CHILTON'S
AUTO REPAIR MANUAL 1989-1993

Publisher and Editor-in-Chief	Kerry A. Freeman, S.A.E.
Managing Editors	Peter M. Conti, Jr. □ W. Calvin Settle, Jr., S.A.E.
Assistant Managing Editor	Nick D'Andrea
Senior Editors	Richard J. Rivele, S.A.E. □ Ron Webb
Project Managers	Ken Grabowski, A.S.E., S.A.E. □ Michael L. Grady
	Martin J. Gunther □ Steven Morgan
	Richard T. Smith □ Jim Taylor
Editorial Staff	Lawrence C. Braun, S.A.E., A.S.C. □ Tom Browne
	Robert E. Doughten □ Sam Fioriani
	Jeff H. Fisher, A.S.E. □ Edward J. Giacomucci, A.S.E.
	Jacques Gordon □ Ben Greisler, S.A.E.
	Jeffrey M. Hoffman □ Joseph T. Lafferty
	Neil Leonard, A.S.E. □ Kevin Maher
	James R. Marotta □ Robert McAnally
	John H. Rutter □ Don Schnell, A.S.E., S.A.E.
	James B. Steele □ Larry E. Stiles
	Anthony Tortorici, A.S.E., S.A.E.
Director of Manufacturing	Mike D'Imperio
Manager of Manufacturing	John F. Butler
Assistant Production Manager	Andrea M. Steiger
Production Assistants	Marsha Park Herman □ Monica Santa Maria
	Margaret Stoner
Mechanical Artists	Lisa Gressen □ Lorraine Martinelli □ Kim Tansey
OFFICERS	
Sr. Vice President	Ronald A. Hoxter

CHILTON BOOK COMPANY

ONE OF THE DIVERSIFIED PUBLISHING COMPANIES,
A PART OF CAPITAL CITIES/ABC, INC.

Manufactured in USA
© 1992 Chilton Book Company
Chilton Way Radnor, Pa. 19089
ISBN 0-8019-7909-9
ISSN 0069-3634

1234567890   1098765432

CAR MODELS

TABLE OF CONTENTS

Car Sections

HOW TO USE THIS MANUAL

Car Section

Car sections are grouped by manufacturer and arranged in alphabetical order. The text and illustrations that comprise the service procedures in each Car Section are arranged in the following order of systems and components: Engine Mechanical, Engine Lubrication, Engine Cooling, Engine Electrical, Emission Controls, Fuel System, Drive Axle, Manual Transmission/Transaxle, Clutch, Automatic Transmission/Transaxle, Front Suspension, Rear Suspension, Steering, Brakes, Chassis Electrical.

Specification charts are always located at the front of each section. All illustrations are located as close as possible to the pertinent text. Procedures are for all models in the particular section unless specifically noted otherwise.

Locating Information

The Table of Contents, at the front of the book, lists the beginning of each Car Section in the manual.

To find where a particular Car Section is located in the book, you need only look in the Table of Contents. Once you have found the proper section, you may wish to find where specific procedures are located in that section. Turn to the Index at the front of the section. At the upper left-hand side is a listing of the main topics within the section and the page number they will be found on. Following the main topics is an alphabetical listing of all the procedures within the section and their page numbers.

Safety Notice

Proper service and repair procedures are vital to the safe, reliable operation of all motor vehicles, as well as the personal safety of those performing repairs. This manual outlines procedures for servicing and repairing vehicles using safe effective methods. The procedures contain many NOTES and CAUTIONS which should be followed along with standard safety procedures to eliminate the possibility of personal injury or improper service which could damage the vehicle or compromise its safety.

It is important to note that repair procedures and techniques, tools and parts for servicing motor vehicles, as well as the skill and experience of the individual performing the work vary widely. It is not possible to anticipate all of the conceivable ways or conditions under which vehicles may be serviced, or to provide cautions as to all of the possible hazards that may result. Standard and accepted safety precautions and equipment should be used when handling toxic or flammable fluids, and safety goggles or other protection should be used during cutting, grinding, chiseling, prying, or any other process that can cause material removal or projectiles.

Some procedures require the use of tools specially designed for a specific purpose. Before substituting another tool or procedure, you must be completely satisfied that neither your personal safety, nor the performance of the vehicle will be endangered.

Part Numbers

Part numbers listed in this book are not recommendations by Chilton for any product by brand name. They are references that can be used with interchange manuals and aftermarket supplier catalogs to locate each brand supplier's discrete part number.

Although information in this manual is based on industry sources and is as complete as possible at the time of publication, the possibility exists that some car manufacturers made later changes which could not be included here. Information on very late models may not be available in some circumstances. While striving for total accuracy, Chilton Book Company cannot assume responsibility for any errors, changes, or omissions that may occur in the compilation of this data.

Copyright Notice

Chrysler/Eagle
Front Wheel Drive

DODGE—Stealth **EAGLE**—Summit • Talon **PLYMOUTH**—Laser

SPECIFICATIONS

VEHICLE IDENTIFICATION CHART

It is important for servicing and ordering parts to be certain of the vehicle and engine identification. The VIN (vehicle identification number) is a 17 digit number visible through the windshield on the driver's side of the dash and contains the vehicle and engine identification codes. The tenth digit indicates model year and the eighth digit indicates engine code. It can be interpreted as follows:

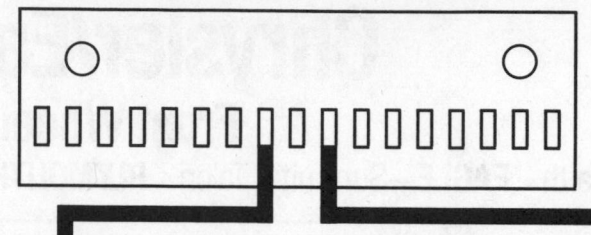

Engine Code

Code	Liters	Cu. In. (cc)	Cyl.	Fuel Sys.	Eng. Mfg.
T	1.8	107 (1754)	4	MPI	Mitsubishi
R	2.0	122 (2000)	4	MPI	Mitsubishi
U	2.0	122 (2000)	4	Turbo	Mitsubishi
X	1.5	92 (1468)	4	MPI	Mitsubishi
Y	1.6	98 (1606)	4	MPI	Mitsubishi
A	1.5	92 (1468)	4	MPI	Mitsubishi
S	3.0	181 (2967)	6	MPI	Mitsubishi
B	3.0	181 (2967)	6	MPI	Mitsubishi
C	3.0	181 (2967)	6	Turbo	Mitsubishi
D	1.8	110 (1834)	4	MPI	Mitsubishi
W	2.4	143.4 (2350)	4	MPI	Mitsubishi

MPI—Multi Point Fuel Injection

Model Year

Code	Year
K	1989
L	1990
M	1991
N	1992
P	1993

ENGINE IDENTIFICATION

Year	Model	Engine Displacement Liters (cc)	Engine Series (ID/VIN)	Fuel System	No. of Cylinders	Engine Type
1989	Eagle Summit	1.5 (1468)	X	MPI	4	SOHC
	Eagle Summit	1.6 (1606)	Y	MPI	4	DOHC
1990	Eagle Summit	1.5 (1468)	X	MPI	4	SOHC
	Eagle Summit	1.6 (1606)	Y	MPI	4	DOHC
	Plymouth Laser	1.8 (1754)	T	MPI	4	SOHC
	Plymouth Laser	2.0 (2000)	R	MPI	4	DOHC
	Plymouth Laser	2.0 (2000)	U	Turbo	4	DOHC
	Eagle Talon	2.0 (2000)	R	MPI	4	DOHC
	Eagle Talon	2.0 (2000)	U	Turbo	4	DOHC
1991	Eagle Summit	1.5 (1468)	A	MPI	4	SOHC
	Plymouth Laser	1.8 (1754)	T	MPI	4	SOHC
	Plymouth Laser	2.0 (2000)	R	MPI	4	DOHC
	Plymouth Laser	2.0 (2000)	U	Turbo	4	DOHC
	Eagle Talon	2.0 (2000)	R	MPI	4	DOHC
	Eagle Talon	2.0 (2000)	U	Turbo	4	DOHC

ENGINE IDENTIFICATION

Year	Model	Engine Displacement Liters (cc)	Engine Series (ID/VIN)	Fuel System	No. of Cylinders	Engine Type
1991	Dodge Stealth	3.0 (2967)	S	MPI	6	SOHC
	Dodge Stealth	3.0 (2967)	B	MPI	6	DOHC
	Dodge Stealth	3.0 (2967)	C	Turbo	6	DOHC
1992-93	Eagle Summit	1.5 (1468)	A	MPI	4	SOHC
	Plymouth Laser	1.8 (1754)	T	MPI	4	SOHC
	Plymouth Laser	2.0 (2000)	R	MPI	4	DOHC
	Plymouth Laser	2.0 (2000)	U	Turbo	4	DOHC
	Eagle Talon	2.0 (2000)	R	MPI	4	DOHC
	Eagle Talon	2.0 (2000)	U	Turbo	4	DOHC
	Dodge Stealth	3.0 (2967)	S	MPI	6	SOHC
	Dodge Stealth	3.0 (2967)	B	MPI	6	DOHC
	Dodge Stealth	3.0 (2967)	C	Turbo	6	DOHC
	Eagle Summit Wagon	1.8 (1834)	D	MPI	4	SOHC
	Eagle Summit Wagon	2.4 (2350)	W	MPI	4	SOHC

MPI—Multi Point Fuel Injection
SOHC—Single Overhead Camshaft
DOHC—Double Overhead Camshaft

GENERAL ENGINE SPECIFICATIONS

Year	Engine ID/VIN	Engine Displacement Liters (cc)	Fuel System Type	Net Horsepower @ rpm	Net Torque @ rpm (ft. lbs.)	Bore × Stroke (in.)	Compression Ratio	Oil Pressure @ rpm
1989	X	1.5 (1472)	MPI	81 @ 5500	91 @ 3000	2.972 × 3.228	9.4:1	54 @ 2000
	Y	1.6 (1606)	MPI	113 @ 6500	99 @ 5000	3.243 × 2.955	9.2:1	54 @ 2000
1990	X	1.5 (1472)	MPI	81 @ 5500	91 @ 3000	2.972 × 3.228	9.4:1	54 @ 2000
	Y	1.6 (1606)	MPI	113 @ 6500	99 @ 5000	3.243 × 2.955	9.2:1	54 @ 2000
	T	1.8 (1712)	MPI	92 @ 5000	105 @ 3500	3.172 × 3.388	9.0:1	41 @ 2000
	R	2.0 (1952)	MPI	135 @ 6000	125 @ 5000	3.349 × 3.467	9.0:1	41 @ 2000
	U	2.0 (1952)	Turbo	190 @ 6000	203 @ 3000	3.349 × 3.467	7.8:1	41 @ 2000
1991	A	1.5 (1468)	MPI	92 @ 6000	93 @ 3000	2.97 × 3.23	9.2:1	54 @ 2000
	T	1.8 (1754)	MPI	92 @ 5000	105 @ 3500	3.17 × 3.39	9.0:1	41 @ 2000
	R	2.0 (2000)	MPI	135 @ 6000	125 @ 5000	3.35 × 3.47	9.0:1	41 @ 2000
	U	2.0 (2000)	Turbo	190 @ 6000	203 @ 3000	3.35 × 3.47	7.8:1	41 @ 2000
	S	3.0 (2967)	MPI	164 @ 5500	185 @ 4000	3.58 × 2.99	8.9:1	30–80 @ 2000
	B	3.0 (2967)	MPI	222 @ 6000	201 @ 4500	3.58 × 2.99	10.0:1	30–80 @ 2000
	C	3.0 (2967)	Turbo	300 @ 6000	307 @ 2500	3.58 × 2.99	8.0:1	30–80 @ 2000
1992-93	A	1.5 (1468)	MPI	92 @ 6000	93 @ 3000	2.97 × 3.23	9.2:1	54 @ 2000
	T	1.8 (1754)	MPI	92 @ 5000	105 @ 3500	3.17 × 3.39	9.0:1	41 @ 2000
	R	2.0 (2000)	MPI	135 @ 6000	125 @ 5000	3.35 × 3.47	9.0:1	41 @ 2000
	U	2.0 (2000)	Turbo	190 @ 6000	203 @ 3000	3.35 × 3.47	7.8:1	41 @ 2000
	S	3.0 (2967)	MPI	164 @ 5500	185 @ 4000	3.58 × 2.99	8.9:1	30–80 @ 2000
	B	3.0 (2967)	MPI	222 @ 6000	201 @ 4500	3.58 × 2.99	10.0:1	30–80 @ 2000
	C	3.0 (2967)	Turbo	300 @ 6000	307 @ 2500	3.58 × 2.99	8.0:1	30–80 @ 2000

GENERAL ENGINE SPECIFICATIONS

Year	Engine ID/VIN	Engine Displacement Liters (cc)	Fuel System Type	Net Horsepower @ rpm	Net Torque @ rpm (ft. lbs.)	Bore × Stroke (in.)	Compression Ratio	Oil Pressure @ rpm
1992–93	D	1.8 (1834)	MPI	113 @ 6000	116 @ 4500	3.19 × 3.50	9.5:1	①
	W	2.4 (2350)	MPI	116 @ 5000	136 @ 3500	3.41 × 3.94	8.5:1	①

NOTE: Horsepower and torque are SAE net figures. They are measured at the rear of the transmission with all accessories installed and operating. Since the figures vary when a given engine is installed in different models, some are representative rather than exact.
MPI—Multi Point Fuel Injection
① 11.4 psi or more at curb idle speed

GASOLINE ENGINE TUNE-UP SPECIFICATIONS

Year	Engine ID/VIN	Engine Displacement Liters (cc)	Spark Plugs Gap (in.)	Ignition Timing (deg.) MT	Ignition Timing (deg.) AT	Fuel Pump (psi)	Idle Speed (rpm) MT	Idle Speed (rpm) AT	Valve Clearance In.	Valve Clearance Ex.
1989	X	1.5 (1472)	0.039–0.043	5B	5B	38	750	750	0.006	0.010
	Y	1.6 (1606)	0.039–0.043	5B	5B	38	750	750	Hyd.	Hyd.
1990	X	1.5 (1472)	0.039–0.043	5B	5B	38	750	750	0.006	0.010
	Y	1.6 (1606)	0.039–0.043	5B	5B	38	750	750	Hyd.	Hyd.
	T	1.8 (1712)	0.039–0.043	5B	5B	38	700	700	Hyd.	Hyd.
	R	2.0 (1952)	0.039–0.043	5B	5B	38	700	700	Hyd.	Hyd.
	U	2.0 (1952)	0.028–0.031	5B	5B	27	750	750	Hyd.	Hyd.
1991	A	1.5 (1472)	0.039–0.043	5B	5B	38	750	750	0.006	0.010
	T	1.8 (1712)	0.039–0.043	5B	5B	38	750	750	Hyd.	Hyd.
	R	2.0 (1952)	0.039–0.043	5B	5B	38	700	700	Hyd.	Hyd.
	U	2.0 (1952)	0.028–0.031	5B	5B	27	750	750	Hyd.	Hyd.
	S	3.0 (2902)	0.039–0.043	5B	5B	38	750	750	Hyd.	Hyd.
	B	3.0 (2902)	0.039–0.043	5B	5B	38	750	750	Hyd.	Hyd.
	C	3.0 (2902)	0.035	5B	5B	34	700	700	Hyd.	Hyd.
1992	A	1.5 (1472)	0.039–0.043	5B	5B	38	750	750	0.006	0.010
	T	1.8 (1712)	0.039–0.043	5B	5B	38	750	750	Hyd.	Hyd.
	R	2.0 (1952)	0.039–0.043	5B	5B	38	700	700	Hyd.	Hyd.
	U	2.0 (1952)	0.028–0.031	5B	5B	27	750	750	Hyd.	Hyd.
	S	3.0 (2902)	0.039–0.043	5B	5B	38	750	750	Hyd.	Hyd.
	B	3.0 (2902)	0.039–0.043	5B	5B	38	750	750	Hyd.	Hyd.
	C	3.0 (2902)	0.035	5B	5B	34	700	700	Hyd.	Hyd.
	D	1.8 (1834)	0.039–0.043	5B	5B	38	750	750	0.004	0.008
	W	2.4 (2350)	0.039–0.043	5B	5B	38	750	750	Hyd.	Hyd.
1993			SEE UNDERHOOD SPECIFICATIONS STICKER							

NOTE: The lowest cylinder pressure should be within 75% of the highest cylinder pressure reading. For example, if the highest cylinder is 134 psi, the lowest should be 101. Engine should be at normal operating temperature with throttle valve in the wide open position.
The underhood specifications sticker often reflects tune-up specification changes in production. Sticker figures must be used if they disagree with those in this chart.
Hyd.—Hydraulic
B—Before Top Dead Center—BTDC

FIRING ORDERS

NOTE: To avoid confusion, always replace spark plugs and wires one at a time.

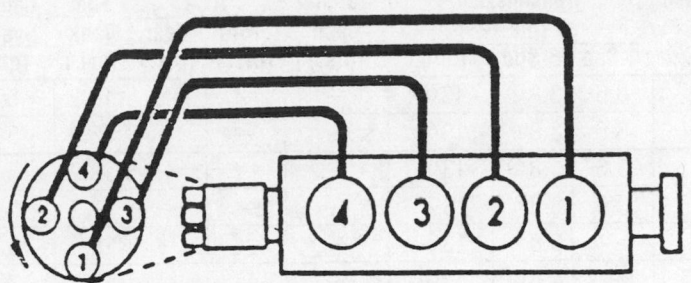

1991–93 1.5L and 1992–93 1.8L (Summit Wagon) Engines
Engine Firing Order: 1–3–4–2
Distributor Rotation: Counterclockwise

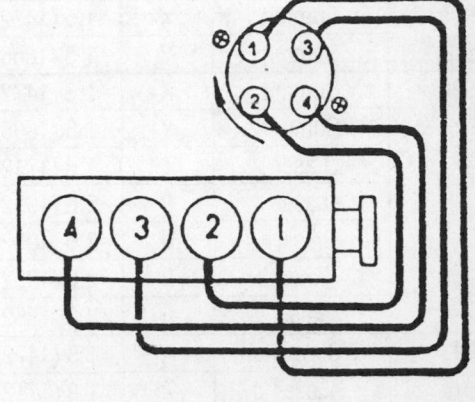

1.8L, 1989–90 1.5L and 1992–93 2.4L Engines
Engine Firing Order: 1–3–4–2
Distributor Rotation: Clockwise

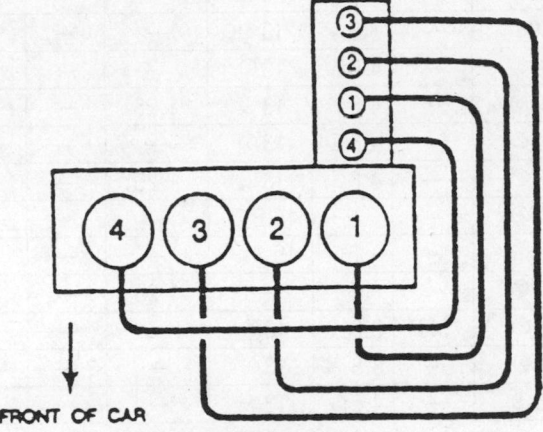

1.6L and 2.0L Engines
Engine Firing Order: 1–3–4–2
Distributorless Ignition System

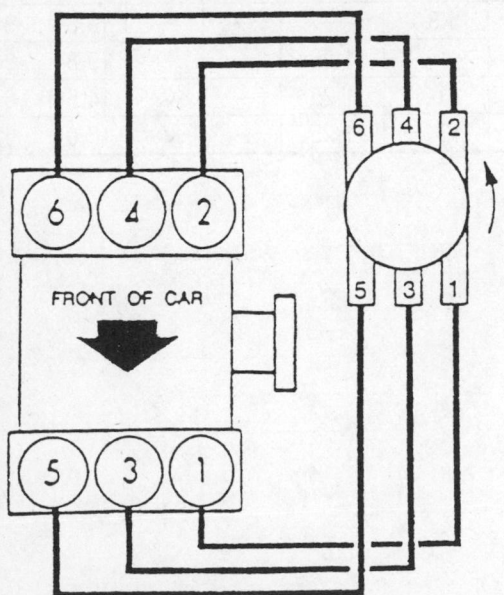

3.0L SOHC Engine
Engine Firing Order: 1–2–3–4–5–6
Distributor Rotation: Counterclockwise

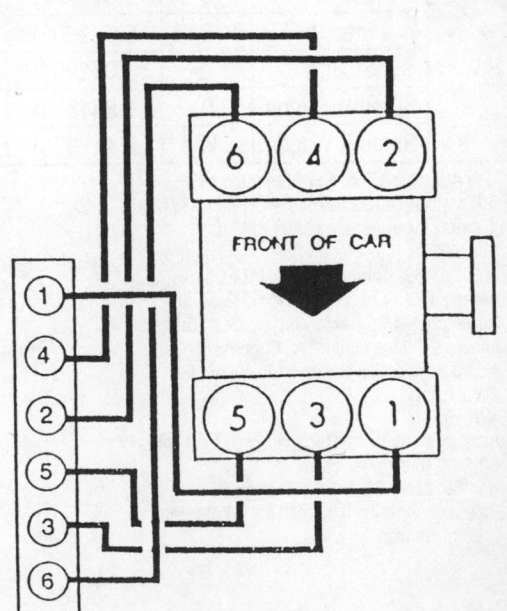

3.0L DOHC Engine
Engine Firing Order: 1–2–3–4–5–6
Distributorless Ignition System

CAPACITIES

Year	Model	Engine ID/VIN	Engine Displacement Liters (cc)	Engine Crankcase with Filter ④	Transmission (pts.) 4-Spd	5-Spd	Auto.	Transfer case (pts.)	Drive Axle Front (pts.)	Rear (pts.)	Fuel Tank (gal.)	Cooling System (qts.)
1989	Summit	X	1.5 (1472)	3.6①	3.6	3.8②	13③	—	—	—	13.2	5.3
	Summit	Y	1.5 (1606)	4.6①	3.6	3.8	13③	—	—	—	13.2	5.3
1990	Summit	X	1.5 (1472)	3.6①	3.6	3.8②	13③	—	—	—	13.2	5.3
	Summit	Y	1.5 (1606)	4.6①	3.6	3.8	13③	—	—	—	13.2	5.3
	Laser	T	1.8 (1712)	4.1①	—	3.8	13③	—	—	—	16.0	6.6
	Laser	R	2.0 (1952)	4.6①	—	4.6⑤	13③	—	—	—	16.0	7.6
	Laser	U	2.0 (1952)	4.6①	—	4.8⑥	13③	1.25	—	⑦	16.0	7.6
	Talon	R	2.0 (1952)	4.6①	—	4.6⑤	13③	—	—	—	16.0	7.6
	Talon	U	2.0 (1952)	4.6①	—	4.8⑥	13③	1.25	—	⑦	16.0	7.6
1991	Summit	A	1.5 (1472)	3.6⑧	3.6	3.8	13③	—	—	—	13.2	5.3
	Laser	T	1.8 (1712)	4.1⑧	—	3.8	13③	—	—	—	16.0	6.6
	Laser	R	2.0 (1952)	4.6⑧	—	4.6⑤	13③	—	—	—	16.0	7.6
	Laser	U	2.0 (1952)	4.6⑧	—	4.8⑥	13③	1.25	—	⑦	16.0	7.6
	Talon	R	2.0 (1952)	4.6⑧	—	4.6⑤	13③	—	—	—	16.0	7.6
	Talon	U	2.0 (1952)	4.6⑧	—	4.8⑥	13③	1.25	—	⑦	16.0	7.6
	Stealth	S	3.0 (2902)	4.7⑧	—	5	15.8③	—	—	—	19.8	8.5
	Stealth	B	3.0 (2902)	4.7⑧	—	5	15.8③	—	—	⑨	19.8	8.5
	Stealth	C	3.0 (2902)	5.2⑧	—	5	—	1.25	—	⑨	19.8	8.5
1992–93	Summit	A	1.5 (1472)	3.6⑧	3.6	3.8	13③	—	—	—	13.2	5.3
	Laser	T	1.8 (1712)	4.1⑧	—	3.8	13③	—	—	—	16.0	6.6
	Laser	R	2.0 (1952)	4.6⑧	—	4.6⑤	13③	—	—	—	16.0	7.6
	Laser	U	2.0 (1952)	4.6⑧	—	4.8⑥	13③	1.25	—	⑦	16.0	7.6
	Talon	R	2.0 (1952)	4.6⑧	—	4.6⑤	13③	—	—	—	16.0	7.6
	Talon	U	2.0 (1952)	4.6⑧	—	4.8⑥	13③	1.25	—	⑦	16.0	7.6
	Stealth	S	3.0 (2902)	4.7⑧	—	5	15.8③	—	—	—	19.8	8.5
	Stealth	B	3.0 (2902)	4.7⑧	—	5	15.8③	—	—	—	19.8	8.5
	Stealth	C	3.0 (2902)	5.2⑧	—	5	—	1.25	—	⑨	19.8	8.5
	Summit Wagon	D	1.8 (1834)	4.0⑧	—	3.8	13③	1.25	—	⑦	14.5	6.3
	Summit Wagon	W	2.4 (2350)	4.1⑧	—	4.8	13③	1.25	—	⑦	16.0	6.8

① Use API class SF or SF/CC engine oil
② 3.8 pts. for transaxle models KM201, KM206.
   4.4 pts. for transaxle model KM210
   See Vehicle Information Code Plate on firewall
   for transaxle number. Manual transaxles, use
   API class GL-4 or higher Hypoid Gear oil
③ Automatic—Use Dexron II type fluid. Quantity
   shown includes converter. Check when hot.
④ Add 0.5 qt. for oil cooler on Turbo models.
⑤ 2WD-Turbo
⑥ 4WD-Turbo
⑦ Rear axle—with 4WD, capacity 0.75 qt. plus
   0.63 qt. in transfer case.
⑧ Use API class SG or SG/CD engine oil.
⑨ Rear axle with 4WD capacity 1.16 qts. plus
   0.69 qt. in transfer case.

CAMSHAFT SPECIFICATIONS

All measurements given in inches.

Year	Engine ID/VIN	Engine Displacement Liters (cc)	Journal Diameter 1	2	3	4	5	Elevation In.	Ex.	Bearing Clearance	Camshaft End Play
1989	X	1.5 (1472)	1.8110	1.8110	1.8110	—	—	1.5318	1.5344	0.0015–0.0031	0.002–0.008
	Y	1.6 (1606)	1.0200	1.0200	1.0200	1.0200	1.0200 ①	1.3858	1.3743	0.0020–0.0035	0.004–0.008
1990	X	1.5 (1472)	1.8110	1.8110	1.8110	—	—	1.5318	1.5344	0.0015–0.0031	0.002–0.008
	Y	1.6 (1606)	1.0200	1.0200	1.0200	1.0200	1.0200 ①	1.3858	1.3743	0.0020–0.0035	0.004–0.008
	T	1.8 (1712)	1.3360–1.3366	1.3360–1.3366	1.3360–1.3366	1.3360–1.3366	1.3360–1.3370	1.4138	1.4138	0.0020–0.0035	0.004–0.008
	R	2.0 (1952)	1.0217–1.0224	1.0217–1.0224	1.0217–1.0224	1.0217–1.0224	1.0217–1.0224 ①	1.3974	1.3858	0.0020–0.0035	0.004–0.008
	U	2.0 (1952)	1.0217–1.0224	1.0217–1.0224	1.0217–1.0224	1.0217–1.0224	1.0217–1.0224 ①	1.3974	1.3858	0.0020–0.0035	0.004–0.008
1991	A	1.5 (1472)	1.8110	1.8110	1.8110	1.8110	—	1.5059–1.5256	1.5197–1.5394	0.0024–0.0055	NA
	T	1.8 (1712)	1.3360–1.3366	1.3360–1.3366	1.3360–1.3366	1.3360–1.3366	1.3360–1.3366	1.4138	1.4138	0.0020–0.0035	0.004–0.008
	R	2.0 (1952)	1.0217–1.0224	1.0217–1.0224	1.0217–1.0224	1.0217–1.0224	1.0217–1.0224 ①	1.3974	1.3858	0.0020–0.0035	0.004–0.008
	U	2.0 (1952)	1.0217–1.0224	1.0217–1.0224	1.0217–1.0224	1.0217–1.0224	1.0217–1.0224–	1.3974	1.3858	0.0020–0.0035	0.004–0.008
	S	3.0 (2902)	1.3400	1.3400	1.3400	1.3400	—	1.6430–1.6440	1.6430–1.6440	0.0020–0.0035	0.004–0.008
	B	3.0 (2902)	1.0200	1.0200	1.0200	1.0200	1.0200	1.3776–1.3972	1.3661–1.3858	0.0020–0.0035	0.004–0.008
	C	3.0 (2902)	1.0200	1.0200	1.0200	1.0200	1.0200	1.3776–1.3972	1.3661–1.3858	0.0020–0.0035	0.004–0.008
1992–93	A	1.5 (1472)	1.8110	1.8110	1.8110	1.8110	—	1.5059–1.5256	1.5197–1.5394	0.0024–0.0055	NA
	T	1.8 (1712)	1.3360–1.3366	1.3360–1.3366	1.3360–1.3366	1.3360–1.3366	1.3360–1.3366	1.4138	1.4138	0.0020–0.0035	0.004–0.008
	R	2.0 (1952)	1.0217–1.0224	1.0217–1.0224	1.0217–1.0224	1.0217–1.0224	1.0217–1.0224 ①	1.3974	1.3858	0.0020–0.0035	0.004–0.008
	U	2.0 (1952)	1.0217–1.0224	1.0217–1.0224	1.0217–1.0224	1.0217–1.0224	1.0217–1.0224 ①	1.3974	1.3858	0.0020–0.0035	0.002–0.008
	S	3.0 (2902)	1.3400	1.3400	1.3400	1.3400	—	1.6430–1.6440	1.6430–1.6440	0.0020–0.0035	0.004–0.008
	B	3.0 (2902)	1.0200	1.0200	1.0200	1.0200	1.0200	1.3776–1.3972	1.3661–1.3858	0.0020–0.0035	0.004–0.008
	C	3.0 (2902)	1.0200	1.0200	1.0200	1.0200	1.0200	1.3776–1.3972	1.3661–1.3858	0.0020–0.0035	0.004–0.008
	D	1.8 (1834)	1.7689–1.7693	1.7689–1.7693	1.7689–1.7693	1.7689–1.7693	1.7689–1.7693	1.4670–1.4880	1.4800–1.4990	0.0020–0.0035	NA
	W	2.4 (2350)	1.3362–1.3366	1.3362–1.3366	1.3362–1.3366	1.3362–1.3366	1.3362–1.3366	1.7335–1.7531	1.7335–1.7531	0.0020–0.0035–	NA

NA—Not available
① 6 journals are used.

Bearing caps Nos. 2–5 are the same shape.
''L'' or ''R'' is stamped on No. 1 bearing cap.

L = Intake side, R = Exhaust side. Bearing caps should be reinstalled at their original locations.

CRANKSHAFT AND CONNECTING ROD SPECIFICATIONS

All measurements are given in inches.

Year	Engine ID/VIN	Engine Displacement Liters (cc)	Crankshaft				Connecting Rod		
			Main Brg. Journal Dia.	Main Brg. Oil Clearance	Shaft End-play	Thrust on No.	Journal Diameter	Oil Clearance	Side Clearance
1989	X	1.5 (1472)	1.890	0.0008–0.0018	0.0020–0.0071	3	1.6500	0.0006–0.0017	0.0039–0.0098
	Y	1.6 (1606)	2.240	0.0008–0.0020	0.0020–0.0071	3	1.7700	0.0008–0.0020	0.0039–0.0098
1990	X	1.5 (1472)	1.890	0.0008–0.0018	0.0020–0.0071	3	1.6500	0.0006–0.0017	0.0039–0.0098
	Y	1.6 (1606)	2.240	0.0008–0.0020	0.0020–0.0071	3	1.7700	0.0008–0.0020	0.0039–0.0098
	T	1.8 (1712)	2.240	0.0008–0.0020	0.0020–0.0070	3	1.7700	0.0008–0.0020	0.0039–0.0098
	R	2.0 (1952)	2.243–2.244	0.0008–0.0020	0.0020–0.0070	3	1.7709–1.7715	0.0008–0.0020	0.0040–0.0098
	U	2.0 (1952)	2.243–2.244	0.0008–0.0020	0.0020–0.0070	3	1.7709–1.7715	0.0008–0.0020	0.0040–0.0098
1991	A	1.5 (1472)	1.890	0.0008–0.0028	0.0020–0.0071	3	1.6500	0.0008–0.0024	0.0039–0.0098
	T	1.8 (1712)	2.240	0.0008–0.0020	0.0020–0.0070	3	1.7700	0.0008–0.0020	0.0039–0.0098
	R	2.0 (1952)	2.243–2.244	0.0008–0.0020	0.0020–0.0070	3	1.7709–1.7715	0.0008–0.0020	0.0040–0.0098
	U	2.0 (1952)	2.243–2.244	0.0008–0.0020	0.0020–0.0070	3	1.7709–1.7715	0.0008–0.0020	0.0040–0.0098
	S	3.0 (2902)	2.358	0.0008–0.0019	0.0020–0.0098	3	1.9650	0.0006–0.0018	0.0040–0.0098
	B	3.0 (2902)	2.358	0.0007–0.0017	0.0020–0.0098	3	1.9650	0.0006–0.0018	0.0040–0.0098
	C	3.0 (2902)	2.358	0.0007–0.0017	0.0020–0.0098	3	1.9650	0.0006–0.0018	0.0040–0.0098
1992–93	A	1.5 (1472)	1.890	0.0008–0.0028	0.0020–0.0071	3	1.6500	0.0008–0.0024	0.0039–0.0098
	T	1.8 (1712)	2.240	0.0008–0.0020	0.0020–0.0070	3	1.7700	0.0008–0.0020	0.0039–0.0098
	R	2.0 (1952)	2.243–2.244	0.0008–0.0020	0.0020–0.0070	3	1.7709–1.7715	0.0008–0.0020	0.0040–0.0098
	U	2.0 (1952)	2.243–2.244	0.0008–0.0020	0.0020–0.0070	3	1.7709–1.7715	0.0008–0.0020	0.0040–0.0098
	S	3.0 (2902)	2.358	0.0008–0.0019	0.0020–0.0098	3	1.9650	0.0006–0.0018	0.0040–0.0098
	B	3.0 (2902)	2.358	0.0007–0.0017	0.0020–0.0098	3	1.9650	0.0006–0.0018	0.0040–0.0098
	C	3.0 (2902)	2.358	0.0007–0.0017	0.0020–0.0098	3	1.9650	0.0006–0.0018	0.0040–0.0098
	D	1.8 (1834)	1.968	0.0008–0.0016	0.0020–0.0070	3	1.7709–1.7715	0.0008–0.0020	0.0040–0.0098
	W	2.4 (2350)	2.243–2.244	0.0008–0.0020	0.0020–0.0070	3	1.7709–1.7717	0.0008–0.0020	0.0039–0.0098

VALVE SPECIFICATIONS

Year	Engine ID/VIN	Engine Displacement Liters (cc)	Seat Angle (deg.)	Face Angle (deg.)	Spring Test Pressure (lbs. @ in.)	Spring Installed Height (in.)	Stem-to-Guide Clearance (in.)		Stem Diameter (in.)	
							Intake	Exhaust	Intake	Exhaust
1989	X	1.5 (1472)	44–45.5	45–45.5	53②	1.756①	0.0008–0.0020	0.0020–0.0035	0.2600	0.2600
	Y	1.6 (1606)	44–44.5	45–45.5	53②	1803③	0.0008–0.0019	0.0020–0.0033	0.2585–0.2586	0.2571–0.2579
1990	X	1.5 (1472)	44–44.5	45–45.5	53②	1.756①	0.0008–0.0020	0.0020–0.0035	0.2600	0.2600
	Y	1.6 (1606)	44–44.5	45–45.5	66②	1.902④	0.0008–0.0019	0.0020–0.0033	0.2585–0.2586	0.2571–0.2579
	T	1.8 (1712)	44–44.5	45–45.5	62②	1.937⑦	0.0012–⑤ 0.0024	0.0020–⑥ 0.0035–	0.3100	0.3100
	R	2.0 (1952)	44–44.5	45–45.5	66②	1.902⑧	0.0008–⑤ 0.0019	0.0020–⑥ 0.0033	0.2585–0.2591	0.2571–0.2579
	U	2.0 (1952)	44–44.5	45–45.5	66②	1.902⑧	0.0008–⑤ 0.0019	0.0020⑥ 0.0033	0.2585–0.2591	0.2571–0.2579
1991	A	1.5 (1472)	44–44.5	45–45.5	② ⑨	⑩	0.0008–0.0020	0.0020–0.0035	0.2585–0.2591	0.2571–0.2579
	T	1.8 (1712)	44–44.5	45–45.5	62②	1.937⑦	0.0012–⑤ 0.0024	0.0020–⑥ 0.0035	0.3100	0.3100
	R	2.0 (1952)	44–44.5	45–45.5	66②	1.902⑧	0.0008–⑤ 0.0019	0.0020–⑧ 0.0033	0.2585–0.2591	0.2571–0.2579
	U	2.0 (1952)	44–44.5	45–45.5	66②	1.902⑧	0.0008–⑤ 0.0019	0.0020–⑥ 0.0033	0.2585–0.2591	0.2571–0.2579
	S	3.0 (2902)	44–44.5	45–45.5	74②	1.600–1.630	0.0012–0.0039	0.0020–0.0059	0.3140	0.3140
	B	3.0 (2902)	44–44.5	45–45.5	62②	1.500–1.530	0.0008–0.0039	0.0020–0.0047	0.2600	0.2600
	C	3.0 (2902)	44–44.5	45–45.5	62②	1.500–1.530	0.0008–0.0039	0.0020–0.0047	0.2600	0.2600
1992-93	A	1.5 (1472)	44–44.5	45–45.5	② ⑨	⑩	0.0008–0.0020	0.0020–0.0035	0.2585–0.2591	0.2571–0.2579
	T	1.8 (1712)	44–44.5	45–45.5	62②	1.937⑦	0.0012–⑤ 0.0024	0.0020–⑥ 0.0035	0.3100	0.3100
	R	2.0 (1952)	44–44.5	45–45.5	66②	1.902⑧	0.0008–⑤ 0.0019	0.0020–⑧ 0.0033	0.2585–0.2591	0.2571–0.2579
	U	2.0 (1952)	44–44.5	45–45.5	66②	1.902⑧	0.0008–⑤ 0.0019	0.0020–⑥ 0.0033	0.2585–0.2591	0.2571–0.2579
	S	3.0 (2902)	44–44.5	45–45.5	74②	1.600–1.630	0.0012–0.0039	0.0020–0.0059	0.3140	0.3140
	B	3.0 (2902)	44–44.4	45–45.5	62②	1.500–1.530	0.0008–0.0039	0.0020–0.0047	0.2600	0.2600
	C	3.0 (2902)	44–44.5	45–45.5	62②	1.500–1.530	0.0008–0.0039	0.0020–0.0047	0.2600	0.2600
	D	1.8 (1834)	43.5–44	45–45.5	132②	⑪	0.0008–0.0020	0.0020–0.0035	0.2350–0.2354	0.2343–0.2350

VALVE SPECIFICATIONS

Year	Engine ID/VIN	Engine Displacement Liters (cc)	Seat Angle (deg.)	Face Angle (deg.)	Spring Test Pressure (lbs. @ in.)	Spring Installed Height (in.)	Stem-to-Guide Clearance (in.)		Stem Diameter (in.)	
							Intake	Exhaust	Intake	Exhaust
1992–93	W	2.4 (2350)	44 44.5	45– 45.5	73 ②	⑫	0.0012– 0.0024	0.0020– 0.0035	0.3100	0.3100

NA—Not available
① Free length, not installed height
   Used limit = 1.717
② At installed height
③ Free length, not installed height
   Used limit = 1.768
④ Free length, not installed height
   Used limit = 1.862

⑤ Used limit = 0.004
⑥ Used limit = 0.006
⑦ Free length, not installed height
   Used limit = 1.898
⑧ Free length, not installed height
   Used limit = 1.862

⑨ Intake: 51
   Exhaust: 64
⑩ Free length, not installed height
   Intake: 1.776–1.815
   Exhaust: 1.803–1.843
⑪ Free length, not installed height—2.004
⑫ Free length, not installed height—1.961

PISTON AND RING SPECIFICATIONS

All measurements are given in inches.

Year	Engine ID/VIN	Engine Displacement Liters (cc)	Piston Clearance	Ring Gap			Ring Side Clearance		
				Top Compression	Bottom Compression	Oil Control	Top Compression	Bottom Compression	Oil Control
1989	X	1.5 (1472)	0.0008– 0.0016	0.0079– 0.0138	0.0079– 0.0138	0.0079– 0.0276	0.0012– 0.0028	0.0008– 0.0024	NA
	Y	1.6 (1606)	0.0008– 0.0016	0.0098– 0.0157	0.0138– 0.0197	0.0079– 0.0276	0.0012– 0.0028	0.0012– 0.0028	NA
1990	X	1.5 (1472)	0.0008– 0.0016	0.0079– 0.0138	0.0079– 0.0138	0.0079– 0.0276	0.0012– 0.0028	0.0008– 0.0024	NA
	Y	1.6 (1606)	0.0008– 0.0016	0.0098– 0.0157	0.0138– 0.0197	0.0079– 0.0276	0.0012– 0.0028	0.0012– 0.0028	NA
	T	1.8 (1712)	0.0004– 0.0012	0.0118– 0.0177	0.0079– 0.0138	0.0080– 0.0280	0.0018– 0.0033	0.0008– 0.0024	NA
	R	2.0 (1952)	0.0008– 0.0016	0.0098– 0.0157	0.0138– 0.0197	0.0079– 0.0276	0.0012– 0.0028	0.0012– 0.0028	NA
	U	2.0 (1952)	0.0012– 0.0020	0.0098– 0.0177	0.0138– 0.0197	0.0079– 0.0276	0.0012– 0.0028	0.0012– 0.0028	NA
1991	A	1.5 (1472)	0.0008– 0.0016	0.0079– 0.0157	0.0079– 0.0138	0.0079– 0.0276	0.0012– 0.0028	0.0008– 0.0024	NA
	T	1.8 (1712)	0.0004– 0.0012	0.0118– 0.0177	0.0079– 0.0138	0.0080– 0.0280	0.0018– 0.0033	0.0008– 0.0024	NA
	R	2.0 (1952)	0.0008– 0.0016	0.0098– 0.0157	0.0138– 0.0197	0.0079– 0.0276	0.0012– 0.0028	0.0012– 0.0028	NA
	U	2.0 (1952)	0.0012– 0.0020	0.0098– 0.0177	0.0138– 0.0197	0.0079– 0.0276	0.0012– 0.0028	0.0012– 0.0028	NA
	S	3.0 (2902)	0.0012– 0.0020	0.0118– 0.0177	0.0098– 0.0157	0.0118– 0.0154	0.0020– 0.0035	0.0008– 0.0024	NA
	B	3.0 (2902)	0.0012– 0.0020	0.0118– 0.0177	0.0177– 0.0236	0.0079– 0.0236	0.0012– 0.0028	0.0008– 0.0024	NA
	C	3.0 (2902)	0.0012– 0.0020	0.0118– 0.0177	0.0177– 0.0236	0.0079– 0.0236	0.0012– 0.0028	0.0008– 0.0024	NA
1992–93	A	1.5 (1472)	0.0008– 0.0016	0.0079– 0.0157	0.0079– 0.0138	0.0079– 0.0276	0.0012– 0.0028	0.0008– 0.0024	NA
	T	1.8 (1712)	0.0004– 0.0012	0.0118– 0.0177	0.0079– 0.0138	0.0080– 0.0280	0.0018– 0.0033	0.0008– 0.0024	NA
	R	2.0 (1952)	0.0008– 0.0016	0.0098– 0.0157	0.0138– 0.0197	0.0079– 0.0276	0.0012– 0.0028	0.0012– 0.0028	NA

PISTON AND RING SPECIFICATIONS
All measurements are given in inches.

| Year | Engine ID/VIN | Engine Displacement Liters (cc) | Piston Clearance | Ring Gap | | | Ring Side Clearance | | |
				Top Compression	Bottom Compression	Oil Control	Top Compression	Bottom Compression	Oil Control
1992–93	U	2.0 (1952)	0.0012–0.0020	0.0098–0.0177	0.0138–0.0197	0.0079–0.0276	0.0012–0.0028	0.0012–0.0028	NA
	S	3.0 (2902)	0.0012–0.0020	0.0118–0.0177	0.0098–0.0157	0.0118–0.0154	0.0020–0.0035	0.0008–0.0024	NA
	B	3.0 (2902)	0.0012–0.0020	0.0118–0.0177	0.0177–0.0236	0.0079–0.0236	0.0012–0.0028	0.0008–0.0024	NA
	C	3.0 (2902)	0.0012–0.0020	0.0118–0.0177	0.0177–0.0236	0.0079–0.0236	0.0012–0.0028	0.0008–0.0024	NA
	D	1.8 (1834)	0.0008–0.0016	0.0098–0.0157	0.0157–0.0217	0.0079–0.0236	0.0012–0.0028	0.0008–0.0024	NA
	W	2.4 (2350)	0.0004–0.0012	0.0098–0.0157	0.0079–0.0157	0.0079–0.0276	0.0012–0.0028	0.0008–0.0024	NA

NA—Not available

TORQUE SPECIFICATIONS
All readings in ft. lbs.

| Year | Engine ID/VIN | Engine Displacement Liters (cc) | Cylinder Head Bolts | Main Bearing Bolts | Rod Bearing Bolts | Crankshaft Damper Bolts | Flywheel Bolts | Manifold | | Spark Plugs | Lug Nut |
								Intake	Exhaust		
1989	X	1.5 (1472)	①	36–40	23–25	51–72②	94–101	11–14	11–14	15–21③	65–80
	Y	1.6 (1606)	④	47–51	36–38	80–94⑤	94–101	18–22	18–22	15–21③	65–80
1990	X	1.5 (1472)	①	36–40	23–25	51–72②	94–101	11–14	11–14	15–21③	65–80
	Y	1.6 (1606)	④	47–51	36–38	80–94⑤	94–101	18–22	18–22	15–21③	65–80
	T	1.8 (1712)	51–54	37–39	24–25	80–94	94–101	13–18	18–22	15–21③	87–101
	R	2.0 (1952)	65–72	47–51	36–38	80–94	94–101	18–22	18–22	15–21③	87–101
	U	2.0 (1952)	65–72	47–51	36–38	80–94	94–101	18–22	18–22	15–21③	87–101
1991	A	1.5 (1472)	①	47–51	36–38	51–72②	94–101	11–14	11–14	15–21③	65–80
	T	1.8 (1712)	51–54	37–39	24–25	80–94	94–101	13–18	18–22	15–21③	87–101
	R	2.0 (1952)	65–72	47–51	36–38	94	94–101	18–22	18–22	15–21③	87–101
	U	2.0 (1952)	65–72	47–51	36–38	94	94–101	18–22	18–22	15–21③	87–101
	S	3.0 (2902)	76–83	58	38	108–116	55	13	13	18③	87–101
	B	3.0 (2902)	76–83	58	38	130–137	55	14	33	18③	87–101
	C	3.0 (2902)	87–94	58	38	130–137	55	9–11	22⑦	18③	87–101
1992–93	A	1.5 (1472)	①	47–51	36–38	51–72②	94–101	11–14	11–14	15–21③	65–80
	T	1.8 (1712)	51–54	37–39	24–25	80–94	94–101	13–18	18–22	15–21③	87–101
	R	2.0 (1952)	65–72	47–51	36–38	94	94–101	18–22	18–22	15–21③	87–101
	U	2.0 (1952)	65–72	47–51	36–38	94	94–101	18–22	18–22	15–21③	87–101
	S	3.0 (2902)	76–83	58	38	108–116	55	13	13	18③	87–101
	B	3.0 (2902)	76–83	58	38	130–137	55	14	33	18③	87–101
	C	3.0 (2902)	87–94	58	38	130–137	55	9–11	22⑦	18③	87–101
	D	1.8 (1834)	⑦	14	14.5	134	72	13	13	18	65–80
	W	2.4 (2350)	⑦	38	38	—	98	13	13	18	65–80

① 51–54 COLD
　58–61 HOT
② Pulley to crankshaft sprocket—9–11
③ Spark plugs used in aluminum heads should always have lubricated threads
④ 65–72 COLD
　72–80 HOT
⑤ Pulley to crankshaft sprocket—14–22
⑥ Torque to 14.5 ft. lbs., back off, torque again to 14.5 ft. lbs., then turn additional ¼ turn
⑦ See text for special sequence

BRAKE SPECIFICATIONS
All measurements in inches unless noted

Year	Model		Master Cylinder Bore	Brake Disc			Brake Drum Diameter			Minimum Lining Thickness	
				Original Thickness	Minimum Thickness	Maximum Runout	Original Inside Diameter	Max. Wear Limit	Maximum Machine Diameter	Front	Rear
1989	Summit ①	—	13/16	0.510	0.449	0.006	7.10	7.2	NA	0.080	0.040
	Summit ②	front	7/8	0.940	0.882	0.006	—	—	—	0.080	0.080
		rear	—	0.390	0.331	0.006	—	—	—	0.080	0.080
1990	Summit ①	—	13/16	0.510	0.449	0.006	7.10	7.2	NA	0.080	0.040
	Summit ②	front	7/8	0.940	0.882	0.006	—	—	—	0.080	0.080
		rear	—	0.390	0.331	0.006	—	—	—	0.080	0.080
	Laser	front	③	0.940	0.882	0.003	—	—	—	0.080	0.080
		rear	—	0.390	0.331	0.003	—	—	—	0.080	0.080
	Talon	front	③	0.940	0.882	0.003	—	—	—	0.080	0.080
		rear	—	0.390	0.331	0.003	—	—	—	0.080	0.080
1991	Summit ④	—	13/16	0.510	0.449	0.006	7.10	7.2	NA	0.080	0.040
	Summit ⑤	—	7/8	0.710	0.646	0.006	7.10	7.2	NA	0.080	0.040
	Laser	front	⑥	0.940	0.882	0.003	—	—	—	0.080	0.080
		rear	—	0.390	0.331	0.003	—	—	—	0.080	0.080
	Talon	front	⑥	0.940	0.882	0.003	—	—	—	0.080	0.080
		rear	—	0.390	0.331	0.003	—	—	—	0.080	0.080
	Stealth ⑦	front	⑨	0.940	0.880	0.003	—	—	—	0.080	0.080
		rear	—	0.710	0.650	0.003	—	—	—	0.080	0.080
	Stealth ⑧	front	1 1/16	1.180	1.120	0.003	—	—	—	0.080	0.080
		rear	—	0.790	0.720	0.003	—	—	—	0.080	0.080
1992–93	Summit ④	—	13/16	0.510	0.449	0.006	7.10	7.2	NA	0.080	0.040
	Summit ⑤	—	7/8	0.710	0.646	0.006	7.10	7.2	NA	0.080	0.040
	Laser	front	⑥	0.940	0.882	0.003	—	—	—	0.080	0.080
		rear	—	0.390	0.331	0.003	—	—	—	0.080	0.080
	Talon	front	⑥	0.940	0.882	0.003	—	—	—	0.080	0.080
		rear	—	0.390	0.331	0.003	—	—	—	0.080	0.080
	Stealth ⑦	front	⑨	0.940	0.880	0.003	—	—	—	0.080	0.080
		rear	—	0.710	0.650	0.003	—	—	—	0.080	0.080
	Stealth ⑧	front	1 1/16	1.180	1.120	0.003	—	—	—	0.080	0.080
		rear	—	0.790	0.720	0.003	—	—	—	0.080	0.080
	Summit Wagon	front	⑩	0.945	0.882	0.003	—	—	—	0.080	0.040
		rear	—	0.394	0.331	0.003	⑪	⑫	—	0.080	0.040

NA—Not available
① 1.5L engine
② 1.6L engine
③ Non-turbocharged engine: 7/8
   Turbocharged engine: 15/16
④ Hatchback
⑤ Sedan

⑥ Non-turbocharged without ABS: 7/8
   Non-turbocharged with ABS: 15/16
   Turbocharged with FWD: 15/16
   Turbocharged with AWD: 1
⑦ FWD—Front Wheel Drive
⑧ AWD—All Wheel Drive
⑨ Without ABS: 1
   With ABS: 1 1/16

⑩ Without ABS: 15/16
   With ABS: 1
⑪ 8 in. drum: 7.992
   9 in. drum: 9.0
⑫ 8 in. drum 8.071
   9 in. drum 9.079

WHEEL ALIGNMENT

Year	Model		Caster Range (deg.)	Caster Preferred Setting (deg.)	Camber Range (deg.)	Camber Preferred Setting (deg.)	Toe-in (in.)	Steering Axis Inclination (deg.)
1989	Summit	front	2P–3P	$2\frac{1}{3}$P	$\frac{1}{2}$N–$\frac{1}{2}$P	0	0	—
		rear	—	—	1N–0	$\frac{2}{3}$N	0	—
1990	Summit	front	2P–3P	$2\frac{1}{3}$P	$\frac{1}{2}$N–$\frac{1}{2}$P	0	0	—
		rear	—	—	1N–0	$\frac{2}{3}$N	0	—
	Laser [1]	front	$1\frac{5}{16}$P–$2\frac{5}{6}$P	$2\frac{1}{3}$P	$\frac{4}{15}$N–$\frac{11}{15}$P	$\frac{7}{30}$	0	—
		rear	—	—	$1\frac{1}{4}$N–$\frac{1}{4}$N	$\frac{3}{4}$N	0	—
	Laser [2]	front	$1\frac{9}{10}$P–$2\frac{9}{10}$P	$2\frac{2}{5}$P	$\frac{5}{12}$N–$\frac{7}{12}$P	$\frac{1}{12}$P	0	—
		rear	—	—	$1\frac{1}{4}$N–$\frac{1}{4}$N	$\frac{3}{4}$N	0	—
	Laser [3]	front	$1\frac{4}{5}$P–$2\frac{4}{5}$P	$2\frac{3}{10}$P	$\frac{1}{3}$N–$\frac{2}{3}$P	$\frac{1}{6}$P	0	—
		rear	—	—	$2\frac{1}{20}$N–$1\frac{1}{20}$N	$1\frac{11}{20}$N	0.14	—
	Talon [2]	front	$1\frac{9}{10}$P–$2\frac{9}{10}$P	$2\frac{2}{5}$P	$\frac{5}{12}$N–$\frac{7}{12}$P	$\frac{1}{12}$P	0	—
		rear	—	—	$1\frac{1}{4}$N–$\frac{1}{4}$P	$\frac{3}{4}$N	0	—
	Talon [3]	front	$1\frac{4}{5}$P–$2\frac{4}{5}$P	$2\frac{3}{10}$P	$\frac{1}{3}$N–$\frac{2}{3}$P	$\frac{1}{6}$P	0	—
		rear	—	—	$2\frac{1}{20}$N–$1\frac{1}{20}$P	$1\frac{11}{20}$N	0.14	—
1991	Summit	front	$1\frac{5}{6}$P–$2\frac{5}{6}$P	$2\frac{1}{3}$P	$\frac{1}{2}$N–$\frac{1}{2}$P	0	0	—
		rear	—	—	$1\frac{1}{6}$N–$\frac{1}{6}$N	$\frac{2}{3}$N	0	—
	Laser [1]	front	$1\frac{5}{16}$P–$2\frac{5}{6}$P	$2\frac{1}{3}$P	$\frac{4}{15}$N–$\frac{11}{15}$P	$\frac{7}{30}$	0	—
		rear	—	—	$1\frac{1}{4}$N–$\frac{1}{4}$N	$\frac{3}{4}$N	0	—
	Laser [2]	front	$1\frac{9}{10}$P–$2\frac{9}{10}$P	$2\frac{2}{5}$P	$\frac{5}{12}$N–$\frac{7}{12}$P	$\frac{1}{12}$P	0	—
		rear	—	—	$1\frac{1}{4}$N–$\frac{1}{4}$N	$\frac{3}{4}$N	0	—
	Laser [3]	front	$1\frac{4}{5}$P–$2\frac{4}{5}$P	$2\frac{3}{10}$P	$\frac{1}{3}$N–$\frac{2}{3}$P	$\frac{1}{6}$P	0	—
		rear	—	—	$2\frac{1}{20}$N–$1\frac{1}{20}$N	$1\frac{11}{20}$N	0.14	—
	Talon [2]	front	$1\frac{9}{10}$P–$2\frac{9}{10}$P	$2\frac{2}{5}$P	$\frac{5}{12}$N–$\frac{7}{12}$P	$\frac{1}{12}$P	0	—
		rear	—	—	$1\frac{1}{4}$N–$\frac{1}{4}$P	$\frac{3}{4}$N	0	—
	Talon [3]	front	$1\frac{4}{5}$P–$2\frac{4}{5}$P	$2\frac{3}{10}$P	$\frac{1}{3}$N–$\frac{2}{3}$P	$\frac{1}{6}$P	0	—
		rear	—	—	$2\frac{1}{20}$N–$1\frac{1}{20}$P	$1\frac{11}{20}$N	0.14	—
	Stealth	front	$3\frac{5}{12}$P–$4\frac{5}{12}$P	$3\frac{11}{12}$P	$\frac{1}{2}$N–$\frac{1}{2}$P	0	0.12	—
		rear	—	—	[4]	[5]	0.01	—
1992–93	Summit	front	$1\frac{5}{6}$P–$2\frac{5}{6}$P	$2\frac{1}{3}$P	$\frac{1}{2}$N–$\frac{1}{2}$P	0	0	—
		rear	—	—	$1\frac{1}{6}$N–$\frac{1}{6}$N	$\frac{2}{3}$N	0	—
	Laser [1]	front	$1\frac{5}{16}$P–$2\frac{5}{6}$P	$2\frac{1}{3}$P	$\frac{4}{15}$N–$\frac{11}{15}$P	$\frac{7}{30}$P	0	—
		rear	—	—	$1\frac{1}{4}$N–$\frac{1}{4}$N	$\frac{3}{4}$N	0	—
	Laser [2]	front	$1\frac{9}{10}$P–$2\frac{9}{10}$P	$2\frac{2}{5}$P	$\frac{5}{12}$N–$\frac{7}{12}$P	$\frac{1}{12}$P	0	—
		rear	—	—	$1\frac{1}{4}$N–$\frac{1}{4}$N	$\frac{3}{4}$N	0	—
	Laser [3]	front	$1\frac{4}{5}$P–$2\frac{4}{5}$P	$2\frac{3}{10}$P	$\frac{1}{3}$N–$\frac{2}{3}$P	$\frac{1}{6}$P	0	—
		rear	—	—	$2\frac{1}{20}$N–$1\frac{1}{20}$N	$1\frac{11}{20}$N	0.14	—
	Talon [2]	front	$1\frac{9}{10}$P–$2\frac{9}{10}$P	$2\frac{2}{5}$P	$\frac{5}{12}$N–$\frac{7}{12}$P	$\frac{1}{12}$P	0	—
		rear	—	—	$1\frac{1}{4}$N–$\frac{1}{4}$P	$\frac{3}{4}$N	0	—
	Talon [3]	front	$1\frac{4}{5}$P–$2\frac{4}{5}$P	$2\frac{3}{10}$P	$\frac{1}{3}$N–$\frac{2}{3}$P	$\frac{1}{6}$P	0	—
		rear	—	—	$2\frac{1}{20}$N–$1\frac{1}{20}$P	$1\frac{11}{20}$N	0.14	—
	Stealth	front	$3\frac{5}{12}$P–$4\frac{5}{12}$P	$3\frac{11}{12}$P	$\frac{1}{2}$N–$\frac{1}{2}$P	0	0.12	—
		rear	—	—	[4]	[5]	0.01	—

WHEEL ALIGNMENT

Year	Model		Caster Range (deg.)	Caster Preferred Setting (deg.)	Camber Range (deg.)	Camber Preferred Setting (deg.)	Toe-in (in.)	Steering Axis Inclination (deg.)
1992-93	Summit Wagon ⑩	front	⑥	⑦	⑧	⑨	0.12	—
		rear	—	—	1N–0	½N	0.08	—

N—Negative
P—Positive
① 1.8L engine
② 2.0L engine with FWD
③ AWD—All Wheel Drive
④ FWD: ½N–½P
   AWD: ⅔N–⅓P

⑤ FWD: 0
   AWD: ⅙N
⑥ FWD: 1½P–2⅚P
   AWD: 1⁵/₁₂P–2¾P
⑦ FWD: 2⅙P
   AWD: 2½P

⑧ FWD: ¹/₁₆N–⁵/₁₆P
   AWD: ⅙P–1¹/₁₆P
⑨ FWD: ⅓P
   AWD: ⅔P
⑩ Camber & Caster are preset and cannot be adjusted. If Camber is not within specifications, check for bent or damaged parts.

ENGINE MECHANICAL

NOTE: Disconnecting the negative battery cable on some vehicles may interfere with the functions of the on board computer systems and may require the computer to undergo a relearning process, once the negative battery cable is reconnected.

Engine Assembly

REMOVAL & INSTALLATION

The following procedure can be used on all vehicles. Slight variations may occur due to extra connections, etc., but the basic procedure should cover all models.

1. Relieve fuel system pressure.
2. Disconnect the negative battery cable. Remove the under cover if equipped.
3. Matchmark the hood and hinges and remove the hood assembly. Remove the air cleaner assembly and all adjoining air intake duct work.
4. Drain the Engine coolant and remove the radiator assembly, coolant reservoir and intercooler.
5. Remove the transaxle and transfer case if equippped with AWD.
6. Disconnect and tag for assembly reference the connections for the accelerator cable, heater hoses, brake vacuum hose, connection for vacuum hoses, high pressure fuel line, fuel return line, oxygen sensor connection, coolant temperature gauge connection, coolant temperature sensor connector, connection for thermo switch sensor, if equipped with automatic transaxle, the connection for the idle speed control, the motor position sensor connector, the throttle position sensor connector, the EGR temperature sensor connection (California vehicles), the fuel injector connectors, the power transistor connector, the ignition coil connector, the condenser and noise filter connector, the distributor and control harness, the connections for the alternator and oil pressure switch wires.

7. Remove the air conditioner drive belt and the air conditioning compressor. Leave the hoses attached. Do not discharge the system. Wire the compressor aside.
8. Remove the power steering pump and wire aside.
9. Remove the exhaust manifold to head pipe nuts. Discard the gasket.
10. Attach a hoist to the Engine and take up the Engine weight. Remove the Engine mount bracket. Remove any torque control brackets (roll stoppers). Note that some Engine mount pieces have arrows on them for proper assembly. Double check that all cables, hoses, harness connectors, etc., are disconnected from the Engine. Lift the Engine slowly from the Engine compartment.

To install:

11. Install the Engine and secure in position. The front lower mount through bolt nut should not be tightened until the full weight of the Engine is on the mount. Tightening the Engine mount bolts as followings:

Summit

Upper mount to Engine nuts and bolts—36–47 ft. lbs. (50–65 Nm)

Upper mount through bolt nut—65–80 ft. lbs. (90–110 Nm)

Lower mount through bolt nut—33–43 ft. lbs. (45–60 Nm)

Summit Wagon

Upper mount to Engine nuts and bolts—42 ft. lbs. (58 Nm)

Upper mount through bolt nut—51 ft. lbs. (70 Nm)

Lower mount through bolt nut FWD—40 ft. lbs. (55 Nm)

Lower mount through bolt nut AWD—38 ft. lbs. (53 Nm)

Laser and Talon

Upper mount to Engine nuts and bolts—36–47 ft. lbs. (50–65 Nm)

Upper mount through bolt nut—43–58 ft. lbs. (60–80 Nm)

Lower mount through bolt nut—33–43 ft. lbs. (45–60 Nm)

Stealth

Upper mount to Engine nuts and bolts—72–87 ft. lbs. (100–120 Nm)

Upper mount through bolt nut—51 ft. lbs. (70 Nm)

Lower mount through bolt nut—36–43 ft. lbs. (47–60 Nm).

12. Install the exhaust pipe, power steering pump and air conditioning compressor.
13. Checking the tags installed during removal, reconnect all electrical and vacuum connections.
14. Install the transaxle to the vehicle and tighten the upper mounting bolts to 65 ft. lbs (90 Nm). Install the starter assembly and tighten both mounting bolts to 54–65 ft. lbs. (75–90 Nm).
15. Install the radiator assembly and intercooler.
16. Install the air cleaner assembly. Install all control brackets, if not already done.
17. Fill the Engine with the proper amount of Engine oil. Connect the negative battery cable.
18. Refill the cooling system. Start the Engine, allow it to reach normal operating temperature. Check for leaks.
19. Check the ignition timing and adjust, if necessary.
20. Install the hood.
21. Road test the vehicle and check all functions for proper operation.

Engine Mounts

REMOVAL & INSTALLATION

1. Disconnect the negative battery cable. Remove the air cleaner and all necessary air duct work.
2. Raise and safely support the Engine so it is not resting on the Engine mount. One suggested way is a block of wood between a floor jack and the oil pan. Use care not to bend or damage any components.
3. Remove the retainer bolt from

the clamp securing the power steering pressure hose and the air conditioning low pressure hose.

4. Remove the Engine mount bracket and body connection through bolt. Take note of the position of the arrow on the oval shaped mounting stopper plate. This is important.

5. Remove the Engine mounting bracket and stopper plate.

6. Lower mounts (roll stoppers) are removed by removing the through bolt, then the frame bolts. On Stealth, the condenser fan assembly and front catalytic converter must first be removed to gain access to the front mount.

To install:

7. Install the Engine mounting bracket and stopper plate. Note the arrows on the stopper plates and make sure they are installed properly. On most Engines the arrows will face the towards the center of the Engine.

8. Install the lower front roll stopper so the part of the bracket with the hole in it is facing the front of the vehicle.

9. The front lower mount through bolt nut should not be tightened until the full weight of the Engine is on the mount. Torque specifications are as follows:

Summit

Upper mount to Engine nuts and bolts—36–47 ft. lbs. (50–65 Nm)

Upper mount through bolt nut—65–80 ft. lbs. (90–110 Nm)

Lower mount through bolt nut—33–43 ft. lbs. (45–60 Nm)

Summit Wagon

Upper mount to Engine nuts and bolts—42 ft. lbs. (58 Nm)

Upper mount through bolt nut—51 ft. lbs. (70 Nm)

Lower mount through bolt nut FWD—40 ft. lbs. (55 Nm)

Lower mount through bolt nut AWD—38 ft. lbs. (53 Nm)

Laser and Talon

Upper mount to Engine nuts and bolts—36–47 ft. lbs. (50–65 Nm)

Upper mount through bolt nut—43–58 ft. lbs. (60–80 Nm)

Lower mount through bolt nut—33–43 ft. lbs. (45–60 Nm)

Stealth

Upper mount to Engine nuts and bolts—72–87 ft. lbs. (100–120 Nm)

Upper mount through bolt nut—51 ft. lbs. (70 Nm)

Lower mount through bolt nut—36–43 ft. lbs. (47–60 Nm).

10. Install the remaining items removed and roadtest the vehicle.

Cylinder Head

REMOVAL & INSTALLATION

1.5L and 1.8L (Laser) Engines

1. Relieve the fuel system pressure. Disconnect the negative battery cable.

2. Drain the cooling system.

3. Remove the air intake hose and the breather hose.

4. Disconnect the accelerator cable. There will be 2 cables, if equipped with cruise-control.

5. Place a shop towel around the high presure fuel line to absorb any residual fuel remaining in the system. Disconnect the high pressure fuel line.

6. Remove the upper radiator hose, the water breather hose, the water bypass hose and the heater hose.

7. Disconnect the PCV hose.

8. Remove the spark plug cables.

9. Disconnect and plug the fuel return line.

10. Disconnect the vacuum line for the brake booster.

11. Disconnect the electrical connections for the oxygen sensor, Engine coolant temperature gauge unit and the water temperature sensor.

12. Disconnect the electrical connections for the idle speed control motor, throttle position sensor, distributor, motor position sensor connector, fuel injectors, EGR temperature sensor (California vehicles), power transistor, condenser and ground cable.

13. Disconnect the Engine control wiring harness.

14. Remove the clamp that holds the power steering pressure hose to the Engine mounting bracket.

15. Place a jack and wood block under the oil pan and carefully lift just enough to take the weight off the Engine mounting bracket. Then remove the bracket.

16. Remove the valve cover, gasket and half-round seal.

17. Remove the timing belt front upper cover.

18. If possible, rotate the crankshaft clockwise until the timing marks on the cam sprocket and belt align. Remove the sprocket bolt and remove the sprocket with the timing belt attached. On 1.8L Engine, place on the timing belt front lower cover. On 1.5L Engine, attach a flexible cord to the hood and suspend the sprocket so it cannot turn. Remove the timing belt rear upper cover.

19. Remove the exhaust pipe self-locking nuts and separate the exhaust pipe from the exhaust manifold. Discard the gasket.

20. Loosen the cylinder head mounting bolts in 3 Steps, starting from the outside and working inward. Lift off the cylinder head assembly and remove the head gasket.

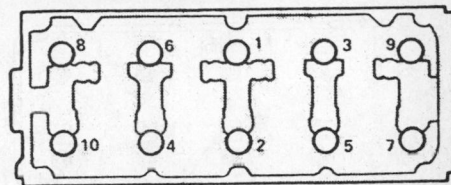

← FRONT OF Engine

Cylinder head torque sequence—1.5L, 1.6L, 1.8L and 2.0L Engines

To install:

21. Thoroughly clean and dry the mating surfaces of the head and block. Check the cylinder head for cracks, damage or Engine coolant leakage. Remove scale, sealing compound and carbon. Clean oil passages throughly. Check the head for flatness. End to end, the head should be within 0.002 in. normally with 0.008 in. the maximum allowed out of true. The total thickness allowed to be removed from the head and block is 0.008 in. maximum.

22. Place a new head gasket on the cylinder block with the identification marks facing upward. Make sure the gasket has the proper identification mark for the Engine. Do not use sealer on the gasket.

23. Carefully install the cylinder head on the block. Using 3 even Steps, torque the head bolts in sequence, to 51–54 ft. lbs. (70–75 Nm).

24. Install a new exhaust pipe gasket and connect the exhaust pipe to the manifold. Install the upper rear timing cover.

25. Align the timing marks and install the cam sprocket. Torque the retaining bolt to 47–54 ft. lbs. (65–75 Nm) on 1.5L Engine or 58–72 ft. lbs. (80–100 Nm) on 1.8L Engine. Check the belt tension and adjust, if necessary. Install the outer timing cover.

26. Apply sealer to the perimeter of the half-round seal. Install a new valve cover gasket. Install the valve cover.

27. Install the Engine mount bracket. Once secure, remove the jack.

28. Install the clamp that holds the power steering pressure hose to the Engine mounting bracket.

29. Connect or install all previously disconnected hoses, cables and electrical connections. Adjust the throttle cable(s).

30. Replace the O-rings and connect the fuel lines.

31. Install the air intake hose. Connect the breather hose.

32. Change the Engine oil and oil filter.

33. Fill the system with coolant.

34. Connect the negative battery cable, run the vehicle until the thermostat opens, fill the radiator completely.

35. Check and adjust the idle speed and ignition timing.

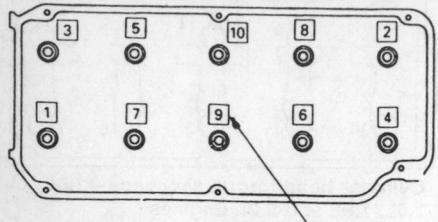

INTAKE SIDE   FRONT OF Engine ⇒

EXHAUST SIDE   LOOSENING ORDER

Cylinder head bolt removal sequence – 1.8L Engine – Summit Wagon

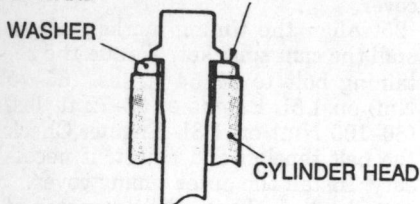

IDENTIFICATION MARK "G9S"

INTAKE SIDE

FRONT OF Engine

EXHAUST SIDE

Install cylinder head gasket with identification mark facing upwards – 1.8L Engine – Summit Wagon

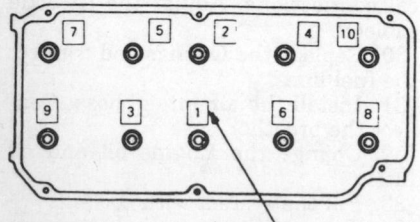

SAGGING SIDE OF WASHER IS FACING UPWARD

WASHER

CYLINDER HEAD

Correct cylinder head bolt washer Installaton – 1.8L Engine – Summit Wagon

INTAKE SIDE   FRONT OF ENGINE ⇒

EXHAUST SIDE   TIGHTENING ORDER

Cylinder head torque sequence – 1.8L Engine – Summit Wagon

36. Once the vehicle has cooled, recheck the coolant level.

1.8L Engine (Summit Wagon)

1. Relieve fuel system pressure. Disconnect the negative battery cable.

2. Drain the cooling system. Disconnect the brake booster vacuum hose and PVC valve connection.

3. Remove the upper radiator hose, overflow tube and the water hose from the thermostat to the throttle body.

4. Disconnect the air flow sensor connector. Remove the air cleaner case cover and the air intake hose.

5. Wrap the connection with a shop towel and disconnect the high pressure fuel line at the fuel rail.

6. Disconnect the fuel return hose and remove the O-ring.

7. Disconnect the accelerator cable connection from the throttle body and position aside.

8. Disconnect the electrical harnesses at the oil pressure switch, oxygen sensor, water temperature sensor connector, distributor, condenser, ISC, TPS, detonation sensor and the fuel injectors.

9. Disconnect the spark plug cables from each spark plug.

10. Unbolt the control harness assembly and position aside.

11. Remove the thermostat housing, thermostat and the thermostat case with O-ring from the Engine.

12. Remove the rocker cover.

13. Remove the timing belt upper cover.

14. Rotate the crankshaft in the forward (right) direction to align the camshaft timing marks. Matchmark the camshaft sprocket and the timing belt. Tie the camshaft sprocket and the timing belt together so the sprocket will not move with respect to the timing belt.

15. While holding the camshaft sprocket in position using the appropriate wrench, remove the camshaft sprocket and with the belt attached. Wire the sprocket and belt aside making sure constant tension is maintained on the belt. Do not allow the belt to slacken or Engine timing may be altered.

NOTE: When removing the camshaft sprocket, do not allow the crankshaft to rotate. If crankshaft rotation did occur, the Engine timing may have been changed. Confirm proper Engine timing during installation.

16. Loosen the cylinder head bolts in 2 or 3 Steps in the appropriate order and remove from the cylinder head.

17. Remove the cylinder head from the Engine.

CAUTION

When placing the removed cylinder head upside down, take care not to bend or damage the plug guide. The plug guide can not be replaced.

---

18. Remove the cylinder head gasket from the block.

To install:

19. Thoroughly clean and dry the mating surfaces of the head and block. Check the cylinder head for cracks, damage or Engine coolant leakage. Remove scale, sealing compound and carbon. Clean oil passages throughly. Check the head for flatness. End to end, the head should be within 0.002 in. normally with 0.008 in. the maximum allowed out of true. The total thickness allowed to be removed from the head and block is 0.008 in. maximum.

20. Place a new head gasket on the cylinder block with the identification marks facing upward. Make sure the gasket has the proper identification mark for the Engine. Do not use sealer on the gasket.

21. Carefully install the cylinder head on the block. Inspect the cylinder head bolt prior to installation, the length below the head of the bolts should be below the limit of 3.795 in. (96.4mm). Apply a small amount of Engine oil to the thread section and the washer of the cylinder head bolt and install so the sagging side made by tapping out the washer is facing upward. (chamfer edge faces up).

22. Tighten the cylinder head bolts in the proper order as follows:

   a. In the proper tightening sequence, torque bolts to 54 ft. lbs. (75 Nm).

   b. In the reverse order of the tightening sequence, fully loosen bolts.

   c. In the proper tightening sequence, torque bolts to 14 ft. lbs. (20 Nm).

   d. In the proper tightening sequence, tighten bolts an additional ¼ turn (90 degrees).

   e. In the proper tightening sequence, tighten bolts an additional ¼ turn (90 degrees).

23. Install the camshaft sprocket and tighten bolt to 65 ft. lbs. (90 Nm), while holding the sprocket in place using the appropriate wrench. Confirm proper timing mark alignment.

24. Install the upper timing belt cover and rocker cover.

25. Loosen the water pipe mounting bolt.

26. Apply a thin bead of sealant MD970389 or equivalent, to the water tube connection on the thermostat case.

27. Apply a small amount of water to the O-ring of the water inlet pipe and

press the thermostat case assembly onto the water inlet pipe. Install the thermostat case assembly mounting bolt tightening to 16 ft. lbs. (22 Nm).

28. Tighten the water pipe mounting bolt.

29. Install the thermostat into the housing so the jiggle valve is located at the top. Tighten the housing bolts to 10 ft. lbs. (14 Nm).

30. Connect the upper radiator hose to the thermostat housing.

31. Connect or install all previously disconnected hoses, cables and electrical connections. Adjust the throttle cable(s).

32. Replace the O-rings and reconnect the fuel lines.

33. Install the air intake hose. Connect the breather hose, air cleaner case cover and air flow sensor connector.

34. Change the Engine oil and oil filter. Reconnect the brake booster and the PCV vacuum hoses.

35. Fill the system with coolant.

36. Connect the negative battery cable, run the vehicle until the thermostat opens, fill the radiator completely.

37. Check and adjust the idle speed and ignition timing.

38. Check all systems for leaks. Allow the Engine to cool and recheck the coolant level.

2.4L Engine

1. Relieve fuel system pressure. Disconnect the negative battery cable.

2. Drain the cooling system.

3. Disconnect the accelerator cable.

4. Remove the radiator.

5. Disconnect the air flow sensor connector and the air intake hose. Remove the air cleaner cover.

6. Disconnect the PCV hose.

7. Disconnect the water hose connection at the throttle body to water inlet pipe.

8. Disconnect the water hose connection at the throttle body to thermostat hose.

9. Wrap the connection with a shop towel and disconnect the high pressure fuel line at the fuel rail.

10. Disconnect the fuel return hose and remove the O-ring.

11. Disconnect the accelerator cables connection at the throttle body.

12. Disconnect the spark plug cables from the spark plugs.

13. Disconnect the electrical connectors from the oxygen sensor, water temperature gauge unit, Engine coolant temperature sensor, TPS, power transistor connector, fuel injectors, ignition coil, distributor, and air conditioner compressor. Label prior to disconnecting to assure correct relocation on assembly.

14. Remove the bolt retaining the power steering hose and air conditioner hose clamp.

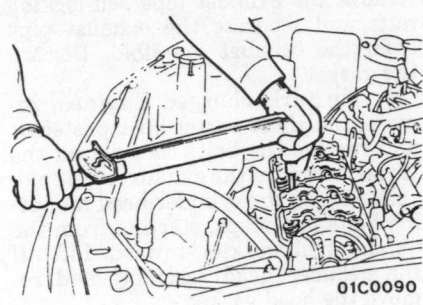

Front of engine ➡
Intake side

4	6	9	7	1
2	8	10	5	3

Exhaust side

Removal sequece of cylinder head bolts—2.4L Engine—Summit Wagon

01C0090

Front of engine ➡
Intake side

4	6	9	7	1
2	8	10	5	3

Exhaust side

Cylinder head bolt torque sequence— 2.4L Engine

Identification mark "64 C" Carved mark

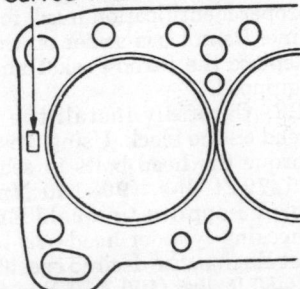

Identification mark to be position on the upper surface during Installation—2.4L Engine

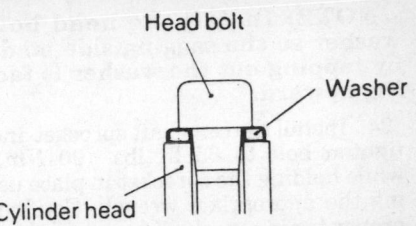

Correct Installation of cylinder head bolt washer—2.4L Engine. Sagging side made by tapping out the washer facing upward.

15. Remove the coolant reservoir. Remove the bolt holding the ground wire to the manifold.

16. Place a jack and wood block under the oil pan and carefully lift just enough to take the weight off the Engine mounting bracket. Then remove the Engine mounting bracket taking note of the position of the mount stopper.

17. Remove the valve cover, gasket and half-round seal.

18. Remove the timing belt front upper cover.

19. If possible, rotate the crankshaft clockwise until the timing marks on the cam sprocket and belt align. Matchmark the timing sprocket to the belt. Remove the sprocket bolt and remove the sprocket with the timing belt attached. Attach a flexible cord to the hood and suspend the sprocket so it cannot turn and there is no slack in the belt. Remove the timing belt rear upper cover.

20. Loosen the head bolts in the correct sequence in 2 or 3 steps. Remove the cylinder head bolts and head assembly from the block.

To install:

21. Thoroughly clean and dry the mating surfaces of the head and block. Check the cylinder head for cracks, damage or Engine coolant leakage. Remove scale, sealing compound and carbon. Clean oil passages throughly. Check the head for flatness. End to end, the head should be within 0.002 in. normally with 0.008 in. the maximum allowed out of true. The total thickness allowed to be removed from the head and block is 0.008 in. maximum.

22. Place a new head gasket on the cylinder block with the identification marks at the top (upward) position. Make sure the gasket has the proper identification mark for the Engine. Do not use sealer on the gasket. Replace the turbo gasket and ring, if equipped.

23. Carefully install the cylinder head on the block. Install the cylinder head bolts and washer torquing in 3 even progressions to 76–83 ft. lbs. (105–115 Nm). This torque applies to a cold Engine.

NOTE: Install the head bolt washer so the sagging side made by tapping out the washer is facing upward.

24. Install the camshaft sprocket and tighten bolt to 65 ft. lbs. (90 Nm), while holding the sprocket in place using the appropriate wrench. Confirm proper timing mark alignment.

25. Apply sealer to the perimeter of the half-round seal and to the lower edges of the half-round portions of the belt-side of the new gasket. Install the valve cover.

26. Install the Engine mount positioning the stopper in the same direction as it was prior to removal.

27. Install the power steering and air conditioning compressor hose clamp in position and secure with the retainer bolt. Tighten the bolt to 9 ft. lbs. (12 Nm).

28. Install the coolant reservoir tank.

29. Reconnect all electrical harness connectors disconnect during disassembly. Connect the ground wire to the manifold.

30. Connect the accelerator cables and the spark plug cables.

31. Replace the O-rings and reconnect the fuel lines.

32. Reconnect the water hoses to throttle body, thermostat and the heater assembly.

33. Install the air intake case cover, air flow sensor connector and the radiator.

34. Fill the system with coolant. Adjust the accelerator cable.

35. Firmly set the parking brake. Start the Engine and allow to idle until the thermostat opens, add coolant as required to fill system to the appropriate level.

36. Check all systems for leaks. Allow the Engine to cool and recheck the coolant level.

1.6L and 2.0L Engines

1. Relieve fuel system pressure. Disconnect the negative battery cable.

2. Drain the cooling system.

3. Disconnect the accelerator cable. There will be 2 cables if equipped with cruise-control.

4. Remove the air cleaner with the air intake hose.

5. Disconnect the oxygen sensor, Engine coolant temperature sensor, the Engine coolant temperature gauge unit and the Engine coolant temperature switch on vehicles with air conditioning.

6. Disconnect the ISC motor, throttle position sensor, crankshaft angle sensor, fuel injectors, ignition coil, power transistor, noise filter, knock sensor on turbocharged Engines, EGR temperature sensor (California vehi-

cles), ground cable and Engine control wiring harness.

7. Remove the upper radiator hose and the overflow tube.

8. Remove the spark plug cable center cover and remove the spark plug cables.

9. Disconnect and plug the high pressure fuel line.

10. Disconnect the small vacuum hoses.

11. Remove the heater hose and water bypass hose.

12. Remove the PCV hose.

13. If turbocharged, remove the vacuum hoses, water line and eyebolt connection for the oil line for the turbo.

14. Disconnect and plug the fuel return hose.

15. Disconnect the brake booster vacuum hose.

16. Remove the timing belt.

17. Remove the valve cover and the half-round seal.

18. On non-turbocharged Engines, remove the exhaust pipe self-locking nuts and separate the exhaust pipe from the exhaust manifold. Discard the gasket.

19. On turbocharged Engines, remove the sheet metal heat protector and remove the bolts that attach the turbocharger to the exhaust manifold.

20. Loosen the cylinder head mounting bolts in 3 steps, starting from the outside and working inward. Lift off the cylinder head assembly and remove the head gasket.

To install:

21. Thoroughly clean and dry the mating surfaces of the head and block. Check the cylinder head for cracks, damage or Engine coolant leakage. Remove scale, sealing compound and carbon. Clean oil passages throughly. Check the head for flatness. End to end, the head should be within 0.002 in. normally with 0.008 in. the maximum allowed out of true. The total thickness allowed to be removed from the head and block is 0.008 in. maximum.

22. Place a new head gasket on the cylinder block with the identification marks at the front top (upward) position. Make sure the gasket has the proper identification mark for the Engine. Do not use sealer on the gasket. Replace the turbo gasket and ring, if equipped.

23. Carefully install the cylinder head on the block. Using 3 even steps, torque the head bolts in sequence to 65-72 ft. lbs. (90-100 Nm). This torque applies to a cold Engine. If checking cylinder head bolt torque on hot Engine, the desired specification is 72-80 ft. lbs. (100-110 Nm).

24. On turbocharged Engine, install the heat shield. On non-turbocharged Engine, install a new exhaust pipe gas-

ket and connect the exhaust pipe to the manifold.

25. Apply sealer to the perimeter of the half-round seal and to the lower edges of the half-round portions of the belt-side of the new gasket. Install the valve cover.

26. Install the timing belt and all related items.

27. Connect or install all previously disconnected hoses, cables and electrical connections. Adjust the throttle cable(s).

28. Install the spark plug cable center cover.

29. Replace the O-rings and connect the fuel lines.

30. Install the air cleaner and intake hose. Connect the breather hose.

31. Change the Engine oil and oil filter.

32. Fill the system with coolant.

33. Connect the negative battery cable, run the vehicle until the thermostat opens, fill the radiator completely.

34. Check and adjust the idle speed and ignition timing.

35. Once the vehicle has cooled, recheck the coolant level.

3.0L SOHC Engine

1. Relieve fuel system pressure. Disconnect the negative battery cable.

2. Drain the cooling system.

3. Remove the air intake hose.

4. Remove the exhaust manifold.

5. Remove the air intake plenum and intake manifold.

6. Remove the timing belt.

7. Remove the camshaft sprocket and rear timing belt cover.

8. Remove the power steering pump bracket. If removing the rear (right) side head, remove the alternator brace.

9. Disconnect the water inlet pipe.

10. Remove the purge pipe assembly.

11. Remove the valve cover.

12. Loosen the cylinder head mounting bolts in 3 steps, starting from the outside and working inward. Lift off the cylinder head assembly and remove the head gasket.

To install:

13. Thoroughly clean and dry the mating surfaces of the head and block. Check the cylinder head for cracks, damage or Engine coolant leakage. Remove scale, sealing compound and carbon. Clean oil passages throughly. Check the head for flatness. End to end, the head should be within 0.002 in. normally with 0.008 in. the maximum allowed out of true. The total thickness allowed to be removed from the head and block is 0.008 in. maximum.

14. Place a new head gasket on the cylinder block making sure the identification mark on the cylinder head gasket is in the front top (upward) loca-

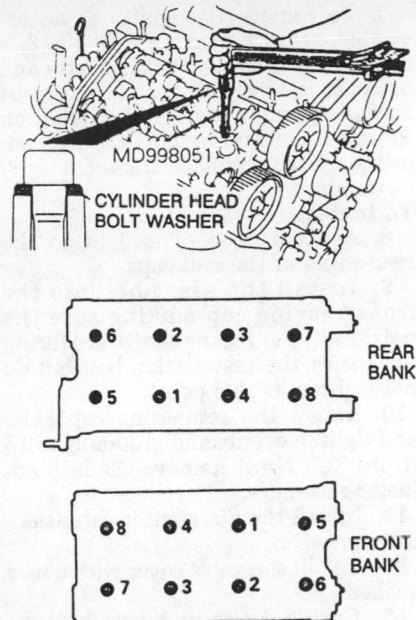

CYLINDER HEAD
BOLT WASHER

REAR
BANK

| ●6 | ●2 | ●3 | ●7 |
| ●5 | ●1 | ●4 | ●8 |

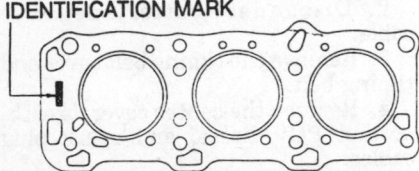

FRONT
BANK

| ●8 | ●4 | ●1 | ●5 |
| ●7 | ●3 | ●2 | ●6 |

**Cylinder head bolt installation
sequence—3.0L Engine**

IDENTIFICATION MARK

**Cylinder head gasket identification
marks—3.0L Engine**

tion. Do not use sealer on the gasket.
Make sure the gasket has the proper
identification mark for the Engine.

15. Carefully install the cylinder
head on the block. Make sure the head
bolt washers are installed with the
chamfered edge upward. Using 3 even
steps, torque the head bolts in sequence, to 76–83 ft. lbs. (105–115
Nm). This torque specifications assumes the Engine is cold.

16. Apply sealer to the lower edges of
the half-round portions of the belt-side
of the new gasket and install the valve
cover.

17. Install the purge pipe assembly.

18. Connect the water inlet pipe.

19. Install the power steering pump
bracket and alternator brace.

20. Install the rear timing belt cover
and cam sprocket. Torque the retaining bolt to 65 ft. lbs. (90 Nm).

21. Install the timing belt and all related items.

22. Using all new gaskets, install the
intake manifold, air intake plenum
and exhaust manifold, following the
proper torque sequences.

23. Install the air intake hose.

24. Change the Engine oil and oil
filter.

REAR BANK

○2		○7		○3	
○6	○11		○10		○9	5
○4		○8		○1	

FRONT BANK

○1		○8		○4	
○5	○9	○10		○11		○6
○3		○7		○2	

**Valve cover bolt installation
sequence—3.0L DOHC Engine**

25. Fill the system with coolant.

26. Connect the negative battery cable, run the vehicle until the thermostat opens, fill the radiator completely.

27. Check and adjust the idle speed
and ignition timing.

28. Once the vehicle has cooled, recheck the coolant level.

3.0L DOHC Engine

1. Relieve fuel system pressure. Disconnect the negative battery cable.

2. Drain the cooling system.

3. Remove the air intake hoses.

4. Remove air intake plenum and
intake manifold.

5. Remove the turbocharger, if
equipped, and exhaust manifold.

6. Remove the timing belt.

7. Remove the triple pipe assembly
across the top of the Engine.

8. Remove the breather hose.

9. Remove the spark plug cable center cover and remove the spark plug
cables.

10. When removing the valve cover,
note that bolts for the front head are
black and bolts for the rear head are
green. Also, all bolts are 10mm long
except the 1 closest to the sprockets on
the rear head which is 20mm long.

11. To remove the intake camshaft
sprocket, hold the camshaft with a
wrench on the hexagon near the end of
the camshaft and remove the bolt.

12. Remove the center rear timing
belt cover.

13. Remove the ignition coil.

14. Disconnect all water hoses from
the thermostat housing and remove
the housing.

15. Disconnect the water inlet from
the front head.

16. Loosen the cylinder head mounting bolts in 3 steps, starting from the
outside and working inward. Lift off
the cylinder head assembly and remove the head gasket.

To install:

17. Thoroughly clean and dry the
mating surfaces of the head and block.
Check the cylinder head for cracks,
damage or Engine coolant leakage. Remove scale, sealing compound and carbon. Clean oil passages throughly.
Check the head for flatness. End to
end, the head should be within 0.002
in. normally with 0.008 in. the maximum allowed out of true. The total
thickness allowed to be removed from
the head and block is 0.008 in.
maximum.

18. Place a new head gasket on the
cylinder block with the identification
marks in the front top (upward) position. Do not use sealer on the gasket.

19. Carefully install the cylinder
head on the block. Make sure the head
bolt washers are installed with the
chamfered edge upward. Using 3 even
steps, torque the head bolts in sequence, to 76–83 ft. lbs. (105–115 Nm)
for non-turbocharged cold Engine or
87–94 ft. lbs. (120–130 Nm) for turbocharged cold Engine.

20. Connect the water inlet to the
front head.

21. Replace the gaskets and install
the thermostat housing and connect
the hoses.

22. Install the ignition coil and center rear timing belt cover.

23. Using the same procedure as in
removal, install the intake camshaft
sprocket. Torque the retaining bolt to
65 ft. lbs. (90 Nm).

24. Apply sealer to the lower edges of
the half-round portions of the belt-side
of the new gasket and install the valve
cover. Make sure green bolts are installed on the rear head and black
bolts are installed on the front head.
Also, make sure the longest bolt is installed in its proper location closest to
the sprockets on the rear head. Tight-
en the bolts in the proper sequence to
26 inch lbs. Then retighten bolts 1–6
to 36 inch lbs.

25. Connect the spark plug cables
and install the center cover.

26. Install the breather hose.

27. Install the triple pipe assembly
across the top of the Engine and
torque the retaining bolts to 7 ft. lbs.
(10 Nm).

28. Install the timing belt and all related items.

29. Using all new gaskets, install the
intake manifold, air intake plenum,
turbocharger and exhaust manifold,
following the proper torque sequences.

30. Install the air intake hoses.

31. Change the Engine oil and oil
filter.

32. Fill the system with coolant.

34. Connect the negative battery cable, run the vehicle until the thermostat opens, fill the radiator completely.

35. Adjust the accelerator cable.
Check and adjust the idle speed and ignition timing.

36. Once the vehicle has cooled, recheck the coolant level.

Valve Lifters

REMOVAL & INSTALLATION

1.6L and 2.0L Engines

1. Release the fuel system pressure. Disconnect the negative battery cable.

2. Disconnect the accelerator cable, PCV hoses, breather hoses, spark plug cables and the remove the valve cover.

3. Rotate the crankshaft clockwise and align the timing marks so No. 1 piston will be at TDC of the compression stroke. At this time the timing marks on the camshaft sprocket and the upper surface of the cylinder head should coincide, and the dowel pin of the camshaft sprocket should be at the upper side.

NOTE: Always rotate the crankshaft in a clockwise direction. Make a mark on the back of the timing belt indicating the direction of rotation so it may be reassembled in the same direction if it is to be reused.

4. Remove the timing belt upper and lower covers.

5. Remove the timing belt.

6. Remove the crank angle sensor.

7. Remove the camshafts.

8. Visually inspect the rocker arm roller and replace if dent, damage or seizure is evident. Check the roller for smooth rotation. Replace if excess play or binding is present. Also, inspect valve contact surface for possible damage or seizure. It is recommended that all rocker arms and lash adjusters be replaced together.

To install:

9. Install the lash adjusters and rocker arms into the cylinder head. Lubricate lightly with clean oil prior to installation.

10. Apply Engine oil to the lobes and journals of each camshaft. Install the camshafts into the cylinder head taking care not to confuse the intake and the exhaust camshaft; the intake camshaft has a slit on its rear end for driving the crank angle sensor. Align shafts so dowel pins on camshaft sprocket end are located on the top.

11. Install and tighten the camshaft bearing caps in the proper sequence torquing to specifications in 3 even progressions.

12. Replace the camshaft oil seals and install the sprockets.

13. Locate the dowel pin on the sprocket end of the intake camshaft at the top position, if not already done.

14. Align the punch mark on the crank angle sensor housing with the notch on the sensor plate. Install the crank angle sensor into the cylinder head.

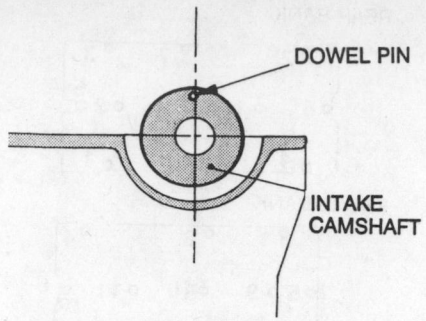

Alignment of the camshaft dowel pin prior to crank angle sensor installaton—1.6L Engine

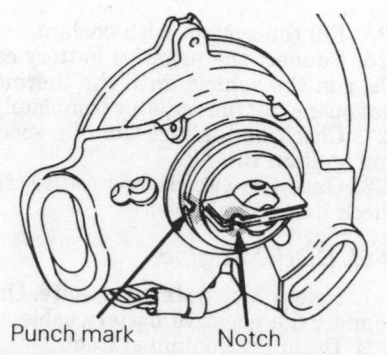

Alignment of the factory marks on crank angle sensor prior to installaton—1.6L Engine

15. Install the timing belt, covers and related components.

16. Install the valve cover using new gasket. Reconnect all related components.

17. Reconnect the negative battery cable.

1.8L, 2.4L and 3.0L SOHC Engine

1. Disconnect the negative battery cable.

2. Remove the valve cover. Install lash adjuster retainer tools MD998443 or equivalent, to the rocker arms.

3. Remove the distributor extension, if necessary.

4. Have a helper hold the rear of the camshaft down. If not, the belt will dislodge and valve timing will be lost. Remove the rear bearing cap.

5. Loosen the remaining camshaft cap retaining bolts but don't remove them from the caps. Do not loosen the forward most camshaft bearing cap bolts.

6. At this point, the shafts can be removed as an assembly for service or service of individual components can be made by sliding component to be replaced off back end of shafts. If the later method of replacement is used, keep all parts in order or removal and install parts in same location.

7. To remove the shafts as an assembly, remove bearing caps No. 2, 3 and 4, rocker arms, rocker shafts and bolts. It is essential that all parts be kept in the same order and orientation for reinstallation. Remove the lash adjuster tools to replace the adjuster(s) as reqiured.

To install:

8. Apply a drop of sealant to the rear edges of the end caps.

9. Install the assembly into the front bearing cap making sure the notches in the rocker shafts are facing up. Insert the installation bolt but do not tighten at this point.

10. Install the remaining cap bolts and tighten evenly and gradually to 15 ft. lbs. (20 Nm). Remove the lash adjuster retainers.

11. Install the distributor extension, if removed.

12. Install the valve cover with a new gasket.

13. Connect the negative battery cable.

3.0L DOHC Engine

1. Relieve the fuel system pressure.

2. Disconnect battery negative cable.

3. Remove the timing belt cover and timing belt.

4. Remove the center cover, breather and PCV hoses, and spark plug cables.

5. Remove the rocker cover, semi-circular packing, throttle body stay, both camshaft sprockets, and oil seals.

6. Remove the crank angle sensor and adaptor.

7. Remove the intake and exhaust camshafts.

8. Remove rocker arms and lash adjusters from the head. It is recommended that all lash adjusters and rockers be replaced at 1 time.

To install:

9. Immerse the lash adjusters in clean diesel fuel. Using a small wire, move the plunger of the lash adjuster up and down 4 or 5 times while pushing down lightly on the check ball in order to bleed out the air. Install the lash adjusters in the cylinder head.

10. Lubricate the camshafts with heavy Engine oil and position the camshafts on the cylinder head.

NOTE: Do not confuse the intake camshaft with the exhaust camshaft. On 1991 models, the intake camshaft has a V stamped on the hexagon of the shaft and the exhaust camshaft is stamped with a C. On 1992–93 models, the intake camshaft has a V or B stamped on the hexagon and the exhaust camshaft has a D or F.

11. Make sure the dowel pin on both

camshaft sprocket ends in the up position.

12. Install the bearing caps. Tighten the caps in sequence and in 2 or 3 steps. Caps 2, 3 and 4 have a front mark. Install with the mark aligned with the front mark on the cylinder head. Intake caps have **I** stamped on the cap and exhaust caps have **E**. Also, make sure the rocker arm is correctly mounted on the lash adjuster and the valve stem end. Torque the retaining bolts to 15 ft. lbs. (20 Nm).

13. Apply a coating of Engine oil to the oil seals and install.

14. Install the timing belt, valve cover and all related parts.

15. Connect the negative battery cable and check for leaks.

Valve Lash

ADJUSTMENT

1.5L and 1.8L (Summit Wagon) Engines

NOTE: Incorrect valve clearances will cause unsteady Engine operation, excessive noise and reduced Engine output. Check the valve clearances and adjust as required while the Engine is hot.

1. Warm the Engine to operating temperature, turn **OFF** and disconnect the negative battery cable.

2. Remove all spark plugs so Engine can be easily turned by hand.

3. Remove the valve cover.

4. Turn the crankshaft clockwise until the notch on the pulley is aligned with the **T** mark on the timing belt lower cover. This brings both No. 1 and No. 4 cylinder pistons to Top Dead Center (TDC).

5. Wiggle the rocker arms on No. 1 and No. 4 cylinders up and down to determine which cylinder is at TDC on the compression stroke. Both rocker arms should move if the piston in that cylinder is at TDC on the compression stroke.

6. Measure the valve clearance with a feeler gauge. When the No. 1 piston is at TDC on the compression stroke, check No. 1 intake and exhaust, No. 2 intake and No. 3 exhaust. Then turn the crankshaft clockwise 1 turn to bring No. 4 to TDC on its compression stroke. With No. 4 on TDC, compression stroke, check No. 2 exhaust, No. 3 intake and No. 4 intake and exhaust.

7. Valve lash specifications for 1.5L Engine: Exhaust–0.0098 in. hot or 0.0067 in. cold; Intake–0.0059 in. hot or 0.0028 in. cold.

8. Valve lash specifications for 1.8L (Summit Wagon) Engine: Intake–0.0035 in. (0.09mm) cold: Exhaust–0.0079 in. (0.20mm) cold.

9. If the valve clearances are out of specification, loosen the rocker arm locknut and adjust the clearance using a feeler gauge while turning the adjusting screw. Be sure to hold the screw to prevent it from turning when tightening the locknut.

10. After adjusting the valves, install the valve cover and spark plugs, and connect the negative battery cable.

Rocker Arms/Shafts

REMOVAL & INSTALLATION

1.5L and 1.8L (Summit Wagon) Engines

1. Disconnect the negative battery cable.

2. Remove the valve cover and discard the gasket.

3. Remove the rocker shaft hold-down bolts gradually and evenly and remove the rocker shaft/arm assemblies.

4. If disassembly is required, keep all parts in the exact order of removal. Inspect the roller surfaces of the rockers. Replace if there are any signs of damage or if the roller does not turn smoothly. Check the inside bore of the rockers and the adjuster tip for wear.

To install:

5. Lubricate the rocker shaft with clean Engine oil and install the rockers and springs in their proper places.

6. Install the rocker shaft assemblies on the Engine and tighten the

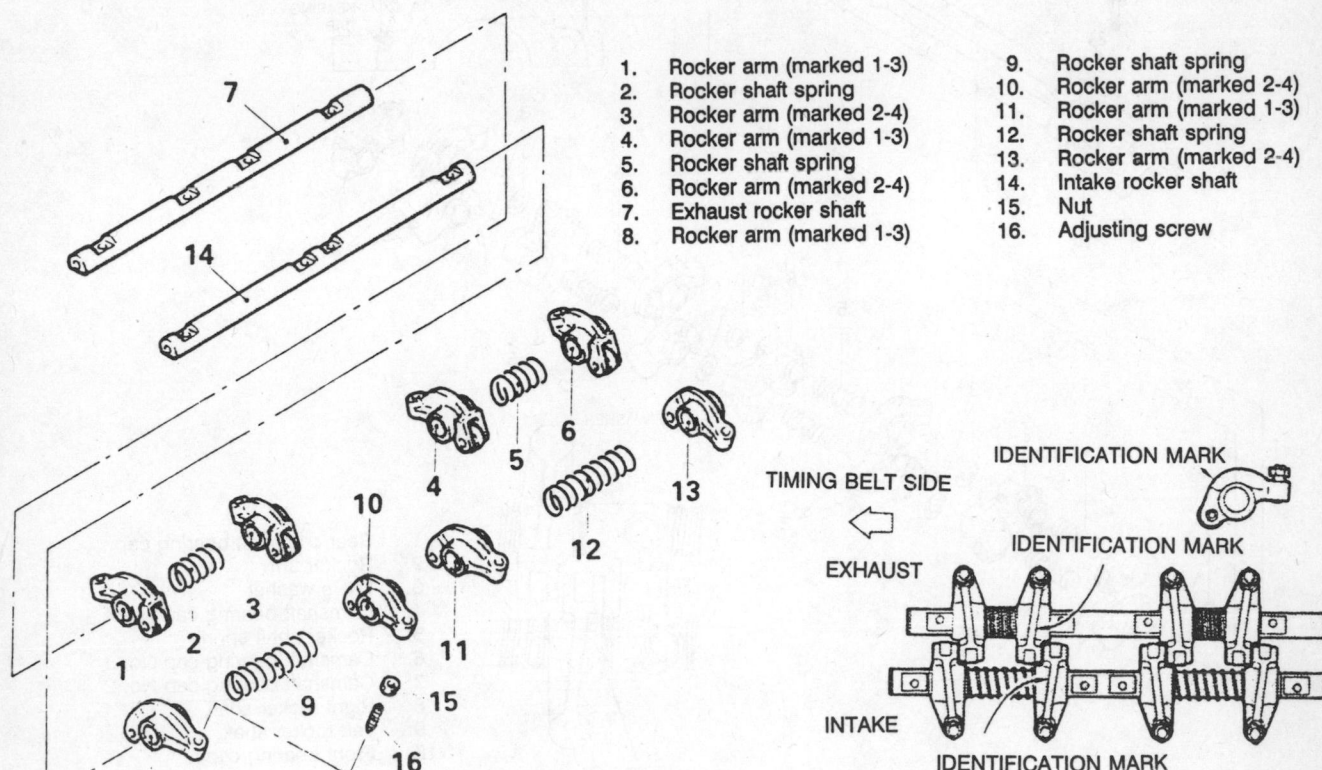

1. Rocker arm (marked 1-3)
2. Rocker shaft spring
3. Rocker arm (marked 2-4)
4. Rocker arm (marked 1-3)
5. Rocker shaft spring
6. Rocker arm (marked 2-4)
7. Exhaust rocker shaft
8. Rocker arm (marked 1-3)
9. Rocker shaft spring
10. Rocker arm (marked 2-4)
11. Rocker arm (marked 1-3)
12. Rocker shaft spring
13. Rocker arm (marked 2-4)
14. Intake rocker shaft
15. Nut
16. Adjusting screw

IDENTIFICATION MARK

TIMING BELT SIDE

IDENTIFICATION MARK

EXHAUST

INTAKE

IDENTIFICATION MARK

Rocker arm and shaft assembly—1989-90 1.5L Engine

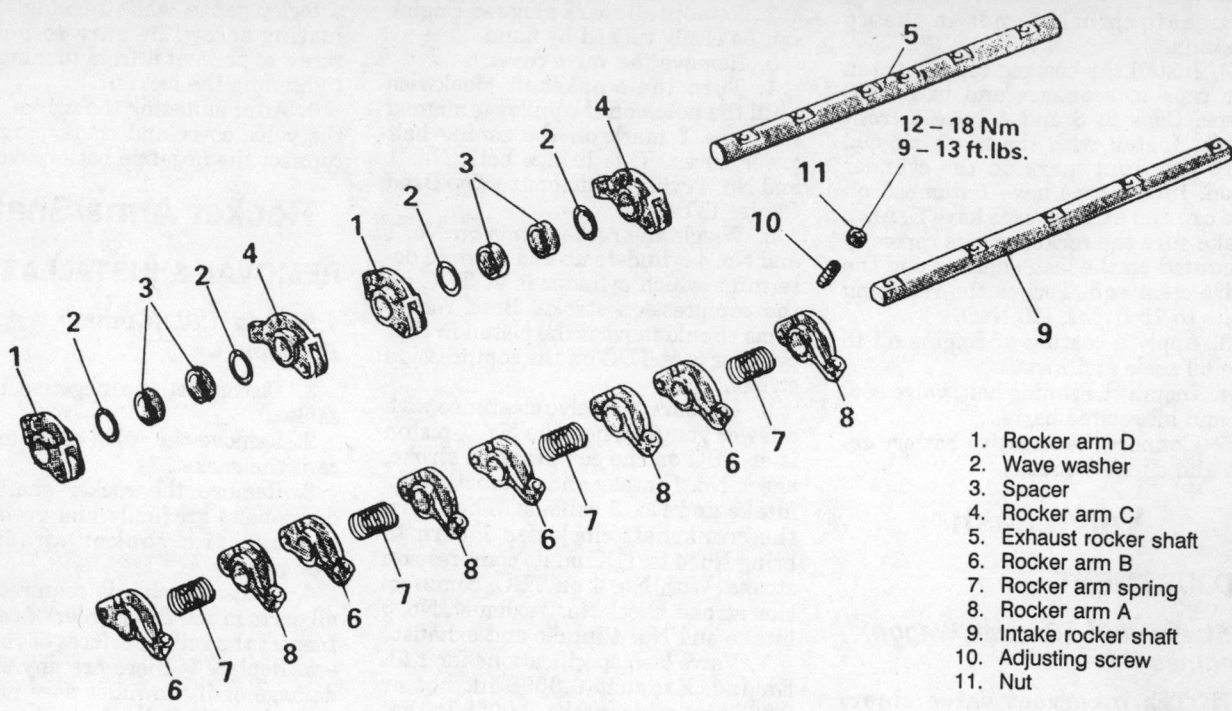

**12 – 18 Nm
9 – 13 ft.lbs.**

1. Rocker arm D
2. Wave washer
3. Spacer
4. Rocker arm C
5. Exhaust rocker shaft
6. Rocker arm B
7. Rocker arm spring
8. Rocker arm A
9. Intake rocker shaft
10. Adjusting screw
11. Nut

Rocker arm and shaft assembly—1991–93 1.5L Engine

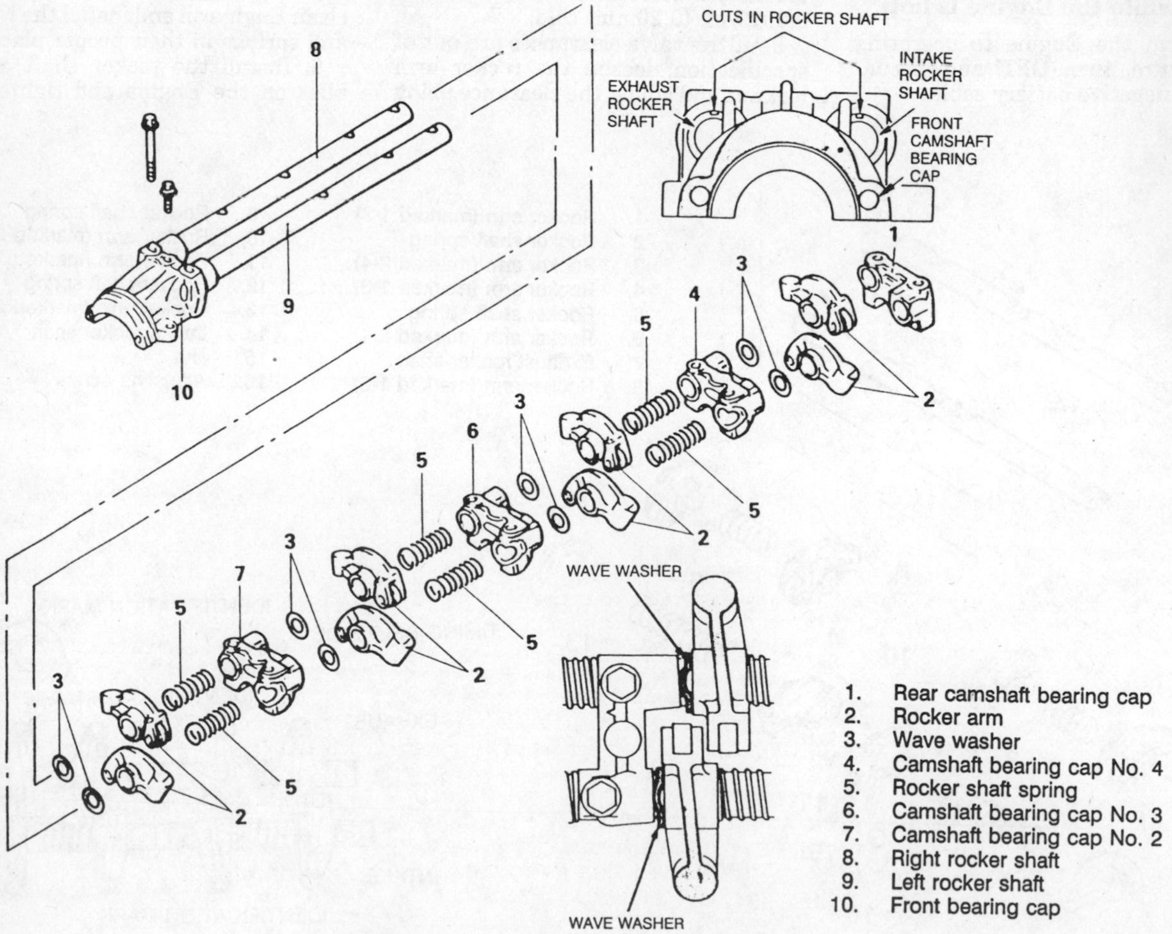

CUTS IN ROCKER SHAFT

EXHAUST ROCKER SHAFT

INTAKE ROCKER SHAFT

FRONT CAMSHAFT BEARING CAP

WAVE WASHER

WAVE WASHER

1. Rear camshaft bearing cap
2. Rocker arm
3. Wave washer
4. Camshaft bearing cap No. 4
5. Rocker shaft spring
6. Camshaft bearing cap No. 3
7. Camshaft bearing cap No. 2
8. Right rocker shaft
9. Left rocker shaft
10. Front bearing cap

Rocker arm and shaft assembly—1.8L Engine

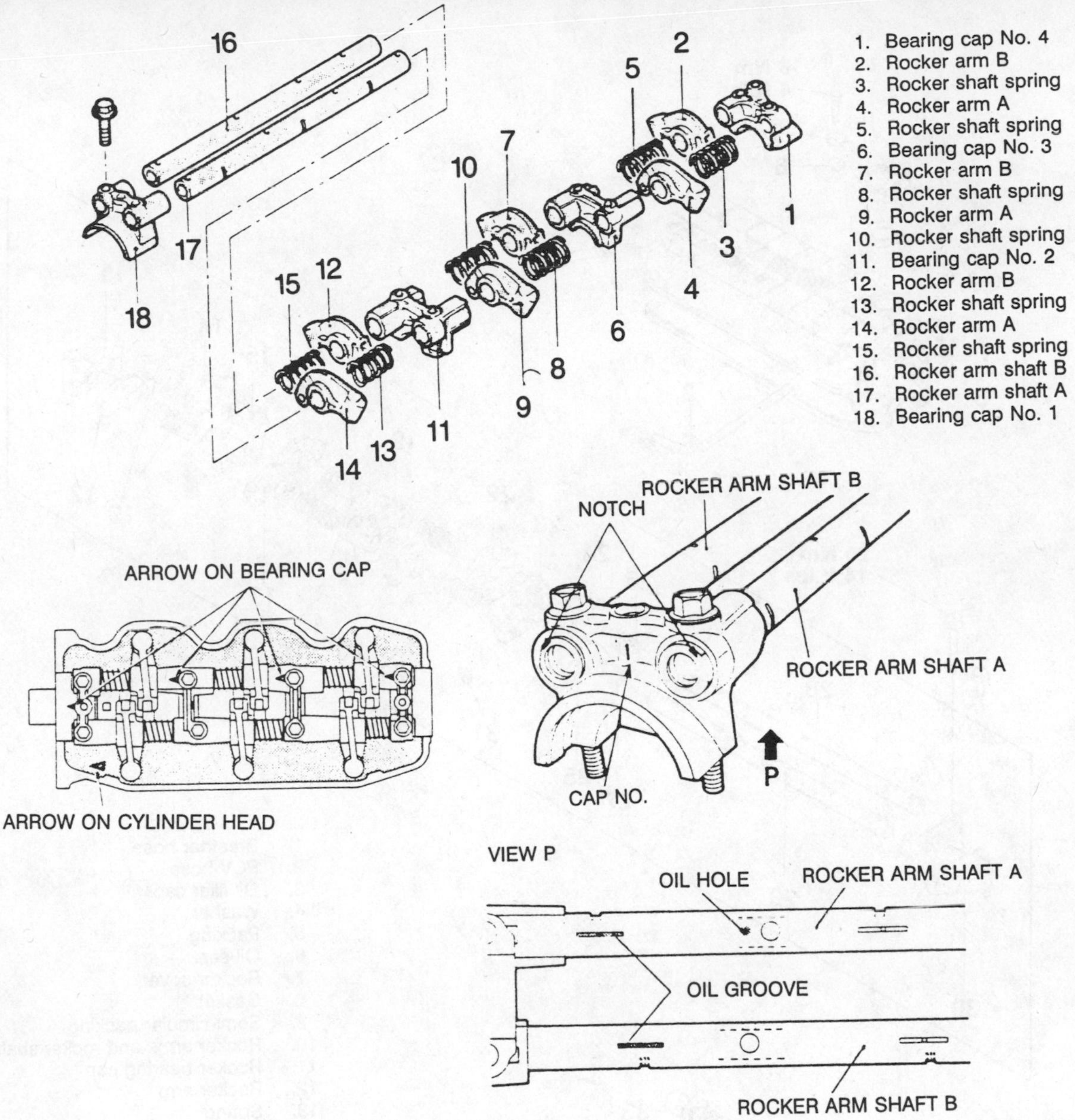

1. Bearing cap No. 4
2. Rocker arm B
3. Rocker shaft spring
4. Rocker arm A
5. Rocker shaft spring
6. Bearing cap No. 3
7. Rocker arm B
8. Rocker shaft spring
9. Rocker arm A
10. Rocker shaft spring
11. Bearing cap No. 2
12. Rocker arm B
13. Rocker shaft spring
14. Rocker arm A
15. Rocker shaft spring
16. Rocker arm shaft B
17. Rocker arm shaft A
18. Bearing cap No. 1

ARROW ON BEARING CAP

ARROW ON CYLINDER HEAD

NOTCH

ROCKER ARM SHAFT B

ROCKER ARM SHAFT A

CAP NO.

P

VIEW P

OIL HOLE   ROCKER ARM SHAFT A

OIL GROOVE

ROCKER ARM SHAFT B

Rocker arm and shaft assembly—3.0L SOHC Engine

bolts gradually and evenly. On 1.5L Engine, torque to 14–20 ft. lbs. (20–27 Nm) on 1989–90 Engines or 21–25 ft. lbs. (29–35 Nm) on 1991–93 Engines. On Summit Wagon equipped with 1.8L Engine, torque the rocker shaft bolts to 23 ft. lbs. (32 Nm).

7. Install the valve cover with a new gasket.

8. Connect the negative battery cable.

1.8L, 2.4L and 3.0L SOHC Engines

1. Disconnect the negative battery cable.

2. Remove the valve cover. Install lash adjuster retainer tools MD998443 or equivalent, to the rocker arms.

3. Remove the distributor extension, if necessary.

4. Have a helper hold the rear of the camshaft down. If not, the belt will dislodge and valve timing will be lost.

5. Loosen the camshaft cap retaining bolts but don't remove them from the caps. Remove the rear bearing cap.

6. Loosen the remaining camshaft cap retaining bolts but don't remove them from the caps. Do not loosen the forward most camshaft bearing cap bolts.

7. At this point, the shafts can be removed as an assembly for service or service of individual components can be made by sliding component to be replaced off back end of shafts. If the later method of replacement is used, only disassembly as far as needed and keep

all parts in order of removal. Installation of parts in the same location and orientation id required.

8. To remove the shafts as an assembly, remove bearing caps No. 2, 3 and 4, rocker arms, rocker shafts and bolts. It is essential that all parts be kept in the same order and orientation for reinstallation. Remove the lash adjuster tools to replace the adjuster(s) as required. Inspect the roller surfaces of the rockers. Replace if there are any signs of damage or if the roller does not turn smoothly. Check the inside bore of the rockers and lifter for wear.

To install:

9. Apply a drop of sealant to the rear edges of the end caps.

10. Install the assembly into the fron bering cap making sure the notches in

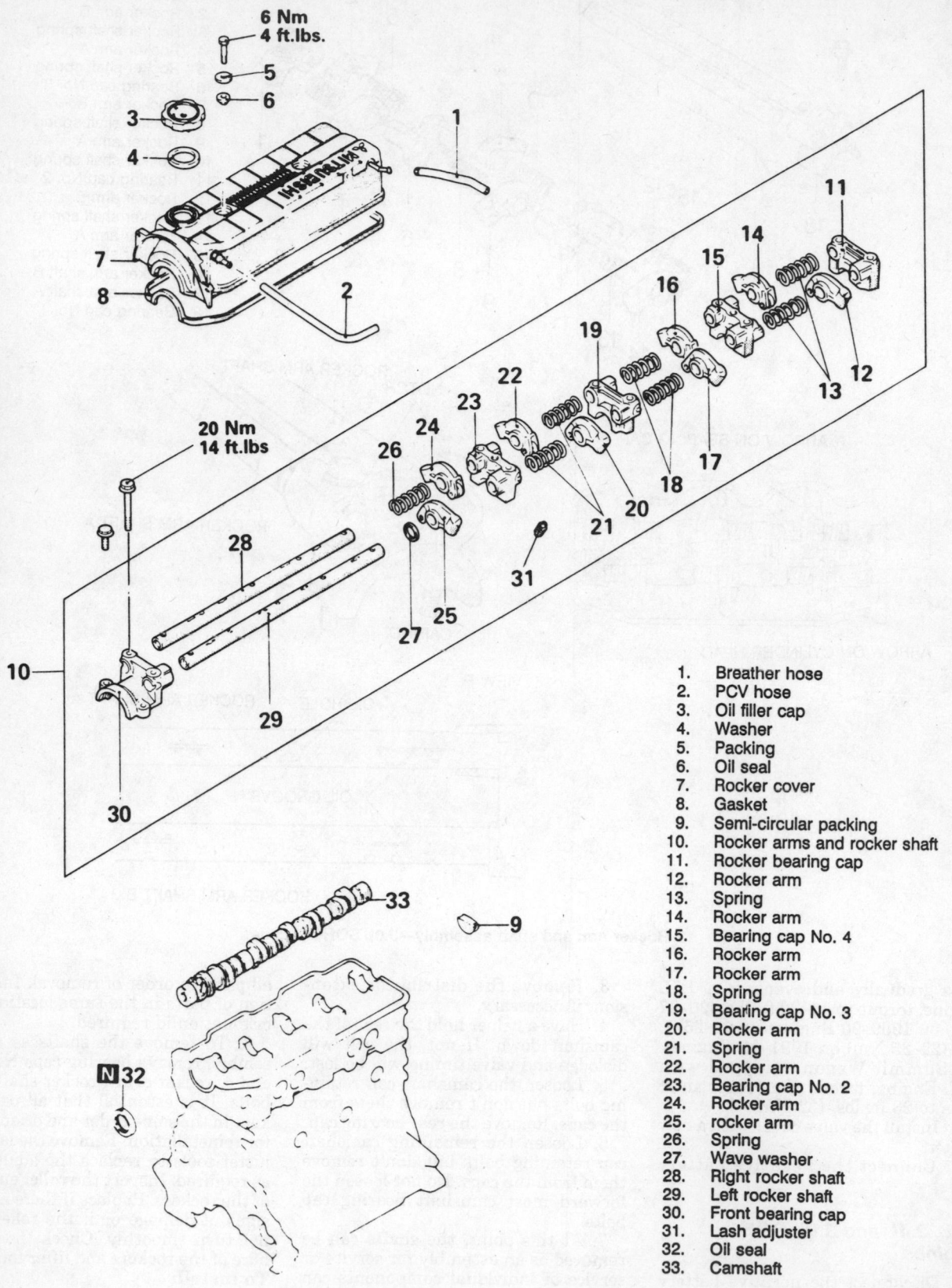

6 Nm
4 ft.lbs.

20 Nm
14 ft.lbs

1. Breather hose
2. PCV hose
3. Oil filler cap
4. Washer
5. Packing
6. Oil seal
7. Rocker cover
8. Gasket
9. Semi-circular packing
10. Rocker arms and rocker shaft
11. Rocker bearing cap
12. Rocker arm
13. Spring
14. Rocker arm
15. Bearing cap No. 4
16. Rocker arm
17. Rocker arm
18. Spring
19. Bearing cap No. 3
20. Rocker arm
21. Spring
22. Rocker arm
23. Bearing cap No. 2
24. Rocker arm
25. rocker arm
26. Spring
27. Wave washer
28. Right rocker shaft
29. Left rocker shaft
30. Front bearing cap
31. Lash adjuster
32. Oil seal
33. Camshaft

Electric cooling fan test—Summit, Summit Wagon, Laser and Talon

the rocker shafts are facing up. Insert the installation bolt but do not tighten at this point.

11. Install the remaining cap bolts and tighten evenly and gradually to 15 ft. lbs. (20 Nm). Remove the lash adjuster retainers.

12. Install the distributor extension, if removed.

13. Install the valve cover with a new gasket.

14. Connect the negative battery cable.

Air Intake Plenum and Intake Manifold

REMOVAL & INSTALLATION

Except 3.0L Engine

1. Relieve the fuel system pressure.
2. Disconnect battery negative cable and drain the cooling system.
3. Disconnect the accelerator cable, breather hose and air intake hose.

4. Disconnect the upper radiator hose, heater hose and water bypass hose.

5. Remove all vacuum hoses and pipes as necessary, including the brake booster vacuum line.

6. Disconnect the high pressure fuel line, fuel return hose and remove throttle control cable brackets.

7. Tag and disconnect the electrical connectors from the oxygen sensor, coolant temperature sensor, thermo switch, idle speed control connection,

1. Fuel rail and injectors
2. Insulator
3. Insulator
4. Bracket
5. Engine hanger
6. Thermostat housing
7. Intake manifold
8. Gasket
9. Throttle body
10. Gasket
11. Bracket
12. Air intake plenum
13. Gasket
14. Cover (except California)
15. Gasket (except California)
16. EGR valve (California vehicles)
17. Gasket (California vehicles)
18. EGR temperature sensor (California vehicles)
19. Thermostat housing
20. Gasket
21. Thermostat

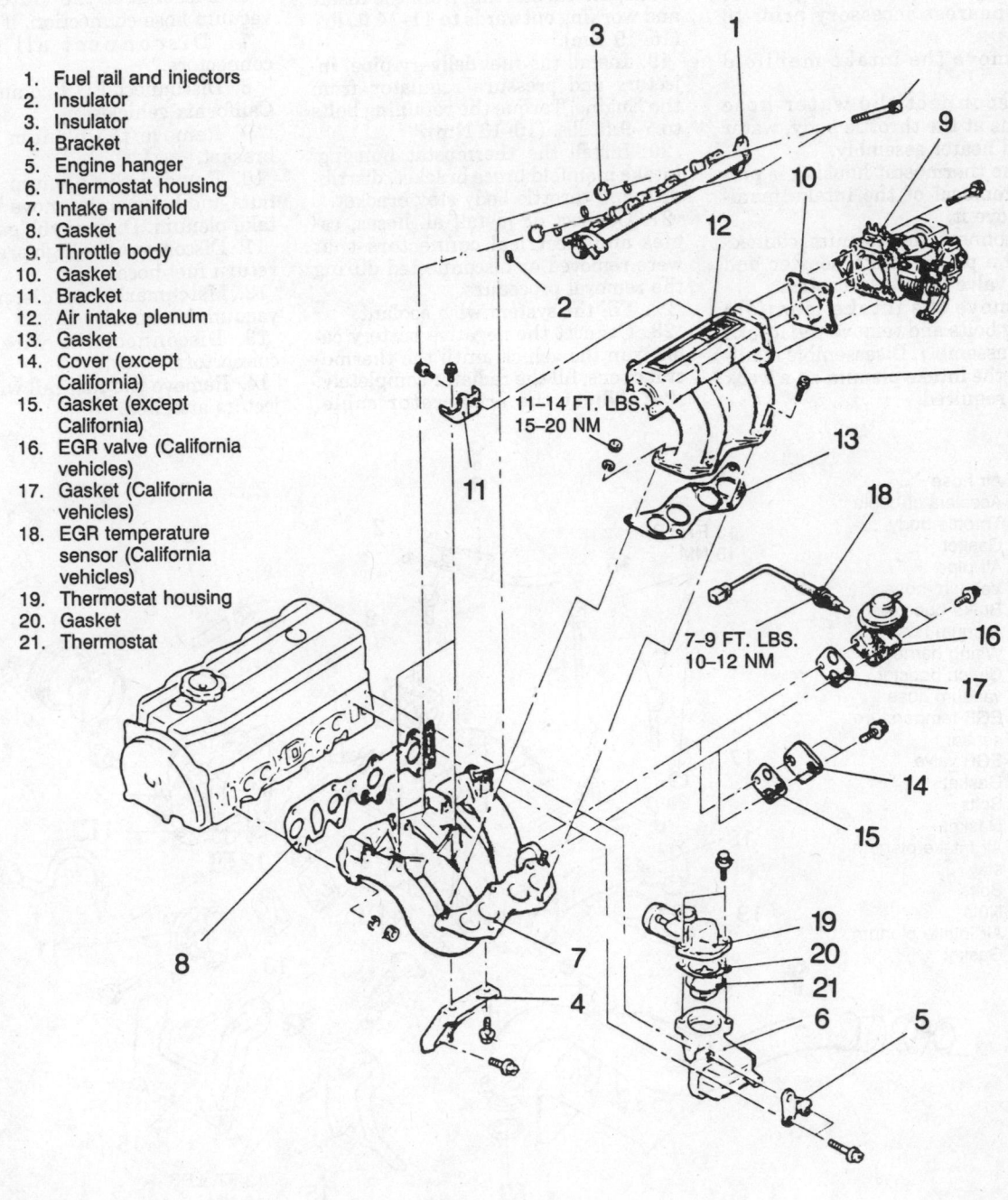

11–14 FT. LBS.
15–20 NM

7–9 FT. LBS.
10–12 NM

Air Intake plenum and Intake manifold—1.8L Engine

EGR temperature sensor, spark plug wires, etc. that may interfere with the manifold removal procedure.

8. Remove the fuel rail, fuel injectors, pressure regulator and insulators.

9. Remove the fuel delivery pipe, injectors and pressure regulator from the Engine.

10. If equipped with 1989–91 Engines, remove the distributor from the Engine if it passes through the manifold. Distributor removal is also necessary on the 1992–93 2.4L Engine. Matchmark the distributor shaft to the housing and the housing to the head or nearest accessory prior to removal.

11. Remove the intake manifold bracket.

12. Disconnect the water hose connctions at the throttle body, water inlet, and heater assembly.

13. If the thermostat housing is preventing removal of the intake manifold, remove it.

14. Disconnect the vacuum connection at the power brake booster and the PCV valve if still connected.

15. Remove the intake manifold mounting bolts and remove the intake manifold assembly. Disassemble manifold from the intake plenum on a work bench as required.

To install:

16. Assemble the intake manifold assembly using all new gaskets. Torque air intake plenum bolts to 11–14 ft. lbs. (15–19 Nm).

17. Clean all gasket material from the cylinder head intake mounting surface and intake manifold assembly. Check both surfaces for cracks or other damage. Check the intake manifold water passages and jet air passages for clogging. Clean if necessary.

18. Install a new intake manifold gasket to the head and install the manifold. Torque the manifold in a crisscross pattern, starting from the inside and working outwards to 11–14 ft. lbs. (15–19 Nm).

19. Install the fuel delivery pipe, injectors and pressure regulator from the Engine. Torque the retaining bolts to 7–9 ft. lbs. (10–13 Nm).

20. Install the thermostat housing, intake manifold brace bracket, distributor and throttle body stay bracket.

21. Connect or install all hoses, cables and electrical connectors that were removed or disconnected during the removal procedure.

22. Fill the system with coolant.

23. Connect the negative battery cable, run the vehicle until the thermostat opens, fill the radiator completely.

24. Adjust the accelerator cable.

Check and adjust the idle speed and ignition timing.

25. Once the vehicle has cooled, recheck the coolant level.

3.0L Engine

1. Relieve the fuel system pressure.

2. Disconnect battery negative cable and drain the cooling system.

3. Remove the air intake hose(s).

4. Disconnect the accelerator control cables from the throttle body.

5. Matchmark and disconnect the vacuum hoses including the brake booster hose.

6. Disconnect the clutch booster vacuum hose connection, if equipped.

7. Disconnect all harness connectors.

8. Disconnect EGR components on California vehicles.

9. Remove the plenum retaining bracket.

10. Remove the plenum retaining nuts and bolts and remove the air intake plenum. Discard the gasket.

11. Disconnect the high pressure and return fuel hoses.

12. Matchmark and disconnect the vacuum hoses.

13. Disconnect the wire harness connectors.

14. Remove the fuel rail with the injectors attached.

1. Air hose
2. Accelerator cable
3. Throttle body
4. Gasket
5. Air pipe
6. Vacuum hose
7. Brake booster vacuum hose
8. Wiring harness
9. Clutch booster vacuum hose
10. EGR temperature sensor
11. EGR valve
12. Gasket
13. Bolts
14. Gasket
15. Air intake plenum stay
16. Bolts
17. Nuts
18. Air intake plenum
19. Gasket

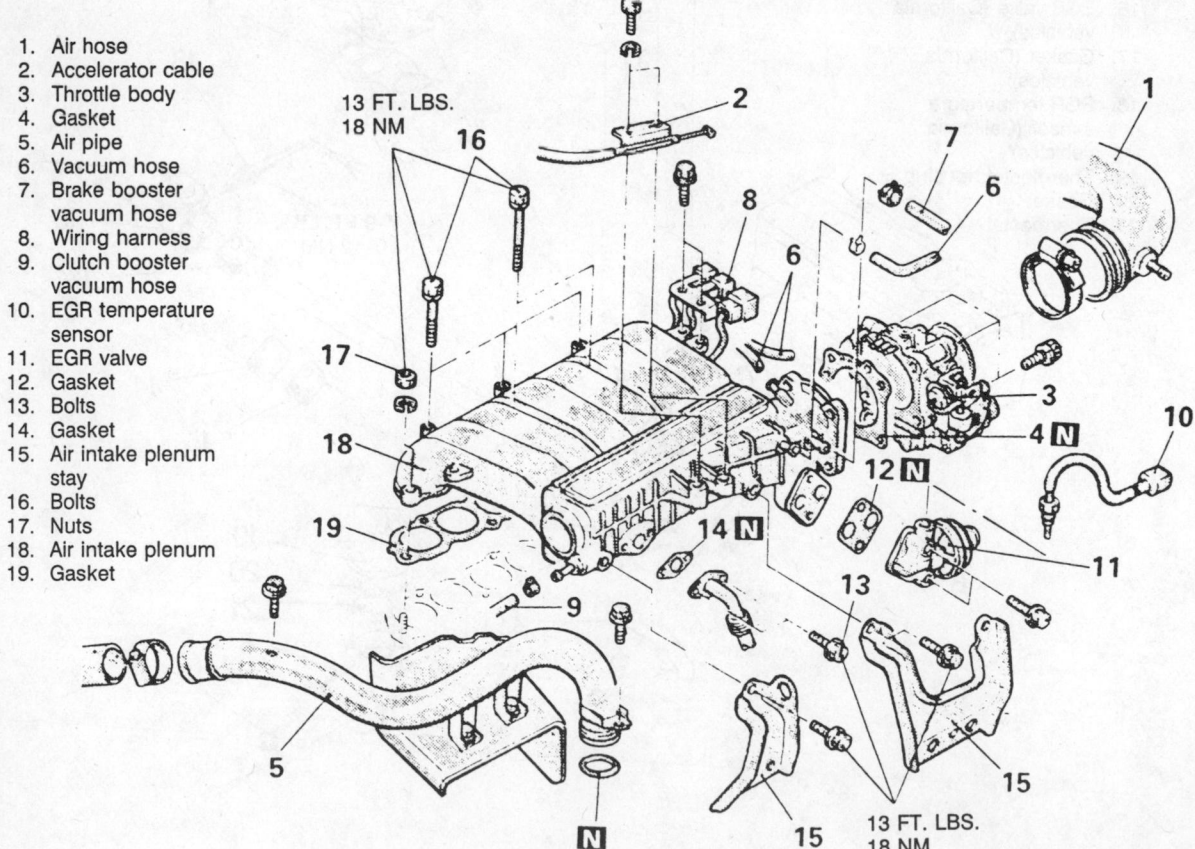

Air intake plenum assembly—turbocharged 3.0L Engine

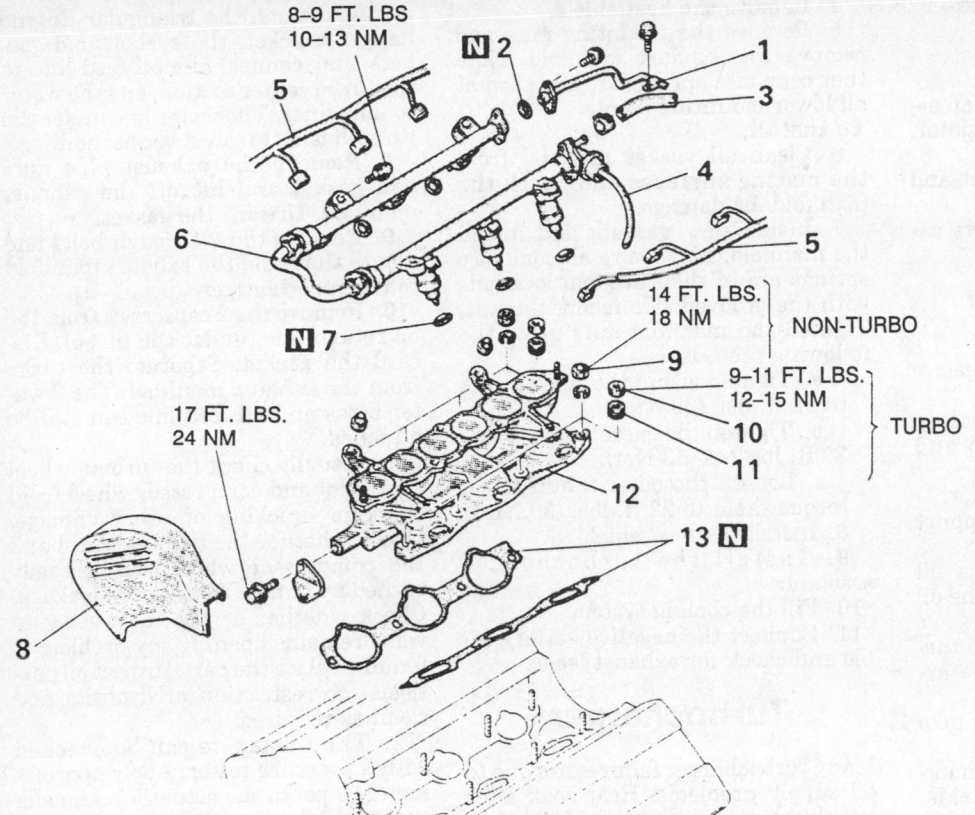

8–9 FT. LBS
10–13 NM

14 FT. LBS.
18 NM — NON-TURBO

9–11 FT. LBS.
12–15 NM — TURBO

17 FT. LBS.
24 NM

1. High pressure fuel hose
2. O-ring
3. Fuel return hose
4. Vacuum hoses
5. Injector copnnector
6. Fuel rail and injectors
7. Insulators
8. Timing belt upper cover
9. Mounting nut (Non-turbocharged engine
10. Mounting nut (turbocharged engine)
11. Cone disc spring (turbocharged engine)
12. Intake manifold
13. Gasket

Intake manifold and related parts – 3.0L Engine

15. On SOHC Engines, disconnect the water hoses. On DOHC Engines, remove the timing belt upper cover.

16. Remove the intake manifold mounting nuts; turbocharged Engines have cone disc springs under some of the nuts which should be removed. Remove the intake manifold and discard the gaskets.

To install:

17. Check all items for cracks, clogging and warpage. Maximum warpage is 0.008 in. (0.2mm). Replace all questionable parts.

18. Thoroughly clean and dry the mating surfaces of the heads, intake manifold and air intake plenum.

19. Install new intake manifold gaskets to the heads with the adhesive side facing up.

20. Place the manifold on the heads and install the cone disc springs and/or lock washers.

21. Lubricate the studs lightly with oil, then install the nuts following this procedure:

  a. Tighten the nuts on the front bank to 26–43 inch lbs. (3–5 Nm).

  b. Tighten the nuts on the rear bank to 9–11 ft. lbs. (12–15 Nm).

  c. Tighten the nuts on the front bank to 9–11 ft. lbs. (12–15 Nm).

  d. Repeat Steps B and C.

  e. On non-turbocharged Engines only, tighten the nuts to a final torque of 13–14 ft. lbs. (18–19 Nm).

22. On SOHC Engines, connect the water hoses. On DOHC Engines, install the timing belt upper cover.

23. Install the fuel rail assembly.

24. Connect the harness connector and vacuum hoses.

25. Replace the O-ring and connect the fuel hoses.

26. Install a new intake air plenum gasket and install the plenum. Tighten the retaining nuts and bolts evenly and gradually to 13 ft. lbs. (18 Nm).

27. Install the retaining bracket.

28. Connect EGR components on California vehicles.

29. Connect the harness connectors and vacuum hoses.

30. Connect and adjust the accelerator cables.

31. Install the air intake hose(s).

32. Fill the system with coolant.

33. Connect the negative battery cable, run the vehicle until the thermostat opens, fill the radiator completely.

34. Check and adjust the idle speed and ignition timing.

35. Once the vehicle has cooled, recheck the coolant level.

Exhaust Manifold

REMOVAL & INSTALLATION
Non-Turbocharged Engines

1. Disconnect battery negative cable.

2. Raise the vehicle and support safely.

3. Remove the exhaust pipe to exhaust manifold nuts and separate exhaust pipe. Discard gasket.

4. Lower vehicle.

5. Remove electric cooling fan assembly, if necessary. If removing the front manifold on 3.0L Engine, remove the dipstick tube. If removing the front manifold from 3.0L DOHC Engine, remove the alternator.

6. Disconnect necessary EGR components.

7. On all except 3.0L Engine, remove outer exhaust manifold heat shield and Engine hanger. Disconnect the electrical connector and remove the oxygen sensor.

8. Remove the exhaust manifold mounting bolts, the inner heat shield and the exhaust manifold.

To install:

9. Clean all gasket material from the mating surfaces and check the manifold for damage.

10. Install a new gasket and install the manifold. Tighten the nuts to in a criss-cross pattern to:

SOHC Engines – 11–14 ft. lbs. (15–20 Nm).

1.6L and 2.0L Engines – 18–22 ft. lbs. (25–30 Nm).

1991 3.0L DOHC Engine – 33 ft. lbs. (45 Nm).

1992–93 3.0L DOHC Engine—22 ft. lbs. (30 Nm).

11. Install the heat shields.

12. Connect EGR components.

13. Install the electric cooling fan assembly, dipstick tube and alternator, as required.

14. Install a new flange gasket and connect the exhaust pipe.

15. Connect the negative battery cable and check for exhaust leaks.

1.6L and 2.0L Turbocharged Engines

1. Disconnect the battery negative cable. Drain the cooling system.

2. Remove the condenser cooling fan and power steering pump and bracket as required.

3. Disconnect the oxygen sensor.

4. Raise the vehicle and support safely.

5. On 2.0L Engine, drain the oil from the crankcase and remove the oil level indicator and tube.

6. Remove the exhaust pipe to turbocharger nuts and separate the exhaust pipe. Discard the gasket.

7. Lower vehicle. Remove air intake and vacuum hose connections.

8. Remove the upper exhaust manifold and turbocharger heat shields. Remove the exhaust manifold to turbocharger attaching bolts and nut.

9. Remove the Engine hanger, water and oil lines from the turbo.

10. Remove the exhaust manifold mounting nuts. Remove the exhaust manifold and gasket.

To install:

11. Clean all gasket material from the mating surfaces and check the manifold for damage.

12. Install new gaskets and install the manifold. Tighten the manifold to head nuts in a criss-cross pattern to 18–22 ft. lbs. (25–30 Nm). Tighten the manifold to turbo nut and bolts to 40–47 ft. lbs. (55–65 Nm).

13. Install the Engine hanger, water and oil lines to the turbocharger.

14. Install the heat shields.

15. Install the new gasket and connect the exhaust pipe.

16. Install the condenser cooling fan and power steering pump. Connect the oxygen sensor harness.

17. Install the oil level indicator and tube replacing O-ring as required.

18. Fill the crankcase with clean oil and refill the cooling system.

19. Connect the negative battery cable and check for exhaust leaks.

3.0L Turbocharged Engine

1. Disconnect the negative battery cable.

2. Drain the Engine coolant.

3. Remove the turbocharger assembly.

4. Remove the heat shield.

5. Remove the mounting nuts and remove the exhaust manifold. Note that cone disc springs are installed at all lower mounting points.

To install:

6. Clean all gasket material from the mating surfaces and check the manifold for damage.

7. Install new gaskets and install the manifold. Make sure all cone disc springs are in their original locations with the grooved side facing the nut. Tighten the manifold nuts using the following procedure:

a. Tighten all but the outer 2 nuts to 22 ft. lbs. (30 Nm).

b. Tighten the outer 2 nuts to 34–38 ft. lbs. (47–53 Nm).

c. Loosen the outer 2 nuts, then torque them to 22 ft. lbs. (30 Nm).

8. Install the heat shield.

9. Install the turbocharger assembly.

10. Fill the cooling system.

11. Connect the negative battery cable and check for exhaust leaks.

Turbocharger

Many turbocharger failures are due to oil supply problems. Heat soak after hot shutdown can cause the Engine oil in the turbocharger and oil lines to "coke." Often the oil feed lines will become partially or completely blocked with hardened particles of carbon, blocking oil flow. Check the oil feed pipe and oil return line for clogging. Clean these tubes well. Always use new gaskets above and below the oil feed eyebolt fitting. Do not allow particles of dirt or old gasket material to enter the oil passage hole and that no portion of the new gasket blocks the passage.

REMOVAL & INSTALLATION

1.6L and 2.0L Engines

1. Disconnect the negative battery cable.

2. Drain the Engine oil, cooling system and remove the radiator. On Laser and Talon with air conditioning, remove the condenser fan assembly with the radiator.

3. Disconnect the oxygen sensor connector and remove the sensor.

4. Remove the oil dipstick and tube on Laser and Talon.

5. Remove the air intake bellows hose, the wastegate vacuum hose, the connections for the air outlet hose, and the upper and lower heat shields.

6. On Laser and Talon, unbolt the power steering pump and bracket assembly and leaving the hoses connected, wire it aside.

7. Remove the self-locking exhaust manifold nuts, the triangular Engine hanger bracket, the eyebolt and gaskets that connect the oil feed line to the turbo center section, and the water cooling lines. The water line under the turbo has a threaded connection.

8. Remove the exhaust pipe nuts and gasket and lift off the exhaust manifold. Discard the gasket.

9. Remove the 2 through bolts and 2 nuts that hold the exhaust manifold to the turbocharger.

10. Remove the 2 capscrews from the oil return line (under the turbo). Discard the gasket. Separate the turbo from the exhaust manifold. The 2 water pipes and oil feed line can still be attached.

11. Visually check the turbine wheel (hot side) and compressor wheel (cold side) for cracking or other damage. Check whether the turbine wheel and the compressor wheel can be easily turned by hand. Check for oil leakage. Check whether or not the wastegate valve remains open. If any problem is found, replace the part. Inspect oil passages for restriction or deposits and clean as required.

12. The wastegate can be checked with a pressure tester. Apply approximately 9 psi to the actuator and make sure the rod moves. Do not apply more than 10.3 psi or the diaphragm in the wastegate may be damaged. Vacuum applied to the wastegate actuator should be maintained, replace if leaks vacuum. Do not attempt to adjust the wastegate valve.

To install:

13. Prime the oil return line with clean Engine oil. Replace all locking nuts. Before installing the threaded connection for the water inlet pipe, apply light oil to the inner surface of the pipe flange. Assemble the turbocharger and exhaust manifold.

14. Install the exhaust manifold using a new gasket.

15. Connect the water cooling lines, oil feed line and Engine hanger.

16. If removed, install the power steering pump and bracket.

17. Install the heat shields, air outlet hose, wastegate hose and air intake bellows.

18. Install the oil dipstick tube and dipstick. Install the oxygen sensor.

19. Install the radiator assembly.

20. Fill the Engine with oil, fill the cooling system and reconnect the negative battery cable.

3.0L Engine
RIGHT SIDE (FRONT) TURBOCHARGER

1. Disconnect the negative battery cable.

2. Remove the radiator.

3. Remove the right side transaxle bracket.

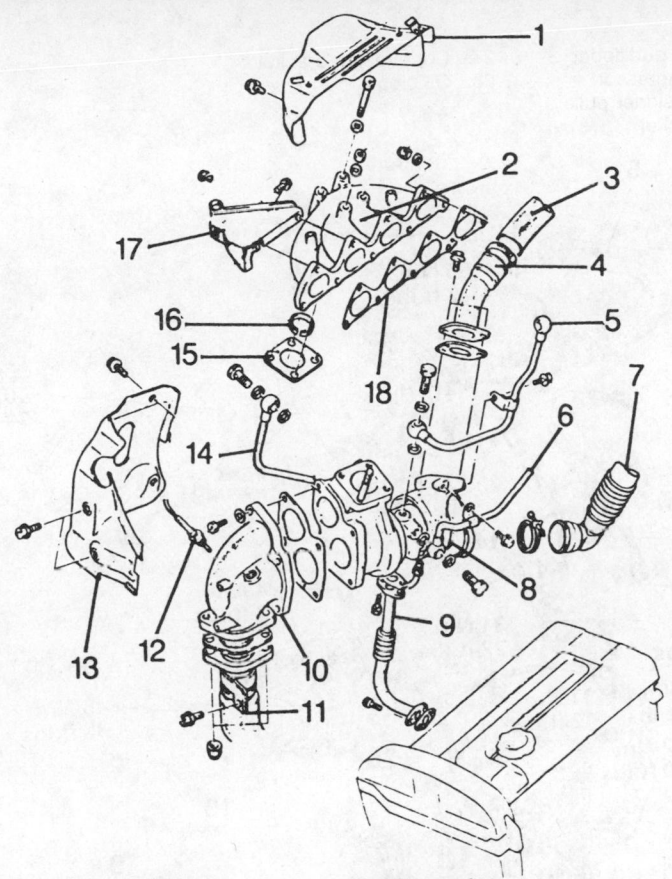

1. Upper heat shield
2. Exhaust manifold
3. Air hose connector
4. Air inlet fitting
5. Oil feed pipe
6. Water line
7. Connection–air intake
8. Turbocharger assembly
9. Oil drainback line
10. Exhaust fitting
11. Exhaust pipe
12. Oxygen sensor
13. Lower heat shield
14. Water line
15. Gasket
16. Ring
17. Brace/bracket
18. Manifold gasket

Turbocharger assembly—1.6L and 2.0L Engines

4. Remove the front exhaust pipe.
5. Carefully matchmark, diagram or photograph all air intake hoses and pipes along the front of the Engine. It is imperative that all of these pieces are installed in the exact same positions when assembling. Remove the hoses and pipes and keep covered in a clean area.
6. Remove the alternator.
7. Remove the oil dipstick tube.
8. Remove the turbocharger heat protector.
9. Remove the water feed pipes.
10. Remove the oxygen sensor.
11. Remove the oil return line.
12. Remove the exhaust extension fitting and bracket.
13. Remove all air conditioning components preventing removal of the turbocharger.
14. Remove the oil feed tube.
15. Remove the turbocharger to exhaust manifold bolts and remove the turbocharger assembly.

To install:
16. Visually check the turbine wheel (hot side) and compressor wheel (cold side) for cracking or other damage. Check whether the turbine wheel and the compressor wheel can be easily turned by hand. Check for oil leakage. Check whether or not the wastegate valve remains open. If any problem is found, replace the part.
17. Clean all mating surfaces. Pour clean Engine oil through the oil pipe feed hole in the turbocharger.
18. Install a new gasket and ring a install the turbocharger to the manifold. Torque the bolts to 40–47 ft. lbs. (55–65 Nm).
19. Replace the eye-bolt rings and install the oil feed pipe.
20. Install the removed air conditioning components.
21. Install the exhaust extension fitting and bracket with a new gasket. Torque the nuts to 40–47 ft. lbs. (55–65 Nm).

22. Install the oil return line with new gaskets.
23. Install the oxygen sensor.
24. Replace the eye-bolt rings and install the water feed pipes.
25. Install the turbocharger heat protector.
26. Install the dipstick tube.
27. Install the alternator.
28. Install all air intake hoses and pipes along the front of the Engine. Make sure all are in their proper positions.
29. Install a new gasket and connect the front exhaust pipe.
30. Install the right side transaxle bracket.
31. Install the radiator.
32. Fill the system with coolant.
33. Connect the negative battery cable and check for exhaust leaks.

LEFT SIDE (REAR) TURBOCHARGER

1. Remove the battery.
2. Drain the coolant.
3. Remove the front exhaust pipe.
4. Disconnect the accelerator cable from the throttle body.
5. Remove the intake air hose, the air pipe across the top of the Engine and its heat shield.
6. Remove the clutch booster vacuum hose and disconnect the accelerator cable from the pedal.
7. Remove the air intake hoses coming from the air cleaner box.
8. Remove the oxygen sensor and the turbocharger heat protector.
9. Remove the EGR pipe, if equipped.
10. Remove the oil feed pipe.
11. Remove the EGR valve, if equipped.
12. Remove the water feed pipes.
13. Remove the exhaust extension fitting and bracket.
14. Remove the inner heat protector.
15. Remove the oil return tube.
16. Remove the turbocharger to exhaust manifold nuts and remove the turbocharger assembly.

To install:
17. Visually check the turbine wheel (hot side) and compressor wheel (cold side) for cracking or other damage. Check whether the turbine wheel and the compressor wheel can be easily turned by hand. Check for oil leakage. Check whether or not the wastegate valve remains open. If any problem is found, replace the part.
18. Clean all mating surfaces. Pour clean Engine oil through the oil pipe feed hole in the turbocharger.
19. Install a new gasket and ring a install the turbocharger to the manifold. Torque the nuts to 40–47 ft. lbs. (55–65 Nm).
20. Install the oil return line with new gaskets.

1. Air hose
2. Air intake hose
3. Air hose
4. Air hose
5. Air hose
6. Air pipe
7. Air hose
8. Air pipe
9. Drive belt
10. Alternator
11. Dipstick tube
12. Heat protector
13. Water pipe
14. Water pipe
15. Oxygen sensor connector
16. Turbocharger and fitting assembly
17. Gasket
18. Ring
19. Oxygen sensor
20. Bracket
21. Exhaust fitting
22. Gasket
23. Oil return pipe
24. Turbocharger assembly
25. Air conditioner compressor
26. Tensioner pulley bracket
27. Compressor bracket
28. Oil pipe

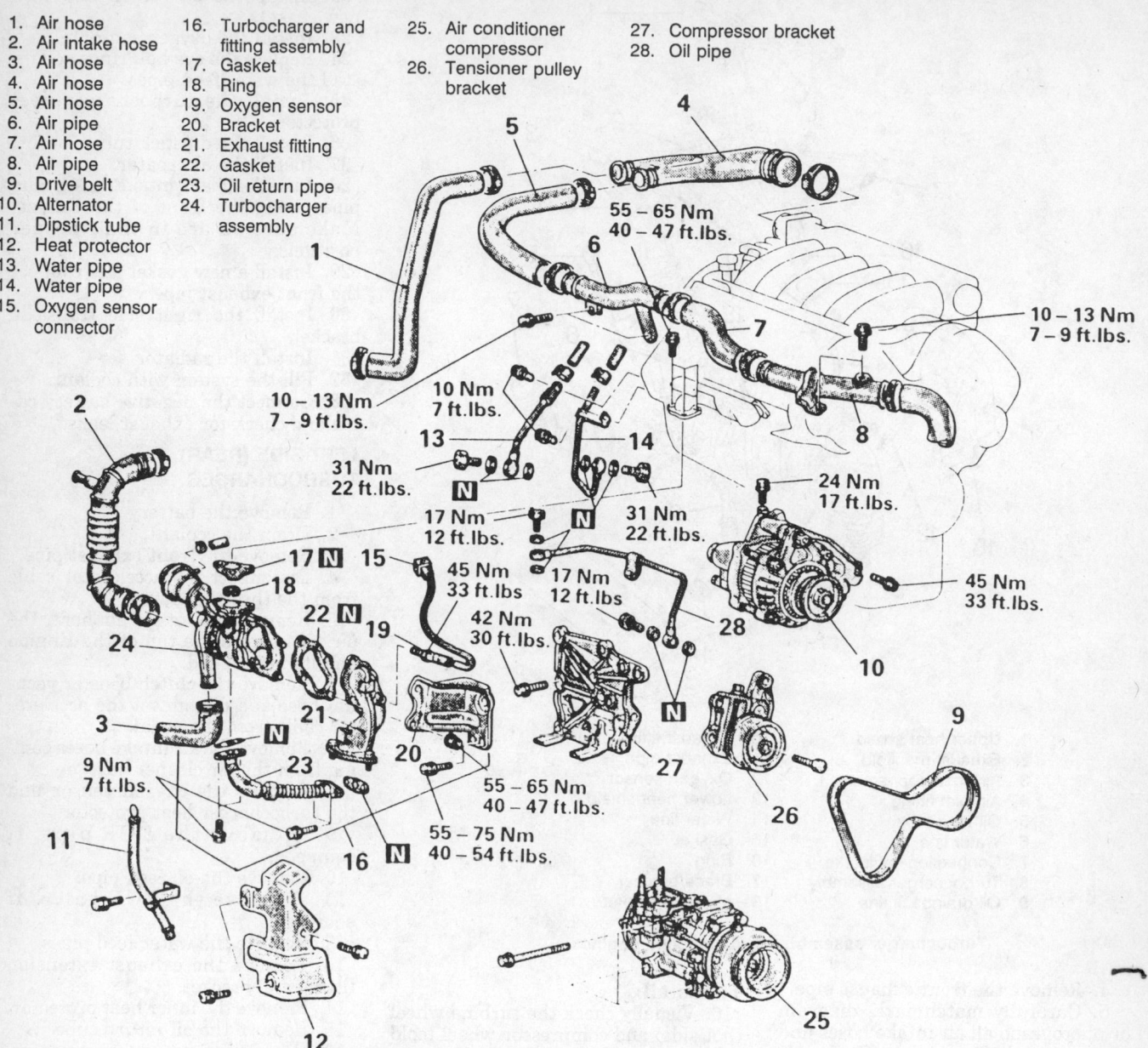

Right side (front) turbocharger and related parts—Stealth

21. Install the inner heat protector.
22. Install the exhaust extension fitting and bracket with a new gasket. Torque the nuts to 40–47 ft. lbs. (55–65 Nm).
23. Replace the eye-bolt rings and install the water feed pipes.
24. Install the EGR valve, if equipped.
25. Replace the eye-bolt rings and install the oil feed pipe.
26. Install the EGR pipe if equipped.
27. Install the turbocharger heat protector and oxygen sensor.
28. Install the air intake hoses coming from the air cleaner box. Make sure the triangular aligning marks are engaged.
29. Connect the accelerator cable to from the pedal and install the clutch booster vacuum hose.
30. Install the heat shield, the air pipe across the top of the Engine and the air intake hose.
31. Connect the accelerator cable to the throttle body.
32. Install a new gasket and connect the front exhaust pipe.
33. Fill the system with coolant.
34. Install the battery.
35. Connect the negative battery cable and check for exhaust leaks.

Timing Belt Front Cover
REMOVAL & INSTALLATION

Except 3.0L Engine

1. Disconnect the negative battery cable.
2. Remove the Engine undercover.
3. On Summit Wagon, remove the coolant reservoir.
4. Using the proper equipment, slightly raise the Engine to take the weight off of the side Engine mount. Remove the Engine mount bracket.

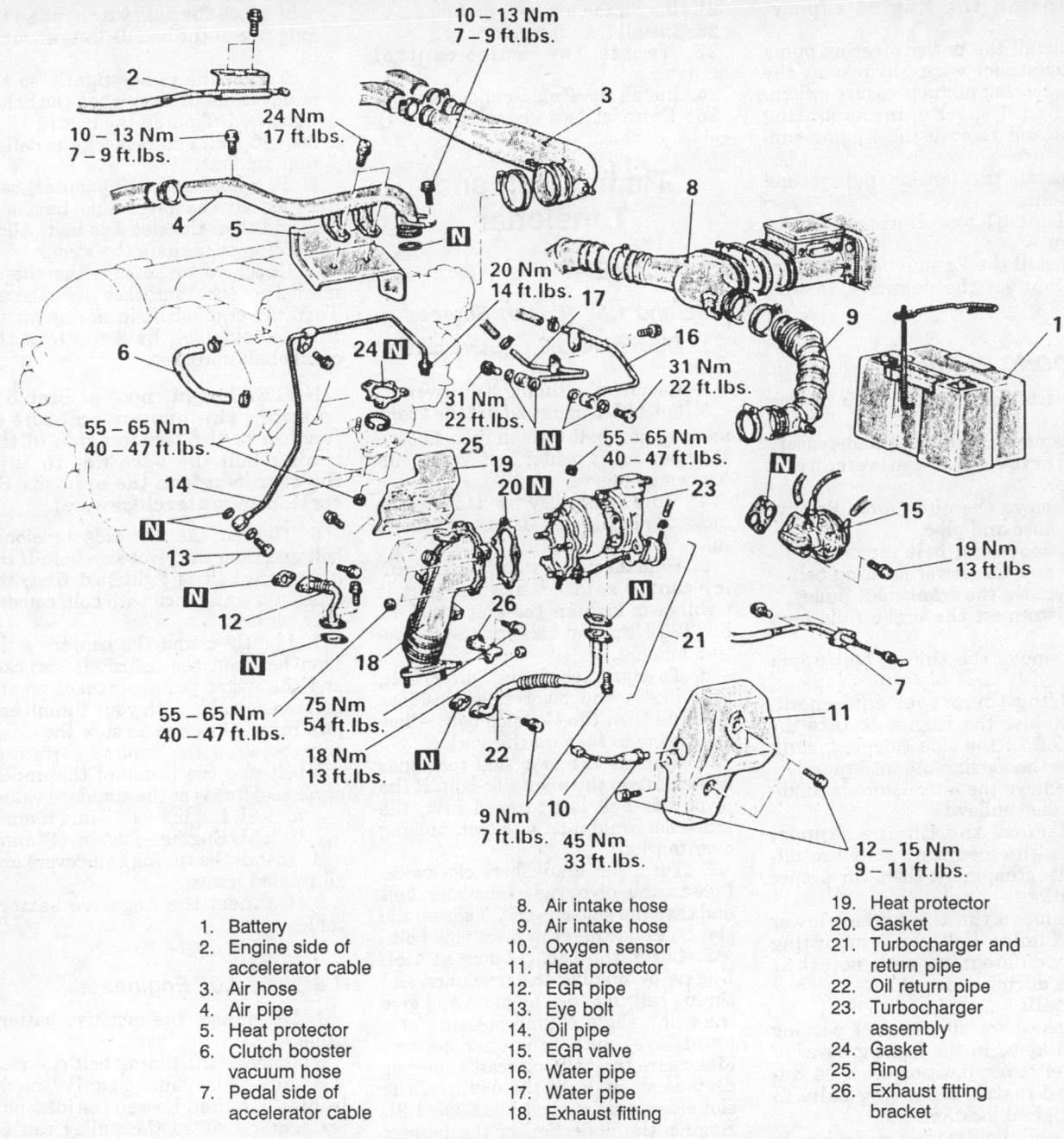

1. Battery
2. Engine side of accelerator cable
3. Air hose
4. Air pipe
5. Heat protector
6. Clutch booster vacuum hose
7. Pedal side of accelerator cable
8. Air intake hose
9. Air intake hose
10. Oxygen sensor
11. Heat protector
12. EGR pipe
13. Eye bolt
14. Oil pipe
15. EGR valve
16. Water pipe
17. Water pipe
18. Exhaust fitting
19. Heat protector
20. Gasket
21. Turbocharger and return pipe
22. Oil return pipe
23. Turbocharger assembly
24. Gasket
25. Ring
26. Exhaust fitting bracket

Left side (rear) turbocharger and related parts—Stealth

5. Remove the drive belts, tension pulley brackets, water pump pulley and crankshaft pulley.

6. Remove all attaching screws and remove the upper and lower timing belt covers.

7. The installation is the reverse of the removal procedure. Make sure all pieces of packing are positioned in the inner grooves of the covers when installing.

3.0L SOHC Engine

1. Disconnect the negative battery cable.

2. Remove the Engine undercover.

3. Remove the cruise control actuator.

4. Remove the accessory drive belts.

5. Remove the air conditioner compressor tension pulley assembly.

6. Remove the tension pulley bracket.

7. Using the proper equipment, slightly raise the Engine to take the weight off of the side Engine mount. Remove the Engine mounting bracket.

8. Disconnect the power steering pump pressure switch connector. Remove the power steering pump and wire aside.

9. Remove the Engine support bracket.

10. Remove the crankshaft pulley.

11. Remove the timing belt cover cap.

12. Remove the timing belt upper and lower covers.

To install:

13. Install the timing covers. Make sure all pieces of packing are positioned in the inner grooves of the covers when installing.

14. Install the crankshaft pulley. Torque the bolt to 108–116 ft. lbs. (150–160 Nm).

15. Install the Engine support bracket.

16. Install the power steering pump and reconnect wire harness at the power steering pump pressure switch.

17. Install the Engine mounting bracket and remove the Engine support fixture.

18. Install the tension pulleys and drive belts.

19. Install the cruise control actuator.

20. Install the Engine undercover.

21. Connect the negative battery cable.

3.0L DOHC Engine

1. Disconnect the negative battery cable.

2. Remove the Engine undercover.

3. Remove the cruise control actuator.

4. Remove the alternator. Remove the air hose and pipe.

5. Remove the belt tensioner assembly and the power steering belt.

6. Remove the crankshaft pulley.

7. Disconnect the brake fluid level sensor.

8. Remove the timing belt upper cover.

9. Using the proper equipment, slightly raise the Engine to take the weight off of the side Engine mount. Remove the Engine mount bracket.

10. Remove the alternator/air conditioner idler pulley.

11. Remove the Engine support bracket. The mounting bolts are different lengths; mark them for proper installation.

12. Remove the timing belt lower cover. Timing bolt cover mounting bolts are different in length, note their position during removal.

To install:

13. Make sure all pieces of packing are positioned in the inner grooves of the lower cover, position cover on Engine and install mounting bolts in their original location.

14. Install the Engine support bracket and secure using mounting bolts in their original location. Lubricate the reaming area of the reamer bolt and tighten slowly.

15. Install the idler pulley.

16. Install the Engine mount bracket. Remove the Engine support fixture.

17. Make sure all pieces of packing are positioned in the inner grooves of the upper cover and install.

18. Connect the brake fluid level sensor.

19. Install the crankshaft pulley. Torque the bolt to 130–137 ft. lbs. (180–190 Nm).

20. Install the belt tensioner assembly and the power steering belt.

21. Install the air hose and pipe.

22. Install the alternator.

23. Install the cruise control actuator.

24. Install the Engine undercover.

25. Connect the negative battery cable.

Timing Belt and Tensioner

ADJUSTMENT

1.5L and 1.8L (Laser) Engines

1. Disconnect the negative battery cable.

2. Remove the timing belt covers.

3. On 1.8L Engine, adjust the silent shaft (inner) belt tension first. Loosen the idler pulley center bolt so the pulley can be moved.

4. Move the pulley by hand so the long side of the belt deflects about ¼ in.

5. Hold the pulley tightly so the pulley cannot rotate when the bolt is tightened. Tighten the bolt to 15 ft. lbs. (20 Nm) and recheck the deflection amount.

6. To adjust the timing (outer) belt, first loosen the pivot side tensioner bolt and then the slot side bolt. Allow the spring to take up the slack.

7. Tighten the slot side tensioner bolt and then the pivot side bolt. If the pivot side bolt is tightened first, the tensioner could turn with bolt, causing over tension.

8. Turn the crankshaft clockwise. Loosen the pivot side tensioner bolt and then the slot side bolt. Tighten the slot bolt and then the pivot side bolt.

9. Check the belt tension on 1.5L Engine by holding the tensioner and timing belt together by hand and give the belt a slight thumb pressure at a point level with tensioner center. Make sure the belt cog crest comes as deep as about ¼ of the width of the slot side tensioner bolt head. On 1.8L Engine, the deflection of the longest span of the belt should be about 0.40 in. Do not manually overtighten the belt or it will howl.

10. Install the timing belt covers and all related items.

11. Connect the negative battery cable.

1.8L and 2.4L Engines

SUMMIT WAGON

1. Disconnect negative battery cable.

2. Remove the timing belt covers.

3. On 2.4L Engine, adjust the silent shaft (inner) belt tension first as follows:

   a. Loosen the idler pulley center bolt so the pulley can be moved.

   b. Move the pulley by hand so the long side of the belt deflects about ¼ in.

   c. Hold the pulley tightly so the pulley cannot rotate when the bolt is tightened. Tighten the bolt to 15 ft. lbs. (20 Nm) and recheck the deflection amount.

4. To adjust the timing (outer) belt, first loosen the pivot side tensioner bolt and then the slot side bolt. Allow the spring to take up the slack.

5. Check to make sure the timing marks on each sprocket are aligned. Turn the crankshaft in normal direction (clockwise), by 2 teeth of the crankshaft sprocket.

NOTE: The purpose of Step 5 is to apply the proper amount of tension to the tension side of the timing belt, be sure not to turn the crankshaft in the opposite direction (counterclockwise).

6. Tighten the slot side tensioner bolt and then the pivot side bolt. If the pivot side bolt is tightened first, the tensioner could turn with bolt, causing over tension.

7. Lightly clamp the center of the span between the camshaft sprocket and the water pump sprocket on the belt tension side with your thumb and forefinger. Check to be sure the clearance between the reverse surface of the belt and the inside of the undercover seal line is at the standard value.

   a. 1.8L Engine—1.18 in. (30mm).

   b. 2.4L Engine—0.55 in. (14mm).

8. Install the timing belt covers and all related items.

9. Connect the negative battery cable.

1.6L and 2.0L Engines

1. Disconnect the negative battery cable.

2. Remove the timing belt covers.

3. Adjust the silent shaft (inner) belt tension first. Loosen the idler pulley center bolt so the pulley can be moved.

4. Move the pulley by hand so the long side of the belt deflects about ¼ in.

5. Hold the pulley tightly so the pulley cannot rotate when the bolt is tightened. Tighten the bolt to 15 ft. lbs. (20 Nm) and recheck the deflection amount.

6. To adjust the timing (outer) belt, turn the crankshaft ¼ turn counterclockwise, then turn it clockwise to move No. 1 cylinder to TDC.

7. Loosen the center bolt. Using tool MD998752 or equivalent and a torque wrench, apply a torque of 1.88–2.03 ft. lbs. (2.6–2.8 Nm). If the body of the vehicle interferes with the special tool and the torque wrench, use a

1. Condenser tank
2. Clamp section of air conditioner and power steering hose
3. Drive belt (power steering and air conditioner)
4. Drive belt (alternator)
5. Crankshaft bolt
6. Crankshaft pulley
7. Timing belt upper cover
8. Timing belt lower cover
9. Flange
10. Timing belt
11. Timing belt tensioner
12. Tensioner spacer
13. Tensioner spring

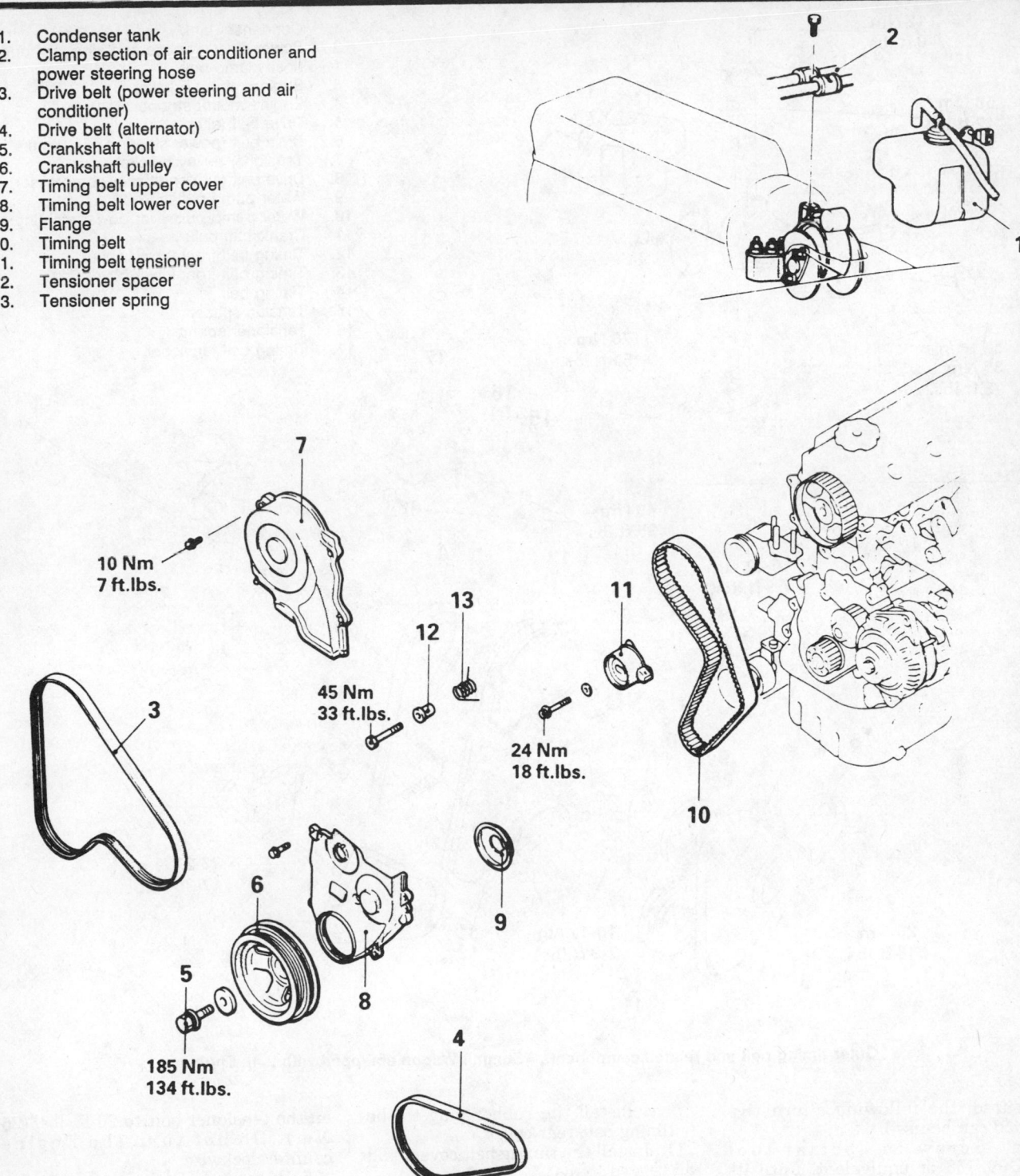

Timing belt and related components—Summit Wagon equipped with 1.8L Engine

jack and slightly raise the Engine assembly. Holding the tensioner pulley, tighten the center bolt.

8. Screw special tool MD998738 or exact equivalent into the Engine left support bracket until its end makes contact with the tensioner arm. At this point, screw the special tool in some more and remove the set wire attached

to the auto tensioner, if wire was not previously removed. Then remove the special tool.

9. Rotate the crankshaft 2 complete turns clockwise and let it sit for approximately 15 minutes. Then, measure the auto tensioner protrusion (the distance between the tensioner arm and auto tensioner body) to en-

sure that it is within 0.15–0.18 in. (3.8–4.5mm). If out of specification, repeat Step 1–4 until the specified value is obtained.

10. If the timing belt tension adjustment is being performed with the Engine mounted in the vehicle, and clearance between the tensioner arm and the auto tensioner body cannot be

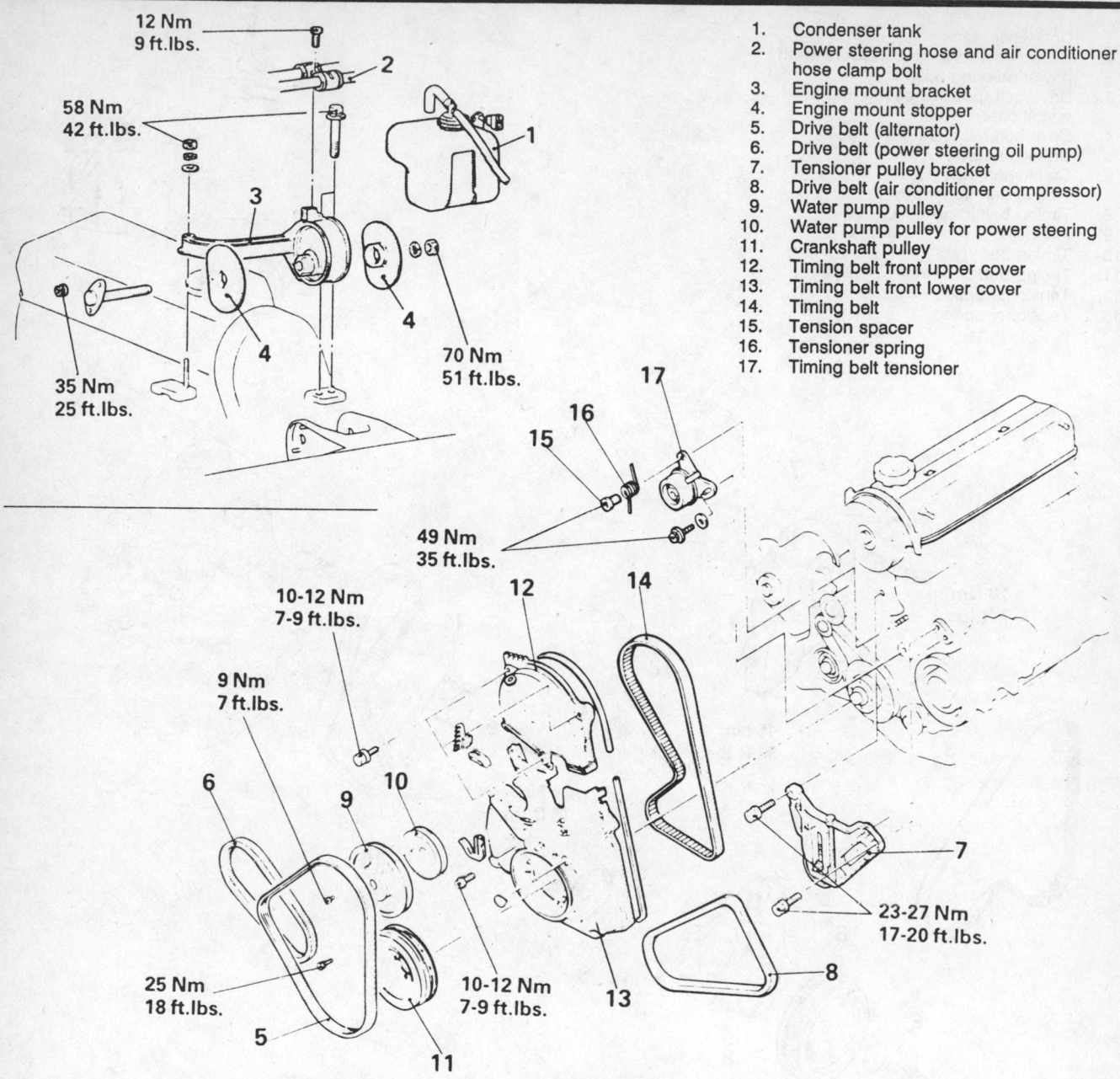

1. Condenser tank
2. Power steering hose and air conditioner hose clamp bolt
3. Engine mount bracket
4. Engine mount stopper
5. Drive belt (alternator)
6. Drive belt (power steering oil pump)
7. Tensioner pulley bracket
8. Drive belt (air conditioner compressor)
9. Water pump pulley
10. Water pump pulley for power steering
11. Crankshaft pulley
12. Timing belt front upper cover
13. Timing belt front lower cover
14. Timing belt
15. Tension spacer
16. Tensioner spring
17. Timing belt tensioner

Outer timing belt and related components—Summit Wagon equipped with 2.4L Engine

measured, the following alternative method can be used:

a. Screw in special tool MD998738 or equivalent, until its end makes contact with the tensioner arm.

b. After the special tool makes contact with the arm, screw it in some more to retract the auto tensioner pushrod while counting the number of turns the tool makes until the tensioner arm is brought into contact with the auto tensioner body. Make sure the number of turns the special tool makes conforms with the standard value of 2½–3 turns.

c. Install the rubber plug to the timing belt rear cover.

11. Install the timing belt covers and all related items.

12. Connect the negative battery cable.

3.0L SOHC Engine

1. Disconnect the negative battery cable.

2. Remove the timing belt covers.

3. Loosen the bolt that holds the tensioner in place and allow the spring to automatically apply tension to the belt.

4. Rotate the crankshaft smoothly, 2 Engine revolutions clockwise. Tight-

en the tensioner bolt to 20 ft. lbs. (25 Nm). Do not turn the Engine counterclockwise.

5. Measure the belt tension between the rear camshaft sprocket and the crankshaft with belt tension gauge. The specification is 46–68 lbs. (210–310 N).

6. Install the timing belt covers and all related items.

7. Connect the negative battery cable.

3.0L DOHC Engine

1. Disconnect the negative battery cable.

2. Remove the timing belt covers.

1. Timing belt
2. Crankshaft sprocket
3. Flange
4. Timing belt B tensioner
5. Timing belt B

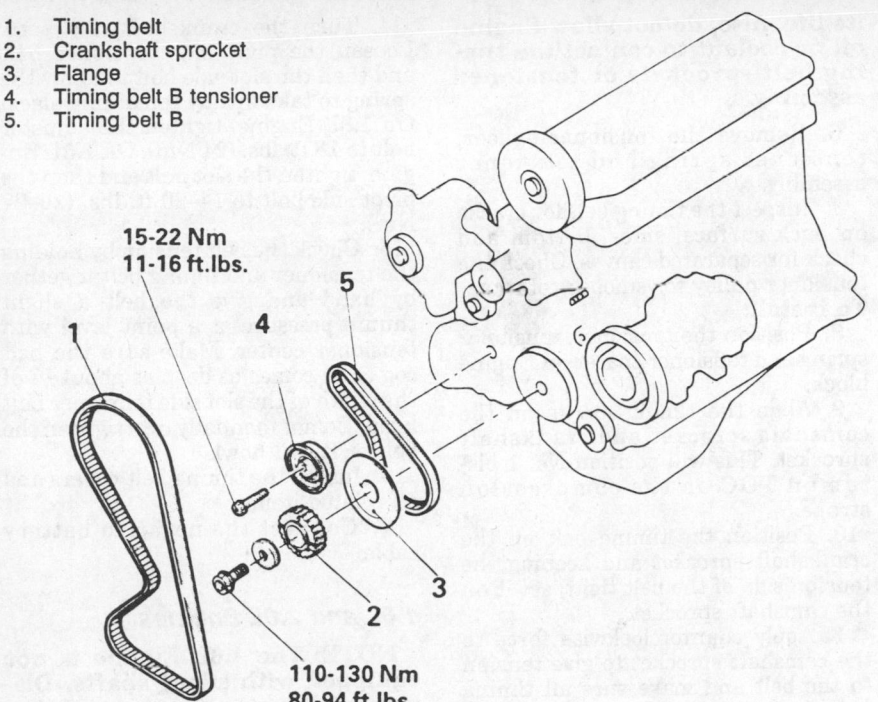

15-22 Nm
11-16 ft.lbs.

110-130 Nm
80-94 ft.lbs.

Inner timing belt and related components—Summit Wagon equipped with 2.4L Engine

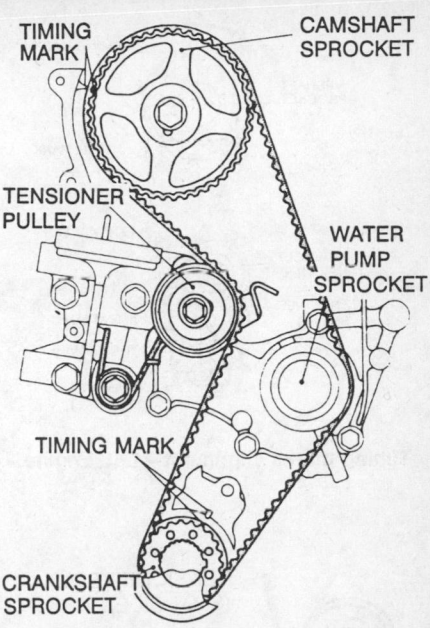

Timing mark alignment—1.8L Engine—(Summit Wagon)

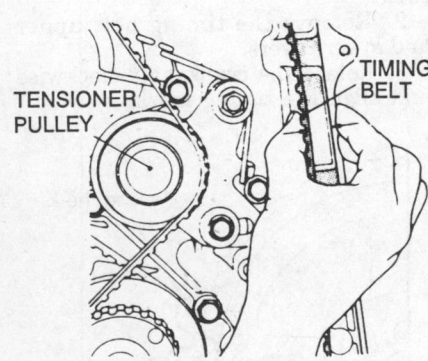

Checking timing belt clearance to assure proper tension—2.4L Engine

NOTE: Even if the set pin can not be easily inserted, the auto tensioner is normal if its rod protrusion is within specification.

7. Measure the auto tensioner protrusion (the distance between the tensioner arm and auto tensioner body) to ensure that it is within 0.15–0.18 in. (3.8–4.5mm). If out of specification, repeat Step 1–4 until the specified value is obtained.

8. Check again that the timing marks on all sprockets are in proper alignment.

9. Install the timing belt covers and all related items.

10. Connect the negative battery cable.

REMOVAL & INSTALLATION

1.8L (Summit Wagon) and 1.5L Engines

1. Disconnect the negative battery cable. Remove the Engine under cover.

2. Raise and safely support the weight of the Engine using the appropriate equipment. Remove the front Engine mount bracket and accessory drive belts.

3. On Summit Wagon, remove the coolant reservoir tank.

4. Remove timing belt upper and lower covers.

5. Make a mark on the back of the timing belt indicating the direction of

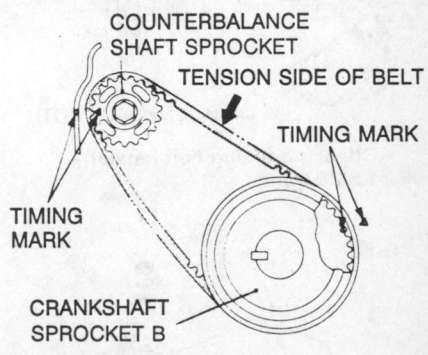

Inner belt timing mark alignment—2.4L Engine

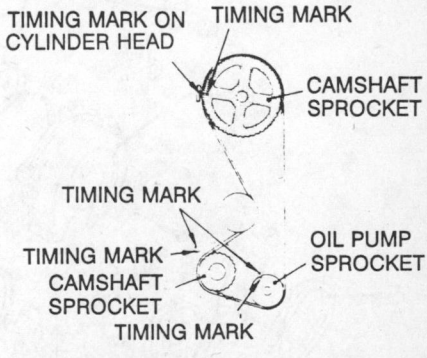

Outer belt timing mark alignment—2.4L Engine

3. Turn the crankshaft ¼ turn counterclockwise, then turn it clockwise until all timing marks are aligned.

4. Loosen the center bolt on the tensioner pulley. Using tool MD998767 or equivalent and a torque wrench, apply a torque of 7.2 ft. lbs. (10 Nm). Tighten the tensioner bolt; make sure the tensioner doesn't rotate with the bolt.

5. Remove the set wire attached to the auto tensioner, if wire was not previously removed.

6. Rotate the crankshaft 2 complete turns clockwise and let it sit for approximately 5 minutes. Then, check that the set pin can easily be inserted and removed from the hole in the auto tensioner.

rotation so it may be reassembled in the same direction if it is to be reused. Loosen the timing belt trensioner and remove the timing belt.

NOTE: If coolant or Engine oil comes in contact with the timing belt, they will drastically shorten

1-35

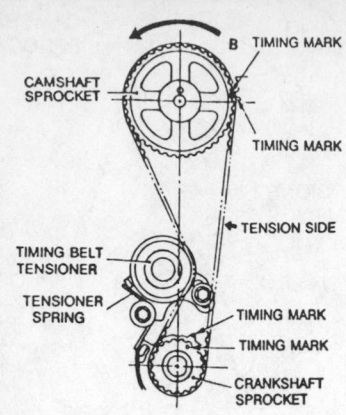

Timing marks alignment—1.5L Engine

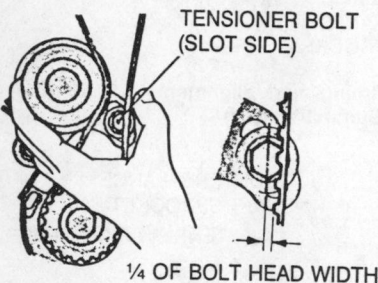

Checking timing belt tension— 1.5L Engine

its life. Also, do not allow Engine oil or coolant to contact the timing belt sprockets or tensioner assembly.

6. Remove the tensioner spacer, tensioner spring and tensioner assembly.

7. Inspect the timing belt for cracks on back surface, sides, bottom and check for separated canvas. Check the tensioner pulley for smooth rotation. **To install:**

8. Position the tensioner, tensioner spring and tensioner spacer on Engine block.

9. Align the timing marks on the camshaft sprocket and crankshaft sprocket. This will position No. 1 piston on TDC on the compression stroke.

10. Position the timing belt on the crankshaft sprocket and keeping the tension side of the belt tight, set it on the camshaft sprocket.

11. Apply counterclockwise force to the camshaft sprocket to give tension to the belt and make sure all timing marks are aligned.

12. Loosen the pivot side tensioner bolt and the slot side bolt. Allow the spring to take up the slack.

13. Tighten the slot side tensioner bolt and then the pivot side bolt. If the pivot side bolt is tightened first, the tensioner could turn with bolt, causing over tension.

14. Turn the crankshaft clockwise. Loosen the pivot side tensioner bolt and then the slot side bolt to allow the spring to take up any remaining slack. On 1.8L Engine, tighten the adjuster bolt to 18 ft. lbs. (24 Nm). On 1.5L Engine, tighten the slot bolt and then the pivot side bolt to 14–20 ft. lbs. (20–27 Nm).

15. Check the belt tension by holding the tensioner and timing belt together by hand and give the belt a slight thumb pressure at a point level with tensioner center. Make sure the belt cog crest comes as deep as about ¼ of the width of the slot side tensioner bolt head. Do not manually overtighten the belt or it will howl.

16. Install the timing belt covers and all related items.

17. Connect the negative battery cable.

1.6L and 2.0L Engines

NOTE: The 1.6L Engine is not equipped with silent shafts. Disregard all instructions pertaining to silent shafts if working on that Engine.

1. Disconnect the negative battery cable.

2. Remove the timing belt upper and lower covers.

3. Rotate the crankshaft clockwise and align the timing marks so No. 1

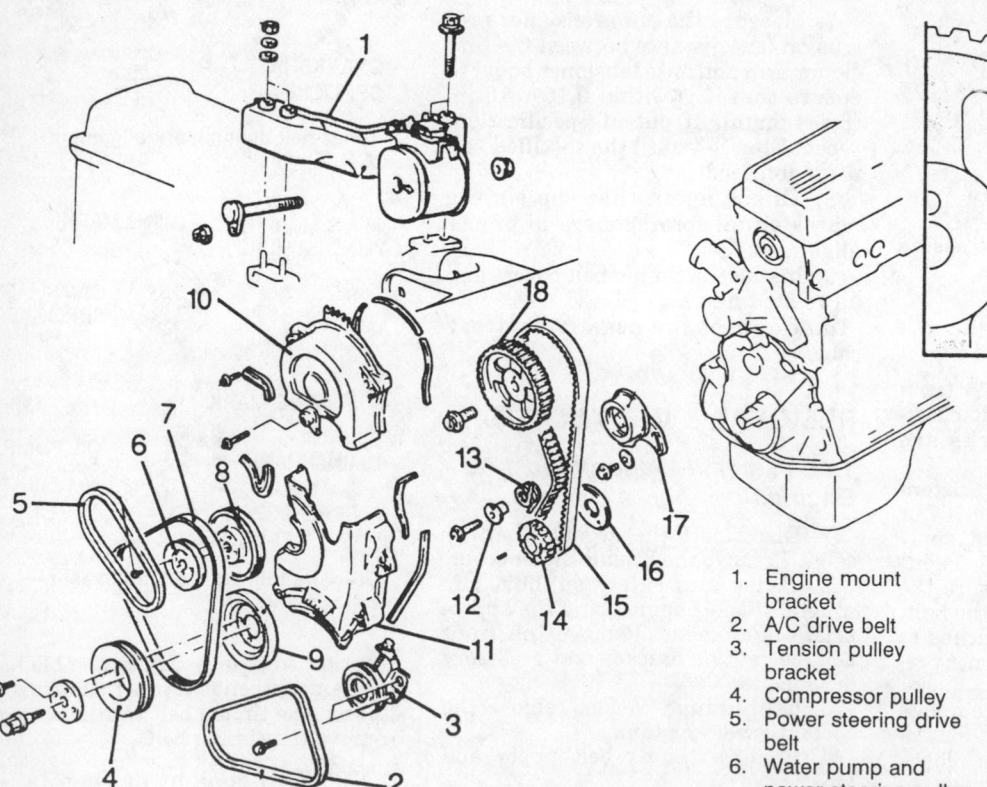

1. Engine mount bracket
2. A/C drive belt
3. Tension pulley bracket
4. Compressor pulley
5. Power steering drive belt
6. Water pump and power steering pulley
7. Alternator belt
8. Water pump pulley
9. Crankshaft pulley
10. Timing belt upper cover
11. Timing belt lower cover
12. Tensioner spacer
13. Tensioner spring
14. Crankshaft sprocket
15. Cam belt
16. Flange
17. Tensioner
18. Cam sprocket

Timing belt and related parts—1.5L Engine

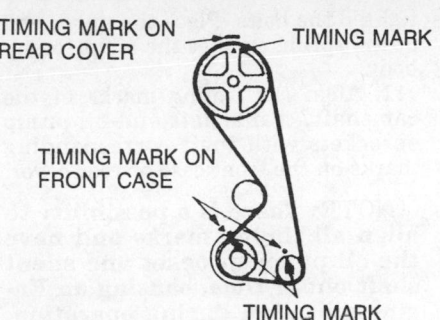

Timing belt timing marks alignment—1.8L Engine

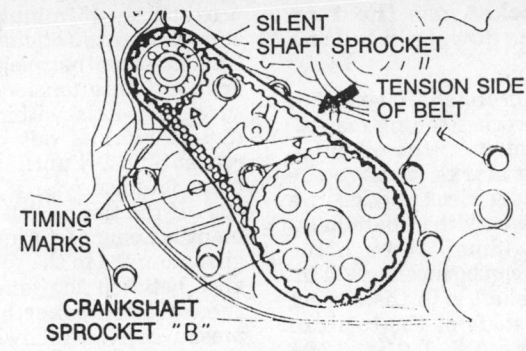

Silent shaft belt timing marks alignment—1.8L and 2.0L Engines

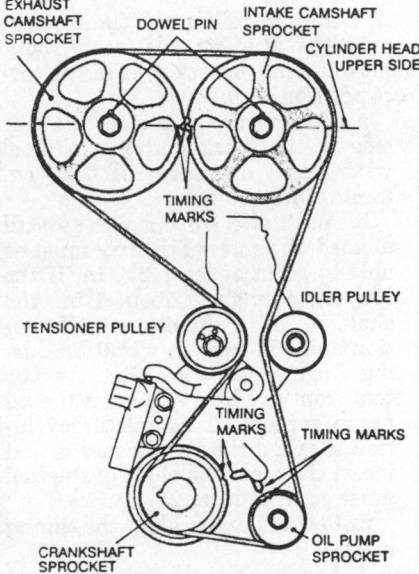

Timing belt and related components—1.6L and 2.0L Engines

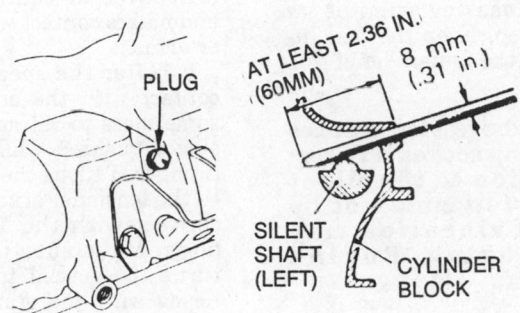

Checking the rear silent shaft for proper positioning

piston will be at TDC of the compression stroke. At this time the timing marks on the camshaft sprocket and the upper surface of the cylinder head should coincide, and the dowel pin of the camshaft sprocket should be at the upper side.

NOTE: Always rotate the crankshaft in a clockwise direction. Make a mark on the back of the timing belt indicating the direction of rotation so it may be reassembled in the same direction if it is to be reused.

4. Remove the auto tensioner and remove the outermost timing belt.
5. Remove the timing belt tensioner pulley, tensioner arm, idler pulley, oil pump sprocket, special washer, flange and spacer.
6. Remove the silent shaft (inner) belt tensioner and remove the belt.

To install:
7. Align the timing marks on the crankshaft sprocket and the silent shaft sprocket. Fit the inner timing belt over the crankshaft and silent shaft sprocket. Ensure that there is no slack in the belt.
8. While holding the inner timing belt tensioner with your fingers, adjust the timing belt tension by applying a force towards the center of the belt, until the tension side of the belt is taut. Tighten the tensioner bolt.

NOTE: When tightening the bolt of the tensioner, ensure that the tensioner pulley shaft does not rotate with the bolt. Allowing it to rotate with the bolt can cause excessive tension on the belt.

9. Check belt for proper tension by depressing the belt on its' long side with your finger and noting the belt deflection. The desired reading is 0.20–0.28 in. (5–7mm). If tension is not correct, readjust and check belt deflection.
10. Install the flange, crankshaft and washer to the crankshaft. The flange on the crankshaft sprocket must be installed towards the inner timing belt sprocket. Tighten bolt to 80–94 ft. lbs. (110–130 Nm).
11. To install the oil pump sprocket, insert a Phillips screwdriver with a shaft 0.31 in. (8mm) in diameter into the plug hole in the left side of the cylinder block to hold the left silent shaft. Tighten the nut to 36–43 ft. lbs. (50–60 Nm).

12. Using a wrench, hold the camshaft at its' hexagon between journal No. 2 and 3 and tighten bolt to 58–72 ft. lbs. (80–100 Nm). If no hexagon is present between journal No. 2 and 3, hold the sprocket stationary with a spanner wrench while tightening the retainer bolt.
13. Carefully push the auto tensioner rod in until the set hole in the rod aligned up with the hole in the cylinder. Place a wire into the hole to retain the rod.
14. Install the tensioner pulley onto the tensioner arm. Locate the pinhole in the tensioner pulley shaft to the left of the center bolt. Then, tighten the center bolt finger-tight.
15. When installing the timing belt, turn the 2 camshaft sprockets so their dowel pins are located on top. Align the timing marks facing each other with the top surface of the cylinder head. When you let go of the exhaust camshaft sprocket, it will rotate 1 tooth in the counterclockwise direction. This should be taken into account when installing the timing belts on the sprocket.

NOTE: Both camshaft sprockets are used for the intake and exhaust camshafts and are provided with 2 timing marks. When the sprocket is mounted on the exhaust camshaft, use the timing mark on the right with the dowel pin hole on top. For the intake

camshaft sprocket, use the 1 on the left with the dowel pin hole on top.

16. Align the crankshaft sprocket and oil pump sprocket timing marks.

17. After alignment of the oil pump sprocket timing marks, remove the plug on the cylinder block and insert a Phillips screwdriver with a shaft diameter of 0.31 in. (8mm) through the hole. If the shaft can be inserted 2.4 in. deep, the silent shaft is in the correct position. If the shaft of the tool can only be inserted 0.8–1.0 in. (20–25mm) deep, turn the oil pump sprocket 1 turn and realign the marks. Reinsert the tool making sure it is inserted 2.4 in. deep. Keep the tool inserted in hole for the remainder of this procedure.

NOTE: The above step assures that the oil pump socket is in correct orientation to the silent shafts. This step must not be skipped or a vibration may develope during Engine operation.

18. Install the timing belt as follows:
   a. Install the timing belt around the intake camshaft sprocket and retain it with 2 spring clips or binder clips.
   b. Install the timing belt around the exhaust sprocket, aligning the timing marks with the cylinder head top surface using 2 wrenches. Retain the belt with 2 spring clips.
   c. Install the timing belt around the idler pulley, oil pump sprocket, crankshaft sprocket and the tensioner pulley. Remove the 2 spring clips.
   d. Lift upward on the tensioner pulley in a clockwise direction and tighten the center bolt. Make sure all timing marks are aligned.
   e. Rotate the crankshaft ¼ turn counterclockwise. Then, turn in clockwise until the timing marks are aligned again.

19. To adjust the timing (outer) belt, turn the crankshaft ¼ turn counterclockwise, then turn it clockwise to move No. 1 cylinder to TDC.

20. Loosen the center bolt. Using tool MD998738 or equivalent and a torque wrench, apply a torque of 1.88–2.03 ft. lbs. (2.6–2.8 Nm). Tighten the center bolt.

21. Screw the special tool into the Engine left support bracket until its end makes contact with the tensioner arm. At this point, screw the special tool in some more and remove the set wire attached to the auto tensioner, if the wire was not previously removed. Then remove the special tool.

22. Rotate the crankshaft 2 complete turns clockwise and let it sit for ap-

proximately 15 minutes. Then, measure the auto tensioner protrusion (the distance between the tensioner arm and auto tensioner body) to ensure that it is within 0.15–0.18 in. (3.8–4.5mm). If out of specification, repeat Step 1–4 until the specified value is obtained.

23. If the timing belt tension adjustment is being performed with the Engine mounted in the vehicle, and clearance between the tensioner arm and the auto tensioner body cannot be measured, the following alternative method can be used:
   a. Screw in special tool MD998738 or equivalent, until its end makes contact with the tensioner arm.
   b. After the special tool makes contact with the arm, screw it in some more to retract the auto tensioner pushrod while counting the number of turns the tool makes until the tensioner arm is brought into contact with the auto tensioner body. Make sure the number of turns the special tool makes conforms with the standard value of 2½–3 turns.
   c. Install the rubber plug to the timing belt rear cover.

24. Install the timing belt covers and all related items.

25. Connect the negative battery cable.

1.8L (Laser) and 2.4L Engines

1. If possible, position the Engine so the No. 1 piston is at TDC.

2. Disconnect the negative battery cable. On Summit Wagon with 2.4L Engine, remove the coolant reservoir and the power steering and air conditioner hose clamp bolt.

3. Remove the timing belt covers.

4. Remove the timing (outer) belt tensioner and remove the outer timing belt.

5. Remove the outer crankshaft sprocket and flange.

6. Remove the silent shaft (inner) belt tensioner and remove the belt.

To install:

7. Align the timing marks of the silent shaft sprockets and the crankshaft sprocket with the timing marks on the front case. Wrap the timing belt around the sprockets so there is no slack in the upper span of the belt and the timing marks are still aligned.

8. Install the tensioner pulley and move the pulley by hand so the long side of the belt deflects about ¼ in.

9. Hold the pulley tightly so the pulley cannot rotate when the bolt is tightened. Tighten the bolt to 15 ft. lbs. (20 Nm) and recheck the deflection amount.

10. Install the timing belt tensioner fully toward the water pump and

tighten the bolts. Place the upper end of the spring against the water pump body.

11. Align the timing marks of the camshaft, crankshaft and oil pump sprockets with their corresponding marks on the front case or rear cover.

NOTE: There is a possibility to align all timing marks and have the oil pump sprocket and silent shaft out of time, causing an Engine vibration during operation. If the following step is not followed exactly, there is a 50 percent chance that the silent shaft alignment will be 180 degrees off.

12. Before installing the timing belt, ensure that the left side (rear) silent shaft (oil pump sprocket) is in the correct position as follows:
   a. Remove the plug from the rear side of the block and insert a tool with shaft diameter of 0.31 in. (8mm) into the hole.
   b. With the timing marks still aligned, the shaft of the tool must be able to go in at least 2⅓ in. If the tool can only go in about 1 in., the shaft is not in the correct orientation and will cause a vibration during Engine operation. Remove the tool from the hole and turn the oil pump sprocket 1 complete revolution. Realign the timing marks and insert the tool. The shaft of the tool must go in at least 2⅓ in.
   c. Recheck and realign the timing marks.
   d. Leave the tool in place to hold the silent shaft while continuing.

13. Install the belt to the crankshaft sprocket, oil pump sprocket, then camshaft sprocket, in that order. While doing so, make sure there is no slack between the sprocket except where the tensioner is installed.

14. Recheck the timing marks' alignment. If all are aligned, loosen the tensioner mounting bolt and allow the tensioner to apply tension to the belt.

15. Remove the tool that is holding the silent shaft and rotate the crankshaft a distance equal to 2 teeth on the camshaft sprocket. This will allow the tensioner to automatically apply the proper tension on the belt. Do not manually overtighten the belt or it will howl.

16. Tighten the lower mounting bolt first, then the upper spacer bolt.

17. To verify correct belt tension, check that the deflection at the longest span of the belt is about ½ in.

18. Install the timing belt covers and all related items.

19. Connect the negative battery cable.

3.0L SOHC Engine

1. If possible, position the Engine so

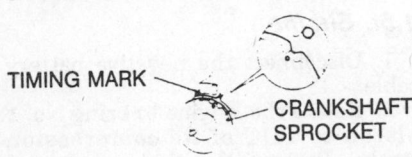

TIMING MARK

CAMSHAFT SPROCKET

TIMING MARK

CRANKSHAFT SPROCKET

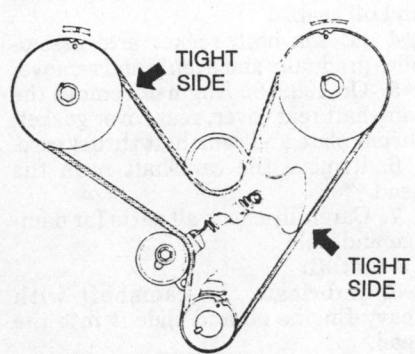

TIGHT SIDE

TIGHT SIDE

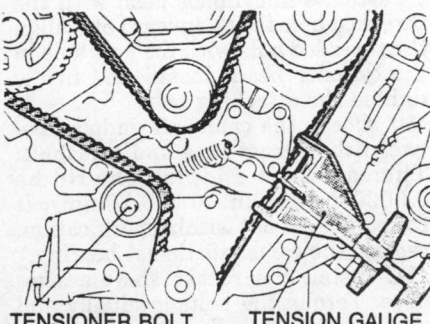

TENSIONER BOLT   TENSION GAUGE

Timing belt and related parts—3.0L SOHC Engine

the No. 1 cylinder is at TDC of its compression stroke. Disconnect the negative battery cable. Remove the timing covers from the Engine.

2. If the same timing belt will be reused, mark the direction of the timing belt's rotation for installation in the same direction. Make sure the Engine is positioned so the No. 1 cylinder is at the TDC of its compression stroke and the sprockets' timing marks are aligned with the Engine's timing mark indicators.

3. Loosen the timing belt tensioner bolt and remove the belt. If the tensioner is not being removed, position it as far away from the center of the Engine as possible and tighten the bolt.

4. If the tensioner is being removed, paint the outside of the spring to ensure that it is not installed backwards. Unbolt the tensioner and remove it along with the spring.

To install:

5. Install the tensioner, if removed, and hook the upper end of the spring to the water pump pin and the lower end to the tensioner in exactly the same position as originally installed. If not already done, position both camshafts so the marks align with those on the rear. Rotate the crankshaft so the timing mark aligns with the mark on the oil pump.

6. Install the timing belt on the crankshaft sprocket and while keeping the belt tight on the tension side, install the belt on the front camshaft sprocket.

7. Install the belt on the water pump pulley, then the rear camshaft sprocket and the tensioner.

8. Rotate the front camshaft counterclockwise to tension the belt between the front camshaft and the crankshaft. If the timing marks became misaligned, repeat the procedure.

9. Install the crankshaft sprocket flange.

10. Loosen the tensioner bolt and allow the spring to apply tension to the belt.

11. Turn the crankshaft 2 full turns in the clockwise direction until the timing marks align again. Now that the belt is properly tensioned, torque the tensioner lock bolt to 21 ft. lbs. (29 Nm). Measure the belt tension between the rear camshaft sprocket and the crankshaft with belt tension gauge. The specification is 46–68 lbs. (210–310 N).

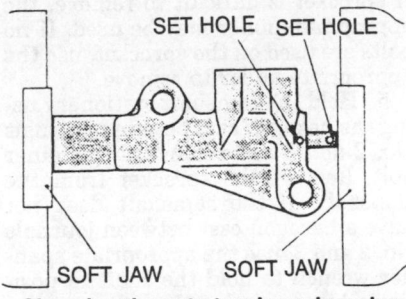

SET HOLE   SET HOLE

SOFT JAW   SOFT JAW

Clamping the auto-tensioner in a vice

12. Install the timing belt covers and all related parts.

13. Connect the negative battery cable and road test the vehicle.

3.0L DOHC Engine

1. If possible, position the Engine so the No. 1 cylinder is at TDC of its compression stroke. Disconnect the negative battery cable. Remove the timing covers from the Engine.

2. If the same timing belt will be reused, mark the direction of the timing belt's rotation for installation in the same direction. Make sure the Engine is positioned so the No. 1 cylinder is at the TDC of its compression stroke and the sprockets' timing marks are aligned with the Engine's timing mark indicators on the valve covers or head.

3. Loosen the timing belt tensioner bolt and remove the belt.

4. Remove the tensioner assembly.

To install:

5. If the auto tensioner rod is fully extended, reset it as follows:

   a. Clamp the tensioner in a soft-jaw vise in level position.

   b. Slowly push the rod in with the vise until the set hole in the rod is aligned with the hole in the cylinder.

   c. Insert a stiff wire into the set holes to retain the position.

   d. Remove the assembly from the vice.

6. Leave the retaining wire in the tensioner and install to the Engine.

7. On 1991 DOHC 3.0L Engines, clean and inspect both auto tensioner mounting bolts. Coat the threads of

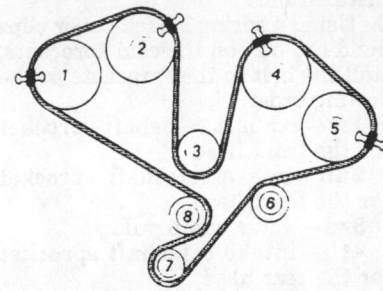

Timing belt installation—3.0L DOHC Engine

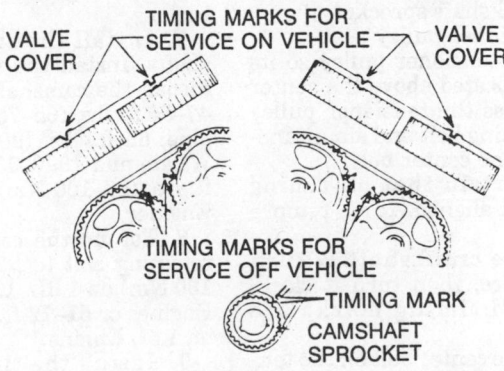

VALVE COVER

TIMING MARKS FOR SERVICE ON VEHICLE

VALVE COVER

TIMING MARKS FOR SERVICE OFF VEHICLE

TIMING MARK

CAMSHAFT SPROCKET

Aligning the timing marks—3.0L DOHC Engine

the old bolts with Mopar thread sealer 4318034. If new bolts are installed, inspect the heads of the new bolts. If there is white paint on the bolt head, no sealer is required. If there is no paint on the head of the bolt, apply a coat of thread sealer to the bolt. Install both bolts and torque to 17 ft. lbs. (24 Nm).

8. If the timing marks of the camshaft sprockets and crankshaft sprocket are not aligned at this point, proceed as follows:

NOTE: Keep fingers out from in between the camshaft sprockets. The sprockets may move unexpectedly because of valve spring pressure and could pinch fingers.

a. Align the mark on the crankshaft sprocket with the mark on the front case. Then move the sprocket 2 teeth clockwise to lower the piston so the valve can't touch the piston when the camshafts are being moved.

b. Turn each camshaft sprocket 1 at a time to align the timing marks with the mark on the valve cover or head. If the intake and exhaust valves of the same cylinder are opened simultaneously, they could interfere with each other. Therefore, if any resistance is felt, turn the other camshaft to move the valve.

c. Align the timing mark of the crankshaft sprocket, then continue 1 tooth farther in the counterclockwise direction to facilitate belt installation.

9. Using 4 spring loaded paper clips to hold the belt on the cam sprockets, install the belt to the sprockets in the following order:

1st—exhuast camshaft sprocket for the front head
2nd—intake camshaft sprocket for the front head
3rd—water pump pulley
4th—intake camshaft sprocket for the rear head
5th—exhuast camshaft sprocket for the rear head
6th—idler pulley
7th—crankshaft sprocket
8th—tensioner pulley

10. Turn the tensioner pulley so its pin holes are located above the center bolt. Then press the tensioner pulley against the timing belt and simultaneously tighten the center bolt.

11. Make certain that all timing marks are still aligned. If so, remove the 4 clips.

12. Turn the crankshaft ¼ turn counterclockwise, then turn it clockwise until all timing marks are aligned.

13. Loosen the center bolt on the tensioner pulley. Using tool MD998767 or

equivalent and a torque wrench, apply a torque of 7.2 ft. lbs. (10 Nm). Tighten the tensioner bolt; make sure the tensioner doesn't rotate with the bolt.

14. Remove the set wire attached to the auto tensioner, if the wire was not previously removed.

15. Rotate the crankshaft 2 complete turns clockwise and let it sit for approximately 5 minutes. Then, make sure the set pin can easily be inserted and removed from the hole in the tensioner.

16. Measure the auto tensioner protrusion (the distance between the tensioner arm and auto tensioner body) to ensure that it is within 0.15–0.18 in. (3.8–4.5mm). If out of specification, repeat Step 1–4 until the specified value is obtained.

17. Install the timing belt covers and all related items.

18. Connect the negative battery cable.

Timing Sprockets and Oil Seals

REMOVAL & INSTALLATION

1. Disconnect the negative battery cable.

2. Remove the valve cover(s) and timing belt(s).

3. Remove the crankshaft pulley retainer bolts and remove the pulley.

4. Remove the crankshaft sprocket retainer bolt and washer from the sprocket, if used, and remove sprocket. If sprocket is difficult to remove, the appropriate puller may be used. If no bolts are used on the sprocket, use the appropriate puller to remove.

5. Hold the camshaft stationary using the hexagon cast between journals No. 2 and 3 and remove the retainer bolt. Remove the sprocket from the camshaft. If the camshaft does not have a hexagon cast between journals No. 2 and 3, use the appropriate spanner wrench to hold the shaft in position while removing the bolt.

6. Pry the seals from the bores and replace using the proper installation tools.

7. Install the sprockets to their shafts. Install the retainer bolts and torque the camshaft sprocket bolt to 47–54 ft. lbs. (65–75 Nm) on 1.5L Engine, 65 ft. lbs. (90 Nm) on Summit Wagon and 1992–93 Stealth or 58–72 ft. lbs. (80–100 Nm) on the remaining Engines.

8. Torque the crankshaft sprocket retaining bolt to 80–94 ft. lbs. (110–130 Nm) on 1.6L, 1.8L, 2.0L and 2.4L Engines or 51–72 ft. lbs. (70–100 Nm) on 1.5L Engine.

9. Install the timing belt(s) and valve cover(s).

10. Connect the negative battery cable and check for leaks.

Camshaft

REMOVAL & INSTALLATION

1.5L Engine

1. Disconnect the negative battery cable.

2. Rotate the Engine to bring No. 1 piston to TDC of its compression stroke. Remove the timing belt and valve cover.

3. Remove the camshaft sprocket and oil seal.

4. Loosen both rocker arm assemblies gradually and evenly and remove.

5. On 1989–90 Engines, remove the camshaft rear cover, rear cover gasket, thrust plate and camshaft thrust case.

6. Remove the camshaft from the head.

7. Carefully check all parts for damage and wear.

To install:

8. Lubricate the camshaft with heavy Engine oil and slide it into the head.

9. If equipped, insert the camshaft thrust case in cylinder head with the threaded hole facing upward and align the threaded hole with the bolt hole in the cylinder head. Install and firmly tighten the attaching bolt.

10. Check the camshaft endplay between the thrust case and camshaft. The camshaft endplay should be 0.0020–0.0080 in. (0.5–0.20mm). If the endplay is not within specification, replace the camshaft thrust bearing.

11. Install the rocker shaft assemblies. Torque the bolts gradually and evenly to 14–20 ft. lbs. (20–27 Nm) on 1989–90 Engines or 21–25 ft. lbs. (29–35 Nm) on 1991–93 Engines.

12. When installing the oil seal, coat the external surface with Engine oil. Position the seal on the camshaft end and drive it into place.

13. Install the camshaft sprocket, timing belt and valve cover with new gasket.

14. Connect the negative battery cable and check for leaks.

1.6L and 2.0L Engines

1. Relieve the fuel system pressure.

2. Disconnect battery negative cable.

3. Disconnect the accelerator cable.

4. Remove the timing belt cover and timing belt.

5. Remove the center cover, breather and PCV hoses, and spark plug cables.

6. Remove the rocker cover, semi-circular packing, throttle body stay, crankshaft angle sensor, both camshaft sprockets, and oil seals.

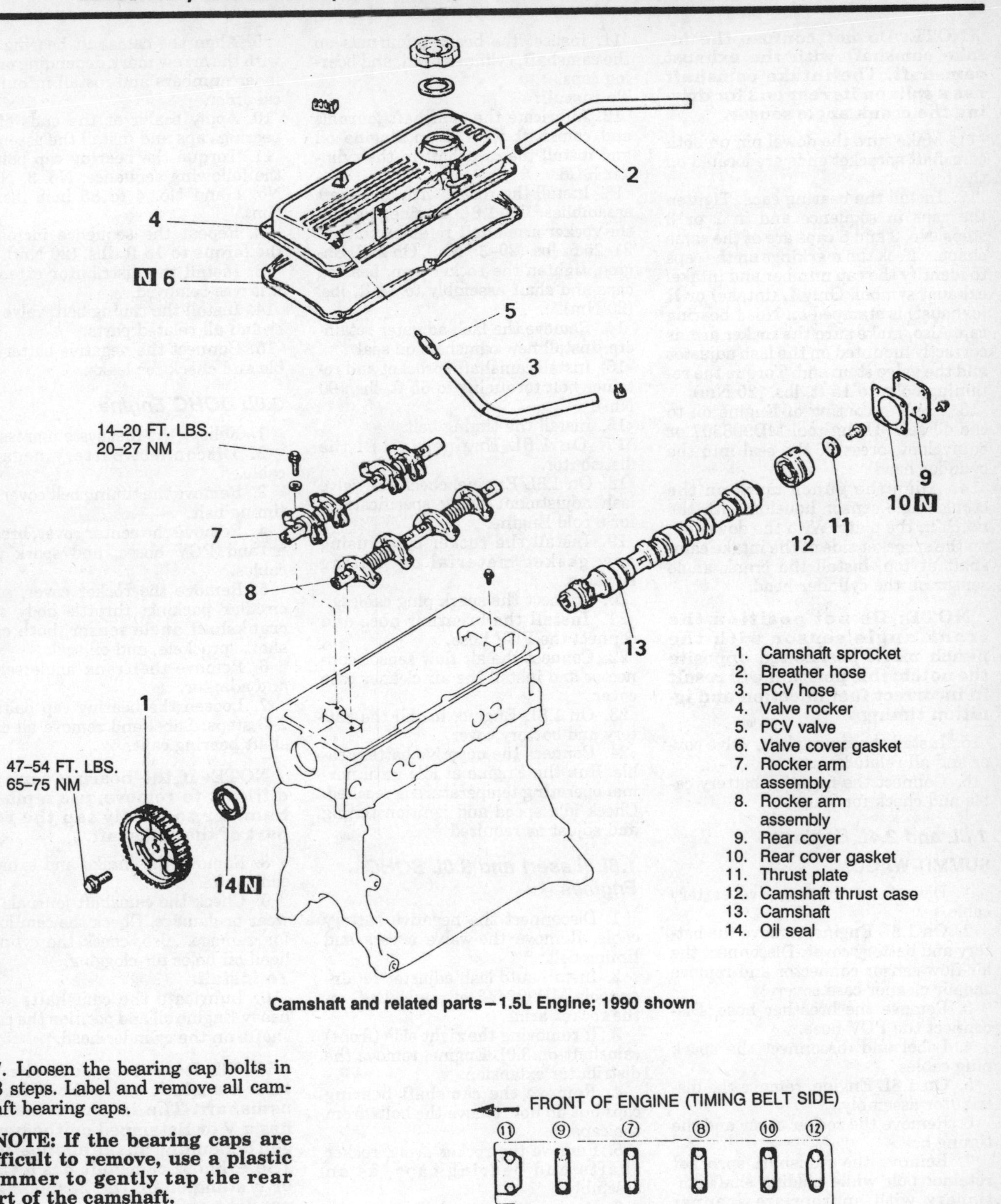

14–20 FT. LBS.
20–27 NM

47–54 FT. LBS.
65–75 NM

1. Camshaft sprocket
2. Breather hose
3. PCV hose
4. Valve rocker
5. PCV valve
6. Valve cover gasket
7. Rocker arm assembly
8. Rocker arm assembly
9. Rear cover
10. Rear cover gasket
11. Thrust plate
12. Camshaft thrust case
13. Camshaft
14. Oil seal

Camshaft and related parts—1.5L Engine; 1990 shown

7. Loosen the bearing cap bolts in 2–3 steps. Label and remove all camshaft bearing caps.

NOTE: If the bearing caps are difficult to remove, use a plastic hammer to gently tap the rear part of the camshaft.

8. Remove the intake and exhaust camshafts.

9. Check the camshaft journals for wear or damage. Check the cam lobes for damage. Also, check the cylinder head oil holes for clogging.

To install:

10. Lubricate the camshafts with heavy Engine oil and position the camshafts on the cylinder head.

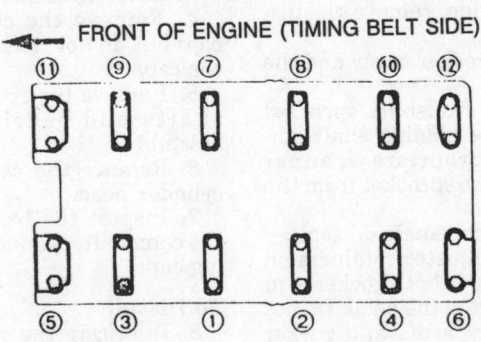

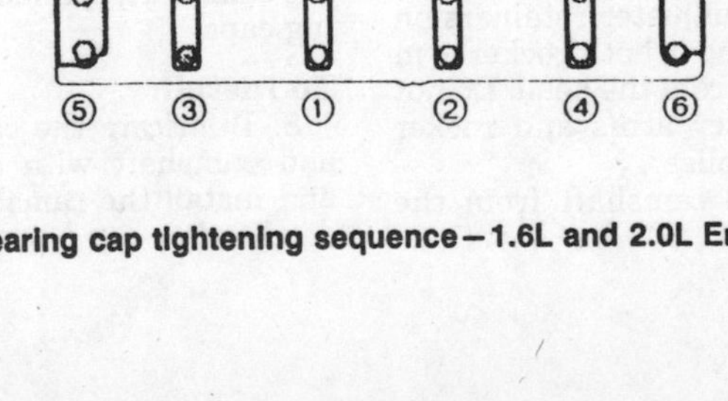

FRONT OF ENGINE (TIMING BELT SIDE)

⑪   ⑨   ⑦   ⑧   ⑩   ⑫

⑤   ③   ①   ②   ④   ⑥

Bearing cap tightening sequence—1.6L and 2.0L Engines

NOTE: Do not confuse the intake camshaft with the exhaust camshaft. The intake camshaft has a split on its rear end for driving the crank angle sensor.

11. Make sure the dowel pin on both camshaft sprocket ends are located on the top.

12. Install the bearing caps. Tighten the caps in sequence and in 2 or 3 steps. No. 2 and 5 caps are of the same shape. Check the markings on the caps to identify the cap number and intake/exhaust symbol. Only L (intake) or R (exhaust) is stamped on No. 1 bearing cap. Also, make sure the rocker arm is correctly mounted on the lash adjuster and the valve stem end. Torque the retaining bolts to 15 ft. lbs. (20 Nm).

13. Apply a coating of Engine oil to the oil seal. Using tool MD998307 or equivalent, press-fit the seal into the cylinder head.

14. Align the punch mark on the crank angle sensor housing with the notch in the plate. With the dowel pin on the sprocket side of the intake camshaft at top, install the crank angle sensor on the cylinder head.

NOTE: Do not position the crank angle sensor with the punch mark positioned opposite the notch; this position will result in incorrect fuel injection and ignition timing.

15. Install the timing belt, valve cover and all related parts.

16. Connect the negative battery cable and check for leaks.

1.8L and 2.4L Engines
SUMMIT WAGON

1. Disconnect the negative battery cable.

2. On 1.8L Engine, remove the battery and battery cover. Disconnect the air flow sensor connector and remove the air cleaner case cover.

3. Remove the breather hose. Disconnect the PCV hose.

4. Label and disconnect the spark plug cables.

5. On 1.8L Engine, remove the distributor assembly.

6. Remove the rocker cover and the timing belt.

7. Remove the camshaft sprocket retainer bolt while holding shaft stationary with appropriate spanner wrench. Remove the sprocket from the shaft.

8. Remove the camshaft oil seal.

9. Install lash adjuster retainers on 2.4L Engine. Remove both rocker arm shaft assemblies from the head. Do not disassemble rocker arms and rocker arm shaft assemblies.

10. Remove the camshaft from the cylinder.

11. Inspect the bearing journals on the camshaft, cylinder head, and bearing caps.

To install:

12. Lubricate the camshaft journals and camshaft with clean Engine oil and install the camshaft in the cylinder head.

13. Install the rocker arm and shaft assemblies. On 1.8L Engine, tighten the rocker arm shaft retainer bolts to 21–25 ft. lbs. (29–35 Nm). On 2.4L Engine, tighten the rocker arm, bearing caps and shaft assembly to 14 ft. lbs. (20 Nm).

14. Remove the lash adjuster retainers. Install new camshaft oil seal.

15. Install camshaft sprocket and retainer bolt torqueing to 65 ft. lbs. (90 Nm).

16. Install the timing belt.

17. On 1.8L Engine, install the distributor.

18. On 1.8L Engine, check the valve lash adjustment using specifications for a cold Engine.

19. Install the rocker cover using new gasket material on mating surfaces.

20. Connect the spark plug cables.

21. Install the breather hose and connect the PCV hose.

22. Connect the air flow sensor connector and install the air cleaner case cover.

23. On 1.8L Engine, install the battery and battery cover.

24. Connect the negative battery cable. Run the Engine at idle until normal operating temperature is reached. Check idle speed and ignition timing and adjust as required.

1.8L (Laser) and 3.0L SOHC Engines

1. Disconnect the negative battery cable. Remove the valve covers and timing belt.

2. Install auto lash adjuster retainer tools MD998443 or equivalent, on the rocker arms.

3. If removing the right side (front) camshaft on 3.0L Engine, remove the distributor extension.

4. Remove the camshaft bearing caps but do not remove the bolts from the caps.

5. Remove the rocker arms, rocker shafts and bearing caps, as an assembly.

6. Remove the camshaft from the cylinder head.

7. Inspect the bearing journals on the camshaft, cylinder head, and bearing caps.

To install:

8. Lubricate the camshaft journals and camshaft with clean Engine oil and install the camshaft in the cylinder head.

9. Align the camshaft bearing caps with the arrow mark depending on cylinder numbers and install in numerical order.

10. Apply sealer at the ends of the bearing caps and install the assembly.

11. Torque the bearing cap bolts in the following sequence: No. 3, No. 2, No. 1 and No. 4 to 85 inch lbs. (10 Nm).

12. Repeat the sequence increasing the torque to 15 ft. lbs. (20 Nm).

13. Install the distributor extension if it was removed.

14. Install the timing belt, valve cover and all related parts.

15. Connect the negative battery cable and check for leaks.

3.0L DOHC Engine

1. Relieve the fuel system pressure.

2. Disconnect battery negative cable.

3. Remove the timing belt cover and timing belt.

4. Remove the center cover, breather and PCV hoses, and spark plug cables.

5. Remove the rocker cover, semicircular packing, throttle body stay, crankshaft angle sensor, both camshaft sprockets, and oil seals.

6. Remove the crank angle sensor and adaptor.

7. Loosen the bearing cap bolts in 2–3 steps. Label and remove all camshaft bearing caps.

NOTE: If the bearing caps are difficult to remove, use a plastic hammer to gently tap the rear part of the camshaft.

8. Remove the intake and exhaust camshafts.

9. Check the camshaft journals for wear or damage. Check the cam lobes for damage. Also, check the cylinder head oil holes for clogging.

To install:

10. Lubricate the camshafts with heavy Engine oil and position the camshafts on the cylinder head.

NOTE: Do not confuse the intake camshaft with the exhaust camshaft. The intake camshaft has a V or B stamped on the hexagon depending on the application. The exhaust camshaft has a C, D or F stamped on the hexagon depending on application.

11. Make sure the dowel pin on both camshaft sprocket ends are located as shown.

12. Install the bearing caps. Tighten the caps in sequence and in 2 or 3 steps. Caps 2, 3 and 4 have a front mark. Install with the mark aligned with the front mark on the cylinder head. Intake caps have **I** stamped on

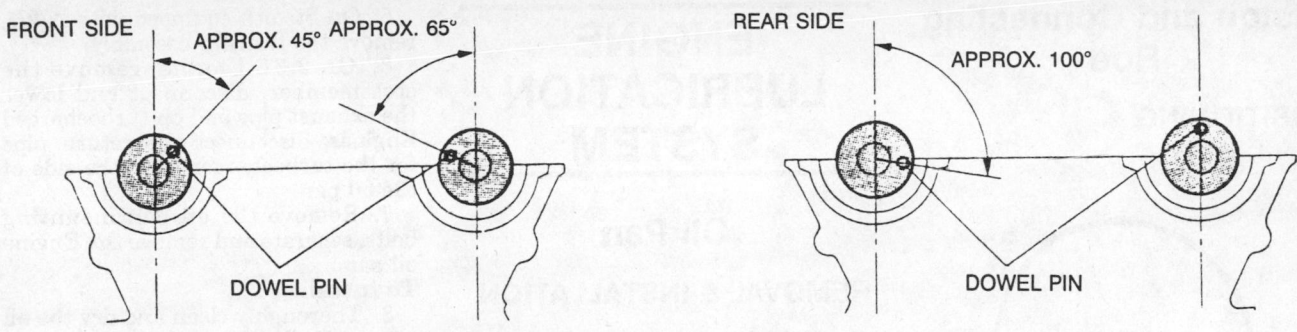

When installing the camshafts, position them so the dowel pins are as shown—3.0L DOHC Engine

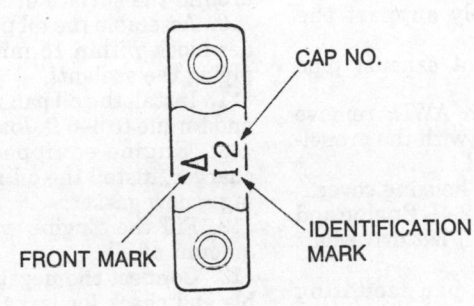

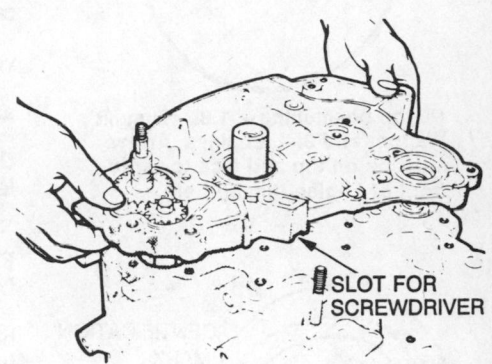

Slot used to remove sticking front case— 1.8L Engine

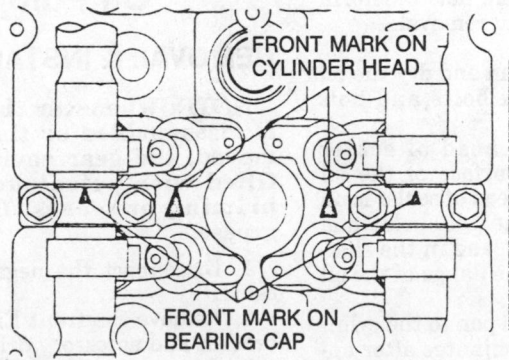

Align the marks on the caps and head as shown—3.0L DOHC Engine

the cap and exhaust caps have E. Also, make sure the rocker arm is correctly mounted on the lash adjuster and the valve stem end. Torque the retaining bolts to 15 ft. lbs. (20 Nm).

13. Apply a coating of Engine oil to the oil seals and install.

14. Install the timing belt, valve cover and all related parts.

15. Connect the negative battery cable and check for leaks.

Silent Shaft

REMOVAL & INSTALLATION

1.8L (Laser) and 2.4L Engines

1. Disconnect the negative battery cable.

2. Remove the oil filter, oil pressure switch, oil gauge sending unit, oil filter mounting bracket and gasket.

3. Raise and safely support the vehicle. Drain Engine oil. Remove Engine oil pan, oil screen and gasket.

4. Lower the vehicle. Remove the timing belts.

5. Remove the front Engine cover which is also the oil pump cover. Different length bolts are used. Take note of their locations. On 1.8L Engine, if the cover sticks to the block, look for a special slot provided and pry with a flat bladded tool. Discard the shaft seal and gasket.

6. Remove the oil pump driven gear flange bolt. When loosening this bolt, first insert a tool approximately ⅜ in. diameter into the plug hole on the left side of the cylinder block to hold the silent shaft. Remove the oil pump gears and remove the front case assembly.

Remove the threaded plug, the oil pressure relief spring and plunger.

7. Remove the silent shaft oil seals, the crankshaft oil seal and front case gasket.

8. Remove the silent shafts.

To install:

9. Carefully install the silent shafts to the block.

10. Install the oil pump components.

11. Install new seals and install the front case with a new gasket.

12. Install the timing belts and all related items. Make sure the orientation of the silent shafts is correct using alignment tool as specified in the timing belt section of this chapter.

NOTE: The timing of the oil pump sprocket and connected silent shaft can be incorrect, even with the timing mark aligned. Incorrect orientation of the silent shaft will result in Engine vibration during operation. Follow the alignment procedure in the timing belt section of this chapter.

13. Install the oil pan, oil filter mounting bracket, oil switches oil filter and oil.

14. Connect the negative battery cable and check for leaks.

Piston and Connecting Rod

POSITIONING

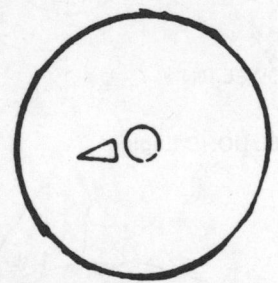

Piston positioning— 1.8L (Summit Wagon) and 2.4L Engines. Arrow must be on top and face towards front of Engine (timing belt).

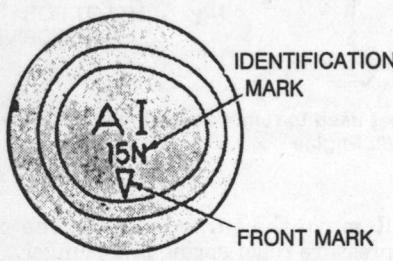

Piston Identification marks—1.5L Engine

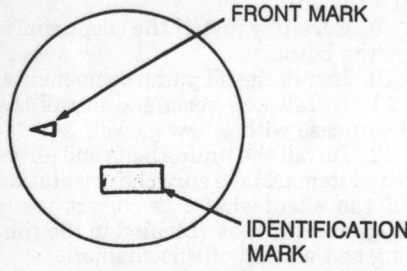

Piston Identification marks—1.6L, 1.8L and 2.0L Engines

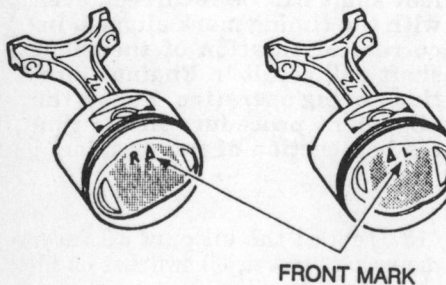

Piston Identification marks—3.0L Engine

ENGINE LUBRICATION SYSTEM

Oil Pan

REMOVAL & INSTALLATION

Summit Wagon

1. Disconnect negative battery cable.
2. Raise and safely support the vehicle.
3. Remove the front exhaust pipe and gasket.
4. If equipped with AWD, remove the transfer assembly with the propeller shaft still installed.
5. Remove the bell housing cover.
6. If equipped with 2.4L Engine and FWD, remove the front left driveshaft from the transaxle.
7. Remove the oil pan mounting bolts and nuts. Remove the oil pan using tool MD998727 or equivalent, and a brass bar. Take care not to deform the pan flange during removal.

To install:

8. Thoroughly clean and dry the oil pan, cylinder block bolts and bolt holes.
9. Apply a thin bead of sealer around the flange surface of the oil pan. Make sure the bead of sealer is on the area between the bolt holes and the inside of the pan, and in the shallow groove around the flange of the oil pan.
10. Assemble the oil pan to the cylinder block within 15 minutes after applying the sealant.
11. Install the oil pan mounting bolts and nuts and tighten to 5 ft. lbs. (7 Nm).
12. Install the bellhousing cover.
13. Install the front driveshaft.
14. Install the transfer assembly.
15. Install the front exhaust pipe.
16. Lower the vehicle and add clean Engine oil to the correct level. Reconnect the negative battery cable and check for leaks.

Except Summit Wagon

1. Disconnect the negative battery cable.
2. Raise the vehicle and support safely.
3. Remove the oil pan drain plug and drain the Engine oil. On 1.6L Engine equipped with turbocharger, remove the oil return pipe and gasket.
4. On 1.8L Engine, disconnect and lower the exhaust pipe.

5. On Stealth equipped with AWD, remove the transfer assembly.
6. On 2.0L Engine, remove the crossmember, disconnect and lower the exhaust pipe and on turbocharged Engines, disconnect the return pipe for the turbocharger from the side of the oil pan.
7. Remove the oil pan mounting bolts, separate and remove the Engine oil pan.

To install:

8. Thoroughly clean and dry the oil pan, cylinder block bolts and bolt holes.
9. Apply a thin bead of sealer around the surface of the oil pan.
10. Assemble the oil pan to the cylinder block within 15 minutes after applying the sealant.
11. Install the oil pan mounting bolts and torque to 4–6 ft. lbs. (6–8 Nm). On 1.6L Engine equipped with turbocharger, install the oil return pipe using a new gasket.
12. Fill the Engine with the proper amount of oil.
13. Connect the negative battery cable and check for leaks.

Oil Pump

REMOVAL & INSTALLATION

NOTE: Whenever the oil pump is disassembled or the cover removed, the gear cavity must be filled with petroleum jelly for priming purposes. Do not use grease.

1. Disconnect the negative battery cable.
2. Remove the front Engine mount bracket and accessory drive belts.
3. Remove timing belt upper and lower covers.
4. Remove the timing belt and crankshaft sprocket.
5. Remove the oil pan.
6. Remove the oil screen and gasket.
7. Remove and tag the front cover mounting bolts. Note the lengths of the mounting bolts as they are removed for proper installation.
8. On 1.6L Engine, remove the plug cap using tool MD998162 or equivalent, and remove the oil pressure switch.
9. Remove the front case cover and oil pump assembly. If necessary, the silent shaft can come out with the assembly. Disassemble as required.

NOTE: On 1.5L Engine, the outer gear does not have any marks indicating its installed direction. Make a mark on the reverse side of the outer gear so it can be reinstalled in its proper position.

1. Oil filter
2. Oil pressure switch
3. Oil pressure gauge unit
4. Oil filter bracket
5. Gasket
6. Drain plug
7. Drain plug gasket
8. Oil pan
9. Oil screen
10. Gasket
11. Oil pump cover
12. Oil seal
13. Gasket
14. Flange bolt
15. Pump driven gear
16. Pump drive gear
17. Front case
18. Plug
19. Relief spring
20. Relief plunger
21. Silent shaft oil seal
22. Crankshaft front seal
23. Gasket
24. Right side silent shaft
25. Left side silent shaft
26. Silent shaft front bearing
27. Silent shaft rear bearing

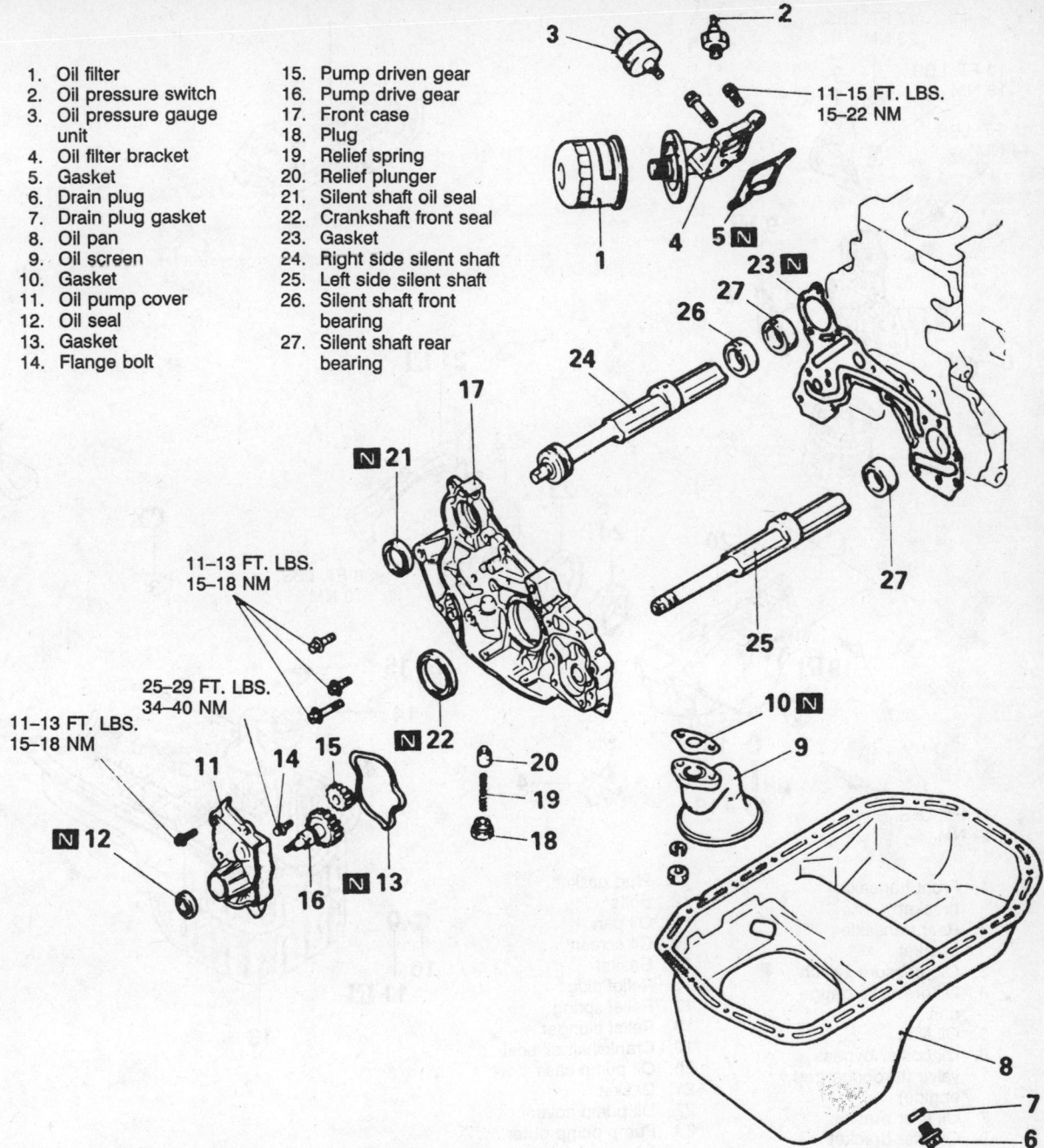

Front case, oil pump and related components—1.8L Engine—1.6L and 2.0L Engines are similar

To install:

10. Thoroughly clean all gasket material from all mounting surfaces.

11. Apply Engine oil to the entire surface of the gears or rotors. On 1.5L Engine, make sure the outer gear is installed in the same direction as before according to the mark made at the time of removal.

12. On Engines with silent shafts and 1.8L (Summit Wagon) Engine, install the drive/driven gears with the 2 timing marks aligned.

13. Assemble the front case cover and oil pump assembly to the Engine block using a new gasket. On 1.6L Engine, assemble the front case cover and oil pump assembly using tool MD998285 or equivalent, on the front end of the crankshaft.

14. Install the oil screen with new gasket.

15. Install the oil pan and timing belts.

16. Connect the negative battery cable and check for adequate oil pressure.

CHECKING

1. After disassembling the oil pump, clean all parts.

2. Assemble the oil pump gear to the front case and rotate it to ensure smooth rotation and no looseness. Make sure there is no ridge wear on the contact surface between the front case and the gear surface of the oil pump front cover.

3. The gear clearance should be checked using the following procedure:

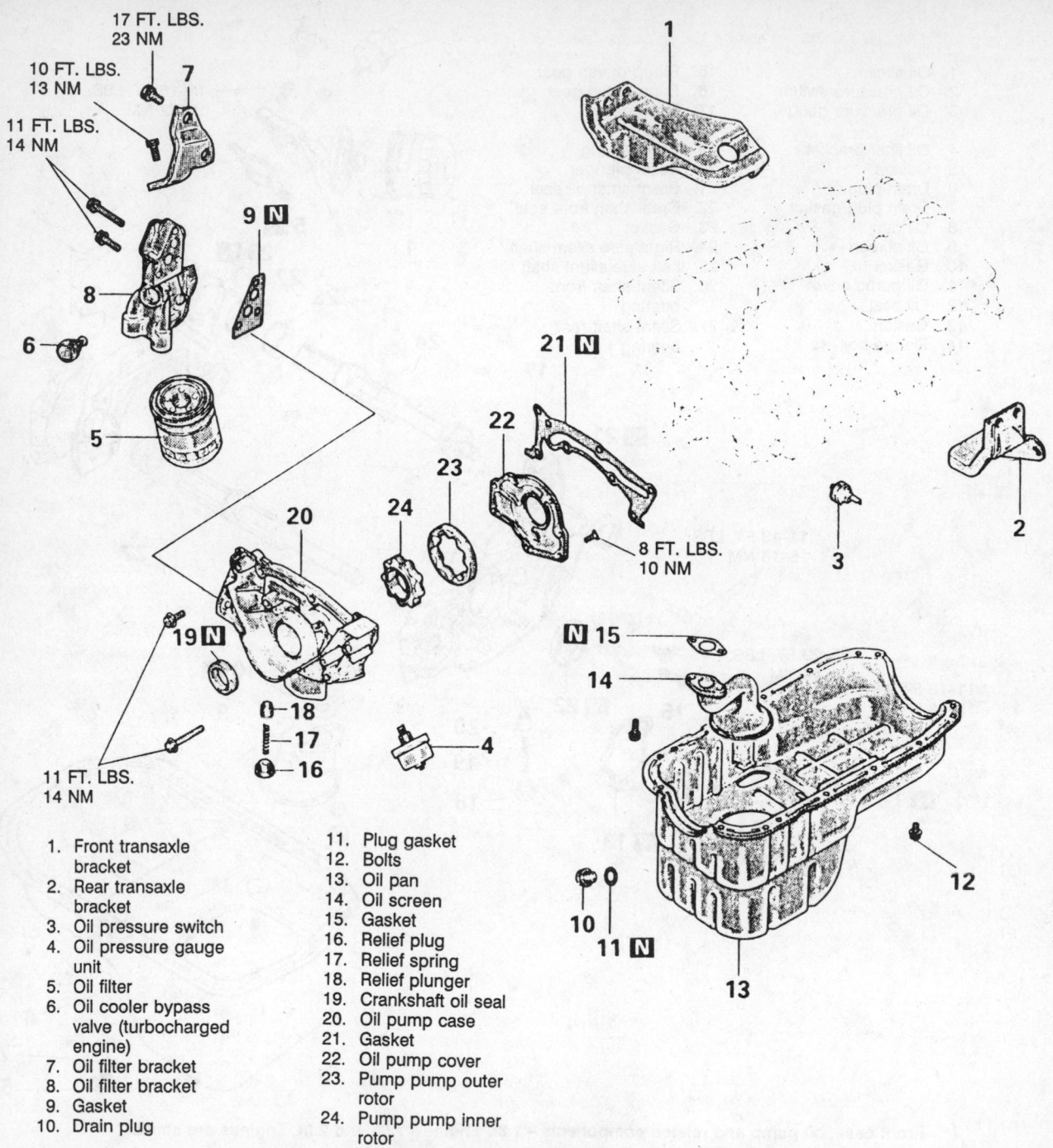

17 FT. LBS.
23 NM

10 FT. LBS.
13 NM

11 FT. LBS.
14 NM

11 FT. LBS.
14 NM

8 FT. LBS.
10 NM

1. Front transaxle
   bracket
2. Rear transaxle
   bracket
3. Oil pressure switch
4. Oil pressure gauge
   unit
5. Oil filter
6. Oil cooler bypass
   valve (turbocharged
   engine)
7. Oil filter bracket
8. Oil filter bracket
9. Gasket
10. Drain plug

11. Plug gasket
12. Bolts
13. Oil pan
14. Oil screen
15. Gasket
16. Relief plug
17. Relief spring
18. Relief plunger
19. Crankshaft oil seal
20. Oil pump case
21. Gasket
22. Oil pump cover
23. Pump pump outer
    rotor
24. Pump pump inner
    rotor

Oil pump and related components – 3.0L Engine – 1.5L Engine is similar

a. On 1.5L Engine, check the outer ring shaped gear. The distance between the outer circumference and the front case should be 0.0039–0.0079 in. The outer gear's side clearance be 0.0016–0.0039 in. The tip clearance or clearance between the outer and inner gear teeth with the inner gear teeth meshed, should be 0.0024–0.0071 in. with a maximum limit of 0.0138 in.

b. On 1.6L and 2.4L Engines, with the drive and driven gears installed in the front case, measure the tip clearance of the gears. The distance between the tips of the drive gear's teeth and the case should be 0.0063–0.0083 in. with a limit of 0.0098 in. The distance between the tips of the driven gear's teeth and the case should be 0.0051–0.0071 in. with a limit of 0.0098 in. The end-play is checked by placing a straight-edge across the machined cover surface and measuring with a feeler gauge. The endplay for the

drive gear should be 0.0031–0.0055 in. with a limit of 0.0098 in. The endplay for the driven gear on 1.6L Engine is 0.0024–0.0047 in. with a limit of 0.0098 in. and 0.0051–0.0071 in. with a limit of 0.0098 in.

c. On 1.8L (Laser) Engine, with the drive and driven gears installed in the front case, measure the tip clearance of the gears. The distance between the tips of the drive gear's teeth and the case should be 0.0024–0.0047 in. with a limit of 0.079 in.

The distance between the tips of the driven gear's teeth and the case should be 0.0039–0.0079 in. with a limit of 0.071 in. The endplay is checked by placing a straight-edge across the machined cover surface and measuring with a feeler gauge. The endplay for the drive gear should be 0.0039–0.0063 in. with a limit of 0.008 in. The endplay for the driven gear is 0.0008–0.0020 in. with a limit of 0.006 in.

d. On 1.8L (Summit Wagon) Engine, with the drive and driven gears installed in the front case, measure the tip clearance of the gears. The distance between the tips of the inner gear's teeth and the case should be 0.0016–0.0039 in. (0.06–0.18mm). The distance between the outer gear and the case should be 0.0039–0.0071 in. (0.10–0.18mm). The distance between the upper portion of the inner gear teeth and the teeth of the outer gear is 0.0024–0.0071 in. (0.06–0.18mm).

e. On 2.0L Engine, with the drive and driven gears installed in the front case, measure the tip clearance of the gears. The distance between the tips of the drive gear's teeth and the case should be 0.0063–0.0083 in. with a limit of 0.0098 in. The distance between the tips of the driven gear's teeth and the case should be 0.0051–0.0071 in. with a limit of 0.0098 in. The endplay is checked by placing a straight-edge across the machined cover surface and measuring with a feeler gauge. The endplay for the drive gear should be 0.0031–0.0055 in. with a limit of 0.0098 in. The endplay for the driven gear is 0.0024–0.0047 in. with a limit of 0.0098 in.

f. On 3.0L Engine, assemble the rotors on the pump housing and check the clearance between the rotors and the housing. The clearance specification is 0.0039–0.0071 in. The side clearance is checked by placing a straight-edge across the machined cover surface and measuring with a feeler gauge. This specification is 0.0016–0.0037 in.

4. If any measurement is beyond specification, replace the entire pump assembly.

Rear Main Bearing Oil Seal

REMOVAL & INSTALLATION

1. Disconnect the negative battery cable.
2. Remove the transaxle from the vehicle.
3. Remove the flywheel/ring gear assembly.
4. Remove the rear Engine plate and the bellhousing cover.
5. If the crankshaft rear oil seal case is leaking, remove it. Otherwise, just remove the oil seal. Some Engines have a separator that should also be removed.

To install:
6. Lubricate the inner diameter of the new seal with clean Engine oil.
7. Install the oil seal in the crankshaft rear oil seal case using tool MD998376 or equivalent. Press the seal all the way in without tilting it. Force the oil separator into the oil seal case so the oil hole in the separator is downward.
8. Install the seal case with a new gasket.
9. Install the flywheel and transaxle.
10. Connect the negative battery cable and check for leaks.

ENGINE COOLING

Radiator

REMOVAL & INSTALLATION

1. Disconnect the negative battery cable.
2. Drain the cooling system.
3. Disconnect the overflow tube. Some vehicles may also require removal of the overflow tank.
4. Disconnect upper and lower radiator hoses.
5. Disconnect electrical connectors for cooling fan and air conditioning condenser fan, if equipped. Remove the fan assembly.
6. Disconnect thermo sensor wires.
7. Disconnect and plug automatic transaxle cooler lines, if equipped with automatic transaxle.
8. Remove the upper radiator mounts and lift out the radiator assembly.
9. Service the lower mounts, as required.
To install:
10. Install the radiator and fan assembly, if removed as an assembly.
11. Connect the automatic transaxle cooler lines, if disconnected.
12. Connect the thermo wires.
13. Install the fan if removed separately.
14. Install the radiator hoses.
15. Install the overflow tube and reservoir, if removed.
16. Fill the system with coolant.
17. Connect the negative battery ca-

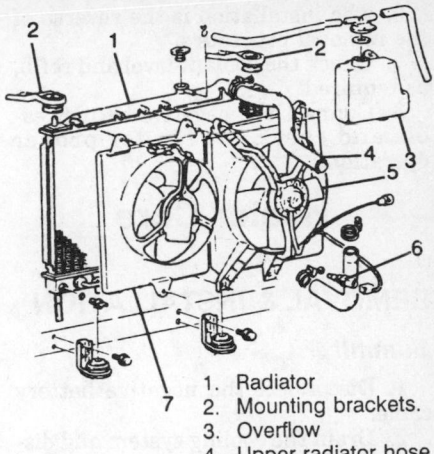

1. Radiator
2. Mounting brackets.
3. Overflow
4. Upper radiator hose
5. Cooling fan
6. Thermo switch
7. A/C condenser fan

Representative electric cooling fan and radiator assembly

ble, run the vehicle until the thermostat opens, fill the radiator completely and check the automatic transaxle fluid level, if equipped.
18. Once the vehicle has cooled, recheck the coolant level.

Electric Cooling Fan

TESTING

———— **CAUTION** ————
Make sure the key is in the OFF position when checking the electric cooling fan. If not, the fan could turn ON at any time, causing serious personal injury.

1. Disconnect the negative battery cable.
2. Disconnect the electrical plug from the fan motor harness.
3. Apply battery voltage to the appropriate terminals and make sure motor runs smoothly, without abnormal noise or vibration.
4. Reconnect the negative battery cable.

REMOVAL & INSTALLATION

1. Disconnect the negative battery cable. Drain the cooling system.
2. Unplug the connector(s). Most of these connectors employ a waterproof connector. When disconnecting, make sure all parts of the connector remain intact.
3. Disconnect the upper radiator hose from the radiator.
4. Remove the fan mounting screws. The radiator and condenser cooling fans are separately removable.
5. Remove the fan assembly and disassemble as required.

6. The installation is the reverse of the removal procedure.

7. Check the coolant level and refill, as required.

8. Connect the negative battery cable and check the fan for proper operation.

Heater Core

REMOVAL & INSTALLATION

Summit

1. Disconnect the negative battery cable.

2. Drain the cooling system and disconnect the heater hoses.

3. Remove the front seats as follows:

   a. Remove the covers over the anchor nuts and bolts and the seat belt guide ring.

   b. Disconnect the seat belt switch wiring harness from under the seat.

   c. Remove the fasteners and lift the front seats from the vehicle.

4. Remove the floor console by first taking out the coin holder and the console box tray. Remove the remote control mirror switch or cover. All of these items require only a plastic trim tool to carefully pry them out.

5. Remove the rear console box assembly.

6. Remove the shift lever knob on manual transaxle vehicles.

7. Remove the front console box assembly.

8. A number of the instrument panel pieces may be retained by pin type fasteners. They may be removed using the following procedure:

   a. This type of clip is removed by pressing down on the center pin with a blunt pointed tool. Press down a little more than $1/16$ in. (2mm); this releases the clip. Pull the clip outward to remove it.

   b. Do not push the pin inward more than necessary because it may damage the grommet or the pin may fall in, if pushed in too far. Once the clips are removed, use a plastic trim stick to pry the piece loose.

9. Remove both lower cowl trim panels (kick panels).

10. Remove the ashtray.

11. Remove the center panel around the radio.

12. Remove the sunglass pocket at the upper left side of panel and the side panel into which it mounts.

13. Remove the hood release handle and the driver's side knee protector.

14. Remove the steering column top and bottom covers.

15. Remove the radio.

16. Remove the glove box assembly and striker.

17. Remove the instrument panel lower cover, 2 small pieces in the center, by pulling forward.

18. Remove the heater control assembly screw.

19. Remove the instrument cluster bezel and pull out the gauge assembly.

20. Remove the speedometer adapter by disconnecting the speedometer cable at the transaxle pulling the cable sightly towards the vehicle interior and giving a slight twist on the adapter to release it.

21. Insert a small flat-tipped tool to open the tab on the gauge cluster connector. Remove the harness connectors.

22. Remove, by prying with a plastic trim tool, the right side speaker cover and the speaker, the upper side defroster grilles and the clock or plug to gain access to some of the instrument panel mounting bolts.

23. Lower the steering column by removing the bolt and nut.

24. Remove the instrument panel bolts and the instrument panel.

25. Disconnect the air selection, temperature and mode selection control cables from the heater box and remove the heater control assembly.

26. Remove the connector for the ECI control relay.

27. Remove both stamped steel instrument panel supports.

28. Remove the heater duct work.

29. Remove the heater box mounting nuts.

30. Remove the automatic transaxle ELC control box.

31. Remove the evaporator mounting nuts and clips.

32. With the evaporator pulled toward the vehicle interior, remove the heater unit. Be careful not to damage the heater tubes or to spill coolant inside the vehicle.

33. Remove the cover plate around the heater tubes and the core fastener

1. Lower cover
2. Screw
3. Cluster bezel
4. Instrument cluster
5. Speedometer cable adaptor
6. Wiring harness
7. Speaker garnish
8. Speaker
9. Side defroster grille
10. Clock or plug
11. Mounting bolts
12. Instrument panel mounting bolts
13. Instrument panel

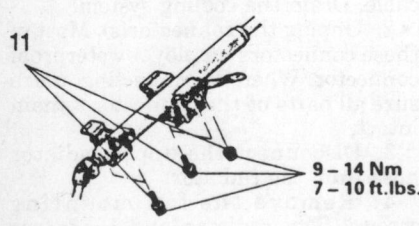

9 – 14 Nm
7 – 10 ft.lbs.

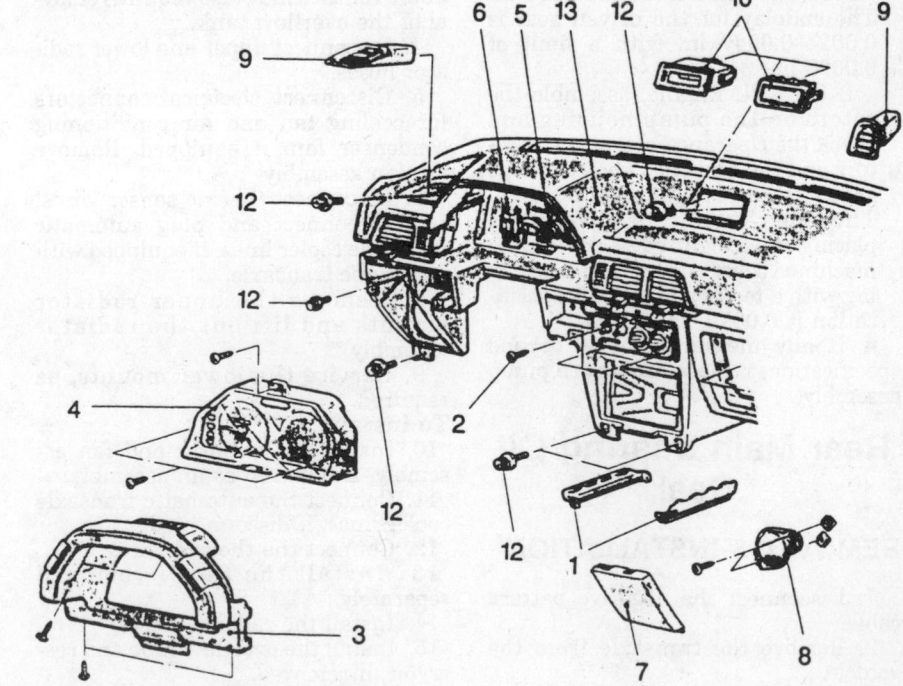

Instrument panel and related parts—Summit

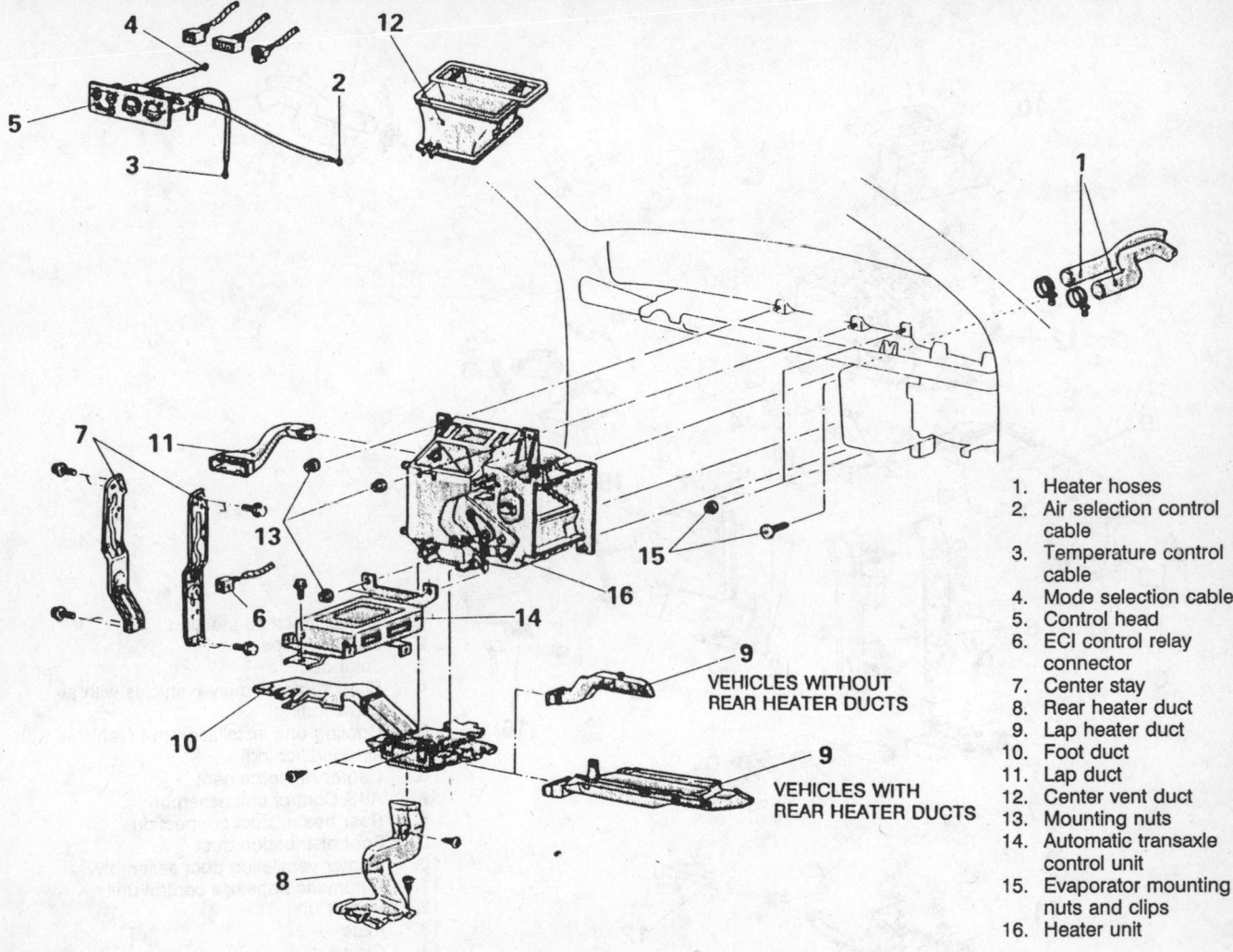

Heater case and related parts—Summit

1. Heater hoses
2. Air selection control cable
3. Temperature control cable
4. Mode selection cable
5. Control head
6. ECI control relay connector
7. Center stay
8. Rear heater duct
9. Lap heater duct
10. Foot duct
11. Lap duct
12. Center vent duct
13. Mounting nuts
14. Automatic transaxle control unit
15. Evaporator mounting nuts and clips
16. Heater unit

clips. Pull the heater core from the heater box, being careful not to damage the fins or tank ends.

To install:

34. Thoroughly clean and dry the inside of the case. Install the heater core to the heater box. Install the clips and cover.

35. Install the heater unit into position on the vehicle while pulling outward on the evaporator.

36. Install the evaporator and heater unit mounting nuts and clips.

37. Install the automatic transaxle ELC box.

38. Connect the air selection, temperature and mode selection control cables from the heater box and install the heater control assembly.

39. Install both stamped steel instrument panel supports. Connect the connector for the ECI control relay.

40. Install the remaining instrument panel components reversing the removal procedure.

41. Install the center console as follows:

a. Install the front console box assembly.

b. Install the shift lever knob on manual transaxle vehicles.

c. Install the rear console box assembly.

d. Install the remote control mirror switch or cover.

e. Install the coin holder and the console box tray.

42. Position the front seats into the vehicle. Install and torque the front seat retainer nuts to 26 ft. lbs. (36 Nm) and the rear mounting bolts to 25–40 ft. lbs. (35–55 Nm).

43. Install fastener covers and connect the wiring harness at the seat.

44. Refill the cooling system.

45. Evacuate and recharge the air conditioning system. Add 2 oz. of refrigerant oil during the recharge, if the evaporator was replaced.

46. Connect the negative battery cable and check the entire climate control system for proper operation. Check the system for leaks.

Summit Wagon

1. Disconnect negative battery cable.

2. Drain the Engine coolant.

3. Remove the hood lock release handle, instrument panel under cover, lower frame, foot duct, lap duct and the lap heater duct.

4. Remove the glove box, speaker harness and the glove box frame.

5. Remove the meter hood and combination meter from the instrument panel. Remove the adapter lock and pull the speedometer cable into the passenger compartment slightly. Remove the rear of the adapter from the cable. Next, turn the adapter so the notched section is aligned with the tab on the cable section and slide adapter outward to remove.

6. Remove the ash tray from the center panel. Remove the mounting screws, radio and the center panel from the vehicle.

7. Remove the center air outlet from instrument panel by removing

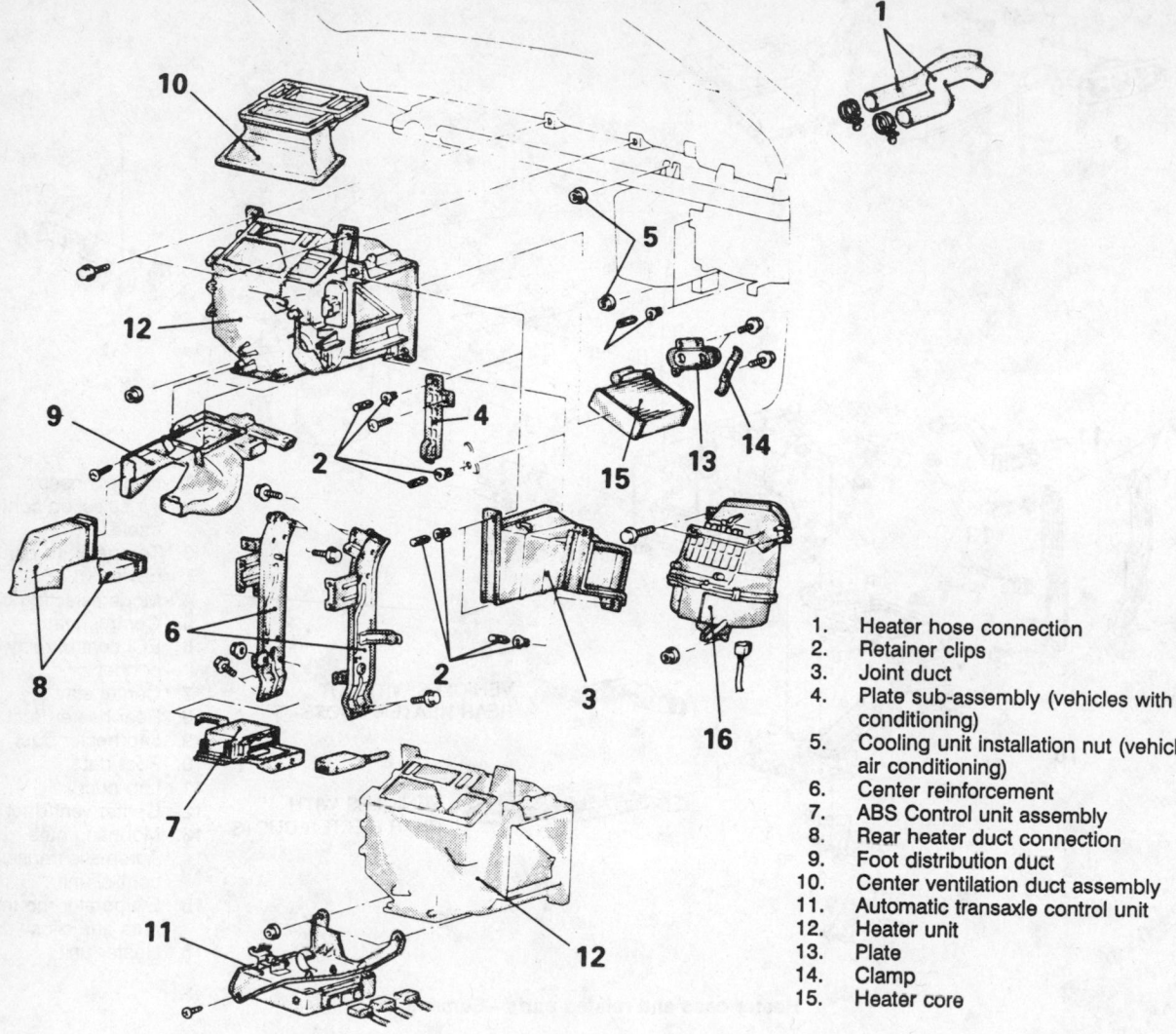

1. Heater hose connection
2. Retainer clips
3. Joint duct
4. Plate sub-assembly (vehicles with air conditioning)
5. Cooling unit installation nut (vehicles with air conditioning)
6. Center reinforcement
7. ABS Control unit assembly
8. Rear heater duct connection
9. Foot distribution duct
10. Center ventilation duct assembly
11. Automatic transaxle control unit
12. Heater unit
13. Plate
14. Clamp
15. Heater core

Heater case and related components—1992–93 Summit Wagon

the clip on the lower section of the outlet. Next insert a flat tipped tool in between the fins and remove the clip on the top section while pulling the lock spring toward the inside. Remove the center air outlet assembly.

8. Disconnect the air selection, temperature and mode selection control cables from the heater box and remove the heater control assembly.

9. Remove the clock or plug from the upper instrument panel. Remove the instrument panel retaining bolt under the plug.

10. Lower the steering column by removing the bolt and nut under the column.

11. Remove the floor console side covers. If equipped with manual transaxle, remove the shifter knob.

12. Remove the floor console switch panel, mounting bolts and the floor console from the vehicle.

13. Remove the instrument panel retainer bolts and the instrument panel.

14. Disconnect the heater hoses at the heater box.

15. Remove the heater joint duct by first removing the pin type retainer clips on the duct using the following procedure:

  a. This type of clip is removed by pressing down on the center pin with a blunt pointed tool. Press down a little more than $1/16$ in. (2mm); this releases the clip. Pull the clip outward to remove it.

  b. Do not push the pin inward more than necessary because it may damage the grommet or the pin may fall in if pushed in too far. Once the clips are removed, use a plastic trim stick to pry the piece loose.

16. Remove the center reinforcement. Remove the cooling unit mount-

ing nut, if equipped with air conditioning.

17. Disconnect and remove the ABS control unit and the automatic transmission ELC control unit.

18. Remove the foot distribution duct and disconnect the rear heater duct connection.

19. Remove both stamped steel instrument panel supports.

20. Remove the mounting bolts and the heater unit from the vehicle. Be careful not to damage the heater tubes or to spill coolant inside the vehicle.

21. Remove the cover plate around the heater tubes and the core fastener clips. Pull the heater core from the heater box, being careful not to damage the fins or tank ends.

To install:

22. Thoroughly clean and dry the inside of the case. Install the heater core

to the heater box. Install the clips and cover.

23. Install the heater unit into position on the vehicle and install the evaporator and heater unit mounting nuts and clips.

24. Install the automatic transaxle ELC box and the ABS control unit.

25. Connect the air selection, temperature and mode selection control cables from the heater box and install the heater control assembly.

26. Install both stamped steel instrument panel supports. Connect the connector for the ECI control relay.

27. Install the remaining instrument panel components reversing the removal procedure.

28. Install the center console as follows:

    a. Install the front console box assembly.

    b. Install the shift lever knob on manual transaxle vehicles.

    c. Install the rear console box assembly.

    d. Install the floor console switch panel

    e. Install the coin holder and the console box tray.

29. Refill the cooling system.

30. Evacuate and recharge the air conditioning system. Add 2 oz. of refrigerant oil during the recharge, if the evaporator was replaced.

31. Connect the negative battery cable and check the entire climate control system for proper operation. Check the system for leaks.

Laser and Talon

1. Disconnect the negative battery cable.

2. Drain the cooling system and discharge the air conditioning system. Disconnect the refrigerant lines from the evaporator, if equipped. Cover the exposed ends of the lines to minimize contamination.

3. Remove the floor console by first removing the plugs, then the screws retaining the side covers and the small cover piece in front of the shifter. Remove the shifter knob, if equipped with manual transmission, and the cup holder. Remove both small pieces of upholstery to gain access to retainer screws. Disconnect both electrical connectors at the front of the console. Remove the shoulder harness guide plates and the console assembly.

4. Locate the rectangular plugs in the knee protector on either side of the steering column. Pry these plugs out and remove the screws. Remove the

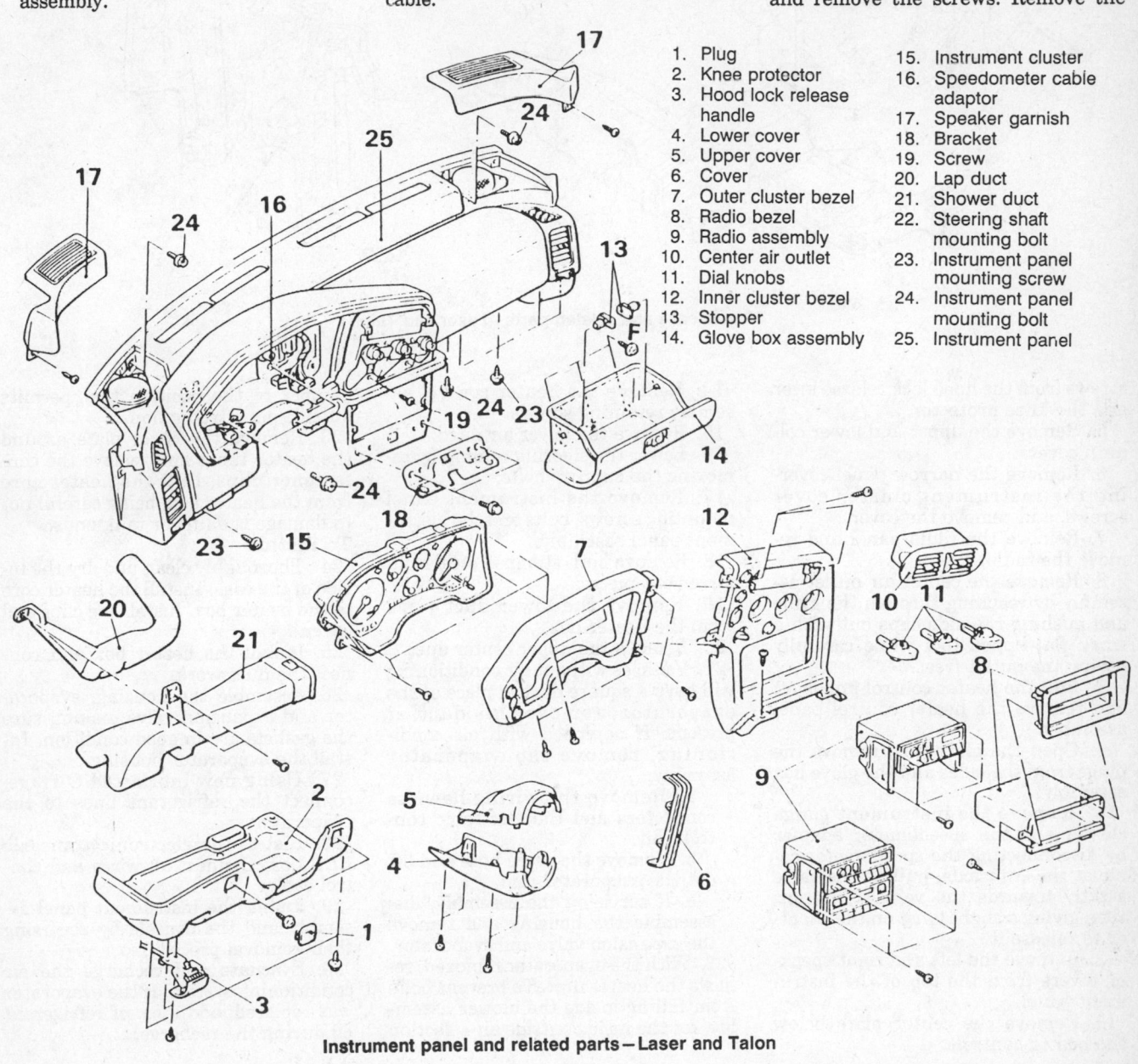

1. Plug
2. Knee protector
3. Hood lock release handle
4. Lower cover
5. Upper cover
6. Cover
7. Outer cluster bezel
8. Radio bezel
9. Radio assembly
10. Center air outlet
11. Dial knobs
12. Inner cluster bezel
13. Stopper
14. Glove box assembly
15. Instrument cluster
16. Speedometer cable adaptor
17. Speaker garnish
18. Bracket
19. Screw
20. Lap duct
21. Shower duct
22. Steering shaft mounting bolt
23. Instrument panel mounting screw
24. Instrument panel mounting bolt
25. Instrument panel

Instrument panel and related parts—Laser and Talon

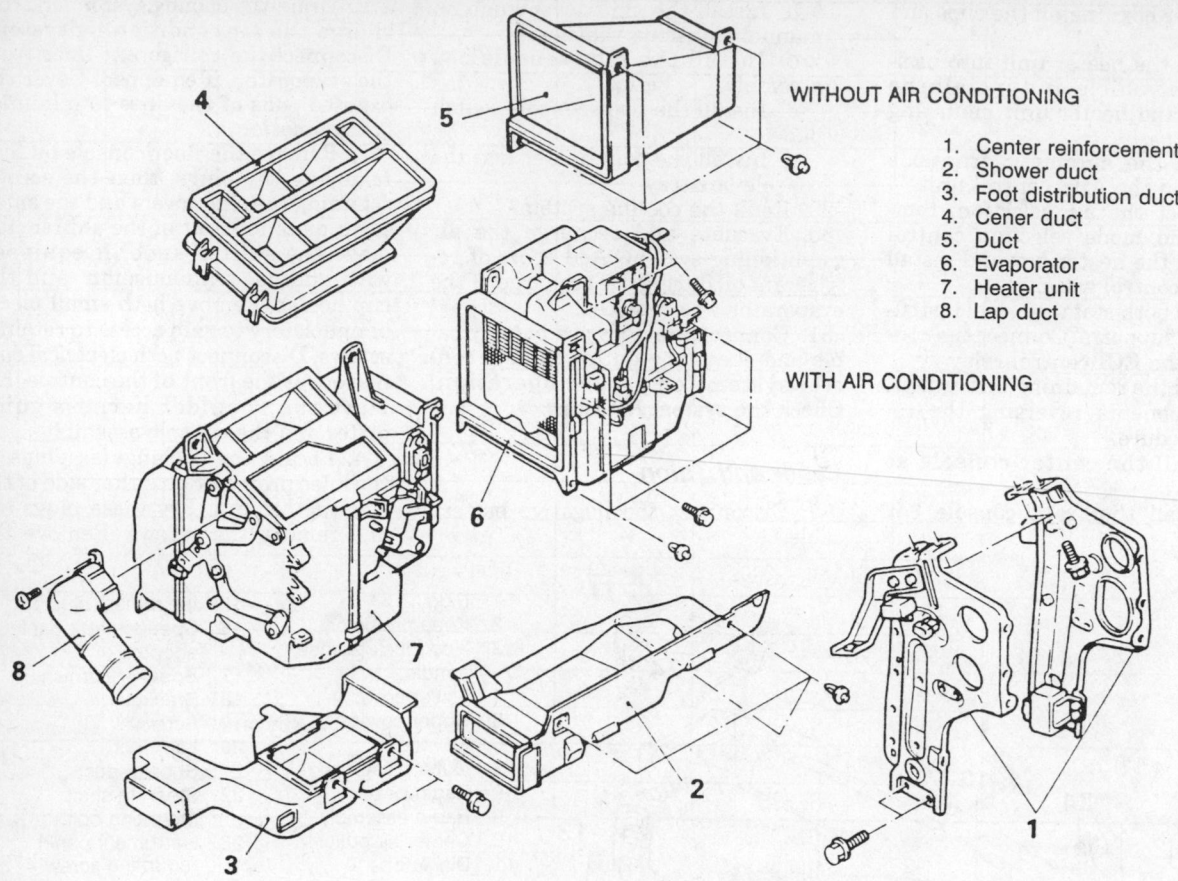

WITHOUT AIR CONDITIONING

1. Center reinforcement
2. Shower duct
3. Foot distribution duct
4. Cener duct
5. Duct
6. Evaporator
7. Heater unit
8. Lap duct

WITH AIR CONDITIONING

Heater case and related parts—Laser and Talon

screws from the hood lock release lever and the knee protector.

5. Remove the upper and lower column covers.

6. Remove the narrow panel covering the instrument cluster cover screws, and remove the cover.

7. Remove the radio panel and remove the radio.

8. Remove the center air outlet assembly by reaching through the grille and pushing the side clips out with a small flat-tipped tool while carefully prying the outlet free.

9. Pull the heater control knobs off and remove the heater control panel assembly.

10. Open the glove box, remove the plugs from the sides and the glove box assembly.

11. Remove the instrument gauge cluster and the speedometer adapter by disconnecting the speedometer cable at the transaxle, pulling the cable sightly towards the vehicle interior, then giving a slight twist on the adapter to release it.

12. Remove the left and right speaker covers from the top of the instrument panel.

13. Remove the center plate below the heater controls.

14. Remove the heater control assembly retaining screws.

15. Remove the lower air ducts.

16. Lower the steering column by removing the support bolts.

17. Remove the instrument panel mounting screws, bolts and the instrument panel assembly.

18. Remove both stamped steel reinforcement pieces.

19. Remove the lower duct work from the heater box.

20. Remove the upper center duct.

21. Vehicles without air conditioning will have a square duct in place of the evaporator; remove this duct, if present. If equipped with air conditioning, remove the evaporator assembly:

a. Remove the wiring harness connectors and the electronic control unit.

b. Remove the drain hose and lift out the evaporator unit.

c. If servicing the assembly, disassemble the housing and remove the expansion valve and evaporator.

22. With the evaporator removed, remove the heater unit. To prevent bolts from falling inside the blower assembly, set the inside/outside air-selection

damper to the position that permits outside air introduction.

23. Remove the cover plate around the heater tubes and remove the core fastener clips. Pull the heater core from the heater box, being careful not to damage the fins or tank ends.

To install:

24. Thoroughly clean and dry the inside of the case. Install the heater core to the heater box. Install the clips and cover.

25. Install the heater box and connect the duct work.

26. Assemble the housing, evaporator and expansion valve making sure the gaskets are in good condition. Install the evaporator housing.

27. Using new lubricated O-rings, connect the refrigerant lines to the evaporator.

28. Install the electronic transaxle ELC box. Connect all wires and control cables.

29. Install the instrument panel assembly and the console by reversing their removal procedures.

30. Evacuate and recharge the air conditioning system. If the evaporator was replaced, add 2 oz. of refrigerant oil during the recharge.

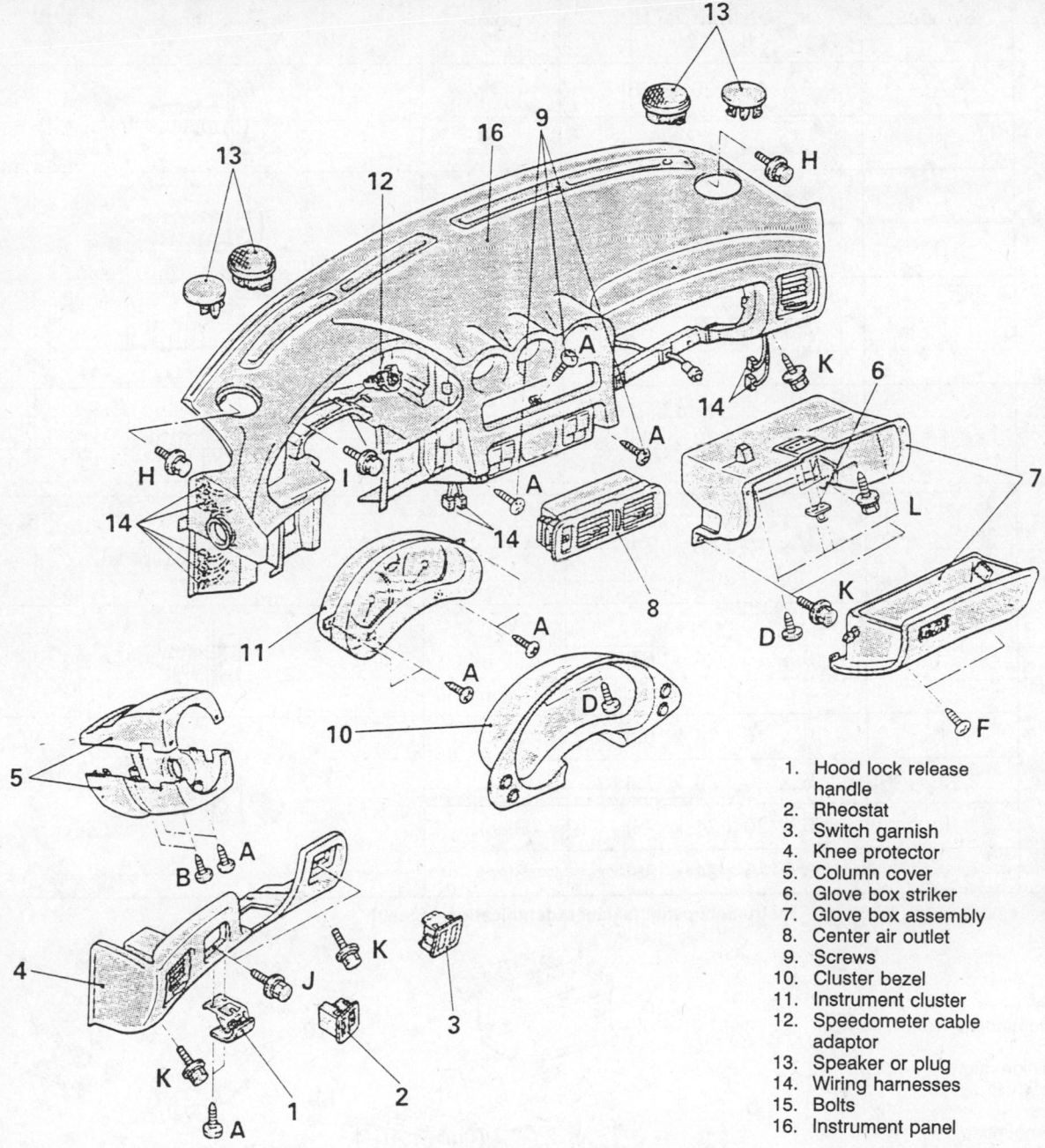

1. Hood lock release handle
2. Rheostat
3. Switch garnish
4. Knee protector
5. Column cover
6. Glove box striker
7. Glove box assembly
8. Center air outlet
9. Screws
10. Cluster bezel
11. Instrument cluster
12. Speedometer cable adaptor
13. Speaker or plug
14. Wiring harnesses
15. Bolts
16. Instrument panel

Instrument panel and related parts—Stealth

31. Connect the negative battery cable and check the entire climate control system for proper operation. Check the system for leaks.

Stealth

NOTE: If equipped with an air bag, be sure to disarm it before starting any repairs on the vehicle.

1. Disconnect the negative battery cable.

2. If equipped with an air bag, disarm as follows:

a. Position the front wheels in the straight-ahead position and place the key in the **LOCK** position. Remove the key from the ignition lock cylinder.

b. Disconnect the negative battery cable and insulate the cable end with high-quality electrical tape or similar non-conductive wrapping.

c. Wait at least 1 minute before working on the vehicle. The air bag system is designed to retain enough

voltage to deploy the air bag for a short period of time even after the battery has been disconnected.

3. Drain the cooling system and disconnect the heater hoses from the core tubes.

4. To remove the console, perform the following:

a. Remove the cup holder and console plug.

b. Remove the rear console.

c. Remove the radio bezels and radio.

d. Remove the switch bezel.

Name	Symbol	Size mm (in.) (D x L)	Color	Shape
Tapping screw	A	5 x 16 (.20 x .63)	–	
	B	5 x 30 (.20 x 1.2)	–	
	C	4 x 12 (.16 x .47)	Black	
	D	5 x 16 (.20 x .63)	Black	
	E	4 x 16 (.16 x .63)	–	
Washer assembled screw	F	5 x 16 (.20 x .63)	–	
	G	4 x 12 (.16 x .47)	–	
Washer assembled bolt	H	6 x 16 (.24 x .63)	–	
	I	6 x 16 (.24 x .63)	–	
	J	6 x 20 (.24 x .79)	–	
	K	6 x 20 (.24 x .79)	Black	
	L	6 x 25 (.24 x .98)	Black	

Instrument panel fastener Identification—Stealth

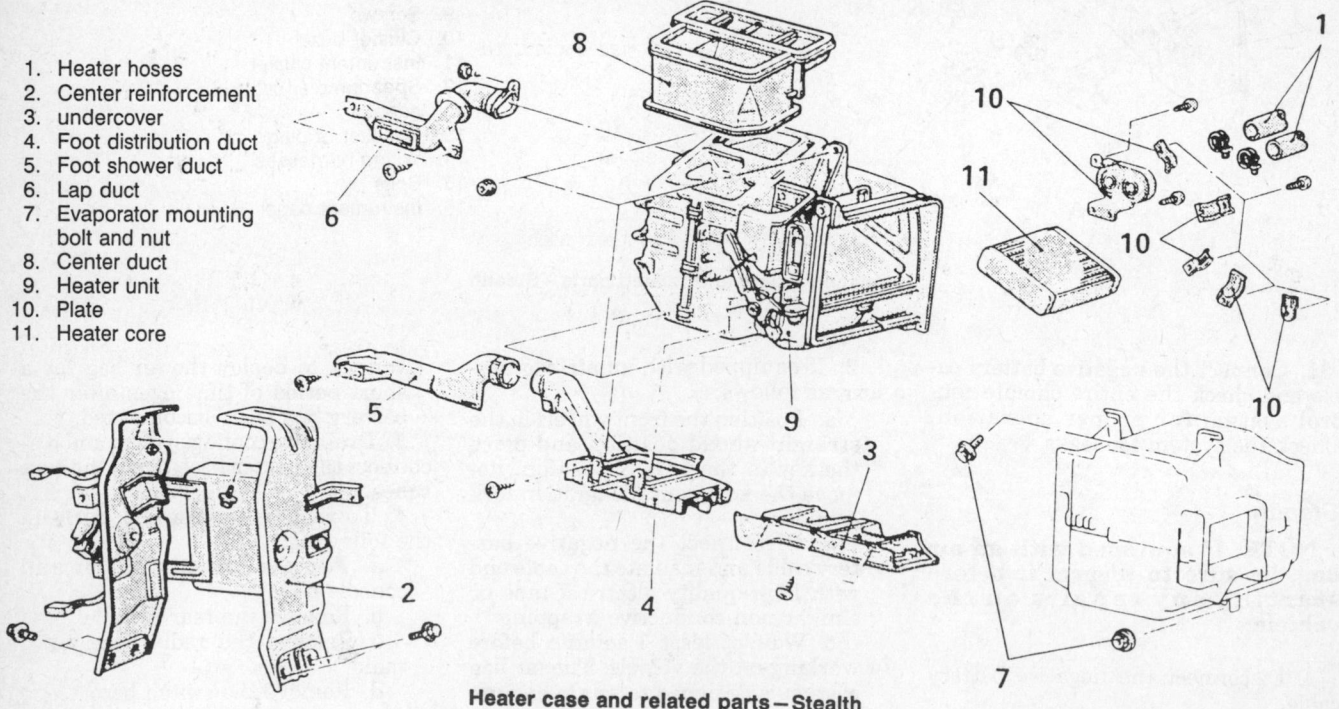

1. Heater hoses
2. Center reinforcement
3. undercover
4. Foot distribution duct
5. Foot shower duct
6. Lap duct
7. Evaporator mounting bolt and nut
8. Center duct
9. Heater unit
10. Plate
11. Heater core

Heater case and related parts—Stealth

e. Remove the side covers and front console garnish.

f. If equipped with a manual transaxle, remove the shifter knob.

g. Remove the mounting screws and remove the console assembly.

5. Remove the hood lock release handle from the instrument panel.

6. Remove the interior and dash lights rheostat and switch bezel to its right.

7. Remove the driver's knee protector. Remove the steering column upper and lower covers.

8. Remove the glove box, glove box door striker and cover.

9. Remove the center air outlet assembly and the climate control switch assembly.

10. Remove the instrument cluster bezel and cluster.

11. If equipped with front speakers, remove them. If not, remove the plug in their place.

12. Disconnect the wiring harnesses on the right side of the instrument panel.

13. Remove the steering shaft support bolts and lower the steering column.

14. Remove the instrument panel mounting hardware and remove the instrument panel from the vehicle.

15. Remove the center reinforcement.

16. Remove the foot warmer ducts and lap duct.

17. If equipped with air conditioning, remove the evaporator case mounting bolt and nut to allow clearance for heater unit removal.

18. Remove the center duct above the heater unit.

19. Remove the heater unit and disassemble on a workbench. Remove the heater core from the heater case.

To install:

20. Thoroughly clean and dry the inside of the case and install the heater core and all related parts.

21. Install the heater unit to the vehicle and install the mounting screws.

22. Install the center duct above the unit.

23. Secure the evaporator case with the bolt and nut.

24. Install the lap duct and foot warmer ducts.

25. Install the center reinforcement.

26. Install the instrument panel by reversing its removal procedure.

27. Install the hood lock release cable handle.

28. Install the console.

29. Fill the cooling system.

30. Connect the negative battery cable and check the entire climate control system for proper operation and leaks.

Water Pump

REMOVAL & INSTALLATION

1. Disconnect the negative battery cable.

2. Drain the cooling system.

3. Remove the Engine undercover.

4. Disconnect the clamp bolt from the power streering hose.

5. Support the Engine with the appropriate equipment and remove the Engine mount bracket.

6. Remove the timing belt(s) from the front of the Engine.

7. Disconnect the coolant hoses from the pump, if equipped.

8. Remove the alternator brace.

9. Remove the water pump, gasket and O-ring where the water inlet pipe(s) joins the pump.

To install:

10. Thoroughly clean and dry both gasket surfaces of the water pump and block.

11. Install a new O-ring into the groove on the front end of the water inlet pipe. Do not apply oils or grease to the O-ring. Wet with water only.

12. Install the gasket and pump assembly and tighten the bolts. Note the marks on the bolt heads. Those marked **4** should be torqued to 9–11 ft. lbs. Those bolts marked **7** should be torqued from 14–20 ft. lbs.

13. Connect the hoses to the pump.

14. Reinstall the timing belt and related parts.

15. Install the Engine undercover.

16. Fill the system with coolant.

17. Connect the negative battery cable, run the vehicle until the thermostat opens and fill the radiator completely.

18. Once the vehicle has cooled, recheck the coolant level.

Thermostat

REMOVAL & INSTALLATION

1. Disconnect the negative battery cable.

2. Drain the cooling system.

3. On Stealth, remove necessary air intake plumbing.

4. Disconnect the upper radiator hose and overflow hose from the thermostat housing.

5. Remove the thermostat housing and gasket.

6. Remove the thermostat taking note of its original position in the housing or intake mnifold.

To install:

7. Install the thermostat so its flange seats tightly in the machined groove in the intake manifold or thermostat case. Refer to its location prior to removal. On Stealth and Summit

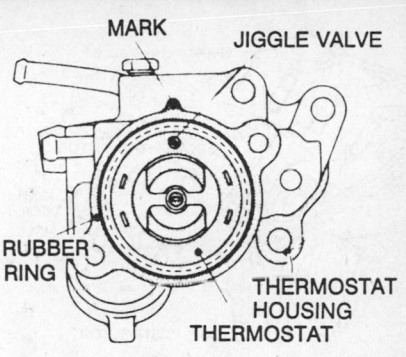

Installation of thermostat so jiggle valve is in alignment with mark on thermostat housing — Summit Wagon

Wagon, align the jiggle valve with the alignment mark on the thermostat housing.

8. Use a new gasket and reinstall the thermostat housing. Torque the housing mounting bolts to 12–14 ft. lbs. (17–20 Nm).

9. Fill the system with coolant.

10. Install removed air intake plumbing.

11. Connect the negative battery cable, run the vehicle until the thermostat opens and fill the radiator completely.

12. Once the vehicle has cooled, recheck the coolant level.

Cooling System Bleeding

All vehicles are equipped with a self-bleeding thermostat. Slowly fill the cooling system in the conventional manner; air will vent through the jiggle valve in the thermostat. Run the vehicle until the thermostat has opened and continue filling the radiator. Recheck the coolant level after the vehicle has cooled.

ENGINE ELECTRICAL

NOTE: Disconnecting the negative battery cable on some vehicles may interfere with the functions of the on board computer systems and may require the computer to undergo a relearning process, once the negative battery cable is reconnected.

Distributor

REMOVAL

1. Disconnect the negative battery

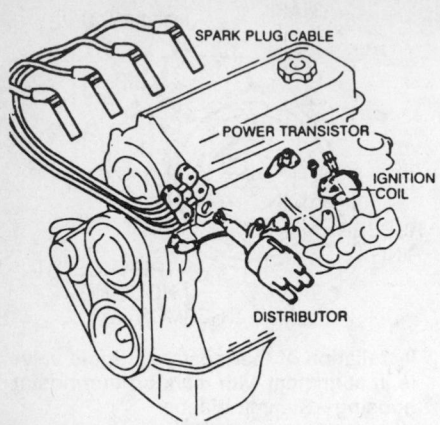

Ignition system—1.8L and 1989–90 1.5L Engines

cable. Remove the ignition wire cover, if equipped.

2. Disconnect the distributor harness electrical connectors.

3. Unscrew the distributor cap hold-down screws or release the clips and lift off the distributor cap with all ignition wires still connected. Remove the coil wire, if necessary.

4. Matchmark the rotor to the distributor housing and the distributor housing to the Engine.

NOTE: Do not crank the Engine during this procedure. If the Engine is cranked, the matchmark must be disregarded.

5. Remove the hold-down nut.

6. Carefully remove the distributor from the Engine.

INSTALLATION

NOTE: Some Engines may be sensitive to the routing of the distributor sensor wires. If routed near the high-voltage coil wire or the spark plug wires, the electromagnetic field surrounding the high voltage wires could generate an occasional disruption of the ignition system operation.

Timing Not Disturbed

1. Install a new distributor housing O-ring and lubricate with clean oil.

2. Install the distributor in the Engine so the rotor is aligned with the matchmark on the housing and the housing is aligned with the matchmark on the Engine. Make sure the distributor is fully seated and the distributor shaft is fully engaged.

3. Install the hold-down nut.

4. Connect the distributor harness connectors.

5. Make sure the sealing O-ring is in place, install the distributor cap and tighten the screws or secure the clips.

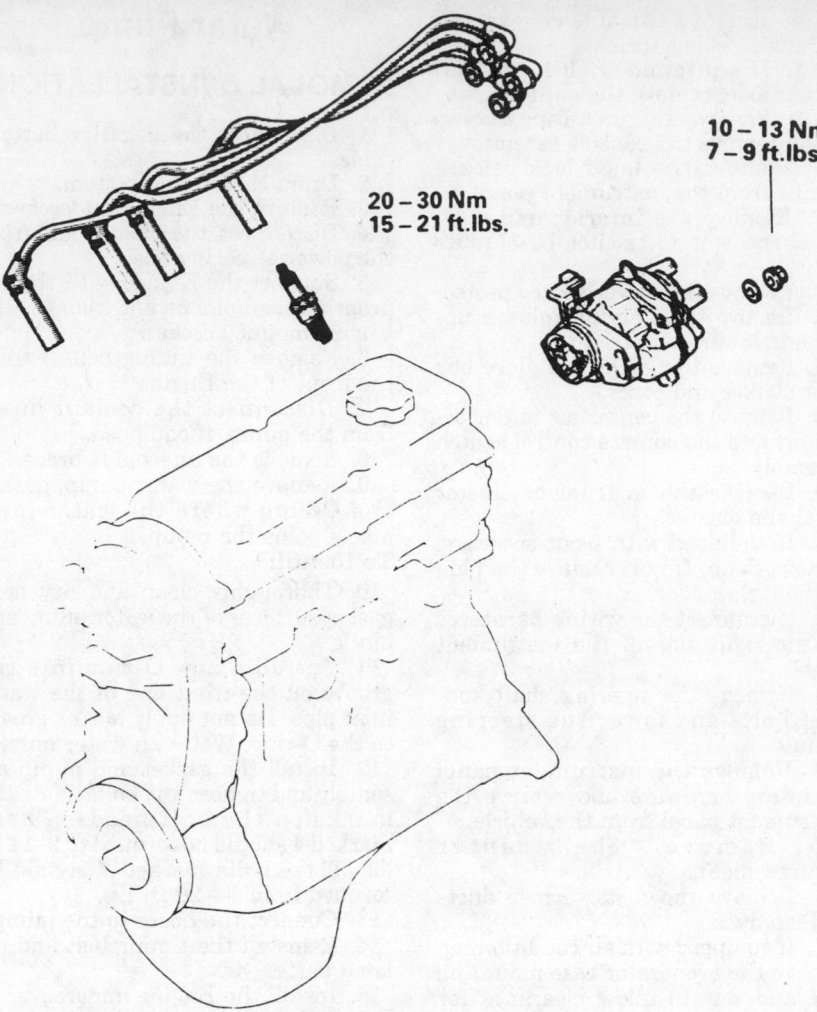

Ignition system components—1992–93 1.5L Engine

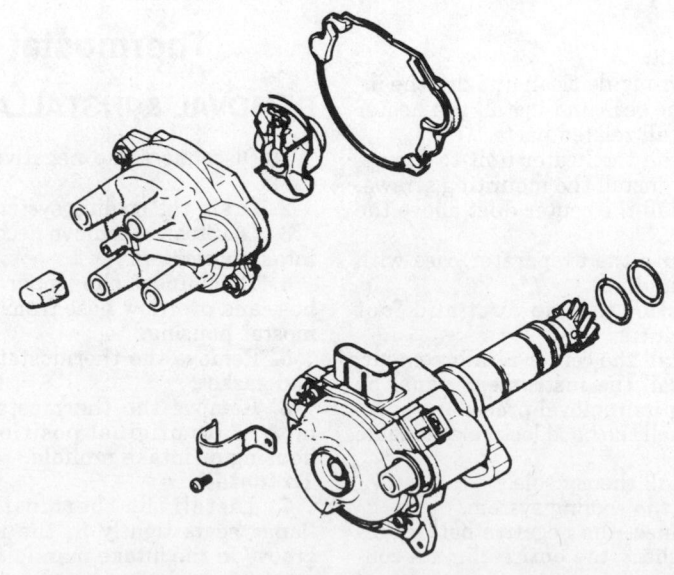

Distributor assembly and related components—1992 1.8L Engine

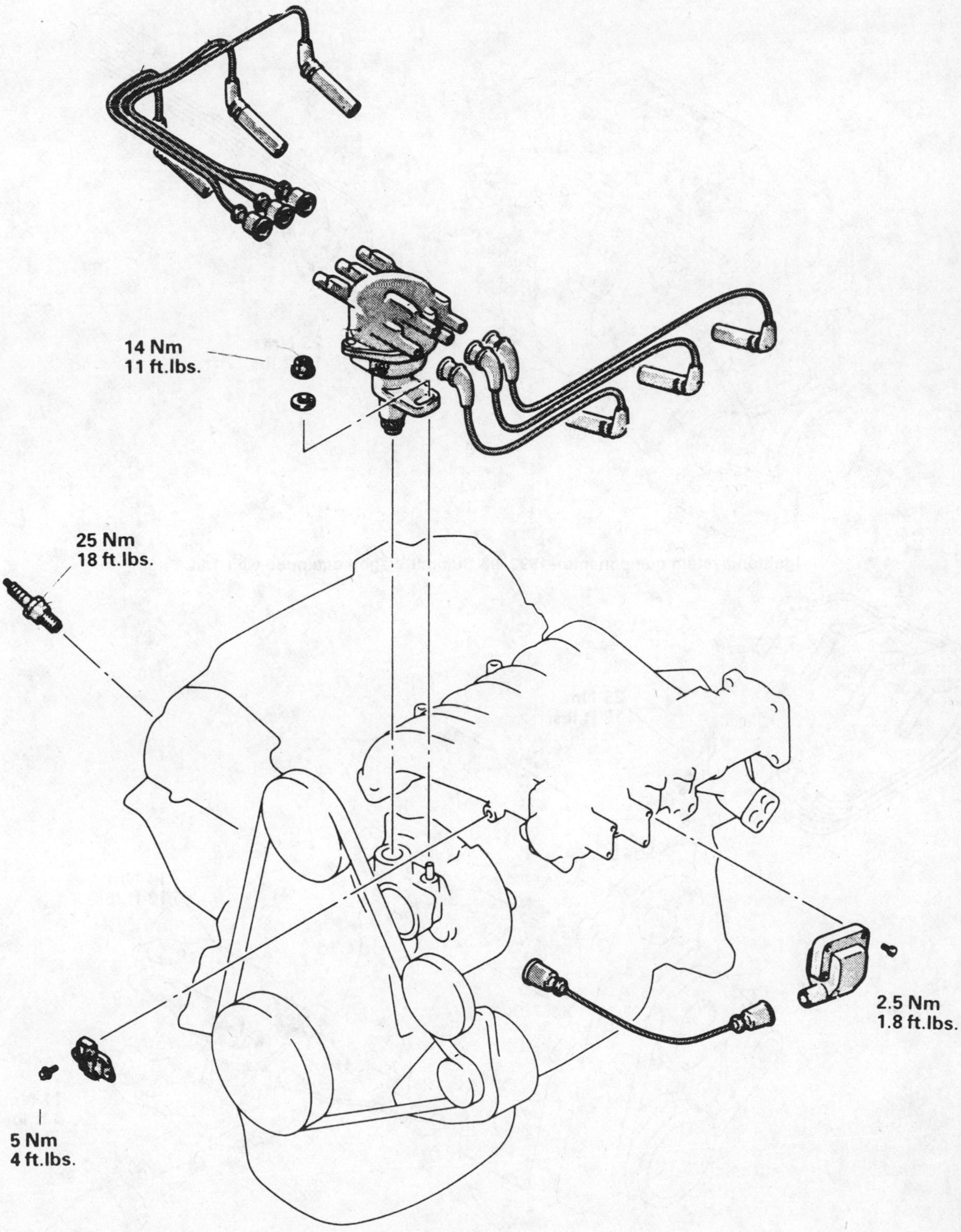

14 Nm
11 ft.lbs.

25 Nm
18 ft.lbs.

2.5 Nm
1.8 ft.lbs.

5 Nm
4 ft.lbs.

Ignition system components—1992–93 3.0L SOHC Engine

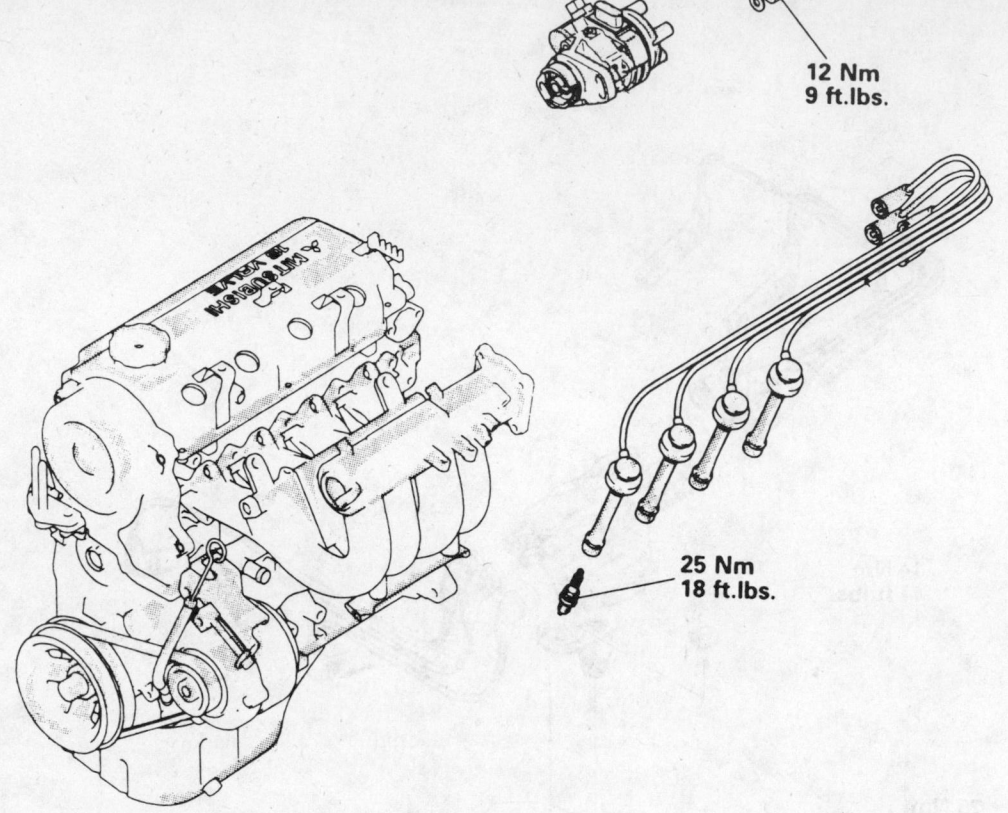

12 Nm
9 ft.lbs.

25 Nm
18 ft.lbs.

Ignition system components—1992–93 Summit Wagon equipped with 1.8L Engine

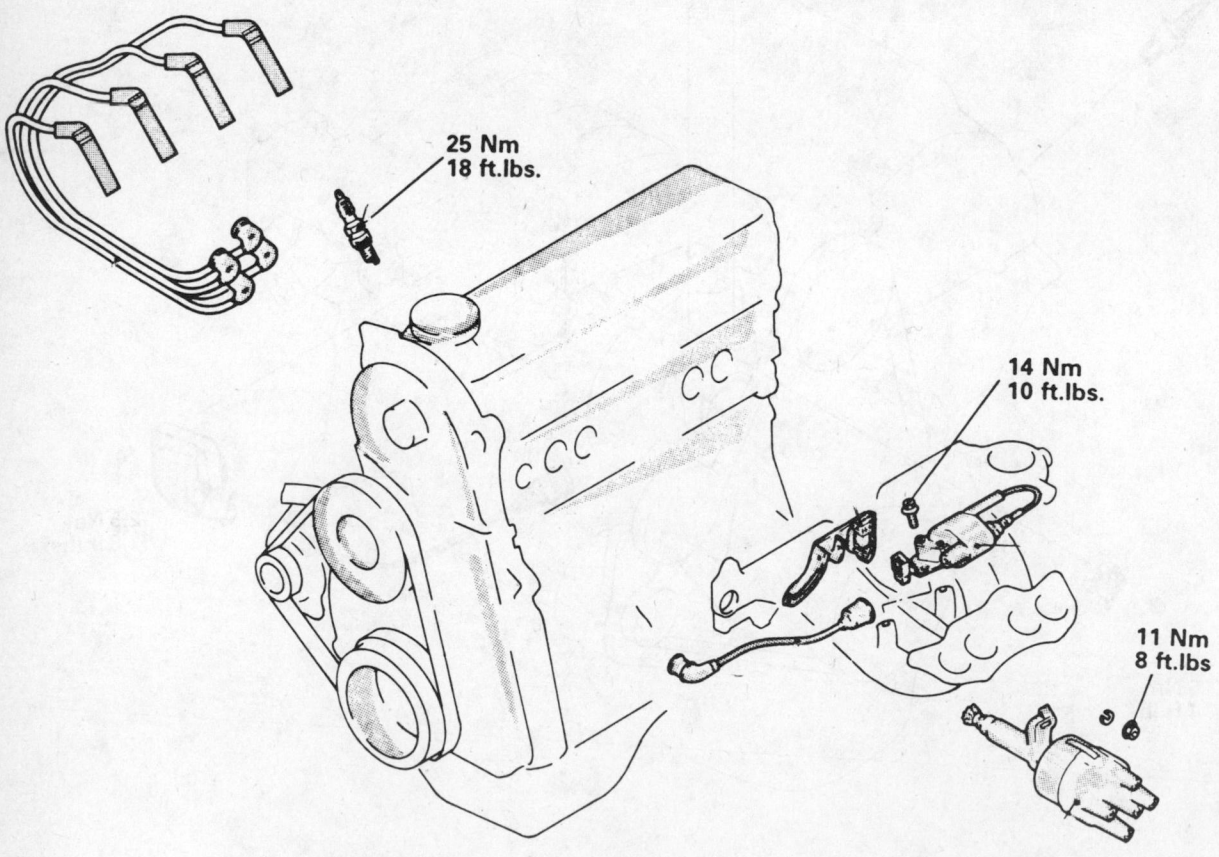

25 Nm
18 ft.lbs.

14 Nm
10 ft.lbs.

11 Nm
8 ft.lbs

Ignition system components—1992–93 Summit Wagon equipped with 2.4L Engine

6. Connect the negative battery cable.

7. Adjust the ignition timing and tighten the hold-down nut.

Timing Disturbed

1. Install a new distributor housing O-ring and lubricate with clean oil.

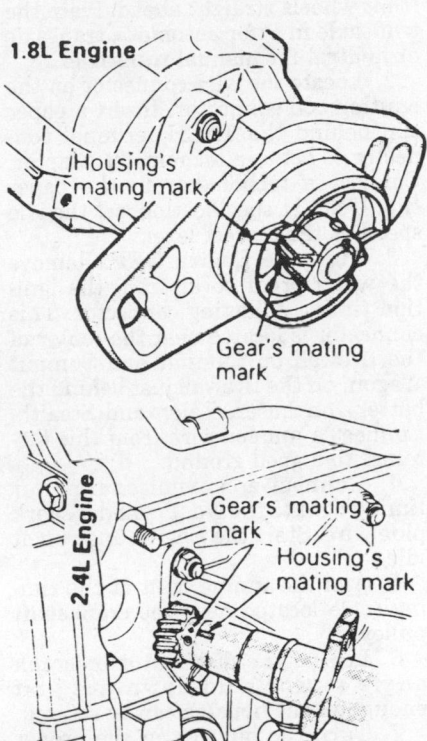

Alignment of factory marks on distributor housing and gear as seen on 1.8L and 2.4L Engines – 1992-93 Summit Wagon. Other models are similar.

2. Position the Engine so the No. 1 piston is at TDC of its compression stroke and the mark on the vibration damper is aligned with **0** on the timing indicator.

3. Align the distributor housing and gear mating marks. Install the distributor in Engine so the slot or groove of the distributor's installation flange aligns with the distributor installation stud in the Engine block. Make sure the distributor is fully seated. Inspect alignment of the distributor rotor making sure the rotor is aligned with the position of the No. 1 ignition wire in the distributor cap.

NOTE: Make sure the rotor is pointing to where the No. 1 runner originates inside the cap, if equipped, and not where the No. 1 ignition wire plugs into the cap.

4. Install the hold-down nut.

5. Connect the distributor harness connectors.

6. Make sure the sealing O-ring is in

place, install the distributor cap and tighten the screws or secure the clips.

7. Connect the negative battery cable.

8. Adjust the ignition timing and tighten the hold-down bolt.

Distributorless Ignition

REMOVAL & INSTALLATION

Crank Angle Sensor

1. Disconnect the negative battery cable.

2. Disconnect the sensor harness connector.

3. Unscrew the cap hold-down screws and lift off the cap.

4. Matchmark the coupling to the sensor housing and the housing to the Engine.

NOTE: Do not crank the Engine during this procedure. If the Engine is cranked, the matchmark must be disregarded.

5. Remove the hold-down nut.

6. Carefully remove the crank angle sensor assembly from the Engine.

To install:

7. If the timing is not disturbed, perform the following procedures:

   a. Install a new housing O-ring and lubricate with clean oil.

   b. Install the assembly in the Engine so the coupling is aligned with the matchmark on the housing and the housing is aligned with the matchmark on the Engine. Make sure the sensor assembly is fully

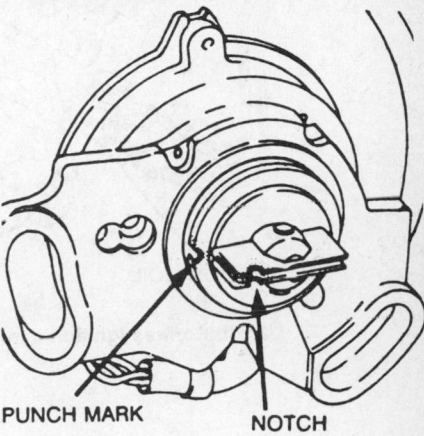

PUNCH MARK   NOTCH

Crank angle sensor factory alignment marks

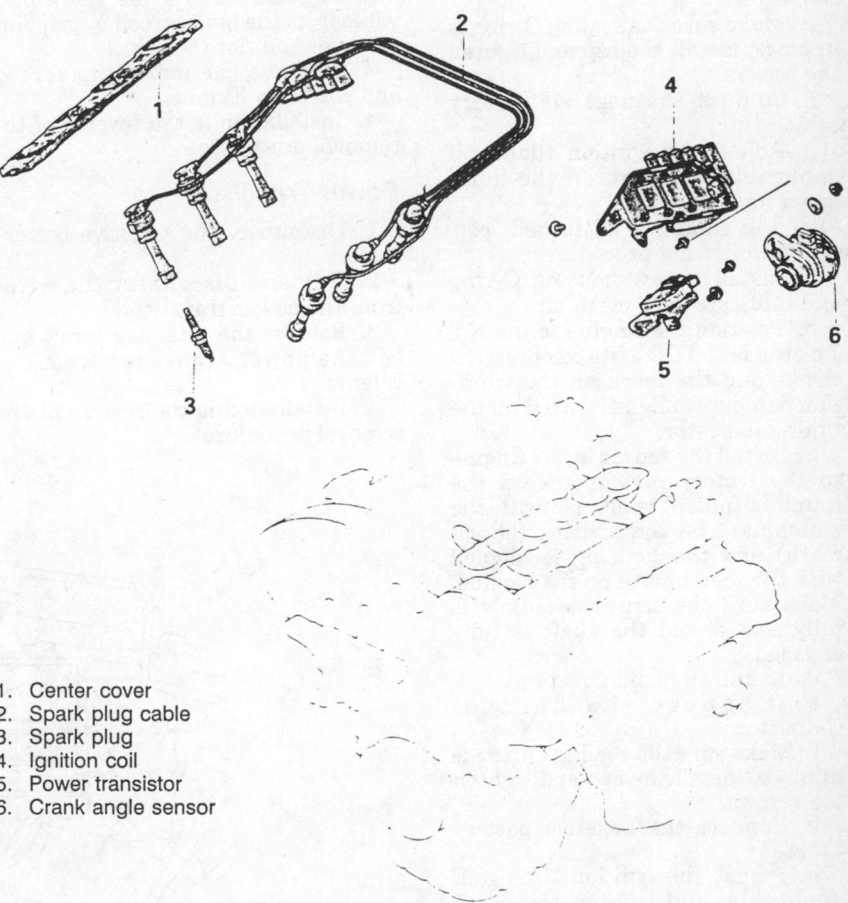

1. Center cover
2. Spark plug cable
3. Spark plug
4. Ignition coil
5. Power transistor
6. Crank angle sensor

Distributorless Ignition system – 3.0L DOHC Engine

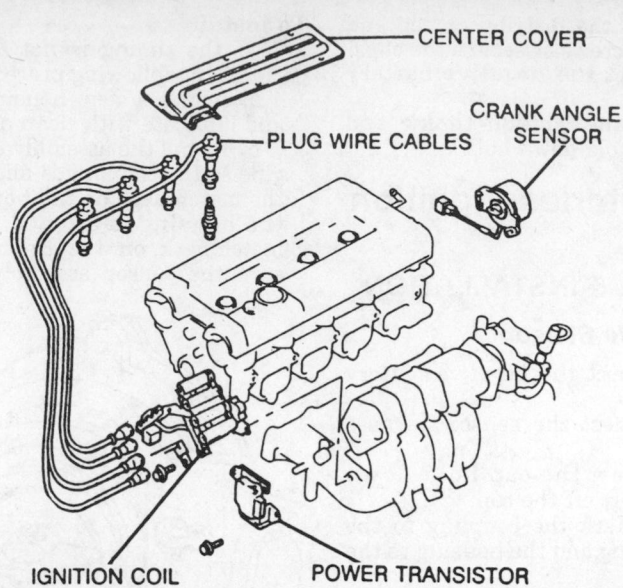

CENTER COVER

CRANK ANGLE SENSOR

PLUG WIRE CABLES

IGNITION COIL

POWER TRANSISTOR

Distributorless ignition system—1.6L and 2.0L Engines

seated and the shaft is fully engaged.

c. Install the hold-down nut.

d. Connect the harness connector.

e. Make sure the sealing O-ring is in place, install the cap and tighten the screws.

f. Connect the negative battery cable.

g. Adjust the ignition timing, if applicable, and tighten the hold-down nut.

8. If the timing is disturbed, perform the following procedures:

a. Install a new housing O-ring and lubricate with clean oil.

b. Position the Engine so the No. 1 piston is at TDC of its compression stroke and the mark on the vibration damper is aligned with **0** on the timing indicator.

c. Install the sensor in the Engine so the factory matchmark on the coupling (notch) is aligned with the matchmark on the housing (punch mark) and the housing is aligned with the matchmark on the Engine. Make sure the sensor assembly is fully seated and the shaft is fully engaged.

d. Install the hold-down nut.

e. Connect the harness connector.

f. Make sure the sealing O-ring is in place, install the cap and tighten the screws.

g. Connect the negative battery cable.

h. Adjust the ignition timing, if applicable, and tighten the hold-down nut.

Ignition Coil

1. Disconnect the negative battery cable.

2. Tag and remove the spark plug wires from the ignition coil by gripping the boot and not the cable.

3. Remove the mounting screws and coil from Engine.

4. Installation is the reverse of the removal procedure.

Power Transistor

1. Disconnect the negative battery cable.

2. Tag and disconnect the wires from the power transistor.

3. Remove the retaining screw and lift the power transistor from the Engine.

4. Installation is the reverse of the removal procedure.

Ignition Timing

ADJUSTMENT

1. Set the parking brake, start and run the Engine until normal operating temperature is obtained. Keep all lights and accessories OFF and the front wheels straight ahead. Place the transaxle in **P** for automatic transaxle or neutral for manual transaxle.

2. Locate the wire connector on the ignition coil connector. Insert a paper clip behind the TACH terminal connector to act as a tachometer adapter. Connect a tachometer to the paper clip. If not at specification, set the idle speed at the correct level.

3. Turn the Engine **OFF**. Remove the water-proof cover from the ignition timing adjusting connector. This connector is located near the center of the firewall on Summit and Summit Wagon, on the firewall just behind the battery on Laser, Talon and Stealth. Connect a jumper wire from this terminal to a good ground.

4. Connect a conventional power timing light to the No. 1 cylinder spark plug wire. Start the Engine and run at idle.

5. Aim the timing light at the timing scale located near the crankshaft pulley.

6. Loosen the distributor or crank angle sensor hold-down nut just enough so the housing can be rotated.

7. Turn the housing in the proper direction until the specified timing is reached. Tighten the hold-down nut and recheck the timing. Turn the Engine **OFF**.

8. Remove the jumper wire from the ignition timing adjusting terminal and install the water-proof cover.

9. Start the Engine and check the actual timing (the timing without the terminal grounded). This reading should be approximately 5 degrees more than the basic timing. Actual timing may increase according to alti-

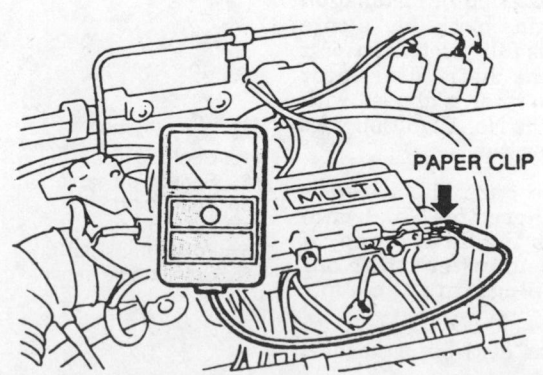

PAPER CLIP

Tachometer connector location common to most Engines

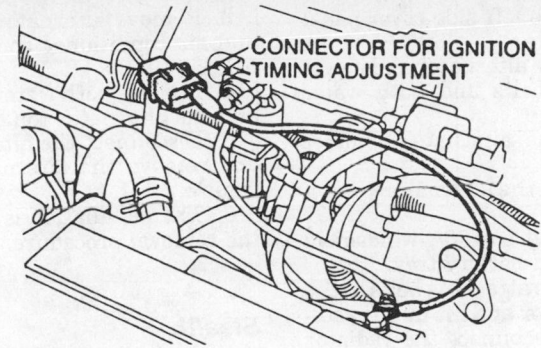

Ignition timing adjustment connector—1.5L Engine

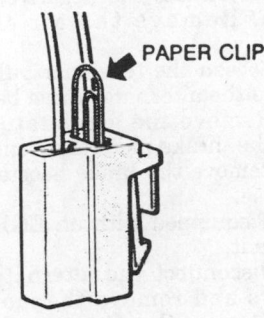

Insert paper clip as shown

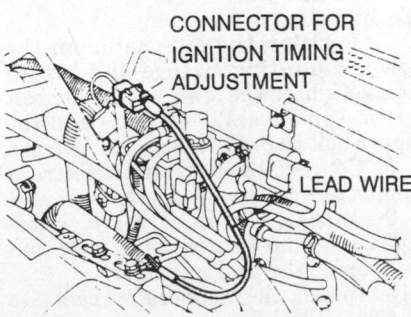

Ignition timing adjustment connector—1.6L Engine

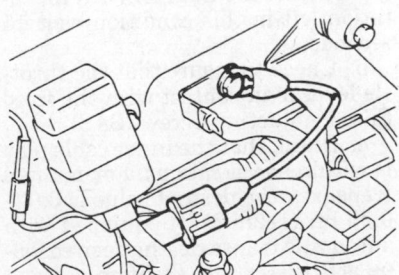

Ignition timing adjustment connector—Laser and Talon

tude. Also, actual timing may fluctuate because of slight variation accomplished by the ECU. As long as the basic timing is correct, the Engine is timed correctly.

10. Turn the Engine **OFF**. Disconnect the timing apparatus and tachometer.

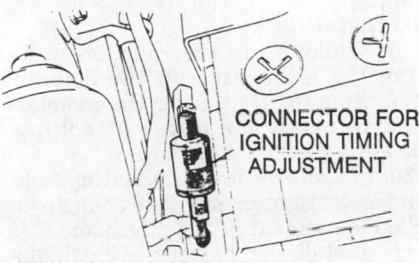

Ignition timing adjustment connector—Stealth

Alternator

PRECAUTIONS

Several precautions must be observed with alternator-equipped vehicles to avoid damage to the unit.

• If the battery is removed for any reason, make sure it is reconnected with the correct polarity. Reversing the battery connections may result in damage to the 1-way rectifiers.

• When utilizing a booster battery as a starting aid, always connect the positive to positive terminals and the negative terminal from the booster battery to a good Engine ground on the vehicle being started.

• Never use a fast charger as a booster to start vehicles.

• Disconnect the battery cables when charging the battery with a fast charger.

• Never attempt to polarize the alternator.

• Do not use test lamps of more than 12 volts when checking diode continuity.

• Do not short across or ground any of the alternator terminals.

• The polarity of the battery, alternator and regulator must be matched and considered before making any electrical connections within the system.

• Never separate the alternator on an open circuit. Make sure all connections within the circuit are clean and tight.

• Disconnect the battery ground

SOHC ENGINE

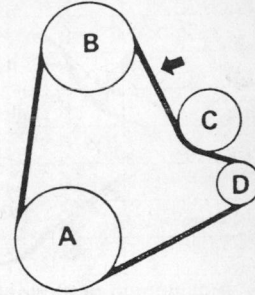

DOHC ENGINE WITHOUT AIR CONDITIONING

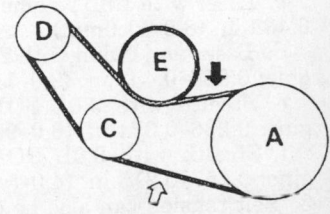

DOHC ENGINE WITH AIR CONDITIONING

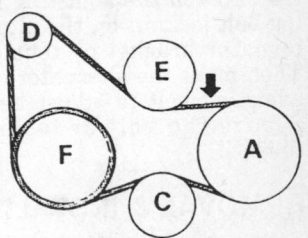

A. Crankshaft pulley
B. Power steering pulley
C. Tensioner pulley
D. Alternator pulley
E. Idler pulley
F. Air conditioner compressor pulley

Serpentine belt layout—Stealth

terminal when performing any service on electrical components.

• Disconnect the battery if arc welding is to be done on the vehicle.

BELT TENSION ADJUSTMENT

1. Place a straightedge along the top edge of the belt and across 2 pulleys. Allow both ends of the straightedge to rest on top of each pulley for support.

2. Measure the deflection of the belt from the straightedge with a force of about 22 lbs. applied midway between the 2 pulleys. Deflection should be:

    a. Summit: 0.217–0.354 in. (5.5–9.0mm)

    b. Summit Wagon: 0.34–0.47 in. (8.5–12mm).

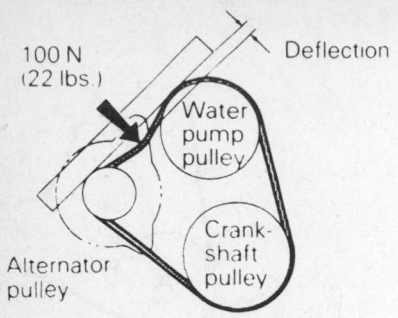

100 N (22 lbs.) Deflection

Water pump pulley

Crankshaft pulley

Alternator pulley

Positioning of straightedge while checking belt tension—1.5L Engine

c. Laser with 1.8L Engine: 0.315–0.433 in. (8.0–11.0mm)

d. Laser and Talon with 2.0L Engine: 0.354–0.453 in. (9.0–11.5mm)

e. Stealth with 3.0L SOHC Engine: 0.236–0.354 in. (6.0–9.0mm)

f. Stealth with 3.0L DOHC Engine: 0.157–0.216 in. (4.0–5.5mm)

3. Belt tension can also be checked with a tension gauge. The desired value should be 55–110 lbs. (250–500 N).

4. Loosen the adjusting bolt or fixing bolt locknut on the alternator, alternator bracket or tension pulley. Then move the alternator or turn the adjusting bolt to adjust belt tension. Secure the bolt or locknut when finished.

REMOVAL & INSTALLATION

Summit and Summit Wagon

1.5L AND 2.4L ENGINES

1. Disconnect the negative battery cable.

2. On Summit, remove the left side cover panel under the vehicle.

3. Remove the drive belts.

4. Remove both water pump pulleys.

5. Remove the alternator upper bracket/brace.

6. Disconnect the alternator electrical connectors and remove alternator.

To install:

7. Position the alternator on the lower mounting fixture and install the lower mounting bolt and nut. Tighten nut just enough to allow for movement of the alternator.

8. Install the alternator upper bracket/brace and connect the alternator electrical harness.

9. Install the water pump pulleys.

10. Install the drive belts and adjust to the proper tension.

11. Install the left side cover panel under the vehicle as required.

12. Connect the negative battery cable and check for proper operation.

1.6L ENGINE

1. Disconnect the negative battery cable.

2. Remove the left side cover panel under the vehicle.

3. Remove the alternator and power steering drive belts and both water pump pulleys.

4. Remove the alternator adjuster brace.

5. Disconnect the alternator electrical connection.

6. Remove the battery, windshield washer tank and battery tray.

7. Remove the attaching bolts at the top of the radiator and lift up the radiator. Do not disconnect the radiator hoses.

8. Remove the alternator from the vehicle.

To install:

9. While lifting the radiator, position the alternator on the Engine mounting fixture. Lower the radiator and reinstall the upper attaching bolts.

10. Install the lower mounting bolt and nut. Tighten nut just enough to allow movement of the alternator.

11. Install the battery, windshield washer tank and battery tray.

12. Connect the alternator electrical connections.

13. Install the alternator adjuster brace.

14. Install both water pump pulleys and tighten mounting bolts to 6–7 ft. lbs. (8–10 Nm).

15. Install the alternator and power steering drive belts and adjust to the proper tension.

16. Install the left side cover panel under the vehicle.

17. Connect the negative battery cable and check for proper operation.

Summit Wagon

1.8L ENGINE

1. Disconnect negative battery cable.

2. Remove the accessory drive belts.

3. Disconnect the electrical harness from the alternator.

4. Remove the alternator mounting nut, bolt and upper brace assembly from the vehicle.

To install:

5. Install the alternator and secure using mounting nuts. Make sure the upper brace assembly is in place.

6. Install and adjust drive belts to the proper tension. Secure all mounting hardware.

7. Reconnect the negative battery cable and check system operation.

Laser and Talon

1. Disconnect the negative battery cable. Remove the left side undercover from the vehicle.

2. If equipped with air conditioning, remove the condenser electric fan motor and shroud assembly.

3. Remove alternator, water pump and air conditioner compressor drive belts.

4. Remove both water pump pulleys and the alternator top brace.

5. Disconnect the alternator wiring and remove the alternator from the vehicle.

6. The installation is the reverse of the removal procedure.

Stealth

3.0L SOHC ENGINE

1. Disconnect the negative battery cable. Remove the air cleaner assembly.

2. Loosen the tensioner pulley and remove the alternator drive belt.

3. Remove the accelerator cable from the intake plenum extension.

4. Remove the brake booster vacuum hose.

5. If equipped with an EGR valve, remove it.

6. Disconnect the alternator connectors and remove the mounting bolts. Remove the alternator from behind the surge tank at the center of the vehicle.

To install:

7. Position the alternator on the lower mounting fixture and install bolts. Tighten the lower mounting bolt to 14–18 ft. lbs. (20–25 Nm) and the upper bolt to 8–11 ft. lbs. (12–15 Nm).

8. Connect the alternator electrical connectors to the alternator.

9. Install the EGR valve, if removed. Connect the vacuum hose connection at the brake booster.

10. Install the accelerator cable to the intake plenum extension. Check the accelerator cable adjustment as follows:

a. Turn the ignition key **ON** but do not start the Engine. With the ignition left in this condition wait 15 seconds.

b. Check to insure that the throttle lever is in contact with the fixed Speed Adjusting Screw (SAS).

c. Check that the inner cable play is within specifications. For manual transaxle, the desired value is 0.04–0.08 in. (1–2mm). If equipped with automatic transaxle, the desired value is 0.12–0.20 in. (3–5mm).

d. If not within the desired value, loosen the adjusting bolts and slide plate so play at the inner cable will fall within the desired value. Retighten the adjusting bolts.

11. Reinstall the drive belt and adjust the tensioner until the proper belt tension is achieved.

12. Install the air cleaner and connect the negative battery cable. Check the charging system for proper operation.

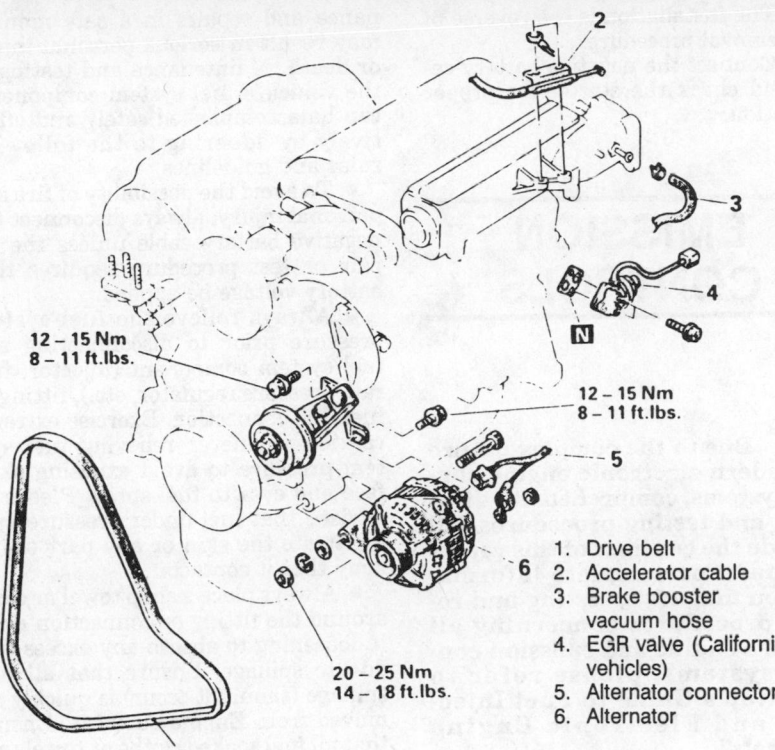

12 – 15 Nm
8 – 11 ft.lbs.

12 – 15 Nm
8 – 11 ft.lbs.

20 – 25 Nm
14 – 18 ft.lbs.

1. Drive belt
2. Accelerator cable
3. Brake booster vacuum hose
4. EGR valve (California vehicles)
5. Alternator connector
6. Alternator

Alternator and related parts – 3.0L SOHC Engine

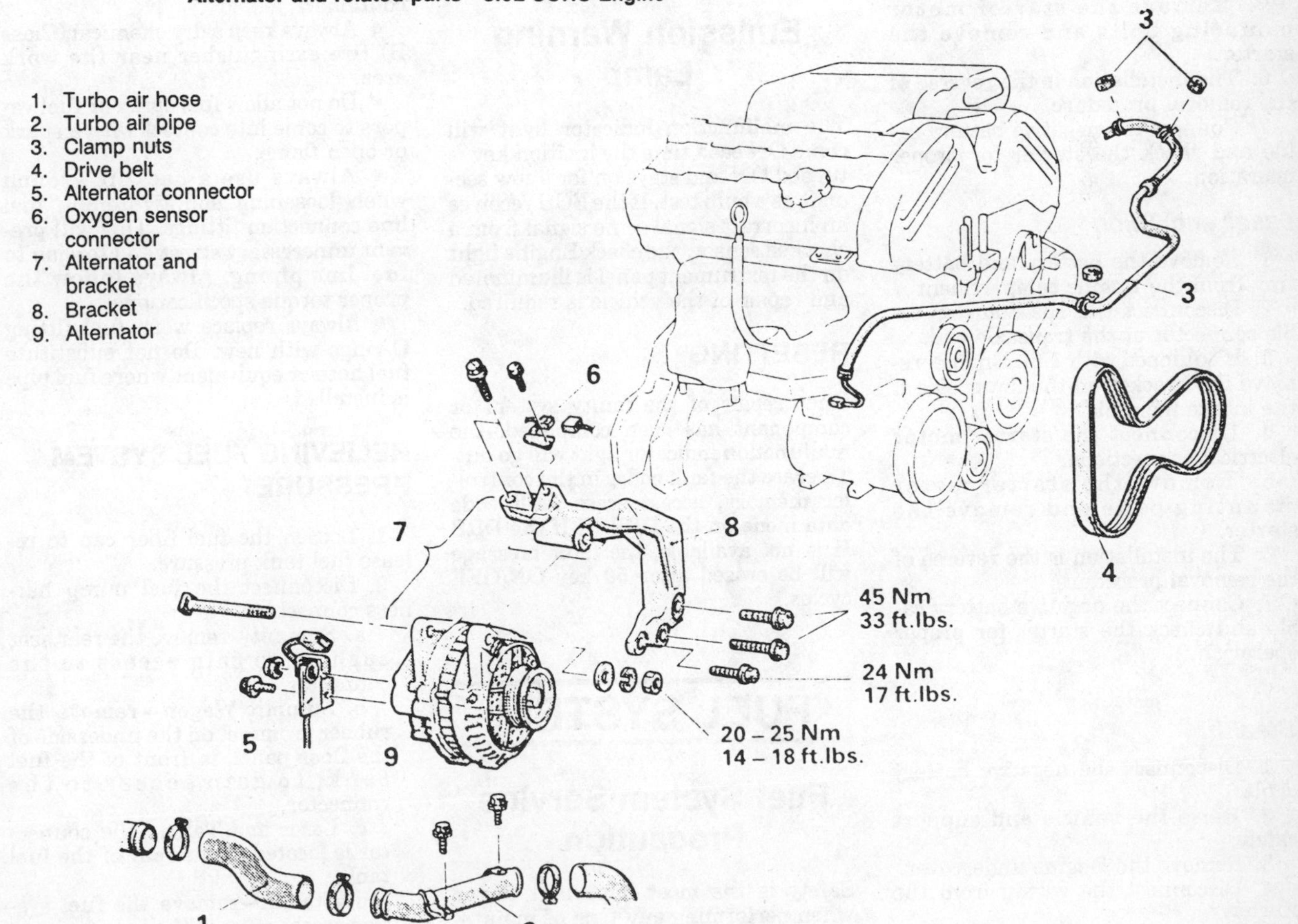

1. Turbo air hose
2. Turbo air pipe
3. Clamp nuts
4. Drive belt
5. Alternator connector
6. Oxygen sensor connector
7. Alternator and bracket
8. Bracket
9. Alternator

3.0L DOHC Engine

1. Disconnect the negative battery cable. Remove the surge tank.

2. Remove the necessary air delivery hoses to gain access to the alternator.

3. If equipped with air conditioning, remove the clamp nut, raise the suction hose and suspend it from the Engine hood.

4. Loosen the tensioner pulley and remove the alternator drive belt.

5. Disconnect the oxygen sensor connector.

6. Disconnect the alternator wiring, remove the alternator bracket mounting bolts and remove the bracket and alternator as an assembly. Separate on a workbench.

To install:

7. Install the alternator onto the bracket and install bracket assembly to the Engine.

8. Connect the oxygen sensor connector.

9. Install the drive belt and adjust to proper tension using the tensioner pulley.

10. Install air conditioning suction hose to its original position and secure using clamp nut.

45 Nm
33 ft.lbs.

24 Nm
17 ft.lbs.

20 – 25 Nm
14 – 18 ft.lbs.

Alternator and related parts – 3.0L DOHC Engine

11. Install the air delivery hose(s) and the surge tank.

12. Reconnect the negative battery cable and check the charging system for proper operation.

Starter

REMOVAL & INSTALLATION

Summit and Summit Wagon

1. Disconnect the negative battery cable.

2. Disconnect the air-flow sensor assembly connector and remove the breather hose. Remove the resonator retaining nuts and remove the air intake hose and resonator assembly as required.

NOTE: Use care when removing the air cleaner cover because the air-flow sensor is attached and is a sensitive component.

3. Remove the heat shield from under the intake manifold on the 1.5L Engine.

4. Disconnect the starter motor electrical connections.

5. Remove the starter motor mounting bolts and remove the starter.

6. The installation is the reverse of the removal procedure.

7. Connect the negative battery cable and check the starter for proper operation.

Laser and Talon

1. Remove the battery and battery tray from the Engine compartment.

2. Disconnect the speedometer cable connector at the transaxle end.

3. If equipped with 1.8L Engine, remove the bracket on the lower side if the intake manifold.

4. Disconnect the starter motor electrical connections.

5. Remove the starter motor mounting bolts and remove the starter.

6. The installation is the reverse of the removal procedure.

7. Connect the negative battery cable and check the starter for proper operation.

Stealth

1. Disconnect the negative battery cable.

2. Raise the vehicle and support safely.

3. Remove the Engine undercover.

4. Disconnect the wiring from the starter.

5. Remove the mounting bolts and starter from the vehicle.

6. The installation is the reverse of the removal procedure.

7. Connect the negative battery cable and check the starter for proper operation.

EMISSION CONTROLS

Due to the complex nature of modern electronic engine control systems, comprehensive diagnosis and testing procedures fall outside the confines of this repair manual. For complete information on diagnosis, testing and repair procedures concerning all modern engine and emission control systems, please refer to "Chilton's Guide to Fuel Injection and Electronic Engine Controls".

Emission Warning Lamp

The malfunction indicator light will come **ON** each time the ignition key is turned **ON** and stays on for a few seconds as a bulb test. If the ECU receives an incorrect signal or no signal from a checked sensor, the check Engine light on the instrument panel is illuminated and repair of the vehicle is required.

RESETTING

Once repair of the faulty system or component has been completed, the malfunction indicator light will go out. To erase the fault codes in the controller memory, access erase fault code data mode on the DRB II. If the DRB II is not available, the fault message will be erased after 50 key ON/OFF cycles.

FUEL SYSTEM

Fuel System Service Precaution

Safety is the most important factor when performing any type of maintenance, especially fuel system maintenance. Failure to conduct mainte-

nance and repairs in a safe manner may result in serious personal injury or death. Maintenance and testing of the vehicle's fuel system components can be accomplished safely and effectively by adhering to the following rules and guidelines.

• To avoid the possibility of fire and personal injury, always disconnect the negative battery cable unless the repair or test procedure requires that battery voltage be applied.

• Always relieve the fuel system pressure prior to disconnecting any fuel system component (injector, fuel rail, pressure regulator, etc.), fitting or fuel line connection. Exercise extreme caution whenever relieving fuel system pressure to avoid exposing skin, face and eyes to fuel spray. Please be advised that fuel under pressure may penetrate the skin or any part of the body that it contacts.

• Always place a shop towel or cloth around the fitting or connection prior to loosening to absorb any excess fuel due to spillage. Ensure that all fuel spillage (should it occur) is quickly removed from Engine surfaces. Ensure that all fuel soaked cloths or towels are deposited into a suitable waste container.

• Always keep a dry chemical (Class B) fire extinguisher near the work area.

• Do not allow fuel spray or fuel vapors to come into contact with a spark or open flame.

• Always use a backup wrench when loosening and tightening fuel line connection fittings. This will prevent unnecessary stress and torsion to fuel line piping. Always follow the proper torque specifications.

• Always replace worn fuel fitting O-rings with new. Do not substitute fuel hose or equivalent where fuel pipe is installed.

RELIEVING FUEL SYSTEM PRESSURE

1. Loosen the fuel filler cap to release fuel tank pressure.

2. Disconnect the fuel pump harness connector:

   a. Summit—remove the rear seat cushion to gain access to the connector.

   b. Summit Wagon—remove the rubber grommet on the underside of the floor panel, in front of the fuel tank, to gain access to the connector.

   c. Laser and Talon—the connector is located at the rear of the fuel tank.

   d. Stealth—remove the fuel system access cover in the luggage compartment to gain access to the connector.

3. Start the vehicle and allow it to run until it stalls from lack of fuel. Turn the key to the **OFF** position.

4. Disconnect the negative battery cable, then reconnect the fuel pump connector.

5. Wrap shop towels around the fitting that is being disconnected to absorb residual fuel in the lines.

Fuel Tank

REMOVAL & INSTALLATION

1. Relieve fuel system pressure.
2. Disconnect the negative battery cable.
3. Raise the vehicle and support safely.
4. Drain the fuel from the fuel tank into an approved container.
5. On Summit Wagon equipped with AWD, remove the propeller shaft as follows:

   a. Remove the center exhaust pipe bracket.

   b. Matchmark the differential companion flange to the propeller flange yoke.

   c. Remove the bolts, washers and nuts from the center support. Remove the propeller shaft assembly in a straight and level manner to avoid damage to the boot caused by pinching.

   d. Install cover into the rear end of the transfer case to prevent the entry of foreign materials.

6. Disconnect the return hose, high pressure hose and all other hoses and connectors connected to the pump/sending unit.

──── **CAUTION** ────

Cover all fuel hose connections with a shop towel, prior to disconnecting, to prevent splash of fuel that could be caused by residual pressure remaining in the fuel line.

1. Fuel pump
2. In-tank filter
3. Fuel gauge tank unit
4. Two-way valve
5. Vapor hose
6. Check valve
7. High pressure hose
8. Return hose
9. Tank drain plug

7. Disconnect the filler and vent hoses. Place a support under the tank and remove the retaining nuts.

8. Lower the tank from the vehicle.

To install:

9. Install the fuel tank and connect the filler and vent hoses. Tighten the tank retaining nuts to 17–22 ft. lbs. (24–31 Nm).

10. Connect the return hose, high pressure hose and all other hoses and connectors connected to the pump/sending unit.

11. Install the propeller shaft aligning the matchmarks prior to installation. Tighten the rear yoke nuts to 22–25 ft. lbs. (30–35 Nm) and the center support self-locking nuts to 22 ft. lbs. (30 Nm). Install the exhaust pipe center bracket.

12. Lower the vehicle and return fuel to the gas tank.

13. Connect the negative battery cable and check the entire system for proper operation and leaks.

Fuel Filter

REMOVAL & INSTALLATION

──── **CAUTION** ────

Do not use conventional fuel filters, hoses or clamps when servicing fuel injection systems. They are not compatible with the injection system and could fail, causing personal injury or damage to the vehicle. Use only hoses and clamps specifically designed for fuel injection.

1. Relieve the fuel pressure.
2. Disconnect the negative battery cable.
3. The filter is located in the Engine compartment, mounted either on the firewall or inner fender panel.

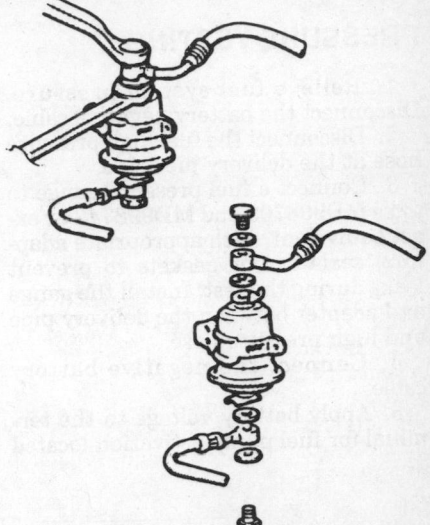

Fuel filter and hoses

4. On Summit Wagon and Stealth, remove the air cleaner assembly and intake hoses. On Stealth, remove the battery and battery tray with washer tank.

5. Hold the fuel filter nut securely with a backup or spanner wrench. Cover the hoses with shop towels and remove the eye bolt. Discard the gaskets.

6. On Stealth, the high pressure hose connection is accomplished with another eye bolt connection; first separate the flare nut connection at the line, then repeat Step 5. Otherwise, separate the flare nut connection at the filter. Discard the gaskets.

7. Remove the mounting bolts and remove the fuel filter from the vehicle.

To install:

8. If equipped with flare fitting, install a new O-ring and tighten the fitting by hand before installing the filter to the vehicle.

9. Install the filter to its bracket only finger-tight. Movement of the filter will ease attachment of the fuel lines.

10. Install new O-rings and connect the high pressure hose and eye bolt, then the main pipe and eye bolt. While holding the fuel filter nut, tighten the eye bolts to 22 ft. lbs. (30 Nm). Tighten the flare nut to 25 ft. lbs. (35 Nm).

11. Tighten the mounting bolts fully.

12. Install the air cleaner assembly, battery and battery tray with washer tank, if removed.

13. Connect the negative battery cable, install the fuel filler cap, turn the key to the **ON** position to pressurize the fuel system and check for leaks. Release the fuel pressure and repair leaks as required.

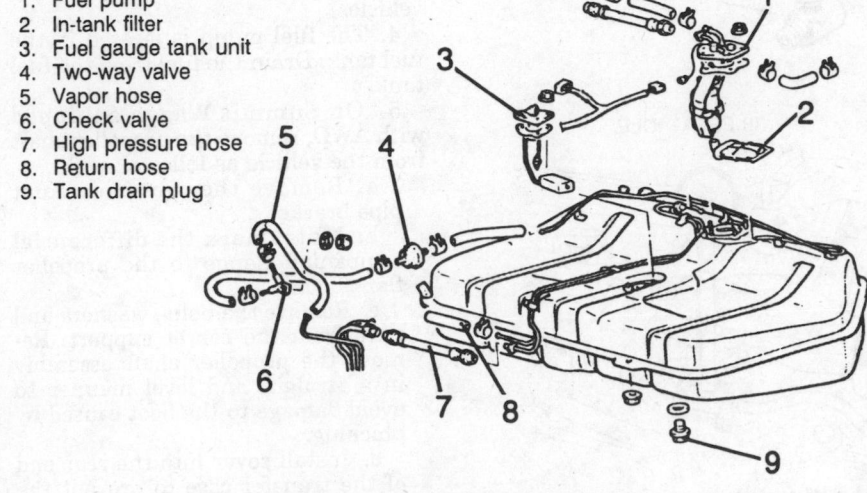

Fuel tank assembly and related parts

Electric Fuel Pump

PRESSURE TESTING

1. Relieve fuel system pressure. Disconnect the battery negative cable.
2. Disconnect the fuel high pressure hose at the delivery pipe side.
3. Connect a fuel pressure gauge to tools MD998709 and MD998742 or exact equivalent, with appropriate adaptors, seals and/or gaskets to prevent leaks during the test. Install the gauge and adapter between the delivery pipe and high pressure hose.
4. Connect the negative battery cable.
5. Apply battery voltage to the terminal for fuel pump activation located in the Engine compartment, to run the fuel pump and check for leaks.
6. Start the Engine and run at curb idle speed.
7. Measure the fuel pressure and compare to specifications.
8. Locate and disconnect the vacuum hose running to the fuel pressure regulator. Plug the end of the hose and record the fuel pressure again. The fuel pressure should have increased approximately 10 psi.
9. Reconnect the vacuum hose the fuel pressure regulator. After the fuel pressure stabilizes, race the Engine 2–3 times and check that the fuel pressure does not fall when the Engine is running at idle.
10. Check to be sure there is fuel pressure in the return hose by gently pressing the fuel return hose with fingers while racing the Engine. There will be no fuel pressure in the return hose when the volume of fuel flow is low.
11. If fuel pressure is too low, check for a clogged fuel filter, a defective fuel pressure regulator or a defective fuel pump, any of which will require replacement.
12. If fuel pressure is too high, the fuel pressure regulator is defective and will have to be replaced or the fuel return is bent or clogged. If the fuel pressure reading does not change when the vacuum hose is disconnected, the hose is clogged or the valve is stuck in the fuel pressure regulator and it will have to be replaced.
13. Stop the Engine and check for changes in the fuel pressure gauge. It should not drop. If the gauge reading does drop, watch the rate of drop. If fuel pressure drops slowly, the likely cause is a leaking injector which will require replacement. If the fuel pressure drops immediately after the Engine is stopped, the check valve in the fuel pump isn't closing and the fuel pump will have to be replaced.
14. Relieve fuel system pressure.
15. Disconnect the high pressure hose and remove the fuel pressure gauge from the delivery pipe.
16. Install a new O-ring in the groove of the high pressure hose. Connect the hose to the delivery pipe and tighten the screws. After installation, apply battery voltage to the terminal for fuel pump activation to run the fuel pump. Check for leaks.

REMOVAL & INSTALLATION
Summit and Summit Wagon

1. Relieve fuel system pressure. Remove the filler cap.
2. Disconnect the negative battery cable.
3. Raise and safely support the vehicle.
4. The fuel pump is located in the fuel tank. Drain the fuel from the fuel tank.
5. On Summit Wagon equipped with AWD, remove the propeller shaft from the vehicle as follows:
   a. Remove the center exhaust pipe bracket.
   b. Matchmark the differential companion flange to the propeller flange yoke.
   c. Remove the bolts, washers and nuts from the center support. Remove the propeller shaft assembly in a straight and level manner to avoid damage to the boot caused by pinching.
   d. Install cover into the rear end of the transfer case to prevent the entry of foreign materials.

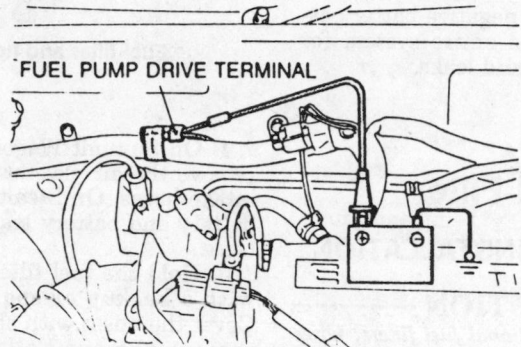

Fuel pump test terminal—Summit and Summit Wagon

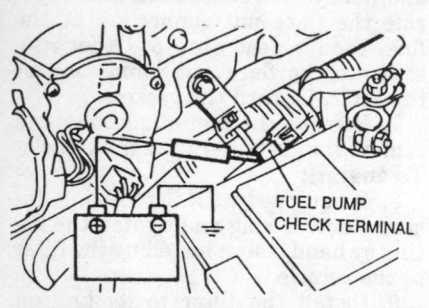

Fuel pump test terminal—Laser and Talon

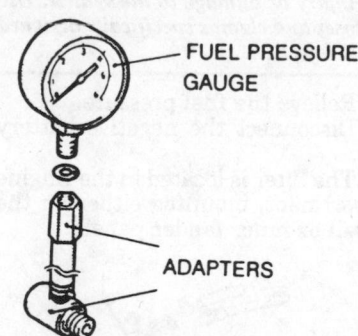

38 PSI AT IDLE

Fuel pump test terminal—Stealth

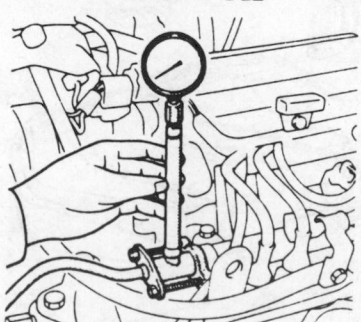

Fuel system pressure testing

6. Disconnect the return hose, high pressure hose and all other hoses and connectors connected to the pump and sending unit.

7. Disconnect the filler and vent hoses. Place a support under the tank and remove the retaining nuts. Lower the tank from vehicle.

8. Remove retaining nuts and remove the fuel pump assembly from tank.

To install:

9. Install the replacement pump using a new gasket. Be certain the pump is installed in the same location, facing the same direction as before.

10. Install the fuel tank and secure the retainer nuts. Connect all electrical harness connectors. Reconnect all vent hoses, fuel supply and fuel return hoses securing with the proper clamps.

11 On Summit Wagon, install the propeller shaft aligning the matchmarks prior to installation. Tighten the rear yoke nuts to 22–25 ft. lbs. (30–35 Nm) and the center support self-locking nuts to 22 ft. lbs. (30 Nm).

12. Install the exhaust pipe center bracket. Check that electrical connectors are properly installed and all fuel hose connections are tight.

13. Connect the negative battery cable and check the entire fuel system for proper operation and leaks. If repairing of a fuel leak is required, release the fuel system pressure prior to repairing system.

Laser and Talon

WITH FWD

1. Relieve fuel system pressure. Remove the filler cap.

2. Disconnect the negative battery cable.

3. Raise and safely support the vehicle.

4. Drain the fuel from the fuel tank.

5. Remove the electrical connector from the fuel pump.

6. Remove the high pressure fuel hose connector.

7. Loosen self-locking nuts on tank support straps to the end of the stud bolts.

8. Remove the right side lateral rod attaching bolt and disconnect the arm from the right body coupling. Lower the lateral rod and suspend from the axle beam.

9. Remove the holding bolt and gasket from the base of the tank and remove the fuel pump assembly.

To install:

10. Align the 3 projections on packing with the holes on the fuel pump and the nipples on the pump facing the same direction as before removal.

11. Install the holding bolt through the bottom of the tank. Make sure the

gasket on the bolt is replaced and is not pinched during installation.

12. Install the right side lateral rod and attaching bolt into the right body coupling.

13. Tighten self-locking nuts on tank support straps. Install the high pressure fuel hose connector.

14. Install the elctrical connector to the fuel pump assembly.

15. Connect the negative battery cable and check the entire system for proper operation and leaks.

WITH AWD

1. Relieve fuel system pressure. Remove the filler cap.

2. Disconnect the negative battery cable.

3. The fuel pump is located in the fuel tank. Remove the hole cover located in the rear floor pan.

4. Remove the electrical connector from the fuel pump. Remove the overfill limiter (two-way valve).

5. Cover the hose connection with a shop towel to prevent any splash of fuel due to residual pressure in the fuel pipe. Remove the high pressure fuel hose connectors.

6. Remove the fuel pump and gauge assembly from the tank.

To install:

7. Align the 3 projections on the packing with the holes on the fuel pump and the nipples on the pump facing the same direction as before removal.

8. Install the high pressure hose connections.

9. Install the overfill limiter (two-way valve) and the electrical connector to the fuel pump.

10. Reconnect the negative battery cable and check the entire system for leaks.

11. Install MOPAR Rope Caulk Sealer part 4026044 to the rear floor pan and install the cover into place.

Stealth

1. Relieve fuel system pressure. Remove the filler cap.

2. Disconnect the negative battery cable.

3. The fuel pump is located in the fuel tank. Drain the fuel from the fuel tank.

4. Remove the fuel gauge cover located in the rear floor pan.

5. Remove the fuel pump and gauge electrical connector. Remove the overfill limiter (two-way valve).

6. Disconnect both sides of the high pressure fuel hose. When disconnecting the fuel pump side of the hose, hold the pump side nut with a wrench while turning the nut on the hose side. This will prevent any damage that will occur to the fittings and the hoses if 2 wrenches are not used.

7. Remove the fuel pump and gauge assembly from the tank.

To install:

8. Align the 3 projections on the packing with the holes on the fuel pump and the nipples on the pump facing the same direction as before removal.

9. Temporarily tighten the flare nut on the high pressure hose by hand. Making sure the hose does not twist, tighten body side nut to 22 ft. lbs. (30 Nm) and the fuel pump side nut to 25 ft. lbs. (35 Nm).

10. Install the overfill limiter (two-way valve) with the long shouldered side of the valve facing the canister.

11. Connect the electrical connector to the pump assembly.

12. Reconnect the negative battery cable and check the entire system for leaks.

13. Install MOPAR Rope Caulk Sealer part 4026044 to the rear floor pan and install the cover into place.

Fuel Injection

IDLE SPEED ADJUSTMENT

NOTE: The idle speed is controlled electronically and adjustment is usually unnecessary. However, the idle speed may be checked using the following procedures.

1.8L (Summit Wagon) and 2.4L Engines

1. Warm the Engine to operating temperature, leave lights, electric cooling fan and accessories **OFF**. The transaxle should be in **N** or **P** for automatic transaxle. The steering wheel in a neutral position for vehicles with power steering.

2. Insert the paper clip into the 1 terminal rpm connector in the Engine compartment, and connect the primary voltage detection type tachometer to the paper clip.

3. Ground the self-diagnostic control terminal of the diagnostic connector with a jumper wire.

4. Remove the waterproof female connector from the ignition timing adjustment connector. Ground the ignition timing adjustment terminal.

5. Start the Engine and run at idle. Check the basic idle speed, the desired value is 650–850 rpm.

6. If the value is not within specifications, turn the Speed Adjusting Screw (SAS) to make the necessary adjustment.

NOTE: If the idle speed is higher than the standard value, inspect the SAS screw for evidence

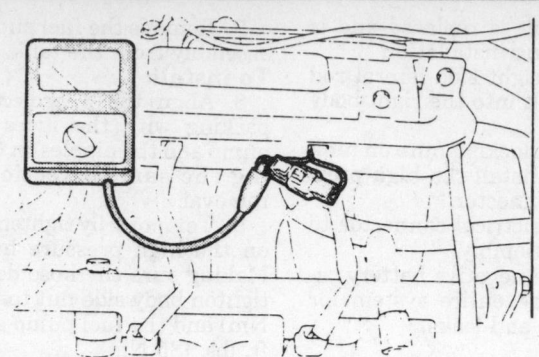

Connecting tachometer to the terminal — 1992–93 Summit Wagon

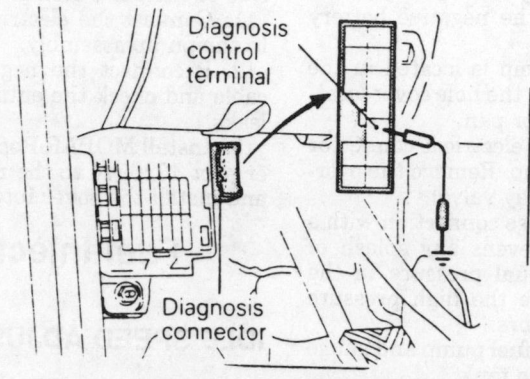

Diagnosis control terminal

Diagnosis connector

Grounding the diagnostic terminal — 1992–93 Summit Wagon

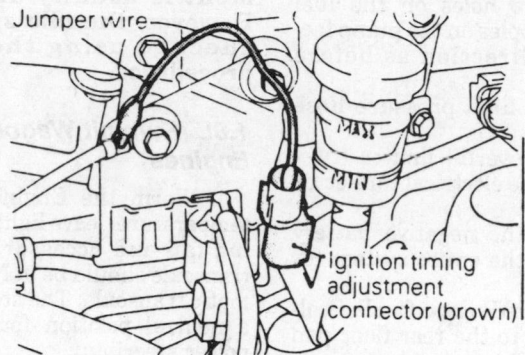

Jumper wire

Ignition timing adjustment connector (brown)

Grounding the ignition timing adjustment terminal — 1992–93 Summit Wagon

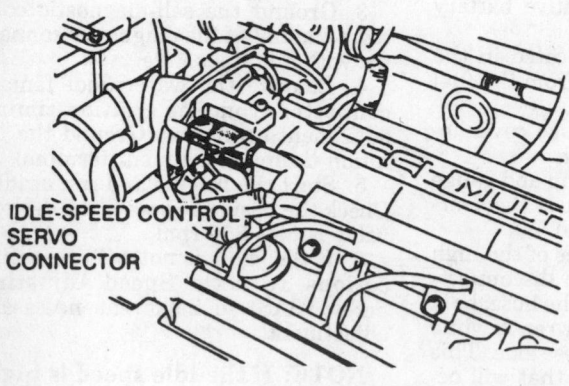

IDLE-SPEED CONTROL SERVO CONNECTOR

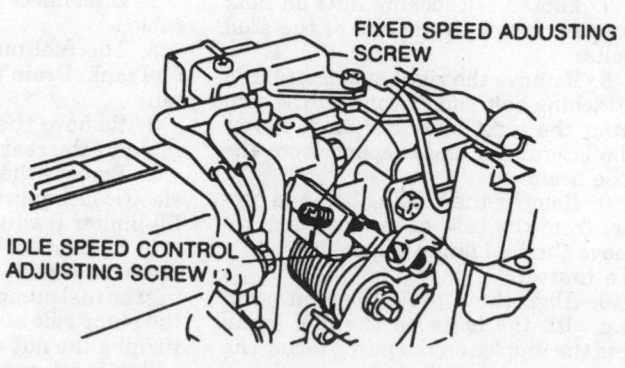

FIXED SPEED ADJUSTING SCREW

IDLE SPEED CONTROL ADJUSTING SCREW

Adjustment points for idle speed — 1.5L and 1.8L Engines

of movement. If there is evidence that the SAS screw has been adjusted, readjust to the proper setting. If the screw does not look as though it has been adjusted, it is possible that there is leakage as a result of deterioration of the Fast Idle Air Valve (FIAV), and, if so the throttle body should be replaced.

7. Turn the ignition OFF. Disconnect and remove the jumper wires from the diagnosis control terminal and the ignition timing adjustment terminal.

8. Start the Engine and let run at idle speed for about 10 minutes, check to be sure the idling condition is normal.

1.5L and 1.8L (Laser) Engines

1. Warm the Engine to operating temperature, leave lights, electric cooling fan and accessories OFF. The transaxle should be in N or P for automatic transaxle. The steering wheel in a neutral position for vehicles with power steering.

2. Check the ignition timing and adjust, if necessary.

3. Connect a tachometer to the CRC filter connector. Use a paper clip for a tach adapter.

4. Run the Engine for more than 10 seconds at 2000–3000 rpm. Allow the Engine to idle for 2 minutes. Check the idle rpm. Curb idle should be 750 ± 100 rpm.

5. If adjustment is required, slacken the accelerator cable.

6. Connect a digital voltmeter between terminal 19 throttle position sensor output voltage) of the Engine control unit and terminal 24 (ground).

7. Set the ignition switch to ON, without starting the Engine, and hold it in that position for 15 seconds or more. Turn the ignition switch OFF.

8. Disconnect the connectors of the idle speed control servo and lock the

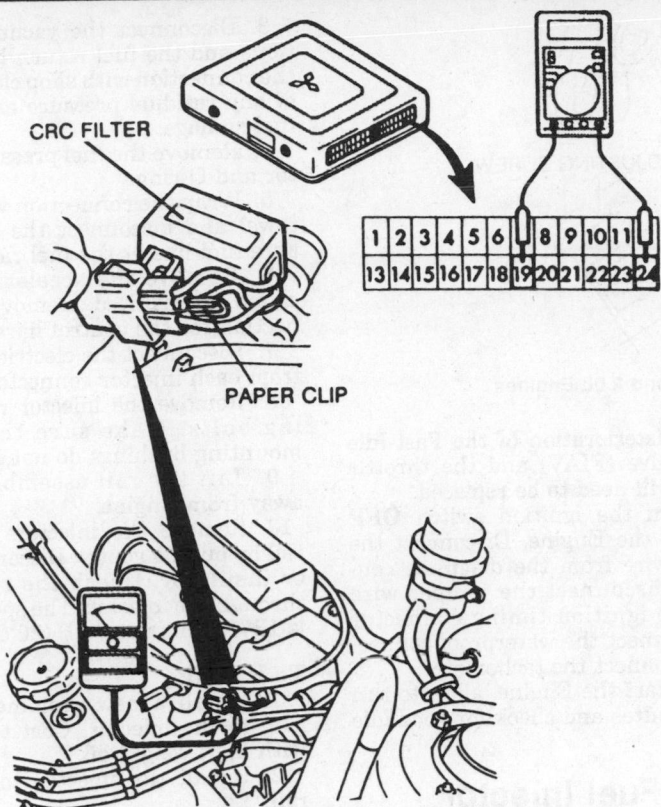

Idle speed check connections—1.5L and 1.8L Engines

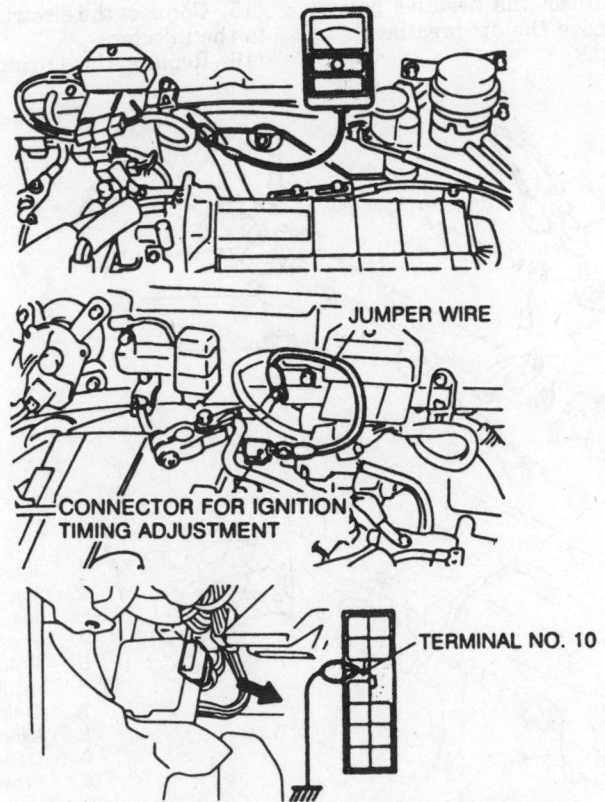

Idle speed check connections—1.6L and 2.0L Engines

idle speed control plunger at the initial position. Back out the fixed Speed Adjusting Screw (SAS).

9. Start the Engine and allow to idle. Basic idle speed should be at specification. A new Engine may idle a little lower. If the vehicle stalls or has a very low idle speed, suspect a deposit buildup on the throttle valve which must be cleaned.

10. If the idle speed is wrong, adjust with the idle speed control adjusting screw. Use a hexagon wrench if possible. Turn in the fixed SAS until the Engine speed rises. Then back out the fixed SAS until the Touch Point where the Engine speed does not fall any longer, is found. Back out the fixed SAS an additional ½ turn from the touch point.

11. Stop the Engine. Turn the ignition switch to **ON** but do not start Engine. Check that the output voltage from the throttle position sensor is 0.48–0.52 volts. If it is out of specification, adjust by loosening the throttle position sensor mounting screws and rotating the throttle position sensor. Turning the throttle position sensor clockwise increases the output voltage. After adjustment, tighten screws firmly.

12. Turn the ignition switch **OFF**.

13. Adjust the free-play of the accelerator cable, reconnect the connectors of the idle speed control servo and remove the voltmeter.

14. Start the Engine and check the curb idle. It should be 700 ± 100 rpm.

15. Turn the ignition switch to **OFF**, disconnect the negative battery cable for more than 10 seconds and reconnect. This clears any trouble codes introduced during testing.

16. Restart the Engine, allow to run for 5 minutes and check for good idle quality.

1.6L, 2.0L and 3.0L Engines

1. Warm the Engine to operating temperature, leave lights, electric cooling fan and accessories **OFF**. The transaxle should be in **N**. The steering wheel in a neutral position for vehicles with power steering.

2. Check the ignition timing and adjust, if necessary.

3. Connect a tachometer to the 1 pin connector under the hood.

4. Run the Engine for more than 10 seconds at 2000–3000 rpm. Allow the Engine to idle for 2 minutes. Check the idle rpm. Curb idle should be 750 ± 50 rpm.

5. If adjustment is required, disconnect the waterproof female connector used for ignition timing adjustment. Connect this terminal to ground using a jumper wire.

6. Locate the self-diagnosis terminal under the dashboard and connect

1-69

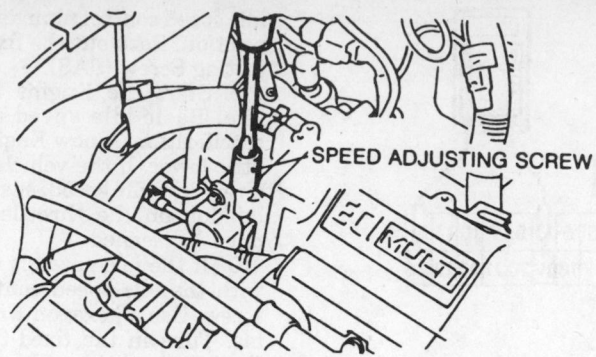

Adjustment point for idle speed—1.6L and 2.0L Engines

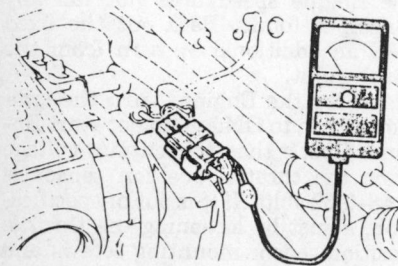

Idle speed check connector—3.0L SOHC Engine

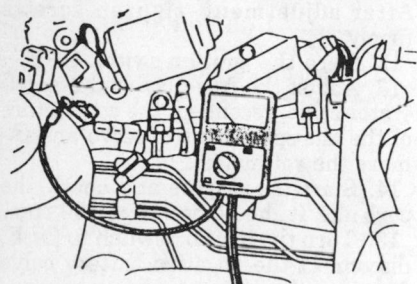

Idle speed check connector—3.0L DOHC Engine

terminal No. **10** to ground with a jumper wire.

7. Start the Engine and allow to idle. Check that the basic idle speed is at specification. On Stealth, the tachometer reading will be $\frac{1}{3}$ of the actual Engine speed. Multiply the reading by 3 to figure the actual Engine speed. If the idle speed deviates from this speed, check the following:

a. A new Engine will idle more slowly. Break-in should take approximately 300 miles.

b. If the vehicle stalls or has a very low idle speed, suspect a deposit buildup on the throttle valve which must be cleaned.

c. If the idle speed is high even though the speed adjusting screw is fully closed, check that the idle position switch (fixed speed adjusting screw) position has changed. If so, adjust the idle position switch.

d. If after all these checks the idle is still out of specification, it is probable that there is leakage resulting

from deterioration of the Fast-Idle Air Valve (FIAV) and the throttle body will need to be replaced.

8. Turn the ignition switch **OFF** and stop the Engine. Disconnect the jumper wire from the diagnosis connector, disconnect the jumper wire from the ignition timing connector and reconnect the waterproof connector. Disconnect the tachometer.

9. Restart the Engine, allow to run for 5 minutes and check for good idle quality.

Fuel Injector

REMOVAL & INSTALLATION

1.5L and 1.8L (Laser) Engines

1. Relieve the fuel system pressure.
2. Disconnect the negative battery cable. Remove the air breather hose, as required.

3. Disconnect the vacuum connections and the fuel return hose. Cover the connection with shop cloths in case of any residual pressure and to avoid fuel spillage.

4. Remove the fuel pressure regulator and O-ring.

5. Wrap the connection with a shop towel and disconnect the high pressure fuel line at the fuel rail.

6. Remove the accelerator cable clamp as required. Remove the connection for the control harness.

7. Disconnect the electrical harness from each injector connector.

8. Remove the injector rail retaining bolts. Make sure the rubber mounting bushings do not get lost.

9. Lift the rail assembly up and away from Engine.

10. Remove the injectors from the rail by pulling gently. Discard the lower insulator. Check the resistance through the injector. The specification is 13–16 ohms at 70°F (20°C).

To install:

11. Install a new grommet and O-ring to the injector. Coat the O-ring with light weight oil.

12. Install the injector to the fuel rail.

13. Install the fuel rail and injectors to the manifold. Make sure the rubber bushings are in place before tightening the mounting bolts.

14. Tighten the retaining bolts to 72 inch lbs. (11 Nm).

15. Connect the electrical connectors to the injectors.

16. Replace the O-ring on the fuel

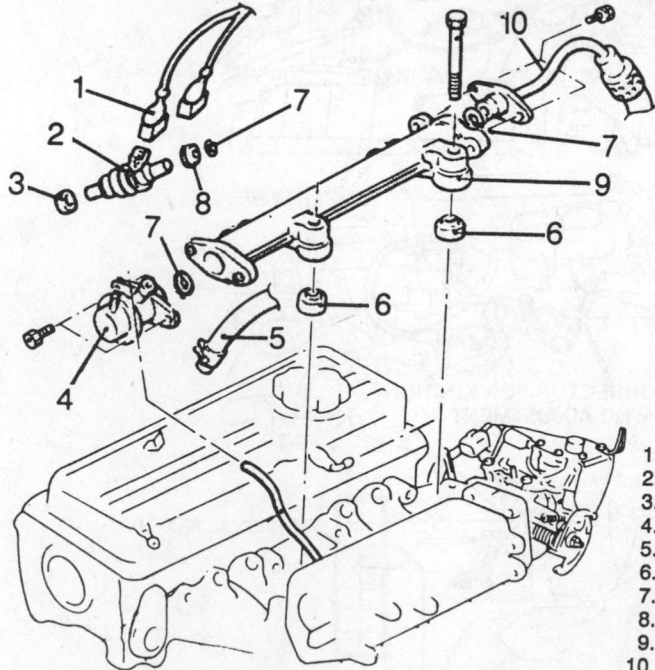

1. Injector harness
2. Injector
3. Insulator
4. Pressure regulator
5. Return hose
6. Insulator
7. O-ring
8. Injector grommet
9. Delivery pipe
10. Pressure line

Fuel rail, Injectors and related parts—1.5L and 1.8L Engines

pressure regulator, lightly lubricate and insert on delivery pipe.

17. Connect the fuel return hose.

18. Replace the O-ring on high pressure fuel line, lightly lubricate it and connect to delivery pipe.

19. Connect the negative battery cable and check the entire system for proper operation and leaks.

1.8L (Summit Wagon) and 2.4L Engines

1. Relieve the fuel system pressure.

2. Disconnect the negative battery cable.

3. Disconnect and remove the air intake hoses, as required.

4. Wrap the connection with a shop towel and disconnect the high pressure fuel line at the fuel rail.

5. Disconnect the fuel return hose and remove the O-ring.

6. Disconnect the accelerator cable connection from the throttle body and position aside.

7. Disconnect the vacuum connection from the fuel pressure regulator.

8. Disconnect the electrical harness connector from each fuel injector.

9. Remove the injector rail retaining bolts. Make sure the rubber mounting insulators do not get lost.

10. Lift the rail assembly up and away from Engine.

11. Remove the injectors from the rail by pulling gently. Discard the lower insulator. Check the resistance through the injector. The specification is 13–16 ohms at 70°F (20°C).

To install:

12. Install a new grommet and O-ring to the injector. Coat the O-ring with light weight oil.

13. Install the injector to the fuel rail.

14. Install the fuel rail and injectors to the manifold. Make sure the rubber bushings are in place before tightening the mounting bolts.

15. Tighten the retaining bolts to 8.7 ft. lbs. (12 Nm).

16. Connect the electrical connectors to the injectors.

17. Replace the O-ring on the fuel pressure regulator, lightly lubricate and install on the delivery pipe. Connect the vacuum hose to the fuel pressure regulator.

18. Connect the fuel return hose.

19. Replace the O-ring on high pressure fuel line, lightly lubricate it and connect to delivery pipe.

21. Reconnect the accelerator cable to the throttler body and adjust to specifications.

22. Connect the negative battery cable and check the entire system for proper operation and leaks.

1.6L and 2.0L DOHC Engines

1. Relieve the fuel system pressure.

2. Disconnect the negative battery cable.

3. Wrap the connection with a shop towel and disconnect the high pressure fuel line at the fuel rail.

4. Disconnect the fuel return hose and remove the O-ring.

5. Disconnect the vacuum hose from the fuel pressure regulator. Remove the fuel pressure regulator and O-ring.

6. Disconnect the PCV hose. On Laser and Talon, remove the center cover.

7. Label and disconnect the electrical connectors from each injector.

8. Remove the injector rail retaining bolts. Make sure the rubber mounting bushings do not get lost.

9. Lift the rail assembly up and away from the Engine.

10. Remove the injectors from the rail by pulling gently. Discard the lower insulator. Check the resistance through the injector. The specification for 2.0L turbocharged Engine is 2–3 ohms at 70°F (20°C). The specification for the others is 13–15 ohms at 70°F (20°C).

To install:

11. Install a new grommet and O-ring to the injector. Coat the O-ring with light oil.

12. Install the injector to the fuel rail.

13. Replace the seats in the intake manifold. Install the fuel rail and injectors to the manifold. Make sure the rubber bushings are in place before tightening the mounting bolts.

14. Tighten the retaining bolts to 72 inch lbs. (11 Nm).

15. Connect the connectors to the injectors and install the center cover. Connect the PCV hose.

16. Replace the O-ring, lightly lubricate it and connect the fuel pressure regulator.

17. Connect the fuel return hose.

18. Replace the O-ring, lightly lubricate it and connect the high pressure fuel line.

19. Connect the negative battery cable and check the entire system for proper operation and leaks.

3.0L Engine

1. Relieve the fuel system pressure.

2. Disconnect the negative battery cable.

3. Drain the cooling system.

4. Disconnect all components from the air intake plenum and remove the plenum from the intake manifold. Discard the gaskets.

5. Wrap the connection with a shop towel and disconnect the high pressure fuel line at the fuel rail.

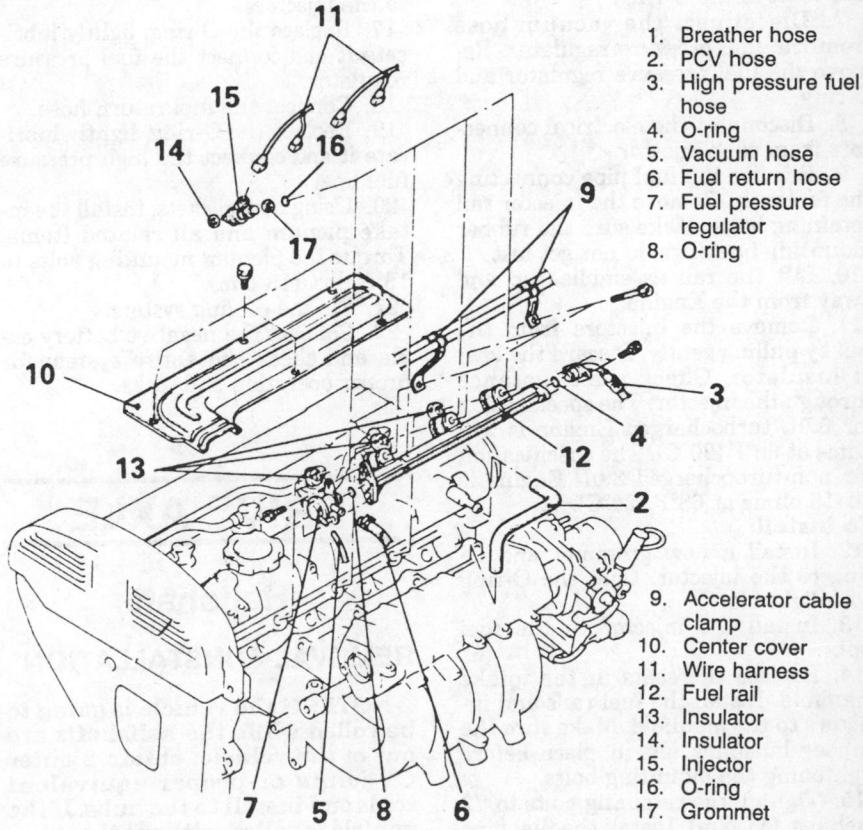

1. Breather hose
2. PCV hose
3. High pressure fuel hose
4. O-ring
5. Vacuum hose
6. Fuel return hose
7. Fuel pressure regulator
8. O-ring
9. Accelerator cable clamp
10. Center cover
11. Wire harness
12. Fuel rail
13. Insulator
14. Insulator
15. Injector
16. O-ring
17. Grommet

Fuel rail, injectors and related parts—1.6L and 2.0L Engines

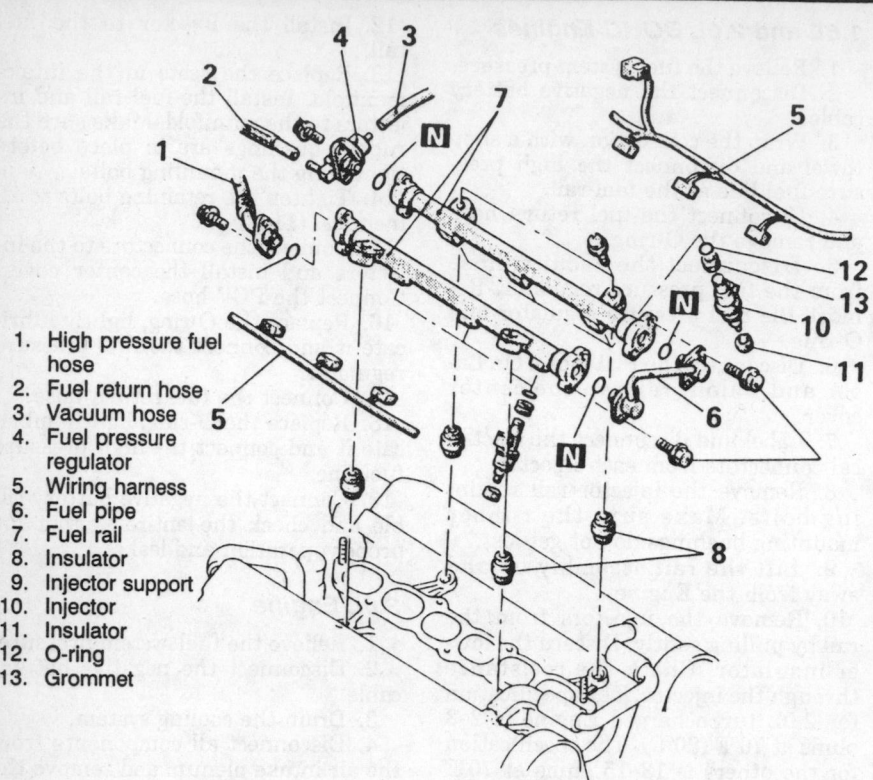

1. High pressure fuel hose
2. Fuel return hose
3. Vacuum hose
4. Fuel pressure regulator
5. Wiring harness
6. Fuel pipe
7. Fuel rail
8. Insulator
9. Injector support
10. Injector
11. Insulator
12. O-ring
13. Grommet

Fuel rail, injectors and related parts—3.0L Engine

6. Disconnect the fuel return hose and remove the O-ring.

7. Disconnect the vacuum hose from the fuel pressure regulator. Remove the fuel pressure regulator and O-ring.

8. Disconnect the electrical connectors from each injector.

9. Remove the fuel pipe connecting the fuel rails. Remove the injector rail retaining bolts. Make sure the rubber mounting bushings do not get lost.

10. Lift the rail assemblies up and away from the Engine.

11. Remove the injectors from the rail by pulling gently. Discard the lower insulator. Check the resistance through the injector. The specification for 3.0L turbocharged Engine is 2–3 ohms at 68°F (20°C). The specification for non-turbocharged 3.0L Engine is 13–15 ohms at 68°F (20°C).

To install:

12. Install a new grommet and O-ring to the injector. Coat the O-ring with light oil.

13. Install the injector to the fuel rail.

14. Replace the seats in the intake manifold. Install the fuel rails and injectors to the manifold. Make sure the rubber bushings are in place before tightening the mounting bolts.

15. Tighten the retaining bolts to 72 inch lbs. (11 Nm). Install the fuel pipe with new gasket.

16. Connect the electrical connectors to the injectors.

17. Replace the O-ring, lightly lubricate it and connect the fuel pressure regulator.

18. Connect the fuel return hose.

19. Replace the O-ring, lightly lubricate it and connect the high pressure fuel line.

20. Using new gaskets, install the intake plenum and all related items. Torque the plenum mounting bolts to 13 ft. lbs. (18 Nm).

21. Fill the cooling system.

22. Connect the negative battery cable and check the entire system for proper operation and leaks.

DRIVE AXLE

Halfshaft

REMOVAL & INSTALLATION

NOTE: If the vehicle is going to be rolled while the halfshafts are out of the vehicle, obtain 2 outer CV-joints or proper equivalent tools and install to the hubs. If the vehicle is rolled without the proper torque applied to the front wheel bearings, the bearings will no longer be usable.

1. Disconnect the negative battery cable.

2. Remove the cotter pin, halfshaft nut and washer.

3. Raise the vehicle and support safely. Remove the lower ball joint and the tie rod end from the steering knuckle.

4. On vehicles with an inner shaft, remove the center support bearing bracket bolts and washers.

5. On vehicles with an inner shaft, remove the halfshaft by setting up a puller on the outside wheel hub and pushing the halfshaft from the front hub. Then tap the shaft union at the joint case with a plastic hammer to remove the halfshaft shaft and inner shaft from the transaxle.

6. On vehicles without an inner shaft, remove the halfshaft by setting up a puller on the outside wheel hub and pushing the halfshaft from the front hub. After pressing the outer shaft, insert a prybar between the transaxle case and the halfshaft and pry the shaft from the transaxle. Do not pull on the shaft; doing so damages the inboard joint. Do not insert the prybar too far or the oil seal in the case may be damaged.

To install:

7. Inspect the halfshaft boot for damage or deterioration. Check the ball joints and splines for wear.

8. Replace the circlips on the ends of the halfshafts.

9. Insert the halfshaft into the transaxle. Make sure it is fully seated.

10. Pull the strut assembly out and install the other end to the hub.

11. Install the center bearing bracket bolts and tighten to 33 ft. lbs. (45 Nm).

12. Install the washer so the chamfered edge faces outward. Install the nut and tighten temporarily.

13. Install the tie rod end and ball joint.

14. Install the wheel and lower the vehicle to the floor. Tighten the axle nut with the brakes applied. Tighten the nut to a maximum torque of 188 ft. lbs. (260 Nm). Install the cotter pin and bend to secure.

CV-Boot

The vehicles use several different types of joints. Engine size, transaxle type, whether the joint is an inboard or outboard joint, even which side of the vehicle is being serviced could make a difference in joint type. Be sure to properly identify the joint before attempting joint or boot replacement. Look for identification numbers at the large end of the boots and/or on the end of the metal retainer bands.

The 4 types of joints used are the Birfield Joint, (B.J.), the Tripod Joint (T.J.), the Double Offset Joint (D.O.J.) and the Rzeppa Joint (R.J.). In addition, some left side shafts will have a round dynamic damper installed on the shaft. Special grease is generally used with these joints and is often supplied with the replacement joint and/or boot. Do not use regular chassis grease.

In most cases, a specification is called out for the distance between the large and small boot bands. This is so the boot will not be installed either too loose or too tight, which could cause early wear and cracking, allowing the grease to get out and water and dirt in, leading to early joint failure.

REMOVAL & INSTALLATION

Except Double Offset Joint

Although joint types vary, the basic procedures are the same, with the exception of the Double Offset Joint. The following is a general procedure which should apply to most applications.

1. Disconnect the negative battery cable. Remove the halfshaft.
2. Remove the snapring next to the tripod joint spider assembly from the halfshaft with snapring pliers and remove the spider assembly from the

CV-JOINT INSTALLED LENGTHS

DISTANCE A—SUMMIT

TRIPOD JOINTS	
1.5L and 1.6L Engine w/AT,	LH Shaft—3.15 in. ±.12 in. (80mm ± 3mm)
	RH Shaft—3.35 in. ±.12 in. (85mm ± 3mm)
1.6L Engine w/MT,	—3.35 in. ±.12 in. (80mm ± 3mm)
DOUBLE OFFSET JOINTS	
1.6L Engine Non Turbo	—2.92 in. ±.12 in. (75mm ± 3mm)
1.6L Engine Turbo	—3.15 in. ±.12 in. (80mm ± 3mm)

DISTANCE A—LASER AND TALON

1.8L Engine up to 4–89	LH Shaft—3.15 in. ±.12 in. (80mm ± 3mm)
1.8L Engine from 5–89	LH Shaft—2.95 in. ±.12 in. (75mm ± 3mm)
1.8L Engine up to 4–89	RH Shaft—3.15 in. ±.12 in. (80mm ± 3mm)
1.8L Engine from 5–89	RH Shaft—3.35 in. ±.12 in. (85mm ± 3mm)
2.0L Engine up to 4–89	2WD-LH Shaft—2.95 in. ±.12 in. (75mm ± 3mm)
2.0L Engine from 5–89	2WD-LH Shaft—3.15 in. ±.12 in. (80mm ± 3mm)
2.0L Engine Turbo	2WD-LH Shaft—3.15 in. ±.12 in. (80mm ± 3mm)
2.0L Engine Non Turbo	2WD-RH Shaft—3.15 in. ±.12 in. (80mm ± 3mm)
2.0L Engine Turbo	2WD-RH Shaft—3.15 in. ±.12 in. (80mm ± 3mm)
2.0L Engine Non Turbo	4WD-LH Shaft—3.35 in. ±.12 in. (85mm ± 3mm)
2.0L Engine Non Turbo	4WD-RH Shaft—3.35 in. ±.12 in. (85mm ± 3mm)

① Automatic transaxle
② Manual transaxle

1. TJ boot band
2. Small boot band
3. TJ case and inner shaft assembly
4. TJ case
5. Seal plate
6. Inner shaft
7. Bracket assembly
8. Outer dust seal
9. Inner dust seal
10. Center bearing
11. Cente bearing bracket
12. Circlip
13. Snapring
14. Spider assembly
15. TJ boot
16. BJ boot band
17. Small boot band
18. BJ boot
19. BJ assembly
20. Dust cover

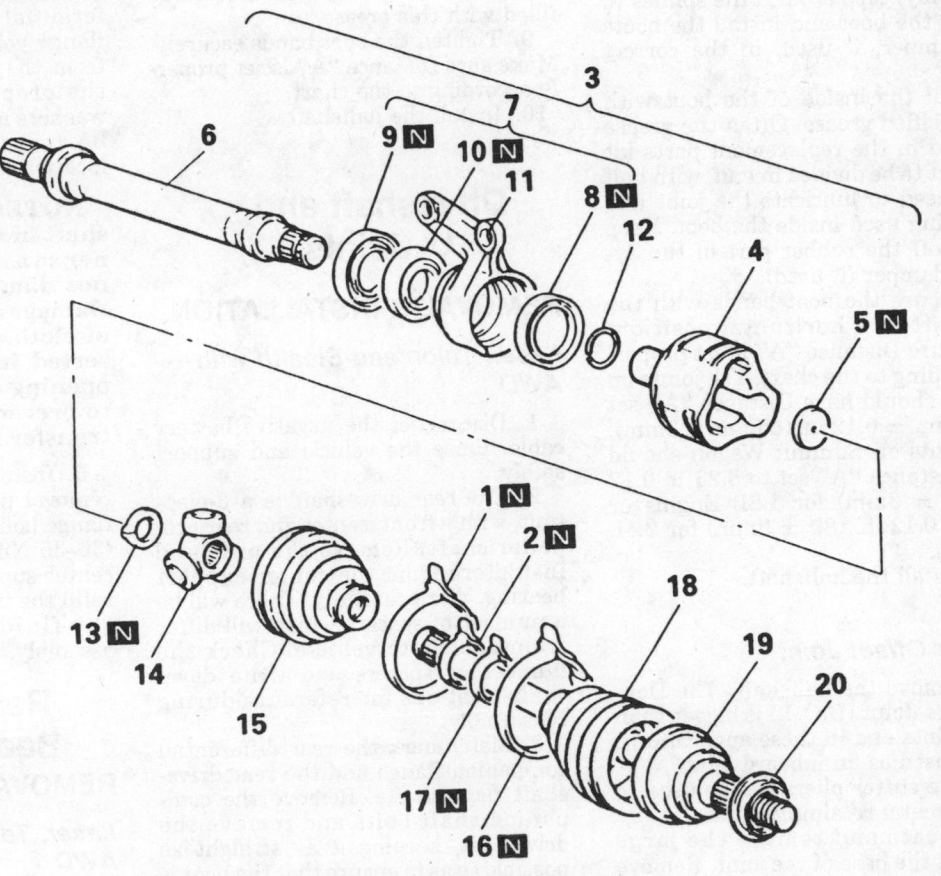

Representative halfshaft and CV-joint assemblies

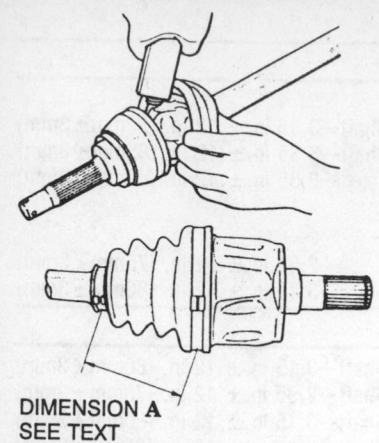

DIMENSION **A**
SEE TEXT

CV-joint and boot assembly with distance A indicated

shaft. Do not disassemble the spider and use care in handling.

3. Side cutter pliers can be used to cut the metal retaining bands.

4. If the boot is be reused, wrap vinyl tape around the spline part of the shaft so the boot will not be damaged when removed. Remove the dynamic damper, if used, and boots from the shaft.

To install:

5. Double check that the correct replacement parts are being installed. Wrap vinyl tape around the splines to protect the boot and install the boots and damper, if used, in the correct order.

6. Fill the inside of the boot with the specified grease. Often the grease supplied in the replacement parts kit is meant to be divided in half, with half being used to lubricate the joint and half being used inside the boot. Keep grease off the rubber part of the dynamic damper (if used).

7. Secure the boot bands with the halfshaft in a horizontal position. Make sure Distance "A" is set properly according to the chart. T.J. joints on Stealth should have Distance "A" set to 3.35 in. ± 0.12 in. (85mm ± 3mm). T.J. joints on Summit Wagon should have Distance "A" set to 3.23 ± 0.12 in. (82 ± 3mm) for 1.8L Engine or 3.15 ± 0.12 in. (80 ± 3mm) for 2.4L Engines.

8. Install the halfshaft.

Double Offset Joint

1. Remove the halfshaft. The Double Offset Joint (D.O.J.) is bigger than other joints and in these applications, is only used as an inboard joint.

2. Side cutter pliers can be used to cut the metal retaining bands.

3. Locate and remove the large circlip at the base of the joint. Remove the outer race (the body of the joint).

4. Matchmark the shaft, D.O.J. inner race and cage. Remove the joint balls and the small snapring from the shaft. With a brass drift pin, tap lightly and evenly around the inner race to remove the race and the inner cage from the shaft.

5. If the boot is to be reused, wipe the grease from the splines and wrap the splines in vinyl tape before sliding the boot from the shaft.

To install:

6. Be sure to tape the shaft splines before installing the boots. Fill the inside of the boot with the specified grease. Often the grease supplied in the replacement parts kit is meant to be divided in half, with half being used to lubricate the joint and half being used inside the boot.

7. Install the cage onto the halfshaft so the small diameter side of the cage is installed first. Align the matchmarks made at disassembly on the inner race and shaft. With a brass drift pin, tap lightly and evenly around the inner race to install the race until it comes into contact with the rib of the shaft. Apply the specified grease to the inner race and cage and fit them together aligning the matchmarks. Insert the balls into the cage.

8. Install the outer race (the body of the joint) after filling with the specified grease. The outer race should be filled with this grease.

9. Tighten the boot bands securely. Make sure Distance "A" is set properly according to the chart.

10. Install the halfshaft.

Driveshaft and U- Joints

REMOVAL & INSTALLATION

Laser, Talon and Stealth with AWD

1. Disconnect the negative battery cable. Raise the vehicle and support safely.

2. The rear driveshaft is a 3-piece unit, with a front, center and rear propeller shaft. Remove the nuts and insulators from the center support bearing. Work carefully. There will be a number of spacers which will differ from vehicle to vehicle. Check the number of spacers and write down their locations for reference during reassembly.

3. Matchmark the rear differential companion flange and the rear driveshaft flange yoke. Remove the companion shaft bolts and remove the driveshaft, keeping it as straight as possible so as to ensure that the boot is not damaged or pinched. Use care to

keep from damaging the oil seal in the output housing of the transfer case.

NOTE: Damage to the boot can be avoided and work will be easier if a piece of cloth or similar material is inserted in the boot.

4. Do not lower the rear of the vehicle or oil will flow from the transfer case. Cover the opening to keep dirt out.

To install:

5. Install the driveshaft to the vehicle and align the matchmarks at the rear yoke. Install the bolts and torque to 22–25 ft. lbs. (30–35 Nm) on Laser and Talon or 36–43 ft. lbs. (50–60 Nm) on Stealth.

6. Install the center support bearing with all spacers in place. Torque the retaining nuts to 22–25 ft. lbs. (30–35 Nm).

7. Check the fluid levels in the transfer case and rear differential case.

Summit Wagon

1. Disconnect the battery negative cable.

2. Raise the vehicle and support safely. Drain the oil from the transfer assembly.

3. Disconnect the front exhaust pipe.

4. Make mating marks on the differential companion flange and the flange yoke. Remove the locking nut from the center support and remove the propeller shaft. Make note of washers and spacers used so they can be reinstalled in their original location.

NOTE: Remove the propeller shaft in a straight and level manner so as to ensure that the boot is not damaged through pinching. Damage can be avoided if a piece of cloth or similar material is inserted into the boot. Cover the opening of the transfer assembly to prevent dirt from entering the transfer assembly.

5. Installation is the reverse of the removal procedure. Tighten the rear flange bolts and nuts to 22–25 ft. lbs. (30–35 Nm), the locking nuts on the center support to 22 ft. lbs. (30 Nm), refill the transfer assembly and check the fluid level in the transaxle assembly.

Rear Axle Shaft, Bearing and Seal

REMOVAL & INSTALLATION

Laser, Talon and Stealth with AWD

1. Disconnect the negative battery

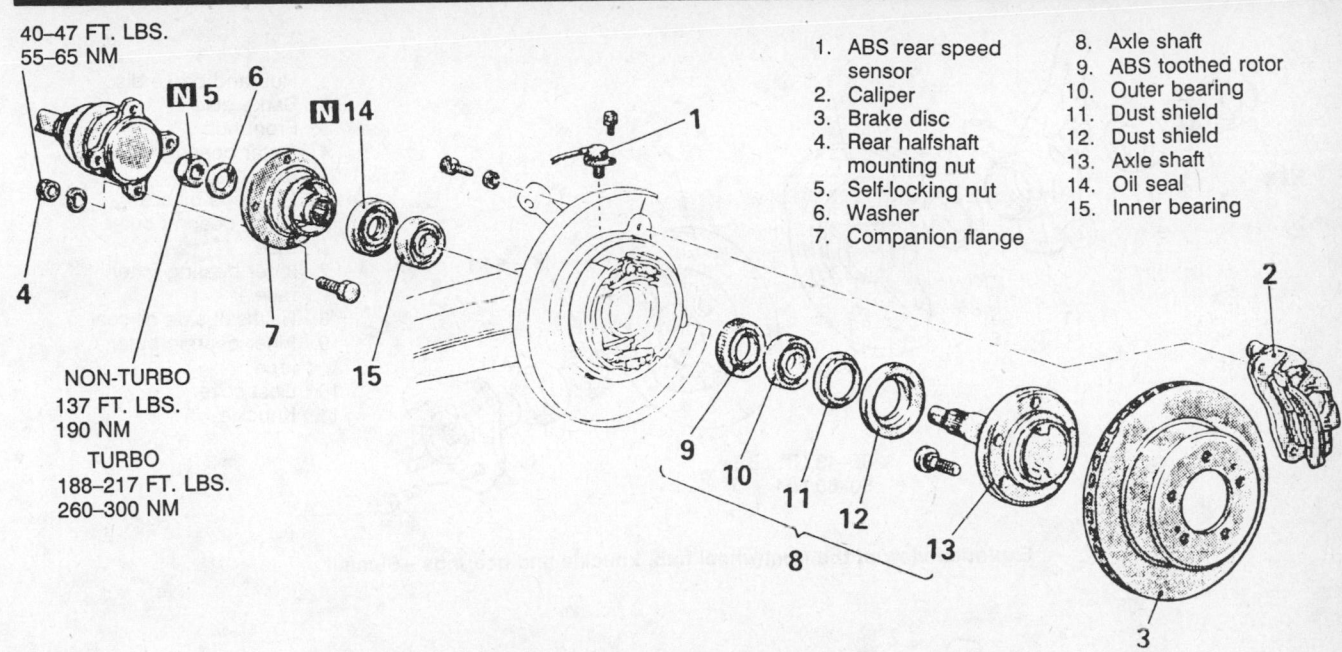

40–47 FT. LBS.
55–65 NM

NON-TURBO
137 FT. LBS.
190 NM

TURBO
188–217 FT. LBS.
260–300 NM

1. ABS rear speed sensor
2. Caliper
3. Brake disc
4. Rear halfshaft mounting nut
5. Self-locking nut
6. Washer
7. Companion flange
8. Axle shaft
9. ABS toothed rotor
10. Outer bearing
11. Dust shield
12. Dust shield
13. Axle shaft
14. Oil seal
15. Inner bearing

Rear axle shaft and related parts—Laser, Talon and Stealth with AWD

cable. Raise the vehicle and support safely.

2. Remove the bolts that attach the rear halfshaft to the companion flange.

3. Use a prybar to pry the inner shaft out of the differential case. Don't insert the prybar too far or the seal could be damage.

4. Remove the rear halfshaft from the vehicle.

5. If equipped with ABS, remove the rear wheel speed sensor.

6. Remove the caliper, pads and brake rotor.

7. Hold the axle shaft stationary and remove the axle shaft self-locking nut and washer.

8. Using a slide hammer, separate the axle shaft from the companion flange and remove.

9. Use a vice and gear puller tool to disassemble the axle shaft and companion flange assemblies.

To install:

10. Assemble the axle shaft and companion shaft assemblies using new parts as required.

11. Install the axle shaft to the housing and slide the axle shaft over it. Install the washer and new self-locking nut. Hold the axle shaft stationary and torque the nut to 116–159 ft. lbs. (160–220 Nm) for Laser, Talon and 1991 non-turbocharged Stealth. Torque to 188–217 ft. lbs. (260–300 Nm) for 1991 turbocharged and 1992-93 Stealth.

12. Install the brake rotor, pads and caliper.

13. Install the ABS rear wheel speed sensor.

14. Replace the circlip and install the rear halfshaft to the differential case. Make sure it snaps in place. Torque the companion flange bolts to 40–47 ft. lbs. (55–65 Nm).

15. Check the fluid level in the rear differential.

Summit Wagon with AWD

1. Disconnect the negative battery cable. Raise the vehicle and support safely.

2. Remove the bolts that attach the rear halfshaft to the rear carrier.

3. Remove the cotter pin, driveshaft nut cover and nut from the rear driveshaft.

NOTE: Do not apply the vehicle weight to the wheel bearing while loosening the driveshaft nut or bearing damage may occur.

4. Separate the shaft from the hub using a puller. Remove the shaft from the flange and lift from the vehicle.

5. Installation is the reverse of the removal procedure. Torque the retainers on the rear carrier to 40–47 ft. lbs. (55–65 Nm) and the shaft end nut to 145–188 ft. lbs. (200–260 Nm).

Front Wheel Hub, Knuckle and Bearing

REMOVAL & INSTALLATION

1. Disconnect the negative battery cable.

2. Remove the cotter pin, halfshaft nut and washer.

3. Raise the vehicle and support safely. If equipped with ABS, remove the front wheel speed sensor. Remove the ball joint and tie rod end from the steering knuckle.

4. Remove the caliper and brake pads and suspend with a wire.

5. On vehicles with an inner shaft, remove the center support bearing bracket bolts and washers. Remove the halfshaft by setting up a puller on the outside wheel hub and pushing the halfshaft from the front hub. Then tap the joint case with a plastic hammer to remove the halfshaft shaft and inner shaft from the transaxle.

6. On vehicles without an inner shaft, remove the halfshaft by setting up a puller on the outside wheel hub and pushing the halfshaft from the front hub. After pressing the outer shaft, insert a prybar between the transaxle case and the halfshaft and pry the shaft from the transaxle.

7. On Stealth with AWD, the front hub/bearing assembly can be serviced at this point as a unit. If the knuckle is being removed, proceed. All others models require knuckle removal for service.

8. Unbolt the lower end of the strut and remove the hub and steering knuckle assembly.

9. Set up a puller with the knuckle/hub in a vise and pull the hub from the knuckle. Do not use a hammer to accomplish this or the bearing will be damaged.

10. Once the hub and outer bearing inner race are removed with a puller, the bearing outer races can be re-

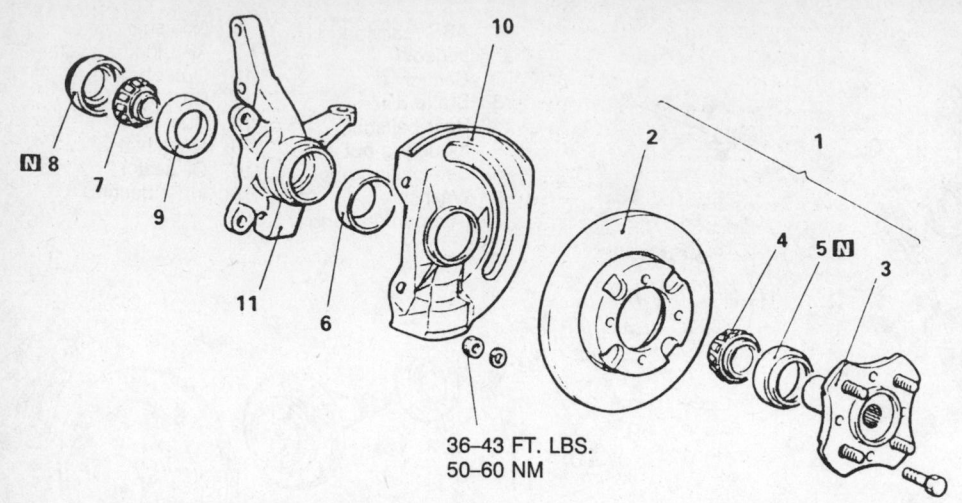

1. Hub and brake disc
2. Barke disc
3. Front hub
4. Outer bearing inner race
5. Hub side oil seal
6. Outer bearing outer race
7. Inner bearing inner race
8. Halfhsaft side oil seal
9. Inner bearing outer race
10. Dust cover
11. Knuckle

36–43 FT. LBS.
50–60 NM

Exploded view of the front wheel hub, knuckle and bearings—Summit

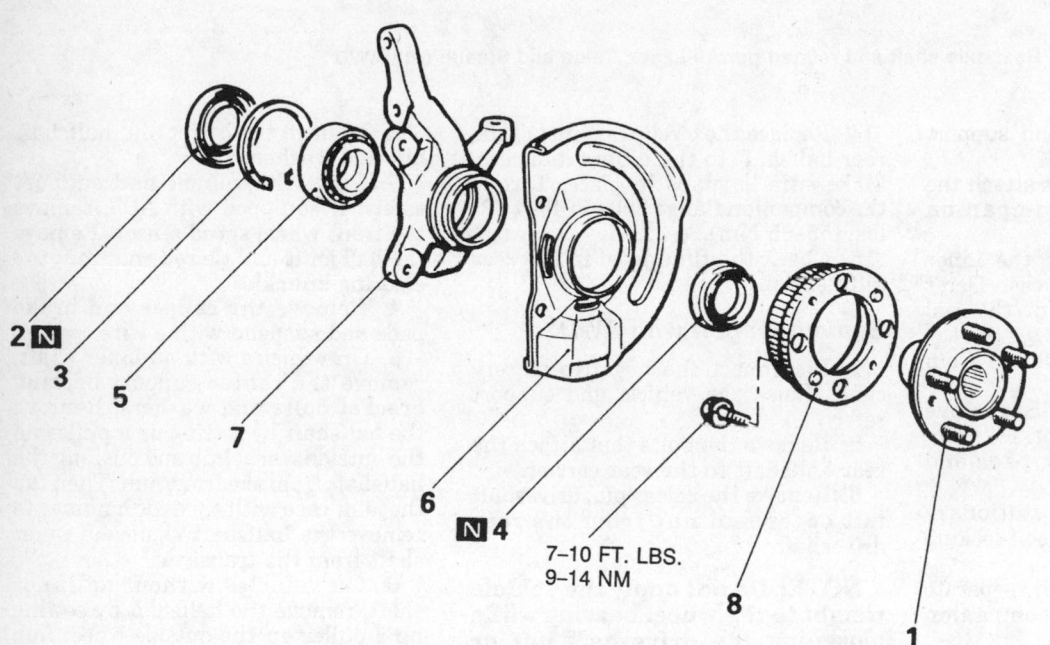

1. Front hub
2. Halfshaft side oil seal
3. Snapring
4. Hub side oil seal
5. Wheel bearing
6. Dust shield
7. Knuckle
8. ABS toothed rotor

7–10 FT. LBS.
9–14 NM

Exploded view of the front wheel hub, knuckle and bearings—except Summit

moved by tapping out with a brass drift pin and a hammer.

To install:

11. Assemble the hub/knuckle assembly with pressing tools, using new parts as required.

12. Install the knuckle assembly to the vehicle and install the strut bolts.

13. On AWD Stealth, torque the front hub/bearing assembly nuts to 76 ft. lbs. (105 Nm).

14. Apply a thin coat of grease to the outside of the outer races and install into the hub with a bearing driver.

15. Apply multi-purpose grease to the bearings, inside surface of the hub and the lip of the grease seal. Place the outside bearing into the knuckle and install the seal with a driver.

16. The hub is assembled to the knuckle with a puller. Draw the parts together firmly to seat the bearings. Use a small torque wrench to check the bearing turning torque. It should be 16 inch lbs. or less for Laser, Talon and Stealth or 11 lbs. or less for Summit. Check that the bearings feel smooth when rotated.

17. Apply a thin coat of grease to the lip of the halfshaft side axle seal and drive into place until it contacts the inner bearing outer race.

18. Replace the circlips on the ends of the halfshafts.

19. Insert the halfshaft into the transaxle. Make sure it is fully seated.

20. Pull the strut assembly out and install the other end to the hub.

21. Install the center bearing bracket bolts and tighten to 33 ft. lbs. (45 Nm).

22. Install the washer so the chamfered edge faces outward. Install the nut and tighten temporarily.

23. Install the tie rod end and ball joint.

24. Install the wheel and lower the vehicle to the floor. Tighten the axle nut with the brakes applied. Tighten the nut to a torque of 145–188 ft. lbs. (200–260 Nm). Install the cotter pin and bend to secure.

1. ABS speed sensor connector
2. Cotter pin
3. Halfshaft end nut
4. Caliper
5. Brake dusc
6. Front hub bearing unit
7. Dust shield
8. Lower ball joint
9. Cotter pin
10. Tie rod end
11. Halfshaft
12. MacPhersonstrut mounting bolt
13. Hub and knuckle
14. Hub

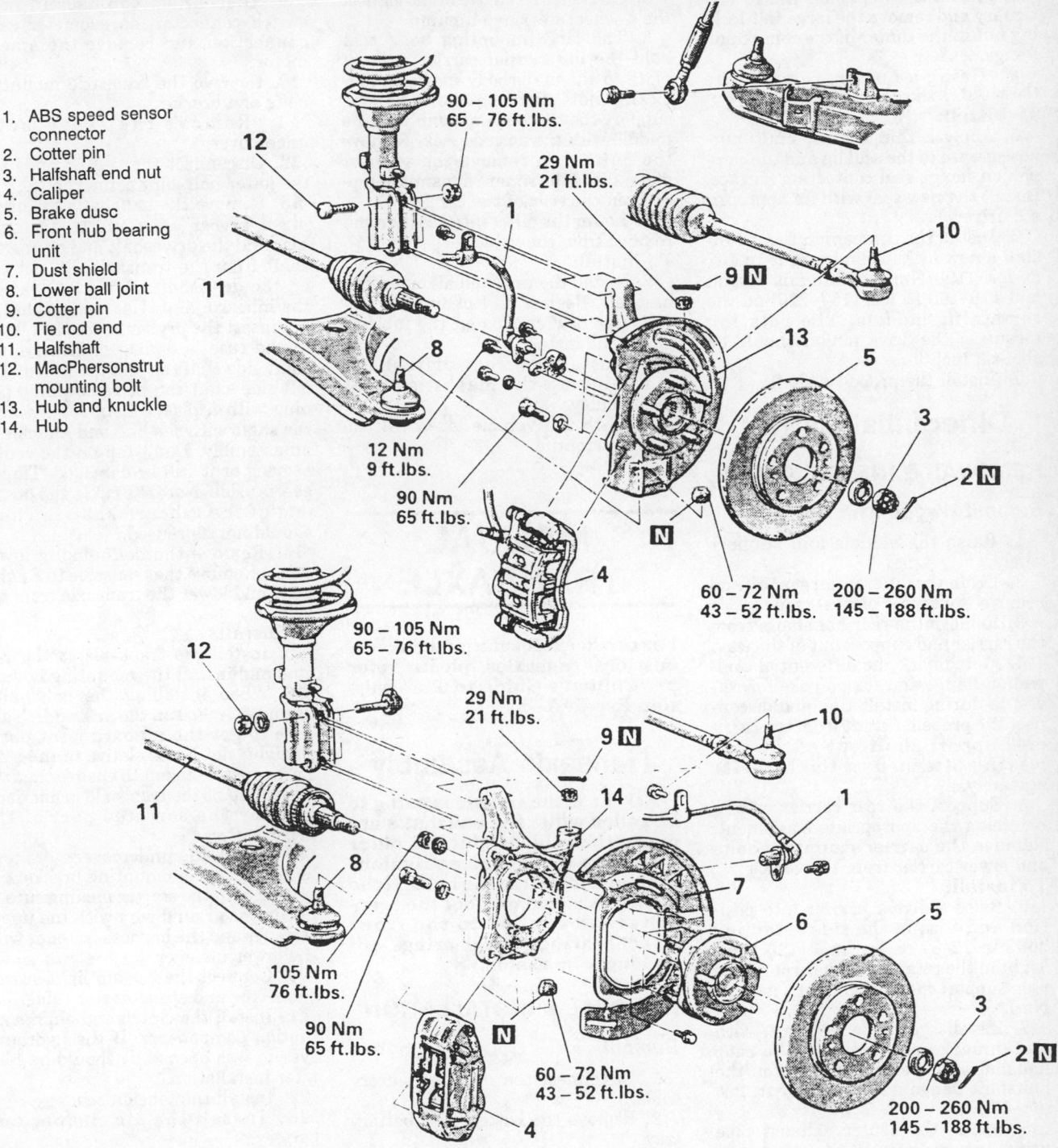

90 – 105 Nm
65 – 76 ft.lbs.

29 Nm
21 ft.lbs.

12 Nm
9 ft.lbs.

90 Nm
65 ft.lbs.

60 – 72 Nm
43 – 52 ft.lbs.

200 – 260 Nm
145 – 188 ft.lbs.

105 Nm
76 ft.lbs.

Front wheel hub, knuckle and bearing. FWD is on top and AWD in on the bottom.

Pinion Seal

REMOVAL & INSTALLATION

Front Differential

1. Disconnect the negative battery cable.
2. Remove the front halfshaft.

3. Using a prying tool, pry the seal from the case.
To install:
4. Apply a thin coat of multi-purpose grease to the seal lip and the seal contact surface.
5. Install the new seal with an appropriate driver.
6. Install the front halfshaft.

Rear Differential

1. Raise the vehicle and support safely.
2. Matchmark the rear propeller shaft and companion flange and remove the shaft. Don't let it hang from the transaxle. Tie it up to the underbody.

3. Hold the companion flange stationary and remove the large self-locking nut in the center of the companion flange.

4. Using a puller, remove the flange. Pry the old seal out.

To install:

5. Apply a thin coat of multi-purpose grease to the seal lip and the companion flange seal contacting surface. Install the new seal with an appropriate driver.

6. Install the companion flange. Install a new locknut and torque to 137 ft. lbs. (190 Nm) on Summit Wagon and 116–160 ft. lbs. (157–220) on the remaining models. The rotation torque of the drive pinion should be about 3 inch lbs.

7. Install the propeller shaft.

Differential Carrier

REMOVAL & INSTALLATION

Summit Wagon with AWD

1. Raise the vehicle and support safely.

2. Drain the differential gear oil and remove the center exhaust pipe.

3. Remove the rear halfshafts from the carrier and support out of the way.

4. Matchmark the differential companion flange and flange yoke for reference during installation and disconnect the propeller shaft from the carrier. Support shaft out of the way leaving attached to the transfer assembly.

5. Support the rear carrier assembly using the appropriate equipment. Remove the carrier mounting bolts and lower carrier from the vehicle.

To install:

6. Raise the rear carrier into position and torque the side retaining bolts to 72–87 ft. lbs. (100–120 Nm). Tighten the retainer bolts through the rear support member to 69 ft. lbs. (95 Nm).

7. Install the propeller shaft, with matchmarks aligned, and the rear halfshafts to the carrier. Tighten the halfshaft flange nuts to 40–47 ft. lbs. (55–65 Nm).

8. Install the center exhaust pipe using new gasket.

9. With the vehicle level, fill the rear differential.

Laser, Talon and Stealth with AWD

1. Raise the vehicle and support safely.

2. Drain the differential gear oil and remove the center exhaust pipe.

3. Matchmark and remove the rear driveshaft.

4. Remove the rear halfshafts.

5. On Stealth, remove or disconnect the 4 wheel steering oil pump.

6. The large mounting bolts that hold the differential carrier support plate to the underbody may use self-locking nuts. Before removing them, support the rear axle assembly in the middle with a transaxle jack. Remove the nuts, then remove the support plate(s) and the square dynamic damper from the rear of the carrier.

7. Lower the differential carrier and remove from the vehicle.

To install:

8. Install the unit and all mounting brackets. Replace all locknuts.

9. Use new circlips on the inboard joints and install.

10. Install the rear driveshaft, matching up the marks made at disassembly.

11. With the vehicle level, fill the rear differential.

MANUAL TRANSAXLE

For further information on transmissions/transaxles, please refer to "Chilton's Guide to Transmission Repair".

Transaxle Assembly

NOTE: If the vehicle is going to be rolled while the halfshafts are out of the vehicle, obtain 2 outer CV-joints or proper equivalent tools and install to the hubs. If the vehicle is rolled without the proper torque applied to the front wheel bearings, the bearings will no longer be usable.

REMOVAL & INSTALLATION

Summit

1. Disconnect the negative battery cable.

2. Remove the battery and battery tray.

3. Remove the air cleaner assembly and air hoses.

4. Raise the vehicle and support safely.

5. Drain the transaxle oil.

6. If equipped with 1.6L Engine, remove the tension rod.

7. Disconnect the shifter cables.

8. Remove the clutch release cylinder and clutch oil line bracket and secure to the body. Do not disconnect the fluid lines. Disconnect the clutch cable, if equipped with cable controlled clutch system.

9. Disconnect the backup lamp switch connector, speedometer cable connection and remove the starter motor.

10. Remove the transaxle mounting bolts and bracket.

11. Remove the sheet metal undercover.

12. Disconnect the tie rod ends and the lower ball joint connections.

13. Remove the halfshafts by inserting a prybar between the transaxle case and the driveshaft and prying the shaft from the transaxle. Do not pull on the driveshaft. Doing so damages the inboard joint. Use the prybar. Do not insert the prybar so far the oil seal in the case is damaged. Remove the right side shaft as just described. The left side shaft can be removed by tapping with a plastic hammer. Remove the shaft with the hub and knuckle as an assembly. Don't tap on the center bearing or it will be damaged. Tie the shafts aside. Note the circle clip on the end of the inboard shafts. These should not be reused.

14. Remove the bellhousing lower cover. Remove the transaxle to Engine bolts and lower the transaxle from the vehicle.

To install:

15. Install the transaxle to the Engine and install the mounting bolts.

16. When installing the halfshafts, use new circlips on the axle ends. Take care to get the inboard joint parts straight, not bent relative to the axle. Care must be taken to ensure that the oil seal lip of the transaxle is not damaged by the serrated part of the driveshaft.

17. Install the undercover.

18. Install the mounting brackets.

19. Install the starter making sure to fasten the ground wire with the upper fastener and the harness fastener with the lower fastener.

20. Connect the backup light switch connector and speedometer cable.

21. Install the clutch and shifter actuation components. If the hydraulic system was opened, it should be bled after installation.

22. Install the tension rod.

23. Install the air cleaner and battery.

24. Make sure the vehicle is level when refilling the transaxle. Use Hypoid gear oil or equivalent, GL-4 or higher.

25. Connect the negative battery cable and check the transaxle for proper operation. Make sure the reverse lights come on when in reverse.

Summit Wagon

1. Disconnect negative battery cable. Support the weight of the Engine using the appropriate fixture.

2. Remove the air cleaner assembly.

Remove the transaxle upper coupling bolts.

3. Raise and safely support the vehicle.

4. Disconnect the control cable connetion from the transaxle.

5. Disconnect the reverse light switch connection.

6. Disconnect the spedometer cable from the transaxle.

7. Remove the starter motor leaving the harness connected and secure aside.

8. Disconnect the tie rod end from the steering knuckle. Disconnect the stabilizer bar.

9. Remove the right side under cover. Drain the transaxle fluid.

10. Insert a prybar between the transaxle case and the driveshaft and pry the shaft from the transaxle. Turn the driveshaft and suspend with a wire so there are no sharp bends in any of the joints. Turn the right side shaft 90 degrees towards the front of the vehicle so it will not be a hindrance.

NOTE: When removing the shaft, use a prybar. Do not pull on the driveshaft; doing so will damage the inboard joint. Do not insert the prybar so deep as to damage the oil seal.

11. Remove the clutch oil line bracket bolt and remove the release cylinder. Suspend cylinder out of the way leaving the oil lines connected.

12. On AWD models, remove the front exhaust pipe and transfer assembly.

13. Remove the center support member.

14. Remove the bellhousing cover. Support the transaxle using a transmission jack.

15. Remove the transaxle mount bolt.

16. Remove the transaxle assembly lower part coupling bolts.

17. Slide the transaxle assembly away from the Engine and remove from the vehicle.

To install:

18. Position the transaxle assembly against the Engine. Install the transaxle assembly lower part coupling bolts.

19. Install the transaxle mount bolt and tighten nut to 51 ft. lbs. (70 Nm).

20. On 1.8L Engine, install the center support member.

21. Remove the transaxle jack. Install the bellhousing cover.

22. Install the clutch oil line bracket bolt and release cylinder.

23. Install the front driveshafts so the inboard joint part of the shaft is straight in relation to the transaxle. Care must be taken to ensure that the oil seal lip part of the transaxle is not

damaged by the serrated part of the driveshaft.

24. Connect the tie rod end from the steering knuckle. Disconnect the stabilizer bar.

25. Install the right side under cover. Install the starter motor.

26. Connect the tie rod ends to the steering knuckle and secure using new cotter pin.

27. Reconnect the speedometer cable, backup switch connector and the control cable connector.

28. Refill the transaxle assembly with Hypoid gear oil or equivalent, GL-4 or higher. Install the air cleaner assembly.

29. Connect the negative battery cable and check the transaxle and transfer case for proper operation. Make sure the reverse lights come ON when in reverse.

Laser and Talon

1. Remove the battery.

2. Remove the auto-cruise actuator and bracket underhood, on the passenger side inner fender wall.

3. Drain the transaxle and transfer case.

4. Remove the air intake hose.

5. Remove the cotter pin securing the select and shift cables and remove the cable ends from the transaxle.

6. Remove the connection for the clutch release cylinder and without disconnecting the hydraulic line, secure aside.

7. Disconnect the backup light switch and the speedometer cable.

8. Disconnect the starter electrical connections and remove the starter motor.

9. Remove the transaxle mount bracket.

10. Raise the vehicle and support safely. Remove the undercover.

11. Remove the cotter pin and disconnect the tie rod end from the steering knuckle.

12. Remove the self-locking nut and remove the lower arm ball joint.

13. Remove the halfshafts by inserting a prybar between the transaxle case and the driveshaft and prying the shaft from the transaxle. Do not pull on the driveshaft. Doing so damages the inboard joint. Use the prybar. Do not insert the prybar so far the oil seal in the case is damaged. On AWD, remove the right side shaft as just described. The left side shaft can be removed by tapping the axle case with a plastic hammer and removing the shaft with the hub and knuckle as an assembly. Don't tap on the center bearing or it will be damaged. Tie the shafts aside. Note the circle clip on the end of the inboard shafts. These should not be reused.

14. On AWD vehicle, disconnect the front exhaust pipe.

15. On AWD vehicle, remove the transfer case by removing the attaching bolts, moving the transfer case to the left and lowering the front side. Remove it from the rear driveshaft. Be careful of the oil seal. Do not allow the prop shaft to hang; tie it up. Cover the transfer case openings to keep out dirt.

16. Remove the underpan from the transaxle bellhousing. On AWD, also remove the crossmember and the triangular gusset.

17. Remove the transaxle lower coupling bolt. It is just above the halfshaft opening on 2WD or transfer case opening on AWD.

18. Remove the transaxle assembly. On turbocharged vehicle, take care to prevent damaging the lower radiator hose with the transaxle housing. Wind tape around the lower hose and put tape on the transaxle housing. Support the transaxle assembly using the proper jack, move the transaxle to the right and lower it.

To install:

19. Install the transaxle to the Engine and install the mounting bolts.

20. Install the transaxle lower coupling bolt.

21. Install the underpan, crossmember and the triangular gusset.

22. Install the transfer case on AWD vehicles and connect the exhaust pipe.

23. When installing the halfshafts, use new circlips on the axle ends. Take care to get the inboard joint parts straight, not bent relative to the axle. Care must be taken to ensure that the oil seal lip of the transaxle is not damaged by the serrated part of the driveshaft.

24. Connect the tie rod and ball joint to the steering knuckle.

25. Install the transaxle mount bracket.

26. Install the starter motor.

27. Connect the backup light switch and the speedometer cable.

28. Install the clutch release cylinder.

29. Connect the select and shift cables and install new cotter pins.

30. Install the air intake hose.

31. Install the auto-cruise actuator and bracket underhood, on the passenger side inner fender wall.

32. Install the battery.

33. Make sure the vehicle is level when refilling the transaxle. Use Hypoid gear oil or equivalent, GL-4 or higher.

34. Connect the negative battery cable and check the transaxle and transfer case for proper operation. Make sure the reverse lights come on when in reverse.

Stealth

1. Remove the battery and battery tray. Raise the vehicle and support safely. Drain the transaxle oil and the oil from the transfer case.

2. If equipped with AWD, disconnect the exhaust pipe. Remove the mounting bolts and lower the transfer case from the vehicle.

3. Remove the left side splash shield and Engine under cover.

4. Remove the air cleaner assembly and all adjoining duct work.

5. Disconnect the shifter control cables and speedometer connector.

6. Remove the clutch release cylinder.

7. Disconnect the reverse light switch.

8. Support the weight of the transaxle and remove the transaxle mount through bolt. Remove the access plug, remove the bolts for the bracket and remove the brackets.

9. Disconnect the transaxle ground cable.

10. Disconnect the tie rod end and ball joint from the steering knuckle.

11. Remove the right frame member.

12. Remove the starter motor.

13. Remove the halfshafts by inserting a prybar between the transaxle case and the driveshaft and prying the shaft from the transaxle. Do not pull on the driveshaft. Doing so damages the inboard joint. Use the prybar. Do not insert the prybar so far the oil seal in the case is damaged. On AWD, remove the right side shaft as just described. The left side shaft can be removed by tapping with a plastic hammer. Remove the shaft with the hub and knuckle as an assembly. Don't tap on the center bearing or it will be damaged. Tie the shafts aside. Note the circle clip on the end of the inboard shafts. These should not be reused.

14. Remove the transaxle brackets.

15. Remove the transaxle assembly. On turbocharged vehicles, take care to prevent damaging the lower radiator hose with the transaxle housing. Wind tape around the lower hose and put tape on the transaxle housing. Support the transaxle assembly using the proper jack, move the transaxle away from the Engine and lower it.

To install:

16. Install the transaxle to the Engine and install the mounting bolts.

17. When installing the halfshafts, use new circlips on the axle ends. Take care to get the inboard joint parts straight, not bent relative to the axle. Care must be taken to ensure that the oil seal lip of the transaxle is not damaged by the serrated part of the driveshaft.

18. Install the starter motor and cover.

19. Install the right side frame member.

20. Install the ball joint and tie rod to the steering knuckle.

21. Connect the transaxle ground cable.

22. Install the side mount brackets and install the access plug.

23. Connect the reverse light switch.

24. Install the clutch release cylinder.

25. Connect the shifter control cables and speedometer connector.

26. Install the transfer case and related items on AWD vehicles.

27. Install the air cleaner assembly and all adjoining duct work.

28. Install the left side splash shield.

29. Install the battery tray and battery.

30. Make sure the vehicle is level when refilling the transaxle. Use Hypoid gear oil or equivalent, GL-4 or higher.

31. Connect the negative battery cable and check the transaxle and transfer case for proper operation. Make sure the reverse lamps come on when in reverse.

LINKAGE ADJUSTMENT

There are 2 cables, the select cable and the shift cable.

1. On the transaxle, put select lever in **N** and move the transaxle shift lever to put it in **4th** gear. Depress the clutch, if necessary, to shift.

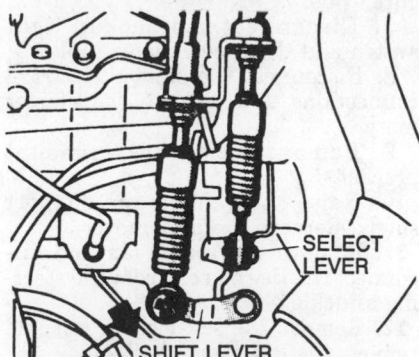

Transaxle shift lever to be moved in the direction shown to set in 4th gear position

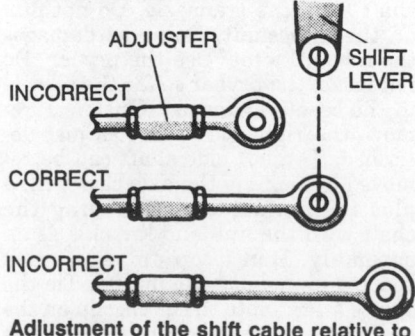

Adjustment of the shift cable relative to the shift lever

2. Move the shift lever in the vehicle to the **4th** gear position until it contacts the stop.

3. Turn the adjuster turn buckle so the shift cable eye aligns with the eye in the gear shift lever. When installing the cable eye, make sure the flange side of the plastic bushing at the shift cable end is on the cotter pin side.

4. The cables should be adjusted so the clearance between the shift lever and the 2 stoppers are equal when the shift lever is moved to 3rd and 4th gear. Move the shift lever to each position and check that the shifting is smooth.

CLUTCH

Clutch Assembly

REMOVAL & INSTALLATION

1. Disconnect the negative battery cable. Raise and safely suport the vehicle.

2. Remove the transaxle assembly from the vehicle.

3. Remove the pressure plate attaching bolts. If the pressure plate is to be reused, loosen the bolts in succession, 1 or 2 turns at a time to prevent warping the the cover flange.

4. Remove the pressure plate release bearing assembly and the clutch disc. Do not use solvent to clean the bearing.

5. Inspect the condition of the clutch components and replace any worn parts.

To install:

6. Inspect the flywheel for heat damage or cracks. Resurface or replace the flywheel as required, using new bolts.

7. Using the proper alignment tool, install the clutch disc to the flywheel. Install the pressure plate assembly and tighten the pressure plate bolts evenly to 14–16 ft. lbs. (19–22 Nm). Remove the alignment tool.

8. Apply a very light coat of high temperature grease to the clutch fork at the ball pivot and where the fork contacts the bearing. Also a little bit of grease can be applied to end of the release cylinder's pushrod and to the pushrod hole on the fork. Apply a light coat of grease on the transaxle input shaft splines.

9. Install a new clutch release bearing. Pack its inner surface with grease.

10. Install the transaxle assembly and check for proper clutch operation.

PEDAL HEIGHT/FREE-PLAY ADJUSTMENT

1. Measure the clutch pedal height from the face of the pedal pad to the firewall. The desired distances are as follows:

    a. Summit—6.61–6.8 in. (168–171mm)

    b. Laser and Talon—6.93–7.17 in. (176–182mm)

    c. Stealth with FWD—6.93–7.17 in. (176–182mm)

    d. Stealth with AWD—7.2–7.4 in. (183–188mm)

    e. Summit Wagon—7.68–7.87 in. (195–200mm)

2. Measure the clutch pedal clevis pin play at the face of the pedal pad. The standard values are as follows:

    a. Summit—0.04–0.12 in. (1–3mm)

    b. Laser and Talon—0.04–0.12 in. (1–3mm)

    c. Stealth with FWD—0.24–0.51 in. (6–13mm)

    d. Stealth with AWD—0.49–0.79 in. (12–20mm)

    e. Summit Wagon—0.04–0.12 in. (1–3mm)

3. If the clutch pedal height or clevis pin play are not within the standard values, adjust as follows:

    a. For vehicles without cruise control, turn and adjust the bolt so the pedal height is the standard value, then tighten the locknut.

    b. Vehicles with auto-cruise control system, disconnect the clutch switch connector and turn the switch to obtain the standard clutch pedal height. Then, lock with the locknut.

    c. Turn the pushrod to adjust the clutch pedal clevis pin play to agree with the standard value and secure the pushrod with the locknut.

NOTE: When adjusting the clutch pedal height or the clutch pedal clevis pin play, be careful not to push the pushrod toward the master cylinder.

    d. Check that when the clutch pedal is depressed all the way, the interlock switch switches over from **ON** to **OFF**.

Clutch Cable

ADJUSTMENT

To adjust the clutch cable, turn the adjusting wheel at the firewall to obtain the proper free-play of about 1 inch.

REMOVAL & INSTALLATION

1. Disconnect the negative battery cable.

2. Remove the cable retaining clamps.

3. Remove the cotter pin from the clutch actuating arm at the transaxle and disconnect the cable.

4. Rotate the adjusting wheel counterclockwise to loosen the cable. Disconnect the cable at the pedal and remove the cable from the vehicle.

5. The installation is the reverse of the removal procedure.

6. Lubricate all pivot points. Adjust the cable to achieve proper freeplay.

Clutch Master Cylinder

REMOVAL & INSTALLATION

1. Disconnect the negative battery cable.

2. Remove necessary underhood components in order to gain access to the clutch master cylinder.

2. Loosen the line at the cylinder and allow the fluid to drain. Use care; brake fluid damages paint.

3. On Summit, Summit Wagon, Laser, Talon and FWD Stealth, remove the clevis pin retainer at the clutch pedal and remove the washer and clevis pin. AWD Stealth has a clutch pedal booster which directly activates the master cylinder.

4. Remove the 2 nuts and pull the cylinder from the firewall. A seal should be between the mounting flange and firewall. This seal should be replaced.

5. The installation is the reverse of the removal procedure.

6. Lubricate all pivot points with grease.

7. Bleed the system at the slave cylinder using DOT 3 brake fluid and check the adjustment of the clutch pedal.

Clutch Release Cylinder

REMOVAL & INSTALLATION

1. Disconnect the negative battery cable. Remove necessary underhood components in order to gain access to the clutch release cylinder.

2. Remove the hydraulic line and allow the system to drain.

3. Remove the bolts and pull the cylinder from the transaxle housing. On some 1.5L Engines, instead of a pushrod bearing against the clutch arm, a clevis pin and yoke is used. Simply remove the circlip, pull out the clevis pin and remove the cylinder.

4. The installation is the reverse of the removal procedure.

5. Lubricate all pivot points with grease.

6. Bleed the system using DOT 3 brake fluid.

Hydraulic Clutch System Bleeding

1. Fill the reservoir with brake fluid.

2. Loosen the bleed screw, have the clutch pedal pressed to the floor.

3. Tighten the bleed screw and release the clutch pedal.

4. Repeat the procedure until the fluid is free of air bubbles.

NOTE: It is suggested to attach a hose to the bleeder and place the other end into a container at least ½ full of brake fluid during the bleeding operation. Do not allow the reservoir to run out of fluid during bleeding.

AUTOMATIC TRANSAXLE

For further information on transmissions/transaxles, please refer to "Chilton's Guide to Transmission Repair".

Transaxle Assembly

NOTE: If the vehicle is going to be rolled while the halfshafts are out of the vehicle, obtain 2 outer CV-joints or proper equivalent tools and install to the hubs. If the vehicle is rolled without the proper torque applied to the front wheel bearings, the bearings will no longer be usable.

REMOVAL & INSTALLATION

Summit

1. Disconnect the negative battery cable.

2. Remove the battery and battery tray.

3. Remove the air pipe and air hose.

4. Raise the vehicle and support safely.

5. Drain the transaxle oil.

6. If equipped with 1.6L Engine, remove the tension rod.

7. Disconnect the control cable and cooler lines.

8. Disconnect the throttle control cable on 3 speed transaxle.

9. Disconnect the shift control solenoid valve connector on 4 speed transaxle.

10. Disconnect the inhibitor switch

and kickdown servo switch on 4 speed transaxle.

11. Disconnect the pulse generator and oil temperature sensor on 4 speed transaxle.

12. Disconnect the speedometer cable and remove the starter.

13. Remove the transaxle mounting bolts and bracket.

14. Remove the under guard pan.

15. Disconnect the steering tie rod end and the ball joint from the steering arm.

16. Remove the halfshafts at the inboard side from the transaxle. Tie the joint assembly aside.

17. Remove the bellhousing cover and remove the driveplate bolts.

18. Remove the transaxle assembly lower connecting bolt, located just over the halfshaft opening.

19. Properly support the transaxle assembly and lower it moving it to the right for clearance.

To install:

20. After the torque converter has been mounted on the transaxle, install the transaxle assembly on the Engine. Tighten the driveplate bolts to 34–38 ft. lbs. (46–53 Nm). Install the bell housing cover.

21. Replace the circlips and install the halfshafts to the transaxle.

22. Install the tie rods and ball joint to the steering arm.

23. Install the underguard and the mounting brackets.

24. Install the starter.

25. Connect the speedometer cable.

26. Connect the control cables, oil cooler lines and electrical connections.

27. Install the tension rod.

28. Install the air pipe and hose, battery tray and battery.

29. Refill with Dexron II, Mopar ATF Plus type 7176 or equivalent, automatic transaxle fluid.

30. Start the Engine and allow to idle for 2 minutes. Apply parking brake and move selector through each gear position, ending in **N**. Recheck fluid level and add if necessary. Fluid level should be between the marks in the **HOT** range.

Summit Wagon

1. Disconnect negative battery cable.

2. Remove the air cleaner assembly.

3. Disconnect the transaxle control lever. Disconnect and plug the oil cooler lines.

4. Disconnect the pulse generator connector, oil temperature connector, kickdown servo switch connector, inhibitor switch connector and solenoid valve connection.

5. Disconnect the speedometer cable connection. Remove the oil level dipstick and tube.

6. Install holding fixture to the top of the Engine to support Engine weight.

7. Remove the top transaxle upper coupling bolts. Raise and safely support the vehicle.

8. Remove the starter motor leaving wire harness attached.

9. Remove the right side under cover. Drain the transaxle fluid.

10. Disconnect the tie rod ends, stabilizer bar and lower ball joints.

11. If equipped with AWD, it will be necessary to remove the right driveshaft from the vehicle.

12. Except AWD vehicles, remove the driveshafts from the transfer case, insert a prybar between the driveshaft and the transaxle case and pry the shaft from the transaxle housing. Swing the shafts out of the way keeping the joints straight and suspend using wire. Turn the right shaft 90 degrees toward the front of the vehicle so that it will not be a hindrance.

NOTE: Do not pull on the shaft during removal from the transaxle; doing so will damage the inboard joint. Do not insert the prybar so deep as to damage the oil seal.

13. Remove the lower bellhousing cover. Scribe a mark on the drive plate and transaxle converter face using chaulk. Remove the drive plate connecting bolts while turning the crankshaft.

14. Support the transaxle using a transmission jack. Remove the center support.

15. Remove the transaxle mount bolt and bracket.

16. If equipped with AWD, disconnect the front exhaust pipe and remove the transfer assembly.

17. Remove the lower transaxle case coupling bolts, press the torque converter towards the transfer case to prevent separation during removal and lower the transfer case from the vehicle.

To install:

18. Install the transaxle into the vehicle and secure using the lower case coupling bolts.

19. Install the transaxle mount bolt and bracket, torque through bolt nut to 51 ft. lbs. (70 Nm).

20. Align the scribe marks on the converter and the driveplate. Install the driveplate connecting bolts torquing to 33–38 ft. lbs. (46–53 Nm).

21. Install the transfer assembly and the center crossmember. Remove the transmission jack.

22. Install the center exhaust pipe.

23. Install the drive axles into the transfer case taking care not to damage the oil seal lip part of the transaxle with the serrated part of the driveshaft.

24. Connect the tie rod ends, stabilizer bar and lower ball joints.

25. Install the right side under cover.

26. Lower the vehicle. Install the upper transaxle coupling bolts.

27. Connect the speedometer cable and the electrical harness connectors disconnected during the removal procedure.

28. Install the starter motor torqueing the retainer bolts to 35 ft. lbs. (49 Nm).

29. Connect the transaxle cooler hoses and the connections for the manual controls.

30. Install the air cleaner assembly and the oil level dipstick and tube.

31. Refill with Dexron II, Mopar ATF Plus type 7176 or equivalent, automatic transaxle fluid.

32. Start the Engine and allow to idle for 2 minutes. Apply parking brake and move selector through each gear position, ending in **N**. Recheck fluid level and add if necessary. Fluid level should be between the marks in the **HOT** range. Check operation of all gauges and meters.

Laser and Talon

1. Remove the battery and battery tray.

2. On 1990–91 equipped with autocruise, remove the control actuator and bracket.

3. Drain the transaxle fluid.

4. Remove the air cleaner assembly, intercooler and air hose.

5. Remove the adjusting nut and disconnect the shift cable.

6. Disconnect and tag the electrical connectors for the solenoid, neutral safety switch (inhibitor switch), the pulse generator kickdown servo switch and oil temperature sensor.

7. Disconnect the speedometer cable and oil cooler lines.

8. Disconnect the wires to the starter motor and remove the starter.

9. Remove the upper transaxle to Engine bolts.

10. Support the transaxle and remove the transaxle mounting bracket.

11. Raise the vehicle and support safely. Remove the sheet metal under guard.

12. Remove the tie rod ends and the ball joints from the steering knuckle.

13. Remove the halfshafts by inserting a prybar between the transaxle case and the driveshaft and prying the shaft from the transaxle. Do not pull on the driveshaft. Doing so damages the inboard joint. Use the prybar. Do not insert the prybar so far the oil seal in the case is damaged. Tie the halfshafts aside.

14. On AWD, disconnect the exhaust pipe, remove the frame pieces, and remove the transfer case.

15. Remove the lower bellhousing cover and remove the special bolts holding the flexplate to the torque converter. To remove, turn the Engine crankshaft with a box wrench and bring the bolts into position appropriate for removal, 1 at a time. After removing the bolts, push the torque converter toward the transaxle so it doesn't stay on the Engine allowing oil to pour out the converter hub or cause damage to the converter.

16. Remove the lower transaxle to Engine bolts and remove the transaxle assembly.

To install:

17. After the torque converter has been mounted on the transaxle, install the transaxle assembly on the Engine. Tighten the driveplate bolts to 34–38 ft. lbs. (46–53 Nm). Install the bellhousing cover.

18. On AWD, install the transfer case and frame pieces. Connect the exhaust pipe using a new gasket.

19. Replace the circlips and install the halfshafts to the transaxle.

20. Install the tie rods and ball joint to the steering arm.

21. Install the transaxle mounting bracket.

22. Install the under guard.

23. Install the starter.

24. Connect the speedometer cable and oil cooler lines.

25. Connect the solenoid, neutral safety switch (inhibitor switch), the pulse generator kickdown servo switch and oil temperature sensor.

26. Install the shift control cable.

27. Install the air hose, intercooler and air cleaner assembly.

28. If equipped with auto-cruise, install the control actuator and bracket.

29. Refill with Dexron II, Mopar ATF Plus type 7176 or equivalent, automatic transaxle fluid.

30. Start the Engine and allow to idle for 2 minutes. Apply parking brake and move selector through each gear position, ending in **N**. Recheck fluid level and add if necessary. Fluid level should be between the marks in the **HOT** range.

Stealth

1. Disarm the air bag, if equipped. Remove the battery, battery tray and washer tank.

2. Remove the air cleaner assembly and adjoining duct work.

3. Disconnect the shifter control cable.

4. Disconnect and plug the oil cooler hoses.

5. Disconnect the inhibitor switch, kickdown servo switch, pulse generator, oil temperature sensor, shift control solenoid valve, and ground cable.

6. Disconnect the speedometer cable.

7. Raise the vehicle and support safely. Remove the undercovers.

8. Support the weight of the transaxle and remove the mount bracket. Remove the upper bellhousing bolts.

9. Disconnect the tie rod end and ball joint from the steering knuckle.

10. Remove the right frame member.

11. Remove the starter.

12. Remove the halfshafts by inserting a prybar between the transaxle case and the driveshaft and prying the shaft from the transaxle. Do not pull on the driveshaft. Doing so damages the inboard joint. Use the prybar. Do not insert the prybar so far the oil seal in the case is damaged. Tie the halfshafts aside.

13. Remove the remaining mounting brackets.

14. Remove the bellhousing cover plate.

15. Remove the special bolts holding the flexplate to the torque converter.

16. After removing the bolts, push the torque converter toward the transaxle so it doesn't stay on the Engine side and allow oil to pour out the converter hub.

17. Remove the lower transaxle to Engine bolts and remove the transaxle assembly.

To install:

18. After the torque converter has been mounted on the transaxle, install the transaxle assembly on the Engine. Tighten the driveplate bolts to 34–38 ft. lbs. (46–53 Nm). Install the bellhousing cover.

19. Install the mounting brackets.

20. Replace the circlips and install the halfshafts to the transaxle.

21. Install the starter and frame member.

22. Install the tie rods and ball joint to the steering arm.

23. Install the upper bellhousing bolts.

24. Install the transaxle mounting bracket.

25. Install the undercovers.

26. Connect the speedometer cable.

27. Connect the inhibitor switch, kickdown servo switch, pulse generator, oil temperature sensor, shift control solenoid valve, and ground cable.

28. Connect the oil cooler hoses.

29. Connect the shifter control cable.

30. Install the air cleaner assembly and adjoining duct work.

31. Install the washer tank, battery tray and battery.

32. Refill with Dexron II, Mopar ATF Plus type 7176 or equivalent, automatic transaxle fluid.

33. Start the Engine and allow to idle for 2 minutes. Apply parking brake and move selector through each gear position, ending in **N**. Recheck fluid level and add if necessary. Fluid level should be between the marks in the **HOT** range.

SHIFTER CONTROL CABLE ADJUSTMENT

1. The shifter cable adjustment is done at the neutral safety switch (inhibitor switch). Locate the switch on the transaxle and note the alignment holes in the arm and the body of the switch. Place the selector lever in **N**. Place the manual lever of the transaxle in the neutral position.

2. Check alignment of the hole in the manual control lever to the hole in the inhibitor switch body. If the holes do not align, adjustment is required.

3. To adjust, loosen the nut on the cable end and pull the cable end by hand until the alignment holes match. Tighten the nut. Check that the transaxle shifts and conforms to the positions of the selector lever.

THROTTLE CONTROL CABLE ADJUSTMENT

Some vehicles do not use a throttle linkage. Instead, the throttle position sensor provides an electric signal to the transaxle, so no linkage adjustment is required.

1. Check that the throttle lever is in the curb idle position, with the Engine **OFF** but at normal operating temperature.

2. At the lower cable bracket, raise the cone shaped cover to uncover a small fitting on the cable. By loosening the locknut and adjuster nut, make the distance between the fitting on the cable and the lower collar is 0.020–0.060 in.

3. With the throttle in the wide open position, check that the cable does not bind.

TRANSFER CASE

Transfer Case Assembly

REMOVAL & INSTALLATION

Laser, Talon and Stealth

1. Disconnect the battery negative cable.

2. Raise the vehicle and support safely. Drain the transfer oil.

3. On Stealth, remove necessary front bumper components.

4. Disconnect the front exhaust pipe.

5. Unbolt the transfer case assembly and remove by sliding it off the rear driveshaft. Be careful not to damage the oil seal in the transfer case output housing. Do not let the rear driveshaft hang; suspend it from a frame piece. Cover the opening in the transaxle and transfer case to keep oil from dripping and to keep dirt out.

To install:

6. Lubricate the driveshaft sleeve yoke and oil seal lip on the transfer extension housing. Install the transfer case assembly to the transaxle. Use care when installing the rear driveshaft to the transfer case output shaft.

7. Tighten the transfer case to transaxle bolts to 40–43 ft. lbs. (55–60 Nm) on Laser and Talon with manual transaxle; 43–58 ft. lbs. (60–80 Nm) on Laser and Talon with automatic transaxle or 64 ft. lbs. (88 Nm) on Stealth.

8. Install the exhaust pipe using a new gasket. Install removed bumper components.

9. Refill the transfer case and check oil levels in transaxle and transfer case.

Summit Wagon

1. Disconnect the battery negative cable.

2. Raise the vehicle and support safely. Drain the oil from the transfer assembly.

3. Disconnect the front exhaust pipe.

4. Make mating marks on the differential companion flange and the flange yoke. Remove the propeller shaft.

NOTE: Remove the propeller shaft in a straight and level manner so as to ensure that the boot is not damaged through pinching. Damage can be avoided if a piece of cloth or similar material is inserted into the boot. Cover the opening of the transfer assembly to prevent dirt from entering the transfer assembly.

5. Remove the transfer assembly mounting bolts and the transfer assembly from the vehicle.

To install:

6. Position the transfer assembly into the vehicle and secure using the mounting bolts, tightened to 51 ft. lbs. (70 Nm).

7. Align the mating marks and install propeller shaft.

8. Attach the front exhaust pipe using new gasket.

9. Reconnect the negative battery and lower the vehicle. Refill the transfer case and check oil levels in transaxle and transfer case.

FRONT SUSPENSION

MacPherson Strut

REMOVAL & INSTALLATION

1. Disconnect the negative battery cable.

2. On Summit Wagon, if removing the right front strut, remove the auto-cuise control actuator.

3. On Summit Wagon, disconnect and remove the daytime running lamp delay and control unit from the mounting bracket located on top of the left strut tower.

4. Raise and safely support vehicle.

5. Remove the brake hose and tube bracket. Do not pry the brake hose and tube clamp away when removing it.

6. If equipped with ABS, disconnect the front speed sensor mounting clamp from the strut.

7. Support the lower arm and remove the strut to knuckle bolts. Use a piece of wire to suspend the knuckle to keep the weight off the brake hose.

8. Before removing the top bolts, make matchmarks on the body and the strut insulator for proper reassembly. If this plate is installed improperly, the wheel alignment will be wrong. Remove the strut upper bolts and remove the strut assembly from the vehicle.

To install:

9. Install the strut to the vehicle and install the top bolts.

10. Connect the ECS connector.

11. Install to the knuckle and install the bolts.

12. Install the brake hose bracket and the ABS clamp.

13. Install the daytime running lamp delay and control unit to the mounting bracket located on top of the left strut tower.

14. Install the auto-cuise control actuator.

15. Install the wheel and tire assembly. Perform a front end alignment.

Lower Ball Joints

INSPECTION

The lower ball joints on these vehicles are not serviceable. If defective, the entire lower arm must be replaced. The ball joints can be checked using the following procedure:

1. Wiggle the ball joint a few times to make sure it is free.

2. Double-nut the stud and use a torque wrench to measure how much torque is required to turn it. Starting torque should be:

a. Summit: 48 inch lbs. (5.5 Nm) or less.

b. Laser and Talon: 26–87 inch lbs. (3–10 Nm).

c. Stealth: 86–191 inch lbs. (10–22 Nm).

d. Summit Wagon: 17–78 inch lbs. (2–9 Nm).

3. If the stud has more resistance than specified, replace the lower arm assembly. If the resistance is less, it may still be reused unless it has excessive play.

4. A new grease boot can be installed using a large socket for a driver.

Lower Control Arm
REMOVAL & INSTALLATION

1. Disconnect the negative battery cable.

2. Raise the vehicle and support safely.

3. Remove sway bar links from lower control arm.

4. Disconnect the ball joint stud from the steering knuckle.

5. Remove the inner mounting frame-through bolt and nut.

6. Remove the rear mount bolts. Remove the clamp if equipped.

7. Remove the rear rod bushing if servicing.

To install:

8. Assemble the control arm and bushing.

9. Install the control arm to the vehicle and install the through bolt. Replace the nut and snug temporarily.

10. Install the rear mount clamp, bolts and replacement nuts. Torque the bolts to 43–58 ft. lbs. (60–80 Nm) on Summit, 51 ft. lbs. on Summit Wagon or 70 ft. lbs. (95 Nm) on Laser, Talon and Stealth. Torque the nuts, if equipped, to 30 ft. lbs. (41 Nm).

11. Connect the ball joint stud to the knuckle. Install a new nut and torque to 43–52 ft. lbs. (60–72 Nm).

12. Install the sway bar and links.

13. Lower the vehicle to the floor for the final torquing of the frame mount through bolt.

14. Once the full weight of the vehicle is on the floor, torque the frame mount through bolt nuts to 78 ft. lbs. (108 Nm) on Summit Wagon or 75–90 ft. lbs. (102–122 Nm) on remaining models.

15. Connect the negative battery cable.

Sway Bar

REMOVAL & INSTALLATION
Summit, Laser and Talon

1. Disconnect the negative battery cable.

2. Raise and safely support vehicle. Remove the front exhaust pipe if necessary.

3. On Summit, remove the tie rod end from the steering knuckle.

4. Remove the center crossmember rear installation bolts.

5. Remove the stabilizer link bolts. On the ball stud type, hold ball stud with a hex wrench and remove the self-locking nut with a box wrench.

6. Remove the stabilizer bar mounts and remove the bar from the vehicle.

7. The installation is the reverse of the removal procedure. Lubricate all rubber parts when installing. Note that the bar brackets are marked left and right.

8. Tighten link bolts with rubber bushings just until the bushings are squashed to the width of the washer.

Summit Wagon

1. Disconnect the negative battery cable.

2. Raise and safely support vehicle. Remove the front exhaust pipe.

3. Remove the stabilizer bar mounting nuts.

4. Remove the bolts from the stabilizer bar mounting fixtures and remove the bar, bushings and fixtures from the vehicle.

5. Installaton is the reverse of the removal procedure. Torque the stabilizer fixture mounting fixtures to 16 ft. lbs. (22 Nm), the stabilizer bar link nuts to 29 ft. lbs. (40 Nm) and the exhaust flange nuts to 33 ft. lbs. (45 Nm).

Stealth

1. Disconnect the negative battery cable.

2. Raise the vehicle and support safely.

3. Remove the front exhaust pipe and Engine undercover.

4. Remove the left and right frame members.

5. On AWD vehicles with automatic transaxle, remove the transfer case bracket and transfer case.

6. Remove the sway bar link.

7. Remove the sway bar brackets and remove the sway bar from the vehicle.

To install:

8. Note that the bar brackets are marked left and right. Lubricate all rubber parts and install the bushings, the sway bar and brackets.

9. Install the sway bar link.

10. Install the transfer case and bracket.

11. Install the frame members.

12. Install the Engine undercover and exhaust pipe.

13. Connect the negative battery cable.

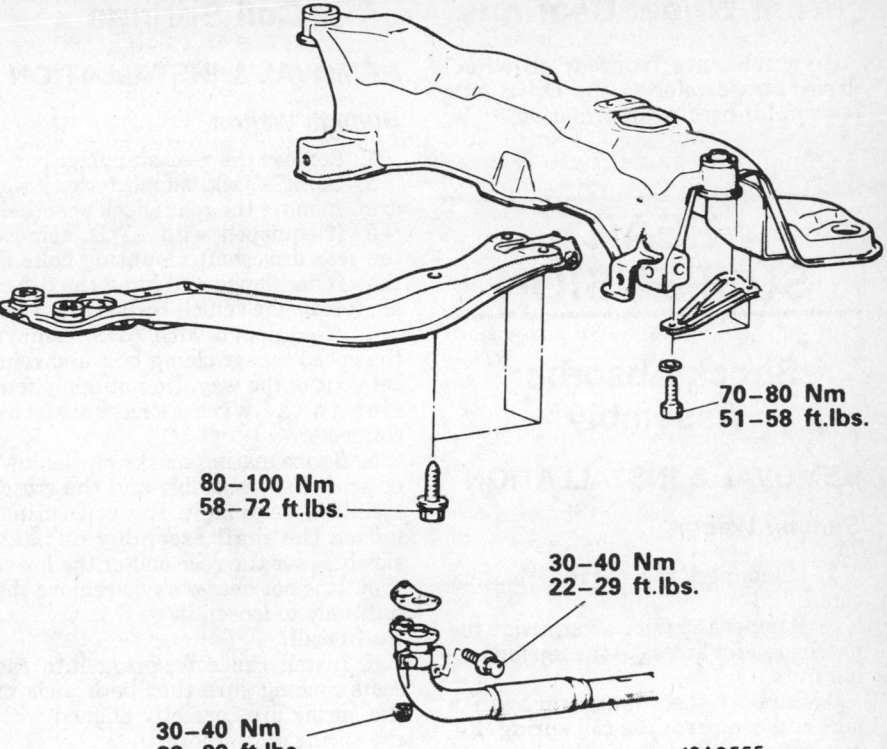

70–80 Nm
51–58 ft.lbs.

80–100 Nm
58–72 ft.lbs.

30–40 Nm
22–29 ft.lbs.

30–40 Nm
22–29 ft.lbs.

12A0555

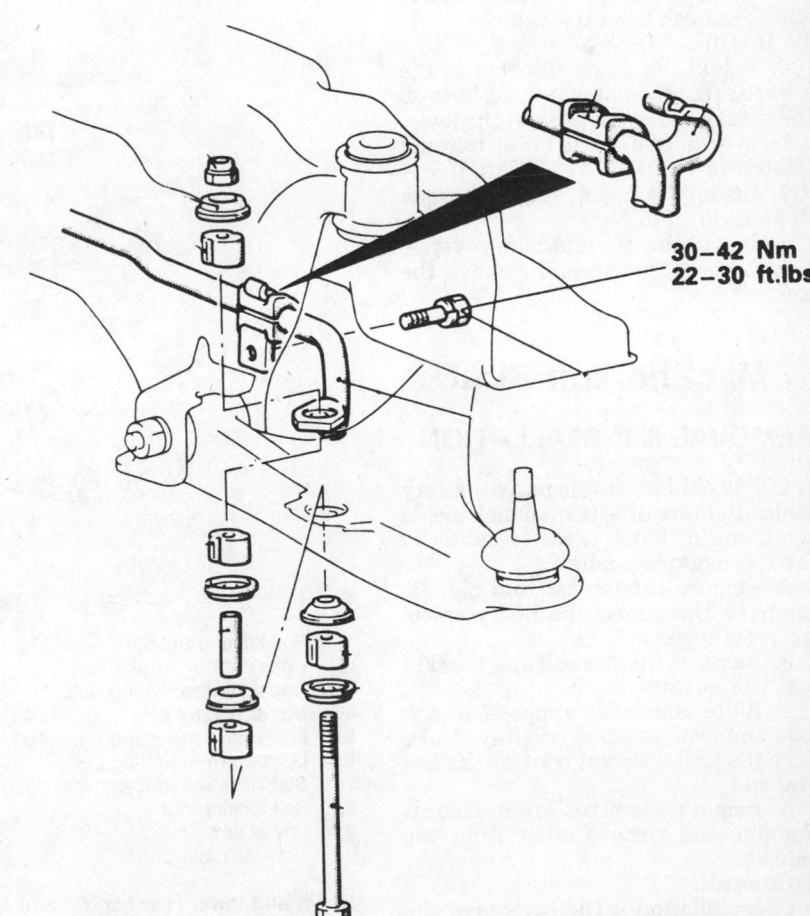

30–42 Nm
22–30 ft.lbs.

Stabilizer bar (rubber bushing type)—1992 FWD Laser and Talon

Front Wheel Bearings

All vehicles are front or all-wheel drive. Please refer to the Drive Axle section for bearing information.

REAR SUSPENSION

Shock Absorber Assembly

REMOVAL & INSTALLATION

Summit Wagon

1. Disconnect the negative battery cable.
2. Remove the trim cover inside the hatch area for access to the top mounting nuts.
3. Support the lower arm with a jack and compress the coil spring. Remove the lower mounting nut.
4. Remove the cap from the upper end of the shock.
5. Remove the upper mounting nut and the shock from the vehicle.

To install:

6. Install the shock absorber to the lower arm so the flat mounting boss on the shock absorber is against the lower control arm. Install the lower nut and tighten to 72 ft. lbs. (100 Nm).
7. Install the upper nut and torque to 33 ft. lbs. (45 Nm).
8. Install the cap and trim cover.
9. Lower the arm and remove the jack.

MacPherson Strut

REMOVAL & INSTALLATION

1. Disconnect the negative battery cable. Remove the trim panel inside the trunk or hatch area for access to the top mounting nuts.
2. Remove the top cap and mounting nuts. Disconnect the ECS connector if equipped.
3. Remove the brake tube bracket bolt if necessary.
4. Raise and safely support torsion axle and arm assembly slightly. Make sure the jack does not contact the lateral rod.
5. Remove the strut lower mounting nut and remove strut from the vehicle.

To install:

6. Installation is the reverse of the removal procedure.

Coil Springs

REMOVAL & INSTALLATION

Summit Wagon

1. Remove the rear stabilizer bar.
2. Using a jack, support the lower arm. Remove the rear shock absorber.
3. If equipped with AWD, remove the rear driveshaft mounting bolts at the carrier flange and hang the driveshaft from the vehicle body using wire.
4. If equipped with ABS, remove the speed sensor clamp bolt and relocate out of the way. Do not apply tension to the wire harness of the connector.
5. Scribe mating marks on the lower arm shaft assembly and the crossmember. To remove the coil spring, loosen the shaft assembly nut and slowly lower the rear end of the lower arm. It is not necessary to remove the nut, only to loosen it.

To install:

6. Install the coil spring into the seats making sure that both ends of the spring are correctly aligned with the spring seat groove.
7. Slowly raise the rear the rear end of the lower arm and align the scribe marks made during disassembly.

Tighten shaft assembly nut to 69 ft. lbs. (95 Nm).

8. Install the speed sensor clamp to its' original location and secure the wire harness making.
9. Install the rear drive shaft to the flange and secure tightening mounting bolts to 40–47 ft. lbs. (55–65 Nm).
10. Reconnect the lower portion of the shock and tighten the retaining bolt to 72 ft. lbs. (100 Nm).
11. Lower the arm and remove the jack.

Rear Control Arms

REMOVAL & INSTALLATION

Laser and Talon with AWD and Stealth

1. Disconnect the negative battery cable. On FWD Stealth, remove the rear strut assembly. Raise and safely support vehicle. Remove the brake line clamp bolt.
2. Remove the ball joint(s) from the rear trailing arm/steering knuckle.
3. If removing the lower arm, disconnect the sway bar link from the arm.
4. Matchmark and remove the inboard lower arm pivot bolt, if neces-

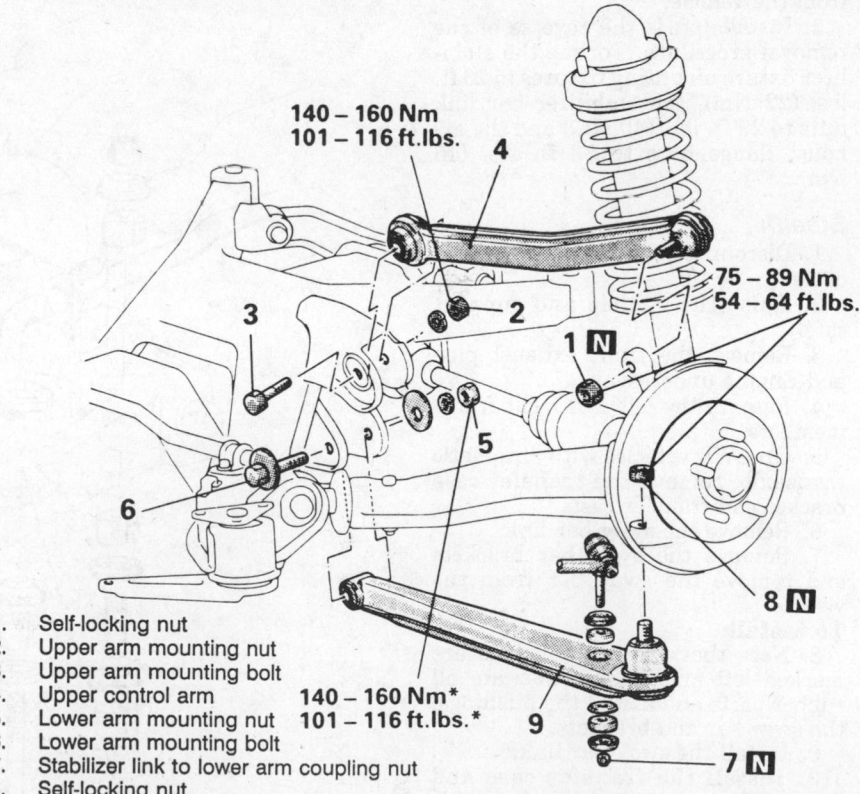

1. Self-locking nut
2. Upper arm mounting nut
3. Upper arm mounting bolt
4. Upper control arm
5. Lower arm mounting nut
6. Lower arm mounting bolt
7. Stabilizer link to lower arm coupling nut
8. Self-locking nut
9. Lower arm
N: Non-reusable parts

140 – 160 Nm
101 – 116 ft.lbs.

75 – 89 Nm
54 – 64 ft.lbs.

140 – 160 Nm*
101 – 116 ft.lbs.*

Upper and lower rear control arm and related components – 1992 Stealth with AWD. Laser and Talon equipped with AWD similar.

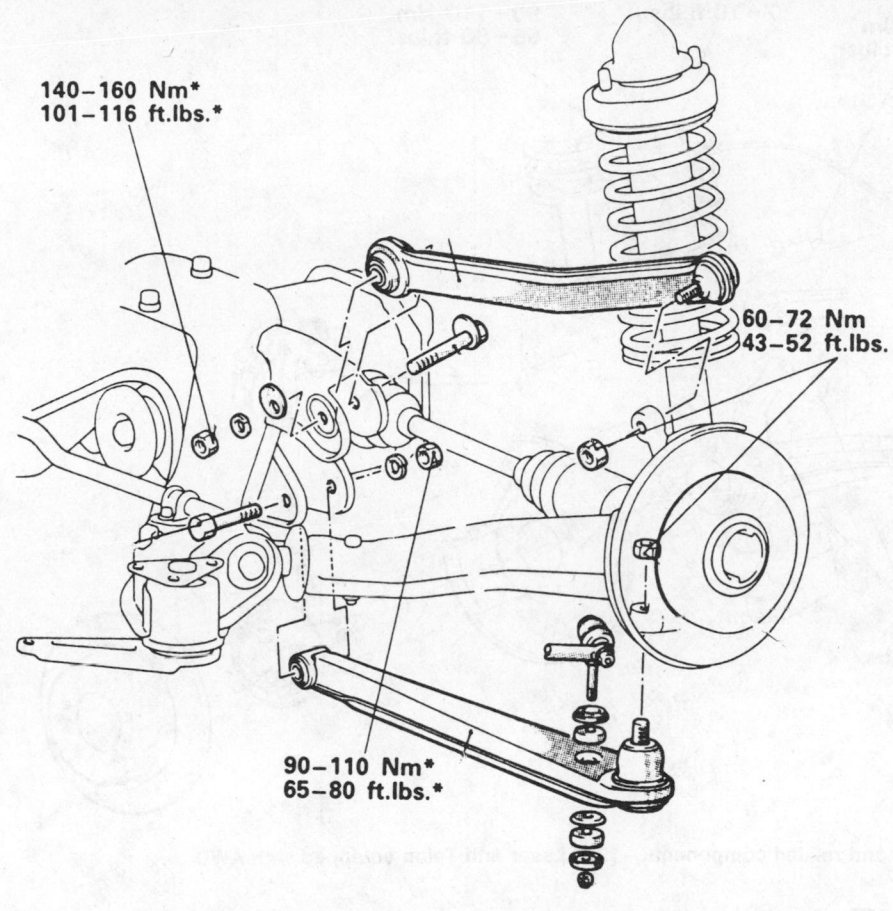

140–160 Nm*
101–116 ft.lbs.*

60–72 Nm
43–52 ft.lbs.

90–110 Nm*
65–80 ft.lbs.*

Rear suspension—upper and lower arm and related components—1992 Laser and Talon equipped with AWD

sary, and remove the arm from the vehicle.

5. Installation is the reverse of the removal procedure. Replace all self-locking nuts. Do not torque the inboard pivot nuts until the full weight of the vehicle is on the ground.

6. On Laser and Talon, torque the lower arm installation nut to 65–80 ft. lbs. (90–110 Nm) and the upper arm installation nut to 101–116 ft. lbs. (140–160 Nm). On Stealth, torque the lower and the upper arm installation nuts to 101–116 ft. lbs. (140–160 Nm).

7. Perform a rear wheel alignment.

Summit Wagon

1. Disconnect negative battery cable.

2. Remove the rear stabilizer bar.

3. If equipped with AWD, remove the rear axle shaft.

3. Remove the rear brake drum.

4. If equipped with ABS, remove the rear caliper assembly and brake disc.

5. Remove the rear hub assembly. If equipped with ABS, take care not to

damage the rotor teeth during hub removal.

6. Disconnect the parking brake cable from the rear brake shoe.

7. If equipped with ABS, disconnect and remove the rear wheel sensor.

NOTE: The speed sensor has a pole piece projecting from it. This exposed tip must be protected from impact or scratches. Do not allow the pole piece to contact the toothed wheel during removal or installation.

8. Remove the rear shock and coil spring.

9. Remove the brake line and parking brake mounting bolts from the lower control arm.

10. Matchmark and remove the inboard lower arm pivot bolt. Remove the flange bolt and the arm from the vehicle.

To install:

11. Install the arm on the vehicle and secure with the flange bolt, temporarily tighten the nut. Install the arm piv-

ot bolt and temporarily tighten the nut.

12. Install the rear shock and coil spring.

13. Install the brake line and parking brake mounting bolts to the lower control arm.

14. Connect the parking brake cable to the rear brake shoe.

15. Install the rear hub assembly.

16. Install the rear brake drum or, if equipped with ABS, install the rear caliper assembly and brake disc.

17. Install the rear axle shaft.

18. Install and connect the rear wheel speed sensor. Use a brass or other non-magnetic feeler gauge to check the air gap between the tip of the pole piece and the toothed wheel. Correct gap is 0.012–0.035 in. (0.3–0.9mm). Tighten the 2 sensor bracket bolts to 10 ft. lbs. (14 Nm) with the sensor located so the gap is the same at several points on the toothed wheel. If the gap is incorrect, it is likely that the toothed wheel is worn or improperly installed.

19. Lower the vehicle and tighten the lower arm flange bolt nut and the arm pivot bolt to 69 ft. lbs. (95 Nm).

20. Install the rear stabilizer bar and reconnect the negative battery cable.

21. Bleed the brake system if any lines where opened. Adjust the parking brake and perform a rear wheel alignment.

Rear Trailing Arm

REMOVAL & INSTALLATION

Laser and Talon with AWD and Stealth

1. Disconnect the negative battery cable. Raise and safely support vehicle.

2. Remove the rear caliper from the brake disc and suspend with a wire. Remove the brake disc. Disconnect the parking brake cable and remove the mounting bolts along the trailing arm.

3. Remove the bolt(s) holding the speed sensor bracket to the knuckle and remove the assembly from the vehicle.

NOTE: The speed sensor has a pole piece projecting from it. This exposed tip must be protected from impact or scratches. Do not allow the pole piece to contact the toothed wheel during removal or installation.

4. On AWD, remove the rear axle to companion flange bolts and nuts and separate the axle from the companion flange. Remove the self-locking nut and remove the axle hub and companion flange. Remove the dust shield.

5. On FWD Stealth, remove the axle hub unit, parking brake shoes and

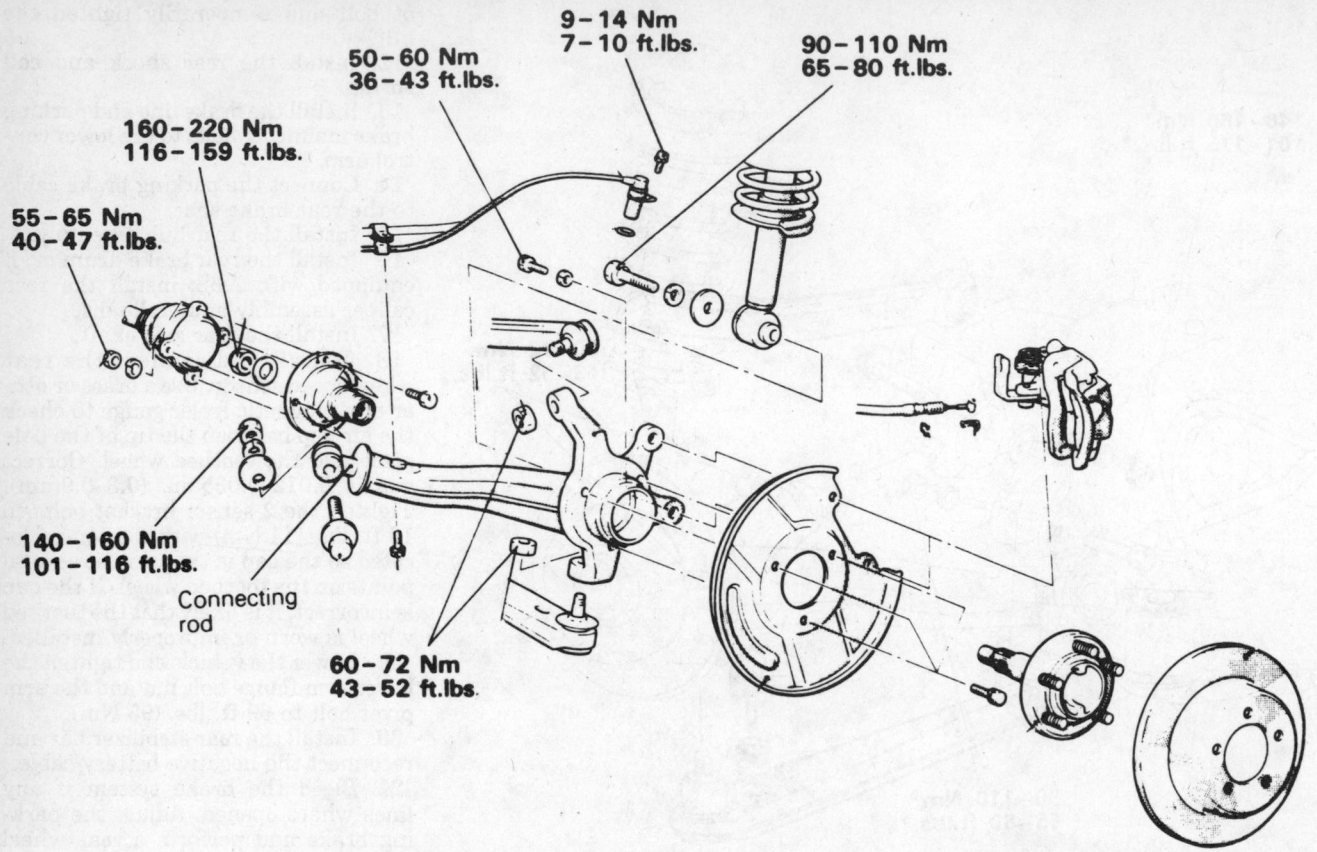

9–14 Nm
7–10 ft.lbs.

90–110 Nm
65–80 ft.lbs.

50–60 Nm
36–43 ft.lbs.

160–220 Nm
116–159 ft.lbs.

55–65 Nm
40–47 ft.lbs.

140–160 Nm
101–116 ft.lbs.

Connecting rod

60–72 Nm
43–52 ft.lbs.

Rear trailing arm assembly and related components—1992 Laser and Talon equipped with AWD

backing plate. Remove the sway bar link bolt.

6. Remove the lower strut mounting bolt.

7. Remove the control arms from the trailing arm.

8. Remove the trailing arm front mounting nuts and bolts and remove the trailing arm from the vehicle. On AWD, remove the connecting rod at the front of the arm using tool MB991254 or equivalent.

To install:

9. Assemble the trailing arm and connecting rod. Install the trailing arm to the vehicle and install the front mounting nuts and bolts. Complete the final tightening of these when the full weight of the vehicle is on the ground.

10. Install the control arms to the trailing arm, using new self-locking nuts.

11. Install the lower strut bolt.

12. On FWD Stealth, install the sway bar link. Install the parking brake parts and axle hub unit.

13. On AWD, install the dust shield, axle hub and companion flange with a new self-locking nut. Connect the rear axle to the companion flange.

14. Temporarily install the speed sensor to the knuckle; tighten the bolts only finger-tight.

15. Route the cable correctly and loosely install the clips and retainers. All clips must be in their original position and the sensor cable must not be twisted. Improper installation may cause cable damage and system failure.

NOTE: The wiring in the harness is easily damaged by twisting and flexing. Use the white stripe on the outer insulation to keep the sensor harness properly placed.

16. Use a brass or other non-magnetic feeler gauge to check the air gap between the tip of the pole piece and the toothed wheel. Correct gap is 0.012–0.035 inch (0.3–0.9mm). Tighten the 2 sensor bracket bolts to 10 ft. lbs. (14 Nm) with the sensor located so the gap is the same at several points on the toothed wheel. If the gap is incorrect, it is likely that the toothed wheel is worn or improperly installed.

17. Install the brake disc, caliper and connect the parking brake cable, if not already done. Install the mounting clamps bolts.

18. Double check everything for correct routing and installation. Lower the vehicle so its full weight is on the floor.

19. On Laser, Talon and FWD Stealth, torque the front trailing arm/spindle assembly mount nuts to 101–116 ft. lbs. (140–160 Nm). On AWD Stealth, tighten front trailing arm/spindle assembly mount nuts to 145–174 ft. lbs. (200–240 Nm).

20. Perform a rear wheel alignment.

Rear Wheel Bearings

REMOVAL & INSTALLATION

Summit

1. Raise the vehicle and support safely.

2. Remove the tire and wheel assembly.

3. If equipped with rear disc brakes, remove the caliper from the disc and remove the brake disc.

4. Remove the dust cap and bearing nut. Do not use an air gun to remove the nut.

5. Remove the outer wheel bearing.

6. Remove the drum and/or axle hub with the inner wheel bearing and the grease seal.

7. Remove the grease seal and remove the inner bearing.

To install:

8. Lubricate the inner bearing and install to the drum or hub.

9. Install a new grease seal.

10. To determine if the self-locking nut is reusable:

a. Screw in the self-locking nut until about $\frac{1}{10}$ in. of the spindle is showing.

b. Measure the torque required to turn the self-locking nut counterclockwise.

c. The lowest allowable torque is 48 inch lbs. (5.5 Nm). If the measured torque is less than the specification, replace the nut.

11. Install the drum and/or hub to the vehicle.

12. Lubricate and install the outer wheel bearing to the spindle.

13. Torque the self-locking nut to 108–145 ft. lbs. (150–200 Nm).

14. Set up a dial indicator and measure the endplay while moving the hub or drum in and out. If the endplay exceeds 0.008 in. (0.002mm), retorque the nut. If still beyond the limit, replace the bearings.

15. Install the grease cap and wheel assembly.

Summit Wagon

1. Raise the vehicle and support safely. Remove the tire and wheel assembly.

2. If equipped with ABS, remove the caliper assembly, brake disc and rear wheel speed sensor from the adapter. If not equipped with ABS, remove the brake drum.

NOTE: The speed sensor has a pole piece projecting from it. This exposed tip must be protected from impact or scratches. Do not allow the pole piece to contact the toothed wheel during removal or installation.

3. Remove the dust cap, nut and tounged washer. Do not use an air gun to remove the nut.

4. Remove the rear hub assembly taking care not to scrape or damage the teeth of the speed rotor, if equipped.

5. Inspect the hub unit bearing for wear or damage. If replacement of the bearing is required, the hub assembly and bearing is to be replaced as a unit. The rear hub unit bearing assembly should should not be dismantled.

6. Installation is the reverse of the removal procedure.

Laser, Talon and Stealth

1. Raise the vehicle and support safely.

2. Remove the tire and wheel assembly.

3. Remove the bolt(s) holding the speed sensor bracket to the knuckle and remove the assembly from the vehicle.

NOTE: The speed sensor has a pole piece projecting from it. This exposed tip must be protected from impact or scratches. Do not allow the pole piece to contact the toothed wheel during removal or installation.

4. Remove the caliper from the brake disc and suspend with a wire.

5. Remove the brake disc.

6. Remove the grease cap, self-locking nut and tounged washer.

7. Remove the rear hub assembly.

NOTE: The rear hub assembly can not be disassembled. If bearing replacement is required, replace the assembly as a unit.

To install:

8. Install the hub assembly.

9. Install the tounged washer and a new self-locking nut. Torque the nut to 144–188 ft. lbs. (200–260 Nm), align with the indentation in the spindle, and crimp.

10. Set up a dial indicator and measure the endplay while moving the hub in and out. If the endplay exceeds 0.004 in. (0.01mm) for Laser and Talon or 0.002 in. (0.005mm) for Stealth, retorque the nut. If still beyond the limit, replace the hub unit.

11. Install the grease cap and brake parts.

12. Temporarily install the speed sensor to the knuckle; tighten the bolts only finger-tight.

13. Route the cable correctly and loosely install the clips and retainers. All clips must be in their original position and the sensor cable must not be twisted. Improper installation may cause cable damage and system failure.

NOTE: The wiring in the harness is easily damaged by twisting and flexing. Use the white stripe on the outer insulation to keep the sensor harness properly placed.

14. Use a brass or other non-magnetic feeler gauge to check the air gap between the tip of the pole piece and the toothed wheel. Correct gap is 0.012–0.035 in. (0.3–0.9mm). Tighten the 2 sensor bracket bolts to 10 ft. lbs. (14 Nm) with the sensor located so the gap is the same at several points on the toothed wheel. If the gap is incorrect, it is likely that the toothed wheel is worn or improperly installed.

15. Install the wheel.

Rear Axle Assembly
REMOVAL & INSTALLATION
Except Summit Wagon

1. Raise the vehicle and support safely.

2. Remove the tire and wheel assembly.

3. If equipped with ABS, remove the bolts holding the speed sensor bracket to the trailing arm and remove the sensor assembly from the vehicle.

NOTE: The speed sensor has a pole piece projecting from it. This exposed tip must be protected from impact or scratches. Do not allow the pole piece to contact the toothed wheel during removal or installation.

4. If equipped with rear disc brakes, remove the caliper from the disc and remove the brake disc.

5. Remove the dust cap and bearing nut. Do not use an air gun to remove the nut.

6. Remove the outer wheel bearing.

7. Remove the drum and/or axle hub with the inner wheel bearing and the grease seal.

8. Remove the parking brake cable, brake hose, tube bracket and brake shoes with backing plate from the axle.

9. Remove the lateral rod mounting bolt and nut and secure the lateral rod to the axle beam with a piece of wire.

10. Using the proper equipment, slightly raise the torsion axle and arm assembly. Remove lower strut mounting bolt.

11. Remove the front trailing arm mount bolts and remove the rear axle assembly.

To install:

12. Install the rear axle assembly to the vehicle and install the strut mounting bolts. Install the front mount bolts and lateral rod bolts. Do not tighten these until the full weight of the vehicle is on the ground.

13. Install the backing plate, brake shoes, cable and hose.

14. On Summit, to determine if the self-locking nut is reusable:

a. Screw in the self-locking nut until about $\frac{1}{10}$ in. of the spindle is showing.

b. Measure the torque required to turn the self-locking nut counterclockwise.

c. The lowest allowable torque is 48 inch lbs. (5.5 Nm). If the measured torque is less than the specification, replace the nut.

15. Install the drum and/or axle hub. On Summit, lubricate and install the outer wheel bearing to the spindle. Torque the self-locking nut to 108–145 ft. lbs. (150–200 Nm).

16. On Laser and Talon, install the tounged washer and a new self-locking nut. Torque the nut to 144–188 ft. lbs. (200–260 Nm), align with the indentation in the spindle, and crimp.

17. Install the grease cap and brake parts.

18. Temporarily install the speed

sensor to the knuckle; tighten the bolts only finger-tight.

19. Route the cable correctly and loosely install the clips and retainers. All clips must be in their original position and the sensor cable must not be twisted. Improper installation may cause cable damage and system failure.

NOTE: The wiring in the harness is easily damaged by twisting and flexing. Use the white stripe on the outer insulation to keep the sensor harness properly placed.

20. Use a brass or other non-magnetic feeler gauge to check the air gap between the tip of the pole piece and the toothed wheel. Correct gap is 0.012–0.035 in. (0.3–0.9mm). Tighten the 2 sensor bracket bolts to 10 ft. lbs. (14 Nm) with the sensor located so the gap is the same at several points on the toothed wheel. If the gap is incorrect, it is likely that the toothed wheel is worn or improperly installed.

21. Install the wheel.

22. Lower the vehicle so the full weight of the vehicle is on the floor.

23. On Summit, torque the front trailing arm bolt to 94–108 ft. lbs. (130–150 Nm). On Laser and Talon, torque the trailing arm bolt to 72–87 ft. lbs. ((100–120 Nm).

24. Torque the axle side lateral rod nut to 58–72 ft. lbs. (80–100 Nm) on Summit or 72–87 ft. lbs. (100–120 Nm) on Laser and Talon.

STEERING

Steering Wheel

NOTE: If equipped with an air bag, be sure to disarm it before starting repairs on the vehicle. Failure to do so could result in personal injury or death.

REMOVAL & INSTALLATION

Summit, Summit Wagon, Laser and Talon

WITHOUT AIR BAG

1. Disconnect the negative battery cable.

2. Remove the horn pad and disconnect horn button connector.

3. Remove steering wheel retaining nut.

4. Matchmark the steering wheel to the shaft.

5. Use a steering wheel puller to remove the steering wheel. Do not hammer on steering wheel to remove it.

The collapsible column mechanism may be damaged.

To install:

6. Line up the matchmarks and install the steering wheel. Torque the retaining nut to 29 ft. lbs. (40 Nm).

7. Install the steering wheel attaching nut and torque to 33 ft. lbs. (45 Nm).

8. Reconnect the horn connector and install the horn pad.

Stealth

1. Disconnect the negative battery cable.

2. Remove the air bag module mounting nut from behind the steering wheel. Matchmark the steering wheel.

3. Disconnect the connector of the clockspring from the air bag module, press the air bag's lock towards the module to spread the lock open. While holding lock in this position, use a small tipped prying tool to gently pry the connector from the module.

4. Store the air bag module in a clean, dry place with the pad cover facing up.

5. Remove the steering wheel retaining nut. Matchmark the steering wheel to the shaft. Use a steering wheel puller to remove the wheel. Do not use a hammer or the collapsible mechanism in the column could be damaged.

To install:

6. Confirm that the front wheels are in a straight-ahead position. Center the clockspring by aligning the NEUTRAL mark on the clockspring with the mating mark on the casing.

7. Line up and install the steering wheel. Torque the retaining nut to 29 ft. lbs. (40 Nm).

Steering Column

NOTE: If equipped with an air bag, be sure to disarm it before starting any repairs on the vehicle.

REMOVAL & INSTALLATION

1. Disconnect the negative battery cable.

2. Remove the instrument panel undercover or knee protector.

3. Remove the trim clip, foot shower duct and lap shower duct.

4. Remove the steering wheel and air bag module as required. Remove the column upper and lower cover. Disconnect the key interlock cable if equipped.

5. Disconnect all connector to column-mounted items.

6. Remove the band from the steering joint cover. Remove the joint assembly and gear box connecting bolt.

7. Remove the screws that attach the rubber seal to the firewall.

8. Remove the lower and upper column mounting bolts.

9. Remove the steering column assembly.

To install:

10. Install the column so the splines are inserted around the rack input shaft. Install the pinch bolt.

11. Install the mounting bolts.

12. Install the rubber seal screws.

13. Connect the connectors and interlock cable.

14. Install the column covers.

15. Install the remaining interior pieces.

16. Connect the negative battery cable and check all column-mounted switches for proper operation.

Manual Steering Rack

ADJUSTMENT

1. Remove the rack and pinion assembly.

2. Mount the rack in a vise and with a small torque wrench and an adapter to connect to the input shaft, position the rack at its center. Tighten the rack support cover, the bottom plug, to 11 ft. lbs. In the neutral position, rotate the shaft clockwise 1 turn in 4–6 seconds. Return the rack support cover 30–60 degrees and adjust the total pinion torque to 5–11 inch lbs.

3. When adjusting, set to the higher side of the specification. Make sure there is no ratcheting or catching when operating the rack. If the rack cannot be adjusted to specification, check the rack support cover components or replace. After adjusting, lock the rack support cover with the locking nut.

REMOVAL & INSTALLATION

Summit

1. Disconnect the battery negative cable. Raise the vehicle and support safely.

2. Remove the pinch bolt holding the lower steering column joint to the rack and pinion input shaft.

3. Remove the cotter pins and disconnect the tie rod ends.

4. Remove the rack and pinion steering assembly and its rubber mounts.

5. The installation is the reverse of the removal procedure.

6. Perform a front end alignment.

Laser and Talon

1. Disconnect the negative battery cable. Raise the vehicle and support safely.

2. Remove the bolt holding lower

steering column joint to the rack and pinion input shaft.

3. Remove the cotter pins and disconnect the tie rod ends.

4. Locate the triangular brace near the stabilizer bar brackets on the crossmember and remove both the brace and the stabilizer bar brackets.

5. Remove the through bolt from the round roll stopper and remove the rear bolts from the center crossmember.

6. Disconnect the front exhaust pipe.

7. Remove the rack and pinion steering assembly and its rubber mounts. Move the rack to the right to remove from the crossmember. Use caution to avoid damaging the boots.

To install:

8. Install the rack and mounting bolts, torquing bolts to 43–58 ft. lbs. (60–80 Nm). When installing the rubber rack mounts, align the projection of the mounting rubber with the indentation in the crossmember. Install the pinch bolt.

9. Connect the exhaust pipe.

10. Install the center member mounting bolts and roll stopper through bolt.

11. Install the stabilizer bar brackets and brace.

12. Connect the tie rod ends.

13. Perform a front end alignment.

Power Steering Rack

ADJUSTMENT

1. Disconnect the negative battery cable.

2. Raise the vehicle and support safely.

3. Remove the steering rack assembly from the vehicle.

NOTE: If equipped with air bag, prior to removal of the steering gear box, center the front wheels and remove the ignition key. Failure to do so may damage the SRS clockspring and render SRS system inoperative, risking serious driver injury.

4. Secure the steering rack assembly in a vise. Do not clamp the vise jaws on the steering housing tubes. Clamp the vise jaws only on the housing cast metal.

5. Remove the steering gear housing end plug from the steering gear shaft bore using tool 6103 or equivalent.

6. Remove the preload adjustment cap locknut from the steering gear housing bore using tool 6097 or equivalent.

7. With rack at center position, check torque on the rack support cover to 11 ft. lbs. (15 Nm).

8. With rack at center position, rotate the shaft clockwise 1 turn in 4–6 seconds. Return the rack support cover 30–60 degrees and adjust the total pinion torque to 5–11 inch lbs. Set the standard value at its highest value when adjusting. Assure no ratcheting or catching when operating the rack towards the shaft direction.

9. Secure the preload adjustment cap with a new locknut using tool 6097 or equivalent. Do not allow the adjustment cap to rotate when tightening the locknut.

10. Install the end plug using tool 6103 or equivalent.

REMOVAL & INSTALLATION

Summit and Summit Wagon

1. Disconnect the battery negative cable. Raise the vehicle and support safely.

2. Remove the pinch bolt holding the lower steering column joint to the rack and pinion input shaft.

3. Remove the cotter pins and disconnect the tie rod ends from the steering knuckle.

4. On Summit Wagon equipped with AWD, remove the transfer case rear bracket.

5. On Summit Wagon equipped with 2.4L Engine and FWD, disconnect the stabilizer bar and remove as reqired.

6. Disconnect the power steering fluid pressure pipe and return hose from the rack fittings.

7. Remove the rack and pinion steering assembly and its rubber mounts.

To install:

8. Install the steering gear into the vehicle and secure using the retainer clamps and bolts.

9. Connect the power steering fluid lines to the rack fitings.

10. Install the stabilizer bar and rear transaxle bracket.

11. Connect the tie rod ends to the steering knuckles.

12. Connect the negative battery cable. Refill the reservoir and bleed the system.

13. Perform a front end alignment.

Laser and Talon

1. Disconnect the negative battery cable. Raise the vehicle and support safely.

2. Remove the bolt holding lower steering column joint to the rack and pinion input shaft.

3. Remove the transfer case, if equipped.

4. Remove the cotter pins and disconnect the tie rod ends.

5. Locate the triangular brace near the stabilizer bar brackets on the

crossmember and remove both the brace and the stabilizer bar brackets.

6. Remove the through bolt from the round roll stopper and remove the rear bolts from the center crossmember.

7. Disconnect the front exhaust pipe.

8. Disconnect the power steering fluid pressure pipe and return hose from the rack fittings.

9. Remove the rack and pinion steering assembly and its rubber mounts. Move the rack to the right to remove from the crossmember. Use caution to avoid damaging the boots.

To install:

10. Install the rack and install the mounting bolts. Torque the mounting bolts to 43–58 ft. lbs. (60–80 Nm). When installing the rubber rack mounts, align the projection of the mounting rubber with the indentation in the crossmember. Install the pinch bolt.

11. Connect the power steering fluid lines to the rack.

12. Connect the exhaust pipe.

13. Install the center member mounting bolts and roll stopper through bolt.

14. Install the stabilizer bar brackets and brace.

15. Connect the tie rod ends.

16. Install the transfer case.

17. Refill the reservoir and bleed the system.

18. Peform a front end alignment.

Stealth

NOTE: If equipped with air bag, prior to removal of the steering gear box, center the front wheels and remove the ignition key. Failure to do so may damage the SRS clockspring and render SRS system inoperative, risking serious driver injury.

1. Disconnect the negative battery cable. Disarm the air bag.

2. Disconnect the front exhaust pipe.

3. If equipped with AWD, remove the transfer case assembly.

4. Remove the bolt holding lower steering column joint to the rack and pinion input shaft.

5. Remove the cotter pins and disconnect the tie rod ends.

6. Remove the left and right frame members.

7. Remove the stabilizer bar bracket.

8. If equipped with 4 wheel steering, disconnect the lines going to the rear pump.

9. Remove the rack and pinion steering assembly and its rubber mounts. Move the rack to the right to

remove from the crossmember. Use caution to avoid damaging the boots.

To install:

10. Install the rack and install the mounting bolts, tightening bolts to 51 ft. lbs. (70 Nm). When installing the rubber rack mounts, align the projection of the mounting rubber with the indentation in the crossmember. Install the pinch bolt.

11. Connect the lines going to the 4 wheel steering rear pump and to the rack itself.

12. Install the frame members and torque the bolts to 50 ft. lbs. (68 Nm).

13. Connect the tie rods and install new cotter pins.

14. Install the transfer case and front exhaust pipe.

15. Refill the reservoir and bleed the system.

16. Peform front end alignment.

Rear Steering Gear

REMOVAL & INSTALLATION

1. Disconnect the negative battery cable. Raise the vehicle and support safely.

2. Drain the power steering fluid.

3. Remove the main muffler assembly.

4. Remove the rear shock absorber lower mounting bolts.

5. Using the proper equipment, support the weight of the rear differential. Remove the 2 small crossmember brackets.

6. Remove the large self-locking crossmember mounting nuts on the differential side.

7. Remove the oil line clamp bolts.

8. Remove the pressure tubes.

9. Hold the tie rod ends stationary and remove the tie rod end nuts. Remove the tie rod ends from the trailing arms.

10. Remove the mounting bolts and remove the rear steering gear.

To install:

11. Secure the unit to the crossmember tightening the bolts to 30 ft. lbs. (42 Nm). Move the power cylinder piston rod over its full stroke to determine its neutral position.

12. Align the tie rod ends with the holes in the trailing arms and install the nuts. Adjust the length of the tie rods with the nuts if necessary. The difference in length between the 2 tie rod ends should not exceed 0.04 in. (1mm). The tie rod nuts' torque specification is 42 ft. lbs. (58 Nm).

13. Replace the O-rings and install the pressure tubes. Clamp in place.

14. Install the large self-locking crossmember mounting nuts on the differential side and torque to 80–94 ft. lbs. (110–130 Nm).

15. Install the 2 small crossmember

brackets. Remove the support equipment.

16. Install the shock mounting bolts.

17. Install the muffler assembly.

18. Refill the reservoir and bleed the system.

19. To check and see if the system is functioning:

   a. Raise the vehicle safely so all 4 wheels turn freely.

   b. Run the vehicle at 50 mph.

   c. Turn the steering wheel quickly to the left and right and make sure the rear wheels steer in the same direction as the front wheels.

20. Perform a rear alignment.

Power Steering Pump

REMOVAL & INSTALLATION

Front

1. Disconnect the battery negative cable.

2. Remove the pressure switch connector from the side of the pump.

3. If the alternator is located under the oil pump, cover it with a shop towel to protect it from oil.

4. Disconnect the return fluid line. Remove the reservoir cap and allow the return line to drain the fluid from the reservoir. If the fluid is contaminated, disconnect the ignition high tension cable and crank the Engine several times to drain the fluid from the gearbox.

5. On Summit Wagon equipped with 2.4L Engine, remove the alternator drive belt and the heat protector.

6. Disconnect the pressure line.

7. Remove the pump drive belt and unbolt the pump from its bracket.

To install:

8. Install the pump, wrap the belt around the pulley and tighten the bolts.

9. Replace the O-rings and connect the pressure line. Connect the pressure line so the notch in the fitting aligns and contacts the pump's guide bracket.

10. Connect the return line.

11. Connect the pressure switch connector.

12. Adjust the belt tension and tighten the adjusting bolts.

13. Refill the reservoir and bleed the system.

Rear

STEALTH WITH FOUR WHEEL STEERING

1. Disconnect the negative battery cable. Raise the vehicle and support safely.

2. Drain the power steering fluid.

3. Remove the main muffler assembly.

4. Remove the rear shock absorber lower mounting bolts.

5. Using the proper equipment, support the weight of the rear differential. Remove the 2 small crossmember brackets.

6. Remove the large self-locking crossmember mounting nuts on the differential side.

7. Disconnect the pressure and suction hoses from the fittings on the pump.

8. Remove the pump retaining bolt and remove the pump from the rear differential assembly. Do not attempt to disassemble the pump; it is not serviceable.

To install:

9. Replace the O-ring and install the pump assembly to the differential. Make sure the housing is fully seated and the gear is fully engaged. Install the retaining bolt.

10. Replace the O-ring and connect the fluid lines to the pump.

11. Install the large self-locking crossmember mounting nuts on the differential side. Torque to 80–94 ft. lbs. (110–130 Nm).

12. Install the 2 small crossmember brackets. Remove the support equipment.

13. Install the shock mounting bolts.

14. Install the muffler assembly.

15. Refill the reservoir and bleed the system.

16. To check and see if the system is functioning:

   a. Raise the vehicle safely so all 4 wheels turn freely.

   b. Run the vehicle at 50 mph.

   c. Turn the steering wheel quickly to the left and right and make sure the rear wheels steer in the same direction as the front wheels.

BELT ADJUSTMENT

1. Press the belt in about the center between the power steering pump pulley and the pulley it shares, usually the water pump pulley. With reasonable pressure applied (about 22 lbs.) the belt should deflect about 1/4–3/8 in.

2. Adjustment can be made by loosening the 3 bolts that hold the pump. Place a suitable bar or lever between the body of the pump and gently pry to get the desired tension.

3. Retighten the 3 bolts and check again.

SYSTEM BLEEDING

Front

1. Raise the vehicle and support safely.

2. Manually turn the pump pulley a few times.

3. Turn the steering wheel all the

way to the left and to the right 5 or 6 times.

4. Disconnect the ignition high tension cable and, while operating the starter motor intermittently, turn the steering wheel all the way to the left and right 5–6 times for 15–20 seconds. During bleeding, make sure the fluid in the reservoir never falls below the lower position of the filter. If bleeding is attempted with the Engine running, the air will be absorbed in the fluid. Bleed only while cranking.

5. Connect ignition high tension cable, start Engine and allow to idle.

6. Turn the steering wheel left and right until there are no air bubbles in the reservoir. Confirm that the fluid is not milky and the level is up to the specified position on the gauge. Confirm that there is is very little change in the fluid level when the steering wheel is turned. If the fluid level changes more than 0.2 in. the air has not been completely bled. Repeat the process.

Rear

1. Bleed the front system as described above.

2. Start the Engine and let it idle. Raise and safely support the vehicle.

3. Loosen the bleeder screw on the left side of the control valve and install special tool MB991230 to the bleeder.

4. Turn the steering wheel all the way to the left, then immediately turn it half way back. Confirm that air has discharged with the fluid.

5. Repeat Step 5 two or three times as required, to remove all air from the rear system. Stop the Engine.

6. Loosen the power cylinder (rear steering gear) bleeder screw about ⅛ turn and install the same special tool with the rotation prevention metal fixtures to prevent the bleeder from opening more. Attach a plastic tube to the bleeder.

7. Start the Engine and run to 50 mph to circulate the fluid.

8. Maintain a speed of 20 mph and turn the steering wheel back and forth. Air should be discharged through the tube of the special tool and into the oil reservoir.

9. Repeat until all air is removed from the power cylinder.

NOTE: If air has not been completely bled from the system, the pump will make a humming noise or an unusual noise will come from the flow control valve: this also contributes to shortened pump life.

Tie Rod Ends

REMOVAL & INSTALLATION

1. Disconnect the battery negative cable.

2. Raise the vehicle and support safely.

3. Wire brush the threads on the tie rod shaft and lubricate with penetrating oil. Loosen the locknut.

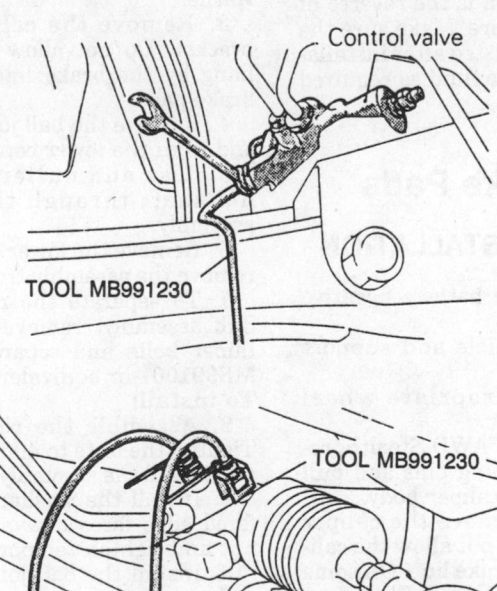

Control valve

TOOL MB991230

TOOL MB991230

Bleeding the rear steering system

4. Remove the cotter pin and nut and press the tie rod end from the steering knuckle.

5. Hold the tie rod shaft with locking pliers and turn the tie rod end off, counting the number of turns for installation.

6. The installation is the reverse of the removal procedure. Install the tie rod end the same number of turns that it took to remove the old 1.

7. Perform front end alignment.

BRAKES

Master Cylinder

REMOVAL & INSTALLATION

1. Disconnect the negative battery cable.

2. Disconnect the fluid level sensor connector.

3. Disconnect the brake lines from the master cylinder. On Laser and Talon, a separate reservoir is used. Plug the lines to prevent drainage.

4. On Stealth, disconnect the low pressure hose.

5. Remove the 2 nuts securing the master cylinder and lift off. On Summit Wagon, slide the proportioning valve assembly off of the master cylinder mounting studs prior to master cylinder removal.

To install:

6. Bench bleed the master cylinder.

7. Install master cylinder and proportioning valve to the studs and install the nuts.

8. Install the brake lines to the master cylinder. Bleed brake system starting at the master cylinder. If air remains in the system continue bleeding the entire system.

9. Connect the negative battery cable and check the brakes for proper operation.

Proportioning Valve

REMOVAL & INSTALLATION

1. Disconnect the negative battery cable.

2. Locate the proportioning valve, usually below the master cylinder.

3. Tag and disconnect the brake lines from the valve.

4. Remove the proportioning valve from the Engine compartment. On

Summit Wagon, remove the master cylinder retainer nuts to remove the proportioning valve assembly.

5. The installation is the reverse of the removal procedure.

6. Bleed the brakes in the following order:

Summit and Summit Wagon
  a. Left rear wheel cylinder or caliper
  b. Right front cylinder
  c. Right rear wheel cylinder or caliper
  d. Left front caliper

Laser and Talon
  a. Right rear caliper
  b. Left front caliper
  c. Left rear caliper
  d. Right front caliper

7. Connect the negative battery cable and check the brakes for proper operation.

Power Brake Booster

REMOVAL & INSTALLATION

1. Disconnect the negative battery cable. On some models, relocate the relay box and the solenoid valve located at the power brake unit.

2. Disconnect the vacuum hose from the booster. Pull it straight off. Prying off the vacuum hose could damage the check valve installed in the brake booster.

3. Disconnect the brake level sensor connector.

4. Remove the nuts attaching the master cylinder to the booster and remove the master cylinder.

5. From inside the passenger compartment, remove the cotter pin and clevis pin that secures the booster pushrod to the brake pedal.

6. Remove the nuts that attach the booster to the dash panel and remove it from the vehicle.

7. The installation is the reverse of the removal procedure.

8. Connect the negative battery cable, bleed the brakes and check for proper operation.

Brake Caliper

REMOVAL & INSTALLATION

Front Brakes

1. Disconnect the negative battery cable.

2. Raise the vehicle and support safely. Remove appropriate wheel assembly.

3. To disconnect the front brake hose, hold the nut on the brake hose side and loosen the flared brake line nut.

4. Remove the caliper lock pins and remove the caliper.

5. The installation is the reverse of the removal procedure. Make sure the brake hose is not twisted after installation. Refill the brake fluid as required and bleed the brakes.

Rear Brakes

SUMMIT, SUMMIT WAGON, LASER AND TALON

1. Disconnect the negative battery cable.

2. Raise the vehicle and support safely. Remove appropriate wheel assembly.

3. Disconnect the parking brake cable from the actuator on the caliper.

4. To disconnect the brake hose, hold the nut on the brake hose side and loosen the flared brake line nut.

5. Remove the retaining bolts and remove rear caliper assembly.

6. The installation is the reverse of the removal procedure. Make sure the brake hose is not twisted after installation.

7. Refill the brake fluid as required and bleed the brakes.

STEALTH

1. Disconnect the negative battery cable.

2. Raise the vehicle and support safely. Remove appropriate wheel assembly.

3. To disconnect the brake hose, hold the nut on the brake hose side and loosen the flared brake line nut.

4. Remove the caliper lock pins and remove the caliper.

5. The installation is the reverse of the removal procedure. Make sure the brake hose is not twisted after installation. Refill the brake fluid as required and bleed the brakes.

Disc Brake Pads

REMOVAL & INSTALLATION

1. Disconnect the battery negative cable.

2. Raise the vehicle and support safely.

3. Remove appropriate wheel assembly.

4. On the front of AWD Stealth, remove the pad retaining pins and pull the pads out of the caliper body.

5. On others, remove the caliper from its adaptor. Do not allow the caliper to hang by the brake line. On some vehicles, the caliper can be flipped up by leaving the upper pin in place and using it as a pivot point. Take note of the clips, pins, anti-squeal shims and other parts for reference at assembly.

6. On vehicles with rear disc brakes, it may help to loosen the parking brake cable from inside the vehicle and dis-connect the parking brake end from the rear caliper.

To install:

7. Use a large C-clamp to compress the piston(s) back into the caliper bore. On rear disc brakes with the parking brake mechanism incorporated into the caliper, a special tool is needed to turn the piston back into the bore.

8. Install the pads and all other small parts. Note that rear disc pads on calipers with the parking brake mechanism incorporated into the caliper should have a projection on the back side of the shoe that fits into the rear caliper piston.

9. Install the caliper. Make sure the brake hose is not twisted after installation. Connect the parking brake cable if disconnected.

10. Install the tire and wheel assembly and connect the negative battery cable. Pump the brake pedal until firm before putting transaxle in gear or moving vehicle.

Brake Rotor

REMOVAL & INSTALLATION

Summit Front Rotor

1. Loosen the large driveshaft nut while the vehicle is still on the ground with the brakes applied. Then raise and safely support vehicle. Remove appropriate wheel assembly.

2. Remove the axle end nut and lock washer.

3. Remove the caliper from its bracket. Do not allow the caliper to hang by the brake line. Remove the brake pads.

4. Remove the ball joint and tie rod end from the lower control arm.

5. Use and puller to push the halfshaft through the rotor/hub assembly.

6. Remove the lower strut bolts and remove the assembly from the vehicle.

7. To separate the rotor from the hub assembly, remove the rotor retainer bolts and separate using tool MB991001 or equivalent.

To install:

8. Assemble the rotor and hub. Tighten the nuts to 40 ft. lbs. (54 Nm) and install the assembly to the vehicle.

9. Install the washer so the chamfered edge faces outward. Install the nut and tighten temporarily.

10. Install the ball joint and tie rod end.

11. Install the brake components.

12. Install the wheel and lower the vehicle to the floor. Tighten the axle nut with the brakes applied to a maximum torque of 188 ft. lbs. (260 Nm). Install the cotter pin and bend to secure.

Except Summit Front Rotor

1. Raise the vehicle and support safely. Remove appropriate wheel assembly.
2. Remove the caliper and brake pads.
3. The rotor on most models is held to the hub by 2 small threaded screws. Remove screws, if equipped, and pull off the rotor.
4. Installation is the reverse of the removal process.

Brake Drum

REMOVAL & INSTALLATION

WItH Rear Hub Assembly

1. Raise the vehicle and support safely.
2. Remove the wheel and tire assembly.
3. Remove the brake drum from the vehicle.
4. The installation is the reverse of the removal procedure.

Without Rear Hub Assembly

1. Raise the vehicle and support safely.
2. Remove the wheel and tire assembly.
3. Remove the dust cap.
4. Remove the self-locking nut.
5. Remove the outer wheel bearing.
6. Remove the drum with the inner wheel bearing from the spindle. Remove the grease seal.

To install:

7. To determine if the self-locking nut is reusable:

a. Screw in the self-locking nut until about $\frac{1}{10}$ in. of the spindle is showing.
b. Measure the torque required to turn the self-locking nut counterclockwise.
c. The lowest allowable torque is 48 inch lbs. (5.5 Nm). If the measured torque is less than the specification, replace the nut.
8. Lubricate and install the inner wheel bearing. Install a new grease seal.
9. Install the drum to the spindle.
10. Lubricate and install the outer wheel bearing.
11. Torque the self-locking nut to 108–145 ft. lbs. (150–200 Nm).
12. Install the grease cap.

Brake Shoes

REMOVAL & INSTALLATION

1. Raise the vehicle and support safely. Remove appropriate wheel assembly.
2. Remove the brake drum. Remove the shoe to shoe spring.
3. Remove the shoe to lever spring and remove the adjuster assembly.
4. Take note of the springs and clips for proper reassembly. Remove the shoe hold-down clips and remove the shoes. Separate the parking brake cable from the rear brake shoe during removal.

To install:

5. Thoroughly clean and dry the backing plate. To prepare the backing plate, lubricate the bosses, anchor pin and parking brake actuating lever piv-

ot surface lightly with lithium-based grease.
6. Remove, clean and dry all parts still on the old shoes. Lubricate the star wheel shaft threads with anti-sieze lubricant and transfer all parts to their proper locations on the new shoes.
7. Install shoes to the vehicle.
8. Connect the parking brake cablc.
9. Adjust the star wheel.
10. To determine if the self-locking nut is reusable:

a. Screw in the self-locking nut until about $\frac{1}{10}$ in. of the spindle is showing.
b. Measure the torque required to turn the self-locking nut counterclockwise.
c. The lowest allowable torque is 48 inch lbs. (5.5 Nm). If the measured torque is less than the specification, replace the nut.
11. Remove any grease from the brake linings and install the drum to the spindle.
12. Lubricate and install the outer wheel bearing.
13. Torque the self-locking nut to 108–145 ft. lbs. (150–200 Nm).
14. Install the grease cap.

Wheel Cylinder

REMOVAL & INSTALLATION

1. Raise the vehicle and support safely.
2. Remove the wheel and the brake drum.
3. Remove the shoe-to-lever spring and the upper shoe-to-shoe spring.

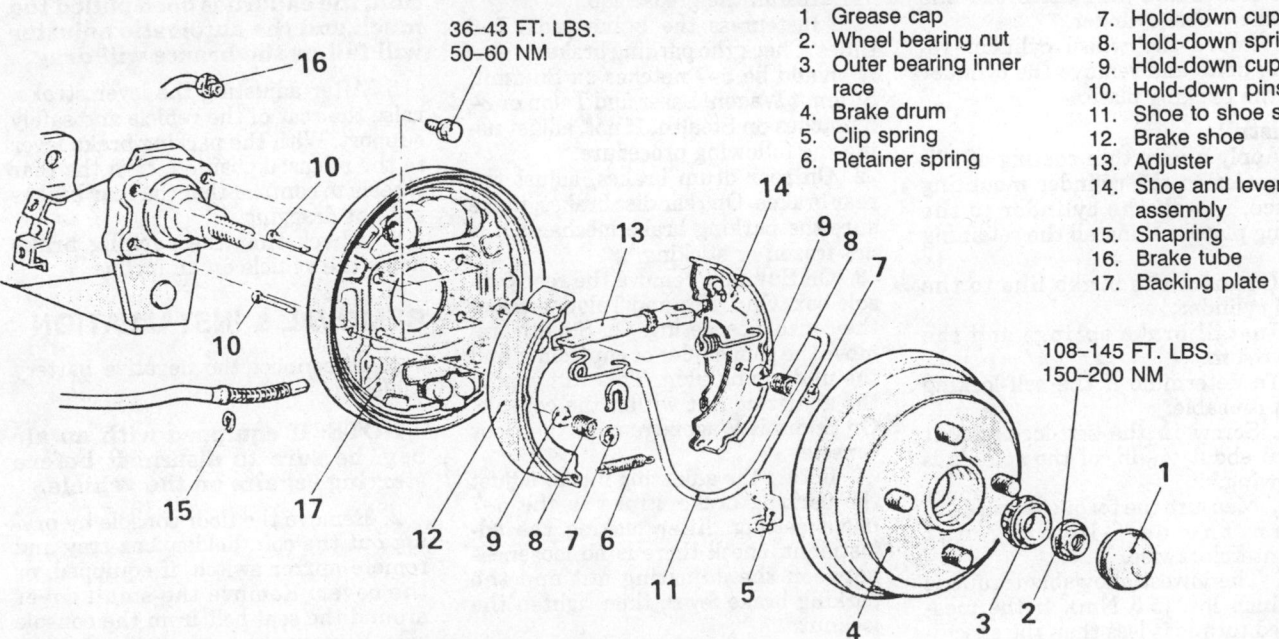

36–43 FT. LBS.
50–60 NM

1. Grease cap
2. Wheel bearing nut
3. Outer bearing inner race
4. Brake drum
5. Clip spring
6. Retainer spring
7. Hold-down cups
8. Hold-down springs
9. Hold-down cups
10. Hold-down pins
11. Shoe to shoe spring
12. Brake shoe
13. Adjuster
14. Shoe and lever assembly
15. Snapring
16. Brake tube
17. Backing plate

108–145 FT. LBS.
150–200 NM

Exploded view of the rear brakes – 1989–90 Summit

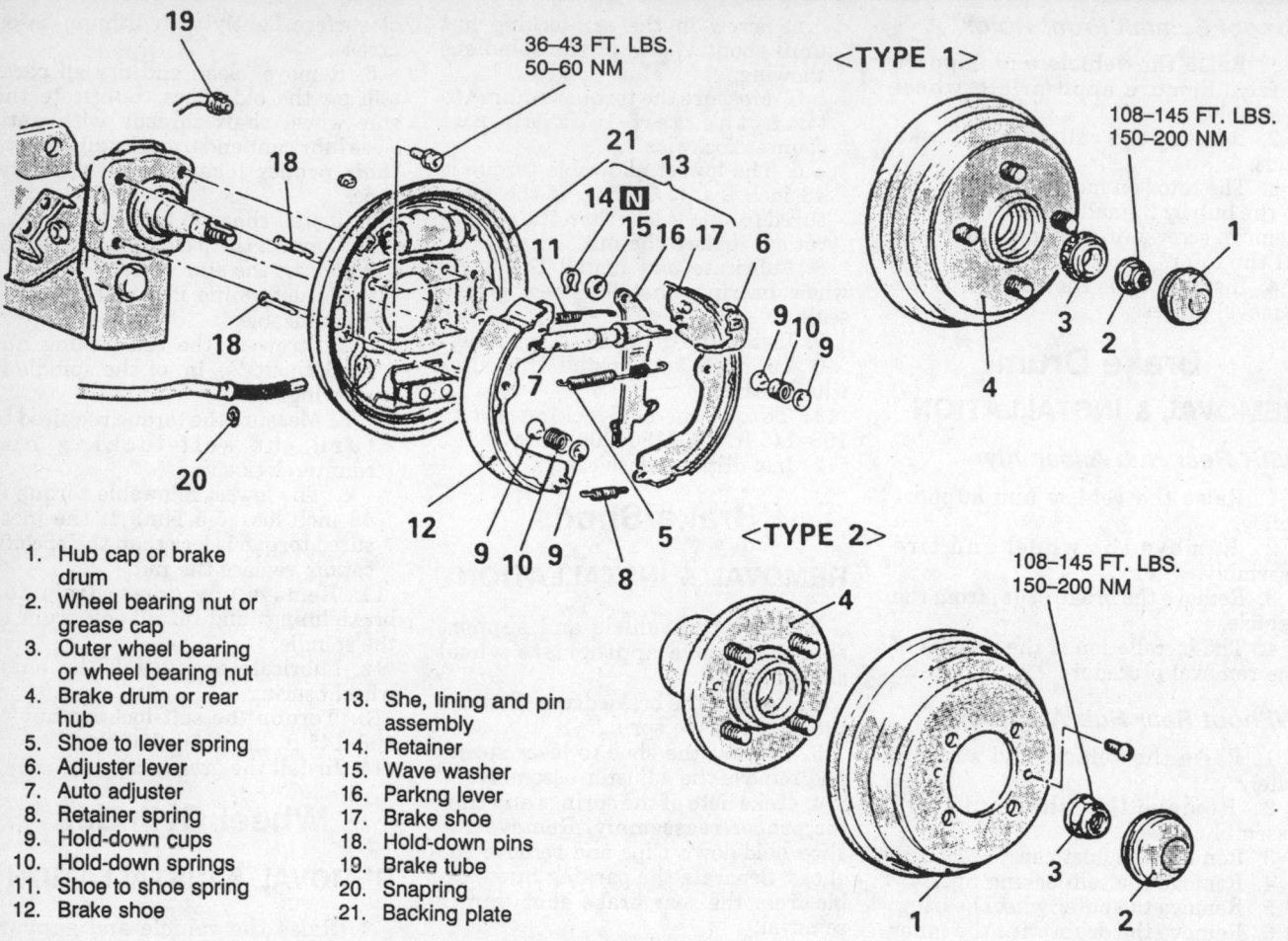

36–43 FT. LBS.
50–60 NM

<TYPE 1>

108–145 FT. LBS.
150–200 NM

<TYPE 2>

108–145 FT. LBS.
150–200 NM

1. Hub cap or brake drum
2. Wheel bearing nut or grease cap
3. Outer wheel bearing or wheel bearing nut
4. Brake drum or rear hub
5. Shoe to lever spring
6. Adjuster lever
7. Auto adjuster
8. Retainer spring
9. Hold-down cups
10. Hold-down springs
11. Shoe to shoe spring
12. Brake shoe
13. She, lining and pin assembly
14. Retainer
15. Wave washer
16. Parkng lever
17. Brake shoe
18. Hold-down pins
19. Brake tube
20. Snapring
21. Backing plate

Exploded view of the rear brakes—1991–93 Summit

Spread the upper portion of the brake shoes slightly.

4. Remove and plug the brake line from the wheel cylinder.

5. Remove the wheel cylinder retaining bolts and remove the cylinder from the backing plate.

To install:

6. Apply a very thin coating of silicone sealer to the cylinder mounting surface, install the cylinder to the backing plate and install the retaining bolts.

7. Connect the brake line to the wheel cylinder.

8. Install brake springs and the brake drum.

9. To determine if the self-locking nut is reusable:

   a. Screw in the self-locking nut until about $\frac{1}{10}$ in. of the spindle is showing.

   b. Measure the torque required to turn the self-locking nut counterclockwise.

   c. The lowest allowable torque is 48 inch lbs. (5.5 Nm). If the measured torque is less than the specification, replace the nut.

10. Torque the self-locking nut to 108–145 ft. lbs. (150–200 Nm) if equipped.

11. Install the grease cap.

12. Instepress the brake pedal 5–6 times. Check the parking brake stroke. It should be 5–7 notches on Summit, Summit Wagon, Laser and Talon or 3–5 notches on Stealth. If not, adjust using the following procedure.

2. On rear drum brakes, adjust the rear brakes. On rear disc brakes, make sure the parking brake mechanism is not frozen or sticking.

3. On Summit, remove the rear console box. On Laser and Talon, remove the console carpeting. On Stealth, remove the coin holder or cup holder and the underlying plug. This will expose the adjusting nut within the console. On Summit Wagon, remove the floor console.

4. Rotate the adjusting nut to adjust the parking brake stroke to the 5–7 notch setting. After making the adjustment, check there is no looseness between the adjusting nut and the parking brake lever, then tighten the locknut.

NOTE: Do not adjust the park-

ing brake too tight. If the number of notches is less than specification, the cable has been pulled too much and the automatic adjuster will fail or the brakes will drag.

5. After adjusting the lever stroke, raise the rear of the vehicle and safely support. With the parking brake lever in the released position, turn the rear wheels to confirm that the rear brakes are not dragging.

6. Check that the parking brake holds the vehicle on an incline.

REMOVAL & INSTALLATION

1. Disconnect the negative battery cable.

NOTE: If equipped with an air bag, be sure to disarm it before starting repairs on the vehicle.

2. Remove the floor console by prying out the coin holder, box tray and remote mirror switch, if equipped, or the cover. Remove the small cover around the seat belt from the console side. Remove the screws from the center section and remove the rear part of the console.

NOTE: If equipped with SRS, when removing the floor console, don't allow any impact or shock to the SRS diagnostic unit.

3. On some vehicles, it will be necessary to remove the rear seat cushion.

4. Remove the center cable clamp and grommet.

5. Raise the vehicle and support safely.

6. At the rear wheel, remove the brake drum or disc and disconnect the cable end from the parking brake strut lever or actuator. If necessary, compress the retaining strips to remove the cable from the backing plate.

7. Unfasten any other frame retainers and remove the cables.

8. The installation is the reverse of the removal procedure.

9. Adjust the rear brakes and parking brake cables.

10. Connect the negative battery cable and check the rear wheels to confirm that the rear brakes are not dragging.

11. Check that the parking brake holds the vehicle on an incline.

Brake System Bleeding

NOTE: If using a pressure bleeder, follow the instructions furnished with the unit and choose the correct adaptor for the application. Do not substitute an adapter that "almost fits" as it will not work and could be dangerous.

Master Cylinder

If the master cylinder is off the vehicle it can be bench bled.

1. Connect 2 short pieces of brake line to the outlet fittings, bend them until the free end is below the fluid level in the master cylinder reservoir.

2. Fill the reservoir with fresh brake fluid. Pump the piston slowly until no more air bubbles appear in the reservoirs.

3. Disconnect the 2 short lines, refill the master cylinder and securely install the cylinder caps.

4. If the master cylinder is on the vehicle, it can still be bled, using a flare nut wrench.

5. Open the brake lines slightly with the flare nut wrench while pressure is applied to the brake pedal by a helper inside the vehicle.

6. Be sure to tighten the line before the brake pedal is released.

7. Repeat the process with both lines until no air bubbles come out.

Calipers and Wheel Cylinders

1. Fill the master cylinder with fresh brake fluid. Check the level often during the procedure.

2. Starting with the wheel farthest from the master cylinder, remove the protective cap from the bleeder and place where it will not be lost. Clean the bleeder screw.

--- CAUTION ---

When bleeding the brakes, keep face away from the brake area. Spewing fluid may cause facial and/or visual damage. Do not allow brake fluid to spill on the car's finish; it will remove the paint.

3. If the system is empty, the most efficient way to get fluid down to the wheel is to loosen the bleeder about ½–¾ turn, place a finger firmly over the bleeder and have a helper pump the brakes slowly until fluid comes out the bleeder. Once fluid is at the bleeder, close it before the pedal is released inside the vehicle.

NOTE: If the pedal is pumped rapidly, the fluid will churn and create small air bubbles, which are almost impossible to remove from the system. These air bubbles will accumulate and a spongy pedal will result.

4. Once fluid has been pumped to the caliper or wheel cylinder, open the bleed screw again, have the helper press the brake pedal to the floor, lock the bleeder and have the helper slowly release the pedal. Wait 15 seconds and repeat the procedure (including the 15 second wait) until no more air comes out of the bleeder upon application of the brake pedal. Remember to close the bleeder before the pedal is released inside the vehicle each time the bleeder is opened. If not, air will be introduced into the system.

5. If a helper is not available, connect a small hose to the bleeder, place the end in a container of brake fluid and proceed to pump the pedal from inside the vehicle until no more air comes out the bleeder. The hose will prevent air from entering the system.

6. Repeat the procedure on remaining wheel cylinders in the following order:
Summit or Summit Wagon
   a. Left rear wheel cylinder or caliper
   b. Right front cylinder
   c. Right rear wheel cylinder or caliper
   d. Left front caliper
Laser, Talon and Stealth
   a. Right rear caliper
   b. Left front caliper
   c. Left rear caliper
   d. Right front caliper

7. Hydraulic brake systems must be totally flushed if the fluid becomes contaminated with water, dirt or other corrosive chemicals. To flush, bleed the entire system until all fluid has been replaced with the correct type of new fluid.

8. Install the bleeder cap on the bleeder to keep dirt out. Always road test the vehicle after brake work of any kind is done.

Anti-lock Brake System Service

PRECAUTIONS

• Certain components within the ABS system are not intended to be serviced or repaired individually. Only those components with removal and installation procedures should be serviced.

• Do not use rubber hoses or other parts not specifically specified for the ABS system. When using repair kits, replace all parts included in the kit. Partial or incorrect repair may lead to functional problems and require the replacement of components.

• Lubricate rubber parts with clean, fresh brake fluid to ease assembly. Do not use lubricated shop air to clean parts; damage to rubber components may result.

• Use only DOT 3 brake fluid from an unopened container.

• If any hydraulic component or line is removed or replaced, it may be necessary to bleed the entire system.

• A clean repair area is essential. Always clean the reservoir and cap thoroughly before removing the cap. The slightest amount of dirt in the fluid may plug an orifice and impair the system function. Perform repairs after components have been thoroughly cleaned; use only denatured alcohol to clean components. Do not allow ABS components to come into contact with any substance containing mineral oil; this includes used shop rags.

• The Anti-Lock control unit is a microprocessor similar to other computer units in the vehicle. Ensure that the ignition switch is **OFF** before removing or installing controller harnesses. Avoid static electricity discharge at or near the controller.

• If any arc welding is to be done on the vehicle, the ALCU connectors should be disconnected before welding operations begin.

Hydraulic Unit

REMOVAL & INSTALLATION

Summit Wagon

1. Disconnect the negative battery

cable. Remove the splash shield from under the vehicle.

2. Use a syringe or similar device to remove as much fluid as possible from the reservoir. Some fluid will be spilled from lines during removal of the hydraulic unit; protect adjacent painted surfaces.

3. Remove the dust cover and the oil reservoir.

4. Disconnect the brake lines from the hydraulic unit. Correct reassembly is critical. Label or identify the lines before removal. Plug each line immediately after removal.

5. Disconnect the hydaulic unit electrical harness connectors.

6. Disconnect the hydraulic unit ground strap from the chassis.

7. Remove the 3 nuts holding the hydraulic unit. Remove the unit upwards.

NOTE: The hydraulic unit is heavy; use care when removing it. The unit must remain in the upright position at all times and be protected from impact and shock.

8. Set the unit upright supported by blocks on the workbench. The hydraulic unit must not be tilted or turned upside down. No component of the hydraulic unit should be loosened or disassembled.

9. The bracket assemblies and relays may be removed if desired.

To install:

10. Install the relays and brackets if removed.

11. Install the hydraulic unit into the vehicle, keeping it upright at all times.

12. Install the retaining nuts and tighten.

13. Connect the ground strap to the chassis bracket. Connect the hydraulic unit wiring harness.

14. Connect the hydaulic unit electrical harness connectors.

15. Install the dust cover and the oil reservoir.

16. Connect each brake line loosely to the correct port and double check the placement. Tighten each line to 10 ft. lbs. (13.5 Nm).

17. Fill the reservoir to the MAX line with brake fluid.

18. Bleed the master cylinder, then bleed the brake lines. Refill the master cylinder and check for proper operation.

Laser and Talon

1. Disconnect the negative battery cable. Use a syringe or similar device to remove as much fluid as possible from the reservoir. Some fluid will be spilled from lines during removal of the hydraulic unit; protect adjacent painted surfaces.

2. On turbocharged Engine, remove the center intercooler duct. Loosen the clamps and remove the bolts holding the duct to the air cleaner.

3. Disconnect the brake lines from the hydraulic unit. Correct reassembly is critical. Label or identify the lines before removal. Plug each line immediately after removal.

4. Remove the cover from the relay box. Disconnect the electrical harness to the hydraulic unit.

5. Disconnect the hydraulic unit ground strap from the chassis.

6. Remove the 3 nuts holding the hydraulic unit. Remove the unit upwards.

NOTE: The hydraulic unit is heavy; use care when removing it. The unit must remain in the upright position at all times and be protected from impact and shock.

7. Set the unit upright supported by blocks on the workbench. The hydraulic unit must not be tilted or turned upside down. No component of the hydraulic unit should be loosened or disassembled.

8. The bracket assemblies and relays may be removed if desired.

To install:

9. Install the relays and brackets if removed.

10. Install the hydraulic unit into the vehicle, keeping it upright at all times.

11. Install the retaining nuts and tighten.

12. Connect the ground strap to the chassis bracket. Connect the hydraulic unit wiring harness.

13. Install the cover on the relay box.

14. Connect each brake line loosely to the correct port and double check the placement. Tighten each line to 10 ft. lbs. (13.5 Nm).

15. Fill the reservoir to the MAX line with brake fluid.

16. Bleed the master cylinder, then bleed the brake lines.

17. If equipped, install the intercooler air duct.

Stealth

1. Disconnect the negative battery cable. Remove the splash shield from beneath the car.

2. Use a syringe or similar device to remove as much fluid as possible from the reservoir. Some fluid will be spilled from lines during removal of the hydraulic unit; protect adjacent painted surfaces.

3. Lift the relay box with the harness attached and position it aside.

4. Remove the air intake duct.

5. Disconnect the brake lines from the hydraulic unit. Correct reassembly is critical. Label or identify the lines before removal. Plug each line immediately after removal. It will be neces-

sary to hold the relay box aside to allow wrench access.

6. Disconnect the wiring harness connections at the hydraulic unit.

7. Disconnect the hydraulic unit ground strap from the chassis.

8. Remove the 3 bolts holding the hydraulic unit bracket. Remove the unit and the bracket.

NOTE: The hydraulic unit is heavy; use care when removing it. The unit must remain in the upright position at all times and be protected from impact and shock.

9. Set the unit upright supported by blocks on the workbench. The hydraulic unit must not be tilted or turned upside down. No component of the hydraulic unit should be loosened or disassembled.

10. Loosen the nut holding the bracket to the hydraulic unit and remove the bracket.

11. Disconnect the external ground wire from the bracket.

To install:

12. Install the bracket if removed. Connect the ground wire to the bracket.

13. Install the hydraulic unit into the vehicle, keeping it upright at all times.

14. Install the retaining nuts and tighten.

15. Connect the hydraulic unit wiring harness.

16. Connect each brake line loosely to the correct port and double check the placement. Tighten each line to 11 ft. lbs. (15 Nm).

17. Fill the reservoir to the MAX line with brake fluid.

18. Bleed the master cylinder, then bleed the brake lines.

19. Secure the relay box in position and install the air duct.

20. Install the splash shield.

Anti-Lock Control Unit

REMOVAL & INSTALLATION

Except Summit Wagon

1. Ensure that the ignition switch is OFF throughout the procedure.

2. Remove the interior right rear quarter trim panel and rear seat back and/or cushion.

3. Release the lock on the bottom of the connector; disconnect the multi-pin connector from the control unit. On Laser and Talon, access may be easier if the external ground is disconnected from the bracket.

4. Remove the retaining nuts and remove the control unit from its bracket. The bracket may be removed if desired.

To install:

5. Place the bracket in position. In-

stall the controller and tighten the retaining nuts.

6. Connect the ground wire to the bracket if removed. Ensure a proper, tight connection. The ground must be connected before the multi-pin harness is connected.

7. Connect the multi-pin connector and secure the lock.

8. Install the rear quarter trim panel and seat.

Summit Wagon

1. Ensure that the ignition switch is **OFF** throughout the procedure.

2. Remove the cup holder in front of the center console.

3. Remove the console side covers.

4. Disconnect the electrical harness from the control unit.

5. Remove the fasteners and the control unit from the vehicle.

6. Installation is the reverse of the removal procedure.

G-Sensor

The G-Sensor is found only on All Wheel Drive (AWD) vehicles.

REMOVAL & INSTALLATION

Summit Wagon

1. Disconnect negative battery cable.

2. Remove the floor console.

3. Disconnect the wiring harness connector from the sensor.

4. Remove the retaining screw and G-sensor from the mounting bracket.

5. Installation is the reverse of the removal procedure.

Laser and Talon

1. Ensure that the ignition switch is **OFF** throughout the procedure.

2. Remove the rear seat cushion.

3. Disconnect the wiring harness to G-sensor.

4. Remove the retaining bolts and remove the sensor.

5. To install, position the sensor, tighten the retaining bolts and connect the harness.

6. Install the rear seat cushion.

Stealth

1. Disconnect the negative battery cable. Remove the rearmost console assembly.

NOTE: If equipped with SRS, when removing the floor console, don't allow any impact or shock to the SRS diagnostic unit.

2. Remove the front console assembly.

3. Disconnect the G-sensor wiring harness.

4. Remove the G-sensor from the bracket. Remove the bracket if desired.

To install:

5. Reinstall the bracket. Tighten the bolts to 4 ft. lbs. (5 Nm.)

6. Install the G-sensor and connect the wiring harness.

7. Install the front and rear console assemblies.

Wheel Speed Sensors
——— CAUTION ———

Vehicles equipped with air bag systems will have wiring and system components in the fender or wheel well area. The ABS components must be correctly identified before beginning repairs. Improper work procedures may cause impaired function of the ABS and/or SRS systems

REMOVAL & INSTALLATION

1. Disconnect the negative battery cable. Raise and safely support the vehicle.

2. Remove the wheel and tire.

3. Remove the inner fender or splash shield.

4. Beginning at the sensor end, carefully disconnect or release each clip and retainer along the sensor wire. Take careful note of the exact position of each clip; they must be reinstalled in the identical position. Rear wheel sensor harnesses will be held by plastic wire ties; these may be cut away but must be replaced at reassembly.

5. Disconnect the sensor connector at the end of the harness.

6. Remove the 2 bolts holding the speed sensor bracket to the knuckle and remove the assembly from the vehicle.

NOTE: The speed sensor has a pole piece projecting from it. This exposed tip must be protected from impact or scratches. Do not allow the pole piece to contact the toothed wheel during removal or installation.

7. Remove the sensor from the bracket.

To install:

8. Assemble the sensor onto the bracket and tighten the bolt to 10 ft. lbs. (14 Nm). Note that the brackets are different for the left and right front wheels. Each bracket has identifying letters stamped on it.

9. Temporarily install the speed sensor to the knuckle; tighten the bolts only finger-tight.

10. Route the cable correctly and loosely install the clips and retainers. All clips must be in their original position and the sensor cable must not be twisted. Improper installation may

cause cable damage and system failure.

NOTE: The wiring in the harness is easily damaged by twisting and flexing. Use the white stripe on the outer insulation to keep the sensor harness properly placed.

11. Use a brass or other non-magnetic feeler gauge to check the air gap between the tip of the pole piece and the toothed wheel. Correct gap is 0.012–0.035 in. (0.3–0.9mm). Tighten the 2 sensor bracket bolts to 10 ft. lbs. (14 Nm) with the sensor located so the gap is the same at several points on the toothed wheel. If the gap is incorrect, it is likely that the toothed wheel is worn or improperly installed.

12. Tighten the screws and bolts for the cable retaining clips.

13. Install the inner fender or splash shield.

14. Install the wheel and tire. Lower the vehicle to the ground.

Front Toothed Wheel Rings

REMOVAL & INSTALLATION

1. Disconnect the negative battery cable. Raise and safely support the vehicle.

2. Remove the wheel and tire.

3. Remove the wheel speed sensor and disconnect sufficient harness clips to allow the sensor and wiring to be moved out of the work area.

NOTE: The speed sensor has a pole piece projecting from it. This exposed tip must be protected from impact or scratches. Do not allow the pole piece to contact the toothed wheel during removal or installation.

4. Remove the front hub and knuckle assembly.

5. Remove the hub from the knuckle.

6. Support the hub in a vise with protected jaws. Remove the retaining bolts from the toothed wheel and remove the toothed wheel.

To install:

7. Fit the new toothed wheel onto the hub and tighten the retaining bolts to 7 ft. lbs. (10 Nm).

8. Assemble the hub to the knuckle.

9. Install the hub and knuckle assembly to the vehicle.

10. Install the wheel speed sensor.

11. Install the wheel and tire.

12. Lower the vehicle to the ground.

Rear Toothed Wheel Rings

REMOVAL & INSTALLATION

Front Wheel Drive

1. Disconnect the negative battery cable. Raise and safely support the vehicle.
2. Remove the wheel and tire.
3. Remove the wheel speed sensor and disconnect sufficient harness clips to allow the sensor and wiring to be moved out of the work area.

NOTE: The speed sensor has a pole piece projecting from it. This exposed tip must be protected from impact or scratches. Do not allow the pole piece to contact the toothed wheel during removal or installation.

4. Remove the hub assembly.
5. Support the hub in a vise with protected jaws. Remove the retaining bolts from the toothed wheel and remove the toothed wheel.

To install:
6. Fit the new toothed wheel onto the hub and tighten the retaining bolts to 7 ft. lbs. (10 Nm).
7. Install the hub assembly to the vehicle.
8. Install the tounged washer and hub nut. Tighten to 166 ft. lbs. (230 Nm) on Summit Wagon or 166–188 ft. lbs. (230–260 Nm) on the remaining models. Crimp at the indentation and install the grease cap.
9. Install the wheel speed sensor.
10. Install the wheel and tire.
11. Lower the vehicle to the ground.

All Wheel Drive

EXCEPT SUMMIT WAGON

1. Disconnect the negative battery cable. Raise and safely support the vehicle.
2. Remove the wheel and tire.
3. Disconnect the parking brake cable at the caliper or shoes.
4. Remove the speed sensor and its O-ring. Disconnect sufficient clamps and wire ties to allow the sensor to be moved well out of the work area.

NOTE: The speed sensor has a pole piece projecting from it. This exposed tip must be protected from impact or scratches. Do not allow the pole piece to contact the toothed wheel during removal or installation.

5. Remove the brake caliper and brake disc.
6. Remove the 3 retaining nuts and bolts holding the outer end of the driveshaft to the companion flange.

Swing the axle shaft away and support it with stiff wire. Do not overextend the joint in the axle; do not allow it to hang of its own weight.
7. Remove the retaining nut and washer on the back of the driveshaft. Use special tool MB990767 or equivalent, to counterhold the hub.
8. Remove the companion flange from the knuckle.
9. Using an axle puller which bolts to the wheel lugs, remove the axle shaft assembly.
10. Fit the shaft assembly in a press with the toothed wheel completely supported by a bearing plate such as special tool MB990560 or equivalent.
11. Press the toothed wheel off the axle shaft.

To install:
12. Press the new toothed wheel onto the shaft with the groove facing the axle shaft flange.
13. Install the axle shaft to the knuckle and fit the companion flange in place.
14. Install the lock washer and a new self-locking nut on the axle shaft. Hold the axle shaft stationary and torque nut to 116–159 ft. lbs. (160–220 Nm) for Laser, Talon and 1991 non-turbocharged Stealth. Torque to 188–217 ft. lbs. (260–300 Nm) for 1991 turbocharged Stealth. On 1992–93 Stealth, torque the nut to 188–217 ft. lbs. (260–300 Nm).
15. Swing the axle assembly into place and install the nuts and bolts. Tighten each to 45 ft. lbs. (61 Nm).
16. Install the brake disc and caliper.
17. Install the wheel speed sensor. Always use a new O-ring.
18. Connect the parking brake cable to the caliper.
19. Install the wheel and tire; lower the vehicle to the ground.

Summit Wagon

1. Disconnect negative battery cable.
2. Raise and safely support the vehicle. Remove the tire and wheel assembly.
3. Remove the cotter pin, cover and driveshaft nut.
4. Remove the speed sensor and its O-ring. Disconnect sufficient clamps and wire ties to allow the sensor to be moved well out of the work area.

NOTE: The speed sensor has a pole piece projecting from it. This exposed tip must be protected from impact or scratches. Do not allow the pole piece to contact the toothed wheel during removal or installation.

5. Remove the rear drive shaft from the vehicle.
6. Fit the shaft assembly in a press with the toothed wheel completely

supported by a bearing plate such as special tool MB990560 or equivalent.
7. Press the toothed wheel off the axle shaft.

To install:
8. Press the new toothed wheel onto the shaft with the groove facing the axle shaft flange.
9. Install the axle on vehicle. Tighten the inner flange retainers to 40–47 ft. lbs. (55–65 Nm).
10. Install the driveshaft nut and torque to 145–188 ft. lbs. (200–260 Nm). Secure using new cotter pin.
11. Install the speed sensor and secure the wiring harness in its' original location. Always use a new O-ring.
12. Install the tire and wheel assembly.

CHASSIS ELECTRICAL

Air Bag

DISARMING

1. Position the front wheels in the straight-ahead position and place the key in the LOCK position. Remove the key from the ignition lock cylinder.
2. Disconnect the negative battery cable and insulate the cable end with high-quality electrical tape or similar non-conductive wrapping.
3. Wait at least 1 minute before working on the vehicle. The air bag system is designed to retain enough voltage to deploy the air bag for a short period of time even after the battery has been disconnected.
4. If necessary, enter the vehicle from the passenger side and turn the key to unlock the steering column.

Heater Blower Motor

REMOVAL & INSTALLATION

Summit and Summit Wagon

1. Disconnect the negative battery cable.
2. Remove the glove box assembly and pry off the speaker cover to the lower right of the glove box.
3. Remove the passenger side lower cowl side trim kick panel.
4. Remove the passenger side knee protector, which is the panel surrounding in the glove box opening.
5. Remove the glove frame along top of glove box opening.
6. Remove the lap heater duct. This is a small piece on vehicles without a

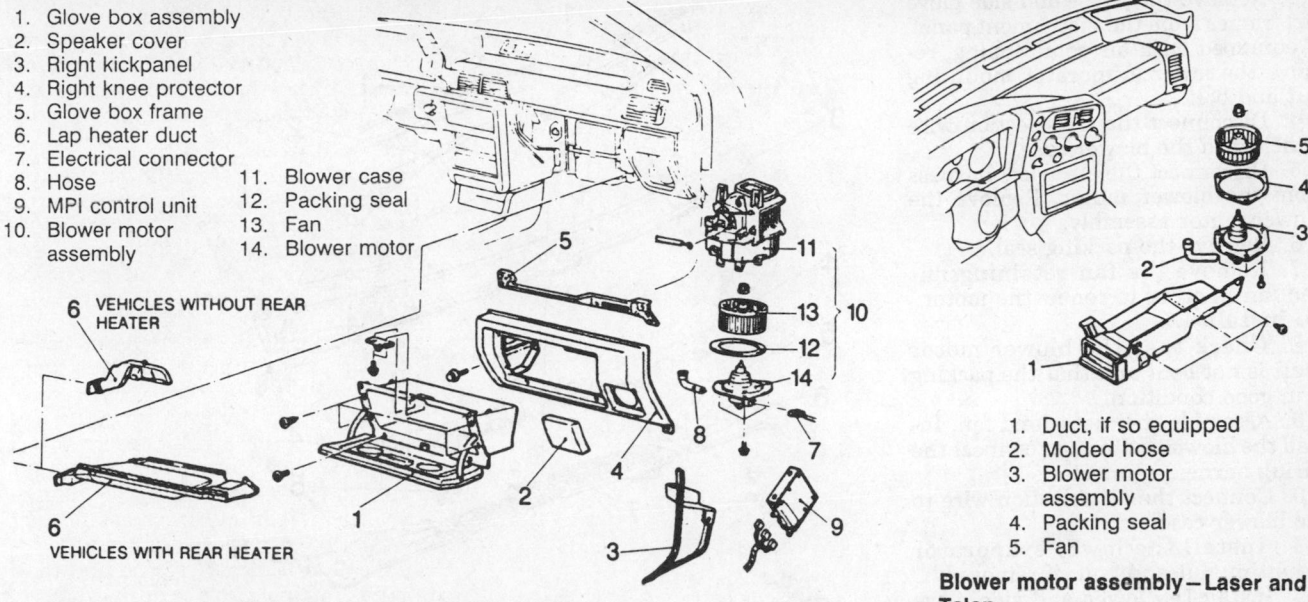

1. Glove box assembly
2. Speaker cover
3. Right kickpanel
4. Right knee protector
5. Glove box frame
6. Lap heater duct
7. Electrical connector
8. Hose
9. MPI control unit
10. Blower motor assembly
11. Blower case
12. Packing seal
13. Fan
14. Blower motor

Blower motor assembly—Summit

1. Duct, if so equipped
2. Molded hose
3. Blower motor assembly
4. Packing seal
5. Fan

Blower motor assembly—Laser and Talon

rear heater and much larger on vehicles with a rear heater.

7. Disconnect the electrical connector from the blower motor.

8. Remove the cooling tube from the blower assembly.

9. On Summit, remove the Multi-Point Injection (MPI) control unit from the lower side of the cowl.

10. Remove the blower motor assembly.

11. Separate the blower assembly case and packing seal from the blower motor flange.

12. Remove the fan retaining nut and fan in order to renew the motor.

To install:

13. Check that the blower motor shaft is not bent and that the packing and blower case are in good condition.

14. Assemble the fan and motor.

15. Install the blower assembly and connect the wiring and cooling tube.

16. Install the MPI control unit as required.

17. Install the lap heater duct.

18. Install the glove box frame, interior trim pieces and glove box assembly.

19. Connect the negative battery cable and check the entire climate control system for proper operation.

Laser and Talon

1. Disconnect the negative battery cable.

NOTE: If equipped with an air bag, be sure to disarm it before working on the vehicle. Failure to disarm an air bag could result in personal injury or death.

2. Remove the right side duct, if equipped.

3. Remove the cooling tube from the blower assembly.

4. Remove the blower motor assembly.

5. Remove the packing seal.

6. Remove the fan retaining nut and fan in order to renew the motor.

To install:

7. Check that the blower motor shaft is not bent and that the packing is in good condition.

8. Assemble the motor and fan. Install the blower motor and connect the wiring harness connector.

9. Install the cooling tube.

10. Install the right side duct, if equipped.

11. Connect the negative battery cable and check the entire climate control system for proper operation.

Stealth

1. Disconnect the negative battery cable.

NOTE: If equipped with an air bag, be sure to disarm it before working on the vehicle. Failure to disarm an air bag could result in personal injury or death.

2. Remove glove box, glove box outer case and the instrument panel undercover.

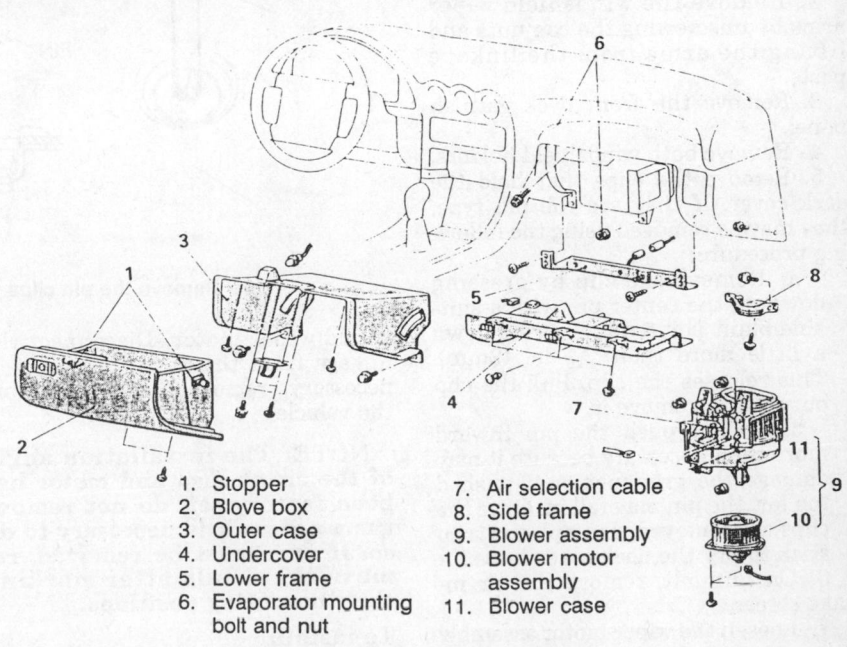

1. Stopper
2. Blove box
3. Outer case
4. Undercover
5. Lower frame
6. Evaporator mounting bolt and nut
7. Air selection cable
8. Side frame
9. Blower assembly
10. Blower motor assembly
11. Blower case

Blower motor assembly—Stealth

3. Remove the lower and side glove box frames from the instrument panel. If equipped with air conditioning, remove the lower evaporator mounting nut and bolt.

4. Disconnect the air selection wire attached to the blower case.

5. Disconnect the electrical harness from the blower motor. Remove the blower motor assembly.

6. Remove the packing seal.

7. Remove the fan retaining nut and fan in order to renew the motor.

To install:

8. Check that the blower motor shaft is not bent and that the packing is in good condition.

9. Assemble the motor and fan. Install the blower motor and connect the wiring harness connector.

10. Connect the air selection wire to the blower case.

11. Install the lower evaporator mounting nut and bolt, if removed.

12. Install the lower and side glove box frames to the instrument panel.

13. Install glove box, glove box outer case and the instrument panel undercover.

14. Reconnect the negative battery cable. Check the entire climate control system for proper operation.

Windshield Wiper Motor

REMOVAL & INSTALLATION

Summit and Summit Wagon

FRONT

1. Disconnect the negative battery cable.

2. Remove the windshield wiper arms by unscrewing the cap nuts and lifting the arms from the linkage posts.

3. Remove the front deck garnish panel.

4. Remove both windshield holders.

5. Remove the clips that hold the deck cover. If they are the pin type, they may be removed using the following procedure:

   a. Remove the clip by pressing down on the center pin with a suitable blunt pointed tool. Press down a little more than $\frac{1}{16}$ in. (2mm). This releases the clip. Pull the clip outward to remove it.

   b. Do not push the pin inward more than necessary because it may damage the grommet or if pushed too far, the pin may fall in. Once the clips are removed, use a plastic trim stick to pry the deck cover loose.

6. On Summit, remove the air intake screen.

7. Loosen the wiper motor assembly mounting bolts and remove the wind-

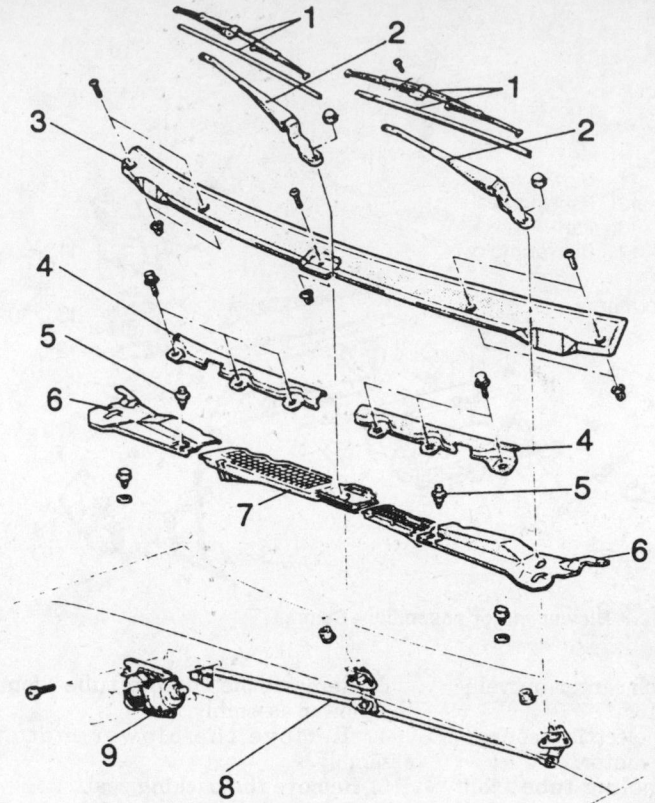

1. Wiper blades
2. Wiper arms
3. Front deck garnish
4. Windshield holder
5. Pin type trim clip
6. Deck cover
7. Air intake screen
8. Wiper linkage
9. Wiper motor

Windshield wiper assembly—Summit

PIN TYPE TRIM CLIP

REMOVAL   INSTALLATION

TRIM

PIN

2 MM (.080 IN.)

GROMMET

Remove the pin clips with care so they can be reused

shield wiper motor. Disconnect the linkage from the motor assembly. If necessary, remove the linkage from the vehicle.

NOTE: The installation angle of the crank arm and motor has been factory set, do not remove them unless it is necessary to do so. If arm must be removed, remove them only after marking their mounting positions.

To install:

8. Install the windshield wiper mo-

tor and connect the linkage. Connect the electrical harness to the motor.

9. When installing the trim and garnish pieces and reusing pin type clips, use the following procedure:

   a. With the pin pulled out, insert the trim clip into the hole in the trim.

   b. Push the pin inward until the pin's head is flush with the grommet.

   c. Check that the trim is secure.

10. Install the wiper arms and tighten nuts to 17 ft. lbs. (24 Nm).

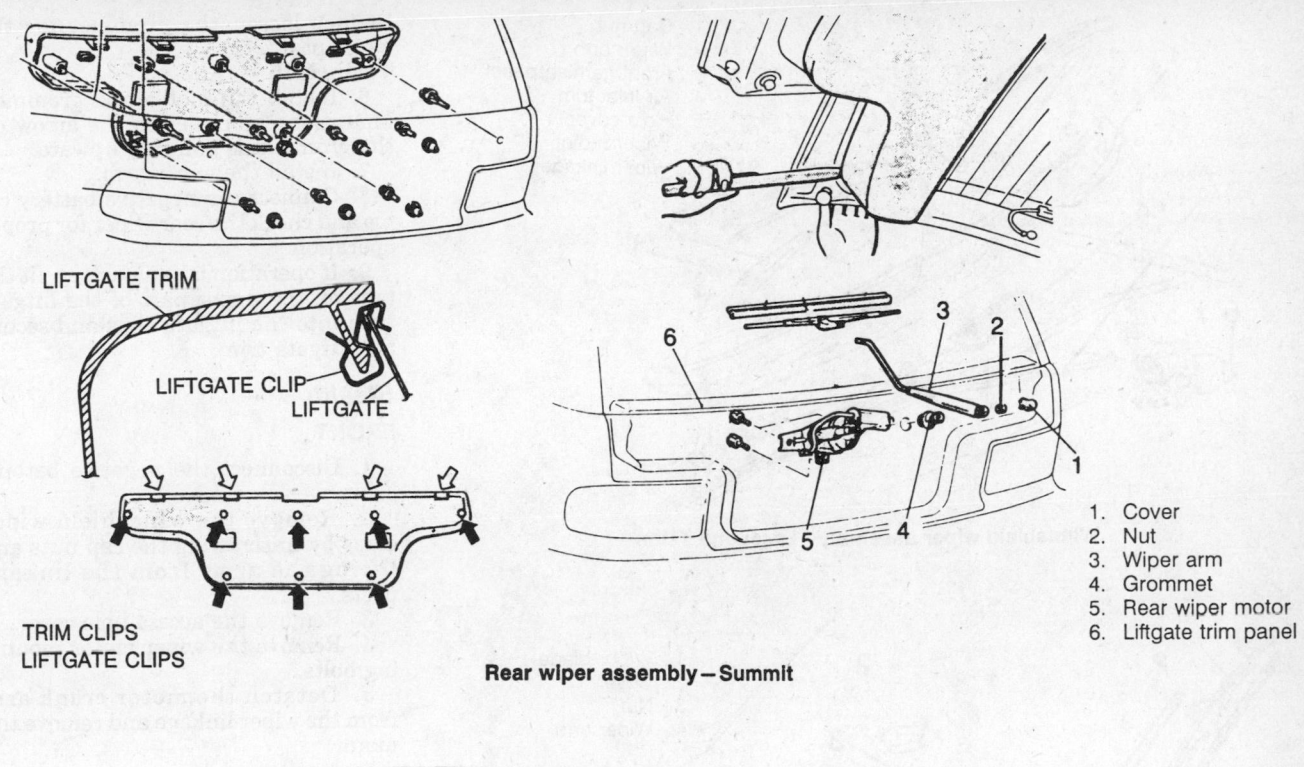

LIFTGATE TRIM

LIFTGATE CLIP

LIFTGATE

TRIM CLIPS
LIFTGATE CLIPS

1. Cover
2. Nut
3. Wiper arm
4. Grommet
5. Rear wiper motor
6. Liftgate trim panel

Rear wiper assembly—Summit

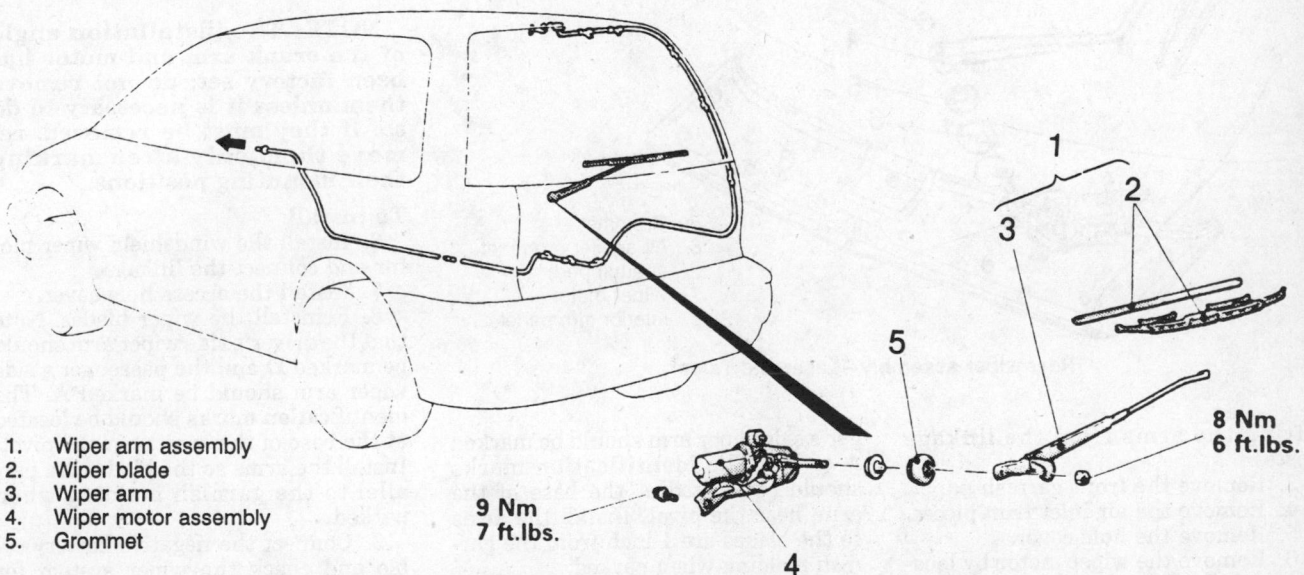

1. Wiper arm assembly
2. Wiper blade
3. Wiper arm
4. Wiper motor assembly
5. Grommet

8 Nm
6 ft.lbs.

9 Nm
7 ft.lbs.

Rear wiper motor and related components—1992–93 Summit Wagon

11. Connect the negative battery cable and check the wiper system for proper operation.

REAR

1. Disconnect the negative battery cable.

2. Remove the rear wiper arm by removing the cap nut cover, unscrewing the cap nut and lifting the arm from the linkage post.

3. Remove the large interior trim panel. Use a plastic trim stick to unhook the trim clips of the liftgate trim.

There will be a row of metal liftgate clips across the top. There will be 2 rows of trim clips that retain the rest of the panel.

4. Disconnect the electrical harness at the wiper motor. Remove the rear wiper assembly. Do not loosen the grommet for the wiper post.

To install:

5. Install the motor and grommet. Mount the grommet so the arrow on the grommet is pointing downward.

6. Install the wiper arm.

7. Connect the negative battery ca-

ble and check rear wiper system for proper operation.

8. If operation is satisfactory, fit the tabs on the upper part of the liftgate trim into the liftgate clips and secure the liftgate trim.

Laser and Talon

FRONT

1. Disconnect the negative battery cable.

2. Remove the windshield wiper arms by unscrewing the cap nuts and

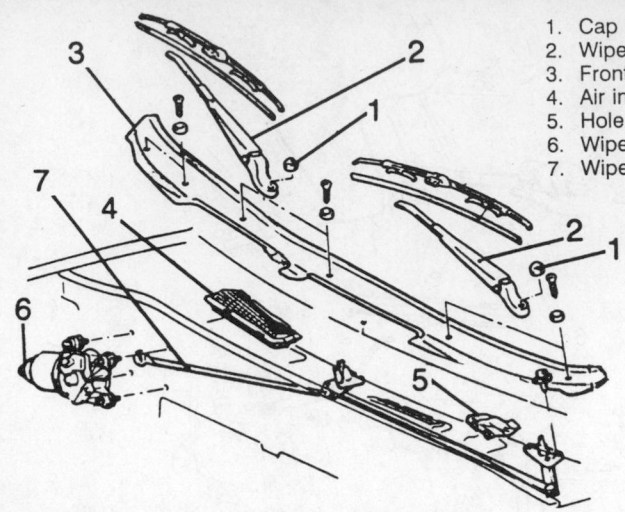

1. Cap nut
2. Wiper arm
3. Front garnish panel
4. Air inlet trim
5. Hole cover
6. Wiper motor
7. Wiper linkage

Windshield wiper assembly—Laser and Talon

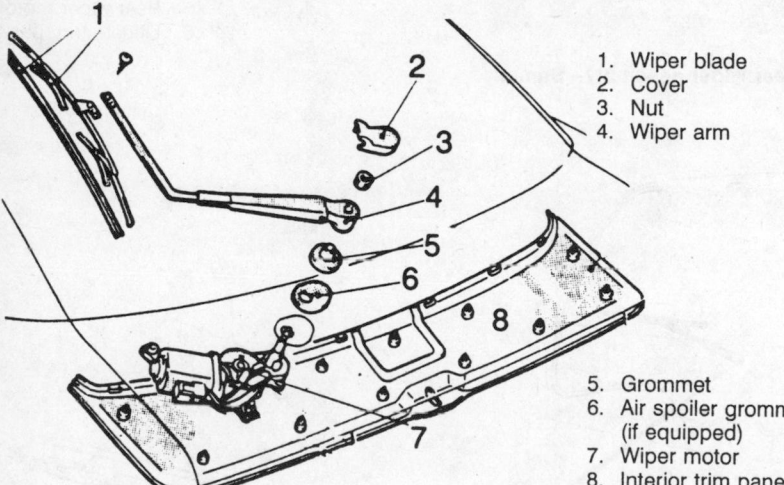

1. Wiper blade
2. Cover
3. Nut
4. Wiper arm

5. Grommet
6. Air spoiler grommet (if equipped)
7. Wiper motor
8. Interior trim panel

Rear wiper assembly—Laser and Talon

lifting the arms from the linkage posts.

3. Remove the front garnish panel.
4. Remove the air inlet trim pieces.
5. Remove the hole cover.
6. Remove the wiper motor by loosening the mounting bolts, removing the motor assembly, then disconnecting the linkage.

NOTE: The installation angle of the crank arm and motor has been factory set; do not remove them unless it is necessary to do so. If they must be removed, remove them only after marking their mounting positions.

To install:

7. Install the windshield wiper motor and connect the linkage.
8. Reinstall all trim pieces.
9. Reinstall the wiper blades. Note that the driver's side wiper arm should be marked **D** or **Dr** and the passen-

ger's side wiper arm should be marked **A** or **As**. The identification marks should be located at the base of the arm, near the pivot. Install the arms so the blades are 1 inch from the garnish molding when parked.
10. Connect the negative battery cable and check the wiper system for proper operation.

REAR

1. Disconnect the negative battery cable.
2. Remove the rear wiper arm by removing the cover, unscrewing the nut and lifting the arm from the linkage post.
3. Remove the large interior trim panel. Use a plastic trim stick to unhook the trim clips of the liftgate trim.
4. If equipped with rear air spoiler, remove the wiper grommet.
5. Remove the rear wiper assembly.

Do not loosen the grommet for the wiper post.

To install:

6. Install the motor and grommet. Mount the grommet so the arrow on the grommet is pointing upward.
7. Install the wiper arm.
8. Connect the negative battery cable and check the rear wiper for proper operation.
9. If operation is satisfactory, fit the tabs on the upper part of the liftgate trim into the liftgate clips and secure the liftgate trim.

Stealth

FRONT

1. Disconnect the negative battery cable.
2. Remove the windshield wiper arms by unscrewing the cap nuts and lifting the arms from the linkage posts.
3. Remove the access hole cover.
4. Remove the wiper motor mounting bolts.
5. Detach the motor crank arm from the wiper linkage and remove the motor.

NOTE: The installation angle of the crank arm and motor has been factory set; do not remove them unless it is necessary to do so. If they must be removed, remove them only after marking their mounting positions.

To install:

6. Install the windshield wiper motor and connect the linkage.
7. Install the access hole cover.
8. Reinstall the wiper blades. Note that the driver's side wiper arm should be marked **D** and the passenger's side wiper arm should be marked **A**. The identification marks should be located at the base of the arm, near the pivot. Install the arms so the blades are parallel to the garnish molding when parked.
9. Connect the negative battery cable and check the wiper system for proper operation.

REAR

1. Disconnect the negative battery cable.
2. Remove the liftgate lower trim. Remove the clips that hold the trim by using the following procedure:
   a. Remove the clip by pressing down on the center pin with a blunt pointed tool. Press down a little more than 1/16 in. (2mm). This releases the clip. Pull the clip outward to remove it.
   b. Do not push the pin inward more than necessary because it may damage the grommet or if pushed too far, the pin may fall in. Once the

1. Wiper blade
2. Wiper arm
3. Deck garnish
4. Right side air inlet garnish
5. Hole cover
6. Wiper cover
7. Linkage
8. Battery
9. Battery tay
10. Washer tank
11. Washer motor
12. Level sensor
13. Washer nozzle
14. Washer tube

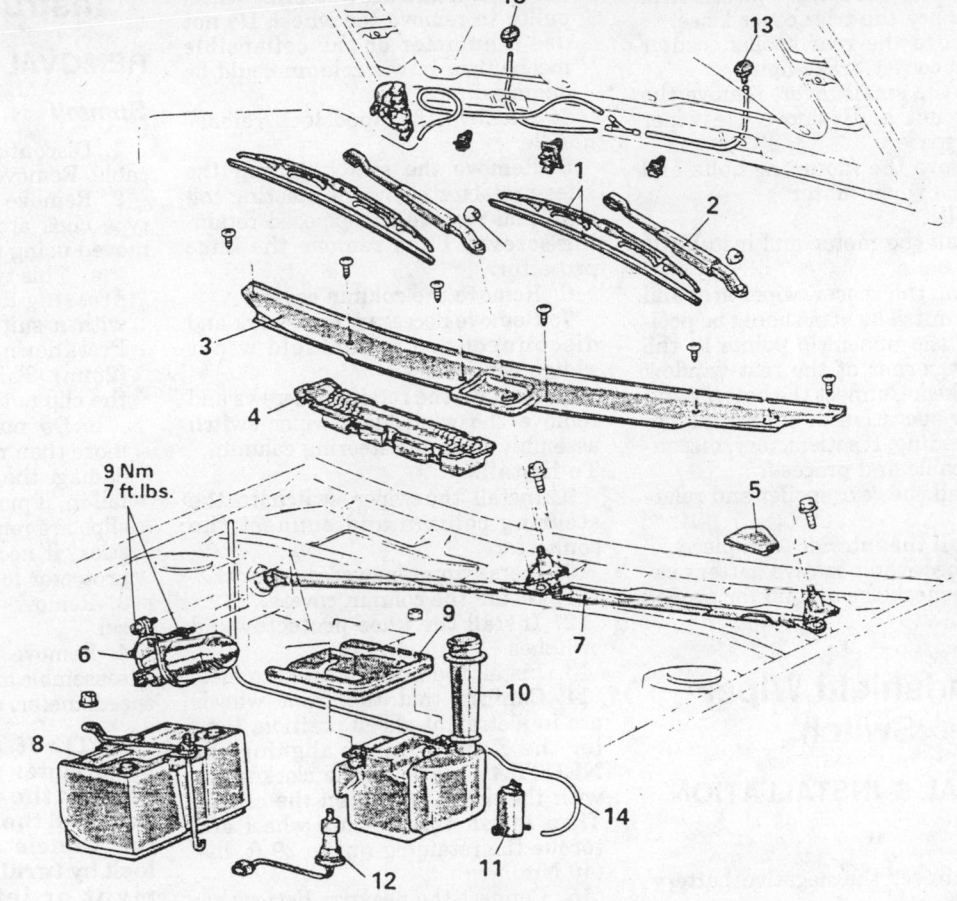

Windshield wiper assembly—Stealth

1. Wiper blade
2. Wiper arm
3. Spacer
4. Wiper motor
5. Cap
6. Washer tank
7. Washer motor
8. Upper liftgate molding
9. Washer nozzle
10. Tube and grommet
11. Washer tube

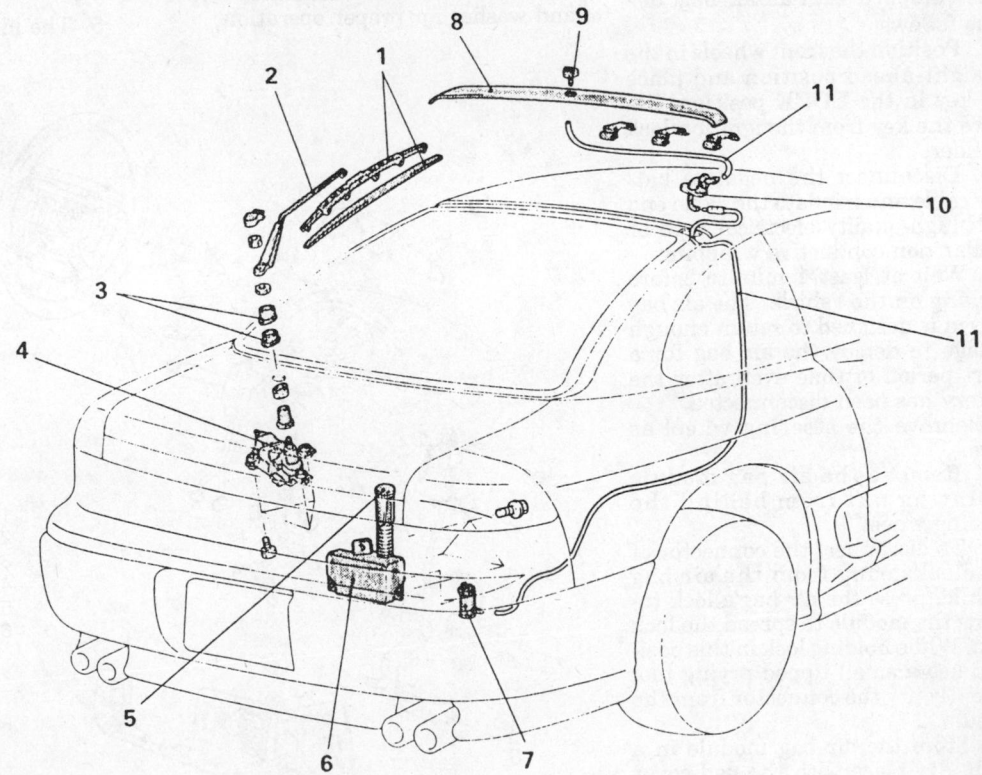

Rear wiper and washer assemblies—Stealth

clips are removed, use a plastic trim stick to pry the trim cover loose.

3. Remove the rear spoiler, center brace and center brake light.

4. Lift the small cover, remove the retaining nut and remove the wiper arm and spacer.

5. Remove the mounting bolts and remove the wiper motor.

To install:

6. Install the motor and install the retaining bolts.

7. Install the spacer, wiper arm and retaining nut. The arm should be positioned so the upper tip points to the upper left corner of the rear window when parked. Connect the battery and check the operation of the motor before proceeding. If satisfactory, disconnect the cable and proceed.

8. Install the rear spoiler and related parts.

9. Install the interior trim piece.

10. Connect the negative battery cable and recheck the system for proper operation.

Windshield Wiper Switch

REMOVAL & INSTALLATION

Stealth

1. Disconnect the negative battery cable.

2. If equipped with an air bag, disarm as follows:

a. Position the front wheels in the straight-ahead position and place the key in the **LOCK** position. Remove the key from the ignition lock cylinder.

b. Disconnect the negative battery cable and insulate the cable end with high-quality electrical tape or similar non-conductive wrapping.

c. Wait at least 1 minute before working on the vehicle. The air bag system is designed to retain enough voltage to deploy the air bag for a short period of time even after the battery has been disconnected.

3. Remove the steering wheel as follows:

a. Remove the air bag module mounting nut from behind the steering wheel.

b. To disconnect the connector of the clockspring from the air bag module, press the air bag's lock towards the module to spread the lock open. While holding lock in this position, use a small tipped prying tool to gently pry the connector from the module.

c. Store the air bag module in a clean, dry place with the pad cover facing up.

d. Remove the steering wheel re-

taining nut and use a steering wheel puller to remove the wheel. Do not use a hammer or the collapsible mechanism in the column could be damaged.

4. Remove the hood lock release handle.

5. Remove the switches from the knee protector below the steering column and remove the exposed retaining screws. Then remove the knee protector.

6. Remove the column covers.

7. Remove necessary duct work and disconnect the windshield wiper switch connectors.

8. Remove the retaining screws and remove the windshield wiper switch assembly from the steering column.

To install:

9. Install the wiper switch to the steering column and connect the connectors.

10. Install any removed duct work.

11. Install the column covers.

12. Install the knee protector and switches.

13. Install the hood release handle.

14. Confirm that the front wheels are in a straight-ahead position. Center the clockspring by aligning the **NEUTRAL** mark on the clockspring with the mating mark on the casing. Then install the steering wheel and torque the retaining nut to 29 ft. lbs. (40 Nm).

15. Connect the negative battery cable and check the windshield wiper and washer for proper operation.

Instrument Cluster

REMOVAL & INSTALLATION

Summit

1. Disconnect the negative battery cable. Remove the center trim panel.

2. Remove the knee protector. If pin type clips are used, they may be removed using the following procedure:

a. This type of clip is removed by pressing down on the center pin with a suitable blunt pointed tool. Press down a little more than $1/16$ in. (2mm). This releases the clip. Pull the clip outward to remove it.

b. Do not push the pin inward more than necessary because it may damage the grommet or the pin may fall in, if pushed in too far. Once the clips are removed, use a plastic trim stick, if necessary, to pry the knee protector loose.

3. Remove the instrument cluster bezel.

4. Remove the instrument cluster. Disassemble and remove gauges or the speedometer, as required.

NOTE: If the speedometer cable adapter requires service, disconnect the cable at the transaxle end. Pull the cable slightly toward the vehicle interior, release the lock by turning the adapter to the right or left and remove the adapter.

5. The installation is the reverse of

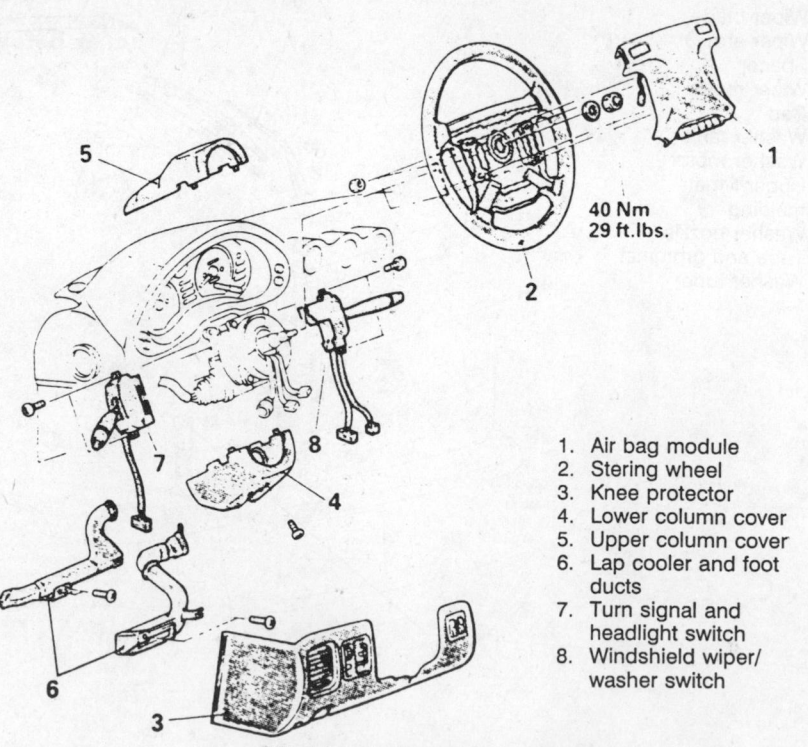

40 Nm
29 ft.lbs.

1. Air bag module
2. Stering wheel
3. Knee protector
4. Lower column cover
5. Upper column cover
6. Lap cooler and foot ducts
7. Turn signal and headlight switch
8. Windshield wiper/ washer switch

Windshield wiper switch—Stealth

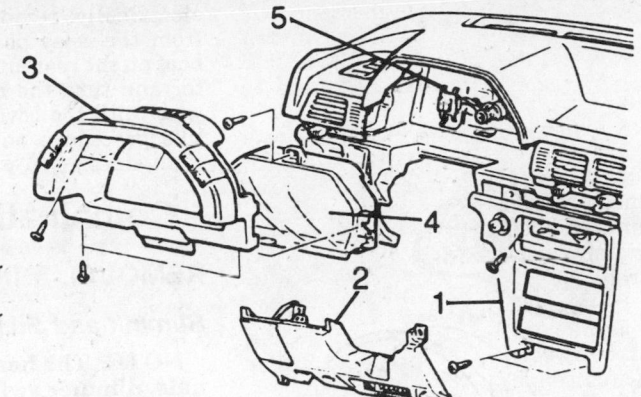

1. Center panel
2. Knee protector
3. Instrument cluster bezel
4. Instrument cluster
5. Speedometer adapter

Instrument cluster assembly—Summit

the removal procedure. Use care not to damage the printed circuit board or any gauge components.

6. Connect the negative battery cable and check all cluster-related items for proper operation.

Summit Wagon

1. Disconnect negative battery cable.

2. Remove the 2 retainer screws on the lower surface of the meter hood.

3. Remove the retainer screws from the under side top portion of the meter hood.

4. Carefully remove the meter hood from the face of the combination meter.

5. Remove the 4 retainer screws and the combination meter assembly with the bezel attached. Remove the front bezel and remove gauges or the speedometer as required.

NOTE: If the speedometer cable adapter requires service, disconnect the cable at the transaxle end. Pull the cable slightly toward the vehicle interior, release the lock by turning the adapter to the right or left and remove the adapter.

6. The installation is the reverse of the removal procedure. Use care not to damage the printed circuit board or any gauge components.

7. Connect the negative battery cable and check all cluster-related items for proper operation.

Laser and Talon

1. Disconnect the negative battery cable.

NOTE: If equipped with an air bag, be sure to disarm it before entering the vehicle.

2. Remove the screw cover on the side of the cluster panel assembly.

3. Remove the front instrument cluster bezel.

4. Remove the instrument cluster. Disassemble and remove gauges or the speedometer as required.

NOTE: If the speedometer cable adapter requires service, disconnect the cable at the transaxle end. Pull the cable slightly toward the vehicle interior, release the lock by turning the adapter to the right or left and remove the adapter.

5. The installation is the reverse of the removal procedure. Use care not to damage the printed circuit board or any gauge components.

6. Connect the negative battery cable and check all cluster-related items for proper operation.

Stealth

1. Disconnect the negative battery cable.

NOTE: If equipped with an air bag, be sure to disarm it before entering the vehicle.

2. Remove the hood lock release handle and switches from the knee protector below the steering column. Then remove the exposed retaining screws and remove the knee protector.

3. Remove the upper and the lower steering column covers.

4. Remove the instrument cluster bezel.

5. Remove the instrument cluster. Disassemble and remove gauges or the speedometer as required.

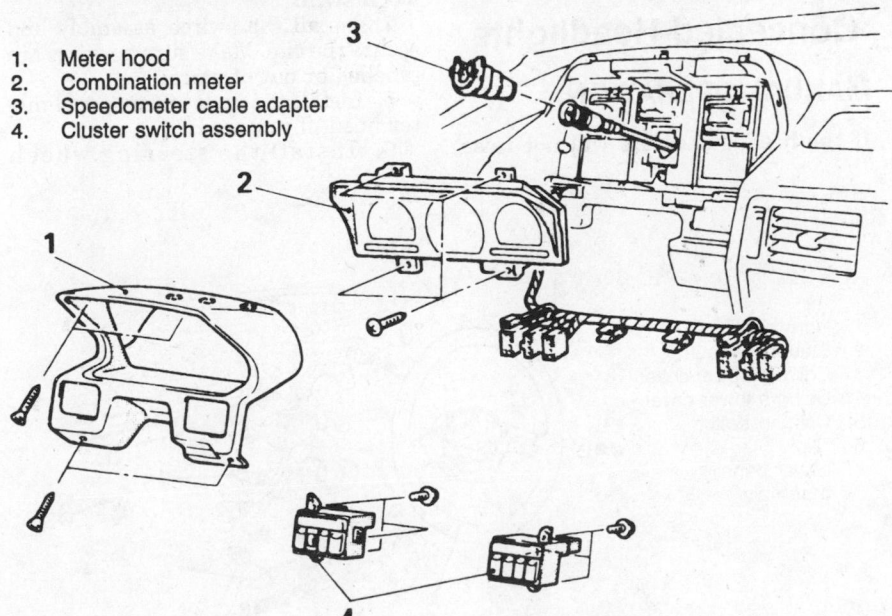

1. Meter hood
2. Combination meter
3. Speedometer cable adapter
4. Cluster switch assembly

Instrument cluster and related components—1992–93 Summit Wagon

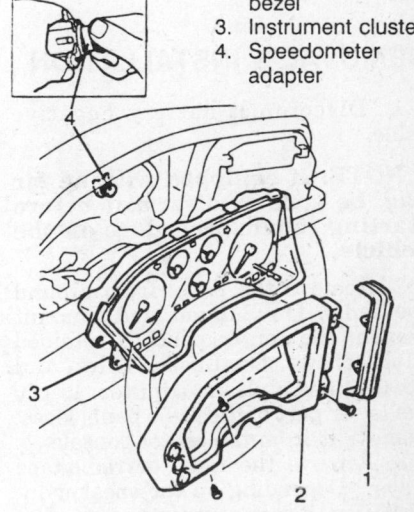

1. Screw cover
2. Instrument cluster bezel
3. Instrument cluster
4. Speedometer adapter

Instrument cluster assembly—Laser and Talon

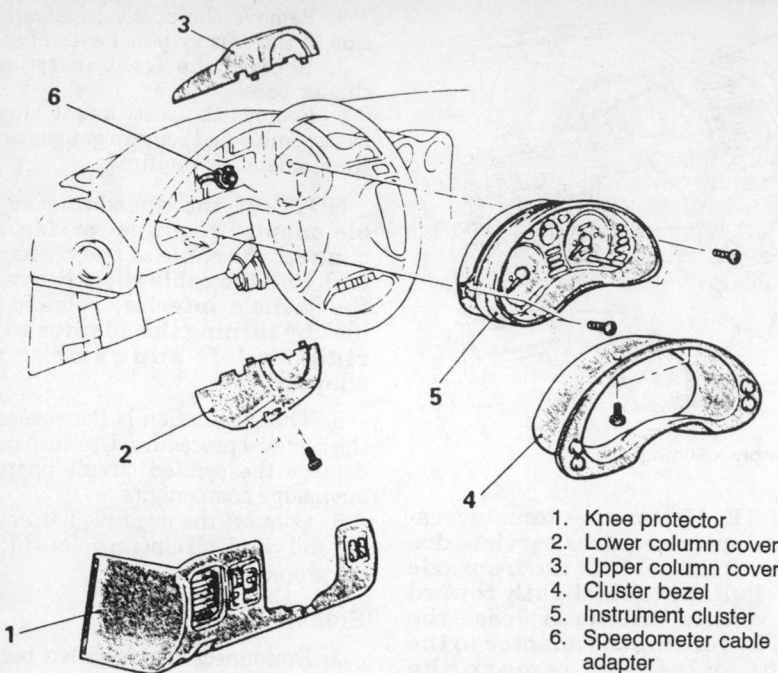

1. Knee protector
2. Lower column cover
3. Upper column cover
4. Cluster bezel
5. Instrument cluster
6. Speedometer cable adapter

Instrument cluster assembly—Stealth

NOTE: If the speedometer cable adapter must be serviced, disconnect the cable at the transaxle end. Pull the cable slightly toward the vehicle interior, release the lock by turning the adapter to the right or left and remove the adapter.

6. The installation is the reverse of the removal procedure. Use care not to damage the printed circuit board or any gauge components.

7. Connect the negative battery cable and check all cluster-related items for proper operation.

Radio

REMOVAL & INSTALLATION

1. Disconnect battery negative cable.

NOTE: If equipped with an air bag, be sure to disarm it before starting repair procedure on the vehicle.

2. Remove the panel from around the radio. On Summit and Summit Wagon, the center panel is retained with screws. On Laser, Talon and Stealth, use a plastic trim tool to pry the lower part of the radio panel loose. Remove it from the center console.

3. Remove the radio or radio/tape player. Depending on the speaker installation, it may save time at installation to identify and tag all wires before they are disconnected.

4. Separate amplifiers and/or CD player can be removed by first removing the side cover of the console box.

5. Remove the mounting brackets from the radio.

To install:

6. The installation is the reverse of the removal procedure. Make all electrical and antenna connections before fastening the radio assembly in place.

7. Install the center panel.

8. Connect the negative battery cable and check the entire audio system for proper operation.

Concealed Headlights

MANUAL OPERATION

If the headlight covers will not raise

electrically, remove the fusible link from the relay box, then remove the boot on the rear area of the pop-up motor and turn the manual knob clockwise until the cover is open. Perform this procedure on both the left and right sides.

Combination Switch

REMOVAL & INSTALLATION

Summit and Summit Wagon

NOTE: The headlights, turn signals, dimmer switch, horn switch, windshield wiper/washer, intermittent wiper switch and on some models, the cruise control function are all built into 1 multi-function combination switch that is mounted on the steering column.

1. Disconnect the negative battery cable.

2. Remove the knee protector panel under the steering column, then the upper and lower column covers. On Summit Wagon, remove the instrument panel under cover.

3. Remove the horn pad by pulling the lower end outward.

4. Matchmark and remove the steering wheel with a steering wheel puller. Do not hammer on the steering wheel to remove it or the collapsible mechanism may be damaged.

5. On Summit Wagon, remove the meter hood to gain clearance between the combination switch and the instrument panel, if required.

6. Disconnect all connectors, remove the wiring clip and remove the column switch assembly.

To install:

7. Install the switch assembly and secure the clip. Make sure no wires are pinched or out of place.

8. Install the instrument panel meter hood, if removed.

9. Install the steering wheel.

1. Horn pad
2. Steering wheel
3. Column upper cover
4. Column lower cover
5. Column switch
6. Clip
7. Lower panel assembly

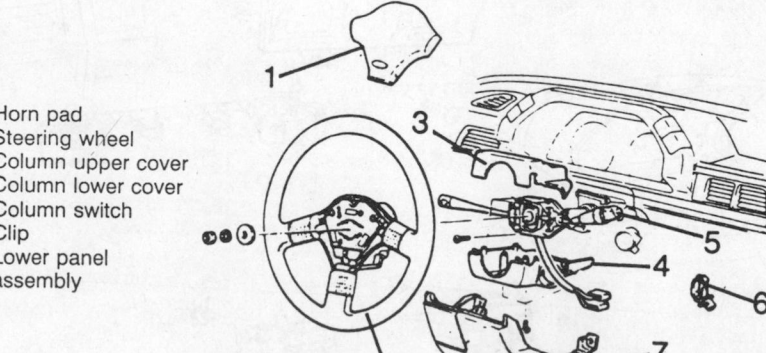

Combination switch assembly—Summit

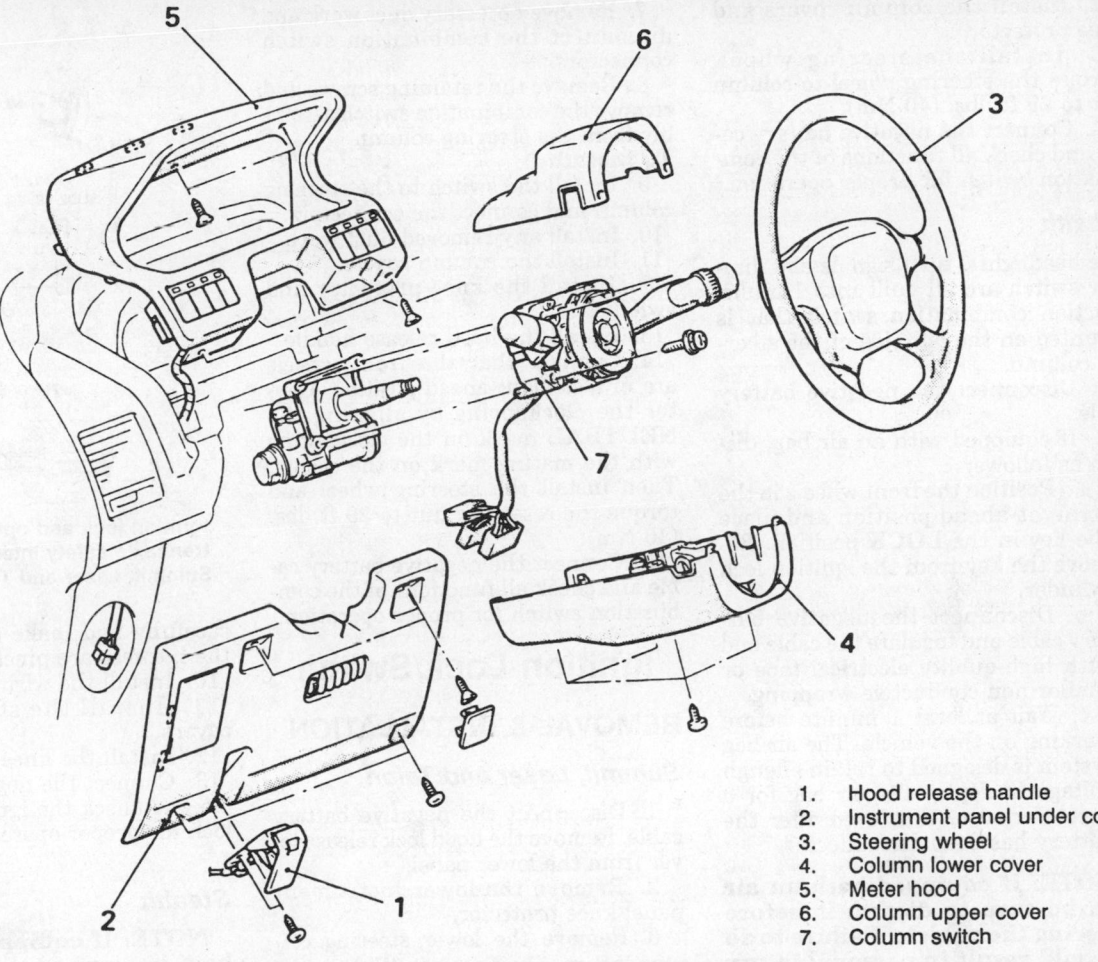

1. Hood release handle
2. Instrument panel under cover
3. Steering wheel
4. Column lower cover
5. Meter hood
6. Column upper cover
7. Column switch

Combination switch and related components—1992–93 Summit Wagon

Torque the steering wheel-to-column nut to 29 ft. lbs. (40 Nm).

10. Install the column covers and knee protector.

11. Connect the negative battery cable and check all functions of the combination switch for proper operation.

Laser and Talon

NOTE: The headlights, turn signals, dimmer switch, windshield/washer and, on some models, the cruise control function are all built into 1 multi-function combination switch that is mounted on the steering column.

1. Disconnect the negative battery cable.

2. Remove the knee protector panel under the steering column, then the upper and lower column covers.

3. Remove the horn pad attaching screw on the under side of the steering wheel and remove the horn pad by pushing the pad upward.

4. Matchmark and remove the steering wheel with a steering wheel puller. Do not hammer on the steering

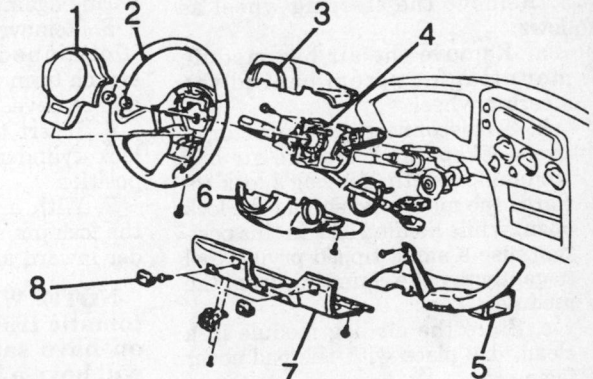

1. Horn pad
2. Steering wheel
3. Column upper cover
4. Column switch
5. Cooler duct
6. Column lower cover
7. Knee protector
8. Screw plugs

Combination switch assembly—Laser and Talon

wheel to remove it or the collapsible mechanism may be damaged.

5. Locate the rectangular plugs in the knee protector on either side of the steering column. Pry these plugs out and remove the screws. Remove the screws from the hood lock release lever and remove the knee protector.

6. Remove the upper and lower column covers.

7. Remove the lap cooler ducts.

8. Remove the band retaining the switch wiring.

9. Disconnect all connectors, remove the wiring clip and remove the column switch assembly.

To install:

10. Install the switch assembly and secure the clip. Make sure no wires are pinched or out of place.

11. Install the lap cooler ducts.

12. Install the column covers and knee protector.

13. Install the steering wheel. Torque the steering wheel-to-column nut to 29 ft. lbs. (40 Nm).

14. Connect the negative battery cable and check all functions of the combination switch for proper operation.

Stealth

The headlights, turn signals and dimmer switch are all built into 1 multifunction combination switch that is mounted on the left side of the steering column.

1. Disconnect the negative battery cable.

2. If equipped with an air bag, disarm as follows:

a. Position the front wheels in the straight-ahead position and place the key in the **LOCK** position. Remove the key from the ignition lock cylinder.

b. Disconnect the negative battery cable and insulate the cable end with high-quality electrical tape or similar non-conductive wrapping.

c. Wait at least 1 minute before working on the vehicle. The air bag system is designed to retain enough voltage to deploy the air bag for a short period of time even after the battery has been disconnected.

NOTE: If equipped with an air bag, be sure to disarm it before entering the vehicle. Failure to do so could result in personal injury or death.

3. Remove the steering wheel as follows:

a. Remove the air bag module mounting nut from behind the steering wheel.

b. To disconnect the connector of the clockspring from the air bag module, press the air bag's lock towards the module to spread the lock open. While holding lock in this position, use a small tipped prying tool to gently pry the connector from the module.

c. Store the air bag module in a clean, dry place with the pad cover facing up.

d. Remove the steering wheel retaining nut and use a steering wheel puller to remove the wheel. Do not use a hammer or the collapsible mechanism in the column could be damaged.

4. Remove the hood lock release handle.

5. Remove the switches from the knee protector below the steering column and remove the exposed retaining screws. Then remove the knee protector.

6. Remove the column covers.

7. Remove necessary duct work and disconnect the combination switch connectors.

8. Remove the retaining screws and remove the combination switch assembly from the steering column.

To install:

9. Install the switch to the steering column and connect the connectors.

10. Install any removed duct work.

11. Install the column covers.

12. Install the knee protector and switches.

13. Install the hood release handle.

14. Confirm that the front wheels are in a straight-ahead position. Center the clockspring by aligning the **NEUTRAL** mark on the clockspring with the mating mark on the casing. Then install the steering wheel and torque the retaining nut to 29 ft. lbs. (40 Nm).

15. Connect the negative battery cable and check all functions of the combination switch for proper operation.

Ignition Lock/Switch

REMOVAL & INSTALLATION

Summit, Laser and Talon

1. Disconnect the negative battery cable. Remove the hood lock release lever from the lower panel.

2. Remove the lower instrument panel knee protector.

3. Remove the lower steering column cover. On Summit Wagon, remove the meter hood.

4. Remove the clip that holds the wiring against the steering column.

5. Remove the key reminder switch, if equipped. Unplug the ignition switch from the steering lock cylinder and remove.

6. Insert the key into the steering lock cylinder and turn to the **ACC** position.

7. With a small pointed tool, push the lock pin of the steering lock cylinder inward and pull the lock out.

NOTE: When equipped with automatic transaxle, Laser and Talon have safety-lock systems and will have a key interlock cable installed in a slide lever on the side of the key cylinder. Carefully unhook the interlock cable from the lock cylinder while withdrawing cylinder from lock housing.

To install:

8. With the ignition key removed, install the slide lever and the interlock cable to the steering lock cylinder. Apply grease to the interlock cable and install cylinder into the lock housing. Check for normal operation of the interlock system.

9. Install the ignition switch plug

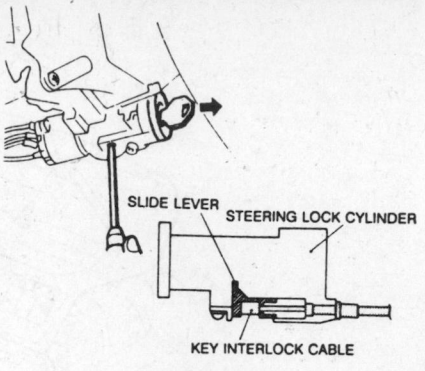

SLIDE LEVER   STEERING LOCK CYLINDER

KEY INTERLOCK CABLE

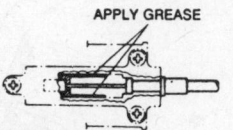

APPLY GREASE

Ignition lock and optional automatic transaxle safety interlock cable— Summit, Laser and Talon

carefully and make sure no wires in the harness are pinched.

10. Install the wiring clip.

11. Install the steering column covers.

12. Install the knee protector.

13. Connect the negative battery cable and check the ignition switch and lock for proper operation.

Stealth

NOTE: If equipped with an air bag, be sure to disarm it before starting any repairs on the vehicle.

1. Disconnect the negative battery cable.

2. If equipped with an air bag, disarm as follows:

a. Position the front wheels in the straight-ahead position and place the key in the **LOCK** position. Remove the key from the ignition lock cylinder.

b. Disconnect the negative battery cable and insulate the cable end with high-quality electrical tape or similar non-conductive wrapping.

c. Wait at least 1 minute before working on the vehicle. The air bag system is designed to retain enough voltage to deploy the air bag for a short period of time even after the battery has been disconnected.

3. If equipped with an air bag, remove the air bag module as follows:

a. Remove the air bag module mounting nut from behind the steering wheel.

b. To disconnect the connector of the clockspring from the air bag module, press the air bag's lock towards the module to spread the lock open. While holding lock in this position, use a small tipped prying tool to gently pry the connector from the module.

c. Store the air bag module in a clean, dry place with the pad cover facing up.

4. Remove the steering wheel retaining nut and use a steering wheel puller to remove the wheel. Do not use a hammer or the collapsible mechanism in the column could be damaged.

5. Remove the hood lock release handle.

6. Remove the switches from the knee protector below the steering column and remove the exposed retaining screws. Then remove the knee protector.

7. Remove the steering column upper and lower covers.

8. Remove necessary duct work and disconnect the windshield wiper and combination switch connectors.

9. Remove the retaining screws and remove the entire column switch/clockspring assembly from the steering column.

10. If damaged, remove the illumination ring, key reminder switch harness and ignition switch harness.

11. To remove the lock cylinder, insert the key and place in the **ACC** position. With a small pointed tool, push the lock pin of the steering lock cylinder inward and pull the lock out.

To install:

12. Install the lock cylinder; make sure the lock pin snaps into place.

13. Install any other removed items, making sure no wires are pinched.

14. Install the column switch/clockspring assembly to the steering column and connect the connectors.

15. Install any removed duct work.

16. Install the column covers.

17. Install the knee protector and switches.

18. Install the hood release handle.

19. Center the clockspring by aligning the **NEUTRAL** mark on the clockspring with the mating mark on the casing. Then install the steering wheel and torque the retaining nut to 29 ft. lbs. (40 Nm).

20. Connect the negative battery cable and check all functions of column-mounted switches and the ignition switch for proper operation.

Stoplight Switch

ADJUSTMENT

1. Disconnect the negative battery cable.

NOTE: If equipped with an air bag, be sure to disarm it before entering the vehicle.

2. The stoplight switch works off the brake pedal lever. To adjust, disconnect the electrical connection and loosen the switch locknut.

3. Screw the switch inward until it contacts the stop on the brake pedal arm. Back out the switch ½–1 full turn. The distance between the end of the switch plunger bore and the brake lever stop should be 0.020–0.040 in. (0.5–1.0mm).

4. Tighten the locknut and connect the wires.

5. Connect the negative battery cable.

6. Make sure the stoplights turn ON when the brake pedal is depressed and go out when the pedal is released. Also, make sure the cruise control system operates properly.

REMOVAL & INSTALLATION

1. Disconnect the negative battery cable.

NOTE: If equipped with an air bag, be sure to disarm it before starting any repairs on the vehicle.

2. Locate the stoplight switch above the brake pedal lever.

3. Disconnect the wiring connectors from the switch and unscrew the switch.

To install:

4. Thread the stop light switch into the switch holding bracket. Adjust the switch to achieve correct operation.

5. Connect the stoplight wires.

6. Connect the negative battery cable.

7. Make sure the stoplights turn ON when the brake pedal is depressed and go out when the pedal is released. Also, make sure the cruise control system operates properly.

Clutch Switch

ADJUSTMENT

The clutch interlock switch is located at the top of the clutch pedal arm. Note that there may be 2 switches; 1 will be a cruise control cut-out switch.

1. Clutch interlock switch adjustment is made with the pedal fully depressed.

2. Measure the gap between the switch plunger and the arm stop. The gap should be 0.140 in. (3.5mm).

3. If adjustment is necessary, loosen the locknut and rotate the switch until the desired clearance is obtained. Tighten locknut to lock switch in place.

4. After completing the adjustment, check that the pedal free-play, measured at the face of the pedal pad is 0.240–0.510 in. (6–13mm). The distance between the pedal pad and the firewall when the clutch is disengaged (applied) should be 2.20 in. or more for Summit and Stealth, 1.77 in. or more on Summit Wagon, 2.80 in. or more for Laser and Talon. If these dimensions are not right, the hydraulic clutch system may need further servicing.

REMOVAL & INSTALLATION

1. Disconnect the negative battery cable.

NOTE: If equipped with an air bag, be sure to disarm it before starting any repairs on the vehicle.

2. Locate the interlock switch above the clutch pedal lever.

3. Disconnect the wiring connectors from the switch and unscrew the switch.

To install:

4. Thread the switch into the mounting bracket and adjust to 0.140 in. (3.5mm) clearance.

5. Reconnect the interlock wires.

6. Make sure the Engine will not start unless the clutch pedal is depressed. Also, make sure the cruise control system operates properly.

Neutral Safety Switch

ADJUSTMENT

1. Locate the neutral safety switch

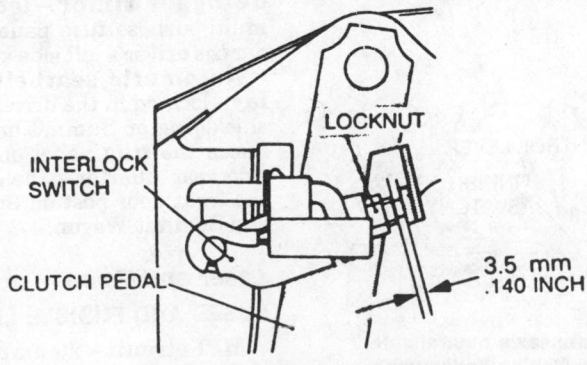

Clutch interlock switch adjustment

on the top of the transaxle. Note that several different cable attaching methods have been used. The procedure here can be used as a general guide for all.

2. Place the selector lever in **N**.

3. Loosen the 2 adjusting nuts to free up the cable and lever.

4. Place the safety switch manual control lever in **N**.

5. Note that 1 end of the safety switch manual control lever has a 12mm wide square end. There is also a 12mm wide tab on the switch body flange. Loosen both retaining bolts and turn the safety switch until these portions align. Tighten the bolts, making sure the switch doesn't move.

6. Loosen the adjuster nuts and gently pull the cable to remove any slack. Gently tighten adjusting nut until it just starts to contact the adjuster. Secure adjusting nut with its locknut then turn nut to lock.

7. Verify that the switch lever moves to positions corresponding to each position of the selector lever.

8. Make sure the Engine only starts in **P** and **N**. Also make sure the reverse lights turn ON in **R**.

REMOVAL & INSTALLATION

1. Disconnect the negative battery cable.

2. Disconnect the selector cable from the lever.

3. Remove the 2 retaining screws and lift off the switch.

4. The installation is the reverse of the removal procedure. Do not tighten the bolts until the switch is adjusted.

5. Make sure the Engine only starts in **P** and **N**. Also make sure the reverse lights turn ON in **R**.

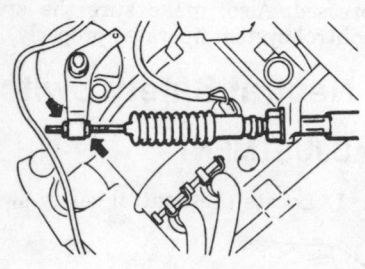

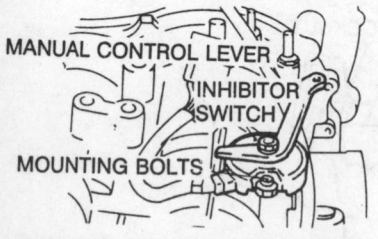

MANUAL CONTROL LEVER

INHIBITOR SWITCH

MOUNTING BOLTS

Automatic transaxle neutral safety (inhibitor) switch and adjustment

Fuses, Fusible Links and Relays

LOCATION

Summit and Summit Wagon

FUSES AND FUSIBLE LINKS

Main fuse panel—passenger's side, under the hood, just behind the battery.

Main relay bank—passenger's side, under the hood, just behind the battery.

Fuse links—passenger's side, under the hood, just behind the battery.

Air conditioning control relay center—driver's side, under the hood, up front behind the headlight.

Multi-purpose fuse block—inside the vehicle, on the left side behind the driver's knee protector.

RELAYS

Headlight relay, power window relay, radiator fan motor relay and alternator relay—passenger's side, under the hood, just behind the battery.

Air conditioner compressor relay, the condenser fan motor relay and the condenser fan motor control relay—under the hood, up front behind the headlight.

Intermittent wiper relay—incorporated into the column switch.

Seat belt warning timer relay—behind the instrument panel to the right of the center air conditioning outlets.

Multi-Point Injection control relay—inside the passenger compartment behind the right kick panel on Summit Wagon or behind the forward part of the console, on the left side on Summit.

Starter relay—right side of the vehicle in the relay box.

Defogger relay—under the driver's left side knee protector.

Door lock relay—behind the driver's side kick panel, at the bottom.

Heater relay, the turn signal and hazard flasher unit and the defogger timer—located in the multi-purpose fuse panel located under the driver's left side knee protector.

Automatic seatbelt motor relay—located in the driver's side windshield post on Summit hatchback, and inside the trim panel on the driver's side rear quarter panel, just behind the front door post on Summit Sedan and Summit Wagon.

Laser and Talon

FUSES AND FUSIBLE LINKS

MPI circuit—20 amp fuse link—under the hood in a centralized junc-

tion with the battery positive cable clamp.

Radiator fan motor circuit—30 amp fuse link—under the hood in a centralized junction with the battery positive cable clamp.

Ignition switch circuit—30 amp fuse link—under the hood in a centralized junction with the battery positive cable clamp.

Secondary fuse panel—located on the passenger side, under the hood, just forward of the strut tower.

Secondary fuse panel—driver's side, under the hood, back against the firewall.

Multi-purpose fuse block—located inside the vehicle, on the left side behind the driver's knee protector.

RELAYS

Taillight relay, headlight relay, radiator fan motor relay, pop-up (retractable light) motor relay, power window relay, alternator relay and fog light relay.—passenger side of vehicle, under the hood, just forward of the strut tower.

Air conditioning condenser fan relays and air conditioning compressor clutch relay—driver's side of vehicle, under the hood, just forward of the strut tower.

Door lock relay, starter relay, defogger timer—interior relay box inside the vehicle passanger compartment.

Stealth

FUSES AND FUSIBLE LINKS

Main fuse panel—located on the passenger side, under the hood, just forward of the air flow box. This panel also contains several fusible links.

Multipurpose fuse block—located under the instrument panel, on the left side behind the driver's knee protector.

RELAYS

Radiator fan relay, air conditioning system relays—centralized fuse/relay panel on the driver side, under the hood, just forward of the strut tower.

Taillight relay, headlight relay, pop-up (retractable light) motor relay, horn relay, alternator relay and fog light relay— Engine compartment in front of the air flow box.

Blower motor and theft alarm horn.—inside the vehicle, above the fuse box.

Computers

LOCATION

Summit and Summit Wagon

Multi-Point Injection (MPI)

control unit—located under the instrument panel at the top of the passenger side kick panel, next to the blower motor.

Air conditioning control unit—mounted behind the glove box.

Automatic transaxle control unit—mounted on the floor at the very front of the console.

Cruise control unit—under the instrument panel behind the driver's side knee protector.

Electric door lock control unit—fastened to the body structure behind the driver's side kick panel.

Automatic seat belt control unit—under the console next to hand brake handle.

ELC 4-speed automatic transaxle control unit—under the instrument panel at center of dash.

Anti-lock Braking System (ABS) control unit—under the instrument panel at center of dash.

Laser and Talon

Multi-Point Injection (MPI) control unit—located under the instrument panel at the front of the center console.

Air conditioning control unit—mounted behind the glove box.

Automatic transaxle control unit—mounted on the floor at the very front of the console.

Cruise control unit—mounted at top of instrument panel structure near where the dash pad and windshield meet.

Electric door lock control unit or theft-alarm control unit—fastened to the body structure behind the passenger's side kick panel.

Automatic seat belt control unit—fastened to the body structure under the trim panel at the base of the driver's side door latch pillar.

Anti-Lock Brake control unit—mounted behind the right side rear quarter trim panel.

Stealth

Multi-Point Injection (MPI) control unit—located under the instrument panel at the front of the center console.

Automatic transaxle control unit—mounted on the floor at the very front of the console.

Air conditioning control unit—mounted at the front of the center console just above the MPI control unit.

Air conditioner compressor lock controller—mounted on the bottom of the heater core housing under the right side of the instrument panel.

Cruise control unit—located behind the right side kick panel.

Electronic Timing and Control

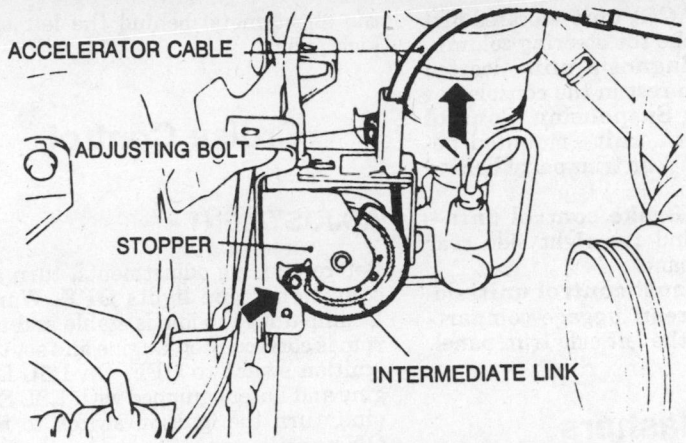

Common cable adjusting point—1990 Summit

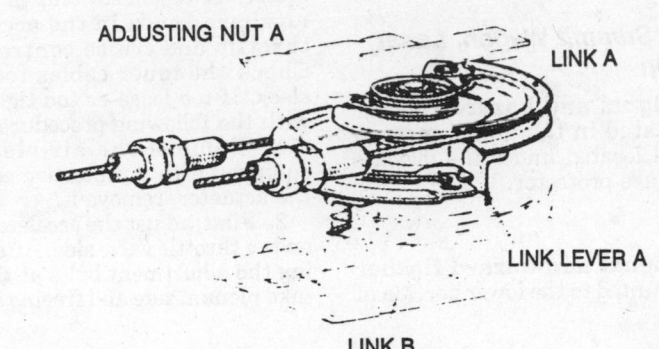

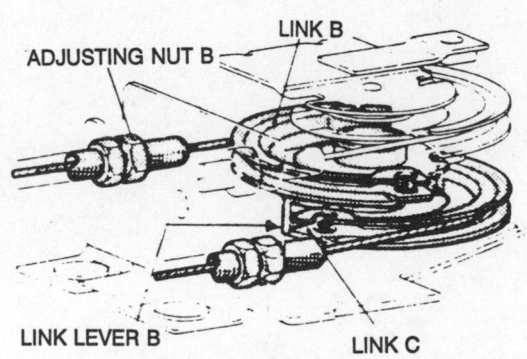

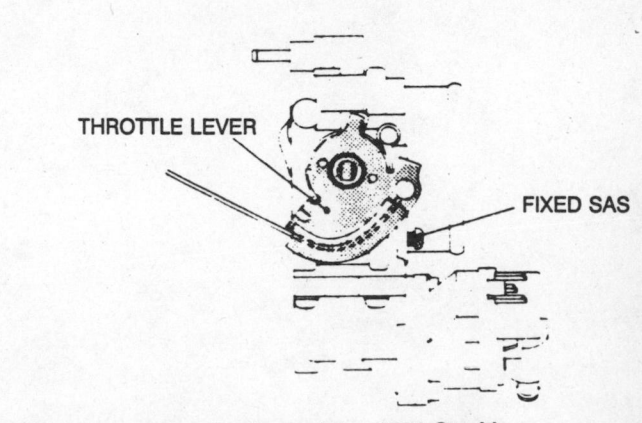

Common cable adjusting points—1992 Stealth

System (ETACS) unit—located just to the left of the the steering column.

Air bag diagnosis unit—located under the arm rest in the console.

Electronic Suspension Control (ECS) control unit—mounted behind the right rear trim panel behind an access door.

Anti-Lock Brake control unit—mounted behind the right side rear quarter trim panel.

Active exhaust control unit—located in the rear luggage compartment, behind the left side trim panel.

Flashers

LOCATION

Summit, Summit Wagon, Laser and Talon

Turn signal and hazard flasher unit—located in the multi-purpose fuse panel located under the driver's left side knee protector.

Stealth

Turn signal and hazard flasher unit—mounted to the lower portion of the sheet metal behind the left side kick panel.

Cruise Control

ADJUSTMENT

Before starting adjustments, turn air conditioner and lights **OFF**. Warm Engine until the idle is stable and the rpm is correct. Stop Engine and set the ignition switch to **OFF**. On 1.5L Engine and Laser equipped with 1.8L Engine, turn the ignition switch to the **ON** position, without starting the Engine. Leave in the position for approximately 15 seconds. Confirm there are no sharp bends in the accelerator, throttle and cruise control cables. Check the inner cables for correct slack. If too loose or too tight, adjust with the following procedure:

1. Remove the air cleaner. If equipped with a protective cover over the actuator, remove it.

2. First, adjust the accelerator cable on the throttle valve side. After loosening the adjustment bolts at the air intake plenum side and freeing the inner cable, use the adjusting bolts that secure the plate so the free-play of the inner cable becomes 0.040–0.080 in. (1–2mm). If there is excessive play of the accelerator cable, when climbing a hill the vehicle speed will drop substantially. If there is no play, the idling speed will increase.

3. After adjusting the accelerator cable, confirm that the throttle lever touches the idle position switch.

4. Next, adjust accelerator cable on the accelerator pedal side. Loosen the adjusting bolt or locknut. While keeping the intermediate link of the actuator in close contact with the stop, adjust the inner cable play of accelerator cable **A** to 0–0.040 in. (0–1mm) for manual transaxle vehicles or 0.080–0.120 in. (2–3mm) for automatic transaxle vehicles.

5. After making the adjustment of the cable, make sure the throttle lever at the Engine side moves 0.040–0.080 in. (1–2mm) when the actuator link is turned. If throttle lever movement is incorrect, adjust by turning adjusting nut **B**.

6. Confirm that the throttle valve fully opens and closes by operating the accelerator pedal.

7. Install the air cleaner.

Chrysler/Eagle
Front Wheel Drive
DODGE—MONACO
EAGLE—MEDALLION • PREMIER

SPECIFICATIONS

VEHICLE IDENTIFICATION CHART

It is important for servicing and ordering parts to be certain of the vehicle and engine identification. The VIN (vehicle identification number) is a 17 digit number visible through the windshield on the driver's side of the dash and contains the vehicle and engine identification codes. The tenth digit indicates model year and the eighth digit indicates engine code. It can be interpreted as follows:

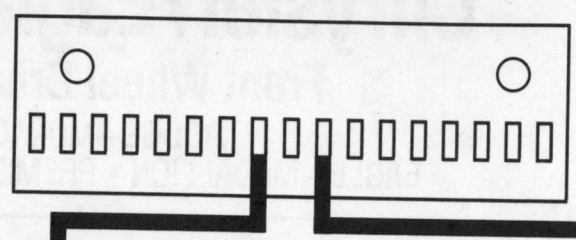

Engine Code							Model Year	
Code	**Liters**	**Cu. In. (cc)**	**Cyl.**	**Fuel Sys.**	**Eng. Mfg.**		**Code**	**Year**
F	2.2	132 (2163)	4	MPI	Renault		K	1989
H	2.5	150 (2459)	4	TBI	AMC		L	1990
U	3.0	180 (2950)	6	MPI	Renault		M	1991
							N	1992

MPI—Multi Port Injection
TBI—Throttle Body Injection

ENGINE IDENTIFICATION

Year	Model	Engine Displacement Liters (cc)	Engine Series (ID/VIN)	Fuel System	No. of Cylinders	Engine Type
1989	Medallion	2.2 (2163)	F	MPI	4	SOHC
	Premier	2.5 (2459)	H	TBI	4	OHV
	Premier	3.0 (2950)	U	MPI	6	SOHC
1990	Premier	3.0 (2950)	U	MPI	6	SOHC
	Monaco	3.0 (2950)	U	MPI	6	SOHC
1991	Premier	3.0 (2950)	U	MPI	6	SOHC
	Monaco	3.0 (2950)	U	MPI	6	SOHC
1992	Premier	3.0 (2950)	U	MPI	6	SOHC
	Monaco	3.0 (2950)	U	MPI	6	SOHC

TBI—Throttle Body Injection
MPI—Multi-Point Fuel Injection
OHV—Overhead Valve Engine
SOHC—Single Overhead Camshaft

GENERAL ENGINE SPECIFICATIONS

Year	Engine ID/VIN	Engine Displacement Liters (cc)	Fuel System Type	Net Horsepower @ rpm	Net Torque @ rpm (ft. lbs.)	Bore × Stroke (in.)	Compression Ratio	Oil Pressure @ rpm
1989	F	2.2 (2163)	MPI	103 @ 5000	124 @ 2500	3.46 × 3.50	9.2:1	44 @ 3000
	H	2.5 (2459)	TBI	111 @ 4750	142 @ 2500	3.88 × 3.19	9.2:1	37 @ 1600
	U	3.0 (2950)	MPI	150 @ 5000	171 @ 3750	3.66 × 2.87	9.3:1	60 @ 4000

GENERAL ENGINE SPECIFICATIONS

Year	Engine ID/VIN	Engine Displacement Liters (cc)	Fuel System Type	Net Horsepower @ rpm	Net Torque @ rpm (ft. lbs.)	Bore × Stroke (in.)	Compression Ratio	Oil Pressure @ rpm
1990	U	3.0 (2950)	MPI	150 @ 5000	171 @ 3750	3.66 × 2.87	9.3:1	60 @ 4000
1991	U	3.0 (2950)	MPI	150 @ 5000	171 @ 3750	3.66 × 2.87	9.3:1	60 @ 4000
1992	U	3.0 (2950)	MPI	150 @ 5000	171 @ 3750	3.66 × 2.87	9.3:1	60 @ 4000

NOTE: Horsepower and torque are SAE net figures. They are measured at the rear of the transmission with all accessories installed and operating. Since the figures vary when a given engine is installed in different models, some are representative rather than exact.

MPI—Multi-Point Fuel Injection
TBI—Throttle Body Injection

GASOLINE ENGINE TUNE-UP SPECIFICATIONS

Year	Engine ID/VIN	Engine Displacement Liters (cc)	Spark Plugs Gap (in.)	Ignition Timing (deg.) MT	Ignition Timing (deg.) AT	Fuel Pump (psi)	Idle Speed (rpm) MT	Idle Speed (rpm) AT	Valve Clearance In.	Valve Clearance Ex.
1989	F	2.2 (2163)	0.035	①	①	34–36	800	700	0.006	0.008
	H	2.5 (2459)	0.035	①	①	14–15	700	750	Hyd.	Hyd.
	U	3.0 (2950)	0.035	①	①	28–30	700	750	Hyd.	Hyd.
1990	U	3.0 (2950)	0.035	①	①	28–30	700	700	Hyd.	Hyd.
1991	U	3.0 (2950)	0.035	①	①	②	①	①	Hyd.	Hyd.
1992	U	3.0 (2950)	0.035	①	①	43	①	①	Hyd.	Hyd.

NOTE: The lowest cylinder pressure should be within 75% of the highest cylinder pressure reading. For example, if the highest cylinder is 134 psi, the lowest should be 101. Engine should be at normal operating temperature with throttle valve in the wide open position.

The underhood specifications sticker often reflects tune-up specification changes in production. Sticker figures must be used if they disagree with those in this chart.

Hyd.—Hydraulic
① Refer to Underhood Specifications Sticker
② Vehicles built before 10-9-91: 28–31 psi
  Vehicles built after 10-9-91: 43 psi

FIRING ORDERS

NOTE: To avoid confusion, always replace spark plugs and wires one at a time.

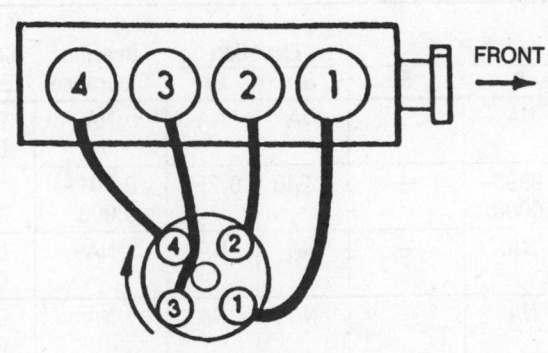

2.5L Engine
Engine Firing Order: 1–3–4–2
Distributor Rotation: Clockwise

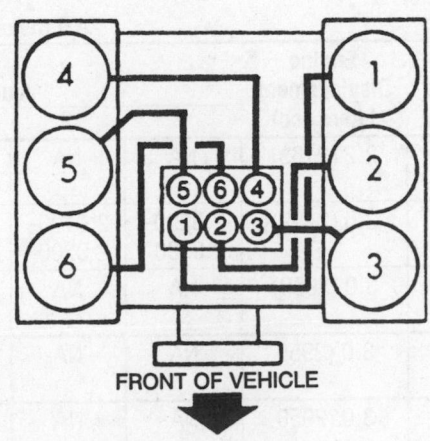

1991–93 3.0L Engine (Built on or after Oct. 9, 1991)
Engine Firing Order: 1–6–3–5–2–4
Distributorless Ignition System

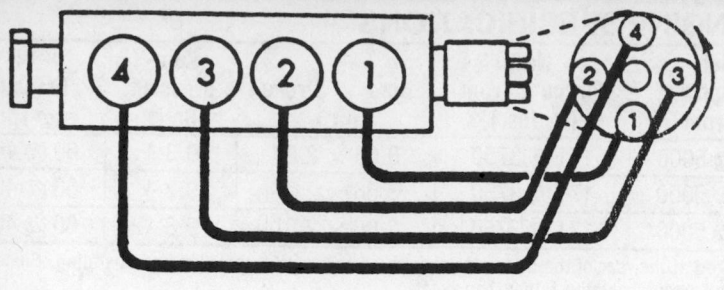

2.2L Engine
Engine Firing Order: 1–3–4–2
Distributor Rotation: Counterclockwise

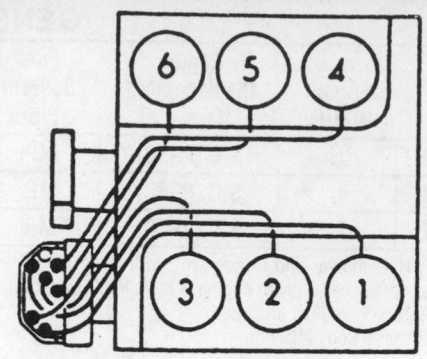

1991 3.0L Engine (Built before Oct. 9, 1991)
Engine Firing Order: 1–6–3–5–2–4
Distributor Rotation: Counterclockwise

CAPACITIES

Year	Model	Engine ID/VIN	Engine Displacement Liters (cc)	Engine Crankcase with Filter (qts.)	Transmission (pts.) 4-Spd	Transmission (pts.) 5-Spd	Transmission (pts.) Auto.	Drive Axle Front (pts.)	Drive Axle Rear (pts.)	Fuel Tank (gal.)	Cooling System (qts.)
1989	Medallion	F	2.2 (2163)	5.0	4.8	—	12.8②	—	—	17	7.0
	Premier	H	2.5 (2459)	5.0	—	—	14.8②	1.32①	—	17	8.6
	Premier	U	3.0 (2950)	6.0	—	—	14.8②	1.32①	—	17	8.6
1990	Premier	U	3.0 (2950)	6.0	—	—	14.7②	1.32①	—	17	8.6
	Monaco	U	3.0 (2950)	6.0	—	—	14.7②	1.32①	—	17	8.6
1991	Premier	U	3.0 (2950)	6.0	—	—	14.7②	1.32①	—	17	8.6
	Monaco	U	3.0 (2950)	6.0	—	—	14.7②	1.32①	—	17	8.6
1992	Premier	U	3.0 (2950)	6.0	—	—	14.7②	1.32①	—	17	8.6
	Monaco	U	3.0 (2950)	6.0	—	—	14.7②	1.32①	—	17	8.6

① The differential requires a synthetic-type SAE grade 75W-140 gear lubricant. It is the only recommended lubricant. It is factory filled and designed to last the life of the differential under normal conditions.

② The ZF-4 transaxle requires Mopar Mercon automatic transmission fluid only. No substitutions are to be made.

CAMSHAFT SPECIFICATIONS

All measurements given in inches.

Year	Engine ID/VIN	Engine Displacement Liters (cc)	Journal Diameter 1	Journal Diameter 2	Journal Diameter 3	Journal Diameter 4	Journal Diameter 5	Elevation In.	Elevation Ex.	Bearing Clearance	Camshaft End Play
1989	F	2.2 (2163)	NA	NA	NA	NA	—	NA	NA	NA	0.002–0.005
	H	2.5 (2459)	2.0290–2.0300	2.0190–2.0200	2.0090–2.0100	1.9990–2.0000	—	0.240	0.250	0.001–0.003	0
	U	3.0 (2950)	NA	NA	NA	NA	—	NA	NA	NA	0.003–0.005
1990	U	3.0 (2950)	NA	NA	NA	NA	—	NA	NA	NA	0.003–0.005
1991	U	3.0 (2950)	NA	NA	NA	NA	—	NA	NA	NA	0.003–0.005
1992	U	3.0 (2950)	NA	NA	NA	NA	—	NA	NA	NA	0.003–0.005

NA—Not available

CRANKSHAFT AND CONNECTING ROD SPECIFICATIONS

All measurements are given in inches.

| Year | Engine ID/VIN | Engine Displacement Liters (cc) | Crankshaft | | | | Connecting Rod | | |
			Main Brg. Journal Dia.	Main Brg. Oil Clearance	Shaft End-play	Thrust on No.	Journal Diameter	Oil Clearance	Side Clearance
1989	F	2.2 (2163)	2.4760	0.0015–0.0035	0.005–0.011	1	2.2060–2.2160	0.0008–0.0030	0.012–0.022
	H	2.5 (2459)	2.4996–2.5001	0.0020	0.002–0.007	2	2.0934–2.0955	0.0015–0.0020	0.010–0.019
	U	3.0 (2950)	2.7576–2.7583	0.0015–0.0035	0.002–0.007	1	2.3611–2.3618	0.0008–0.0030	0.008–0.015
1990	U	3.0 (2950)	2.7576–2.7583	0.0015–0.0035	0.002–0.007	1	2.3611–2.3618	0.0008–0.0030	0.008–0.015
1991	U	3.0 (2950)	2.7576–2.7583	0.0015–0.0035	0.002–0.007	1	2.3611–2.3618	0.0008–0.0030	0.008–0.015
1992	U	3.0 (2950)	2.7576–2.7583	0.0015–0.0035	0.002–0.007	1	2.3611–2.3618	0.0008–0.0030	0.008–0.015

VALVE SPECIFICATIONS

| Year | Engine ID/VIN | Engine Displacement Liters (cc) | Seat Angle (deg.) | Face Angle (deg.) | Spring Test Pressure (lbs. @ in.) | Spring Installed Height (in.) | Stem-to-Guide Clearance (in.) | | Stem Diameter (in.) | |
							Intake	Exhaust	Intake	Exhaust
1989	F	2.2 (2163)	②	②	NA	NA	0.004	0.004	0.315	0.315
	H	2.5 (2459)	①	45	200 @ 1.210	1¹¹⁄₁₆	0.001–0.003	0.001–0.003	0.311–0.312	0.311–0.312
	U	3.0 (2950)	45	45	155 @ 1.220	1¹³⁄₁₆	NA	NA	0.315	0.315
1990	U	3.0 (2950)	45	45	155 @ 1.220	1¹³⁄₁₆	NA	NA	0.315	0.315
1991	U	3.0 (2950)	45	45	155 @ 1.220	1¹³⁄₁₆	NA	NA	0.315	0.315
1992	U	3.0 (2950)	45	45	155 @ 1.220	1¹³⁄₁₆	NA	NA	0.315	0.315

NA—Not available
① Intake—44.5
  Exhaust—40.5
② Intake—60
  Exhaust—45

PISTON AND RING SPECIFICATIONS

All measurements are given in inches.

| Year | Engine ID/VIN | Engine Displacement Liters (cc) | Piston Clearance | Ring Gap | | | Ring Side Clearance | | |
				Top Compression	Bottom Compression	Oil Control	Top Compression	Bottom Compression	Oil Control
1989	F	2.2 (2163)	NA	①	①	①	NA	NA	NA
	H	2.5 (2459)	0.0013–0.0021	0.010–0.020	0.010–0.020	0.015–0.055	0.0010–0.0032	0.0010–0.0032	0.0010–0.0085
	U	3.0 (2950)	NA	0.016–0.022	0.016–0.022	NA	0.0010–0.0020	0.0010–0.0020	0.0015–0.0035
1990	U	3.0 (2950)	NA	0.016–0.022	0.016–0.022	NA	0.0010–0.0020	0.0010–0.0020	0.0015–0.0035
1991	U	3.0 (2950)	NA	0.016–0.022	0.016–0.022	NA	0.0010–0.0020	0.0010–0.0020	0.0015–0.0035
1992	U	3.0 (2950)	NA	0.016–0.022	0.016–0.022	NA	0.0010–0.0020	0.0010–0.0020	0.0015–0.0035

NA—Not available
① Factory specifies only 1 type of ring. Ring gap is pre-adjusted.

TORQUE SPECIFICATIONS

All readings in ft. lbs.

Year	Engine ID/VIN	Engine Displacement Liters (cc)	Cylinder Head Bolts	Main Bearing Bolts	Rod Bearing Bolts	Crankshaft Damper Bolts	Flywheel Bolts	Manifold Intake	Manifold Exhaust	Spark Plugs	Lug Nut ④
1989	F	2.2 (2163)	①	69	46	96	44	11	13	11	90
	H	2.5 (2459)	②	80	33	80	48–54	⑤	⑤	22	90
	U	3.0 (2950)	②	③	35	133	48–54	11	13	11	90
1990	U	3.0 (2950)	②	③	35	133	48–54	11	13	11	90
1991	U	3.0 (2950)	②	③	35	133	48–54	11	13	11	90
1992	U	3.0 (2950)	②	③	35	133	48–54	11	13	11	90

① Torque in 3 steps, in sequence:
  1st—37 ft. lbs.
  2nd—59 ft. lbs.
  3rd—69 ft. lbs.
  Run engine for 15 minutes, shut off and allow
  to cool for 6 hours and recheck, should be
  65–72 ft. lbs.
② See text
③ Tighten in 2 steps, in sequence:
  1st—20 ft. lbs.
  2nd—Angular torque 75 degrees
④ Specification given for aluminum wheels.
  Tighten steel wheels to 63 ft. lbs.
⑤ Torque bolts 1, 6, 7, 8 to 30 ft. lbs.
  2, 3, 4, 5 to 23 ft. lbs.
  9 and 10 to 14 ft. lbs.

BRAKE SPECIFICATIONS

All measurements in inches unless noted.

Year	Model		Master Cylinder Bore	Brake Disc Original Thickness	Brake Disc Minimum Thickness	Maximum Runout	Brake Drum Diameter Original Inside Diameter	Max. Wear Limit	Maximum Machine Diameter	Minimum Lining Thickness Front	Minimum Lining Thickness Rear
1989	Medallion		0.810	0.756	0.697	0.002	8.941	9.000	NA	0.06	0.06
	Premier		0.945	0.866	0.807	0.003	8.858	8.917	NA	0.06	0.06
1990	Premier	front	0.945	0.941	0.807	0.003	—	—	NA	0.06	0.06
		rear	—	0.393	0.374	0.003	8.858	8.917	NA	0.06	0.06
	Monaco	front	0.945	0.941	0.807	0.003	—	—	NA	0.06	0.06
		rear	—	0.393	0.374	0.003	8.858	8.917	NA	0.06	0.06
1991	Premier	front	0.945	0.941	0.890	0.003	—	—	NA	0.06	0.06
		rear	—	0.393	0.374	0.003	8.858	8.917	NA	0.06	0.06
	Monaco	front	0.945	0.941	0.890	0.003	—	—	NA	0.06	0.06
		rear	—	0.393	0.374	0.003	8.858	8.917	NA	0.06	0.06
1992	Premier	front	0.945	0.941	0.890	0.003	—	—	NA	0.06	0.06
		rear	—	0.393	0.374	0.003	8.858	8.917	NA	0.06	0.06
	Monaco	front	0.945	0.941	0.890	0.003	—	—	NA	0.06	0.06
		rear	—	0.393	0.374	0.003	8.858	8.917	NA	0.06	0.06

NA—Not available

WHEEL ALIGNMENT

Year	Model	Caster Range (deg.)	Caster Preferred Setting (deg.)	Camber Range (deg.)	Camber Preferred Setting (deg.)	Toe-out (in.)	Steering Axis Inclination (deg.)
1989	Medallion	1½P–3½P	2½P	1/16P–13/16P	7/16P	5/64	12¾
	Premier	1½P–3½P	2⅛P	9/16N–1/16N	5/16N	1/8	NA
1990	Premier	1½P–2½P	2P	9/16N–1/16N	5/16N	0	NA
	Monaco	1½P–2½P	2P	9/16N–1/16N	5/16N	0	NA
1991	Premier	1½P–2½P	2P	9/16N–1/16N	5/16N	0	NA
	Monaco	1½P–2½P	2P	9/16N–1/16N	5/16N	0	NA
1992	Premier	1½P–2½P	2P	9/16N–1/16N	5/16N	0	NA
	Monaco	1½P–2½P	2P	9/16N–1/16N	5/16N	0	NA

NA—Not applicable
N—Negative
P—Positive

ENGINE MECHANICAL

NOTE: Disconnecting the negative battery cable on some vehicles may interfere with the functions of the on-board computer systems and may require the computer to undergo a relearning process, once the negative battery cable is reconnected.

Engine Assembly

REMOVAL & INSTALLATION

The following procedure can be used on all vehicles. Slight variations may occur due to extra connections, etc., but the basic procedure should cover all models.

1. Relieve fuel system pressure.
2. Disconnect the negative battery cable.
3. Matchmark the hood and hinges and remove the hood assembly. Remove the air cleaner assembly and all adjoining air intake duct work.
4. Drain the engine coolant.
5. Disconnect and tag for assembly reference the connections for the accelerator cable, heater hoses, brake vacuum hose, connection for vacuum hoses, high pressure fuel line, fuel return line and electrical harness connectors.
6. Remove the grille. Remove the screws retaining the front facia panel and radiator support and remove.
7. Remove the radiator and cooling fan. If equipped with air conditioning, safely discharge the air conditioning system and remove the condenser and the radiator as an assembly.

8. Disconnect the electrical leads to the unit ECU or SBEC.
9. Remove the bolts that attach the exhaust head pipes to the exhaust manifold.
10. Remove the heater hoses and on automatic transaxle equipped vehicles, remove the cooler lines.
11. Raise the vehicle and safely support. Remove the underbody splash shield.
12. Remove the power steering pump mounting bolts and support the pump to the side. Remove the header pipe to converter bolts and remove the converter.
13. If equipped with automatic transaxle, disconnect the shifter linkages. On manual transaxle vehicles, disconnect the clutch cable at the transaxle.
14. Remove the wheel assemblies and remove the front stabilizer bar. Remove the brake calipers and support aside. Disconnect the tie rod ends from the steering knuckle. Remove the halfshaft retaining pin and remove the halfshaft assembly. Remove the strut-to-steering knuckle bolts.
15. Loosen the upper strut mounting bolts and swing the axle/strut assembly aside. Support the axles safely.
16. Disconnect the speedometer cable. Disconnect the vapor canister and remove it.
17. Loosen the bolts attaching the transmission support to the engine cradle. Remove the bolts attaching the left and right halves of the crossmember to the transaxle. Lower the vehicle.
18. Attach a lifting device to the engine lifting eyes and lift the engine slightly. Remove the engine support bolts and remove the engine/transaxle assembly. Lift the engine out at an angle, make sure the transaxle clears the

engine compartment. Separate the engine from the transaxle.

To install:

19. Position the engine/transaxle assembly in the vehicle and align the engine mounts.
20. If equipped with 2.2L engine, tighten the right yoke thru bolt and the lower yoke nut to 100 ft. lbs. (133 Nm).
21. If equipped with 2.5L engine, install the engine mount bolts and tighten as follows:
   a. Front engine mount mounting nuts—50 ft. lbs. (65 Nm).
   b. Rear engine mount bolt—49 ft. lbs. (67 Nm).
   c. Rear crossmember mounting bolts—31 ft. lbs. (43 Nm).
   d.Right yoke thru bolt and the lower yoke nut to 100 ft. lbs. (133 Nm).
22. If equipped with 3.0L engine, install the engine mount bolts and tighten as follows:
   a. Lower engine mount-to-cradle thru bolt—32 ft. lbs. (43 Nm).
   b. Lower engine mount retainer nut—35 ft. lbs. (48 Nm).
   c. Front damper mounting bracket retainer bolts—20 ft. lbs. (27 Nm).
   d. Front damper-to-damper mounting bracket bolt—20 ft. lbs. (27 Nm).
   e. Rear crossmember cushion mount thru bolt—49 ft. lbs. (67 Nm).
23. Once all engine mounting bolts are installed and tightened, remove the lifting device. Install the left and right sections of the crossmember, if removed.
24. Position and install the halfshafts to the transaxle, use new retaining pins. Install the shock absorber to steering knuckle bolts and attach

the tie rod ends. Attach the front stabilizer bar.

25. Install the converter to the header pipe. Install the power steering pump and adjust the belt tension. Connect the shift linkage and throttle cables.

26. Reconnect all electrical harness connectors and vacuum hoses to their original location. Install the canister and the air cleaner assemblies. Reconnect the fuel lines and coolant hoses.

27. Install the radiator and fan assemblies. Attach the front facia and support assembly. Install the grille.

28. Install the hood making sure the matchmarks made during removal are aligned.

29. Check and fill all fluid levels to the proper level.

30. Connect the negative battery cable. Start the engine, allow it to reach normal operating temperature. Check for leaks.

31. Road test the vehicle.

Engine Mounts

REMOVAL & INSTALLATION

Except 3.0L Engine

1. Disconnect the negative battery cable.

2. Remove the engine mount upper attaching bolt.

3. Remove the engine pitch restrictor and bracket.

4. Raise the vehicle and support it safely.

5. Remove the engine mount bottom attaching bolt.

6. Carefully raise the engine and remove the engine mount.

7. Installation is the reverse of the removal procedure.

8. If equipped with 2.2L engine, tighten the right yoke thru bolt and the lower yoke nut to 100 ft. lbs. (133 Nm).

9. If equipped with 2.5L engine, tighten the front engine mount mounting nuts to 50 ft. lbs. (65 Nm) and the rear engine mount bolt to 49 ft. lbs. (67 Nm). Tighten the rear crossmember mounting bolts to 31 ft. lbs. (43 Nm), and the yoke nut to 100 ft. lbs. (133 Nm).

3.0L Engine

FRONT MOUNTS

1. Disconnect the negative battery cable.

2. Raise the vehicle and support it safely.

3. Remove the engine mount stud locknut.

4. Disconnect the front engine damper and raise the engine enough to remove the mount.

5. Remove the mount through bolt and remove the mount.

6. The installation is the reverse of the removal procedure. Observe the following torque values:

   a. Lower engine mount-to-cradle thru bolt—32 ft. lbs. (43 Nm).

   b. Lower engine mount retainer nut—35 ft. lbs. (48 Nm).

   c. Front damper mounting bracket retainer bolts—20 ft. lbs. (27 Nm).

   d. Front damper-to-damper mounting bracket bolt—20 ft. lbs. (27 Nm).

   e. Engine mount nut to 48 ft. lbs. (65 Nm).

REAR MOUNT/CUSHION

1. Disconnect the negative battery cable.

2. Raise the vehicle and support it safely.

3. Remove the underbody splash shield.

4. Using the proper equipment, support the weight of the transaxle.

5. Remove the nuts that attach the crossmember to the engine cradle.

6. Remove the large bolt that attaches the rear cushion to the support bracket.

7. Remove the bolt that attaches the exhaust pipe bracket to rear cushion.

8. Remove the crossmember and the rear cushion.

9. Remove the support bracket bolts and remove the bracket from the transaxle.

To install:

10. Install the support bracket to the transaxle and torque to 30 ft. lbs. (40 Nm).

11. Position the exhaust bracket on the rear cushion.

12. Install the rear cushion and the crossmember. Align the cushion to bracket bolt and nut. Leave it loose at this point.

13. Install, but don't tighten the exhaust bracket bolts.

14. Tighten the rear cushion to support bracket bolt to 49 ft. lbs. (67 Nm).

15. Tighten the exhaust bracket to rear cushion bolts to 23 ft. lbs. (31 Nm).

16. Install the bolts and nuts that attach the crossmember to the studs on the engine cradle. Torque to 44 ft. lbs. (60 Nm).

17. Remove the support apparatus from the transaxle.

18. Lower the vehicle. Connect the negative battery cable.

Cylinder Head

REMOVAL & INSTALLATION

2.2L Engine

1. Relieve the fuel system pressure.

2. Disconnect the negative battery cable and drain the cooling system. Remove the air inlet tube from the throttle body.

3. Remove the accessory drive belts. Remove the timing belt cover.

4. Loosen the bolts on the timing belt tensioner and remove the timing belt. Remove the spark plugs and wires.

5. Remove any hoses attached to the rocker cover and remove the rocker arm cover. Remove the distributor from the rear of the head.

6. Remove all of the cylinder head bolts except for the bolt at position No. 10 in the tightening sequence. Loosen the bolt at position No. 10 and pivot the cylinder head on that bolt. This can be done by tapping the opposite end of the head with an block of wood. This is necessary to free the cylinder head from the cylinder liners.

NOTE: When the cylinder head has been removed, retain the cylinder liners in the block with a liner hold-down clamp. This tool is designed to prevent the cylinder liners from being knocked out of position. If this happens, the sealing rings will dislodge or rip.

7. Once the head is free, remove the last bolt and remove the cylinder head. Clean all gasket material from mating surfaces.

To install:

8. Place the new cylinder head gasket on the block using the alignment dowel on the block to hold it in place.

9. Position the cylinder head on the block and insert the cylinder head bolts. Following tightening sequence, torque cylinder head bolts in 3 steps as follows:

   Step 1—37 ft. lbs. (51 Nm)
   Step 2—59 ft. lbs. (80 Nm)
   Step 3—69 ft. lbs. (94 Nm).

10. Install the distributor to the head. Install the rocker arm cover, using a new gasket. Tighten the rocker cover bolts to 35 inch lbs.

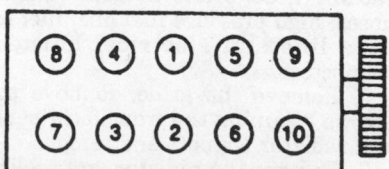

Cylinder head bolt torque sequence—2.2L engine

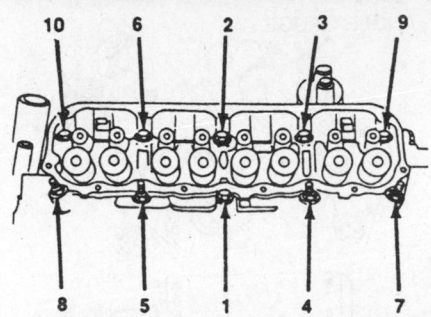

Cylinder head bolt torque sequence— 2.5L engine

11. Install the timing belt and adjust the belt tension. Install the timing belt cover. Install the spark plugs and wires.

12. Install the accessory drive belts and reconnect all hoses that were disconnected.

13. Install the air inlet tube. Fill the cooling system.

14. Connect the negative battery cable. Run the engine and bleed the cooling system. Check for leaks.

2.5L Engine

1. Relieve the fuel system pressure.

2. Disconnect the negative battery cable and drain the cooling system.

3. Loosen the accessory drive belt and remove.

4. Remove the bolts attaching the air conditioning compressor and without disconnecting the pressure lines, move the compressor aside.

5. Disconnect the upper radiator hose and the heater hoses.

6. Remove the rocker arm cover. Remove the rocker arm assembly, keeping all of the valve train components in their original order for installation.

7. Remove the intake and exhaust manifolds.

8. Remove the cylinder head bolts and remove the cylinder head.

9. Clean all gasket material from mating surfaces.

To install:

10. Place the new cylinder head gasket on the block with the numbers facing UP.

NOTE: The cylinder head gasket used on this engine is a composite gasket and does not require the use of any sealing compound.

11. Place the cylinder head on the block and install the bolts. Following the proper sequence, tighten the bolts in the following steps:

  a. Torque all 10 bolts to 22 ft. lbs. (30 Nm)

  b. Torque all 10 bolts to 45 ft. lbs. (61 Nm)

  c. Retorque all 10 bolts to 45 ft. lbs. (61 Nm)

  d. Torque bolts No. 1–6 to 110 ft. lbs. (149 Nm)

  e. Torque bolt No. 7 to 100 ft. lbs. (136 Nm)

  f. Torque bolts No. 8–10 to 110 ft. lbs. (149 Nm)

  g. Retorque each bolt to its proper torque. Pay special attention to bolt No. 7; it should be overtorqued.

12. Install the valve train components in their original sequence. Place a new gasket on the cylinder head and install the rocker cover.

13. Connect all of the hoses removed and install the air conditioning compressor, tighten the mounting bolts to 20 ft. lbs. (27 Nm). Route the accessory drive belt and adjust the tension.

14. Connect the battery cable and fill the cooling system. Run the engine and bleed the cooling system. Check for leaks.

3.0L Engine

1. Relieve the fuel system pressure.

2. Disconnect the negative battery cable and drain the cooling system.

3. Remove the accessory drive belt and remove the air conditioning compressor from the cylinder head cover.

4. Remove the intake and exhaust manifolds.

5. Remove the spark plug wires. Remove the rocker arm cover.

6. Remove the alternator mounting bracket and remove the top timing case bolts that thread into the cylinder head.

NOTE: The timing sprocket and chain must be supported in place and not allowed to drop into the timing case. If the chain and sprocket slip into the case the timing case will have to be removed.

7. Turn the crankshaft until the camshaft sprocket dowel is straight up. A special tool is available called a timing chain support bracket. This support bracket and dummy bearing attaches to the timing case cover. On the left cylinder head, remove the distributor assembly.

8. Remove the threaded plug on the front of the timing case cover to gain access to the camshaft sprocket bolt.

9. Remove the cylinder head bolts. Remove the rocker shaft assembly.

10. Remove the rear camshaft cover and gasket at the rear of the cylinder head.

11. Loosen the camshaft thrust plate screw, located behind the timing sprocket, and move the thrust plate up. This will allow the camshaft to move back in the head as the sprocket bolt is removed.

12. Loosen the camshaft sprocket bolt and pull the camshaft back until the bolt is free from the camshaft, the bolt will stay in the sprocket. Use an old pushrod or a long thin drift punch as a tool and insert it into the front and rear cylinder head bolt holes on the exhaust manifold side of the head. Tap the dowel down below the head gasket. The reason for this is that the cylinder head is not to be removed by pulling straight upward which would pull the cylinder liners loose from the block. It is to be bumped sideways to break the seal.

NOTE: Do not pull straight up on the cylinder head to remove it. This will cause the cylinder liners to come out of the block.

13. Position a block of wood on the intake manifold side of the head and strike it with a hammer, do the same on the exhaust manifold side of the head. Repeat this until the cylinder head is loose. Remove the cylinder head.

NOTE: When the cylinder head has been removed, retain the cylinder liners in the block with a liner hold-down clamp. This tool is designed to prevent the cylinder liners from being knocked out of position. If this happens, the sealing rings will dislodge or rip. Do not rotate the engine with the liner clamps in place.

14. Remove the cylinder head gasket and clean all gasket material from mating surfaces. Remove the cylinder head locating dowels. Check that the cylinder liners protrude between 0.002–0.005 in.

To install:

15. When installing, cut the gasket flush with the cylinder head gasket face at the back of the timing case cover and remove the pieces. Clean the back of the timing cover. Cut sections of new gasket to replace the pieces removed and attach them with adhesive. Install a small punch into the hole in the block below the locating dowel bolt holes. This will act as a stop for the dowel. Push the dowel into the block until it contacts the punch.

16. Install a new cylinder head gasket over the alignment dowels on the head. Place a small bead of RTV or equivalent, at the point where the head gasket meets the timing case cover.

17. Place the cylinder head on the block and install the top timing case

cover-to-cylinder head bolts finger-tight.

18. Remove the timing sprocket support tool. Position the camshaft into the sprocket and align the dowel to the slot in the camshaft. Install the sprocket bolt and lightly tighten it. Slide the thrust plate into position and tighten the thrust plate bolt to 9 ft. lbs. (12 Nm).

19. Install the rocker shaft assembly. Install new cylinder head bolts. If the original cylinder head bolts are to be used, inspect all bolts for necking prior to bolt installation.

NOTE: It is recommended that the cylinder head bolts be replaced during installation. If the original bolts are to be used, inspect the threads of the bolts for necking prior to installation. Necking can be checked by holding a straightedge against the threads. If all threads do not contact the straight edge, the bolt should be replaced.

20. Using the proper sequence, tighten the cylinder head bolts on engines built after code 89616 as follows:

a. Starting with bolt No. 1, torque all bolts to 44 ft. lbs. (60 Nm).

b. The following is performed on all bolts, one at a time. Starting with bolt No. 1, loosen the bolt completely, then tighten to 30 ft. lbs. (41 Nm).

c. Place an angle adapter on the torque wrench between the socket and wrench and angle tighten each bolt, in sequence, an additional 180 degrees ± 20 degrees.

d. Repeat Step C to ensure proper torque.

e. Check each bolt for at least 52 ft. lbs. (70 Nm) of torque.

21. On engines built before code 89616, tighten the cylinder head bolts as follows:

a. Starting with bolt No. 1, torque all bolts to 44 ft. lbs. (60 Nm).

b. The following is performed on all bolts, one at a time. Starting with bolt No. 1, loosen the bolt completely, then tighten to 15 ft. lbs. (20 Nm).

c. Place an angle adapter on the torque wrench between the socket and wrench and angle tighten each bolt, in sequence, an additional 106 degrees ± 20 degrees.

d. Repeat the procedure for all bolts in the above sequence.

22. Install the rocker covers, intake and exhaust manifolds.

23. Install the timing case plug, spark plug wires and the air conditioning compressor. Reconnect all hoses and fill the cooling system.

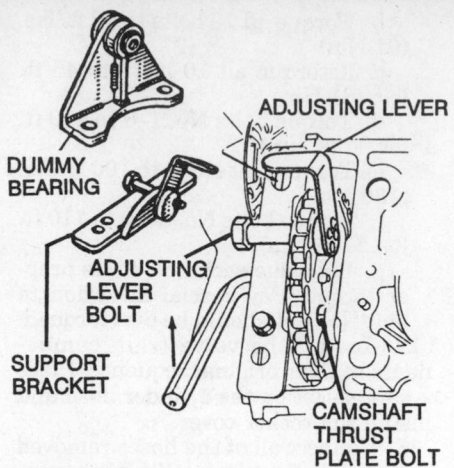

Special tools are recommended to retain cam drive when head is removed—3.0L engine

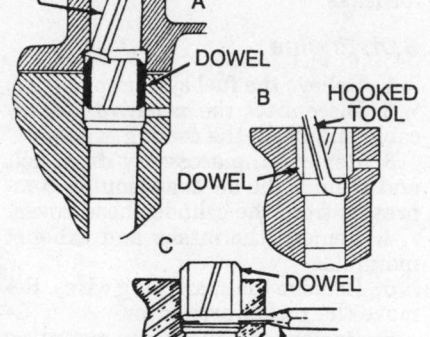

A—Push locating dowel below head gasket level so head can be bumped sideways to remove; B—Pull dowel out with hook shaped tool; C—Use pin punch to gauge depth of dowel at installation—3.0L engine

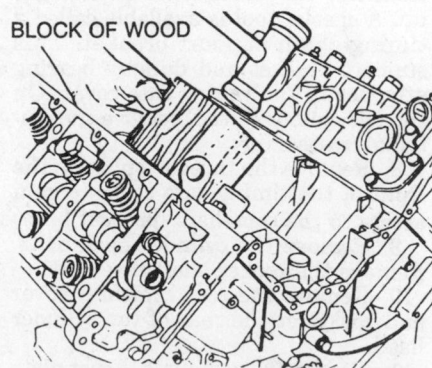

Lifting the head could dislodge the cylinder liner on 3.0L engine; instead, bump sideways as shown

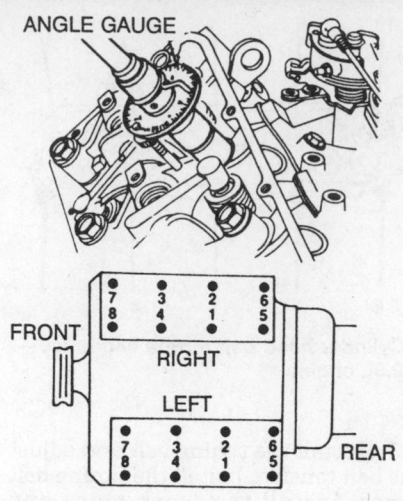

Head bolt torque sequence and torque angle gauge—3.0L engine

24. Install the distributor assembly on the left cylinder head. Install the accessory drive belt and adjust the tension. Connect the negative battery terminal. Start the engine and bleed the cooling system. Check for leaks.

Valve Lifters

REMOVAL & INSTALLATION

2.5L Engine

1. Disconnect the negative battery cable. Remove the valve cover, the bridge and pivot assemblies, and the rocker arms.

NOTE: To avoid damaging the bridges, alternately loosen each bridge bolt a turn at a time.

2. Remove the pushrods, keeping them in their respective order.

3. Remove the cylinder head assembly and manifolds.

4. Remove the lifters through the pushrod openings, with a lifter removal tool. Retain the lifters in their respective removed order.

To install:

5. Dip each lifter in clean engine oil before installation. Install used lifters into their original bores.

6. Install the cylinder head assembly onto the engine block using a new head gasket. Tighten in sequence to the proper torque specification. Install the manifolds, if removed separately.

7. Install the pushrods into their original positions and install the rocker arms and bridges and the pivot assemblies. Tighten the bridge bolts a turn at a time, alternately, to avoid damaging the bridges.

8. Pour the remaining oil supplement over the valve train.

9. Install the valve cover and related parts.

10. Connect the negative battery cable and check for leaks.

3.0L Engine

1. Disconnect the negative battery cable.

2. Remove the rocker cover and the rocker shaft assembly.

3. On the rocker shaft, remove the retaining screw from the end of the shaft and carefully disassemble the rocker shaft components.

4. Remove the lifter and the lifter thrust washer from the rocker arm. Check the lifters for excess wear and check the rocker arm for blocked oil passages.

To install:

5. Lightly coat the lifter and thrust washer with clean engine oil. Install the lifter in the rocker arm.

NOTE: The lifter may tend to fall from the rocker arm. To prevent this use masking tape or wire to hold the tappet in place until the shaft assembly is installed.

6. Assemble the rocker shaft components in the order they were disassembled. Install the rocker shaft assembly on the cylinder head.

7. Install the rocker arm cover.

8. Connect the negative battery cable and check for leaks.

Valve Lash

ADJUSTMENT

2.2L Engine

1. Warm the engine to normal operating temperature.

2. Stop the engine and remove the valve cover.

3. Using tool MOT–647 or equivalent, loosen the locknut on the adjuster and turn the adjuster to obtain the proper clearance. Specification are 0.006 in. for intake valves and 0.008 in. for exhaust valves. Make sure the valve is not in any mode of operation, fully closed or at top dead center of its' compression stroke.

NOTE: Check the adjuster to be sure it is aligned evenly with the valve stem. If it is not aligned, valve damage could occur.

4. Rotate the crankshaft to bring each set of valves to the TDC of its compression stroke and adjust them in the same manner.

5. When adjustment is complete, install the valve cover and check engine operation.

Rocker Arms/Shafts

REMOVAL & INSTALLATION

2.2L Engine

1. Relieve the fuel system pressure. Disconnect the negative battery cable.

2. Remove the rocker arm cover retaining bolts and remove the rocker cover.

3. Remove the bolts retaining the rocker arm shaft to the cylinder head.

To install:

4. Position the rocker shaft assembly on cylinder head and tighten the rocker shaft retaining bolts to 66 inch lbs. (7.5 Nm).

5. Install the rocker cover using a new gasket.

6. Connect the negative battery cable and check engine operation.

2.5L Engine

1. Disconnect the negative battery cable.

2. Disconnect and mark all vacuum hoses and electrical connections as required.

3. Remove the vacuum switch and bracket assembly. Remove the diverter valve and bracket assembly.

4. Remove the valve cover.

5. Remove the bolts at each bridge and pivot assembly. Alternately loosen each bolt a turn at a time to avoid damaging the bridges.

6. Remove the bridges, pivots and corresponding pairs of rocker arms keeping them in the order of removal.

To install:

7. Lubricate all parts to be installed using clean engine oil. Install the rocker arms, pivots and bridges keeping in the same order as removal.

8. Install mounting bolts and tighten alternately a turn at a time to avoid damage to the bridge. Torque to 19 ft. lbs. (26 Nm).

9. Install the valve cover, vacuum switch and bracket assembly and disconneted vacuum hoses.

10. Connect the electrical harness connectors and the negative battery cable.

3.0L Engine

1. Relieve the fuel system pressure. Disconnect the negative battery cable.

2. Remove the engine cover mounting bolts and remove the engine cover.

3. Disconnect the vacuum hoses and electrical connectors, as required.

4. Remove the spark plug wire holder and loosen the accessory drive belt.

5. Remove the air conditioning compressor mounting bolts and position the compressor aside, if required.

6. Remove the power steering reservoir, idle speed regulator bracket, accelerator cable and bracket.

7. Remove the rocker arm cover attaching bolts and remove the rocker cover.

8. Label the rocker shaft assemblies. Remove the rocker arm shaft attaching bolts and remove the shaft assembly.

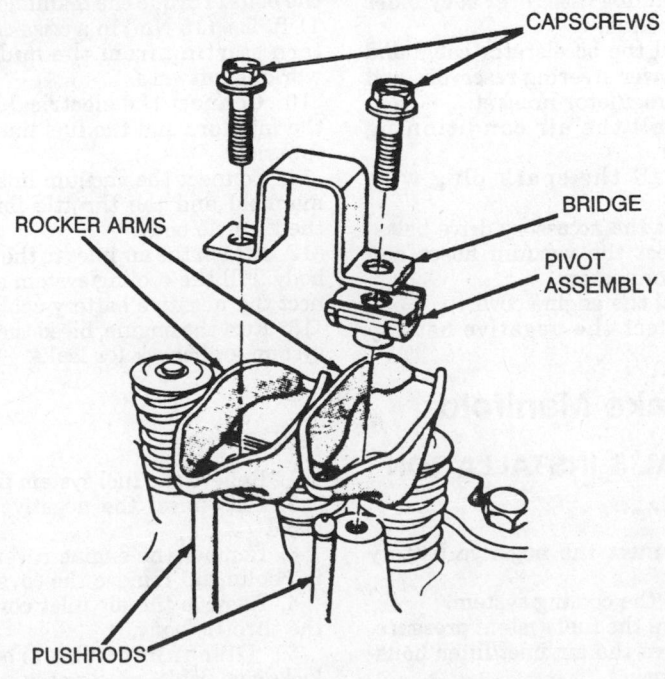

Rocker arm and bridge—2.5L engine

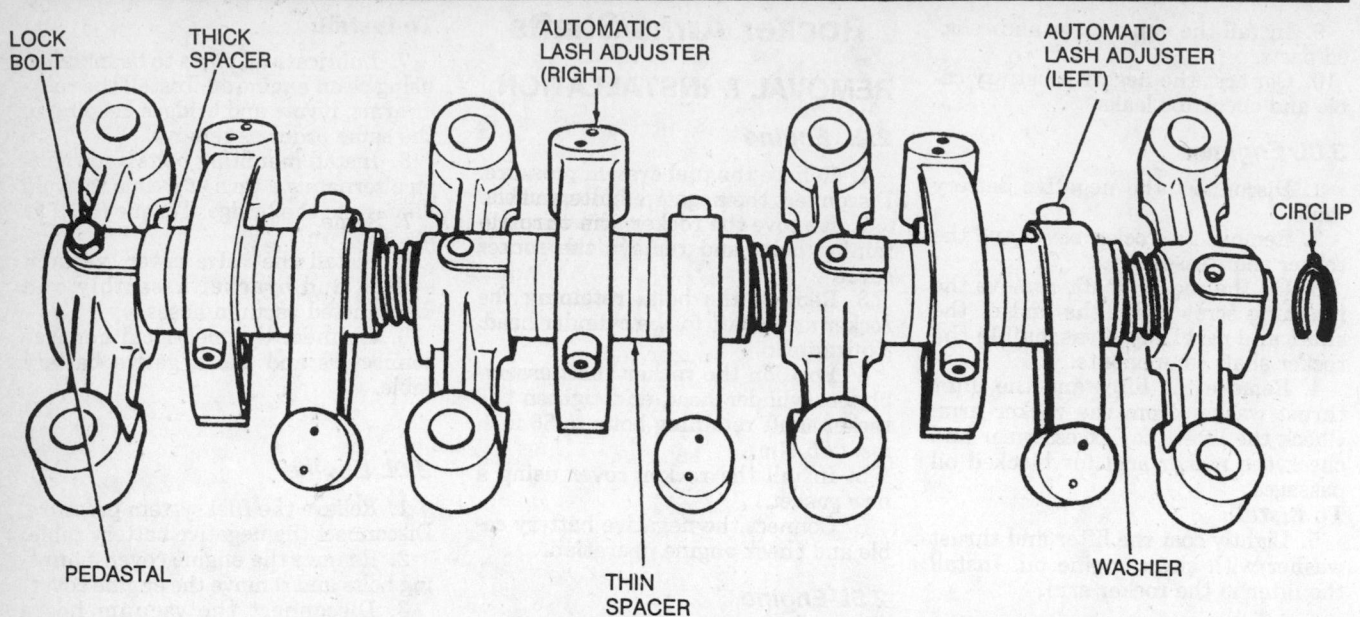

LOCK BOLT   THICK SPACER   AUTOMATIC LASH ADJUSTER (RIGHT)   AUTOMATIC LASH ADJUSTER (LEFT)   CIRCLIP

PEDASTAL   THIN SPACER   WASHER

Rocker shaft assembly—3.0L engine

NOTE: Both left and right rocker shaft assemblies are identical and can be interchanged between cylinder heads. Always install them on the same cylinder head that they were removed from.

To install:

9. Lightly coat the rocker shaft assembly with clean engine oil and position on the cylinder head. Tighten the attaching bolts to 53 inch lbs. (6 Nm).

10. Before installing the rocker cover, apply a light coating of sealer to the top of the timing case cover at cylinder head joints area.

11. Install the accelerator cable and bracket, power steering reservoir, and idle speed regulator bracket.

12. Install the air conditioning compressor.

13. Install the spark plug wire holder.

14. Adjust the accessory drive belt.

15. Connect the vacuum hoses and electrical connectors.

16. Install the engine cover.

17. Connect the negative battery cable.

Intake Manifold

REMOVAL & INSTALLATION

2.2L Engine

1. Disconnect the negative battery cable.

2. Drain the cooling system.

3. Relieve the fuel system pressure.

4. Remove the air inlet/filter housing and tube.

5. Disconnect the fuel lines at the injector rail. Disconnect the vacuum lines at the intake manifold.

6. Disconnect the throttle linkage at the throttle body. Remove the electrical connectors from the injectors.

7. Remove the intake manifold retaining bolts and remove the intake manifold.

8. Clean the gasket mating surfaces.

To install:

9. Position the intake manifold on the head using a new gasket and insert the bolts. Torque the manifold bolts to 11 ft. lbs. (15 Nm) in a criss-cross pattern starting from the middle and working outward.

10. Connect the electrical leads to the injectors and the fuel lines to the fuel rail.

11. Connect the vacuum lines at the manifold and the throttle linkage at the throttle body.

12. Attach the air inlet to the throttle body. Fill the cooling system and connect the negative battery cable.

13. Run the engine, bleed the cooling system and check for leaks.

3.0L Engine

1. Relieve the fuel system pressure.

2. Disconnect the negative battery cable.

3. Remove the engine cover retaining bolts and remove the cover.

4. Remove the air inlet cover from the throttle body.

5. Disconnect the transaxle kickdown cable, accelerator cable and cruise control cable from the throttle body. Remove the vacuum hoses from the intake manifold.

6. Remove the electrical connector from the throttle position sensor. Disconnect and tag the electrical connectors from the fuel injectors and lay the harness aside.

7. Remove the EGR tube. Remove the wire from the air temperature sensor.

8. Remove the fuel lines from the injector rails.

9. Remove the 4 bolts retaining the intake manifold and remove the manifold. Remove the O-rings from the cylinder heads and discard them.

NOTE: When the intake manifold has been removed the O-rings in the cylinder heads must be replaced.

10. Clean all gasket mating surfaces.

To install:

11. Use new O-rings and install the intake manifold. Torque the retaining bolts to 11 ft. lbs. (15 Nm) in an "X" pattern.

12. Install the fuel lines to the fuel rail assembly. Connect the electrical connectors to the fuel injectors. Connect all of the electrical connectors and vacuum hoses removed.

13. Connect the EGR tube. Connect the transaxle kickdown cable, accelerator and cruise control cables. Connect the negative battery cable.

14. Install the air inlet to the throttle body. Install the engine cover.

15. Connect the negative battery cable.

16. Run the engine and check for leaks.

Exhaust Manifold

REMOVAL & INSTALLATION

2.2L Engine

1. Disconnect the negative battery cable.
2. Remove the exhaust manifold heat shield and hot air tube.
3. Remove the EGR tube from the manifold.
4. Remove the bolts retaining the header pipe to the manifold.
5. Remove the manifold mounting nuts. Remove the manifold and gaskets.

To install:

6. Place the manifold gaskets and the manifold on the block. Tighten the mounting nuts to 13 ft. lbs. (18 Nm) in a criss-cross pattern starting from the middle and working outward.
7. Install the heat shield and the EGR tube.
8. Connect the negative battery cable and check for exhaust leaks.

3.0L Engine

1. Disconnect the negative battery cable.
2. Disconnect the EGR tube from the right side manifold.
3. Raise the vehicle and support safely.
4. Remove the nuts retaining the header pipe to the manifolds.
5. On the right manifold, remove the nuts securing the dipstick tube to the manifold. On the left manifold, remove the starter heat shield and the heat stove.
6. Lower the vehicle.
7. Remove the manifold mounting nuts and remove the manifolds.

To install:

8. Install the manifold and the mounting nuts. Tighten nut to 13 ft. lbs. (18 Nm) starting in the center of the maifold and working out.
9. Raise and safely support the vehicle.
10. Install te starter heat shield and the dipstick retainer nut as required.
11. Install the header pipe to the manifolds and secure.
12. Install the EGR tube, if removed. Connect the negative battery cable.
13. Start the engine and check for leaks.

Combination Manifold

REMOVAL & INSTALLATION

2.5L Engine

1. Relieve the fuel system pressure.
2. Disconnect the negative battery cable.

3. Remove the air inlet cover and hose from the throttle body.
4. Loosen the accessory drive belt and remove it. Remove the power steering pump and brackets. Support the pump to the side but do not disconnect the pressure lines.
5. Disconnect the fuel lines and the accelerator cable from the throttle body. Disconnect the electrical connectors for the idle speed sensor, throttle position sensor, coolant temperature sensor, air intake temperature sensor and the oxygen sensor.
6. Disconnect the electrical plug from the fuel injector. Disconnect the vacuum lines at the intake manifold.
7. Remove the bolts supporting the EGR tube to the exhaust manifold. Remove the heater hoses from the intake manifold.
8. Remove the intake/exhaust manifold mounting bolts and remove the manifolds from the engine.

To install:

9. Clean all of the gasket mounting surfaces.
10. Position the new intake manifold gasket and the new exhaust manifold spacers over the locating dowels. Install the manifold to the head and tighten the mounting bolts as follows:
   a. Centermost upper manifold bolt – 30 ft. lbs. (41 Nm).
   b. Lower outermost bolts – 30 ft. lbs. (41 Nm).
   c. Remaining mounting bolts – 23 ft. lbs. (31 Nm).
11. Install the EGR tube to the exhaust manifold. Connect the heater and vacuum hoses. Attach the fuel lines to the throttle body.
12. Reconnect all electrical connectors. Install the power steering pump and brackets.
13. Connect the accelerator cable. Install the accessory drive belt and adjust the tension. Install the air inlet tube and cover.
14. Connect the negative battery cable and fill the cooling system.
15. Run the engine and bleed the cooling system. Check for leaks.

Timing Chain Front Cover

REMOVAL & INSTALLATION

2.5L Engine

1. Disconnect the negative battery cable.
2. Remove the drive belts, engine fan and hub assembly, vibration damper, pulley and key.
3. Remove the alternator bracket. If equipped with air conditioning, remove the compressor.

4. Remove the oil pan-to-cover bolts and the cover-to-engine block bolts.
5. Remove the front cover assembly from the engine.
6. Cut off the oil pan side gasket end tabs flush with the front face of the cylinder block and remove the gasket tabs.
7. Remove the oil seal from the timing cover and clean all gasket material from the sealing surface.

To install:

8. Apply sealant to both sides of the gasket and install on the cover sealing surface.
9. Cut the end tabs from the replacement oil pan side gasket and cement the tabs on the oil pan.
10. Install a new oil seal into the cover assembly.

NOTE: The oil seal can be installed after the cover has been installed on the engine block, depending upon whether the cover aligning tools are available.

11. Coat the front cover seal end tab recesses with RTV sealant and position the seal on the cover bottom.
12. Position the cover on the engine block and position an alignment tool into the crankshaft opening.

NOTE: Two different types of alignment tools are available, without seal in housing or with seal in housing.

13. Install the cover-to-engine block bolts and the oil pan-to-cover bolts. Tighten the cover-to-engine block bolts to 5 ft. lbs. (7 Nm) and the oil pan-to-cover bolts to 11 ft. lbs. (15 Nm).
14. If not already done, install the seal.
15. Install the vibration damper.
16. Install the compressor and alternator bracket.
17. Install the engine fan and hub assembly. Install the belts and adjust.
18. Connect the negative battery cable and check for leaks.

3.0L Engine

1. Disconnect the negative battery cable.
2. Remove the rocker covers. Hold the camshaft sprocket in place and remove the distributor drive/camshaft sprocket bolt. Remove the distributor assembly.
3. Remove the accessory drive belt. Remove the nuts retaining the front engine vibration damper to the engine and move it toward the radiator.
4. Remove the crankshaft pulley nut and remove the crankshaft pulley.

NOTE: The crankshaft pulley nut is put on with a threaded lock

installed with the nut. It may be necessary to strike the pulley with a brass hammer to loosen it.

5. Remove the timing cover mounting bolts. Place a prying tool between the cylinder block and a special boss on the front cover and gently pry off the cover. Discard the gaskets.

6. Remove the oil seal from the cover.

To install:

7. To prevent the key from falling into the oil pan, rotate the crankshaft so the keyway points upward.

8. Apply a bead of RTV sealer to the points where the cylinder heads meet the block and the lower case meets the block.

9. Install the cover with new gasket over the alignment dowels. Tighten the bolts to 9 ft. lbs. (12 Nm).

10. Install the distributor assembly and install the rocker covers.

11. Install the crankshaft pulley, apply thread locking compound to the threads of the pulley nut and tighten to 133 ft. lbs. (180 Nm).

12. Install the accessory drive belt and adjust the belt tension.

NOTE: It is very important the accessory drive belt is routed correctly. If it is incorrectly routed the water pump could be driven in the wrong direction, causing the engine to overheat.

13. Install the engine vibration damper.

14. Connect the negative battery cable and check for leaks.

Timing Chain and Sprockets

REMOVAL & INSTALLATION

2.5L Engine

1. Disconnect the negative battery cable.

2. Remove the fan shroud assembly, accessory drive belts, water pump pulley, crankshaft vibration damper and timing case cover.

NOTE: It is a good practice to either remove the radiator or cover the radiator core area when working around the radiator, as damage can result to the radiator core.

3. Rotate the crankshaft until the **0** timing mark on the crankshaft sprocket aligns with the timing mark on the cover.

4. Remove the oil slinger from the crankshaft.

5. Remove the camshaft retaining bolt, the sprocket and chain assembly.

6. If the timing chain tensioner is to be replaced, the oil pan must also be removed.

To install:

7. Turn the tensioner lever to the **UNLOCK** position and pull the tensioner block toward the tensioner lever to compress the spring. Hold the block and turn the tensioner lever to the lock **UP** position.

8. Install the crankshaft/camshaft sprockets and timing chain. Make sure the timing marks are aligned as indicated in Step 3.

9. Install the camshaft sprocket retaining bolt and washer. Torque the bolt to 80 ft. lbs. (108 Nm).

NOTE: To verify correct installation of the timing chain, rotate the crankshaft until the camshaft sprocket timing mark is approximately at the 1 o'clock position. There should be 20 pins (2 per link) between the marks.

10. Install the oil slinger.

11. Install the timing case cover and all related parts.

12. Connect the negative battery cable and check engine for proper operation.

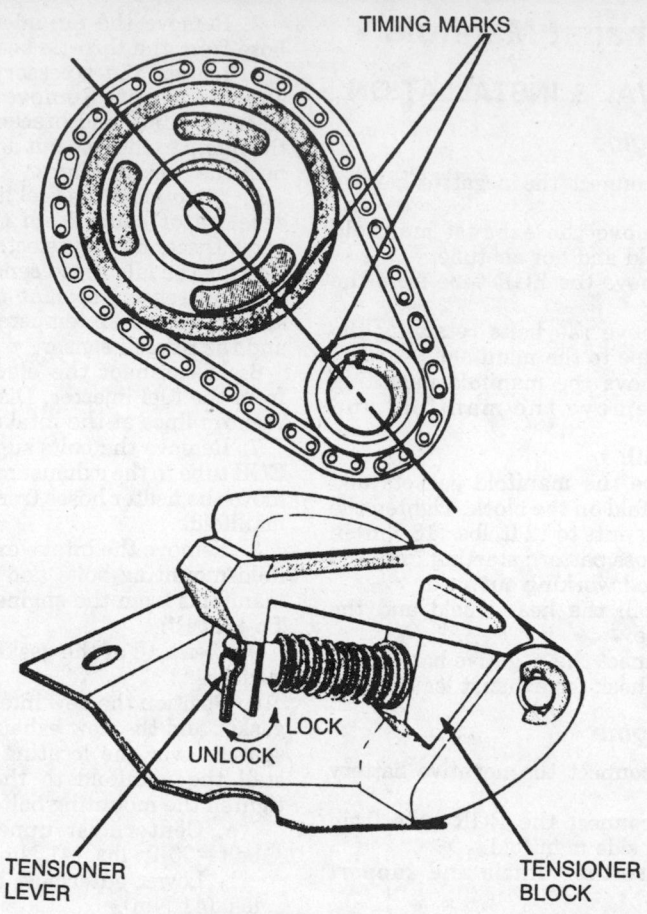

Timing mark alignment—2.5L engine

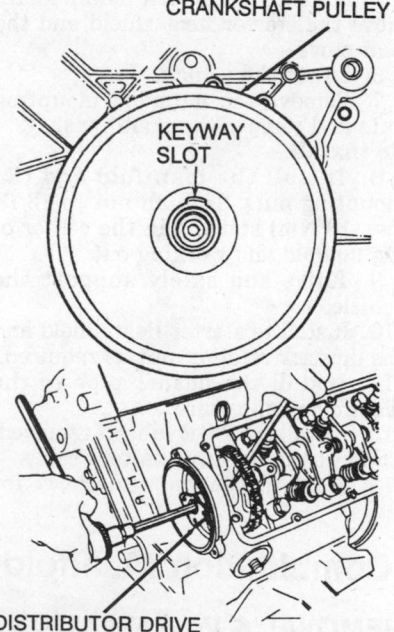

When removing crank pulley, turn keyway to top keeping key from falling into engine, and hold cam gear as shown—3.0L engine

3.0L Engine

1. Disconnect the negative battery cable. Remove the cylinder head cover.

2. Inspect the chain and sprocket for wear by pulling on the top of the chain. This will produce a gap between the bottom of the timing chain and the bottom of the area between the 2 sprocket teeth. The maximum gap is 0.067 in. (0.17mm). This must not be exceeded. This gap corresponds to a travel of 0.866 in. (2.19mm) by the timing chain tensioner plunger.

3. Use the solid end of a No. 51 drill bit (0.067 in. diameter) to gauge the gap. If the solid end of the drill bit fits into the gap between the timing chain and the 2 sprocket teeth, then the following parts must be replaced: timing chain shoes, tensioners, guides, sprockets, tensioner shoes. Use the following procedure.

4. Disconnect the negative battery cable.

5. Remove the front cover assembly. Turn the crankshaft until piston No. 1 is at TDC of the compression stroke.

NOTE: Keep all of the components from each side together. This will aid in assembly.

6. Remove the oil pump sprocket retaining bolts and remove the sprocket/chain assembly.

7. Remove the bolt attaching the right side camshaft sprocket to the camshaft. Remove the right side tensioner and let the tensioner shoe hang down.

8. Remove the right side timing chain and sprocket. Remove the right side chain guide and tensioner shoe.

9. Remove the bolt attaching the left side camshaft sprocket to the camshaft. Remove the left side tensioner and let the tensioner shoe hang down.

10. Remove the left side timing chain and sprocket. Remove the left side chain guide and tensioner shoe.

To install:

NOTE: Inspect the timing chain tensioner. An opening shows the tensioner lock inside. This tensioner lock should not be removed. The lock is held in place by a spring that pushes a steel ball against the lock finger. If the lock is removed accidentally, replace the tensioner assembly because there is no way of checking the position of the lock finger in relation to the steel ball. When installing a tensioner use a thin blade tool to turn the ratchet counterclockwise. Then push the tensioner arm in. Position the tensioner over the filter and the tensioner shoe into the arm.

Cylinder block and front cover boss—3.0L engine

11. To install, place the left and right chain guides into position and tighten the bolts to 48 inch lbs. (5.4 Nm). Install the tensioner shoes and tighten the mounting bolts to 9 ft. lbs. (12 Nm)

12. Turn the left camshaft until the keyway slot is in the 11 o'clock position. Turn the right camshaft so the keyway is in the 8 o'clock position.

13. Turn the crankshaft until the keyway is aligned with the centerline of the left cylinder head.

NOTE: The crankshaft has 3 sprockets on it. A sprocket each for the left and right timing chains and 1 for the oil pump drive. The timing mark is located on the center sprocket.

14. Install the left camshaft sprocket. Install the left timing chain on the crankshaft. Position the single painted link of the timing chain on the tooth of the rear sprocket which is directly behind the timing mark of the center sprocket.

15. Install the left timing chain over the camshaft sprocket. The chain must be positioned with the unpainted link which is between 2 painted links aligned with the stamped timing mark on the camshaft sprocket.

16. Once the left chain is positioned, install the tensioner shoe and turn the tensioner arm inward. Tighten the

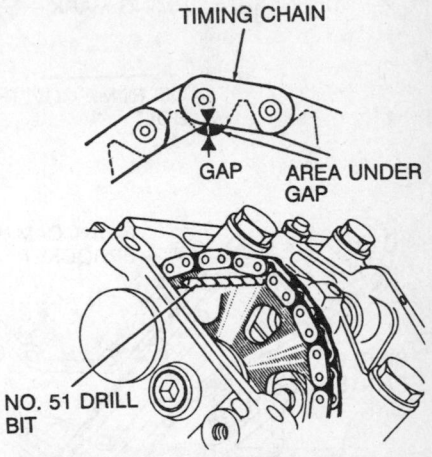

Measuring chain wear using a No. 51 drill as gauge—3.0L engine

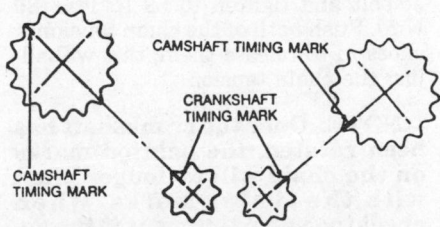

Align crank and right cam mark (A); turn crank 90 degrees and check left cam mark (B)

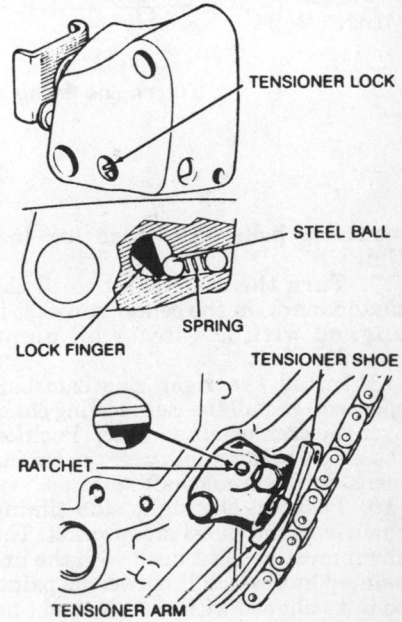

Engine chain tensioner—3.0L engine

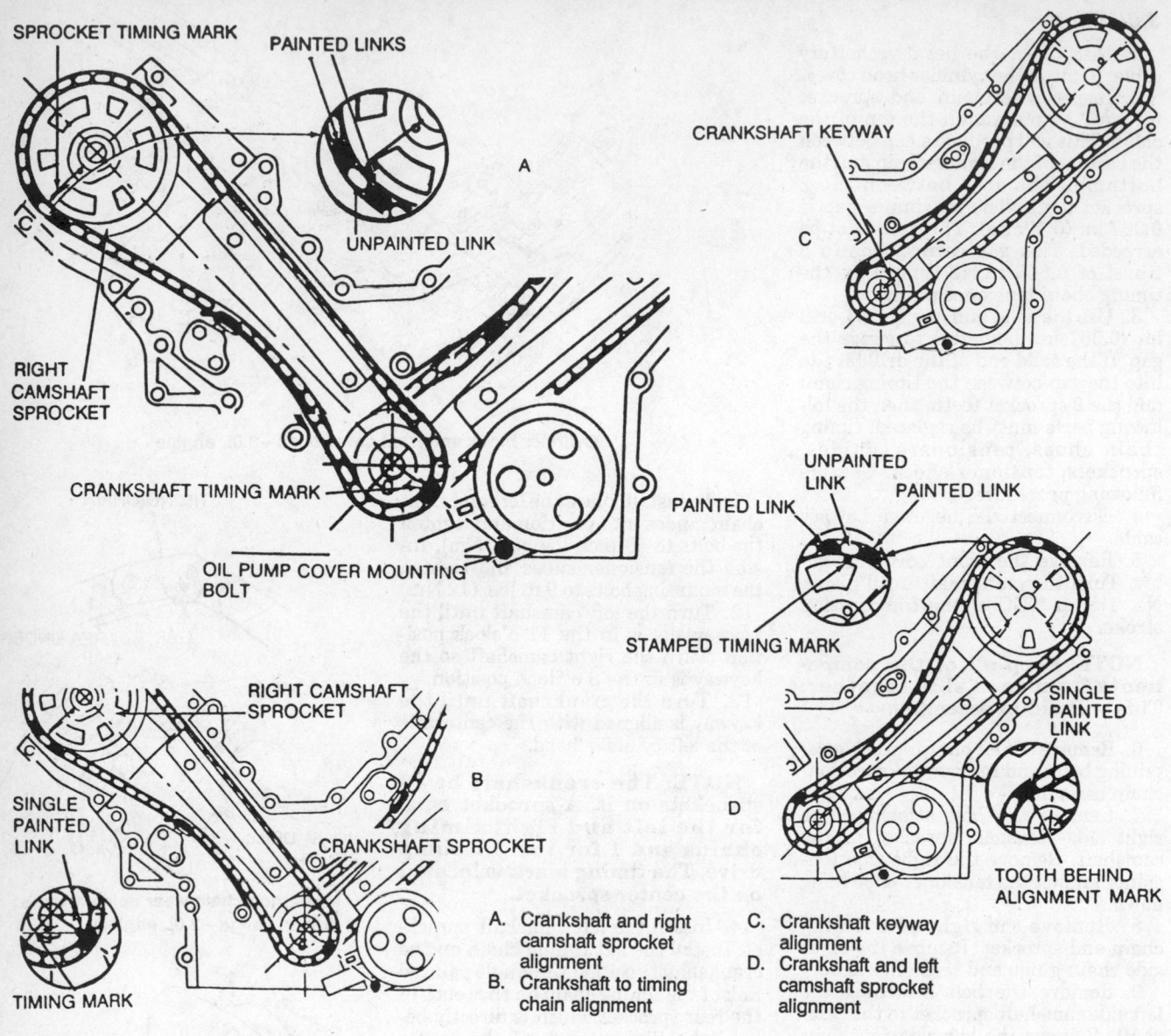

SPROCKET TIMING MARK

PAINTED LINKS

UNPAINTED LINK

A

RIGHT CAMSHAFT SPROCKET

CRANKSHAFT TIMING MARK

OIL PUMP COVER MOUNTING BOLT

CRANKSHAFT KEYWAY

C

UNPAINTED LINK

PAINTED LINK

PAINTED LINK

STAMPED TIMING MARK

RIGHT CAMSHAFT SPROCKET

B

CRANKSHAFT SPROCKET

SINGLE PAINTED LINK

TIMING MARK

D

SINGLE PAINTED LINK

TOOTH BEHIND ALIGNMENT MARK

A. Crankshaft and right camshaft sprocket alignment
B. Crankshaft to timing chain alignment
C. Crankshaft keyway alignment
D. Crankshaft and left camshaft sprocket alignment

3.0L engine timing chains and marks are complex; locate and note marks before removal

mounting bolts to 48 inch lbs. (5.4 Nm).

17. Turn the crankshaft until the timing mark on the center sprocket is aligned with the lower oil pump mounting bolt.

18. Install the right side camshaft sprocket. Install the right timing chain over the crankshaft sprocket. Position the single painted link over the timing mark on the crankshaft sprocket.

19. Position the right side timing chain over the camshaft sprocket. The chain must be positioned with the unpainted link which is between 2 painted links aligned with the stamped timing mark on the camshaft sprocket.

20. Once the right side chain is posi-

tioned, install the tensioner shoe and turn the tensioner arm inward. Tighten the mounting bolts to 48 inch lbs. (5.4 Nm).

21. Install the right camshaft sprocket bolt and tighten to 59 ft. lbs. (80 Nm). Push both of the chain tensioner shoes in to release them; this will adjust the chain tension.

NOTE: Once the crankshaft has been rotated, the painted marks on the chain will no longer align with the timing marks. When checking valve timing, it is the relation of the timing marks to each other that is used, not the position of the paint marks on the

chains. To check, rotate the crankshaft 180 degrees. Check that the right camshaft sprocket timing mark and the crankshaft sprocket timing mark are aligned. Rotate the crankshaft another 90 degrees. Check that the left camshaft sprocket timing mark and the crankshaft sprocket timing mark are aligned.

22. Install the oil pump sprocket and chain, apply a thread locking compound to the retaining bolts, and tighten to 48 inch lbs. (5.4 Nm).

23. Install the front cover assembly. Connect the negative battery cable. Check timing.

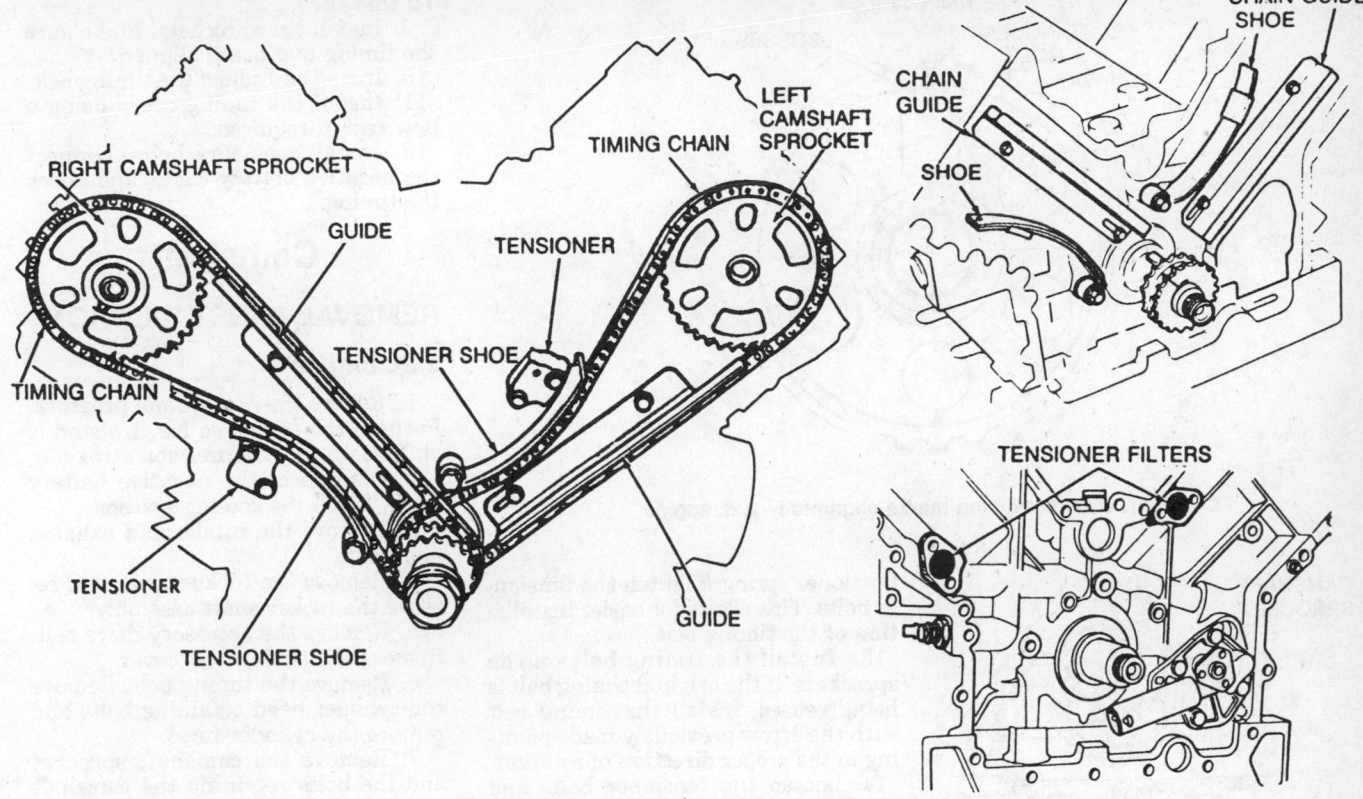

Timing chain and tensioner layout—3.0L engine

Timing Belt Front Cover

REMOVAL & INSTALLATION

2.2L Engine

1. Disconnect the negative battery cable. Remove the drive belts, fan and pulley.
2. Remove the vibration damper.
3. Remove the oil pan-to-cover bolts and cover-to-block bolts.
4. Raise the cover and pull the oil pan front seal up far enough to extract the tabs from the holes in the cover.

NOTE: If this isn't done, the oil pan will have to be removed to get the seals into place.

5. Remove the cover gasket from block. Cut off the seal tab flush with the front face of the block.
To install:
6. Clean all mating surfaces and remove the oil seal.
7. Install a new front oil seal.
8. Install a new neoprene seal in the front of the oil pan, cutting off the protruding tabs to match the original. Use sealer on the tab ends and the gasket surfaces.
9. Position the cover on the block and install the bolts. Tighten the cover

bolts to 4–6 ft. lbs. (5–8 Nm). The 4 lower bolts are tightened to 10–12 ft. lbs. (14–16 Nm).
10. Install the vibration damper and belts.
11. Connect the negative battery cable.

OIL SEAL REPLACEMENT

1. Disconnect the negative battery cable. Remove the timing belt cover.
2. Thoroughly clean and dry the cover.
3. Drive out the old seal. Install a new seal with a round driver.
4. Reinstall timing belt cover.

NOTE: The front oil seal can be installed with the cover in place only if the proper tool or equivalent is available.

Timing Belt and Tensioner

ADJUSTMENT

1. Rotate the crankshaft clockwise 2 complete turns.
2. Loosen the tensioner bolts ¼ turn.
3. The spring loaded timing belt tensioner will automatically adjust to the correct position.

4. Tighten the bottom tensioner bolt first, then the upper bolt. Torque both bolts to 18 ft. lbs. (24 Nm).
5. Check timing belt deflection. It should be 0.216–0.276 in. (5.5–7.0mm).

REMOVAL & INSTALLATION

2.2L Engine

1. Disconnect the negative battery cable.
2. Remove the drive belts, vibration damper, pulley and key.
3. Remove the alternator bracket. If equipped with air conditioning, remove the compressor.
4. Remove the timing belt cover.
5. Make a mark on the back of the timing belt indicating the direction of rotation so it may be reassembled in the same direction if it is to be reused.
6. Loosen the timing belt tensioner pivot bolt and locking bolt.
7. Remove the timing belt.

NOTE: If coolant or engine oil comes in contact with the timing belt, they will drastically shorten its life. Also, do not allow engine oil or coolant to contact the timing belt sprockets or tensioner assembly.

To install:
8. Inspect all parts for damage and

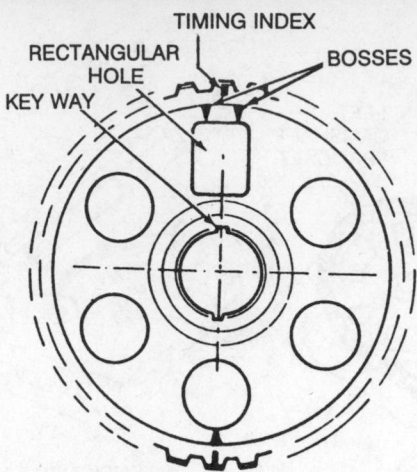

Camshaft sprocket timing marks alignment—2.2L engine

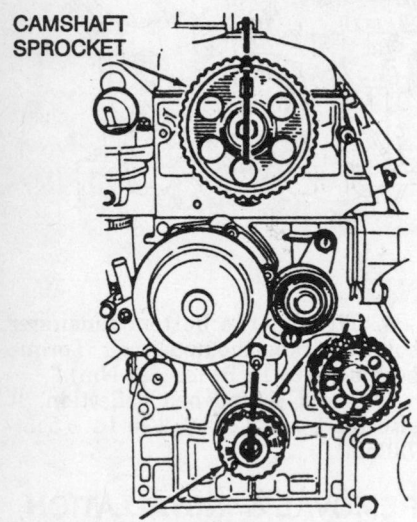

Timing index and timing marks alignment—2.2L engine

wear. If any of the following is found, replacement is necessary:

a. Timing belt—cracks on back surface, sides, bottom and separated canvas.

b. Tensioner pulleys—turn the pulleys and check for binding, excessive play, unusual noise or if there is a grease leak.

9. Position the camshaft sprocket timing index in line with the static timing mark.

10. Position the crankshaft so No. 1 piston is at TDC on the compression stroke.

11. Remove the access hole plug in the cylinder block and insert the special tool used to apply pressure to the tensioner.

12. Loosen the timing belt tensioner bolts. Push the tensioner pulley towards the water pump to compress the

tensioner spring. Tighten the tensioner bolts. This allows for easier installation of the timing belt.

13. Install the timing belt on the sprockets. If the original timing belt is being reused, install the timing belt with the arrow previously made pointing in the proper direction of rotation.

14. Loosen the tensioner bolts and allow the spring loaded tensioner to contact the belt. This will automatically tension the belt. Then, tighten the tensioner retaining bolts.

15. Position the timing belt cover over the sprockets and check the position of the camshaft sprocket timing mark with the index on the cover.

16. Install cylinder block plug, check the timing belt tension adjustment.

17. Install the compressor and alternator bracket.

18. Install vibration damper and drive belts.

19. Connect the negative battery cable and check the engine for proper operation.

Timing Sprockets

REMOVAL & INSTALLATION

1. Disconnect battery negative cable.

2. Turn crankshaft until piston No. 1 is at TDC of the compression stroke.

3. Remove the accessory drive belts.

4. Remove crankshaft vibration damper.

5. Remove the timing belt cover.

6. Remove the timing belt.

7. Make sure the camshaft sprocket has the rectangular hole upwards and timing mark is at the 12 o'clock position.

8. Loosen the camshaft sprocket bolt and gently tap the sprocket from the rear to remove.

To install:

9. Install the sprockets. Make sure the timing marks are aligned.

10. Install and adjust the timing belt.

11. Install the timing cover using a new seal, if required.

12. Install accessory belts, connect the negative battery cable, and check the timing.

Camshaft

REMOVAL & INSTALLATION

2.2L Engine

1. Relieve the fuel system pressure. Position the engine so No. 1 piston is at TDC on the compression stroke.

2. Disconnect the negative battery cable. Drain the cooling system.

3. Remove the intake and exhaust manifolds.

4. Remove the rocker cover and remove the rocker shaft assembly.

5. Remove the accessory drive belt. Remove the timing belt cover.

6. Remove the timing belt. Remove the cylinder head retaining bolts and remove the cylinder head.

7. Remove the camshaft sprocket and the bolts retaining the camshaft thrust plate.

8. Pry the oil seal out from around the camshaft and slide the camshaft from the head. Use care not to damage the camshaft lobes or the bearings.

To install:

9. Lubricate the camshaft with heavy oil and slide it into the head.

10. Install the camshaft thrust plate. Install a new camshaft oil seal using tool MOT–791–10 or equivalent. Install the camshaft sprocket and tighten the retaining bolt to 37 ft. lbs. (51 Nm).

11. Replace the gasket and install the cylinder head.

12. Install the timing belt and adjust the tension. Install the timing belt cover.

13. Install the rocker shaft assembly. Install the rocker cover, intake and exhaust manifolds.

14. Install the accessory drive belt and fill the cooling system.

15. Connect the negative battery cable. Run the engine and bleed the cooling system.

2.5L Engine

1. Relieve the fuel system pressure. Position the engine so No. 1 piston is at TDC on the compression stroke.

2. Disconnect the negative battery cable. Drain the cooling system.

3. Remove the radiator.

4. Remove the fan and water pump pulley.

5. Remove the grille, if necessary for clearance.

6. Remove the rocker cover, rocker arms and pushrods keeping in order of removal so they can be reinstalled in their original location.

7. Remove the distributor, spark plugs and fuel pump.

8. Remove the lifters.

9. Remove the crankshaft hub and timing gear cover.

10. Remove the 2 camshaft thrust plate screws by working through the holes in the gear.

11. Remove the camshaft and gear assembly by pulling it through the front of the block. Be careful not to damage the bearings.

To install:

12. Lubricate the camshaft with heavy oil and install it into the block.

13. Install the timing chain and sprockets. Install the timing case cover.

14. Install the valve lifters and related components. Install the rocker cover.

15. Install the crankshaft hub and the water pump pulley. Install the accessory drive belts.

16. Position the distributor and tighten the hold-down bolt. Install the spark plugs.

17. Install the grille.

18. Connect the negative battery cable and check the timing.

3.0L Engine

The camshafts used in this engine are removed from the rear of the cylinder heads after the cylinder heads have been removed.

1. Relieve the fuel system pressure. Position the engine so No. 1 piston is at TDC on the compression stroke.

2. Disconnect the negative battery cable.

3. Drain the cooling system.

4. Remove the cylinder head(s).

5. Remove the camshaft cover at the rear of the cylinder head. Loosen the camshaft retainer bolt and slide the retainer away from the camshaft.

6. Slide the camshaft out of the head. Use care not to damage the camshaft lobes or bearings.

To install:

7. Coat the camshaft with heavy oil and slide it into the head. Position the retainer in the grove of the camshaft and tighten the mounting bolt to 9 ft. lbs. (12 Nm).

8. Push the camshaft to the front and check the camshaft endplay by inserting a feeler gauge between the retainer and the front of the camshaft. The endplay must be 0.0030–0.0055 in. (0.07–0.14mm).

9. Install the camshaft cover using a new gasket. Coat the threads of the bolt with Loctite 271® or equivalent, and tighten the bolts to 53 inch lbs. (6 Nm).

10. Install the cylinder heads and all related parts.

11. Install the timing chains and sprockets.

12. Install the front cover assembly and the accessory drive belt.

13. Install the rocker shaft assemblies and the rocker covers.

14. Fill the cooling system and connect the negative battery cable. Install the air inlet tube.

15. Run the engine and bleed the cooling system.

Intermediate Shaft

REMOVAL & INSTALLATION

2.2L Engine

1. Disconnect the negative battery cable.

2. Remove the timing belt cover and the timing belt.

3. Remove the oil pump driveshaft cover, located on the side of the block.

4. Screw a piece of threaded rod into the top of oil pump driveshaft and remove it.

5. Remove the bolt retaining the intermediate shaft sprocket and remove the intermediate shaft sprocket.

6. Remove the bolts from the intermediate shaft cover. Remove the cover and gasket. Remove the bolt from the intermediate shaft retainer and pivot the retainer. Remove the intermediate shaft by pulling it from the block.

To install:

7. Coat the shaft with heavy oil and slide it into the block. Pivot the retainer into position and tighten the bolt. Install the shaft cover and loosely install the retaining bolts.

8. Install the shaft oil seal and align the cover using tool MOT–790 or equivalent. Tighten the cover retaining bolts.

9. Install the sprocket and bolt. Tighten the bolt to 37 ft. lbs. (51 Nm).

10. Install the oil pump driveshaft and cover.

11. Install the timing belt and cover, and check the belt tension.

12. Connect the negative battery cable.

Piston and Connecting Rod

POSITIONING

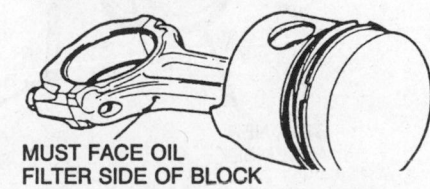

MUST FACE OIL
FILTER SIDE OF BLOCK

Piston positioning—2.2L engine

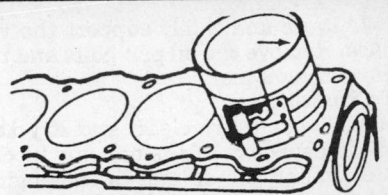

2.5L engine—oil squirt holes face the camshaft and the arrow on the top of the piston must face the front of the engine

LEFT BANK

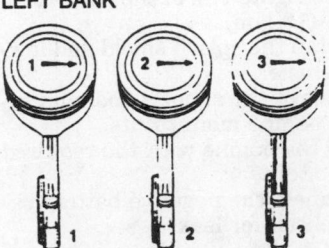

RIGHT BANK

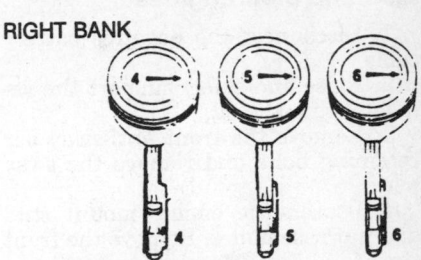

Piston positioning—3.0L engine

ENGINE LUBRICATION

Oil Pan

REMOVAL & INSTALLATION

2.2L Engine

1. Disconnect the negative battery cable.

2. Raise and safely support the vehicle.

3. Remove the underbody splash shield and drain the engine oil.

4. Remove the engine mount cushion nuts.

5. Lower the vehicle and position engine support tool MS–1900 or equivalent, on the inner fender flanges.

6. Tighten the support tool until the engine is raised enough to remove the oil pan.

NOTE: There are 3 sizes of bolts used to retain the oil pan on this engine. Note the location of each bolt when it is removed.

7. Raise and safely support the vehicle. Remove the oil pan bolts and remove the oil pan.

To install:

8. Thoroughly clean and dry the mating surfaces of the pan and block.

9. Install the oil pan to the engine block using a new gasket. Do not use any sealer on the gasket; it must be installed dry.

10. Tighten the oil pan bolts attaching the pan to the clutch/converter housing first, then tighten the remaining bolts. Tighten all of the bolts to 88 inch lbs. (10 Nm).

11. Install the splash shield and lower the vehicle.

12. Remove the support tool and install the engine mount nuts.

13. Fill the engine with the required amount of oil.

14. Connect the negative battery cable and check for leaks.

2.5L and 3.0L Engines

1. Disconnect the negative battery cable.

2. Raise and safely support the vehicle. Drain the oil.

3. Remove the front anti-sway bar retaining bolts and remove the sway bar.

4. Loosen the engine mount stud and nut assemblies. Remove the front tires.

5. Remove the lower ball joint retaining bolts and disengage the lower ball joints from the steering knuckles.

6. Remove the nuts at the center of the transaxle crossmember securing the rear of the transaxle to the crossmember.

7. Lower the vehicle and attach engine support tool MS-1900 to the engine.

8. With the vehicle lowered, loosen the 4 sub-frame attaching nuts. Remove the front 2 first, allowing the sub-frame to pivot to the ground. Support the rear of the sub-frame and remove the 2 rear nuts. Lower the sub-frame away from the vehicle.

9. Raise and support the vehicle. Remove the oil pan retaining bolts and remove the oil pan.

To install:

10. Thoroughly clean and dry the mating surfaces of the pan and block.

11. Install the oil pan to the engine block using a new gasket. Do not use any sealer on the gasket; it must be installed dry. Tighten all of the retaining bolts to 9 ft. lbs. (12 Nm).

12. Install the sub-frame assembly and tighten the mounting nuts to 92 ft. lbs. (125 Nm).

13. Connect the lower ball joints and tighten the attaching nut to 77 ft. lbs. (104 Nm). Tighten the transaxle-to-crossmember bolts to 20 ft. lbs. (27 Nm).

14. Remove the engine support tool. Attach the anti-sway bar and install the front wheels.

15. Lower the vehicle. Fill the crankcase with the appropriate quantity and grade of oil.

16. Connect the negative battery cable and check for leaks.

Oil Pump

REMOVAL & INSTALLATION

2.2L Engine

1. Disconnect the negative battery cable.

2. Remove the oil pump drive cover plate bolts and remove the cover.

3. Using a threaded rod, thread it into the top of the pump driveshaft. Remove the pump driveshaft by pulling it out of the block.

4. Raise and safely support the vehicle. Drain the oil.

5. Remove the oil pan. Remove the oil pump mounting bolts and remove the pump.

To install:

6. Install the oil pump using a new gasket. Tighten the mounting bolts to 33 ft. lbs. (45 Nm).

7. Install the oil pan. Fill the crankcase with the correct grade and quantity of oil.

8. Install the oil pump driveshaft and cover.

9. Connect the negative battery cable and check for leaks. Check for sufficient oil pressure.

2.5L Engine

1. Disconnect the negative battery cable.

2. Raise the vehicle and support safely. Drain the engine oil and remove the oil pan.

3. Remove the oil pump retaining bolts, the oil pump and gasket.

NOTE: The oil pump removal and installation will not affect the distributor timing because the distributor drive gear remains meshed with the camshaft. Do not disturb the position of the oil inlet tube and strainer assembly in the pump body. If the tube is moved in the body, a replacement tube and strainer must be installed to assure an airtight seal.

4. To ensure self priming, fill the gear cavity with petroleum jelly before installing the cover.

To install:

5. Install the pump with a new gasket. Tighten the short bolts to 10 ft. lbs. (14 Nm) and the long bolts to 17 ft. lbs. (23 Nm).

6. Install the oil pan and related parts using new gaskets and seals.

7. Fill the crankcase with the correct grade and quantity of oil.

8. Connect the negative battery cable and check for leaks. Check for sufficient oil pressure.

3.0L Engine

1. Disconnect the negative battery cable.

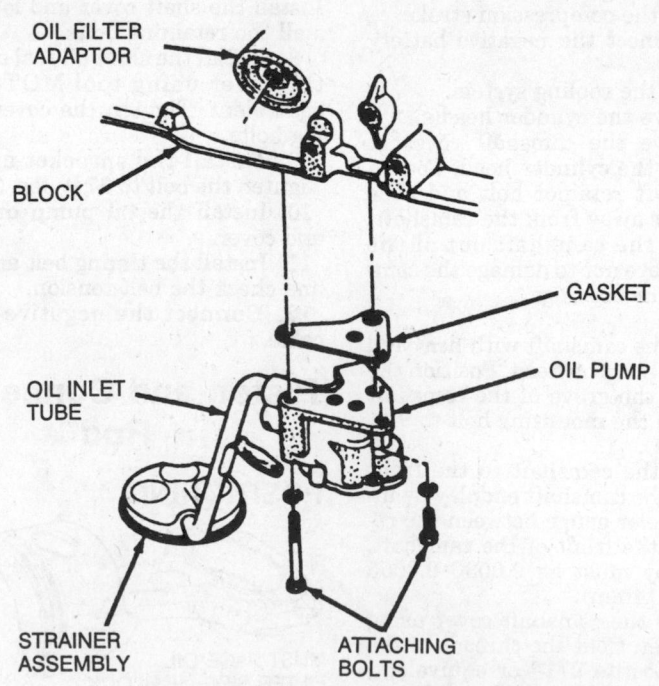

Oil pump and related parts—2.5L engine

2. Remove the timing chain cover assembly. Turn the crankshaft so the key is facing **UP**.

3. Remove the bolts retaining the oil pump drive sprocket. Remove the sprocket and the oil pump drive chain.

4. Remove the oil pump mounting bolts and remove the oil pump. Inspect the components for wear and replace pump assembly if worn.

To install:

5. Thoroughly clean and dry the mating surfaces of the pump and block. Install the oil pump to the block using a new gasket. Tighten the bolts to 9 ft. lbs. (12 Nm).

NOTE: Prime the oil pump by squirting oil through the hole below the oil filter connector shaft on the oil filter mounting surface.

6. Install the oil pump drive sprocket and chain. Coat the threads of the sprocket bolts with a thread locking compound and torque them to 53 inch lbs. (6 Nm).

7. Install the timing chain cover. Fill the oil filter with clean engine oil and install.

8. Connect the negative battery cable and check for leaks. Check for sufficient oil pressure.

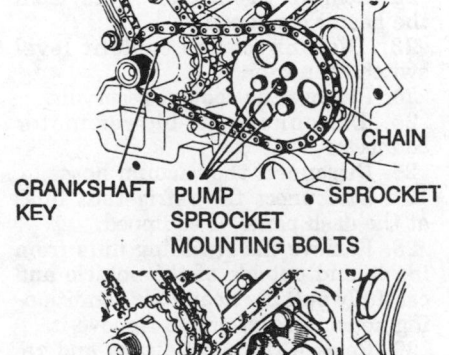

CRANKSHAFT KEY
PUMP SPROCKET MOUNTING BOLTS
CHAIN
SPROCKET

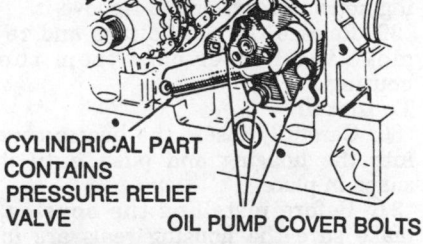

CYLINDRICAL PART CONTAINS PRESSURE RELIEF VALVE
OIL PUMP COVER BOLTS

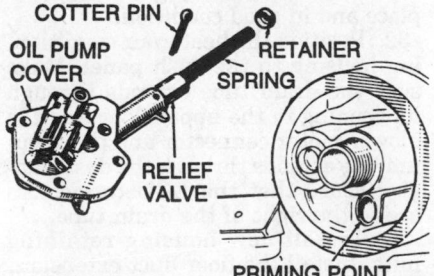

COTTER PIN
OIL PUMP COVER
RETAINER
SPRING
RELIEF VALVE
PRIMING POINT

Engine oil pump drive, mount, components and priming point—3.0L engine

Rear Main Oil Seal

REMOVAL & INSTALLATION

2.2L and 2.5L Engines

The rear main oil seal is a single unit and may be removed without removing the oil pan or crankshaft.

1. Disconnect the negative battery cable.

2. Remove the transaxle and flywheel.

3. Remove the rear main oil seal with a small prying tool. Be extremely careful not to scratch the crankshaft.

To install:

4. Lubricate the lips of the new seal with clean engine oil. Install the new seal by hand onto the rear crankshaft flange. The helical lip side of the seal should face the engine. Make sure the seal is firmly and evenly installed.

5. The new seal is installed with a special installer. Use the tool as follows:

a. Back the plastic wing nut off until it contacts the cap nut on the end of the shaft.

b. Lightly lubricate both the inside and outside edges of the seal.

c. Install the seal on the tool with the dust shield facing toward the plastic wing nut.

d. Fit the tool pilot in the center of the front surface of the installer into the pilot hole in the back of the crankshaft; the small dowel at the top of the front surface of the tool must fit into the corresponding small hole in the crankshaft at the same time. Hold the tool in this position and thread the 2 attaching screws into the crankshaft.

e. Turn the plastic wing nut in until it bottoms out to fully seat the seal. Unscrew the attaching nuts and remove the seal installer.

f. Inspect the dust shield all around to make sure it is not curled under. If it is, gently to pull the lip out.

6. Install the flywheel and transaxle.

7. Connect the negative battery cable and check for leaks.

3.0L Engine

1. Disconnect the negative battery cable.

2. Remove the transaxle assembly.

3. Remove the bolts from the lower rear main seal housing.

4. Remove the rear main seal housing bolts and remove the housing.

5. Remove the old rear main seal from the housing.

To install:

6. Thoroughly clean and dry the gasket mating surfaces.

7. Using a new gasket, install the rear main seal housing on the block.

8. Tighten the seal housing-to-block bolts first, then tighten the lower bolts. Torque all bolts to 9 ft. lbs. (12 Nm).

9. Install the new rear seal to tool MOT–259–01 or equivalent, and lightly coat the inner edges of the seal with oil. Install the seal to the seal housing by lightly tapping on the installation tool.

10. Remove the installation tool.

11. Install the transaxle assembly.

12. Connect the negative battery cable and check for leaks.

ENGINE COOLING

Radiator

REMOVAL & INSTALLATION

NOTE: Keep coolant off of the accessory drive belt and pulleys. Cover the belt and pulley with shop cloths prior to working on them. If coolant contacts the belts or pulleys, flush with water. Do not remove radiator cap or block drains when the system is hot.

Monaco and Premier

1. Disconnect the battery negative cable.

2. Remove the electric cooling fan assembly.

3. Attach one end of a ¼ in. hose about 3 feet long to the end of the radiator drain, the other end in a clean container. Open the drain and remove the radiator cap to drain the system.

4. Disconnect upper and lower hoses from the radiator.

5. Remove the front grille then disconnect the radiator from the air conditioning condenser by removing the top and bottom attaching screws. Lift out the radiator.

6. The installation is the reverse of the removal installation. Note that the radiator is equipped with alignment dowels on the bottom that fit into holes in the body crossmembers. Align these dowels when at installing.

7. Fill the radiator with coolant and bleed the system.

8. Connect the negative battery cable and check for leaks.

Medallion

1. Disconnect the negative battery cable.

2. Drain the coolant.

3. Matchmark and remove the hood.

4. If equipped with air conditioning, properly discharge the system.

5. Remove the 5 grille mounting screws and remove the grille.

6. Remove the radiator support and facia panel.

7. Disconnect hoses from the radiator.

8. Disconnect the connectors from the cooling fans and thermo switch.

9. If equipped with air conditioning, disconnect the refrigerant lines from the condenser. Cover the exposed ends of the lines to minimize contamination.

10. Remove any remaining mounting hardware and lift the radiator, condenser and cooling fans from the engine compartment as an assembly. Separate the components as required.

To install:

11. Assemble the components and position in the engine compartment. Install mounting hardware.

12. Replace the O-rings and connect the refrigerant lines to the condenser, if equipped.

13. Connect the electrical connectors.

14. Connect the hoses to the radiator.

15. Install the facia panel, radiator support, grille and hood.

16. Fill the radiator with coolant and bleed the system.

17. Evacuate and recharge the air conditioning system.

18. Connect the negative battery cable and check the entire climate control system for proper operation.

Electric Cooling Fan

TESTING

—————— CAUTION ——————

Make sure the key is in the OFF position when checking the electric cooling fan. If not, the fan could turn ON at any time, causing serious personal injury.

1. Unplug the fan connector.

2. Using a jumper wire, connect the ground terminal of the fan connector to the negative battery terminal.

3. The fan should turn ON when the hot terminal is connected to the positive battery terminal.

4. If not, the fan is defective and should be replaced.

REMOVAL & INSTALLATION

Monaco and Premier

1. Disconnect the negative battery cable.

2. Remove the radiator support bracket screws. Remove the vibration cushion nuts.

3. Remove the upper radiator crossmember mounting screws and the crossmember.

4. Disconnect the electrical connectors from the fan. Remove the cooling fan and shroud mounting bolts and the fan by lifting upwards.

To install:

5. Install the fan into position and install the mounting bolts.

6. Install the radiator crossmember and support bracket.

7. Connect the negative battery cable and check the fan for proper operation.

Medallion

1. Disconnect the negative battery cable.

2. Unplug the connector.

3. Remove the mounting screws.

4. Remove the fan assembly.

5. The installation is the reverse of the removal procedure.

6. Connect the negative battery cable and check the fan for proper operation.

Heater Core

REMOVAL & INSTALLATION

Monaco and Premier

1. Disconnect the negative battery cable.

2. Drain the coolant. Properly discharge the air conditioning system, if equipped.

3. Remove the instrument panel lower trim cover, which is retained by 3 screws.

4. Remove the instrument panel support rod. Remove the screw attaching the steering column wiring harness bulkhead connector.

5. Disconnect the automatic transaxle shift cable from the lever.

   a. Compress the cable retainer tangs with pliers and slide the cable from the column mounting bracket.

   b. Loosen the screw that holds the anchoring bracket in place, move the bracket to the keyhole position and remove it from its mounting bracket.

6. Lift the indicator wire off of the pulley.

7. Pull the plastic sleeve down to expose the steering column universal joint.

8. Make a reference mark on the steering column shaft and intermediate shaft.

9. Remove the bolt from the intermediate shaft.

10. Remove the 4 bolts and nuts that hold the steering column to the instrument panel and carefully lower to the vehicle floor.

11. Separate the steering column shaft from the intermediate shaft and remove the steering column assembly from the vehicle.

12. Remove the defroster grille from the top of the instrument panel.

13. Loosen but do not remove the nut located near the parking brake release handle and the nut which is located on the passenger side kick panel.

14. Remove the screws and lower the parking brake release handle.

15. Remove the ashtray.

16. Disconnect the cigarette lighter connectors.

17. Remove the screw from the ashtray cavity.

18. Disconnect all electrical connections.

19. Remove the bolts that hold the instrument panel to the center floor bracket.

20. Disconnect the interior temperature sensor.

21. Remove the floor duct extension.

NOTE: The heater core inlet and outlet tubes are made of plastic and may break if too much pressure is applied.

22. Remove the heater hoses from the heater core spouts.

23. Disconnect the coolant level switch connector.

24. Remove the coolant reservoir.

25. Disconnect the blower motor connector.

26. Disconnect the vacuum hoses.

27. Disconnect the refrigerant lines at the dash panel, if equipped.

28. Remove the retaining nuts from inside and outside of the vehicle and carefully pull the heater/air conditioning housing rearward to remove it.

29. Release the plastic tabs and remove the heater core from the housing.

To install:

30. Carefully insert the heater core into the housing and push until it snaps in place.

31. Before installing the housing, make sure the housing seals are in place and in good condition.

32. Position the heater/air conditioning housing to the dash panel. Make sure the drain tube extends through its opening in the upper floor and the blower motor connector and the vacuum line extends through the dash panel. Ensure that the ECU connectors are to the right of the drain tube.

33. Install new housing retaining nuts. Install the floor duct extension.

34. Install new O-rings on the refrigerant lines and lubricate with clean refrigerant oil. Press each line into its connector until it snaps into place.

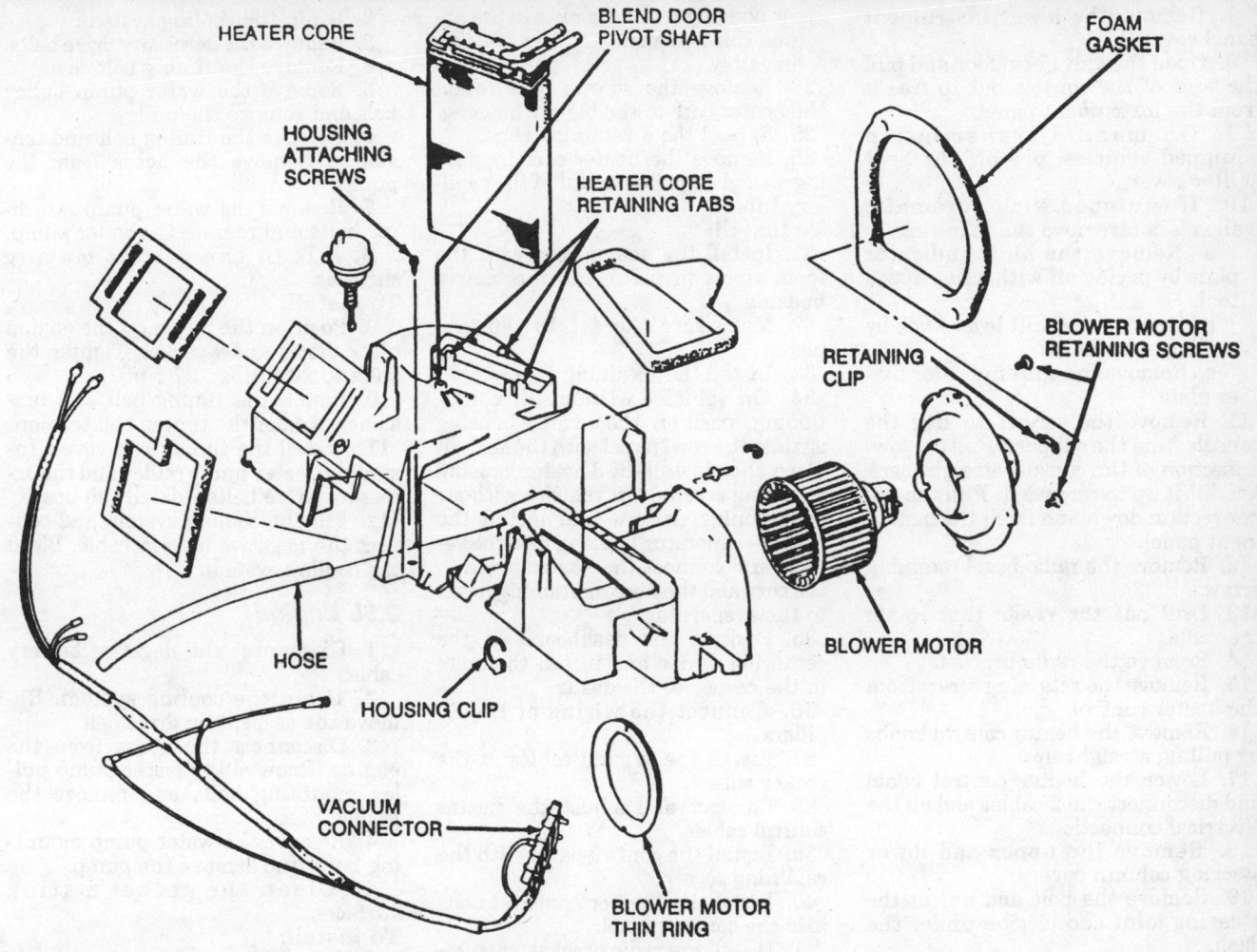

HEATER CORE

BLEND DOOR PIVOT SHAFT

FOAM GASKET

HOUSING ATTACHING SCREWS

HEATER CORE RETAINING TABS

BLOWER MOTOR RETAINING SCREWS

RETAINING CLIP

BLOWER MOTOR

HOSE

HOUSING CLIP

VACUUM CONNECTOR

BLOWER MOTOR THIN RING

Heater core and upper air conditioning housing parts—Monaco and Premier

35. Connect the vacuum hose and the blower electrical connector.

36. Install the coolant reservoir bracket and reservoir.

37. Reconnect the coolant level switch connector.

38. Carefully reconnect the heater hoses to the core.

39. Place the instrument panel into position so the mounting brackets engage the studs on the kick panels. Make sure the wiring harness is behind the center mounting bracket and connect all electrical connections.

40. Install the bolt to the brake support.

41. Install the screw into the ashtray cavity.

42. Install the 2 bolts to the center support bracket.

43. Connect the cigarette lighter connectors and the ashtray.

44. Tighten the nut located near the parking brake release handle and the nut located on the passenger side kick panel.

45. Install the parking brake release handle.

46. Install the bolts under the defroster grille, then install the grille.

47. Position and install the steering column shaft in the intermediate steering shaft U-joint. Align the 2 shafts using the reference marks made during removal. Install but do not tighten the U-joint bolt.

48. Attach the steering column to the instrument panel and tighten the bolts/nuts to 35 ft. lbs. (47 Nm).

49. Tighten the bolt in the intermediate steering shaft U-joint and move the plastic sleeve into position.

50. Snap the shift cable into the mounting bracket.

51. Snap the shift cable head onto the mounting ball in the shift arm.

52. Loop the shift indicator wire over the pulley. Position the anchoring bracket over the screw.

53. Move the gearshift lever into **N** and check the position of the shift indicator. If the pointer is not aligned with the **N** mark on the display, slide the bracket forward/rearward to align the indicator. Tighten the screw.

54. Install the bulkhead connector

and install the connector attaching screw.

55. Install the instrument panel support rod securely.

56. Install the instrument panel lower trim cover.

57. Evacuate and recharge the air conditioning system, if equipped.

58. Connect the negative battery cable and check the entire climate control system for proper operation. Check the system for leaks.

Medallion

1. Disconnect the negative battery cable.

2. Drain the cooling system. If equipped with air conditioning, properly discharge the system.

3. Remove the left and right rocker trim panels.

4. Disconnect the instrument panel wiring at the A-pillars.

5. Disconnect the ground cables at the rocker sills.

6. Disconnect the fuse panel and door buzzer.

7. Remove the lower instrument panel cover.

8. Open the glove box door and pull the edge of the console out to free it from the instrument panel.

9. On manual transmission equipped vehicles, pry off the boot shifter cover.

10. If equipped with automatic transmission remove the following:

a. Remove the shift indicator plate by prying off with a flat tipped tool.

b. Remove the shift lever knob by pulling straight off.

c. Remove the shift indicator cover plate.

11. Remove the screws to free the console from the support. Pull the lower section of the console straight back and lift it up to remove it. Pull the upper section down and from the instrument panel.

12. Remove the radio bezel retaining screws.

13. Drill out the rivets that retain the radio.

14. Remove the radio bracket.

15. Remove the retaining screw from the heater control.

16. Remove the heater control knobs by pulling straight up.

17. Lower the heater control panel and disconnect the 2 cables and all the electrical connections.

18. Remove the upper and lower steering column covers.

19. Remove the bolt and nut at the steering joint connection under the dash.

20. Remove the 4 hex head bolts and 1 large Torx® head bolt holding the steering column in place.

21. Pull the steering column forward slightly and it will drop down. Disconnect the instrument panel wiring and remove the steering column.

22. Remove the speaker covers at the upper corners of the dash.

23. Remove the dash attaching bolts at each corner and remove the dash assembly.

24. Disconnect all electrical connections.

25. Disconnect and plug the heater hoses from the core.

26. On vehicles without air conditioning, remove the 3 remaining screws which retain the heater blower housing to the cowl panel and the housing by pulling it rearward.

27. On vehicles with air conditioning, perform the following:

a. Disconnect the refrigerant lines from the expansion valve.

b. Remove the heater evaporator housing retaining screws from inside the passenger compartment.

c. Remove the vacuum reservoir from the bracket on the engine compartment side of the dash panel.

d. Remove the 2 heater/evapora-tor housing retaining nuts in the engine compartment and the housing assembly.

28. Remove the screws that retain the heater core to the blower housing.

29. Spread the 4 retaining clips.

30. Remove the heater core by pulling straight up. Be careful of the capillary tube.

To install:

31. Install the heater core with the foam strips in place into the blower housing.

32. Make sure the 4 tabs clip into place.

33. Install the retaining screws.

34. On vehicles without air conditioning, position the heater housing against the cowl panel with the seals in place, then install the 3 heater housing retaining screws. On vehicles with air conditioning, mount and install the heater/evaporator housing into the vehicle and connect the heater hoses to the core and the air conditioning hoses to the evaporator.

35. Position the dashboard on the centering device and install the bolts in the corner of the dash.

36. Connect the wiring at the A-pillars.

37. Install the ground cables at the rocker sills.

38. Connect and adjust the heater control cables.

39. Install the control panel with the retaining screw.

40. Install the heater control knobs into the control panel.

41. Install the radio bracket, then secure the radio with rivets.

42. Install the lower console assembly.

43. Install the radio bezel and retaining screws.

44. Assemble the steering joint to the steering column.

45. Connect the speedometer cable.

46. Install the lower instrument panel cover.

47. Install the fuse panel and door buzzer.

48. Install the rocker trim panels.

49. On the vehicles without air conditioning, connect the heater hoses to the heater core.

50. Fill and bleed the cooling system.

51. Evacuate and recharge the air conditioning system, if equipped.

52. Connect the negative battery cable and check the entire climate control system for proper operation. Check the system for leaks.

Water Pump

REMOVAL & INSTALLATION

2.2L Engine

1. Disconnect the negative battery cable.

2. Drain the cooling system.

3. Remove the accessory drive belts.

4. Remove the timing belt cover.

5. Remove the water pump pulley bolt and remove the pulley.

6. Remove the timing belt and tensioner. Remove the hoses from the pump.

7. Remove the water pump attaching bolts and remove the water pump.

8. Clean the gasket mating surfaces.

To install:

9. Position the pump on the engine block using a new gasket. Tighten the bolts to 20 ft. lbs. (27 Nm).

10. Install the timing belt and tensioner. Adjust the timing belt tension.

11. Install the timing belt cover. Install the water pump pulley and the accessory drive belts. Install the hoses.

12. Fill the cooling system and connect the negative battery cable. Bleed the cooling system.

2.5L Engine

1. Disconnect the negative battery cable.

2. Drain the cooling system. Remove the serpentine drive belt.

3. Disconnect the hoses from the engine. Remove the water pump pulley mounting bolts and remove the pulley.

4. Remove the water pump mounting bolts and remove the pump.

5. Clean the gasket mating surfaces.

To install:

6. Install the water pump using a new gasket. Tighten the bolts to 13 ft. lbs. (16 Nm).

7. Install the hoses and the water pump pulley. Tighten the pulley retaining bolts to 20 ft. lbs. (27 Nm).

8. Install the accessory drive belt.

NOTE: It is important that the serpentine belt is installed correctly. If it is incorrectly routed, the water pump could be rotated in the wrong direction, causing the engine to overheat.

9. Fill the cooling system. Connect the negative battery cable. Start the engine and bleed the cooling system.

3.0L Engine

1. Disconnect the negative battery cable.

2. Drain the cooling system.

3. Remove the spark plug wire holder from the top of the thermostat housing.

4. Remove the accessory drive belt. Remove the upper and lower radiator hoses from the radiator.

5. Disconnect the electrical lead to the coolant temperature sensor.

6. Remove the front damper mounting bracket nuts and push the

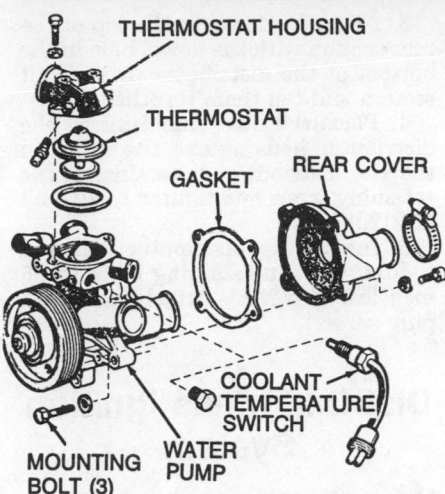

THERMOSTAT HOUSING

THERMOSTAT

GASKET

REAR COVER

COOLANT TEMPERATURE SWITCH

MOUNTING BOLT (3)

WATER PUMP

Water pump and thermostat assembly— 3.0L engine

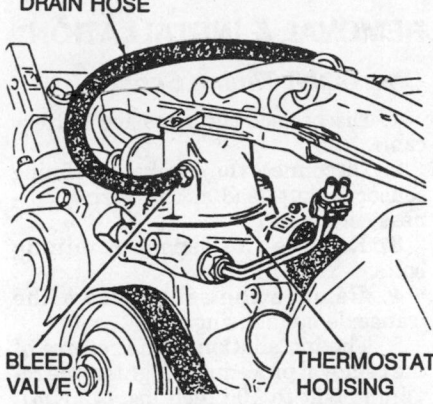

DRAIN HOSE

BLEED VALVE

THERMOSTAT HOUSING

Cooling system bleed valve—3.0L engine

bracket towards the the radiator but do not contact radiator fins. Remove the nuts holding the engine damper to the engine and remove.

7. At the back of the water pump, disconnect the hoses to the cylinder heads and the heater hoses.

8. If replacing the pump on an early 1991 engine, remove the water pump pulley. Remove the water pump mounting bolts.

NOTE: On 1991 Monaco or Premier built before October 9, 1991, it will be necessary to remove the pulley from the water pump to access the lower pump mounting bolts. Remember to install the pump onto the engine prior to installing the pulley. The lower mounting bolts can not be installed with the pulley pressed onto the water pump shaft.

9. Remove the water pump from the engine.

To install:

10. Position the water pump to the block and tighten the mounting bolts

to 13 ft. lbs. (16 Nm). On 1991 Monaco or Premier built prior to October 9, 1991, press the pulley onto the water pump shaft.

11. Connect all of the hoses to the water pump, making sure they are not kinked. Connect the electrical lead to the coolant temperature sensor.

12. Install the accessory drive belt, engine damper and damper bracket. Adjust the drive belt tension.

13. Install the spark plug wire holder to the thermostat housing.

14. Fill the cooling system.

15. Connect the negative battery cable. Start the engine and bleed the cooling system. Check for leaks.

Thermostat

REMOVAL & INSTALLATION

1. Disconnect negative battery cable.

2. Drain the coolant until below the level of the thermostat housing. If useable, save it in a clean container.

3. Disconnect the coolant temperature sensor wire connector from the sensor.

4. Some engines have a spark plug wire holder on the top of the housing which should be moved.

5. Place shop towels on the serpentine belt. Chemicals deteriorate the synthetic materials in the belt. Always protect the belt and pulleys with clean shop towels.

6. Remove the thermostat housing and pull out the thermostat. Leave the radiator hose connected.

To install:

7. Clean gasket surfaces well. Inspect housing ports for blockage. Install a new thermostat and gasket.

8. Install the thermostat housing.

9. Install the spark plug wire holder on top of the housing.

10. Connect the coolant temperature sensor wire.

11. Fill the cooling system.

12. Connect the negative battery cable. Start the engine and bleed the cooling system. Check for leaks.

Cooling System Bleeding

3.0L Engine

NOTE: This procedure should be followed after any cooling system component has been replaced or removed and installed. It is essential that coolant does not contact the accessory drive belt or pulleys. Chemicals deteriorate the synthetic materials in the belt. Always protect the the serpentine belt and pulleys with

clean shop towels. When installing the drain hose to the air bleed valve on the thermostat housing, route the hose away from the belt, pulleys and cooling fan.

1. Attach one end of a 4-foot-long ¼ in. hose to the air bleed on the thermostat housing. Route the hose away from the drive belt and pulleys. Place the other end of the hose in a clean container. The purpose of this hose is to keep coolant away from the belt and pulleys.

2. Open the bleed valve.

3. Slowly fill the coolant pressure bottle until a steady stream of coolant flows from the hose attached to the bleed valve. Close the bleed valve and continue filling to the full mark on the bottle. The full mark is the top of the post inside the bottle. Install the cap tightly on the coolant pressure bottle.

4. Remove the hose from the bleed valve, start and run the engine until the upper radiator hose is warm to the touch.

5. Turn the engine **OFF**. Reattach the drain hose to the bleed valve. Be sure to route the hose away from the belt and pulleys. Open the bleed valve until a steady stream of coolant flows from the hose. Close the bleed valve and remove the hose.

6. Check that the coolant pressure bottle is at or slightly above the full mark, at the top of the post inside the coolant pressure bottle. The full mark on the coolant pressure bottle is the correct coolant level for a cold engine. A hot engine will normally have a coolant level higher than the full mark.

ENGINE ELECTRICAL

NOTE: Disconnecting the negative battery cable on some vehicles may interfere with the functions of the on board computer systems and may require the computer to undergo a relearning process, once the negative battery cable is reconnected.

Distributor

REMOVAL

2.2L and 2.5L Engines

1. Disconnect the negative battery cable. Remove the distributor cap with the wires attached.

2. Matchmark the position of the rotor tip to the distributor housing and the housing the the engine.

3. Disconnect the harness connector from the distributor.

4. Remove the distributor hold-down bolt and pull the distributor up out of the engine. Note the position of the rotor in relation to the engine as the rotor stops rotating.

5. Do not rotate the engine with the distributor removed.

3.0L Engine

1. Disconnect the negative battery cable.

2. Remove accessory drive belt, if required.

3. Remove the timing belt cover.

4. Remove the spark plug wires from the spark plugs.

5. Remove the screws retaining the distributor cap.

6. Remove the screws that attach the distributor drive to the rotor and remove the rotor. Remove the dust shield from inside the housing.

7. Separate the distributor drive front and rear sections. Remove the distributor housing attaching bolts and remove the housing and seal.

INSTALLATION

NOTE: Some engines may be sensitive to the routing of the distributor sensor wires. If routed near the high-voltage coil wire or spark plug wires, the electromagnetic field surrounding the high-voltage wires could generate an occasional disruption of the ignition system operation.

Timing Not Disturbed

2.2L AND 2.5L ENGINES

1. Install the distributor with both matchmarks aligned.

2. Install the distributor cap, hold-down clamp and nut. Tighten the nut hand-tight.

3. Connect the distributor wiring and negative battery cable. Run the engine until normal operating temperature is reached and adjust the ignition timing.

4. Tighten the hold-down nut and recheck ignition timing.

3.0L ENGINE

1. Lightly coat the seal lips with clean engine oil and install the seal and housing.

2. Install the distributor drive rear section through the back of the cover, past the seal and into the housing.

3. Align the dowel in the top of the rear section with the dowel hole in the bottom of the distributor drive front section and press together.

4. Place the dust shield inside the distributor housing and the rotor on the the distributor drive. Install the retaining screw and tighten to 26 inch lbs. (2.9 Nm).

5. Install the distributor cap and tighten the cap retaining bolts to 35 inch lbs. (4.0 Nm).

6. Connect the spark plug wires.

Timing Disturbed

2.2L ENGINE

1. Position the engine so the No. 1 piston is at TDC of its compression stroke and the mark on the vibration damper is aligned with 0 on the timing indicator.

2. Install the distributor in the engine so the rotor is aligned with the position of the No. 1 ignition wire in the distributor cap and the housing is aligned with the matchmark on the engine. Make sure the distributor is fully seated and the distributor shaft is fully engaged.

NOTE: Make sure the rotor is pointing to where the No. 1 runner originates inside the cap, if equipped, and not where the No. 1 ignition wire plugs into the cap.

3. Install the hold-down nut.

4. Connect the distributor harness connectors.

5. Make sure the sealing O-ring is in place, install the distributor cap and tighten the screws or secure the clips.

6. Connect the negative battery cable.

7. Adjust the ignition timing and tighten the hold-down bolt.

2.5L ENGINE

1. Rotate the engine until the No. 1 piston is at TDC of the compression stroke.

2. Using an appropriate tool inserted in the distributor hole, rotate the oil pump gear so the slot in the oil pump shaft is slightly past the 3 o'clock position, relative to the length of the engine block.

3. With the distributor cap removed, install the distributor with the rotor at the 5 o'clock position, relative to the oil pump gear shaft slot. When the distributor is completely in place, the rotor should be at the 6 o'clock position. If not, remove the distributor and perform the entire procedure again.

4. Check the timing and tighten the lock bolt.

3.0L ENGINE

1. Position the engine so the No. 1 piston is at TDC of its compression stroke and the mark on the vibration damper is aligned with 0 on the timing indicator.

2. Install the distributor drive rear section through the back of the cover, past the seal and into the housing.

3. Align the dowel in the top of the rear section with the dowel hole in the bottom of the distributor drive front section and tap them together.

4. Place the dust shield inside the distributor housing and the rotor on the the distributor drive. Install the retaining screw and tighten to 26 inch lbs. (2.9 Nm).

5. Install the distributor cap and tighten the cap retaining bolts to 35 inch lbs. (4.0 Nm). Attach the spark plug wires.

Distributorless Ignition System

Monaco or Premier built on or after October 9, 1991, as well as 1992–93 models are equipped with distributorless ignition systems.

REMOVAL & INSTALLATION

Crankshaft Timing Sensor

1. Disconnect the negative battery cable.

2. Disconnect the crankshaft timing sensor pickup lead at the wiring harness connector.

3. Remove the sensor retaining bolts.

4. Remove the sensor from the transaxle bellhousing.

5. The installation is the reverse of the removal procedure. Tighten the retaining bolt to 105 inch lbs. (12 Nm).

Camshaft Position Sensor

1. Disconnect the negative battery cable.

2. Disconnect the camshaft position sensor lead at the wiring harness.

3. Remove the retaining bolt and remove the sensor from the cylinder head.

To install:

4. Install the sensor with the tab facing the rear of the engine.

5. Install the retaining bolt and tighten to 105 inch lbs. (12 Nm).

6. Connect the camshaft position sensor lead at the wiring harness.

Ignition Coil

1. Disconnect the negative battery cable.

2. Remove the spark plug wires from the coil by gripping the boot and not the cable.

3. Disconnect the electrical connector.

4. Remove the coil fasteners and the coil from the engine.

5. The installation is the reverse of the removal procedure.

Ignition Timing

ADJUSTMENT

Ignition timing is adjusted by the vehicle's Electronic Control Unit (ECU) based on inputs from various engine sensors and is not adjustable.

Alternator

PRECAUTIONS

Several precautions must be observed with alternator equipped vehicles to avoid damage to the unit.
- If the battery is removed for any reason, make sure it is reconnected with the correct polarity. Reversing the battery connections may result in damage to the one-way rectifiers.
- When utilizing a booster battery as a starting aid, always connect the positive to positive terminals and the negative terminal from the booster battery to a good engine ground on the vehicle being started.
- Never use a fast charger as a booster to start vehicles.
- Disconnect the battery cables when charging the battery with a fast charger.
- Never attempt to polarize the alternator.
- Do not use test lamps of more than 12 volts when checking diode continuity.
- Do not short across or ground any of the alternator terminals.
- The polarity of the battery, alternator and regulator must be matched and considered before making any electrical connections within the system.
- Never separate the alternator on an open circuit. Make sure all connections within the circuit are clean and tight.
- Disconnect the battery ground terminal when performing any service on electrical components.
- Disconnect the battery if arc welding is to be done on the vehicle.

BELT TENSION ADJUSTMENT

A single serpentine belt is used to drive all engine accessories. On the 2.2L engine, the drive belt tension is adjusted with the belt tension adjuster bolt, next to the alternator. On the 2.5L engine, the drive belt tension is adjusted with the power steering pump. On Premier the 3.0L engine, the drive belt tension is adjusted with the alternator. If replacement of drive belt is required, make sure the belt is routed

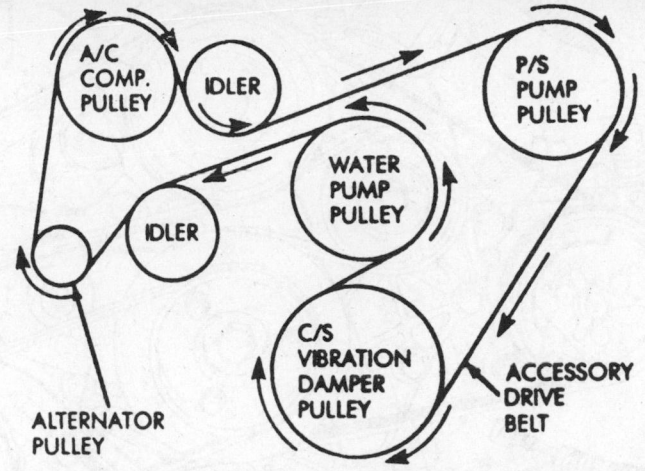

WITH A/C

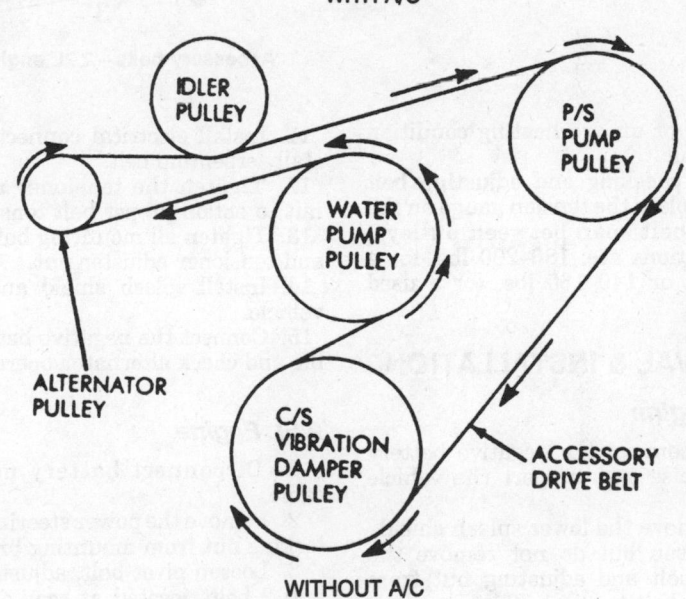

WITHOUT A/C

Serpentine belt arrangement—2.5L engine

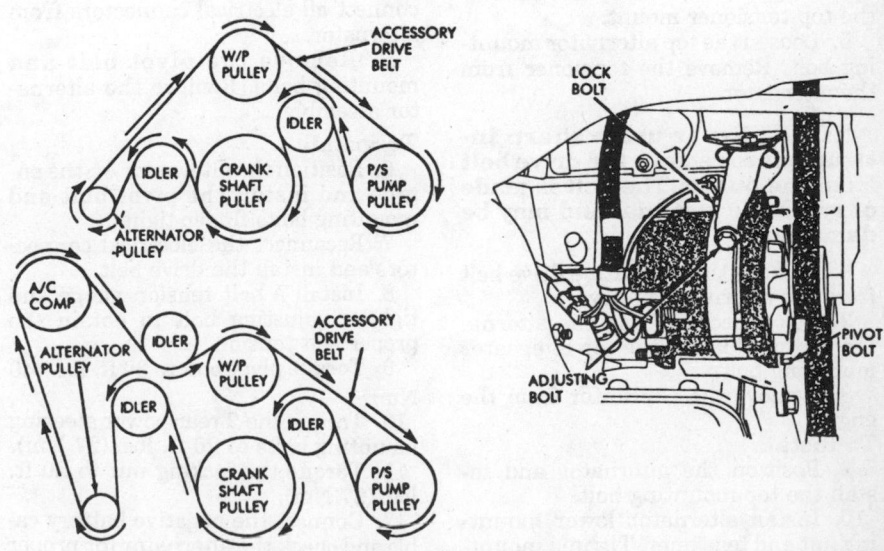

Serpentine belt and alternator adjust points—3.0L engine

Accessory belts—2.2L engine

1. Power steering belt
2. Serpentine belt
3. Serpentine belt adjustment nut
4. Water pump

correctly or an overheating condition may result.

When checking and adjusting belt tension, place the tension gauge on the longest belt span between pulleys. Specifications are: 180–200 lbs. for a new belt or 140–160 lbs. for a used belt.

REMOVAL & INSTALLATION

2.2L Engine

1. Disconnect the negative battery cable. Raise and support the vehicle safely.
2. Remove the lower splash shield.
3. Loosen but do not remove the locking bolt and adjusting nut from the drive belt tension adjuster.
4. Remove the lower alternator mounting nut. The nut is also used by the top tensioner mount.
5. Loosen the top alternator mounting bolt. Remove the tensioner from the alternator.

NOTE: Never use a sharp instrument to remove the drive belt from the pulley. The belt is made of synthetic material and may be damaged.

6. Remove the serpentine drive belt from the alternator pulley.
7. Disconnect and tag the alternator wiring. Remove the top alternator mounting bolt.
8. Remove the alternator from the engine.
To install:
9. Position the alternator and install the top mounting bolt.
10. Install alternator lower mounting nut and tensioner. Tighten mounting nut finger-tight.

11. Install electrical connectors. Install serpentine belt.
12. Tighten the tensioner adjuster nut to obtain proper belt tension.
13. Tighten all mounting bolts, nuts and tensioner adjuster nut.
14. Install splash shield and lower vehicle.
15. Connect the negative battery cable and check alternator operation.

2.5L Engine

1. Disconnect battery negative cable.
2. Remove the power steering pump locking nut from mounting bracket.
3. Loosen pivot bolt, adjusting bolt and 2 bolts located at rear of power steering pump.
4. Remove the drive belt and disconnect all electrical connectors from alternator.
5. Remove the pivot bolt and mounting bolts. Remove the alternator assembly.
To install:
6. Position the alternator on the engine and install the pivot bolt and mounting bolts finger-tight.
7. Reconnect the electrical connectors and install the drive belt.
8. Install a belt tension gauge and tighten adjusting bolt to obtain the proper belt tension.
9. Torque pivot bolt to 30 ft. lbs. (40 Nm).
10. Torque the 2 rear power steering mounting bolts to 20 ft. lbs. (27 Nm).
11. Torque the locking nut to 20 ft. lbs. (27 Nm).
12. Connect the negative battery cable and check the alternator for proper operation.

3.0L Engine

1. Disconnect the negative battery cable.
2. Raise and safely support the vehicle.
3. Remove the lower splash shield.
4. Loosen the alternator adjusting bolt and relieve the belt tension. Remove alternator drive belt, mounting bolt and pivot bolt.
5. Disconnect all electrical connectors from the alternator and remove from engine.
To install:
6. Position the alternator on the engine and install pivot bolt and mounting bolts finger-tight.
7. Reconnect the electrical connectors and install the drive belt.
8. Torque the pivot bolt to 37 ft. lbs. (50 Nm).
9. Tighten the adjusting bolt to obtain the proper belt tension.
10. Torque the mounting bolt to 20 ft. lbs. (27 Nm).
11. Install the lower splash shield and lower the vehicle.
12. Connect the negative battery cable and check the alternator for proper operation.

Starter

REMOVAL & INSTALLATION

Premier and Monaco

1. Disconnect the negative battery cable. Raise and support the vehicle safely.
2. Disconnect and tag the starter motor wiring.
3. On 2.5L engine, remove the

starter motor mounting bolts. Remove the starter motor and shim from the engine.

4. On 3.0L engine, remove the starter motor mounting bolts. Remove the starter motor and mounting plate from the engine.

5. The installation is the reverse of the removal procedure.

6. Connect the negative battery cable and check the starter for proper operation.

Medallion

1. Disconnect the negative battery cable. Raise and support the vehicle safely.

2. Remove the starter motor mounting bracket bolts and bracket from the starter motor.

3. With the bracket removed, disconnect and tag the starter motor wiring.

4. Remove the rear starter motor mounting bolts.

5. Support the starter motor and remove the front mounting bolt.

6. Remove the starter motor and locating bushing from the engine.

7. Transfer the rear mount from the old starter motor to the new motor.

To install:

8. Place the bushing in the front starter motor mount on the engine.

9. Install the starter motor on engine and tighten the mounting bolts.

10. Connect the starter motor wiring harness.

11. Install the starter motor mounting bracket.

12. Lower the vehicle.

13. Connect the negative battery cable and check starter for proper operation.

EMISSION CONTROLS

Due to the complex nature of modern electronic engine control systems, comprehensive diagnosis and testing procedures fall outside the confines of this repair manual. For complete information on diagnosis, testing and repair procedures concerning all modern engine and emission control systems, please refer to "Chilton's Guide to Fuel Injection and Electronic Engine Controls".

Emission Warning Lamps

RESETTING

A Vehicle Maintenance Monitor (VMM) is installed on most vehicles. The dashboard display is activated at 7500 mile intervals to remind the vehicle owner that regular service and maintenance is due. Perform the required service and then press the **RESET** button located on the left side of the instrument panel on the monitor display.

FUEL SYSTEM

Fuel System Service Precautions

Safety is an important factor when servicing the fuel system. Failure to conduct maintenance and repairs in a safe manner may result in serious personal injury. Maintenance and testing of the vehicle's fuel system components can be accomplished safely and effectively by adhering to the following rules and guidelines.

● To avoid the possibility of fire and personal injury, always disconnect the negative battery cable unless the repair or test procedure requires that battery voltage be applied.

● Always relieve the fuel system pressure prior to disconnecting any fuel system component (injector, fuel rail, pressure regulator, etc.), fitting or fuel line connection. Exercise extreme caution whenever relieving fuel system pressure to avoid exposing skin, face and eyes to fuel spray. Please be advised that fuel under pressure may penetrate the skin or any part of the body that it contacts.

● Always place a shop towel or cloth around the fitting or connection prior to loosening to absorb any excess fuel due to spillage. Ensure that all fuel spillage is quickly removed from engine surfaces. Ensure that all fuel soaked cloths or towels are deposited into a suitable waste container.

● Always keep a dry chemical (Class B) fire extinguisher near the work area.

● Do not allow fuel spray or fuel vapors to come into contact with a spark or open flame.

● Always use a backup wrench when loosening and tightening fuel line connection fittings. This will prevent unnecessary stress and torsion to fuel line piping. Always follow the proper torque specifications.

● Always replace worn fuel fitting O-rings. Do not substitute fuel hose where fuel pipe is installed.

FUEL TUBES AND QUICK-CONNECT FITTINGS

Monaco and Premier

The fuel system in these vehicles utilize plastic fuel tubes with quick-connect fittings that have sealed O-rings; these O-rings do not have to be replaced when the fittings are disconnected. The quick-connect fitting consists of the O-rings, a retainer and the casing. When the fuel tube nipple is inserted into the quick-connect fitting, the shoulder of the nipple is locked in place by the retainer, and the O-rings seal the tube. The fuel tube nipples must first be lubricated with clean 30 weight engine oil prior to reconnecting the quick-connect fitting.

When the fittings are disconnected, the retainer will stay on the nipple of the component that the tube is being disconnected from. A fuel tube should never be inserted into a quick-connect fitting without the retainer being either on the tube or already in the quick-connect fitting. In either case, care must be taken to ensure that the retainer is locked securely into the quick-connect fitting.

If the quick-connect fitting has windows in the side of the casing, the retainer locking ears and the shoulder (stop bead) on the tube must be visible in the windows, or the retainer is not properly installed. After connecting a quick-connect fitting, the connection should be verified by pulling on the lines to ensure that the lock is secure.

There is a factory tool that can be used at the 3.0L engine fuel rail and fuel pressure regulator to remove the quick-connect fitting and retainer as

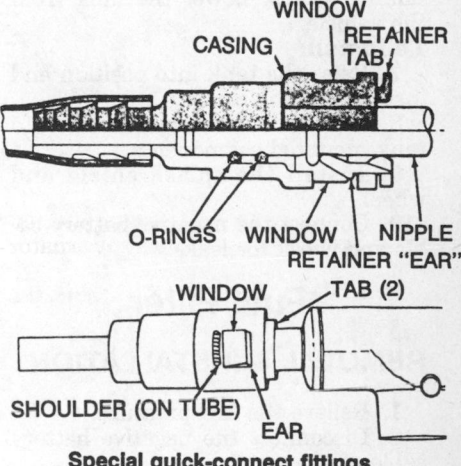

Special quick-connect fittings

an assembly. The retainer will remain in the fitting in the correct position. To install the fuel tube, push it over the nipple until a click is heard. Pull back on the tube to ensure that the connector is locked in place.

RELIEVING FUEL SYSTEM PRESSURE

NOTE: Always wear eye protection when servicing the fuel system. Do not smoke or allow open flame near the fuel system or components during fuel system service.

1. Loosen the fuel filler cap to release fuel tank pressure.
2. Disconnect the fuel pump harness connector located in the rear of the vehicle near the fuel tank.
3. Start the vehicle and allow it to run until it stalls from lack of fuel. Turn the key to the OFF position.
4. Disconnect the negative battery cable, then reconnect the fuel pump connector.
5. Wrap shop towels around the fitting that is being disconnected to absorb residual fuel in the lines.

Fuel Tank

REMOVAL & INSTALLATION

1. Relieve the fuel system pressure.
2. Disconnect the negative battery cable.
3. Drain the fuel from the fuel tank.
4. Raise and safely support the vehicle. Remove the right rear wheel and inner fender splash shield.
5. Disconnect the fuel lines at the fuel filter and the electrical connectors from the tank. Disconnect the fuel tank vent tube from the filler neck. Disconnect the ground wire from the body.
6. Place a jack under the tank to support it's weight and remove the retaining straps. Lower the tank from the vehicle.
To install:
7. Raise the tank into position and install the tank straps.
8. Connect all hoses and wires to tank-mounted components.
9. Install the splash shield and wheel.
10. Connect the negative battery cable and check for leaks.

Fuel Filter

REMOVAL & INSTALLATION

1. Relieve the fuel pressure.
2. Disconnect the negative battery cable.

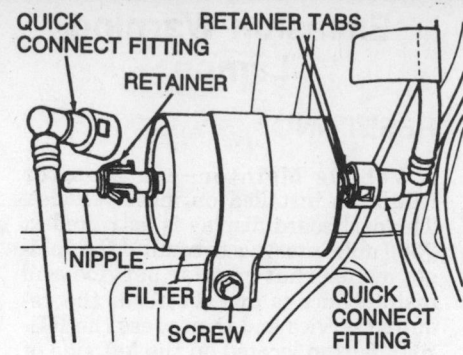

Fuel filter with special fittings

3. The filter is located on the frame rail near the rear of the vehicle.
4. Depress the retainer tabs together and slowly pull the connectors from the fuel filter. Note the retainer tabs stay on the fuel filter nipples.
5. Remove the screw holding the fuel filter in place and remove the filter.
To install:
6. Carefully remove the retainers from the fuel filter nipples with a thin straight blade tool. Insert the tool between the filter nipple and the wedge portion of the retainer that seats against the shoulder of the nipple. Press the wedge back and slip the wedge over the nipple shoulder. Repeat this on the other side of the retainer and then pull the retainer off the nipple.
7. Push the retainers back into the fuel line quick-connect fittings. Ensure that the locking ears and the shoulder (stop bead) on the fuel tube are completely visible in the windows on the side of the quick-connect fitting.
8. The fuel filter may be marked IN and OUT at the nipple ends. The side marked IN is connected to the fuel line from the fuel tank. The side of the filter marked OUT is connected to the fuel line that runs to the engine. After determining the proper direction, install the fuel filter with the attaching screw.
9. Use a clean cloth to wipe the tube ends clean and lightly lubricate the fuel tube ends with clean 30 weight motor oil. The connectors contain O-rings which do not have to be replaced when the fittings are disconnected. Push the quick-connect fitting over the fuel tube until a click is heard. If the quick-connect fitting is type that has windows on the side, ensure that the locking ears on the retainer and the shoulder (stop bead) on the fuel tube are completely visible in the windows. Do not rely on the audible click to confirm that a secure connection has been made. Pull back on the quick-connect fitting to further ensure that

the connection is complete and the connector is locked in place.
10. Connect the negative battery cable, install the fuel filler cap, turn the key to the ON position to pressurize the fuel system and check for leaks.

Electric Fuel Pump

PRESSURE TESTING

2.2L Engine

1. Relieve the fuel system pressure.
2. Disconnect the hose from the fuel pressure regulator to the fuel rail.
3. Disconnect the vacuum hose from the pressure regulator and connect it to a vacuum pump.
4. Connect a fuel gauge to the fuel rail and start the engine.
5. Check the fuel pressure readings and compare against the specification.
6. Apply 15 in. Hg of vacuum to the pressure regulator. The pressure should drop about 3 psi.
7. Turn the ignition OFF. Remove the fuel gauge from fuel rail.
8. Reconnect the vacuum hose to the pressure regulator and hose from the pressure regulator to the fuel rail.

2.5L Engine

NOTE: The throttle body has 2 port plugs on it. The test port is located on the side of the fuel pressure regulator next to the fuel return tube connection.

1. Allow the engine to cool down before removing the test port.
2. Relieve the fuel system pressure.
3. Place a shop towel over the test port to catch fuel and slowly remove the test port plug from the throttle body.
4. Install fuel pressure test adapter along with a 0–30 psi (0–207 kPa) gauge into test port.
5. Start the engine and let it idle. Check the fuel pressure reading. If the pressure is not within specifications adjust the fuel pressure regulator as followed:

   a. Locate the fuel pressure regulator adjusting screw behind the aluminum plug in the nose of the fuel pressure regulator casing.
   b. Lightly tap the plug with a small punch and hammer until it pops out.
   c. Run the engine at 750–800 rpm, then turn the adjustment screw until the fuel pressure is within specifications.
6. Turn the ignition switch OFF. Disconnect the fuel gauge and pressure test adapter.
7. Install the plug in test port. Install the aluminum plug in front of the regulator adjusting screw.

8. Replace the fuel tank filler cap.

3.0L Engine

1. Relieve the fuel system pressure.
2. Remove the black fuel supply tube from the fuel rail using tool 6182 or equivalent. Slide the tool over the nipple and up into the connector until the handle fits the connector. Pull the fuel supply tube off the fuel rail.
3. Install fuel tube adapter 6175 or equivalent and a 0–60 psi gauge. Push the adapter female end with the quick connect fitting over the fuel rail. Push the male end with the nipple into the black fuel supply tube.
4. Start the engine and check the fuel pressure against the specification.
5. If the fuel pressure is not within specifications, check items such as a restricted fuel return hose, pressure regulator vacuum hose for leaks, faulty fuel pump or a faulty pressure regulator.
6. Remove the fuel tube adapter 6175 or equivalent.
7. Lightly lubricate the ends of the fuel supply tube with clean engine oil. Install the black fuel supply tube to fuel rail and grey fuel return tube to the pressure regulator.

REMOVAL & INSTALLATION

2.2L Engine

The fuel pump used on the 2.2L engine is mounted on a plate located under the vehicle in front of the rear axle assembly.

1. Release the fuel system pressure.
2. Disconnect the battery negative cable.
3. Raise and support the vehicle safely.
4. Disconnect the electrical connectors from pump.
5. Plug the pump inlet and outlet hoses to prevent fuel flow.
6. Disconnect fuel pump hoses. Wrap a shop towel around the hoses and remove them from the fuel pump.
7. Remove the pump retaining strap and remove the fuel pump.
8. Installation is the reverse of the removal procedure.

NOTE: The pump terminals are different sizes to ensure the pump rotates in the correct direction.

9. Connect the negative battery cable and check for proper operation.

2.5L and 3.0L Engines

1. Relieve the fuel system pressure.
2. Disconnect the negative battery cable.
3. Drain the fuel from the fuel tank.
4. Raise and safely support the vehicle. Remove the right rear wheel and inner fender splash shield.

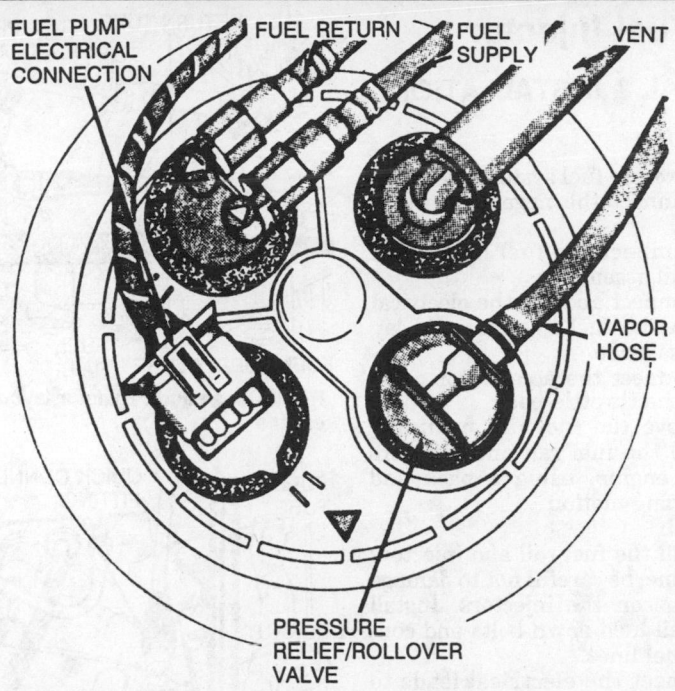

Top view of the fuel pump unit—Late 1991–92 Monaco and Premier

5. Disconnect the fuel lines at the fuel filter and the electrical connectors from the tank. Disconnect the fuel tank vent tube from the filler neck. Disconnect the ground wire from the body.
6. Place a jack under the tank to support it's weight and remove the retaining straps. Lower the tank from the vehicle.
7. On vehicles built before October 9, 1991, remove the bolts holding the tank sending unit to the tank. On vehicles built on or after October 9, 1991, remove the fuel pump module retaining clamp. Pull the sending unit/pump from the tank, noting the position of the gasket.
8. Late 1991–92 modules cannot be disassembled and must be replaced as an assembly. On 1989 to early 1991 vehicles, disconnect the electrical connectors from the terminals on fuel pump and remove the pump holding bracket.
9. Disconnect the hose clamp at inlet port. Unscrew hose clamp and remove fuel pump.

NOTE: On some vehicles, there may be a tray in the bottom of the fuel tank that is contoured to hold the fuel filter. When installing the pump/sending unit, make sure the filter correctly fits into the tray.

To install:
10. Position the gasket so the holes in the gasket align with bolt holes in the fuel tank.
11. Install the sending unit/pump into the fuel tank and install the retaining bolts or clamp.
12. Install the fuel tank and all related items to the vehicle.
13. Connect the negative battery cable and check the entire system for proper operation and leaks.

Fuel Injection

IDLE SPEED ADJUSTMENT

The idle speed on fuel injected vehicles is controlled by the ECU through the use of an Idle Speed Control motor (ISC) or an idle speed regulator. The ISC motor does not require periodic adjustment.

On 2.5L engine, if the ISC is removed or replaced, it should be adjusted to establish the initial position of the plunger. To adjust the ISC, use the following procedure:
1. Start the engine and allow it to reach normal operating temperature.
2. Disconnect the ISC motor wire connector.
3. Locate the diagnostic terminals on the right side inner fender well. Connect a tachometer to terminals **D1–1** and **D1–3** of the diagnostic connector.
4. An adapter may be required to connect to the ISC motor. Fully extend the ISC motor plunger.
5. Adjust the plunger screw until the engine is running at 3500 rpm.
6. Remove adapter and reconnect the idle speed motor electrical connector. Idle speed should automatically return to normal.

Fuel Injector

REMOVAL & INSTALLATION

2.2L Engine

1. Relieve the fuel system pressure.
2. Disconnect the negative battery cable.
3. Disconnect the fuel lines from the fuel rail assembly.
4. Disconnect and tag the electrical leads from the fuel injectors and lay the harness aside.
5. Disconnect the accelerator cable from the the throttle body.
6. Remove the fuel rail mounting bolts. Pull the fuel rail and injectors from the engine, using a back and forth twisting motion.

To install:

7. Install the fuel rail and injectors to the engine, be careful not to damage the O-rings on the injectors. Install the fuel rail hold-down bolts and connect the fuel lines.
8. Connect the electrical leads to the injectors. Connect the throttle cable.
9. Connect the negative battery cable. Turn the ignition to the **ON** position to pressurize the fuel system. Check for leaks.

2.5L Engine

1. Relieve the fuel system pressure.
2. Disconnect the negative battery cable.
3. Remove the air inlet tube from the throttle body. Disconnect the electrical lead from the fuel injector.
4. Remove the screws attaching the injector hold-down plate and remove the hold-down plate.
5. Using an appropriate tool, grasp the top of the injector and pull the injector out of the throttle body.

NOTE: The pintle at the bottom of the injector must be kept clean and undamaged. If the injector is dropped on the pintle, do not re-use the injector.

6. Remove the upper O-ring, injector alignment washer and the lower O-ring. Discard the O-rings.

To install:

7. Install new O-rings and install the alignment washer on the injector. Install the injector into the throttle body by pushing down on the injector.
8. Install the injector hold-down plate. Connect the electrical connector.
9. Install the air inlet tube and connect the negative battery cable.

3.0L Engine

1. Relieve the fuel system pressure.
2. Disconnect the negative battery cable.

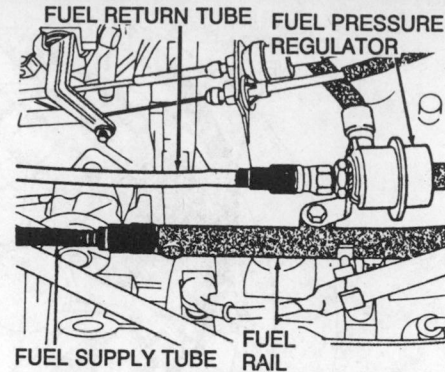

Return hose and regulator layout—3.0L engine

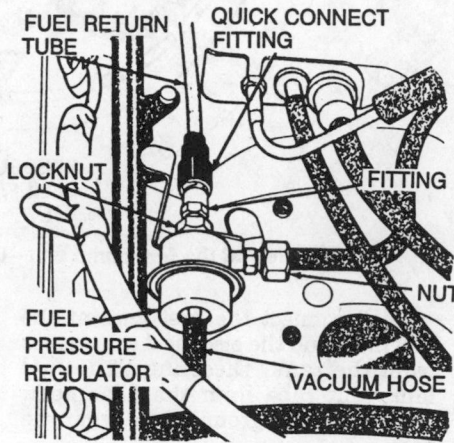

Fuel lines and routing—3.0L engine

3. Disconnect the fuel lines from the fuel rail assembly.
4. Disconnect and tag the electrical leads from the fuel injectors and lay the harness aside.
5. Disconnect the cruise and accelerator cables from the the throttle body.
6. Remove the 4 screws attaching the engine cover and remove the cover.
7. Remove the fuel rail mounting bolts and disconnect the vacuum line from the fuel pressure regulator. Pull the fuel rail and injectors from the engine, using a back and forth twisting motion.
8. Remove the retaining clip and separate the injectors from the fuel rail.

To install:

9. Assemble the fuel rail. Install the fuel rail and injectors to the engine, be careful not to damage the O-rings on the injectors. Install the fuel rail hold-down bolts and connect the fuel lines.
10. Connect the electrical leads to the injectors. Connect the throttle cable. Install the engine cover plate.
11. Connect the negative battery cable. Turn the ignition to the **ON** position to pressurize the fuel system and check for leaks.

DRIVE AXLE

Halfshaft

REMOVAL & INSTALLATION

The halfshafts are comprised of an inner CV-joint, an interconnecting shaft and an outer Rzeppa CV-joint with a stub shaft. The inner tripod CV-joint can be disassembled but must be replaced as a unit. The outer Rzeppa joint CV-joint cannot be disassembled and must also be replaced as a unit. The protective rubber boots and clamps that cover each CV-joint are replaceable components.

1. Disconnect the negative battery cable. Raise the vehicle and support safely.
2. Remove the wheels.
3. Remove the brake caliper but do not disconnect the brake hose from the caliper. Wire it aside. Do not allow the brake hose to support the weight of the caliper.
4. Remove the halfshaft hub nut. A holding fixture may be required to hold the wheel hub/rotor when removing the nut.
5. Spiral wound roll pin(s) are used to retain each halfshaft at the transaxle. Using a drift type tool, remove the halfshaft-to-transaxle roll pin(s).

NOTE: Before proceeding to the next step, be certain the front suspension is hanging free. The strut body to suspension knuckle bolts are splined. Remove the bolts only as instructed in the following steps.

6. Remove the 2 splined bolts that attach the strut body to the suspension knuckle. Do this by first loosening and turning the nuts (do not turn the bolt heads) until they are almost at the end of the bolt threads. Tap the nuts with a brass hammer to loosen the bolts and disengage the splines. Remove the nuts and slide the bolts out of the strut body and suspension knuckle.
7. Place a drain pan under the transaxle end of the halfshaft.
8. Wrap a shop towel around the halfshaft outer rubber boot to prevent damaging the boot.
9. Tilt the suspension knuckle out and away from the strut body and remove the halfshaft. If the halfshaft cannot be pushed through the hub by hand, use a puller.

To install:

10. Install the halfshaft to the transaxle shaft and align the roll pin holes in each shaft.

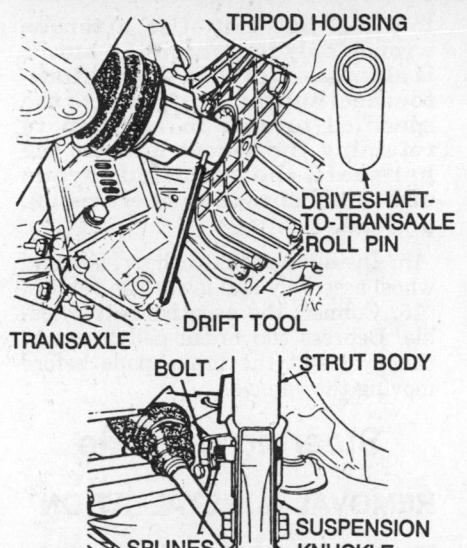

Remove the halfshaft by driving out the roll pin and removing from knuckle

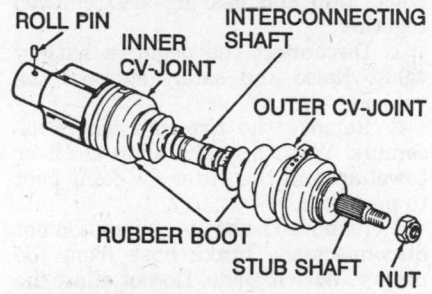

Halfshaft assembly and related components

NOTE: One side of the roll pin hole in the transaxle shaft is beveled. Align the beveled side of that hole with the side of the hole in the CV-joint housing that is located in the housing "valley."

11. Insert the roll pin(s) and seat with a hammer and a drift type tool.
12. Insert the halfshaft end through the hub.
13. Tilt the knuckle back into position and install the bolts. Hold the bolt heads with a wrench to prevent them from turning and tighten the nuts to 123 ft. lbs. (167 Nm).
14. Install the halfshaft end nut and tighten to 181 ft. lbs. (245 Nm), while holding the rotor and hub in place.
15. Install the brake caliper.
16. Check the differential fluid level. Fill with recommended synthetic gear oil.
17. Install the wheels.
18. Connect the negative battery cable.

CV-Joint Boot

The protective rubber boots and clamps that cover each CV-joint are replaceable components. The applicable CV-joint must be removed from the interconnecting shaft to replace a rubber boot.

REMOVAL & INSTALLATION

Outer CV-Joint

1. Disconnect the negative battery cable. Remove the halfshaft.
2. Side cutter pliers can be used to cut the metal retaining bands. If the rubber boot is re-useable, use care when cutting the clamps. Do not accidentally cut the boot when cutting the clamps.
3. Slide the rubber boot off of the CV housing for access to the plastic retainer.
4. Spread the plastic retainer at the seam with snapring pliers.
5. Tap the outer CV-joint with a plastic mallet to disengage the interconnecting shaft from the retainer.
6. Separate the outer CV-joint from the interconnecting shaft. Using heavy tape, wrap the splines on the end of the shaft to prevent damage to the boot during removal. Slide off the rubber boot. Inspect the boot for excess wear or damage and replace as required.

To install:

7. Inspect the plastic retainer in the outer CV-joint. Replace the retainer if it is damaged or defective. If a replacement retainer must be installed, ensure that it is installed correctly. The tapered end mates with the shaft and the segmented end mates with the CV-joint.
8. Install the rubber boot on the shaft. Thoroughly lubricate the CV-joint and the inside of the boot with the proper lubricant which is usually supplied with the service kit.

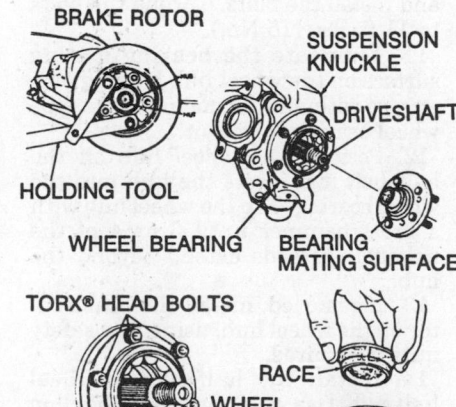

Front wheel bearing removal—Monaco and Premier

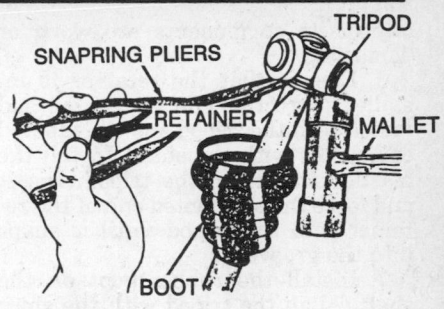

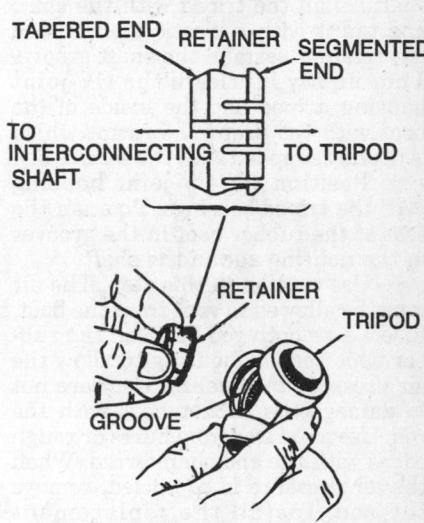

Joint removal and retainer orientation

9. Align the shaft with the plastic retainer and the CV-joint, then tap the CV-joint onto the shaft with a plastic mallet. Continue tapping the CV-joint until the segmented end of the retainer snaps into position on the shaft.
10. Position the rubber boot on the clamp grooves machined in the CV-joint and in the shaft. Install the replacement clamps and crimp with the special tool.
11. Install the halfshaft in the vehicle.

Inner CV-Joint

1. Disconnect the negative battery cable. Remove the halfshaft.
2. Side cutter pliers can be used to cut the metal retaining bands. If the rubber boot is reuseable, use care when cutting the clamps. Do not accidentally cut the boot when cutting the clamps.
3. Slide the rubber boot off the CV-joint housing. Remove the inner CV-joint housing by pulling it straight away from the tripod.
4. Spread the plastic retainer with snapring pliers and tap the tripod with a plastic mallet to remove it from the shaft. If necessary, cut the retainer to remove it. Slide the rubber boot from the shaft. Inspect the boot for damage. If damaged, replace the boot.

To install:

5. Replace the complete CV-joint if

any of its components are worn or damaged.

6. Ensure that the retainer is installed correctly. The segmented end mates with the tripod and the tapered end mates with the shaft. Install the plastic retainer in the tripod. Insert and force the segmented end of the retainer into the tripod until it snaps into the groove.

7. Install the rubber boot on the shaft. Align the tripod with the shaft and tap it with a plastic mallet until the retainer seats in the shaft groove. Thoroughly lubricate the CV-joint housing, tripod and the inside of the boot with the proper lubricant which is usually supplied with the service kit.

8. Position the CV-joint housing over the tripod/bearings. Position the seat of the rubber boot in the grooves in the housing and in the shaft.

9. Use caution in this step. The air must be allowed to vent from the boot. Insert a smooth rod between the rubber boot and the housing to allow the air pressure to equalize. Use care not to damage the rubber boot with the rod. Use a rod free from burrs or rough edges with the end chamferred. When the air pressure is equalized, remove the rod. Install the replacement clamps and crimp with the special crimping tool.

10. Install the halfshaft in the vehicle.

Front Wheel Hub and Bearings

REMOVAL & INSTALLATION

The front wheel hub can be removed without removing the bearing from the steering knuckle. However, the wheel hub must be removed before the bearing can be removed from the knuckle. The wheel hub and bearing are independently replaceable.

When servicing the steering knuckle, the wheel hub and bearing should be removed as a unit. Although the wheel bearing components can be disassembled for inspection, the bearing must be replaced as a unit only. If any of the bearing components are worn, damaged or defective, the complete bearing must be replaced.

1. Disconnect the negative battery cable. Raise and safely support the vehicle.

2. Remove the halfshaft end nut. Push the halfshaft inward and disengage the shaft splines from the wheel hub splines. If it does not push out easily, use a screw type puller to press the shaft from the hub.

3. Install a puller plate that can be used with a slide hammer and pull the rotor/hub assembly from the steering

knuckle. Use care to keep dirt and debris from the bearing as the hub assembly is removed.

4. If necessary, the rotor and hub can be separated by removing the rotor safety nuts. If these safety nuts are damaged by removal, replace with new ones.

5. Remove the Torx® bolts that attach the wheel bearing to the knuckle. Remove the bearing.

6. If the wheel hub and/or bearing are being replaced without the other, remove the outer race from the hub with a shop press and the appropriate adapters.

To install:

7. If a new wheel hub is being installed, force the original bearing outer race on the replacement hub with a shop press and a length of steel pipe that has the correct inside diameter to fit around the hub. If a new bearing is being installed, do the same with the new race.

8. If the original wheel bearing is being installed, pack the bearing and lubricate both races (inner and outer) with an extreme pressure type wheel bearing lubricant.

9. If a replacement wheel bearing is being installed, prepare the bearing as follows:

   a. Remove and discard the plastic protective covers.

   b. Locate, remove and discard the plastic protective sleeve from the replacement bearing bore.

   c. Remove the inner and outer bearing races from the bearing.

   d. Pack the bearing with lubricant which may be supplied with the replacement bearing.

   e. Insert the bearing inner race in the bearing and force the bearing outer race on the wheel hub with a press and a length of steel pipe.

10. Install the bearing to the knuckle and install the bolts. Torque the bolts to 11 ft. lbs. (15 Nm).

11. Lubricate the bearing mating surface on the wheel hub bearing outer race with an extreme pressure type wheel bearing lubricant.

12. Position the wheel hub on the halfshaft and insert the hub into the wheel bearing. Tap the wheel hub with a brass hammer until 3 or 4 of the halfshaft threads extend beyond the hub.

13. If removed, install the brake rotor on the wheel hub, using new safety nuts if required.

14. Install the halfshaft-to-wheel hub nut. Use an appropriate holding tool to keep the hub from rotating while tightening the nut to 181 ft. lbs. (245 Nm) torque.

NOTE: Do not use an impact wrench to tighten the driveshaft-

to-wheel hub nut. Use a torque wrench only to tighten the nut. It is also essential that the halfhaft-to-wheel hub nut be tighten to the specified torque. In addition to retaining the wheel hub on the halfshaft, the specified torque also establishes the wheel bearing preload.

15. Install the brake caliper, tire and wheel assembly and lower the vehicle.

16. Connect the negative battery cable. Depress the brake pedal several times to seat the brake pads before moving the vehicle.

Steering Knuckle

REMOVAL & INSTALLATION

The front wheel hub and bearing must be removed as a unit before the suspension knuckle can be removed. This is the only service situation where the wheel hub and bearing are removed together.

1. Disconnect the negative battery cable. Raise and safely support the vehicle.

2. Remove the tire and wheel assembly. Wrap a heavy shop cloth or towel around the outer CV-joint boot to protect it.

3. Remove the brake caliper. Do not disconnect the brake hose from the caliper. Wire it aside. Do not allow the brake hose to support the caliper weight.

4. Remove the halfshaft hub nut. A holding fixture may be required to hold the wheel hub/rotor when removing the nut.

5. Push the halfshaft inward, to disengage the shaft splines from the wheel hub splines. If it does not push out easily, use a screw type puller to press the shaft from the hub.

6. Install a puller plate that can be used with a slide hammer and pull the rotor/hub assembly from the suspension knuckle. Use care to keep dirt and debris from the bearing as the hub assembly is removed.

7. Remove the rotor from the hub by removing the rotor safety nuts. If these safety nuts are damaged by removal, always replace with new ones.

8. Rotate the wheel hub as necessary and use the access hole in the hub to remove each wheel bearing-to-suspension knuckle Torx® head bolt. Reinstall the brake rotor, attach a puller plate to it that can be used with a slide hammer and pull the rotor/hub assembly from the suspension knuckle. Use care to keep dirt and debris from the bearing as the hub assembly is removed.

9. Loosen but do not remove the stabilizer bar inner bracket retaining

bolts at the engine cradle. Remove the stabilizer bar outer bracket retaining nuts at the suspension arm and remove the bracket from the retaining bolts. Note that the stabilizer bar outer bracket retaining nuts also retain the ball joint to the suspension arm. Move the stabilizer bar away from the suspension arm and reinstall one of the nuts on either of the ball joint retaining bolts.

10. Loosen but do remove the nuts and bolts at the bushings that attach the suspension arm to the engine cradle.

11. Remove the ball joint stud pinch bolt and disengage the ball joint stud from the suspension knuckle.

12. Note that the 2 bolts that hold the bottom of the MacPherson strut to the suspension knuckle have splines under the bolt head. This keeps the bolt from rotating. Turn the nuts (not the bolt heads) until they are almost at the end of the bolt threads. Tap the nuts with a brass hammer to loosen the bolts and disengage the splines. Remove the nuts and pull out the bolts. Remove the knuckle from the halfshaft.

To install:

13. Position the steering knuckle over the halfshaft and insert the ball joint stud into the knuckle. Install the pinch bolt. Note that there is a recess, groove or keyway machined into the ball joint stud. The pinch bolt must be seated in this groove. Torque to 77 ft. lbs. (104 Nm).

14. Position the knuckle to the strut and install the through bolts. Note that the splines under the bolt heads must be properly aligned in the strut hole. Tap the bolts in place and install the nuts. Use a wrench on the bolt head to keep the bolt from turning and stripping the splines when the nut is tightened.

15. Remove the ball joint retaining nut and position the stabilizer bar at the suspension arm. Position the outer bracket on the stabilizer bar and install the nuts but do not tighten yet. The ball joint nuts must not be tightened until the vehicle is lowered and the tire and wheel assembly is installed and supporting the weight of the vehicle.

16. Position the wheel bearing and hub over the halfshaft and insert into the knuckle with the hub splines mated with the halfshaft splines.

17. Remove the brake rotor from the hub. Rotate the hub, as necessary, and use the access hole in the hub to install each wheel bearing-to-knuckle Torx® head bolt. Tighten each bolt to 11 ft. lbs. (15 Nm). Install the brake rotor.

18. Install the halfshaft-to-wheel hub nut. Use an appropriate holding tool to keep the hub from rotating while tightening the nut to 181 ft. lbs. (245 Nm) torque.

NOTE: Do not use an impact wrench to tighten the halfshaft-to-wheel hub nut. Use a torque wrench only to tighten the nut. It is also essential that the halfshaft-to-wheel hub nut be tighten to the specified torque. In addition to retaining the wheel hub on the halfshaft, the specified torque also establishes the wheel bearing preload.

19. Install the brake caliper, tire and wheel assembly and lower the vehicle.

20. With the vehicle weight being supported by the tire and wheels, torque the suspension arms-to-engine cradle nuts and bolts at the bushings to 103 ft. lbs. (140 Nm), torque the stabilizer bar outer bracket retaining nuts to 60 ft. lbs. (81 Nm) and tighten the stabilizer bar inner bracket retaining bolts to 21 ft. lbs. (29 Nm).

21. Connect the negative battery cable. Depress the brake pedal several times to seat the brake pads before moving the vehicle.

Transaxle Output Shaft Seal

REMOVAL & INSTALLATION

1. Raise the vehicle and support it safely.

2. Remove the tires and wheels.

3. Remove the halfshaft.

4. Remove the differential drain plug and drain the lubricant into a clean container for reuse.

5. With a flat tipped tool, pry out the dust cover from the output shaft.

6. Loosen the shaft bolt in the center of the output shaft and pull the short shaft and bearing out of the transaxle case. Pry out the shaft seal.

7. Installation is the reverse of removal. Torque the short output shaft center bolt to 18 ft. lbs. (24 Nm).

8. Refill the differential with synthetic-type 75W–140 hypoid gear lubricant. Add oil until it starts to flow out of the fill plug opening.

Manual Transaxle

For further information on transmissions/transaxles, please refer to "Chilton's Guide to Transmission Repair".

Transaxle Assembly

REMOVAL & INSTALLATION

1. Disconnect the negative battery cable.

2. Disconnect and remove the flexible heat tube from the engine.

3. Remove the TDC sensor retaining bolt and remove the sensor.

4. Remove the bolts retaining the steering bracket and remove the bracket.

5. Remove the bolts attaching the crossmember to the side sill and body.

6. Raise and safely support the vehicle.

7. Remove the front wheels. Disconnect and remove the passenger side tie rod.

8. Loosen the bolt retaining the coolant expansion tank and move the tank aside.

9. Attach an engine support tool to the engine and take up the engine weight.

10. Remove the bolts attaching the exhaust head pipe to the manifold. Remove the bolts attaching the exhaust head pipe to the converter and remove the head pipe.

11. Remove the crossmember by turning it and taking it out through the passenger side wheel well.

12. Disengage the clutch cable. Remove the upper steering knuckle mounting bolt and loosen the lower bolt.

13. Remove the halfshaft retaining pin. Swing each rotor and steering knuckle outward and remove the halfshafts from the transaxle.

14. Disconnect the reverse lockout cable and disconnect the shift rod from the lever. Disconnect the speedometer cable. Disconnect the ground strap at the transaxle.

15. Support the transaxle. Remove the transaxle support cushion nuts. Remove the bolts that attach the 2 transaxle mounting brackets to the transaxle.

16. Disconnect the wiring harness connector and remove the starter. Remove the bolts attaching the clutch housing to the engine.

17. Pull the transaxle straight back until the clutch shaft is clear of the engine and lower the transaxle.

To install:

18. Raise and position the transaxle in the vehicle. Align the release bearing and the release fork.

19. Install the transaxle-to-engine mounting bolts. Tighten to 37 ft. lbs. (51 Nm).

20. Install the starter and connect the electrical connectors. Slightly raise the transaxle and install the mounting brackets. Align the transaxle support

cushion bolts and install the retaining nuts.

21. Connect the speedometer cable and the shift rods. Connect the clutch cable.

22. Install the halfshafts by tilting the steering knuckle in, then install the upper bolt and tighten both bolts to 148 ft. lbs. (200 Nm).

23. Install the axle retaining pins. Connect the ground strap to the case.

24. Install the crossmember through the wheel well opening and position it on the side sills. Install and tighten the bolts.

25. Connect the tie rods to the steering bracket and tighten the mounting bolts to 25 ft. lbs. (34 Nm). Connect the steering gear bracket to the steering rack and tighten the bolts to 30 ft. lbs. (41 Nm).

26. Install the front wheels. Install the TDC sensor and the heat tube. Connect the exhaust header pipe to the converter and manifold.

27. Check and fill the transaxle.

28. Remove the engine support tool.

29. Connect the negative battery cable and check the transaxle for proper operation. Make sure the reverse lights come on when in R.

CLUTCH

Clutch Assembly

REMOVAL & INSTALLATION

1. Disconnect the negative battery cable.

2. Remove the transaxle assembly from the vehicle.

3. Remove the pressure plate attaching bolts. If the pressure plate is to be reused, loosen the bolts in succession, 1 or 2 turns at a time to prevent warping the cover.

4. Remove the pressure plate release bearing assembly and the clutch disc. Do not use solvent to clean the bearing.

To install:

5. Inspect the condition of the clutch components and replace any worn parts.

NOTE: The release bearing and pressure plate are not serviced separately. The bearing is permanently attached to the pressure plate diaphragm fingers. The pressure plate and bearing must be serviced as an assembly.

6. Inspect the flywheel for heat damage or cracks. Replace if damaged.

7. Install the clutch disc to the flywheel using alignment tool EMB–786–01 or equivalent. Install the pressure plate assembly and tighten the pressure plate bolts evenly to 18 ft. lbs. (25 Nm). Remove the alignment tool.

8. Install the transaxle assembly and check the clutch operation.

Clutch Cable

ADJUSTMENT

The Medallion is equipped with a cable-operated self-adjusting clutch mechanism. The adjustment is automatically set during operation by a quadrant mechanism on the clutch pedal assembly.

AUTOMATIC TRANSAXLE

For further information on transmissions/transaxles, please refer to "Chilton's Guide to Transmission Repair".

Transaxle Assembly

REMOVAL & INSTALLATION

Premier and Monaco

AR-4 TRANSAXLE

1. Disconnect the negative battery cable. Remove the windshield washer reservoir.

2. Disconnect the connectors at the control unit.

3. Disconnect and plug the fluid cooler hoses.

4. Remove the engine timing sensor.

5. Raise the vehicle and support safely. Remove the front wheels.

6. Remove the pins attaching the halfshafts to the transaxle output shafts.

7. Remove the upper steering knuckle mounting nut, remove the bolt, and loosen the lower bolt. Tilt the knuckles outward and slide the halfshafts from the transaxle.

8. Remove the transaxle splash shield.

9. Remove the brackets, retainers, tie straps or clips securing the transaxle electrical wiring to the vehicle body. Leave all components in place for transaxle removal.

10. Remove the starter and heat shield.

11. Remove the converter housing access plug and remove the converter bolts.

12. Remove the exhaust pipe clamp and bracket.

13. Using the proper equipment, support the weight of the transaxle.

14. Remove the bolts and nuts that attach the transaxle crossmember to the engine cradle. Remove the bolt attaching the rear mount to the transaxle bracket. Remove the crossmember and mount as an assembly.

15. Disconnect the shift cable from the bellcrank and remove the brace rod.

16. Move the bellcrank, link rod and bracket, and shift cable and bracket aside for clearance.

17. Remove the transaxle mount bracket.

18. Remove the transaxle to engine bolts. Note that 2 of these bolts are reversed.

19. Pull the transaxle back and away from the engine and remove from the engine.

To install:

NOTE: When installing, make sure the dowel pins are seated in the converter housing before tightening any bolts. Also, make sure the converter is aligned in the driveplate timing wheel. The timing wheel timing segments can be damaged if misaligned.

20. Lubricate the hub bore of the driveplate with with chassis grease. Install the converter.

21. Mount the transaxle on a transaxle jack and raise into position.

22. Align the converter housing with the driveplate and engine dowel pins and slide the transaxle onto the engine.

23. Install the transaxle to engine mounting bolts.

24. Coat the threads with Loctite® and install the converter bolts. Tighten to 24 ft. lbs. (33 Nm). Install the access plug.

25. Install the transaxle mount bracket and tighten the bolts to 29 ft. lbs. (40 Nm).

26. Install the bellcrank and bracket. Connect the bellcrank link rod to the shift lever.

27. Position the shift cable bracket on the case but do not tighten the bolts yet.

28. Attach the brace rod to the bellcrank and shift cable brackets. Tighten all bolts.

29. Snap the shift cable onto the bellcrank.

30. Install the transaxle crossmember but do not tighten the bolts yet.

31. Attach the transaxle bracket to the rear mount.

32. Tighten the transaxle bracket-to-rear mount bolt to 49 ft. lbs. (67 Nm). Tighten the crossmember bolts to 31

ft. lbs. (43 Nm). Remove the support equipment.

33. Install the exhaust pipe bracket and clamp. Install the starter and heat shield.

34. Verify that the transaxle output shaft O-rings are in position and are not damaged. Replace if necessary. Install the halfshafts and install the retaining pins.

35. Install the halfshafts. Tilt the steering knuckles in and install the top bolts. Tighten the nuts to 148 ft. lbs. (200 Nm). Install the front wheels.

36. Install the engine timing sensor.

37. Connect the transaxle cooling hoses. Fill the differential section of the unit with synthetic type 75W–140 gear oil.

38. Route the wire harness properly and secure. Install the splash shield.

39. Fill the transmission section of the transaxle with Mobil Universal automatic transmission fluid. Connect the control unit harness.

40. Connect the negative battery cable and check the transaxle for proper operation. Check and adjust the shift cable as required.

ZF-4 TRANSAXLE

1. Disconnect the negative battery cable.

2. Loosen the throttle valve cable adjusting nut and remove the cable from the engine bracket.

3. Remove the upper steering knuckle mounting nut, remove the bolt, and loosen the lower bolt.

4. Remove the halfshaft retaining pin. Swing each rotor and steering knuckle outward and slide the halfshafts from the transaxle.

5. Remove the underbody splash shield. Loosen the nut attaching the fill tube to the pan and drain the transaxle. When fluid has drained, tighten the nut.

6. Remove the converter housing covers. Remove the converter-to-flexplate bolts. Support the transaxle.

7. Remove the nuts attaching the crossmember to the side sills. Remove the large bolt and nut that attach the rear cushion to the support bracket.

8. Remove the support bracket and rear cushion.

9. Disconnect the header pipes from the exhaust manifold and the catalytic converter.

10. Loosen the engine cradle bolts only until there is ½–⅞ in. clearance between the cradle and the side sill.

11. Remove the front exhaust pipe. Remove the starter, plate and dowel.

12. Disconnect the shift cable from the transaxle lever. Remove the cable bracket bolts and separate the bracket from the case. Remove the brace rod.

13. Disconnect and remove the TDC sensor, speedometer sensor, and engine speed sensor. Disconnect and plug the transaxle cooling lines.

14. Using a transaxle jack, support the weight of the transaxle. Remove the transaxle-to-engine bolts, then pull the transaxle back and away from the engine.

To install:

15. Position the transaxle to the engine. Install the transaxle-to-engine bolts and tighten to 31 ft. lbs. (42 Nm).

16. Install removed sensors and connect all electrical leads. Connect the transaxle cooler lines. Install the brace rod.

17. Attach the shift bracket to the case and tighten the bolts to 125 inch lbs. (14 Nm). Install the shift cable to the bracket.

18. Install the starter. Connect the exhaust head pipes to the manifolds and the converter.

19. Install the rear support and cushion, install the mounting bolts and tighten to 49 ft. lbs. (66 Nm).

20. Tighten the engine cradle bolts to 92 ft. lbs. (125 Nm). Install the halfshafts.

21. Coat the threads with Loctite® and install the converter-to-flexplate bolts. Tighten to 24 ft. lbs. (33 Nm). Install the converter housing covers.

22. Install the halfshafts. Tilt the steering knuckles in and install the top bolts. Tighten the nuts to 148 ft. lbs. (200 Nm).

23. Install the front wheels. Install the under body splash shield. Attach the throttle valve cable.

24. Fill the transmission side of the transaxle with Mopar Mercon™ transaxle fluid. Check the differential fluid level. If it is low, fill with synthetic type 75W–140 gear oil.

25. Connect the negative battery cable and check the transaxle for proper operation.

Medallion

1. Disconnect the negative battery cable.

2. Disconnect and remove the flexible heat tube from the engine.

3. Remove the TDC sensor retaining bolt and remove the sensor.

4. Remove the bolts retaining the steering bracket and remove the bracket.

5. Remove the bolts attaching the crossmember to the side sill and body.

6. Raise and safely support the vehicle.

7. Remove the front wheels. Disconnect and remove the passenger side tie rod.

8. Loosen the bolt retaining the coolant expansion tank and move the tank aside.

9. Attach an engine support tool to take up the weight of the engine.

10. Remove the bolts attaching the exhaust head pipe to the manifold. Remove the bolts attaching the exhaust head pipe to the converter and remove the head pipe. Disconnect the coolant lines to the heat exchanger, if equipped.

11. Remove the crossmember by turning it and taking out through the passenger side wheel well.

12. Disengage the shift cable and support it to the side. Remove the upper steering knuckle mounting bolt and loosen the lower bolt.

13. Remove the halfshaft retaining pin. Swing each rotor and steering knuckle outward and slide the halfshafts from the transaxle.

14. Disconnect the speedometer cable. Disconnect the ground strap at the transaxle. Disconnect the BVA module harness.

15. Support the transaxle. Remove the transaxle support cushion nuts. Remove the bolts that attach the 2 transaxle mounting brackets to the transaxle.

16. Disconnect the wiring harness connector and remove the starter. Remove the converter-to-flywheel bolts. Remove the transaxle-to-engine bolts.

17. Pull the transaxle straight back until the converter is clear of the engine and lower the transaxle. Install converter retainer BVI–465 or equivalent, to keep the converter from falling out.

To install:

18. Raise and position the transaxle into the vehicle. Apply a small amount of grease to the torque converter pilot. Align the painted marks on the converter with the painted marks on the flywheel. Coat the threads with Loctite® and install the converter to flywheel bolts. Tighten to 34 ft. lbs. (46 Nm).

19. Install the transaxle-to-engine mounting bolts.

20. Install the starter and connect the electrical connectors. Slightly raise the transaxle and install the mounting brackets. Align the transaxle support cushion bolts and install the retaining nuts.

21. Connect the speedometer cable and the shift cable.

22. Install the halfshafts by tilting the steering knuckle in, install the upper bolt and tighten both the nuts to 148 ft. lbs. (200 Nm).

23. Install the axle retaining pins. Connect the ground strap to the case.

24. Install the crossmember through the wheel well opening and position it on the side sills. Install and tighten the bolts.

25. Connect the tie rods to the steering bracket and tighten the mounting bolts to 25 ft. lbs. (34 Nm). Connect the steering gear bracket to the steer-

ing rack and tighten the bolts to 30 ft. lbs. (41 Nm). Connect the cooling lines.

26. Install the front wheels. Install the TDC sensor and the heat tube. Connect the exhaust header pipe to the converter and manifold. Connect the BVA wiring.

27. Check and fill the transaxle fluid. Remove the engine support tool and connect the negative battery cable.

SHIFT LINKAGE ADJUSTMENT

Premier and Monaco

1. Disconnect the negative battery cable.

2. Shift into the **P** detent.

3. Remove the shifter cover and locate the shift cable cross-lock where the cable meets the shifter bracket. Release the shift cable cross-lock by pulling it upward.

4. Move the transaxle shift lever all the way rearward into the **P** detent. Be sure the lever is centered in the detent. Verify positive engagement of the park lock by attempting to rotate the halfshafts. The shafts cannot be turned if the park lock is properly engaged.

5. On 2.5L engine, adjust by performing the following:

a. Grasp the shift cable and pull it rearward until the distance between the back of the lock tab and the seat (exposed threads) is 0.30 in. (7.62mm).

b. If adjustment is not correct, and the column shifter was biased toward the **D** gate, decrease the clearance by 0.040 in. (1mm) increments until correct.

c. If adjustment is not correct, and the column shifter was biased toward the **N** gate, increase the clearance by 0.040 in. (1mm) increments until correct.

6. On 3.0L engine, adjust by performing the following:

a. Verify that the cable is proper-

ly routed and secured and the cable grommet is fully seated in the floor pan. Press the cable cross-lock downward until it snaps in place.

b. Position the cable self-adjusting unit in the fork of the lower cable mounting bracket at the transaxle. Use the index key to properly index and seat the cable within the bracket.

c. Seat the cable core end fitting onto the transaxle operating lever pin.

d. At the transaxle end fitting, push the core-adjust slider mechanism until it snaps into a locked position. This will properly adjust and lock the gearshift cable.

7. Check the shift cable adjustment. The engine should start in **P** and **N** only.

THROTTLE VALVE CABLE ADJUSTMENT

1. Disconnect negative battery cable.

2. Loosen the cable locknuts and lift the threaded shank of the cable out of the engine bracket.

3. Place the throttle lever in the curb idle position.

4. An accurate measurement must now be made. Vernier calipers are suggested. If accurate calipers are not available, fabricate a cable adjustment gauge from a small piece of sheet stock or other material that can be slipped over the throttle cable wire. The gauge must be 1.55 in. (39.5mm) long.

5. Pull the cable wire forward and position the vernier calipers or fabricated gauge on the wire between the cable connector and cable end.

6. Pull the cable shank rearward to the detent position but not to the wide open throttle position; the detent position feels similar to a stop when reached.

7. Hold the cable shank at the detent position, then insert the cable shank into the cable bracket and tighten the cable locknuts.

8. Remove the vernier calipers or gauge and verify the adjustment. The cable detent position should be reached when the cable wire travels 1.55 in. ± 0.039 in. (39.5mm ± 1mm).

POSITION VERNIER CALIPERS OR FABRICATED GAUGE HERE

CABLE WIRE

CABLE CONNECTOR

CABLE END

THROTTLE LEVER

CABLE LOCKNUTS

1.55 IN. (39.5MM)

ENGINE BRACKET

DETENT POSITION SHOULD BE REACHED AT CABLE TRAVEL OF 1.55 IN. ± 0.039 IN. (39.5MM ± 1MM)

Throttle valve cable adjustment—Premier and Monaco

FRONT SUSPENSION

MacPherson Strut

REMOVAL & INSTALLATION

1. Raise and safely support vehicle.

Do not support vehicle by placing supports under the suspension arms.

2. Remove the wheel and tire assemblies.

3. Remove the outer tie rod ends with a screw type puller.

--- CAUTION ---

Do not remove the strut strut-to-tower cushion locknut (the center nut). The coil spring is compressed and has very strong tension. Bodily injury could result.

4. Remove the 3 strut tower cushion-to-tower attaching bolts.

NOTE: Before proceeding to the next step, make sure the suspension is hanging free. There must not be any pressure or tension on any front suspension components. Note too that the strut body-to-knuckle bolts are splined. Do not try to turn the bolt head. Turn the nuts only. Follow the procedure below.

Also, make sure brake hoses and/or ABS wiring will not be damaged.

5. Remove the splined bolts by loosening the nuts until they are almost at the end of the bolt threads. Tap the nuts with a brass hammer to loosen the bolts and disengage the splines. Remove the nuts, then the bolts.

6. For protection, wrap the halfshaft boot with heavy shop towels. Then press down on the suspension arm and pull the strut out of the wheel well.

To install:

7. Carefully route the strut into place and install the 3 upper strut tower cushion-to-body bolts finger-tight. Make sure the splines are aligned on the bolts and tap into place. Tighten the nuts only. Do not allow the bolt heads to turn or the splines will strip. Hold the bolt heads with a wrench while the nuts are tightened. Torque the nuts to 123 ft. lbs. (167 Nm).

8. Torque the 3 upper bolts to 17 ft. lbs. (23 Nm).

9. Install the tie rod end and install the wheel.

10. Perform a front end alignment.

Lower Ball Joints

Inspect the lower ball joint and replace if the protective boot is torn or the ball joint is worn or damaged.

REMOVAL & INSTALLATION

1. Disconnect the negative battery cable. Raise and safely support vehicle.

2. Remove the wheel and tire assemblies.

3. Wrap a heavy shop cloth or towel around the halfshaft outer boot to protect it.

4. Loosen but do not remove the stabilizer bar inner bracket retaining bolts at the engine cradle. Remove the stabilizer bar outer bracket nuts at the suspension arm and remove the bracket. Note that the outer bracket nuts and bolts also fasten the ball joint to the suspension arm.

5. Remove the ball joint pinch bolt from the suspension knuckle. Loosen but do not remove the nuts and bolts at the bushings that attach the suspension arm to the engine cradle.

6. Disengage the ball joint stud from the suspension knuckle and remove the plastic washer from the stud. Remove the ball joint from the suspension arm by removing the bolts and tapping upward on it with a brass hammer.

To install:

7. Install the replacement ball joint assembly to the suspension arm. Crimp the sleeves, but do not tighten the nuts yet. Install a new plastic washer on the stud.

8. Install to the knuckle. When installing the pinch bolt that holds the ball joint stud to the knuckle, make sure the bolt aligns with the groove in the stud. Torque to 77 ft. lbs. (105 Nm).

9. Do not tighten the stabilizer bar nuts or bolts until the vehicle is lowered and the tires are supporting the weight of the vehicle. At that time, torque the suspension arm-to-engine cradle nuts and bolts to 103 ft. lbs. (140 Nm), the stabilizer outer bracket nuts to 60 ft. lbs. (81 Nm), and the stabilizer bar inner bracket nuts to 21 ft. lbs. (29 Nm).

10. Perform a front end alignment.

Lower Control Arms

REMOVAL & INSTALLATION

1. Raise and safely support vehicle.
2. Remove the wheel and tire assemblies.
3. Wrap a heavy shop cloth or towel around the halfshaft outer boot to protect it.
4. Loosen but do not remove the stabilizer bar inner bracket retaining bolts at the engine cradle. Remove the stabilizer bar outer bracket nuts at the suspension arm and remove the bracket. Note that the outer bracket nuts and bolts also fasten the ball joint to the suspension arm. Reinstall a nut to keep the ball joint from separating from the arm.
5. Remove the ball joint pinch bolt from the suspension knuckle. Remove the nuts and bolts at the bushings that

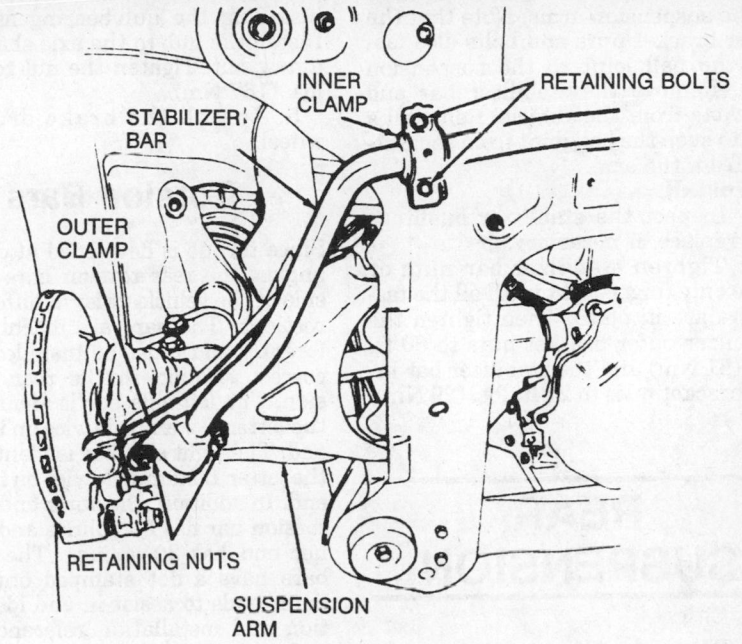

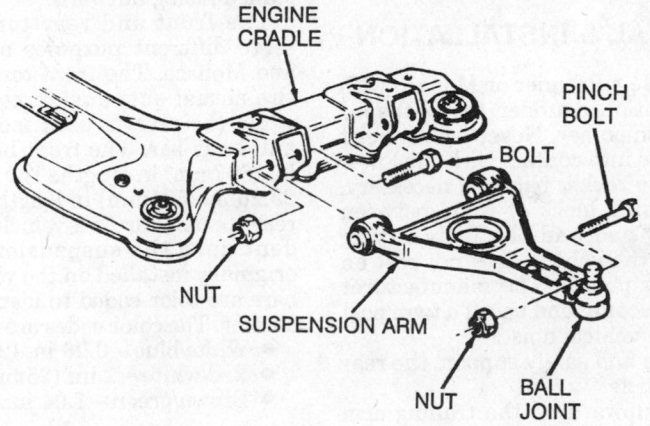

Control arm and sway bar assemblies

attach the suspension arm to the engine cradle.

6. Disengage the ball joint stud from the suspension knuckle, remove the plastic washer from the stud and remove the arm from the vehicle.

To install:

7. If reuseable, transfer the ball joint. Inspect the suspension arm bushings and replace if necessary. Install the cradle bolts, but do not tighten until the full weight of the vehicle is on the ground.

8. Install the ball joint stud to the knuckle. When installing the pinch bolt that holds the ball joint stud to the knuckle, make sure the bolt aligns with the groove in the stud. Torque to 77 ft. lbs. (105 Nm).

9. Do not tighten the stabilizer bar nuts or bolts until the vehicle is lowered and the tires are supporting the

weight of the vehicle. At that time, torque the suspension arm-to-engine cradle nuts and bolts to 103 ft. lbs. (140 Nm), the stabilizer outer bracket nuts to 60 ft. lbs. (81 Nm) and the stabilizer bar inner bracket nuts to 21 ft. lbs. (29 Nm).

Sway Bar

REMOVAL & INSTALLATION

1. For ease of stabilizer bar (sway bar) removal and installation, do not raise the vehicle. Leave the vehicle's weight on the tires.
2. Remove the bolts that hold the stabilizer bar inner brackets to the engine cradle.
3. Remove the retaining nuts from the stabilizer bar outer bracket bolts

at the suspension arms. Note that the outer bracket nuts and bolts also fasten the ball joint to the suspension arm. Remove the stabilizer bar and brackets from the vehicle. Reinstall a nut to keep the ball joint from separating from the arm.

To install:

4. Inspect the stabilizer bushings and replace, if necessary.

5. Tighten stabilizer bar nuts or bolts only finger-tight until all the fasteners are in place. Then tighten the stabilizer outer bracket nuts to 60 ft. lbs. (81 Nm) and the stabilizer bar inner bracket nuts to 21 ft. lbs. (29 Nm).

REAR SUSPENSION

Shock Absorbers

REMOVAL & INSTALLATION

Never raise a Premier or Monaco with a lift positioned under the V-shaped rear crossmember. Never let the hoist arms come into contact with the lower edge of the rocker panel. If necessary, place a small block of wood between the hoist pad and the body lifting points so the vehicle does not rest on the rocker panels. The manufacturer does not recommend use of a twin post under-the-vehicle hoist.

1. Raise and safely support the rear of the vehicle.

2. Lift upward on the trailing arm to relieve the weight from the shock absorber.

3. Remove the top and bottom bolts and remove the shock absorber.

4. Installation is the reverse of removal. Torque the top bolt to 60 ft. lbs. (81 Nm) and the bottom bolt to 85 ft. lbs. (115 Nm).

Rear Wheel Bearings

REMOVAL & INSTALLATION

The rear wheel bearings and hubs are replaced as assemblies only. They are non-adjustable. The maximum allowable bearing endplay is 0.001 in. If the endplay exceeds this, the bearing/hub assembly should be replaced.

1. Raise and safely support the rear of the vehicle. Remove the wheel.

2. Remove the brake drum from the axle shaft hub.

3. Remove the axle shaft hub nut and remove the hub/bearing assembly.

To install:

4. Lightly oil the axle shaft before installing the hub/bearing assembly. Install the hub to the axle shaft using a new nut. Tighten the nut to 123 ft. lbs. (167 Nm).

5. Install the brake drum and wheel.

Torsion Bars

Since torque is developed at different angles, the rear torsion bars at each side of the vehicle twist in different directions. The bars are machined differently and must be installed at the correct location in the rear suspension. The left side bar is identified by the letter **G** stamped twice on its outer end. The right side bar is identified by the letter **D** stamped twice on its outer end. In addition, the outer end of each torsion bar has 31 splines and the inner end has 30 splines. The torsion bars have a dot stamped onto their outer ends to assist in end identification and installation reference. This end with the dot must always be installed facing outward.

The front and rear torsion bars serve different purposes on Premier and Monaco. The front torsion bar is the actual suspension component, while the rear is used mostly as an anti-sway bar. The front bar is 26.25 in. (667mm) in length. The rear bar is 23.26 in. (591mm) in length. Also, the rear torsion bar in a vehicle is dependent upon the suspension package originally installed on the vehicle. The bars are color-coded to identify its diameter. The color codes are as follows:

- White/blue—0.96 in. (24mm)
- Red/white—1 in. (25mm)
- Brown/green—1.04 in. (26mm)

Never raise a Premier or Monaco with a lift positioned under the V-shaped rear crossmember. Never let the hoist arms come into contact with the lower edge of the rocker panel. If necessary, place a small block of wood between the hoist pad and the body lifting points so the vehicle does not rest on the rocker panels. The manufacturer does not recommend use of a twin post under-the-vehicle hoist.

REMOVAL & INSTALLATION

1. Disconnect the negative battery cable.

2. Raise the vehicle and support it safely.

3. Remove the both rear wheels and shocks.

4. Pry the protective end caps and remove them from the front torsion bars.

5. Unthread the protective end caps and remove them from the rear torsion bars.

6. Pry the retaining clips away from the ends of the torsion bars and remove.

NOTE: Each torsion bar bracket has an existing dot stamped into it that provides a reference for the initial installation position of the front torsion bar. An additional installation position mark must be punched into the trailing suspension arm before the bar is removed from the crossmember.

7. Place a straightedge on the centerline of the 2 torsion bar installation

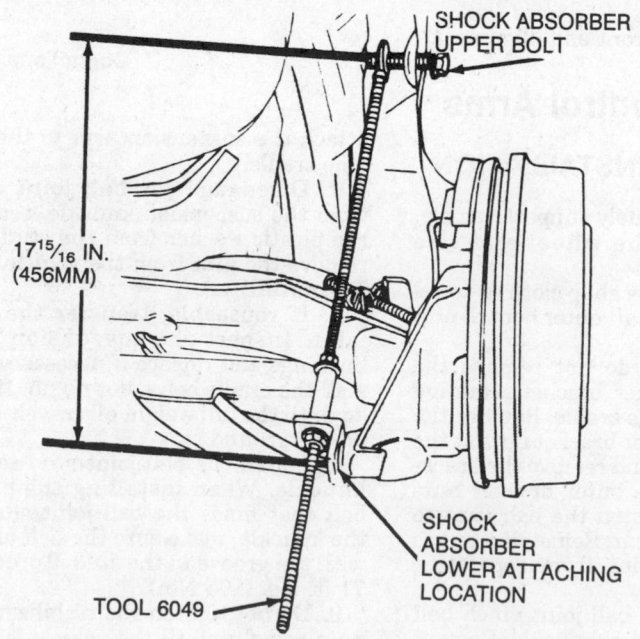

SHOCK ABSORBER UPPER BOLT

17 15/16 IN. (456MM)

TOOL 6049

SHOCK ABSORBER LOWER ATTACHING LOCATION

Special threaded tool installation

holes and punch a dot into the trailing suspension arm adjacent to the rear torsion bar spline groove.

8. Note and record the relative positions of the installation reference dots on the ends of the torsion bars in respect to the dots on the torsion bar support bracket and the trailing suspension arm. In other words, count the number of splines between the dot on the bar and the dot made on the bracket or trailing arm. These dots will ensure that the proper "initial twist" is applied to the torsion bar upon installation, according to the suspension package originally installed in the vehicle.

9. Loosen and extract the front torsion bars using a slide hammer. Pull the bars out far enough to disengage the splines from the connecting link and the torsion support brackets.

10. Loosen and extract the rear torsion bars using a slide hammer. Pull the bars out far enough to disengage the splines from the connecting link and the trailing suspension arms.

11. The crossmember must be lowered before the torsion bars can be removed from it. Using the proper equipment, support the weight of the rear crossmember. Do not apply lifting force to the crossmember.

12. Loosen both torsion support bracket front bolts about 4 turns. Do not remove these bolts.

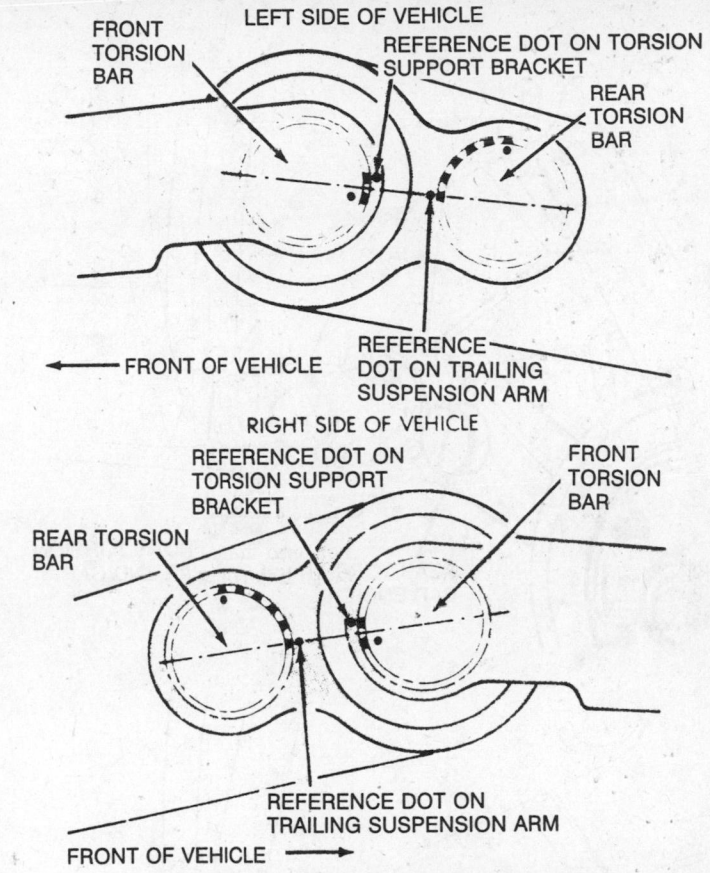

Example of rear torsion bar installation positions

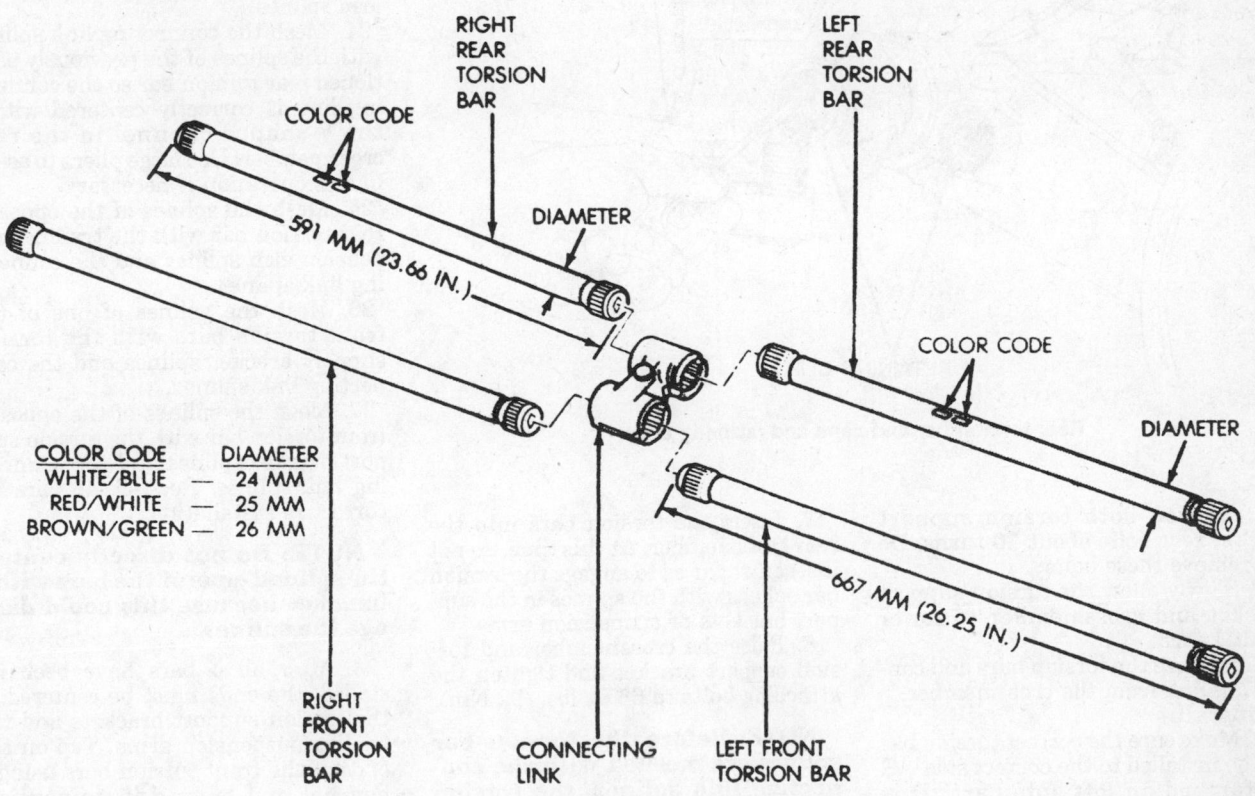

COLOR CODE	DIAMETER
WHITE/BLUE	24 MM
RED/WHITE	25 MM
BROWN/GREEN	26 MM

Rear torsion bars and identifying codes

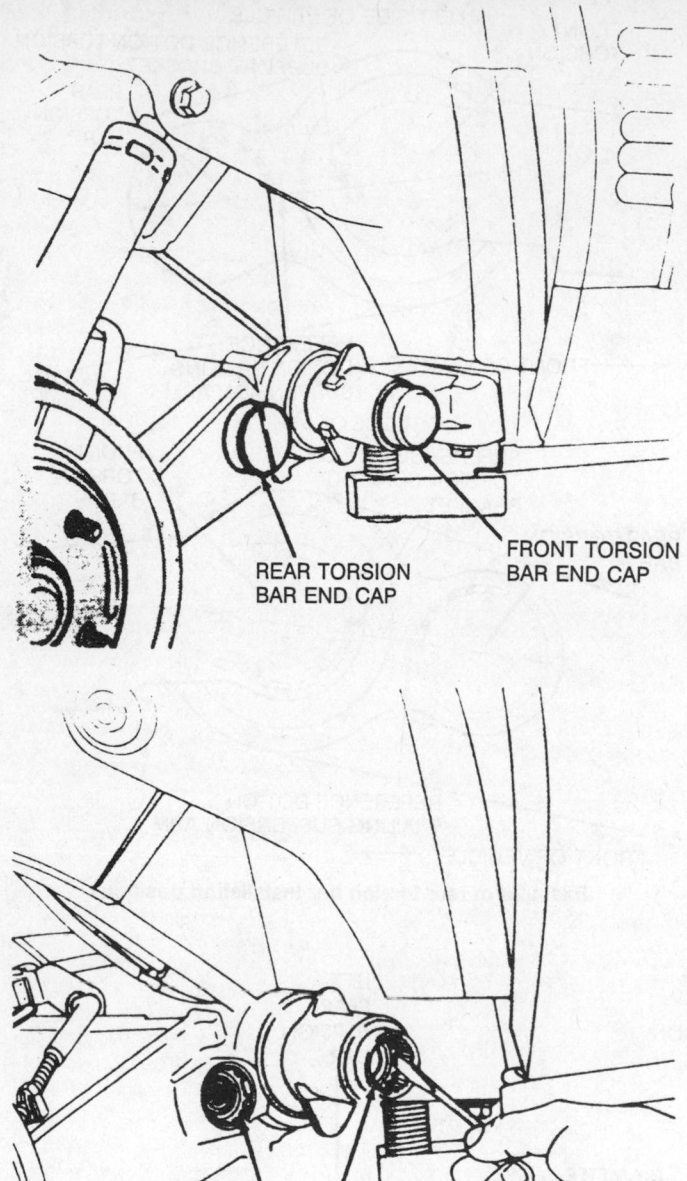

REAR TORSION
BAR END CAP

FRONT TORSION
BAR END CAP

RETAINING CLIPS

Rear torsion bar end caps and retaining clips

13. Loosen both torsion support bracket rear bolts about 10 turns. Do not remove these bolts.

14. Slowly allow the torsion support bracket and crossmember to lower about 1 inch.

15. Remove the torsion bars and connecting link from the crossmember.
To install:

16. Make sure the correct torsion bar will be installed to the correct side—G is stamped on left side bars; D is stamped on right side bars.

17. Insert the torsion bars into the rear crossmember. At this time, do not insert it so far as to engage the torsion bar splines with the splines in the support brackets or suspension arms.

18. Raise the crossmember and torsion support bracket and tighten the attaching bolts to 68 ft. lbs. (92 Nm).

NOTE: Before the torsion bar splines are meshed with the connecting link splines, the torsion support bracket splines and the

trailing suspension arm splines must be positioned at the correct location in relation to the vehicle chassis.

19. Position the trailing suspension arms in the correct location on each side of the vehicle using 2 sets of special tool 6049 (threaded rod). Two spacers from tool set 7466 must also be used. Adjust each positioning tool so the distance between the center of the rod eyelet and the center of the hub is on the adjusting bracket is $17^{15}/_{16}$ in. (456mm).

20. After the distance has been properly set, install the positioning tools where the rear shocks are installed.

21. Insert the upper attaching bolt through the eyelet and loosely tighten it. Insert the spacer into the lower shock attaching bolt hole and insert the adjustable bracket hub into the spacer.

22. Liberally apply all-purpose lubricant to all torsion bar splines.

NOTE: If the bars are not being replaced, they must be installed in their exact original locations. The dot reference positions must be the same on both sides of the vehicle to prevent added stress from being applied to the bars.

23. Refer to the previously made torsion bar dot reference positions and correctly mesh the splines of the torsion bars with the trailing suspension arm splines.

24. Mesh the connecting link splines with the splines of the previously positioned rear torsion bar so the connecting link is correctly centered within the V-shaped channel in the rear crossmember. Use large pliers to assist in this operation if necessary.

25. Mesh the splines of the opposite rear torsion bar with the trailing suspension arm splines and the connecting link splines.

26. Mesh the splines of one of the front torsion bars with the torsion support bracket splines and the connecting link splines.

27. Mesh the splines of the opposite front torsion bar with the torsion support bracket splines and the connecting link splines. Recheck all bars for correct re-installation.

NOTE: Do not directly contact the splined ends of the bars with a hammer because this could damage the splines.

28. After all 4 bars have been installed, the ends must be centered in the torsion support brackets and the trailing suspension arms. Tap on the ends of the front torsion bars using a hammer and brass drift to position. Adjust so the outer end of each bar is

recessed $^{13}/_{16}$ in. $\pm$ $^{1}/_{16}$ in. (20.6mm $\pm$ 1.6mm) from the outer edge of the torsion support bracket boss.

29. Tap on the ends of the rear torsion bars using a hammer and brass drift to position. Adjust so the outer end of each bar is recessed $^{1}/_{4}$ in. $\pm$ $^{1}/_{16}$ in. (6.3mm $\pm$ 1.6mm) from the outer edge of the trailing suspension arm.

30. Position and press the retaining clips inward against the ends of the torsion bars.

31. Install the protective caps.

32. Remove the position tools from the vehicle and install the shock absorbers.

33. Install the wheels and lower the vehicle.

34. Measure the vehicle height using the following procedure:

   a. The vehicle should be unloaded, on a flat level surface, with a full tank of fuel, and with the tires all adjusted to the same proper pressure.

   b. Measure from the centerline of the front wheel hubs to the ground (H1) and from the rear wheel hubs to the ground (H4).

   c. Measure from the engine cradle at the wheel hub vertical centerline to the ground on each side (H2).

   d. Measure from the front torsion bar horizontal center line to the ground on each side (H3).

   e. Subtract H2 from H1. This value should be 3.36–3.98 in. (85–101mm). If this height is not within specification, replace worn front end parts.

   f. Subtract H3 from H4. This value should be 1.25–1.87 in. (31.5–47.5mm).

35. If the rear vehicle height is not within specification, reposition the front torsion bar(s). This is accomplished by adjusting the length of special tool 6049 (threaded rod) when reinstalling the bar (Step 19 in the procedure). Do not attempt to adjust vehicle height with the rear torsion bars.

36. Connect the negative battery cable and road test the vehicle.

Rear Axle Assembly

REMOVAL & INSTALLATION

1. Raise and safely support the vehicle.

2. Remove the rear wheels.

3. Remove the parking brake cables from the body support.

4. Disconnect and plug the brake hoses at the axle. Remove the shock absorbers.

5. Support the axle assembly and remove the support bracket bolts. Lower the axle assembly and remove.

To install:

6. Installation is the reverse of removal. Position the axle under the vehicle and raise it into place. Install and tighten the support bracket bolts, tighten to 68 ft. lbs. (92 Nm).

7. Connect the brake hoses at the axle. Connect the parking brake cables. Install the shock absorbers, tighten the upper shock bolt to 60 ft. lbs. (81 Nm) and the lower bolt to 85 ft. lbs. (115 Nm).

8. Install the rear wheels, bleed the brake system and adjust the parking brake cable.

STEERING

Steering Wheel

REMOVAL & INSTALLATION

1. Disconnect the negative battery cable.

2. Unsnap the horn button and disconnect the wires. Remove the horn button.

3. Note the position of the reference mark on the end of the steering shaft. Matchmark the steering wheel to the shaft to emphisize the alignment.

4. Remove the nut and slide the wheel off the shaft. If required, use a suitable steering wheel puller. Disconnect the speed control wire connector, if equipped.

To install:

5. Install the electrical connector. Align the pin on the turn signal cam with the pin bore in the steering wheel and slide the wheel into place.

6. Align the wheel with the reference mark on the steering shaft and install the nut. Tighten the nut to 52 ft. lbs. (71 Nm).

7. Connect the negative battery cable.

Steering Column

REMOVAL & INSTALLATION

1. Disconnect battery negative cable.

2. Remove the screws that attach the instrument panel lower trim cover to the instrument panel. Remove the cover.

3. Remove the screws that attach the instrument panel support rod to the instrument panel. Remove the rod.

4. Disconnect the steering column wire harness connector.

5. Remove the screw that attaches the dash panel wire harness connector to the dash panel.

6. If equipped with a steering column gearshift mechanism, perform the following:

   a. Disconnect the automatic transaxle shift cable receptacle from the shift lever ball joint with a small prybar.

   b. Disconnect the shift cable retainer from the steering column bracket by depressing the cable retainer lock tabs with pliers.

   c. Slide the shift cable retainer out of the steering column bracket.

   d. Remove the screw that attaches the shift position indicator bracket to the steering column and remove the indicator wire from the pivot pin.

7. Detach the steering column boot from the steering column. Slide the upper half of the 2-piece boot downward over the lower half of the boot for access to the steering column shaft and intermediate shaft U-joint.

8. Matchmark the steering column shaft and the intermediate shaft U-joint coupling for installation alignment reference.

9. Remove the bolt from the intermediate steering shaft U-joint coupling clamp.

10. Remove the bolts and nuts that attach the steering column to the instrument panel.

11. Carefully lower the steering column to the vehicle floor. Disconnect the steering shaft from the intermediate shaft and remove the column from the vehicle.

To install:

12. Align the reference marks and insert the steering shaft into the intermediate shaft U-joint coupling clamp.

13. Install but do not tighten the intermediate shaft U-joint clamp bolt.

14. Place the steering column into position, install the nuts and bolts and torque to 33 ft. lbs. (45 Nm). Tighten the intermediate shaft U-bolt clamp bolt to 30 ft. lbs. (41 Nm).

15. Reassemble the shift mechanism. Check shift indicator alignment. Place the gearshift in N and observe the position of the shift indicator pointer. If the pointer is not aligned, loosen the shift position indicator bracket screw and move the bracket forward or backward to correctly align the pointer with the N on the quadrant. Tighten the screw.

16. Align the 2 halves of the steering shaft boot. Rotate the upper half of the boot until the X mark on the lower half is centered in the oval alignment cutout (window) in the upper half of the boot. Verify that the alignment mark on the metal boot flange is at the 6 o'clock position.

17. Install instrument panel components.

18. Connect the negative battery ca-

ble and check all column-mounted components for proper operation.

Power Steering Rack and Pinion

REMOVAL & INSTALLATION

1. Disconnect the negative battery cable. Remove the instrument panel lower cover.

2. Unsnap the steering shaft boot flange from the dash panel opening and slide the boot upward.

3. Remove the U-joint coupling clamp bolt. Matchmark the steering column shaft and the intermediate shaft U-joint coupling for installation alignment reference.

4. In the engine compartment, remove the splash shield from the dash panel.

5. Remove the fluid lines from their retaining block slots. Position a drain pan under the tubes and disconnect them from the steering gear.

6. Remove the front attaching nut from the right side bracket.

7. Raise the vehicle and support safely. Remove the left front wheel.

8. Disconnect the tie rod ends from the strut body brackets.

9. Remove the 3 bolts that attach the steering gear brackets to the cross member support.

10. Tie the tie rods to the steering gear to keep them parallel to the rack. Remove the steering gear and tie rods through the left side of the vehicle.

To install:

11. Remove the tie rod ends from the steering gear to aid installation. Install the gear through the left opening. Position on the support and install the bracket attaching nut and bolts. Tighten to 40 ft. lbs. (55 Nm).

12. Attach the tie rod ends to the strut body brackets. Tighten the nuts to 35 ft. lbs. (48 Nm).

13. Connect the tie rods to the rack shaft spacer block and tighten the bolts to 55 ft. lbs. (75 Nm). Bend the lock tabs over the bolt flats.

14. Replace the O-rings and connect the fluid lines to the rack. Insert the lines into their slots.

15. Install the splash shield onto the dash panel.

16. Align the reference marks and insert the steering shaft into the intermediate shaft U-joint coupling clamp. Install the intermediate shaft U-joint clamp bolt. Tighten the intermediate shaft U-bolt clamp bolt to 30 ft. lbs. (41 Nm).

17. Lower the boot and install the instrument panel lower cover.

18. Fill the pump reservoir with power steering fluid.

19. Perform a front end alignment.

Power Steering Pump

REMOVAL & INSTALLATION

1. Disconnect the negative battery cable.

2. Raise and safely support the vehicle.

3. Remove the underbody splash shield. Loosen the accessory drive belt.

4. Disconnect and plug the power steering fluid lines.

5. Remove the pump mounting bolts and remove the pump.

To install:

6. Install the pump to the engine.

7. Replace the O-rings and connect the pressure lines.

8. Install the accessory drive belt and adjust the tension.

9. Lower the vehicle. Fill and bleed the system.

Belt Adjustment

1. Proper belt tension for serpentine accessory drive belt is 180–200 ft. lbs. Inspect the tension with gauge and adjust as required.

2. Loosen the power steering locknut and pivot bolt.

3. Loosen the power steering pump rear mounting bolts. Loosen or tighten the adjusting nut as required to correct tension.

4. Secure all mounting bolts.

System Bleeding

1. With the wheels turned all the way to the left, add power steering fluid to the **COLD** mark on the fluid level indicator or until the reservoir is full.

2. Start the engine and run at fast idle momentarily, then shut the engine **OFF** and recheck fluid level. If necessary, add fluid.

3. Start the engine and bleed the system by turning the wheels from side to side without hitting the stops.

NOTE: Fluid with air in it has a red milky appearance.

4. Return the wheels to the center position and keep the engine running for 2–3 minutes.

5. Road test the vehicle and recheck the fluid level making sure it is at the **HOT** mark or the reservoir is full.

Tie Rod Ends

The rack and pinion system is mounted high in the body. The steering tie rods are connected to the steering rack shaft via a spacer block located at the center of the steering rack body. The tie rods are connected to strut body brackets.

REMOVAL & INSTALLATION

1. Raise and safely support vehicle.

2. Remove the wheel and tire assemblies.

3. Remove the nuts attaching the tie rod end ball studs to the strut body brackets.

4. Loosen the locknuts that secure the tie rod ends to the tie rods. A wire brush and solvent will help clear the threads of road debris.

5. Disconnect the tie rod ends with an appropriate press type tool.

6. Unscrew the tie rod ends. Counting the turns will make installation easier and get the front end alignment close.

7. Installation is the reverse of removal.

8. Torque the tie rod ends-to-strut bracket nuts to 35 ft. lbs. (48 Nm).

9. Perform a front end alignment.

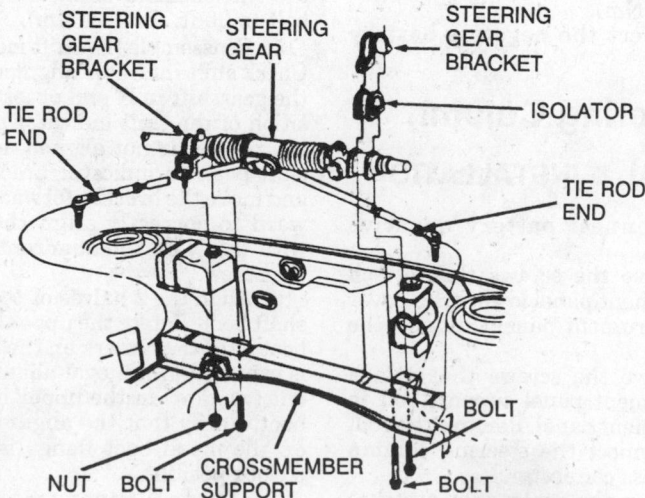

Rack and pinion steering gear and related parts

BRAKES

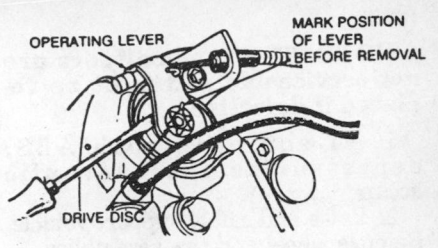

CAUTION

The ABS pump/motor assembly will keep the hydraulic accumulator charged to a pressure of 1600–200 psi (11,000–14,000 kPa) any time the ignition switch is in the ON position. The pump cannot run if the ignition switch is in the OFF position or if the negative battery cable is disconnected.

If equipped with ABS, depressurize the hydraulic accumulator before disassembling or disconnecting any part of the hydraulic system. Failure to do so could result in serious personal injury.

If the engine is hot, do not attempt brake system work inside the engine compartment. If brake fluid comes in contact with a hot engine, combustion is possible.

Master Cylinder

REMOVAL & INSTALLATION

Except ABS

1. Disconnect the negative battery cable.
2. Disconnect the fluid sensor electrical connector, if equipped.
3. Disconnect the brake lines from the master cylinder and plug the brake line openings. Cover the master cylinder outlet ports and brake lines to prevent the entry of dirt.
4. If equipped with manual brake, disconnect the master cylinder pushrod at the brake pedal.
5. Remove the master cylinder retaining bolts or nuts.
6. Remove the proportioning valve bracket, if required.
7. Remove the master cylinder from the vehicle.

To install:

8. Bench bleed the master cylinder and install onto the mounting studs. Install the nuts and tighten to 13 ft. lbs. (18 Nm).
9. Install the lines to the master cylinder loosely. While a helper slowly pushes the brake pedal to the floor, tighten both lines at the master cylinder. Make sure the pedal does not move up prior to tightening the lines at the cylinder.
10. If equipped with manual brake, connect the master cylinder pushrod at the brake pedal.
11. Connect the fluid sensor electrical connector, if equipped.
12. Connect the negative battery cable, fill the master cylinder with clean

brake fluid and bleed the brake system as required.

Proportioning Valve

REMOVAL & INSTALLATION

1. Disconnect the negative battery cable.
2. Disconnect and plug the brake lines from the proportioning valve.
3. Remove the bolt and nut attaching the valve to the bracket.
4. Remove the valve from the vehicle.
5. Installation is the reverse of removal.
6. Bleed the brakes after installation.

Power Brake Booster

REMOVAL & INSTALLATION

1. Disconnect the negative battery cable.
2. Disconnect the vacuum line from the booster.
3. Remove the clip retaining the throttle cables to the bracket on the booster. Remove the master cylinder.
4. Inside the vehicle, disconnect the connector from the brake light switch. Remove the pushrod from the brake pedal.
5. Remove the booster retaining nuts and remove the booster. Inspect the seal for damage.

To install:

6. Transfer parts to the replacement booster. Install the booster to the firewall and connect the pushrod to the brake pedal. Connect the brake light switch.
7. Install the master cylinder and clip the throttle cables in place.
8. Connect the negative battery cable and bleed the brake system.

Brake Caliper

REMOVAL & INSTALLATION

Front

1. If equipped with ABS, depressurize the hydraulic accumulator.
2. Raise and safely support vehicle. Remove wheel and tire assemblies.
3. Disconnect the brake hose from the caliper.
4. Remove caliper slide pins and lift caliper up and out of the bracket.
5. The installation is the reverse of removal. Replace the copper washers that seal the brake hoses is necessary.
6. Bleed the brakes after installation. Pump brake pedal to seat the brakes before moving the vehicle.

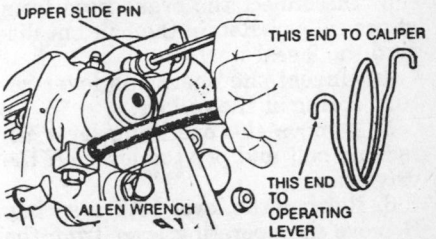

Rear disc brake caliper assembly— Monaco and Premier

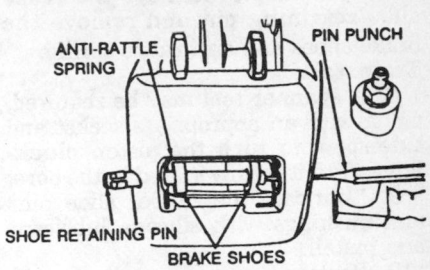

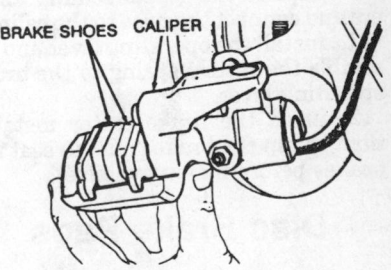

Rear caliper retaining pins—Monaco and Premier

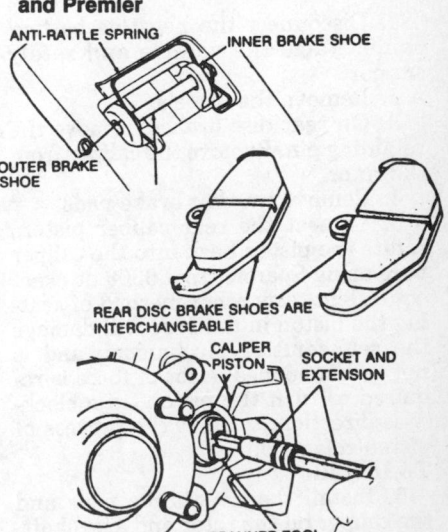

Rear brake pads with cranking piston back into the bore

Rear

NOTE: The rear calipers are not serviceable and must be replaced if defective.

1. If equipped with ABS, depressurize the hydraulic accumulator.
2. Raise and safely support vehicle. Remove wheel and tire assemblies.
3. Disconnect the brake hose from at the caliper. Retain the bolt but discard the 2 seal washers.
4. Unseat the operating lever return spring at the caliper.
5. Remove the operating lever attaching bolt and pry the lever off the drive disc.
6. Remove the lever return spring. Remove the operating lever from the parking brake cable.
7. Remove caliper slide pins and remove the caliper. Remove the brake shoe retaining pin and remove the brake shoes and anti-rattle spring.

To install:

8. A spanner tool may be required, along with an appropriate socket and extension, to turn the piston **clockwise** until it is fully seated in the bore.
9. Lubricate the caliper slide pins and bushings with silicone lubricant and install.
10. Replace the copper sealing washers and connect the hose to the caliper.
11. Install the operating lever and assemble the return spring to the brake operating lever.
12. Bleed the brakes after installation. Pump the brake pedal to seat the brakes before moving vehicle.

Disc Brake Pads

REMOVAL & INSTALLATION

1. Disconnect the negative battery cable. Raise the vehicle and safely support.
2. Remove the wheels.
3. On rear disc brakes, remove the retaining pin. Remove the caliper from the rotor.
4. Remove the disc brake pads.
5. To seat the rear caliper piston, rotate the piston back into the caliper bore using Spanner tool 6366 or exact equivalent. Any other method of seating the piston in the bore will damage the self adjuster mechanism, and is not recommended. A lot of force is required to turn the piston, in a clockwise direction, to start the process of piston retraction.

To install:

6. Install the new brake pads and the caliper on the rotor and axle shaft. Secure using the caliper slide pins, making sure the pins go through the ends of each anti-rattle clip. Tighten

the small diameter pin to 21 ft. lbs. (28 Nm) and torque the larger diameter pin to 36 ft. lbs. (48 Nm) torque.

7. Install the parking brake cable in the caliper flange and position the return spring onto the caliper with the round end on the operating lever and the square end on the caliper.
8. Install the operating lever on the parking brake cable. Pull the parking brake cable rearward and install the operating lever on the caliper drive disc.
9. Connect the return spring to the operating lever first, and then to the caliper.
10. Install the tire and wheel assembly. Lower the vehicle and pump the brakes to seat the pads against the rotors.

Brake Rotor

REMOVAL & INSTALLATION

1. If equipped with ABS, depressurize the hydraulic accumulator.
2. Raise and safely support vehicle. Remove wheel and tire assemblies.
3. Remove caliper and brake pads. Do not allow the brake hose to take the weight of the caliper.

4. Remove the bolts attaching the caliper bracket to the steering knuckle.
5. Remove the rotor retaining nuts and pull the rotor from the hub.

To install:

6. Installation is the reverse of removal. Torque the caliper bracket bolts to 70 ft. lbs. (95 Nm).
7. Pump brake pedal to seat caliper pistons and brakes before moving the vehicle.
8. Check the brake fluid level.

Brake Drums

REMOVAL & INSTALLATION

1. Raise and safely support vehicle.
2. Remove wheel and tire assemblies.
3. Remove drum retaining nuts and pull the drum from the hub.
4. If the drum is difficult to remove, the brake shoes are probably holding the drum in place and must be backed off. Remove the access plug from the backing plate. Unseat the adjuster lever with a small pointed tool and back off the adjuster screw with a brake tool.
5. Installation is the reverse of re-

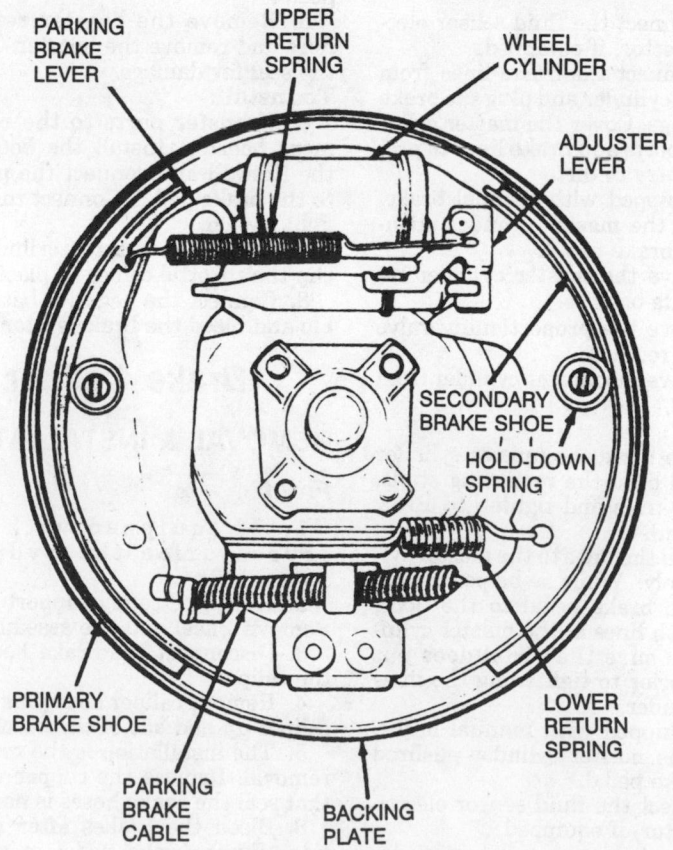

Drum brake components

moval. Adjust the brake shoes as necessary.

Brake Shoes

REMOVAL & INSTALLATION

1. Raise and safely support vehicle.
2. Remove wheel and tire assemblies.
3. Remove the brake drum and hub as an assembly. Do this by removing the hub cap but not the drum retaining nuts. Remove the large center hub nut and pull off the hub/drum.
4. If the drum is difficult to remove, the brake shoes are probably holding the drum in place and must be backed off. Remove the backing plate plug. Unseat the adjuster lever with a small pointed tool and back off the adjuster screw with a brake tool.
5. Remove the upper return spring with brake pliers. Install a wheel cylinder clamp to hold the piston in place. Remove the lower return spring.
6. Remove the parking brake adjuster cross lever (strut). Disengage the parking brake cable by moving the end of the cable away from the lever with expanding type snapring pliers and disengage the cable from the lever.
7. Remove the adjuster screw. Remove the secondary hold-down springs and the secondary brake shoe. Remove the horseshoe clip and remove the parking brake lever from the brake shoe.
8. Remove the primary brake shoe hold-down spring and remove the shoe.

To install:

9. Clean and lubricate the shoe contact surfaces on the backing plate, the parking brake lever pivot and the adjuster screw threads with moly grease.
10. Insert the parking brake lever pivot in the secondary shoe. Install the clip and crimp in place. Attach the parking brake lever to the lever.
11. Position the secondary shoe and lever on the backing plate and install the hold-down spring and pin.
12. Install the primary shoe and hold-down spring and pin.
13. When installing the adjuster screw, be sure the adjuster position is correct. The large notch in the adjuster screw goes to the brake shoe. The small notch goes to the adjuster lever. The long end goes to the secondary shoe.
14. Install the adjuster lever on the primary shoe pin and seat the lever in the adjuster screw. Make sure the adjuster lever is seated in the small notch of the adjuster screw.
15. Install the return springs. Sand the brakes clean.
16. Adjust the brake shoes and install the drum.

Wheel Cylinder

REMOVAL & INSTALLATION

1. Disconnect the negative battery cable. Raise and safely support vehicle.
2. Remove wheel and tire assemblies.
3. Remove drum retaining nuts and pull the drum from the hub.
4. Remove the brake shoe upper return spring and spread the shoes slightly to make room for cylinder removal.
5. Disconnect the brake line at the cylinder, remove the cylinder attaching bolts and remove the cylinder from the backing plate.
6. Installation is the reverse of removal. Torque the retaining bolts to 11 ft. lbs. (15 Nm).
7. Bleed the brake system. Adjust the brake shoes and parking brakes.

Parking Brake Cable

ADJUSTMENT

1. Adjust the rear brakes if necessary.
2. Apply and release the parking brake 5 times to center the shoes in the drums. Set the pedal on the first notch from the released position.
3. Raise and support the vehicle safely.
4. Tighten the cable at the equalizer so the wheels can just barely be turned forward, then loosen 1 turn. Be sure to hold the end of the cable screw to prevent the cable from turning.
5. Release the parking brake and check for rear brake drag. The wheels should rotate freely with the parking brake not applied.

REMOVAL & INSTALLATION

Front

1. Disconnect the negative battery cable.
2. Raise the vehicle and support safely.
3. Remove the jam nut and adjusting nut from the front cable. Lower the vehicle.
4. Remove the left side sill trim, driver's seat and lower dash trim cover.
5. Remove the rear seat cushion. Roll the carpeting aside for access to the cable.
6. Pull the cable through the holes in the floor pan and remove the cable from the actuating pedal.
7. The installation is the reverse of the removal procedure. Make sure the cable is routed properly before installing interior parts.
8. Adjust the rear brakes and cable.

Rear

1. Raise and safely support the vehicle.
2. Loosen the cable adjusting nut at the equalizer.
3. Remove the cotter pin for the cable to be replaced from the equalizer. Then remove the retaining clip attaching the cable to the frame.
4. If only replacing the right side, remove the bolts attaching the cable to the rear axle housing. Disconnect the cable at the frame bracket.
5. If equipped with rear drums, remove the rear wheels and brake drum. Remove the shoes. Compress the locking tabs at the backing plate with a hose clamp or box wrench and remove the cable.
6. If equipped with rear disc brakes, disconnect the cable from the actuating arm and remove from the bracket.
7. Installation is the reverse of the removal process. Use a new cotter pin for the connection to the equalizer. Adjust the rear brakes and cable.

Brake System Bleeding

Except Anti-Lock Brakes

NOTE: If using a pressure bleeder, follow the instructions furnished with the unit and choose the correct adaptor for the application. Do not substitute an adapter that "almost fits" as it will not work and could be dangerous.

MASTER CYLINDER

If the master cylinder is off the vehicle, it can be bench bled.

1. Connect 2 short pieces of brake line to the outlet fittings, bend them until the free end is below the fluid level in the master cylinder reservoirs.
2. Fill the reservoir with fresh brake fluid. Pump the piston slowly until no more air bubbles appear in the reservoirs.
3. Disconnect the 2 short lines, refill the master cylinder and securely install the cylinder caps.
4. If the master cylinder is on the vehicle, it can still be bled, using a flare nut wrench.
5. Open the brake lines slightly with the flare nut wrench while pressure is applied to the brake pedal by a helper inside the vehicle.
6. Be sure to tighten the line before the brake pedal is released.
7. Repeat the process with both lines until no air bubbles come out.

CALIPERS AND WHEEL CYLINDERS

1. Fill the master cylinder with

fresh brake fluid. Check the level often during the procedure.

2. Starting with the right rear wheel, remove the protective cap from the bleeder, if equipped, and place where it will not be lost. Clean the bleed screw.

CAUTION

When bleeding the brakes, keep face away from the brake area. Spewing fluid may cause facial and/or visual damage. Do not allow brake fluid to spill on the car's finish; it will remove the paint.

3. If the system is empty, the most efficient way to get fluid down to the wheel is to loosen the bleeder about ½–¾ turn, place a finger firmly over the bleeder and have a helper pump the brakes slowly until fluid comes out the bleeder. Once fluid is at the bleeder, close it before the pedal is released inside the vehicle.

NOTE: If the pedal is pumped rapidly, the fluid will churn and create small air bubbles, which are almost impossible to remove from the system. These air bubbles will eventually congregate and a spongy pedal will result.

4. Once fluid has been pumped to the caliper or wheel cylinder, open the bleed screw again, have the helper press the brake pedal to the floor, lock the bleeder and have the helper slowly release the pedal. Wait 15 seconds and repeat the procedure (including the 15 second wait) until no more air comes out of the bleeder upon application of the brake pedal. Remember to close the bleeder before the pedal is released inside the vehicle each time the bleeder is opened. If not, air will be induced into the system.

5. If a helper is not available, connect a small hose to the bleeder, place the end in a container of brake fluid and proceed to pump the pedal from inside the vehicle until no more air comes out the bleeder. The hose will prevent air from entering the system.

6. Repeat the procedure on remaining wheel cylinder and calipers in order:
   a. Left rear
   b. Right front
   c. Left front

7. Hydraulic brake systems must be totally flushed if the fluid becomes contaminated with water, dirt or other corrosive chemicals. To flush, bleed the entire system until all fluid has been replaced with the correct type of new fluid.

8. Install the bleeder cap(s) on the bleeder to keep dirt out. Always road test the vehicle after brake work of any kind is done.

Anti-Lock Brakes
PRESSURE BLEEDING

The brake lines may be pressure bled, using a standard diaphragm type pressure bleeder. Only diaphragm type pressure bleeding equipment should be used to bleed the system.

1. The ignition should be turned **OFF** and remain **OFF** throughout this procedure.

2. Depressurize the hydraulic accumulator.

CAUTION

Failure to depressurize the hydraulic accumulator prior to performing this operation, may result in personal injury and/or damage to the painted surfaces.

3. Remove the reservoir caps.
4. Install the pressure bleeder adapter.
5. Attach the bleeding equipment to the bleeder adapter. Charge the pressure bleeder to approximately 20 psi (138 kPa).
6. Connect a transparent hose to the caliper bleed screw. Submerge the free end of the hose in a clear glass container, which is partially filled with clean, fresh brake fluid.
7. With the pressure turned **ON**, open the caliper bleed screw ½–¾ turn and allow fluid to flow into the container. Leave the bleed screw open until clear, bubble-free fluid slows from the hose. If the reservoir has been drained or the hydraulic assembly removed from the vehicle prior to the bleeding operation, slowly pump the brake pedal 1–2 times while the bleed screw is open and fluid is flowing. This will help purge air from the hydraulic assembly. Tighten the bleeder screw to 7.5 ft. lbs. (10 Nm).
8. Repeat Step 7 at all calipers. Calipers should be bled in the following order:
   a. Left rear
   b. Right rear
   c. Left front
   d. Right front
9. After bleeding all 4 calipers, remove the pressure bleeding equipment and bleeder adapter by closing the pressure bleeder valve and slowly unscrewing the bleeder adapter from the hydraulic assembly reservoir. Failure to release pressure in the reservoir will cause spillage of brake fluid and could result in injury or damage to painted surfaces.
10. Using a syringe or equivalent method, remove excess fluid from the reservoir to bring the fluid level to full level.
11. Install the reservoir caps and connect the fluid level sensor connector. Turn the ignition **ON** and allow the pump to charge the accumulator.

MANUAL BLEEDING

1. Depressurize the hydraulic accumulator.

CAUTION

Failure to depressurize the hydraulic accumulator, prior to performing this operation may result in personal injury and/or damage to the painted surfaces.

2. Connect a transparent hose to the caliper bleed screw. Submerge the free end of the hose in a clear glass container, which is partially filled with clean, fresh brake fluid.
3. Slowly pump the brake pedal several times, using full strokes of the pedal and allowing approximately 5 seconds between pedal strokes. After 2 or 3 strokes, continue to hold pressure on the pedal, keeping it at the bottom of its travel.
4. With pressure on the pedal, open the bleed screw ½–¾ turn. Leave bleed screw open until fluid no longer flows from the hose. Tighten the bleed screw and release the pedal.
5. Repeat this procedure until clear, bubble-free fluid flows from the hose.
6. Repeat all steps at each of the calipers. Calipers should be bled in the following order:
   a. Left rear
   b. Right rear
   c. Left front
   d. Right front

Anti-Lock Brake System Service

PRECAUTIONS

Failure to observe the following precautions may result in system damage.

• Before performing electric arc welding on the vehicle, disconnect the ABS controller and the hydraulic modulator connectors.

• When performing painting work on the vehicle, do not expose the ABS controller to temperatures in excess of 185°F (85°C) for longer than 2 hrs. The system may be exposed to temperatures up to 200°F (95°C) for less than 15 min.

• Never disconnect or connect the ABS controller or hydraulic modulator connectors with the ignition switch ON.

• Never disassemble any component of the Anti-Lock Brake System (ABS) which is designated non-serviceable; the component must be replaced as an assembly.

• When filling the master cylinder, always use brake fluid which meets DOT-3 specifications; petroleum base fluid will destroy the rubber parts.

DEPRESSURIZING THE HYDRAULIC ACCUMULATOR

1. With the ignition **OFF**, pump the brake pedal a minimum of 40 times, using approximately 50 lbs. (222 N) pedal force. A noticeable change in pedal feel will occur when the accumulator is discharged.

2. When a definite increase in pedal effort is felt, stroke the pedal a few additional times. Disconnect the negative battery cable.

Pump/Motor Assembly

REMOVAL & INSTALLATION

1. Disconnect the negative battery cable. Depressurize the hydraulic accumulator.

— **CAUTION** —

Failure to depressurize the hydraulic accumulator, prior to performing this operation may result in personal injury and/or damage to the painted surfaces.

2. Disconnect all electrical connectors to the pump motor.
3. Disconnect and plug the high and low pressure hoses from the hydraulic assembly.
4. Remove the connector body from the engine mount.
5. Remove the heat shield.
6. Remove the retainer bolts that are used to mount the pump/motor.
7. Lift the pump/motor assembly off of the studs and out of the vehicle.
To install:
8. Position the assembly and install the retaining bolts.
9. Install the heat shield.

10. Install the connector body to the engine mount.
11. Connect the high and low pressure hoses to the hydraulic assembly.
12. Connect all electrical connectors to the pump motor.
13. Connect the negative battery cable and check the brakes for proper operation.

Hydraulic Assembly

REMOVAL & INSTALLATION

1. Disconnect the negative battery cable. Depressurize the hydraulic accumulator.

— **CAUTION** —

Failure to depressurize the hydraulic accumulator, prior to performing this operation may result in personal injury and/or damage to the painted surfaces.

2. Remove the fresh air intake ducts.
3. Disconnect all electrical connectors from the hydraulic unit and pump/motor.
4. Remove as much of the fluid as possible from the reservoir on the hydraulic assembly.
5. Remove the pressure hose fitting from the hydraulic assembly.
6. Disconnect the return hose from the filter nipple. Cap the spigot on the reservoir.
7. Disconnect all brake tubes from the hydraulic assembly.
8. Remove the driver's side lower panel.
9. Disconnect the pushrod from the brake pedal.
10. Remove the 4 under-dash hydraulic assembly mounting nuts.
11. Remove the hydraulic assembly.
To install:
12. Have a helper position the hy-

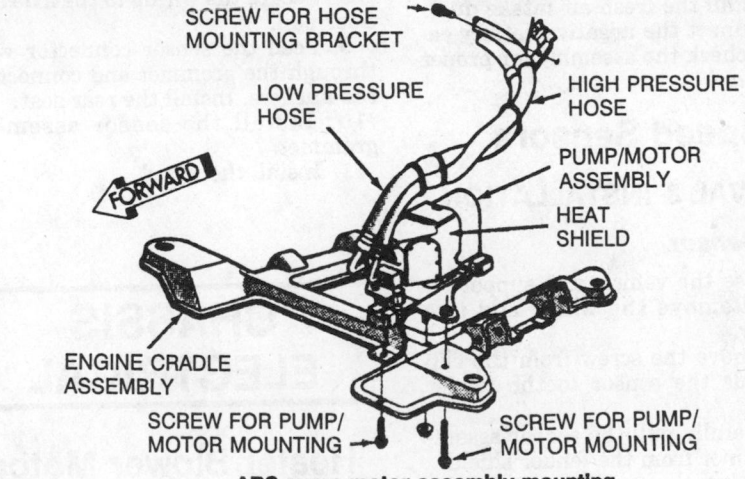

ABS pump motor assembly mounting

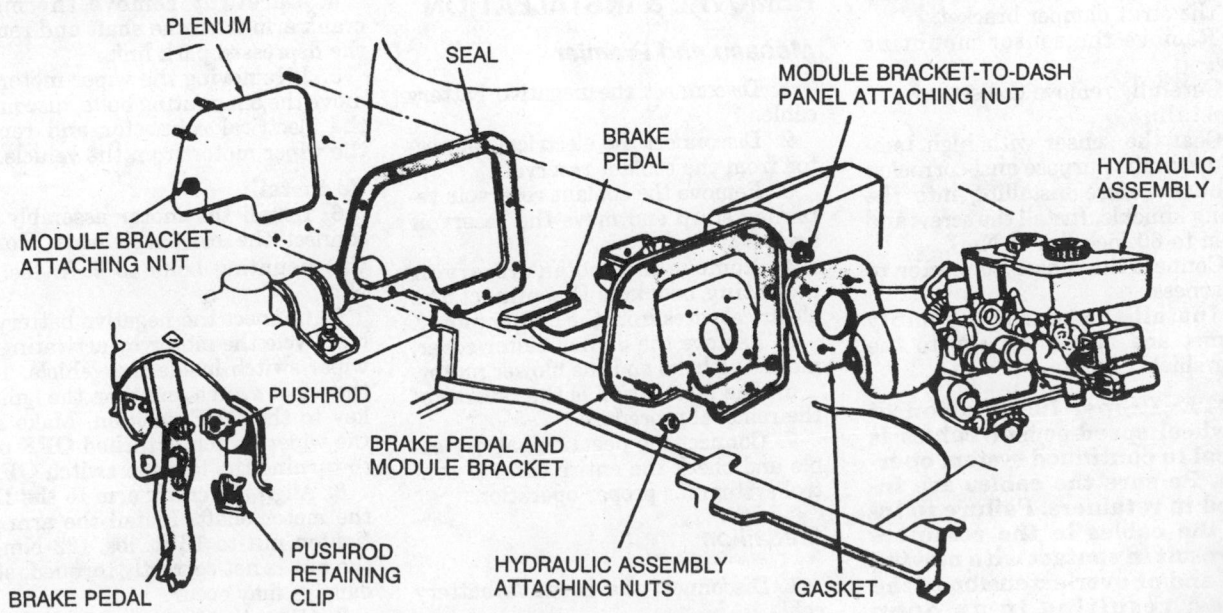

ABS hydraulic assembly mounting

draulic assembly on the vehicle and hold in place.

13. Install and torque the mounting nuts to 21 ft. lbs. (28 Nm).

14. Using Lubriplate® or equivalent, coat the bearing surface of the pedal pin.

15. Connect the pushrod to the pedal and install a new retainer clip.

16. Install the high pressure hose to the hydrailic assembly and tighten the hose to the hydraulic assembly fitting to 12 ft. lbs. (16 Nm).

17. Install the return hose to the nipple on the filter.

18. Connect the hydraulic brake lines. If the proportioning valves were removed from the hydraulic assembly, install and tighten to 30 ft. lbs. (40 Nm).

19. Fill the reservoir to the top of the screen.

20. Connect all electrical connectors to the hydraulic assembly.

21. Bleed the entire brake system.

22. Install the fresh air intake duct.

23. Connect the negative battery cable and check the assembly for proper operation.

Speed Sensors

REMOVAL & INSTALLATION

Front Sensor

1. Raise the vehicle and support it safely. Remove the wheel and tire assembly.

2. Remove the screw from the clip that holds the sensor to the fender shield.

3. Carefully pull the sensor assembly grommet from the fender shield.

4. Unplug the connector from the harness. Remove the retainer clip from the strut damper bracket.

5. Remove the sensor mounting screw.

6. Carefully remove the sensor.

To install:

7. Coat the sensor with high temperature multi-purpose anti-corrosion compound before installing into the steering knuckle. Install the screw and tighten to 60 inch lbs. (7 Nm).

8. Connect the sensor connector to the harness.

9. Install the sensor assembly grommet and attach the clip to the fender shield.

NOTE: Proper installation of the wheel speed sensor cables is critical to continued system operation. Be sure the cables are installed in retainers. Failure to install the cables in the retainers may result in contact with moving parts and/or over-extension of the cables, resulting in an open circuit.

10. Install the wheel and tire assembly.

Rear Sensor

1. Raise the vehicle and support it safely. Remove the wheel and tire assembly.

2. Remove the rear seat and disconnect the sensor connector.

3. Carefully pull the sensor assembly grommet from the underbody and pull the harness through the hole.

4. Remove the screws that retain the wiring to the rear axle and floorpan.

5. Remove the bolt that retains the sensor to the rear bearing retainer.

6. Carefully remove the sensor.

To install:

7. Coat the sensor with high temperature multi-purpose anti-corrosion compound before installing into the bearing retainer. Install the screw and tighten to 60 inch lbs. (7 Nm).

8. Secure the wiring to the axle and floor pan.

9. Feed the sensor connector wire through the grommet and connect to the harness. Install the rear seat.

10. Install the sensor assembly grommet.

11. Install the wheel.

CHASSIS ELECTRICAL

Heater Blower Motor

REMOVAL & INSTALLATION

Monaco and Premier

1. Disconnect the negative battery cable.

2. Disconnect the electrical connector from the coolant reservoir.

3. Remove the coolant reservoir retaining strap and move the reservoir aside.

4. Remove the coolant reservoir mounting bracket. Disconnect the electrical wires from the blower motor.

5. Remove the blower motor cover, mounting bolts and the blower motor.

6. The installation is the reverse of the removal procedure.

7. Connect the negative battery cable and check the entire climate control system for proper operation.

Medallion

1. Disconnect the negative battery cable.

2. Remove the glove box door straps

and the glove box door. Remove the inner glove box.

3. Unclip the ventilator outlet from the right side of the blower housing. Disconnect the electrical connector from the blower motor.

4. Remove the blower housing retaining screws and the housing.

5. Remove the fan assembly from the blower housing.

To install:

6. Install the fan assembly into the blower housing and install the retaining screws. Connect the electrical connector and the ventilator outlet.

7. Install the inner glove box and the glove box door.

8. Connect the negative battery cable and check the entire climate control system for proper operation.

Windshield Wiper Motor

REMOVAL & INSTALLATION

Premier and Monaco

1. Disconnect the negative battery cable.

2. Remove the wiper arms. Remove the screws retaining the left and right cowl screens and remove both screens.

3. Disconnect the ball end of the link. Move the link to the right to expose the nut. While holding the motor crank arm, remove the center shaft locknut and spacer from the wiper motor.

NOTE: Do not hit the shaft or crank arm as damage can occur to the internal mechanism of the motor shaft.

4. Carefully remove the motor crank arm from the shaft and remove the depressed park link.

5. If removing the wiper motor, remove the 3 mounting bolts, disconnect the electrical connector and remove the wiper motor from the vehicle.

To install:

6. Install the motor assembly and connect the electrical leads. Torque the mounting bolts to 7 ft. lbs. (10 Nm).

7. Connect the negative battery cable. Cycle the motor by activating the wiper switch inside the vehicle. Turn the wiper switch and then the ignition key to the OFF position. Make sure the wiper switch is turned OFF prior to turning the ignition switch OFF.

8. Align the crank arm to the D on the motor shaft. Install the arm and tighten nut to 16 ft. lbs. (22 Nm). If the nut is not correctly torqued, shaft damage may occur.

9. Cover the cap end of the link with shop rag to prevent damage and snap

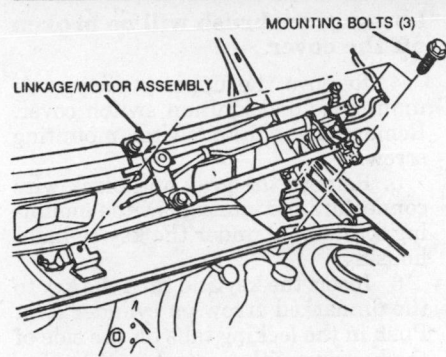

MOUNTING BOLTS (3)

LINKAGE/MOTOR ASSEMBLY

Wiper transmission and motor assembly—Monaco and Premier

the cap of the link over the ball. Place the other end of the depression park link over the ball.

10. Install the cowl screens by tucking under the weatherstrip and secure with fasteners. Inspect weatherstrip to ensure full engagement to the upper lip of the dash panel.

11. Connect the washer hoses to the appropriate wiper arm and install the arms onto the vehicle.

12. Connect the negative battery cable if not already done, and check the wipers for proper operation.

Medallion

1. Disconnect the negative battery cable. Remove the wiper arms.

2. Remove the screws retaining the cowl in front of the windshield and remove the cowl.

3. Disconnect the electrical plug at the wiper motor.

4. Remove the screws retaining the wiper motor and wiper transmission and remove the assembly.

To install:

5. Install the wiper and transmission assembly. Connect the electrical plug to the wiper motor.

6. Install the cowl and the wiper arms.

7. Connect the negative battery cable and check the wipers for proper operation.

Instrument Cluster

REMOVAL & INSTALLATION

Premier and Monaco

1. Disconnect the negative battery cable.

2. On 1989 models, remove the instrument panel lower cover. Remove the shift indicator cable anchor and remove the wire from the rear of the shift lever pulley.

3. Remove the screws retaining the instrument cluster bezel and remove the bezel.

4. Remove the cluster retaining screws and tilt the cluster forward. Place the gear shift lever and the steering wheel, if equipped with tilt wheel, in the extreme downward position. Disconnect the electrical connectors and the speedometer cable and remove the cluster from the instrument panel.

5. Installation is the reverse of the removal procedure. Connect the negative battery cable and check operation of all gauges, speedometer and dash mounted warning lights.

Medallion

1. Disconnect the negative battery cable.

2. Remove the instrument glare shield retaining screws. Press the holding tabs in and remove the glare shield.

3. Open the fuse panel access door, reach through the fuse panel door and remove the speedometer cable from the rear of the instrument cluster.

4. Remove the instrument cluster mounting screws and pull the cluster forward. Disconnect the electrical wiring and remove the cluster from the vehicle.

5. Install the cluster and connect the electrical wiring. Install the glare shield. Connect the speedometer cable and connect the negative battery cable.

Speedometer and Tachometer

REMOVAL & INSTALLATION

1. Disconnect the negative battery cable.

2. Remove the instrument cluster.

NOTE: Wear clean gloves when handling the cluster dial and gauge assembly. Finger prints and nails will mar the surface.

3. Remove the clear lens and black mask. Remove the mounting screws and remove the dial and gauge assembly from the cluster housing.

4. Grasp the pointer hub and slowly rotate the pointer assembly back and forth until the pointer contacts the trip reset shaft, while gently pulling upward of the hub away from the dial surface. Repeat this procedure as many times as it takes to remove the pointer from the shaft.

5. Remove the retaining screws and remove the speedometer from the faceplate.

To install:

6. Position the speedometer and secure with the screws.

7. Grasp the pointer by hand and

gently place the bushing onto the movement shaft. The pointer tip should be indicating approximately 90 mph.

8. Rotate the pointer assembly counterclockwise while gently pushing down on the hub toward the dial surface—a slight resistance should be felt. Clearance between the underside of the hub and the dial surface should be 0.020–0.060 in. (0.5–1.5mm) before the pointer tip is aligned with the zero horizontal graduation.

9. If the pointer is not properly aligned to the horizontal graduation, perform either of the following:

a. Pointer too **high**—continue rotating the assembly counterclockwise until alignment is achieved.

b. Pointer too **low**—Rotate the pointer clockwise until rotational resistance is felt—this does not refer to contact with the trip reset shaft. Continue rotating in the direction of resistance to compensate for initial misalignment. Release the hub, allowing the pointer to rotate back to its rest position.

c. If alignment is not achieved, repeat the above as required.

10. Place the gauge faceplate and secure with the nuts. Install the retaining screws.

11. Position the black mask and clear lens and secure with screws.

12. Install the instrument cluster.

13. Connect the negative battery cable and check gauge for proper operation.

Radio

REMOVAL & INSTALLATION

1. Disconnect the battery negative cable.

2. Remove the instrument cluster bezel by removing the screws.

3. Remove the radio mounting screws.

4. Disconnect the electrical connector, the ground wire and unplug the antenna. Remove the radio.

5. The installation is the reverse of the removal procedure.

6. Connect the negative battery cable and check all radio functions for proper operation.

Combination Switch

REMOVAL & INSTALLATION

Premier and Monaco

The windshield wiper, turn signal, headlight and dimmer switches are all combined in the combination switch on the left side of the steering column.

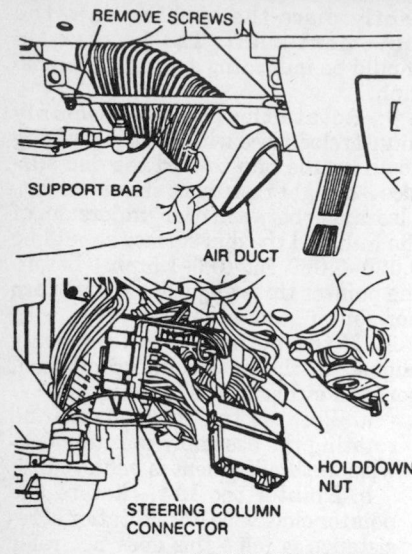

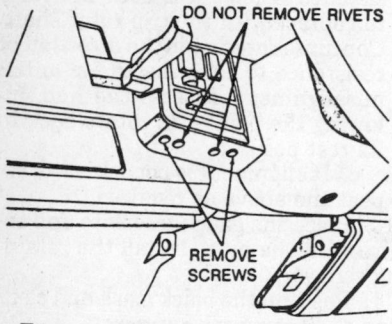

To remove the combination switch, remove the duct, electrical connection and pod screws

1. Disconnect the negative battery cable.
2. Remove the lower instrument panel cover.
3. Remove the screws and the lower support rod. Pull the air duct aside.
4. Cut the harness plastic tie-wrap straps.
5. Loosen the hold-down nut in the center of the steering column electrical connector and separate the connector.
6. Separate the left side pod switch connector from the steering column connector by placing a flat blade tool between the connectors to disengage the locking tab. Push on the wire side of the left side pod switch connector and slide the connector out of the channels of the steering column connector.
7. Disconnect the electrical connector, then remove the bottom 2 screws (not the rivets) from the pod assembly.
8. To gain access to the inside of the pod, remove the screws from the back of the left side switch pod assembly and remove the switch pod housing back cover.

NOTE: There are small retaining clips on the left side pod that

may fall off when the switch is removed.

9. Carefully pull the switch pod far enough from the housing to expose the 2 screws, remove them and gently pull the switch forward and pull the harness out through the housing to remove the switch.
To install:
10. Route the switch assembly connector through the housing and along the underside of the steering column.
11. Connect the switch connector.
12. Connect the steering column connector and install the hold-down nut. Secure with a new tie.
13. Position the switch and secure with the screws.
14. Connect the air duct.
15. Install the lower support bar and the lower instrument cover.
16. Connect the negative battery cable and check all functions of the combination switch for proper operation.

Medallion

1. Disconnect the negative battery cable.
2. Remove the screws from the lower steering column cover and remove the cover.
3. If equipped with cruise control, pull down on the piece of wire at the forward edge of the cover. This will pull the spring loaded cruise control commutator into its housing.
4. Remove the upper and lower steering column covers.
5. Remove the 2 retaining screws and remove the switch.
6. Disconnect the wire connectors.
To install:
7. Install the switch to the column and install the retaining screws.
8. Connect the wire harness connector.
9. Install the steering column covers.
10. Connect the negative battery cable and check all functions of the combination switch for proper operation.

Ignition Lock/Switch

REMOVAL & INSTALLATION

Medallion

1. Disconnect battery negative cable.
2. Remove 4 screws from lower steering column cover.
3. On cruise control equipped vehicles, pull down on the wire at the forward edge of the lower cover. This allow the spring loaded commutator brush to be pull into its housing.

NOTE: If the lower steering cover is removed before the commutator brush is pulled into its

housing, the brush will be broken off the cover.

4. Remove the upper steering column cover and ignition switch cover. Remove the ignition switch mounting screw.
5. Remove the gray and black wire connectors and ignition switch mounting screw from under the key cylinder housing.
6. Insert the key and turn the key to the unmarked arrow on cylinder lock. Push in the locking tabs on the side of the housing with a punch and remove the switch.
7. Separate the switch from the wires by removing the screw retaining the connector. Feed the wiring harness through the lock cylinder hole.
8. Separate the tumbler by removing the 2 attaching screws.
To install:
9. Assemble the tumbler and connect the wiring to the switch.
10. Guide the wire harness through the lock cylinder hole and slide the switch into the hole. Press both locking tabs inward and slide the switch into place until it locks.
11. Install the ignition switch mounting screw at the bottom of cylinder housing and reconnect electrical connectors.
12. Install the ignition switch cover and steering column covers.
13. Connect the negative battery cable and check all functions of the ignition switch for proper operation.

Ignition Lock

REMOVAL & INSTALLATION

Premier and Monaco

1. Disconnect the negative battery cable. Detach the horn contact cover from the steering wheel and disconnect the horn connector wire.
2. Note the position of the alignment reference mark on the end of the steering shaft hub and remove the steering shaft hub nut.
3. Disconnect the speed control wire connector, if equipped, and remove the steering wheel from the steering column.
4. Remove the turn signal cancelling cam, unlock the tabs, and slide the canceller off the steering shaft.
5. If equipped with a tilt wheel, remove the tilt control lever.
6. Remove the screws retaining the right and left switch pods. Remove the ignition switch trim ring.
7. Remove the screws from the pod housing/column cover. Remove the pod housing/column cover by pulling it up, then guide the pods through the cover and remove the cover.

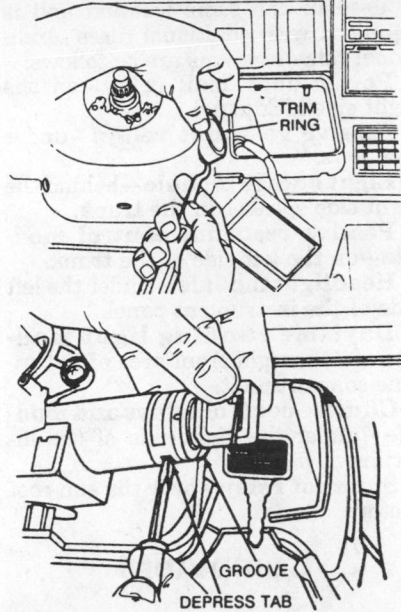

Ignition lock repair requires trim ring removal and pushing the lock tab

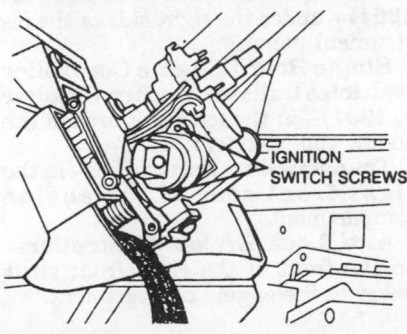

Ignition switch retaining screws—Monaco and Premier

8. Insert the key into the ignition and align the key with groove in the lock cylinder housing. Push in the locking tab on the bottom of the housing with a punch and remove the cylinder. Separate the switch from the wires by removing the screw retaining the connector.

To install:

9. Insert the key into the ignition and align key with groove in lock cylinder housing.

10. Depress the tab and install the lock cylinder.

11. Install the pod housing/column cover and install the pods.

12. Install the ignition switch trim ring.

NOTE: The retaining clips on the left and right switch pods must be in place when the switches are installed.

13. Install the tilt lever, if equipped. Install the turn signal cam with pin

bore in the steering wheel. Reconnect the electrical connector.

14. Install the steering wheel, position the reference mark in the same position prior to removal and align the pin on the turn signal cam with the pin bore on the steering wheel.

15. Connect the negative battery cable and check for proper operation.

Ignition Switch

REMOVAL & INSTALLATION

Premier and Monaco

1. Disconnect battery negative cable.

2. Remove instrument panel lower cover attaching screws and remove cover.

3. Remove the horn pad. Disconnect the wires and remove the horn button.

4. Remove the steering wheel and the turn signal cancel cam.

5. If equipped with tilt wheel, use a small wrench to unscrew the tilt lever.

6. Remove the screws retaining the right and left switch pods. Remove the ignition switch trim ring.

7. Remove the screws from the pod housing/column cover. Remove the pod housing/column cover by pulling it up, guide the pods through the cover and remove the cover.

8. Remove the lower column shroud attaching screws and remove lower shroud.

9. Remove the upper column shroud attaching screws and remove upper shroud.

10. Remove the ignition switch retaining screws and separate the switch from cylinder housing.

11. Cut the tie straps and remove the harness anchor.

12. Loosen the retaining nut in the center of the steering column connector and separate the switch pod connector by disengaging locking tabs.

13. Remove the electrical harness from the channels of steering column connector and remove the ignition switch assembly.

To install:

14. Slide the switch pod connectors into the ignition switch connector and install the nut.

15. Install the ignition switch and secure with its retaining screws.

16. Route the wiring harness along the underside of steering column and secure with new tie straps. Install the harness anchor and secure with its retaining screw.

17. Install the pod housing/column cover and install the pods.

18. Install the ignition switch trim ring.

NOTE: The retaining clips on

the left and right switch pods must be in place when the switches are installed.

19. Install the tilt lever, if equipped. Install the turn signal cam with pin bore in the steering wheel. Reconnect the electrical connector.

20. Install the steering wheel, aligning the pin on the turn signal cam with the pin bore on the steering wheel.

21. Connect the negative battery cable and check all functions of the ignition switch for proper operation.

Stoplight Switch

Two different switches are used. Without cruise control, the switch is attached to the brake pedal by the pushrod bolt. If equipped with cruise control, the switch is attached to a bracket on the brake support. Neither switch requires adjustment.

REMOVAL & INSTALLATION

1. Disconnect the negative battery cable.

2. Remove the bolt retaining the master cylinder pushrod to the brake pedal.

3. Disconnect the electrical wires from the stoplight switch and remove the switch.

To install:

4. Install the switch and the master cylinder pushrod to the brake pedal and install the retaining bolt.

5. Connect the electrical wires to the switch.

6. Connect the negative battery cable and check the operation of the brake lights.

Neutral Safety Switch

REMOVAL & INSTALLATION

Premier and Monaco

1. Disconnect battery negative cable.

2. Disconnect the neutral switch harness connector located in the engine compartment.

3. Raise and support the vehicle safely. Remove the splash shield.

4. Remove the bolt attaching the switch bracket to transaxle case and remove switch from case. Replace the O-ring.

5. The installation is the reverse of the removal procedure.

6. Connect the negative battery cable and check the switch for proper operation.

Medallion

A multi-function switch located on the

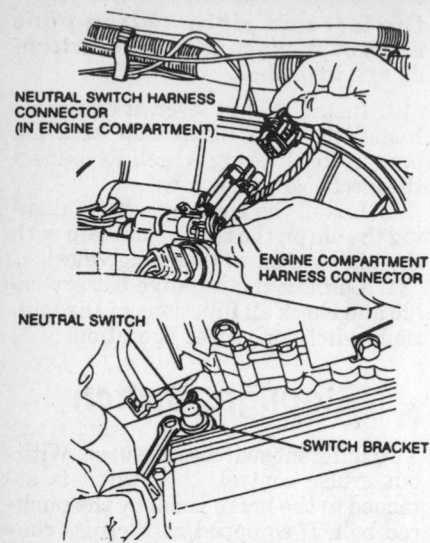

NEUTRAL SWITCH HARNESS
CONNECTOR
(IN ENGINE COMPARTMENT)

ENGINE COMPARTMENT
HARNESS CONNECTOR

NEUTRAL SWITCH

SWITCH BRACKET

Neutral safety switch location

transaxle assembly allows the vehicle to start only in **N** and **P** positions.

1. Disconnect the negative battery cable.

2. Remove the electrical connection from switch.

3. Remove the switch mounting screws and remove the switch.

4. The installation is the reverse of the removal procedure.

5. Connect the negative battery cable and check the switch for proper operation.

Fuses, Circuit Breakers and Relays

LOCATION

Fuses

Power Distribution Center—located on the left side of the engine compartment on vehicles built on or after October 9, 1991.

Main fuse panel—located under the instrument panel, above the parking brake release lever.

Fusible Links

Fusible links are used to prevent major wire harness damage in the event of a short circuit or an overload condition in the wiring circuits which are normally not fused, due to carrying high amperage loads or because of their locations within the wiring harness. The fuse links are located in the wiring harness near the battery. Each fusible link is of a fixed value for a specific electrical load and should a link fail, the cause of the failure must be determined and repaired prior to installing a new fusible link of the same value.

Circuit Breakers

Circuit breakers are an integral part of the headlight switch, the wiper switch and the air conditioning circuit. They are used to protect each circuit from an overload. Other circuit breakers are on the fuse panel.

Relays

Relays are used throughout the system in various locations. When replacing a protective electrical relay, be very sure to install the same type of relay. Verify that the schematic imprinted on the original and replacement relays are identical. Relay part numbers may change. Do not rely on them for identification. Instead, use the schematic imprinted on the relay for positive identification.

On vehicles built before October 9, 1991, a relay bank is located on the left side of the engine compartment. On vehicles built on or after October 9, 1991, the Power Distribution Center is used in the same location and is equipped with additional fuses. Additional relay locations are as follows:

Power door lock relay—on the right side kick panel.

Passive restraint relays—under the seats.

Light outage module—behind the right side speaker in the trunk.

Passive restraint control module—on the left side of the trunk.

Headlight module—under the left side of the instrument panel.

Daytime running light module—in the right front area of the engine compartment.

Climate control relays and module—under the right side of the instrument panel.

Sun roof relay—near the sun roof motor.

Computers

LOCATION

Engine Control Unit (except vehicles built after October 9, 1991)—under the right side of the instrument panel.

Single Board Engine Controller (vehicles built on or after October 9, 1991)—in the left front area of the engine compartment.

Transmission Controller—in the right front area of the engine compartment.

Anti Lock Brakes Controller—on the front of the right front strut tower in the engine compartment.

Flashers

LOCATION

Turn Signal Flasher—behind the left side of the instrument panel.

Hazard Flasher—behind the left side of the instrument panel.

Chrysler Corp.
Front Wheel Drive

"A" Body—Spirit, Acclaim, LeBaron Landau   **"E" Body**—600, Caravelle, New Yorker   **"G" Body**—Daytona   **"H" Body**—Lancer, LeBaron GTS   **"J" Body**—LeBaron   **"K" Body**—Aries, Reliant, LeBaron   **"P" Body**—Shadow, Sundance **TC** by Maserati

SPECIFICATIONS

VEHICLE IDENTIFICATION CHART

It is important for servicing and ordering parts to be certain of the vehicle and engine identification. The VIN (vehicle identification number) is a 17 digit number visible through the windshield on the driver's side of the dash and contains the vehicle and engine identification codes. The tenth digit indicates model year and the eighth digit indicates engine code. It can be interpreted as follows:

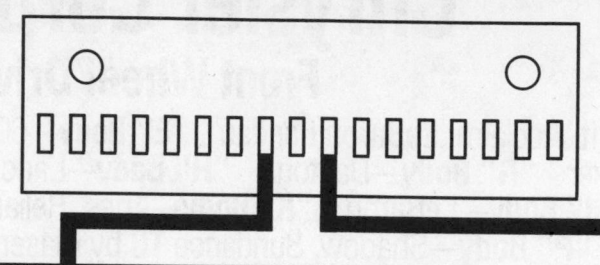

Engine Code							Model Year	
Code	Liters	Cu. In. (cc)	Cyl.	Fuel Sys.	Eng. Mfg.		Code	Year
A (1989)	2.2	135 (2213)	4	Turbo II	Chrysler		K	1989
A (1991–93)	2.2	135 (2213)	4	Turbo III	Chrysler		L	1990
C	2.2	135 (2213)	4	Turbo IV	Chrysler		M	1991
D	2.2	135 (2213)	4	EFI	Chrysler		N	1992
E	2.2	135 (2213)	4	Turbo	Chrysler		P	1993
J	2.5	153 (2507)	4	Turbo I	Chrysler			
K	2.5	153 (2507)	4	EFI	Chrysler			
3	3.0	181 (2966)	6	MPI	Mitsubishi			

EFI—Electronic Fuel Injection
MPI—Multi-Point Fuel Injection

VEHICLE IDENTIFICATION CHART
TC Maserati

It is important for servicing and ordering parts to be certain of the vehicle and engine identification. The VIN (vehicle identification number) is a 17 digit number visible through the windshield on the driver's side of the dash and contains the vehicle and engine identification codes. The tenth digit indicates model year and the fifth digit indicates engine code. It can be interpreted as follows:

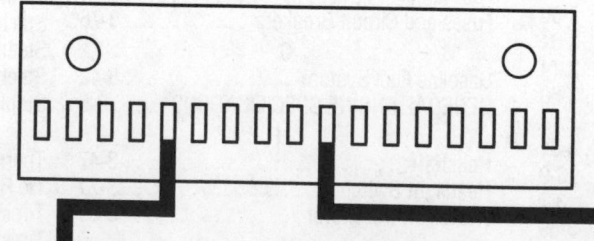

Engine Code							Model Year	
Code	Liters	Cu. In. (cc)	Cyl.	Fuel Sys.	Eng. Mfg.		Code	Year
A	2.2	135 (2213)	4	Turbo	Chrysler		K	1989
R	2.2	135 (2213)	4	Turbo	Chrysler ①		L	1990
S	3.0	181 (2966)	6	EFI	Mitsubishi		M	1991
							N	1992
							P	1993

EFI—Electronic Fuel Injection
① Cylinder Head and Related Parts by Maserati

ENGINE IDENTIFICATION

Year	Model	Engine Displacement Liters (cc)	Engine Series (ID/VIN)	Fuel System	No. of Cylinders	Engine Type
1989	Aries	2.2 (2213)	D	EFI	4	SOHC
	Aries	2.5 (2507)	K	EFI	4	SOHC
	Reliant	2.2 (2213)	D	EFI	4	SOHC
	Reliant	2.5 (2507)	K	EFI	4	SOHC
	Daytona	2.2 (2213)	A	Turbo II	4	SOHC
	Daytona	2.5 (2507)	J	Turbo I	4	SOHC
	Daytona	2.5 (2507)	K	EFI	4	SOHC
	LeBaron	2.2 (2213)	A	Turbo II	4	SOHC
	LeBaron	2.5 (2507)	J	Turbo I	4	SOHC
	LeBaron	2.5 (2507)	K	EFI	4	SOHC
	LeBaron GTS	2.2 (2213)	D	EFI	4	SOHC
	LeBaron GTS	2.2 (2213)	A	Turbo II	4	SOHC
	LeBaron GTS	2.5 (2507)	J	Turbo I	4	SOHC
	LeBaron GTS	2.5 (2507)	K	EFI	4	SOHC
	Lancer	2.2 (2213)	D	EFI	4	SOHC
	Lancer	2.2 (2213)	A	Turbo II	4	SOHC
	Lancer	2.5 (2507)	J	Turbo I	4	SOHC
	Lancer	2.5 (2507)	K	EFI	4	SOHC
	Shadow	2.5 (2507)	J	Turbo I	4	SOHC
	Shadow	2.5 (2507)	K	EFI	4	SOHC
	Shadow	2.2 (2213)	D	EFI	4	SOHC
	Shadow	2.2 (2213)	A	Turbo II	4	SOHC
	Sundance	2.2 (2213)	D	EFI	4	SOHC
	Sundance	2.5 (2507)	J	Turbo I	4	SOHC
	Sundance	2.5 (2507)	K	EFI	4	SOHC
	Spirit	2.5 (2507)	J	Turbo I	4	SOHC
	Spirit	2.5 (2507)	K	EFI	4	SOHC
	Spirit	3.0 (2966)	3	MPI	6	SOHC
	Acclaim	2.5 (2507)	J	Turbo I	4	SOHC
	Acclaim	2.5 (2507)	K	EFI	4	SOHC
	Acclaim	3.0 (2966)	3	MPI	6	SOHC
	TC	2.2 (2213)	A	Turbo II	4	SOHC
	TC	2.2 (2213)	R	Turbo	4	DOHC
1990	Daytona	2.5 (2507)	J	Turbo I	4	SOHC
	Daytona	2.2 (2213)	C	Turbo IV	4	SOHC
	Daytona	3.0 (2966)	3	MPI	6	SOHC
	LeBaron	2.5 (2507)	J	Turbo I	4	SOHC
	LeBaron	2.5 (2507)	K	EFI	4	SOHC
	LeBaron	2.2 (2213)	C	Turbo IV	4	SOHC
	LeBaron	3.0 (2966)	3	MPI	6	SOHC
	LeBaron Landau	3.0 (2966)	3	MPI	6	SOHC
	Shadow	2.2 (2213)	D	EFI	4	SOHC
	Shadow	2.2 (2213)	C	Turbo IV	4	SOHC
	Shadow	2.5 (2507)	J	Turbo I	4	SOHC

ENGINE IDENTIFICATION

Year	Model	Engine Displacement Liters (cc)	Engine Series (ID/VIN)	Fuel System	No. of Cylinders	Engine Type
1990	Shadow	2.5 (2507)	K	EFI	4	SOHC
	Sundance	2.2 (2213)	D	EFI	4	SOHC
	Sundance	2.5 (2507)	J	Turbo I	4	SOHC
	Sundance	2.5 (2507)	K	EFI	4	SOHC
	Spirit	2.5 (2507)	J	Turbo I	4	SOHC
	Spirit	2.5 (2507)	K	EFI	4	SOHC
	Spirit	3.0 (2966)	3	MPI	6	SOHC
	Acclaim	2.5 (2507)	J	Turbo I	4	SOHC
	Acclaim	2.5 (2507)	K	EFI	4	SOHC
	Acclaim	3.0 (2966)	3	EFI	6	SOHC
	TC	2.2 (2213)	R	Turbo	4	DOHC
	TC	3.0 (2966)	S	EFI	6	SOHC
1991	Daytona	2.5 (2507)	J	Turbo I	4	SOHC
	Daytona	2.5 (2507)	K	EFI	4	SOHC
	Daytona	3.0 (2966)	3	MPI	6	SOHC
	LeBaron	2.5 (2507)	J	Turbo I	4	SOHC
	LeBaron	2.5 (2507)	K	EFI	4	SOHC
	LeBaron	3.0 (2966)	3	MPI	6	SOHC
	LeBaron Landau	3.0 (2966)	3	MPI	6	SOHC
	Shadow	2.2 (2213)	D	EFI	4	SOHC
	Shadow	2.5 (2507)	J	Turbo I	4	SOHC
	Shadow	2.5 (2507)	K	EFI	4	SOHC
	Sundance	2.2 (2213)	D	EFI	4	SOHC
	Sundance	2.5 (2507)	J	Turbo I	4	SOHC
	Sundance	2.5 (2507)	K	EFI	4	SOHC
	Spirit	2.5 (2507)	J	Turbo I	4	SOHC
	Spirit	2.5 (2507)	K	EFI	4	SOHC
	Spirit	3.0 (2966)	3	MPI	6	SOHC
	Spirit R/T	2.2 (2213)	A	Turbo III	4	DOHC
	Acclaim	2.5 (2507)	K	EFI	4	SOHC
	Acclaim	3.0 (2966)	3	MPI	6	SOHC
	TC	3.0 (2966)	S	EFI	6	SOHC
1992–93	Daytona	2.5 (2507)	J	Turbo I	4	SOHC
	Daytona	2.5 (2507)	K	EFI	4	SOHC
	Daytona	3.0 (2966)	3	MPI	6	SOHC
	Daytona	2.2 (2213)	A	Turbo III	4	DOHC
	LeBaron	2.5 (2507)	J	Turbo I	4	SOHC
	LeBaron	2.5 (2507)	K	EFI	4	SOHC
	LeBaron	3.0 (2966)	3	MPI	6	SOHC
	Shadow	2.2 (2213)	D	EFI	4	SOHC
	Shadow	2.5 (2507)	J	Turbo I	4	SOHC
	Shadow	2.5 (2507)	K	EFI	4	SOHC
	Acclaim	2.5 (2507)	K	EFI	4	SOHC
	Acclaim	3.0 (2966)	3	MPI	6	SOHC

ENGINE IDENTIFICATION

Year	Model	Engine Displacement Liters (cc)	Engine Series (ID/VIN)	Fuel System	No. of Cylinders	Engine Type
1992–93	Spirit R/T	2.2 (2213)	A	Turbo III	4	DOHC
	Spirit	2.5 (2507)	J	Turbo I	4	SOHC
	Spirit	2.5 (2507)	K	MPI	4	SOHC
	Spirit	3.0 (2966)	3	EFI	6	SOHC
	Sundance	2.2 (2213)	D	EFI	4	SOHC
	Sundance	2.5 (2507)	K	EFI	4	SOHC

DOHC—Double Overhead Camshaft
SOHC—Single Overhead Camshaft
EFI—Electronic Fuel Injection
MPI—Multi-Point Fuel Injection

GENERAL ENGINE SPECIFICATIONS

Year	Engine ID/VIN	Engine Displacement Liters (cc)	Fuel System Type	Net Horsepower @ rpm	Net Torque @ rpm (ft. lbs.)	Bore × Stroke (in.)	Compression Ratio	Oil Pressure @ rpm
1989	A	2.2 (2213)	Turbo	174 @ 5200	170 @ 3600	3.44 × 3.62	8.1:1	30–80 @ 3000
	D	2.2 (2213)	EFI	99 @ 5600	121 @ 3200	3.44 × 3.62	9.5:1	30–80 @ 3000
	K	2.5 (2507)	EFI	100 @ 4800	135 @ 2800	3.44 × 4.09	8.9:1	30–80 @ 3000
	J	2.5 (2507)	Turbo	150 @ 4800	180 @ 2000	3.44 × 4.09	7.8:1	30–80 @ 3000
	3	3.0 (2966)	EFI	141 @ 5000	171 @ 2000	3.59 × 2.99	8.6:1	30–80 @ 3000
	R	2.2 (2213)	Turbo	200 @ 5500	220 @ 3400	3.44 × 3.62	7.4:1	30–80 @ 3000
1990	C	2.2 (2213)	Turbo	174 @ 5200	210 @ 2400	3.44 × 3.62	8.0:1	30–80 @ 3000
	D	2.2 (2213)	EFI	99 @ 5600	121 @ 3200	3.44 × 3.62	9.5:1	30–80 @ 3000
	K	2.5 (2507)	EFI	100 @ 4800	135 @ 2800	3.44 × 4.09	8.9:1	30–80 @ 3000
	J	2.5 (2507)	Turbo	150 @ 4800	180 @ 2000	3.44 × 4.09	7.8:1	30–80 @ 3000
	3	3.0 (2966)	EFI	141 @ 5000	171 @ 2000	3.59 × 2.99	8.9:1	30–80 @ 3000
	S	3.0 (2966)	EFI	141 @ 5000	170 @ 2800	3.59 × 2.99	8.9:1	30–80 @ 3000
	R	2.2 (2213)	Turbo	200 @ 5500	220 @ 3400	3.44 × 3.62	7.4:1	30–80 @ 3000
1991	D	2.2 (2213)	EFI	99 @ 5600	121 @ 3200	3.44 × 3.62	9.5:1	30–80 @ 3000
	K	2.5 (2507)	EFI	100 @ 4800	135 @ 2800	3.44 × 4.09	8.9:1	30–80 @ 3000
	J	2.5 (2507)	Turbo	150 @ 4800	180 @ 2000	3.44 × 4.09	7.8:1	30–80 @ 3000
	3	3.0 (2966)	EFI	141 @ 5000	171 @ 2000	3.59 × 2.99	8.9:1	30–80 @ 3000
	S	3.0 (2966)	EFI	141 @ 5000	170 @ 2800	3.59 × 2.99	8.9:1	30–80 @ 3000
	A	2.2 (2213)	Turbo	224 @ 2800	217 @ 6000	3.44 × 3.62	8.5:1	30–80 @ 3000
1992–93	D	2.2 (2213)	EFI	93 @ 4800	121 @ 3200	3.44 × 3.62	9.5:1	30–80 @ 3000
	A	2.2 (2213)	Turbo	224 @ 6000	217 @ 5600	3.44 × 3.62	8.5:1	30–80 @ 3000
	K	2.5 (2507)	EFI	100 @ 4800	135 @ 2800	3.44 × 4.09	8.9:1	30–80 @ 3000
	J	2.5 (2507)	Turbo	152 @ 4800	219 @ 2400	3.44 × 4.09	7.8:1	30–80 @ 3000
	3	3.0 (2966)	MPI	141 @ 5000	171 @ 2800	3.59 × 2.99	8.9:1	30–80 @ 3000

NOTE: Horsepower and torque are SAE net figures. They are measured at the rear of the transmission with all accessories installed and operating. Since the figures vary when a given engine is installed in different models, some are representative rather than exact.
EFI—Electronic Fuel Injection
MPI—Multi-Point Fuel Injection

GASOLINE ENGINE TUNE-UP SPECIFICATIONS

Year	Engine ID/VIN	Engine Displacement Liters (cc)	Spark Plugs Gap (in.)	Ignition Timing (deg.) MT	AT	Fuel Pump ② (psi)	Idle Speed (rpm) MT	AT	Valve Clearance In.	Ex.
1989	A	2.2 (2213)	0.035	12B	—	55	900	—	Hyd.	Hyd.
	D	2.2 (2213)	0.035	12B	12B	14.5	850	850	Hyd.	Hyd.
	K	2.5 (2507)	0.035	12B	12B	14.5	850	850	Hyd.	Hyd.
	J	2.5 (2507)	0.035	12B	12B	55	900	720	Hyd.	Hyd.
	3	3.0 (2966)	0.040	—	12B	48	—	700	Hyd.	Hyd.
	R	2.2 (2213)	0.030	12B	—	55	900	—	0.012	0.010
1990	C	2.2 (2213)	0.035	12B	—	55	900	—	Hyd.	Hyd.
	D	2.2 (2213)	0.035	12B	12B	14.5	850	850	Hyd.	Hyd.
	K	2.5 (2507)	0.035	12B	12B	14.5	850	850	Hyd.	Hyd.
	J	2.5 (2507)	0.035	12B	12B	55	900	720	Hyd.	Hyd.
	3	3.0 (2966)	0.040	—	12B	48	—	700	Hyd.	Hyd.
	S	3.0 (2966)	0.040	—	12B	48	—	700	Hyd.	Hyd.
	R	2.2 (2213)	0.030	12B	—	55	900	—	0.012	0.010
1991	D	2.2 (2213)	0.035	12B	12B	39	850	850	Hyd.	Hyd.
	K	2.5 (2507)	0.035	12B	12B	39①	850	850	Hyd.	Hyd.
	J	2.5 (2507)	0.035	12B	12B	55	900	850	Hyd.	Hyd.
	3	3.0 (2966)	0.040	—	12B	48	—	700	Hyd.	Hyd.
	S	3.0 (2966)	0.040	—	12B	48	—	700	Hyd.	Hyd.
	A	2.2 (2213)	0.035	NA	—	55	850	—	Hyd.	Hyd.
1992	D	2.2 (2213)	0.035	12B	12B	39	850	850	Hyd.	Hyd.
	A	2.2 (2213)	0.035	—	—	55	850	—	Hyd.	Hyd.
	K	2.5 (2507)	0.035	12B	12B	39	850	850	Hyd.	Hyd.
	J	2.5 (2507)	0.035	12B	12B	55	900	850	Hyd.	Hyd.
	3	3.0 (2966)	0.040	—	12B	48	—	700	Hyd.	Hyd.
1993				SEE UNDERHOOD SPECIFICATIONS STICKER						

NOTE: The lowest cylinder pressure should be within 75% of the highest cylinder pressure reading. For example, if the highest cylinder is 134 psi, the lowest should be 101. Engine should be at normal operating temperature with throttle valve in the wide open position.

The underhood specifications sticker often reflects tune-up specification changes in production. Sticker figures must be used if they disagree with those in this chart.

Hyd.—Hydraulic

① Early 1991 Shadow Convertible: 14.5 psi
② The specifications listed reflect system pressures with the vacuum line at the pressure regulator disconnected

FIRING ORDERS

NOTE: To avoid confusion, always replace spark plug wires one at a time.

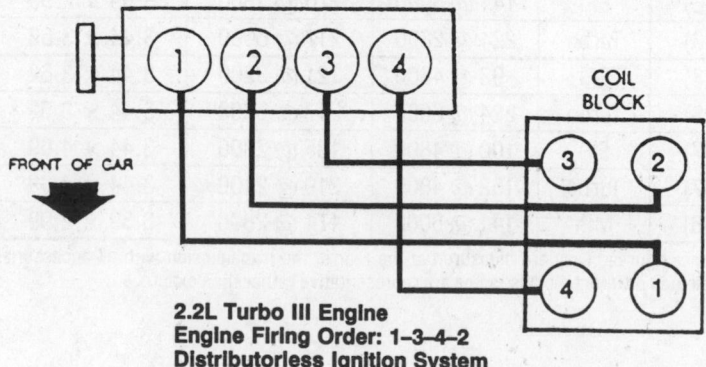

2.2L Turbo III Engine
Engine Firing Order: 1-3-4-2
Distributorless Ignition System

FIRING ORDERS

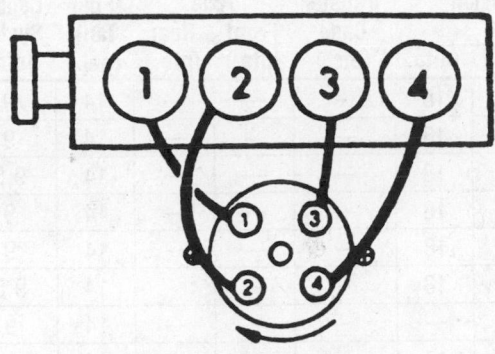

2.2L and 2.5L Engines (Except Turbo III)
Engine Firing Order: 1–3–4–2
Distributor Rotation: Clockwise

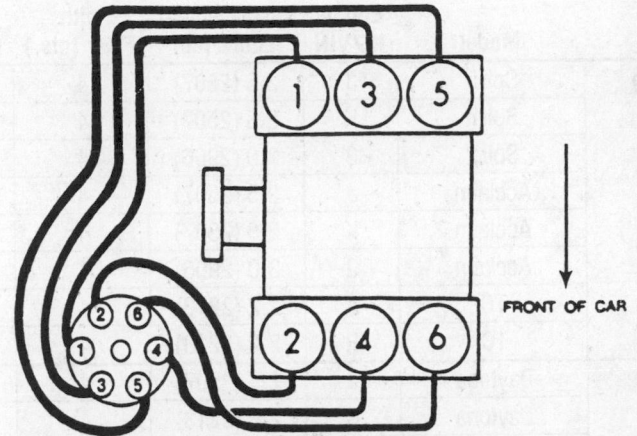

FRONT OF CAR

3.0L Engine
Engine Firing Order: 1–2–3–4–5–6
Distributor Rotation: Counterclockwise

CAPACITIES

Year	Model	Engine ID/VIN	Engine Displacement Liters (cc)	Engine Crankcase with Filter (qts.)	Transmission (pts.) 4-Spd	5-Spd	Auto.	Transfer Case (pts.)	Drive Axle Front (pts.)	Rear (pts.)	Fuel Tank (gal.)	Cooling System (qts.)
1989	Aries	D	2.2 (2213)	4	—	5	18	—	—	—	14	9
	Aries	K	2.5 (2507)	4	—	5	18	—	—	—	14	9
	Reliant	D	2.2 (2213)	4	—	5	18	—	—	—	14	9
	Reliant	K	2.5 (2507)	4	—	5	18	—	—	—	14	9
	Daytona	A	2.2 (2213)	4	—	5	—	—	—	—	14	9
	Daytona	J	2.5 (2507)	4	—	5	18	—	—	—	14	9
	Daytona	K	2.5 (2507)	4	—	5	18	—	—	—	14	9
	LeBaron	A	2.2 (2213)	4	—	5	—	—	—	—	14	9
	LeBaron	J	2.5 (2507)	4	—	5	18	—	—	—	14	9
	LeBaron	K	2.5 (2507)	4	—	5	18	—	—	—	14	9
	LeBaron GTS	D	2.2 (2213)	4	—	5	18	—	—	—	14	9
	LeBaron GTS	A	2.2 (2213)	4	—	5	—	—	—	—	14	9
	LeBaron GTS	J	2.5 (2507)	4	—	5	—	—	—	—	14	9
	LeBaron GTS	K	2.5 (2507)	4	—	5	—	—	—	—	14	9
	Lancer	D	2.2 (2213)	4	—	5	18	—	—	—	14	9
	Lancer	A	2.2 (2213)	4	—	5	18	—	—	—	14	9
	Lancer	J	2.5 (2507)	4	—	5	18	—	—	—	14	9
	Lancer	K	2.5 (2507)	4	—	5	18	—	—	—	14	9
	Shadow	J	2.5 (2507)	4	—	5	18	—	—	—	14	9
	Shadow	K	2.5 (2507)	4	—	5	18	—	—	—	14	9
	Shadow	D	2.2 (2213)	4	—	5	18	—	—	—	14	9
	Shadow	A	2.2 (2213)	4	—	5	—	—	—	—	14	9
	Sundance	D	2.2 (2213)	4	—	5	18	—	—	—	14	9
	Sundance	J	2.5 (2507)	4	—	5	18	—	—	—	14	9
	Sundance	K	2.5 (2507)	4	—	5	18	—	—	—	14	9

CAPACITIES

Year	Model	Engine ID/VIN	Engine Displacement Liters (cc)	Engine Crankcase with Filter (qts.)	Transmission (pts.)			Transfer Case (pts.)	Drive Axle		Fuel Tank (gal.)	Cooling System (qts.)
					4-Spd	5-Spd	Auto.		Front (pts.)	Rear (pts.)		
1989	Spirit	J	2.5 (2507)	4	—	5	18	—	—	—	14	9
	Spirit	K	2.5 (2507)	4	—	5	18	—	—	—	14	9
	Spirit	3	3.0 (2966)	4	—	—	18	—	—	—	14	9.5
	Acclaim	J	2.5 (2507)	4	—	5	18	—	—	—	14	9
	Acclaim	K	2.5 (2507)	4	—	5	18	—	—	—	14	9
	Acclaim	3	3.0 (2966)	4	—	—	18	—	—	—	14	9.5
	TC	A	2.2 (2213)	4	—	5	—	—	—	—	14	9
	TC	R	2.2 (2213)	4	—	5	18	—	—	—	14	9
1990	Daytona	J	2.5 (2507)	4	—	5	18	—	—	—	14	9
	Daytona	C	2.2 (2213)	4	—	5	—	—	—	—	14	9
	Daytona	3	3.0 (2966)	4	—	—	18	—	—	—	14	9.5
	LeBaron	J	2.5 (2507)	4	—	5	18	—	—	—	14	9
	LeBaron	K	2.5 (2507)	4	—	5	18	—	—	—	14	9
	LeBaron	C	2.2 (2213)	4	—	5	—	—	—	—	14	9.5
	LeBaron	3	3.0 (2966)	4	—	—	18	—	—	—	14	9.5
	LeBaron Landau	3	3.0 (2966)	4	—	—	18	—	—	—	14	9
	Shadow	D	2.2 (2213)	4	—	5	18	—	—	—	14	9
	Shadow	C	2.2 (2213)	4	—	5	—	—	—	—	14	9
	Shadow	J	2.5 (2507)	4	—	5	18	—	—	—	14	9
	Shadow	K	2.5 (2507)	4	—	5	18	—	—	—	14	9
	Sundance	D	2.2 (2213)	4	—	5	18	—	—	—	14	9
	Sundance	J	2.5 (2507)	4	—	5	18	—	—	—	14	9
	Sundance	K	2.5 (2507)	4	—	5	18	—	—	—	14	9
	Spirit	J	2.5 (2507)	4	—	5	18	—	—	—	14	9
	Spirit	K	2.5 (2507)	4	—	5	18	—	—	—	14	9
	Spirit	3	3.0 (2966)	4	—	—	18	—	—	—	14	9.5
	Acclaim	J	2.5 (2507)	4	—	5	18	—	—	—	14	9
	Acclaim	K	2.5 (2507)	4	—	5	18	—	—	—	14	9
	Acclaim	3	3.0 (2966)	4	—	—	18	—	—	—	14	9.5
	TC	R	2.2 (2213)	4.5	—	5	18	—	—	—	14	9.5
	TC	S	3.0 (2966)	4	—	5	18	—	—	—	14	9
1991	Daytona	J	2.5 (2507)	4.5	—	5	18	—	—	—	14	9
	Daytona	K	2.5 (2507)	4.5	—	5	—	—	—	—	14	9
	Daytona	3	3.0 (2966)	4.5	—	—	18	—	—	—	14	9.5
	LeBaron	J	2.5 (2507)	4.5	—	5	18	—	—	—	14	9
	LeBaron	K	2.5 (2507)	4.5	—	5	18	—	—	—	14	9
	LeBaron	3	3.0 (2966)	4.5	—	—	18	—	—	—	14	9.5
	LeBaron Landau	3	3.0 (2966)	4.5	—	—	18	—	—	—	16	9.5
	Shadow	D	2.2 (2213)	4.5	—	5	18	—	—	—	14	9
	Shadow	J	2.5 (2507)	4.5	—	5	18	—	—	—	14	9
	Shadow	K	2.5 (2507)	4.5	—	5	18	—	—	—	14	9
	Sundance	D	2.2 (2213)	4.5	—	5	18	—	—	—	14	9
	Sundance	J	2.5 (2507)	4.5	—	5	18	—	—	—	14	9

CAPACITIES

Year	Model	Engine ID/VIN	Engine Displacement Liters (cc)	Engine Crankcase with Filter (qts.)	Transmission (pts.) 4-Spd	5-Spd	Auto.	Transfer Case (pts.)	Drive Axle Front (pts.)	Rear (pts.)	Fuel Tank (gal.)	Cooling System (qts.)
1991	Sundance	K	2.5 (2507)	4.5	—	5	18	—	—	—	14	9
	Spirit	J	2.5 (2507)	4.5	—	5	18	—	—	—	14	9
	Spirit	K	2.5 (2507)	4.5	—	5	18	—	—	—	16	9
	Spirit	3	3.0 (2966)	4.5	—	—	18	—	—	—	16	9.5
	Spirit R/T	A	2.2 (2213)	4.5	—	5	—	—	—	—	16	9.5
	Acclaim	K	2.5 (2507)	4.5	—	5	18	—	—	—	16	9
	Acclaim	3	3.0 (2966)	4.5	—	—	18	—	—	—	16	9.5
	TC	S	3.0 (2966)	4.5	—	—	18	—	—	—	14	9.5
1992-93	Daytona	J	2.5 (2507)	4.5	—	5	18	—	—	—	14	9
	Daytona	K	2.5 (2507)	4.5	—	5	18	—	—	—	14	9
	Daytona	3	3.0 (2966)	4.5	—	—	18	—	—	—	14	9.5
	Daytona	A	2.2 (2213)	4.5	—	5	—	—	—	—	14	9
	LeBaron	J	2.5 (2507)	4.5	—	5	18	—	—	—	14	9
	LeBaron	K	2.5 (2507)	4.5	—	5	18	—	—	—	14	9
	LeBaron	3	3.0 (2966)	4.5	—	—	18	—	—	—	16	9.5
	Shadow	D	2.2 (2213)	4.5	—	5	18	—	—	—	14	9
	Shadow	J	2.5 (2507)	4.5	—	5	18	—	—	—	14	9
	Shadow	K	2.5 (2507)	4.5	—	5	18	—	—	—	14	9
	Acclaim	K	2.5 (2507)	4.5	—	5	18	—	—	—	16	9
	Acclaim	3	3.0 (2966)	4.5	—	—	18	—	—	—	16	9.5
	Spirit R/T	A	2.2 (2213)	4.5	—	5	—	—	—	—	16	9
	Spirit	J	2.5 (2507)	4.5	—	5	18	—	—	—	16	9
	Spirit	K	2.5 (2507)	4.5	—	—	18	—	—	—	16	9
	Spirit	3	3.0 (2966)	4.5	—	5	18	—	—	—	16	9.5
	Sundance	D	2.2 (2213)	4.5	—	5	18	—	—	—	14	9
	Sundance	K	2.5 (2507)	4.5	—	5	18	—	—	—	14	9

CAMSHAFT SPECIFICATIONS

All measurements given in inches.

Year	Engine ID/VIN	Engine Displacement Liters (cc)	Journal Diameter 1	2	3	4	5	Elevation In.	Ex.	Bearing Clearance	Camshaft End Play
1989	A	2.2 (2213)	1.375–1.376	1.375–1.376	1.375–1.376	1.375–1.376	1.375–1.376	NA	NA	—	0.005–0.020
	D	2.2 (2213)	1.375–1.376	1.375–1.376	1.375–1.376	1.375–1.376	1.375–1.376	NA	NA	—	0.005–0.020
	K	2.5 (2507)	1.375–1.376	1.375–1.376	1.375–1.376	1.375–1.376	1.375–1.376	NA	NA	—	0.005–0.020
	J	2.5 (2507)	1.375–1.376	1.375–1.376	1.375–1.376	1.375–1.376	1.375–1.376	NA	NA	—	0.005–0.020
	3	3.0 (2966)	NA	NA	NA	NA	NA	①	①	—	NA
	R	2.2 (2213)	NA	NA	NA	NA	NA	NA	NA	—	NA

CAMSHAFT SPECIFICATIONS

All measurements given in inches.

Year	Engine ID/VIN	Engine Displacement Liters (cc)	Journal Diameter 1	2	3	4	5	Elevation In.	Ex.	Bearing Clearance	Camshaft End Play
1990	C	2.2 (2213)	1.375–1.376	1.375–1.376	1.375–1.376	1.375–1.376	1.375–1.376	NA	NA	—	0.005–0.020
	D	2.2 (2213)	1.375–1.376	1.375–1.376	1.375–1.376	1.375–1.376	1.375–1.376	NA	NA	—	0.005–0.020
	K	2.5 (2507)	1.375–1.376	1.375–1.376	1.375–1.376	1.375–1.376	1.375–1.376	NA	NA	—	0.005–0.020
	J	2.5 (2507)	1.375–1.376	1.375–1.376	1.375–1.376	1.375–1.376	1.375–1.376	NA	NA	—	0.005–0.020
	3	3.0 (2966)	NA	NA	NA	NA	NA	①	①	—	NA
	S	3.0 (2966)	NA	NA	NA	NA	NA	①	①	—	NA
	R	2.2 (2213)	NA	NA	NA	NA	NA	NA	NA	—	NA
1991	D	2.2 (2213)	1.395–1.396	1.395–1.396	1.395–1.396	1.395–1.396	1.395–1.396	NA	NA		0.005–0.020
	K	2.5 (2507)	1.395–1.396	1.395–1.396	1.395–1.396	1.395–1.396	1.395–1.396	NA	NA	—	0.005–0.020
	J	2.5 (2507)	1.395–1.396	1.395–1.396	1.395–1.396	1.395–1.396	1.395–1.396	NA	NA	—	0.005–0.020
	3	3.0 (2966)	NA	NA	NA	NA	NA	①	①	—	NA
	S	3.0 (2966)	NA	NA	NA	NA	NA	①	①	—	NA
	A	2.2 (2213)	1.886–1.887	1.886–1.887	1.886–1.887	1.886–1.887	1.886–1.887	NA	NA	—	0.001–0.020
1992–93	D	2.2 (2213)	1.395–1.396	1.395–1.396	1.395–1.396	1.395–1.396	1.395–1.396	NA	NA	—	0.005–0.013
	A	2.2 (2213)	1.886–1.887	1.886–1.887	1.886–1.887	1.886–1.887	1.886–1.887	NA	NA	—	0.001–0.020
	K	2.5 (2507)	1.395–1.396	1.395–1.396	1.395–1.396	1.395–1.396	1.395–1.396	NA	NA	—	0.005–0.013
	J	2.5 (2507)	1.395–1.396	1.395–1.396	1.395–1.396	1.395–1.396	1.395–1.396	NA	NA	—	0.001–0.020
	3	3.0 (2966)	NA	NA	NA	NA	NA	①	①	—	NA

NA—Not available   ① Standard value: 1.624 in.   Wear limit: 1.604 in.

CRANKSHAFT AND CONNECTING ROD SPECIFICATIONS

All measurements are given in inches.

Year	Engine ID/VIN	Engine Displacement Liters (cc)	Crankshaft Main Brg. Journal Dia.	Main Brg. Oil Clearance	Shaft End-play	Thrust on No.	Connecting Rod Journal Diameter	Oil Clearance	Side Clearance
1989	A	2.2 (2213)	2.362–2.363	0.0004–0.0040	0.002–0.014	3	1.9680–1.9690	0.0008–0.0040	0.005–0.013
	D	2.2 (2213)	2.362–2.363	0.0004–0.0040	0.002–0.014	3	1.9680–1.9690	0.0008–0.0040	0.005–0.013
	K	2.5 (2507)	2.362–2.363	0.0004–0.0040	0.002–0.014	3	1.9680–1.9690	0.0008–0.0040	0.005–0.013
	J	2.5 (2507)	2.362–2.363	0.0004–0.0040	0.002–0.014	3	1.9680–1.9690	0.0008–0.0040	0.005–0.013

CRANKSHAFT AND CONNECTING ROD SPECIFICATIONS

All measurements are given in inches.

Year	Engine ID/VIN	Engine Displacement Liters (cc)	Crankshaft				Connecting Rod		
			Main Brg. Journal Dia.	Main Brg. Oil Clearance	Shaft End-play	Thrust on No.	Journal Diameter	Oil Clearance	Side Clearance
	3	3.0 (2966)	2.361–2.362	0.0006–0.0020	0.002–0.010	3	1.9680–1.9690	0.0008–0.0028	0.004–0.010
	R	2.2 (2213)	2.362–2.363	0.0011–0.0031	0.002–0.007	3	1.9695–1.9705	0.0006–0.0016	0.006–0.009
1990	C	2.2 (2213)	2.362–2.363	0.0004–0.0040	0.002–0.014	3	1.9680–1.9690	0.0008–0.0040	0.005–0.013
	D	2.2 (2213)	2.362–2.363	0.0004–0.0040	0.002–0.014	3	1.9680–1.9690	0.0008–0.0040	0.005–0.013
	K	2.5 (2507)	2.362–2.363	0.0004–0.0040	0.002–0.014	3	1.9680–1.9690	0.0008–0.0040	0.005–0.013
	J	2.5 (2507)	2.362–2.363	0.0004–0.0040	0.002–0.014	3	1.9680–1.9690	0.0008–0.0040	0.005–0.013
	3	3.0 (2966)	2.361–2.362	0.0006–0.0020	0.002–0.010	3	1.9680–1.9690	0.0008–0.0028	0.004–0.010
	S	3.0 (2966)	2.361–2.363	0.0006–0.0020	0.002–0.010	3	1.9680–1.9690	0.0008–0.0028	0.004–0.010
	R	2.2 (2213)	2.362–2.363	0.0011–0.0031	0.002–0.007	3	1.9695–1.9705	0.0006–0.0016	0.006–0.009
1991	D	2.2 (2213)	2.362–2.363	0.0004–0.0040	0.002–0.014	3	1.9680–1.9690	0.0008–0.0040	0.005–0.013
	K	2.5 (2507)	2.362–2.363	0.0004–0.0040	0.002–0.014	3	1.9680–1.9690	0.0008–0.0040	0.005–0.013
	J	2.5 (2507)	2.362–2.363	0.0004–0.0040	0.002–0.014	3	1.9680–1.9690	0.0008–0.0040	0.005–0.013
	3	3.0 (2966)	2.361–2.362	0.0006–0.0020	0.002–0.010	3	1.9680–1.9690	0.0008–0.0028	0.004–0.010
	S	3.0 (2966)	2.361–2.363	0.0006–0.0020	0.002–0.010	3	1.9680–1.9690	0.0008–0.0028	0.004–0.010
	A	2.2 (2213)	2.362–2.363	0.0004–0.0040	0.002–0.014	3	1.9680–1.9690	0.0008–0.0034	0.005–0.013
1992–93	D	2.2 (2213)	2.362–2.363	0.0004–0.0040	0.002–0.014	3	1.9680–1.9690	0.0008–0.0030	0.005–0.013
	A	2.2 (2213)	2.362–2.363	0.0004–0.0040	0.002–0.014	3	1.9680–1.9690	0.0008–0.0030	0.005–0.013
	K	2.5 (2507)	2.362–2.363	0.0004–0.0040	0.002–0.014	3	1.9680–1.9690	0.0008–0.0030	0.005–0.013
	J	2.5 (2507)	2.362–2.363	0.0004–0.0040	0.002–0.014	3	1.9680–1.9690	0.0008–0.0030	0.005–0.013
	3	3.0 (2966)	2.361–2.362	0.0006–0.0020	0.002–0.010	3	1.9680–1.9690	0.0006–0.0020	0.004–0.010

VALVE SPECIFICATIONS

Year	Engine ID/VIN	Engine Displacement Liters (cc)	Seat Angle (deg.)	Face Angle (deg.)	Spring Test Pressure (lbs. @ in.)	Spring Installed Height (in.)	Stem-to-Guide Clearance (in.) Intake	Exhaust	Stem Diameter ① (in.) Intake	Exhaust
1989	A	2.2 (2213)	45	45	114 @ 1.65	1.65	0.001–0.003	0.0030–0.0047	0.3124	0.3103
	D	2.2 (2213)	45	45	114 @ 1.65	1.65	0.001–0.003	0.0030–0.0047	0.3124	0.3103
	K	2.5 (2507)	45	45	114 @ 1.65	1.65	0.001–0.003	0.0030–0.0047	0.3124	0.3103
	J	2.5 (2507)	45	45	114 @ 1.65	1.65	0.001–0.003	0.0030–0.0047	0.3124	0.3103
	3	3.0 (2966)	44.5	45.5	73 @ 1.59	1.59	0.001–0.002	0.0020–0.0030	0.3130–0.3140	0.3120–0.3130
	R	2.2 (2213)	NA	NA	NA	②	0.001–0.002	0.0010–0.0030	0.2750–0.2760	0.2750–0.2760
1990	C	2.2 (2213)	45	45	114 @ 1.65	1.65	0.001–0.003	0.0030–0.0047	0.3124	0.3103
	D	2.2 (2213)	45	45	114 @ 1.65	1.65	0.001–0.003	0.0030–0.0047	0.3124	0.3103
	K	2.5 (2507)	45	45	114 @ 1.65	1.65	0.001–0.003	0.0030–0.0047	0.3124	0.3103
	J	2.5 (2507)	45	45	114 @ 1.65	1.65	0.001–0.003	0.0030–0.0047	0.3124	0.3103
	3	3.0 (2966)	44.5	45.5	73 @ 1.59	1.59	0.001–0.002	0.0020–0.0030	0.3130–0.3140	0.3120–0.3130
	S	3.0 (2966)	44.5	45.5	180 @ 1.59	1.59	0.001–0.002	0.0020–0.0030	0.3130–0.3140	0.3120–0.3130
	R	2.2 (2213)	NA	NA	NA	②	0.001–0.002	0.0010–0.0030	0.2750–0.2760	0.2750–0.2760
1991	D	2.2 (2213)	45	45	114 @ 1.65	1.65	0.001–0.003	0.0030–0.0047	0.3124	0.3103
	K	2.5 (2507)	45	45	114 @ 1.65	1.65	0.001–0.003	0.0030–0.0047	0.3124	0.3103
	J	2.5 (2507)	45	45	114 @ 1.65	1.65	0.001–0.003	0.0030–0.0047	0.3124	0.3103
	3	3.0 (2966)	44.5	45.5	73 @ 1.59	1.59	0.001–0.002	0.0020–0.0030	0.3130–0.3140	0.3120–0.3130
	S	3.0 (2966)	44.5	45.5	180 @ 1.59	1.59	0.001–0.004	0.0020–0.0040	0.3130–0.3140	0.3120–0.3130
	A	2.2 (2213)	45	45	225 @ 1.34	1.34	0.001–0.004	0.0020–0.0040	0.2740	0.2730
1992–93	D	2.2 (2213)	45	45	114 @ 1.65	1.65	0.001–0.003	0.0030–0.0047	0.3124	0.3103
	A	2.2 (2213)	45	45	225 @ 1.34	1.34	0.001–0.004	0.0020–0.0040	0.2740	0.2730
	K	2.5 (2507)	45	45	114 @ 1.65	1.65	0.001–0.003	0.0030–0.0047	0.3124	0.3103
	J	2.5 (2507)	45	45	114 @ 1.65	1.65	0.001–0.003	0.0030–0.0047	0.3124	0.3103
	3	3.0 (2966)	44	45–45.5	73 @ 1.56	1.59	0.001–0.004	0.0020–0.0030	0.3130–0.3140	0.3120–0.3125

NA—Not available ① If no range is given, the specification is the minimum allowable diameter.

PISTON AND RING SPECIFICATIONS
All measurements are given in inches.

Year	Engine ID/VIN	Engine Displacement Liters (cc)	Piston Clearance	Ring Gap Top Compression	Ring Gap Bottom Compression	Ring Gap Oil Control	Ring Side Clearance Top Compression	Ring Side Clearance Bottom Compression	Ring Side Clearance Oil Control
1989	A	2.2 (2213)	0.0005–0.0027	0.010–0.039	0.009–0.037	0.015–0.074	0.0016–0.0030	0.0016–0.0035	0.0002–0.0080
	D	2.2 (2213)	0.0005–0.0027	0.010–0.039	0.011–0.039	0.015–0.074	0.0015–0.0040	0.0015–0.0040	0.0002–0.0080
	K	2.5 (2507)	0.0010–0.0027	0.010–0.039	0.011–0.039	0.015–0.074	0.0015–0.0040	0.0015–0.0040	0.0002–0.0080
	J	2.5 (2507)	0.0006–0.0030	0.010–0.039	0.009–0.037	0.015–0.074	0.0016–0.0030	0.0016–0.0035	0.0002–0.0080
	3	3.0 (2966)	0.0008–0.0015	0.012–0.018	0.010–0.016	0.012–0.035	0.0020–0.0035	0.0008–0.0020	NA
	R	2.2 (2213)	0.0005–0.0015	0.010–0.039	0.010–0.039	0.015–0.074	0.0015–0.0031	0.0015–0.0016	0.0002–0.0080
1990	C	2.2 (2213)	0.0005–0.0027	0.010–0.039	0.009–0.037	0.015–0.074	0.0016–0.0030	0.0016–0.0035	0.0002–0.0080
	D	2.2 (2213)	0.0005–0.0027	0.010–0.039	0.011–0.039	0.015–0.074	0.0015–0.0040	0.0015–0.0040	0.0002–0.0080
	J	2.5 (2507)	0.0006–0.0030	0.010–0.039	0.009–0.037	0.015–0.074	0.0016–0.0030	0.0016–0.0035	0.0002–0.0080
	K	2.5 (2507)	0.0010–0.0027	0.010–0.039	0.011–0.039	0.015–0.074	0.0015–0.0040	0.0015–0.0040	0.0002–0.0080
	3	3.0 (2966)	0.0012–0.0020	0.012–0.018	0.010–0.016	0.012–0.035	0.0020–0.0035	0.0008–0.0020	NA
	S	3.0 (2966)	0.0012–0.0020	0.012–0.018	0.010–0.016	0.012–0.035	0.0020–0.0035	0.0008–0.0020	NA
	R	2.2 (2213)	0.0005–0.0015	0.010–0.039	0.010–0.039	0.012–0.035	0.0015–0.0031	0.0015–0.0016	0.0002–0.0080
1991	D	2.2 (2213)	0.0005–0.0027	0.010–0.039	0.011–0.039	0.015–0.074	0.0015–0.0040	0.0015–0.0040	0.0002–0.0080
	K	2.5 (2507)	0.0010–0.0027	0.010–0.039	0.011–0.039	0.015–0.074	0.0015–0.0040	0.0015–0.0040	0.0002–0.0080
	J	2.5 (2507)	0.0006–0.0030	0.010–0.039	0.009–0.037	0.015–0.074	0.0016–0.0030	0.0016–0.0035	0.0002–0.0080
	3	3.0 (2966)	0.0012–0.0020	0.012–0.018	0.010–0.016	0.012–0.035	0.0020–0.0035	0.0008–0.0020	NA
	S	3.0 (2966)	0.0012–0.0020	0.012–0.018	0.010–0.016	0.012–0.035	0.0020–0.0035	0.0008–0.0020	NA
	A	2.2 (2213)	0.0018–0.0039	0.014–0.039	0.014–0.039	0.010–0.039	0.0016–0.0030	0.0016–0.0030	0.0002–0.0040
1992–93	D	2.2 (2213)	0.0005–0.0027	0.010–0.039	0.011–0.039	0.015–0.074	0.0015–0.0040	0.0015–0.0040	0.0002–0.0080
	A	2.2 (2213)	0.0018–0.0039	0.014–0.039	0.014–0.039	0.010–0.039	0.0015–0.0040	0.0015–0.0040	0.0002–0.0080
	K	2.5 (2507)	0.0012–0.0020	0.012–0.018	0.010–0.016	0.012–0.035	0.0020–0.0035	0.0008–0.0020	NA
	J	2.5 (2507)	0.0006–0.0030	0.010–0.039	0.009–0.037	0.015–0.074	0.0016–0.0030	0.0016–0.0035	0.0002–0.0080
	3	3.0 (2966)	0.0012–0.0020	0.012–0.018	0.010–0.016	0.012–0.035	0.0020–0.0035	0.0008–0.0020	NA

NA—Not available

TORQUE SPECIFICATIONS
All readings in ft. lbs.

Year	Engine ID/VIN	Engine Displacement Liters (cc)	Cylinder Head Bolts	Main Bearing Bolts	Rod Bearing Bolts	Crankshaft Damper Bolts	Flywheel Bolts	Manifold Intake	Manifold Exhaust	Spark Plugs	Lug Nut
1989	A	2.2 (2213)	①	30 ③	40 ③	50	70	17	17	26	95
	D	2.2 (2213)	①	30 ③	40 ③	50	70	17	17	26	95
	K	2.5 (2507)	①	30 ③	40 ③	50	70	17	17	26	95
	J	2.5 (2507)	①	30 ③	40 ③	50	70	17	17	26	95
	3	3.0 (2966)	80	60	38	112	70	17	17	20	95
	R⑥	2.2 (2213)	②	④	⑤	80	70	17	18	13	95
1990	C	2.2 (2213)	①	30 ③	40 ③	85	70	17	17	26	95
	D	2.2 (2213)	①	30 ③	40 ③	85	70	17	17	26	95
	K	2.5 (2507)	①	30 ③	40 ③	85	70	17	17	26	95
	J	2.5 (2507)	①	30 ③	40 ③	85	70	17	17	26	95
	3	3.0 (2966)	80	60	38	112	70	17	17	20	95
	S	3.0 (2966)	80	60	38	112	70	17	17	20	95
	R⑥	2.2 (2213)	②	④	⑤	80	70	17	18	13	95
1991	D	2.2 (2213)	①	30 ③	40 ③	85	70	17	17	26	95
	K	2.5 (2507)	①	30 ③	40 ③	85	70	17	17	26	95
	J	2.5 (2507)	①	30 ③	40 ③	85	70	17	17	26	95
	3	3.0 (2966)	80	60	38	112	70	17	17	20	95
	S	3.0 (2966)	80	60	38	112	70	17	17	20	95
	A	2.2 (2213)	①	④	48	80	70	17	17	18	95
1992–93	D	2.2 (2213)	①	30 ③	40 ③	85	70	17	17	26	95
	A	2.2 (2213)	①	30 ③	50	80	70	17	17	20	95
	K	2.5 (2507)	①	30 ③	40 ③	85	70	17	17	26	95
	J	2.5 (2507)	①	30 ③	40 ③	85	70	17	17	26	95
	3	3.0 (2966)	80	60	38	112	70	17	17	20	95

① Sequence: 45, 65, 65, plus ¼ turn
② Sequence: 32, 50, 65 plus ¼ turn
③ Plus ¼ turn
④ Sequence: 32, 43, 76
⑤ Sequence: 32, 47
⑥ TC Turbo

BRAKE SPECIFICATIONS
All measurements in inches unless noted

Year	Model		Master Cylinder Bore	Brake Disc Original Thickness	Brake Disc Minimum Thickness	Maximum Runout	Brake Drum Diameter Original Inside Diameter	Brake Drum Diameter Max. Wear Limit	Brake Drum Diameter Maximum Machine Diameter	Minimum Lining Thickness Front	Minimum Lining Thickness Rear
1989	Aries		0.827	0.935	0.882	0.005	7.87	NA	NA	0.30	0.06
	Reliant		0.827	0.861	0.803	0.005	7.87	NA	NA	0.30	0.06
	Lancer		0.827	0.935	0.882	0.005	7.87	NA	NA	0.30	0.06
	LeBaron GTS		0.827	0.861	0.803	0.005	7.87	NA	NA	0.30	0.06
	Shadow		0.827	0.935	0.882	0.005	7.87	NA	NA	0.30	0.06
	Sundance		0.827	0.861	0.803	0.005	7.87	NA	NA	0.30	0.06
	Spirit		0.827	0.935	0.882	0.005	7.87	NA	NA	0.30	0.06
	Acclaim		0.827	0.861	0.803	0.005	7.87	NA	NA	0.30	0.06

BRAKE SPECIFICATIONS

All measurements in inches unless noted

Year	Model		Master Cylinder Bore	Brake Disc Original Thickness	Brake Disc Minimum Thickness	Maximum Runout	Brake Drum Diameter Original Inside Diameter	Brake Drum Diameter Max. Wear Limit	Brake Drum Diameter Maximum Machine Diameter	Minimum Lining Thickness Front	Minimum Lining Thickness Rear
1989	Daytona	front	0.827	0.861	0.803	0.005	—	—	—	0.30	—
		solid rear disc	—	0.468	0.409	0.005	—	—	—	—	0.28
		vented rear disc	—	0.856	0.797	0.005	—	—	—	—	0.28
	LeBaron	front	0.827	0.861	0.803	0.005	—	—	—	0.30	—
		solid rear disc	—	0.468	0.409	0.005	—	—	—	—	0.28
		vented rear disc	—	0.856	0.797	0.005	—	—	—	—	0.28
	TC	front	NA	NA	0.882	0.005	—	—	—	0.30	—
		rear disc	—	NA	0.291	0.003	—	—	—	—	0.28
1990	LeBaron Landau		0.827	0.861	0.803	0.005	7.87	NA	NA	0.30	0.06
	Shadow		0.827	0.935	0.882	0.005	7.87	NA	NA	0.30	0.06
	Sundance		0.827	0.861	0.803	0.005	7.87	NA	NA	0.30	0.06
	Spirit		0.827	0.935	0.882	0.005	7.87	NA	NA	0.30	0.06
	Acclaim		0.827	0.861	0.803	0.005	7.87	NA	NA	0.30	0.06
	Daytona	front	0.827	0.861	0.803	0.005	—	—	—	0.30	—
		solid rear disc	—	0.468	0.409	0.003	—	—	—	—	0.28
		vented rear disc	—	0.856	0.797	0.003	—	—	—	—	0.28
	LeBaron	front	0.827	0.861	0.803	0.005	—	—	—	0.30	—
		solid rear disc	—	0.468	0.409	0.003	—	—	—	—	0.28
		vented rear disc	—	0.856	0.797	0.003	—	—	—	—	0.28
	TC	front	NA	NA	0.882	0.005	—	—	—	0.30	—
		rear disc	—	NA	0.291	0.003	—	—	—	—	0.28
1991	LeBaron Landau	front	0.827	0.861	0.803	0.005	—	—	—	0.30	—
		rear disc	—	0.856	0.797	0.003	—	—	—	—	0.28
	Shadow		0.827	0.935	0.882	0.005	7.87	NA	NA	0.30	0.06
	Sundance		0.827	0.861	0.803	0.005	7.87	NA	NA	0.30	0.06
	Spirit	front	0.827	0.861	0.803	0.005	—	—	—	0.30	—
		rear disc	—	0.856	0.797	0.005	—	—	—	—	0.28
	Acclaim	front	0.827	0.861	0.803	0.005	—	—	—	0.30	—
		rear disc	—	0.856	0.797	0.005	—	—	—	—	0.28
	Daytona	front	0.827	0.861	0.803	0.005	—	—	—	0.30	—
		solid rear disc	—	0.468	0.409	0.003	—	—	—	—	0.28
		vented rear disc	—	0.856	0.797	0.003	—	—	—	—	0.28
	LeBaron	front	0.827	0.861	0.803	0.005	—	—	—	0.30	—
		solid rear disc	—	0.468	0.409	0.003	—	—	—	—	0.28
		vented rear disc	—	0.856	0.797	0.003	—	—	—	—	0.28
	TC	front	NA	NA	0.882	0.005	—	—	—	0.30	—
		rear disc	—	NA	0.291	0.003	—	—	—	—	0.28

BRAKE SPECIFICATIONS
All measurements in inches unless noted

Year	Model		Master Cylinder Bore	Brake Disc Original Thickness	Brake Disc Minimum Thickness	Brake Disc Maximum Runout	Brake Drum Diameter Original Inside Diameter	Brake Drum Diameter Max. Wear Limit	Brake Drum Diameter Maximum Machine Diameter	Minimum Lining Thickness Front	Minimum Lining Thickness Rear
1992–93	Shadow		0.827	0.935	0.882	0.005	7.87	NA	NA	0.30	0.06
	Sundance		0.827	0.861	0.803	0.005	7.87	NA	NA	0.30	0.06
	Spirit	front	0.827	0.861	0.803	0.005	—	—	—	0.30	—
		rear disc	—	0.856	0.797	0.005	—	—	—	—	0.28
	Acclaim	front	0.827	0.861	0.803	0.005	—	—	—	0.30	—
		rear disc	—	0.856	0.797	0.005	—	—	—	—	0.28
	Daytona	front	0.827	0.861	0.803	0.005	—	—	—	0.30	—
		solid rear disc	—	0.468	0.409	0.003	—	—	—	—	0.28
		vented rear disc	—	0.856	0.797	0.003	—	—	—	—	0.28
	LeBaron	front	0.827	0.861	0.803	0.005	—	—	—	0.30	—
		solid rear disc	—	0.468	0.409	0.003	—	—	—	—	0.28
		vented rear disc	—	0.856	0.797	0.003	—	—	—	—	0.28

NA—Not available

WHEEL ALIGNMENT

Year	Model		Caster Range (deg.)	Caster Preferred Setting (deg.)	Camber Range (deg.)	Camber Preferred Setting (deg.)	Toe-in (in.)	Steering Axis Inclination (deg.)
1989	Aries	front	①	$1^3/_{16}$P	$^1/_4$N–$^3/_4$P	$^5/_{16}$P	$^1/_{16}$	$13^5/_{16}$
		rear	—	—	$1^1/_4$N–$^1/_4$N	$^1/_2$N	0	—
	Reliant	front	①	$1^3/_{16}$P	$^1/_4$N–$^3/_4$P	$^5/_{16}$P	$^1/_{16}$	$13^5/_{16}$
		rear	—	—	$1^1/_4$N–$^1/_4$N	$^1/_2$N	0	—
	Daytona	front	①	$1^3/_{16}$P	$^1/_4$N–$^3/_4$P	$^5/_{16}$P	$^1/_{16}$	$13^5/_{16}$
		rear	—	—	$1^1/_4$N–$^1/_4$N	$^1/_2$N	0	—
	LeBaron	front	①	$1^3/_{16}$P	$^1/_4$N–$^3/_4$P	$^5/_{16}$P	$^1/_{16}$	$13^5/_{16}$
		rear	—	—	$1^1/_4$N–$^1/_4$N	$^1/_2$N	0	—
	Lancer	front	①	$1^3/_{16}$P	$^1/_4$N–$^3/_4$P	$^5/_{16}$P	$^1/_{16}$	$13^5/_{16}$
		rear	—	—	$1^1/_4$N–$^1/_4$N	$^1/_2$N	0	—
	LeBaron GTS	front	①	$1^3/_{16}$P	$^1/_4$N–$^3/_4$P	$^5/_{16}$P	$^1/_{16}$	$13^5/_{16}$
		rear	—	—	$1^1/_4$N–$^1/_4$N	$^1/_2$N	0	—
	Shadow	front	①	$1^3/_{16}$P	$^1/_4$N–$^3/_4$P	$^5/_{16}$P	$^1/_{16}$	$13^5/_{16}$
		rear	—	—	$1^1/_4$N–$^1/_4$N	$^1/_2$N	0	—
	Sundance	front	①	$1^3/_{16}$P	$^1/_4$N–$^3/_4$P	$^5/_{16}$P	$^1/_{16}$	$13^5/_{16}$
		rear	—	—	$1^1/_4$N–$^1/_4$N	$^1/_2$N	0	—
	Spirit	front	①	$1^3/_{16}$P	$^1/_4$N–$^3/_4$P	$^5/_{16}$P	$^1/_{16}$	$13^5/_{16}$
		rear	—	—	$1^1/_4$N–$^1/_4$N	$^1/_2$N	0	—
	Acclaim	front	①	$1^3/_{16}$P	$^1/_4$N–$^3/_4$P	$^5/_{16}$P	$^1/_{16}$	$13^5/_{16}$
		rear	—	—	$1^1/_4$N–$^1/_4$N	$^1/_2$N	0	—
	TC	front	①	$1^3/_{16}$P	$^1/_4$N–$^3/_4$P	$^5/_{16}$P	$^1/_{16}$	$13^5/_{16}$
		rear	—	—	$1^1/_4$N–$^1/_4$N	$^1/_2$N	0	—

WHEEL ALIGNMENT

Year	Model		Caster Range (deg.)	Caster Preferred Setting (deg.)	Camber Range (deg.)	Camber Preferred Setting (deg.)	Toe-in (in.)	Steering Axis Inclination (deg.)
1990	Daytona	front	①	1³/₁₆P	¼N–¾P	⁵/₁₆P	¹/₁₆	13⁵/₁₆
		rear	—	—	1¼N–¼N	½N	0	—
	LeBaron	front	①	1³/₁₆P	¼N–¾P	⁵/₁₆P	¹/₁₆	13⁵/₁₆
		rear	—	—	1¼N–¼N	½N	0	—
	LeBaron Landau	front	①	1³/₁₆P	¼N–¾P	⁵/₁₆P	¹/₁₆	13⁵/₁₆
		rear	—	—	1¼N–¼N	½N	0	—
	Shadow	front	①	1³/₁₆P	¼N–¾P	⁵/₁₆P	¹/₁₆	13⁵/₁₆
		rear	—	—	1¼N–¼N	½N	0	—
	Sundance	front	①	1³/₁₆P	¼N–¾P	⁵/₁₆P	¹/₁₆	13⁵/₁₆
		rear	—	—	1¼N–¼N	½N	0	—
	Spirit	front	①	1³/₁₆P	¼N–¾P	⁵/₁₆P	¹/₁₆	13⁵/₁₆
		rear	—	—	1¼N–¼N	½N	0	—
	Acclaim	front	①	1³/₁₆P	¼N–¾P	⁵/₁₆P	¹/₁₆	13⁵/₁₆
		rear	—	—	1¼N–¼N	½N	0	—
	TC	front	①	1³/₁₆P	¼N–¾P	⁵/₁₆P	¹/₁₆	13⁵/₁₆
		rear	—	—	1¼N–¼N	½N	0	—
1991	Daytona	front	①	2¾P	¼N–¾P	⁵/₁₆P	¹/₁₆	12½
		rear	—	—	1¼N–¼N	½N	0	—
	LeBaron	front	①	2¾P	¼N–¾P	⁵/₁₆P	¹/₁₆	12½
		rear	—	—	1¼N–¼N	½N	0	—
	LeBaron Landau	front	①	2¾P	¼N–¾P	⁵/₁₆P	¹/₁₆	12½
		rear	—	—	1¼N–¼N	½N	0	—
	Shadow	front	①	2¾P	¼N–¾P	⁵/₁₆P	¹/₁₆	12½
		rear	—	—	1¼N–¼N	½N	0	—
	Sundance	front	①	2¾P	¼N–¾P	⁵/₁₆P	¹/₁₆	12½
		rear	—	—	1¼N–¼N	½N	0	—
	Spirit	front	①	2¾P	¼N–¾P	⁵/₁₆P	¹/₁₆	12½
		rear	—	—	1¼N–¼N	½N	0	—
	Acclaim	front	①	2¾P	¼N–¾P	⁵/₁₆P	¹/₁₆	12½
		rear	—	—	1¼N–¼N	½N	0	—
	TC	front	①	1³/₁₆P	¼N–¾P	⁵/₁₆P	¹/₁₆	13⁵/₁₆
		rear	—	—	1¼N–¼N	½N	0	—
1992-93	Daytona	front	①	2¾P	¼N–¾P	⁵/₁₆P	¹/₁₆	12½
		rear	—	—	1¼N–¼N	½N	0	—
	LeBaron	front	①	2¾P	¼N–¾P	⁵/₁₆P	¹/₁₆	12½
		rear	—	—	1¼N–¼N	½N	0	—
	Shadow	front	①	2¾P	¼N–¾P	⁵/₁₆P	¹/₁₆	12½
		rear	—	—	1¼N–¼N	½N	0	—
	Sundance	front	①	2¾P	¼N–¾P	⁵/₁₆P	¹/₁₆	12½
		rear	—	—	1¼N–¼N	½N	0	—
	Spirit	front	①	2¾P	¼N–¾P	⁵/₁₆P	¹/₁₆	12½
		rear	—	—	1¼N–¼N	½N	0	—
	Acclaim	front	①	2¾P	¼N–¾P	⁵/₁₆P	¹/₁₆	12½
		rear	—	—	1¼N–¼N	½N	0	—

N—Negative   P—Positive   ① Not adjustable; variation between sides should not exceed 1.5°

ENGINE MECHANICAL

NOTE: Disconnecting the negative battery cable on some vehicles may interfere with the functions of the on board computer systems and may require the computers to undergo a relearning process, once the negative battery cable is reconnected.

Engine Assembly

REMOVAL & INSTALLATION

2.2L and 2.5L Engines

1. Disconnect the negative battery cable and all engine ground straps. Relieve the fuel pressure.
2. Mark the hood hinge outline on the hood and remove the hood.
3. Drain the cooling system. Remove the radiator hoses, fan assembly, radiator and intercooler, if equipped.
4. Remove the air cleaner, duct hoses and oil filter.
5. If equipped with air conditioning, unbolt the air conditioning compressor and position it aside. It is not necessary to disconnect the refrigerant lines from the compressor.
6. Remove the power steering pump mounting bolts and position the pump aside, without disconnecting any fluid lines.
7. Label and disconnect all electrical connectors from the engine, alternator and fuel injection system.
8. Disconnect and plug the fuel lines and heater hoses.
9. Disconnect the throttle linkage.
10. Remove the alternator.
11. Raise the vehicle and support safely.
12. Disconnect the exhaust pipe from the manifold. Remove the right inner fender shield.
13. If equipped with a manual transaxle, remove the transaxle.
14. If equipped with an automatic transaxle, perform the following procedu006157UF100
a. Remove the lower cover from the transaxle case.
b. Remove the starter and set it aside.
c. Matchmark the flexplate to the torque converter for installation purposes.
d. Remove the torque converter bolts. Separate the converter from the flexplate. Remove the lower bellhousing bolts.

15. Lower the vehicle and support the transaxle, if still in the vehicle, with a floor jack or equivalent. Attach an engine lifting device to the engine.
16. Remove the remaining bellhousing bolts.

NOTE: If removing the insulator-to-rail screws, first mark the position of the insulator on the side rail to insure proper alignment during reinstallation.

17. Remove the front engine mount nut/bolt and the left insulator through bolt or the insulator bracket to transaxle bolts.
18. Lift and remove the engine from the vehicle.
To install:
19. Lower the engine into the engine compartment. Make sure the lifting device is supporting the full weight of the engine and loosely install all of the mounting bolts until all are threaded. Then tighten all bolts.
20. Remove the lifting device.
21. Raise the vehicle and support safely.
22. If equipped with a manual transaxle, install the transaxle.
23. If equipped with an automatic transaxle, align the mating marks and install the torque converter bolts. Torque bolts to 55 ft. lbs. (75 Nm). Install the torque converter inspection plate and the starter.
24. Connect the exhaust pipe. Lower the vehicle.
25. Install the alternator, power steering pump and air conditioning compressor, if equipped.
26. Connect the fuel lines and heater hoses.
27. Connect the throttle linkage.
28. Connect all remaining electrical connectors.
29. Install the air cleaner assembly and oil filter.
30. Install the radiator, fan assembly, hoses and intercooler, if equipped.
31. Fill the engine with the proper amount of engine oil. Connect the negative battery cable.
32. Refill the cooling system. Start the engine, allow it to reach normal operating temperature. Check for leaks.
33. Check the ignition timing and adjust if necessary.
34. Install the hood aligning the matchmarks made during the removal procedure.

3.0L Engine

1. Disconnect the negative battery cable. Relieve the fuel pressure.
2. Matchmark the hinge-to-hood position and remove the hood.
3. Drain the cooling system. Disconnect and label all engine electrical connections.

4. Remove the coolant hoses from the radiator and engine. Remove the radiator and cooling fan assembly.
5. Remove the air cleaner assembly. Disconnect the fuel lines from the engine. Disconnect the accelerator cable from the throttle body.
6. Raise the vehicle and support safely. Drain the engine oil.
7. Remove the air conditioning compressor mounting bolts, the drive belts and position the compressor aside. Disconnect the exhaust pipe from the exhaust manifold.
8. Remove the transaxle inspection cover, matchmark the converter to the flexplate, and remove the torque converter bolts.
9. Remove the power steering pump mounting bolts and set the pump aside, upright, with the fluid lines attached.
10. Remove the lower bellhousing bolts. Disconnect and label the starter motor wiring and remove the starter motor from the engine.
11. Lower the vehicle. Disconnect and label all electrical connectors from the engine, alternator and fuel injection system, vacuum hoses, and engine ground straps.
12. Support the transaxle with a floor jack or equivalent. Attach an engine lifting device to the engine.
13. Remove the upper transaxle-to-engine bolts.
14. To separate the engine mounts from the insulators, mark the right insulator-to-right frame support and remove the mounting bolts. Remove the front engine mount through bolt. Remove the left insulator through bolt from inside the wheel housing. Remove the insulator bracket-to-transaxle bolts.
15. Lift and remove the engine from the vehicle.
To install:
16. Lower the engine into the engine compartment. Align the engine mounts and install the bolts; do not tighten the bolts until all bolts have been installed. Torque the through bolts to 75 ft. lbs. (102 Nm).
17. Install the upper transaxle-to-engine mounting bolts and torque to 75 ft. lbs. (102 Nm). Remove the engine lifting fixture from the engine.
18. Raise the vehicle and support safely.
19. Align the converter marks, and install the torque converter bolts. Install the transaxle inspection cover.
20. Connect the exhaust pipe to the exhaust manifold. Install the starter motor and connect the wiring.
21. Install the power steering pump and air conditioning compressor. Adjust the drive belt tension, if necessary.
22. Lower the vehicle. Reconnect all

vacuum hoses and electrical connections to the engine.

23. Connect the fuel lines and accelerator cable.

24. Install the radiator and fan assembly. Connect the fan motor wiring. Connect the radiator hoses and refill the cooling system.

25. Refill the engine with the proper oil to the correct level.

26. Connect the engine ground straps. Install the hood aligning the matchmarks made during removal. Connect the negative battery cable.

27. Start and run the engine until normal operating temperature is reached. Check for fluid leaks. Adjust the transaxle linkage, if necessary.

Engine Mounts

REMOVAL & INSTALLATION

2.2L and 2.5L Engines

RIGHT SIDE MOUNT

1. Disconnect the negative battery cable.

2. Matchmark the engine mount to its frame mounting location.

3. Remove the load on the engine motor mounts by carefully supporting the engine and transmission assembly with a floor jack.

4. Remove the through bolt from the insulator assembly and remove the insulator.

5. Installation is the reverse of the removal procedure. Make sure the matchmarks are aligned before tightening bolts.

6. Tighten the lower yoke nut first, then the through bolt nut, then the body mounting bolts.

FRONT MOUNT

1. Disconnect the negative battery cable.

2. Matchmark the engine mount to its frame mounting location.

3. Remove the load on the engine motor mounts by carefully supporting the engine and transmission assembly so it will rotate.

4. Remove the bolt from the insulator and front crossmember bracket.

5. Remove the front engine mount bracket to front crossmember screws and nuts. Remove the insulator assembly.

6. Installation is the reverse of removal procedure.

3.0L Engine

1. Raise the vehicle and support safely, if necessary. Using the proper equipment, support the weight of the engine.

2. Remove all bolts and nuts that attach the mount to the engine strut,

transaxle or body and remove the mount assembly from the vehicle.

3. Remove the through bolt and separate the insulator from the yoke bracket as required.

4. The installation is the reverse of the removal procedure. Make sure the matchmarks are aligned before tightening bolts.

5. Tighten the lower yoke nut first, then the through bolt nut, then the body mounting bolts.

Cylinder Head

REMOVAL & INSTALLATION

2.2L and 2.5L Except DOHC Engines

1. Disconnect the negative battery cable from the battery and cylinder head. Relieve the fuel pressure. Drain the cooling system. Remove the dipstick bracket nut from the thermostat housing and remove the ignition coil from the thermostat housing if installed there.

2. Remove the air cleaner assembly. Remove the upper radiator hose and disconnect the heater hoses.

3. Disconnect and label the vacuum lines, hoses and wiring connectors from the manifold(s), throttle body and from the cylinder head.

4. Disconnect all linkages and the fuel line from the throttle body. Unbolt the cable bracket. Remove the ground strap attaching screw from the firewall.

5. If equipped with air conditioning, remove the air conditioning compressor from the mounting bracket and position aside. The factory recommends that the compressor mounting bracket be removed prior to removing the cylinder head, however, if the upper compressor mounting bolts that thread into the cylinder head are removed from the compressor mounting bracket, in most cases, the cylinder head can be removed with the bracket in place.

If the bracket is to be removed, perform the following procedure:

a. Remove the alternator pivot bolt and remove the alternator from the bracket. Turn the alternator so the wire connections are facing up and disconnect the harness connectors from the rear of the alternator.

b. Remove the air conditioning compressor belt idler.

c. Remove the right engine mount yoke screw securing engine mount support strut to the engine.

d. Remove the 5 side mounting bolts retaining the bracket to the front of the engine.

e. Remove the front mounting nut. Remove the front bolt and strut and rotate the solid mount bracket away from the engine. Slide the bracket on the stud until free of the mounting studs and remove from the engine.

6. Remove the upper timing belt cover. Raise the vehicle and support safely. Disconnect the exhaust pipe from the exhaust manifold. Disconnect the water hose and oil drain from the turbocharger, if equipped.

7. Rotate the engine by hand until the timing marks align. The No. 1 piston should be at TDC of its compression stroke. Lower the vehicle.

8. With the timing marks aligned, remove the camshaft sprocket. The camshaft sprocket can be suspended to keep the timing intact. Remove the spark plug wires from the spark plugs.

9. Remove the valve cover and curtain. Remove the cylinder head bolts and washers, starting from the outside and working inward.

10. Remove the cylinder head from the engine.

11. Clean the cylinder head gasket mating surfaces. Clean and inspect all cylinder head bolt threads for necking. If necking has occured, the threads on the bolts will not be uniform and straight when help up against a straightedge. It is recommended that all head bolts be replaced with new pri-

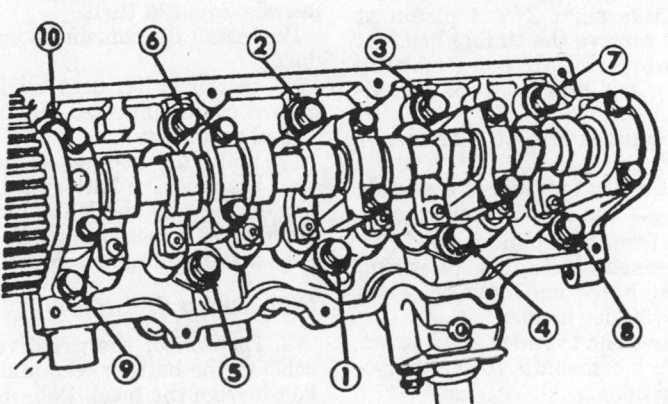

Cylinder head bolt torque sequence—2.2L and 2.5L SOHC engines

or to installation of the cylinder head.

To install:

NOTE: Head bolt diameter is 11mm. These bolts are identified with the number "11" on the head of the bolt. The 10mm bolts used on previous vehicles will thread into an 11mm bolt hole, but will permanently damage the cylinder block. Make sure the correct bolts are used when replacing head bolts.

12. Using new gaskets and seals, install the head to the engine.

13. Using new head bolts of the correct diameter, assembled with the old washers, torque the cylinder head bolts in sequence to 45 ft. lbs. (61 Nm). Repeating the sequence, torque the bolts to 65 ft. lbs. (88 Nm). With the bolts at 65 ft. lbs., turn each bolt an additional ¼ turn.

14. Install the timing belt and covers. Install the solid mount compressor bracket, if removed.

15. Install the upper air conditioning compressor mounting bracket bolts, if removed. Install the air conditioning compressor to the mounting bracket and secure with the mounting nuts.

16. Raise and safely support the vehicle. Reconnect the exhaust pipe to the manifold using a new gasket as required.

17. Connect the remaining hoses, linkage and electrical harness connectors disconnected during the removal procedure.

18. Refill the cooling system. Connect the negative battery cable. Start the engine and check for leaks using the DRB II to activate the fuel pump. Adjust the timing, as required.

2.2L DOHC Engine

TC

1. Disconnect the negative battery cable and unbolt it from the head. Relieve the fuel pressure. Drain the cooling system.

2. Remove the timing belt covers/. Rotate the engine by hand until the timing marks align (No. 1 piston at TDC) and remove the timing belt.

3. Remove the air conditioning compressor and bracket from the cylinder head.

4. Disconnect the turbocharger coolant lines.

5. Remove the air cleaner assembly and separate the intake and exhaust manifolds from the cylinder head.

6. Disconnect and label all wiring connectors, hoses and ignition wires from the cylinder head.

7. Remove the cylinder head cover. Remove both camshafts to expose cylinder head bolts.

8. Remove the cylinder head bolts

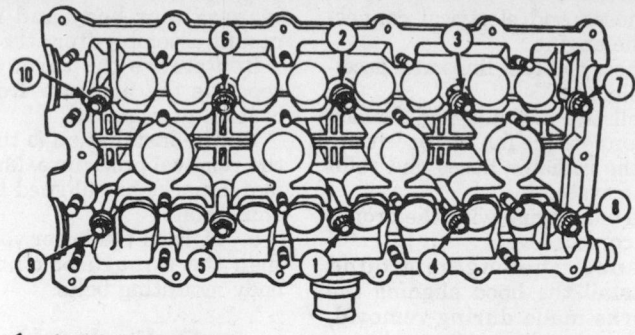

⟸ TIMING BELT END

Cylinder head bolt torque sequence—2.2L DOHC engine—TC

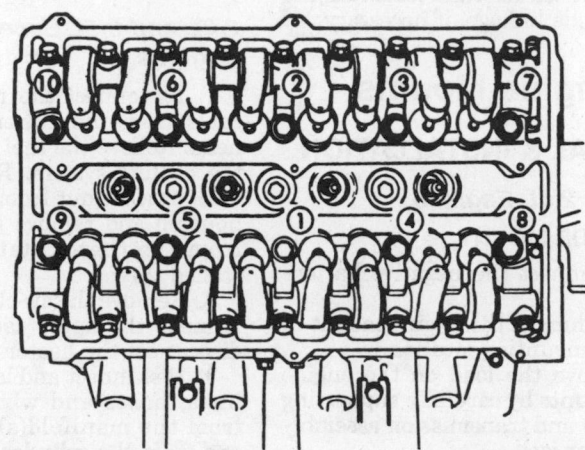

Cylinder head bolt torque sequence—2.2L Turbo III engine

and washers, starting from the outside and working inward.

9. Remove the cylinder head and gasket from the engine.

10. Clean the cylinder head gasket mating surfaces.

To install:

11. Using new gaskets and seals, install the head to the engine. Using new head bolts assembled with the old washers, torque the cylinder head bolts in sequence, to 32 ft. lbs. (44 Nm). Repeating the sequence, torque the bolts to 50 ft. lbs. (69 Nm). Repeating the sequence a third time, torque the bolts to 65 ft. lbs. (88 Nm). With the bolts at 65 ft. lbs., tighten each bolt an additional ¼ turn.

12. Install the camshafts and timing belt.

13. Install or connect all items removed or disconnected during the removal procedure.

14. Refill the cooling system. Connect the negative battery cable. Start the engine and check for leaks using the DRB II to activate the fuel pump. Adjust the timing as required.

2.2L Turbo III Engine

1. Disconnect the negative battery cable at the battery terminal and unbolt it from the head. Relieve the fuel pressure. Drain the cooling system.

2. Remove the air cleaner assembly with all ductwork.

3. Remove the timing belt covers. Rotate the engine by hand until the timing marks align (No. 1 piston at TDC). Remove the timing belt.

4. Remove the air conditioning compressor and bracket from the cylinder head.

5. Disconnect the turbocharger coolant lines and separate the intake and exhaust manifolds from the cylinder head.

6. Remove the ignition cable cover and valve covers. Disconnect and label all wiring connectors, hoses and ignition wires from the cylinder head.

7. Remove the cylinder head and gasket from the engine.

8. Clean the cylinder head gasket mating surfaces. Clean and inspect all cylinder head bolt threads for necking. If necking has occured, the threads on the bolts will not be uniform or straight when help up against a straight edge, and will require replacement. It is recommended that all head bolts be replaced with new prior to installation of the cylinder head.

To install:

NOTE: The head gasket used on the Turbo III engine is unique to that engine. Make sure the replacement head gasket is identical to the original gasket before installing.

Head bolt diameter is 11mm and the head bolts are unique to this engine. These bolts are identified with the number 11 on the head of the bolt and are not interchangeable with other engines. Make sure the correct head bolts are used when replacing head bolts.

9. Using new gaskets and seals, install the head to the engine. Using new head bolts assembled with the old washers, torque the cylinder head bolts in sequence, to 45 ft. lbs. (61 Nm). Repeating the sequence, torque the bolts to 65 ft. lbs. (88 Nm). With the bolts at 65 ft. lbs., turn each bolt an additional ¼ turn. Final torque must be over 90 ft. lbs. (122 Nm).

10. Install the timing belt and all related items.

11. Install the intake and exhaust manifolds.

12. Install the air conditioning compressor and bracket the cylinder head.

13. Install the valve covers and torque the bolts to 105 inch lbs. (12 Nm).

14. Install the air cleaner assembly and all ductwork.

15. Refill the cooling system. Connect the negative battery cable. Start the engine and check for leaks.

3.0L Engine

1. Disconnect the negative battery cable. Relieve the fuel pressure. Drain the cooling system.

2. Remove the drive belt and the air conditioning compressor from its mount and support it aside. Using a ½ in. drive breaker bar, insert it into the square hole of the serpentine drive belt tensioner, rotate it counterclockwise to reduce the belt tension and remove the belt. Remove the alternator and power steering pump from the brackets and move them aside.

3. Raise the vehicle and support safely. Remove the right front wheel assembly and the right inner splash shield.

4. Remove the crankshaft pulleys and the torsional damper.

5. Lower the vehicle. Using a floor jack and a block of wood positioned under the oil pan, raise the engine slightly. Remove the engine mount bracket from the timing cover end of the engine and the timing belt covers.

6. To remove the timing belt, perform the following procedures:

a. Rotate the crankshaft to position the No. 1 cylinder on the TDC of its compression stroke; the crankshaft sprocket timing mark should align with the oil pan timing indicator and the camshaft sprockets timing marks (triangles) should align

with the rear timing belt covers timing marks.

b. Mark the timing belt in the direction of rotation for reinstallation purposes.

c. Loosen the timing belt tensioner and remove the timing belt.

NOTE: When removing the timing belt from the camshaft sprocket, make sure the belt does not slip off the other camshaft sprocket. Support the belt so it can not slip off the crankshaft sprocket and opposite side camshaft sprocket.

7. Remove the air cleaner assembly. Label and disconnect the spark plug wires and the vacuum hoses.

8. Remove the valve cover.

9. Install auto lash adjuster retainer tools MD998443 or equivalent, on the rocker arms.

10. If removing the front cylinder head, matchmark the distributor rotor-to-distributor housing and the housing-to-distributor extension locations. Remove the distributor and the distributor extension.

11. Remove the camshaft bearing assembly to cylinder head bolts (do not remove the bolts from the assembly). Remove the rocker arms, rocker shafts and bearing caps as an assembly, as required. Remove the camshafts from the cylinder head and inspect them for damage, if necessary.

12. Remove the intake manifold assembly.

13. Remove the exhaust manifold.

14. Remove the cylinder head bolts, starting from the outside and working inward. Remove the cylinder head from the engine.

15. Clean the gasket mounting surfaces and check the heads for warpage; the maximum warpage allowed is 0.008 in. (0.20mm).

To install:

16. Install the new cylinder head gaskets over the dowels on the engine block.

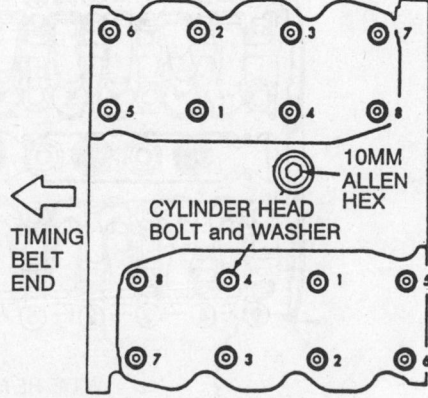

Cylinder head bolt torque sequence— 3.0L engine

17. Install the cylinder heads on the engine and torque the cylinder head bolts in sequence using 3 even steps to 70 ft. lbs. (95 Nm) on 1989–91 engines or 80 ft. lbs. (108 Nm) on 1992–93 engines.

18. Install or connect all items removed or disconnected during the removal procedure.

19. When installing the timing belt over the camshaft sprocket, use care not to allow the belt to slip off the opposite camshaft sprocket.

20. Make sure the timing belt is installed on the camshaft sprocket in the same position as when removed.

21. Refill the cooling system. Connect the negative battery cable. Start the engine and check for leaks using the DRB II to activate the fuel pump. Adjust the timing as required.

Valve Lifters

REMOVAL & INSTALLATION

2.2L and 2.5L Engines Except DOHC

1. Disconnect the negative battery cable.

2. Remove the valve cover and curtain. If removing all lifters, remove the camshaft and rocker arms.

3. If only removing 1 lifter, rotate the crankshaft until the low point of the desired cam lobe is contacting the rocker arm.

4. Using the special valve spring compressor tool 4682 or equivalent, depress the valve spring without dislodging the keepers and slide the rocker arm out.

5. Remove the valve lifter(s) from the bore(s).

6. The installation is the reverse of the removal procedure. Lubricate the lifter(s) and their bore(s) with clean engine oil prior to installation.

2.2L Turbo III Engine

1. Disconnect the negative battery cable.

2. Remove the valve cover(s).

3. Remove the rocker arm shaft(s).

4. Slide the rocker arm(s) off the shaft and remove the lash adjuster from the rocker arm.

5. The installation is the reverse of the removal procedure.

6. Connect the negative battery cable.

3.0L Engine

1. Disconnect the negative battery cable. Remove the air cleaner assembly.

2. Remove the valve cover.

3. Using the valve lifter retainer tools MD998443 or equivalent, install

them on the rocker arms to keep the lifters from falling out.

4. On the right side cylinder head, remove the distributor extension.

5. Have a helper hold the rear end of the camshaft down. If the rear of the camshaft cannot be held down, the belt will dislodge and the valve timing will be lost. Loosen the camshaft cap bolts but do not remove them from the caps. Remove the caps, arms, shafts and bolts all as an assembly.

6. Remove the lifter(s) from the rocker arm(s).

7. Lubricate the lifter(s) and their bore(s) with clean engine oil.

To install:

8. Install the lifter into the rocker arms and install the retaining tool.

9. Install the camshaft bearing caps, arms, shafts and bolts all as an assembly and secure.

10. Install the distributor extension, if removed.

11. Remove the valve lifter retaining tools and install the valve cover, using a new gasket.

12. Reconnect the negative battery cable, start the engine and check for leaks.

Valve Lash

ADJUSTMENT

2.2L DOHC Engine

TC

1. Disconnect the negative battery cable.

2. Remove the valve cover.

3. Check the clearance of all valves by inserting a feeler gauge between the camshaft and adjusting disc when the cam lobe is pointing straight up. Record all measurements.

4. The specifications are:
   Intake – 0.012 in. (0.30mm)
   Exhaust – 0.016 in. (0.40mm)

5. If not at specifications, remove the camshaft(s) and use the appropriate adjusting discs to bring clearance to specification.

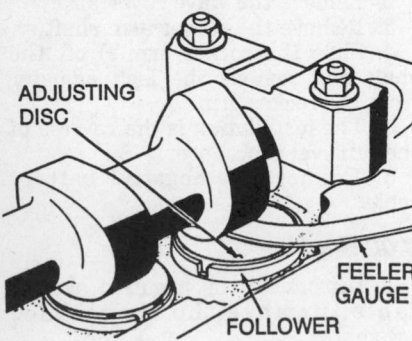

Checking valve clearance –
2.2L DOHC engine

Rocker Arms/Shafts

REMOVAL & INSTALLATION

2.2L and 2.5L Engines Except Turbo III

1. Disconnect the negative battery cable.

2. Remove the valve cover.

3. Rotate the crankshaft until the low point of the desired cam lobe is contacting the rocker arm.

4. Using the special valve spring compressor tool or equivalent, depress the valve spring without dislodging the keepers and slide the rocker arm out.

5. The installation is the reverse of the removal procedure.

2.2L Turbo III Engine

1. Disconnect the negative battery cable.

2. Remove the valve cover(s).

3. Remove the rocker arm retaining bolts in the proper removal sequence.

4. Remove the rocker shaft assembly from the cylinder head.

5. Keep all parts in order and disassemble as required. Inspect the lash adjusters carefully.

To install:

6. Lubricate and assemble the rocker arms to the shaft.

7. Make sure the lash adjusters are at least partially full of oil. This is indicated by little or no plunger travel when depressing. Install to the rocker arms.

8. Install the assembly and tighten the bolts in the proper sequence to 18 ft. lbs. (24 Nm).

9. Install the valve cover(s).

10. Connect the negative battery cable.

3.0L Engine

1. Disconnect the negative battery cable. Remove the air cleaner assembly.

2. Remove the valve cover.

3. Install auto lash adjuster retainer tools MD998443 or equivalent, on the rocker arms to keep the lash adjusters from falling out.

4. On the right side cylinder head, remove the distributor extension.

5. Have a helper hold the rear end of the camshaft down. If the rear of

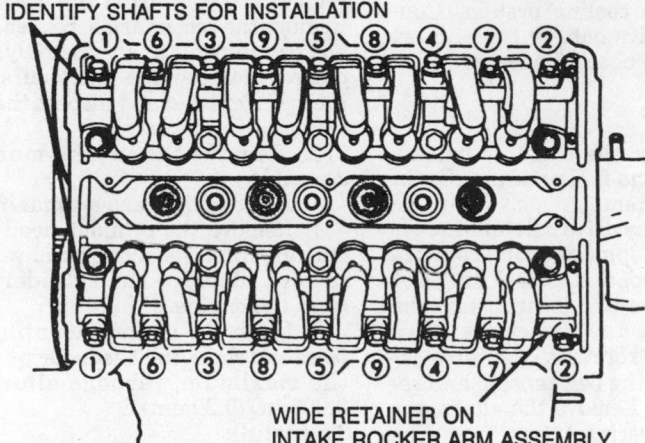

IDENTIFY SHAFTS FOR INSTALLATION

WIDE RETAINER ON
INTAKE ROCKER ARM ASSEMBLY

Rocker shaft retaining bolt removal sequence – 2.2L Turbo III engine

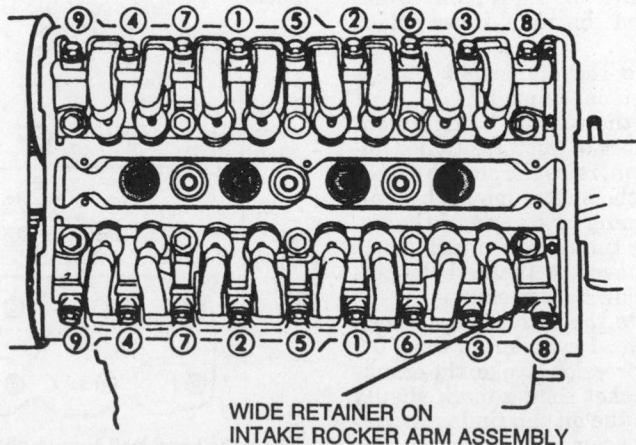

WIDE RETAINER ON
INTAKE ROCKER ARM ASSEMBLY

Rocker shaft retaining bolt installation sequence – 2.2L Turbo III engine

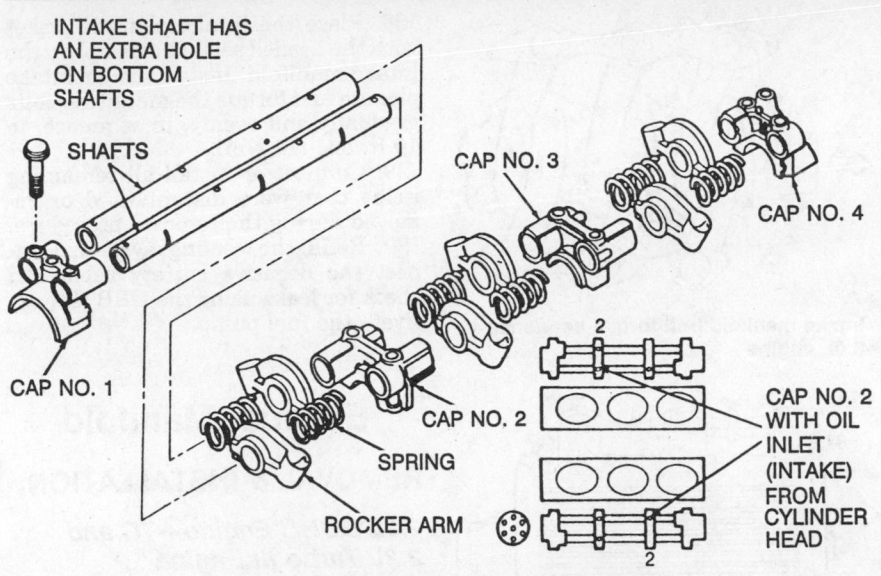

INTAKE SHAFT HAS AN EXTRA HOLE ON BOTTOM SHAFTS

SHAFTS

CAP NO. 3

CAP NO. 4

CAP NO. 1

CAP NO. 2

SPRING

ROCKER ARM

CAP NO. 2 WITH OIL INLET (INTAKE) FROM CYLINDER HEAD

Rocker shafts/arms assembly—3.0L engine

OIL HOLE (TO IDENTIFY INLET FROM OUTLET SHAFT)

INLET SIDE

EXHAUST SIDE

OIL IS TRANSFERRED TO THE EXHAUST SHAFT THROUGH THE CAM BEARING CAP

Identifying rocker shafts— 3.0L engine

the camshaft cannot be held down, the belt will dislodge and the valve timing will be lost. Loosen the camshaft cap bolts but do not remove them from the caps. Remove the caps, arms, shafts and bolts all as an assembly.

6. Disassemble the unit keeping all parts in order and repair as required.

7. When assembling, apply a drop of sealant to the rear edge of the rear cap.

To install:

8. Install the caps, arms and shafts assembly to the engine. Torque the cap bolts first to 85 inch lbs. (19 Nm), then to 180 inch lbs. (19 Nm) in the following order: No. 3 cap, No. 2 cap, No. 1 cap, No. 4 cap.

9. Remove the hydraulic lash adjuster retainer tools and install the rocker covers. Torque the cover retainer bolts to 88 inch lbs. (10 Nm).

10. Install the air cleaner assembly, connect the negative battery cable and check for fluid leaks.

Intake Manifold

REMOVAL & INSTALLATION

2.2L DOHC Engine—TC

1. Disconnect the negative battery cable. Relieve the fuel system pressure.

2. Drain the coolant system.

3. Using the proper equipment, support the weight of the engine. Remove the front engine mount through bolt and rotate the top of the engine away from the cowl.

4. Remove the upper radiator hose, bypass hose and thermostat housing.

5. Disconnect and plug the fuel hoses from the fuel tubes.

6. Remove the air cleaner assembly and all duct work.

7. Disconnect the linkage from the throttle body and disconnect the throttle body support bracket from the engine.

8. Label and disconnect all vacuum hoses from the intake manifold.

9. Disconnect the Throttle Position Sensor (TPS) and Automatic Idle Speed (AIS) motor wiring connectors from the throttle body.

10. Disconnect wiring from the fuel injectors, charge temperature, coolant temperature and knock sensors.

11. Remove the air conditioning compressor bracket to intake manifold attaching bolt.

12. Remove the intake manifold strut bolt.

13. Remove the intake manifold attaching nuts and remove the manifold from the cylinder head.

14. Discard the intake manifold gasket. Clean the mating surfaces and inspect for damage and distortion. The mating surfaces must be flat within

0.006 in. (0.15mm) per foot of manifold length.

To install:

15. Install a new intake manifold gasket. Do not use sealer of any kind.

16. Position the manifold on the studs and install the retaining nuts. Starting at the center and working outwards, torque the nuts gradually and evenly to 17 ft. lbs. (23 Nm).

17. Install the strut bolt and torque to 21 ft. lbs. (29 Nm). Install the air conditioning compressor bracket bolt and torque to 21 ft. lbs. (29 Nm).

18. Install the front engine mount through bolt.

19. Connect all hoses and wiring that was disconnected during the removal procedure.

20. Install the throttle body bracket and connect the linkage.

21. Install the upper radiator hose, bypass hose and thermostat housing.

22. Refill the cooling system. Connect the negative battery cable. Start the engine and check for leaks using the DRB II to activate the fuel pump.

2.2L Turbo III Engine

1. Disconnect the negative battery cable. Relieve the fuel system pressure. Drain the cooling system.

2. Remove the fresh air duct from the air filter housing. Remove the inlet hose from the intercooler.

3. Remove the radiator hose from the thermostat housing.

4. Remove the DIS ignition coil from the intake manifold.

5. Disconnect the throttle and speed control cables from the throttle body.

6. Disconnect the intercooler-to-throttle body outlet hose. Disconnect the vacuum hoses from the throttle body and carefully remove the harness.

7. Disconnect the AIS motor and TPS wiring connectors.

8. Remove the PCV breather/separator box and vacuum harness assembly. Remove the brake booster hose, vacuum vapor harness and fuel pressure regulator from the intake manifold.

9. Disconnect the fuel injector wiring harness and charge temperature sensor.

10. Wrap shop towels around the fittings and disconnect the fuel supply and return fuel lines.

11. Remove the intake manifold retaining bolts and remove the manifold from the cylinder head.

To install:

12. Inspect the manifold for damage of any kind. Thoroughly clean and dry the mating surfaces.

13. Install the new gasket and manifold to the cylinder head. Starting at the center and working outwards,

torque the bolts gradually and evenly to 17 ft. lbs. (23 Nm).

14. Lubricate the quick connect fuel fittings with oil and connect to the chassis tubes. Ensure they are locked by pulling on them.

15. Install the PCV breather/separator box and vacuum harness assembly. Connect the brake booster hose, vacuum vapor harness and fuel pressure regulator to the intake manifold.

16. Connect the fuel injector wiring harness and charge temperature sensor. Connect the AIS motor and TPS wiring connectors.

17. Connect the vacuum hoses from the throttle body and carefully remove the harness. Connect the intercooler-to-throttle body outlet hose.

18. Connect the throttle and speed control cables from the throttle body.

19. Install the DIS ignition coil to the intake manifold.

20. Connect the radiator hose to the thermostat housing.

21. Install the inlet hose to the intercooler. Install the fresh air duct to the air filter housing.

22. Refill and bleed the cooling system. Connect the negative battery cable. Start the engine and check for leaks.

3.0L Engine

1. Disconnect the negative battery cable. Relieve the fuel system pressure.

2. Drain the cooling system.

3. Remove the throttle body to air cleaner hose.

4. Remove the throttle body and transaxle kickdown linkage.

5. Remove the AIS motor and TPS wiring connectors from the throttle body.

6. Remove and label the vacuum hose harness from the throttle body.

7. Remove the PCV and brake booster hoses from the intake plenum. Remove the EGR tube flange from the air intake plenum, if equipped.

8. Disconnect and label the charge and temperature sensor wiring at the intake manifold.

9. Remove the vacuum connections from the air intake plenum vacuum connector.

10. Remove the fuel hoses from the fuel rail.

11. Remove the air intake plenum mounting bolts and remove the plenum.

12. Remove the vacuum hoses from the fuel rail and pressure regulator.

13. Disconnect the fuel injector wiring harness from the engine wiring harness.

14. Remove the fuel pressure regulator mounting bolts and remove the regulator from the fuel rail.

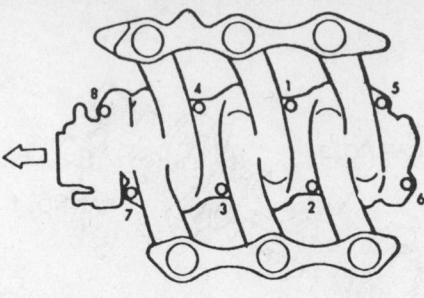

Intake manifold bolt torque sequence—3.0L engine

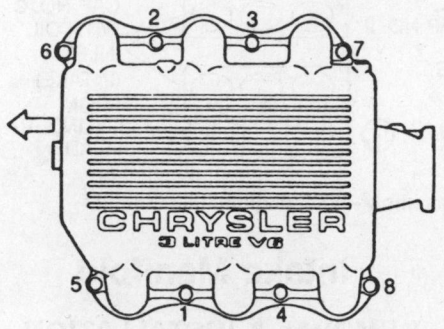

Air intake plenum bolt torque sequence—3.0L engine

15. Remove the fuel rail mounting bolts and remove the fuel rail from the intake manifold.

16. Separate the radiator hose from the thermostat housing and heater hoses from the heater pipe.

17. Remove the intake manifold mounting bolts and remove the manifold from the engine.

18. Clean the gasket mounting surfaces on the engine and intake manifold.

To install:

19. Using new gaskets, position the intake manifold on the engine and install the mounting nuts and washers.

20. Torque the mounting nuts gradually and evenly, in sequence, to 15 ft. lbs. (20 Nm).

21. Make sure the injector holes are clean. Lubricate the injector O-rings with a drop of clean engine oil and install the injector assembly onto the engine.

22. Install and torque the fuel rail mounting bolts to 10 ft. lbs. (14 Nm).

23. Install the fuel pressure regulator onto the fuel rail.

24. Install the fuel supply and return tube and the vacuum crossover hold-down bolt.

25. Connect the fuel injection wiring harness to the engine wiring harness.

26. Connect the vacuum harness to the fuel pressure regulator and fuel rail assembly.

27. Remove the cover from the lower intake manifold and clean the mating surface.

28. Place the intake plenum gasket with the beaded sealant side up, on the intake manifold. Install the air intake plenum and torque the mounting bolts gradually and evenly, in sequence, to 10 ft. lbs. (14 Nm).

29. Connect or install all remaining items that were disconnected or removed during the removal procedure.

30. Refill the cooling system. Connect the negative battery cable and check for leaks using the DRB II to activate the fuel pump.

Exhaust Manifold

REMOVAL & INSTALLATION

2.2L DOHC Engine—TC and 2.2L Turbo III Engine

1. Disconnect the negative battery cable.

2. Remove the turbocharger assembly.

3. Remove the coolant tube from the cylinder head.

4. Remove the exhaust manifold retaining nuts and remove the manifold.

4. Clean the gasket mounting surfaces. Inspect the manifolds for cracks, flatness and/or damage.

To install:

5. Install a new exhaust manifold gasket. Do not use sealer of any kind.

6. Position the manifold on the studs and install the retaining nuts. Starting at the center and working outwards, torque the nuts gradually and evenly to 17 ft. lbs. (23 Nm).

7. Using a new gasket, connect the coolant tube to the cylinder head.

8. Install the turbocharger assembly.

9. Start the engine and check for exhaust leaks.

3.0L Engine

1. Disconnect the negative battery cable. Raise the vehicle and safely support.

2. Disconnect the exhaust pipe from the rear exhaust manifold, at the articulated joint.

3. Disconnect the EGR tube from the rear manifold and disconnect the oxygen sensor wire.

4. Remove the crossover pipe to manifold bolts.

5. Remove the rear manifold to cylinder head nuts and the manifold.

6. Lower the vehicle and remove the heat shield from the manifold.

7. Remove the front manifold to cylinder head nuts and remove the manifold.

8. Clean the gasket mounting surfaces. Inspect the manifolds for cracks, flatness and/or damage.

To install:

9. When installing, the numbers 1–3–5 on the gaskets are used with the rear cylinders and 2–4–6 are on the gasket for the front cylinders. Torque the manifold to cylinder head nuts to 14 ft. lbs. (19 Nm).

10. Install the crossover pipe to the manifold.

11. Connect the EGR tube and oxygen sensor wire.

12. Connect the exhaust pipe to the rear exhaust manifold, at the articulated joint.

13. Connect the negative battery cable and check the manifolds for leaks.

Combination Manifold

REMOVAL & INSTALLATION

2.2L and 2.5L Engines Except DOHC

WITHOUT TURBOCHARGER

NOTE: On some vehicles, some of the manifold attaching bolts are not accessible or too heavily sealed from the factory and cannot be removed on the vehicle. Head removal would be necessary in these situations.

1. Disconnect the negative battery cable.

2. Relieve the fuel system pressure.

3. Drain the cooling system.

4. Remove the air cleaner and disconnect all vacuum lines, electrical wiring and fuel lines from the throttle body.

5. Disconnect the throttle linkage.

6. Loosen the power steering pump and remove the drive belt.

7. Remove the power brake vacuum hose from the intake manifold.

8. Remove the water hoses from the water crossover.

9. Raise and safely support the vehicle. Disconnect the exhaust pipe from the exhaust manifold.

10. Remove the power steering pump

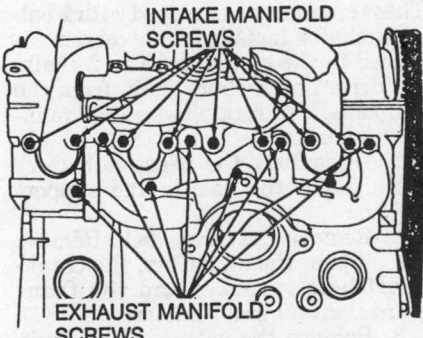

INTAKE MANIFOLD SCREWS

EXHAUST MANIFOLD SCREWS

Combination manifold attaching nuts and bolts—2.2L and 2.5L non-turbocharged engines

from its mounting bracket and set it aside.

11. Remove the intake manifold support bracket, if equipped.

12. Remove the EGR tube, if equipped.

13. Remove the intake manifold bolts.

14. Lower the vehicle.

15. Remove the intake manifold.

16. Remove the exhaust manifold retainer nuts.

17. Remove the exhaust manifold.

To install:

18. Install a new combination manifold gasket. Coat steel gasket lightly with gasket sealer on the manifold side. Do not coat a compression gasket with sealer.

19. Install the manifold assembly. Starting from the middle and working outwards, install the mounting nuts and torque to 13–17 ft. lbs. (18–23 Nm). Install the heat cowl to the exhaust manifold.

20. Install the intake manifold. Starting from the middle and working outward, torque the bolts to 17 ft. lbs. (23 Nm.) .

21. Install the EGR tube, if removed.

22. Install the intake support bracket, if equipped.

23. Install the power steering pump.

24. Raise the vehicle and support safely. Install the exhaust pipe to the exhaust manifold.

25. Install the water hoses to the water crossover.

26. Install the power brake vacuum hose to the intake manifold.

27. Connect the throttle linkage.

28. Install all vacuum lines, electrical wiring and fuel lines to the carburetor or throttle body.

29. Install the air cleaner assembly.

30. Refill the cooling system.

31. Connect the negative battery cable and check the manifolds for leaks.

WITH TURBOCHARGER

NOTE: On some vehicles, some of the manifold attaching bolts are not accessible or too heavily sealed from the factory and cannot be removed from the vehicle. Head removal would be necessary in these situations.

1. Disconnect the negative battery cable. Drain the cooling system. Raise and safely support the vehicle.

2. Disconnect the exhaust pipe at the articulated joint. Disconnect the oxygen sensor at the electrical connection.

3. Remove the turbocharger to engine support bracket.

4. Loosen the oil drain back tube connector hose clamps. Move the tube down on the engine block fitting.

5. Disconnect the turbocharger coolant inlet tube from the engine

block and disconnect the tube support bracket.

6. Remove the air cleaner assembly, including the throttle body adaptor, hose and air cleaner box with support bracket.

7. Disconnect the accelerator linkage, injector wiring harness, throttle body electrical connector and vacuum hoses.

8. Remove the bracket to intake manifold screws and the bracket to heat shield retainer clips. remove the heat shield.

9. Remove the fuel return and supply lines at the fuel rail. Cover hose connections with a rag to absorb any fuel spray caused by residual pressure in the lines prior to disconnecting.

10. Remove the fuel rail retaining bolts. Remove the fuel rail from the vehicle, with injectors attached, by pulling straight upward.

11. Disconnect the turbocharger oil feed line at the oil sending unit tee fitting. Remove the turbocharger from the engine.

12. Remove the 8 intake manifold retainer screws and washers and remove the intake manifold.

13. Remove the 8 exhaust manifold retainer nuts and remove the exhaust manifold.

To install:

14. Place a new 2-sided Grafoil type intake/exhaust manifold gasket; do not use sealant.

15. Position the exhaust manifold on the cylinder head. Apply anti-seize compound to the stud threads, install and torque the retaining nuts, starting at center and progressing outward in both directions, to 17 ft. lbs. (23 Nm). Repeat this procedure until all nuts are at 17 ft. lbs. (23 Nm).

16. Position the intake manifold on the cylinder head. Install and torque the retaining screws, starting at center and progressing outward in both directions, to 19 ft. lbs. (26 Nm). Repeat this procedure until all screws are at 19 ft. lbs. (26 Nm).

17. Connect the turbocharger outlet to the intake manifold inlet tube. Position the turbocharger on the exhaust manifold. Apply anti-seize compound to threads and torque the retainer nuts to 30 ft. lbs. (41 Nm). Torque the connector tube clamps to 30 inch lbs. (3 Nm).

18. Install the cowl mounted heat shield.

19. Install the tube support bracket to the cylinder head.

20. Install the throttle body air horn into the turbocharger inlet tube. Install and torque the throttle body to intake manifold screws to 21 ft. lbs. (28 Nm). Torque the tube clamp to 30 inch lbs.

21. Reconnect the turbocharger oil

feed line to the oil sending unit tee fitting and bearing housing, if disconnected. Torque the tube nuts to 10 ft. lbs. (14 Nm).

22. Install the air cleaner assembly. Connect the vacuum lines and accelerator cables.

23. Install the fuel rail and injectors to the engine and secure with the mounting bolts. Connect the fuel rail supply and return lines.

24. Install the air shield to bracket clips, if not already done.

25. Connect the turbocharger inlet coolant tube to the engine block. Torque the tube nut to 30 ft. lbs. (41 Nm). Install the tube support bracket.

26. Install the turbocharger housing-to-engine block support bracket and the screws hand tight. Torque the block screw 1st to 40 ft. lbs. (54 Nm). Torque the screw to the turbocharger housing to 20 ft. lbs. (27 Nm).

27. Reposition the drain back hose connector and tighten the hose clamps. Reconnect the exhaust pipe.

28. Refill the cooling system.

29. Connect the negative battery cable and check the manifolds for leaks.

Turbocharger

REMOVAL & INSTALLATION

NOTE: On some vehicles, some of the turbocharger to exhaust manifold nuts are not accessible enough to loosen and cannot be removed from the vehicle. Head removal would be necessary in these situations.

1. Disconnect negative battery cable.

2. From above the vehicle, perform the following removal procedures:

   a. Remove the front engine mount through bolt and rotate the top of the engine forward away from the cowl.

   b. Separate the coolant line from the water box and turbocharger housing.

   c. Separate the oil feed line from the turbocharger housing.

   d. Remove the waste gate rod-to-gate retainer clip. Remove the 3 upper and 1 lower driver's side nuts retaining the turbocharger to the manifold.

   e. Disconnect the vacuum lines at the electrical lead from the oxygen sensor.

3. Raise and safely support the vehicle.

4. Remove the right front wheel and tire assembly.

5. Remove the right halfshaft assembly.

6. Remove the turbocharger to block support bracket. Separate the oil

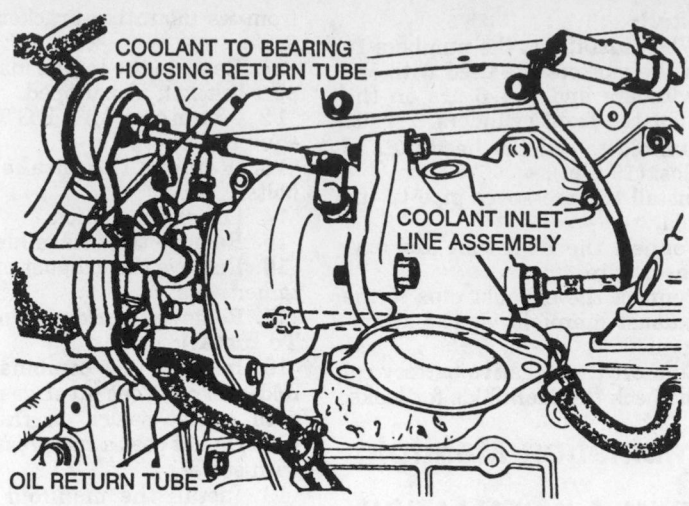

COOLANT TO BEARING HOUSING RETURN TUBE

COOLANT INLET LINE ASSEMBLY

OIL RETURN TUBE

Coolant and oil tube connections on turbo—2.2L Turbo III engine; others similar

drain back tube fitting from the turbocharger housing and remove the fitting and hose.

7. Remove the remaining turbocharger to manifold retaining nuts.

8. Disconnect the articulated exhaust pipe joint from the turbocharger housing.

9. Remove the lower coolant line and the turbocharger inlet fitting.

10. Lift the turbocharger off the manifold mounting studs and lower assembly from the vehicle.

To install:

NOTE: Before installing the turbocharger assembly to the engine, be sure it is first charged with oil. Failure to do this may cause damage to the turbocharger assembly.

11. Position the turbocharger on the exhaust manifold. Apply an anti-seize compound, Loctite® 771–64 or equivalent, to the threads and torque the retaining nuts to 40 ft. lbs. (54 Nm). Connect the vacuum hose.

12. Install the lower coolant line. Install the oil drain back tube into the turbocharger housing with new gasket in place.

13. Install and tighten turbocharger to block support bracket finger tight. First, tighten the block screw to 40 ft. lbs. (54 Nm), then tighten screw to turbocharger housing to 20 ft. lbs. (27 Nm).

14. Reposition exhaust pipe to the manifold and secure with the retainer bolts. Torque the shouldered bolts 20 ft. lbs. (28 Nm).

15. Install the right driveshaft and the wheel and tire assembly to the vehicle.

16. Lower the vehicle and perform the following installation procedures:

   a. Install the 3 turbocharger to

manifold retainer nuts torqueing to 40 ft. lbs. (54 Nm).

   b. Reconnect the oxygen sensor lead and the vacuum harness if still disconnected.

   c. Attach the oil feed line to the turbocharger bearing housing tightening fitting to 10 ft. lbs. (14 Nm).

   d. Apply thread sealant to the water box and turbocharger return coolant line end fittings. Install the coolant line fittings and tighten to 30 ft. lbs. (41 Nm).

   e. Align the front engine mount in the crossmember bracket.

   f. Install the through bolt and tighten to 40 ft. lbs. (54 Nm).

17. Refill the cooling system. Connect the negative battery cable and check the turbocharger for proper operation.

Timing Chain Front Cover

REMOVAL & INSTALLATION

2.2L Turbo III and 2.5L Engines

These engines are equipped with 2 balance shafts installed in a carrier attached to the crankcase. The 2 shafts are driven by a short chain from the crankshaft, to rotate twice the crankshaft speed.

1. Disconnect the negative battery cable. Raise the vehicle and support safely.

2. Remove the timing belt. Remove the oil pan, the oil pickup, the crankshaft belt sprocket and the front crankshaft oil seal retainer.

3. Remove the balance shaft chain cover, the guide and the tensioner.

4. Remove the balance shaft sprocket-to-shaft bolt, the gear cover to bal-

ance shaft bolt and the crankshaft sprocket-to-crankshaft bolts, then the sprockets with the balance shaft chain.

To install:

5. Install the balance chain sprocket and torque the sprocket to crankshaft bolts to 11 ft. lbs. (13 Nm).

6. Rotate the crankshaft to position the No. 1 cylinder on the TDC of the compression stroke; the timing marks on the chain sprocket should align with the parting line on the left side of the No. 1 main bearing cap.

7. Position the balance shaft sprocket into the balance chain so the sprocket (yellow dot) timing mark mates with the yellow link on the chain.

8. Install the balance chain/sprocket assembly onto the crankshaft and the balance shaft.

NOTE: The timing marks on the sprocket, the lower nickle plated link and the arrow on the side of the gear cover should line up when the balance shafts are correctly timed.

9. Torque the sprocket to shaft bolts to 21 ft. lbs. (28 Nm). If necessary to secure the crankshaft while tightening the bolts, place a block of wood between the crankcase and the crankshaft counterbalance.

10. Loosely install the chain tensioners and place a shim (0.039 in. × 2.75 in.) between the chain and the tensioner. Apply firm pressure, to reduce the chain slack, to the tensioner shoe. Torque the tensioner to front gear cover bolts to 8.5 ft. lbs. (12 Nm).

11. Install the chain cover and the rear cover to the carrier housing and torque the bolts to 8.5 ft. lbs. (12 Nm).

12. Replace the crankshaft retainer seal, apply silicone sealer to the mating surface and install the retainer.

13. Install the oil pickup and oil pan.

14. Install the crankshaft sprocket and the timing belt.

15. Connect the negative battery cable, add fluids to the correct level and road test the vehicle.

Timing Belt Cover

REMOVAL & INSTALLATION

2.2L and 2.5L Engines

UPPER COVER

1. Disconnect the negative battery cable.

2. Remove the nuts and bolts that attach the upper cover to the valve cover, block or cylinder head.

3. Remove the bolt that attaches the upper cover to the lower cover.

4. Remove the upper cover.

5. Installation is the reverse of the removal procedure.

LOWER COVER

1. Disconnect the negative battery cable.

2. Raise the vehicle and support safely.

3. Remove the right tire and wheel assembly. Remove the right side inner splash shield.

4. Remove the crankshaft pulley, water pump pulley and the accessory drive belt(s).

5. Remove the lower cover attaching bolts and the cover from the engine.

6. The installation is the reverse of the removal procedure.

3.0L Engine

1. Disconnect the negative battery cable.

2. If equipped with air conditioning, remove the air conditioning compressor mounting bolts and position compressor aside. It is not necessary to remove the refrigerant lines from the compressor.

3. Remove the air conditioning compressor bracket mounting screws and remove the bracket and adjustable drive belt tensioner from the engine block.

4. Remove the power steering/alternator belt tensioner mounting bolt and remove the tensioner.

5. Remove the power steering pump mounting bolts and position the pump assembly out of the way.

6. Raise the vehicle and safely support. Remove the right inner fender splash shield.

7. Remove the crankshaft pulley bolt and the pulley/damper assembly from the crankshaft.

8. Lower the vehicle and place a floor jack under the engine to support it.

9. Separate the front engine mount insulator from the bracket. Raise the engine slightly and remove the mount bracket.

10. Remove the timing belt cover bolts and the upper and lower covers from the engine.

To install:

11. Install the timing belt covers and retainer bolts to the engine.

12. While aligning the engine position and the mount, lower the engine into the front support and secure with the retaining bolts and nuts.

13. Install the crankshaft pulley bolt and the pulley/damper assembly to the crankshaft.

14. With the engine securely in place, install the right inner splash shield.

15. Install the power steering pump, air conditioner compressor mounting bracket, air conditioning compressor

and the belt adjuster brackets. Install the accessory drive belts.

16. Connect the negative battery cable.

Timing Belt and Tensioner

ADJUSTMENT

2.2L and 2.5L Engines Except Turbo III

1. Disconnect the negative battery cable.

2. Raise the vehicle and support safely. Remove the right front inner splash shield.

3. Remove the tensioner cover.

4. Place the special tensioning tool C–4703 on the hex of the tensioner so the weight is at about the 10 o'clock position. Loosen the adjuster retainer bolt.

5. The tensioner should drop to the 9 o'clock position. Reposition the tool as required in order to have it end up at the 9 o'clock position (parallel to the ground, hanging toward the rear of the vehicle) ± 15 degrees.

6. Hold the tool in position and tighten the tensioner retainer bolt. Do not pull the tool past the position achieved by the tension adjustment tool or the belt will be too tight, causing a howling noise during operation or possible belt breakage.

7. Install the cover and the splash shield.

2.2L Turbo III Engine

1. Disconnect the negative battery cable.

2. Remove the timing covers.

3. Install a belt tension gauge on the timing belt between the camshaft sprockets. For the reading the be accu-

SPECIAL TOOL

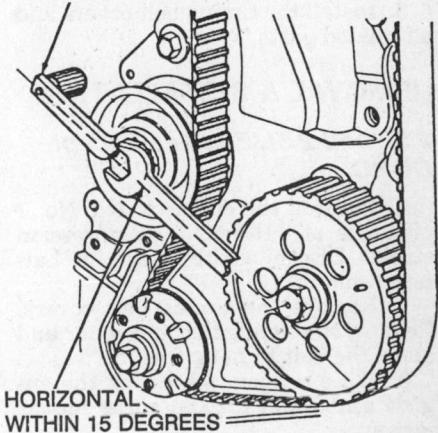

HORIZONTAL WITHIN 15 DEGREES

Adjusting the timing bolt tension—2.2L and 2.5L engines except Turbo III

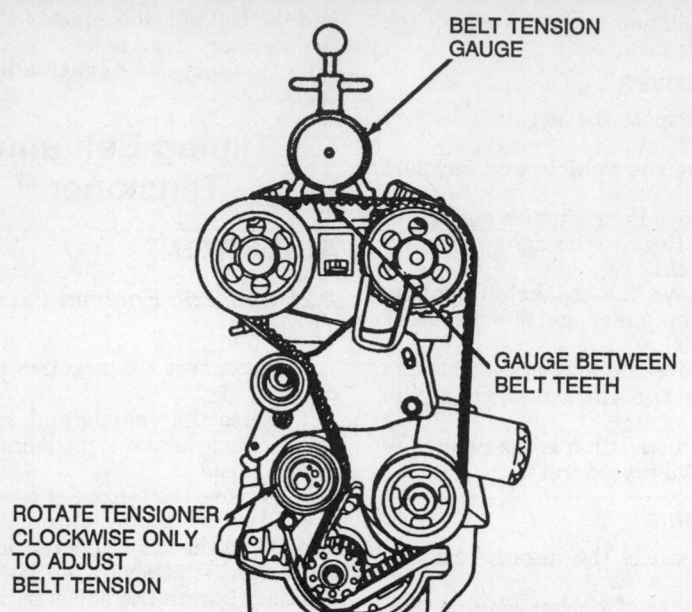

BELT TENSION GAUGE

GAUGE BETWEEN BELT TEETH

ROTATE TENSIONER CLOCKWISE ONLY TO ADJUST BELT TENSION

Checking the belt tension—2.2L Turbo III engine

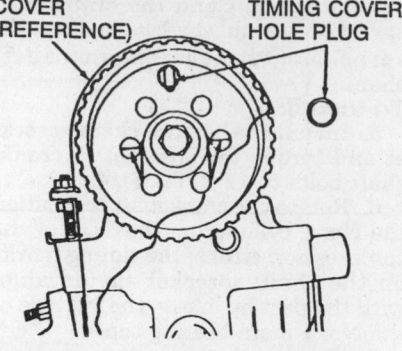

COVER (REFERENCE)

TIMING COVER HOLE PLUG

Alignment of arrows on the camshaft sprocket with the camshaft cap to cylinder head mounting line—2.2L and 2.5L SOHC engines

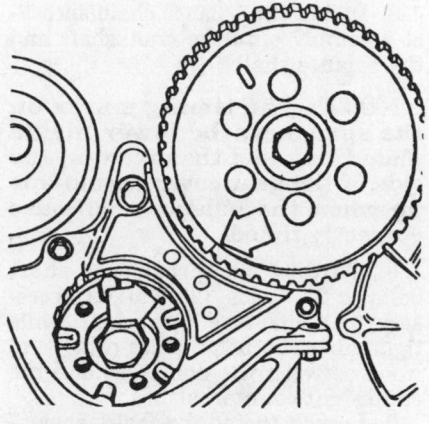

Alignment of the crankshaft sprocket and intermediate shaft sprocket—2.2L and 2.5L engines except Turbo III

rate, make sure the tension gauge is between the teeth on the belt.

4. Rotate the tensioner clockwise to adjust the belt tension to 110 lbs. (445 N) for new belt or 70 lbs. (311 N) for used belt.

5. Rotate the crankshaft clockwise 2 revolutions and recheck the tension. Adjust as required.

6. Install the timing covers and related components.

3.0L Engine

1. Disconnect the negative battery cable.

2. Remove the timing belt covers.

3. Loosen the bolt that holds the timing belt tensioner in place.

4. Allow the spring only to pull the tensioner in automatically. Do not manually move the tensioner or the belt will be too tight.

5. Tighten the tensioner locking bolt.

6. Install the timing belt covers and all related parts.

REMOVAL & INSTALLATION

2.2L and 2.5L Engines Except DOHC

1. Position the engine so the No. 1 piston is at TDC of its compression stroke. Disconnect the negative battery cable.

2. Remove the timing belt covers. Remove the timing belt tensioner and allow the belt to hang free.

3. Place a floor jack under the engine and separate the right motor mount.

4. Remove the air conditioning compressor belt idler pulley, if

equipped, and remove the mounting stud. Remove the compressor/alternator bracket as follows:

a. Remove the alternator pivot bolt and remove the alternator from the bracket. Turn the alternator so the wire connections are facing up and disconnect the harness connectors from the rear of the alternator.

b. Remove the air conditioning compressor belt idler.

c. Remove the right engine

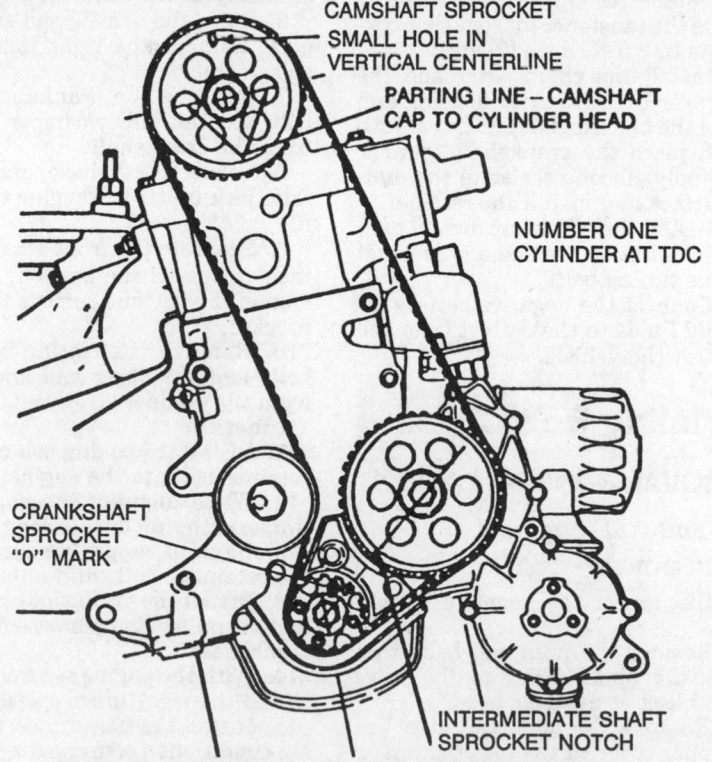

CAMSHAFT SPROCKET SMALL HOLE IN VERTICAL CENTERLINE

PARTING LINE—CAMSHAFT CAP TO CYLINDER HEAD

NUMBER ONE CYLINDER AT TDC

CRANKSHAFT SPROCKET "0" MARK

INTERMEDIATE SHAFT SPROCKET NOTCH

Timing belt installation—2.2L and 2.5L SOHC engines

mount yoke screw securing engine mount support strut to the engine.

d. Remove the 5 side mounting bolts retaining the bracket to the front of the engine.

e. Remove the front mounting nut. Remove the front bolt and strut and rotate the solid mount bracket away from the engine. Slide the bracket on the stud until free of the mounting studs and remove from the engine.

5. Remove the timing belt from the vehicle.

To install:

6. Turn the crankshaft sprocket and intermediate shaft sprocket until the marks are in line. Use a straight-edge from bolt to bolt to confirm alignment.

7. Turn the camshaft until the small hole in the sprocket is at the top and the arrows on the hub are in line with the camshaft cap to cylinder head mounting lines. When looking through the hole on top of the cam-shaft sprocket, the uppermost center nipple of the valve cover end seal should be at the center of the hole. Use a mirror to check the alignment of the arrows so it is viewed straight on and not at an angle from above. Install the belt but let it hang free at this point.

8. Install the air conditioning com-pressor/alternator bracket, idler pul-ley and motor mount. Remove the floor jack. Raise the vehicle and sup-port safely. Have the tensioner at an arm's reach because the timing belt will have to be held in position with one hand.

9. To properly install the timing belt, reach up and engage it with the camshaft sprocket. Turn the interme-diate shaft counterclockwise slightly, then engage the belt with the interme-diate shaft sprocket. Hold the belt against the intermediate shaft sprock-et and turn clockwise to take up all tension; if the timing marks are out of alignment, repeat until alignment is correct.

10. Using a wrench, turn the crank-shaft sprocket counterclockwise slightly and wrap the belt around it. Turn the sprocket clockwise so there is no slack in the belt between sprockets; if the timing marks are out of align-ment, repeat until alignment is correct.

NOTE: If the timing marks are in line but slack exists in the belt between either the camshaft and intermediate shaft sprockets or the intermediate and crankshaft sprockets, the timing will be in-correct when the belt is ten-sioned. All slack must be only be-tween the crankshaft and cam-shaft sprockets.

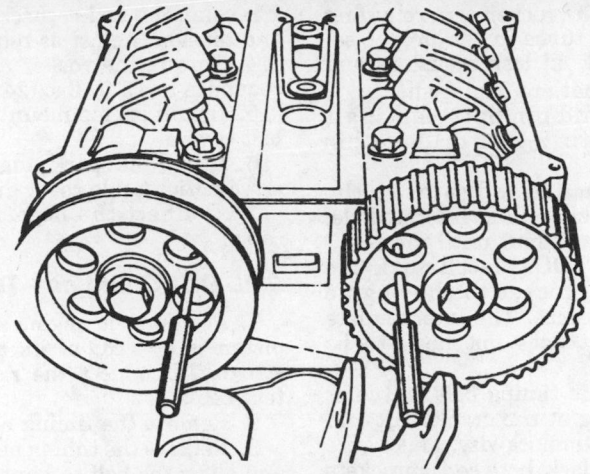

Camshaft pinned in position—2.2L Turbo III engine

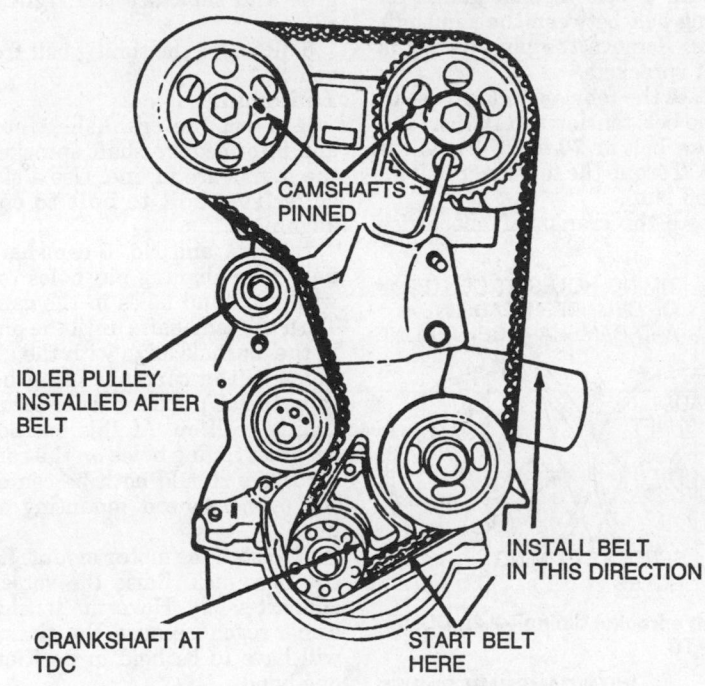

Timing belt properly installed—2.2L Turbo III engine

11. Install the tensioner and install the mounting bolt loosely. Place the special tensioning tool C–4703 on the hex of the tensioner so the weight is at about the 9 o'clock position (parallel to the ground, hanging toward the rear of the vehicle) ± 15 degrees.

12. Hold the tool in position and tighten the bolt to 45 ft. lbs. (61 Nm). Do not pull the tool past the 9 o'clock position; this will make the belt too tight and will cause it to howl or possi-bly break.

13. Lower the vehicle and recheck the camshaft sprocket positioning. If it is correct install the timing belt covers and all related parts.

14. Connect the negative battery ca-ble and road test the vehicle.

2.2L Turbo III Engine

1. Disconnect the negative battery cable.

2. Remove the timing belt covers.

3. Install appropriate engine sup-port tool and lift the engine slightly. Separate the right motor mount.

4. Raise the vehicle and support safely. Remove the lower accessory drive belt idler pulley bracket assembly.

5. Loosen the timing belt tensioner and remove the timing belt and idler pulley.

To install:

6. Remove the air cleaner fresh air duct, ignition cable cover, spark plugs and valve covers.

7. Loosen the rocker arm retaining bolts about 3 turns in the proper sequence. Check all lash adjusters and replace any that are damaged.

8. Align and pin both camshaft sprockets with $\frac{3}{32}$ in. drills or pin punches.

9. Install a dial indicator so the plunger is in the No. 1 spark plug hole. Rotate the crankshaft until the No. 1 piston is at TDC. Matchmark the crankshaft sprocket to the engine block for reference. The intermediate shaft sprocket does not need to be timed.

10. Install the timing belt and idler pulley starting at the crankshaft and working counterclockwise. Make sure there is no slack between sprockets when installing.

11. Install a belt tension gauge on the timing belt between the camshaft sprockets. Remove the pins from the camshaft sprockets.

12. Rotate the tensioner clockwise to adjust the belt tension to 110 lbs. (445 N) for new belt or 70 lbs. (311 N) for used belt. Torque the tensioner bolt 39 ft. lbs. (53 Nm).

13. Rotate the crankshaft clockwise

TIMING HOLES AT CENTER
OF CYLINDER HEAD LINE
AND CAMSHAFT CENTERLINE

Camshaft sprocket timing—2.2L DOHC engine—TC

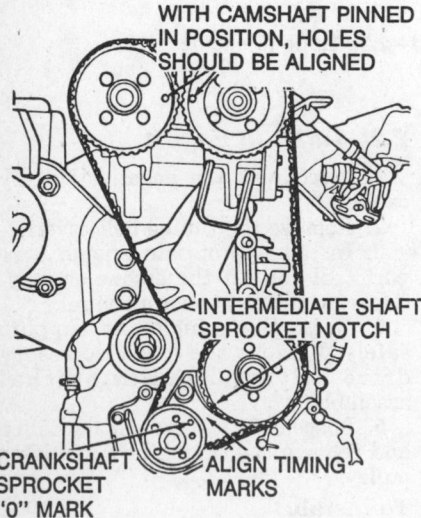

Timing belt installation—2.2L DOHC engine—TC

2 revolutions and recheck the timing and tension. Adjust as required.

14. Torque the rocker arm bolts in sequence to 18 ft. lbs. (24 Nm).

15. Install engine mount and timing belt covers.

16. Install the spark plugs, valve covers, ignition cable cover and air duct.

17. Connect the negative battery cable.

2.2L DOHC Engine—TC

1. Position the engine so the No. 1 piston is at TDC of its compression stroke. Disconnect the negative battery cable.

2. Remove the timing belt covers.

3. Remove the timing belt tensioner and allow the belt to hang free.

4. Place a floor jack under the engine and separate the right motor mount.

5. Remove the timing belt from the vehicle.

To install:

6. Turn the crankshaft sprocket and intermediate shaft sprocket until the marks are in line. Use a straight-edge from bolt to bolt to confirm alignment.

7. No. 1 and No. 6 camshaft journals have aligning pin holes to index with the blind holes in the camshaft. Turn the camshafts until the pin holes in the journals align with the aligning holes in the corresponding bearing caps. Install pin punches to secure this timing position. At this position, the sprocket timing holes on the camshaft sprockets should both be centered at the cylinder head mounting surface line.

8. Install the motor mount. Remove the floor jack. Raise the vehicle and support safely. Have the tensioner at arm's reach because the timing belt will have to be held in position with one hand.

9. To properly install the timing belt, reach up and engage it with the camshaft sprockets, leaving no tension between sprockets. Turn the intermediate shaft counterclockwise slightly, then engage the belt with the intermediate shaft sprocket. Hold the belt against the intermediate shaft sprocket and turn clockwise to take up all tension; if the timing marks are out of alignment, repeat until alignment is correct.

10. Using a wrench, turn the crankshaft sprocket counterclockwise slightly and wrap the belt around it. Turn the sprocket clockwise so there is no slack in the belt between sprockets; if the timing marks are out of alignment, repeat until alignment is correct.

NOTE: If the timing marks are in line but slack exists in the belt

anywhere except on the tensioner side, the timing will be incorrect when the belt is tensioned. All slack must be only between the crankshaft and exhaust camshaft sprockets.

11. Install the tensioner and install the mounting bolt loosely. Remove the pin punches from the camshafts. Place the special tensioning tool C–4703 on the hex of the tensioner so the weight is at about the 9 o'clock position (parallel to the ground, hanging toward the rear of the vehicle) ± 15 degrees.

12. Hold the tool in position and tighten the bolt to 45 ft. lbs. (61 Nm). Do not pull the tool past the 9 o'clock position; this will make the belt too tight and will cause it to howl or possibly break.

13. Rotate the crankshaft 2 full revolutions. With the No. 1 cylinder at TDC, all timing marks must be in line. Repeat the procedure if the timing is not correct.

14. Install the timing belt covers and all related parts.

15. Connect the negative battery cable and road test the vehicle.

3.0L Engine

1. If possible, position the engine so the No. 1 cylinder is at TDC of its compression stroke. Disconnect the negative battery cable. Remove the timing covers from the engine.

2. If the same timing belt will be reused, mark the direction of the timing belt's rotation for installation in the same direction. Make sure the engine is positioned so the No. 1 cylinder is at the TDC of its compression stroke and the sprockets timing marks are aligned with the engine's timing mark indicators.

3. Loosen the timing belt tensioner and remove the belt. If not removing the tensioner, position it as far away from the center of the engine as possible and tighten the bolt.

4. If the tensioner is being removed, paint the outside of the spring to ensure it is not installed backwards. Unbolt the tensioner and remove it along with the spring.

To install:

5. Install the tensioner if removed, and hook the upper end of the spring to the water pump pin and the lower end to the tensioner in exactly the same position as originally installed. If not already done, position both camshafts so the marks align with those on the alternator bracket (rear bank) and inner timing cover (front bank). Rotate the crankshaft so the timing mark aligns with the mark on the oil pump.

6. Install the timing belt on the crankshaft sprocket and while keeping

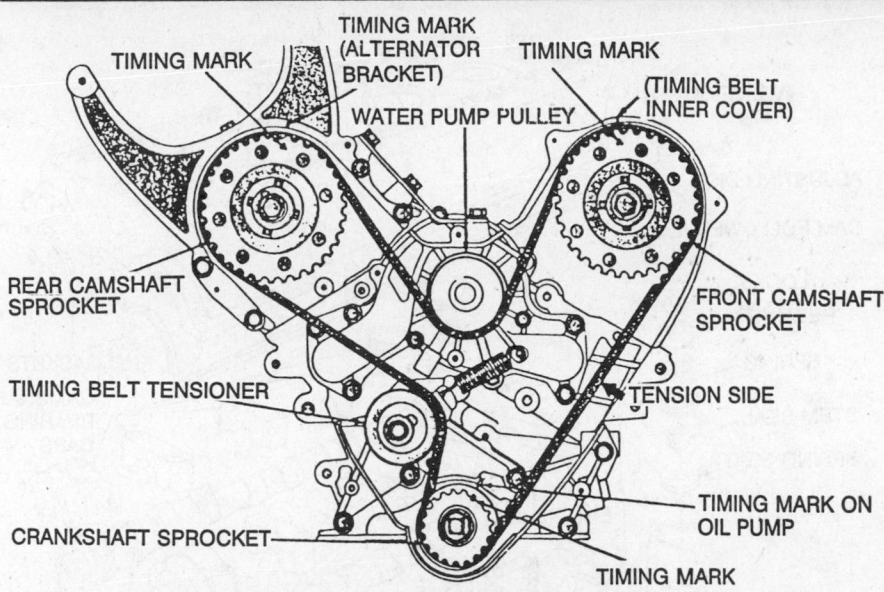

TIMING MARK
TIMING MARK (ALTERNATOR BRACKET)
TIMING MARK
WATER PUMP PULLEY
(TIMING BELT INNER COVER)
REAR CAMSHAFT SPROCKET
FRONT CAMSHAFT SPROCKET
TIMING BELT TENSIONER
TENSION SIDE
CRANKSHAFT SPROCKET
TIMING MARK ON OIL PUMP
TIMING MARK

Timing belt installation—3.0L engine

the belt tight on the tension side (right side), install the belt on the front camshaft sprocket.

7. Install the belt on the water pump pulley, then the rear camshaft sprocket and the tensioner.

8. Rotate the front camshaft counterclockwise to tension the belt between the front camshaft and the crankshaft. If the timing marks came out of line, repeat the procedure.

9. Install the crankshaft sprocket flange.

10. Loosen the tensioner bolt and allow the spring to tension the belt.

11. Turn the crankshaft 2 full turns in the clockwise direction only until the timing marks are aligned and torque the tensioner lock bolt to 21 ft. lbs. (29 Nm).

12. Install the timing belt covers and all related parts.

13. Connect the negative battery cable and road test the vehicle.

Timing Sprockets

REMOVAL & INSTALLATION

2.2L and 2.5L Engines

1. Disconnect the negative battery cable. Remove the timing belt.

2. Remove the crankshaft sprocket bolt. Using the puller tool C–4685 or equivalent and the button from tool L–4524 or equivalent, remove the crankshaft sprocket.

3. Using the tool C–4687 or equivalent, hold the camshaft and/or intermediate shaft sprocket, remove the center bolt and the sprocket(s).

4. Replace the seal(s) if leaking.

5. The installation is the reverse of the removal procedure. Torque the camshaft and intermediate sprocket

bolts to 65 ft. lbs. (88 Nm) and the crankshaft sprocket bolt to 50 ft. lbs. (68 Nm) on 1989 engine or 85 ft. lbs. (115 Nm) on 1990–93 engine.

3.0L Engine

1. Disconnect the negative battery cable.

2. Remove the timing belt.

3. To remove the camshaft sprocket, hold the sprocket with tool MB990775 or equivalent, and remove the retaining bolt and washer.

4. To remove the crankshaft sprocket, remove the bolt and remove the sprocket from the crankshaft. Replace any leaking seals.

5. The installation is the reverse of the removal procedure. Torque the camshaft sprocket bolt to 70 ft. lbs. (95 Nm) while holding the sprocket with the holding tool. Torque the crankshaft sprocket bolt. to 110 ft. lbs. (150 Nm).

Camshaft

REMOVAL & INSTALLATION

2.2L and 2.5L Engines Except DOHC

1. Disconnect the negative battery cable.

2. Turn the crankshaft so the No. 1 piston is at the TDC of the compression stroke. Remove the upper timing belt cover.

3. Remove the camshaft sprocket bolt and the sprocket and suspend tightly so the belt does not lose tension. If it does, the belt timing will have to be reset.

4. Remove the valve cover.

5. If the rocker arms are being re-

used, mark them for installation identification and loosen the camshaft bearing bolts, evenly and gradually.

6. Using a soft mallet, tap the rear of the camshaft a few times to break the bearing caps loose.

7. Remove the bolts, bearing caps and the camshaft with seals.

NOTE: Take note of the color of the paint stripe on the rear camshaft seal. These stripes differentiate seal sizes. If a seal with a different color stripe is installed, a severe leak will develop if the seal is too small or the cap will not be able to be fully installed if the seal is too big.

Also, oversized components can be identified as follows: the top of the bearing caps are painted green and "O/SJ" is stamped behind the oil galley plug on the end of the head. The barrel of an oversized camshaft is also painted green and "O/SJ" is stamped on the end of the shaft. If normal sized parts are installed in place of oversized ones, oil pressure will be significantly reduced.

8. Check the oil passages for blockages and the parts for wear and damage and replace parts, as required. Clean the gasket mounting surfaces.
To install:

9. Transfer the sprocket key to the new camshaft. New rocker arms and a new camshaft sprocket bolt are normally included with the camshaft package. Install the rocker arms, lubricate the camshaft and install with end seals installed.

10. Place the bearing caps with No. 1 at the timing belt end and No. 5 at the transaxle end. The camshaft bearing caps are numbered and have arrows facing forward. Torque the camshaft bearing bolts evenly and gradually to 18 ft. lbs. (24 Nm).

NOTE: Apply RTV silicone gasket material to the No. 1 and 5 bearing caps. Install the bearing caps before the seals are installed.

11. Mount a dial indicator to the front of the engine and check the camshaft endplay. Play should not exceed 0.020 in.

12. Install the camshaft sprocket and the new bolt.

13. Install the valve cover with a new gasket.

14. Connect the negative battery cable and check for leaks.

2.2L Turbo III Engine

1. Disconnect the negative battery cable.

2. Remove the cylinder head.

3. Remove the rocker shaft assemblies.

4. The thrust plates in the rear of the head are not interchangeable; the intake camshaft uses a wider plate. Identify the plates and remove them.

5. To remove the cam seal, push the cam toward the seal end and the seal will be pushed out of its bore in the head.

6. Carefully pull the camshaft from the head. The intake and exhaust camshafts are not interchangeable. If both are being removed, identify them for installation purposes.

To install:

7. Inspect the camshaft for wear and replace any parts that are damaged.

8. Lubricate the journals with fresh engine oil and insert the camshaft into the head.

9. Install the thrust plates and tighten the retaining nuts to 55–70 inch lbs. (6–8 Nm).

10. Install new camshaft seals flush with the head surface using installation tool C–4680.

11. Move the camshaft as far rearward as possible. Use a dial indicator and measure the endplay. Endplay specification is 0.001–0.008 in. (0.026–0.206mm).

12. Install the rocker shaft assemblies.

13. Install the cylinder head.

14. Connect the negative battery cable.

2.2L DOHC Engine—TC

1. Disconnect the negative battery cable.

2. Turn the crankshaft so the No. 1 piston is at the TDC of the compression stroke. With all timing marks aligned, remove the timing belt.

3. Remove the valve cover.

4. Remove the camshaft bearing caps nuts and washers.

5. Using a soft mallet, rap the camshaft caps a few times to break them loose.

6. Check the oil passages for blockages and the parts for wear and damage and replace parts, as required. Clean the gasket mounting surfaces.

To install:

7. Transfer the sprocket and key to the new camshaft.

8. Lubricate the camshaft and journals with clean engine oil and position the camshaft in the cylinder head.

9. Apply RTV silicone gasket material to the No. 1 and 6 bearing caps. The camshaft bearing caps are numbered. Place the bearing caps on the cylinder head with Nos. 1 and 6 at the timing belt end and Nos. 5 and 10 at the transaxle end. Torque the camshaft bearing bolts evenly and gradu-

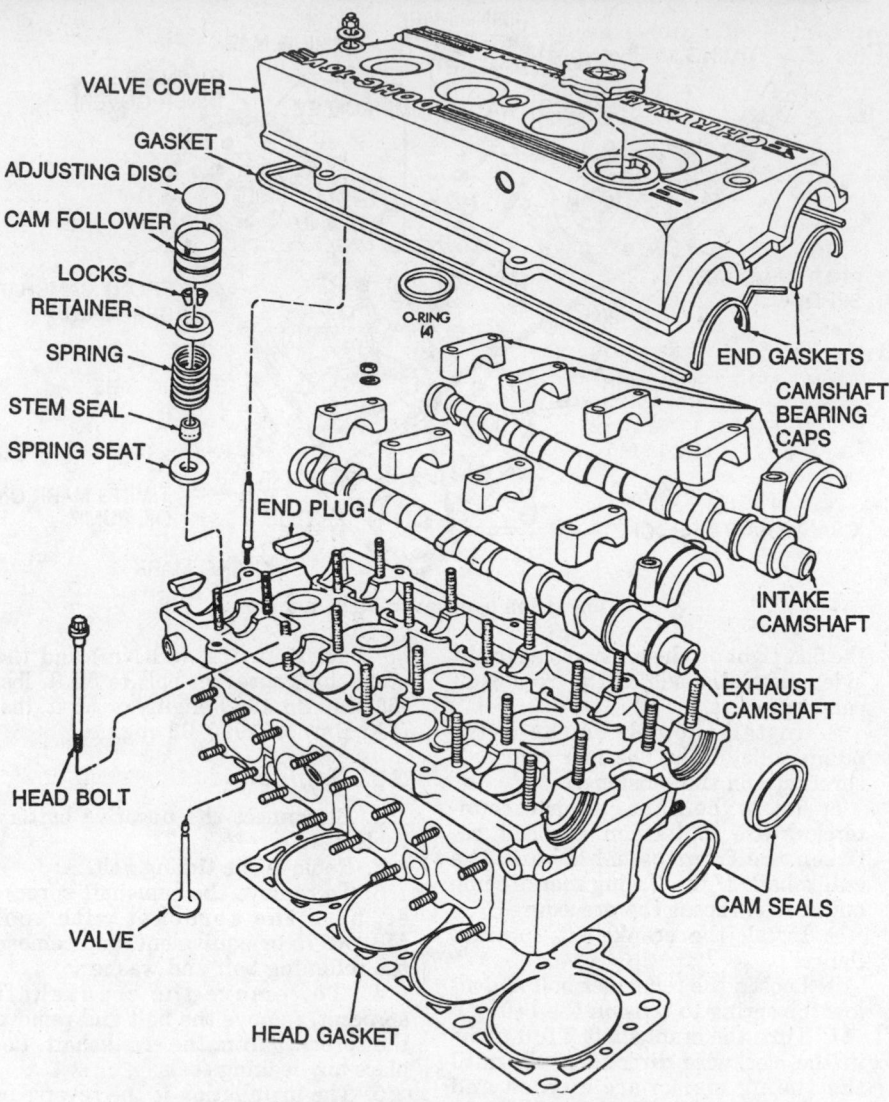

Cylinder head and valve assembly—2.2L DOHC engine—TC

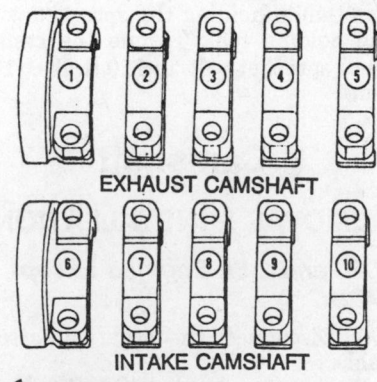

Camshaft bearing caps installation—2.2L DOHC engine

ally to 20 ft. lbs. (24 Nm) starting from the middle and working outward.

10. Check all valve clearances and adjust, if necessary. Install new camshaft end seals using tool C–4680.

11. Install the timing belt.

12. Install the valve cover with new seals.

13. Connect the negative battery cable and check for leaks.

3.0L Engine

1. Disconnect the negative battery cable. Remove the air cleaner assembly and valve covers.

2. Install auto lash adjuster retainer tools MD998443 or equivalent, on the rocker arms.

3. If removing the right side (front) camshaft, remove the distributor extension.

4. Loosen the camshaft bearing caps but do not remove the bolts from the caps.

5. Remove the rocker arms, rocker shafts and bearing caps, as an assembly.

6. Remove the camshaft from the cylinder head.

7. Inspect the bearing journals on

the camshaft, cylinder head and bearing caps.

To install:

8. Lubricate the camshaft journals and camshaft with clean engine oil and install the camshaft in the cylinder head.

9. Align the camshaft bearing caps with the arrow mark (depending on cylinder numbers) and in numerical order.

10. Apply sealer at the ends of the bearing caps and install the assembly.

11. Torque the bearing cap bolts, in the following sequence: No. 3, No. 2, No. 1 and No. 4 to 85 inch lbs. (10 Nm).

12. Repeat the sequence increasing the torque to 175–180 inch lbs. (18–20 Nm).

13. Install the distributor extension, if removed.

14. Install the valve cover and all related parts.

15. Connect the negative battery cable.

Intermediate Shaft

REMOVAL & INSTALLATION

2.2L and 2.5L Engines

1. Disconnect the negative battery cable.

2. Crank the engine so the No. 1 piston is at TDC of its compression stroke. Remove the timing belt covers to confirm that all timing marks are aligned.

3. Remove the distributor, if equipped. Looking down at the oil pump, the slot in the shaft must be parallel with the center line of the crankshaft. Remove the oil pump.

4. Remove the timing belt and the intermediate shaft sprocket.

5. Remove the intermediate shaft retainer bolts and remove the retainer from the block.

6. Remove the intermediate shaft from the engine.

7. If necessary, remove the front bushing using tool C–4697–2 and the rear bushing using tool C–4686–2.

To install:

8. Install the front bushing using tool C–4697–1 until the tool is flush with the block. Install the rear bushing using tool C–4686–1 until the tool is flush with the block.

9. Lubricate the distributor drive gear, if equipped, and install the intermediate shaft.

10. Replace the seal in the retainer and apply silicone sealer to the mating surface of the retainer. Install the retainer to the block and torque the bolts to 10 ft. lbs. (12 Nm).

11. Install the intermediate shaft sprocket and the timing belt.

12. With the timing belt properly installed, install the oil pump so the slot is parallel to the center line of the crankshaft. If equipped, install the distributor so the rotor is aligned with the No. 1 spark plug wire tower on the cap.

13. Connect the negative battery cable, check for leaks and adjust the ignition timing, as required.

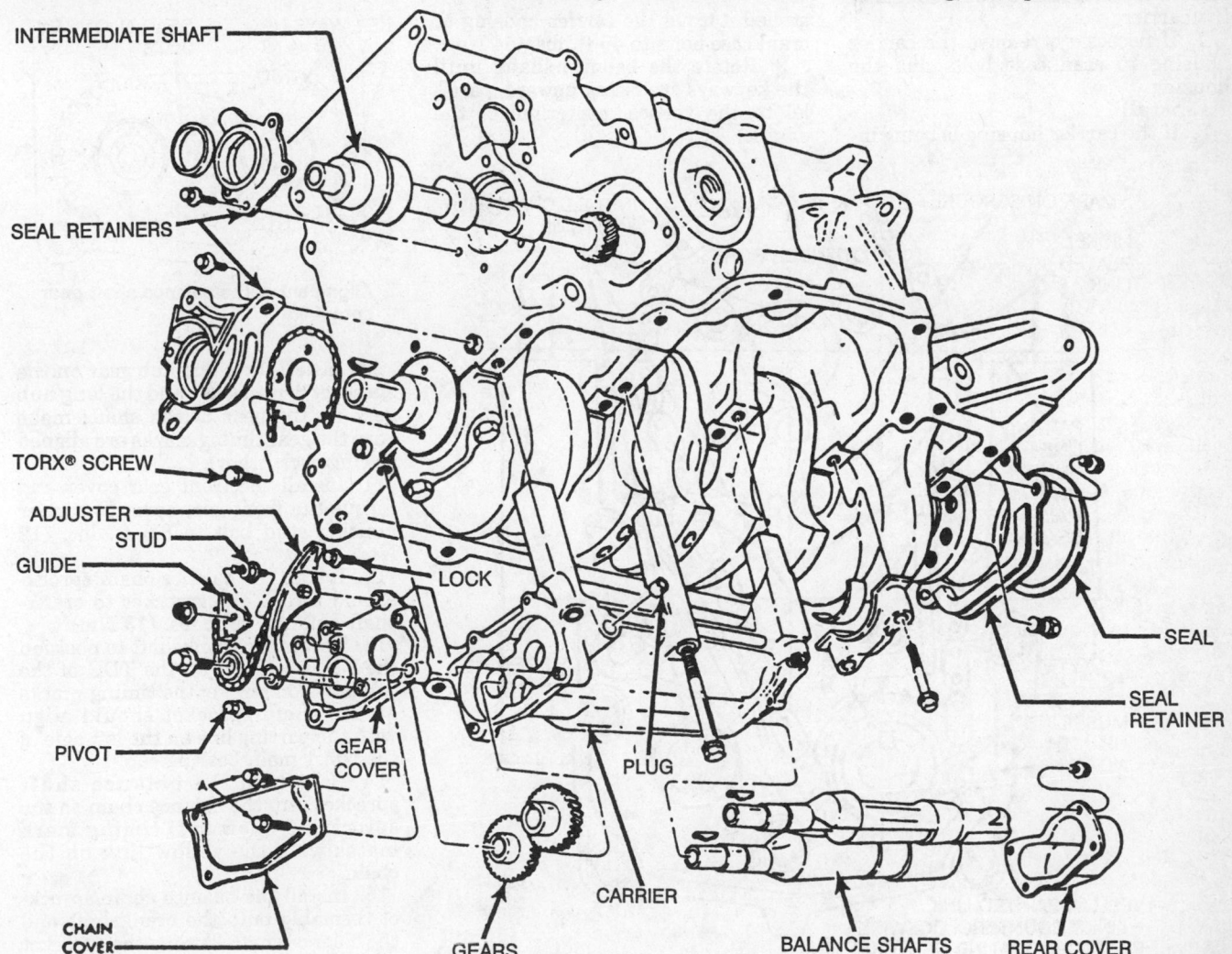

INTERMEDIATE SHAFT

SEAL RETAINERS

TORX® SCREW

ADJUSTER

STUD

GUIDE

PIVOT

LOCK

GEAR COVER

PLUG

SEAL

SEAL RETAINER

CHAIN COVER

GEARS

CARRIER

BALANCE SHAFTS

REAR COVER

Exploded view of the balance shafts and related parts

Balance Shafts

REMOVAL & INSTALLATION

2.5L Engine and 2.2L Turbo III and IV Engines

1. Disconnect the negative battery cable. Raise the vehicle and support safely.

2. Remove the timing belt. Remove the oil pan, the oil pickup, the crankshaft belt sprocket and the front crankshaft oil seal retainer.

3. Remove the balance shaft chain cover, chain guide and the tensioner.

4. Remove the balance shaft sprocket-to-shaft bolt, the gear cover to balance shaft bolt and the crankshaft sprocket-to-crankshaft bolts, then the sprockets with the balance shaft chain.

5. Remove the front gear cover-to-carrier housing stud, the gear cover and the balance shaft drive gears.

6. Remove the rear gear cover-to-carrier housing bolts, the rear cover and the balance shafts from the rear of the carrier.

7. If necessary, remove the carrier housing to crankcase bolts and the housing.

To install:

8. If the carrier housing is being in-

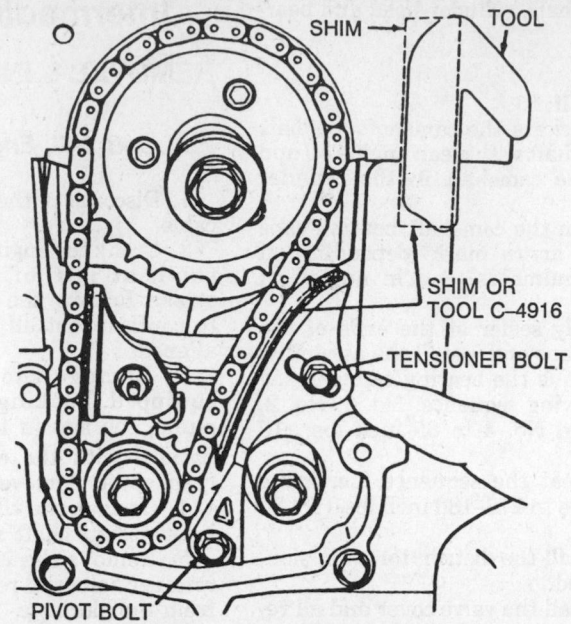

Adjusting the balance shaft chain tensioner

stalled, torque the carrier housing to crankcase bolts to 40 ft. lbs. (54 Nm).

9. Rotate the balance shafts until the keyways are facing upward, parallel to the vertical centerline of the engine.

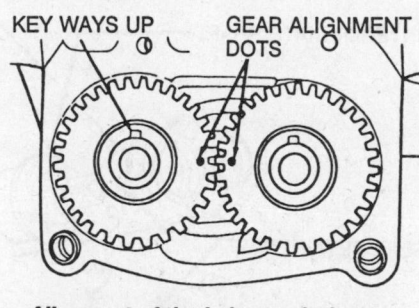

Alignment of the balance shaft gear sprockets

10. Install the short hub gear on the sprocket driven shaft and the long hub gear on the gear driven shaft; make sure the gear timing marks are aligned (facing each other).

11. Install the front gear cover and torque the front gear cover to carrier housing stud bolt to 8.5 ft. lbs. (12 Nm).

12. Install the balance chain sprocket and torque the sprocket to crankshaft bolts to 11 ft. lbs. (13 Nm).

13. Rotate the crankshaft to position the No. 1 cylinder on the TDC of the compression stroke; the timing marks on the chain sprocket should align with the parting line on the left side of the No. 1 main bearing cap.

14. Position the balance shaft sprocket into the balance chain so the sprocket (yellow dot) timing mark mates with the yellow link on the chain.

15. Install the balance chain/sprocket assembly onto the crankshaft and the balance shaft. Torque the sprocket to shaft bolts to 21 ft. lbs. (28 Nm). If necessary to secure the crankshaft

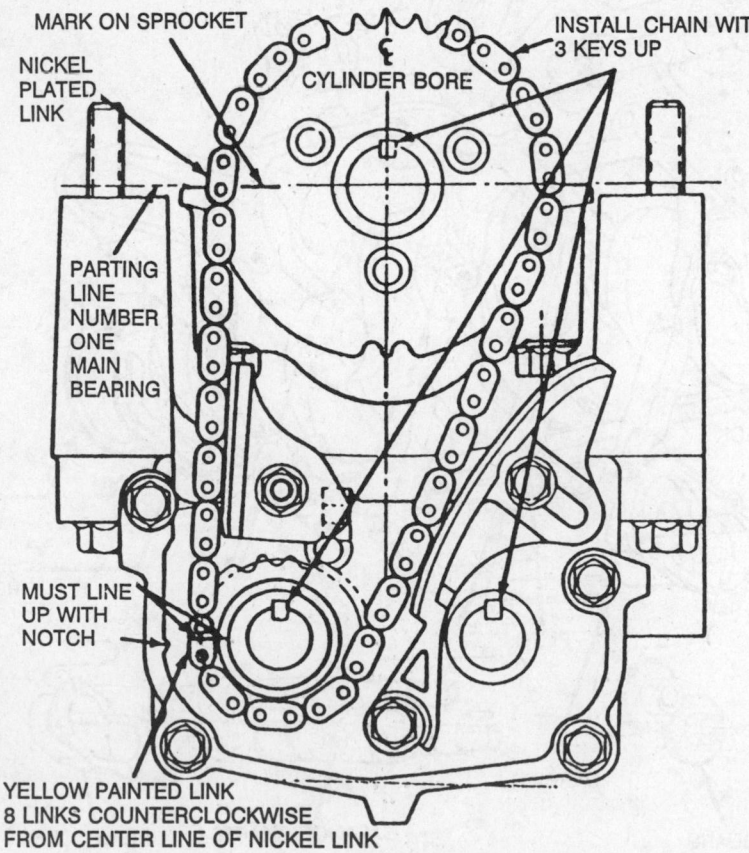

Balance shaft sprocket and crankshaft sprocket timing

while tightening the bolts, place a block of wood between the crankcase and the crankshaft counterbalance.

16. Loosely, install the chain tensioners and place a shim (0.039 in. × 2.75 in.) between the chain and the tensioner. Apply firm pressure, to reduce the chain slack, to the tensioner shoe. Torque the tensioner upper bolt first, and then the lower pivot bolt to 8.5 ft. lbs. (12 Nm). Remove the shim from the tensioner.

17. Install the chain cover and the rear cover to the carrier housing and torque the bolts to 8.5 ft. lbs. (12 Nm).

18. Replace the crankshaft retainer seal, apply silicone sealer to the mating surface and install the retainer.

19. Install the oil pickup and oil pan.

20. Install the crankshaft sprocket, timing belt and related components.

21. Connect the negative battery cable, correct all engine fluid levels and road test the vehicle.

Piston and Connecting Rod

POSITIONING

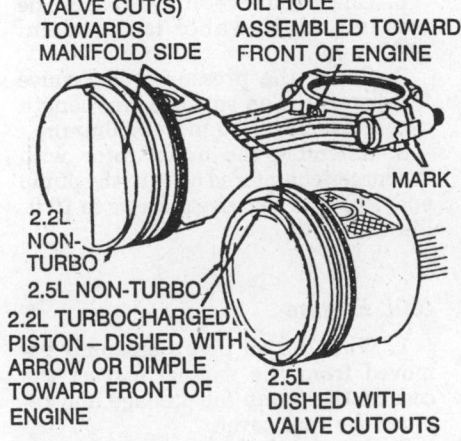

Piston and rod positioning—2.2L and 2.5L non-turbocharged engines

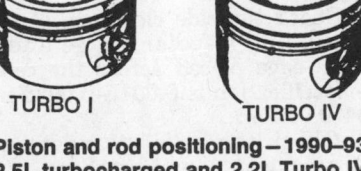

Piston and rod positioning—1990–93 2.5L turbocharged and 2.2L Turbo IV engines

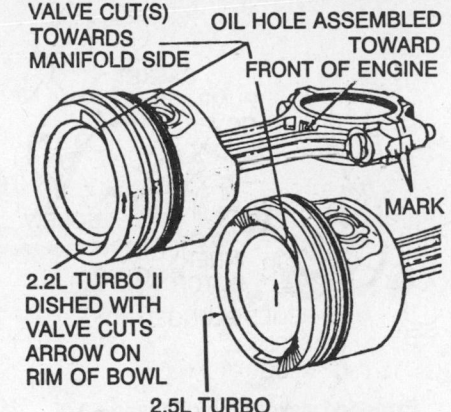

Piston and rod positioning—2.2L Turbo II and 1989 2.5L turbocharged engines

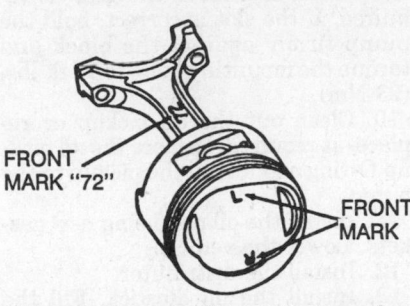

Piston and rod positioning—3.0L engine

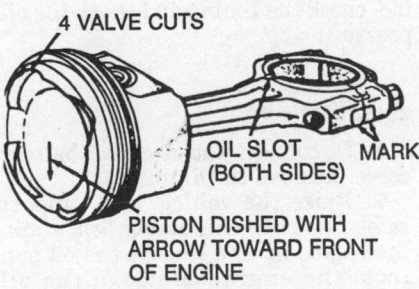

Piston and rod positioning—TC, 2.2L DOHC engine and 2.2L Turbo III engines

ENGINE LUBRICATION

Oil Pan

REMOVAL & INSTALLATION

2.2L and 2.5L Engines

1. Disconnect the negative battery cable. Remove the oil dipstick.

2. Raise the vehicle and support safely.

3. Drain the engine oil.

4. Remove the engine to transaxle struts, if equipped.

5. Remove the torque converter or clutch inspection cover.

6. Remove the oil pan retaining screws, oil pan and side seals.

To install:

7. Thoroughly clean and dry all sealing surfaces, bolts and bolt holes.

8. Apply silicone sealer to the 4 end seal-to-block corners and install the end seals making sure the corners are not twisted.

9. Apply silicone to the 4 pan-to-block corners. Install a new pan gasket or apply silicone sealer to the sealing surface of the pan and install to the engine making sure not to dislodge the end seals.

10. Install the retaining screws and torque to 17 ft. lbs. (23 Nm).

11. Install the torque converter inspection cover and engine to transaxle struts, if equipped. Lower the vehicle.

12. Install the dipstick. Fill the engine with the proper amount of oil.

13. Connect the negative battery cable and check for leaks.

3.0L Engine

1. Disconnect the negative battery cable.

2. Raise the vehicle and support safely.

3. Remove the torque converter bolt access cover.

4. Drain the engine oil.

5. Remove the oil pan retaining screws and remove the oil pan and gasket.

To install:

6. Thoroughly clean and dry all sealing surfaces, bolts and bolt holes.

7. Apply silicone sealer to the chain cover to block mating seam and the rear main seal retainer to block seam, if equipped.

8. Install a new pan gasket or apply silicone sealer to the sealing surface of the pan and install to the engine.

9. Install the retaining screws and torque to 50 inch lbs. (6 Nm).

10. Install the torque converter bolt access cover, if equipped. Lower the vehicle.

11. Install the dipstick. Fill the engine with the proper amount of oil.

12. Connect the negative battery cable and check for leaks.

Oil Pump

REMOVAL & INSTALLATION

2.2L and 2.5L Engines

NOTE: Many of the following

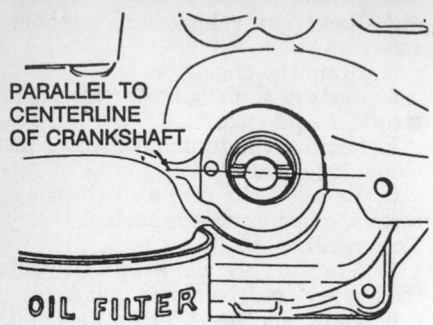

PARALLEL TO
CENTERLINE
OF CRANKSHAFT

OIL FILTER

Aligning the slot in the oil pump shaft—2.2L and 2.5L engines

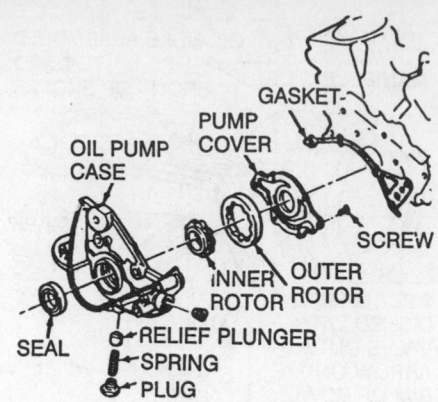

GASKET

PUMP COVER

OIL PUMP CASE

SCREW

INNER ROTOR

OUTER ROTOR

SEAL

RELIEF PLUNGER

SPRING

PLUG

Exploded view of the oil pump—3.0L engine

steps pertain to engines with a distributor. Disregard these steps when working on Turbo III engine. Since that engine does not have a distributor, the oil pump can be installed without timing the distributor gear. The oil pump on all other engines must be properly timed.

1. Crank the engine so the No. 1 piston is at TDC of its compression stroke. Disconnect the negative battery cable.
2. Matchmark the rotor to the block and remove the distributor. Confirm that the slot in the oil pump shaft is parallel to the centerline of the crankshaft. Matchmark the slot to the distributor bore, if desired.
3. Remove the dipstick. Raise the vehicle and support safely. Drain the engine oil and remove the pan.
4. Remove the screw on the pump cover holding the oil pick-up tube to the oil pump and remove the tube.
5. Remove the 2 oil pump mounting bolts and remove the oil pump from the engine.
To install:
6. Prime the pump by pouring fresh oil into the pump intake and turning the driveshaft until oil comes out the pressure port. Repeat a few times until no air bubbles are present.
7. Apply Loctite® 515 or equivalent, to the pump body to block machined surface interface. Lubricate the oil pump and distributor driveshaft.
8. Align the timing mark on the intermediate sprocket so it is aligned with the timing mark on the crankshaft sprocket. Install the pump fully and rotate back and forth to ensure proper positioning between the pump mounting surface and the machined surface of the block.
9. Install the mounting bolts finger-tight and lower the vehicle to confirm that the slot in the oil pump is parallel with the centerline of the crankshaft when the intermediate shaft and the crankshaft are properly aligned. If the slot is not properly positioned, raise

the vehicle and move the gear as required. If the slot is correct, hold the pump firmly against the block and torque the mounting bolts to 17 ft. lbs. (23 Nm).
10. Clean out the oil pickup or replace, as required. Replace the oil pick-up O-ring and install the pickup to the pump.
11. Install the oil pan using new gaskets. Lower the vehicle.
12. Install the distributor.
13. Install the oil dipstick. Fill the engine with the proper amount of oil.
14. Connect the negative battery cable, check the timing and check the oil pressure.

3.0L Engine

1. Disconnect the negative battery cable. Remove the dipstick.
2. Raise the vehicle and support safely. Remove the timing belt, drain the engine oil and remove the oil pan from the engine. Remove the oil pickup.
3. Remove the oil pump mounting bolts and remove the pump from the front of the engine. Note the different length bolts and their positions for installation.
To install:
4. Clean the gasket mounting surfaces of the pump and engine block.
5. Prime the pump by packing the inside of the oil pump with non—medicated petroleum jelly. Using a new gasket, install the oil pump on the engine and torque all bolts to 10 ft. lbs. (13 Nm).
6. Install the balancer and crankshaft sprocket to the end of the crankshaft.
7. Clean out the oil pickup or replace, as required. Replace the oil pick-up gasket ring and install the pickup to the pump.

8. Install the timing belt, oil pan and all related parts.
9. Install the dipstick. Fill the engine with the proper amount of oil.
10. Connect the negative battery cable and check the oil pressure.

CHECKING

2.2L and 2.5L Engines

1. Remove the cover from the oil pump.
2. Check endplay of the inner rotor using a feeler gauge and a straight-edge placed across the pump body. The specification is 0.001–0.004 in. (0.03–0.09mm).
3. Measure the clearance between the inner and outer rotors. The maximum clearance is 0.008 in. (0.20mm).
4. Measure the clearance between the outer rotor and the pump body. The maximum clearance is 0.014 in. (0.35mm).
5. The minimum thickness of the outer rotor is 0.944 in. (23.96mm). The minimum diameter of the outer rotor is 2.77 in. (62.70mm). The minimum thickness of the inner rotor is 0.943 in. (23.95mm).
6. Check the cover for warpage. The maximum allowable is 0.003 in. (0.076mm).
7. Check the pressure relief valve for damage. The spring's free length specification is 1.95 in. (49.50mm).
8. Assemble the outer rotor with the larger chamfered edge in the pump body. Torque the cover screws to 10 ft. lbs. (12 Nm).

3.0L Engine

1. With the oil pump assembly removed from the engine, inspect the case of the pump for damage and remove the rear cover.
2. Remove the pump rotors and inspect the case for excessive wear.
3. Measure the diameter of the inner rotor hub that sits in the case. Measure the inside diameter of the inner rotor hub bore. Subtract the first measurement from the second; if the result is over 0.006 in. (0.15mm), replace the oil pump assembly.
4. Measure the clearance between the outer rotor and the case. The specification is 0.004–0.007 in. (0.10–0.18mm).
5. Check the side clearance of the rotors using a feeler gauge and a straight-edge placed across the case. The specification is 0.0015–0.0035 in. (0.04–0.09mm).
6. Check the relief plunger and spring for damage and breakage.
7. Install the rear cover to the case.

Rear Main Bearing Oil Seal

REMOVAL & INSTALLATION

1. Disconnect the negative battery cable.
2. Remove the transaxle. Remove the flywheel or flexplate.
3. If there is leakage coming from the rear seal retainer, drain the engine oil and remove the oil pan, if necessary. Remove the rear main oil seal retainer.
4. Remove the seal from the retainer.
To install:
5. Lightly coat the seal outer diameter with Loctite® Stud N' Bearing Mount or equivalent.
6. Install the seal to the retainer.
7. If the retainer was removed, thoroughly clean and dry the retainer to block sealing surfaces and install a new gasket or apply silicone sealer and install the retainer. Install the pan, if it was removed.
8. Install the flywheel or flex plate and the transaxle.
9. Connect the negative battery cable, correct all engine fluid levels and check for leaks.

ENGINE COOLING

Radiator

REMOVAL & INSTALLATION

1. Disconnect the negative battery cable.
2. Drain the coolant.
3. Remove the upper hose and coolant reserve tank hose from the radiator.
4. Remove the electric cooling fan.
5. Raise the vehicle and support safely. Remove the lower hose from the radiator.
6. Disconnect the automatic transaxle cooler hoses, if equipped, and plug them. Lower the vehicle.
7. Remove the mounting brackets and carefully lift the radiator out of the engine compartment.
To install:
8. Lower the radiator into position.
9. Install the mounting brackets.
10. Raise the vehicle, if necessary, and support safely. Connect the automatic transaxle cooler lines, if equipped.

11. Lower the vehicle and connect the lower hose.
12. Install the electric cooling fan.
13. Connect the upper hose and coolant reserve tank hose.
14. Fill the system with coolant.
15. Connect the negative battery cable, run the vehicle until the thermostat opens, fill the radiator completely and check the automatic transaxle fluid level, if equipped.
16. Once the vehicle has cooled, recheck the coolant level.

Electric Cooling Fan

TESTING

— CAUTION —
Make sure the key is in the OFF position when checking the electric cooling fan. If not, the fan could turn ON at any time, causing serious personal injury.

1. Unplug the fan connector.
2. Using a jumper wire, connect the terminals of the fan connector to a good 12 volt source observing correct polarity. The female terminal on the fan motor is normally the negative terminal.
3. The fan should come ON with the circuit completed and should run smoothly and free of vibrations.
4. If not, the fan is defective and should be replaced.

REMOVAL & INSTALLATION

1. Disconnect the negative battery cable.
2. Unplug the connector.
3. Remove the mounting screws.
4. Remove the fan assembly from the vehicle.
5. The installation is the reverse of the removal procedure.

Heater Core

REMOVAL & INSTALLATION

Without Air Conditioning

1. Disconnect the negative battery cable. Drain the cooling system.
2. Clamp off the heater hoses near the heater core and remove the hoses from the core tubes. Plug the hose ends and the core tubes to prevent spillage of coolant.
3. Remove the glove box, right side kick and sill panels and all modules, relay panels and computer components in the vicinity of the heater housing.
4. Remove the lower instrument panel silencers and reinforcements. Remove the radio and other dash-

mounted optional equipment, as required.
5. Remove the floor console, if equipped. Remove the floor and defroster distribution ducts.
6. Remove the bolt holding the right side instrument panel to the right cowl.
7. Disconnect the blower motor wiring, antenna, resistor wiring and the temperature control cable.
8. On 1990–93 Daytona and LeBaron, using a cutting device, cut the instrument panel along the indented line along the padded cover to the right of the glove box opening. Cut only plastic, not metal. Remove the reinforcement and the piece of instrument panel that is riveted to it.
9. Disconnect the demister hoses from the top of the housing, if equipped.
10. Disconnect the hanger strap from the package and rotate it aside.
11. Remove the retaining nuts from the package mounting studs at the firewall.
12. Fold the carpeting and insulation back to provide a little more working room and to prevent spillage from staining the carpeting. Pull the right side of the instrument panel out as far as possible.
13. Remove the heater housing from under the dash panel and remove it from the passenger compartment. If the passenger seat is preventing removal, remove it.
14. Disassemble the housing assembly as follows:
   a. Locate and remove the 1 retaining nut from the blend air door pivot shaft.
   b. Remove the crank arm by squeezing the retainer away from the shaft and pulling straight upward.
   c. Disconnect the vacuum lines from the defroster and panel mode vacuum actuators and position them aside.
   d. Remove the heater unit cover attaching screws going upward at the defroster outlet chamber.
   e. Remove the 2 heater unit cover attaching screws going upward at the air inlet plenum.
   f. Remove the remaining heater unit cover attaching screws going downward into the housing and remove the cover.
15. Remove the retaining screw from the heater core and remove the core from the housing assembly.

To install:
16. Remove the temperature control door from the housing and clean the unit out with solvent. Lubricate the lower pivot rod and its well and install. Wrap the heater core with foam tape

and place it in position. Secure it with its screw.

17. Assemble the housing, making sure all cover screws were installed.

18. Connect the demister hoses. Install the nuts to the firewall and connect the hanger strap inside the passenger compartment.

19. Fold the carpeting back into position.

20. Install the bolt that attaches the right side of the instrument panel to the cowl.

21. Connect the blower motor wiring, antenna, resistor wiring and the temperature control cable.

22. Install the air distribution ducts.

23. Install the floor console, if equipped.

24. Install the radio and all other dash mounted items that were removed during the disassembly procedure.

25. Install the lower instrument panel reinforcements and silencers.

26. Install all modules, relay panels and computer components that were removed during disassembly.

27. Install the glove box and right side kick and sill panels. Install the passenger seat if removed.

28. Connect the heater hoses to the heater core tubes.

29. Fill the cooling system.

30. Connect the negative battery cable and check the entire climate control system for proper operation and leakage.

With Air Conditioning

1. Disconnect the negative battery cable. Properly discharge the air conditioning system. Drain the cooling system.

2. Clamp off the heater hoses near the heater core and remove the hoses from the core tubes. Plug the hose ends and the core tubes to prevent spillage of coolant.

3. Disconnect the H-valve connection at the valve and remove the H-valve. Remove the condensation tube.

4. Disconnect the vacuum lines at the brake booster and water valve.

5. Remove the glove box, right side kick, sill panels and all modules, relay panels and computer components in the vicinity of the housing. Remove the blower motor from the housing.

6. Remove the lower instrument panel silencers and reinforcements. Remove the radio, cigar lighter, ash tray receiver and the heater and air conditioning control unit from the instrument panel. If equipped with Automatic Temperature Control (ATC), disconnect the instrument wiring from the rear face of the ATC control unit.

7. Remove the floor console, if

equipped. Remove the floor and center air distribution ducts.

8. Remove the bolt holding the right side instrument panel to the right cowl.

9. Disconnect the blower motor wiring, antenna, resistor wiring and the temperature control cable. Disconnect the vacuum harness at the connection at the top of the housing.

10. On 1990–93 Daytona and LeBaron, using a cutting device, cut the instrument panel along the indented line along the padded cover to the right of the glove box opening. Cut only plastic, do not cut through the metal dash support. Remove the reinforcement and the piece of instrument panel that is riveted to it.

11. Disconnect the demister hoses from the top of the housing, if equipped.

12. Disconnect the hanger strap from the package and rotate it aside.

13. Remove the retaining nuts from the package mounting studs at the firewall.

14. Fold the carpeting and insulation back to provide a little more working room and to prevent spillage from staining the carpeting. Pull the right side of the instrument panel out as far as possible.

15. Remove the air conditioning and heater housing assembly from under the dash panel and remove it from the passenger compartment. Remove the passenger seat if more clearance is required.

16. Disassemble the housing assembly as follows:

   a. Locate and remove the 1 retaining nut from the blend air door pivot shaft.

   b. Remove the crank arm by squeezing the retainer away from the shaft and pulling straight upward.

   c. Disconnect the vacuum lines from the defroster and panel mode vacuum actuators and position them aside.

   d. Remove the heater air conditioning unit cover attaching screws going upward at the defroster outlet chamber.

   e. Remove the 2 heater air conditioning unit cover attaching screws going upward at the air inlet plenum.

   f. Remove the remaining air conditioning unit cover attaching screws going downward into the housing and remove the cover.

17. Remove the retaining screw from the heater core and remove the core from the housing assembly.

To install:

18. Remove the temperature control door from the housing and clean the unit out with solvent. Lubricate the

lower pivot rod and its well and install. Wrap the heater core with foam tape and place it in position. Secure it with its screw.

19. Assemble the housing, making sure all vacuum tubing is properly routed. Install the crank arm onto shaft and secure using the retainer clip.

20. Feed the vacuum lines through the hole in the firewall and install the assembly to the vehicle. Connect the vacuum harness and demister hoses. Install the nuts to the firewall and connect the hanger strap inside the passenger compartment.

21. Fold the carpeting and installation back into position.

22. Install the bolt that attaches the right side of the instrument panel to the cowl.

23. Connect the blower motor wiring, antenna, resistor wiring and the temperature control cable. If equipped with ATC, reconnect the wire harness to the rear of the control assembly.

24. Install the center and floor distribution ducts.

25. Install the floor console, if equipped.

26. Install the radio and all other dash mounted items that were removed during the disassembly procedure.

27. Install the lower instrument panel reinforcements and silencers.

28. Install all modules, relay panels and computer components removed during disassembly.

29. Install the glove box and right side kick and sill panels. Install the passenger seat, if removed.

30. Connect the vacuum lines at the brake booster and water valve.

31. Using new gaskets, install the H-valve and condensation tube.

32. Connect the heater hoses to the core tubes at the firewall.

33. Using the proper equipment, evacuate and recharge the air conditioning system.

34. Fill the cooling system.

35. Connect the negative battery cable and check the entire climate control system for proper operation and leakage.

Water Pump

REMOVAL & INSTALLATION

2.2L and 2.5L Engines

1. Disconnect the negative battery cable.

2. Drain the cooling system.

3. If equipped with air conditioning, remove the compressor from the bracket and position it aside. It is not necessary to discharge the air conditioning system.

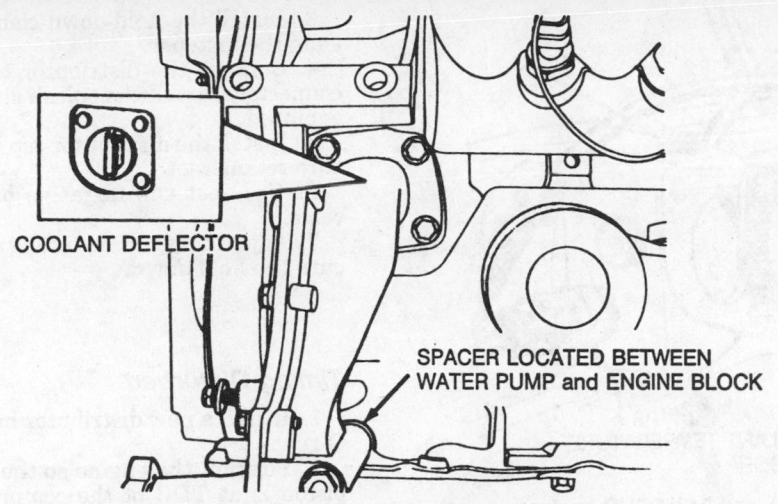

Water pump assembly—2.2L Turbo III engine

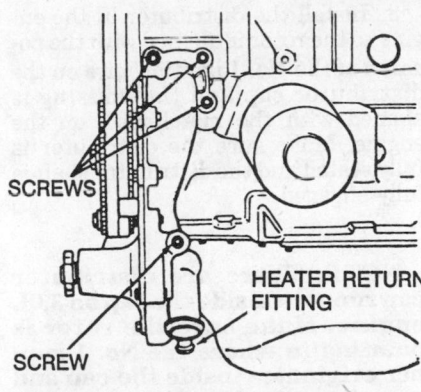

Water pump assembly—2.2L and 2.5L engines. Note differences on 2.2L Turbo III engine

Water pump assembly—3.0L engine

4. Remove the alternator and bracket from the engine. Have a drain pan under the side mounting stud because the stud screws into a water jacket, and coolant will spill out when it is removed. Remove the pulley and belt from the water pump.

5. Disconnect the lower radiator hose and heater hose from the water pump.

6. Remove the water pump housing attaching screws and remove the assembly from the vehicle. Discard the O-ring. The 2.2L Turbo III engine is equipped with a spacer between the pump housing and block on the lower mounting stud.

7. Remove the water pump from the housing. The 2.2L Turbo III engine is equipped with a coolant deflector which an be re-used.

To install:

8. Using a new gasket or silicone sealer, install the water pump to the housing.

9. On 2.2L Turbo III engine, install the coolant deflector to the block and install the spacer to the lower stud. In-

stall a new O-ring to the housing and install to the engine. Torque the 3 upper bolts to 21 ft. lbs. (30 Nm) and the lower nut to 50 ft. lbs. (68 Nm).

10. Install the water pump pulley and torque the bolts to 21 ft. lbs. (30 Nm). Connect the radiator hose and heater hose to the water pump.

11. Install the alternator and compressor bracket to the engine. Install the alternator and the air conditioning compressor. Adjust the accessory drive belts.

12. Remove the hex-head plug on the top of the thermostat housing. Fill the radiator with coolant until the coolant comes out the plug hole. Install the plug and continue to fill the radiator.

13. Connect the negative battery cable, run the vehicle until the thermostat opens, fill the radiator completely and check for leaks.

14. Once engine has cooled, recheck the coolant level and add as required.

3.0L Engine

1. Disconnect the negative battery cable.

2. Drain the cooling system.

3. Remove the timing cover. If the same timing belt will be reused, mark the direction of the timing belt's rotation, for installation in the same direction. Make sure the engine is positioned so the No. 1 cylinder is at the TDC of its compression stroke and the sprockets timing marks are aligned with the engine's timing mark indicators.

4. Loosen the timing belt tensioner bolt and remove the belt. Position the tensioner as far away from the center of the engine as possible and tighten the bolt. Remove the water pump mounting bolts, separate the pump from the water inlet pipe and remove the pump from the engine.

To install:

5. Install the water pump to the engine with new gasket in place. Torque the water pump mounting bolts to 20 ft. lbs. (27 Nm).

6. If not already done, position both camshafts so the marks align with those on the alternator bracket (rear bank) and inner timing cover (front bank). Rotate the crankshaft so the timing mark aligns with the mark on the oil pump.

7. Install the timing belt on the crankshaft sprocket and while keeping the belt tight on the tension side (right side), install the belt on the front camshaft sprocket.

8. Install the belt on the water pump pulley, then the rear camshaft sprocket and the tensioner.

9. Rotate the front camshaft counterclockwise to tension the belt between the front camshaft and the crankshaft. If the timing marks are not aligned, repeat the procedure.

10. Install the crankshaft sprocket flange.

11. Loosen the tensioner bolt and allow the spring to tension the belt.

12. Turn the crankshaft 2 full turns in the clockwise direction only until the timing marks are aligned and torque the tensioner lock bolt to 21 ft. lbs. (29 Nm).

13. Refill the cooling system. This system uses a self-bleeding thermostat, so there is no need to bleed the system. Connect the negative battery cable, road test the vehicle and check for leaks.

Thermostat

REMOVAL & INSTALLATION

1. Disconnect the negative battery cable. Drain the coolant down to thermostat level or below.

2. Remove the thermostat housing.

3. Remove the thermostat and discard the gasket. Clean the housing

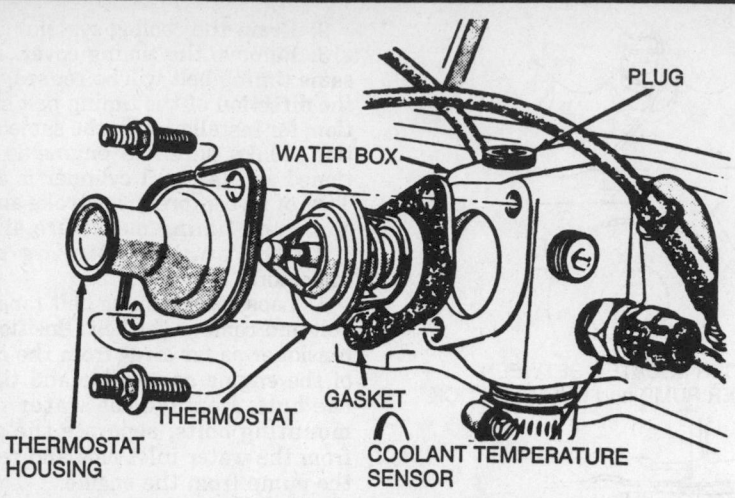

Thermostat and related items—2.2L and 2.5L SOHC engines

mating surfaces and install a new gasket.

To install:

4. Install the thermostat into the housing and position the housing on the engine.

5. Add coolant to the proper level.

6. On 2.2L and 2.5L engines, remove the plug on top of the thermostat housing. On 2.2L Turbo III engine, remove the coolant temperature sensor on top of the housing. Fill the radiator with coolant until the coolant comes out the hole. Install the plug or sensor and continue to fill the radiator. The 3.0L engine thermostat is self-bleeding.

7. Connect the negative battery cable, run the vehicle until the thermostat opens, fill the radiator completely and check for leaks.

8. Once the vehicle has cooled, recheck the coolant level.

COOLING SYSTEM BLEEDING

To bleed air from the 2.2L and 2.5L engines, remove the plug or sensor on the top of the thermostat housing. Fill the radiator with coolant until the coolant comes out the hole. Install the plug and continue to fill the radiator. This will vent all trapped air from the engine.

The thermostat in the 3.0L engine is equipped with a small air vent valve that allows trapped air to bleed from the system during refilling. This valve negates the need for cooling system bleeding in those engines.

ENGINE ELECTRICAL

NOTE: Disconnecting the nega-

tive battery cable on some vehicles may interfere with the functions of the on board computer systems and may require the computers to undergo a relearning process, once the negative battery cable is reconnected.

Distributor

REMOVAL

1. Disconnect the negative battery cable.

2. Disconnect the distributor pickup lead wires. Remove the splash shield, if equipped.

3. Unscrew the distributor cap hold-down screws and lift off the distributor cap with all ignition wires still connected. Remove the coil wire, if necessary.

4. Matchmark the rotor to the distributor housing and the distributor housing to the engine.

NOTE: Do not crank the engine during this procedure. If the engine is cranked, the matchmark must be disregarded.

5. Remove the hold-down bolt and clamp or nut.

6. Remove the distributor from the engine.

INSTALLATION

Timing Not Disturbed

1. Install a new distributor housing O-ring.

2. Install the distributor in the engine so the rotor is aligned with the matchmark on the housing and the housing is aligned with the matchmark on the engine. Make sure the distributor is fully seated and the distributor shaft is fully engaged.

3. Install the hold-down clamp and snug the fastener.

4. Connect the distributor harness connector. Install the splash shield, if equipped.

5. Install the distributor cap and secure retainers.

6. Connect the negative battery cable.

7. Adjust the ignition timing and secure the hold-down.

Timing Disturbed

1. Install a new distributor housing O-ring.

2. Position the engine so the No. 1 piston is at TDC of the compression stroke and the mark on the vibration damper is aligned with 0 on the timing indicator.

3. Install the distributor in the engine so the rotor is aligned with the position of the No. 1 ignition wire on the distributor cap and the housing is aligned with the matchmark on the engine. Make sure the distributor is fully seated and the distributor shaft is fully engaged.

NOTE: There are distributor cap runners inside the cap on 3.0L engine. Make sure the rotor is pointing to where the No. 1 runner originates inside the cap and not where the No. 1 ignition wire plugs into the cap.

4. Install the hold-down clamp and snug retainer.

5. Connect the distributor wire harness connector. Install the splash shield, if equipped.

6. Install the distributor cap and tighten the screws.

7. Connect the negative battery cable.

8. Adjust the ignition timing and tighten the hold-down bolt.

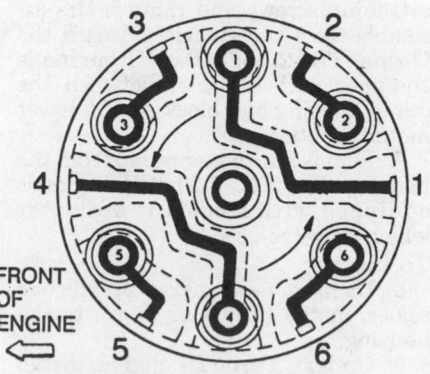

Distributor cap terminal routing—3.0L engine

Distributorless Ignition System

REMOVAL & INSTALLATION

Crankshaft Sensor

1. Disconnect negative battery cable.
2. Remove the inter-cooler to turbocharger air hose.
3. Disconnect the crankshaft sensor wiring harness connector.
4. Remove the timing sensor retaining bolts and lift the sensor straight up and out of the transaxle housing.

To install:

5. Install the sensor into the transaxle. Apply a downward pressure on the sensor until contact with the transaxle housing is made and secure with the mounting bolt. Tighten bolt to a torque of 145 inch lbs. (16 Nm).
6. Connect the sensor electrical harness and the negative battery cable.
7. Install air inlet hose.

Camshaft Sensor

1. Disconnect negative battery cable.
2. Disconnect the cam reference sensor lead at the wiring harness connector.
3. Remove the sensor retainer bolt and remove the sensor.
4. If installing the original sensor, clean off the old spacer from the sensor face. A new spacer must be installed during installation. If installing a new sensor, confirm that a new paper spacer is installed on the sensor prior to installation.

To install:

5. Install the sensor into the cylinder head and push the sensor downward until contact is made with the camshaft gear. While holding the sensor in this position, install and tighten the retainer bolt to 145 inch lbs. (16 Nm).
6. Connect the sensor wire harness connector and the negative battery cable.

Ignition Coil

1. Remove the ignition cables from the coil pack.
2. Disconnect the harness connector from the coil pack.
3. Remove the ignition coil fasteners and the coil pack from the engine.
4. Installation is the reverse of the removal procedure. Torque the fasteners to 105 inch lbs. (12 Nm).

Ignition Timing

The ignition timing can not be set or adjusted on the 2.2L Turbo III engine.

ADJUSTMENT

1. Start the engine, set the parking brake and run the engine until at normal operating temperature. Keep all lights and accessories **OFF**.
2. If a magnetic timing unit is available, insert the probe into the receptacle near the timing scale. The scale is located on the top of the bellhousing on 2.2L and 2.5L engines or near the crankshaft pulley on the 3.0L engine.
3. If a magnetic timing unit is not available, connect a conventional power timing light to the No. 1 cylinder spark plug wire.
4. If a Diagnostic Readout Box II (DRB II) is available, access the Basic Timing Mode.
5. If the DRB II is not available, disconnect the coolant sensor. This sensor is located on the side of the thermostat housing on 2.2L and 2.5L engines and between the distributor or thermostat housing on 3.0L engine. The Check Engine light on the instrument panel must be **ON**.
6. Aim the timing light at the timing scale or read the magnetic timing unit.
7. Loosen the distributor hold-down bolt or nut enough so the distributor can be rotated.
8. Turn the distributor in the proper direction until the specified timing according to the VECI label is reached. Tighten the hold-down bolt or nut and recheck the timing.
9. Turn the engine **OFF**. Connect the coolant sensor and check to make sure the Check Engine light does not come ON when the vehicle is restarted. Disconnect the timing apparatus.
10. If the coolant temperature sensor was disconnected, erase the created fault code using the Erase Fault Code mode on the DRB II.

Alternator

PRECAUTIONS

Several precautions must be observed when working with the alternator to avoid damage to the unit.

- If the battery is removed for any reason, make sure it is reconnected with the correct polarity. Reversing the battery connections may result in damage to the one-way rectifiers.
- When utilizing a booster battery as a starting aid, always connect the positive to positive terminals and the negative terminal from the booster battery to a good engine ground on the vehicle being started.
- Never use a fast charger as a booster to start vehicles.
- Disconnect the battery cables when charging the battery with a fast charger.
- Never attempt to polarize the alternator.
- Do not use test lights of more than 12 volts when checking diode continuity.
- Do not short across or ground any of the alternator terminals.
- The polarity of the battery, alternator and regulator must be matched and considered before making any electrical connections within the system.
- Never separate the alternator on an open circuit. Make sure all connections within the circuit are clean and tight.
- Disconnect the battery ground terminal when performing any service on electrical components.
- Disconnect the battery if arc welding is to be done on the vehicle.

BELT TENSION ADJUSTMENT

NOTE: The belt tension is automatically adjusted by a dynamic tensioner on the 2.2L Turbo III and 3.0L engines. Periodic adjustment is not necessary.

1. Loosen the pivot bolt slightly.
2. Raise the vehicle and support safely. Remove the splash shield. Loosen the "T" bolt locknut enough so the alternator can be moved.
3. Tighten the adjusting bolt down until the belt deflects about ¼ in. under a 10 lb. load.
4. Tighten the "T" bolt locknut and pivot bolt.

REMOVAL & INSTALLATION

2.2L and 2.5L Engines

EXCEPT TURBO III

1. Disconnect the negative battery cable. Remove the accessory drive belt(s).
2. If equipped with air conditioning, it may be necessary to remove the air conditioning compressor to gain access to the alternator. Position the compressor aside without disconnecting the refrigerant lines.
3. Remove the oil filter to allow the alternator to be removed from above.
4. Remove all mounting bolts, spacers and adjuster bolt, if equipped, and remove the alternator from the brackets. Disconnect the wire harness from the rear of the alternator and remove alternator from the vehicle.
5. Installation is the reverse of the removal procedure. Connect the negative battery cable and check for proper operation of the charging system.

2.2L TURBO III ENGINE

1. Disconnect negative battery cable.

2. Remove the alternator/air conditioning drive belt.

3. Remove the air conditioner compressor mounting bolts and remove compressor from the mounting bracket. Position the compressor aside to allow for alternator removal. It is not necessary to disconnect the refrigerant hoses from the compressor.

4. Remove the alternator mounting bracket bolts and separate the alternator from the mounting bracket. Remove the B+ terminal nut, field terminal nuts and ground wire harness hold down nuts. Remove the wire harness connectors from the alternator.

5. Remove the alternator from the vehicle.

To install:

6. Install the alternator into position and reattach the wire harness connectors using the appropriate fasteners.

7. Align the mounting ears on the alternator to the mounting bracket and secure using the alternator mounting bolts.

8. Install the air conditioning compressor to the bracket and install the mounting bolts.

9. Install the accessory drive belt.

10. Connect the negative battery cable and check for proper operation of the charging system.

3.0L Engine

1. Disconnect negative battery cable.

2. Release the dynamic belt tensioner using a ½ in. breaker bar and remove the alternator drive belt.

3. Remove the alternator mounting bolts and position the alternator so the wire terminals are accessible. Remove the wire connector fasteners, harness and the alternator from the vehicle.

4. Installation is the reverse of the removal procedure. Connect the negative battery cable and check for proper operation of the charging system.

Starter

REMOVAL & INSTALLATION

1. Disconnect the negative battery cable.

2. On 2.2L and 2.5L engines, remove the attaching nut and bolt at the top of the bellhousing. Raise the vehicle and support safely.

3. Remove the rear mount from the starter, if equipped. If equipped with 2.2L or 2.5L engine, remove the heat shield retainer clip and the shield from the starter.

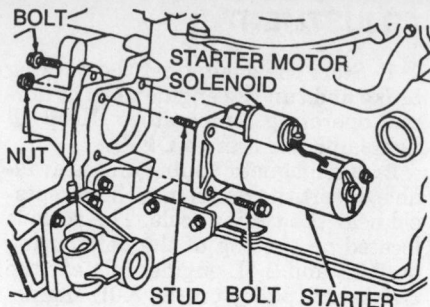

Removing or installing the starter—2.2L and 2.5L engines

4. Unbolt the starter and remove from the bellhousing. Position the starter so the wire harness connectors are accessible, remove the retainers and the wire harness from the starter solenoid.

5. Remove the starter motor from the vehicle.

To install:

6. Connect the wire harness to the starter assembly. If equipped with a 2.2L or 2.5L engine, position the heat shield on the starter assembly and secure in place using the shield retainer clip.

7. On the 2.2L and 2.5L engines, install the lower bolt loosely, then lower the vehicle and install the uppermost nut and bolt from above. Torque starter retainer bolts to 40 ft. lbs. (54 Nm). Raise the vehicle again and torque the bottom mounting bolt to the same value. Install the rear mount to the starter as required.

8. On the 3.0L engine, install all mounting bolts and torque to 40 ft. lbs. (54 Nm) evenly.

9. Connect the negative battery cable and check the starter for proper operation.

FUEL SYSTEM

Fuel System Service Precautions

Safety is the most important factor when performing not only fuel system maintenance but any type of maintenance. Failure to conduct maintenance and repairs in a safe manner may result in serious personal injury or death. Maintenance and testing of the vehicle's fuel system components can be accomplished safely and effec-

tively by adhering to the following rules and guidelines.

● To avoid the possibility of fire and personal injury, always disconnect the negative battery cable unless the repair or test procedure requires that battery voltage be applied.

● Always relieve the fuel system pressure prior to disconnecting any fuel system component (injector, fuel rail, pressure regulator, etc.), fitting or fuel line connection. Exercise extreme caution whenever relieving fuel system pressure to avoid exposing skin, face and eyes to fuel spray. Please be advised that fuel under pressure may penetrate the skin or any part of the body that it contacts.

● Always place a shop towel or cloth around the fitting or connection prior to loosening to absorb any excess fuel due to spillage. Ensure that all fuel spillage (should it occur) is quickly removed from engine surfaces. Ensure that all fuel soaked cloths or towels are deposited into a suitable waste container.

● Always keep a dry chemical (Class B) fire extinguisher near the work area.

● Do not allow fuel spray or fuel vapors to come into contact with a spark or open flame.

● Always use a backup wrench when loosening and tightening fuel line connection fittings. This will prevent unnecessary stress and torsion to fuel line piping. Always follow the proper torque specifications.

● Always replace worn fuel fitting O-rings with new. Do not substitute fuel hose or equivalent where fuel pipe is installed.

RELIEVING FUEL SYSTEM PRESSURE

1. Loosen the fuel filler cap to release fuel tank pressure.

2. Locate and disconnect the fuel injector harness connector.

3. Connect a jumper wire from terminal No. 1 of the appropriate connector to ground.

4. Being careful not to allow contact between the jumper leads, connect a

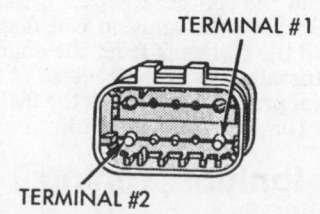

Injector harness connector—1992–93 3.0L engine

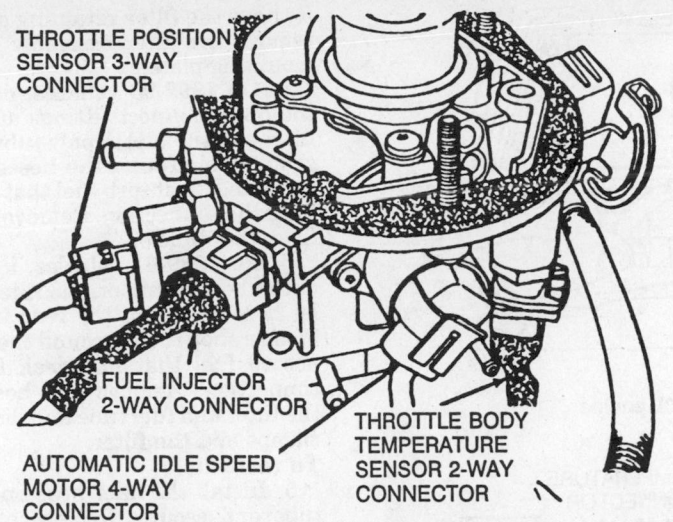

THROTTLE POSITION
SENSOR 3-WAY
CONNECTOR

FUEL INJECTOR
2-WAY CONNECTOR

THROTTLE BODY
TEMPERATURE
SENSOR 2-WAY
CONNECTOR

AUTOMATIC IDLE SPEED
MOTOR 4-WAY
CONNECTOR

Fuel injector harness location—2.2L and 2.5L non-turbocharged engine

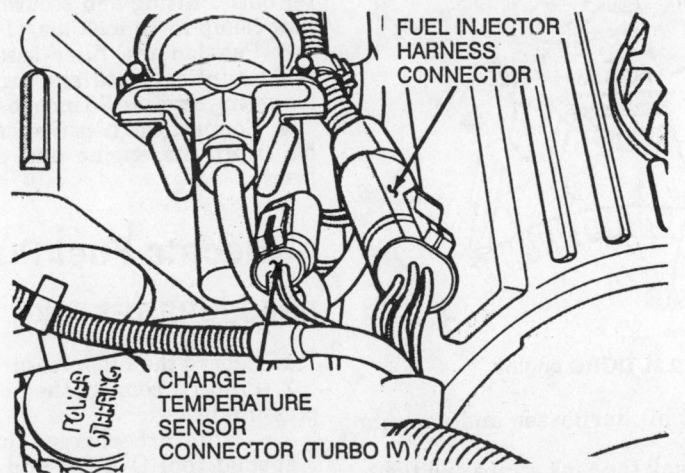

FUEL INJECTOR
HARNESS
CONNECTOR

CHARGE
TEMPERATURE
SENSOR
CONNECTOR (TURBO IV)

**Fuel injectors harness location—turbocharged engine, except TC and Turbo III.
The connector may vary slightly between vehicles**

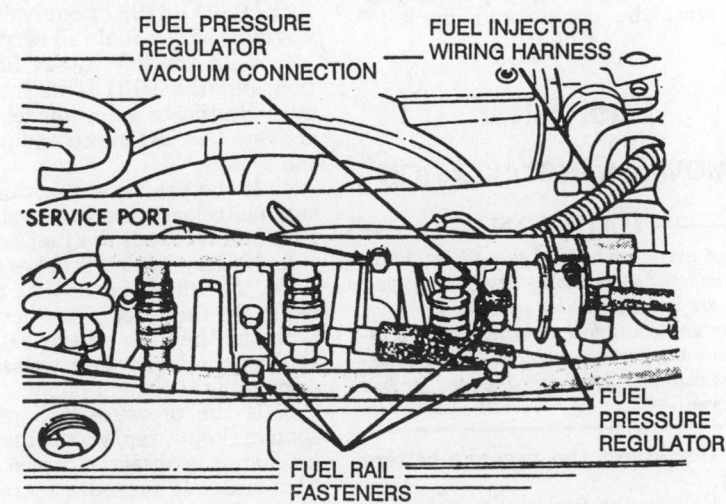

FUEL PRESSURE
REGULATOR
VACUUM CONNECTION

FUEL INJECTOR
WIRING HARNESS

SERVICE PORT

FUEL
PRESSURE
REGULATOR

FUEL RAIL
FASTENERS

Fuel injectors wiring harness—2.2L Turbo III engine

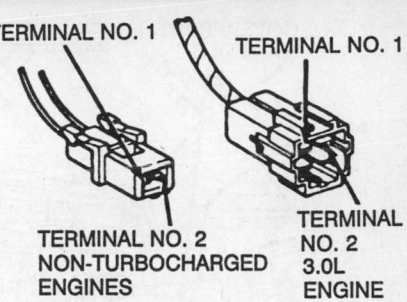

TERMINAL NO. 1

TERMINAL NO. 1

TERMINAL NO. 2
NON-TURBOCHARGED
ENGINES

TERMINAL
NO. 2
3.0L
ENGINE

TERMINAL NO. 1

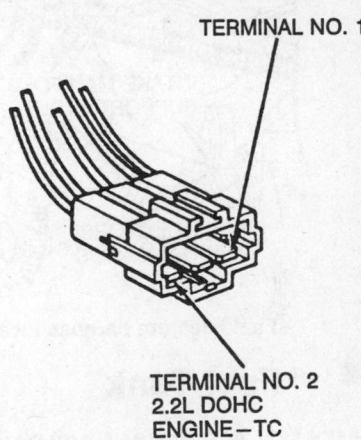

TERMINAL NO. 2
TURBOCHARGED
ENGINES—1990–92
EXCEPT TC

TERMINAL NO. 1

TERMINAL NO. 2
2.2L DOHC
ENGINE—TC

TERMINAL NO. 1

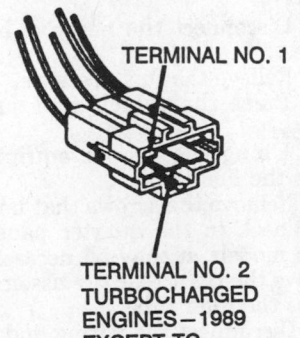

TERMINAL NO. 2
TURBOCHARGED
ENGINES—1989
EXCEPT TC

**Fuel injector harness connector
terminals**

jumper wire to terminal No. 2 of the connector and touch the other end of the jumper to the positive battery post for no longer than 5 seconds. This will relieve fuel pressure.

5. Remove the jumper wires, disconnect the negative battery cable and continue with fuel system service.

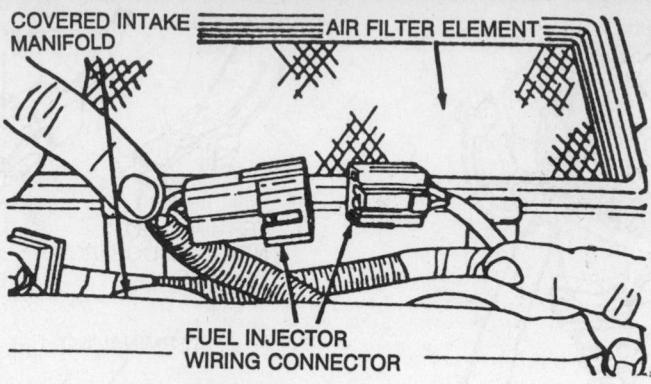

Fuel injectors harness location – 3.0L engine

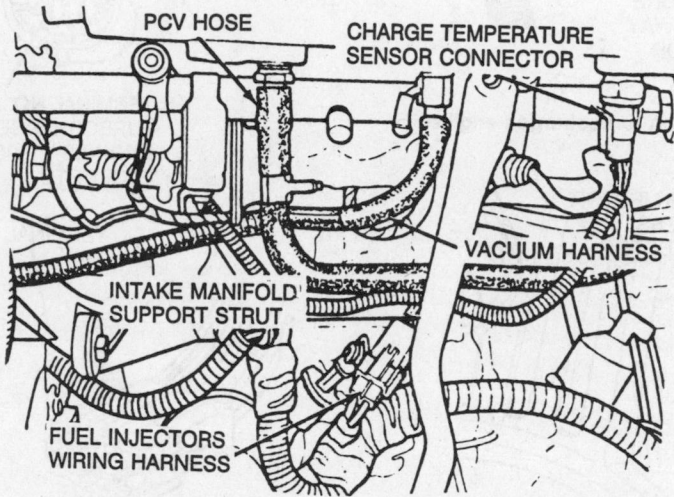

Fuel injectors harness location – TC with 2.2L DOHC engine

Fuel Tank

REMOVAL & INSTALLATION

1. Disconnect the negative battery cable.
2. Relieve the fuel pressure.
3. Raise the vehicle and support safely.
4. Using the proper equipment, drain the fuel tank.
5. Remove the screws that hold the filler neck to the quarter panel. On some models, it may be necessary to remove the right rear tire assembly to access the filler tube.
6. Disconnect the wiring and hoses from the tank.
7. Place a transmission jack or equivalent, under the center of the tank and apply slight pressure. Remove the tank straps.
8. Remove the filler tube from the tank.
9. Lower the tank and disconnect the vapor separator rollover valve hose. Remove the fuel tank from the vehicle.

To install:

10. Raise the tank into position and connect all harnesses and vacuum hoses.
11. Install the tank straps and tighten the retaining nuts.
12. Install the screws that hold the filler neck to the quarter panel.
13. Connect the negative battery cable, start the engine and check for leaks.

Fuel Filter

REMOVAL & INSTALLATION

— CAUTION —

Do not use conventional fuel filters, hoses or clamps when servicing this fuel system. They are not compatible with the injection system and could fail, causing personal injury or damage to the vehicle. Use only hoses and clamps specifically designed for fuel injection.

1. Disconnect the negative battery cable.
2. Relieve the fuel pressure.
3. The filter is located on the frame rail toward the rear of the vehicle. Raise the vehicle and support safely.

Remove the filter retaining screw and remove the filter assembly from the mounting plate.

4. On 1992-93 vehicles, disconnect the quick connect fittings at the fuel filter and the fuel supply tube. Wrap a shop towel around the hoses prior to removing, to absorb fuel that may leak from the connection. Remove the filter from the vehicle.

5. On 1989-91 vehicles. loosen the outlet hose clamp on the filter and inlet hose clamp on the rear fuel tube. Wrap a shop towel around the hoses to absorb fuel that may leak from the connection. Remove the hoses from the filter and fuel tube and discard the clamps and the filter.

To install:

6. Install the inlet hose on the fuel tube and secure. Replace old clamp with new and tighten to 10 inch lbs. (1 Nm).

7. Install the outlet hose on the filter outlet fitting and secure. Tighten new clamp to 10 inch lbs. (1 Nm).

8. Position the filter assembly on the mounting plate and tighten the mounting screw to 75 inch lbs. (8 Nm).

9. Connect the negative battery cable, start the engine and check for leaks.

Electric Fuel Pump

PRESSURE TESTING

1. Relieve the fuel pressure.
2. Properly connect the fuel system pressure tester:
   a. Non-turbocharged engines – special tool C–4799 and adaptor 6539 or equivalent, is installed between the fuel supply hose and the engine fuel line assembly.
   b. Turbocharged engines – special tool C–4799 or equivalent, is installed to the fuel rail service valve.
3. With the key in the **RUN** position, put the DRB II in the activate auto shutdown relay mode; this will activate the fuel pump and pressurize the system.
4. If the pressure is within specifications, release the fuel system pressure and reinstall the fuel hose.
5. If fuel pressure is below specifications, install the tester with the adaptor in the fuel supply line between the tank and the filter and repeat the test. Release the fuel system pressure prior to opening the fuel system.
6. If the pressure is 5 psi higher than in Step 5, replace the fuel filter. If no change is observed, squeeze the return hose. If pressure increases, replace the pressure regulator. If no change is observed, the problem is either a plugged in-tank sock filter or a defective pump.

7. If fuel pressure is above specifications, remove the fuel return line hose from the chassis line at the fuel tank and connect a 3 foot piece of fuel hose to the return line. Put the other end into a 2 gallon minimum capacity approved gasoline container. Repeat the test. If pressure is now correct, replace the fuel pump assembly.

8. If fuel pressure is still above specifications, release the fuel system pressure and remove the fuel return line hose from the chassis fuel tubes close to the engine.

9. Attach fuel pressure tester to the fuel return hose, place the other end of the hose into an approved gasoline container and repeat the test.

10. If the pressure is now correct, check for a restricted fuel return line. If the fuel pressure did not change, replace the fuel pressure regulator.

REMOVAL & INSTALLATION

1. Disconnect the negative battery cable.

2. Relieve the fuel system pressure.

3. Raise the vehicle and support safely.

4. Using the proper equipment, drain the fuel tank.

5. Remove the screws that hold the filler neck to the quarter panel.

6. Disconnect the wiring and hoses from the tank.

7. Place a transmission jack under the center of the tank and apply slight pressure. Remove the tank straps.

8. Remove the filler tube from the tank.

9. Lower the tank and disconnect the vapor separator rollover valve hose. Remove the fuel tank from the vehicle.

10. Using a hammer and a brass drift, tap the lock ring counterclockwise to release the pump.

11. Partially pull the pump assembly out of the tank until the return line hose connection is visible at the of the pump assembly.

12. Disconnect the fuel fitting by pressing in on the ears.

13. Remove the pump from the tank with the O-ring. Discard the O-ring, pump inlet filter and inlet seal. Disassemble as required.

To install:

14. Install a new inlet seal, filter and strainer O-ring onto the pump. When installing strainer onto the pump reservoir body, make sure the locking tabs on the reservoir body lock over the locking tangs on the strainer.

15. Install the pump into the tank so the fuel return hose is not kinked.

16. Install the lock ring with a hammer and brass punch turning the ring clockwise. Overtightening of the lock ring may result in a leak.

17. Install the fuel tank and remaining components into position.

18. Connect the negative battery cable, start the engine and check the fuel system for leaks.

Fuel Injection

IDLE SPEED ADJUSTMENT

The idle speed is controlled by the Automatic Idle Speed motor (AIS). The AIS is controlled by the SMEC or SBEC, which receives data from various sensors and switches in the system and adjusts the engine idle to a predetermined speed. Idle speed specifications can be found on the Vehicle Emission Control Information (VECI) label located in the engine compartment. If the idle speed is not within specifications and there are no problems with the system, the throttle body should be replaced.

IDLE MIXTURE ADJUSTMENT

There is no idle mixture adjustment provided with any Chrysler fuel injection system.

Fuel Injector

REMOVAL & INSTALLATION

2.2L and 2.5L Non—Turbocharged Engines

1. Disconnect the negative battery cable.

2. Remove the air cleaner assembly.

3. Relieve the fuel pressure.

4. Remove the injector hold-down Torx® screw and the hold-down.

5. Using a pair of small flat-tipped tools, lift the cap off the injector.

6. Gently pry the injector from its pod.

7. Remove the lower O-ring from the pod.

To install:

8. Install the new lower O-ring on the injector.

9. Align the injector terminal housing with the locating socket in the injector cap.

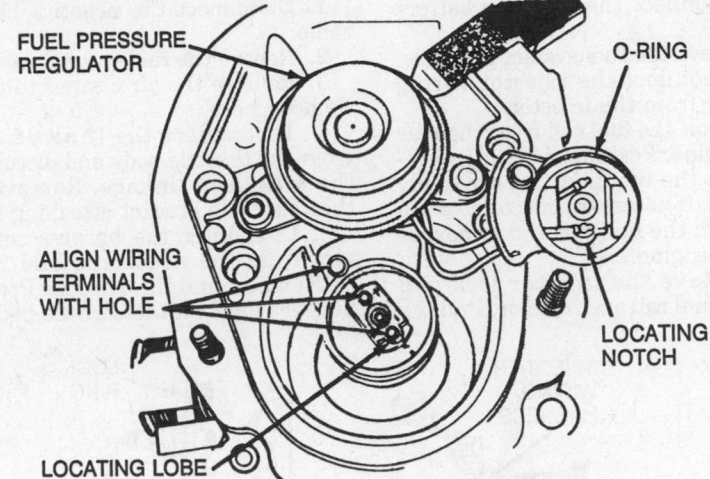

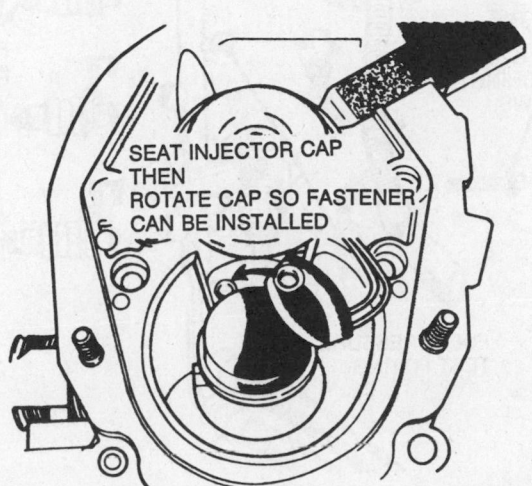

Installing the injector to the cap—2.2L and 2.5L non-turbocharged engines

10. Press the injector cap so the upper O-ring flange is flush with the lower surface of the cap.

11. Spray the inner surfaces of the injector pod with a carburetor parts cleaner to remove residual varnish and gasoline.

12. Lubricate the O-rings sparingly with unmedicated petroleum jelly.

13. Place the injector and cap into the injector pod and align the cap locating pin with the locating hole in the casting.

14. Press firmly on the injector cap until it is flush with the casting surface.

15. Align the hole in the hold-down with the pin on the cap and install.

16. Push down on the cap, install the screw and torque to 35 inch lbs. (4 Nm).

17. Connect the negative battery cable and check for leaks using the DRB II to activate the fuel pump.

18. Install the air cleaner.

2.2L and 2.5L Turbocharged Engines

1. Disconnect the negative battery cable.

2. Relieve the fuel system pressure.

3. Disconnect the injector wiring connector from the injector.

4. Unbolt the fuel rail from the rear of the engine. Position the fuel rail assembly so the fuel injectors are easily accessible. If necessary, disconnect the hoses from the fuel rail and remove it from the engine.

5. Remove the injector lock clip from the fuel rail and injector. Pull the injector straight out of the fuel rail receiver cup.

6. Check the injector O-ring for damage. If the O-ring is damaged, replace it. If the injector is being reused, install a protective cap on the injector tip to prevent damage.

7. Repeat the procedure for the remaining injectors.

To install:

8. Before installing an injector the rubber O-ring should be lubricated with a drop of clean engine oil to aid in installation.

9. Install injector top end into fuel rail receiver cup.

10. Install injector clip by sliding the open end into top slot of the injector and onto the receiver cup ridge into the side slots of clip.

11. Repeat the steps for the remaining injectors.

12. Install the fuel rail.

13. Connect the negative battery cable and check for leaks using the DRB II to activate the fuel pump.

3.0L Engine

1. Disconnect the negative battery cable.

2. Relieve the fuel system pressure.

3. Remove the air cleaner to throttle body hose.

4. Disconnect the throttle cable from the throttle body and disconnect the kickdown linkage. Remove the throttle cable bracket attaching bolts.

5. Disconnect the harness connectors from the Automatic Idle Speed (AIS) motor and the Throttle Position Sensor (TPS) on the throttle body.

6. Matchmark and carefully remove the vacuum hoses from the throttle body.

7. Remove the PCV and brake booster hoses from the air intake plenum.

8. Remove the ignition coil from the intake plenum, if mounted there.

9. Remove the EGR tube flange from the intake plenum, if equipped.

10. Unplug the coolant temperature sensor and charge temperature sensor, if equipped.

11. Remove the vacuum connection from the air intake plenum vacuum connector.

12. Remove the fuel hoses from the fuel rail and plug them.

13. Remove the air intake plenum to intake manifold bolts and remove the plenum and gaskets. Cover the intake manifold openings.

14. Remove the vacuum hoses from the fuel rail.

15. Label and disconnect the fuel injector wiring harness from each injector.

16. Remove the fuel rail attaching bolts and remove the fuel rail with the wiring harness from the vehicle. Position the rail on the bench upside down so the injectors are easily accessible.

17. Remove the retainer clip from the slot on the fuel injector and remove by pulling the injector straight out off of the rail.

To install:

18. Lubricate the rubber O-ring with clean oil and install to the rail receiver cap. Install the injector clip to the **TOP** slot of the injector, plug in the connector and install the connector clip.

19. Install the fuel rail to the vehicle and plug in the injector harness. Connect the vacuum hoses to the fuel rail.

20. Install new intake plenum gaskets with the beaded sealer side up and install the intake plenum. Torque the attaching bolts and nuts to 115 inch lbs. (13 Nm).

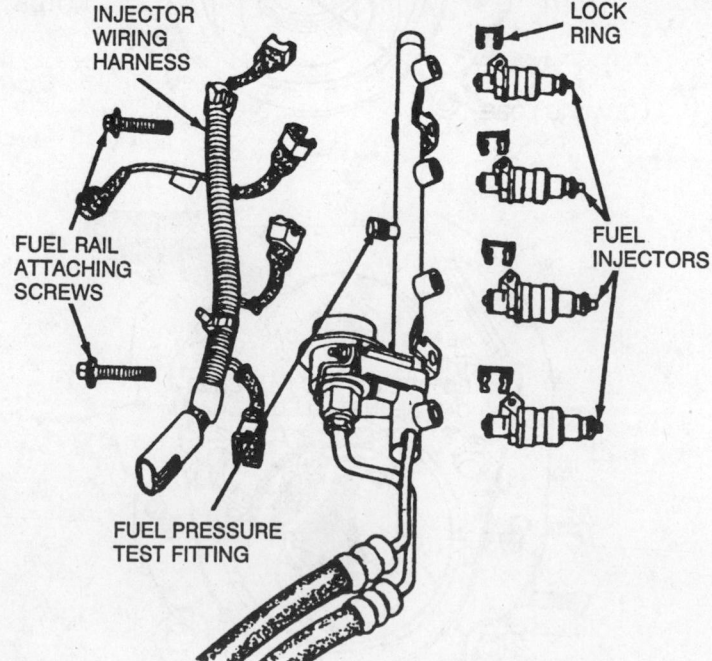

INJECTOR WIRING HARNESS
LOCK RING
FUEL RAIL ATTACHING SCREWS
FUEL INJECTORS
FUEL PRESSURE TEST FITTING

Fuel Injector removal and installation—turbocharged engine

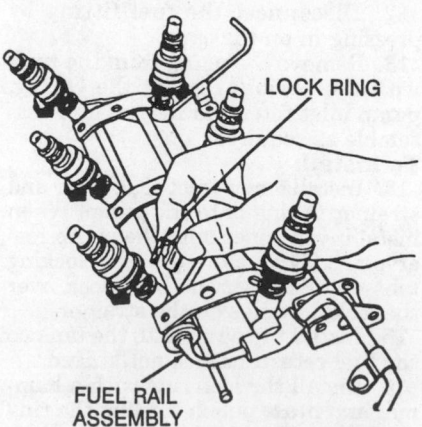

LOCK RING
FUEL RAIL ASSEMBLY

Fuel rail assembly—3.0L engine

21. Install the fuel hoses to the fuel rail.

22. Connect remaining items that were attached to the intake plenum and throttle body.

23. Connect the negative battery cable and check for leaks using the DRB II to activate the fuel pump.

DRIVE AXLE

Halfshaft

REMOVAL & INSTALLATION

1. Disconnect the negative battery cable.

2. Remove the cotter pin, nut lock and spring washer from the end of the halfshaft. Apply the brakes and loosen the hub nut while the vehicle is on the floor.

3. Raise the vehicle and support safely. Remove the tire and wheel assembly.

4. Remove the axle nut and washer.

5. Remove the ball joint retaining bolt and pry the control arm down to release the ball stud from the steering knuckle.

6. If removing the right halfshaft, remove the speedometer pinion retainer nut from the extension on the right side of the transaxle and remove the pinion.

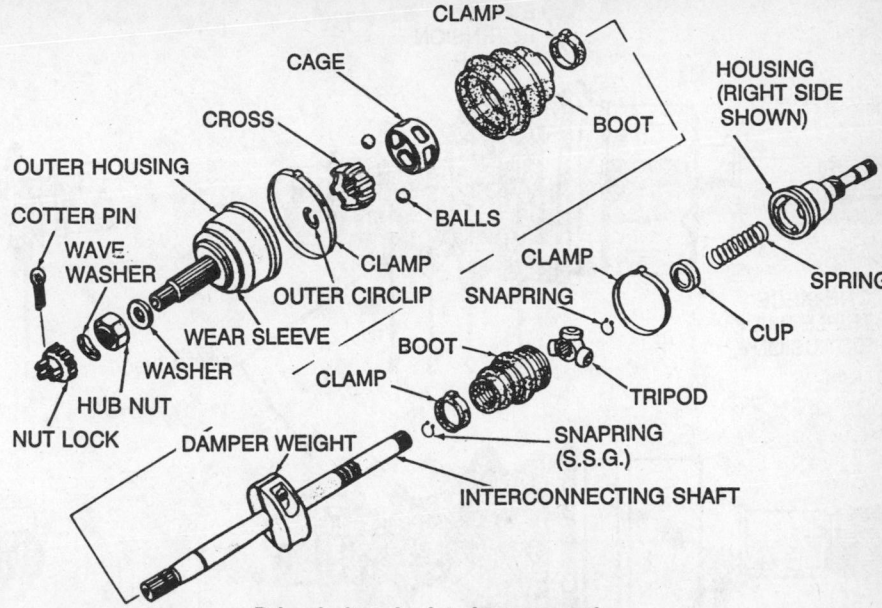

Driveshaft and related components

7. Position a drainpan under the transaxle where the halfshaft enters the differential or extension housing. Remove the halfshaft from the steering knuckle and then the transaxle or center bearing by pulling on the inner joint. Unbolt the center bearing from the block and remove the intermediate shaft from the transaxle, if equipped.

To install:

8. Install the halfshaft or intermediate shaft to the transaxle, being careful not to damage the side seals. Make sure the inner joint clicks into place inside the differential. Install the center bearing retaining bolts if equipped, then install the outer shaft to the center bearing.

9. Pull the front strut out and insert the outer joint into the front hub.

10. If necessary, turn the ball joint stud to position the bolt retaining indent to the inside of the vehicle. Install the ball joint stud into the steering knuckle. Install the retaining bolt and nut and torque to 70 ft. lbs. (95 Nm). This nut and bolt combination is unique to this application and should not be replaced with conventional hardware. Use original equipment parts if replacing.

11. Install the speedometer pinion to the extension on the transaxle and secure using the mounting bolt.

12. Install the axle nut washer and nut and torque the nut to 180 ft. lbs. (244 Nm). Install the spring washer, nut lock and a new cotter pin.

13. Install the tire and wheel assembly.

CV-Boot

REMOVAL & INSTALLATION

NOTE: Use only clamps provided with the replacement package when servicing. Plastic wire ties and other straps will not clamp tightly enough and grease will sling out, causing costly damage to the joint.

Inner Joint

1. Remove the halfshaft from the vehicle.

2. If cutting the boot away, mark and note the boot positioning on the

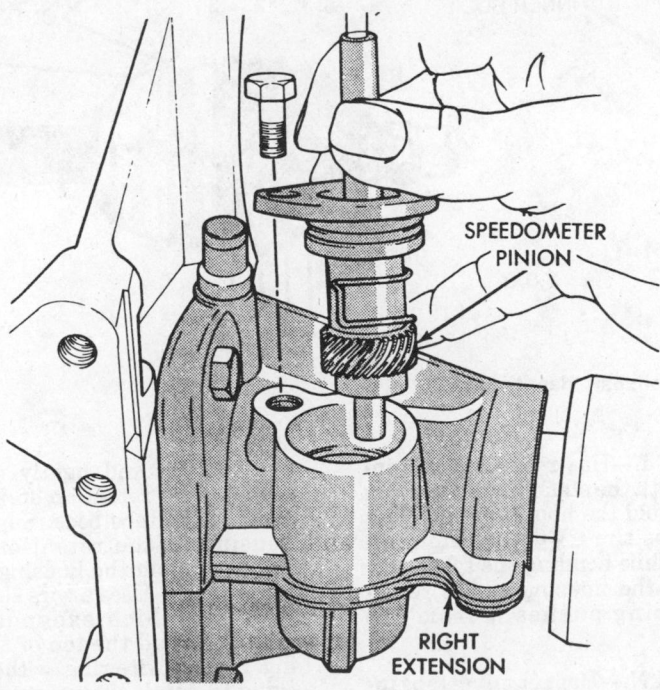

Removing speedometer pinion from axle housing

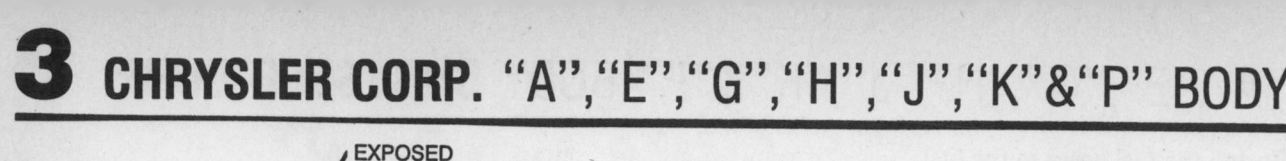

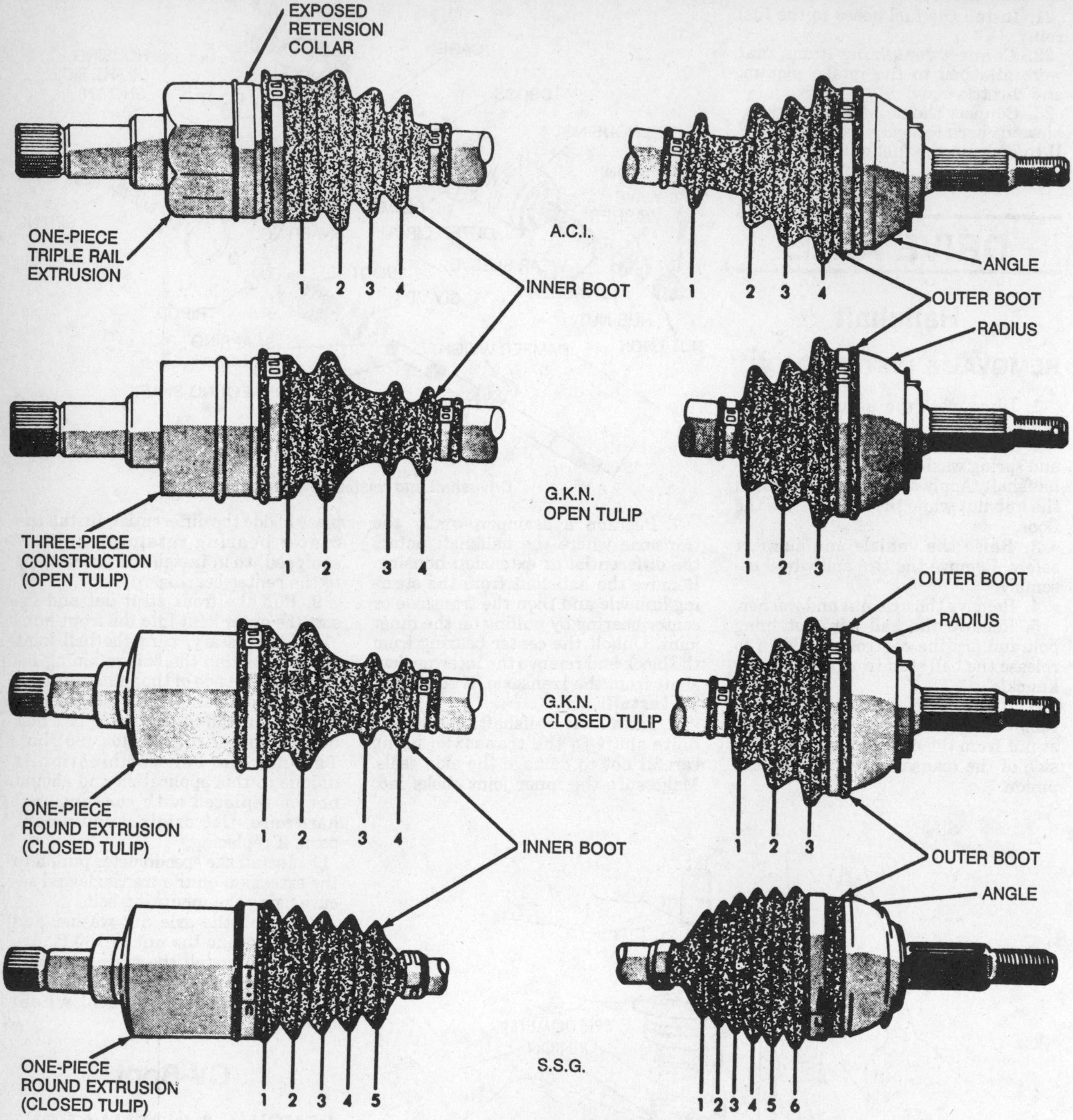

EXPOSED
RETENSION
COLLAR

ONE-PIECE
TRIPLE RAIL
EXTRUSION

A.C.I.

INNER BOOT

1 2 3 4

ANGLE

OUTER BOOT

RADIUS

THREE-PIECE
CONSTRUCTION
(OPEN TULIP)

1 2 3 4

G.K.N.
OPEN TULIP

1 2 3

OUTER BOOT

RADIUS

ONE-PIECE
ROUND EXTRUSION
(CLOSED TULIP)

1 2 3 4

G.K.N.
CLOSED TULIP

INNER BOOT

1 2 3

OUTER BOOT

ANGLE

ONE-PIECE
ROUND EXTRUSION
(CLOSED TULIP)

1 2 3 4 5

S.S.G.

1 2 3 4 5 6

Halfshaft Identification.

shaft relative to the raised shoulders. Remove the boot clamps to gain access to the tripod retention system.

3. Separate the housing from the tripod according to the following:

NOTE: Hold the rollers in place when removing the housing from the tripod or the needle bearings may fall out.

a. A.C.I.—Has retaining tabs integral with the staked boot retaining collar. Hold the housing and lightly compress the CV-joint retention spring while bending the tabs back. Support the housing as the retention spring pushes it from the housing.

b. G.K.N.—Has retaining tabs integral with the housing cover. Hold

the housing and lightly compress the CV-joint retention spring while bending the tabs back. Support the housing as the retention spring pushes it from the housing.

c. S.S.G.—Uses a wire ring tripod retainer which expands into a groove around the top of the housing. Pry the wire ring, without damaging it, out of the groove and slide the tripod from the housing.

4. Remove the snapring ring from the end of the shaft and remove the tripod.

5. If not already done, mark the boot positioning on the shaft relative to the raised shoulders. Remove the boot from the shaft.

6. Remove as much old grease as possible from the joint. Inspect all parts for wear or damage.

NOTE: Do not use petroleum based solvents on the joints, shaft or boot to clean; it will ruin hidden rubber seals within the joint. Use only chlorine based cleaner or hot soapy water to clean the joint, if necessary. Make sure the joint is completely dry before assembling.

To install:

7. On right inner joint of shafts of turbocharged vehicles, slide a new rubber washer seal over the stub shaft and down into the groove provided.

8. If the clamping device is not a staight strap, install it on the shaft first, then install the boot to the shaft in the proper position. Using the proper tool, C-4975 for crimping with plastic boot, C-4124 for crimping with rubber boot or C-4653 for clamping a strap, secure the clamp.

9. Slide the tripod on the shaft:

   a. A.C.I.—Slide the tripod on the shaft with the non-chamfered edge facing the tripod retainer ring groove.

   b. G.K.N.—Slide the tripod on the shaft with the non-chamfered edge facing the tripod retainer ring groove.

   c. S.S.G.—Place the wire ring tripod retainer over the shaft, then slide the tripod. The tripod may installed either way; both ends are the same.

10. Install the snapring into its groove on the shaft to lock the tripod in position.

11. Distribute the grease provided in the grease package as follows or according to the instructions in the package:

   a. A.C.I.—Distribute 1 of the 2 packets of grease into the boot and the remaining packet into the housing.

   b. G.K.N—If equipped with 3 packets of grease, distribute 2 of the 3 packets into the boot and the remaining packet into the housing. Otherwise, distribute ½ of the packet of grease into the boot and the remaining amount into the housing.

   c. S.S.G.—Distribute ½ of the packet of grease into the boot and the remaining amount into the housing.

12. Position the spring in the housing spring pocket with the spring cup attached to the exposed end of the spring. Place a dab of grease on the concave surface of the spring cup.

13. Keeping the spring centered, install the housing to the tripod as follows:

   a. A.C.I.—Slip the housing onto the tripod. Do not bend the retaining tabs back into their original position. Instead, secure the boot to hold the housing. The tripod must be re-engaged to the housing with the shaft installed on the vehicle.

   b. G.K.N—Slip the housing onto the tripod. Bend the retaining tabs back into their original positions. Check for proper retention ability.

   c. S.S.G.—Slip the housing onto the tripod and install the tripod wire retaining ring. Check for proper retention ability.

14. Position the larger end of the boot over the housing.

15. Using the proper tool, C-4975 for crimping with plastic boot, C-4124 for crimping with rubber boot or C-4653 for clamping a strap, secure the clamp.

16. Install the halfshaft to the vehicle. Fill the transaxle if fluid was lost when removing the halfshaft.

17. Road test the vehicle.

Outer Joint

1. Remove the halfshaft from the vehicle.

2. Mark and note the boot positioning on the shaft, relative to the raised shoulders, if cutting the boot away. Remove the boot clamps to gain access to the joint retention system.

3. Separate the housing from the tripod according to the following:

   a. A.C.I.—Using a soft-jaw vise, support the halfshaft. Strike the joint assembly sharply with a soft-face hammer to dislodge the internal circlip and remove from the shaft.

   b. G.K.N—Using a soft-jaw vise, support the halfshaft. Strike the joint assembly sharply with a soft-face hammer to dislodge the internal circlip and remove from the shaft.

   c. S.S.G.—Loosen the damper weight bolts and slide it and the boot toward the inner joint. Expand the snapring and slide the joint from the shaft. Reinstall the damper weight and torque the bolts to 21 ft. lbs. (28 Nm).

4. If damaged, remove the wear sleeve from the CV-joint machined ledge.

5. Remove the circlip from the groove.

6. If not already done, mark the boot positioning on the shaft relative to the raised shoulders and remove the boot from the shaft.

7. Remove as much old grease as possible from the joint. Inspect all parts for wear or damage.

NOTE: Do not use petroleum based solvents on the joints, shaft or boot to clean; it will ruin hidden rubber seals within the joint. Use only chlorine based cleaner or hot soapy water to clean the joint, if necessary. Make sure the joint it completely dry before assembling.

To install:

8. If the clamping device is not a staight strap, install it on the shaft first, then install the boot to the shaft in the proper position. Using the proper tool, C-4975 for crimping with plastic boot, C-4124 for crimping with rubber boot or C-4653 for clamping a strap, secure the clamp.

9. Install new circlip if provided in the replacement package.

10. Position the outer joint on the shaft with hub nut installed, engage the splines and strike sharply with a soft-face hammer to install. Make sure the circlip did not become dislodged.

11. Position the larger end of the boot over the housing.

12. Using the proper tool C-4975 for crimping with plastic boot, C-4124 for crimping with rubber boot or C-4653 for clamping a strap, secure the clamp.

13. Install the halfshaft to the vehicle. Fill the transaxle if fluid was lost when removing the halfshaft.

14. Road test the vehicle.

Front Wheel Hub and Bearing

REMOVAL & INSTALLATION

Pressed In (Two-Piece Hub and Bearing)

NOTE: Some hub and bearing replacement packages include the one-piece unit. If this is the case, follow the installation steps for one-piece unit instead of for the two-piece unit.

1. Loosen the hub nut while the vehicle is on the floor and the brakes are applied. Raise and safely support the vehicle.

2. Remove the tire and wheel assembly. Remove the brake caliper from the adaptor and remove the adaptor. Remove the brake disc.

3. Remove the hub nut and the washer from the stub shaft.

4. Disconnect the tie rod end from the steering arm using the appropriate puller.

5. Remove the clamp bolt securing the ball joint stud into the steering knuckle and separate.

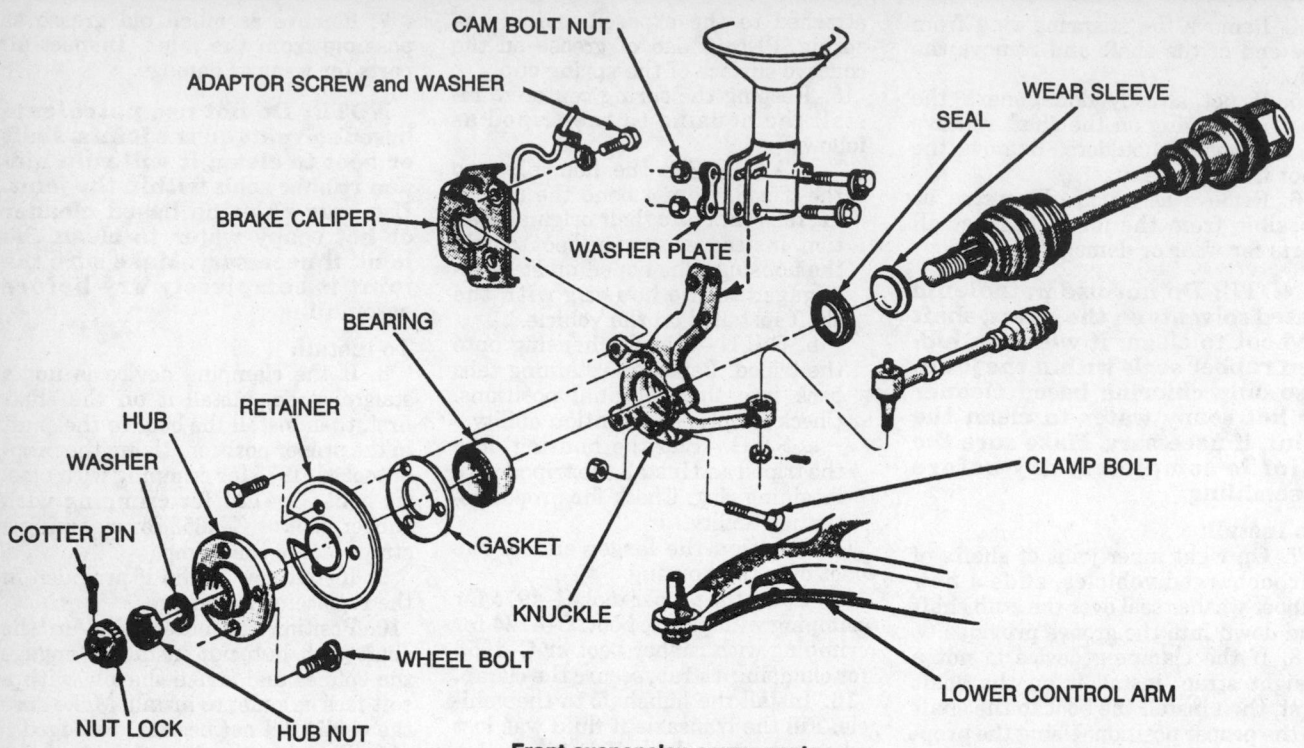

CAM BOLT NUT
ADAPTOR SCREW and WASHER
SEAL
WEAR SLEEVE
BRAKE CALIPER
WASHER PLATE
BEARING
HUB
RETAINER
WASHER
CLAMP BOLT
COTTER PIN
GASKET
KNUCKLE
WHEEL BOLT
NUT LOCK
HUB NUT
LOWER CONTROL ARM

Front suspension components

6. Matchmark the lower strut mount to the knuckle. Remove the 2 strut clamp bolts and remove the knuckle from the vehicle.

7. Attach the hub removal tool C–4811 or equivalent, and the triangular adapter, to the 3 rear threaded holes of the steering knuckle housing with the thrust button inside the hub bore.

8. Tighten the bolt in the center of the tool, to press the hub from the steering knuckle. Remove the removal tools.

9. Remove the bolts and bearing retainer from the outside the steering knuckle.

10. Carefully pry the bearing seal from the machined recess of the steering knuckle and clean the recess.

11. Insert tool C–4811 or equivalent through the hub bearing and install bearing removal adapter to the outside of the steering knuckle. Tighten the tool to press the hub bearing from the steering knuckle. Discard the bearing and the seal.

To install:

12. Use tool C–4811 or equivalent, and the bearing installation adapter to press in the hub bearing into the steering knuckle.

13. Install a new seal, the bearing retainer and the bolts to the steering knuckle. Torque the bearing retainer bolts to 20 ft. lbs. (27 Nm).

14. Use the tool C–4811 or equivalent, and the hub installation adapter, to press the hub into the hub bearing.

15. Using the bearing installation

tool C–4698 or equivalent, drive the new dust seal into the rear of the steering the hub and bearing from the knuckle as required.

16. Install the steering knuckle onto the vehicle guiding the halfshaft through the hub and install the 2 strut strut bolts. Align the matchmarks made during disassembly and tighten the nuts. The vehicle will require a front end alignment.

17. Install the ball joint stud into the steering knuckle and secure with the original knuckle clamp bolt tightened to 105 ft. lbs. (145 Nm) torque.

18. Install the tie rod end to the steering knuckle. Tighten the attaching nut to 35 ft. lbs. (47 Nm) and install new cotter pin.

19. Install the brake disc and caliper to the knuckle assembly.

20. Clean all foreign material from the threads of the axle stub shaft and install the washer and hub nut. With the brakes applied, torque the nut to 180 ft. lbs. (244 Nm) torque.

21. Install the spring washer, nut lock and new cotter pin. Wrap the prongs of the cotter pin tightly around the nut lock.

22. Install the tire and wheel assembly and tighten the lug nuts to 95 ft. lbs. (129 Nm).

23. Align the front end of the vehicle and road test.

Bolt In (One-Piece Hub and Bearing)

NOTE: Knuckle removal is not

necessary for bearing and hub replacement. If the hub and bearing assembly requires replacement, it is to be replaced as an assembly.

1. Loosen the hub nut while the vehicle is on the floor and the brakes are applied. Raise and safely support the vehicle.

2. Remove the tire and wheel assembly from the vehicle.

3. Remove the hub nut and the washer from the stub shaft.

4. Disconnect the tie rod end from the steering arm using the appropriate puller.

5. Remove the clamp bolt securing the ball joint stud into the steering knuckle and separate.

6. Remove the caliper guide pin bolts and separate the caliper assembly from the braking disc. Support the caliper with wire hook and not by the hydraulic hose.

7. Separate the steering knuckle assembly from the ball joint stud. Pull the knuckle assembly out and away from the halfshaft.

NOTE: Care must be taken when separating the halfshaft from the knuckle, do not separate the inner C/V joint during this operation. Do not allow the halfshaft to hang by the inner C/V joint, it must be supported.

8. Remove the 4 hub and bearing assembly mounting bolts from the

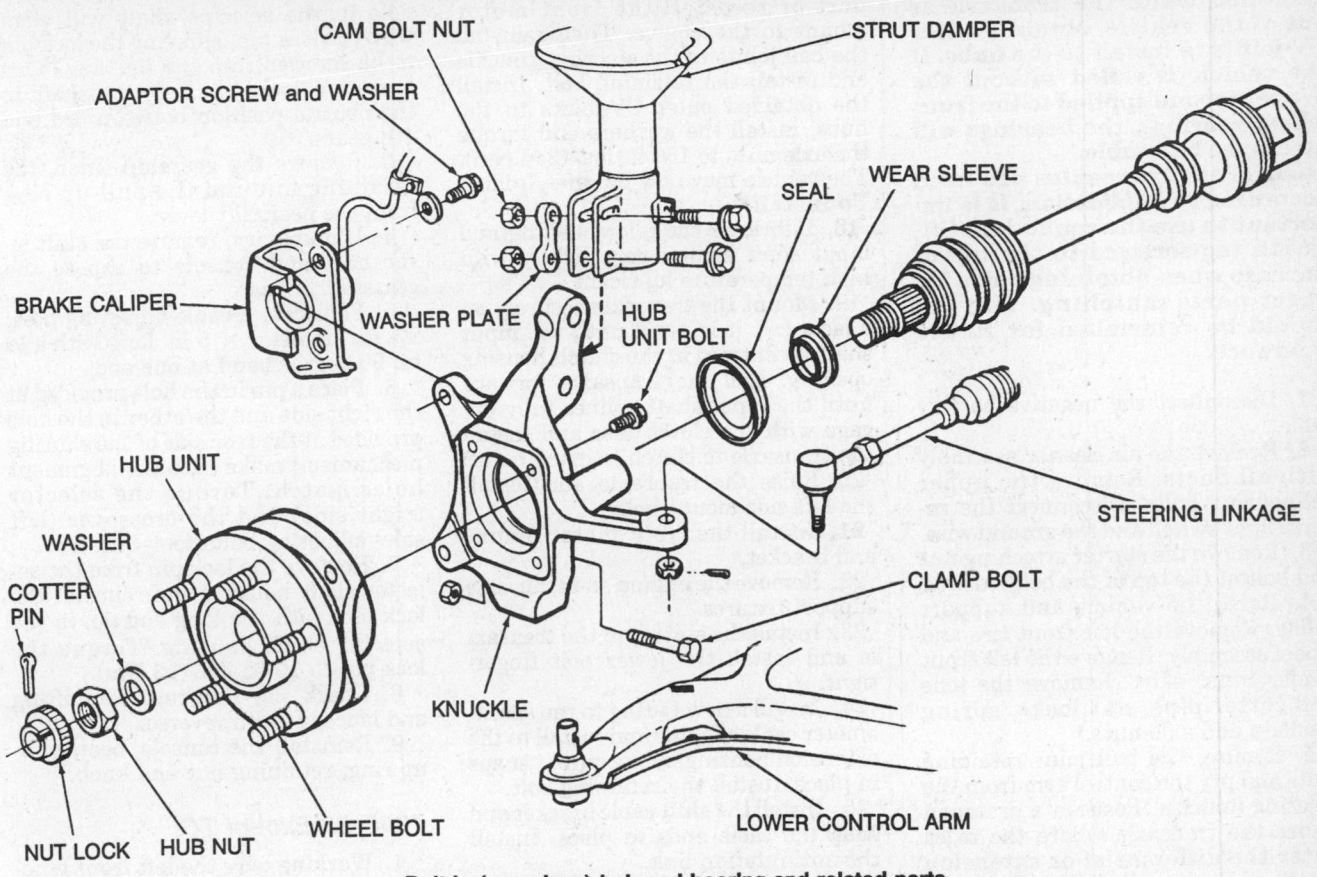

CAM BOLT NUT

ADAPTOR SCREW and WASHER

STRUT DAMPER

SEAL

WEAR SLEEVE

BRAKE CALIPER

WASHER PLATE

HUB UNIT BOLT

STEERING LINKAGE

HUB UNIT

WASHER

COTTER PIN

CLAMP BOLT

KNUCKLE

NUT LOCK HUB NUT

WHEEL BOLT

LOWER CONTROL ARM

Bolt-in (one-piece) hub and bearing and related parts

rear of the knuckle and remove the assembly from the knuckle.

9. Carefully pry the bearing seal from the machined recess of the steering knuckle and clean the recess.

10. Thoroughly clean and dry the knuckle and bearing mating surfaces and the seal installation area.

To install:

11. Install the hub and bearing assembly to the knuckle and torque the bolts in a criss-cross pattern to 45 ft. lbs. (65 Nm).

12. Install a new seal and wear sleeve. Lubricate the circumferences of the seal and sleeve liberally with grease.

13. Install the ball joint stud to the steering knuckle assembly and secure with the original knuckle clamp bolt tightened to 105 ft. lbs. (145 Nm) torque.

14. Install the tie rod end to the steering knuckle. Tighten the attaching nut to 35 ft. lbs. (47 Nm) and install new cotter pin.

15. Install the brake disc and caliper to the knuckle assembly.

16. Clean all foreign material from the threads of the axle stub shaft and install the washer and hub nut. With the brakes applied, torque the nut to 180 ft. lbs. (244 Nm) torque.

17. Install the spring washer, nut

lock and new cotter pin. Wrap the prongs of the cotter pin tightly around the nut lock.

18. Install the tire and wheel assembly and tighten the lug nuts to 95 ft. lbs. (129 Nm).

Differential Case

REMOVAL & INSTALLATION

1. Disconnect the negative battery cable.

2. Remove the transaxle from the vehicle.

3. Remove the right side extension housing from the transaxle.

4. Remove the differential cover retaining bolt and the cover from the transaxle.

5. Remove the differential bearing retainer bolts and the side differential bearing retainer, located on the left side of the transaxle, using tool L-4435 or equivalent. Use caution and take note of shims and their positioning, they can be dislodged during removal.

6. Remove the differential case from the transaxle.

To install:

7. Install the differential case into the transaxle and secure by installing

the differential bearing retainer and 3 retainer bolts.

8. Apply RTV sealant around the inner surface of the extension housing under the O-ring and install to the transaxle. Install the 2 extension housing retainer bolts.

9. Apply a bead of sealer around the mating surface of the differential cover and install to the transaxle.

10. Install the remaining differential bearing retainer bolts and install the transaxle into the vehicle.

11. Connect the negative battery cable, fill the transaxle with the proper oil and road test the vehicle.

MANUAL TRANSAXLE

For further information on transmission/transaxles, please refer to "Chilton's Guide to Transmission Repair".

Transaxle Assembly

REMOVAL & INSTALLATION

NOTE: If the vehicle is going to

be rolled while the transaxle is out of the vehicle, obtain 2 outer CV-joints to install to the hubs. If the vehicle is rolled without the proper torque applied to the front wheel bearings, the bearings will no longer be usable.

Different transaxles are used according to application. It is important to use the round identification tag screwed to the top of the case when obtaining parts for exact parts matching. The tag should be reinstalled for future reference.

1. Disconnect the negative battery cable.

2. Remove the air cleaner assembly with all ducts. Remove the upper bellhousing bolts. Disconnect the reverse light switch and the ground wire.

3. Remove the starter attaching nut and bolt at the top of the bellhousing.

4. Raise the vehicle and support safely. Remove the left front tire and wheel assembly. Remove the left front fender inner skirt. Remove the axle end cotter pins, nut locks, spring washers and axle nuts.

5. Remove the ball joint retaining bolts and pry the control arm from the steering knuckle. Position a drainpan under the transaxle where the axles enter the differential or extension housing. Remove the axles from the transaxle or center bearing. Unbolt the center bearing and remove the intermediate axle from the transaxle, if equipped.

6. Remove the anti-rotation link from the crossmember. Disconnect the shifter cables from the transaxle and unbolt the cable bracket.

7. Remove the speedometer gear adaptor bolt and remove the adaptor from the transaxle.

8. Remove the rear mount from the starter, unbolt the starter and position aside.

9. Using the proper equipment, support the weight of the engine.

10. Remove the front motor mount and bracket.

11. Position a transaxle jack under the transaxle assembly.

12. Remove the lower bellhousing bolts.

13. Remove the left side splash shield. Remove the transaxle mount bolts.

14. Carefully pry the transaxle from the engine.

15. Slide the transaxle rearward until the input shaft clears the clutch disc.

16. Pull the transaxle completely away from the clutch housing and remove it from the vehicle.

17. To prepare the vehicle for rolling, support the engine with a suitable sup-

port or reinstall the front motor mount to the engine. Then reinstall the ball joints to the steering knuckle and install the retaining bolt. Install the obtained outer CV-joints to the hubs, install the washers and torque the axle nuts to 180 ft. lbs. (244 Nm). The vehicle may now be safely rolled.

To install:

18. Lubricate the pilot bushing and input shaft splines very lightly with high temperature lubricant.

19. Mount the transaxle securely on a jack. Lift it in place until the input shaft is centered in the clutch housing opening. Roll the transaxle forward until the input shaft splines fully engage with the clutch disc and install the transaxle to clutch housing bolts.

20. Raise the transaxle and install the left side mount bolts.

21. Install the front motor mount and bracket.

22. Remove the engine and transaxle support fixtures.

23. Install the starter to the transaxle and install the lower bolt finger-tight.

24. Install a new O-ring to the speedometer cable adaptor and install to the extension housing; make sure it snaps in place. Install the retaining bolt.

25. Install the shift cable bracket and snap the cable ends in place. Install the anti-rotation link.

26. Install the axles and center bearing, if equipped. Install the ball joints to the steering knuckles. Torque the axle nuts to 180 ft. lbs. (244 Nm) and install new cotter pins. Fill the transaxle with SAE 5W-30 engine oil until the level is even with the bottom of the filler hole. Install the splash shield and install the wheels. Lower the vehicle.

27. Install the upper bellhousing bolts.

28. Install the starter attaching nut and bolt at the top of the bellhousing. Raise the vehicle and tighten the starter bolt from under the vehicle. Lower the vehicle.

29. Connect the reverse light switch and the ground wire.

30. Install the air cleaner assembly.

31. Connect the negative battery cable and check the transaxle for proper operation. Make sure the reverse lights are on when the transaxle is in R.

CABLE ADJUSTMENT

1989 Except TC

1. Working over the left front fender, remove the lock pin from the transaxle selector shaft housing.

2. Reverse the lock pin so the long end is down and insert it into the same threaded hole while pushing the selector shaft into the selector housing. A

hole in the selector shaft will align with the lock pin, allowing the lock pin to be screwed into the housing. This operation locks the selector shaft in the neutral position between 3rd and 4th gears.

3. Remove the gearshift knob, the retaining nut and the pull-up ring from the gearshift lever.

4. If necessary, remove the shift lever boot and console to expose the gearshift linkage.

5. Fabricate 2 cable adjusting pins: $^3/_{16}$ in. diameter × 5 in. long with a ½ in. 90 degree bend at one end.

6. Place a pin in the hole provided at the right side and the other in the hole provided at the rear side of the shifting mechanism; make sure the alignment holes match. Torque the selector (right side) and the crossover (left side) adjusting bolts to 4–5 ft. lbs.

7. Remove the lock pin from the selector shaft housing and reinstall the lock pin, with the long end up, in the selector shaft housing. Torque the lock pin to 10 ft. lbs. (12 Nm).

8. Check the first/reverse shifting and blockout into reverse.

9. Reinstall the console, boot, pull-up ring, retaining nut and knob.

1990–93 Except TC

1. Working over the left front fender, remove the lock pin from the transaxle selector shaft housing.

2. Reverse the lock pin so the long end is down and insert it into the same threaded hole while pushing the selector shaft into the selector housing. A hole in the selector shaft will align with the lock pin, allowing the lock pin to be screwed into the housing. This operation locks the selector shaft in the neutral position between 3rd and 4th gears.

3. Remove the gearshift knob, the retaining nut and the pull-up ring from the gearshift lever.

4. If necessary, remove the shift lever boot and console to expose the gearshift linkage. The selector cable is not adjustable.

5. Loosen the crossover cable adjusting screw and allow the cable to move in the slot. Tighten the screw to 70 inch lbs. (8 Nm).

6. Remove the lock pin from the selector shaft housing and reinstall the lock pin, with the long end up, in the selector shaft housing. Torque the lock pin to 10 ft. lbs. (12 Nm).

7. Check the first/reverse shifting and blockout into reverse.

8. Reinstall the console, boot, pull-up ring, retaining nut and knob.

1989–91 TC

1. Disconnect the negative battery cable.

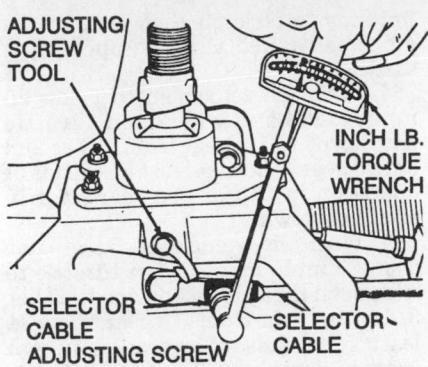

ADJUSTING SCREW TOOL

INCH LB. TORQUE WRENCH

SELECTOR CABLE ADJUSTING SCREW

SELECTOR CABLE

Adjusting the shifter cables—TC

2. Remove the console assembly to gain access to the cable ends.

3. Place the selector shaft in the neutral position.

4. Loosen the selector and crossover cables adjusting screws enough so the cables are free to move.

5. Install screw tool with tethered spacer block, which is taped to the shifter support bracket, to the support bracket.

6. Torque the cable adjusting screws to 70 inch lbs. (8 Nm).

7. Remove the tethered adjusting tool and attach it to the bracket for future use.

8. Install the console assembly.

9. Road test the vehicle and check for smooth shifting.

CLUTCH

Clutch Assembly

REMOVAL & INSTALLATION

1. Disconnect the negative battery cable. Remove the transaxle.

2. Matchmark the pressure plate cover to the flywheel. To avoid the clutch plate from falling and becoming damaged during removal, insert a clutch aligning tool into the pressure plate and through the clutch plate.

3. Loosen the flywheel to pressure plate bolts gradually and evenly to avoid warpage.

4. Remove the pressure plate and clutch assembly from the flywheel.

5. Sand or replace the flywheel scoring, cracks or heat damaged is present.

6. Sparingly apply anti-sieze compound to the input shaft and clutch disc splines. Install a new release bearing.

To install:

7. Install the clutch disc assembly to the flywheel and, using a clutch disc

alignment tool, align the disc on the flywheel and cover.

8. Torque the pressure plate/clutch assembly mounting bolts to the flywheel gradually and evenly to 21 ft. lbs. (28 Nm).

9. Install the transaxle to the vehicle.

10. Connect the negative battery cable, correct fluid levels as required and check the clutch and reverse lights for proper operation.

PEDAL FREE-PLAY ADJUSTMENT

All vehicles are equipped with a self-adjusting cable operated mechanism and no adjustment is provided. The mechanism is located above the clutch pedal, where the cable and pivot points may be lubricated.

Clutch Cable

REMOVAL & INSTALLATION

1. Disconnect the negative battery cable.

2. Remove the retainer from the clutch release lever at the transaxle by pulling on the tail of the ball stud.

3. Pry out the ball end of the cable from the positioner adjuster on the back of the brake pedal and remove the cable, passing it through the hoop in the shock tower mounting bracket.

4. Installation is the reverse of the removal procedure. After installation, push and lift the clutch pedal 2 or 3 times to allow the mechanism to adjust the cable.

AUTOMATIC TRANSAXLE

For further information on transmission/transaxles, please refer to "Chilton's Guide to Transmission Repair".

Transaxle Assembly

REMOVAL & INSTALLATION

NOTE: If the vehicle is going to be rolled while the transaxle is out of the vehicle, obtain 2 outer CV-joints to install to the hubs. If the vehicle is rolled without the proper torque applied to the front wheel bearings, the bearings will no longer be usable.

1. Disconnect the negative battery cable. If equipped with 3.0L engine, drain the coolant and remove the coolant return extension. Remove the dipstick.

2. Remove the air cleaner assembly if it is preventing access to the upper bellhousing bolts. Remove the upper bellhousing bolts and water tube, where applicable. Unplug all electrical connectors from the transaxle.

3. If equipped with a 2.2L or 2.5L engine, remove the starter attaching nut and bolt at the top of the bellhousing.

4. Disconnect the transaxle control cable at the transaxle. Raise the vehicle and support safely.

5. Remove the tire and wheel assemblies. Remove the axle end cotter

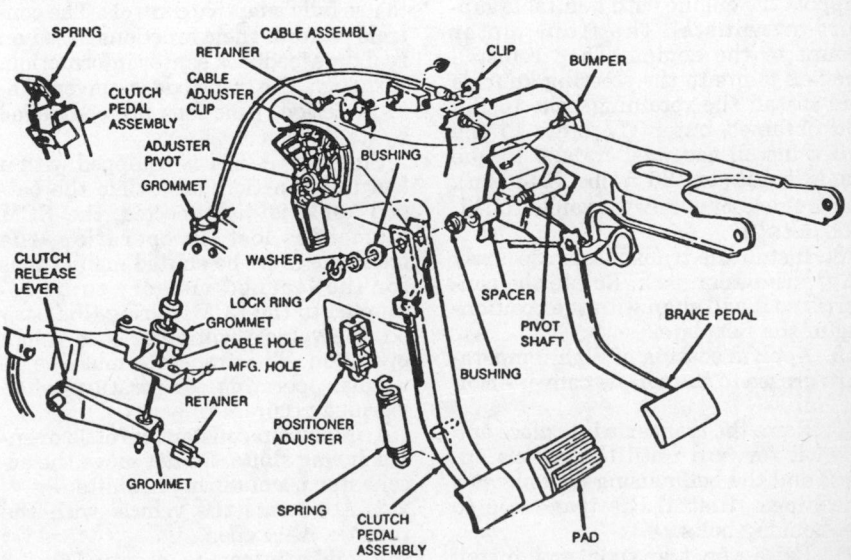

SPRING

CABLE ASSEMBLY

RETAINER

CLIP

BUMPER

CLUTCH PEDAL ASSEMBLY

CABLE ADJUSTER CLIP

ADJUSTER PIVOT

BUSHING

GROMMET

CLUTCH RELEASE LEVER

WASHER

SPACER

LOCK RING

PIVOT SHAFT

GROMMET

BRAKE PEDAL

CABLE HOLE

MFG. HOLE

BUSHING

RETAINER

POSITIONER ADJUSTER

GROMMET

SPRING

CLUTCH PEDAL ASSEMBLY

PAD

Clutch pedal, cable and related parts

pins, nut locks, spring washers and axle nuts.

6. Remove the ball joint retaining bolts and pry the control arm from the steering knuckle. Position a drain pan under the transaxle where the axles enter the differential or extension housing. Remove the axles from the transaxle or center bearing. Unbolt the center bearing and remove the intermediate axle from the transaxle, if equipped.

7. Drain the transaxle. Disconnect and plug the fluid cooler hoses. If equipped with Direct Ignition System (DIS), disconnect the harness connector and remove the crankshaft position sensor from the transaxle bellhousing.

8. Remove the speedometer cable adaptor bolt and remove the adaptor from the transaxle.

9. Remove the starter. Remove the torque converter inspection cover, matchmark the torque converter to the flexplate and remove the torque converter bolts.

10. Using the proper equipment, support the weight of the engine. Remove the front motor mount and bracket.

11. Position a transaxle jack under the transaxle.

12. Remove the lower bellhousing bolts.

13. Remove the left side splash shield. Remove the transaxle mount bolts.

14. Carefully pry the transaxle from the engine.

15. Slide the transaxle rearward until dowels disengage from the mating holes in the transaxle case.

16. Pull the transaxle completely away from the engine and remove it from the vehicle.

17. To prepare the vehicle for rolling, support the engine with a suitable support or reinstall the front motor mount to the engine. Then reinstall the ball joints to the steering knuckle and install the retaining bolt. Install the obtained outer CV-joints to the hubs, install the washers and torque the axle nuts to 180 ft. lbs. (244 Nm). The vehicle may now be safely rolled.

To install:

18. Install the transmission securely on transmission jack. Rotate the converter so it will align with the positioning of the flexplate.

19. Apply a coating of high temperature grease to the torque converter pilot hub.

20. Raise the transaxle into place and push it forward until the dowels engage and the bellhousing is flush with the block. Install the transaxle to bellhousing bolts.

21. Raise the transaxle and install the left side mount bolts. Install the torque converter bolts and torque to 55 ft. lbs. (74 Nm).

22. Install the front motor mount and bracket. Remove the engine and transaxle support fixtures.

23. Install the starter to the transaxle. Install the bolt finger-tight if equipped with a 2.2L or 2.5L engine.

24. Install a new O-ring to the speedometer cable adaptor and install to the extension housing; make sure it snaps in place. Install the retaining bolt.

25. Connect the shifter and kickdown linkage to the transaxle, if equipped.

26. Install the axles and center bearing, if equipped. Install the ball joints to the steering knuckles. Torque the axle nuts to 180 ft. lbs. (244 Nm) and install new cotter pins. Install the splash shield and wheels. Lower the vehicle. Install the dipstick.

27. Install the upper bellhousing bolts and water pipe, if removed.

28. If equipped with 2.2L or 2.5L engine, install the starter attaching nut and bolt at the top of the bellhousing. Raise the vehicle again and tighten the starter bolt from under the vehicle. Lower the vehicle.

29. Connect all electrical wiring to the transaxle.

30. Install the air cleaner assembly, if removed. Fill the transaxle with the proper amount of Mopar ATF Plus Type 7176 or conventional Dexron®II.

31. Connect the negative battery cable and check the transaxle for proper operation.

UPSHIFT AND KICKDOWN LEARNING PROCEDURE

A-604 Ultradrive Transaxle

In 1989, the A-604 4 speed, electronic transaxle was introduced; it is the first to use fully adaptive controls. The controls perform their functions based on real time feedback sensor information. Although, the transaxle is conventional in design, functions are controlled by its ECM.

Since the A-604 is equipped with a learning function, each time the battery cable is disconnected, the ECM memory is lost. In operation, the transaxle must be shifted many times for the learned memory to be re-inputed to the ECM; during this period, the vehicle will experience rough operation. The transaxle must be at normal operating temperature when learning occurs.

1. Maintain constant throttle opening during shifts. Do not move the accelerator pedal during upshifts.

2. Accelerate the vehicle with the throttle ⅛-½ open.

3. Make fifteen to twenty 1/2, 2/3 and 3/4 upshifts. Accelerating from a full stop to 50 mph each time at the aforementioned throttle opening is sufficient.

4. With the vehicle speed below 25 mph, make 5-8 wide open throttle kickdowns to 1st gear from either 2nd or 3rd gear. Allow at least 5 seconds of operation in 2nd or 3rd gear prior to each kickdown.

5. With the vehicle speed greater than 25 mph, make 5 part throttle to wide open throttle kickdowns to either 3rd or 2nd gear from 4th gear. Allow at least 5 seconds of operation in 4th gear, preferably at road load throttle prior to performing the kickdown.

SHIFT LINKAGE ADJUSTMENT

1. Apply the parking brake. Place the shifter in the **P** detent.

2. Loosen the clamp bolt on the gearshift cable bracket.

3. Pull the shift lever all the way to the front detent position and tighten the lock screw.

4. Check for proper neutral safety switch operation.

THROTTLE PRESSURE CABLE ADJUSTMENT

1. Run the engine until it reaches normal operating temperature.

2. Loosen the cable mounting bracket lock screw.

3. Position the bracket so both alignment tabs are touching the transaxle case surface and tighten the lock screws.

4. Release the cross lock on the cable assembly by pulling the cross lock up.

5. To ensure proper adjustment, the cable must be free to slide all the way toward the engine against its stop after the cross lock is released.

6. Move the transaxle throttle control lever fully clockwise and press the cross lock down until it snaps into position.

7. Road test the vehicle and check the shift points.

THROTTLE PRESSURE ROD ADJUSTMENT

1. Run the engine until it reaches normal operating temperature.

2. Loosen the adjustment swivel lock screw.

3. To ensure proper adjustment, the swivel must be free to slide along the flat end of the throttle rod. Disassembly, clean and lubricate as required.

4. Hold the transaxle throttle con-

trol lever firmly toward the engine and tighten the swivel screw.

5. Road test the vehicle and check the shift points.

FRONT SUSPENSION

MacPherson Strut

REMOVAL & INSTALLATION

1. Remove the 3 mounting nuts from the shock tower under the hood.
2. Raise the vehicle and support safely.
3. Remove the brake hose bracket screw from the strut.
4. Matchmark the lower strut mount to the knuckle and remove the strut to knuckle bolts, nuts and nut plate.
5. The installation is the reverse of the removal procedure. Torque the upper mounting nuts to 20 ft. lbs. (27 Nm). Do not fully tighten the lower mounting bolts until the front end alignment has been completed.
6. Perform a front end alignment. Torque the strut to knuckle nuts to final torque of 75 ft. lbs. (100 Nm) plus ¼ turn.

Lower Ball Joints

INSPECTION

To inspect the ball joints, grasp the grease fitting by hand with the vehicle on the ground. If the grease fitting can be moved at all by hand, the ball joint should be replaced.

REMOVAL & INSTALLATION

1. Raise the vehicle and support safely. Remove the tire and wheel assembly.
2. Remove the lower control arm from the vehicle.
3. Pry off the ball joint seal. Position the receiver cup tool C—46992 or equivalent, to support the lower control arm while receiving the ball joint assembly.
4. Press against the ball joint upper housing to remove the ball joint from the lower control arm.
To install:
5. By hand, position the ball joint assembly into the bore in the lower control arm. Be sure the ball joint is not cocked in the bore of the control arm.

6. Position arm assembly in press with installer tool C—46992 or equivalent, supporting the control arm.
7. Apply pressure against the ball joint assembly until the joint is fully seated against the bottom of the control arm. Do not apply excessive pressure against the control arm.
8. Position a new seal over the stud of the ball joint so it is against the ball joint housing, and using a 1½ in. socket, press the seal onto ball joint housing until it is seated against the top surface of the control arm.
9. Install the control arm on the vehicle.
10. Install the tire and wheel assembly.

Lower Control Arms

REMOVAL & INSTALLATION

1. Raise the vehicle and support safely. Remove the tire and wheel assembly.
2. Remove the sway bar to lower control arm retainer on both sides of the vehicle. Rotate the bar down away from the control arm.
3. Remove the ball joint stud retaining bolt and nut.
4. Pry the lower control arm from the steering knuckle.
5. Remove the control arm to crossmember bolts, nuts bushings and retainers.
6. Remove the control arm from the vehicle.

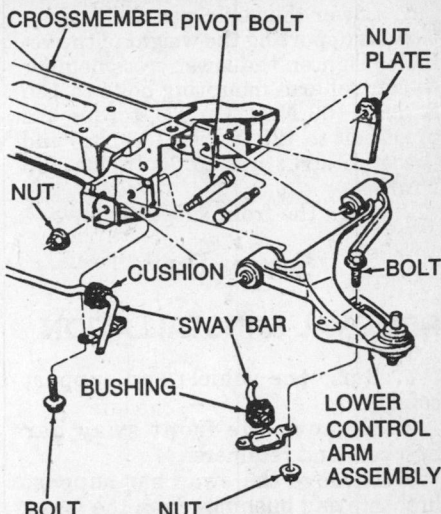

Lower control arm and related components—except TC

7. Transfer all reusable parts to the new control arm and lubricate.
8. Position the control arm onto the vehicle and install the attaching bolts. Loosely assemble the nuts to the attaching bolts.
9. Install the ball joint to the steering knuckle and tighten the retaining nut and bolt to 105 ft. lbs. (145 Nm).
10. Position the sway bar against the lower control arm and install the retainers, torqueing to 50 ft. lbs. (70 Nm). Install the tire and wheel assembly.

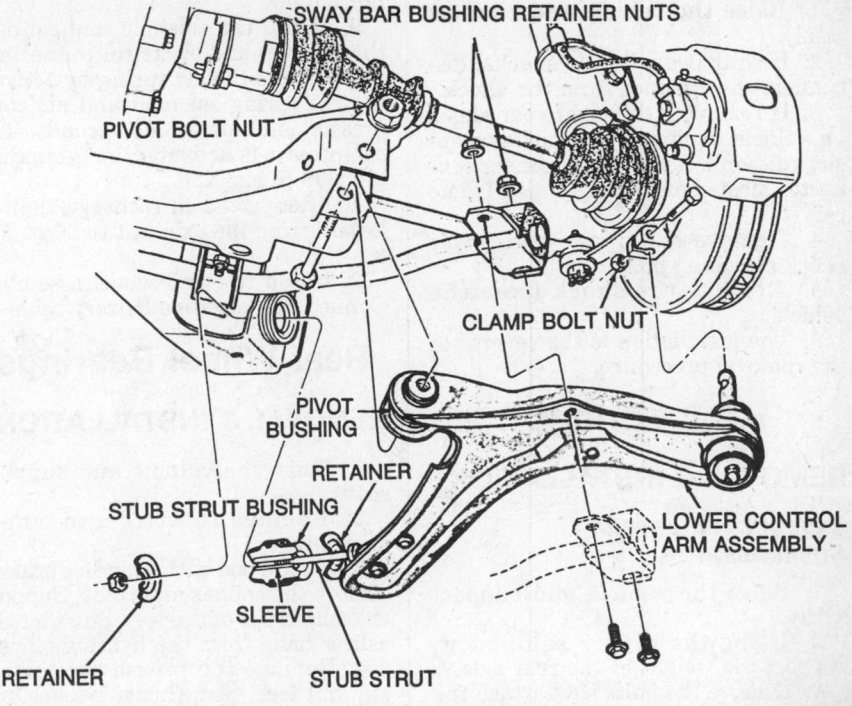

Lower control arm and related parts—TC

11. Lower the vehicle so the suspension is supporting the weight of the vehicle. Tighten the lower crossmember to control arm mounting bolts to 125 ft. lbs. (169 Nm). On TC, torque the pivot bolt to 120 ft. lbs. (163 Nm) and the stub strut nut to 70 ft. lbs. (95 Nm).

12. Align the front suspension.

Sway Bar

REMOVAL & INSTALLATION

1. Raise the vehicle and support safely.

2. Remove the front sway bar brackets and retainers.

3. Remove the sway bar support brackets and bushings from the lower control arm. Remove the sway bar from the vehicle.

4. The installation is the reverse of the removal procedure. Lubricate the sway bar bushings liberally with grease before assembling and torque retainers to 50 ft. lbs. (70 Nm).

REAR SUSPENSION

Shock Absorbers

REMOVAL & INSTALLATION

1. Raise the vehicle and support safely.

2. If equipped with air shocks, disconnect the air lines from the shock.

3. If removing the right rear shock on vehicle equipped with air suspension, disconnect the height sensor connector located on the right rear frame rail.

4. Remove the upper and lower shock attaching bolts.

5. Remove the shock from the vehicle.

6. The installation is the reverse of the removal procedure.

Coil Springs

REMOVAL & INSTALLATION

Except Load Leveling Suspension

1. Raise the vehicle and support safely.

2. Using the proper equipment, support the weight of the rear axle.

3. Remove the bolts that attach the shock to the lower mounting bracket.

4. Lower the axle assembly until the spring and upper isolater can be removed. Do not streatch the brake hose.

5. Remove the 2 screws holding the cup to the rail and remove the assembly.

To install:

6. Position the cup to the rail and install the 2 attaching screws.

7. Install the isolator over the jounce bumper and install the spring.

8. Raise the axle and loosely assemble both shock absorber attaching bolts. Remove the rear axle support and lower the vehicle.

9. With the suspension supporting the weight of the vehicle, tighten both lower shock bolts to 45 ft. lbs. (61 Nm).

Load Leveling Susupension

1. Disconnect negative battery cable.

2. Raise and safely support the vehicle. Remove the wheel and tire assembly.

3. Disconnect the air lines and the electrical connectors from the solenoid. Remove the solenoid.

4. Release the upper air spring retainer clips. Remove the lower spring to axle nut.

5. Pry assembly down to pull the alignment studs through the retaining clips and remove the assembly.

To install:

6. Position assembly lower stud into the axle seat and upper alignment pins through the frame rail adaptor.

7. Install the upper retainer clips.

8. Install the lower spring to axle nut loosely.

9. Install the solenoid and connect the air lines and electrical connector.

10. Charge the air spring by activating the spring solenoid and air compressor. Add air for 60 seconds. The compressor is activated by grounding pin **S08** to pin **X20**.

11. After partial air recharge, tighten lower spring the axle nut to 50 ft. lbs. (68 Nm).

12. Install tire and wheel assembly. Connect the negative battery cable.

Rear Wheel Bearings

REMOVAL & INSTALLATION

1. Raise the vehicle and support safely.

2. Remove the tire and wheel assembly.

3. If equipped with rear disc brakes, remove the caliper and rotor. Support the caliper out of the way, don't let the caliper hang from the hydraulic hose.

4. Remove the grease cap, cotter pin, nut lock, nut, thrust washer and outer wheel bearing.

5. Carefully slide the hub or drum from the spindle. Using the appropriate tool, remove the grease seal and inner bearing from the drum or hub and replace as required.

To install:

6. Coat the stub axle shaft with multi-purpose grade 2 EP grease and slide the hub onto the shaft. Do not drag the seal or inner bearing over the threaded area of the stub axle.

7. Install the outer bearing, thrust washer and nut. Tighten the nut to 20–26 ft. lbs. (27–34 Nm).

8. Back the adjuster nut off ¼ turn, then tighten finger-tight only. Position the nut lock over the nut and install a new cotter pin.

9. Install the grease cap, tire and wheel assembly.

Rear Axle Assembly

REMOVAL & INSTALLATION

1. Raise the vehicle and support safely.

2. Disconnect the parking brake cable at the connection. Detach the cable housing from the hanger bracket.

3. Disconnect the brake tubes from the hoses and unclip the brake tubes from the axle housing. Disconnect the rear wheel speed sensors, if equipped with anti-lock brakes.

4. Using the proper equipment, support the weight of the axle.

5. Remove the lower bolt from the shock absorbers and remove the track bar to axle pivot bolt. Suspend the track bar with a wire.

6. Lower the axle and remove the springs.

7. Support pivot bushing ends of the trailer arms. Remove the pivot bushing hanger bracket to frame screws. Lower and remove the axle from the vehicle.

To install:

8. Raise and support the axle. Attach the pivot bushing hanger brackets to frame rail. Tighten screws to 45 ft. lbs. (61 Nm).

9. Install the rear spring and insulators. Raise the rear axle and install the shock absorber and track bar through bolts loosely.

10. Reconnect the brake tubes and attach the hose mounting brackets.

11. Connect parking brake cable and speed sensor, if equipped.

12. Install the tire and wheel assembly. Bleed the brake system.

13. With the suspension supporting the weight of the vehicle, tighten the lower shock absorber bolts to 45 ft. lbs. (61 Nm) and the track bar bolt to 70 ft. lbs. (95 Nm).

STEERING

Steering Wheel

--- **CAUTION** ---

On vehicles equipped with the air bag system, the system must be disarmed prior to removing the steering wheel. Failure to disarm the air bag system may result in accidental deployment of the air bag module and possible personal injury.

REMOVAL & INSTALLATION

Without Airbag

1. Disconnect the negative battery cable.
2. Straighten the steering wheel so the front tires are pointing straight-ahead.
3. Remove the horn pad.
4. Remove the steering wheel hold-down nut and remove the damper, if equipped. Matchmark the steering wheel to the shaft.
5. Using a steering wheel puller, pull the steering wheel off the shaft.
6. The installation is the reverse of the removal procedure. Torque the hold-down nut to 45 ft. lbs. (60 nm).

With Airbag

1. Disconnect the negative battery cable and isolate using an appropriate insulator. Allow the system capacitor to discharge for 2 minutes prior to starting repairs on the vehicle.
2. Straighten the steering wheel so the front tires are pointing straight-ahead.
3. Remove the 4 nuts located on the back side of the steering wheel that attach the airbag module to the steering wheel.
4. Lift the module and disconnect the connectors. Remove the speed control switch, if equipped.

NOTE: All columns except Acustar are equipped with a clockspring set screw held by a plastic tether on the steering wheel. Acustar-mounted clocksprings are auto-locking. If the steering column is not an Acustar and is lacking the set screw, obtain one before proceeding.

5. If equipped with the set screw, place it in the clockspring to ensure proper positioning when the steering wheel is removed.
6. Remove the steering wheel hold-down nut and remove the damper, if equipped. Matchmark the steering wheel to the shaft.
7. Using a steering wheel puller, pull the steering wheel off the shaft.

To install:

8. Position the steering wheel on the steering column. Make sure the flats on the hub of the steering wheel are aligned with the formations on the clockspring.
9. Pull the airbag and speed control connectors through the lower, larger hole in the steering wheel and pull the horn wire through the smaller hole at the top. Make sure the wires are not pinched anywhere.
10. Install the damper, if equipped.
11. Install the hold-down nut and torque to 45 ft. lbs. (60 Nm).
12. If equipped with a clockspring set screw, remove the screw and place it in its storage location on the steering wheel.
13. Connect the horn wire.
14. Connect the speed control wire and install the speed control switch.
15. Connect the clockspring lead wire to the airbag module and install module to steering wheel.

NOTE: Do not allow anyone to enter the vehicle from this point on, until this procedure is completed.

16. Connect the DRB II to the Airbag System Diagnostic Module (ASDM) connector located to the right of the console.
17. From the passenger side of the vehicle, turn the key to the **ON** position and exit the vehicle.
18. Check to make sure no one has entered the vehicle. Connect the negative battery cable.
19. Using the DRB II, read and record any active fault data or stored codes.
20. If any active fault codes are present, perform the proper diagnostic procedures before continuing.
21. If there are no active fault codes, erase the stored fault codes; if there are active codes, the stored codes will not erase.
22. From the passenger side of the vehicle, turn the key **OFF**, then **ON** and observe the instrument cluster airbag warning light. It should come on for 6–8 seconds, then go out, indicating the system is functioning normally. If the warning light either fails to come ON or stays lit, there is a system malfunction and further diagnostics are needed.

Steering Column

REMOVAL & INSTALLATION

Acustar Column

1. Disconnect the negative battery cable. Disarm the air bag system, if equipped.
2. Straighten the steering wheel so the front tires are pointing straight-ahead.
3. Remove the steering wheel hold-down nut and remove the damper, if equipped. Matchmark the steering wheel to the shaft.
4. Using a steering wheel puller, pull the steering wheel off the shaft.
5. If equipped with column shift, disconnect the transaxle shift cable from the steering column by prying it out of the grommet in the shift lever.
6. If equipped with pointer type gear indicator, loosen the set screw on the lower side of the steering column and remove the pointer needle.
7. If equipped with a cable actuated gear shift indicator, place the gear shift lever in the **N** or **P** position and remove the PRNDL indicator actuation cable from the steering column actuator arm. Swing the lock bar located on the lower portion of the insert upward and squeeze the legs together. Remove the insert from the steering column.
8. Disconnect all wiring connectors from below the instrument panel that lead up into the steering column.
9. Remove the nuts that attach the steering column assembly to the instrument panel support.
10. On 1989–90 vehicles, firmly grasp the steering column assembly and pull rearward, disconnecting the lower stub shaft from the steering gear coupling. Do not remove the rool pin to remove the steering column.
11. On 1991–93 vehicles, remove the retaining pin in the upper to lower steering coupler retaining bolt. Remove the upper to lower steering coupler retaining nut and pinch bolt from the coupling and separate the stub shaft from the steering gear coupling.
12. Remove the column from the vehicle.

To install:

13. Install new cable attaching grommet into the steering column shift lever. Install the steering column into the vehicle. Guide the stub shaft into the steering gear coupling and install the pinch bolt and nut, if equipped.
14. Install the nuts that attach the steering column assembly to the instrument panel support. Torque the steering column assembly to support bracket nuts to 105 inch. lbs. (12 Nm).
15. Connect the wire harness connectors at the base of the steering column.
16. If equipped with a cable actuated gear shift indicator, route the PRNDL actuator assembly under the left column wing and along the left side of the steering column. Insert the flange of

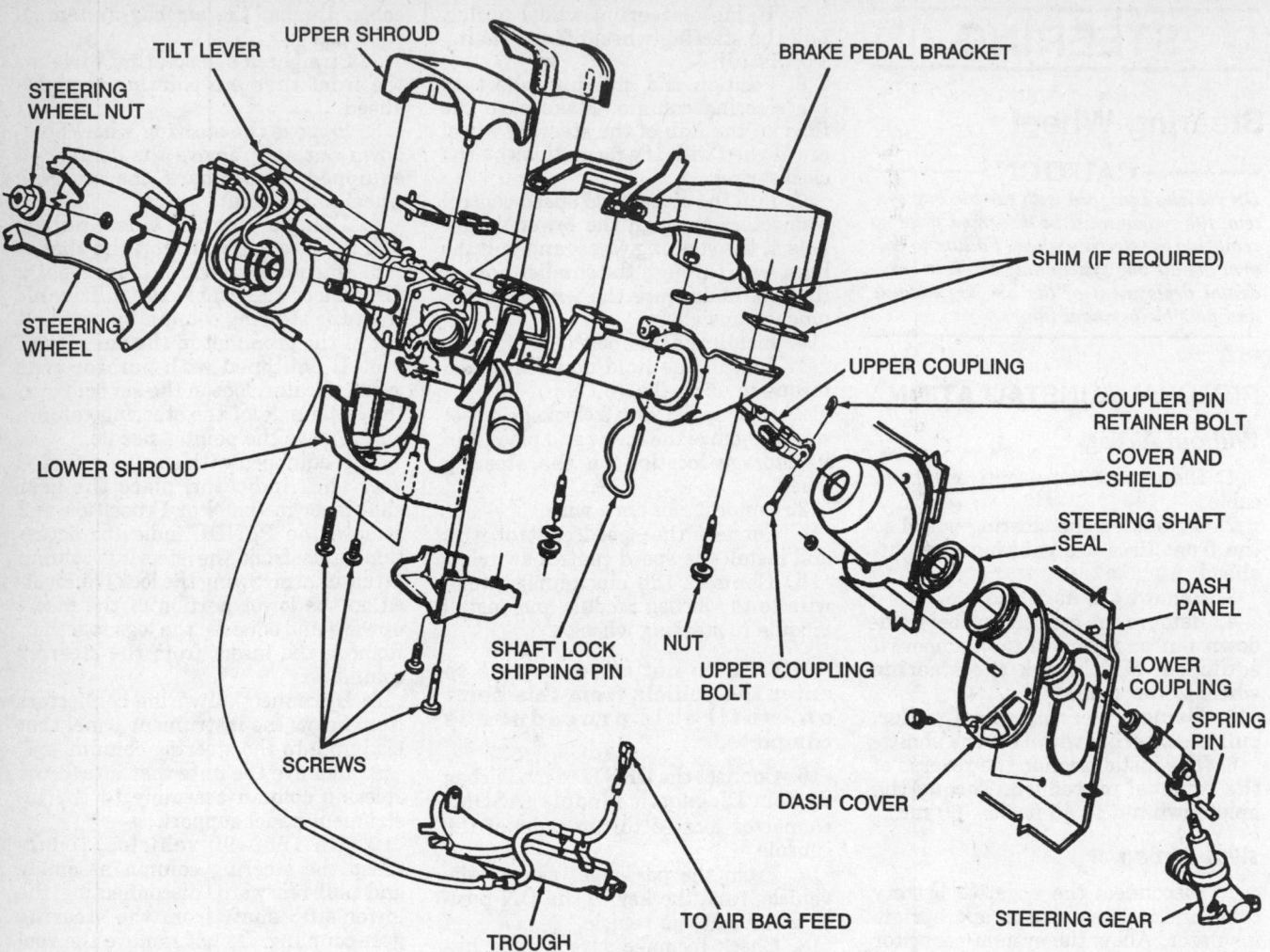

STEERING WHEEL NUT

STEERING WHEEL

TILT LEVER

UPPER SHROUD

BRAKE PEDAL BRACKET

SHIM (IF REQUIRED)

UPPER COUPLING

COUPLER PIN RETAINER BOLT

COVER AND SHIELD

STEERING SHAFT SEAL

DASH PANEL

LOWER COUPLING

SPRING PIN

STEERING GEAR

DASH COVER

TO AIR BAG FEED

TROUGH

SCREWS

SHAFT LOCK SHIPPING PIN

NUT

UPPER COUPLING BOLT

LOWER SHROUD

Exploded view of Acustar steering column

the actuator assembly into the steering column jacket. Engage the lock bar to secure the actuator assembly to the housing. Hook the cable to the steering column actuator arm. Move the shifter to **N** and check for proper pointer location. If the pointer is misaligned, adjust the pointer arm using a ⁹⁄₆₄ Allen head screwdriver.

17. If equipped with pointer type gear shift indicator, install the pointer into the indicator housing and the steering column and secure.

18. Connect the transaxle shift cable to the shift lever on the steering column. Readjust the transaxle shift linkage.

19. Install the clockspring, steering wheel and remaining components removed during disassembly.

20. Connect the negative battery cable and check the steering column and all related components for proper operation.

Manual Rack and Pinion Steering Gear

REMOVAL & INSTALLATION

1. Disconnect the negative battery cable.

2. Raise the vehicle and support safely.

3. Remove front wheel assemblies.

4. Remove the cotter pins, castellated nuts and tie rod ends from the steering knuckles.

5. Support the front crossmember using a transmission jack. Remove the front suspension crossmember attaching bolts and nuts.

6. Lower the crossmember.

7. Remove the tie rod inner boot shields.

8. Remove the steering gear bolts from the front suspension crossmember.

9. Remove the steering gear from the left side of the vehicle.

To install:

10. Transfer the required parts to the new rack, as required.

11. Place the rack on the crossmember and torque the steering gear attaching bolts to 21 ft. lbs. (29 Nm). Attach the boot shields.

12. Have a helper inside the vehicle remove the trim boot and align the stub shaft with the coupling while the crossmember is raised into position. If a helper is not available, the steering column will have to be unbolted so the steering shaft can be inserted into the coupling. The right rear crossmember bolt is a pilot bolt that correctly locates the crossmember; tighten it first. Torque the crossmember bolts to 90 ft. lbs. (122 Nm).

13. Install the tie rod ends to the steering knuckle and torque the nut to

45 ft. lbs. (61 Nm). Install a new cotter pin.

14. Insert the stub shaft shim where the stub shaft goes into the coupling.

15. Connect the negative battery cable and check the gear for proper operation.

Power Rack and Pinion Steering Gear

REMOVAL & INSTALLATION

1. Disconnect the negative battery cable.

2. Raise the vehicle and support safely.

3. Remove both front wheel assemblies.

4. Remove the cotter pins, castellated nuts and tie rod ends from the steering knuckles.

5. If equipped, remove the anti-rotational link from the crossmember. The lower universal joint is removed with the steering gear.

6. Disconnect and plug the oil pressure line from the rack. Disconnect and plug the return hose from the line coming from the rack.

7. Support the front crossmember using a transmission jack. Remove the front suspension crossmember attaching bolts and nuts.

8. Lower the crossmember.

9. Remove the tie rod inner boot shields.

10. Remove the steering gear bolts from the front suspension crossmember.

11. Remove the steering gear from the left side of the vehicle.

To install:

12. Transfer the required parts to the new rack, as required.

13. Place the rack on the crossmember and torque the steering gear attaching bolts to 50 ft. lbs. (68 Nm). Attach the fluid lines and the boot shields.

14. Have a helper inside the vehicle remove the trim boot and align the stub shaft with the coupling while the crossmember is raised into position. If a helper is not available, the steering column will have to be unbolted so the steering shaft can be inserted into the coupling. The right rear crossmember bolt is a pilot bolt that correctly locates the crossmember, tighten it first. Torque the crossmember bolts to 90 ft. lbs. (122 Nm).

15. Install the anti-rotational link.

16. Install the tie rod ends to the steering knuckle and torque the nut to 45 ft. lbs. (61 Nm). Install a new cotter pin.

17. Insert the stub shaft shim where the stub shaft goes into the coupling.

18. Refill the power steering pump.

19. Connect the negative battery cable and check the gear for proper operation.

Power Steering Pump

REMOVAL & INSTALLATION

1. Disconnect the negative battery cable.

2. Position a drain pan under the power steering pump. Raise and safely support the vehicle.

3. Disconnect the fluid hoses from the pump and plug them. On 3.0L engine, remove the tube and dipstick assembly from the pump.

4. Remove the front bracket attaching bolts and remove the belt from the pulley.

5. On 3.0L engine, disconnect the front exhaust pipe from the exhaust manifold and position aside. This is required for clearance to remove the pump.

6. Loosen the rear pump-to-bracket nut. Remove the bolt attaching the pulley side of the power steering pump to the mounting bracket.

7. On 3.0L engine, remove the nut holding the power steering pump rear support bracket to the pump. Remove the the 2 bolts mounting the power steering pump support bracket to the engine and remove the bracket.

8. Lower the vehicle. Remove the remaining retaining bolts and the rear mounting nut. Remove the power steering pump from the vehicle.

9. Remove the pulley from the pump with the proper puller. Install the pulley on the new pump using the special installation tools.

To install:

10. Install the pump to the engine making sure, on 3.0L engine, that the stud on the back of the pump is in the slotted hole in the bracket.

11. Install the mounting screws. Install the tube and dipstick assembly on the pump, if equipped.

12. Install the exhaust pipe to the manifold using a new gasket where required.

13. Install the power steering pump drive belt and adjust the tension as required.

14. Refill the pump using the correct fluid and bleed the system.

BELT ADJUSTMENT

NOTE: The belt tension is automatically adjusted by a dynamic tensioner on the 3.0L engine. Adjustment is not possible.

1. Loosen the bracket mounting bolts.

2. On 1989 vehicles, use a ½ in. drive breaker bar in the square hole provided in the bracket to move the pump away from the engine. On 1990–93 vehicles, tighten the adjusting nut until the pump is in the desired position. Do not pry against the fluid reservoir.

3. With the pump moved enough so the belt deflects about ¼–½ in. under a 10 lb. load, tighten the bolts.

SYSTEM BLEEDING

1. Fill the reservoir with power steering fluid. Do not add transmission fluid in the power steering pump.

2. Turn the wheels to the full left turn position and add fluid until the reservoir is full.

3. Start the engine and add fluid to bring the level to the correct level.

4. To purge the system of air, turn

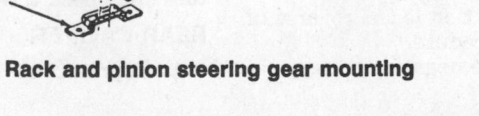

Rack and pinion steering gear mounting

the steering wheel from side to side without contacting the stops.

5. Return the wheel to the straight-ahead position and operate the engine for 2 minutes before road testing.

Tie Rod Ends

REMOVAL & INSTALLATION

1. Raise the vehicle and support safely. Remove the cotter pin and nut from the tie rod end.

2. Using a puller, remove the tie rod from the steering knuckle.

3. Loosen the sleeve clamp nut and bolt, if equipped, and unscrew the tie rod end from the sleeve or inner tie rod.

4. The installation is the reverse of the removal procedure. Torque the stud nuts to 45 ft. lbs. (61 Nm) and install a new cotter pin.

5. Perform a front end alignment as required.

BRAKES

Master Cylinder

REMOVAL & INSTALLATION

Except TC with Anti-Lock Brakes

1. Disconnect the negative battery cable.

2. Disconnect brake lines from the master cylinder and plug master cylinder fluid outlets.

3. Remove the nuts attaching the master cylinder to the power booster.

4. Disconnect the electrical connector from the master cylinder, if equipped. Remove the master cylinder from the mounting studs.

5. Remove the fluid reservoir from the cylinder as required.

To install:

6. Bench bleed the master cylinder as follows:

   a. Mount master cylinder in a vise.

   b. Attach tube to the fluid outlets on the master cylinder and bend tube so the outlet end of the tubes will be below the surface of brake fluid in each reservoir.

   c. Fill both reservoirs with brake fluid conforming to DOT 3 specifications.

d. Slowly depress the piston and then allow the piston to return to the released position. Repeat this procedure until no bubbles are present in the fluid exiting the tubes.

   e. Remove the tubes from the master cylinder and refill the reservoir with fluid.

7. Install the master cylinder to the mounting studs and install the retainer nuts.

8. Install the brake lines to the master cylinder loosely. Have a helper slowly depress the brake pedal from inside the vehicle. While the pedal is being depressed, tighten the fluid lines to the master cylinder.

9. Connect the negative battery cable and check the brakes for proper operation.

Combination Valve

REMOVAL & INSTALLATION

1. Disconnect the negative battery cable.

2. Raise the vehicle and support safely.

3. Tag and disconnect the brake lines from the valve.

4. Disconnect the wires to the pressure switch.

5. Remove the combination valve from the frame bracket.

6. The installation is the reverse of the removal procedure.

7. Bleed the brakes in the following order:

   a. Right rear wheel cylinder or caliper

   b. Left rear wheel cylinder or caliper

   c. Right front caliper

   d. Left front caliper

8. Connect the negative battery cable and check the brakes for proper operation.

Power Brake Booster

REMOVAL & INSTALLATION

1. Disconnect the negative battery cable. Disconnect the vacuum hose(s) from the booster.

2. Remove the nuts attaching the master cylinder to the booster and move the master cylinder aside.

3. From inside of the vehicle, remove the clip that secures the booster pushrod to the brake pedal and remove the nuts that attach the booster to the dash panel. Remove the booster from the vehicle.

4. The installation is the reverse of the removal procedure.

5. Connect the negative battery ca-

ble and check the brakes for proper operation.

Brake Caliper

REMOVAL & INSTALLATION

Except TC With Anti-Lock Brakes

1. Raise the vehicle and support safely.

2. Remove the tire and wheel assembly.

3. Remove the caliper mounting bolts.

4. Lift the caliper off the adapter and away from the disc. Remove the outer pad from the caliper.

5. Remove the brake hose retaining bolt from the caliper.

To install:

6. Install the brake hose to the caliper using new copper washers.

7. Position the caliper over the rotor so the caliper engages the adaptor correctly. Install the mounting bolts. Install the hold-down spring, if equipped.

8. Fill the master cylinder and bleed the brakes. Make sure the brake hose is not twisted after installation.

TC

FRONT CALIPER

1. Depressurize the hydraulic accumulator. Remove some of the fluid from the master cylinder.

2. Raise the vehicle and support safely. Remove the tire and wheel assemblies.

3. Remove the hold-down spring from the caliper assembly by pushing in at the middle of the spring and pushing it outward.

4. Loosen the guide pins and remove the caliper from the brake disc.

5. Remove the inboard shoe from the caliper by pulling the shoe and lining assembly away from the piston.

6. Disconnect the brake hose from the caliper and remove the caliper from the vehicle.

To install:

7. Connect the brake hose to the caliper using new gasket.

8. Install the inboard shoe to the caliper and install the caliper to the adapter.

9. Install the guide pins and tighten to 18–26 ft. lbs. (25–35 Nm). Install the hold-down spring.

10. Install the wheel and tire assembly, lower the vehicle, pump the break pedal to seat the pads against the rotors and check the brake fluid level.

REAR CALIPER

1. Depressurize the hydraulic accu-

mulator. Remove some of the fluid from the master cylinder.

2. Raise the vehicle and support safely. Remove the tire and wheel assemblies.

3. Clean the back of the caliper around the access plug and remove plug from the caliper.

4. Insert a 4mm Allen wrench through hole and turn the retraction shaft counterclockwise a few turns to increase clearance between pads and rotor.

5. Remove the anti-rattle spring from outboard pad taking care not to damage it.

6. Back the caliper guide pins out just enough to free caliper from adapter.

7. Remove the caliper from the adapter. Remove the inboard brake pad from the caliper by pulling pad away from the piston.

8. Disconnect the brake hose from the caliper.
To install:
9. Connect the brake hose to the caliper using new gasket.

10. Install the inboard shoe to the caliper and install the caliper to the adapter.

11. Install the guide pins and tighten to 18–26 ft. lbs. (25–35 Nm). Install the hold-down spring.

12. Install the wheel and tire assembly, lower the vehicle, pump the break pedal to seat the pads against the rotors and check the brake fluid level.

Disc Brake Pads

REMOVAL & INSTALLATION

Except TC with Anti-Lock Brakes

1. Remove some of the fluid from the master cylinder.

2. Raise the vehicle and support safely. Remove the tire and wheel assemblies.

3. Remove the hold-down spring if necessary. Remove the caliper and remove the outer pad from the caliper.

4. Remove the inner pad from the adaptor.
To install:
5. Use a large C-clamp to compress the piston back into the caliper bore.

6. Install the inner pad to the adaptor.

7. Position the caliper over the rotor so the caliper engages the adaptor correctly and install the retainer pin(s).

8. Install the hold-down spring, if removed.

9. Refill the master cylinder.

TC

1. Depressurize the hydraulic accumulator. Remove ⅔ of brake fluid from the master cylinder.

2. Remove access plug and insert a 4mm Allen wrench through hole.

3. Turn the retraction shaft counterclockwise a few turns to increase clearance between pads and rotor.

4. Remove the anti-rattle spring from outboard pad taking care not to damage it.

5. Back the caliper guide pins out just enough to free caliper from adapter.

6. Lift the caliper off rotor and carefully suspend with wire.

7. Remove the brake pads.

8. Insert the Allen wrench through access hole and turn counterclockwise, if necessary, to retract piston further to increase clearance for new pads.
To install:
9. Install new inner and outer pads.

NOTE: The outboard pads are marked for right and left sides and must be properly installed.

10. Lower the caliper over rotor and pads.

11. Install the guide pins and tighten to proper torque.

12. Insert the Allen wrench through the access hole and turn clockwise until snug (no clearance between pads and rotors) then back off ⅓ turn to obtain proper clearance.

13. Check the brake fluid level and add, if necessary.

Brake Rotor

REMOVAL & INSTALLATION

1. Raise the vehicle and support safely. Remove the tire and wheel assembly.

2. Remove the caliper and brake pads.

3. Remove the factory installed clips, if equipped. It is not necessary to reinstall these clips.

4. Remove the rotor from the hub.

5. The installation is the reverse of the removal procedure.

Brake Drum

REMOVAL & INSTALLATION

1. Raise the vehicle and support safely.

2. Remove the wheel and tire assembly.

3. Remove the dust cap.

4. Remove the cotter pin and nut lock.

5. Remove the wheel bearing nut and washer from the spindle.

6. Remove the outer wheel bearing.

7. Remove the drum with the inner wheel bearing from the spindle. If the drum is difficult to remove, remove the plug from the rear of the backing plate and push the self adjuster lever away from the star wheel. Rotate the star wheel with an upward motion to retract the shoes and remove the drum. Remove the grease seal.
To install:
8. Lubricate and install the inner wheel bearing. Install a new grease seal.

9. Install the drum to the spindle.

10. Lubricate and install the outer wheel bearing, washer and nut. When the bearing preload is properly set, install the nut lock and a new cotter pin.

11. Install the grease cap.

12. Install the wheel and tire assembly. Adjust the rear brakes as required.

Brake Shoes

REMOVAL & INSTALLATION

1. Raise the vehicle and support safely. Remove the wheel and tire assemblies and the drums.

2. Remove the automatic adjuster spring and lever.

3. Rotate the automatic adjuster star wheel enough so both shoes move out far enough to be free of the wheel cylinder boots.

4. Disconnect the parking brake cable from the actuating lever.

5. Remove the lower shoe to shoe or shoe to anchor spring(s).

6. With the shoes held together by the upper shoe to shoe spring, remove them from the backing plate.
To install:
7. Thoroughly clean and dry the backing plate. To prepare the backing plate, lubricate the bosses, anchor pin and parking brake actuating lever pivot surface lightly with lithium based grease.

8. Remove, clean and dry all parts still on the old shoes. Lubricate the star wheel shaft threads with antisieze lubricant and transfer all parts to their proper locations on the new shoes.

9. Install the lower spring(s).

10. Connect the parking brake cable.

11. Install the automatic adjuster lever and spring.

12. Adjust the star wheel.

13. Remove any grease from the linings and install the drum.

14. Complete the brake adjustment with the wheels installed.

Wheel Cylinder

REMOVAL & INSTALLATION

1. Raise the vehicle and support safely.
2. Remove the wheel, drum and brake shoes.
3. Remove and plug the brake line from the wheel cylinder.
4. Remove the wheel cylinder bolts and remove the cylinder from the backing plate.

To install:

5. Apply a very thin coating of silicone sealer to the cylinder mounting surface, install the cylinder to the backing plate and install the retaining bolts.
6. Connect the brake line to the wheel cylinder.
7. Install all brake parts that were removed.
8. Install the tire and wheel assembly.
9. Bleed the brakes.

Parking Brake Cable

ADJUSTMENT

Except 1990–93 Daytona and LeBaron

1. Release the parking brakes fully.
2. Raise the vehicle and support safely.
3. Adjust the rear brakes.
4. Loosen the adjusting nut until there is slack in all the cables.
5. Rotate the rear wheels and tighten the cable adjusting nut until there is a slight drag at the wheels.
6. Continue to rotate the rear wheels and loosen the nut until all drag is eliminated.
7. Back off the nut an additional 2 turns.
8. Apply and release the parking brake several times. Upon the least release, verify there is no drag at the wheels.
9. To check the operation, make sure the parking brake holds on an incline.

1990–93 Daytona and LeBaron
The parking brake hand lever contains a self-adjusting loaded clockspring feature. Routine parking brake adjustment is not required.

REMOVAL & INSTALLATION

Front Cable

EXCEPT 1990–93 DAYTONA AND LEBARON

1. Loosen the adjusting nut from

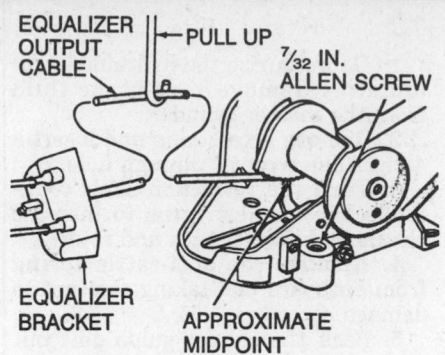

EQUALIZER OUTPUT CABLE ← PULL UP   7/32 IN. ALLEN SCREW

EQUALIZER BRACKET   APPROXIMATE MIDPOINT

Self-adjusting parking brake lever assembly — 1990–93 Daytona and LeBaron

under the vehicle. On TC, disconnect the cable from the equalizer bracket.
2. Lift the carpet and floor matting and remove the floor pan seal.
3. Pull the cable end forward and disconnect from the clevis.
4. Pull the cable through the hole and remove.
5. The installation is the reverse of the removal procedure.
6. Connect the negative battery cable and check the parking brakes for proper operation.

1990–93 DAYTONA AND LEBARON

──── CAUTION ────

The parking brake hand lever contains a self-adjusting loaded clockspring loaded to about 30 lbs. Care must be taken when handling components in the vicinity of the hand lever or serious personal injury may result.

1. Disconnect the negative battery cable.
2. Disengage the cable from the equalizer bracket in the console.
4. Lift the carpet and floor matting and remove the floor pan seal.
5. Separate the cable from the rear parking brake shoes lever.
6. Pull the cable through the hole and remove.

To install:

7. Install the cable and connect to the rear shoes and equalizer bracket. Install the floor pan seal and position the carpet.
8. To reload, lockout and adjust the system:
   a. Pull on the equalizer output cable with at least 30 lbs. pressure to wind up the spring. Continue until the self-adjuster lockout pawl is positioned about midway between the self-adjuster sector.
   b. Rotate the lockout pawl into the self-adjuster sector by turning the Allen screw clockwise. This action requires very little effort; do not force the screw.
   c. Adjust the rear drum-in-hat parking brake shoes.

d. Turn the Allen screw counterclockwise about 15 degrees. When turning the lockout device, self-adjuster release is a snapping noise followed by a detent that should be felt. Very light effort is required to seat the lockout device into the detent. Make sure to follow through into the detent.
   e. Cycle the lever a few times to complete the adjustment. The wheels should rotate freely.
9. Connect the negative battery cable and check the parking brakes for proper operation.

Rear Cable

EXCEPT TC

REAR DRUM BRAKES

1. Raise the vehicle and support safely. Loosen the cable adjusting nut to provide slack in the cable.
2. Remove the tire and wheel assembly.
3. Remove the drake drums. Disconnect the cable from the actuating lever on the rear brake shoe assembly.
4. Remove the retaining clip from the cable at the support bracket and pull the cable from the trailing arm assembly.
5. The installation is the reverse of the removal procedure.

REAR DISC BRAKES

1. Raise the vehicle and support safely. Loosen the cable adjusting nut to provide slack in the cable.
2. Remove the tire and wheel assembly. Remove the disc brake caliper and rotor from the rear hub.
3. Disconnect the cable from the actuating lever on the rear brake shoe assembly.
4. Remove the retaining clip from the cable at the support bracket and pull the cable from the trailing arm assembly.
5. The installation is the reverse of the removal procedure.

TC

1. Raise the vehicle and support safely. Remove the wheels.
2. Loosen the adjusting nut and disconnect the rear cable from the connector.
3. Remove the brake cable retaining clips from the hanger bracket and caliper.
4. Disconnect the cable from the parking brake lever on the caliper. Remove the cable guide from the trailing arm.
5. Pull the cable assembly from the hanger bracket.
6. The installation is the reverse of the removal procedure.

Brake System Bleeding

Except Anti-Lock Brakes

NOTE: If using a pressure bleeder, follow the instructions furnished with the unit and choose the correct adaptor for the application. Do not substitute an adapter that "almost fits" as it will not work and could be dangerous.

MASTER CYLINDER

If the master cylinder is off the vehicle, it can be bench bled.

1. Connect 2 short pieces of brake line to the outlet fittings, bend them until the free end is below the fluid level in the master cylinder reservoirs.
2. Fill the reservoir with fresh brake fluid. Pump the piston slowly until no more air bubbles appear in the reservoirs.
3. Disconnect the 2 short lines, refill the master cylinder and securely install the cylinder caps.
4. If the master cylinder is on the vehicle, it can still be bled, using a flare nut wrench.
5. Open the brake lines slightly with the flare nut wrench while pressure is applied to the brake pedal by a helper inside the vehicle.
6. Be sure to tighten the line before the brake pedal is released.
7. Repeat the procedure with both lines until no air bubbles appear.

CALIPERS AND WHEEL CYLINDERS

1. Fill the master cylinder with fresh brake fluid. Check the level often during the procedure.
2. Starting with the right rear wheel, remove the protective cap from the bleeder, if equipped, and place where it will not be lost. Clean the bleed screw.

CAUTION
When bleeding the brakes, keep face away from the brake area. Spewing fluid may cause facial and/or visual damage. Do not allow brake fluid to spill on the car's finish; it will remove the paint.

3. If the system is empty, the most efficient way to get fluid down to the wheel is to loosen the bleeder about ½–¾ turn, place a finger firmly over the bleeder and have a helper pump the brakes slowly until fluid comes out the bleeder. Once fluid is at the bleeder, close it before the pedal is released inside the vehicle.

NOTE: If the pedal is pumped rapidly, the fluid will churn and create small air bubbles, which are almost impossible to remove

from the system. These air bubbles will eventually congregate and a spongy pedal will result.

4. Once fluid has been pumped to the caliper or wheel cylinder, open the bleed screw again, have the helper press the brake pedal to the floor, lock the bleeder and have the helper slowly release the pedal. Wait 15 seconds and repeat the procedure (including the 15 second wait) until no more air comes out of the bleeder upon application of the brake pedal. Remember to close the bleeder before the pedal is released inside the vehicle each time the bleeder is opened. If not, air will be induced into the system.
5. If a helper is not available, connect a small hose to the bleeder, place the end in a container of brake fluid and proceed to pump the pedal from inside the vehicle until no more air comes out the bleeder. The hose will prevent air from entering the system.
6. Repeat the procedure on remaining wheel cylinders in order:
    a. Left rear
    b. Right front
    c. Left front
7. Hydraulic brake systems must be totally flushed if the fluid becomes contaminated with water, dirt or other corrosive chemicals. To flush, bleed the entire system until all fluid has been replaced with the correct type of new fluid.
8. Install the bleeder cap(s), if equipped, on the bleeder to keep dirt out. Always road test the vehicle after brake work of any kind is done.

Anti-Lock Brakes

The brake system must be bled any time air is permitted to enter the system through loosened or disconnected lines or hoses, or anytime the modulator is removed. Excessive air within the system will cause a soft or spongy feel in the brake pedal.

When bleeding any part of the system, the reservoir must remain close to **FULL** at all times. Check the level frequently and top off fluid as needed.

The Bendix Anti-lock 6 brake system must be bled as 2 separate brake systems. Proper procedures must be followed if the system is to work correctly. The normal portion of the brake system is bled in the usual fashion with either pressure or manual bleeding equipment and must be fully and properly bled before bleeding the modulator.

BLEEDING THE MODULATOR ASSEMBLY

To bleed the ABS unit, the battery must be relocated outside the vehicle and connected to the vehicle with jumper cables. This allows access to

the 4 bleeder screws on top of the modulator assembly. Additionally, the DRB II must be connected to the diagnostic plug before bleeding begins; the DRB II is used to activate the system(s) during the procedure. The 4 components to be bled within the modulator are (in order) the secondary sump, the primary sump, the primary accumulator and the secondary accumulator. Use the following procedure to bleed the modulator assembly.

CAUTION
Wear eye protection when bleeding the modulator assembly and always use a hose on the bleed screw to direct the flow of fluid away from painted surfaces. Bleeding the modulator may result in the release of very high pressure fluid.

1. Connect a clear hose to the secondary sump bleeder screw and route the hose to a clear container.
2. Either install and pressurize the pressure bleeding equipment at the master cylinder or have an assistant provide light and constant pressure on the brake pedal.
3. Open the bleeder screw about ½–¾ turn. Use the DRB II to select the ACTUATE VALVES test; actuate the left front build/decay valve.
4. Bleed until the fluid flows free of air bubbles or until the brake pedal bottoms.
5. Tighten the bleeder screw and release the brake pedal if it was being held.
6. Repeat Steps 2 through 5 until the fluid is free of air bubbles. Remember to check the fluid reservoir level periodically.
7. Select and actuate the right rear build/decay valve and perform Steps 2–5 until the fluid flows without air bubbles.
8. Move the bleeder tube to the primary sump bleeder screw.
9. Pressurize the pressure bleeding equipment at the master cylinder or have an assistant provide light and constant pressure on the brake pedal.
10. Open the bleeder screw about ½–¾ turn. Using the DRB II, actuate the right front build/decay valve.
11. Bleed until the fluid flows free of air bubbles or until the brake pedal bottoms.
12. Tighten the bleeder screw and release the brake pedal if it was being held.
13. Repeat Steps 2 through 5 until the fluid is free of air bubbles. Remember to check the fluid reservoir level periodically.
14. Select and actuate the left rear build/decay valve. Perform Steps 2–5 until the fluid runs free of air bubbles.
15. Move the bleeder tube to the primary accumulator bleeder screw.
16. Pressurize the pressure bleeding

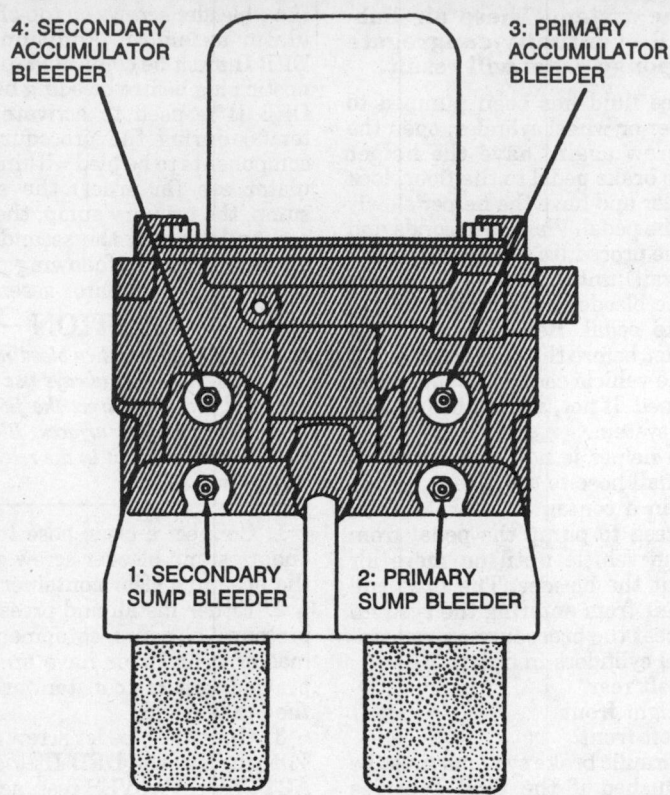

4: SECONDARY ACCUMULATOR BLEEDER

3: PRIMARY ACCUMULATOR BLEEDER

1: SECONDARY SUMP BLEEDER

2: PRIMARY SUMP BLEEDER

Bleeder locations for the ABS modulator assembly—Daytona, LeBaron, LeBaron Landau, Spirit and Acclaim

equipment at the master cylinder or have an assistant provide light and constant pressure on the brake pedal.

17. Open the bleeder screw about ½–¾ turn. Using the DRB II, actuate the right front/left rear isolation valve.

18. Bleed until the fluid flows free of air bubbles or until the brake pedal bottoms.

19. Tighten the bleeder screw and release the brake pedal if it was being held.

20. Repeat Steps 2 through 5 until the fluid is free of air bubbles. Check the fluid reservoir level periodically.

21. Select and actuate the right front build/decay valve. Perform Steps 2–5 until the fluid runs free of air bubbles.

22. Move the bleeder tube to the secondary accumulator bleeder screw.

23. Pressurize the pressure bleeding equipment at the master cylinder or have an assistant provide light and constant pressure on the brake pedal.

24. Open the bleeder screw about ½–¾ turn. Using the DRB II, actuate the left front/right rear isolation valve.

25. Bleed until the fluid flows free of air bubbles or until the brake pedal bottoms.

26. Tighten the bleeder screw and release the brake pedal if it was being held.

27. Repeat Steps 2 through 5 until

the fluid is free of air bubbles. Check the fluid reservoir level periodically.

28. Select and actuate the left front build/decay valve. Perform Steps 2–5 until the fluid runs free of air bubbles.

29. Remove the bleeding apparatus; fill the brake fluid reservoir to the correct level and install the cap.

TC With Anti-Lock Brakes
BOOSTER BLEEDING

1. Depressurize the hydraulic accumulator by turning the ignition to the **OFF** position and pumping the brake pedal approximately 20 times until a hard brake pedal is obtained.

2. Connect all pump/motor and hydraulic assembly electrical connections. Be sure all brake lines and hose connections are tight.

3. Fill the reservoir to the full level.

4. Connect a transparent hose to the bleeder screw location on the right side of the hydraulic assembly. Place the other end of the hose into a clear container to receive brake fluid.

5. Open the bleeder screw ½–¾ of a turn.

6. Turn the ignition switch to the **ON** position. The pump/motor should run, discharging fluid into the container. After a good volume of fluid has been forced through the hose, an air-

free flow in the plastic hose and container will indicate a good bleed.

7. Turn the ignition switch **OFF**.

NOTE: If the brake fluid does not flow, it may be due to a lack of prime to the pump/motor. Try shaking the return hose to break up air bubbles that may be present within the hose.

Should the brake fluid still not flow, turn the ignition switch OFF. Remove the return hose from the reservoir and cap nipple on the reservoir. Manually fill the return hose with brake fluid and connect to the reservoir. Repeat the bleeding process.

8. Remove the hose from the bleeder screw. Tighten the bleeder screw to 7.5 ft. lbs. (10 Nm). Do not overtighten.

9. Top off the reservoir to the correct fluid level.

10. Turn the ignition switch to the **ON** position. Allow the pump to charge the accumulator, which should stop after approximately 30 seconds.

PRESSURE BLEEDING

The brake lines may be pressure bled, using a standard diaphragm type pressure bleeder. Only diaphragm type pressure bleeding equipment should be used to bleed the system.

1. The ignition should be turned **OFF** and remain **OFF** throughout this procedure.

2. Depressurize the hydraulic accumulator.

--- **CAUTION** ---

Failure to depressurize the hydraulic accumulator, prior to performing this operation may result in personal injury and/or damage to the painted surfaces.

3. Remove the electrical connector from fluid level sensor on the reservoir cap and remove the reservoir cap.

4. Install the pressure bleeder adapter.

5. Attach the bleeding equipment to the bleeder adapter. Charge the pressure bleeder to approximately 20 psi (138 kPa).

6. Connect a transparent hose to the caliper bleed screw. Submerge the free end of the hose in a clear glass container, which is partially filled with clean, fresh brake fluid.

7. With the pressure turned **ON**, open the caliper bleed screw ½–¾ turn and allow fluid to flow into the container. Leave the bleed screw open until clear, bubble-free fluid flows from the hose. If the reservoir has been drained or the hydraulic assembly removed from the vehicle prior to the bleeding operation, slowly pump the brake pedal 1–2 times while the bleed screw is open and fluid is flowing. This

will help purge air from the hydraulic assembly. Tighten the bleeder screw to 7.5 ft. lbs. (10 Nm).

8. Repeat Step 7 at all calipers. Calipers should be bled in the following order:

   a. Left rear
   b. Right rear
   c. Left front
   d. Right front

9. After bleeding all 4 calipers, remove the pressure bleeding equipment and bleeder adapter by closing the pressure bleeder valve and slowly unscrewing the bleeder adapter from the hydraulic assembly reservoir. Failure to release pressure in the reservoir will cause spillage of brake fluid and could result in injury or damage to painted surfaces.

10. Using a syringe or equivalent method, remove excess fluid from the reservoir to bring the fluid level to full level.

11. Install the reservoir cap and connect the fluid level sensor connector. Turn the ignition **ON** and allow the pump to charge the accumulator.

MANUAL BLEEDING

1. Depressurize the hydraulic accumulator.

——— CAUTION ———
Failure to depressurize the hydraulic accumulator, prior to performing this operation may result in personal injury and/or damage to the painted surfaces.

2. Connect a transparent hose to the caliper bleed screw. Submerge the free end of the hose in a clear glass container, which is partially filled with clean, fresh brake fluid.

3. Slowly pump the brake pedal several times, using full strokes of the pedal and allowing approximately 5 seconds between pedal strokes. After 2–3 strokes, continue to hold pressure on the pedal, keeping it at the bottom of its travel.

4. With pressure on the pedal, open the bleed screw ½–¾ turn. Leave bleed screw open until fluid no longer flows from the hose. Tighten the bleed screw and release the pedal.

5. Repeat this procedure until clear, bubble-free fluid flows from the hose.

6. Repeat all steps at each of the calipers. Calipers should be bled in the following order:

   a. Left rear
   b. Right rear
   c. Left front
   d. Right front

Anti-Lock Brake System Service

PRECAUTIONS

Failure to observe the following precautions may result in system damage.

● Before performing electric arc welding on the vehicle, disconnect the control module and the hydraulic unit connectors.

● When performing painting work on the vehicle, do not expose the control module to temperatures in excess of 185°F (85°C) for longer than 2 hrs. The system may be exposed to temperatures up to 200°F (95°C) for less than 15 min.

● Never disconnect or connect the control module or hydraulic modulator connectors with the ignition switch ON.

● Never disassemble any component of the Anti-Lock Brake System (ABS) which is designated nonservicable; the component must be replaced as an assembly.

● When filling the master cylinder, always use brake fluid which meets DOT-3 specifications; petroleum-based fluid will destroy the rubber parts.

DEPRESSURIZING THE HYDRAULIC ACCUMULATOR

TC

1. With the ignition **OFF**, pump the brake pedal a minimum of 20 times, using approximately 50 lbs. (222 N) pedal force. A noticeable change in pedal feel will occur when the accumulator is discharged.

2. When a definite increase in pedal effort is felt, stroke the pedal a few additional times. This should remove all hydraulic pressure from the system.

Pump/Motor Assembly
REMOVAL & INSTALLATION

Except TC

The pump and motor assembly used

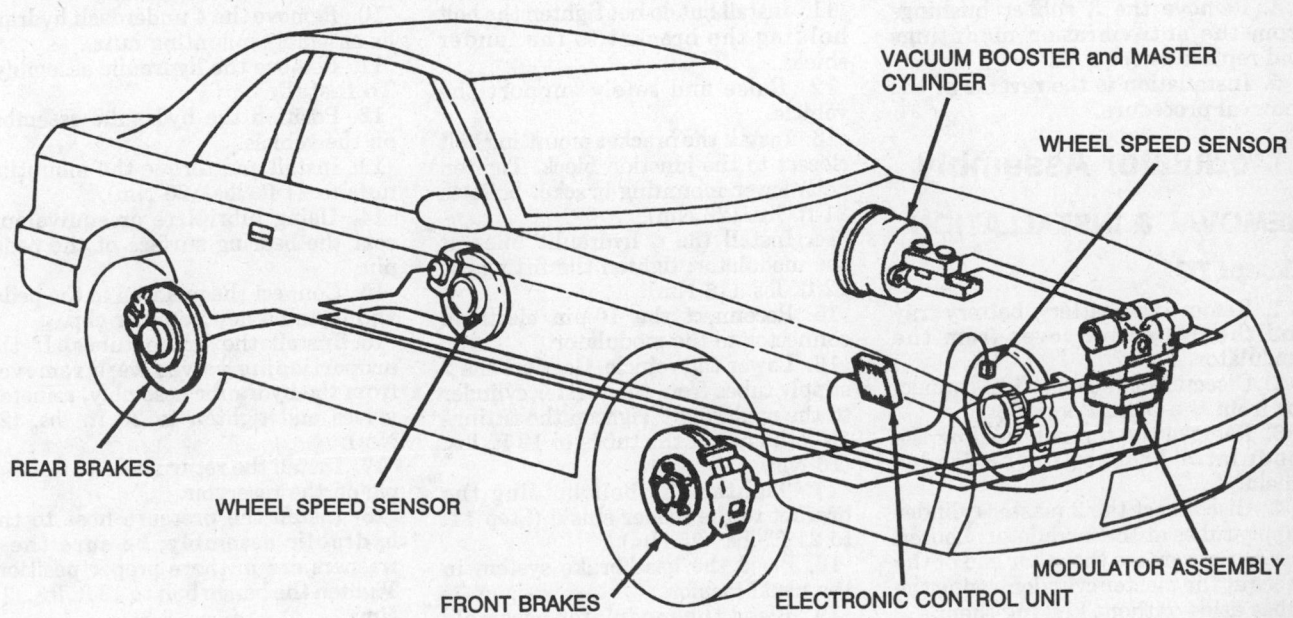

VACUUM BOOSTER and MASTER CYLINDER

WHEEL SPEED SENSOR

REAR BRAKES

WHEEL SPEED SENSOR

FRONT BRAKES

ELECTRONIC CONTROL UNIT

MODULATOR ASSEMBLY

Anti-lock brake system components—Daytona, LeBaron, LeBaron Landau, Spirit and Acclaim

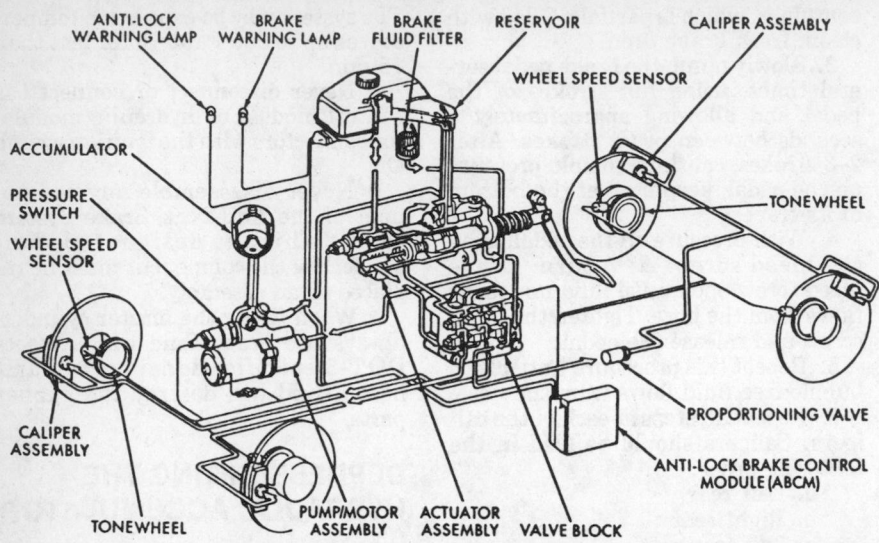

ANTI-LOCK WARNING LAMP   BRAKE WARNING LAMP   BRAKE FLUID FILTER   RESERVOIR   CALIPER ASSEMBLY

WHEEL SPEED SENSOR

ACCUMULATOR

PRESSURE SWITCH

WHEEL SPEED SENSOR

TONEWHEEL

CALIPER ASSEMBLY

TONEWHEEL

PUMP/MOTOR ASSEMBLY   ACTUATOR ASSEMBLY   VALVE BLOCK

PROPORTIONING VALVE

ANTI-LOCK BRAKE CONTROL MODULE (ABCM)

Anti-lock brake system components—TC

on the Bendix Anti-lock 6 brake system is not removable. If the pump or motor fails, the modulator assembly must be replaced.

TC

1. Depressurize the hydraulic accumulator.

—— CAUTION ——

Failure to depressurize the hydraulic accumulator prior to performing this operation may result in personal injury and/or damage to the painted surfaces.

2. Remove the hydraulic assembly from the vehicle.
3. Loosen the pump and motor mounting screws and remove from the front anchor pin.
4. Remove the 3 rubber bushings from the anti-vibration mountings and replace as required.
5. Installation is the reverse of the removal procedure.

Modulator Assembly

REMOVAL & INSTALLATION

Except TC

1. Remove the battery, battery tray and the protective cover from the modulator.
2. Disconnect the electrical connector from the Delta P switch.
3. Remove the top bolt holding the modulator bracket to the fender shield.
4. Disconnect the 2 master cylinder supply tubes at the modulator. Loosen but do not remove the other end of the tubes at the master cylinder; swing the tubes aside without kinking them.
5. Raise and safely support the vehicle.

6. From below, disconnect the modulator 10-pin electrical connector. Remove the remaining 4 brake tubes from the modulator assembly.
7. Remove the modulator bracket mounting bolt which is closest to the hydraulic junction block.
8. Loosen but do not fully remove the bracket mounting bolt closest to the radiator.
9. Lower the vehicle; lift the modulator assembly and bracket out of the vehicle.

To install:

10. Install the modulator and bracket into position. Use the protruding tab on the modulator to locate and hold the assembly. Make certain the bracket is held by the front mounting bolt.
11. Install but do not tighten the bolt holding the bracket to the fender shield.
12. Raise and safely support the vehicle.
13. Install the bracket mounting bolt closest to the junction block. Tighten both lower mounting bracket bolts to 21 ft. lbs. (28 Nm).
14. Install the 4 hydraulic lines at the modulator; tighten the fittings to 12 ft. lbs. (16 Nm).
15. Reconnect the 10-pin electrical connector to the modulator.
16. Lower the vehicle. Connect the 2 supply tubes from the master cylinder to the modulator. Tighten the fittings at both ends of the tubes to 12 ft. lbs. (16 Nm).
17. Tighten the bolt holding the bracket to the fender shield (Step 11) to 21 ft. lbs. (28 Nm).
18. Bleed the base brake system in the usual fashion.
19. Bleed the modulator assembly following the correct sequences and procedure.

20. Install the protective cover on the modulator assembly.
21. Install the battery tray and battery. Connect the battery cables.

Hydraulic Assembly

REMOVAL & INSTALLATION

TC

1. Depressurize the hydraulic accumulator.

—— CAUTION ——

Failure to depressurize the hydraulic accumulator prior to performing this operation may result in personal injury and/or damage to the painted surfaces.

2. Remove the fresh air intake ducts.
3. Disconnect all electrical connectors from the hydraulic unit and pump/motor.
4. Disconnect the ground cable from the hydraulic unit.
5. Remove as much of the fluid as possible from the reservoir on the hydraulic assembly.
6. Remove the pressure hose fitting (banjo bolt) from the hydraulic assembly. Use care not to drop the 2 washers used to seal the pressure hose fitting to the hydraulic assembly inlet.
7. Disconnect the return hose from the reservoir nipple. Cap the spigot on the reservoir.
8. Disconnect all brake tubes from the hydraulic assembly.
9. Remove the driver's side sound insulation panel. Disconnect the pushrod from the brake pedal.
10. Remove the 4 underdash hydraulic assembly mounting nuts.
11. Remove the hydraulic assembly.

To install:

12. Position the hydraulic assembly on the vehicle.
13. Install and torque the mounting nuts to 21 ft. lbs. (28 Nm).
14. Using lubriplate or equivalent, coat the bearing surface of the pedal pin.
15. Connect the pushrod to the pedal and install a new retainer clip.
16. Install the brake tubes. If the proportioning valves were removed from the hydraulic assembly, reinstall valves and tighten to 20 ft. lbs. (27 Nm).
17. Install the return hose to the nipple on the reservoir.
18. Install the pressure hose to the hydraulic assembly; be sure the 2 washers are in there proper position. Tighten the bango bolt to 13 ft. lbs. (18 Nm).
19. Fill the reservoir to the top of the screen.

20. Connect all electrical connectors to the hydraulic assembly.
21. Bleed the entire brake system.
22. Install the crosscar brace, if disturbed. Install the fresh air intake duct.

Sensor Block

REMOVAL & INSTALLATION

TC

1. Depressurize the hydraulic accumulator.

————— **CAUTION** —————
Failure to depressurize the hydraulic accumulator, prior to performing this operation may result in personal injury and/or damage to the painted surfaces.

2. Disconnect all electrical connectors from the reservoir on the hydraulic assembly.
3. Working from under the dash, disconnect the pushrod from the brake pedal.
4. Remove the driver's side sound insulator panel.
5. Remove the 4 hydraulic assembly mounting nuts.
6. Working from under the hood, pull the hydraulic assembly away from the dash panel and rotate the assembly enough to gain access to the sensor block cover.

NOTE: The brake lines should not be removed or deformed during this procedure.

7. Remove the sensor block cover retaining bolt and remove the sensor block cover. Care should be used not to damage the cover gasket during removal.
8. Disengage the locking tabs and disconnect the valve block connector (12 pin) from the sensor block.
9. Disengage the reed block connector, marked PUSH, by carefully pulling outward on the orange connector body. The connector is partially retained by a plastic clip and will only move outward approximately ½ in. (13mm).
10. Remove the 3 block retaining bolts.
11. Carefully disengage the sensor block pressure port from the hydraulic assembly and remove the sensor block from the vehicle. The sensor block pressure port is sealed with an O-ring and extra care should be taken to prevent damage to the seal.
12. Inspect the sensor block pressure port O-ring for damage. Replace the O-ring if cut or damaged. Check the sensor block wiring for any mispositioning or damage. Correct any

damage or replace the sensor block if damage cannot be corrected.

To install:
13. Pull the reed block connector (2 pin) outward to the disengage position prior to installing the sensor block on the hydraulic unit.
14. Throughly lubricate the sensor block pressure port O-ring with fresh, clean brake fluid. Carefully insert the pressure port into the hydraulic assembly's orifice, taking care not to cut or damage the O-ring. Position the sensor block for installation of the mounting bolts.
15. Install the sensor block mounting bolts. Tighten to 11 ft. lbs. (15 Nm).
16. Engage the reed block connector by pressing on the orange connector body marked PUSH.
17. Connect the valve block connector (12 pin) to the sensor block.
18. Install the sensor block cover, gasket and mounting bolt.
19. Connect the sensor block and control pressure switch connectors.
20. Install the hydraulic assembly.

Wheel Speed Sensors

REMOVAL & INSTALLATION

Except TC
FRONT WHEEL

1. Raise and safely support the vehicle. Remove the wheel and tire.

2. Remove the clip holding the wiring grommet to the fender well.
3. Remove the screws holding the sensor wiring tube to the fender well.
4. Carefully remove the grommet from the fender shield.
5. Make certain the ignition switch is **OFF**. Disconnect the sensor wiring from the ABS harness.
6. Remove the triangular retaining clip from the bracket on the strut. Not all vehicles have this clip.
7. Remove the sensor wiring grommets from the bracket.
8. Remove the fastener holding the sensor head.
9. Carefully remove the sensor head from the steering knuckle. Do not use pliers on the sensor head; if it is seized in place, use a hammer and small punch to tap the edge of the sensor ear. The tapping and side-to-side motion will free the unit.

To install:
10. Connect the speed sensor to the ABS harness.
11. Push the sensor assembly grommet into the the hole in the fender shield. Install the retainer clip and screw.
12. Install the sensor wiring tube and tighten the retaining bolts to 35 inch lbs. (4 Nm).
13. Install the sensor grommets into the brackets on the fender shield and strut. Install the retainer clip at the strut.
14. Install the sensor to the knuckle.

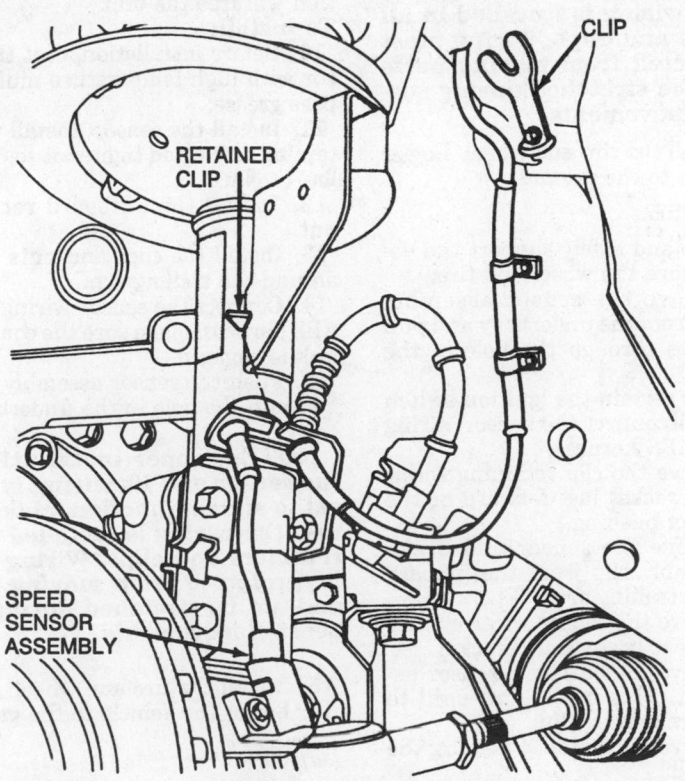

Front wheel speed sensor

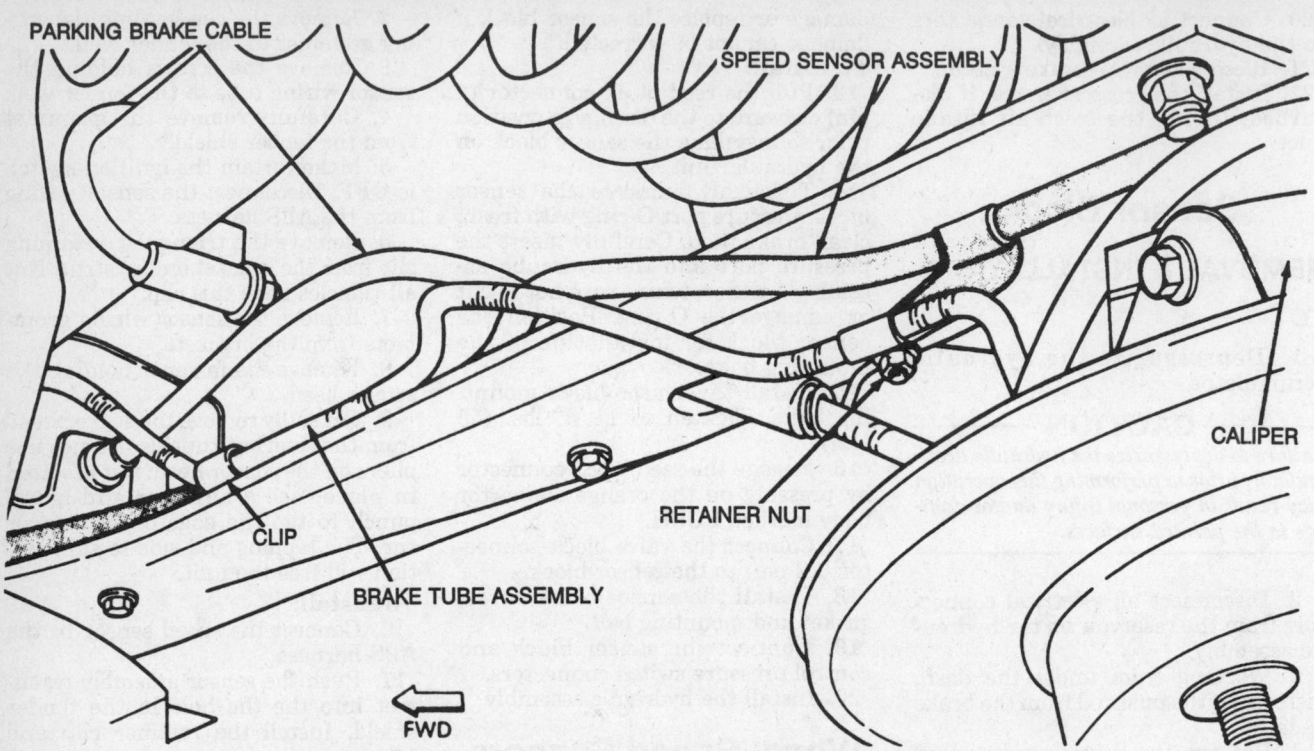

PARKING BRAKE CABLE

SPEED SENSOR ASSEMBLY

CALIPER

RETAINER NUT

CLIP

BRAKE TUBE ASSEMBLY

FWD

Rear wheel speed sensor—Daytona, LeBaron, LeBaron Landau, Spirit and Acclaim

Install the retaining screw and tighten it to 60 inch lbs. (7 Nm).

NOTE: Proper installation of the sensor and its wiring is critical to system function. Make certain the wiring is installed in all retainers and clips. Wiring must be protected from moving parts and not be stretched during suspension movements.

15. Install the tire and wheel. Lower the vehicle to the ground.

REAR WHEEL

1. Raise and safely support the vehicle. Remove the wheel and tire.

2. Remove the sensor assembly grommet from the underbody and pull the harness through the hole in the body.

3. Make certain the ignition switch is **OFF**. Disconnect the sensor wiring from the ABS harness.

4. Remove the clip retaining screw from the bracket just forward of the trailing arm bushing.

5. Remove the sensor and brake tube assembly clip from the inboard side of the trailing arm.

6. Remove the sensor wire retainer from the rear brake hose bracket.

7. Remove the outboard sensor assembly nut. This nut is also used to hold the brake tube clip.

8. Remove the fastener holding the sensor head.

9. Carefully remove the sensor head

from the adapter assembly. Do not use pliers on the sensor head; if it is seized in place, use a hammer and small punch to tap the edge of the sensor ear. The tapping and side-to-side motion will free the unit.

To install:

10. Before installation, coat the sensor with high temperature multi-purpose grease.

11. Install the sensor; install the retaining screw and tighten it to 60 inch lbs. (7 Nm).

12. Install the outboard retaining nut.

13. Install the clips and nuts at and around the trailing arm.

14. Connect the sensor wiring to the ABS harness; make sure the connector lock is engaged.

15. Push the sensor assembly grommet into the hole in the underbody.

NOTE: Proper installation of the sensor and its wiring is critical to system function. Make certain the wiring is installed in all retainers and clips. Wiring must be protected from moving parts and not be stretched during suspension movements.

16. Install the tire and wheel.
17. Lower the vehicle to the ground.

TC

1. Raise the vehicle and support

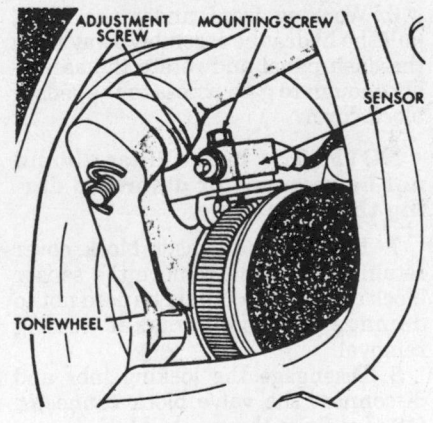

ADJUSTMENT SCREW

MOUNTING SCREW

SENSOR

TONEWHEEL

Front wheel speed sensor—TC

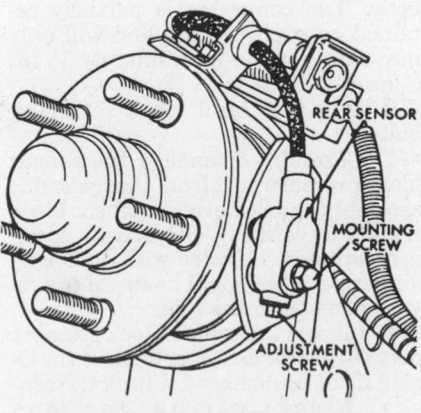

REAR SENSOR

MOUNTING SCREW

ADJUSTMENT SCREW

Rear wheel speed sensor—TC

safely. Remove the wheel and tire assembly.

2. Remove the sensor cable from the retainer clips.

3. Carefully pull the sensor assembly grommet from the floor pan.

4. Unplug the connector from the harness.

5. Remove the sensor mounting screw. Do not disturb the adjustment screw.

6. Carefully remove the sensor.

To install:

7. To install, coat the sensor with high temperature multi-purpose anti-corrosion compound at all areas it contacts the bracket before installing into the steering knuckle. Install the screw and tighten to 85 inch lbs. (10 Nm).

8. Connect the sensor connector to the harness and install the sensor connector lock.

9. Install the sensor assembly grommet.

NOTE: Proper installation of the wheel speed sensor cables is critical to continued system operation. Be sure the cables are installed in retainers. Failure to install the cables in the retainers may result in contact with moving parts and/or over-extension of the cables, resulting in an open circuit.

CHASSIS ELECTRICAL

Air Bag

Disarming

NOTE: Before attempting any repair procedure that is located in the area of an air bag sensor or wire harness, it is recommended that the air bag system be disarmed. Failure to disarm the air bag system may result in accidental deployment of the air bag module and possible personal injury.

To disarm the air bag system, disconnect the negative battery cable and isolate using an appropriate insulator. Allow the system capacitor to discharge for 2 minutes prior to starting repairs on the vehicle.

Heater Blower Motor

REMOVAL & INSTALLATION

1. Disconnect the negative battery cable.

2. Remove the glove box assembly, lower right side instrument panel trim cover and right cowl trim panel, as required. Disconnect the blower lead wire connector.

3. If equipped with air conditioning, disconnect the 2 vacuum lines at the recirculating air door actuator.

4. Remove the 2 screws at the top of the blower housing that secure it to the unit cover.

5. Remove the 5 screws from around the blower housing and separate the blower housing from the heater unit.

6. Remove the 3 screws that secure the blower and wheel assembly to the heater or air conditioning housing and remove the assembly from the unit. Remove the fan from the blower motor.

To install:

7. Install the fan onto the blower motor and position motor assembly in housing. Secure motor using 3 mounting screws.

8. Install the blower housing and the heater unit and secure with screws.

9. Connect the 2 vacuum hoses to the recirculating air door actuator as required.

10. Connect the blower lead wire connector.

11. Install the glove box assembly, lower right side instrument panel trim cover and right cowl trim panel, as required.

12. Connect the negative battery cable and check the blower motor for proper operation.

Windshield Wiper Motor

REMOVAL & INSTALLATION

1. Disconnect the negative battery cable.

2. Remove the wiper arms and the blades. Disconnect hoses from connector at the base of each arm. Remove the cowl top plastic cover and screen.

3. Remove the wiper motor cover, if equipped. Disconnect the motor wiring harness connector.

4. Remove the wiper motor mounting nuts. Remove the wiper motor, pivot and links from the vehicle as an assembly.

5. Installation is the reverse of the removal procedure.

6. Connect the negative battery cable and check the wiper motor for proper operation.

Liftgate Wiper Motor

REMOVAL & INSTALLATION

Daytona

1. Disconnect the negative battery cable.

2. To remove the wiper arm, lift the arm against its spring tension and release the latch. Lift the arm off of the motor shaft.

3. Open the liftgate and remove the trim panel. Disconnect the connector from the motor.

4. Remove the grommet from the liftgate glass.

5. Remove the screws that fasten the bracket to the liftgate and remove the motor assembly from the vehicle.

To install:

6. Install a new grommet in the liftgate glass.

7. Position the motor to the liftgate and secure tightening 2 retaining screws to 70 inch lbs. (8 Nm).

8. Connect the electrical harness to the wiper motor.

9. Install the interior rear trim panel.

10. Reconnect the negative battery cable and check the rear wiper assembly for proper operation.

Windshield Wiper Switch

REMOVAL & INSTALLATION

1989 Vehicles with Standard Column

1. Disconnect the negative battery cable and insulate to prevent accidental contact with battery post.

2. Remove the lower steering column cover, if equipped.

3. Straighten the steering wheel so the tires are pointing straight-ahead.

NOTE: If equipped with an airbag, it is imperative that the air bag system be disarmed prior to starting repair procedures and the steering wheel removal and installation procedure under Steering be followed.

4. Remove the steering wheel.

5. Remove the plastic wiring channel from the under the steering column.

6. Disconnect the wiper switch connector, intermittent wipe module connector and cruise control connector, as equipped.

7. Remove the side lock housing cover.

8. Remove the slotted hex-head screw that attaches the wiper switch

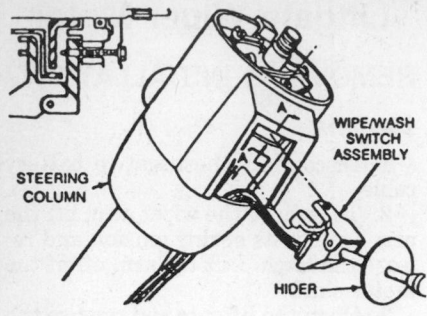

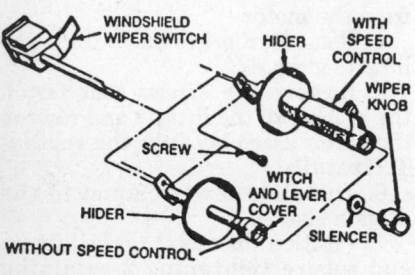

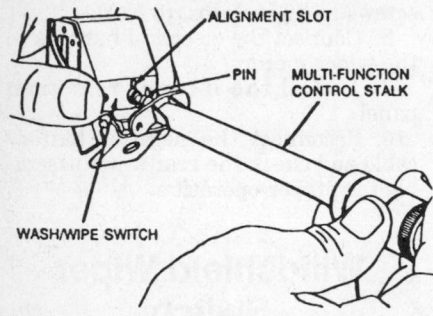

Removing the windshield wiper switch—standard column

to the turn signal switch, then remove the switch.

9. Remove the control knob from the end of the stalk. Pull the round nylon hider up the control stalk and remove the revealed screws that attach the control stalk sleeve to the wiper switch.

10. Rotate the control stalk shaft to the full clockwise position and remove the shaft from the wiper switch by pulling it straight out.

To install:

11. Install the control shaft to the wiper switch, install the screws, the hider and the control knob.

12. Run the wiring through the opening and down the steering column, position the switch and install the hex-head screw. Make sure the dimmer switch rod is properly engaged.

13. Install the side lock housing cover.

14. Connect the wires and install the wiring channel.

15. Install the steering wheel torque the nut to 45 ft. lbs. (61 Nm).

16. Install the horn pad and the lower steering column cover.

17. Connect the negative battery cable and check the wiper and washer, cruise control, turn signal switch and dimmer switch for proper operation.

Maserati TC and 1989 Vehicles with Tilt Wheel

1. Disconnect the negative battery cable and insulate to protect against accidental contact with the battery post.

2. Remove the lower steering column cover and remove the plastic wiring channel from the under the steering column.

3. Position the steering wheel so the tires are pointing straight-ahead.

NOTE: If equipped with an airbag, it is imperative that the steering wheel removal and installation procedure is followed.

4. Remove the steering wheel.

5. Depress the lockplate with the proper depressing tool, remove the retaining ring from its groove and remove the tool, ring, lockplate, cancelling cam and spring.

6. Remove the switch stalk actuator screw and arm.

7. Remove the hazard switch knob.

8. Disconnect the turn signal switch, wiper switch, intermittent module and cruise control connectors, if equipped.

9. Remove the 3 screws and remove the turn signal switch. Tape the connector to the wires to aid in removal.

10. Remove the ignition key light.

11. Place the key in the **LOCK** position and remove the key. Insert a thin tool into the slot next to the switch mounting screw boss, depress the spring latch at the bottom of the slot releasing the lock. Remove the lock cylinder.

12. Remove the buzzer switch and wedge spring.

13. Remove the 3 housing cover screws and remove the housing cover.

14. Remove the wiper switch pivot pin with a punch and remove the switch.

15. Remove the control knob from the end of the stalk. Pull the round nylon hider up the control stalk and remove the revealed screws that attach the control stalk sleeve to the wiper switch.

16. Rotate the control stalk shaft to the full clockwise position and remove the shaft from the wiper switch by pulling it straight out.

To install:

17. Install the control shaft to the wiper switch, install the screws, the hider and the control knob.

18. Run the wiring through the opening and down the steering column, position the switch and install the wiper switch pivot pin.

19. Install the housing cover.

20. Install the buzzer switch and wedge spring.

21. Install the lock cylinder.

22. Install the ignition key light.

23. Install the turn signal switch, switch stalk actuator arm and hazard switch knob.

24. Install the spring, cancelling cam, lockplate and ring on the steering shaft. Depress the plate with the depressing tool and install the ring securely in the groove. Remove the tool slowly.

25. Connect the turn signal switch, wiper switch, intermittent module and cruise control connectors, if equipped. Install the channel.

26. Install the steering wheel and torque the nut to 45 ft. lbs. (61 Nm).

27. Install the horn pad.

28. Connect the negative battery cable and check the wiper and washer, cruise control, turn signal switch and dimmer switch for proper operation.

29. Install the lower column cover, if equipped.

1990–93 Daytona and LeBaron
WITH POD MOUNTED SWITCH

1. Disarm the air bag system as follows:

   a. Disconnect the negative battery cable and isolate using an appropriate insulator.

   b. Allow the system capacitor to discharge for 2 minutes prior to starting repairs on the vehicle.

NOTE: Failure to disarm the air bag system may result in accidental deployment of the air bag module and possible personal injury.

2. Remove the panel vent grille above the switch pod assembly and remove the 2 revealed pod mounting screws.

3. If equipped with tilt wheel, position the steering wheel in the lowest position.

4. Remove the 2 remaining screws under the pod and pull the pod from the instrument clustster. Disconnect the wiring harnesses and remove the pod.

5. Unhook the switch linkage from the buttons, remove the switch mounting screws and the switch.

To install:

6. Latch the switch linkage in the up position. Insert the switch into the pod and install the mounting screws. Unlatch the linkage and install onto the push buttons.

7. Operate all switch modes checking for correct operation.

8. Reinstall the inner switch pod

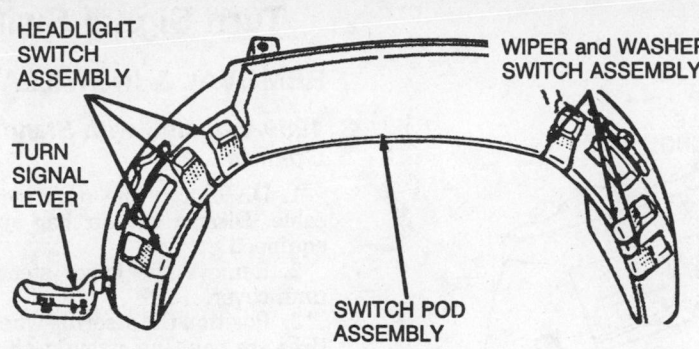

HEADLIGHT SWITCH ASSEMBLY

TURN SIGNAL LEVER

WIPER and WASHER SWITCH ASSEMBLY

SWITCH POD ASSEMBLY

Instrument panel switch pod assembly—1990–93 Daytona and LeBaron

Radio

REMOVAL & INSTALLATION

NOTE: If removing a compact disc player, the procedures outlined for radio removal and installation will apply.

1. Disconnect the negative battery cable.
2. Remove the console or cluster front trim bezel, as required. If equipped with a full center console, remove the right side panel cover.
3. Remove the screws that attach the radio to the instrument panel.
4. Pull the radio out slightly and disconnect the harness connectors, ground cable and antenna. Remove the radio from the vehicle.
5. The installation is the reverse of the removal procedure.

Concealed Headlights

MANUAL OPERATION

1. Disconnect the negative battery cable.
2. Locate the manual override knob, which is accessible through a flap cover hole in the sight shield between the bumper fascia, and under the hood.
3. Remove the protective cover boot.
4. Rotate the manual override knob to raise the headlight cover(s). Several revolutions may be required to start movement of the doors.
5. Connect the negative battery cable.

Headlight Switch

REMOVAL & INSTALLATION

Except 1990–93 Daytona and LeBaron

1. Disconnect the negative battery cable.
2. Remove the headlight switch bezel or cluster bezel, as required.
3. Remove the screws securing the headlight switch mounting plate to the instrument panel. Pull the assembly out and disconnect the connectors from the switch.
4. Depress the spring button and remove the headlight switch knob and stem.
5. Remove the escutcheon, if equipped, and remove the nut that attaches the switch to the mounting plate.
6. The installation is the reverse of the removal procedure.

panel retainer screws and install the pod assembly into the instrument cluster. Secure pod with the retainer screws.

9. Install the steering wheel, the panel vent grille and connect the negative battery cable. Check for proper operation of the switch.

Instrument Cluster

REMOVAL & INSTALLATION

Except 1990–93 Daytona and LeBaron

1. Disconnect the negative battery cable. Disarm the air bag system if equipped.
2. Remove the instrument cluster bezel. Cluster removal is not necessary if just removing gauges.
3. When only removing gauge(s) or the speedometer, remove the trip odometer reset knob, if necessary, remove the mask and lens assembly and remove the desired gauge from the cluster. Disconnect the speedometer cable, if equipped, when removing the speedometer.
4. If equipped with automatic transaxle and column shift lever, remove the upper and lower column covers and disconnect the gear indicator cable.
5. Remove the screws attaching the cluster assembly to the instrument panel.
6. Pull the cluster out and disconnect all harness wiring connectors and the speedometer cable, if equipped. Remove the cluster from the vehicle.
To install:
7. Position the cluster and feed the gear indicator cable through its slot.
8. Connect all wiring and install the speedometer cable to the speedometer, if removed; make sure the cable end is securely clicked in place.
9. Install the cluster retaining screws. Connect the gearshift indicator cable.
10. Install the upper and lower steer-

ing column covers and the cluster bezel.
11. Connect the negative battery cable, check all gauges and the speedometer for proper operation. Make sure the gearshift indicator is properly aligned.

1990–93 Daytona and LeBaron

1. Disconnect the negative battery cable. Disarm the air bag system, if equipped.
2. Remove the panel vent grille above the switch pod assembly and remove the 2 revealed pod mounting screws.
3. Remove the 2 remaining screws under the pod and pull the pod out to disconnect the wiring harnesses. Remove the pod from the instrument panel.
4. Unscrew the tilt column lever, if equipped, remove the screws from under the upper steering column shrouds and remove the shrouds.
5. Pull rearward to disengage the cluster trim bezel retaining clips and remove the bezel.
6. When only removing gauges or the speedometer, remove the mask and lens assembly and remove the desired assembly from the cluster.
7. Remove the screws attaching the cluster to the instrument panel.
8. Pull the cluster out and disconnect all wiring harnesses and the turbo gauge hose, if equipped. Remove the cluster from the vehicle.
To install:
9. Position the cluster and connect all wiring and the turbo hose, if it was disconnected.
10. Install the cluster mounting screws.
11. Install the cluster trim bezel.
12. Install the steering column shrouds and the tilt lever, if equipped.
13. Install the switch pod assembly and panel vent grille.
14. Connect the negative battery cable and check all gauges, switches and the speedometer for proper operation.

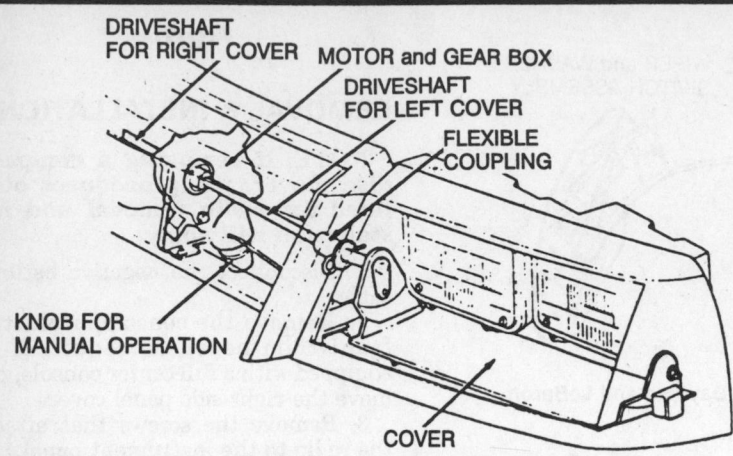

DRIVESHAFT FOR RIGHT COVER — MOTOR and GEAR BOX — DRIVESHAFT FOR LEFT COVER — FLEXIBLE COUPLING — KNOB FOR MANUAL OPERATION — COVER

Manual override knob—LeBaron

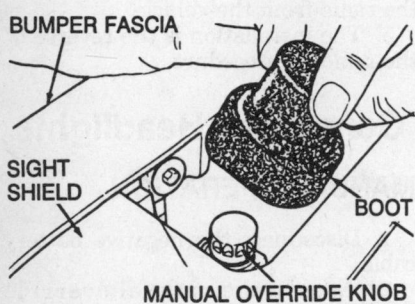

BUMPER FASCIA — SIGHT SHIELD — BOOT — MANUAL OVERRIDE KNOB

Manual override knob—Daytona

7. Connect the negative battery cable and check the switch for proper operation.

1990–93 Daytona and LeBaron

1. Disconnect the negative battery cable.
2. Remove the panel vent grille above the switch pod assembly and remove the 2 revealed pod mounting screws.
3. Remove the 2 remaining screws under the pod and pull the pod out to disconnect the wiring harnesses. Remove the pod from the instrument panel.
4. Remove the turn signal switch lever by pulling it straight out of the pod.
5. Remove the inner panel from the pod. Remove the turn signal switch in order to gain access to the headlight switch retainers.
6. Remove the switch mounting screws.
7. Disconnect the switch linkage from the buttons by pulling the linkage straight up. Remove the switch.
To install:
8. Latch the switch linkage in the up position. Insert the dimmer shaft into the dimmer knob while alinging the switch to the pod assembly.

9. Install the switch attaching screws.
10. Unlatch linkage and install onto push buttons. Operate the switch to assure correct installation.
11. Reconnect the wiring for the turn signal switch, if disconnected, and install switch to it's original position. Make sure switch wiring is properly clipped into position.
12. Place together the inner and the outer bezel sections and install the inner switch pod panel retainer screws from underneath the switch pod.
13. Install the turn signal lever by pushing straight into the switch assembly.
14. Install the switch pod assembly into the instrument panel.
15. Reconnect the negative battery terminal and check for proper system function.

Dimmer Switch

REMOVAL & INSTALLATION

Maserati TC and 1989 Vehicles

NOTE: The dimmer switch is incorporated into the combination switch on 1990–93 LeBaron Landau, Shadow, Sundance, Spirit and Acclaim. On 1990–93 Daytona and LeBaron, it is incorporated with the remote turn signal switch.

1. Disconnect the negative battery cable.
2. Remove the lower steering column cover, if equipped.
3. Unplug the switch, located on the lower portion of the steering column.
4. Holding the actuating rod against its upper seat, remove the bolts that attach the switch to the column, and remove the switch.
5. The installation is the reverse of the removal procedure. Adjust the switch as required.

Turn Signal Switch

REMOVAL & INSTALLATION

1989 Vehicles with Standard Column

1. Disconnect the negative battery cable. Disarm the air bag system, if equipped.
2. Remove the lower steering column cover.
3. Position the steering wheel so the tires are pointing straight-ahead.

NOTE: If equipped with an airbag, it is imperative that the steering wheel removal and installation procedure is followed.

4. Remove the steering wheel.
5. Remove the plastic wiring channel from the under the steering column and disconnect the turn signal switch connector.
6. Remove the hazard switch knob. Remove the slotted hex-head screw that attaches the wiper switch to the turn signal switch.
7. Remove the 3 screws and pull the turn signal switch out of the column.
To install:
8. Run the wiring through the opening and down the steering column, position the switch and install the hex-head screw. Make sure the dimmer switch rod is properly engaged.
9. Install the 3 screws and the hazard switch knob.
10. Connect the wires and install the wiring channel.
11. Install the steering wheel and torque the nut to 45 ft. lbs. (61 Nm).
12. Install the horn pad.
13. Connect the negative battery cable and check the turn signal switch and dimmer switch for proper operation.
14. Install the lower column cover, if equipped.

Maserati TC and 1989 Vehicles with Tilt Wheel

1. Disconnect the negative battery cable. Disarm the air bag system, if equipped.
2. Remove the lower steering column cover, if equipped and remove the plastic wiring channel from the under the steering column.
3. Position the steering wheel so the tires are pointing straight-ahead.

NOTE: If equipped with an airbag, it is imperative that the steering wheel removal and installation procedure is followed.

4. Remove the steering wheel.
5. Depress the lockplate with the proper depressing tool, remove the re-

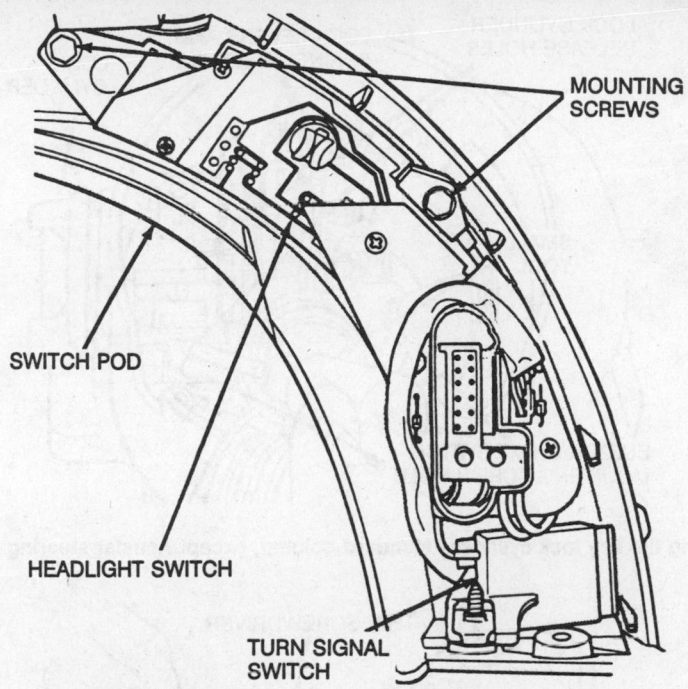

Turn signal switch location—1990–93 Daytona and LeBaron

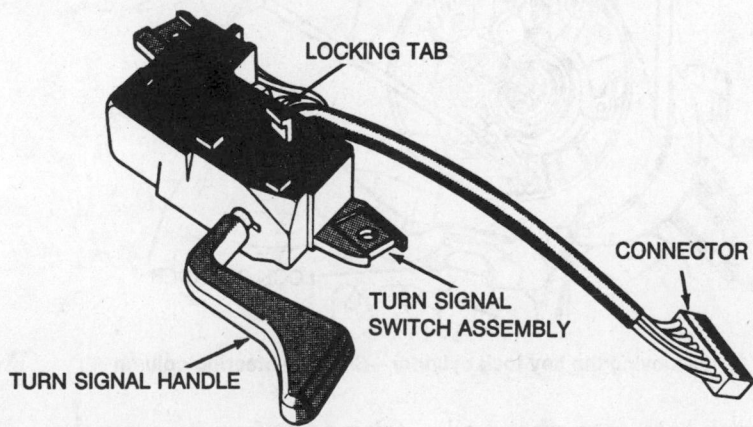

Remote turn signal switch assembly—1993 Daytona and LeBaron

taining ring from its groove and remove the tool, ring, lockplate, cancelling cam and spring.

6. Remove the stalk actuator screw and arm.

7. Remove the hazard switch knob.

8. Disconnect the turn signal switch connector.

9. Remove the 3 screws and remove the turn signal switch. Tape the connector to the wires to aid in removal.

To install:

10. Run the wiring through the opening and down the steering column, install the turn signal switch, switch stalk actuator arm and hazard switch knob.

11. Install the spring, cancelling cam, lockplate and ring on the steering shaft. Depress the plate with the depressing tool and install the ring securely in the groove. Remove the tool slowly.

12. Connect the turn signal switch connector and install the channel.

13. Install the steering wheel and torque the nut to 45 ft. lbs. (61 Nm).

14. Install the horn pad.

15. Connect the negative battery cable and check the turn signal switch and dimmer switch for proper operation.

16. Install the lower column cover.

1990–93 Daytona and LeBaron
REMOTE MOUNTED SWITCH

1. Disconnect the negative battery cable.

2. Remove the panel vent grille above the switch pod assembly and remove the 2 revealed pod mounting screws.

3. Remove the 2 remaining screws under the pod and pull the pod out to disconnect the wiring harnesses. Remove the pod from the instrument panel.

4. Remove the turn signal switch lever by pulling it straight out of the pod.

5. Remove the inner panel from the pod.

6. Remove the turn signal switch mounting screws and slide the switch out of the slot.

7. Unplug the switch harness from the 8 way connector and remove the switch.

To install:

8. Connect the wire connector, install the switch into the switch pod and secure with the switch retainer screws.

9. Install the turn signal control lever into the switch. Install the pod assembly into the instrument panel.

10. Connect the negative battery terminal and check for proper operation of all switch controlled systems.

Combination Switch

REMOVAL & INSTALLATION

1990–93 LeBaron Landau, Shadow, Sundance, Spirit and Acclaim

1. Disconnect the negative battery

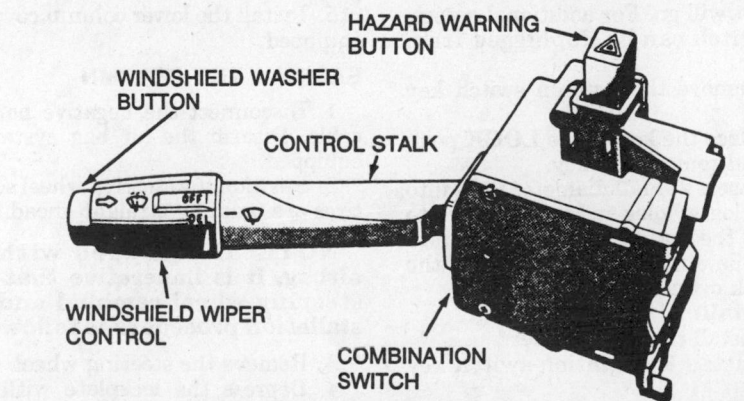

Combination switch—1990–93 LeBaron Landau, Shadow, Sundance, Spirit and Acclaim

cable. Disarm the air bag system, if equipped.

2. Remove the tilt lever, if equipped.

3. Remove the upper and the lower steering column covers.

4. Remove the combination switch tamper-proof mounting screws. Gently pull the switch away from the steering column and loosen the connector screw; the screw will remain in the connector. Disconnect the connector from the switch.

To install:

5. Install the wiring connector to the switch and tighten the connector to 17 inch lbs. (2 Nm).

6. Mount the combination switch to the column and torque the retainers to 17 inch lbs. (2 Nm).

7. Install both the upper and the lower steering column covers.

8. Install the tilt lever if removed.

9. Connect the negative battery cable and check switch for proper operation.

Ignition Lock

REMOVAL & INSTALLATION

Standard Column

EXCEPT ACUSTAR COLUMN

NOTE: The Acustar column can be identified by the "halo" light around the ignition key cylinder.

1. Disconnect the negative battery cable. Disarm the air bag system, if equipped.

2. Position the steering wheel so the tires are pointing straight-ahead.

NOTE: If equipped with an airbag, it is imperative that the steering wheel removal and installation procedure is followed.

3. Remove the steering wheel.

4. Remove the hazard switch knob. Remove the slotted hex-head screw that attaches the wiper switch to the turn signal switch.

5. Remove the 3 screws and pull the turn signal switch out of the column as far as it will go. For additional access, the switch can be unplugged from below.

6. Remove the ignition switch key light.

7. Place the key in the **LOCK** position and remove the key.

8. Insert 2 small-diameter tools into both release holes and push inward to release the spring loaded lock retainers while simultaneously pulling the key lock cylinder out of its bore.

To install:

9. Install the key cylinder.

10. Install the ignition switch key light.

11. Install the turn signal switch and

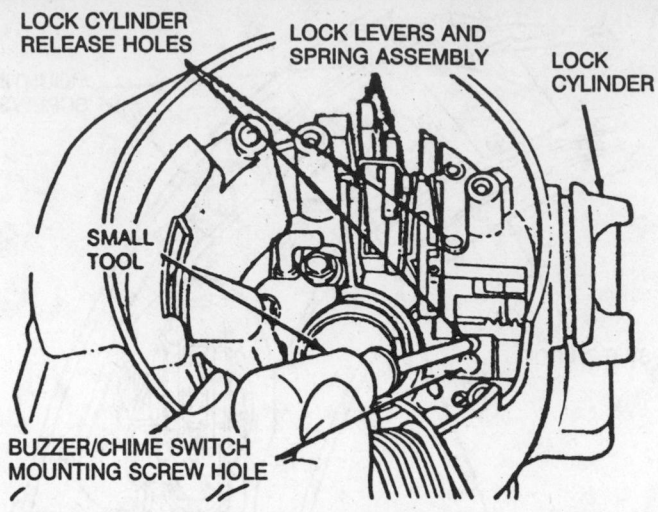

LOCK CYLINDER RELEASE HOLES

LOCK LEVERS AND SPRING ASSEMBLY

LOCK CYLINDER

SMALL TOOL

BUZZER/CHIME SWITCH MOUNTING SCREW HOLE

Removing the key lock cylinder—standard column, except Acustar steering column

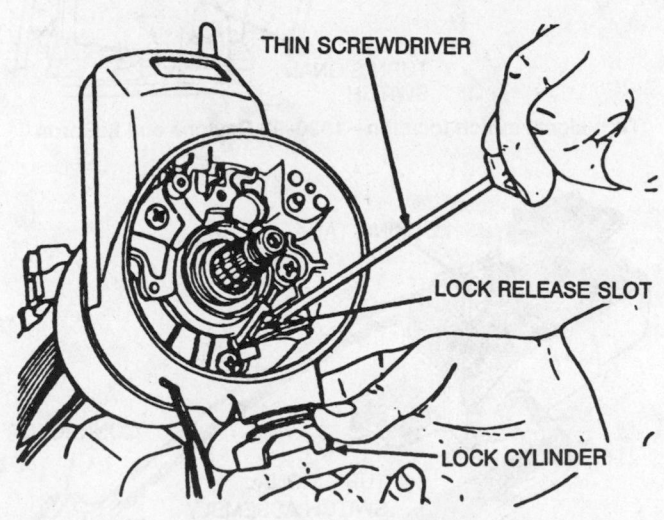

THIN SCREWDRIVER

LOCK RELEASE SLOT

LOCK CYLINDER

Removing the key lock cylinder—Saginaw steering column

hazard switch knob, then connect all wiring.

12. Install the steering wheel and torque the nut to 45 ft. lbs. (61 Nm).

13. Install the horn pad.

14. Connect the negative battery cable and check the lock cylinder for proper operation.

15. Install the lower column cover, if equipped.

SAGINAW TILT COLUMN

1. Disconnect the negative battery cable. Disarm the air bag system if equipped.

2. Position the steering wheel so the tires are pointing straight-ahead.

NOTE: If equipped with an airbag, it is imperative that the steering wheel removal and installation procedure is followed.

3. Remove the steering wheel.

4. Depress the lockplate with the proper depressing tool, remove the re-

taining ring from its groove, then remove the tool, ring, lockplate, cancelling cam and spring.

5. Remove the stalk actuator screw and arm.

6. Remove the hazard switch knob.

7. Remove the turn signal switch mounting screws and pull the switch out of the column as far as the wires will allow. Unplug harness from below if necessary.

8. Remove the ignition key light.

9. Place the key in the **LOCK** position and remove the key. Insert a thin tool into the slot next to the switch mounting screw boss, depress the spring latch at the bottom of the slot releasing the lock and remove the lock cylinder.

To install:

10. Install the lock cylinder.

11. Install the ignition key light.

12. Install the turn signal switch, switch stalk actuator arm and hazard switch knob.

13. Install the spring, cancelling cam, lockplate and ring on the steering shaft. Depress the plate with the depressing tool and install the ring securely in the groove. Remove the tool slowly making sure the ring is properly seated in the groove on the shaft.

14. Connect the electrical harness at the base of the steering column if disconnected.

15. Install the steering wheel and torque the nut to 45 ft. lbs. (61 Nm).

16. Install the horn pad.

17. Connect the negative battery cable and check the turn signal switch for proper operation.

18. Install the lower column cover.

Ignition Switch

REMOVAL & INSTALLATION

Except Acustar Steering Column

NOTE: The Acustar column can be identified by the "halo" light around the ignition key cylinder.

1. Disconnect the negative battery cable. Disarm the air bag system if equipped.

2. Remove the lower steering column cover.

3. Remove the steering column retaining nuts and lower the steering column so the steering wheel is resting on the driver's seat.

4. Remove the 2 screws that attach the ignition switch to the steering column.

5. Rotate the switch 90 degrees and pull up to disengage it from the ignition switch rod.

To install:

6. Engage the switch with the rod, rotate the switch 90 degrees and push down until fully engaged.

7. Install the mounting screws finger-tight.

8. Place the key in the **LOCK** position and remove the key. Adjust the switch by pushing up gently on the switch to take up all slack in the rod and secure in this position by tightening the mounting screws.

9. Raise the steering column and loosely tighten the mounting nuts. Reconnect the negative battery cable and check the switch for proper operation in all positions.

10. Secure the column mounting nuts to 105 inch lbs. (12 Nm). Install the steering column cover.

Ignition Lock/Switch

REMOVAL & INSTALLATION

Acustar Steering Column

NOTE: The Acustar column can

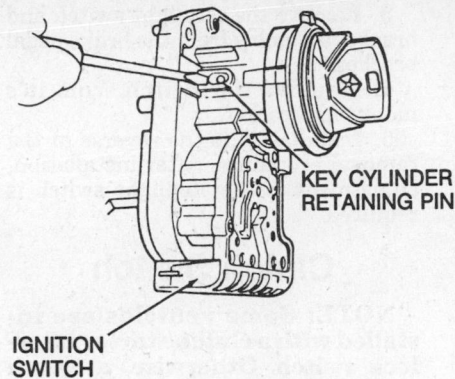

KEY CYLINDER RETAINING PIN

IGNITION SWITCH

Depressing the key cylinder retaining pin—Acustar column

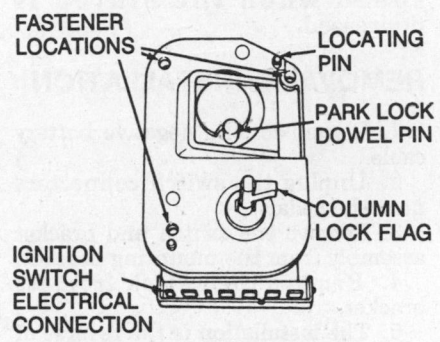

FASTENER LOCATIONS

LOCATING PIN

PARK LOCK DOWEL PIN

COLUMN LOCK FLAG

IGNITION SWITCH ELECTRICAL CONNECTION

Preparing the ignition switch for installation—Acustar column

be identified by the "halo" light around the ignition key cylinder.

1. Disconnect the negative battery cable. Disarm the air bag, if equipped.

NOTE: Failure to disarm the air bag system may result in accidental deployment of the air bag module and possible personal injury.

2. Remove the tilt lever, if equipped.

3. Remove the upper and lower column covers.

4. Remove the 3 ignition switch Torx® screws; APEX 440–TX20H or equivalent required.

5. Pull the switch away from the column. Release the connector locks on the 2 wiring connectors and disconnect them from the switch.

6. Remove the key lock cylinder from the ignition switch as follows:

a. Insert the key and turn the switch to the **LOCK** position. Using a small tool, depress the key cylinder retaining pin until flush with the key cylinder surface.

b. Rotate the key clockwise to the **OFF** position to unseat the key cylinder from the ignition switch assembly. The cylinder bezel should be about ⅛ in. above the ignition switch halo light ring. Do not attempt to remove the key cylinder at this point.

c. With the key cylinder unseated, rotate the key and cylinder counterclockwise to the **LOCK** position and remove the key.

d. Remove the key cylinder from the ignition switch.

To install:

7. If equipped with floor mounted gear shifter, place the selector in the **P** position.

8. Connect the electrical harness to the ignition switch making sure the locking tabs are fully seated in the wiring connectors.

9. Place the gear shift lever in the **P** position. Mount the ignition switch to the column as follows:

a. Place the ignition switch in the **LOCK** position. The switch is in the lock position when the column lock flag is parallel to the ignition switch terminals.

b. Position the ignition switch lock dowel pin so it will engage the steering column park lock slider linkage.

c. Apply a light coat of grease to

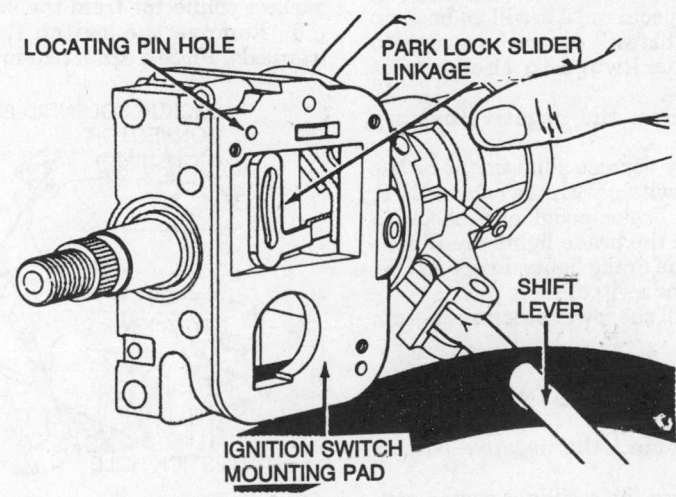

LOCATING PIN HOLE

PARK LOCK SLIDER LINKAGE

SHIFT LEVER

IGNITION SWITCH MOUNTING PAD

Ignition switch mounting pad—Acustar column

the column lock flag and the park lock dowel pin. Place the ignition against the lock housing opening on the steering column. Ensure ignition switch park lock dowel pin enters the slot in the park lock slider linkage in the steering column.

d. Install the ignition switch mounting screws and torque to 17 inch lbs. (2 Nm).

10. Install the steering column covers. If equipped with tilt wheel, install the tilt lever.

11. Install the ignition key to the lock cylinder as follows:

a. With the key cylinder and ignition switch in the **LOCK** position, key not in cylinder, gently insert the key cylinder into the ignition switch until it bottoms.

b. Insert the ignition key into the ignition cylinder. Simultaneously, push in on the cylinder and rotate the key to the end of travel. The ignition cylinder should now be fully seated in the ignition switch.

12. Connect the negative battery cable.

13. Check the push-to-lock and park lock functions, halo lighting and all ignition switch positions for proper operation.

Stoplight Switch

ADJUSTMENT

1. Disconnect the negative battery cable. Disarm the air bag system, if equipped.

2. Remove the lower steering column cover.

3. Push the switch and retainer bracket forward towards the brake pedal as far as it will go. The brake pedal should move forward slighty.

4. Gently pull back on the brake pedal bringing the striker back toward the switch. Continue to pull back on the brake pedal until it will go back no further. This will cause the switch to ratchet backward to the correct position.

5. Connect the negative battery cable.

6. Verify correct adjustment of the stoplight switch; with the engine OFF, apply the brake pedal and check to make sure the brake lights are illuminated. If the brake lights do not go ON, readjust the switch.

7. Install the lower steering column cover.

REMOVAL & INSTALLATION

1. Disconnect the negative battery cable.

2. Unplug the stoplight switch connectors above the brake pedal.

3. Remove the stoplight switch and bracket assembly from the brake pedal bracket.

4. Remove the switch from it's mounting bracket.

5. Installation is the reverse of the removal procedure. After installation, adjustment of the stoplight switch is required.

Clutch Switch

NOTE: Some vehicles are installed with a clutch/starter interlock switch. Otherwise, a clutch switch is installed on vehicles equipped with speed control only. Its function is to cancel the set speed when the clutch is depressed.

REMOVAL & INSTALLATION

1. Disconnect the negative battery cable.

2. Unplug the switch connectors near the pedals.

3. Remove the switch and bracket assembly from the mounting bracket.

4. Remove the switch from its bracket.

5. The installation is the reverse of the removal procedure.

6. Connect the negative battery cable and check the speed control system for proper operation.

Neutral Safety Switch

REMOVAL & INSTALLATION

1. Disconnect the negative battery cable.

2. Locate the neutral safety switch at the left rear corner of the automatic transaxle. The neutral safety switch is the black switch located to the right of the PRNDL switch. Unplug the switch harness connector from the switch.

3. Remove the switch from the transaxle. Place a drain pan under the

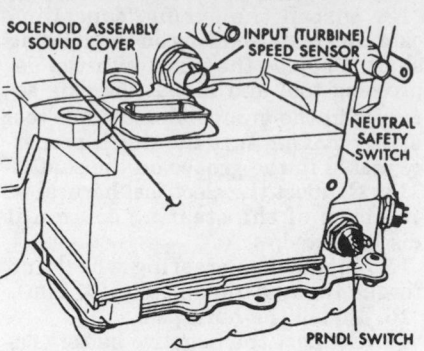

Neutral safety switch location—A604 automatic transaxle

switch to catch any transaxle fluid that may leak out during switch removal.

4. The installation is the reverse of the removal procedure. Torque the switch to 25 ft. lbs. (34 Nm).

5. Connect the negative battery cable and check the switch for proper operation.

Fuses, Circuit Breakers and Relays

Location

Aries and Reliant

The fuse block is located behind a re-

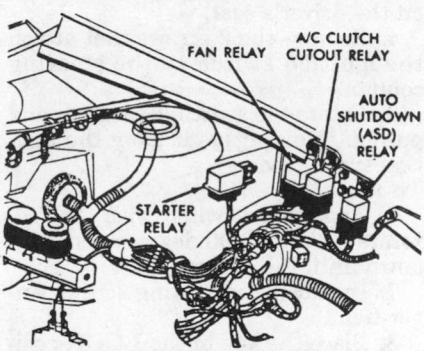

Relay identification—1989-90 vehicles and early 1991 Shadow Convertible

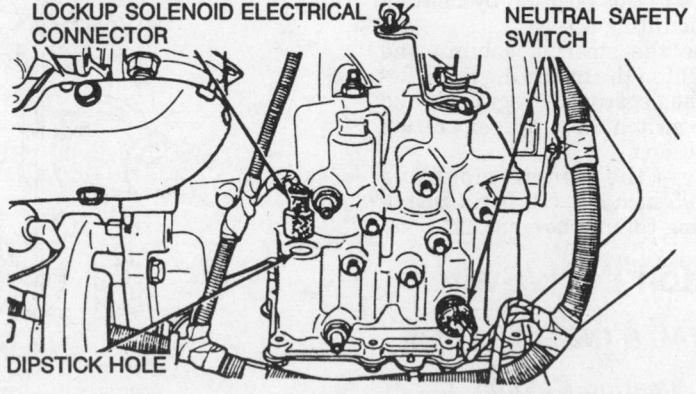

Neutral safety switch location—A413 automatic transaxle

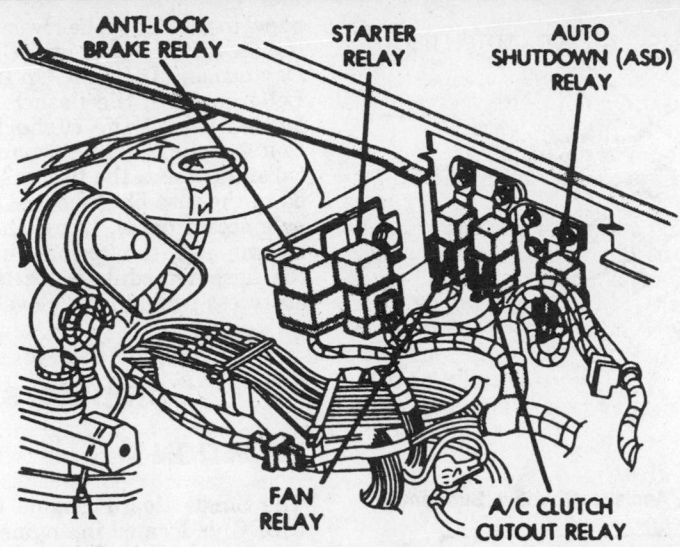

Relay identification—1991 vehicles without Power Distribution Center

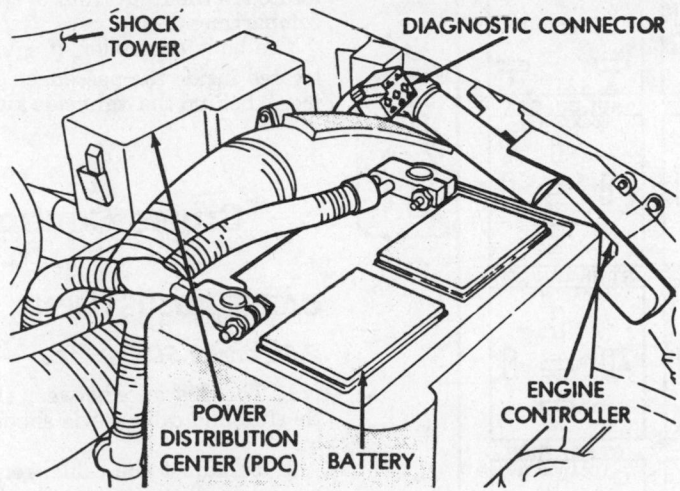

Power distribution center—1992–93 Daytona

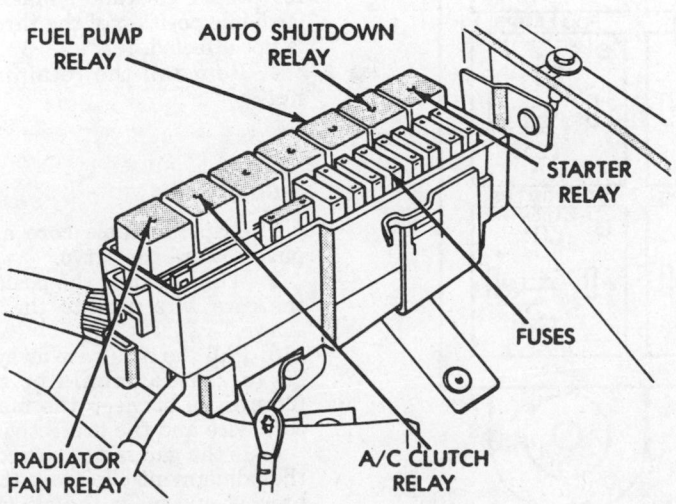

Relay identification—1992–93 Daytona

moveable access panel, below the steering column. The hazard and turn signal flashers along with the time delay and horn relays are also located behind the panel. Additional relays are mounted on the inner fender panel near the battery.

Spirit, Acclaim, Shadow and Sundance

The fuse block is located behind the steering column cover, accessible by removing the fuse access panel above the hood latch release lever. The relay and flasher module is located behind an access panel in the glovebox. Included in the module are the hazard and turn signal flashers along with the time delay and horn relays. Additional relays are mounted on the inner fender panel near the battery and strut tower.

Lancer and LeBaron GTS

The fuse block is located behind the glove box door, accessible by removing the fuse access panel. The relay and flasher module is located behind the cupholder in the center of the instrument panel. The entire module can be removed by pushing it up and off of its mounting bracket. Included in the module are the hazard and turn signal flashers along with the time delay and horn relays. Additional relays are mounted on the inner fender panel near the battery and strut tower.

Daytona, LeBaron and TC

The fuse block is located behind a removeable access panel to the left of the lower portion of the steering column. On TC and 1989 Daytona and LeBaron, the time delay and horn relays are also located behind the panel.

On 1990–93 Daytona and LeBaron, a relay bank is located on the left side kick panel. The Power Distribution Center, which contains additional relays and fuses, is located in the engine compartment behind the battery. Each item is identified on the cover.

Flashers

LOCATION

The hazard and turn signal flashers are located behind a removeable access

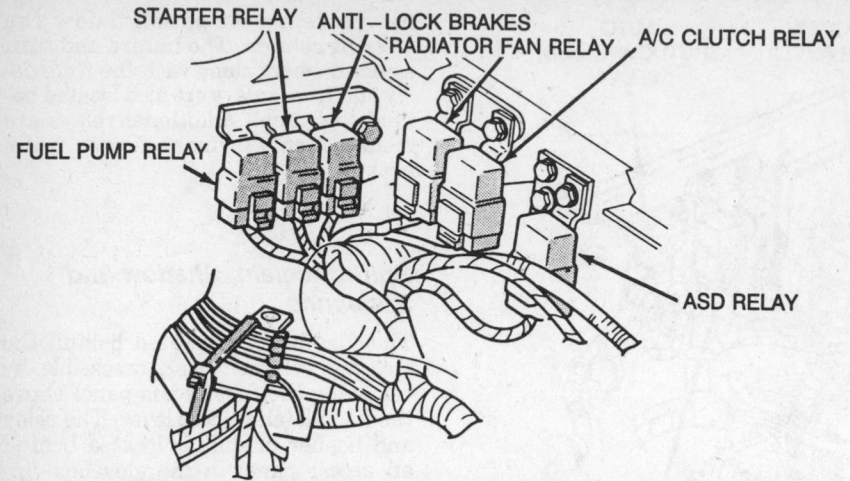

Power Identification—1992–93 LeBaron, Spirit, Acclaim, Shadow, Sundance

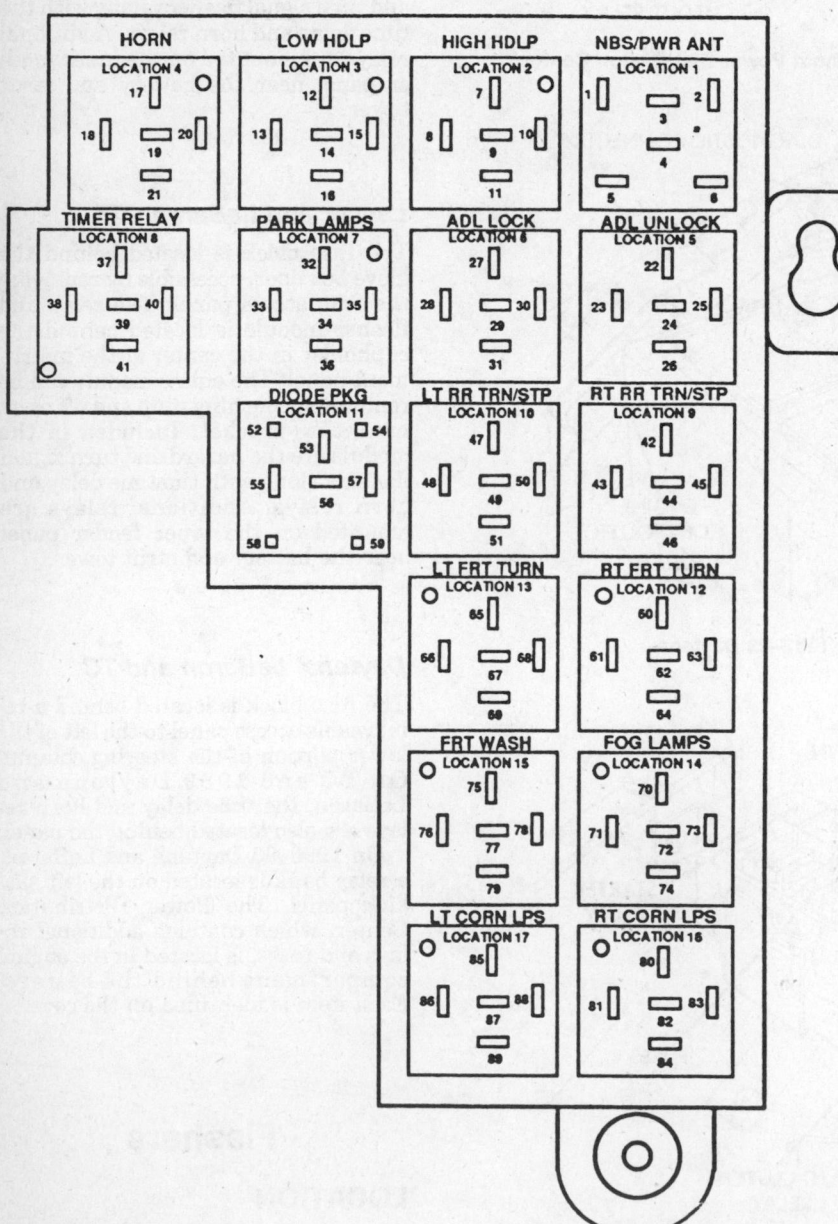

Relay Identification. Wire-end view of the relay bank on the left side kick panel—1990–92 Daytona and LeBaron

panel to the left of the lower portion of the steering column on TC and 1989 Daytona and LeBaron. On Lancer and LeBaron GTS, the flasher module is located behind the cupholder in the center of the instrument panel. On Aries and Reliant, the flashers are located in the fuse block behind a removeable access panel, below the steering column. On the rermaining models, the flasher module is located behind an access panel in the glovebox.

Computers

LOCATION

The Single Board Engine Controller (SBEC) is located in engine compartment, to the left of the battery.

If equipped with the A604 automatic transaxle, the transaxle controller is located in the right front of the engine compartment.

The body controller, if equipped, is located inside the passenger compartment, behind the right side kick panel.

Cruise Control

CABLE ADJUSTMENT

2.2L and 2.5L Engines

1. The clearance between the throttle stud and cable clevis should be $\frac{1}{16}$ in.

2. To adjust the cable, remove the retaining clip or loosen the retaining clamp nut at the throttle bracket.

3. Pull all slack out of the cable using a $\frac{1}{16}$ in. diameter tool to account for proper clearance. Make sure the curb idle position of the throttle blade is not affected.

4. Reinstall the retaining clip or nut.

3.0L Engine

1. Grip the cable core and lightly push toward the servo.

2. While holding the position, mark the core wire next to the protective sleeve.

3. Pull the core wire away from the servo. There should be a 0.24 in. (6mm) gap between the mark on the core wire and the protective sleeve.

4. If the gap is not correct, remove the adjustment clip from the throttle bracket and move the sleeve to bring the gap into specification.

5. Reinstall the clip.

Chrysler Corp.

Front Wheel Drive

CHRYSLER—Imperial • New Yorker
DODGE—Dynasty

SPECIFICATIONS

VEHICLE IDENTIFICATION CHART

It is important for servicing and ordering parts to be certain of the vehicle and engine identification. The VIN (vehicle identification number) is a 17 digit number visible through the windshield on the driver's side of the dash and contains the vehicle and engine identification codes. The tenth digit indicates model year and the eighth digit indicates engine code. It can be interpreted as follows:

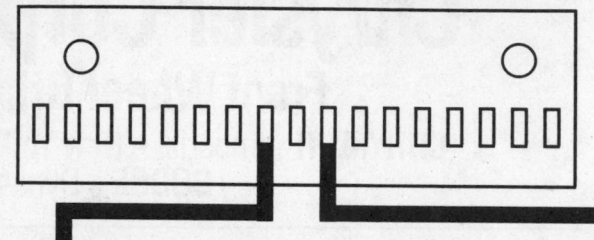

		Engine Code					Model Year	
Code	Liters	Cu. In. (cc)	Cyl.	Fuel Sys.	Eng. Mfg.		Code	Year
K	2.5	153 (2507)	4	EFI	Chrysler		K	1989
3	3.0	181 (2966)	6	MPI	Mitsubishi		L	1990
R	3.3	201 (3294)	6	MPI	Chrysler		M	1991
L	3.8	231 (3786)	6	MPI	Chrysler		N	1992
							P	1993

EFI—Electronic Fuel Injection
MPI—Multipoint Fuel Injection

ENGINE IDENTIFICATION

Year	Model	Engine Displacement Liters (cc)	Engine Series (ID/VIN)	Fuel System	No. of Cylinders	Engine Type
1989	Dynasty	2.5 (2507)	K	EFI	4	OHC
	Dynasty	3.0 (2966)	3	MPI	6	OHC
	New Yorker Landau	3.0 (2966)	3	MPI	6	OHC
1990	Dynasty	2.5 (2507)	K	EFI	4	OHC
	Dynasty	3.0 (2966)	3	MPI	6	OHC
	Dynasty	3.3 (3294)	R	MPI	6	OHV
	New Yorker Landau	3.0 (2966)	3	MPI	6	OHC
	New Yorker Landau	3.3 (3294)	R	MPI	6	OHV
	New Yorker Salon	3.0 (2966)	3	MPI	6	OHC
	New Yorker Salon	3.3 (3294)	R	MPI	6	OHV
	New Yorker 5th Avenue	3.3 (3294)	R	MPI	6	OHV
	Imperial	3.3 (3294)	R	MPI	6	OHV
1991	Dynasty	2.5 (2507)	K	EFI	4	OHC
	Dynasty	3.0 (2966)	3	MPI	6	OHC
	Dynasty	3.3 (3294)	R	MPI	6	OHV
	New Yorker Salon	3.3 (3294)	R	MPI	6	OHV
	New Yorker 5th Avenue	3.3 (3294)	R	MPI	6	OHV
	New Yorker 5th Avenue	3.8 (3786)	L	MPI	6	OHV
	Imperial	3.8 (3786)	L	MPI	6	OHV

ENGINE IDENTIFICATION

Year	Model	Engine Displacement Liters (cc)	Engine Series (ID/VIN)	Fuel System	No. of Cylinders	Engine Type
1992-93	Dynasty	2.5 (2507)	K	EFI	4	OHC
	Dynasty	3.0 (2966)	3	MPI	6	OHC
	Dynasty	3.3 (3294)	R	MPI	6	OHV
	New Yorker Salon	3.3 (3294)	R	MPI	6	OHV
	New Yorker 5th Avenue	3.3 (3294)	R	MPI	6	OHV
	New Yorker 5th Avenue	3.8 (3786)	L	MPI	6	OHV
	Imperial	3.8 (3786)	L	MPI	6	OHV

OHC—Overhead Camshaft
OHV—Overhead Valve
MPI—Multipoint Fuel Injection
EFI—Electronic Fuel Injection

GENERAL ENGINE SPECIFICATIONS

Year	Engine ID/VIN	Engine Displacement Liters (cc)	Fuel System Type	Net Horsepower @ rpm	Net Torque @ rpm (ft. lbs.)	Bore × Stroke (in.)	Compression Ratio	Oil Pressure @ rpm
1989	K	2.5 (2507)	EFI	100 @ 2800	135 @ 2800	3.44 × 4.09	8.9:1	30–80 @ 3000
	3	3.0 (2966)	MPI	141 @ 5000	171 @ 2800	3.59 × 2.99	8.9:1	30–80 @ 3000
1990	K	2.5 (2507)	EFI	100 @ 2800	135 @ 2800	3.44 × 4.09	8.9:1	30–80 @ 3000
	3	3.0 (2966)	MPI	141 @ 5000	171 @ 2800	3.59 × 2.99	8.9:1	30–80 @ 3000
	R	3.3 (3294)	MPI	147 @ 4800	183 @ 3600	3.66 × 3.19	8.9:1	30–80 @ 3000
1991	K	2.5 (2507)	EFI	100 @ 2800	135 @ 2800	3.44 × 4.09	8.9:1	30–80 @ 3000
	3	3.0 (2966)	MPI	141 @ 5000	171 @ 2800	3.59 × 2.99	8.9:1	30–80 @ 3000
	R	3.3 (3294)	MPI	147 @ 4800	183 @ 3600	3.66 × 3.19	8.9:1	30–80 @ 3000
	L	3.8 (3786)	MPI	150 @ 4400	203 @ 3200	3.78 × 3.42	9.0:1	30–80 @ 3000
1992-93	K	2.5 (2507)	EFI	100 @ 2800	135 @ 2800	3.44 × 4.09	8.9:1	30–80 @ 3000
	3	3.0 (2966)	MPI	141 @ 5000	171 @ 2800	3.59 × 2.99	8.9:1	30–80 @ 3000
	R	3.3 (3294)	MPI	147 @ 4800	183 @ 3600	3.66 × 3.19	8.9:1	30–80 @ 3000
	L	3.8 (3786)	MPI	150 @ 4400	203 @ 3200	3.78 × 3.42	9.0:1	30–80 @ 3000

NOTE: Horsepower and torque are SAE net figures. They are measured at the rear of the transmission with all accessories installed and operating. Since the figures vary when a given engine is installed in different models, some are representative rather than exact.
EFI—Electronic Fuel Injection
MPI—Multipoint Fuel Injection

GASOLINE ENGINE TUNE-UP SPECIFICATIONS

Year	Engine ID/VIN	Engine Displacement Liters (cc)	Spark Plugs Gap (in.)	Ignition Timing (deg.) MT	Ignition Timing (deg.) AT	Fuel Pump (psi)	Idle Speed (rpm) MT	Idle Speed (rpm) AT	Valve Clearance In.	Valve Clearance Ex.
1989	K	2.5 (2507)	0.035	—	12B	15	—	850	Hyd.	Hyd.
	3	3.0 (2966)	0.040	—	12B	48①	—	700	Hyd.	Hyd.
1990	K	2.5 (2507)	0.035	—	12B	15	—	850	Hyd.	Hyd.
	3	3.0 (2966)	0.040	—	12B	48①	—	700	Hyd.	Hyd.
	R	3.3 (3294)	0.050	—	12B	48①	—	750	Hyd.	Hyd.

GASOLINE ENGINE TUNE-UP SPECIFICATIONS

Year	Engine ID/VIN	Engine Displacement Liters (cc)	Spark Plugs Gap (in.)	Ignition Timing (deg.)		Fuel Pump (psi)	Idle Speed (rpm)		Valve Clearance	
				MT	AT		MT	AT	In.	Ex.
1991	K	2.5 (2507)	0.035	—	12B	15	—	850	Hyd.	Hyd.
	3	3.0 (2966)	0.040	—	12B	48①	—	700	Hyd.	Hyd.
	R	3.3 (3294)	0.050	—	12B	48①	—	750	Hyd.	Hyd.
	L	3.8 (3786)	0.050	—	12B	48①	—	750	Hyd.	Hyd.
1992	K	2.5 (2507)	0.035	—	12B	15	—	850	Hyd.	Hyd.
	3	3.0 (2966)	0.040	—	12B	48①	—	700	Hyd.	Hyd.
	R	3.3 (3294)	0.050	—	12B	48①	—	750	Hyd.	Hyd.
	L	3.8 (3786)	0.050	—	12B	48①	—	750	Hyd.	Hyd.
1993	REFER TO UNDERHOOD SPECIFICATIONS STICKER									

NOTE: The lowest cylinder pressure should be within 75% of the highest cylinder pressure reading. For example, if the highest cylinder is 134 psi, the lowest should be 101. Engine should be at normal operating temperature with throttle valve in the wide open position.
The underhood specifications sticker often reflects tune-up specification changes in production. Sticker figures must be used if they disagree with those in this chart.
Hyd.—Hydraulic
① This reading measured with the vacuum hose disconnected from the fuel pressure regulator.

FIRING ORDERS

NOTE: To avoid confusion, always replace spark plug wires one at a time.

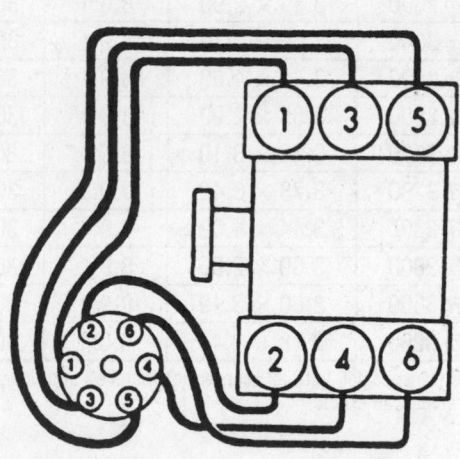

3.0L Engine
Engine Firing Order: 1–2–3–4–5–6
Distributor Rotation: Counterclockwise

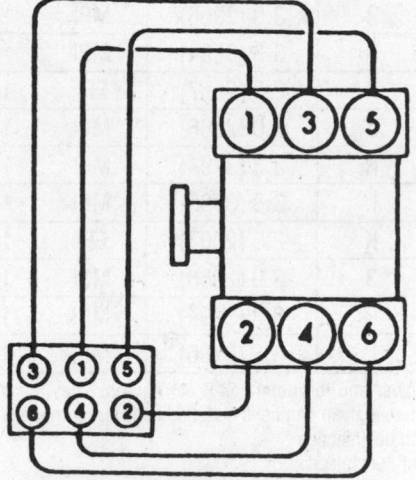

3.3L and 3.8L Engines
Engine Firing Order: 1–2–3–4–5–6
Distributorless Ignition System

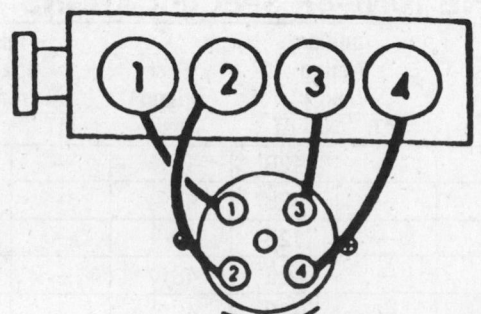

2.5L Engine
Engine Firing Order: 1–3–4–2
Distributor Rotation: Clockwise

CAPACITIES

Year	Model	Engine ID/VIN	Engine Displacement Liters (cc)	Engine Crankcase (qts.) with Filter	Transmission (pts.) 4-Spd	5-Spd	Auto.	Transfer case (pts.)	Drive Axle Front (pts.)	Rear (pts.)	Fuel Tank (gal.)	Cooling System (qts.)
1989	Dynasty	K	2.5 (2507)	4	—	—	18	—	—	—	16	9.0
	Dynasty	3	3.0 (2966)	4	—	—	18	—	—	—	16	9.5
	New Yorker Landau	3	3.0 (2966)	4	—	—	18	—	—	—	16	9.5
1990	Dynasty	K	2.5 (2507)	4	—	—	18	—	—	—	16	9.0
	Dynasty	3	3.0 (2966)	4	—	—	18	—	—	—	16	9.5
	Dynasty	R	3.3 (3294)	4	—	—	18	—	—	—	16	9.5
	New Yorker Landau	3	3.0 (2966)	4	—	—	18	—	—	—	16	9.5
	New Yorker Landau	R	3.3 (3294)	4	—	—	18	—	—	—	16	9.5
	New Yorker Salon	3	3.0 (2966)	4	—	—	18	—	—	—	16	9.5
	New Yorker Salon	R	3.3 (3294)	4	—	—	18	—	—	—	16	9.5
	New Yorker 5th Avenue	R	3.3 (3294)	4	—	—	18	—	—	—	16	9.5
	Imperial	R	3.3 (3294)	4	—	—	18	—	—	—	16	9.5
1991	Dynasty	K	2.5 (2507)	4	—	—	18	—	—	—	16	9.0
	Dynasty	3	3.0 (2966)	4	—	—	18	—	—	—	16	9.5
	Dynasty	R	3.3 (3294)	4	—	—	18	—	—	—	16	9.5
	New Yorker Salon	R	3.3 (3294)	4	—	—	18	—	—	—	16	9.5
	New Yorker 5th Avenue	R	3.3 (3294)	4	—	—	18	—	—	—	16	9.5
	New Yorker 5th Avenue	L	3.8 (3786)	4	—	—	18	—	—	—	16	9.5
	Imperial	L	3.8 (3786)	4	—	—	18	—	—	—	16	9.5
1992–93	Dynasty	K	2.5 (2507)	4	—	—	18	—	—	—	16	9.0
	Dynasty	3	3.0 (2966)	4	—	—	18	—	—	—	16	9.5
	Dynasty	R	3.3 (3294)	4	—	—	18	—	—	—	16	9.5
	New Yorker Salon	R	3.3 (3294)	4	—	—	18	—	—	—	16	9.5
	New Yorker 5th Avenue	R	3.3 (3294)	4	—	—	18	—	—	—	16	9.5
	New Yorker 5th Avenue	L	3.8 (3786)	4	—	—	18	—	—	—	16	9.5
	Imperial	L	3.8 (3786)	4	—	—	18	—	—	—	16	9.5

CAMSHAFT SPECIFICATIONS

All measurements given in inches.

Year	Engine ID/VIN	Engine Displacement Liters (cc)	Journal Diameter 1	2	3	4	5	Elevation In.	Ex.	Bearing Clearance	Camshaft End Play
1989	K	2.5 (2507)	1.375–1.376	1.375–1.376	1.375–1.376	1.375–1.376	1.375–1.376	NA	NA	—	0.005–0.020
	3	3.0 (2966)	NA	NA	NA	NA	—	①	①	—	NA
1990	K	2.5 (2507)	1.375–1.376	1.375–1.376	1.375–1.376	1.375–1.376	1.375–1.376	NA	NA	—	0.005–0.020
	3	3.0 (2966)	NA	NA	NA	NA	—	①	①	—	NA
	R	3.3 (3294)	1.997–1.999	1.980–1.982	1.965–1.967	1.949–1.952	—	0.400	0.400	0.001–0.005	0.005–0.012

CAMSHAFT SPECIFICATIONS

All measurements given in inches.

| Year | Engine ID/VIN | Engine Displacement Liters (cc) | Journal Diameter | | | | | Elevation | | Bearing Clearance | Camshaft End Play |
			1	2	3	4	5	In.	Ex.		
1991	K	2.5 (2507)	1.395–1.396	1.395–1.396	1.395–1.396	1.395–1.396	1.395–1.396	NA	NA	—	0.005–0.020
	3	3.0 (2966)	NA	NA	NA	NA	—	①	①	—	NA
	R	3.3 (3294)	1.997–1.999	1.980–1.982	1.965–1.967	1.949–1.952	—	0.400	0.400	0.001–0.005	0.005–0.012
	L	3.8 (3786)	1.997–1.999	1.980–1.982	1.965–1.967	1.949–1.952	—	0.400	0.400	0.001–0.004	0.005–0.012
1992–93	K	2.5 (2507)	1.395–1.396	1.395–1.396	1.395–1.396	1.395–1.396	1.395–1.396	NA	NA	—	0.005–0.020
	3	3.0 (2966)	NA	NA	NA	NA	—	①	①	—	NA
	R	3.3 (3294)	1.997–1.999	1.980–1.982	1.965–1.967	1.949–1.952	—	0.400	0.400	0.001–0.005	0.005–0.012
	L	3.8 (3786)	1.997–1.999	1.980–1.982	1.965–1.967	1.949–1.952	—	0.400	0.400	0.001–0.004	0.005–0.012

NA—Not available
① Standard Value: 1.624 in.
 Wear limit: 1.604 in.

CRANKSHAFT AND CONNECTING ROD SPECIFICATIONS

All measurements are given in inches.

| Year | Engine ID/VIN | Engine Displacement Liters (cc) | Crankshaft | | | | Connecting Rod | | |
			Main Brg. Journal Dia.	Main Brg. Oil Clearance	Shaft End-play	Thrust on No.	Journal Diameter	Oil Clearance	Side Clearance
1989	K	2.5 (2507)	2.362–3.363	0.0004–0.0040	0.002–0.014	3	1.968–1.969	0.0008–0.0040	0.005–0.013
	3	3.0 (2966)	2.361–2.362	0.0006–0.0020	0.002–0.010	3	1.968–1.969	0.0008–0.0028	0.004–0.010
1990	K	2.5 (2507)	2.362–3.363	0.0004–0.0040	0.002–0.014	3	1.968–1.969	0.0008–0.0040	0.005–0.013
	3	3.0 (2966)	2.361–2.362	0.0006–0.0020	0.002–0.010	3	1.968–1.969	0.0008–0.0028	0.004–0.010
	R	3.3 (3294)	2.519	0.0007–0.0022	0.001–0.007	2	2.283	0.0008–0.0030	0.005–0.015
1991	K	2.5 (2507)	2.362–3.363	0.0004–0.0040	0.002–0.014	3	1.968–1.969	0.0008–0.0040	0.005–0.013
	3	3.0 (2966)	2.361–2.362	0.0006–0.0020	0.002–0.010	3	1.968–1.969	0.0008–0.0028	0.004–0.010
	R	3.3 (3294)	2.519	0.0007–0.0022	0.001–0.007	2	2.283	0.0008–0.0030	0.005–0.015
	L	3.8 (3786)	2.519	0.0007–0.0022	0.003–0.009	2	2.283	0.0008–0.0030	0.005–0.015
1992–93	K	2.5 (2507)	2.362–3.363	0.0004–0.0040	0.002–0.014	3	1.968–1.969	0.0008–0.0040	0.005–0.013
	3	3.0 (2966)	2.361–2.362	0.0006–0.0020	0.002–0.010	3	1.968–1.969	0.0008–0.0028	0.004–0.010
	R	3.3 (3294)	2.519	0.0007–0.0022	0.001–0.007	2	2.283	0.0008–0.0030	0.005–0.015
	L	3.8 (3786)	2.519	0.0007–0.0022	0.003–0.009	2	2.283	0.0008–0.0030	0.005–0.015

VALVE SPECIFICATIONS

Year	Engine ID/VIN	Engine Displacement Liters (cc)	Seat Angle (deg.)	Face Angle (deg.)	Spring Test Pressure (lbs. @ in.)	Spring Installed Height (in.)	Stem-to-Guide Clearance (in.)		Stem Diameter (in.)	
							Intake	Exhaust	Intake	Exhaust
1989	K	2.5 (2507)	45	45	114 @ 1.65	1.65	0.0010–0.0030	0.0030–0.0047	0.3124	0.3103
	3	3.0 (2966)	44.5	45.5	73 @ 1.59	1.59	0.0010–0.0020	0.0020–0.0030	0.3130–0.3140	0.3120–0.3130
1990	K	2.5 (2507)	45	45	114 @ 1.65	1.65	0.0010–0.0030	0.0030–0.0047	0.3124	0.3103
	3	3.0 (2966)	44.5	45.5	73 @ 1.59	1.59	0.0010–0.0020	0.0020–0.0030	0.3130–0.3140	0.3120–0.3130
	R	3.3 (3294)	45	44.5	60 @ 1.56	1.56	0.0020–0.0160	0.0020–0.0160	0.3130–0.3140	0.3120–0.3130
1991	K	2.5 (2507)	45	45	114 @ 1.65	1.65	0.0010–0.0030	0.0030–0.0047	0.3124	0.3103
	3	3.0 (2966)	44.5	45.5	73 @ 1.59	1.59	0.0010–0.0020	0.0020–0.0030	0.3130–0.3140	0.3120–0.3130
	R	3.3 (3294)	45	44.5	60 @ 1.56	1.56	0.0020–0.0160	0.0020–0.0160	0.3130–0.3140	0.3120–0.3130
	L	3.8 (3786)	45	44.5	60 @ 1.56	1.56	0.0010–0.0030	0.0020–0.0160	0.3120–0.3130	0.3110–0.3120
1992–93	K	2.5 (2507)	45	45	114 @ 1.65	1.65	0.0010–0.0030	0.0030–0.0047	0.3124	0.3103
	3	3.0 (2966)	44.5	45.5	73 @ 1.59	1.59	0.0010–0.0020	0.0020–0.0030	0.3130–0.3140	0.3120–0.3130
	R	3.3 (3294)	45	44.5	60 @ 1.56	1.56	0.0020–0.0160	0.0020–0.0160	0.3130–0.3140	0.3120–0.3130
	L	3.8 (3786)	45	44.5	60 @ 1.56	1.56	0.0010–0.0030	0.0020–0.0160	0.3120–0.3130	0.3110–0.3120

PISTON AND RING SPECIFICATIONS

All measurements are given in inches.

Year	Engine ID/VIN	Engine Displacement Liters (cc)	Piston Clearance	Ring Gap			Ring Side Clearance		
				Top Compression	Bottom Compression	Oil Control	Top Compression	Bottom Compression	Oil Control
1989	K	2.5 (2507)	0.0010–0.0027	0.0100–0.0390	0.0110–0.0390	0.015–0.074	0.0010–0.0030	0.0010–0.0030	0.0006–0.0089
	3	3.0 (2966)	0.0012–0.0020	0.0120–0.0310	0.0100–0.0310	0.012–0.039	0.0020–0.0035	0.0008–0.0020	NA
1990	K	2.5 (2507)	0.0010–0.0027	0.0100–0.0390	0.0110–0.0390	0.015–0.074	0.0010–0.0030	0.0010–0.0030	0.0006–0.0089
	3	3.0 (2966)	0.0012–0.0020	0.0120–0.0310	0.0100–0.0300	0.012–0.039	0.0020–0.0039	0.0008–0.0039	NA
	R	3.3 (3294)	0.0009–0.0022	0.0118–0.0217	0.0118–0.0217	0.010–0.039	0.0012–0.0037	0.0012–0.0037	0.0006–0.0089

PISTON AND RING SPECIFICATIONS

All measurements are given in inches.

| Year | Engine ID/VIN | Engine Displacement Liters (cc) | Piston Clearance | Ring Gap | | | Ring Side Clearance | | |
				Top Compression	Bottom Compression	Oil Control	Top Compression	Bottom Compression	Oil Control
1991	K	2.5 (2507)	0.0010–0.0027	0.0100–0.0390	0.0110–0.0390	0.015–0.074	0.0010–0.0040	0.0010–0.0040	0.0006–0.0089
	3	3.0 (2966)	0.0012–0.0020	0.0120–0.0310	0.0100–0.0300	0.012–0.039	0.0020–0.0039	0.0008–0.0039	NA
	R	3.3 (3294)	0.0009–0.0022	0.0118–0.0217	0.0118–0.0217	0.010–0.039	0.0012–0.0037	0.0012–0.0037	0.0005–0.0089
	L	3.8 (3786)	0.0009–0.0022	0.0118–0.0217	0.0118–0.0217	0.010–0.039	0.0012–0.0037	0.0012–0.0037	0.0005–0.0089
1992–93	K	2.5 (2507)	0.0010–0.0027	0.0100–0.0390	0.0110–0.0390	0.015–0.074	0.0010–0.0040	0.0010–0.0040	0.0006–0.0089
	3	3.0 (2966)	0.0012–0.0020	0.0120–0.0310	0.0100–0.0300	0.012–0.039	0.0020–0.0039	0.0008–0.0039	NA
	R	3.3 (3294)	0.0009–0.0022	0.0118–0.0217	0.0118–0.0217	0.010–0.039	0.0012–0.0037	0.0012–0.0037	0.0005–0.0089
	L	3.8 (3786)	0.0009–0.0022	0.0118–0.0217	0.0118–0.0217	0.010–0.039	0.0012–0.0037	0.0012–0.0037	0.0005–0.0089

NA—Not available

TORQUE SPECIFICATIONS

All readings in ft. lbs.

| Year | Engine ID/VIN | Engine Displacement Liters (cc) | Cylinder Head Bolts | Main Bearing Bolts | Rod Bearing Bolts | Crankshaft Damper Bolts | Flywheel Bolts | Manifold | | Spark Plugs | Lug Nut |
								Intake	Exhaust		
1989	K	2.5 (2507)	①	30③	40③	85	70	17	17	26	80–110
	3	3.0 (2966)	80	60	38	112	70	17	17	20	80–110
1990	K	2.5 (2507)	①	30③	40③	85	70	17	17	26	80–110
	3	3.0 (2966)	80	60	38	112	70	17	17	20	80–110
	R	3.3 (3294)	②	30③	40③	110	70	17	17	20	80–110
1991	K	2.5 (2507)	①	30③	40③	85	70	17	17	26	80–110
	3	3.0 (2966)	80	60	38	112	70	17	17	20	80–110
	R	3.3 (3294)	②	30③	40③	—	70	17	17	20	80–110
	L	3.8 (3786)	②	30③	40③	—	70	17	17	20	80–110
1992–93	K	2.5 (2507)	①	30③	40③	85	70	17	17	26	80–110
	3	3.0 (2966)	80	60	38	112	70	17	17	20	80–110
	R	3.3 (3294)	②	30③	40③	—	70	17	17	20	80–110
	L	3.8 (3786)	②	30③	40③	—	70	17	17	20	80–110

① Sequence: 45, 65, 65, plus ¼ turn
② Sequence: 45, 65, 65, plus ¼ turn
  Torque the small bolt in the rear of the cylinder head to 25 ft. lbs. (34 Nm) last
③ Plus ¼ turn

BRAKE SPECIFICATIONS

All measurements in inches unless noted.

Year	Model		Master Cylinder Bore	Brake Disc Original Thickness	Brake Disc Minimum Thickness	Maximum Runout	Brake Drum Diameter Original Inside Diameter	Brake Drum Diameter Max. Wear Limit	Brake Drum Diameter Maximum Machine Diameter	Minimum Lining Thickness Front	Minimum Lining Thickness Rear
1989	Dynasty		0.827	0.935	0.882	0.005	7.87	NA	NA	0.30	0.06
	New Yorker Landau	front	0.827	0.935	0.882	0.005	7.87	NA	NA	0.30	0.06
		rear	—	0.354	0.339	0.005	—	—	—	—	0.28
1990	Dynasty	front	0.827	0.935	0.882	0.005	7.87	NA	NA	0.30	0.06
		rear	—	0.354	0.339	0.005	—	—	—	—	0.28
	New Yorker Landau	front	0.827	0.935	0.882	0.005	7.87	NA	NA	0.30	0.06
		rear	—	0.354	0.339	0.005	—	—	—	—	0.28
	New Yorker Salon	front	0.827	0.935	0.882	0.005	7.87	NA	NA	0.30	0.06
		rear	—	0.354	0.339	0.005	—	—	—	—	0.28
	New Yorker 5th Avenue	front	0.827	0.935	0.882	0.005	7.87	NA	NA	0.30	0.06
		rear	—	0.354	0.339	0.005	—	—	—	—	0.28
	Imperial	front	0.827	0.935	0.882	0.005	7.87	NA	NA	0.30	0.06
		rear	—	0.354	0.339	0.005	—	—	—	—	0.28
1991	Dynasty	front	0.827	0.935	0.882	0.005	7.87	NA	NA	0.30	0.06
		rear	—	0.354	0.339	0.005	—	—	—	—	0.28
	New Yorker Salon	front	0.827	0.935	0.882	0.005	7.87	NA	NA	0.30	0.06
		rear	—	0.354	0.339	0.005	—	—	—	—	0.28
	New Yorker 5th Avenue	front	0.827	0.935	0.882	0.005	7.87	NA	NA	0.30	0.06
		rear	—	0.354	0.339	0.005	—	—	—	—	0.28
	Imperial	front	0.827	0.935	0.882	0.005	7.87	NA	NA	0.30	0.06
		rear	—	0.354	0.339	0.005	—	—	—	—	0.28
1992–93	Dynasty	front	0.827	0.861	0.803	0.005	—	—	—	0.30	—
		rear	—	0.354	0.339	0.005	—	—	—	—	0.28
	New Yorker Salon	front	0.827	0.861	0.803	0.005	—	—	—	0.30	—
		rear	—	0.354	0.339	0.005	—	—	—	—	0.28
	New Yorker 5th Avenue	front	0.827	0.861	0.803	0.005	—	—	—	0.30	—
		rear	—	0.354	0.339	0.005	—	—	—	—	0.28
	Imperial	front	0.827	0.861	0.803	0.005	—	—	—	0.30	—
		rear	—	0.354	0.339	0.005	—	—	—	—	0.28

WHEEL ALIGNMENT

Year	Model		Caster Range (deg.)	Caster Preferred Setting (deg.)	Camber Range (deg.)	Camber Preferred Setting (deg.)	Toe-in (in.)	Steering Axis Inclination (deg.)
1989	Dynasty	front	①	1 3/16	1/4N–3/4P	5/16P	1/16	13 5/16
		rear	—	—	1 1/4N–1/4N	1/2N	0	—
	New Yorker Landau	front	①	1 3/16	1/4N–3/4P	5/16P	1/16	13 5/16
		rear	—	—	1 1/4N–1/4N	1/2N	0	—

WHEEL ALIGNMENT

Year	Model		Caster Range (deg.)	Caster Preferred Setting (deg.)	Camber Range (deg.)	Camber Preferred Setting (deg.)	Toe-in (in.)	Steering Axis Inclination (deg.)
1990	Dynasty	front	①	1³/₁₆	¼N–¾P	⁵/₁₆P	¹/₁₆	13⁵/₁₆
		rear	—	—	1¼N–¼N	½N	0	—
	New Yorker Landau	front	①	1³/₁₆	¼N–¾P	⁵/₁₆P	¹/₁₆	13⁵/₁₆
		rear	—	—	1¼N–¼N	½N	0	—
	New Yorker Salon	front	①	1³/₁₆	¼N–¾P	⁵/₁₆P	¹/₁₆	13⁵/₁₆
		rear	—	—	1¼N–¼N	½N	0	—
	New Yorker 5th Avenue	front	①	1³/₁₆	¼N–¾P	⁵/₁₆P	¹/₁₆	13⁵/₁₆
		rear	—	—	1¼N–¼N	½N	0	—
	Imperial	front	①	1³/₁₆	¼N–¾P	⁵/₁₆P	¹/₁₆	13⁵/₁₆
		rear	—	—	1¼N–¼N	½N	0	—
1991	Dynasty	front	①	2¾	¼N–¾P	⁵/₁₆P	¹/₁₆	12½
		rear	—	—	1¼N–¼N	½N	0	—
	New Yorker Salon	front	①	2¾	¼N–¾P	⁵/₁₆P	¹/₁₆	12½
		rear	—	—	1¼N–¼N	½N	0	—
	New Yorker 5th Avenue	front	①	2¾	¼N–¾P	⁵/₁₆P	¹/₁₆	12½
		rear	—	—	1¼N–¼N	½N	0	—
	Imperial	front	①	3	¼N–¾P	⁵/₁₆P ②	¹/₁₆	12½
		rear	—	—	1¼N–¼N	½N	0	—
1992–93	Dynasty	front	①	2¾	¼N–¾P	⁵/₁₆P	¹/₁₆	12½
		rear	—	—	1¼N–¼N	½N	0	—
	New Yorker Salon	front	①	2¾	¼N–¾P	⁵/₁₆P	¹/₁₆	12½
		rear	—	—	1¼N–¼N	½N	0	—
	New Yorker 5th Avenue	front	①	2¾	¼N–¾P	⁵/₁₆P	¹/₁₆	12½
		rear	—	—	1¼N–¼N	½N	0	—
	Imperial	front	①	3	¼N–¾P	⁵/₁₆P ②	¹/₁₆	12½
		rear	—	—	1¼N–¼N	½N	0	—

N—Negative
P—Positive

① Not adjustable—variation between sides should not exceed 1½°

② With air suspension—¹/₁₀ in.

ENGINE MECHANICAL

Disconnecting the negative battery cable on some vehicles may interfere with the functions of the on board computer systems and may require the computer to undergo a relearning process, once the negative battery cable is reconnected.

Engine Assembly

REMOVAL & INSTALLATION

2.5L Engine

1. Disconnect the negative battery cable and all engine ground straps. Relieve the fuel pressure.
2. Mark the hood hinge outline on the hood and remove the hood.
3. Drain the cooling system. Remove the radiator hoses, fan assembly and radiator.
4. Remove the air cleaner, duct hoses and oil filter.
5. Unbolt the air conditioning compressor from its mount, and position it aside.
6. Remove the power steering pump mounting bolts and position the pump aside. Disconnecting the fluid lines from the pump is not necessary.
7. Label and disconnect all electrical connectors from the engine, alternator and fuel injection system.
8. Disconnect and plug the fuel lines and heater hoses.
9. Disconnect the throttle linkage.
10. Remove the alternator.

11. Raise the vehicle and support safely.
12. Disconnect the exhaust pipe from the manifold.
13. Remove the right inner fender shield. Remove the lower cover from the transaxle case.
14. Remove the starter and set it aside. Matchmark the flexplate to the torque converter for installation purposes. Remove the torque converter bolts. Separate the converter from the flexplate. Remove the lower bellhousing bolts.
15. Lower the vehicle and support the transaxle with a floor jack or equivalent. Attach an engine lifting device to the engine.
16. Remove the remaining bellhousing attaching bolts.

NOTE: If removing the insulator-to-rail screws, first mark the position of the insulator on the side rail to ensure proper alignment during reinstallation.

17. Remove the front engine mount nut/bolt and the left insulator through bolt or the insulator bracket to transaxle bolts.

18. Lift the engine from the vehicle and remove.

To install:

19. Lower the engine into the engine compartment. Make sure the lifting device is supporting the full weight of the engine and loosely install all of the mounting bolts until all are threaded. Then tighten all bolts.

20. Remove the lifting device.

21. Raise the vehicle and support safely.

22. If equipped with an automatic transaxle, install the torque converter bolts and torque to 55 ft. lbs. (75 Nm).

23. Install the torque converter inspection plate and starter.

24. Connect the exhaust pipe. Lower the vehicle.

25. Install the alternator, power steering pump and air conditioning compressor.

26. Connect the fuel lines and heater hoses.

27. Connect the throttle linkage.

28. Connect all remaining electrical connectors.

29. Install the air cleaner assembly and oil filter.

30. Install the radiator, fan assembly and hoses.

31. Fill the engine with the proper amount of engine oil. Connect the negative battery cable.

32. Refill the cooling system. Start the engine, allow it to reach normal operating temperature and check all fluids for leaks.

33. Check the ignition timing and adjust if necessary.

34. Install the hood making sure to realign with the marks during disassembly.

3.0L, 3.3L and 3.8L Engines

1. Disconnect the negative battery cable. Release the fuel system pressure.

2. Matchmark the hinge-to-hood position and remove the hood.

3. Drain the cooling system. Disconnect and label all engine electrical connections.

4. Remove the coolant hoses from the radiator and engine. Remove the radiator and cooling fan assembly.

5. Remove the air cleaner assembly. Disconnect the fuel lines from the engine. Disconnect the accelerator cable from the engine.

6. Raise the vehicle and support safely. Drain the engine oil.

7. Remove the air conditioning

compressor mounting bolts, the drive belts and position the compressor to the side. Disconnect the exhaust pipe from the exhaust manifold.

8. Remove the transaxle inspection cover, matchmark the converter to the flexplate and remove the torque converter bolts.

9. Remove the power steering pump mounting bolts and set the pump aside, upright, with the fluid lines attached.

10. Remove the lower bellhousing bolts. Disconnect and label the starter motor wiring and remove the starter motor from the engine.

11. Lower the vehicle. Disconnect and label the vacuum hoses and engine ground straps.

12. Support the transaxle with a floor jack or equivalent. Attach an engine lifting device to the engine.

13. Remove the upper transaxle-to-engine bolts.

14. To separate the engine mounts from the insulators, mark the right insulator-to-right frame support and remove the mounting bolts. Remove the front engine mount through bolt. Remove the left insulator through bolt, from inside the wheel housing. Remove the insulator bracket-to-transaxle bolts.

15. Lift and remove the engine from the vehicle.

To install:

16. Lower the engine into the engine compartment. Align the engine mounts and install the bolts; do not tighten the bolts until all bolts have been installed. Torque the through bolts to 75 ft. lbs. (102 Nm).

17. Install the upper transaxle-to-engine mounting bolts and torque to 75 ft. lbs. (102 Nm). Remove the engine lifting fixture from the engine.

18. Raise the vehicle and support safely.

19. Align the converter marks, install the torque converter bolts and tightening to 55 ft. lbs. (75 Nm). Install the transaxle inspection cover.

20. Connect the exhaust pipe to the exhaust manifold. Install the starter motor and connect the wiring.

21. Install the power steering pump and air conditioning compressor. Adjust the drive belt tension, if necessary.

22. Lower the vehicle. Reconnect all vacuum hoses and electrical connections to the engine.

23. Connect the fuel lines and accelerator cable.

24. Install the radiator and fan assembly. Connect the fan motor wiring. Connect the radiator hoses and refill the cooling system.

25. Refill the engine with the proper oil to the correct level.

26. Connect the engine ground

straps. Install the hood and align the matchmarks. Connect the battery.

27. Start and run the engine until it reaches normal operating temperatures and check for leaks. Adjust the transaxle linkage, if necessary.

Engine Mounts

REMOVAL & INSTALLATION

2.5L Engine

RIGHT SIDE MOUNT

1. Disconnect the negative battery cable.

2. Matchmark the engine mount to its frame mounting location.

3. Remove the load on the engine motor mounts by carefully supporting the engine and transmission assembly with a floor jack.

4. Remove the through bolt from the insulator assembly and remove the insulator.

To install:

5. Install the insulator to its position and install the retaining bolts loosely.

6. Tighten the lower yoke nut first, then the through bolt nut and then the body mounting bolts. Make sure the matchmarks are aligned before tightening bolts.

FRONT MOUNT

1. Disconnect the negative battery cable.

2. Matchmark the engine mount to its frame mounting location.

3. Remove the load on the engine motor mounts by carefully supporting the engine and transmission assembly with a floor jack so it will rotate.

4. Remove the bolt from the insulator and front crossmember bracket.

5. Remove the front engine mount bracket to front crossmember screws and nuts. Remove the insulator assembly.

6. Installation is the reverse of the removal procedure.

3.0L, 3.3L and 3.8L Engines

1. Raise the vehicle and support safely, if necessary. Using the proper equipment, support the weight of the engine.

2. Remove all bolts and nuts that attach the mount to the engine strut, transaxle or body and remove the mount assembly from the vehicle.

3. Remove the through bolt and separate the insulator from the yoke bracket as required.

4. The installation is the reverse of the removal procedure. Make sure the matchmarks are aligned before tightening bolts.

5. Tighten the lower yoke nut first,

then the through bolt nut, then the body mounting bolts.

Cylinder Head

REMOVAL & INSTALLATION

2.5L Engine

1. Relieve the fuel pressure. Disconnect the negative battery cable and unbolt it from the head. Drain the cooling system.
2. Remove the dipstick bracket nut from the thermostat housing. Remove the ignition coil from the thermostat housing if mounted there.
3. Remove the air cleaner assembly. Remove the upper radiator hose and disconnect the heater hoses.
4. Disconnect and label the vacuum lines, hoses and wiring connectors from the manifolds, throttle body and from the cylinder head.
5. Disconnect the all linkages and the fuel line from the throttle body. Unbolt the cable bracket. Remove the ground strap attaching screw from the firewall.
6. Remove the air conditioning compressor from the mounting bracket. It is not necessary to disconnect the refrigerant hoses from the air compressor.
7. Remove the upper air conditioning compressor/alternator mount bolts that thread into the cylinder head. The cylinder head can be remove with the bracket mounted on the engine.
8. Remove the upper timing belt cover.
9. Raise the vehicle and support safely. Disconnect the exhaust pipe from the exhaust manifold.
10. Rotate the engine by hand, until the timing marks align. The No. 1 piston should be at TDC of its compression stroke. Lower the vehicle.
11. With the timing marks aligned, remove the camshaft sprocket and disconnect the timing belt. Remove the spark plug wires from the spark plugs.
12. Remove the valve cover and curtain. Remove the cylinder head bolts and washers, starting from the outside and working inward.
13. Remove the cylinder head from the engine.
14. Clean the cylinder head gasket mating surfaces.

To install:

15. Using new gaskets and seals, install the cylinder head to the engine block. Using new head bolts assembled with the old washers, torque the cylinder head bolts in sequence, to 45 ft. lbs. (61 Nm). Repeating the sequence, torque the bolts to 65 ft. lbs. (88 Nm). With the bolts at 65 ft. lbs., turn each bolt an additional ¼ turn.

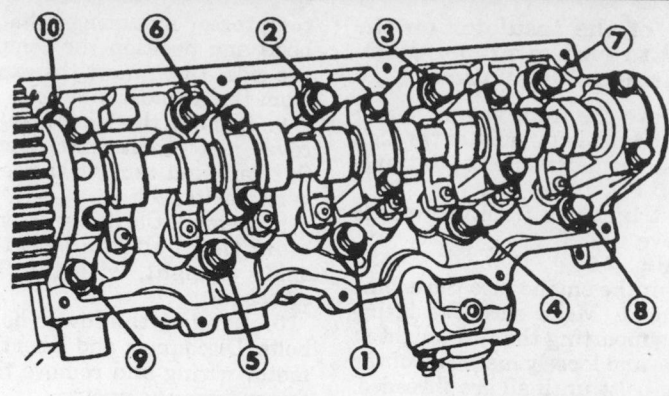

Cylinder head bolt torque sequence—2.5L engine

16. Install the camshaft sprocket and the timing belt.
17. Raise and safely support the vehicle. Connect the exhaust pipe to the exhaust manifold replacing the gasket as required.
18. Install the air conditioning compressor and the alternator to the mounting bracket and reconnect all electrical connectors.
19. Install the accessory drive belt and adjust tension as required.
20. Apply form-in-place Mopar Silicone Rubber Adhesive Sealant or equivalent gasket material to the rocker cover and replace both cover end seals.
21. Install to rocker cover to the engine and secure with the retainer bolts tightened to 105 inch lbs. (12 Nm).
22. Refill the cooling system. Connect the negative battery cable. Start the engine and check for leaks using the DRB I or II to activate the fuel pump.
23. Adjust the timing as required.

3.0L Engine

1. Release the fuel system pressure. Disconnect the negative battery cable. Drain the cooling system.
2. Remove the compressor drive belt and the air conditioning compressor from its mount and support it aside.
3. Using a ½ in. drive breaker bar, insert it into the square hole of the serpentine drive belt tensioner, rotate it counterclockwise to reduce the belt tension and remove the belt.
4. Remove the alternator and power steering pump from the brackets and position them aside.
5. Raise the vehicle and support safely. Remove the right front wheel and the inner splash shield.
6. Remove the crankshaft pulleys and the torsional damper.
7. Lower the vehicle. Using a floor jack and a block of wood positioned under the oil pan, raise the engine slightly. Remove the engine mount bracket

from the timing cover end of the engine.
8. To remove the timing belt, perform the following procedures:
   a. Rotate the crankshaft to position the No. 1 cylinder on the TDC of its compression stroke; the crankshaft sprocket timing mark should align with the oil pan timing indicator and the camshaft sprockets timing marks (triangles) should align with the timing marks on the rear timing belt covers.
   b. Remove the timing belt covers.
   c. Mark the timing belt in the direction of rotation for reinstallation purposes.
   d. Loosen the timing belt tensioner and remove the timing belt.

NOTE: When removing the timing belt from the camshaft sprocket, make sure the belt does not slip off the other camshaft sprocket. Support the belt so it cannot slip off the crankshaft sprocket and opposite side camshaft sprocket.

9. Remove the air cleaner assembly. Label and disconnect the spark plug wires and the vacuum hoses.
10. Remove the valve cover.
11. Install auto lash adjuster retainer tools MD998443 or equivalent, on the rocker arms.
12. If removing the front cylinder head, matchmark the distributor rotor to the distributor housing and the housing to distributor extension locations. Remove the distributor and the distributor extension.
13. Remove the camshaft bearing assembly to cylinder head bolts but do not remove the bolts from the assembly. Remove the rocker arms, rocker shafts and bearing caps as an assembly, as required. Remove the camshafts from the cylinder head and inspect them for damage.
14. Remove the intake manifold assembly.
15. Remove the exhaust manifold.
16. Remove the cylinder head bolts,

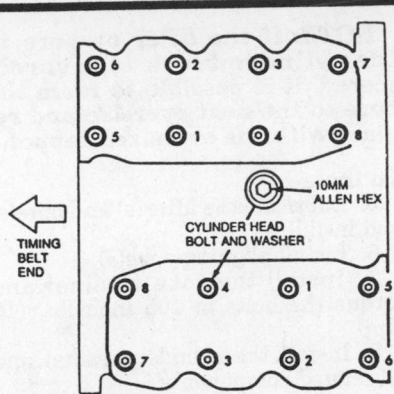

Cylinder head bolt torque sequence— 3.0L engine

starting from the outside and working inward. Remove the cylinder head from the engine.

17. Clean the gasket mounting surfaces and check the heads for warpage; maximum warpage is 0.008 in. (0.20mm).

To install:

18. Install the new cylinder head gasket(s) over the dowels on the engine block.

19. Install the cylinder head(s) on the engine and torque the cylinder head bolts, in sequence, using 3 even steps, to 70 ft. lbs. (95 Nm).

20. Installing the timing belt over the camshaft sprocket, use care not to allow the belt to slip off the opposite camshaft sprocket. Make sure the timing belt is installed on the camshaft sprocket in the same position as when removed.

21. Install the intake and exhaust manifolds to the engine using new gaskets where applicable.

22. Install the engine mounting bolts.

23. Raise and safely support the vehicle. Connect the exhaust pipe to the manifold.

24. Connect the remaining electrical connector disconnected during the cylinder head removal.

25. Refill the cooling system. Connect the negative battery cable. Start the engine and check for leaks using the DRB II to activate the fuel pump.

26. Adjust the timing as required.

3.3L and 3.8L Engines

1. Relieve the fuel pressure. Disconnect the negative battery cable. Drain the cooling system.

2. Remove the intake manifold with the throttle body.

3. Disconnect the coil wires, coolant temperature sending unit wire, heater hoses and bypass hose.

4. Remove the closed ventilation system hoses, evaporation control system hoses and valve cover.

5. Remove the exhaust manifold.

6. Remove the rocker arm and shaft assemblies. Remove the pushrods and identify them in ensure installation in their original positions.

7. Remove the head bolts and remove the cylinder head from the block.

To install:

8. Clean the gasket mounting surfaces and install a new head gasket to the block.

9. Install the head to the block. Before installing the head bolts, inspect them for stretching at the threads. Hold a straight-edge up to the threads. If the threads are not all even and in alignment, the bolt is stretched and should be replaced.

10. Torque the bolts in sequence to 45 ft. lbs. (61 Nm). Repeat the sequence and torque the bolts to 65 ft. lbs. (88 Nm). With the bolts at 65 ft. lbs., turn each bolt an additional ¼ turn.

NOTE: Cylinder head bolt final torque should be at least 90 ft. lbs. (122 Nm). If this torque is not achieved, the cylinder head bolts are to be replaced.

11. Torque the lone head bolt in the rear of the head to 25 ft. lbs. (33 Nm) after the other 8 bolts have been properly torqued.

12. Install the pushrods, rocker arms and shafts and torque the bolts to 21 ft. lbs. (28 Nm).

13. Place a drop of silicone sealer onto each of the 4 manifold to cylinder head gasket corners.

— CAUTION —

The intake manifold gasket is composed of very thin and sharp metal. Handle this gasket with care or damage to the gasket or personal injury could result.

14. Install the intake manifold gasket and torque the end retainers to 105 inch lbs. (12 Nm).

15. Install the intake manifold and torque the bolts in sequence to 10 inch lbs. Repeat the sequence increasing the torque to 17 ft. lbs. (23 Nm) and recheck each bolt for 17 ft. lbs. After the bolts are torqued, inspect the seals to ensure that they have not become dislodged.

16. Lubricate the injector O-rings with clean oil and position the fuel rail in place. Install the rail mounting bolts.

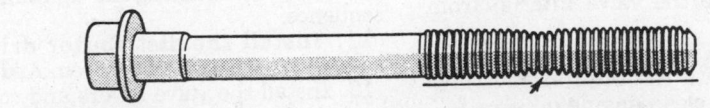

STRETCHED BOLT   THREADS ARE NOT STRAIGHT ON LINE

THREADS ARE STRAIGHT ON LINE

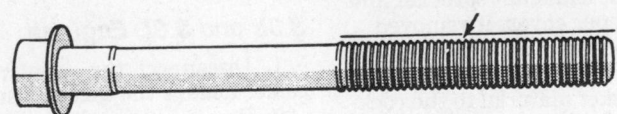

UNSTRETCHED BOLT

Checking bolts for stretching (necking)

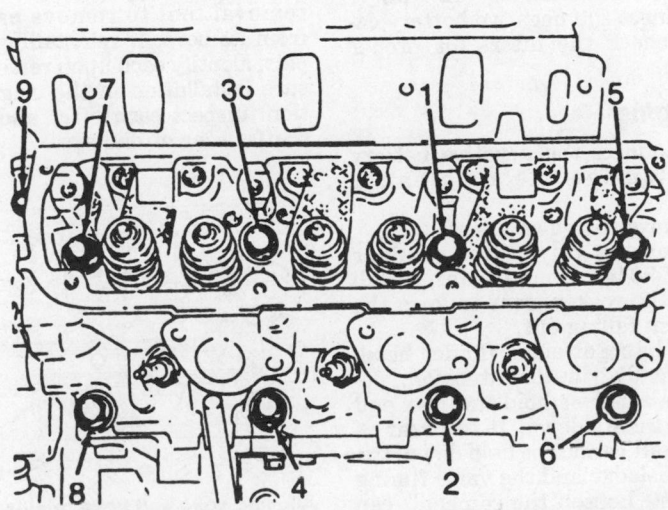

Cylinder head bolt torque sequence—3.3L and 3.8L engines

17. Install the valve cover with a new gasket. Install the exhaust manifold.

18. Install or connect all remaining items removed or disconnected during the removal procedure.

19. Refill the cooling system. Connect the negative battery cable. Start the engine and check for leaks using the DRB I or II to activate the fuel pump.

Valve Lifters

REMOVAL & INSTALLATION

2.5L Engine

1. Disconnect the negative battery cable.

2. Remove the valve cover and curtain. If removing all lifters, remove the upper timing belt cover, camshaft and rocker arms.

3. If only removing 1 lifter, rotate the crankshaft until the low point of the desired cam lobe is contacting the rocker arm.

4. Using the special valve spring compressor tool 4682 or equivalent, depress the valve spring without dislodging the keepers and slide the rocker arm out.

5. Remove the valve lifter(s) from the bore(s).

To install:

6. Lubricate the lifter(s) and their bore(s) with clean engine oil.

7. Install the lifter(s) into the appropriate bore, keeping in the original location, and install the rocker arms.

8. Install the camshaft sprocket and timing belt upper cover, if removed.

9. Apply form-in-place Mopar Silicone Rubber Adhesive Sealant or equivalent gasket material to the rocker cover and replace both cover end seals.

10. Install to rocker cover to the engine and secure with the retainer bolts tightened to 105 inch lbs. (12 Nm).

11. Connect the negative battery cable and check the lifters for proper operation.

3.0L Engine

1. Disconnect the negative battery cable. Remove the air cleaner assembly.

2. Remove the valve cover.

3. Using the valve lifter retainer tools MD998443 or equivalent, install them on the rocker arms to keep the lifters from falling out.

4. On the right side cylinder head, remove the distributor extension.

5. Have a helper hold the rear end of the camshaft down. If the rear of the camshaft cannot be held down, the belt will dislodge and the valve timing will be lost. Loosen the camshaft cap bolts but do not remove them from the

caps. Remove the caps, arms, shafts and bolts all as an assembly. It is not necessary to disassemble the shaft to replace lifter(s).

6. Remove the retainers and the lifter(s) from the rocker arm(s).

To install:

7. Lubricate the lifter(s) and their bore(s) with clean engine oil.

8. Install the lifter(s) into the rocker arm(s) and install the retainers.

9. Install the shaft assembly onto the engine. Apply Mopar Silicone Rubber Adhesive Sealant or equivalent, under the outside corners of both outermost camshaft bearing caps. (No. 1 and No. 4) prior to installation.

NOTE: On shaft assembly installation, make sure the arrow on the cylinder head is facing the same direction as the arrow on the corresponding rocker arm shaft bearing cap. The direction of the arrow marks on the front and the rear assemblies are opposite to each other.

10. Torque the bearing cap bolts to 85 inch lbs. (10 Nm) tightening No. 3 first, No. 2 second, No. 1 third and No. 4 last. Increase the torque to 180 inch lbs. (20 Nm), following the tightening sequence.

11. Install the distributor drive adapter and distributor, if removed.

12. Install the valve covers and connect the negative battery cable.

13. Start the engine, check for leaks and check the lifters for proper operation.

3.3L and 3.8L Engines

1. Disconnect the negative battery cable. Relieve the fuel pressure.

2. Remove the cylinder head(s) to gain access to the valve lifter(s).

3. Remove the yoke retainer and aligning yoke(s).

4. Use an appropriate valve lifter removal tool to remove each lifter from its bore. If reinstalling the tappets, identify each upon removal to ensure installation in the original position. Inspect each lifter and bore for scuffs, wear or damage.

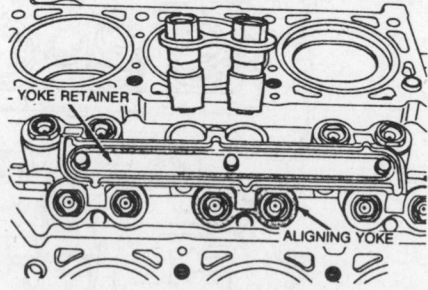

Aligning yoke and yoke retainer for roller lifters—3.3L and 3.8L engines

NOTE: If the lifter or bore in the cylinder block is severely scored, it is possible to ream the bore to the next oversize and replace with the oversized tappet.

To install:

5. Lubricate the lifter(s) and bore(s) and install.

6. Install aligning yoke(s).

7. Install the yoke retainer and torque the bolts to 105 inch lbs. (12 Nm).

8. Install the cylinder head(s) and all related components.

9. Connect the negative battery cable and check the lifters for proper operation.

Rocker Arms/Shafts

REMOVAL & INSTALLATION

2.5L Engine

1. Disconnect the negative battery cable.

2. Remove the valve cover.

3. Rotate the crankshaft until the low point of the desired cam lobe is contacting the rocker arm.

4. Use special valve spring compressor tool C-4682A or equivalent, to depress the valve spring without dislodging the keepers, and slide the rocker arm out from under the camshaft.

5. The installation is the reverse of the removal procedure.

3.0L Engine

1. Disconnect the negative battery cable. Remove the air cleaner assembly.

2. Remove the valve cover.

3. Install the auto lash adjuster retainer tools MD998443 or equivalent, on the rocker arms to keep the lash adjusters from falling out during removal.

4. Remove the distributor extension, if necessary.

5. Have a helper hold the rear end of the camshaft down. If the rear of the camshaft cannot be held down, the belt will dislodge and the valve timing will be lost. Loosen the camshaft cap bolts but do not remove them from the caps. Remove the caps, arms, shafts and bolts all as an assembly.

6. Disassemble the unit, keeping all parts in order and repair as required.

To install:

7. Install the shaft assembly to the engine. Apply Mopar Silicone Rubber Adhesive Sealant or equivalent, under the outside corners of both outermost camshaft bearing caps. (No. 1 and No. 4) prior to installation.

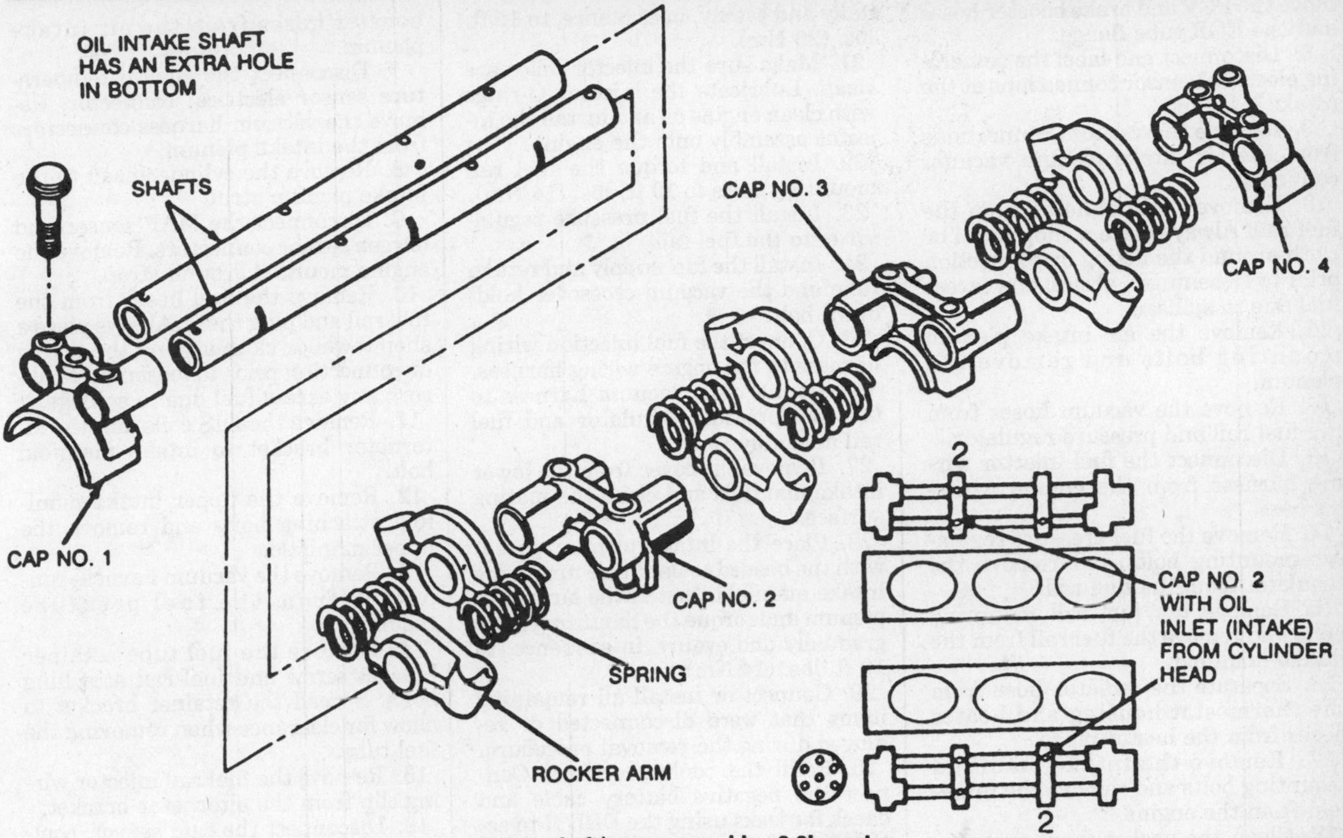

OIL INTAKE SHAFT
HAS AN EXTRA HOLE
IN BOTTOM

SHAFTS

CAP NO. 3

CAP NO. 4

CAP NO. 1

CAP NO. 2

CAP NO. 2
WITH OIL
INLET (INTAKE)
FROM CYLINDER
HEAD

SPRING

ROCKER ARM

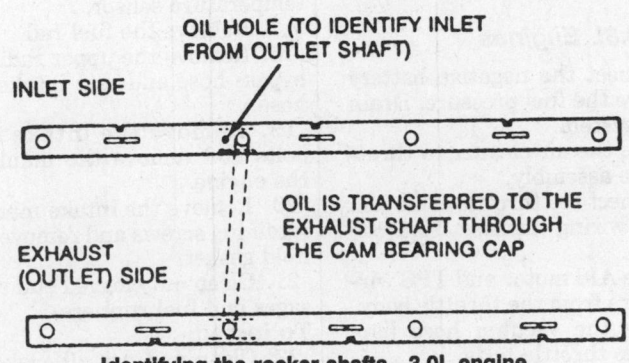

Rocker shaft/arms assembly—3.0L engine

OIL HOLE (TO IDENTIFY INLET
FROM OUTLET SHAFT)

INLET SIDE

OIL IS TRANSFERRED TO THE
EXHAUST SHAFT THROUGH
THE CAM BEARING CAP

EXHAUST
(OUTLET) SIDE

Identifying the rocker shafts—3.0L engine

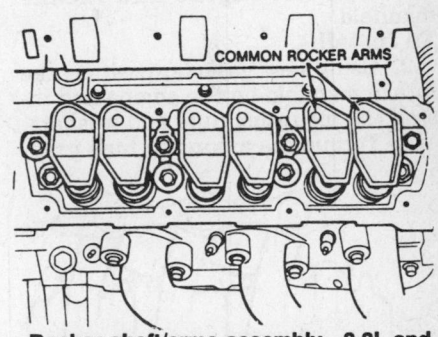

COMMON ROCKER ARMS

Rocker shaft/arms assembly—3.3L and
3.8L engines

NOTE: On shaft assembly installation, make sure the arrow on the cylinder head is facing the same direction as the arrow on the corresponding rocker arm shaft bearing cap. The direction of the arrow marks on the front and the rear assemblies are opposite to each other.

8. Torque the bearing cap bolts to 85 inch lbs. (10 Nm) tightening No. 3 first, No. 2 second, No. 1 third and No. 4 last. Increase the torque to 180 inch lbs. (20 Nm), following the tightening sequence.

9. Install the distributor drive adapter and distributor if removed.

10. Install the valve covers and connect the negative battery cable.

11. Start the engine, check for leaks and check the lifters for proper operation.

3.3L and 3.8L Engines

1. Disconnect the negative battery cable.

2. Remove the upper intake manifold assembly and valve cover.

3. Remove the rocker shaft retaining bolts and retainers.

4. Remove the rocker shaft and arm assembly. Disassemble and repair as required.

5. The installation is the reverse of the removal procedure. Torque the retaining bolts gradually and evenly to 21 ft. lbs. (28 Nm).

6. Allow 20 minutes tappet-bleed-down time after rocker shaft installation before starting the engine.

Intake Manifold

REMOVAL & INSTALLATION

3.0L Engine

1. Disconnect the negative battery cable. Relieve the fuel system pressure.

2. Drain the cooling system.

3. Remove the throttle body to air cleaner hose.

4. Remove the throttle body and transaxle kickdown linkage.

5. Remove the AIS motor and TPS wiring connectors from the throttle body.

6. Remove and label the vacuum hose harness from the throttle body.

7. From the air intake plenum, re-

move the PCV and brake booster hoses and the EGR tube flange.

8. Disconnect and label the remaining electrical sensor connections at the intake manifold.

9. Remove the vacuum connections from the air intake plenum vacuum connector.

10. Remove the fuel hoses from the fuel rail. Always place a shop towel or cloth around the fitting or connection prior to loosening to absorb any excess fuel due to spillage.

11. Remove the air intake plenum mounting bolts and remove the plenum.

12. Remove the vacuum hoses from the fuel rail and pressure regulator.

13. Disconnect the fuel injector wiring harness from the engine wiring harness.

14. Remove the fuel pressure regulator mounting bolts and remove the regulator from the fuel rail.

15. Remove the fuel rail mounting bolts and remove the fuel rail from the intake manifold.

16. Separate the radiator hose from the thermostat housing and heater hoses from the heater pipe.

17. Remove the intake manifold mounting bolts and remove the manifold from the engine.

18. Clean the gasket mounting surfaces on the engine and intake manifold.

To install:

19. Using new gaskets, position the intake manifold on the engine and install the mounting nuts and washers.

20. Torque the mounting nuts gradually and evenly, in sequence, to 15 ft. lbs. (20 Nm).

21. Make sure the injector holes are clean. Lubricate the injector O-rings with clean engine oil and install the injector assembly onto the engine.

22. Install and torque the fuel rail mounting bolts to 10 ft. lbs. (14 Nm).

23. Install the fuel pressure regulator onto the fuel rail.

24. Install the fuel supply and return tube and the vacuum crossover holddown bolt.

25. Connect the fuel injection wiring harness to the engine wiring harness.

26. Connect the vacuum harness to the fuel pressure regulator and fuel rail assembly.

27. Remove the cover from the lower intake manifold and clean the mating surface.

28. Place the intake plenum gasket with the beaded sealant side up, on the intake manifold. Install the air intake plenum and torque the mounting bolts gradually and evenly, in sequence, to 10 ft. lbs. (14 Nm).

29. Connect or install all remaining items that were disconnected or removed during the removal procedure.

30. Refill the cooling system. Connect the negative battery cable and check for leaks using the DRB II to activate the fuel pump.

3.3L and 3.8L Engines

1. Disconnect the negative battery cable. Relieve the fuel pressure. Drain the cooling system.

2. Remove the air cleaner to throttle body hose assembly.

3. Disconnect the throttle cable and remove the wiring harness from the bracket.

4. Remove AIS motor and TPS wiring connectors from the throttle body.

5. Remove the vacuum hose harness from the throttle body.

6. Remove the PCV and brake booster hoses from the air intake plenum.

7. Disconnect the charge temperature sensor electrical connector. Remove the vacuum harness connectors from the intake plenum.

8. Remove the cylinder head to the intake plenum strut.

9. Disconnect the MAP sensor and oxygen sensor connectors. Remove the engine mounted ground strap.

10. Remove the fuel hoses from the fuel rail and plug them. Always place a shop towel or cloth around the fitting or connection prior to loosening to absorb any excess fuel due to spillage.

11. Remove the DIS coils and the alternator bracket to intake manifold bolt.

12. Remove the upper intake manifold attaching bolts and remove the upper manifold.

13. Remove the vacuum harness connector from the fuel pressure regulator.

14. Remove the fuel tube retainer bracket screw and fuel rail attaching bolts. Spread the retainer bracket to allow for clearance when removing the fuel tube.

15. Remove the fuel rail injector wiring clip from the alternator bracket.

16. Disconnect the cam sensor, coolant temperature sensor and engine temperature sensor.

17. Remove the fuel rail.

18. Remove the upper radiator hose, bypass hose and rear intake manifold hose.

19. Remove the intake manifold bolts and remove the manifold from the engine.

20. Remove the intake manifold seal retaining screws and remove the manifold gasket.

21. Clean out clogged end water passages and fuel runners.

To install:

22. Clean and dry all gasket mating surfaces.

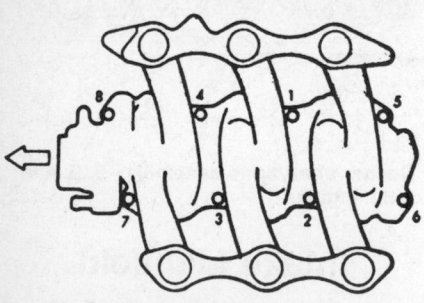

Intake manifold bolt torque sequence—3.0L engine

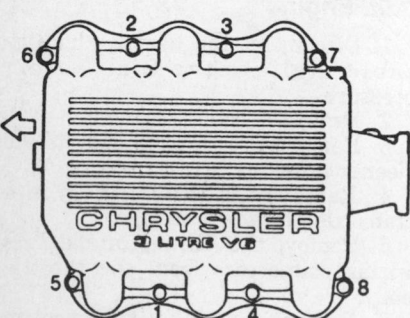

Air Intake plenum bolt torque sequence—3.0L engine

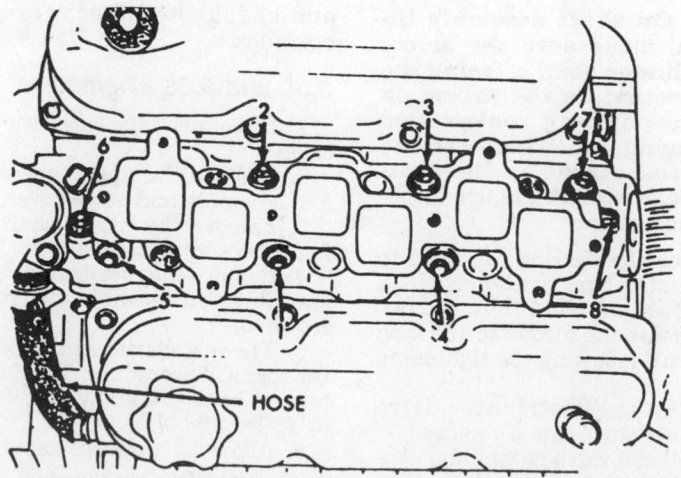

Intake manifold bolt torque sequence—3.3L and 3.8L engines

23. Place a drop of silicone sealer onto each of the 4 manifold-to-cylinder head gasket corners.

— CAUTION —

The intake manifold gasket is composed of very thin and sharp metal. Handle this gasket with care or damage to the gasket or personal injury could result.

24. Install the intake manifold gasket and torque the end retainers to 10 ft. lbs. (12 Nm).

25. Install the intake manifold and torque the bolts in sequence to 10 inch lbs. Repeat the sequence increasing the torque to 17 ft. lbs. (23 Nm) and recheck each bolt for 17 ft. lbs. of torque. After the bolts are torqued, inspect the seals to ensure that they have not become dislodged.

26. Lubricate the injector O-rings with clean oil and position the fuel rail in place. Install the rail mounting bolts.

27. Connect the cam sensor, coolant temperature sensor and engine temperature sensor.

28. Install the fuel rail injector wiring clip to the alternator bracket.

29. Install the fuel rail attaching bolts and fuel tube retainer bracket screw.

30. Install the vacuum harness to the pressure regulator.

31. Install the upper intake manifold with a new gasket. Install the bolts only finger-tight. Install the alternator bracket to intake manifold bolt and the cylinder head to intake manifold strut and bolts. Torque the intake manifold mounting bolts to 21 ft. lbs. (28 Nm) starting from the middle and working outward. Torque the bracket and strut bolts to 40 ft. lbs. (54 Nm).

32. Install or connect all items that were removed or disconnected from the intake manifold and throttle body.

33. Connect the fuel hoses to the rail. Push the fittings in until they click in place.

34. Install the air cleaner assembly.

35. Connect the negative battery cable and check for leaks using the DRB II to activate the fuel pump.

Exhaust Manifold

REMOVAL & INSTALLATION

3.0L Engine

1. Disconnect the negative battery cable. Raise the vehicle and support safely.

2. Disconnect the exhaust pipe from the rear exhaust manifold at the articulated joint.

3. Disconnect the EGR tube from the rear manifold and unplug the oxygen sensor wire.

4. Remove the crossover pipe to manifold bolts.

5. Remove the rear manifold to cylinder head nuts and the manifold.

6. Lower the vehicle and remove the heat shield from the manifold.

7. Remove the front manifold to cylinder head nuts and the manifold.

8. Clean the gasket mounting surfaces. Inspect the manifolds for cracks, flatness and/or damage.

To install:

9. When installing, the numbers 1–3–5 on the gaskets are used with the rear cylinders and 2–4–6 are on the gasket for the front cylinders. Torque the manifold to cylinder head nuts to 14–17 ft. lbs. (19–23 Nm).

10. Install the crossover pipe to the manifold.

11. Connect the EGR tube and oxygen sensor wire.

12. Connect the exhaust pipe to the rear exhaust manifold, at the articulated joint.

13. Connect the negative battery cable and check the manifolds for leaks.

3.3L and 3.8L Engines

1. Disconnect the negative battery cable.

2. If removing the rear manifold, raise the vehicle and support safely. Disconnect the exhaust pipe at the articulated joint from the rear exhaust manifold.

3. Separate the EGR tube from the rear manifold and disconnect the oxygen sensor wire.

4. Remove the alternator/power steering support strut.

5. Remove the bolts attaching the crossover pipe to the manifold.

6. Remove the bolts attaching the manifold to the head and remove the manifold.

7. If removing the front manifold, remove the heat shield, bolts attaching the crossover pipe to the manifold and the nuts attaching the manifold to the head.

8. Remove the manifold from the engine.

To install:

9. Install the manifold to the engine and secure using the mounting bolts and nuts tightened to 17 ft. lbs. (23 Nm). Install the heat shield, if removed.

10. Install the crossover pipe to the manifold.

11. Connect the EGR tube and oxygen sensor wire.

12. Connect the exhaust pipe to the rear exhaust manifold, at the articulated joint.

13. Connect the negative battery cable and check the manifolds for leaks.

Combination Manifold

REMOVAL & INSTALLATION

2.5L Engine

NOTE: In some cases, some of the manifold attaching bolts are not accessible or too heavily sealed from the factory and cannot be removed on the vehicle. Head removal would be necessary in these situations.

1. Disconnect the negative battery cable.

2. Relieve the fuel system pressure.

3. Drain the cooling system.

4. Remove the air cleaner and disconnect all vacuum lines, electrical wiring and fuel lines from the throttle body.

5. Disconnect the throttle linkage.

6. Loosen the power steering pump and remove the drive belt.

7. Remove the power brake vacuum hose from the intake manifold.

8. Remove the water hoses from the water crossover.

9. Raise the vehicle and support safely.

10. Disconnect the exhaust pipe from the exhaust manifold.

11. Remove the power steering pump from its mounting bracket and set it aside. It is not necessary to remove the fluid lines.

12. Remove the EGR tube.

13. Remove the intake manifold bolts.

14. Lower the vehicle.

15. Remove the intake manifold.

16. Remove the exhaust manifold nuts.

17. Remove the exhaust manifold.

To install:

18. Install a new combination manifold gasket.

19. Install the exhaust manifold assembly. Install the mounting nuts and torque to 17 ft. lbs. (23 Nm.) starting from the middle and working outward. Install the heat cowl to the exhaust manifold.

20. Install the intake manifold. Torque the bolts to 17 ft. lbs. (23 Nm.) starting from the middle and working outward.

21. Install the EGR tube, if removed.

22. Install the intake support bracket, if equipped.

23. Install the power steering pump.

24. Raise the vehicle and support safely. Install the exhaust pipe to the exhaust manifold.

25. Install the water hoses to the water crossover.

26. Install the power brake vacuum hose to the intake manifold.

27. Connect the throttle linkage.

28. Install all vacuum lines, electrical

wiring and fuel lines to the throttle body.

29. Install the air cleaner assembly.

30. Refill the cooling system.

31. Connect the negative battery cable and check the manifolds for leaks.

Timing Chain Front Cover

REMOVAL & INSTALLATION

3.3L and 3.8L Engines

1. Disconnect the negative battery cable. Drain the cooling system.

2. Support the engine using the proper equipment and remove the right side motor mount.

3. Raise the vehicle and support safely. Drain the engine oil and remove the oil pan.

4. Remove the right wheel and splash shield.

5. Remove the drive belt.

6. Unbolt the air conditioning compressor and position it to the side. Remove the compressor mounting bracket.

7. Remove the crankshaft pulley bolt and remove the pulley using a puller.

8. Remove the idler pulley from the engine bracket and remove the bracket.

9. Remove the cam sensor from the timing chain cover.

10. Remove the cover mounting bolts and the cover from the engine. Make sure the oil pump inner rotor does not fall out. Remove the 3 O-rings from the coolant passages and the oil pump outlet.

To install:

11. Thoroughly clean and dry the gasket mating surfaces. Install new O-rings to the block.

12. Remove the crankshaft oil seal from the cover. The seal must be removed from the cover when installing to ensure proper oil pump engagement.

13. Using a new gasket, install the chain case cover to the engine.

14. Make certain the oil pump is engaged onto the crankshaft before proceeding or there will be no oil pressure. Install the attaching bolts and torque to 20 ft. lbs. (27 Nm).

15. Use tool C-4992 to install the crankshaft oil seal. Install the crankshaft pulley using a 5.9 in. bolt used with thrust bearing and washer plate L-4524. Make sure the pulley bottoms out on the inner diameter of the crankshaft seal. Install the bolt and torque to 40 ft. lbs. (54 Nm).

16. Install the engine bracket and torque the bolts to 40 ft. lbs. (54 Nm). Install the idler pulley to the engine bracket.

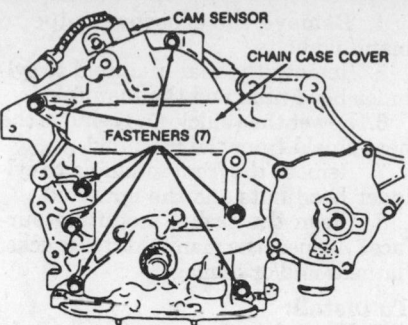

Timing chain cover—3.3L and 3.8L engines

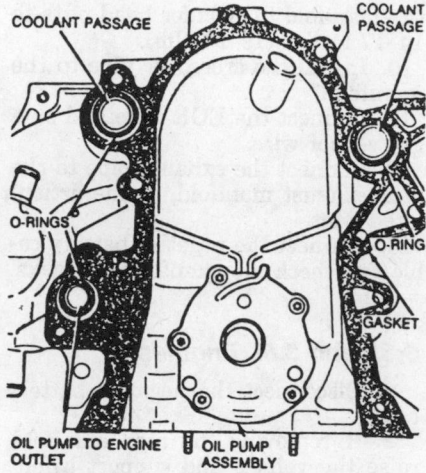

Timing cover removed—3.3L and 3.8L engines

17. To install the cam sensor, perform the following:

   a. Clean off the old spacer from the sensor face completely. A new spacer must be attached to the cam sensor prior to installation; if a new spacer is not used, engine performance will be adversely affected.

   b. Inspect the O-ring for damage and replace, if necessary. Lubricate the O-ring lightly with oil and push the sensor into its bore in the chain case cover until contact is made with the cam timing gear. Hold in this position and tighten the bolt to 9 ft. lbs. (12 Nm).

18. Install the air conditioning compressor and bracket.

19. Install the drive belt.

20. Install the inner splash shield and wheel.

21. Install the oil pan with a new gasket.

22. Install the motor mount.

23. Remove the engine temperature sensor and fill the cooling system until the level reaches the vacant sensor hole. Install the sensor and continue to fill the radiator. Fill the engine with the proper amount of oil.

24. Connect the negative battery cable and check for leaks.

Front Cover Oil Seal

REPLACEMENT

3.3L and 3.8L Engines

1. Disconnect the negative battery cable.

2. Raise the vehicle and support safely. Remove the right front wheel and the inner splash shield.

3. Remove the drive belt.

4. Remove the crankshaft bolt. Using a puller, remove the crankshaft pulley.

5. Use tool C-4991 to remove the seal.

To install:

6. Clean out the bore. Place the seal with the spring toward the engine. Install the new seal using tool C-4992 until it is flush with the cover.

7. Install the crankshaft pulley using a 5.9 in. bolt with thrust bearing and washer plate L-4524. Make sure the pulley bottoms out on the inner diameter of the crankshaft seal. Install the bolt and torque to 40 ft. lbs. (54 Nm).

8. Install the drive belt.

9. Install the splash shield and wheel.

10. Connect the negative battery cable and check for leaks.

Timing Chain and Gears

REMOVAL & INSTALLATION

3.3L and 3.8L Engines

1. If possible, position the engine so the No. 1 piston is at TDC of its compression stroke. Disconnect the negative battery cable. Drain the coolant.

2. Remove the timing chain case cover.

3. Remove the camshaft sprocket attaching bolt. Remove the camshaft sprocket and timing chain together.

4. Using the appropriate puller, remove the crankshaft sprocket taking care not to damage the crankshaft surface.

To install:

5. Position the new crankshaft sprocket onto the crankshaft using soft mallet and appropriate driver. Be sure to fully seat the sprocket in position.

6. If not already done, rotate the crankshaft so the timing mark is at the 12 o'clock position. Place the timing chain around the camshaft sprocket and place the timing mark to the 6 o'clock position.

7. Place the timing chain around the crankshaft sprocket and install the camshaft sprocket to the engine.

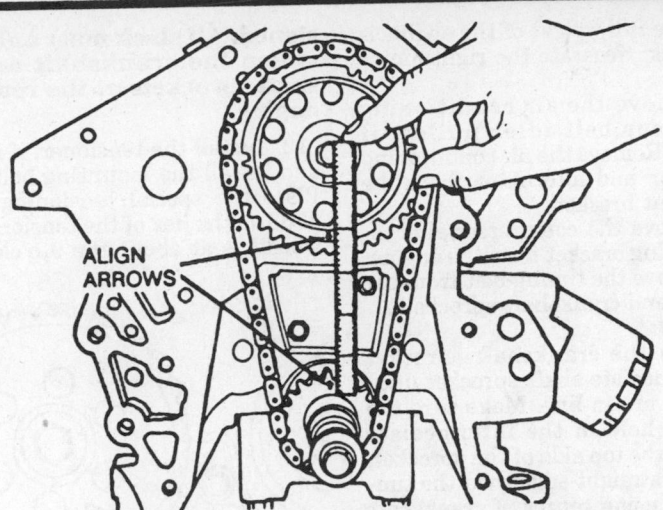

ALIGN ARROWS

Aligning the timing marks—3.3L and 3.8L engines

8. Using a straightedge check the alignment of the timing marks.

9. Install the camshaft bolt and washer and tighten to 35 ft. lbs. (47 Nm).

10. Rotate the crankshaft 2 revolutions and check for proper alignment of the timing marks. If the marks do not line up, remove the camshaft sprocket and realign.

11. Check the camshaft end-play. New thrust plate specifications are 0.005–0.012 in. or 0.012 in. for an old thrust plate. Replace the thrust plate if not within specifications.

12. Install the timing chain snubber and tighten the retainer screws to 105 inch lbs. (12 Nm).

13. Thoroughly clean and dry the gasket mating surfaces.

14. Install new O-rings to the block.

15. Remove the crankshaft oil seal from the cover. The seal must be removed from the cover when installing to ensure proper oil pump engagement.

16. Using a new gasket, install the chain case cover to the engine.

17. Make certain that the oil pump is engaged onto the crankshaft before proceeding or severe engine damage will result. Install the attaching bolts and torque to 20 ft. lbs. (27 Nm).

18. Use tool C–4992 to install the crankshaft oil seal. Install the crankshaft pulley using a 5.9 in. suitable bolt and thrust bearing and washer plate L–4524. Make sure the pulley bottoms out on the crankshaft seal diameter. Install the bolt and torque to 40 ft. lbs. (54 Nm).

19. Install all other parts removed during the chain case cover removal procedure.

20. To install the cam sensor, first clean off the old spacer from the sensor face completely. Inspect the O-ring for damage and replace, if necessary. A new spacer must be attached to the cam sensor prior to installation; if a new spacer is not used, engine performance will be adversely affected. Oil the O-ring lightly and push the sensor into its bore in the chain case cover until contact is made with the cam timing gear. Hold in this position and tighten the bolt to 10 ft. lbs. (12 Nm).

21. Refill the cooling system and fill the engine with oil.

22. Connect the negative battery cable, road test the vehicle and check for leaks.

Timing Belt Front Cover

REMOVAL & INSTALLATION

2.5L Engine
UPPER COVER

1. Disconnect the negative battery cable.

2. Remove the bolt that attach the upper cover to the valve cover.

3. Remove the nuts that attaches the upper cover to the lower cover.

4. Remove the upper cover by lifting upward. Guide the cover front inner lip past the timing belt and valve cover during removal.

5. Installation is the reverse of the removal procedure.

LOWER COVER

1. Disconnect the negative battery cable.

2. Remove the bolt that attaches the upper cover to the lower cover.

3. Raise the vehicle and support safely. Remove the right side splash shield.

4. Remove the crankshaft pulley, water pump pulley and drive belts.

5. Remove the lower cover attaching bolts and remove the lower cover.

6. The installation is the reverse of the removal procedure.

3.0L Engine

1. Disconnect the negative battery cable.

2. To remove the air conditioning compressor belt, loosen the adjustment pulley locknut, turn the screw counterclockwise to reduce the drive belt tension and remove the belt.

3. To remove the serpentine drive belt, insert a ½ in. breaker bar in to the square hole of the tensioner pulley, rotate it counterclockwise to reduce the drive belt tension and remove the belt.

4. Remove the air conditioning compressor and the air compressor bracket, power steering pump and alternator from the mounts and support them to the side. Remove power steering pump/alternator automatic belt tensioner bolt and the tensioner.

5. Raise the vehicle and support safely. Remove the right inner fender splash shield.

6. Remove the crankshaft pulley bolt and the pulley/damper assembly from the crankshaft.

7. Lower the vehicle and place a floor jack under the engine to support it.

8. Separate the front engine mount insulator from the bracket. Raise the engine slightly and remove the mount bracket.

9. Remove the timing belt cover bolts and the upper and lower covers from the engine.

To install:

10. Install the timing covers and bolts.

11. Install the engine mount bracket. The engine mount through bolt must be torqued to 100 ft. lbs. (136 Nm) with the engine support removed and the engine's weight on the mount.

12. Install the pulley damper assembly to the crankshaft. Torque the bolt to 110 ft. lbs. (149 Nm). Install the splash shield.

13. Install the power steering pump/alternator automatic belt tensioner.

14. Install the air conditioning compressor bracket, compressor, power steering pump and alternator.

15. Install the belts.

16. Connect the negative battery cable and check all disturbed components for proper operation.

Timing Belt and Tensioner

ADJUSTMENT

2.5L Engine

1. Disconnect the negative battery cable.

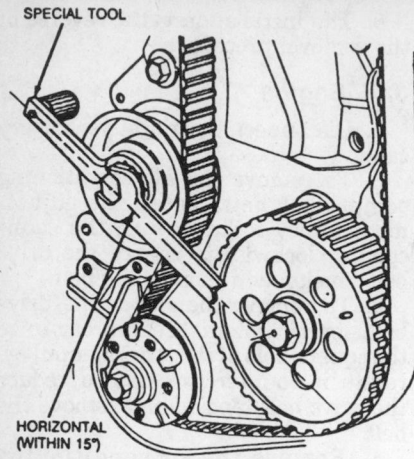

SPECIAL TOOL

HORIZONTAL
(WITHIN 15°)

Adjusting the timing belt—2.5L engine

2. Raise the vehicle and support safely. Remove the right front inner splash shield.

3. Remove the tensioner cover.

4. Place the special tensioning tool C–4703 on the hex of the tensioner so the weight is at about the 10 o'clock position, then loosen the bolt.

5. The tensioner should drop to the 9 o'clock position. Reposition the tool as required in order to have it end up at the 9 o'clock position, parallel to the ground, hanging toward the rear of the vehicle, ± 15 degrees.

6. Hold the tool in position and tighten the bolt. Do not pull the tool past the 9 o'clock position or the belt will be too tight and will cause howling or possible breakage.

7. Install the cover and the splash shield.

3.0L Engine

1. Disconnect the negative battery cable.

2. Remove the timing belt covers.

3. Loosen the bolt that holds the timing belt tensioner in place.

4. Allow the spring only to pull the tensioner in automatically. Do not manually move the tensioner or the belt will be too tight.

5. Tighten the tensioner locking bolt.

6. Install the timing belt covers and all related parts.

REMOVAL & INSTALLATION

2.5L Engine

1. If possible, position the engine so the No. 1 piston is at TDC of its compression stroke. Disconnect the negative battery cable.

2. Remove the timing belt covers. Loosen the timing belt tensioner retainer bolt, remove the belt from the tensioner and allow it to hang free.

3. Place a floor jack under the en-gine so the full weight of the engine is on the jack. Separate the right motor mount.

4. Remove the air conditioning compressor belt idler pulley, if equipped. Remove the air conditioning compressor and alternator from the solid mount bracket.

5. Remove the compressor/alterna-tor mounting bracket from the engine.

6. Remove the timing belt from the camshaft and crankshaft sprockets.

To install:

7. Turn the crankshaft sprocket and intermediate shaft sprocket until the marks are in line. Make sure the elongated hole in the intermediate shaft is at the top side of the sprocket. Position a straight-edge thru the timing marks using center of crankshaft and intermediate sprocket retainer bolt heads as a guide for straightness, and confirm alignment.

8. Turn the camshaft until the small hole in the sprocket is at the top and rows on the hub are in line with the camshaft cap to cylinder head mounting lines. If necessary, use a mirror to see the alignment so it is viewed straight on and not at an angle from above. Install the belt around each timing sprocket in the approximate position of installation.

9. Install the air conditioning compressor/alternator bracket, idler pulley and motor mount. Remove the floor jack. Raise the vehicle and support safely. Have the tensioner at an arm's reach because the timing belt will have to be held in position with one hand.

10. To properly install the timing belt, reach up and position on the camshaft sprocket. Turn the intermediate shaft counterclockwise slightly (1–2 teeth), then engage the belt with the intermediate shaft sprocket. Hold the belt against the intermediate shaft sprocket and turn clockwise to take up all tension; if the timing marks are out of alignment, repeat until alignment is correct.

11. Using a wrench, turn the crank-shaft sprocket counterclockwise slightly (1–2 teeth), and position belt on sprocket. Turn the sprocket clock-wise so there is no slack in the belt between sprockets; if the timing marks between the crankshaft and the inter-mediate shaft or the timing marks on the camshaft sprocket are out of align-ment, repeat until alignment is correct.

NOTE: If the timing marks are in line but slack exists in the belt between either the camshaft and intermediate shaft sprockets or the intermediate and crankshaft sprockets, the timing will be in-correct when the belt is ten-sioned. All slack must only be be-tween the crankshaft and cam-shaft sprockets at the rear of the engine.

12. Install the tensioner, if removed, and install the mounting bolt loosely. Place the special tensioning tool C–4703 on the hex of the tensioner so the weight is at about the 9 o'clock posi-

Alignment of the crankshaft sprocket and intermediate shaft sprocket—2.5L engine

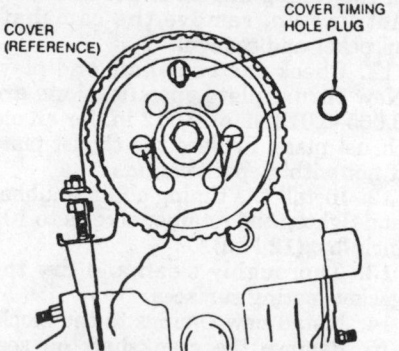

COVER
(REFERENCE)

COVER TIMING
HOLE PLUG

Alignment of the arrows on the camshaft sprocket with the camshaft cap-to-cylinder-mounting line—2.5L engine

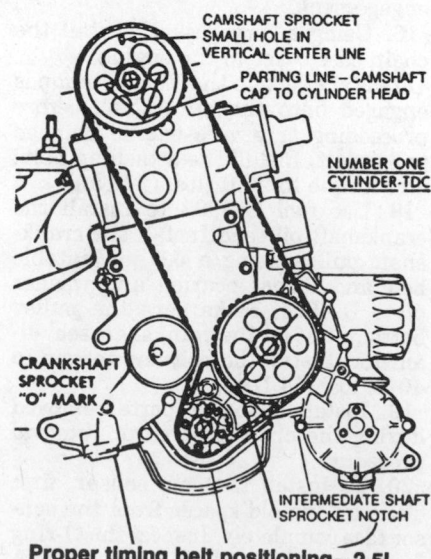

CAMSHAFT SPROCKET
SMALL HOLE IN
VERTICAL CENTER LINE

PARTING LINE—CAMSHAFT
CAP TO CYLINDER HEAD

NUMBER ONE
CYLINDER-TDC

CRANKSHAFT
SPROCKET
"O" MARK

INTERMEDIATE SHAFT
SPROCKET NOTCH

Proper timing belt positioning—2.5L engine

tion, parallel to the ground, hanging toward the rear of the vehicle, ± 15 degrees.

13. Hold the tool in position and tighten the bolt to 45 ft. lbs. (61 Nm). Do not pull the tool past the 9 o'clock position; this will make the belt too tight and will cause it to howl or possibly break.

14. Lower the vehicle and recheck all timing sprockets to assure correct alignment. If correct, install the timing belt covers, crankshaft pulleys and the remaining components removed.

15. Connect the negative battery cable. Start the engine and run until normal operating temperature is reached. Check the ignition timing, adjust as required and road test the vehicle.

3.0L Engine

1. If possible, position the engine so the No. 1 cylinder is at TDC of its compression stroke. Disconnect the negative battery cable. Remove the timing covers from the engine.

2. If the same timing belt will be reused, mark the direction of the timing belt's rotation, for installation in the same direction. Make sure the engine is positioned so the No. 1 cylinder is at the TDC of its compression stroke and the sprockets timing marks are aligned with the engine's timing mark indicators.

3. Loosen the timing belt tensioner bolt and remove the belt. If not removing the tensioner, position it as far away from the center of the engine as possible and tighten the bolt.

4. If the tensioner is being removed, paint the outside of the spring to ensure that it is not installed backwards. Unbolt the tensioner and remove it along with the spring.

To install:

5. Install the tensioner, if removed, and hook the upper end of the spring to the water pump pin and the lower end to the tensioner in exactly the same position as originally installed. If not already done, position both camshafts so the marks line up with those on the alternator bracket (rear bank) and inner timing cover (front bank). Rotate the crankshaft so the timing mark aligns with the mark on the oil pump.

6. Install the timing belt on the crankshaft sprocket and while keeping the belt tight on the tension side (right side), install the belt on the front camshaft sprocket.

7. Install the belt on the water pump pulley, then the rear camshaft sprocket and the tensioner.

8. Rotate the front camshaft counterclockwise to tension the belt between the front camshaft and the crankshaft. If the timing marks be-

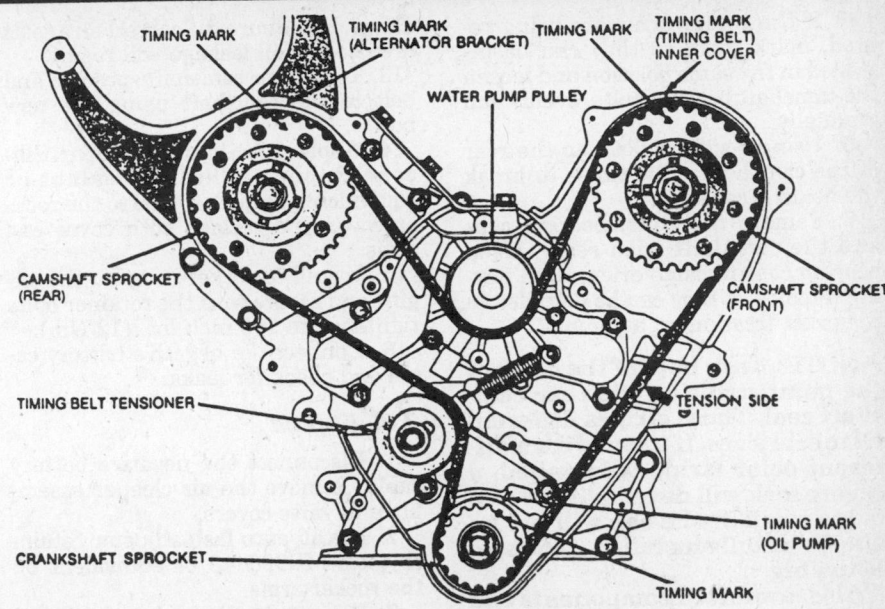

Proper timing belt positioning—3.0L engine

came misaligned, repeat the procedure.

9. Install the crankshaft sprocket flange.

10. Loosen the tensioner bolt and allow the spring to tension the belt.

11. Turn the crankshaft 2 full turns in the clockwise direction only until the timing marks align again. Now that the belt is properly tensioned, torque the tensioner lock bolt to 21 ft. lbs. (29 Nm).

12. Install the timing belt covers and all related parts.

13. Connect the negative battery cable and road test the vehicle.

Timing Sprockets

REMOVAL & INSTALLATION

2.5L Engine

1. Disconnect the negative battery cable. Remove the timing belt.

2. Remove the crankshaft sprocket bolt. Using the puller tool C–4685 or equivalent, and the button from tool L–4524 or equivalent, remove the crankshaft sprocket.

3. Using the tool C–4687 or equivalent, hold the camshaft and/or intermediate sprocket, remove the center bolt and the sprocket(s).

4. The installation is the reverse of the removal procedure. Torque the camshaft and intermediate sprocket bolts to 65 ft. lbs. (88 Nm) and the crankshaft sprocket bolt to 85 ft. lbs. (115 Nm).

5. Connect the negative battery cable and road test the vehicle.

3.0L Engine

1. Disconnect the negative battery cable.

2. Remove the timing belt.

3. To remove the camshaft sprocket, hold the sprocket with tool MB990775 or equivalent, and remove the retaining bolt and washer.

4. To remove the crankshaft sprocket, remove the bolt and remove the sprocket from the crankshaft.

5. The installation is the reverse of the removal procedure. Torque the camshaft sprocket bolt to 70 ft. lbs. (95 Nm) while holding the sprocket with the holding tool. Torque the crankshaft sprocket bolt. to 112 ft. lbs. (151 Nm).

6. Connect the negative battery cable and road test the vehicle.

Camshaft

REMOVAL & INSTALLATION

2.5L Engine

1. Disconnect the negative battery cable.

2. Turn the crankshaft so the No. 1 piston is at the TDC of its compression stroke. Remove the upper timing belt cover.

3. Remove the valve cover.

4. Remove the camshaft sprocket bolt and the sprocket from the end of the camshaft, taking care not to allow the timing belt to loosen. Suspend the camshaft timing sprocket, with the belt in place tightly so the belt does not lose tension. If it does, the belt timing will have to be reset.

5. If the rocker arms are being re-used, mark them so they can be installed in the same position and loosen the camshaft bearing bolts, evenly and gradually.

6. Using a soft mallet, tap the rear of the camshaft a few times to break the bearing caps loose.

7. Remove the bolts, bearing caps and the camshaft with seals. Keep bearing caps in same orientation during removal so they can be installed in the exact location on assembly.

NOTE: Take note of the color of the paint stripe on the rear camshaft seal. These stripes differentiate seal sizes. If a seal with a different color stripe is installed, a severe leak will develop if the seal is too small or the cap will not be able to be fully installed if the seal is too big.

Also, oversized components can be identified as follows: the top of the bearing caps are painted green and "O/SJ" is stamped behind the oil galley plug on the end of the head. The barrel of an oversized camshaft is also painted green and "O/SJ" is stamped on the end of the shaft. If normal sized parts are installed in place of oversized ones, oil pressure will be significantly reduced.

8. Check the oil passages for blockages and all parts for wear and damage and replace parts as required. Clean the gasket mounting surfaces.

To install:

9. Transfer the camshaft sprocket key to the new camshaft. New rocker arms and a new camshaft sprocket bolt are normally included with the camshaft package. Install the rocker arms, lubricate the camshaft journals and lobes with clean engine oil and install on the cylinder head.

NOTE: Apply RTV silicone gasket material to the No. 1 and 5 bearing caps. Install the bearing caps before the seals are installed.

10. Install the bearing caps in the same orientation as prior to removal. The bearing cap with No. 1 should be at the timing belt end and No. 5 at the transaxle end. The camshaft bearing caps are numbered and have arrows facing forward. Torque the camshaft bearing bolts evenly and gradually to 18 ft. lbs. (24 Nm).

11. Mount a dial indicator to the front of the engine and check the camshaft end-play. Play should not exceed 0.020 in.

12. Install the front and the rear camshaft end seals into position in the bearing caps using the appropriate

driver. Make sure the correct size seals are used or oil leakage will result.

13. Install the camshaft sprocket and belt to the camshaft using the new bolt.

14. Apply form-in-place Mopar Silicone Rubber Adhesive Sealant or equivalent gasket material to the rocker cover and replace both cover end seals.

15. Install to rocker cover to the engine and secure with the retainer bolts tightened to 105 inch lbs. (12 Nm).

16. Connect the negative battery cable and check for leaks.

3.0L Engine

1. Disconnect the negative battery cable. Remove the air cleaner assembly and valve covers.

2. Install auto lash adjuster retainer tools MD998443 or equivalent on the rocker arms.

3. If removing the right side (front) camshaft, remove the distributor extension.

4. Remove the camshaft bearing caps but do not remove the bolts from the caps.

5. Remove the rocker arms, rocker shafts and bearing caps, as an assembly.

6. Remove the camshaft from the cylinder head.

7. Inspect the bearing journals on the camshaft, cylinder head and bearing caps.

To install:

8. Lubricate the camshaft journals and camshaft with clean engine oil and install the camshaft in the cylinder head.

9. Align the camshaft bearing caps with the arrow mark depending on cylinder numbers and install in numerical order.

10. Apply sealer at the ends of the bearing caps and install the assembly.

11. Torque the bearing cap bolts, in the following sequence: No. 3, No. 2, No. 1 and No. 4 to 85 inch lbs. (10 Nm).

12. Repeat the sequence increasing the torque to 175 inch lbs. (18 Nm).

13. Install the distributor extension, if removed.

14. Install the valve cover and all related components.

15. Connect the negative battery cable and road test the vehicle.

3.3L and 3.8L Engines

1. Relieve the fuel pressure. Disconnect the negative battery cable.

2. Remove the engine from the vehicle. Remove the intake manifold, cylinder heads, timing chain cover and timing chain from the engine.

3. Remove the rocker arm and shaft assemblies.

4. Label and remove the pushrods and lifters.

5. Remove the camshaft thrust plate.

6. Install a long bolt into the front of the camshaft to facilitate its removal. Remove the camshaft being careful not to damage the cam bearings with the cam lobes.

To install:

7. Install the camshaft to within 2 in. of its final installation position.

8. Install the camshaft thrust plate and 2 bolts and torque to 10 ft. lbs. (12 Nm).

9. Place both camshaft and crankshaft gears on the bench with the timing marks on the exact imaginary center line through both gear bores as they are installed on the engine. Place the timing chain around both sprockets.

10. Turn the crankshaft and camshaft so the keys line up with the keyways in the gears when the timing marks are in proper position.

11. Slide both gears over their respective shafts and use a straight-edge to check timing mark alignment.

12. Measure camshaft end-play. If not within specifications, replace the thrust plate.

13. If the camshaft was not replaced, lubricate and install the lifters in their original locations. If the camshaft was replaced, new lifters must be used.

14. Install the pushrods and rocker shaft assemblies.

15. Install the timing chain cover, cylinder heads and intake manifold.

16. Install the engine in the vehicle.

17. After engine and all related components are installed, change the engine oil and replace the oil filter.

NOTE: If the camshaft or lifters have been replaced, add 1 pint of Mopar crankcase conditioner or equivalent, when replenishing the oil to aid in break in. This mixture should be left in the engine for a minimum of 500 miles and drained at the next normal oil change.

18. Fill the radiator with coolant.

19. Connect the negative battery cable, set all adjustments to specifications and check for leaks.

Intermediate Shaft

REMOVAL & INSTALLATION

2.5L Engine

1. Disconnect the negative battery cable.

2. Crank the engine around until the No. 1 piston is at TDC of its compression stroke. Remove the timing

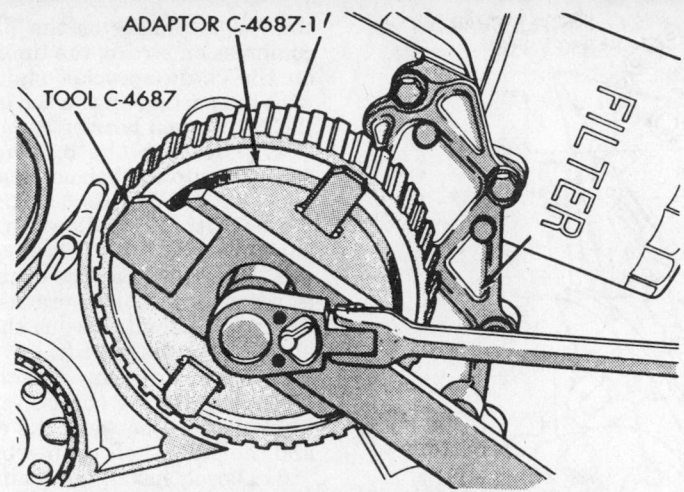

Removing intermediate shaft sprocket—1992-93 2.5L engine

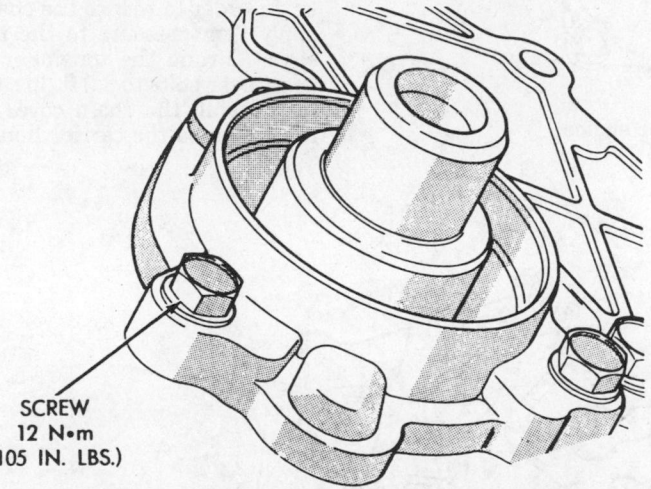

Intermediate shaft retainer—1992-93 2.5L engine

belt covers and confirm that all timing marks are in line.

3. Remove the distributor from the engine.

4. Looking down at the oil pump, the slot in the shaft must be parallel with the center line of the crankshaft. Drain the engine oil, remove the oil pan and remove the oil pump.

5. Loosen the timing belt tensioner and remove the timing belt.

6. Remove the intermediate sprocket retainer bolt while holding the sprocket stationary using tools C–4687 and adapter C–4687–1. Remove the sprocket from the shaft.

7. Remove the shaft retainer screws and the retainer from the block.

8. Remove the intermediate shaft from the engine.

9. If necessary, remove the front bushing using tool C–4697–2 and the rear bushing using tool C–4686–2.
To install:

10. Install the front bushing using tool C–4697–1 until the tool is flush with the block. Install the rear bush-

ing using tool C–4686–1 until the tool is flush with the block.

11. Lubricate the distributor drive gear and install the intermediate shaft into the block.

12. Replace the seal in the retainer and apply silicone sealer to the mating surface of the retainer. Install the retainer to the block and torque the bolts to 10 ft. lbs. (12 Nm).

13. Install the intermediate shaft sprocket and the timing belt.

14. With the timing belt properly installed, install the oil pump so the slot is parallel to the center line of the crankshaft. Install the distributor so the rotor is aligned with the No. 1 spark plug wire tower on the cap.

15. Install the remaining components removed during the removal procedure.

16. Connect the negative battery cable, add clean engine oil to the correct level, start the vehicle and check the oil pressure for the proper pressure reading.

17. Allow the engine to run until nor-

mal operating temperature is reached. Check and adjust the ignition timing and inspect for leaks. Road test the vehicle.

Balance Shafts

REMOVAL & INSTALLATION

2.5L Engine

1. Disconnect the negative battery cable. Raise the vehicle and support safely.

2. Remove the timing belt. Remove the oil pan, the oil pickup, the crankshaft belt sprocket and the front crankshaft oil seal retainer.

3. Remove the balance shaft chain cover, the guide and the tensioner.

4. Remove the balance shaft sprocket-to-shaft bolt, the gear cover-to-balance shaft bolt and the crankshaft sprocket-to-crankshaft bolts, then the sprockets with the balance shaft chain.

5. Remove the front gear cover-to-carrier housing stud, the gear cover and the balance shaft drive gears.

6. Remove the rear gear cover-to-carrier housing bolts, the rear cover and the balance shafts from the rear of the carrier.

7. If necessary, remove the carrier housing-to-crankcase bolts and the housing.
To install:

8. If the carrier housing is being installed, torque the carrier housing-to-crankcase bolts to 40 ft. lbs. (54 Nm).

9. Rotate the balance shafts until the keyways are facing upward, parallel to the vertical centerline of the engine.

10. Install the short hub gear on the sprocket driven shaft and the long hub gear on the gear driven shaft; make sure the gear timing marks are aligned facing each other.

11. Install the front gear cover and torque the front gear cover-to-carrier housing stud bolt to 8.5 ft. lbs. (12 Nm).

12. Install the balance chain sprocket and torque the sprocket-to-crankshaft bolts to 11 ft. lbs. (13 Nm).

13. Rotate the crankshaft to position

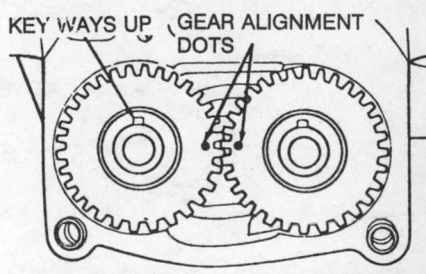

Aligning the balance shaft gear timing marks—2.5L engine

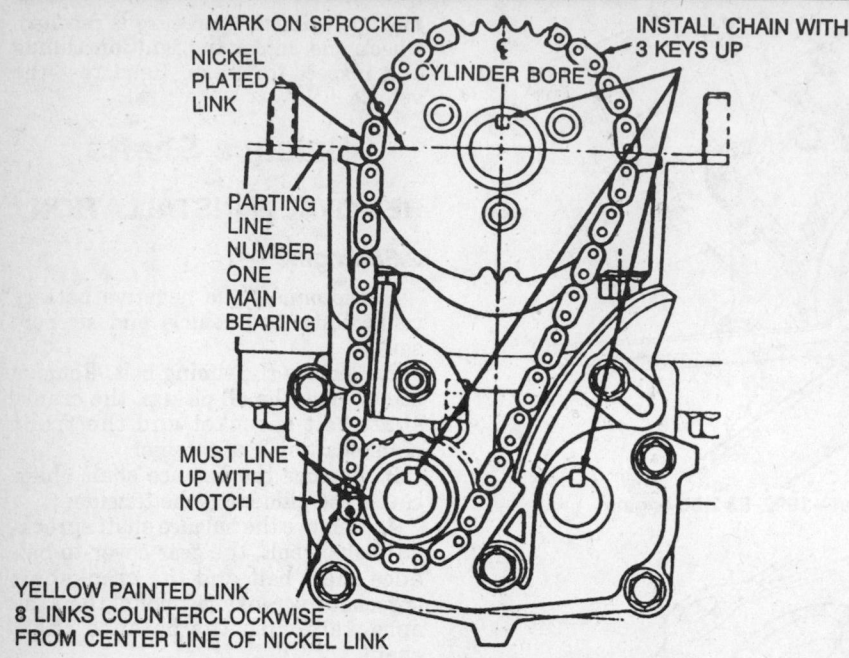

Balance shaft chain installation—2.5L engine

the No. 1 cylinder on the TDC of its compression stroke; the timing marks on the chain sprocket should align with the parting line on the left side of the No. 1 main bearing cap.

14. Position the balance shaft sprocket into the balance chain so the sprocket (yellow dot) timing mark mates with the yellow link on the chain.

15. Install the balance chain/sprocket assembly onto the crankshaft and the balance shaft. Torque the sprocket-to-shaft bolts to 21 ft. lbs. (28 Nm). If necessary to secure the crankshaft while tightening the bolts, place a block of wood between the crankcase and the crankshaft counterbalance.

16. Loosely install the chain tensioners and place a shim (0.039 in. × 2.75 in.) between the chain and the tensioner. In order to reduce the chain slack, apply firm pressure to the tensioner shoe. Torque the tensioner-to-front gear cover bolts to 8.5 ft. lbs. (12 Nm).

17. Install the chain cover and the rear cover to the carrier housing and

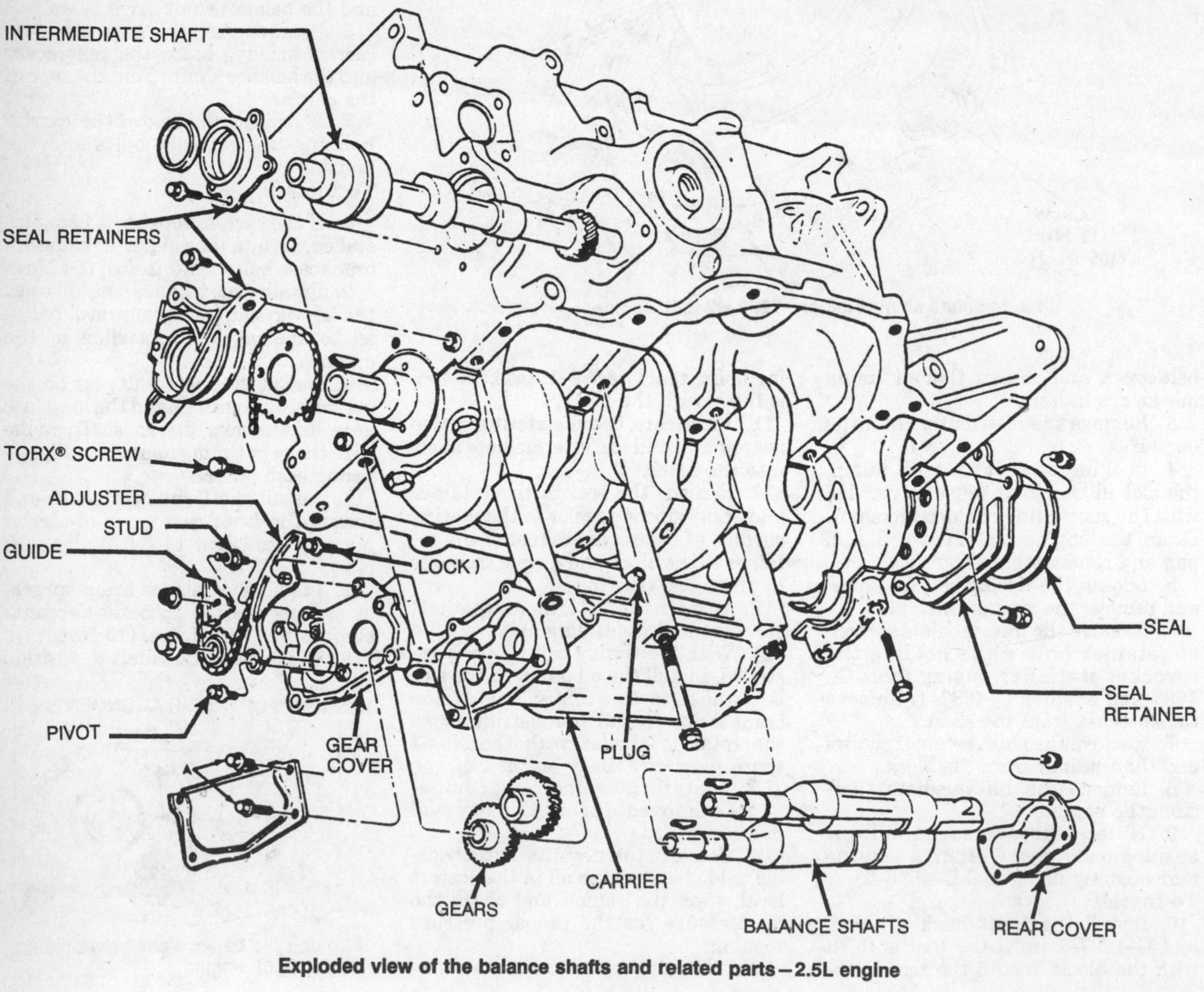

Exploded view of the balance shafts and related parts—2.5L engine

torque the bolts to 8.5 ft. lbs. (12 Nm).

18. Replace the crankshaft retainer seal, apply silicone sealer to the mating surface and install the retainer.

19. Install the oil pickup and oil pan.

20. Install the crankshaft sprocket and the timing belt.

21. Add clean engine oil to fill the crankcase to the proper level. Connect the negative battery cable, start the vehicle and check for proper oil pressure. Allow the engine to idle until normal operating temperature is reached. Check and adjust the ignition timing as required. Road test the vehicle.

Piston and Connecting Rod

POSITIONING

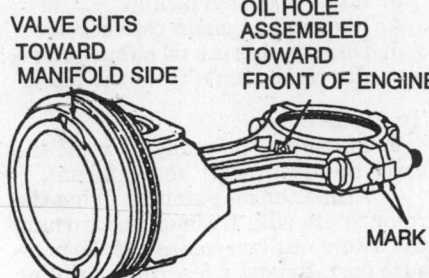

VALVE CUTS TOWARD MANIFOLD SIDE

OIL HOLE ASSEMBLED TOWARD FRONT OF ENGINE

MARK

Piston positioning—2.5L engine

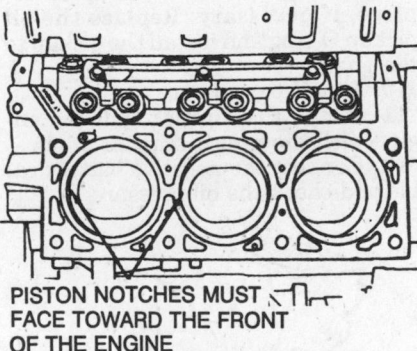

PISTON NOTCHES MUST FACE TOWARD THE FRONT OF THE ENGINE

Piston positioning—3.0L engine

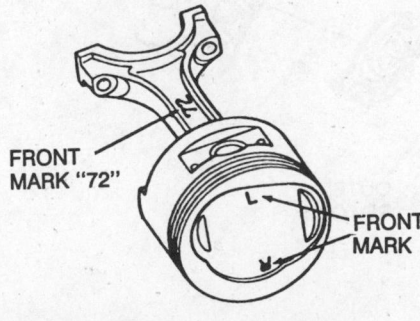

FRONT MARK "72"

FRONT MARK

Piston positioning—3.3L and 3.8L engines

ENGINE LUBRICATION

Oil Pan

REMOVAL & INSTALLATION

2.5L Engine

1. Disconnect the negative battery cable. Remove the oil dipstick.

2. Raise the vehicle and support safely.

3. Drain the engine oil.

4. Remove the engine to transaxle struts and the bellhousing inspection cover.

5. Remove the oil pan retaining screws. Remove the oil pan and the side seals from the engine block.

To install:

6. Thoroughly clean and dry all sealing surfaces, bolts and bolt holes.

7. Apply silicone sealer to the 4 end seal to block corners and install the end seals making sure the corners are not twisted.

8. Apply silicone to the 4 pan to block corners. Install a new pan gasket or apply silicone sealer to the sealing surface of the pan.

9. Install the oil pan to the engine block making sure not to dislodge the end seals.

10. Install the retaining screws and torque to 17 ft. lbs. (23 Nm).

11. Install the bellhousing inspection cover and engine to transaxle struts. Lower the vehicle.

12. Install the dipstick. Fill the engine with the proper amount of clean engine oil.

13. Connect the negative battery cable and check for leaks.

3.0L, 3.3L and 3.8L Engines

1. Disconnect the negative battery cable.

2. Raise the vehicle and support safely.

3. Remove the torque converter bolt access cover.

4. Drain the engine oil.

5. Remove the oil pan retaining screws and remove the oil pan and gasket.

To install:

6. Thoroughly clean and dry all sealing surfaces, bolts and bolt holes.

7. Apply silicone sealer to the chain cover-to-block mating seam and the rear main seal retainer-to-block seam, if equipped.

8. Install a new pan gasket or apply silicone sealer to the sealing surface of the pan, and install to the engine.

9. Install the retaining screws and torque to 50 inch lbs. (6 Nm).

10. Install the torque converter bolt access cover, if equipped. Lower the vehicle.

11. Install the dipstick. Fill the engine with the proper amount of clean engine oil.

12. Connect the negative battery cable and check for leaks.

Oil Pump

REMOVAL & INSTALLATION

2.5L Engine

1. Crank the engine around so the No. 1 piston is at TDC of its compression stroke. Disconnect the negative battery cable.

2. Matchmark the rotor to the block and remove the distributor. Confirm that the slot in the oil pump shaft is parallel to the centerline of the crankshaft. Matchmark the slot to the distributor bore, if desired.

3. Remove the oil dipstick. Raise the vehicle and support safely. Drain the engine oil and remove the pan.

4. Remove the oil pickup.

5. Remove the 2 mounting bolts and remove the oil pump from the engine.

To install:

6. Prime the pump by pouring fresh oil into the pump intake and turning the driveshaft until oil comes out the pressure port. Repeat a few times until no air bubbles are present.

7. Apply Loctite® 515 or equivalent, to the pump body-to-block machined surface interface. Lubricate the oil pump and distributor driveshaft.

8. Align the slot so it will be in the same position as when it was removed. If it is not, the distributor will not be timed correctly. Install the pump fully and rotate back and forth to ensure proper positioning between the pump mounting surface and the machined surface of the block.

9. Install the mounting bolts finger-tight and lower the vehicle to confirm proper slot positioning. If the slot is not properly positioned, raise the vehicle and move the gear, as required. If the slot is correct, hold the pump firmly against the block and torque the mounting bolts to 17 ft. lbs. (23 Nm).

10. Clean out the oil pickup or replace if necessary. Replace the oil pickup O-ring and install the pickup to the pump.

11. Install the oil pan using new gaskets. Lower the vehicle.

12. Install the distributor.

13. Install the dipstick. Add clean engine oil to fill the crankcase to the proper level.

14. Connect the negative battery cable, start the vehicle and check for

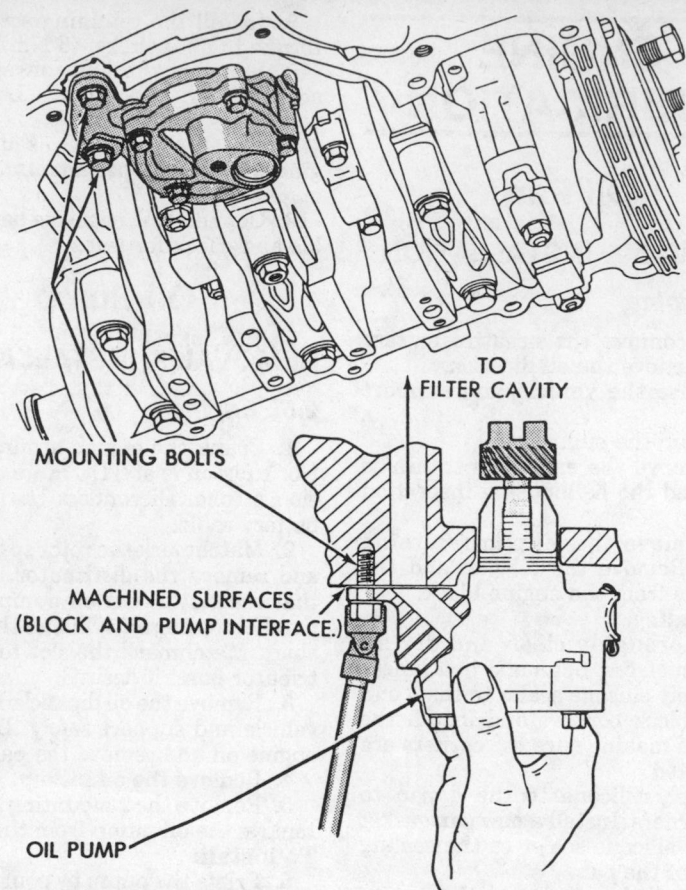

Aligning the slot in the oil pump shaft—2.5L engine

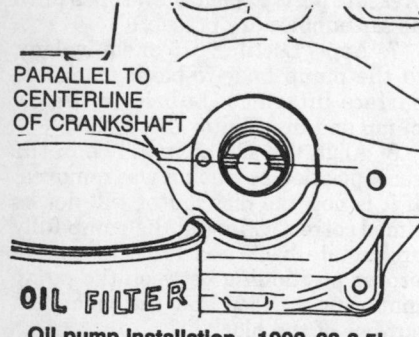

PARALLEL TO CENTERLINE OF CRANKSHAFT

OIL FILTER

Oil pump installation—1992-93 2.5L engine

proper oil pressure. Allow the engine to idle until normal operating temperature is reached. Check and adjust the ignition timing as required. Road test the vehicle.

3.0L Engine

1. Disconnect the negative battery cable. Remove the dipstick.
2. Raise the vehicle and support safely. Remove the timing belt, drain the engine oil and remove the oil pan from the engine. Remove the oil pickup.
3. Remove the oil pump mounting bolts and remove the pump from the front of the engine. Note the different

length bolts and their position in the pump for installation.

To install:
4. Clean the gasket mounting surfaces of the pump and engine block.
5. Prime the pump by pouring fresh oil into the pump and turning the rotors. Using a new gasket, install the oil

pump on the engine and torque all bolts to 11 ft. lbs. (15 Nm).
6. Install the balancer and crankshaft sprocket to the end of the crankshaft.
7. Clean out the oil pickup or replace, if necessary. Replace the oil pickup gasket ring and install the pickup to the pump.
8. Install the timing belt, oil pan and all related parts.
9. Install the dipstick. Fill the engine with the proper amount of oil.
10. Connect the negative battery cable and check the oil pressure.

3.3L and 3.8L Engines

1. Disconnect the negative battery cable. Remove the dipstick.
2. Raise the vehicle and support safely. Drain the oil and remove the oil pan.
3. Remove the oil pickup.
4. Remove the chain case cover.
5. Disassemble the oil pump and remove its components from the block.

To install:
6. Assemble the pump. Torque the cover screws to 10 ft. lbs. (12 Nm).
7. Prime the oil pump by filling the rotor cavity with fresh oil and turning the rotors until oil comes out the pressure port. Repeat a few times until no air bubbles are present.
8. Install the chain case cover.
9. Clean out the oil pickup or replace, if necessary. Replace the oil pickup O-ring and install the pickup to the pump.
10. Install the oil pan.
11. Install the dipstick. Fill the engine with the proper amount of oil.
12. Connect the negative battery cable and check the oil pressure.

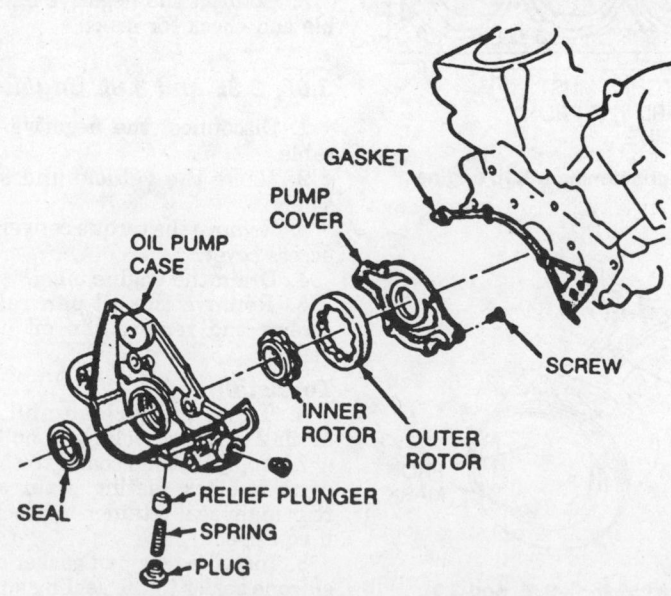

Exploded view of the oil pump—3.0L engine

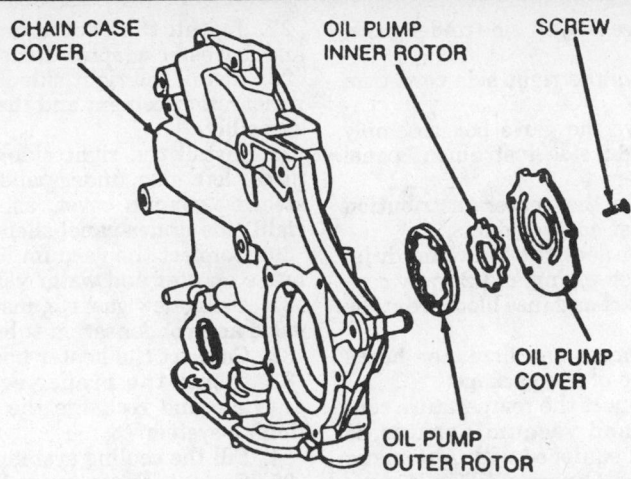

CHAIN CASE COVER · OIL PUMP INNER ROTOR · SCREW · OIL PUMP COVER · OIL PUMP OUTER ROTOR

Oil pump components—3.3L and 3.8L engines

CHECKING

2.5L Engine

1. Remove the cover from the oil pump.
2. Check end-play of the inner rotor using a feeler gauge and a straight-edge placed across the pump body. The specification is 0.001–0.004 in. (0.03–0.09mm).
3. Measure the clearance between the inner and outer rotors. The maximum clearance is 0.008 in. (0.20mm).
4. Measure the clearance between the outer rotor and the pump body. The maximum clearance is 0.014 in. (0.35mm).
5. The minimum thickness of the outer rotor is 0.944 in. (23.96mm). The minimum diameter of the outer rotor is 2.77 in. (62.70mm). The minimum thickness of the inner rotor is 0.943 in. (23.95mm).
6. Check the cover for warpage. The maximum allowable is 0.003 in. (0.076mm).
7. Check the pressure relief valve for damage. The spring's free length specification is 1.95 in. (49.50mm).
8. Assemble the outer rotor with the larger chamfered edge in the pump body. Torque the cover screws to 10 ft. lbs. (12 Nm).

3.0L Engine

1. Remove the rear cover.
2. Remove the pump rotors and inspect the case for excessive wear.
3. Measure the diameter of the inner rotor hub that sits in the case. Measure the inside diameter of the inner rotor hub bore. Subtract the first measurement from the second; if the result is over 0.006 in. (0.15mm), replace the oil pump assembly.
4. Measure the clearance between the outer rotor and the case. The specification is 0.004–0.007 in. (0.10–0.18mm).

5. Check the side clearance of the rotors using a feeler gauge and a straight-edge placed across the case. The specification is 0.0015–0.0035 in. (0.04–0.09mm).
6. Check the relief plunger and spring for damage and breakage.
7. Install the rear cover to the case.

3.3L and 3.8L Engines

1. Thoroughly clean and dry all parts. The mating surface of the chain case cover should be smooth. Replace the pump cover if it is scratched or grooved.
2. Lay a straight-edge across the pump cover surface. If a 0.003 in. (0.076mm) feeler gauge can be inserted between the cover and straight-edge, the cover should be replaced.
3. The minimum thickness of either rotor is 0.301 in. (7.63mm). The minimum diameter of the outer rotor is 3.14 in. (79.78mm).
4. Install the outer rotor onto the chain case cover, press to one side and measure the clearance between the rotor and case. If the measurement exceeds 0.022 in. (56mm) and the rotor is good, replace the chain case cover.
5. Install the inner rotor to the chain case cover and measure the clearance between the rotors. If the clearance exceeds 0.008 in. (0.203mm), replace both rotors.
6. Place a straight-edge over the chain case cover between bolt holes. If a 0.004 in. (0.102mm) thick feeler gauge can be inserted under the straight-edge, replace the pump assembly.
7. Inspect the relief valve plunger for scoring and freedom of movement. Small marks may be removed with 400 grit wet or dry sandpaper.
8. The relief valve spring should have a free length of 1.95 in.
9. Assemble the pump using new parts where necessary.

Rear Main Bearing Oil Seal

REMOVAL & INSTALLATION

1. Disconnect the negative battery cable.
2. Remove the transaxle. Remove the flexplate.
3. If there is any leakage coming from the rear seal retainer, drain the engine oil and remove the oil pan, if necessary. Remove the rear main oil seal retainer.
4. Remove the seal from the retainer.
To install:
5. Lightly coat the seal outer diameter with Loctite® Stud N' Bearing Mount or equivalent.
6. Install the seal to the retainer.
7. If the retainer was removed, thoroughly clean and dry the retainer to block sealing surfaces and install a new gasket or apply silicone sealer and install the retainer. Install the pan, if removed.
8. Install the flexplate and transaxle.
9. Connect the negative battery cable and check for leaks.

ENGINE COOLING

Radiator

REMOVAL & INSTALLATION

1. Disconnect the negative battery cable.
2. Drain the coolant.
3. Remove the upper hose and coolant reserve tank hose from the radiator.
4. Remove the electric cooling fan.
5. Raise the vehicle and support safely. Remove the lower hose from the radiator.
6. If the cooler is in the radiator, disconnect and plug the automatic transaxle cooler hoses. Lower the vehicle.
7. Remove the mounting brackets and carefully lift the radiator out of the engine compartment.
To install:
8. Lower the radiator into position.
9. Install the mounting brackets.
10. Raise the vehicle and support safely. Connect the automatic transaxle cooler lines, if disconnected.
11. Connect the lower hose. Lower the vehicle.

12. Install the electric cooling fan.

13. Connect the upper hose and coolant reserve tank hose.

14. Fill the system with coolant and bleed.

15. Connect the negative battery cable, run the vehicle until the thermostat opens, fill the radiator completely and check the automatic transaxle fluid level.

16. Once cooled, recheck the coolant level.

Electric Cooling Fan

CAUTION

Make sure the key is in the OFF position when working the electric cooling fan. If not, the fan could turn ON at any time, causing serious personal injury.

TESTING

1. Unplug the fan connector.

2. Using a jumper wire, connect the female terminal of the fan connector to the negative battery terminal.

3. The fan should come ON when the male terminal is connected to the positive battery terminal.

4. If not, the fan is defective and should be replaced.

REMOVAL & INSTALLATION

1. Disconnect the negative battery cable.

2. Unplug the vehicle harness connector from the fan connector.

3. Remove the mounting screws.

4. Remove the fan assembly from the vehicle.

5. The installation is the reverse of the removal procedure.

Heater Core

REMOVAL & INSTALLATION

1. Disconnect the negative battery cable. Properly discharge the air conditioning system. Drain the cooling system.

2. Clamp off the heater hoses near the heater core and remove the hoses from the core tubes. Plug the hose ends and the core tubes to prevent spillage of coolant.

3. Disconnect the H-valve connection at the valve and remove the H-valve. Remove the condensation tube.

4. Disconnect the vacuum lines at the brake booster and water valve, if equipped.

5. Remove the right upper and lower under-panel silencers.

6. Remove the steering column cover and the ash tray.

7. Remove the left side under-panel silencer.

8. Remove the right side cowl trim piece.

9. Remove the glove box assembly and the right side instrument panel reinforcement.

10. Remove the center distribution and defroster adaptor ducts.

11. Disconnect the relay module, blower motor wiring and 25-way connector bracket and fuse block from the panel.

12. Disconnect the demister hoses from the top of the package.

13. Disconnect the temperature control cable and vacuum harness, if equipped. If equipped with Automatic Temperature Control (ATC), disconnect the instrument panel wiring from the rear of the ATC unit.

14. Disconnect the hanger strap from the package and rotate it out of the way.

15. Remove the retaining nuts from the package mounting studs at the firewall.

16. Fold the carpeting and insulation back to provide a little more working room and to prevent spillage from staining the carpeting.

17. Move the package rearward to clear the mounting studs and lower.

18. Pull the right side of the instrument panel out as far as possible. Rotate the package while removing it from under the instrument panel.

19. To disassemble the housing assembly, remove the vacuum diaphragm, if equipped. Then remove the retaining screws from the cover and remove the cover.

20. Remove the retaining screw from the heater core and remove the core from the housing assembly.

To install:

21. Remove the temperature control door from the housing and clean the unit out with solvent. Lubricate the lower pivot rod and its well and install. Wrap the heater core with foam tape and place it in position. Secure it with its screw.

22. Assemble the package, making sure all vacuum tubing is properly routed.

23. If equipped, feed the vacuum lines through the hole in the firewall and install the assembly to the vehicle. Connect the vacuum harness and demister hoses. Install the nuts to the firewall and connect the hanger strap inside the passenger compartment.

24. Fold the carpeting back into position.

25. Connect the wiring to the ATC unit, if equipped.

26. Install the fuse block. Connect the 25-way connector, relay module and blower motor wiring.

27. Install the center distribution and defroster adaptor ducts.

28. Install the right side instrument panel reinforcement and the glove box assembly.

29. Install the right side cowl trim piece, left side under-panel silencer, steering column cover, ash tray and right side under-panel silencers.

30. Connect the vacuum lines at the brake booster and water valve.

31. Using new gaskets, install the H-valve and condensation tube.

32. Connect the heater hoses.

33. Using the proper equipment, evacuate and recharge the air conditioning system.

34. Fill the cooling system.

35. Connect the negative battery cable and check the entire climate control system for proper operation and leakage.

Water Pump

REMOVAL & INSTALLATION

2.5L Engine

1. Disconnect the negative battery cable.

2. Drain the cooling system.

3. Remove the air conditioning compressor from the bracket and position it to the side. It is not necessary to remove the refrigerant hoses from the compressor.

4. Remove the alternator and the solid bracket from the engine.

5. Remove the pulley from the water pump.

6. Disconnect the lower radiator hose and heater hose from the water pump.

7. Remove the water pump housing attaching screws and remove the assembly from the vehicle. Discard the O-ring.

8. Remove the water pump from the housing.

To install:

9. Using a new gasket or silicone sealer, install the water pump to the housing.

10. Install a new O-ring to the housing and install to the engine. Torque the bolts to 21 ft. lbs. (30 Nm).

11. Install the water pump pulley and torque the bolts to 21 ft. lbs. (30 Nm). Connect the radiator hose and heater hose to the water pump.

12. Install all items removed to gain access to the water pump, then adjust the belts.

13. Remove the hex-head plug on the top of the thermostat housing. Fill the radiator with coolant until the coolant comes out the plug hole. Install the plug and continue to fill the radiator.

14. Connect the negative battery cable, run the vehicle until the thermo-

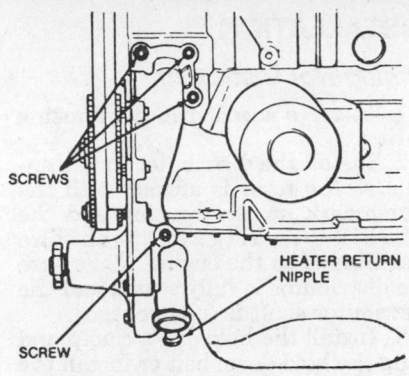

Water pump assembly—2.5L engine

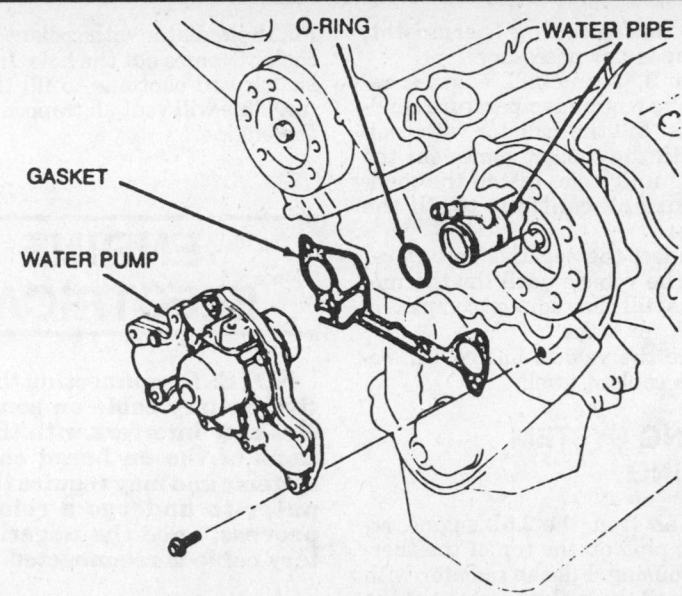

Water pump assembly—3.0L engine

stat opens, fill the radiator completely and check for leaks.

15. Once the vehicle has cooled, recheck the coolant level.

3.0L Engine

1. Disconnect the negative battery cable.
2. Drain the cooling system.
3. Remove the timing cover. If the same timing belt will be reused, mark the direction of the timing belt's rotation, for installation in the same direction. Make sure the engine is positioned so the No. 1 cylinder is at the TDC of its compression stroke and the sprockets timing marks are aligned with the engine's timing mark indicators.
4. Loosen the timing belt tensioner bolt and remove the belt. Position the tensioner as far away from the center of the engine as possible and tighten the bolt. Remove the water pump mounting bolts, separate the pump from the water inlet pipe and remove the pump from the engine.

To install:

5. Install the pump with a new gasket to the engine. Torque the water pump mounting bolts to 20 ft. lbs. (27 Nm).
6. If not already done, position both camshafts so the marks line up with those on the alternator bracket (rear bank) and inner timing cover (front bank). Rotate the crankshaft so the timing mark aligns with the mark on the oil pump.
7. Install the timing belt on the crankshaft sprocket and while keeping the belt tight on the tension side (right side), install the belt on the front camshaft sprocket.
8. Install the belt on the water pump pulley, then the rear camshaft sprocket and the tensioner.
9. Rotate the front camshaft counterclockwise to tension the belt between the front camshaft and the crankshaft. If the timing marks became misaligned, repeat the procedure.

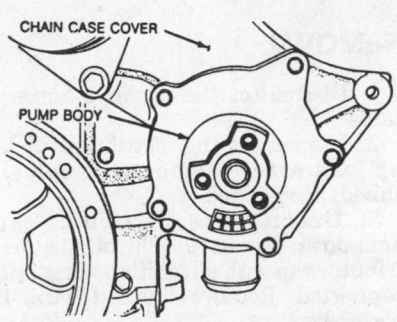

Water pump assembly—3.3L and 3.8L engines

10. Install the crankshaft sprocket flange.
11. Loosen the tensioner bolt and allow the spring to tension the belt.
12. Turn the crankshaft 2 full turns in the clockwise direction only until the timing marks align again. Now that the belt is properly tensioned, torque the tensioner lock bolt to 21 ft. lbs. (29 Nm).
13. Refill the cooling system. This system uses a self-bleeding thermostat, so there is no need to bleed the system. Connect the negative battery cable and road test the vehicle.

3.3L and 3.8L Engines

1. Disconnect the negative battery cable.
2. Drain the cooling system.
3. Remove the serpentine belt.
4. Raise the vehicle and support safely. Remove the right front tire and wheel assembly and lower fender shield.
5. Remove the water pump pulley.
6. Remove the 5 mounting screws and remove the pump from the engine.
7. Discard the O-ring.

To install:

8. Using a new O-ring, install the pump to the engine. Torque the mounting bolts to 9 ft. lbs. (12 Nm).
9. Install the water pump pulley.
10. Install the fender shield, tire and wheel assembly. Lower the vehicle.
11. Install the serpentine belt.
12. Remove the engine temperature sending unit. Fill the radiator with coolant until the coolant comes out the sending unit hole. Install the sending unit and continue to fill the radiator.
13. Connect the negative battery cable, run the vehicle until the thermostat opens, fill the radiator completely and check for leaks.
14. Once cooled, recheck the coolant level.

Thermostat

REMOVAL & INSTALLATION

1. Disconnect the negative battery cable. Drain the coolant down to thermostat level or below.
2. Remove the thermostat housing retaining bolts and the housing.
3. Remove the thermostat and discard the gasket.
4. Clean the housing mating surfaces and use a new gasket.
5. Install the thermostat into the housing with new gasket in place and secure using fasteners.
6. Fill the system with coolant as follows:
   a. On the 2.5L engine, remove the hex-head plug on the thermostat housing. Fill the radiator with coolant until the coolant comes out the plug hole. Install the plug and continue to fill the radiator.
   b. The 3.0L engine is equipped

with a self-bleeding thermostat; bleeding is not necessary.

    c. On 3.3L and 3.8L engines, remove the engine temperature sending unit. Fill the radiator with coolant until the coolant comes out the sending unit hole. Install the sending unit and continue to fill the radiator.

7. Connect the negative battery cable, run the vehicle until the thermostat opens, fill the radiator completely and check for leaks.

8. Once the vehicle has cooled, recheck the coolant level.

COOLING SYSTEM BLEEDING

To bleed air from the 2.5L engine, remove the plug on the top of the thermostat housing. Fill the radiator with coolant until the coolant comes out the hole. Install the plug and continue to fill the radiator. This will vent all trapped air from the engine.

    The thermostat in the 3.0L engine is equipped with a small air vent valve that allows trapped air to bleed from the system during refilling. This valve negates the need for cooling system bleeding in those engines.

    On 3.3L and 3.8L engines, remove the engine temperature sending unit.

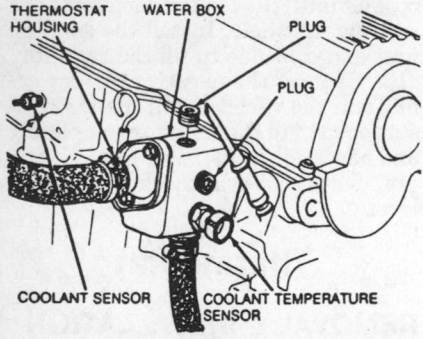

Cooling system bleed plug—2.5L engine

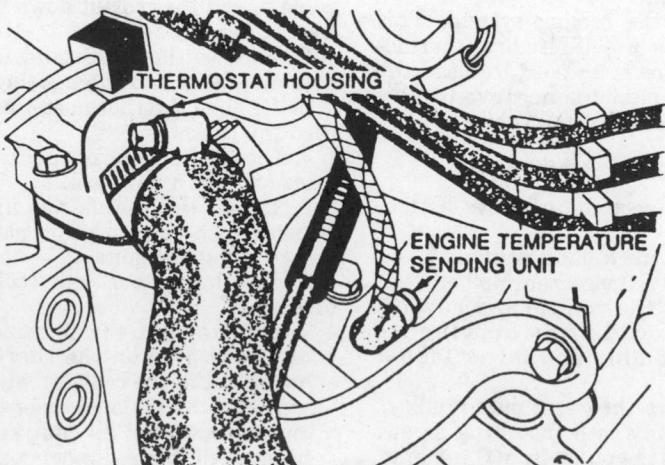

Coolant temperature sending unit location—3.3L and 3.8L engines

Fill the radiator with coolant until the coolant comes out the hole. Install the switch and continue to fill the radiator. This will vent all trapped air from the engine.

ENGINE ELECTRICAL

    NOTE: Disconnecting the negative battery cable on some vehicles may interfere with the functions of the on board computer systems and may require the computer to undergo a relearning process, once the negative battery cable is reconnected.

Distributor

REMOVAL

1. Disconnect the negative battery cable.
2. Disconnect the distributor pickup lead wires. Remove the splash shield, if equipped.
3. Unscrew the distributor cap hold-down screws and lift off the distributor cap with all ignition wires still connected. Remove the coil wire, if necessary.
4. Matchmark the rotor to the distributor housing and the distributor housing to the engine.

    NOTE: Do not crank the engine during this procedure. If the engine is cranked, the matchmark must be disregarded.

5. Remove the hold-down bolt and clamp or nut.
6. Remove the distributor from the engine.

INSTALLATION

Timing Not Disturbed

1. Install a new distributor housing O-ring.
2. Install the distributor in the engine so the rotor is aligned with the matchmark on the housing and the housing is aligned with the matchmark on the engine. Make sure the distributor is fully seated and the distributor shaft is fully engaged.
3. Install the hold-down clamp and snug the hold-down bolt or install the nut.
4. Connect the distributor pickup lead wires. Install the splash shield, if equipped.
5. Install the distributor cap and tighten the screws.
6. Connect the negative battery cable.
7. Adjust the ignition timing and tighten the hold-down bolt.

Timing Disturbed

1. Install a new distributor housing O-ring.
2. Position the engine so No. 1 piston is at TDC of the compression stroke and the mark on the vibration damper is aligned with **0** on the timing indicator.
3. Install the distributor in the engine so the rotor is aligned with the position of the No. 1 ignition wire on the distributor cap and the housing is aligned with the matchmark on the engine. Make sure the distributor is fully seated and the distributor shaft is fully engaged.

    NOTE: There are distributor cap runners inside the cap on 3.0L engine. Make sure the rotor is pointing to where the No. 1 runner originates inside the cap and not where the No. 1 ignition wire plugs into the cap.

4. Install the hold-down clamp and snug the hold-down bolt or install the nut.

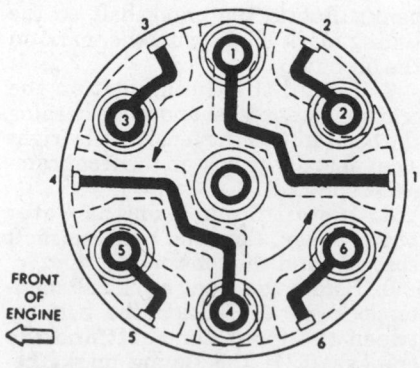

Distributor cap terminal routing—3.0L engine

5. Connect the distributor pickup lead wires. Install the splash shield, if equipped.

6. Install the distributor cap and tighten the screws.

7. Connect the negative battery cable.

8. Adjust the ignition timing and tighten the hold-down nut or bolt.

Distributorless Ignition System

REMOVAL & INSTALLATION

Ignition Coil

1. Disconnect the negative battery cable.

2. Remove the spark plug wires from the coil.

3. Disconnect the electrical connector.

4. Remove the coil mounting screws.

5. Remove the coil from the engine.

6. The installation is the reverse of the removal procedure.

Crankshaft Position Sensor

1. Disconnect the negative battery cable.

2. Disconnect the sensor lead at the harness connector.

3. Remove the sensor retaining bolt.

4. Pull the sensor straight up out the transaxle housing.

5. If the sensor is being reinstalled, remove any remains of the old spacer completely and attach a new spacer to the sensor. If a new spacer is not used, the sensor will not function properly. New sensors are packaged with a new spacer.

To install:

6. Install the sensor to the tranaxle housing and push the sensor down until it contacts the driveplate.

7. Hold in this position and install the retaining bolt. Torque to 9 ft. lbs. (12 Nm).

8. Connect the sensor lead wire and the negative battery cable.

Camshaft Position Sensor

1. Disconnect the negative battery cable.

2. Disconnect the sensor lead at the harness connector.

3. Loosen the sensor retaining bolt sufficiently to allow the slotted mounting surface to slide past the bolt.

4. Pull the sensor straight up and out of the chain case cover. Resistance may be high due to the rubber O-ring.

5. If the sensor is being reinstalled, remove any remains of the old spacer completely and attach a new spacer to the sensor. If a new spacer is not used,

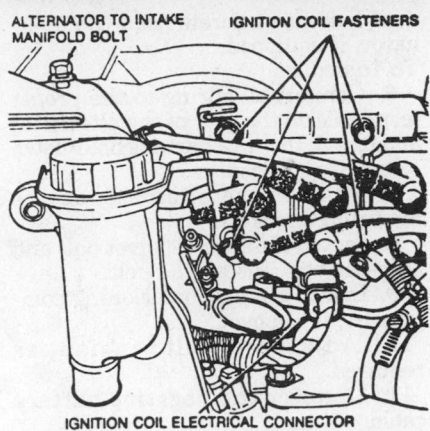

Ignition coil removal and installation— 3.3L and 3.8L engines

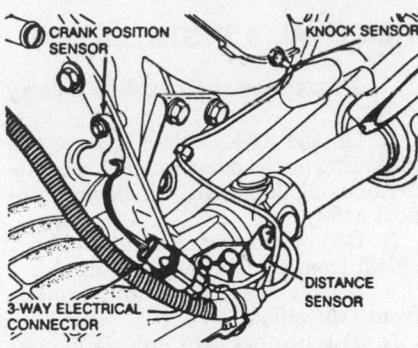

Crankshaft position sensor location— 3.3L and 3.8L engines

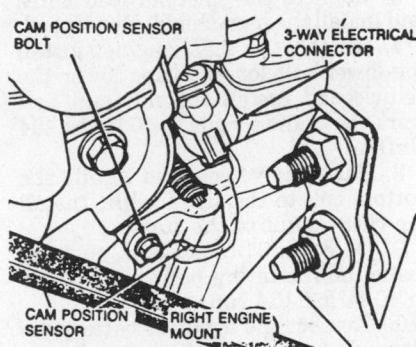

Camshaft position sensor location—3.3L and 3.8L engines

the sensor will not function properly. New sensors are packaged with a new spacer.

To install:

6. Inspect the O-ring for damage and replace, if necessary.

7. Lubricate the O-ring with oil. Install the sensor to the chain case cover and push the sensor into its bore until contact is made with the cam timing gear.

8. Hold in this position and tighten the bolt to 9 ft. lbs. (12 Nm).

9. Connect the wire and rout it away from the accessory drive belt.

Ignition Timing

ADJUSTMENT

NOTE: The ignition timing on the distributorless 3.3L and 3.8L engines cannot be changed or set.

1. Start the engine, set the parking brake and run the engine until at normal operating temperature. Keep all lights and accessories OFF.

2. If a magnetic timing unit is available, insert the probe into the receptacle near the timing scale. The scale is located on the top of the bellhousing on the 2.5L engine and near the crankshaft pulley on the 3.0L engine.

3. If a magnetic timing unit is not available, connect a conventional power timing light to the No. 1 cylinder spark plug wire.

4. Connect the red lead of a tachometer to the negative primary terminal of the coil and connect the black lead to a good ground.

5. Connect the Diagnostic Readout Box II (DRB II) and access the Basic Timing Mode. If the DRB II is not available, disconnect the coolant sensor located near the thermostat housing. The Check Engine light on the instrument panel must be ON.

6. Aim the timing light at the timing scale or read the magnetic timing unit.

7. Loosen the distributor hold-down bolt just enough so the distributor can be rotated.

8. Turn the distributor in the proper direction until the specified timing according to the VECI label is reached. Tighten the hold-down bolt or nut and recheck the timing.

9. Turn the engine OFF. Connect the coolant sensor. Make sure the Check Engine light does not come ON when the vehicle is restarted. Disconnect the timing apparatus and tachometer.

10. If the coolant temperature sensor was disconnected, erase the created fault code using the Erase Fault Code mode on the DRB II.

Alternator

PRECAUTIONS

Several precautions must be observed when working with the alternator to avoid damaging the unit.

● If the battery is removed for any reason, make sure it is reconnected with the correct polarity. Reversing the battery connections may result in damage to the one-way rectifiers.

● When utilizing a booster battery as a starting aid, always connect the positive to positive terminals and the negative terminal from the booster battery to a good engine ground on the vehicle being started.

• Never use a fast charger as a booster to start vehicles.

• Disconnect the battery cables when charging the battery with a fast charger.

• Never attempt to polarize the alternator.

• Do not use test lights of more than 12 volts when checking diode continuity.

• Do not short across or ground any of the alternator terminals.

• The polarity of the battery, alternator and regulator must be matched and considered before making any electrical connections within the system.

• Never separate the alternator on an open circuit. Make sure all connections within the circuit are clean and tight.

• Disconnect the battery ground terminal when performing any service on electrical components.

• Disconnect the battery if arc welding is to be done on the vehicle.

BELT TENSION ADJUSTMENT

NOTE: The belt tension is automatically adjusted by a dynamic tensioner on the 3.0L, 3.3L and 3.8L engines. Periodic adjustment is not necessary.

1. Loosen the pivot bolt slightly.
2. Raise the vehicle and support safely. Remove the splash shield. Loosen the "T" bolt locknut enough so the alternator can be moved.
3. Tighten the adjusting bolt until the belt deflects about ¼ in. under a 10 lb. load.
4. Tighten the "T" bolt locknut to 40 ft. lbs. (54 Nm).

REMOVAL & INSTALLATION

1. Disconnect the negative battery cable.
2. On the 2.5L engine, remove the air conditioning compressor and position it to the side.
3. On 3.0L, 3.3L and 3.8L engines, release the dynamic belt tensioner and remove the accessory drive belt. On 2.5L engine, loosen the mounting bolts, move the alternator toward the engine and remove the drive belt(s).
4. Remove the mounting bolts and spacers and remove the alternator from the brackets.
5. Remove the battery positive, field and ground terminals from the rear of the alternator. Remove the wire har-

ness hold-down screw from the alternator, if equipped.

To install:

6. Connect all wiring to the proper terminals on the rear of the alternator and install the wire harness hold-down screw, if equipped.
7. Position the alternator in the mounting brackets.
8. Install the spacers, pivot bolt and adjuster bolt. Install the belt.
9. Install the air conditioning compressor, if removed.
10. Adjust the belt tension, as required.
11. Connect the negative battery cable.

Starter

REMOVAL & INSTALLATION

1. Disconnect the negative battery cable.
2. On the 2.5L engine, remove the attaching nut and bolt at the top of the bellhousing. Raise the vehicle and support safely.
3. Remove the rear mount and heat shield from the starter, if equipped.
4. Unbolt the starter and remove from the vehicle.
5. Disconnect the solenoid lead wires from the starter.

To install:

6. Connect the solenoid lead wires and install the heat shield, if equipped.
7. On the 2.5L engine, install the lower bolt loosely, then lower the vehicle and install the nut and bolt from above and torque to 40 ft. lbs. (54 Nm).
8. Raise the vehicle and torque the bottom bolt to the same value. Install the rear mount to the starter.
9. On 3.0L, 3.3L and 3.8L engines, install all mounting bolts and torque to 40 ft. lbs. (54 Nm) evenly.
10. Connect the negative battery cable and check the starter for proper operation.

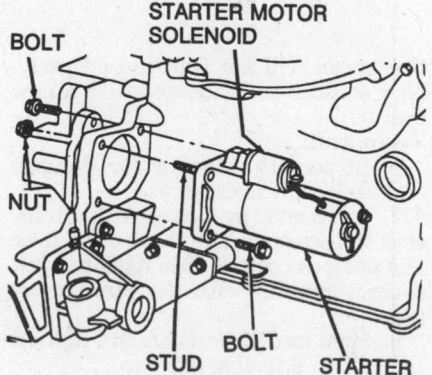

Starter mounting – 2.5L engine

EMISSION CONTROLS

Due to the complex nature of modern electronic engine control systems, comprehensive diagnosis and testing procedures fall outside the confines of this repair manual. For complete information on diagnosis, testing and repair procedures concerning all modern engine and emission control systems, please refer to "Chilton's Guide to Fuel Injection and Electronic Engine Controls".

Emission Warning Lamps

RESETTING

In order to reset the Emission Warning Lamp, actuate erase fault code data using the DRB II tester connected to the diagnostic connector located in the engine compartment near the engine controller.

FUEL SYSTEM

Fuel System Service Precautions

Safety is the most important factor when performing not only fuel system maintenance but any type of maintenance. Failure to conduct maintenance and repairs in a safe manner may result in serious personal injury or death. Maintenance and testing of the vehicle's fuel system components can be accomplished safely and effectively by adhering to the following rules and guidelines.

• To avoid the possibility of fire and personal injury, always disconnect the negative battery cable unless the repair or test procedure requires that battery voltage be applied.

• Always relieve the fuel system pressure prior to disconnecting any fuel system component (injector, fuel rail, pressure regulator, etc.), fitting or fuel line connection. Exercise extreme caution whenever relieving fuel system pressure to avoid exposing skin, face and eyes to fuel spray. Please be advised that fuel under pressure may penetrate the skin or any part of the body that it contacts.

• Always place a shop towel or cloth

around the fitting or connection prior to loosening to absorb any excess fuel due to spillage. Ensure that all fuel spillage (should it occur) is quickly removed from engine surfaces. Ensure that all fuel soaked cloths or towels are deposited into a suitable waste container.

● Always keep a dry chemical (Class B) fire extinguisher near the work area.

● Do not allow fuel spray or fuel vapors to come into contact with a spark or open flame.

● Always use a backup wrench when loosening and tightening fuel line connection fittings. This will prevent unnecessary stress and torsion to fuel line piping. Always follow the proper torque specifications.

● Always replace worn fuel fitting O-rings with new. Do not substitute fuel hose or equivalent where fuel pipe is installed.

RELIEVING FUEL SYSTEM PRESSURE

1. Loosen the fuel filler cap to release fuel tank pressure.
2. Locate and disconnect the fuel injector harness connector.

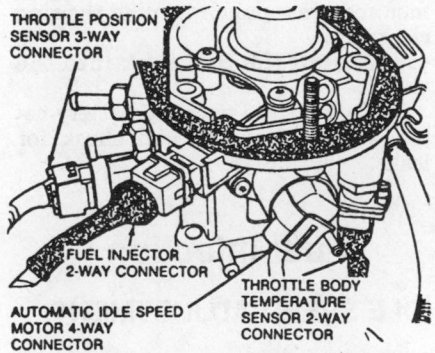

Fuel Injector harness location—2.5L engine

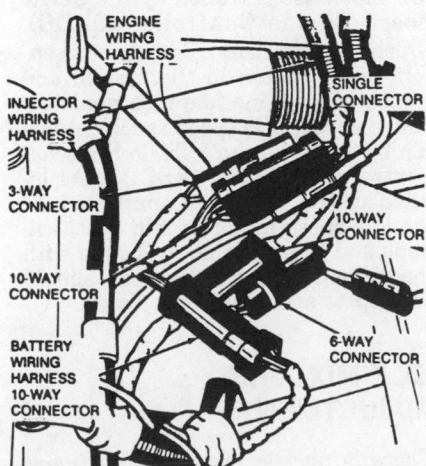

Fuel Injector harness location—3.3L and 3.8L engines

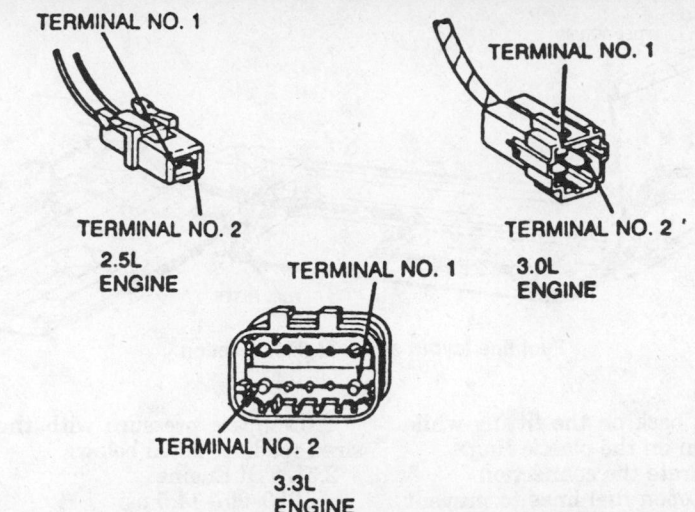

Fuel Injector harness connector terminal identification

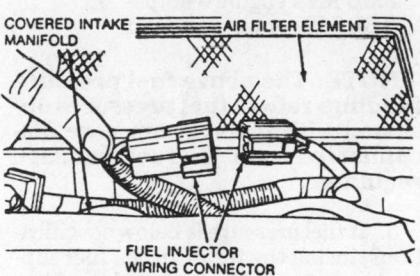

Fuel Injector harness location—3.0L engine

3. Connect a jumper wire from terminal No. 1 of the appropriate connector to ground.

4. Being careful not to allow contact between the jumper leads, connect a jumper wire to terminal No. 2 of the connector and touch the other end of the jumper to the positive battery post for no longer than 5 seconds. This will relieve fuel pressure.

5. Remove the jumper wires and continue with fuel system service.

Fuel Tank

REMOVAL & INSTALLATION

1. Disconnect the negative battery cable.
2. Release the fuel system pressure.
3. Raise the vehicle and support safely.
4. Using the proper equipment, drain the fuel tank.
5. Remove the screws that hold the filler neck to the quarter panel.
6. Disconnect the electrical wiring harness and fuel hoses from the tank.
7. Place a transmission jack or equivalent, under the center of the tank and apply slight pressure. Loosen the tank straps, lower the tank slightly and disconnect the hose from the pres-

sure relief rollover valve. Carefully remove the filler tube from the tank.

8. Remove the tank staps and lower the tank from the vehicle.

To install:
9. Raise the tank into position and connect all harnesses, fuel hoses and vacuum hoses.
10. Install the tank straps and tighten the retaining nuts.
11. Install the screws that hold the filler neck to the quarter panel.
12. Connect the negative battery cable, start the engine and check for leaks.

Fuel Filter

REMOVAL & INSTALLATION

——— CAUTION ———
Do not use conventional fuel filters, hoses or clamps when servicing this fuel system. They are not compatible with the injection system and could fail, causing personal injury or damage to the vehicle. Use only hoses and clamps specifically designed for fuel injection.

1. Disconnect the negative battery cable.
2. Release the fuel system pressure.
3. The filter is located on the frame rail toward the rear of the vehicle. Raise the vehicle and support safely. Remove the filter retaining screw and remove the filter assembly from the mounting plate.
4. Wrap a shop towel around the hoses to absorb fuel. Remove the hoses from the filter and fuel tube and discard the clamps and the filter. If equipped with Quick Connect fuel fittings, disconnect as follows:
   a. Remove any loose dirt from the fitting.

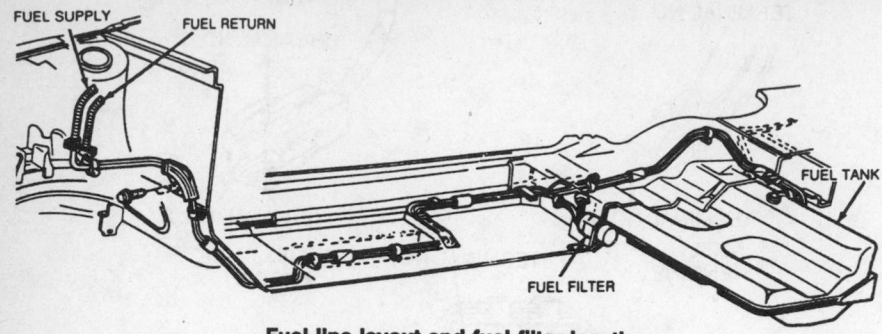

FUEL SUPPLY   FUEL RETURN

FUEL TANK

FUEL FILTER

Fuel line layout and fuel filter location

b. Pull back on the fitting while pushing in on the plastic ring.

c. Separate the connection.

5. Cover open fuel lines to prevent contamination.

To install:

6. Install the inlet hose on the fuel tube and tighten the new clamp to 10 inch lbs. If equipped with Quick Connect fittings, install as follows:

a. Lubricate the fuel tube nipple with clean 30W engine oil.

b. Insert the nipple into the Quick Connect fitting. The tube should be locked in place, if the connection is correctly made. If the tube will not lock, inspect the connection making sure the black plastic release is not causing the locking retainer to jam in the release position.

c. Using the DRB II, actuate the ASD Fuel System Test to pressurize the fuel system. Inspect the Quick Connect fitting for leaks.

7. Install the outlet hose on the filter outlet fitting and tighten the new clamp to 10 inch lbs.

8. Position the filter assembly on the mounting plate and tighten the mounting screw to 75 inch lbs. (8 Nm).

9. Connect the negative battery cable, start the engine and check for leaks.

Electric Fuel Pump

PRESSURE TESTING

1. Relieve the fuel pressure.

2. Properly connect the fuel system pressure tester:

a. 2.5L and 3.0L engines—special tool C-4799A or equivalent, is installed between the fuel supply hose and the engine fuel line assembly.

b. 3.3L and 3.8L engines—special tool C-4799A or equivalent, is installed to the fuel rail service valve.

3. With the key in the **RUN** position, put the DRB II in the activate auto shutdown relay mode; this will activate the fuel pump and pressurize the system.

4. Compare pressure with the desired readings listed below:

2.5L TBI Engine
1989–90—14.5 psi
1991–93—39 psi
3.0L MPI engine—48 psi
3.3L MPI engine—48 psi
3.8L MPI engine—48 psi

NOTE: The above fuel pressure readings reflect fuel pressures obtained with the vacuum hose disconnected from the fuel pressure regulator.

5. If fuel pressure is below specifications, install the tester in the fuel supply line between the tank and the filter and repeat the test.

6. If the pressure is 5 psi higher than in Step 5, replace the fuel filter. If no change is observed, squeeze the return hose. If pressure increases, replace the pressure regulator. If no change is observed, the problem is either a plugged in-tank sock filter or a defective pump.

7. If fuel pressure is above specifications, remove the fuel return line hose from the chassis line at the fuel tank and connect a 3 foot piece of fuel hose to the return line. Put the other end into a 2 gallon minimum capacity approved gasoline container. Repeat the test. If pressure is now correct, check the in-tank return hose for kinking. Replace the fuel pump assembly if the in-tank reservoir check valve or aspirator jet is obstructed.

8. If pressure is still above specifications, remove the fuel return hose from the throttle body. Connect a substitute hose to the throttle body return nipple and place the other end of the hose in a clean container. Repeat the test. If pressure is now correct, check for a restricted fuel return line. If no change is observed, replace the fuel pressure regulator.

REMOVAL & INSTALLATION

1. Disconnect the negative battery cable.

2. Release the fuel system pressure.

3. Raise the vehicle and support safely.

4. Using the proper equipment, drain the fuel tank.

5. Remove the fuel tank from the vehicle

6. Using a hammer and a brass drift, tap the lock ring counterclockwise to release the pump.

7. Partially pull the pump assembly, only 1 hose goes to the pump, which is bigger than the sending unit, out of the tank until the return line hose connection is visible at the bottom of the pump assembly.

8. Disconnect the fuel fitting.

9. Remove the pump from the tank with the O-ring. Discard the O-ring, pump inlet filter and inlet seal. Disassemble as required.

To install:

10. Install a new inlet seal and filter on the end of the pump.

11. Install a new O-ring to the pump.

12. Connect the reservoir hose to the pump assembly at the suction end of the pump. Press the female fitting onto the pump assembly male end until the ears snap in place.

13. Install the pump into the tank so the fuel return hose is not kinked.

14. Install the lock ring with a hammer and brass punch turning the ring clockwise.

15. Install the fuel tank into the vehicle.

16. Connect the negative battery cable, start the engine and check for leaks.

Fuel Injection

IDLE SPEED ADJUSTMENT

The idle speed is controlled by the Automatic Idle Speed (AIS) motor. The AIS motor is controlled by the Single Board Engine Controller (SBEC), which receives data from various sensors and switches in the system and adjusts the engine idle to a predetermined speed. Idle speed specifications can be found on the Vehicle Emission Control Information (VECI) label located in the engine compartment. If the idle speed is not within specifications and there are no problems with the system, the throttle body should be suspect and possibly replaced.

IDLE MIXTURE ADJUSTMENT

There is no idle mixture adjustment provided with any Chrysler fuel injection system.

Fuel Injector

REMOVAL & INSTALLATION

2.5L Engine

1. Disconnect the negative battery cable.
2. Remove the air cleaner assembly.
3. Relieve the fuel pressure.
4. Remove the injector hold-down Torx® screw and the hold-down.
5. Using a small flat-tipped tool, lift the cap off of the injector.
6. Using the same tool, gently pry the injector from its pod.
7. Remove the lower O-ring from the pod.

To install:

8. Install the new lower O-ring on the injector.
9. Align the injector terminal housing with the locating socket in the injector cap.
10. Press the injector cap so the upper O-ring flange is flush with the lower surface of the cap.
11. Spray the inner surfaces of the injector pod with carburetor parts cleaner to remove residual varnish and gasoline.
12. Lubricate the O-rings sparingly with clean oil.
13. Place the injector and cap into the injector pod and align the cap locating pin with the locating hole in the casting.

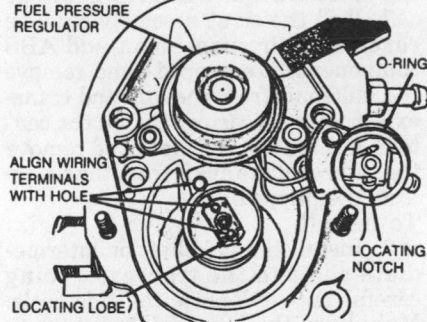

Fuel Injector Installation—2.5L engine

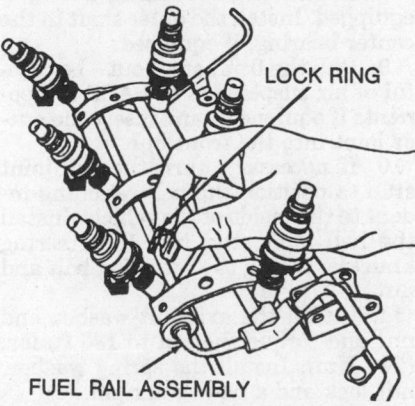

Fuel rail assembly—3.0L engine

14. Press firmly on the injector cap until it is flush with the casting surface.
15. Align the hole in the hold-down with the pin on the cap and install.
16. Push down on the cap, install the screw and torque to 35 inch lbs. (4 Nm).
17. Connect the negative battery cable and check for leaks using the DRB II to activate the fuel pump.
18. Install the air cleaner.

3.0L Engine

1. Disconnect the negative battery cable.
2. Relieve the fuel pressure.
3. Remove the air cleaner to throttle body hose.
4. Disconnect the throttle cable from the throttle body and disconnect the kickdown linkage. Remove the throttle cable bracket attaching bolts.
5. Disconnect the connectors to the throttle body.
6. Matchmark and carefully remove the vacuum hoses from the throttle body.
7. Remove the PCV and brake booster hoses from the air intake plenum.
8. Remove the ignition coil from the intake plenum, if mounted there.
9. Remove the EGR tube flange from the intake plenum, if equipped.
10. Unplug the coolant temperature sensor and charge temperature sensor, if equipped.
11. Remove the vacuum connection from the air intake plenum vacuum connector.
12. Remove the fuel hoses from the fuel rail and plug them.
13. Remove the air intake plenum to intake manifold bolts and remove the plenum and gaskets. Cover the intake manifold openings.
14. Remove the vacuum hoses from the fuel rail.
15. Disconnect the fuel injector wiring harness.
16. Remove the fuel rail attaching bolts and remove the fuel rail with the wiring harness from the vehicle. Position the rail on the bench upside down so the injectors are easily accessible.
17. Remove the small connector retainer clip and unplug the injector. Remove the injector clip off the fuel rail and injector. Pull the injector straight out of the rail.

To install:

18. Lubricate the rubber O-ring with clean oil and install to the rail receiver cap. Install the injector clip to the **TOP** slot of the injector, plug in the connector and install the connector clip.
19. Install the fuel rail to the vehicle and plug in the injector harness. Connect the vacuum hoses to the fuel rail.

20. Install new intake plenum gaskets with the beaded sealer side up and install the intake plenum. Torque the attaching bolts and nuts to 115 inch lbs. (13 Nm).
21. Install the fuel hoses to the fuel rail.
22. Install or connect all items that were removed or disconnected from the intake plenum and throttle body.
23. Connect the negative battery cable and check for leaks using the DRB I or II to activate the fuel pump.

3.3L and 3.8L Engines

1. Disconnect the negative battery cable.
2. Release the fuel system pressure.
3. Remove the air cleaner and hose assembly.
4. Disconnect the throttle cable. Remove the wiring harness from the throttle cable bracket and intake manifold water tube.
5. Remove the vacuum hose harness from the throttle body.
6. Remove the PCV and brake booster hoses from the air intake plenum.
7. Remove the EGR tube flange from the intake plenum, if equipped.
8. Unplug the charge temperature sensor and unplug all vacuum hoses from the intake plenum.
9. Remove the cylinder head to intake plenum strut.
10. Disconnect the MAP sensor and oxygen sensor connector. Remove the engine mounted ground strap.
11. Release the fuel hose quick disconnect fittings and remove the hoses from the fuel rail. Plug the hoses to prevent contamination of the system. Always place a shop towel or cloth around the fitting or connection prior to loosening to absorb any excess fuel due to spillage.
12. Remove the Direct Ignition System (DIS) coils and the alternator bracket-to-intake manifold bolt.
13. Remove the intake manifold bolts and rotate the manifold back over the rear valve cover. Cover the intake manifold.
14. Remove the vacuum harness from the pressure regulator.
15. Remove the fuel tube retainer bracket screw and fuel rail attaching bolts. Spread the retainer bracket to allow for clearance when removing the fuel tube.
16. Remove the fuel rail injector wiring clip from the alternator bracket.
17. Disconnect the cam sensor, coolant temperature sensor and engine temperature sensor.
18. Remove the fuel rail from the engine taking care not to damage or drop injectors during removal.
19. Position the rail on a work bench so the injectors are easily accessible.

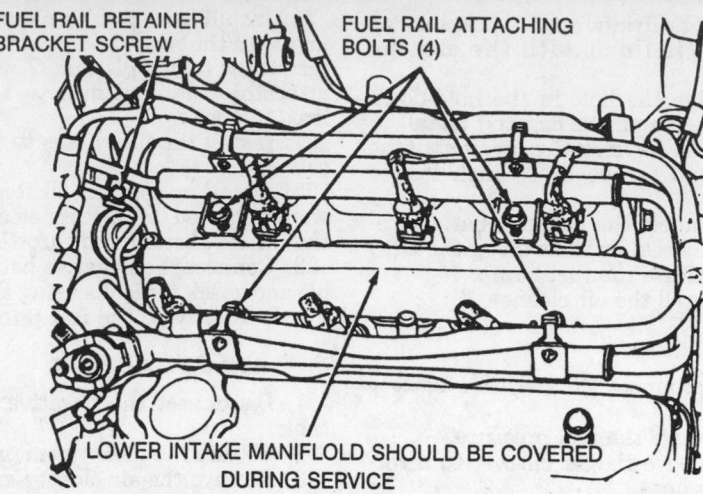

FUEL RAIL RETAINER
BRACKET SCREW

FUEL RAIL ATTACHING
BOLTS (4)

LOWER INTAKE MANIFLOLD SHOULD BE COVERED
DURING SERVICE

Fuel rail assembly—3.3L and 3.8L engines

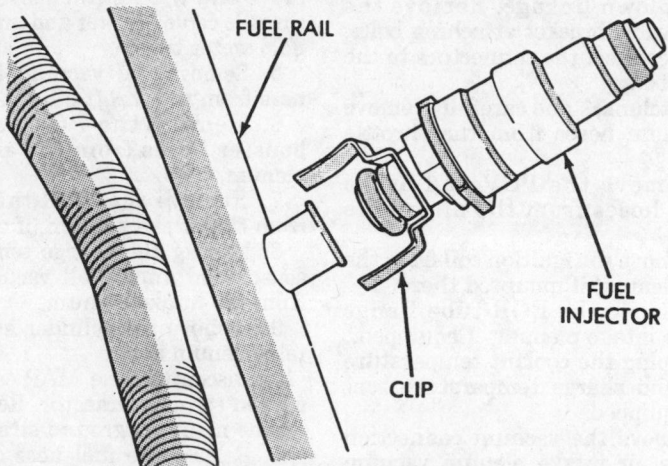

FUEL RAIL

FUEL
INJECTOR

CLIP

Fuel injector removal—1992–93 3.3L and 3.8L engines

20. On 1989–91 engines, remove the injectors from the fuel rail by removing the small connector retainer clip. Pull the injector straight out of the rail.

21. On 1992–93 engines, remove the injectors from the fuel rail by rotating while lightly pulling the injector from the fuel rail. The retainer spring clip will stay on the injector. Inspect the clip, if damaged it will require replacement.

To install:

22. Lubricate the rubber O-ring on the injector with clean oil.

23. On 1989–91 engines, install the injector to the fuel rail receiver cap and install the clip to the slot in the injector, plug in the connector and install the connector retainer clip.

24. On 1992–93 engines, install the injector retainer clip by sliding the open end into the **TOP SLOT** of the injector. The edge of the receiver cup will slide into the side slots in the clip. Install the injector top end into the fuel rail receiver cup taking care not to damage the O-ring during installation.

25. Install the fuel rail to the engine. Connect the harness connectors to each injector.

26. Connect the cam sensor, coolant temperature sensor and engine temperature sensor.

27. Install the fuel rail injector wiring clip to the alternator bracket.

28. Install the fuel rail attaching bolts and fuel tube retainer bracket screw.

29. Install the vacuum harness to the pressure regulator.

30. Install the intake manifold with a new gasket. Install the bolts only finger-tight. Install the alternator bracket to intake manifold bolt and the cylinder head to intake manifold strut and bolts. Torque the intake manifold mounting bolts to 21 ft. lbs. (28 Nm) starting from the middle and working outward. Torque the bracket and strut bolts to 40 ft. lbs. (54 Nm).

31. Install or connect all items that were removed or disconnected from the intake manifold and throttle body.

32. Connect the fuel hoses to the rail. Push the fittings in until they click in place.

33. Install the air cleaner assembly.

34. Connect the negative battery cable and check for leaks using the DRB II to activate the fuel pump.

DRIVE AXLE

Halfshaft

REMOVAL & INSTALLATION

1. Disconnect the negative battery cable.

2. Raise the vehicle and support safely. Remove the tire and wheel assembly.

3. Remove the cotter pin from the end of the halfshaft. Remove the nut lock, spring washer, axle nut and washer.

4. Remove the speedometer pinion retainer bolt from the extension housing on the transaxle and remove the pinion by pulling upward. The pinion must be removed prior to removing the right side halfshaft or damage to the speedometer pinion may occur.

5. Remove the ball joint retaining bolt and pry the control arm down to release the ball stud from the steering knuckle.

6. Position a drain pan under the transaxle where the halfshaft enters the differential or extension housing.

7. Pull the strut assembly out—be careful of air suspension and ABS components if equipped—and remove the halfshaft from the hub and transaxle or center bearing. Unbolt the center bearing from the block and remove the intermediate shaft from the transaxle, if equipped.

To install:

8. Install the halfshaft or intermediate shaft to the transaxle, being careful not to damage the side seals. Make sure the inner joint clicks into pace inside the differential. Install the center bearing retaining bolts, if equipped. Install the outer shaft to the center bearing, if equipped.

9. Pull the front strut out—be careful of air suspension and ABS components if equipped—and insert the outer joint into the front hub.

10. If necessary, turn the ball joint stud to position the bolt retaining indent to the inside of the vehicle. Install the ball joint stud into the steering knuckle. Install the retaining bolt and nut.

11. Install the axle nut washer and nut and torque the nut to 180 ft. lbs. (244 Nm). Install the spring washer, nut lock and a new cotter pin.

12. Install the tire and wheel assembly.

CV-Boot

REMOVAL & INSTALLATION

NOTE: Use only clamps provided with the replacement package when servicing. Plastic wire ties and other straps will not clamp tightly enough and grease will sling out causing costly damage to the joint.

Inner Joint

1. Raise the vehicle and support safely. Remove the halfshaft from the vehicle.
2. If cutting the boot away, mark and note the boot positioning on the shaft relative to the raised shoulders. Remove the boot clamps to gain access to the tripod retention system.
3. Separate the housing from the tripod according to the following:

NOTE: Always hold the rollers in place when removing the housing from the tripod or the needle bearing may fall out.

   a. G.K.N. — Has retaining tabs integral with the housing cover. Hold the housing and lightly compress the CV-joint retention spring while bending the tabs back. Support the housing as the retention spring pushes it from the housing.

   b. S.S.G. — Uses a wire ring tripod retainer which expands into a groove around the top of the housing. Use a tool to pry the wire ring, without damaging it, out of the groove and slide the tripod from the housing.

4. Remove the snapring from the end of the shaft and remove the tripod.
5. If not already done, mark the boot positioning on the shaft, relative

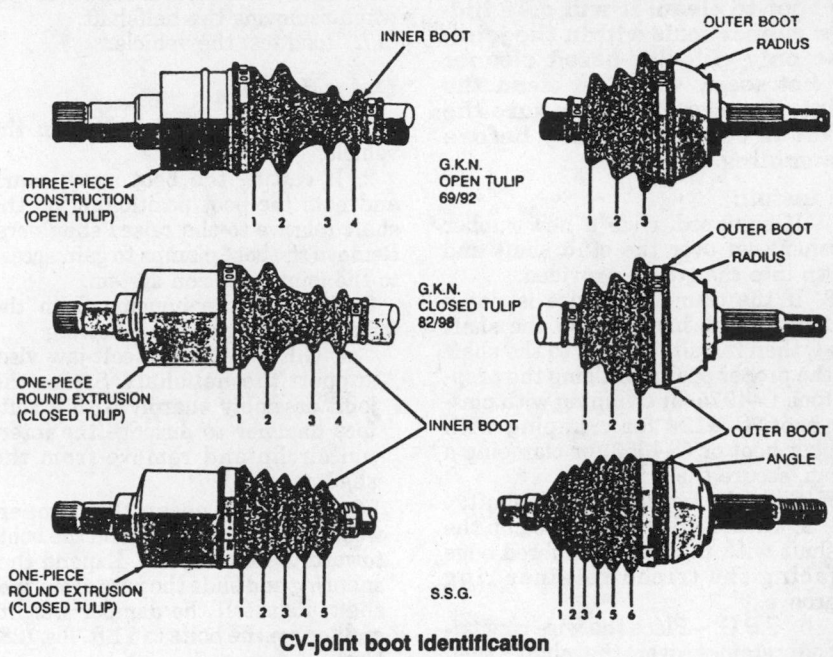

CV-joint boot identification

Exploded view of a typical halfshaft

to the raised shoulders and remove the boot from the shaft.

6. Remove as much old grease as possible from the joint. Inspect all parts for wear or damage.

NOTE: Do not use petroleum-based solvents on the joints, shaft or boot to clean; it will ruin hidden rubber seals within the joint. Use only chlorine-based cleaner or hot soapy water to clean the joint, if necessary. Make sure the joint is completely dry before assembling.

To install:

7. If equipped, slide a new rubber washer seal over the stub shaft and down into the groove provided.

8. If the clamping device is not a straight strap, install it on the shaft first, then install the boot to the shaft in the proper position. Using the proper tool, C–4975 for crimping with plastic boot, C–4124 for crimping with rubber boot or C–4653 for clamping a strap, secure the clamp.

9. Slide the tripod onto the shaft:

a. G.K.N – Slide the tripod on the shaft with the non-chamfered edge facing the tripod retainer ring groove.

b. S.S.G. – Place the wire ring tripod retainer over the shaft, then slide the tripod. The tripod may installed either way; both ends are the same.

10. Install the snapring into its groove on the shaft to lock the tripod in position.

11. Distribute the grease provided in the grease package as follows, or according to the instructions in the package:

a. G.K.N – If equipped with 3 packets of grease, distribute 2 of the 3 packets into the boot and the remaining packet into the housing. Otherwise, distribute ½ of the packet of grease into the boot and the remaining amount into the housing.

b. S.S.G. – Distribute ½ of the packet of grease into the boot and the remaining amount into the housing.

12. Position the spring in the housing spring pocket with the spring cup attached to the exposed end of the spring. Place a dab of grease on the concave surface of the spring cup.

13. Keeping the spring centered, install the housing to the tripod as follows:

a. G.K.N – Slip the housing onto the tripod. Bend the retaining tabs back into their original positions. Check for proper retention ability.

b. S.S.G. – Slip the housing onto the tripod and install the tripod wire retaining ring. Check for proper retention ability.

14. Position the larger end of the boot over the housing.

15. Using the proper tool, C–4975 for crimping with plastic boot, C–4124 for crimping with rubber boot or C–4653 for clamping a strap, secure the clamp.

16. Install the halfshaft to the vehicle. Fill the transaxle if fluid was lost when removing the halfshaft.

17. Road test the vehicle.

Outer Joint

1. Remove the halfshaft from the vehicle.

2. If cutting the boot away, mark and note the boot positioning on the shaft relative to the raised shoulders. Remove the boot clamps to gain access to the joint retention system.

3. Separate the housing from the tripod according to the following:

a. G.K.N – Using a soft-jaw vise, support the halfshaft. Strike the joint assembly sharply with a soft-face hammer to dislodge the internal circlip and remove from the shaft.

b. S.S.G. – Loosen the damper weight bolts and slide it and the boot toward the inner joint. Expand the snapring and slide the joint from the shaft. Reinstall the damper weight and torque the bolts to 21 ft. lbs. (28 Nm).

4. If damaged, remove the wear sleeve from the CV-joint machined ledge.

5. Remove the circlip from the groove.

6. If not already done, mark the boot positioning on the shaft, relative to the raised shoulders and remove the boot from the shaft.

7. Remove as much old grease as possible from the joint. Inspect all parts for wear or damage.

NOTE: Do not use petroleum-based solvents on the joints, shaft or boot to clean; it will ruin hidden rubber seals within the joint. Use only chlorine-based cleaner or hot soapy water to clean the joint, if necessary. Make sure the joint is completely dry before assembling.

To install:

8. If the clamping device is not a straight strap, install it on the shaft first, then install the boot to the shaft in the proper position. Using the proper tool, C–4975 for crimping with plastic boot, C–4124 for crimping with rubber boot or C–4653 for clamping a strap, secure the clamp.

9. Install a new circlip if provided in the replacement package. Fill the boot with the proper amount of grease according to the instructions provided with the package.

10. Position the outer joint on the shaft with hub nut installed, engage the splines and strike sharply with a soft-face hammer to install. Make sure the circlip did not become dislodged.

11. Position the larger end of the boot over the housing.

12. Using the proper tool, C–4975 for crimping with plastic boot, C–4124 for crimping with rubber boot or C–4653 for clamping a strap, secure the clamp.

13. Install the halfshaft to the vehicle. Fill the transaxle if fluid was lost during halfshaft removal.

14. Road test the vehicle.

Front Wheel Hub and Bearing

REMOVAL & INSTALLATION

Pressed In (Two-Piece Hub and Bearing)

NOTE: Some hub and bearing replacement packages include the one-piece unit described below. If this is the case, follow the installation steps for one-piece unit instead of for the two-piece unit described here.

1. Loosen the hub nut while the vehicle is on the floor and the brakes are applied. Raise and safely support the vehicle.

2. Remove the tire and wheel assembly. Remove the brake caliper from the adaptor and remove the adaptor. Remove the brake disc.

3. Remove the hub nut and the washer from the stub shaft.

4. Disconnect the tie rod end from the steering arm using the appropriate puller.

5. Remove the clamp bolt securing the ball joint stud into the steering knuckle and separate.

6. Matchmark the lower strut mount to the knuckle. Remove the 2 strut clamp bolts and remove the knuckle from the vehicle.

7. Attach the hub removal tool C–4811 or equivalent, and the triangular adapter, to the 3 rear threaded holes of the steering knuckle housing with the thrust button inside the hub bore.

8. Tighten the bolt in the center of the tool, to press the hub from the steering knuckle. Remove the removal tools.

9. Remove the bolts and bearing retainer from the outside of the steering knuckle.

10. Carefully pry the bearing seal from the machined recess of the steering knuckle and clean the recess.

11. Insert tool C–4811, or equivalent through the hub bearing and install bearing removal adapter to the outside of the steering knuckle. Tighten the

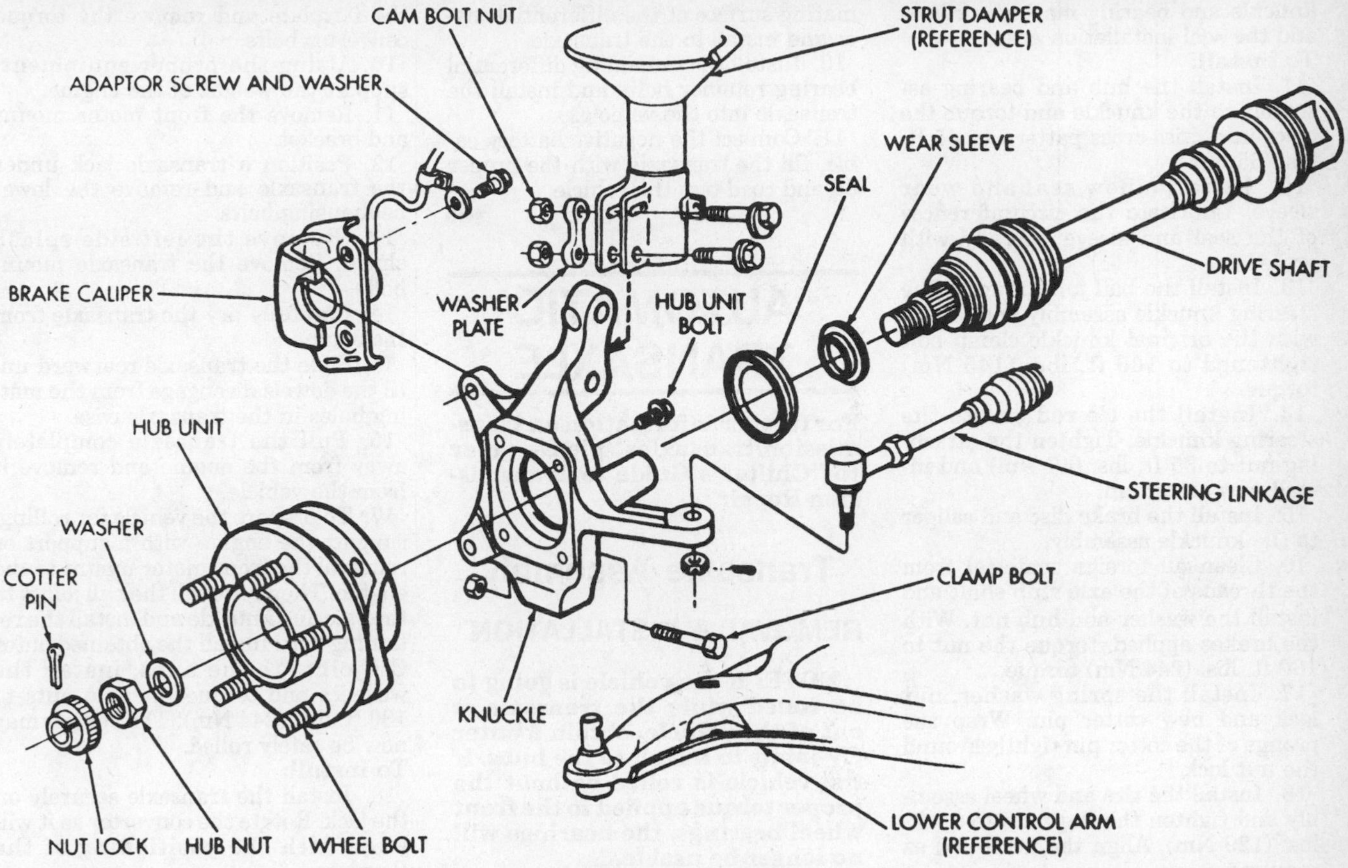

Front suspension components

Labels: CAM BOLT NUT, ADAPTOR SCREW AND WASHER, STRUT DAMPER (REFERENCE), WEAR SLEEVE, SEAL, BRAKE CALIPER, DRIVE SHAFT, WASHER PLATE, HUB UNIT BOLT, HUB UNIT, STEERING LINKAGE, WASHER, COTTER PIN, CLAMP BOLT, NUT LOCK, HUB NUT, WHEEL BOLT, KNUCKLE, LOWER CONTROL ARM (REFERENCE)

tool to press the hub bearing from the steering knuckle. Discard the bearing and the seal.

To install:

12. Use tool C–4811 or equivalent, and the bearing installation adapter to press in the hub bearing into the steering knuckle.

13. Install a new seal, the bearing retainer and the bolts to the steering knuckle. Torque the bearing retainer bolts to 20 ft. lbs. (27 Nm).

14. Use the tool C–4811 or equivalent, and the hub installation adapter, to press the hub into the hub bearing.

15. Using the bearing installation tool C–4698 or equivalent, drive the new dust seal into the rear of the steering the hub and bearing from the knuckle as required.

16. Install the steering knuckle onto the vehicle guiding the halfshaft through the hub and install the 2 strut strut bolts. Align the matchmarks made during disassembly and tighten the nuts. The vehicle will require a front end alignment.

17. Install the ball joint stud into the steering knuckle and secure with the original knuckle clamp bolt tightened to 70 ft. lbs. (95 Nm).

18. Install the tie rod end to the steering knuckle. Tighten the attach-

ing nut to 35 ft. lbs. (47 Nm) and install new cotter pin.

19. Install the brake disc and caliper to the knuckle assembly.

20. Clean all foreign material from the threads of the axle stub shaft and install the washer and hub nut. With the brakes applied, torque the nut to 180 ft. lbs. (244 Nm) torque.

21. Install the spring washer, nut lock and new cotter pin. Wrap the prongs of the cotter pin tightly around the nut lock.

22. Install the tire and wheel assembly and tighten the lug nuts to 95 ft. lbs. (129 Nm).

23. Align the front end of the vehicle and road test.

Bolt In (One-Piece Hub and Bearing)

NOTE: Knuckle removal is not necessary for bearing and hub replacement. If the hub and bearing assembly requires replacement, it is to replaced as an assembly.

1. Loosen the hub nut while the vehicle is on the floor and the brakes are applied. Raise and safely support the vehicle.

2. Remove the tire and wheel assembly from the vehicle.

3. Remove the hub nut and the washer from the stub shaft.

4. Disconnect the tie rod end from the steering arm using the appropriate puller.

5. Remove the clamp bolt securing the ball joint stud into the steering knuckle and separate.

6. Remove the caliper guide pin bolts and separate the caliper assembly from the braking disc. Support the caliper with wire hook and not by the hydraulic hose.

7. Separate the steering knuckle assembly from the ball joint stud. Pull the knuckle assembly out and away from the halfshaft.

NOTE: Care must be taken when separating the halfshaft from the knuckle, do not separate the inner CV-joint during this operation. Do not allow the halfshaft to hang by the inner CV-joint, it must be supported.

8. Remove the 4 hub and bearing assembly mounting bolts from the rear of the knuckle and remove the assembly from the knuckle.

9. Carefully pry the bearing seal from the machined recess of the steering knuckle and clean the recess.

10. Thoroughly clean and dry the

knuckle and bearing mating surfaces and the seal installation area.

To install:

11. Install the hub and bearing assembly to the knuckle and torque the bolts in a criss-cross pattern to 45 ft. lbs. (65 Nm).

12. Install a new seal and wear sleeve. Lubricate the circumferences of the seal and sleeve liberally with grease.

13. Install the ball joint stud to the steering knuckle assembly and secure with the original knuckle clamp bolt tightened to 105 ft. lbs. (145 Nm) torque.

14. Install the tie rod end to the steering knuckle. Tighten the attaching nut to 35 ft. lbs. (47 Nm) and install new cotter pin.

15. Install the brake disc and caliper to the knuckle assembly.

16. Clean all foreign material from the threads of the axle stub shaft and install the washer and hub nut. With the brakes applied, torque the nut to 180 ft. lbs. (244 Nm) torque.

17. Install the spring washer, nut lock and new cotter pin. Wrap the prongs of the cotter pin tightly around the nut lock.

18. Install the tire and wheel assembly and tighten the lug nuts to 95 ft. lbs. (129 Nm). Align the front end as required.

Differential Case

REMOVAL & INSTALLATION

1. Disconnect the negative battery cable.

2. Remove the transaxle from the vehicle.

3. Remove the right side extension housing from the transaxle.

4. Remove the differential cover retaining bolt and the cover from the transaxle.

5. Remove the differential bearing retainer bolts and the side differential bearing retainer, located on the left side of the transaxle, using tool L–4435 or equivalent. Use caution and take note of shims and their positioning, they can be dislodged during removal.

6. Remove the differential case from the transaxle.

To install:

7. Install the differential case into the transaxle and secure by installing the differential bearing retainer and 3 retainer bolts.

8. Apply RTV sealant around the inner surface of the extension housing under the O-ring and install to the transaxle. Install the 2 extension housing retainer bolts.

9. Apply a bead of sealer around the

mating surface of the differential cover and install to the transaxle.

10. Install the remaining differential bearing retainer bolts and install the transaxle into the vehicle.

11. Connect the negative battery cable, fill the transaxle with the proper oil and road test the vehicle.

AUTOMATIC TRANSAXLE

For further information on transmission/transaxles, please refer to "Chilton's Guide to Transmission Repair".

Transaxle Assembly

REMOVAL & INSTALLATION

NOTE: If the vehicle is going to be rolled while the transaxle is out of the vehicle, obtain 2 outer CV-joints to install to the hubs. If the vehicle is rolled without the proper torque applied to the front wheel bearings, the bearings will no longer be usable.

1. Disconnect the negative battery cable. Drain the coolant. Remove the transaxle fluid dipstick.

2. Remove the air cleaner assembly if it is preventing access to the upper bellhousing bolts. Remove the upper bellhousing bolts and water tube, where applicable. Unplug all electrical connectors from the transaxle.

3. If equipped with 2.5L engine, remove the upper starter attaching nut and bolt at the top of the bellhousing.

4. Raise the vehicle and support safely. Remove the wheels. Remove the axle end cotter pins, nut locks, spring washers and axle nuts.

5. Remove the speedometer cable adaptor bolt and remove the adaptor from the transaxle extension housing.

6. Remove the ball joint retaining bolts and pry the control arm from the steering knuckle.

7. Position a drainpan under the transaxle where the axles enter the differential or extension housing. Remove the axles from the transaxle or center bearing. Unbolt the center bearing and remove the intermediate axle from the transaxle, if equipped.

8. Drain the transaxle. Disconnect and plug the fluid cooler hoses. Disconnect the shifter and kickdown linkage from the transaxle, if equipped.

9. Remove the starter. Remove the torque converter inspection cover, matchmark the torque converter to

the flexplate and remove the torque converter bolts.

10. Using the proper equipment, support the weight of the engine.

11. Remove the front motor mount and bracket.

12. Position a transaxle jack under the transaxle and remove the lower bellhousing bolts.

13. Remove the left side splash shield. Remove the transaxle mount bolts.

14. Carefully pry the transaxle from the engine.

15. Slide the transaxle rearward until the dowels disengage from the mating holes in the transaxle case.

16. Pull the transaxle completely away from the engine and remove it from the vehicle.

17. To prepare the vehicle for rolling, support the engine with a support or reinstall the front motor mount to the engine. Then reinstall the ball joints to the steering knuckle and install the retaining bolt. Install the obtained outer CV-joints to the hubs, install the washers and torque the axle nuts to 180 ft. lbs. (244 Nm). The vehicle may now be safely rolled.

To install:

18. Install the transaxle securely on the jack. Rotate the converter so it will align with the positioning of the flexplate.

19. Apply a light coating of high temperature grease to the torque converter pilot hub.

20. Raise the transaxle into place and push it forward until the dowels engage and the bellhousing is flush with the block. Install the transaxle to bellhousing bolts.

21. Raise the transaxle and install the left side mount bolts. Install the torque converter bolts and torque to 55 ft. lbs. (74 Nm).

22. Install the front motor mount and bracket. Remove the engine and transaxle support fixtures.

23. Install the starter to the transaxle. Install the bolt finger tight, if equipped with 2.5L engine.

24. Install the axles making sure to install new retainer clips at the transaxle end of each shaft. Install the ball joints to the steering knuckles. Torque the axle nuts to 180 ft. lbs. (244 Nm) and install new cotter pins.

25. Connect the shifter and kickdown linkage to the transaxle, if equipped. Install a new O-ring to the speedometer cable adaptor and install to the extension housing; make sure it snaps in place. Install the retaining bolt.

26. Install the splash shield and install the wheels.

27. Install the upper bellhousing bolts and water pipe, if removed.

28. If equipped with 2.5L engine, in-

stall the starter attaching nut and bolt at the top of the bellhousing. Raise the vehicle again and tighten the starter bolt from under the vehicle.

29. Connect all electrical wiring to the transaxle. Lower the vehicle. Install the dipstick.

30. Install the air cleaner assembly, if removed. Fill the transaxle with the proper amount of Mopar ATF Plus Type 7176.

31. Connect the negative battery cable and check the transaxle for proper operation.

UPSHIFT AND KICKDOWN LEARNING PROCEDURE

A–604 Ultra-Drive Transaxle

In 1989, the A–604 4 speed, electronic transaxle was introduced; it is the first to use fully adaptive controls. The controls perform their functions based on real time feedback sensor information. Although, the transaxle is conventional in design, its functions are controlled by the ECM.

Since the A–604 is equipped with a learning function, each time the battery cable is disconnected, the ECM memory is lost. In operation, the transaxle must be shifted many times for the learned memory to be reinputed in the ECM; during this period, the vehicle will experience rough operation. The transaxle must be at normal operating temperature when learning occurs.

1. Maintain constant throttle opening during shifts. Do not move the accelerator pedal during upshifts.

2. Accelerate the vehicle with the throttle ⅛–½ open.

3. Make fifteen to twenty 1/2, 2/3 and 3/4 upshifts. Accelerating from a full stop to 50 mph each time at the aforementioned throttle opening is sufficient.

4. With the vehicle speed below 25 mph, make 5–8 wide open throttle kickdowns to 1st gear from either 2nd or 3rd gear. Allow at least 5 seconds of operation in 2nd or 3rd gear prior to each kickdown.

5. With the vehicle speed greater than 25 mph, make 5 part throttle to wide open throttle kickdowns to either 3rd or 2nd gear from 4th gear. Allow at least 5 seconds of operation in 4th gear (preferably at road load throttle) prior to performing the kickdown.

SHIFT LINKAGE ADJUSTMENT

1. Place the shifter in the **P** detent.
2. Loosen the clamp bolt on the gearshift cable bracket.
3. Pull the shift lever all the way to

the front detent position and tighten the lock screw.

4. Check for proper neutral safety switch operation.

THROTTLE PRESSURE CABLE ADJUSTMENT

1. Run the engine until it reaches normal operating temperature.

2. Loosen the cable mounting bracket lock screw.

3. Position the bracket so both alignment tabs are touching the transaxle case surface and tighten the lock screws.

4. Release the cross lock on the cable assembly by pulling the cross lock up.

5. To ensure proper adjustment, the cable must be free to slide all the way toward the engine against its stop after the cross lock is released.

6. Move the transaxle throttle control lever fully clockwise and press the cross lock down until it snaps into position.

7. Road test the vehicle and check the shift points.

FRONT SUSPENSION

MacPherson Strut

REMOVAL & INSTALLATION

Except With Automatic Air Suspension

1. Remove the 3 mounting nuts from the shock tower under the hood.

2. Raise the vehicle and support safely.

3. Remove the brake hose bracket screw from the strut.

4. Matchmark the lower strut location to the steering knuckle and remove the strut to knuckle bolts, nuts and nut plate.

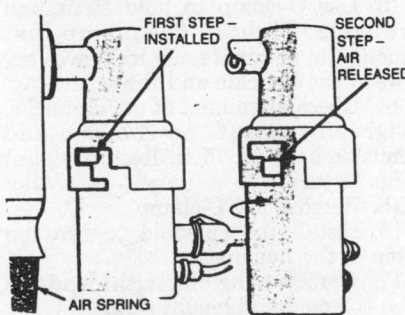

Air suspension spring solenoid positions – 1990 vehicle

5. The installation is the reverse of the removal procedure. Torque the upper mounting nuts to 20 ft. lbs. (27 Nm). Tighten but do not torque the lower mounting bolts until the front end alignment has been completed.

6. Perform a front end alignment. Torque the strut to knuckle nuts to 75 ft. lbs. (100 Nm) plus ¼ turn.

Air Suspension Strut

REMOVAL & INSTALLATION

1. Disconnect the negative battery cable.

2. Raise the vehicle and support safely. Remove the wheel and tire assembly.

3. To disconnect the air line, pull back on the plastic ring and pull the air line from the fitting.

4. Disconnect the electrical leads from the solenoid and the height sensor.

5. The solenoid has a molded square tang that fits into stepped notches in the air spring housing to provide for exhaust and a retaining positions. To vent the air spring:

   a. Release the retaining clip.

   b. Rotate the solenoid to the first

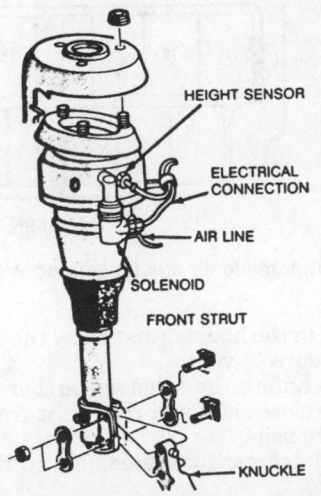

Air suspension strut assembly

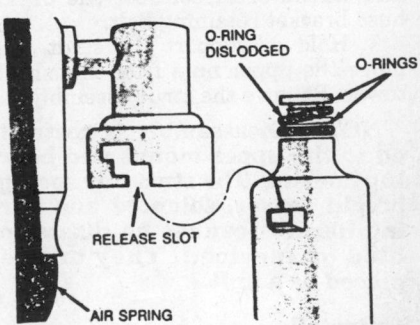

Air suspension solenoid removed – 1990 vehicle

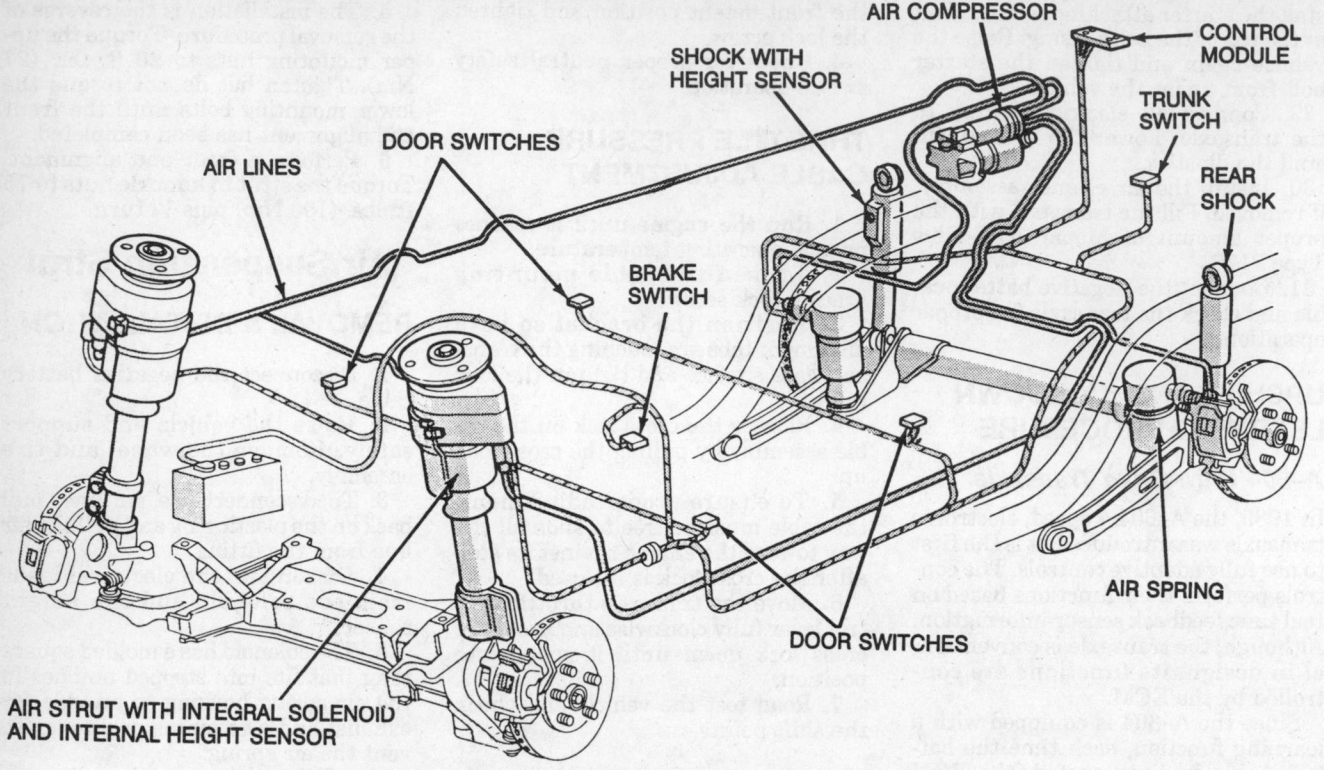

Automatic air suspension system components—1992-93 vehicle

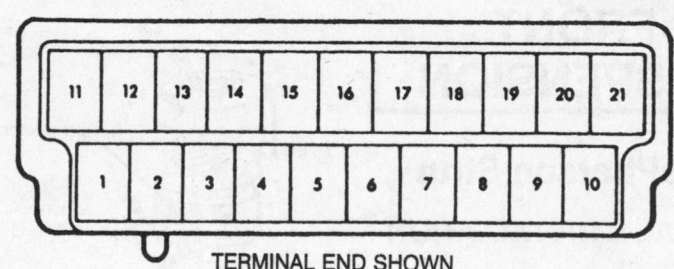

TERMINAL END SHOWN

Automatic air suspension controller connector terminals (terminal end)

step in the housing and allow the air pressure to vent.

c. Rotate the solenoid farther to the release slot and remove it from the housing.

6. Matchmark the assembly to the knuckle.

7. Remove cam bolt, knuckle bolt, and washers. Disconnect the brake hose bracket retaining bolt.

8. Hold or support the strut. Remove the upper nuts from the shock tower. Remove the strut assembly.

NOTE: Disassembly is restricted to the upper mount and bearing housing. The strut, air spring, height sensor, solenoid and wiring harness cannot be disassembled or serviced. They are replaced as a unit.

To install:

9. Install the strut assembly into the fender reinforcement, then install the retaining nuts and washers. Tighten to 20 ft. lbs. (27 Nm).

10. Position the knuckle into strut. Install washers with cam and knuckle bolts.

11. Attach brake hose retainer and tighten to 10 ft. lbs. (13 Nm).

12. Index the strut to the marks made during removal.

13. Use C-clamp to hold strut and knuckle. Tighten the clamp just enough to eliminate any looseness between the knuckle and the strut.

14. Check alignment of matchmarks. Tighten the nuts on the cam and knuckle bolts to 75 ft. lbs. (100 Nm) plus ¼ turn.

15. Remove the C-clamp.

16. Install the solenoid to the top step in the housing.

17. Connect the electrical leads to the solenoid and height sensor.

18. Connect the air line by pushing it into place; it will lock in place.

19. Connect the negative battery cable.

20. Recharge the air spring on 1990-93 vehicles as follows:

a. To activate the left front spring solenoid, ground Pin S31 to Pin X20 of the controller connector.

b. To activate the right front spring solenoid, ground Pin S30 to Pin X20 of the controller connector.

c. To activate the right rear spring solenoid, ground Pin S32 to Pin X20 of the controller connector.

d. Run the compressor for 60 seconds by jumping from pin No. S08 to pin No. X20 of the controller connector.

21. Install the wheel and tire.

22. Check the system for proper operation.

Lower Ball Joints

INSPECTION

To inspect the ball joints, grasp the grease fitting by hand with the vehicle on the ground. If the grease fitting can be moved at all by hand, the ball joint should be replaced.

REMOVAL & INSTALLATION

1. Raise the vehicle and support safely. Remove the tire and wheel assembly.

2. Remove the lower control arm from the vehicle.

3. Pry off the ball joint seal. Position the receiver cup tool C–46992 or equivalent, to support the lower control arm while receiving the ball joint assembly.

4. Press against the ball joint upper housing to remove the ball joint from the lower control arm.

To install:

5. By hand, position the ball joint assembly into the bore in the lower control arm. Be sure the ball joint is not cocked in the bore of the control arm.

6. Position arm assembly in press with installer tool C–46992 or equivalent, supporting the control arm.

7. Apply pressure against the ball joint assembly until the joint is fully seated against the bottom of the control arm. Do not apply excessive pressure against the control arm.

8. Position a new seal over the stud of the ball joint so it is against the ball joint housing, and using a 1½ in. socket, press the seal onto ball joint housing until it is seated against the top surface of the control arm.

9. Install the control arm on the vehicle.

10. Install the tire and wheel assembly.

Lower Control Arms

REMOVAL & INSTALLATION

1. Raise the vehicle and support safely. Remove the tire and wheel assembly.

2. Remove the sway bar to lower control arm retainer on both sides of the vehicle. Rotate the bar down away from the control arm.

3. Remove the ball joint stud retaining bolt and nut.

4. Pry the lower control arm from the steering knuckle.

5. Remove the control arm to crossmember bolts, nuts bushings and retainers.

6. Remove the control arm from the vehicle.

7. Transfer all reusable parts to the new control arm and lubricate.

8. Position the control arm onto the vehicle and install the attaching bolts. Loosely assemble the nuts to the attaching bolts.

9. Install the ball joint to the steering knuckle and tighten the retaining nut and bolt to 105 ft. lbs. (145 Nm).

10. Position the sway bar against the lower control arm and install the retainers, torqueing to 50 ft. lbs. (70 Nm). Install the tire and wheel assembly.

11. Lower the vehicle so the suspen-

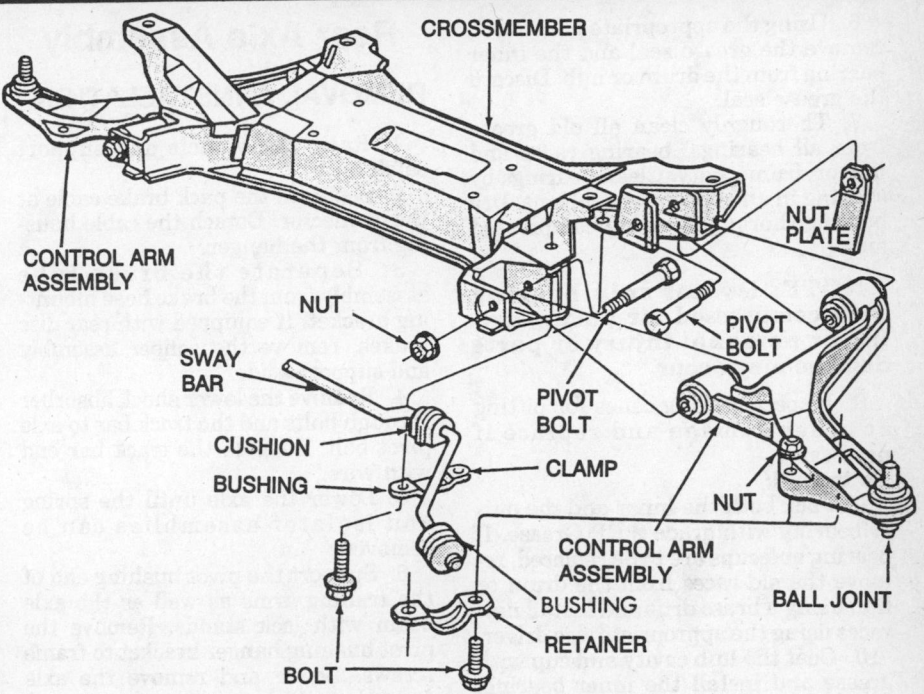

Front lower control arm and related components—1992–93 vehicles

sion is supporting the weight of the vehicle. Tighten the lower crossmember to control arm mounting bolts to 125 ft. lbs. (169 Nm).

12. Align the front suspension.

Sway Bar

REMOVAL & INSTALLATION

1. Raise the vehicle and support safely.

2. Remove the front sway bar brackets and retainers.

3. Remove the sway bar support brackets and bushings from the lower control arm. Remove the sway bar from the vehicle.

4. The installation is the reverse of the removal procedure. Lubricate the sway bar bushings liberally with grease before assembling.

REAR SUSPENSION

Shock Absorbers

REMOVAL & INSTALLATION

1. Raise the vehicle and support safely. Disconnect the height sensor and air line, if equipped. The air line is released by pulling back on the plastic retaining ring.

2. Remove the bolts that attach the shock to the frame or bracket.

3. Remove the shock from the vehicle.

4. The installation is the reverse of the removal procedure.

Coil Springs

REMOVAL & INSTALLATION

1. Raise the vehicle and support safely.

2. Using the proper equipment, support the weight of the rear axle.

3. Remove the bolts that attach the shock to the lower mounting bracket.

4. Slowly lower the axle and remove the coil spring from the vehicle.

5. The installation is the reverse of the removal procedure.

Air Springs

REMOVAL & INSTALLATION

1. Disconnect the negative battery cable.

2. Raise the vehicle and support safelyper out of the way using wire. Do not let the caliper hang from the brake hose.

4. Remove the grease cap, cotter pin, nut lock, nut, thrust washer and outer wheel bearing.

5. Carefully slide the drum or hub from the spindle making sure not to drag the inner bearing or grease seal over the threaded stub axle or damage may occur.

6. Using the appropriate puller tool, remove the grease seal and the inner bearing from the drum or hub. Discard the grease seal.

7. Thoroughly clean all old grease from all bearings, bearing races and hub or drum cavity. Clean bearings by soaking in an appropriate solvent. Dry bearing thoroughly using compressed air.

NOTE: Do not spin bearing with compressed air during drying or personal injury or parts damage may occur.

8. Inspect bearing cones for pitting or other damage and replace if necessary.

To install:

9. Pack both the inner and the outer bearing with grade 2 EP Grease. If bearing and cups are to be replaced, remove the old races from the drum or hub using a brass drift and install new races using the appropriate size driver.

10. Coat the hub cavity and cup with grease and install the inner bearing. Install the grease seal using the appropriate size driver.

11. Before installing the hub or drum, inspect the stub axle for burrs or rough surfaces and smooth out all rough surfaces.

12. Slide the drum or hub assembly onto the stub axle shaft. Install the outer bearing, washer and nut.

13. Tighten the wheel bearing nut to 20–25 ft. lbs. (27–34 Nm) while rotating the wheel. Back off the adjuster nut ¼ turn, then retighten finger tight only.

14. Position the nut lock over the flats of the adjusting nut and install a new cotter pin. Install the grease cap.

15. Install the tire and wheel assembly and lower the vehicle.

ADJUSTMENT

1. Raise the vehicle and support safely.

2. Remove the tire and wheel assembly.

3. If equipped with rear disc brakes, remove the caliper and the rotor. Support the caliper out of the way using wire. Do not let the caliper hang from the brake hose.

4. Remove the grease cap, cotter pin and nut lock.

5. Tighten the wheel bearing nut to 20–25 ft. lbs. (27–34 Nm) while rotating the wheel. Back off the adjuster nut ¼ turn, then retighten finger tight only.

6. Position the nut lock over the flats of the adjusting nut and install a new cotter pin. Install the grease cap.

7. Install the tire and wheel assembly and lower the vehicle.

Rear Axle Assembly

REMOVAL & INSTALLATION

1. Raise the vehicle and support safely.

2. Separate the park brake cable at the connector. Detach the cable housing from the hanger.

3. Separate the brake tube asssembly from the brake hose mounting bracket. If equipped with rear disc brakes, remove the caliper assembly and support aside.

4. Remove the lower shock absorber through bolts and the track bar to axle pivot bolt. Support the track bar end with wire.

5. Lower the axle until the spring and isolator assemblies can be removed.

6. Support the pivot bushing end of the trailing arms as well as the axle beam with jack stands. Remove the pivot bushing hanger bracket to frame screws. Lower and remove the axle from the vehicle.

To install:

7. Raise the axle in position and support the axle on jack stands.

8. Install the shock absorber and track bar through bolts loosely.

9. Install the brake assemblies and related components to the axle assembly, if removed, and adjust bearing preload.

10. Attach parking brake mechanism to the rear suspension and brake actuators.

11. Install the brake hose and fitting into the bracket and install the lock. Attach the brake tube to the hose fitting and tighten to 140 inch lbs. (16 Nm).

12. Install the tire and wheel assemblies. Lower the vehicle so the weight of the vehicle is resting on the suspension. Tighten the lower shock absorber bolts to 45 ft. lbs. (61 Nm) and the track bar bolt to 70 ft. lbs. (95 Nm).

13. Adjust the rear brakes and the parking brake cable. Bleed the brake system.

STEERING

Steering Wheel

— CAUTION —
On vehicles equipped with the air bag system, the system must be disarmed prior to removing the steering wheel. Failure to disarm the air bag system may result in accidental deployment of the air bag module and possible personal injury.

REMOVAL & INSTALLATION

Without Airbag

1. Disconnect the negative battery cable.

2. Straighten the steering wheel so the front tires are pointing straight ahead.

2. Remove the horn pad.

3. Remove the steering wheel hold-down nut and remove the damper, if equipped. Matchmark the steering wheel to the shaft.

4. Using a steering wheel puller, pull the steering wheel off the shaft.

5. The installation is the reverse of the removal procedure. Torque the hold-down nut to 45 ft. lbs. (60 nm).

WITH AIRBAG

1. Disconnect the negative battery cable and isolate using an appropriate insulator. Allow the system capacitor to discharge for 2 minutes prior to starting repairs on the vehicle.

2. Straighten the steering wheel so the front tires are pointing straight forward.

3. Remove the 4 nuts located on the back side of the steering wheel that attach the airbag module to the steering wheel.

4. Lift the module and disconnect the connectors. Remove the speed control switch, if equipped.

NOTE: All columns except Acustar are equipped with a clockspring set screw held by a plastic tether on the steering wheel. Acustar mounted clocksprings are auto-locking. If the steering column is not an Acustar and is lacking the set screw, obtain one before proceeding.

5. If equipped with the set screw, place it in the clockspring to ensure proper positioning when the steering wheel is removed.

6. Remove the steering wheel hold-down nut and damper, if equipped. Matchmark the steering wheel to the shaft.

Air bag module and related components

7. Using a steering wheel puller, pull the steering wheel off the shaft.
To install:

8. Position the steering wheel on the steering column. Make sure the flats on the hub of the steering wheel are aligned with the formations on the clockspring.

9. Pull the airbag and speed control connectors through the lower, larger hole in the steering wheel and pull the horn wire through the smaller hole at the top. Make sure the wires are not pinched anywhere.

10. Install the damper, if equipped.

11. Install the hold-down nut and torque to 45 ft. lbs. (60 Nm).

12. If equipped with a clockspring set screw, remove the screw and place it in its storage location on the steering wheel.

13. Connect the horn wire.

14. Connect the speed control wire and install the speed control switch.

15. Connect the clockspring lead wire to the airbag module and install module to steering wheel.

NOTE: Do not allow anyone to enter the vehicle from this point on, until this procedure is completed.

16. Connect the DRB II to the Airbag System Diagnostic Module (ASDM) connector located to the right of the console.

17. From the passenger side of the vehicle, turn the key to the **ON** position.

18. Check to make sure nobody has entered the vehicle. Connect the negative battery cable.

19. Using the DRB II, read and record any active fault data or stored codes.

20. If any active fault codes are present, perform the proper diagnostic procedures before continuing.

21. If there are no active fault codes, erase the stored fault codes. If there are active codes, the stored codes will not erase.

22. From the passenger side of the vehicle, turn the key **OFF**, then **ON** and observe the instrument cluster airbag warning light. It should come on for 6–8 seconds, then go out, indicating the system is functioning normally. If the warning light either fails to come **ON** or stays lit, there is a system malfunction and the proper diagnostic procedures should be performed.

Steering Column

REMOVAL & INSTALLATION

Acustar Column

1. Disconnect the negative battery

cable. Disarm the air bag system, if equipped.

2. Straighten the steering wheel so the front tires are pointing straight-ahead.

3. Remove the steering wheel hold-down nut and remove the damper, if equipped. Matchmark the steering wheel to the shaft.

4. Using a steering wheel puller, pull the steering wheel off the shaft.

5. If equipped with column shift, disconnect the transaxle shift cable from the steering column by prying it out of the grommet in the shift lever.

6. If equipped with pointer type gear indicator, loosen the set screw on the lower side of the steering column and remove the pointer needle.

7. If equipped with a cable actuated gear shift indicator, place the gear shift lever in the **N** or **P** position and

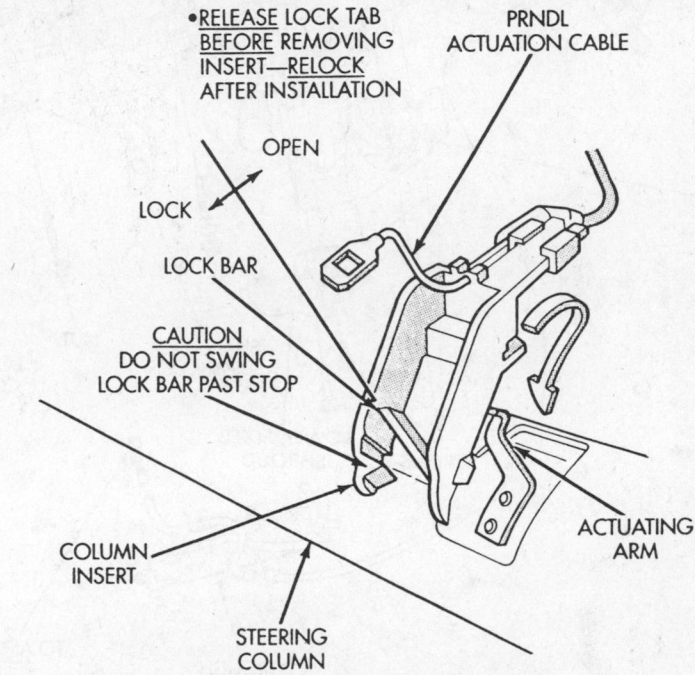

PRNDL cable removal—1992 vehicle

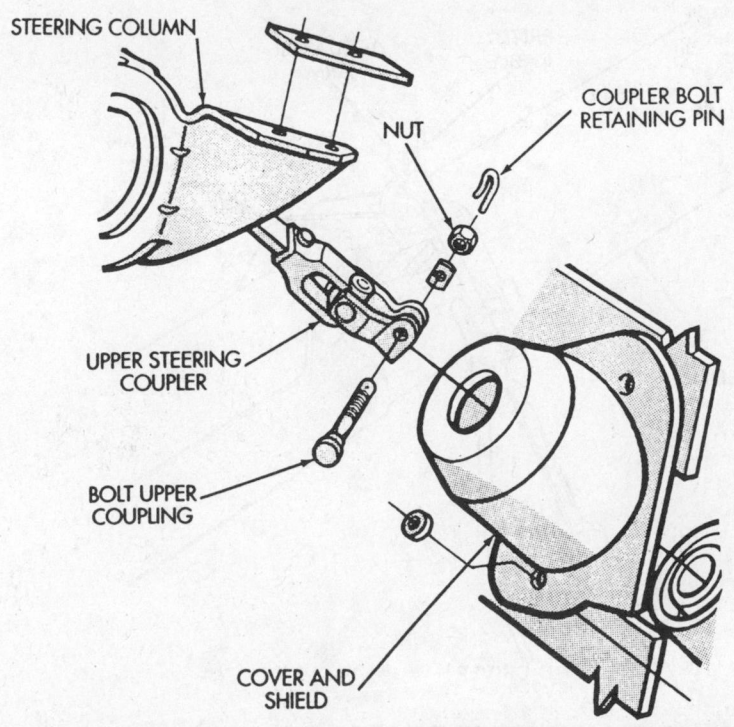

Steering column coupler removal and installation—1992 vehicle

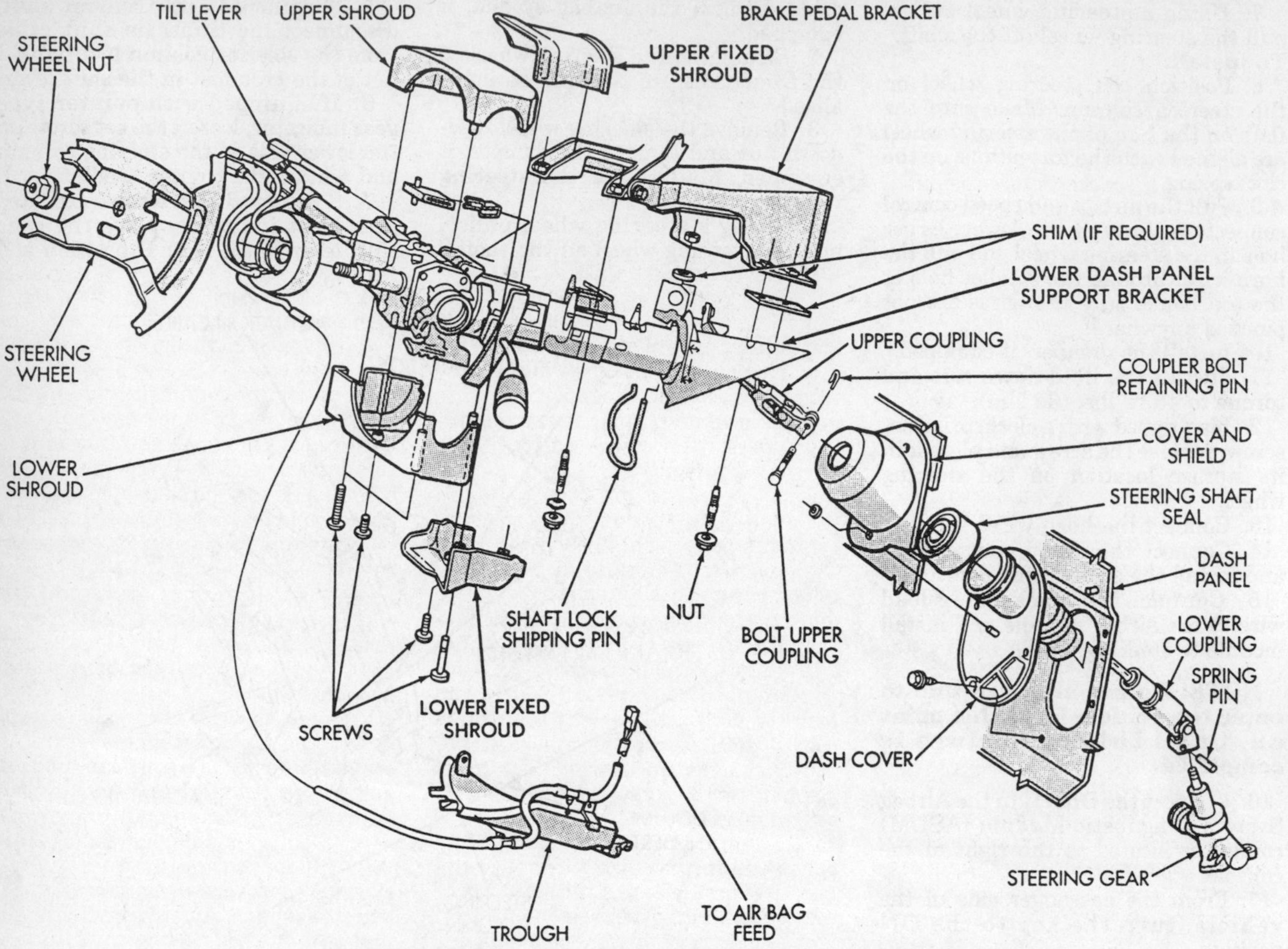

STEERING WHEEL NUT

TILT LEVER

UPPER SHROUD

UPPER FIXED SHROUD

BRAKE PEDAL BRACKET

SHIM (IF REQUIRED)

LOWER DASH PANEL SUPPORT BRACKET

UPPER COUPLING

COUPLER BOLT RETAINING PIN

COVER AND SHIELD

STEERING SHAFT SEAL

DASH PANEL

LOWER COUPLING

SPRING PIN

STEERING WHEEL

LOWER SHROUD

SHAFT LOCK SHIPPING PIN

NUT

BOLT UPPER COUPLING

SCREWS

LOWER FIXED SHROUD

DASH COVER

STEERING GEAR

TROUGH

TO AIR BAG FEED

Acustar Standard and tilt steering column—1992-93 vehicles

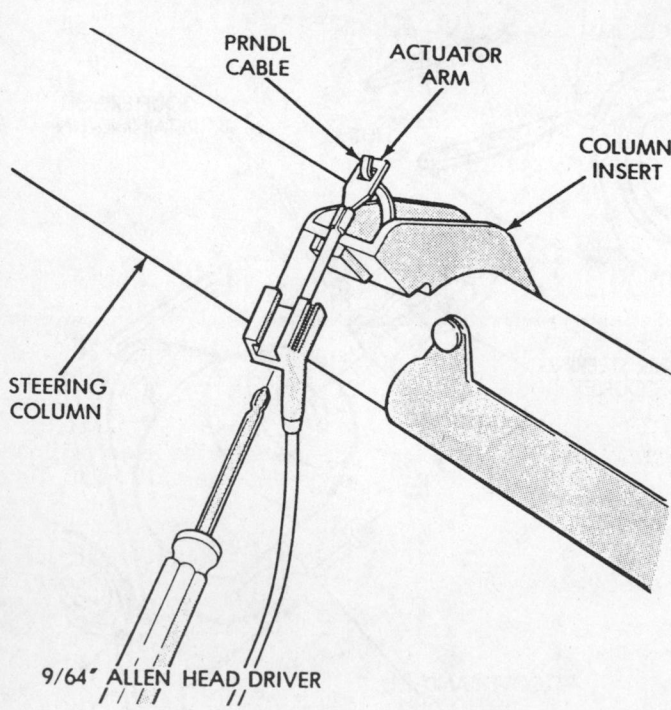

PRNDL CABLE

ACTUATOR ARM

COLUMN INSERT

STEERING COLUMN

9/64″ ALLEN HEAD DRIVER

Adjusting PRNDL actuator cable

remove the PRNDL indicator actuation cable from the steering column actuator arm. Swing the lock bar located on the lower portion of the PRNDL insert upward and squeeze the legs together. Remove the insert from the steering column.

8. Disconnect all wiring connectors from below the instrument panel that lead up into the steering column.

9. Remove the nuts that attach the steering column assembly to the instrument panel support.

10. On 1989–90 vehicles, firmly grasp the steering column assembly and pull rearward, disconnecting the lower stub shaft from the steering gear coupling. Do not remove the roll pin to remove the steering column.

11. On 1991–93 vehicles, remove the retaining pin in the upper to lower steering coupler retaining bolt. Remove the upper to lower steering coupler retaining nut and pinch bolt from the coupling and separate the stub shaft from the steering gear coupling.

12. Remove the column from the vehicle.

To install:

13. Install new cable attaching grom-

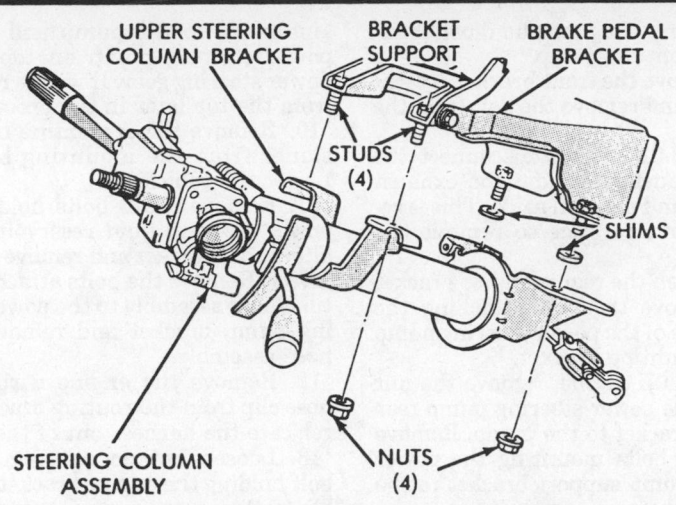

Steering column mounting—1992 vehicle

met into the steering column shift lever. Install the steering column into the vehicle. Guide the stub shaft into the steering gear coupling and install the pinch bolt and nut, if equipped.

14. Install the nuts that attach the steering column assembly to the instrument panel support. Torque the steering column assembly to support bracket nuts to 105 inch. lbs. (12 Nm).

15. Connect the wire harness connectors at the base of the steering column.

16. If equipped with a cable actuated

gear shift indicator, route the PRNDL actuator assembly under the left column wing and along the left side of the steering column. Insert the flange of the actuator assembly into the steering column jacket. Engage the lock bar to secure the actuator assembly to the housing. Hook the cable to the steering column actuator arm. Move the shifter to **N** and check for proper pointer location. If the pointer is misaligned, adjust the pointer arm using a 9/64 Allen head screwdriver.

17. If equipped with pointer type

gear shift indicator, install the pointer into the indicator housing and the steering column and secure.

18. Connect the transaxle shift cable to the shift lever on the steering column. Readjust the transaxle shift linkage.

19. Install the clockspring, steering wheel and remaining components removed during disassembly.

20. Connect the negative battery cable and check the steering column and all related components for proper operation.

Power Rack and Pinion

NOTE: **The power steering gear should not be serviced. If a malfunction or fluid leak occurs, the complete assembly should be replaced.**

REMOVAL & INSTALLATION

1. Disconnect the negative battery cable.

2. Raise the vehicle and support safely.

3. Remove the front tire and wheel assemblies.

4. Remove the cotter pins, castellated nuts and tie rod ends from the steering knuckles.

5. Disconnect the engine damper

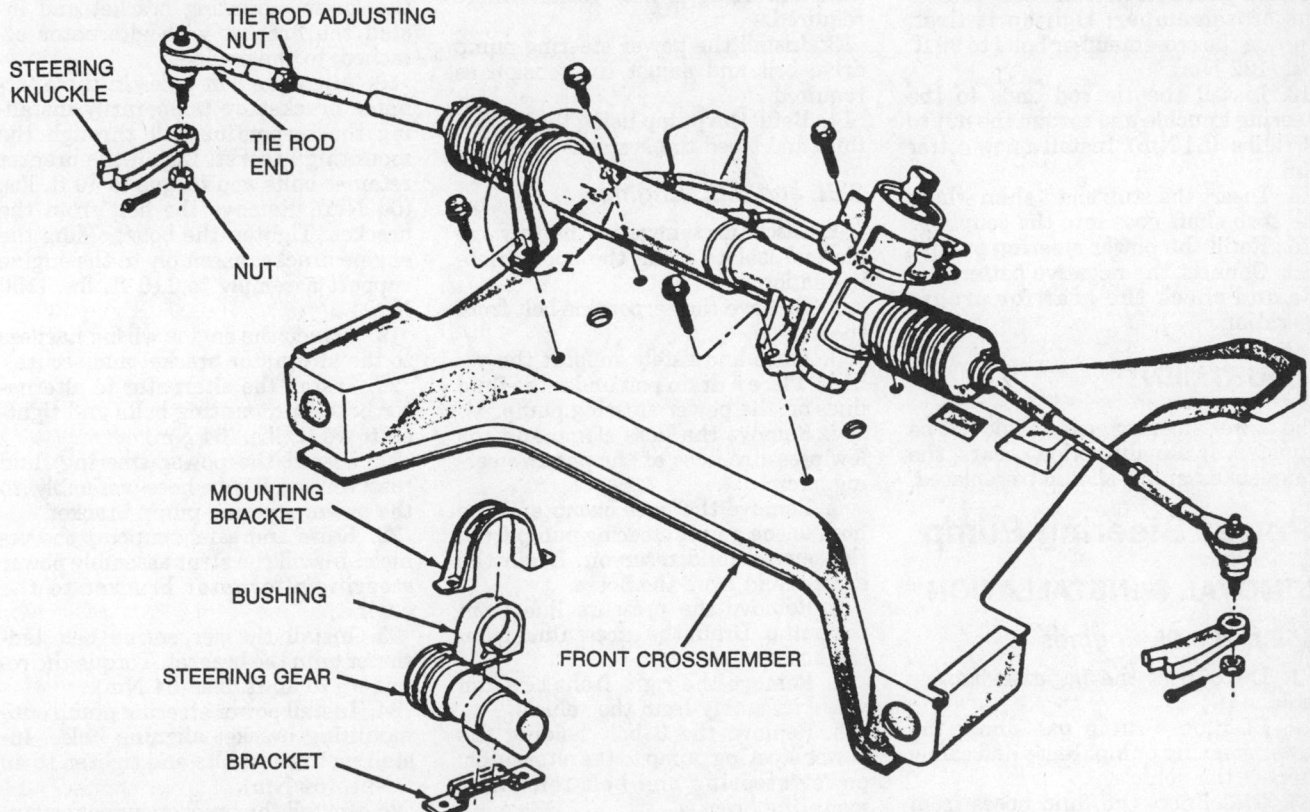

Rack and pinion steering gear mounting to the crossmember

strut from the crossmember if equipped.

6. Place a transmission jack under the front crossmember and apply a slight upward pressure on the crossmember. Remove the front suspension crossmember attaching bolts and lower the crossmember using the jack. Disconnect the steering gear from the steering column at the stub shaft while lowering the crossmember from the vehicle.

7. Disconnect and plug the oil pressure line from the rack. Disconnect and plug the return hose from the line coming from the rack.

8. Remove the tie rod inner boot shields.

9. Remove the steering gear bolts from the front suspension crossmember.

10. Remove the steering gear from the left side of the vehicle.

To install:

11. Place the rack on the crossmember and torque the steering gear attaching bolts to 21 ft. lbs. (29 Nm). Attach the fluid lines and the boot shields.

12. Have a helper inside the vehicle remove the trim boot and align the stub shaft with the coupling while the crossmember is raised into position. If a helper is not available, the steering column will have to be unbolted so the steering shaft can be inserted into the coupling. The right rear crossmember bolt is a pilot bolt that correctly locates the crossmember; tighten it first. Torque the crossmember bolts to 90 ft. lbs. (122 Nm).

13. Install the tie rod ends to the steering knuckle and torque the nut to 45 ft. lbs. (61 Nm). Install a new cotter pin.

14. Insert the stub shaft shim where the stub shaft goes into the coupling.

15. Refill the power steering pump.

16. Connect the negative battery cable and check the gear for proper operation.

ADJUSTMENT

The power steering gear should not be adjusted. If a malfunction occurs, the complete assembly should be replaced.

Power Steering Pump

REMOVAL & INSTALLATION

2.5L and 3.0L Engines

1. Disconnect the negative battery cable.

2. Position a drain pan under the power steering pump. Raise and safely support the vehicle.

3. Disconnect the fluid hoses from the pump and plug them. On 3.0L en-

gine, remove the tube and dipstick assembly from the pump.

4. Remove the front bracket attaching bolts and remove the belt from the pulley.

5. On 3.0L engine, disconnect the front exhaust pipe from the exhaust manifold and position aside. This is required for clearance to remove the pump.

6. Loosen the rear pump-to-bracket nut. Remove the bolt attaching the pulley side of the power steering pump to the mounting bracket.

7. On 3.0L engine, remove the nut holding the power steering pump rear support bracket to the pump. Remove the the 2 bolts mounting the power steering pump support bracket to the engine and remove the bracket.

8. Lower the vehicle. Remove the remaining retaining bolts and the rear mounting nut. Remove the power steering pump from the vehicle.

9. Remove the pulley from the pump with the proper puller. Install the pulley on the new pump using the special installation tools.

To install:

10. Install the pump to the engine making sure, on 3.0L engine, that the stud on the back of the pump is in the slotted hole in the bracket.

11. Install the mounting screws. Install the tube and dipstick assembly on the pump, if equipped.

12. Install the exhaust pipe to the manifold using a new gasket where required.

13. Install the power steering pump drive belt and adjust the tension as required.

14. Refill the pump using the correct fluid and bleed the system.

3.3L and 3.8L Engines

1. Disconnect negative battery cable and isolate using the appropriate insulation.

2. Remove the serpentine belt from the engine.

3. Raise and safely support the vehicle. Place a drain pan under the fluid lines on the power steering pump.

4. Remove the hose clamp and the low pressure hose at the power steering pump.

5. Remove the hose clamp and the hose to the power steering pump from the remote fluid reservoir. Drain the excess fluid from the hoses.

6. Remove the pressure line from the pump. Drain the excess fluid from the hose.

7. Remove the right front tire and wheel assembly from the vehicle.

8. Remove the 3 bolt holding the power steering pump to the alternator, power steering and belt tensioner mounting bracket.

9. Remove the strut from the en-

gine block to the pump and lay the power steering pump on top of the power steering gear. It will be removed from the top later in the procedure.

10. Remove the serpentine belt tensioner from the mounting bracket. Lower the vehicle.

11. Remove the 2 bolts holding the power steering fluid reservoir to the alternator bracket and remove the reservoir. Remove the bolts attaching the tube/hose assembly to the power steering pump bracket and remove tube/hose assembly.

12. Remove the engine wiring harness clip from the routing bracket and relocate the harness out of the way.

13. Loosen but do not remove the bolt holding the engine bracket assembly to the engine support assembly.

14. Remove the upper alternator to alternator bracket mounting bolts and rotate the assembly back toward the dash panel. Remove the alternator from the mounting bracket and remove the mounting bracket from the engine. Lay the alternator on top of the intake manifold.

15. Remove the power steering pump through the top in the area of the alternator. Transfer parts as required.

To install:

16. Install the power steering pump in the vehicle., laying it on the steering gear.

17. Install the alternator back onto the lower mounting bracket and install the bracket with alternator attached, to the engine.

18. Align the bolt holes in the alternator bracket by temporarily installing the serpentine belt through the mounting bracket. Install the bracket retainer bolts and torque to 40 ft. lbs. (54 Nm). Remove the bolt from the bracket. Tighten the bolt holding the engine bracket assembly to the engine support assembly to 110 ft. lbs. (150 Nm).

19. Attach the engine wiring harness to the alternator bracket and secure.

20. Install the alternator to alternator bracket mounting bolts and tighten to 40 ft. lbs. (54 Nm).

21. Install the power steering fluid reservoir and tube/hose assembly to the power steering pump bracket.

22. Raise and safely support the vehicle. Install the strut assembly power steering/alternator bracket to the engine.

23. Install the serpentine belt tensioner onto the bracket. Torque the retainers to 40 ft. lbs. (54 Nm).

24. Install power steering pump onto mounting bracket aligning holes. Install mounting bolts and tighten to 40 ft. lbs. (54 Nm).

25. Install the bracket support strut. Install the power steering fluid pres-

sure line with new O-ring in place and tighten the fitting to 275 inch lbs. (31 Nm).

26. Install the power steering pump low pressure line to the pump and the reservoir. Be sure all hose clamps are reinstalled.

27. Secure right front tire and wheel assembly on vehicle and lower.

28. Install the serpentine belt making sure positioning on all pulleys is correct.

29. Fill the reservoir to the correct level using the proper fluid, do not use automatic transmission fluid.

30. Start the engine and add fluid to bring the level to the correct level.

31. To purge the system of air, turn the steering wheel from side to side without contacting the stops.

32. Return the wheel to the straight-ahead position and operate the engine for 2 minutes before road testing.

BELT ADJUSTMENT

NOTE: The belt tension is automatically adjusted by a dynamic tensioner on 3.0L, 3.3L and 3.8L engines. Adjustment is not possible.

1. Loosen the bracket mounting bolts.

2. On 1989 vehicles, use a ½ in. drive breaker bar in the square hole provided in the bracket to move the pump away from the engine. On 1990–91 vehicles, tighten the adjusting nut until the pump is in the desired position. Do not pry against the fluid reservoir.

3. With the pump moved enough so the belt deflects about ¼–½ in. under a 10 lb. load, tighten the bolts.

SYSTEM BLEEDING

1. Fill the reservoir with power steering fluid.

2. Turn the wheels to the full left turn position and add fluid until the reservoir is full.

3. Start the engine and add fluid to bring the level to the correct level.

4. To purge the system of air, turn the steering wheel from side to side without contacting the stops.

5. Return the wheel to the straight-ahead position and operate the engine for 2 minutes before road testing.

Tie Rod Ends

REMOVAL & INSTALLATION

1. Raise the vehicle and support safely.

2. Remove the cotter pin and nut from the tie rod end.

3. Using a puller, separate the tie rod from the steering knuckle.

4. Loosen the sleeve clamp nut and bolt, if equipped, and unscrew the tie rod end from the sleeve or inner tie rod.

5. The installation is the reverse of the removal procedure. Torque the stud nuts to 45 ft. lbs. (61 Nm) and install a new cotter pin.

6. Perform a front end alignment, as required.

BRAKES

Master Cylinder

REMOVAL & INSTALLATION

Except Anti-Lock Brakes

1. Disconnect the negative battery cable.

2. Disconnect and plug the brake lines from the master cylinder.

3. Remove the nuts attaching the master cylinder to the power booster.

4. Remove the master cylinder from the mounting studs.

5. Remove the fluid reservoir from the cylinder.

To install:

6. Fill the master cylinder with clean brake fluid and bench bleed.

7. Install cylinder to the mounting studs on the booster and secure.

8. Install the brake lines to the master cylinder loosely. Have a helper slowly depress the brake pedal while the lines at the master cylinder are tightened.

9. Connect the negative battery cable, add brake fluid to fill reservoir to the appropriate level and check the brakes for proper operation.

Combination Valve

REMOVAL & INSTALLATION

1. Disconnect the negative battery cable. Raise the vehicle and support safely.

2. Tag and disconnect the brake lines from the valve.

3. Disconnect the wires to the pressure switch.

4. Remove the combination valve from the frame bracket.

5. Installation is the reverse of the removal procedure.

6. Bleed the brakes in the following order:

a. Right rear wheel cylinder or caliper

b. Left rear wheel cylinder or caliper

c. Right front caliper

d. Left front caliper

Power Brake Booster

REMOVAL & INSTALLATION

1. Disconnect the negative battery cable. Disconnect the vacuum hose(s) from the booster.

2. Remove the master cylinder from the brake booster.

3. From inside the passenger compartment, remove the clip that secures the booster pushrod to the brake pedal.

4. Remove the nuts that attach the booster to the dash panel. Remove the booster from the vehicle.

5. The installation is the reverse of the removal procedure.

6. Connect the negative battery cable and check the brakes for proper operation.

Brake Caliper

REMOVAL & INSTALLATION

1. Raise the vehicle and support safely.

2. Remove the tire and wheel assembly.

3. Remove the caliper mounting pins.

4. Lift the caliper off the rotor. Remove the outer pad from the caliper.

5. Remove the brake hose retaining bolt from the caliper.

To install:

6. Install the brake hose to the caliper using new copper washers.

7. Position the caliper over the rotor so the caliper engages the adaptor correctly. Install the mounting pins and tighten to 35 ft. lbs. (47 Nm).

8. Fill the master cylinder to the appropriate level and bleed the brakes.

Disc Brake Pads

REMOVAL & INSTALLATION

All Front Brakes and 1991–93 Rear Brakes

1. Depressurize the hydraulic accumulator, if equipped with anti-lock brakes. Remove some of the fluid from the master cylinder.

2. Raise the vehicle and support safely. Remove the tire and wheel assemblies.

3. Remove the caliper and remove the outer pad from the caliper.

4. Remove the inner pad from the adaptor.

To install:

5. Use a large C-clamp to compress the piston back into the caliper bore.

6. Install the inboard shoe by inserting the retaining clip into the piston cavity. Install the outboard brake shoe by sliding the retaining clip over the caliper fingers.

7. Position the caliper over the rotor so the caliper engages the adaptor correctly and install the retainer pin(s).

8. Install the hold-down spring, if removed.

9. Refill the master cylinder. Pump the brake pedal until a firm pedal is achieved prior to moving the vehicle. This will seat the brakes against the rotors.

1989–90 Rear Disc Brakes

1. Depressurize the hydraulic accumulator, if equipped with anti-lock brakes. Disconnect negative battery cable.

2. Raise the vehicle and support safely. Remove the tire and wheel assemblies.

3. Release the parking brake and cycle the brake pedal. Make sure cable is not binding, causing the parking brakes to drag.

4. Manually pull the caliper toward the outside of the vehicle so the piston will be retracted.

5. Drive the brake shoe retainer pin from the caliper and remove the 2 mounting bolts.

6. Lift the caliper away from the disc. Be careful not to loose the anti-rattle clips for they may become dislodged during caliper removal.

7. Supoport the caliper using wire. Do not allow the caliper to hang from the hydraulic hose.

8. Remove the disc brake pads from the adapter.

To install:

9. Lubricate the mating surfaces of the adapter assembly lightly with multi-purpose grease. Install the pads to the adapter.

10. Install the caliper onto the adapter. The lower end of the caliper must be installed onto the adapter first.

11. Insert the anti-rattle clip through the inspection opening in the top of the caliper and install placing the lower end of the clip in position first.

12. Install the brake shoe retainer pin while pushing down on the caliper slightly. Align and install the upper caliper retainer bolt first, then install the lower retainer bolt. Tighten bolts to 19 ft. lbs. (25 Nm).

13. Install the tire and wheel assem-

bly, lower the vehicle and pump the brake pedal until a firm pedal is obtained. Check the fluid in the master cylinder and fill to the appropriate level.

Brake Rotor

REMOVAL & INSTALLATION

1. Raise the vehicle and support safely. Remove the tire and wheel assembly.

2. Remove the caliper and brake pads.

3. Remove the factory installed clips, if equipped. It is not necessary to reinstall these clips.

4. Remove the adaptor, if necessary. Remove the rotor from the hub.

5. The installation is the reverse of the removal procedure.

Brake Drum

REMOVAL & INSTALLATION

1. Raise the vehicle and support safely.

2. Remove the wheel and tire assembly.

3. Remove the dust cap.

4. Remove the cotter pin and nut lock.

5. Remove the wheel bearing nut and washer from the spindle.

6. Remove the outer wheel bearing.

7. Remove the drum with the inner wheel bearing from the spindle. If the drum is difficult to remove, remove the plug from the rear of the backing plate and push the self adjuster lever away from the star wheel. Rotate the star wheel to retract the shoes. Remove the grease seal.

To install:

8. Lubricate and install the inner wheel bearing. Install a new grease seal.

9. Install the drum to the spindle.

10. Lubricate and install the outer wheel bearing, washer and nut. When the bearing preload is properly set, install the nut lock and a new cotter pin.

11. Install the grease cap.

12. Install the wheel and tire assembly. Adjust the rear brakes as required.

Brake Shoes

REMOVAL & INSTALLATION

1. Raise the vehicle and support safely. Remove the wheel and tires and the brake drums.

2. Remove the automatic adjuster spring and lever.

3. Rotate the automatic adjuster star wheel so both shoes move out far enough to be free of the wheel cylinder boots.

4. Disconnect the parking brake cable from the actuating lever.

5. Remove the lower shoe-to-shoe or shoe-to-anchor spring(s).

6. With the shoes held together by the upper shoe-to-shoe spring, remove them from the backing plate.

To install:

7. Thoroughly clean and dry the backing plate. To prepare the backing plate, lubricate the bosses, anchor pin and parking brake actuating lever pivot surface lightly with lithium based grease.

8. Remove, clean and dry all parts still on the old shoes. Lubricate the star wheel shaft threads with anti-sieze lubricant and transfer all parts to their proper locations on the new shoes.

9. Install the lower spring(s).

10. Connect the parking brake cable to the brake shoe.

11. Install the automatic adjuster lever and spring.

12. Adjust the star wheel so a slight resistance is felt when installing the drum to the spindle.

13. Remove any grease from the linings, install the brake drum, wheel bearing washer and end nut to the spindle. Adjust the bearing pre-load and install new cotter pin.

14. Install the tire and wheel assembly.

15. Complete the brake adjustment with the wheels installed.

Wheel Cylinder

REMOVAL & INSTALLATION

1. Raise the vehicle and support safely.

2. Remove the wheel, drum and brake shoes.

3. Remove and plug the brake line from the wheel cylinder.

4. Remove the wheel cylinder bolts and remove the cylinder from the backing plate.

To install:

5. Apply a very thin coating of silicone sealer to the cylinder mounting surface, install the cylinder to the backing plate and install the retaining bolts.

6. Connect the brake line to the wheel cylinder.

7. Install all brake parts that were removed.

8. Install the tire and wheel assembly.

9. Bleed the brake system.

Parking Brake Cables

ADJUSTMENT

Drum Brakes

1. Release the parking brakes fully.
2. Raise the vehicle and support safely.
3. Adjust the rear brakes.
4. Loosen the adjusting nut until there is slack in all the cables.
5. Rotate the rear wheels and tighten the cable adjusting nut until there is a slight drag at the wheels.
6. Continue to rotate the rear wheels and loosen the nut until all drag is eliminated.
7. Back off the nut an additional 2 turns.
8. Apply and release the parking brake several times. Upon the least release, verify there is no drag at the wheels.
9. To check the operation, make sure the parking brake holds on an incline.

Rear Disc Brakes

1. Fully release the parking brakes and pump the brakes several times. Raise the vehicle and support safely.
2. Tighten the cable adjusting nut until a very slight drag is felt at each rear wheel.
3. Loosen the adjusting nut 5 turns.
4. Actuate the parking brake lever on the rear calipers by manually pulling down and releasing each rear parking brake cable at the rear of the vehicle.
5. The parking brake lever should be touching the stop pin on both rear calipers. If not, loosen the adjusting nut 1 turn.
6. Repeat Steps 4 and 5 until the parking brake lever returns against the stop pin on both calipers.
7. When the adjustment is complete, the actuating levers on both calipers should return against the stop pins when the parking brakes are released and the wheels must rotate freely.
8. To confirm proper operation, make sure the parking brake holds on an incline.

REMOVAL & INSTALLATION

Front Cable

1. Disconnect the negative battery cable.
2. Loosen the adjusting nut and disengage the front cable from the equalizer bracket.
4. Lift the carpet and floor matting and remove the floor pan seal.
5. Pull the cable end forward and disconnect from the clevis.

6. Pull the cable through the hole and remove.
7. The installation is the reverse of the removal procedure.
8. Adjust the cables, connect the negative battery cable and check the parking brakes for proper operation.

Rear Cable

DRUM BRAKES

1. Disconnect the negative battery cable. Raise the vehicle and support safely.
2. Remove the rear wheels. Back off the adjusting nut enough to provide slack in all cables and disconnect cables from the cable connectors.
3. Remove the brake drums. Disconnect the cable from the brake shoe lever.
4. Compress the retaining clips on the end of the cable housing and pull the cable from the backing plate.
5. Remove the retaining clip at the support bracket and remove the cable from the trailing arm assembly.
6. The installation is the reverse of the removal procedure.
7. Adjust the cables, connect the negative battery cable and check the parking brakes for proper operation.

DISC BRAKES

1. Disconnect the negative battery cable. Raise the vehicle and support safely. Remove the rear wheels.
2. Remove the brake cable retaining clips from the hanger bracket and caliper.
3. Disconnect the cable from the parking brake lever on the caliper.
4. Remove the cable guide attaching nut and screw.
5. Pull the cable assembly out from the hanger bracket and caliper.
6. The installation is the reverse of the removal procedure.
7. Adjust the cables, connect the negative battery cable and check the parking brakes for proper operation.

Brake System Bleeding

Except Anti-Lock Brakes

NOTE: If using a pressure bleeder, follow the instructions furnished with the unit and choose the correct adaptor for the application. Do not substitute an adapter that "almost fits" as it will not work and could be dangerous.

MASTER CYLINDER

If the master cylinder is off the vehicle it can be bench bled.
1. Connect 2 short pieces of brake line to the outlet fittings, bend them

until the free end is below the fluid level in the master cylinder reservoirs.
2. Fill the reservoir with fresh brake fluid. Pump the piston slowly until no more air bubbles appear in the reservoirs.
3. Disconnect the 2 short lines, refill the master cylinder and securely install the cylinder caps.
4. If the master cylinder is on the vehicle, it can still be bled, using a flare nut wrench.
5. Open the brake lines slightly with the flare nut wrench while pressure is applied to the brake pedal by a helper inside the vehicle.
6. Be sure to tighten the line before the brake pedal is released.
7. Repeat the process with both lines until no air bubbles come out.

CALIPERS AND WHEEL CYLINDERS

1. Fill the master cylinder with fresh brake fluid. Check the level often during the procedure.
2. Starting with the right rear wheel, remove the protective cap from the bleeder, and place where it will not be lost. Clean the bleed screw.

--- CAUTION ---

When bleeding the brakes, keep face away from the brake area. Spewing fluid may cause facial and/or visual damage. Do not allow brake fluid to spill on the car's finish; it will remove the paint.

3. If the system is empty, the most efficient way to get fluid down to the wheel is to loosen the bleeder about ½–¾ turn, place a finger firmly over the bleeder and have a helper pump the brakes slowly until fluid comes out the bleeder. Once fluid is at the bleeder, close it before the pedal is released inside the vehicle.

NOTE: If the pedal is pumped rapidly, the fluid will churn and create small air bubbles, which are almost impossible to remove from the system. These air bubbles will eventually congregate and a spongy pedal will result.

4. Once fluid has been pumped to the caliper or wheel cylinder, open the bleed screw again, have the helper press the brake pedal to the floor, lock the bleeder and have the helper slowly release the pedal. Wait 15 seconds and repeat the procedure (including the 15 second wait) until no more air comes out of the bleeder upon application of the brake pedal. Remember to close the bleeder before the pedal is released inside the vehicle each time the bleeder is opened. If not, air will be induced into the system.
5. If a helper is not available, connect a small hose to the bleeder, place

the end in a container of brake fluid and proceed to pump the pedal from inside the vehicle until no more air comes out the bleeder. The hose will prevent air from entering the system.

6. Repeat the procedure on remaining wheel cylinders in order:
   a. Left rear
   b. Right front
   c. Left front

7. Hydraulic brake systems must be totally flushed if the fluid becomes contaminated with water, dirt or other corrosive chemicals. To flush, bleed the entire system until all fluid has been replaced with new fluid.

8. Install the bleeder cap(s) on the bleeder to keep dirt out. Always road test the vehicle after brake work of any kind is done.

Anti-Lock Brakes

BOOSTER BLEEDING—BOSCH ABS III

1. The hydraulic accumulator must be depressurized.

2. Connect all pump/motor and hydraulic assembly electrical connections, if previously disconnected. Be sure all brake lines and hose connections are tight.

3. Fill the reservoir to the full level.

4. Connect a transparent hose to the bleeder screw location on the right side of the hydraulic assembly. Place the other end of the hose into a clear container to receive brake fluid.

5. Open the bleeder screw ½–¾ of a turn.

6. Turn the ignition switch to the ON position. The pump/motor should run, discharging fluid into the container. After a good volume of fluid has been forced through the hose, an air-free flow in the plastic hose and container will indicate a good bleed.

7. Turn the ignition switch OFF.

NOTE: If the brake fluid does not flow, it may be due to a lack of prime to the pump/motor. Try shaking the return hose to break up air bubbles that may be present within the hose.

Should the brake fluid still not flow, turn the ignition switch to the OFF position. Remove the return hose from the reservoir and cap nipple on the reservoir. Manually fill the return hose with brake fluid and connect to the reservoir. Repeat the bleeding process.

8. Remove the hose from the bleeder screw. Tighten the bleeder screw to 7.5 ft. lbs. (10 Nm). Do not overtighten.

9. Top off the reservoir to the correct fluid level.

10. Turn the ignition switch to the ON position. Allow the pump to charge the accumulator, which should stop after approximately 30 seconds.

Pressure Bleeding

The brake lines may be pressure bled, using a standard diaphragm type pressure bleeder. Only diaphragm type pressure bleeding equipment should be used to bleed the system.

1. The ignition should be turned OFF and remain OFF throughout this procedure.

2. Depressurize the hydraulic accumulator as follows:
   a. Disconnect the negative battery cable.
   b. Pump the brake pedal a minimum of 40 times.
   c. A noticeable difference in pressure should be noticed. When this occurs, press the pedal an additional 10 times.

--- CAUTION ---

Failure to depressurize the hydraulic accumulator, prior to performing this operation may result in personal injury and/or damage to the painted surfaces.

3. Remove the electrical connector from fluid level sensor on the reservoir cap(s) and remove the reservoir cap(s).

4. Install the pressure bleeder adapter.

5. Attach the bleeding equipment to the bleeder adapter. Charge the pressure bleeder to approximately 20 psi (138 kPa).

6. Connect a transparent hose to the caliper bleed screw. Submerge the free end of the hose in a clear glass container, which is partially filled with clean, fresh brake fluid.

7. With the pressure turned ON, open the caliper bleed screw ½–¾ turn and allow fluid to flow into the container. Leave the bleed screw open until clear, bubble-free fluid slows from the hose. If the reservoir has been drained or the hydraulic assembly removed from the vehicle prior to the bleeding operation, slowly pump the brake pedal 1–2 times while the bleed screw is open and fluid is flowing. This will help purge air from the hydraulic assembly. Tighten the bleeder screw to 7.5 ft. lbs. (10 Nm).

8. Repeat Step 7 at all calipers. Calipers should be bled in the following order:
   a. Left rear
   b. Right rear
   c. Left front
   d. Right front

9. After bleeding all 4 calipers, remove the pressure bleeding equipment and bleeder adapter by closing the pressure bleeder valve and slowly unscrewing the bleeder adapter from the hydraulic assembly reservoir. Failure to release pressure in the reservoir will cause spillage of brake fluid and could result in injury or damage to painted surfaces.

10. Using a syringe or equivalent method, remove excess fluid from the reservoir to bring the fluid level to full level.

11. Install the reservoir cap and connect the fluid level sensor connector. Turn the ignition ON and allow the pump to charge the accumulator.

Manual Bleeding

1. Depressurize the hydraulic accumulator as follows:
   a. Disconnect the negative battery cable.
   b. Pump the brake pedal a minimum of 40 times.
   c. A noticeable difference in pressure should be noticed. When this occurs, press the pedal an additional 10 times.

--- CAUTION ---

Failure to depressurize the hydraulic accumulator, prior to performing this operation may result in personal injury and/or damage to the painted surfaces.

2. Connect a transparent hose to the caliper bleed screw. Submerge the

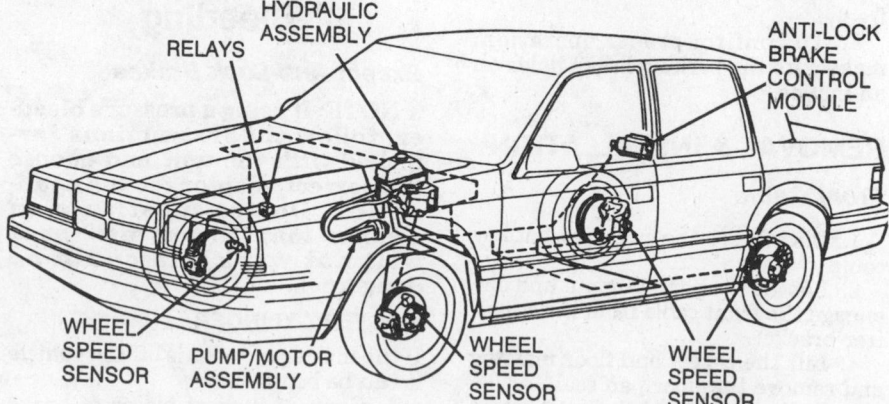

Bosch ABS III anti-lock brake system schematic—1989–90 vehicles

free end of the hose in a clear glass container, which is partially filled with clean, fresh brake fluid.

3. Slowly pump the brake pedal several times, using full strokes of the pedal and allowing approximately 5 seconds between pedal strokes. After 2 or 3 strokes, continue to hold pressure on the pedal, keeping it at the bottom of its travel.

4. With pressure on the pedal, open the bleed screw ½–¾ turn. Leave the bleed screw open until fluid no longer flows from the hose. Tighten the bleed screw and release the pedal.

5. Repeat this procedure until clear, bubble-free fluid flows from the hose.

6. Repeat all steps at each of the calipers. Calipers should be bled in the following order:
   a. Left rear
   b. Right rear
   c. Left front
   d. Right front

7. Fill the hydraulic assembly to the proper level using clean brake fluid meeting DOT 3 brake fluid.

8. Install both reservoir caps. Turn the ignition to the **RUN** position to allow the pump/motor to recharge the system.

Anti-Lock Brake System Service

PRECAUTIONS

Failure to observe the following precautions may result in system damage.
- Before performing electric arc welding on the vehicle, disconnect the Electronic Brake Control Module (EBCM) and the hydraulic modulator connectors.
- When performing painting work on the vehicle, do not expose the Electronic Brake Control Module (EBCM) to temperatures in excess of 185°F (85°C) for longer than 2 hrs. The system may be exposed to temperatures up to 200°F (95°C) for less than 15 min.
- Never disconnect or connect the Electronic Brake Control Module (EBCM) or hydraulic modulator connectors with the ignition switch ON.
- Never disassemble any component of the Anti-Lock Brake System (ABS) which is designated non-servicable; the component must be replaced as an assembly.
- When filling the master cylinder, always use brake fluid which meets DOT-3 specifications; petroleum-based fluid will destroy the rubber parts.

DEPRESSURIZING THE HYDRAULIC ACCUMULATOR

1. With the ignition **OFF**, pump the brake pedal a minimum of 40 times, using approximately 50 lbs. (222 N) pedal force. A noticeable change in pedal feel will occur when the accumulator is discharged.

2. When a definite increase in pedal effort is felt, stroke the pedal 10 additional times. This should remove all hydraulic pressure from the system.

Pump/Motor Assembly

REMOVAL & INSTALLATION

1989–90 Vehicles

1. Disconnect the negative battery cable. Depressurize the hydraulic accumulator.

—————— **CAUTION** ——————
Failure to depressurize the hydraulic accumulator, prior to performing this operation may result in personal injury and/or damage to the painted surfaces.

2. Remove the fresh air intake ducts.

3. Disconnect all electrical connectors to the pump motor.

4. Disconnect the high and low pressure hoses from the hydraulic assembly. Cap the spigot on the reservoir.

5. Disconnect the shift selection cable bracket from the transaxle and move it aside.

6. Loosen the nuts on the 2 studs that position the pump/motor to the transaxle differential cover.

7. Remove the retainer bolts that are used to mount hose bracket and pump/motor. The engine inlet water extension pipe is also held in position by these bolts.

NOTE: Do not disturb the inlet water extension pipe, or engine coolant will leak out.

8. Disconnect the wiring harness retaining clip from the hose bracket.

9. Lift the pump/motor assembly off the studs and out of the vehicle.

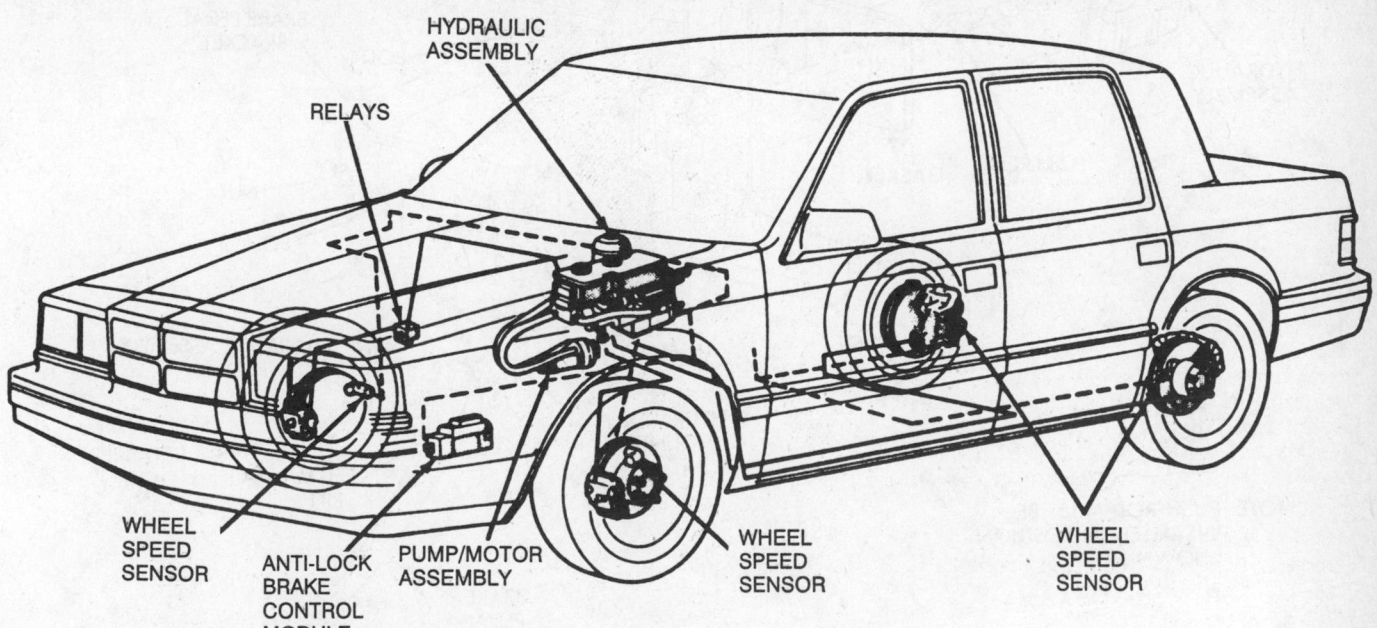

HYDRAULIC ASSEMBLY

RELAYS

WHEEL SPEED SENSOR

ANTI-LOCK BRAKE CONTROL MODULE

PUMP/MOTOR ASSEMBLY

WHEEL SPEED SENSOR

WHEEL SPEED SENSOR

Bendix System 10 anti-lock brake system schematic—1991–93 vehicles

10. Remove the heat shield from the pump/motor, if equipped and discard.

To install:

11. Install a new heat shield to the pump/motor bracket, using fasteners provided.

12. Install the pump/motor assembly onto the studs and secure.

13. Connect the high and low pressure hoses to the hydraulic assembly.

14. Connect the shift selection cable bracket to the transaxle and adjust.

15. Connect the fresh air intake ducts.

16. Connect the negative battery cable and check the assembly for proper operation.

1991–93 Vehicles

1. Disconnect the negative battery cable.

2. Depressurize the hydraulic accumulator.

--------- **CAUTION** ---------

Failure to depressurize the hydraulic accumulator, prior to performing this operation may result in personal injury and/or damage to the painted surfaces.

3. Remove the fresh air intake ducts from the engine.

4. Remove the clip holding the high pressure line to the battery tray or body of the vehicle.

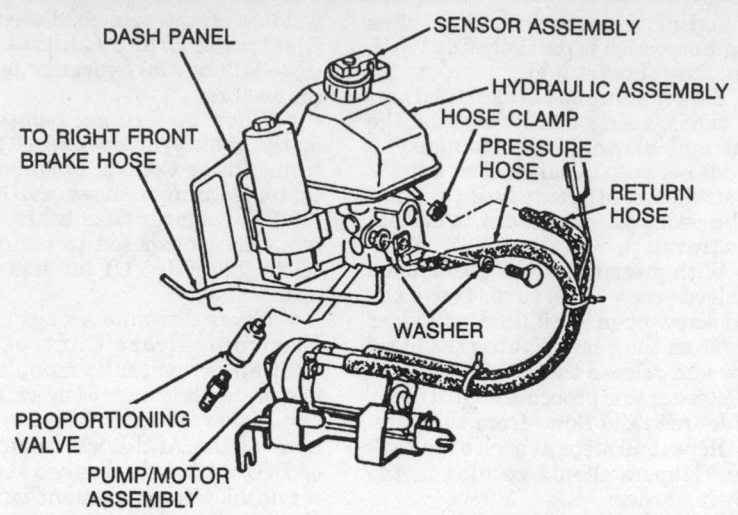

Hydraulic assembly, pump/motor assembly and related parts—1989–90 vehicles

5. Disconnect the electrical connectors running across the engine compartment in the vicinity of the pump/motor high and low pressure hoses. One of these connectors is the one for the pump/motor assembly.

6. Disconnect the high and low pressure hoses from the hydraulic assembly. Cap or plug the reservoir fitting.

7. Disconnect the pump/motor electrical connector from the engine mount.

8. Remove the heat shield bolt from the front of the pump bracket. Remove the heat shield.

9. Lift the pump/motor assembly from the bracket and lift assembly out of the vehicle.

To install:

10. Fit the pump motor assembly

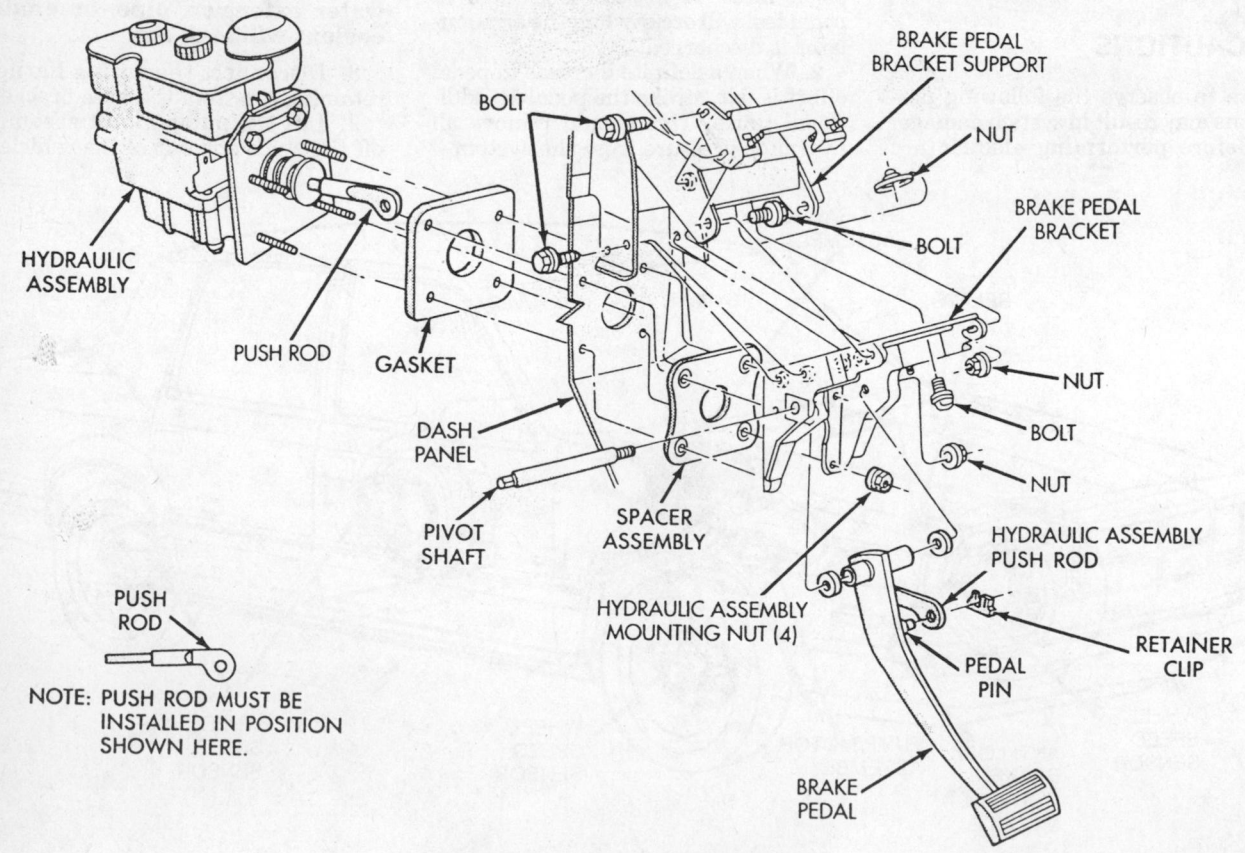

NOTE: PUSH ROD MUST BE INSTALLED IN POSITION SHOWN HERE.

Hydraulic assembly—1992–93 vehicles

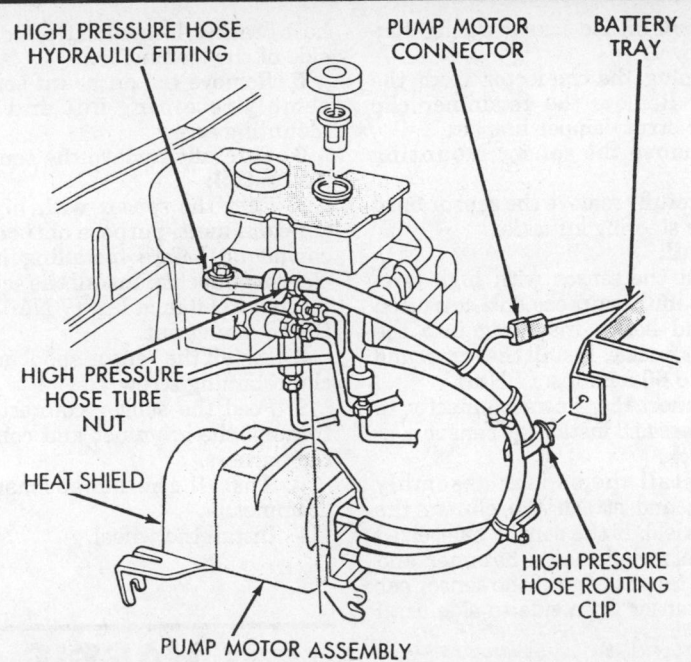

HIGH PRESSURE HOSE HYDRAULIC FITTING

PUMP MOTOR CONNECTOR

BATTERY TRAY

HIGH PRESSURE HOSE TUBE NUT

HEAT SHIELD

HIGH PRESSURE HOSE ROUTING CLIP

PUMP MOTOR ASSEMBLY

Brake tube and hose routing at hydraulic unit—1992 vehicle equipped with ABS

onto the bracket; install the heat shield and its retaining bolt.

11. Install the pump/motor electrical connector to the engine mount.

12. Connect the high and low pressure hose to the hydraulic assembly. Tighten the high pressure line to 145 inch lbs. (16 Nm). Tighten the hose clamp on the low pressure hose to 10 inch lbs (1 Nm).

13. Connect the electrical connectors removed for access.

14. Install the high pressure line retaining clip to the battery tray if removed.

15. Install the fresh air intake ducts.

16. Bleed the brake system.

Hydraulic Assembly

REMOVAL & INSTALLATION

1. Disconnect the negative battery cable. Depressurize the hydraulic accumulator.

— **CAUTION** —

Failure to depressurize the hydraulic accumulator, prior to performing this operation may result in personal injury and/or damage to the painted surfaces.

2. Remove the fresh air intake ducts.

3. Disconnect all electrical connectors from the hydraulic unit and pump/motor.

4. Remove as much of the fluid as possible from the reservoir on the hydraulic assembly.

5. Remove the pressure hose fitting (banjo bolt) from the hydraulic assembly. Use care not to drop the 2 washers

used to seal the pressure hose fitting to the hydraulic assembly inlet.

6. Disconnect the return hose from the reservoir nipple. Cap the spigot on the reservoir.

7. Disconnect all brake tubes from the hydraulic assembly.

8. Remove the driver's side sound insulation panel.

9. Disconnect the pushrod from the brake pedal by using a small, flat tool to release the retainer clip on the brake pedal pin. The center tang on the clip must be moved back enough to allow the lock tab to clear the pin. Disconnect the pushrod from the pedal pin.

10. Remove the 4 underdash hydraulic assembly mounting nuts.

11. Remove the hydraulic assembly.

To install:

12. Position the hydraulic assembly on the vehicle.

13. Install and torque the mounting nuts to 21 ft. lbs. (28 Nm).

14. Using Lubriplate® or equivalent, coat the bearing surface of the pedal pin.

15. Connect the pushrod to the pedal and install a new retainer clip.

16. Install the brake tubes. If the proportioning valves were removed from the hydraulic assembly, reinstall valves and tighten to 30 ft. lbs. (40 Nm).

17. Install the return hose to the nipple on the reservoir.

18. Install the pressure hose to the hydraulic assembly; be sure the 2 washers are in there proper position. Tighten the bango bolt to 13 ft. lbs. (18 Nm).

19. Fill the reservoir to the top of the screen.

20. Connect all electrical connectors to the hydraulic assembly.

21. Bleed the entire brake system.

22. Install the crosscar brace, if disturbed. Install the fresh air intake duct.

23. Connect the negative battery cable and check the assembly for proper operation.

Sensor Block

REMOVAL & INSTALLATION

1989–90 Vehicles

1. Disconnect the negative battery cable. Depressurize the hydraulic accumulator.

— **CAUTION** —

Failure to depressurize the hydraulic accumulator, prior to performing this operation may result in personal injury and/or damage to the painted surfaces.

2. Disconnect all electrical connectors from the reservoir on the hydraulic assembly.

3. Working from under the dash, disconnect the pushrod from the brake pedal.

4. Remove the driver's side sound insulator panel.

5. Remove the 4 hydraulic assembly mounting nuts.

6. Working from under the hood, pull the hydraulic assembly away from the dash panel and rotate the assembly enough to gain access to the sensor block cover.

NOTE: The brake lines should not be removed or deformed during this procedure.

7. Remove the sensor block cover retaining bolt and remove the sensor block cover. Care should be used not to damage the cover gasket during removal.

8. Disengage the locking tabs and disconnect the valve block connector (12 pin) from the sensor block.

9. Disengage the reed block connector, marked PUSH, by carefully pulling outward on the orange connector body. The connector is partially retained by a plastic clip and will only move outward approximately ½ in. (13mm).

10. Remove the 3 block retaining bolts.

11. Carefully disengage the sensor block pressure port from the hydraulic assembly and remove the sensor block from the vehicle. The sensor block pressure port is sealed with an O-ring and extra care should be taken to prevent damage to the seal.

12. Inspect the sensor block pressure port O-ring for damage. Replace the O-ring if cut or damaged. Check the sensor block wiring for any mispositioning or damage. Correct any damage or replace the sensor block, if damage cannot be corrected.

To install:

13. Pull the reed block connector (2 pin) outward to the disengage position prior to installing the sensor block on the hydraulic unit.

14. Throughly lubricate the sensor block pressure port O-ring with fresh, clean brake fluid. Carefully insert the pressure port into the hydraulic assembly's orifice, taking care not to cut or damage the O-ring. Position the sensor block for installation of the mounting bolts.

15. Install the sensor block mounting bolts. Tighten to 11 ft. lbs. (15 Nm).

16. Engage the reed block connector by pressing on the orange connector body marked **PUSH.**

17. Connect the valve block connector (12 pin) to the sensor block.

18. Install the sensor block cover, gasket and mounting bolt.

19. Connect the sensor block and control pressure switch connectors.

20. Install the hydraulic assembly by reversing the removal procedure.

21. Connect the negative battery cable and check the sensor block for proper operation.

Wheel Speed Sensors

REMOVAL & INSTALLATION

Front Sensor

1. Raise the vehicle and support safely. Remove the wheel and tire assembly.

2. Remove the screw from the clip that holds the sensor to the fender shield.

3. Carefully pull the sensor assembly grommet from the fender shield.

Do not pull on the sensor wiring during removal.

4. Unplug the connector from the harness. Remove the retaininer clip from the strut damper bracket.

5. Remove the sensor mounting screw.

6. Carefully remove the sensor head from the steering knuckle.

To install:

7. Coat the sensor with high temperature multi-purpose anti-corrosion compound before installing into the steering knuckle. Install the screw and tighten to 60 inch lbs. (7 Nm).

8. Connect the sensor connector to the harness and install the sensor connector lock.

9. Install the sensor assembly grommet and attach the clip to the fender shield. If the sensor has seized due to corrosion, use a hammer and punch to tap the edge of the sensor ear rocking sensor from side to side until free.

NOTE: Proper installation of the wheel speed sensor cables is critical to continued system operation. Be sure the cables are installed in retainers. Failure to install the cables in the retainers may result in contact with moving parts and/or over-extension of the cables, resulting in an open circuit.

10. Install the wheel.

Rear Sensor

1. Raise the vehicle and support safely. Remove the wheel and tire assembly.

2. Carefully pull the sensor assembly grommet from the underbody and pull the harness through the hole.

3. Unplug the connector from the harness. Remove the retaininer clip from the strut damper bracket.

4. Remove the sensor spool grommet clip retaining screw from the body

hose bracket, located in front of the inside of the trailing arm.

5. Remove the outboard sensor assembly retaining nut and sensor mounting screw.

6. Carefully remove the sensor.

To install:

7. Coat the sensor with high temperature multi-purpose anti-corrosion compound before installing into the steering knuckle. Install the screw and tighten to 60 inch lbs. (7 Nm). Install the retaining nut.

8. Install the sensor spool grommet clip retaining screw.

9. Feed the sensor connector wire through the grommet and connect to the harness.

10. Install the sensor assembly grommet.

11. Install the wheel.

CHASSIS ELECTRICAL

Air Bag

DISARMING

NOTE: Before attempting any repair procedure that is located in the area of an air bag sensor or wire harness, it is recommended that the air bag system be disarmed. Failure to disarm the air bag system may result in accidental deployment of the air bag module and possible personal injury.

To disarm the air bag system, disconnect the negative battery cable and isolate using an appropriate insulator. Allow the system capacitor to discharge for 2 minutes prior to starting repairs on the vehicle.

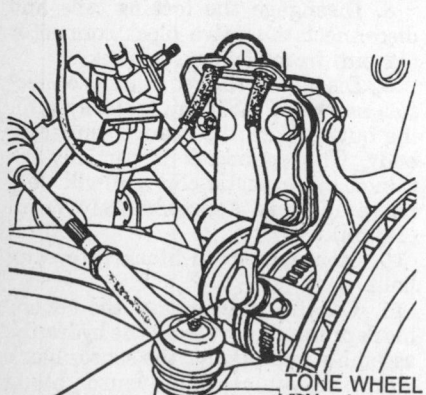

Front wheel speed sensor location

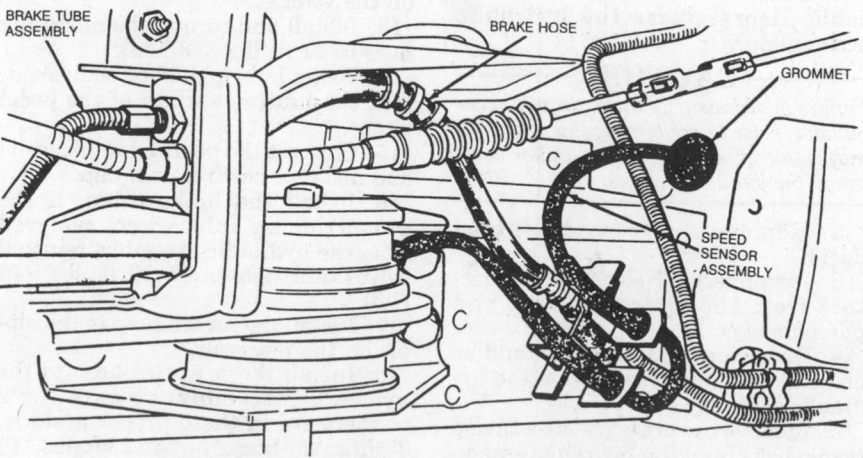

Rear speed sensor wiring routing along the body

Heater Blower Motor

REMOVAL & INSTALLATION

1. Disconnect the negative battery cable.
2. Remove the glove box assembly, lower right side instrument panel trim cover and right cowl trim panel, as required. Disconnect the blower lead wire connector.
3. If equipped with air conditioning, disconnect the 2 vacuum lines from the recirculating door actuator and position the actuator to the side.
4. Remove the 2 screws at the top of the blower housing that secure it to the unit cover.
5. Remove the 5 screws from around the blower housing and separate the blower housing from the unit.
6. Remove the 3 screws that secure the blower assembly to the heater or air conditioning housing and remove the assembly from the unit. Remove the fan from the blower motor.

To install:
7. Install the fan onto the blower motor and position motor assembly in housing. Secure motor using 3 mounting screws.
8. Install the blower housing and the heater unit and secure with screws.
9. Connect the 2 vacuum hoses to the recirculating air door actuator as required.
10. Connect the blower lead wire connector.
11. Install the glove box assembly, lower right side instrument panel trim cover and right cowl trim panel, as required.
12. Connect the negative battery cable and check the blower motor for proper operation.

Windshield Wiper Motor

REMOVAL & INSTALLATION

1. Disconnect the negative battery cable.
2. Remove the wiper arms, blades and the plastic cowl top cover.
3. Remove the attaching screws from each pivot assembly.
4. Remove the motor mounting bracket retainer bolts and disconnect the wiper motor harness connector.
5. Remove the wiper motor, pivot and links from the vehicle as an assembly.
6. Clamp the wiper motor in a vise and remove the nut from the end of the motor shaft. Do not allow the shaft of the motor to turn from the PARK position.

To install:
7. Assemble the linkage to the motor. Make sure the crank fits over the D slot on the motor shaft. Tighten the motor shaft nut to 90 inch lbs. (10 Nm).
8. Make sure the motor is still in the PARK position prior to installing the wiper linkage. If not, temporarily connect the motor to the wiring harness and operate the switch to position the motor in the PARK position. Connect the linkage to the motor.
9. Install the wiper motor, pivot and links to the vehicle as an assembly.
10. Secure the mounting bracket retainer bolts to 70 inch. lbs. (8 Nm). Attach the wiper motor harness.
11. Cycle the switch and turn OFF to assure motor is in the PARK position. Install the cowl top plastic cover and wiper arms tightening the retaining nuts to 150 inch lbs. (17 Nm).
12. Connect the negative battery cable and check for proper operation of the wipers.

Windshield Wiper Switch

REMOVAL & INSTALLATION

NOTE: On 1990–93 vehicles, the windshield wiper switch is part of the combination switch.

1989 Vehicles

STANDARD COLUMN

1. Disconnect the negative battery cable.
2. Remove the lower steering column cover.
3. Straighten the steering wheel so the tires are pointing straight-ahead.

NOTE: If equipped with an airbag, it is imperative that the steering wheel removal and installation procedure under Steering is followed.

4. Remove the steering wheel.
5. Remove the plastic wiring channel from the underside of the steering column.
6. Disconnect the wiper switch connector, intermittent wipe module connector and cruise control connector, if equipped.
7. Remove the side lock housing cover.
8. Remove the slotted hex-head screw that attaches the wiper switch to the turn signal switch and remove the switch.
9. Remove the control knob from the end of the stalk. Pull the round nylon hider up the control stalk and remove the revealed screws that attach the control stalk sleeve to the wiper switch.

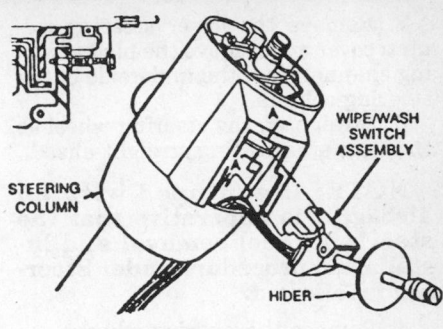

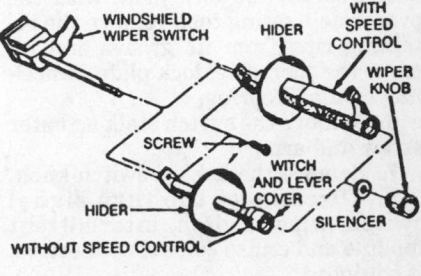

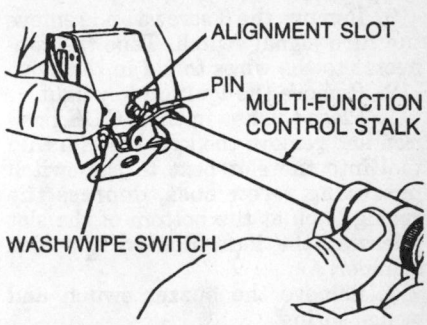

Removing the wiper switch—1989 standard column

10. Rotate the control stalk shaft to the full clockwise position and remove the shaft from the wiper switch by pulling it straight out.

To install:
11. Install the control shaft to the wiper switch, install the screws, the hider and the control knob.
12. Run the wiring through the opening and down the steering column, position the switch and install the hex-head screw. Make sure the dimmer switch rod is properly engaged.
13. Install the side lock housing cover.
14. Connect the wires and install the wiring channel.
15. Install the steering wheel and torque the nut to 45 ft. lbs. (61 Nm).
16. Install the horn pad.
17. Connect the negative battery cable and check the wiper and washer, cruise control, turn signal switch and dimmer switch for proper operation.
18. Install the lower column cover.

TILT COLUMN

1. Disconnect the negative battery cable.

2. Remove the lower steering column cover and remove the plastic wiring channel from the underside of the steering column.

3. Straighten the steering wheel so the tires are pointing straight-ahead.

NOTE: If equipped with an airbag, it is imperative that the steering wheel removal and installation procedure under Steering is followed.

4. Remove the steering wheel.

5. Depress the lock plate with the proper depressing tool, remove the retaining ring from its groove and remove the tool, ring, lock plate, cancelling cam and spring.

6. Remove the switch stalk actuator screw and arm.

7. Remove the hazard switch knob.

8. Disconnect the turn signal switch, wiper switch, intermittent module and cruise control connectors, if equipped.

9. Remove the 3 screws and remove the turn signal switch. Tape the connector to the wires to aid in removal.

10. Remove the ignition key light.

11. Place the key in the **LOCK** position and remove the key. Insert a thin tool into the slot next to the switch mounting screw boss, depress the spring latch at the bottom of the slot releasing the lock. Remove the lock cylinder.

12. Remove the buzzer switch and wedge spring.

13. Remove the 3 housing cover screws and remove the housing cover.

14. Remove the wiper switch pivot pin with a punch and remove the switch.

15. Remove the control knob from the end of the stalk. Pull the round nylon hider up the control stalk and remove the revealed screws that attach the control stalk sleeve to the wiper switch.

16. Rotate the control stalk shaft to the full clockwise position and remove the shaft from the wiper switch by pulling it straight out.

To install:

17. Install the control shaft to the wiper switch, install the screws, the hider and the control knob.

18. Run the wiring through the opening and down the steering column, position the switch and install the wiper switch pivot pin.

19. Install the housing cover.

20. Install the buzzer switch and wedge spring.

21. Install the lock cylinder.

22. Install the ignition key light.

23. Install the turn signal switch, switch stalk actuator arm and hazard switch knob.

24. Install the spring, cancelling cam, lock plate and ring on the steering shaft. Depress the plate with the depressing tool and install the ring securely in the groove. Remove the tool slowly.

25. Connect the turn signal switch, wiper switch, intermittent module and cruise control connectors, if equipped. Install the wiring channel.

26. Install the steering wheel and torque the nut to 45 ft. lbs. (61 Nm).

27. Install the horn pad.

28. Connect the negative battery cable and check the wiper and washer, cruise control, turn signal switch and dimmer switch for proper operation.

29. Install the lower column cover.

Instrument Cluster

REMOVAL & INSTALLATION

1. Disconnect the negative battery cable and disarm the air bag system, if equipped. Move the gear selector lever to the lowest position.

2. Remove the 5 screws retaining the upper bezel and 4 screws attaching the lower bezel to the instrument panel. Remove bezels from the instrument panel.

3. When only removing gauge(s) or the speedometer, remove the trip odometer reset knob by pulling straight back. Remove the mask and lens assembly and the desired gauge from the cluster.

4. Disconnect the gear indicator cable. On 1991–93 models equipped with PRNDL indicator assembly, disconnect and remove PRNDL as follows:

a. Move the shifter to the PARK position.

b. Remove the guide tube from behind the fuse block and disconnect the eyelet from the column actuating arm.

c. Release the lock lever on the lower end of the column insert and squeeze the legs together.

d. Remove the insert from the steering column and secure out of the way.

5. Remove the rear window defogger bezel and the radio bezel. Remove the upper steering column cover.

6. Remove the 4 screws attaching the cluster housing to the base panel and pull the cluster out. Disconnect the 2 wiring harnesses and remove the cluster from the vehicle.

To install:

7. Connect the wiring harness. Install cluster assembly and connect the gear indicator cable. If equipped with PRNDL assembly, install as follows:

a. Route the PRNDL guide tube through the access hole in the base of the panel. Release the guide tube behind the fuse block.

b. Insert the flange of the column insert into the column, squeeze the legs together with the tabs under column jacket and engage the lock bar to secure the insert.

c. Hook the eyelet to the steering column actuator and check the pointer, which should be pointing to N position.

d. If alignment is incorrect, adjust pointer to align with the center of the N by turning the adjuster screw located by the cable actuator arm.

8. Install the upper and lower steering column cover, radio bezel, rear window defroster bezel and the cluster bezel.

9. Install the retaining screws.

10. Connect the negative battery cable and check all gauges and the speedometer for proper operation. Make sure the gearshift indicator is properly aligned.

Radio

REMOVAL & INSTALLATION

1. Disconnect the negative battery cable.

2. Remove the cluster bezel.

3. Remove the screws that attach the radio to the instrument panel.

4. Pull the radio out, disconnect the connectors, ground cable and antenna and remove the radio.

5. The installation is the reverse of the removal procedure.

6. Connect the negative battery cable and check the radio for proper operation.

Concealed Headlights

MANUAL OPERATION

1. Disconnect the negative battery cable.

2. Locate the manual override knob located under the center of the front bumper.

3. Rotate the manual override knob to raise the headlight cover(s).

4. Connect the negative battery cable.

Headlight Switch

REMOVAL & INSTALLATION

1. Disconnect the negative battery cable. Remove the headlight cluster bezel.

2. Remove the screws securing the headlight and heated rear window switch module to the instrument panel. Pull the assembly out to disconnect the connectors from the switch.

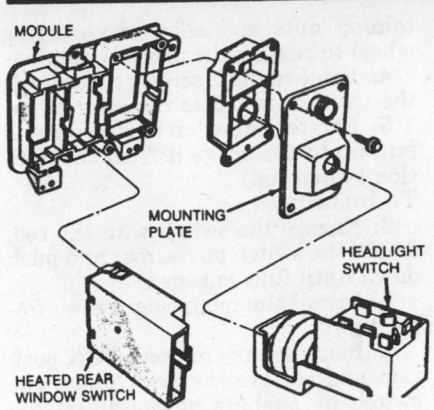

Headlight and heated rear window switches

3. Depress the spring button and remove the headlight switch knob and stem.

4. Remove the escutcheon and remove the nut that attaches the switch to the mounting plate.

5. The installation is the reverse of the removal procedure.

Dimmer Switch

REMOVAL & INSTALLATION

NOTE: On 1990–93 vehicles, the dimmer switch is part of the combination switch.

1989 Vehicles

1. Disconnect the negative battery cable.

2. Remove the lower steering column cover, if equipped.

3. Unplug the switch, located on the lower portion of the steering column.

4. Holding the actuating rod against its upper seat, remove the bolts that attach the switch to the column and remove the switch.

5. The installation is the reverse of the removal procedure. Adjust the switch as required.

Turn Signal Switch

NOTE: On 1990–93 vehicles, the turn signal switch is part of the combination switch.

REMOVAL & INSTALLATION

1989 Vehicles

STANDARD COLUMN

1. Disconnect the negative battery cable.

2. Remove the lower steering column cover.

3. Straighten the steering wheel so the tires are pointing straight-ahead.

NOTE: If equipped with an airbag, it is imperative that the steering wheel removal and installation procedure under Steering is followed.

4. Remove the steering wheel.

5. Remove the plastic wiring channel from the underside of the steering column and disconnect the turn signal switch connector.

6. Remove the hazard switch knob. Remove the slotted hex-head screw that attaches the wiper switch to the turn signal switch.

7. Remove the 3 screws and pull the turn signal switch out of the column.

To install:

8. Run the wiring through the opening and down the steering column, position the switch and install the hex-head screw. Make sure the dimmer switch rod is properly engaged.

9. Install the 3 screws and the hazard switch knob.

10. Connect the wires and install the wiring channel.

11. Install the steering wheel and torque the nut to 45 ft. lbs. (61 Nm).

12. Install the horn pad.

13. Connect the negative battery cable and check the turn signal switch and dimmer switch for proper operation.

14. Install the lower column cover.

TILT COLUMN

1. Disconnect the negative battery cable.

2. Remove the lower steering column cover and remove the plastic wiring channel from the underside of the steering column.

3. Straighten the steering wheel so the tires are pointing straight-ahead.

NOTE: If equipped with an airbag, it is imperative that the steering wheel removal and installation procedure under Steering is followed.

4. Remove the steering wheel.

5. Depress the lock plate with the proper depressing tool, remove the retaining ring from its groove and remove the tool, ring, lock plate, cancelling cam and spring.

6. Remove the stalk actuator screw and arm.

7. Remove the hazard switch knob.

8. Disconnect the turn signal switch connector.

9. Remove the 3 screws and remove the turn signal switch. Tape the connector to the wires to aid in removal.

To install:

10. Run the wiring through the opening and down the steering column, install the turn signal switch, switch stalk actuator arm and hazard switch knob.

11. Install the spring, cancelling cam, lock plate and ring on the steering shaft. Depress the plate with the depressing tool and install the ring securely in the groove. Remove the tool slowly.

12. Connect the turn signal switch connector and install the channel.

13. Install the steering wheel and torque the nut to 45 ft. lbs. (61 Nm).

14. Install the horn pad.

15. Connect the negative battery cable and check the turn signal switch and dimmer switch for proper operation.

16. Install the lower column cover.

Combination Switch

REMOVAL & INSTALLATION

1990–93 Vehicles

1. Disconnect the negative battery cable.

2. Remove the tilt lever, if equipped.

3. Remove the steering column covers.

4. Remove the combination switch tamper-proof mounting screws and pull the switch away from the steering column.

5. Loosen the connector screw; the screw will remain in the connector.

6. Disconnect the connector from the switch.

To install:

8. Install the wiring connector to the switch and tighten the connector retainer screw to 17 inch lbs. (2 Nm).

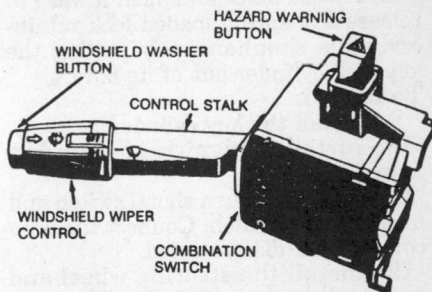

Combination switch—1990–93 vehicles

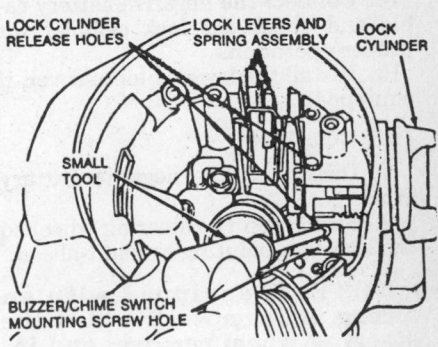

Removing the key lock cylinder—1989 standard column

9. Mount the combination switch to the column and tighten the retaining screws to 17 inch lbs. (2 Nm).

10. Install the tilt lever to the column, if equipped.

11. Connect the negative battery cable and check for proper operation of all switch functions.

Ignition Lock

REMOVAL & INSTALLATION

1989 Vehicles

STANDARD COLUMN

1. Disconnect the negative battery cable.

2. Straighten the steering wheel so the tires are pointing straight-ahead.

NOTE: If equipped with an airbag, it is imperative that the steering wheel removal and installation procedure under Steering is followed.

3. Remove the steering wheel.

4. Remove the hazard switch knob. Remove the slotted hex-head screw that attaches the wiper switch to the turn signal switch.

5. Remove the 3 screws and pull the turn signal switch out of the column as far as it will go. Unplug it below if necessary.

6. Remove the ignition switch key light.

7. Place the key in the LOCK position and remove the key.

8. Insert 2 small diameter tools into both release holes and push inward to release the spring loaded lock retainers while simultaneously pulling the key lock cylinder out of its bore.

To install:

9. Install the key cylinder.

10. Install the ignition switch key light.

11. Install the turn signal switch and hazard switch knob. Connect the wire connector if disconnected.

12. Install the steering wheel and torque the nut to 45 ft. lbs. (61 Nm).

13. Install the horn pad.

14. Connect the negative battery cable and check the lock cylinder for proper operation.

15. Install the lower column cover, if equipped.

TILT COLUMN

1. Disconnect the negative battery cable.

2. Straighten the steering wheel so the tires are pointing straight-ahead.

NOTE: If equipped with an airbag, it is imperative that the steering wheel removal and installation procedure under Steering is followed.

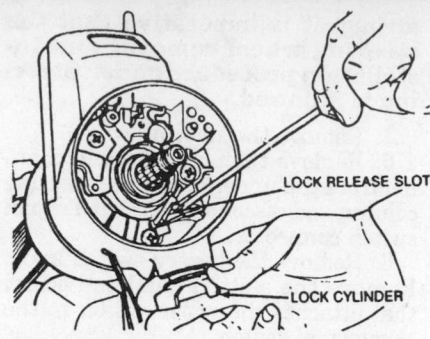

Removing the key lock cylinder—1989 tilt column

3. Remove the steering wheel.

4. Depress the lock plate with the proper depressing tool, remove the retaining ring from its groove and remove the tool, ring, lock plate, cancelling cam and spring.

5. Remove the stalk actuator screw and arm.

6. Remove the hazard switch knob.

7. Remove the 3 screws and pull the turn signal switch out of the column as far as it will go. Unplug it below if necessary.

8. Remove the ignition key light.

9. Place the key in the LOCK position and remove the key. Insert a thin tool into the slot next to the switch mounting screw boss, depress the spring latch at the bottom of the slot releasing the lock and remove the lock cylinder.

To install:

10. Install the lock cylinder.

11. Install the ignition key light.

12. Install the turn signal switch, switch stalk actuator arm and hazard switch knob.

13. Install the spring, cancelling cam, lock plate and ring on the steering shaft. Depress the plate with the depressing tool and install the ring securely in the groove. Remove the tool slowly.

14. Connect the wire connectors, if disconnected.

15. Install the steering wheel and torque the nut to 45 ft. lbs. (61 Nm).

16. Install the horn pad.

17. Connect the negative battery cable and check the turn signal switch for proper operation.

18. Install the lower column cover.

Ignition Switch

REMOVAL & INSTALLATION

1989 Vehicle

1. Disconnect the negative battery cable.

2. Remove the lower steering column cover.

3. Remove the steering column re-

taining nuts and allow the steering wheel to rest on the driver's seat.

4. Remove the 2 screws that attach the ignition switch to the column.

5. Rotate the switch 90 degrees and pull up to disengage it from the ignition switch rod.

To install:

6. Engage the switch with the rod, rotate the switch 90 degrees and push down until fully engaged.

7. Install the mounting screws finger tight.

8. Place the key in the LOCK position and remove the key. Adjust the switch by pushing up gently on the switch to take up all slack in the rod.

9. Tighten the mounting screws and check the switch for proper operation in all positions.

10. Install the steering column and cover.

Ignition Lock/Switch

REMOVAL & INSTALLATION

1990–93 Vehicles

1. Disconnect the negative battery cable.

2. Remove the tilt lever, if equipped.

3. Remove the upper and lower column covers.

4. Remove the 3 ignition switch tamper-proof Torx® screws; APEX 440–TX20H or equivalent is required.

5. Pull the switch away from the column. Release the connector locks on the 2 wiring connectors and disconnect them from the switch.

6. Remove the key lock cylinder from the ignition switch by performing the following:

a. Insert the key and turn the switch in the LOCK position. Using a small tool, depress the key cylinder retaining pin flush with the key cylinder surface.

b. Rotate the key clockwise to the OFF position to unseat the key cylinder from the ignition switch assembly. The cylinder bezel should be about ⅛ in. above the ignition switch halo light ring. Do not at-

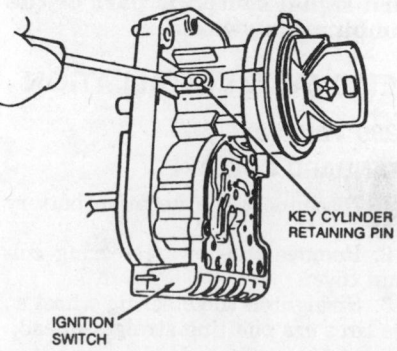

Depressing the key cylinder retaining pin

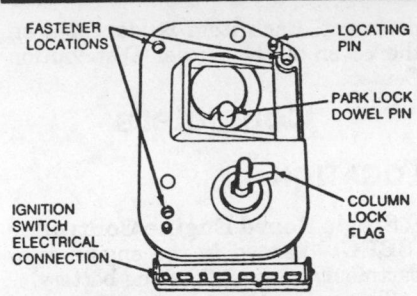

Preparing the ignition switch for Installation

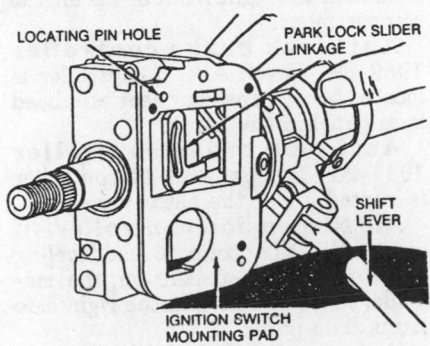

Ignition switch mounting pad

tempt to remove the key cylinder at this point.

c. With the key cylinder in the unseated position, rotate the key counterclockwise to the **LOCK** position and remove the key.

d. Remove the key cylinder from the ignition switch.

To install:

7. Connect the wiring connectors.

8. Mount ignition switch to the column by performing the following:

a. Position the shifter in **PARK** position. The park lock dowel pin on the ignition switch assembly must engage with the column park lock slider linkage.

b. Verify that the ignition switch is in the **LOCK** position. The flag should be parallel to the ignition switch terminals. Apply a small amount of grease to the flag and pin.

c. Position the park lock link to mid-travel.

d. Align the locating pin hole and its pin and position the ignition switch against the lock housing face, make sure the pin is inserted into the park lock link contour slot. Torque the retaining screws to 17 inch lbs. (2 Nm).

9. With the key cylinder and ignition switch in the **LOCK** position, key not in cylinder, gently insert the key cylinder into the ignition switch until it bottoms.

10. Insert the key. Simultaneously push in on the cylinder and rotate the key to the **RUN** position. This action should fully seat the cylinder in the ignition switch.

11. Install the column covers and the tilt lever, if equipped.

12. Connect the negative battery cable and check the push-to-lock and park lock functions, halo lighting and all ignition switch positions for proper operation.

Stoplight Switch

ADJUSTMENT

1. Disconnect the negative battery cable. Disarm the air bag system, if equipped.

2. Remove the lower steering column cover.

3. Push the switch and retainer bracket forward towards the brake pedal as far as it will go. The brake pedal should move forward slightly.

4. Gently pull back on the brake pedal bringing the striker back toward the switch. Continue to pull back on the brake pedal until it will go back no further. This will cause the switch to ratchet backward to the correct position.

5. Connect the negative battery cable.

6. Verify correct adjustment of the stoplight switch; with the engine OFF, apply the brake pedal and check to make sure the brake lights are illuminated. If the brake lights do not go on, readjust the switch as outlined above.

7. Install the lower steering column cover.

REMOVAL & INSTALLATION

1. Disconnect the negative battery cable.

2. Unplug the stoplight switch connectors near the brake pedal.

3. Remove the switch and bracket assembly from the brake pedal bracket.

4. Remove the switch from its bracket.

To install:

5. Install the switch and bracket assembly to the brake pedal bracket and push the switch forward as far as it will go; the brake pedal should move forward slightly.

6. Pull back on the brake pedal bringing the striker toward the switch until the pedal will not go back any farther.

7. This will cause the switch to ratchet backward into position and automatic adjustment is complete.

8. Connect the negative battery cable and check the switch for proper operation. Also, make sure the speed control system functions properly, if equipped.

Neutral Safety Switch

REMOVAL & INSTALLATION

1. Disconnect the negative battery cable.

2. Locate the neutral safety switch at the left rear corner of the automatic transaxle, in the left front of engine compartment. Do not confuse with the white PRNDL switch on the A604 automatic transaxle. Unplug the switch connector.

3. Remove the switch from the transaxle.

4. The installation is the reverse of the removal procedure. Torque the switch to 25 ft. lbs. (34 Nm).

5. Connect the negative battery cable and check the switch for proper operation.

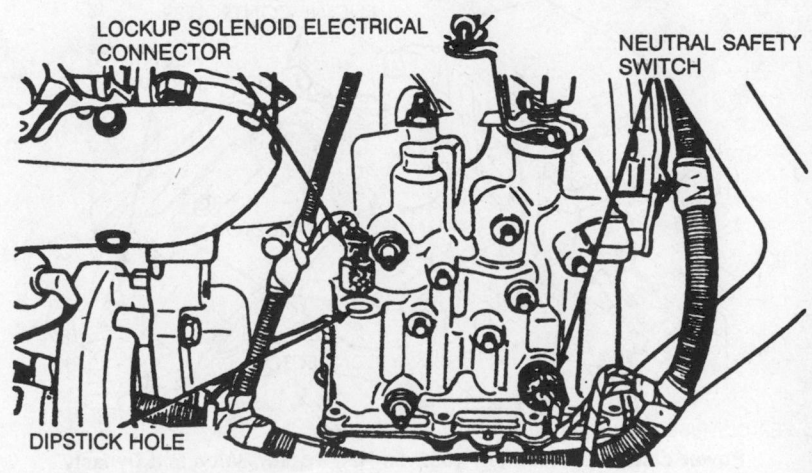

Neutral safety switch identification—A413 automatic transaxle

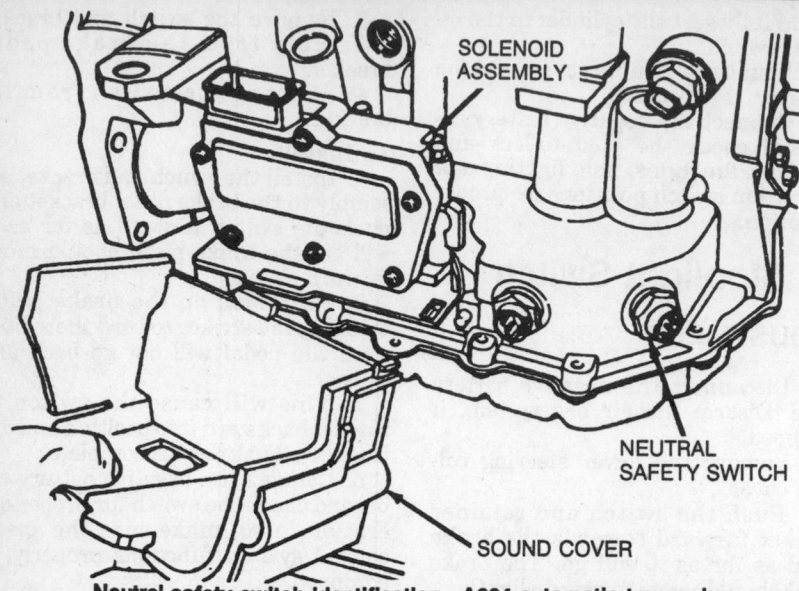

Neutral safety switch identification—A604 automatic transaxle

Fuses, Circuit Breakers, Relays and Flashers

LOCATION

Fusible Links

On vehicles without a Power Distribution Center, fusible links are part of the the large wiring harness behind the battery. On vehicles with a Power Distribution Center, fusible links in the form of cartridge fuses, which resemble small relays but serve as fusible links, are located in the Center. Each item is identified on the cover of the Power Distribution Center.

Fuse Panels

The fuse panel, which contains fuses and circuit breakers, is located behind the glove box door. To remove the panel, pull it out from the bottom and slide the tabs out from the top. Additional fuses are in the Power Distribution Center located near the left side strut tower in the engine compartment. Each item is identified on the cover of the Power Distribution Center.

Relays, Flashers and Circuit Breakers

The relay and flasher module is located behind the cupholder, which also contains circuit breakers. The entire module can be removed by pushing it up and off of its mounting bracket. Additional relays are in the Power Distribution Center located near the left side strut tower in the engine com-

partment. Each item is identified on the cover of the Power Distribution Center.

Computers

LOCATION

Single Board Engine Controller (SBEC)—located in the engine compartment, to the left of the battery.
Transaxle controller—if equipped with the A604 automatic transaxle, the transaxle controller is located in the right front of the engine compartment.
Anti-lock brake controller 1989–90—Bosch ABS 3 controller is located behind the rear seat bulkhead trim panel in the trunk.
Anti-lock brake controller 1991–93—Bendix ABS 10 controller is located under the battery tray.
Air suspension controller—if equipped with automatic load leveling or automatic air suspension, the controller is located behind the right side trunk trim panel.
Body controller—located inside the passenger compartment, behind the right side kick panel.

Cruise Control

ADJUSTMENT

2.5L Engine

1. The clearance between the throttle stud and cable clevis should be $\frac{1}{16}$ in.
2. To adjust the cable, remove the retaining clip or loosen the retaining clamp nut at the throttle bracket.
3. Pull all slack out of the cable using a suitable $\frac{1}{16}$ in. diameter tool to account for proper clearance. Make sure the curb idle position of the throttle blade is not affected.
4. Reinstall the retaining clip or nut.

3.0L, 3.3L and 3.8L Engines

1. Grip the cable core and lightly push toward the servo.
2. While holding the position, mark the core wire next to the protective sleeve.
3. Pull the core wire away from the servo. There should be a 0.24 in. (6mm) gap between the mark on the core wire and the protective sleeve.
4. If the gap is not correct, remove the adjustment clip from the throttle bracket and move the sleeve to bring the gap into specification.
5. Reinstall the clip.

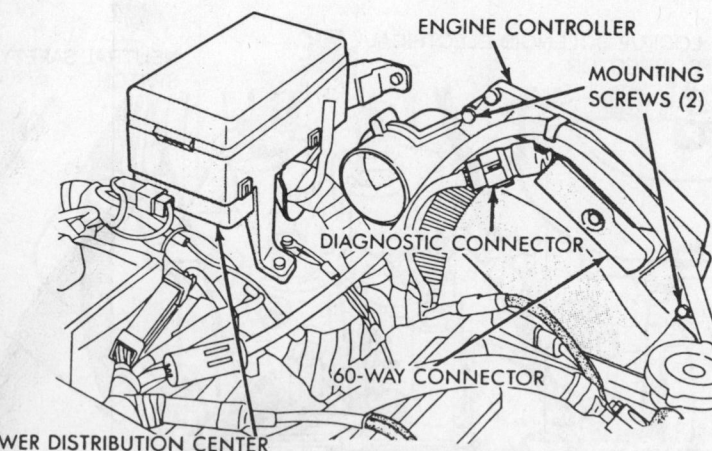

Power distribution center—1992–93 New Yorker/Salon and Dynasty

Chrysler Corp.
Front Wheel Drive
DODGE—Omni
PLYMOUTH—Horizon

SPECIFICATIONS

VEHICLE IDENTIFICATION CHART

It is important for servicing and ordering parts to be certain of the vehicle and engine identification. The VIN (vehicle identification number) is a 17 digit number visible through the windshield on the driver's side of the dash and contains the vehicle and engine identification codes. The tenth digit indicates model year and the eighth digit indicates engine code. It can be interpreted as follows:

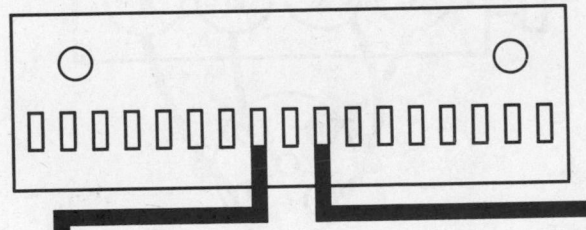

Engine Code						Model Year	
Code	Liters	Cu. In. (cc)	Cyl.	Fuel Sys.	Eng. Mfg.	Code	Year
D	2.2	135 (2200)	4	EFI	Chrysler	K	1989
						L	1990

EFI—Electronic Fuel Injection

ENGINE IDENTIFICATION

Year	Model	Engine Displacement Liters (cc)	Engine Series Identification (ID/VIN)	Fuel System	No. of Cylinders	Engine Type
1989	Horizon	2.2 (2200)	D	EFI	4	OHC
	Omni	2.2 (2200)	D	EFI	4	OHC
1990	Horizon	2.2 (2200)	D	EFI	4	OHC
	Omni	2.2 (2200)	D	EFI	4	OHC

EFI—Electronic Fuel Injection
OHC—Overhead Cam

GENERAL ENGINE SPECIFICATIONS

Year	Engine ID/VIN	Engine Displacement Liters (cc)	Fuel System Type	Net Horsepower @ rpm	Net Torque @ rpm (ft. lbs.)	Bore × Stroke (in.)	Compression Ratio	Oil Pressure @ rpm
1989	D	2.2 (2200)	EFI	99 @ 5600	121 @ 3200	3.44 × 3.62	9.5:1	30–80 @ 3000
1990	D	2.2 (2200)	EFI	99 @ 5600	121 @ 3200	3.44 × 3.62	9.5:1	30–80 @ 3000

NOTE: Horsepower and torque are SAE net figures. They are measured at the rear of the transmission with all accessories installed and operating. Since the figures vary when a given engine is installed in different models, some are representative rather than exact.
EFI—Electronic Fuel Injection

GASOLINE ENGINE TUNE-UP SPECIFICATIONS

Year	Engine ID/VIN	Engine Displacement Liters (cc)	Spark Plugs Gap (in.)	Ignition Timing (deg.) MT	Ignition Timing (deg.) AT	Fuel Pump (psi)	Idle Speed (rpm) MT	Idle Speed (rpm) AT	Valve Clearance In.	Valve Clearance Ex.
1989	D	2.2 (2200)	0.035	12B	12B	15	850	850	Hyd.	Hyd.
1990	D	2.2 (2200)	0.035	12B	12B	15	850	850	Hyd.	Hyd.

NOTE: The lowest cylinder pressure should be within 75% of the highest cylinder pressure reading. For example, if the highest cylinder is 134 psi, the lowest should be 101. Engine should be at normal operating temperature with throttle valve in the wide open position.
The underhood specifications sticker often reflects tune-up specification changes in production. Sticker figures must be used if they disagree with those in this chart.
Hyd.—Hydraulic
① Minimum

FIRING ORDERS

NOTE: To avoid confusion, always replace spark plug wires one at a time.

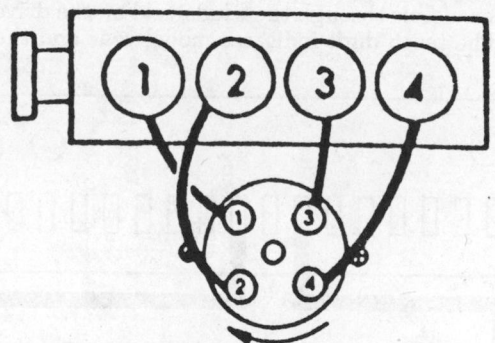

2.2L Engine
Engine Firing Order: 1–3–4–2
Distributor Rotation: Clockwise

CAPACITIES

Year	Model	Engine ID/VIN	Engine Displacement Liters (cc)	Engine Crankcase (qts.) with Filter	Transmission (pts.) 4-Spd	Transmission (pts.) 5-Spd	Transmission (pts.) Auto.	Drive Axle (pts.)	Fuel Tank (gal.)	Cooling System (qts.)
1989	Horizon	D	2.2 (2200)	4	—	4.8	18	—	13	9
	Omni	D	2.2 (2200)	4	—	4.8	18	—	13	9
1990	Horizon	D	2.2 (2200)	4	—	4.8	18	—	13	9
	Omni	D	2.2 (2200)	4	—	4.8	18	—	13	9

CAMSHAFT SPECIFICATIONS

All measurements given in inches.

| Year | Engine ID/VIN | Engine Displacement Liters (cc) | Journal Diameter | | | | | Elevation | | Bearing Clearance | Camshaft End Play |
			1	2	3	4	5	In.	Ex.		
1989	D	2.2 (2200)	1.375–1.376	1.375–1.376	1.375–1.376	1.375–1.376	1.375–1.376	NA	NA	—	0.005–0.020
1990	D	2.2 (2200)	1.375–1.376	1.375–1.376	1.375–1.376	1.375–1.376	1.375–1.376	NA	NA	—	0.005–0.020

NA—Not available

CRANKSHAFT AND CONNECTING ROD SPECIFICATIONS

All measurements are given in inches.

| Year | Engine ID/VIN | Engine Displacement Liters (cc) | Crankshaft | | | | Connecting Rod | | |
			Main Brg. Journal Dia.	Main Brg. Oil Clearance	Shaft End-play	Thrust on No.	Journal Diameter	Oil Clearance	Side Clearance
1989	D	2.2 (2200)	2.362–2.363	0.0003–0.0040	0.002–0.014	3	1.968–1.969	0.0008–0.0040	0.005–0.013
1990	D	2.2 (2200)	2.362–2.363	0.0003–0.0040	0.002–0.014	3	1.968–1.969	0.0008–0.0040	0.005–0.013

VALVE SPECIFICATIONS

| Year | Engine ID/VIN | Engine Displacement Liters (cc) | Seat Angle (deg.) | Face Angle (deg.) | Spring Test Pressure (lbs. @ in.) | Spring Installed Height (in.) | Stem-to-Guide Clearance (in.) | | Stem Diameter (in.) | |
							Intake	Exhaust	Intake	Exhaust
1989	D	2.2 (2200)	45	45	95 @ 1.65	1.65	0.001–0.003	0.0030–0.0047	0.3124	0.3103
1990	D	2.2 (2200)	45	45	95 @ 1.65	1.65	0.001–0.003	0.0030–0.0047	0.3124	0.3103

PISTON AND RING SPECIFICATIONS

All measurements are given in inches.

| Year | Engine ID/VIN | Engine Displacement Liters (cc) | Piston Clearance | Ring Gap | | | Ring Side Clearance | | |
				Top Compression	Bottom Compression	Oil Control	Top Compression	Bottom Compression	Oil Control
1989	D	2.2 (2200)	0.0005–0.0027	0.0100–0.0390	0.0110–0.0390	0.0150–0.0740	0.0015–0.0040	0.0015–0.0040	0.0002–0.0080
1990	D	2.2 (2200)	0.0005–0.0027	0.0100–0.0390	0.0110–0.0390	0.0150–0.0740	0.0015–0.0040	0.0015–0.0040	0.0002–0.0080

TORQUE SPECIFICATIONS
All readings in ft. lbs.

Year	Engine ID/VIN	Engine Displacement Liters (cc)	Cylinder Head Bolts	Main Bearing Bolts	Rod Bearing Bolts	Crankshaft Pulley Bolts	Flywheel Bolts	Manifold Intake	Manifold Exhaust	Spark Plugs	Lug Nut
1989	D	2.2 (2200)	①	30②	40②	50	70	17	17	26	95
1990	D	2.2 (2200)	①	30②	40②	50	70	17	17	26	95

① Sequence:
1st step 45 ft. lbs.
2nd step 65 ft. lbs.
3rd step plus ¼ turn
② Plus ¼ turn

BRAKE SPECIFICATIONS
All measurements in inches unless noted.

Year	Model	Master Cylinder Bore	Brake Disc Original Thickness	Brake Disc Minimum Thickness	Brake Disc Maximum Runout	Brake Drum Original Inside Diameter	Brake Drum Max. Wear Limit	Brake Drum Maximum Machine Diameter	Minimum Lining Thickness Front	Minimum Lining Thickness Rear
1989	Horizon	0.827	NA	0.431	0.005	7.87	NA	NA	0.06	0.06
	Omni	0.827	NA	0.431	0.005	7.87	NA	NA	0.06	0.06
1990	Horizon	0.827	NA	0.431	0.005	7.87	NA	NA	0.06	0.06
	Omni	0.827	NA	0.431	0.005	7.87	NA	NA	0.06	0.06

NA—Not available

WHEEL ALIGNMENT

Year	Model		Caster Range (deg.)	Caster Preferred Setting (deg.)	Camber Range (deg.)	Camber Preferred Setting (deg.)	Toe-in (in.)	Steering Axis Inclination (deg.)
1989	Horizon	Front	①	1⁹⁄₁₀P	¼N–¾P	⁵⁄₁₆P	¹⁄₁₆	13³⁄₈
		Rear	—	—	1¼N–¼N	¾N	³⁄₃₂	13³⁄₈
	Omni	Front	①	1⁹⁄₁₀P	¼N–¾P	⁵⁄₁₆P	¹⁄₁₆	13³⁄₈
		Rear	—	—	1¼N–¼N	¾N	³⁄₃₂	13³⁄₈
1990	Horizon	Front	①	1⁹⁄₁₀P	¼N–¾P	⁵⁄₁₆P	¹⁄₁₆	13³⁄₈
		Rear	—	—	1¼N–¼N	¾N	³⁄₃₂	13³⁄₈
	Omni	Front	①	1⁹⁄₁₀P	¼N–¾P	⁵⁄₁₆P	¹⁄₁₆	13³⁄₈
		Rear	—	—	1¼N–¼N	¾N	³⁄₃₂	13³⁄₈

N—Negative
P—Positive
① Variation between sides not to exceed 1½P

Chrysler Corp.
Rear Wheel Drive
CHRYSLER—Fifth Avenue • Newport
DODGE—Diplomat
PLYMOUTH—Caravelle • Gran Fury

SPECIFICATIONS

VEHICLE IDENTIFICATION CHART

It is important for servicing and ordering parts to be certain of the vehicle and engine identification. The VIN (vehicle identification number) is a 17 digit number visible through the windshield on the driver's side of the dash and contains the vehicle and engine identification codes. The tenth digit indicates model year and the eighth digit indicates engine code. It can be interpreted as follows:

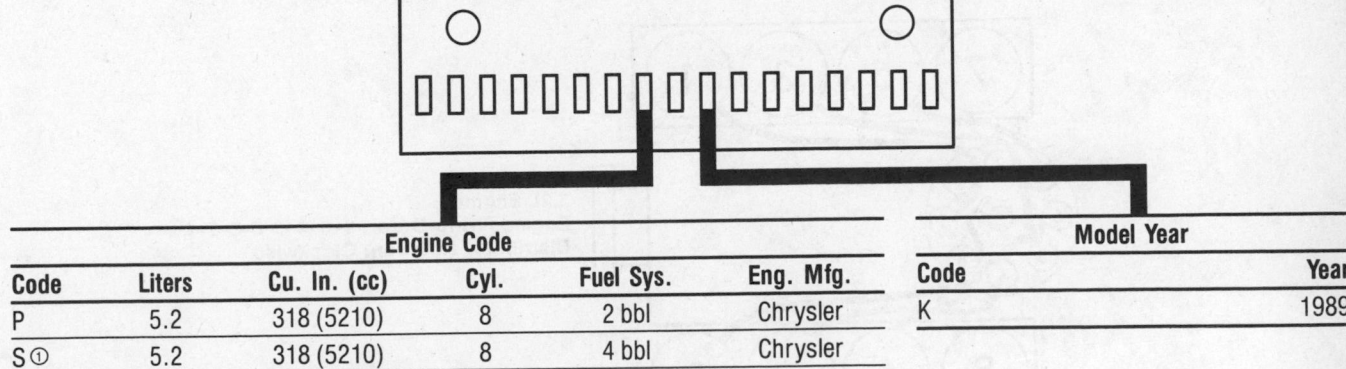

Engine Code						Model Year	
Code	Liters	Cu. In. (cc)	Cyl.	Fuel Sys.	Eng. Mfg.	Code	Year
P	5.2	318 (5210)	8	2 bbl	Chrysler	K	1989
S①	5.2	318 (5210)	8	4 bbl	Chrysler		
4	5.2	318 (5210)	8	4 bbl	Chrysler		

① HD—Heavy duty

6-1

ENGINE IDENTIFICATION

Year	Model	Engine Displacement Liters (cc)	Engine Series (ID/VIN)	Fuel System	No. of Cylinders	Engine Type
1989	Diplomat	5.2 (5210)	P	2 bbl.	8	OHV
	Gran Fury/Caravelle ①	5.2 (5210)	P	2 bbl.	8	OHV
	Gran Fury/Caravelle ①	5.2 (5210)	4	4 bbl.	8	OHV
	Gran Fury/Caravelle ①	5.2 (5210)	S ②	4 bbl.	8	OHV
	Fifth Avenue/Newport	5.2 (5210)	P	2 bbl.	8	OHV
	Fifth Avenue/Newport	5.2 (5210)	4	4 bbl.	8	OHV
	Fifth Avenue/Newport	5.2 (5210)	S ②	4 bbl.	8	OHV

OHV—Overhead Valves
① Caravelle—Canada only
② Heavy Duty

GENERAL ENGINE SPECIFICATIONS

Year	Engine ID/VIN	Engine Displacement Liters (cc)	Fuel System Type	Net Horsepower @ rpm	Net Torque @ rpm (ft. lbs.)	Bore × Stroke (in.)	Compression Ratio	Oil Pressure @ rpm
1989	P	5.2 (5210)	2 bbl	140 @ 3600	265 @ 1600	3.910 × 3.310	9.0:1	80 @ 3000
	4	5.2 (5210)	4 bbl	140 @ 3600	265 @ 2000	3.910 × 3.310	9.0:1	80 @ 3000
	S ①	5.2 (5210)	4 bbl	175 @ 4000	250 @ 3200	3.910 × 3.310	8.0:1	80 @ 3000

NOTE: Horsepower and torque are SAE net figures. They are measured at the rear of the transmission with all accessories installed and operating. Since the figures vary when a given engine is installed in different models, some are representative rather than exact.
① Heavy Duty

TUNE-UP SPECIFICATIONS

Year	Engine ID/VIN	Engine Displacement Liters (cc)	Spark Plugs Gap (in.)	Ignition Timing (deg.) MT	AT	Fuel Pump (psi)	Idle Speed (rpm) MT	AT	Valve Clearance In.	Ex.
1989	P	5.2 (5210)	0.035	—	7B	5.75–7.25	—	680	Hyd.	Hyd.
	4	5.2 (5210)	0.035	—	16B	5.75–7.25	—	750	Hyd.	Hyd.
	S	5.2 (5210)	0.035	—	16B	5.75–7.25	—	750	Hyd.	Hyd.

NOTE: The lowest cylinder pressure should be within 75% of the highest cylinder pressure reading. For example, if the highest cylinder is 134 psi, the lowest should be 101. Engine should be at normal operating temperature with throttle valve in the wide open position.
The underhood specifications sticker often reflects tune-up specification changes in production. Sticker figures must be used if they disagree with those in this chart.
Hyd.—Hydraulic

FIRING ORDERS

NOTE: To avoid confusion, always replace spark plug wires one at a time.

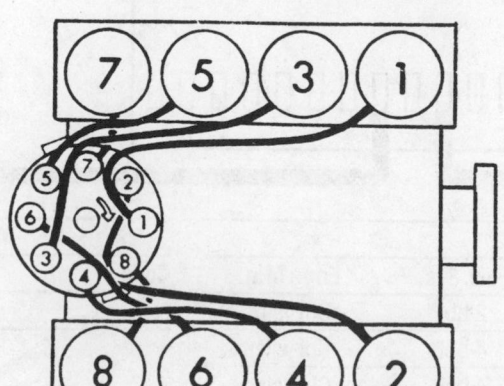

5.2L Engine
Engine Firing Order: 1–8–4–3–6–5–7–2
Distributor Rotation: Clockwise

CAPACITIES

Year	Model	Engine ID/VIN	Engine Displacement Liters (cc)	Engine Crankcase with Filter	Transmission (pts.) 4-Spd	5-Spd	Auto.	Drive Axle (pts.)	Fuel Tank (gals.)	Cooling System (qts.)
1989	Diplomat	P	5.2 (5210)	5	—	—	16.4	②	18	15.5 ③
	Diplomat	4	5.2 (5210)	5	—	—	16.3	16.4	18	15.5 ③
	Diplomat	S	5.2 (5210)	5	—	—	16.3	16.4	18	15.5 ③
	Gran Fury/ Caravelle ①	P	5.2 (5210)	5	—	—	16.4	②	18	15.5 ③
	Gran Fury/ Caravelle ①	4	5.2 (5210)	5	—	—	16.3	16.4	18	15.5 ③
	Gran Fury/ Caravelle ①	S	5.2 (5210)	5	—	—	16.3	16.4	18	15.5 ③
	Fifth Avenue/ Newport	P	5.2 (5210)	5	—	—	16.4	②	18	15.5 ③
	Fifth Avenue/ Newport	4	5.2 (5210)	5	—	—	16.3	16.4	18	15.5 ③
	Fifth Avenue/ Newport	S	5.2 (5210)	5	—	—	16.3	16.4	18	15.5 ③

① Caravelle-Canada only
② 7¼ in. axle—2.5 pts.
   8¼ in. axle—4.4 pts.
   9¼ in. axle—4.5 pts.
③ Add 1 qt. for vehicles with air conditioning

CAMSHAFT SPECIFICATIONS

All measurements given in inches.

Year	Engine ID/VIN	Engine Displacement Liters (cc)	Journal Diameter 1	2	3	4	5	Elevation In.	Ex.	Bearing Clearance	Camshaft End Play
1989	P	5.2 (5210)	1.998–1.999	1.982–1.983	1.967–1.968	1.951–1.952	1.5605–1.5615	0.373	0.400	0.001–0.003	0.002–0.010
	4	5.2 (5210)	1.998–1.999	1.982–1.983	1.967–1.968	1.951–1.952	1.5605–1.5615	0.373	0.400	0.001–0.003	0.002–0.010
	S	5.2 (5210)	1.998–1.999	1.982–1.983	1.967–1.968	1.951–1.952	1.5605–1.5615	0.373	0.400	0.001–0.003	0.002–0.010

CRANKSHAFT AND CONNECTING ROD SPECIFICATIONS

All measurements are given in inches.

Year	Engine ID/VIN	Engine Displacement Liters (cc)	Crankshaft Main Brg. Journal Dia.	Main Brg. Oil Clearance	Shaft End-play	Thrust on No.	Connecting Rod Journal Diameter	Oil Clearance	Side Clearance
1989	P	5.2 (5210)	2.4995–2.5005	①	0.002–0.010	3	2.1240–2.1250	0.0005–0.0022	0.006–0.014
	4	5.2 (5210)	2.4995–2.5005	①	0.002–0.010	3	2.1240–2.1250	0.0005–0.0022	0.006–0.014
	S	5.2 (5210)	2.4995–2.5005	①	0.002–0.010	3	2.1240–2.1250	0.0005–0.0022	0.006–0.014

① No. 1—0.0005–0.0015;
   No. 2-5—0.0005–0.0020

VALVE SPECIFICATIONS

Year	Engine ID/VIN	Engine Displacement Liters (cc)	Seat Angle (deg.)	Face Angle (deg.)	Spring Test Pressure (lbs. @ in.)	Spring Installed Height (in.)	Stem-to-Guide Clearance (in.) Intake	Stem-to-Guide Clearance (in.) Exhaust	Stem Diameter (in.) Intake	Stem Diameter (in.) Exhaust
1989	P	5.2 (5210)	45	45	177 @ 1.31	$1^{21}/_{32}$	0.0010–0.0030	0.0020–0.0040	0.3725	0.3715
	4	5.2 (5210)	45	45	177 @ 1.31	$1^{21}/_{32}$	0.0010–0.0030	0.0020–0.0040	0.3725	0.3715
	S	5.2 (5210)	45	45	193 @ 1.25	$1^{21}/_{32}$	0.0015–0.0035	0.0025–0.0045	0.3720	0.3710

PISTON AND RING SPECIFICATIONS
All measurements are given in inches.

Year	Engine ID/VIN	Engine Displacement Liters (cc)	Piston Clearance	Ring Gap Top Compression	Ring Gap Bottom Compression	Ring Gap Oil Control	Ring Side Clearance Top Compression	Ring Side Clearance Bottom Compression	Ring Side Clearance Oil Control
1989	P	5.2 (5210)	0.0005–0.0015 ①	0.0100–0.0200	0.0100–0.0200	0.0150–0.0550	0.0015–0.0030	0.0015–0.0030	0.0002–0.0050
	4	5.2 (5210)	0.0005–0.0015 ①	0.0100–0.0200	0.0100–0.0200	0.0150–0.0550	0.0015–0.0030	0.0015–0.0030	0.0002–0.0050
	S	5.2 (5210)	0.0005–0.0015 ①	0.0100–0.0200	0.0100–0.0200	0.0150–0.0550	0.0015–0.0030	0.0015–0.0030	0.0002–0.0050

① High Performance engines—0.001–0.002

TORQUE SPECIFICATIONS
All readings in ft. lbs.

Year	Engine ID/VIN	Engine Displacement Liters (cc)	Cylinder Head Bolts	Main Bearing Bolts	Rod Bearing Bolts	Crankshaft Pulley Bolts	Flywheel Bolts	Manifold Intake	Manifold Exhaust	Spark Plugs	Lug Nut
1989	P	5.2 (5210)	105	85	45	100	55	45	①	30	85
	4	5.2 (5210)	105	85	45	100	55	45	①	30	85
	S	5.2 (5210)	105	85	45	100	55	45	①	30	85

① Nuts—15 ft. lbs., bolts—20 ft. lb.

BRAKE SPECIFICATIONS
All measurements in inches unless noted.

Year	Model	Master Cylinder Bore	Brake Disc Original Thickness	Brake Disc Minimum Thickness	Brake Disc Maximum Runout	Brake Drum Diameter Original Inside Diameter	Brake Drum Diameter Max. Wear Limit	Brake Drum Diameter Maximum Machine Diameter	Minimum Lining Thickness Front	Minimum Lining Thickness Rear
1989	All	0.827 ①	1.000	0.940	0.004	10.000 ②	10.090 ③	10.060 ④	1/8	1/8

① Heavy Duty—1.03 ③ Heavy Duty—11.090
② Heavy Duty—11.000 ④ Heavy Duty—11.060

WHEEL ALIGNMENT

Year	Model	Caster Range (deg.)	Caster Preferred Setting (deg.)	Camber Range (deg.)	Camber Preferred Setting (deg.)	Toe-in (in.)	Steering Axis Inclination (deg.)
1989	All	$1^{1}/_{4}$P–$3^{3}/_{4}$P	$2^{1}/_{2}$P	$^{1}/_{4}$N–$1^{1}/_{4}$P	$^{1}/_{2}$P	1/8	8

N—Negative
P—Positive

Ford Motor Co.
Rear Wheel Drive
FORD—Mustang • Thunderbird
LINCOLN—Mark VII **MERCURY**—Cougar

SPECIFICATIONS

VEHICLE IDENTIFICATION CHART

It is important for servicing and ordering parts to be certain of the vehicle and engine identification. The VIN (vehicle identification number) is a 17 digit number visible through the windshield on the driver's side of the dash and contains the vehicle and engine identification codes. The tenth digit indicates model year and the eighth digit indicates engine code. It can be interpreted as follows:

Engine Code

Code	Liters	Cu. In. (cc)	Cyl.	Fuel Sys.	Eng. Mfg.
A	2.3	140 (2295)	4	EFI	Ford
M	2.3	140 (2295)	4	EFI	Ford
4	3.8	232 (3801)	6	SEFI	Ford
R	3.8	232 (3801)	6	SEFI	Ford
C	3.8	232 (3801)	6	SEFI	Ford
E	5.0	302 (4943)	8	SEFI	Ford
T	5.0	302 (4943)	8	SEFI	Ford

Model Year

Code	Year
K	1989
L	1990
M	1991
N	1992
P	1993

EFI—Electronic Fuel Injection   SEFI—Sequential Electronic Fuel Injection

ENGINE IDENTIFICATION

Year	Model	Engine Displacement Liters (cc)	Engine Series (ID/VIN)	Fuel System	No. of Cylinders	Engine Type
1989	Mustang	2.3 (2295)	A	EFI	4	OHC
	Mustang	5.0 (4943)	E	SEFI	8	OHV
	Thunderbird	3.8 (3801)	4	SEFI	6	OHV
	Thunderbird SC	3.8 (3801)	R①	SEFI	6	OHV
	Cougar	3.8 (3801)	4	SEFI	6	OHV
	Cougar XR7	3.8 (3801)	R①	SEFI	6	OHV
	Mark VII	5.0 (4943)	E	SEFI	8	OHV
1990	Mustang	2.3 (2295)	A	EFI	4	OHC
	Mustang	5.0 (4943)	E	SEFI	8	OHV
	Thunderbird	3.8 (3801)	4	SEFI	6	OHV
	Thunderbird SC	3.8 (3801)	R	SEFI	6	OHV
	Cougar	3.8 (3801)	4	SEFI	6	OHV
	Cougar XR7	3.8 (3801)	R	SEFI	6	OHV
	Mark VII	5.0 (4943)	E	SEFI	8	OHV
1991	Mustang	2.3 (2295)	M	EFI	4	OHC
	Mustang	5.0 (4943)	E	SEFI	8	OHV
	Thunderbird	3.8 (3801)	4	SEFI	6	OHV
	Thunderbird SC	3.8 (3801)	R	SEFI	6	OHV
	Thunderbird	5.0 (4943)	T	SEFI	8	OHV
	Cougar	3.8 (3801)	4	SEFI	6	OHV
	Cougar	5.0 (4943)	T	SEFI	8	OHV
	Mark VII	5.0 (4943)	E	SEFI	8	OHV

ENGINE IDENTIFICATION

Year	Model	Engine Displacement Liters (cc)	Engine Series (ID/VIN)	Fuel System	No. of Cylinders	Engine Type
1992–93	Mustang	2.3 (2295)	M	EFI	4	OHC
	Mustang	5.0 (4943)	E	SEFI	8	OHV
	Thunderbird	3.8 (3801)	4	SEFI	6	OHV
	Thunderbird SC	3.8 (3801)	R	SEFI	6	OHV
	Thunderbird	5.0 (4943)	T	SEFI	8	OHV
	Cougar	3.8 (3801)	4	SEFI	6	OHV
	Cougar	5.0 (4943)	T	SEFI	8	OHV
	Mark VII	5.0 (4943)	E	SEFI	8	OHV

EFI—Electronic Fuel Injection
SEFI—Sequential Electronic Fuel Injection
OHC—Overhead Cam
OHV—Overhead Valve
① Early production could be Code C

GENERAL ENGINE SPECIFICATIONS

Year	Engine ID/VIN	Engine Displacement Liters (cc)	Fuel System Type	Net Horsepower @ rpm	Net Torque @ rpm (ft. lbs.)	Bore × Stroke (in.)	Compression Ratio	Oil Pressure @ rpm
1989	A	2.3 (2295)	EFI	88 @ 4000	132 @ 2600	3.78 × 3.12	9.5:1	40–60 @ 2000 ①
	4	3.8 (3801)	SEFI	140 @ 3800	215 @ 2400	3.81 × 3.39	9.0:1	40–60 @ 2500 ①
	R	3.8 (3801)	SEFI	210 @ 4000	315 @ 2600	3.81 × 3.39	8.2:1	40–60 @ 2500 ①
	C	3.8 (3801)	SEFI	210 @ 4000	315 @ 2600	3.81 × 3.39	8.2:1	40–60 @ 2500 ①
	E	5.0 (4943)	SEFI	225 @ 4200	300 @ 3200	4.00 × 3.00	9.0:1	40–60 @ 2000 ①
1990	A	2.3 (2295)	EFI	88 @ 4000	132 @ 2600	3.78 × 3.12	9.5:1	40–60 @ 2000 ①
	4	3.8 (3801)	SEFI	140 @ 3800	215 @ 2400	3.81 × 3.39	9.0:1	40–60 @ 2500 ①
	R	3.8 (3801)	SEFI	210 @ 4000	315 @ 2600	3.81 × 3.39	8.2:1	40–60 @ 2500 ①
	E	5.0 (4943)	SEFI	225 @ 4200	300 @ 3200	4.00 × 3.00	9.0:1	40–60 @ 2000 ①
1991	M	2.3 (2295)	EFI	105 @ 4600	135 @ 2600	3.78 × 3.12	9.5:1	40–60 @ 2000 ①
	4	3.8 (3801)	SEFI	140 @ 3800	215 @ 2400	3.81 × 3.39	9.0:1	40–60 @ 2500 ①
	R	3.8 (3801)	SEFI	210 @ 4000	315 @ 2600	3.81 × 3.39	8.2:1	40–60 @ 2500 ①
	E	5.0 (4943)	SEFI	225 @ 4200	300 @ 3200	4.00 × 3.39	9.0:1	40–60 @ 2000 ①
	T	5.0 (4943)	SEFI	200 @ 4000	275 @ 3000	4.00 × 3.39	9.0:1	40–60 @ 2000 ①
1992–93	M	2.3 (2295)	EFI	105 @ 4600	135 @ 2600	3.78 × 3.12	9.5:1	40–60 @ 2000 ①
	4	3.8 (3801)	SEFI	140 @ 3800	215 @ 2400	3.81 × 3.39	9.0:1	40–60 @ 2500 ①
	R	3.8 (3801)	SEFI	210 @ 4000	315 @ 2600	3.81 × 3.39	8.2:1	40–60 @ 2500 ①
	E	5.0 (4943)	SEFI	225 @ 4200	300 @ 3200	4.00 × 3.00	9.0:1	40–60 @ 2000 ①
	T	5.0 (4943)	SEFI	200 @ 4000	275 @ 3000	4.00 × 3.39	9.0:1	40–60 @ 2000 ①

NOTE: Horsepower and torque are SAE net figures. They are measured at the rear of the transmission with all accessories installed and operating. Since the figures vary when a given engine is installed in different models, some are representative rather than exact.
EFI—Electronic Fuel Injection
SEFI—Sequential Electronic Fuel Injection
① With engine at normal operating temperature

GASOLINE ENGINE TUNE-UP SPECIFICATIONS

Year	Engine ID/VIN	Engine Displacement Liters (cc)	Spark Plugs Gap (in.)	Ignition Timing (deg.) MT	Ignition Timing (deg.) AT	Fuel Pump (psi)②	Idle Speed (rpm) MT	Idle Speed (rpm) AT	Valve Clearance In.	Valve Clearance Ex.
1989	A	2.3 (2295)	0.044	10B	10B	35–45	①	①	Hyd.	Hyd.
	4	3.8 (3801)	0.054	—	10B	35–45	—	①	Hyd.	Hyd.
	R	3.8 (3801)	0.054	10B	10B	35–40	700–800	550–650	Hyd.	Hyd.
	C	3.8 (3801)	0.054	10B	10B	35–40	700–800	550–650	Hyd.	Hyd.
	E	5.0 (4943)	0.054	10B	10B	35–45	①	①	Hyd.	Hyd.
1990	A	2.3 (2295)	0.044	10B	10B	35–40	①	①	Hyd.	Hyd.
	4	3.8 (3801)	0.054	—	10B	35–40	—	①	Hyd.	Hyd.
	R	3.8 (3801)	0.054	10B	10B	35–40	700–800	550–650	Hyd.	Hyd.
	E	5.0 (4943)	0.054	10B	10B	35–40	①	①	Hyd.	Hyd.
1991	M	2.3 (2295)	0.044	10B	10B	35–40	①	①	Hyd.	Hyd.
	4	3.8 (3801)	0.054	—	10B	35–40	—	①	Hyd.	Hyd.
	R	3.8 (3801)	0.054	10B	10B	35–40	750	550	Hyd.	Hyd.
	E	5.0 (4943)	0.054	10B	10B	35–40	①	①	Hyd.	Hyd.
	T	5.0 (4943)	0.054	—	10B	35–40	—	①	Hyd.	Hyd.
1992	M	2.3 (2295)	0.044	10B	10B	35–40	①	①	Hyd.	Hyd.
	4	3.8 (3801)	0.054	—	10B	35–40	①	①	Hyd.	Hyd.
	R	3.8 (3801)	0.054	10B	10B	35–40	①	①	Hyd.	Hyd.
	E	5.0 (4943)	0.054	10B	10B	35–40	①	①	Hyd.	Hyd.
	T	5.0 (4943)	0.054	—	10B	35–40	①	①	Hyd.	Hyd.
1993	REFER TO UNDERHOOD SPECIFICATIONS STICKER									

NOTE: The lowest cylinder pressure should be within 75% of the highest cylinder pressure reading. For example, if the highest cylinder is 134 psi, the lowest should be 101. Engine should be at normal operating temperature with throttle valve in the wide open position.
The underhood specifications sticker often reflects tune-up specification changes in production. Sticker figures must be used if they disagree with those in this chart.
B—Before Top Dead Center
Hyd.—Hydraulic
① Refer to Vehicle Emission Information Label
② Key on, engine off

FIRING ORDERS

NOTE: To avoid confusion, always replace spark plug wires one at a time.

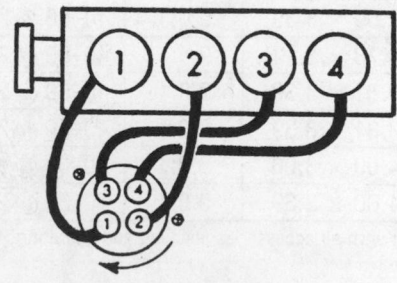

1989–90 2.3L Engine
Engine Firing Order: 1–3–4–2
Distributor Rotation: Clockwise

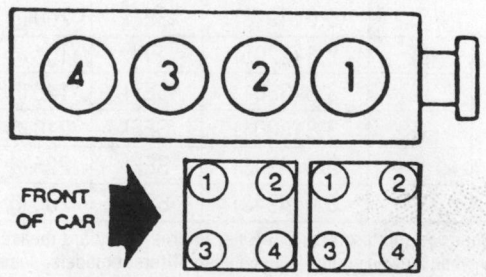

1991–93 2.3L Engine
Engine Firing Order: 1–3–4–2
Distributorless Ignition System

FIRING ORDERS

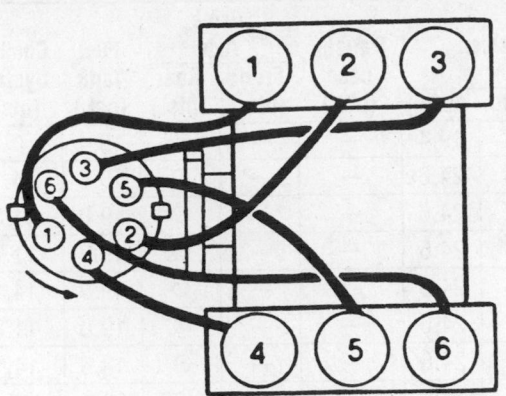

3.8L (except SC) Engine
Engine Firing Order: 1–4–2–5–3–6
Distributor Rotation: Counterclockwise

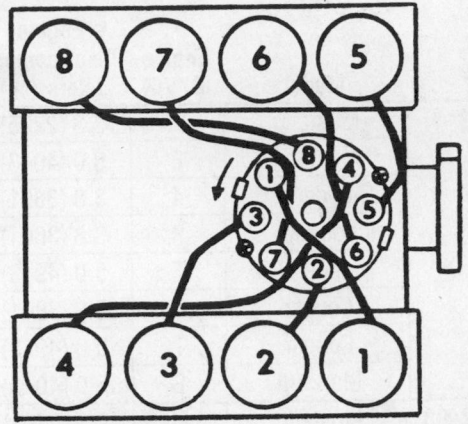

5.0L Engine
Engine Firing Order: 1–3–7–2–6–5–4–8
Distributor Rotation: Counterclockwise

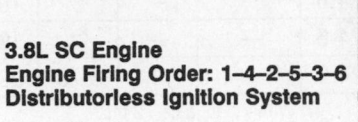
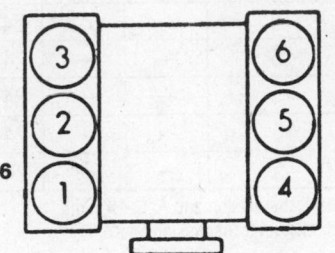

3.8L SC Engine
Engine Firing Order: 1–4–2–5–3–6
Distributorless Ignition System

CAPACITIES

Year	Model	Engine ID/VIN	Engine Displacement Liters (cc)	Engine Crankcase with Filter (qts.)	Transmission (pts.) 4-Spd	5-Spd	Auto.	Transfer case (pts.)	Drive Axle Front (pts.)	Rear (pts.)	Fuel Tank (gal.)	Cooling System (qts.)
1989	Mustang	A	2.3 (2295)	5	—	5.6	20	—	—	①	15.4	②
	Mustang	E	5.0 (4943)	5	—	5.6	20	—	—	①	15.4	14.1
	Thunderbird	4	3.8 (3801)	5	—	—	24.6	—	—	③	18.8	11.8
	Thunderbird SC	R	3.8 (3801)	5	—	6.3	24.6	—	—	③	18.8	11.9
	Thunderbird SC	C	3.8 (3801)	5	—	6.3	24.6	—	—	③	18.8	11.9
	Cougar	4	3.8 (3801)	5	—	—	24.6	—	—	③	18.8	11.8
	Cougar XR7	R	3.8 (3801)	5	—	6.3	24.6	—	—	③	18.8	11.9
	Cougar XR7	C	3.8 (3801)	5	—	6.3	24.6	—	—	③	18.8	11.9
	Mark VII	E	5.0 (4943)	5	—	—	24.6	—	—	3.75	22.1	14.1
1990	Mustang	A	2.3 (2295)	5	—	5.6	19.4	—	—	①	15.4	②
	Mustang	E	5.0 (4943)	5	—	5.6	24.6	—	—	①	15.4	14.1
	Thunderbird	4	3.8 (3801)	5	—	—	24.6	—	—	③	18.8	11.8
	Thunderbird SC	R	3.8 (3801)	5	—	6.3	24.6	—	—	③	18.8	11.9
	Cougar	4	3.8 (3801)	5	—	—	24.6	—	—	③	18.8	11.8
	Cougar XR7	R	3.8 (3801)	5	—	6.3	24.6	—	—	③	18.8	11.9
	Mark VII	E	5.0 (4943)	5	—	—	24.6	—	—	3.75	22.1	14.1

CAPACITIES

Year	Model	Engine ID/VIN	Engine Displacement Liters (cc)	Engine Crankcase with Filter (qts.)	Transmission (pts.) 4-Spd	5-Spd	Auto.	Transfer case (pts.)	Drive Axle Front (pts.)	Rear (pts.)	Fuel Tank (gal.)	Cooling System (qts.)
1991	Mustang	M	2.3 (2295)	5	—	5.6	19.4	—	—	①	15.4	②
	Mustang	E	5.0 (4943)	5	—	5.6	24.6	—	—	①	15.4	14.1
	Thunderbird	4	3.8 (3801)	5	—	—	24.6	—	—	③	19.0	11.8
	Thunderbird SC	R	3.8 (3801)	5	—	6.3	24.6	—	—	③	19.0	11.9
	Thunderbird	T	5.0 (4943)	5	—	—	24.6	—	—	③	19.0	14.1
	Cougar	4	3.8 (3801)	5	—	—	24.6	—	—	③	19.0	11.8
	Cougar	T	5.0 (4943)	5	—	—	24.6	—	—	③	19.0	14.1
	Mark VII	E	5.0 (4943)	5	—	—	24.6	—	—	3.75	22.1	14.1
1992–93	Mustang	M	2.3 (2295)	5	—	5.6	19.4	—	—	①	15.4	②
	Mustang	E	5.0 (4943)	5	—	5.6	24.6	—	—	①	15.4	14.1
	Thunderbird	4	3.8 (3801)	5	—	—	24.6	—	—	③	19.0	11.8
	Thunderbird SC	R	3.8 (3801)	5	—	6.3	24.6	—	—	③	19.0	11.9
	Thunderbird	T	5.0 (4943)	5	—	—	24.6	—	—	③	19.0	14.1
	Cougar	4	3.8 (3801)	5	—	—	24.6	—	—	③	19.0	11.8
	Cougar	T	5.0 (4943)	5	—	—	24.6	—	—	③	19.0	14.1
	Mark VII	E	5.0 (4943)	5	—	—	24.6	—	—	3.75	22.1	14.1

① With 7.5 in. axle—3.5 pts.
With 7.5 in. limited slip, 8.8 in. standard and limited slip axles—3.75 pts.

② With manual transmission and A/C—9.7 qts.
Except with manual transmission and A/C—10 qts.

③ With 7.5 in. axle—3 pts.
With 7.5 in. limited slip axle—2.75 pts.
With 8.8 in. standard and limited slip axles—3.25 pts.

CAMSHAFT SPECIFICATIONS

All measurements given in inches.

Year	Engine ID/VIN	Engine Displacement Liters (cc)	Journal Diameter 1	2	3	4	5	Elevation In.	Ex.	Bearing Clearance	Camshaft End Play
1989	A	2.3 (2295)	1.7713-1.7720	1.7713-1.7720	1.7713-1.7720	1.7713-1.7720	—	0.4000	0.4000	0.001-0.006	0.0010-0.0090
	4	3.8 (3801)	2.0505-2.0515	2.0505-2.0515	2.0505-2.0515	2.0505-2.0515	—	0.2400-0.2450	0.2540-0.2590	0.001-0.003	①
	R	3.8 (3801)	2.0505-2.0515	2.0505-2.0515	2.0505-2.0515	2.0505-2.0515	—	0.2400-0.2450	0.2540-0.2590	0.001-0.003	①
	C	3.8 (3801)	2.0505-2.0515	2.0505-2.0515	2.0505-2.0515	2.0505-2.0515	—	0.2400-0.2450	0.2540-0.2590	0.001-0.003	①
	E	5.0 (4943)	2.0805-2.0815	2.0655-2.0665	2.0505-2.0515	2.0355-2.0365	2.0205-2.0215	0.2780	0.2780	0.001-0.006	0.0005-0.0090
1990	A	2.3 (2295)	1.7713-1.7720	1.7713-1.7720	1.7713-1.7720	1.7713-1.7720	—	0.4000	0.4000	0.001-0.006	0.0010-0.0090
	4	3.8 (3801)	2.0505-2.0515	2.0505-2.0515	2.0505-2.0515	2.0505-2.0515	—	0.2400-0.2450	0.2540-0.2590	0.001-0.003	①
	R	3.8 (3801)	2.0505-2.0515	2.0505-2.0515	2.0505-2.0515	2.0505-2.0515	—	0.2400-0.2450	0.2540-0.2590	0.001-0.003	①
	E	5.0 (4943)	2.0805-2.0815	2.0655-2.0665	2.0505-2.0515	2.0355-2.0365	2.0205-2.0215	0.2780	0.2780	0.001-0.006	0.0005-0.0090

CAMSHAFT SPECIFICATIONS
All measurements given in inches.

Year	Engine ID/VIN	Engine Displacement Liters (cc)	Journal Diameter 1	2	3	4	5	Elevation In.	Ex.	Bearing Clearance	Camshaft End Play
1991	M	2.3 (2295)	1.7713–1.7720	1.7713–1.7720	1.7713–1.7720	1.7713–1.7720	—	0.2381	0.2381	0.001–0.006	0.0010–0.0090
	4	3.8 (3801)	2.0505–2.0515	2.0505–2.0515	2.0505–2.0515	2.0505–2.0515	—	0.2400–0.2450	0.2540–0.2590	0.001–0.003	0.0010–0.0060
	R	3.8 (3801)	2.0505–2.0515	2.0505–2.0515	2.0505–2.0515	2.0505–2.0515	—	0.2400–0.2450	0.2540–0.2590	0.001–0.003	0.0010–0.0060–
	E	5.0 (4943)	2.0805–2.0815	2.0655–2.0665	2.0505–2.0515	2.0355–2.0365	2.0205–2.0215	0.2780	0.2780	0.001–0.006	0.0005–0.0090
	T	5.0 (4943)	2.0805–2.0815	2.0655–2.0665	2.0505–2.0515	2.0355–2.0365	2.0205–2.0215	0.2780	0.2780	0.001–0.006	0.0005–0.0090
1992–93	M	2.3 (2295)	1.7713–1.7720	1.7713–1.7720	1.7713–1.7720	1.7713–1.7720	—	0.2381	0.2381	0.001–0.006	0.0010–0.0090
	4	3.8 (3801)	2.0505–2.0515	2.0505–2.0515	2.0505–2.0515	2.0505–2.0515	—	0.2400–0.2450	0.2540–0.2590	0.001–0.003	0.0010–0.0060
	R	3.8 (3801)	2.0505–2.0515	2.0505–2.0515	2.0505–2.0515	2.0505–2.0515	—	0.2400–0.2450	0.2540–0.2590	0.001–0.003	0.0010–0.0060–
	E	5.0 (4943)	2.0805–2.0815	2.0655–2.0665	2.0505–2.0515	2.0355–2.0365	2.0205–2.0215	0.2780	0.2780	0.001–0.006	0.0005–0.0090
	T	5.0 (4943)	2.0805–2.0815	2.0655–2.0665	2.0505–2.0515	2.0355–2.0365	2.0205–2.0215	0.2780	0.2780	0.001–0.006	0.0005–0.0090

① The endplay is controlled by the button and spring on the camshaft end.

CRANKSHAFT AND CONNECTING ROD SPECIFICATIONS
All measurements are given in inches.

Year	Engine ID/VIN	Engine Displacement Liters (cc)	Crankshaft Main Brg. Journal Dia.	Main Brg. Oil Clearance	Shaft End-play	Thrust on No.	Connecting Rod Journal Diameter	Oil Clearance	Side Clearance
1989	A	2.3 (2295)	2.3982–2.3990	0.0008–0.0026	0.004–0.012	3	2.0465–2.0472	0.0008–0.0026	0.0035–0.0140
	4	3.8 (3801)	2.5190–2.5198	0.0005–0.0023	0.004–0.008	3	2.3103–2.3111	0.0009–0.0027	0.0047–0.0140
	R	3.8 (3801)	①	②	0.004–0.008	3	2.3103–2.3111	0.0009–0.0027	0.0047–0.0140
	C	3.8 (3801)	①	②	0.004–0.008	3	2.3103–2.3111	0.0009–0.0028	0.0047–0.0140
	E	5.0 (4943)	2.2482–2.2490	0.0004–0.0021	0.004–0.012	3	2.1228–2.1236	0.0008–0.0024	0.0100–0.0230
1990	A	2.3 (2295)	2.3982–2.3990	0.0008–0.0026	0.004–0.012	3	2.0465–2.0472	0.0008–0.0026	0.0035–0.0140
	4	3.8 (3801)	2.5190–2.5198	0.0005–0.0023	0.004–0.008	3	2.3103–2.3111	0.0009–0.0027	0.0047–0.0140
	R	3.8 (3801)	③	④	0.004–0.008	3	2.3103–2.3111	0.0009–0.0027	0.0047–0.0140
	E	5.0 (4943)	2.2482–2.2490	0.0004–0.0021	0.004–0.012	3	2.1228–2.1236	0.0008–0.0024	0.0100–0.0230

CRANKSHAFT AND CONNECTING ROD SPECIFICATIONS

All measurements are given in inches.

Year	Engine ID/VIN	Engine Displacement Liters (cc)	Crankshaft Main Brg. Journal Dia.	Crankshaft Main Brg. Oil Clearance	Crankshaft Shaft End-play	Crankshaft Thrust on No.	Connecting Rod Journal Diameter	Connecting Rod Oil Clearance	Connecting Rod Side Clearance
1991	M	2.3 (2295)	2.2051–2.2059	0.0008–0.0026	0.003–0.012	3	2.0462–2.0472	0.0008–0.0026	0.0035–0.0140
	4	3.8 (3801)	2.5190–2.5198	0.0005–0.0023	0.004–0.008	3	2.3103–2.3111	0.0009–0.0027	0.0047–0.0140
	R	3.8 (3801)	③	④	0.004–0.Q08	3	2.3103–2.3111	0.0009–0.0027	0.0047–0.0140
	E	5.0 (4943)	2.2482–2.2490	0.0004–0.0021	0.004–0.012	3	2.1228–2.1236	0.0008–0.0024	0.0100–0.0230
	T	5.0 (4943)	2.2482–2.2490	0.0004–0.0021	0.004–0.012	3	2.1228–2.1236	0.0008–0.0024	0.0100–0.0230
1992–93	M	2.3 (2295)	2.2051–2.2059	0.0008–0.0026	0.003–0.012	3	2.0462–2.0472	0.0008–0.0026	0.0035–0.0140
	4	3.8 (3801)	2.5190–2.5198	0.0005–0.0023	0.004–0.008	3	2.3103–2.3111	0.0009–0.0027	0.0047–0.0140
	R	3.8 (3801)	③	④	0.004–0.008	3	2.3103–2.3111	0.0009–0.0027	0.0047–0.0140
	E	5.0 (4943)	2.2482–2.2490	0.0004 0.0021	0.004–0.012	3	2.1228–2.1236	0.0008–0.0024	0.0100–0.0230
	T	5.0 (4943)	2.2482–2.2490	0.0004–0.0021	0.004–0.012	3	2.1228–2.1236	0.0008–0.0024	0.0100–0.0230

① No. 1, 2 & 3—2.5186–2.5194
No. 4—2.5092–2.5100
② No. 1, 2 & 3—0.0009–0.0026
No. 4—0.0014–0.0032
③ No. 1, 2 & 3—2.5190–2.5198
No. 4—2.5096–2.5104
④ No. 1, 2 & 3—0.0005–0.0023
No. 4—0.0010–0.0028

VALVE SPECIFICATIONS

Year	Engine ID/VIN	Engine Displacement Liters (cc)	Seat Angle (deg.)	Face Angle (deg.)	Spring Test Pressure (lbs. @ in.)	Spring Installed Height (in.)	Stem-to-Guide Clearance (in.) Intake	Stem-to-Guide Clearance (in.) Exhaust	Stem Diameter (in.) Intake	Stem Diameter (in.) Exhaust
1989	A	2.3 (2295)	45	44	128.1–141.6 @ 1.12	1.52	0.0010–0.0027	0.0015–0.0032	0.3416–0.3423	0.3411–0.3418
	4	3.8 (3801)	44.5	45.8	220 @ 1.18	1.65	0.0010–0.0028	0.0015–0.0033	0.3415–0.3423	0.3410–0.3418
	R	3.8 (3801)	44.5	45.8	220 @ 1.18	1.65	0.0010–0.0028	0.0015–0.0033	0.3415–0.3423	0.3410–0.3418
	C	3.8 (3801)	44.5	45.8	220 @ 1.18	1.65	0.0010–0.0028	0.0015–0.0033	0.3415–0.3423	0.3410–0.3418
	E	5.0 (4943)	45	44	①	②	0.0010–0.0027	0.0015–0.0032	0.3416–0.3423	0.3411–0.3418
1990	A	2.3 (2295)	45	44	128.1–141.6 @ 1.12	1.52	0.0010–0.0027	0.0015–0.0032	0.3416–0.3423	0.3411–0.3418
	4	3.8 (3801)	44.5	45.8	220 @ 1.18	1.65	0.0010–0.0028	0.0015–0.0033	0.3415–0.3423	0.3410–0.3418
	R	3.8 (3801)	44.5	45.8	220 @ 1.18	1.65	0.0010–0.0028	0.0015–0.0033	0.3415–0.3423	0.3410–0.3418
	E	5.0 (4943)	45	44	①	②	0.0010–0.0027	0.0015–0.0032	0.3416–0.3423	0.3411–0.3418

VALVE SPECIFICATIONS

Year	Engine ID/VIN	Engine Displacement Liters (cc)	Seat Angle (deg.)	Face Angle (deg.)	Spring Test Pressure (lbs. @ in.)	Spring Installed Height (in.)	Stem-to-Guide Clearance (in.) Intake	Stem-to-Guide Clearance (in.) Exhaust	Stem Diameter (in.) Intake	Stem Diameter (in.) Exhaust
1991	M	2.3 (2295)	45	44	128–142 @ 1.12	1.52	0.0010–0.0027	0.0015–0.0032	0.3416–0.3423	0.3411–0.3418
	4	3.8 (3801)	44.5	45.8	220 @ 1.18	1.65	0.0010–0.0028	0.0015–0.0033	0.3415–0.3423	0.3410–0.3418
	R	3.8 (3801)	44.5	45.8	220 @ 1.18	1.65	0.0010–0.0028	0.0015–0.0033	0.3415–0.3423	0.3410–0.3418
	E	5.0 (4943)	45	44	①	②	0.0010–0.0027	0.0015–0.0032	0.3416–0.3423	0.3411–0.3418
	T	5.0 (4943)	45	44	①	②	0.0010–0.0027	0.0015–0.0032	0.3416–0.3423	0.3411–0.3418
1992–93	M	2.3 (2295)	45	44	128–142 @ 1.12	1.52	0.0010–0.0027	0.0015–0.0032	0.3416–0.3423	0.3411–0.3418
	4	3.8 (3801)	44.5	45.8	220 @ 1.18	1.65	0.0010–0.0028	0.0015–0.0033	0.3415–0.3423	0.3410–0.3418
	R	3.8 (3801)	44.5	45.8	220 @ 1.18	1.65	0.0010–0.0028	0.0015–0.0033	0.3415–0.3423	0.3410–0.3418
	E	5.0 (4943)	45	44	①	②	0.0010–0.0027	0.0015–0.0032	0.3416–0.3423	0.3411–0.3418
	T	5.0 (4943)	45	44	①	②	0.0010–0.0027	0.0015–0.0032	0.3416–0.3423	0.3411–0.3418

① Intake: 211–230 @ 1.33
  Exhaust: 200–226 @ 1.15
② Intake: 1.75–1.80 in.
  Exhaust: 1.58–1.64 in.

PISTON AND RING SPECIFICATIONS

All measurements are given in inches.

Year	Engine ID/VIN	Engine Displacement Liters (cc)	Piston Clearance	Ring Gap Top Compression	Ring Gap Bottom Compression	Ring Gap Oil Control	Ring Side Clearance Top Compression	Ring Side Clearance Bottom Compression	Ring Side Clearance Oil Control
1989	A	2.3 (2295)	0.0030–0.0038	0.010–0.020	0.010–0.020	0.010–0.049	0.0020–0.0040	0.0020–0.0040	Snug
	4	3.8 (3801)	0.0014–0.0032	0.011–0.012	0.009–0.020	0.015–0.058	0.0016–0.0034	0.0016–0.0034	Snug
	R	3.8 (3801)	0.0040–0.0045	0.011–0.012	0.009–0.020	0.015–0.058	0.0016–0.0034	0.0016–0.0034	Snug
	C	3.8 (3801)	0.0040–0.0045	0.011–0.012	0.009–0.020	0.015–0.058	0.0016–0.0034	0.0016–0.0034	Snug
	E	5.0 (4943)	0.0030–0.0038	0.010–0.020	0.010–0.020	0.015–0.055	0.0020–0.0040	0.0020–0.0040	Snug
1990	A	2.3 (2295)	0.0030–0.0038	0.010–0.020	0.010–0.020	0.010–0.049	0.0020–0.0040	0.0020–0.0040	Snug
	4	3.8 (3801)	0.0014–0.0032	0.011–0.012	0.009–0.020	0.015–0.058	0.0016–0.0034	0.0016–0.0034	Snug
	R	3.8 (3801)	0.0040–0.0045	0.011–0.012	0.009–0.020	0.015–0.058	0.0016–0.0034	0.0016–0.0034	Snug
	E	5.0 (4943)	0.0030–0.0038	0.010–0.020	0.010–0.020	0.015–0.055	0.0020–0.0040	0.0020–0.0040	Snug

PISTON AND RING SPECIFICATIONS

All measurements are given in inches.

| Year | Engine ID/VIN | Engine Displacement Liters (cc) | Piston Clearance | Ring Gap | | | Ring Side Clearance | | |
				Top Compression	Bottom Compression	Oil Control	Top Compression	Bottom Compression	Oil Control
1991	M	2.3 (2295)	0.0024–0.0033	0.010–0.020	0.010–0.020	0.015–0.049	0.0016–0.0033	0.0016–0.0033	Snug
	4	3.8 (3801)	0.0014–0.0032	0.011–0.012	0.009–0.020	0.015–0.058	0.0016–0.0034	0.0016–0.0034	Snug
	R	3.8 (3801)	0.0040–0.0045	0.011–0.012	0.009–0.020	0.015–0.058	0.0016–0.0034	0.0016–0.0034	Snug
	E	5.0 (4943)	0.0030–0.0038	0.010–0.020	0.010–0.020	0.015–0.055	0.0020–0.0040	0.0020–0.0040	Snug
	T	5.0 (4943)	0.0030–0.0038	0.010–0.020	0.010–0.020	0.015–0.055	0.0020–0.0040	0.0020–0.0040	Snug
1992–93	M	2.3 (2295)	0.0019–0.0029	0.010–0.020	0.015–0.025	0.010–0.040	0.0016–0.0033	0.0016–0.0033	Snug
	4	3.8 (3801)	0.0014–0.0032	0.011–0.012	0.009–0.020	0.015–0.058	0.0016–0.0034	0.0016–0.0034	Snug
	R	3.8 (3801)	0.0015–0.0025	0.011–0.012	0.009–0.020	0.015–0.058	0.0016–0.0034	0.0016–0.0034	Snug
	E	5.0 (4943)	0.0030–0.0038	0.010–0.020	0.010–0.020	0.015–0.055	0.0020–0.0040	0.0020–0.0040	Snug
	T	5.0 (4943)	0.0030–0.0038	0.010–0.020	0.010–0.020	0.015–0.055	0.0020–0.0040	0.0020–0.0040	Snug

TORQUE SPECIFICATIONS

All readings in ft. lbs.

| Year | Engine ID/VIN | Engine Displacement Liters (cc) | Cylinder Head Bolts | Main Bearing Bolts | Rod Bearing Bolts | Crankshaft Damper Bolts | Flywheel Bolts | Manifold | | Spark Plugs | Lug Nut |
								Intake	Exhaust		
1989	A	2.3 (2295)	①	②	③	103–133	56–64	20–29	④	5–10	85–105
	4	3.8 (3801)	⑤	65–81	31–36	93–121	54–64	⑥	15–22	5–11	85–105
	R	3.8 (3801)	⑤	65–81	31–36	93–121	54–64	⑦	15–22	5–11	85–105
	C	3.8 (3801)	⑤	65–81	31–36	93–121	54–64	⑦	15–22	5–11	85–105
	E	5.0 (4943)	⑧	60–70	19–24	70–90	75–85	⑨	18–24	5–10	85–105
1990	A	2.3 (2295)	①	②	③	103–133	56–64	20–29	④	5–10	85–105
	4	3.8 (3801)	⑩	65–81	31–36	103–132	54–64	⑥	15–22	5–11	85–105
	R	3.8 (3801)	⑪	65–81	31–36	103–132	54–64	⑦	15–22	5–11	85–105
	E	5.0 (4943)	⑧	60–70	19–24	70–90	75–85	⑨	18–24	5–10	85–105
1991	M	2.3 (2295)	①	②	③	114–151	56–64	19–28	④	5–10	85–105
	4	3.8 (3801)	⑩	65–81	31–36	103–132	54–64	⑥	15–22	5–11	85–105
	R	3.8 (3801)	⑪	65–81	31–36	103–132	54–64	⑦	15–22	5–11	85–105
	E	5.0 (4943)	⑧	60–70	19–24	70–90	75–85	⑨	18–24	5–10	85–105
	T	5.0 (4943)	⑧	60–70	19–24	70–90	75–85	⑨	18–24	5–10	85–105

TORQUE SPECIFICATIONS

All readings in ft. lbs.

Year	Engine ID/VIN	Engine Displacement Liters (cc)	Cylinder Head Bolts	Main Bearing Bolts	Rod Bearing Bolts	Crankshaft Damper Bolts	Flywheel Bolts	Manifold Intake	Manifold Exhaust	Spark Plugs	Lug Nut
1992–93	M	2.3 (2295)	①	②	③	114–151	56–64	19–28	④	5–10	85–105
	4	3.8 (3801)	⑩	65–81	31–36	103–132	54–64	⑦	15–22	5–11	85–105
	R	3.8 (3801)	⑪	65–81	31–36	103–132	54–64	⑦	15–22	5–11	85–105
	E	5.0 (4943)	⑧	60–70	19–24	70–90	75–85	⑫	18–24	5–10	85–105
	T	5.0 (4943)	⑧	60–70	19–24	70–90	75–85	⑫	18–24	5–10	85–105

① Tighten in 2 steps:
Step 1: 50–60 ft. lbs.
Step 2: 80–90 ft. lbs.
② Tighten in 2 steps:
Step 1: 50–60 ft. lbs.
Step 2: 75–85 ft. lbs.
③ Tighten in 2 steps:
Step 1: 25–30 ft. lbs.
Step 2: 30–36 ft. lbs.
④ Tighten in 2 steps:
Step 1: 178–204 inch lbs.
Step 2: 20–30 ft. lbs.
⑤ Tighten in 7 steps:
Step 1: 37 ft. lbs.
Step 2: 45 ft. lbs.
Step 3: 52 ft. lbs.
Step 4: 59 ft. lbs.
Step 5: Back off all bolts 2–3 turns

Step 6: Tighten, in sequence to 52 ft. lbs.
Step 7: Turn bolts, in sequence, 90–110 degrees
⑥ Tighten in 3 steps:
Step 1: 7.5 ft. lbs.
Step 2: 15 ft. lbs.
Step 3: 24 ft. lbs.
⑦ Tighten in 2 steps:
Step 1: 7.5 ft. lbs.
Step 2: 11 ft. lbs.
⑧ Tighten in 2 steps:
Step 1: 55–65 ft. lbs.
Step 2: 65–72 ft. lbs.
⑨ Tighten in 3 steps:
Step 1: 15–20 ft. lbs.
Step 2: 23–25 ft. lbs.
Step 3: Retorque with engine hot
⑩ Tighten in 6 steps:
Step 1: 37 ft. lbs.

Step 2: 45 ft. lbs.
Step 3: 52 ft. lbs.
Step 4: 59 ft. lbs.
Step 5: Back off all bolts 2–3 turns
Step 6: Tighten to 11–18 ft. lbs., rotate long bolts an additional 85–105 degrees, short bolts 65–85 degrees, go to next bolt in sequence.
⑪ Tighten in 6 steps:
Step 1: 37 ft. lbs.
Step 2: 45 ft. lbs.
Step 3: 52 ft. lbs.
Step 4: 59 ft. lbs.
Step 5: Back off all bolts 2–3 turns
Step 6: Tighten to 48–55 ft. lbs., rotate bolts an additional 90–110 degrees, go to next bolt in sequence.
⑫ Tighten in 2 steps:
Step 1: 15–20 ft. lbs.
Step 2: 23–25 ft. lbs.

BRAKE SPECIFICATIONS

All measurements in inches unless noted.

Year	Model	Master Cylinder Bore	Brake Disc Original Thickness	Brake Disc Minimum Thickness	Brake Disc Maximum Runout	Brake Drum Diameter Original Inside Diameter	Brake Drum Diameter Max. Wear Limit	Brake Drum Diameter Maximum Machine Diameter	Minimum Lining Thickness Front	Minimum Lining Thickness Rear
1989	Mustang	0.872	①	②	0.003	9.000	9.060	NA	0.125	0.031
	Thunderbird	0.872③	④	⑤	0.003	9.843	9.904	NA	0.125	⑥
	Cougar	0.872③	④	⑤	0.003	9.843	9.904	NA	0.125	⑥
	Mark VII	1.125	⑦	⑧	⑨	—	—	—	0.125	0.125
1990	Mustang	0.872	①	②	0.003	9.000	9.060	NA	0.125	0.031
	Thunderbird	0.938③	④	⑤	0.003	9.843	9.904	NA	0.125	⑥
	Cougar	0.938③	④	⑤	0.003	9.843	9.904	NA	0.125	⑥
	Mark VII	1.125	⑦	⑧	⑨	—	—	—	0.125	0.125
1991	Mustang	0.872	①	②	0.003	9.000	9.060	NA	0.125	0.031
	Thunderbird	0.938③	④	⑤	0.003	9.843	9.904	NA	0.125	⑥
	Cougar	0.938③	④	⑤	0.003	9.843	9.904	NA	0.125	⑥
	Mark VII	1.125	⑦	⑧	⑩	—	—	—	0.125	0.123
1992–93	Mustang	0.872	①	②	0.003	9.000	9.060	NA	0.125	0.031
	Thunderbird	0.938③	④	⑪	0.003	9.843	9.904	NA	0.125	⑥
	Cougar	0.938③	④	⑪	0.003	9.843	9.904	NA	0.125	⑥
	Mark VII	1.125	⑦	⑧	⑨	—	—	—	0.125	0.123

NA—Not available
① 2.3L Engine—0.870 in.
5.0L Engine—1.03 in.
② 2.3L Engine—0.810 in.
5.0L Engine—1.972 in.
③ Except ABS equipped

④ Front—1.024 in.
Rear—0.945 in.
⑤ Front—0.935 in.
Rear—0.896 in.
⑥ With drum brakes—0.031 in.
With disc brakes—0.123 in.

⑦ Front—1.03 in.
Rear—0.945 in.
⑧ Front—0.972 in.
Rear—0.895 in.
⑨ Front—0.003 in.
Rear—0.004 in.

⑩ Front—0.003 in.
Rear—0.002 in.
⑪ Front—0.974 in.
Rear—0.896 in.

WHEEL ALIGNMENT

Year	Model		Caster Range (deg.)	Caster Preferred Setting (deg.)	Camber Range (deg.)	Camber Preferred Setting (deg.)	Toe-in (in.)	Steering Axis Inclination (deg.)
1989	Mustang	Exc. 5.0L GT	13/32P–1 29/32P	1 3/16P	27/32N–21/32P	3/32N	3/16	15 23/32
		5.0L GT	1/2P–2P	1 9/32P	5/8N–29/32P	5/32P	3/16	15 23/32
	Thunderbird	Front	4 3/4P–6 1/4P	5 1/2P	1 1/4N–1/4P	1/2N	1/8	15 23/32
		Rear	—	—	1N–0	1/2N	1/16	—
	Cougar	Front	4 3/4P–6 1/4P	5 1/2P	1 1/4N–1/4P	1/2N	1/8	15 23/32
		Rear	—	—	1N–0	1/2N	1/16	—
	Mark VII	—	5/8P–2 3/4P	1 1/2P	3/4N–3/4P	0	1/8	11
1990	Mustang	Exc. 5.0L GT	1 5/32P–2 5/8P	1 29/32P	1 1/4N–1/4P	1/2N	1/8 ①	15 23/32
		5.0L GT	1 5/32P–2 5/8P	1 29/32P	1 3/8N–1/8P	5/8N	1/8 ①	15 23/32
	Thunderbird	Front	4 3/4P–6 1/4P	5 1/2P	1 1/4N–1/4P	1/2N	1/8	15 23/32
		Rear	—	—	1N–0	1/2N	1/16	—
	Cougar	Front	4 3/4P–6 1/4P	5 1/2P	1 1/4N–1/4P	1/2N	1/8	15 23/32
		Rear	—	—	1N–0	1/2N	1/16	—
	Mark VII	—	5/8P–2 3/4P	1 1/2P	3/4N–3/4P	0	1/8	11
1991	Mustang	Exc. 5.0L GT	1 5/32P–2 5/8P	1 29/32P	1 1/4N–1/4P	1/2N	1/8 ①	15 23/32
		5.0L GT	1 5/32P–2 5/8P	1 29/32P	1 3/8N–1/8P	5/8N	1/8 ①	15 23/32
	Thunderbird	Front	4 3/4P–6 1/4P	5 1/2P	1 1/4N–1/4P	1/2N	1/8	15 23/32
		Rear	—	—	1N–0	1/2N	1/16	—
	Cougar	Front	4 3/4P–6 1/4P	5 1/2P	1 1/4N–1/4P	1/2N	1/8	15 23/32
		Rear	—	—	1N–0	1/2N	1/16	—
	Mark VII	—	5/8P–2 3/4P	1 1/2P	3/4N–3/4P	0	1/8	11
1992–93	Mustang	Exc. 5.0L GT	1 5/32P–2 5/8P	1 29/32P	1 1/4N–1/4P	1/2N	1/8 ①	15 23/32
		5.0L GT	1 5/32P–2 5/8P	1 29/32P	1 3/8N–1/8P	5/8N	1/8 ①	15 23/32
	Thunderbird	Front	4 3/4P–6 1/4P	5 1/2P	1 1/4N–1/4P	1/2N	1/8	15 23/32
		Rear	—	—	1N–0	1/2N	1/16	—
	Cougar	Front	4 3/4P–6 1/4P	5 1/2P	1 1/4N–1/4P	1/2N	1/8	15 23/32
		Rear	—	—	1N–0	1/2N	1/16	—
	Mark VII	—	5/8P–2 3/4P	1 1/2P	3/4N–3/4P	0	1/8	11

N—Negative
P—Positive
① Toe-out

ENGINE MECHANICAL

NOTE: Disconnecting the negative battery cable on some vehicles may interfere with the functions of the on board computer systems and may require the computer to undergo a relearning process, once the negative battery cable is reconnected.

Engine Assembly

REMOVAL & INSTALLATION

2.3L Engine

1. Disconnect the negative battery cable and relieve the fuel system pressure.
2. Drain the cooling system and the crankcase.
3. Mark the position of the hood on the hinges and remove the hood.
4. Remove the air cleaner outlet hose.
5. Remove the radiator upper and lower hoses. Disconnect the electrical connector to the cooling fan and remove the fan and shroud. If equipped with automatic transmission, disconnect the oil cooler lines from the radiator. Remove the radiator.
6. Disconnect the heater hose from the heater core. Tag and disconnect the wires from the alternator and starter. Disconnect the accelerator cable from the throttle body.

7. If equipped with air conditioning, remove the compressor from the mounting bracket and position it aside, leaving the refrigerant lines attached.

8. If equipped with power steering, remove the pump and position aside, leaving the hoses attached.

9. Disconnect the flexible fuel line at the fuel rail and plug the fuel line.

10. Disconnect the coil primary wire, the water temperature sending unit connector and the injector wiring harness connectors from the main wiring harness.

11. Remove the starter and remove the engine mount bolts.

12. Raise and safely support the vehicle. Remove the flywheel or converter housing upper retaining bolts.

13. Disconnect the muffler inlet pipe at the exhaust manifold. Disconnect the engine right and left mounts at the No. 2 crossmember pedestals. Remove the flywheel or converter housing cover.

14. If equipped with a manual transmission, remove the flywheel housing lower retaining bolts. If equipped with an automatic transmission, disconnect the converter from the flywheel and disconnect the transmission oil cooler lines, if attached to the engine at the pan rail. Remove the converter housing lower retaining bolts.

15. Lower the vehicle. Support the transmission and flywheel or converter housing with a jack.

16. Attach suitable engine lifting equipment to the engine lifting brackets. Carefully lift the engine out of the engine compartment and install on a work stand.

To install:

17. Install the clutch, if removed.

18. Carefully lower the engine into the engine compartment. Make sure the studs on the exhaust manifold are aligned with the holes in the muffler inlet pipe.

19. If equipped with an automatic transmission, start the converter pilot into the crankshaft. If equipped with a manual transmission, start the transmission input shaft into the clutch disc. It may be necessary to adjust the position of the transmission in relation to the engine if the input shaft will not enter the clutch disc.

NOTE: If the engine hangs up after the shaft enters, turn the crankshaft slowly in a clockwise direction, with the transmission in gear, until the shaft splines mesh with the clutch disc splines.

20. Install the flywheel or converter housing upper retaining bolts. Remove the engine lifting equipment.

21. Remove the jack from the trans-

mission. Raise and safely support the vehicle.

22. Install the flywheel or converter housing lower retaining bolts. If equipped with an automatic transmission, attach the converter to the flywheel and tighten the retaining nuts to 20–34 ft. lbs. (27–46 Nm).

23. Install the flywheel or converter housing dust cover. Install the left and right engine mounts to the No. 2 crossmember pedestal. Tighten the nuts and bolts to 80–106 ft. lbs.

24. Connect the muffler inlet pipe to the manifold. Connect the fuel line to the fuel rail.

25. Install the starter and connect the starter cable.

26. Lower the vehicle. Connect the oil pressure and water temperature sending unit connectors. Connect the coil and alternator wires. Connect the accelerator cable and the heater hoses.

27. If equipped with air conditioning, install the compressor in the mounting bracket. If equipped with power steering, install the pump. Install the drive belt.

28. Install the radiator, cooling fan and shroud. Connect the fan electrical connector. If equipped with automatic transmission, connect the oil cooler lines to the radiator. Install the upper and lower radiator hoses.

29. Install the air cleaner outlet hose.

30. Fill the crankcase with the proper type and quantity of oil. Fill and bleed the cooling system.

31. Connect the negative battery cable, start the engine and bring to normal operating temperature. Check for leaks. Check all fluid levels.

32. Align the hood on the hinges with the marks that were made during removal. Secure with the mounting bolts.

3.8L Engine

1. Disconnect the negative battery cable. Drain the crankcase and the cooling system.

2. Relieve the fuel system pressure and discharge the air conditioning system.

3. Disconnect the electrical connector to the underhood lamp. Mark the position of the hood on the hinges and remove the hood.

4. Remove the left cowl vent screen and wiper module. On non-supercharged engines, disconnect the alternator to voltage regulator wiring assembly.

5. On supercharged engines, remove the upper intercooler tube at the supercharger and cooler assemblies. Remove the bolt retaining the cooler tube to the alternator bracket and remove the tube.

6. Remove the radiator upper sight shield. Release the belt tension and remove the drive and accessory/supercharger belts. Remove the air cleaner-to-throttle body tube.

7. On supercharged engines, disconnect the cooling fan electrical connector and remove the cooling fan/shroud assembly. On non-supercharged engines, remove the fan and shroud.

8. Remove the upper radiator hose and disconnect the heater hoses. If equipped with an automatic transmission, disconnect the oil cooler lines from the radiator.

9. Disconnect the lower radiator hose at the water pump. Remove the radiator. On supercharged engines it will also be necessary to remove the 2 push pins retaining the intercooler to the radiator assembly.

10. Disconnect the power steering pressure hose assembly. On non-supercharged engines, remove the power steering pump and bracket assembly and position aside.

11. Disconnect the air conditioner compressor clutch wire. Disconnect and plug the refrigerant lines. Remove the compressor.

12. Remove the coolant recovery reservoir and remove the wiring shield. Remove the accelerator cable mounting bracket and position aside.

13. Disconnect the fuel lines from the fuel rail. Tag and disconnect the engine control module wiring, engine feed harnesses and vacuum hoses.

14. On non-supercharged engines, disconnect the ground and coil wires. On supercharged engines, disconnect the DIS module wiring, remove the coil pack retaining bolts and position the coil pack aside.

15. On supercharged engines, remove the nuts retaining the lower intercooler tube to the supercharger elbow and lower intercooler tube bracket and remove the intercooler tube retaining bolt and nut at the alternator bracket.

16. On supercharged engines, remove the alternator bracket bolts, disconnect the alternator wiring and remove the alternator. Remove the power steering pump bracket assembly and position aside.

17. Disconnect the canister purge line and disconnect 1 end of the throttle control valve cable.

18. Raise and safely support the vehicle. Remove the oil filter element.

19. On supercharged engines, remove the 2 nuts retaining the lower intercooler tube to the intercooler and remove the intercooler and intercooler tube.

20. Remove the exhaust pipe-to-manifold nuts and remove the left ex-

haust shield. Disconnect the oxygen sensors.

21. If equipped with an automatic transmission, remove the inspection plug and remove the torque converter bolts.

22. Remove the engine-to-transmission bolts and remove the engine mount through bolts. On supercharged engines, remove the left mount retaining strap bolt.

23. Remove the crankshaft pulley assembly.

NOTE: If the crankshaft pulley and vibration damper have to be separated, mark the damper and pulley so they may be reassembled in the same relative position. This is important as the damper and pulley are initially balanced as a unit. If the crankshaft damper is being replaced, check if the original damper has balance pins installed. If so, new balance pins must be installed on the new damper in the same position as the original damper.

24. Remove the starter. Remove the ground cable and remove the left and right starter harness retainers.

25. Disconnect the oil level indicator sensor and partially lower the vehicle. Disconnect the oil pressure sending unit gauge assembly.

26. Position a floor jack under the transmission and position suitable engine lifting equipment.

27. Remove the engine from the vehicle and position on a workstand.

To install:

28. Remove the engine assembly from the workstand and install engine lifting equipment.

29. Position the engine in the vehicle and install 2 engine-to-transmission bolts. Lower the engine onto the mounting seats, left side first, and remove the lifting equipment. Remove the jacks.

30. Tighten the 2 engine-to-transmission bolts to 40–50 ft. lbs. (55–68 Nm) and connect the oil pressure sending unit gauge assembly. Raise and safely support the vehicle.

31. Install the remaining engine-to-transmission bolts and tighten to 40–50 ft. lbs. (55–68 Nm).

32. Install the torque converter bolts and tighten to 20–34 ft. lbs. (27–46 Nm). Install the inspection plug.

33. Install and tighten the engine mount through bolts to 35–50 ft. lbs. (47–68 Nm). On supercharged engines, install the left mount retaining strap bolt and tighten to 33–45 ft. lbs. (45–61 Nm).

34. Install the starter. Install the starter harness retainer, ground cable and transmission oil cooler line brack-

et. Install the exhaust pipe-to-manifold nuts.

35. Install the crankshaft pulley assembly and tighten the bolts to 20–28 ft. lbs. (26–30 Nm).

36. Connect the oxygen sensors and the oil level indicator sensor. Install a new oil filter and lower the vehicle.

37. Connect the throttle control valve cable and the canister purge line.

38. On supercharged engines, perform the following:

   a. Install the lower intercooler tube, intercooler and power steering pump bracket assembly.

   b. Install the alternator, connect the wiring and install the alternator bracket bolts.

   c. Install the intercooler tube bolts at the power steering bracket and install the nuts retaining the lower intercooler tube to the lower intercooler tube bracket and supercharger elbow.

   d. Install the coil pack and retaining bolts.

39. Install the coolant recovery reservoir.

40. Connect the alternator-to-voltage regulator wiring, the engine control module wiring assembly and engine feed harnesses. Connect the vacuum hoses.

41. On non-supercharged engines, connect the wiring assembly ground and coil wire. On supercharged engines, connect the DIS module wiring.

42. Connect the fuel lines to the fuel rail. Install the accelerator cable mounting bracket and the wiring shield.

43. Install the air conditioning compressor and retaining bolts. Tighten the bolts to 30–45 ft. lbs. (41–61 Nm).

44. Remove the plugs from the air conditioner compressor lines and connect the lines to the compressor. Connect the compressor clutch wire.

45. On non-supercharged engines, install the power steering pump bracket assembly. Connect the power steering hoses.

46. Install the radiator. On supercharged engines, install the intercooler to the radiator and install the retaining push pins.

47. Connect the lower radiator hose to the water pump and install the heater hoses. If equipped with an automatic transmission, install the oil cooler lines to the radiator.

48. Install the upper radiator hose and the fan and fan shroud. On supercharged engines, connect the cooling fan electrical connector.

49. Position the drive belts and the accessory/supercharger belts. Install the radiator sight shield.

50. On supercharged engines, install the intercooler tube and bolts retaining the tube to the power steering

bracket. Install the upper intercooler tube to the supercharger and cooler assemblies.

51. Install the cowl vent screen and wiper module. Install the hood, aligning the marks that were made during removal. Connect the underhood lamp wiring.

52. Fill the crankcase with the proper type and quantity of engine oil. Fill and bleed the cooling system.

53. Connect the negative battery cable, start the engine and bring to normal operating temperature. Check for leaks. Check all fluid levels.

54. Leak test, evacuate and charge the air conditioning system according to the proper procedure. Observe all safety precautions.

5.0L Engine

MUSTANG AND MARK VII

1. Disconnect the negative battery cable. Drain the crankcase and the cooling system.

2. Relieve the fuel system pressure and discharge the air conditioning system.

3. Mark the position of the hood on the hinges and remove the hood. Disconnect the battery ground cables from the cylinder block.

4. Remove the air intake duct.

5. Disconnect the upper radiator hose from the thermostat housing and the lower hose from the water pump. If equipped with an automatic transmission, disconnect the oil cooler lines from the radiator.

6. Remove the bolts attaching the radiator fan shroud to the radiator. Remove the radiator. Remove the fan, belt, pulley and shroud.

7. Remove the alternator bolts and position the alternator aside.

8. Disconnect the oil pressure sending unit wire from the sending unit and, if equipped, the low oil level sensor wire from the left side of the oil pan. Disconnect the flexible fuel line at the fuel tank line. Plug the fuel tank line.

9. Disconnect the accelerator cable from the throttle body. Disconnect the TV rod if equipped with an automatic transmission. Disconnect the cruise control cable, if equipped.

10. Disconnect the transmission filler tube bracket from the cylinder block.

11. If equipped with air conditioning, disconnect the lines and electrical connectors at the compressor and remove the compressor. Plug the lines and the compressor fittings to prevent the entrance of dirt and moisture.

12. Disconnect the power steering pump bracket from the cylinder head. Position the power steering pump

aside in a position that will prevent the fluid from leaking.

13. Disconnect the power brake vacuum line from the intake manifold.

14. Disconnect the heater hoses from the heater tubes. Disconnect the electrical connector from the coolant temperature sending unit.

15. Remove the flywheel or converter housing-to-engine upper bolts.

16. Disconnect the wiring harness at the two 10-pin connectors.

17. Raise and safely support the vehicle. Disconnect the starter cable from the starter and remove the starter.

18. Disconnect the muffler inlet pipes from the exhaust manifolds. Disconnect the engine mounts from the chassis. Disconnect the downstream thermactor tubing and check valve from the right exhaust manifold stud, if equipped.

19. If equipped with automatic transamission, disconnect the transmission cooler lines from the retainer and remove the converter housing inspection cover. Disconnect the flywheel from the converter and secure the converter assembly in the housing.

20. Remove the remaining converter or flywheel housing-to-engine bolts.

21. Lower the vehicle and then support the transmission. Attach engine lifting equipment and hoist the engine.

22. Raise the engine slightly and carefully pull it from the transmission. Carefully lift the engine out of the engine compartment. Avoid bending or damaging the rear cover plate or other components. Install the engine on a workstand.

To install:

23. Attach the engine lifting equipment and remove the engine from the workstand.

24. Lower the engine carefully into the engine compartment. Make sure the exhaust manifolds are properly aligned with the muffler inlet pipes.

25. Start the converter pilot, or manual transmission input shaft, into the crankshaft. Align the paint mark on the flywheel to the paint mark on the torque converter.

26. Install the flywheel or converter housing upper bolts, making sure the dowels in the cylinder block engage the housing.

27. Install the engine mount-to-chassis attaching fasteners and remove the engine lifting equipment.

28. Raise and safely support the vehicle. Connect both muffler inlet pipes to the exhaust manifolds. Install the starter and connect the starter cable.

29. If equipped with automatic transmission, remove the retainer holding the converter in the housing. Attach the converter to the flywheel.

Install the converter housing inspection cover.

30. Install the remaining flywheel or converter housing attaching bolts. Remove the support from the transmission and lower the vehicle.

31. Connect the wiring harness at the two 10-pin connectors.

32. Connect the coolant temperature sending unit wire and connect the heater hoses. Connect the wiring to the sensors.

33. Connect the transmission filler tube bracket, if equipped with automatic transmission.

34. Connect the acclerator cable and TV cable. Connect the cruise control cable, if equipped.

35. Remove the plug from the fuel tank line and connect the fuel line and the oil pressure sending unit wire.

36. Install the pulley, water pump belt and fan/clutch assembly.

37. Position the alternator bracket and install the alternator bolts. Connect the alternator and ground cables.

38. Install the air conditioning compressor. Unplug and connect the refrigerant lines and connect the electrical connector to the compressor.

39. Install the power steering pump bracket and the accessory drive belt. Connect the power brake vacuum line.

40. Place the shroud over the fan and install the radiator. Connect the radiator hoses and the transmission oil cooler lines. Position the shroud and install the bolts.

41. Connect the heater hoses to the heater tubes. Fill and bleed the cooling system. Fill the crankcase with the proper type and quantity of engine oil. Adjust the transmission throttle linkage, if equipped with automatic transmission.

42. Connect the negative battery cable. Start the engine and bring to normal operating temperature. Check for leaks. Check all fluid levels.

43. Install the air intake duct assembly. Install the hood, aligning the marks that were made during removal.

44. Leak test, evacuate and charge the air conditioning system according to the proper procedure. Observe all safety precautions.

THUNDERBIRD AND COUGAR

1. Disconnect the negative battery cable. Drain the crankcase and the cooling system.

2. Relieve the fuel system pressure and discharge the air conditioning system.

3. Disconnect the electrical connector for the underhood lamp. Mark the position of the hood on the hinges and remove the hood.

4. Remove the oil dipstick. Disconnect and plug the refrigerant lines at the air conditioning compressor.

5. Disconnect the compressor clutch and power steering pressure switch electrical connectors. Disconnect the alternator wiring harness from the alternator and position the harness aside.

6. Remove the fan shroud and the fan. Remove the upper radiator hose.

7. Remove the air cleaner-to-throttle body tube. Disconnect and plug the transmission oil cooler lines at the radiator.

8. Disconnect the throttle and kickdown cables from the throttle body and remove the cable bracket retaining bolts. Position the cable and bracket assembly aside.

9. Tag and disconnect the vacuum lines at the upper intake manifold vacuum tree, air conditioning control panel vacuum supply hose, thermactor valve and EGR valve. Disconnect the electrical connector at the EGR valve.

10. Remove the upper intake manifold as follows:

   a. Disconnect the electrical connectors at the idle air bypass valve, throttle position sensor and EGR position sensor.

   b. Disconnect the vacuum line from the fuel pressure regulator and the PCV hose from the fitting on the rear of the upper manifold.

   c. Remove the upper intake manifold retaining bolts and remove the manifold.

11. Disconnect the main engine wiring harness connectors at the right side of the dash panel. Position the engine wiring harness so it can be removed with the engine.

12. Disconnect the heater hoses at the engine. Disconnect the wiring harness from the coil and distributor and position the harness aside.

13. Disconnect and plug the fuel lines at the fuel supply manifold.

14. Disconnect the lower radiator hose from the water pump. Remove the radiator retaining bolts and remove the radiator.

15. Raise and safely support the vehicle. Remove the oil filter.

16. Remove the starter. Disconnect the oxygen sensors for the right and left catalytic converters. Disconnect the negative battery cable from the left side of the engine.

17. On the right side of the engine, disconnect the brackets for the transmission cooler lines, engine-to-body ground straps and the starter wiring harness.

18. Remove the torque converter inspection cover and mark 1 of the converter studs to the flywheel for alignment during reassembly. Remove the torque converter attaching nuts.

19. Remove the exhaust manifold

heat shield at the left manifold flange and disconnect the exhaust pipe from the flange. Disconnect the right exhaust manifold flange.

20. Loosen the transmission mount retaining nut. Remove the converter housing to engine bolts and the motor mount through bolts.

21. Lower the vehicle and disconnect the power steering lines. Cap the lines to prevent contamination.

22. Support the transmission with a floor jack. Install suitable engine lifting equipment on the engine lifting eyes.

23. Lift the engine assembly clear of the engine mounts and remove the engine from the vehicle. Place the engine on a workstand.

To install:

24. Install suitable engine lifting equipment on the engine lifting eyes and lift the engine from the workstand.

25. Carefully lower the engine into the engine compartment. Make sure the exhaust manifolds are properly aligned with the muffler inlet pipes.

26. Start the converter pilot into the crankshaft. Align the mark on the flywheel to the mark on the torque converter.

27. Position the retaining clip for the left oxygen sensor wiring near the left upper transmission-to-engine bolt. Install the converter housing upper bolts. Make sure the dowels in the cylinder block engage the converter housing.

28. Raise and safely support the vehicle. Install the remaining converter housing bolts and install the motor mount through bolts. Tighten the transmission mount retaining nut to 65–85 ft. lbs. (88–115 Nm).

29. Connect the right exhaust manifold flange. Connect the exhaust pipe to the left exhaust manifold flange and install the heat shield.

30. Install the torque converter retaining nuts and the inspection cover.

31. On the right side of the engine, install the brackets for the transmission cooler lines, engine-to-body ground strap and the starter wiring harness.

32. Connect the negative battery cable to the left side of the engine. Connect the oxygen sensors for the catalytic converters.

33. Install the starter. Install a new oil filter and the oil pan drain plug. Lower the vehicle and connect the power steering lines.

34. Install the radiator. Connect the coolant overflow hose and the lower radiator hose.

35. Connect the fuel lines to the fuel supply manifold.

36. Position and connect the wiring harness for the coil and distributor.

Connect the heater hoses at the engine. Connect the main engine wiring harness connectors at the right side of the dash panel.

37. Install the upper intake manifold in the reverse order of removal. Be sure to use a new gasket.

38. Connect the vacuum lines at the upper intake manifold vacuum tee, air conditioning control panel vacuum supply hose, thermactor valve and EGR valve. Connect the electrical connector to the EGR valve.

39. Connect the throttle and kickdown cables to the throttle body and install the cable bracket retaining bolts.

40. Connect the transmission oil cooler lines and the upper radiator hose. Install the fan shroud and the fan. Install the air cleaner-to-throttle body tube assembly.

41. Position and connect the wiring harness for the alternator. Connect the compressor clutch electrical connector and connect the refrigerant lines to the compressor.

42. Install the hood, aligning the marks that were made during removal. Connect the wiring connector for the underhood lamp.

43. Fill the engine with the proper type and quantity of engine oil. Fill and bleed the cooling system. Install the dipstick.

44. Fill the power steering system with the proper type and quantity of fluid. Connect the negative battery cable.

45. Start the engine and bring to normal operating temperature. Check for leaks. Check all fluid levels.

46. Leak test, evacuate and charge the air conditioning system according to the proper procedure. Observe all safety precautions.

Engine Mounts

REMOVAL & INSTALLATION

2.3L Engine

FRONT

1. Disconnect the negative battery cable. Raise and safely support the vehicle. Support the engine using a wood block and jack placed under the engine.

2. Remove the through bolts attaching both mounts to the No. 2 crossmember pedestal bracket. On convertible, remove the nuts.

3. Disconnect shift linkage.

4. Raise the engine sufficiently to disengage the mount from the crossmember pedestal bracket.

5. Remove the bolts attaching the mount to the engine and remove the mount.

To install:

6. Position the mount on the engine and install the attaching bolts. Tighten to 35–46 ft. lbs. (47–63 Nm).

7. Lower the engine into position making sure the mounts are seated flat on the No. 2 crossmember. Hand start the bolts, lower the engine completely, then tighten the through bolts to 35–46 ft. lbs. (47–63 Nm).

8. On convertible, tighten the flange nut to 73–106 ft. lbs. (98–144 Nm).

9. Install shift linkage. Lower the vehicle and connect the negative battery cable.

REAR

1. Disconnect the negative battery cable. Raise and safely support the vehicle.

2. Support the transmission with a jack and a wood block. Remove the nut(s) retaining the rear mount to the crossmember.

3. Remove the 2 bolts and nuts retaining the crossmember to the body brackets. Remove the crossmember by raising the transmission slightly with the jack.

4. Remove the 2 bolts retaining the rear mount to the transmission and remove the mount and retainer. If equipped with automatic transmission, remove the 2 bolts retaining the rear mount to the intermediate bracket.

To install:

5. Position the rear mount and retainer on the transmission. Install the 2 retaining bolts and tighten to 51–70 ft. lbs. (68–95 Nm). If equipped with automatic transmission, tighten the 2 bolts to 35–50 ft. lbs. (47–68 Nm).

6. Install the crossmember to the body brackets. Tighten the retaining nuts and bolts to 35–50 ft. lbs. (47–68 Nm).

7. Lower the transmission and install the mount to crossmember retaining nuts. Tighten to 26–35 ft. lbs. (34–48 Nm). If equipped with automatic transmission, tighten the nut to 65–87 ft. lbs. (88–119 Nm).

8. Lower the vehicle. Connect the negative battery cable.

3.8L Engine

FRONT

1. Disconnect the negative battery cable.

2. Remove fan shroud retaining screws. Remove the air tube to the remote air cleaner.

3. Raise and safely support the vehicle. Support engine using a jack and wood block placed under the engine.

4. Remove the engine mount through bolt. On supercharged en-

gines, remove the retaining strap bolt from the left side.

5. Remove shift linkage.

6. Raise engine high enough to clear clevis brackets.

NOTE: Raise the engine carefully so as not to damage the lines and hoses at the rear of the engine.

7. Remove any accessory and oil cooler line retaining clips from the engine support brackets.

8. Remove bolts retaining the engine mount and bracket assembly to engine. Remove the mount and bracket assembly.

NOTE: The left hand front engine mount removal on the supercharged engine may require lowering the front sub frame.

To install:

9. Position the engine mount and bracket assembly to the engine, install the retaining bolts and tighten to 26–34 ft. lbs. (34–47 Nm).

10. Install the accessories to the lower front engine mount support bracket stud. Tighten to 26–34 ft. lbs. (34–47 Nm).

11. Lower the engine into position and make sure the engine mounts are seated flat on the front sub frame; the left mount must seat first. Install the through-bolt and tighten to 35–50 ft. lbs. (47–68 Nm). On supercharged engines, install the retaining strap bolt and tighten to 34–44 ft. lbs. (45–61 Nm).

12. Lower the vehicle and install the air tube and the fan shroud retaining screws. Connect the negative battery cable.

REAR

1. Disconnect the negative battery cable. Raise and safely support the vehicle.

2. Support the transmission with a jack and a wood block. Remove the rear nut attaching the mount-to-crossmember. Keep transmission weight on the mount during nut removal.

3. Remove the 2 bolts retaining the crossmember-to-body brackets. Remove the crossmember by raising the transmission slightly with the jack.

4. Remove the bolts retaining the rear engine mount to the transmission. Remove the mount.

To install:

5. Position the engine mount and retainer on the transmission. Install the 2 retaining bolts and tighten to 35–50 ft. lbs. (47–68 Nm).

6. Install the crossmember-to-body brackets. Tighten the retaining bolts or nuts to 34–47 ft. lbs. (45–65 Nm).

7. Lower the transmission. Install

the mount-to-crossmember nut. Tighten to 65–84 ft. lbs. (88–115 Nm).

8. Lower the vehicle and connect the negative battery cable.

5.0L Engine

FRONT

1. Disconnect the negative battery cable. Remove fan shroud attaching screws.

2. Raise and safely support the vehicle. Support the engine using a jack and wood block placed under the engine.

3. Remove the nuts or bolts attaching the mounts to the No. 2 crossmember. On Thunderbird and Cougar, remove the through bolts.

4. Disconnect shift linkage on all except Thunderbird and Cougar.

5. Raise the engine sufficiently with the jack to disengage the mount from the crossmember. If equipped, remove the transmission brace attached at the left or right engine mount bracket.

6. Remove the engine mount and bracket assembly to the cylinder block attaching bolts. Remove the engine mount.

To install:

7. Position the mount on the engine and install the attaching bolts. Tighten the bolts to 45–59 ft. lbs. (61–81 Nm).

8. Attach the transmission brace to the right or left engine mount, if equipped. Tighten the nut to 45–59 ft. lbs. (60–81 Nm).

9. Lower the engine into position making sure the mounts are seated flat on the No. 2 crossmember and the insulator studs are at the bottom of the slots.

NOTE: On Thunderbird and Cougar, the left mount, with the locating pin, must seat before the right mount.

10. Install and tighten the mount nuts to 73–106 ft. lbs. (98–144 Nm). On Thunderbird and Cougar, install the through bolts and tighten to 35–45 ft. lbs. (45–61 Nm).

11. Lower the vehicle and install the fan shroud attaching screws. Connect the negative battery cable.

Mustang

REAR

1. Disconnect the negative battery cable. Raise and safely support the vehicle.

2. Support the transmission with a jack and wood block. Remove the 2 nuts attaching the mount to the crossmember.

3. Remove the 2 bolts and nuts attaching the crossmember to the body brackets and remove the crossmember

by raising the transmission slightly with the jack.

4. Remove the 2 bolts attaching the rear mount to the transmission and remove the mount and retainer.

To install:

5. Position the rear mount and retainer on the transmission. Install the 2 attaching bolts and tighten to 51–70 ft. lbs. (68–95 Nm).

6. Install the crossmember to the body brackets. Tighten the attaching nuts to 35–50 ft. lbs. (47–68 Nm).

7. Lower the transmission and install the mount-to-crossmember attaching nuts. Tighten to 26–35 ft. lbs. (34–48 Nm).

8. Lower the vehicle and connect the negative battery cable.

Thunderbird and Cougar

REAR

1. Disconnect the negative battery cable. Raise and safely support the vehicle.

2. Remove the nut attaching the rear mount-to-crossmember.

NOTE: This must be done while the transmission weight is still on the mount.

3. Support the transmission with a jack and a wood block. Remove the bolts that attach the crossmember to the body brackets and remove the crossmember.

4. Remove the bolts attaching the mount to the transmission bracket and remove the mount.

To install:

5. Position the mount on the transmission bracket. Install the bolts and tighten to 35–50 ft. lbs. (47–68 Nm).

6. Install the crossmember to the body brackets and tighten the bolts to 34–47 ft. lbs. (45–65 Nm).

7. Lower the transmission and install the nut. Tighten the nut to 65–85 ft. lbs. (88–115 Nm).

8. Lower the vehicle and connect the negative battery cable.

Mark VII

REAR

1. Disconnect the negative battery cable. Raise and safely support the vehicle.

2. Support the transmission with a jack and wood block. Remove the bolts that attach the rear mounts and crossmember to the transmission.

3. Remove the lower rebound mount.

4. Raise the transmission slightly with the jack. Remove the upper mounts.

To install:

5. Position the upper mounts between the crossmember and the transmission.

6. Position the lower mounts and hand start the attaching bolts. Lower the transmission and tighten the crossmember-to-body bolts to 45–70 ft. lbs. (60–95 Nm) and the crossmember-to-transmission bolts to 35–50 ft. lbs. (47–68 Nm).

7. Lower the vehicle and connect the negative battery cable.

Cylinder Head

REMOVAL & INSTALLATION

2.3L Engine

1. Disconnect the negative battery cable. Drain the cooling system and relieve the fuel system pressure.

2. Remove the air cleaner assembly.

3. Remove the engine and alternator wiring harnesses. Remove the heater hose retaining screw from the rocker arm cover, if equipped.

4. Tag and disconnect the spark plug wires from the spark plugs. Remove the spark plug wires and, if equipped, the distributor cap. Remove the spark plugs.

5. Tag and disconnect the required vacuum hoses. Remove the dipstick and disconnect the dipstick tube from the bracket.

6. Remove the upper intake manifold and throttle body as follows:

   a. Tag and disconnect the electrical connectors and vacuum hoses.

   b. Disconnect the throttle linkage, cruise control and kickdown cable. Unbolt the accelerator cable from the bracket and position the cable aside.

   c. Disconnect the crankcase vent hose. Disconnect the PCV hose from the fitting on the underside of the upper intake manifold.

   d. Disconnect the EGR tube from the EGR valve. Remove the upper intake manifold mounting bolts and the manifold.

7. Remove the rocker cover retaining bolts and remove the cover. Remove the intake manifold retaining bolts.

8. Remove the accessory drive belt, loosen the retaining bolt and swing the alternator aside.

9. Remove the upper radiator hose. Remove the timing belt cover retaining bolts and remove the cover.

10. Loosen the timing belt idler retaining bolts. Position the idler in the unloaded position and tighten the retaining bolts.

11. Remove the timing belt from the camshaft sprocket and the auxiliary sprocket.

12. Remove the exhaust manifold retaining bolts. Remove the timing belt idler and 2 bracket bolts. Remove the timing belt idler spring stop from the cylinder head.

13. Disconnect the oil sending unit wire, if necessary.

14. Remove the cylinder head bolts and the cylinder head. Clean all gasket mating surfaces and blow the oil out of the cylinder head bolt block holes.

15. Check the cylinder head for flatness using a straight-edge and a feeler gauge. If the head gasket surface is warped greater than 0.006 in., it must be resurfaced. Do not grind more than 0.010 in. from the cylinder head.

To install:

16. Position the head gasket on the block. Position the camshaft with the pin approximateley 30 degrees to the right of the 6 o' clock position when facing the front of the cylinder head. The camshaft must be positioned this way to protect protruding valves.

17. Position the cylinder head on the block and install the cylinder head bolts. Tighten the bolts, in sequence, in 2 steps, first to 50–60 ft. lbs. (60–81 Nm) and then to 80–90 ft. lbs. (108–122 Nm).

18. Connect the oil sending unit wire, if necessary. Install the timing belt tensioner spring stop to the cylinder head.

19. Position the timing belt tensioner and tensioner spring to the cylinder head and install the retaining bolts. Rotate the tensioner against the spring with belt tensioner tool T74P-6254–A or equivalent, and temporarily tighten.

20. Install the exhaust manifold retaining bolts. Tighten the bolts, in sequence, in 2 steps, first to 178–204 inch lbs. (20–23 Nm) and then to 20–30 ft. lbs. (27–40 Nm).

21. If equipped with a distributor, align the distributor rotor with the No. 1 plug location on the distributor cap. Align the camshaft sprocket with the pointer and align the crankshaft pulley with the pointer on the timing belt cover.

22. Install the timing belt over the sprockets. Loosen the tensioner retaining bolts, rotate the engine by hand 1 complete revolution and check the timing alignment.

23. Tighten the 10mm tensioner bolt to 28–40 ft. lbs. (38–54 Nm) and the 8mm bolt to 14–21 ft. lbs. (19–29 Nm).

24. Install the timing belt cover and tighten the retaining bolts to 6–9 ft. lbs. (8–12 Nm).

25. Install the rocker arm cover and tighten the retaining bolts to 62–97 inch lbs. (7–11 Nm).

26. Install the intake manifold. Tighten the bolts, in sequence, to 19–28 ft. lbs. (26–38 Nm).

27. Install the upper intake manifold and throttle body in the reverse order of removal. Tighten the upper intake-

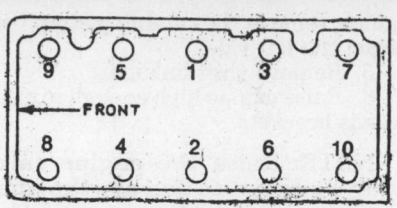

Cylinder head bolt torque sequence—2.3L engine

to-lower intake bolts, in sequence, to 15–22 ft. lbs. (20–30 Nm).

28. Position the alternator and install the drive belt. Install the upper radiator hose.

29. Install the dipstick and connect the necessary vacuum hoses. Install the spark plugs, spark plug wires and distributor cap, if equipped.

30. Position and connect the engine and alternator wiring harnesses. Install the hose from the air cleaner to the throttle body. If equipped, install the retaining heater hose screw to the rocker cover.

31. Fill and bleed the cooling system. Connect the negative battery cable, start the engine and bring to normal operating temperature. Check for leaks. If equipped with distributor ignition, check the ignition timing.

3.8L Engine

1. Disconnect the negative battery cable.

2. Relieve the fuel system pressure. Drain the cooling system.

3. Remove air cleaner assembly including the air intake duct and heat tube.

4. Loosen accessory drive belt idler. Remove drive belt.

5. If the left cylinder head is being removed, perform the following:

   a. On supercharged engines, remove the intercooler and intercooler tubes.

   b. Remove oil fill cap.

   c. Remove the power steering pump front mounting bracket attaching bolts.

   d. Remove the alternator assembly and accessory drive belt main idler.

   e. Remove the power steering/pump alternator bracket retaining bolts.

   f. Leaving the hoses connected, place the power steering pump/alternator bracket assembly aside in a position to prevent the fluid from leaking out.

6. If the right cylinder head is being removed, perform the following:

   a. If equipped, disconnect the thermactor tube support bracket from the rear of the cylinder head. Remove the thermactor pump pulley and remove the pump.

b. If equipped, remove the air conditioner compressor belt and main drive belt.

c. If equipped, remove the compressor mounting bracket retaining bolts. Leave the hoses connected and position the compressor aside.

d. Remove the PCV valve.

7. On supercharged engines, remove the supercharger. On non-supercharged engines, remove the upper intake manifold as follows:

a. Disconnect the electrical connectors at the idle air bypass valve, throttle position sensor and EGR position sensor.

b. Disconnect the throttle and transmission linkage from the throttle body. Remove the cable bracket from the manifold and position the bracket and cables aside.

c. Tag and disconnect the vacuum lines at the upper manifold vacuum tree, EGR valve and fuel pressure regulator.

d. Disconnect the PCV hose from the fitting at the rear of the upper manifold.

e. Remove the retaining bolts and remove the upper intake manifold.

8. Remove valve rocker arm cover attaching screws. Remove the fuel rail and the lower intake manifold.

9. Remove the exhaust manifold(s).

10. Loosen rocker arm fulcrum attaching bolts enough to allow the rocker arm to be lifted off the pushrod and rotated to 1 side.

11. Remove the pushrods. Identify the position of each rod. The rods should be installed in their original position during assembly.

12. Remove the cylinder head attaching bolts and discard.

13. Remove the cylinder head(s). Clean all gasket mating surfaces.

14. Check the flatness of the cylinder head gasket surface using a straight edge and a feeler gauge. The allowable warpage is 0.003 in. for every 6.0 inches. Do not machine more than 0.010 in.

To install:

NOTE: Lightly oil all bolt and stud bolt threads before installation except those specifying special sealant.

15. Position new head gasket(s) on the cylinder block using the dowels for alignment.

16. Position the cylinder head(s) on the block.

17. Install new cylinder head bolts.

NOTE: Always use new cylinder head bolts to assure a leak-tight assembly. Torque retention with used bolts can vary, which may result in coolant or compression

leakage at the cylinder head mating surface area.

18. On 1989 vehicles tighten the new cylinder head attaching bolts in sequence as follows:

a. 37 ft. lbs. (50 Nm)

b. 45 ft. lbs. (60 Nm)

c. 52 ft. lbs. (70 Nm)

d. 59 ft. lbs. (80 Nm)

e. Back-off the attaching bolts 2–3 turns

f. In sequential order, tighten the bolts to 52 ft. lbs. (70 Nm)

g. In sequential order, rotate the bolts an additional 90–110 degrees

NOTE: When cylinder head attaching bolts have been tightened using multi-step torque procedure, it is not necessary to retighten the bolts after extended engine operation.

19. On 1990–93 vehicles tighten the new cylinder head attaching bolts in numerical sequence as follows:

a. 37 ft. lbs. (50 Nm)

b. 45 ft. lbs. (60 Nm)

c. 52 ft. lbs. (70 Nm)

d. 59 ft. lbs. (80 Nm)

e. Back-off the attaching bolts 2–3 turns

f. On supercharged engines, tighten each long and short bolt to 48–55 ft. lbs. (65–75 Nm), rotate an additional 90–110 degrees, then go to the next bolt in sequence.

g. On non-supercharged engines, tighten each long bolt to 11–18 ft. lbs. (15–25 Nm), rotate an additional 85–105 degrees, then go to the next bolt in sequence. Do the same for each short bolt except only rotate the short bolts 65–85 degrees.

NOTE: When cylinder head attaching bolts have been tightened using multi-step torque procedure, it is not necessary to retighten the bolts after extended engine operation.

20. Lubricate each pushrod with heavy engine oil and install, in their original positions.

21. For each valve, rotate the crankshaft until the lifter rests on the base circle of the camshaft lobe, before tightening the fulcrum attaching bolts to 43 inch lbs. (5 Nm).

22. Lubricate the rocker arm assemblies with heavy engine oil and final tighten the fulcrum bolts to 19–25 ft. lbs. (25–35 Nm). Fulcrums must be fully seated in cylinder head and pushrods must be seated in rocker arm sockets prior to final tightening. Final tightening can be done with the camshaft in any position.

NOTE: If the original valve train components are being in-

stalled, a valve clearance check is not required. If a component has been replaced, perform a valve clearance check.

23. Install the exhaust manifold(s).

24. Install the lower intake manifold and the fuel rail.

25. Position cover and new gasket on the cylinder head and install attaching bolts. Note the location of spark plug wire routing clip stud bolts. Tighten attaching bolts to 80–106 inch lbs. (9–12 Nm).

26. Install the upper intake manifold. On supercharged engines, install the supercharger.

27. Install the spark plugs, if removed.

28. Connect the spark plug wires to the spark plugs.

29. If the left cylinder head is being installed, perform the following:

a. Install the oil filler cap.

b. Install the alternator/power steering pump mounting bracket.

c. Install the alternator assembly.

d. Install the main accessory drive belt tensioner assembly.

e. Install the power steering pump assembly.

f. Install the power steering pump support bracket.

g. On supercharged engines, install the intercooler tubes.

30. If the right cylinder head is being installed, perform the following:

a. Install PCV valve.

b. If equipped with air conditioning, install the compressor mounting and support brackets and install the compressor.

c. If equipped, install the thermactor pump and pump pulley.

d. If equipped, install the accessory drive belt idler pulley.

e. If equipped, install the thermactor air control valve or air bypass valve hose. Tighten the clamps securely to the air pump assembly.

31. Install the accessory drive belt. If equipped, attach the thermactor

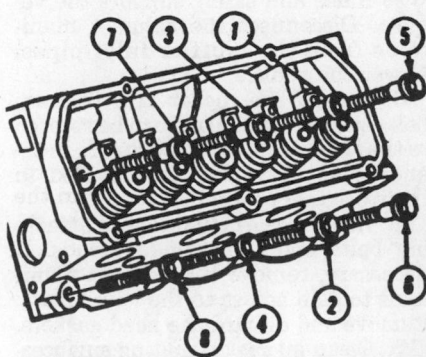

Cylinder head bolt torque sequence—3.8L engine

tube(s) support bracket to the rear of the cylinder head. Tighten attaching bolts to 30–40 ft. lbs. (40–55 Nm).

32. Connect the negative battery cable.

33. Fill and bleed the cooling system.

34. Start engine and check for coolant, fuel and oil leaks.

35. Check and, if necessary, adjust the curb idle speed.

36. Install the air cleaner assembly including the air intake duct and heat tube.

5.0L Engine

1. Disconnect the negative battery cable.

2. Drain the cooling system and relieve the fuel system pressure.

3. Remove the upper and lower intake manifold and throttle body assembly.

4. If the left cylinder head is to be removed and the vehicle is equipped with air conditioning, proceed as follows:

   a. Discharge the air conditioning system.

   b. Disconnect and plug the refrigerant lines at the compressor. Cap the openings on the compressor.

   c. Disconnect the electrical connector to the compressor.

   d. Remove the compressor and the necessary mounting brackets.

5. If the left cylinder head is to be removed, disconnect the power steering pump bracket from the cylinder head. Position the pump aside in a position that will prevent the oil from draining out.

6. Disconnect the oil level indicator tube bracket from the exhaust manifold stud.

7. If the right cylinder head is to be removed, remove the alternator mounting bracket from the cylinder head.

8. Remove the thermactor crossover tube from the rear of the cylinder heads. Remove the fuel line from the clip at the front of the right cylinder head.

9. Raise and safely support the vehicle. Disconnect the exhaust manifolds from the muffler inlet pipes. Lower the vehicle.

10. Loosen the rocker arm fulcrum bolts so the rocker arms can be rotated to the side. Remove the pushrods in sequence so they may be installed in their original positions.

11. Remove the cylinder head attaching bolts and the cylinder heads. If necessary, remove the exhaust manifolds to gain access to the lower bolts. Remove and discard the head gaskets.

12. Clean all gasket mating surfaces. Check the flatness of the cylinder head using a straight-edge and a feeler gauge. The cylinder head must not be warped any more than 0.003 in. in any 6.0 in.; 0.006 in. overall. Machine as necessary.

To install:

13. Position the new cylinder head gasket over the dowels on the block. Position the cylinder heads on the block and install the attaching bolts.

14. Tighten the bolts, in sequence, in 2 steps, first to 55–65 ft. lbs. (75–88 Nm), then to 65–72 ft. lbs. (88–97 Nm).

NOTE: When the cylinder head bolts have been tightened following this procedure, it is not necessary to retighten the bolts after extended operation.

15. If removed, install the exhaust manifolds. Tighten the retaining bolts to 18–24 ft. lbs. (24–32 Nm).

16. Clean the pushrods, making sure the oil passages are clean. Check the ends of the pushrods for wear. Visually check the pushrods for straightness or check for runout using a dial indicator. Replace pushrods, as necessary.

17. Apply a suitable grease to the ends of the pushrods and install them in their original positions. Position the rocker arms over the pushrods and the valves.

18. Before tightening each fulcrum bolt, bring the lifter for the fulcrum bolt to be tightened onto the base circle of the camshaft by rotating the engine. When the lifter is on the base circle of the camshaft, tighten the fulcrum bolt to 18–25 ft. lbs. (24–34 Nm).

NOTE: If all the original valve train parts are reinstalled, a valve clearance check is not necessary. If any valve train components are replaced, a valve clearance check must be perforemed.

19. Install new rocker arm cover gaskets on the rocker arm covers and install the covers on the cylinder heads. Tighten the retaining bolts to 10–13 ft. lbs. (14–18 Nm), wait 2 minutes, then retighten to the same specification.

20. Raise and safely support the vehicle. Connect the exhaust manifolds to the muffler inlet pipes. Lower the vehicle.

21. If necessary, install the air conditioning compressor and brackets. Connect the refrigerant lines and electrical connector to the compressor.

22. If necessary, install the alternator bracket.

23. If the left cylinder head was removed, install the power steering pump.

24. Install the drive belt. Install the thermactor tube at the rear of the cylinder heads.

25. Install the intake manifold. Fill and bleed the cooling system.

26. Connect the negative battery cable, start the engine and bring to normal operating temperature. Check for leaks. Check all fluid levels.

27. If necessary, leak test, evacuate and charge the air conditioning system according to the proper procedure. Observe all safety precautions.

Valve Lifters

REMOVAL & INSTALLATION

2.3L Engine

The 2.3L engine is equipped with hydraulic lash adjusters which, while not being exactly the same as a conventional hydraulic lifter, perform the same function—maintain proper valve train clearance.

1. Disconnect the negative battery cable.

2. If equipped with distributor ignition, tag and disconnect the spark plug wires from the spark plugs. Move the wires out of the way.

3. Remove the hose and the retaining bolts from the rocker arm cover and remove the cover.

4. Rotate the camshaft so the base circle of the cam is facing the cam follower to be removed.

5. Using valve spring compressor tool T88T-6565-BH or equivalent, compress the lash adjuster as required and/or depress the valve spring if necessary and slide the cam follower over the lash adjuster and out.

6. Lift out the hydraulic lash adjuster.

To install:

7. Rotate the camshaft so the base circle of the camshaft is facing the lash adjuster and cam follower to be installed. Lubricate the hydraulic lash adjuster with clean engine oil and position it in the bore.

8. Using valve spring compressor tool T88T-6565-BH or equivalent, compress the lash adjuster, as necessary, to position the cam follower over the lash adjuster and the valve stem.

9. Before rotating the camshaft to the next position, make sure the lash adjuster just installed is fully compressed and released.

10. Clean the gasket mating surface of the rocker arm cover and cylinder head. Install a new gasket and the rocker arm cover. Install the mounting screws and tighten to 62–97 inch lbs. (7–11 Nm).

11. Install the remaining components in the reverse order of removal. Start the engine and check for oil leaks.

3.8L Engine

NOTE: Before replacing a lifter for noisy operation, be sure the noise is not caused by improper valve to rocker arm clearance or by worn rocker arms or pushrods.

1. Disconnect the negative battery cable. Tag and disconnect the spark plug wires at the spark plugs.
2. Remove plug wire routing clips from the studs on the rocker arm cover attaching bolts. Lay the plug wires, with the routing clips toward the front of the engine.
3. Remove the upper intake manifold. On supercharged engine, remove the supercharger.
4. Remove the rocker arm covers. Remove the lower intake manifold.
5. Sufficiently loosen each rocker arm fulcrum attaching bolt to allow the rocker arm to be lifted off the pushrod and rotated to 1 side.
6. Remove the pushrods. The location of each pushrod should be identified. When the engine is assembled each rod should be installed in its original position.
7. Remove the 4 bolts holding the 2 guide plate retainers in place; the bolts are held captive in the retainers. Remove the 6 guide plates from the adjacent lifters.
8. Remove the lifters using a magnet. The location of each lifter should be identified. When the engine is assembled, each lifter should be installed in its original position.

NOTE: If the lifters are stuck in the bores due to excessive varnish or gum deposits, it may be necessary to use a claw-type tool to aid removal. When using a remover tool, rotate the lifter back and forth to loosen it from gum or varnish that may have formed on the lifter.

To install:

9. Clean the rocker arm cover and cylinder head mating surfaces.
10. Install each lifter in the bore from which it was removed. If new lifters are being installed, check the new lifters for free fit in the bores.
11. Align the flats on the side of the lifters and install the 6 guide plates between the adjacent lifters. Make sure the word UP is showing. Install the 2 guide plate retainers and tighten the 4 captive bolts to 7–10 ft. lbs. (9–14 Nm).
12. Dip each pushrod in heavy engine oil and install in its original position.
13. For each valve, rotate the crankshaft until the lifter rests on the base circle of the camshaft lobe. Position the rocker arms over the pushrods. Install the fulcrums and tighten the bolts to 5–11 ft. lbs. (7–15 Nm).

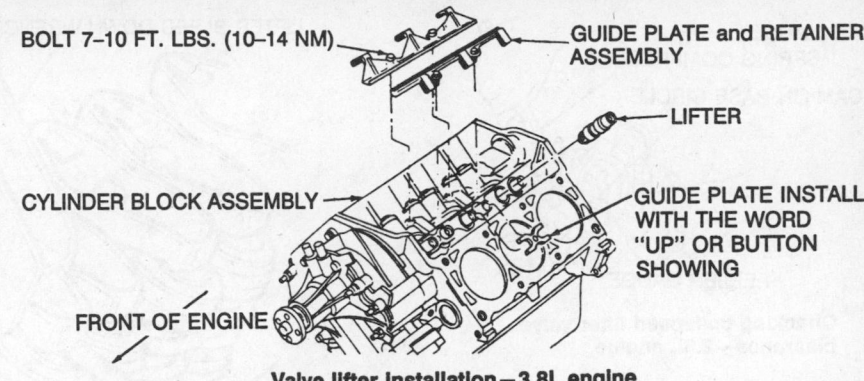

BOLT 7–10 FT. LBS. (10–14 NM) — GUIDE PLATE and RETAINER ASSEMBLY

— LIFTER

CYLINDER BLOCK ASSEMBLY —

GUIDE PLATE INSTALL WITH THE WORD "UP" OR BUTTON SHOWING

FRONT OF ENGINE

Valve lifter installation – 3.8L engine

14. Lubricate all rocker arm assemblies with heavy engine oil. Final tighten the fulcrum bolts to 19–25 ft. lbs. (25–35 Nm). For final tightening the camshaft may be in any position.

NOTE: The fulcrums must be fully seated in the cylinder head and the pushrods must be seated in the rocker arm sockets prior to final tightening.

15. Install the lower intake manifold and the rocker arm covers. On non-supercharged engines, install the upper intake manifold. On supercharged engines, install the supercharger.
16. Install the spark plug wire routing clips and connect the wires to the spark plugs. Connect the negative battery cable, start the engine and check for oil and coolant leaks.

5.0L Engine

1. Disconnect the negative battery cable. Remove the intake manifold and related parts.
2. Disconnect the necessary hoses from the rocker arm covers. Tag and disconnect the spark plug wires, then remove the wires and brackets from the rocker arm cover attaching studs. Remove the upper intake manifold.
3. Remove the rocker arm covers. Loosen the rocker arm fulcrum bolts and rotate the rocker arms to the side.
4. Remove the valve pushrods and identify them so they can be installed in their original position.
5. Remove the lifter guide retainer bolts. Remove the retainer and lifter guide plates. Identify the guide plates so they may be reinstalled in their original positions.
6. Using a magnet, remove the lifters and place them in a rack so they can be installed in their original bores.

NOTE: If the lifters are stuck in the bores due to excessive varnish or gum deposits, it may be necessary to use a claw-type tool to aid removal. When using a remover tool, rotate the lifter back and forth to loosen it from gum or var-

nish that may have formed on the lifter.

To install:

7. Lubricate the lifters and install them in their original bores. If new lifters are being installed, check them for free fit in their respective bores.
8. Install the lifter guide plates in their original positions, then install the guide plate retainer.
9. Install the pushrods in their original positions. Apply grease to the ends prior to installation.
10. Lubricate the rocker arms and fulcrum seats with heavy engine oil. Position the rocker arms over the pushrods and install the fulcrum bolts.
11. Before tightening each fulcrum bolt, rotate the crankshaft until the lifter is on the base circle of the cam. Tighten the fulcrum bolt to 18–25 ft. lbs. (24–34 Nm). Check the valve clearance.
12. Install the rocker arm covers and the intake manifold. Connect the negative battery cable, start the engine and check for leaks.

Valve Lash

ADJUSTMENT

2.3L Engine

1. Disconnect the negative battery cable.
2. Remove the valve cover assembly.
3. Position the camshaft so the base circle of the lobe is facing the cam follower of the valve to be checked.
4. Using valve spring compressor tool T88T-6565-BH or equivalent, slowly apply pressure to the cam follower until the the lash adjuster is completely collapsed.
5. With follower collapsed, insert a feeler gauge between the base circle of the camshaft and follower. The clearance should not be more than 0.035–0.055 in.
6. If the clearance is excessive, re-

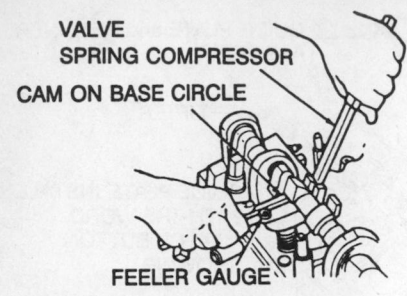

Checking collapsed lifter valve clearance—2.3L engine

move the cam follower and inspect for damage.

7. If the cam follower appears to be intact and not excessively worn, measure the valve spring assembled height to make sure the valve is not sticking.

8. If the valve spring assembled height is correct, check the camshaft for wear. If the camshaft dimensions are correct, replace the lash adjuster.

9. Install the valve cover and all remaining components.

3.8L Engine

The valve lash is not adjustable. If the collapsed lifter clearance is found to be incorrect, there are replacement pushrods available to compensate for excessive or insufficient clearance.

1. Disconnect the negative battery cable.

2. Remove the valve cover assembly on the side to be checked.

3. Turn the engine until the No. 1 piston is at TDC on the compression stroke.

4. The following valves can be checked with the engine in this position:
   a. No. 1 intake—No. 1 exhaust
   b. No. 3 intake—No. 2 exhaust
   c. No. 6 intake—No. 4 exhaust

5. Rotate the engine 360 degrees and check the following valves:
   a. No. 2 intake—No. 3 exhaust
   b. No. 4 intake—No. 5 exhaust
   c. No. 5 intake—No. 6 exhaust

6. Check each of the lifters by placing hydraulic lifter compressor tool T71P–6513–B or equivalent, on the rocker arm and slowly applying pressure to the lifter, until the lifter is collapsed.

7. Hold the lifter in this position and check the clearance between the rocker arm and the valve stem tip. The clearance should be 0.09–0.19 in. (2.25–4.79mm).

8. Repeat this operation for each valve to be checked.

9. If the clearance is greater than specification, replace the pushrod with a longer one. If the clearance is less than specified, replace the pushrod with a shorter one.

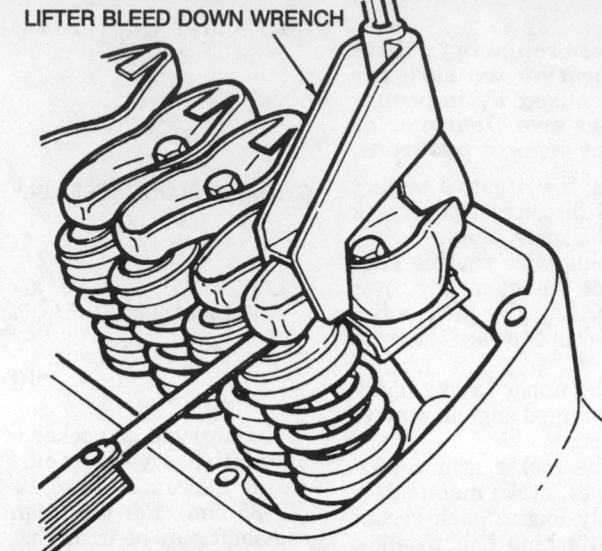

Checking collapsed lifter valve clearance—3.8L and 5.0L engines

5.0L Engine

The valve lash is not adjustable. If the collapsed lifter clearance is found to be incorrect, there are replacement pushrods available to compensate for excessive or insufficient clearance.

1. Install an auxiliary starter switch. Crank the engine with the ignition switch OFF until the No. 1 piston is at TDC on the compression stroke.

2. With the crankshaft in the positions designated in Steps 4, 5 and 6, position lifter bleed down wrench tool T71P–6513–B or equivalent, on the rocker arm. Slowly apply pressure to bleed down the lifter until the plunger is completely bottomed. Hold the lifter in this position and check the available clearance between the rocker arm and the valve stem tip with a feeler gauge.

3. The clearance should be 0.123–0.146 in. If the clearance is less than specification, install a shorter pushrod. If the clearance is greater than specification, install a longer pushrod.

4. The following valves can be checked with the engine in position 1, No. 1 piston at TDC on the compression stroke.
   a. No. 1 intake—No. 1 exhaust
   b. No. 4 intake—No. 3 exhaust
   c. No. 8 intake—No. 7 exhaust

5. Rotate the engine 360 degrees (1 revolution) from the 1st position and check the following valves:
   a. No. 3 intake—No. 2 exhaust
   b. No. 7 intake—No. 6 exhaust

6. Rotate the engine 90 degrees (¼ revolution) from the 2nd position and check the following valves:
   a. No. 2 intake—No. 4 exhaust
   b. No. 5 intake—No. 5 exhaust
   c. No. 6 intake—No. 8 exhaust

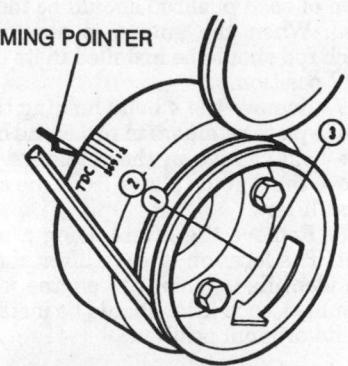

POSITION 1—NO. 1 AT TDC ON COMPRESSION STROKE
POSITION 2—ROTATE THE CRANKSHAFT 360 DEGREES (1 REVOLUTION) CLOCKWISE FROM POSITION 1
POSITION 3—ROTATE THE CRANKSHAFT 90 DEGREES (¼ REVOLUTION) CLOCKWISE FROM POSITION 2

Engine valve adjusting positions—5.0L engine

Rocker Arms

REMOVAL & INSTALLATION

2.3L Engine

1. Disconnect the negative battery cable.

2. If equipped with distributor ignition, tag and disconnect the spark plug wires from the spark plugs. Move the wires aside.

3. Remove the hose and the retaining bolts from the rocker arm cover and remove the cover.

4. Rotate the camshaft so the base circle of the cam is facing the cam follower to be removed.

5. Using valve spring compressor tool T88T-6565-BH or equivalent, compress the lash adjuster as required and/or depress the valve spring if necessary and slide the cam follower over the lash adjuster and out.

To install:

6. Using valve spring compressor tool T88T-6565-BH or equivalent, compress the lash adjuster, as necessary, to position the cam follower over the lash adjuster and the valve stem.

7. Before rotating the camshaft to the next position, make sure the lash adjuster just installed is fully compressed and released.

8. Clean the gasket mating surface of the rocker arm cover and cylinder head. Install a new gasket and the rocker arm cover. Install the mounting screws and tighten to 62–97 inch lbs. (7–11 Nm).

9. Install the remaining components in the reverse order of removal. Start the engine and check for oil leaks.

3.8L Engine

1. Disconnect the negative battery cable.

2. Disconnect the spark plug wires from the spark plugs. Remove the spark plug wire routing clips from the rocker arm cover attaching bolt studs.

3. To remove the left rocker arm cover, proceed as follows:

    a. Remove the oil fill cap.

    b. On 1990–93 vehicles, remove the crankcase vent tube.

    c. On supercharged engines, remove the intercooler tubes and the oil cooler inlet tube.

4. To remove the right rocker arm cover, proceed as follows:

    a. Remove the PCV valve.

    b. Position the air cleaner assembly aside, if necessary.

    c. On supercharged engines, remove the air inlet tube and remove the throttle body assembly.

5. Remove the rocker arm cover attaching screws and remove the rocker arm covers.

6. Remove the rocker arm, fulcrum and bolt assemblies. Keep each assembly together and identify the assemblies so they may be reinstalled in their original positions.

To install:

7. Clean all gasket mating surfaces on the rocker arm covers and cylinder heads. Clean the rocker arms and fulcrums and inspect for wear or damage. Replace as necessary.

8. Apply grease to the pushrod tips and valve stem tips. Lubricate the fulcrums and rocker arms with heavy engine oil and install them over the pushrods and valve stems.

9. For each valve, rotate the crankshaft until the lifter is on the base cir-

cle of the camshaft. Install the fulcrum bolt and tighten to 5–11 ft. lbs. (7–15 Nm). Make sure the pushrod and fulcrum are fully seated prior to tightening.

10. Lubricate all rocker arm assemblies with engine oil. Final tighten the fulcrum bolts to 19–25 ft. lbs. (25–35 Nm). When final tightening, the camshaft may be in any position. Make sure the pushrod and fulcrum are fully seated prior to tightening.

11. Position new gaskets on the cylinder heads and install the rocker arm covers. Tighten the attaching bolts to 80–106 inch lbs. (9–12 Nm). Note the location of the spark plug wire routing clip stud bolts prior to installation.

12. After installing the left rocker arm cover, proceed as follows:

    a. Install the oil fill cap.

    b. On 1990–93 vehicles, install the crankcase vent tube.

    c. On supercharged engines, install the intercooler tubes and the oil cooler inlet tube.

13. After installing the right valve cover, proceed as follows:

    a. Install the PCV valve.

    b. Install the air cleaner assembly, if necessary.

    c. On supercharged engines, install the air inlet tube and the throttle body assembly.

14. Install the spark plug wire routing clips and connect the wires to the spark plugs.

15. Connect the negative battery cable, start the engine and check for leaks.

5.0L Engine

1. Disconnect the negative battery cable.

2. Before removing the right rocker arm cover, disconnect the PCV closure tube from the oil fill stand pipe at the rocker cover.

3. Remove the thermactor bypass valve and air supply hoses as necessary to provide clearance.

4. Tag and disconnect the spark plug wires from the spark plugs. Remove the wires and bracket assembly from the rocker arm cover attaching stud and position the wires aside.

5. Remove the upper intake manifold as follows:

    a. Disconnect the electrical connectors at the idle air bypass valve, throttle position sensor and EGR position sensor.

    b. Disconnect the throttle and transmission linkage from the throttle body. Remove the cable bracket from the manifold and position the cables and bracket aside.

    c. Tag and disconnect the vacuum lines at the upper intake manifold vacuum tree, EGR valve, fuel pres-

sure regulator and evaporative canister.

    d. Disconnect the PCV hose from the fitting on the rear of the upper manifold and disconnect the PCV vent closure tube at the throttle body.

    e. Partially drain the cooling system and remove the 2 EGR coolant lines from the fittings on the EGR spacer.

    f. Remove the retaining bolts and remove the upper intake manifold and throttle body assembly.

6. Remove the attaching bolts and remove the covers.

7. Remove the rocker arm fulcrum bolt, fulcrum seat and rocker arm. Keep all rocker arm assemblies together. Identify each assembly so it may be reinstalled in its original position.

To install:

8. Clean all gasket mating surfaces of the rocker arm covers and cylinder heads. Clean and inspect the rocker arm assemblies for wear and/or damage. Replace as necessary.

9. Apply grease to the pushrod and valve stem tips and the underside of the fulcrum seats.

10. Rotate the crankshaft until the lifter is on the camshaft base circle and install the rocker, fulcrum seat and fulcrum bolt. Tighten the bolts to 18–25 ft. lbs. (24–34 Nm). Make sure the pushrod and fulcrum are fully seated prior to tightening.

11. Position new rocker arm cover gaskets and install the rocker arm covers. Tighten the bolts to 10–13 ft. lbs. (14–18 Nm), wait 2 minutes and tighten again to the same specification.

12. Install the crankcase ventilation tube in the right cover. Install the upper intake manifold in the reverse order of removal. Tighten the retaining bolts to 12–17 ft. lbs. (16–24 Nm).

13. Install the spark plug wires and bracket assembly on the rocker cover attaching stud. Connect the spark plug wires.

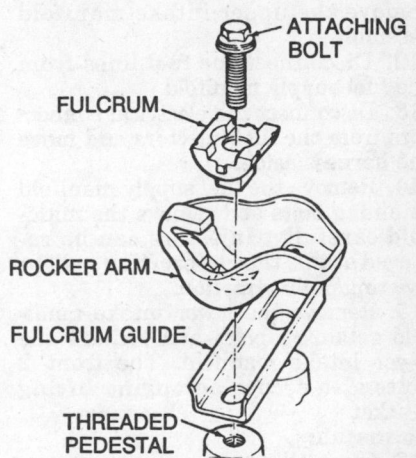

Rocker arm assembly—5.0L engine

14. Install the air cleaner intake duct assembly. Install the thermactor by-pass valve and air supply hoses, if required.

15. Connect the negative battery cable, start the engine and check for leaks.

Intake Manifold

REMOVAL & INSTALLATION

2.3L Engine

1. Disconnect the negative battery cable.
2. Relieve the fuel system pressure and drain the cooling system.
3. Disconnect and label the electrical connectors at the following:
   a. Air bypass valve
   b. Throttle positioning sensor
   c. Injector wiring harness
   d. Air charge temperature sensor
   e. Engine coolant temperature sensor
   f. EGR valve, if necessary
   g. Fan switch, if necessary
   h. Ignition control assembly, if equipped
4. Tag and disconnect the necessary vacuum lines.
5. Remove the throttle linkage shield. Disconnect the throttle linkage and if equipped, the cruise control and kickdown cables. Unbolt the accelerator cable from the bracket and position the cable out of the way.
6. Disconnect the air intake hose and crankcase vent hose.
7. Disconnect the PCV system hose from the fitting on the underside of the upper intake manifold.
8. Disconnect the water bypass hose at the lower intake manifold.
9. Loosen the EGR flange nut and disconnect the EGR tube.
10. Remove the engine oil dipstick bracket retaining bolt.
11. Remove the upper intake manifold retaining bolts and/or studs and remove the upper intake manifold assembly.
12. Disconnect the fuel lines from the fuel supply manifold.
13. Disconnect the electrical connectors from the fuel injectors and move the harness aside.
14. Remove the fuel supply manifold retaining bolts and remove the manifold carefully. Injectors can be removed at this time by exerting a slight twisting/pulling motion.
15. Remove the lower intake manifold retaining bolts and remove the lower intake manifold. The front 2 bolts also secure an engine lifting bracket.

To install:

16. Clean all gasket mating syrfaces. Clean and oil the manifold bolt

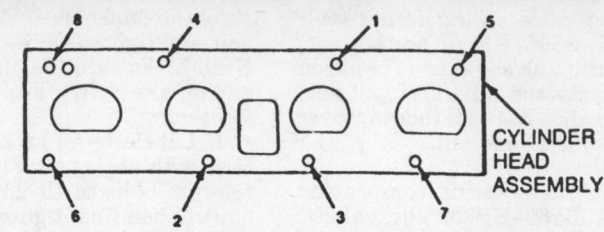

Intake manifold-to-cylinder head torque sequence—1989 2.3L engine

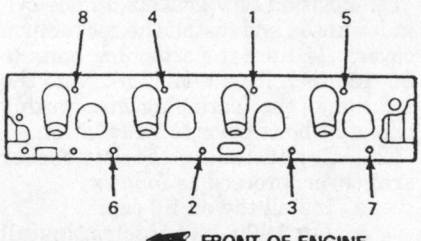

FRONT OF ENGINE

Intake manifold-to-cylinder head torque sequence—1990–93 2.3L engine

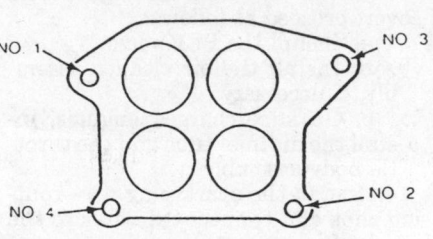

Upper intake manifold bolt torque sequence—1989 2.3L engine

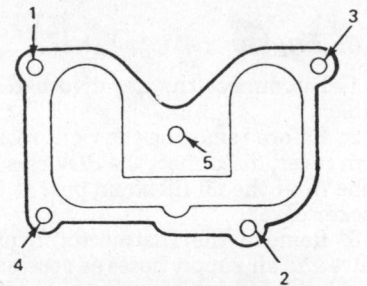

Upper intake manifold bolt torque sequence—1990–93 2.3L engine

threads. Install a new intake manifold gasket.

17. Position the lower intake manifold to the head with the engine lift bracket. Install the manifold retaining bolts finger-tight.
18. On 1989–90 vehicles, tighten the manifold retaining bolts, in sequence, in 2 steps, first to 5–7 ft. lbs. (7–10 Nm) and then to 20–29 ft. lbs. (26–38 Nm). On 1991–93 vehicles, tighten the manifold retaining bolts, in sequence, to 15–22 ft. lbs. (20–30 Nm).
19. Install the fuel supply manifold and injectors. Connect the electrical connectors to the injectors.

20. Install a new gasket and the upper intake manifold. Tighten the bolts to 15–22 ft. lbs. (20–30 Nm) in the proper sequence. Connect the fuel lines to the fuel supply manifold.
21. Install the engine oil dipstick and retaining bolt. Connect the EGR tube, water bypass line and PCV hose.
22. Connect the electrical connectors and vacuum lines to their original locations. Connect the throttle linkage.
23. Fill and bleed the cooling system. Connect the negative battery cable, start the engine and check for leaks.

3.8L Engine

1. Disconnect the negative battery cable.
2. Drain the cooling system and relieve the fuel system pressure.
3. Remove the air cleaner assembly or air inlet tube.
4. Disconnect the accelerator cable at the throttle body. Disconnect the cruise control cable, if equipped.
5. If equipped with an automatic transmission, disconnect the transmission linkage at the upper intake manifold. Remove the retaining bolts from the accelerator cable mounting bracket and position the cables aside.
6. If equipped, disconnect the thermactor air supply hose at the check valve. The valve is located in the Y-pipe assembly.
7. Disconnect the fuel lines. If equipped, remove the supercharger.
8. Disconnect the radiator hose at the thermostat housing and the coolant bypass hose at the manifold.
9. Disconnect the heater tube at the intake manifold and remove the tube support bracket retaining nut. Remove the heater hose at the rear of the heater tube. Loosen the hose clamp at the heater elbow and remove the heater tube with the hose attached. Remove the heater tube with the lines attached and set the assembly aside.
10. Tag and disconnect the vacuum lines at the fuel rail assembly and intake manifold. Tag and disconnect the necessary electrical connectors.
11. If equipped with air conditioning, remove the compressor support bracket. Disconnect the 1 PCV line at the upper intake manifold and at the valve. Remove the second PCV line from the left rocker arm cover.

12. Remove the throttle body assembly. Remove the EGR valve assembly from the upper manifold.

13. Remove the retaining nut and remove the wiring retainer bracket located at the left front of the intake manifold and set aside with the spark plug wires.

14. Remove the upper intake manifold retaining bolts/studs and remove the upper intake manifold.

15. Remove the injectors and fuel rail assembly. Remove the heater water outlet hose.

16. Remove the lower intake manifold retaining bolts/studs and remove the lower intake manifold.

NOTE: The manifold is sealed at each end with RTV-type sealer. To break the seal, it may be necessary to pry on the front of the manifold with a small prybar. If it is necessary to pry on the manifold, use care to prevent damage to the machined surfaces.

To install:

17. Clean all gasket mating surfaces. Lightly oil all retaining bolt and stud threads.

18. Apply a dab of gasket adhesive to each cylinder head mating surface. Press new intake manifold gaskets in place, using location pins as necessary to aid in installation.

19. Apply a ⅛ in. bead of silicone sealer at each corner where the cylinder head joins the cylinder block. Install the front and rear intake manifold end seals.

20. Carefully lower the intake manifold into place on the cylinder heads and cylinder block. Use locating pins as necessary to guide the manifold.

21. Install the bolts and stud bolts in their original locations. On 1989–91 non-supercharged engines, tighten the bolts, in sequence, in 3 steps, first to 8 ft. lbs. (10 Nm), then to 15 ft. lbs. (20 Nm), and finally to 24 ft. lbs. (32 Nm).

22. On all supercharged engines and 1992–93 non-supercharged engines, tighten the bolts, in sequence, in 2 steps, first to 8 ft. lbs. (11 Nm) and then to 11 ft. lbs. (15 Nm).

23. Connect the rear PCV line to the upper intake tube. Install the front PCV tube so the mounting bracket sits over the lower intake manifold stud. Tighten the nut on the stud to 15–22 ft. lbs. (20–30 Nm).

24. Install the injectors and the fuel rail. On non-supercharged engines, install the upper intake manifold assembly. Install the bolts and stud bolts in their original locations. Tighten the 4 center bolts and then the end bolts in 3 steps, first to 8 ft. lbs. (10 Nm), then to 15 ft. lbs. (20 Nm), and finally to 24 ft. lbs. (32 Nm).

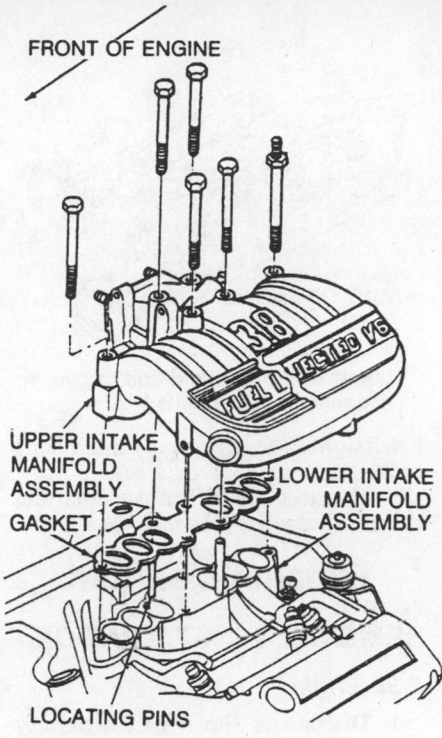

FRONT OF ENGINE

UPPER INTAKE MANIFOLD ASSEMBLY
GASKET
LOWER INTAKE MANIFOLD ASSEMBLY
LOCATING PINS

Upper intake manifold installation— 3.8L engine

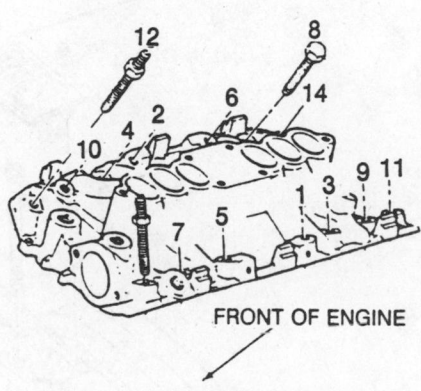

FRONT OF ENGINE

Lower intake manifold bolt torque sequence—3.8L engine

25. On supercharged engines, install the supercharger.

26. Install the EGR valve. Install the throttle body and cross-tighten the retaining nuts to 15–22 ft. lbs. (20–30 Nm).

27. Connect the rear PCV line at the PCV valve on the upper intake manifold. If equipped with air conditioning, install the compressor support bracket.

28. Connect the necessary electrical connectors and vacuum hoses. Connect the heater tube hose to the heater elbow and position the heater tube support bracket. Tighten the retaining nut to 15–22 ft. lbs. (20–30 Nm).

29. Connect the heater hose to the heater tube and connect the coolant bypass hose and radiator upper hose.

30. Connect the fuel lines. Position the accelerator cable mounting bracket and tighten the mounting bolts to 15–22 ft. lbs. (20–30 Nm).

31. Connect the transmission linkage at the upper intake manifold. If equipped, connect the cruise control cable.

32. Fill and bleed the cooling system. Connect the negative battery cable, start the engine and check for leaks.

33. Check and if necessary, adjust the engine idle speed, transmission throttle linkage and cruise control.

5.0L Engine

1. Disconnect the negative battery cable.

2. Drain the cooling system and relieve the fuel system pressure.

3. Disconnect the acclerator cable and cruise control linkage, if equipped, from the throttle body. Disconnect the TV cable, if equipped. Tag and disconnect the vacuum lines at the intake manifold fitting.

4. Tag and disconnect the spark plug wires from the spark plugs. Remove the wires and bracket assembly from the rocker arm cover attaching stud. Remove the distributor cap and wires assembly.

5. Disconnect the fuel lines and the distributor wiring connector. Mark the position of the rotor on the distributor housing and the distributor housing in the block. Remove the hold-down bolt and remove the distributor.

6. Disconnect the upper radiator hose at the thermostat housing and the water temperature sending unit wire at the sending unit. Disconnect the heater hose from the intake manifold and disconnect the 2 throttle body cooler hoses.

7. Disconnect the water pump bypass hose from the thermostat housing. Tag and disconnect the connectors from the engine coolant temperature, air charge temperature, throttle position and EGR sensors and the idle speed control solenoid. Disconnect the injector wire connections and the fuel charging assembly wiring.

8. Remove the PCV valve from the grommet at the rear of the lower intake manifold. Disconnect the fuel evaporative purge hose from the plastic connector at the front of the upper intake manifold.

9. Remove the upper intake manifold cover plate and upper intake bolts. Remove the upper intake manifold.

10. Remove the heater tube assembly from the lower intake manifold.

11. Remove the lower intake manifold retaining bolts and remove the lower intake manifold.

NOTE: If it is necessary to pry the intake manifold away from

the cylinder heads, be careful to avoid damaging the gasket sealing surfaces.

To install:

12. Clean all gasket mating surfaces. Apply a ⅛ in. bead of silicone sealer to the points where the cylinder block rails meet the cylinder heads.

13. Position new seals on the cylinder block and new gaskets on the cylinder heads with the gaskets interlocked with the seal tabs. Make sure the holes in the gaskets are aligned with the holes in the cylinder heads.

14. Apply a ¹/₁₆ in. bead of sealer to the outer end of each intake manifold seal for the full width of the seal.

15. Using guide pins to ease installation, carefully lower the intake manifold into position on the cylinder block and cylinder heads.

NOTE: After the intake manifold is in place, run a finger around the seal area to make sure the seals are in place. If the seals are not in place, remove the intake manifold and position the seals.

16. Make sure the holes in the manifold gaskets and the manifold are in alignment. Remove the guide pins. Install the intake manifold attaching bolts and tighten, in sequence, to 23–25 ft. lbs. (31–34 Nm) on 1989–91 vehicles or 15–20 ft. lbs. (20–27 Nm) on 1992–93 vehicles.

17. Install the heater tube assembly to the lower intake manifold.

18. Install the water pump bypass hose on the thermostat housing. Install the hoses to the heater tubes.

19. Connect the upper radiator hose and connect the heater hose at the intake manifold. Connect the fuel lines.

20. Install the distributor, aligning the housing and rotor with the marks that were made during removal. Install the distributor cap. Position the spark plug wires in the harness brackets on the rocker arm cover attaching stud and connect the wires to the spark plugs.

21. Install a new gasket and the upper intake manifold. Tighten the bolts to 12–18 ft. lbs. (16–24 Nm). Install the cover plate and connect the crankcase vent tube.

22. Connect the TV cable and cruise control cable, if equipped, to the throttle body. Connect the electrical connectors and vacuum lines.

23. Connect the coolant hoses to the EGR spacer. Fill and bleed the cooling system.

24. Connect the negative battery cable, start the engine and check for leaks. Check the ignition timing.

25. Operate the engine at fast idle. When engine temperatures have stabi-

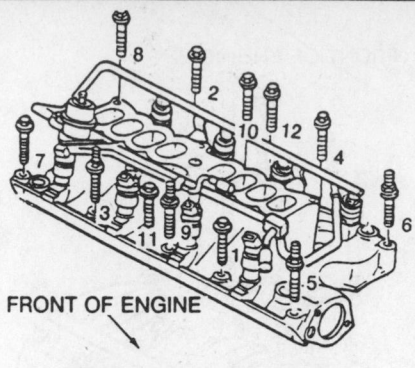

FRONT OF ENGINE

Lower intake manifold bolt torque sequence—5.0L engine

lized, tighten the intake manifold bolts to 23–25 ft. lbs. (31–34 Nm).

26. Connect the air intake duct and the crankcase vent hose.

Exhaust Manifold

REMOVAL & INSTALLATION

2.3L Engine

1. Disconnect the negative battery cable.

2. Remove the air cleaner and duct assembly.

3. Remove the EGR tube at the exhaust manifold and loosen at the EGR valve.

4. Disconnect and, if necessary, remove the oxygen sensor from the exhaust manifold.

5. Raise and safely support the vehicle. Remove the 2 exhaust pipe bolts and lower the vehicle.

6. Remove the 8 exhaust manifold bolts and remove the exhaust manifold.

7. Installation is the reverse of the removal procedure. Tighten the manifold bolts, in sequence, in 2 steps, first to 15–17 ft. lbs. (20–30 Nm) and then to 20–30 ft. lbs. (27–41 Nm). Tighten the exhaust pipe bolts to 25–34 ft. lbs. (36–46 Nm).

3.8L Engine

LEFT SIDE

1. Disconnect the negative battery cable. Remove oil level dipstick tube support bracket.

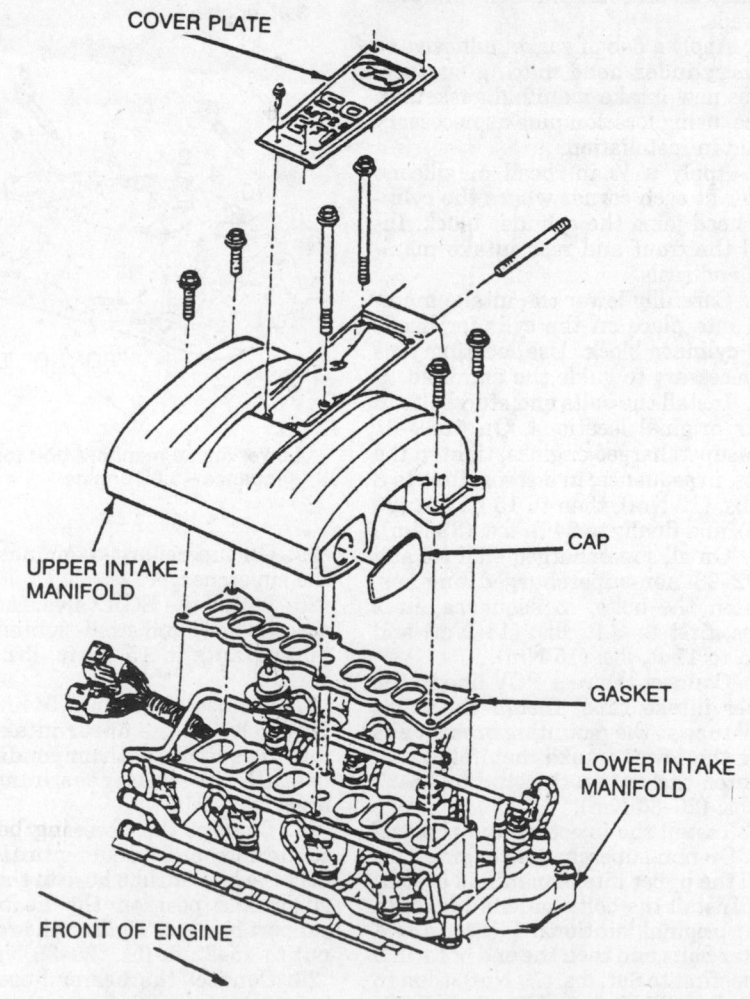

COVER PLATE

UPPER INTAKE MANIFOLD

CAP

GASKET

LOWER INTAKE MANIFOLD

FRONT OF ENGINE

Upper intake manifold installation—5.0L engine

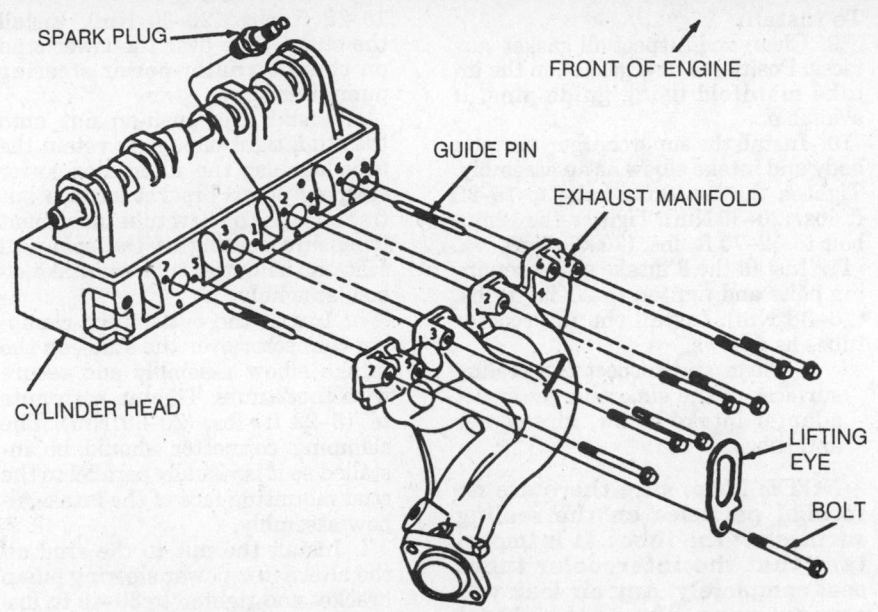

Exhaust manifold installation and torque sequence—2.3L engine

2. Disconnect the oxygen sensor at the wiring connector.

3. Tag and disconnect the wires from the spark plugs.

4. Raise and safely support the vehicle.

5. Remove the manifold to exhaust pipe attaching nuts.

6. Lower the vehicle.

7. On supercharged engines, remove the intercooler tubes and remove the oil cooler tube and dipstick tube support brackets from the studs.

8. Remove exhaust manifold attaching bolts and manifold.

9. Installation is the reverse of the removal procedure. Tighten the manifold retaining bolts to 15–22 ft. lbs. (20–30 Nm).

RIGHT SIDE

1. Disconnect the negative battery cable. On supercharged engines, remove the air cleaner inlet tube.

2. On non-supercharged engines, disconnect the coil secondary wire from the coil. Tag and disconnect the wires from the spark plugs.

3. On non-supercharged engines, remove the spark plugs and the outer heat shield.

4. Raise and safely support the vehicle. Disconnect the EGR tube.

5. If equipped with automatic transmission, remove the dipstick tube.

6. On 1989–90 vehicles, remove the thermactor downstream air tube. Use cutters to cut the tube clamp at the catalytic converter.

7. Remove the manifold-to-exhaust pipe retaining nuts and lower the vehicle.

8. Remove the exhaust manifold retaining bolts and remove the manifold.

9. Installation is the reverse of the removal procedure. Tighten the exhaust manifold retaining bolts to 15–22 ft. lbs. (20–30 Nm).

5.0L Engine

THUNDERBIRD AND COUGAR

1. Disconnect the negative battery cable.

2. If removing the left manifold, remove the oil dipstick tube nut and pull the bracket from the manifold stud.

3. Raise and safely support the vehicle.

4. Carefully tap upward on the dipstick tube and remove it from the vehicle.

5. If removing the left manifold, disconnect the oxygen sensor connector.

6. Disconnect the exhaust manifold(s) from the exhaust pipe(s). Lower the vehicle.

7. If removing the right exhaust manifold, disconnect the electrical connector from the mass air flow sensor, located on the air cleaner assembly. Remove the air cleaner and inlet duct assembly.

8. Tag and disconnect the spark plug wires.

9. If removing the right exhaust manifold, remove the alternator rear brace and the thermactor hose assembly and EGR tube.

10. Remove the retaining bolts and remove the exhaust manifold(s) through the top of the engine compartment.

11. Installation is the reverse of the removal procedure. Clean the manifold and cylinder head mating surfaces prior to installation. Working from the center to the ends, tighten the exhaust

manifold-to-cylinder head bolts to 18–24 ft. lbs. (24–32 Nm).

MUSTANG AND MARK VII

1. Disconnect the negative battery cable.

2. If removing the right exhaust manifold, remove the thermactor hardware.

3. Tag and disconnect the spark plug wires. Remove the spark plugs.

4. Raise and safely support the vehicle.

5. Disconnect the exhaust pipe(s) from the manifold(s). Lower the vehicle.

6. Remove the retaining bolts and remove the exhaust manifold(s).

7. Installation is the reverse of the removal procedure. Clean the manifold and cylinder head mating surfaces prior to installation. Working from the center to the ends, tighten the exhaust manifold attaching bolts to 18–24 ft. lbs. (24–32 Nm).

Supercharger

REMOVAL & INSTALLATION

3.8L SC Engine

NOTE: Before beginning any supercharger service, clean the area around the supercharger assembly. Cover the engine and supercharger openings while the supercharger is removed, to prevent damage by foreign material.

1. Disconnect the negative battery cable and partially drain the cooling system.

2. Remove the throttle body air inlet tube and the cowl vent screens.

3. Tag and disconnect the right side spark plug wires at the coil and position aside. Tag and disconnect the electrical connections at the air bypass valve, throttle position sensor and air charge temperature sensors.

4. Tag and disconnect the vacuum lines from the inlet/plenum assembly. If equipped, remove the EGR transducer from the bracket and disconnect the vacuum line. Disconnect the PCV tube.

5. Disconnect the throttle linkage at the throttle housing. Remove the linkage bracket retaining bolts and position the bracket aside. Disconnect the cruise control, if equipped.

6. Remove the 2 EGR valve attaching bolts and move the EGR valve away from the intake assembly, if equipped. Disconnect the coolant hoses from the throttle body, if equipped.

7. Remove the supercharger drive belt. Remove the intercooler inlet and outlet tubes as follows:

   a. Disconnect the inlet tube from

7 FORD MOTOR CO. THUNDERBIRD/COUGAR

the supercharger outlet adapter using spanner nut wrench tool T89P–6634–A or equivalent. Remove the 4 nuts retaining the inlet and outlet tubes to the intercooler.

b. Remove the nut and push-on nut retaining the inlet tube to the alternator-power steering pump bracket. Remove the stud from the alternator-power steering pump bracket. Remove the inlet tube.

NOTE: Use exreme care during removal and installation of the intercooler tubes so as not to scratch, nick or contaminate the sealing surfaces.

c. Remove the 2 nuts retaining the outlet tube to the intake elbow assembly. Raise and safely support the vehicle.

d. Remove the bolt retaining the outlet tube to the cylinder block front upper support bracket. Loosen, but do not remove the support bracket.

NOTE: The bracket must be close to the front face of the cylinder block to allow the bracket to pivot during outlet tube reinstallation.

e. Remove the nut and push-on nut retaining the outlet tube to the alternator-power steering pump bracket. Remove the power steering pump drive belt.

f. Tag and disconnect the spark plug wires from the coil. Remove the power steering pump bracket brace to water pump retaining stud nuts. Remove 2 power steering pump bracket to cylinder head retaining bolts and 1 stud nut.

g. Install a 10 × 1.5mm × 170mm bolt, 6½ in. long into the top hole in the power steering pump bracket. Thread the bolt into the cylinder head approximately 5 turns. This will aid in holding the power steering pump bracket in position.

h. Remove the power steering pump filler cap. Slide the power steering pump bracket assembly forward on the stud and bolt that was installed in the previous step.

i. Remove the outlet tube by pulling underneath the power steering pump bracket assembly and up through the engine compartment. It may be necessary to pivot the outlet tube clamping connector to gain clearance during removal.

8. Remove the 3 intake elbow retaining bolts and the 3 supercharger retaining bolts. Lift the supercharger and intake elbow assembly from the vehicle as a unit.

To install:
9. Clean and inspect all gasket surfaces. Position a new gasket on the intake manifold using guide pins, if available.

10. Install the supercharger, throttle body and intake elbow as an assembly. Tighten the two 8mm bolts to 15–22 ft. lbs. (20–30 Nm). Tighten the 12mm bolt to 52–70 ft. lbs. (70–95 Nm).

11. Install the 3 intake elbow retaining bolts and tighten to 20–28 ft. lbs. (26–38 Nm). Install the intercooler tubes as follows:

a. Clean and inspect the sealing surfaces of the supercharger outlet adapter intake elbow, intercooler and tubes.

NOTE: Make sure there are no foreign particles on the sealing surfaces of the tubes. It is important that the intercooler tubes seal completely. Any air leak will cause poor operation and performance.

b. Install gasket sealant tape ESE–M4G168–B or equivalent, circumferentially to the spherical seat surfaces of the intercooler tubes. Install the tape approximately ⅛ in. (3mm) from the inner diameter of the tubes. Overlap the tape ends approximately ¼ in. (6mm). Do not stretch the tape during installation or the seal may leak. During proper installation, a slight wrinkling will occur on the tape edge at the inner diameter.

NOTE: The system must be torqued in sequence and to the specification for that step. This is required for proper alignment of the system to ensure sealing of the intercooler tubes.

c. Guide the outlet tube down through the engine compartment and underneath the power steering pump bracket assembly. It may be necessary to rotate the lower outlet tube clamping connector to gain clearance.

NOTE: Use extreme care during installation of the intercooler tubes so as not to scratch, nick or contaminate the sealing surfaces.

d. Slide the power steering pump bracket assembly into position. Install the power steering pump bracket retaining stud nut and tighten to 30–40 ft. lbs. (40–55 Nm).

e. Remove the bolt installed in Step 7g of the removal procedure. Install the power steering pump bracket to cylinder head bolts and tighten to 30–40 ft. lbs. (40–55 Nm).

f. Install the power steering pump bracket brace to water pump retaining stud nuts and tighten to

15–22 ft. lbs. (20–30 Nm). Install the outlet tube over the lower stud on the alternator-power steering pump bracket.

g. Install the push-on nut onto the stud, tight enough to retain the tube against the alternator-power steering pump bracket surface but free enough to allow tube movement to ensure seating of the spherical seat on the outlet tube to intake elbow assembly.

h. Install the outlet tube clamping connector over the studs on the intake elbow assembly and secure with the 2 nuts. Tighten both nuts to 15–22 ft. lbs. (20–30 Nm). The clamping connector should be installed so it is visually parallel to the stud mounting face of the intake elbow assembly.

i. Install the nut to the stud on the alternator-power steering pump bracket and tighten to 30–40 ft. lbs. (40–55 Nm). Install the bolt to secure the outlet tube to the cylinder block support bracket and tighten to 30–40 ft. lbs. (40–55 Nm). Tighten the support bracket to front of cylinder block retaining nut to 15–22 ft. lbs. (20–30 Nm) and bolt to 52–70 ft. lbs. (70–95 Nm).

j. Apply anti-seize compound to the inner backside spherical seat surface and threads of the supercharger outlet adapter collar. Position the inlet tube, then install the upper stud into the alternator-power steering pump bracket.

k. Install the push-on nut onto the stud, tight enough to retain the tube against the alternator-power steering pump bracket surface but free enough to allow tube movement to ensure seating of the spherical seat on the inlet tube to supercharger outlet adapter.

l. Fully hand tighten the supercharger outlet adapter collar onto the threaded tube end of the inlet tube assembly. Install the intercooler assembly to the inlet and outlet tubes. Install the nuts to the studs tight enough to retain the intercooler and tubes together but free enough to allow movement on the spherical seats. Do not tighten at this time.

m. Tighten the supercharger outlet adapter collar to inlet tube to 48 ft. lbs. (65 Nm) on 1989 vehicles or 148 ft. lbs. (200 Nm) on 1990–93 vehicles.

n. Wait 10 minutes minimum and retighten the supercharger outlet collar to 48 ft. lbs. (65 Nm) on 1989 vehicles or 148 ft. lbs. (200 Nm) on 1990–93 vehicles.

NOTE: When first compressed, the sealant tape flows and forms

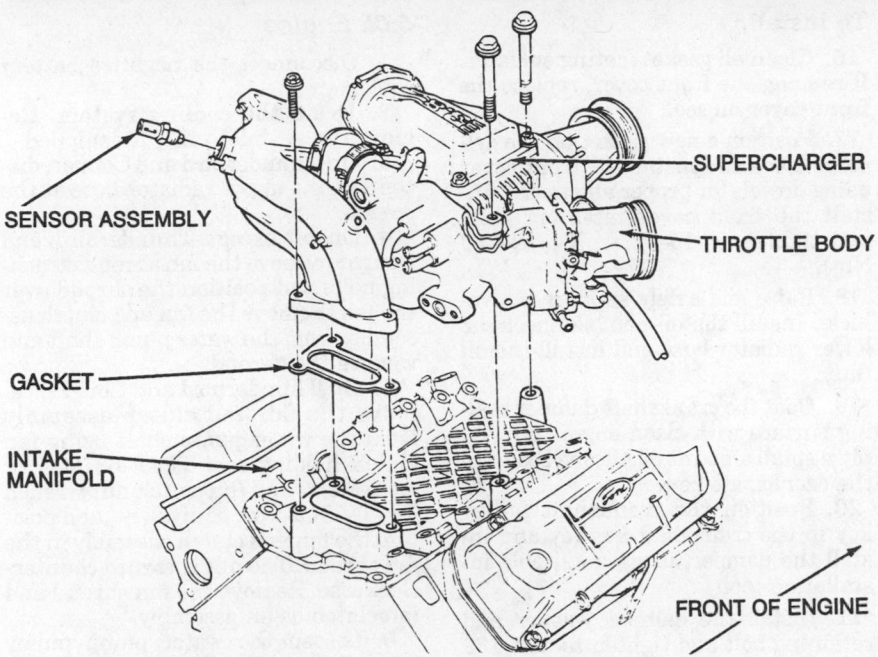

SUPERCHARGER

THROTTLE BODY

SENSOR ASSEMBLY

GASKET

INTAKE MANIFOLD

FRONT OF ENGINE

Removing the supercharger assembly—3.8L SC engine

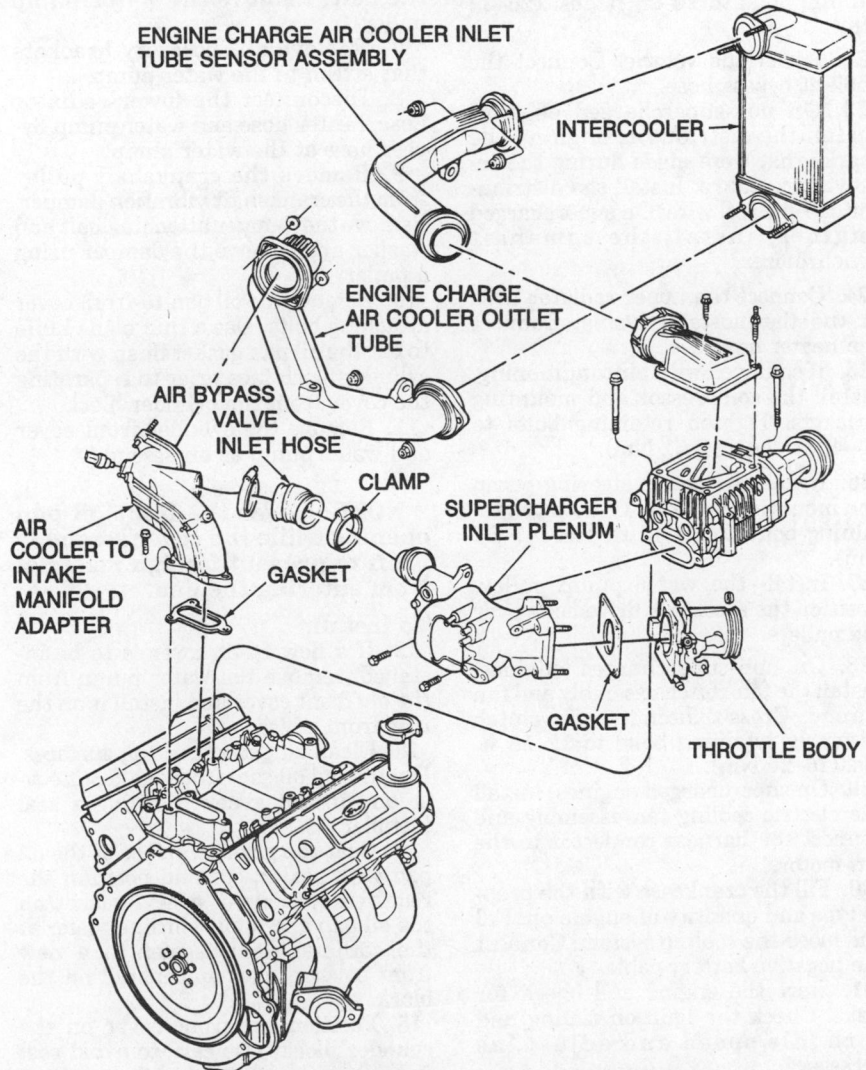

ENGINE CHARGE AIR COOLER INLET TUBE SENSOR ASSEMBLY

INTERCOOLER

ENGINE CHARGE AIR COOLER OUTLET TUBE

AIR BYPASS VALVE INLET HOSE

CLAMP

AIR COOLER TO INTAKE MANIFOLD ADAPTER

SUPERCHARGER INLET PLENUM

GASKET

GASKET

THROTTLE BODY

Supercharger system components—3.8L SC engine

to the sealing surface. If the collar is not retightened, the torque of the collar will drop causing a leak at this joint.

   o. Tighten the inlet and outlet tube to intercooler nuts to 15–22 ft. lbs. (20–30 Nm). The clamping connectors should be installed so they are visually parallel to the stud mounting face of the intercooler assembly.

   p. Install the nut retaining the inlet tube to the alternator-power steering pump support bracket and tighten to 30–40 ft. lbs. (40–55 Nm).

12. Install the supercharger drive belt. Connect the coolant hoses to the throttle body, if equipped.

13. Connect the EGR valve with a new gasket to the intake manifold, if equipped. Tighten the retaining bolts to 14–22 ft. lbs. (20–30 Nm).

14. Install the throttle linkage bracket and connect the throttle linkage. Tighten to 10–15 ft. lbs. (14–20 Nm).

15. Connect the vacuum lines to the inlet assembly and connect the PCV tube. If equipped, connect the vacuum line to the EGR transducer and install the transducer in the bracket.

16. Install the right side spark plug wires. Connect the electrical connectors at the air bypass valve, throttle position sensor and air charge temperature sensor.

17. Install the cowl covers and the throttle body air inlet tube.

18. Fill and bleed the cooling system. Connect the negative battery cable. Start the engine and check for leaks and proper operation.

Timing Chain Front Cover

REMOVAL & INSTALLATION

3.8L Engine

1. Disconnect the negative battery cable and drain the cooling system.

2. Remove the air cleaner assembly and air intake duct.

3. On non-supercharged engines, remove the fan/clutch assembly and shroud. On supercharged engines, remove the electric cooling fan assembly.

4. Remove the accessory drive belt idlers, drive belts and the water pump pulley.

5. Remove the power steering pump bracket retaining bolts. Leaving the hoses connected, place the pump/bracket assembly aside in a position to prevent fluid from leaking out.

6. If equipped with air conditioning, remove the compressor front support bracket but leave the compressor in place.

7. Disconnect the coolant bypass hose and heater hose at the water pump. Disconnect the upper radiator hose at the thermostat housing.

8. On non-supercharged engines, disconnect the coil wire from the distributor cap and remove the cap with the secondary wires attached.

9. On non-supercharged engines, mark the position of the rotor in relation to the distributor housing and mark the position of the distributor housing on the front cover. Remove the distributor hold-down clamp and lift the distributor out of the front cover.

10. On supercharged engines, remove the hold-down clamp and lift the camshaft synchronizer from the front cover.

11. Raise and safely support the vehicle. Remove the crankshaft damper and pulley using a puller.

NOTE: If the crankshaft pulley and vibration damper have to be separated, mark the damper and pulley so they may be reassembled in the same relative position. This is important as the damper and pulley are initially balanced as a unit. If the crankshaft damper is being replaced, check if the original damper has balance pins installed. If so, new balance pins must be installed on the new damper in the same position as the original damper. The crankshaft pulley, new or original, must also be installed in the same relative position as originally installed.

12. Remove the oil filter. On supercharged engines, remove the oil cooler.

13. Disconnect the lower radiator hose at the water pump. Remove the oil pan.

NOTE: The front cover cannot be removed without lowering the oil pan.

14. Lower the vehicle. Remove the front cover retaining bolts. It is not necessary to remove the water pump.

NOTE: Do not overlook the cover retaining bolt located behind the oil filter adapter. The front cover will break if pried on and all retaining bolts are not removed.

15. Remove the front cover and water pump as an assembly. Remove and discard the cover gasket.

NOTE: The front cover contains the oil pump and water pump. If a new front cover is to be installed, remove the water pump and oil pump from the old front cover.

To install:

16. Clean all gasket mating surfaces. If reusing the front cover, replace the front cover oil seal.

17. Position a new gasket on the cylinder block and install the front cover using dowels for proper alignment. Install the front cover retaining bolts and tighten to 15–22 ft. lbs. (20–30 Nm).

18. Raise and safely support the vehicle. Install the oil pan. Connect the lower radiator hose and install the oil filter.

19. Coat the crankshaft damper sealing surface with clean engine oil. Apply a small amount of silicone sealer to the crankshaft keyway.

20. Position the crankshaft pulley key in the crankshaft keyway and install the damper, using a suitable installation tool.

21. Install the damper washer and retaining bolt and tighten to 103–132 ft. lbs. (140–180 Nm). Install the crankshaft pulley and tighten the retaining bolts to 20–28 ft. lbs. (26–38 Nm).

22. Lower the vehicle. Connect the coolant bypass hose.

23. On non-supercharged engines, install the distributor, aligning the marks that were made during the removal procedure. Install the distributor cap and coil wire. On supercharged engines, install the camshaft synchronizer.

24. Connect the upper radiator hose at the thermostat housing. Connect the heater hose.

25. If equipped with air conditioning, install the compressor and mounting brackets. Tighten retaining bolts to 30–45 ft. lbs. (41–61 Nm).

26. Install the power steering pump and mounting bracket. Tighten the retaining bolts to 30–45 ft. lbs. (41–61 Nm).

27. Install the water pump pulley. Position the accessory drive belts over the pulleys.

28. On non-supercharged engines, install the fan/clutch assembly and fan shroud. Cross-tighten the fan/clutch assembly retaining bolts to 12–18 ft. lbs. (16–24 Nm).

29. On supercharged engines, install the electric cooling fan assembly and connect the harness connector to the fan motor.

30. Fill the crankcase with the proper type and quantity of engine oil. Fill and bleed the cooling system. Connect the negative battery cable.

31. Start the engine and check for leaks. Check the ignition timing and curb idle speed and adjust, as necessary.

5.0L Engine

1. Disconnect the negative battery cable.

2. Drain the cooling system. Remove the air inlet tube, if equipped.

3. On Thunderbird and Cougar, disconnect the upper radiator hose at the engine.

4. On all except Thunderbird and Cougar, remove the fan shroud attaching bolts and position the shroud over the fan. Remove the fan and clutch assembly from the water pump shaft and remove the shroud.

5. On Thunderbird and Cougar, remove the fan and clutch assembly from the water pump shaft using fan clutch holding tool T84T–6312–C or equivalent, and fan clutch nut wrench T84T–6312–D or equivalent, and position the fan and clutch assembly in the fan shroud. The nut is turned counterclockwise. Remove the fan shroud and fan/clutch as an assembly.

6. Loosen the water pump pulley bolts. Rotate the tensioner away from the accessory drive belt and remove the belt. Remove the water pump pulley.

7. Remove all accessory brackets that attach to the water pump.

8. Disconnect the lower radiator hose, heater hose and water pump bypass hose at the water pump.

9. Remove the crankshaft pulley from the crankshaft vibration damper. Remove the damper attaching bolt and washer and remove the damper using a puller.

10. Remove the oil pan-to-front cover attaching bolts. Use a thin blade knife to cut the oil pan gasket flush with the cylinder block face prior to separating the cover from the cylinder block.

11. Remove the cylinder front cover and water pump as an assembly.

NOTE: Cover the front oil pan opening while the cover assembly is off to prevent foreign material from entering the pan.

To install:

12. If a new front cover is to be installed, remove the water pump from the old front cover and install it on the new front cover.

13. Clean all gasket mating surfaces. Pry the old oil seal from the front cover and install a new 1, using a seal installer.

14. Coat the gasket surface of the oil pan with sealer, cut and position the required sections of a new gasket on the oil pan and apply silicone sealer at the corners. Apply sealer to a new front cover gasket and install on the block.

15. Position the front cover on the cylinder block. Use care to avoid seal damage or gasket mislocation. It may

be necessary to force the cover downward to slightly compress the pan gasket. Use front cover aligner tool T61P–6019–B or equivalent to assist the operation.

16. Coat the threads of the front cover attaching screws with pipe sealant and install. While pushing in on the alignment tool, tighten the oil pan to cover attaching screws to 9–12 ft. lbs. (12–16 Nm).

17. Tighten the front cover to cylinder block attaching bolts to 12–18 ft. lbs. (16–24 Nm). Remove the alignment tool.

18. Apply multi-purpose grease to the sealing surface of the vibration damper. Apply silicone sealer to the keyway of the vibration damper.

19. Line up the vibration damper keyway with the crankshaft key and install the damper using a suitable installation tool. Tighten the retaining bolt to 70–90 ft. lbs. (95–122 Nm). Install the crankshaft pulley.

20. Install the remaining components in the reverse order of their removal.

21. Fill the crankcase with the proper type and quantity of engine oil. Fill and bleed the cooling system.

22. Connect the negative battery cable, start the engine and check for leaks.

Front Cover Oil Seal

REPLACEMENT

3.8L Engine

1. Disconnect the negative battery cable.

2. On non-supercharged engines, remove the fan shroud and position it back over the fan. Remove the fan/clutch assembly and shroud.

3. On supercharged engines, disconnect the electric cooling fan connector and remove the fan assembly.

4. Loosen the accessory drive belt idlers. Raise and safely support the vehicle.

5. Disengage the drive belts and remove the crankshaft pulley. On supercharged engines, remove the upper and lower crankshaft shields.

6. Remove the crankshaft damper retaining bolt and remove the damper using a puller.

7. Using a small prybar, remove the seal from the front cover. Use care to prevent damage to the cover and crankshaft.

To install:

8. Inspect the front cover and crankshaft damper for damage, nicks, burrs or other roughness which may cause the seal to fail. Service or replace components as necessary.

9. Lubricate the seal lip using clean engine oil. Install the seal using a suitable seal installer.

10. Lubricate the seal surface on the damper with clean engine oil. Install the damper using a suitabel installation tool.

11. Install the damper retaining bolt and tighten to 103–132 ft. lbs. (140–180 Nm). Install the crankshaft pulley and tighten the retaining bolts to 20–28 ft. lbs. (26–38 Nm).

12. Install the remaining components in the reverse order of their removal. Connect the negative battery cable, start the engine and check for leaks.

5.0L Engine

1. Disconnect the negative battery cable.

2. Remove the fan shroud and position it back over the fan. Remove the fan/clutch assembly and shroud.

3. Remove the accessory drive belts.

4. Remove the crankshaft pulley from the damper and remove the damper retaining bolt. Remove the damper using a puller.

5. Remove the seal using a seal removal tool.

To install:

6. Lubricate the seal lip with clean engine oil and install using a seal installer.

7. Apply clean engine oil to the sealing surface of the vibration damper. Line up the crankshaft damper keyway with the crankshaft key and install the damper using a damper installation tool.

8. Install the damper retaining bolt and tighten to 70–90 ft. lbs. (95–122 Nm).

9. Install the remaining components in the reverse order of their removal.

Timing Chain and Sprockets

REMOVAL & INSTALLATION

3.8L Engine

1. Disconnect the negative battery cable and drain the cooling system.

2. Remove the air cleaner assembly and air intake duct.

3. On non-supercharged engines, remove the fan/clutch assembly and shroud. On supercharged engines, remove the electric cooling fan assembly.

4. Remove the accessory drive belt idlers, drive belts and the water pump pulley.

5. Remove the power steering pump bracket retaining bolts. Leaving the hoses connected, place the pump/bracket assembly aside in a position to prevent fluid from leaking out.

6. If equipped with air conditioning, remove the compressor front support bracket but leave the compressor in place.

7. Disconnect the coolant bypass hose and heater hose at the water pump. Disconnect the upper radiator hose at the thermostat housing.

8. On non-supercharged engines, disconnect the coil wire from the distributor cap and remove the cap with the secondary wires attached.

9. On non-supercharged engines, remove the distributor hold-down clamp and lift the distributor out of the front cover.

10. On supercharged engines, remove the hold-down clamp and lift the camshaft synchronizer from the front cover.

11. Raise and safely support the vehicle. Remove the crankshaft damper and pulley using a puller.

NOTE: If the crankshaft pulley and vibration damper have to be separated, mark the damper and pulley so they may be reassembled in the same relative position. This is important as the damper and pulley are initially balanced as a unit. If the crankshaft damper is being replaced, check if the original damper has balance pins installed. If so, new balance pins must be installed on the new damper in the same position as the original damper. The crankshaft pulley, new or original, must also be installed in the same relative position as originally installed.

12. Remove the oil filter. On supercharged engines, remove the oil cooler.

13. Disconnect the lower radiator hose at the water pump. Remove the oil pan.

NOTE: The front cover cannot be removed without lowering the oil pan.

14. Lower the vehicle. Remove the front cover retaining bolts. It is not necessary to remove the water pump.

NOTE: Do not overlook the cover retaining bolt located behind the oil filter adapter. The front cover will break if pried on and all retaining bolts are not removed.

15. Remove the front cover and water pump as an assembly. Remove and discard the cover gasket.

NOTE: The front cover contains the oil pump and water pump. If a new front cover is to be installed, remove the water pump and oil pump from the old front cover.

16. Remove the camshaft bolt and washer from the end of the camshaft.

17. Remove the distributor drive gear, camshaft sprocket, crankshaft sprocket and timing chain.

NOTE: If the crankshaft sprocket is difficult to remove, pry the sprocket off the shaft using a pair of large prybars positioned on both sides of the sprocket.

To install:

18. Clean all gasket mating surfaces. If reusing the front cover, replace the front cover oil seal.

19. Rotate the crankshaft to position the No. 1 piston at TDC and the crankshaft keyway at the 12 o' clock position.

20. Lubricate the timing chain with engine oil.

21. Install the camshaft sprocket, crankshaft sprocket and timing chain. Make sure the timing marks align.

22. Install the distributor drive gear. Install the bolt and washer assembly on the end of the camshaft and tighten to 15–22 ft. lbs. (20–30 Nm) on 1989 vehicles or 30–37 ft. lbs. (40–50 Nm) on 1990–93 vehicles.

23. Position a new gasket on the cylinder block and install the front cover using dowels for proper alignment. Install the front cover retaining bolts and tighten to 15–22 ft. lbs. (20–30 Nm).

24. Raise and safely support the vehicle. Install the oil pan. Connect the lower radiator hose and install the oil filter.

25. Coat the crankshaft damper sealing surface with clean engine oil. Apply a small amount of silicone sealer to the crankshaft keyway.

26. Position the crankshaft pulley key in the crankshaft keyway and install the damper, using a suitable installation tool.

27. Install the damper washer and retaining bolt and tighten to 103–132 ft. lbs. (140–180 Nm). Install the crankshaft pulley and tighten the retaining bolts to 20–28 ft. lbs. (26–38 Nm).

28. Lower the vehicle. Connect the coolant bypass hose.

29. On non-supercharged engines, install the distributor with the rotor pointing at the No. 1 distributor cap tower. Install the distributor cap and coil wire. On supercharged engines, install the camshaft synchronizer.

30. Connect the upper radiator hose at the thermostat housing. Connect the heater hose.

31. If equipped with air conditioning, install the compressor and mounting brackets. Tighten retaining bolts to 30–45 ft. lbs. (41–61 Nm).

32. Install the power steering pump and mounting bracket. Tighten the retaining bolts to 30–45 ft. lbs. (41–61 Nm).

33. Install the water pump pulley. Position the accessory drive belts over the pulleys.

34. On non-supercharged engines, install the fan/clutch assembly and fan shroud. Cross-tighten the fan/clutch assembly retaining bolts to 12–18 ft. lbs. (16–24 Nm).

35. On supercharged engines, install the electric cooling fan assembly and connect the harness connector to the fan motor.

36. Fill the crankcase with the proper type and quantity of engine oil. Fill and bleed the cooling system. Connect the negative battery cable.

37. Start the engine and check for leaks. Check the ignition timing and curb idle speed and adjust, as necessary.

5.0L Engine

1. Disconnect the negative battery cable and drain the cooling system.

2. Remove the timing chain front cover.

3. Rotate the crankshaft until the timing marks on the sprockets are aligned.

4. Remove the camshaft retaining bolt, washer and eccentric, if equipped. Slide both sprockets and the timing

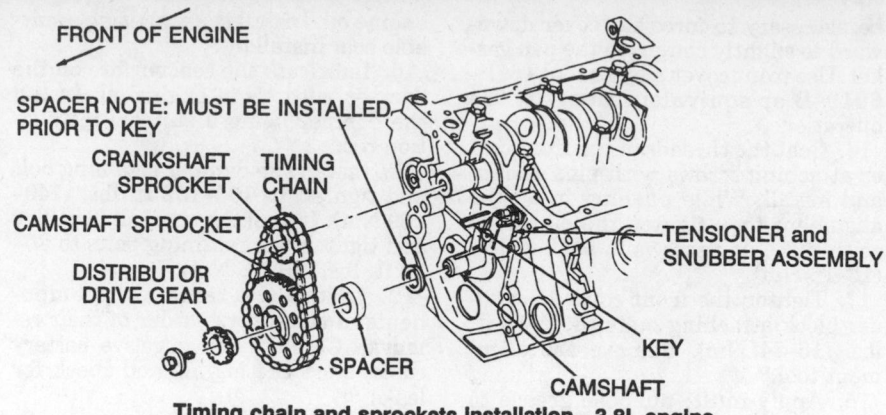

FRONT OF ENGINE

SPACER NOTE: MUST BE INSTALLED PRIOR TO KEY

CRANKSHAFT SPROCKET

TIMING CHAIN

CAMSHAFT SPROCKET

DISTRIBUTOR DRIVE GEAR

TENSIONER and SNUBBER ASSEMBLY

KEY

SPACER

CAMSHAFT

Timing chain and sprockets Installation—3.8L engine

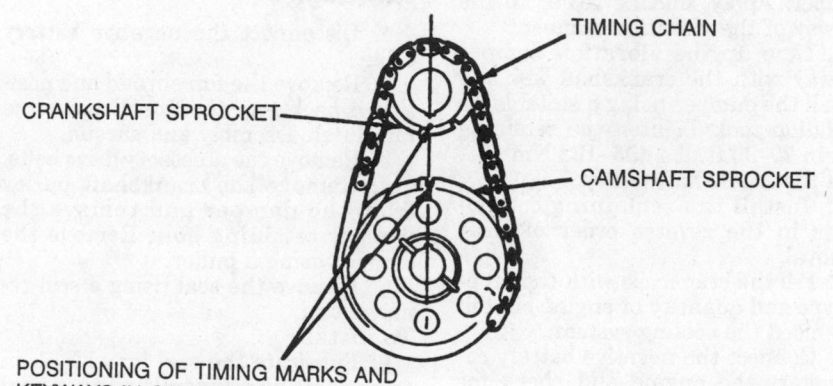

TIMING CHAIN

CRANKSHAFT SPROCKET

CAMSHAFT SPROCKET

POSITIONING OF TIMING MARKS AND KEYWAYS IN CAMSHAFT AND CRANKSHAFT SPROCKETS MUST BE IN LINE AS SHOWN WITH NO. 1 PISTON AT TDC FIRING

Timing chain sprocket alignment—3.8L engine

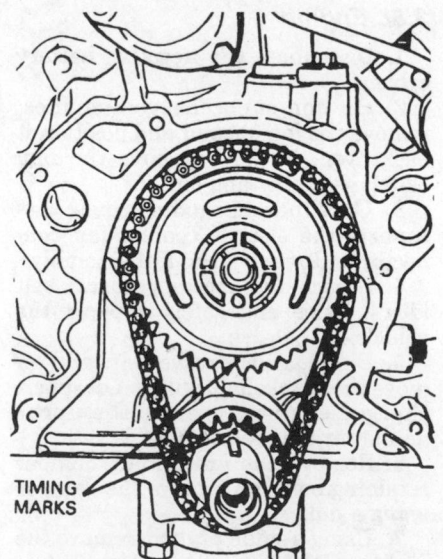

TIMING MARKS

Timing chain sprocket alignment—5.0L engine

chain forward and remove them as an assembly.

To install:

5. Position the sprockets and timing chain on the camshaft and crankshaft simultaneously. Make sure the timing marks on the sprockets are aligned.

6. Install the washer, eccentric if equipped, and camshaft sprocket retaining bolt. Tighten the bolt to 40–45 ft. lbs. (54–61 Nm).

7. Install the timing chain front cover and remaining components.

8. Fill and bleed the cooling system. Connect the negative battery cable, start the engine and check for leaks.

9. Check and adjust the ignition timing and idle speed, as necessary.

Timing Belt Front Cover

REMOVAL & INSTALLATION

2.3L Engine

1. Disconnect the negative battery cable and drain the cooling system. Remove the 4 water pump pulley bolts.

2. Remove the automatic belt tensioner and accessory drive belt. Remove the upper radiator hose.

3. Remove the crankshaft pulley

bolt and pulley. Remove the thermostat housing and gasket.

4. Remove the timing belt outer cover retaining bolt(s). Release the cover interlocking tabs, if equipped, and remove the cover.

To install:

5. Position the timing belt front cover. Snap the interlocking tabs into place, if necessary. Install the timing belt outer cover retaining bolt(s) and tighten to 71–106 inch lbs. (8–12 Nm).

6. Install the thermostat housing and a new gasket. Install the upper radiator hose.

7. Install the crankshaft pulley and retaining bolt. Tighten to 103–133 ft. lbs. (140–180 Nm) on 1989–90 vehicles or 114–151 ft. lbs. (155–205 Nm) on 1991–93 vehicles.

8. Install the water pump pulley and the automatic belt tensioner. Install the accessory drive belt.

9. Connect the negative battery cable, start the engine and check for leaks.

OIL SEAL REPLACEMENT

2.3L Engine

1. Disconnect the negative battery cable.

2. Remove the timing belt front cover and timing belt.

3. Use a suitable puller to remove the crankshaft, camshaft and auxiliary shaft sprockets, as necessary.

4. Use seal remover tool T74P-6700–B or equivalent, to remove the crankshaft, camshaft and auxiliary shaft seals, as necessary. Position the tool so the jaws are gripping the thin edge of the seal. Operate the jackscrew on the tool to remove the seal.

To install:

5. Lubricate the lips of the new seal(s) with clean engine oil.

6. Use seal replacer tool T74P-6150–A or equivalent, to install the seal(s).

7. Install the crankshaft, camshaft and auxiliary shaft sprockets, as necessary. Tighten the camshaft sprocket retaining bolt to 52–70 ft. lbs. (70–95 Nm) and the auxiliary sprocket retaining bolt to 30–41 ft. lbs. (40–55 Nm).

8. Install the timing belt and timing belt front cover.

9. Connect the negative battery cable, start the engine and check for leaks.

Timing Belt and Tensioner

REMOVAL & INSTALLATION

2.3L Engine

1. Disconnect the negative battery cable.

2. Remove the timing belt front cover.

3. Loosen the belt tensioner adjustment screw, position belt tensioner tool T74P-6254–A or equivalent, on the tension spring roll pin and release the belt tensioner. Tighten the adjustment screw to hold the tensioner in the released position.

4. On 1991–93 vehicles, remove the bolts holding the timing sensor in place and pull the sensor assembly free of the dowel pin.

5. Remove the crankshaft pulley, hub and belt guide. Remove the timing belt. If the belt is to be reused, mark the direction of rotation so it may be reinstalled in the same direction.

To install:

6. Position the crankshaft sprocket to align with the TDC mark and the camshaft sprocket to align with the camshaft timing pointer. On 1989–90 vehicles, remove the distributor cap and set the rotor to the No. 1 firing position by turning the auxiliary shaft.

7. Install the timing belt over the crankshaft sprocket and then counterclockwise over the auxiliary and camshaft sprockets. Align the belt fore-and-aft on the sprockets.

8. Loosen the tensioner adjustment bolt to allow the tensioner to move

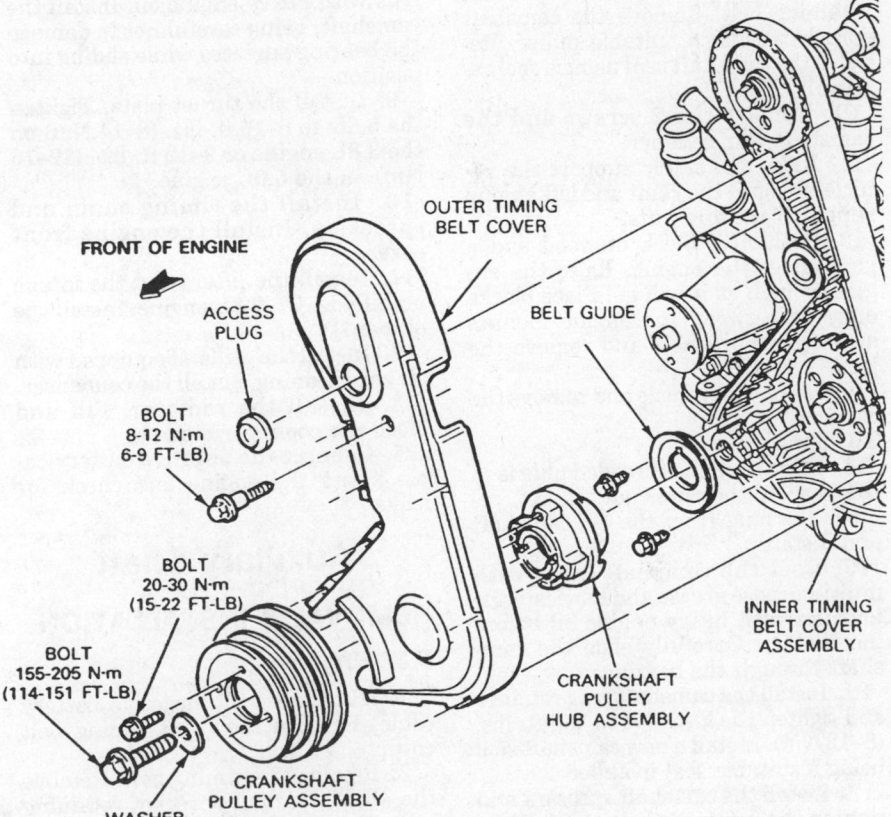

FRONT OF ENGINE

ACCESS PLUG

OUTER TIMING BELT COVER

BELT GUIDE

BOLT 8-12 N·m (6-9 FT-LB)

BOLT 20-30 N·m (15-22 FT-LB)

BOLT 155-205 N·m (114-151 FT-LB)

WASHER

CRANKSHAFT PULLEY ASSEMBLY

CRANKSHAFT PULLEY HUB ASSEMBLY

INNER TIMING BELT COVER ASSEMBLY

Timing belt front cover installation—1991–93 2.3L engine

against the belt. If the spring does not have enough tension to move the roller against the belt, it may be necessary to manually push the roller against the belt and tighten the bolt.

9. To make sure the belt does not jump time during rotation in Step 10, remove a spark plug from each cylinder.

10. Rotate the crankshaft 2 complete turns in the direction of normal rotation to remove the slack from the belt. Tighten the tensioner adjustment to 29–40 ft. lbs. (40–55 Nm) and pivot bolts to 14–22 ft. lbs. (20–30 Nm). Check the alignment of the timing marks.

11. Install the crankshaft belt guide.

12. On 1989–90 vehicles, install the crankshaft pulley and tighten the retaining bolt to 103–133 ft. lbs. (140–180 Nm). On 1991–93 vehicles, proceed as follows:

    a. Install the timing sensor onto the dowel pin and tighten the 2 longer bolts to 14–22 ft. lbs. (20–30 Nm).

    b. Rotate the crankshaft 45 degrees couterclockwise and install the crankshaft pulley and hub assembly. Tighten the bolt to 114–151 ft. lbs. (155–205 Nm).

    c. Rotate the crankshaft 90 degrees clockwise so the vane of the crankshaft pulley engages with timing sensor positioner tool T89P-6316–A or equivalent. Tighten the 2 shorter sensor bolts to 14–22 ft. lbs. (20–30 Nm).

    d. Rotate the crankshaft 90 degrees counterclockwise and remove the sensor positioner tool.

    e. Rotate the crankshaft 90 degrees clockwise and measure the outer vane to sensor air gap. The air gap must be 0.018–0.039 in. (0.458–0.996mm).

13. Install the timing belt front cover, spark plugs and remaining components.

14. Connect the negative battery cable, start the engine and check the ignition timing.

Timing Sprockets

REMOVAL & INSTALLATION

2.3L Engine

1. Disconnect the negative battery cable.

2. Remove the timing belt front cover and the timing belt.

3. Remove the camshaft and auxiliary shaft sprocket retaining bolts. Remove the crankshaft, camshaft and auxiliary shaft sprockets using suitable pullers.

To install:

4. Install the crankshaft, camshaft and auxiliary shaft sprockets. Tighten

the camshaft sprocket retaining bolt to 52–70 ft. lbs. (70–95 Nm) and the auxiliary sprocket retaining bolt to 30–41 ft. lbs. (40–55 Nm).

5. Install the timing belt and timing belt front cover.

6. Connect the negative battery cable.

Camshaft

REMOVAL & INSTALLATION

2.3L Engine

1. Disconnect the negative battery cable and drain the cooling system.

2. Remove the air intake and the throttle body.

3. Disconnect the radiator hoses. Remove the cooling fan, shroud and radiator assembly.

4. Tag and disconnect the spark plug wires and position aside.

5. Tag and disconnect the necessary electrical connectors and vacuum lines and position aside.

6. Remove the rocker cover retaining bolts and the rocker cover.

7. Remove the timing belt front cover and the timing belt.

8. Compress the valve springs using valve spring compressor lever T88T-6565–BH or equivalent and remove the cam followers.

9. Remove the camshaft sprocket retaining bolt. Remove the camshaft sprocket using a suitable puller. Remove the camshaft seal using a seal removal tool.

10. Remove the 2 screws and the camshaft rear retainer.

11. Raise and safely support the vehicle. Remove the right and left engine support bolts and nuts.

12. Position a block of wood and a jack under the engine. Raise the engine as high as it will go. Place blocks of wood between the engine mounts and chassis brackets and remove the jack.

13. Lower the vehicle and remove the camshaft.

To install:

14. Make sure the threaded plug is in the rear of the camshaft. If not, remove the plug from the old camshaft and install.

15. Coat the camshaft lobes with multi-purpose grease and lubricate the journals with heavy engine oil before installation. Carefully slide the camshaft through the bearings.

16. Install the camshaft rear retainer and tighten the 2 screws to 6–9 ft. lbs. (8–12 Nm). Install a new camshaft seal using a suitable seal installer.

17. Install the camshaft sprocket and tighten the retaining bolt to 52–70 ft. lbs. (70–95 Nm).

18. Install the timing belt and timing belt front cover.

19. Raise and safely support the vehicle. Position a block of wood and a jack and raise the engine. Remove the blocks of wood, lower the engine and remove the jack.

20. Install the engine support bolts and nuts and lower the vehicle.

21. Install the remaining components in the reverse order of removal.

22. Connect the negative battery cable, start the engine and check for leaks. Check the ignition timing, if necessary.

3.8L and 5.0L Engines

1. Disconnect the negative battery cable and drain the cooling system.

2. Relieve the fuel system pressure and discharge the air conditioning system.

3. Remove the radiator. If equipped with air conditioning, remove the condenser.

4. Remove the grille.

5. Remove the intake manifolds and the lifters. On the 3.8L engine, remove the oil pan.

6. Remove the timing chain front cover, the timing chain and spacer.

7. Remove the thrust plate. Remove the camshaft, being careful not to damage the bearing surfaces.

To install:

8. Lubricate the cam lobes and journals with heavy engine oil. Install the camshaft, being careful not to damage the bearing surfaces while sliding into position.

9. Install the thrust plate. Tighten the bolts to 6–10 ft. lbs. (8–14 Nm) on the 3.8L engine or 9–12 ft. lbs. (12–16 Nm) on the 5.0L engine.

10. Install the timing chain and sprockets. Install the engine front cover.

11. Install the lifters and the intake manifolds. On 3.8L engine, install the oil pan.

12. Install the grille. If equipped with air conditioning, install the condenser.

13. Install the radiator. Fill and bleed the cooling system.

14. Connect the negative battery cable. Start the engine and check for leaks.

Auxiliary Shaft

REMOVAL & INSTALLATION

2.3L Engine

1. Disconnect the negative battery cable. Remove the front timing belt cover.

2. Remove the timing belt. Remove the auxiliary shaft sprocket retaining bolt. Remove the sprocket using a puller.

3. On 1989–90 vehicles, mark the position of the distributor housing in the engine block and remove the distributor.

4. Remove the auxiliary shaft cover and thrust plate.

5. Withdraw the auxiliary shaft from the block being careful not to damage the bearings.

To install:

6. Dip the auxiliary shaft in engine oil before installing. Slide the auxiliary shaft into the cylinder block, being careful not to damage the bearings.

7. Install the thrust plate. Tighten the thrust plate screws to 6–9 ft. lbs. (8–12 Nm).

8. Install a new gasket and auxiliary shaft cover. Tighten the cover screws to 6–9 ft. lbs. (8–12 Nm).

NOTE: The auxiliary shaft cover and cylinder front cover share a common gasket. Cut off the old gasket around the cylinder cover and use half of the new gasket on the auxiliary shaft cover.

9. Insert the distributor, aligning the housing-to-engine block marks, and install the auxiliary shaft sprocket.

10. Align the timing marks and install the timing belt.

11. Install the timing belt cover.

12. Check the ignition timing.

Piston and Connecting Rod

POSITIONING

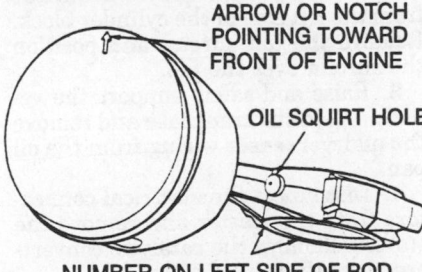

ARROW OR NOTCH POINTING TOWARD FRONT OF ENGINE

OIL SQUIRT HOLE

NUMBER ON LEFT SIDE OF ROD

Piston and rod assembly—2.3L engine

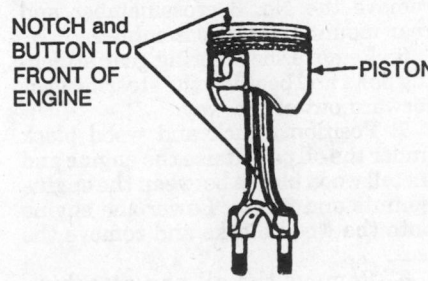

NOTCH and BUTTON TO FRONT OF ENGINE

PISTON

Piston and rod assembly—3.8L engine

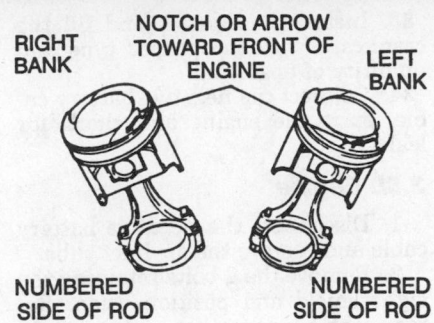

NOTCH OR ARROW TOWARD FRONT OF ENGINE

RIGHT BANK

LEFT BANK

NUMBERED SIDE OF ROD

NUMBERED SIDE OF ROD

Piston and rod assembly—5.0L engine

ENGINE LUBRICATION

Oil Pan

REMOVAL & INSTALLATION

2.3L Engine

1989–90

1. Disconnect the negative battery cable and drain the cooling system.

2. Disconnect the electrical connector to the cooling fan and remove the fan and shroud assembly. Disconnect the radiator hoses at the radiator. If equipped with an automatic transmission, disconnect the oil cooler lines at the radiator.

3. Raise and safely support the vehicle. Drain the crankcase and disconnect the low oil level sensor, if equipped.

4. Remove the right and left engine mount through bolts, except convertible. On convertible, remove the nuts. Using a jack and a block of wood, raise the engine as high as it will go. Place wood blocks between the mounts and the pedestal brackets. Remove the jack.

5. Remove the shake brace. Remove the sway bar retaining bolts and lower the sway bar.

6. Disconnect the cable at the starter and remove the starter. Remove the steering gear retaining bolts and lower the gear.

7. Remove the oil pan retaining bolts and allow the oil pan to drop to the crossmember. Rotate the crankshaft to position No. 4 piston up in the cylinder bore so the oil pan clears the crankshaft throw. Remove the oil pan.

8. Clean the oil pan and the gasket mating surfaces. Remove and clean the oil pickup tube and screen assembly.

To install:

9. Install the oil pickup tube and screen assembly.

10. Apply gasket adhesive to the oil pan and install the oil pan gasket to the pan. Apply silicone sealer to the area where the front cover meets the engine block.

11. Position the oil pan and pan reinforcements to the cylinder block and install the retaining bolts. Tighten to 71–106 inch lbs. (8–12 Nm).

12. Position the steering gear and install the bolts and nuts. Install the starter and connect the cable.

13. Raise the engine enough to remove the wood blocks. Lower the engine and remove the jack. Install the shake brace.

14. Install the right and left engine through bolts, except convertible. Tighten the bolts to 65–85 ft. lbs. (88–119 Nm). On convertible, install the right and left engine support nuts. Tighten the nuts to 80–106 ft. lbs. (108–144 Nm).

15. Install the sway bar. Connect the low oil level sensor, if equipped. Install a new oil filter.

16. Lower the vehicle. Install the cooling fan and shroud assembly. Connect the cooling fan electrical connector and the radiator hoses. If equipped with an automatic transmission, connect the oil cooler lines.

17. Fill the engine with the proper type and quantity of engine oil. Fill and bleed the cooling system.

18. Connect the negative battery cable, start the engine and check for leaks.

1991–93

1. Disconnect the negative battery cable. Remove the air cleaner outlet tube at the throttle body.

2. Remove the engine oil dipstick.

3. Install engine support fixture D88L–6000–A or equivalent.

4. Raise and safely support the vehicle.

5. Remove the engine mount through bolts.

6. Drain the engine oil.

7. Disconnect the cable from the starter and remove the starter.

8. Disconnect the exhaust manifold tube to the inlet pipe bracket and disconnect the catalytic converter at the inlet pipe.

9. Remove the transmission. If equipped with manual transmission, remove the clutch pressure plate and disc.

10. Remove the flywheel retaining bolts and remove the flywheel.

11. If equipped with automatic transmission, remove the oil cooler lines from the retainer at the block.

12. Lower the vehicle. Raise the engine using the engine support fixture,

then raise and safely support the vehicle.

13. Remove the oil pan attaching bolts and lower the oil pan to the chassis. Remove the oil pump and pickup tube and lay the assembly in the oil pan.

14. Remove the pan and pump from the vehicle.

15. Clean the oil pan and all gasket mating surfaces. Clean the oil pump exterior and pickup tube screen.

To install:

16. Install the oil pan gasket in the groove in the oil pan.

17. Lay the oil pump and pickup tube assembly in the oil pan and position the pan on the crossmember.

18. Install the oil pump and pickup tube assembly. Tighten the oil pump mounting bolts to 14–21 ft. lbs. (19–29 Nm) and the oil pump strap nut to 30–41 ft. lbs. (40–55 NM).

19. Apply silicone sealer to the points where the rear main bearing cap meets the cylinder block, to the corners of the engine front cover and to where the front cover meets the cylinder block.

20. Install the oil pan assembly. Install the oil pan flange bolts tight enough to compress the oil pan gasket to the point that the 2 transmission holes are aligned with the 2 tapped holes in the oil pan, but loose enough to allow movement of the pan, relative to the block.

21. Install the 2 oil pan/transmission bolts and tighten to 30–36 ft. lbs. (40–50 Nm) to align the oil pan with the transmission, then loosen the bolts ½ turn.

22. Tighten all oil pan flange bolts to 90–120 inch lbs. (10–13 Nm). Tighten the 2 oil pan/transmission bolts to 30–39 ft. lbs. (40–54 Nm).

23. Install a new oil filter.

24. Lower the vehicle. Lower the engine onto the engine mounts, then raise and safely support the vehicle.

25. Install the flywheel and tighten the attaching bolts to 54–64 ft. lbs. (73–87 Nm). If equipped with manual transmission, install the clutch pressure plate and disc assembly.

26. Install the transmission.

27. Install the engine mount through bolts and tighten to 65–85 ft. lbs. (88–115 Nm).

28. If equipped with automatic transmission, connect the oil cooler line retainer clip to the engine.

29. Connect the exhaust pipe and the inlet pipe.

30. Install the starter and connect the starter cable.

31. Lower the vehicle. Remove the engine support fixture.

32. Connect the air cleaner outlet tube to the throttle body.

33. Install the dipstick and fill the crankcase with the proper type and quantity of engine oil.

34. Connect the negative battery cable, start the engine and check for leaks.

3.8L Engine

1. Disconnect the negative battery cable and remove the air inlet tube.

2. Remove the 2 bolts retaining the sight shield and position aside. Remove the hood weather seal.

3. Remove the wipers. Remove the left cowl vent screen and the wiper module. On supercharged engines, remove the intercooler tubes.

4. Install engine support fixture tool D88L-6000-A or equivalent. Raise and safely support the vehicle.

5. Remove the engine mount through bolts. On supercharged engine, remove the left mount retaining strap bolt.

6. Partially lower the vehicle and raise the engine with the support fixture.

7. Raise and safely support the vehicle. Remove the starter.

8. Drain the crankcase and remove the oil filter.

9. Remove the wire loom, ground strap and automatic transmission oil cooler lines, if equipped.

10. Remove the oil pan-to-bellhousing bolts and the bolts at the crankshaft position sensor shield, if equipped. Remove the remaining oil pan retaining bolts.

11. Remove the steering shaft pinch bolts and separate the steering shaft. Position a jack under the front of the sub-frame.

12. Remove the 6 rearward bolts on the front of the sub-frame. Loosen the 2 front sub-frame bolts.

13. Remove the lower strut-to-control arm bolts and nuts and lower the sub-frame. Remove the oil pan.

To install:

14. Clean the gasket mating surfaces and the oil pan. Apply silicone sealer to the oil pan.

15. Fit the oil pan to the cylinder block. Make sure enough clearance has been provided to allow the oil pan to be installed without sealer being scraped off under the cylinder block.

16. Install the oil pan retaining bolts at the cylinder block and bell housing and install the lower crankshaft sensor shield, if equipped. Tighten the bolts to 80–106 inch lbs. (9–12 Nm).

17. Raise the sub-frame into position and install the lower strut mount-to-control arm bolts. Tighten to 103–144 ft. lbs. (140–195 Nm).

18. Install the 2 front sub-frame bolts and the 6 bolts at the rear of the front sub-frame member. Install a ¾ in. outside diameter pipe or equivalent, into both front left and right sub-frame and body alignment holes. Tighten 1 bolt at each corner. Remove the alignment tools and tighten the bolts to 70–95 ft. lbs. (95–130 Nm).

19. Connect the steering shaft and install the pinch bolt. Tighten to 30–42 ft. lbs. (41–57 Nm).

20. Install the transmission cooler lines, wire loom and ground strap. Install a new oil filter.

21. Install the starter and partially lower the vehicle.

22. Lower the engine with the support fixture. Seat the left side locating pin before the right. Partially raise the vehicle and support safely.

23. Install the engine mount through bolts and tighten to 35–50 ft. lbs. (47–68 Nm). On supercharged engine, install the left mount retaining strap bolt and tighten to 33–45 ft. lbs. (45–61 Nm). Lower the vehicle.

24. Remove the engine support fixture. On supercharged engine, install the intercooler tubes.

25. Install the wiper module and the left cowl vent screen. Install the wipers and the hood weather seal.

26. Install the sight shield and the 2 retaining bolts. Install the air duct assembly. Fill the crankcase with the proper type and quantity of engine oil.

27. Connect the negative battery cable, start the engine and check for leaks.

5.0L Engine
MUSTANG AND MARK VII

1. Disconnect the negative battery cable and remove the air cleaner tube.

2. Remove the oil level indicator from the left side of the cylinder block. Remove the fan shroud and position the shroud over the fan.

3. Raise and safely support the vehicle. Drain the crankcase and remove the oil level sensor wiring from the oil pan.

4. Disconnect the electrical connectors from the starter and remove the starter. Remove the catalytic converter and muffler inlet pipes.

5. Remove the engine mount-to-No. 2 crossmember attaching bolts or nuts. Support the transmission and remove the No. 3 crossmember and rear mount support assemblies.

6. Remove the steering gear attaching bolts and position the steering gear forward out of the way.

7. Position a jack and wood block under the oil pan. Raise the engine and install wood blocks between the engine mounts and frame. Lower the engine onto the wood blocks and remove the jack.

8. Remove the oil pan attaching bolts and lower the pan to the crossmember. Remove the oil pump and

pickup tube assembly and allow to drop into the pan. Remove the pan.

To install:

9. Clean the oil pan and the gasket mating surfaces. Clean the oil pump exterior amd pickup tube screen. Apply gasket sealer to the gasket mating surfaces and install new oil pan gaskets.

10. With the oil pump and pickup tube assembly positioned in the oil pan, raise the pan onto the crossmember. Install the oil pump and then the pan. Tighten the oil pan bolts to 9 ft. lbs. (12 Nm).

11. Position the oil pan and the wood block under the oil pan. Raise the engine and remove the wood blocks. Lower the engine and remove the jack. Install the engine mount-to-No. 2 crossmember attaching nuts or bolts. Tighten to 80–106 ft. lbs. (108–144 Nm).

12. Position the steering gear and install the retaining bolts. Install the starter and connect the electrical connectors. Connect the oil level sensor wire to the oil pan.

13. Install the rear mount and the No. 3 crossmember. Tighten the attaching bolts to 80–106 ft. lbs. (108–144 Nm). Install the catalytic converter and muffler inlet pipes. Lower the vehicle.

14. Install the fan shroud and install the oil level indicator to the side of the cylinder block. Install the air cleaner assembly.

15. Fill the crankcase with the proper type and quantity of engine oil. Connect the negative battery cable, start the engine and check for leaks.

THUNDERBIRD AND COUGAR

1. Disconnect the negative battery cable and remove the oil level dipstick. Disconnect the air cleaner cover retaining clips to allow free movement when the engine is raised.

2. Remove the 2 bolts retaining the radiator shroud to the radiator and pull the shroud loose from the lower retaining clips.

3. Install engine support fixture tool D88L–6000–A or equivalent. Raise and safely support the vehicle.

4. Drain the crankcase and remove the engine mount through bolts. Loosen the transmission mount nut to allow the mount to move when the engine is raised. Partially lower the vehicle.

5. Raise the engine approximately 2 in. using the support fixture. Raise and safely support the vehicle.

6. Remove the power steering cooler line retaining clips. Remove the bolt securing the transmission lines to the right side of the engine block.

7. Disconnect the electrical connector from the low oil level sensor locat-

ed in the oil pan, if equipped. Remove the oil pan retaining bolts.

8. Remove the steering shaft pinch bolt and separate the steering shaft from the power steering rack assembly.

9. Position 2 jack stands under the engine support sub-frame. Remove the lower strut-to-control arm bolts and nuts from both sides.

10. While supporting the engine support sub-frame on jack stands, remove the 6 rearward bolts on the sub-frame. Loosen the 2 froward bolts on the sub-frame. Lower the sub-frame.

11. Remove the oil pump/pickup tube assembly and place it in the oil pan. Remove the pan.

To install:

12. Clean the oil pan and the gasket mating surfaces. Clean the oil pump exterior and the pickup tube screen.

13. Apply a thin coat of silicone sealer to the engine block and to the engine block side of a new oil pan gasket. Allow the adhesive to set-up for approximately 5 minutes, before positioning the gasket to the engine.

14. Place the oil pump and pickup tube assembly in the oil pan and position the pan on the sub-frame. Install the oil pump/pickup tube and oil pump drive to the engine. Tighten the oil pump retaining bolts to 22–32 ft. lbs. (30–43 Nm).

15. Position the oil pan to the engine and install all the pan bolts hand tight, then tighten the bolts evenly to 9 ft. lbs. (12 Nm). Connect the electrical connector to the low oil level sensor, if equipped.

16. Raise the sub-frame into position while supporting the sub-frame on the jackstands. Install a ¾ in. outside diameter pipe or equivalent, into both front left and right sub-frame and body alignment holes. Tighten 1 bolt at each corner. Remove the alignment tools and tighten the bolts to 70–95 ft. lbs. (95–130 Nm).

17. Install the lower strut-to-control arm bolts and nuts and tighten to 103–144 ft. lbs. (140–195 Nm). Remove the 2 jackstands used for installing the sub-frame.

18. Connect the steering shaft and install the steering shaft pinch bolt. Tighten the pinch bolt to 30–42 ft. lbs. (41–57 Nm). Install the bolt securing the transmission lines to the right side of the engine block.

19. Secure the power steering cooler line retaining clips and partially lower the vehicle. Lower the engine onto the engine mounts and remove the engine support fixture.

20. Raise and safely support the vehicle. Tighten the transmission mount nut to 65–85 ft. lbs. (88–115 Nm). Install the engine mount through bolts.

21. Install a new oil filter and lower

the vehicle. Position the fan shroud into the lower retaining clips and install the 2 bolts. Connect the air filter cover retaining clips.

22. Fill the crankcase with the proper type and quantity of engine oil. Install the dipstick and connect the negative battery cable. Start the engine and check for leaks.

Oil Pump

REMOVAL & INSTALLATION

Except 3.8L Engine

1. Disconnect the negative battery cable. Remove the oil pan.

2. Remove the oil pump inlet tube and screen assembly.

3. Remove the oil pump attaching bolts and gasket. Remove the oil pump intermediate shaft.

To install:

4. Prime the oil pump by filling either the inlet or outlet ports with engine oil and rotating the pump shaft to distribute the oil within the pump body.

5. Position the intermediate driveshaft into the distributor socket. With the shaft firmly seated in the distributor socket, the stop on the shaft should touch the roof of the crankcase. Remove the shaft and position the stop, as necessary.

6. Position a new gasket on the pump body, insert the intermediate shaft into the oil pump and install the pump and shaft as an assembly.

NOTE: Do not attempt to force the pump into position if it will not seat readily. The driveshaft hex may be misaligned with the distributor shaft. To align, rotate the intermediate shaft into a new position.

7. Tighten the oil pump attaching screws to 14–21 ft. lbs. (19–29 Nm) on the 2.3L engine or 22–32 ft. lbs. (30–43 Nm) on the 5.0L engine.

8. Clean and install the oil pump inlet tube and screen assembly.

9. Install the oil pan and the remaining components.

3.8L Engine

NOTE: The timing chain front cover houses the oil pump on the 3.8L engine. If the oil pump housing is scored, worn or grooved, the entire front cover will have to be replaced.

1. Disconnect the negative battery cable. Raise and safely support the vehicle.

2. Remove the oil filter.

3. Remove the cover/filter mount

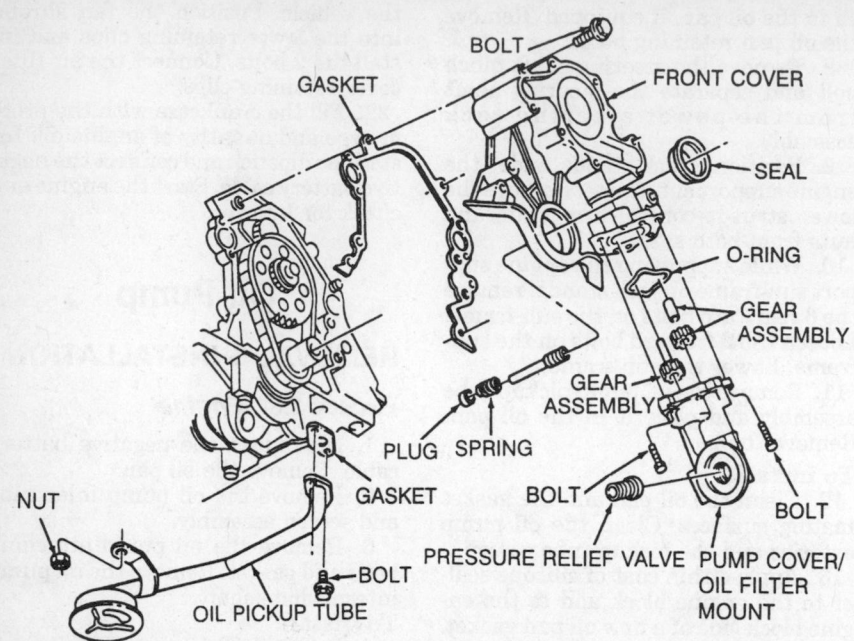

BOLT
GASKET
FRONT COVER
SEAL
O-RING
GEAR ASSEMBLY
GEAR ASSEMBLY
PLUG   SPRING
NUT
GASKET
BOLT
BOLT
BOLT
OIL PICKUP TUBE
PRESSURE RELIEF VALVE
PUMP COVER/ OIL FILTER MOUNT

Oil pump and timing chain front cover exploded view—3.8L engine

assembly. On supercharged engines, remove the oil cooler assembly.

4. Lift the pump gears from their mounting pocket in the front cover.

5. Clean all gasket mounting surfaces.

6. Inspect the mounting pocket for wear. If excessive wear is present, complete timing cover assembly replacement is necessary.

7. Inspect the cover/filter mount gasket to timing cover surface for flatness. Place a straight edge across the flat and check clearance with a feeler gauge. If the measured clearance exceeds 0.0016 in. (0.04mm), replace the cover/filter mount.

8. Replace the pump gears if wear is excessive.

9. Remove the plug from the end of the pressure relief valve passage using a small drill and slide hammer. Use caution when drilling.

10. Remove the spring and valve from the bore. Clean all dirt and metal chips from the bore and valve. Inspect all parts for wear. Replace as necessary.

To install:

11. Install the valve and spring after lubricating them with engine oil. The end with the smaller diameter goes in first.

12. Install a new plug. The plug can be tapped into the bore using a plastic tipped hammer. Make sure the plug is 0–0.010 in. (0–0.25mm) below the machined surface.

13. Lightly pack the gear pocket with petroleum jelly. Install the gears in the cover pocket, making sure petroleum jelly fills all the voids between the gears and pockets.

NOTE: Failure to properly coat the oil pump gears may result in failure of the pump to prime when the engine is started.

14. Position the pump body O-ring seal and install the pump body to the front cover using alignment dowels on the front cover.

15. Tighten the pump body retaining bolts to 18–22 ft. lbs. (25–30 Nm) for M8 bolts and 30–40 ft. lbs. (40–55 Nm) for M10 bolts.

16. Install the oil cooler on supercharged engine. Install a new oil filter.

17. Connect the negative battery cable, start the engine and check for leaks and proper oil pressure.

CHECKING

1. Check the inside of the pump housing and the inner and outer gears for damage or excessive wear.

2. Check the mating surface of the pump cover for wear. Minor scuff marks are normal, but if the cover, gears or housing surfaces are excessively worn, scored or grooved, replace the pump. Inspect the rotor for nicks, burrs or score marks. Remove minor imperfections with an oil stone.

3. Measure the inner to outer rotor tip clearance. With the rotor assembly removed from the pump and resting on a flat surface, the inner and outer rotor tip clearance must not exceed 0.012 in. (0.30mm) with the feeler gauge inserted 0.5 in. (13mm) minimum.

4. With the rotor assembly installed in the housing, place a straight-edge over the rotor assembly and the hous-

ing. Measure the rotor endplay between the straight edge and both the inner and outer race. The maximum clearance must not exceed 0.005 in. (0.13mm).

5. Inspect the relief valve spring to see if it is collapsed or worn. Check the relief valve spring tension. Specifications are as follows:

2.3L engine—12.6–14.5 lbs. at 1.20 in.

3.8L engine—15.2–17.1 lbs. at 1.20 in.

5.0L engine—10.6–12.2 lbs. at 1.704 in.

6. If the spring tension is not within specification and/or the spring is worn or damaged, replace the pump. Check the relief valve piston for free operation in the bore.

NOTE: Except on the 3.8L engine, internal oil pump components are not serviced. If any component is out of specification, the entire pump must be replaced.

Rear Main Bearing Oil Seal

REMOVAL & INSTALLATION

1. Disconnect the negative battery cable. Remove the transmission. If equipped with manual transmission, remove the clutch and flywheel.

2. Punch 2 holes in the crankshaft rear oil seal on opposite sides of the crankshaft, just above the bearing cap to cylinder block split line. Install a sheet metal screw in each of the holes or use a small slide hammer and pry the crankshaft rear main oil seal from the block.

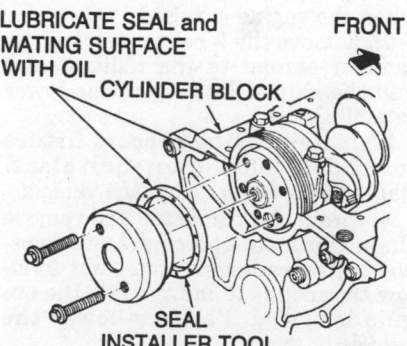

LUBRICATE SEAL and MATING SURFACE WITH OIL
FRONT
CYLINDER BLOCK
SEAL INSTALLER TOOL

NOTE: REAR FACE OF SEAL MUST BE WITHIN 0.005 in. (0.127mm) OF THE REAR FACE OF THE BLOCK SEAL (INSTALL WITH SPRING SIDE TOWARD ENGINE)

Rear main bearing oil seal installation

NOTE: Use extreme caution not to scratch the crankshaft oil seal surface.

3. Clean the oil seal recess in the cylinder block and main bearing cap.

4. Coat the seal and all of the seal mounting surfaces with oil. Position the seal on rear main seal installer T82L–6701–A or equivalent, and position the tool and seal to the rear of the engine.

5. Alternate bolt tightening to seat the seal properly. The rear face of the seal must be within 0.005 in. (0.127mm) of the rear face of the block.

ENGINE COOLING

Radiator

REMOVAL & INSTALLATION

Except 3.8L SC Engine

1. Disconnect the negative battery cable.

2. Remove the radiator cap. Place a drain pan under the radiator, open the draincock and drain the coolant.

— CAUTION —

Never remove the radiator cap while the engine is running or personal injury from scalding hot coolant or steam may result. If possible, wait until the engine has cooled to remove the radiator cap. If this is not possible, wrap a thick cloth around the radiator cap and turn it slowly to the first stop. Step back while the pressure is released from the cooling system. When it is certain all the pressure has been released, press down on the cap, still with the cloth, and turn and remove it.

3. Disconnect the upper, lower and overflow hoses at the radiator.

4. If equipped with an automatic transmission, disconnect the fluid cooler lines at the radiator.

5. On Mustang with 2.3L engine, remove the electric cooling fan/shroud assembly. On all other vehicles, remove the 2 upper fan shroud retaining bolts at the radiator support, lift the fan shroud sufficiently to disengage the lower retaining clips and lay the shroud back over the fan.

6. Remove the radiator upper support retaining bolts and remove the supports. Lift the radiator from the vehicle.

To install:

7. If a new radiator is to be installed, transfer the petcock from the old radiator to the new one. If equipped with automatic transmission, transfer the fluid cooler line fittings from the old radiator.

8. Position the radiator assembly into the vehicle. Install the upper supports and the retaining bolts. If equipped with automatic transmission, connect the fluid cooler lines.

9. On Mustang with the 2.3L engine, install the electric cooling fan/shroud assembly. On all other vehicles, place the fan shroud into the clips on the lower radiator support and install the 2 upper shroud retaining bolts. Position the shroud to maintain approximately 0.38 in. (9.7mm) radial clearance between the fan blades and the shroud.

10. Connect the radiator hoses. Close the radiator petcock. Fill and bleed the cooling system.

11. Start the engine and bring to operating temperature. Check for coolant and transmission fluid leaks.

12. Check the coolant and transmission fluid levels.

3.8L SC Engine

1. Disconnect the negative battery cable.

2. Remove the intercooler.

3. Remove the radiator cap. Place a drain pan under the radiator, open the draincock and drain the coolant.

— CAUTION —

Never remove the radiator cap while the engine is running or personal injury from scalding hot coolant or steam may result. If possible, wait until the engine has cooled to remove the radiator cap. If this is not possible, wrap a thick cloth around the radiator cap and turn it slowly to the first stop. Step back while the pressure is released from the cooling system. When it is certain all the pressure has been released, press down on the cap, still with the cloth, and turn and remove it.

4. Disconnect the upper and lower radiator hoses and the overflow hose at the radiator.

5. If equipped with an automatic transmission, disconnect the fluid cooler lines at the radiator.

6. Remove the overflow hose from the clip on the fan shroud. Remove the 2 shroud upper retaining bolts at the radiator support and remove the wiring harness retaining clip from the fan shroud. Lift the electric cooling fan/shroud assembly from the radiator, disengaging the shroud from the lower retaining clips.

7. Remove the 2 bolts retaining the top of the air duct to the intercooler and remove the upper 2 radiator retaining bolts. Tilt the radiator and support assembly toward the engine and lift the radiator from the vehicle.

To install:

8. If a new radiator is to be installed and the vehicle is equipped with automatic transmission, transfer the fluid cooler line fittings from the old radiator.

9. Position the radiator and support assembly in the vehicle and install the 2 upper retaining bolts.

10. Cut the retaining strap from the air duct. The duct should spring out from the support assembly. Lift the top of the duct and insert the tabs on the bottom of the duct into the clips at the bottom of the intercooler. Install the 2 bolts that retain the top of the duct to the intercooler.

11. Connect the fluid cooler lines to the radiator. Position the engine cooling fan and stud assembly into the radiator lower clips. Attach the top of the radiator to the top of the support with the 2 bolts.

12. Connect the radiator and overflow hoses to the radiator. Route the overflow hose through the retaining clip. Make sure the draincock is closed and fill the cooling system.

13. Install the intercooler. Connect the cooling fan electrical connector and install the harness clip to the fan shroud.

14. Start the engine and bring to operating temperature. Check for coolant and transmission fluid leaks.

15. Check the coolant and transmission fluid levels.

Electric Cooling Fan

TESTING

1. Disconnect the electrical connector at the cooling fan motor.

2. Connect a jumper wire between the negative motor lead and ground.

3. Connect another jumper wire between the positive motor lead and the positive terminal of the battery.

4. If the cooling fan motor does not run, it must be replaced.

REMOVAL & INSTALLATION

Mustand With 2.3L Engine

1. Disconnect the negative battery cable.

2. Remove the fan wiring harness from the routing clip. Disconnect the wiring harness from the fan motor connector by pulling up on the single lock finger to separate the connectors.

3. Remove the 4 mounting bracket attaching screws and remove the fan assembly from the vehicle.

4. Remove the retaining clip from the end of the motor shaft and remove the fan.

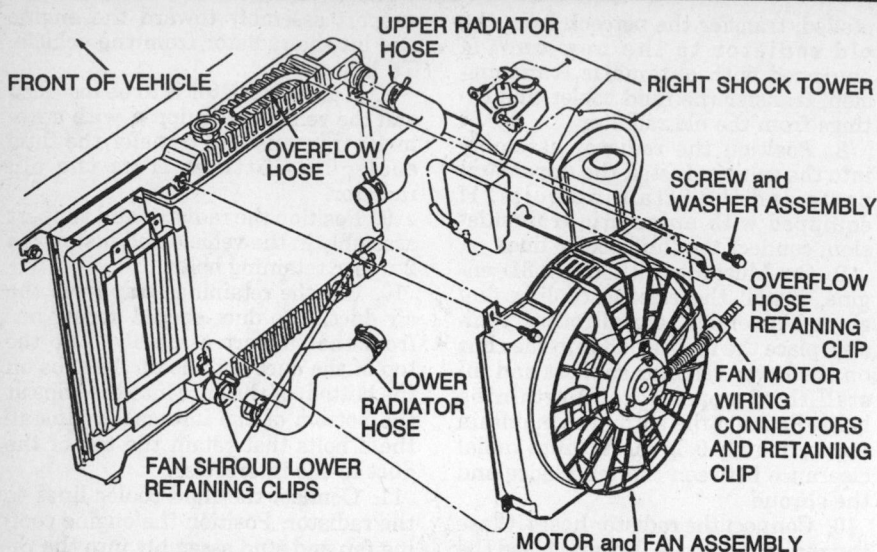

UPPER RADIATOR HOSE

FRONT OF VEHICLE

OVERFLOW HOSE

RIGHT SHOCK TOWER

SCREW and WASHER ASSEMBLY

OVERFLOW HOSE RETAINING CLIP

FAN MOTOR WIRING CONNECTORS AND RETAINING CLIP

LOWER RADIATOR HOSE

FAN SHROUD LOWER RETAINING CLIPS

MOTOR and FAN ASSEMBLY

Electric cooling fan installation—Thunderbird and Cougar with 3.8L SC engine

NOTE: A metal burr may be present on the motor after the retaining clip is removed. Deburring of the shaft may be required to remove the fan.

5. Remove the nuts attaching the fan motor to the mounting bracket.

6. Installation is the reverse of the removal procedure.

Thunderbird and Cougar With 3.8L SC Engine

1. Disconnect the negative battery cable.

2. Disconnect the fan motor wiring connector at the side of the fan shroud. Remove the male terminal connector retaining clip from the shroud mounting tab.

3. Remove the overflow hose from the fan shroud retaining clip and remove the 2 shroud upper retaining bolts at the radiator support.

4. Lift the cooling fan module past the radiator, disengaging the shroud from the 2 lower retaining clips.

5. Installation is the reverse of the removal procedure. Tighten the shroud retaining bolts to 36 inch lbs. (4 Nm).

Heater Core

REMOVAL & INSTALLATION

Without Air Conditioning

MUSTANG

1. Disconnect the negative battery cable.

2. Remove the floor console and instrument panel as follows:

   a. Remove the 2 access covers at the rear of the console by snapping them out. Remove the 4 armrest-to-floor bracket retaining bolts and remove the armrest assembly by snapping it out of the console.

   b. Remove the gear shift lever opening finish panel by snapping out. If equipped with a manual transmission, the shift boot is attached to the bottom of the finish panel. Remove the shift knob and slide the boot and finish panel up the shift lever to remove.

   c. Pull up the emergency brake lever. Remove the 4 retaining screws and lift up the top finish panel. Disconnect the necessary wire connectors.

   d. Remove the 2 console-to-rear floor bracket retaining screws. Insert a small prybar into the 2 notches at the bottom of the front upper finish panel and snap it out.

   e. Remove the radio assembly. Open the glove compartment door and drop the glove compartment assembly down. Remove the 2 console-to-instrument panel retaining screws.

   f. Remove the 4 console-to-bracket retaining screws and remove the console.

   g. Disconnect all underhood wiring connectors from the main wiring harness. Disengage the rubber grommet seal from the dash panel and push the wiring harness and connectors into the passenger compartment.

   h. On 1989 vehicles, remove the 2 screws attaching the steering column shroud to the dash panel and remove the shroud. On 1990–93 vehicles, remove the 3 bolts attaching the steering column opening cover and reinforcement panel. Remove the cover.

   i. On 1989 vehicles, remove the 3

screws and the steering column cover assembly. On 1990–93 vehicles, remove the steering column opening reinforcement by removing 2 bolts, remove the 2 bolts retaining the lower steering column opening reinforcement and remove the reinforcement.

   j. Remove the 6 steering column retaining nuts. Two are retaining the hood release mechanism and 4 retain the column to the lower brake pedal support. Lower the steering column to the floor.

   k. On 1989 vehicles, remove the 4 screws retaining the steering column brace to the cowl side. On 1990–93 vehicles, remove the steering column upper and lower shrouds and disconnect the wiring from the combination switch.

   l. Remove the brake pedal support nut and snap out the defroster grille.

   m. Remove the screws from the speaker covers. Snap out the speaker covers. Remove the front screws retaining the right and left scuff plates at the cowl trim panel. Remove the right and left side cowl trim panels.

   n. Disconnect the wiring at the right and left cowl sides. Remove the cowl side retaining bolts, 1 on each side.

   o. Open the glove compartment door and flex the glove compartment bin tabs inward. Drop down the glove compartment door assembly.

   p. Remove the 5 cowl top screw attachments. Gently pull the instrument panel away from the cowl. Disconnect the speedometer cable and wire connectors.

3. Drain the coolant from the cooling system and remove the hoses from the heater core. Plug the hoses and the core.

4. Remove the screw attaching the air inlet duct and blower housing assembly support bracket to the cowl top panel.

5. Disconnect the black vacuum supply hose from the in-line vacuum check valve in the engine compartment.

6. Disconnect the blower motor wire harness from the resistor and motor head.

7. Working under the hood, remove the 2 nuts retaining the heater assembly to the dash panel.

8. In the passenger compartment, remove the screw attaching the heater assembly support bracket to the cowl top panel. Remove the 1 screw retaining the bracket below the heater assembly to the dash panel.

9. Carefully pull the heater assembly away from the dash panel and remove from the vehicle.

10. Remove the 4 heater core access cover attaching screws and remove the access cover from the case.

11. Lift the heater core and seal from the case. Remove the seal from the heater core tubes.

To install:

12. Install the heater core tube seal on the heater core tubes. Inspect the heater core sealer in the heater case and replace, if necessary.

13. Install the heater core in the case with the seals on the outside of the case. Position the heater core access cover on the case and install the 4 attaching screws.

14. Position the heater assembly in the vehicle. Install the screw attaching the heater assembly support bracket to the cowl top panel.

15. Check the heater assembly drain tube to make sure it is through the dash panel and is not pinched or kinked.

16. Working under the hood, install the 2 nuts retaining the heater assembly to the dash panel. Install the air inlet duct and blower housing support bracket attaching screw. Install 1 screw to the retainer bracket below the heater assembly to the dash panel.

17. Connect the blower motor ground wire to ground and the harness to the resistor and blower motor lead.

18. Connect the black vacuum supply hose to the vacuum check valve in the engine compartment.

19. Install the instrument panel and floor console by reversing the removal procedure.

20. Connect the heater hoses to the heater core and fill the cooling system. Check the system for proper operation.

THUNDERBIRD AND COUGAR

1. Disconnect the negative battery cable.

2. Remove the instrument panel as follows:

a. Disconnect the underhood wiring at the left side of the dash panel.

b. Disengage the wiring connector from the dash panel and push the wiring harness into the passenger compartment.

c. Remove the steering column lower trim cover by removing the 3 screws at the bottom, 1 screw on the left side and pulling to disengage the 5 snap-in retainers across the top.

d. Remove the steering column lower opening reinforcement. 6 screws retain the reinforcement to the instrument panel.

e. Remove the steering column upper and lower shrouds and disconnect the wiring from the steering column.

f. Remove the shift interlock switch and disconnect the steering column lower universal joint.

g. Support the steering column and remove the 4 nuts retaining the column to the support. Remove the column from the vehicle.

h. Remove the 1 screw retaining the left side of the instrument panel to the parking brake bracket.

i. Install the steering column lower opening reinforcement using the 4 screws, 1 at each corner. This will prevent the instrument panel from twisting when being removed.

j. Remove the right and left cowl side trim panels.

k. Remove the console assembly and remove the 2 nuts retaining the center of the instrument panel to the floor.

l. Open the glove compartment, squeeze the sides of the bin and lower to the full open position. From under the instrument panel and through the glove compartment opening, disconnect the wiring, vacuum lines and control cables.

m. Remove 2 screws from the right side and 2 screws from the left side retaining the instrument panel to the cowl side.

n. Remove the right and left upper finish panels by pulling up to disengage the snap-in retainers. There are 3 on the right side, 4 on the left side.

o. Remove the 4 screws retaining the instrument panel to the cowl top. Remove the right and left roof rail trim panel. Remove the door frame weatherstrip.

p. Carefully pull the instrument panel away from the cowl and disconnect any remaining wiring or controls.

3. Remove the right instrument panel brace located above the heater case and attached to the cowl.

4. Drain the coolant from the cooling system and remove the hoses from the heater core. Plug the hoses and the core.

5. Disconnect the black vacuum supply hose from the in-line vacuum check valve in the engine compartment.

6. Disconnect the blower motor wire harness from the resistor and motor lead.

7. Working under the hood, remove the 3 nuts retaining the heater assembly to the dash panel.

8. In the passenger compartment, remove the screw attaching the heater assembly support bracket to the cowl top panel.

9. Remove the 1 screw retaining the bracket below the heater assembly to the dash panel.

10. Carefully pull the heater assembly away from the dash panel and re-

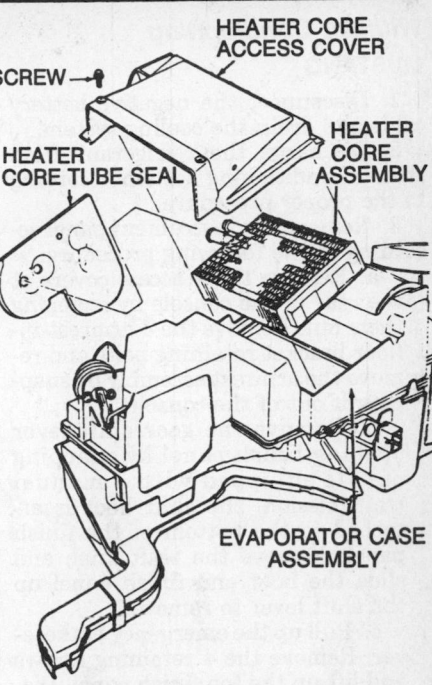

Heater core Installation—Mustang

move the heater assembly from the vehicle.

11. Remove the 4 heater core access cover attaching screws and remove the access cover.

12. Remove the seal from the heater core tubes and pull the heater core from the case.

To install:

13. Inspect the heater core sealer in the case and replace, if necessary.

14. Install the heater core in the case with the seals on the outside of the case. Install the heater core tube seal on the heater core tubes.

15. Position the heater core access cover and seal on the case and install the 4 attaching screws.

16. Position the heater assembly in the vehicle. Install the screw attaching the heater assembly support bracket to the cowl top panel.

17. Working under the hood, install the 3 nuts retaining the heater assembly to the dash panel.

18. Install 1 screw to retain the bracket below the heater assembly to the dash panel.

19. Connect the blower motor and the harness to the resistor and blower motor lead.

20. Connect the black vacuum supply hose to the vacuum check valve in the engine compartment.

21. Install the right instrument panel brace and install the instrument panel by reversing the removal procedure.

22. Connect the heater hoses to the heater core and fill the cooling system. Check heater operation.

With Air Conditioning

MUSTANG

1. Disconnect the negative battery cable and drain the cooling system.
2. Discharge the refrigerant from the air conditioning system according to the proper procedure.
3. Remove the instrument panel according to the following procedure:

   a. Remove the 2 access covers at the rear of the console by snapping them out. Remove the 4 armrest-to-floor bracket retaining bolts and remove the armrest assembly by snapping it out of the console.

   b. Remove the gear shift lever opening finish panel by snapping out. If equipped with a manual transmission, the shift boot is attached to the bottom of the finish panel. Remove the shift knob and slide the boot and finish panel up the shift lever to remove.

   c. Pull up the emergency brake lever. Remove the 4 retaining screws and lift up the top finish panel. Disconnect the necessary wire connectors.

   d. Remove the 2 console-to-rear floor bracket retaining screws. Insert a small prybar into the 2 notches at the bottom of the front upper finish panel and snap it out.

   e. Remove the radio assembly. Open the glove compartment door and drop the glove compartment assembly down. Remove the 2 console-to-instrument panel retaining screws.

   f. Remove the 4 console-to-bracket retaining screws and remove the console.

   g. Disconnect all underhood wiring connectors from the main wiring harness. Disengage the rubber grommet seal from the dash panel and push the wiring harness and connectors into the passenger compartment.

   h. On 1989 vehicles, remove the 2 screws attaching the steering column shroud to the dash panel and remove the shroud. On 1990–93 vehicles, remove the 3 bolts attaching the steering column opening cover and reinforcement panel. Remove the cover.

   i. On 1989 vehicles, remove the 3 screws and the steering column cover assembly. On 1990–93 vehicles, remove the steering column opening reinforcement by removing 2 bolts, remove the 2 bolts retaining the lower steering column opening reinforcement and remove the reinforcement.

   j. Remove the 6 steering column retaining nuts. 2 are retaining the hood release mechanism and 4 retain the column to the lower brake pedal support. Lower the steering column to the floor.

   k. On 1989 vehicles, remove the 4 screws retaining the steering column brace to the cowl side. On 1990–93 vehicles, remove the steering column upper and lower shrouds and disconnect the wiring from the combination switch.

   l. Remove the brake pedal support nut and snap out the defroster grille.

   m. Remove the screws from the speaker covers. Snap out the speaker covers. Remove the front screws retaining the right and left scuff plates at the cowl trim panel. Remove the right and left side cowl trim panels.

   n. Disconnect the wiring at the right and left cowl sides. Remove the cowl side retaining bolts, 1 on each side.

   o. Open the glove compartment door and flex the glove compartment bin tabs inward. Drop down the glove compartment door assembly.

   p. Remove the 5 cowl top screw attachments. Gently pull the instrument panel away from the cowl. Disconnect the speedometer cable and wire connectors.

4. Disconnect the liquid line and the accumulator/drier inlet tube from the evaporator core at the dash panel. Cap the refrigerant lines and evaporator core tube to prevent the entrance of dirt and moisture.
5. Disconnect the heater hoses from the heater core tubes and plug the hoses and tubes.
6. Remove the screw attaching the air inlet duct and blower housing assembly support brace to the cowl top panel.
7. Disconnect the black vacuum supply hose from the in-line vacuum check valve in the engine compartment. Disconnect the blower motor wires from the wire harness and disconnect the wire harness from the blower motor resistor.
8. Working under the hood, remove the 2 nuts retaining the evaporator case to the dash panel. Inside the passenger compartment, remove the 2 screws attaching the evaporator case support brackets to the cowl top panel.
9. Remove the 1 screw retaining the bracket below the evaporator case to the dash panel. Carefully pull the evaporator case away from the dash panel and remove the evaporator case assembly from the vehicle.

NOTE: Whenever an evaporator case is replaced, it will be necessary to replace the suction accumulator/drier.

10. Remove the 4 heater core access cover attaching screws and remove the cover from the case.
11. Lift the heater core and seal from the case. Remove the seal from the heater core tubes.

To install:

12. Install the heater core tube seal on the heater core tubes.
13. Inspect the heater core sealer in the evaporator case. Replace with suitable caulking cord, if necessary.
14. Install the heater core in the case with the seals on the outside of the case. Position the heater core access cover on the case and install the 4 attaching screws.
15. Position the evaporator case assembly in the vehicle. Install the screws attaching the evaporator case support brackets to the cowl top panel. Check the evaporator case drain tube to make sure it is through the dash panel and is not pinched or kinked.
16. Install 1 screw retaining the bracket below the evaporator case to the dash panel. Working under the hood, install the 2 nuts retaining the evaporator case to the dash panel. Tighten the 4 nuts and 2 screws in the engine compartment. Tighten the 2 screws in the passenger compartment and the 2 support bracket attaching screws.
17. Connect the blower motor wire harness to the resistor and blower motor. Connect the black vacuum supply hose to the vacuum check valve in the engine compartment.
18. Using new O-rings lubricated with clean refrigerant oil, connect the liquid line and suction accumulator inlet to the evaporator core tubes. Tighten each connection using a backup wrench to prevent component damage.
19. Install the instrument panel by reversing the removal procedure.
20. Connect the heater hoses to the heater core and fill the cooling system.
21. Connect the negative battery cable. Leak test, evacuate and charge the refrigerant system according to the proper procedure. Observe all safety precautions.
22. Check the system for proper operation.

THUNDERBIRD AND COUGAR

1. Disconnect the negative battery cable and drain the cooling system.
2. Discharge the refrigerant from the air conditioning system according to the proper procedure.
3. Remove the instrument panel according to the following procedure:

   a. Disconnect the underhood wiring at the left side of the dash panel.

   b. Disengage the wiring connector from the dash panel and push the wiring harness into the passenger compartment.

   c. Remove the steering column

lower trim cover by removing the 3 screws at the bottom, 1 screw on the left side and pulling to disengage the 5 snap-in retainers across the top.

d. Remove the 6 retaining screws and the steering column lower opening reinforcement.

e. Remove the steering column upper and lower shrouds and disconnect the wiring from the steering column.

f. Remove the shift interlock switch and disconnect the steering column lower universal joint.

g. Support the steering column and remove the 4 nuts retaining the column to the support. Remove the column from the vehicle.

h. Remove the 1 screw retaining the left side of the instrument panel to the parking brake bracket.

i. Install the steering column lower opening reinforcement using the 4 screws, 1 at each corner. This will prevent the instrument panel from twisting when being removed.

j. Remove the right and left cowl side trim panels.

k. Remove the console assembly and remove the 2 nuts retaining the center of the instrument panel to the floor.

l. Open the glove compartment, squeeze the sides of the bin and lower to the full open position. From under the instrument panel and through the glove compartment opening, disconnect the wiring, vacuum lines and control cables.

m. Remove 2 screws from the right side and 2 screws from the left side retaining the instrument panel to the cowl side.

n. Remove the right and left upper finish panels by pulling up to disengage the snap-in retainers. There are 3 on the right side, 4 on the left side.

o. Remove the 4 screws retaining the instrument panel to the cowl top. Remove the right and left roof rail trim panel. Remove the door frame weather-strip.

p. Carefully pull the instrument panel away from the cowl and disconnect any remaining wiring or controls.

4. Disconnect the liquid line and accumulator/drier inlet tube from the evaporator core at the dash panel. Cap the refrigerant lines and evaporator core to prevent the entrance of dirt and moisture.

5. Disconnect the refrigerant lines and wiring connector from the suction accumulator/drier. Remove the suction accumulator/drier and bracket.

6. If necessary, remove the throttle cable bracket and position aside.

7. Disconnect the heater hoses from the heater core. Plug the hoses and heater core tubes.

8. Disconnect the black vacuum supply hose from the in-line vacuum check valve in the engine compartment. Disconnect the blower motor wiring.

9. Working under the hood, remove the nuts retaining the evaporator case to the dash panel. In the passenger compartment, remove the screw attaching the evaporator case support bracket to the cowl top panel.

10. Remove 1 nut retaining the bracket below the evaporator case to the dash panel. Carefully pull the evaporator case away from the dash panel and remove the evaporator case assembly from the vehicle.

NOTE: Whenever an evaporator case is removed, it will be necessary to replace the suction accumulator/drier.

11. Remove the 4 heater core access cover attaching screws and remove the access cover from the evaporator case.

12. Remove the tube seal from the heater core tubes. Slide the heater core and seals from the evaporator case.

To install:

13. Install the heater core in the evaporator case with the tube seal on the outside of the case.

14. Position the heater core access cover on the evaporator case and install the 4 attaching screws.

15. Position the evaporator case assembly in the vehicle and install the screw attaching the evaporator case support bracket to the cowl top panel. Check the evaporator case drain tube to make sure it is through the dash panel and is not pinched or kinked.

16. Install 1 nut retaining the mounting bracket at the left end of the evaporator case to the dash panel and another nut to retain the bracket below the evaporator case to the dash panel.

17. Working under the hood, install the nuts retaining the evaporator case to the dash panel. Tighten the 4 nuts, 2 in the engine compartment and 2 in the passenger compartment and the 1 support bracket attaching screw.

18. Connect the black vacuum supply hose to the vacuum check valve in the engine compartment.

19. Install the suction accumulator/drier and bracket. Using new O-rings lubricated with clean refrigerant oil, connect the refrigerant lines to the suction accumulator/drier. Connect the wire harness to the pressure switch.

20. Install the throttle cable bracket, if removed.

21. Using new O-rings lubricated with clean refrigerant oil, connect the liquid line and suction accumulator inlet tube to the evaporator core.

22. Install the instrument panel by reversing the removal procedure.

23. Connect the heater hoses to the heater core and fill the cooling system.

24. Leak test, evacuate and charge the system according to the proper procedure. Observe all safety precautions.

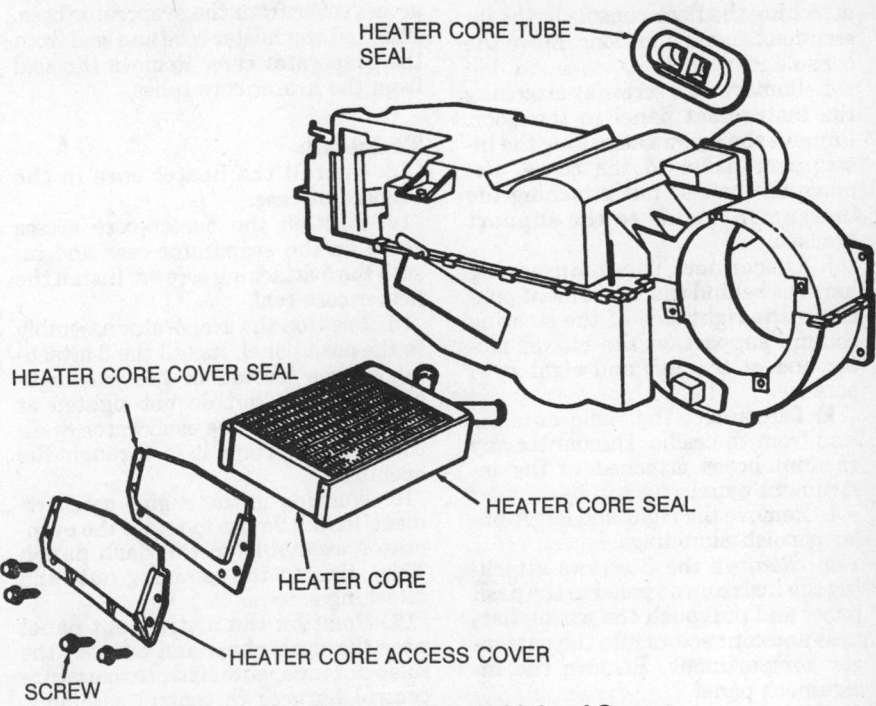

Heater core Installation—Thunderbird and Cougar

25. Check the system for proper operation.

MARK VII

1. Disconnect the negative battery cable and drain the cooling system. Remove the air intake duct.

2. Discharge the refrigerant from the air conditioning system according to the proper procedure.

3. Remove the instrument panel as follows:

   a. Disconnect all underhood electrical connectors of the main wiring harness. Disengage the rubber grommet from the dash panel.

   b. Remove the right and left sound insulator assemblies from under the instrument panel. Remove the bulb and socket assemblies, if necessary.

   c. Remove the steering column opening trim cover and the lower steel reinforcement.

   d. Remove the left and right cowl trim panels. Remove the screws attaching the hood release to the cowl panel before removing the left trim panel.

   e. Remove the steering column trim shroud screws and remove the shrouds.

   f. Disconnect all electrical connector quick couplers from the steering column switches.

   g. Remove the 4 nuts attaching the steering column to the support. Lower the column to rest on the seat cushion.

   h. Snap out the defroster opening grille panel and remove the screws attaching the floor console to the instrument panel and floor. Move the console rearward.

   i. Remove the screw(s) attaching the instrument panel to the floor. Remove the screws attaching the instrument panel to the cowls. Remove the bolt or nut attaching the instrument panel to the support bracket.

   j. Disconnect the main wiring harness behind the instrument panel, on the right side of the steering column support, at the blower motor and at the left and right cowl panels.

   k. Disconnect the radio antenna lead from the radio. Disconnect any vacuum hoses attached to the instrument panel.

   l. Remove the right and left A-pillar garnish mouldings.

   m. Remove the 3 screws attaching the instrument panel to the dash panel and pull/push the wiring harness and connectors into the passenger compartment. Remove the instrument panel.

4. Disconnect the heater hoses from the heater core. Plug the hoses and the core. Disconnect the wire harness connector from the clutch cycling pressure switch, located on top of the suction accumulator/drier.

5. Disconnect the liquid line and the accumulator/drier inlet tube from the evaporator core tubes. Use a backup wrench to prevent component damage. Cap all fittings to prevent the entrance of dirt and moisture.

6. Working under the hood, remove the 2 nuts retaining the accumulator/drier bracket to the dash panel. Position the accumulator/drier and liquid line aside and remove the 2 evaporator assembly retaining nuts.

7. Disconnect the wiring harness connectors, as necessary. Disconnect the harness connectors from the blower motor wires and blower motor speed controller.

8. Disconnect the automatic temperature control sensor hose and elbow from the evaporator case. Disconnect the automatic temperature control harness at the control assembly.

9. Disconnect the rear seat duct adapter from the floor duct. Remove the 3 evaporator attaching screws and remove the evaporator assembly from the vehicle.

NOTE: Whenever an evaporator case is removed, it will be necessary to replace the suction accumulator/drier.

11. Remove the 5 heater core access cover attaching screws and remove the access cover from the evaporator case.

12. Lift the heater core and seal from the evaporator case. Remove the seal from the heater core tubes.

To install:

13. Install the heater core in the evaporator case.

14. Position the heater core access cover on the evaporator case and install the 5 attaching screws. Install the heater core seal.

15. Position the evaporator assembly to the dash panel. Install the 3 attaching screws located in the passenger compartment, but do not tighten at this time. Check the evaporator drain tube to be certain it is through the opening.

16. Working in the engine compartment, install 2 nuts to retain the evaporator assembly to the dash panel. Then, tighten the retaining nuts and attaching screws.

17. Position the instrument panel near the dash panel and connect the radio antenna, automatic temperature control harness to control assembly, harness to blower motor speed controller and blower motor wires. Also attach any additional wire harness connectors disconnected during removal.

18. Move the instrument panel into position and install the attaching screws. Connect the automatic temperature control sensor hose and elbow assembly.

NOTE: Make sure the air conditioning plenum (attached to the instrument panel) is correctly aligned and sealed at the evaporator outlet opening. Air leakage to the floor area will result if the plenum is not sealed at the evaporator case outlet.

19. Install the nut retaining the instrument panel to the brake pedal and steering column support. Position the steering column to the brake pedal and steering column support and install the retaining nuts.

20. Install the steering column opening reinforcement and shroud. Install the screws to attach the lower center of the instrument panel to the floor brace.

21. Install the defroster opening grille and the right and left side cowl trim panels. Install the right and left instrument panel sound insulators.

22. Install the rear seat duct adapter and the console assembly. Install the instrument panel right hand finish panel and the steering column opening cover.

23. Position the accumulator/drier mounting bracket over the studs on the dash panel and loosely install the 2 nuts.

24. Connect the accumulator/drier inlet tube to the evaporator core outlet tube using a new O-ring lubricated with clean refrigerant oil. Do not tighten the connection.

25. Connect the liquid line to the evaporator core inlet tube using a new O-ring lubricated with clean refrigerant oil. Do not tighten the connection.

26. Tighten the 2 nuts retaining the accumulator/drier to the dash panel. Tighten the 2 refrigerant line connections at the evaporator core. Use a backup wrench to prevent component damage.

27. Connect the harness connector to the clutch cycling pressure switch. Connect the heater hoses to the heater core and fill the cooling system.

28. Connect the negative battery cable. Leak test, evacuate and charge the refrigerant system according to the proper procedure. Observe all safety precautions.

29. Check the automatic temperature control system and all instrument panel functions for proper operation.

Water Pump

REMOVAL & INSTALLATION

2.3L Engine

1. Disconnect the negative battery cable and drain the cooling system.
2. Remove the 4 bolts retaining the pulley to the water pump shaft. Remove the fan and shroud.
3. Remove the air conditioning and power steering belts. Remove the water pump pulley.
4. Remove the heater hose to the water pump and the lower radiator hose.
5. Remove the timing belt outer cover bolt, release the interlocking tabs and remove the cover.
6. Remove the water pump retaining bolts and remove the water pump.
7. Installation is the reverse of the removal procedure. Clean all gasket mating surfaces prior to installation. Apply pipe sealant to the water pump bolts and tighten to 14–21 ft. lbs. (20–30 Nm). Tighten the pulley retaining bolts to 15–22 ft. lbs. (20–30 Nm).
8. Fill and bleed the cooling system. Operate the engine until normal operating temperatures have been reached and check for leaks.

3.8L Engine

1. Disconnect the negative battery cable and drain the cooling system.
2. On all except supercharged engine, remove the fan/clutch assembly and shroud.
3. Rotate the main accessory drive belt tensioner. Remove the main drive belt and water pump pulley.
4. Remove the power steering pump pulley and remove the water pump to power steering pump brace.

NOTE: **On supercharged engines, it may be necessary to remove the intercooler to gain access to the power steering pump pulley.**

5. On all except supercharged engine, disconnect the coolant bypass hose(s) and the heater hose at the water pump. On supercharged engine, disconnect the oil cooler tube and bypass hose and remove the upper crankshaft sensor cover.
6. Disconnect the lower radiator hose. Remove the water pump retaining bolts and the pump. If a prybar is used to assist removal, be careful not to damage the mating surfaces.
7. Installation is the reverse of the removal procedure. Clean all gasket mating surfaces prior to installation. Tighten the water pump retaining bolts to 15–22 ft. lbs. (20–30 Nm). Fill and bleed the cooling system. Operate

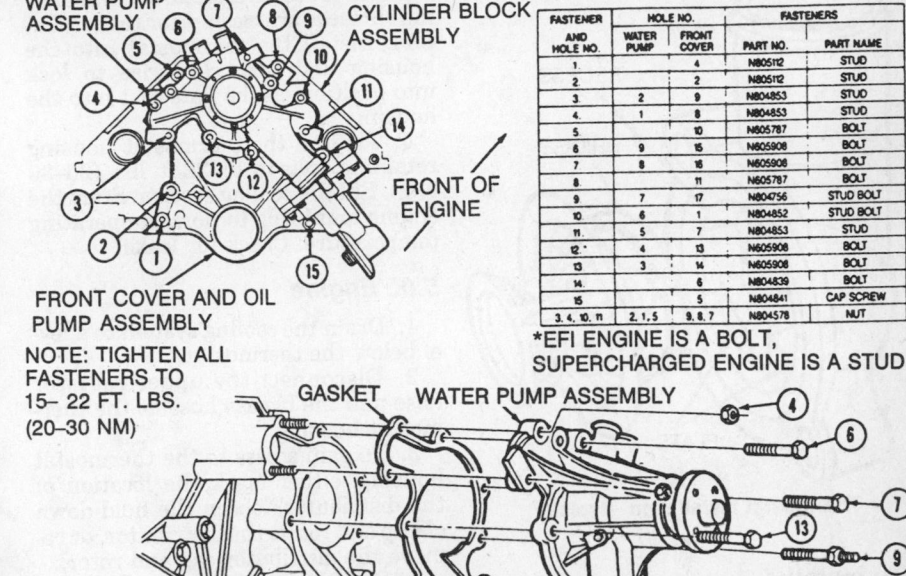

FASTENER AND HOLE NO.	HOLE NO.		FASTENERS	
	WATER PUMP	FRONT COVER	PART NO.	PART NAME
1.		4	N805112	STUD
2.		2	N805112	STUD
3.	2	9	N804853	STUD
4.	1	8	N804853	STUD
5.		10	N805787	BOLT
6.	9	16	N605908	BOLT
7.	8	15	N605908	BOLT
8.		11	N605787	BOLT
9.	7	17	N804756	STUD BOLT
10.	6	1	N804852	STUD BOLT
11.	5	7	N804853	STUD
12.	4	13	N605908	BOLT
13.	3	14	N605908	BOLT
14.		6	N804839	BOLT
15.		5	N804841	CAP SCREW
3, 4, 10, 11	2, 1, 5	9, 8, 7	N604578	NUT

WATER PUMP ASSEMBLY — CYLINDER BLOCK ASSEMBLY — FRONT OF ENGINE

FRONT COVER AND OIL PUMP ASSEMBLY

NOTE: TIGHTEN ALL FASTENERS TO 15–22 FT. LBS. (20–30 NM)

*EFI ENGINE IS A BOLT, SUPERCHARGED ENGINE IS A STUD

GASKET — WATER PUMP ASSEMBLY — STUDS — FRONT COVER AND OIL PUMP ASSEMBLY

Water pump fastener and hole location—3.8L engine

the engine until normal operating temperatures have been reached and check for leaks.

NOTE: **The threads of the No. 1 water pump retaining bolt must be coated with pipe sealant before installing.**

5.0L Engine

1. Disconnect the negative battery cable.
2. Drain the cooling system. Remove the air inlet tube, if equipped.
3. On Thunderbird and Cougar, disconnect the upper radiator hose at the engine.
4. On all except Thunderbird and Cougar, remove the fan shroud attaching bolts and position the shroud over the fan. Remove the fan and clutch assembly from the water pump shaft and remove the shroud.
5. On Thunderbird and Cougar, remove the fan and clutch assembly from the water pump shaft using fan clutch holding tool T84T–6312–C or equivalent, and fan clutch nut wrench T84T–6312–D or equivalent, and position the fan and clutch assembly in the fan shroud. The nut is turned counterclockwise. Remove the fan shroud and fan/clutch as an assembly.
6. Loosen the water pump pulley bolts. Rotate the tensioner away from the accessory drive belt and remove the belt. Remove the water pump pulley.

7. Remove all accessory brackets that attach to the water pump.
8. Disconnect the lower radiator hose, heater hose and water pump bypass hose at the water pump.
9. Remove the water pump attaching bolts and remove the water pump. Discard the gasket.
10. Installation is the reverse of the removal procedure. Clean all gasket mating surfaces prior to installation. Tighten the water pump attaching bolts to 12–18 ft. lbs. (16–24 Nm).
11. Fill and bleed the cooling system. Operate the engine until normal operating temperatures have been reached and check for leaks.

Thermostat

REMOVAL & INSTALLATION

2.3L Engine

1. Drain the cooling system to a level below the thermostat.
2. Remove the upper radiator hose and disconnect the heater hose at the thermostat housing located on the left front lower side of the engine.
3. Remove the thermostat housing retaining bolts and remove the housing. Remove the thermostat by rotating counterclockwise in the housing until the thermostat becomes free to remove. Do not pry out the thermostat.
4. Remove and discard the gasket.

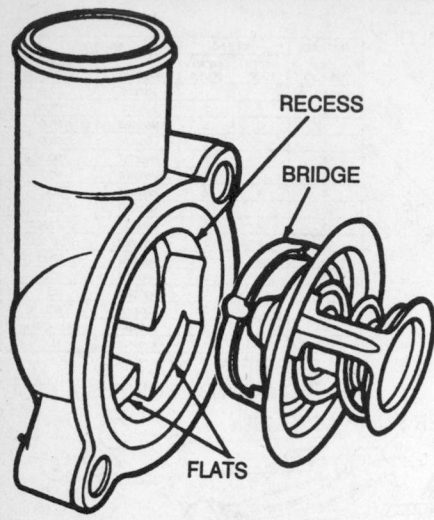

Thermostat Installation—typical

To install:

5. Clean all gasket mating surfaces and position a new gasket on the cylinder head opening. The gasket must be positioned on the cylinder head, before the thermostat is installed.

6. Install the thermostat into the housing with the bridge section in the housing. Turn the thermostat clockwise to lock it into position on the flats cast into the housing.

NOTE: It is important that the rubber thermostat gasket be pressed and the correct thermostat installation alignment be made to provide coolant flow to the heater. Insert and rotate the thermostat to the left or right until it stops in the thermostat housing. Visually check for full width of heater outlet tube opening to be visible within the thermostat port in assembly. This port alignment at assembly is required to provide maximum coolant flow to the heater.

7. Position the thermostat housing against the gasket on the cylinder head. Install and tighten the retaining bolts to 14–21 ft. lbs. (19–29 Nm).

8. Connect the upper radiator hose and the heater hose to the thermostat housing. Fill the cooling system. Start the engine and bring to normal operating temperature. Check for leaks.

3.8L Engine

1. Drain the cooling system to a level below the thermostat.

2. Disconnect the upper radiator hose at the thermostat housing.

3. Remove the 2 thermostat housing retaining bolts and remove the thermostat housing and gasket. Remove the thermostat.

4. Installation is the reverse of the removal procedure. Make sure all mating surfaces are clean prior to installation. Install the thermostat into the housing and turn clockwise to lock into position on the flats cast into the housing.

5. Tighten the thermostat housing retaining bolts to 15–22 ft. lbs. (20–30 Nm). Fill the cooling system. Start the engine and bring to normal operating temperature. Check for leaks.

5.0L Engine

1. Drain the cooling system to a level below the thermostat.

2. Disconnect the upper radiator hose and the bypass hose at the thermostat housing.

3. To gain access to the thermostat housing, either mark the location of the distributor, loosen the hold-down clamp and rotate the distributor, or remove the distributor cap and rotor.

4. Remove the thermostat housing retaining bolts and the housing and gasket. Remove the thermostat.

To install:

5. Clean the gasket mating surfaces. Position a new gasket on the intake manifold.

6. Install the thermostat in the housing, rotating slightly to lock the thermostat in place on the flats cast into the housing. Install the housing on the manifold and tighten the bolts to 12–18 ft. lbs. (16–24 Nm).

7. Install the distributor cap and rotor, or reposition the distributor for correct ignition timing, as necessary. Tighten the hold-down bolt to 17–25 ft. lbs. (23–34 Nm).

8. Connect the bypass hose and the upper radiator hose to the thermostat housing. Fill the cooling system.

9. Start the engine and bring to normal operating temperature. Check for leaks.

Cooling System Bleeding

When the entire cooling system is drained, the following procedure should be used to ensure a complete fill.

1. Install the block drain plug, if removed and close the draincock. On 1991–93 3.8L engine, remove the vent plug on the intake manifold behind the thermostat housing. With the engine OFF, add a 50/50 mixture of water and anti-freeze to the radiator until it reaches the radiator filler neck seat.

NOTE: On Mustang equipped with the 2.3L engine, disconnect the heater hose at the connection on the thermostat housing. Fill the radiator until coolant is visible at the connection in the thermostat housing or the coolant level in the radiator reaches the radiator filler neck seat. Install the heater hose and tighten the hose clamps.

2. Install the radiator cap to the first notch to keep spillage to a minimum. On 1991–93 3.8L engine, install the vent plug.

3. Start the engine and let it idle until the upper radiator hose is warm. This indicates that the thermostat is open and coolant is flowing through the entire system.

4. Carefully remove the radiator cap and top off the radiator with the water/anti-freeze mixture. Install the cap on the radiator securely.

5. Fill the coolant recovery reservoir to the FULL HOT mark with the water/anti-freeze mixture. Install the reservoir cap.

ENGINE ELECTRICAL

NOTE: Disconnecting the negative battery cable on some vehicles may interfere with the functions of the on board computer

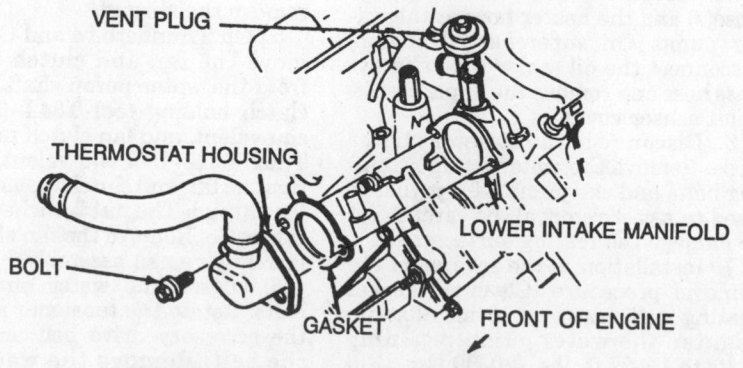

Vent plug location—1991–93 3.8L engine

systems and may require the computer to undergo a relearning process, once the negative battery cable is reconnected.

Distributor

REMOVAL

1. Disconnect the negative battery cable.

2. Mark the position of the No. 1 cylinder wire tower on the distributor base.

NOTE: This reference is necessary in case the engine is disturbed while the distributor is removed.

3. Remove the distributor cap and position the cap and ignition wires to the side. Disconnect the wiring harness plug from the distributor connector.

4. Scribe a mark on the distributor body to indicate the position of the rotor tip. Scribe a mark on the distributor housing and engine block or timing cover to indicate the position of the distributor in the engine.

5. Remove the hold-down bolt and clamp located at the base of the distributor. Remove the distributor from the engine. Note the direction the rotor tip points if it moves from the No. 1 position when the drive gear disengages. For reinstallation purposes, the rotor should be at this point to insure proper gear mesh and timing.

6. Cover the distributor opening in the engine to prevent the entry of dirt or foreign material.

7. Avoid turning the crankshaft, if possible, while the distributor is removed. If the engine is disturbed, the No. 1 cylinder piston will have to be brought to TDC on the compression stroke before the distributor is installed.

INSTALLATION

NOTE: Before installing, visually inspect the distributor. The drive gear should be free of nicks, cracks and excessive wear. The distributor drive shaft should move freely, without binding. The O-ring should fit tightly and be free of cuts.

Timing Not Disturbed

1. Position the distributor in the engine, aligning the rotor and distributor housing with the marks that were made during removal. If the distributor does not fully seat in the engine block or timing cover, it may be because the distributor is not engaging properly with the oil pump intermediate shaft. Remove the distributor and, using a suitable tool, turn the intermediate shaft until the distributor will seat properly.

2. Install the hold-down clamp and bolt. Snug the mounting bolt so the distributor can be turned for ignition timing purposes.

3. Install the distributor cap and connect the distributor to the wiring harness.

4. Connect the negative battery cable. Check and, if necessary, adjust the ignition timing.

5. After the timing has been set, tighten the distributor hold-down clamp bolt to 14–21 ft. lbs. (19–28 Nm) on the 2.3L engine, 20–29 ft. lbs. (27–40 Nm) on the 3.8L engine or 18–26 ft. lbs. (24–35 Nm) on the 5.0L engine. Recheck the ignition timing after tightening the bolt.

Timing Disturbed

1. Disconnect the No. 1 cylinder spark plug wire and remove the No. 1 cylinder spark plug.

2. Place a finger over the spark plug hole and crank the engine slowly until compression is felt.

3. Align the TDC mark on the crankshaft pulley with the pointer on the timing cover. This places the piston in No. 1 cylinder at TDC on the compression stroke.

4. Turn the distributor shaft until the rotor points to the distributor cap No. 1 spark plug tower, as marked during the removal procedure.

5. Install the distributor in the engine, aligning the rotor and distributor housing with the marks that were made during removal. If the distributor does not fully seat in the engine block or timing cover, it may be because the distributor is not engaging properly with the oil pump intermediate shaft. Remove the distributor and, using a suitable tool, turn the intermediate shaft until the distributor will seat properly.

6. Install the hold-down clamp and bolt. Snug the mounting bolt so the distributor can be turned for ignition timing purposes.

7. Install the No. 1 cylinder spark plug and connect the spark plug wire. Install the distributor cap and connect the distributor to the wiring harness.

8. Connect the negative battery cable and set the ignition timing.

9. After the timing has been set, tighten the distributor hold-down clamp bolt to 14–21 ft. lbs. (19–28 Nm) on the 2.3L engine, 20–29 ft. lbs. (27–40 Nm) on the 3.8L engine or 18–26 ft. lbs. (24–35 Nm) on the 5.0L engine. Recheck the ignition timing after tightening the bolt.

Distributorless Ignition System (DIS)

The 3.8L SC and 1991–93 2.3L engines are equipped with distributorless ignition systems. The DIS consists of the following components: crankshaft sensor, ignition module, ignition coil pack, the spark angle portion of the ECU and the related wiring. The system used on the 3.8L SC engine includes a camshaft sensor.

The DIS eliminates the need for a distributor by using multiple ignition coils. Each coil fires 2 spark plugs at the same time. The plugs are paired so as 1 fires during the compression cycle, the other fires during the exhaust stroke. The next time the coil is fired, the plug that was on exhaust will be on compression and the 1 that was on compression will be on exhaust. The spark in the exhaust cylinder is wasted but little of the coil energy is lost. The ignition coils are mounted together in coil packs. There are 2 coil packs used on the 2.3L engine, each containing 2 ignition coils. The 3.8L SC engine uses 1 coil pack containing 3 separate ignition coils.

The crankshaft sensor is a Hall effect magnetic switch, activated by vanes on the crankshaft damper and pulley assembly. The signal generated by this sensor is called the Profile Ignition Pickup (PIP). The PIP signal provides base timing and rpm information to the ECU. In addition, the crankshaft sensor on the 2.3L engine provides a Cylinder Identification (CID) signal. The CID signal is used to synchronize the ignition coils.

The camshaft sensor used on the 3.8L SC engine is a Hall effect magnetic switch, activated by a single vane which is driven by the camshaft. This sensor provides CID information for the ignition coil and for fuel system synchronization.

The ignition module is a microprocessor that receives input from the crankshaft and camshaft sensors in regards to engine position, base timing and engine speed and input from the ECU pertaining to spark advance. The ignition module uses this information to direct which coil to fire and to calculate the turn on and turn off times of the coils required to achieve the correct dwell and spark advance.

REMOVAL & INSTALLATION

Crankshaft Sensor

2.3L ENGINE

1. Disconnect the negative battery cable.

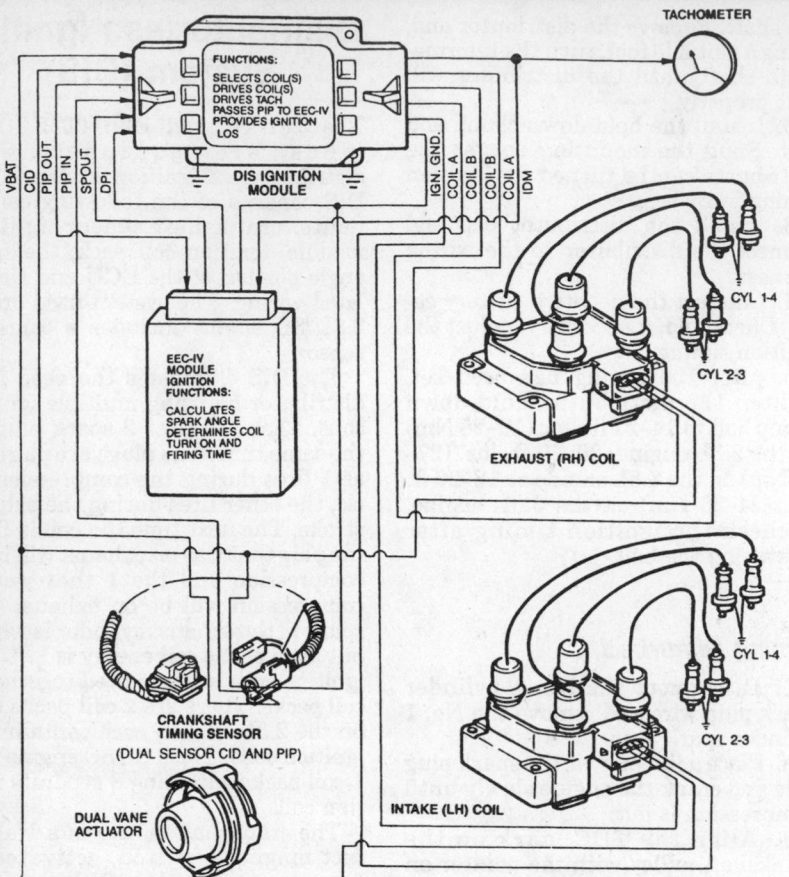

Distributorless ignition system—2.3L engine

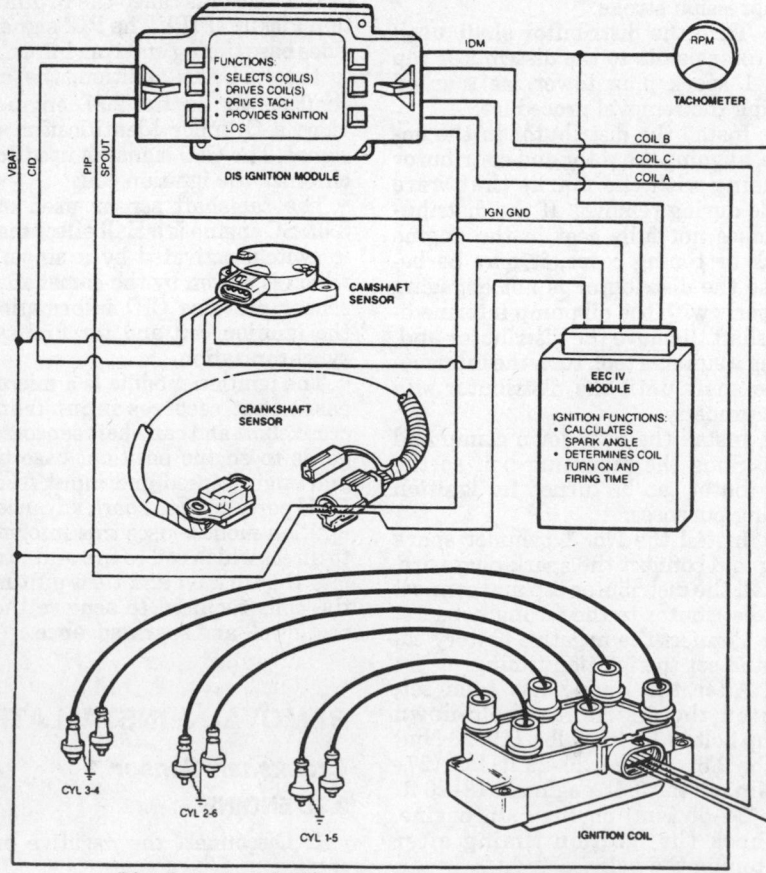

Distributorless ignition system—3.8L SC engine

2. Disconnect the sensor electrical connectors from the engine harness.

3. Remove the large electrical connector from the sensor by prying out the red retaining clip and removing the 4 wires.

4. Remove the accessory drive belts and the 4 bolts retaining the crankshaft pulley to the crankshaft pulley hub. Remove the crankshaft pulley.

5. Remove the timing belt outer cover.

6. Rotate the crankshaft so the keyway is at the 10 o'clock position to place the vane window of both inner and outer vane cups over the crankshaft timing sensor assembly.

NOTE: The vane cups are attached to the crankshaft pulley hub assembly.

7. Remove the 2 sensor retaining bolts and the plastic wire harness retainer that secures the sensor harness to it's mounting bracket. Remove the sensor, sliding the electrical wires out from behind the inner timing belt cover.

To install:

8. Remove the large electrical connector from the new crankshaft timing sensor.

9. Slide the electrical wires behind the inner timing belt cover and position the sensor. Hold the sensor loosely in place with the retaining bolts, but do not tighten at this time.

10. Install the large electrical connector onto the sensor.

NOTE: Make sure the 4 wires to the large electrical connector are installed in the proper locations as indicated. The sensor will not function properly if the wires are installed in the wrong locations.

11. Reconnect both sensor electrical connectors to the engine harness.

12. Rotate the crankshaft so the outer vane on the crankshaft pulley hub assembly engages both sides of the crankshaft Hall effect sensor positioner T89P–6316–A or equivalent, and tighten the sensor retaining bolts.

13. Rotate the crankshaft so the vane on the crankshaft pulley hub is no longer engaged in the positioning tool. Remove the tool.

14. Install the new plastic wire harness retainer to secure the sensor harness to it's mounting bracket. Trim off the excess.

15. Install the timing belt outer cover.

16. Install the crankshaft pulley and tighten the 4 attaching bolts to 15–22 ft. lbs. (20–30 Nm). Install the accessory drive belts.

3.8L SC ENGINE

1. Disconnect the negative battery cable.

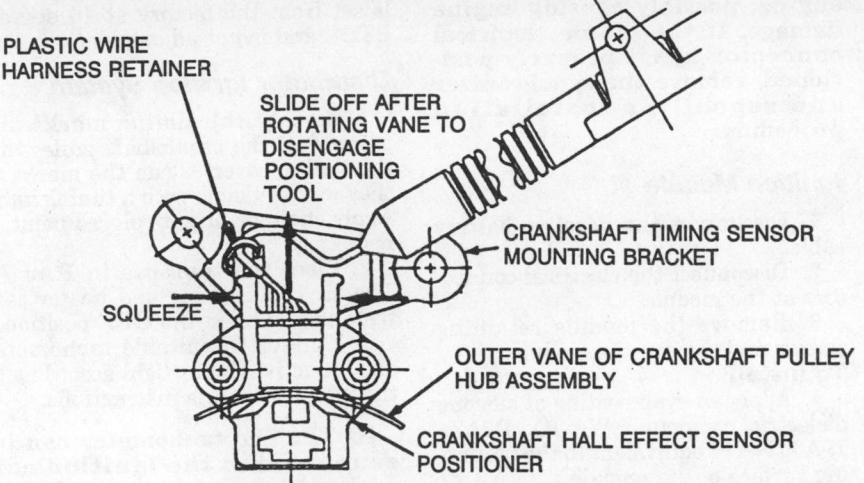

Crankshaft Hall effect sensor positioning—2.3L engine

2. Disconnect the sensor electrical connectors from the engine wiring harness.

3. Raise and safely support the vehicle.

4. Remove the upper and lower damper shield assemblies.

5. Rotate the crankshaft by hand to position the metal vane of the shutter, attached to the rear of the damper, outside of the sensor air gap.

6. Remove the crankshaft sensor retaining screws and remove the sensor.

To install:

7. Position the crankshaft sensor assembly on the bracket.

8. Install 2 sensor retaining screws but do not tighten at this time.

9. Install crankshaft sensor gauge T89P-6316-AH or equivalent, to the outside surface of 1 vane of the shutter.

NOTE: The gauge is magnetic and will conform to the shape of the vane.

10. Rotate the crankshaft by hand to align the shutter vane with the gauge into the sensor air gap.

11. Push the sensor housing inward to contact the gauge and tighten the screws to 22–31 inch lbs. (2.5–3.5 Nm).

NOTE: This is a critical torque. Overtightening can cause damage to the timing sensor.

12. Rotate the crankshaft by hand to position the shutter vane with the gauge outside of the air gap. Remove the magnetic gauge.

13. Install the upper and lower damper shields and tighten the nuts to 9–11 ft. lbs. (12–15 Nm) and the bolts to 6–8.5 ft. lbs. (8–11.5 Nm).

14. Lower the vehicle.

15. Route the sensor wiring harness and connect both electrical connectors.

16. Connect the negative battery cable.

Camshaft Sensor
3.8L SC ENGINE

1. Disconnect the negative battery cable.

2. Disconnect the camshaft sensor electrical connector.

3. Remove the camshaft sensor retaining screws and remove the sensor.

4. Installation is the reverse of the removal procedure. Tighten the retaining screws to 22–31 inch lbs. (2.5–3.5 Nm).

Synchronizer Assembly
3.8L SC ENGINE

The synchronizer assembly mounts in place of the distributor. It provides the mechanical link between the camshaft sensor and the camshaft.

NOTE: Before starting this procedure, set the No. 1 cylinder to 26 degrees after TDC on the compression stroke. Then note the position of the camshaft sensor electrical connector. The installation procedure requires that the connector be located in the same position.

1. Disconnect the negative battery cable.

2. Remove the camshaft sensor assembly.

3. Remove the synchronizer clamp, bolt and washer.

4. Remove the synchronizer from the front engine cover, by pulling it out. The oil pump intermediate shaft will come out with the assembly.

To install:

NOTE: If the replacement synchronizer does not contain a plastic locator cover tool, a special service tool such as synchro positioner tool T89P-12200-A or equivalent, must be used to install the synchronizer. Failure to use this special tool will cause the synchronizer timing to be out of adjustment, and could lead to engine damage.

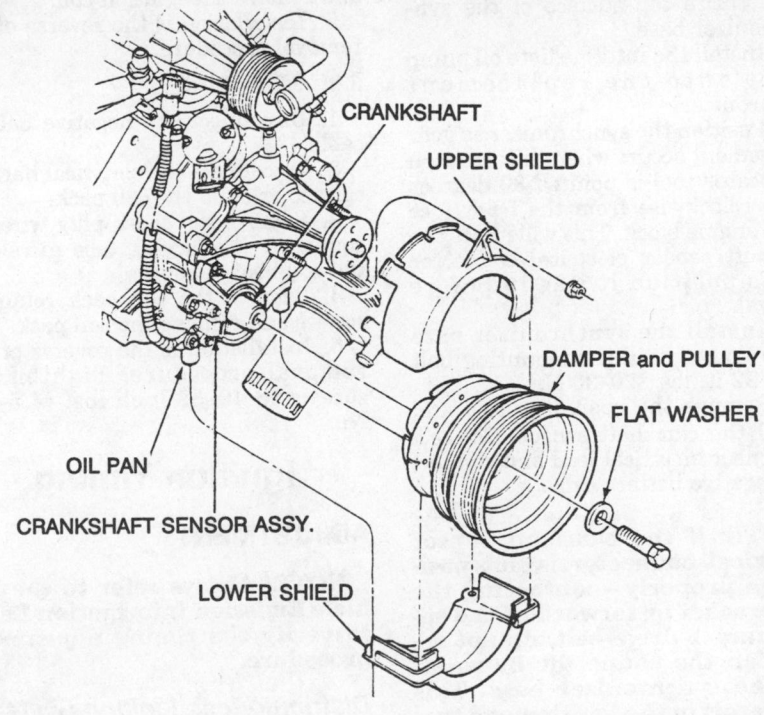

Crankshaft sensor removal and installation—3.8L SC engine

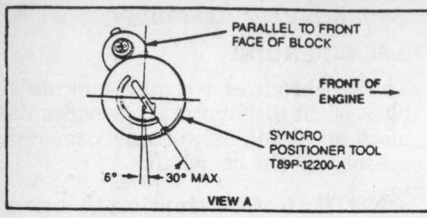

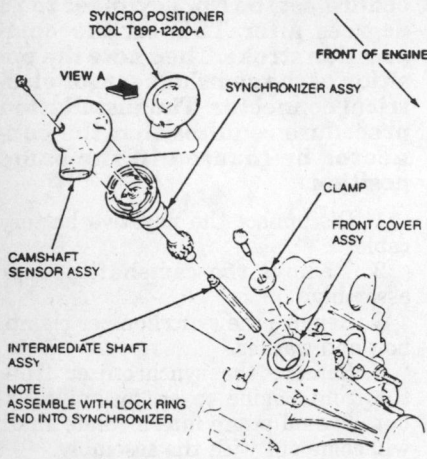

Synchronizer assembly Installation— 3.8L SC engine

5. If the plastic locator cover tool is not attached to the replacement synchronizer, attach synchro positioner tool T89P–12200–A or equivalent, as follows:

   a. Engage the synchronizer vane into the tool's radial slot.

   b. Rotate the tool on the synchronizer base until the tool boss engages the base notch. The cover tool should be square and in contact with the entire top surface of the synchronizer base.

6. Install the intermediate oil pump shaft onto the replacement synchronizer.

7. Position the synchronizer so gear engagement occurs when the arrow on the locator tool is pointed 30 degrees counterclockwise from the front face of the engine block. This will locate the camshaft sensor electrical connector to the position it was in before removal.

8. Install the synchronizer base clamp and tighten the mounting bolt to 15–22 ft. lbs. (20–30 Nm).

9. Remove the positioner tool and install the camshaft sensor. Connect the sensor electrical lead and connect the negative battery cable.

NOTE: If the camshaft sensor electrical connector is not positioned properly—contacting the A/C bracket or forward of the supercharger drive belt, do not reposition the connector by rotating the synchronizer base. This will result in the ignition and fuel systems being out of time with the

engine, possibly causing engine damage. If the sensor electrical connector is not properly positioned, remove the synchronizer and repeat the installation procedure.

Ignition Module

1. Disconnect the negative battery cable.

2. Disconnect the electrical connectors at the module.

3. Remove the module retaining screws and remove the module.
To install:

4. Apply an even coating of silicone dielectric compound WA–IO, D7AZ–19A331–A or equivalent to the mounting surface of the module.

5. Install the module and the retaining screws. Tighten the screws to 22–31 inch lbs. (2.5–3.5 Nm).

6. Connect the electrical connectors to the module and connect the negative battery cable.

Ignition Coil Pack

2.3L ENGINE

1. Disconnect the negative battery cable.

2. Squeeze the locking tabs of the coil wire retainer by hand and remove the spark plug wires with a twisting and pulling motion. Do not pull on the wire.

3. Disconnect the engine harness electrical connector from the ignition coil assembly.

4. Remove the 4 retaining screws and remove the ignition coil.

5. Installation is the reverse of the removal procedure.

3.8L SC ENGINE

1. Disconnect the negative battery cable.

2. Disconnect the electrical harness connector from the coil pack.

3. Remove the spark plug wires by squeezing the locking tabs to release the coil boot retainers.

4. Remove the coil pack retaining screws and remove the coil pack.

5. Installation is the reverse of the removal procedure. Tighten the screws to 40–62 inch lbs. (4.5–7.0 Nm).

Ignition Timing

ADJUSTMENT

NOTE: Always refer to the Vehicle Emission Information Label to verify the timing adjustment procedure.

Distributorless Ignition Systems

Base timing for distributorless engines

is set from the factory at 10 degrees BTDC and is not adjustable.

Distributor Ignition System

1. Locate the timing marks and pointer on the crankshaft pulley and the timing cover. Clean the marks so they will be visible with a timing light. Apply chalk or bright-colored paint, if necessary.

2. Place the transaxle in **P** or **N**. The air conditioning and heater controls should be in the **OFF** position.

3. Connect a suitable tachometer and inductive timing light according to the manufacturer's instructions.

NOTE: The tachometer can be connected to the ignition coil without removing the coil connector. Insert an alligator clip into the back of the connector, onto the dark green/yellow dotted wire. Do not let the clip accidently ground to a metal surface as it may permanently damage the coil.

4. Disconnect the single wire in-line SPOUT connector or remove the shorting bar from the double wire SPOUT connector.

5. Start the engine and allow it to warm up to operating temperature.

NOTE: To set timing correctly, a remote starter should not be used. Use the ignition key only to start the vehicle. Disconnecting the start wire at the starter relay will cause the TFI module to revert to start mode timing after the vehicle is started. Reconnecting the start wire after the vehicle is running will not correct the timing.

6. With the engine at the timing rpm specified, check the initial timing by aiming the timing light at the timing marks and pointer. Refer to the underhood Vehicle Emission Information Label for specifications.

7. If the marks align, shut OFF the engine and proceed to Step 8. If the marks do not align, shut OFF the engine and loosen the distributor hold-down clamp bolt. Start the engine, aim the timing light and turn the distributor until the timing marks align. Shut OFF the engine and tighten the distributor hold-down clamp bolt. Recheck the timing after the bolt has been tightened.

8. Reconnect the single wire in-line SPOUT connector or reinstall the shorting bar on the double wire SPOUT connector. Check the timing advance to verify the distributor is advancing beyond the initial setting.

9. Remove the inductive timing light and tachometer.

Alternator
PRECAUTIONS

Several precautions must be observed with alternator equipped vehicles to avoid damage to the unit.

• If the battery is removed for any reason, make sure it is reconnected with the correct polarity. Reversing the battery connections may result in damage to the one-way rectifiers.

• When utilizing a booster battery as a starting aid, always connect the positive to positive terminals and the negative terminal from the booster battery to a good engine ground on the vehicle being started.

• Never use a fast charger as a booster to start vehicles.

• Disconnect the battery cables when charging the battery with a fast charger.

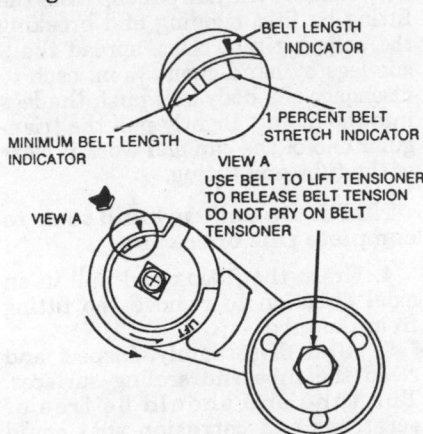

Belt tensioner—3.8L and 5.0L engines

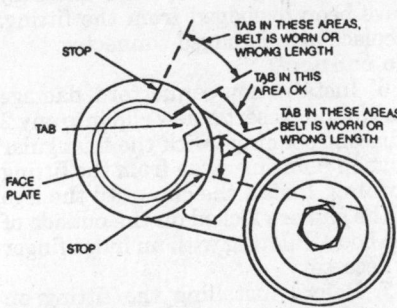

Belt replacement checking—3.8L and 5.0L engines

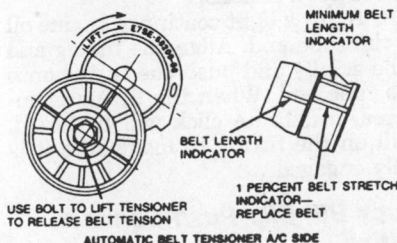

• Never attempt to polarize the alternator.

• Do not use test lamps of more than 12V when checking diode continuity.

• Do not short across or ground any of the alternator terminals.

• The polarity of the battery, alternator and regulator must be matched and considered before making any electrical connections within the system.

• Never separate the alternator on an open circuit. Make sure all connections within the circuit are clean and tight.

• Disconnect the battery ground terminal when performing any service on electrical components.

• Disconnect the battery if arc welding is to be done on the vehicle.

BELT TENSION ADJUSTMENT

All vehicles are equipped with an automatic belt tensioner. No adjustment is necessary or possible. The belt tensioner is equipped with a belt wear indicator; when 1 percent belt stretch is indicated, the drive belt must be replaced. If the wear indicator is difficult to see on the 3.8L or 5.0L engines, locate the tab on the tensioner face plate. The tab should be approximately between the stops.

REMOVAL & INSTALLATION

1. Disconnect the negative battery cable.
2. Tag and disconnect the wiring connectors from the rear of the alternator.
3. Loosen the alternator pivot bolt and remove the adjusting bolt. Disengage the drive belt from the alternator pulley.
4. Remove the alternator pivot bolt and the alternator.
5. Installation is the reverse of the removal procedure.

Voltage Regulator
REMOVAL & INSTALLATION

1. Disconnect the negative battery cable.
2. Disconnect the wire connectors, remove the regulator mounting screws and remove the regulator.

NOTE: Always disconnect the connector plug from the regulator before removing the mounting screws.

3. Installation is the reverse of the removal procedure.

Starter
REMOVAL & INSTALLATION

1. Disconnect the negative battery cable.
2. Raise the vehicle and support it safely.
3. Disconnect the starter cable from the starter. If equipped with starter mounted solenoid, disconnect the push-on connector from the solenoid.

NOTE: To disconnect the hardshell connector from the solenoid S terminal, grasp the plastic shell and pull off; do not pull on the wire. Pull straight off to prevent damage to the connector and S terminal.

4. Remove the starter bolts and the starter.
5. Position the starter to the engine and tighten the mounting bolts to 15–20 ft. lbs. (20–27 Nm).
6. Reconnect the starter cable and, if equipped, solenoid wire. Connect the negative battery cable.

EMISSION CONTROLS

Due to the complex nature of modern electronic engine control systems, comprehensive diagnosis and testing procedures fall outside the confines of this repair manual. For complete information on diagnosis, testing and repair procedures concerning all modern engine and emission control systems, please refer to "Chilton's Guide to Fuel Injection and Electronic Engine Controls".

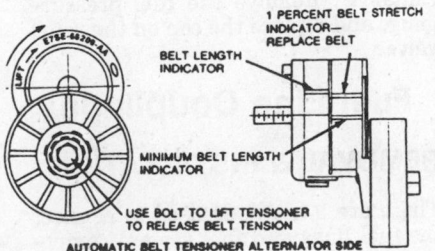

Belt wear indicator marks—2.3L engine

Emission Warning Lamps

RESETTING

These vehicles have a CHECK ENGINE lamp that will light when there is a fault in the engine control system. This light cannot be reset without diagnosing the fault in the system. When the system has been diagnosed and the problem corrected, the light will go out.

Service Lamp

Thunderbird and Cougar

The optional Vehicle Maintenance Monitor (VMM) alerts the vehicle operator to when engine oil needs to be changed and when fuel, oil, coolant and washer fluids are low. To reset the VMM after an oil change, proceed as follows:

1. Turn the ignition key **OFF**, then turn it **ON**, but do not start the engine.
2. Within 16 seconds of turning the key to **ON**, stick a straightened paperclip into the reset switch hole and firmly push in the switch. The left side of the display will now flash.

NOTE: The reset switch is very small and is located to the left of the word "OK" on the VMM panel.

3. Keep pushing down on the reset switch with the paperclip until the left side of the display stops flashing. The VMM is now reset. Do not stop pushing in the switch until the display stops flashing, or the VMM will not be reset.

FUEL SYSTEM

Fuel System Service Precautions

Safety is the most important factor when performing not only fuel system maintenance but any type of maintenance. Failure to conduct maintenance and repairs in a safe manner may result in serious personal injury or death. Maintenance and testing of the vehicle's fuel system components can be accomplished safely and effectively by adhering to the following rules and guidelines.

• To avoid the possibility of fire and personal injury, always disconnect the negative battery cable unless the repair or test procedure requires that battery voltage be applied.

• Always relieve the fuel system pressure prior to disconnecting any fuel system component (injector, fuel rail, pressure regulator, etc.), fitting or fuel line connection. Exercise extreme caution whenever relieving fuel system pressure to avoid exposing skin, face and eyes to fuel spray. Please be advised that fuel under pressure may penetrate the skin or any part of the body that it contacts.

• Always place a shop towel or cloth around the fitting or connection prior to loosening to absorb any excess fuel due to spillage. Ensure that all fuel spillage (should it occur) is quickly removed from engine surfaces. Ensure that all fuel soaked cloths or towels are deposited into a suitable waste container.

• Always keep a dry chemical (Class B) fire extinguisher near the work area.

• Do not allow fuel spray or fuel vapors to come into contact with a spark or open flame.

• Always use a backup wrench when loosening and tightening fuel line connection fittings. This will prevent unnecessary stress and torsion to fuel line piping. Always follow the proper torque specifications.

• Always replace worn fuel fitting O-rings with new. Do not substitute fuel hose or equivalent where fuel pipe is installed.

RELIEVING FUEL SYSTEM PRESSURE

Fuel supply lines on all fuel injected engines will remain pressurized for some period of time after the engine is shut OFF. This pressure must be relieved before servicing the fuel system. Pressure is relieved through the fuel pressure relief valve.

To relieve the fuel system pressure, first remove the fuel tank cap to relieve pressure in the tank, then remove the cap on the fuel pressure relief valve, located on the fuel rail. Attach fuel pressure gauge T80L–9974–A or equivalent, and drain the system through the drain tube into a suitable container. Remove the fuel pressure gauge and replace the cap on the relief valve.

Fuel Line Couplings

REMOVAL & INSTALLATION

There are 3 methods used to connect the fuel lines and fuel system components, the hairpin clip push connect fitting, the duck bill clip push connect fitting and the spring lock coupling. Each requires a different procedure to disconnect and connect.

Hairpin Clip Push Connect Fitting

1. Inspect the visible internal portion of the fitting for dirt accumulation. If more than a light coating of dust is present, clean the fitting before disassembly.
2. Some adhesion between the seals in the fitting and the tubing will occur with time. To separate, twist the fitting on the tube, then push and pull the fitting until it moves freely on the tube.

NOTE: Use care when separating 90 degree elbow connectors, as excessive side loading could break the connector body.

3. Remove the hairpin clip from the fitting by first bending and breaking the shipping tab. Next, spread the 2 clip legs by hand about ⅛ in. each to disengage the body and push the legs into the fitting. Lightly pull the triangular end of the clip and work it clear of the tube and fitting.

NOTE: Do not use hand tools to complete this operation.

4. Grasp the fitting and pull in an axial direction to remove the fitting from the tube.
5. After disassembly, inspect and clean the tube end sealing surfaces. The tube end should be free of scratches and corrosion that could provide leak paths. Inspect the inside of the fitting for any internal parts such as O-rings and spacers that may have been dislodged from the fitting. Replace any damaged connector.

To connect:

6. Install a new connector if damage was found. Insert a new clip into any 2 adjacent openings with the triangular portion pointing away from the fitting opening. Install the clip until the legs of the clip are locked on the outside of the body. Piloting with an index finger is necessary.
7. Before installing the fitting on the tube, wipe the tube end with a clean cloth. Inspect the inside of the fitting to make sure it is free of dirt and/or obstructions.
8. Apply a light coating of engine oil to the tube end. Align the fitting and tube axially and push the fitting onto the tube end. When the fitting is engaged, a definite click will be heard. Pull on the fitting to make sure it is fully engaged.

Duck Bill Clip Push Connect Fitting

1. Inspect the visible internal por-

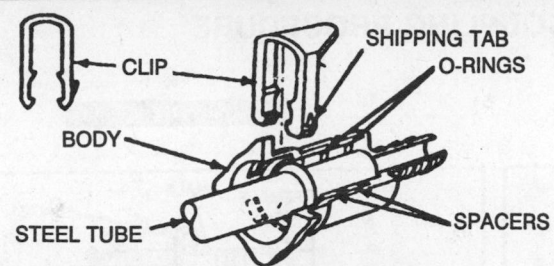

CLIP — BODY — STEEL TUBE — SHIPPING TAB — O-RINGS — SPACERS

Hairpin clip push connect fitting

tion of the fitting for dirt accumulation. If more than a light coating of dust is present, clean the fitting before disassembly.

2. Some adhesion between the seals in the fitting and the tubing will occur with time. To separate, twist the fitting on the tube, then push and pull the fitting until it moves freely on the tube.

3. Align the slot on push connect disassembly tool T82L–9500–AH or equivalent, with either tab on the clip, 90 degrees from the slots on the side of the fitting and insert the tool. This disengages the duck bill retainer from the tube.

4. Holding the tool and the tube with 1 hand, pull the fitting away from the tube.

NOTE: Use hands only. Only moderate effort is required if the tube has been properly disengaged.

5. After disassembly, inspect and clean the tube end sealing surfaces. The tube end should be free of scratches and corrosion that could provide leak paths. Inspect the inside of the fitting for any internal parts such as O-rings and spacers that may have been dislodged from the fitting. Replace any damaged connector.

6. Some fuel tubes have a secondary bead which aligns with the outer surface of the clip. These beads can make tool insertion difficult. If there is extreme difficulty, use the following disassembly method:

a. Using pliers with a jaw width of 0.2 in. (5mm) or less, align the jaws with the openings in the side of the fitting case and compress the portion of the retaining clip that engages the fitting case. This disengages the retaining clip from the case. Often 1 side of the clip will disengage before the other. The clip must be disengaged from both openings.

b. Pull the fitting off the tube by hand only. Only moderate effort is required if the retaining clip has been properly disengaged.

c. After disassembly, inspect and clean the tube end sealing surfaces. The tube end should be free of

scratches and corrosion that could provide leak paths. Inspect the inside of the fitting for any internal parts such as O-rings and spacers that may have been dislodged from the fitting. Replace any damaged connector.

d. The retaining clip will remain on the tube. Disengage the clip from the tube bead and remove.

To connect:

7. Install a new connector if damage was found. Install the new replacement clip into the body by inserting 1 of the retaining clip serrated edges on the duck bill portion into 1 side of the window openings. Push on the other side until the clip snaps into place.

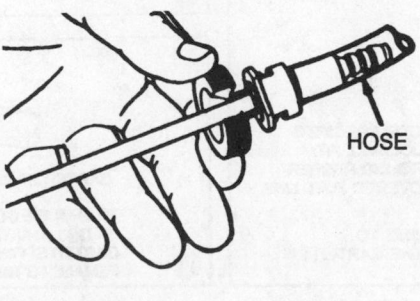

HOSE

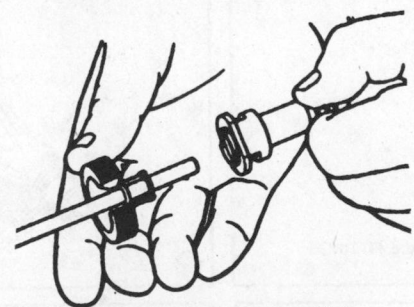

Duck bill clip push connect fitting disconnect tool

8. Before installing the fitting on the tube, wipe the tube end with a clean cloth. Inspect the inside of the fitting to make sure it is free of dirt and/or obstructions.

9. Apply a light coating of engine oil to the tube end. Align the fitting and tube axially and push the fitting onto the tube end. When the fitting is engaged, a definite click will be heard. Pull on the fitting to make sure it is fully engaged.

Spring Lock Coupling

The spring lock coupling is a fuel line coupling held together by a garter spring inside a circular cage. When the coupling is connected together, the flared end of the female fitting slips behind the garter spring inside the cage of the male fitting. The garter spring and cage then prevent the flared end of the female fitting from pulling out of the cage. As an additional locking feature, most vehicles have a horseshoe shaped retaining clip that improves the retaining reliability of the spring lock coupling.

Fuel Tank
REMOVAL & INSTALLATION

1. Disconnect the negative battery cable and relieve the fuel system pressure.

2. Siphon or pump as much fuel as possible out through the fuel filler pipe.

NOTE: All vehicles have reservoirs inside the fuel tank to maintain fuel near the fuel pickup during cornering and under low fuel operating conditions. These reservoirs could block siphon tubes or hoses from reaching the bottom of the fuel tank. Repeated attempts using different hose orientations can overcome this obstacle.

3. Raise and safely support the vehicle.

4. On Thunderbird and Cougar, remove the exhaust pipe and exhaust shield. Disconnect the fuel fill and vent hoses connecting the filler pipe to the tank. Disconnect 1 end of the vapor

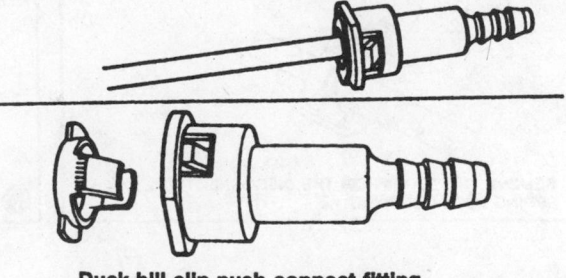

Duck bill clip push connect fitting

SPRING LOCK COUPLING PROCEDURE

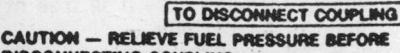

TO DISCONNECT COUPLING

CAUTION — RELIEVE FUEL PRESSURE BEFORE DISCONNECTING COUPLING

CLIP

① REMOVE CLIP FROM COUPLING

USE SPECIFIED TOOL OR EQUIVALENT

TOOL:
— 3/8 INCH
— 1/2 INCH

CAGE OPENING

② FIT TOOL TO COUPLING SO THAT TOOL CAN ENTER CAGE OPENING TO RELEASE THE GARTER SPRING.

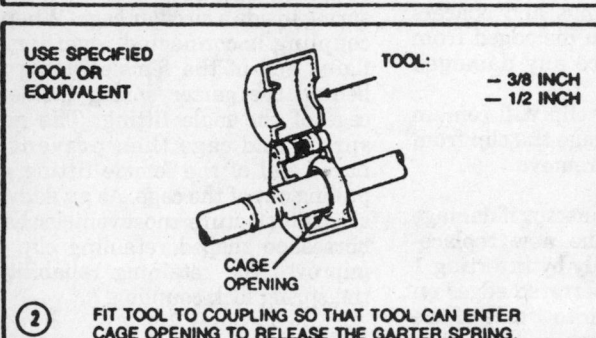

PUSH TOOL INTO CAGE OPENING

NOTE: SPECIFIED TOOL WILL FIT AROUND RUBBER COVERED FUEL LINE.

PUSH THE TOOL INTO THE CAGE OPENING TO RELEASE THE FEMALE FITTING FROM THE GARTER SPRING

③

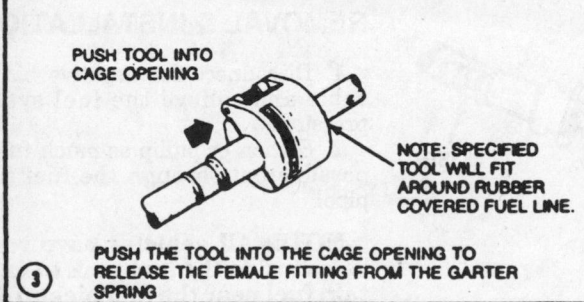

④ PULL THE COUPLING MALE AND FEMALE FITTINGS APART

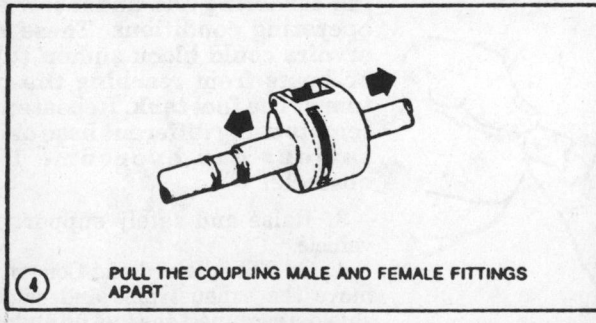

⑤ REMOVE THE TOOL FROM THE DISCONNECTED SPRING LOCK COUPLING

TO CONNECT COUPLING

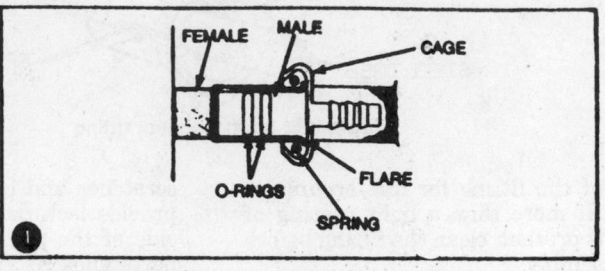

FEMALE   MALE   CAGE

O-RINGS   FLARE   SPRING

①

REPLACEMENT O-RINGS (3/8 INCH DIA., 2 PER FITTING) (1/2 INCH DIA., 2 PER FITTING)

USE ONLY SPECIFIED FUEL RESISTANT O-RINGS (COLOR: BROWN)

CHECK FOR CORROSION

LUBRICATE O-RINGS WITH CLEAN ENGINE OIL

CLEAN FITTINGS WITH SOLVENT. CHECK FOR MISSING OR DAMAGED O-RINGS. REPLACE MISSING O-RINGS. IF EITHER O-RING IS DAMAGED, REPLACE BOTH O-RINGS.
REPLACEMENT GARTER SPRINGS:
3/8-INCH —
1/2-INCH —

②

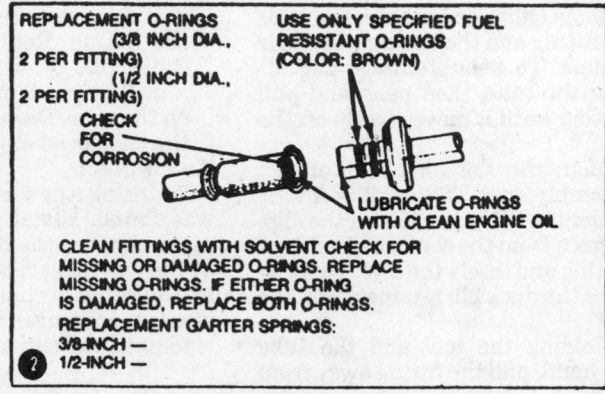

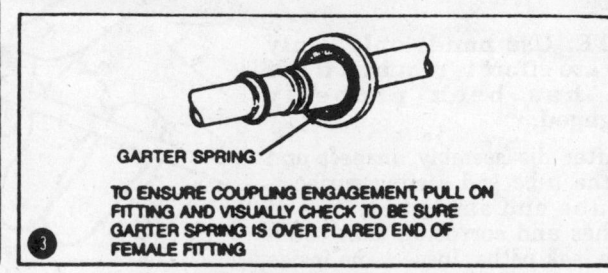

GARTER SPRING

TO ENSURE COUPLING ENGAGEMENT, PULL ON FITTING AND VISUALLY CHECK TO BE SURE GARTER SPRING IS OVER FLARED END OF FEMALE FITTING

③

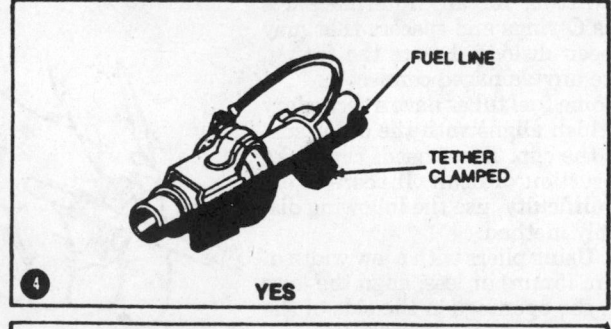

FUEL LINE

TETHER CLAMPED

④ YES

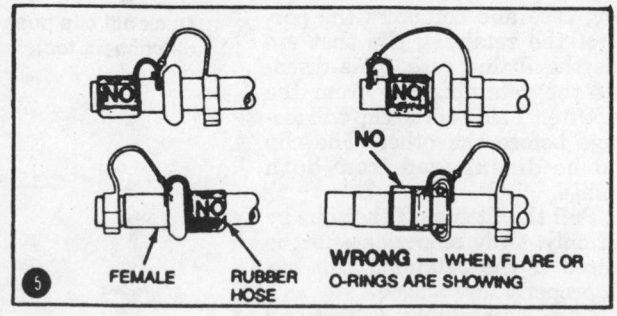

NO   NO

NO

FEMALE   RUBBER HOSE

WRONG — WHEN FLARE OR O-RINGS ARE SHOWING

⑤

crossover hose at the rear over the driveshaft.

5. If equipped with a metal retainer that fastens the filler pipe to the fuel tank, remove the screw attaching the retainer to the fuel tank flange.

6. Disconnect the fuel lines and the electrical connector to the fuel tank sending unit. On some vehicles, these are inaccessible on top of the tank. In these cases they must be disconnected with the tank partially removed.

7. Place a safety support under the fuel tank and remove the bolts from the fuel tank straps. Allow the straps to swing out of the way. Be careful not to deform the fuel tank.

8. Partially remove the tank and disconnect the fuel lines and electrical connector from the sending unit, if required.

9. Remove the tank from the vehicle.

To install:

10. Raise the fuel tank into position in the vehicle. Connect the fuel lines and sending unit electrical connector if it is necessary to connect them before the tank is in the final installed position.

11. Lubricate the fuel filler pipe with water base tire mounting lubricant and install the tank onto the filler pipe, then bring the tank into final position. Be careful not to deform the tank.

12. Bring the fuel tank straps around the tank and start the retaining nut or bolt. Align the tank with the straps. If equipped, make sure the fuel tank shields are installed with the straps and are positioned correctly on the tank. On Thunderbird and Cougar, align the tank with the driveshaft.

13. Check the hoses and wiring mounted on the tank top to make sure they are correctly routed and will not be pinched between the tank and body. On Thunderbird and Cougar, make sure the fuel vent hose is positioned above the vent retainer and not contacting the driveshaft.

14. Tighten the fuel tank strap retaining nuts or bolts to 22–30 ft. lbs. (29–41 Nm).

15. If not already connected, connect the fuel hoses and lines which were disconnected. Make sure the fuel supply, fuel return, if present, and vapor vent connections are made correctly. If not already connected, connect the sending unit electrical connector.

16. On Thunderbird and Cougar, install the exhaust pipe shield and exhaust pipe.

17. Lower the vehicle. Replace the fuel that was drained from the tank. Check all connections for leaks.

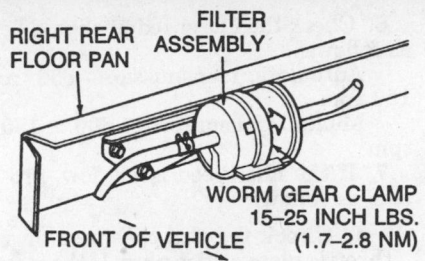

In-line fuel filter location

Fuel Filter

REMOVAL & INSTALLATION

1. Disconnect the negative battery cable and relieve the fuel system pressure.

2. Raise and safely support the vehicle.

3. Remove the push connect fittings at both ends of the filter. Install new retainer clips in each push connect fitting.

4. Remove the fuel filter from the bracket by loosening the worm gear clamp. Note the direction of the flow arrow as installed in the bracket to ensure proper direction of fuel flow through the replacement filter.

To install:

5. Install the fuel filter into the bracket, ensuring the proper direction of flow. Tighten the worm gear clamp to 15–25 inch lbs. (1.7–2.8 Nm).

6. Install the push connect fittings onto the filter ends. Start the engine and check for leaks.

7. Lower the vehicle.

Electric Fuel Pump

PRESSURE TESTING

1. Relieve the fuel system pressure and connect a fuel pressure gauge to the valve on the fuel rail.

2. Ground the fuel pump lead of the self-test connector through a jumper wire at the **FP** lead.

3. Turn the ignition key to the **RUN** position to operate the fuel pump.

4. Observe the fuel pressure gauge. The indicated pressure should be 35–40 psi.

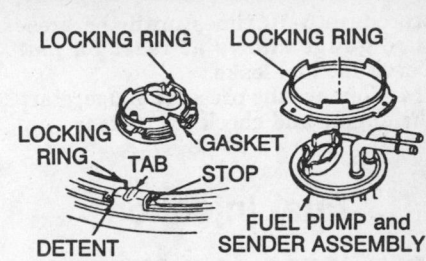

Electric fuel pump installation

5. Remove the fuel pressure gauge and the jumper wire.

REMOVAL & INSTALLATION

1. Disconnect the negative battery cable and relieve the fuel system pressure.

2. Remove the fuel tank and place it on a bench.

3. Remove any dirt that has accumulated around the fuel pump retaining flange so it will not enter the tank during pump removal and installation.

4. Turn the fuel pump locking ring counterclockwise and remove the locking ring.

5. Remove the fuel pump and bracket assembly. Remove and discard the seal ring.

To install:

6. Clean the fuel pump mounting flange, fuel tank mounting surface and seal ring groove.

7. Apply a light coating of grease on a new seal ring to hold it in place during assembly and install in the seal ring groove.

8. Install the fuel pump and bracket assembly carefully to ensure the filter is not damaged. Make sure the locating keys are in the keyways and the seal ring remains in the groove.

9. Hold the pump assembly in place and install the locking ring finger-tight. Make sure all the locking tabs are under the tank lock ring tabs.

10. Rotate the locking ring clockwise until the ring is against the stops.

11. Install the fuel tank in the vehicle. Add a minimum of 10 gallons of fuel to the tank and check for leaks.

12. Install a suitable fuel pressure gauge to the valve on the fuel rail.

13. Turn the ignition switch from **OFF** to **ON** for 3 seconds. Repeat this

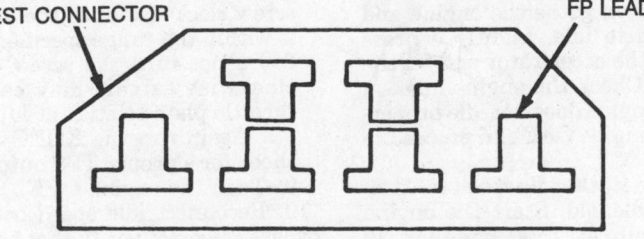

Self-test connector terminal location

procedure 5–10 times until the pressure gauge shows at least 35 psi. Check for fuel leaks.

14. Remove the pressure gauge, start the engine and check for leaks.

Fuel Injection

IDLE SPEED ADJUSTMENT

2.3L Engine

1989–90

1. Place the transmission in **N** or **P**. Apply the parking brake.

2. Bring the engine to normal operating temperature. Place the air conditioner/heater selector to the **OFF** position. Check and, if necessary, adjust the ignition timing.

3. Disconnect the negative battery terminal for 5 minutes, then reconnect. Start the engine and stabilize for 2 minutes, then goose the engine and let it return to idle. Lightly depress and release the accelerator and let the engine idle. Check the engine idle.

4. If the engine does not idle properly, shut the engine OFF and proceed to Step 5.

5. Disconnect the idle speed control-air bypass solenoid. Start the engine and let it run at 1500 rpm for 30 seconds.

6. Turn the throttle plate stop screw and set the idle speed to the following specification:

Automatic transmission – 650 ± 25 rpm

Manual transmission – 600 ± 25 rpm

7. Shut OFF the engine and reconnect the idle speed control-air bypass solenoid. Make sure the throttle is not stuck in the bore and the linkage is not preventing the throttle from closing.

1991

1. Place the transmission in **N** or **P**. Apply the parking brake.

2. Bring the engine to normal operating temperature. Place the air conditioner/heater selector to the **OFF** position. Check and, if necessary, adjust the ignition timing.

3. Disconnect the negative battery terminal for 5 minutes, then reconnect. Start the engine and stabilize for 2 minutes, then goose the engine and let it return to idle. Lightly depress and release the accelerator and let the engine idle. Check the engine idle.

4. If the engine does not idle properly, shut the engine OFF and proceed to Step 5.

5. Disconnect the idle speed control-air bypass solenoid. Start the engine and let it run at 1500 rpm for 30 seconds.

6. Check the idle speed; it should be as follows:

Automatic transmission – 650 ± 150 rpm

Manual transmission – 600 ± 150 rpm

7. If the idle speed is too low, proceed as follows:

a. Check for the presence of a throttle plate orifice plug. If there is no plug, turn the screw clockwise to the desired rpm, ± 25 rpm.

b. If there is a plug from previous service, remove the plug and adjust the screw in either direction, as required. The screw must be in contact with the lever pad after adjustment.

8. If the idle speed is too high, proceed as follows:

a. Turn the engine **OFF** and disconnect the air cleaner hose.

b. Block off the orifice in the throttle plate temporarily with tape. If the orifice already has a plug from previous service, proceed to Step d.

c. Restart the engine and check the idle speed. Mass air engines will require the air cleaner hose to be reattached before the idle speed check. If the engine stalled, crack open the throttle plate with the stop screw. Do not over adjust.

d. If the idle speed continues to be fast, connect a suitable scan tool to the Self-Test connector and perform the Key On Engine Off (KOEO) Self-Test. Check for a Throttle Position Sensor (TPS) output code.

e. If the output code is within range, remove the tape and check for vacuum leaks, throttle linkage binding, or other causes for excessive high idle.

f. If the output code is out of range, adjust the throttle screw to obtain the proper code. The lever pad must be in contact with the screw after adjustment.

g. If the idle speed drops to within the range specified in Step 6 or below, or the engine stalls, turn the engine **OFF**, disconnect the air cleaner hose and remove the tape. Install the proper plug in the throttle plate orifice.

h. Connect the air cleaner hose and start the engine. Check the idle speed. Turn the throttle plate stop screw clockwise until the idle speed is within the range specified in Step 6. Do not turn the screw counterclockwise as this may cause the throttle plate to stick at idle.

i. Again run the KOEO test and check for a proper TPS output code.

9. Turn the engine **OFF**.

10. Reconnect idle speed control-air bypass solenoid, verify that the throttle is not stuck in the bore and linkage is not preventing the throttle from closing.

11. Start engine and let stabilize for 2 minutes, then quickly open throttle and let return to idle, lightly depress and release accelerator. Check idle speed.

1992–93

1. Connect the SUPER STAR II tester, tool number 007–00028 or other suitable scan tool to the Self-Test connector. Activate the Key On Engine Running (KOER) Self-Test.

2. After Code 1 or 111 has been displayed, unlatch and within 4 seconds, latch the STI button.

3. A single pulse code indicates the entry mode, then observe the Self-Test Ouput (STO) on the tester for the following:

a. A constant tone, solid light or **STO LO** readout means the base idle speed is within the correct range. To exit the test, unlatch the STI button, then wait 4 seconds for reinitialization. After 10 minutes, the tool will exit by itself.

b. A beeping tone, flashing light or **STO LO** readout at 8 Hz indicates the Throttle Position Sensor (TPS) is out of range due to over adjustment. Adjustment may be required.

c. A beeping tone, flashing light or **STO LO** readout at 4 Hz indicates the base idle speed is too fast and adjustment is required. Proceed to Step 5.

d. A beeping tone, flashing light or **STO LO** readout at 1 Hz indicates the base idle speed is too low and adjustment is required. Proceed to Step 4.

4. If the idle speed is too low, check for the presence of a throttle plate orifice plug. If there is no plug, turn the throttle screw clockwise until the conditions in Step 3a exist. If there is a plug from previous service, remove the plug and then adjust the screw in either direction, as required. The screw must be in contact with the lever pad after adjustment.

5. If the idle speed is too high, proceed as follows:

a. Turn the engine **OFF**.

b. Block off the orifice in the throttle plate temporarily with tape. If the orifice already has a plug, proceed to Step d.

c. Reattach the air intake hose. Restart the engine and check the idle speed using the Self-Test. If the engine stalled, crack open the plate with the throttle return screw.

d. If the idle speed continues to be fast, run the Key On Engine Off (KOEO) Self-Test and check for a TPS output code.

e. If the output code is within

range, remove the tape and check for vacuum leaks, throttle linkage binding, or other causes for excessive high idle.

f. If the output code is out of range, adjust the throttle screw to obtain the proper code. The lever pad must be in contact with the screw after adjustment.

g. If the idle speed drops to or below the desired level, as indicated by the Self-Test Output tone, turn the engine **OFF**, disconnect the air cleaner hose and remove the tape.

h. Install the proper plug in the throttle plate orifice.

i. Reconnect the air cleaner hose. Start the engine and turn the throttle plate stop screw clockwise until the conditions in Step 3a exist. Do not turn the screw counterclockwise as this may cause the throttle plate to stick at idle.

6. Run the KOEO Self-Test for proper TPS output code.

7. Make sure the throttle is not stuck in the bore and the linkage is not preventing the throttle from closing.

3.8L Engine, Except SC

1989–90

1. Place the transmission in **N** or **P**. Apply the emergency brake and block the wheels. If equipped with automatic brake release, disconnect the vacuum hose and plug it.

2. Bring the engine to normal operating temperature. Place the air conditioner/heater selector to the **OFF** position. Check and, if necessary, adjust the ignition timing.

3. Disconnect the negative battery terminal for 5 minutes, then reconnect. Start the engine and stabilize for 2 minutes, then goose the engine and let it return to idle. Lightly depress and release the accelerator and let the engine idle. Check the engine idle.

4. If the engine does not idle properly, shut the engine OFF and proceed to Step 5.

5. Back out the throttle plate stop screw clear off the throttle lever pad. With a 0.010 in. feeler gauge between the throttle plate stop screw and the throttle lever pad, turn the screw in until contact is made, then turn an additional 1½ turns.

6. Start the engine and stabilize for 2 minutes, then goose the engine and let it return to idle. Lightly depress and release the accelerator and let the engine idle.

1991–93

1. Place the transaxle in **P** and apply the parking brake.

2. Start the engine and bring to normal operating temperature. Make sure

the heater, air conditioning and all other accessories are OFF.

3. Check and if necessary, adjust the ignition timing.

4. Make sure the fuel pressure is correct. Any indicated vehicle malfunction service codes should be resolved before proceeding further.

5. Connect the SUPER STAR II tester, tool number 007–00028 or other suitable scan tool to the Self-Test connector. Activate the Key On Engine Running (KOER) Self-Test.

6. After Code 1 or 111 has been displayed, unlatch and within 4 seconds, latch the STI button.

7. A single pulse code indicates the entry mode, then observe the Self-Test Ouput (STO) on the tester for the following:

a. A constant tone, solid light or **STO LO** readout means the base idle speed is within the correct range. To exit the test, unlatch the STI button, then wait 4 seconds for reinitialization. After 10 minutes, the tool will exit by itself.

b. A beeping tone, flashing light or **STO LO** readout at 8 Hz indicates the Throttle Position Sensor (TPS) is out of range due to over adjustment. Adjustment may be required.

c. A beeping tone, flashing light or **STO LO** readout at 4 Hz indicates the base idle speed is too fast and adjustment is required. Proceed to Step 9.

d. A beeping tone, flashing light or **STO LO** readout at 1 Hz indicates the base idle speed is too low and adjustment is required. Proceed to Step 8.

8. If the idle speed is too low, check for the presence of a throttle plate orifice plug. If there is no plug, turn the throttle screw clockwise until the conditions in Step 7a exist. If there is a plug from previous service, remove the plug and then adjust the screw in either direction, as required. The screw must be in contact with the lever pad after adjustment.

9. If the idle speed is too high, proceed as follows:

a. Turn the engine **OFF**.

b. Block off the orifice in the throttle plate temporarily with tape. If the orifice already has a plug, proceed to Step d.

c. Reattach the air intake hose. Restart the engine and check the idle speed using the Self-Test. If the engine stalled, crack open the plate with the throttle return screw.

d. If the idle speed continues to be fast, run the Key On Engine Off (KOEO) Self-Test and check for a TPS output code.

e. If the output code is within range, remove the tape and check

for vacuum leaks, throttle linkage binding, or other causes for excessive high idle.

f. If the output code is out of range, adjust the throttle screw to obtain the proper code. The lever pad must be in contact with the screw after adjustment.

g. If the idle speed drops to or below the desired level, as indicated by the Self-Test Output tone, turn the engine **OFF**, disconnect the air cleaner hose and remove the tape.

h. Install the proper plug in the throttle plate orifice.

i. Reconnect the air cleaner hose. Start the engine and turn the throttle plate stop screw clockwise until the conditions in Step 7a exist. Do not turn the screw counterclockwise as this may cause the throttle plate to stick at idle.

10. Run the KOEO Self-Test for proper TPS output code.

11. Make sure the throttle is not stuck in the bore and the linkage is not preventing the throttle from closing.

12. Check the Throttle Valve (TV) pressure adjustment.

3.8L SC Engine

1989–90

1. Place the transmission in **N** or **P**. Apply the emergency brake and block the wheels. If equipped with automatic brake release, disconnect the vacuum hose and plug it.

2. Bring the engine to normal operating temperature. Place the air conditioner/heater selector to the **OFF** position. Check and, if necessary, adjust the ignition timing.

3. Disconnect the negative battery terminal for 5 minutes, then reconnect. Start the engine and stabilize for 2 minutes, then goose the engine and let it return to idle. Lightly depress and release the accelerator and let the engine idle. Check the engine idle.

4. If the engine does not idle properly, shut the engine OFF and proceed to Step 5.

5. Back out the throttle plate stop screw clear off the throttle lever pad. With a 0.010 in. feeler gauge between the throttle plate stop screw and the throttle lever pad, turn the screw in until contact is made, then turn an additional 1½ turns.

6. Start the engine and stabilize for 2 minutes, then goose the engine and let it return to idle. Lightly depress and release the accelerator and let the engine idle.

1991–93

1. Place the transaxle in **P** and apply the parking brake.

2. Start the engine and bring to normal operating temperature. Make sure

the heater, air conditioning and all other accessories are OFF.

3. Check and if necessary, adjust the ignition timing.

4. Make sure the fuel pressure is correct. Any indicated vehicle malfunction service codes should be resolved before proceeding further.

5. Connect the SUPER STAR II tester, tool number 007-00028 or other suitable scan tool to the Self-Test connector. Activate the Key On Engine Running (KOER) Self-Test.

6. After Code 1 or 111 has been displayed, unlatch and within 4 seconds, latch the STI button.

7. A single pulse code indicates the entry mode, then observe the Self-Test Ouput (STO) on the tester for the following:

a. A constant tone, solid light or **STO LO** readout means the base idle speed is within the correct range. To exit the test, unlatch the STI button, then wait 4 seconds for reinitialization. After 10 minutes, the tool will exit by itself.

b. A beeping tone, flashing light or **STO LO** readout at 8 Hz indicates the Throttle Position Sensor (TPS) is out of range due to over adjustment. Adjustment may be required.

c. A beeping tone, flashing light or **STO LO** readout at 4 Hz indicates the base idle speed is too fast and adjustment is required. Proceed to Step 9.

d. A beeping tone, flashing light or **STO LO** readout at 1 Hz indicates the base idle speed is too low and adjustment is required. Proceed to Step 8.

8. If the idle speed is too low, do not clean the throttle body. Turn the air trim screw counterclockwise until the conditions in Step 7a are satisfied.

9. If the idle speed is too high, do not clean the throttle body. Turn the air trim screw clockwise until the conditions in Step 7a are satisfied.

5.0L Engine

1989–90

1. Place the transmission in **N** or **P**. Apply the emergency brake and block the wheels. If equipped with automatic brake release, disconnect the vacuum hose and plug it.

2. Bring the engine to normal operating temperature. Place the air conditioner/heater selector to the **OFF** position. Check and, if necessary, adjust the ignition timing.

3. Disconnect the negative battery terminal for 5 minutes, then reconnect. Start the engine and stabilize for 2 minutes, then goose the engine and let it return to idle. Lightly depress

and release the accelerator and let the engine idle. Check the engine idle.

4. If the engine does not idle properly, shut the engine OFF and proceed to Step 5.

5. Back out the throttle plate stop screw clear off the throttle lever pad. With a 0.010 in. feeler gauge between the throttle plate stop screw and the throttle lever pad, turn the screw in until contact is made, then turn an additional 1½ turns on the HO engine or 1⅞ turns on the non-HO engine.

6. Start the engine and stabilize for 2 minutes, then goose the engine and let it return to idle. Lightly depress and release the accelerator and let the engine idle.

1991–93 THUNDERBIRD AND COUGAR

1. Place the transaxle in **P** and apply the parking brake.

2. Start the engine and bring to normal operating temperature. Make sure the heater, air conditioning and all other accessories are OFF.

3. Check and if necessary, adjust the ignition timing.

4. Make sure the fuel pressure is correct. Any indicated vehicle malfunction service codes should be resolved before proceeding further.

5. Connect the SUPER STAR II tester tool 007-00028 or other suitable scan tool, to the Self-Test connector. Activate the Key On Engine Running (KOER) Self-Test.

6. After Code 1 or 111 has been displayed, unlatch and within 4 seconds, latch the STI button.

7. A single pulse code indicates the entry mode, then observe the Self-Test Ouput (STO) on the tester for the following:

a. A constant tone, solid light or **STO LO** readout means the base idle speed is within the correct range. To exit the test, unlatch the STI button, then wait 4 seconds for reinitialization. After 10 minutes, the tool will exit by itself.

b. A beeping tone, flashing light or **STO LO** readout at 8 Hz indicates the Throttle Position Sensor (TPS) is out of range due to over adjustment. Adjustment may be required.

c. A beeping tone, flashing light or **STO LO** readout at 4 Hz indicates the base idle speed is too fast and adjustment is required. Proceed to Step 9.

d. A beeping tone, flashing light or **STO LO** readout at 1 Hz indicates the base idle speed is too low and adjustment is required. Proceed to Step 8.

8. If the idle speed is too low, do not clean the throttle body. Turn the air

trim screw counterclockwise until the conditions in Step 7a are satisfied.

9. If the idle speed is too high, do not clean the throttle body. Turn the air trim screw clockwise until the conditions in Step 7a are satisfied.

1991–93 MUSTANG AND MARK VII

1. Place the transaxle in **P** and apply the parking brake.

2. Start the engine and bring to normal operating temperature. Make sure the heater, air conditioning and all other accessories are OFF.

3. Check and if necessary, adjust the ignition timing.

4. Make sure the fuel pressure is correct. Any indicated vehicle malfunction service codes should be resolved before proceeding further.

5. Disconnect the negative battery terminal for 5 minutes, then reconnect. Start the engine and stabilize for 2 minutes, then goose the engine and let it return to idle. Lightly depress and release the accelerator and let the engine idle. Check the engine idle.

6. If the engine does not idle properly, shut the engine OFF and place a 0.025 in. feeler gauge between the throttle plate stop screw and throttle lever.

7. Start the engine and let it idle. Check the idle speed; it should be 675 ± 50 rpm.

8. If the idle speed is too low, proceed as follows:

a. Shut the engine OFF. Do not clean the throttle body, but check the throttle plate for an orifice plug.

b. If there is no plug, start the engine and let it idle for 2 minutes, then adjust the idle to the desired speed, ± 25 rpm.

c. If there is a plug, remove it, then start the engine and let it idle for 2 minutes. Adjust the idle to the desired speed, ± 25 rpm.

d. The screw must be in contact with the lever pad after adjustment.

9. If the idle speed is too high, proceed as follows:

a. Shut the engine OFF and disconnect the air cleaner hose.

b. Block off the orifice in the throttle plate temporarily with tape. If the orifice already has a plug, proceed to Step d.

c. Reattach the air intake hose. Restart the engine and check the idle speed. If the engine stalled, crack open the plate with the throttle return screw.

d. If the idle speed continues to be fast, connect a suitable scan tool and run the Key On Engine Off (KOEO) Self-Test and check for a TPS output code.

e. If the output code is within range, remove the tape and check for vacuum leaks, throttle linkage binding, or other causes for excessive high idle.

f. If the output code is out of range, adjust the throttle screw to obtain the proper code. The lever pad must be in contact with the screw after adjustment.

g. If the idle speed drops to or below the desired level, turn the engine **OFF**, disconnect the air cleaner hose and remove the tape.

h. Install the proper plug in the throttle plate orifice.

i. Reconnect the air cleaner hose. Start the engine and turn the throttle plate stop screw clockwise to the nominal idle speed, ± 25 rpm. Do not turn the screw counterclockwise as this may cause the throttle plate to stick at idle.

10. Remove the feeler gauge from between the throttle plate stop screw and throttle lever.

11. Shut the engine OFF and disconnect the battery for 10 minutes minimum.

12. Run the KOEO Self-Test for proper TPS output code.

13. Start the engine and let the idle stabilize for 2 minutes. Rev the engine and let it return to idle. Lightly depress and release the accelerator; let the engine idle.

14. If equipped with automatic overdrive transmission, check the throttle valve pressure adjustment.

IDLE MIXTURE ADJUSTMENT

The idle mixture is controlled by the electronic control unit and cannot be adjusted.

Fuel Injector

REMOVAL & INSTALLATION

2.3L Engine

1. Disconnect the negative battery cable.

2. Remove the fuel tank cap and relieve the fuel system pressure.

3. Disconnect the air intake, electrical connectors, throttle linkage, vacuum lines and EGR tube from the upper intake manifold and throttle body. Tag the electrical connectors and vacuum lines prior to removal for installation reference.

4. Remove the upper intake manifold retaining bolts and remove the upper intake manifold and throttle body assembly.

5. Disconnect the electrical connectors from the injectors.

6. Disconnect the fuel lines from the fuel supply manifold.

7. Remove the fuel supply manifold retaining bolts, carefully disengage the manifold and fuel injectors from the engine and remove the manifold and injectors.

8. Remove the fuel injectors from the manifold.

To install:

9. Lubricate new O-rings with clean light grade oil and install 2 on each injector.

NOTE: Never use silicone grease as it will clog the injectors.

10. Install the fuel supply manifold and injectors into the intake manifold. Push the fuel rail down to make sure all the fuel injector O-rings are fully seated in the fuel rail cups and intake manifold.

11. Install the fuel manifold assembly retaining bolts and tighten to 15–22 ft. lbs. (20–30 Nm) while holding the assembly down.

12. Connect the fuel lines to the manifold assembly.

13. After the fuel rail assembly has been installed and before the fuel injector wire connectors have been connected, connect the negative battery cable and turn the key to the **ON** position. This will cause the fuel pump to run for 2–3 seconds and pressurize the system.

14. Check for fuel leaks, especially where the fuel injector is installed into the fuel rail.

15. Disconnect the negative battery cable.

16. Install the upper intake manifold in the reverse order of removal. Tighten the retaining bolts, in sequence, to 15–22 ft. lbs. (20–30 Nm).

17. Connect the fuel injector wire connectors.

18. Connect the negative battery cable. Start the engine and let it idle.

19. Turn the engine **OFF** and check for fuel leaks.

3.8L Engine

EXCEPT SUPERCHARGED ENGINE

1. Disconnect the negative battery cable.

2. Remove the fuel tank cap and relieve the fuel system pressure.

3. Disconnect the electrical connectors at the air bypass valve, TP sensor and EGR position sensor.

4. Disconnect the throttle linkage at the throttle ball and the transmission linkage from the throttle body.

5. Remove the 2 bolts securing the bracket to the intake manifold and position the bracket with the cables aside.

6. Disconnect all the vacuum lines from the upper intake manifold and throttle assembly. Tag all lines prior to removal for ease of reinstallation.

7. Remove the upper intake mani-

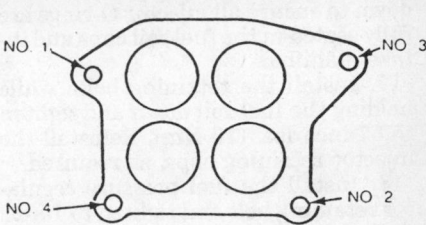

Upper intake manifold bolt torque sequence—1989 2.3L engine

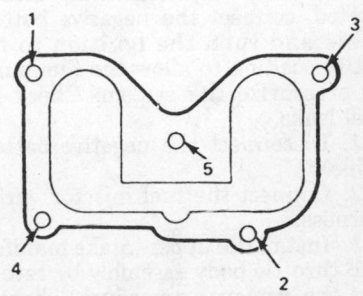

Upper intake manifold bolt torque sequence—1990-93 2.3L engine

fold retaining bolts and remove the upper intake manifold and throttle body assembly.

8. Disconnect the fuel lines from the fuel rail assembly.

9. Remove the fuel pressure regulator.

10. Disconnect the electrical connectors from the fuel injectors. Remove the injector retaining clips, as required.

11. Remove the fuel rail retaining bolts. Carefully disengage the fuel rail from the fuel injectors and remove the fuel rail.

NOTE: It may be easier to remove the injectors with the fuel rail as an assembly.

12. Grasping the injector body, pull while gently rocking the injector from side-to-side to remove the injector from the fuel rail or the intake manifold.

13. Inspect the pintle protection cap (plastic hat) and washer for signs of deterioration. Replace the complete injector, as required. If the cap is missing, look for it in the intake manifold.

NOTE: The pintle protection cap is not available as a separate part.

To install:

14. Lubricate new O-rings with light grade oil and install 2 on each injector.

NOTE: Never use silicone grease as it will clog the injectors.

15. Install the injectors in the intake manifold using a light, twisting pushing motion.

16. Install the fuel rail, pushing it

down to ensure all injector O-rings are fully seated in the fuel rail cups and intake manifold.

17. Install the retaining bolts while holding the fuel rail down and tighten to 87 inch lbs. (10 Nm). Reinstall the injector retaining clips, as required.

18. Install the fuel pressure regulator retaining bolt and tighten to 15–22 ft. lbs. (20–30 Nm).

19. Connect the fuel lines to the fuel rail.

20. With the injector wiring disconnected, connect the negative battery cable and turn the ignition to the **RUN** position to allow the fuel pump to pressurize the system. Check for fuel leaks.

21. Disconnect the negative battery cable.

22. Connect the fuel injector wiring harness.

23. Install the upper intake manifold and throttle body assembly by reversing the removal procedure. Tighten the upper intake manifold retaining bolts to 24 ft. lbs. (32 Nm).

24. Connect the negative battery cable, start the engine and check for fuel leaks.

SUPERCHARGED ENGINE

1. Disconnect the negative battery cable.

2. Remove the fuel tank cap and relieve the fuel system pressure.

3. Remove the supercharger assembly.

4. Disconnect the fuel lines from the fuel rail assembly.

5. Remove the 4 fuel rail assembly retaining bolts and remove the fuel pressure regulator bracket retaining bolt.

6. Disconnect the electrical connectors from the injectors.

7. Carefully disengage the fuel rail from the fuel injectors and remove the fuel rail.

NOTE: It may be easier to remove the injectors with the fuel rail as an assembly.

8. Grasping the injector body, remove the injector from the fuel rail or intake manifold by pulling while gently rocking the injector from side-to-side.

9. Inspect the pintle protection cap (plastic hat) and washer for signs of deterioration. Replace the complete injector, as required. If the cap is missing, look for it in the intake manifold.

NOTE: The pintle protection cap is not available as a separate part.

To install:

10. Lubricate new O-rings with light grade oil and install 2 on each injector.

NOTE: Never use silicone grease as it will clog the injectors.

11. Install the injectors, using a light, twisting, pushing motion.

12. Place the fuel rail assembly over each of the injectors and seat the injectors into the fuel rail.

NOTE: It may be easier to seat the injectors in the fuel rail and then seat the entire assembly in the lower intake manifold.

13. Install the fuel rail assembly retaining bolts and tighten to 70–97 inch lbs. (8–11 Nm). Install the fuel pressure regulator bracket retaining bolt and tighten to 15–22 ft. lbs. (20–30 Nm).

14. Install the supercharger assembly.

15. Connect the negative battery cable. Turn the ignition from **OFF** to **ON** several times without starting the engine to check for fuel leaks. Check all connections at the fuel rail and injectors.

16. Start the engine and warm to operating temperature. Check for fuel or coolant leaks.

5.0L Engine

1. Disconnect the negative battery cable.

2. Remove the fuel tank cap and relieve the fuel system pressure.

3. Partially drain the cooling system into a suitable container.

4. Disconnect the electrical connectors at the air bypass valve, TP sensor and EGR sensor.

5. Disconnect the throttle linkage at the throttle ball and transmission linkage from the throttle body. Remove the 2 bolts securing the bracket the bracket to the intake manifold and position the bracket with the cables aside.

6. Disconnect the upper intake manifold vacuum fitting connections by disconnecting all vacuum lines to the vacuum tree, vacuum lines to the EGR valve, vacuum line to the fuel pressure regulator and canister purge line.

7. Disconnect the PCV system by disconnecting the hose from the fitting on the rear of the upper manifold and disconnect the PCV vent closure tube at the throttle body.

8. Remove the 2 EGR coolant lines from the fittings on the EGR spacer.

9. Remove the 6 upper intake manifold retaining bolts.

10. Remove the upper intake and throttle body as an assembly from the lower intake manifold.

11. Disconnect the fuel lines from the fuel rail.

12. Remove the 4 fuel rail assembly retaining bolts.

13. Disconnect the electrical connectors from the injectors.

14. Carefully disengage the fuel rail from the fuel injectors.

NOTE: It may be easier to remove the injectors with the fuel rail as an assembly.

15. Grasping the injector body, pull up while gently rocking the injector from side-to-side to remove the injector from the fuel rail or intake manifold.

16. Inspect the pintle protection cap (plastic hat) and washer for signs of deterioration. Replace the complete injector, as required. If the cap is missing, look for it in the intake manifold.

NOTE: The pintle protection cap is not available as a separate part.

To install:

17. Lubricate new O-rings with light grade oil and install 2 on each injector.

NOTE: Never use silicone grease as it will clog the injectors.

18. Install the injectors using a light, twisting, pushing motion.

19. Install the fuel rail, pushing it down to ensure all the injector O-rings are fully seated in the fuel rail cups and intake manifold.

20. Install the retaining bolts while holding the fuel rail down and tighten to 70–105 inch lbs. (8–12 Nm).

21. Connect the fuel lines to the fuel rail.

22. With the injector wiring disconnected, connect the negative battery cable and turn the ignition switch to the **RUN** position to allow the fuel pump to pressurize the system.

23. Check for fuel leaks.

24. Disconnect the negative battery cable.

25. Connect the electrical connectors to the injectors.

26. Install the upper intake manifold and throttle body assembly by reversing the removal procedure. Tighten the retaining bolts to 12–17 ft. lbs. (16–24 Nm).

27. Refill the cooling system and connect the negative battery cable.

28. Start the engine and let it idle for 2 minutes. Turn the engine **OFF** and check for leaks.

DRIVE AXLE

Rear Halfshaft

REMOVAL & INSTALLATION

Thunderbird and Cougar

NOTE: Before removing the

rear halfshafts, new inboard CV-joint stub shaft circlips, new differential oil seals and new hub retainer nuts must be available for assembly.

1. Remove the wheelcover/hub cover and remove the hub retainer nut. Loosen the wheel nuts.

2. Raise and support the vehicle safely by the frame only. Remove the wheel nuts and remove the wheel and tire assembly.

3. If equipped with drum brakes, remove the brake drum.

4. If equipped with disc brakes, perform the following:

   a. Remove the anti-lock brake sensors, if equipped.

   b. Use needle-nose pliers to slide the parking brake cable adjusting clip downward until the cable is free.

   c. Remove the parking brake cable from the brake caliper.

   d. Remove the upper and lower caliper retaining bolts and remove the caliper. Support the caliper out of the way with a wire, do not allow it to hang from the brake hose.

   e. Remove the brake rotor.

5. Remove the upper control arm nuts and bolt. Wire the upper control arm to the top of the shock absorber, out of the way.

6. Using a paint marker, mark the position of the lower control arm in relation to the knuckle with the lower bushings in the relaxed position.

NOTE: Failure to mark this relationship will result in bushing wind-up on assembly and incorrect ride height, causing misalignment and premature tire wear.

7. Use a suitable puller to free the halfshaft from the hub.

8. Remove the lower control arm to knuckle attaching bolts. Remove the knuckle assembly while supporting the outboard CV-joint and boot. Carefully rest the halfshaft on the lower control arm.

9. If equipped with drum brakes, wire the knuckle assembly to the top of the shock. Do not allow the knuckle assembly to hang from the brake hose.

10. Remove the halfshaft from the differential using CV-joint remover tool T89P–3514–A or equivalent. Push the tool outward until the CV-joint is freed from the differential side gear.

NOTE: Be careful not to damage the differential oil seal, differential housing and/or CV-joint boot.

11. Remove the halfshaft from the vehicle. Insert plugs into the differential housing to prevent fluid loss.

To install:

12. Remove the differential plugs and install new differential oil seals.

13. Install a new circlip on the halfshaft. Start the ends in the groove and push the circlip into the groove, to prevent over expanding the circlip.

14. Lightly lubricate the stub shaft splines and carefully align the splines on the shaft with the splines in the differential.

15. Push the halfshaft inward to seat the circlip in the differential side gear groove. Use care not to damage the seal.

16. Engage the hub splines with the outboard CV-joint splines.

17. Install the lower control arm bolts and nuts. Align the paint marks and tighten the bolts to 119–147 ft. lbs. (160–200mm).

18. Install a new hub retaining nut and pull the CV-joint into the hub as far as possible by hand.

19. Install the upper arm retaining bolt and nut and tighten to 119–147 ft. bs. (160–200 Nm).

20. If equipped with drum brakes, install the brake drum. If equipped with disc brakes, proceed as follows:

   a. Install the brake rotor.

   b. Install the brake caliper assembly to the rotor with the outer brake shoe against the rotor's braking surface. This prevents pinching the piston boot between the inner brake shoe and the piston.

   c. Install the upper and lower caliper retaining bolts and tighten to 80–99 ft. lbs. (108–135 Nm).

   d. Install the parking brake cable to the brake caliper. Install the cable adjustment clip.

   e. Install the anti-lock brake sensor, if equipped. Tighten the retaining bolts to 15–19 ft. lbs. (19–27 Nm).

21. Check inboard CV-joint circlip engagement by attempting to pull the inboard CV-joint from the axle. If the CV-joint circlip is not seated, push the CV-joint in until the circlip is fully engaged in the side gear.

22. Check the axle lube level and fill, as necessary.

23. Install the wheel and tire assembly and tighten the wheel nuts to 80–106 ft. lbs. (108–144 Nm). Lower the vehicle.

24. Tighten the hub nut to 250 ft. lbs. (340 Nm). Install the wheelcover/hub cover.

CV-Boot

REMOVAL & INSTALLATION

Thunderbird and Cougar

1. Remove the halfshaft from the vehicle and clamp in a vise. Do not allow the vise jaws to contact the boot or its clamp.

NOTE: The vise should be equipped with jaw caps to prevent damage to any machined surfaces.

2. Cut and remove both boot clamps and slide the boot back on the shaft.

3. Slide the outer race off the tripod.

NOTE: When replacing damaged CV-joint boots, the grease should be checked for contamination or gritty feeling. If the CV-joints are operating satisfactory and the grease does not feel contaminated, add grease and replace the boot. If the grease appears contaminated, the CV-joint should be disassembled and inspected.

4. Move the stop ring back on the shaft using snapring pliers.

5. Move the tripod back on the shaft to allow access to the circlip.

6. Remove the circlip and the tripod from the shaft.

7. Remove the stop ring and remove the inboard CV-joint boot.

8. Reposition the halfshaft in the vise and remove the outboard CV-joint boot.

NOTE: The outboard CV-joint is permanently retained to the inter-connecting shaft and cannot be disassembled. Outboard CV-joints are serviced as an assembly, including the inter-connecting shaft, boot, clamps grease and circlips.

To install:

9. Slide the outboard boot on the shaft. Before positioning the boot over the CV-joint, pack the CV-joint and boot with grease. On 1989–91 vehicles, the total amount of grease required is 7.05 ounces (200 grams) for vehicles without anti-lock brakes or 8.82 ounces (250 grams) for vehicles equipped with anti-lock brakes. On 1992–93 vehicles, the total amount of grease required is 7.05 ounces (200 grams) for vehicles with 3.8L engine or 8.82 ounces (250 grams) for vehicles equipped with 3.8L SC or 5.0L engine.

10. Position the boot on the CV-joint and install the boot clamps.

11. Slide the inboard CV-joint boot on the shaft.

12. With the stop ring installed past the splines, install the tripod assembly with the chamfered side toward the stop ring.

13. Start 1 end of a new circlip in the groove of the halfshaft and work the circlip over the stub shaft end and into the groove. This will avoid over-expanding the circlip.

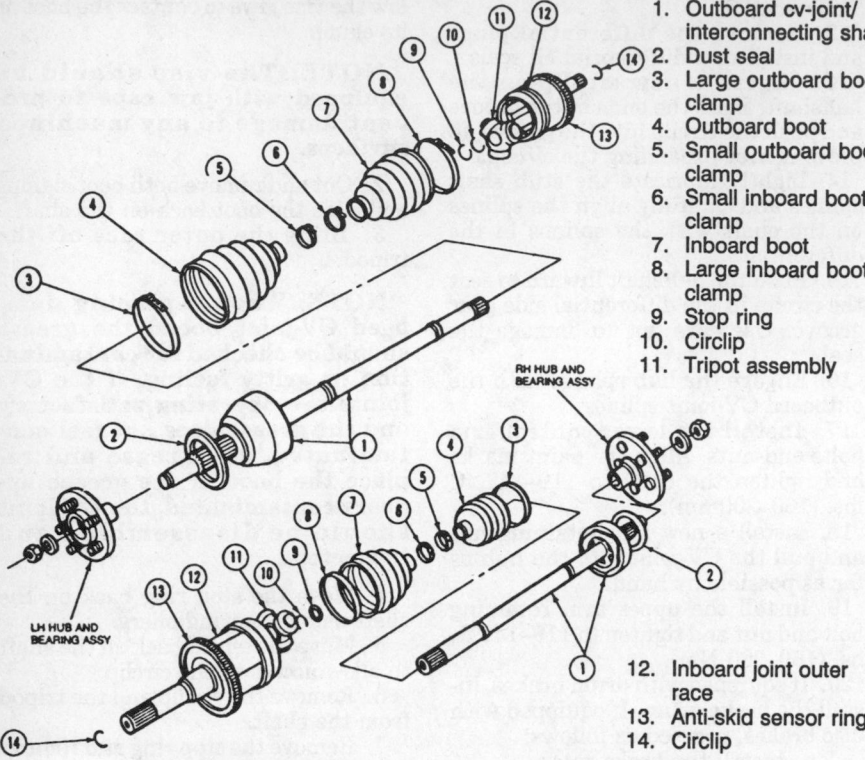

1. Outboard cv-joint/interconnecting shaft
2. Dust seal
3. Large outboard boot clamp
4. Outboard boot
5. Small outboard boot clamp
6. Small inboard boot clamp
7. Inboard boot
8. Large inboard boot clamp
9. Stop ring
10. Circlip
11. Tripot assembly

12. Inboard joint outer race
13. Anti-skid sensor ring
14. Circlip

Disassembled view of the halfshafts—Thunderbird and Cougar

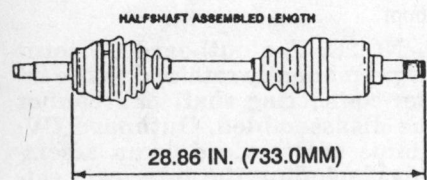

Halfshaft assembled length—Thunderbird and Cougar

14. Compress the circlip and slide the tripod assembly forward over the circlip to expose the stop ring groove.

15. Move the stop ring into the groove using snapring pliers and make sure it is fully seated in the groove.

16. Fill the CV-joint outer race and boot with grease. The total amount of grease required is 9 ounces (250 grams) for vehicles without anti-lock brakes or 10.58 ounces (300 grams) for vehicles equipped with anti-lock brakes.

17. Install the outer race on the tripod assembly.

18. Position the boot over the CV-joint. Move the CV-joint in and out, as necessary, to adjust to the proper length.

19. Release any air pressure by inserting a small prybar with a dulled blade between the boot and the outer bearing race.

20. Seat the boot in the groove and clamp in position without cutting the boot.

Driveshafts and U-Joints

REMOVAL & INSTALLATION

Except Thunderbird and Cougar

1. Raise and safely support the vehicle. Matchmark the rear driveshaft yoke and the companion flange so they can be reassembled in the same position to maintain balance.

NOTE: Mark VII vehicles may have a balance weight attached to 1 of the flange bolts. This bolt should be reinstalled in it's original position.

2. Remove the flange bolts and disconnect the driveshaft from the axle companion flange.

3. Allow the rear of the driveshaft to drop down slightly. Pull the driveshaft and slip yoke out of the transmission extension housing.

4. Plug the transmission to prevent fluid leakage.

To install:

5. Lubricate the yoke splines and install the yoke into the transmission extension housing, aligning the splines. Be careful not to bottom the slip yoke hard against the transmission seal.

6. Rotate the pinion flange, as necessary, to align the matchmarks made during removal. Install the driveshaft

yoke to the pinion flange. Install the bolts and tighten to 71–95 ft. lbs. (95–130 Nm).

Thunderbird and Cougar

1. Drain the fuel tank.

2. Raise and safely support the vehicle by the frame.

3. Remove the crossmember on the forward side of the fuel tank.

4. Remove the exhaust pipe at the muffler. Lower the pipe and support with a wire.

5. Remove the exhaust pipe rear insulator from the exhaust pipe hanger stud.

6. Remove the muffler insulator from the hanger stud. Remove the exhaust system from the vehicle.

7. Remove the driveshaft hoop on the rear side of the tank.

8. Remove the fuel tank filler tube retaining bolt from the right frame rail.

9. Carefully place a transmission jack under the fuel tank and remove the front heat shield.

10. Remove the support on the forward side of the fuel tank.

11. Remove the fuel tank support straps and lower the tank approximately 6 in.

12. Locate the original paint mark on the axle companion flange and mark the driveshaft flange in the same location. If the original mark is not visible matchmark both flanges.

13. Remove the driveshaft retaining bolts and separate the driveshaft from the axle companion flange. Pull the driveshaft rearward to remove. Install a plug in the extension housing to prevent fluid loss.

To install:

14. Lubricate the slip yoke splines and remove the plug from the transmission extension. Install the driveshaft assembly. Do not allow the slip yoke to bottom on the output shaft with excessive force.

15. Align the marks on the driveshaft with the axle companion flange. Install and tighten the bolts to 71–95 ft. lbs. (95–130 Nm).

16. Raise the fuel tank and install the support straps. Tighten the retaining bolts to 21–29 ft. lbs. (28–40 Nm).

17. Install the fuel tank filler tube retaining bolt. Tighten to 36–48 inch lbs. (4.0–5.5 Nm).

18. Install the driveshaft hoop and tighten the retaining bolts to 30–44 ft. lbs. (40–61 Nm).

19. Install the support on the forward side of the fuel tank and tighten the bolts to 30–44 ft. lbs. (40–61 Nm).

20. Raise the exhaust pipe and support with wire. Install the muffler and exhaust pipe insulators on the hanger studs.

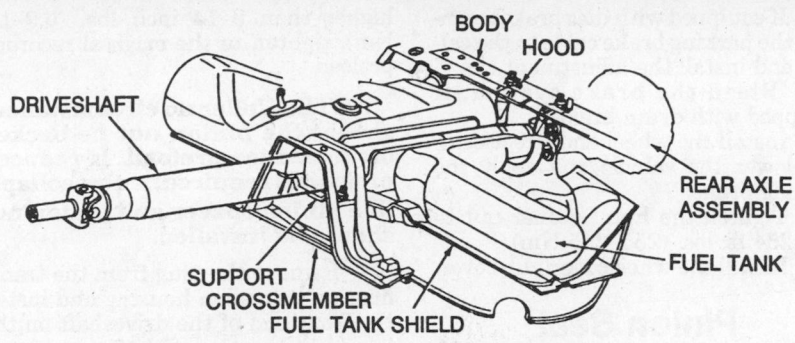

Driveshaft Installation—Thunderbird and Cougar

21. Install the exhaust pipe to the muffler and tighten the bolts to 21–29 ft. lbs. (28–40 Nm).

22. Install the crossmember on the forward side of the fuel tank and tighten the bolts to 12–17 ft. lbs. (16–24 Nm).

23. Lower the vehicle.

Rear Axle Shaft, Bearing and Seal

REMOVAL & INSTALLATION

Except Thunderbird and Cougar

1. Raise and safely support the vehicle. Remove wheel and tire assembly and remove brake drum or brake rotor.

2. If equipped, remove the anti-lock brake speed sensor.

3. Clean all dirt from the area of the carrier cover. Drain the axle lubricant by removing the housing cover.

4. Remove differential pinion shaft lock bolt and pinion shaft.

5. Push flanged end of axle shafts toward the center of the vehicle and remove the C-lock from button end of the axle shaft. Remove the axle shaft from the housing, being careful not to damage the oil seal.

6. Insert wheel bearing and seal replacer tool T85L–1225–AH or equivalent, in the bore and position it behind the bearing so the tangs on the tool engage the bearing outer race. Remove bearing and seal as a unit using an impact slide hammer.

To install:

7. Lubricate the new bearing with rear axle lubricant. Install the bearing into the housing bore using a suitable bearing installer.

8. Install a new axle seal using a seal installer.

NOTE: On 8.8 in. axle, check for the presence of an axle shaft O-ring on the spline end of the shaft and install, if not present.

9. Carefully slide the axle shaft into the axle housing, without damaging the bearing or seal assembly. Start the splines into the side gear and push firmly until the button end of the axle shaft can be seen in the differential case.

10. Install the C-lock on the button end of the axle shaft splines, then push the shaft outboard until the shaft splines engage and the C-lock seats in the counterbore of the differential side gear.

11. Insert the differential pinion shaft through the case and pinion gears, aligning the hole in the shaft with the lock bolt hole. Apply a suitable locking compound to the lock bolt and install in the case and pinion shaft. Tighten to 15–30 ft. lbs. (20–41 Nm).

12. Cover the inside of the differential case with a shop rag and clean the machined surface of the carrier and cover. Remove the shop rag.

13. Apply a bead of silicone sealer to the cover and install on the carrier. Tighten the bolts in a criss-cross pattern. Final torque the cover retaining bolts to 25–34 ft. lbs. (34–47 Nm) if the cover is metal or 15–19 ft. lbs. (20–27 Nm) if the cover is plastic.

14. Add rear axle lubricant to the carrier to a level 1/4–9/16 in. below the bottom of the fill hole. Install the filler plug and tighten to 15–30 ft. lbs. (20–41 Nm).

15. Install the anti-lock speed sensor, if equipped. Tighten the retaining bolt to 40–60 inch lbs. (4.5–6.8 Nm).

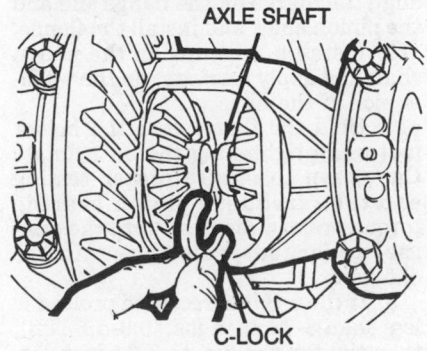

Removing the axle shaft C-locks

16. Install the brake calipers and rotors or the brake drums, as required. Install the wheel and tire assembly and lower the vehicle.

Thunderbird and Cougar

NOTE: A new hub retainer nut must be used in this procedure.

1. Remove the wheelcover/hub cover from the wheel and tire assembly and loosen the lug nuts.

2. Remove and discard the hub nut and washer.

3. Raise and safely support the vehicle. Remove the wheel and tire assembly.

4. Use needle-nose pliers to slide the parking brake cable adjusting clip downward, until the cable is free.

5. If equipped with disc brakes, remove the parking brake cable from the caliper.

6. Remove the caliper from the disc brake rotor, leaving the brake hose connected. Wire the caliper to the brake line junction bracket; do not let it hang by the brake hose.

7. Remove the brake rotor or brake drum.

8. If equipped with disc brakes, remove the splash shield.

9. If equipped with drum brakes, disconnect the parking brake cable and disconnect the brake line from the wheel cylinder.

10. Remove the upper control arm nut and bolt. Wire the upper control arm to the body to prevent damage to the CV-joint boots when the knuckle and hub assembly is removed.

11. Attach hub removal tool T81P–1104–C or other equivalent puller tool, to the hub studs and turn the tool shaft until the halfshaft is free in the hub.

12. Mark the position of the control arm in relation to the knuckle with the bushings in the relaxed position. When the upper control arm bolt is removed from the knuckle, the lower arm bushings will return to the relaxed position.

NOTE: Failure to mark the position will cause bushing wind up at assembly resulting in improper ride height. This can cause incorrect alignment and tire wear.

13. If the knuckle is being replaced, note the approximate angle of the knuckle in the relaxed position by measuring the distance from the upper bushing to a point on the vehicle body.

14. Remove the lower control arm-to-knuckle retaining bolts and nuts and remove the knuckle assembly from the halfshaft.

15. Position the knuckle and hub assembly in a vise.

16. If equipped with drum brakes, remove the brake shoes, springs and adjuster from the backing plate. Remove the screws retaining the backing plate to the knuckle.

17. Position a suitable 3-jaw puller on the knuckle and press the hub out of the knuckle.

18. Remove the backing plate and remove the bearing retainer snapring.

19. Position the knuckle and bearing assembly on a press and, using suitable tools, press the bearing from the knuckle.

To install:

20. Place the knuckle in the press and position the bearing in the knuckle bore. Press the bearing into the knuckle using suitable tools.

21. Install the bearing retainer snapring.

22. Position the backing plate on the knuckle with the retaining bolts. Tighten the bolts to 45–59 ft. lbs. (61–81 Nm).

23. Support the knuckle on a suitable fixture. Position the hub on the bearing and press into place using suitable tools.

24. If equipped with drum brakes, install the brake shoes, springs and adjuster.

25. Using a hammer and chisel, drive the bearing dust seal from the outer CV-joint. Using a suitable installation tool, install a new seal on the CV-joint, making sure the seal flange faces out toward the bearing.

26. Place the knuckle and hub assembly on the halfshaft splines and install the lower control arm-to-knuckle bolts and nuts. Position the knuckle so the marks made during the removal procedure align with the marks on the control arm. If a new knuckle is being installed, set the knuckle at the approximate angle noted during removal before tightening the bolts.

27. Push the knuckle and hub assembly firmly onto the halfshaft splines. Install the upper control arm bolt and nut and tighten the nut to 118–148 ft. lbs. (160–200 Nm).

28. Install a new hub nut and washer and tighten by hand.

29. If equipped with disc brakes, install the splash shield to the knuckle and tighten the retaining bolts to 45–59 ft. lbs. (61–81 Nm).

30. If equipped with drum brakes, connect the brake line to the wheel cylinder and connect the parking brake cable.

31. Install the brake rotor or drum.

32. If equipped with disc brakes, install the caliper over the rotor with the outer brake pad against the rotor, to prevent pinching the piston boot between the inner pad and piston. Install the caliper-to-knuckle bolts and tighten to 44–60 ft. lbs. (59–81 Nm).

33. If equipped with disc brakes, connect the parking brake cable to the caliper and install the adjustment clip.

34. Bleed the brake system, if equipped with drum brakes.

35. Install the wheel and tire assembly, lower the vehicle and apply the parking brake.

36. Tighten the hub retainer nut to 188–254 ft. lbs. (255–345 Nm).

37. Install the wheelcover/hub cover.

Pinion Seal

REMOVAL & INSTALLATION

Except Thunderbird and Cougar

1. Raise and safely support the vehicle. Matchmark the rear driveshaft yoke and the axle flange so they may be reassembled in the same position to maintain balance.

2. Disconnect the driveshaft from the rear axle companion flange, remove the driveshaft and remove the driveshaft from the extension housing. Plug the extension housing to prevent leakage.

3. Install an inch pound torque wrench on the pinion nut and record the torque required to maintain rotation of the pinion through several revolutions.

4. While holding the companion flange with holder tool T78P–4851–A or equivalent, remove the pinion nut.

5. Clean the area around the oil seal and place a pan under the seal.

6. Mark the companion flange in relation to the pinion shaft so the flange can be installed in the same position.

7. Remove the rear axle companion flange using tool T65L–4851–B or equivalent.

8. Pry the seal out of the housing using a prybar.

To install:

9. Clean the oil seal seat surface and install the seal in the carrier using seal replacer tool T79P–4676–A or equivalent. Apply lubricant to the lips of the seal.

10. Apply a small amount of lubricant to the companion flange splines, align the marks on the flange and and the pinion shaft and install the flange.

11. Install a new nut on the pinion shaft and apply lubricant on the washer side of the nut.

12. Hold the flange with the holder tool while tightening the nut. Rotate the pinion to ensure proper seating and take frequent pinion bearing torque preload readings until the original recorded preload reading is obtained.

13. If the original recorded preload is less than 8–14 inch lbs. (0.9–1.6 Nm), then tighten the nut to 8–14 inch lbs. (0.9–1.6 Nm). If the original preload is higher than 8–14 inch lbs. (0.9–1.6 Nm), tighten to the original recorded preload.

NOTE: Under no circumstances should the pinion nut be backed off to reduce preload. If reduced preload is required, a new collapsible pinion spacer and pinion nut should be installed.

14. Remove the plug from the transmission extension housing and install the front end of the driveshaft on the transmission output shaft.

15. Connect the rear end of the driveshaft to the axle companion flange, aligning the scribe marks and tighten the 4 bolts to 71–95 ft. lbs. (95–130 Nm).

16. Add lubricant to the axle until it is ¼–⁹⁄₁₆ in. below the bottom of the fill hole with the axle in operating position.

17. Make sure the axle vent is not plugged with debris.

Thunderbird and Cougar

1. Raise and safely support the vehicle on the frame.

2. Place a screw type jackstand under the rear axle pinion nose and remove the rear axle mount to axle cover retaining bolts and nuts.

3. Install the rear axle mount bolt in the lower bolt hole to allow the axle to pivot forward.

4. Mark the driveshaft in relation to the companion flange and remove the driveshaft retaining bolts.

5. Slide the driveshaft forward and rest on the driveshaft hoop.

6. Remove the front axle mount retaining nuts. Slowly lower the axle to gain access to the companion flange.

NOTE: The axle must always be supported.

7. Install an inch pound torque wrench on the pinion nut and record the torque required to maintain rotation of the pinion through several revolutions.

8. While holding the companion flange with holder tool T78P–4851–A or equivalent, remove the pinion nut.

9. Mark the companion flange in relation to the pinion shaft so the flange can be installed in the same position.

10. Place a pan under the companion flange.

11. Remove the rear axle companion flange using tool T65L–4851–B or equivalent.

12. Pry the seal out of the housing using a prybar.

To install:

13. Clean the pinion seal seat surface and install the seal in the carrier using seal replacer tool T79P–4676–A or

equivalent. Apply lubricant to the lips of the seal.

14. Apply a small amount of lubricant to the companion flange splines, align the marks on the flange and and the pinion shaft and install the flange.

15. Install a new nut on the pinion shaft and apply lubricant on the washer side of the nut.

16. Hold the flange with the holder tool while tightening the nut. Rotate the pinion to ensure proper seating and take frequent pinion bearing torque preload readings until the original recorded preload reading is obtained.

17. If the original recorded preload is less than 8–14 inch lbs. (0.9–1.6 Nm), then tighten the nut to 8–14 inch lbs. (0.9–1.6 Nm). If the original preload is higher than 8–14 inch lbs. (0.9–1.6 Nm), tighten to the original recorded preload.

NOTE: Under no circumstances should the pinion nut be backed off to reduce preload. If reduced preload is required, a new collapsible pinion spacer and pinion nut should be installed.

18. Using a jack stand, raise and locate the axle on the front mounting bolts.

19. Install the front mounting nuts and tighten to 68–100 ft. lbs. (92–136 Nm).

20. Remove the rear mount bolt from the pivot position.

21. Install the rear mount bolts in the axle cover mount and tighten to 80–100 ft. lbs. (108–136 Nm).

22. Align the marks on the driveshaft and the companion flange, install the retaining bolts and tighten to 70–95 ft. lbs. (95–129 Nm).

23. Fill the rear axle with lubricant to level with the bottom of the filler hole. Install the filler plug and tighten to 20–30 ft. lbs. (28–40 Nm).

24. Lower the vehicle.

Axle Housing

REMOVAL & INSTALLATION

Except Thunderbird and Cougar

1. Raise and safely support the vehicle. Position saftey stands under the rear frame crossmember.

2. Remove the cover and drain the axle lubricant.

3. Remove the wheel and tire assemblies. Remove the brake drums or brake rotors.

4. Remove the lock bolt from the pinion shaft and remove the shaft.

5. Remove the anti-lock brake sensor before removing the axle shafts, if equipped.

6. Push the axle shafts inward to remove the C-locks and remove the axle shafts.

7. If necessary, remove the bolt attaching the brake junction block to rear cover.

8. Remove the 4 retaining nuts from each backing plate and wire the backing plate to the underbody.

9. Matchmark the driveshaft yoke and companion flange. Disconnect the driveshaft at the companion flange and wire it to the underbody.

10. Support the axle housing with jackstands. Disengage the brake line from the clips that retain the line to the axle housing.

12. Disconnect the vent from the rear axle housing.

NOTE: Some axle vents may be secured to the housing assembly through the brake junction block. At assembly, a thread lock/sealer must be applied to ensure retension.

13. If equipped with air springs, proceed as follows:

a. Disconnect the negative battery cable. Turn **OFF** the air suspension switch located in the trunk.

b. Disconnect the electrical connector and the air line from the air spring solenoid, located on the air spring.

c. Remove the solenoid clip and rotate the solenoid counterclockwise to the first stop.

d. Pull the solenoid straight out slowly to the second stop to bleed the air from the system.

——— CAUTION ———

Do not fully release the solenoid until the air is completely bled from the air spring, or personal injury may result.

e. After the air is fully bled from the system, rotate the solenoid counterclockwise to the 3rd stop and remove the solenoid from the solenoid housing.

f. Remove the bolts retaining the springs to the lower arms.

14. Disconnect the lower shock absorber studs from the mounting brackets on the axle housing. If equipped, disconnect the quad shock from the quad shock bracket.

15. Disconnect the upper arms from the mountings on the axle housing ear brackets.

16. Lower the axle housing assembly until the coil springs are released and lift out the coil springs.

17. Disconnect the suspension lower arms at the axle housing.

18. Lower the axle housing and remove it from the vehicle.

To install:

19. Position the axle housing under

the vehicle and raise the axle with a hoist or jack. Conect the lower suspension arms to their mounting brackets on the axle housing. Do not tighten the bolts and nuts at this time.

20. Reposition the rear coil springs or air springs, as required.

21. Raise the housing into position.

22. Connect the uppper arms to the mounting ears on the housing. Tighten the nuts and bolts to 100 ft. lbs. (135 Nm). Tighten the lower arm bolts and nuts to 100 ft. lbs. (35 Nm).

23. Connect the air springs to the axle housing.

24. Install the axle vent and the the brake line to the clips that retain the line to the axle housing. If equipped with air springs, proceed as follows:

a. Check the solenoid O-rings for damage and replace, as required. Lightly grease the O-ring area of the solenoid and the larger solenoid housing O-ring with silicone dielectric compound.

b. Insert the solenoid into the air spring end cap and rotate clockwise to the 3rd stop, push in to the 2nd stop, then rotate clockwise to the 1st stop.

c. Install the solenoid clip. Connect the air line and the electrical connector.

25. Install the brake backing plates on the axle housing flanges.

26. Connect the lower shock absorber studs to the mounting bracket on the axle housing. If equipped, connect the quad shock to the quad shock bracket.

27. Connect the driveshaft to the companion flange and tighten the bolts and nuts to 70–95 ft. lbs. (95–130 Nm).

28. Slide the rear axle shafts into the housing until the splines enter the side gear. Push the axle shafts inward and install the C-lock at the end of each shaft spline. Pull the shafts outboard until the C-lock enters the recess in the side gears.

29. Install the pinion shaft. Apply Loctite® to the pinion shaft lock bolt and tighten to 15–30 ft. lbs. (20–41 Nm).

30. Install the anti-lock sensor, if equipped.

31. Install the rear brake drums or disc brake rotors and calipers.

32. Install the rear carrier cover using new silcone sealer. Tighten the retaining bolts on metal covers to 25–34 ft. lbs. (34–47 Nm) or 15–19 ft. lbs. (20–27 Nm) on plastic covers.

33. Install the brake junction block on the carrier cover and tighten to 11–17 ft. lbs. (14–24 Nm).

34. Fill the axle with lubricant to the bottom of the filler hole. Install the filler plug and tighten to 15–30 ft. lbs. (20–41 Nm).

35. If equipped with air springs, proceed as follows:

a. Connect the negative battery cable and turn ON the air suspension switch. Leave the diagnostic pigtail ungrounded.

b. Connect a suitable battery charger to the battery.

c. Open the drivers door, but leave all other doors shut. Turn the ignition switch to the RUN position for 5 seconds minimum, then turn the switch OFF.

d. Connect a jumper wire between the diagnostic pigtail and ground. The pigtail must remain grounded for the remainder of the spring fill procedure.

e. Leaving the driver s door open, apply the brakes and turn the ignition switch to RUN, but do not start the engine. The warning indicator will blink continuously once every 2 seconds, to indicate the spring pump sequence has been entered.

f. Close and open the drivers door once. After a 6 second delay, the rear spring will be filled for 60 seconds.

g. After completing the spring fill, turn the air suspension switch OFF to prevent deflation of the air springs while the vehicle is raised. Inspect the air springs for proper inflation: no folds or creases.

36. Lower the vehicle. If equipped with air suspension, turn the air suspension switch ON.

NOTE: If equipped with air suspension, any further leveling will be done during normal vehicle operation on the ground.

Thunderbird and Cougar

NOTE: Before removing the rear halfshafts, new inboard CV-joint stub shaft circlips, new differential oil seals and new hub retainer nuts must be available for assembly.

1. Remove the right wheelcover/hub cover and remove the hub retainer nut. Loosen the wheel nuts.

2. Raise and support the vehicle safely by the frame only. Remove the wheel nuts and remove the right wheel and tire assembly.

3. If equipped with drum brakes, remove the right brake drum.

4. If equipped with disc brakes, perform the following:

a. Remove the anti-lock brake sensor, if equipped.

b. Use needle-nose pliers to slide the parking brake cable adjusting clip downward until the cable is released.

c. Remove the parking brake cable from the brake caliper.

d. Remove the retaining bolts and remove the right caliper. Support the caliper from the brake junction bracket with a wire; do not allow it to hang from the brake hose.

e. Remove the right brake rotor.

5. Remove the right upper control arm nut and bolt. Wire the upper control arm to the top of the shock absorber, out of the way.

6. Using a paint marker, mark the position of the right lower control arm in relation to the knuckle with the lower bushings in the relaxed position.

NOTE: Failure to mark this relationship will result in bushing wind-up on assembly and incorrect ride height, causing misalignment and premature tire wear.

7. If equipped with drum brakes, proceed as follows:

a. Use hub remover tool T81P-1104-C or other suitable puller to free the right halfshaft from the hub.

b. Remove the lower control arm-to-knuckle attaching bolts.

c. Remove the right knuckle assembly from the halfshaft.

d. Carefully rest the halfshaft on the lower arm and wire the knuckle assembly to the top of the shock. Do not allow the knuckle assembly to hang from the brake hose.

e. Remove the right halfshaft from the differential using CV-joint remover tool T89P-3514-A or equivalent. Push the tool inward until the CV-joint is freed from the differential side gear.

NOTE: Be careful not to damage the differential oil seal, differential housing and/or CV-joint boot.

f. Remove the halfshaft from the vehicle. Insert a plug into the differential housing to prevent fluid loss.

8. If equipped with disc brakes, proceed as follows:

a. Remove the lower control arm-to-knuckle attaching bolts.

b. Remove the right halfshaft from the differential using CV-joint remover tool T89P-3514-A or equivalent. Push the tool inward until the CV-joint is freed from the differential side gear.

NOTE: Be careful not to damage the differential oil seal, differential housing and/or CV-joint boot.

c. Remove the halfshaft and knuckle assembly from the vehicle.

d. Insert a plug into the differential housing to prevent fluid loss.

9. Mark the driveshaft in relation to the companion flange. Remove the driveshaft retaining bolts, slide the driveshaft forward and let it rest on the driveshaft hoop.

10. With a jack supporting the rear axle, remove the rear axle mount to crossmember retaining nuts. Remove the rear mount from the axle cover.

11. Remove the axle front retaining bolts, nuts, bushings and washers.

12. Remove the inboard CV-joint of the left halfshaft from the differential housing using CV-joint remover tool T89P-3514-A or equivalent, by pushing the tool inward, toward the carrier.

13. Partially lower the axle assembly. While lowering the axle, move it to the right and disengage the axle from the left stub shaft. Be careful not to damage the CV-joint boot.

14. Install a plug into the left side of the differential and lower the axle from the vehicle.

To install:

15. Replace the differential oil seals. Install a new circlip on the left inboard stub shaft.

16. Position the axle on the jack and partially raise to align the left CV-joint stub shaft into the differential side gear. Lightly lubricate the stub shaft splines prior to installation.

NOTE: Be careful not to damage the differential pilot bearing or oil seal during halfshaft installation and spline alignment.

17. Locate the axle on the front mounting bolts and push in the CV-joint until the circlip seats in the differential side gear.

18. Install the bushings, washers and nuts on the front differential mount. Tighten the retaining nuts to 68–100 ft. lbs. (92–136 Nm). The bushings must be installed properly.

19. Install the rear mount to the differential cover. Tighten to 80–100 ft. lbs. (108–136 Nm).

20. Install the rear mount-to-crossmember retaining bolts and nuts. Tighten to 122–156 ft. lbs. (165–211 Nm).

21. Align the marks on the driveshaft and companion flange. Install the retaining bolts and tighten to 70–95 ft. lbs. (95–129 Nm).

22. Install a new circlip on the right inboard stub shaft, by sliding it into the groove on the splined end of the shaft.

23. Lightly lubricate the stub shaft splines and carefully align the splines on the shaft with the splines in the differential.

24. Push the halfshaft inward to seat the circlip in the differential side gear groove. Use care not to damage the seal.

25. If equipped with drum brakes, proceed as follows:

a. Engage the hub splines with the outboard CV-joint splines.

b. Install the lower control arm bolts and nuts. Align the paint marks and tighten the bolts to 119–147 ft. lbs. (160–200mm).

c. Install a new hub retaining nut and pull the CV-joint into the hub as far as possible by hand.

d. Install the upper arm retaining bolt and nut and tighten to 119–147 ft. lbs. (160–200 Nm).

e. Install the brake drum.

26. If equipped with disc brakes, proceed as follows:

a. Install the lower control arm bolts and nuts. Align the paint marks and tighten the bolts to 119–147 ft. lbs. (160–200mm).

b. Install the upper arm retaining bolt and nut and tighten to 119–147 ft. lbs. (160–200 Nm).

c. Install the brake rotor.

d. Install the brake caliper assembly to the rotor with the outer brake shoe against the rotor's braking surface. This prevents pinching the piston boot between the inner brake shoe and the piston.

e. Install the caliper retaining bolts and tighten to 45–65 ft. lbs. (60–90 Nm).

f. Install the parking brake cable to the brake caliper. Install the cable adjustment clip.

g. Install the anti-lock brake sensor, if equipped. Tighten the retaining bolts to 14–20 ft. lbs. (19–27 Nm).

27. Fill the axle with the proper type and quantity of lubricant. Install the differential fill plug and tighten to 20–30 ft. lbs. (28–40 Nm).

28. Install the wheel and tire assembly and tighten the wheel nuts to 80–106 ft. lbs. (108–144 Nm). Lower the vehicle.

29. If equipped with drum brakes, tighten the hub nut to 250 ft. lbs. (340 Nm). Install the wheelcover/hub cover.

MANUAL TRANSMISSION

For further information on transmission/transaxles, please refer to "Chilton's Guide to Transmission Repair".

Transmission Assembly

REMOVAL & INSTALLATION

Mustang

1. Disconnect the negative battery cable.

2. Raise and support the vehicle safely.

3. Mark the position of the driveshaft on the axle flange so it can be reinstalled in the same position. Disconnect the driveshaft from the flange. Slide the driveshaft off the transmission output shaft and install a suitable plug to prevent lubricant from leaking.

4. Remove the catalytic converter.

5. Remove the 2 nuts attaching the rear transmission support to the crossmember. Remove the bolts.

6. Support the engine and transmission with a suitable jack.

7. Remove the 2 nuts from the crossmember bolts. Remove the bolts, raise the jack slightly and remove the crossmember.

8. Lower the transmission to expose the 2 bolts securing the shift handle to the shift tower. Remove the 2 nuts and bolts and remove the shift handle.

9. Disconnect the wiring harness from the backup lamp switch. On the 5.0L engine, disconnect the neutral sensing switch.

10. Remove the bolt from the speedometer cable retainer and remove the speedometer driven gear from the transmission.

11. Remove the 4 bolts that secure the transmission to the flywheel housing.

12. Move the transmission and jack rearward until the transmission input shaft clears the flywheel housing. If necessary lower the engine enough to obtain clearance for removing the transmission.

NOTE: Do not depress the clutch while the transmission is removed.

To install:

13. Make sure the mounting surface of the transmission and flywheel housing are clean and free of dirt, paint and burrs.

14. Install 2 guide pins in the flywheel housing lower mounting bolt holes. Raise the transmission and move forward on the guide pins until the input shaft splines enter the clutch hub splines and the case is positioned against the flywheel housing.

15. Install the 2 upper transmission-to-flywheel housing mounting bolts snug and remove the 2 guide pins. Install the 2 lower mounting bolts and tighten all the bolts to 45–65 ft. lbs. (61–88 Nm).

16. Raise the transmission with a jack until the shift handle can be secured to the shift tower. Install and tighten the attaching bolts and washers to 23–32 ft. lbs. (31–43 Nm).

17. Connect the speedometer cable to the extension housing and tighten the attaching screw to 54–115 inch lbs. (6–13 Nm).

18. Raise the rear of the transmission with the jack and install the transmission support. Install and tighten the attaching bolts to 36–50 ft. lbs. (48–68 Nm).

19. With the transmission extension housing resting on the engine rear support, install the attaching bolts and tighten to 35 ft. lbs. (48 Nm).

20. Connect the backup lamp switch wiring harness. On 5.0L engine, connect the neutral sensing switch to the wiring harness.

21. Install the catalytic converter. Tighten the attaching bolts to 20–30 ft. lbs. (27–41 Nm).

22. Remove the extension housing installation tool and slide the forward end of the driveshaft over the transmission output shaft. Connect the driveshaft to the axle flange. Make sure the marks align that were made during removal. Tighten the U-bolt nuts to 42–57 ft. lbs. (56–77 Nm).

23. Fill the transmission with the proper type and quantity of fluid.

24. Lower the vehicle. Check the shift and crossover motion for full shift engagement and smooth crossover operation.

Thunderbird and Cougar

1. Disconnect the negative battery cable.

2. Shift the transmission into the **N** position.

3. Remove the shift knob and the console top cover.

4. Remove the 2 shifter retaining bolts and remove the shifter.

5. Raise and support the vehicle safely.

6. Remove the drain plug and drain the oil from the transmission.

7. Remove the body reinforcement in front of the axle.

8. Disconnect the rear exhaust assembly from the resonator.

9. Remove the 4 bolts retaining the driveshaft to the companion flange. The rear driveshaft yoke and companion flange are marked for reassembly.

10. Position an axle stand under the front axle housing and remove the forward retaining nuts and bushings. Loosen the rear retaining nuts to allow the axle to tilt for driveshaft removal.

11. Pull the vent tube from the hole in the sub-frame.

12. Lower the front of the axle housing with the axle stand and slide the driveshaft out of the transmission above the axle housing. Let the driveshaft rest on the front driveshaft support and axle assembly.

13. Remove the catalytic converter.

14. Disconnect the hydraulic clutch line.

15. Disconnect the electrical connectors and remove the starter.

16. Position a transmission jack under the transmission. Remove the crossmember and the bellhousing to engine bolts.

17. Move the transmission to the rear until the input shaft clears the flywheel and lower the transmission from the vehicle.

To install:

18. Install guide studs in the engine block and raise the transmission until the input shaft splines are aligned with the clutch disc splines.

19. Slide the transmission forward on the guide studs until it is against the bellhousing. Install the bellhousing-to-engine retaining bolts and tighten to 28–38 ft. lbs. (38–51 Nm).

20. Install the crossmember and tighten the bolts to 35–50 ft. lbs. (47–68 Nm). Remove the transmission jack.

21. Install the starter and connect the electrical connectors. Connect the hydraulic clutch line.

22. Install the catalytic converter assembly.

23. Lubricate the splines with grease and slide the driveshaft into the transmission.

24. Raise the axle housing with the axle stand and install the bushings and retaining nuts. Tighten the retaining nuts to 68–100 ft. lbs. (92–136 Nm) and remove the axle stand.

25. Position the vent tube in the hole of the sub-frame.

26. Align the driveshaft yoke and companion flange and install the retaining bolts. Tighten to 71–95 ft. lbs. (95–129 Nm).

27. Connect the exhaust pipe muffler assembly to the resonator. Lower the vehicle.

28. Position the shifter and install the retaining bolts. Tighten to 18–24 ft. lbs. (24–33 Nm). Install the console top cover and the shifter knob.

29. Connect the negative battery cable. Check transmission operation.

CLUTCH

Clutch Assembly

REMOVAL & INSTALLATION

Mustang

1. Disconnect the negative battery cable. Lift the clutch pedal to its uppermost position to disengage the pawl and quadrant. Push quadrant forward, unhook cable from quadrant and allow quadrant to slowly swing rearward.

2. Raise and safely support the vehicle. Remove the dust shield, if equipped.

3. Disconnect cable from the release lever. Remove the retaining clip and remove the clutch cable from the flywheel housing.

4. Remove the starter. If equipped with 5.0L engine, remove the bolts that secure engine rear plate to front lower part of flywheel housing. If equipped with 2.3L engine, remove the flywheel housing-to-oil pan bolts.

5. Remove the transmission, then the flywheel housing.

6. Remove the clutch release lever boot. Remove clutch release lever from housing by pulling it through the window in housing until retainer spring is disengaged from pivot. Remove release bearing from release lever.

7. Loosen the pressure plate cover attaching bolts evenly to release spring tension gradually and avoid distorting cover. If same pressure plate and cover are to be installed, mark cover and flywheel so pressure plate can be installed in its original position.

8. Inspect the flywheel for scoring, cracks or other damage and machine or replace, as necessary. Inspect the pilot bearing for damage and free movement. Replace, as necessary.

To install:

9. If removed, install the flywheel. Make sure the mating surfaces of the flywheel and the crankshaft flange are clean prior to installation. Tighten the flywheel bolts to 56–64 ft. lbs. (73–87 Nm) on 2.3L engines or 75–85 ft. lbs. (102–115 Nm) on 5.0L engine.

10. Position the clutch disc and pressure plate assembly on the flywheel. The 3 dowel pins on the flywheel must be properly aligned with the pressure plate. Bent, damaged or missing dowels must be replaced. Start the pressure plate bolts but do not tighten them.

11. Align the clutch disc using a suitable alignment tool inserted in the pilot bearing. Alternately tighten the bolts a few turns at a time, until they are all tight. Final torque the bolts to 12–24 ft. lbs. (17–32 Nm). Remove the alignment tool.

12. Apply a light coating of multipurpose long-life grease to the release bearing contact surface of the transmission bearing retainer, the pressure plate fingers contact surface of the release bearing, the release lever pivot pocket, release lever fork and flywheel housing pivot ball. Fill the grease groove of the release bearing hub with the same grease. Clean all excess grease from the inside bore of the bearing hub.

13. Install the release bearing on the release lever and install the lever in the flywheel housing. Install the boot.

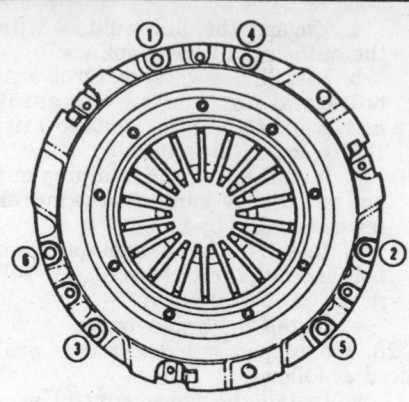

Pressure plate bolt torque sequence— Thunderbird and Cougar

14. Install the flywheel housing. Tighten the bolts to 29–38 ft. lbs. (38–52 Nm) on the 2.3L engine or 38–55 ft. lbs. (52–74 Nm) on the 5.0L engine.

15. Install the remaining components in the reverse order of removal.

Thunderbird and Cougar

1. Disconnect the negative battery cable.

2. Disconnect the clutch hydraulic system master cylinder from the clutch pedal.

3. Raise and support the vehicle safely.

4. Remove the starter.

5. Disconnect the hydraulic coupling at the transmission with tool T88T–70522–A or equivalent, by sliding the white plastic sleeve toward the slave cylinder and applying a slight tug on the tube.

6. Remove the transmission.

7. Matchmark the assembled position of the pressure plate to the flywheel.

8. Loosen the pressure plate attaching bolts evenly until the pressure plate springs are expanded, and remove the bolts. Be sure to support the pressure plate before removing the last bolt.

9. Remove the pressure plate and clutch disc from the flywheel.

10. Inspect the flywheel for scoring, cracks or other damage and machine or replace, as necessary. Inspect the pilot bearing for damage and free movement. Replace, as necessary.

To install:

11. If removed, install the flywheel. Make sure the mating surfaces of the flywheel and the crankshaft flange are clean prior to installation. Tighten the flywheel bolts to 54–64 ft. lbs. (73–87 Nm).

12. Position the clutch disc on the flywheel so a suitable alignment tool can enter the clutch pilot bearing and align the disc.

13. If reinstalling the original pressure plate, align the matchmarks. Po-

sition the pressure plate on the flywheel and install the retaining bolts hand tight. Tighten the bolts, in sequence, to 20–28 ft. lbs. (27–39 Nm). Remove the alignment tool.

14. Install the remaining components in the reverse order of removal. Tighten the flywheel housing-to-engine bolts to 40–49 ft. lbs. (54–67 Nm).

NOTE: Reuse the aluminum washers under the attaching bolts to prevent galvanic corrosion.

Clutch Cable

REMOVAL & INSTALLATION

Mustang

NOTE: Whenever the clutch cable is disconnected, it is mandatory that the proper method for installing the clutch cable be followed.

1. Lift the clutch pedal to its upward most position to disengage the pawl and quadrant. Push the quadrant forward, unhook the cable from the quadrant and allow it to slowly swing rearward.
2. Remove the screw that holds the cable insulator to the dash panel and pull the cable through the dash panel and into the engine compartment.
3. Remove the cable bracket screw from the fender apron.
4. Raise and support the vehicle safely.
5. On 5.0L engine, remove the dust cover from the bellhousing.
6. Remove the clip retainer holding the cable to the bellhousing.
7. On the 5.0L engine, slide the ball on the end of the cable through the hole in the clutch release lever and remove the cable.
8. On the 2.3L engine, remove the hairpin clip, clevis pin and clevis from the end of the cable.

To install:

NOTE: The clutch pedal must be lifted to disengage the adjusting mechanism during cable installation. Failure to do so will cause damage the self-adjuster mechanism. A prying instrument should never be used to install the cable into the quadrant.

9. Slide the cable through the hole in the bellhousing and through the hole in the the release lever. On the 5.0L engine, slide the ball on the end of the cable assembly into the cable ball pocket on the clutch release lever. On the 2.3L engine, place the cable ball into the clevis. Install the clevis and

clevis pin onto the clutch release lever and into the clevis pin.
10. Install the clutch cable retaining clip on the bellhousing.
11. On the 5.0L engine, install the dust shield on the bellhousing.
12. Push the cable assembly into the engine compartment and lower the vehicle. Install the cable bracket screw in the fender apron.
13. Push the cable into the hole in the dash panel and secure the insulator with a screw.
14. Install the cable assembly by lifting the clutch pedal to disengage the pawl and quadrant. Then, pushing the quadrant forward, hook the end of the cable over the rear of the quadrant.
15. Depress the clutch pedal several times to adjust the cable.

Clutch Master Cylinder

REMOVAL & INSTALLATION

Thunderbird and Cougar

1. Disconnect the negative battery cable.

2. Disconnect the clutch pedal from the pushrod.
3. Disconnect the hydraulic line from the slave cylinder by depressing the white retainer bushing with tool T88T–70522–A or equivalent, while pulling slightly on the line.
4. Remove the 2 push pins retaining the clutch master cylinder reservoir to the left shock tower.
5. Rotate the master cylinder 45 degrees counterclockwise, then carefully pull the master cylinder through the dash panel, noting the routing of the hydraulic line to the slave cylinder.
6. If the master cylinder is to be replaced, position the master cylinder in a vise and drive out the roll pin using a drift. Remove the O-ring from the tube connection of the master cylinder.

To install:

7. Install a new O-ring onto the clutch tube and install the tube into the master cylinder. Install the roll pin.
8. Position the clutch master cylinder in the engine compartment and route the hydraulic line to the slave cylinder.

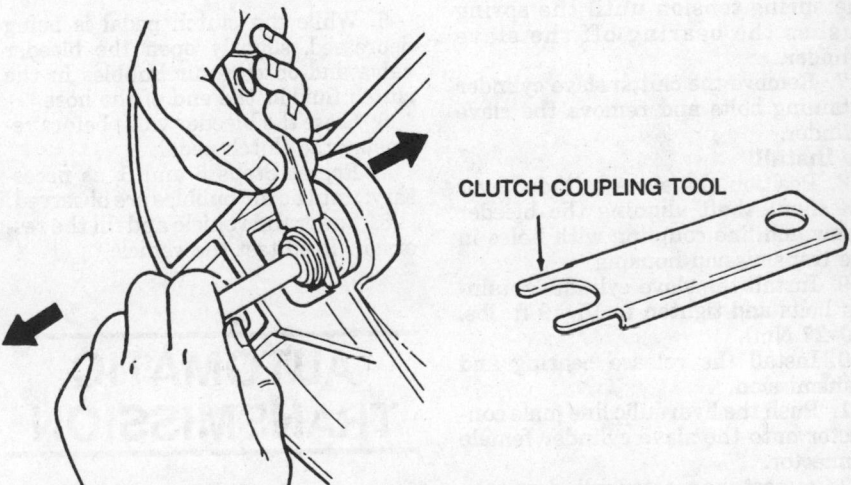

CLUTCH COUPLING TOOL

Disconnecting the clutch hydraulic line from the slave cylinder—Thunderbird and Cougar

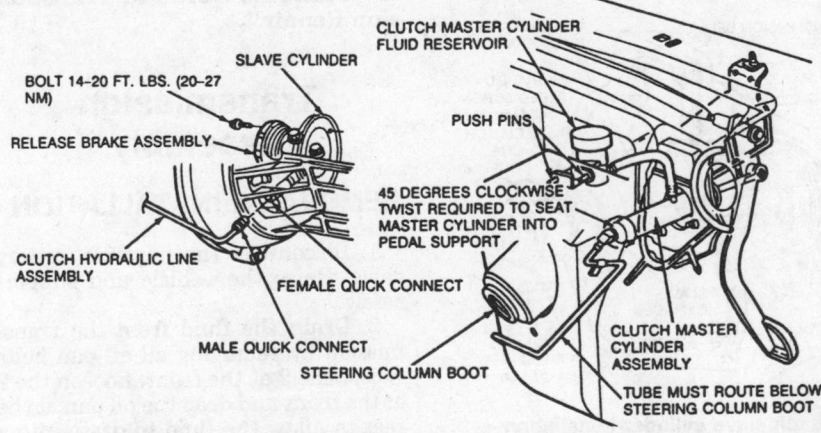

BOLT 14–20 FT. LBS. (20–27 NM)

RELEASE BRAKE ASSEMBLY

SLAVE CYLINDER

CLUTCH HYDRAULIC LINE ASSEMBLY

FEMALE QUICK CONNECT

MALE QUICK CONNECT

STEERING COLUMN BOOT

CLUTCH MASTER CYLINDER FLUID RESERVOIR

PUSH PINS

45 DEGREES CLOCKWISE TWIST REQUIRED TO SEAT MASTER CYLINDER INTO PEDAL SUPPORT

CLUTCH MASTER CYLINDER ASSEMBLY

TUBE MUST ROUTE BELOW STEERING COLUMN BOOT

Clutch master cylinder installation—Thunderbird and Cougar

9. Install the master cylinder to the dash panel and install the clutch master cylinder fluid reservoir.

10. Push the hydraulic line male connector onto the slave cylinder female connector. Connect the pushrod to the clutch pedal.

11. Fill the reservoir and bleed the system.

Clutch Slave Cylinder

REMOVAL & INSTALLATION

Thunderbird and Cougar

1. Disconnect the negative battery cable.

2. Disconnect the master cylinder pushrod from the clutch pedal.

3. Raise and support the vehicle safely.

4. Disconnect the hydraulic line from the slave cylinder by depressing the white retainer bushing with tool T88T-70522-A or equivalent, while pulling slightly on the line.

5. Remove the transmission.

6. Remove the clutch release bearing by rotating the assembly against the spring tension until the spring pushes the bearing off the slave cylinder.

7. Remove the clutch slave cylinder retaining bolts and remove the slave cylinder.

To install:

8. Position the slave cylinder over the input shaft aligning the bleeder screw and line coupling with holes in the transmission housing.

9. Install the slave cylinder retaining bolts and tighten to 15–19 ft. lbs. (20–27 Nm).

10. Install the release bearing and transmission.

11. Push the hydraulic line male connector onto the slave cylinder female connector.

12. Connect the master cylinder pushrod to the clutch pedal. Bleed the system.

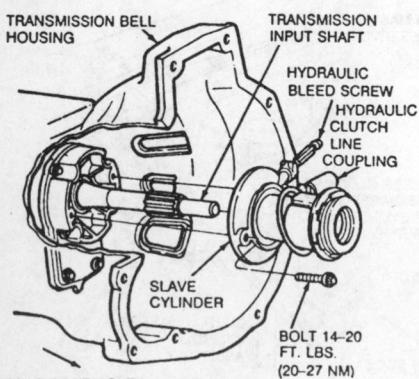

TRANSMISSION BELL HOUSING
TRANSMISSION INPUT SHAFT
HYDRAULIC BLEED SCREW
HYDRAULIC CLUTCH LINE COUPLING
SLAVE CYLINDER
BOLT 14–20 FT. LBS. (20–27 NM)
FRONT OF VEHICLE

Clutch slave cylinder installation— Thunderbird and Cougar

Hydraulic Clutch System Bleeding

THUNDERBIRD and COUGAR

NOTE: Be sure to pump the clutch at least 30 times to make sure air is in the system. If the slave cylinder is pushed off the clutch plate, a similar pedal feel may occur. Pumping the clutch pushes fluid from the clutch reservoir into the slave cylinder, pushing it out to meet the clutch plate.

1. Clean all dirt and grease from the cap to make sure no foreign substances enter the system.

2. Remove the cap and diaphragm and fill the reservoir to the top with the proper fluid.

3. Raise and support the vehicle safely.

4. Attach a hose to the bleeder valve at the slave cylinder.

NOTE: Keep the clutch fluid reservoir full at all times to prevent air from being pulled into the system.

5. While the clutch pedal is being depressed, slightly open the bleeder valve and observe air bubbles in the clutch fluid at the end of the hose.

6. Close the bleeder valve before releasing the clutch pedal.

7. Repeat Steps 5 and 6, as necessary, until no air bubbles are observed.

8. Lower the vehicle and fill the reservoir. Road test the vehicle.

AUTOMATIC TRANSMISSION

For further information on transmission/transaxles, please refer to "Chilton's Guide to Transmission Repair".

Transmission Assembly

REMOVAL & INSTALLATION

1. Disconnect the negative battery cable. Raise the vehicle and support safely.

2. Drain the fluid from the transmission by removing all oil pan bolts except the 2 at the front. Loosen the 2 at the front and drop the oil pan at the rear to allow the fluid to drain into a container. When drained, reinstall a few of the bolts to hold the pan in place.

3. Remove the access cover and remove the converter drain plug, if equipped, to allow the converter to drain. After the converter has drained, reinstall the drain plug and tighten. Remove the converter to flywheel nuts by turning the converter to expose the bolts.

NOTE: Crank the engine over with a wrench on the crankshaft pulley attaching bolt. On belt driven OHC engines, never rotate the pulley in a counterclockwise direction as viewed from the front.

4. On Mustang and Mark VII, mark the position of the driveshaft on the axle flange so it can be reinstalled in the same position. Disconnect the driveshaft from the flange and slide the driveshaft from the transmission. Install a suitable plug in the extension housing to prevent fluid leakage.

5. On Thunderbird and Cougar, proceed as follows:

   a. Remove the catalytic converter.

   b. Remove the body reinforcement.

   c. Remove the exhaust pipe and muffler assembly.

   d. Mark the position of the driveshaft on the axle flange so it can be reinstalled in the same position. Disconnect the driveshaft from the flange.

   e. Loosen the differential housing assembly rear mounting nuts approximately ¼ in.

   f. Position an axle stand under the front of the differential housing and remove the forward mounting nuts and bushings. Pull the vent tube from the hole in the sub-frame.

   g. Lower the front of the differential housing with the axle stand and slide the driveshaft out of the transmission above the axle housing. Let the drive shaft rest on the front driveshaft support and axle assembly.

6. Remove the speedometer cable or sensor from the extension housing.

7. Disconnect the manual control shift rod or cable and the downshift rod or cable from the transmission control levers.

8. Remove the starter cable and remove the starter.

9. Remove the electrical wires and vacuum lines, as required from the transmission assembly. Remove the bellcrank bracket, if equipped, from the converter housing.

10. Place a support under the transmission and slightly raise it. It may be necessary to raise the engine hood and loosen the fan shroud.

11. Remove the rear crossmember and engine rear support. Disconnect and remove any interfering exhaust components.

12. Lower the transmission to expose the oil cooler line fittings. Disconnect the lines from the transmission.

13. Support the engine and remove the dipstick tube and all the bell housing retaining bolts except for the top 2.

14. Chain the transmission to the jack or support unit for safety.

15. Remove the 2 top bolts from the converter housing and move the transmission rearward and down from under the vehicle. Hold the converter in place to avoid having it drop from the transmission.

To install:

16. Tighten the converter drain plug to 8–28 ft. lbs. (11–38 Nm).

17. Position the converter to the transmission and rotate into position to make sure the drive flats are fully engaged in the pump gear.

NOTE: Lubricate the pilot with chassis grease.

18. Raise the converter and transmission assembly into position. Rotate the converter until the studs and drain plug are in alignment with the holes in the flywheel. Align the orange balancing marks on the converter stud and flywheel bolt hole if balancing marks are present.

NOTE: The converter face must rest squarely against the flywheel. This indicates that the converter pilot is not binding in the engine crankshaft. To ensure the converter is properly seated, grasp a converter stud. It should move freely back and forth in the flywheel hole. If the converter will not move, the transmission must be removed and the converter repositioned so the impeller hub is properly engaged in the pump gear.

19. Install the transmission-to-engine attaching bolts. Tighten the bolts to 40–50 ft. lbs. (55–68 Nm) on all except 2.3L engine. On 2.3L engine, tighten the bolts to 28–38 ft. lbs. (38–51 Nm).

20. Remove the safety chain from around the transmission.

21. Install a new O-ring on the lower end of the transmission filler tube, if equipped. Install the tube to the transmission case and secure with the retaining bolt.

22. Connect the speedometer cable to the transmission case, if equipped.

23. Connect the oil cooler lines to the right side of the transmission case.

24. Position the crossmember on the side supports. Position the rear mount on the crossmember and install the attaching bolts and/or nuts.

25. Secure the engine rear support to the extension housing.

26. Install any exhaust system components, if removed.

27. Lower the transmission and remove the jack.

28. Secure the crossmember to the side supports with the attaching bolts.

29. Connect the TV linkage rod or cable and the manual linkage rod.

30. Install the converter to flywheel attaching nuts and tighten to 20–34 ft. lbs. (27–46 Nm). Install the converter housing cover.

31. Secure the starter motor in place and connect all electrical connections.

32. Install the driveshaft, making sure the index marks are aligned. On Thunderbird and Cougar, proceed as follows:

   a. Raise the differential housing with the axle stand and install the bushings and retaining nuts. Tighten to 68–100 ft. lbs. (92–136 Nm). Remove the axle stand.

   b. Tighten the differential rear retaining nuts to 122–156 ft. lbs. (165–211 Nm).

   c. Position the vent tube in the hole of the sub-frame.

   d. Align the driveshaft yoke and companion flange and install the retaining bolts. Tighten to 70–95 ft. lbs. (95–129 Nm).

   e. Install the catalytic converter, exhaust pipe and muffler.

   f. Install the body reinforcement.

33. Lower the vehicle. Fill the transmission with the proper type and quantity of fluid, start the engine and check the transmission for leakage. Adjust the linkage as required.

MANUAL LINKAGE ADJUSTMENT

1. Position the transmission selector lever in the **OVERDRIVE** position.

NOTE: The shift lever should be held against the rearward OVERDRIVE stop when the linkage is adjusted.

2. Raise and safely support the vehicle. Loosen the manual lever shift cable or rod retaining nut. Move the transmission manual lever to the **OVERDRIVE** position.

3. With the transmission selector lever and manual lever in the **OVERDRIVE** position, tighten the retaining nut to 10–18 ft. lbs. (13–25 Nm).

4. Check the operation of the transmission in each selector lever position.

THROTTLE VALVE CABLE ADJUSTMENT

Automatic Overdrive Transmission

1. Set the parking brake and place the shift selector in **N**.

2. Remove the air cleaner cover and inlet tube from the throttle body inlet to access the throttle lever and cable.

3. Using a small prybar, pry the grooved pin on the cable assembly out of the grommet on the throttle body. Then push out the white locking tab.

4. Check the plastic block with pin and tab; it should slide freely on the notched rod. If not, the white tab may not be pushed out far enough.

5. While holding the throttle lever firmly against the idle stop, push the grooved pin into the grommet on the throttle lever as far as it will go.

6. Make sure the throttle lever does not move while pushing the pin into the grommet.

7. Install the air cleaner cover and inlet tube.

FRONT SUSPENSION

NOTE: If equipped with the level ride air suspension, power to the air system must be shut OFF before servicing the suspension. The switch is located in the luggage compartment, on the drivers side rear fender well.

MacPherson Strut

REMOVAL & INSTALLATION

Mustang

1. Disconnect the negative battery cable.

2. Place the ignition switch in the **UNLOCKED** position to permit free movement of the front wheels.

3. Raise the vehicle by the lower control arms until the wheels are just off the ground. From the engine compartment, remove and discard the 3 upper mount retaining nuts. Do not remove the pop-rivet holding the camber plate position.

4. Continue to raise the front of the vehicle by the lower control arms and position safety stands under the frame jacking pads, rearward of the wheels.

5. Remove the wheel and tire assembly and remove the brake caliper. Support the caliper with a length of wire; do not let the caliper hang by the brake hose.

6. Remove the 2 lower nuts that attach the strut to the spindle, leaving the bolts in place. Carefully remove both spindle-to-strut bolts, push the bracket free of the spindle and remove the strut.

7. Compress the strut to clear the upper mount of the body mounting pad. Remove the upper mount and jounce bumper, if necessary.

To install:

8. Install the upper mount and jounce bumper, if removed.

9. Position the 3 upper mount studs into the body mounting pad and camber plate and start 3 new nuts.

10. Compress the strut and position into the spindle. Install 2 new lower retaining bolts and hand start the nuts. Remove the suspension load from the control arms by lowering the vehicle. Tighten the lower retaining nuts to 140–200 ft. lbs. (190–271 Nm).

11. Raise the suspension control arms and tighten the 3 new upper mount retaining nuts to 45–59 ft. lbs. (60–81 Nm).

12. Install the brake caliper and the wheel and tire assembly.

13. Lower the vehicle to the ground and check the front end alignment.

Thunderbird and Cougar

1. Remove the plastic cover at the upper strut mount, if equipped. If equipped with automatic ride control, remove the actuator assembly as follows:

   a. Make sure the vehicle is level. Turn the ignition switch **OFF**.

   b. Disconnect the actuator connector from the wiring harness connector. Remove the actuator cover by snapping off.

   c. Slide the actuator connector off the cover by inserting a small prybar tip between the connector and track to separate the 2 parts prior to sliding the connector off.

   d. Squeeze the 2 actuator retaining tabs firmly inward with 1 hand and lift the actuator off the mounting bracket with the other hand.

   e. Grasp the piston rod end at the 9mm hex with a socket wrench.

   f. Loosen the nut retaining the actuator mounting bracket to the strut with a 19mm box wrench while holding the socket wrench.

   g. Remove the nut and mounting bracket.

2. Remove the 3 upper strut retaining nuts and collar plate from the mounting studs in the engine compartment.

3. Raise and safely support the vehicle. Remove the wheel and tire assembly.

4. Remove the lower strut mounting bolt and nut and remove the nut at the stabilizer link upper mounting stud. Separate the link from the spindle using a suitable joint separator tool.

5. Support the lower control arm with a jack. Raise the control arm and spindle with the jack until the stabilizer link can be completely separated from the spindle. Position the link aside.

6. Remove and discard the spindle to upper control arm retaining nut and bolt. Lower the jack to separate the spindle from the upper control arm. Support the spindle with a length of wire; do not let it hang free.

7. Lower the support for the lower control arm and remove the strut assembly from the vehicle.

To install:

8. Position the strut over the lower arm. Insert the lower strut bolt into the control arm.

9. Using a jack, raise the control arm and strut into position. Align upper strut mounting studs with the holes.

10. Remove the wire supporting the spindle and position the spindle to the upper control arm. Raise the lower control arm using the jack and attach the spindle to the upper control arm.

11. Install a new spindle retaining bolt from the front of the vehicle and install the nut. Tighten to 59–66 ft. lbs. (80–90 Nm).

12. Position the stabilizer bar link and lower the spindle assembly until the link can be installed. Install the nut on the link stud and tighten to 48–55 ft. lbs. (65–75 Nm).

13. Remove the jack from the lower arm. Install the lower strut nut, but do not tighten at this time.

14. Install the wheel and tire assembly and lower the vehicle. Make sure the upper strut mounting studs are aligned with the holes.

15. Install the collar plate and 3 nuts to the upper mounting studs. Tighten to 17–22 ft. lbs. (22–31 Nm).

16. Install the washer, nut and automatic ride actuator, if equipped. Install the plastic cover, if equipped.

17. Neutralize the front suspension bushings by pushing down and releasing on the front of the vehicle. Then tighten the lower strut nut to 140–162 ft. lbs. (190–220 Nm).

NOTE: The lower strut nut must be tightened with the vehicle weight on the wheels.

Mark VII

1. Turn the air suspension switch **OFF**.

2. Turn the ignition switch to the **UNLOCKED** position to allow free movement of the front wheels.

3. From inside the engine compartment, loosen but do not remove, the 1 strut-to-upper mount retaining nut. A small prybar positioned in the slot will hold the rod stationary while loosening the nut.

4. Raise the vehicle and position safety stands under the lower control arms as far outboard as possible, verifying the lower sensor mounting bracket is clear. Lower the vehicle until vehicle weight is supported by the lower arms.

5. Remove the wheel and tire assembly. Remove the brake caliper and support with a length of wire. Do not let the caliper hang by the brake hose.

6. Remove and discard the strut-to-upper mount retaining nut and then the 2 lower nuts and bolts attaching the strut to the spindle.

NOTE: The strut should be held firmly during removal of the last bolt since the gas pressure will cause the strut to fully extend when removed.

7. Lift the strut up from the spindle to compress the rod and then remove the strut. Remove the jounce bumper.

To install:

8. Prime the new strut by extending and compressing the strut 5 times. Install the jounce bumper.

9. Place the strut rod through the upper mount and hand start a new nut. Tighten the nut to 55–92 ft. lbs. (75–125 Nm).

10. Compress the strut and position onto the spindle. Install 2 new lower retaining bolts and hand start the nuts.

11. Raise the vehicle to remove the vehicle load from the lower control arms. Tighten the lower retaining nuts to 140–200 ft. lbs. (190–271 Nm).

12. Install the brake caliper and the wheel and tire assembly. Remove the safety stand and lower the vehicle to the ground.

13. Turn the air suspension switch **ON**. Check the front end alignment.

Coil Springs

REMOVAL & INSTALLATION

Mustang

1. Raise and safely support the vehicle, allowing the control arms to hang free.

2. Remove the wheel and tire assembly and the brake caliper. Suspend the caliper with a length of wire; do not let the caliper hang by the brake hose.

3. Disconnect the tie rod end from the steering spindle and disconnect the stabilizer link from the lower arm.

4. Remove the steering gear bolts, if

necessary and position the gear so the suspension arm bolt can be removed.

5. If equipped with 2.3L engine, use spring compressor tool T82P–5310–A or equivalent to place the upper plate in position into the spring pocket cavity on the crossmember. The hooks on the plate should be facing the center of the vehicle.

6. If equipped with 5.0L engine, use spring compressor tool D78P–5310–A or equivalent, to install a plate between the coils near the toe of the spring. Mark the location of the upper plate on the coils for installation.

7. Install the compression rod into the lower arm spring pocket hole, through the coil spring and into the upper plate.

8. Install the lower plate, lower ball nut, thrust washer and bearing and forcing nut onto the compression rod. Tighten the forcing nut until a drag on the nut is felt.

9. Remove the suspension arm-to-crossmember nuts and bolts. The compressor tool forcing nut may have to be tightened or loosened for easy bolt removal.

10. Loosen the compression rod forcing nut until spring tension is relieved and remove the forcing nut. Remove the compression rod and coil spring.

To install:

11. Place the insulator on top of the spring. Position the spring into the lower arm pocket. Make sure the spring pigtail is positioned between the 2 holes in the lower arm spring pocket.

12. Position the spring into the upper spring seat in the crossmember.

13. If equipped with 2.3L engine, insert the compression rod through the control arm and spring, then hook it to the upper plate. The upper plate is installed with the hooks facing the center of the vehicle.

14. If equipped with 5.0L engine, install the upper plate between the coils in the location marked during removal.

15. Install the lower plate, ball nut, thrust washer and bearing and forcing nut onto the compression rod.

16. Tighten the forcing nut, position the lower arm into the crossmember and install new lower arm-to-crossmember bolts and nuts. Do not tighten at this time.

17. Remove the spring compressor tool from the vehicle. Raise the suspension arm to a normal attitude position with a jack. Tighten the lower arm-to-crossmember attaching nuts to 110–150 ft. lbs. (149–203 Nm). Remove the jack.

18. Install the steering gear-to-crossmember bolts and nuts, if removed. Hold the bolts and tighten the nuts to 90–100 ft. lbs. (122–135 Nm).

19. Connect the stabilizer bar link to the lower suspension arm. Tighten the attaching nut to 6–17 ft. lbs. (8–24 Nm).

20. Position the tie rod into the steering spindle and install the retaining nut. Tighten the nut to 35 ft. lbs. (47 Nm) and continue tightening the nut to align the next castellation with the hole in the stud. Install a new cotter pin.

21. Install the brake caliper and the wheel and tire assembly. Lower the vehicle.

Thunderbird and Cougar

1. Remove the strut assembly from the vehicle.

NOTE: The upper strut mount cannot be rotated when the strut and spring are assembled. Mark the position of the upper mount to the coil spring with chalk or paint, prior to disassembly. If the upper mount is not properly positioned during assembly, it will not install in the vehicle.

2. Position the strut assembly in spring compressor tool 086–00029 or equivalent.

3. Compress the spring. Remove the strut nut and washer and remove the upper mount.

4. Release the spring compressor to remove the coil spring.

To install:

5. If installing a new spring or upper mount, transfer the reference marks from the removed part to the new part.

6. Position the strut and the spring in the spring compressor tool and compress the spring to install the upper mount.

7. Install the upper mount, aligning the refernce marks. Install the washer and nut and tighten to 37–52 ft. lbs. (50–71 Nm).

8. Release the spring compressor, making sure the spring is properly seated at top and bottom.

9. Install the strut assembly in the vehicle.

Air Springs

REMOVAL & INSTALLATION

Mark VII

1. Turn the air suspension switch **OFF**.

2. Raise and safely support the vehicle on the frame. The suspension must be at full rebound.

3. Remove the wheel and tire assembly. Remove the air spring solenoid as follows:
   a. Disconnect the electrical con-

nector and then disconnect the air line.
   b. Remove the solenoid clip.
   c. Rotate the solenoid counterclockwise to the first stop.
   d. Pull the solenoid straight out slowly to the second stop to bleed air from the system.

NOTE: Do not fully release the solenoid until the air is completely bled from the air spring.

   e. After the air is fully bled from the system, rotate counterclockwise to the third stop and remove the solenoid from the solenoid housing. Remove the large O-ring from the solenoid housing.

4. Remove the clip retaining the spring to the lower arm. Push down on the spring clip on the collar of the air spring and rotate the collar counterclockwise to release the spring from the body spring seat.

5. Remove the air spring.

To install:

6. Install the air spring solenoid as follows:
   a. Check the solenoid O-rings for cuts or abrasion. Replace the O-rings as required. Lightly grease the O-ring area of the solenoid and the larger solenoid housing O-ring with silicone dielectric compound.
   b. Insert the solenoid into the air spring end cap and rotate clockwise to the third stop, push in to the second stop, then rotate clockwise to the first stop.
   c. Install the solenoid clip. Inspect the wire harness connector and ensure the rubber gasket is in place at the bottom of the connector cavity.

7. For left side installations, position the notch on the collar to be in-line with the centerline of the solenoid. For right side installations, the flat on the collar is to be in-line with the centerline of the solenoid.

8. Install the air spring into the body spring seat, taking care to keep the solenoid air and electrical connections clean and free of damage. Rotate the air spring collar until the spring clip snaps into place. Make sure the air spring collar is retained by the 3 rolled tabs on the body spring seat.

9. Connect the air line and electrical connector to the solenoid.

10. Align and secure the lower arm-to-spring attachment with the suspension at full rebound and supported by the shock absorbers.

NOTE: The air springs may be damaged if the suspension is allowed to compress before the spring is inflated.

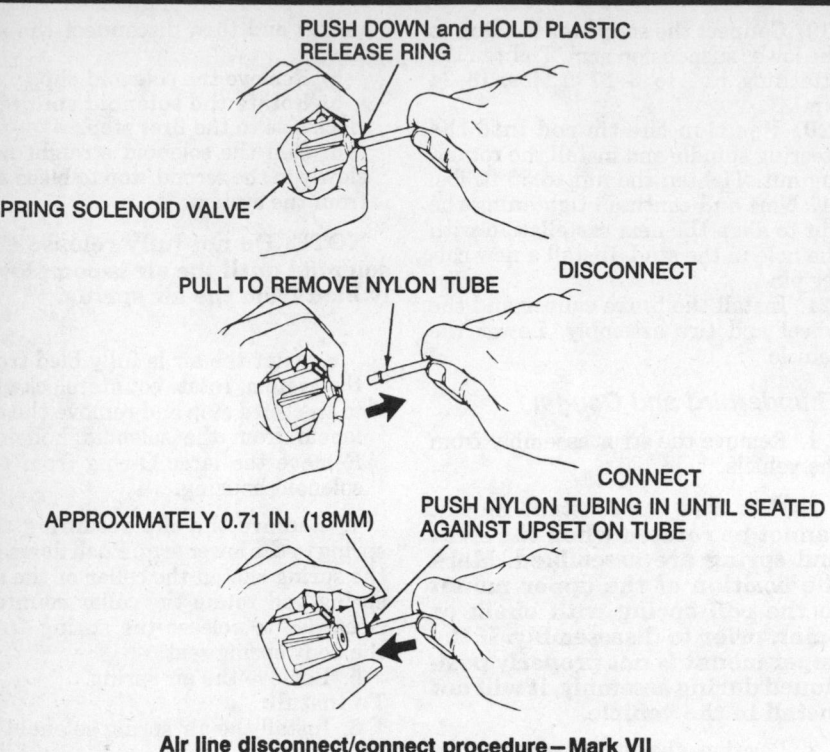

Air line disconnect/connect procedure—Mark VII

PUSH DOWN and HOLD PLASTIC RELEASE RING

SPRING SOLENOID VALVE

PULL TO REMOVE NYLON TUBE   DISCONNECT

APPROXIMATELY 0.71 IN. (18MM)

CONNECT
PUSH NYLON TUBING IN UNTIL SEATED AGAINST UPSET ON TUBE

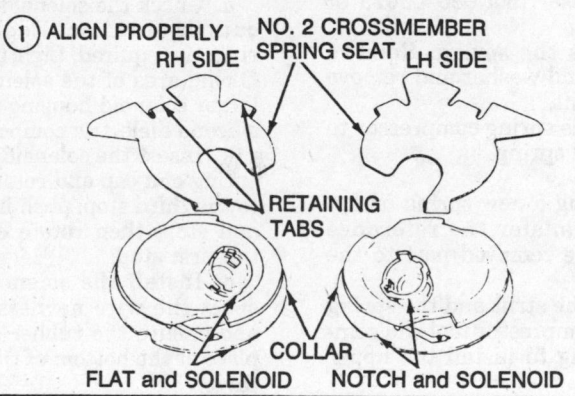

① ALIGN PROPERLY RH SIDE   NO. 2 CROSSMEMBER SPRING SEAT LH SIDE

RETAINING TABS

COLLAR
FLAT and SOLENOID   NOTCH and SOLENOID

② POSITION INTO SPRING SEAT

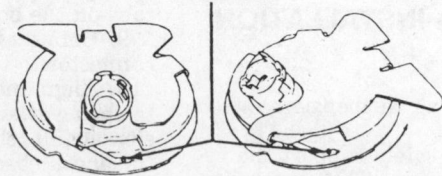

③ ROTATE COLLAR AS SHOWN UNTIL SPRING CLIP SNAPS INTO PLACE

SPRING CLIP

Air spring-to-body spring seat installation—Mark VII

11. Refill the air spring as follows:

a. Turn the air suspension switch **ON**. Leave the diagnostic pigtail ungrounded.

b. Connect a battery charger to reduce battery drain.

c. Turn the ignition switch from the **OFF** to the **RUN** position, hold in the **RUN** position for a minimum of 5 seconds, then return to the **OFF** position. The drivers door must be open but all other doors must be shut.

d. Ground the diagnostic pigtail by connecting a jumper wire from the pigtail to vehicle ground. The pigtail must remain grounded during the spring fill sequence.

e. While applying the brakes, turn the ignition switch to the **RUN** position. The door must be open but do not start the vehicle. The warning indicator will blink continuously once every 2 seconds to indicate the spring pump sequence has been entered.

f. To fill the front spring(s), close and open the door twice. After a 6 second delay, the front spring will be filled for 60 seconds.

g. Immediately after completion of the air spring fill, turn the air suspension switch **OFF** to prevent deflation of the air springs while the vehicle is raised. Inspect all springs for proper inflation; no folds or creases.

12. Install the wheel and tire assembly and lower the vehicle. Turn the air suspension switch **ON**.

NOTE: Any further vehicle leveling will be done when the vehicle is in normal operation on the ground.

Upper Ball Joints

INSPECTION

Thunderbird and Cougar

1. Raise the vehicle and place jacks under the sub-frame. This will minimize the load on the ball joints.

2. Attach a dial indicator in such a way as to measure the lateral movement between the spindle and the arm.

3. Grasp the tire at the top and bottom and slowly move the tire in and out. Note the reading on the dial indicator. If the reading exceeds 0.015 in. (0.4mm), replace the ball joint.

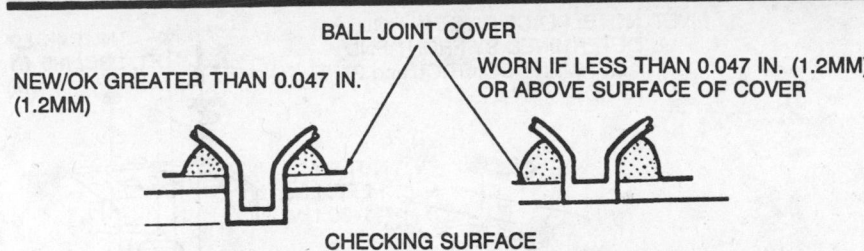

NEW/OK GREATER THAN 0.047 IN. (1.2MM)

BALL JOINT COVER

WORN IF LESS THAN 0.047 IN. (1.2MM) OR ABOVE SURFACE OF COVER

CHECKING SURFACE

Lower ball joint cover checking surface—Mustang and Mark VII

REMOVAL & INSTALLATION

Thunderbird and Cougar

The ball joint is an integral part of the upper control arm. If the ball joint is defective, the entire upper control arm must be replaced.

Lower Ball Joints

INSPECTION

Mustang and Mark VII

1. Support the vehicle in normal driving position with ball joints loaded.
2. Wipe the wear indicator and ball joint cover checking surface clean.
3. The checking surface should project outside the cover. If the checking surface is inside the cover, replace the lower arm assembly.

Thunderbird and Cougar

1. Raise the vehicle and place jacks under the sub-frame. This will minimize the load on the ball joints.
2. Attach a dial indicator in such a way as to measure the lateral movement between the spindle and the arm.
3. Grasp the tire at the top and bottom and slowly move the tire in and out. Note the reading on the dial indicator. If the reading exceeds 0.015 in. (0.4mm), replace the ball joint.

REMOVAL & INSTALLATION

Mustang and Mark VII

The ball joint is an integral part of the lower control arm. If the ball joint is defective, the entire lower control arm must be replaced.

Thunderbird and Cougar

1. Remove the lower control arm.
2. Remove and discard the joint boot seal.
3. Press out the ball joint using ball joint remover tool D89P-3010-A and cup tool D84P-3395-A4 or equivalent, and a suitable press.
To install:
4. When installing a new ball joint,

leave the protective cover in place during installation to protect the ball joint seal. It may be necessary to cut off the end of the cover to allow it to pass through the receiving cup.
5. Install the ball joint with ball joint replacer tool D89P-3010-B, cup tool D84P-3395-A4 or equivalent, and a suitable press.
6. Make sure the ball joint is fully seated in the control arm and the ball joint seal is free of cuts or tears.
7. Install the lower control arm. Check the front end alignment.

Upper Control Arms

REMOVAL & INSTALLATION

Thunderbird and Cougar

1. Raise and safely support the vehicle. Remove the wheel and tire assembly.
2. Remove and discard the upper spindle-to-ball joint bolt and nut. Slightly spread the spindle at the slot and remove the ball joint.
3. Lower the vehicle. Break off the flags on the upper control arm pivot bolt heads.
4. Remove the upper control arm bolts and the control arm.
To install:
5. Position the upper control arm and install new bolts without the flags and nuts.

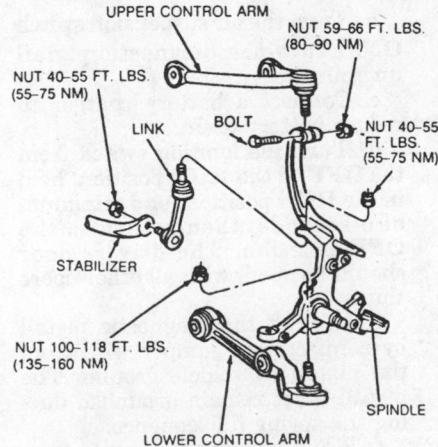

UPPER CONTROL ARM

NUT 59-66 FT. LBS. (80-90 NM)

NUT 40-55 FT. LBS. (55-75 NM)

LINK   BOLT

NUT 40-55 FT. LBS. (55-75 NM)

STABILIZER

NUT 100-118 FT. LBS. (135-160 NM)

LOWER CONTROL ARM

SPINDLE

Front suspension assembly— Thunderbird and Cougar

6. Hold the upper control arm at a horizontal position and tighten the nuts to 72-88 ft. lbs. (98-120 Nm).

NOTE: If it is necessary to tighten the bolts, due to nut access, tighten the bolts to 82-88 ft. lbs. (110-120 Nm).

7. Raise the vehicle. Attach the spindle to the upper control arm. Install a new bolt and nut from the front of the vehicle and tighten to 59-66 ft. lbs. (80-90 Nm).
8. Install the wheel and tire assembly and lower the vehicle. Check the front end alignment.

Lower Control Arms

REMOVAL & INSTALLATION

Mustang and Mark VII

1. On Mark VII, turn the air suspension switch **OFF**.
2. Raise and safely support the vehicle. Allow the control arms to hang free. Remove the wheel and tire assembly.
3. If necessary, remove the brake caliper and suspend with a length of wire; do not let the caliper hang by the brake hose. Remove the brake rotor and dust shield.
4. Disconnect the tie rod end from the steering spindle. Disconnect the stabilizer bar link from the lower arm.
5. Remove the steering gear bolts and lower the gear out of the way to provide clearance, if necessary, for suspension arm bolt removal.
6. On Mark VII, disconnect the lower end of the height sensor from the lower control arm sensor mounting stud. Remove the sensor mounting stud and screw from the lower arm, noting the position of the stud on the lower arm bracket.
7. Remove the cotter pin and loosen the lower ball joint stud nut 1-2 turns. Do not remove the nut at this time. Tap the spindle boss sharply to relieve the stud pressure.
8. On Mustang, install a suitable spring compressor and compress the spring so it is free in the seat. On Mark VII, proceed as follows:
    a. Disconnect the electrical connector and then disconnect the air line.
    b. Remove the solenoid clip.
    c. Rotate the solenoid counterclockwise to the first stop.
    d. Pull the solenoid straight out slowly to the second stop to bleed the air from the system.
    e. Push in, then rotate clockwise to the first stop.
    f. Install the solenoid clip. Inspect the wire harness connector and en-

sure the rubber gasket is in place at the bottom of the connector cavity.

g. Remove and discard the air spring-to-lower arm fastener clip.

9. Remove and discard the ball joint nut and raise the entire strut and spindle assembly. Wire out of the way to obtain working room.

10. Remove and discard the control arm-to-crossmember nuts and bolts. Remove the lower control arm and, on Mustang, remove the coil spring.

To install:

11. On Mustang, position the coil spring into the lower arm pocket. Make sure the spring pigtail is positioned between the 2 holes in the pocket.

12. Position the lower arm to the crossmember and install new arm-to-crossmember bolts and nuts. Do not tighten at this time.

13. Remove the wire from the strut and spindle assembly and attach the spindle to the ball joint stud. Install a new ball joint stud nut, but do not tighten at this time.

14. On Mustang, raise the control arm with a jack to a normal attitude position and remove the spring compressor.

15. On Mark VII, position the air spring in the arm and install the new fastener. Install the sensor mounting stud and screw to the lower arm in the same position as on the replaced arm. Connect the lower end of the sensor to the lower arm mounting stud. Raise the control arm to curb height with a jack.

16. With the jack in place, tighten the lower arm-to-crossmember attaching nuts to 110–150 ft. lbs. (149–203 Nm).

17. Tighten the ball joint stud nut to 100–120 ft. lbs. (136–163 Nm) and install a new cotter pin. Remove the jack.

18. Install the dust shield, rotor and brake caliper, if removed. Install the steering gear-to-crossmember bolts and nuts, if removed. Hold the bolts and tighten the nuts to 90–100 ft. lbs. (122–136 Nm).

19. Position the tie rod into the steering spindle and install the retaining nut. Tighten the nut to 35 ft. lbs. (47 Nm) and continue tightening the nut to align the next castellation with the hole in the stud. Install a new cotter pin.

20. Connect the stabilizer bar link to the lower control arm. Tighten the retaining nut to 6–17 ft. lbs. (8–24 Nm).

21. On Mustang, install the wheel and tire assembly and lower the vehicle. Check the front end alignment.

22. On Mark VII, proceed as follows:

a. Connect the air line and then the electrical connector to the air spring solenoid.

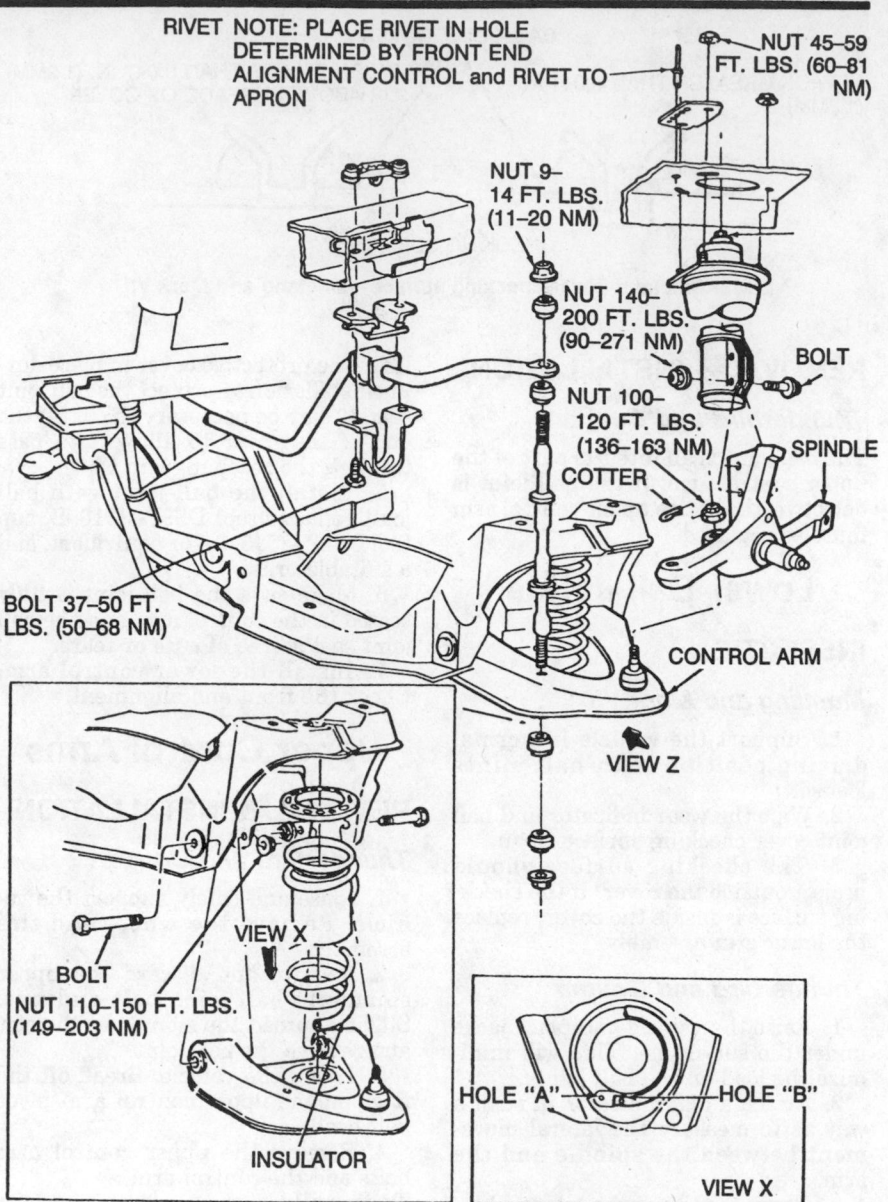

RIVET NOTE: PLACE RIVET IN HOLE DETERMINED BY FRONT END ALIGNMENT CONTROL and RIVET TO APRON

NUT 45–59 FT. LBS. (60–81 NM)

NUT 9–14 FT. LBS. (11–20 NM)

NUT 140–200 FT. LBS. (90–271 NM)

BOLT

NUT 100–120 FT. LBS. (136–163 NM)

COTTER

SPINDLE

CONTROL ARM

VIEW Z

BOLT 37–50 FT. LBS. (50–68 NM)

VIEW X

BOLT

NUT 110–150 FT. LBS. (149–203 NM)

INSULATOR

HOLE "A"   HOLE "B"

VIEW X

END OF SPRING MUST CLEAR HOLE "A" AND COVER HOLE "B"

Front suspension assembly—Mustang

b. Turn the air suspension switch **ON**. Leave the diagnostic pigtail ungrounded.

c. Connect a battery charger to reduce battery drain.

d. Turn the ignition switch from the **OFF** to the **RUN** position, hold in the **RUN** position for a minimum of 5 seconds, then return to the **OFF** position. The drivers door should be open, with all other doors shut.

e. Ground the diagnostic pigtail by connecting a jumper wire from the pigtail to vehicle ground. The pigtail must remain grounded during the spring fill sequence.

f. While applying the brakes, turn the ignition switch to the **RUN** position. The door must be open; do not start the vehicle. The warning indicator will blink continuously once every 2 seconds to indicate the spring pump sequence has been entered.

g. To fill the front spring(s), close and open the door twice. After a 6 second delay, the front spring will be filled for 60 seconds.

h. Immediately after completion of the air spring fill, turn the air suspension switch **OFF** to prevent deflation of the air springs while the vehicle is raised. Inspect all springs for proper inflation; no folds or creases.

i. Install the wheel and tire assembly and lower the vehicle. Turn the air suspension switch **ON**. Check the front end alignment.

NOTE: Any further vehicle leveling will be done when the vehicle is in normal operation on the ground.

Thunderbird and Cougar

1. Raise and safely support the vehicle. Remove the wheel and tire assembly.

2. Loosen the ball joint nut 3–4 turns. Rap the spindle to separate the ball joint. Leave the nut attached.

3. Support the spindle with a wire. Mark the position of the camber adjusting cam. Remove and discard the nut attaching the tension strut to the control arm.

4. Remove the lower strut bolt and remove the pivot bolt.

5. Remove the ball joint nut and remove the control arm.

To install:

6. Position the control arm in the vehicle and loosely install the pivot bolt and new nut.

7. Install the tension strut washer and insulators and loosely install the strut to control arm attaching nut.

8. Loosely install a new ball joint nut. Install a new lower strut bolt and nut, but do not tighten at this time.

9. Tighten the ball joint nut to 82–118 ft. lbs. (110–160 Nm). Tighten the tension strut to control arm nut to 103–118 ft. lbs. (140–160 Nm).

10. Remove the wire holding the spindle. Install the wheel and tire assembly and lower the vehicle.

11. Push down on the front of the vehicle and release to neutralize the suspension. Tighten the lower strut nut to 140–162 ft. lbs. (190–220 Nm).

NOTE: **The lower strut nut must be tightened with the vehicle weight on the wheels.**

12. Align the camber marks at the pivot bolt and tighten the nut to 98–114 ft. lbs. (135–155 Nm).

13. Check the front end alignment.

Stabilizer Bar

REMOVAL & INSTALLATION

Mustang and Mark VII

1. On Mark VII, turn the air suspension switch **OFF**.

2. Raise the front of the vehicle and place jackstands under the lower control arms.

3. Disconnect the stabilizer bar from the links and the insulator mounting clamps. Remove the stabilizer bar.

4. Cut the worn insulators from the stabilizer bar.

5. Installation is the reverse of the removal procedure. Coat the necessary parts of the stabilizer bar with rubber lubricant prior to installation.

Thunderbird and Cougar

1. Disconnect the negative battery cable.

2. Remove the air inlet tube. Remove the stabilizer bar retaining bracket bolts and brackets.

3. Remove the serpentine drive belt. Raise and safely support the vehicle.

4. Remove the wheel and tire assemblies. Remove the crankshaft vibration damper.

5. Remove the cotter pins and nuts from the tie rod ends. Separate the tie rod ends from the spindles.

6. Remove the transmission oil cooler line bracket. Remove the stabilizer bar to lower link retaining nuts.

7. Remove the stabilizer bar link from the stabilizer bar using joint separator tool D88L-3006-A or equivalent. Be careful not to damage the ball joint seal.

8. Remove the stabilizer bar through the right wheel opening. Remove the bushings from the stabilizer bar.

To install:

9. Install the bushings onto the stabilizer bar and position the bar in the vehicle.

10. Attach the stabilizer links to the bar and tighten the retaining nuts to 48–55 ft. lbs. (65–75 Nm).

11. Install the stabilizer bar bracket and retaining bolts. Tighten to 48–55 ft. lbs. (65–75 Nm).

12. Install the transmission oil cooler lines. Install the tie rod ends to the spindles. Tighten the nuts to 39–54 ft. lbs. (53–73 Nm) and install new cotter pins.

13. Install the crankshaft damper.

Install the wheel and tire assemblies and lower the vehicle.

14. Install the serpentine drive belt and the air inlet tube. Connect the negative battery cable.

Front Wheel Bearings

ADJUSTMENT

Mustang and Mark VII

1. On Mark VII, turn the air suspension switch **OFF**.

2. Raise and safely support the front of the vehicle.

3. Remove the wheel cover and grease cap.

4. Remove the cotter pin and nut retainer.

5. Loosen the adjusting nut 3 turns and rock the wheel back and forth a few times to release the brake pads from the rotor.

6. While rotating the wheel and hub assembly in a counterclockwise direction, tighten the adjusting nut to 17–25 ft. lbs. (23–34 Nm).

7. Back off the adjusting nut ½ turn, then retighten to 10–28 inch lbs. (1.1–3.2 Nm).

8. Install the nut retainer and a new cotter pin. Check the wheel rotation. If it is noisy or rough, the bearings either need to be cleaned and repacked or replaced. After adjustment is completed, replace the grease cap.

9. Lower the vehicle. Before driving the vehicle, pump the brake pedal several times to restore normal brake pedal travel. On Mark VII, turn the air suspension switch **ON**.

Thunderbird and Cougar

The front wheel bearings are of a hub

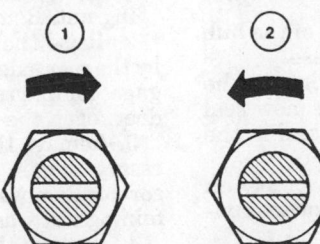

WITH HUB ROTATING, TORQUE ADJUSTING NUT TO 17–25 FT. LBS. (23–34 NM)

BACK ADJUSTING NUT OFF ½ TURN

TIGHTEN ADJUSTING NUT TO 10–28 INCH LBS. (1.1–3.2 NM)

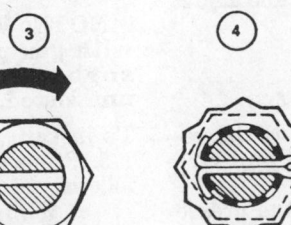

INSTALL THE RETAINER and NEW COTTER PIN

Wheel bearing adjustment procedure

unit design and are pregreased, sealed and require no maintenance. The bearings are preset and cannot be adjusted.

REMOVAL & INSTALLATION

Mustang and Mark VII

1. On Mark VII, turn the air suspension switch OFF.

2. Raise and support the vehicle safely. Remove the wheel and tire assembly and the caliper. Suspend the caliper with a length of wire; do not let it hang from the brake hose.

3. Pry off the dust cap. Remove the cotter pin, nut retainer, adjusting nut and flatwasher. Remove the outer roller bearing assembly.

4. Pull off the brake disc and wheel hub assembly.

5. Remove the inner grease seal using a prybar. Remove the inner roller bearing assembly.

6. Clean the bearings with solvent and inspect them for pits, scratches and excessive wear. Wipe all the old grease from the hub and inspect the bearing races. If either bearings or races are damaged, the bearing races must be removed and the bearings and races replaced as an assembly.

7. If the bearings are to be replaced, drive out the races from the hub using a brass drift.

8. Make sure the spindle, hub and bearing assemblies are clean prior to installation.

To install:

9. If the bearing races were removed, install new ones using a suitable bearing race installer. Pack the bearings with a bearing packer. If a packer is not available, work as much grease as possible between the rollers and cages.

10. Coat the inner surface of the hub and bearing races with grease.

11. Install the inner bearing in the hub. Lubricate the lips of a new seal with grease and install the seal in the hub, using a seal installer.

12. Install the hub/disc assembly on the spindle, being careful not to damage the oil seal.

13. Install the outer bearing, washer and spindle nut. Install the caliper and the wheel and tire assembly and adjust the bearings.

Thunderbird and Cougar

1. Raise and safely support the vehicle. Remove the wheel and tire assembly.

2. Remove and discard the grease cap from the hub.

3. Remove the brake caliper. Suspend the caliper with a length of wire; do not let it hang from the brake hose.

4. Remove the rotor. Remove and discard the wheel hub nut.

5. Remove the hub and bearing assembly.

To install:

6. Install the hub and bearing assembly. Install a new wheel hub nut and tighten to 238 ft. lbs. (322 Nm).

7. Install the rotor and a new grease cap. Install the brake caliper.

8. Install the wheel and tire assembly and lower the vehicle.

REAR SUSPENSION

Shock Absorbers

REMOVAL & INSTALLATION

1. On Mark VII, turn the air suspension switch OFF. On Thunderbird and Cougar, proceed as follows to remove the actuation assembly, if equipped with automatic ride control:

   a. Make sure the vehicle is on a flat surface and the ignition is in the OFF position.

   b. Remove the luggage compartment side trim panel and disconnect the actuator wiring connector.

   c. Squeeze the 2 actuator retaining tabs firmly inward with 1 hand and lift the actuator off the mounting bracket with the other hand.

   d. Grasp the actuator mounting bracket with water pump pliers and hold firmly. While holding the bracket, loosen the bracket retaining nut. Remove the bracket.

2. Raise the vehicle and support it by the rear axle housing. Open the luggage compartment. On Mustang 3-door, open the hatch back door.

3. Remove the trim panels, as necessary, to gain access to the shock absorber. Remove the shock absorber retaining nut washer and insulator.

4. Remove the shock absorber bolt washer and nut at the lower arm and remove the shock absorber.

NOTE: Vehicles are equipped with gas pressurized shock absorbers which will extend unassisted.

To install:

5. Prime the new shock absorber as follows:

   a. With the shock absorber right side up, extend it fully.

   b. Turn the shock upside down and fully compress it.

   c. Repeat the previous 2 steps at

least 3 times to make sure any trapped air has been expelled.

6. Place the inner washer and insulator on the upper retaining stud and position the stud through the shock tower mounting hole.

7. Attach the lower end of the shock absorber with the retaining bolt and nut. Tighten the bolt to 45–60 ft. lbs. (61–81 Nm) on Mark VII and Mustang with handling package or 57–70 ft. lbs. (76–95 Nm) on Mustang without handling package. Tighten the nut to 72–97 ft. lbs. (97–132 Nm) on Thunderbird and Cougar.

8. Install the upper insulator, washer and retaining nut and tighten to 20–25 ft. lbs. (26–35 Nm) on Mustang and Mark VII or 27–35 ft. lbs. (37–47 Nm) on Thunderbird and Cougar.

9. On Thunderbird and Cougar, install the shock actuator, if necessary.

10. Lower the vehicle. On Mark VII, turn the air suspension switch ON.

Coil Springs

REMOVAL & INSTALLATION

Mustang

1. Raise and safely support the vehicle. Support the body at the rear body crossmember.

2. Remove the stabilizer bar, if equipped.

3. Support the axle with a suitable jack or jackstands.

4. Place another jack under the lower arm axle pivot bolt. Remove and discard the bolt and nut. Lower the jack slowly until the coil spring load is relieved.

5. Remove the coil spring and insulator from the vehicle.

To install:

6. Place the upper spring insulator on top of the spring. Place the lower spring insulator on the lower arm.

7. Position the coil spring on the lower arm spring seat, so the pigtail on the lower arm is at the rear of the vehicle and pointing toward the left side of the vehicle.

8. Slowly raise the jack until the arm is in position. Insert a new rear pivot bolt and nut with the nut facing outward. Do not tighten at this time.

9. Raise the axle to curb height. Tighten the lower arm-to-axle pivot bolt to 70–100 ft. lbs. (95–135 Nm).

10. Install the stabilizer bar, if equipped. Remove the crossmember supports and lower the vehicle.

Thunderbird and Cougar

1. Raise and safely support the vehicle. Remove the rear wheel and tire assembly.

2. Remove the rear stabilizer bar

link nuts at both ends of the bar. Rotate the bar up and out of the way.

3. Disconnect the parking brake cable at the brake caliper.

4. Install 3 spring cage tools 086-00031 or equivalent to the rear spring as follows:

   a. Install 1 spring cage without an adjuster link to the inboard side, the innermost "bend" of the spring.

   b. Install 2 more spring cages, with adjusters, at 120 degree angles to the previously installed cage.

5. Place a jack under the lower rear control arm as far outboard as possible.

6. Support the rear knuckle and caliper assembly by wiring the upper control arm to the body.

7. Remove the lower shock absorber mounting bolt and nut. Mark the toe adjustment cam-to-subframe position and loosen both inboard pivot bolts on the lower control arm.

NOTE: The control arm must not be lowered until the pivot bolts are loose. Do not attempt to remove the plastic cap on the front pivot nut.

8. Remove the 2 bolts and nuts attaching the lower control arm to the knuckle. Lower the control arm by lowering the jack. Make sure the spring cages properly seat on the spring as the control arm is dropped.

9. Remove the jack, pull the control arm down fully by hand and remove the rear spring with the cages in place. Remove the spring insulators, if necessary.

10. If the springs are to be replaced, use a suitable coil spring compressor to compress the spring and remove the spring cages.

To install:

11. If a new spring is to be installed, it first must be compressed and caged. Compress the spring to the length of the original spring. If replacing a broken spring, compress the spring to approximately 10½ in. (267mm).

12. Install the spring insulators, if removed. Install the spring, with the cages in place, onto the upper and lower control arm seats.

NOTE: The short cage, without the adjuster, must be inboard. the spring pigtails may be in any position.

13. Position 2 jack stands under the front bumper reinforcement to prevent the rear of the vehicle lifting off the hoist.

14. Position a jack under the lower control arm and raise the lower control arm up to the knuckle bores. Make sure the spring seats properly. Install the bolts and nuts attaching the lower control arm to the knuckle and tighten

the bolts to 118–148 ft. lbs. (160–200 Nm).

15. Remove the wire supporting the knuckle, caliper and upper control arm. Install the lower shock absorber mount bolt and nut and tighten the nut to 110–120 ft. lbs. (150–162 Nm).

16. Remove the jack and the jack stands. Remove the spring cages.

17. Connect the parking brake cable to the caliper. Install the rear stabilizer bar links and retaining nuts.

18. Install the wheel and tire assembly and lower the vehicle.

19. Set the toe adjustment cam to the mark made at the time of removal. Tighten the front lower control arm-to-sub-frame nut to 185–228 ft. lbs. (250–310 Nm). Tighten the rear lower control arm-to-sub-frame nut to 126–169 ft. lbs. (170–230 Nm).

20. Check the rear wheel toe setting and adjust as necessary.

Air Springs

REMOVAL & INSTALLATION

Mark VII

1. Turn the air suspension switch **OFF**.

2. Raise and safely support the vehicle on the frame. The suspension must be at full rebound.

3. Remove the wheel and tire assembly. Remove the air spring solenoid as follows:

   a. Disconnect the electrical connector and then disconnect the air line.

   b. Remove the solenoid clip.

   c. Rotate the solenoid counterclockwise to the first stop.

   d. Pull the solenoid straight out slowly to the second stop to bleed air from the system.

NOTE: Do not fully release the solenoid until the air is completely bled from the air spring.

   e. After the air is fully bled from the system, rotate counterclockwise to the third stop and remove the solenoid from the solenoid housing. Remove the large O-ring from the solenoid housing.

4. Remove the bolts retaining the spring to the lower arm. Push down on the spring clip on the collar of the air spring and rotate the collar counterclockwise to release the spring from the body spring seat.

5. Remove the air spring.

To install:

6. Install the air spring solenoid as follows:

   a. Check the solenoid O-rings for cuts or abrasion. Replace the O-rings as required. Lightly grease the

O-ring area of the solenoid and the larger solenoid housing O-ring with silicone dielectric compound.

   b. Insert the solenoid into the air spring end cap and rotate clockwise to the third stop, push in to the second stop, then rotate clockwise to the first stop.

   c. Install the solenoid clip. Inspect the wire harness connector and ensure the rubber gasket is in place at the bottom of the connector cavity.

7. For left side installations, position the notch on the collar to be in-line with the centerline of the solenoid. For right side installations, the flat on the collar is to be in-line with the centerline of the solenoid.

8. Install the air spring into the body spring seat, taking care to keep the solenoid air and electrical connections clean and free of damage. Rotate the air spring collar until the spring clip snaps into place. Make sure the air spring collar is retained by the 3 rolled tabs on the body spring seat.

9. Connect the air line and electrical connector to the solenoid.

10. Align and secure the lower arm-to-spring attachment with the suspension at full rebound and supported by the shock absorbers.

NOTE: The air springs may be damaged if the suspension is allowed to compress before the spring is inflated.

11. Refill the air spring as follows:

   a. Turn the air suspension switch **ON**. Leave the diagnostic pigtail ungrounded.

   b. Connect a battery charger to reduce battery drain.

   c. Turn the ignition switch from the **OFF** to the **RUN** position, hold in the **RUN** position for a minimum of 5 seconds, then return to the **OFF** position. The drivers door should be open with all other doors shut.

   d. Ground the diagnostic pigtail by connecting a jumper wire from the pigtail to vehicle ground. The pigtail must remain grounded during the spring fill sequence.

   e. While applying the brakes, turn the ignition switch to the **RUN** position. The door must be open; do not start the vehicle. The warning indicator will blink continuously once every 2 seconds to indicate the spring pump sequence has been entered.

   f. To fill the rear spring(s), close and open the door once. After a 6 second delay, the rear spring will be filled for 60 seconds.

   g. Immediately after completion of the air spring fill, turn the air suspension switch **OFF** to prevent deflation of the air springs while the vehicle is raised. Inspect all springs for proper inflation; no folds or creases.

12. Install the wheel and tire assembly and lower the vehicle. Turn the air suspension switch **ON**.

NOTE: Any further vehicle leveling will be done when the vehicle is in normal operation on the ground.

Rear Control Arms

REMOVAL & INSTALLATION

Mustang

UPPER ARM

NOTE: If 1 arm needs to be replaced, replace the other arm also.

1. Raise and safely support the vehicle at the rear crossmember.
2. Remove and discard the upper arm pivot bolts and nuts and remove the control arm.
To install:
3. Place the upper arm into the bracket of the body side rail. Install a new pivot bolt and nut with the nut facing outboard. Do not tighten at this time.
4. Using a jack, raise the suspension until the upper arm-to-axle pivot hole is in position with the hole in the axle bushing. Install a new pivot bolt and nut with the nut facing inboard. Do not tighten at this time.
5. Raise the suspension to curb height. Tighten the front upper arm bolt to 77–105 ft. lbs. (104–142 Nm) and the rear upper arm bolt to 70–100 ft. lbs. (95–135 Nm).
6. Remove the supports and lower the vehicle.

LOWER ARM

NOTE: If 1 arm needs to be replaced, replace the other arm also.

1. Raise and safely support the vehicle at the rear crossmember.
2. Remove the stabilizer bar, if equipped.
3. Place a jack under the lower arm-to-axle pivot bolt. Remove and discard the bolt and nut. Lower the jack slowly until the coil spring can be removed.
4. Remove and discard the lower arm-to-frame pivot bolt and nut. Remove the lower arm.
To install:
5. Position the lower arm assembly into the front arm bracket. Install a new pivot bolt and nut with the nut facing outwards. Do not tighten at this time.
6. Position the coil spring on the

lower arm spring seat, so the pigtail on the lower arm is at the rear of the vehicle and pointing toward the left side of the vehicle.
7. Slowly raise the jack until the arm is in position. Insert a new rear pivot bolt and nut with the nut facing outward. Do not tighten at this time.
8. Raise the axle to curb height. Tighten the lower arm front bolt to 77–105 ft. lbs. (104–142 Nm) and the rear bolt to 70–100 ft. lbs. (95–135 Nm).
9. Install the stabilizer bar, if equipped. Remove the crossmember supports and lower the vehicle.

Thunderbird and Cougar

UPPER ARM

1. Raise and safely support the vehicle. Remove the rear wheel and tire assembly.
2. Support the knuckle and hub assembly so it cannot swing outward.
3. Remove the inner and outer pivot bolts and nuts at the upper control arm and remove the arm.
To install:
4. Install the upper arm. Loosely install the bolts and nuts.

NOTE: The inner pivot bolt used for camber adjustment has a specially shaped washer under the bolt head. Make sure fasteners are used in the correct locations.

5. Install the wheel and tire assembly and lower the vehicle.
6. Tighten the outboard nut to 118–148 ft. lbs. (160–200 Nm).
7. Set the camber and tighten the inner pivot nut to 81–98 ft. lbs. (110–133 Nm).

LOWER ARM

1. Remove the coil spring.
2. Remove the inner control arm pivot bolts and nuts and remove the arm.

NOTE: Do not attempt to remove the plastic cap on the front pivot nut.

3. Remove the toe compensating link from the control arm.
To install:
4. Inspect the large nut used at the inner front arm attachment for condition of plastic cap. Use a new nut if the cap is cracked, loose or missing.
5. Install the toe compensating link on the arm.
6. Install the lower control arm to the sub-frame and loosely install the pivot bolts and nuts.
7. Tighten the toe compensating link nut to 118–148 ft. lbs. (160–200 Nm).

8. Install the spring and reattach the control arm at the knuckle.
9. Check and adjust the rear toe.

Mark VII

UPPER ARM

NOTE: If 1 arm needs to be replaced, replace the other arm also.

1. Turn the air suspension switch **OFF**.
2. Raise and safely support the vehicle. Allow the suspension to be at full rebound.
3. On the right side, disconnect the rear height sensor from the side arm. Note position of the sensor adjustment bracket on the upper arm.
4. Remove and discard the upper arm pivot bolts and nuts and remove the upper arm.
To install:
5. Place the upper arm into position and install new pivot bolts and nuts. At the body bracket, the nut must face outboard. At the axle, the nut must face inboard. Do not tighten at this time.
6. Connect the rear height sensor to the arm. Set the adjustment bracket to the same position as on the replaced arm and tighten the nut to 7–10 ft. lbs. (8–14 Nm).
7. Using a suitable jack, raise the axle to curb height. Tighten the front upper arm bolt to 80–105 ft. lbs. (108–142 Nm) and the rear upper arm bolt to 70–100 ft. lbs. (95–135 Nm).
8. Remove the supports and lower the vehicle. Turn the air suspension switch **ON**.

LOWER ARM

NOTE: If 1 arm needs to be replaced, replace the other arm also.

1. Turn the air suspension switch **OFF**.
2. Raise and safely support the vehicle. Allow the suspension to be at full rebound.
3. Remove the wheel and tire assembly.
4. Vent the air springs to atmospheric pressure as follows:
   a. Disconnect the electrical connector and then disconnect the air line.
   b. Remove the solenoid clip.
   c. Rotate the solenoid counterclockwise to the first stop.
   d. Pull the solenoid straight out slowly to the second stop to bleed the air from the system.
   e. Push in, then rotate clockwise to the first stop.
   f. Install the solenoid clip. Inspect the wire harness connector and ensure the rubber gasket is in place at the bottom of the connector cavity.

g. Reconnect the air line and electrical connector.

5. Remove and discard the 2 air spring-to-lower control arm bolts and remove the air spring from the lower arm.

6. Remove and discard the bolts and remove the arm from the vehicle.

To install:

6. Position the control arm and install new pivot bolts and nuts with the nuts facing outward. Do not tighten at this time.

7. Install 2 new air spring-to-arm bolts, but do not tighten at this time.

8. Using a jack, raise the axle to curb height. Tighten the lower arm front bolt to 80–105 ft. lbs. (108–142 Nm) and the rear bolt to 70–100 ft. lbs. (95–135 Nm).

9. Tighten the air spring-to-arm bolt to 25–35 ft. lbs. (34–48 Nm). Make sure the air spring piston is flat on the lower arm. Remove the jack.

10. Refill the air spring as follows:

a. Turn the air suspension switch **ON**. Leave the diagnostic pigtail ungrounded.

b. Connect a battery charger to reduce battery drain.

c. Turn the ignition switch from the **OFF** to the **RUN** position, hold in the **RUN** position for a minimum of 5 seconds, then return to the **OFF** position. The drivers door should be open with all other doors shut.

d. Ground the diagnostic pigtail by connecting a jumper wire from the pigtail to vehicle ground. The pigtail must remain grounded during the spring fill sequence.

e. While applying the brakes, turn the ignition switch to the **RUN** position. The door must be open; do not start the vehicle. The warning indicator will blink continuously once every 2 seconds to indicate the spring pump sequence has been entered.

f. To fill the rear spring(s), close and open the door once. After a 6 second delay, the rear spring will be filled for 60 seconds.

g. Immediately after completion of the air spring fill, turn the air suspension switch **OFF** to prevent deflation of the air springs while the vehicle is raised. Inspect all springs for proper inflation; no folds or creases.

11. Install the wheel and tire assembly and lower the vehicle. Turn the air suspension switch **ON**.

NOTE: Any further vehicle leveling will be done when the vehicle is in normal operation on the ground.

STEERING

Steering Wheel

Mustang and Mark VII With Air Bag

1. Center the front wheels in the straight-ahead position.

2. On 1990–91 vehicles, disarm the air bag system as follows:

a. Disconnect the negative battery cable.

b. Open the glove compartment door, press in the sides and lower the door down past the stops. Remove the heater duct, if necessary. Disconnect the electrical connector from the backup power supply (blue box, 1 connector).

NOTE: The backup power supply allows air bag deployment if the battery or battery cables are damaged in an accident before the crash sensors close. The power supply is a capacitor that will leak down in approximately 15 minutes after the battery is disconnected or in 1 minute if the battery positive cable is grounded. The backup power supply must be disconnected before any air bag related service is performed.

c. Remove the 4 nut and washer assemblies retaining the driver air bag module and remove the steering wheel.

d. Disconnect the driver air bag module connector and attach a jumper wire to the air bag terminals on the clockspring.

3. On 1992–93 vehicles, disarm the air bag system as follows:

a. Disconnect the positive battery cable. Wait 1 minute for the backup power supply in the diagnostic monitor to deplete its stored energy.

b. Remove the 4 nut and washer assemblies retaining the driver air bag module to the steering wheel and remove the air bag module.

c. Disconnect the driver air bag connector. Connect air bag simulator tool 105–00008 or equivalent, to the vehicle harness at the top of the steering wheel.

4. Disconnect the cruise control

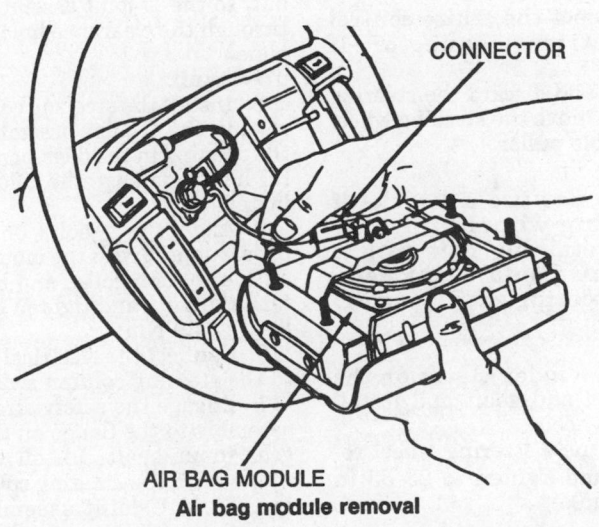

CONNECTOR

AIR BAG MODULE
Air bag module removal

wire harness from the steering wheel, if equipped.

5. Remove and discard the steering wheel bolt. Remove the steering wheel using a suitable puller. Route the contact assembly wire harness through the steering wheel as the wheel is lifted off the shaft.

NOTE: Do not use a knock-off type steering wheel puller or strike the retaining bolt with a hammer. This could cause damage to the steering shaft bearing.

To install:

6. Make sure the front wheels are in the straight-ahead position.

7. Route the contact assembly wire harness through the steering wheel opening at the 3 o'clock position and install the steering wheel on the steering shaft. The steering wheel and shaft alignment marks should be aligned. Make sure the air bag contact wire is not pinched.

8. Install a new steering wheel retaining bolt and tighten to 23–33 ft. lbs. (31–48 Nm).

9. If equipped, connect the cruise control wire harness to the wheel and snap the connector assembly into the steering wheel clip. Make sure the wiring does not get trapped between the steering wheel and contact assembly.

10. Connect the air bag wire harness to the air bag module and install the module to the steering wheel. Tighten the module retaining nuts to 3–4 ft. lbs. (4–6 Nm).

11. Connect the air bag backup power supply and battery cable. Verify the air bag warning indicator.

Except Mustang and Mark VII With Air Bag

1. Disconnect the negative battery cable.

2. Remove the horn pad and cover assembly. Disconnect the horn electrical connector.

3. Disconnect the cruise control switch electrical connector, if equipped.

4. Remove and discard the steering wheel bolt. Remove the steering wheel using a suitable puller.

NOTE: Do not use a knock-off type steering wheel puller or strike the retaining bolt with a hammer. This could cause damage to the steering shaft bearing.

To install:

5. Align the index marks on the steering wheel and shaft and install the steering wheel.

6. Install a new steering wheel retaining bolt and tighten to 23–33 ft. lbs. (31–45 Nm).

7. Connect the cruise control electrical connector, if equipped.

8. Connect the horn electrical connector and install the horn pad and cover.

9. Connect the negative battery cable.

Steering Column

REMOVAL & INSTALLATION

Mustang and 1989 Mark VII

1. Disconnect the negative battery cable. On 1992–93 Mustang equipped with an air bag, disconnect the positive battery cable and wait 1 minute for the backup power supply in the diagnostic monitor to deplete its stored energy. On 1990–91 Mustang equipped with an air bag, disconnect the air bag backup power supply.

NOTE: If equipped with an air bag, do not remove the steering column wheel and air bag module as an assembly unless the column is locked or the steering shaft is secured to keep it from turning. This will avoid damage to the clockspring assembly.

2. Remove the 2 nuts that attach the flexible coupling to the flange on the steering input shaft. Disengage the safety strap and bolt assembly from the flexible coupling.

3. Remove the steering column trim shrouds.

4. Remove the steering column cover and hood release mechanism directly under the column.

5. Disconnect the electrical connectors to the steering column switches.

6. Remove the 4 screws that attach the dust boot to the dash panel.

7. Remove the 4 attaching nuts holding the column to the brake pedal support. Lower the column to clear the 4 mounting bolts and pull the column out, so the U-joint assembly will pass through the clearance hole in the dash panel.

To install:

8. Install the steering column by inserting the U-joint assembly through the opening in the dash panel. Be careful not to damage the column during installation.

9. Align the 4 bolts on the brake pedal support with the mounting holes on the column collar and bracket. Attach the nuts and tighten to 20–37 ft. lbs. (27–50 Nm).

10. Connect the electrical connectors to the steering column switches.

11. Engage the safety strap and bolt assembly to the flange on the steering gear input shaft. Install the 2 nuts that attach the steering column lower shaft and U-joint assembly to the

flange on the steering gear input shaft. Tighten the nuts to 20–37 ft. lbs. (27–50 Nm).

NOTE: The safety strap must be properly positioned to prevent metal-to-metal contact after tightening the nuts. The flexible coupling must not be distorted when the nuts are tightened. Pry the steering shaft up or down with a suitable prybar to achieve ± ⅛ in. (3mm) coupling insulator flatness.

12. Engage the dust boot at the base of the steering column to the dash panel opening. Install the 4 screws that attach the dust boot to the dash panel.

13. Install the steering wheel and the trim shrouds.

14. Install the hood release mechanism and steering column cover beneath the steering column.

15. Connect the battery cable(s). Check the steering column for proper operation.

1990–93 Mark VII

1. Make sure the front wheels are in the straight-ahead position. Disconnect the negative battery cable. On 1990–91 vehicles, disconnect the air bag backup power supply. On 1992–93 vehicles, disconnect the positive battery cable and wait 1 minute for the backup power supply in the diagnostic monitor to deplete its stored energy.

2. Remove the steering wheel.

3. Remove the right and left lower mouldings from the instrument panel by pulling up and snapping out of the retainers.

4. Remove the instrument panel lower trim cover.

5. Remove the air bag clockspring contact assembly as follows:

a. Disconnect the contact assembly wire harness.

b. Apply 2 strips of tape across the contact assembly stator and rotor to prevent accidental rotation.

c. Remove the 3 contact assembly retaining screws and pull the contact assembly off the column shaft.

6. Unscrew the tilt lever from the column.

7. Place the ignition lock cylinder in the **RUN** position. Using an ⅛ in. drift, depress the lock cylinder retaining pin through the access hole and remove the lock cylinder.

8. Remove the 4 retaining screws and remove the column shrouds.

9. Remove the 2 retaining bolts and remove the instrument panel reinforcement.

10. Remove the 2 interlock cable retaining screws and remove the cable.

11. Remove the 2 combination

switch retaining screws and set the combination switch aside.

12. Remove the parking brake vacuum release assembly or disconnect the hoses at the switch.

13. Remove the pinch bolt from the steering shaft flex coupling.

14. Remove the interlock cable retaining screws and cable end assembly.

15. While supporting the column assembly, remove the 4 column assembly retaining nuts. Remove the column from the vehicle.

To install:

16. Align the column lower universal joint to the lower shaft. Install 1 bolt and tighten to 29–41 ft. lbs. (40–56 Nm).

17. Install the interlock cable retaining screws and cable end assembly.

18. Position the steering column assembly to the column support bracket. Install the 4 retaining nuts and tighten to 10–14 ft. lbs. (13–19 Nm).

19. Install the combination switch with the 2 retaining screws. Tighten to 18–26 inch lbs. (2–3 Nm). Connect all electrical connectors.

20. Install the instrument panel reinforcement brace and tighten the bolts to 25–38 ft. lbs. (34–52 Nm).

21. Install the lock cylinder and the tilt lever.

22. Install the air bag clockspring contact assembly as follows:

   a. Make sure the front wheels are in the straight-ahead position and the steering column shaft alignment mark is at the 12 o'clock position.

   b. Align the contact assembly to the column shaft and mounting bosses and slide the contact assembly onto the shaft.

   c. Install the 3 retaining screws and tighten to 18–26 inch lbs. (2–3 Nm). Remove the tape strips.

   d. Route the contact assembly down the column assembly and connect to the wire harness.

NOTE: If a new contact assembly is being installed, remove the plastic lock mechanism after the contact assembly is secured to the column.

23. Install the shroud assembly and the lower instrument panel cover and snap the right and left lower instrument panel mouldings into place.

24. Install the steering wheel. Install a new bolt and tighten to 23–33 ft. lbs. (31–48 Nm).

25. Position the air bag module to the wheel and install the 4 retaining nuts. Tighten to 3–4 ft. lbs. (4–6 Nm).

26. Connect the battery cable(s) and the air bag backup power supply. Verify the air bag warning indicator.

Thunderbird and Cougar

1. Disconnect the negative battery cable.

2. Remove lower left finish panel retaining bolts.

3. Carefully pull the lower left finish panel to disengage the retaining clips.

4. Remove the lower left reinforcement panel retaining bolts and remove the reinforcement panel.

5. Remove the steering column upper and lower shroud retaining screws and remove the shroud.

6. Disconnect the electrical connectors for the ignition key courtesy lamp, cruise control, ignition switch, combination switch and steering shock absorber sensor.

7. Remove the steering universal shaft pinch bolt.

8. Remove the steering column retaining nuts.

9. Disconnect the hazard warning wire connector.

10. Remove the brake shift interlock switch retaining screw and remove the switch.

11. Remove the steering column from the vehicle.

To install:

12. Position the steering column and loosely install 1 retaining nut.

13. Install the brake shift interlock switch and connect the hazard warning wire connector.

14. Install the steering column upper shroud.

15. Align the steering column universal.

16. Install the steering column retaining nuts.

17. Install the universal pinch bolt and tighten to 30–42 ft. lbs. (41–57 Nm).

18. Connect the wire conectors to the steering shock absorber sensor, combination switch, ignition switch, cruise control and ignition key courtesy lamp.

19. Position the steering column harness wiring and secure in place.

20. Install the lower steering column shroud and retaining screws.

21. Position the lower left reinforcement panel and install the retaining bolts.

22. Position the lower left finish panel and install the retaining bolts.

23. Connect the negative battery cable and check column operation.

Power Rack and Pinion

ADJUSTMENT

Rack Yoke Plug Clearance

The rack yoke plug clearance adjustment is not a normal service adjustment. It is only required when the input shaft and valve assembly is removed.

1. Clean the exterior of the steering rack thoroughly.

2. Install 2 long bolts and washers through the bushings and attach the rack to bench mounted holding fixture T57L–500–B or equivalent.

3. Do not remove the external pressure lines, unless they are leaking or damaged. If the lines are removed, install new seals. If the lines are damaged, they must be replaced.

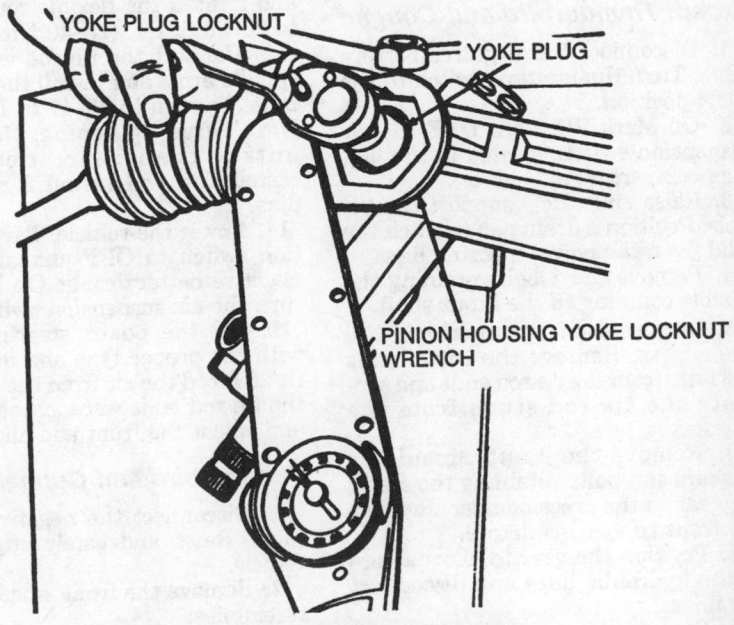

Rack yoke plug clearance adjustment

4. Drain the power steering fluid by rotating the input shaft lock-to-lock twice using pinion shaft torque adapter tool T74P–3504–R or equivalent. Cover the ports on the valve housing with a shop cloth while draining the gear to avoid possible oil sparay.

5. Insert an inch pound torque wrench with a maximum capacity of 30–60 inch lbs. (3.39–6.77 Nm) into the pinion shaft torque adapter tool. Position the adapter and wrench on the input shaft splines.

6. Loosen the yoke plug locknut with pinion housing locknut wrench T78P–3504–H or equivalent. Loosen the yoke plug with a ¾ in. socket wrench.

7. With the rack at the center of travel, tighten the yoke plug to 45–50 inch lbs. (5.0–5.6 Nm). Clean the threads of the yoke plug prior to tightening to prevent a false reading.

8. Back off the yoke plug approximately ⅛ turn, 44 degrees minimum to 54 degrees maximum, until the torque required to initiate and sustain rotation of the input shaft is 7–18 inch lbs. (0.79–2.03 Nm) for base power steering or 7–24 inch lbs. (0.79–2.71 Nm) for handling package.

9. Place pinion housing yoke locknut wrench T78P–3504–H or equivalent, on the yoke plug locknut. While holding the yoke plug, tighten the locknut to 44–66 ft. lbs. (60–89 Nm).

NOTE: Do not allow the yoke plug to move while tightening or the preload will be affected.

10. Install the steering rack in the vehicle.

REMOVAL & INSTALLATION

Except Thunderbird and Cougar

1. Disconnect the negative battery cable. Turn the ignition switch to the **RUN** position.

2. On Mark VII, turn **OFF** the air suspension switch, located in the luggage compartment.

3. Raise and safely support the vehicle. Position a drain pan to catch the fluid from the power steering lines.

4. Remove the 1 bolt retaining the flexible coupling to the input shaft.

5. Remove the front wheel and tire assemblies. Remove the cotter pins and nuts from the tie rod ends and separate the tie rod studs from the spindles.

6. Remove the 2 nuts, insulator washers and bolts retaining the steering gear to the crossmember. Remove the front rubber insulators.

7. Position the gear to allow access to the hydraulic lines and disconnect the lines.

8. Remove the steering gear.

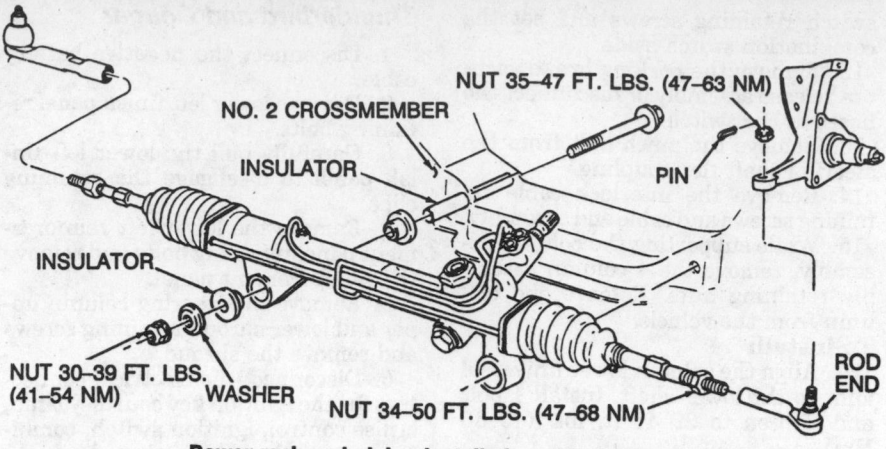

Power rack and pinion Installation—Mark VII

NUT 35–47 FT. LBS. (47–63 NM)
NO. 2 CROSSMEMBER
INSULATOR
PIN
INSULATOR
NUT 30–39 FT. LBS. (41–54 NM)
WASHER
NUT 34–50 FT. LBS. (47–68 NM)
ROD END

To install:

9. Install new plastic seals on the hydraulic line fittings.

10. Install the gear on the mounting spikes and install the hydraulic lines. Tighten the fittings to 10–15 ft. lbs. (14–20 Nm) on 1989 vehicles or 20–25 ft. lbs. (27–33 Nm) on 1990–93 vehicles.

NOTE: The hoses are designed to swivel when properly tightened. Do not attempt to eliminate looseness by over-tightening the fittings.

11. Install the front rubber insulators. Make sure all rubber insulators are pushed completely inside the gear housing before installing the mounting bolts.

12. Insert the input shaft into the flexible coupling. Install the mounting bolts, insulator washers and nuts. Tighten the nuts to 30–40 ft. lbs. (41–54 Nm) while holding the bolts. Install and tighten the flexible coupling bolt to 20–30 ft. lbs. (28–40 Nm).

13. Connect the tie rod ends to the spindle arms and install the retaining nuts. Tighten to 35–47 ft. lbs. (48–63 Nm). After tightening, tighten the nuts to their nearest cotter pin castellation and install 2 new cotter pins.

14. Lower the vehicle. Turn the ignition switch to **OFF** and connect the negative battery cable. On Mark VII, turn the air suspension switch **ON**.

15. Fill the power steering system with the proper type and quantity of fluid. Bleed the air from the system. If the tie rod ends were loosened, check and adjust the front end alignment.

Thunderbird and Cougar

1. Disconnect the negative battery cable. Raise and safely support the vehicle.

2. Remove the front wheel and tire assemblies.

3. Remove the cotter pins and nuts from the tie rod ends. Separate the tie rods from the spindles using a suitable tool.

4. Place a drain pan under the vehicle. Disconnect and plug the power steering return line hose. Disconnect the power steering pressure line at the intermediate fitting and position aside.

5. Remove the steering shaft retaining bolt. Remove the rack-to-subframe bolts and nuts. The nuts are accessed through the hole in the front crossmember.

6. Lower the rack as necessary to remove the pressure line inlet tube. Remove and discard the plastic seal on the inlet tube. Cut the tie strap securing the pressure line to each tube.

7. Remove the steering rack from the vehicle.

To install:

8. Install a new seal on the pressure line inlet tube.

9. Install the insulators from the rear side of the rack housing making sure they are fully seated. Use a suitable rubber lubricant to aid in installation.

10. Install and position the rack to the front crossmember. Install the pressure line inlet tube to the rack.

11. Align the steering shaft to allow the rack to completely seat on the crossmember. Install the steering rack retaining bolts and nuts. Tighten the bolts to 100–144 ft. lbs. (135–195 Nm).

12. Install the steering shaft retaining bolt and tighten to 20–30 ft. lbs. (28–40 Nm).

13. Secure the pressure line to the rack tube with a new tie strap. Connect the power steering pressure line.

14. Connect the power steering return line and tighten the clamp to 12–18 inch lbs. (1.4–2.0 Nm).

15. Install the outer tie rod ends to the spindles. Install the nuts and tighten to 39 ft. lbs. (53 Nm). Continue to tighten the nuts until the castellations line up with the stud bores, then install new cotter pins.

16. Install the front wheel and tire assemblies and lower the vehicle.

17. Fill the power steering system with the proper type and quantity of fluid. Bleed the air from the system. If the tie rods were loosened, check and adjust the front end alignment.

Power Steering Pump

REMOVAL & INSTALLATION

NOTE: On the 3.8L SC engine, the intercooler and intercooler tubes must be removed to gain access to the power steering pump.

1. Disconnect the negative battery cable.

2. Disconnect the fluid return hose at the reservoir and drain the fluid into a container.

3. Remove the pressure hose from the pump fitting, but do remove the fitting from the pump.

4. Remove the pump mounting bracket. Disconnect the belt from the pulley and remove the pump.

5. On engines with the fixed pump system, remove the pulley before removing the pump.

To install:

6. On non-fixed pump systems, install the pulley on the pump, if removed.

7. Place the pump on the mounting bracket and install the bolts at the front of the pump. Tighten to 30–45 ft. lbs. (40–62 Nm).

8. On fixed pump systems, install the pulley.

9. Place the belt on the pump pulley and adjust the tension, if necessary.

10. Install the pressure hose to the pump fitting. Tighten the tube nut with a tube nut wrench rather than with an open-end wrench. Tighten to 20–25 ft. lbs. (27–34 Nm).

NOTE: Do not overtighten this fitting. Swivel and/or end-play of the fitting is normal and does not indicate a loose fitting. Overtightening the tube nut can collapse the tube nut wall, resulting in a leak and requiring replacement of the entire pressure hose assembly. Use of an open-end wrench to tighten the nut can deform the tube nut hex which may result in improper torque and may make further servicing of the system difficult.

11. Connect the return hose to the pump and tighten the clamp. Fill the reservoir with the proper type and quantity of fluid. Bleed the air from the system.

BELT ADJUSTMENT

All vehicles are equipped with an automatic belt tensioner. No adjustment is necessary or possible. The belt tensioner is equipped with a belt wear indicator; when 1 percent belt stretch is indicated, the drive belt must be replaced. If the wear indicator is difficult to see on the 3.8L or 5.0L HO engines, locate the tab on the tensioner face plate. The tab should be approximately between the stops.

SYSTEM BLEEDING

1. Disconnect the ignition coil.

2. Raise and safely support the vehicle so the front wheels are off the floor.

3. Fill the power steering fluid reservoir.

4. Crank the engine with the starter and add fluid until the level remains constant.

5. While cranking the engine, rotate the steering wheel from lock-to-lock.

NOTE: The front wheels must be off the floor during lock-to-lock rotation of the steering wheel.

6. Check the fluid level and add fluid, if necessary.

7. Connect the ignition coil wire. Start the engine and allow it to run for several minutes.

8. Rotate the steering wheel from lock-to-lock.

9. Shut off the engine and check the fluid level. Add fluid, if necessary.

10. If air is still present in the system, purge the system of air using power steering pump air evacuator tool 021–00014 or equivalent, as follows:

a. Make sure the power steering pump reservoir is full to the COLD FULL mark on the dipstick.

b. Tightly insert the rubber stopper of the air evacuator assembly into the pump reservoir fill neck.

c. Apply 15 in. Hg maximum vacuum on the pump reservoir for a minimum of 3 minutes with the engine idling. As air purges from the system, vacuum will fall off. Maintain adequate vacuum with the vacuum source.

d. Release the vacuum and remove the vacuum source. Fill the reservoir to the COLD FULL mark.

e. With the engine idling, apply 15 in. Hg vacuum to the pump reservoir. Slowly cycle the steering wheel from lock-to-lock every 30 seconds for approximately 5 minutes. Do not hold the steering wheel on the stops while cycling. Maintain adequate vacuum with the vacuum source as the air purges.

f. Release the vacuum and remove the vacuum source. Fill the reservoir to the COLD FULL mark.

g. Start the engine and cycle the steering wheel. Check for oil leaks at all connections. In severe cases of aeration, it may be necessary to repeat Steps 10b–10f.

Tie Rod Ends

REMOVAL & INSTALLATION

1. Raise and safely support the vehicle.

2. Remove the cotter pin and nut from the tie rod end ball stud. Disconnect the tie rod end from the spindle using ball stud remover tool 3290–D or equivalent.

3. Holding the tie rod end with a wrench, loosen the tie rod jam nut. Grip the tie rod end with pliers and remove the assembly from the tie rod, but first note the depth to which the tie rod was located by using the jam nut as a marker.

To install:

4. Clean the tie rod threads.

5. Thread the new tie rod end onto the tie rod to the same depth as the removed tie rod end.

6. Place the tie rod end ball stud into the spindle and install the nut. Make sure the front wheels are in the straight-ahead position.

7. Tighten the nut to 35 ft. lbs. (48 Nm) and continue tightening the nut to align the next castellation of the nut with the cotter pin hole in the stud. Install a new cotter pin.

8. Set the toe to specification. Tighten the jam nut to 35–50 ft. lbs. (48–68 Nm).

BRAKES

Master Cylinder

REMOVAL & INSTALLATION

Except Mark VII, Thunderbird and Cougar With Anti-Lock Brakes

NOTE: The master cylinder on Mark VII, Thunderbird and Cougar with anti-lock brakes is part of the hydraulic actuation assembly and cannot be removed separately.

1. Disconnect the negative battery cable.

2. Remove the brake lines from the

primary and secondary outlet ports of the master cylinder.

3. Disconnect the brake warning indicator connector.

4. Remove the nuts attaching master cylinder to the brake booster assembly.

5. Slide the master cylinder forward and upward from the vehicle.

To install:

6. Position the master cylinder over the booster pushrod and onto the 2 studs on the booster. Install the retaining nuts and tighten to 14–25 ft. lbs. (18–34 Nm).

7. Install short brake lines in the master cylinder outlet ports and position them so they point back into the reservoir and the ends of the lines are submerged in brake fluid.

8. Fill the reservoir with brake fluid and cover the reservoir with a shop towel.

9. Pump the brakes until clear, bubble-free fluid comes out of both brake lines. If any brake fluid spills on the paint, wash it off immediately with water.

10. Remove the short brake lines and connect the vehicle brake lines to the master cylinder. Bleed each brake line at the master cylinder using the following procedure:

a. Have an assistant pump the brake pedal 10 times and then hold firm pressure on the pedal.

b. Crack the rear most brake line fitting with a tubing wrench until a stream of brake fluid comes out. Have the assistant maintain pressure on the brake pedal until the brake line fitting is tightened again.

c. Repeat this operation until clear, bubble free fluid comes out from around the brake line fitting.

d. Repeat this bleeding operation at the front brake line fitting.

11. Connect the brake warning indicator switch connector.

12. Bleed the system. Operate the brakes several times, then check for external hydraulic leaks.

Brake Control Valves

There are several types of valves in use. Not all valves perform the same function nor are they located in the same place on every vehicle.

Mustang—a brake control valve which contains a proportioning valve and shuttle valve located on the fender apron.

Thunderbird and Cougar—Vehicles without anti-lock brakes have 2 pressure control valves housed in the master cylinder. Vehicles with anti-lock brakes have a control valve which is located on a bracket below the hydraulic actuation unit.

Mark VII—a proportioning valve is located in the rear outlet port of the hydraulic actuator.

REMOVAL & INSTALLATION

1. Disconnect the negative battery cable.

2. Disconnect the brake line(s) from the valve. Disconnect the electrical connector, if equipped.

3. Unscrew the valve from the master cylinder or remove the mounting screw from the frame or fender apron, as required.

4. Installation is the reverse of the removal procedure. Bleed the brake system.

Power Brake Booster

REMOVAL & INSTALLATION

1. Disconnect the negative battery cable. Remove the air cleaner.

2. On Mustang equipped with the 2.3L engine, perform the following:

a. Relieve the fuel system pressure.

b. Disconnect the accelerator cable from the throttle body. Remove the screw that secures the accelerator cable to the accelerator shaft bracket and remove the cable from the bracket.

c. Remove the screws that secure the accelerator shaft bracket to the manifold and rotate the bracket toward the engine. Remove the horn.

d. Disconnect the 2 manifold injector connectors located near the oil dipstick retaining bracket. Disconnect the 2 fuel hoses to the fuel supply manifold.

e. Remove the 3 bolts holding the oil dipstick bracket to the upper intake manifold. Remove the dipstick and bracket.

f. Remove the windshield wiper motor and remove the vacuum hoses directly over the brake booster at the dash panel vacuum tee.

g. Remove the bolt holding the clutch cable stand, move the bracket to the side rail at the fender inner panel.

h. If equipped with cruise control, move the cruise control cable aside to clear the booster.

3. Disconnect the manifold vacuum hose from the booster check valve.

4. Disconnect the brake lines from the master cylinder, remove the master cylinder-to-booster retaining nuts and remove the master cylinder.

5. Working inside the vehicle below the instrument panel, remove the stoplight switch connector. Remove the switch retaining pin and slide the switch off the brake pedal pin just far

enough for the outer arm to clear the pin, then remove the switch. Be careful not to damage the switch.

6. Remove the booster-to-dash panel attaching nuts.

7. On Mustang equipped with cruise control, remove and set aside the control amplifier which is mounted to the lower outboard booster stud.

8. Slide the booster pushrod, washers and bushing off the brake pedal pin. Remove the booster.

9. Installation is the reverse of the removal procedure. Tighten the booster-to-dash panel attaching nuts and the master cylinder attaching nuts to 14–25 ft. lbs. (18–34 Nm). Bleed the brake system.

Brake Caliper

REMOVAL & INSTALLATION

Front

1. Raise and safely support the vehicle. Remove the front wheel and tire assembly.

2. On all except Mustang with 2.3L engine, remove the hollow brake hose retaining bolt and plug the brake hose.

3. On Mustang with 2.3L engine, loosen the brake line fitting that connects the brake hose to the brake line at the frame bracket. Remove the retaining clip from the hose and bracket and disengage the hose from the bracket. Unscrew the hose from the caliper.

4. Remove the caliper locating pins and remove the caliper. If removing both calipers, mark the right and left sides so they may be reinstalled correctly.

To install:

5. Install the caliper over the rotor with the outer brake shoe against the rotor's braking surface. On Thunderbird and Cougar, make sure the anti-rattle spring is under the arm of the knuckle.

6. Lubricate the inside of the locating pin insulators with silicone dialectric grease. Install the caliper locating pins and start the threads by hand. Tighten to 45–65 ft. lbs. (61–88 Nm) on Mustang and Mark VII. On Thunderbird and Cougar, tighten the locating pins to 19–25 ft. lbs. (25–34 Nm).

NOTE: On Mustang with 2.3L engine, new caliper locating pins must be used.

7. On all except Mustang with 2.3L engine, install new copper washers on each side of the brake hose fitting outlet and install the bolt, through the hose fitting and into the caliper. Tighten the bolt to 30–44 ft. lbs. (40–60 Nm) on Thunderbird and Cougar. On Mus-

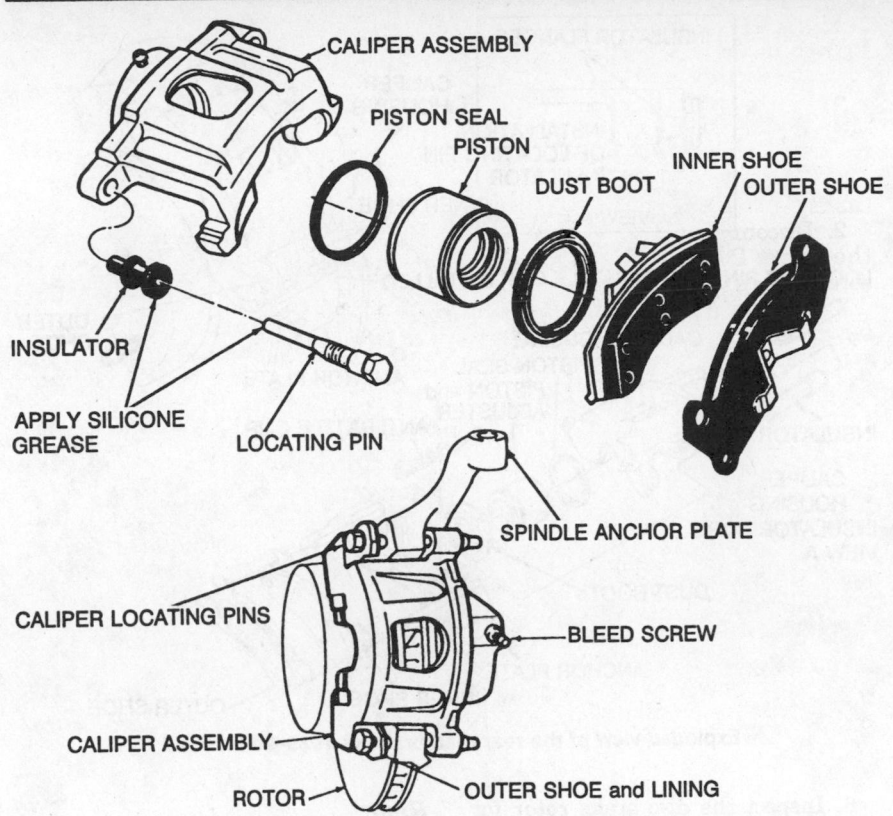

Front disc brake assembly—Mark VII

tang and Mark VII, tighten the bolt to 17–25 ft. lbs. (23–34 Nm).

8. On Mustang with 2.3L engine, thread the brake hose into the caliper and tighten to 20–30 ft. lbs. (28–41 Nm).

NOTE: This is a special self-sealing fitting that does not require a gasket. When the hose is correctly tightened, there should be 1 or 2 threads of the fitting still showing at the caliper. It is not necessary for the hose fitting to be flush with the caliper for sealing, so do not over-tighten.

9. On Mustang with 2.3L engine, position the brake hose in its bracket and install the retaining clip. Connect the brake line to the hose and tighten the line fitting nut.

10. Bleed the brake system, install the wheel and tire assembly and lower the vehicle.

11. To position the brake pads, apply the brake pedal several times before moving the vehicle.

Rear

THUNDERBIRD, COUGAR AND 1991–93 MARK VII

1. Raise and safely support the vehicle. Remove the rear wheel and tire assembly.

2. Remove the brake hose from the caliper.

3. Release the parking brake cable tension, if necessary. Remove the cable retaining clip and disconnect the cable end from the lever.

4. Hold the slider pin hex heads with an open end wrench and remove the pinch bolts.

5. Lift the caliper assembly away from the anchor plate. Remove the slider pins and boots from the anchor plate.

To install:

6. Apply silicone dialectric compound to the inside of the slider pin boots and to the slider pins.

7. Position the slider pins and boots in the anchor plate. Position the caliper assembly on the anchor plate. Make sure the brake shoes and anti-rattle springs are installed correctly.

8. Remove the residue from the pinch bolt threads and apply locking compound. Install the pinch bolts and tighten to 23–26 ft. lbs. (31–35 Nm) while holding the slider pins with an open end wrench.

9. Attach the cable end to the parking brake lever and install the cable retaining clip. Adjust the parking brake.

10. Using new washers, connect the brake flex hose to the caliper. Tighten the retaining bolt to 30–45 ft. lbs. (40–60 Nm).

11. Bleed the brake system, install the wheel and tire assembly and lower the vehicle.

12. Pump the brake pedal prior to moving the vehicle to position the linings.

1989–90 MARK VII

1. Raise and safely support the vehicle. Remove the rear wheel and tire assembly.

2. Disconnect the parking brake cable from the lever and bracket. Be careful to avoid kinking or cutting the cable or return spring.

3. Remove the caliper locating pins. Lift the caliper away from the anchor plate by pushing the caliper upward toward the anchor plate and then rotate the lower end out of the anchor plate.

4. If insufficient clearance between the caliper and the brake pads prevents removal of the caliper, proceed as follows:

a. Lower the vehicle and remove ½ of the brake fluid from the master cylinder.

b. Raise and safely support the vehicle. Loosen the caliper parking brake end retainer ½ turn, maximum, to allow the piston to be forced back into its bore.

c. To loosen the end retainer, remove the parking brake lever, then mark the end retainer and caliper housing to make sure the end retainer is not loosened more than ½ turn. Force the piston back in its bore and then remove the caliper.

NOTE: If the retainer must be loosened more than ½ turn, the seal between the thrust screw and the housing may be broken and brake fluid may leak into the parking brake mechanism chamber. In this case, the end retainer must be removed and the caliper overhauled.

To install:

5. If the end retainer has been loosened only ½ turn, install the caliper in the anchor plate without the brake pads. Tighten the end retainer to 75–96 ft. lbs. (101–130 Nm).

6. Install the parking brake lever on its keyed spline. The lever arm must point down and rearward. The parking brake cable will then pass freely under the axle. Tighten the retainer screw to 16–22 ft. lbs. (22–29 Nm). The parking brake lever must rotate freely after tightening the retainer screw. Remove the caliper from the anchor plate.

7. Install the brake pads.

8. Install the flexible hose by placing a new washer on each side of the fitting outlet and install the attaching bolt through the washers and fitting. Tighten to 20–30 ft. lbs. (27–40 Nm).

9. Position the upper tab of the caliper housing on the anchor plate upper abutment surface. Rotate the caliper housing until it is completely over the rotor. Be careful not to damage the piston boot.

10. Lubricate the locating pins and inside of the insulator with silicone dielectric compound. Apply threadlocking compound to the locating pin threads.

11. Hand start the locating pins through the caliper insulators and into the anchor plate. Tighten to 29–37 ft. lbs. (40–50 Nm).

12. Connect the parking brake cable to the bracket and the lever on the caliper. Bleed the brake system and fill the master cylinder.

13. Adjust the caliper as follows:

a. With the engine running, pump the service brake lightly about 40 times. Allow at least 1 second between pedal applications.

b. Check the parking brake for excessive travel or very light effort. In either case, repeat pumping the service brake pedal or check the parking brake cable for proper tension. The calipers must return to the OFF position when the parking brake is released.

c. If the parking brake cable bracket has been removed or loosened, apply the service brake pedal lightly with the engine, running. While the service brake pedal is being applied, rotate the parking brake bracket until the bracket lever stop contacts the actuating lever. Hold the parking brake bracket in this position while tightening the bolts to 30–37 ft. lbs. (40–50 Nm).

14. Install the wheel and tire assembly and lower the vehicle. Make sure a firm brake pedal application is obtained.

Disc Brake Pads

REMOVAL & INSTALLATION

Front

1. Remove and discard half the brake fluid from the master cylinder reservoir.

2. Raise and safely support vehicle. Remove the front wheel and tire assemblies.

3. Remove the caliper locating pins and remove the caliper from the anchor plate and rotor, but do not disconnect the brake hose.

4. Lift the caliper assembly from the knuckle or spindle.

5. Remove the outer brake pad from the caliper assembly and remove the inner brake pad from the caliper piston.

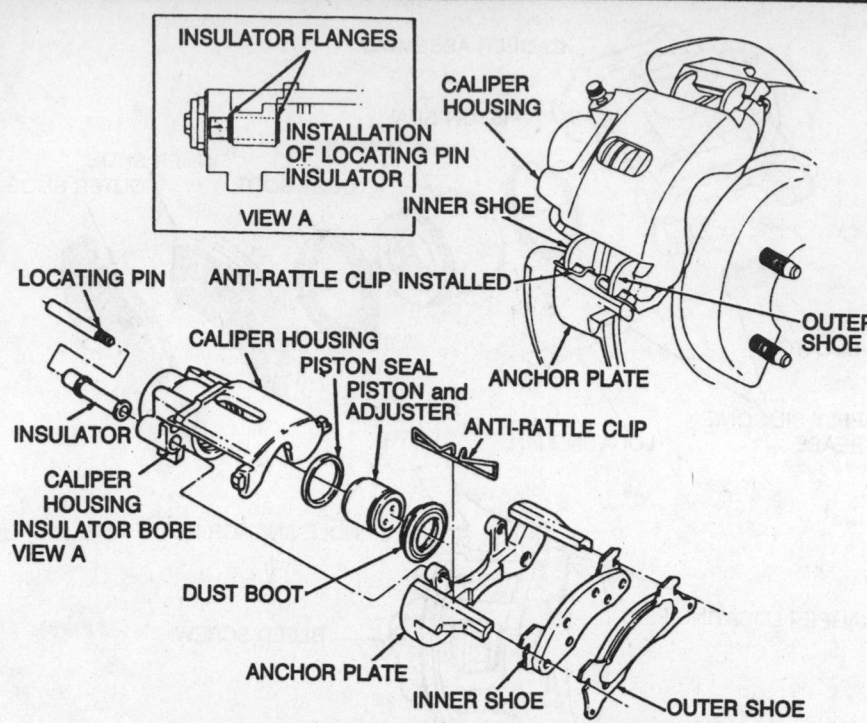

Exploded view of the rear disc brakes—1989–90 Mark VII

6. Inspect the disc brake rotor for scoring and wear. Replace or machine, as necessary. If machining, observe the minimum thickness specification.

7. Suspend the caliper inside the fender housing with a length of wire. Do not let the caliper hang by the brake hose.

To install:

8. Use a large C-clamp and wood block to push the caliper piston back into its bore.

9. Install the inner brake pad, then the outer brake pad, making sure the clips are properly seated.

10. Install the caliper and the wheel and tire assembly. Lower the vehicle.

11. Pump the brake pedal prior to moving the vehicle to seat the brake pads. Refill the master cylinder.

Rear

THUNDERBIRD, COUGAR AND 1991–93 MARK VII

1. Remove and discard half the brake fluid from the master cylinder.

2. Raise and safely support vehicle. Remove the rear wheel and tire assembly.

3. Remove the caliper from the anchor plate and rotor, but do not disconnect the brake hose. Suspend the caliper inside the fender housing with a length of wire. Do not let the caliper hang by the brake hose.

4. Remove the brake pads from the anchor plate.

5. Inspect the disc brake rotor for scoring and wear. Replace or machine, as necessary. If machining, observe the minimum thickness specification.

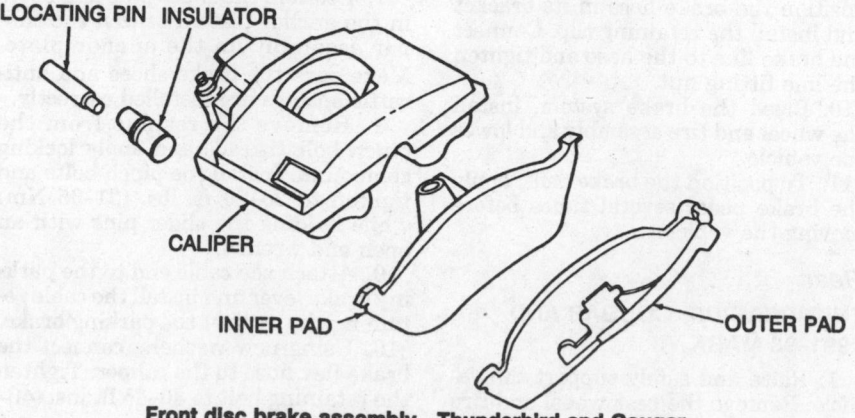

Front disc brake assembly—Thunderbird and Cougar

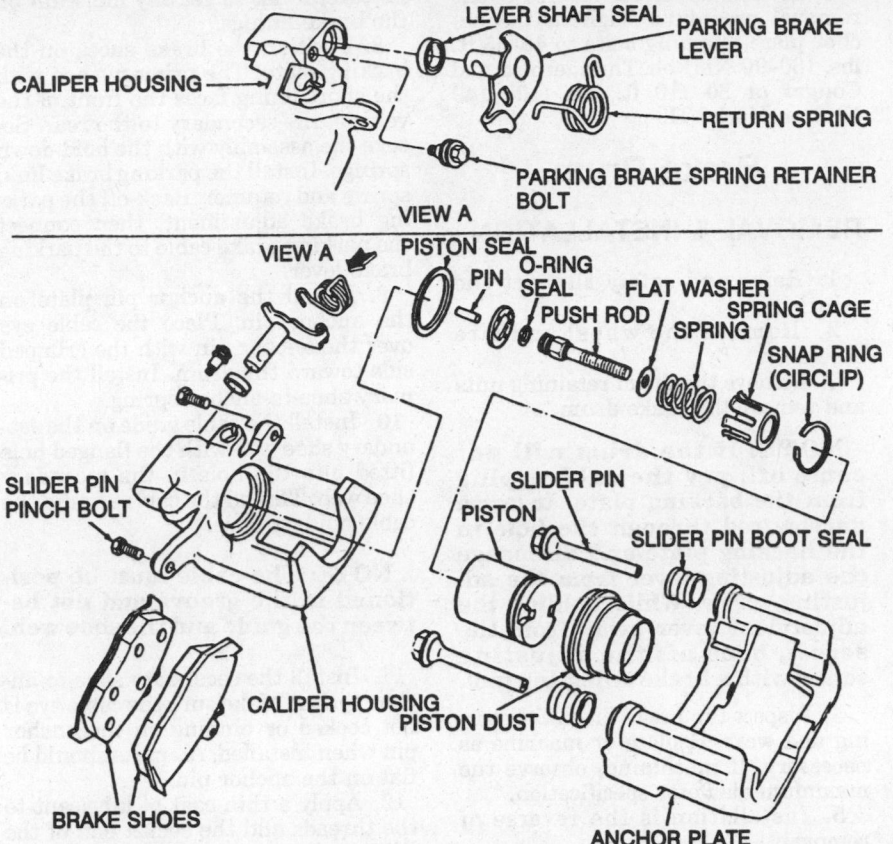

CALIPER HOUSING

LEVER SHAFT SEAL

PARKING BRAKE LEVER

RETURN SPRING

PARKING BRAKE SPRING RETAINER BOLT

VIEW A

VIEW A

PISTON SEAL

PIN

O-RING SEAL

PUSH ROD

FLAT WASHER

SPRING CAGE

SPRING

SNAP RING (CIRCLIP)

SLIDER PIN PINCH BOLT

SLIDER PIN

PISTON

SLIDER PIN BOOT SEAL

CALIPER HOUSING

PISTON DUST

BRAKE SHOES

ANCHOR PLATE

Exploded view of the rear disc brakes—Thunderbird, Cougar and 1991–93 Mark VII

To install:

6. Using brake piston turning tool T87P-2588-A or equivalent, rotate the caliper piston clockwise until it is fully seated. Make sure 1 of the 2 slots in the piston face is positioned so it will engage the nib on the brake pad.

7. Install the brake pads on the anchor plate. Install the caliper and wheel and tire assembly and lower the vehicle.

8. Pump the brake pedal prior to moving the vehicle to seat the brake pads. Refill the master cylinder.

1989–90 MARK VII

1. Remove and discard half the brake fluid from the master cylinder.

2. Raise and safely support vehicle. Remove the rear wheel and tire assemblies.

3. Remove the caliper from the anchor plate and rotor, but do not disconnect the brake hose. Suspend the caliper inside the fender housing with a length of wire. Do not let the caliper hang by the brake hose.

4. Remove and discard the caliper pin insulators. Remove the disc brake pads and the rotor.

5. Inspect the disc brake rotor for scoring and wear. Replace or machine, as necessary. If machining, observe the minimum thickness specification.

To install:

6. Install new pin insulators in the caliper housing. Make sure both insulator flanges straddle the housing holes.

7. Install the caliper on the anchor plate, without the disc brake pads or rotor in position. Install tool T75P-2588-B or equivalent on the caliper.

8. While holding the tool shaft, rotate the tool handle counterclockwise until the tool is firmly seated against the piston.

9. Loosen the tool handle ¼ turn. While holding the handle, rotate the tool shaft clockwise until the piston is fully bottomed in its bore. The piston will continue to turn even after it is bottomed. When there is no further inward movement of the piston and the tool handle is rotated until there is firm seating force, the piston is bottomed. Remove the tool and the caliper from the anchor plate.

10. Lubricate the anchor plate sliding ways with disc brake caliper slide grease. Do not get any lubricant on the braking surfaces.

11. Install the anti-rattle clip on the lower rail of the anchor plate. Install the inner brake pad on the anchor plate with the lining toward the rotor. Install the rotor.

12. Install the outer brake pad with the lining toward the rotor. Position the upper tab of the caliper housing on the anchor plate upper abutment surface. Rotate the caliper housing until it is completely over the rotor. Be careful not to damage the piston boot.

13. Adjust the piston position as follows:

a. Pull the caliper outboard until the inner pad is firmly seated against the rotor. Measure the clearance between the outer pad and the caliper. The clearance must be $^1/_{32}$–$^3/_{32}$ in. (0.8–2.4mm).

b. If the clearance is not as specified, remove the caliper and readjust the piston to obtain the required gap. Follow the procedures in Steps 7–9 and rotate the shaft counterclockwise to narrow the gap or clockwise to widen the gap. A ¼ turn of the piston moves it approximately $^1/_{16}$ in. (1.6mm).

NOTE: A clearance greater than $^3/_{32}$ in. (2.4mm) may allow the adjuster to be pulled out of the piston when the service brake is applied. This will cause the parking brake mechanism to fail to adjust. It is then necessary to replace the piston/adjuster assembly.

14. Lubricate the locating pins and inside of the insulator with silicone dielectric compound. Apply threadlocking compound to the locating pin threads.

15. Hand start the locating pins through the caliper insulators and into the anchor plate. Tighten to 29–37 ft. lbs. (40–50 Nm).

16. Connect the parking brake cable to the bracket and the lever on the caliper.

17. Adjust the caliper as follows:

a. With the engine running, pump the service brake lightly about 40 times. Allow at least 1 second between pedal applications.

b. Check the parking brake for excessive travel or very light effort. In either case, repeat pumping the service brake pedal or check the parking brake cable for proper tension. The calipers must return to the OFF position when the parking brake is released.

c. If the parking brake cable bracket has been removed or loosened, apply the service brake pedal lightly with the engine, running. While the service brake pedal is being applied, rotate the parking brake bracket until the bracket lever stop contacts the actuating lever. Hold the parking brake bracket in this position while tightening the bolts to 30–37 ft. lbs. (40–50 Nm).

18. Install the wheel and tire assem-

bly and lower the vehicle. Make sure a firm brake pedal application is obtained.

Brake Rotor

REMOVAL & INSTALLATION

Front

MUSTANG AND MARK VII

1. Raise and safely support the vehicle. Remove the wheel and tire assembly.
2. Remove the caliper, but do not disconnect the brake hose. Suspend the caliper inside the fender housing with a length of wire. Do not let the caliper hang by the brake hose.
3. Remove the grease cap from the hub and remove the cotter pin, nut lock, adjusting nut and flatwasher.
4. Remove the outer roller bearing assembly and remove the hub and rotor assembly.
5. Inspect the rotor for scoring and wear. Replace or machine as necessary. If machining, observe the minimum thickness specification.
6. Installation is the reverse of removal. Make sure the grease in the rotor is clean and adequate. Adjust the wheel bearings.

THUNDERBIRD AND COUGAR

1. Raise and safely support the vehicle. Remove the wheel and tire assembly.
2. Remove the caliper, but do not disconnect the brake hose. Suspend the caliper inside the fender housing with a length of wire. Do not let the caliper hang by the brake hose.
3. Remove the rotor retaining push nuts, if equipped, and remove the rotor from the hub.
4. Inspect the rotor for scoring and wear. Replace or machine as necessary. If machining, observe the minimum thickness specification.
5. Installation is the reverse of the removal procedure.

Rear

1. Raise and safely support the vehicle. Remove the wheel and tire assembly.
2. Remove the caliper, but do not disconnect the brake hose. Suspend the caliper inside the fender housing with a length of wire. Do not let the caliper hang by the brake hose.
3. Remove the caliper anchor plate.
4. Remove the rotor retaining push nuts, if equipped, and remove the rotor from the hub.
5. Inspect the rotor for scoring and wear. Replace or machine as necessary. If machining, observe the minimum thickness specification.

6. Installation is the reverse of the removal procedure. Tighten the anchor plate retaining bolts to 45–65 ft. lbs. (60–90 Nm) on Thunderbird and Cougar or 80–110 ft. lbs. (108–149 Nm) on Mark VII.

Brake Drum

REMOVAL & INSTALLATION

1. Raise and safely support the vehicle.
2. Remove the wheel and tire assembly.
3. Remove the drum retaining nuts and remove the brake drum.

NOTE: If the drum will not come off, pry the rubber plug from the backing plate. Insert a narrow rod through the hole in the backing plate and disengage the adjusting lever from the adjusting screw. While holding the adjustment lever away from the screw, back off the adjusting screw with a brake adjusting tool.

4. Inspect the brake drum for scoring and wear. Replace or machine as necessary. If machining, observe the maximum diameter specification.
5. Installation is the reverse of removal.

Brake Shoes

REMOVAL & INSTALLATION

Mustang

1. Raise and safely support the vehicle. Remove the rear wheel and tire assembly. Remove the brake drum.
2. Remove the shoe-to-anchor springs and unhook the cable eye from the anchor pin. Remove the anchor pin plate.
3. Remove the shoe hold-down springs, shoes, adjusting screw, pivot nut, socket and automatic adjustment parts.
4. Remove the parking brake link, spring and retainer. Disconnect the parking brake cable from the parking brake lever.
5. After removing the rear brake secondary shoe, disassemble the parking brake lever from the shoe by removing the retaining clip and spring washer.
To install:
6. Before installing the rear brake shoes, assemble the parking brake lever to the secondary shoe and secure it with the spring washer and retaining clip.
7. Apply a light coating of caliper slide grease at the points where the brake shoes contact the backing plate.

Be careful not to get any lubricant on the brake linings.
8. Position the brake shoes on the backing plate. The primary shoe with the short lining faces the front of the vehicle, the secondary to the rear. Secure the assembly with the hold-down springs. Install the parking brake link, spring and retainer. Back-off the parking brake adjustment, then connect the parking brake cable to the parking brake lever.
9. Install the anchor pin plate on the anchor pin. Place the cable eye over the anchor pin with the crimped side toward the drum. Install the primary shoe-to-anchor spring.
10. Install the cable guide on the secondary shoe web with the flanged hole fitted into the hole in the secondary shoe web. Thread the cable around the cable guide groove.

NOTE: The cable must be positioned in the groove and not between the guide and the shoe web.

11. Install the secondary shoe-to-anchor spring. Make sure the cable eye is not cocked or binding on the anchor pin when installed. All parts should be flat on the anchor pin.
12. Apply a thin coat of lubricant to the threads and the socket end of the adjusting screw. Turn the adjusting screw into the adjusting pivot nut to the limit of the threads, then back-off ½ turn.

NOTE: Make sure the socket end of the adjusting screw is stamped with an R or L, indicating the right or left side of the vehicle. The adjusting screw assemblies must be installed on the correct side for proper brake shoe adjustment.

13. Place the adjusting socket on the screw and install the assembly between the shoe ends with the adjusting screw toothed wheel nearest the secondary shoe.
14. Hook the cable hook into the hole in the adjusting lever. The adjusting levers are stamped with an R or L to indicate their installation on the right or left side.
15. Position the hooked end of the adjuster spring completely into the large hole in the primary shoe web. Connect the loop end of the spring to the adjuster lever hole.
16. Pull the adjuster lever, cable and automatic adjuster spring down and toward the rear, engaging the pivot hook in the large hole of the secondary shoe web.
17. Make sure the upper ends of the brake shoes are seated against the anchor pin and the shoes are centered on the backing plate.

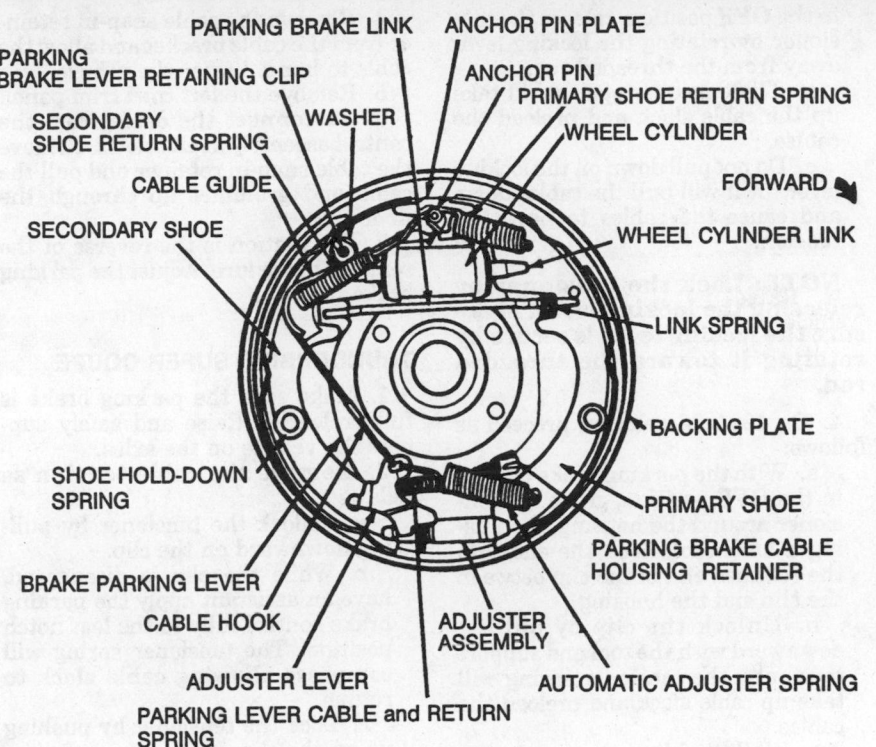

PARKING BRAKE LINK
ANCHOR PIN PLATE
PARKING BRAKE LEVER RETAINING CLIP
ANCHOR PIN
SECONDARY SHOE RETURN SPRING
WASHER
PRIMARY SHOE RETURN SPRING
WHEEL CYLINDER
CABLE GUIDE
SECONDARY SHOE
FORWARD
WHEEL CYLINDER LINK
LINK SPRING
BACKING PLATE
SHOE HOLD-DOWN SPRING
PRIMARY SHOE
PARKING BRAKE CABLE HOUSING RETAINER
BRAKE PARKING LEVER
CABLE HOOK
ADJUSTER ASSEMBLY
ADJUSTER LEVER
AUTOMATIC ADJUSTER SPRING
PARKING LEVER CABLE and RETURN SPRING

Brake shoe assembly—Mustang

18. Adjust the brakes using brake adjustment gauge D81L–1103–A or equivalent.

19. Install the brake drum, wheel and tire assemblies and lower the vehicle.

20. Apply the brakes several times while backing up the vehicle. After each stop, the vehicle must be moved forward.

Thunderbird and Cougar

1. Raise and safely support the vehicle. Remove the rear wheel and tire assembly. Remove the brake drum.

2. Disconnect the parking brake cable from the parking brake lever.

3. Remove the 2 brake shoe hold-down retainers, springs and pins.

4. Spread the brake shoes over the piston shoe guide slots. Lift the brake shoes, springs and adjuster off the backing plate as an assembly. Be careful not to bend the adjusting lever.

5. Remove the adjuster spring. To separate the shoes, remove the retracting springs.

6. Remove the parking brake lever retaining clip and spring washer. Remove the lever from the pin.

To install:

7. Apply a light coating of caliper slide grease to the backing plate brake shoe contact areas.

8. Apply a light coat of lubricant to the threaded areas of the adjuster

screw and socket. Assemble the brake adjuster with the stainless steel washer. Turn the socket all the way down on the screw, then back off ½ turn.

9. Install the parking brake lever to the trailing shoe with the spring washer and new retaining clip. Crimp the clip to securely retain the lever.

10. Position the trailing shoe on the

backing plate and attach the parking brake cable. Position the leading shoe on the backing plate and attach the lower retracting spring to the brake shoes.

11. Install the adjuster assembly to the slots in the brake shoes. The socket end must fit into the wider slot in the leading shoe. The slot in the adjuster nut must fit into the slots in the trailing shoe and parking brake lever.

12. Install the adjuster lever on the pin on the leading shoe and to the slot in the adjuster socket.

13. Install the upper retracting spring in the slot on the trailing shoe and the slot in the adjuster lever. The adjuster lever should contact the star and adjuster assembly.

14. Install the brake shoe anchor pins, springs and retainers.

15. Adjust the brake shoes using brake adjusting gauge D81L–1103–A or equivalent.

16. Install the brake drum, wheel and tire assemblies and lower the vehicle.

17. Apply the brakes several times while backing up the vehicle. After each stop, the vehicle must be moved forward.

Wheel Cylinder

REMOVAL & INSTALLATION

1. Remove the wheel and tire assembly and the brake drum.

2. Remove the brake shoe assembly.

3. Disconnect the brake line from the wheel cylinder at the backing plate.

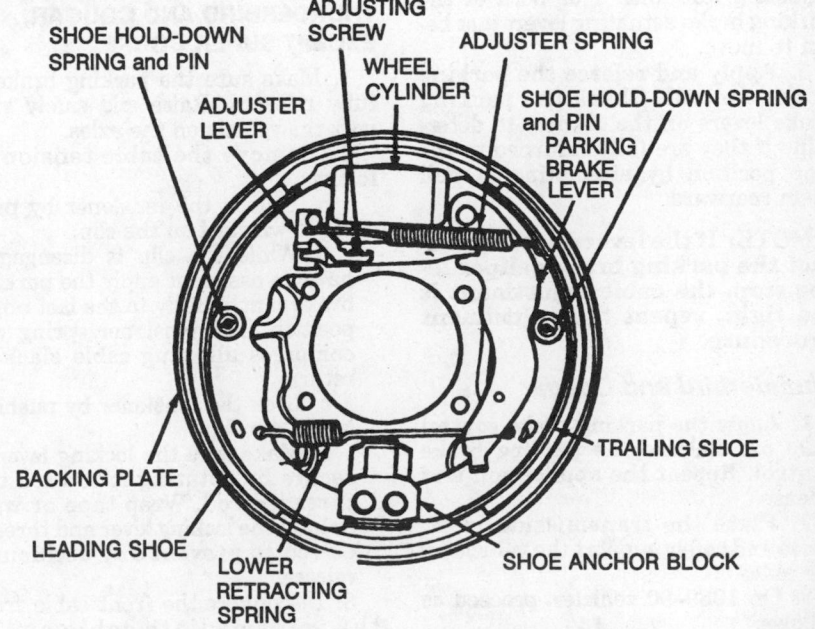

SHOE HOLD-DOWN SPRING and PIN
ADJUSTING SCREW
ADJUSTER SPRING
WHEEL CYLINDER
ADJUSTER LEVER
SHOE HOLD-DOWN SPRING and PIN
PARKING BRAKE LEVER
TRAILING SHOE
BACKING PLATE
LEADING SHOE
LOWER RETRACTING SPRING
SHOE ANCHOR BLOCK

Brake shoe assembly—Thunderbird and Cougar

4. Remove the wheel cylinder attaching bolts and remove the wheel cylinder.

5. Installation is the reverse of the removal procedure. Tighten the wheel cylinder attaching bolts to 10–20 ft. lbs. (14–28 Nm) on Mustang. On Thunderbird and Cougar, tighten the attaching bolts to 106–160 inch lbs. (12–18 Nm).

6. Bleed the brake system.

Parking Brake Cable

ADJUSTMENT

Mustang and 1991–93 Mark VII

1. Make sure the parking brake is fully released.

2. Place the transmission in N. Raise and safely support the vehicle.

3. Tighten the adjusting nut against the cable equalizer, causing a rear wheel brake drag. Loosen the adjusting nut until the rear brakes are fully released. There should be no brake drag.

4. Lower the vehicle and check the operation of the parking brake.

1989–90 Mark VII

1. Raise and safely support the vehicle.

2. Back off the parking brake cable adjusting nut until the cables are loose.

3. Make sure each rear disc brake is properly adjusted by moving the caliper lever in the applied direction. If the lever moves more than 20 degrees, using hand pressure of approximately 50 lbs. maximum, adjust the brake pads.

4. Tighten the parking brake cable adjusting nut until 1 or both of the parking brake actuating levers just begin to move.

5. Apply and release the parking brake control. Check the parking brake levers on the calipers to determine if they are fully returned to the stop position by attempting to pull them rearward.

NOTE: If the lever does not contact the parking brake caliper lever stop, the cable adjustment is too tight, repeat the adjustment procedure.

Thunderbird and Cougar

1. Apply the parking brake control fully on. Release the parking brake control. Repeat the application and release.

2. Place the transmission in N. Raise and safely support the vehicle by the axles.

3. On 1989–90 vehicles, proceed as follows:

    a. With the parking brake control in the OFF position, release the tensioner by rotating the locking lever away from the threaded rod.

    b. The tensioner spring will take up the cable slack and preload the cables.

    c. Do not pull down on the locking lever for it will pull the cables down and cause the cables to have low tension.

NOTE: Lock the tensioner by releasing the locking lever. Make sure the locking lever is secure by rotating it toward the threaded rod.

4. On 1991–93 vehicles, proceed as follows:

    a. With the parking brake control in the OFF position, grasp the tensioner around the housing, then using a hook tool, hook the end into the rounded end of the clip between the clip and the housing.

    b. Unlock the clip by pulling downward with the tool and support tensioner; the tensioner spring will take up cable slack and preload the cables.

    c. While holding the tensioner, lock the clip by pushing up on the bottom of the clip. If the clip does not slide up, move the assembly slightly to align the closest groove on the adjuster rod to the clip.

5. Examine the tensioner for remaining cable take up capability. If none is present, check all cables, parking brake control and brackets for possible damage or deflection.

REMOVAL & INSTALLATION

Front Cable

THUNDERBIRD AND COUGAR, EXCEPT SUPER COUPE

1. Make sure the parking brake is fully released. Raise and safely support the vehicle on the axles.

2. Remove the cable tension as follows:

    a. Unlock the tensioner by pulling downward on the clip.

    b. While the clip is disengaged, have an assistant apply the parking brake control fully to the last notch position. The tensioner spring will compress allowing cable slack to return.

    c. Lock the tensioner by pushing up on the clip.

    d. Make sure the locking lever is secure by rotating it toward the threaded rod. Wrap tape or wire around the locking lever and threaded rod to prevent any accidental release.

3. Disconnect the front cable from the intermediate cable at the connector.

4. Remove the cable snap-in retainer from the cable bracket and allow the cable to hang. Lower the vehicle.

5. Remove the left cowl trim panel.

6. Disconnect the cable from the control assembly at the clevis. Remove the cable snap-in retainer and pull the cable and grommet up through the floor pan.

7. Installation is the reverse of the removal procedure. Adjust the parking brake.

THUNDERBIRD SUPER COUPE

1. Make sure the parking brake is fully released. Raise and safely support the vehicle on the axles.

2. Remove the cable tension as follows:

    a. Unlock the tensioner by pulling downward on the clip.

    b. While the clip is disengaged, have an assistant apply the parking brake control fully to the last notch position. The tensioner spring will compress allowing cable slack to return.

    c. Lock the tensioner by pushing up on the clip.

    d. Make sure the locking lever is secure by rotating it toward the threaded rod. Wrap tape or wire around the locking lever and threaded rod to prevent any accidental release.

3. Disconnect the front cable from the right rear cable at the connector.

4. Remove the cable snap-in retainer from the tensioner housing. Remove the cable routing clip from the body rear crossmember by squeezing the clip together between the cable and crossmember. Allow the cable to hang.

5. Lower the vehicle. Remove the rear seat and the console.

6. Disconnect the cable from the control at the clevis hook. Remove the cable snap-in retainer from the hand control assembly.

7. Pull the cable and grommet up through the rear floor. Pull the cable out from under the carpet.

MARK VII

1. Raise and safely support the vehicle. Loosen the adjusting nut at the adjuster.

2. Disconnect the front cable from the equalizer lever assembly and remove the cable from the body bracket. Lower the vehicle.

3. Inside the passenger compartment, remove the retainer holding the cable conduit to the parking brake control and remove the cable.

4. Installation is the reverse of the removal procedure. Adjust the parking brake.

Intermediate Cable

THUNDERBIRD AND COUGAR, EXCEPT SUPER COUPE

1. Make sure the parking brake is fully released. Raise and safely support the vehicle on the axles.
2. Remove the cable tension as follows:
   a. Unlock the tensioner by pulling downward on the clip.
   b. While the clip is disengaged, have an assistant apply the parking brake control fully to the last notch position. The tensioner spring will compress allowing cable slack to return.
   c. Lock the tensioner by pushing up on the clip.
   d. Make sure the locking lever is secure by rotating it toward the threaded rod. Wrap tape or wire around the locking lever and threaded rod to prevent any accidental release.
3. Disconnect the intermediate cable from the right rear cable and front cable at the connector.
4. Remove the cable snap-in retainer from the tensioner housing and body bracket.
5. Remove the cable routing clips for body side rails and rear crossmember by squeezing the clip together between the cable and the crossmembers. Remove the cable.
6. Installation is the reverse of the removal procedure. Adjust the parking brake.

MARK VII

1. Raise and safely support the vehicle. Remove the cable adjusting nut.
2. Disconnect the intermediate cable ends from the left rear and the transverse cable.
3. Remove the cotter pin, washer and spring from the pin protruding through the equalizer lever assembly and remove the lever.

NOTE: The intermediate cable cannot be separated from the lever assembly.

4. Installation is the reverse of the removal procedure. Adjust the parking brake.

Transverse Cable

MARK VII

1. Raise and safely support the vehicle. Loosen the adjusting nut on the adjusting rod until it is off the rod.
2. Remove the cable ends from the right rear and intermediate cables.
3. Remove hairpin clips or conduit bracket, as required, to remove the transverse cable from the vehicle.
4. Installation is the reverse of the removal procedure. Adjust the parking brake.

Rear Cables

MUSTANG

1. Place the parking brake control in the released position. Release the cable tension as follows:
   a. Remove the floor console.
   b. With an assistant inside the vehicle, raise and safely support the vehicle.
   c. Have another assistant pull the equalizer rearward approximately 1–2½ in. to rotate the self-adjuster reel backward.
   d. Insert a steel lockpin through the holes in the lever and control assembly. This locks the ratchet wheel in the cable released position.

NOTE: Do not remove the steel lockpin until the cables are connected to the equalizer. Pin removal releases the tension in the ratchet wheel causing the spring to unwind and release tension. If the pin is removed without the cables attached, the entire assembly must be removed to reset the spring tension.

2. Raise and safely support the vehicle. Remove the rear cables from the equalizer.
3. Remove the cable snap fitting from the body. Remove the retaining clip that attaches the cable to the underbody.
4. Remove the wheel and tire assemblies and the brake drums.
5. Remove the self adjuster springs and remove the cable retainers from the backing plates.
6. Disconnect the cable ends from the parking brake levers, compress the cable retainer prongs and pull the cable ends from the backing plates.
7. Installation is the reverse of the removal procedure. Adjust the parking brake.

THUNDERBIRD AND COUGAR WITH DRUM BRAKES

1. Make sure the parking brake is fully released. Raise and safely support the vehicle on the axles.
2. Remove the cable tension as follows:
   a. Unlock the tensioner by pulling downward on the clip.
   b. While the clip is disengaged, have an assistant apply the parking brake control fully to the last notch position. The tensioner spring will compress allowing cable slack to return.
   c. Lock the tensioner by pushing up on the clip.
   d. Make sure the locking lever is secure by rotating it toward the

threaded rod. Wrap tape or wire around the locking lever and threaded rod to prevent any accidental release.
3. Remove the wheel and tire assemblies and the brake drums.
4. Disconnect the parking brake cable end from the parking brake actuating lever. Depress the conduit retaining prongs and remove the cable and pronged fitting from the backing plate.
5. Remove the cable snap-in retainer from the frame bracket.
6. Disconnect the cable end from the tensioner or intermediate cable at the connector. Remove the rear cable by sliding the cable through the clip on the lower control arm.
7. Installation is the reverse of the removal procedure. Adjust the parking brake.

THUNDERBIRD AND COUGAR WITH DISC BRAKES

1. Make sure the parking brake is fully released. Raise and safely support the vehicle on the axles.
2. Remove the cable tension as follows:
   a. Unlock the tensioner by pulling downward on the clip.
   b. While the clip is disengaged, have an assistant apply the parking brake control fully to the last notch position. The tensioner spring will compress allowing cable slack to return.
   c. Lock the tensioner by pushing up on the clip.
   d. Make sure the locking lever is secure by rotating it toward the threaded rod. Wrap tape or wire around the locking lever and threaded rod to prevent any accidental release.
3. Disconnect the rear cable end from the tensioner or intermediate/front cable at the connector.
4. Remove the cable snap-in retainer from the frame bracket. Disconnect the rear cable end from the caliper housing and remove the cable from the parking brake lever arm on the caliper.
5. Remove the cable retainer from the rear stabilizer bar.
6. Installation is the reverse of the removal procedure. Adjust the parking brake.

MARK VII

1. Raise and safely support the vehicle. Loosen the adjusting nut at the adjuster assembly.
2. With the cables slackened, disconnect the rear cables from the right and left rear cable connectors. The left cable connects to the end of the intermediate cable, The right cable connects to the transverse cable.
3. Disconnect the rear cables from the body brackets or caliper brackets.

4. Slide the cable out of the brake lever arm and remove from the vehicle.

5. Installation is the reverse of the removal procedure. Adjust the parking brake.

Brake System Bleeding

Without Anti-Lock Brakes

1. Clean all dirt from the master cylinder filler cap.

2. If the master cylinder is known or suspected to have air in the bore, it must be bled before any of the wheel cylinders or calipers. To bleed the master cylinder, loosen the upper secondary left front outlet fitting approximately ¾ turn. Have an assistant depress the brake pedal slowly through it's full travel. Close the outlet fitting and let the pedal return slowly to the fully released position. Wait 5 seconds and then repeat the operation until all air bubbles disappear.

3. Repeat Step 2 with the right-hand front outlet fitting.

4. Continue to bleed the brake system by removing the rubber dust cap from the wheel cylinder bleeder fitting or caliper fitting at the right-hand rear of the vehicle. Place a suitable box wrench on the bleeder fitting and attach a rubber drain tube to the fitting. The end of the tube should fit snugly around the bleeder fitting. Submerge the other end of the tube in a container partially filled with clean brake fluid and loosen the fitting ¾ turn.

5. Have an assistant push the brake pedal down slowly through it's full travel. Close the bleeder fitting and allow the pedal to slowly return to it's full release position. Wait 5 seconds and repeat the procedure until no bubbles appear at the submerged end of the bleeder tube. Secure the bleeder fitting and remove the bleeder tube. Install the rubber dust cap on the bleeder fitting.

6. Repeat the procedure in Steps 4 and 5 in the following sequence: left front, left rear and right front. Refill the master cylinder reservoir after each wheel cylinder or caliper has been bled and install the master cylinder cover and gasket. When brake bleeding is completed, the fluid level should be filled to the maximum level indicated on the reservoir.

7. Always make sure the disc brake pistons are returned to their normal positions by depressing the brake pedal several times until normal pedal travel is established. If the pedal feels spongy, repeat the bleeding procedure.

With Anti-Lock Brakes

The front brakes can be bled in the same manner as a vehicle without anti-lock brakes or they can be bled with a pressure bleeder. The rear brakes must be bled with a pressure bleeder or with a fully charged accumulator.

PRESSURE BLEEDING

1. Clean all dirt from the reservoir filler cap area. Attach a suitable pressure bleeder to the reservoir cap opening.

2. Maintain 35 psi pressure on the system through the pressure bleeder.

3. Remove the dust cap from the right front caliper bleeder fitting. Attach a rubber drain tube to the fitting, making sure the tube fits snugly.

4. With the ignition switch in the OFF position and the brake pedal in the fully released position, open the bleeder fitting for 10 seconds at a time until an air-free stream of brake fluid flow is observed.

5. Repeat the procedure at the left front, right rear and left rear calipers, in that order.

6. Place the ignition switch in the RUN position and pump the brake pedal several times to complete the bleeding procedure and to fully charge the accumulator.

7. Turn the ignition switch to the OFF position and remove the pressure bleeder. Siphon off the excess fluid in the reservoir to adjust the level to the MAX mark with a fully charged accumulator.

REAR BRAKE BLEEDING WITH A FULLY CHARGED ACCUMULATOR

1. Remove the dust cap from the right rear caliper bleeder fitting. Attach a rubber drain tube to the fitting, making sure the tube fits snugly.

2. Turn the ignition switch to the RUN position. This will turn on the electric pump to charge the accumulator, as required.

3. Have an assistant hold the brake pedal in the applied position. Open the bleeder fitting for 10 seconds at a time until an air-free stream of brake fluid flow is observed.

— CAUTION —

To prevent possible injury, care must be used when opening the bleeder screws due to the high pressures available from a fully charged accumulator.

4. Repeat the procedure at the left rear caliper.

5. Pump the brake pedal several times to complete the bleeding procedure.

6. Adjust the fluid level in the reservoir to the MAX mark with a fully charged accumulator.

NOTE: If the pump motor is allowed to run continuously for approximately 20 minutes, a thermal safety switch inside the motor may shut the motor off to prevent it from overheating. If that happens, a 2–10 minute cool down period is typically required before normal operation can resume.

Anti-Lock Brake System Service

PRECAUTIONS

● Before servicing any high pressure component, discharge the hydraulic pressure from the system.

● Do not allow brake fluid to contact any electrical connections.

● Use care when opening the bleeder screws due to the high system pressure from the accumulator.

RELIEVING ANTI-LOCK BRAKE SYSTEM PRESSURE

— CAUTION —

Before servicing any component which contains high pressure, it is mandatory that the hydraulic pressure in the system be discharged or personal injury could result.

To discharge the system, turn the ignition OFF and pump the brake pedal a minimum of 20 times until an increase in pedal force is clearly felt.

Hydraulic Control Unit (HCU)

REMOVAL & INSTALLATION

The hydraulic actuation assembly contains all the anti-lock brake hydraulic components: master cylinder and fluid reservoir, hydraulic pump motor and accumulator and solenoid valve block assembly.

1. Discharge the hydraulic pressure in the system.

2. Disconnect the negative battery cable.

3. On Thunderbird and Cougar, remove the air cleaner housing and duct assembly.

4. Tag and disconnect the electrical connectors from the fluid level indicator, main valve, solenoid valve block, pressure warning switch, hydraulic pump motor and ground connector from the master cylinder portion of the assembly.

5. Disconnect the brake line fittings. Immediately plug each port to prevent fluid loss and contamination.

NOTE: Do not allow brake fluid

to come in contact with any electrical connectors.

6. On Mark VII, remove the accumulator. On Thunderbird and Cougar, remove the trim panel under the steering column.

7. Disconnect the actuation assembly pushrod from the brake pedal by removing the hairpin connector next to the stoplight switch. Slide the switch, pushrod and plastic bushings off the pedal pin.

8. Remove the 4 retaining nuts that hold the actuation assembly to the brake pedal support bracket.

9. Remove the actuation assembly.

To install:

10. Mount the actuation assembly with the rubber boot and foam gasket to the engine side of the dash panel with the 4 mounting studs and pushrod inserted in the proper holes.

11. Working in the passenger compartment, loosely start 4 retaining locknuts attaching the actuation assembly to the pedal support bracket.

12. Connect the pushrod to the brake pedal pin by sliding the flanged plastic bushing, pushrod and washer onto the brake pedal pin. Position the stoplight switch so the slot on the switch bracket straddles the pushrod on the brake pedal pin, with the hole on the opposite leg of the switch bracket just clearing the pin. Slide the switch onto the pedal pin until it bottoms. Install the outer nylon bushing and secure the assembly with the hairpin retainer.

13. Tighten the 4 locknuts to 13–25 ft. lbs. (18–34 Nm).

14. From the engine compartment, connect the brake tubes and tighten the nuts to 10–15 ft. lbs. (13–20 Nm). Connect the electrical connectors.

15. On Mark VII, screw in the accumulator, making sure the O-ring is in place. Tighten to 30–34 ft. lbs. (40–46 Nm). On Thunderbird and Cougar, install the air cleaner and duct assembly.

16. Connect the negative battery cable and bleed the brake system.

Front Wheel Speed Sensor

REMOVAL & INSTALLATION

Thunderbird and Cougar

1. Disconnect the negative battery cable. Raise and safely support the vehicle.

2. From underside of vehicle, up front near radiator support, disconnect sensor electrical connector for right or left front sensor.

3. Remove routing clips along wiring harness.

4. Remove Torx® head screw securing sensor to front spindle.

NOTE: If the toothed speed indicator ring is damaged, replace it.

To install:

5. Install sensor into hole in spindle. No adjustment is necessary. Install Torx® head screw and tighten to 40–60 inch lbs. (4.5–6.8 Nm).

6. Route wiring using clips previously removed. Ensure wiring is routed properly as shown.

7. Connect sensor wiring connector to harness connector.

Mark VII

1. Disconnect the negative battery cable.

2. From inside engine compartment, disconnect sensor electrical connector for right or left front sensor.

3. Raise and safely support the vehicle. Disengage wire grommet at right or left shock tower and pull sensor cable connector through hole. Use care not to damage connector.

4. Remove sensor wire from bracket on shock strut and side rail.

5. Remove wheel and tire assembly.

6. Loosen 5mm setscrew holding sensor to sensor bracket post. Remove sensor through hole in disc brake splash shield.

7. To remove sensor bracket or sensor bracket post in case of damage, the caliper and hub and rotor assembly must be removed. After removing the hub and rotor assembly, remove 2 brake splash shield attaching bolts that attach sensor bracket.

NOTE: Replace the toothed sensor ring, if damaged.

To install:

8. Install sensor bracket with sensor bracket post, if removed. Tighten sensor retaining bolt to 40–53 inch lbs. (4.5–6.0 Nm) and splash shield attaching bolts to 10–15 ft. lbs. (13–20 Nm). Install hub and rotor assembly and caliper.

9. If a sensor is to be reused or adjusted, pole face must be clean of all foreign material. Carefully scrape pole face with a dull knife or similar tool, to ensure that sensor slides freely on the post. Glue a new front paper spacer on pole face, front paper spacer is marked with an **F** and is 0.051 in. (1.3mm) thick. Also, the steel sleeve around post bolt must be rotated to provide a new surface for setscrew to indent and lock into.

10. Install sensor through brake shield onto sensor bracket post. Ensure paper spacer on sensor is intact and does not come off during installation.

11. Push sensor toward toothed sensor ring until new paper sensor contacts the ring. Hold sensor against sensor ring and tighten the 5mm setscrew to 21–26 inch lbs. (2.4–3.0 Nm).

12. Insert sensor cable into bracket on shock strut, rail bracket; then through inner fender apron to engine compartment and seat grommet. Install wheel and tire assembly.

13. Lower vehicle and from inside

FLUID RESERVOIR

FLUID LEVEL INDICATOR 5-PIN PLUG (CANNOT BE SEEN IN THIS VIEW)

ACCUMULATOR

SOLENOID VALVE BODY

SOLENOID VALVE BLOCK ASSEMBLY

MAIN VALVE 2-PIN PLUG

ACTUATION ASSEMBLY (INCLUDES MAIN VALVE)

PRESSURE WARNING SWITCH 5-PIN PLUG (ON PRESSURE WARNING SWITCH)

HYDRAULIC PUMP MOTOR

PUMP MOTOR 5-PIN PLUG

Hydraulic actuation assembly—Thunderbird and Cougar

engine compartment, connect sensor electrical connection. Connect the negative battery cable.

Rear Wheel Speed Sensor

REMOVAL & INSTALLATION

Thunderbird and Cougar

1. Disconnect the negative battery cable.

2. From inside luggage compartment, disconnect wheel sensor electrical connector located rearward of wheel well, behind carpeting on sides of luggage compartment.

3. Lift luggage compartment carpet and push sensor wire grommet through hole in luggage compartment floor.

4. Raise and safely support the vehicle.

5. Remove plastic clip holding sensor wire to axle carrier housing. Do not bend the clip open more than the amount necessary to remove the clip from the axle housing.

6. Remove wheel sensor retaining bolt using a ½ in. socket.

To install:

7. Align sensor locating tab and bolt hole with axle housing and push into position.

8. Install sensor retaining bolt and tighten to 14–20 ft. lbs. (19–27 Nm).

9. Install plastic clip retaining sensor wire to axle carrier housing and push electrical connector through hole in floor into luggage compartment. Ensure that rubber grommet is properly seated in hole in floor.

10. Lower the vehicle. Connect sensor electrical connector to connector on harness.

Mark VII

1989–90

1. Disconnect the negative battery cable.

2. From inside the luggage compartment, disconnect the wheel sensor electrical connector located behind the forward luggage compartment trim panel.

3. Lift the luggage compartment carpet and push the sensor wire grommet through the hole in the luggage compartment floor.

4. Raise the vehicle and remove the appropriate wheel and tire assembly.

5. Carefully remove the wheel sensor wiring from the axle shaft housing. The wiring harness has 3 different types of retainers:

    a. The inboard retainer is a clip located on top of the differential housing. Bend the clip out of the

way enough to remove the wiring harness.

    b. The second retainer is a C-clip located in the center of the axle shaft housing. Pull rearward on the clip to disengage the clip from the axle housing.

NOTE: Do not bend the clip open beyond the amount necessary to remove the clip from the axle housing.

    c. The third clip is at the connection between the rear wheel brake tube and the flexible hose. Remove the hold-down bolt and open the clip to remove the wiring harness.

6. Remove the rear wheel caliper and rotor assemblies.

7. Remove the wheel sensor E8 Torx® head retaining bolt. Slip the grommet out of the rear brake splash shield and pull the sensor wire outward through the hole.

8. Inspect the sensor bracket for possible damage. If damaged, remove the two 6mm self-tapping screws attaching the bracket to the axle adapter and remove the bracket.

NOTE: Replace the toothed sensor ring, if damaged.

To install:

9. Install the sensor bracket, if removed. Tighten the screws to 11–15 ft. lbs. (15–20 Nm)

10. Loosen the 5mm setscrew on the sensor and ensure that the sensor slides freely on the sensor bracket post.

11. If a sensor is to be reused or adjusted, the pole face must be clean of all foreign material. Carefully scrape the pole face with a dull knife or similar tool. Glue a new rear paper spacer on the pole face. Rear paper spacer is marked with an **R** and is 0.043-inch thick. If desired, a feeler gauge may be used instead of a paper spacer. If used, remove paper spacer prior to adjusting. Also, the steel sleeve around the post bolt must be rotated to provide a new surface for the setscrew to indent and lock into.

12. Insert the sensor into large hole in the sensor bracket and install the E8 Torx® head retaining bolt into the snesor bracket post. Tighten the bolt to 40–60 inch lbs. (4.5–6.8 Nm).

13. Push the sensor toward the toothed ring until the new paper sensor makes contact with the sensor ring. Hold the sensor against the toothed ring and tighten the 5mm setscrew to 21–26 inch lbs. (2.4–3.0 Nm).

14. Install the caliper and rotor.

15. Push the wire and connector through the splash shield hole and engage the grommet into the shield eyelet. Install the sensor wire in the retainers along the axle housing.

16. Push the connector through the hole in the luggage compartment and seat the grommet in the luggage compartment floorpan.

17. From inside the luggage compartment, connect the cable electrical connector. Install the carpet as necessary.

18. Check the function of the sensor by driving the vehicle and observing the "Check Anti-Lock Brakes" light in the overhead console.

1991–93

1. Disconnect the negative battery cable.

2. From inside the luggage compartment, disconnect the wheel sensor electrical connector located behind the forward luggage compartment trim panel.

3. Lift the luggage compartment carpet and push the sensor wire grommet through the hole in the luggage compartment floor.

4. Raise the vehicle and remove the appropriate wheel and tire assembly.

5. Carefully remove the wheel sensor wiring from the axle shaft housing. The wiring harness has 3 different types of retainers:

    a. The inboard retainer is a clip located on top of the differential housing. Bend the clip out of the way enough to remove the wiring harness.

    b. The second retainer is a C-clip located in the center of the axle shaft housing. Pull rearward on the clip to disengage the clip from the axle housing.

NOTE: Do not bend the clip open beyond the amount necessary to remove the clip from the axle housing.

    c. The third clip is at the connection between the rear wheel brake tube and the flexible hose. Remove the hold-down bolt and open the clip to remove the wiring harness.

6. Remove the sensor retaining bolt and remove the sensor.

NOTE: Replace the toothed sensor ring, if damaged.

To install:

7. Install the sensor in the rear brake adapter and tighten the retaining screws to 11–15 ft. lbs. (15–20 Nm).

8. Install the sensor wire in the retainers along the axle housing. Push the connector through the hole in the luggage compartment and seat the grommet in the luggage compartment floorpan.

9. Install the wheel and tire assembly and lower the vehicle.

10. From inside the luggage compartment, connect the cable electrical

connector. Install the carpet, as necessary.

11. Check the sensor function by driving the vehicle and observing the "Check Anti-Lock Brakes" indicator.

CHASSIS ELECTRICAL

Air Bag

DISARMING

1990–91

1. Disconnect the negative battery cable.

2. Open the glove compartment door, press in the sides and lower the door down past the stops. Remove the heater duct, if necessary. Disconnect the electrical connector from the back-up power supply (blue box, 1 connector).

NOTE: The backup power supply allows air bag deployment if the battery or battery cables are damaged in an accident before the crash sensors close. The power supply is a capacitor that will leak down in approximately 15 minutes after the battery is disconnected or in 1 minute if the battery positive cable is grounded. The backup power supply must be disconnected before any air bag related service is performed.

3. Remove the 4 nut and washer assemblies retaining the driver air bag module to the steering wheel.

—————— CAUTION ——————
When carrying a live air bag, make sure the bag and trim cover are pointed away from the body. In the unlikely event of an accidental deployment, the bag will then deploy with minimal chance of injury. When placing a live air bag on a bench or other surface, always face the bag and trim cover up, away from the surface. This will reduce the motion of the module if it is accidently deployed.

4. Disconnect the driver air bag module connector and attach a jumper wire to the air bag terminals on the clockspring.

1992–93

1. Disconnect the positive battery cable. Wait 1 minute for the backup power supply in the diagnostic monitor to deplete its stored energy.

2. Remove the 4 nut and washer assemblies retaining the driver air bag module to the steering wheel.

—————— CAUTION ——————
When carrying a live air bag, make sure the bag and trim cover are pointed away from the body. In the unlikely event of an accidental deployment, the bag will then deploy with minimal chance of injury. When placing a live air bag on a bench or other surface, always face the bag and trim cover up, away from the surface. This will reduce the motion of the module if it is accidently deployed.

3. Disconnect the driver air bag connector. Connect air bag simulator tool 105–00008 or equivalent, to the vehicle harness at the top of the steering wheel.

Heater Blower Motor

REMOVAL & INSTALLATION

Mustang

1989–91

1. Disconnect the negative battery cable. Loosen glove compartment assembly by squeezing the sides together to disengage the retainer tabs.

2. Squeeze the sides of the glove compartment and let the glove compartment door hang down in front of instrument panel. Remove blower motor cooling hose.

3. Disconnect electrical wiring harness. Remove 4 screws attaching motor to housing. Pull motor and wheel out of housing.

4. Installation is the reverse of the removal procedure. Connect the negative battery cable.

1992–93

1. Disconnect the negative battery cable.

2. Squeeze the sides of the glove compartment together to disengage the retaining tabs. Let the glove compartment hang down in front of the instrument panel.

3. Disconnect the blower motor electrical connector and the vacuum hose from the outside-recirc door vacuum motor.

4. Remove the housing assembly-to-bracket case retaining nut. Close the glove compartment door and remove the 2 lower screws from the blower motor housing.

5. Lift the blower motor housing and air inlet duct/recirc door assemblies away from the heater case. Removing the lower right trim panel will allow for easier removal.

6. Disconnect the cooling tube from the blower motor.

7. Remove the retaining screws and pull the blower motor and wheel from the housing.

8. Remove the pushnut from the blower motor shaft and remove the wheel.

To install:

9. Install gasket material, jumper wire harness, wheel and pushnut onto a new blower motor.

10. Install the blower motor into the housing and secure with the screws.

11. Connect the blower motor cooling tube.

12. Tape the blower motor power lead to the air inlet duct to keep the wire away from the blower outlet during installation.

13. Install the air inlet duct and blower housing to the evaporator case, inserting the flange at the top of the blower outlet into the opening in the evaporator case.

14. Install 2 lower blower motor housing-to-heater case retaining screws.

15. Use a suitable vacuum pump to hold the outside-recirc door open and rotate the blower wheel to make sure it rotates freely. If there is interference, remove the blower motor and wheel and correct the problem.

16. Connect the blower motor power lead to the harness connector and connect the vacuum hose to the outside-recirc door vacuum motor.

17. Make sure the blower motor functions properly and make sure there are no air leaks between the blower motor housing and heater case.

18. Install the blower housing-to-bracket retaining nut. Install the lower right trim panel, if removed.

Thunderbird and Cougar

1. Disconnect the negative battery cable.

2. Remove the glove compartment liner to gain access to the blower motor mounting screws.

3. Remove the 4 retaining screws and remove the blower motor and wheel assembly from the blower housing.

4. Remove the pushnut from the blower motor shaft and remove the blower wheel from the shaft.

5. Installation is the reverse of removal. Connect the negative battery cable.

Mark VII

1. Disconnect the negative battery cable.

2. Remove the recirc duct assembly and disconnect the blower electrical connector.

3. Remove the 4 retaining screws and remove the blower motor and wheel assembly from the blower housing.

4. Remove the pushnut from the blower motor shaft and remove the blower wheel from the shaft.

5. Installation is the reverse of removal. Connect the negative battery cable.

Windshield Wiper Motor

REMOVAL & INSTALLATION

Mustang

1. Disconnect the negative battery cable.

2. Remove the right hand wiper arm assembly as follows:

  a. Raise the wiper blade off the windshield.

  b. Move the slide latch away from the pivot shaft and slowly lower the arm onto the latch. This unlocks the arm from the pivot shaft and holds the blade off the glass.

  c. Pull the arm from the pivot shaft. The use of tools is unnecessary.

3. Remove the cowl top grille retaining screws and grille.

4. Disconnect the linkage drive arm from the motor crankpin after removing the clip.

5. Disconnect the electrical connector from the wiper motor, remove the 3 retaining bolts and remove the motor from the vehicle.

To install:

6. Install the motor and tighten the bolts to 60–80 inch lbs. (7–9 Nm). Connect the electrical connector.

7. Connect the linkage drive arm to the motor crankpin and install the clip.

8. Install the cowl top grille and secure with the screws.

9. Make sure the motor is in the PARK position. Install the wiper arm so the blade is 2.3–3.5 in. (58.42–88.90mm) from the bottom windshield moulding. Install the arm as follows:

  a. Install the arm head over the pivot shaft.

  b. While applying downward pressure on the arm head, raise the other end of the arm enough to let the latch slide under the pivot shaft to the latched position, using finger pressure only to slide the latch.

  c. Lower the blade. If the blade does not touch the windshield, the slide latch is not completely in place.

Thunderbird and Cougar

1. Disconnect the negative battery cable.

2. With the wipers in the PARK position, remove the arm and blade assemblies as follows:

  a. Raise the wiper blade off the windshield.

  b. Move the slide latch away from the pivot shaft and slowly lower the arm onto the latch. This unlocks the arm from the pivot shaft and holds the blade off the glass.

  c. Pull the arm from the pivot shaft. The use of tools is unnecessary.

3. Remove the left-hand cowl vent screen.

4. Remove the vacuum manifolds from the wiper module and disconnect the electrical connectors.

5. Remove the 5 screws and 1 nut from the wiper module and remove the wiper module.

6. Disconnect the linkage drive arm from the motor crankpin after removing the clip.

7. Remove the 3 wiper motor retaining screws and pull the motor from the opening.

To install:

8. Install the motor and secure with the retaining screws.

9. Connect the linkage arm to the motor crankpin and install the clip.

10. Install the wiper module and secure with the screws and nut.

11. Connect the electrical connectors and install the vacuum manifolds. Install the left-hand cowl vent screen.

12. Make sure the motor is in the PARK position. Install the wiper arms as follows:

  a. Align the keyway on the pivot shaft with the wiper arm and install the arm head over the pivot shaft.

  b. While applying downward pressure on the arm head, raise the other end of the arm enough to let the latch slide under the pivot shaft to the latched position, using finger pressure only to slide the latch.

  c. Lower the blade. If the blade does not touch the windshield, the slide latch is not completely in place.

Mark VII

1. Turn the wipers ON until they reach full travel on the windshield then turn the key **OFF**.

2. Disconnect the negative battery cable and remove the arm and blade assemblies as follows:

  a. Raise the wiper blade off the windshield.

  b. Move the slide latch away from the pivot shaft and slowly lower the arm onto the latch. This unlocks the arm from the pivot shaft and holds the blade off the glass.

  c. Pull the arm from the pivot shaft. The use of tools is unneccessary.

3. Remove the left hand cowl vent screen.

4. Disconnect the linkage drive arm from the motor crankpin after removing the clip.

5. Disconnect the electrical connector from the wiper motor, remove the 3 retaining bolts and remove the motor from the vehicle.

To install:

6. Install the motor and tighten the retaining bolts to 60–80 inch lbs. (7–9 Nm). Connect the electrical connector.

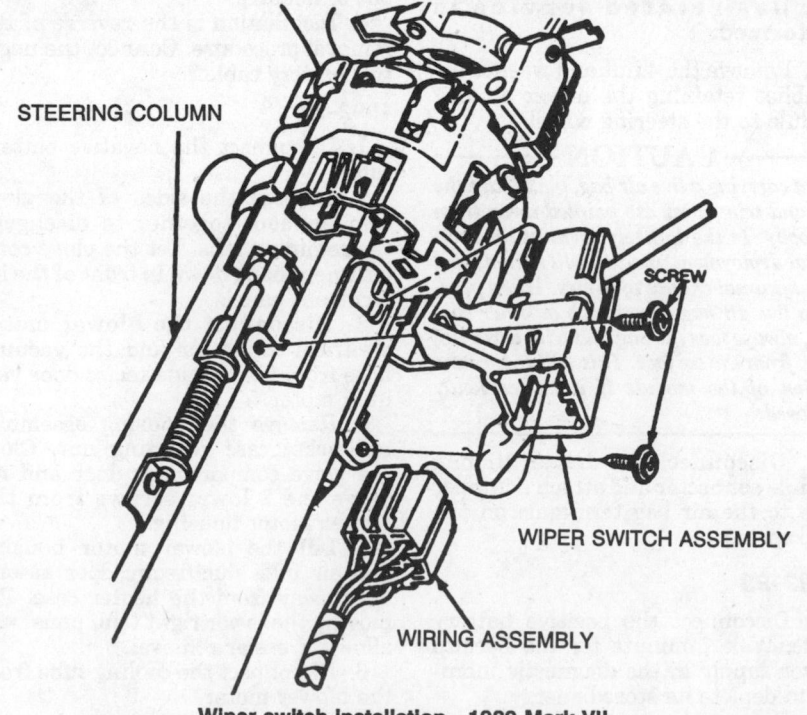

Wiper switch installation–1989 Mark VII

STEERING COLUMN

SCREW

WIPER SWITCH ASSEMBLY

WIRING ASSEMBLY

7. Connect the linkage arm to the motor crankpin and install the clip.

8. Install the left-hand cowl vent screen.

9. Connect the negative battery cable and turn the wiper switch **ON**. Let the motor move the pivot shafts 3–4 cycles, then turn the wiper switch **OFF**. The pivot shafts will now be in the PARK position.

10. Install the arms so the wiper blades are 0–0.83 in. (0–21mm) from the bottom windshield moulding. Install the wiper arms as follows:

a. Install the arm head over the pivot shaft.

b. While applying downward pressure on the arm head, raise the other end of the arm enough to let the latch slide under the pivot shaft to the latched position, using finger pressure only to slide the latch.

c. Lower the blade. If the blade does not touch the windshield, the slide latch is not completely in place.

Wiper Switch

REMOVAL & INSTALLATION

Except 1989 Mark VII

Windshield wiper function is controlled by the combination switch on all vehicles except 1989 Mark VII.

1989 Mark VII

1. Disconnect the negative battery cable.

2. Remove the 4 steering column shroud retaining screws. Separate the top and bottom shroud halves.

3. Remove the wiper switch retaining screws and remove the switch.

4. Disconnect the electrical connector.

5. The installation of the wiper switch is the reverse of the removal procedure.

Instrument Cluster

REMOVAL & INSTALLATION

Standard Cluster
MUSTANG

1. Disconnect the negative battery cable.

2. Remove the switch assembly on the right and left sides of the cluster assembly.

3. Remove the 2 upper and 3 lower retaining screws from the instrument cluster trim cover and remove the trim cover.

4. Remove the 4 retaining screws from the instrument cluster to panel.

5. Pull the cluster away from the instrument panel. Reach behind the instrument cluster to disconnect the speedometer cable. Disconnect the cable by pressing on the flat surface of the plastic connector (quick disconnect).

6. Pull the cluster further away from the instrument panel and disconnect the cluster printed circuit connectors from their receptacles in the cluster backplate.

7. Remove the cluster.

8. Installation is the reverse of the removal procedure. Apply a $3/16$ in. (4.6mm) diameter ball of silicone damping grease in the drive hole of the speedometer head prior to installation.

THUNDERBIRD AND COUGAR

1. Disconnect the negative battery cable.

2. Remove the 2 retaining screws and remove the cluster trim panel.

3. Remove the 4 cluster mounting screws.

4. Pull the bottom of the cluster toward the steering wheel.

5. Reach behind and under the cluster and unplug the 2 connectors. On Thunderbird SC, disconnect the vacuum line for the boost gauge.

6. Remove the cluster by swinging the bottom of the cluster out to clear the top of the steering column shroud.

7. Installation is the reverse of removal.

MARK VII LSC

1. Disconnect the negative battery cable.

2. Remove the instrument cluster finish panel, disconnecting the warning indicator module connectors.

3. Remove the instrument panel binnacle moulding.

4. Remove the 5 mask to backplate retaining screws. Do not remove the 3 top screws securing the lens to the mask. Remove the mask and lens assembly.

5. Lift the main dial assembly from the backplate. Some effort may be required to pull the quick connect terminals from the clips.

6. Installation is the reverse of the removal procedure.

Electronic Cluster
THUNDERBIRD AND COUGAR

1. Disconnect the negative battery cable.

2. Remove the headlight switch knob.

3. Remove the cluster finish panel by removing 2 screws on the upper inside surface. Carefully pull away the finish panel while detaching the spring clips surrounding the finish panel.

4. Unplug the connector on the rear of the switch assembly. If equipped, disconnect the autolamp module.

5. Place a clean, soft cloth over the steering column shroud to prevent scratching or damage. Remove the 4 cluster retaining screws.

6. Pull the bottom of the cluster toward the steering wheel. Place a clean, soft cloth over the lens to prevent potential scratches.

7. Reach behind and under the cluster to unplug the 2 connectors. Swing the bottom of the cluster out to clear the crash pad and remove the cluster.

8. Installation is the reverse of the removal procedure.

1989–90 MARK VII

1. Disconnect the negative battery cable. Remove the screws retaining instrument finish panel and rotate top of panel toward steering wheel. Disconnect electrical and air sensor connectors at right-hand portion of finish panel. Remove panel.

2. Remove 6 screws retaining instrument panel pad and rotate pad toward steering wheel and remove.

3. Remove 4 screws retaining instrument cluster to instrument panel and remove.

4. Disconnect electrical connector at lower left rear corner of cluster.

5. Installation is the reverse order of the removal procedure.

1991–93 MARK VII

1. Disconnect the negative battery cable.

2. Remove the instrument cluster trim bezel. Remove the headlight switch knob.

3. Remove the screws retaining the instrument panel pad and rotate the pad toward the steering wheel and remove. Remove the headlight switch trim panel.

4. Remove the 4 screws retaining the instrument cluster to the instrument panel and remove the cluster.

5. Disconnect the electrical connector at the lower left rear corner of the cluster.

6. Installation is the reverse of the removal procedure.

Speedometer

REMOVAL & INSTALLATION

Except Electronic Cluster
MUSTANG, THUNDERBIRD AND COUGAR

1. Disconnect the negative battery cable.

2. Remove the instrument cluster assembly.

3. Remove the 7 screws retaining the mask and lens assembly.

4. Remove the speedometer head assembly retaining screws and remove the speedometer.

5. Installation is the reverse of the removal procedure.

MARK VII LSC

1. Disconnect the negative battery cable.
2. Remove the instrument cluster finish panel, disconnecting the warning indicator module connectors.
3. Remove the instrument panel binnacle moulding.
4. Remove the 5 mask to backplate retaining screws. Do not remove the 3 top screws securing the lens to the mask. Remove the mask and lens assembly.
5. Lift the main dial assembly from the backplate. Some effort may be required to pull the quick connect terminals from the clips.
6. Remove the screws retaining the fuel gauge, temperature gauge and tachometer. The speedometer is integral with the main dial.
7. Installation is the reverse of the removal procedure.

Electronic Cluster

The speedometer is an integral part of the electronic cluster and cannot be removed separately.

Radio

REMOVAL & INSTALLATION

Except 1989 Mark VII

1. Disconnect the negative battery cable.
2. Install radio removal tools T87P–19061–A or equivalent into the radio face plate. Push the tools in approximately 1 in. (25.4mm) to release the retaining clips.

NOTE: Do not use excessive force when installing the radio removal tools, as this will damage the retaining clips, making radio removal difficult.

3. Apply a slight spreading force on the tools and pull the radio from the dash.
4. Disconnect the power, antenna and speaker leads and remove the radio.
5. Installation is the reverse of the removal procedure.

1989 Mark VII

1. Disconnect the negative battery cable.
2. Remove the center instrument trim panel.
3. Remove the 4 screws retaining the radio and mounting bracket to the instrument panel.
4. Push the radio to the front and raise the back end of the radio slightly

so the rear support bracket clears the clip in the instrument panel. Pull the radio out of the instrument panel slowly.
5. Disconnect the wiring connectors and antenna cable.
6. Installation is the reverse of the removal procedure.

Headlight Switch

REMOVAL & INSTALLATION

Mustang

1. Disconnect the negative battery cable.
2. Disengage the 2 locking tabs on the left side of the switch, under the paddles, by pushing the tabs in with a small prybar and pulling on the paddles.
3. Using a small prybar, pry the right side of the switch out of the instrument panel.
4. Pull the switch out of the opening and disconnect the 2 connectors.
5. To install, assemble the connectors, insert the switch into the panel opening and push until the locking tabs on both sides of the switch snap into place.

Thunderbird and Cougar

1. Disconnect the negative battery cable.
2. Remove the 2 cluster finish panel retaining screws.
3. Pull the headlight switch knob off.
4. Unsnap the cluster finish panel.
5. Disconnect the electrical connector to the headlight dimmer sensor assembly.
6. Through the opening in the instrument panel, depress the shaft release button on the switch and remove the shaft. The switch must be in the full **ON** position to release the shaft.

7. Remove the headlight switch retaining nut and pull the switch through the opening to disconnect the wiring connector.
8. Installation is the reverse of removal.

Mark VII

1989

1. Disconnect the negative battery cable. Remove the lens assembly attaching screws and then the lens assembly.
2. Remove the screws securing the switch to the instrument panel and pull the switch out from the panel.

NOTE: If equipped with auto lamp/auto dimmer system, remove this control first.

3. Disconnect the electrical connector and remove the switch from the vehicle.
4. Installation is the reverse order of the removal procedure.

1990–93

1. Disconnect the negative battery cable.
2. Remove the center moulding and the headlight switch knob.
3. Remove the 5 screws retaining the cluster finish panel and snap out the headlight switch lens.
4. Remove the 2 screws retaining the headlight switch. Remove the switch from the instrument panel and disconnect the electrical connector.
5. Installation is the reverse of the removal procedure.

Combination Switch

The combination switch incorporates the turn signal, dimmer and wiper switch functions on all except 1989 Mark VII. Only the turn signal and dimmer function is controlled by the combination switch on 1989 Mark VII.

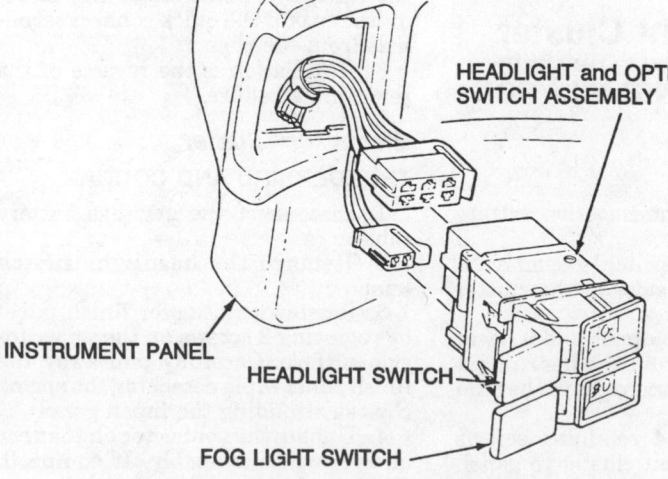

HEADLIGHT and OPTIONAL FOG LIGHT SWITCH ASSEMBLY

INSTRUMENT PANEL

HEADLIGHT SWITCH

FOG LIGHT SWITCH

Headlight switch Installation – Mustang

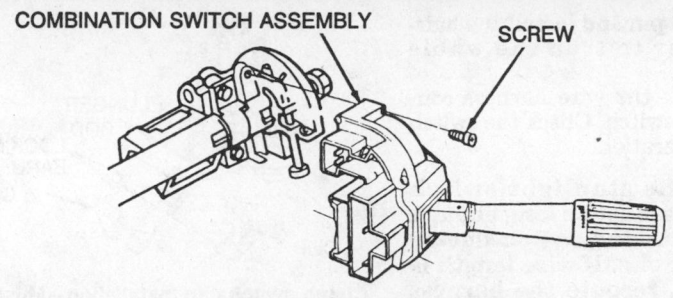

COMBINATION SWITCH ASSEMBLY   SCREW

Combination switch—Mustang

REMOVAL & INSTALLATION

Mustang, Thunderbird and Cougar

1. Disconnect the negative battery cable.
2. Remove the shroud retaining screws and remove the upper and lower shrouds.
3. Remove the switch retaining screws and lift up the switch assembly.
4. With the wiring connectors exposed, carefully lift the connector retainer tabs and disconnect the connectors.
5. Installation is the reverse of the removal procedure.

Mark VII

1989

1. Disconnect the negative battery cable.
2. Remove the switch lever by grasping and pulling straight out.
3. Remove the steering column cover retaining screws and remove the cover.
4. With the wiring connectors exposed, carefully lift the connector retainer tabs and disconnect the connectors.
5. Remove the switch retaining screws and lift up the switch assembly.
6. Installation is the reverse of the removal procedure.

1990–93

1. Disconnect the negative battery cable.
2. If equipped with tilt column, move to the lowest position and remove the tilt lever.
3. Remove the ignition lock cylinder.
4. Remove the shroud screws and remove the upper and lower shrouds.
5. Remove the 2 self-tapping screws attaching the combination switch to the steering column casting and remove the switch.
6. Disconnect the 2 electrical connectors.
7. Installation is the reverse of the removal procedure.

Ignition Lock

REMOVAL & INSTALLATION

Functional Lock

The following procedure is for vehicles with functioning lock cylinders. Ignition keys are available for these vehicles, or the ignition key numbers are known and the proper key can be made.

1. Disconnect the negative battery cable. If equipped, properly disarm the air bag system.
2. On Thunderbird, Cougar and 1989 Mark VII and Mustang equipped with tilt column, remove the upper extension shroud by unsnapping the shroud retaining clip at the 9 o'clock position.
3. On all except 1990–93 Mark VII, remove the trim shroud halves by removing the attaching screws. Remove the electrical connector from the key warning switch.
4. Place the gear shift lever in **P**, for column shift only, and turn the ignition to the **RUN** position.
5. Place a ⅛ in. diameter wire pin or small drift punch in the hole in the casting surrounding the lock cylinder and depress the retaining pin while pulling out on the lock cylinder to remove it from the column housing.

To install:

6. To install the lock cylinder, turn it to the **RUN** position and depress the retaining pin. Insert the lock cylinder into its housing in the lock cylinder casting.
7. Make sure the cylinder is fully seated and aligned in the interlocking washer before turning the key to the **OFF** position. This action will permit the cylinder retaining pin to extend into the hole in the lock cylinder housing.
8. Using the ignition key, rotate the cylinder to ensure the correct mechanical operation in all positions.
9. Check for proper start in **P** or **N**. Also make sure the start circuit cannot be actuated in **D** or **R** positions and that the column is locked in the **LOCK** position.

10. Connect the key warning buzzer electrical connector and install the trim shrouds, if required.

Non-Functional Lock

The following procedure is for vehicles with non-functioning locks. On these vehicles, the lock cylinder cannot be rotated due to a lost or broken key, the key number is not known, or the lock cylinder cap is damaged and/or broken, preventing the lock cylinder from rotating.

1. Disconnect the negative battery cable. If equipped, properly disarm the air bag system.
2. Remove the steering wheel.
3. On Thunderbird, Cougar and 1989 Mark VII and Mustang equipped with tilt column, remove the upper extension shroud by unsnapping the shroud retaining clip at the 9 o'clock position.
4. On all except 1990–93 Mark VII, remove the trim shroud halves by removing the attaching screws. Remove the electrical connector from the key warning switch.
5. Drill out the retaining pin using a ⅛ in. diameter drill, being careful not to drill deeper than ½ in.
6. Position a chisel at the base of the ignition lock cylinder. Strike the chisle with sharp blows, using a hammer, to break the cap away from the lock cylinder.
7. Drill approximately 1¾ in. down the middle of the ignition key slot, using a ⅜ in. diameter drill bit, until the lock cylinder breaks loose from the breakaway base of the lock cylinder. Remove the lock cylinder and drill shavings from the lock cylinder housing.
8. Remove the snapring or retainer, washer and steering column lock gear. Thoroughly clean all drill shavings and other foreign materials from the casting.
9. Inspect the lock cylinder housing for damage and replace, as necessary.

To install:

10. Install the ignition lock drive gear, washer and retainer.
11. Install the ignition lock cylinder and check for smooth operation.
12. Connect the electrical connector to the key warning switch.
13. Install the trim shrouds, if necessary.
14. Install the new lock cylinder housing assembly.
15. Install the steering wheel and connect the negative battery cable.

Ignition Switch
REMOVAL & INSTALLATION

1. Disconnect the negative battery cable.

2. Remove the steering column shroud. On 1990–93 Mark VII, remove the steering column opening trim cover and remove the cover.

3. Disconnect the switch electrical connector.

4. Turn the ignition lock cylinder to **RUN**.

5. Remove the screws attaching the switch and disengage the switch from the actuator.

To install:

6. Adjust the new ignition switch by sliding the carrier to the **RUN** position.

7. Make sure the ignition key lock cylinder is in the **RUN** position. The **RUN** position is achieved by rotating the key lock cylinder approximately 90 degrees from the **LOCK** position.

8. Install the ignition switch onto the actuator pin or install the switch pin in the column hole, as required.

9. Align the switch mounting holes and install the attaching screws. Tighten the screws to 50–69 inch lbs. (5.6–7.9 Nm).

10. Connect the electrical connector to the ignition switch.

11. Connect the negative battery cable. Check the ignition switch for proper function in **START** and **ACC** positions. Make sure the column is locked in the **LOCK** position.

12. Install the remaining components in the reverse order of removal.

Stoplight Switch

REMOVAL & INSTALLATION

1. Disconnect the negative battery cable.

2. Disconnect the wire harness at the connector from the switch. The locking tab on the connector must be lifted before the connector can be removed.

3. Remove the hairpin retainer. Slide the stoplight switch, the pushrod and the nylon washers and bushings away from the pedal and remove the switch.

NOTE: Since the switch side plate nearest the brake pedal is slotted, it is not necessary to remove the brake master cylinder pushrod and 1 washer from the brake pedal pin.

To install:

4. Position the switch so the U-shaped side is nearest the pedal and directly over/under the pin. Then slide the switch down/up trapping the master cylinder pushrod and black bushing between the switch side plates. Push the switch and pushrod assembly firmly toward the brake pedal arm. Assemble the outside white plastic washer to the pin and install the hairpin retainer to trap the whole assembly.

5. Assemble the wire harness connector to the switch. Check the switch for proper operation.

NOTE: The stoplight switch wire harness must be long enough to travel with the switch during full pedal stroke. If wire length is insufficient, reroute the harness or service, as required.

Clutch Switch

ADJUSTMENT

1. If necessary, remove the panel above the clutch pedal.

2. Disconnect the electrical connector at the switch.

3. Using test light, make sure the switch is open with the clutch pedal up (clutch engaged) and closed at approximately 1 in. from the clutch pedal full-down position (clutch disengaged).

4. If the switch does not operate as specified, check if the self-adjusting clip is out of position on the rod; it should be near the end of the rod.

5. If the clip is out of position, remove it and reposition about 1 in. from the end of the rod. Reset the switch by pushing the clutch pedal to the floor.

6. Repeat Step 3. If the switch is damaged or the clips do not stay in place, replace the switch.

REMOVAL & INSTALLATION

Mustang

1. Disconnect the negative battery cable. Disconnect wiring connector.

2. Remove retaining pin from clutch pedal.

3. Remove switch bracket attaching screw.

4. Lift switch and bracket assembly upward to disengage tab from pedal support.

5. Move the switch outward to disengage actuating rod eyelet from clutch pedal pin and remove switch from vehicle.

To install:

NOTE: Always install the switch with the self-adjusting clip about 1.0 in. (25.4mm) from the end of the rod. The clutch pedal must be fully up (clutch engaged). Otherwise, the switch may be misadjusted.

6. Place eyelet end of rod onto pivot pin.

7. Swing switch assembly around to line up hole in mounting boss with hole in bracket.

8. Install attaching screw.

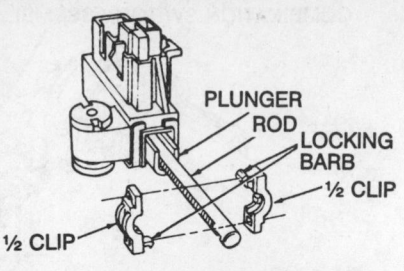

Clutch switch clip installation—Mustang

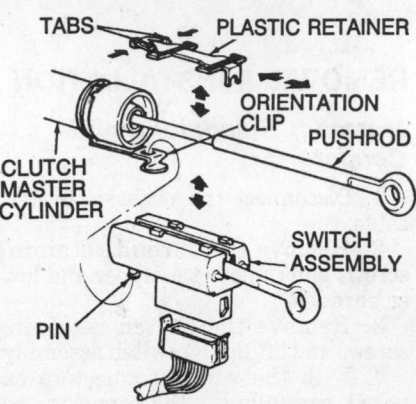

Clutch switch installation—Thunderbird

9. Replace retaining pin on clutch pedal.

10. Connect wiring connector.

Thunderbird and Cougar

1. Disconnect the negative battery cable.

2. Disconnect wiring connector from the switch.

3. Remove the C-clip from the clutch pedal switch pin and slide the pushrod off the pin.

4. Remove the C-clip from the end of the clutch pedal switch rod.

5. Remove the switch pushrod from the switch.

6. Disconnect the switch from the plastic bracket.

7. Installation is the reverse of removal. Check switch operation.

Neutral Safety Switch

REMOVAL & INSTALLATION

Mustang With 2.3L Engine

1. Disconnect the negative battery cable.

2. Disconnect the switch wiring harness connector.

3. Remove the neutral safety switch and O-ring using socket tool T74P-77247–A or equivalent.

NOTE: Use of different tools could crush or puncture the walls of the switch.

To install:

4. Install the neutral safety switch and new O-ring using socket tool T74P-77247-A or equivalent.

5. Tighten the switch to 7–10 ft. lbs. (10–14 Nm).

6. Connect the neutral safety switch to the wiring harness.

7. Connect the negative battery cable.

8. Check that the vehicle starts only in the **N** or **P** position.

Mustang With 5.0L Engine, Thunderbird, Cougar and Mark VII

1. Place the selector lever in the manual **L** position.

2. Disconnect the negative battery cable.

3. Raise and support the vehicle safely.

4. Disconnect the neutral safety switch electrical harness from the switch by pushing the harness straight up off the switch using a small long-bladed prybar under the rubber plug section of the harness.

5. Install socket tool T74P-77247-A or equivalent, and rachet on the neutral safety switch. Once the ratchet and socket tool are over the switch, reach from the rear of the transmission over the extension housing area and remove the neutral safety switch and O-ring.

NOTE: Use of different tools could crush or puncture the walls of the switch.

To install:

6. Install the neutral safety switch and new O-ring using socket tool T74P-77247-A or equivalent.

7. Tighten the switch to 8–11 ft. lbs. (11–15 Nm).

8. Connect the neutral safety switch to the wiring harness.

9. Lower the vehicle and connect the negative battery cable.

10. Check that the vehicle starts only in the **N** or **P** position.

Fuses, Circuit Breakers and Relays

LOCATION

Fuses

All vehicles are equipped with a fuse panel located on the left side of the lower instrument panel. In addition, Thunderbird and Cougar are equipped with a high-current fuse box located in the engine compartment on the left fender apron.

Fuse Links

Fuse links are used to protect the main wiring harness and selected branches from complete burn-out, should a short circuit or electrical overload occur. A fuse link is a short length of insulated wire, integral with the engine compartment wiring harness. It is several wire gauges smaller than the circuit it protects and generally located in-line directly from the positive terminal of the battery.

Circuit Breakers

Circuit breakers are used on certain electrical components requiring high amperage. The advantage of the circuit breaker is its ability to open and close the electrical circuit as the load demands, rather than the necessity of a part replacement.

MUSTANG

Windshield Wiper Circuit—one 8.25 amp circuit breaker located on the fuse panel.

Power Windows—one 20 amp circuit breaker located on the fuse panel.

Power Windows, Power Seats, Power Door Locks—one 20 amp circuit breaker located at the starter relay.

Headlight and High Beam—one 22 amp circuit breaker incorporated in the lighting switch.

Convertible Top—one 25 amp circuit breaker located at the lower instrument panel-reinforcement.

THUNDERBIRD AND COUGAR

Windshield Wiper Circuit—one 8.25 amp circuit breaker located on the fuse panel.

Power Windows and Moon Roof Motor—one 20 amp circuit breaker located on the fuse panel.

Power Seats, Door Locks and Fuel Door Release Solenoid—one 20 amp circuit breaker located on the fuse panel.

Cigar Lighter and High Beam—one 20 amp circuit breaker located on the fuse panel.

MARK VII

Windshield Wiper Circuit—one 6 amp circuit breaker located on the fuse panel.

Cigar Lighters/Horns—one 20 amp circuit breaker located on the fuse panel.

Power Windows and Sun Roof—one 20 amp circuit breaker located on the fuse panel.

Power Windows, Seats and Door Locks—one 20 amp circuit breaker located at the starter relay.

Headlight and High Beam—one 22 amp circuit breaker incorporated in the lighting switch.

Relays

MUSTANG

Air Conditioner WOT Cut-Out Relay—located in the left side of the engine compartment on 1989 vehicles and on the right fender apron on 1990–93 vehicles.

Convertible Top Lower and Raise Relays—located in luggage compartment, behind rear seat.

EEC Power Relay—located on the EEC module bracket in the lower right cowl on 1989–90 vehicles and behind the right cowl panel, above the EEC control module on 1991–93 vehicles.

Fuel Pump Relay—located under the driver's seat on 1989–91 vehicles and on the right side of the engine compartment, on the lower front of the wheelwell on 1992–93 vehicles.

Horn Relay—located behind the instrument panel near the instrument cluster on 1989–90 vehicles and behind the center of the instrument panel, above the warning chime module on 1991–93 vehicles.

LCD illumination Relay—located behind the center of the instrument panel on 1990–93 vehicles.

Low Oil Warning Relay—located on left instrument panel shake brace on 1989–90 vehicles and behind the left side of the instrument panel, to the left of the steering column brace on 1991–93 vehicles.

Rear Defrost Control Relay—located at left side of instrument panel near fuse panel.

Starter Relay—located at the left front fender apron.

Window Safety Relay—located behind left cowl panel.

THUNDERBIRD AND COUGAR

Air Conditioner WOT Cut-Out Relay—located at the right front of the firewall, on the relay bracket.

Anti-Lock Hydraulic Pump Motor Relay—located at the right front of the firewall, on the relay bracket.

Anti-Lock Power Relay—located at the right front of the firewall, on the relay bracket.

Anti-Theft Alarm Relay—located in the left rear of the trunk, near the anti-theft module on 1989 vehicles.

Anti-Theft Disarm Relay—located in the left rear of the trunk, near the anti-theft horn relay on 1989 vehicles.

Anti-Theft Horn Relay—located in the left rear of the trunk, behind the wheel well on 1989 vehicles.

Autolamp Dual Coil Relay—located behind the center of the instrument panel, to the left of the glove box on 1989–90 vehicles and at the left side of the instrument panel, to the right of the steering column on 1991–93 vehicles.

EEC Power Relay—located at the left fender apron, inside the power distribution box.

Fuel Pump Relay—located in the left side of the trunk, behind the wheel well.

Hard Ride Relay—located under the rear package tray.

Hi-Lo Beam Relay—located behind the left side of the instrument panel, to the right of the steering column on 1989–90 vehicles.

Horn Relay—located in the left side of the engine compartment, inside the power distribution box.

LCD Illumination Relay—located behind the left side of the instrument panel, near the steering column.

Soft Ride Relay—located under the rear package tray.

Starter Relay—located on the left fender apron.

Starter Interrupt Relay—located under the left side of the instrument panel on 1989–90 vehicles.

MARK VII

Air Conditioning WOT Cut-Out Realy—located on the left fender apron, near the shock tower.

Air Suspension Compressor Relay—located on the left fender apron, near the shock tower.

Anti-Lock Brake Hydraulic Pump Motor Relay—located in front of the firewall, behind the brake master cylinder.

Anti-Lock Power Relay—located in front of the firewall, behind the brake master cylinder.

Anti-Theft Alarm Relay—located under the right side of the rear package tray on 1989–90 vehicles.

Anti-Theft Inverter Relay—located under the right side of the rear package tray on 1989–90 vehicles.

Anti-Theft Starter Interrupt Relay—located under the left side of the instrument panel near the ground bus bracket on 1989–90 vehicles.

ATC Feedback Isolation Relay—located behind the right side of the instrument panel, near the rear of the glove box on 1989–90 vehicles and behind the left side of the instrument panel, to the right of the steering column on 1991–93 vehicles.

Autolamp Relay—located on the top rear of the shake brace on 1989 vehicles, behind the instrument panel, to the left of the panel defrost actuator on 1990 vehicles and behind the left side of the instrument panel, to the right of the steering column on 1991–93 vehicles.

EEC Power Relay—located at the right hand dash panel on 1989 vehicles, on the right fender apron on 1990

vehicles and in the right rear of the engine compartment on 1991–93 vehicles.

Flash-to-Pass Relay—located at left side of instrument panel, to the right of the steering column on 1989 vehicles.

Fuel Pump Relay—located at the outside of the left deck lid hinge support.

Hi-Lo Beam Relay—located to the right of the steering column, behind the instrument panel.

Horn Relay—located on the right fender apron, near the right front height sensor on 1989–91 vehicles and in the right rear corner of the engine compartment on the firewall on 1992–93 vehicles.

Interior Lamp Relay—located behind the center of the instrument panel on 1989 vehicles.

Keyless/Anti-Theft Disarm Relay—located under right side of rear package tray on 1989–90 vehicles.

Left Hand Cornering Lamp Relay—located at the left side of the instrument panel, near the steering column on 1989 vehicles.

Low Oil Level Relay—located at the right of the instrument panel, behind the glove compartment on 1989–90 vehicles and behind the left side of the instrument panel on 1991–93 vehicles.

Moonroof Relay—located at the center rear of the roof, above the headliner, on 1991–93 vehicles.

Right Hand Cornering Lamp Relay—located at the left side of the instrument panel, near the steering column on 1989 vehicles.

Starter Relay—located on the left fender apron.

Computers

LOCATION

The engine electronic control module is located behind the right cowl panel. The anti-lock brake control module is located under the center of the rear package tray. The automatic temperature control module is located behind the center of the instrument panel. The air bag diagnostic module is located behind the lower center of the instrument panel on Mustang and 1990 Mark VII and behind the top right side of the instrument panel, above the glove compartment, on 1991–93 Mark VII.

Turn Signal and Hazard Flashers

LOCATION

The turn signal and hazard flashers

are attached to the fuse panel, or the instrument panel reinforcement over the fuse panel, on Mustang and Mark VII. On Thunderbird and Cougar, an electronic flasher is located behind the left side of the instrument panel, to the right of the steering column.

Cruise Control

ADJUSTMENT

Actuator Cable

1. Remove the cable retaining clip.
2. Push the cable through the adjuster until a slight tension is felt.
3. Insert the cable retaining clip and snap into place.

Vacuum Dump Valve

The vacuum dump valve is movable in its mounting bracket. It should be adjusted so it is closed (no vacuum leaks) when the brake pedal is in its normal release position (not depressed) and open when the pedal is depressed. Use a hand vacuum pump to make this adjustment.

Clutch Switch

MUSTANG

1. Prop the clutch pedal in the full-up position, pawl fully released from the sector.
2. Loosen the switch retaining screw.
3. Slide the switch forward toward the clutch pedal until the switch plunger cap is 0.030 in. (0.76mm) from contacting the switch housing. Then, tighten the retaining screw.
4. Remove the prop from the clutch pedal and test drive for clutch switch cancellation of cruise control.

THUNDERBIRD

1. Disconnect the wiring harness from the switch.
2. Using a volt-ohmmeter, probe the switch terminals with the switch installed and the clutch pedal at the up, or clutch engaged position.
3. The EFI switch, terminals 5 and 6, should be normally open and close within approximately 2 in. (50mm) of clutch pedal travel.
4. The cruise control release switch, terminals 3 and 4, should be normally closed and open within approximately 2 in. (50mm) of clutch travel.
5. The clutch interlock switch, terminals 1 and 2, should be normally open and close when the clutch pedal has been moved to approximately 1 in. (25mm) from full travel.
6. Replace the clutch switch if any of the conditions in Steps 3, 4 and 5 are not as specified.

Ford Motor Co.
Rear Wheel Drive

FORD—Crown Victoria   **LINCOLN**—Town Car
MERCURY—Grand Marquis

SPECIFICATIONS

VEHICLE IDENTIFICATION CHART

It is important for servicing and ordering parts to be certain of the vehicle and engine identification. The VIN (vehicle identification number) is a 17 digit number visible through the windshield on the driver's side of the dash and contains the vehicle and engine identification codes. The tenth digit indicates model year and the eighth digit indicates engine code. It can be interpreted as follows:

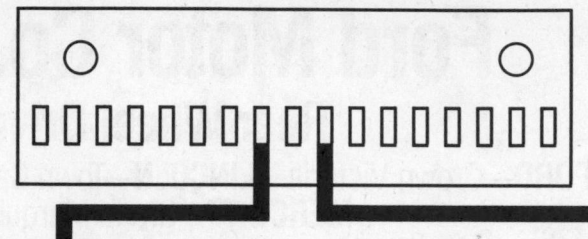

Engine Code						Model Year	
Code	Liters	Cu. In. (cc)	Cyl.	Fuel Sys.	Eng. Mfg.	Code	Year
W	4.6	280 (4593)	8	SEFI	Ford	K	1989
F	5.0	302 (4943)	8	SEFI	Ford	L	1990
G	5.8	351 (5767)	8	VV	Ford	M	1991
						N	1992
						P	1993

SEFI—Sequential Electronic Fuel Injection
VV—Variable Venturi Carburetor

ENGINE IDENTIFICATION

Year	Model	Engine Displacement Liters (cc)	Engine Series (ID/VIN)	Fuel System	No. of Cylinders	Engine Type
1989	Crown Victoria	5.0 (4943)	F	SEFI	8	OHV
	Crown Victoria	5.8 (5767)	G	VV	8	OHV
	Grand Marquis	5.0 (4943)	F	SEFI	8	OHV
	Grand Marquis	5.8 (5767)	G	VV	8	OHV
	Town Car	5.0 (4943)	F	SEFI	8	OHV
1990	Crown Victoria	5.0 (4943)	F	SEFI	8	OHV
	Crown Victoria	5.8 (5767)	G	VV	8	OHV
	Grand Marquis	5.0 (4943)	F	SEFI	8	OHV
	Grand Marquis	5.8 (5767)	G	VV	8	OHV
	Town Car	5.0 (4943)	F	SEFI	8	OHV
1991	Crown Victoria	5.0 (4943)	F	SEFI	8	OHV
	Crown Victoria	5.8 (5767)	G	VV	8	OHV
	Grand Marquis	5.0 (4943)	F	SEFI	8	OHV
	Grand Marquis	5.8 (5767)	G	VV	8	OHV
	Town Car	4.6 (4593)	W	SEFI	8	OHC
1992-93	Crown Victoria	4.6 (4593)	W	SEFI	8	OHC
	Grand Marquis	4.6 (4593)	W	SEFI	8	OHC
	Town Car	4.6 (4593)	W	SEFI	8	OHC

SEFI—Sequential Electronic Fuel Injection
VV—Variable Venturi Carburetor
OHV—Overhead Valve
OHC—Overhead Camshaft

GENERAL ENGINE SPECIFICATIONS

Year	Engine ID/VIN	Engine Displacement Liters (cc)	Fuel System Type	Net Horsepower @ rpm	Net Torque @ rpm (ft. lbs.)	Bore × Stroke (in.)	Compression Ratio	Oil Pressure @ rpm③
1989	F	5.0 (4943)	SEFI	①	②	4.00 × 3.00	8.9:1	40–60 @ 2000
	G	5.8 (5767)	VV	180 @ 3600	285 @ 2400	4.00 × 3.50	8.3:1	40–60 @ 2000
1990	F	5.0 (4943)	SEFI	①	②	4.00 × 3.00	8.9:1	40–60 @ 2000
	G	5.8 (5767)	VV	180 @ 3600	285 @ 2400	4.00 × 3.50	8.3:1	40–60 @ 2000
1991	W	4.6 (4593)	SEFI	④	⑤	3.55 × 3.54	9.0:1	20–45 @ 1500
	F	5.0 (4943)	SEFI	①	②	4.00 × 3.00	8.9:1	40–60 @ 2000
	G	5.8 (5767)	VV	180 @ 3600	285 @ 2400	4.00 × 3.50	8.3:1	40–60 @ 2000
1992–93	W	4.6 (4593)	SEFI	④	⑤	3.55 × 3.54	9.0:1	20–45 @ 1500

NOTE: Horsepower and torque are SAE net figures. They are measured at the rear of the transmission with all accessories installed and operating. Since the figures vary when a given engine is installed in different models, some are representative rather than exact.

SEFI—Sequential Electronic Fuel Injection
VV—Variable Venturi Carburetor
① Single exhaust: 150 @ 3200
   Dual exhaust: 160 @ 3400
② Single exhaust: 270 @ 2000
   Dual exhaust: 280 @ 2200
③ Engine at normal operating temperature
④ Single exhaust: 190 @ 4200
   Dual exhaust: 210 @ 4600
⑤ Single exhaust: 260 @ 3200
   Dual exhaust: 270 @ 3400

GASOLINE ENGINE TUNE-UP SPECIFICATIONS

Year	Engine ID/VIN	Engine Displacement Liters (cc)	Spark Plugs Gap (in.)	Ignition Timing (deg.) MT	Ignition Timing (deg.) AT	Fuel Pump (psi)	Idle Speed (rpm) MT	Idle Speed (rpm) AT	Valve Clearance In.	Valve Clearance Ex.
1989	F	5.0 (4943)	0.050	—	10B	35–40③	—	①	Hyd.	Hyd.
	G	5.8 (5767)	0.044	—	14B	6–8	—	①	Hyd.	Hyd.
1990	F	5.0 (4943)	0.050	—	10B	35–40③	—	①	Hyd.	Hyd.
	G	5.8 (5767)	0.044	—	14B	6–8	—	①	Hyd.	Hyd.
1991	W	4.6 (4593)	0.054	—	10B	35–40	—	560②	Hyd.	Hyd.
	F	5.0 (4943)	0.050	—	10B	35–40③	—	①	Hyd.	Hyd.
	G	5.8 (5767)	0.044	—	14B	6–8	—	①	Hyd.	Hyd.
1992	W	4.6 (4593)	0.054	—	10B	35–40	—	560②	Hyd.	Hyd.
1993	SEE UNDERHOOD SPECIFICATIONS STICKER									

NOTE: The lowest cylinder pressure should be within 75% of the highest cylinder pressure reading. For example, if the highest cylinder is 134 psi, the lowest should be 101. Engine should be at normal operating temperature with throttle valve in the wide open position.
The underhood specifications sticker often reflects tune-up specification changes in production. Sticker figures must be used if they disagree with those in this chart.
Hyd.—Hydraulic
B—Before Top Dead Center
① Refer to the underhood specifications sticker
② Transmission in drive
③ Key on, engine off

FIRING ORDERS

NOTE: To avoid confusion, always replace spark plug wires one at a time.

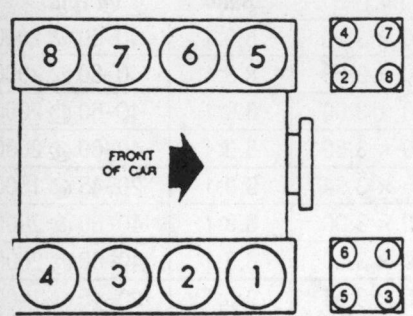

4.6L Engine
Engine Firing Order: 1–3–7–2–6–5–4–8
Distributorless Ignition System

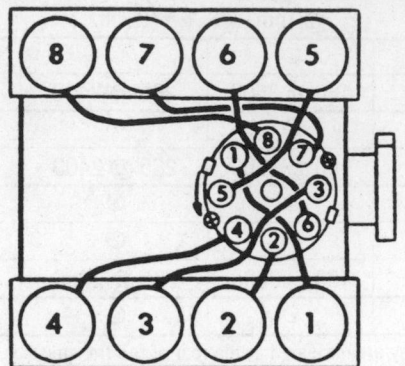

5.0L Engine
Engine Firing Order: 1–5–4–2–6–3–7–8
Distributor Rotation: Counterclockwise

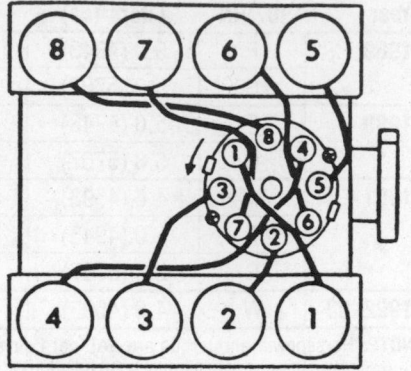

5.8L Engine
Engine Firing Order: 1–3–7–2–6–5–4–8
Distributor Rotation: Counterclockwise

CAPACITIES

Year	Model	Engine ID/VIN	Engine Displacement Liters (cc)	Engine Crankcase with Filter (qts.)	Transmission (pts.) 4-Spd	5-Spd	Auto.	Transfer case (pts.)	Drive Axle Front (pts.)	Rear (pts.)	Fuel Tank (gal.)	Cooling System (qts.)
1989	Crown Victoria	F	5.0 (4943)	5	—	—	24.6	—	—	4.0	18.0	14.1
	Crown Victoria	G	5.8 (5767)	5	—	—	24.6	—	—	4.0	20.0	14.1
	Grand Marquis	F	5.0 (4943)	5	—	—	24.6	—	—	4.0	18.0	14.1
	Grand Marquis	G	5.8 (5767)	5	—	—	24.6	—	—	4.0	20.0	14.1
	Town Car	F	5.0 (4943)	5	—	—	24.6	—	—	4.0	22.3	14.1
1990	Crown Victoria	F	5.0 (4943)	5	—	—	24.6	—	—	4.0	18.0	14.1
	Crown Victoria	G	5.8 (5767)	5	—	—	24.6	—	—	4.0	20.0	14.1
	Grand Marquis	F	5.0 (4943)	5	—	—	24.6	—	—	4.0	18.0	14.1
	Grand Marquis	G	5.8 (5767)	5	—	—	24.6	—	—	4.0	20.0	14.1
	Town Car	F	5.0 (4943)	5	—	—	24.6	—	—	4.0	18.0	14.1
1991	Crown Victoria	F	5.0 (4943)	5	—	—	24.6	—	—	4.0	18.0	14.1
	Crown Victoria	G	5.8 (5767)	5	—	—	24.6	—	—	4.0	20.0	14.1
	Grand Marquis	F	5.0 (4943)	5	—	—	24.6	—	—	4.0	18.0	14.1
	Grand Marquis	G	5.8 (5767)	5	—	—	24.6	—	—	4.0	20.0	14.1
	Town Car	W	4.6 (4593)	5	—	—	24.6	—	—	4.0	20.0	14.1
1992–93	Crown Victoria	W	4.6 (4593)	5	—	—	24.6	—	—	4.0	20.0	14.1
	Grand Marquis	W	4.6 (4593)	5	—	—	24.6	—	—	4.0	20.0	14.1
	Town Car	W	4.6 (4593)	5	—	—	24.6	—	—	4.0	20.0	14.1

CAMSHAFT SPECIFICATIONS

All measurements given in inches.

Year	Engine ID/VIN	Engine Displacement Liters (cc)	Journal Diameter 1	2	3	4	5	Elevation In.	Ex.	Bearing Clearance	Camshaft End Play
1989	F	5.0 (4943)	2.0805–2.0815	2.0655–2.0665	2.0505–2.0515	2.0355–2.0365	2.0205–2.0215	0.2325–0.2375	0.2424–0.2474	0.0010–0.0060	0.0005–0.0090
	G	5.8 (5767)	2.0805–2.0815	2.0655–2.0665	2.0505–2.0515	2.0355–2.0365	2.0205–2.0215	0.2730–0.2780	0.2780–0.2830	0.0010–0.0060	0.0010–0.0090

CAMSHAFT SPECIFICATIONS

All measurements given in inches.

Year	Engine ID/VIN	Engine Displacement Liters (cc)	Journal Diameter 1	2	3	4	5	Elevation In.	Ex.	Bearing Clearance	Camshaft End Play
1990	F	5.0 (4943)	2.0805-2.0815	2.0655-2.0665	2.0505-2.0515	2.0355-2.0365	2.0205-2.0215	0.2325-0.2375	0.2424-0.2474	0.0010-0.0060	0.0005-0.0090
	G	5.8 (5767)	2.0805-2.0815	2.0655-2.0665	2.0505-2.0515	2.0355-2.0365	2.0205-2.0215	0.2730-0.2780	0.2780-0.2830	0.0010-0.0060	0.0010-0.0090
1991	W	4.6 (4593)	1.0605-1.0615	1.0605-1.0615	1.0605-1.0615	1.0605-1.0615	1.0605-1.0615	0.2590	0.2590	0.0010-0.0047	0.0010-0.0070
	F	5.0 (4943)	2.0805-2.0815	2.0655-2.0665	2.0505-2.0515	2.0355-2.0365	2.0205-2.0215	0.2325-0.2375	0.2424-0.2474	0.0010-0.0060	0.0005-0.0090
	G	5.8 (5767)	2.0805-2.0815	2.0655-2.0665	2.0505-2.0515	2.0355-2.0365	2.0205-2.0215	0.2730-0.2780	0.2780-0.2830	0.0010-0.0060	0.0005-0.0090
1992-93	W	4.6 (4593)	1.0605-1.0615	1.0605-1.0615	1.0605-1.0615	1.0605-1.0615	1.0605-1.0615	0.2590	0.2590	0.0010-0.0047	0.0010-0.0070

CRANKSHAFT AND CONNECTING ROD SPECIFICATIONS

All measurements are given in inches.

Year	Engine ID/VIN	Engine Displacement Liters (cc)	Crankshaft Main Brg. Journal Dia.	Main Brg. Oil Clearance	Shaft End-play	Thrust on No.	Connecting Rod Journal Diameter	Oil Clearance	Side Clearance
1989	F	5.0 (4943)	2.2482-2.2490	0.0004-0.0021	0.004-0.012	3	2.1228-2.1236	0.0008-0.0024	0.010-0.023
	G	5.8 (5767)	2.9994-3.0002	0.0008-0.0026	0.004-0.012	3	2.3103-2.3111	0.0007-0.0025	0.010-0.023
1990	F	5.0 (4943)	2.2482-2.2490	0.0004-0.0021	0.004-0.012	3	2.1228-2.1236	0.0008-0.0024	0.010-0.023
	G	5.8 (5767)	2.9994-3.0002	0.0008-0.0026	0.004-0.012	3	2.3103-2.3111	0.0007-0.0025	0.010-0.023
1991	W	4.6 (4593)	2.6575	0.0011-0.0025	0.005-0.010	5	2.0866	0.0011-0.0027	0.006-0.019
	F	5.0 (4943)	2.2482-2.2490	0.0004-0.0024	0.004-0.012	3	2.1228-2.1236	0.0008-0.0026	0.010-0.023
	G	5.8 (5767)	2.9994-3.0002	0.0008-0.0025	0.004-0.012	3	2.3103-2.3111	0.0007-0.0025	0.010-0.023
1992-93	W	4.6 (4593)	2.6578-2.6598	0.0011-0.0025	0.005-0.010	5	2.0866	0.0011-0.0027	0.006-0.019

VALVE SPECIFICATIONS

Year	Engine ID/VIN	Engine Displacement Liters (cc)	Seat Angle (deg.)	Face Angle (deg.)	Spring Test Pressure (lbs. @ in.)	Spring Installed Height (in.)	Stem-to-Guide Clearance (in.) Intake	Exhaust	Stem Diameter (in.) Intake	Exhaust
1989	F	5.0 (4943)	45	44	①	②	0.0010-0.0027	0.0015-0.0032	0.3416-0.3423	0.3411-0.3418
	G	5.8 (5767)	45	44	195-215 @ 1.05	②	0.0010-0.0027	0.0015-0.0032	0.3416-0.3423	0.3411-0.3418

VALVE SPECIFICATIONS

Year	Engine ID/VIN	Engine Displacement Liters (cc)	Seat Angle (deg.)	Face Angle (deg.)	Spring Test Pressure (lbs. @ in.)	Spring Installed Height (in.)	Stem-to-Guide Clearance (in.)		Stem Diameter (in.)	
							Intake	Exhaust	Intake	Exhaust
1990	F	5.0 (4943)	45	44	①	②	0.0010–0.0027	0.0015–0.0032	0.3416–0.3423	0.3411–0.3418
	G	5.8 (5767)	45	44	195–215 @ 1.05	②	0.0010–0.0027	0.0015–0.0032	0.3416–0.3423	0.3411–0.3418
1991	W	4.6 (4593)	45	45.5	132 @ 1.10	1.57	0.0008–0.0027	0.0018–0.0037	0.2746–0.2754	0.2736–0.2744
	F	5.0 (4943)	45	44	①	②	0.0010–0.0027	0.0015–0.0032	0.3416–0.3423	0.3411–0.3418
	G	5.8 (5767)	45	44	195–215 @ 1.05	②	0.0010–0.0027	0.0015–0.0032	0.3416–0.3423	0.3411–0.3418
1992–93	W	4.6 (4593)	45	45.5	132 @ 1.10	1.57	0.0008–0.0027	0.0018–0.0037	0.2746–0.2754	0.2736–0.2744

① Intake: 194–214 @ 1.36
  Exhaust: 190–210 @ 1.20
② Intake: 1.75–1.80
  Exhaust: 1.58–1.64

PISTON AND RING SPECIFICATIONS

All measurements are given in inches.

Year	Engine ID/VIN	Engine Displacement Liters (cc)	Piston Clearance	Ring Gap			Ring Side Clearance		
				Top Compression	Bottom Compression	Oil Control	Top Compression	Bottom Compression	Oil Control
1989	F	5.0 (4943)	0.0014–0.0022	0.010–0.020	0.010–0.020	0.015–0.055	0.0020–0.0040	0.0020–0.0040	Snug
	G	5.8 (5767)	0.0018–0.0026	0.010–0.020	0.010–0.020	0.015–0.055	0.0020–0.0040	0.0020–0.0040	Snug
1990	F	5.0 (4943)	0.0014–0.0022	0.010–0.020	0.010–0.020	0.015–0.055	0.0020–0.0040	0.0020–0.0040	Snug
	G	5.8 (5767)	0.0018–0.0026	0.010–0.020	0.010–0.020	0.015–0.055	0.0020–0.0040	0.0020–0.0040	Snug
1991	W	4.6 (4593)	0.0008–0.0018	0.009–0.019	0.009–0.019	0.010–0.030	0.0016–0.0035	0.0012–0.0031	Snug
	F	5.0 (4943)	0.0014–0.0022	0.010–0.020	0.010–0.020	0.015–0.055	0.0020–0.0040	0.0020–0.0040	Snug
	G	5.8 (5767)	0.0018–0.0026	0.010–0.020	0.010–0.020	0.015–0.055	0.0020–0.0040	0.0020–0.0040	Snug
1992–93	W	4.6 (4593)	0.0008–0.0018	0.009–0.019	0.009–0.019	0.010–0.030	0.0016–0.0035	0.0012–0.0031	Snug

TORQUE SPECIFICATIONS

All readings in ft. lbs.

Year	Engine ID/VIN	Engine Displacement Liters (cc)	Cylinder Head Bolts	Main Bearing Bolts	Rod Bearing Bolts	Crankshaft Damper Bolts	Flywheel Bolts	Manifold		Spark Plugs	Lug Nut
								Intake	Exhaust		
1989	F	5.0 (4943)	①	60–70	19–24	70–90	75–85	23–25 ②	18–24	5–10	85–105
	G	5.8 (5767)	③	90–105	40–45	70–90	75–85	23–25 ②	18–24	10–15	85–105
1990	F	5.0 (4943)	①	60–70	19–24	70–90	75–85	23–25 ②	18–24	5–10	85–105
	G	5.8 (5767)	③	90–105	40–45	70–90	75–85	23–25 ②	18–24	10–15	85–105

TORQUE SPECIFICATIONS

All readings in ft. lbs.

Year	Engine ID/VIN	Engine Displacement Liters (cc)	Cylinder Head Bolts	Main Bearing Bolts	Rod Bearing Bolts	Crankshaft Damper Bolts	Flywheel Bolts	Manifold Intake	Manifold Exhaust	Spark Plugs	Lug Nut
1991	W	4.6 (4593)	④	⑤	⑥	114–121	54–64	15–22	15–22	7	85–105
	F	5.0 (4943)	①	60–70	19–24	70–90	75–85	23–25②	18–24	5–10	85–105
	G	5.8 (5767)	③	95–105	40–45	70–90	75–85	23–25②	18–24	10–15	85–105
1992–93	W	4.6 (4593)	④	⑤	⑥	114–121	54–64	15–22	15–22	7	85–105

① Tighten in 2 steps:
  Step 1: 55–65 ft. lbs.
  Step 2: 65–72 ft. lbs.
② Retorque with engine hot
③ Tighten in 3 steps:
  Step 1: 85 ft. lbs.
  Step 2: 95 ft. lbs.
  Step 3: 105–112 ft. lbs.

④ Tighten in 3 steps:
  Step 1: 15–22 ft. lbs.
  Step 2: Turn each bolt 85–95 degrees, in sequence
  Step 3: Turn each bolt 85–95 degrees, in sequence

⑤ Tighten in 2 steps:
  Step 1: 22–25 ft. lbs.
  Step 2: Turn each bolt 85–95 degrees
⑥ Tighten in 2 steps:
  Step 1: 18–25 ft. lbs.
  Step 2: Turn each bolt 85–95 degrees

BRAKE SPECIFICATIONS

All measurements in inches unless noted.

Year	Model	Master Cylinder Bore	Brake Disc Original Thickness	Brake Disc Minimum Thickness	Maximum Runout	Brake Drum Diameter Original Inside Diameter	Brake Drum Diameter Max. Wear Limit	Brake Drum Diameter Maximum Machine Diameter	Minimum Lining Thickness Front	Minimum Lining Thickness Rear
1989	Crown Victoria	1.00	1.03	0.972	0.003	①	NA	②	0.125	0.031
	Grand Marquis	1.00	1.03	0.972	0.003	①	NA	②	0.125	0.031
	Town Car	1.00	1.03	0.972	0.003	10.000	NA	10.060	0.125	0.031
1990	Crown Victoria	1.00	1.03	0.972	0.003	①	NA	②	0.125	0.031
	Grand Marquis	1.00	1.03	0.972	0.003	①	NA	②	0.125	0.031
	Town Car	1.00	1.03	0.972	0.003	10.000	NA	10.060	0.125	0.031
1991	Crown Victoria	1.00	1.03	0.972	0.003	①	NA	②	0.125	0.031
	Grand Marquis	1.00	1.03	0.972	0.003	①	NA	②	0.125	0.031
	Town Car	1.00	③	④	0.003	—	—	—	0.125	0.123
1992–93	Crown Victoria	1.00	③	④	⑤	—	—	—	0.125	0.123
	Grand Marquis	1.00	③	④	⑤	—	—	—	0.125	0.123
	Town Car	1.00	③	④	⑤	—	—	—	0.125	0.123

NA—Not available
① Sedan except Police, Taxi and trailer tow:
  10.000
  Station Wagon, Police, Taxi and trailer tow:
  11.030
② Sedan except Police, Taxi and trailer tow:
  10.060
  Station Wagon, Police, Taxi and trailer tow:
  11.090
③ Front: 1.03
  Rear: 0.50
④ Front: 1.03
  Rear: 0.44
⑤ Front: 0.002
  Rear: 0.003

WHEEL ALIGNMENT

Year	Model	Caster Range (deg.)	Caster Preferred Setting (deg.)	Camber Range (deg.)	Camber Preferred Setting (deg.)	Toe-in (in.)	Steering Axis Inclination (deg.)
1989	Crown Victoria	2½P–4½P	3½P	1¼N–¼P	½N	1/16	11
	Grand Marquis	2½P–4½P	3½P	1¼N–¼P	½N	1/16	11
	Town Car	2½P–4½P	3½P	1¼N–¼P	½N	1/16	11
1990	Crown Victoria	2½P–4½P	3½P	1¼N–¼P	½N	1/16	11
	Grand Marquis	2½P–4½P	3½P	1¼N–¼P	½N	1/16	11
	Town Car	2½P–4½P	3½P	1¼N–¼P	½N	1/16	11
1991	Crown Victoria	2½P–4½P	3½P	1¼N–¼P	½N	1/16	11
	Grand Marquis	2½P–4½P	3½P	1¼N–¼P	½N	1/16	11
	Town Car	4¾P–6¼P	5½P	1¼N–¼P	½N	1/16	11
1992–93	Crown Victoria	4¾P–6¼P	5½P	1¼N–¼P	½N	1/16	11
	Grand Marquis	4¾P–6¼P	5½P	1¼N–¼P	½N	1/16	11
	Town Car	5¼P–6¾P	6P	1¼N–¼P	½N	1/16	11

N—Negative
P—Positive

ENGINE MECHANICAL

NOTE: Disconnecting the negative battery cable on some vehicles may interfere with the functions of the on board computer systems and may require the computer to undergo a relearning process, once the negative battery cable is reconnected.

Engine Assembly

REMOVAL & INSTALLATION

4.6L Engine

1. Disconnect the battery cables. Drain the crankcase and the cooling system.
2. Relieve the fuel system pressure and discharge the air conditioning system.
3. Mark the position of the hood on the hinges and remove the hood.
4. Remove the cooling fan, shroud and radiator.
5. Remove the wiper module and support bracket. Remove the air inlet tube.
6. Remove the 42-pin connector from the retaining bracket on the brake vacuum booster. Disconnect the 42-pin connector and transmission harness connector and position aside.
7. Disconnect the accelerator and cruise control cables. Disconnect the throttle valve cable.
8. Disconnect the electrical connector and vacuum hose from the purge solenoid. Disconnect the power supply from the power distribution box and starter relay.
9. Disconnect the vacuum supply hose from the throttle body adapter vacuum port. Disconnect the heater hoses.
10. Disconnect the alternator harness from the fender apron and junction block. Disconnect the air conditioning hoses from the compressor.
11. Disconnect the EVO sensor connector from the power steering pump and disconnect the body ground strap from the dash panel.
12. Raise and safely support the vehicle.
13. Disconnect the exhaust system from the exhaust manifolds and support with wire hung from the crossmember.
14. Remove the retaining nut from the transmission line bracket and remove the 3 bolts and stud retaining the engine to the transmission knee braces.
15. Remove the starter. Remove the 4 bolts retaining the power steering pump to the engine block and position aside.
16. Remove the plug from the engine block to access the torque converter retaining nuts. Rotate the crankshaft until each of the 4 nuts is accessible and remove the nuts.
17. Remove the 6 transmission-to-engine retaining bolts. Remove the engine mount through bolts, 2 on the left mount and 1 on the right mount.
18. Lower the vehicle. Support the transmission with a floor jack and remove the bolt retaining the right engine mount to the lower engine bracket.
19. Install an engine lifting bracket to the left cylinder head on the front and the right cylinder head on the rear. Connect engine lifting equipment to the lifting brackets.
20. Raise the engine slightly and carefully separate the engine from the transmission.
21. Carefully lift the engine out of the engine compartment and position on a workstand. Remove the engine lifting equipment.
To install:
22. Install engine lifting brackets as in Step 19. Connect engine lifting equipment to the brackets and remove the engine from the workstand.
23. Carefully lower the engine into the engine compartment. Start the converter pilot into the flexplate and align the paint marks on the flexplate and torque converter. Make sure the studs on the torque converter align with the holes in the flexplate.
24. Fully engage the engine to the transmission and lower onto the mounts. Remove the engine lifting equipment and brackets. Install the bolt retaining the right engine mount to the frame.
25. Raise and safely support the vehicle. Install the 6 engine-to-transmission bolts and tighten to 30–44 ft. lbs. (40–60 Nm).
26. Install the engine mount through bolts and tighten to 15–22 ft. lbs. (20–30 Nm). Install the 4 torque converter retaining nuts and tighten to 22–25 ft.

lbs. (20–30 Nm). Install the plug into the access hole in the engine block.

27. Position the power steering pump on the engine block and install the 4 retaining nuts. Tighten to 15–22 ft. lbs. (20–30 Nm). Install the starter.

28. Position the engine to transmission braces and install the 3 bolts and 1 stud. Tighten the bolts and stud to 18–31 ft. lbs. (25–43 Nm).

29. Position the transmission line bracket to the knee brace stud and install the retaining nut. Tighten to 15–22 ft. lbs. (20–30 Nm).

30. Cut the wire and position the exhaust system to the manifolds. Install the 4 nuts and tighten to 20–30 ft. lbs. (27–41 Nm).

NOTE: Make sure the exhaust system clears the No. 3 crossmember. Adjust as necessary.

31. Lower the vehicle and connect the EVO sensor.

32. Connect the air conditioner lines to the compressor and connect the alternator harness from the fender apron and junction block.

33. Connect the heater hoses and connect the vacuum supply hose to the throttle body adapter vacuum port.

34. Connect the power supply to the power distribution box and starter relay. Connect the electrical connector and vacuum hose to the purge solenoid.

35. Connect and if necessary, adjust the throttle valve cable. Connect the accelerator and cruise control cables.

36. Connect the 42-pin engine harness connector and transmission harness connector. Install the 42-pin connector to the retaining bracket on the brake vacuum booster.

37. Install the wiper module and support bracket. Connect the fuel lines.

38. Install the radiator, cooling fan and shroud. Install the air inlet tube.

39. Fill the crankcase with the proper type and quantity of engine oil. Fill and bleed the cooling system.

40. Install the hood, aligning the marks that were made during removal. Connect the battery cables.

41. Start the engine and bring to operating temperature. Check for leaks. Check all fluid levels. Leak test, evacuate and charge the air conditioning system according to the proper procedure. Observe all safety precautions.

5.0L and 5.8L Engines

1. Disconnect the battery cables. Drain the crankcase and the cooling system.

2. Relieve the fuel system pressure and discharge the air conditioning system.

3. Mark the position of the hood on the hinges and remove the hood. Disconnect the battery ground cables from the cylinder block.

4. Remove the air intake duct and the air cleaner, if engine mounted.

5. Disconnect the upper radiator hose from the thermostat housing and the lower hose from the water pump. Disconnect the oil cooler lines from the radiator.

6. Remove the bolts attaching the radiator fan shroud to the radiator. Remove the radiator. Remove the fan, belt pulley and shroud.

7. Remove the alternator bolts and position the alternator aside.

8. Disconnect the oil pressure sending unit wire from the sending unit. Disconnect the flexible fuel line at the fuel tank line. Plug the fuel tank line.

9. Disconnect the accelerator cable from the carburetor or throttle body. Disconnect the TV rod. Disconnect the cruise control cable, if equipped.

10. Disconnect the throttle valve vacuum line from the intake manifold, if equipped. Disconnect the transmission filler tube bracket from the cylinder block.

11. Disconnect the air conditioning lines and electrical connectors at the compressor and remove the compressor. Plug the lines and the compressor fittings to prevent the entrance of dirt and moisture.

12. Disconnect the power steering pump bracket from the cylinder head. Remove the drive belt. Position the power steering pump aside in a position that will prevent the fluid from leaking.

13. Disconnect the power brake vacuum line from the intake manifold.

14. On 5.0L engines, disconnect the heater hoses from the heater tubes. On 5.8L engines, disconnect the heater hoses from the water pump and intake manifold. Disconnect the electrical connector from the coolant temperature sending unit.

15. Remove the converter housing-to-engine upper bolts.

16. On 5.8L engines, disconnect the primary wiring connector from the ignition coil. Disconnect the wiring to the solenoid on the left rocker cover. Remove the wire harness from the left rocker arm cover and position the wires aside. Disconnect the ground strap from the block.

17. On 5.0L engines, disconnect the wiring harness at the two 10-pin connectors.

18. Raise and safely support the vehicle. Disconnect the starter cable from the starter and remove the starter.

19. Disconnect the muffler inlet pipes from the exhaust manifolds. Disconnect the engine mounts from the chassis. Disconnect the downstream thermactor tubing and check valve from the right exhaust manifold stud, if equipped.

20. Disconnect the transmission cooler lines from the retainer and remove the converter housing inspection cover. Disconnect the flywheel from the converter and secure the converter assembly in the housing. Remove the remaining converter housing-to-engine bolts.

21. Lower the vehicle and then support the transmission. Attach engine lifting equipment and hoist the engine.

22. Raise the engine slightly and carefully pull it from the transmission. Carefully lift the engine out of the engine compartment. Avoid bending or damaging the rear cover plate or other components. Install the engine on a workstand.

To install:

23. Attach the engine lifting equipment and remove the engine from the workstand.

24. Lower the engine carefully into the engine compartment. Make sure the exhaust manifolds are properly aligned with the muffler inlet pipes.

25. Start the converter pilot into the crankshaft. Align the paint mark on the flywheel to the paint mark on the torque converter.

26. Install the converter housing upper bolts, making sure the dowels in the cylinder block engage the converter housing.

27. Install the engine mount-to-chassis attaching fasteners and remove the engine lifting equipment.

28. Raise and safely support the vehicle. Connect both muffler inlet pipes to the exhaust manifolds. Install the starter and connect the starter cable.

29. Remove the retainer holding the converter in the housing. Attach the converter to the flywheel. Install the converter housing inspection cover and install the remaining converter housing attaching bolts.

30. Remove the support from the transmission and lower the vehicle.

31. On 5.8L engines, connect the wiring harness to the left rocker arm cover and connect the coil wiring connector. On 5.0L engines, connect the wiring harness at the two 10-pin connectors.

32. Connect the coolant temperature sending unit wire and connect the heater hoses. Connect the wiring to the metal heater tubes and the engine coolant temperature, air charge temperature and oxygen sensors.

33. Connect the transmission filler tube bracket. Connect the manual shift rod and the retracting spring. Connect the throttle valve vacuum line, if equipped.

34. Connect the accelerator cable and

TV cable. Connect the cruise control cable, if equipped.

35. Remove the plug from the fuel tank line and connect the fuel line and the oil pressure sending unit wire.

36. Install the pulley, water pump belt and fan/clutch assembly.

37. Position the alternator bracket and install the alternator bolts. Connect the alternator and ground cables. Adjust the drive belt tension.

38. Install the air conditioning compressor. Unplug and connect the refrigerant lines and connect the electrical connector to the compressor.

39. Install the power steering drive belt and power steering pump bracket. Connect the power brake vacuum line.

40. Place the shroud over the fan and install the radiator. Connect the radiator hoses and the transmission oil cooler lines. Position the shroud and install the bolts.

41. Connect the heater hoses to the heater tubes. Fill and bleed the cooling system. Fill the crankcase with the proper type and quantity of engine oil. Adjust the transmission throttle linkage.

42. Connect the negative battery cable. Start the engine and bring to normal operating temperature. Check for leaks. Check all fluid levels.

43. Install the air intake duct assembly. Install the hood, aligning the marks that were made during removal.

44. Leak test, evacuate and charge the air conditioning system according to the proper procedure. Observe all safety precautions.

Engine Mounts

REMOVAL & INSTALLATION

4.6L Engine

FRONT

1. Disconnect the battery cables. Drain the cooling system, relieve the fuel system pressure and discharge the air conditioning system.

2. Remove the air inlet tube and the cooling fan and shroud. Remove the upper radiator hose.

3. Disconnect the fuel lines from the fuel rail. Remove the wiper module and support bracket.

4. Disconnect the air conditioning compressor outlet hose at the compressor and remove the bolt retaining the hose assembly to the right coil bracket.

5. Remove the 42-pin engine harness connector from the retaining bracket on the brake vacuum booster. Disconnect the 42-pin connector and transmission harness connector.

6. Disconnect the throttle valve ca-

ble from the throttle body. Disconnect the heater outlet hose.

7. Remove the upper stud and loosen the lower bolt retaining the heater outlet hose to the right cylinder head and position aside.

8. Remove the blower motor resistor. Remove the bolt retaining the right engine mount to the lower engine bracket.

9. Disconnect the vacuum hoses from the EGR valve and EGR tube. Remove the 2 bolts retaining the EGR valve to the intake manifold. Disconnect both oxygen sensors.

10. Raise and safely support the vehicle. Remove the engine mount through bolts, 2 from the left side and 1 from the right.

11. Remove the EGR tube line nut from the right exhaust manifold and remove the EGR valve and tube assembly.

12. Disconnect the exhaust pipes from the manifolds. Lower the exhaust and hang the pipes with wire from the crossmember.

13. Position a jack and a block of wood under the oil pan, rearward of the oil drain hole. Raise the engine approximately 4 in. (100mm).

14. Install a block of wood under the oil pan and lower the engine onto the wood block. Remove 3 retaining bolts each from the right and left engine mounts and remove the mounts.

To install:

15. Position the mounts on the engine block, install 3 retaining bolts and tighten to 45–60 (60–81 Nm). Raise the engine and remove the wood block.

16. Lower the engine onto the mounts. Position and connect the EGR valve and tube assembly to the exhaust manifold. Tighten the line nut to 26–33 ft. lbs.

NOTE: Loosen the line nut at the EGR valve prior to installing the assembly onto the vehicle. This will allow enough movement to align the EGR valve retaining bolts.

17. Install the engine mount through bolts and tighten to 15–22 ft. lbs. (20–30 Nm).

18. Cut the wire and position the exhaust manifolds. Install the 4 nuts and tighten to 20–30 ft. lbs. (27–41 Nm). Make sure the exhaust system clears the No. 3 crossmember; adjust as necessary.

19. Lower the vehicle and connect the oxygen sensors. Install the bolt retaining the right engine mount to the frame. Tighten to 45–60 ft. lbs. (60–81 Nm).

20. Install a new gasket on the EGR valve and position to the intake manifold. Install the 2 EGR valve retaining

bolts and tighten to 15–22 ft. lbs. (20–30 Nm).

21. Tighten the EGR tube line nut at the EGR valve to 26–33 ft. lbs. (35–45 Nm). Connect the vacuum hoses to the EGR valve and tube.

22. Install the blower motor resistor. Position the heater outlet hose. Install the upper stud and tighten the upper stud and lower bolt to 15–22 ft. lbs. (20–30 Nm). Install the gound strap onto the stud and tighten the nut to 15–22 ft. lbs. (20–30 Nm). Connect the heater outlet hose.

23. Connect and if necessary, adjust the throttle valve cable. Connect the 42-pin connector and transmission harness connector. Install the 42-pin engine harness connector to the retaining bracket on the brake vacuum booster.

24. Connect the air conditioning compressor outlet hose to the compressor and install the bolt retaining the hose assembly to the right coil bracket.

25. Install the upper radiator hose and connect the fuel lines. Install the wiper module and retaining bracket.

26. Install the cooling fan and shroud. Install the air inlet tube.

27. Fill and bleed the cooling system. Connect the battery cables, start the engine and check for leaks. Leak test, evacuate and charge the air conditioning system according to the proper procedure. Observe all safety precautions.

REAR

1. Disconnect the negative battery cable. Raise and safely support the vehicle.

2. Support the transmission with a jack and wood block. Remove the 2 nuts attaching the rear mount to the crossmember.

3. Remove the 2 bolts attaching the mount to the transmission.

4. Raise the transmission with the jack and remove the mount.

To install:

5. Position the mount on the transmission. Install the 2 retaining bolts and tighten to 50–70 ft. lbs. (68–95 Nm).

6. Lower the transmission. Install the rear mount-to-crossmember retaining nuts and tighten to 35–50 ft. lbs. (48–68 Nm).

7. Lower the vehicle and connect the negative battery cable.

5.0L and 5.8L Engines

FRONT

1. Disconnect the negative battery cable. Remove fan shroud attaching screw.

2. Raise and safely support the vehicle. Support the engine using a jack

and wood block placed under the engine.

3. Remove the through bolts attaching the mounts to the mount support bracket.

4. Remove the bolts attaching the mount to the frame.

5. Raise the engine slightly with the jack and remove the mount.

To install:

6. Position the mount to the frame and install the attaching bolts. Tighten the bolts to 26–38 ft. lbs. (35–52 Nm).

7. Lower the engine into position and install the mount-to-mount support bracket through bolts. Tighten the through bolts to 45–65 ft. lbs. (61–88 Nm).

8. Lower the vehicle. Connect the negative battery cable and install the fan shroud attaching screws.

REAR

1. Disconnect the negative battery cable. Raise and safely support the vehicle.

2. Support the transmission with a jack and wood block. Remove the 2 nuts attaching the mount to the crossmember.

3. Remove the 2 bolts attaching the mount to the transmission.

4. Raise the transmission with the jack and remove the mount.

To install:

5. Position the mount on the transmission. Install the 2 retaining bolts and tighten to 50–70 ft. lbs. (68–95 Nm).

6. Lower the transmission. Install the mount-to-crossmember retaining nuts and tighten to 35–50 ft. lbs. (48–68 Nm).

7. Lower the vehicle and connect the negative battery cable.

Cylinder Head

REMOVAL & INSTALLATION

4.6L Engine

1. Disconnect the negative battery cable.

2. Drain the cooling system and remove the cooling fan and shroud.

3. Relieve the fuel system pressure and disconnect the fuel lines.

4. Remove the air inlet tube and the wiper module. Release the belt tensioner and remove the accessory drive belt.

5. Tag and disconnect the ignition wires from the spark plugs. Disconnect the ignition wire brackets from the camshaft cover studs and remove the 2 bolts retaining the ignition wire tray to the coil brackets.

6. Remove the bolt retaining the air conditioner high pressure line to the right coil bracket. Disconnect both ignition coils and CID sensor.

7. Remove the nuts retaining the coil brackets to the front cover. Slide the ignition coil brackets and ignition wire assembly off the mounting studs and remove from the vehicle.

8. Remove the water pump pulley. Disconnect the alternator wiring harness from the junction block, fender apron and alternator. Disconnect the bolts retaining the alternator to the intake manifold and engine block and remove the alternator.

9. Disconnect the positive battery cable at the power distribution box. Remove the retaining bolt from the positive battery cable bracket located on the side of the right cylinder head.

10. Disconnect the vent hose from the canister purge solenoid and position the positive battery cable out of the way. Disconnect the canister purge solenoid vent hose from the PCV valve and remove the PCV valve from the camshaft cover.

11. Remove the 42-pin engine harness connector from the retaining bracket on the brake vacuum booster, disconnect and position out of the way.

12. Disconnect the HDR sensor, air conditioning compressor clutch and canister purge solenoid connectors.

13. Raise and safely support the vehicle.

14. Remove the bolts retaining the power steering pump to the engine block and front cover. The front lower bolt on the power steering pump will not come all the way out. Wire the power steering pump out of the way.

15. Remove the 4 bolts retaining the oil pan to the front cover. Remove the crankshaft damper retaining bolt and remove the damper, using a suitable puller.

16. Disconnect the EVO sensor and oil sending unit. Position the EVO sensor and oil pressure sending unit harness out of the way.

17. Disconnect the EGR tube from the right exhaust manifold. Disconnect the exhaust pipes from the exhaust manifolds. Lower the exhaust pipes and hang with wire from the crossmember.

18. Remove the bolt retaining the starter wiring harness to the rear of the right cylinder head. Lower the vehicle.

19. Remove the bolts and stud bolts retaining the camshaft covers to the cylinder heads and remove the covers.

20. Disconnect the accelerator, cruise control and throttle valve cables. Remove the accelerator cable bracket from the intake manifold and position out of the way.

21. Disconnect the vacuum hose from the throttle body elbow vacuum port, both oxygen sensors and the heater supply hose.

22. Remove the 2 bolts retaining the thermostat housing to the intake manifold and position the upper hose and thermostat housing out of the way.

NOTE: Two thermostat housing bolts also retain the intake manifold.

23. Remove the 9 bolts retaining the intake manifold to the cylinder heads and remove the intake manifold and gaskets.

24. Remove the 7 stud bolts and 4 bolts retaining the front cover to the engine and remove the front cover.

25. Remove the timing chains.

26. Remove the 10 bolts retaining the left cylinder head to the engine block and remove the head.

NOTE: The lower rear bolt cannot be removed due to interference with the brake vacuum booster. Use a rubber band to hold the bolt away from the engine block.

27. Remove the ground strap, 1 stud and 1 bolt retaining the heater return line to the right cylinder head.

28. Remove the 10 bolts retaining the right cylinder head to the engine block and remove the head.

NOTE: The lower rear bolt cannot be removed due to interference with the evaporator housing. Use a rubber band to hold the bolt away from the engine block.

29. Clean all gasket mating surfaces. Check the cylinder head and engine block for flatness. Check the cylinder head for scratches near the coolant passage and combustion chamber that could provide leak paths. Machine as necessary.

To install:

30. Rotate the crankshaft counterclockwise 45 degrees. The crankshaft keyway should be at the 9 o'clock position viewed from the front of the engine. This ensures that all pistons are below the top of the engine block deck face.

31. Rotate the camshaft to a stable position where the valves do not extend below the head face.

32. Position new head gaskets on the engine block. Install the lower rear bolts on both cylinder heads and retain with rubber bands as explained during the removal procedure.

33. Position the cylinder heads on the engine block dowels, being careful not to score the surface of the head face. Apply clean oil to the head bolts, remove the rubber band from the lower rear bolt and install all bolts handtight.

34. Tighten the head bolts as follows:
   a. Tighten the bolts, in sequence, to 15–22 ft. lbs. (20–30 Nm).

b. Rotate each bolt, in sequence, 85–95 degrees.

c. Rotate each bolt, in sequence, an additional 85–95 degrees.

35. Position the heater return hose and install the 2 bolts. Rotate the camshafts using the flats matched at the center of the camshaft until both are in time. Install cam positioning tools T91P–6256–A or equivalent, on the flats of the camshafts to keep them from rotating.

36. Rotate the crankshaft clockwise 45 degrees to position the crankshaft at TDC on No. 1 cylinder.

NOTE: The crankshaft must only be rotated in the clockwise direction and only as far as TDC.

37. Install the timing chains according to the proper procedure.

38. Install a new front cover seal and gasket. Apply silicone sealer to the lower corners of the cover where it meets the junction of the oil pan and cylinder block and to the points where the cover contacts the junction of the cylinder block and cylinder head.

39. Install the front cover and the stud bolts and bolts. Tighten to 15–22 ft. lbs. (20–30 Nm).

40. Position new intake manifold gaskets on the cylinder heads. Make sure the alignment tabs on the gaskets are aligned with the holes in the cylinder heads.

NOTE: Before installing the intake manifold, inspect it for nicks and cuts that could provide leak paths.

41. Position the intake manifold on the cylinder heads and install the retaining bolts. Tighten the bolts, in sequence, to 15–22 ft. lbs. (20–30 Nm).

42. Install the thermostat and O-ring, then position the thermostat housing and upper hose and install the 2 bolts. Tighten to 15–22 ft. lbs. (20–30 Nm).

43. Connect the heater supply hose and both oxygen sensors. Connect the vacuum hose to the throttle body adapter vacuum port.

44. Connect and, if necessary, adjust the throttle valve cable. Install the accelerator cable bracket on the intake manifold and connect the accelerator and cruise control cables to the throttle body.

45. Apply silicone sealer to both places where the front cover meets the cylinder head. Install new gaskets on the camshaft covers.

46. Install the camshaft covers on the cylinder heads. Install the bolts and stud bolts and tighten to 6.0–8.8 ft. lbs. (8–12 Nm).

47. Raise and safely support the vehicle. Position the starter wiring harness to the right cylinder head and install the retaining bolt.

48. Cut the wire and position the exhaust pipes to the exhaust manifolds. Tighten the 4 nuts to 20–30 ft. lbs. (27–41 Nm).

NOTE: Make sure the exhaust system clears the No. 3 crossmember. Adjust as necessary.

49. Connect the EGR tube to the right exhaust manifold and tighten the line nut to 26–33 ft. lbs. (35–45 Nm). Connect the EVO sensor and oil sending unit.

50. Apply a small amount of silicone sealer in the rear of the keyway on the damper. Position the damper on the crankshaft, making sure the crankshaft key and keyway are aligned.

51. Using damper installer T74P–6316–B or equivalent, install the crankshaft damper. Install the damper bolt and washer and tighten to 114–121 ft. lbs. (155–165 Nm).

52. Install the 4 bolts retaining the oil pan to the front cover and tighten to 15–22 ft. lbs. (20–30 Nm).

53. Position the power steering pump on the engine and install the 4 retaining bolts. Tighten to 15–22 ft. lbs. (20–30 Nm). Lower the vehicle.

54. Connect the air conditioning compressor, HDR sensor and canister purge solenoid.

55. Connect the 42-pin engine harness connector and transmission harness connector. Install the 42-pin connector on the retaining bracket on the vacuum brake booster.

56. Install the PCV valve in the right camshaft cover and connect the canister purge solenoid vent hose.

57. Position the positive battery cable harness on the right cylinder head and install the bolt retaining the cable bracket to the cylinder head. Connect the positive battery cable at the power distribution box and battery.

58. Position the alternator and install the 2 retaining bolts. Tighten to 15–22 ft. lbs. (20–30 Nm). Install the 2 bolts retaining the alternator brace to the intake manifold and tighten to 6–8 ft. lbs. (8–12 Nm).

59. Install the water pump pulley and tighten the bolts to 15–22 ft. lbs. (20–30 Nm).

60. Position the ignition coil brackets and ignition wire assembly onto the mounting studs. Install the 7 nuts retaining the coil brackets to the front cover and tighten to 15–22 ft. lbs. (20–30 Nm).

61. Install the 2 bolts retaining the ignition wire tray to the coil bracket and tighten to 6.0–8.8 ft. lbs. (8–12 Nm). Connect both ignition coils and CID sensor.

62. Position the air conditioner high pressure line on the right coil bracket and install the bolt. Connect the ignition wires to the spark plugs and install the bracket onto the camshaft cover studs.

63. Install the accessory drive belt and the wiper module. Connect the fuel lines and install the cooling fan and shroud. Fill and bleed the cooling system.

64. Install the air inlet tube and connect the negative battery cable. Start the engine and bring to normal operating temperature. Check for leaks. Check all fluid levels.

5.0L and 5.8L Engines

1. Disconnect the negative battery cable.

2. Drain the cooling system and relieve the fuel system pressure.

3. On 5.0L engine, remove the upper and lower intake manifold and throttle body assembly. On 5.8L engine, remove the intake manifold and carburetor assembly.

4. If the air conditioning compressor is in the way of a cylinder head that is to be removed, proceed as follows:

a. Discharge the air conditioning system.

b. Disconnect and plug the refrigerant lines at the compressor. Cap the openings on the compressor.

c. Disconnect the electrical connector to the compressor.

d. Remove the compressor and the necessary mounting brackets.

5. If the left cylinder head is to be removed, disconnect the power steering pump bracket from the cylinder head and remove the drive belt from the pump pulley. Position the pump out of the way in a position that will prevent the oil from draining out.

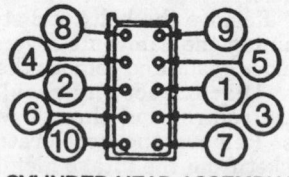

RIGHT CYLINDER HEAD ASSEMBLY

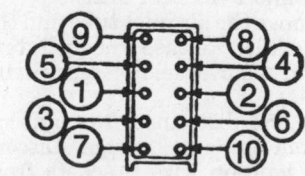

LEFT CYLINDER HEAD ASSEMBLY

FRONT OF Engine

Cylinder head bolt torque sequence—4.6L Engine

6. Disconnect the oil level dipstick tube bracket from the exhaust manifold stud, if necessary.

7. If the right cylinder head is to be removed, on some vehicles it is necessary to disconnect the alternator mounting bracket from the cylinder head.

8. Remove the thermactor crossover tube from the rear of the cylinder heads. If equipped, remove the fuel line from the clip at the front of the right cylinder head.

9. Raise and safely support the vehicle. Disconnect the exhaust manifolds from the muffler inlet pipes. Lower the vehicle.

10. Loosen the rocker arm fulcrum bolts so the rocker arms can be rotated to the side. Remove the pushrods in sequence so they may be installed in their original positions.

11. Remove the cylinder head attaching bolts and the cylinder heads. If necessary, remove the exhaust manifolds to gain access to the lower bolts. Remove and discard the head gaskets.

12. Clean all gasket mating surfaces. Check the flatness of the cylinder head using a straightedge and a feeler gauge. The cylinder head must not be warped any more than 0.003 in. in any 6.0 in. span; 0.006 in. overall. Machine as necessary.

To install:

13. Position the new cylinder head gasket over the dowels on the block. Position the cylinder heads on the block and install the attaching bolts.

14. On 5.0L engine, tighten the bolts, in sequence, in 2 steps, first to 55–65 ft. lbs. (75–88 Nm), then to 65–72 ft. lbs. (88–97 Nm). On 5.8L engine, tighten the bolts, in sequence, in 2 steps, first to 95–105 ft. lbs. (129–142 Nm), then to 105–112 ft. lbs. (142–152 Nm).

NOTE: When the cylinder head bolts have been tightened following this procedure, it is not necessary to retighten the bolts after extended operation.

15. If removed, install the exhaust manifolds. Tighten the retaining bolts to 18–24 ft. lbs. (24–32 Nm).

16. Clean the pushrods, making sure the oil passages are clean. Check the ends of the pushrods for wear. Visually check the pushrods for straightness or check for runout using a dial indicator. Replace pushrods, as necessary.

17. Apply a suitable grease to the ends of the pushrods and install them in their original positions. Position the rocker arms over the pushrods and the valves.

18. Before tightening each fulcrum bolt, bring the lifter for the fulcrum bolt to be tightened onto the base circle of the camshaft by rotating the engine. When the lifter is on the base circle of the camshaft, tighten the fulcrum bolt to 18–25 ft. lbs. (24–34 Nm).

NOTE: If all the original valve train parts are reinstalled, a valve clearance check is not necessary. If any valve train components are replaced, a valve clearance check must be performed.

19. Install new rocker arm cover gaskets on the rocker arm covers and install the covers on the cylinder heads.

20. Raise and safely support the vehicle. Connect the exhaust manifolds to the muffler inlet pipes. Lower the vehicle.

21. If necessary, install the air conditioning compressor and brackets. Connect the refrigerant lines and electrical connector to the compressor.

22. If necessary, install the alternator bracket.

23. If the left cylinder head was removed, install the power steering pump.

24. Install the drive belts. Install the thermactor tube at the rear of the cylinder heads.

25. Install the intake manifold. Fill and bleed the cooling system.

26. Connect the negative battery cable, start the engine and bring to normal operating temperature. Check for leaks. Check all fluid levels.

27. If necessary, leak test, evacuate and charge the air conditioning system according to the proper procedure. Observe all safety precautions.

Valve Lifters

REMOVAL & INSTALLATION

4.6L Engine

The 4.6L engine is equipped with hydraulic lash adjusters which, while not being exactly the same as a conventional hydraulic lifter, perform the same function—maintain proper valve train clearance.

1. Disconnect the negative battery cable.

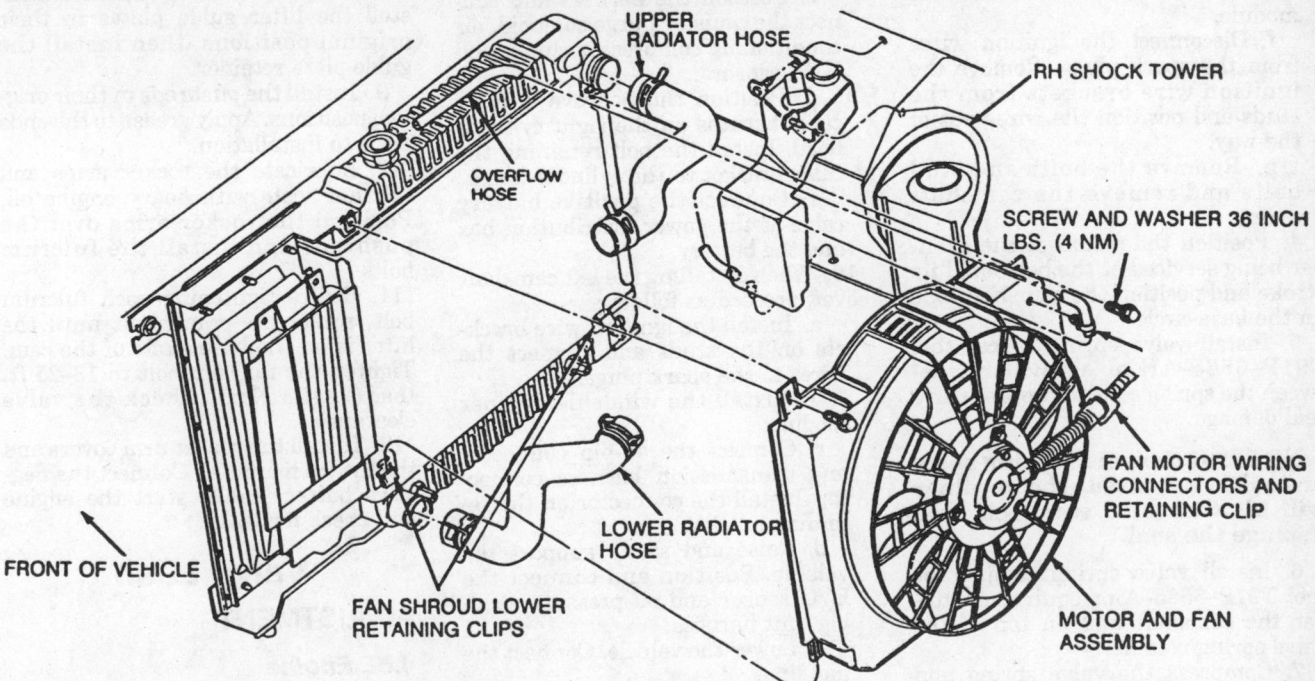

UPPER RADIATOR HOSE

RH SHOCK TOWER

OVERFLOW HOSE

SCREW AND WASHER 36 INCH LBS. (4 NM)

FAN MOTOR WIRING CONNECTORS AND RETAINING CLIP

FRONT OF VEHICLE

FAN SHROUD LOWER RETAINING CLIPS

LOWER RADIATOR HOSE

MOTOR AND FAN ASSEMBLY

Cylinder head bolt torque sequence—5.0L and 5.8L engines

2. Remove the right camshaft cover as follows:

a. Disconnect the positive battery cable at the battery and at the power distribution box. Remove the retaining bolt from the positive battery cable bracket located on the side of the right cylinder head.

b. Disconnect the High Data Rate (HDR) sensor, air conditioning compressor clutch and canister purge solenoid connectors. Position the harness out of the way.

c. Disconnect the vent hose from the purge solenoid and position the positive battery cable out of the way.

d. Disconnect the ignition wires from the spark plugs. Remove the ignition wire brackets from the camshaft cover studs and position the wires out of the way.

e. Remove the PCV valve from the camshaft cover grommet and position out of the way.

f. Remove the bolts and stud bolts and remove the camshaft cover.

3. Remove the left camshaft cover as follows:

a. Remove the air inlet tube. Relieve the fuel system pressure and disconnect the fuel lines.

b. Raise and safely support the vehicle.

c. Disconnect the EVO sensor and oil pressure sending unit and position the harness out of the way. Lower the vehicle.

d. Remove the 42-pin engine harness connector from the retaining bracket on the brake vacuum booster. Disconnect and position out of the way.

e. Remove the windshield wiper module.

f. Disconnect the ignition wires from the spark plugs. Remove the ignition wire brackets from the studs and position the wires out of the way.

g. Remove the bolts and stud bolts and remove the camshaft cover.

4. Position the piston of the cylinder being serviced at the bottom of its stroke and position the camshaft lobe on the base circle.

5. Install valve spring spacer tool T91P–6565–AH or equivalent, between the spring coils to prevent valve seal damage.

NOTE: If the valve spring spacer tool is not used, the retainer will hit the valve stem seal and damage the seal.

6. Install valve spring compressor tool T91P–6565–A or equivalent, under the camshaft and on top of the valve spring retainer.

7. Compress the valve spring and remove the roller follower. Remove the valve spring compressor and spacer.

8. Remove the hydraulic lash adjuster.

To install:

9. Check the hydraulic lash adjusters. They must have no more than 1.5mm of plunger travel prior to installation.

10. Apply engine oil to the valve stem and tip, roller follower contact surfaces and lash adjuster bore. Install the lash adjusters.

11. Install valve spring spacer tool T91P–6565–AH or equivalent, between the spring coils. Compress the valve spring using valve spring compressor tool T91P–6565–A or equivalent, and install the roller follower.

NOTE: The piston must be at the bottom of its stroke and the camshaft at the base circle.

12. Remove the valve spring compressor and spacer.

13. Clean the sealing surfaces of the camshaft covers and cylinder heads. Apply silicone sealer to the places where the front cover meets the cylinder head.

14. Position new gaskets onto the camshaft covers and install the covers. Install the bolts and stud bolts and tighten to 6.0–8.8 ft. lbs. (8–12 Nm).

15. When installing the right camshaft cover, proceed as follows:

a. Install the PCV valve into the camshaft cover grommet.

b. Install the ignition wire brackets on the studs and connect the wires to the spark plugs.

c. Position the harness and connect the canister purge solenoid, air conditioning compressor clutch and HDR sensor.

d. Position the positive battery cable harness on the right cylinder head. Install the bolt retaining the cable bracket to the cylinder head.

e. Connect the positive battery cable at the power distribution box and the battery.

16. When installing the left camshaft cover, proceed as follows:

a. Install the ignition wire brackets on the studs and connect the wires to the spark plugs.

b. Install the windshield wiper module.

c. Connect the 42-pin connector and transmission harness connector. Install the connector on the retaining bracket.

d. Raise and safely support the vehicle. Position and connect the EVO sensor and oil pressure sending unit harness.

e. Lower the vehicle. Connect the fuel lines.

17. Connect the negative battery ca-ble. Start the engine and check for leaks.

5.0L and 5.8L Engines

1. Disconnect the negative battery cable. Remove the intake manifold and related parts.

2. Remove the crankcase ventilation hoses, PCV valve and elbows from the valve rocker arm covers.

3. Remove the valve rocker arm covers. Loosen the valve rocker arm fulcrum bolts and rotate the rocker arms to the side.

4. Remove the valve pushrods and identify them so they can be installed in their original position.

5. If equipped with roller lifters, remove the lifter guide retainer bolts. Remove the retainer and lifter guide plates. Identify the guide plates so they may be reinstalled in their original positions.

6. Using a magnet, remove the lifters and place them in a rack so they can be installed in their original bores.

NOTE: If the lifters are stuck in the bores due to excessive varnish or gum deposits, it may be necessary to use a claw-type tool to aid removal. When using a remover tool, rotate the lifter back and forth to loosen it from gum or varnish that may have formed on the lifter.

To install:

7. Lubricate the lifters and install them in their original bores. If new lifters are being installed, check them for free fit in their respective bores.

8. If equipped with roller lifters, install the lifter guide plates in their original positions, then install the guide plate retainer.

9. Install the pushrods in their original positions. Apply grease to the ends prior to installation.

10. Lubricate the rocker arms and fulcrum seats with heavy engine oil. Position the rocker arms over the pushrods and install the fulcrum bolts.

11. Before tightening each fulcrum bolt, rotate the crankshaft until the lifter is on the base circle of the cam. Tighten the fulcrum bolt to 18–25 ft. lbs. (24–34 Nm). Check the valve clearance.

12. Install the rocker arm covers and the intake manifold. Connect the negative battery cable, start the engine and check for leaks.

Valve Lash

ADJUSTMENT

4.6L Engine

The valve lash is not adjustable. If the

collapsed lash adjuster clearance is incorrect, check the camshaft, roller follower and valve for wear or damage.

1. Disconnect the negative battery cable.

2. Remove the camshaft covers.

3. Rotate the crankshaft until the camshaft base circle is contacting the roller follower.

4. Use a suitable tool to bleed down the lash adjuster. Slowly compress the lash adjuster until the plunger is bottomed.

5. Use a feeler gauge to check the clearance between the camshaft and the roller follower. The clearance should be 0.018–0.033 in. (0.45–0.85mm).

5.0L Engine

The valve lash is not adjustable. If the collapsed lifter clearance is found to be incorrect, there are replacement pushrods available to compensate for excessive or insufficient clearance.

1. Install an auxiliary starter switch. Crank the engine with the ignition switch off until the No. 1 piston is at TDC on the compression stroke.

2. With the crankshaft in the positions designated in Steps 4, 5 and 6, position lifter bleed down wrench tool T71P-6513-B or equivalent, on the rocker arm. Slowly apply pressure to bleed down the lifter until the plunger is completely bottomed. Hold the lifter in this position and check the available clearance between the rocker arm and the valve stem tip with a feeler gauge.

3. The clearance should be 0.071–0.171 in. If the clearance is less than specification, install a shorter pushrod. If the clearance is greater than specification, install a longer pushrod.

4. The following valves can be checked with the engine in position 1, No. 1 piston at TDC on the compression stroke.

   a. No. 1 intake—No. 1 exhaust

   b. No. 7 intake—No. 5 exhaust

   c. No. 8 intake—No. 4 exhaust

5. Rotate the engine 360 degrees (1 revolution) from the 1st position and check the following valves:

   a. No. 5 intake—No. 2 exhaust

   b. No. 4 intake—No. 6 exhaust

6. Rotate the engine 90 degrees (¼ revolution) from the 2nd position and check the following valves:

   a. No. 2 intake—No. 7 exhaust

   b. No. 3 intake—No. 3 exhaust

   c. No. 6 intake—No. 8 exhaust

5.8L Engine

The valve lash is not adjustable. If the collapsed lifter clearance is found to be incorrect, there are replacement pushrods available to compensate for excessive or insufficient clearance.

1. Install an auxiliary starter

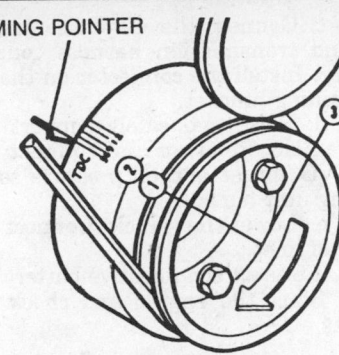

TIMING POINTER

POSITION 1—NO. 1 AT TDC ON COMPRESSION STROKE
POSITION 2—ROTATE THE CRANKSHAFT 360 DEGREES (1 REVOLUTION) CLOCKWISE FROM POSITION 1
POSITION 3—ROTATE THE CRANKSHAFT 90 DEGREES (¼ REVOLUTION) CLOCKWISE FROM POSITION 2

Engine valve adjusting positions—5.0L and 5.8L engines

switch. Crank the engine with the ignition switch off until the No. 1 piston is at TDC on the compression stroke.

2. With the crankshaft in the positions designated in Steps 4, 5 and 6, position lifter bleed down wrench tool T71P-6513-B or equivalent, on the rocker arm. Slowly apply pressure to bleed down the lifter until the plunger is completely bottomed. Hold the lifter in this position and check the available clearance between the rocker arm and the valve stem tip with a feeler gauge.

3. The clearance should be 0.092–0.192 in. If the clearance is less than specification, install a shorter pushrod. If the clearance is greater than specification, install a longer pushrod.

4. The following valves can be checked with the engine in position 1, No. 1 piston at TDC on the compression stroke.

   a. No. 1 intake—No. 1 exhaust

   b. No. 4 intake—No. 3 exhaust

   c. No. 8 intake—No. 7 exhaust

5. Rotate the engine 360 degrees (1 revolution) from the 1st position and check the following valves:

   a. No. 3 intake—No. 2 exhaust

   b. No. 7 intake—No. 6 exhaust

6. Rotate the engine 90 degrees (¼ revolution) from the 2nd position and check the following valves:

   a. No. 2 intake—No. 4 exhaust

   b. No. 5 intake—No. 5 exhaust

   c. No. 6 intake—No. 8 exhaust

Rocker Arms

REMOVAL & INSTALLATION

4.6L Engine

1. Disconnect the negative battery cable.

2. Remove the right camshaft cover as follows:

   a. Disconnect the positive battery cable at the battery and at the power distribution box. Remove the retaining bolt from the positive battery cable bracket located on the side of the right cylinder head.

   b. Disconnect the High Data Rate (HDR) sensor, air conditioning compressor clutch and canister purge solenoid connectors. Position the harness out of the way.

   c. Disconnect the vent hose from the purge solenoid and position the positive battery cable out of the way.

   d. Disconnect the ignition wires from the spark plugs. Remove the ignition wire brackets from the camshaft cover studs and position the wires out of the way.

   e. Remove the PCV valve from the camshaft cover grommet and position out of the way.

   f. Remove the bolts and stud bolts and remove the camshaft cover.

3. Remove the left camshaft cover as follows:

   a. Remove the air inlet tube. Relieve the fuel system pressure and disconnect the fuel lines.

   b. Raise and safely support the vehicle.

   c. Disconnect the EVO sensor and oil pressure sending unit and position the harness out of the way. Lower the vehicle.

   d. Remove the 42-pin engine harness connector from the retaining bracket on the brake vacuum booster. Disconnect and position out of the way.

   e. Remove the windshield wiper module.

   f. Disconnect the ignition wires from the spark plugs. Remove the ignition wire brackets from the studs and position the wires out of the way.

   g. Remove the bolts and stud bolts and remove the camshaft cover.

4. Position the piston of the cylinder being serviced at the bottom of its stroke and position the camshaft lobe on the base circle.

5. Install valve spring spacer tool T91P-6565-AH or equivalent, between the spring coils to prevent valve seal damage.

NOTE: If the valve spring spacer tool is not used, the retainer will hit the valve stem seal and damage the seal.

6. Install valve spring compressor tool T91P-6565-A or equivalent, under the camshaft and on top of the valve spring retainer.

7. Compress the valve spring and remove the roller follower. Remove

the valve spring compressor and spacer.

To install:

8. Apply engine oil to the valve stem and tip and roller follower contact surfaces.

9. Install valve spring spacer tool T91P–6565–AH or equivalent, between the spring coils. Compress the valve spring using valve spring compressor tool T91P–6565–A or equivalent, and install the roller follower.

NOTE: The piston must be at the bottom of its stroke and the camshaft at the base circle.

10. Remove the valve spring compressor and spacer.

11. Clean the sealing surfaces of the camshaft covers and cylinder heads. Apply silicone sealer to the places where the front cover meets the cylinder head.

12. Position new gaskets onto the camshaft covers and install the covers. Install the bolts and stud bolts and tighten to 6.0–8.8 ft. lbs. (8–12 Nm).

13. When installing the right camshaft cover, proceed as follows:

a. Install the PCV into the camshaft cover grommet.

b. Install the ignition wire brackets on the studs and connect the wires to the spark plugs.

c. Position the harness and connect the canister purge solenoid, air conditioning compressor clutch and HDR sensor.

d. Position the positive battery cable harness on the right cylinder head. Install the bolt retaining the cable bracket to the cylinder head.

e. Connect the positive battery cable at the power distribution box and the battery.

14. When installing the left camshaft cover, proceed as follows:

a. Install the ignition wire brackets on the studs and connect the wires to the spark plugs.

b. Install the windshield wiper module.

Camshaft follower removal—4.6L Engine

c. Connect the 42-pin connector and transmission harness connector. Install the connector on the retaining bracket.

d. Raise and safely support the vehicle. Position and connect the EVO sensor and oil pressure sending unit harness.

e. Lower the vehicle. Connect the fuel lines.

15. Connect the negative battery cable. Start the engine and check for leaks.

5.0L Engine

1. Disconnect the negative battery cable.

2. Before removing the right rocker arm cover, disconnect the PCV closure tube from the oil fill stand pipe at the rocker cover.

3. Remove the thermactor bypass valve and air supply hoses as necessary to provide clearance.

4. Disconnect the spark plug wires from the spark plugs. Remove the wires and bracket assembly from the rocker arm cover attaching stud and position the wires out of the way.

5. Remove the upper intake manifold as follows:

a. Tag and disconnect the electrical connectors at the air bypass valve, throttle position sensor and EGR position sensor.

b. Disconnect the throttle and transmission linkage at the throttle body. Remove the cable bracket from the intake manifold and position the bracket and cables aside.

c. Tag and disconnect the vacuum lines from the vacuum tree, EGR valve, fuel pressure regulator and evaporative canister.

d. Disconnect the PCV hose from the fitting on the rear of the upper manifold and disconnect the PCV vent closure tube at the throttle body.

e. Remove the 2 EGR coolant lines from the EGR spacer.

f. Remove the 6 retaining bolts and remove the upper intake manifold.

6. Remove the attaching bolts and remove the rocker arm covers.

7. Remove the rocker arm fulcrum bolt, fulcrum seat and rocker arm. Keep all rocker arm assemblies together. Identify each assembly so it may be reinstalled in its original position.

To install:

8. Clean all gasket mating surfaces of the rocker arm covers and cylinder heads. Clean and inspect the rocker arm assemblies for wear and/or damage. Replace as necessary.

9. Apply grease to the pushrod and valve stem tips and the underside of the fulcrum seats.

10. Rotate the crankshaft until the lifter is on the camshaft base circle and install the rocker, fulcrum seat and fulcrum bolt. Tighten the bolts to 18–25 ft. lbs. (24–34 Nm).

11. Position new rocker arm cover gaskets and install the rocker arm covers. Tighten the bolts to 10–13 ft. lbs. (14–18 Nm), wait 2 minutes and tighten again to the same specification.

12. Install the crankcase ventilation tube in the right cover. Install the upper intake manifold in the reverse order of removal.

13. Install the spark plug wires and bracket assembly on the rocker cover attaching stud. Connect the spark plug wires.

14. Install the air cleaner and intake duct assembly. Install the thermactor bypass valve and air supply hoses, if required.

15. Connect the negative battery cable, start the engine and check for leaks.

5.8L Engine

1. Disconnect the negative battery cable.

2. Before removing the right rocker arm cover, remove the air cleaner assembly. Disconnect the automatic choke heat chamber air inlet hose from the inlet tube near the right rocker arm cover, if equipped.

3. Remove the crankcase ventilation fresh air tube from the rocker arm cover.

4. Remove the thermactor bypass valve and air supply hoses as necessary to provide clearance.

5. Disconnect the spark plug wires from the spark plugs. Remove the wires and bracket assembly from the rocker arm cover attaching stud and position the wires out of the way.

6. On the left side rocker arm cover, remove the wire harness from the retaining clips. Disconnect the wires at the solenoid mounted on the left rocker cover.

7. Remove the rocker arm cover attaching bolts and remove the rocker arm cover. Remove the rocker arm fulcrum bolt, fulcrum seat and rocker arm. Keep all rocker arm assemblies together. Identify each assembly so it may be reinstalled in its original position.

To install:

8. Clean all gasket mating surfaces of the rocker arm covers and cylinder heads. Clean and inspect the rocker arm assemblies for wear and/or damage. Replace as necessary.

9. Apply grease to the pushrod and valve stem tips and the underside of the fulcrum seats.

10. Rotate the crankshaft until the lifter is on the camshaft base circle and install the rocker, fulcrum seat and

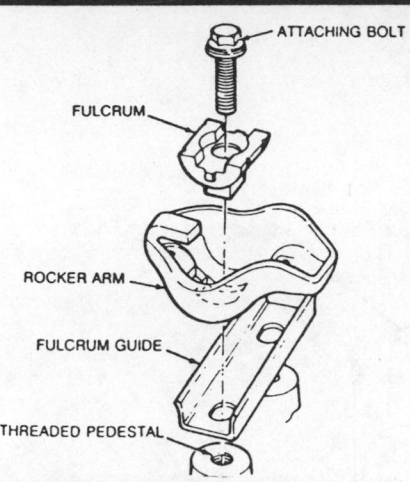

Rocker arm assembly—5.0L and 5.8L engines

fulcrum bolt. Tighten the bolts to 18–25 ft. lbs. (24–34 Nm).

11. Position new rocker arm cover gaskets and install the rocker arm covers. Tighten the bolts to 3–5 ft. lbs. (4–7 Nm) on 1989–90 vehicles or 10–13 ft. lbs. (14–18 Nm) on 1991 vehicles, wait 2 minutes and tighten again to the same specification.

12. Install the crankcase ventilation hoses on the rocker arm covers.

13. Install the spark plug wires and bracket assembly on the rocker arm cover attaching stud. Connect the spark plug wires.

14. Install the air cleaner, the thermactor bypass valve and air supply hoses.

15. Connect the negative battery cable, start the engine and check for leaks.

Intake Manifold

REMOVAL & INSTALLATION

4.6L Engine

1. Disconnect the negative battery cable.

2. Drain the cooling system. Relieve the fuel system pressure and disconnect the fuel lines.

3. Remove the wiper module and the air inlet tube. Release the belt tensioner and remove the accessory drive belt.

4. Tag and disconnect the ignition wires from the spark plugs. Disconnect the ignition wire brackets from the camshaft cover studs.

5. Disconnect both ignition coils and CID sensor. Tag and disconnect all ignition wires from both ignition coils. Remove the 2 bolts retaining the ignition wire tray to the coil brackets and remove the ignition wire assembly.

6. Disconnect the alternator wiring harness from the junction block at the fender apron and alternator. Remove

the bolts retaining the alternator brace to the intake manifold and the alternator to the engine block and remove the alternator.

7. Raise and safely support the vehicle. Disconnect the oil sending unit and EVO harness sensor and position the wiring harness out of the way.

8. Disconnect the EGR tube from the right exhaust manifold and lower the vehicle.

9. Remove the 42-pin engine harness connector from the retaining bracket on the vacuum brake booster and disconnect the connector.

10. Disconnect the air conditioning compressor, HDR sensor and canister purge solenoid.

11. Remove the PCV valve from the camshaft cover and disconnect the canister purge vent hose from the PCV valve.

12. Disconnect the accelerator and cruise control cables from the throttle body. Remove the accelerator cable bracket from the intake manifold and position out of the way.

13. Disconnect the throttle valve cable from the throttle body and the vacuum hose from the throttle body adapter port.

14. Disconnect both oxygens sensors and the heater supply hose.

15. Remove the 2 bolts retaining the thermostat housing to the intake manifold and position the upper hose and thermostat housing out of the way.

NOTE: The 2 thermostat housing bolts also retain the intake manifold.

16. Remove the bolts retaining the intake manifold to the cylinder heads and remove the intake manifold. Remove and discard the gaskets.

To install:

17. Clean all gasket mating surfaces. Position new intake manifold gaskets on the cylinder heads. Make sure the alignment tabs on the gaskets are aligned with the holes in the cylinder heads.

18. Install the intake manifold and the retaining bolts. Tighten the bolts, in sequence, to 15–22 ft. lbs. (20–30 Nm).

19. Inspect and if necessary, replace the O-ring seal on the thermostat housing. Position the housing and upper hose and install the 2 bolts. Tighten to 15–22 ft. lbs. (20–30 Nm).

20. Connect the heater supply hose and connect both oxygens sensors.

21. Connect the vacuum hose to the throttle body adapter vacuum port. Connect and, if necessary, adjust the throttle valve cable.

22. Install the accelerator cable bracket on the intake manifold and connect the accelerator and cruise control cables to the throttle body.

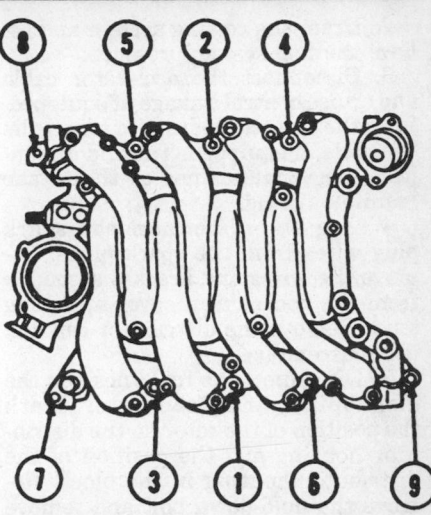

Intake manifold bolt torque sequence— 4.6L Engine

23. Install the PCV valve in the camshaft cover and connect the canister purge solenoid vent hose. Connect the air conditioning compressor, HDR sensor and canister purge solenoid.

24. Connect the 42-pin engine harness connector. Install the connector on the retaining bracket on the vacuum brake booster.

25. Raise and safely support the vehicle. Connect the EGR tube to the right exhaust manifold and tighten the line nut to 26–33 ft. lbs. (35–45 Nm).

26. Connect the EVO sensor and oil sending unit. Lower the vehicle.

27. Position the alternator and install the retaining bolts. Tighten to 15–22 ft. lbs. (20–30 Nm). Install the 2 bolts retaining the alternator brace to the intake manifold and tighten to 6.0–8.8 ft. lbs. (8–12 Nm).

28. Connect the alternator wiring harness to the alternator, right-hand fender apron and junction block.

29. Position the ignition wire assembly on the engine and install the 2 bolts retaining the ignition wire tray to the coil brackets. Tighten the bolts to 6.0–8.8 ft. lbs. (8–12 Nm).

30. Connect the ignition wires to the ignition coils in their proper positions. Connect the ignition wires to the spark plugs.

31. Connect the ignition wire brackets on the camshaft cover studs. Connect both ignition coils and CID sensor.

32. Install the accessory drive belt and the air inlet tube. Install the wiper module and connect the fuel lines.

33. Fill and bleed the cooling system. Connect the negative battery cable, start the engine and check for leaks.

5.0L Engine

1. Disconnect the negative battery cable.

2. Drain the cooling system and relieve the fuel system pressure.

3. Disconnect the acclerator cable and cruise control linkage, if equipped, from the throttle body. Disconnect the TV cable, if equipped. Tag and disconnect the vacuum lines at the intake manifold fitting.

4. Tag and disconnect the spark plug wires from the spark plugs. Remove the wires and bracket assembly from the rocker arm cover attaching stud. Remove the distributor cap and wires assembly.

5. Disconnect the fuel lines and the distributor wiring connector. Mark the position of the rotor on the distributor housing and the position of the distributor housing in the block. Remove the hold-down bolt and remove the distributor.

6. Disconnect the upper radiator hose at the thermostat housing and the water temperature sending unit wire at the sending unit. Disconnect the heater hose from the intake manifold and disconnect the 2 throttle body cooler hoses.

7. Disconnect the water pump bypass hose from the thermostat housing. Tag and disconnect the connectors from the engine coolant temperature, air charge temperature, throttle position and EGR sensors and the idle speed control solenoid. Disconnect the injector wire connections and the fuel charging assembly wiring.

8. Remove the PCV valve from the grommet at the rear of the lower intake manifold. Disconnect the fuel evaporative purge hose from the plastic connector at the front of the upper intake manifold.

9. Remove the upper intake manifold cover plate and upper intake bolts. Remove the upper intake manifold.

10. Remove the heater tube assembly from the lower intake manifold studs. Remove the alternator and air conditioner braces from the intake studs. Disconnect the heater hose from the lower intake manifold.

11. Remove the lower intake manifold retaining bolts and remove the lower intake manifold.

Upper Intake manifold Installation—5.0L Engine

NOTE: If it is necessary to pry the intake manifold away from the cylinder heads, be careful to avoid damaging the gasket sealing surfaces.

To install:

12. Clean all gasket mating surfaces. Apply a 1/8 in. bead of silicone sealer to the points where the cylinder block rails meet the cylinder heads.

13. Position new seals on the cylinder block and new gaskets on the cylinder heads with the gaskets interlocked with the seal tabs. Make sure the holes in the gaskets are aligned with the holes in the cylinder heads.

14. Apply a 1/16 in. bead of sealer to the outer end of each intake manifold seal for the full width of the seal.

15. Using guide pins to ease installation, carefully lower the intake manifold into position on the cylinder block and cylinder heads.

NOTE: After the intake manifold is in place, run a finger around the seal area to make sure the seals are in place. If the seals are not in place, remove the intake manifold and position the seals.

16. Make sure the holes in the manifold gaskets and the manifold are in alignment. Remove the guide pins. Install the intake manifold attaching bolts and tighten, in sequence, to 23–25 ft. lbs. (31–34 Nm).

17. If required, install the heater tube assembly to the lower intake manifold studs.

18. Install the water pump bypass hose and upper radiator hose on the thermostat housing. Install the hoses to the heater tubes and intake manifold. Connect the fuel lines.

19. Install the distributor, aligning the housing and rotor with the marks that were made during removal. Install the distributor cap. Position the spark plug wires in the harness brackets on the rocker arm cover attaching stud and connect the wires to the spark plugs.

20. Install a new gasket and the upper intake manifold. Tighten the bolts to 12–18 ft. lbs. (16–24 Nm). Install

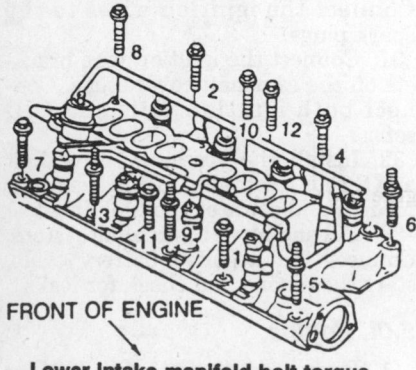

Lower Intake manifold bolt torque sequence—5.0L Engine

the cover plate and connect the crank-case vent tube.

21. Connect the accelerator, TV cable and cruise control cable, if equipped, to the throttle body. Connect the electrical connectors and vacuum lines.

22. Connect the coolant hoses to the EGR spacer. Fill and bleed the cooling system.

23. Connect the negative battery cable, start the engine and check for leaks. Check the ignition timing.

24. Operate the engine at fast idle. When engine temperatures have stabilized, tighten the intake manifold bolts to 23–25 ft. lbs. (31–34 Nm).

25. Connect the air intake duct and the crankcase vent hose.

5.8L Engine

1. Disconnect the negative battery cable and drain the cooling system.

2. Remove the air cleaner, crankcase ventilation hose and intake duct assembly. If equipped, disconnect the automatic choke heat tube.

3. Disconnect the accelerator cable and cruise control linkage, if equipped, from the carburetor. Disconnect the TV rod, if equipped, and remove the accelerator cable bracket.

4. Tag and disconnect the vacuum lines at the intake manifold and the wires from the coil.

5. Tag and disconnect the spark plug wires from the spark plugs. Remove the wires and bracket assembly from the rocker arm cover attaching stud. Remove the distributor cap and spark plug wires assembly.

6. Remove the carburetor fuel inlet line.

7. Disconnect the vacuum hoses and the wiring connector from the distributor. Mark the position of the rotor on the distributor housing and the position of the distributor housing in the block. Remove the hold-down bolt and remove the distributor.

8. Disconnect the upper radiator hose at the thermostat housing and the water temperature sending unit wire at the sending unit. Disconnect the heater hose from the intake manifold. Disconnect the EGR cooler T-fitting from the heater return hose, if equipped.

9. Disconnect the water pump bypass hose at the thermostat housing. Disconnect the crankcase vent hose at the rocker arm cover. Disconnect the fuel evaporative purge tube, if equipped.

10. Remove the intake manifold and carburetor as an assembly.

NOTE: If it is necessary to pry the intake manifold away from the cylinder heads, be careful to avoid damaging the gasket sealing surfaces.

To install:

11. Clean all gasket mating surfaces. Apply a ⅛ in. bead of silicone sealer to the points where the cylinder block rails meet the cylinder heads.

12. Position new seals on the cylinder block and new gaskets on the cylinder heads with the gaskets interlocked with the seal tabs. Make sure the holes in the gaskets are aligned with the holes in the cylinder heads.

13. Apply a $^1/_{16}$ in. bead of sealer to the outer end of each intake manifold seal for the full width of the seal.

14. Using guide pins to ease installation, carefully lower the intake manifold into position on the cylinder block and cylinder heads.

NOTE: After the intake manifold is in place, run a finger around the seal area to make sure the seals are in place. If the seals are not in place, remove the intake manifold and position the seals.

15. Make sure the holes in the manifold gaskets and the manifold are in alignment. Remove the guide pins. Install the intake manifold attaching bolts and tighten, in sequence, to 23–25 ft. lbs. (31–34 Nm).

16. Install the water pump bypass hose on the thermostat housing. Connect the upper radiator hose and the heater hose. Install the carburetor fuel line.

17. Install the distributor, aligning the distributor housing and rotor with the marks that were made during removal. Install the distributor cap. Position the spark plug wires in the harness brackets on the rocker arm cover attaching stud and connect the wires to the spark plugs.

18. Connect the crankcase vent tube. Connect the coil wire and primary wiring connector.

19. Connect the accelerator cable and cable bracket. Connect the TV rod and the cruise control, if equipped.

20. Connect all electrical connections and vacuum lines disconnected during removal. Fill and bleed the cooling system.

21. Connect the negative battery cable, start the engine and check for leaks. Adjust the ignition timing and connect the vacuum hoses to the distributor.

22. Operate the engine at fast idle. When engine temperatures have stabilized, tighten the intake manifold bolts to 23–25 ft. lbs. (31–34 Nm).

23. Connect the air cleaner and intake duct assembly and the crankcase vent hose.

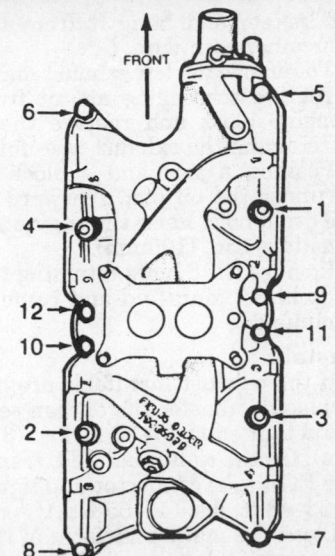

Intake manifold bolt torque sequence—5.8L Engine

Exhaust Manifold

REMOVAL & INSTALLATION

4.6L Engine

1. Disconnect the battery cables. Remove the air inlet tube.

2. Drain the cooling system and remove the cooling fan and shroud. Relieve the fuel system pressure and disconnect the fuel lines.

3. Remove the upper radiator hose. Remove the wiper module and support bracket.

4. Discharge the air conditioning system. Disconnect and plug the compressor outlet hose at the compressor and remove the bolt retaining the hose assembly to the right coil bracket. Cap the compressor opening.

5. Remove the 42-pin engine harness connector from the retaining bracket on the brake vacuum booster. Disconnect the connector.

6. Disconnect the throttle valve cable from the throttle body. Disconnect the heater outlet hose.

7. Remove the nut retaining the ground strap to the right cylinder head. Remove the upper stud and lower bolt retaining the heater outlet hose to the right cylinder head and position out of the way.

8. Remove the blower motor resistor and remove the bolt retaining the right engine insulator to the lower engine bracket. Disconnect both oxygen sensors.

9. Raise and safely support the vehicle. Remove the engine mount through bolts.

10. Remove the EGR tube line nut from the right exhaust manifold.

11. Disconnect the exhaust pipes from the manifolds. Lower the ex-

haust system and hang it from the crossmember with wire.

12. To remove the left exhaust manifold, remove the engine mount from the engine block and remove the 8 bolts retaining the exhaust manifold.

13. Position a jack and a block of wood under the oil pan, rearward of the oil drain hole. Raise the engine approximately 4 in. (100mm).

14. Remove the 8 bolts retaining the right exhaust manifold and remove the manifold.

To install:

15. If the exhaust manifolds are being replaced, transfer the oxygen sensors and tighten to 27–33 ft. lbs. (37–45 Nm). On the right manifold, transfer the EGR tube connector and tighten to 33–48 ft. lbs. (45–65 Nm).

16. Clean the mating surfaces of the exhaust manifolds and cylinder heads.

17. Position the exhaust manifolds to the cylinder heads and install the retaining bolts. Tighten, in sequence, to 15–22 ft. lbs. (20–30 Nm).

18. Position and connect the EGR valve and tube assembly to the exhaust manifold. Tighten the line nut to 26–33 ft. lbs. (35–45 Nm).

19. Install the left engine mount and tighten the bolts to 15–22 ft. lbs. (20–30 Nm). Lower the engine onto the mounts and remove the jack. Install the engine mount through bolts and tighten to 15–22 ft. lbs. (20–30 Nm).

20. Cut the wire and position the exhaust system. Tighten the nuts to 20–30 ft. lbs. (27–41 Nm).

NOTE: Make sure the exhaust system clears the No. 3 crossmember. Adjust as necessary.

21. Lower the vehicle. Connect both oxygen sensors and install the bolt retaining the right engine mount to the frame. Tighten to 15–22 ft. lbs. (20–30 Nm).

22. Install the blower motor resistor. Position the heater outlet hoses. Install the upper stud and lower bolt and tighten to 15–22 ft. lbs. (20–30 Nm). Install the ground strap onto the stud and tighten the nut to 15–22 ft. lbs. (20–30 Nm).

23. Connect the heater outlet hose. Connect and if necessary, adjust the throttle valve cable.

24. Connect the 42-pin connector and transmission harness connector. Install the connector to the retaining bracket on the brake vacuum booster.

25. Connect the air conditioning compressor outlet hose to the compressor and install the bolt retaining the hose assembly to the right coil bracket.

26. Install the upper radiator hose and connect the fuel lines. Install the wiper module and retaining bracket.

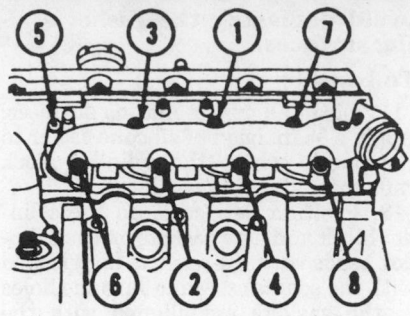

NOTE: ENGINE REMOVED FOR CLARITY
NOTE: LEFT EXHAUST MANIFOLD SHOWN, RIGHT EXHAUST MANIFOLD TYPICAL

Exhaust manifold bolt torque sequence— 4.6L Engine

27. Install the cooling fan and shroud. Install the air inlet tube. Connect the battery cables, start the engine and check for leaks.

28. Leak test, evacuate and charge the air conditioning system according to the proper procedure. Observe all safety precautions.

5.0L and 5.8L Engines

1. Disconnect the negative battery cable.

2. Remove the thermactor hardware from the right exhaust manifold. Remove the air cleaner and inlet duct, if necessary.

3. Tag and disconnect the spark plug wires. Remove the spark plugs.

4. Disconnect the engine oil dipstick tube from the exhaust manifold stud.

5. Raise and safely support the vehicle. Disconnect the exhaust pipes from the exhaust manifolds.

6. Remove the engine oil dipstick tube by carefully tapping upward on the tube. Disconnect the oxygen sensor connector.

7. Lower the vehicle.

8. Remove the attaching bolts and washers and remove the exhaust manifolds.

9. Installation is the reverse of the removal procedure. Working from the center to the ends, tighten the exhaust manifold attaching bolts to 18–24 ft. lbs. (24–32 Nm).

Timing Chain Front Cover

REMOVAL & INSTALLATION

4.6L Engine

1. Disconnect the negative battery cable.

2. Remove the cooling fan and shroud. Loosen the water pump pulley bolts, remove the accessory drive belt and remove the water pump pulley.

3. Raise and safely support the vehicle.

4. Remove the bolts retaining the power steering pump to the engine block and cylinder front cover. The lower front bolt on the power steering pump will not come all the way out. Wire the power steering pump out of the way.

5. Remove the 4 bolts retaining the oil pan to the front cover. Remove the crankshaft damper retaining bolt and washer. Remove the damper using a puller.

6. Lower the vehicle. Remove the bolt retaining the air conditioner high pressure line to the right coil bracket.

7. Remove the front bolts and loosen the remaining bolts on the camshaft covers. Using plastic wedges or similar tools, prop up both camshaft covers. Disconnect both ignition coils and CID sensor.

8. Remove the 3 nuts retaining the right coil bracket to the front cover. Position the power steering hose out of the way.

9. Remove the 4 nuts retaining the left coil bracket to the front cover. Slide both coil brackets and ignition wires off the mounting studs and lay the assembly on top of the engine.

10. Disconnect the High Data Rate (HDR) sensor. Remove the 7 stud bolts and 4 bolts retaining the front cover to the engine and remove the front cover.

To install:

11. Inspect and replace the front cover seal as necessary and clean the sealing surfaces of the cylinder block. Apply silicone sealer to the oil pan where it meets the cylinder block and to the points where the cylinder head meets the cylinder block.

12. Install the front cover and the attachings studs and bolts. Tighten to 15–22 ft. lbs. (20–30 Nm). Connect the HDR sensor.

13. Position the coil brackets and ignition wires as an assembly onto the mounting studs. Position the power steering hose and install the 7 nuts retaining the coil brackets to the front cover. Tighten the nuts to 15–22 ft. lbs. (20–30 Nm). Connect both ignition coils and CID sensor.

14. Remove the plastic wedges holding up the camshaft covers. Apply silicone sealer where the front cover meets the cylinder head and make sure the camshaft cover gaskets are properly positioned. Install the front retaining bolts into the camshaft cover and tighten the bolts to 6.0–8.8 ft. lbs. (8–12 Nm).

15. Position the air conditioner high pressure line on the right coil bracket and install the bolt. Raise and safely support the vehicle.

16. Apply a small amount of silicone sealer in the rear of the keyway in the

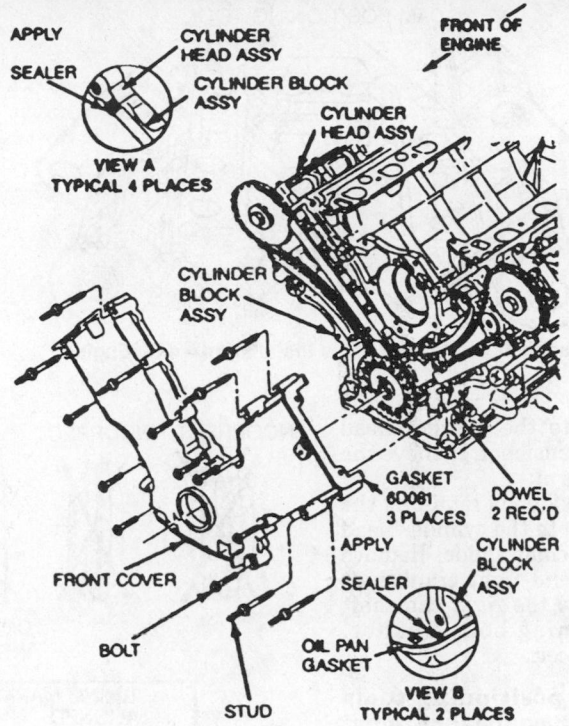

Timing chain front cover installation—4.6L Engine

damper. Position the damper on the crankshaft and install, using a suitable installation tool. Install the damper bolt and washer and tighten to 114–121 ft. lbs. (155–165 Nm).

17. Install the 4 bolts retaining the oil pan to the front cover. Tighten to 15–22 ft. lbs. (20–30 Nm).

18. Position the power steering pump on the engine and install the 4 retaining bolts. Tighten to 15–22 ft. lbs. (20–30 Nm). Lower the vehicle.

19. Install the water pump pulley with the 4 bolts. Tighten to 15–22 ft. lbs. (20–30 Nm). Install the accessory drive belt and the cooling fan and shroud.

20. Connect the negative battery cable, start the engine and check for leaks.

5.0L and 5.8L Engines

1. Disconnect the negative battery cable.

2. Drain the cooling system. Remove the air inlet tube.

3. Remove the fan shroud attaching bolts and position the shroud over the fan. Remove the fan and clutch assembly from the water pump shaft and remove the shroud.

4. Remove the air conditioner drive belt and idler pulley bracket. Remove the alternator and power steering drive belts. Remove the power steering pump and position aside, leaving the hoses attached. Remove all accessory brackets that attach to the water pump.

5. Remove the water pump pulley. Disconnect the lower radiator hose, heater hose and water pump bypass hose at the water pump.

6. Remove the crankshaft pulley from the crankshaft vibration damper. Remove the damper attaching bolt and washer and remove the damper using a puller.

7. On 5.8L engines, disconnect the fuel pump outlet line from the fuel pump. Remove the fuel pump attaching bolts and lay the pump to 1 side with the flexible fuel line still attached.

8. Remove the fuel line from the clip on the front cover, if equipped.

9. Remove the oil pan-to-front cover attaching bolts. Use a thin blade knife to cut the oil pan gasket flush with the cylinder block face prior to separating the cover from the cylinder block.

10. Remove the cylinder front cover and water pump as an assembly.

NOTE: Cover the front oil pan opening while the cover assembly is off to prevent foreign material from entering the pan.

To install:

11. If a new front cover is to be installed, remove the water pump from the old front cover and install it on the new front cover.

12. Clean all gasket mating surfaces. Pry the old oil seal from the front cover and install a new 1, using a seal installer.

13. Coat the gasket surface of the oil

pan with sealer, cut and position the required sections of a new gasket on the oil pan and apply silicone sealer at the corners. Apply sealer to a new front cover gasket and install on the block.

14. Position the front cover on the cylinder block. Use care to avoid seal damage or gasket mislocation. It may be necessary to force the cover downward to slightly compress the pan gasket. Use front cover aligner tool T61P-6019–B or equivalent to assist the operation.

15. Coat the threads of the front cover attaching screws with pipe sealant and install. While pushing in on the alignment tool, tighten the oil pan to cover attaching screws to 9–11 ft. lbs. (12–15 Nm).

16. Tighten the front cover to cylinder block attaching bolts to 15–18 ft. lbs. (20–24 Nm). Remove the alignment tool.

17. Apply multi-purpose grease to the sealing surface of the vibration damper. Apply silicone sealer to the keyway of the vibration damper.

18. Line up the vibration damper keyway with the crankshaft key and install the damper using a suitable installation tool. Tighten the retaining bolt to 70–90 ft. lbs. (95–122 Nm). Install the crankshaft pulley.

19. On 5.8L engines, install the fuel pump with a new gasket. Connect the fuel pump outlet line.

20. Install the remaining components in the reverse order of their removal.

21. Fill the crankcase with the proper type and quantity of engine oil. Fill and bleed the cooling system.

22. Connect the negative battery cable, start the engine and check for leaks.

Front Cover Oil Seal

REPLACEMENT

4.6L Engine

1. Disconnect the negative battery cable.

2. Release the belt tensioner and remove the accessory drive belt.

3. Raise and safely support the vehicle.

4. Remove the crankshaft damper retaining bolt and washer. Remove the damper using a puller.

5. Using a small prybar, remove the front cover seal.

To install:

6. Lubricate the seal bore in the front cover and seal lip with clean engine oil. Install the seal, using a seal installer.

7. Apply a small amount of silicone sealer to the rear of the damper key-

way. Using a damper installer, install the crankshaft damper. Be sure the key on the crankshaft aligns with the keyway in the damper.

8. Install the crankshaft damper retaining bolt and washer and tighten to 114–121 ft. lbs. (155–165 Nm).

9. Lower the vehicle and install the accessory drive belt.

10. Connect the negative battery cable, start the engine and check for leaks.

5.0L and 5.8L Engines

1. Disconnect the negative battery cable.

2. Remove the fan shroud and position it back over the fan. Remove the fan/clutch assembly and shroud.

3. Remove the accessory drive belts.

4. Remove the crankshaft pulley from the damper and remove the damper retaining bolt. Remove the damper using a puller.

5. Remove the seal using a seal removal tool.

To install:

6. Lubricate the seal lip with clean engine oil and install using a seal installer.

7. Apply clean engine oil to the sealing surface of the vibration damper. Apply a small amount of silicones ealer to the damper keyway. Line up the crankshaft damper keyway with the crankshaft key and install the damper using a damper installation tool.

8. Install the damper retaining bolt and tighten to 70–90 ft. lbs. (95–122 Nm).

9. Install the remaining components in the reverse order of their removal.

Timing Chain and Sprockets

REMOVAL & INSTALLATION

4.6L Engine

NOTE: This is not a free wheeling engine. If it has "jumped time," there will be damage to the valves and/or pistons and will require the removal of the cylinder heads.

1. Disconnect the negative battery cable.

2. Remove the camshaft covers and the timing chain front cover.

3. Remove the High Data Rate (HDR) wheel.

4. Rotate the engine to set the No. 1 piston at TDC on the compression stroke.

5. Install cam positioning tools T91P–6256–A or equivalent, on the flats of the camshaft. This will prevent accidental rotation of the camshafts.

Camshaft positioning tools installation—4.6L Engine

6. Remove the 2 bolts retaining the right tensioner to the cylinder head and remove the tensioner. Remove the right tensioner arm.

7. Remove the 2 bolts retaining the right chain guide to the cylinder head and remove the chain guide. Remove the right chain and right crankshaft sprocket. Remove the right camshaft sprocket retaining bolt, washer, sprocket and spacer.

NOTE: Cam positioning tools T91P–6256–A or equivalent, must be installed on the camshaft to prevent the camshaft from rotating.

8. Remove the 2 bolts retaining the left tensioner to the cylinder head and remove the tensioner. Remove the left tensioner arm.

9. Remove the 2 bolts retaining the left chain guide to the cylinder head and remove the chain guide. Remove the left chain and left crankshaft sprocket. Remove the left camshaft sprocket retaining bolt, washer, sprocket and spacer.

NOTE: Cam positioning tools T91P–6256–A or equivalent, must be installed on the camshaft to prevent the camshaft from rotating.

10. Inspect the friction material on the tensioner arms and chain guides. If worn or damaged, remove and clean the oil pan and replace the oil pickup tube.

NOTE: At no time, when the timing chains are removed and the cylinder heads are installed, may the crankshaft and/or camshafts be rotated. Failure to follow these directions will result in valve and/or piston damage.

To install:

11. Make sure cam positioning tools T91P–6256–A or equivalent, are installed on the camshafts to prevent them from rotating.

12. Position the camshaft spacers and sprockets on the camshafts and install the washers and retaining

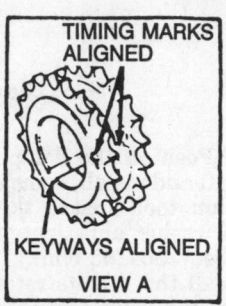

Crankshaft sprocket positioning—4.6L Engine

bolts. Tighten the retaining bolts to 81–95 ft. lbs. (110–130 Nm).

13. Install the left crankshaft sprocket with the tapered part of the sprocket facing away from the engine block.

NOTE: The crankshaft sprockets are identical. They may only be installed 1 way, with the tapered part of the sprocket facing each other.

14. Install the left timing chain on the camshaft and crankshaft sprockets. Make sure the copper links of the chain line up with the timing marks of the sprockets.

NOTE: If the copper links of the timing chain are not visible, pull the chain taught until the opposite sides of the chain contact 1 another and lay it on a flat surface. Mark the links at each end of the chain and use them in place of the copper links.

15. Install the right crankshaft sprocket with the tapered part of the sprocket facing the left crankshaft sprocket.

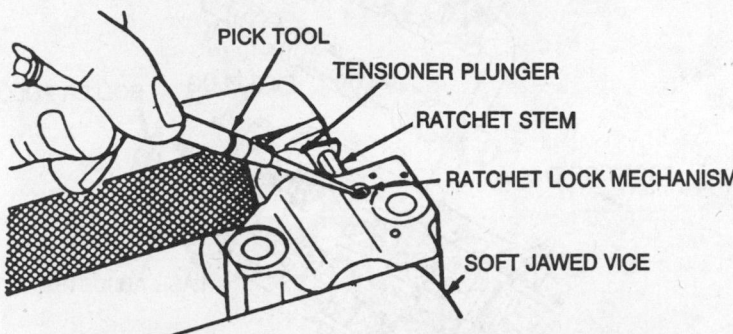

NOTE: WITH EITHER CHAIN POSITIONED
AS SHOWN, MARK EACH END and USE
THE MARKS AS TIMING MARKS

Alternate timing chain marking procedure—4.6L Engine

PICK TOOL

TENSIONER PLUNGER

RATCHET STEM

RATCHET LOCK MECHANISM

SOFT JAWED VICE

Timing chain tensioner bleeding procedure—4.6L Engine

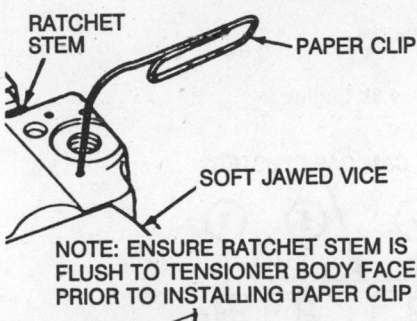

RATCHET
STEM

PAPER CLIP

SOFT JAWED VICE

NOTE: ENSURE RATCHET STEM IS
FLUSH TO TENSIONER BODY FACE
PRIOR TO INSTALLING PAPER CLIP

**Timing chain tensioner locking
procedure—4.6L Engine**

16. Install the right timing chain on the camshaft and crankshaft sprockets. Make sure the copper links of the chain line up with the timing marks of the sprockets.

17. It is necessary to bleed the timing chain tensioners before installation. Proceed as follows:

a. Position the timing chain tensioner in a soft-jawed vice.

b. Using a small pick or similar tool, hold the ratchet lock mechanism away from the ratchet stem and slowly compress the tensioner plunger by rotating the vise handle.

NOTE: The tensioner must be compressed slowly or damage to the internal seals will result.

c. Once the tensioner plunger bottoms in the tensioner bore, continue to hold the ratchet lock mechanism and push down on the ratchet stem until flush with the tensioner face.

d. While holding the ratchet stem flush to the tensioner face, release the ratchet lock mechanism and install a paper clip or similar tool in the tensioner body to lock the tensioner in the collapsed position.

e. The paper clip must not be removed until the timing chain, tensioner, tensioner arm and timing chain guide are completely installed on the engine.

18. Lubricate the tensioner arm contact surfaces with engine oil and install the right and left tensioner arms on their dowels.

19. Install the right and left timing chain tensioners and secure with 2 bolts on each. Tighten the bolts to 15–22 ft. lbs. (20–30 Nm).

20. Install the right and left timing chain guides and secure with 2 bolts on each. Tighten the bolts to 6.0–8.8 ft. lbs. (8–12 Nm).

21. Remove the paper clips from the timing chain tensioners and make sure all timing marks are aligned.

22. Remove the camshaft positioning tools.

23. Installation of the remaining components is the reverse of removal.

24. Connect the negative battery cable, start the engine and check for leaks and proper operation.

5.0L and 5.8L Engines

1. Disconnect the negative battery cable and drain the cooling system.

2. Remove the timing chain front cover.

3. Rotate the crankshaft until the timing marks on the sprockets are aligned.

4. Remove the camshaft retaining bolt, washer and eccentric. Slide both sprockets and the timing chain forward and remove them as an assembly.

To install:

5. Position the sprockets and timing chain on the camshaft and crankshaft simultaneously. Make sure the timing marks on the sprockets are aligned.

6. Install the washer, eccentric and camshaft sprocket retaining bolt. Tighten the bolt to 40–45 ft. lbs. (54–61 Nm).

7. Install the timing chain front cover and remaining components.

8. Fill and bleed the cooling system. Connect the negative battery cable, start the engine and check for leaks.

9. Check and adjust the ignition timing and idle speed, as necessary.

Camshaft

REMOVAL & INSTALLATION

4.6L Engine

1. Disconnect the negative battery cable and drain the cooling system. Relieve the fuel system pressure.

2. Remove the right and left camshaft covers.

3. Remove the timing chain front cover. Remove the timing chains.

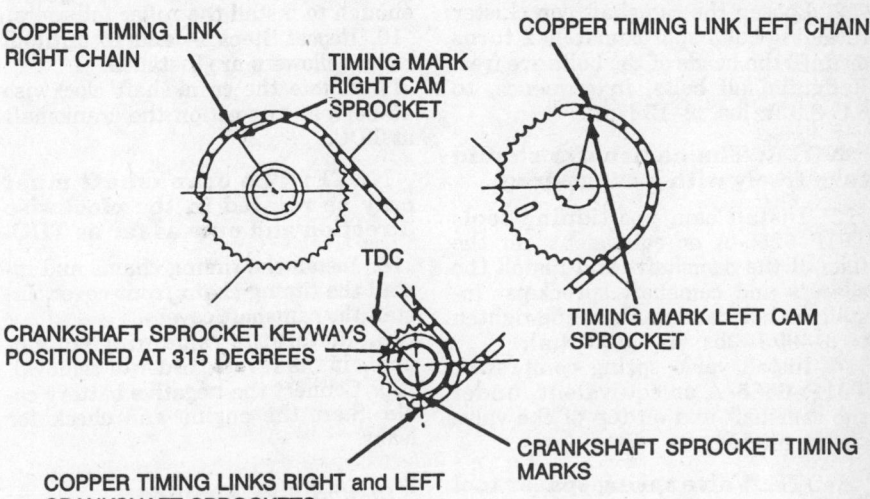

COPPER TIMING LINK
RIGHT CHAIN

TIMING MARK
RIGHT CAM
SPROCKET

COPPER TIMING LINK LEFT CHAIN

TIMING MARK LEFT CAM
SPROCKET

TDC

CRANKSHAFT SPROCKET KEYWAYS
POSITIONED AT 315 DEGREES

CRANKSHAFT SPROCKET TIMING
MARKS

COPPER TIMING LINKS RIGHT and LEFT
CRANKSHAFT SPROCKETS

Timing chain and sprockets alignment—4.6L Engine

4. Rotate the crankshaft counter-clockwise 45 degrees from TDC to make sure all pistons are below the top of the engine block deck face.

NOTE: The crankshaft must be in this position prior to rotating the camshafts or damage to the pistons and/or valve train will result.

5. Install valve spring compressor tool T91P–6565–A or equivalent, under the camshaft and on top of the valve spring retainer.

NOTE: Valve spring spacer tool T91P–6565–AH or equivalent, must be installed between the spring coils and the camshaft must be at the base circle before compressing the valve spring.

6. Compress the valve spring far enough to remove the roller follower. Repeat Steps 5 and 6 until all roller followers are removed.

7. Remove the bolts retaining the camshaft cap cluster assemblies to the cylinder heads. Tap upward on the camshaft caps at points near the upper bearing halves and gradually lift the camshaft clusters from the cylinder heads.

8. Remove the camshafts straight upward to avoid bearing damage.

To install:

9. Apply heavy engine oil to the camshaft journals and lobes. Position the camshafts on the cylinder heads.

10. Install and seat the camshaft cap cluster assemblies. Hand start the bolts.

11. Tighten the camshaft cluster retaining bolts in sequence to 6.0–8.8 ft. lbs. (8–12 Nm).

NOTE: Each camshaft cap cluster assembly is tightened individually.

12. Loosen the camshaft cap cluster retaining bolts approximately 2 turns or until the heads of the bolts are free. Retighten all bolts, in sequence, to 6.0–8.8 ft. lbs. (8–12 Nm).

NOTE: The camshafts should turn freely with a slight drag.

13. Install cam positioning tools T91P–6256–A or equivalent, on the flats of the camshafts and install the spacers and camshaft sprockets. Install the bolts and washers and tighten to 81–95 ft. lbs. (110–130 Nm).

14. Install valve spring compressor tool T91P–6565–A or equivalent, under the camshaft and on top of the valve spring retainer.

NOTE: Valve spring spacer tool T91P–6565–AH or equivalent, must be installed between the spring coils and the camshaft

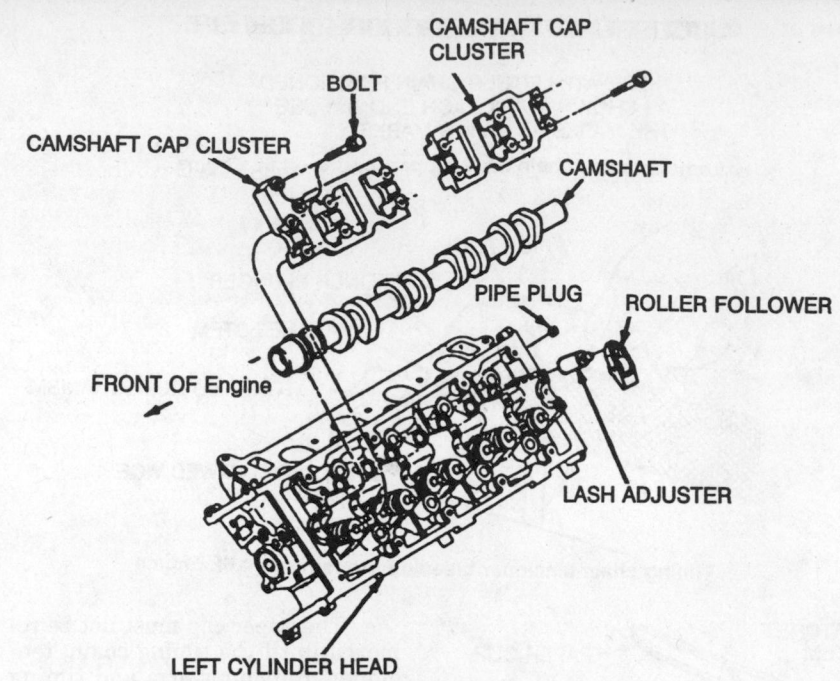

Camshaft Installation—4.6L Engine

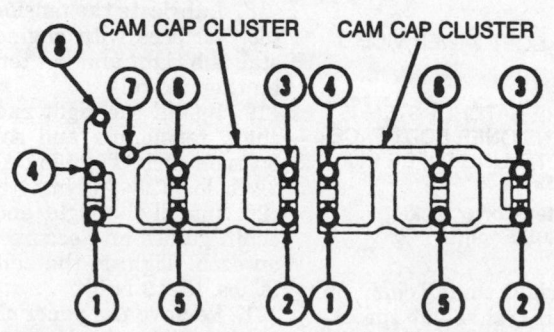

Camshaft cap cluster bolt torque sequence—4.6L Engine

must be at the base circle before compressing the valve spring.

15. Compress the valve spring far enough to install the roller followers.

16. Repeat Steps 14 and 15 until all roller followers are installed.

17. Rotate the crankshaft clockwise 45 degrees to position the crankshaft at TDC.

NOTE: The crankshaft must only be rotated in the clockwise direction and only as far as TDC.

18. Install the timing chains and install the timing chain front cover. Install the camshaft covers.

19. Install the remaining components in the reverse order of removal.

20. Connect the negative battery cable. Start the engine and check for leaks.

5.0L and 5.8L Engines

1. Disconnect the negative battery cable and drain the cooling system.

2. Relieve the fuel system pressure and discharge the air conditioning system.

3. Remove the radiator and air conditioner condenser.

4. Remove the grille.

5. Remove the intake manifold and the lifters.

6. Remove the timing chain front cover, the timing chain and camshaft sprocket.

7. Check the camshaft endplay as follows:

a. Position a dial indicator on the front of the engine, with the indicator foot resting on the end of the camshaft.

b. Push the camshaft toward the rear of the engine and set the indicator pointer to 0.

c. Pull the camshaft forward and release it. Check the dial indicator reading.

d. If endplay exceeds 0.009 in., replace the thrust plate.

e. Recheck the endplay with the

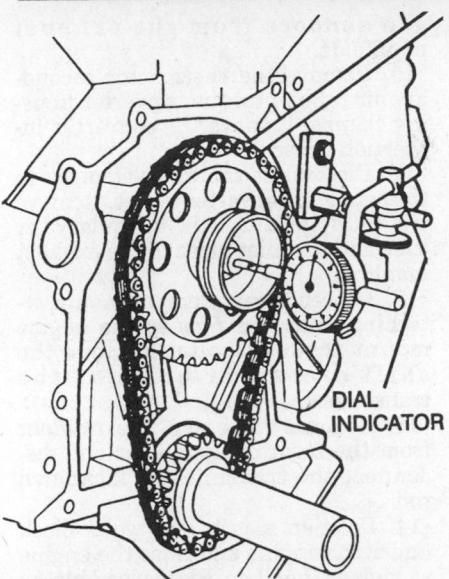

Checking camshaft endplay—5.0L and 5.8L engines

new thrust plate installed. If endplay is still excessive, check the camshaft and rear camshaft bore plug.

8. Remove the thrust plate. Remove the camshaft, being careful not to damage the bearing surfaces.

To install:

9. Lubricate the cam lobes and journals with heavy engine oil. Install the camshaft, being careful not to damage the bearing surfaces while sliding into position.

10. Install the thrust plate. Tighten the bolts to 9–12 ft. lbs. (12–16 Nm).

11. Install the timing chain and sprockets. Install the engine front cover.

12. Install the lifters and the intake manifolds.

13. Install the grille and the air conditioner condenser.

14. Install the radiator. Fill and bleed the cooling system.

15. Connect the negative battery cable. Start the engine and check for leaks.

16. Evacuate and recharge the air conditioning system.

Piston and Connecting Rod

POSITIONING

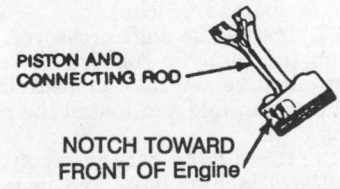

Piston and rod assembly—4.6L Engine

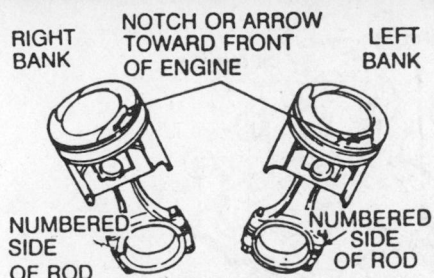

Piston and rod assembly—5.0L and 5.8L engines

ENGINE LUBRICATION

Oil Pan

REMOVAL & INSTALLATION

4.6L Engine

1. Disconnect the battery cables and remove the air inlet tube.

2. Drain the cooling system and remove the cooling fan and shroud. Releive the fuel system pressure and disconnect the fuel lines.

3. Remove the upper radiator hose. Remove the wiper module and support bracket.

4. Discharge the air conditioning system. Disconnect and plug the compressor outlet hose at the compressor and remove the bolt retaining the hose assembly to the right coil bracket. Cap the compressor outlet.

5. Remove the 42-pin engine harness connector from the retaining bracket on the brake vacuum booster and disconnect the connector and transmission harness connector.

6. Disconnect the throttle valve cable from the throttle body and disconnect the heater outlet hose.

7. Remove the nut retaining the ground strap to the right cylinder head. Remove the upper stud and loosen the lower bolt retaining the heater outlet hose to the right cylinder head and position out of the way.

8. Remove the blower motor resistor. Remove the bolt retaining the right engine mount to the lower engine bracket.

9. Disconnect the vacuum hoses from the EGR valve and tube. Remove the 2 bolts retaining the EGR valve to the intake manifold.

10. Raise and safely support the vehicle. Drain the crankcase and remove the engine mount through bolts.

11. Remove the EGR tube line nut from the right exhaust manifold and remove the EGR valve and tube assembly.

12. Disconnect the exhaust from the exhaust manifolds. Lower the exhaust system and support it with wire from the crossmember.

13. Position a jack and a block of wood under the oil pan, rearward of the oil drain hole. Raise the engine approximately 4 in. and insert 2 wood blocks approximately 2½ in. thick under each engine mount. Lower the engine onto the wood blocks and remove the jack.

14. Remove the 16 bolts retaining the oil pan to the engine block and remove the oil pan.

NOTE: It may be necessary to loosen, but not remove, the 2 nuts on the rear tranmission mount and with a jack, raise the transmission extension housing slightly to remove the pan.

To install:

15. Clean the oil pan and the gasket mating surfaces.

16. Position a new gasket on the oil pan. Apply silicone sealer to where the front cover meets the cylinder block and rear seal retainer meets the cylinder block. Position the oil pan on the engine and install the bolts. Tighten the bolts, in sequence, to 15–22 ft. lbs. (20–30 Nm).

17. Position the jack and wood block under the oil pan, rearward of the oil drain hole and raise the engine enough to remove the wood blocks. Lower the engine and remove the jack.

18. Install the engine mount through bolts and tighten to 15–22 ft. lbs. (20–30 Nm).

19. Position the EGR valve and tube assembly in the vehicle and connect to the exhaust manifold. Tighten the line nut to 26–33 ft. lbs. (35–45 Nm).

NOTE: Loosen the line nut at the EGR valve prior to installing the assembly into the vehicle. This will allow enough movement to align the EGR valve retaining bolts.

20. Cut the wire and position the exhaust system to the manifolds. Install the 4 nuts and tighten to 20–30 ft. lbs. (27–41 Nm). Make sure the exhaust system clears the crossmember. Adjust as necessary.

21. Install a new oil filter and lower the vehicle.

22. Install the bolt retaining the right engine mount to the lower engine bracket. Tighten to 15–22 ft. lbs. (20–30 Nm).

23. Install a new gasket on the EGR valve and position on the intake manifold. Install the 2 bolts retaining the EGR valve to the intake manifold and tighten to 15–22 ft. lbs. (20–30 Nm).

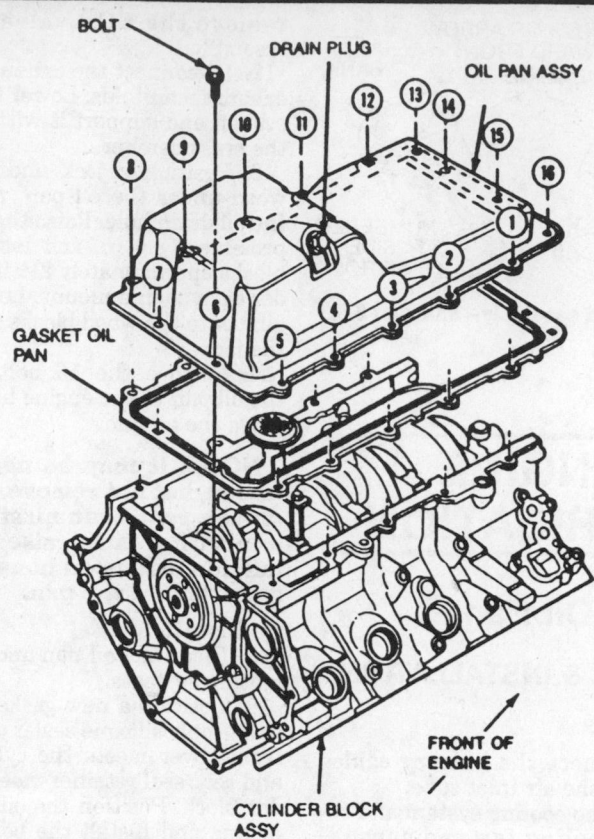

Oil pan bolt torque sequence—4.6L Engine

Tighten the EGR tube line nut at the EGR valve to 26–33 ft. lbs. (35–45 Nm). Connect the vacuum hoses to the EGR valve and tube.

24. Install the blower motor resistor. Position the heater outlet hose, install the upper stud and tighten the upper and lower bolts to 15–22 ft. lbs. (20–30 Nm). Install the gound strap on the stud and tighten to 15–22 ft. lbs. (20–30 Nm).

25. Connect the heater outlet hose and the throttle valve cable. If necessary, adjust the throttle valve cable.

26. Connect the 42-pin connector and tranmission harness connector. Install the harness connector on the brake vacuum booster.

27. Connect the air conditioning compressor outlet hose to the compressor and install the bolt retaining the hose to the right coil bracket.

28. Install the upper radiator hose and connect the fuel lines. Install the wiper module and retaining bracket.

29. Install the cooling fan and shroud and fill the cooling system. Fill the crankcase with the proper type and quantity of engine oil.

30. Connect the negative battery cable and install the air inlet tube. Start the engine and check for leaks.

31. Evacuate and recharge the air conditioning system.

5.0L and 5.8L Engines

1. Disconnect the negative battery cable. Relieve the fuel system pressure.

2. On 5.8L engine, remove the air cleaner assembly and air ducts.

3. Disconnect the accelerator and TV cables at the throttle body or carburetor. On 5.8L engine, remove the accelerator mounting bracket retaining bolts and remove the bracket.

4. Remove the fan shroud attaching bolts, positioning the fan shroud back over the fan. Remove the dipstick and tube assembly.

5. Disconnect the wiper motor electrical connector and remove the wiper motor. Disconnect the windshield washer hose and remove the wiper motor mounting cover.

6. Remove the thermactor air dump tube retaining clamp on 5.0L engine. Remove the thermactor crossover tube at the rear of the vehicle.

7. Raise and safely support the vehicle. Drain the crankcase. Remove the filler tube from the oil pan and drain the transmission.

8. Disconnect the starter cable and remove the starter. Disconnect the fuel line.

9. Disconnect the exhaust system from the manifolds. Remove the oxygen sensors from the exhaust manifolds.

10. Remove the thermactor secondary air tube to torque converter housing clamps. Remove the converter inspection cover.

11. Disconnect the exhaust pipes to the catalytic converter outlet. Remove the catalytic converter secondary air tube and the inlet pipes to the exhaust manifold.

12. Loosen the rear engine mount attaching nuts and remove the engine mount through bolts. Remove the shift crossover bolts at the transmission.

13. Remove the brake line retainer from the front crossmember and disconnect the transmission kickdown rod.

14. Position a jack and wood block under the engine and raise the engine as high as it will go. Place wood blocks between the engine mounts and the chassis brackets, lower the engine and remove the jack.

15. Remove the oil pan retaining bolts and lower the oil pan. Remove the 2 bolts retaining the oil pump pickup tube and screen to the oil pump and the nut from the main bearing cap stud. Allow the pickup tube to drop into the oil pan.

16. Rotate the crankshaft, as required, for clearance and remove the oil pan from the vehicle.

To install:

17. Clean the oil pan and the gasket mating surfaces. Clean the oil pump pickup tube and screen assembly.

18. Install a new oil filter. Position a new oil pan gasket on the cylinder block. Place the oil pickup tube and screen in the oil pan and position the oil pan on the crossmember.

19. Install the pickup tube and screen with a new gasket. Install the bolts and tighten to 12–18 ft. lbs. (16–24 Nm). Position the oil pan and install the retaining bolts. Tighten to 7–10 ft. lbs. (9–14 Nm).

20. Position the jack and wood block under the engine and raise the engine enough to remove the wood blocks. Lower the engine and remove the jack. Install the engine mount through bolts and tighten to 33–46 ft. lbs. (45–62 Nm).

21. Connect the fuel lines. Install the converter inspection cover. Tighten the rear mount attaching nuts to 35–50 ft. lbs. (48–68 Nm).

22. Install the shift crossover. Position the catalytic converters, secondary air tube and inlet pipes to the exhaust manifold and install the retaining nuts.

23. Install the catalytic converter outlet attaching bolts and install the secondary air tube on the converter

housing. Install the starter and connect the starter cable.

24. Install the oxygen sensors and lower the vehicle. Install the dipstick and tube. Install the thermactor air dump valve to exhaust manifold clamp.

25. Connect the windshield wiper hose and install the wiper motor mounting plate. Install the wiper motor.

26. Install the accelerator cable mounting bracket with the attaching screws on 5.8L engine. Connect the accelerator and TV cables to the throttle body or carburetor.

27. Position the shroud and install the retaining bolts. Install the thermactor tube to the rear of the engine. Install the air cleaner assembly and air ducts.

28. Fill the crankcase with the proper type and quantity of engine oil. Fill the transmission with the proper type and quantity of tranmission fluid.

29. Connect the negative battery cable. Start the engine and check for leaks.

Oil Pump

REMOVAL & INSTALLATION

4.6L Engine

1. Disconnect the negative battery cable.

2. Remove the camshaft covers, front cover, and oil pan.

3. Remove the timing chains.

4. Remove the 4 bolts retaining the oil pump to the cylinder block and remove the pump.

5. Remove the 2 bolts retaining the oil pickup tube to the oil pump and remove the bolt retaining the oil pickup tube to the main bearing stud spacer. Remove the pickup tube.

To install:

6. Clean the oil pickup tube and replace the O-ring.

7. Position the tube on the oil pump and hand-start the 2 bolts. Install the bolt retaining the pickup tube to the main bearing stud spacer hand tight.

8. Tighten the pickup tube-to-oil pump bolts to 6.0–8.8 ft. lbs. (8–12 Nm). Tighten the pickup tube to main bearing stud spacer bolt to 15–22 ft. lbs. (20–30 Nm).

9. Rotate the inner rotor of the oil pump to align with the flats on the crankshaft and install the oil pump flush with the cylinder block. Install the 4 retaining bolts and tighten to 6.0–8.8 ft. lbs. (8–12 Nm).

10. Install a new oil filter. Install the timing chains.

11. Install the oil pan, front cover and camshaft covers.

12. Fill the crankcase with the proper type and quantity of engine oil. Connect the negative battery cable, start the engine and check for leaks.

5.0L and 5.8L Engines

1. Disconnect the negative battery cable. Remove the oil pan.

2. Remove the oil pump inlet tube and screen assembly.

3. Remove the oil pump attaching bolts and gasket. Remove the oil pump intermediate shaft.

To install:

4. Prime the oil pump by filling either the inlet or outlet ports with engine oil and rotating the pump shaft to distribute the oil within the pump body.

5. Position the intermediate driveshaft into the distributor socket. With the shaft firmly seated in the distributor socket, the stop on the shaft should touch the roof of the crankcase. Remove the shaft and position the stop, as necessary.

6. Position a new gasket on the pump body, insert the intermediate shaft into the oil pump and install the pump and shaft as an assembly.

NOTE: Do not attempt to force the pump into position if it will not seat readily. The driveshaft hex may be misaligned with the distributor shaft. To align, rotate the intermediate shaft into a new position.

7. Tighten the oil pump attaching bolts to 22–32 ft. lbs. (30–43 Nm).

8. Clean and install the oil pump inlet tube and screen assembly.

9. Install the oil pan and the remaining components.

CHECKING

5.0L and 5.8L Engines

1. Check the inside of the pump housing and the inner and outer gears for damage or excessive wear.

2. Check the mating surface of the pump cover for wear. Minor scuff marks are normal, but if the cover, gears or housing surfaces are excessively worn, scored or grooved, replace the pump. Inspect the rotor for nicks, burrs or score marks. Remove minor imperfections with an oil stone.

3. Measure the inner to outer rotor tip clearance. With the rotor assembly removed from the pump and resting on a flat surface, the inner and outer rotor tip clearance must not exceed 0.012 in. (0.30mm) with the feeler gauge inserted 0.5 in. (13mm) minimum.

4. With the rotor assembly installed in the housing, place a straightedge over the rotor assembly and the housing. Measure the rotor endplay between the straight edge and both the inner and outer race. The maximum clearance must not exceed 0.005 in. (0.13mm).

5. Inspect the relief valve spring to see if it is collapsed or worn. Check the relief valve spring tension. Specifications are as follows:

    5.0L engine – 10.6–12.2 lbs. at 1.704 in.

    5.8L engine – 18.2–20.2 lbs. at 2.49 in.

6. If the spring tension is not within specification and/or the spring is worn or damaged, replace the pump. Check the relief valve piston for free operation in the bore.

NOTE: Internal oil pump components are not serviced. If any component is out of specification, the entire pump must be replaced.

Rear Main Bearing Oil Seal

REMOVAL & INSTALLATION

1. Disconnect the negative battery cable. Remove the transmission.

2. Punch 2 holes in the crankshaft rear oil seal on opposite sides of the crankshaft, just above the bearing cap to cylinder block split line. Install a sheet metal screw in each of the holes or use a small slide hammer and pry the crankshaft rear main oil seal from the block.

NOTE: Use extreme caution not to scratch the crankshaft oil seal surface.

3. Clean the oil seal recess in the cylinder block and main bearing cap.

4. Coat the seal and all of the seal mounting surfaces with oil. Position the seal on rear main seal installer T82L–6701–A or equivalent, and position the tool and seal to the rear of the engine.

5. Alternate bolt tightening to seat the seal properly. The rear face of the

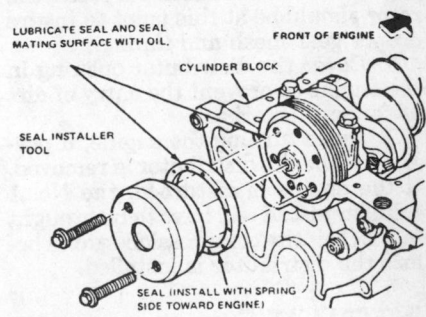

Rear main bearing oil seal Installation

seal must be within 0.005 in. (0.127mm) of the rear face of the block.

ENGINE ELECTRICAL

NOTE: Disconnecting the negative battery cable on some vehicles may interfere with the functions of the on board computer systems and may require the computer to undergo a relearning process, once the negative battery cable is reconnected.

Distributor

REMOVAL

1. Disconnect the negative battery cable.
2. Mark the position of the No. 1 cylinder wire tower on the distributor base.

NOTE: This reference is necessary in case the engine is disturbed while the distributor is removed.

3. Remove the distributor cap and position the cap and ignition wires to the side. Disconnect the wiring harness plug from the distributor connector. Disconnect and plug the vacuum hoses from the vacuum diaphragm assembly, if equipped.
4. Scribe a mark on the distributor body to indicate the position of the rotor tip. Scribe a mark on the distributor housing and engine block or timing cover to indicate the position of the distributor in the engine.
5. Remove the hold-down bolt and clamp located at the base of the distributor. Remove the distributor from the engine. Note the direction the rotor tip points if it moves from the No. 1 position when the drive gear disengages. For reinstallation purposes, the rotor should be at this point to insure proper gear mesh and timing.
6. Cover the distributor opening in the engine to prevent the entry of dirt or foreign material.
7. Avoid turning the engine, if possible, while the distributor is removed. If the engine is disturbed, the No. 1 cylinder piston will have to be brought to TDC on the compression stroke before the distributor is installed.

INSTALLATION

NOTE: Before installing, visually inspect the distributor. The drive gear should be free of nicks, cracks and excessive wear. The distributor drive shaft should move freely, without binding. If equipped with an O-ring, it should fit tightly and be free of cuts.

Timing Not Disturbed

1. Position the distributor in the engine, aligning the rotor and distributor housing with the marks that were made during removal. If the distributor does not fully seat in the engine block or timing cover, it may be because the distributor is not engaging properly with the oil pump intermediate shaft. Remove the distributor and, using a suitable tool, turn the intermediate shaft until the distributor will seat properly.
2. Install the hold-down clamp and bolt. Snug the mounting bolt so the distributor can be turned for ignition timing purposes.
3. Install the distributor cap and connect the distributor to the wiring harness.
4. Connect the negative battery cable. Check and, if necessary, set the ignition timing. Tighten the distributor hold-down clamp bolt to 18–26 ft. lbs. (24–35 Nm) on the 5.0L engine. Recheck the ignition timing after tightening the bolt.
5. If equipped, connect the vacuum diaphragm hoses.

Timing Disturbed

1. Disconnect the No. 1 cylinder spark plug wire and remove the No. 1 cylinder spark plug.
2. Place a finger over the spark plug hole and crank the engine slowly until compression is felt.
3. Align the TDC mark on the crankshaft pulley with the pointer on the timing cover. This places the piston in No. 1 cylinder at TDC on the compression stroke.
4. Turn the distributor shaft until the rotor points to the distributor cap No. 1 spark plug tower.
5. Install the distributor in the engine, aligning the rotor and distributor housing with the marks that were made during removal. If the distributor does not fully seat in the engine block or timing cover, it may be because the distributor is not engaging properly with the oil pump intermediate shaft. Remove the distributor and, using a suitable tool, turn the intermediate shaft until the distributor will seat properly.
6. Install the hold-down clamp and bolt. Snug the mounting bolt so the distributor can be turned for ignition timing purposes.
7. Install the No. 1 cylinder spark plug and connect the spark plug wire.

Install the distributor cap and connect the distributor to the wiring harness.
8. Connect the negative battery cable and set the ignition timing.
9. After the timing has been set, tighten the distributor hold-down clamp bolt to 18–26 ft. lbs. (24–35 Nm). Recheck the ignition timing after tightening the bolt.
10. If equipped, connect the vacuum diaphragm hoses.

Distributorless Ignition System (DIS)

The 4.6L engine is equipped with a distributorless ignition system. The DIS consists of the following components: crankshaft sensor, ignition module, ignition coil pack, the spark angle portion of the ECU and the related wiring.

The DIS eliminates the need for a distributor by using multiple ignition coils. Each coil fires 2 spark plugs at the same time. The plugs are paired so as 1 fires during the compression cycle, the other fires during the exhaust stroke. The next time the coil is fired, the plug that was on exhaust will be on compression and the 1 that was on compression will be on exhaust. The spark in the exhaust cylinder is wasted but little of the coil energy is lost. The ignition coils are mounted together in coil packs. There are 2 coil packs used, each containing 2 ignition coils.

The crankshaft sensor is a variable reluctance-type sensor triggered by a 36-minus-1 tooth trigger wheel configuration pressed onto the rear of the crankshaft damper. The signal generated by this sensor is called a Variable Reluctance Sensor (VRS) signal. The VRS signal provides engine position and rpm information to the ignition module.

The ignition module is a microprocessor that receives input from the crankshaft sensor in regards to engine position, base timing and engine speed and input from the ECU pertaining to spark advance. The ignition module uses this information to direct which coil to fire and to calculate the turn and turn off times of the coils required to achieve the correct dwell and spark advance.

REMOVAL & INSTALLATION

Crankshaft Sensor

1. Disconnect the negative battery cable.
2. Remove the serpentine belt.
3. Raise and safely support the vehicle.
4. Disconnect the crankshaft sensor and air conditioning compressor elec-

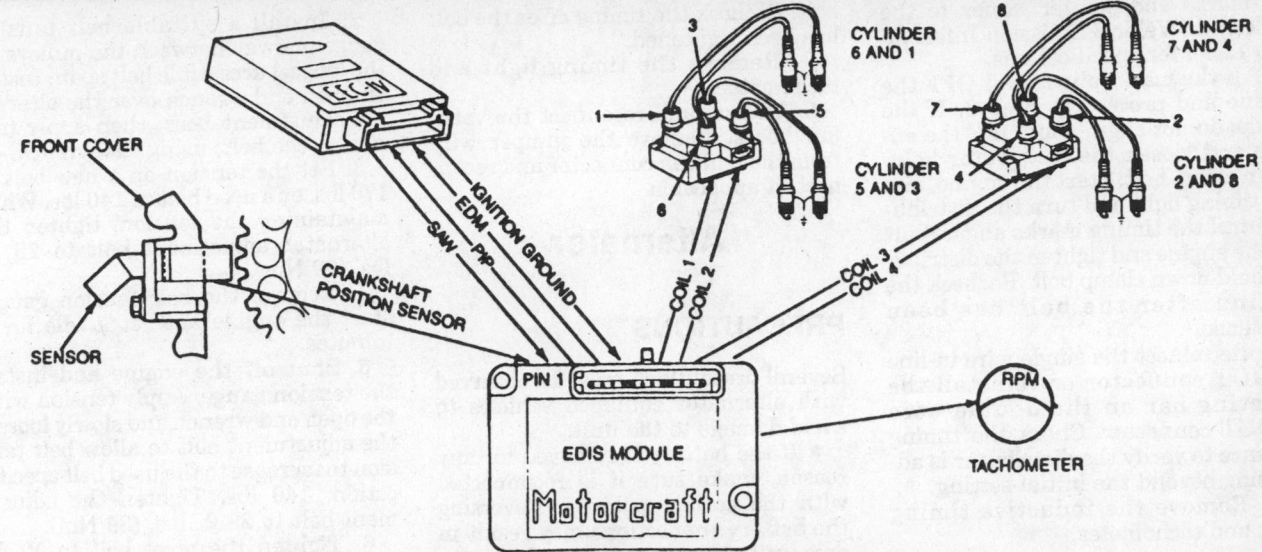

Distributorless ignition system — 4.6L Engine

trical connectors from the engine wiring harness.

5. Properly discharge the air conditioning system and remove the air conditioning compressor.

6. Remove the crankshaft position sensor retaining screw and remove the sensor.

To install:

7. Make sure the sensor mounting surface is clean and the sensor O-ring is in the proper location on the sensor assembly.

8. Position the sensor assembly and install the retaining screw. Tighten to 71–106 inch lbs. (8–12 Nm).

NOTE: Do not overtighten the screw.

9. Install the air conditioning compressor. Evacuate and recharge the system according to the proper procedure.

10. Properly route the engine wiring harness and connect the electrical connectors to the air conditioning compressor and crankshaft sensor.

11. Lower the vehicle.

12. Install the serpentine belt and connect the negative battery cable.

Ignition Module

1. Disconnect the negative battery cable.

2. Disconnect the electrical connectors at the module by pushing in on the connector finger ends while grasping the connector body and pulling away from the module.

3. Remove the module retaining screws and remove the module.

To install:

4. Install the module and the retaining screws. Tighten the screws to 24–35 inch lbs. (3–4 Nm).

5. Connect the electrical connectors

to the module by pushing until the connector fingers are locked over the locking wedge feature on the module.

NOTE: Locking the connector is important to ensure sealing of the connector/module interface.

6. Connect the negative battery cable.

Ignition Coil Pack

1. Disconnect the negative battery cable.

2. Disconnect the electrical connectors from the coil pack and capacitor.

3. Disconnect the spark plug wires by squeezing the locking tabs and twisting while pulling upward.

4. Remove the 4 coil pack retaining bolts and remove the coil pack and capacitor. Save the capacitor for installation with the new coil pack.

5. Installation is the reverse of the removal procedure. Tighten the retaining bolts to 40–61 inch lbs. (5–7 Nm). Apply silicone dielectric compound D7AZ–19A331–A or equivalent, to all spark plug wire boots prior to installation.

Ignition Timing

ADJUSTMENT

NOTE: Always refer to the Vehicle Emission Information Label to verify the timing adjustment procedure.

4.6L Engine

Base timing for the distributorless engine is set from the factory at 10 degrees BTDC and is not adjustable.

5.0L Engine

1. Locate the timing marks and pointer on the crankshaft pulley and the timing cover. Clean the marks so they will be visible with a timing light. Apply chalk or bright-colored paint, if necessary.

2. Place the transaxle in **P** or **N**. The air conditioning and heater controls should be in the **OFF** position.

3. Connect a suitable tachometer and inductive timing light according to the manufacturer's instructions.

NOTE: The tachometer can be connected to the ignition coil without removing the coil connector. Insert an alligator clip into the back of the connector, onto the dark green/yellow dotted wire. Do not let the clip accidently ground to a metal surface as it may permanently damage the coil.

4. Disconnect the single wire in-line SPOUT connector or remove the shorting bar from the double wire SPOUT connector.

5. Start the engine and allow it to warm up to operating temperature.

NOTE: To set timing correctly, a remote starter should not be used. Use the ignition key only to start the vehicle. Disconnecting the start wire at the starter relay will cause the TFI module to revert to start mode timing after the vehicle is started. Reconnecting the start wire after the vehicle is running will not correct the timing.

6. With the engine at the timing rpm specified, check the initial timing by aiming the timing light at the tim-

ing marks and pointer. Refer to the underhood Vehicle Emission Information Label for specifications.

7. If the marks align, shut OFF the engine and proceed to Step 8. If the marks do not align, shut OFF the engine and loosen the distributor hold-down clamp bolt. Start the engine, aim the timing light and turn the distributor until the timing marks align. Shut off the engine and tighten the distributor hold-down clamp bolt. Recheck the timing after the bolt has been tightened.

8. Reconnect the single wire in-line SPOUT connector or reinstall the shorting bar on the double wire SPOUT connector. Check the timing advance to verify the distributor is advancing beyond the initial setting.

9. Remove the inductive timing light and tachometer.

5.8L Engine

1. Locate the timing marks and pointer on the crankshaft pulley and the timing cover. Clean the marks so they will be visible with a timing light. Apply chalk or bright-colored paint, if necessary.

2. Place the transaxle in **P** or **N**. The air conditioning and heater controls should be in the **OFF** position.

3. Disconnect the vacuum hoses from the distributor vacuum advance connection at the distributor and plug the hoses.

4. Connect a suitable inductive timing light and a tachometer according to the manufacturer's instructions.

NOTE: The tachometer can be connected to the ignition coil without removing the coil connector. Insert an alligator clip into the TACH TEST cavity and connect the tachometer lead to the alligator clip.

5. If equipped with a barometric pressure switch, disconnect it from the ignition module and place a jumper wire across the pins at the ignition module connector (yellow and black wires).

6. Start the engine and allow it to warm up to operating temperature.

7. With the engine at the timing rpm specified, check the initial timing by aiming the timing light at the timing marks and pointer. Refer to the underhood Vehicle Emission Information Label for specifications.

8. If the marks align, proceed to Step 9. If the marks do not align, shut OFF the engine and loosen the distributor hold-down clamp bolt. Start the engine, aim the timing light and turn the distributor until the timing marks align. Shut OFF the engine and tighten the distributor hold-down clamp

bolt. Recheck the timing after the bolt has been tightened.

9. Remove the timing light and tachometer.

10. Unplug and reconnect the vacuum hoses. Remove the jumper wire from the ignition connector and reconnect, if applicable.

Alternator

PRECAUTIONS

Several precautions must be observed with alternator equipped vehicles to avoid damage to the unit.

● If the battery is removed for any reason, make sure it is reconnected with the correct polarity. Reversing the battery connections may result in damage to the one-way rectifiers.

● When utilizing a booster battery as a starting aid, always connect the positive to positive terminals and the negative terminal from the booster battery to a good engine ground on the vehicle being started.

● Never use a fast charger as a booster to start vehicles.

● Disconnect the battery cables when charging the battery with a fast charger.

● Never attempt to polarize the alternator.

● Do not use test lamps of more than 12V when checking diode continuity.

● Do not short across or ground any of the alternator terminals.

● The polarity of the battery, alternator and regulator must be matched and considered before making any electrical connections within the system.

● Never separate the alternator on an open circuit. Make sure all connections within the circuit are clean and tight.

● Disconnect the battery ground terminal when performing any service on electrical components.

● Disconnect the battery if arc welding is to be done on the vehicle.

BELT TENSION ADJUSTMENT

4.6L Engine

Vehicles with the 4.6L engine are equipped with an automatic belt tensioner. No adjustment is necessary or possible. To remove the drive belt, rotate the tensioner away from the belt using a ½ in. breaker bar.

5.0L and 5.8L Engines

1. Loosen the alternator pivot and adjustment bolts.

2. Install a suitable belt tension gauge midway between the pulleys on the longest accessible belt span. Install an open end wrench over the alternator adjustment boss, then apply tension to the belt, using the wrench.

3. Set the tension on a new belt to 170 lbs. or a used belt to 140 lbs. While maintaining the tension, tighten the alternator adjustment bolt to 29 ft. lbs. (39 Nm).

4. Remove the belt tension gauge, start the engine and let it idle for 5 minutes.

5. Shut off the engine and install the tension gauge. Apply tension with the open end wrench and slowly loosen the adjustment bolt to allow belt tension to increase to the used belt specification, 140 lbs. Tighten the adjustment bolt to 29 ft. lbs. (39 Nm).

6. Tighten the pivot bolt to 50 ft. lbs. (68 Nm).

REMOVAL & INSTALLATION

1. Disconnect the negative battery cable.

2. Tag and disconnect the wiring connectors from the rear of the alternator. To disconnect push-on type terminals, depress the lock tab and pull straight off.

3. Loosen the alternator pivot bolt and remove the adjusting bolt. Disengage the drive belt from the alternator pulley.

4. Remove the alternator pivot bolt and the alternator.

5. Installation is the reverse of the removal procedure. Adjust the belt tension.

Voltage Regulator

REMOVAL & INSTALLATION

1. Disconnect the negative battery cable.

2. Remove the regulator mounting screws, unlock the wire connectors and remove the regulator.

NOTE: Always disconnect the connector plug from the regulator before removing the mounting screws.

3. Installation is the reverse of the removal procedure.

Starter

REMOVAL & INSTALLATION

1. Disconnect the negative battery cable.

2. Raise the vehicle and support it safely.

3. Disconnect the starter cable from the starter. If equipped with starter mounted solenoid, disconnect the push-on connector from the solenoid.

NOTE: To disconnect the hardshell connector from the solenoid S terminal, grasp the plastic shell and pull off; do not pull on the wire. Pull straight off to prevent damage to the connector and S terminal.

4. Remove the starter bolts and the starter.

To install:

5. Position the starter to the engine and tighten the mounting bolts to 15–20 ft. lbs. (20–27 Nm).

6. Reconnect the electrical leads. Connect the negative battery cable.

EMISSION CONTROLS

Due to the complex nature of modern electronic engine control systems, comprehensive diagnosis and testing procedures fall outside the confines of this repair manual. For complete information on diagnosis, testing and repair procedures concerning all modern engine and emission control systems, please refer to "Chilton's Guide to Fuel Injection and Electronic Engine Controls".

Emission Warning Lamps

RESETTING

These vehicles have an CHECK ENGINE lamp that will light when there is a fault in the engine control system. This light cannot be reset without diagnosing the fault in the system. When the system has been diagnosed and the problem corrected, the light will go out.

FUEL SYSTEM

Fuel System Service Precautions

Safety is the most important factor when performing not only fuel system maintenance but any type of mainte-

nance. Failure to conduct maintenance and repairs in a safe manner may result in serious personal injury or death. Maintenance and testing of the vehicle's fuel system components can be accomplished safely and effectively by adhering to the following rules and guidelines.

- To avoid the possibility of fire and personal injury, always disconnect the negative battery cable unless the repair or test procedure requires that battery voltage be applied.
- Always relieve the fuel system pressure prior to disconnecting any fuel system component (injector, fuel rail, pressure regulator, etc.), fitting or fuel line connection. Exercise extreme caution whenever relieving fuel system pressure to avoid exposing skin, face and eyes to fuel spray. Please be advised that fuel under pressure may penetrate the skin or any part of the body that it contacts.
- Always place a shop towel or cloth around the fitting or connection prior to loosening to absorb any excess fuel due to spillage. Ensure that all fuel spillage (should it occur) is quickly removed from engine surfaces. Ensure that all fuel soaked cloths or towels are deposited into a suitable waste container.
- Always keep a dry chemical (Class B) fire extinguisher near the work area.
- Do not allow fuel spray or fuel vapors to come into contact with a spark or open flame.
- Always use a backup wrench when loosening and tightening fuel line connection fittings. This will prevent unnecessary stress and torsion to fuel line piping. Always follow the proper torque specifications.
- Always replace worn fuel fitting O-rings with new. Do not substitute fuel hose or equivalent where fuel pipe is installed.

RELIEVING FUEL SYSTEM PRESSURE

Fuel supply lines on all fuel injected engines will remain pressurized for some period of time after the engine is shut OFF. This pressure must be relieved before servicing the fuel system. Pressure is relieved through the fuel pressure relief valve, located on the fuel rail.

To relieve the fuel system pressure, first remove the fuel tank cap to relieve pressure in the tank, then remove the cap on the fuel pressure relief valve. Attach fuel pressure gauge T80L–9974–A or equivalent, and drain the system through the drain tube into a suitable container. Remove the fuel pressure gauge and replace the cap on the relief valve.

Fuel Line Couplings

REMOVAL & INSTALLATION

There are 3 methods in use to connect the fuel lines and fuel system components, the hairpin clip push connect fitting, the duck bill clip push connect fitting and the spring lock coupling. Each requires a different procedure to disconnect and connect.

Hairpin Clip Push Connect Fitting

1. Inspect the visible internal portion of the fitting for dirt accumulation. If more than a light coating of dust is present, clean the fitting before disassembly.

2. Some adhesion between the seals in the fitting and the tubing will occur with time. To separate, twist the fitting on the tube, then push and pull the fitting until it moves freely on the tube.

3. Remove the hairpin clip from the fitting by first bending and breaking the shipping tab. Next, spread the 2 clip legs by hand about ⅛ in. each to disengage the body and push the legs into the fitting. Lightly pull the triangular end of the clip and work it clear of the tube and fitting.

NOTE: Do not use hand tools to complete this operation.

4. Grasp the fitting and pull in an axial direction to remove the fitting from the tube. Be careful on 90 degree elbow connectors, as excessive side loading could break the connector body.

5. After disassembly, inspect and clean the tube end sealing surfaces. The tube end should be free of scratches and corrosion that could provide leak paths. Inspect the inside of the fitting for any internal parts such as O-rings and spacers that may have been dislodged from the fitting. Replace any damaged connector.

To connect:

6. Install a new connector if damage was found. Insert a new clip into any 2 adjacent openings with the triangular portion pointing away from the fitting opening. Install the clip until the legs of the clip are locked on the outside of the body. Piloting with an index finger is necessary.

7. Before installing the fitting on the tube, wipe the tube end with a clean cloth. Inspect the inside of the fitting to make sure it is free of dirt and/or obstructions.

8. Apply a light coating of engine oil to the tube end. Align the fitting and tube axially and push the fitting onto the tube end. When the fitting is engaged, a definite click will be heard.

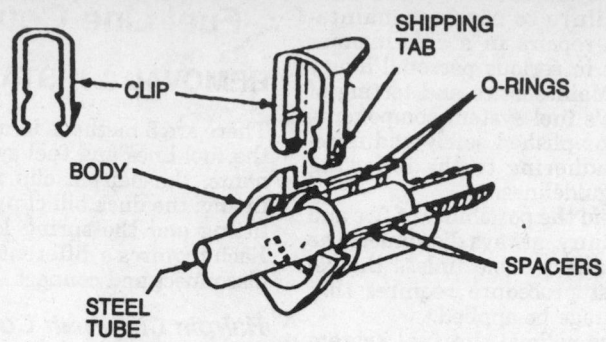

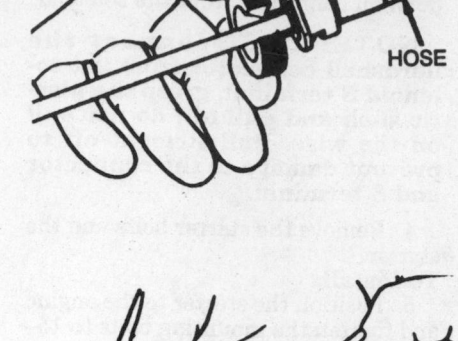

Hairpin clip push connect fitting

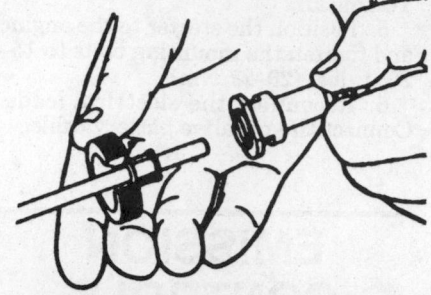

Duck bill clip push connect fitting disconnect tool

Pull on the fitting to make sure it is fully engaged.

Duck Bill Clip Push Connect Fitting

1. Inspect the visible internal portion of the fitting for dirt accumulation. If more than a light coating of dust is present, clean the fitting before disassembly.

2. Some adhesion between the seals in the fitting and the tubing will occur with time. To separate, twist the fitting on the tube, then push and pull the fitting until it moves freely on the tube.

3. Align the slot on push connect disassembly tool T90T–9550–B or T90T–9550–C or equivalent, with either tab on the clip, 90 degrees from the slots on the side of the fitting and insert the tool. This disengages the duck bill retainer from the tube.

4. Holding the tool and the tube with 1 hand, pull the fitting away from the tube.

NOTE: Use hands only. Only moderate effort is required if the tube has been properly disengaged.

5. After disassembly, inspect and clean the tube end sealing surfaces. The tube end should be free of scratches and corrosion that could provide leak paths. Inspect the inside of the fitting for any internal parts such as O-rings and spacers that may have been dislodged from the fitting. Replace any damaged connector.

6. Some fuel tubes have a secondary bead which aligns with the outer surface of the clip. These beads can make tool insertion difficult. If there is extreme difficulty, use the following disassembly method:

a. Using pliers with a jaw width of 0.2 in. (5mm) or less, align the jaws with the openings in the side of the fitting case and compress the portion of the retaining clip that en-

gages the fitting case. This disengages the retaining clip from the case. Often 1 side of the clip will disengage before the other. The clip must be disengaged from both openings.

b. Pull the fitting off the tube by hand only. Only moderate effort is required if the retaining clip has been properly disengaged.

c. After disassembly, inspect and clean the tube end sealing surfaces. The tube end should be free of scratches and corrosion that could provide leak paths. Inspect the inside of the fitting for any internal parts such as O-rings and spacers that may have been dislodged from the fitting. Replace any damaged connector.

d. The retaining clip will remain on the tube. Disengage the clip from the tube bead and remove.

To connect:

7. Install a new connector if damage was found. Install the new replacement clip into the body by inserting 1 of the retaining clip serrated edges on the duck bill portion into 1 side of the window openings. Push on the other side until the clip snaps into place.

8. Before installing the fitting on the tube, wipe the tube end with a clean cloth. Inspect the inside of the fitting to make sure it is free of dirt and/or obstructions.

9. Apply a light coating of engine oil to the tube end. Align the fitting and tube axially and push the fitting onto the tube end. When the fitting is engaged, a definite click will be heard. Pull on the fitting to make sure it is fully engaged.

Spring Lock Coupling

The spring lock coupling is a fuel line coupling held together by a garter spring inside a circular cage. When the coupling is connected together, the flared end of the female fitting slips behind the garter spring inside the cage of the male fitting. The garter spring and cage then prevent the flared end of the female fitting from pulling out of the cage. As an additional locking feature, most vehicles have a horseshoe shaped retaining clip that improves the retaining reliability of the spring lock coupling.

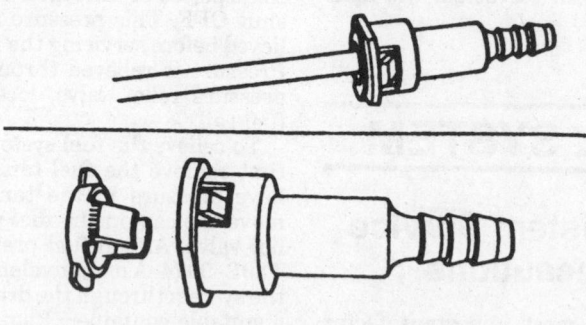

Duck bill clip push connect fitting

SPRING LOCK COUPLING CONNECT and DISCONNECT PROCEDURE

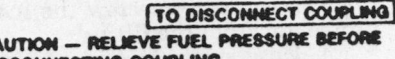

TO DISCONNECT COUPLING

CAUTION — RELIEVE FUEL PRESSURE BEFORE DISCONNECTING COUPLING

CLIP

① REMOVE CLIP FROM COUPLING

USE SPECIFIED TOOL OR EQUIVALENT

TOOL:
— 3/8 INCH
— 1/2 INCH

CAGE OPENING

② FIT TOOL TO COUPLING SO THAT TOOL CAN ENTER CAGE OPENING TO RELEASE THE GARTER SPRING.

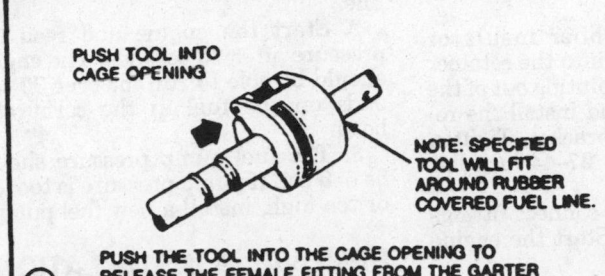

PUSH TOOL INTO CAGE OPENING

NOTE: SPECIFIED TOOL WILL FIT AROUND RUBBER COVERED FUEL LINE.

③ PUSH THE TOOL INTO THE CAGE OPENING TO RELEASE THE FEMALE FITTING FROM THE GARTER SPRING

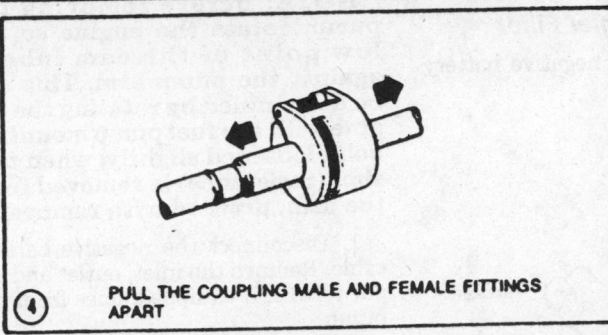

④ PULL THE COUPLING MALE AND FEMALE FITTINGS APART

⑤ REMOVE THE TOOL FROM THE DISCONNECTED SPRING LOCK COUPLING

TO CONNECT COUPLING

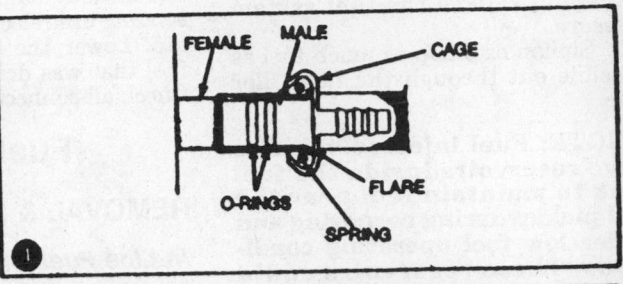

FEMALE · MALE · CAGE

O-RINGS · FLARE · SPRING

①

REPLACEMENT O-RINGS (3/8 INCH DIA., 2 PER FITTING) (1/2 INCH DIA., 2 PER FITTING)

USE ONLY SPECIFIED FUEL RESISTANT O-RINGS (COLOR: BROWN)

CHECK FOR CORROSION

LUBRICATE O-RINGS WITH CLEAN ENGINE OIL

CLEAN FITTINGS WITH SOLVENT. CHECK FOR MISSING OR DAMAGED O-RINGS. REPLACE MISSING O-RINGS. IF EITHER O-RING IS DAMAGED, REPLACE BOTH O-RINGS.

REPLACEMENT GARTER SPRINGS:
3/8-INCH —
1/2-INCH —

②

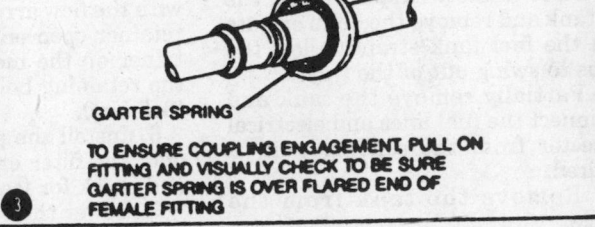

GARTER SPRING

③ TO ENSURE COUPLING ENGAGEMENT, PULL ON FITTING AND VISUALLY CHECK TO BE SURE GARTER SPRING IS OVER FLARED END OF FEMALE FITTING

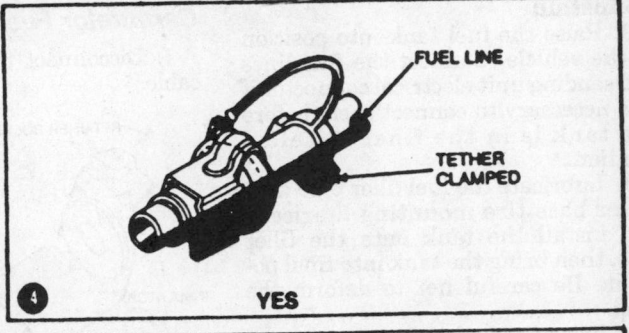

FUEL LINE

TETHER CLAMPED

④ YES

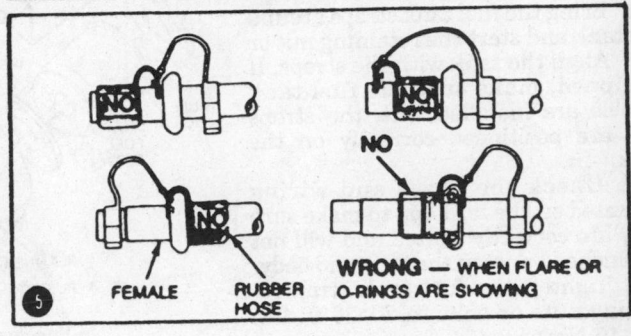

FEMALE · RUBBER HOSE

WRONG — WHEN FLARE OR O-RINGS ARE SHOWING

⑤

Fuel Tank

REMOVAL & INSTALLATION

1. Disconnect the negative battery cable and relieve the fuel system pressure.
2. Siphon or pump as much fuel as possible out through the fuel filler pipe.

NOTE: Fuel injected vehicles have reservoirs inside the fuel tank to maintain fuel near the fuel pickup during cornering and under low fuel operating conditions. These reservoirs could block siphon tubes or hoses from reaching the bottom of the fuel tank. Repeated attempts using different hose orientations can overcome this obstacle.

3. Raise and safely support the vehicle.
4. If equipped with a metal retainer that fastens the filler pipe to the fuel tank, remove the screw attaching the retainer to the fuel tank flange.
5. Disconnect the fuel lines and the electrical connector to the fuel tank sending unit. On some vehicles, these are inaccessible on top of the tank. In these cases they must be disconnected with the tank partially removed.
6. Place a safety support under the fuel tank and remove the bolts or nuts from the fuel tank straps. Allow the straps to swing out of the way.
7. Partially remove the tank and disconnect the fuel lines and electrical connector from the sending unit, if required.
8. Remove the tank from the vehicle.
To install:
9. Raise the fuel tank into position in the vehicle. Connect the fuel lines and sending unit electrical connector if it is necessary to connect them before the tank is in the final installed position.
10. Lubricate the fuel filler pipe with water base tire mounting lubricant and install the tank onto the filler pipe, then bring the tank into final position. Be careful not to deform the tank.
11. Bring the fuel tank straps around the tank and start the retaining nut or bolt. Align the tank with the straps. If equipped, make sure the fuel tank shields are installed with the straps and are positioned correctly on the tank.
12. Check the hoses and wiring mounted on the tank top to make sure they are correctly routed and will not be pinched between the tank and body.
13. Tighten the fuel tank strap retaining nuts or bolts to 20–30 ft. lbs. (28–40 Nm).

14. If not already connected, connect the fuel hoses and lines which were disconnected. Make sure the fuel supply, fuel return, if present, and vapor vent connections are made correctly. If not already connected, connect the sending unit electrical connector.
15. Lower the vehicle. Replace the fuel that was drained from the tank. Check all connections for leaks.

Fuel Filter

REMOVAL & INSTALLATION

In-Line Fuel Filter

1. Disconnect the negative battery cable and relieve the fuel system pressure.
2. Raise and safely support the vehicle.
3. Remove the push connect fittings at both ends of the filter. Install new retainer clips in each push connect fitting.
4. Remove the fuel filter and retainer from the metal bracket. Remove the filter from the retainer. Note that the direction of the flow arrow points to the open end of the retainer. Remove the rubber insulator rings.
To install:
5. Install the rubber insulator rings, place the filter into the retainer with the flow arrow pointing out of the retainer open end, and install the retainer on the metal bracket. Tighten the retaining bolts to 27–44 inch lbs. (3–5 Nm).
6. Install the push connect fittings onto the filter ends. Start the engine and check for leaks.
7. Lower the vehicle.

Carburetor Fuel Inlet Filter

1. Disconnect the negative battery cable.

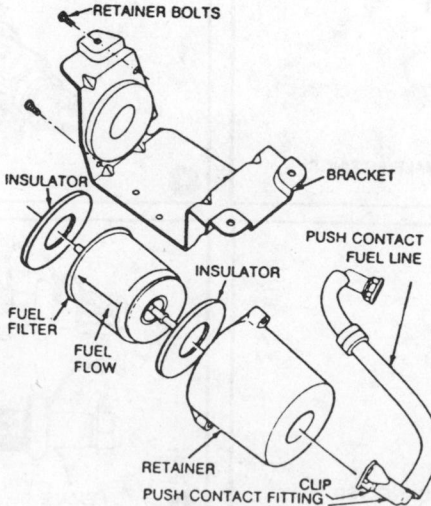

In-line fuel filter

2. Place a rag under the carburetor inlet fitting to catch fuel spillage.
3. Hold the inlet fitting with a back-up wrench and unscrew the fuel line tube nut from the fitting.
4. Unscrew the fuel inlet fitting and remove the gasket, filter and spring. Discard the gasket and filter.
To install:
5. Install the spring, new filter and gasket.
6. Hand start the fuel inlet fitting into the carburetor. Tighten to 90–125 inch lbs. (10–14 Nm).
7. Apply engine oil to the fuel tube nut threads and tube flare. Hand start the fuel line tube nut into the fuel inlet fitting, approximately 2 threads.
8. Use a backup wrench on the fuel inlet fitting while tightening the fuel line tube nut to 15–18 ft. lbs. (20–24 Nm).
9. Start the engine and check for leaks. Install the air cleaner.

Mechanical Fuel Pump

PRESSURE TESTING

1. Connect a suitable pressure gauge to the carburetor end of the fuel line.
2. Start the engine and read the pressure after 10 seconds. The engine should be able to run for over 30 seconds on the fuel in the carburetor bowl.
3. The fuel pump pressure should be 6–8 psi. If pump pressure is too low or too high, install a new fuel pump.

REMOVAL & INSTALLATION

NOTE: Before removing the pump, rotate the engine so the low point of the cam lobe is against the pump arm. This can be determined by rotating the engine with the fuel pump mounting bolts loosened slightly; when tension (resistance) is removed from the arm, proceed with removal.

1. Disconnect the negative battery cable. Remove the inlet, outlet and vapor return, if equipped, lines from the pump.
2. Remove the fuel pump mounting bolts and remove the pump and gasket.
To install:
3. Clean all gasket material from the pump mounting surface on the engine and apply a coat of oil-resistant sealer to the new gasket.
4. Install the retaining bolts into the fuel pump and install the gasket on the bolts. Position the pump on the engine. Turn the retaining bolts alternately and evenly and tighten to 19–27 ft. lbs. (26–37 Nm).

5. Reinstall the fuel lines, start the engine and check for leaks.

Electric Fuel Pump

PRESSURE TESTING

1. Relieve the fuel system pressure and connect a fuel pressure gauge to the valve on the fuel rail.
2. Ground the fuel pump lead of the self-test connector through a jumper wire at the **FP** lead.
3. Turn the ignition key to the **RUN** position to operate the fuel pump.
4. Observe the fuel pressure gauge. the indicated pressure should be 35–40 psi.
5. Remove the fuel pressure gauge and the jumper wire.

REMOVAL & INSTALLATION

1. Disconnect the negative battery cable and relieve the fuel system pressure.
2. Remove the fuel tank and place it on a bench.
3. Remove any dirt that has accumulated around the fuel pump retaining flange so it will not enter the tank during pump removal and installation.
4. Turn the fuel pump locking ring counterclockwise and remove the locking ring.
5. Remove the fuel pump and bracket assembly. Remove and discard the seal ring.

To install:

6. Clean the fuel pump mounting flange, fuel tank mounting surface and seal ring groove.
7. Apply a light coating of grease on a new seal ring to hold it in place during assembly and install in the seal ring groove.
8. Install the fuel pump and bracket assembly carefully to ensure the filter is not damaged. Make sure the locating keys are in the keyways and the seal ring remains in the groove.
9. Hold the pump assembly in place and install the locking ring finger-tight. Make sure all the locking tabs are under the tank lock ring tabs.

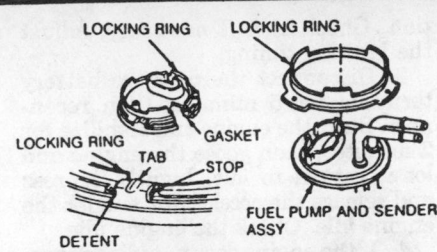

In-tank electric fuel pump installation

10. Rotate the locking ring clockwise until the ring is against the stops.
11. Install the fuel tank in the vehicle. Add a minimum of 10 gallons of fuel to the tank and check for leaks.
12. Install a suitable fuel pressure gauge to the valve on the fuel rail.
13. Turn the ignition switch from **OFF** to **ON** for 3 seconds. Repeat this procedure 5–10 times until the pressure gauge shows at least 35 psi. Check for fuel leaks.
14. Remove the pressure gauge, start the engine and check for leaks.

Carburetor

REMOVAL & INSTALLATION

1. Disconnect the negative battery cable. Remove the air cleaner.
2. Remove the throttle cable and transmission kickdown levers from the throttle lever. Tag and disconnect all vacuum lines, emission hoses, the fuel line and electrical connections.
3. Remove the carburetor retaining nuts; then remove the carburetor. Remove the carburetor mounting gasket spacer, if equipped, and lower gasket from the intake manifold.
4. Installation is the reverse of the removal procedure.
5. To prevent leakage, distortion or damage to the carburetor body flange, snug the nuts; then, alternately tighten each nut in a criss-cross pattern to 12–15 ft. lbs. (16–20 Nm).
6. Adjust engine idle speed.

IDLE SPEED ADJUSTMENT

1. Place the transmission in **N** or **P**. Apply the parking brake and block the wheels. If equipped with automatic

brake release, disconnect the vacuum hose and plug it.
2. Bring the engine to normal operating temperature. Place the air conditioner/heater selector to the **OFF** position.
3. Disconnect the vacuum hose at the EGR valve and plug.
4. Place the fast idle adjustment on the second step of the fast idle cam. Check and/or adjust fast idle rpm to specification. Refer to the emission calibration label.
5. Rev engine momentarily and repeat Step 4. Remove plug from EGR vacuum hose and reconnect.
6. Disconnect and plug the vacuum hose at the throttle kicker and place the transmission in the idle setting position specified on the emission calibration label. If adjustment is required, turn the curb idle speed screw and set the idle to the speed specified on the emission calibration label.
7. Put the transmission in **N** or **P**, increase the engine speed momentarily and recheck.
8. Apply a slight pressure on top of the nylon nut located on the accelerator pump to take up the linkage clearance. Turn the nut on the accelerator pump rod clockwise until a clearance of 0.010 in. ± 0.005 in. is obtained between the top of the accelerator pump and the pump lever.
9. Turn the accelerator pump rod 1 turn counterclockwise to set the lever lash preload. Remove the plug from the throttle kicker vacuum hose and reconnect.
10. Disconnect and plug the vacuum hose at the Vacuum Operated Throttle Modulator (VOTM) kicker. Connect an external vacuum source providing a minimum of 10 in. Hg to the VOTM kicker. With the transmission in the specified position, check/adjust the VOTM kicker speed.
11. If adjustment is required, turn the VOTM kicker speed adjusting screw. Remove external vacuum source and reconnect VOTM kicker hose.

IDLE MIXTURE ADJUSTMENT

The normal propane enrichment method of adjusting the idle mixture is not possible on the 7200VV carburetor.

SERVICE ADJUSTMENTS

For all carburetor service adjustment procedures and specifications, please refer to "Carburetor Service" in the Unit Repair section.

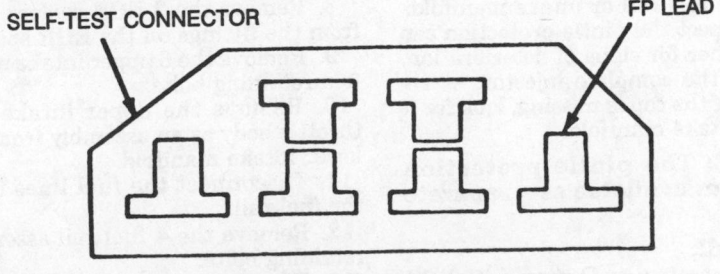

Self-test connector terminal location

Fuel Injection

IDLE SPEED ADJUSTMENT
4.6L Engine

1. Place the transaxle in **P** and apply the parking brake.
2. Start the engine and bring to normal operating temperature. Make sure the heater, air conditioning and all other accessories are OFF.
3. Check and if necessary, adjust the ignition timing.
4. Make sure the fuel pressure is correct. Any indicated vehicle malfunction service codes should be resolved before proceeding further.
5. Connect the SUPER STAR II tester, tool number 007–00028 or other suitable scan tool to the Self-Test connector. Activate the Key On Engine Running (KOER) Self-Test.
6. After Code 1 or 111 has been displayed, unlatch and within 4 seconds, latch the STI button.
7. A single pulse code indicates the entry mode, then observe the Self-Test Ouput (STO) on the tester for the following:
   a. A constant tone, solid light or **STO LO** readout means the base idle speed is within the correct range. To exit the test, unlatch the STI button, then wait 4 seconds for reinitialization. After 10 minutes, the tool will exit by itself.
   b. A beeping tone, flashing light or **STO LO** readout at 8 Hz indicates the Throttle Position Sensor (TPS) is out of range due to over adjustment. Adjustment may be required.
   c. A beeping tone, flashing light or **STO LO** readout at 4 Hz indicates the base idle speed is too fast and adjustment is required. Proceed to Step 9.
   d. A beeping tone, flashing light or **STO LO** readout at 1 Hz indicates the base idle speed is too low and adjustment is required. Proceed to Step 8.
8. If the idle speed is too low, do not clean the throttle body. Turn the air trim screw counterclockwise until the conditions in Step 7a are satisfied.
9. If the idle speed is too high, do not clean the throttle body. Turn the air trim screw clockwise until the conditions in Step 7a are satisfied.

5.0L Engine

1. Place the transmission in **N** or **P**. Apply the emergency brake and block the wheels. If equipped with automatic brake release, disconnect the vacuum hose and plug it.
2. Bring the engine to normal operating temperature. Place the air conditioner/heater selector to the OFF position. Check and, if necessary, adjust the ignition timing.
3. Disconnect the negative battery terminal for 5 minutes, then reconnect. Start the engine and stabilize for 2 minutes, then goose the engine and let it return to idle. Lightly depress and release the accelerator and let the engine idle. Check the engine idle.
4. If the engine does not idle properly, shut the engine OFF and proceed to Step 5.
5. Back out the throttle plate stop screw clear off the throttle lever pad. With a 0.010 in. feeler gauge between the throttle plate stop screw and the throttle lever pad, turn the screw in until contact is made, then turn an additional 1⅛ turns.
6. Start the engine and stabilize for 2 minutes, then goose the engine and let it return to idle. Lightly depress and release the accelerator and let the engine idle.

IDLE MIXTURE ADJUSTMENT

The idle mixture is controlled by the electronic control unit and cannot be adjusted.

Fuel Injector

REMOVAL & INSTALLATION
4.6L Engine

1. Disconnect the negative battery cable.
2. Remove the fuel tank cap and relieve the fuel system pressure.
3. Disconnect the vacuum line at the pressure regulator.
4. Disconnect the fuel lines from the fuel rail.
5. Disconnect the electrical connectors from the injectors.
6. Remove the fuel rail assembly retaining bolts.
7. Carefully disengage the fuel rail from the fuel injectors and remove the fuel rail.

NOTE: It may be easier to remove the injectors with the fuel rail as an assembly.

8. Grasping the injector body, pull while gently rocking the injector from side-to-side to remove the injector from the fuel rail or intake manifold.
9. Inspect the pintle protection cap and washer for signs of deterioration. Replace the complete injector, as required. If the cap is missing, look for it in the intake manifold.

NOTE: The pintle protection cap is not available as a separate part.

To install:

10. Lubricate new O-rings with light grade oil and install 2 on each injector.

NOTE: Never use silicone grease as it will clog the injectors.

11. Install the injectors using a light, twisting, pushing motion.
12. Install the fuel rail, pushing it down to ensure all injector O-rings are fully seated in the fuel rail cups and intake manifold.
13. Install the retaining bolts while holding the fuel rail down and tighten to 71–106 inch lbs. (8–12 Nm).
14. Connect the fuel lines to the fuel rail and the vacuum line to the pressure regulator.
15. With the injector wiring disconnected, connect the negative battery cable and turn the ignition switch to the **RUN** position to allow the fuel pump to pressurize the system.
16. Check for fuel leaks.
17. Disconnect the negative battery cable.
18. Connect the electrical connectors to the fuel injectors.
19. Connect the negative battery cable and start the engine. Let it idle for 2 minutes.
20. Turn the engine **OFF** and check for leaks.

5.0L Engine

1. Disconnect the negative battery cable.
2. Remove the fuel tank cap and relieve the fuel system pressure.
3. Partially drain the cooling system into a suitable container.
4. Disconnect the electrical connectors at the air bypass valve, throttle position sensor and EGR sensor.
5. Disconnect the throttle linkage at the throttle ball and transmission linkage from the throttle body. Remove the 2 bolts securing the bracket the bracket to the intake manifold and position the bracket with the cables aside.
6. Disconnect the upper intake manifold vacuum fitting connections by disconnecting all vacuum lines to the vacuum tree, EGR valve, fuel pressure regulator and evaporative canister.
7. Disconnect the PCV hose from the fitting on the rear of the upper manifold and disconnect the PCV vent closure tube at the throttle body.
8. Remove the 2 EGR coolant lines from the fittings on the EGR spacer.
9. Remove the 6 upper intake manifold retaining bolts.
10. Remove the upper intake and throttle body as an assembly from the lower intake manifold.
11. Disconnect the fuel lines from the fuel rail.
12. Remove the 4 fuel rail assembly retaining bolts.
13. Disconnect the electrical connectors from the injectors.

14. Carefully disengage the fuel rail from the fuel injectors.

NOTE: It may be easier to remove the injectors with the fuel rail as an assembly.

15. Grasping the injector body, pull up while gently rocking the injector from side-to-side to remove the injector from the fuel rail or intake manifold.

16. Inspect the pintle protection cap and washer for signs of deterioration. Replace the complete injector, as required. If the cap is missing, look for it in the intake manifold.

NOTE: The pintle protection cap is not available as a separate part.

To install:

17. Lubricate new O-rings with light grade oil and install 2 on each injector.

NOTE: Never use silicone grease as it will clog the injectors.

18. Install the injectors using a light, twisting, pushing motion.

19. Install the fuel rail, pushing it down to ensure all the injector O-rings are fully seated in the fuel rail cups and intake manifold.

20. Install the retaining bolts while holding the fuel rail down and tighten to 70–105 inch lbs. (8–12 Nm).

21. Connect the fuel lines to the fuel rail.

22. With the injector wiring disconnected, connect the negative battery cable and turn the ignition switch to the **RUN** position to allow the fuel pump to pressurize the system.

23. Check for fuel leaks.

24. Disconnect the negative battery cable.

25. Connect the electrical connectors to the injectors.

26. Install the upper intake manifold and throttle body assembly by reversing the removal procedure. Use a new gasket and tighten the retaining bolts to 12–18 ft. lbs. (16–24 Nm).

27. Refill the cooling system and connect the negative battery cable.

28. Start the engine and let it idle for 2 minutes. Turn the engine **OFF** and check for leaks.

DRIVE AXLE

Driveshafts and U-Joints

REMOVAL & INSTALLATION

1. Raise and safely support the ve-

hicle. Mark the position of the driveshaft yoke on the axle companion flange so they can be reassembled in the same way to maintain balance.

2. Remove the flange bolts and disconnect the driveshaft from the axle companion flange.

3. Allow the rear of the driveshaft to drop down slightly. Pull the driveshaft and slip yoke out of the transmission extension housing.

4. Plug the transmission to prevent fluid leakage.

To install:

5. Lubricate the yoke splines and install the yoke into the transmission extension housing, aligning the splines. Be careful not to bottom the slip yoke hard against the transmission seal.

6. Rotate the axle flange, as necessary, to align the marks made during removal. Install the driveshaft yoke to the axle flange. Install the bolts and tighten to 71–95 ft. lbs. (95–130 Nm).

Rear Axle Shaft, Bearing and Seal

REMOVAL & INSTALLATION

1. Raise and safely support the vehicle. Remove wheel and tire assembly and remove brake drum or brake rotor.

2. If equipped, remove the anti-lock brake speed sensor.

3. Clean all dirt from the area of the carrier cover. Drain the axle lubricant by removing the housing cover.

4. Remove differential pinion shaft lock bolt and pinion shaft.

5. Push flanged end of axle shafts toward the center of the vehicle and remove the C-lock from button end of the axle shaft. Remove the axle shaft from the housing, being careful not to damage the oil seal.

6. Insert wheel bearing and seal replacer tool T85L–1225–AH or equivalent, in the bore and position it behind the bearing so the tangs on the tool engage the bearing outer race. Remove bearing and seal as a unit using an impact slide hammer.

To install:

7. Lubricate the new bearing with rear axle lubricant. Install the bearing into the housing bore using a suitable bearing installer.

8. Install a new axle seal using a seal installer.

NOTE: Check for the presence of an axle shaft O-ring on the spline end of the shaft and install, if not present.

9. Carefully slide the axle shaft into the axle housing, without damaging the bearing or seal assembly. Start the

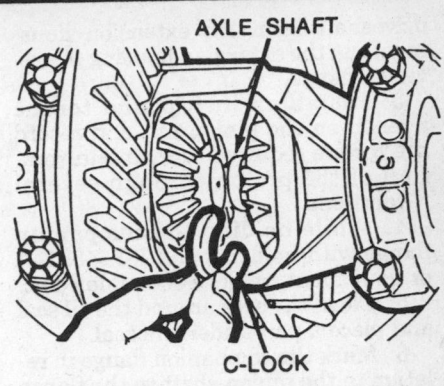

AXLE SHAFT

C-LOCK

Removing the axle shaft C-locks

splines into the side gear and push firmly until the button end of the axle shaft can be seen in the differential case.

10. Install the C-lock on the button end of the axle shaft splines, then push the shaft outboard until the shaft splines engage and the C-lock seats in the counterbore of the differential side gear.

11. Insert the differential pinion shaft through the case and pinion gears, aligning the hole in the shaft with the lock bolt hole. Apply locking compound to the lock bolt and install in the case and pinion shaft. Tighten to 15–30 ft. lbs. (20–41 Nm).

12. Cover the inside of the differential case with a shop rag and clean the machined surface of the carrier and cover. Remove the shop rag.

13. Apply a bead of silicone sealer to the cover and install on the carrier. Tighten the bolts in a criss-cross pattern. Final torque the cover retaining bolts to 25–35 ft. lbs. (34–47 Nm).

14. Add rear axle lubricant to the carrier to a level 1/4–9/16 in. below the bottom of the fill hole. If equipped with limited slip, add friction modifier C8AZ–19B564–A or equivalent. Install the filler plug and tighten to 15–30 ft. lbs. (20–41 Nm).

15. Install the anti-lock speed sensor, if equipped. Tighten the retaining bolt to 40–60 inch lbs. (4.5–6.8 Nm).

16. Install the brake calipers and rotors or the brake drums, as required. Install the wheel and tire assembly and lower the vehicle.

Pinion Seal

REMOVAL & INSTALLATION

1. Raise and safely support the vehicle. Mark the position of the driveshaft yoke on the axle companion flange so they may be reassembled in the same way to maintain balance.

2. Disconnect the driveshaft from the rear axle companion flange, remove the driveshaft and remove the

driveshaft from the extension housing. Plug the extension housing to prevent leakage.

3. Install an inch pound torque wrench on the pinion nut and record the torque required to maintain rotation of the pinion through several revolutions.

4. While holding the companion flange with holder tool T78P–4851–A or equivalent, remove the pinion nut.

5. Clean the area around the oil seal and place a pan under the seal.

6. Mark the companion flange in relation to the pinion shaft so the flange can be installed in the same position.

7. Remove the rear axle companion flange using tool T65L–4851–B or equivalent.

8. Pry the seal out of the housing using a prybar.

To install:

9. Clean the oil seal seat surface and install the seal in the carrier using seal replacer tool T79P–4676–A or equivalent. Apply lubricant to the lips of the seal.

10. Apply a small amount of lubricant to the companion flange splines, align the marks on the flange and and the pinion shaft and install the flange.

11. Install a new nut on the pinion shaft and apply lubricant on the washer side of the nut.

12. Hold the flange with the holder tool while tightening the nut. Rotate the pinion to ensure proper seating and take frequent pinion bearing torque preload readings until the original recorded preload reading is obtained.

13. If the original recorded preload is less than 8–14 inch lbs. (0.9–1.6 Nm), then tighten the nut to 8–14 inch lbs. (0.9–1.6 Nm). If the original preload is higher than 8–14 inch lbs. (0.9–1.6 Nm), tighten to the original recorded preload.

NOTE: Under no circumstances should the pinion nut be backed off to reduce preload. If reduced preload is required, a new collapsible pinion spacer and pinion nut should be installed.

14. Remove the plug from the transmission extension housing and install the front end of the driveshaft on the transmission output shaft.

15. Connect the rear end of the driveshaft to the axle companion flange, aligning the scribe marks. Tighten the 4 bolts to 71–95 ft. lbs. (95–130 Nm).

16. Add lubricant to the axle until it is ¼–⁹⁄₁₆ in. below the bottom of the fill hole with the axle in operating position. If equipped with limited slip, add friction modifier C8AZ–19B564–A or equivalent.

17. Make sure the axle vent is not plugged with debris.

Axle Housing

REMOVAL & INSTALLATION

1. Raise and safely support the vehicle. If equipped, turn the air suspension switch **OFF**. Position safety stands under the rear frame crossmember.

2. Remove the cover and drain the axle lubricant.

3. Remove the wheel and tire assemblies. Remove the brake drums or brake rotors.

4. Remove the lock bolt from the pinion shaft and remove the shaft.

5. Remove the anti-lock brake sensor before removing the axle shafts, if equipped.

6. Push the axle shafts inward to remove the C-locks and remove the axle shafts.

7. If equipped with drum brakes, remove the 4 retaining nuts from each backing plate and wire the backing plate to the underbody.

8. If equipped with disc brakes, remove the disc brake adapter bracket, bolts and J-nuts. Remove the 4 retaining nuts from each adapter and wire the adapters to the underbody.

9. Mark the position of the driveshaft yoke on the axle companion flange. Disconnect the driveshaft at the companion flange and wire it to the underbody.

10. Support the axle housing with jackstands. Disengage the brake line from the clips that retain the line to the axle housing.

11. Disconnect the vent from the rear axle housing.

12. If equipped with air springs, proceed as follows:

a. Disconnect the negative battery cable. Make sure the air suspension switch, located in the trunk, is **OFF**.

b. Remove the heat shield and spring retainer clip from the top of the air spring.

c. Disconnect the electrical connector and the air line from the air spring solenoid, located on the air spring.

d. Remove the solenoid clip and rotate the solenoid counterclockwise to the first stop.

e. Pull the solenoid straight out slowly to the second stop to bleed the air from the system.

—— **CAUTION** ——

Do not fully release the solenoid until the air is completely bled from the air spring, or personal injury may result.

f. After the air is fully bled from the system, rotate the solenoid counterclockwise to the 3rd stop and remove the solenoid from the solenoid housing.

g. Insert air spring removal tool T90P–5310–A or equivalent, between the axle tube and spring seat on the forward side of the axle.

h. Position the tool so its flat end rests on the piston knob. Push downward, forcing the piston and retainer clip off the axle spring seat.

i. Remove the air spring.

13. Disconnect the lower shock absorber studs from the mounting brackets on the axle housing.

14. Disconnect the upper arms from the mountings on the axle housing ear brackets.

15. Lower the axle housing assembly until the springs are released and lift out the springs.

16. Disconnect the suspension lower arms at the axle housing.

17. Lower the axle housing and remove it from the vehicle.

To install:

18. Position the axle housing under the vehicle and raise the axle with a hoist or jack. Conect the lower suspension arms to their mounting brackets on the axle housing. Do not tighten the bolts and nuts at this time.

19. Reposition the rear springs.

20. Raise the housing into position.

21. Connect the uppper arms to the mounting ears on the housing. Tighten the nuts and bolts to 103–133 ft. lbs. (140–180 Nm). Tighten the lower arm bolts and nuts to 103–133 ft. lbs. (140–180 Nm).

22. Install the axle vent and install the brake line to the clips that retain the line to the axle housing. If equipped with air springs, proceed as follows:

a. Check the solenoid O-rings for damage and replace, as required. Lightly grease the O-ring area of the solenoid and the larger solenoid housing O-ring with silicone dielectric compound.

b. Insert the solenoid into the air spring end cap and rotate clockwise to the 3rd stop, push in to the 2nd stop, then rotate clockwise to the 1st stop.

c. Install the solenoid clip. Connect the air line and the electrical connector.

d. Install the air spring into the frame spring seat. Connect the spring retainer clip to the knob of the spring cap from the top side of the frame spring seat.

e. Align the air spring piston with the axle seats. Squeeze to increase pressure and push downward on the piston, snapping the piston to the axle seat.

23. If equipped with drum brakes, install the brake backing plates on the axle housing flanges. If equipped with

disc brakes, install the disc brake adapters and tighten the nuts to 20–29 ft. lbs. (27–40 Nm). Install the disc brake adapter brackets, bolts and J-nuts. Tighten to 20–39 ft. lbs. (27–54 Nm).

24. Connect the lower shock absorber studs to the mounting bracket on the axle housing.

25. Connect the driveshaft to the companion flange and tighten the bolts and nuts to 70–95 ft. lbs. (95–130 Nm).

26. Slide the rear axle shafts into the housing until the splines enter the side gear. Push the axle shafts inward and install the C-lock at the end of each shaft spline. Pull the shafts outboard until the C-lock enters the recess in the side gears.

27. Install the pinion shaft. Apply locking compound to the pinion shaft lock bolt. Install and tighten to 15–30 ft. lbs. (20–41 Nm).

28. Install the anti-lock sensor, if equipped.

29. Install the rear brake drums or disc brake rotors and calipers.

30. Install the rear carrier cover using new silicone sealer. Tighten to 25–35 ft. lbs. (34–47 Nm).

31. Add rear axle lubricant to the carrier to a level ¼–⁹⁄₁₆ in. below the bottom of the fill hole. If equipped with limited slip, add friction modifier C8AZ–19B564–A or equivalent. Install the filler plug and tighten to 15–30 ft. lbs. (20–41 Nm).

32. If equipped, fill the air springs as follows before lowering the vehicle:

a. Turn the air suspension switch **ON**. The ignition switch must be **ON** and the engine running or a battery charger must be connected to the battery to reduce battery drain.

b. Remove the right luggage compartment trim panel and connect Super Star II tester 007-0041–A or equivalent to the air suspension diagnostic connector.

c. Set the tester to EEC-IV/MCU mode. Also set the tester to FAST mode. Release the tester button to the HOLD (up) position and turn the tester **ON**.

d. Depress the tester button to TEST (down) position. A Code 10 will be displayed. Within 2 minutes a Code 13 will be displayed. After Code 13 is displayed, release the tester button to HOLD (up) position, wait 5 seconds and depress the tester button to TEST (down) position. Ignore any codes displayed.

e. Release the tester button to the HOLD (up) position. Wait at least 20 seconds, then depress the tester button to TEST (down) position. Within 10 seconds, the following codes will be displayed in the order shown.

f. Within 4 seconds after Code 26

AIR SUSPENSION CODE CHART

Code	Description
23	Vent Rear
26	Compress Rear
31	Cycle Compressor On and Off Repeatedly
32	Cycle Vent Solenoid Valve Open and Closed Repeatedly
33	Cycle Spring Solenoid Valves Open and Closed Repeatedly

is displayed, release the tester button to the HOLD (up) position. Waiting longer than 4 seconds may result in Functional Test 31 being entered. The compressor will fill the air springs with air as long as the tester button is in the HOLD (up) position. To stop filling the air springs, depress the tester button to the TEST (down) position.

NOTE: It is possible to overheat the compressor during this operation. If the compressor overheats, the self-resetting circuit breaker in the compressor will open and remain open for about 15 minutes. This allows the compressor to cool down.

g. To exit Functional Test 26, disconnect the tester and turn the ignition switch **OFF**.

33. Lower the vehicle.

AUTOMATIC TRANSMISSION

For further information on transmission/transaxles, please refer to "Chilton's Guide to Transmission Repair".

Transmission Assembly

REMOVAL & INSTALLATION

1. Disconnect the negative battery cable. Raise the vehicle and support safely.

2. Drain the fluid from the transmission by removing all oil pan bolts except the 2 at the front. Loosen the 2 at the front and drop the oil pan at the rear to allow the fluid to drain into a container. When drained, reinstall a few of the bolts to hold the pan in place.

3. Remove the converter bottom cover and remove the converter drain plug, to allow the converter to drain. After the converter has drained, reinstall the drain plug and tighten. Remove the converter to flywheel nuts by turning the converter to expose the nuts.

NOTE: Crank the engine over with a wrench on the crankshaft pulley attaching bolt.

4. Mark the position of the driveshaft on the rear axle flange and remove the driveshaft. Install a suitable plug in the transmission extension housing to prevent fluid leakage.

5. Disconnect the starter cable and remove the starter. Disconnect the wiring from the neutral safety switch.

6. Remove the mount-to-crossmember and crossmember-to-frame bolts. Remove the mount-to-transmission bolts.

7. Disconnect the shift and throttle valve cables from the transmission.

8. Remove the bellcrank bracket from the converter housing.

9. Position a suitable jack and raise the transmission. Remove the transmission mount and crossmember.

NOTE: It may be necessary to disconnect or remove interfering exhaust system components.

10. Lower the transmission to gain access to the oil cooler lines. Disconnect the oil cooler lines from the transmission.

11. Disconnect the speedometer cable from the extension housing.

12. Remove the transmission dipstick tube-to-engine block retaining bolt and remove the tube and dipstick from the transmission.

13. Secure the transmission to the jack with a chain and remove the transmission-to-engine bolts.

14. Carefully pull the transmission and converter assembly rearward and lower them from the vehicle.

To install:

15. Tighten the converter drain plug to 8–28 ft. lbs. (11–38 Nm).

16. If removed, position the converter on the transmission and rotate into position to make sure the drive flats are fully engaged in the pump gear.

NOTE: Lubricate the pilot with chassis grease.

17. Raise the converter and transmission assembly into position. Rotate the converter until the studs and drain plug are in alignment with the holes in the flywheel. Align the orange balancing marks on the converter stud and flywheel bolt hole if balancing marks are present.

NOTE: The converter face must rest squarely against the flywheel. This indicates that the converter pilot is not binding in the engine crankshaft. To ensure the converter is properly seated, grasp a converter stud. It should move freely back and forth in the flywheel hole. If the converter will not move, the transmission must be removed and the converter repositioned so the impeller hub is properly engaged in the pump gear.

18. Install the transmission-to-engine attaching bolts. Tighten the bolts to 40–50 ft. lbs. (55–68 Nm).

19. Remove the safety chain from around the transmission.

20. Install a new O-ring on the lower end of the transmission dipstick tube and install the tube to the transmission case.

21. Connect the speedometer cable to the transmission case.

22. Connect the oil cooler lines to the right side of the transmission case.

23. Position the crossmember on the side supports. Position the rear mount on the crossmember and install the attaching bolt/nut.

24. Secure the engine rear support to the transmission extension housing.

25. Install any exhaust system components, if removed.

26. Lower the transmission and remove the jack.

27. Secure the crossmember to the side supports with the attaching bolts.

28. Connect the TV linkage and the manual linkage rod. Connect the shift cable.

29. Install the converter to flywheel attaching nuts and tighten to 20–34 ft. lbs. (27–46 Nm). Install the converter housing cover.

30. Secure the starter motor in place and connect all electrical connections.

31. Install the driveshaft, aligning the marks that were made during removal.

32. Lower the vehicle. Fill the transmission with the proper type and quantity of fluid, start the engine and check the transmission for leakage. Adjust the linkage as required.

MANUAL LINKAGE ADJUSTMENT

1989

1. Place the selector lever in the **OVERDRIVE** position, tight against the overdrive stop. An 8 lb. weight should be hung on the selector lever to ensure the lever remains against the overdrive stop during the linkage adjustment.

2. Loosen the shift rod adjusting bolt.

3. Shift the transmission into **OVERDRIVE** by pushing the column shift rod downward to the lowest position and pulling up 3 detents.

4. Make sure the selector lever has not moved from the overdrive stop. Tighten the bolt to 14–23 ft. lbs. (19–31 Nm).

5. Check the transmission operation for all selector lever detent positions.

1990–93

1. Loosen the adjusting stud nut at the transmission lever.

2. From the passenger compartment, place the steering column selector lever in **OVERDRIVE** and hold the selector lever in position by placing a 3 lb. weight on the lever.

3. Rotate the transmission lever clockwise to low and return it 2 detent positions counterclockwise to the **OVERDRIVE** position.

4. Align the flats of the adjusting stud with the flats of the cable slot and install the cable on the stud.

NOTE: Do not push or pull on the rod while assembling the rod to the stud.

5. Tighten the adjusting stud nut and washer assembly to 10–18 ft. lbs. (13–25 Nm).

6. Check the shift lever for proper operation.

THROTTLE VALVE CABLE ADJUSTMENT

Automatic Overdrive Transmission

1. Set the parking brake and place the shift selector in **N**.

2. Remove the air cleaner cover and inlet tube from the throttle body inlet to access the throttle lever and cable.

3. Using a small prybar, pry the grooved pin on the cable assembly out of the grommet on the throttle body lever. Push out the white locking tab.

4. Check the plastic block with pin and tab; it should slide freely on the notched rod. If not, the white tab may not be pushed out far enough.

5. While holding the throttle lever firmly against the idle stop, push the grooved pin into the grommet on the throttle lever as far as it will go.

6. Make sure the throttle lever does not move while pushing the pin into the grommet.

7. Install the air cleaner cover and inlet tube.

FRONT SUSPENSION

NOTE: If equipped with the level ride air suspension, power to the air system must be shut OFF before servicing the suspension. The switch is located in the luggage compartment, on the drivers side rear fender well.

Shock Absorbers

REMOVAL & INSTALLATION

NOTE: Purge a new shock of air by repeatedly extending it in its normal position and compressing it while inverted.

1. Remove the nut, washer and

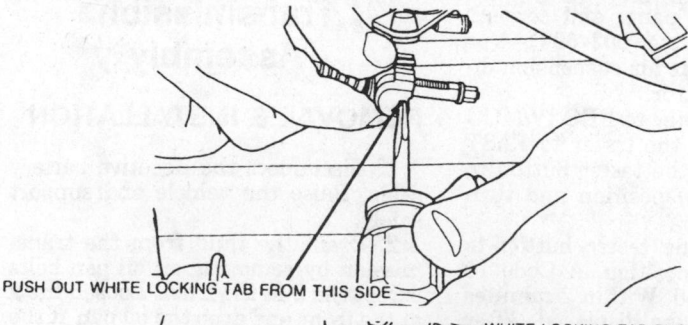

PUSH OUT WHITE LOCKING TAB FROM THIS SIDE

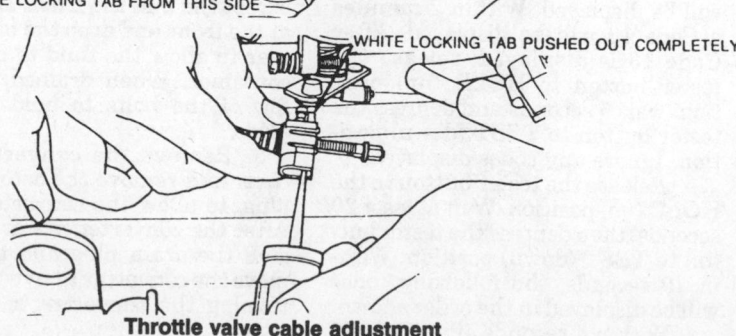

WHITE LOCKING TAB PUSHED OUT COMPLETELY

Throttle valve cable adjustment

bushing from the upper end of the shock absorber.

2. Raise and safely support the vehicle by the frame rails allowing the front wheels to hang.

3. Remove the 2 bolts securing the shock absorber to the lower control arm and remove the shock absorber.

To install:

4. Install a new bushing and washer on the top of the shock absorber and position the unit inside the front spring. Install the 2 lower attaching bolts and torque them to 12–18 ft. lbs. (16–24 Nm).

5. Lower the vehicle.

6. Place a new bushing and washer on the shock absorber top stud and install a new attaching nut. Tighten to 22–26 ft. lbs. (30–41 Nm).

Coil Springs

REMOVAL & INSTALLATION

1. Raise and safely support the vehicle. Remove the wheel and tire assembly.

2. On 1989–91 Crown Victoria and Grand Marquis and 1989–90 Town Car, disconnect the stabilizer bar link from the lower arm.

3. Remove the shock absorber. Remove the steering link from the pitman arm.

4. Using spring compressor tool D78P–5310–A or equivalent, install 1 plate with the pivot ball seat facing downward into the coils of the spring. Rotate the plate, so it is flush with the upper surface of the lower arm.

5. Install the other plate with the pivot ball seat facing upward into the coils of the spring. Insert the upper ball nut through the coils of the spring, so the nut rests in the upper plate.

6. Insert the compression rod into the opening in the lower arm, through the upper and lower plate and upper ball nut. Insert the securing pin through the upper ball nut and compression rod.

NOTE: This pin can only be inserted 1 way into the upper ball nut because of a stepped hole design.

7. With the upper ball nut secured, turn the upper plate so it walks up the coil until it contacts the upper spring seat. Then back off ½ turn.

8. Install the lower ball nut and thrust washer on the compression rod and screw on the forcing nut. Tighten the forcing nut until the spring is compressed enough so it is free in its seat.

9. Remove the 2 lower arm pivot bolts, disengage the lower arm from the frame crossmember and remove the spring.

10. If a new spring is to be installed, perform the following:

   a. Mark the position of the upper and lower plates on the spring with chalk.

   b. With an assistant, compress a new spring for installation and measure the compressed length and the amount of curvature of the old spring.

11. Loosen the forcing nut to relieve the spring tension and remove the tools from the spring.

To install:

12. Assemble the spring compressor and locate in the same position as indicated in Step 10a.

13. Before compressing the coil spring, make sure the upper ball nut securing the pin is inserted properly.

14. Compress the coil spring until the spring height reaches the dimension obtained in Step 10b.

15. Position the coil spring assembly into the lower arm and reverse the removal procedure.

Upper Ball Joints

INSPECTION

1. Raise the vehicle and place floor jacks beneath the lower control arms.

2. Make sure the front wheel bearings are properly adjusted.

3. Have an assistant grasp the bottom of the tire and move the wheel in and out.

4. As the wheel is being moved, observe the upper control arm where the spindle attaches to it. Any movement between the upper part of the spindle and the upper control arm indicates a bad ball joint which must be replaced.

REMOVAL & INSTALLATION

1989–91 Crown Victoria and Grand Marquis, 1989–90 Town Car

NOTE: Ford Motor Company recommends replacement of the control arm and ball joint as an assembly. However, aftermarket replacement parts are available, which can be installed using the following procedure.

1. Raise the vehicle and support on frame points so the front wheels fall to their full down position. Remove the wheel and tire assembly.

2. Drill a ⅛ in. hole completely through each ball joint attaching rivet.

3. Using a large chisel, cut off the head of each rivet and drive them from the arm.

4. Place a jack under the lower arm and raise to compress the coil spring.

5. Remove the cotter pin and attaching nut from the ball joint stud.

6. Using a ball joint removal tool, loosen the ball joint stud from the spindle and remove the ball joint from the arm.

To install:

7. Clean all metal burrs from the arm and install the new ball joint, using the service part nuts and bolts to attach the ball joint. Do not attempt to rivet the ball joint once it has been removed.

8. Install the ball joint stud into the spindle. Tighten the ball joint-to-upper spindle nut to 60–90 ft. lbs. (81–122 Nm). Continue to tighten until the slot for the cotter pin is aligned. Install a new cotter pin.

9. Install the wheel and tire assembly and lower the vehicle. Check front end alignment.

1992–93 Crown Victoria and Grand Marquis, 1991–93 Town Car

1. Raise and safely support the vehicle with safety stands under the frame behind the lower arm. Remove the wheel and tire assembly.

2. Position a floor jack under the lower arm at the lower ball joint area. The floor jack will support the spring load on the lower arm.

3. Remove the retaining nut and pinch bolt from the upper ball joint stud.

4. Mark the position of the alignment cams. When replacing the ball joint this will approximate the current alignment.

5. Remove the 2 nuts retaining the ball joint to the upper arm. Remove the ball joint and spread the slot with a suitable prybar to separate the ball joint stud from the spindle.

To install:

NOTE: The upper ball joints differ from side to side. Be sure to use the proper ball joint on each side.

6. Position the ball joint on the upper arm and insert the ball stud into the spindle.

7. Install the pinch bolt and retaining nut. Tighten to 51–67 ft. lbs. (68–92 Nm).

8. Install the alignment cams to the approximate position at removal. If not marked, install in neutral position.

9. Install the 2 nuts attaching the ball joint to the arm. Hold the cams and tighten the nuts to 90–109 ft. lbs. (122–149 Nm).

10. Remove the floor jack from the lower arm and install the wheel and tire assembly. Remove the safety stands and lower the vehicle.

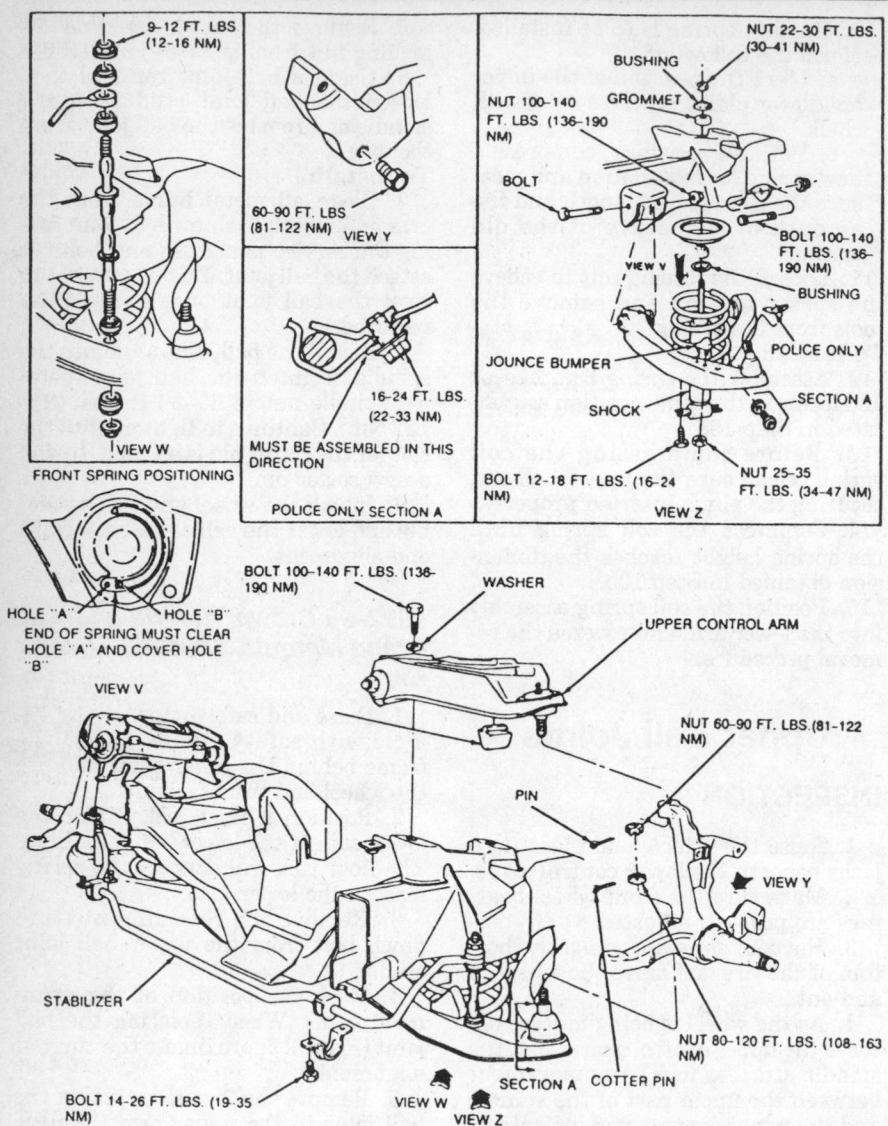

Front suspension assembly—1989–91 Crown Victoria and Grand Marquis and 1989–90 Town Car

11. Check and adjust the front end alignment.

Lower Ball Joints

INSPECTION

1. Support the vehicle in normal driving position with ball joints loaded.
2. Wipe the wear indicator and ball joint cover checking surface clean.

3. The checking surface should project outside the cover. If the checking surface is inside the cover, replace the lower arm assembly.

REMOVAL & INSTALLATION

The ball joint is an integral part of the lower control arm. If the ball joint is defective, the entire lower control arm must be replaced.

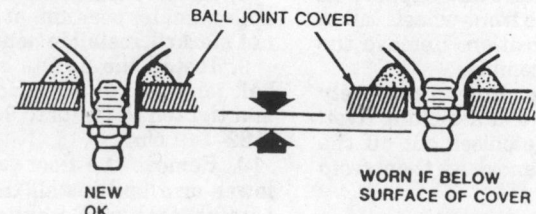

Lower ball joint cover checking surface

Upper Control Arms

REMOVAL & INSTALLATION

1989–91 Crown Victoria and Grand Marquis, 1989–90 Town Car

1. Raise and safely support the vehicle on safety stands positioned on the frame just behind the lower arm. Remove the wheel and tire assembly.
2. Remove the cotter pin from the upper ball joint stud nut. Loosen the nut a few turns but do not remove.
3. Install ball joint press T57P-3006–B or equivalent, between the upper and lower ball joint studs with the adapter screw on top.

NOTE: This tool should be seated firmly against the ends of both studs, not against the nuts or lower stud cotter pin.

4. With a wrench, turn the adapter screw until the tool places the stud under compression. Tap the spindle near the upper stud with a hammer to loosen the stud in the spindle.

NOTE: Do not loosen the stud from the spindle with tool pressure only. Do not contact the boot seal with the hammer.

5. Remove the tool from between the ball joint studs and place a floor jack under the lower arm.
6. Remove the upper arm attaching bolts and the upper arm.

To install:

7. Transfer the rebound bumper from the old arm to the new arm, or replace the bumper if worn or damaged.
8. Position the upper arm shaft to the frame bracket. Install the 2 attaching bolts and washers. Tighten to 100–140 ft. lbs. (136–190 Nm).
9. Connect the upper ball joint stud to the spindle and install the attaching nut. Tighten the nut to 60–90 ft. lbs. (81–122 Nm). Continue to tighten the nut until the slot for the cotter pin is aligned. Install a new cotter pin.
10. Install the wheel and tire assembly and lower the vehicle. Check the front end alignment.

1992–93 Crown Victoria and Grand Marquis, 1991–93 Town Car

1. Raise and safely support the vehicle on safety stands positioned on the frame just behind the lower arm.
2. Remove the wheel and tire assembly and position a floor jack under the lower arm.
3. Remove the retaining nut from the upper ball joint stud to spindle pinch bolt. Tap the pinch bolt to remove from the spindle.

4. Using a suitable prybar, spread the slot to allow the ball joint stud to release out of the spindle.

5. Remove the upper arm retaining bolts and the upper arm.

To install:

6. Transfer the rebound bumper from the old arm to the new arm, or replace the bumper if worn or damaged.

7. Use reference marks from the camber and caster cams as initial settings.

8. Position the upper arm shaft to the frame bracket. Install the 2 retaining bolts and washers. Position the arm in the center of the slot adjustment range and tighten to 100 ft. lbs. (136 Nm).

9. Connect the upper ball joint stud to the spindle and install the retaining pinch bolt and nut. Tighten the nut to 52–66 ft. lbs. (70–90 Nm).

10. Install the wheel and tire assembly and lower the vehicle. Check the front end alignment.

Lower Control Arms

REMOVAL & INSTALLATION

1. Raise the front of the vehicle and position safety stands on the frame behind the lower control arms. Remove the wheel and tire assembly.

2. Remove the brake caliper and suspend with a length of wire; do not let the caliper hang by the brake hose. Remove the brake rotor and dust shield. Remove the anti-lock brake sensor, if equipped.

3. Remove the jounce bumper; inspect and save for installation if in good condition. Remove the shock absorber.

4. On 1989–91 Crown Victoria and Grand Marquis and 1989–90 Town Car, disconnect the stabilizer link from the lower arm.

5. Disconnect the steering center link from the pitman arm.

6. Remove the cotter pin and loosen the lower ball joint stud nut 1–2 turns.

NOTE: Do not remove the nut at this time.

7. Install a suitable ball joint press tool to place the ball joint stud under compression. With the stud under compression, tap the spindle sharply with a hammer to loosen the stud in the spindle. Remove the ball joint press tool.

8. Place a floor jack under the lower arm and install a suitable spring compression tool.

9. Remove the coil spring, the ball joint nut and remove the lower control arm.

To install:

10. Position the arm assembly ball joint stud into the spindle and install the nut. Tighten to 80–120 ft. lbs. (108–163 Nm). Continue to tighten until the slot for the cotter pin is aligned. Install a new cotter pin.

11. Position the coil spring into the upper spring pocket and raise the lower arm, aligning the holes in the arm with the holes in the crossmember. Install the bolts and nuts with the washer installed on the front bushing. Do not tighten at this time.

NOTE: Make sure the pigtail of the lower coil of the spring is in the proper location of the seat on the lower arm, between the 2 holes.

12. Remove the spring compressor tool.

13. Connect the steering center link at the pitman arm and install the nut. Tighten to 43–47 ft. lbs. (59–63 Nm). Continue to tighten until the slot for the cotter pin is aligned. Install a new cotter pin.

14. Install the shock absorber and the jounce bumper.

15. Install the dust shield, rotor and caliper. Install the anti-lock brake sensor, if equipped.

16. On 1989–91 Crown Victoria and Grand Marquis and 1989–90 Town Car, position the stabilizer link to the lower control arm and install the link, bushing and retaining nut. Tighten to 9–15 ft. lbs. (12–20 Nm).

17. Install the wheel and tire assembly and lower the vehicle. With the vehicle supported on the wheels and tires at normal curb height, tighten the lower control arm-to-crossmember bolts to 100–140 ft. lbs. (136–190 Nm).

18. Check the front end alignment.

Stabilizer Bar

REMOVAL & INSTALLATION

1. Raise the front of the vehicle and place jackstands under the lower control arms.

2. On 1989–91 Crown Victoria and Grand Marquis and 1989–90 Town Car, remove the link nuts and disconnect the stabilizer bar from the links.

3. On 1992–93 Crown Victoria and Grand Marquis and 1991–93 Town Car, remove the retaining nuts from the pinch bolts at the spindles. Spread the slots in the spindles with a prybar to free the ball studs.

4. Remove the stabilizer bar brackets from the frame and remove the stabilizer bar. If worn, cut the insulators from the stabilizer bar.

5. On 1992–93 Crown Victoria and Grand Marquis and 1991–93 Town Car, remove the retaining nuts from the ball joint studs at the end of the bar. Use removal tool 3290-D or equivalent to separate the links from the ends of the stabilizer bar.

To install:

6. Coat the necessary parts of the stabilizer bar with rubber lubricant. Slide new insulators onto the stabilizer bar.

7. On 1992–93 Crown Victoria and Grand Marquis and 1991–93 Town Car, install the ball joint links into the ends of the bar with the retaining nuts. Tighten to 30–40 ft. lbs. (40–55 Nm).

8. On 1989–91 Crown Victoria and Grand Marquis and 1989–90 Town Car, attach the ends of the stabilizer bar to the lower control arm with new nuts and links. Tighten the nuts to 9–15 ft. lbs. (12–20 Nm). Install the insulator brackets and tighten the bolts to 14–26 ft. lbs. (19–35 Nm).

9. On 1992–93 Crown Victoria and Grand Marquis and 1991–93 Town Car, position the bar under the vehicle and engage the upper ball joint links to the spindles. Install the insulator brackets with the retaining nuts. Tighten the pinch bolts and nuts at the spindles to 30–40 ft. lbs. (40–55 Nm) Tighten the bracket-to-frame nuts to 44–59 ft. lbs. (59–81 Nm).

Front Wheel Bearings

ADJUSTMENT

1989–91 Crown Victoria and Grand Marquis, 1989–90 Town Car

1. Raise and safely support the front of the vehicle.

2. Remove the wheel cover and grease cap.

3. Remove the cotter pin and nut retainer.

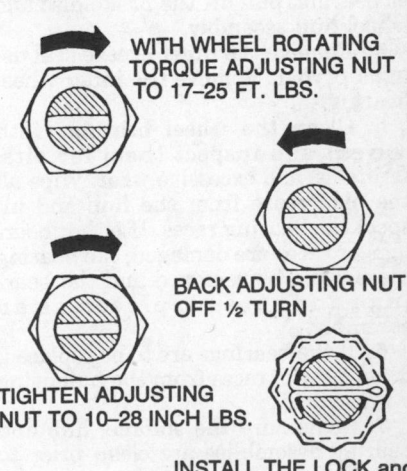

WITH WHEEL ROTATING TORQUE ADJUSTING NUT TO 17–25 FT. LBS.

BACK ADJUSTING NUT OFF ½ TURN

TIGHTEN ADJUSTING NUT TO 10–28 INCH LBS.

INSTALL THE LOCK and NEW COTTER PIN

Wheel bearing adjustment procedure— 1989–91 Crown Victoria and Grand Marquis and 1989–90 Town Car

4. Loosen the adjusting nut 3 turns and rock the wheel in and out a few times to release the brake pads from the rotor.

5. While rotating the wheel and hub assembly in a counterclockwise direction, tighten the adjusting nut to 17–25 ft. lbs. (23–34 Nm).

6. Back off the adjusting nut ½ turn, then retighten to 10–28 inch lbs. (1.1–3.2 Nm).

7. Install the nut retainer and a new cotter pin. Check the wheel rotation. If it is noisy or rough, the bearings either need to be cleaned and repacked or replaced. After adjustment is completed, replace the grease cap.

8. Lower the vehicle. Before driving the vehicle, pump the brake pedal several times to restore normal brake pedal travel.

1992–93 Crown Victoria and Grand Marquis, 1991–93 Town Car

The front wheel bearings are of a hub unit design and are pregreased, sealed and require no maintenance. The bearings are preset and cannot be adjusted.

REMOVAL & INSTALLATION

1989–91 Crown Victoria and Grand Marquis, 1989–90 Town Car

1. Raise and support the vehicle safely. Remove the wheel and tire assembly and the caliper. Suspend the caliper with a length of wire; do not let it hang from the brake hose.

2. Pry off the dust cap. Tap out and discard the cotter pin. Remove the nut retainer.

3. Being careful not to drop the outer bearing, pull off the brake disc and wheel hub assembly.

4. Remove the inner grease seal using a prybar. Remove the inner wheel bearing.

5. Clean the wheel bearings with solvent and inspect them for pits, scratches and excessive wear. Wipe all the old grease from the hub and inspect the bearing races. If either bearings or races are damaged, the bearing races must be removed and the bearings and races replaced as an assembly.

6. If the bearings are to be replaced, drive out the races from the hub using a brass drift.

7. Make sure the spindle, hub and bearing assemblies are clean prior to installation.
To install:
8. If the bearing races were removed, install new ones using a suitable bearing race installer. Pack the

bearings with a bearing packer. If a packer is not available, work as much grease as possible between the rollers and cages.

9. Coat the inner surface of the hub and bearing races with grease.

10. Install the inner bearing in the hub. Using a seal installer, install a new grease seal into the hub. Lubricate the lip of the seal with grease.

11. Install the hub/disc assembly on the spindle, being careful not to damage the oil seal.

12. Install the outer bearing, washer and spindle nut. Install the caliper and the wheel and tire assembly. Adjust the bearings.

1992–93 Crown Victoria and Grand Marquis, 1991–93 Town Car

1. Raise and safely support the vehicle. Remove the wheel and tire assembly.

2. Remove and discard the grease cap from the hub.

3. Remove the brake caliper. Suspend the caliper with a length of wire; do not let it hang from the brake hose.

4. Remove the rotor. Remove and discard the wheel hub nut.

5. Remove the hub and bearing assembly.
To install:
6. Install the hub and bearing assembly. Install a new wheel hub nut and tighten to 238 ft. lbs. (322 Nm).

7. Install the rotor and a new grease cap. Install the brake caliper.

8. Install the wheel and tire assembly and lower the vehicle.

REAR SUSPENSION

Shock Absorbers

REMOVAL & INSTALLATION

Without Automatic Leveling

1. If equipped with air suspension, turn the air suspension switch **OFF**.

2. Raise and safely support the vehicle. Make sure the rear axle is supported.

3. Remove the shock absorber retaining nut, washer and insulator from the stud on the upper side of the frame. Discard the nut. Compress the shock to clear the hole in the frame and remove the inner insulator and washer from the upper retaining stud.

NOTE: All vehicles, except po-

lice applications, are equipped with gas pressurized shock absorbers which will extend unassisted.

4. Remove the self-locking retaining nut and disconnect the shock absorber lower stud from the mounting bracket on the rear axle.
To install:
5. Prime the new shock absorber as follows:

   a. With the shock absorber right side up, extend it fully.

   b. Turn the shock upside down and fully compress it.

   c. Repeat the previous 2 steps at least 3 times to make sure any trapped air has been expelled.

6. Place the inner washer and insulator on the upper retaining stud and position the shock absorber with the stud through the hole in the frame.

7. While holding the shock absorber in position, install the outer insulator, washer and a new stud nut on the upper side of the frame. Tighten the nut to 21 ft. lbs. (29 Nm).

8. Extend the shock absorber and place the lower stud in the mounting bracket hole on the rear axle housing. Install a new self-locking nut and tighten to 52–85 ft. lbs. (70–115 Nm).

9. Lower the vehicle and, if equipped, turn the air suspension switch **ON**.

With Automatic Leveling

NOTE: Disconnect the height sensor connector link before allowing the rear axle to hang free. Then, raise the vehicle on a hoist so the suspension arms hang free with the ignition switch in the OFF position. The rear shock absorbers will vent air through the compressor and a hissing noise will be heard. When the noise stops, the air lines can be disconnected. A residual pressure of 8–24 psi will remain in the air lines.

1. Disconnect the air line by pushing in on the retainer ring and pulling the line out.

2. Remove the top retaining nut, washer and bushing.

3. Remove the bottom retaining nut and washer. Remove the shock absorber.
To install:
4. Position the shock absorber and install the bottom retaining washer and nut. Tighten to 52–85 ft. lbs. (70–115 Nm).

5. Install the top bushing, washer and retaining nut. Tighten to 14–26 ft. lbs. (19–35 Nm).

NOTE: Check the rubber sleeve on the shock absorber to be sure it is not wrapped up. To assist in

identifying wrap-up during installation, a white stripe is on the rubber sleeve and on the shock absorber body. The stripes should align. To correct a wrap-up condition, loosen the upper shock retaining nut and turn the shock to align the stripes. Retaighten the retaining nut.

6. Connect the air line to the shock absorber by pushing in on the retainer ring and installing the air line.

7. Connect the height sensor connecting link and lower the vehicle.

Coil Springs

REMOVAL & INSTALLATION

1. Raise the vehicle and support the rear axle housing. Place jack stands under the frame side rails.

2. Remove the rear stabilizer bar, if equipped.

3. Disconnect the lower studs of both rear shock absorbers from the mounting brackets on the axle tube.

4. Unsnap the right parking brake cable from the right upper arm retainer before lowering the axle.

5. Lower the axle housing until the coil springs are released. Remove the springs and insulators.

To install:

6. Position the spring in the upper and lower seats with an insulator between the upper end of the spring and frame seat.

7. Raise the axle and connect the shock absorbers to the mounting brackets. Install new retaining nuts and tighten to 52–85 ft. lbs. (70–115 Nm).

8. Snap the right parking cable into the upper arm retainer. Install the stabilizer bar, if equipped.

9. Remove the jack stands and lower the vehicle.

Air Springs

REMOVAL & INSTALLATION

1. Turn the air suspension switch **OFF**.

2. Raise and safely support the vehicle on the frame. The suspension must be at full rebound.

3. Remove the heat shield, as required. Remove the spring retainer clip. Remove the air spring solenoid as follows:

a. Disconnect the electrical connector and then disconnect the air line.

b. Remove the solenoid clip.

c. Rotate the solenoid counterclockwise to the first stop.

d. Pull the solenoid straight out

slowly to the second stop to bleed air from the system.

CAUTION

Do not fully release the solenoid until the air is completely bled from the air spring or personal injury may result.

---

e. After the air is fully bled from the system, rotate counterclockwise to the third stop and remove the solenoid from the solenoid housing. Remove the large O-ring from the solenoid housing.

4. Remove the spring piston-to-axle spring seat as follows:

a. Insert air spring removal tool T90P–5310–A or equivalent, between the axle tube and the spring seat on the forward side of the axle.

b. Position the tool so its flat end rests on the piston knob. Push downward, forcing the piston and retainer clip off the axle spring seat.

5. Remove the air spring.

To install:

6. Install the air spring solenoid as follows:

a. Check the solenoid O-rings for cuts or abrasion. Replace the O-rings as required. Lightly grease the O-ring area of the solenoid and the larger solenoid housing O-ring with silicone dielectric compound.

b. Insert the solenoid into the air spring end cap and rotate clockwise to the third stop, push in to the second stop, then rotate clockwise to the first stop.

c. Install the solenoid clip. Inspect the wire harness connector

and ensure the rubber gasket is in place at the bottom of the connector cavity.

7. Install the air spring into the frame spring seat, taking care to keep the solenoid air and electrical connections clean and free of damage.

8. Connect the push on spring retainer clip to the knob of the spring cap from the top side of the frame spring seat.

9. Connect the air line and electrical connector to the solenoid. Install the heat shield to frame spring seat, if required.

10. Align the air spring piston to axle seats. Squeeze to increase pressure and push downward on the piston, snapping the piston to axle seat at rebound and supported by the shock absorber.

NOTE: The air springs may be damaged if the suspension is allowed to compress before the spring is inflated.

11. Refill the air spring as follows:

a. Turn the air suspension switch **ON**. The ignition switch must be **ON** and the engine running or a battery charger must be connected to the battery to reduce battery drain.

b. Remove the right luggage compartment trim panel and connect Super Star II tester 007–0041–A or equivalent to the air suspension diagnostic connector.

c. Set the tester to EEC-IV/MCU mode. Also set the tester to FAST mode. Release the tester button to the HOLD (up) position and turn the tester **ON**.

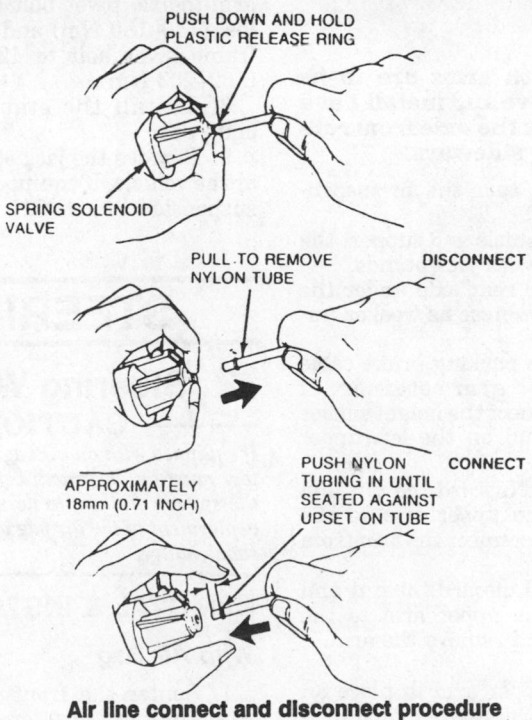

PUSH DOWN AND HOLD PLASTIC RELEASE RING

SPRING SOLENOID VALVE

PULL TO REMOVE NYLON TUBE   DISCONNECT

APPROXIMATELY 18mm (0.71 INCH)

PUSH NYLON TUBING IN UNTIL SEATED AGAINST UPSET ON TUBE   CONNECT

Air line connect and disconnect procedure

d. Depress the tester button to TEST (down) position. A Code 10 will be displayed. Within 2 minutes a Code 13 will be displayed. After Code 13 is displayed, release the tester button to HOLD (up) position, wait 5 seconds and depress the tester button to TEST (down) position. Ignore any codes displayed.

e. Release the tester button to the HOLD (up) position. Wait at least 20 seconds, then depress the tester button to TEST (down) position. Within 10 seconds, the following codes will be displayed in the order shown.

f. Within 4 seconds after Code 26 is displayed, release the tester button to the HOLD (up) position. Waiting longer than 4 seconds may result in Functional Test 31 being entered. The compressor will fill the air springs with air as long as the tester button is in the HOLD (up) position. To stop filling the air springs, depress the tester button to the TEST (down) position.

NOTE: It is possible to overheat the compressor during this operation. If the compressor overheats, the self-resetting circuit breaker in the compressor will open and remain open for about 15 minutes. This allows the compressor to cool down.

g. To exit Functional Test 26, disconnect the tester and turn the ignition switch OFF.

Rear Control Arms

REMOVAL & INSTALLATION

Upper Arm

NOTE: If both arms are to be replaced, remove and install 1 at a time to prevent the axle from rolling or slipping sideways.

1. If equipped, turn the air suspension switch OFF.
2. Raise the vehicle and support the frame side rails with jack stands.
3. Support the rear axle under the differential pinion nose as weel as under the axle.
4. Unsnap the parking brake cable from the upper arm retainer. If equipped, disconnect the height sensor from the ball stud on the left upper control arm.
5. Remove and discard the nut and bolt retaining the upper arm to the axle housing. Disconnect the arm from the housing.
6. Remove and discard the nut and bolt retaining the upper arm to the frame bracket and remove the arm.
To install:
7. Hold the upper arm in place on the front arm bracket and install a

new retaining bolt and self-locking nut. Do not tighten at this time.
8. Secure the upper arm to the axle housing with new retaining bolts and nuts. The bolts must be pointed toward the front of the vehicle.
9. Raise the suspension with a jack until the upper arm rear pivot hole is in position with the hole in the axle bushing. Install a new pivot bolt and nut with the nut facing inboard.
10. Tighten the upper arm-to-axle pivot bolts to 103–133 ft. lbs. (140–180 Nm) and upper arm-to-frame pivot bolts to 120–150 ft. lbs. (162–203 Nm).
11. Snap the parking brake cable into the upper arm retainer. Connect the height sensor to the ball stud on the left upper arm, if equipped.
12. Remove the supports from the frame and axle and lower the vehicle. If equipped, turn the air suspension switch ON.

Lower Arm

1. If equipped, turn the air suspension switch OFF.
2. Raise the vehicle and support the frame side rails with jack stands.
3. Remove the stabilizer bar, if equipped.
4. Support the axle with jack stands under the differential pinion nose as well as under the axle.
5. Remove and discard the lower arm pivot bolts and nuts and remove the lower arm.
To install:
6. Position the lower arm to the frame bracket and axle. Install new bolts and nuts.
7. Raise the axle. Tighten the lower arm-to-axle pivot bolt to 103–133 ft. lbs. (140–180 Nm) and lower arm-to-frame pivot bolt to 120–150 ft. lbs. (162–203 Nm).
8. Install the stabilizer bar, if equipped.
9. Remove the jack stands and lower the vehicle. If equipped, turn the air suspension switch ON.

STEERING

Steering Wheel
CAUTION
If equipped with an air bag, the air bag system must be disarmed, before working on the system. Failure to do so may result in deployment of the air bag and possible personal injury.

REMOVAL & INSTALLATION

With Air Bag

1. Center the front wheels in the straight-ahead position.

2. On 1990–91 vehicles, disarm the air bag system as follows:
a. Disconnect the negative battery cable.
b. Open the glove compartment door, press in the sides and lower the door down past the stops. Remove the heater duct, if necessary. Disconnect the electrical connector from the backup power supply (blue box, 1 connector).

NOTE: The backup power supply allows air bag deployment if the battery or battery cables are damaged in an accident before the crash sensors close. The power supply is a capacitor that will leak down in approximately 15 minutes after the battery is disconnected or in 1 minute if the battery positive cable is grounded. The backup power supply must be disconnected before any air bag related service is performed.

c. Remove the 4 nut and washer assemblies retaining the driver air bag module and remove the steering wheel.

CAUTION
When carrying a live air bag, make sure the bag and trim cover are pointed away from the body. In the unlikely event of an accidental deployment, the bag will then deploy with minimal chance of injury. When placing a live air bag on a bench or other surface, always face the bag and trim cover up, away from the surface. This will reduce the motion of the module if it is accidently deployed.

d. Disconnect the driver air bag module connector and attach a jumper wire to the air bag terminals on the clockspring.
3. On 1992–93 vehicles, disarm the air bag system as follows:
a. Disconnect the positive battery cable. Wait 1 minute for the backup power supply in the diagnostic monitor to deplete its stored energy.
b. Remove the 4 nut and washer assemblies retaining the driver air bag module to the steering wheel and remove the air bag module.

CAUTION
When carrying a live air bag, make sure the bag and trim cover are pointed away from the body. In the unlikely event of an accidental deployment, the bag will then deploy with minimal chance of injury. When placing a live air bag on a bench or other surface, always face the bag and trim cover up, away from the surface. This will reduce the motion of the module if it is accidently deployed.

c. Disconnect the driver air bag connector. Connect air bag simula-

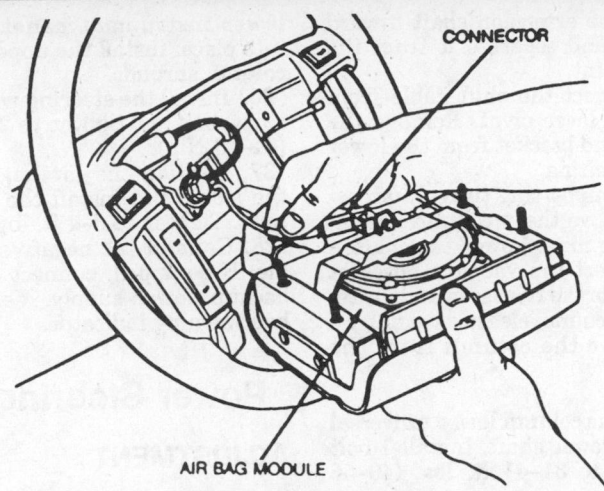

Air bag module removal

tor tool 105–00008 or equivalent, to the vehicle harness at the top of the steering wheel.

4. Disconnect the cruise control wire harness from the steering wheel, if equipped.

5. Remove and discard the steering wheel bolt. Remove the steering wheel using a suitable puller. Route the contact assembly wire harness through the steering wheel as the wheel is lifted off the shaft.

NOTE: Do not use a knock-off type steering wheel puller or strike the retaining bolt with a hammer. This could cause damage to the steering shaft bearing.

To install:

6. Make sure the front wheels are in the straight-ahead position.

7. Route the contact assembly wire harness through the steering wheel the steering wheel on the steering shaft. The steering wheel and shaft alignment marks should be aligned. Make sure the air bag contact wire is not pinched.

8. Install a new steering wheel retaining bolt and tighten to 23–33 ft. lbs. (31–48 Nm).

9. If equipped, connect the cruise control wire harness to the wheel and snap the connector assembly into the steering wheel clip. Make sure the wiring does not get trapped between the steering wheel and contact assembly.

10. Connect the air bag wire harness to the air bag module and install the module to the steering wheel. Tighten the module retaining nuts to 3–4 ft. lbs. (4–6 Nm).

11. Connect the air bag backup power supply and negative battery cable. Verify the air bag warning indicator.

Without Air Bag

1. Disconnect the negative battery cable.

2. Remove the horn pad and cover assembly. Disconnect the horn electrical connector.

3. Disconnect the cruise control switch electrical connector, if equipped.

4. Remove and discard the steering wheel bolt. Remove the steering wheel using a suitable puller.

NOTE: Do not use a knock-off type steering wheel puller or strike the retaining bolt with a hammer. This could cause damage to the steering shaft bearing.

To install:

5. Align the index marks on the steering wheel and shaft and install the steering wheel.

6. Install a new steering wheel retaining bolt and tighten to 30 ft. lbs. (41 Nm).

7. Connect the cruise control electrical connector, if equipped.

8. Connect the horn electrical connector and install the horn pad and cover.

9. Connect the negative battery cable.

Steering Column

REMOVAL & INSTALLATION

1989

1. Disconnect the negative battery cable.

2. Remove the bolt attaching the steering column shaft to the lower steering shaft assembly. Disengage the U-joint stub shaft from the column shaft by collapsing the intermediate shaft assembly. Disconnect the transmission shift rod from the transmission control selector lever, at the bottom of the shift tube.

3. Remove the shift linkage grommet and replace with new, using shift linkage insulator tool T67P–7341–A or equivalent.

4. Remove the steering column trim shrouds.

5. Remove the steering column cover and hood release mechanism directly under the column.

6. Disconnect the electrical connectors to the steering column switches.

7. Loosen the 4 nuts holding the column to the brake pedal support, allowing the column to be lowered enough for access to the shift indicator lever and cable assembly.

NOTE: Be careful not to lower the column too far, so the plastic lever or cable is not damaged due to the weight of the column.

8. Reach between the steering column and instrument panel and gently lift the shift indicator cable off the cleat on the shift indicator lever. Remove the shift indicator cable clamp from the steering column tube.

9. Remove the 4 screws that attach the dust boot to the dash panel.

10. Remove the 4 attaching nuts holding the column to the brake pedal support. Lower the column to clear the 4 mounting bolts and pull the column out.

To install:

11. Install the steering column by inserting the lower end of the steering column through the opening in the dash panel. Be careful not to damage the column during installation.

12. Align the 4 bolts on the brake pedal support with the mounting holes on the column collar and bracket. Attach the nuts loosely, so the column will hang with a clearance between the column and instrument panel.

13. Loosely assemble the shift indicator cable clamp to the steering column outer tube.

14. Reach between the steering column and instrument panel and attach the shift indicator cable onto the shift indicator lever by slipping the loop on the cable over the cleat on the lever.

15. Tighten the 4 column-to-brake pedal support nuts to 20–37 ft. lbs. (27–50 Nm).

16. Move the shift selector into the **D** position against the drive stop on the insert plate. Rotate the shift indicator bracket, located approximately midpoint on the steering column outer tube, clockwise or counterclockwise until the shift indicator pointer in the instrument cluster centers on the letter D. Tighten the nut on the bracket.

17. Connect the electrical connectors to the steering column switches.

18. Slide the lower steering shaft assembly into the steering column shaft and attach with the bolt and nut. Tighten to 35–45 ft. lbs. (48–61 Nm). Pry the lower shaft back and forth un-

til there is ⅛ in. (3mm) coupling insulator flatness. The stone shield must be removed to gain access to the coupling insulator.

19. Connect the shift rod to the shift lever on the lower end of the steering column in the engine compartment using shift linkage insulator tool T67P-7341-A or equivalent. Make sure the grommet has been replaced before the rod is installed. Adjust the shift linkage.

20. Engage the dust boot at the base of the steering column to the dash panel opening. Install the 4 screws that attach the dust boot to the dash panel.

21. Install the steering column trim shrouds.

22. Install the hood release mechanism and steering column cover beneath the steering column.

23. Connect the negative battery cable. Check the steering column for proper operation.

1990–93

1. Make sure the front wheels are in the straight-ahead position. Properly disarm the air bag system.

2. Remove the steering wheel.

3. Remove the right and left lower mouldings from the instrument panel by pulling up and snapping out.

4. Remove the instrument panel lower trim panel and lower steering column shroud.

5. Remove the air bag clockspring contact assembly as follows:

   a. Disconnect the contact assembly wire harness.

   b. Apply 2 strips of tape across the contact assembly stator and rotor to prevent accidental rotation.

   c. Remove the 3 contact assembly retaining screws and pull the contact assembly off the steering column shaft.

6. Unscrew the tilt lever from the column.

7. Place the ignition lock cylinder in the **RUN** position. Using an ⅛ in. drift, depress the lock cylinder retaining pin through the access hole and remove the lock cylinder.

8. Remove the 4 retaining screws from the lower column shroud and remove the column shrouds.

9. Remove the 2 instrument panel reinforcement brace bolts and remove the reinforcement.

10. Remove the steering column to parking brake control shake brace. Disconnect the shift indicator cable from the actuator housing by removing 1 screw.

11. Remove the 2 combination switch retaining screws and set the combination switch aside.

12. Remove the pinch bolt from the steering column to extension shaft.

Compress the extension shaft toward the engine and separate it from the column U-joint.

13. Disconnect the shift cable from the selector lever pivot. Remove the shift cable and bracket from the lower column mounting.

14. While supporting the column assembly, remove the 4 column assembly retaining nuts. Lower the column and disconnect the vacuum hoses at the parking brake release switch or remove the vacuum release assembly.

15. Remove the column from the vehicle.

To install:

16. Align the column lower universal joint to the lower shaft. Install 1 bolt and tighten to 31–41 ft. lbs. (40–56 Nm).

17. Connect the parking brake release vacuum hoses.

18. Position the steering column assembly to the column support bracket. Install the 4 retaining nuts and tighten to 9–14 ft. lbs. (13–19 Nm).

19. Position the shift cable bracket, with the shift cable attached, to the lower 2 screws of the column. Tighten to 5–8 ft. lbs. (7–11 Nm). Snap the shift cable onto the shift selector pivot ball.

20. Install the combination switch with the 2 retaining screws. Tighten to 18–26 inch lbs. (2–3 Nm). Connect all electrical connectors.

21. Attach the shift indicator cable loop on the shift selector hook and install the shift indicator cable bracket to the actuator housing. Install the steering column to parking brake control shake brace.

22. Install the instrument panel reinforcement brace and tighten the bolts.

23. Install the lock cylinder and the tilt lever.

24. Install the air bag clockspring contact assembly as follows:

   a. Make sure the front wheels are in the straight-ahead position and the steering column shaft alignment mark is at the 12 o'clock position.

   b. Align the contact assembly to the column shaft and mounting bosses and slide the contact assembly onto the shaft.

   c. Install the 3 retaining screws and tighten to 18–26 inch lbs. (2–3 Nm). Remove the tape strips.

   d. Route the contact assembly down the column assembly and connect to the wire harness.

NOTE: If a new contact assembly is being installed, remove the plastic lock mechanism after the contact assembly is secured to the column.

25. Install the lower instrument panel cover and snap the right and left

lower instrument panel mouldings into place. Install the upper and lower column shrouds.

26. Install the steering wheel. Install a new bolt and tighten to 23–33 ft. lbs. (31–48 Nm).

27. Position the air bag module to the wheel and install the 4 retaining nuts. Tighten to 3–4 ft. lbs. (4–6 Nm).

28. Connect the negative battery cable. If equipped, connect the air bag backup power supply. Verify the air bag warning indicator.

Power Steering Gear

ADJUSTMENT

Adjust the total-over-center position load to eliminate excessive lash between the sector and rack teeth as follows:

1. Disconnect the pitman arm from the sector shaft.

2. Disconnect the fluid return line at the reservoir. Cap the rservoir return line pipe.

3. Place the end of the return line in a clean container and turn the steering wheel from left stop to right stop several times to discharge the fluid from the gear.

4. Turn the steering wheel to 45 degrees from the left stop.

5. Using a feet pound torque wrench on the steering wheel nut, determine the torque required to rotate the shaft slowly approximately ¼ turn from the 45 degree position. If equipped with tilt column, place the steering wheel in the center tilt position.

6. Turn the steering wheel back to center and determine the torque required to rotate the shaft back and forth across the center position. If the reading is not to specification, loosen the nut and turn the adjuster screw until the reading is to specification. Tighten the wheel nut while holding the screw in place.

7. Check the readings and replace the pitman arm and steering wheel hub cover.

8. Connect the fluid return line to the reservoir and fill the reservoir. Check the belt tension and adjust, if necessary.

REMOVAL & INSTALLATION

1. Disconnect the negative battery cable.

2. Remove the stone shield.

3. Tag the pressure and return lines so they may be reassembled in their original positions.

4. Disconnect the pressure and return lines from the steering gear. Plug

POWER STEERING GEAR ADJUSTMENT SPECIFICATIONS

Vehicles With 0-8045 km (0-5000 miles)	
Checking: Reset if total meshload over mechanical center is not 1.69-2.71 N-m (15-24 lb-in)	**Reset:** Set torque measured rocking across center to a value 1.24-1.69 N-m (11-15 lb-in) greater than that measured 45 degrees from the right stop.
Vehicles With More Than 8045 km (5000 miles) Or Where The Sector Shaft Has Been Replaced	
Checking: Reset if meshload measured while rocking input shaft over center is less than 1.2 N-m (10 lb-in) greater than the torque 45 degrees from the right stop.	**Reset:** Set torque measured rocking across center to a value 1.13-1.58 N-m (10-14 lb-in) greater than that measured 45 degrees from the right stop.

the lines and ports in the gear to prevent the entry of dirt.

5. Remove the clamp bolts retaining the flexible coupling to the steering gear.

6. Raise and safely support the vehicle. Remove the nut from the sector shaft.

7. Remove the pitman arm from the sector shaft with pitman arm remover tool T64P-3590-F or equivalent. Remove the tool from the pitman arm.

NOTE: Do not damage the seals and/or gear housing. Do not use a non-approved tool such as a pickle fork.

8. Support the steering gear and remove the steering gear retaining bolts.

9. Work the gear free of the flex coupling and remove the gear.

10. If the flex coupling did not come off with the gear, lift it off the shaft.
To install:

11. Turn the steering wheel to the straight-ahead position.

12. Center the steering gear input shaft with the indexing flat facing downward on 1989-91 Crown Victoria and Grand Marquis and 1989-90 Town Car. On 1991-93 Town Car and 1992-93 Crown Victoria and Grand Marquis, center the steering gear input shaft with the centerline of the 2 indexing flats at 4 o'clock.

13. Slide the steering gear input shaft into the flex coupling and into place on the frame side rail. Install the retaining bolts and tighten to 50-65 ft. lbs. (68-88 Nm).

14. Make sure the wheels are in the straight-ahead position. Install the pitman arm on the sector shaft and install the lockwasher and nut. Tighten the nut to 200-250 ft. lbs. (271-339 Nm). Install and tighten the sector shaft and retaining bolts.

15. Move the flex coupling into place on the steering gear input shaft. Install the retaining bolt and tighten to 20-30 ft. lbs. (27-41 Nm).

16. Connect the prssure and return lines to the steering gear and tighten the lines. Fill the reservoir and turn the steering wheel from stop-to-stop to distribute the fluid. Check the fluid level and add fluid, if necessary.

17. Start the engine and turn the steering wheel from left to right. Check for leaks. Install the stone shield.

Power Steering Pump

REMOVAL & INSTALLATION

1. Disconnect the negative battery cable.

2. Disconnect the fluid return hose at the pump and drain the fluid into a container.

3. Remove the pressure hose from the pump and, if necessary, drain the fluid into a container. Do not remove the fitting from the pump.

4. Disconnect the belt from the pulley. On 5.0L and 5.8L engine, use pulley removal tool T69L-10300-B or equivalent, to remove the pulley.

5. Remove the mounting bolts and remove the pump.
To install:

6. On 5.0L and 5.8L engine, place the pump on the mounting bracket and install the bolts at the front of the pump. Tighten to 30-45 ft. lbs. (40-62 Nm).

7. On 4.6L engine, place the pump on the mounting bosses of the engine block and install the bolts at the side of the pump. Tighten to 15-22 ft. lbs. (20-30 Nm).

8. On 5.0L and 5.8L engines, install the pump pulley using pulley replacer tool T65P-3A733-C or equivalent.

9. Place the belt on the pump pulley and adjust the tension, if necessary.

10. Install the pressure hose to the pump fitting. Tighten the tube nut with a tube nut wrench rather than with an open-end wrench. Tighten to 20-25 ft. lbs. (27-34 Nm).

NOTE: Do not overtighten this fitting. Swivel and/or end play of the fitting is normal and does not indicate a loose fitting. Overtightening the tube nut can collapse the tube nut wall, resulting in a leak and requiring replacement of the entire pressure hose assembly. Use of an open-end wrench to tighten the nut can deform the tube nut hex which may

result in improper torque and may make further servicing of the system difficult.

11. Connect the return hose to the pump and tighten the clamp. Fill the reservoir with the proper type and quantity of fluid. Bleed the air from the system.

BELT ADJUSTMENT

4.6L Engine

The 4.6L engine is equipped with an automatic belt tensioner. No adjustment is necessary or possible. The belt tensioner is equipped with a belt wear indicator; when 1 percent belt stretch is indicated, the drive belt must be replaced.

5.0L and 5.8L Engines

NOTE: The power steering pump and alternator are driven by the same belt. Belt adjustment is made using the alternator.

1. Loosen the alternator pivot and adjustment bolts.

2. Install a suitable belt tension gauge midway between the pulleys on the longest accessible belt span. Install an open end wrench over the alternator adjustment boss, then apply tension to the belt, using the wrench.

3. Set the tension on a new belt to 170 lbs. or a used belt to 140 lbs. While maintaining the tension, tighten the alternator adjustment bolt to 29 ft. lbs. (39 Nm).

4. Remove the belt tension gauge, start the engine and let it idle for 5 minutes.

5. Shut off the engine and install the tension gauge. Apply tension with the open end wrench and slowly loosen the adjustment bolt to allow belt tension to increase to the used belt specification, 140 lbs. Tighten the adjustment bolt to 29 ft. lbs. (39 Nm).

6. Tighten the pivot bolt to 50 ft. lbs. (68 Nm).

SYSTEM BLEEDING

1. Disconnect the ignition coil.

Raise and safely support the vehicle so the front wheels are off the floor.

2. Fill the power steering fluid reservoir.

3. Crank the engine with the starter and add fluid until the level remains constant.

4. While cranking the engine, rotate the steering wheel from lock-to-lock.

NOTE: The front wheels must be off the floor during lock-to-lock rotation of the steering wheel.

5. Check the fluid level and add fluid, if necessary.

6. Connect the ignition coil wire. Start the engine and allow it to run for several minutes.

7. Rotate the steering wheel from lock-to-lock.

8. Shut off the engine and check the fluid level. Add fluid, if necessary.

9. If air is still present in the system, purge the system of air using power steering pump air evacuator tool 021–00014 or equivalent, as follows:

a. Make sure the power steering pump reservoir is full to the COLD FULL mark on the dipstick or to just above the minimum indication on the reservoir.

b. Tightly insert the rubber stopper of the air evacuator assembly into the pump reservoir fill neck.

c. Apply 15 in. Hg maximum vacuum on the pump reservoir for a minimum of 3 minutes with the engine idling. As air purges from the system, vacuum will fall off. Maintain adequate vacuum with the vacuum source.

d. Release the vacuum and remove the vacuum source. Fill the reservoir to the COLD FULL mark or to just above the minimum indication on the rservoir.

e. With the engine idling, apply 15 in. Hg vacuum to the pump reservoir. Slowly cycle the steering wheel from lock-to-lock every 30 seconds for approximately 5 minutes. Do not hold the steering wheel on the stops while cycling. Maintain adequate vacuum with the vacuum source as the air purges.

f. Release the vacuum and remove the vacuum source. Add fluid, if necessary.

g. Start the engine and cycle the steering wheel. Check for oil leaks at all connections. In severe cases of aeration, it may be necessary to repeat Steps 9b–9f.

Tie Rod Ends

REMOVAL & INSTALLATION

1. Raise fond support the vehicle safely.

2. Remove the cotter pin and nut from the tie rod end ball stud.

3. Loosen the tie rod adjusting sleeve clamp bolts and remove the rod end from the spindle arm or center link, using ball stud remover tool 3290–D or equivalent.

4. Remove the tie rod end from the sleeve, counting the exact number of turns required to do so.

To install:

5. Install the new tie rod end into the sleeve, using the exact number of turns it took to remove the old one. Install the tie rod end ball studs into the spindle arm or center link.

6. Install the stud and stud nut. Tighten to 43–47 ft. lbs. (59–63 Nm), then continue tightening the nut to align its next catellation with the cotter pin hole in the stud. Install a new cotter pin.

NOTE: Never loosen the nut to align the nut castellation and cotter pin hole.

7. Check the toe and adjust if necessary. Loosen the clamps from the sleeve and oil the sleeve, clamps, bolts and nuts. Position the adjusting sleeve clamps so the bolts are horizontal, with the threaded end pointing toward the front of the vehicle, and tighten the clamp nuts to 20–22 ft. lbs. (27–29 Nm).

BRAKES

Master Cylinder

REMOVAL & INSTALLATION

1. Disconnect the negative battery cable.

2. If equipped with anti-lock brakes, depress the brake pedal several times to exhaust all vacuum in the system.

3. Remove the brake lines from the primary and secondary outlet ports of the master cylinder.

4. Disconnect the brake warning indicator connector.

5. If equipped with anti-lock brakes, disconnect the Hydraulic Control Unit (HCU) supply hose at the master cylinder and secure in a position to prevent loss of brake fluid.

6. Remove the nuts attaching master cylinder to the brake booster assembly.

7. Slide the master cylinder forward and upward from the vehicle.

To install:

8. If equipped with anti-lock brakes, install a new seal in the groove in the master cylinder mounting face.

9. Install the master cylinder on the booster studs and install the mounting

nuts. Tighten the nuts to 13–25 ft. lbs. (18–34 Nm) on all except vehicles with anti-lock brakes. If equipped with anti-lock brakes, tighten the nuts to 16–21 ft. lbs. (21–29 Nm).

10. Install short brake lines in the master cylinder outlet ports and position them so they point back into the reservoir and the ends of the lines are submerged in brake fluid.

11. Fill the reservoir with brake fluid and cover the reservoir with a shop towel.

12. Pump the brakes until clear, bubble-free fluid comes out of both brake lines. If any brake fluid spills on the paint, wash it off immediately with water.

13. Remove the short brake lines and connect the vehicle brake lines to the master cylinder. Bleed each brake line at the master cylinder using the following procedure:

a. Have an assistant pump the brake pedal 10 times and then hold firm pressure on the pedal.

b. Crack the rear most brake line fitting with a tubing wrench until a stream of brake fluid comes out. Have the assistant maintain pressure on the brake pedal until the brake line fitting is tightened again.

c. Repeat this operation until clear, bubble free fluid comes out from around the brake line fitting.

d. Repeat this bleeding operation at the front brake line fitting.

14. Attach the HCU supply hose to the master cylinder.

15. Connect the brake warning indicator switch connector.

16. Bleed the system. Operate the brakes several times, then check for external hydraulic leaks.

Brake Control Valves

There are several types of valves in use. Not all valves perform the same function nor are they located in the same place on every vehicle.

Town Car—1989 vehicles use a 3-way brake control valve containing a pressure differential valve, metering valve and proportioning valve located on the frame. 1990–93 vehicles use a brake pressure control valve that contains twin brake proportioning valves located on the frame.

Crown Victoria and Grand Marquis—a pressure control valve is screwed into the master cylinder. In addition, some vehicles have a metering valve located on the frame. Vehicles with anti-lock brakes have a proportioning valve located on the frame.

REMOVAL & INSTALLATION

1. Disconnect the negative battery cable.

2. Disconnect the brake line(s) from the valve. Disconnect the electrical connector, if equipped.

3. Unscrew the valve from the master cylinder or remove the mounting screw from the frame or fender apron, as required.

4. Installation is the reverse of the removal procedure. Bleed the brake system.

Power Brake Booster

REMOVAL & INSTALLATION

1. Disconnect the negative battery cable.

2. If equipped with anti-lock brakes, pump the brake pedal several times until all vacuum is removed from the booster.

3. Remove the master cylinder from the booster and move it aside without disconnecting the brake lines. Be careful not to kink the brake lines.

4. Disconnect the manifold vacuum hose from the booster check valve.

5. Working inside the vehicle below the instrument panel, remove the stoplight switch connector. Remove the switch retaining pin and slide the switch off the brake pedal pin just far enough for the outer arm to clear the pin, then remove the switch. Be careful not to damage the switch.

6. Remove the booster-to-dash panel attaching nuts.

7. Slide the booster pushrod, washers and bushing off the brake pedal pin. Remove the booster.

8. Installation is the reverse of removal procedure. Tighten the booster-to-dash panel attaching nuts and the master cylinder attaching nuts to 13–25 ft. lbs. (18–34 Nm).

Brake Caliper

REMOVAL & INSTALLATION

Front

1. Raise and safely support the vehicle. Remove the front wheel and tire assembly.

2. Loosen the brake line fitting that connects the brake hose to the brake line at the frame bracket. Remove the retaining clip from the hose and bracket and disengage the hose from the bracket. Remove the hose from the caliper.

3. Remove the caliper locating pins and remove the caliper. If removing both calipers, mark the right and left sides so they may be reinstalled correctly.

To install:

4. Install the caliper over the rotor with the outer brake shoe against the rotor's braking surface.

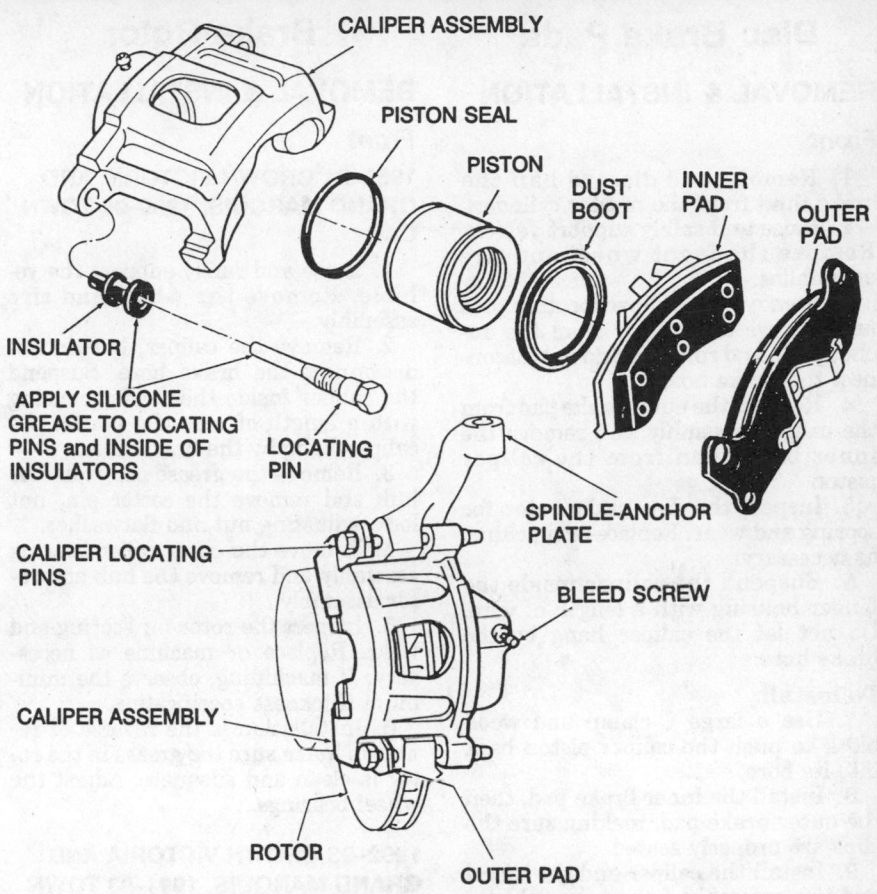

Front disc brake assembly

5. Lubricate the inside of the locating pin insulators with silicone dialectric grease. Install the caliper locating pins and tighten to 45–60 ft. lbs. (61–81 Nm).

6. Install new sealing washers on each side of the brake hose fitting outlet and install the bolt, through the hose fitting and into the caliper. Tighten the bolt to 30 ft. lbs. (41 Nm).

7. Position the other end of the brake hose in the bracket and install the retaining clip. Make sure the hose is not twisted.

8. Connect the brake line to the brake hose and tighten the fitting nut.

9. Bleed the brake system, install the wheel and tire assembly and lower the vehicle.

10. Apply the brake pedal several times before moving the vehicle, to position the brake pads.

Rear

1. Raise and safely support the vehicle. Remove the rear wheel and tire assembly.

2. Remove the brake fitting retaining bolt from the caliper and disconnect the flexible brake hose from the caliper. Plug the hose and the caliper fitting.

3. Remove the caliper locating pins. Lift the caliper off the rotor and anchor plate using a rotating motion.

NOTE: Do not pry directly against the plastic piston or damage to the piston will occur.

To install:

4. Position the caliper assembly above the rotor with the anti-rattle spring located on the lower adapter support arm. Install the caliper over the rotor with a rotating motion. Make sure the inner pad is properly positioned.

5. Install the caliper locating pins and start them in the threads by hand. Tighten them to 19–25 ft. lbs. (26–34 Nm).

6. Install the brake hose on the caliper with a new gasket on each side of the fitting outlet. Insert the retaining bolt and tighten to 30–40 ft. lbs. (40–54 Nm).

7. Bleed the brake system, install the wheel and tire assembly and lower the vehicle.

8. Pump the brake pedal prior to moving the vehicle to position the linings.

Disc Brake Pads

REMOVAL & INSTALLATION

Front

1. Remove and discard half the brake fluid from the master cylinder.
2. Raise and safely support vehicle. Remove the front wheel and tire assemblies.
3. Remove the caliper locating pins and remove the caliper from the anchor plate and rotor, but do not disconnect the brake hose.
4. Remove the outer brake pad from the caliper assembly and remove the inner brake pad from the caliper piston.
5. Inspect the disc brake rotor for scoring and wear. Replace or machine, as necessary.
6. Suspend the caliper inside the fender housing with a length of wire. Do not let the caliper hang by the brake hose.

To install:

7. Use a large C-clamp and wood block to push the caliper piston back into its bore.
8. Install the inner brake pad, then the outer brake pad, making sure the clips are properly seated.
9. Install the caliper and the wheel and tire assembly. Lower the vehicle.
10. Pump the brake pedal prior to moving the vehicle to seat the brake pads. Refill the master cylinder.

Rear

1. Remove and discard half the brake fluid from the master cylinder.
2. Raise and safely support vehicle. Remove the rear wheel and tire assemblies.
3. Remove the caliper locating pins and remove the caliper from the anchor plate and rotor, but do not disconnect the brake hose.
4. Remove the inner and outer brake pads.
5. Inspect the disc brake rotor for scoring and wear. Replace or machine, as necessary.
6. Suspend the caliper inside the fender housing with a length of wire. Do not let the caliper hang by the brake hose.

To install:

7. Use a large C-clamp and wood block to push the caliper piston back into its bore.
8. Install the inner brake pad, then the outer brake pad, making sure the clips are properly seated.
9. Install the caliper and the wheel and tire assembly. Lower the vehicle.
10. Pump the brake pedal prior to moving the vehicle to seat the brake pads. Refill the master cylinder.

Brake Rotor

REMOVAL & INSTALLATION

Front

1989–91 CROWN VICTORIA AND GRAND MARQUIS, 1989–90 TOWN CAR

1. Raise and safely support the vehicle. Remove the wheel and tire assembly.
2. Remove the caliper, but do not disconnect the brake hose. Suspend the caliper inside the fender housing with a length of wire. Do not let the caliper hang by the brake hose.
3. Remove the grease cap from the hub and remove the cotter pin, nut lock, adjusting nut and flatwasher.
4. Remove the outer roller bearing assembly and remove the hub and rotor assembly.
5. Inspect the rotor for scoring and wear. Replace or machine as necessary. If machining, observe the minimum thickness specification.
6. Installation is the reverse of removal. Make sure the grease in the rotor is clean and adequate. Adjust the wheel bearings.

1992–93 CROWN VICTORIA AND GRAND MARQUIS, 1991–93 TOWN CAR

1. Raise and safely support the vehicle. Remove the wheel and tire assembly.
2. Remove the caliper, but do not disconnect the brake hose. Suspend the caliper inside the fender housing with a length of wire. Do not let the caliper hang by the brake hose.
3. Remove the rotor retaining push nuts, if equipped, and remove the rotor from the hub.
4. Inspect the rotor for scoring and wear. Replace or machine as necessary. If machining, observe the minimum thickness specification.
5. Installation is the reverse of the removal procedure.

Rear

1. Raise and safely support the vehicle. Remove the wheel and tire assembly.
2. Remove the caliper, but do not disconnect the brake hose. Suspend the caliper inside the fender housing with a length of wire. Do not let the caliper hang by the brake hose.
3. Remove the rotor retaining push nuts and remove the rotor from the hub.
4. Inspect the rotor for scoring and wear. Replace or machine as necessary. If machining, observe the minimum thickness specification.

5. Installation is the reverse of the removal procedure.

Rear Brake Drum

REMOVAL & INSTALLATION

1. Raise and safely support the vehicle.
2. Remove the wheel and tire assembly.
3. Remove the drum retaining nuts and remove the brake drum.

NOTE: If the drum will not come off, pry the rubber plug from the backing plate. Insert a narrow rod through the hole in the backing plate and disengage the adjusting lever from the adjusting screw. While holding the adjustment lever away from the screw, back off the adjusting screw with a brake adjusting tool.

4. Inspect the brake drum for scoring and wear. Replace or machine as necessary. If machining, observe the maximum diameter specification.
5. Installation is the reverse of removal.

Rear Brake Shoes

REMOVAL & INSTALLATION

1. Raise and safely support the vehicle. Remove the rear wheel and tire assemblies. Remove the brake drum.
2. Remove the shoe-to-anchor springs and unhook the cable eye from the anchor pin. Remove the anchor pin plate.
3. Remove the shoe hold-down springs, shoes, adjusting screw, pivot nut, socket and automatic adjustment parts.
4. Remove the parking brake link, spring and retainer. Disconnect the parking brake cable from the parking brake lever.
5. After removing the rear brake secondary shoe, disassemble the parking brake lever from the shoe by removing the retaining clip and spring washer.

To install:

6. Before installing the rear brake shoes, assemble the parking brake lever to the secondary shoe and secure it with the spring washer and retaining clip.
7. Apply a light coating of caliper slide grease at the points where the brake shoes contact the backing plate. Be careful not to get any lubricant on the brake linings.
8. Position the brake shoes on the backing plate. The primary shoe with the short lining faces the front of the vehicle, the secondary shoe with the

long lining, to the rear. Secure the assembly with the hold-down springs. Install the parking brake link, spring and retainer. Back-off the parking brake adjustment, then connect the parking brake cable to the parking brake lever.

9. Install the anchor pin plate on the anchor pin. Place the cable eye over the anchor pin with the crimped side toward the drum. Install the primary shoe to the anchor pin.

10. Install the cable guide on the secondary shoe web with the flanged hole fitted into the hole in the secondary shoe web. Thread the cable around the cable guide groove.

NOTE: The cable must be positioned in the groove and not between the guide and the shoe web.

11. Install the secondary shoe-to-anchor spring. Make sure the cable eye is not cocked or binding on the anchor pin when installed. All parts should be flat on the anchor pin.

12. Apply a thin coat of lubricant to the threads and the socket end of the adjusting screw. Turn the adjusting screw into the adjusting pivot nut to the limit of the threads, then back-off ½ turn.

NOTE: Make sure the socket end of the adjusting screw is stamped with an R or L, indicating the right or left side of the vehicle. The adjusting screw assemblies must be installed on the correct side for proper brake shoe adjustment.

13. Place the adjusting socket on the screw and install the assembly between the shoe ends with the adjusting screw toothed wheel nearest the secondary shoe.

14. Hook the cable hook into the hole in the adjusting lever. The adjusting levers are stamped with an R or L to indicate their installation on the right or left side.

15. Position the hooked end of the adjuster spring completely into the large hole in the primary shoe web. Connect the loop end of the spring to the adjuster lever hole.

16. Pull the adjuster lever, cable and automatic adjuster spring down and toward the rear, engaging the pivot hook in the large hole of the secondary shoe web.

17. Make sure the upper ends of the brake shoes are seated against the anchor pin and the shoes are centered on the backing plate.

18. Adjust the brakes using brake adjustment gauge D81L–1103–A or equivalent.

19. Install the brake drum, wheel and tire assemblies and lower the vehicle.

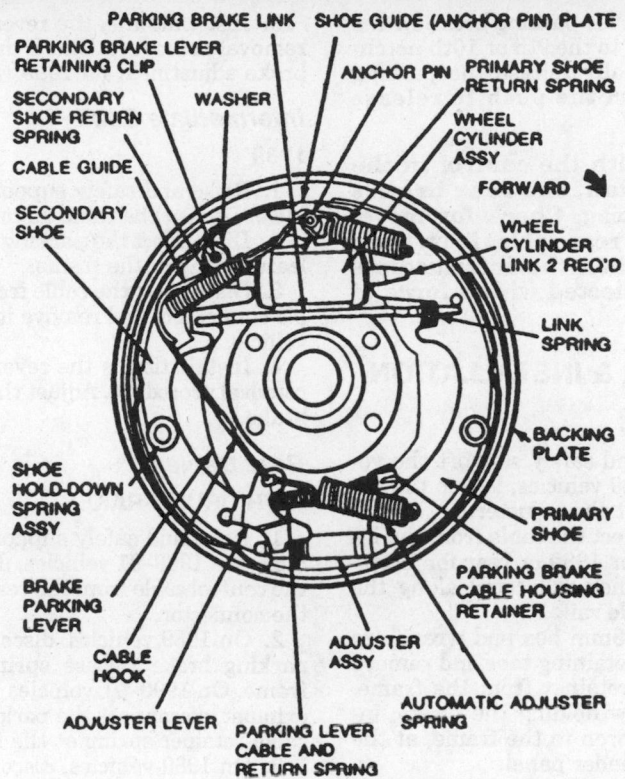

Brake shoe assembly

20. Apply the brakes several times while backing up the vehicle. After each stop, the vehicle must be moved forward.

Wheel Cylinder

REMOVAL & INSTALLATION

1. Remove the wheel and tire assembly and the brake drum.
2. Remove the brake shoe assembly.
3. Disconnect the brake line from the wheel cylinder at the backing plate.
4. Remove the wheel cylinder attaching bolts and remove the wheel cylinder.
5. Installation is the reverse of the removal procedure. Tighten the wheel cylinder attaching bolts to 10–20 ft. lbs. (14–28 Nm).
6. Bleed the brake system.

Parking Brake Cable

ADJUSTMENT

1989

1. Make sure the parking brake is fully released.
2. Place the transmission in N. Raise and safely support the vehicle.
3. Tighten the adjusting nut against the cable equalizer, causing a rear wheel brake drag. Loosen the adjusting nut until the rear brakes are fully released. There should be no brake drag.
4. Lower the vehicle and check the operation of the parking brake.

1990–93

NOTE: The following procedure is to be used only if a new parking brake control assembly is installed. All components of the parking brake system must be installed prior to the adjustment procedure. The parking brake control with automatic tensioning is preset by means of a shipping clip. The following procedure must be followed in sequence and must be done with the vehicle weight on the axle.

1. Verify removal of the shipping clip. The take up reel will apply tension to the system.
2. Depress the parking brake control to the 8th notch.
3. Push the parking brake control pedal to release.
4. Check function as follows:
   a. Apply the parking brake with a full stroke, to the 9th or 10th notch.
   b. Release the parking brake by shifting the vehicle into a forward gear with the engine running. The control must release.

c. Apply the parking brake with a full stroke, to the 9th or 10th notch.

d. Manually release the parking brake with the push to release feature.

NOTE: With the control in the OFF position, the rear brakes must not drag. Check for movement of the rear cables from their conduits when the intermediate cable is deflected with a force of 10–15 lbs.

REMOVAL & INSTALLATION

Front Cable

1. Raise and safely support the vehicle. On 1989 vehicles, loosen the adjusting nut at the adjuster.

2. Disconnect the cable from the intermediate for 1989 or rear for 1990–93 cable connector located along the left frame side rail.

3. Use a 13mm box end wrench to depress the retaining tabs and remove the conduit retainer from the frame. Remove screw holding the plastic inner fender apron to the frame, at the rear of the fender panel.

4. Pull back the fender apron. If equipped, remove the spring clip retainer that holds the parking brake cable to the frame.

5. Pull the cable through the frame and let it hang in the wheel housing. Lower the vehicle.

6. Inside the passenger compartment, remove the sound deadener cover from the cable at the dash panel.

7. On 1989 vehicles, remove the spring retainer and cable end from the clevis at the parking brake control.

8. On 1990–93 vehicles, pull the cable until the parking brake control take up spring tang is at full clockwise position. Use a fabricated tool to retain the reel spring and disconnect the cable from the take up reel.

9. Using a 13mm box end wrench, depress the retaining tabs and remove the conduit from the cable (carbureted)assembly. Push the cable down through the dash panel and remove cable from inside the wheel housing.

10. Installation is the reverse of the removal procedure. Check the parking brake adjustment on 1989 vehicles.

Intermediate Cable

1989

1. Raise and safely support the vehicle. Loosen the cable adjusting nut.

2. Disconnect the parking brake release spring at the frame.

3. Disconnect the cable from the cable connectors and remove it from the vehicle.

4. Installation is the reverse of the removal procedure. Adjust the parking brake.

Rear Cables

WITH DRUM BRAKES

1. Raise and safely support the vehicle. On 1990–91 vehicles, disconnect the control cable from the rear cable at the connector.

2. On 1989 vehicles, disconnect the parking brake release spring at the frame. On 1990–91 vehicles with dual exhaust, disconnect the parking brake cable retainer spring at the frame.

3. On 1989 vehicles, disconnect the left cable from the intermediate cable connector. On 1990–91 vehicles, disconnect the left cable from the right cable at the adjuster bracket.

4. On 1989 vehicles, use a 13mm box end wrench to depress the tabs and remove the left conduit retainer from the rod adjuster. Remove the cable retainer from the left lower arm.

5. Release the right cable tabbed conduit retainer from the frame, using a 13mm box end wrench.

6. On 1989 vehicles, remove the clip retaining the right cable to the frame crossmember. Remove the cable retainer from the right lower arm and disconnect the cable from the retainer on the right upper arm.

7. On 1990–91 vehicles, remove the cable retainer from the left shock bracket and disconnect the cable from the retainer on the crossmember and upper control arm clip.

8. Remove the wheel and tire assemblies and the brake drums.

9. Working on the wheel side of the rear brake, remove the brake automatic adjuster spring. Compress the prongs on the parking brake cable so they can pass through the hole in the backing plate. Pull the cable retainer through the hole.

10. With the tension off the cable spring at the parking brake lever, lift the cable end out of the slot in the lever. Remove the cable through the backing plate hole.

11. Installation is the reverse of the removal procedure. Adjust the parking brake, if necessary.

WITH DISC BRAKES

1. Raise and safely support the vehicle. Disconnect the control cable from the rear cable at the connector.

2. Disconnect the parking brake cable retainer spring at the frame, if equipped with dual exhaust.

3. Disconnect the left cable from the right cable at the adjuster bracket. Release the right cable tabbed conduit retainer from the frame, using a 13mm box end wrench.

4. Remove the cable retainer from the left shock bracket, the wire retainer on the left axle bracket and disconnect the cable from the retainer on the right axle tube by removing the bolt and retainer.

5. Remove the cable retaining E-clip and cable eyelet from the brake lever. Pull the cable out of the disc brake adapter boss. Remove the cables.

6. Installation is the reverse of the removal procedure. Check parking brake operation.

Brake System

BLEEDING

Without Anti-Lock Brakes

1. Clean all dirt from the master cylinder filler cap.

2. If the master cylinder is known or suspected to have air in the bore, it must be bled before any of the wheel cylinders or calipers. To bleed the master cylinder, loosen the upper secondary left front outlet fitting approximately ¾ turn. Have an assistant depress the brake pedal slowly through it's full travel. Close the outlet fitting and let the pedal return slowly to the fully released position. Wait 5 seconds and then repeat the operation until all air bubbles disappear.

3. Repeat Step 2 with the right-hand front outlet fitting.

4. Continue to bleed the brake system by removing the rubber dust cap from the wheel cylinder bleeder fitting or caliper fitting at the right-hand rear of the vehicle. Place a suitable box wrench on the bleeder fitting and at-

47.6mm (1.875 INCH)
3.2mm (0.125 INCH)
9.5mm (0.325 INCH)
3.2mm (0.125 INCH)
3.2mm (0.125 INCH)

Fabricated reel spring retaining tool

tach a rubber drain tube to the fitting. The end of the tube should fit snugly around the bleeder fitting. Submerge the other end of the tube in a container partially filled with clean brake fluid and loosen the fitting ¾ turn.

5. Have an assistant push the brake pedal down slowly through it's full travel. Close the bleeder fitting and allow the pedal to slowly return to it's full release position. Wait 5 seconds and repeat the procedure until no bubbles appear at the submerged end of the bleeder tube. Secure the bleeder fitting and remove the bleeder tube. Install the rubber dust cap on the bleeder fitting.

6. Repeat the procedure in Steps 4 and 5 in the following sequence: left rear, right front, left front. Refill the master cylinder reservoir after each wheel cylinder or caliper has been bled and install the master cylinder cover and gasket. When brake bleeding is completed, the fluid level should be filled to the maximum level indicated on the reservoir.

7. Always make sure the disc brake pistons are returned to their normal positions by depressing the brake pedal several times until normal pedal travel is established. If the pedal feels spongy, repeat the bleeding procedure.

With Anti-Lock Brakes

NOTE: The anti-lock brake system must be bled in 2 steps.

1. The master cylinder and hydraulic control unit must be bled using the Rotunda Anti-Lock Brake Breakout Box/Bleeding Adapter tool T90P-50-ALA or equivalent. If this procedure is not followed, air will be trapped in the hydraulic control unit which will eventually lead to a spongy brake pedal. To bleed the master cylinder and the hydraulic control unit, disconnect the 55-pin plug from the electronic control unit and install the Anti-Lock Brake Breakout Box/Bleeding Adapter to the wire harness 55-pin plug.

a. Place the Bleed/Harness switch in the **BLEED** position.

b. Turn the ignition to the **ON** position. At this point the red off light should come **ON**.

c. Push the motor button on the adapter down to start the pump motor. The red OFF light will turn OFF and the green ON light will turn ON. The pump motor will run for 60 seconds after the motor button is pushed. If the pump motor is to be turned off for any reason before the 60 seconds has elapsed, push the abort button to turn the pump motor off.

d. After 20 seconds of pump motor operation, push and hold the valve button down. Hold the valve button down for 20 seconds and then release it.

e. The pump motor will continue to run for an additional 20 seconds after the valve button is released.

2. The brake lines can now be bled in the normal fashion. Bleed the brake system by removing the rubber dust cap from the caliper fitting at the right-hand rear of the vehicle. Place a suitable box wrench on the bleeder fitting and attach a rubber drain tube to the fitting. The end of the tube should fit snugly around the bleeder fitting. Submerge the other end of the tube in a container partially filled with clean brake fluid and loosen the fitting ¾ turn.

3. Have an assistant push the brake pedal down slowly through it's full travel. Close the bleeder fitting and allow the pedal to slowly return to it's full release position. Wait 5 seconds and repeat the procedure until no bubbles appear at the submerged end of the bleeder tube. Secure the bleeder fitting and remove the bleeder tube. Install the rubber dust cap on the bleeder fitting.

4. Repeat the bleeding procedure at the left front, left rear and right front in that order. Refill the master cylinder reservoir after each caliper has been bled and install the master cylinder and gasket. When brake bleeding is completed, the fluid level should be filled to the maximum level indicated on the reservoir.

5. Always make sure the disc brake pistons are returned to their normal positions by depressing the brake pedal several times until normal pedal travel is established. If the pedal feels spongy, repeat the bleeding procedure.

Anti-Lock Brake System Service

PRECAUTIONS

- Before servicing any high pressure component, discharge the hydraulic pressure from the system.
- Do not allow brake fluid to contact any electrical connections.
- Use care when opening the bleeder screws due to the high system pressure.

RELIEVING ANTI-LOCK BRAKE SYSTEM PRESSURE

— **CAUTION** —

Before servicing any component which contains high pressure, it is mandatory that the hydraulic pressure in the system be discharged or personal injury could result.

To discharge the system, turn the ignition **OFF** and pump the brake pedal a minimum of 20 times until an increase in pedal force is clearly felt.

Hydraulic Control Unit (HCU)

REMOVAL & INSTALLATION

1. Disconnect the negative battery cable.
2. Remove the air cleaner and air outlet tube.
3. Disconnect the 19-pin connector from the HCU to the wiring harness and disconnect the 4-pin connector from the HCU to the pump motor relay.

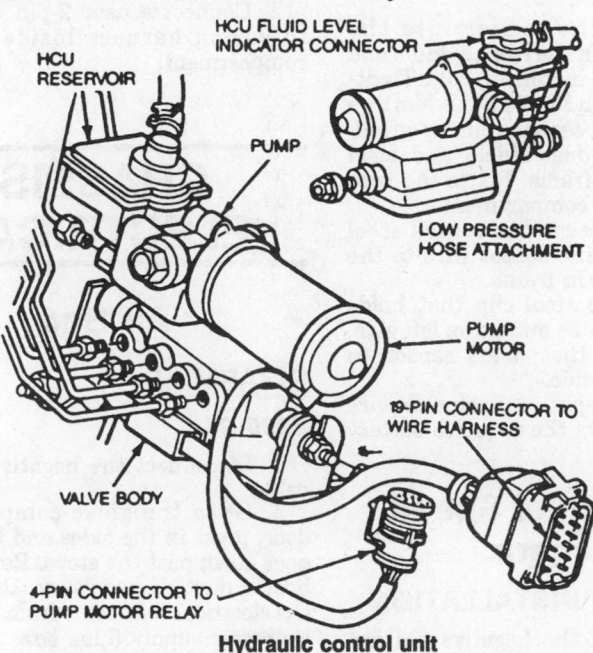

Hydraulic control unit

4. Remove the 2 lines from the inlet ports and the 4 lines from the outlet ports of the HCU. Plug each port to prevent brake fluid from spilling onto the paint and wiring.

5. Remove the 3 nuts retaining the HCU assembly to the mounting bracket and remove the assembly from the vehicle. The nut on the front of the HCU also retains the relay mounting bracket.

6. Install in the reverse order of removal. Tighten the 3 retaining nuts to 12–18 ft. lbs. (16–24 Nm) and the brake lines to 10–18 ft. lbs. (14–24 Nm). Bleed the brake system and check for fluid leaks.

Front Wheel Speed Sensor

REMOVAL & INSTALLATION

1. Disconnect the negative battery cable.

2. From inside engine compartment, disconnect sensor assembly 2-pin connector from the wiring harness.

3. Remove the steel routing clip attaching the sensor wire to the tube bundle on the left sensor or remove the plastic routing clip attaching the sensor wire to the frame on the right sensor.

4. Remove the rubber coated spring steel clip holding the sensor wire to the frame.

5. Remove the sensor wire from the steel routing clip on the frame and from the dust shield.

6. Remove the sensor attaching bolt from the front spindle and slide the sensor out of the mounting hole.

To install:

7. Install the sensor into the mounting hole in the front spindle and attach with the mounting bolt. Tighten to 40–60 inch lbs. (4.5-6.8 Nm).

8. Insert the sensor routing grommets into the dust shield and steel bracket on the frame. Route the wire into the engine compartment.

9. Install the rubber coated steel clip that holds the sensor wire to the frame into hole in frame.

10. Install the steel clip that holds sensor wire to tube bundle on left side, or plastic clip that holds sensor to frame on right side.

11. Connect 2-pin connector to wire harness. Connect the negative battery cable.

Rear Wheel Speed Sensor

REMOVAL & INSTALLATION

1. Disconnect the negative battery cable.

2. From inside luggage compartment disconnect 2-pin sensor connector from wiring harness and push sensor wire through hole in floor.

3. From below vehicle, remove sensor wire from routing bracket located on top of rear axle carrier housing, and remove steel clip holding sensor wire and brake tube against axle housing.

4. Remove screw from clip holding sensor wire and brake tube to bracket on axle.

5. On 1990 vehicles, remove sensor from bracket in rear brake backing plate by spreading open steel split ring with a small prybar or similar tool, and pulling sensor out of bracket.

6. On 1991–93 vehicles, remove sensor to rear adapter retaining bolt and remove sensor.

To install:

7. On 1990 vehicles, ensure that steel split ring is located in groove properly. Opening in ring must not line up with notch in tube shaped sensor retainer. Insert sensor into bracket with notch correctly aligned with bracket. Push sensor in until split ring locks sensor into place.

8. On 1991–93 vehicles, insert sensor adapter and install retaining bolt. Tighten to 40–60 inch lbs. (4.5–6.8 Nm).

9. Attach clip holding sensor and brake tube to bracket on axle housing and secure with screw. Tighten to 40–60 inch lbs. (4.5–6.8 Nm).

10. Install steel clip around axle tube that holds sensor wire and brake tube against axle tube and push spool-shaped grommet into clip located on top of axle carrier housing.

11. Push sensor wire connector up through hole in floor and seat large round grommet into hole.

12. Connect sensor 2-pin connector to wiring harness inside luggage compartment.

CHASSIS ELECTRICAL

Air Bag

DISARMING

1990–91

1. Disconnect the negative battery cable.

2. Open the glove compartment door, press in the sides and lower the door down past the stops. Remove the heater duct, if necessary. Disconnect the electrical connector from the back-up power supply (blue box, 1 connector). If equipped with a passenger air

bag, disconnect the passenger air bag connector.

NOTE: The backup power supply allows air bag deployment if the battery or battery cables are damaged in an accident before the crash sensors close. The power supply is a capacitor that will leak down in approximately 15 minutes after the battery is disconnected or in 1 minute if the battery positive cable is grounded. The backup power supply must be disconnected before any air bag related service is performed.

3. Remove the 4 nut and washer assemblies retaining the driver air bag module to the steering wheel.

------------ CAUTION ------------

When carrying a live air bag, make sure the bag and trim cover are pointed away from the body. In the unlikely event of an accidental deployment, the bag will then deploy with minimal chance of injury. When placing a live air bag on a bench or other surface, always face the bag and trim cover up, away from the surface. This will reduce the motion of the module if it is accidently deployed.

4. Disconnect the driver air bag module connector and attach a jumper wire to the air bag terminals on the clockspring.

1992–93

1. Disconnect the positive battery cable. Wait 1 minute for the backup power supply in the diagnostic monitor to deplete its stored energy.

2. Remove the 4 nut and washer assemblies retaining the driver air bag module to the steering wheel.

------------ CAUTION ------------

When carrying a live air bag, make sure the bag and trim cover are pointed away from the body. In the unlikely event of an accidental deployment, the bag will then deploy with minimal chance of injury. When placing a live air bag on a bench or other surface, always face the bag and trim cover up, away from the surface. This will reduce the motion of the module if it is accidently deployed.

3. Disconnect the driver air bag connector. Connect air bag simulator tool 105–00008 or equivalent, to the vehicle harness at the top of the steering wheel.

4. If equipped with a passenger air bag, proceed as follows:

a. Remove the right-hand instrument panel lower moulding.

b. Remove the cluster finish panel retaining screws and remove the panel.

c. Open the glove compartment, press the sides inward and lower the glove compartment to the floor.

d. Remove the air bag module retaining bolts. Disconnect the electrical connector and remove the module.

e. Connect air bag simulator tool 105-00008 or equivalent, to the vehicle harness connector.

Heater Blower Motor

REMOVAL & INSTALLATION

1. Disconnect the negative battery cable.

2. Disconnect the blower motor lead connector from the wiring harness connector.

3. Remove the blower motor cooling tube from the blower motor.

4. Remove the 4 retaining screws.

5. Turn the motor and wheel assembly slightly to the right so the bottom edge of the mounting plate follows the contour of the wheel well splash panel. Lift up on the blower and remove it from the blower housing.

6. Installation is the reverse of removal. Connect the negative battery cable.

Windshield Wiper Motor

REMOVAL & INSTALLATION

1989–91 Crown Victoria and Grand marquis, 1989 Town Car

1. Disconnect the negative battery cable.

2. Disconnect the 2 push-on wire connectors from the motor.

3. Remove the hood seal. Remove the right wiper arm and blade assembly from the pivot shaft as follows:

a. Raise the wiper blade off the windshield.

b. Move the slide latch away from the pivot shaft and slowly lower the arm onto the latch. This unlocks the arm from the pivot shaft and holds the blade off the glass.

c. Pull the arm from the pivot shaft. The use of tools is unnecessary.

4. Remove the windshield wiper linkage cover by removing the 2 attaching screws and hose clip.

5. Remove the linkage retaining clip from the operating arm on the motor by lifting the locking tab up and pulling the clip away from the pin.

6. Remove the 3 bolts that retain the motor to the dash panel extension and remove the motor.

7. Installation is the reverse of the removal procedure. Make sure the

blades are 1½ in. from the lower windshield moulding when the wipers are in the PARK position.

1992–93 Crown Victoria and Grand Marquis, 1990–93 Town Car

1. Disconnect the negative battery cable.

2. Remove the rear hood seal. Remove the wiper arm assemblies as follows:

a. Raise the wiper blade off the windshield.

b. Move the slide latch away from the pivot shaft and slowly lower the arm onto the latch. This unlocks the arm from the pivot shaft and holds the blade off the glass.

c. Pull the arm from the pivot shaft. The use of tools is unnecessary.

3. Remove the cowl vent screws and disconnect the washer hoses from the washer jets.

4. Disconnect the electrical connectors from the wiper motor.

5. Remove the wiper assembly attaching screws, lift the assembly out and disconnect the washer hose.

6. Unsnap and remove the linkage cover.

7. Remove the linkage retaining clip from the motor operating arm by lifting the locking tab and pulling the clip away from the pin.

8. Remove the motor retaining screws and remove the motor from the vehicle.

9. Installation is the reverse of removal. Install the wiper arms as follows:

a. Align the wiper arm key with the pivot shaft keyway.

b. Install the arm head over the pivot shaft.

c. While applying downward pressure on the arm head, raise the other end of the arm enough to let the latch slide under the pivot shaft to the latched position, using finger pressure only to slide the latch.

d. Lower the blade. If the blade does not touch the windshield, the slide latch is not completely in place.

Wiper Switch

REMOVAL & INSTALLATION

1989

1. Disconnect the negative battery cable.

2. Remove the split steering column cover retaining screws.

3. Separate the halves and remove the wiper switch retaining screws.

4. Disconnect the electrical connector and remove the wiper switch.

5. The installation of the wiper switch is the reverse of the removal procedure.

1990–93

Windshield wiper control is a function of the combination switch.

Instrument Cluster

REMOVAL & INSTALLATION

Standard Cluster

CROWN VICTORIA, GRAND MARQUIS AND 1989 TOWN CAR

1. Disconnect the negative battery cable.

2. On 1989 vehicles, disconnect the speedometer cable. On 1989 Crown Victoria and Grand Marquis, remove the headlight switch knob and shaft assembly.

3. Remove the instrument cluster trim cover attaching screws and remove the trim cover.

4. Except 1992–93 Grand Marquis, remove the lower steering column cover retaining screws and remove the lower cover. On 1992–93 Grand Marquis, remove the knee bolster retaining screws and remove the knee bolster.

5. On all except 1992–93 Grand Marquis, remove the lower half of the steering column shroud.

6. Remove the screw holding the transmission indicator column bracket to the steering column. Detach the cable loop from the pin and cane shift lever. Remove the column bracket from the column.

7. Remove the 4 cluster retaining screws. Disconnect the cluster feed plugs from the receptacle and remove the cluster assembly.

8. Installation is the reverse of the removal procedure.

Electronic Cluster

1992–93 CROWN VICTORIA AND GRAND MARQUIS, 1990–93 TOWN CAR

1. Disconnect the negative battery cable and set the parking brake.

2. Unsnap the center moulding on the left and right sides of the instrument panel. Remove the steering column cover and column shroud.

3. Remove the knobs from the auto dim and auto lamp switches, if equipped. Remove the 13 screws retaining the instrument panel and pull the panel out.

4. Move the shift lever to the 1 position, if required, for easier access.

5. Disconnect the electrical connectors from the warning lamp module,

switch module and center panel switches, if equipped.

6. Remove the instrument cluster carefully so as not to scratch the cluster lens. Disconnect the electrical connector from the front of the cluster.

7. Disconnect the transmission indicator assembly from the cluster by carefully bending the bottom tab down and pulling the indicator assembly forward.

8. Pull the cluster out and disconnect the electrical connectors on the rear of the cluster. Remove the instrument cluster.

9. Installation is the reverse of the removal procedure.

1989 TOWN CAR

1. Disconnect the negative battery cable.

2. Remove the steering column cover and lower instrument panel trim cover. Remove the keyboard trim panel and trim panel on left side of column.

3. Remove the 10 instrument cluster trim cover screws and remove trim cover.

4. Remove the speedometer cable from the clip at the accelerator bracket stud.

5. Remove the 4 screws retaining the instrument cluster to the instrument panel and pull cluster forward. Reach behind the cluster, disconnect both feed plugs and ground wire from their receptacles in the cluster backplate.

6. Disconnect the speedometer cable by pressing on the flat surface of the plastic connector (quick disconnect).

7. Remove the attaching screw from the transmission indicator cable bracket to the steering column. Detach the cable loop from the pin on the shift cane lever of the steering column.

8. Remove the plastic clamp from around steering column. Remove the cluster.

9. Installation is the reverse order of the removal procedure.

Speedometer

REMOVAL & INSTALLATION

Except Electronic Cluster

1989 CROWN VICTORIA, GRAND MARQUIS AND TOWN CAR

1. Disconnect the negative battery cable.

2. Remove the instrument cluster assembly.

3. Remove the screws attaching the lens and mask assembly to the cluster backplate. Remove the lens and mask assembly.

4. Remove the insulator from the rear of the speedometer at the back of the instrument cluster.

5. Remove the terminal nuts from the housing studs on the back of the speedometer.

6. Remove the screws attaching the speedometer to the cluster backplate and remove the speedometer assembly.

7. Installation is the reverse of the removal procedure.

1990–93 CROWN VICTORIA AND GRAND MARQUIS

1. Disconnect the negative battery cable.

2. Remove the instrument cluster assembly.

3. Keeping the cluster face up, remove the lens and mask retaining screws.

4. Remove the lens and mask assembly. Use caution handling the mask to prevent scratches.

5. Remove the transmission indicator assembly. Lift the temperature gauge and fuel gauge from the cluster. Set the face up to avoid damage.

6. Lift the speedometer assembly out of the cluster.

7. Installation is the reverse of the removal procedure.

Electronic Cluster

The speedometer is an integral part of the electronic cluster and cannot be removed separately.

Radio

REMOVAL & INSTALLATION

1989

CROWN VICTORIA AND GRAND MARQUIS

1. Disconnect the battery ground cable.

2. Remove the screws attaching the bezel to the instrument panel. Remove the radio attaching screws.

3. Pull the radio to disengage it from the lower rear support bracket. Disconnect the power antenna and speaker leads and remove the radio.

4. Remove the lower rear support retaining nut and remove the support.

5. Installation is the reverse of the removal procedure.

TOWN CAR

1. Disconnect the negative battery cable.

2. Remove the 3 screws attaching the radio plate to the instrument panel.

3. Pull the radio with the front mounting plate attached rearward un-

til the radio rear support bracket is clear of the instrument panel.

4. Disconnect the radio power feed 8-way connector and speaker 8-way shielded connector from the rear of the radio connectors.

5. Remove the antenna plug from the radio chassis. Remove the radio with the front mounting plate attached.

6. Remove the 2 screws attaching the radio to the front mounting plate and remove the radio. Remove the rear support bracket retaining nut and remove the bracket.

7. Installation is the reverse of the removal procedure.

1990–93

1. Disconnect the negative battery cable.

2. Install radio removal tools T87P-19061–A or equivalent into the radio face plate. Push the tools in approximately 1 in. (25.4mm) to release the retaining clips.

NOTE: Do not use excessive force when installing the radio removal tools, as this will damage the retaining clips, making radio removal difficult.

3. Apply a slight spreading force on the tools and pull the radio from the dash.

4. Disconnect the power, antenna and speaker leads and remove the radio.

5. Installation is the reverse of the removal procedure.

Headlight Switch

REMOVAL & INSTALLATION

1989 Town Car

1. Disconnect the negative battery cable.

2. Remove the headlight switch knob.

3. Remove the auto dimmer bezel and the autolamp delay bezel, if equipped.

4. Remove the steering column lower shroud.

5. Remove the lower left instrument panel trim bezel.

6. Remove the 5 screws that retain the headlight switch mounting bracket to the instrument panel.

7. Carefully pull the switch and bracket from the instrument panel and disconnect the wiring connector(s) from the headlight switch.

8. Remove the locknut and screw that retain the headlight switch to the switch bracket.

9. Installation is the reverse of the removal procedure.

1990–93 Town Car

1. Disconnect the negative battery cable.
2. Remove the headlight switch knob and auto dimmer knob, if equipped.
3. Remove the right and left mouldings from the instrument panel by pulling away from the instrument panel and snapping out of the retainers. Remove 12 screws retaining the finish panel and remove the panel.
4. Remove the 2 headlight switch bracket retaining screws and pull the bracket and switch from the instrument panel.
5. Remove the nut retaining the switch to the bracket, disconnect the connector and remove the switch.
6. Remove the nut retaining the switch to the bracket, disconnect the connector and remove the switch.
7. Installation is the reverse of the removal procedure.

1989 Crown Victoria and Grand Marquis

1. Disconnect the negative battery cable.
2. Pull the headlight switch shaft out to the headlight **ON** position.
3. From under the instrument panel, depress the headlight switch knob and shaft retainer button on the headlight switch. Hold the button in and pull the knob and shaft assembly straight out.
4. Remove the autolamp control bezel and remove the locknut.
5. From under the instrument panel, move the switch toward the front of the vehicle while tilting it downward.
6. Disconnect the wiring from the switch and remove the switch from the vehicle.
7. Installation is the reverse of removal.

1990–93 Crown Victoria and Grand Marquis

1. Disconnect the negative battery cable.
2. Remove the right and left mouldings from the instrument panel by pulling up and snapping out of the retainers.
3. Remove the screws retaining the finish panel to the instrument panel.
4. Remove the headlight switch knob from the shaft and remove the finish panel.
5. Remove the 2 headlight bracket retaining screws and pull the bracket and switch from from the instrument panel.
6. Remove the nut retaining the switch to the bracket.
7. Disconnect the electrical connector and remove the switch.
8. Installation is the reverse of removal.

Combination Switch

The combination switch incorporates the turn signal, dimmer and wiper switch functions on 1990–93 vehicles.

The combination switch incorporates only the turn signal and dimmer function on 1989 vehicles.

REMOVAL & INSTALLATION

1989

1. Disconnect the negative battery cable.
2. Remove the switch lever by grasping and pulling straight out.
3. Remove the steering column cover retaining screws and remove the cover.
4. Remove the shroud retaining screws and remove the shroud.
5. With the wiring connectors exposed, carefully lift the connector retainer tabs and disconnect the connectors.
6. Remove the switch retaining screws and lift up the switch assembly.
7. Installation is the reverse of the removal procedure.

1990–93

1. Disconnect the negative battery cable.
2. If equipped with tilt column,

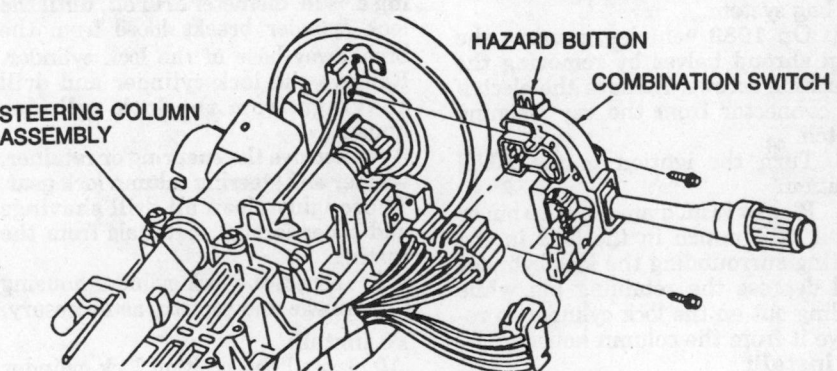

HAZARD BUTTON
COMBINATION SWITCH
STEERING COLUMN ASSEMBLY

Combination switch installation—1990–93

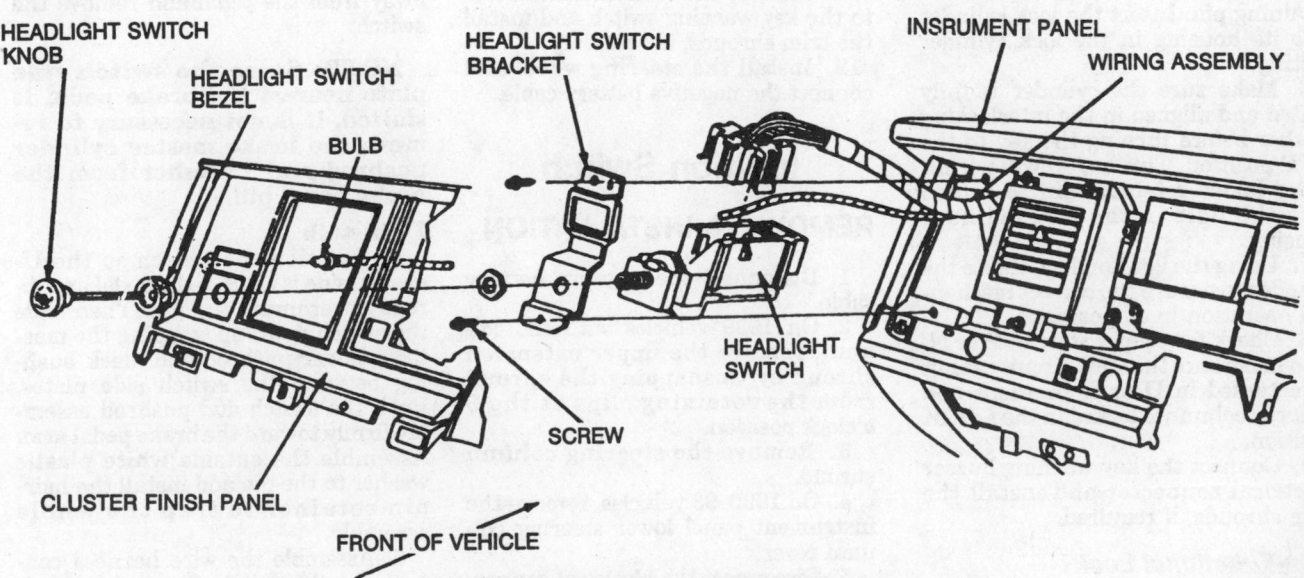

HEADLIGHT SWITCH KNOB
HEADLIGHT SWITCH BEZEL
HEADLIGHT SWITCH BRACKET
BULB
INSRUMENT PANEL
WIRING ASSEMBLY
HEADLIGHT SWITCH
CLUSTER FINISH PANEL
SCREW
FRONT OF VEHICLE

Headlight switch installation—1990–93 Town Car

move to the lowest position and remove the tilt lever.

3. Remove the ignition lock cylinder.

4. Remove the shroud screws and remove the upper and lower shrouds.

5. Remove the 2 self-tapping screws attaching the combination switch to the steering column casting and remove the switch.

6. Remove the wiring harness retainer and disconnect the 2 electrical connectors.

7. Installation is the reverse of the removal procedure.

Ignition Lock

REMOVAL & INSTALLATION

Functional Lock

The following procedure is for vehicles with functioning lock cylinders. Ignition keys are available for these vehicles or the ignition key numbers are known and the proper key can be made.

1. Disconnect the negative battery cable. If equipped, properly disarm the air bag system.

2. On 1989 vehicles, remove the trim shroud halves by removing the attaching screws. Remove the electrical connector from the key warning switch.

3. Turn the ignition to the RUN position.

4. Place a 1/8 in. diameter wire pin or small drift punch in the hole in the casting surrounding the lock cylinder and depress the retaining pin while pulling out on the lock cylinder to remove it from the column housing.

To install:

5. To install the lock cylinder, turn it to the RUN position and depress the retaining pin. Insert the lock cylinder into its housing in the lock cylinder casting.

6. Make sure the cylinder is fully seated and aligned in the interlocking washer before turning the key to the OFF position. This action will permit the cylinder retaining pin to extend into the hole in the lock cylinder housing.

7. Using the ignition key, rotate the cylinder to ensure the correct mechanical operation in all positions.

8. Check for proper start in P or N. Also make sure the start circuit cannot be actuated in D or R positions and that the column is locked in the LOCK position.

9. Connect the key warning buzzer electrical connector and install the trim shrouds, if required.

Non-Functional Lock

The following procedure is for vehicles with non-functioning locks. On these vehicles, the lock cylinder cannot be rotated due to a lost or broken key, the key number is not known, or the lock cylinder cap is damaged and/or broken, preventing the lock cylinder from rotating.

1. Disconnect the negative battery cable. If equipped, properly disarm the air bag system.

2. Remove the steering wheel.

3. On 1989 vehicles, remove the trim shroud halves by removing the attaching screws. Remove the electrical connector from the key warning switch.

4. On 1989–90 vehicles, drill out the retaining pin using a 1/8 in. diameter drill, being careful not to drill deeper than 1/2 in. Position a chisel at the base of the ignition lock cylinder. Strike the chisel with sharp blows, using a hammer, to break the cap away from the lock cylinder.

5. On 1991–93 vehicles, use channel lock or vise grip type pliers to twist the lock cylinder cap until it separates from the lock cylinder.

6. Drill approximately 1¾ in. down the middle of the ignition key slot, using a ⅜ in. diameter drill bit, until the lock cylinder breaks loose from the breakaway base of the lock cylinder. Remove the lock cylinder and drill shavings from the lock cylinder housing.

7. Remove the snapring or retainer, washer and steering column lock gear. Thoroughly clean all drill shavings and other foreign materials from the casting.

8. Inspect the lock cylinder housing for damage and replace, as necessary.

To install:

9. Install the ignition lock cylinder and check for smooth operation.

10. Connect the electrical connector to the key warning switch and install the trim shrouds, if necessary.

11. Install the steering wheel and connect the negative battery cable.

Ignition Switch

REMOVAL & INSTALLATION

1. Disconnect the negative battery cable.

2. On 1989 vehicles with tilt column, remove the upper extension shroud by unsnapping the shroud from the retaining clips at the 9 o'clock position.

3. Remove the steering column shroud.

4. On 1990–93 vehicles, remove the instrument panel lower steering column cover.

5. Disconnect the electrical connector from the ignition switch.

6. Rotate the ignition key lock cylinder to the RUN position.

7. Remove the 2 screws attaching the ignition switch.

8. Disengage the ignition switch from the actuator pin and remove the switch.

To install:

9. Adjust the new ignition switch by sliding the carrier to the RUN position.

10. Check to ensure that the ignition key lock cylinder is in the RUN position. The RUN position is achieved by rotating the key lock cylinder approximately 90 degrees from the LOCK position.

11. Install the ignition switch onto the actuator pin.

12. Align the switch mounting holes and install the attaching screws. Tighten the screws to 50–69 inch lbs. (5.6–7.9 Nm).

13. Connect the electrical connector to the ignition switch.

14. Connect the negative battery cable. Check the ignition switch for proper function in START and ACC positions. Make sure the column is locked in the LOCK position.

15. Install the remaining components in the reverse order of removal.

Stoplight Switch

REMOVAL & INSTALLATION

1. Disconnect the negative battery cable.

2. Disconnect the electrical connector at the switch. The locking tab on the connector must be lifted before the connector can be removed.

3. Remove the hairpin retainer, slide the stoplight switch, the pushrod and the nylon washers and bushings away from the pedal and remove the switch.

NOTE: Since the switch side plate nearest the brake pedal is slotted, it is not necessary to remove the brake master cylinder pushrod and 1 washer from the brake pedal pin.

To install:

4. Position the switch so the U-shaped side is nearest the pedal and directly over/under the pin. Then slide the switch down/up trapping the master cylinder pushrod and black bushing between the switch side plates. Push the switch and pushrod assembly firmly toward the brake pedal arm. Assemble the outside white plastic washer to the pin and install the hairpin retainer to trap the whole assembly.

5. Assemble the wire harness connector to the switch. Check the switch for proper operation.

Ford Motor Co.

Front Wheel Drive

FORD—Escort • Tempo
MERCURY—Topaz

SPECIFICATIONS

VEHICLE IDENTIFICATION CHART

It is important for servicing and ordering parts to be certain of the vehicle and engine identification. The VIN (vehicle identification number) is a 17 digit number visible through the windshield on the driver's side of the dash and contains the vehicle and engine identification codes. The tenth digit indicates model year and the eighth digit indicates engine code. It can be interpreted as follows:

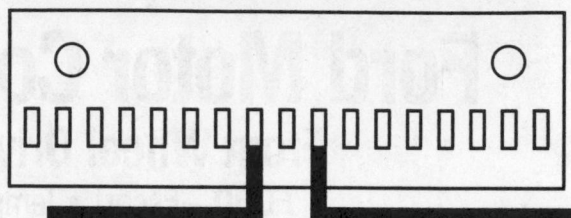

		Engine Code					Model Year	
Code	Liters	Cu. In. (cc)	Cyl.	Fuel Sys.	Eng. Mfg.		Code	Year
8	1.8	112 (1844)	4	EFI	Mazda		K	1989
9	1.9	114 (1859)	4	CFI	Ford		L	1990
J	1.9	114 (1859)	4	EFI	Ford		M	1991
X	2.3	142 (2326)	4	EFI	Ford		N	1992
S	2.3	142 (2326)	4	EFI	Ford		P	1993
U	3.0	181 (2971)	6	EFI	Ford			

CFI—Central Fuel Injection
EFI—Electronic Fuel Injection

ENGINE IDENTIFICATION

Year	Model	Engine Displacement Liters (cc)	Engine Series (ID/VIN)	Fuel System	No. of Cylinders	Engine Type
1989	Escort	1.9 (1859)	9	CFI	4	OHC
	Escort	1.9 (1859)	J	EFI	4	OHC
	Tempo	2.3 (2326)	X	EFI	4	OHV
	Tempo	2.3 (2326)	S	EFI	4	OHV
	Topaz	2.3 (2326)	X	EFI	4	OHV
	Topaz	2.3 (2326)	S	EFI	4	OHV
1990	Escort	1.9 (1859)	9	CFI	4	OHC
	Escort	1.9 (1859)	J	EFI	4	OHC
	Tempo	2.3 (2326)	X	EFI	4	OHV
	Tempo	2.3 (2326)	S	EFI	4	OHV
	Topaz	2.3 (2326)	X	EFI	4	OHV
	Topaz	2.3 (2326)	S	EFI	4	OHV
1991	Escort	1.8 (1844)	8	EFI	4	DOHC
	Escort	1.9 (1859)	J	EFI	4	OHC
	Tempo	2.3 (2326)	X	EFI	4	OHV
	Tempo	2.3 (2326)	S	EFI	4	OHV
	Topaz	2.3 (2326)	X	EFI	4	OHV
	Topaz	2.3 (2326)	S	EFI	4	OHV
1992–93	Escort	1.8 (1844)	8	EFI	4	DOHC
	Escort	1.9 (1859)	J	EFI	4	OHC
	Tempo	2.3 (2326)	X	EFI	4	OHV

ENGINE IDENTIFICATION

Year	Model	Engine Displacement Liters (cc)	Engine Series (ID/VIN)	Fuel System	No. of Cylinders	Engine Type
	Tempo	3.0 (2971)	U	EFI	6	OHV
	Topaz	2.3 (2326)	X	EFI	4	OHV
	Topaz	3.0 (2971)	U	EFI	6	OHV

CFI—Central Fuel Injection   OHV—Overhead Valve
EFI—Electronic Fuel Injection   DOHC—Double Overhead Cam
OHC—Overhead Cam

GENERAL ENGINE SPECIFICATIONS

Year	Engine ID/VIN	Engine Displacement Liters (cc)	Fuel System Type	Net Horsepower @ rpm	Net Torque @ rpm (ft. lbs.)	Bore × Stroke (in.)	Compression Ratio	Oil Pressure @ rpm
1989	9	1.9 (1859)	CFI	90 @ 4600	106 @ 3400	3.23 × 3.46	9.0:1	35–65 @ 2000 ①
	J	1.9 (1859)	EFI	110 @ 5400	115 @ 4200	3.23 × 3.46	9.0:1	35–65 @ 2000 ①
	X	2.3 (2326)	EFI	98 @ 4400	124 @ 2200	3.70 × 3.30	9.0:1	55–70 @ 2000 ①
	S	2.3 (2326)	EFI	100 @ 4400	130 @ 2600	3.70 × 3.30	9.0:1	55–70 @ 2000 ①
1990	9	1.9 (1859)	CFI	90 @ 4600	106 @ 3400	3.23 × 3.46	9.0:1	35–65 @ 2000 ①
	J	1.9 (1859)	EFI	110 @ 5400	115 @ 4200	3.23 × 3.46	9.0:1	35–65 @ 2000 ①
	X	2.3 (2326)	EFI	98 @ 4400	124 @ 2200	3.70 × 3.30	9.0:1	55–70 @ 2000 ①
	S	2.3 (2326)	EFI	100 @ 4400	130 @ 2600	3.70 × 3.30	9.0:1	55–70 @ 2000 ①
1991	8	1.8 (1844)	EFI	127 @ 6500	114 @ 4500	3.27 × 3.35	9.0:1	43–57 @ 3000 ①
	J	1.9 (1859)	EFI	88 @ 4400	108 @ 3800	3.23 × 3.46	9.0:1	35–65 @ 2000 ①
	X	2.3 (2326)	EFI	98 @ 4400	124 @ 2200	3.70 × 3.30	9.0:1	55–70 @ 2000 ①
	S	2.3 (2326)	EFI	100 @ 4400	130 @ 2600	3.70 × 3.30	9.0:1	55–70 @ 2000 ①
1992–93	8	1.8 (1844)	EFI	127 @ 6500	114 @ 4500	3.27 × 3.35	9.0:1	43–57 @ 3000 ①
	J	1.9 (1859)	EFI	88 @ 4400	108 @ 3800	3.23 × 3.46	9.0:1	35–65 @ 2000 ①
	X	2.3 (2326)	EFI	96 @ 4400	128 @ 2600	3.70 × 3.30	9.0:1	55–70 @ 2000 ①
	U	3.0 (2971)	EFI	②	③	3.50 × 3.14	9.3:1	40–60 @ 2500 ①

NOTE: Horsepower and torque are SAE net figures. They are measured at the rear of the transmission with all accessories installed and operating. Since the figures vary when a given engine is installed in different models, some are representative rather than exact.
CFI—Central Fuel Injection
EFI—Electronic Fuel Injection
① Oil at normal operating temperature
② Manual transaxle 140 @ 4800
   Automatic transaxle 135 @ 5500
③ Manual transaxle 150 @ 3250
   Automatic transaxle 150 @ 4200

GASOLINE ENGINE TUNE-UP SPECIFICATIONS

Year	Engine ID/VIN	Engine Displacement Liters (cc)	Spark Plugs Gap (in.)	Ignition Timing (deg.) MT	Ignition Timing (deg.) AT	Fuel Pump (psi)	Idle Speed (rpm) MT	Idle Speed (rpm) AT	Valve Clearance In.	Valve Clearance Ex.
1989	9	1.9 (1859)	0.044	10B	10B	13–17 ①	760–840	760–840	Hyd.	Hyd.
	J	1.9 (1859)	0.044	10B	10B	35–45 ①	②	②	Hyd.	Hyd.
	X	2.3 (2326)	0.054	15B	15B	50–60 ①	820–880	690–750	Hyd.	Hyd.
	S	2.3 (2326)	0.054	15B	15B	50–60 ①	810–890	680–760	Hyd.	Hyd.

GASOLINE ENGINE TUNE-UP SPECIFICATIONS

Year	Engine ID/VIN	Engine Displacement Liters (cc)	Spark Plugs Gap (in.)	Ignition Timing (deg.) MT	Ignition Timing (deg.) AT	Fuel Pump (psi)	Idle Speed (rpm) MT	Idle Speed (rpm) AT	Valve Clearance In.	Valve Clearance Ex.
1990	9	1.9 (1859)	0.044	10B	10B	13–17 ①	760–840	760–840	Hyd.	Hyd.
	J	1.9 (1859)	0.054	10B	10B	35–40 ①	②	②	Hyd.	Hyd.
	X	2.3 (2326)	0.054	15B	15B	50–60 ①	820–880	690–750	Hyd.	Hyd.
	S	2.3 (2326)	0.054	15B	15B	50–60 ①	810–890	680–760	Hyd.	Hyd.
1991	8	1.8 (1844)	0.041	10B	10B	64–85 ①	700–800	700–800	Hyd.	Hyd.
	J	1.9 (1859)	0.054	10B	10B	35–40 ①	②	②	Hyd.	Hyd.
	X	2.3 (2326)	0.054	15B	15B	50–60 ①	820–880	690–750	Hyd.	Hyd.
	S	2.3 (2326)	②	②	②	50–60 ①	②	②	Hyd.	Hyd.
1992	8	1.8 (1844)	0.041	10B	10B	64–85 ①	700–800	700–800	Hyd.	Hyd.
	J	1.9 (1859)	0.054	10B	10B	35–40 ①	②	②	Hyd.	Hyd.
	X	2.3 (2326)	0.054	10B	10B	50–60 ①	②	②	Hyd.	Hyd.
	U	3.0 (2971)	0.044	10B	10B	35–40 ①	②	②	Hyd.	Hyd.
1993	SEE UNDERHOOD SPECIFICATIONS STICKER									

NOTE: The lowest cylinder pressure should be within 75% of the highest cylinder pressure reading. For example, if the highest cylinder is 134 psi, the lowest should be 101. Engine should be at normal operating temperature with throttle valve in the wide open position.
The underhood specifications sticker often reflects tune-up specification changes in production. Sticker figures must be used if they disagree with those in this chart.
B—Before Top Dead Center
Hyd.—Hydraulic
① Key on, engine off
② Refer to vehicle emission control information label

FIRING ORDERS

NOTE: To avoid confusion, always replace spark plug wires one at a time.

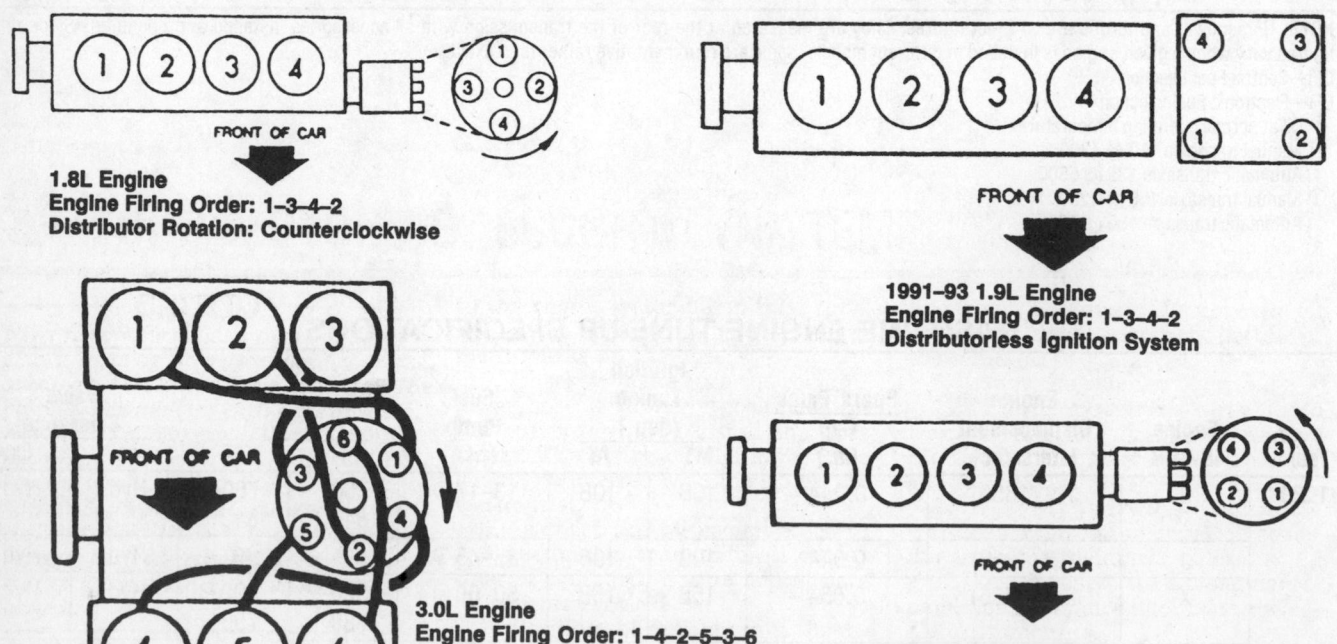

1.8L Engine
Engine Firing Order: 1–3–4–2
Distributor Rotation: Counterclockwise

1991–93 1.9L Engine
Engine Firing Order: 1–3–4–2
Distributorless Ignition System

3.0L Engine
Engine Firing Order: 1–4–2–5–3–6
Distributor Rotation: Clockwise

1989–90 1.9L Engine
Engine Firing Order: 1–3–4–2
Distributor Rotation: Counterclockwise

CAPACITIES

Year	Model	Engine ID/VIN	Engine Displacement Liters (cc)	Engine Crankcase with Filter	Transmission (pts.) 4-Spd	5-Spd	Auto.	Transfer case (pts.)	Drive Axle Front (pts.)	Rear (pts.)	Fuel Tank (gal.)	Cooling System (qts.)
1989	Escort	9	1.9 (1859)	4.0	6.1	6.1	16.6	—	①	—	13	②
	Escort	J	1.9 (1859)	4.0	—	6.1	16.6	—	①	—	13	②
	Tempo	X	2.3 (2326)	5.0	—	6.1	③	①	①	1.3	④	⑤
	Tempo	S	2.3 (2326)	5.0	—	6.1	③	①	①	1.3	④	⑤
	Topaz	X	2.3 (2326)	5.0	—	6.1	③	①	①	1.3	④	⑤
	Topaz	S	2.3 (2326)	5.0	—	6.1	③	①	①	1.3	④	⑤
1990	Escort	9	1.9 (1859)	4.0	6.1	6.1	16.6	—	①	—	⑥	②
	Escort	J	1.9 (1859)	4.0	—	6.1	16.6	—	①	—	⑥	②
	Tempo	X	2.3 (2326)	5.0	—	6.1	③	①	①	1.3	④	⑤
	Tempo	S	2.3 (2326)	5.0	—	6.1	③	①	①	1.3	④	⑤
	Topaz	X	2.3 (2326)	5.0	—	6.1	③	①	①	1.3	④	⑤
	Topaz	S	2.3 (2326)	5.0	—	6.1	③	①	①	1.3	④	⑤
1991	Escort	8	1.8 (1844)	4.0	—	7.2	13.4	—	①	—	13.2	⑦
	Excort	J	1.9 (1859)	4.0	—	5.6	13.4	—	①	—	11.9	⑦
	Tempo	X	2.3 (2326)	5.0	—	6.1	③	①	①	1.3	④	⑤
	Tempo	S	2.3 (2326)	5.0	—	6.1	③	①	①	1.3	④	⑤
	Topaz	X	2.3 (2326)	5.0	—	6.1	③	①	①	1.3	④	⑤
	Topaz	S	2.3 (2326)	5.0	—	6.1	③	①	①	1.3	④	⑤
1992–93	Escort	8	1.8 (1844)	4.0	—	7.2	13.4	—	①	—	13.2	⑦
	Excort	J	1.9 (1859)	4.0	—	5.6	13.4	—	①	—	11.9	⑦
	Tempo	X	2.3 (2326)	5.0	—	6.1	16.6	—	①	—	15.9	⑧
	Tempo	U	3.0 (2971)	4.5	—	6.1	16.6	—	①	—	15.9	⑧
	Topaz	X	2.3 (2326)	5.0	—	6.1	16.6	—	①	—	15.9	⑧
	Topaz	U	3.0 (2971)	4.5	—	6.1	16.6	—	①	—	15.9	⑧

① Included in transaxle capacity
② Without A/C—8.3 qts.
  With A/C
   Manual transaxle—6.8 qts.
   Automatic transaxle—7.3 qts.
③ Except 4WD—16.6 pts.
  With 4WD—20.0 pts.
④ Except 4WD—15.9 gal.
  With 4WD—14.2 gal.
⑤ Manual transaxle—7.3 qts.
   Automatic transaxle—7.8 qts.
⑥ Standard—13 gal.
  Optional—11.5 gal.
⑦ Manual transaxle—5.3 qts.
  Automatic transaxle—6.3 qts.
⑧ Manual transaxle—7.8 qts.
  Automatic transaxle—8.4 qts.

CAMSHAFT SPECIFICATIONS

All measurements given in inches.

Year	Engine ID/VIN	Engine Displacement Liters (cc)	Journal Diameter 1	2	3	4	5	Elevation In.	Ex.	Bearing Clearance	Camshaft End Play
1989	9	1.9 (1859)	1.8007–1.8017	1.8007–1.8017	1.8007–1.8017	1.8007–1.8017	1.8007–1.8017	0.235–0.240	0.235–0.240	0.0013–0.0033	0.002–0.006
	J	1.9 (1859)	1.8007–1.8017	1.8007–1.8017	1.8007–1.8017	1.8007–1.8017	1.8007–1.8017	0.260–0.265	0.260–0.265	0.0013–0.0033	0.002–0.006
	X	2.3 (2326)	2.006–2.009	2.006–2.009	2.006–2.009	2.006–2.009	—	0.245–0.249	0.235–0.239	0.001–0.003	0.009
	S	2.3 (2326)	2.006–2.009	2.006–2.009	2.006–2.009	2.006–2.009	—	0.258–0.262	0.258–0.262	0.001–0.003	0.009

CAMSHAFT SPECIFICATIONS

All measurements given in inches.

Year	Engine ID/VIN	Engine Displacement Liters (cc)	Journal Diameter 1	2	3	4	5	Elevation In.	Ex.	Bearing Clearance	Camshaft End Play
1990	9	1.9 (1859)	1.8007-1.8017	1.8007-1.8017	1.8007-1.8017	1.8007-1.8017	1.8007-1.8017	0.235-0.240	0.235-0.240	0.0013-0.0033	0.002-0.006
	J	1.9 (1859)	1.8007-1.8017	1.8007-1.8017	1.8007-1.8017	1.8007-1.8017	1.8007-1.8017	0.260-0.265	0.260-0.265	0.0013-0.0033	0.002-0.006
	X	2.3 (2326)	2.006-2.009	2.006-2.009	2.006-2.009	2.006-2.009	—	0.245-0.249	0.235-0.239	0.001-0.003	0.009
	S	2.3 (2326)	2.006-2.009	2.006-2.009	2.006-2.009	2.006-2.009	—	0.258-0.262	0.258-0.262	0.001-0.003	0.009
1991	8	1.8 (1844)	1.0213-1.0222	1.0213-1.0222	1.0213-1.0222	1.0213-1.0222	1.0213-1.0222	1.7281-① 1.7360	1.7480-① 1.7560	0.0014-0.0032	0.0028-0.0075
	J	1.9 (1859)	1.8007-1.8017	1.8007-1.8017	1.8007-1.8017	1.8007-1.8017	1.8007-1.8017	0.235-0.240	0.235-0.240	0.0013-0.0033	0.002-0.006
	X	2.3 (2326)	2.006-2.009	2.006-2.009	2.006-2.009	2.006-2.009	—	0.245-0.249	0.235-0.239	0.001-0.003	0.009
	S	2.3 (2326)	2.006-2.009	2.006-2.009	2.006-2.009	2.006-2.009	—	0.258-0.262	0.258-0.262	0.001-0.003	0.009
1992-93	8	1.8 (1844)	1.0213-1.0222	1.0213-1.0222	1.0213-1.0222	1.0213-1.0222	1.0213-1.0222	1.7281-① 1.7360	1.7480-① 1.7560	0.0014-0.0032	0.0028-0.0075
	J	1.9 (1859)	1.8007-1.8017	1.8007-1.8017	1.8007-1.8017	1.8007-1.8017	1.8007-1.8017	0.240-0.245	0.240-0.245	0.0013-0.0033	0.002-0.006
	X	2.3 (2326)	2.006-2.009	2.006-2.009	2.006-2.009	2.006-2.009	—	0.245-0.249	0.235-0.239	0.001-0.003	0.009
	U	3.0 (2971)	2.0074-2.0084	2.0074-2.0084	2.0074-2.0084	2.0074-2.0084	—	0.255-0.260	0.255-0.260	0.001-0.003	0.001-0.005

① Specification is for cam lobe height

CRANKSHAFT AND CONNECTING ROD SPECIFICATIONS

All measurements are given in inches.

Year	Engine ID/VIN	Engine Displacement Liters (cc)	Crankshaft Main Brg. Journal Dia.	Main Brg. Oil Clearance	Shaft End-play	Thrust on No.	Connecting Rod Journal Diameter	Oil Clearance	Side Clearance
1989	9	1.9 (1859)	2.2827-2.2835	①	0.0040-0.0080	3	1.7279-1.7287	0.0008-0.0026	0.0040-0.0140
	J	1.9 (1859)	2.2827-2.2835	①	0.0040-0.0080	3	1.7279-1.7287	0.0008-0.0026	0.0040-0.0140
	X	2.3 (2326)	2.2489-2.2490	0.0008-0.0024	0.0040-0.0080	3	2.1232-2.1240	0.0008-0.0024	0.0035-0.0140
	S	2.3 (2326)	2.2489-2.2490	0.0008-0.0024	0.0040-0.0080	3	2.1232-2.1240	0.0008-0.0024	0.0035-0.0140
1990	9	1.9 (1859)	2.2827-2.2835	①	0.0040-0.0080	3	1.7279-1.7287	0.0008-0.0026	0.0040-0.0140
	J	1.9 (1859)	2.2827-2.2835	①	0.0040-0.0080	3	1.7279-1.7287	0.0008-0.0026	0.0040-0.0140
	X	2.3 (2326)	2.2489-2.2490	0.0008-0.0024	0.0040-0.0080	3	2.1232-2.1240	0.0008-0.0024	0.0035-0.0140
	S	2.3 (2326)	2.2489-2.2490	0.0008-0.0024	0.0040-0.0080	3	2.1232-2.1240	0.0008-0.0024	0.0035-0.0140

CRANKSHAFT AND CONNECTING ROD SPECIFICATIONS

All measurements are given in inches.

Year	Engine ID/VIN	Engine Displacement Liters (cc)	Crankshaft Main Brg. Journal Dia.	Crankshaft Main Brg. Oil Clearance	Crankshaft Shaft End-play	Crankshaft Thrust on No.	Connecting Rod Journal Diameter	Connecting Rod Oil Clearance	Connecting Rod Side Clearance
1991	8	1.8 (1844)	1.9661–1.9668	0.0007–0.0014	0.0031–0.0120	4	1.7692–1.7699	0.0011–0.0027	0.0043–0.0120
	J	1.9 (1859)	2.2827–2.2835	①	0.0040–0.0080	3	1.7279–1.7287	0.0008–0.0026	0.0040–0.0140
	X	2.3 (2326)	2.2489–2.2490	0.0008–0.0024	0.0040–0.0080	3	2.1232–2.1240	0.0008–0.0024	0.0035–0.0140
	S	2.3 (2326)	2.2489–2.2490	0.0008–0.0024	0.0040–0.0080	3	2.1232–2.1240	0.0008–0.0024	0.0035–0.0140
1992–93	8	1.8 (1844)	1.9661–1.9668	0.0007–0.0014	0.0031–0.0120	4	1.7692–1.7699	0.0011–0.0027	0.0043–0.0120
	J	1.9 (1859)	2.2827–2.2835	①	0.0040–0.0080	3	1.7279–1.7287	0.0008–0.0024	0.0040–0.0140
	X	2.3 (2326)	2.2489–2.2490	0.0008–0.0024	0.0040–0.0080	3	2.1232–2.1240	0.0008–0.0024	0.0035–0.0140
	U	3.0 (2971)	2.5190–2.5198	0.0005–0.0023	0.0040–0.0080	3	2.1253–2.1261	0.0009–0.0027	0.0060–0.0140

① Without cylinder head—0.0018–0.0034
With cylinder head—0.0011–0.0027

VALVE SPECIFICATIONS

Year	Engine ID/VIN	Engine Displacement Liters (cc)	Seat Angle (deg.)	Face Angle (deg.)	Spring Test Pressure (lbs. @ in.)	Spring Installed Height (in.)	Stem-to-Guide Clearance (in.) Intake	Stem-to-Guide Clearance (in.) Exhaust	Stem Diameter (in.) Intake	Stem Diameter (in.) Exhaust
1989	9	1.9 (1859)	45	45.6	200 @ 1.09	1.44–1.48	0.0008–0.0027	0.0018–0.0037	0.3159–0.3167	0.3149–0.3156
	J	1.9 (1859)	45	45.6	216 @ 1.016	1.44–1.48	0.0008–0.0027	0.0018–0.0037	0.3159–0.3167	0.3149–0.3156
	X	2.3 (2326)	44–45	44–45	174–188 @ 1.088	1.49	0.0018	0.0023	0.3415–0.3422	0.3411–0.3418
	S	2.3 (2326)	44–45	44–45	174–188 @ 1.088	1.49	0.0018	0.0023	0.3415–0.3422	0.3411–0.3418
1990	9	1.9 (1859)	45	45.6	200 @ 1.09	1.44–1.48	0.0008–0.0027	0.0018–0.0037	0.3159–0.3167	0.3149–0.3156
	J	1.9 (1859)	45	45.6	216 @ 1.016	1.44–1.48	0.0008–0.0027	0.0018–0.0037	0.3159–0.3167	0.3149–0.3156
	X	2.3 (2326)	44–45	44–45	174–188 @ 1.088	1.49	0.0018	0.0023	0.3415–0.3422	0.3411–0.3418
	S	2.3 (2326)	44–45	44–45	174–188 @ 1.088	1.49	0.0018	0.0023	0.3415–0.3422	0.3411–0.3418
1991	8	1.8 (1844)	45	45	NA①	NA	0.0010–0.0024	0.0012–0.0026	0.2350–0.2356	0.2348–0.2354
	J	1.9 (1859)	45	45.6	200 @ 1.09	1.44–1.48	0.0008–0.0027	0.0018–0.0037	0.3159–0.3167	0.3149–0.3156
	X	2.3 (2326)	44–45	44–45	174–188 @ 1.088	1.49	0.0018	0.0023	0.3415–0.3422	0.3411–0.3418
	S	2.3 (2326)	44–45	44–45	174–188 @ 1.088	1.49	0.0018	0.0023	0.3415–0.3422	0.3411–0.3418

VALVE SPECIFICATIONS

Year	Engine ID/VIN	Engine Displacement Liters (cc)	Seat Angle (deg.)	Face Angle (deg.)	Spring Test Pressure (lbs. @ in.)	Spring Installed Height (in.)	Stem-to-Guide Clearance (in.)		Stem Diameter (in.)	
							Intake	Exhaust	Intake	Exhaust
1992–93	8	1.8 (1844)	45	45	NA①	NA	0.0010–0.0024	0.0012–0.0026	0.2350–0.2356	0.2348–0.2354
	J	1.9 (1859)	45	45.6	200 @ 1.09	1.44–1.48	0.0008–0.0027	0.0018–0.0037	0.3159–0.3167	0.3149–0.3156
	X	2.3 (2326)	44–45	44–45	179–194 @ 1.088	1.49	0.0018	0.0023	0.3415–0.3422	0.3411–0.3418
	U	3.0 (2971)	45	44	180 @ 1.16	1.58	0.0010–0.0028	0.0015–0.0033	0.3126–0.3134	0.3121–0.3129

① Check valve spring free length and out-of-square
  Free length: 1.555–1.821 in.
  Out-of-square: 0.064 in. maximum

PISTON AND RING SPECIFICATIONS

All measurements are given in inches.

Year	Engine ID/VIN	Engine Displacement Liters (cc)	Piston Clearance	Ring Gap			Ring Side Clearance		
				Top Compression	Bottom Compression	Oil Control	Top Compression	Bottom Compression	Oil Control
1989	9	1.9 (1859)	0.0016–0.0024	0.010–0.020	0.010–0.020	0.016–0.055	0.0015–0.0032	0.0015–0.0035	Snug
	J	1.9 (1859)	0.0016–0.0024	0.010–0.020	0.010–0.020	0.016–0.055	0.0015–0.0032	0.0015–0.0035	Snug
	X	2.3 (2326)	0.0012–0.0022	0.008–0.016	0.008–0.016	0.015–0.055	0.0020–0.0040	0.0020–0.0040	Snug
	S	2.3 (2326)	0.0012–0.0022	0.008–0.016	0.008–0.016	0.015–0.055	0.0020–0.0040	0.0020–0.0040	Snug
1990	9	1.9 (1859)	0.0016–0.0024	0.010–0.020	0.010–0.020	0.016–0.055	0.0015–0.0032	0.0015–0.0035	Snug
	J	1.9 (1859)	0.0016–0.0024	0.010–0.020	0.010–0.020	0.016–0.055	0.0015–0.0032	0.0015–0.0035	Snug
	X	2.3 (2326)	0.0012–0.0022	0.008–0.016	0.008–0.016	0.015–0.055	0.0020–0.0040	0.0020–0.0040	Snug
	S	2.3 (2326)	0.0012–0.0022	0.008–0.016	0.008–0.016	0.015–0.055	0.0020–0.0040	0.0020–0.0040	Snug
1991	8	1.8 (1844)	0.0015–0.0020	0.006–0.012	0.006–0.012	0.008–0.028	0.0012–0.0026	0.0012–0.0028	Snug
	J	1.9 (1859)	0.0016–0.0024	0.010–0.020	0.010–0.020	0.016–0.055	0.0015–0.0032	0.0015–0.0035	Snug
	X	2.3 (2326)	0.0011–0.0022	0.008–0.016	0.008–0.016	0.015–0.055	0.0020–0.0040	0.0020–0.0040	Snug
	S	2.3 (2326)	0.0011–0.0022	0.008–0.016	0.008–0.016	0.015–0.055	0.0020–0.0040	0.0020–0.0040	Snug
1992–93	8	1.8 (1844)	0.0015–0.0020	0.006–0.012	0.006–0.012	0.008–0.028	0.0012–0.0028	0.0012–0.0028	Snug
	J	1.9 (1859)	0.0016–0.0024	0.010–0.020	0.010–0.020	0.016–0.055	0.0015–0.0032	0.0015–0.0032	Snug
	X	2.3 (2326)	0.0011–0.0022	0.008–0.016	0.008–0.016	0.015–0.055	0.0020–0.0040	0.0020–0.0040	Snug
	U	3.0 (2971)	0.0014–0.0022	0.010–0.020	0.010–0.020	0.010–0.049	0.0012–0.0031	0.0012–0.0031	Snug

TORQUE SPECIFICATIONS
All readings in ft. lbs.

Year	Engine ID/VIN	Engine Displacement Liters (cc)	Cylinder Head Bolts	Main Bearing Bolts	Rod Bearing Bolts	Crankshaft Damper Bolts	Flywheel Bolts	Manifold Intake	Manifold Exhaust	Spark Plugs	Lug Nut
1989	9	1.9 (1859)	①	67–80	26–30	81–96	54–64	12–15	15–20	8–15	85–105
	J	1.9 (1859)	①	67–80	26–30	81–96	54–64	12–15	15–20	8–15	85–105
	X	2.3 (2326)	②	51–66	21–26	140–170	54–64	15–22	③	6–10	85–105
	S	2.3 (2326)	②	51–66	21–26	140–170	54–64	15–22	③	6–10	85–105
1990	9	1.9 (1859)	①	67–80	26–30	81–96	54–64	12–15	15–20	8–15	85–105
	J	1.9 (1859)	①	67–80	26–30	81–96	54–64	12–15	15–20	8–15	85–105
	X	2.3 (2326)	②	51–66	21–26	140–170	54–64	15–22	③	6–10	85–105
	S	2.3 (2326)	②	51–66	21–26	140–170	54–64	15–22	③	6–10	85–105
1991	8	1.8 (1844)	56–60	40–43	35–37	80–87④	71–76	14–19	28–34	11–17	65–87
	J	1.9 (1859)	①	67–80	26–30	81–96	54–64	12–15	16–19	8–15	65–87
	X	2.3 (2326)	②	51–66	21–26	140–170	54–64	⑤	③	6–10	85–105
	S	2.3 (2326)	②	51–66	21–26	140–170	54–64	⑤	③	6–10	85–105
1992–93	8	1.8 (1844)	56–60	40–43	35–37	80–87④	71–76	14–19	28–34	11–17	65–87
	J	1.9 (1859)	①	67–80	26–30	81–96	54–64	12–15	16–19	8–15	65–87
	X	2.3 (2326)	②	51–66	21–26	140–170	54–64	⑤	③	6–10	85–105
	U	3.0 (2971)	⑥	55–63	26	93–121	59	⑦	15–22	5–11	85–105

① Tighten in sequence to 44 ft. lbs.
Loosen 2 turns
Retighten in sequence to 44 ft. lbs.
Turn all bolts, in sequence, 90 degrees
Turn all bolts, in sequence, an additional 90 degrees

② Tighten, in sequence, in 2 steps:
52–59 ft. lbs.
70–76 ft. lbs.
③ Tighten in 2 steps: 5–7 ft. lbs.
20–30 ft. lbs.
④ Specification is for sprocket bolt

⑤ Tighten in 2 steps: 5–7 ft. lbs.
20–30 ft. lbs.
⑥ Tighten, in sequence, to 52–66 ft. lbs.
Loosen 1 turn
Tighten, in sequence, to 33–41 ft. lbs.
Tighten, in sequence, to 63–73 ft. lbs.
⑦ Tighten in 2 steps: 15–22 ft. lbs.
19–24 ft. lbs.

BRAKE SPECIFICATIONS
All measurements in inches unless noted

Year	Model	Master Cylinder Bore	Brake Disc Original Thickness	Brake Disc Minimum Thickness	Brake Disc Maximum Runout	Brake Drum Diameter Original Inside Diameter	Brake Drum Diameter Max. Wear Limit	Brake Drum Diameter Maximum Machine Diameter	Minimum Lining Thickness Front	Minimum Lining Thickness Rear
1989	Escort	①	0.945	0.882	0.003	②	③	NA	0.125	④
	Tempo	①	0.945	0.882	0.003	8.059	8.119	NA	0.125	④
	Topaz	①	0.945	0.882	0.003	8.059	8.119	NA	0.125	④
1990	Escort	①	0.945	0.882	0.003	②	③	NA	0.125	④
	Tempo	①	0.945	0.882	0.003	8.059	8.119	NA	0.125	④
	Topaz	①	0.945	0.882	0.003	8.059	8.119	NA	0.125	④
1991	Escort	0.875	⑤	⑥	0.004	9.000	9.040	NA	0.080	0.040
	Tempo	①	0.945	0.882	0.003	8.059	8.119	NA	0.125	④
	Topaz	①	0.945	0.882	0.003	8.059	8.119	NA	0.125	④
1992–93	Escort	0.875	⑤	⑥	0.004	9.000	9.040	NA	0.080	0.040
	Tempo	①	0.945	0.882	0.003	8.059	8.119	NA	0.125	④
	Topaz	①	0.945	0.882	0.003	8.059	8.119	NA	0.125	④

NA—Not available
① Primary bore—1.12
Secondary bore—0.776
② Escort 2DR Hatchback without styled steel wheels—7.145 in.
Except Escort 2DR Hatchback without styled steel wheels—8.059 in.

③ Escort 2DR Hatchback without styled steel wheels—7.205 in.
Except Escort 2DR Hatchback without styled steel wheels—8.119 in.
④ Riveted linings—to within 0.031 in. of rivet head
Bonded linings—0.060

⑤ Front—0.870 in.
Rear—0.350 in.
⑥ Front—0.790 in.
Rear—0.280 in.

WHEEL ALIGNMENT

Year	Model		Caster Range (deg.)	Caster Preferred Setting (deg.)	Camber Range (deg.)	Camber Preferred Setting (deg.)	Toe-in (in.)	Steering Axis Inclination (deg.)
1989	Escort	Front	$1\frac{5}{8}$P–$3\frac{1}{8}$P	$2\frac{3}{8}$P	①	②	$\frac{1}{4}$N–0	③
		Rear	—	—	$1\frac{3}{16}$N–$\frac{1}{2}$P	$\frac{5}{16}$N	0–$\frac{3}{8}$P	—
	Tempo	Front	$1\frac{11}{16}$P–$3\frac{3}{16}$P	$2\frac{7}{16}$P	④	⑤	$\frac{1}{4}$N–0	③
		Rear	—	—	⑥	⑦	$\frac{3}{16}$N–$\frac{3}{16}$P	—
	Topaz	Front	$1\frac{11}{16}$P–$3\frac{3}{16}$P	$2\frac{7}{16}$P	④	⑤	$\frac{1}{4}$N–0	③
		Rear	—	—	⑥	⑦	$\frac{3}{16}$N–$\frac{3}{16}$P	—
1990	Escort	Front	$1\frac{5}{8}$P–$3\frac{1}{8}$P	$2\frac{3}{8}$P	①	②	$\frac{1}{4}$N–0	③
		Rear	—	—	$1\frac{3}{16}$N–$\frac{1}{2}$P	$\frac{5}{16}$N	0–$\frac{3}{8}$P	—
	Tempo	Front	$1\frac{11}{16}$P–$3\frac{3}{16}$P	$2\frac{7}{16}$P	④	⑤	$\frac{1}{4}$N–0	③
		Rear	—	—	⑥	⑦	$\frac{3}{16}$N–$\frac{3}{16}$P	—
	Topaz	Front	$1\frac{11}{16}$P–$3\frac{3}{16}$P	$2\frac{7}{16}$P	④	⑤	$\frac{1}{4}$N–0	③
		Rear	—	—	⑥	⑦	$\frac{3}{16}$N–$\frac{3}{16}$P	—
1991	Escort	Front	1P–$2\frac{7}{8}$P	$1\frac{15}{16}$P	$\frac{27}{32}$N–$1\frac{1}{16}$P	$\frac{3}{32}$N	$\frac{1}{32}$N–$\frac{7}{32}$P	$23\frac{13}{16}$
		Rear	—	—	$1\frac{3}{32}$N–$\frac{7}{16}$P	$\frac{11}{32}$N	$\frac{1}{32}$N–$\frac{7}{32}$P	—
	Tempo	Front	$1\frac{11}{16}$P–$3\frac{3}{16}$P	$2\frac{7}{16}$P	④	⑤	$\frac{1}{4}$N–0	③
		Rear	—	—	⑥	⑦	$\frac{3}{16}$N–$\frac{3}{16}$P	—
	Topaz	Front	$1\frac{11}{16}$P–$3\frac{3}{16}$P	$2\frac{7}{16}$P	④	⑤	$\frac{1}{4}$N–0	③
		Rear	—	—	⑥	⑦	$\frac{3}{16}$N–$\frac{3}{16}$P	—
1992–93	Escort	Front	1P–$2\frac{7}{8}$P	$1\frac{15}{16}$P	$\frac{27}{32}$N–$1\frac{1}{16}$P	$\frac{3}{32}$N	$\frac{1}{32}$N–$\frac{7}{32}$P	$23\frac{13}{16}$
		Rear	—	—	$1\frac{3}{32}$N–$\frac{7}{16}$P	$\frac{11}{32}$N	$\frac{1}{32}$N–$\frac{7}{32}$P	—
	Tempo	Front	$1\frac{11}{16}$P–$3\frac{3}{16}$P	$2\frac{7}{16}$P	④	⑤	$\frac{1}{4}$N–0	③
		Rear	—	—	⑥	⑦	$\frac{3}{16}$N–$\frac{3}{16}$P	—
	Topaz	Front	$1\frac{11}{16}$P–$3\frac{3}{16}$P	$2\frac{7}{16}$P	④	⑤	$\frac{1}{4}$N–0	③
		Rear	—	—	⑥	⑦	$\frac{3}{16}$N–$\frac{3}{16}$P	—

N—Negative
P—Positive

① Left wheel: $\frac{3}{8}$P–$1\frac{7}{8}$P
Right wheel: 0–$1\frac{1}{2}$P
② Left wheel: $1\frac{1}{8}$P
Right wheel: $\frac{3}{4}$P

③ Left wheel: $14\frac{21}{32}$
Right wheel: $15\frac{3}{32}$
④ Left wheel: $\frac{21}{32}$P–$2\frac{5}{32}$P
Right wheel: $\frac{7}{32}$P–$1\frac{23}{32}$P
⑤ Left wheel: $1\frac{13}{32}$P
Right wheel: $\frac{31}{32}$P

⑥ Front wheel drive: $\frac{29}{32}$N–$\frac{19}{32}$P
All wheel drive: $\frac{13}{32}$N–$\frac{13}{32}$P
⑦ Front wheel drive: $\frac{5}{32}$N
All wheel drive: $\frac{11}{32}$P

ENGINE MECHANICAL

NOTE: Disconnecting the negative battery cable on some vehicles may interfere with the functions of the on board computer systems and may require the computer to undergo a relearning process, once the negative battery cable is reconnected.

Engine Assembly

REMOVAL & INSTALLATION

1.8L Engine

WITH AUTOMATIC TRANSAXLE

The 1.8L engine can be removed without removing the transaxle from the vehicle. The engine can be split from the transaxle and lifted out of the engine compartment.

1. Disconnect the negative battery cable.
2. Mark the position of the hood hinges and remove the hood.
3. If equipped with air conditioning, properly discharge the system.
4. Drain the cooling system and engine oil.
5. Remove the air duct connecting the throttle body and resonance chamber.
6. Disconnect the power brake vacuum supply hose from the power booster.
7. If equipped with cruise control, disconnect the necessary vacuum hoses from the intake plenum.
8. Disconnect the electrical connectors from the power steering pump, water thermoswitch, temperature sending unit, oil pressure switch, fuel injector wiring harness, exhaust gas oxygen sensor, throttle position sensor and distributor.

NOTE: Mark the position of the connectors prior to removal to ease reinstallation.

9. Disconnect all engine ground straps.
10. Disconnect the ignition coil high-tension lead from the distributor.
11. Disconnect the accelerator and kickdown cables from the throttle cam.
12. Remove the accelerator and kickdown cable bracket from the intake plenum and set the assembly aside.
13. Disconnect the heater core inlet and outlet hoses at the bulkhead.

14. Relieve the fuel system pressure.

15. Remove the necessary fuel line clips and disconnect the fuel pressure and return lines.

16. Remove the upper radiator hose.

17. Disconnect the electrical connectors from the cooling fan and the radiator thermoswitch.

18. Remove the starter motor.

19. Raise and safely support the vehicle.

20. Remove the right upper and both left and right lower splash shields.

21. Remove the radiator lower hose.

22. Disconnect the 2 transaxle cooling lines from the radiator and plug the lines.

23. If necessary, remove the air conditioner line routing bracket from the radiator and position the line aside.

24. Remove the halfshaft bearing support.

25. Remove the inspection plate from the oil pan, place a wrench on the crankshaft pulley, and rotate the crankshaft to gain access to the torque converter nuts. Remove the nuts.

26. Remove the power steering and, if equipped, air conditioner drive belt.

27. Remove the crankshaft pulley.

28. Remove the exhaust flex-pipe and mounting flange assembly from the exhaust manifold.

29. If equipped with air conditioning, remove the compressor.

30. Remove the power steering pump and bracket assembly with the hoses still connected. Suspend the pump with wire, aside of the work area.

31. Remove all accessible transaxle-to-engine bolts from the engine block.

32. Lower the vehicle.

33. Remove the radiator mounting brackets and the resonance duct.

34. Remove the radiator, fan and shroud assembly from the vehicle.

35. Remove the vacuum chamber canister located next to the intake plenum.

36. Remove the pressure regulator and bracket assembly and set it aside.

37. Remove the shutter valve actuator and bracket assembly and set it aside.

38. Remove the alternator and water pump drive belt and remove the alternator.

39. Install a suitable engine removal sling onto the engine lifting brackets. Place a suitable engine hoist into position and support the engine.

40. Remove the oil pan-to-transaxle attaching bolts and the remaining transaxle-to-engine bolts from the engine block.

41. Remove the engine vibration dampener.

42. Remove the engine mount and the transaxle-to-engine upper right-hand bolt.

43. Carefully separate the engine from the transaxle, then remove the engine from the vehicle.

44. Install the engine onto a suitable engine stand.

To install:

45. Install a suitable engine removal sling onto the engine lifting brackets.

46. Place a suitable engine hoist into position and install the engine sling. Remove the engine from the engine stand and lower it into the engine compartment.

47. Install the transaxle-to-engine upper right bolt and tighten to 41–59 ft. lbs. (55–80 Nm).

NOTE: Make sure the torque converter studs are properly seated in the flexplate mounting holes.

48. Install the engine mount. Tighten the bolt and nuts to 49–69 ft. lbs. (67–93 Nm).

49. Install the engine vibration dampener. Tighten the bolt and nuts to 41–59 ft. lbs. (55–80 Nm).

50. Remove the engine sling from the lifting brackets and remove the engine hoist.

51. Install the remaining transaxle-to-engine bolts and tighten to 41–59 ft. lbs. (55–80 Nm).

52. Install the alternator and the alternator and water pump drive belt.

53. Install the shutter valve actuator and bracket assembly.

54. Install the pressure regulator and bracket assembly.

55. Install the vacuum chamber canister located next to the intake plenum.

56. Place the power steering pump and bracket assembly into its mounting position.

57. Place the radiator, fan and shroud assembly into its mounting position.

58. Install the radiator mounting brackets along with the resonance duct. Tighten the mounting bolts to 69–95 inch lbs. (7.8–11.0 Nm).

59. Connect the cooling fan and radiator thermoswitch electrical connectors.

60. Raise and safely support the vehicle.

61. Install the oil pan-to-transaxle attaching bolts and tighten to 27–38 ft. lbs. (37–52 Nm).

62. Install the power steering pump and bracket assembly. Tighten the bolts to 27–38 ft. lbs. (37–52 Nm).

63. Install the lower radiator hose and clamps.

64. Connect the 2 transaxle cooling lines to the radiator.

65. If equipped, install the air conditioning compressor.

66. Install the air conditioning hose routing bracket to the radiator, if equipped. Tighten the bracket attaching nuts to 56–82 inch lbs. (6.4–9.3 Nm).

67. Install the crankshaft pulley and tighten the bolts to 109–152 inch lbs. (12–17 Nm).

68. Place a wrench on the crankshaft pulley and rotate the crankshaft to gain access to the torque converter studs. Install the torque converter nuts and tighten to 25–36 ft. lbs. (34–49 Nm). Install the transaxle inspection plate.

69. Install the power steering and air conditioning drive belt.

70. Install the halfshaft bearing support and tighten the bolts to 31–46 ft. lbs. (42–62 Nm).

71. Install the starter motor.

72. Connect the heater core inlet and outlet hoses at the bulkhead.

73. Install the exhaust flex-pipe, with a new gasket, to the exhaust manifold. Tighten the pipe-to-converter attaching nuts to 23–34 ft. lbs. (31–46 Nm).

74. Install the right and left lower splash shields and the right upper splash shield. Tighten the bolts to 69–95 inch lbs. (7.8–11.0 Nm).

75. Lower the vehicle.

76. Install the upper radiator hose and clamps.

77. Unplug the fuel pressure and return lines and connect them to the fuel rail. Install the necessary fuel line clips.

78. Install the accelerator and kickdown cable bracket onto the intake plenum. Tighten the bolts to 69–95 inch lbs. (7.8–11.0 Nm). Install the accelerator and kickdown cables onto the throttle cam.

79. Connect the power brake vacuum supply hose to the vacuum booster.

80. If equipped, connect the cruise control vacuum hoses to the intake plenum.

81. Connect all engine ground straps.

82. Connect all remaining electrical connectors to their original locations, as marked during the removal procedure.

83. Connect the ignition coil high-tension lead into the distributor.

84. Install the air duct between the throttle body and resonance chamber assembly.

85. Fill the cooling system. Fill the crankcase with the proper type and quantity of engine oil.

86. If equipped, recharge the air conditioning system according to the proper procedure.

87. Install the hood, aligning the marks that were made during the removal procedure.

88. Connect the negative battery cable.

89. Start the engine and check for leaks. Stop the engine and check the fluid levels.

WITH MANUAL TRANSAXLE

The engine and transaxle must be removed as an assembly. Lift the assembly out of the engine compartment.

1. Disconnect the negative battery cable.
2. Mark the position of the hood on the hinges and remove the hood.
3. If equipped with air conditioning, properly discharge the system.
4. Drain the cooling system and the engine oil.
5. Remove the resonance duct and the air cleaner assembly.
6. Remove the battery and the battery tray.
7. Disconnect the accelerator cable from the throttle cam and remove the accelerator cable bracket from the intake plenum.
8. Remove the upper radiator hose and disconnect the radiator overflow hose from the radiator filler neck.
9. Disconnect the radiator thermoswitch and cooling fan electrical connectors.
10. Remove the attaching nuts to the radiator mounting brackets and remove the brackets.
11. Disconnect the alternator, oil pressure switch, throttle position sensor, idle speed control, manual lever position switch, fuel injector wiring harness, backup light switch, water thermoswitch, oxygen sensor, power steering pump and distributor electrical connectors.

NOTE: Mark the position of the connectors prior to removal to ease reinstallation.

12. Disconnect all engine ground straps.
13. Disconnect the ignition coil high-tension lead from the distributor.
14. Properly relieve the fuel system pressure.
15. Disconnect the fuel pressure and return lines.
16. Disconnect the heater core inlet and outlet, power brake vacuum supply, purge control vacuum and, if equipped, cruise control vacuum hoses.

NOTE: Mark the position of the hoses prior to removal to ease reinstallation.

17. Raise and safely support the vehicle.
18. Remove the right upper and lower splash shields.
19. Remove the clutch slave cylinder pipe bracket from the transaxle with the hose still connected. Position the slave cylinder aside.

NOTE: Be careful not to damage the pipe or the hose.

20. Disconnect the shift control rod and the extension bar from the transaxle.
21. Remove the battery duct.
22. Remove the radiator lower hose.
23. Remove the power steering and, if equipped, air conditioning compressor drive belt.
24. Remove the power steering pump and bracket assembly with the hoses still connected. Suspend the pump with wire aside of the work area.
25. Remove the air conditioning hose routing bracket, if equipped, from the transaxle crossmember and position the air conditioning hose aside.
26. If equipped, remove the air conditioning compressor with the hoses still connected. Suspend the compressor with wire aside of the work area.
27. Disconnect the speedometer cable from the transaxle.
28. Remove the exhaust pipe front mounting flange and support bracket from the exhaust manifold.
29. Mark the location and disconnect the wires from the starter motor.
30. Remove the stabilizer bar.
31. Remove the tie rod ends from the steering knuckles.
32. Remove the halfshafts from the transaxle.
33. Remove the transaxle front and rear mount attaching nuts from the crossmember.
34. Lower the vehicle.
35. Remove the radiator, fan and shroud assembly from the vehicle.
36. Install a suitable engine removal sling onto the engine lifting brackets.
37. Place a suitable engine hoist into position and support the engine.
38. Remove the engine vibration dampener.
39. Remove the engine mount, transaxle upper mount and the transaxle support bracket.
40. Remove the engine and transaxle assembly.
41. Remove the intake plenum support bracket.
42. Remove the starter motor.
43. Remove the transaxle front mount.
44. Remove all oil pan-to-transaxle bolts and transaxle-to-engine attaching bolts from the engine block and separate the transaxle from the engine.
45. Remove the clutch assembly from the engine.
46. Install the engine onto a suitable engine stand.

To install:

47. Install a suitable engine removal sling onto the engine lifting brackets. Place a suitable engine hoist into position and install the engine sling.

48. Remove the engine from the engine stand and lower the engine with the hoist still supporting it.
49. Install the clutch assembly.
50. Install the transaxle onto the engine.
51. Install the transaxle-to-engine bolts and tighten to 47–66 ft. lbs. (64–89 Nm).
52. Install the oil pan-to-transaxle attaching bolts and tighten to 27–38 ft. lbs. (37–52 Nm).
53. Position the transaxle front mount onto the transaxle and install the attaching bolts. Tighten the bolts to 27–38 ft. lbs. (37–52 Nm).
54. Position the starter motor into the transaxle housing and install the mounting bolts. Tighten the bolts to 27–38 ft. lbs. (37–52 Nm).
55. Install the intake plenum support bracket. Tighten the bolts to 27–38 ft. lbs. (37–52 Nm) and the nut to 14–19 ft. lbs. (19–25 Nm).
56. Using the engine hoist, position the engine and transaxle assembly into the engine compartment and align the engine mounting points with the engine mount and the mounting holes in the transaxle crossmember.
57. Install the attaching nuts to the transaxle front and rear mounts and the transaxle crossmember.
58. Position the engine mount into the vehicle.
59. Install the engine mount through-bolt and nut. Tighten them to 49–69 ft. lbs. (67–93 Nm).
60. Install the engine mount-to-engine attaching nuts. Tighten the nuts to 54–76 ft. lbs. (74–103 Nm).
61. Install the engine mount vibration dampener and attaching bolt and nut. Tighten the bolt and nut to 41–59 ft. lbs. (55–80 Nm).
62. Place the clutch slave cylinder and pipe assembly into its proper mounting position.
63. Install the transaxle support bracket and attaching bolts. Tighten the bolts to 41–59 ft. lbs. (55–80 Nm).
64. Install the transaxle upper mount and install the attaching bolts. Tighten the bolts to 32–45 ft. lbs. (43–61 Nm).
65. Install the transaxle upper mount attaching nuts. Tighten the nuts to 49–69 ft. lbs. (67–93 Nm).
66. Place the radiator, fan and shroud assembly into its mounting position.
67. Install the radiator mounting brackets and tighten the nuts to 69–95 inch lbs. (7.8–11.0 Nm).
68. Install the upper radiator hose and connect the expansion reservoir overflow tube to the radiator filler neck.
69. Connect the cooling fan and radiator thermoswitch electrical connectors.

70. Raise and safely support the vehicle.

71. Install the lower radiator hose.

72. Install the halfshafts.

73. Install the tie rod ends into the steering knuckle.

74. Install the stabilizer bar.

75. Connect the wires to the starter motor according to their positions as marked during the removal procedure.

76. Install the exhaust front mounting flange to the exhaust manifold while making sure to install a new gasket. Tighten the flange-to-manifold attaching nuts to 23–34 ft. lbs. (31–46 Nm).

77. Install the exhaust pipe support bracket. Tighten the bracket attaching bolts to 27–38 ft. lbs. (37–52 Nm).

78. Install the speedometer cable into the transaxle.

79. If equipped, install the air conditioning compressor. Tighten the mounting bolts to 15–22 ft. lbs. (20–30 Nm).

80. Install the air conditioning routing bracket, if equipped, to the transaxle crossmember. Tighten the bolt to 56–82 inch lbs. (6.4–9.3 Nm).

81. Install the power steering pump and bracket assembly. Tighten the pump mounting bolts to 27–38 ft. lbs. (37–52 Nm).

82. Install the power steering and air conditioning drive belt.

83. Install the battery duct and tighten the attaching bolts to 69–95 inch lbs. (7.8–11.0 Nm).

84. Install the extension bar to the transaxle and tighten the attaching nut to 23–34 ft. lbs. (31–46 Nm).

85. Connect the shift control rod to the transaxle and tighten the attaching nut to 12–17 ft. lbs. (16–23 Nm).

86. Install the clutch slave cylinder attaching bolts and tighten to 12–17 ft. lbs. (16–23 Nm).

87. Position the slave cylinder pipe and install the routing bracket and attaching bolt. Tighten the bolt to 12–17 ft. lbs. (16–23 Nm).

88. Install the right upper and lower splash shields. Tighten the bolts to 69–95 inch lbs. (7.8–11.0 Nm).

89. Lower the vehicle.

90. Connect the heater core and vacuum hoses according to their original positions as marked during the removal procedure.

91. Connect the fuel pressure and return lines.

92. Connect the ignition coil high tension lead into the distributor.

93. Connect all engine ground straps.

94. Connect all remaining electrical connectors according to the locations marked during the removal procedure.

95. Install the accelerator cable bracket to the intake plenum and connect the accelerator cable to the throttle cam.

96. Install the battery tray and the battery.

97. Install the air cleaner assembly and the resonance duct.

98. Fill the cooling system. Fill the engine with the proper type and quantity of oil.

99. If equipped, recharge the air conditioning system.

100. Install the hood, aligning the marks that were made during the removal procedure.

101. Connect the negative battery cable.

102. Start the engine and check for leaks. Stop the engine and check the fluid levels.

1989–90 1.9L Engine

1. Mark position of the hood on the hinges and remove the hood.

2. Relieve the fuel system pressure. Remove air cleaner, air intake duct and heat tube.

3. Disconnect negative battery cable.

4. Drain the cooling system. Remove the secondary wire from the ignition coil.

5. Remove alternator air intake tube and the alternator drive belt. Remove alternator mounting bolts and lay alternator aside.

6. Disconnect the radiator hoses and heater hoses at the engine. Disconnect the oil cooler lines, if equipped with automatic transaxle.

7. Remove radiator cooling fan and shroud as an assembly.

8. Remove the transaxle cooler line routing clip located at the radiator, if equipped with automatic transaxle. Remove the radiator and disconnect the heater at the metal tube.

9. Identify, tag and disconnect the electrical connections and vacuum hoses as necessary. Disconnect the fuel upply and return lines. If equipped with power assist brakes, disconnect the power boost vacuum hose at the engine.

10. Disconnect kickdown rod at the fuel charging assembly, if equipped with automatic transaxle.

11. Disconnect accelerator cable at the fuel charging assembly and remove the cable routing bracket attaching screws. Disconnect the vapor hose at the carbon canister tube.

12. Raise and safely support the vehicle.

13. Remove the clamp from the heater supply and return hose. Remove the starter brace at front of starter motor and remove battery cable from starter. Remove the starter motor.

14. Disconnect exhaust inlet pipe at manifold.

15. Remove support bracket in front of converter cover, if equipped with automatic transaxle or inspection cover, if equipped with manual transaxle. Remove the converter or inspection cover.

16. Remove crankshaft pulley and damper.

17. Remove torque converter to flywheel nuts, if equipped with automatic transaxle.

18. Remove timing belt cover lower attaching bolts, if equipped with manual transaxle.

19. Remove converter housing, if equipped with automatic transaxle, or flywheel housing, if equipped with manual transaxle, attaching bolts.

20. Remove 2 oil pan-to-transaxle attaching bolts. Disconnect coolant bypass hose from intake manifold. Remove the bolt attaching the battery negative cable to the cylinder block.

21. Remove nut and bolt attaching insulator bracket to the engine bracket at front of engine.

22. Lower the vehicle.

23. Install suitable lifting brackets on engine.

24. Use a suitable lifting device connected to the engine lifting brackets and raise engine just enough to remove the through bolt from the front engine insulator and remove insulator.

25. Remove the remaining timing belt cover bolts and remove the cover, if equipped with manual transaxle.

26. Remove insulator attaching bracket from engine.

27. Position a jack under the transaxle. Raise jack just enough to support the weight of the transaxle.

28. Remove the converter housing or flywheel housing upper attaching bolts.

29. Remove engine assembly from vehicle.

To install:

30. Carefully lower engine into the vehicle using a suitable lifting device.

31. Join the engine and the transaxle, making sure the alignment dowels on the back of the engine engage the transaxle housing.

NOTE: If equipped with an manual transaxle, make sure the transaxle input shaft engages the clutch disc. If equipped with an automatic transaxle, make sure the torque converter studs engage the flywheel.

32. Install the converter or flywheel housing upper attaching bolts.

33. Install 2 oil pan to transaxle attaching bolts and tighten to 30–40 ft. lbs. (40–54 Nm). Then loosen bolts ½ turn.

34. Remove jack from under the transaxle.

35. Position engine insulator attaching casting on the engine and install the attaching bolt and nut.

36. Attach the nuts to the insulator to casting.

37. Remove lifting device and the lifting brackets.

38. Connect electrical connectors, vacuum hoses and carbon canister vapor hose.

39. If equipped with an automatic transaxle, connect the kickdown rod.

40. Connect the heater hoses.

41. Connect the fuel supply and return lines.

42. If equipped with power brakes, connect the vacuum hose to the power booster.

43. Position the accelerator cable routing bracket and install the attaching bolts.

44. Connect the accelerator cable to the fuel charging assembly.

45. Connect the coolant bypass hose, if equipped with an manual transaxle.

46. Install radiator.

47. Install the negative battery cable to cylinder block attaching bolt.

48. Attach the lower cooler line, if equipped with an automatic transaxle.

49. Connect the lower radiator hose.

50. Attach the upper cooler line, if equipped with an automatic transaxle.

51. Install radiator cooling fan and shroud assembly. Connect the cooling fan electrical connector.

52. Connect the upper radiator hose.

53. Raise and safely support the vehicle.

54. Tighten the casting-to-insulator attaching nuts.

55. Install the torque converter-to-flywheel attaching bolts.

56. Install the crankshaft damper.

57. Install lower attaching bolts to converter housing, if equipped with automatic transaxle; flywheel housing if equipped with manual transaxle.

58. Install the converter or inspection cover.

59. Install support bracket.

60. Install starter motor and connect battery cable.

61. Install starter brace at the front of the starter motor.

62. Connect the exhaust inlet pipe.

63. Install the cooler line routing bracket, if equipped with automatic transaxle.

64. Lower the vehicle.

65. Install the timing belt cover, if equipped with manual transaxle.

66. Install alternator and drive belt.

67. Connect negative battery cable.

68. Install alternator air intake tube.

69. Fill cooling system, overflow bottle and bleed the cooling system.

70. Fill the crankcase to the proper level.

71. Install the hood, aligning the marks that were made during removal.

72. Start engine and check for coolant, oil and fuel leaks.

73. Install air cleaner assembly with the intake duct and heat tube and connect the vacuum hoses.

1991–93 1.9L Engine

WITH AUTOMATIC TRANSAXLE

The engine is removed without the transaxle attached. The engine is lifted from the engine compartment with the transaxle assembly remaining in the vehicle, attached to the mounts.

1. Mark the position of the hood on the hinges and remove the hood.

2. Disconnect the negative battery cable.

3. Drain the cooling system and the engine oil.

4. Remove the air intake duct.

5. Remove the crankcase ventilation hose from the valve cover and the vacuum hose from the bottom side of the throttle body.

6. Disconnect the power brake booster supply hose.

7. Disconnect the following electrical connectors:

    a. Fuel charging harness, located at the right shock tower.

    b. Alternator harness, from the back side of the alternator.

    c. Oxygen sensor.

    d. Ignition coil.

    e. Radio suppressor, mounted on the coil bracket.

    f. Coolant temperature sensor, cooling fan sensor and temperature gauge sending unit, mounted on a common water tube near the thermostat housing.

    g. Radiator cooling fan.

NOTE: Mark the position of the electrical connectors prior to removal to aid reinstallation.

8. Remove the idle air bypass valve.

9. Remove the ground strap from the stud on the left side of the cylinder head near the ignition coil.

10. Disconnect the accelerator cable and the transaxle kickdown cable from the throttle lever. Remove the cable bracket from the intake manifold and position aside.

11. Disconnect both heater hoses at the engine compartment bulkhead.

12. Properly relieve the fuel system pressure and disconnect the fuel supply and return hoses at the fuel supply manifold.

13. Remove the upper radiator hose.

14. Raise and safely support the vehicle.

15. Remove the right side and the right and left front splash shields.

16. Remove the lower radiator hose from the radiator.

17. Position a drain pan under the radiator and remove the lower transaxle oil cooler line.

18. Remove the 2 oil cooler line retaining bracket bolts from the bottom of the radiator.

19. Remove the radiator fan shroud lower mounting bolts.

20. Lower the vehicle.

21. Remove the radiator fan shroud upper mounting bolts and remove the fan and shroud assembly from the vehicle.

22. Remove the upper transaxle oil cooler line from the radiator and remove the radiator from the vehicle.

23. If equipped with air conditioning, properly discharge the system.

24. Disconnect the air conditioning suction line at the suction accumulator/drier. Plug or cap the openings to prevent the entrance of dirt and moisture.

25. Remove the accessory drive belt.

26. Remove the power steering return hose from the pump reservoir and the high-pressure hose from the power steering pump.

27. Remove the power steering and air conditioner line retainer bracket bolts from the alternator bracket. Position the hoses aside.

28. Remove the accessory drive belt automatic tensioner assembly.

29. Raise and safely support the vehicle.

30. Remove the drive belt idler pulley.

31. If equipped, remove the 4 air conditioning compressor mounting bolts. Remove the compressor assembly with the lines attached and position aside. Safety wire the compressor to the vehicle sub-frame.

32. Remove the catalytic converter inlet pipe.

33. Remove the transaxle kickdown cable support bracket from the back side of the engine block. Position the cable and the bracket aside.

34. Disconnect the oil pressure switch.

35. Disconnect the relay wire and the positive battery cable from the starter.

36. Remove the flywheel inspection shield.

37. Remove the 4 torque converter attaching nuts.

38. Remove the crankshaft dampener.

39. Remove the 5 engine-to-transaxle bolts.

40. Lower the vehicle.

41. Remove the 3 starter motor mounting bolts and remove the starter out of the top of the engine compartment.

42. Remove the 2 transaxle-to-engine mounting bolts.

43. Connect an engine removal sling to suitable engine lifting brackets. Position a suitable engine hoist and suport the engine.

44. Remove the right engine mount dampener and mount assembly.

45. With the engine assembly supported by the engine hoist, carefully separate the assembly from the transaxle.

46. Lift the engine assembly out of the vehicle.

47. Install the engine onto a suitable engine stand.

To install:

48. Attach the engine removal sling to the engine lifting brackets and remove the engine from the stand with the engine hoist.

49. Carefully lower the engine into the vehicle and join the engine to the transaxle. Make sure the torque converter studs correctly engage the flywheel and the alignment dowels engage the transaxle housing.

50. Install the 2 transaxle-to-engine bolts, but do not fully tighten them at this time.

51. Install the right engine mount insulator and dampener.

52. Position the engine hoist aside and remove the sling from the engine lifting brackets.

53. Raise and safely support the vehicle.

54. Install the 5 engine-to-transaxle bolts, but do not fully tighten them at this time.

55. Install the crankshaft dampener and tighten the attaching bolt to 81–96 ft. lbs. (110–130 Nm).

56. Install the 4 torque converter attaching nuts and tighten to 25–36 ft. lbs. (34–49 Nm). Install the flywheel inspection plate.

57. Connect the oil pressure switch.

58. Install the kickdown cable support bracket.

59. If equipped, position the air conditioning compressor on the bracket and install the 4 mounting bolts. Tighten the bolts to 15–22 ft. lbs. (20–30 Nm).

60. Install the catalytic converter inlet pipe.

61. Lower the vehicle.

62. From above, position the starter motor and install the 3 mounting bolts. Connect the positive battery cable and the relay wire to the starter.

63. Tighten the 2 transaxle-to-engine bolts to 40–59 ft. lbs. (55–80 Nm).

64. Install the power steering high-pressure hose on the pump.

65. Install the accessory drive belt idler pulley and automatic tensioner.

66. Install the power steering return hose on the pump reservoir.

67. Install the power steering hose retainer bracket on the alternator bracket.

68. Install the accessory drive belt.

69. If equipped, connect the air conditioner suction line to the accumulator.

70. Install the radiator assembly.

71. Connect the upper transaxle oil cooler line at the radiator.

72. Position the cooling fan and shroud assembly and install the upper mounting bolts.

73. Raise and safely support the vehicle.

74. Install the lower shroud bolts and connect the lower transaxle oil cooler line.

75. Install the oil cooler line retaining bracket bolts.

76. Install the lower radiator hose.

77. Tighten the 5 engine-to-transaxle bolts to 27–38 ft. lbs. (37–52 Nm).

78. Install the left and right front splash shields and the right side splash shield.

79. Lower the vehicle.

80. Install the upper radiator hose.

81. Connect both heater hoses at the engine compartment bulkhead.

82. Install the accelerator cable bracket and attach the accelerator and kickdown cables to the throttle lever.

83. Install the idle air bypass valve.

84. Install the ground strap on the stud at the front left side of the cylinder head, near the ignition coil.

85. Connect the remaining electrical connectors according to the positions marked during the removal procedure.

86. Connect the fuel supply and return lines. Be sure to install the fuel line safety clips.

87. Connect the power brake suply hose, the vacuum hose on the bottom side of the throttle body, and the crankcase ventilation hose to the valve cover.

88. Install the air intake duct.

89. Connect the negative battery cable.

90. Fill the cooling system. Fill the crankcase with the proper type and quantity of engine oil.

91. Install the hood, aligning the marks that were made during the removal procedure.

92. Start the engine and check for leaks. Stop the engine and check the fluid levels.

93. If equipped, evacuate and recharge the air conditioning system according to the proper procedure.

WITH MANUAL TRANSAXLE

The engine is removed with the transaxle attached. The engine is lifted out of the engine compartment.

1. Mark the position of the hood on the hinges and remove the hood.

2. Disconnect the battery cables and remove the battery and the battery tray.

3. Drain the cooling system and the engine oil.

4. Remove the air cleaner.

5. Disconnect the crankcase ventilation hose from the valve cover and the vacuum hose from the bottom side of the throttle body.

6. Remove the power brake supply hose.

7. Disconnect the following electrical connectors:

   a. Fuel charging harness, located at the right shock tower.

   b. Alternator harness, from the back side of the alternator.

   c. Oxygen sensor.

   d. Ignition coil.

   e. Radio suppressor, mounted on the coil bracket.

   f. Coolant temperature sensor, cooling fan sensor and temperature gauge sending unit, mounted on a common water tube near the thermostat housing.

   g. Radiator cooling fan.

NOTE: Mark the position of the electrical connectors prior to removal to aid reinstallation.

8. Remove the idle air bypass valve.

9. Remove the ground strap from the stud on the left side of the cylinder head near the ignition coil.

10. Disconnect the accelerator cable from the throttle lever. Remove the cable bracket from the intake manifold and position aside.

11. Disconnect both heater hoses at the engine compartment bulkhead.

12. Properly relieve the fuel system pressure and disconnect the fuel supply and return hoses at the fuel supply manifold.

13. Remove the upper radiator hose.

14. If equipped, properly discharge the air conditioning system and disconnect the suction line at the accumulator.

15. Remove the accessory drive belt and the automatic tensioner and idler pulley.

16. Disconnect the power steering return hose from the pump reservoir and the high pressure hose from the pump.

17. Remove the power steering hose and air conditioning line retainer brackets from the alternator bracket.

18. Raise and safely support the vehicle.

19. Remove the right and left side and front splash shields.

20. Disconnect the lower radiator hose from the radiator and remove the radiator fan shroud lower mounting bolts.

21. If equipped, remove the 4 air conditioning compressor mounting bolts.

Remove the compressor assembly with the lines attached and position aside. Safety wire the compressor to the vehicle sub-frame.

22. Remove the catalytic converter inlet pipe.

23. Disconnect the oil pressure switch.

24. Disconnect the relay wire and the positive battery cable at the starter.

25. Remove the transaxle extension bar and shift control rod.

26. Remove the crankshaft dampener.

27. Remove the front wheel and tire assemblies.

28. Remove both halfshaft assemblies.

29. Install suitable transaxle plugs into the differential side gears.

NOTE: Failure to install the transaxle plugs may allow the differential side gears to move out of position. Should the gears become misaligned, the differential will have to be removed from the transaxle to align the gears.

30. Disconnect the speedometer cable and the neutral switch on the transaxle.

31. Remove the clutch slave cylinder and line as an assembly from the transaxle and set it aside.

32. Remove the transaxle front and rear mount bolts.

33. Lower the vehicle.

34. Remove the radiator fan shroud upper mounting bolts and remove the fan shroud assembly from the vehicle.

35. Connect a suitable engine removal sling to the engine lifting brackets. Connect the sling to a suitable engine hoist, position the hoist and support the engine.

36. Remove the right engine mount dampener and mount assembly.

37. Remove the transaxle upper mount.

38. Lift the engine and transaxle assembly out of the vehicle and set it down on the floor.

To install:

39. Carefully lower the engine and transaxle assembly into the vehicle with the engine hoist.

40. Position the transaxle on its mounts and install the transaxle upper mount.

41. Install the right engine mount and mount damper.

42. Remove the engine removal sling and the hoist.

43. Position the fan shroud assembly and install the upper mounting bolts.

44. Raise and safely support the vehicle.

45. Install the front and rear transaxle mount bolts.

46. Install the clutch slave cylinder and line assembly.

47. Connect the neutral switch and the speedometer cable.

48. Remove the transaxle plugs and install the halfshaft assemblies.

49. Install the crankshaft dampener and tighten the bolt to 81–96 ft. lbs. (110–130 Nm).

50. Install the transaxle extension bar and shift control rod.

51. Connect the relay wire and the positive battery cable to the starter.

52. Connect the oil pressure switch.

53. Install the catalytic converter inlet pipe.

54. If equipped, position the air conditioning compressor on its bracket and install the 4 mounting bolts.

55. Install the radiator fan shroud lower mounting bolts and install the lower radiator hose.

56. Install the left and right side and front splash shields.

57. Lower the vehicle.

58. Install the power steering hoses and install the power steering hose and air conditioner line retainer brackets.

59. Install the accessory drive belt idler pulley and automatic tensioner and install the accessory drive belt.

60. If equipped, connect the air conditioner suction line.

61. Install the upper radiator hose.

62. Connect the fuel supply and return hoses to the fuel supply manifold.

63. Connect both heater hoses.

64. Install the accelerator cable bracket on the intake manifold and connect the cable to the throttle lever.

65. Install the ground strap on the stud at the front left side of the cylinder head.

66. Install the idle air bypass valve.

67. Connect the remaining electrical connectors according to the positions marked during the removal procedure.

68. Connect the power brake supply hose, the crankcase ventilation hose and the vacuum line at the bottom of the throttle body.

69. Install the air cleaner assembly.

70. Install the battery tray and the battery. Connect the battery cables.

71. Fill the cooling system. Fill the crankcase with the proper type and quantity of oil.

72. Install the hood, aligning the marks that were made during the removal procedure.

73. Start the engine and check for leaks. Stop the engine and check the fluid levels.

74. If equipped, evacuate and recharge the air conditioning system according to the proper procedure.

2.3L Engine

NOTE: This procedure describes the removal and installation of the engine and transaxle as an assembly.

1. Mark the position of the hood on the hinges and remove the hood.

2. Disconnect the negative battery cable.

3. Properly relieve the fuel system pressure. Remove the air cleaner.

4. Remove lower radiator hose to drain the engine coolant.

5. Remove upper radiator hose and disconnect transaxle cooler lines at rubber hoses below radiator, if equipped with automatic transaxle.

6. Disconnect the coolant fan at the electrical connection.

7. Remove radiator shroud and cooling fan as an assembly. Remove radiator.

8. Discharge air conditioning system, if equipped and remove pressure and suction lines from compressor.

—————— CAUTION ——————

Use extreme care when discharging air conditioning system, as the refrigerant is under high pressure and may cause personal injury.

9. Identify, tag and disconnect all electrical and vacuum lines as necessary.

10. If equipped, disconnect the TV linkage at the automatic transaxle. If equipped, disconnect the clutch cable from the shift lever on the transaxle.

11. Disconnect accelerator linkage and fuel lines.

12. Remove coil and brackets assembly.

13. Disconnect power steering lines at pump and remove the bracket at the cylinder head, if equipped.

14. Install 2 engine lifting eyes and install engine support tool D88L–6000–A or equivalent, to engine lifting eyes.

15. Raise and safely support the vehicle.

16. Remove battery cable from starter and remove hose from catalytic converter.

17. Remove bolt attaching exhaust pipe bracket to oil pan and 2 exhaust pipe to manifold attaching nuts.

18. Remove exhaust inlet pipe-to-exhaust manifold retaining nuts, pull exhaust system out of rubber insulating grommets and set aside.

19. Remove speedometer cable from transaxle.

20. Remove one heater hose from water pump inlet tube and the other from the steel heater inlet tube.

21. Remove the clamp retaining bolts or nuts at the underside of the oil pan and remove the inlet tube.

22. Remove bolts attaching control arms to body. Remove stabilizer bar brackets retaining bolts and remove brackets.

23. Remove both halfshaft assemblies. After removing the halfshafts,

install transaxle plugs T81P–1177–B or equivalent, in the differential side gears.

NOTE: Failure to install the plugs can result in dislocation of the differential side gears. If the gears become misaligned, the differential must be removed from the transaxle to realign the gears.

24. On manual transaxle equipped vehicles, remove roll restrictor nuts from transaxle. Pull roll restrictor from mounting bracket.
25. On manual transaxle equipped vehicles, remove shift stabilizer bar to transaxle attaching bolts. Remove shift mechanism to shift shaft attaching nut and bolt at transaxle.
26. On automatic transaxle equipped, disconnect manual shift cable clip from lever on transaxle. Remove manual shift linkage bracket bolts from transaxle and remove bracket.
27. Remove the left rear insulator mount bracket from body bracket.
28. Remove the left front insulator to transaxle mounting bolts.
29. Lower the vehicle. Install lifting equipment to the 2 lifting eyes on engine.

NOTE: Do not allow front wheels to touch floor.

30. Remove the th engine support tool.
31. Remove right No. 3A insulator intermediate bracket-to-engine bracket bolts, intermediate bracket-to-insulator attaching nuts and the nut on the bottom of the double ended stud which attaches the intermediate bracket-to-engine bracket. Remove bracket.
32. Carefully lower engine and transaxle assembly to the floor.
To install:
33. Raise and safely support the vehicle.
34. Position engine and transaxle assembly directly below engine compartment.
35. Slowly lower vehicle over engine and transaxle assembly.

NOTE: Do not allow the front wheels to touch the floor.

36. Install lifting equipment to both existing engine lifting eyes on engine.
37. Raise engine and transaxle assembly up through engine compartment and position accordingly.
38. Install right side No. 3A insulator intermediate attaching nuts to intermediate bracket. Tighten to 55–75 ft. lbs. (75–100 Nm). Attach intermediate bracket to engine bracket bolts. Tighten to 52–70 ft. lbs. (70–95 Nm). Install nut on bottom of double-ended stud that attaches the intermediate

bracket-to-engine bracket. Tighten to 60–90 ft. lbs. (80–120 Nm).
39. Install engine support tool D88L–6000–A or equivalent, to engine lifting eye.
40. Remove lifting equipment.
41. Raise and safely support the vehicle.
42. Position transaxle jack under engine. Raise engine and transaxle assembly into mounted position.
43. Install insulator-to-bracket nut and tighten to 45–65 ft. lbs. (61–68 Nm). Tighten the left rear No. 4 insulator bracket-to-body bracket nuts to 45–65 ft. lbs. (61–68 Nm).
44. If equipped with manual transaxle, position roll restrictor onto starter studs. Install nuts attaching roll restrictor to transaxle and tighten to 25–39 ft. lbs. (35–50 Nm).
45. Install starter cable to starter. Install water pump inlet tube and tighten the fastener to 71–97 inch lbs. (8–11 Nm).
46. Install lower radiator hose.
47. If equipped with manual transaxle, install shift stabilizer bar-to-transaxle attaching bolt. Tighten to 23–35 ft. lbs. (31–47 Nm).
48. If equipped with manual transaxle, install shift mechanism-to-input shift shaft (on transaxle) bolt and nut. Tighten to 7–10 ft. lbs. (9–13 Nm).
49. If equipped with automatic transaxle, install manual shift linkage bracket bolts to transaxle. Install cable clip to lever on transaxle.
50. Install lower radiator hose to radiator.
51. Install speedometer cable to transaxle.
52. Position exhaust system up and into insulating rubber grommets located at rear of vehicle.
53. Install exhaust pipe-to-exhaust manifold studs. Install exhaust pipe bracket-to-oil pan bolt.
54. Connect pulse air hose to catalytic converter.
55. Place stabilizer bar and control arm assembly into position. Install control arm-to-body attaching bolts. Install stabilizer bar brackets and tighten all fasteners.
56. Install the halfshaft assemblies.
57. Lower vehicle.
58. Remove engine support tool.
59. Connect any remaining electrical and vacuum lines.
60. Install heater hose.
61. Install air conditioning discharge and suction lines to compressor, if equipped. Do not charge at this time.
62. Connect fuel supply and return lines to engine.
63. Connect accelerator cable.
64. Install power steering pressure and return lines.
65. If equipped with automatic

transaxle, connect TV linkage at transaxle.
66. If equipped with manual transaxle, connect clutch cable to shift lever on transaxle. Check clutch adjustment.
67. Install radiator shroud and coolant fan assembly. Connect the coolant fan electrical connector and install the upper radiator hose.
68. If equipped with automatic transaxle, connect transaxle cooler lines to rubber hoses below radiator.
69. Fill cooling system.
70. Install the coil and the air cleaner assembly.
71. Connect the negative battery cable.
72. Install the hood, aligning the marks made during the removal procedure.
73. Charge air conditioning system, if equipped.
74. Check all fluid levels.
75. Start the engine and check for leaks.

3.0L Engine

1. Disconnect the battery cables and remove the battery. Remove the battery tray with the air cleaner assembly attached.
2. Drain the cooling system.
3. If equipped, properly discharge the air conditioning system.
4. Mark the position of the hood on its hinges and remove the hood.
5. Properly relieve the fuel system pressure, then disconnect the fuel lines and position them aside.
6. Remove the upper radiator hose.
7. Tag and disconnect all necessary electrical connectors and vacuum lines.
8. Disconnect the lines from the power steering pump and remove the power steering reservoir.
9. Disconnect the air conditioning lines from the condenser, leaving the manifold lines attached to the compressor.
10. Disconnect the accelerator linkage, transaxle throttle valve linkage and cruise control cable, if equipped.
11. Disconnect the speedometer cable.
12. If equipped with automatic transaxle, disconnect the transaxle cooler lines from the radiator.
13. Remove the coolant overflow bottle and the lower radiator hose.
14. Remove the power steering lines at the rear of the engine above the transaxle.
15. Raise and safely support the vehicle.
16. Drain the engine oil and remove the heater hoses.
17. Remove the front wheel and tire assemblies.

18. Support the exhaust system and remove the exhaust Y-pipe.

19. Remove the bolt retaining the air conditioner line to the engine block.

20. Disconnect the tie rod ends from the spindles.

21. Disconnect the lower ball joints and pull down on the control arms to disengage them from the spindles.

22. Remove both halfshaft assemblies. After removing the halfshafts, install transaxle plugs T81P–1177–B or equivalent, in the differential side gears.

NOTE: Failure to install the plugs can result in dislocation of the differential side gears. If the gears become misaligned, the differential must be removed from the transaxle to realign the gears.

23. Lower the vehicle.

24. Remove the ignition coil bracket bolts and position the coil assembly aside.

25. Install suitable engine lifting eyes to the engine at the front of the right cylinder and at the rear of the left cylinder head. Attach suitable engine lifting equipment to the lifting eyes.

26. Remove the through bolts from the engine mounts.

27. Carefully lift the engine from the vehicle. The engine must be tilted to clear the master cylinder.

To install:

28. Carefully lower the engine into the engine compartment, being careful to clear the master cylinder.

29. Position the engine and install the through bolts in the engine mounts.

30. Remove the engine lifting equipment and the lifting eyes.

31. Position the ignition coil/bracket assembly and install the attaching bolts.

32. Raise and safely support the vehicle.

33. Remove the plugs and install the halfshaft assemblies.

34. Connect the lower ball joints and the tie rod ends to the spindles.

35. Install the bolt retaining the air conditioning line to the engine block.

36. Install the exhaust Y-pipe.

37. Install the front wheel and tire assemblies.

38. Connect the heater hoses.

39. Lower the vehicle.

40. Connect the power steering lines at the rear of the engine above the transaxle.

41. Install the lower radiator hose and the coolant overflow bottle.

42. If equipped with automatic transaxle, connect the transaxle cooler lines to the radiator.

43. Connect the speedometer cable.

44. Connect the accelerator linkage,

transaxle throttle valve linkage and cruise control cable, if equipped.

45. Connect the air conditioning lines to the condenser.

46. Install the power steering fluid reservoir and connect the lines to the power steering pump.

47. Connect all vacuum lines and electrical connectors that were marked and disconnected during the removal procedure.

48. Install the upper radiator hose.

49. Connect the fuel lines.

50. Install the hood on the hinges, aligning the marks that were made during the removal procedure.

51. Install the battery tray and battery. Connect the battery cables.

52. Fill the cooling system.

53. Start the engine and bring to normal operating temperature. Check for leaks and check all fluid levels.

54. If equipped, properly evacuate and charge the air conditioning system.

Engine Mounts

REMOVAL & INSTALLATION

Tempo, Topaz and 1989–90 Escort

RIGHT ENGINE INSULATOR (NO. 3A)

1. Disconnect the negative battery cable. Place a floor jack and a block of wood under the engine oil pan. Raise the engine approximately ½ in. or enough to take the load off of the insulator.

2. On 1989–90 Escort and 1989–91 Tempo and Topaz, proceed as follows:

a. Remove the lower support bracket attaching nut, bottom of the double ended stud. Remove the insulator-to-support bracket attaching nuts. Do not remove the nut on top of the double ended stud.

b. Remove the insulator support bracket from the vehicle. Remove the insulator attaching nuts through the right side front wheel opening.

c. Remove the insulator attaching bolts through the engine compartment. Work the insulator out of the body and remove it from the vehicle.

3. On 1992–93 Tempo and Topaz, proceed as follows:

a. Remove the insulator attaching nut from the bottom of the double-ended stud.

b. Remove the insulator lower retaining bolt through the engine compartment.

c. If equipped with 2.3L engine, remove the 2 bolts attaching the insulator-to-engine bracket.

d. If equipped with 3.0L engine, remove the 2 nuts and 1 bolt attaching the insulator-to-engine bracket.

e. Remove the insulator from the vehicle.

To install:

4. On 1989–90 Escort and 1989–91 Tempo and Topaz, proceed as follows:

a. Work insulator into the body opening.

b. Position the insulator and loosely install the attaching nuts and bolts. Tighten the nuts to 75–100 ft. lbs. (100–135 Nm) and tighten the bolts to 37–55 ft. lbs. (50–75 Nm).

c. Install insulator support casting on top of the insulator and engine support bracket. Make sure the double-edged stud is through the hole in the engine bracket.

d. Loosely install the insulator-to-support bracket nuts and bolts.

e. Tighten the insulator support casting-to-insulator attaching nuts to 55–75 ft. lbs. (75–100 Nm). Install and tighten lower support bracket nut to 60–90 ft. lbs. (80–120 Nm).

9. On Escort, install the insulator casting-to-engine bracket bolt and tighten to 60–90 ft. lbs. (80–120 Nm).

5. On 1992–93 Tempo and Topaz, proceed as follows:

a. Position the insulator into the body opening.

b. Loosely install the retaining nuts and bolts. Tighten the nuts to 73–97 ft. lbs. (98–132 Nm) and bolts to 40–53 ft. lbs. (53–71 Nm).

c. If equipped with 2.3L engine, loosely install the retaining bolts and nut. Tighten the bolts and nut to 65–87 ft. lbs. (88–118 Nm).

d. If equipped with 3.0L engine, loosely install the retaining nuts, attaching bolt and retaining lower nut. Tighten to 51–67 ft. lbs. (68–92 Nm), 22–29 ft. lbs. (30–40 Nm) and 65–87 ft. lbs. (88–118 Nm).

6. Lower the engine and remove the jack. Connect the negative battery cable.

RIGHT ENGINE INSULATOR (NO. 2A – 3.0L ENGINE)

1. Disconnect the negative battery cable. Place a floor jack and a block of wood under the engine oil pan. Raise the engine approximately ½ in. or enough to take the load off of insulator.

2. Remove the insulator lower nut.

3. Remove the stabilizer bar bracket bolts.

4. Remove the insulator-to-A/C bracket bolt.

5. Remove the insulator from the vehicle.

To install:

6. Position the insulator onto the A/C bracket and loosely attach the bolt. Tighten the bolt to 26–36 ft. lbs. (34–46 Nm).

7. Position the insulator onto the stabilizer bar bracket and loosely attach the nut. Loosely attach the stabilizer bar bracket bolts and tighten to 40–53 ft. lbs. (53–72 Nm). Tighten the nut to 26–36 ft. lbs. (34–46 Nm).

8. Lower the engine and remove the jack. Connect the negative battery cable.

LEFT REAR ENGINE INSULATOR (NO. 4)

1. Disconnect the negative battery cable. Raise the vehicle and support safely. Place a transaxle jack and a block of wood under the transaxle.

2. Raise the transaxle approximately ½ in. or enough to take the load off of the insulator.

3. Remove the insulator attaching nuts from the support bracket. Remove the 2 through bolts and remove the insulator from the transaxle.

To install:

4. Install the insulator over the left rear transaxle housing and support bracket studs.

5. Install the 2 insulator through bolts and tighten to 30–40 ft. lbs. (41–54 Nm).

6. Install 2 insulator-to-support bracket attaching nuts. Tighten to 73–97 ft. lbs. (98–132 Nm).

7. Lower vehicle and remove floor jack. Connect negative battery cable.

NOTE: To remove the left rear support bracket, remove the left rear engine insulator No. 4. Then remove the support bracket attaching bolts. When installing the support bracket, torque the attaching bolts to 51–67 ft. lbs. (68–92 Nm).

LEFT FRONT ENGINE INSULATOR (NO. 1)

1. Disconnect the negative battery cable. Raise and the vehicle and support safely. Place a transaxle jack and a block of wood under the transaxle. Raise the transaxle approximately ½ in. or enough to take the load off of the insulator.

2. Remove the insulator-to-support bracket attaching nut(s). Remove the insulators and transaxle attaching bolts and remove the insulator from the vehicle.

3. Complete the installation of the insulator by reversing the removal procedure. Torque the insulator to transaxle attaching bolts to 26–36 ft. lbs. (34–46 Nm). Torque the insulator-to-support bracket nut to 80–100 ft. lbs. (108–136 Nm) on 1989–91 vehi-

cles or the insulator-to-support bracket nuts to 26–36 ft. lbs. (34–46 Nm) on 1992–93 vehicles.

Cylinder Head

REMOVAL & INSTALLATION

1.8L Engine

1. Properly relieve the fuel system pressure.

2. Disconnect the negative battery cable.

3. Drain the cooling system.

4. Remove the bolts from the timing belt upper and middle covers. Remove the covers and gaskets.

5. Rotate the crankshaft by hand in the direction of normal engine rotation and align the timing marks located on the camshaft pulleys and seal plate.

6. Loosen the timing belt tensioner lock bolt and temporarily secure the tensioner spring in the fully extended position.

7. Remove the timing belt from the camshaft pulleys and secure it aside to prevent damage during the removal and installation of the cylinder head.

NOTE: Do not allow the timing belt to become contaminated by oil or grease. Mark the direction of rotation on the timing belt prior to removal so it can be reinstalled in the same direction.

8. Tag and disconnect the vacuum hoses from the cylinder head cover.

9. Tag and disconnect the spark plug wires from the spark plugs and position the wires aside.

10. Remove the cylinder head cover and gasket.

11. Remove the air duct from the resonance chamber and throttle body.

12. Disconnect the accelerator cable and, if equipped with automatic transaxle, the kickdown cable from the throttle cam. Remove the cable bracket from the intake plenum.

13. Tag and disconnect all vacuum lines from the intake plenum.

14. Tag and disconnect all necessary electrical connectors from the cylinder head, exhaust manifold, intake plenum, and throttle body. Disconnect the ground straps.

15. Remove the upper radiator hose.

16. Remove the transaxle-to-engine block upper-right bolt.

17. Disconnect the fuel pressure and return lines and plug the lines.

18. Disconnect the ignition coil high-tension lead from the distributor.

19. Tag and disconnect the necessary hoses connected to the cylinder head and intake plenum.

20. Remove the 2 bolts from the transaxle vent tube routing brackets.

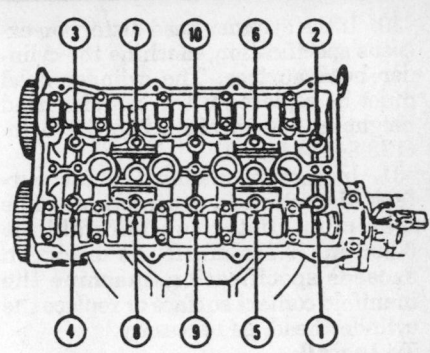

Cylinder head bolt removal sequence— 1.8L Engine

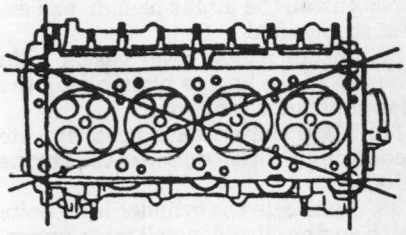

Cylinder head warpage measuring locations—1.8L Engine

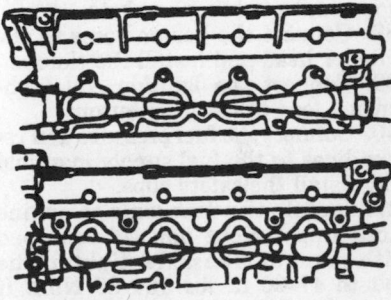

Manifold contact surface warpage measuring location—1.8L Engine

21. Raise and safely support the vehicle.

22. Remove the bolt from the water pump-to-cylinder head hose bracket.

23. Remove the exhaust front mounting flange and exhaust pipe support bracket from the exhaust manifold.

24. Remove the intake plenum support bracket.

25. Lower the vehicle.

26. Remove the cylinder head bolts in the proper sequence.

27. Remove the cylinder head assembly, with the intake plenum and exhaust manifold attached, from the vehicle.

28. Remove the intake plenum and exhaust manifold.

29. Inspect the cylinder head for damage, cracks, and leakage of water and oil. Measure the cylinder head for warpage in 6 directions. The maximum distortion allowable is 0.004 in. (0.10mm).

30. If the cylinder head distortion exceeds specification, machine the cylinder head surface. The cylinder head must be replaced if the cylinder head height is not within 5.268–5.276 in. (133.8–134.0mm).

31. Inspect the manifold contact surface distortion in 4 directions. The maximum distortion allowable is 0.006 in. (0.15mm). If the distortion exceeds specification, machine the manifold contact surface or replace the cylinder head, as necessary.

To install:

32. Remove all dirt, oil and old gasket material from all gasket contact surfaces.

33. Install the intake plenum and exhaust manifold.

34. Install a new head gasket onto the top of the engine block, using the dowel pins for reference.

35. Place the cylinder head into its mounting position on top of the engine block.

36. Lubricate the cylinder head bolts with engine oil and install them finger-tight. Tighten the bolts in the proper sequence to 56–60 ft. lbs. (76–81 Nm).

37. Install the 2 bolts to the transaxle vent tube routing brackets.

38. Connect the heater hoses to the cylinder head and install the clamps.

39. Connect the ignition coil high-tension lead to the distributor.

40. Connect the fuel pressure and return lines to the fuel supply manifold and install the safety clips.

41. Install the transaxle-to-engine block upper-right bolt. If equipped with manual transaxle, tighten the bolt to 47–66 ft. lbs. (64–89 Nm). If equipped with automatic transaxle, tighten the bolt to 41–59 ft. lbs. (55–80 Nm).

42. Install the upper radiator hose and clamps.

43. Connect the ground straps and connect the electrical connectors that were disconnected at the cylinder head, exhaust manifold, intake plenum, and throttle body.

44. Connect the vacuum lines to the intake plenum.

45. Install the accelerator and kickdown cable bracket onto the intake plenum and tighten the bolts to 69–95 inch lbs. (7.8–11.0 Nm). Connect the cable(s) to the throttle cam.

46. Install the cylinder head cover and gasket, then connect the hose running from the plenum to the cylinder head cover. Tighten the cover bolts to 43–78 inch lbs. (4.9–8.8 Nm).

47. Install the air duct to the resonance chamber and throttle body and tighten the clamps. Connect the hose going from the air duct to the cylinder head cover.

48. Install and connect the spark plug wires.

49. Raise and safely support the vehicle.

50. Install the intake plenum support bracket. Tighten the bolts to 27–38 ft. lbs. (37–52 Nm) and the nut to 14–19 ft. lbs. (19–25 Nm).

51. Install the bolt to the water pump-to-cylinder head hose bracket.

52. Install the exhaust front mounting flange with a new gasket to the exhaust manifold. Tighten the flange-to-manifold attaching nuts to 23–34 ft. lbs. (31–46 Nm).

53. Install the exhaust pipe support bracket. Tighten the bracket attaching bolts to 27–38 ft. lbs. (37–52 Nm).

54. Make sure the yellow ignition timing mark on the crankshaft pulley is aligned with the TDC mark on the timing belt cover.

55. Lower the vehicle.

56. Make sure the timing marks on the camshaft pulleys and seal plate are aligned. Install the timing belt, in the original direction of rotation, so there is no looseness at the idler pulley side or between the 2 camshaft pulleys.

NOTE: Do not turn the crankshaft counterclockwise.

57. Turn the crankshaft 2 turns clockwise by hand and verify that the yellow ignition timing mark on the crankshaft pulley is aligned with the timing mark on the timing belt cover. Verify that the timing marks on the camshaft pulley and seal plate are aligned.

NOTE: If the timing marks are not aligned, remove the timing belt and repeat the procedure beginning with Step 54.

58. Turn the crankshaft $1^5/_6$ turns clockwise by hand and align the 4th tooth to the right of the I and E timing marks on the camshaft pulleys with the seal plate alignment marks.

59. Loosen the timing belt tensioner lock bolt and apply tension to the timing belt. Tighten the tensioner lock bolt to 27–38 ft. lbs. (37–52 Nm).

60. Turn the crankshaft $2^1/_6$ turns clockwise and verify that the timing marks on the camshaft pulleys and the seal plate are aligned.

61. Install new gaskets onto the timing belt upper and middle covers and install the covers. Tighten the mounting bolts to 69–95 inch lbs. (8–11 Nm).

62. Fill the cooling system.

63. Connect the negative battery cable.

64. Start the engine and check for leaks.

1.9L Engine

1989–90

NOTE: The engine must be cold

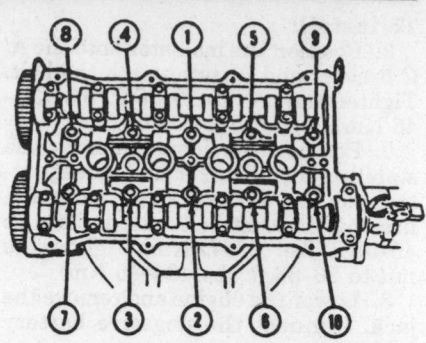

Cylinder head bolt torque sequence—1.8L Engine

before removing the cylinder head, to reduce the possibility of warpage or distortion.

1. Disconnect the negative battery cable. Properly relieve the fuel system pressure.

2. Drain the cooling system and disconnect the heater hose at the fitting located under the intake manifold.

3. Disconnect the radiator upper hose at the cylinder head.

4. Disconnect the wiring terminal from the cooling fan switch.

5. Remove the air cleaner assembly.

6. Remove the PCV hose.

7. Identify, tag and disconnect the required vacuum hoses.

8. Remove the rocker arm cover.

9. Disconnect all accessory drive belts.

10. Remove the crankshaft damper.

11. Remove the timing belt cover.

12. Set the No. 1 cylinder to TDC on the compression stroke prior to removing the timing belt.

13. Remove the distributor cap and spark plug wires as an assembly.

14. Loosen both belt tensioner attaching bolts using torque wrench adapter tool T81P-6254-A or equivalent.

15. Secure the belt tensioner as far left toward the front of the vehicle as possible.

16. Remove the timing belt.

NOTE: Do not allow the timing belt to become contaminated by oil or grease. Mark the direction of rotation on the timing belt prior to removal so it can be reinstalled in the same direction.

17. Disconnect the EGR tube at the EGR valve.

18. Disconnect the fuel supply and return lines at the metal connectors, located on the right side of the engine; set rubber lines aside.

19. Disconnect the accelerator cable and, if equipped, the cruise control cable.

20. Disconnect the alternator wiring harness.

21. Remove the alternator and its mounting bracket.
22. Raise and safely support the vehicle.
23. Disconnect the exhaust system at the exhaust pipe.
24. Lower the vehicle.
25. Remove the cylinder head bolts and washers. Discard the bolts.

NOTE: Do not reuse the cylinder head retaining bolts. Use new bolts when installing head.

26. Remove the cylinder head with the exhaust and intake manifolds attached. Discard the cylinder head gasket.

NOTE: Do not lay the cylinder head flat. Damage to the spark plug or gasket contact surfaces may result.

To install:
27. Clean all gasket material from the mating surfaces on the cylinder head and block and clean out the head bolt holes in the block.
28. Before final installation of the

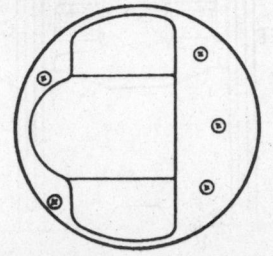

EFI

CYLINDER HEAD

SQUISH HEIGHT DIMENSION

CYLINDER BLOCK

HEAD GASKET

SQUISH HEIGHT DIMENSION
0.046–0.060 INCH
(1.156–1.527MM)

EFI HO

SQUISH HEIGHT DIMENSION

SQUISH HEIGHT DIMENSION

HEAD GASKET

CYLINDER BLOCK

SQUISH HEIGHT DIMENSION
0.039–0.070 INCH (1.0–1.77MM)

Piston squish height— 1989–90 1.9L Engine

Solder locations to measure piston squish height

cylinder head to the engine, check the piston squish height as follows:

NOTE: Squish height is the clearance of the piston dome to the combustion chamber at piston TDC. No cylinder block deck machining or use of replacement crankshaft, piston or connecting rod causing the assembled squish height to be over or under tolerance specification, is permitted. If no parts other than the head gasket are replaced, the squish height should be within specification. If parts other than the head gasket are replaced, check the squish height. If the squish height is out of specification, replace the parts again and recheck the squish height.

a. Place a small amount of soft lead solder or shot of an appropriate thickness on the piston spherical areas shown.
b. Rotate the crankshaft to lower the piston in the bore and install the head gasket and cylinder head.

NOTE: A compressed (used) head gasket is preferred.

c. Install used head bolts and tighten the head bolts to 30–44 ft. lbs. (40–60 Nm) following the proper sequence.
d. Rotate the crankshaft to move the piston through its TDC position.
e. Remove the cylinder head and measure the thickness of the compressed solder to determine squish height at TDC. The solder should be 0.039–0.070 in. (1.0–1.77mm) for EFI HO engines or 0.046–0.060 in. (1.156–1.527mm) for EFI engine.
29. If the camshaft has been turned or removed or if installing a replacement cylinder head, rotate the camshaft until the camshaft gear pointer is aligned with the timing mark on the cylinder head and the camshaft keyway is at the 6 o'clock.
30. Position the No. 1 piston 90 degrees BTDC, pulley keyway at 9 o'clock position, during the cylinder head installation.
31. Position the cylinder head gasket on the cylinder block.
32. Install the cylinder head and install new bolts and washers in the following order:
a. Apply a light coat of engine oil to the threads of the new cylinder head bolts and install the new bolts into the head.
b. Torque the cylinder head bolts, in sequence, to 44 ft. lbs. (60 Nm).
c. Loosen the cylinder head bolts approximately 2 turns and then torque again to 44 ft. lbs. (60 Nm) using the same torque sequence.
d. After setting the torque again,

turn the head bolts 90 degrees in sequence and to complete the head bolt installation, turn the head bolts an additional 90 degrees in the same torque sequence.

NOTE: The cylinder head attaching bolts cannot be tightened to the specified torque more than once and must therefore be replaced when installing a cylinder head.

33. Raise and safely support the vehicle.
34. Connect the exhaust system at the exhaust pipe.
35. Lower the vehicle.
36. Install the alternator mounting bracket and the alternator. Connect the alternator wiring harness.
37. Connect the accelerator cable

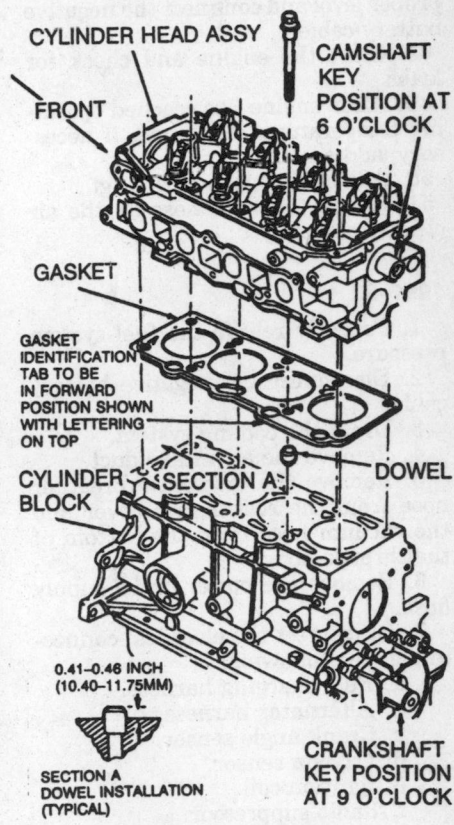

CYLINDER HEAD ASSY

CAMSHAFT KEY POSITION AT 6 O'CLOCK

FRONT

GASKET

GASKET IDENTIFICATION TAB TO BE IN FORWARD POSITION SHOWN WITH LETTERING ON TOP

CYLINDER BLOCK

SECTION A

DOWEL

0.41–0.46 INCH (10.40–11.75MM)

SECTION A
DOWEL INSTALLATION (TYPICAL)

CRANKSHAFT KEY POSITION AT 9 O'CLOCK

Cylinder head Installation— 1.9L Engine

TIGHTENING SEQUENCE CYLINDER HEAD ATTACHING BOLTS

9	3	1	5	7	
○	○	○	○	○	INTAKE
○	○	○	○	○	EXHAUST
8	6	2	4	10	

Cylinder head bolt torque sequence— 1.9L Engine

and, if equipped, the cruise control cable.

38. Connect the fuel supply and return lines at the metal connector, located on the right side of the engine.

39. Connect the EGR tube to the EGR valve.

40. Install the timing belt. Install the timing belt cover and the crankshaft pulley.

41. Install the distributor cap and spark plug wires.

42. Install the rocker arm cover.

43. Connect the required vacuum hoses.

44. Connect the wiring terminal to the cooling fan switch.

45. Connect the radiator upper hose at the cylinder head.

46. Connect the heater hose to the fitting located below the intake manifold.

47. Fill the cooling system to the proper level and connnect the negative battery cable.

48. Start the engine and check for leaks.

49. After engine has reached operating temperature, check and, if necessary, add coolant.

50. Adjust the ignition timing.

51. Install the PCV hose on the air cleaner assembly.

1991–93

1. Properly relieve the fuel system pressure.

2. Disconnect the negative battery cable.

3. Drain the cooling system.

4. Remove the air intake duct.

5. Remove the crankcase breather hose from the rocker arm cover and the vacuum hose from the bottom of the throttle body.

6. Remove the power brake supply hose.

7. Disconnect the electrical connectors at the following:
   a. Fuel charging harness.
   b. Alternator harness.
   c. Crank angle sensor.
   d. Oxygen sensor.
   e. Ignition coil.
   f. Radio suppressor.
   g. Coolant temperature sensor, cooling fan sensor and temperature sending unit.

NOTE: Tag the connectors prior to removal to aid reinstallation.

8. Remove the ground strap from the stud on the left side of the cylinder head.

9. Disconnect the accelerator and the transaxle kickdown cables from the throttle lever and remove the cable bracket from the intake manifold.

10. Disconnect the heater hose containing the coolant temperature switches at the bulkhead.

11. Remove the upper radiator hose.

12. Disconnect the fuel supply and return lines.

13. Remove the oil level indicator tube mounting nut from the cylinder head stud.

14. Remove the power steering hose and the air conditioner line retainer bracket bolts from the alternator bracket.

15. Remove the accessory drive belt, alternator, and the drive belt automatic tensioner.

16. Raise and safely support the vehicle.

17. Remove the right side splash shield and remove the crankshaft dampener.

18. Remove the catalytic converter inlet pipe.

19. Remove the starter wiring harness from the retaining clip below the intake manifold.

20. Set the engine No. 1 cylinder on TDC.

21. Lower the vehicle.

22. Support the engine with a suitable floor jack.

23. Remove the right engine mount dampener and the right engine mount retaining bolts from the mount bracket on the engine. Loosen the right engine mount thru-bolt and roll the mount back aside.

24. Remove the timing belt cover.

25. Loosen the belt tensioner attaching bolt and pry the tensioner as far toward the rear of the engine as possible. Tighten the attaching bolt while in this position.

26. Remove the timing belt.

NOTE: Do not allow the timing belt to become contaminated by oil or grease. Mark the direction of rotation on the timing belt prior to removal so it can be reinstalled in the same direction.

27. Roll the right engine mount back into position and install the mounting bolts. Lower the floor jack.

28. Remove the heater hose support bracket retaining bolt and the alternator bracket-to-cylinder head mounting bolt.

29. Remove the rocker arm cover.

30. Remove and discard the cylinder head bolts.

31. Remove the cylinder head with the exhaust and intake manifolds attached. Discard the cylinder head gasket.

NOTE: Do not lay the cylinder head flat. Damage to the spark plugs, valves or gasket surfaces may result.

To install:

32. Clean all gasket material from the mating surfaces on the cylinder head and block and clean out the head bolt holes in the block.

33. Before final installation of the cylinder head to the engine, check the piston squish height as follows:

NOTE: Squish height is the clearance of the piston dome to the combustion chamber at piston TDC. No cylinder block deck machining or use of replacement crankshaft, piston or connecting rod causing the assembled squish height to be over or under tolerance specification, is permitted. If no parts other than the head gasket are replaced, the squish height should be within specification. If parts other than the head gasket are replaced, check the squish height. If the squish height is out of specification, replace the parts again and recheck the squish height.

   a. Place a small amount of soft lead solder or shot of an appropriate thickness on the piston spherical areas shown.
   b. Rotate the crankshaft to lower the piston in the bore and install the head gasket and cylinder head.

NOTE: A compressed (used) head gasket is preferred.

   c. Install used head bolts and tighten the head bolts to 30–44 ft. lbs. (40–60 Nm) following the proper sequence.
   d. Rotate the crankshaft to move the piston through its TDC position.
   e. Remove the cylinder head and measure the thickness of the compressed solder to determine squish height at TDC. The solder should be

SQUISH HEIGHT DIMENSION 0.039–0.070 IN. (1.0–1.77MM)

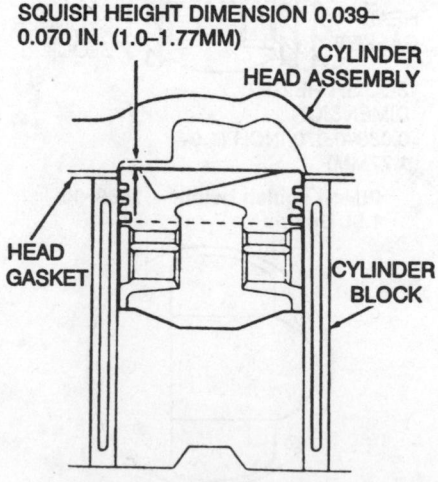

Piston squish height—1991–93 1.9L Engine

0.039–0.070 in. (1.0–1.77mm) for all engines.

34. Install the dowels in the cylinder block, if removed. Check the dowel height, it should be 0.41–0.46 in. (10.40–11.75mm) above the surface of the block. A dowel that is too long will not allow the cylinder head to sit properly.

35. Position the cylinder head gasket on the cylinder block.

36. Install the cylinder head and install new bolts and washers in the following order:

a. Apply a light coat of engine oil to the threads of the new cylinder head bolts and install the new bolts into the head.

b. Torque the cylinder head bolts in sequence to 44 ft. lbs. (60 Nm).

c. Loosen the cylinder head bolts approximately 2 turns and then torque again to 44 ft. lbs. (60 Nm) using the same torque sequence.

d. After setting the torque again, turn the head bolts 90 degrees in sequence and to complete the head bolt installation, turn the head bolts an additional 90 degrees in the same torque sequence.

NOTE: The cylinder head attaching bolts cannot be tightened to the specified torque more than once and must therefore be replaced when installing a cylinder head.

37. Install the rocker arm cover and the alternator bracket-to-cylinder head bolt.

38. Support the engine with a suitable floor jack.

39. Remove the right engine mount-to-mount bracket bolts. Roll the mount aside.

40. Make sure cylinder No. 1 is at TDC.

41. Install the timing belt and the timing belt cover.

42. Roll the right engine mount into place and install the 2 mounting bolts and the mount dampener. Remove the floor jack.

43. Raise and safely support the vehicle.

44. Install the crankshaft dampener.

45. Install the starter wiring harness on the retaining clip below the intake manifold.

46. Install the catalytic converter inlet pipe and the right side splash shield.

47. Lower the vehicle.

48. Install the alternator and the accessory drive belt automatic tensioner. Install the accessory drive belt.

49. Install both the power steering hose and air conditioner line retainer bracket bolts. Install the oil level indicator tube retainer bolt.

50. Connect the fuel supply and return lines.

51. Install the upper radiator hose and connect the heater hose at the engine compartment bulkhead. Install the heater hose support bracket retaining bolt.

52. Install the accelerator cable bracket on the intake manifold and connect the accelerator and kickdown cables to the throttle lever.

53. Install the ground strap at the left side of the cylinder head.

54. Connect all remaining electrical connectors according to their positions marked during the removal procedure.

55. Connect the power brake supply hose, crankcase breather hose and the vacuum line at the bottom of the throttle body.

56. Install the air intake duct.

57. Connect the negative battery cable.

58. Fill and bleed the cooling system.

59. Start the engine and check for leaks. Stop the engine and check the coolant level.

2.3L Engine

1. Disconnect the negative battery cable.

2. Disconnect the electric cooling fan switch at the plastic connector.

3. Drain the cooling system at the lower radiator hose.

4. Disconnect the heater hose at the heater inlet tube and disconnect the adapter hose at the water outlet connector.

5. Disconnect the upper radiator hose at the cylinder head.

6. Remove the air cleaner assembly.

7. Tag and disconnect the required electrical connectors and vacuum hoses.

8. Remove the distributor cap and spark plug wires as an assembly. Tag the spark plug wires prior to removal.

9. Disconnect all accessory drive belts.

10. Remove the rocker arm cover and gasket.

11. Remove the rocker arm fulcrum retaining bolts and remove the fulcrum, rocker arms and pushrods. Mark the location of each rocker arm, pushrod and fulcrum for reinstallation in its original position.

12. Properly relieve the fuel system pressure, then disconnect the fuel supply and return lines at the fuel rail.

13. Disconnect the accelerator cable and cruise control cable, if equipped.

14. Raise and safely support the vehicle.

15. Disconnect the exhaust system at the exhaust pipe and the hose at the tube.

16. Lower the vehicle.

17. Remove the cylinder head bolts.

18. Remove the cylinder head and gasket with the exhaust and intake manifolds attached.

NOTE: Do not lay the cylinder head flat. Damage to spark plugs or gasket surfaces may result.

To install:

19. Clean all gasket material from the mating surfaces of the cylinder head and block.

20. Position the head gasket on the cylinder block.

NOTE: Before installing the cylinder head, thread 2 cylinder head alignment studs T84P–6065–A or equivalent, into the block at opposite corners.

21. Install the cylinder head over the alignment studs onto the cylinder block. Start and run down several head bolts until snug. Remove the alignment studs and install the remaining head bolts. Tighten the bolts in sequence in 2 steps, first to 52–59 ft. lbs. (70–80 Nm) and then to 70–76 ft. lbs. (95–103 Nm).

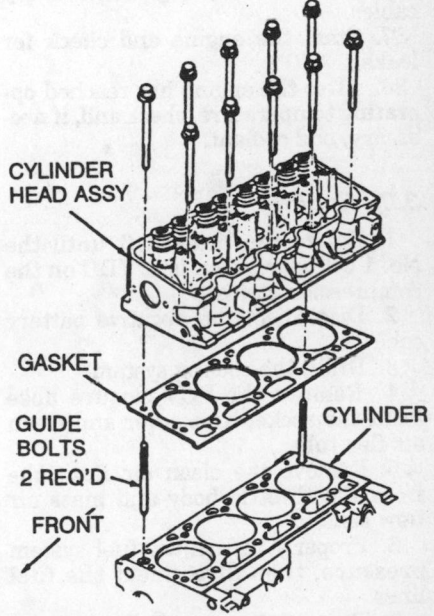

Cylinder head installation—2.3L Engine

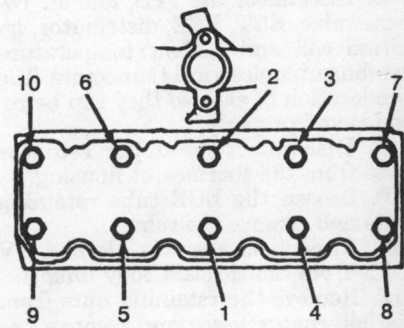

Cylinder head bolt torque sequence—2.3L Engine

22. Raise and safely support the vehicle.

23. Connect the exhaust system at the exhaust pipe and the hose to the metal tube.

24. Lower the vehicle.

25. Connect the accelerator cable and cruise control cable, if equipped.

26. Connect the fuel supply and return lines.

27. Install the fulcrums, rocker arms and pushrods in their original positions. Tighten the fulcrum bolts to 20–26 ft. lbs. (26–38 Nm).

28. Install the rocker arm cover gasket and cover.

29. Install the distributor cap and spark plug wires as an assembly.

30. Connect the accessory drive belts.

31. Connect the required electrical connectors and vacuum hoses.

32. Install the air cleaner assembly.

33. Connect the cooling fan switch at the plastic connector.

34. Connect the upper radiator hose and the heater hose.

35. Fill the cooling system.

36. Connect the negative battery cable.

37. Start the engine and check for leaks.

38. After the engine has reached operating temperature, check and, if necessary, add coolant.

3.0L Engine

1. Rotate the crankshaft until the No. 1 cylinder piston is at TDC on the compression stroke.

2. Disconnect the negative battery cable.

3. Drain the cooling system.

4. Remove the PCV closure hose from the rocker arm cover and clean air flex tube.

5. Remove the clean air flex tube from the throttle body and mass air flow sensor.

6. Properly relieve the fuel system pressure, then disconnect the fuel lines.

7. Tag and disconnect all necessary vacuum lines.

8. Disconnect the TPS, idle air bypass valve, ECT, PFE, distributor, ignition coil and coolant temperature sending unit electrical connectors. Tag the location of each so they can be reconnected properly.

9. Disconnect the upper radiator hose from the thermostat housing.

10. Loosen the EGR tube retaining nuts and remove the tube.

11. Disconnect the throttle and TV cable from the throttle body linkage.

12. Remove the retaining nuts from the alternator brace and remove the brace.

13. Remove the 6 throttle body retaining bolts and remove the throttle body.

14. Disconnect the fuel injector harness retaining stand-offs from the inboard rocker arm cover studs. Carefully disconnect the electrical connections at each injector and remove the harness from the engine.

15. Disconnect the heater hose.

16. Disconnect the ignition wires from the spark plugs, then remove the harness retaining stand-offs from the rocker arm cover studs.

17. Remove the distributor cap. Mark the position of the distributor rotor in relation to the distributor body and the position of the distributor body in relation to the engine block. Remove the distributor holddown bolt and remove the distributor.

18. Remove the oil cooler tube assembly retaining bolt from the ignition coil bracket. Remove the ignition coil from the left cylinder head.

19. Remove the rocker arm covers.

20. Remove the rocker arms and pushrods. Keep all rocker arms, fulcrums and pushrods in order so they can be reinstalled in their original locations.

NOTE: Regardless of the cylinder head being removed, the No. 3 cylinder intake valve rocker arm and pushrod must be removed in order to remove the intake manifold.

21. Remove the intake manifold retaining bolts. Wedge a prybar between the manifold and engine block and pry upward to break the manifold-to-engine block seal, using the area between the thermostat and transaxle as a leverage point.

NOTE: The intake manifold may be removed with the fuel supply manifold and injectors in place.

22. If removing the right (rear) cylinder head, proceed as follows:

a. Remove the accessory and water pump drive belts.

b. Remove the water pump to front cover hose.

c. Raise and safely support the vehicle.

d. Remove the lower water pump tube. Loosen and remove the retaining nut from the upper bracket and the bolt from the lower bracket. Gently grasp the tube at the water pump end and pull the tube out of the water pump. Set the assembly aside.

e. Loosen and remove the exhaust inlet pipe flange retaining nuts from the exhaust manifold studs.

f. Lower the vehicle.

g. Remove the heater hose from the rear of the water pump.

h. Remove the water pump pulley shield. Remove the nut from the stud nut.

i. Remove the water pump from the bracket.

j. Remove the exhaust manifold heat shield and the exhaust manifold.

23. If removing the left (front) cylinder head, proceed as follows:

a. Remove the accessory drive belt.

b. Remove the power steering pulley shield and the accessory belt tensioner.

c. Remove the 3 alternator bracket to cylinder head retaining bolts.

d. Remove the upper alternator retaining bolt.

e. Remove the 3 A/C brace retaining bolts and remove the brace.

f. Move the assembly away from the cylinder head slightly.

g. Remove the exhaust inlet pipe flange retaining nuts from the exhaust manifold studs.

h. Remove the 2 exhaust manifold heat shield retaining nuts and remove the shield.

i. Remove the engine oil dipstick tube or rotate it aside.

j. Remove the exhaust manifold retaining bolts and studs and remove the exhaust manifold.

24. Remove and discard the cylinder head bolts.

25. Remove the cylinder head(s). If the cylinder head is stuck to the gasket, place a prybar into the intake port and rock the cylinder head to break the seal.

NOTE: When breaking the seal, be careful not to damage machined surfaces or the intake valve.

26. Remove the cylinder head and discard the gasket.

27. If any coolant leaked into the cylinder bores from the cylinder head removal, immediately wipe the cylinder dry and apply a light coating of engine oil to the cylinder bore surface.

NOTE: Engine coolant is corrosive to engine bearing material and piston rings.

To install:

28. Lightly oil all bolt and stud threads prior to installation. Always use new cylinder heads bolts.

29. Place shop rags in the lifter valley, cylinder bores and cylinder block coolant passages to catch any dirt or gasket material. Clean the sealing surfaces of the cylinder head, intake manifold, rocker arm covers and cylinder block.

30. If the cylinder head was removed

for head gasket replacement, check the cylinder head and block for flatness using a straight-edge and feeler gauge. Warpage should not exceed 0.003 in. in 6 in. span. Replace or machine the cylinder head, as necessary. If machining, do not grind off more than 0.010 in. (0.254mm).

31. Position new head gasket(s) on the cylinder block, with the V-cut toward the front of the engine. Use dowels to align and hold the gasket in place.

NOTE: Replace any dowels that are damaged or loose.

32. Install and hand tighten the new cylinder head bolts. Tighten as follows:

   a. Tighten, in sequence, to 52–66 ft. lbs. (70–90 Nm).

   b. Back off all bolts 1 turn.

   c. Tighten, in sequence, to 33–41 ft. lbs. (45–55 Nm).

   d. Tighten, in sequence, to 63–73 ft. lbs. (85–99 Nm).

33. Apply a ¼ in. (6mm) drop of silicone sealer at the intersection of the cylinder block and cylinder head at the 4 corners of the lifter valley.

34. Position the intake gaskets on the cylinder heads and align the locking tabs to the cylinder head gaskets.

35. Install the front and rear intake manifold seals and secure with the retaining features.

36. Carefully lower the intake manifold into position, aligning the manifold bolt holes with the holes in the cylinder heads. Be careful not to disturb the sealer.

37. Install the No. 1, 2, 3 and 4 bolts and hand tighten. Install the remaining bolts and tighten all bolts, in sequence, in 2 steps. First tighten to 15–22 ft. lbs. (20–30 Nm), then again in sequence, to 19–24 ft. lbs. (26–32 Nm).

38. Lubricate the distributor gear teeth and the distributor O-ring with engine oil. Install the distributor, aligning the marks that were made during the removal procedure. Install the hold-down bolt and snug.

39. Lubricate the pushrods and rocker arms with engine oil, then install them in their original locations. Snug the retaining bolts.

40. Rotate the crankshaft 1 turn clockwise. Tighten the rocker arm retaining bolts on the No. 1 intake valve, No. 2 exhaust valve, No. 4 intake valve and No. 5 exhaust valve to 5–11 ft. lbs. (7–15 Nm), making sure the rocker arms are seated on the pushrods and the rocker arm fulcrums are seated on the cylinder head.

41. Rotate the crankshaft 120 degrees clockwise. Tighten the remaining rocker arm retaining bolts to 5–11 ft. lbs. (7–15 Nm), making sure the rocker arms are seated on the push-

rods and the rocker arm fulcrums are seated on the cylinder head.

42. Final tighten the rocker arm retaining bolts to 19–28 ft. lbs. (26–38 Nm) with the crankshaft in any position.

43. Install the rocker arm covers.

44. If the right (rear) cylinder head was removed, proceed as follows:

   a. Install the exhaust manifold and tighten the retaining bolts and studs to 15–22 ft. lbs. (20–30 Nm). Install the heat shield and tighten the retaining nuts to 12–15 ft. lbs. (16–20 Nm).

   b. Install the water pump to the bracket and tighten the retaining bolts and stud to 15–22 ft. lbs. (20–30 Nm).

   c. Install the water pump pulley shield and tighten the retaining nut to 7–10 ft. lbs. (9–14 Nm).

   d. Connect the heater hose at the fitting on the rear of the water pump and tighten the clamp.

   e. Raise and safely support the vehicle.

   f. Lubricate the water pump end of the water pump tube with soapy water and install it into the water pump. Install the retaining nut to the upper bracket stud bolt and tighten to 5 ft. lbs. (7 Nm). Install the lower tube bracket retaining bolt and tighten to 71–106 inch lbs. (8–12 Nm).

   g. Install the exhaust pipe flange nuts and tighten to 25–34 ft. lbs. (34–47 Nm).

   h. Lower the vehicle.

   i. Install the water pump to the front cover hose and tighten the clamp.

   j. Install the water pump drive belt. If the left (front) cylinder head was not removed, at this time install the accessory drive belt.

45. If the left (front) cylinder head was removed, proceed as follows:

   a. Install the exhaust manifold and tighten the retaining bolts and studs to 15–22 ft. lbs. (20–30 Nm).

   b. Rotate into position or install the engine oil dipstick tube, as required.

   c. Install the exhaust manifold heat shield and tighten the retaining nuts to 12–15 ft. lbs. (16–20 Nm).

   d. Install the exhaust pipe flange nuts and tighten to 25–34 ft. lbs. (34–47 Nm).

   e. Install the alternator bracket to the cylinder head and tighten the retaining bolts to 30–41 ft. lbs. (40–55 Nm).

   f. Install the A/C brace and the retaining bolts and upper alternator bolt. Tighten the long bolts to 30–41 ft. lbs. (40–55 Nm) and the remaining bolt to 15–22 ft. lbs. (20–30 Nm).

   g. Install the accessory belt ten-

sioner and tighten the retaining bolt to 30–41 ft. lbs. (40–55 Nm).

   h. Install the accessory drive belt.

   i. Install the power steering pulley shield and tighten the retaining bolts to 6–8 ft. lbs. (8.5–11.0 Nm).

46. Install the fuel injector electrical harness to the injectors and secure the harness with the stand-offs to the inboard rocker arm cover studs.

47. Install the ignition coil and tighten the retaining bolts to 15–22 ft. lbs. (20–30 Nm).

48. Install the distributor cap and ignition wires. Install the wire harness stand-offs to the rocker arm cover studs and connect the wires to the spark plugs and ignition coil.

49. Install the throttle body, using a new gasket. Tighten the throttle body mounting bolts to 15–22 ft. lbs. (20–30 Nm).

50. Install the alternator brace to the throttle body and alternator bracket. Tighten the nuts to 12 ft. lbs. (16 Nm).

51. Connect the PCV hose to the tube under the throttle body.

52. Install the EGR tube from the exhaust manifold to the EGR valve. Tighten the retaining nuts to 26–48 ft. lbs. (36–65 Nm).

53. Connect the fuel lines to the fuel supply manifold. Install the fuel line safety clips.

54. Install the upper radiator hose and heater hose and tighten the clamps.

55. Connect all removed vacuum lines to their original locations as marked during the removal procedure.

56. Connect the electrical connectors at the TPS, idle air bypass valve, ECT, PFE, distributor, ignition coil and coolant temperature sending unit.

57. Connect the throttle and TV cables to the throttle body linkage.

58. Fill and bleed the cooling system.

59. Drain the crankcase and fill with the proper type and quantity of engine oil.

NOTE: Engine coolant is corrosive to all engine bearing material. Changing the oil after the replacement of a coolant carrying component prevents failure later.

60. Install the air cleaner tube between the throttle body and mass air flow sensor. Tighten the clamps to 24–35 inch lbs. (2.7–4.0 Nm).

61. Install the PCV closure hose to the rocker arm cover and clean air flex tube.

62. Connect the negative battery cable. Start the engine and check for leaks.

63. Check, and if necessary, adjust the ignition timing.

64. Install the idle air bypass shield.

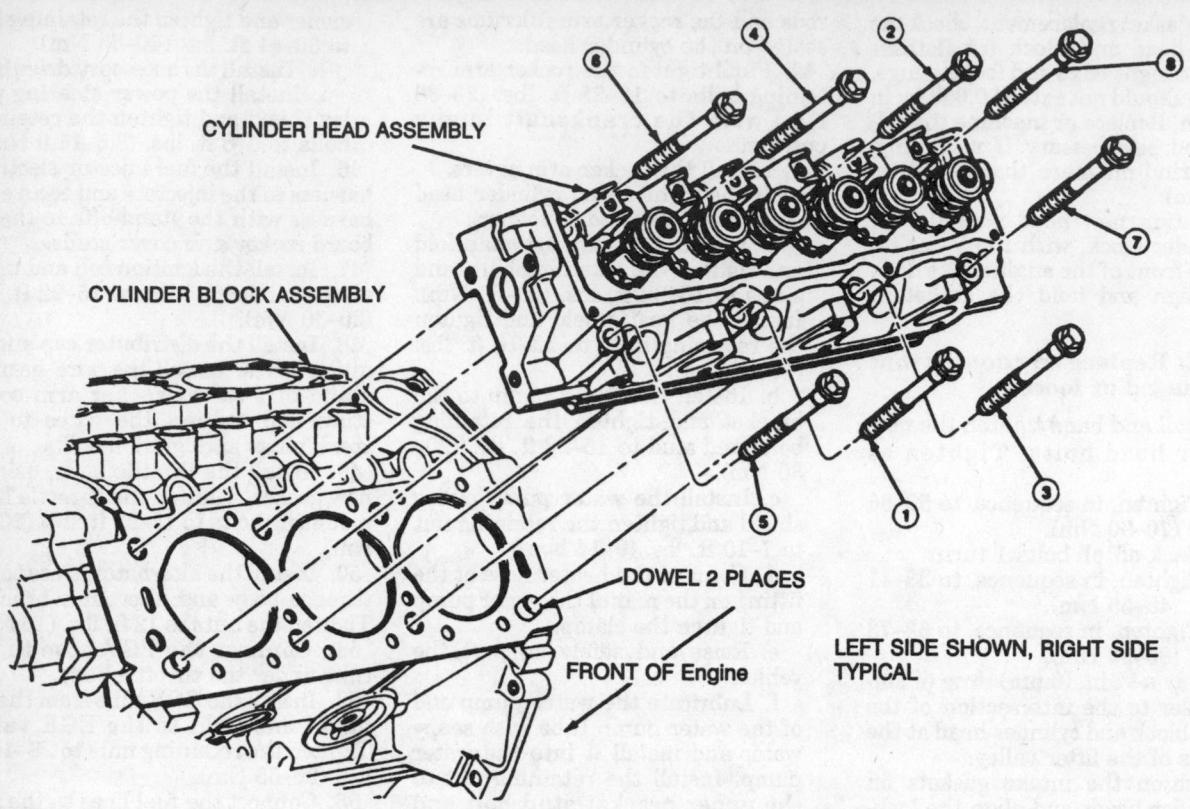

CYLINDER HEAD ASSEMBLY

CYLINDER BLOCK ASSEMBLY

DOWEL 2 PLACES

FRONT OF Engine

LEFT SIDE SHOWN, RIGHT SIDE TYPICAL

Cylinder head bolt torque sequence—3.0L Engine

Valve Lifters

REMOVAL & INSTALLATION

1.8L Engine

NOTE: Hydraulic lash adjusters are used on the 1.8L engine between the valve stem and the camshaft to reduce noise and to provide maintenance-free valve clearance.

1. Disconnect the negative battery cable.
2. Remove the camshafts.
3. Mark the hydraulic lash adjusters and the cylinder head with alignment marks so the hydraulic lash adjusters can be installed in their original mounting positions.
4. Remove the hydraulic lash adjusters from the cylinder head.

To install:

5. Apply clean engine oil to the hydraulic lash adjuster friction surfaces.
6. If the hydraulic lash adjusters are being reused, install them in the positions from which they were removed.
7. Make sure the hydraulic lash adjusters move smoothly in their bores.
8. Install the camshafts.
9. Connect the negative battery cable.

1.9L Engine

1. Disconnect the negative battery cable.
2. Remove air cleaner assembly. Remove valve cover and gasket.
3. Remove rocker arms, lifter guides, lifter retainers and lifters.

NOTE: Always return lifters to the original bores unless they are being replaced.

To install:

4. Lubricate each lifter bore with engine oil.
5. Install the lifters with the plunger upward and position guide flats of lifters to be parallel with centerline of camshaft. If equipped, color orientation dots on lifters should be opposite the oil feed holes in cylinder head.
6. If equipped with roller lifters, install the lifter guide plates over the lifter guide flats with notch toward exhaust side.
7. Lubricate lifter plunger cap and valve tip with engine oil.
8. Install lifter guide plates retainers into rocker arm fulcrum slots, in both intake and exhaust side. On 1989–91 vehicles, the notch to be with exhaust valve lifter. On 1992–93 vehicles, the tab should be located on the intake seal fulcrum slot.

9. Install 4 rocker arms in lifter position No's 3, 6, 7 and 8.
10. Lubricate rocker arm surface that will contact fulcrum surface with engine oil.
11. Install 4 fulcrums. Fulcrums must be fully seated in slots of cylinder head.
12. Install 4 bolts. Tighten to 17–22 ft. lbs. (23–30 Nm).
13. Rotate the engine until the camshaft sprocket keyway is in the 6 o'clock position.
14. Repeat steps 9–12 in lifter position No's 1, 2, 4 and 5.
15. Install valve cover and gasket. Install air cleaner assembly.
16. Connect negative battery cable.

2.3L Engine

NOTE: Before replacing a lifter for noisy operation, make sure the noise is not caused by improper collapsed lifter gap, worn rocker arms, pushrods or valve tips.

1. Disconnect the negative battery cable. Remove the cylinder head and related parts.
2. Using a magnet, remove the lifters. Identify, tag and place the lifters in a rack so they can be installed in their original positions.
3. If the lifters are stuck in their bores by excessive varnish or gum, it

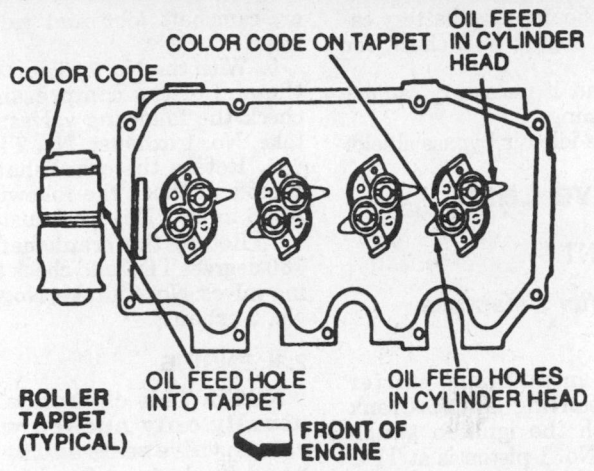

COLOR CODE

COLOR CODE ON TAPPET

OIL FEED IN CYLINDER HEAD

OIL FEED HOLE INTO TAPPET

OIL FEED HOLES IN CYLINDER HEAD

ROLLER TAPPET (TYPICAL)

FRONT OF ENGINE

Roller lifter assembly Installation—1.9L Engine

may be necessary to use a hydraulic lifter puller tool to remove the lifters. Rotate the lifters back and forth to loosen any gum and varnish which may have formed.

To install:

4. Install the hydraulic lifters through the pushrod openings with a magnet.

5. Install the cylinder head and related parts.

6. Connect negative battery cable.

3.0L Engine

NOTE: Before replacing a lifter for noisy operation, make sure the noise is not caused by improper collapsed lifter gap, worn rocker arms, pushrods or valve tips.

1. Rotate the crankshaft until the No. 1 cylinder piston is at TDC on the compression stroke.

2. Disconnect the negative battery cable.

3. Drain the cooling system.

4. Remove the PCV closure hose from the rocker arm cover and clean air flex tube.

5. Remove the clean air flex tube from the throttle body and mass air flow sensor.

6. Properly relieve the fuel system pressure, then disconnect the fuel lines.

7. Tag and disconnect all necessary vacuum lines.

8. Disconnect the TPS, idle air by-pass valve, ECT, PFE, distributor, ignition coil and coolant temperature sending unit electrical connectors. Tag the location of each so they can be reconnected properly.

9. Disconnect the upper radiator hose from the thermostat housing.

10. Loosen the EGR tube retaining nuts and remove the tube.

11. Disconnect the throttle and TV cable from the throttle body linkage.

12. Remove the retaining nuts from the alternator brace and remove the brace.

13. Remove the 6 throttle body retaining bolts and remove the throttle body.

14. Disconnect the fuel injector harness retaining stand-offs from the inboard rocker arm cover studs. Carefully disconnect the electrical connections at each injector and remove the harness from the engine.

15. Disconnect the heater hose.

16. Disconnect the ignition wires from the spark plugs, then remove the harness retaining stand-offs from the rocker arm cover studs.

17. Remove the distributor cap. Mark the position of the distributor rotor in relation to the distributor body and the position of the distributor body in relation to the engine block. Remove the distributor hold-down bolt and remove the distributor.

18. Remove the oil cooler tube assembly retaining bolt from the ignition coil bracket. Remove the ignition coil from the left cylinder head.

19. Remove the rocker arm covers.

20. Regardless of the lifter(s) being removed, the No. 3 cylinder intake valve rocker arm and pushrod must be removed in order to remove the intake manifold.

21. Remove the intake manifold retaining bolts. Wedge a prybar between the manifold and engine block and pry upward to break the manifold-to-engine block seal, using the area between the thermostat and transaxle as a leverage point.

NOTE: The intake manifold may be removed with the fuel supply manifold and injectors in place.

22. Remove the rocker arm, fulcrum and pushrod of the lifter(s) being replaced. Keep the rocker arms, fulcrums and pushrods in order so they

can be reinstalled in their original positions.

23. Loosen the 2 roller lifter guide plate retaining bolts and remove the guide plate retainer assembly from the lifter valley.

24. Remove the lifter guide plate(s) from the lifters by lifting straight up.

25. Remove the lifter by grasping it and pulling in line with the bore. If the lifter(s) are stuck in the bore(s) due to excessive varnish or gum deposits, it may be necessary to use a claw-type tool to aid removal. Rotate the lifter back and forth to loosen it from the deposits.

To install:

26. Lightly oil all retaining bolt and stud threads prior to installation.

27. Clean the gasket mating surfaces of the intake manifold and cylinder head. Before scraping, lay a clean cloth in the lifter valley to catch any gasket material. After scraping, remove the cloth, being careful not to let any particles fall into the drain holes or cylinder head.

28. Lubricate the lifter(s) and bore(s) with clean engine oil and install the lifter(s) into the bore(s).

29. Align the lifter flats and install the lifter guide plate. Install the plate with the word **UP** and or button visible.

30. Install the guide plate retainer assembly over the guide plates with the 2 retainer bolts. Tighten the bolts to 8–10 ft. lbs. (10–14 Nm).

31. Apply a ¼ in. (6mm) drop of silicone sealer to the intersection of the cylinder block and cylinder head at the 4 corners of the lifter valley.

32. Position the intake gaskets on the cylinder heads and align the locking tabs to the cylinder head gaskets.

33. Install the front and rear intake manifold seals and secure with the retaining features.

34. Carefully lower the intake manifold into position, aligning the manifold bolt holes with the holes in the cylinder heads. Be careful not to disturb the sealer.

35. Install the No. 1, 2, 3 and 4 bolts and hand tighten. Install the remaining bolts and tighten all bolts, in sequence, in 2 steps. First tighten to 15–22 ft. lbs. (20–30 Nm), then again in sequence, to 19–24 ft. lbs. (26–32 Nm).

36. Lubricate the distributor gear teeth and the distributor O-ring with engine oil. Install the distributor, aligning the marks that were made during the removal procedure. Install the hold-down bolt and snug.

37. Lubricate the pushrods and rocker arms with engine oil, then install them in their original locations. Snug the retaining bolts.

38. Before tightening each retaining bolt, rotate the crankshaft until the

lifter is on the base circle of the camshaft lobe. Tighten the retaining bolt to 5–11 ft. lbs. (7–15 Nm), making sure the rocker arm is fully seated on the pushrod and the fulcrum is fully seated on the cylinder head. Final tighten the retaining bolt to 19–28 ft. lbs. (26–38 Nm).

39. Install the rocker arm covers.

40. Install the fuel injector electrical harness to the injectors and secure the harness with the stand-offs to the inboard rocker arm cover studs.

41. Install the ignition coil and tighten the retaining bolts to 15–22 ft. lbs. (20–30 Nm). If equipped, install the oil cooler tube assembly bracket to the ignition coil bracket and tighten the retaining bolt to 15–22 ft. lbs. (20–30 Nm).

42. Install the distributor cap and ignition wires. Install the wire harness stand-offs to the rocker arm cover studs and connect the wires to the spark plugs and ignition coil.

43. Install the throttle body, using a new gasket. Tighten the throttle body mounting bolts to 15–22 ft. lbs. (20–30 Nm).

44. Install the alternator brace to the throttle body and alternator bracket. Tighten the nuts to 12 ft. lbs. (16 Nm).

45. Connect the PCV hose to the tube under the throttle body.

46. Install the EGR tube from the exhaust manifold to the EGR valve. Tighten the retaining nuts to 26–48 ft. lbs. (36–65 Nm).

47. Connect the fuel lines to the fuel supply manifold. Install the fuel line safety clips.

48. Install the upper radiator hose and heater hose and tighten the clamps.

49. Connect all removed vacuum lines to their original locations as marked during the removal procedure.

50. Connect the electrical connectors at the TPS, idle air bypass valve, ECT, PFE, distributor, ignition coil and coolant temperature sending unit.

51. Connect the throttle and TV cables to the throttle body linkage.

52. Fill and bleed the cooling system.

53. Drain the crankcase and fill with the proper type and quantity of engine oil.

NOTE: Engine coolant is corrosive to all engine bearing material. Changing the oil after the replacement of a coolant carrying component prevents failure later.

54. Install the air cleaner tube between the throttle body and mass air flow sensor. Tighten the clamps to 24–35 inch lbs. (2.7–4.0 Nm).

55. Install the PCV closure hose to the rocker arm cover and clean air flex tube.

56. Connect the negative battery cable. Start the engine and check for leaks.

57. Check, and if necessary, adjust the ignition timing.

58. Install the idle air bypass shield.

Valve Lash

ADJUSTMENT

Collapsed Lifter Clearance

1.9L ENGINE

1. Connect an auxiliary starter switch in the starting circuit. Crank the engine with the ignition switch **OFF** until the No. 1 piston is at TDC on the compression stroke.

2. With the crankshaft in position, place hydraulic lifter compressor tool T81P–6500–A or equivalent, on the rocker arm. Slowly apply pressure to bleed down the lifter until it completely bottoms. Hold the lifter in this position and check the available clearance between the rocker arm and the valve stem tip with a feeler gauge. The feeler gauge width must not exceed ⅜ in., in order to fit between the rails on the rocker arm.

3. The clearance should be as follows:

1989 EFI engine: 1.2–3.5mm.

1989 EFI-HO engine: 1.5–3.8mm.

1990 EFI with flat tappet: 0.7–5.2mm, 2.9mm normal.

1990–93 EFI with roller tappet: 0–4.5mm, 2.2mm normal.

1990 EFI-HO with flat tappet: 1.2–5.6mm, 3.4mm normal.

1990 EFI-HO with roller tappet: 0.5–4.9mm, 2.7mm normal.

4. If the clearance is not within specifications, check the fulcrum, lifter, camshaft lobe and valve tip for wear.

5. With the No. 1 piston on TDC at the end of the compression stroke check the following valves: No. 1 intake, No. 1 exhaust, No. 2 intake.

6. Rotate the crankshaft 180 degrees and check the following valves: No. 3 intake, No. 3 exhaust.

7. Rotate the crankshaft another 180 degrees TDC and check the following valves: No. 4 intake, No. 4 exhaust, No. 2 exhaust.

2.3L ENGINE

NOTE: This clearance check is usually only needed when the valves, valve seats and/or cylinder head gasket surface have been machined or new parts have been installed. Clearance must be checked when the lifter is completely collapsed.

1. Disconnect the negative battery cable.

2. Remove the rocker arm cover.

3. Rotate the engine until the No. 1 cylinder is at TDC of its compression stroke. The timing marks on the camshaft and crankshaft gears will be together. Check the clearance on No. 1 intake, No. 1 exhaust, No. 2 intake and No. 3 exhaust valves.

4. To check the clearance, use lifter bleed down wrench T71P–6513–B or equivalent, to push down on the rocker arm and bleed the oil from the lifter.

5. Insert the appropriate thickness feeler gauge between the rocker arm and valve stem to check the clearance.

6. Rotate the crankshaft 1 complete turn. Check the clearance on No. 2 exhaust, No. 3 intake, No. 4 intake and No. 4 exhaust.

7. The clearance between the rocker

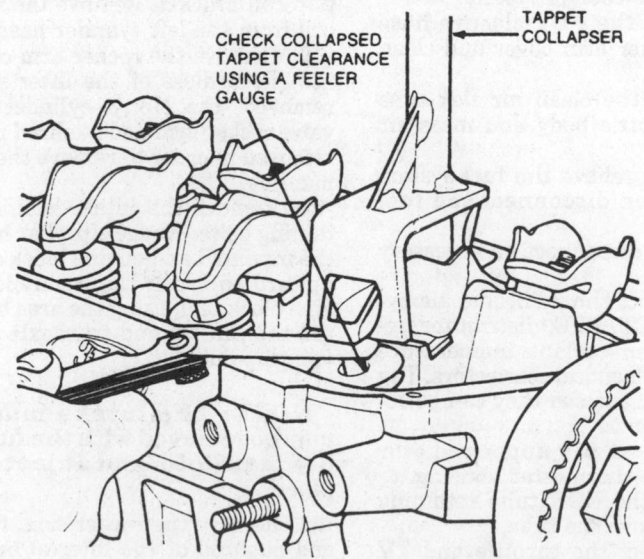

CHECK COLLAPSED TAPPET CLEARANCE USING A FEELER GAUGE

TAPPET COLLAPSER

Checking collapsed lifter clearance—1.9L Engine

arm and the valve stem tip should be 0.072–0.174 in. (1.80–4.34mm) with the lifter on the base circle of the cam.

8. If the clearance is less than specified, shorter pushrods are available to correct the problem. If the clearance is greater than specified, longer pushrods are available.

3.0L ENGINE

NOTE: **This clearance check is usually only needed when the valves, valve seats and/or cylinder head gasket surface have been machined or new parts have been installed. Clearance must be checked when the lifter is completely collapsed.**

1. Disconnect the negative battery cable.
2. Remove the rocker arm covers.
3. Rotate the engine until the No. 1 cylinder is at TDC of its compression stroke and check the clearance between the rocker arm and the following valves: No. 1 intake and exhaust, No. 2 exhaust, No. 3 intake, No. 4 exhaust and No. 6 intake.
4. To check the clearance, use lifter bleed down wrench T71P–6513–B or equivalent, to push down on the rocker arm and bleed the oil from the lifter.
5. Insert the appropriate thickness feeler gauge between the rocker arm and valve stem to check the clearance.
6. Rotate the crankshaft 360 degrees and check the clearance between the rocker arm and the following valves: No. 2 intake, No. 3 exhaust, No. 4 intake, No. 5 intake and exhaust and No. 6 exhaust.
7. The clearance should be 0.09–0.19 in. (2.3–4.8mm).
8. If the clearance is less than specified, shorter pushrods are available to correct the problem. If the clearance is greater than specified, longer pushrods are available.

Rocker Arms

REMOVAL & INSTALLATION

1.9L Engine

1. Disconnect the negative battery cable and remove the air cleaner assembly.
2. Remove and tag all necessary vacuum hoses from the rocker cover. Remove the spark plug wire retainers, if equipped. Remove the rocker cover from the cylinder head.
3. Remove the rocker cover and gasket from the engine.
4. Remove the rocker arm nuts, fulcrums, rocker arms and fulcrum washers. Keep all parts in order so they can be reinstalled to their original position.

To install:
5. Before installation, coat the valve tips, rocker arm and fulcrum contact areas with Lubriplate® or equivalent.
6. Rotate the engine until the lifter is on the base circle of the cam (valve closed).

NOTE: **Be sure to turn the engine only in the normal rotation. Backward rotation will cause the camshaft belt to slip or lose teeth, altering the valve timing and causing serious engine damage.**

7. Install the rocker arm and components and torque the rocker arm bolts to 17–22 ft. lbs. (23–30 Nm). Be sure the lifter is on the base circle of the cam for each rocker arm as it is installed.
8. On 1989–90 vehicles, install guide pins into the cylinder head and guide the gasket and rocker arm cover over the pins. Start 2 screw and washer assemblies and remove the guide pins. Install the retaining screws and washer and torque the screws to 7–10 ft. lbs. (9.5–13.5 Nm).
9. On 1991–93 vehicles, install a new gasket and the rocker arm cover. Install the 3 retaining bolts and tighten to 4–9 ft. lbs. (5–12 Nm).

NOTE: **Do not use any type of sealer with the rocker arm cover silicone gasket.**

10. Connect all vacuum hoses and install the spark plug wire retainers, if equipped.
11. Connect the negative battery cable.

2.3L Engine

1. Disconnect the negative battery cable.
2. Remove and tag all necessary vacuum hoses from the rocker cover.

Remove the oil fill cap and set it aside. Disconnect the PCV hose and set it aside.
3. Remove the rocker arm cover bolts. Remove the rocker cover from the engine.
4. Remove the rocker arm bolts, fulcrums, rocker arms and fulcrum washers. Keep all parts in order so they can be reinstalled to their original position.

To install:
5. Before installation, coat the valve tips, rocker arm and fulcrum contact areas with Lubriplate® or equivalent.
6. For each valve, rotate the engine until the lifter is on the base circle of the cam (valve closed).
7. Install the rocker arm and components and torque the rocker arm bolts in 2 steps: the first to 4.5–7.5 ft. lbs. (6–10 Nm) and the second torque to 20–26 ft. lbs. (26–38 Nm). Be sure the lifter is on the base circle of the cam for each rocker arm as it is installed. For the final tightening, the camshaft may be in any position.
8. Clean the rocker cover rail on the cylinder head.

NOTE: **The rocker arm cover has a reusable "mould in place gasket". If the gasket is damaged by a cut/nick of about ⅛ in. (maximum 2 places), the damaged area may be filled in with RTV sealer. If the gasket is damaged by cuts longer than ⅛ in. or by more than 2 cuts/nicks, replace the rocker arm cover.**

9. Install the rocker arm cover with the retaining bolts and tighten to 5.9–8.5 ft. lbs. (8.0–11.5 Nm). Apply suitable threadlock adhesive to the bolts if they are being reused, to prevent leaks.

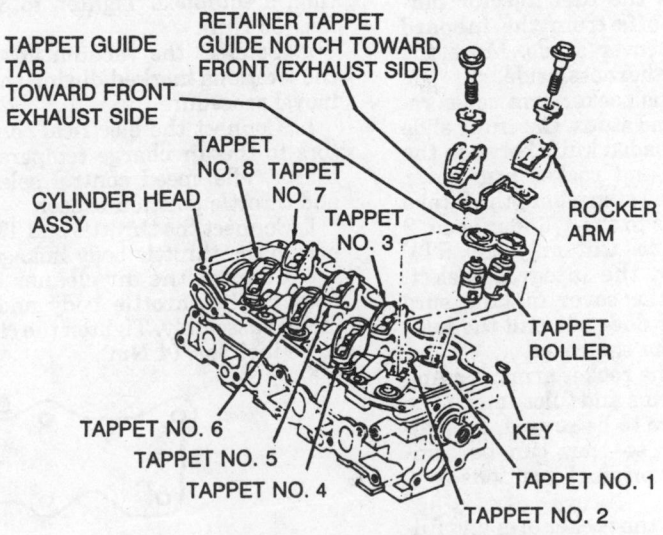

Rocker arm removal—1.9L Engine

10. Install oil fill cap, all necessary vacuum hoses and the PCV hose.

11. Connect negative battery cable.

3.0L Engine

1. Disconnect the negative battery cable.

2. Disconnect the ignition wires from the spark plugs. Remove the ignition wire/separator assembly from the rocker arm cover retaining studs and move aside.

3. If the left rocker arm cover is being removed, proceed as follows:

    a. Disconnect the air cleaner closure system hose.

    b. Remove the fuel injector harness stand-offs from the inboard rocker arm cover studs. Move the harness aside.

4. If the right rocker arm cover is being removed, proceed as follows:

    a. Remove the air cleaner duct hose from the throttle body.

    b. Remove the idle speed control solenoid shield.

    c. Disconnect the throttle and TV cable from the throttle body linkage.

    d. Tag and disconnect the necessary vacuum hoses from the throttle body.

    e. Loosen the EGR tube nuts, if equipped, at the EGR valve and exhaust manifold fitting. Remove or rotate the tube aside.

    f. Remove the PCV hose from the tube under the throttle body.

    g. Disconnect the electrical connectors at the air charge temperature sensor, idle speed control solenoid and throttle position sensor.

    h. Remove the retaining nuts from the alternator brace and remove the brace.

    i. Remove the throttle body mounting bolts and remove the throttle body. Discard the gasket.

    j. Remove the fuel injector harness stand-offs from the inboard rocker arm cover studs. Move the fuel injector harness aside.

5. Loosen the rocker arm cover retaining bolts and studs. Carefully slide a sharp, thin bladed knife between the cylinder head and rocker arm cover gasket at the rail step where the intake manifold mates to the cylinder head, 2 places each side. Cut only the RTV sealer and not the integral gasket, then remove the cover making sure the RTV sealer does not pull the integral gasket from the cover.

6. Remove the rocker arm retaining bolts, rocker arms and fulcrums. If the rocker arms are to be reused, keep all parts in order so they can be reinstalled in their original positions.

To install:

7. Lubricate the rocker arm and fulcrum contact surfaces and the valve stem tips with clean engine oil. Install the rocker arms and fulcrums in their original locations and snug the retaining bolts.

8. Before tightening each retaining bolt, rotate the crankshaft until the lifter is on the base circle of the camshaft lobe. Tighten the retaining bolt to 5–11 ft. lbs. (7–15 Nm), making sure the rocker arm is fully seated on the pushrod and the fulcrum is fully seated on the cylinder head. Final tighten the retaining bolt to 19–28 ft. lbs. (26–38 Nm).

9. Apply a bead of silicone sealer at the cylinder head to intake manifold rail step, 2 places per rail.

10. Position the cover on the cylinder head and hand tighten the retaining bolts and studs. Then, tighten in sequence to 8–10 ft. lbs. (10–14 Nm).

11. If the left rocker arm cover is being installed, proceed as follows:

    a. Connect the air cleaner closure system hose to the nipple.

    b. Install the fuel injector harness stand-offs to the appropriate inboard rocker arm cover studs.

12. If the right rocker arm cover is being installed, proceed as follows:

    a. Install the fuel injector harness stand-offs to the appropriate inboard rocker arm cover studs.

    b. Clean the gasket mating surfaces of the intake manifold and throttle body.

    c. Install the throttle body, using a new gasket and tighten the mounting bolts to 15–22 ft. lbs. (20–30 Nm).

    d. Install the alternator brace the throttle body and alternator bracket. Tighten the nuts to 12 ft. lbs. (16 Nm).

    e. Connect the PCV hose to the tube under the throttle body.

    f. Install the EGR tube to the EGR valve and exhaust manifold fitting, if equipped. Tighten to 37 ft. lbs. (50 Nm).

    g. Connect the vacuum hoses to the locations marked during the removal procedure.

    h. Connect the electrical connectors to the air charge temperature sensor, idle speed control solenoid and throttle position sensor.

    i. Connect the throttle and TV cables to the throttle body linkage.

    j. Connect the air cleaner duct hose to the throttle body and air cleaner assembly. Tighten the clamp to 36 inch lbs. (4 Nm).

    k. Check the TV cable adjustment.

    l. Install the shield on the idle speed control solenoid.

13. Connect the ignition wires to the spark plugs. Install the ignition wire separator stand-offs to the appropriate rocker arm cover studs.

14. Connect the negative battery cable, start the engine and check for oil and vacuum leaks.

Intake Manifold

REMOVAL & INSTALLATION

1.8L Engine

1. Properly relieve the fuel system pressure.

2. Disconnect the negative battery cable.

3. Tag and disconnect the necessary vacuum hoses from the intake manifold and plenum.

4. Remove the vacuum chamber canister from the intake plenum.

5. Disconnect the idle speed control and bypass air hoses from the intake plenum.

6. Disconnect the accelerator cable and, if equipped with automatic transaxle, the kickdown cable from the throttle cam. Remove the cable bracket from the intake plenum.

7. Tag and disconnect the throttle body electrical connectors.

8. Disconnect the fuel pressure and return line spring lock couplings.

9. Disconnect the PCV hose from the intake plenum and cylinder head cover.

10. Disconnect the fuel pressure regulator vacuum hose and the fuel injector wiring harness electrical connectors.

11. Remove the fuel rail mounting bolts and remove the fuel rail.

12. Remove the 2 bolts from the transaxle vent tube and remove the vent tube from the intake plenum.

13. Remove the intake manifold upper mounting nuts.

14. Raise and safely support the vehicle.

15. Remove the intake plenum support bracket and the intake manifold lower mounting nuts.

16. Lower the vehicle.

17. Remove the intake manifold, intake plenum and throttle body as an assembly from the vehicle.

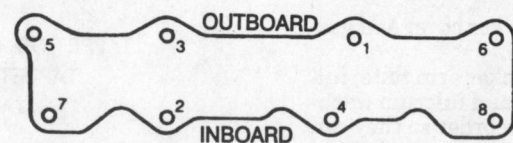

Rocker arm cover bolt torque sequence – 3.0L Engine

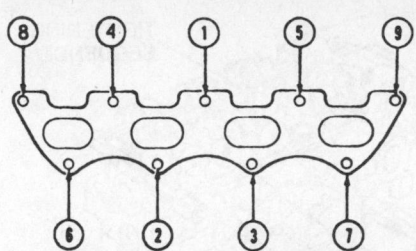

Intake manifold bolt torque sequence—1.8L Engine

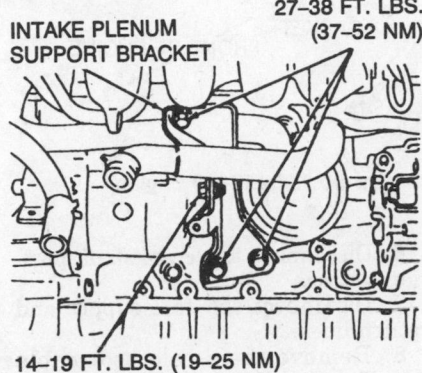

INTAKE PLENUM SUPPORT BRACKET

27–38 FT. LBS. (37–52 NM)

14–19 FT. LBS. (19–25 NM)

Intake plenum support bracket torque specifications—1.8L Engine

18. Remove the intake manifold gasket.

19. If necessary, separate the intake plenum and throttle body from the intake manifold.

20. Clean all gasket mating surfaces.

To install:

21. If necessary, install the throttle body and intake plenum onto the intake manifold.

22. Install the intake manifold gasket.

23. Install the intake manifold, intake plenum and throttle body assembly onto the intake manifold mounting studs.

24. Install the mounting nuts and tighten to 14–19 ft. lbs. (19–25 Nm) in the proper sequence.

25. Raise and safely support the vehicle.

26. Install the intake plenum support bracket and tighten the bolts to specification.

27. Lower the vehicle.

28. Place the fuel rail into position and install the mounting bolts. Tighten the bolts to 14–19 ft. lbs. (19–25 Nm).

29. Connect the fuel injector wiring harness electrical connectors and connect the vacuum hose to the pressure regulator.

30. Connect the PCV hose to the intake plenum and cylinder head cover.

31. Connect the fuel pressure and return line spring lock couplings.

32. Install the transaxle vent tube and vacuum chamber cansister.

33. Connect the electrical connectors to the throttle body and the necessary vacuum hoses to the intake plenum and throttle body.

34. Connect the idle speed control and bypass air hoses to the intake plenum.

35. Install the cable bracket onto the intake plenum and connect the accelerator and, if equipped, kickdown cables to the throttle cam.

36. Install the inlet air duct that connects to the throttle body and the resonance chamber.

37. Connect the negative battery cable.

1989–90 1.9L CFI Engine

1. Properly relieve the fuel system pressure. Disconnect the negative battery cable.

2. Partially drain the cooling system and disconnect the heater hose at the fitting located on the side of the intake manifold.

3. Remove air cleaner assembly.

4. Identify, tag and disconnect the necessary vacuum hoses.

5. Identify, tag and disconnect wiring connectors at the coolant temperature sensor and air charge temperature sensor.

6. Remove EGR supply tube.

7. Raise and safely support the vehicle.

8. Remove the PVS hose connectors. Label the connectors and set aside.

9. Remove the bottom 4 intake manifold retaining nuts, locations 2, 3, 6 and 7.

10. Lower the vehicle.

11. Disconnect fuel lines at the the throttle body.

12. Disconnect accelerator and, if equipped, the cruise control cable.

13. Disconnect the throttle valve linkage at the throttle body and remove the cable bracket attaching bolts on vehicles equipped with automatic transaxle.

14. Remove the remaining 3 intake manifold attaching nuts, intake manifold and gasket.

NOTE: Do not lay the intake manifold flat as the gasket surfaces may be damaged.

To install:

15. Make sure the mating surfaces on the intake manifold and the cylinder head are clean and free of gasket material.

16. Install a new intake manifold gasket.

17. Position the intake manifold on the engine and install the attaching nuts. Tighten the nuts, in sequence, to 12–15 ft. lbs. (16–20 Nm).

18. Connect throttle valve linkage and install the cable bracket attaching bolts, if removed, on vehicles with automatic transaxle.

19. Connect accelerator cable and, if equipped, the cruise control cable.

20. Connect fuel lines at the fuel charging assembly.

21. Raise and safely support the vehicle.

22. Connect heater hose to the fitting located on side of the intake manifold.

23. Lower vehicle.

24. Connect EGR supply tube.

25. Connect the wiring connectors at the coolant temperature sensor and air charge temperature sensor.

26. Connect vacuum hoses.

27. Install air cleaner assembly.

28. Fill the cooling system.

29. Connect the negative battery cable.

30. Start the engine and bring to normal operating temperature. Check for fuel and coolant leaks.

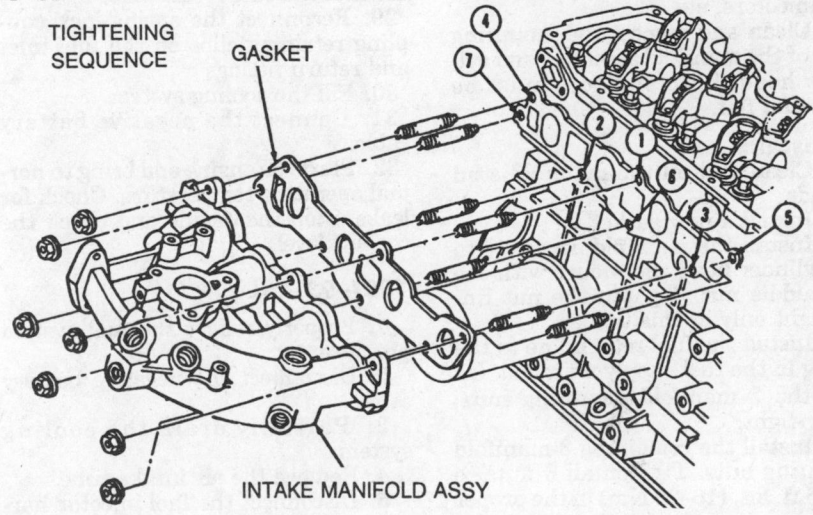

TIGHTENING SEQUENCE   GASKET

INTAKE MANIFOLD ASSY

Intake manifold nut torque sequence—1989–90 1.9L CFI Engine

1989-90 1.9L EFI-HO Engine

1. Disconnect the negative battery cable.
2. Properly relieve the fuel system pressure.
3. Remove the engine air cleaner outlet tube between the vane air meter and the air throttle body by loosening the 2 clamps.
4. Disconnect and remove the accelerator and cruise control cables, if equipped, from the accelerator mounting bracket and throttle lever.
5. Disconnect the top manifold vacuum fitting connections by disconnecting the rear vacuum line to the dash panel vacuum tree and the vacuum line at the intake manifold tee.
6. Disconnect the PCV system by disconnecting the hoses from the PCV valve at the intake manifold connection.
7. Disconnect the EGR vacuum line at the EGR valve. Disconnect the EGR tube from the upper intake manifold by supporting the connector while loosening the compression nut.
8. Disconnect the upper support manifold bracket by removing the top bolt only. Leave the bottom bolts attached.
9. Disconnect the electrical connectors at the main engine harness, near the No. 1 runner, and at the ECT sensor located in the heater supply tube.
10. Remove the fuel supply and return lines.
11. Remove the 6 manifold mounting nuts.
12. Disconnect the lower support manifold bracket by removing the top bolt only. Leave the bottom bolts attached.
13. Remove the manifold with the wiring harness and gasket.
14. If necessary, at this time remove subassemblies from the intake manifold such as the throttle body, fuel rail, fuel injectors, etc.
15. Clean and inspect the mounting faces of the manifold assembly and cylinder head. Both surfaces must be clean and flat.

To install:

16. Clean and oil the manifold stud threads.
17. Install a new gasket.
18. Install the manifold assembly to the cylinder head and secure with the top middle nut. Tighten the nut finger-tight only at this time.
19. Install the fuel return line to the fitting in the fuel supply manifold. Install the 2 manifold mounting nuts, finger-tight.
20. Install the remaining 3 manifold mounting nuts. Tighten all 6 nuts to 12–15 ft. lbs. (16–20 Nm) in the proper sequence.
21. Connect the upper and lower

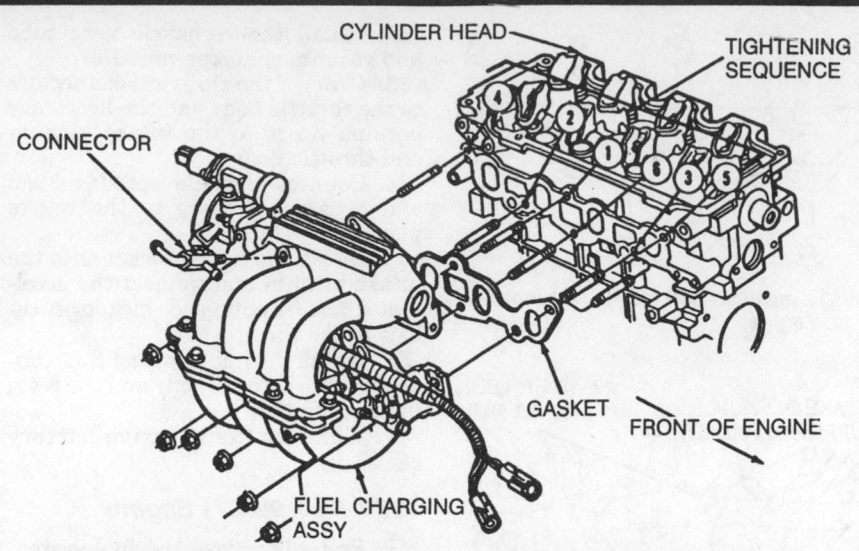

Intake manifold nut torque sequence—1989–90 1.9L EFI-HO Engine

manifold support brackets and tighten the bolts to 15–22 ft. lbs. (20–30 Nm).
22. Install the EGR tube with oil-coated compression nut tightened to 29.5–40.5 ft. lbs. (40–55 Nm).
23. Connect the vacuum line to the throttle body port and connect the large PCV vacuum line to the upper manifold fitting.
24. Connect the rear manifold vacuum connections at the dash panel vacuum tree and connect the vacuum line(s) to the upper manifold.
25. Connect the accelerator and, if equipped, cruise control cables.
26. Install the air supply tube. Tighten the clamps to 12–20 inch lbs. (1.4–2.3 Nm).
27. Connect the wiring harness at the ECT sensor in the heater supply tube and the main engine harness, near the No. 1 runner.
28. Connect the fuel supply hose from the fuel filter to the fuel rail and connect the fuel return line.
29. Reconnect the spring-lock coupling retaining clips on the fuel inlet and return fittings.
30. Fill the cooling system.
31. Connect the negative battery cable.
32. Start the engine and bring to normal operating temperature. Check for leaks. Stop the engine and check the coolant level.

1991-93 1.9L Engine

1. Properly relieve the fuel system pressure.
2. Disconnect the negative battery cable.
3. Partially drain the cooling system.
4. Remove the air intake tube.
5. Disconnect the fuel injector harness from the engine control harness at the right shock tower.

6. Disconnect the crankshaft position sensor.
7. Disconnect the fuel supply and return lines.
8. Remove the accelerator cable and, if equipped with automatic transaxle, kickdown cable from the throttle lever. Remove the cable bracket from the intake manifold and position the cables aside.
9. Remove the power brake supply hose, PCV line and the vacuum line from the bottom of the throttle body.
10. Remove the 7 attaching nuts from the intake manifold studs, slide the manifold assembly off the studs and remove it from the cylinder head. Remove and discard the intake manifold gasket.

To install:

11. Clean and inspect the mounting faces of the intake manifold and cylinder head. Both surfaces must be clean and flat.
12. Clean and oil the manifold studs and position a new gasket over them.
13. Install the intake manifold and the attaching nuts. Tighten the nuts to 12–15 ft. lbs. (16–20 Nm).
14. Install the vacuum line on the bottom of the throttle body, the power brake supply hose and the PCV line.
15. Install the accelerator cable bracket and connect the accelerator cable and, if equipped, kickdown cable on the throttle lever.
16. Connect the crankshaft position sensor electrical connector.
17. Connect the fuel supply and return lines. Install the fuel line retaining clips.
18. Connect the 2 fuel injector harness connectors to the engine control harness at the right shock tower.
19. Install the air intake tube.
20. Refill the cooling system.

21. Connect the negative battery cable.

22. Start the engine and bring to normal operating temperature. Check for leaks. Stop the engine and check the coolant level.

2.3L Engine

1. Disconnect the negative battery cable.

2. Properly relieve the fuel system pressure.

3. Remove the air duct from between the throttle body and air cleaner.

4. Disconnect the accelerator and, if equipped, cruise control cables from the mounting bracket and throttle lever.

5. Tag and disconnect the rear vacuum line to the dash panel vacuum tree, the vacuum line at the intake manifold, MAP sensor vacuum line and fuel pressure regulator vacuum line.

6. Disconnect the hoses from the PCV valve at the intake manifold.

7. Disconnect the EGR vacuum line at the EGR valve and EGR tube. Disconnect the EGR tube from the upper intake manifold by supporting the connector while loosening the compression nut.

8. Disconnect the upper support manifold bracket by removing the top bolt only. Leave the bottom bolts attached.

9. Tag and disconnect the electrical connectors at the main engine harness, near the No. 4 runner.

10. Disconnect the fuel supply and return lines.

11. Remove the 8 manifold mounting fasteners.

12. Disconnect the lower support manifold bracket by removing the top bolt only. Leave the bottom bolts attached.

13. Remove the manifold with the wiring harness. Discard the gasket.

To install:

14. Clean and inspect the mounting faces of the manifold and cylinder head. Both surfaces must be clean and flat.

15. Install a new gasket and the manifold assembly. Install and finger-tighten the fasteners.

16. Connect the fuel return line to the fitting in the fuel supply manifold.

17. Tighten all manifold fasteners, in sequence, to 15–22 ft. lbs. (20–30 Nm).

18. Connect the upper and lower manifold support brackets and tighten to 15–22 ft. lbs. (20–30 Nm).

19. Install the EGR tube with the oil-coated compression nut and tighten to 30–40 ft. lbs. (40–55 Nm).

20. Connect the large PCV vacuum line to the upper manifold fitting.

21. Connect the rear manifold vacuum connections at the dash panel vacuum tree and connect the vacuum line(s) to the upper manifold.

22. Connect the accelerator and, if equipped, the cruise control cables.

23. Connect the wiring harness at the electronic engine control harness.

24. Connect the fuel supply hose from the filter to the fuel supply manifold.

25. Connect the negative battery cable. Start the engine and check for fuel and/or vacuum leaks.

3.0L Engine

1. Disconnect the negative battery cable.

2. Drain the cooling system.

3. Remove the PCV closure hose from the rocker arm cover and clean air flex tube.

4. Remove the clean air flex tube from the throttle body and mass air flow sensor.

5. Properly relieve the fuel system pressure, then disconnect the fuel lines.

6. Tag and disconnect all necessary vacuum lines.

7. Disconnect the TPS, idle air bypass valve, ISC, ECT, PFE, distributor, ignition coil and coolant temperature sending unit electrical connectors. Tag the location of each so they can be reconnected properly.

8. Disconnect the upper radiator hose from the thermostat housing.

9. Loosen the EGR tube retaining nuts and remove the tube.

10. Disconnect the throttle and TV cable from the throttle body linkage.

11. Remove the retaining nuts from the alternator brace and remove the brace.

12. Remove the 6 throttle body retaining bolts and remove the throttle body.

13. Disconnect the fuel injector harness retaining stand-offs from the inboard rocker arm cover studs. Carefully disconnect the electrical connections at each injector and remove the harness from the engine.

14. Disconnect the heater hose.

15. Disconnect the ignition wires from the spark plugs, then remove the harness retaining stand-offs from the rocker arm cover studs.

16. Remove the distributor cap.

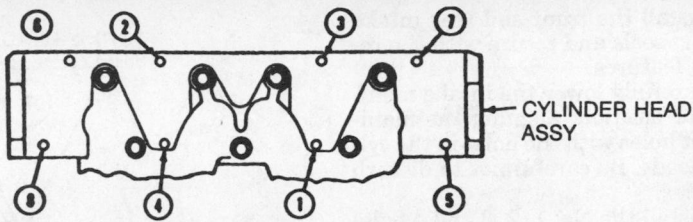

Intake manifold bolt torque sequence—2.3L Engine

Mark the position of the distributor rotor in relation to the distributor body and the position of the distributor body in relation to the engine block. Remove the distributor hold-down bolt and remove the distributor.

17. Remove the oil cooler tube assembly retaining bolt from the ignition coil bracket. Remove the ignition coil from the left cylinder head.

18. Remove the rocker arm covers.

19. Remove the No. 3 cylinder intake valve rocker arm and pushrod.

20. Remove the intake manifold retaining bolts. Wedge a prybar between the manifold and engine block and pry upward to break the manifold-to-engine block seal, using the area between the thermostat and transaxle as a leverage point.

NOTE: The intake manifold may be removed with the fuel supply manifold and injectors in place.

To install:

21. Lightly oil all retaining bolt and stud threads prior to installation.

22. Clean the gasket mating surfaces of the intake manifold and cylinder head. Before scraping, lay a clean cloth in the lifter valley to catch any gasket material. After scraping, remove the cloth, being careful not to let any particles fall into the drain holes or cylinder head.

23. If installing a new intake manifold, transfer the ECT sensor, thermostat gasket and housing, heater hose elbow and coolant temperature sending unit to the new manifold.

24. If removed, install the fuel supply manifold. Apply light grade oil to the fuel injector O-rings prior to installation. Install the injectors into the fuel supply manifold and carefully align the assembly to the intake manifold injector holes. Push 1 side into place at a time until the manifold "clicks" into place. Install the fuel supply manifold retaining bolts and tighten to 71–106 inch lbs. (8–12 Nm).

25. Apply a ¼ in. (6mm) drop of silicone sealer to the intersection of the cylinder block and cylinder head at the 4 corners of the lifter valley.

26. Position the intake gaskets on the cylinder heads and align the locking tabs to the cylinder head gaskets.

27. Install the front and rear intake manifold seals and secure with the retaining features.

28. Carefully lower the intake manifold into position, aligning the manifold bolt holes with the holes in the cylinder heads. Be careful not to disturb the sealer.

29. Install the No. 1, 2, 3 and 4 bolts and hand tighten. Install the remaining bolts and tighten all bolts, in sequence, in 2 steps. First tighten to 15–22 ft. lbs. (20–30 Nm), then again in sequence, to 19–24 ft. lbs. (26–32 Nm).

30. Lubricate the distributor gear teeth and the distributor O-ring with engine oil. Install the distributor, aligning the marks that were made during the removal procedure. Install the hold-down bolt and snug.

31. Lubricate the No. 3 cylinder intake valve pushrod and rocker arm with engine oil, then install. Snug the retaining bolt.

32. Before tightening the retaining bolt, rotate the crankshaft until the lifter is on the base circle of the camshaft lobe. Tighten the retaining bolt to 5–11 ft. lbs. (7–15 Nm), making sure the rocker arm is fully seated on the pushrod and the fulcrum is fully seated on the cylinder head. Final tighten the retaining bolt to 19–28 ft. lbs. (26–38 Nm).

33. Install the rocker arm covers.

34. Install the fuel injector electrical harness to the injectors and secure the harness with the stand-offs to the inboard rocker arm cover studs.

35. Install the ignition coil and tighten the retaining bolts to 15–22 ft. lbs. (20–30 Nm). If equipped, install the oil cooler tube assembly bracket to the ignition coil bracket and tighten the retaining bolt to 15–22 ft. lbs. (20–30 Nm).

36. Install the distributor cap and ignition wires. Install the wire harness stand-offs to the rocker arm cover studs and connect the wires to the spark plugs and ignition coil.

37. Install the throttle body, using a new gasket. Tighten the throttle body mounting bolts to 15–22 ft. lbs. (20–30 Nm).

38. Install the alternator brace to the throttle body and alternator bracket. Tighten the nuts to 12 ft. lbs. (16 Nm).

39. Connect the PCV hose to the tube under the throttle body.

40. Install the EGR tube from the exhaust manifold to the EGR valve. Tighten the retaining nuts to 26–48 ft. lbs. (36–65 Nm).

41. Connect the fuel lines to the fuel supply manifold. Install the fuel line safety clips.

42. Install the upper radiator hose and heater hose and tighten the clamps.

43. Connect all removed vacuum

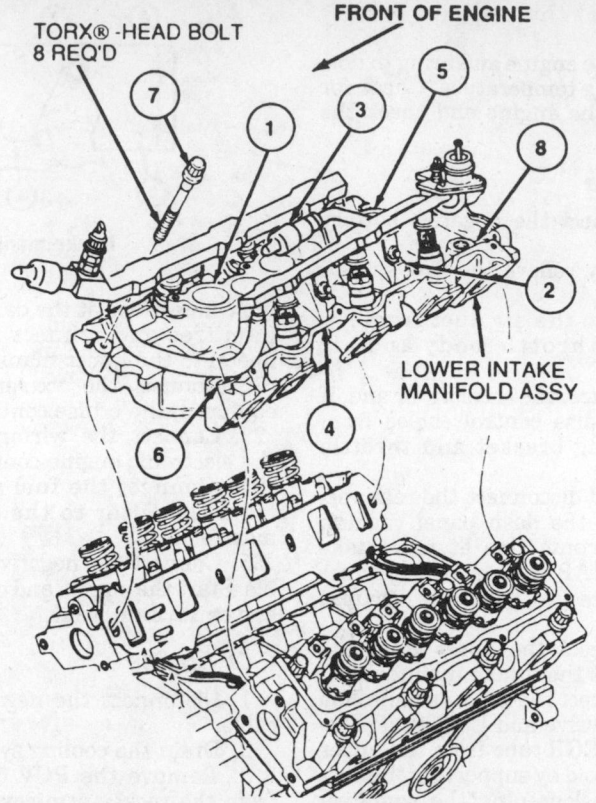

TORX® -HEAD BOLT 8 REQ'D

FRONT OF ENGINE

LOWER INTAKE MANIFOLD ASSY

Intake manifold bolt torque sequence—3.0L Engine

lines to their original locations as marked during the removal procedure.

44. Connect the electrical connectors at the TPS, idle air bypass valve, ECT, PFE, distributor, ignition coil and coolant temperature sending unit.

45. Connect the throttle and TV cables to the throttle body linkage.

46. Fill and bleed the cooling system.

47. Drain the crankcase and fill with the proper type and quantity of engine oil.

NOTE: Engine coolant is corrosive to all engine bearing material. Changing the oil after the replacement of a coolant carrying component prevents failure later.

48. Install the air cleaner tube between the throttle body and mass air flow sensor. Tighten the clamps to 24–35 inch lbs. (2.7–4.0 Nm).

49. Install the PCV closure hose to the rocker arm cover and clean air flex tube.

50. Connect the negative battery cable. Start the engine and check for leaks.

51. Check, and if necessary, adjust the ignition timing.

52. Install the idle air bypass shield.

Exhaust Manifold

REMOVAL & INSTALLATION

1.8L Engine

1. Disconnect the negative battery cable.

2. Remove the resonance duct.

3. Partially drain the cooling system and disconnect the upper radiator hose.

4. Remove the cooling fan.

5. Raise and safely support the vehicle.

6. Remove the exhaust pipe from the exhaust manifold and remove the gasket.

7. Remove the 2 bolts from the exhaust pipe support bracket.

8. Remove the left lower splash shield.

9. Lower the vehicle.

10. Disconnect the oxygen sensor electrical connector.

11. Remove the exhaust manifold heat shield mounting bolts and remove the shield.

12. Remove the exhaust manifold mounting nuts and remove the assembly.

13. Remove all gasket material from

the cylinder head and exhaust manifold.

To install:

14. Install a new gasket onto the exhaust manifold mounting studs.

15. Place the exhaust manifold onto the mounting studs and install the manifold mounting nuts. Tighten the nuts to 28–34 ft. lbs. (38–46 Nm).

16. Place the heat shield into its mounting position and install the shield mounting bolts. Tighten the bolts to 69–95 inch lbs. (7.8–11.0 Nm).

17. Connect the oxygen sensor electrical connector.

18. Install the cooling fan.

19. Connect the upper radiator hose.

20. Install the resonance duct.

21. Raise and safely support the vehicle.

22. Install the exhaust pipe support bracket.

23. Install a new gasket and install the exhaust pipe to the exhaust manifold. Tighten the attaching nuts to 23–34 ft. lbs. (31–46 Nm).

24. Install the left lower splash shield and tighten the bolts to 69–95 inch lbs. (7.8–11.0 Nm).

25. Lower the vehicle.

26. Refill the cooling system.

27. Connect the negative battery cable.

1.9L Engine

1989–90

1. Disconnect the negative battery cable.

2. Remove the air cleaner assembly.

3. Disconnect the electric fan wire.

4. Remove the radiator shroud bolts and radiator shroud.

5. Disconnect the EGR tube at the exhaust manifold.

6. Remove the air conditioning hose bracket.

7. Remove exhaust manifold heat stove. Remove the oxygen sensor from the exhaust manifold.

8. Remove exhaust manifold retaining nuts.

9. Raise and safely support the vehicle.

10. Remove the anti-roll brace.

11. Disconnect the water tube brackets.

12. Disconnect the exhaust pipe at the catalytic converter.

13. Remove the exhaust manifold and gasket. Discard the gasket and replace with new.

To install:

14. Clean the exhaust manifold gasket contact areas.

15. Position the gasket and exhaust manifold.

16. Install exhaust pipe to the catalyst.

17. Install anti-roll brace. Install water tube brackets.

18. Lower vehicle.

19. Install exhaust manifold retaining nuts. Tighten to 16–19 ft. lbs. (21–26 Nm).

20. Install exhaust manifold heat stove.

21. Install oxygen sensor in exhaust manifold. Tighten to 30–40 ft. lbs. (40–50 Nm).

22. Connect the EGR tube.

23. Install air conditioning hose brackets.

24. Position shroud and fan assembly on radiator and install bolts.

25. Connect electric fan wire.

26. Connect battery cable.

27. Install air cleaner assembly.

1991–93

1. Disconnect the negative battery cable.

2. Remove the accessory drive belt.

3. Remove the alternator.

4. Remove the radiator cooling fan and the shroud assembly.

5. Remove the exhaust manifold heat shield.

6. Raise and safely support the vehicle.

7. Remove the 2 catalytic converter inlet pipe-to-exhaust manifold attaching nuts.

8. Lower the vehicle.

9. Remove the 8 exhaust manifold attaching nuts and remove the exhaust manifold and gasket.

To install:

10. Clean the cylinder head and exhaust manifold gasket surfaces.

11. Position the new gasket onto the manifold mounting studs.

12. Position the exhaust manifold on the cylinder head and install the attaching nuts. Tighten the nuts to 16–19 ft. lbs. (21–26 Nm).

13. Raise and safely support the vehicle.

14. Install the catalytic converter inlet pipe-to-exhaust manifold attaching nuts.

15. Lower the vehicle.

16. Install the exhaust manifold heat shield.

17. Install the radiator cooling fan and shroud assembly.

18. Install the alternator and the accessory drive belt.

19. Connect the negative battery cable.

2.3L Engine

1. Disconnect the negative battery cable.

2. Properly relieve the fuel system pressure.

3. Drain the cooling system.

4. Remove the accelerator cable and position to the side.

5. Remove air cleaner assembly and heat stove tube at heat shield.

6. Identify, tag and disconnect all necessary vacuum lines.

7. Disconnect the exhaust pipe-to-exhaust manifold retaining nuts.

8. Remove exhaust manifold heat shield. Disconnect the oxygen sensor wire at the connector.

9. Disconnect the throttle linkage.

10. Disconnect the cruise control cable, if equipped.

11. Disconnect the fuel supply and return lines at the rubber connector.

12. Disconnect EGR tube from the EGR valve.

13. Remove the intake manifold.

14. Remove the exhaust manifold retaining nuts. Remove the exhaust manifold from the vehicle.

To install:

15. Position exhaust manifold to the cylinder head using guide bolts in holes 2 and 3.

16. Install the attaching bolts in the remaining holes.

17. Tighten the attaching bolts until snug, then remove guide bolts and install the remaining attaching bolts.

18. Tighten all exhaust manifold bolts to specification using the following tightening procedure: torque retaining bolts in sequence to 5–7 ft. lbs. (7–10 Nm) then retorque, in sequence, to 20–30 ft. lbs. (27–41 Nm).

19. Install the intake manifold gasket and bolts. Torque the intake manifold retaining bolts, in the proper sequence to 15–22 ft. lbs. (20–30 Nm).

20. Connect the oxygen sensor wire at the connector.

21. Connect the EGR tube to EGR valve.

22. Install exhaust manifold studs.

23. Connect exhaust pipe to exhaust manifold.

24. Connect the fuel supply and return lines.

25. Install vacuum lines.

26. Install air cleaner assembly.

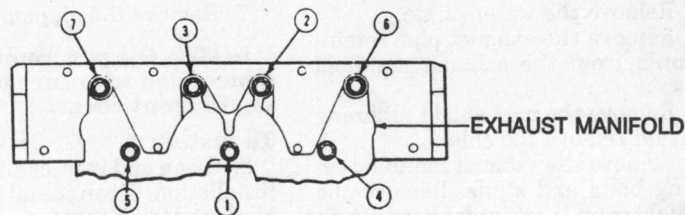

Exhaust manifold bolt torque sequence–2.3L Engine

27. Install accelerator cable and cruise control cable, if equipped.
28. Connect the negative battery cable.
29. Fill the cooling system.
30. Start engine and check for leaks.

3.0L Engine

LEFT SIDE

1. Disconnect the negative battery cable.
2. Remove the 2 retaining nuts and remove the heat shield.
3. Remove the engine oil dipstick tube or rotate it out of the way.
4. Remove the exhaust pipe retaining nuts from the exhaust manifold studs.
5. Remove the exhaust manifold retaining bolts and stud.
6. Remove the manifold from the cylinder head, being careful not to damage the spark plugs.

To install:

7. Lightly oil all bolt and stud threads.
8. Clean the mating surfaces of the cylinder head, manifold and exhaust pipe.
9. Align the exhaust manifold studs with the exhaust pipe flange and install the exhaust manifold to the cylinder head. Install the retaining bolts and stud and tighten to 15–22 ft. lbs. (20–30 Nm).
10. Install the exhaust pipe retaining nuts and tighten to 25–34 ft. lbs. (34–47 Nm).
11. Rotate or install the dipstick tube bracket to the manifold retaining stud and tighten the nut to 11–14 ft. lbs. (15–20 Nm).
12. Install the heat shield and tighten the retaining nuts to 12–14 ft. lbs. (16–20 Nm).
13. Connect the negative battery cable. Start the engine and check for exhaust and oil leaks.

RIGHT SIDE

1. Disconnect the negative battery cable.
2. Drain the cooling system.
3. Disconnect the Pressure Feedback EGR (PFE) sensor hose connection to the EGR tube.
4. Loosen the EGR supply tube nuts at the manifold and EGR valve and remove the tube.
5. Remove the water pump.
6. Remove the exhaust pipe retaining nuts from the exhaust manifold studs.
7. Remove the heat shield retaining nuts and remove the shield.
8. Remove the exhaust manifold retaining bolts and studs. Remove the manifold from the cylinder head, being careful not to damage the spark plugs.

To install:

9. Lightly oil all bolt and stud threads.
10. Clean the mating surfaces of the cylinder head, manifold, exhaust pipe and EGR tube.
11. If installing a new manifold, install the EGR tube adapter/orifice, noting the small hole end (orifice) goes to the manifold.
12. Align the exhaust manifold studs with the exhaust pipe flange and install the exhaust manifold to the cylinder head. Install the retaining bolts and stud and tighten to 15–22 ft. lbs. (20–30 Nm).
13. Install the exhaust pipe retaining nuts and tighten to 25–34 ft. lbs. (34–47 Nm).
14. Install the heat shield and tighten the retaining nuts to 12–15 ft. lbs. (16–20 Nm).
15. Install the water pump.
16. Install the EGR tube and tighten the nuts to 26–48 ft. lbs. (35–65 Nm).
17. Connect the PFE hose to the EGR tube.
18. Fill and bleed the cooling system.
19. Connect the negative battery cable. Start the engine and check for coolant and exhaust leaks.

Timing Chain Front Cover

REMOVAL & INSTALLATION

2.3L Engine

1. Remove the engine and transaxle from the vehicle as an assembly and position in a suitable holding fixture. Remove the dipstick.
2. Remove accessory drive pulley, if equipped, Remove the crankshaft pulley attaching bolt and washer and remove pulley.
3. Remove front cover attaching bolts from front cover. Pry the top of the front cover away from the block.
4. Clean any gasket material from the surfaces.
5. Check timing chain and sprockets for excessive wear. If the timing chain and sprockets are worn, replace with new.
6. Check timing chain tensioner blade for wear depth. If the wear depth exceeds 0.060 in. (1.5mm), replace tensioner.
7. Remove the oil pan.

NOTE: Oil pan removal is recommended to ensure proper sealing to front cover.

To install:

8. Clean and inspect all parts before installation. Clean the oil pan, cylinder block and front cover of gasket material and dirt.

9. Apply oil resistant sealer to a new front cover gasket and position gasket into front cover.
10. Remove the front cover oil seal and position the front cover on the engine.
11. Position front cover alignment tool T84P–6019–C or equivalent, onto the end of the crankshaft, ensuring the crank key is aligned with the keyway in the tool. Bolt the front cover to the engine and torque bolts to 6–9 ft. lbs. (8–12 Nm). Remove the front cover alignment tool.
12. Replace the front cover seal with new. Lubricate the hub of the crankshaft pulley with multi-purpose grease to prevent damage to the seal during installation and initial engine start. Install crankshaft pulley.
13. Install the oil pan.
14. Install the accessory drive pulley, if equipped.
15. Install crankshaft pulley attaching bolt and washer. Tighten to 140–170 ft. lbs. (190–230 Nm).
16. Remove engine from work stand and install in vehicle.

3.0L Engine

1. Remove the engine assembly and install on a suitable workstand.
2. Remove the accessory drive belts.
3. Remove the oil pan.
4. Remove the water pump-to-front cover hose.
5. Remove both belt tensioner assemblies.
6. Remove the vibration damper using a suitable puller.
7. Remove the front cover retaining bolts and remove the front cover. If replacing the front cover, transfer the engine mount to the cover mounting pad.

To install:

8. Lightly oil all bolt and stud threads except those specifying special sealant.

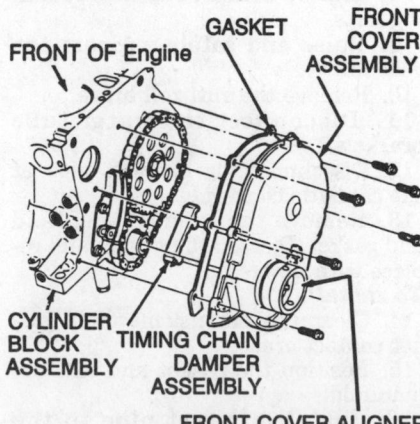

Front cover removal and Installation—2.3L Engine

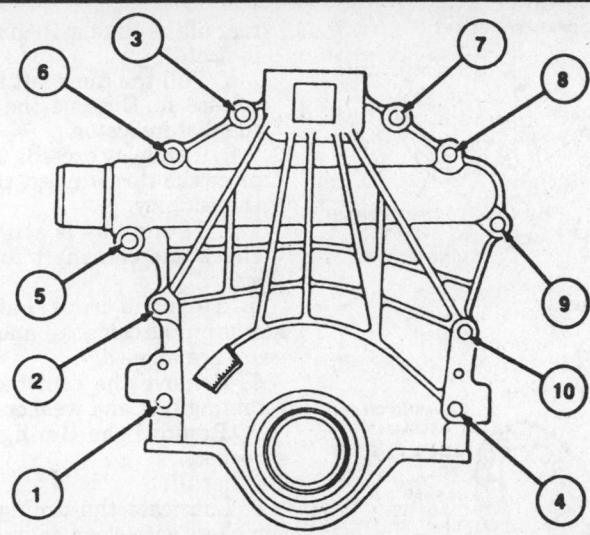

Timing chain front cover bolt torque sequence—3.0L Engine

9. Carefully clean all gasket material and sealant from the timing cover, cylinder block and oil pan.

10. Pry out the crankshaft seal from the timing cover. Lubricate and install a new seal, using a seal installer.

11. Install a new timing cover gasket over the cylinder block dowels.

12. Install the timing cover, being careful not to damage the crankshaft seal.

13. Hand start the timing cover retaining bolts. Apply pipe sealant to bolt No. 1, 2 and 3 prior to installation.

14. Tighten the retaining bolts, in sequence, to 15–22 ft. lbs. (20–30 Nm).

15. Clean the oil pan and install, using new gaskets. Tighten the bolts to 9 ft. lbs. (12 Nm).

16. Install the crankshaft damper and pulley. Lubricate the seal mating surface prior to installation. Tighten the damper bolt to 107 ft. lbs. (145 Nm) and the 4 pulley bolts to 26 ft. lbs. (35 Nm).

17. Install the automatic belt tensioners. Tighten the retaining nuts and bolt to 35 ft. lbs. (48 Nm).

18. Install the accessory drive belts.

19. Install the water pump to the front cover hose.

20. Install the engine assembly.

21. Start the engine and check for coolant, exhaust and oil leaks.

Front Cover Oil Seal

REPLACEMENT

NOTE: The removal and installation of the front cover oil seal on the 2.3L and 3.0L engines can only be accomplished with the engine removed from the vehicle.

2.3L Engine

1. Remove the engine from the vehicle and position in a suitable holding fixture.

2. Remove bolt and washer at crankshaft pulley.

3. Remove the crankshaft pulley using a suitable puller.

4. Using a suitable tool, remove the front cover oil seal.

To install:

5. Coat a new seal with grease. Using a suitable installation tool, install the seal into the cover. Drive the seal in until it is fully seated. Check the seal after installation to be sure the spring is properly positioned in the seal.

6. Install crankshaft pulley, attaching bolt and washer. Torque the crankshaft pulley bolt to 140–170 ft. lbs. (190–230 Nm).

7. Install the engine in the vehicle.

3.0L Engine

1. Remove the engine assembly and install on a suitable workstand.

2. Remove the accessory drive belts.

3. Remove the crankshaft damper retaining bolt and washer.

4. Remove the damper from the crankshaft using a suitable puller.

5. Using a small prybar, pry the seal from the front cover. Be careful not to damage the crankshaft or front cover.

To install:

6. Inspect the front cover and shaft seal surface of the crankshaft damper for damage, nicks, burrs or other roughness which may cause the seal to fail. Service as necessary.

7. Clean the crankshaft and front cover of all dirt and old sealer.

8. Lubricate the seal lip with clean engine oil and install the seal using a suitable seal installer.

9. Coat the crankshaft damper sealing surface with clean engine oil. Apply silicone sealer to the damper key-

way prior to installation. Install the damper using installation tool T82L–6316–A or equivalent.

10. Install the damper retaining bolt and washer. Tighten to 93–121 ft. lbs. (125–165 Nm).

11. Install the accessory drive belts.

12. Install the engine in the vehicle. Start the engine and check for leaks.

Timing Chain and Sprockets

REMOVAL & INSTALLATION

2.3L Engine

1. Disconnect negative battery cable.

2. Remove engine and transaxle from vehicle as an assembly and position in a suitable holding fixture. Remove the dipstick.

3. Remove the front cover from the engine.

4. Check timing chain deflection as follows:

   a. Rotate crankshaft counterclockwise, as viewed from the front of the engine, to take up slack on the left side of chain.

   b. Make a reference mark on the block at approximately mid-point of chain. Measure from this point to chain.

   c. Rotate crankshaft in opposite direction to take up slack on the right side of the chain. Force left side of chain out with fingers and measure distance between reference point and chain. The deflection is the difference between the 2 measurements.

   d. If deflection measurement exceeds 0.5 in. (12.7mm), replace timing chain and sprockets. If wear on tensioner face exceeds 0.06 in. (1.5mm), replace tensioner.

5. Turn engine over until the timing marks are aligned. Remove camshaft sprocket attaching bolt and washer. Slide both sprockets and timing chain forward and remove as an assembly.

6. If equipped, check timing chain vibration damper for excessive wear and replace if necessary. The damper is located inside the front cover.

7. Remove the oil pan.

NOTE: Oil pan removal is recommended to ensure proper sealing to front cover upon installation.

To install:

8. Clean and inspect all parts before installation. Clean the oil pan, cylinder block and front cover of gasket material and dirt.

9. Slide both sprockets and timing

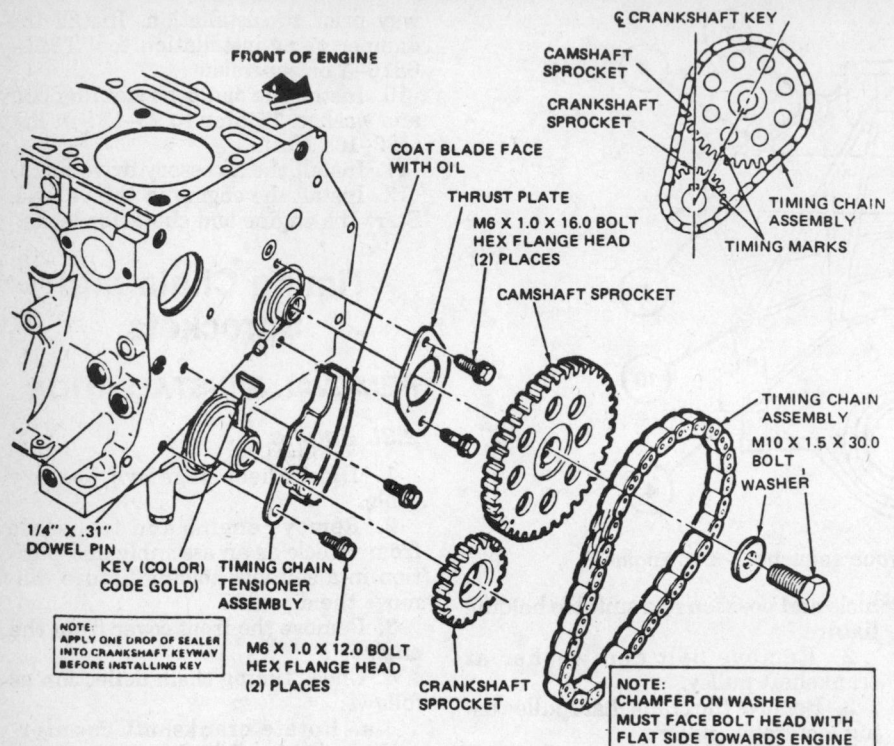

Timing chain tensioner, sprockets and timing chain installation—2.3L Engine

chain onto the camshaft and crankshaft with timing marks aligned. Install camshaft bolt and washer and tighten 41–56 ft. lbs. (55–75 Nm). Oil timing chain, sprockets and tensioner after installation with clean engine oil.

10. Install the front cover.
11. Install the oil pan.
12. Install the accessory drive pulley, if equipped.
13. Install crankshaft pulley attaching bolt and washer. Tighten to 140–170 ft. lbs. (190–230 Nm).
14. Remove engine from work stand and install in vehicle.
15. Connect negative battery cable.

3.0L Engine

1. Remove the engine assembly and install on a suitable workstand.
2. Check the timing chain deflection as follows:
    a. Remove the left rocker arm cover.
    b. Loosen the No. 5 exhaust rocker arm and rotate to 1 side.
    c. Install a dial indicator on the end of the pushrod.
    d. Turn the crankshaft clockwise until the No. 1 piston is at TDC. The damper timing mark should point to TDC on the timing degree indicator. This will take up slack on the right side of the chain.
    e. Zero the dial indicator.
    f. Slowly turn the crankshaft counterclockwise until the slightest

movement is seen on the dial indicator. Stop, and observe the damper timing mark for the number of degrees of travel from TDC.
    g. If the reading on the timing degree indicator exceeds 6 degrees, replace the timing chain and sprockets.
3. Remove the front cover.
4. Check the camshaft endplay as follows:
    a. Remove the rocker arm covers.
    b. Back off all rocker arm retaining bolts to relieve the valve train load on the camshaft.
    c. Attach a suitable dial indicator to the front of the engine. Position the indicator foot on the camshaft retaining bolt.
    d. Push the camshaft toward the

rear of the engine, then zero the dial indicator.
    e. Pull the camshaft forward and release it. Observe the reading on the dial indicator.
    f. If endplay exceeds 0.005 in., replace the thrust plate, then recheck the endplay.
    g. If endplay is still excessive, check the camshaft for excessive wear.
5. Turn the crankshaft until the marks on the camshaft and crankshaft gears are aligned.
6. Remove the camshaft sprocket retaining bolt and washer.
7. Remove the timing chain and sprockets.

To install:
8. Lubricate the timing chain and sprockets with clean engine oil and install as an assembly. Make sure the marks are aligned.
9. Inspect the camshaft sprocket retaining bolt for blockage of the drilled oil passages and clean, as necessary. Install the bolt and washer and tighten to 37–51 ft. lbs. (50–70 Nm).

NOTE: Do not replace the camshaft sprocket retaining bolt with a standard bolt or severe engine damage will result. This bolt is an oil carrying, precision component.

10. Install the front cover and install the engine in the vehicle.
11. Fill and bleed the cooling system. Fill the crankcase with the proper type and quantity of engine oil.
12. Start the engine and check for oil, coolant and exhaust leaks.

Timing Belt Front Cover

REMOVAL & INSTALLATION

1.8L Engine

1. Disconnect the negative battery cable.

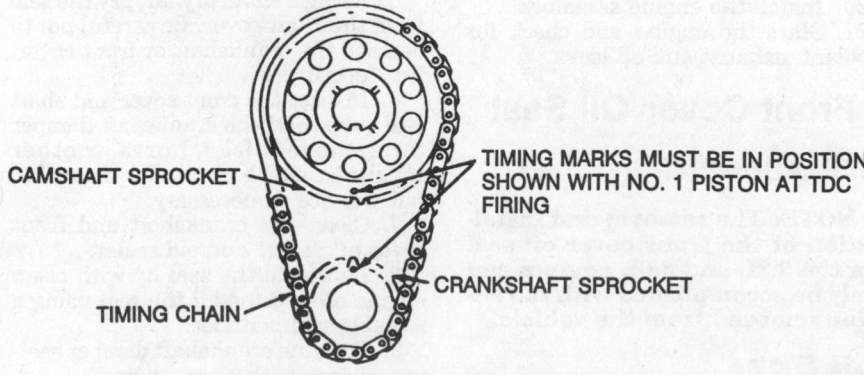

CAMSHAFT SPROCKET

TIMING MARKS MUST BE IN POSITION SHOWN WITH NO. 1 PISTON AT TDC FIRING

CRANKSHAFT SPROCKET

TIMING CHAIN

Timing sprockets alignment—3.0L Engine

2. Remove the timing belt upper cover and gasket.

3. Loosen the water pump pulley bolts.

4. Remove the alternator and water pump accessory drive belt.

5. Remove the water pump pulley bolts and remove the pulley.

6. Raise and safely support the vehicle.

7. Remove the right wheel and tire assembly.

8. Remove the right upper and lower splash shields.

9. Remove the air conditioning, if equipped, and power steering accessory drive belt.

10. Remove the crankshaft pulley, crankshaft pulley guide plate and timing belt outer and inner guide plates.

11. Remove the timing belt middle and lower covers along with the gaskets.

To install:

12. Install the timing belt middle and lower covers along with the gaskets.

13. Install the timing belt inner and outer guide plates, the crankshaft pulley and the crankshaft pulley guide plate. Tighten the bolts to 109–152 inch lbs. (12–17 Nm).

14. Install the air conditioning, if equipped, and power steering accessory drive belt.

15. Install the splash shields and tighten the bolts to 69–95 inch lbs. (7.8–11.0 Nm).

16. Install the water pump pulley and tighten the bolts to 69–95 inch lbs. (7.8–11.0 Nm).

17. Install the alternator and water pump accessory drive belt.

18. Install the right wheel and tire assembly and lower the vehicle.

19. Install the timing belt upper cover and gasket. Tighten the bolts to 69–95 inch lbs. (7.8–11.0 Nm).

20. Connect the negative battery cable.

1.9L Engine

1. Disconnect the negative battery cable.

2. Remove the accessory drive belt.

3. Remove the drive belt automatic tensioner, if equipped.

4. Remove the timing cover retaining nuts.

5. Installation is the reverse of the removal procedure. Tighten the retaining nuts to 3–5 ft. lbs. (5–7 Nm).

OIL SEAL REPLACEMENT

1.8L Engine

1. Disconnect the negative battery cable.

2. Remove the timing belt.

3. Remove the crankshaft oil seal as follows:

a. Remove the crankshaft sprocket locking bolt and remove the crankshaft sprocket. If necessary, use a suitable puller.

b. Remove the Woodruff® key.

c. If necessary, cut the lip of the crankshaft oil seal to ease removal.

d. Use a suitable prying tool to remove the crankshaft oil seal.

4. Remove the camshaft oil seal(s) as follows:

a. Tag and disconnect the vacuum hoses at the cylinder head cover.

b. Disconnect the ignition wires from the spark plugs and position aside.

c. Remove the cylinder head cover mounting bolts and remove the cover.

d. Hold the camshaft with a wrench and remove the camshaft sprocket lock bolt. Remove the camshaft sprocket.

e. Remove the seal plate mounting bolts and remove the seal plate.

f. Remove the camshaft seal using a suitable tool.

To install:

5. Install the new crankshaft oil seal as follows:

a. Lubricate the lip of the new crankshaft oil seal with clean engine oil.

b. Using a suitable installation tool, install the seal evenly until it is flush with the edge of the oil pump body.

c. Install the crankshaft sprocket onto the shaft, making sure to match the alignment grooves.

d. Install the Woodruff® key with the tapered end facing the oil pump.

e. Install the crankshaft sprocket locking bolt. Tighten the locking bolt to 80–87 ft. lbs. (108–118 Nm).

6. Install the new camshaft oil seal(s) as follows:

a. Apply a small amount of clean engine oil to the lip of a new camshaft oil seal.

b. Install the seal, using a suitable seal installer.

c. Install the seal plate and tighten the mounting bolts to 69–95 inch lbs. (7.8–11.0 Nm).

d. Install the camshaft sprocket with the timing mark aligned with the timing mark on the seal plate.

e. Hold the camshaft with a wrench and install the lock bolt. Tighten to 36–45 ft. lbs. (49–61 Nm).

f. Install the cylinder head cover with a new gasket. Tighten the cylinder head cover bolts to 43–78 inch lbs. (4.9–8.8 Nm).

g. Connect the ignition wires and the vacuum hoses.

7. Install the timing belt.

8. Connect the negative battery cable.

1.9L Engine

1989–90

1. Disconnect the negative battery cable.

2. Remove the accessory drive belts.

3. Remove the timing belt cover.

4. Connect engine support tool D88L–6000–A or equivalent to the engine.

5. With the engine supported, remove the right side engine mount.

6. Lower the engine at the right side until the crankshaft damper bolt clears the frame rail and remove the damper bolt.

7. Raise the engine and remove the damper.

8. Remove the timing belt.

9. Remove the crankshaft and/or camshaft sprocket.

10. Use a suitable tool and remove the crankshaft and/or camshaft seal.

To install:

11. Coat the new seal with clean engine oil.

12. Install the seal using a suitable seal installer.

13. Install the crankshaft and/or camshaft sprocket. Tighten the camshaft sprocket bolt to 71–84 ft. lbs. (95–115 Nm).

14. Install the timing belt.

15. Install the crankshaft damper. Tighten the attaching bolt to 81–96 ft. lbs. (110–130 Nm).

16. Install the timing belt cover.

17. Install the accessory drive belts.

18. Connect negative battery cable.

1991–93

1. Disconnect the negative battery cable.

2. Remove the accessory drive belt.

3. Raise and safely support the vehicle.

4. Remove the right side splash shield.

5. Remove the flywheel inspection shield.

6. Use a suitable tool to hold the flywheel in place.

7. Remove the crankshaft bolt and washer and remove the crankshaft dampener.

8. Remove the timing belt.

9. Remove the crankshaft sprocket and belt guide and/or camshaft sprocket.

10. Using a suitable seal remover, remove the crankshaft and/or camshaft seal.

To install:

11. Lubricate the lip of the new seal with clean engine oil.

12. Install the new seal using a suitable installation tool.

13. Install the belt guide and crankshaft sprocket and/or camshaft sprocket. Tighten the camshaft

sprocket bolt to 71–84 ft. lbs. (95–115 Nm).

14. Install the timing belt.

15. Position the crankshaft damper-er on the crankshaft. Install the attaching bolt and washer and tighten to 81–96 ft. lbs. (110–130 Nm).

16. Remove the flywheel holding tool and install the inspection shield.

17. Install the right splash shield and lower the vehicle.

18. Install the accessory drive belt.

19. Connect the negative battery cable.

20. Start the engine and check for leaks.

Timing Belt and Tensioner

ADJUSTMENT

1.8L Engine

1. Disconnect the negative battery cable.

2. Remove the timing belt upper and middle covers and gaskets.

3. Place a wrench onto the crankshaft sprocket and rotate the crankshaft clockwise so the timing marks located on the camshaft sprocket and the seal plate are aligned.

4. Rotate the crankshaft clockwise 2 complete revolutions and align the timing marks on the camshaft sprockets and seal plate.

5. Make sure the yellow ignition timing mark on the crankshaft sprocket is aligned with the TDC mark on the timing belt cover.

6. Measure the timing belt deflection by applying 22 lbs. of pressure on the belt, at a point between the camshaft sprockets. The timing belt deflection should be 0.35–0.45 in. (9.0–11.5mm).

7. If the deflection is not within specification, loosen the tensioner lock bolt. Using a suitable prying tool to move the tensioner, tighten or loosen the belt, as required, so the deflection will meet specification. Tighten the tensioner lock bolt to 27–38 ft. lbs. (37–52 Nm) and recheck the timing belt deflection beginning with Step 3.

8. If the timing belt will not meet specification, it must be replaced.

9. Install new gaskets onto the timing belt covers and install. Tighten the bolts to 69–95 inch lbs. (7.8–11.0 Nm).

1.9L Engine

The timing belt tensioner is spring-loaded on the 1.9L engine. The spring automatically maintains the proper tension and periodic belt tension adjustments are not necessary.

REMOVAL & INSTALLATION

1.8L Engine

1. Disconnect the negative battery cable.

2. Remove the timing belt covers.

3. Rotate the crankshaft and align the timing marks located on the camshaft sprockets and the seal plate.

4. If the timing belt is to be reused, mark an arrow on the belt to indicate its rotational direction for installation reference.

5. Loosen the timing belt tensioner lock bolt and remove the timing belt.

To install:

6. Temporarily secure the timing belt tensioner in the far left position with the spring fully extended, then tighten the lock bolt.

7. Make sure the timing marks on the timing belt sprocket and the engine block are aligned.

8. Make sure the timing marks on the camshaft sprockets and the seal plate are aligned.

9. Install the timing belt.

10. Loosen the tensioner lock bolt. Using a prybar, position the timing belt tensioner so the timing belt is taut, then tighten the tensioner lock bolt.

11. Turn the crankshaft 2 turns clockwise and align the timing belt sprocket mark with the mark on the engine block.

12. Make sure the camshaft sprocket marks are aligned with the seal plate marks.

NOTE: If the timing marks are not aligned, remove the belt and repeat the procedure.

13. Turn the crankshaft 1 5/6 turns clockwise and align the timing belt sprocket mark with the tension set mark, at approximately the 10 o'clock position.

14. Apply tension to the timing belt tensioner and install the tensioner lock bolt. Tighten the bolt to 27–38 ft. lbs. (37–52 Nm).

15. Turn the crankshaft 2 1/6 turns clockwise and make sure the timing marks are aligned.

16. Measure the timing belt deflection by applying 22 lbs. of pressure on the belt between the camshaft sprockets. The timing belt deflection should be 0.35–0.45 in. (9.0–11.5mm). If necessary, adjust the timing belt deflection.

17. Turn the crankshaft 2 turns

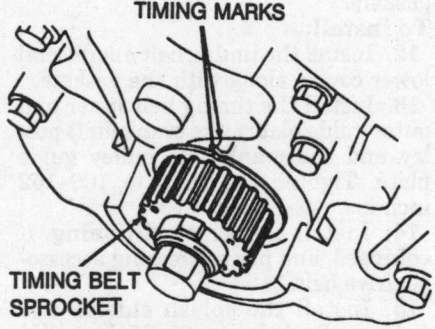

Crankshaft sprocket alignment marks – 1.8L Engine

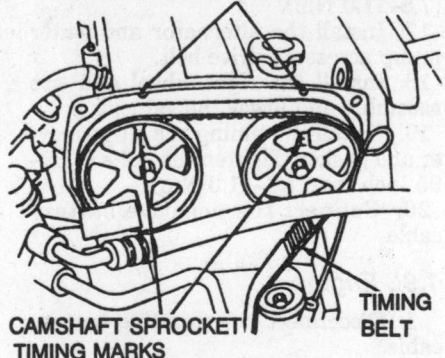

Camshaft sprocket alignment marks – 1.8L Engine

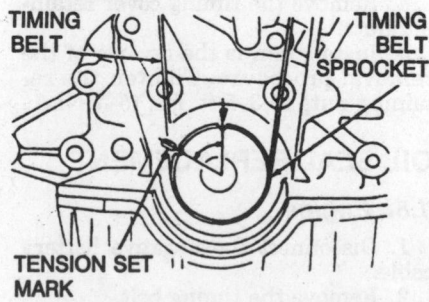

Timing belt tension set position – 1.8L Engine

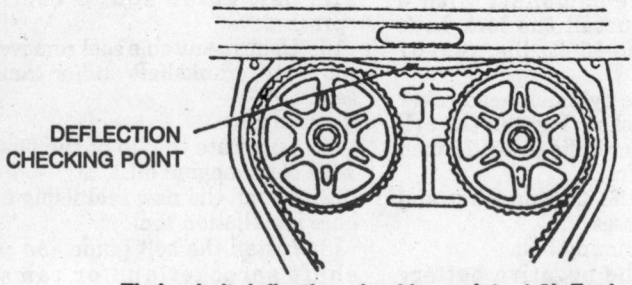

Timing belt deflection checking point – 1.8L Engine

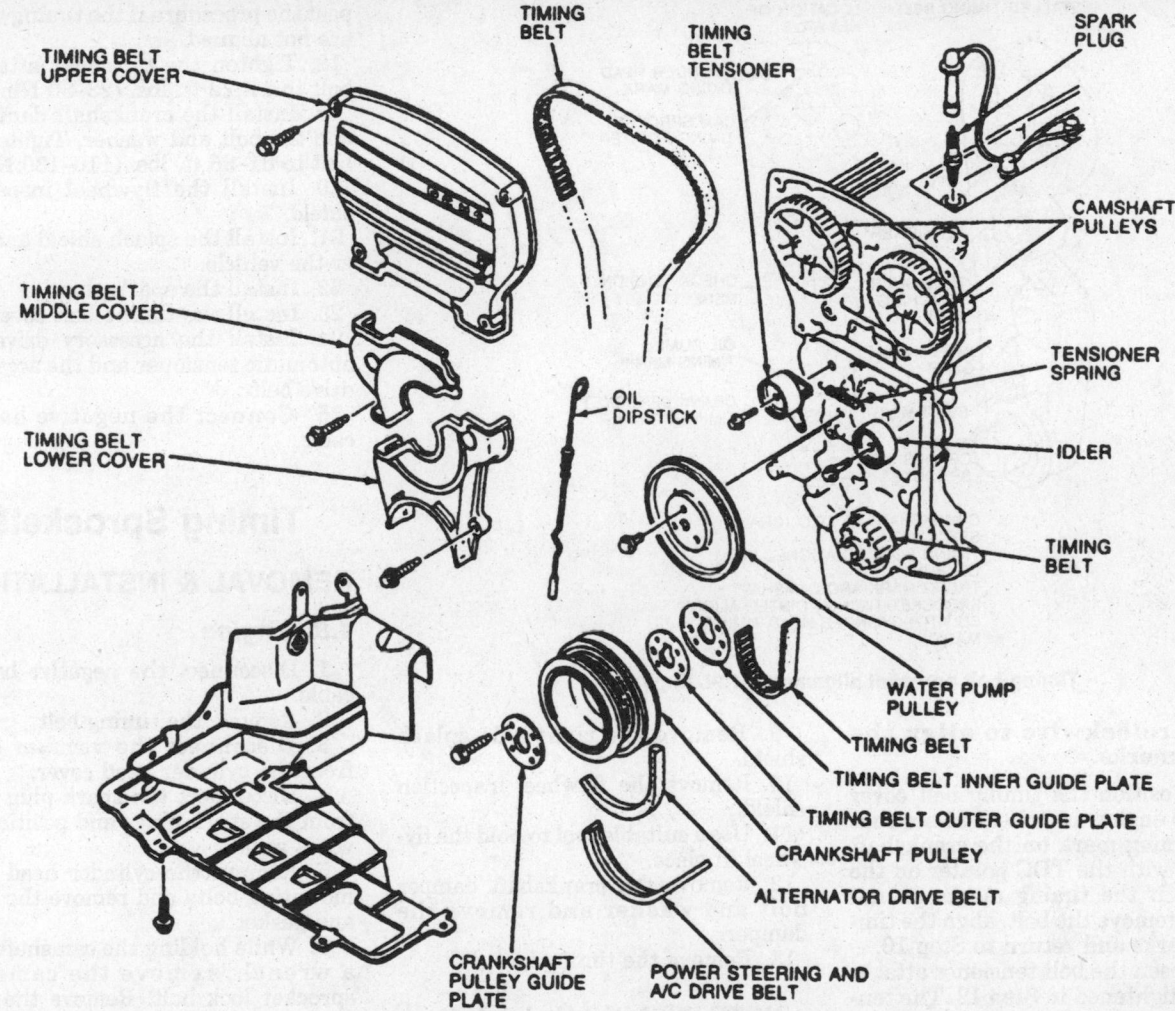

Timing belt removal and installation—1.8L Engine

clockwise and make sure the timing marks are aligned.

NOTE: If the timing marks are not aligned, repeat the procedure beginning at Step 9.

18. Install the timing belt covers and the remaining components according to the proper procedure.

19. Connect the negative battery cable.

1.9L Engine

1989–90

1. Disconnect the negative battery cable.

2. Remove the timing belt cover.

3. Align the timing mark on the camshaft sprocket with the timing mark on the cylinder head.

4. Install the timing belt cover and confirm that the timing mark on the crankshaft damper aligns with the TDC on the front cover.

5. Remove the timing belt cover.

6. Loosen both timing belt tensioner attaching bolts.

7. Pry the belt tensioner away from the belt as far as possible and tighten 1 of the tensioner attaching bolts.

8. Remove crankshaft damper as follows:

    a. Properly support the engine and remove the right side engine mount bolt.

    b. Lower the engine at the right side until the crankshaft damper bolt clears the frame rail and remove the damper bolt.

    c. Raise the engine and remove the damper.

9. Remove the timing belt. If the belt is to be reused, mark the direction of rotation on the belt so it can be reinstalled in the same direction.

NOTE: With the timing belt removed and the No. 1 piston at TDC, Do not rotate the camshaft. If the camshaft must be rotated, align the crankshaft dampener 90 degrees BTDC.

To install:

10. Install the timing belt over the sprockets in a counterclockwise direction starting at the crankshaft. Keep the belt span from the crankshaft to the camshaft tight as the belt is installed over the remaining sprocket.

11. Loosen belt tensioner attaching bolts and allow the tensioner to snap against the belt.

12. Tighten 1 of the tensioner attaching bolts.

13. Install the crankshaft damper, driveplate and damper attaching bolt. Hold the crankshaft damper stationary and tighten the attaching bolt to 81–96 ft. lbs. (110–130 Nm).

14. To seat the belt on the sprocket teeth, proceed as follows:

    a. Connect the negative battery terminal.

    b. Crank engine several revolutions.

    c. Disconnect the negative battery terminal.

    d. Turn camshaft, as necessary, to align the timing pointer on the cam sprocket with the timing mark on the cylinder head.

NOTE: Do not turn the engine

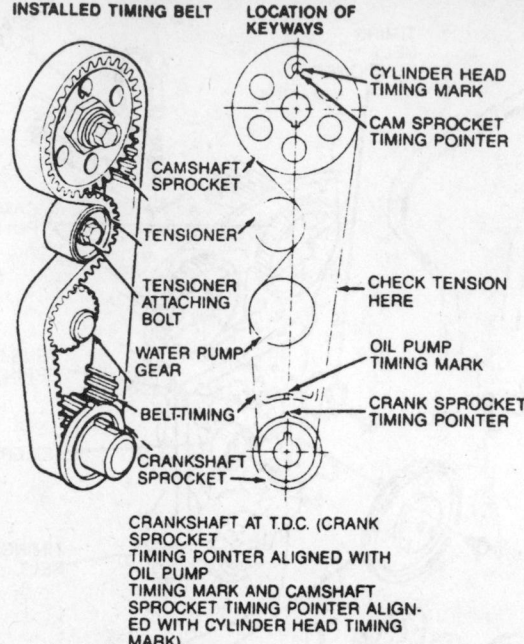

INSTALLED TIMING BELT   LOCATION OF KEYWAYS

CYLINDER HEAD TIMING MARK

CAM SPROCKET TIMING POINTER

CAMSHAFT SPROCKET

TENSIONER

TENSIONER ATTACHING BOLT

CHECK TENSION HERE

WATER PUMP GEAR

OIL PUMP TIMING MARK

BELT-TIMING

CRANK SPROCKET TIMING POINTER

CRANKSHAFT SPROCKET

CRANKSHAFT AT T.D.C. (CRANK SPROCKET TIMING POINTER ALIGNED WITH OIL PUMP TIMING MARK AND CAMSHAFT SPROCKET TIMING POINTER ALIGNED WITH CYLINDER HEAD TIMING MARK).

Timing belt sprocket alignment—1.9L Engine

counterclockwise to align the timing marks.

e. Position the timing belt cover on the engine and check to see that the timing mark on the crankshaft aligns with the TDC pointer on the cover. If the timing marks do not align, remove the belt, align the timing marks and return to Step 10.

15. Loosen the belt tensioner attaching bolt tightened in Step 12. The tensioner spring will apply the proper load on the belt. Tighten the belt tensioner bolt.

NOTE: The engine must be at room temperature. Do not set belt tension on a hot engine.

16. Install timing belt cover.
17. Install accessory drive belts.
18. Connect negative battery cable.

1991–93

1. Disconnect the negative battery cable.
2. Remove the accessory drive belt automatic tensioner and the accessory drive belt.
3. Remove the timing belt cover.
4. Align the timing mark on the camshaft sprocket with the timing mark on the cylinder head.
5. Confirm that the timing mark on the crankshaft sprocket is aligned with the timing mark on the oil pump housing.
6. Loosen the belt tensioner attaching bolt, pry the tensioner away from the timing belt and retighten the bolt.
7. Remove the spark plugs.
8. Raise and safely support the vehicle.

9. Remove the right side splash shield.
10. Remove the flywheel inspection shield.
11. Use a suitable tool to hold the flywheel in place.
12. Remove the crankshaft damper bolt and washer and remove the damper.
13. Remove the timing belt.

NOTE: With the timing belt removed and the No. 1 piston at TDC, do not rotate the camshaft. If the camshaft must be rotated, align the crankshaft damper 90 degrees BTDC.

To install:

14. Install the timing belt over the sprockets in a counterclockwise direction starting at the crankshaft. Keep the belt span from the crankshaft to the camshaft tight while installing over the remaining sprocket.
15. Loosen the belt tensioner attaching bolt, allowing the tensioner to snap against the belt.
16. Rotate the crankshaft clockwise 2 complete revolutions, stopping at TDC. This will allow the tensioner spring to load the timing belt.

NOTE: Do not turn the engine counterclockwise to align the timing marks. Do not rotate the crankshaft with the spark plugs installed.

17. Recheck the camshaft and crankshaft timing marks for alignment, to make sure the timing belt has not skipped a tooth during rotation. Re-

peat the procedure if the timing marks are not aligned.
18. Tighten the tensioner attaching bolt to 17–22 ft. lbs. (23–30 Nm).
19. Install the crankshaft dampener and the bolt and washer. Tighten the bolt to 81–96 ft. lbs. (110–130 Nm).
20. Install the flywheel inspection shield.
21. Install the splash shield and lower the vehicle.
22. Install the spark plugs.
23. Install the timing belt cover.
24. Install the accessory drive belt automatic tensioner and the accessory drive belt.
25. Connect the negative battery cable.

Timing Sprockets

REMOVAL & INSTALLATION

1.8L Engine

1. Disconnect the negative battery cable.
2. Remove the timing belt.
3. Disconnect the vacuum hoses from the cylinder head cover.
4. Disconnect the spark plug wires from the spark plugs and position the wires aside.
5. Remove the cylinder head cover mounting bolts and remove the cover and gasket.
6. While holding the camshaft with a wrench, remove the camshaft sprocket lock bolt. Remove the camshaft sprocket.
7. Remove the timing belt crankshaft sprocket locking bolt.
8. Remove the timing belt sprocket. If necessary, use a suitable puller.
9. Remove the Woodruff® key from the crankshaft.

To install:

10. Install the timing belt sprocket onto the crankshaft while making sure to match the alignment grooves.
11. Install the Woodruff® key with the tapered end facing the oil pump.
12. Install the timing belt sprocket locking bolt and tighten to 80–87 ft. lbs. (108–118 Nm).
13. Install the camshaft sprocket with the timing mark aligned with the timing mark on the seal plate.
14. While holding the camshaft with a wrench, install the camshaft sprocket lock bolt. Tighten the bolt to 36–45 ft. lbs. (49–61 Nm).
15. Install a new cylinder head cover gasket onto the cylinder head.
16. Place the cylinder head cover into its mounting position and install the mounting bolts. Tighten the cylinder head cover bolts to 43–78 inch lbs. (4.9–8.8 Nm).
17. Connect the spark plug wires to

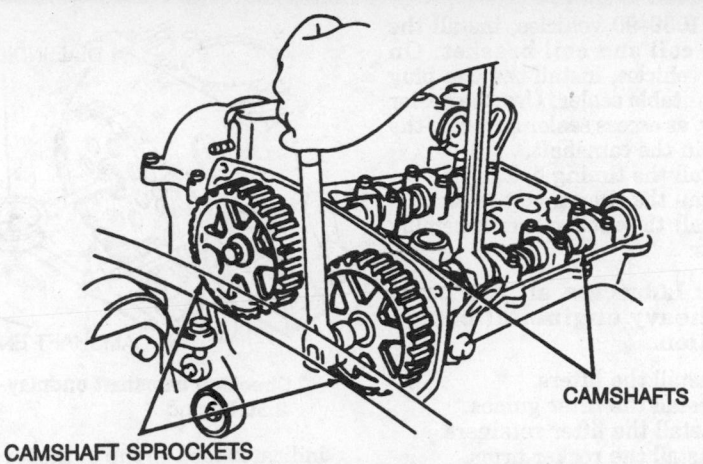

Hold the camshaft with a wrench when removing or installing the camshaft sprocket lock bolt—1.8L Engine

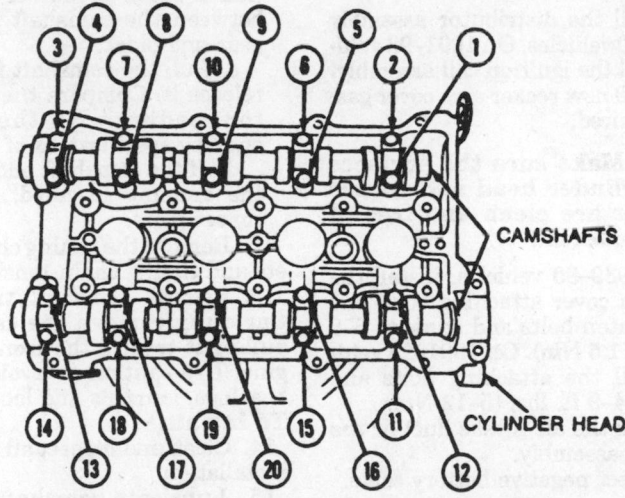

Camshaft cap bolt loosening sequence—1.8L Engine

the spark plugs and connect the vacuum hoses to the cylinder head cover.
18. Install the timing belt and timing belt covers.

1.9L Engine

1. Disconnect the negative battery cable.
2. Remove the timing belt cover and timing belt.

NOTE: With the timing belt removed and pistons at TDC, do not rotate the engine. If the camshaft must be rotated, align the crankshaft sprocket to 90 degrees BTDC.

3. Remove the camshaft sprocket attaching bolt and washer and camshaft sprocket.
4. Remove the crankshaft sprocket.
To install:
5. Install the camshaft sprocket and attaching bolt and washer. Tighten to 71–84 ft. lbs. (95–115 Nm).
6. Install the crankshaft sprocket.

7. Install the timing belt and cover.
8. Connect the negative battery cable.

Camshaft
REMOVAL & INSTALLATION

1.8L Engine

1. Disconnect the negative battery cable.

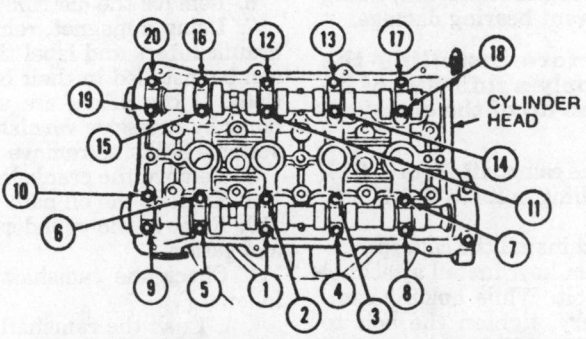

Camshaft cap bolt torque sequence—1.8L Engine

2. Remove the distributor assembly.
3. Remove the camshaft sprockets.
4. Remove the seal plate mounting bolts and remove the seal plate.
5. Loosen the camshaft cap bolts in the correct sequence.
6. Remove the camshaft caps and note their mounting locations for installation reference.

NOTE: The camshaft caps are numbered and have arrow marks for installation and direction reference.

7. Remove the camshaft and camshaft oil seal.
To install:
8. Apply clean engine oil to the camshaft journals and bearings.
9. Place the camshaft into its mounting position.

NOTE: The exhaust camshaft has a groove which must be installed into the distributor drive gear.

10. Apply silicone sealant to the required areas.
11. Install the camshaft caps according to the cap numbers and arrow marks.
12. Install the camshaft cap bolts and tighten them in the proper sequence to 100–126 inch lbs. (11.3–14.2 Nm).
13. Apply a small amount of clean engine oil to the lip of a new camshaft oil seal. Using a suitable installation tool, install the new seal.
14. Place the seal plate into its

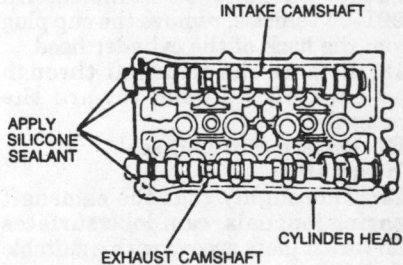

Silicone sealer application points—1.8L Engine

mounting position and install the mounting bolts. Tighten the bolts to 69–95 inch lbs. (7.8–11.0 Nm).

15. Install the camshaft sprockets and the distributor assembly.

16. Connect the negative battery cable.

1.9L Engine

1. Disconnect the negative battery cable.

2. Remove the air cleaner or air intake duct.

3. Remove the accessory drive belts and crankshaft damper.

4. Remove the timing belt cover and rocker arm cover.

5. Set the engine No. 1 cylinder at TDC prior to removing timing belt.

NOTE: Make sure the crankshaft is positioned at TDC and do not turn the crankshaft until the timing belt is installed.

6. Remove rocker arms and lifters as follows:

   a. Remove hex flange bolts.
   b. Remove fulcrums.
   c. Remove rocker arms.
   d. Remove lifter guide retainers.
   e. Remove lifters guides.
   f. Remove lifters.

7. Remove the distributor assembly on 1989–90 vehicles. On 1991–93 vehicles, remove the ignition coil assembly.

8. Remove timing belt.

9. Remove the camshaft sprocket and key.

10. Remove the camshaft thrust plate.

11. Remove the ignition coil and coil bracket on 1989–90 vehicles. On 1991–93 vehicles, remove the cup plug from the back of the cylinder head.

12. Remove the camshaft through the back of the head toward the transaxle.

13. Replace camshaft seal.

To install:

14. Thoroughly coat the camshaft bearing journals, cam lobe surfaces and thrust plate groove with a suitable lubricant.

15. Install the camshaft through the rear of the cylinder head. Rotate the camshaft during installation, being careful to prevent bearing damage.

NOTE: Before installing the camshaft, apply a thin film of lubricant to the lip of the camshaft seal.

16. Install the camshaft thrust plate. Tighten attaching bolts to 6–9 ft. lbs. (8–13 Nm).

17. Align and install the cam sprocket over the cam key. Install attaching washer and bolt. While holding camshaft stationary, tighten the bolt to 71–84 ft. lbs. (95–115 Nm).

18. On 1989–90 vehicles, install the ignition coil and coil bracket. On 1991–93 vehicles, install the cup plug using a suitable sealer. Use the sealer sparingly, as excess sealer may clog the oil holes in the camshaft.

19. Install the timing belt.

20. Install the timing belt cover.

21. Install the rocker arm assembly as follows:

NOTE: Lubricate all the parts with a heavy engine oil before installation.

   a. Install the lifters.
   b. Install the lifter guides.
   c. Install the lifter retainers.
   d. Install the rocker arms.
   e. Install the fulcrums.
   f. Install the rocker arm bolts. Tighten to 17–22 ft. lbs. (23–30 Nm).

22. Install the distributor assembly on 1989–90 vehicles. On 1991–93 vehicles, install the ignition coil assembly.

23. Install new rocker arm cover gasket, if required.

NOTE: Make sure the surfaces on the cylinder head and rocker arm cover are clean and free of sealant material.

24. On 1989–90 vehicles, install the rocker arm cover attaching bolts and studs. Tighten bolts and studs to 6–8 ft. lbs. (8–11.5 Nm). On 1991–93 vehicles, install the attaching bolts and tighten to 4–9 ft. lbs. (5–12 Nm).

25. Install the air intake duct or the air cleaner assembly.

26. Connect negative battery cable.

2.3L Engine

1. Disconnect the negative battery cable.

2. Drain the cooling system and crankcase. Properly relieve the fuel system pressure.

3. Remove the engine from the vehicle and position in a suitable holding fixture. Remove the engine oil dipstick.

4. Remove necessary drive belts and pulleys.

5. Remove the cylinder head.

6. Remove the distributor.

7. Using a magnet, remove the hydraulic lifters and label them so they can be installed in their original positions. If the lifters are stuck in the bores by excessive varnish, etc., use a suitable puller to remove them.

8. Remove the crankshaft pulley.

9. Remove the oil pan.

10. Remove the cylinder front cover and gasket.

11. Check the camshaft endplay as follows:

   a. Push the camshaft toward the rear of the engine and install a dial

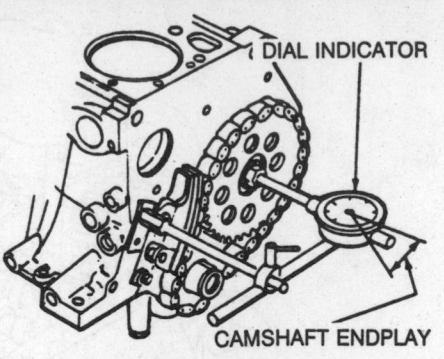

Checking camshaft endplay— 2.3L Engine

indicator tool, so the indicator foot is positioned on the camshaft sprocket attaching bolt.

   b. Zero the dial indicator. Position a small prybar or equivalent, between the camshaft sprocket or gear and block.

   c. Pull the camshaft forward and release it. Compare the dial indicator reading with the camshaft endplay specification of 0.009 in.

   d. If the camshaft endplay is over the amount specified, replace the thrust plate.

12. Remove the timing chain, sprockets and timing chain tensioner.

13. Remove camshaft thrust plate. Carefully remove the camshaft by pulling it toward the front of the engine. Use caution to avoid damaging bearings, journals and lobes.

To install:

14. Clean and inspect all parts before installation.

15. Lubricate camshaft lobes and journals with heavy engine oil. Carefully slide the camshaft through the bearings in the cylinder block.

16. Install the thrust plate. Tighten attaching bolts to 6–9 ft. lbs (8–12 Nm).

17. Install the timing chain, sprockets and timing chain tensioner according to the proper procedure.

18. Install the cylinder front cover and crankshaft pulley.

19. Clean the oil pump inlet tube screen, oil pan and cylinder block gasket surfaces. Prime oil pump by filling the inlet opening with oil and rotate the pump shaft until oil emerges from the outlet tube. Install oil pump, oil pump inlet tube screen and oil pan.

20. Install the accessory drive belts and pulleys.

21. Lubricate the lifters and lifter bores with heavy engine oil. Install lifters into their original bores.

22. Install cylinder head.

23. Position No. 1 piston at TDC after the compression stroke. Position distributor in the block with the rotor at the No. 1 firing position. Install distributor retaining clamp.

24. Install engine in vehicle.
25. Connect engine temperature sending unit wire. Connect coil primary wire. Install distributor cap. Connect spark plug wires and the coil high tension lead.
26. Fill the cooling system and crankcase to the proper levels.
27. Connect negative battery cable.
28. Start the engine. Check and adjust ignition timing. Check for leaks.

3.0L Engine

1. Remove the engine from the vehicle and position on a suitable workstand.
2. Rotate the crankshaft until the piston in No. 1 cylinder is at TDC on the compression stroke.
3. Remove the intake manifold.
4. Remove the lifters.
5. Remove the oil pan.
6. Remove the timing chain cover.
7. Check the camshaft endplay as follows:
    a. Attach a suitable dial indicator to the front of the engine. Position the indicator foot on the camshaft retaining bolt.
    b. Push the camshaft toward the rear of the engine, then zero the dial indicator.
    c. Pull the camshaft forward and release it. Observe the reading on the dial indicator.
    d. If endplay exceeds 0.005 in., replace the thrust plate, then recheck the endplay.
    e. If endplay is still excessive, check the camshaft for excessive wear.
8. Remove the timing chain and sprockets.
9. Remove the 2 camshaft thrust plate retaining bolts and the thrust plate.
10. Remove the camshaft by pulling it slowly toward the front of the engine, being careful not to damage the camshaft bearings, journals or lobes.
To install:
11. Clean all gasket mating surfaces. Clean and inspect all components and replace, as necessary.
12. Lubricate the camshaft lobes, journals and distributor drive gear with clean engine oil. Carefully slide the camshaft through the bearings into the cylinder block.
13. Lubricate the camshaft thrust plate with clean engine oil and install with the 2 retaining bolts. Tighten the bolts to 7 ft. lbs. (10 Nm).
14. Install the timing chain and sprockets.
15. Install the timing chain cover.
16. Install the oil pan.
17. Install the lifters.
18. Install the intake manifold, pushrods, rocker arms, rocker arm covers and distributor.

19. Install the engine assembly in the vehicle.
20. Fill the crankcase with the proper type and quantity of engine oil. Fill and bleed the cooling system.
21. Start the engine and check for coolant, oil, exhaust, vacuum and fuel leaks. Check and, if necessary, adjust the timing.

Piston and Connecting Rod

Positioning

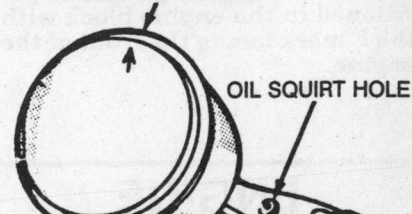

Piston and rod assembly—2.3L Engine

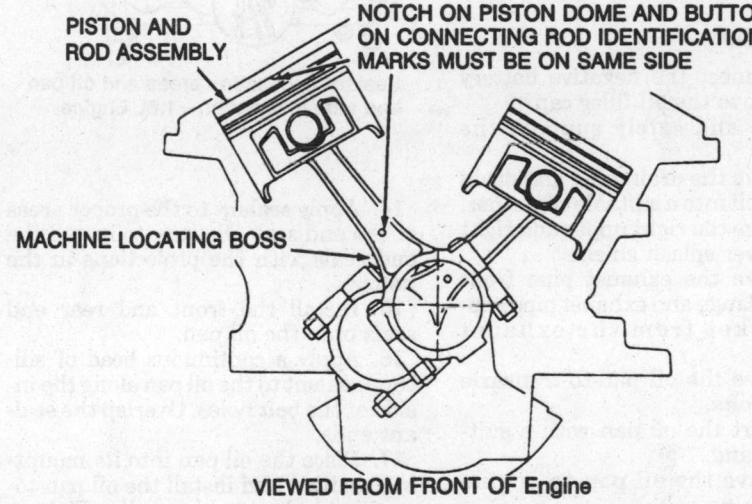

Piston and rod assembly—3.0L Engine

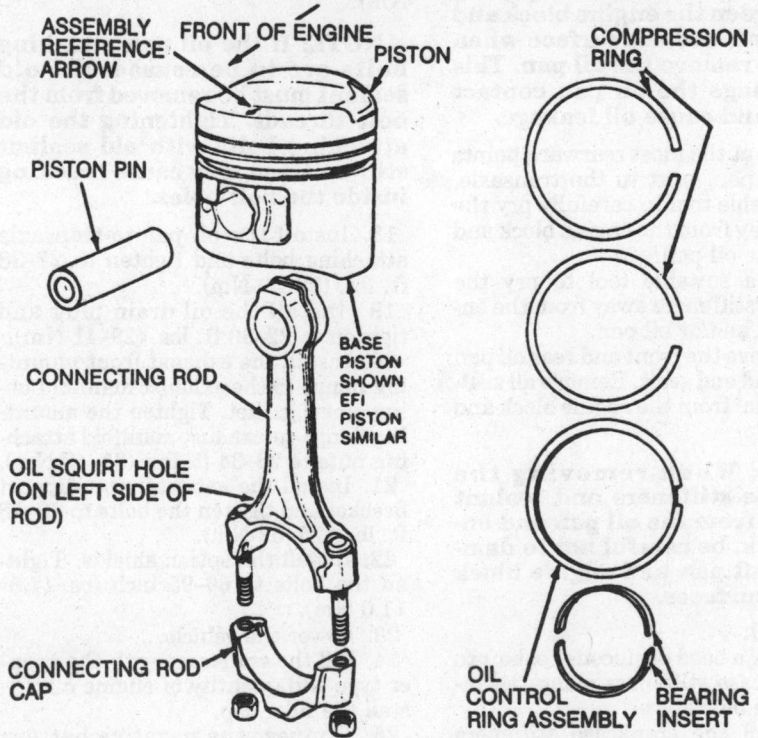

Piston and rod assembly—1.9L Engine

NOTE: On 1.8L engine, the piston and rod assembly must be positioned in the engine block with the F mark facing the front of the engine.

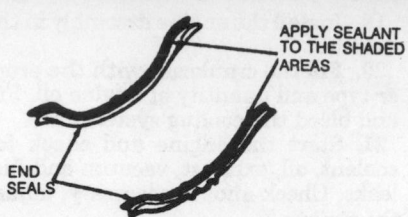

APPLY SEALANT TO THE SHADED AREAS

END SEALS

ENGINE LUBRICATION

Oil Pan

REMOVAL & INSTALLATION

1.8L Engine

1. Disconnect the negative battery cable. Remove the oil filler cap.
2. Raise and safely support the vehicle.
3. Remove the drain plug and drain the engine oil into a suitable container.
4. Remove the right upper and right and left lower splash shields.
5. Remove the exhaust pipe front mounting flange and exhaust pipe support bracket from the exhaust manifold.
6. Remove the oil pan-to-transaxle attaching bolts.
7. Support the oil pan with a suitable jack stand.
8. Remove the oil pan-to-engine block attaching bolts.

NOTE: Do not force a prying tool between the engine block and the oil pan contact surface when trying to remove the oil pan. This may damage the oil pan contact surface and cause oil leakage.

9. Only at the most rearward points of the oil pan, next to the transaxle, use a suitable tool to carefully pry the oil pan away from the engine block and remove the oil pan.
10. Use a suitable tool to pry the crankcase stiffeners away from the engine block and/or oil pan.
11. Remove the front and rear oil pan gaskets and end seals. Remove all sealant material from the engine block and oil pan.

NOTE: When removing the crankcase stiffeners and sealant material from the oil pan and engine block, be careful not to damage the oil pan and engine block contact surfaces.

To install:
12. Apply a bead of silicone sealant to the crankcase stiffeners along the inside of the bolt holes.
13. Install the crankcase stiffeners onto the oil pan.

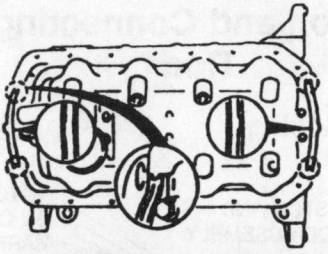

Sealant application areas and oil pan end seal installation — 1.8L Engine

14. Apply sealant to the proper areas of the end seals. Be sure to install the end seals with the projections in the notches.
15. Install the front and rear end seals onto the oil pan.
16. Apply a continuous bead of silicone sealant to the oil pan along the inside of the bolt holes. Overlap the sealant ends.
17. Place the oil pan into its mounting position and install the oil pan-to-engine block attaching bolts. Tighten the bolts to 69–95 inch lbs. (7.8–11.0 Nm).

NOTE: If the oil pan attaching bolts are to be reused, the old sealant must be removed from the bolt threads. Tightening the old attaching bolts with old sealant still on them may cause cracking inside the bolt holes.

18. Install the oil pan-to-transaxle attaching bolts and tighten to 27–38 ft. lbs. (37–52 Nm).
19. Install the oil drain plug and tighten to 22–30 ft. lbs. (29–41 Nm).
20. Install the exhaust front mounting flange to the exhaust manifold using a new gasket. Tighten the mounting flange-to-exhaust manifold attaching nuts to 23–34 ft. lbs. (31–46 Nm).
21. Install the exhaust pipe support bracket and tighten the bolts to 27–38 ft. lbs. (37–52 Nm).
22. Install the splash shields. Tighten the bolts to 69–95 inch lbs. (7.8–11.0 Nm).
23. Lower the vehicle.
24. Fill the crankcase with the proper type and quantity of engine oil. Install the filler cap.
25. Connect the negative battery cable.

1.9L Engine

1. Disconnect negative battery cable.
2. Raise the vehicle and support safely.
3. Drain the crankcase.
4. On 1989–90 vehicles, disconnect cable at the starter, remove starter-brace located at the front of the starter and remove starter attaching bolts and starter.
5. Remove the 2 oil pan-to-transaxle bolts.
6. Disconnect the exhaust inlet pipe at the manifold and converter. Remove pipe.
7. Remove oil pan retaining bolts and oil pan.
8. Remove oil pan gasket and discard.

To install:
9. Clean the oil pan gasket surface and the mating surface on the cylinder block. Wipe the oil pan rail with a solvent-soaked cloth to remove oil traces.
10. Remove and clean the oil pump pick up tube and screen assembly. Install tube and screen assembly using a new gasket.
11. Apply a bead of silicone rubber sealer at the corner of the block and at the seating point of the oil pump and the rear seal retainer joint.
12. Install the gasket in oil pan ensuring press fit tabs are fully engaged in oil pan gasket channel.
13. Install the oil pan and the attaching bolts. Tighten the bolts lightly until the 2 oil pan-to-transmission bolts can be installed.

NOTE: If the oil pan is installed on the engine outside of the vehicle, a transaxle case or equivalent fixture must be bolted to the block to line the oil pan up, flush with the rear face of the block.

14. Tighten the 2 pan-to-transaxle bolts to 30–40 ft. lbs. (40–54 Nm), then loosen ½ turn.
15. Tighten the oil pan flange-to-cylinder block bolts to 15–22 ft. lbs. (20–30 Nm) in the proper sequence. Retighten the 2 oil pan-to-transaxle bolts to 30–40 ft. lbs. (40–55 Nm).
16. Install the transaxle inspection plate.
17. On 1989–90 vehicles, install the starter, starter brace at the starter and connect the starter cable.
18. Install the exhaust inlet pipe. Lower the vehicle and fill the crankcase with the proper type and quantity of engine oil.
19. Connect negative battery cable.
20. Start the engine and check for oil leaks.

2.3L Engine

1. Disconnect the negative battery

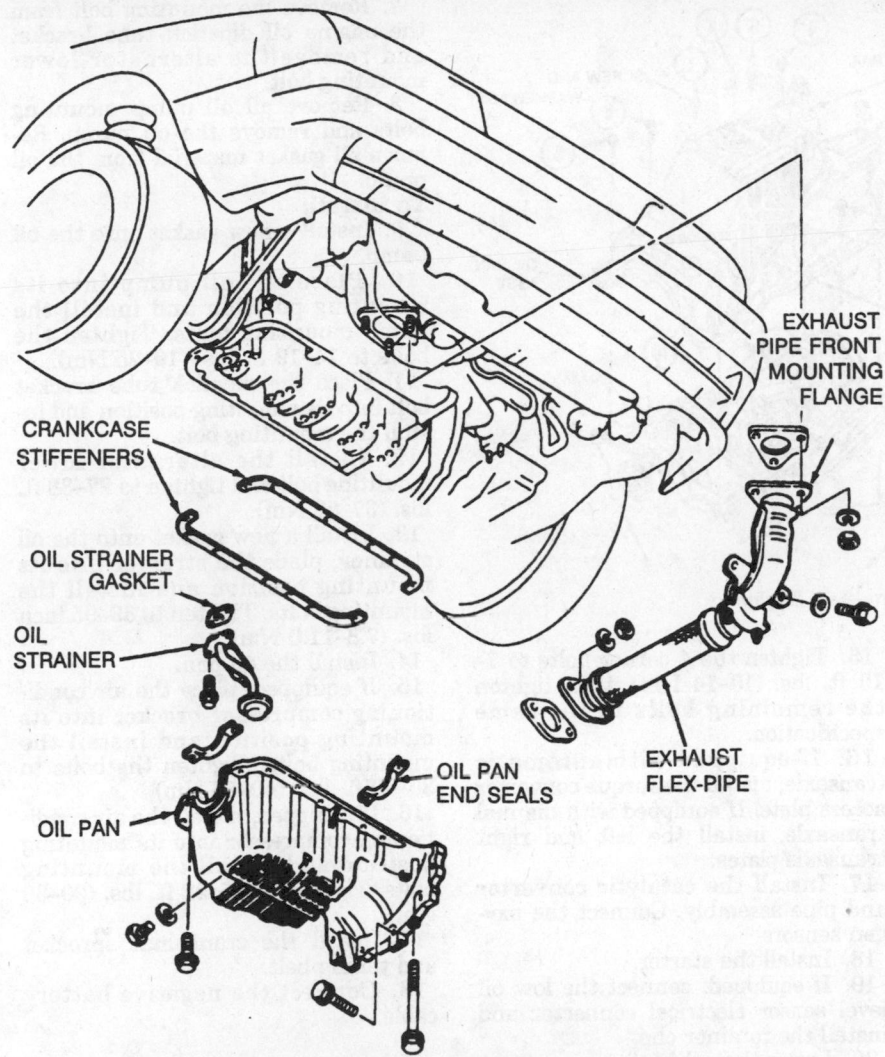

Oil pan removal and installation—1.8L Engine

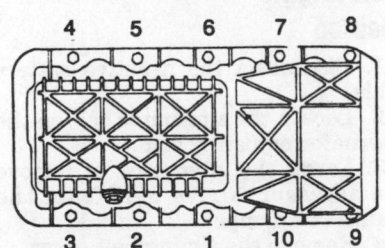

Oil pan attaching bolt torque sequence—1989–90 1.9L Engine

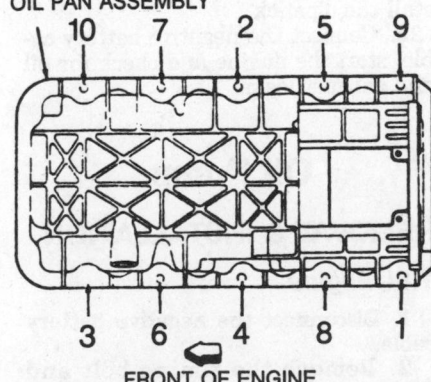

FRONT OF ENGINE

Oil pan attaching bolt torque sequence—1991–93 1.9L Engine

cable. Raise the vehicle and support safely.

2. Drain the crankcase and drain the cooling system by removing the lower radiator hose.

3. Remove the roll restrictor on manual transaxle equipped vehicles.

4. Disconnect the starter cable.

5. Remove the starter.

6. Disconnect the exhaust pipe from oil pan.

7. Remove the engine coolant tube from the lower radiator hose, water

pump and at the tabs on the oil pan. Position air conditioner line off to the side. Remove the retaining bolts and remove the oil pan.

To install:

8. Clean both mating surfaces of oil pan and cylinder block making certain

all traces of RTV sealant are removed. Ensure that the block rails, front cover and rear cover retainer are also clean.

9. Remove and clean oil pump pick-up tube and screen assembly. After cleaning, install tube and screen assembly.

10. Apply RTV E8AZ–19562–A Sealer or equivalent, in oil pan groove. Completely fill oil pan groove with sealer. Sealer bead should be 0.200 in. (5mm) wide and 0.080–0.150 in. (2.0–3.8mm) high (above oil pan surface) in all areas except the half-rounds. The half-rounds should have a bead 0.200 in. (5mm) wide and 0.150–0.200 in. (3.8–5.1mm) high, above the oil pan surface.

NOTE: **Applying RTV in excess of the specified amount will not improve the sealing of the oil pan, and could cause the oil pickup screen to become clogged with sealer. Use adequate ventilation when applying sealer.**

11. Install oil pan to cylinder block within 5 minutes to prevent skinning over. RTV needs to cure completely before coming in contact with any engine oil, about 1 hour at ambient temperature between 65–75°F.

12. Install oil pan bolts lightly until the 2 oil pan-to-transmission bolts can be installed.

NOTE: **If oil pan is installed on engine outside of vehicle, a transaxle case or equivalent, fixture must be bolted to the block to lin the oil pan up, flush with the rear face of block.**

13. Install 2 oil pan-to-transaxle bolts. Tighten to 30–39 ft. lbs. (40–54 Nm) to align oil pan with transaxle. Loosen bolts ½ turn.

14. Tighten all oil pan flange bolts to 15–22 ft. lbs. (20–30 Nm).

15. Tighten 2 oil pan-to-transmission bolts to 30–39 ft. lbs. (40–54 Nm).

16. If required, rework exhaust bracket to fit to oil pan.

17. Replace water inlet tube O-ring and install tube.

18. Install roll restrictor, if equipped.

19. Lower vehicle.

20. Fill the crankcase with the proper type and quantity of engine oil. Fill and bleed the cooling system.

21. Connect negative battery cable.

22. Start engine and check for coolant and oil leaks.

3.0L Engine

1. Disconnect the negative battery cable.

2. Remove the engine oil dipstick.

3. Raise and safely support the vehicle.

4. If equipped, remove the low oil

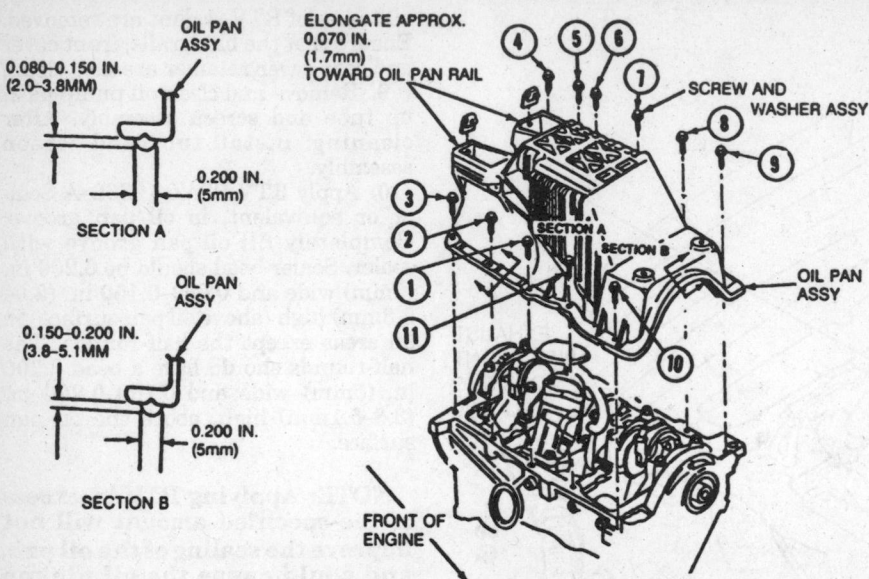

Oil pan Installation—2.3L Engine

level sensor retainer clip and disconnect the electrical connector at the sensor.

5. Drain the engine oil from the crankcase into a suitable container.

6. Remove the starter.

7. Disconnect the exhaust gas oxygen sensors.

8. Remove the catalytic converter and exhaust pipe assembly.

9. If equipped with automatic transaxle, remove the torque converter access plate from the transaxle. If equipped with manual transaxle, remove the left and right transaxle support plates.

10. Remove the oil pan retaining bolts and remove the oil pan, making sure the internal pan baffle does not snag on the oil pump pickup tube and screen. Remove and discard the oil pan gasket.

To install:

11. Clean the oil pan and all gasket mating surfaces.

12. Install a new oil pan gasket on the cylinder block using the retaining features and a suitable gasket adhesive. Snug retaining bolts at the 4 corners and 2 middle places on the cylinder block to support the gasket until the adhesive cures.

13. Apply a $3/16$ in. bead of silicone sealer to the junction of the rear main bearing cap and cylinder block and the junction of the front cover and cylinder block.

NOTE: Do not let the sealer cure longer than 4 minutes prior to oil pan installation or 7 total minutes before bolts are tightened to specification.

14. Position the oil pan and install the retaining bolts, hand tight.

15. Tighten the 4 corner bolts to 7–10 ft. lbs. (10–14 Nm), then tighten the remaining bolts to the same specification.

16. If equipped with automatic transaxle, install the torque converter access plate. If equipped with manual transaxle, install the left and right transaxle plates.

17. Install the catalytic converter and pipe assembly. Connect the oxygen sensors.

18. Install the starter.

19. If equipped, connect the low oil level sensor electrical connector and install the retainer clip.

20. Lower the vehicle.

21. Fill the crankcase with the proper type and quantity of engine oil. Install the dipstick.

22. Connect the negative battery cable, start the engine and check for oil and exhaust leaks.

Oil Pump

REMOVAL & INSTALLATION

1.8L Engine

1. Disconnect the negative battery cable.

2. Remove the timing belt and crankshaft sprocket.

3. Remove the oil pan.

4. Remove the oil strainer mounting bolts and remove the oil strainer and gasket.

5. If equipped, remove the air conditioning compressor mounting bolts and position the compressor so it is free from the work area.

6. Remove the air conditioning compressor mounting bracket.

7. Remove the mounting bolt from the engine oil dipstick tube bracket and remove the alternator lower mounting bolt.

8. Remove all oil pump mounting bolts and remove the oil pump. Remove all gasket material from the oil pump.

To install:

9. Install a new gasket onto the oil pump.

10. Place the oil pump into its mounting position and install the pump mounting bolts. Tighten the bolts to 14–19 ft. lbs. (19–25 Nm).

11. Place the dipstick tube bracket bolt into its mounting position and install the mounting bolt.

12. Install the alternator lower mounting bolt and tighten to 27–38 ft. lbs. (37–52 Nm).

13. Install a new gasket onto the oil strainer, place the strainer into its mounting position and install the mounting bolts. Tighten to 69–95 inch lbs. (7.8–11.0 Nm).

14. Install the oil pan.

15. If equipped, place the air conditioning compressor bracket into its mounting position and install the mounting bolts. Tighten the bolts to 30–40 ft. lbs. (40–55 Nm).

16. If equipped, install the air conditioning compressor into its mounting position and install the mounting bolts. Tighten to 15–22 ft. lbs. (20–30 Nm).

17. Install the crankshaft sprocket and timing belt.

18. Connect the negative battery cable.

1.9L Engine

1989–90

1. Disconnect the negative battery cable.

2. Loosen the alternator bolt on the alternator adjusting arm.

3. Lower the alternator to remove the accessory drive belt from the crankshaft damper.

4. Remove the timing belt cover.

5. Set No. 1 cylinder at TDC. Loosen both belt tensioner attaching bolts. Using a prybar or other suitable tool, pry the tensioner away from the belt. While holding the tensioner away from the belt, tighten one of the tensioner attaching bolts.

6. Disengage timing belt from camshaft sprocket, water pump sprocket and crankshaft sprocket.

7. Raise and safely support the vehicle.

8. Drain the crankcase.

9. Properly support the engine, then remove the right side engine mount bolt. Lower the engine at the right side until the crankshaft damper

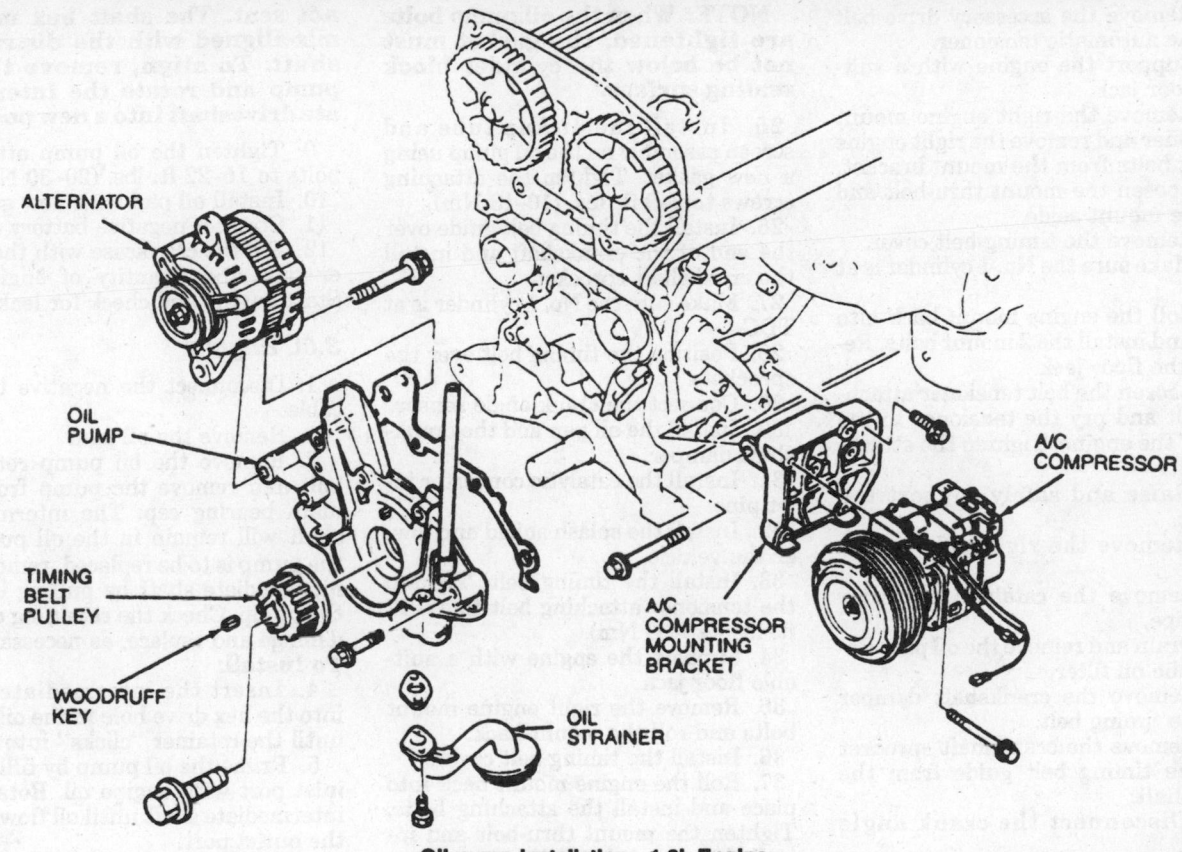

ALTERNATOR

OIL PUMP

TIMING BELT PULLEY

WOODRUFF KEY

A/C COMPRESSOR

A/C COMPRESSOR MOUNTING BRACKET

OIL STRAINER

Oil pump Installation—1.8L Engine

bolt clears the frame rail. Remove the crankshaft damper attaching bolt.

10. Remove the timing belt.

11. Remove the crankshaft driveplate assembly.

12. Remove the crankshaft damper.

13. Remove the crankshaft sprocket.

14. Disconnect the starter cable at the starter.

15. Remove the starter-brace from the engine.

16. Remove the starter.

17. Remove 2 oil pan-to-transaxle bolts.

18. Remove oil pan retaining bolts and oil pan.

19. Remove the 1 piece oil pan gasket.

20. Remove oil pump attaching bolts.

21. Remove oil pump and gasket.

22. Remove oil pump seal.

To install:

23. Make sure the mating surfaces on the cylinder block and the oil pump are clean and free of gasket material.

24. Remove the oil pickup tube and screen assembly from the pump for cleaning.

25. Lubricate the outside diameter of the oil pump seal with clean engine oil.

26. Install the oil pump seal using a suitable seal installer tool.

27. Install pickup tube and screen assembly on the oil pump using a new

gasket. Tighten attaching bolts to 6–9 ft. lbs (8–12 Nm).

28. Lubricate the oil pump seal lip with light engine oil.

29. Position the oil pump gasket over the locating dowels.

30. Prime the oil pump, then position it on the engine. Install attaching bolts and tighten to 6–8 ft. lbs. (8–11 Nm).

31. Apply a bead of sealer approximately ⅛ in. (3.0mm) wide at the corners of the block and at the seating point of the oil pump and the rear seal retainer joint.

32. Install gasket in oil pan ensuring press fit tabs are fully engaged in the oil pan gasket channel.

33. Position the oil pan on the cylinder block. Install oil pan attaching bolts. Tighten lightly until 2 oil pan-to-transmission bolts can be installed.

NOTE: If oil pan is installed on engine outside of vehicle, a transaxle case or equivalent, fixture must be bolted to the block to lin the oil pan up, flush with the rear face of block.

34. Install transaxle inspection plate.

35. Tighten two pan-to-transaxle bolts to 30–40 ft. lbs. (40–54 Nm), then loosen ½ turn.

36. Tighten oil pan flange-to-cylin-

der block bolts to 15–22 ft. lbs. (20–30 Nm).

37. Tighten 2 pan-to-transaxle bolts to 30–40 ft. lbs. (40–54 Nm).

38. Install starter, starter-brace and connect the starter cable.

39. Install crankshaft sprocket and crankshaft damper. Install the crankshaft driveplate assembly.

40. Install timing belt over the crankshaft damper and camshaft.

41. Lower the engine until the crankshaft damper clears the frame and install the damper bolt. Tighten to 81–96 ft. lbs. (110–130 Nm). Raise the engine into position and install the right side engine mount bolt.

42. Lower the vehicle and install the engine front timing cover.

43. Position the accessory drive belts over the alternator and crankshaft damper and tighten.

44. Connect the negative battery cable and fill the crankcase with the proper type and quantity of engine oil.

45. Start the engine and check for oil leaks. Make sure the oil pressure indicator light goes out. If the light remains on, immediately shut OFF the engine and determine the cause.

1991–93

1. Disconnect the negative battery cable.

2. Remove the accessory drive belt and the automatic tensioner.

3. Support the engine with a suitable floor jack.

4. Remove the right engine mount dampener and remove the right engine mount bolts from the mount bracket.

5. Loosen the mount thru-bolt and roll the mount aside.

6. Remove the timing belt cover.

7. Make sure the No. 1 cylinder is at TDC.

8. Roll the engine mount back into place and install the 2 mount bolts. Remove the floor jack.

9. Loosen the belt tensioner attaching bolt and pry the tensioner to the rear of the engine. Tighten the attaching bolt.

10. Raise and safely support the vehicle.

11. Remove the right side splash shield.

12. Remove the catalytic converter inlet pipe.

13. Drain and remove the oil pan. Remove the oil filter.

14. Remove the crankshaft damper and the timing belt.

15. Remove the crankshaft sprocket and the timing belt guide from the crankshaft.

16. Disconnect the crank angle sensor.

17. Remove the 6 oil pump-to-engine bolts and remove the oil pump assembly from the engine. Remove and discard the gasket.

18. Remove the crankshaft seal from the pump and discard.

To install:

19. Make sure the pump mating surfaces on the cylinder block and oil pump are clean and free of gasket material.

20. Remove the oil pickup tube and screen assembly from the pump for cleaning.

21. Lubricate the outside diameter of the crankshaft seal with engine oil and install the seal with a suitable installation tool. Lubricate the seal lip with engine oil.

22. Position the oil pump gasket on the cylinder block.

23. Prime the oil pump with engine oil and position the pump over the crankshaft. Using a suitable tool, position the pump drive gear to allow the pump to pilot over the crankshaft and seat firmly on the cylinder block.

NOTE: The pump drive gear can be accessed through the oil pickup hole in the body of the pump. Do not install the oil pump pickup tube and screen until the pump has been correctly installed on the cylinder block.

24. Install the 6 oil pump bolts and tighten to 8–12 ft. lbs. (11–16 Nm).

NOTE: When the oil pump bolts are tightened, the gasket must not be below the cylinder block sealing surface.

25. Install the pickup tube and screen assembly on the oil pump using a new gasket. Tighten the attaching screws to 7–9 ft. lbs. (10–13 Nm).

26. Install the timing belt guide over the end of the crankshaft and install the crankshaft sprocket.

27. Make sure the No. 1 cylinder is at TDC.

28. Position the timing belt over the sprockets.

29. Connect the crank angle sensor.

30. Install the oil pan and the crankshaft damper.

31. Install the catalytic converter inlet pipe.

32. Install the splash shield and lower the vehicle.

33. Install the timing belt. Tighten the tensioner attaching bolt to 17–22 ft. lbs. (23–30 Nm).

34. Support the engine with a suitable floor jack.

35. Remove the right engine mount bolts and roll the mount back.

36. Install the timing belt cover.

37. Roll the engine mount back into place and install the attaching bolts. Tighten the mount thru-bolt and install the mount damper.

38. Remove the floor jack.

39. Install the accessory drive belt automatic tensioner and the accessory drive belt.

40. Fill the crankcase with the proper type and quantity of engine oil.

41. Connect the negative battery cable, start the engine and check for leaks.

2.3L Engine

1. Disconnect the negative battery cable.

2. Raise and safely support the vehicle.

3. Remove oil pan.

4. Remove oil pump attaching bolts and remove oil pump and intermediate driveshaft.

To install:

5. Prime oil pump by filling inlet port with engine oil. Rotate pump shaft until oil flows from outlet port.

6. If screen and cover assembly have been removed, replace gasket. Clean screen and reinstall screen and cover assembly and tighten attaching bolts and nut.

7. Position intermediate driveshaft into distributor socket.

8. Insert intermediate driveshaft into oil pump. Install pump and shaft as an assembly.

NOTE: Do not attempt to force the pump into position if it will

not seat. The shaft hex may be mis-aligned with the distributor shaft. To align, remove the oil pump and rotate the intermediate driveshaft into a new position.

9. Tighten the oil pump attaching bolts to 15–22 ft. lbs. (20–30 Nm).

10. Install oil pan with new gasket.

11. Connect negative battery cable.

12. Fill the crankcase with the proper type and quantity of engine oil. Start engine and check for leaks.

3.0L Engine

1. Disconnect the negative battery cable.

2. Remove the oil pan.

3. Remove the oil pump retaining bolt and remove the pump from the main bearing cap. The intermediate shaft will remain in the oil pump. If the pump is to be replaced, remove the intermediate shaft by pulling it from the pump. Check the retaining clip for damage and replace, as necessary.

To install:

4. Insert the intermediate shaft into the hex drive hole in the oil pump until the retainer "clicks" into place.

5. Prime the oil pump by filling the inlet port with engine oil. Rotate the intermediate shaft until oil flows from the outlet port.

6. Install the oil pump with the intermediate shaft through the intermediate shaft hole in the rear main bearing cap. Position the pump over the locating pins.

7. Install the retaining bolt and tighten to 30–40 ft. lbs. (40–55 Nm).

8. Install the oil pan.

9. Fill the crankcase with the proper type and quantity of engine oil.

10. Connect the negative battery cable. Start the engine and check for leaks.

CHECKING

1.8L Engine

1. Remove the oil pump from the vehicle.

2. Disassemble the pump, clean all parts with a suitable solvent and allow to dry.

3. Use a suitable feeler gauge to check the outer rotor tooth tip clearance. The maximum allowable clearance is 0.0079 in. (0.20mm).

4. Use a suitable feeler gauge to inspect the outer rotor-to-pump body clearance. The maximum allowable clearance is 0.0087 in. (0.22mm).

5. Use a straightedge and a feeler gauge to inspect the oil pump side clearance. The maximum allowable side clearance is 0.0055 in. (0.14mm).

6. Inspect the pressure spring for breakage or weak retraction. Inspect

the pressure spring free length; it should be 1.791 in. (45.5mm).

7. If the pump is damaged or tolerances are not within specification, replace the oil pump.

1.9L Engine

1. Remove the oil pump from the vehicle.

2. Disassemble the pump, clean all parts with a suitable solvent and allow to dry.

3. Use a suitable feeler gauge to check the inner-to-outer gear tip clearance. The maximum allowable clearance is 0.007 in. (0.18mm).

4. Use a suitable feeler gauge to inspect the outer gear-to-housing clearance. The maximum allowable clearance is 0.0063 in. (0.161mm).

5. Use a straightedge and a feeler gauge to inspect the inner and outer gear-to-cover clearance (endplay). The maximum allowable clearance is 0.0035 in. (0.089mm).

6. Inspect the relief valve spring for breakage or weak retraction. The spring tension should be 9.3–10.3 lbs. (41.4–45.8 N) at 1.11 in. (28.1mm).

7. If the pump is damaged or tolerances are not within specification, replace the oil pump.

2.3L and 3.0L Engines

1. Remove the oil pump from the vehicle.

2. Disassemble the pump and clean all parts in solvent. Allow to dry.

3. Inspect the inside of the pump housing for damage or excessive wear.

4. Check the mating surface for wear. Minor scuff marks are normal, but if the cover, gears or housing are excessively worn, scored or grooved, replace the pump.

5. Inspect the rotor for nicks, burrs or score marks. Remove minor imperfections with an oil stone.

6. Measure the inner-to-outer rotor tip clearance. The clearance must not exceed 0.012 in. (0.30mm) with a feeler gauge inserted ½ in. minimum with the rotors removed from the pump housing.

7. With the rotor assembly installed in the housing, place a straightedge across the rotor assembly and housing. Measure the rotor endplay or clearance, between the straightedge and both the inner rotor and outer race. Maximum clearance must not exceed 0.005 in. (0.13mm).

8. Check the relief valve spring tension. On the 2.3L engine, the tension should be 14.2–16.2 lbs. (63.5–72.1 N) at 1.2 in. (30.4mm). On the 3.0L engine, the tension should be 9.1–10.1 lbs. (40.5–44.9 N) at 1.11 in. (28.2mm). If the spring is worn or

damaged, replace the pump. Check the relief valve piston for freedom of movement in the bore.

9. If the pump is damaged or tolerances are not within specification, replace the oil pump.

Rear Main Bearing Oil Seal

REMOVAL & INSTALLATION

1.8L Engine

1. Disconnect the negative battery cable.

2. Remove the transaxle assembly.

3. If equipped with manual transaxle, remove the clutch disc and pressure plate assembly. Remove the flywheel.

4. If necessary, remove the rear cover mounting bolts and remove the rear cover.

5. Using a suitable prybar, remove the crankshaft rear oil seal. Be careful not to damage the crankshaft seal surface or seal housing.

To install:

6. If removed, install the rear cover and attaching bolts. Tighten the bolts to 69–95 inch lbs. (7.8–11.0 Nm).

7. Lubricate the lip of a new seal and install, using a suitable installation tool.

8. Install the flywheel. Tighten the flywheel bolts to 71–76 ft. lbs. (96–103 Nm).

9. Install the transaxle.

10. Connect the negative battery cable.

1.9L Engine

1. Disconnect the negative battery cable.

2. Raise the vehicle and support it safely. Remove the transaxle.

3. Remove flywheel and the engine cover plate.

4. With a suitable tool, remove the oil seal.

NOTE: Use caution to avoid damaging the oil seal surface.

To install:

5. Inspect the crankshaft seal area for any damage which may cause the seal to leak. If damage is evident, service or replace the crankshaft, as necessary.

6. Coat the crankshaft seal area and the seal lip with engine oil.

7. Using a suitable seal installer tool, install the seal.

8. Install the engine cover plate and the flywheel. Tighten the flywheel attaching bolts to 54–64 ft. lbs. (73–87 Nm).

9. Install the transaxle assembly.

10. Connect the negative battery ca-

ble, start the engine and check for leaks.

2.3L Engine

1. Disconnect the negative battery cable.

2. Remove transaxle.

3. Remove flywheel.

4. Remove rear cover plate.

5. Insert a suitable tool into seal cavity and pry out old seal.

NOTE: Use caution to avoid damaging the oil seal surface.

To install:

6. Inspect the crankshaft seal area for any damage which may cause the seal to leak. If damage is evident, service or replace the crankshaft, as necessary.

7. Coat the crankshaft seal area and the seal lip with engine oil.

8. Using a suitable seal installer tool, install the seal.

9. Install rear cover plate and 2 dowels.

10. Install the flywheel. Tighten attaching bolts to 54–64 ft. lbs. (73–87 Nm).

11. Install the transaxle assembly.

12. Connect the negative battery cable, start the engine and check for leaks.

3.0L Engine

1. Remove the engine and position on a suitable workstand.

2. Using a sharp awl, punch a hole into the seal metal surface between the lip and the block. Thread a screw into the hole and remove the seal, using a slide hammer.

NOTE: Use care to prevent scratching or damaging the oil seal surface.

To install:

3. Apply clean engine oil to the outer lips and inner edge of a new seal.

4. Install the seal, using suitable seal installer.

5. Install the engine.

ENGINE COOLING

Radiator

REMOVAL & INSTALLATION

Except 1991–93 Escort

1. Disconnect the negative battery cable. Remove the radiator cap.

---— **CAUTION** ——

Never remove the radiator cap while the engine is running or personal injury from scalding hot coolant or steam may result. If possible, wait until the engine has cooled to remove the radiator cap. If this is not possible, wrap a thick cloth around the radiator cap and turn it slowly to the first stop. Step back while the pressure is released from the cooling system. When it is certain all the pressure has been released, press down on the cap, still with the cloth, and turn and remove it.

---

2. Position a suitable container under the radiator and open the draincock to drain the radiator.

3. On the the Escort, remove the air intake tube from the radiator support.

4. Remove the upper hose from the radiator.

5. Remove the 2 fasteners retaining the upper end of the fan shroud to the radiator.

NOTE: If equipped with air conditioning, remove the nut and screw retaining the upper end of the fan shroud to the radiator at the cross support and nut and screw at the inlet end of the tank.

6. Disconnect the electric cooling fan motor wires and air conditioning discharge line, if equipped, from the shroud and remove the fan shroud from the vehicle.

7. Loosen the hose clamp and disconnect the radiator lower hose from the radiator.

8. Disconnect the overflow hose from the radiator filler neck.

9. If equipped with an automatic transaxle, disconnect the oil cooler hoses at the transaxle using quick-disconnect tool T82L-9500-AH or equivalent. Cap the oil tubes and plug the oil cooler hoses.

10. Remove the 2 nuts retaining the top of the radiator to the radiator support. If the stud loosens, make sure it is tightened before the radiator is installed. Tilt the top of the radiator rearward to allow clearance with the upper mounting stud and lift the radiator from the vehicle. Make sure the mounts do not stick to the radiator lower mounting brackets.

To install:
11. Make sure the lower radiator isomounts are installed over the bolts on the radiator support.

12. Position the radiator to the radiator support making sure the radiator lower brackets are positioned properly on the lower mounts.

13. Position the top of the radiator to the mounting studs on the radiator support and install 2 retaining nuts. Tighten to 5–7 ft. lbs. (7–9.5 Nm).

14. Connect the radiator lower hose to the engine water pump inlet tube. Install the hose clamp between alignment marks on the hose.

15. Check to make sure the radiator lower hose is properly positioned on the outlet tank and install the hose clamp. The stripe on the lower hose should be indexed with the rib on the tank outlet.

16. Connect the oil cooler hoses to the automatic transaxle oil cooler lines, if equipped. Use an appropriate oil resistant sealer.

17. Position the fan shroud to the radiator lower mounting bosses. On 1989–91 vehicles with air conditioning, insert the lower edge of the shroud into the clip at the lower center of the radiator. Install 2 screws or nuts and bolts retaining the upper end of the fan shroud to the radiator. Tighten the fasteners on Tempo/Topaz to 35–41 inch lbs. (3.9–4.6 Nm). On Escort, tighten to 23–33 inch lbs. (2.6–3.7 Nm). Do not overtighten.

18. Connect the electric cooling fan motor wires to the wire harness.

19. Connect the upper hose to the radiator inlet tank fitting and install the hose clamp.

20. Connect the overflow hose to the nipple just below the radiator filler neck.

21. Install the air intake tube, if necessary.

22. Connect the negative battery cable.

23. Refill the cooling system. Start the engine and allow to come to normal operating temperature. Check for leaks. Confirm the operation of the electric cooling fan.

1991–93 Escort

1. Disconnect the negative battery cable. Remove the radiator cap.

---— **CAUTION** ——

Never remove the radiator cap while the engine is running or personal injury from scalding hot coolant or steam may result. If possible, wait until the engine has cooled to remove the radiator cap. If this is not possible, wrap a thick cloth around the radiator cap and turn it slowly to the first stop. Step back while the pressure is released from the cooling system. When it is certain all the pressure has been released, press down on the cap, still with the cloth, and turn and remove it.

---

2. Position a suitable container under the radiator and open the draincock to drain the radiator.

3. Raise and safely support the vehicle.

4. Remove the right side and front splash shields and remove the lower radiator hose.

5. If equipped with automatic transaxle, remove the lower oil cooler line from the radiator. Remove the oil cooler line brackets from the bottom of the radiator.

6. Lower the vehicle.

7. If equipped with automatic transaxle and air conditioning, remove the seal located between the radiator and fan shroud.

8. If equipped with automatic transaxle, remove the upper oil cooler line from the radiator.

9. If equipped with 1.8L engine, remove the resonance duct from the radiator isomounts.

10. Disconnect the cooling fan motor electrical connector and the cooling fan thermoswitch electrical connector.

11. Remove the 3 fan shroud attaching bolts and remove the shroud assembly by pulling it straight up.

12. Remove the upper radiator hose and the 2 upper radiator isomounts. Remove the radiator by lifting it straight up.

To install:
13. Make sure the radiator lower isomounts are installed over the bolts on the radiator support.

14. Position the radiator to the radiator support, making sure the radiator lower brackets are positioned properly on the lower isomounts.

15. Install the radiator upper isomounts, making sure the radiator locating pegs are positioned correctly. Install the upper radiator hose.

16. Lower the cooling fan shroud assembly into place and install the 3 shroud attaching bolts.

17. Connect the cooling fan motor electrical connector and thermoswitch electrical connector.

18. If equipped with 1.8L engine, install the resonance duct on the radiator isomounts.

19. Install the upper oil cooler line on the radiator.

20. If equipped with automatic transaxle and air conditioning, install the seal between the radiator and fan shroud.

21. Raise and safely support the vehicle. If equipped with automatic transaxle, install the lower oil cooler line on the radiator.

22. Install the lower radiator hose and install the right side and front splash shields.

23. Lower the vehicle and fill the cooling system.

24. Connect the negative battery cable, start the engine and check for coolant leaks.

Electric Cooling Fan

TESTING

Except 1991–93 Escort

1. Check the fuse or circuit breaker for power to the cooling fan motor.

2. Remove the connector(s) at the cooling fan motor(s). Connect a jumper wire and apply battery voltage to the positive terminal of the cooling fan motor.

3. Using an ohmmeter, check for continuity in the cooling fan motor.

NOTE: Remove the cooling fan connector at the fan motor before performing continuity checks. Perform continuity check of the motor windings only. The cooling fan control circuit is connected electrically to the ECM through the cooling fan relay center. Ohmmeter battery voltage must not be applied to the ECM.

4. Ensure proper continuity of the cooling fan motor ground circuit at the chassis ground connector.

1991–93 Escort

1. Make sure the ignition key is OFF.

2. Apply 12 volts to the **Y** wire at the cooling fan motor on all except 1.8L engine vehicles equipped with 4EAT automatic transaxle or 1.9L engine vehicles equipped with air conditioning. Replace the motor if it does not run.

3. On 1.8L engine vehicles equipped with 4EAT automatic transaxle or 1.9L engine vehicles equipped with air conditioning, apply 12 volts to the **BL** wire on the 1.8L engine or the **LG/Y** wire on the 1.9L engine at the cooling fan motor. Replace the motor if it does not run.

REMOVAL & INSTALLATION

Except 1991–93 Escort

NOTE: On 1992–93 Tempo and Topaz, the cooling fan motors for the 2.3L and 3.0L engines are similar in design, but cannot be interchanged. If the incorrect fan motor is installed, the vehicle may overheat or the fan motor may burnout.

1. Disconnect the negative battery cable.

2. Disconnect the wiring connector from the fan motor. Disconnect the wire loom from the clip on the shroud by pushing down on the lock fingers and pulling the connector from the motor end.

3. Remove the fasteners retaining the fan motor and shroud assembly and remove from the vehicle.

4. Remove the fan motor retaining screws.

5. Remove the retaining clip from the motor shaft and remove the fan.

NOTE: A metal burr may be present on the motor shaft after the retaining clip has been removed. If necessary, remove burr to facilitate fan removal.

6. Unbolt and withdraw the fan motor from the shroud.
To install:

7. Install the fan motor in position in the fan shroud. Install the retaining nuts and washers or screws and tighten to 44–66 inch lbs. (5.0–7.5 Nm).

8. Position the fan assembly on the motor shaft and install the retaining clip.

9. Position the fan, motor and shroud as an assembly in the vehicle. Install the retaining nuts or screws and tighten nut to 35–41 inch lbs. (3.9–4.6 Nm) and screw to 23–33 inch lbs. (2.6–3.7 Nm) on Escort; 31–41 inch lbs. (3.5–4.6 Nm) on Tempo and Topaz.

10. Install the fan motor wire loom in the clip provided on the fan shroud. Connect the wiring connector to the fan motor. Be sure the lock fingers on the connector snap firmly into place.

11. Reconnect the battery cable.

12. Check the fan for proper operation.

1991–93 Escort

1. Disconnect the negative battery cable.

2. On 1.8L engine equipped vehicles, remove the resonance duct from the radiator isomounts.

3. Disconnect the cooling fan motor electrical connector.

4. Remove the 3 shroud attaching bolts and remove the cooling fan shroud assembly by pulling it straight up.

5. Working on a bench, remove the cooling fan retainer clip. Remove the cooling fan from the motor shaft.

6. Unclip the cooling fan motor electrical harness retainers and remove the harness from the retainers.

7. Remove the cooling fan motor attaching screws and remove the cooling fan motor from the shroud assembly.
To install:

8. Position the cooling fan motor on the shroud assembly and install the attaching screws.

9. Position the cooling fan motor electrical harness in the harness retainers and clip the retainers shut.

10. Install the cooling fan on the cooling motor shaft and install the retainer clip.

11. Carefully lower the cooling fan shroud assembly into place and install the attaching bolts. Connect the cooling fan motor electrical connector.

12. If equipped with 1.8L engine, install the resonance duct on the radiator isomounts.

13. Connect the negative battery cable.

Heater Core

REMOVAL & INSTALLATION

Tempo and Topaz

1. Disconnect the negative battery cable.

2. Drain the cooling system.

3. Disconnect the heater hoses from the heater core.

4. From inside the vehicle, remove the 2 screws retaining floor duct to the plenum. Remove one screw retaining floor duct to instrument panel. Remove floor duct.

5. Remove the 4 screws attaching the heater core cover to the heater case assembly.

6. Remove the heater core and cover from the plenum.

7. Installation is the reverse of the removal procedure. Check the system for proper operation.

1989–90 Escort

WITHOUT AIR CONDITIONING

1. Disconnect the negative battery cable.

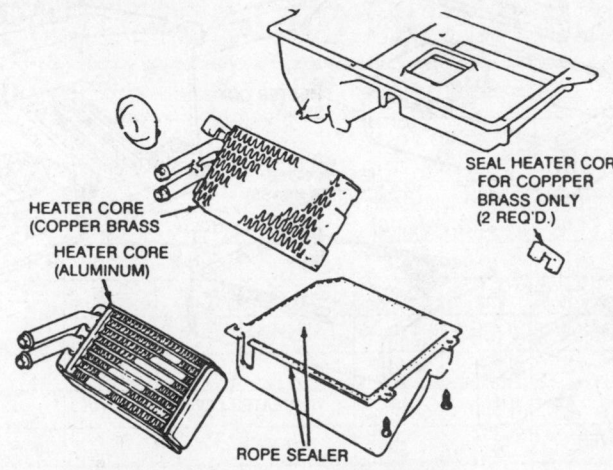

HEATER CORE (COPPER BRASS)

HEATER CORE (ALUMINUM)

SEAL HEATER CORE FOR COPPER BRASS ONLY (2 REQ'D.)

ROPE SEALER

Heater core removal—Tempo and Topaz

2. Drain the cooling system.

3. Loosen the heater hose clamps at the heater core tubes and disconnect the heater hoses from the heater core tubes. Cap the tubes to prevent spilling coolant into the passenger compartment.

4. Remove the glove compartment door, liner and lower reinforcement.

5. Move the temperature control lever to the **WARM** position.

6. Remove the 4 screws attaching the heater core cover to the heater assembly and remove the cover.

7. Working in the engine compartment, loosen the 2 nuts attaching heater case assembly to the dash panel.

8. Push the heater core tubes toward the passenger compartment to loosen the heater core from the heater case assembly.

9. Pull the heater core from the heater case assembly and remove the heater core through the glove compartment opening.

To install:

10. Position the heater core in the core opening in the case assembly with the heater core tubes on the top side of the end tank.

11. Slide the heater core into the opening of the heater case assembly.

12. Position the heater core cover to the heater case assembly. Install the 4 attaching screws.

13. Tighten the 2 nuts attaching heater case assembly to the dash panel.

14. Connect the heater hoses to the heater core tubes. Tighten the hose clamps.

15. Fill the cooling system to the proper level.

16. Install the glove compartment door, liner and hinge bar.

17. Check the heater for proper operation. Check the coolant level after the engine reaches normal operating temperature.

WITH AIR CONDITIONING

1. Disconnect the negative battery cable.

2. Drain cooling system.

3. Loosen the heater hose clamps at the heater core tubes and disconnect the heater hoses from the heater core tubes.

4. Working inside the vehicle, remove the screws attaching the floor duct to the plenum, instrument panel and evaporator assembly and remove the floor duct.

5. Remove the 4 screws attaching the heater core cover to the evaporator case.

6. Remove the heater core and cover from the plenum.

To install:

7. Position the heater core and cover to the evaporator case. Insert the heater core tubes through the dash panel seal holes.

8. Support the heater core and cover in place. Install the 4 attaching screws.

9. Position the floor duct to the evaporator case and instrument panel. Install the 4 attaching screws.

10. Connect the heater hoses to the heater core and tighten the hose clamps.

11. Fill the radiator with coolant to

the proper level and check the system for proper operation.

1991–93 Escort

1. Disconnect the negative battery cable and drain the cooling system.

2. Disconnect the heater hoses at the bulkhead.

3. Remove the instrument panel as follows:

a. Remove the 4 bolts securing the steering column to the instrument panel frame. Lower the steering column.

b. Disconnect the speedometer cable from the instrument panel.

c. Remove the cap screws securing the instrument cluster bezel to the instrument panel and remove the instrument cluster bezel.

d. Remove the screws and bolts securing the instrument cluster to the instrument panel. Pull the instrument cluster out slightly and disconnect the electrical connectors from the rear of the instrument cluster.

e. Remove the instrument cluster from the instrument panel.

f. Detach the hood release cable from the left lower dash trim panel. Carefully pry out both dash side panels.

g. Remove the 4 retaining screws and the left lower dash trim panel. Disconnect all necessary electrical connectors.

h. Remove the 2 hinge-to-instrument panel retaining screws and remove the glove compartment.

i. Remove the climate control assembly and the ash tray.

j. Remove the 7 accessory console retaining screws. Disconnect the radio antenna, radio wire connectors and cigarette lighter connector.

k. Remove the retaining screws and the right lower dash trim panel. Disconnect the 3 amplifier wire connectors.

l. Remove the 4 bolts attaching the instrument panel frame to the floor pan. Remove the bolts from both of the lower instrument panel mounts.

m. Remove the 2 bolts from both of the upper instrument panel mounts. Remove the retaining screw and the defroster duct bezel.

n. Remove the 3 mounting bolts that attach the upper instrument panel to the cowl.

o. Pull the instrument panel slightly away from its mounting position and make sure all electrical connectors are disconnected.

p. Remove the instrument panel from the vehicle.

NOTE: Use care to prevent any

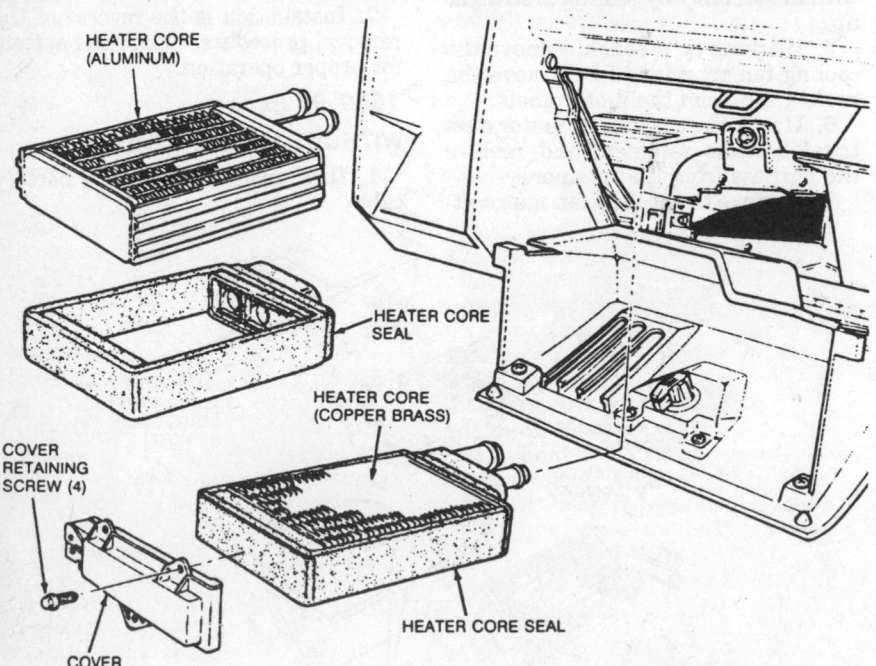

Heater core removal – 1989–90 Escort without air conditioning

HEATER CORE (ALUMINUM)

HEATER CORE SEAL

HEATER CORE (COPPER BRASS)

COVER RETAINING SCREW (4)

COVER

HEATER CORE SEAL

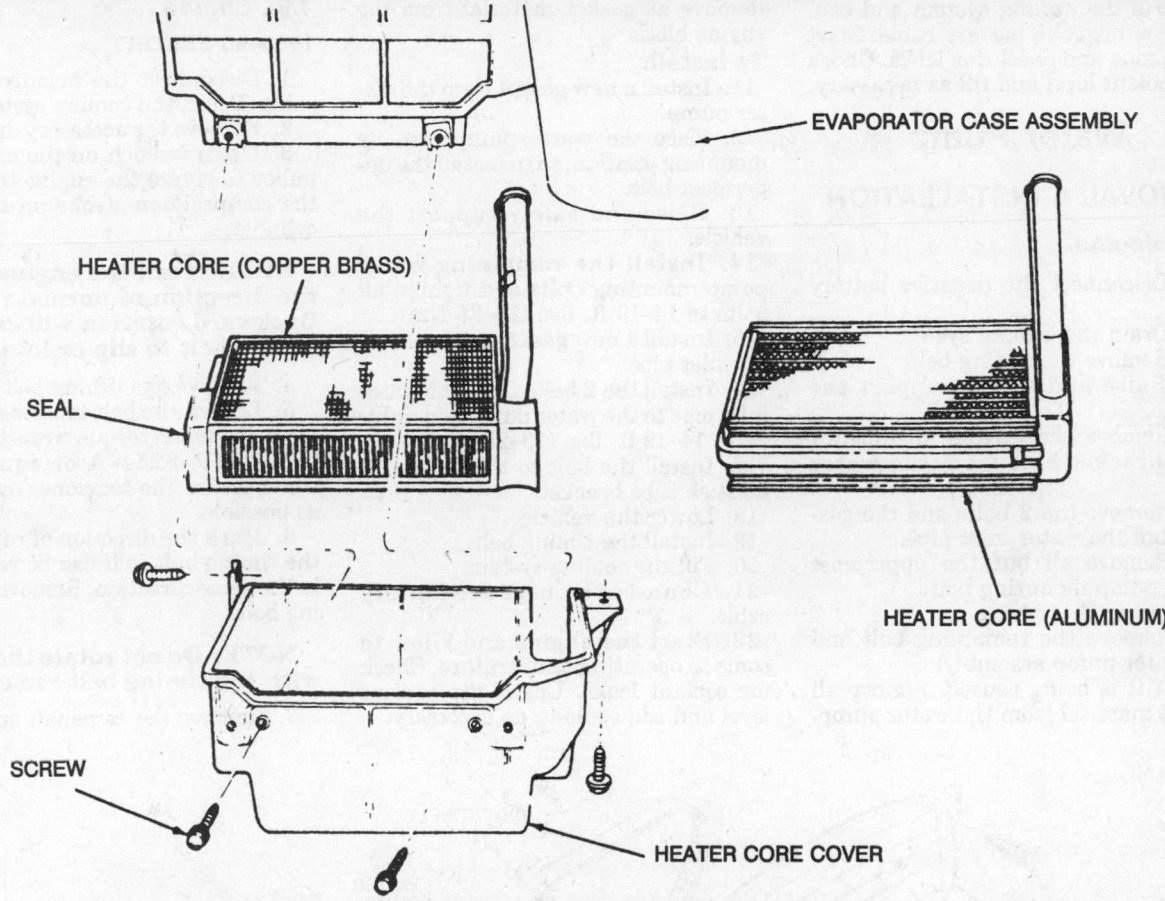

EVAPORATOR CASE ASSEMBLY

HEATER CORE (COPPER BRASS)

SEAL

HEATER CORE (ALUMINUM)

SCREW

HEATER CORE COVER

Heater core removal—1989–90 Escort with air conditioning

damage to the instrument panel or the surrounding interior trim.

4. Disconnect the mode selector and temperature control cables from the cams and retaining clips.

5. Remove the necessary defroster duct screws and loosen the capscrew that secures the heater-to-blower clamp.

6. Remove the 3 heater unit mounting nuts and disconnect the antenna lead from the retaining clip. Remove the heater unit.

7. Remove the insulator and the 4 brace capscrews. Remove the brace.

8. Remove the heater core from the heater unit.

To install:

9. Install the heater core into the heater unit and install the brace.

10. Install the brace capscrews and the insulator.

NOTE: If a new heater unit is being installed, save the keys that are found on the new unit for mode selector and temperature control cable adjustment.

11. Position the heater unit and attach the defroster and floor ducting.

Install the heater unit mounting nuts.

12. Tighten the heater-to-blower clamp capscrew and install the defroster duct screws. Connect the antenna lead to the retaining clip.

13. Install the instrument panel by reversing the removal procedure.

14. Connect the mode selector cable and adjust as follows:

    a. Move the mode selector lever to the **DEFROST** position on the climate control assembly.

    b. Insert cable locating key PN E7GH–18C408–A or equivalent, through the mode cam key slot and heater case key boss opening to secure the cam in the proper position.

    c. Remove the trim panel below the glove compartment, if equipped.

    d. Disconnect the cable from the retaining clip next to the mode selector cam. The mode selector cam is located on the right side of the heater unit.

    e. Move the mode selector lever to the **DEFROST** position.

    f. Connect the cable straight to the retaining clip. Do not exert any force on the cam during cable installation.

    g. Remove the cable locating key.

    h. Install the trim panel, if equipped.

    i. Make sure the mode selector lever moves its full stroke. If after performing the adjustment, air bleeds through the panel vents when in the **FLOOR, MIX** or **DEFROST** position, lengthen the adjustment rod 1–2 turns.

15. Connect the temperature control cable and adjust as follows:

    a. Move the temperature control lever to the **COLD** position on the climate control assembly.

    b. To secure the cam in the proper position, insert cable locating key PN E7GH–18G408–A or equivalent, through the cam key slot to the heater case key boss opening.

    c. Disconnect the cable from the retaining clip next to the temperature control cam. The temperature control cam is located on the left side of the heater unit.

    d. Connect the cable to the retaining clip.

    e. Remove the cable locating key.

    f. Make sure the temperature control lever moves its full stroke.

16. Connect the heater hoses at the bulkhead.

17. Fill the cooling system and connect the negative battery cable. Start the engine and check for leaks. Check the coolant level and fill as necessary.

Water Pump

REMOVAL & INSTALLATION

1.8L Engine

1. Disconnect the negative battery cable.
2. Drain the cooling system.
3. Remove the timing belt.
4. Raise and safely support the vehicle.
5. Remove the engine oil dipstick tube bracket bolt from the water pump.
6. Remove the 2 bolts and the gasket from the water inlet pipe.
7. Remove all but the uppermost water pump mounting bolt.
8. Lower the vehicle.
9. Remove the remaining bolt and the water pump assembly.
10. If it is being reused, remove all gasket material from the water pump.

Remove all gasket material from the engine block.

To install:

11. Install a new gasket onto the water pump.
12. Place the water pump into its mounting position, then install the uppermost bolt.
13. Raise and safely support the vehicle.
14. Install the remaining water pump mounting bolts and tighten all bolts to 14–19 ft. lbs. (19–25 Nm).
15. Install a new gasket onto the water inlet pipe.
16. Install the 2 bolts from the water inlet pipe to the water pump and tighten to 14–19 ft. lbs. (19–25 Nm).
17. Install the bolt to the engine oil dipstick tube bracket.
18. Lower the vehicle.
19. Install the timing belt.
20. Fill the cooling system.
21. Connect the negative battery cable.
22. Start the engine and allow to come to operating temperature. Check for coolant leaks. Check the coolant level and add coolant, as necessary.

1.9L Engine

1989–90 ESCORT

1. Disconnect the negative battery cable. Drain the cooling system.
2. Remove the accessory drive belts.
3. Use a wrench on the crankshaft pulley to rotate the engine to TDC on the compression stroke on the No. 1 cylinder.

NOTE: Turn the engine only in the direction of normal rotation. Backward rotation will cause the timing belt to slip or lose teeth.

4. Remove the timing belt cover.
5. Loosen the belt tensioner attaching bolts, using torque wrench adapter tool T81P-6254-A or equivalent. Then secure the tensioner over as far as possible.
6. Mark the direction of rotation on the timing belt so it can be reinstalled in the same direction. Remove the timing belt.

NOTE: Do not rotate the engine with the timing belt removed.

7. Remove the camshaft sprocket.

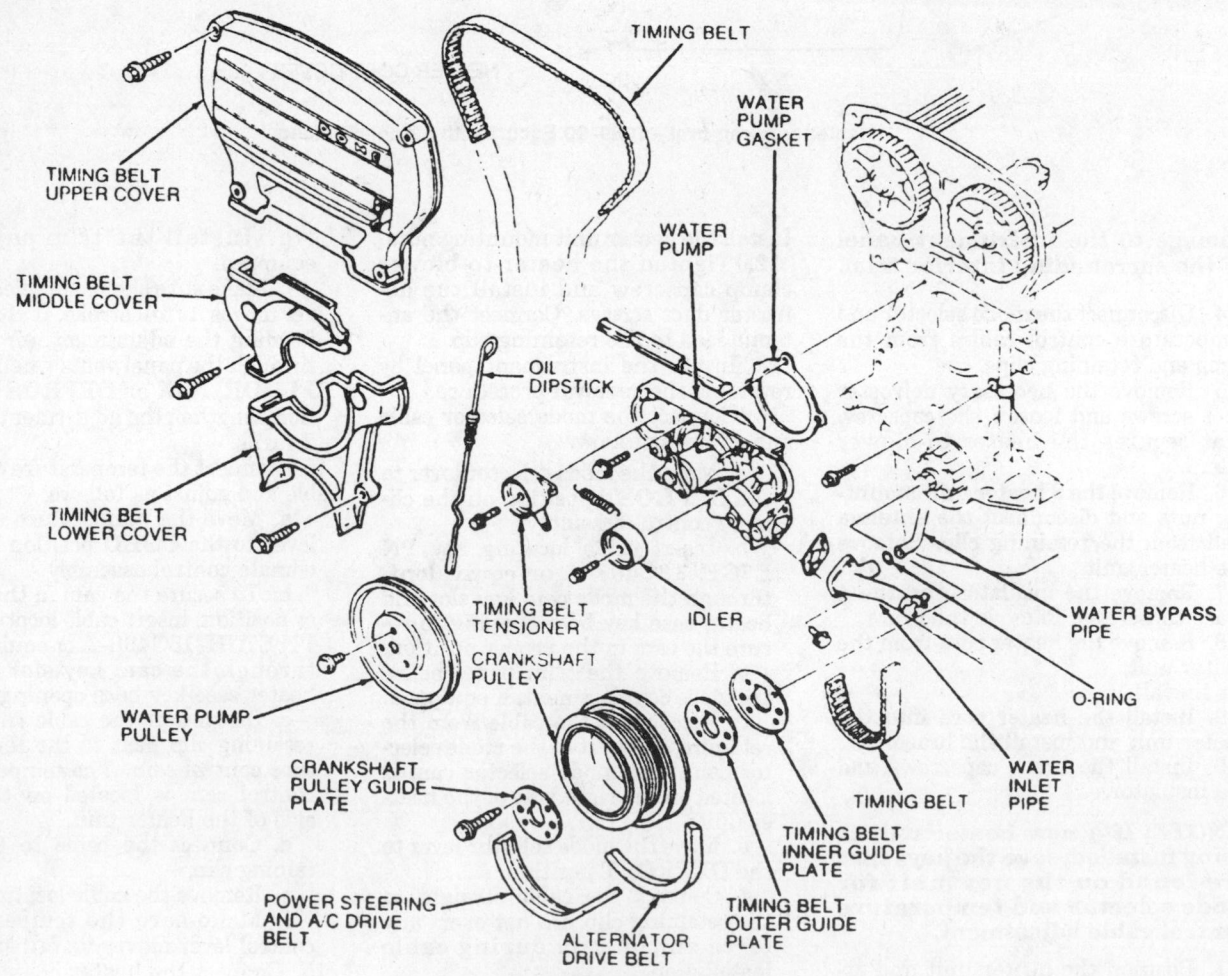

Water pump installation—1.8L Engine

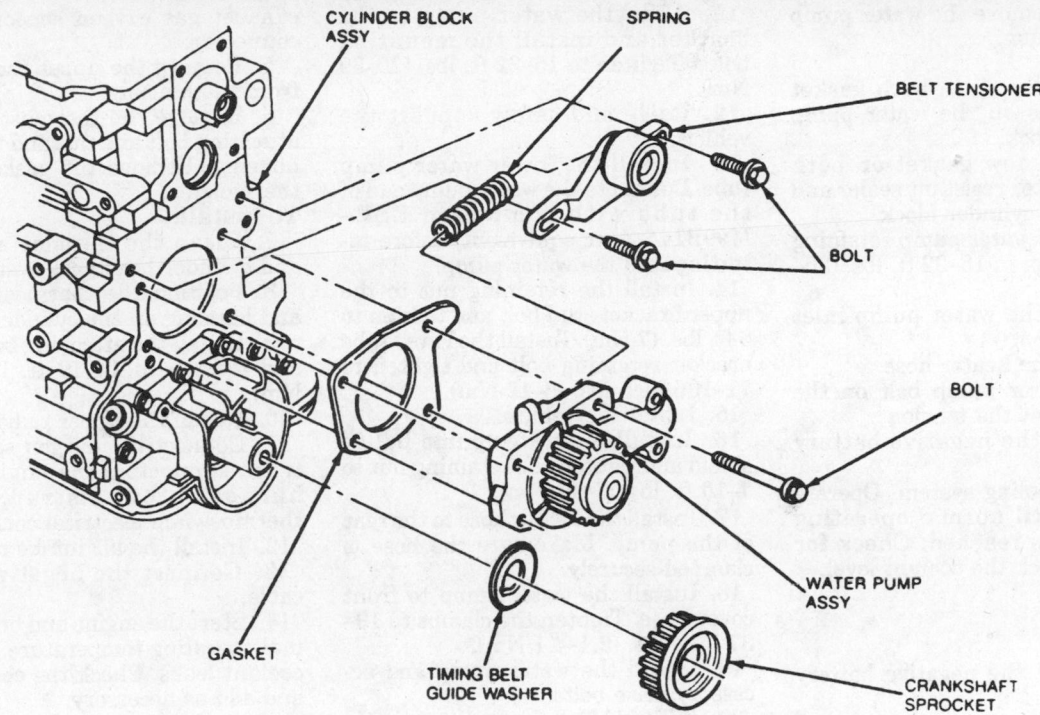

Water pump installation—1.9L engine, 1989–90 Escort

8. Remove the rearward front timing cover stud.

9. Remove the water pump inlet tube fasteners and the inlet tube and gasket.

10. Remove the water pump to cylinder block bolts and remove the water pump and its gasket.

To install:

11. Make certain the mating surfaces on the pump, inlet tube flange and the block are clean.

12. Place the water pump inlet tube bolts through the flange. Install the water pump inlet tube gasket over the bolts.

13. Place the water pump assembly and new gasket to the cylinder block and through the water pump inlet tube bolts. Apply pipe sealant with Teflon® D8AZ–19554–A or equivalent, to the water pump attaching bolts and tighten the bolts to 6.0–8.5 ft. lbs. (8.0–11.5 Nm). Make sure the pump impeller turns freely.

14. Install the water pump inlet tube nuts and tighten to 6–8 ft. lbs. (8.0–11.5 Nm).

15. Install the rearward front timing cover stud.

16. Align and install the camshaft sprocket over the cam key.

17. Install the timing belt.

18. Refill the cooling system and connect the negative battery cable.

19. Start the engine and allow to reach normal operating temperature. Check for coolant leaks. Check the coolant level and add, as necessary.

1991–93 ESCORT

1. Disconnect the negative battery cable.

2. Drain the cooling system.

3. Remove the accessory drive belt and its automatic tensioner.

4. Remove the timing belt cover and the timing belt.

5. Raise and safely support the vehicle.

6. Remove the lower radiator hose and remove the heater hose from the water pump.

7. Lower the vehicle.

8. Support the engine with a suitable floor jack.

9. Remove the right engine mount attaching bolts and roll the engine mount aside.

10. Remove the water pump attaching bolts.

11. Using the floor jack, raise the engine enough to provide clearance for removing the water pump.

12. Remove the water pump and the gasket from the engine through the top of the engine compartment.

To install:

13. Make sure the mating surfaces of the cylinder block and water pump are clean and free of gasket material.

14. If the water pump is to be replaced, transfer the timing belt tensioner components to the new water pump.

15. With the engine supported and raised with a suitable floor jack, place the water pump and the gasket on the

cylinder block and install the 4 attaching bolts. Tighten the bolts to 15–22 ft. lbs. (20–30 Nm).

16. Install the timing belt and cover.

17. Roll the right engine mount into position and install the mount bolts. Remove the floor jack.

18. Raise and safely support the vehicle.

19. Install the lower radiator hose and install the heater hose on the pump.

20. Install the crankshaft dampener and the splash shield.

21. Lower the vehicle.

22. Install the accessory drive belt automatic tensioner and the accessory drive belt.

23. Connect the negative battery cable.

24. Refill the cooling system.

25. Start the engine and allow to come to normal operating temperature. Check for coolant leaks. Check the coolant level and add as necessary.

2.3L Engine

1. Drain the cooling system.

2. Disconnect the negative battery cable.

3. Loosen the water pump idler pulley and remove the belt from the water pump pulley.

4. Disconnect the heater hose at the water pump inlet tube.

5. Disconnect the water pump inlet tube.

6. Remove the 3 water pump retain-

ing bolts and remove the water pump from its mounting.

To install:

7. Thoroughly clean both gasket mating surfaces on the water pump and cylinder block.

8. Coat the new gasket on both sides with a water resistant sealer and position on the cylinder block.

9. Install the water pump retaining bolts and tighten to 15–22 ft. lbs. (20–30 Nm).

10. Connect the water pump inlet tube.

11. Connect the heater hose.

13. Install water pump belt on the pulley and adjust the tension.

14. Connect the negative battery cable.

15. Fill the cooling system. Operate the engine until normal operating temperature is reached. Check for leaks and recheck the coolant level.

3.0L Engine

1. Disconnect the negative battery cable.

2. Drain the cooling system.

3. Remove the water pump drive belt as follows:

a. Mark the direction of rotation on the accessory drive belt so it can be reinstalled in the same direction.

b. Remove the plastic belt shield from the power steering pump.

c. Using a ½ in. drive breaker bar or equivalent, inserted in the idler pulley tensioner, release the tension on the accessory drive belt and remove the belt.

d. Raise and safely support the vehicle.

e. Mark the direction of rotation on the water pump drive belt so it can be reinstalled in the same direction.

f. Use a suitable wrench to turn the water pump belt idler pulley tensioner clockwise and release the tension on the belt. Remove the water pump drive belt.

4. Lower the vehicle and remove the water pump to front cover hose.

5. Raise and safely support the vehicle.

6. Loosen and remove the retaining nut from the upper bracket and the bolt from the lower bracket. Gently grasp the tube at the water end and pull the tube out of the water pump. Remove the lower water pump tube.

7. Lower the vehicle.

8. Remove the heater hose from the rear of the water pump and remove the water pump pulley shield.

9. Remove the water pump from the bracket.

To install:

10. If replacing the water pump, transfer the pulley to the new pump.

11. Align the water pump to the bracket and install the mounting bolts. Tighten to 15–22 ft. lbs. (20–30 Nm).

12. Raise and safely support the vehicle.

13. Install the lower water pump tube. Lubricate the water pump end of the tube with compound ESE-M99B144-A or equivalent, before inserting into the water pump.

14. Install the retaining nut to the upper bracket stud bolt and tighten to 5 ft. lbs. (7 Nm). Install the lower tube bracket retaining bolt and tighten to 71–106 inch lbs. (8–12 Nm).

15. Lower the vehicle.

16. Install the water pump pulley shield and tighten the retaining nut to 7–10 ft. lbs. (9–14 Nm).

17. Install the heater hose to the rear of the pump. Make sure the hose is clamped securely.

18. Install the water pump to front cover hose. Tighten the clamps to 19–37 inch lbs. (2.1–4.1 Nm).

19. Install the water pump and accessory drive belts.

20. Fill and bleed the cooling system.

21. Connect the negative battery cable, start the engine and check for leaks.

Thermostat

REMOVAL & INSTALLATION

1.8L Engine

1. Disconnect the negative battery cable.

2. Drain the cooling system.

3. Remove the air intake tube.

4. Disconnect the water thermoswitch connector, the engine wiring harness ground strap from the connector above the housing, and the exhaust gas oxygen sensor electrical connector.

5. Remove the upper radiator hose from the housing.

6. Remove the thermostat housing attaching bolt and nut and remove the housing. Remove the gasket and the thermostat.

To install:

7. Clean the thermostat housing and cylinder head gasket surfaces.

8. Position the thermostat, gasket and housing on the cylinder head.

9. Install the attaching bolt and nut and tighten to 14–19 ft. lbs. (19–26 Nm).

10. Install the upper radiator hose.

11. Connect the oxygen sensor electrical connector, the engine wiring harness ground strap, and the thermoswitch electrical connector.

12. Install the air intake tube.

13. Connect the negative battery cable.

14. Start the engine and bring to normal operating temperature. Check for coolant leaks. Check the coolant level and add as necessary.

2.3L and 1989–90 1.9L Engines

1. Disconnect the negative battery cable.

2. Disconnect the wiring connector from the thermal switch in the thermostat housing.

3. Drain the cooling system to a corresponding level just below the water outlet connection.

4. Loosen the top hose clamp at the radiator, remove the water outlet connection retaining bolts, lift clear of the engine and remove the thermostat.

NOTE: Do not pry the housing off.

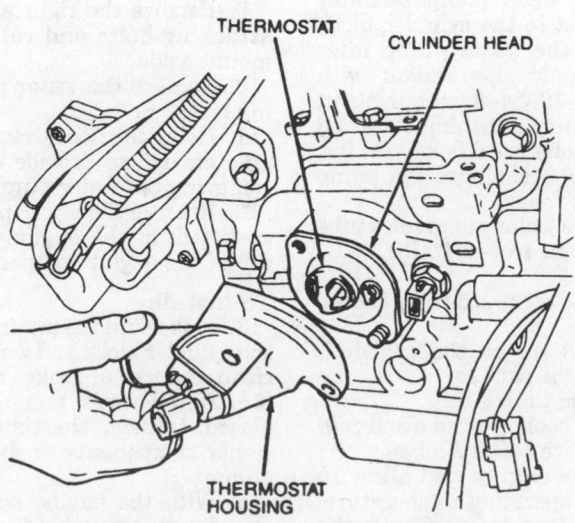

Thermostat Installation—1.8L Engine

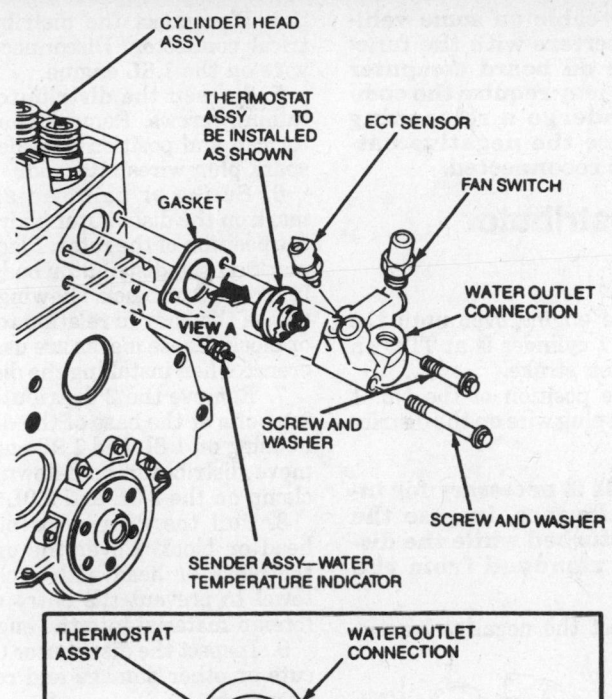

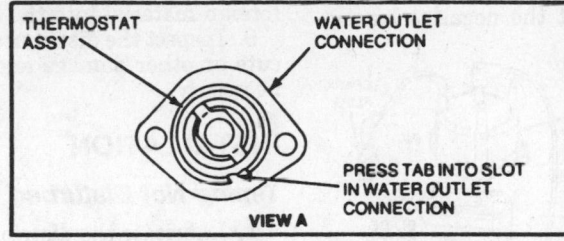

Thermostat Installation—2.3L Engine

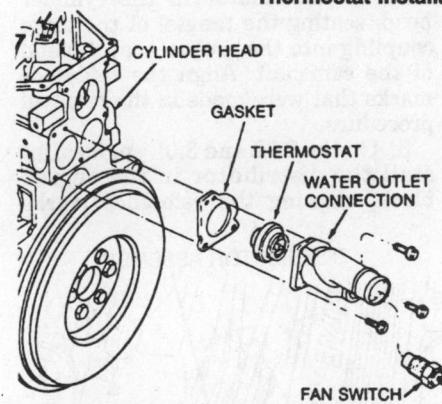

**Thermostat Installation—1989-90
1.9L Engine**

To install:

5. Make sure the water outlet connection pocket and cylinder head mating surfaces are clean and free of gasket material.

6. Place the thermostat in position, fully inserted to compress the gasket. Position the water outlet connection to the cylinder head and tighten the bolts to 6–8 ft. lbs. (8–11 Nm) on the 1.9L engine or 12–18 ft. lbs. (16–24 Nm) on the 2.3L engine.

7. Position the top hose to the radiator and tighten the clamps.

8. Refill the cooling system and connect the negative battery cable.

9. Start the engine and bring to normal operating temperature. Check for coolant leaks. Check the coolant level and add as necessary.

1991–93 1.9L Engine

1. Disconnect the negative battery cable.

2. Drain the cooling system.

3. Remove the air intake tube, crankcase breather and PCV hose.

4. Remove the ignition coil pack and bracket.

5. Remove the upper radiator hose.

6. Remove the heater hose inlet

tube bracket bolt and remove the heater hose inlet tube from the thermostat housing.

7. Remove the 3 thermostat housing attaching bolts and remove the thermostat housing and gasket.

NOTE: Do not pry off the housing.

8. Remove the thermostat and the rubber seal from the housing.

To install:

9. Clean the thermostat housing pocket and cylinder head mating surfaces.

10. Place the thermostat into position, fully inserted to compress the rubber seal inside the housing.

NOTE: Make sure the thermostat tabs engage properly into the housing slots.

11. Position the thermostat housing and gasket on the cylinder head.

12. Install the 3 attaching bolts and tighten to 6.0–8.5 ft. lbs. (8.0–11.5 Nm).

13. Install the heater hose inlet pipe and the heater hose inlet pipe bracket bolt.

14. Install the upper radiator hose.

15. Install the ignition coil and bracket.

16. Install the crankcase breather, PCV hoses and the air intake tube.

17. Connect the negative battery cable.

18. Refill the cooling system.

19. Start the engine and bring to normal operating temperature. Check for coolant leaks. Check the coolant level and add as necessary.

3.0L Engine

1. Disconnect the negative battery cable.

2. Drain the cooling system.

3. Remove the upper radiator hose from the thermostat housing.

4. Remove the mounting bolts and

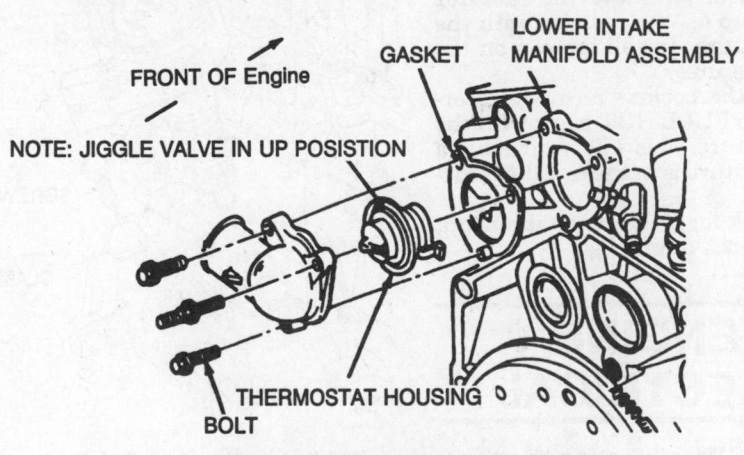

Thermostat Installation—3.0L Engine

remove the thermostat housing and thermostat as an assembly.

5. Clean the gasket mating surfaces, being careful not to gouge the metal.

To install:

6. Install the thermostat into the housing, making sure the jiggle valve is facing up.

7. Install a new gasket onto the thermostat housing. Install the housing and tighten the bolts to 9 ft. lbs. (12 Nm).

8. Install the upper radiator hose and tighten the clamp to 20–30 inch lbs. (2.3–3.4 Nm).

9. Fill and bleed the cooling system.

10. Connect the negative battery cable, start the engine and check for leaks.

Cooling System Bleeding

When the entire cooling system is drained, the following procedure should be used to ensure a complete fill.

1. Install the block drain plug, if removed, and close the draincock. With the engine OFF, add a 50/50 mixture of anti-freeze and water to the radiator until it reaches the radiator filler neck seat. Wait several minutes, as the coolant level in the radiator drops, and continue to add the 50/50 mixture until the radiator remains full.

NOTE: 1991–93 1.9L engines have a float/seat de-gas system in the water outlet connection that improves coolant fill when the thermostat is closed.

2. Install the radiator cap to the first notch to keep spillage to a minimum.

3. Start the engine and let it idle until the upper radiator hose is warm. This indicates that the thermostat is open and coolant is flowing through the entire system.

4. Carefully remove the radiator cap and top off the radiator with the 50/50 mixture. Install the cap on the radiator securely.

5. Fill the coolant recovery reservoir to the FULL HOT mark with the 50/50 mixture. This will ensure that a proper mixture is in the coolant recovery bottle.

6. Check for leaks at the draincock and the block drain plug.

ENGINE ELECTRICAL

NOTE: Disconnecting the nega-

tive battery cable on some vehicles may interfere with the functions of the on board computer systems and may require the computer to undergo a relearning process, once the negative battery cable is reconnected.

Distributor

REMOVAL

1. Turn the engine over until the piston in No. 1 cylinder is at TDC on the compression stroke.

2. Mark the position of the No. 1 cylinder spark plug wire on the distributor base.

NOTE: This is necessary for installation reference, in case the timing is disturbed while the distributor is removed from the engine.

3. Disconnect the negative battery cable.

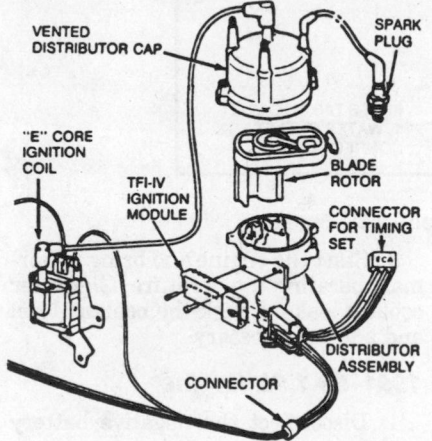

Distributor ignition system components

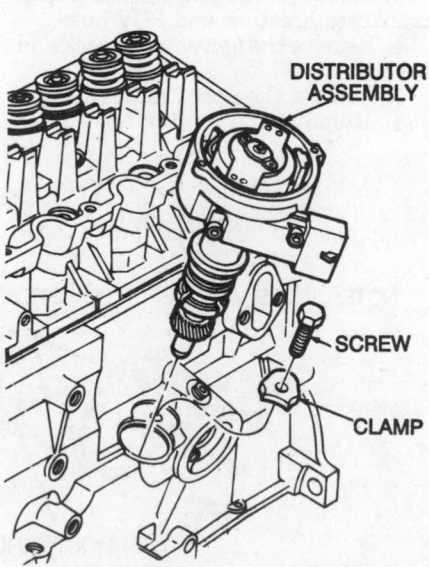

Distributor mounting—2.3L Engine

4. Disconnect the distributor electrical connector. Disconnect the coil wire on the 1.8L engine.

5. Loosen the distributor cap retaining screws. Remove the distributor cap and position it aside with the spark plug wires attached.

6. Scribe or paint an alignment mark on the distributor body, showing the position of the rotor. Place another mark on the distributor body and cylinder head or block, showing the position of the body in relation to the head or block. These marks are used for reference when installing the distributor.

7. Remove the 2 distributor retaining bolts at the base of the distributor housing on 1.8L and 1.9L engines. Remove distributor hold-down bolt and clamp on the 2.3L and 3.0L engines.

8. Pull the distributor out of the head or block. Cover the opening in the block or head with a clean shop towel to prevent the entry of dirt or foreign material into the engine.

9. Inspect the distributor O-ring for cuts or other damage and replace, as necessary.

INSTALLATION

Timing Not Disturbed

1. Lubricate the distributor O-ring.

2. On the 1.8L and 1.9L engines, install the distributor in the cylinder head, seating the tang(s) of the drive coupling into the groove(s) at the end of the camshaft. Align the reference marks that were made in the removal procedure.

3. On the 2.3L and 3.0L engines, install the distributor in the engine block, aligning the reference marks

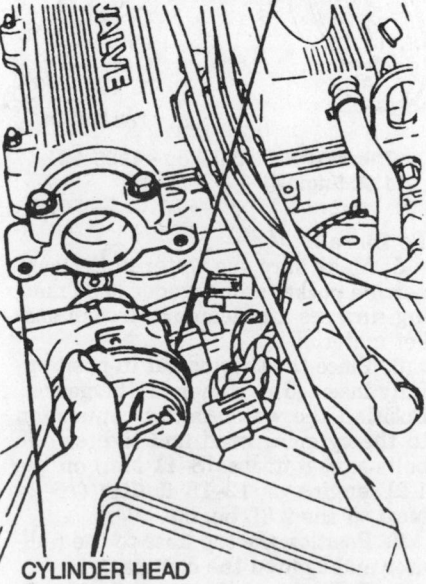

Distributor installation—1.8L Engine

that were made during the removal procedure.

4. Install the distributor hold-down bolt(s). Tighten the bolt(s) enough so the distributor is not loose but can still be moved by hand for ignition timing purposes.

5. Install the distributor cap and connect the distributor electrical connector. Connect the coil wire on 1.8L engine.

6. Connect the negative battery cable.

7. Check and if necessary, adjust the ignition timing.

8. After the timing has been set, tighten the distributor hold-down bolt(s) to 14–19 ft. lbs. (19–25 Nm) on 1.8L engine, 44–62 inch lbs. (5–7 Nm) on 1.9L engine or 17–25 ft. lbs. (23–34 Nm) on 2.3L and 3.0L engines.

Timing Disturbed

1. If the crankshaft was rotated while the distributor was removed, the piston in No. 1 cylinder must be brought to TDC on the compression stroke.

2. Disconnect the No. 1 cylinder spark plug wire and remove the spark plug. Place a finger over the spark plug hole and rotate the crankshaft slowly in the direction of normal rotation, until engine compression is felt.

NOTE: Turn the engine only in the direction of normal rotation.

3. When engine compression is felt at the spark plug hole, indicating that the piston is approaching TDC, continue to turn the crankshaft until the timing mark on the pulley is aligned with the **0** mark on the engine front cover or the timing pointer on the engine front cover is aligned with the **0** mark on the damper, as applicable.

4. Turn the distributor shaft until the ignition rotor is aligned with the mark made on the distributor base during Step 2 of the removal procedure.

5. On the 1.8L and 1.9L engines, install the distributor in the cylinder head, seating the tang(s) of the drive coupling into the groove(s) at the end of the camshaft. Align the distributor body-to-cylinder head reference marks that were made in the removal procedure.

6. On the 2.3L and 3.0L engines, install the distributor in the engine block, aligning the distributor body-to-engine block reference marks that were made during the removal procedure.

7. Install the distributor hold-down bolt(s). Tighten the bolt(s) enough so the distributor is not loose but can still

be moved by hand for ignition timing purposes.

8. Install the distributor cap and connect the distributor electrical connector. Connect the coil wire on 1.8L engine.

9. Install the spark plug in the No. 1 cylinder and tighten to 11–17 ft. lbs. (14–23 Nm) on 1.8L engine, 8–15 ft. lbs. (11–20 Nm) on 1.9L engine, 6–10 ft. lbs. (7–14 Nm) on 2.3L engine or 5–11 ft. lbs. (7–15 Nm) on 3.0L engine. Connect the spark plug wire to the spark plug.

10. Connect the negative battery cable.

11. Check and adjust the ignition timing.

12. After the timing has been set, tighten the distributor hold-down bolt(s) to 14–19 ft. lbs. (19–25 Nm) on 1.8L engine, 44–62 inch lbs. (5–7 Nm) on 1.9L engine or 17–25 ft. lbs. (23–34 Nm) on 2.3L and 3.0L engines.

Distributorless Ignition

Beginning in 1991, the 1.9L engine is equipped with a Distributorless Ignition System (DIS). The DIS consists of the following components: crankshaft sensor, ignition module, ignition coil pack, the spark angle portion of the ECU and the related wiring.

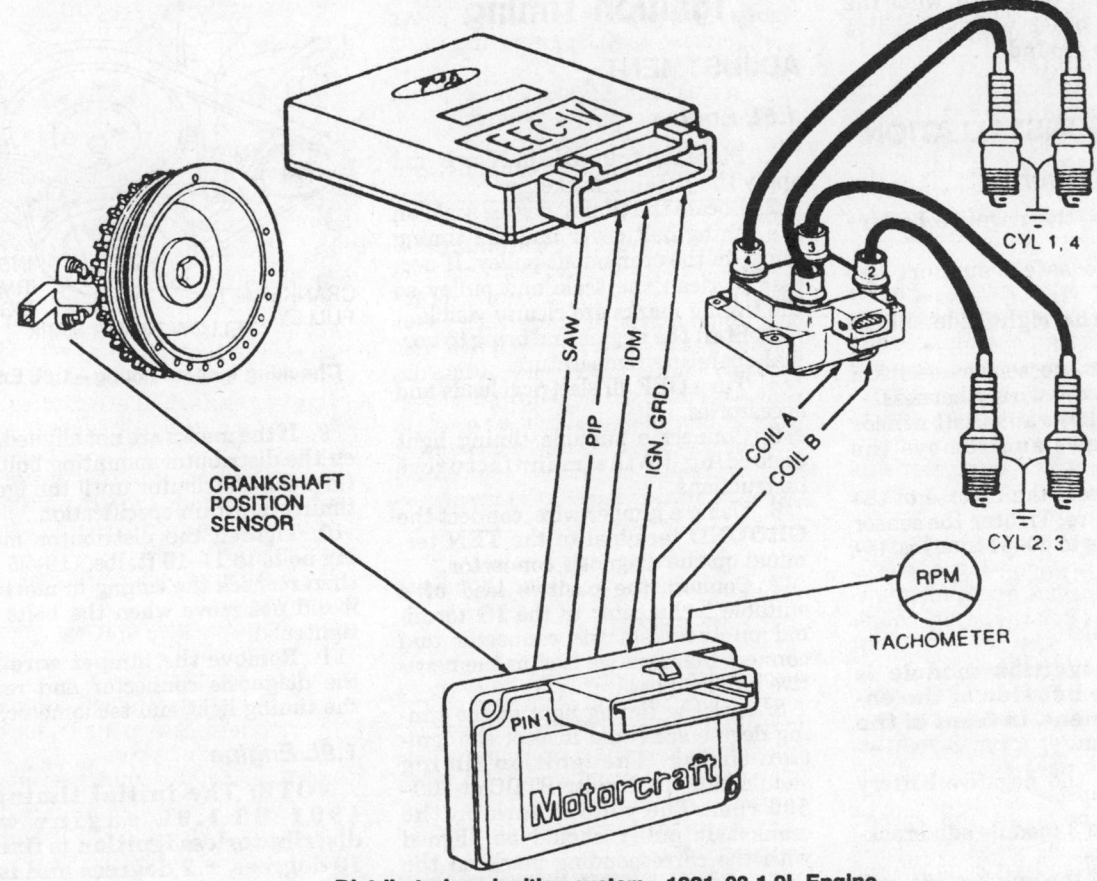

Distributorless Ignition system—1991–93 1.9L Engine

The crankshaft sensor is a variable reluctance-type sensor triggered by a 36-minus-1 tooth trigger wheel configuration pressed onto the rear of the crankshaft dampener. The signal generated by this sensor is called a Variable Reluctance Sensor (VRS) signal. The VRS signal provides engine position and rpm information to the ignition module.

The ignition module is a micro-processor that recieves input from the crankshaft sensor in regards to engine position and engine speed and input from the ECU pertaining to spark advance. The ignition module uses this information to direct which coil to fire and to calculate the turn on and turn off times of the coils required to achieve the correct dwell and spark advance.

The ignition coil pack contains 2 separate ignition coils. Each ignition coil fires 2 cylinders simultaneously. When 1 cylinder is firing on the compression stroke, the other is firing on the exhaust stroke. During the next engine revolution, the reverse occurs. The spark plug fired on the exhaust stroke uses very little of the ignition coil's stored energy; the majority of the energy is used by the spark plug on the compression stroke. Since these 2 spark plugs are connected in series, the firing voltage of 1 plug will be negative with respect to ground, while the voltage of the other will be positive with respect to ground.

REMOVAL & INSTALLATION

Crankshaft Sensor

1. Disconnect the negative battery cable.
2. Raise and safely support the vehicle.
3. Remove the right side splash shield.
4. Disconnect the sensor electrical connector from the wiring harness.
5. Remove the crankshaft sensor mounting screws and remove the sensor.
6. Installation is the reverse of the removal procedure. Tighten the sensor attaching screws to 40–61 inch lbs. (5–7 Nm).

Ignition Module

NOTE: The ignition module is located on the left side of the engine compartment, in front of the left strut tower.

1. Disconnect the negative battery cable.
2. Remove the 3 module sub-bracket attaching nuts.
3. Gently pull the sub-bracket and module assembly straight up and disconnect the module electrical harness.
4. Remove the 2 module attaching screws from the sub-bracket. Remove the ignition module from the sub-bracket.
5. Installation is the reverse of the removal procedure. Tighten the module attaching screws to 24–35 inch lbs. (3–4 Nm). Tighten the sub-bracket attaching nuts to 62–88 inch lbs. (7–10 Nm).

Ignition Coil Pack

1. Disconnect the negative battery cable.
2. Disconnect the electrical connector from the coil pack.
3. Remove the spark plug wires by squeezing the locking tabs to release the coil boot retainers. Tag the wires and mark their position on the coil pack prior to removal.
4. Remove the coil pack attaching bolts and remove the coil pack.

NOTE: Save the capacitor for installation with the new coil pack.

5. Installation is the reverse of the removal procedure. Tighten the attaching bolts to 40–62 inch lbs. (5–7 Nm).

Ignition Timing

ADJUSTMENT

1.8L Engine

1. Place the transaxle in N or P and apply the parking brake.
2. Locate the timing degree scale on the timing belt cover and the timing mark on the crankshaft pulley. If necessary, clean the scale and pulley so the timing marks are clearly visible.
3. Start the engine and bring to normal operating temperature.
4. Turn OFF all electrical loads and accessories.
5. Connect a suitable timing light according to the manufacturers instructions.
6. Using a jumper wire, connect the GROUND terminal to the TEN terminal on the diagnosis connector.
7. Connect the positive lead of a suitable tachometer to the IG terminal on the diagnosis connector and connect the negative lead to the negative battery post.
8. Aim the timing light at the timing degree scale and inspect the ignition timing. The ignition timing should be 9–11 degrees BTDC at 700–800 rpm. The yellow mark on the crankshaft pulley should be aligned with the corresponding mark on the timing belt cover.

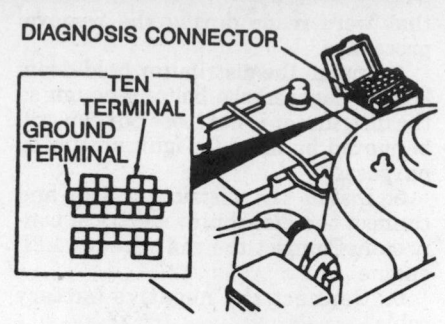

Diagnosis connector location—1.8L Engine

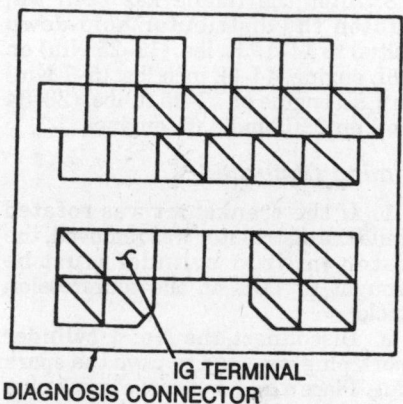

Diagnosis connector terminals—1.8L Engine

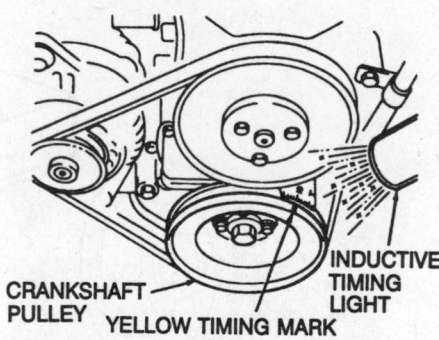

Checking ignition timing—1.8L Engine

9. If the marks are not aligned, loosen the distributor mounting bolts and turn the distributor until the ignition timing is within specification.
10. Tighten the distributor mounting bolts to 14–19 ft. lbs. (19–25 Nm), then recheck the timing to make sure it did not move when the bolts were tightened.
11. Remove the jumper wire from the diagnosis connector and remove the timing light and tachometer.

1.9L Engine

NOTE: The initial timing on 1991–93 1.9L engine with distributorless ignition is fixed at 10 degrees ± 2 degrees and is not adjustable.

1. Ignition timing marks consist of a notch on the crankshaft pulley and a graduated scale molded into the camshaft belt cover. The number of degrees before or after TDC represented by each mark in the scale can be interpreted according to the decal affixed to the top of the belt cover.

2. With white paint or chalk, mark the notch in the crankshaft pulley and the appropriate mark in the degree scale. See the underhood emission control decal for timing specifications.

3. Place the transaxle in **P** or **N**, apply the parking brake and block the wheels. Place the air conditioning/heater control switch in the **OFF** position.

4. Connect a suitable inductive timing light to the engine. Connect a suitable tachometer to the engine.

5. Disconnect the single wire in-line SPOUT connector or remove the shorting bar from the double wire SPOUT connector.

6. Start the engine and bring to normal operating temperature. Make sure the idle speed is as specified on the emission control information label.

7. Aim the timing light at the timing marks. If they are not aligned, loosen the distributor clamp bolts slightly and rotate the distributor body until the marks are aligned.

NOTE: To set timing correctly, a remote starter should not be used. Use the ignition key only to start the vehicle. Disconnecting the start wire at the starter relay will cause the TFI module to revert to start mode timing after the vehicle is started. Reconnecting the start wire after the vehicle is running will not correct the timing.

8. Tighten the distributor clamp bolts, then recheck the timing to make sure it did not change when the bolts were tightened.

9. Connect the SPOUT connector and check the timing to verify distributor advance beyond initial setting.

10. Shut the engine **OFF** and remove all test equipment.

2.3L and 3.0L Engines

On the 2.3L engine, the timing marks are located on the flywheel and are visible through an access hole in the transaxle case. If equipped with manual transaxle, the timing cover plate must be removed in order to view the timing marks and adjust the timing.

On the 3.0L engine, the timing marks are located on the crankshaft damper and timing chain cover.

1. Place the transaxle in **P** or **N** and apply the parking brake. Make sure the A/C and heater are OFF.

2. Open the hood, locate the timing marks and clean with a stiff brush or solvent. If equipped with 2.3L engine and manual transaxle, it will be necessary to remove the cover plate which allows access to to the timing marks.

3. Using white chalk or paint, mark the specified timing mark and pointer.

4. Remove the in-line SPOUT connector or remove the shorting bar from the double wire SPOUT connector.

5. Connect a suitable inductive timing light and a tachometer according to the manufacturers instructions.

6. Start the engine and bring to normal operating temperature.

7. Check the engine idle speed and adjust if it is not within specifications. Aim the timing light at the timing marks. If they are not aligned, loosen the distributor clamp bolt slightly and rotate the distributor body until the marks are aligned.

NOTE: To set timing correctly, a remote starter should not be used. Use the ignition key only to start the vehicle. Disconnecting the start wire at the starter relay will cause the TFI module to revert to start mode timing after the vehicle is started. Reconnecting the start wire after the vehicle is running will not correct the timing.

8. Tighten the distributor clamp bolt, then recheck the ignition timing to make sure it did not change when the bolt was tightened.

9. Shut the engine **OFF** and remove all test equipment. Reconnect the in-line SPOUT connector or reinstall the shorting bar on the double wire SPOUT connector.

10. If equipped with 2.3L engine and manual transaxle, reinstall the cover plate.

Alternator

PRECAUTIONS

Several precautions must be observed with alternator equipped vehicles to avoid damage to the unit.

- If the battery is removed for any reason, make sure it is reconnected with the correct polarity. Reversing the battery connections may result in damage to the one-way rectifiers.
- When utilizing a booster battery as a starting aid, always connect the positive to positive terminals and the negative terminal from the booster battery to a good engine ground on the vehicle being started.
- Never use a fast charger as a booster to start vehicles.

- Disconnect the battery cables when charging the battery with a fast charger.
- Never attempt to polarize the alternator.
- Do not use test lights of more than 12 volts when checking diode continuity.
- Do not short across or ground any of the alternator terminals.
- The polarity of the battery, alternator and regulator must be matched and considered before making any electrical connections within the system.
- Never separate the alternator on an open circuit. Make sure all connections within the circuit are clean and tight.
- Disconnect the battery ground terminal when performing any service on electrical components.
- Disconnect the battery if arc welding is to be done on the vehicle.

BELT TENSION ADJUSTMENT

1.8L Engine

1. Loosen the alternator adjusting bolt.
2. Raise and safely support the vehicle.
3. Loosen the alternator mounting bolt.

NOTE: Do not pry against the stator frame. Position the prybar against a stronger point, such as the area around a case bolt.

4. Position a suitable belt tension gauge on the longest accessible span of belt and tighten the belt. Adjust the tension to 85.8–103.4 lbs. for a new belt or 68.2–85.8 lbs. for a used belt.

NOTE: A belt is considered used if it has been in use for more than 10 minutes

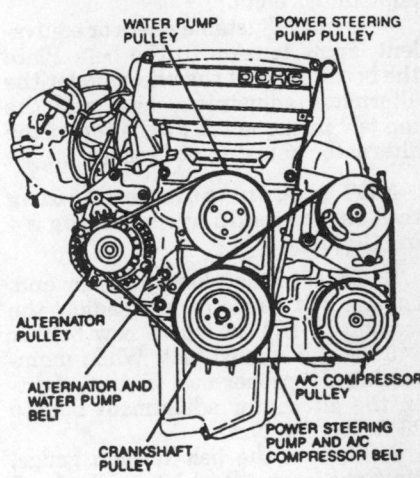

Drive belt arrangement—1.8L Engine

5. If a belt tension gauge is not available, adjust the tension to 0.31–0.35 in. (8–9mm) deflection for a new belt or 0.35–0.39 in. (9–10mm) deflection for a used belt.

6. Tighten the alternator adjusting bolt to 14–19 ft. lbs. (19–25 Nm).

7. Tighten the alternator mounting bolt to 27–38 ft. lbs. (37–52 Nm).

8. Lower the vehicle.

1.9L Engine

NOTE: An automatic tensioner maintains correct belt tension during operation on the 1991–93 1.9L engine. No adjustment is necessary.

1. Loosen the alternator pivot and adjustment bolts.

2. Install a ½ inch breaker bar or equivalent, to the support bracket that is located behind the alternator.

3. Apply tension to the belt using the breaker bar. Using a belt tension gauge, adjust the tesnsion to 140–180 lbs. for a new belt or 120–140 lbs. for a used belt. While maintaining proper belt tension, tighten the alternator adjustment bolt to 30 ft. lbs. (40 Nm).

4. Remove the belt tension gauge and breaker bar, start the engine and let it idle for 5 minutes.

6. Stop the engine and check the belt tension. If the tension is below 120 lbs., retension the belt to 120–140 lbs. and then tighten the adjustment bolt.

7. Tighten the alternator pivot bolt to 50 ft. lbs. (68 Nm) and the support bracket bolt to 35 ft. lbs. (47 Nm).

2.3L Engine

NOTE: An automatic tensioner maintains correct belt tension during operation on the 1992–93 2.3L engine. No adjustment is necessary.

1. Loosen the alternator pivot and adjustment bolts.

2. Using adjustable pliers or equivalent, apply tension to the belt. Place the bottom jaw of the pliers under the alternator adjustment boss and the top jaw in the notch at the top of the alternator adjustment bracket.

NOTE: A suitable tensioning tool can be made by modifying a 4 in. C-clamp.

3. Squeeze the pliers together and, using a belt tension gauge, adjust the tension to 160 lbs. for a new belt or 140 lbs. for a used belt. While maintaining the proper belt tension, tighten the alternator adjustment bolt to 26 ft. lbs. (35 Nm).

4. Remove the belt tension gauge, start the engine and let it idle for 5 minutes.

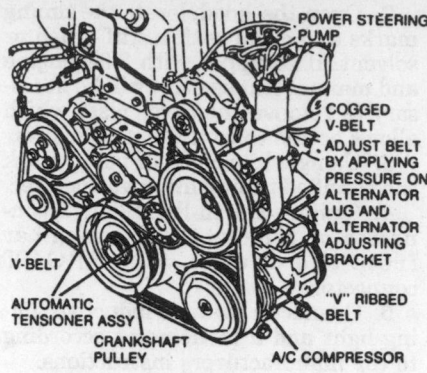

Drive belt arrangement—2.3L Engine

POWER STEERING PUMP
COGGED V-BELT
ADJUST BELT BY APPLYING PRESSURE ON ALTERNATOR LUG AND ALTERNATOR ADJUSTING BRACKET
V-BELT
AUTOMATIC TENSIONER ASSY
CRANKSHAFT PULLEY
"V" RIBBED BELT
A/C COMPRESSOR

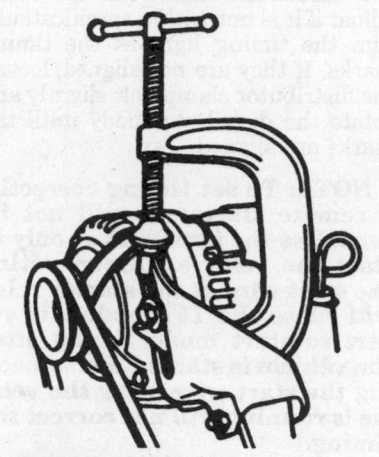

Adjusting alternator belt tension with modified C-clamp—1989–91 2.3L Engine

5. Stop the engine and recheck the belt tension. Adjust to the proper specifications and retighten the adjustment bolt.

6. Tighten the alternator pivot bolt to 52 ft. lbs. (70 Nm).

3.0L Engine

An automatic tensioner maintains correct belt tension during operation on the 3.0L engine. No adjustment is necessary.

REMOVAL & INSTALLATION

Except 1991–93 Escort

1. Disconnect the negative battery cable.

2. Disconnect the wire harness attachments to the integral alternator/regulator assembly. Pull the 2 connectors straight out.

3. Loosen the alternator pivot bolt. Remove the adjustment arm bolt from the alternator.

4. Disengage the alternator drive belt from the alternator pulley.

5. Remove the alternator pivot bolt and alternator/regulator assembly.

6. Remove the alternator fan shield, if equipped.

To install:

7. Position the integral alternator/regulator assembly on the engine.

8. Install the alternator pivot and adjuster arm bolts. Do not tighten the bolts until the belt is tensioned.

9. Install the drive belt over the alternator pulley.

10. Adjust the belt tension according to the proper procedure.

11. Connect wiring harness to the alternator/regulator assembly. Push both connectors straight in.

12. Attach the alternator fan shield to the alternator, if equipped.

13. Connect the negative battery cable.

1991–93 Escort

1.8L ENGINE

1. Disconnect the negative battery cable.

2. Remove the nut securing the wiring connector to the alternator.

3. Remove the field terminal wiring connector.

4. Remove the upper mounting bolt securing the alternator to the alternator to the alternator bracket.

5. Loosen the lower alternator mounting bolt and pivot the alternator forward.

6. Remove the alternator belt from the pulley and position the belt aside.

7. Raise and safely support the vehicle.

8. Remove the lower splash shield located under the accessory belts.

9. Remove the alternator lower mounting bolt and remove the alternator from the vehicle.

To install:

10. Position the alternator into the vehicle and install the lower mounting bolt.

11. Install the lower splash shield.

12. Lower the vehicle.

13. Position the alternator belt onto the pulley and adjust the belt according to the proper procedure.

14. Tighten the upper mounting bolt to 14–19 ft. lbs. (19–25 Nm) and the lower mounting bolt to 27–38 ft. lbs. (37–52 Nm).

15. Install the field terminal wiring connector.

16. Position the wiring connector to the alternator and secure it with the nut.

17. Connect the negative battery cable.

1.9L ENGINE

1. Disconnect the negative battery cable.

2. Using a ⅜ in. drive ratchet or breaker bar inserted in the automatic tensioner, pull the tool toward the

front of the vehicle. While releasing the belt tension, remove the drive belt from the alternator.

3. Remove the nut securing the wiring connector to the alternator.

4. Remove the 2 snap-in type wiring connectors at the alternator.

5. Remove the air conditioning hose bracket from the alternator bracket and position it aside.

6. Remove the alternator mounting bolts.

7. Remove the bolts securing the power steering reservoir and position it aside.

8. Remove the alternator from it's bracket.

To install:

9. Position the alternator onto its bracket.

10. Position the power steering reservoir and secure it with the bolts.

11. Install the alternator upper mounting bolt and tighten to 14–22 ft. lbs. (20–30 Nm). Install the alternator lower mounting bolt and tighten to 29–40 ft. lbs. (40–55 Nm).

12. Position the air conditioning hose bracket onto the alternator bracket and secure it with the bolts.

13. Install the 2 snap-in type wiring connectors into the alternator.

14. Position the wiring connector onto the alternator and secure it with the nut.

15. Install the accessory drive belt.

16. Connect the negative battery cable.

Starter

REMOVAL & INSTALLATION

Except 1991–92 Escort

1. Disconnect the negative battery cable.

2. Raise and safely support the vehicle.

3. Disconnect the starter cable at the starter terminal. On 1991–93 vehicles, disconnect the electrical connector at the solenoid.

NOTE: When disconnecting the plastic hard shell connector at the solenoid S terminal, grasp the plastic connector, depress the plastic tab and pull off the lead assembly. Do not pull on the lead wire or damage may result.

4. Remove the 2 bolts attaching the starter rear support bracket, if equipped. Remove the bracket.

5. If equipped with roll restrictor brace-to-starter studs on the transaxle housing, remove the nuts and remove the brace. On 1989–90 Tempo and Topaz, remove the cable support.

6. Remove the starter retaining bolts and remove the starter.

7. For installation, reverse the removal procedure. Tighten the attaching studs or bolts to 30–40 ft. lbs. (41–54 Nm) on all except 1991–93 Tempo and Topaz. On 1991–93 Tempo and Topaz, tighten the attaching bolts to 16–20 ft. lbs. (21–27 Nm).

1991–93 Escort

1.8L ENGINE

1. Disconnect the negative battery cable.

2. Remove the air duct that connects to the throttle body and resonance chamber.

3. Remove the starter motor upper mounting bolts.

4. Raise and safely support the vehicle.

5. Remove the intake plenum support bracket mounting bolts and remove the bracket.

6. Disconnect the S terminal connector from the starter solenoid.

NOTE: When disconnecting the plastic hard shell connector at the solenoid S terminal, grasp the plastic connector, depress the plastic tab and pull off the lead assembly. Do not pull on the lead wire or damage may result.

7. Remove the B terminal attaching nut and disconnect the cable from the terminal.

8. Remove the starter motor lower mounting bolt and remove the starter motor.

To install:

9. Place the starter motor into its mounting position and install the lower mounting bolt. Tighten the bolt to 15–20 ft. lbs. (20.3–27.0 Nm).

10. Connect the cable to the starter solenoid B terminal and install the attaching nut to the terminal. Tighten the nut to 80–120 inch lbs. (9.0–13.5 Nm).

11. Connect the electrical connector to the starter solenoid S terminal.

12. Install the intake plenum support bracket and tighten the attaching bolts to 27–38 ft. lbs. (37–52 Nm) and the attaching nut to 14–19 ft. lbs. (19–25 Nm).

13. Lower the vehicle.

14. Install the starter motor upper mounting bolts and tighten to 15–20 ft. lbs. (20.3–27.0 Nm).

15. Install the air duct that connects to the throttle body and resonance chamber.

16. Connect the negative battery cable.

1.9L ENGINE

1. Disconnect the negative battery cable.

2. If equipped with an automatic

transaxle, remove the kickdown cable routing bracket from the engine block.

3. Disconnect the wire from the starter solenoid S terminal.

NOTE: When disconnecting the plastic hard shell connector at the solenoid S terminal, grasp the plastic connector, depress the plastic tab and pull off the lead assembly. Do not pull on the lead wire or damage may result.

4. Remove the attaching nut from the starter solenoid B terminal and disconnect the cable from the terminal.

5. Remove the starter motor mounting bolts and remove the starter motor.

To install:

6. Place the starter motor into its mounting position and install the mounting bolts. Tighten the bolts to 15–20 ft. lbs. (20.3–27.0 Nm).

7. Connect the cable to the starter solenoid B terminal and install the attaching nut. Tighten the nut to 80–120 inch lbs. (9–13.5 Nm).

8. Connect the wire to the starter solenoid S terminal.

9. If equipped with an automatic transaxle, install the kickdown cable routing bracket to the engine block.

10. Connect the negative battery cable.

EMISSION CONTROLS

Due to the complex nature of modern electronic engine control systems, comprehensive diagnosis and testing procedures fall outside the confines of this repair manual. For complete information on diagnosis, testing and repair procedures concerning all modern engine and emission control systems, please refer to "Chilton's Guide to Fuel Injection and Electronic Engine Controls".

Emission Warning Lamps

RESETTING

These vehicles have a "CHECK ENGINE" or "SERVICE ENGINE SOON" light that will light when there is a fault in the engine control system. Depending upon the system or sensor involved, the light may go out if the fault is intermittent. However, the fault code will remain stored in the ECU until the system is serviced and the ECU memory cleared. When a fault is detected in certain systems or sensors, the light will remain lit until the system is serviced. When the system has been diagnosed, the problem corrected and the ECU memory cleared, the light will go out.

FUEL SYSTEM

Fuel System Service Precautions

Safety is the most important factor when performing not only fuel system maintenance but any type of maintenance. Failure to conduct maintenance and repairs in a safe manner may result in serious personal injury or death. Maintenance and testing of the vehicle's fuel system components can be accomplished safely and effectively by adhering to the following rules and guidelines.

• To avoid the possibility of fire and personal injury, always disconnect the negative battery cable unless the repair or test procedure requires that battery voltage be applied.

• Always relieve the fuel system pressure prior to disconnecting any fuel system component (injector, fuel rail, pressure regulator, etc.), fitting or fuel line connection. Exercise extreme caution whenever relieving fuel system pressure to avoid exposing skin, face and eyes to fuel spray. Please be advised that fuel under pressure may penetrate the skin or any part of the body that it contacts.

• Always place a shop towel or cloth around the fitting or connection prior to loosening to absorb any excess fuel due to spillage. Ensure that all fuel spillage (should it occur) is quickly removed from engine surfaces. Ensure that all fuel soaked cloths or towels are deposited into a suitable waste container.

• Always keep a dry chemical (Class B) fire extinguisher near the work area.

• Do not allow fuel spray or fuel vapors to come into contact with a spark or open flame.

• Always use a backup wrench when loosing and tightening fuel line connection fittings. This will prevent unnecessary stress and torsion to fuel line piping. Always follow the proper torque specifications.

• Always replace worn fuel fitting O-rings with new. Do not substitute

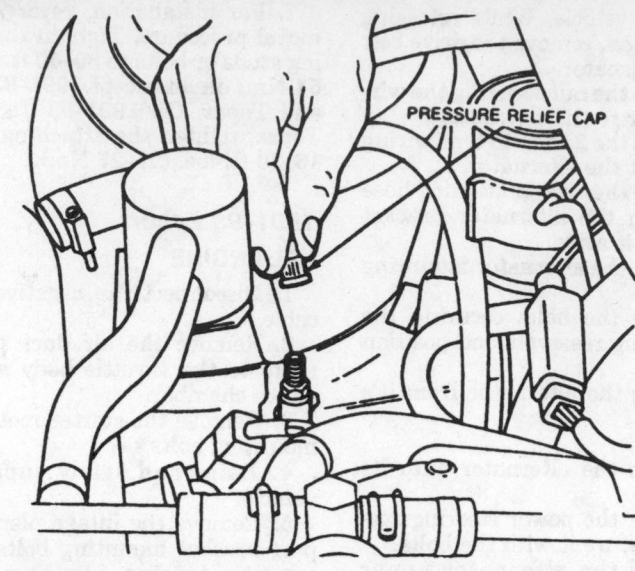

Removing the cap from the pressure relief valve—1989–90 1.9L EFI Engine

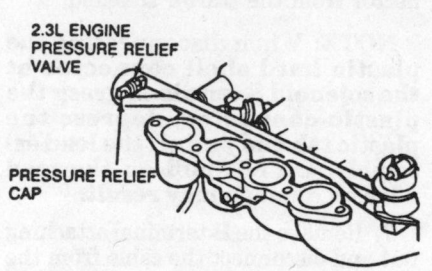

Pressure relief valve location— 2.3L Engine

fuel hose or equivalent, where fuel pipe is installed.

RELIEVING FUEL SYSTEM PRESSURE

The pressure in the fuel system must be released before disconnecting any fuel lines or components.

Except 1.9L Engine With Central Fuel Injection and 1991–93 Escort

1. Disconnect the negative battery cable.
2. A special valve is incorporated in the fuel rail assembly for the purpose of relieving the pressure in the fuel system.
3. Remove the fuel tank cap and remove the cap from the pressure relief valve.
4. **Attach pressure gauge tool T80L–9974–B or equivalent, to the fuel pressure valve on the fuel rail assembly and release the pressure from the system into a suitable container.**

1.9L Engine With Central Fuel Injection

1. Remove the electrical connector at the inertia switch located on the left side of the luggage compartment.
2. Release the fuel system pressure by cranking the engine for 15 seconds.

1991–93 Escort

1. Start the engine.
2. Remove the rear seat cushion and disconnect the fuel pump electrical connectors.
3. Wait for the engine to stall, then turn **OFF** the ignition switch.
4. Connect the fuel pump electrical connectors and install the rear seat cushion.

Fuel Line Couplings

REMOVAL & INSTALLATION

There are several methods used to connect the fuel lines and fuel system components. The hairpin clip push connect fitting, the duck bill clip push connect fitting and the spring lock coupling each require a different procedure to disconnect and connect.

Hairpin Clip Fitting

1. Inspect the internal portion of the fitting for dirt accumulation. If more than a light coating of dust is present, clean the fitting before disassembly.
2. Remove the hairpin clip from the fitting by first bending the shipping tab downward so it will clear the body. This is done, using hands only, by spreading the 2 clip legs about ⅛ in. (3.2mm) each to disengage the body

and pushing the legs into the fitting. Complete removal is accomplished by lightly pulling from the triangular end of the clip and working it clear of the tube and fitting.

NOTE: Do not use any tools when disconnecting the clip.

3. Grasp the fitting and hose assembly and pull in an axial direction to remove the fitting from the steel tube. Adhesion between sealing surfaces may occur. A slight twist of the fitting may be required to break this adhesion for easier removal.

NOTE: On 90 degree elbow connectors, excessive side loading could break the connector body.

4. When the fitting is removed from the tube end, inspect the clip to make sure it has not been damaged. If damaged, replace the clip. If undamaged, immediately install the clip to prevent loss or damage. To install the clip, insert the clip into any 2 adjacent openings with the triangular portion pointing away from the fitting opening. Install the clip to fully engage the body—legs of the hairpin clip locked on the outside of the body. Piloting with an index finger is necessary.

To install:

5. Before installing the fitting on the tube, wipe the tube end with a clean cloth. Inspect the inside of the fitting to make sure it is free of dirt and/or obstructions. Apply a light coat of engine oil to the tube end for ease of assembly.

6. To install the fitting onto the tube, align the fitting and tube axial and push the fitting onto the tube end. When the fitting is engaged, a definite click will be heard. Pull on the fitting to make sure it is fully engaged.

Duck Bill Clip Fitting

1. To disenage the tube from the fitting, align the slot on the quick connect/disconnect tool T82L–9500–AH or equivalent, with either tab on the clip, 90 degrees from the slots on the side of the fitting, and insert the tool.

2. This disengages the duck bill from the tube. Holding the tool and the tube with 1 hand, pull the fitting away from the tube.

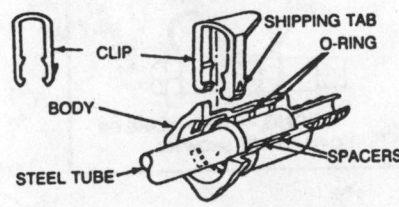

Hairpin clip push connect fitting

DUCK BILL CLIP

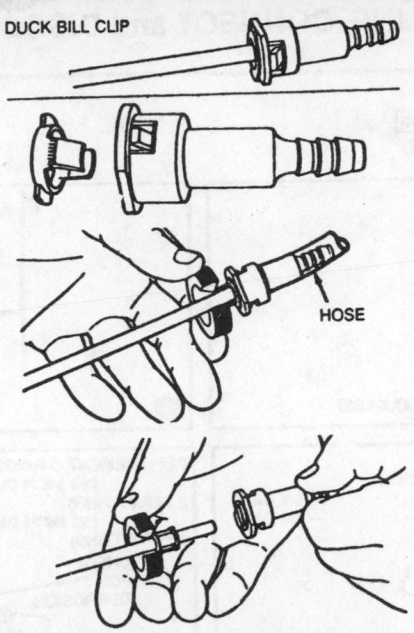

HOSE

Duck bill clip push connect fitting

NOTE: Only moderate effort is required if the tube has been properly disengaged. Use hands only.

3. After disassembly, inspect and clean the tube sealing surface. Also inspect the inside of the fitting for damage to the retaining clip. If the retaining clip appears to be damaged, replace it.

NOTE: Some fuel tubes have a secondary bead which aligns with the outer surface of the clip. These beads can make tool insertion difficult. If there is extreme difficulty, use the ½ in. (12.7mm) fitting method as an alternative.

To install:

4. Install the clip into the body by inserting 1 of the retaining clip serrated edges on the duck bill portion into 1 of the window openings. Push on the other side until the clip snaps into place. Slide the fuel line back into the clip.

Spring Lock Coupling

The spring lock coupling is a fuel line coupling held together by a garter spring inside a circular cage. When the coupling is connected together, the flared end of the female fitting slips behind the garter spring inside the cage of the male fitting. The garter spring and cage then prevent the flared end of the female fitting from pulling out of the cage. As an additional locking feature, most vehicles have a horseshoe shaped retaining clip that improves the retaining reliability of the spring lock coupling.

Fuel Tank

REMOVAL & INSTALLATION

Except 1991–93 Escort

1. Disconnect the negative battery cable.

2. Relieve the fuel system pressure.

3. Fuel should be drained from the tank as completely as possible prior to tank removal. This is accomplished by siphoning or pumping fuel out through the fuel filler neck.

NOTE: There are reservoirs inside the fuel tank to maintain fuel near the fuel pickup during vehicle cornering maneuvers and under low fuel operating conditions. These reservoirs could block siphon tubes or hoses from reaching the bottom of the fuel tank. This situation can be overcome with a few repeated attempts using different hose orientations.

4. Disconnect the fuel hoses and tubes. Disconnect the push connect fittings according to the proper procedure.

5. Disconnect the electrical hookup to the fuel tank sender unit. On some vehicles, the electrical connection is inaccessible on top of the tank and no intermediate connection point is provided. In these cases, the electrical connector must be disconnected from the fuel sender with the tank partially removed from the vehicle.

6. On Tempo and Topaz equipped with all-wheel drive, perform the following procedure to gain access to the fuel tank:

   a. Remove the exhaust system.

   b. Position a suitable jack under the rear axle.

   c. Remove the bolts from the torque tube support bracket.

   d. Remove 1 bolt each from the left and center differential support brackets.

   e. Lower the differential approximately 6–8 in.

   f. Remove 2 horizontal bolts retaining the axle pinion support crossmember.

7. On all vehicles, place a safety support under the fuel tank and remove the bolts or nuts from 1 end of the fuel tank straps. The straps are hinged at 1 end. Remove the bolts from the unhinged end and swing the straps aside.

8. Partially remove the tank and disconnect the fuel lines and the electrical connector from the fuel gauge sender, if required.

9. Remove the tank from the vehicle.

SPRING LOCK COUPLING CONNECT and DISCONNECT PROCEDURE

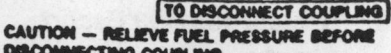

TO DISCONNECT COUPLING

CAUTION — RELIEVE FUEL PRESSURE BEFORE DISCONNECTING COUPLING

CLIP

① REMOVE CLIP FROM COUPLING

USE SPECIFIED TOOL OR EQUIVALENT

TOOL:
— 3/8 INCH
— 1/2 INCH

CAGE OPENING

② FIT TOOL TO COUPLING SO THAT TOOL CAN ENTER CAGE OPENING TO RELEASE THE GARTER SPRING.

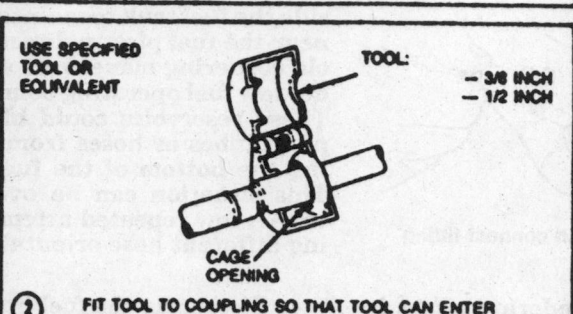

PUSH TOOL INTO CAGE OPENING

NOTE: SPECIFIED TOOL WILL FIT AROUND RUBBER COVERED FUEL LINE.

③ PUSH THE TOOL INTO THE CAGE OPENING TO RELEASE THE FEMALE FITTING FROM THE GARTER SPRING

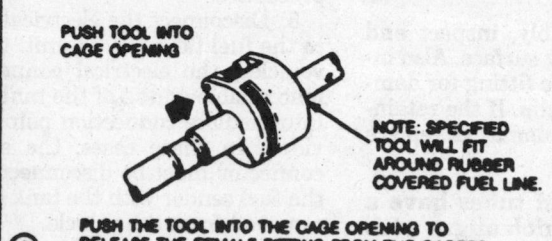

④ PULL THE COUPLING MALE AND FEMALE FITTINGS APART

⑤ REMOVE THE TOOL FROM THE DISCONNECTED SPRING LOCK COUPLING

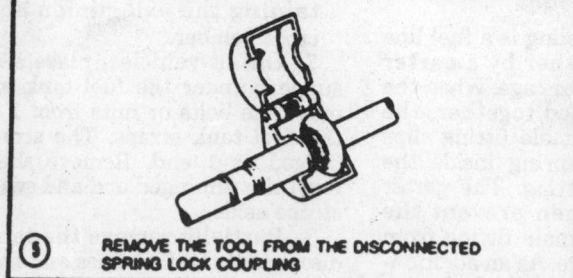

TO CONNECT COUPLING

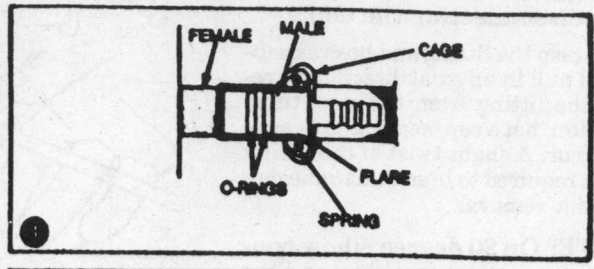

FEMALE   MALE   CAGE

O-RINGS   FLARE   SPRING

①

REPLACEMENT O-RINGS (3/8 INCH DIA., 2 PER FITTING) (1/2 INCH DIA., 2 PER FITTING)

USE ONLY SPECIFIED FUEL RESISTANT O-RINGS (COLOR: BROWN)

CHECK FOR CORROSION

LUBRICATE O-RINGS WITH CLEAN ENGINE OIL

CLEAN FITTINGS WITH SOLVENT CHECK FOR MISSING OR DAMAGED O-RINGS. REPLACE MISSING O-RINGS. IF EITHER O-RING IS DAMAGED, REPLACE BOTH O-RINGS.

REPLACEMENT GARTER SPRINGS:
3/8-INCH —
1/2-INCH —

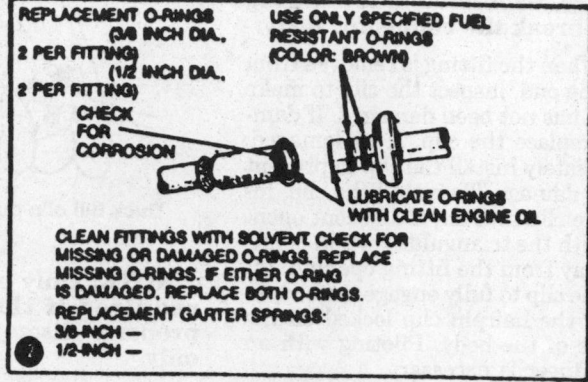

②

GARTER SPRING

③ TO ENSURE COUPLING ENGAGEMENT, PULL ON FITTING AND VISUALLY CHECK TO BE SURE GARTER SPRING IS OVER FLARED END OF FEMALE FITTING

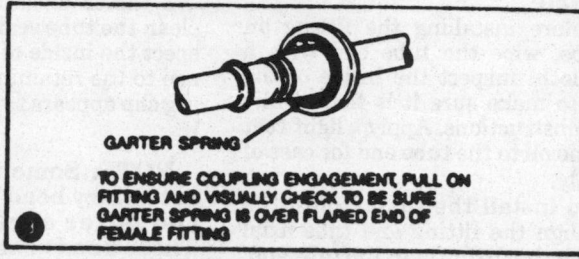

FUEL LINE

TETHER CLAMPED

④ YES

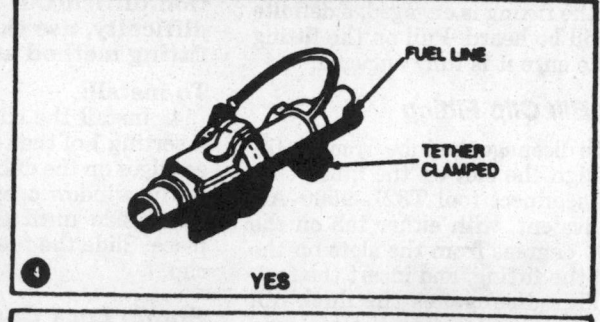

NO   NO

NO

FEMALE   RUBBER HOSE

WRONG — WHEN FLARE OR O-RINGS ARE SHOWING

⑤

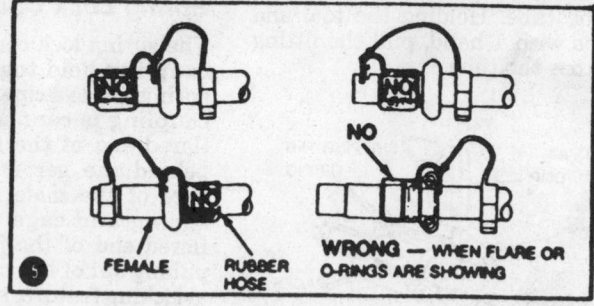

To install:

10. Before proceeding, check the following:

   a. Leak check the sender unit. If necessary, use fuel tank sender wrench T74P-9275-A or equivalent.

   b. Make sure the fuel vapor separator valve is installed completely on the tank top.

   c. Make all required fuel line, fuel return line, vapor vent and electrical connections which will be inaccessible after the tank is installed.

11. Position the fuel tank in the vehicle.

12. Bring the fuel tank straps around the tank and start attaching the nut or bolt. Align the tank with the straps.

13. Check the hoses and wiring mounted on the tank top, to make sure they are correctly routed and will not be pinched between tank and body.

14. Tighten the fuel tank strap attaching bolts to 21–29 ft. lbs. (28–40 Nm) on Escort or 25–39 ft. lbs. (34–54 Nm) on Tempo and Topaz.

15. Connect the fuel tank hoses and lines. Verify that the fuel supply, fuel return and vapor vent connections are made correctly.

16. Connect the electrical connections.

17. Install the fuel filler hoses that connect the fuel tank to the fuel filler pipe. Install new hose clamps and tighten.

18. On Tempo and Topaz with all-wheel drive, perform the following procedure:

   a. Position the crossmember axle pinion support and install 2 retaining bolts.

   b. Raise the differential assembly into position.

   c. Install the bolts retaining the left and center differential support brackets.

   d. Install the torque tube support bracket retaining bolts.

   e. Remove the jack.

   f. Install the exhaust system.

19. Replace the fuel that was drained from the tank.

20. Check all connections for leaks.

21. Connect the negative battery cable.

22. Turn the ignition key **ON** to run the fuel pump and pressurize the system. Check for fuel leaks.

1991–93 Escort

1. Relieve the fuel system pressure.

2. Disconnect the negative battery cable.

3. Completely drain the fuel tank by siphoning or pumping out the fuel through the fuel filler hose.

4. Remove the rear seat cushion.

5. Remove the ground strap retain-ing screw and the 3 remaining fuel pump assembly cover screws.

6. Remove the fuel pump assembly cover.

7. Remove the clips from the fuel hoses.

8. Disconnect the fuel hoses from the fuel pump assembly.

9. Raise and safely support the vehicle.

10. Loosen the filler neck clamp and disconnect the filler neck hose from the filler neck.

11. Loosen the clamp and disconnect the filler neck overflow hose from the overflow tube.

12. Disconnect the vapor hoses from the vapor tubes.

13. Remove the exhaust middle pipe heat shield.

14. Support the fuel tank with a suitable jack.

15. Remove the mounting bolts from the fuel tank straps, unclip the straps and remove them.

16. Remove the 3 fuel tank heat shield attaching bolts from the fuel tank and remove the fuel tank.

To install:

17. Place the fuel tank onto the fuel tank heat shield and install the heat shield attaching bolts into the fuel tank.

18. Clip the fuel tank straps into their mounting positions.

19. Install the fuel tank strap mounting bolts and tighten to 27–38 ft. lbs. (37–52 Nm).

20. Remove the support jack from under the fuel tank.

21. Install the exhaust middle pipe heat shield.

22. Connect the vapor hoses to the vapor tubes.

23. Connect the filler neck hose to the filler neck and install the attaching clamp.

24. Connect the filler neck overflow hose to the overflow tube and install the attaching clamp.

25. Lower the vehicle.

26. Connect the fuel hoses to the fuel pump assembly.

27. Install the clips onto the fuel hoses.

28. Position the fuel pump assembly cover and ground strap and install the retaining screws.

29. Connect the fuel pump assembly electrical connector.

30. Install the rear seat cushion.

31. Replace the fuel that was drained from the tank during the removal procedure. Check for leaks.

32. Connect the negative battery cable.

33. Turn the ignition switch **ON** to run the fuel pump and pressurize the system. Check for fuel leaks.

Fuel Filter

REMOVAL & INSTALLATION

Except 1991–93 Escort

1. Disconnect the negative battery cable.

2. Properly relieve the fuel system pressure.

3. Remove the push connect fittings according to the proper procedure. Install new retainer clips in each connector fitting.

NOTE: The flow arrow direction should be noted to ensure proper flow of fuel through the replacement filter.

4. Remove the filter from the bracket by loosening the filter retaining clamp enough to allow the filter to pass through.

To install:

5. Install the filter in the bracket, ensuring the proper direction of flow, as noted earlier. Tighten the clamp to 15–25 inch lbs. (1.7–2.8 Nm).

6. Install push connect fittings at both ends of the filter.

7. Connect the negative battery cable.

8. Start the engine and inspect for leaks.

1991–93 Escort

1. Properly relieve the fuel system pressure.

2. Disconnect the negative battery cable.

3. Position a suitable container below the fuel filter to collect any excess fuel that may leak from the filter and lines.

4. Remove the retaining clip from the fuel filter upper hose.

5. Disconnect the upper hose from the fuel filter and drain any excess fuel into the container. Plug the hose.

6. Loosen the fuel filter mounting clamp.

7. Raise and safely support the vehicle.

8. Remove the retaining clip from the fuel filter lower hose.

9. Disconnect the lower hose from the fuel filter and drain any excess fuel into the container. Plug the hose.

10. Lower the vehicle.

11. Remove the fuel filter.

To install:

12. Position the fuel filter and tighten the filter mounting clamp.

13. Connect the filter upper hose to the filter and install the upper hose retaining clip.

14. Raise and safely support the vehicle.

15. Connect the filter lower hose to

the filter and install the lower hose retaining clip.

16. Lower the vehicle.

17. Connect the negative battery cable.

18. Start the engine and check for leaks.

Electric Fuel Pump

PRESSURE TESTING

Except 1.8L Engine

1. Make sure the ignition key is in the **OFF** position.

2. Properly relieve the fuel system pressure.

3. Disconnect the fuel pump output line and connect a suitable pressure tester.

4. Ground the fuel pump lead of the Self-Test connector through a jumper wire at the **FP** lead.

5. Turn the ignition key **ON**, to operate the fuel pump, and observe the fuel pressure.

6. The fuel pressure should be 13–17 psi on the 1.9L CFI engine, 50–60 psi on the 2.3L engine or 35–40 psi on the 1.9L EFI and 3.0L engines.

7. Turn the ignition key **OFF** and remove the jumper wire.

8. Properly relieve the fuel system pressure and remove the pressure tester.

9. Reconnect the fuel line.

1.8L Engine

1. Make sure the ignition key is in the **OFF** position.

2. Properly relieve the fuel system pressure.

3. Install a suitable fuel pressure tester in the fuel line between the fuel filter and the fuel rail.

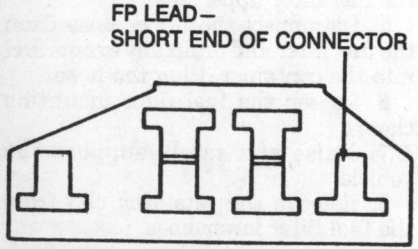

FP LEAD—
SHORT END OF CONNECTOR

Self-Test connector—except 1.8L Engine

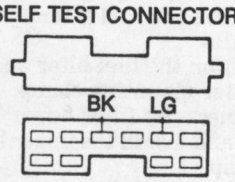

SELF TEST CONNECTOR

BK   LG

Fuel pump test connector terminals—1.8L Engine

4. Jump the fuel pump test connector terminals together, terminal **LG** and terminal **BK** at the Self-Test connector.

5. Turn the ignition key to **RUN**, to operate the fuel pump, and observe the fuel pressure.

6. The fuel pressure should be 64–85 psi.

7. Turn the ignition key **OFF** and remove the jumper wire.

8. Properly relieve the fuel system pressure and remove the pressure tester.

REMOVAL & INSTALLATION

NOTE: The fuel pump is mounted on the fuel sender assembly inside the fuel tank.

Except 1991–93 Escort

1. Properly relieve the fuel system pressure.

2. Disconnect the negative battery cable.

3. Remove the fuel tank.

4. Remove any dirt that has accumulated around the fuel pump retaining flange so it will not enter the fuel tank during removal and installation.

5. Turn the fuel pump locking ring counterclockwise using fuel tank sender wrench D84P-9257-A or equivalent, and remove the lock ring.

6. On all except all-wheel drive vehicles, remove the fuel pump and bracket assembly and remove the seal gasket and discard.

7. On all-wheel drive vehicles, proceed as follows:

   a. Partially lift up the sender unit and disconnect the jet pump line and the electrical connector to the resistor.

   b. Remove the fuel pump and bracket assembly and remove the seal gasket and discard.

   c. Remove the jet pump assembly attaching screw and remove the jet pump assembly.

To install:

8. Clean the fuel pump mounting flange and fuel tank mounting surface and seal ring groove.

9. Put a light coating of multi-purpose lubricant C1AZ-19590-BA or equivalent, on a new seal ring to hold it in place during assembly and install it in the fuel ring groove.

10. On all-wheel drive vehicles, install the jet pump assembly and attaching screw. Tighten the screw to 10–15 ft. lbs. (14–20 Nm).

11. Install the fuel pump and sender assembly carefully to ensure that the filter is not damaged. Make sure the locating keys are in the keyways and the seal ring remains in place.

12. On all-wheel drive vehicles, con-

nect the jet pump line and the electrical connector to the resistor. Make sure the locating keyways and seal ring remain in place.

13. Hold the assembly in place and install the locking ring finger-tight. Make sure all locking tabs are under the tank lock ring tabs.

14. Rotate the locking ring clockwise using fuel tank sender wrench D84P-9275-A or equivalent, until the ring stops against the stops.

15. Install the fuel tank into the vehicle according to the proper procedure.

16. Connect the negative battery cable.

1991–93 Escort

1. Properly relieve the fuel system pressure.

2. Disconnect the negative battery cable.

3. Remove the rear seat cushion. Disconnect the electrical connector at the fuel pump.

4. Remove the ground strap retaining screw and the 3 remaining fuel pump assembly cover screws.

5. Remove the fuel pump assembly cover.

6. Remove the clips from the fuel hoses.

7. Disconnect the fuel hoses from the fuel pump assembly.

8. Using a suitable removal tool, carefully remove and, if necessary, discard the fuel pump assembly spanner nut.

9. Remove the fuel pump assembly and discard the gasket.

To install:

10. Install a new gasket and position the fuel pump assembly in the tank.

11. Install the fuel pump assembly spanner nut.

12. Connect the fuel hoses to the fuel pump assembly and install the clips.

13. Position the fuel pump assembly cover and ground strap and install the retaining screws.

14. Connect the fuel pump assembly electrical connector.

15. Connect the negative battery cable.

16. Turn the ignition switch **ON** to run the fuel pump and pressurize the fuel system. Check for fuel leaks.

17. Install the rear seat cushion.

Fuel Injection

IDLE SPEED ADJUSTMENT

1.8L Engine

1. Apply the parking brake and make sure the vehicle is in **N** or **P**.

2. Start the engine and warm it to normal operating temperature.

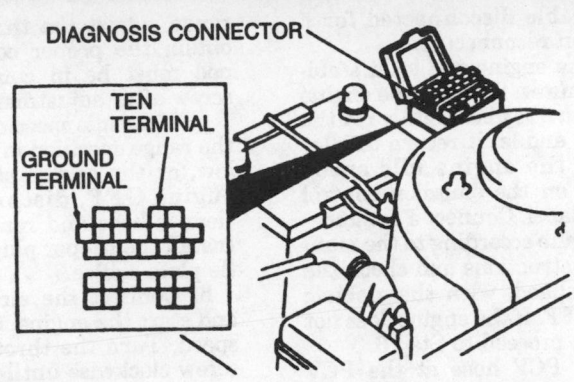

Diagnosis connector location—1991-93 Escort with 1.8L Engine

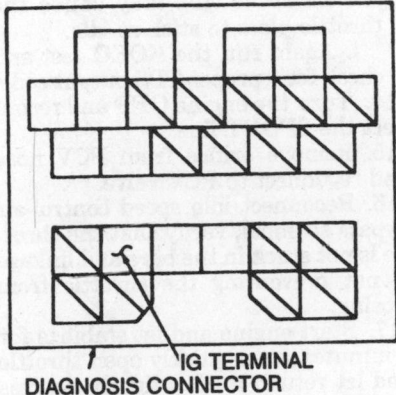

IG terminal location—1991-93 Escort with 1.8L Engine

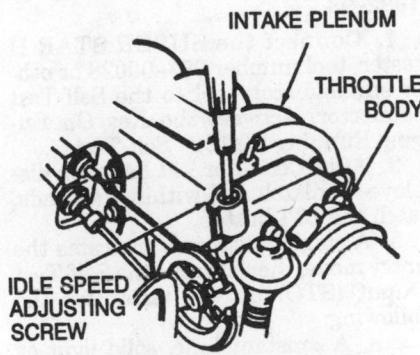

Idle speed adjusting screw location— 1991-93 Escort with 1.8L Engine

3. Turn OFF all electrical loads and accessories.

4. Using a jumper wire, connect the **GROUND** terminal to the **TEN** terminal on the diagnosis connector.

5. Connect the positive lead of a suitable tachometer to the **IG** terminal on the diagnosis connector and the tachometer negative lead to the negative battery terminal.

6. Check the vehicle idle speed when the electric cooling fan is not operating. The idle speed should be 700-800 rpm.

NOTE: When the parking brake is not applied, the idle speed for automatic transaxle vehicles sold in Canada is approximately 800 rpm.

7. If the idle speed is not within specification, adjust the idle speed by turning the idle speed adjusting screw until the idle speed is within specification.

8. Remove the jumper wire from the diagnosis connector and remove the tachometer.

1.9L CFI Engine

1. Place the transaxle in **P** or **N** and apply the parking brake. Make sure the heater and all engine accessories are OFF.

2. Start the engine and bring to normal operating temperature. Check and, if necessary, adjust the ignition timing.

3. Turn the engine **OFF** and disconnect the negative battery cable. Leave the cable disconnected for 5 minutes, then reconnect it.

4. Start the engine and let it stabilize for 2 minutes, then rev the engine and let it return to idle. Lightly rev the engine again and let it return to idle.

5. Check the engine idle speed specification on the emission control information label. Connect a tachometer to the engine according to the manufacturers instructions and check the engine idle speed, with the electric cooling fan OFF. If the engine does not idle properly, proceed to Step 6.

6. Turn the engine **OFF** and remove air cleaner. Connect a jumper wire between the Self-Test Input (STI) and signal return pin on the self-test connector.

7. Turn ignition key **ON** but do not the start engine. Wait for the ISC plunger to retract; approximately 10–15 seconds.

8. Disconnect vehicle harness from the ISC motor. Turn ignition key **OFF** and remove jumper wire.

9. Start the engine and check the idle speed. If the idle speed is 600 ± 50 rpm, proceed to Step 12. If not continue with Step 10.

10. If not already removed, remove the plug that covers the throttle stop adjusting screw. It is necessary to remove the CFI assembly from the vehicle to remove the plug. After removing the plug, install a new throttle stop adjusting screw.

11. Adjust the throttle stop adjusting screw until the engine idle speed is 600 ± 50 rpm.

12. Shut the engine **OFF** and reconnect the wiring harness to the ISC motor. Reinstall the air cleaner.

1.9L EFI Engine

1989–90

1. Place the transaxle in **P** or **N** and apply the parking brake. Make sure the heater and all engine accessories are OFF.

2. Start the engine and bring to normal operating temperature. Check and, if necessary, adjust the ignition timing.

3. Turn the engine **OFF** and disconnect the negative battery cable. Leave the cable disconnected for 5 minutes, then reconnect it.

4. Start the engine and let it stabilize for 2 minutes, then rev the engine and let it return to idle. Lightly rev the engine again and let it return to idle.

5. Check the engine idle speed specification on the emission control information label. Connect a tachometer to the engine according to the manufacturers instructions and check the engine idle speed, with the electric cooling fan OFF. If the engine does not idle properly, proceed to Step 6.

6. Shut the engine **OFF**. Disconnect idle speed control-air bypass solenoid.

7. Start engine and run at 2000 rpm for 60 seconds.

8. Check/adjust idle rpm to 950 ± 50 on all except 1990 1.9L SEFI MA engine. On 1990 1.9L SEFI MA engine, check/adjust idle rpm to 650 ± 50. Adjust by turning the throttle plate stop screw.

9. Shut engine **OFF**, reconnect idle speed control-air bypass solenoid. Verify the throttle is not stuck in the bore and linkage is not preventing the throttle from closing.

10. Start the engine and let stabilize for 2 minutes, then quickly open throttle and let return to idle, lightly depress and release accelerator. Check idle speed.

1991

1. Place the transaxle in **P** or **N** and apply the parking brake. Make sure the heater and all engine accessories are OFF.

2. Start the engine and bring to normal operating temperature. Check

and, if necessary, adjust the ignition timing.

3. Turn the engine OFF and disconnect the negative battery cable. Leave the cable disconnected for 5 minutes, then reconnect it.

4. Start the engine and let stabilize for 2 minutes, then rev the engine and let it return to idle. Lightly rev the engine and release the accelerator; let the engine idle.

5. Check the engine idle speed specification on the emission control information label. Connect a tachometer to the engine according to the manufacturers instructions and check the engine idle speed, with the electric cooling fan OFF. If the engine does not idle properly, proceed to Step 6.

6. Stop the engine and disconnect the idle speed control air bypass solenoid.

7. Start the engine and run it at 2000 rpm for 60 seconds.

8. After the engine returns to idle, check the idle speed. It should be 600 ± 150 rpm.

9. If the idle rpm is incorrect, turn the plate stop screw until the idle speed is within specification.

10. Turn the engine OFF and reconnect the idle speed control-air bypass solenoid. Verify the throttle is not stuck in the bore and the linkage is not preventing the throttle from closing.

11. Start the engine and let it stabilize for 2 minutes, then rev the engine and let it return to idle; lightly depress and release the accelerator and let the engine idle. Check idle speed.

1992–93

The idle speed on 1992–93 vehicles with the 1.9L engine is not adjustable. If the idle speed is incorrect, check for low battery and charging system, idle speed control device contamination, throttle bore contamination, fuel contamination, improper fuel octane rating, low engine operating temperature, low coolant level or leaking cooling system, clogged PCV system, faulty clutch or transmission, brakes not releasing, ignition system fault, exhaust system or EGR fault, or vacuum leaks.

2.3L Engine

1989–91

1. Place the transaxle in P or N and apply the parking brake. Make sure the heater and all engine accessories are OFF.

2. Start the engine and bring to normal operating temperature. Check and, if necessary, adjust the ignition timing, leaving the SPOUT line unplugged.

3. Turn the engine OFF and disconnect the negative battery cable.

Leave the cable disconnected for 5 minutes, then reconnect it.

4. Start the engine and let it stabilize for 2 minutes, then rev the engine and let it return to idle. Lightly rev the engine again and let it return to idle.

5. Check the engine idle speed specification on the emission control information label. Connect a tachometer to the engine according to the manufacturers instructions and check the engine idle speed, with the electric cooling fan OFF. If the engine does not idle properly, proceed to Step 6.

6. Remove PCV hose at the PCV valve and install 0.200 in. diameter orifice, tool T86P–9600–A or equivalent.

7. Disconnect the idle speed control-air bypass solenoid.

8. Start engine and run at 2500 rpm for 30 seconds.

9. Place automatic transaxle in D or manual transaxle in N.

10. On 1989–90 vehicles, check/adjust idle rpm to 1025 ± 50 for automatic transaxle or 1550 ± 50 for manual transaxle. Adjust by turning the throttle plate stop screw.

11. On 1991 vehicles, check the idle speed. It should be 950 ± 150 rpm with automatic transaxle or 1550 ± 200 rpm on manual transaxle.

12. On 1991 vehicles, if the idle speed is too low, proceed as follows:

a. Check for the presence of a throttle plate orifice plug. If there is no plug, turn the screw clockwise to the desired rpm, ± 25 rpm.

b. If there is a plug from previous service, remove the plug and adjust the screw in either direction, as required. The screw must be in contact with the lever pad after adjustment.

13. On 1991 vehicles, if the idle speed is too high, proceed as follows:

a. Turn the engine OFF and disconnect the air cleaner hose.

b. Block off the orifice in the throttle plate temporarily with tape. If the orifice already has a plug from previous service, proceed to Step d.

c. Restart the engine and check the idle speed. Mass air engines will require the air cleaner hose to be reattached before the idle speed check. If the engine stalled, crack open the throttle plate with the stop screw. Do not over adjust.

d. If the idle speed continues to be fast, connect a suitable scan tool to the Self-Test connector and perform the Key On Engine Off (KOEO) Self-Test. Check for a Throttle Position Sensor (TPS) output code.

e. If the output code is within range, remove the tape and check for vacuum leaks, throttle linkage binding or other causes for excessive high idle.

f. If the output code is out of

range, adjust the throttle screw to obtain the proper code. The lever pad must be in contact with the screw after adjustment.

g. If the idle speed drops to within the range specified in Step 11 or below, or the engine stalls, turn the engine OFF, disconnect the air cleaner hose and remove the tape. Install the proper plug in the throttle plate orifice.

h. Connect the air cleaner hose and start the engine. Check the idle speed. Turn the throttle plate stop screw clockwise until the idle speed is within the range specified in Step 11. Do not turn the screw counterclockwise as this may cause the throttle plate to stick at idle.

i. Again run the KOEO test and check for a proper TPS output code.

14. Turn the engine OFF and reconnect the SPOUT line.

15. Remove orifice from PCV hose and reconnect to PCV valve.

16. Reconnect idle speed control-air bypass solenoid, verify that the throttle is not stuck in the bore and linkage is not preventing the throttle from closing.

17. Start engine and let stabilize for 2 minutes, then quickly open throttle and let return to idle, lightly depress and release accelerator. Check idle speed.

1992–93

1. Connect the SUPER STAR II tester, tool number 007–00028 or other suitable scan tool to the Self-Test connector. Activate the Key On Engine Running (KOER) Self-Test.

2. After Code 1 or 111 has been displayed, unlatch and within 4 seconds, latch the STI button.

3. A single pulse code indicates the entry mode, then observe the Self-Test Ouput (STO) on the tester for the following:

a. A constant tone, solid light or STO LO readout means the base idle speed is within the correct range. To exit the test, unlatch the STI button, then wait 4 seconds for reinitialization. After 10 minutes, the tool will exit by itself.

b. A beeping tone, flashing light or STO LO readout at 8 Hz indicates the Throttle Position Sensor (TPS) is out of range due to over adjustment. Adjustment may be required.

c. A beeping tone, flashing light or STO LO readout at 4 Hz indicates the base idle speed is too fast and adjustment is required. Proceed to Step 5.

d. A beeping tone, flashing light or STO LO readout at 1 Hz indicates the base idle speed is too low and adjustment is required. Proceed to Step 4.

4. If the idle speed is too low, check for the presence of a throttle plate orifice plug. If there is no plug, turn the throttle screw clockwise until the conditions in Step 3a exist. If there is a plug from previous service, remove the plug and then adjust the screw in either direction, as required. The screw must be in contact with the lever pad after adjustment.

5. If the idle speed is too high, proceed as follows:

   a. Turn the engine **OFF**.

   b. Block off the orifice in the throttle plate temporarily with tape. If the orifice already has a plug, proceed to Step d.

   c. Reattach the air intake hose. Restart the engine and check the idle speed using the Self-Test. If the engine stalled, crack open the plate with the throttle return screw.

   d. If the idle speed continues to be fast, run the Key On Engine Off (KOEO) Self-Test and check for a TPS output code.

   e. If the output code is within range, remove the tape and check for vacuum leaks, throttle linkage binding, or other causes for excessive high idle.

   f. If the output code is out of range, adjust the throttle screw to obtain the proper code. The lever pad must be in contact with the screw after adjustment.

   g. If the idle speed drops to or below the desired level, as indicated by the Self-Test Output tone, turn the engine **OFF**, disconnect the air cleaner hose and remove the tape.

   h. Install the proper plug in the throttle plate orifice.

   i. Reconnect the air cleaner hose. Start the engine and turn the throttle plate stop screw clockwise until the conditions in Step 3a exist. Do not turn the screw counterclockwise as this may cause the throttle plate to stick at idle.

6. Run the KOEO Self-Test for proper TPS output code.

7. Make sure the throttle is not stuck in the bore and the linkage is not preventing the throttle from closing.

3.0L Engine

1. Connect the SUPER STAR II tester, tool number 007-00028 or other suitable scan tool to the Self-Test connector. Activate the Key On Engine Running (KOER) Self-Test.

2. After Code 1 or 111 has been displayed, unlatch and within 4 seconds, latch the STI button.

3. A single pulse code indicates the entry mode, then observe the Self-Test Ouput (STO) on the tester for the following:

   a. A constant tone, solid light or **STO LO** readout means the base idle speed is within the correct range. To exit the test, unlatch the STI button, then wait 4 seconds for reinitialization. After 10 minutes, the tool will exit by itself.

   b. A beeping tone, flashing light or **STO LO** readout at 8 Hz indicates the Throttle Position Sensor (TPS) is out of range due to over adjustment. Adjustment may be required.

   c. A beeping tone, flashing light or **STO LO** readout at 4 Hz indicates the base idle speed is too fast and adjustment is required. Proceed to Step 5.

   d. A beeping tone, flashing light or **STO LO** readout at 1 Hz indicates the base idle speed is too low and adjustment is required. Proceed to Step 4.

4. If the idle speed is too low, check for the presence of a throttle plate orifice plug. If there is no plug, turn the throttle screw clockwise until the conditions in Step 3a exist. If there is a plug from previous service, remove the plug and then adjust the screw in either direction, as required. The screw must be in contact with the lever pad after adjustment.

5. If the idle speed is too high, proceed as follows:

   a. Turn the engine **OFF**.

   b. Block off the orifice in the throttle plate temporarily with tape. If the orifice already has a plug, proceed to Step d.

   c. Reattach the air intake hose. Restart the engine and check the idle speed using the Self-Test. If the engine stalled, crack open the plate with the throttle return screw.

   d. If the idle speed continues to be fast, run the Key On Engine Off (KOEO) Self-Test and check for a TPS output code.

   e. If the output code is within range, remove the tape and check for vacuum leaks, throttle linkage binding or other causes for excessive high idle.

   f. If the output code is out of range, adjust the throttle screw to obtain the proper code. The lever pad must be in contact with the screw after adjustment.

   g. If the idle speed drops to or below the desired level, as indicated by the Self-Test Output tone, turn the engine **OFF**, disconnect the air cleaner hose and remove the tape.

   h. Install the proper plug in the throttle plate orifice.

   i. Reconnect the air cleaner hose. Start the engine and turn the throttle plate stop screw clockwise until the conditions in Step 3a exist. Do not turn the screw counterclockwise as this may cause the throttle plate to stick at idle.

6. Run the KOEO Self-Test for proper TPS output code.

7. Make sure the throttle is not stuck in the bore and the linkage is not preventing the throttle from closing.

IDLE MIXTURE ADJUSTMENT

Idle mixture is controlled by the Electronic Control Unit and is not adjustable.

Fuel Injector

REMOVAL & INSTALLATION

1.8L Engine

1. Properly relieve the fuel system pressure.

2. Disconnect the negative battery cable.

3. Disconnect the fuel pressure and return lines from the fuel rail.

4. Disconnect the PCV hose from the intake plenum and cylinder head cover.

5. Disconnect the fuel pressure regulator vacuum hose and the fuel injector wiring harness electrical connectors.

6. Remove the fuel rail mounting bolts and remove the fuel rail.

7. Remove the fuel injectors, grommets and insulators.

8. Installation is the reverse of the removal procedure. Lubricate new O-rings with clean engine oil and install them on the fuel injectors prior to installation.

1.9L CFI Engine

1. Disconnect the negative battery cable.

2. Disconnect the electrical connector from the injector top.

3. Remove the fuel injector retaining screw and retainer.

4. Remove the injector and lower O-ring. Discard the O-ring.

To install:

5. Lubricate a new lower O-ring and the injector seat area with clean engine oil. Do not use transmission oil.

6. Install the lower O-ring on the injector.

7. Lubricate the upper O-ring and clean and lubricate the throttle body O-ring seat.

8. Install the injector by centering and applying a steady downward pressure with a slight rotational force.

9. Install the injector retainer and retaining screw. Tighten the retaining screws to 28–32 inch lbs. (3.2–3.6 Nm).

10. Connect the electrical connector.

11. Connect the negative battery cable.

1.9L EFI Engine

1. Relieve the fuel system pressure and disconnect the negative battery cable.

2. Remove spring-lock coupling retainer clips from fuel inlet and return fittings.

3. Disconnect fuel supply and return lines.

3. Remove vacuum line from fuel pressure regulator.

4. Disconnect the fuel injector wiring harness.

5. Carefully remove connectors from individual injectors(s) as required.

6. Remove the 2 bolts securing the injector manifold assembly and remove the assembly.

7. Grasping the injector's body, pull up while gently rocking the injector from side-to-side.

8. Inspect the injector O-rings (2 per injector) for signs of deterioration. Replace as required.

9. Inspect the injector "plastic hat" (covering the injector pintle) and washer for signs of deterioration. Replace as required. If hat is missing, look for it in intake manifold.

To install:

10. Use a light grade oil to lubricate new O-rings and install 2 on each injector .

11. Install the injector(s). Use a light, twisting, pushing motion to install the injector(s).

12. Carefully seat the fuel injector manifold assembly on the injectors and secure the manifold with the attaching bolts. Tighten to 15–22 ft. lbs. (20–30 Nm).

13. Connect the vacuum line to the fuel pressure regulator.

14. Connect fuel supply and fuel return lines.

15. Reconnect spring-lock coupling retaining clips on fuel inlet and return fittings.

16. Check entire assembly for proper alignment and seating.

17. Connect the negative battery cable. With the fuel injector electrical connectors disconnected, turn the ignition switch to the **RUN** position and let the fuel pump pressurize the system. Check for fuel leaks and correct, as necessary.

18. Turn the ignition switch **OFF**.

19. Connect the fuel injector wiring harness connectors.

20. Start the engine and check for leaks.

2.3L Engine

1. Properly relieve the fuel system pressure.

2. Disconnect the engine air cleaner outlet tube from the air intake throttle body and the throttle position sensor from the wiring harness.

3. Disconnect the vacuum lines from the upper manifold and disconnect the EGR tube at the manifold connection.

4. Disconnect the air bypass valve connector, remove the accelerator and, if equipped, speed control cables and remove the manifold upper support bracket top bolt.

5. Remove the fuel supply manifold shield and the 4 upper manifold retaining bolts and 1 retaining shoulder stud.

6. Remove the upper manifold assembly and gasket and set it aside.

7. Disconnect the fuel supply and return lines and the vacuum line at the pressure regulator.

8. Disconnect the fuel injector wiring harness and disconnect the connectors from the injectors.

9. Remove the fuel supply manifold retaining bolts and remove the fuel supply manifold.

10. Grasping the injector body, pull up while gently rocking the injector from side-to-side.

11. Inspect the injector O-rings, the injector plastic hat and washer for signs of deterioration. Replace as necessary. If the hat is missing, look for it in the intake manifold.

12. Installation is the reverse of the removal procedure. Lubricate new O-rings with light engine oil and install on the injectors prior to installation. Tighten the fuel supply manifold retaining bolts and the upper intake manifold retaining bolts to 15–22 ft. lbs. (20–30 Nm).

3.0L Engine

1. Disconnect the negative battery cable.

2. Properly relieve the fuel system pressure.

3. Remove the air intake throttle body as follows:

a. Remove the air cleaner tube from the throttle body. Remove the idle speed control solenoid shield.

b. Disconnect the throttle cable and, if equipped, throttle valve cable.

c. Tag and disconnect all necessary vacuum hoses and electrical connectors.

d. Loosen the EGR tube nuts, if equipped, at the EGR and exhaust manifold fitting. Remove or rotate the tube out of the way.

e. Remove the PCV hose from the tube under the throttle body.

f. Remove the retaining nuts from the alternator brace and remove the brace.

g. Remove the 6 throttle body attaching bolts and remove the throttle body.

4. Perform the following before removing the fuel supply manifold:

a. Scribe an alignment mark on the base of the distributor and lower intake manifold.

b. Remove the distributor hold-down clamp.

c. Lift the distributor enough to allow the fuel supply manifold crossover tube to clear the distributor housing and lower intake manifold.

5. Disconnect the fuel supply and return lines.

6. Disconnect the wiring harness from the injectors.

7. Disconnect the vacuum line from the fuel pressure regulator.

8. Remove the 4 fuel injector manifold retaining bolts.

9. Carefully disengage the fuel supply manifold from the fuel injectors by lifting and gently rocking the rail.

10. Remove the injectors by lifting while gently rocking from side-to-side.

To install:

11. Lubricate new O-rings with engine oil and install 2 on each injector.

12. Make sure the injector cups are clean and undamaged.

13. Install the injectors in the fuel supply manifold using a light twisting-pushing motion.

14. Perform the following:

a. Lift the distributor enough to allow the fuel supply manifold crossover tube to clear the distributor housing and lower intake manifold and position the fuel supply manifold.

b. Lower the distributor into position.

c. Install the distributor hold-down clamp and align the scribe marks. Tighten the hold-down clamp bolt to 18 ft. lbs. (24 Nm).

15. Carefully install the fuel supply manifold and injectors into the lower intake manifold, 1 side at a time. Make sure the O-rings are seated by pushing down on the fuel supply manifold.

16. While holding the fuel supply manifold in place, install the 2 retaining bolts and tighten to 7 ft. lbs. (10 Nm).

17. Connect the fuel supply and return lines.

18. Before connecting the fuel injector harness, connect the negative battery cable and turn the ignition switch to the **ON** position. This will pressurize the fuel system.

19. Using a clean paper towel, check for leaks where the injector connects to the fuel supply manifold. Correct any leaks, as necessary.

20. Turn the ignition switch **OFF** and disconnect the negative battery cable.

21. Connect the fuel injector wiring harness and connect the vacuum line to the fuel pressure regulator.

22. Install the air intake throttle body in the reverse order of removal. Use a new gasket and tighten the 6 attaching bolts to 15–22 ft. lbs. (20–30 Nm).

23. Connect the negative battery cable.

DRIVE AXLE

Halfshaft

REMOVAL & INSTALLATION

Except 1991–93 Escort and All Wheel Drive Rear Halfshaft

NOTE: Halfshaft assembly removal and installation procedures are the same for automatic and manual transaxles, except on the automatic transaxle, the right side halfshaft must be removed first. Differential rotator tool T81P–4026–A or equivalent, is then inserted into the transaxle to drive the left side inboard CV-joint assembly from the transaxle. If only the left side halfshaft assembly is to be removed for service, remove the right side halfshaft assembly from the transaxle only. After removal, support it with a length of wire, then drive the left side halfshaft assembly from the transaxle.

1. Remove the cap from the hub and loosen the hub nut. Set the parking brake. The nut must be loosened without unstaking; the use of a chisel or similar tool may damage the spindle thread.

2. Raise and safely support the vehicle. Remove the wheel and tire assembly. Remove the hub nut/washer and discard the nut.

3. Remove the brake hose routing clip-to-strut bolt.

4. Remove the nut from the ball joint-to-steering knuckle bolt. Using a hammer and a punch, drive the bolt from the steering knuckle and discard the bolt/nut.

5. Using a prybar, separate the ball joint from the steering knuckle. Position the end of the prybar outside of the bushing pocket to avoid damage to the bushing; be careful not to damage the ball joint or CV-joint boot.

NOTE: The lower control arm ball joint fits into a pocket formed in the plastic disc brake rotor shield; bend the shield away from the ball joint while prying the ball joint from the steering knuckle.

6. Using a prybar, pry the halfshaft from the differential housing. Position the prybar between the differential housing and the CV-joint assembly. Be careful not to damage the differential oil seal, case, CV-joint boot or the transaxle.

NOTE: Shipping plugs T81P–1177–B or equivalent, must be installed in the differential housing after halfshaft removal. Failure to do so can result in dislocation of the differential side gears. Should the gears become misaligned, the differential will have to be removed from the transaxle to re-align the gears.

7. Using a piece of wire, support the end of the shaft from a convenient underbody component.

NOTE: Do not allow the shaft to hang unsupported, as damage to the outboard CV-joint may result.

8. Using a front hub removal tool, press the halfshaft's outboard CV-joint from the hub.

NOTE: Never use a hammer to separate the outboard CV-joint stub shaft from the hub. Damage to the CV-joint internal components may result.

To install:

9. Install a new circlip onto the inboard CV-joint stub shaft; the outboard CV-joint stub shaft does not have a circlip. To install the circlip properly, start one end in the groove and work the circlip over the stub shaft end and into the groove; this will avoid over expanding the circlip.

NOTE: Do not reuse the old circlip. A new circlip must be installed each time the inboard CV-joint is installed into the differential.

10. Carefully, align the splines of the inboard CV-joint stub shaft with the splines in the differential. Push the CV-joint into the differential until the circlip is seated in the differential side gear. Use care to prevent damage to the differential oil seal.

NOTE: A non-metallic mallet may be used to aid in seating the circlip into the differential side gear groove; if a mallet is necessary, tap only on the outboard CV-joint stub shaft.

11. Carefully, align the outboard CV-joint stub shaft splines with the hub splines and push the shaft into the hub, as far as possible.

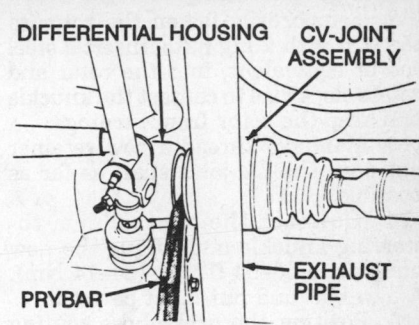

Removing halfshaft from transaxle

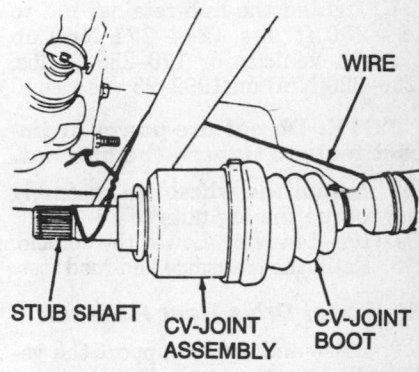

Support halfshaft by wiring to body

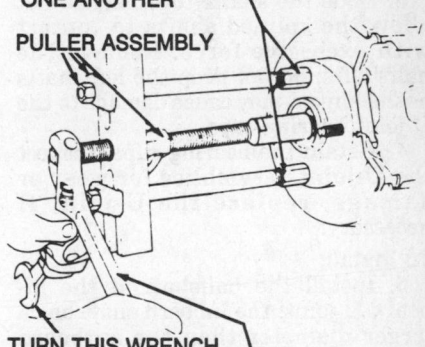

Removing hub from shaft assembly—except 1991–93 Escort

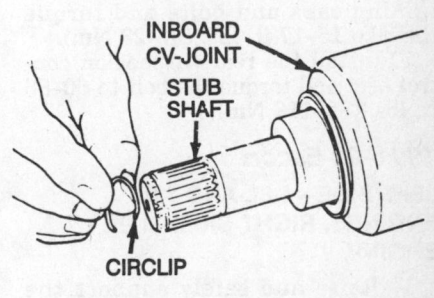

Stub shaft circlip installation

12. Temporarily fasten the rotor to the hub with 2 lug nuts. Insert a steel rod or equivalent, into the rotor and rotate clockwise to contact the knuckle and keep the rotor from turning.

13. Manually thread a new retainer nut onto the CV-joint shaft as far as possible.

14. Connect the control arm-to-steering knuckle and torque the new nut/bolt to 40–54 ft. lbs. (54–74 Nm). A new bolt and nut must be used.

15. Position the brake hose routing clip on the suspension strut and torque the bolt to 8 ft. lbs. (11 Nm).

16. Tighten the hub retainer nut to 180–200 ft. lbs. (244–271 Nm) on 1989–91 vehicles or 170–236 ft. lbs. (230–320 Nm) on 1992–93 vehicles.

NOTE: Do not use power or impact tools to tighten the hub nut.

17. Install the wheel/tire assembly and torque the lug nuts to 80–105 ft. lbs. (108–144 Nm). Lower the vehicle.

18. Refill the transaxle and road test.

All Wheel Drive Rear Halfshaft

1. Raise and safely support the vehicle. Remove the rear suspension control arm bolt.

2. Remove the outboard U-joint retaining bolts and straps. Remove the inboard U-joint retaining bolts and straps.

3. Slide the shafts together; do not allow the splined shafts to contact with excessive force. Remove the halfshafts; do not drop the halfshafts as the impact may cause damage to the U-joint bearing cups.

4. Retain the bearing cups. Inspect the U-joint assemblies for wear or damage, replace the U-joint if necessary.

To Install:

5. Install the halfshaft at the inboard U-joint; the inboard shaft has a larger diameter than the outboard shaft. Install the U-joint retaining caps and bolts and torque them to 15–17 ft. lbs. (21–23 Nm).

NOTE: Be sure to apply Loctite® to the U-joint bolts.

6. Install the halfshaft at the outboard U-joint. Install the U-joint retaining caps and bolts and torque them to 15–17 ft. lbs. (21–23 Nm).

7. Install the rear suspension control arm and torque the bolt to 60–86 ft. lbs. (82–116 Nm).

1991–93 Escort

LEFT SIDE—1.8L AND 1.9L ENGINES, RIGHT SIDE—1.9L ENGINE

1. Raise and safely support the vehicle.

2. Remove the wheel and tire assembly.

3. Remove the splash shield.

4. Carefully raise the staked portion of the halfshaft retaining nut using a suitable small chisel. Remove and discard the retaining nut.

5. Remove the cotter pin and nut from the tie rod end and remove the tie rod end from the steering knuckle using a suitable removal tool.

6. Remove the lower ball joint clamp bolt. Carefully pry down on lower control arm to separate the ball joint from the steering knuckle.

7. Pull outward on the steering knuckle/brake assembly. Carefully pull the halfshaft from the steering knuckle and position it aside.

8. Removal of the left side halfshaft requires removal of the crossmember to allow access with a prybar. If the left side halfshaft is being removed, proceed as follows:

   a. Support the transaxle with a suitable transmission jack.

   b. Remove the 4 transaxle mount-to-crossmember attaching nuts.

   c. Remove the 2 crossmember attaching nuts at the rear of the crossmember.

   d. While supporting the rear of the crossmember, remove the 2 front mounting bolts. Remove the crossmember.

9. Position a drain pan under the transaxle.

10. Insert a prybar between the halfshaft and the transaxle case. Gently pry outward to release the halfshaft from the differential side gears. Be careful no to damage the transaxle case, oil seal, CV-joint or CV-joint boot.

11. Remove the halfshaft.

NOTE: Install suitable plugs after removing the halfshafts to prevent the differential side gears from becoming mispositioned. Should the gears become misaligned, the differential will have to be removed from the transaxle to align the gears.

To install:

12. Position the circlip on the inner CV-joint spline so the circlip gap is at the top. Lubricate the splines lightly with suitable grease.

13. Remove the plugs that were installed in the differential side gears.

14. Position the halfshaft so the CV-joint splines are aligned with the differential side gear splines. Push the halfshaft into the differential.

NOTE: When seated properly, the circlip can be felt as it snaps into the differential side gear groove.

15. Pull outward on the steering knuckle/brake assembly and insert the halfshaft into the steering knuckle.

16. Pry downward on the control arm and position the lower ball joint in the steering knuckle.

17. For left side halfshaft installation, proceed as follows:

   a. Position the crossmember in place.

   b. Install the 2 mounting bolts and the 2 attaching nuts. Tighten the nuts and bolts to 47–66 ft. lbs. (64–89 Nm).

   c. Install the 4 transaxle mount-to-crossmember attaching nuts. Tighten the nuts to 27–38 ft. lbs. (37–52 Nm).

   d. Remove the transmission jack.

18. Install the lower ball joint clamp bolt and tighten to 32–43 ft. lbs. (43–59 Nm).

19. Install the tie rod end in the steering knuckle. Install the nut to the tie rod end and tighten to 31–42 ft. lbs. (42–57 Nm). Install a new cotter pin.

20. Install a new halfshaft retaining nut and tighten to 174–235 ft. lbs. (235–319 Nm). Stake the halfshaft retaining nut using a suitable chisel with a rounded cutting edge.

NOTE: If the nut splits or cracks after staking, replace it with a new nut.

21. Install the splash shield.

22. Install the wheel and tire assembly and lower the vehicle.

23. Check and refill the transaxle with the proper type and quantity of fluid.

RIGHT SIDE—1.8L ENGINE

NOTE: The right side halfshaft assembly is a 2 piece shaft with a bearing support bracket positioned between the 2 halves. The bearing support bracket is mounted on the cylinder block and must be unbolted if the entire halfshaft assembly is to be removed. If only the CV-joints/boots are to be serviced, the outboard shaft assembly may be removed, leaving the bearing support bracket mounted on the engine cylinder block.

1. Raise and safely support the vehicle.

2. Remove the right front wheel and tire assembly.

3. Remove the splash shield.

4. Carefully raise the staked portion of the halfshaft retaining nut using a suitable small chisel. Remove and discard the retaining nut.

5. Remove the cotter pin and nut from the tie rod end and remove the tie rod end from the steering knuckle using a suitable removal tool.

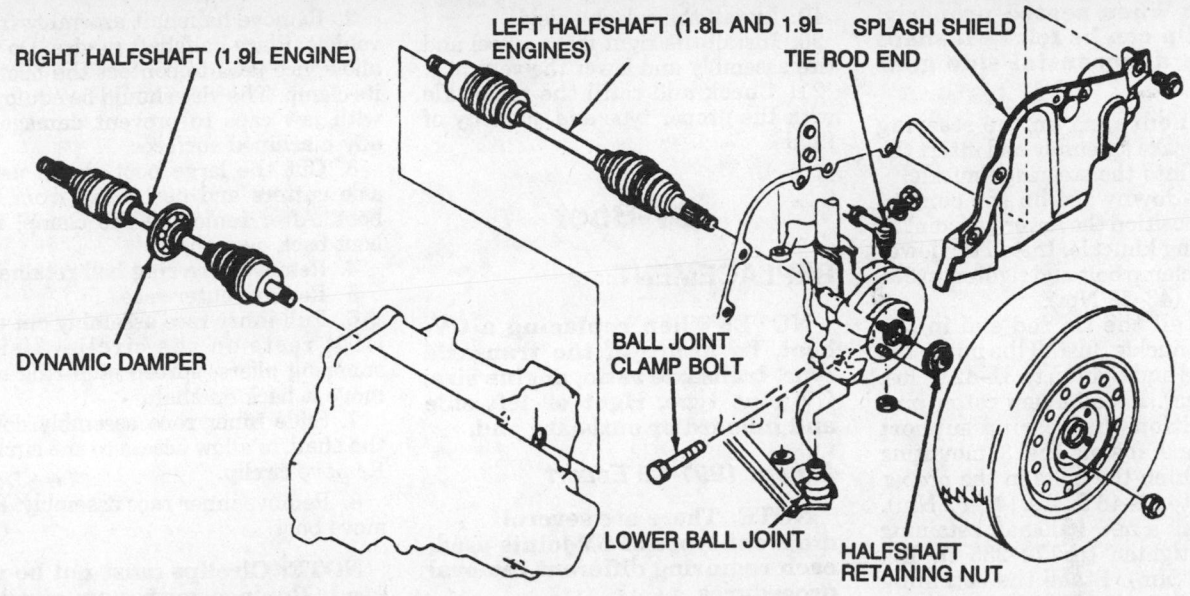

RIGHT HALFSHAFT (1.9L ENGINE)

LEFT HALFSHAFT (1.8L AND 1.9L ENGINES)

SPLASH SHIELD

TIE ROD END

DYNAMIC DAMPER

BALL JOINT CLAMP BOLT

LOWER BALL JOINT

HALFSHAFT RETAINING NUT

Halfshaft removal and installation—left side, 1.8L and 1.9L engines and right side, 1.9L Engine

6. Remove the lower ball joint clamp bolt. Carefully pry down on the lower control arm to separate the ball joint from the steering knuckle.

7. Pull outward on the steering knuckle/brake assembly. Carefully pull the halfshaft from the steering knuckle and position it aside.

8. Position a drain pan under the transaxle.

9. Remove the 3 bearing support bracket mounting bolts.

10. Insert a prybar between the bearing support bracket and the starter bracket. Gently pry outward on the damper until the halfshaft disengages from the differential side gear.

11. Remove the halfshaft assembly.

Install an appropriate differential plug in the differential side gear.

NOTE: If both halfshafts are removed, plugs must be installed to keep the differential side gears from becoming mispositioned. If the gears become misaligned, the differential will have to be removed from the transaxle to align the gears.

To install:

12. Position the circlip on the inner CV-joint spline so the circlip gap is at the top. Lubricate the splines lightly with a suitable grease.

13. Remove the differential plug from the side gear. Position the

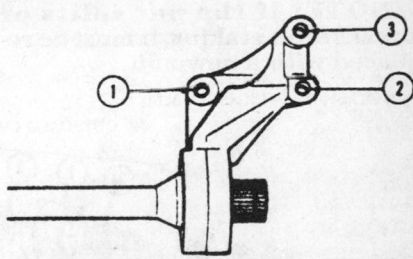

Bearing support bracket torque sequence

halfshaft assembly so the shaft splines are aligned with the differential side gear splines. Push the halfshaft into the differential.

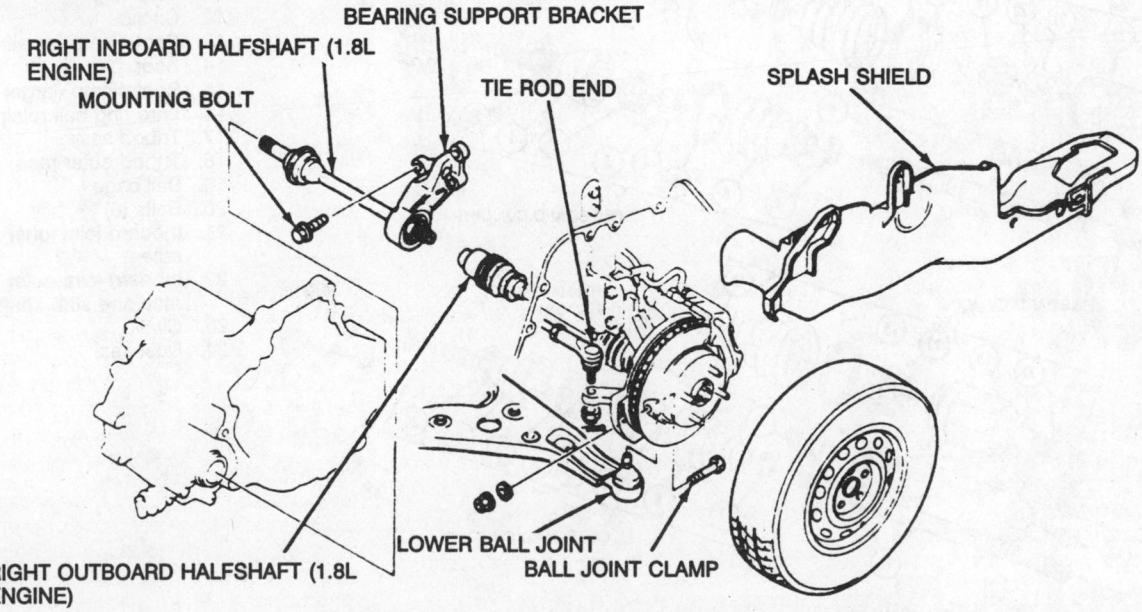

RIGHT INBOARD HALFSHAFT (1.8L ENGINE)

MOUNTING BOLT

BEARING SUPPORT BRACKET

TIE ROD END

SPLASH SHIELD

RIGHT OUTBOARD HALFSHAFT (1.8L ENGINE)

LOWER BALL JOINT

BALL JOINT CLAMP

Halfshaft removal and installation—right side, 1.8L Engine

NOTE: When seated properly, the circlip can be felt as it snaps into the differential side gear groove.

14. Pull outward on the steering knuckle/brake assembly and insert the halfshaft into the steering knuckle.

15. Pry downward on the control arm and position the lower ball joint in the steering knuckle. Install the lower ball joint clamp bolt and tighten to 32–43 ft. lbs. (43–59 Nm).

16. Install the tie rod end in the steering knuckle. Install the nut to the tie rod end and tighten to 31–42 ft. lbs. (42–57 Nm). Install a new cotter pin.

17. Position the bearing support bracket and install the 3 mounting bolts. Tighten the bolts in the proper sequence to 31–46 ft. lbs. (42–62 Nm).

18. Install a new halfshaft retaining nut and tighten to 174–235 ft. lbs. (235–319 Nm). Stake the retaining nut using a suitable chisel with the cutting edge rounded off.

NOTE: If the nut splits or cracks after staking, it must be replaced with a new nut.

19. Install the splash shield.
20. Install the right front wheel and tire assembly and lower the vehicle.
21. Check and refill the transaxle with the proper type and quantity of fluid.

CV-Boot

REPLACEMENT

NOTE: When replacing a CV-boot, be aware of the transaxle type, transaxle ratio, engine size, CV-joint type, right or left side and inboard or outboard end.

Except 1991–93 Escort

NOTE: There are several different types of CV-joints used, each requiring different removal procedures.

DOUBLE OFFSET JOINT INBOARD CV-JOINT BOOT

1. Disconnect the negative battery cable.

2. Remove halfshaft assembly from vehicle. Place halfshaft in vise. Do not allow vice jaws to contact the boot or its clamp. The vise should be equipped with jaw caps to prevent damage to any machined surfaces.

3. Cut the large boot clamp using side cutters and peel away from the boot. After removing the clamp, roll boot back over shaft.

4. Remove wire ring ball retainer.

5. Remove outer race.

6. Pull inner race assembly out until it rests on the circlip. Using snapring pliers, spread stop ring and move it back on shaft.

7. Slide inner race assembly down the shaft to allow access to the circlip. Remove circlip.

8. Remove inner race assembly. Remove boot.

NOTE: Circlips must not be reused. Replace with new circlips before assembly.

9. When replacing damaged CV-boots, the grease should be checked for contamination. If the CV-joints were operating satisfactorily and the grease

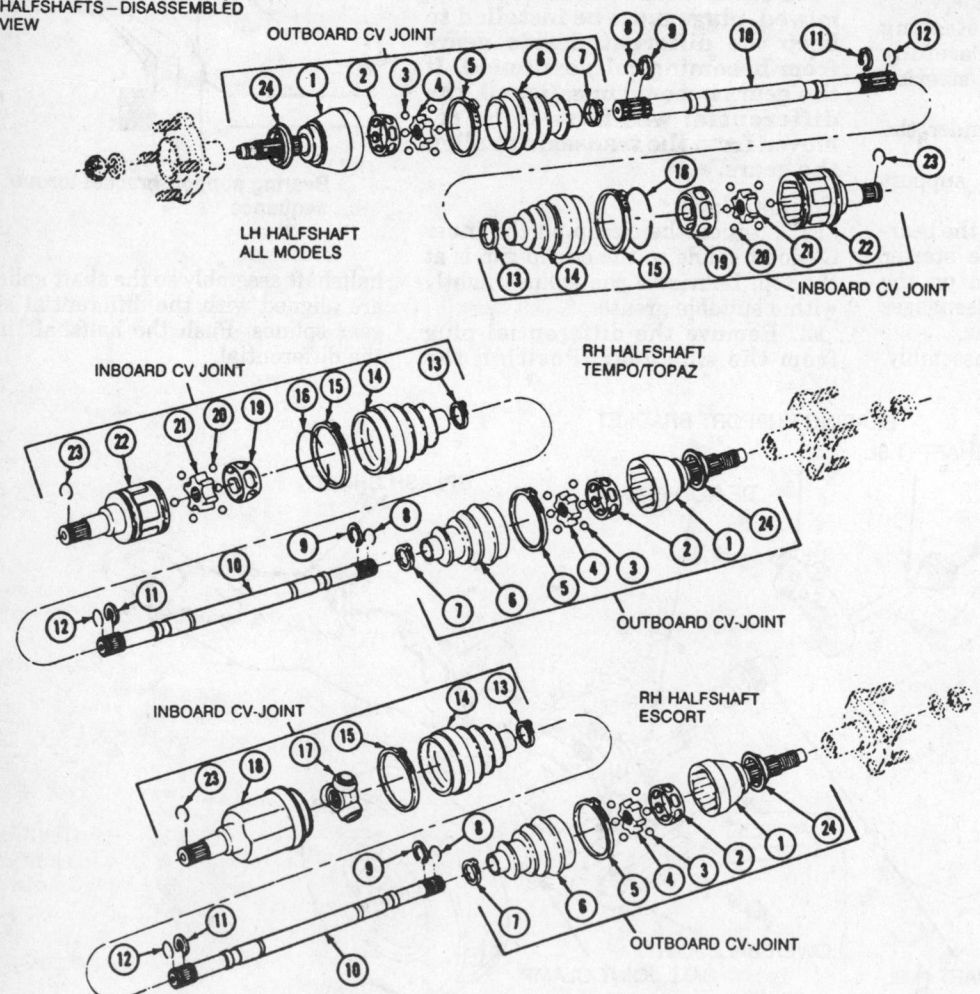

HALFSHAFTS – DISASSEMBLED VIEW

1. Outboard joint outer race and stub shaft
2. Ball cage
3. Balls (6)
4. Outboard joint inner race
5. Boot clamp (large)
6. Boot
7. Boot clamp (small)
8. Circlip
9. Stop ring
10. Interconnecting shaft
11. Stop ring
12. Circlip
13. Boot clamp (small)
14. Boot
15. Boot clamp (large)
16. Wire ring ball retainer
17. Tripod assy
18. Tripod outer race
19. Ball cage
20. Balls (6)
21. Inboard joint inner race
22. Inboard joint outer race and stub shaft
23. Circlip
24. Dust seal

Exploded view of halfshafts—1989–91 Tempo/Topaz and 1989–90 Escort

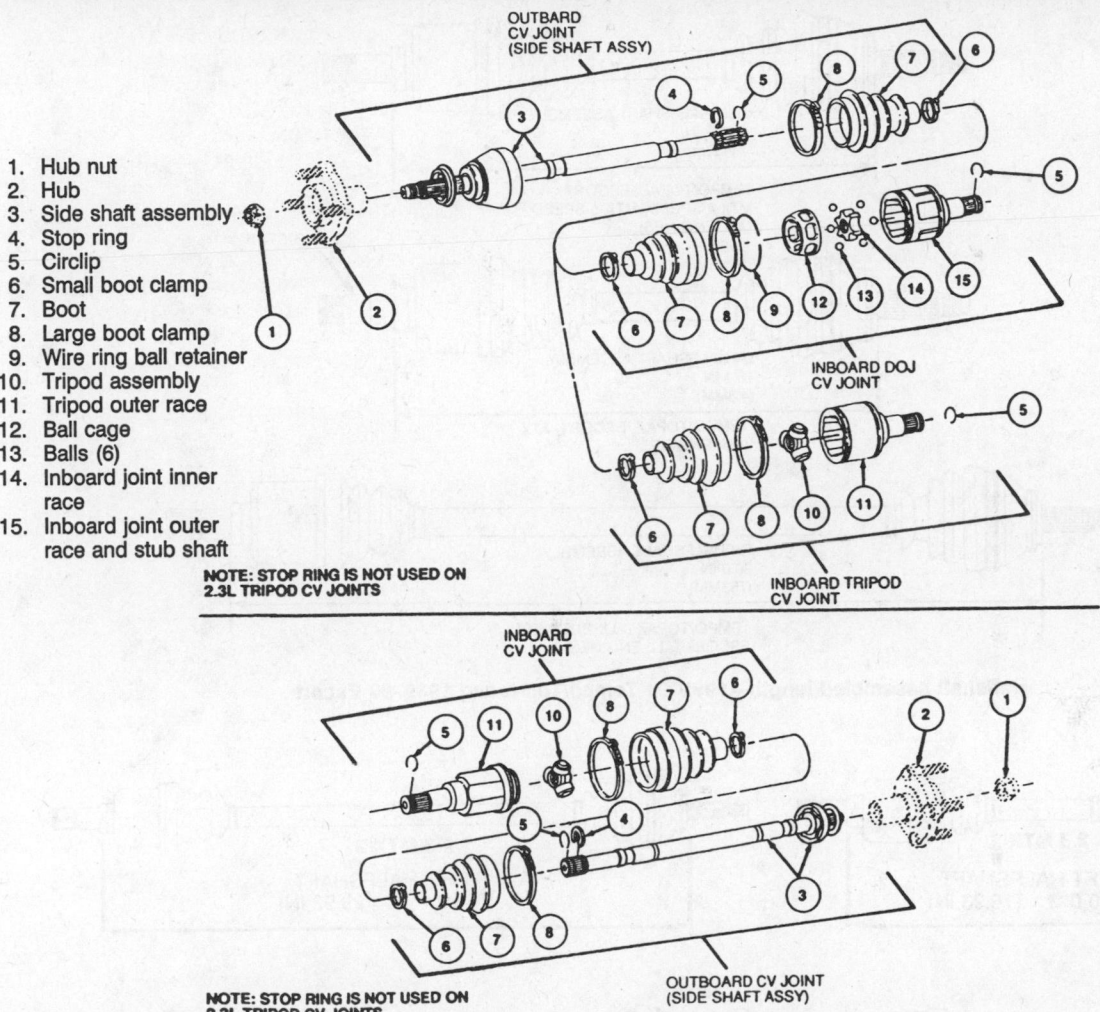

1. Hub nut
2. Hub
3. Side shaft assembly
4. Stop ring
5. Circlip
6. Small boot clamp
7. Boot
8. Large boot clamp
9. Wire ring ball retainer
10. Tripod assembly
11. Tripod outer race
12. Ball cage
13. Balls (6)
14. Inboard joint inner race
15. Inboard joint outer race and stub shaft

NOTE: STOP RING IS NOT USED ON 2.3L TRIPOD CV JOINTS

NOTE: STOP RING IS NOT USED ON 2.3L TRIPOD CV JOINTS

Exploded view of halfshafts—1992-93 Tempo/Topaz

does not appear to be contaminated, add grease and replace the boot. If the lubricant appears contaminated, proceed with a complete CV-joint disassembly and inspection.

10. Remove balls by prying from cage.

NOTE: Exercise care to prevent scratching or other damage to the inner race or cage.

11. Rotate inner race to align lands with cage windows. Lift inner race out through the wider end of the cage.
To install:
12. Clean all parts (except boots) in a suitable solvent.
13. Inspect all CV-joint parts for excessive wear, looseness, pitting, rust and cracks.

NOTE: CV-joint components are matched during assembly. If inspection reveals damage or wear the entire joint must be replaced as an assembly. Do not replace a joint merely because the

parts appear polished. Shiny areas in ball races and on the cage spheres are normal.

14. Install a new circlip, supplied with the service kit, in groove nearest end of shaft. Do not over-expand or twist circlip during installation.
15. Install inner race in the cage. The race is installed through the large end of the cage with the circlip counterbore facing the large end of the cage.
16. With the cage and inner race properly aligned, install the balls by pressing through the cage windows with the heel of the hand.
17. Assemble inner race and cage assembly in outer race.
18. Push the inner race and cage assembly by hand, into the outer race. Install with inner race chamfer facing out.
19. Install ball retainer into groove inside of outer race.
20. Install new CV-boot.
21. Tighten clamp securely but not to the point where the clamp bridge is cut or the boot is damaged.

22. Position stop ring and new circlip into grooves on shaft.
23. Fill CV-joint outer race with 3.2 oz. (90 grams) of grease, then spread 1.4 oz. (40 grams) of grease evenly inside boot for a total combined fill of 4.6 oz. (130 grams).
24. With boot peeled back, install CV-joint using soft tipped hammer. Ensure splines are aligned prior to installing CV-joint onto shaft.
25. Remove all excess grease from the CV-joint external surfaces.
26. Position boot over CV-joint. Before installing boot clamp, move CV-joint in or out, as necessary, to adjust to the proper length.

NOTE: Insert a suitable tool between the boot and outer bearing race and allow the trapped air to escape from the boot. The air should be released from the boot only after adjusting to the proper dimensions.

27. Ensure boot is seated in its groove and clamp in position.

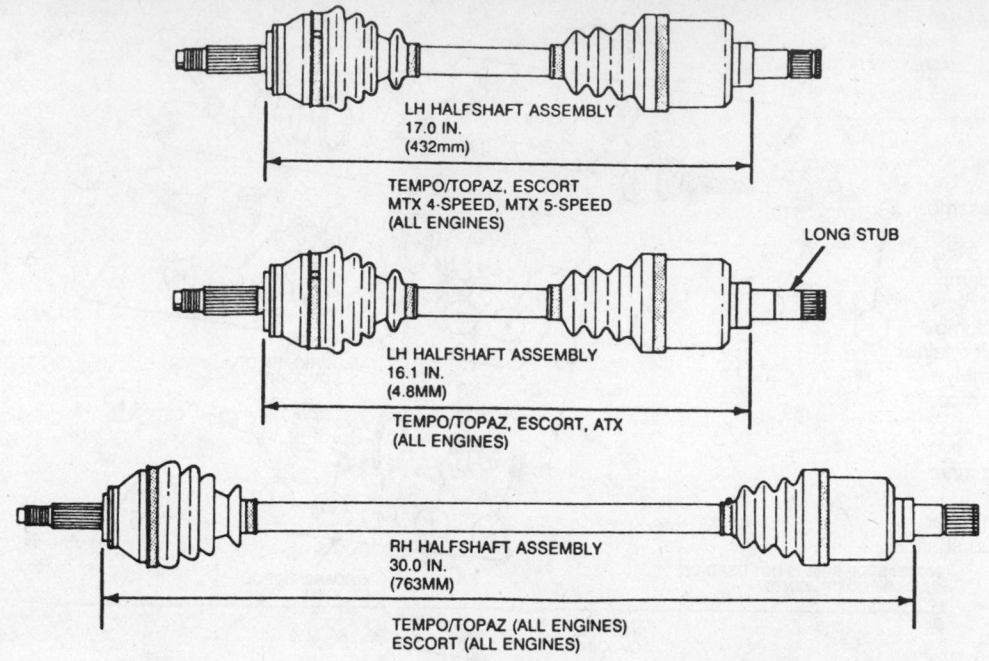

LH HALFSHAFT ASSEMBLY
17.0 IN.
(432mm)

TEMPO/TOPAZ, ESCORT
MTX 4-SPEED, MTX 5-SPEED
(ALL ENGINES)

LONG STUB

LH HALFSHAFT ASSEMBLY
16.1 IN.
(4.8MM)

TEMPO/TOPAZ, ESCORT, ATX
(ALL ENGINES)

RH HALFSHAFT ASSEMBLY
30.0 IN.
(763MM)

TEMPO/TOPAZ (ALL ENGINES)
ESCORT (ALL ENGINES)

Halfshaft assembled length—1989–91 Tempo/Topaz and 1989–90 Escort

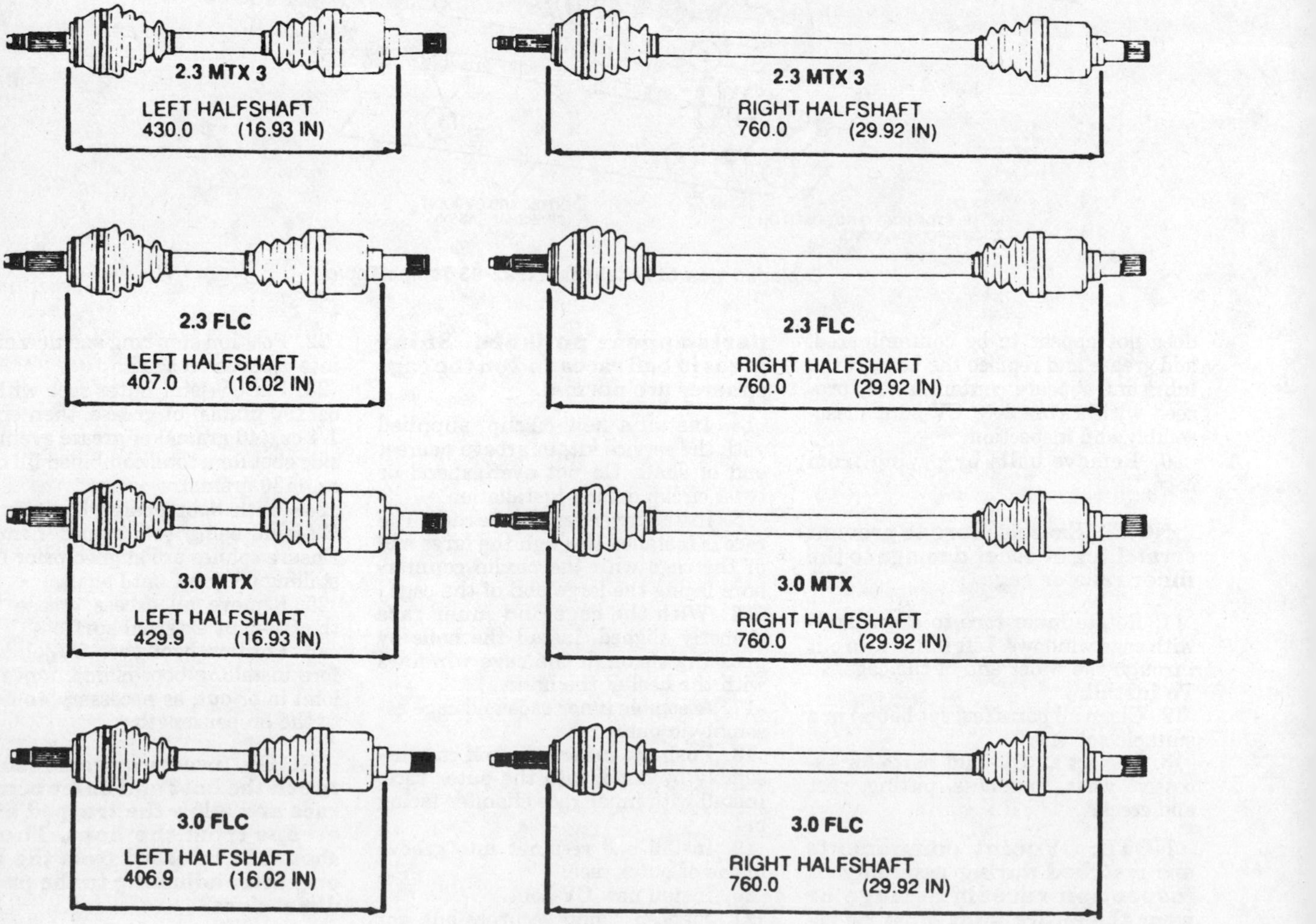

2.3 MTX 3

LEFT HALFSHAFT
430.0   (16.93 IN)

2.3 MTX 3

RIGHT HALFSHAFT
760.0   (29.92 IN)

2.3 FLC

LEFT HALFSHAFT
407.0   (16.02 IN)

2.3 FLC

RIGHT HALFSHAFT
760.0   (29.92 IN)

3.0 MTX

LEFT HALFSHAFT
429.9   (16.93 IN)

3.0 MTX

RIGHT HALFSHAFT
760.0   (29.92 IN)

3.0 FLC

LEFT HALFSHAFT
406.9   (16.02 IN)

3.0 FLC

RIGHT HALFSHAFT
760.0   (29.92 IN)

Halfshaft assembled lengths—1992–93 Tempo/Topaz

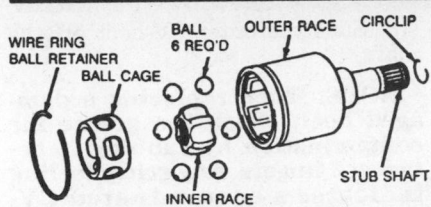

Double offset CV-joint

28. Tighten clamp securely but not to the point where the clamp bridge is cut or the boot is damaged.
29. Install halfshaft assembly in vehicle.
30. Connect negative battery cable.

TRIPOD INBOARD CV-JOINT BOOT

1. Disconnect the negative battery cable.
2. Remove halfshaft assembly from vehicle. Place halfshaft in vice. Do not allow vise jaws to contact the boot or its clamp. The vise should be equipped with jaw caps to prevent damage to any machined surfaces.
3. Cut the large boot clamp using side cutters and peel away from the boot. After removing the clamp, roll boot back over shaft.
4. Bend retaining tabs back slightly to allow for tripod removal.
5. Separate outer race from tripod.
6. On all except 1992–93 vehicles with 2.3L engine, move stop ring back on shaft using snapring pliers. On 1992–93 vehicles with 2.3L engine, remove the tripod snapring.
7. On all except 1992–93 vehicles with 2.3L engine, move tripod assembly back on shaft to allow access to circlip. Remove the circlip and stop ring from the shaft.
8. Remove tripod assembly from shaft.
9. Remove the boot.
10. When replacing damaged CV-boots, the grease should be checked for contamination. If the CV-joints were operating satisfactorily and the grease does not appear to be contaminated, add grease and replace the boot. If the lubricant appears contaminated, proceed with a complete CV-joint disassembly and inspection.

To install:

11. Clean all parts (except boots) in a suitable solvent.
12. Inspect all CV-joint parts for excessive wear, looseness, pitting, rust and cracks.

NOTE: CV-joint components are matched during assembly. If inspection reveals damage or wear the entire joint must be replaced as an assembly. Do not replace a joint merely because the parts appear polished. Shiny

areas in ball races and on the cage spheres are normal.

13. Install new CV-boot.
14. Tighten clamp securely but not to the point where the clamp bridge is cut or the boot is damaged.
15. If equipped, install the stop ring. Install tripod assembly on shaft with chamfered side inboard.
16. Install new circlip or snapring, as required.

NOTE: To install the circlip, start 1 end in the groove and work the circlip over the stub shaft end and into the groove. This will avoid overexpanding the circlip. A new circlip must be used.

17. If equipped, compress circlip and slide tripod assembly forward over circlip to expose stop ring groove. Move stop ring into groove using snapring pliers, making sure it is fully seated in groove.
18. Fill CV-joint outer race with 3.5 oz. (100 grams) of grease and fill CV-boot with 2.1 oz. (60 grams) of grease.
19. Install outer race over tripod assembly and bend 6 retaining tabs back into their original position.
20. Remove all excess grease from CV-joint external surfaces. Position boot over CV-joint. Move CV-joint in and out as necessary, to adjust to proper length.

NOTE: Insert a suitable tool between the boot and outer bearing race and allow the trapped air to escape from the boot. The air should be released from the boot only after adjusting to the proper dimensions.

21. Ensure boot is seated in its groove and clamp in position.
22. Tighten clamp securely but not to the point where the clamp bridge is cut or the boot is damaged.
23. Install a new circlip, supplied with service kit, in groove nearest end of shaft by starting one end in the groove and working clip over stub shaft end and into groove.

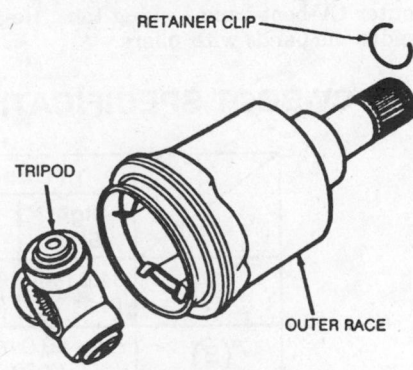

Tripod CV-joint

24. Install halfshaft assembly in vehicle.
25. Connect negative battery cable.

OUTBOARD CV-JOINT BOOT— 1989–91 VEHICLES

1. Disconnect the negative battery cable.
2. Remove halfshaft assembly from vehicle.
3. Place halfshaft in vice. Do not allow vise jaws to contact the boot or its clamp. The vise should be equipped with jaw caps to prevent damage to any machined surfaces.
4. Cut the large boot clamp using side cutters and peel away from the boot. After removing the clamp, roll boot back over shaft.
5. Support the interconnecting shaft in a soft jaw vise and angle the CV-joint to expose inner bearing race.
6. Using a brass drift and hammer, give a sharp tap to the inner bearing race to dislodge the internal circlip and separate the CV-joint from the interconnecting shaft. Take care not to drop the CV-joint at separation.
7. Remove the boot.
8. When replacing damaged CV-boots, the grease should be checked for contamination. If the CV-joints were operating satisfactorily and the grease does not appear to be contaminated, add grease and replace the boot. If the lubricant appears contaminated, proceed with a complete CV-joint disassembly and inspection.
9. Remove circlip located near the end of the shaft. Discard the circlip. Use new clip supplied with boot replacement kit and CV-joint overhaul kit.
10. Clamp CV-joint stub shaft in a vise with the outer face facing up. Care should be taken not to damage dust seal. The vise must be equipped with jaw caps to prevent damage to the shaft splines.
11. Press down on inner race until it tilts enough to allow removal of ball. A tight assembly can be tilted by tapping the inner race with wooden dowel and hammer. Do not hit the cage.
12. With cage sufficiently tilted, remove ball from cage. Remove all 6 balls in this manner.
13. Pivot cage and inner race assembly until it is straight up and down in outer race. Align cage windows with outer race lands while pivoting the bearing cage. With the cage pivoted and aligned, lift assembly from the outer race.
14. Rotate inner race up and out of the cage.

To install:

15. Clean all parts (except boots) in a suitable solvent.
16. Inspect all CV-joint parts for ex-

cessive wear, looseness, pitting, rust and cracks.

NOTE: CV-joint components are matched during assembly. If inspection reveals damage or wear the entire joint must be replaced as an assembly. Do not replace a joint merely because the parts appear polished. Shiny areas in ball races and on the cage spheres are normal.

17. Apply a light coating of grease on inner and outer ball races. Install the inner race in cage.
18. Install inner race and cage assembly in the outer race.
19. Install the assembly vertically and pivot 90 degrees into position.
20. Align cage and inner race with outer race. Tilt inner race and cage and install one of the 6 balls. Repeat this process until the remaining balls are installed.
21. Install new CV-joint boot.
22. Tighten clamp securely but not to the point where the clamp bridge is cut or the boot is damaged.
23. Install the stop ring, if removed. If not removed, make sure the stop ring is properly seated in its groove.
24. Install a new circlip, supplied with the service kit, in groove nearest the end of the shaft.

NOTE: To install the circlip, start 1 end in the groove and work the circlip over the stub shaft end and into the groove. This will avoid overexpanding the circlip. A new circlip must be used.

25. Pack CV-joint with suitable grease. Total amount of grease required is 3.17 oz.
26. With the boot "peeled" back, position CV-joint on shaft and tap into position using a plastic tipped hammer.
27. Remove all excess grease from the CV-joint external surfaces.
28. Position boot over CV-joint.
29. Ensure boot is seated in its groove and clamp into position.
30. Tighten clamp securely but not to the point where the clamp bridge is cut or the boot is damaged.
31. Install halfshaft assembly in vehicle.
32. Connect negative battery cable.

OUTBOARD CV-JOINT BOOT — 1992–93 VEHICLES

The outboard CV-joint cannot be removed from the shaft on these vehicles. If it is necessary to replace the outboard CV-joint boot, the inboard CV-joint and boot must be removed.

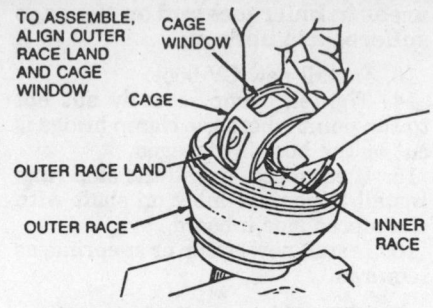

TO ASSEMBLE, ALIGN OUTER RACE LAND AND CAGE WINDOW

CAGE WINDOW

CAGE

OUTER RACE LAND

OUTER RACE

INNER RACE

Outboard CV-joint—1989–91 Tempo/Topaz and 1989–90 Escort

1991–93 Escort

1. Raise and safely support the vehicle.
2. Remove the halfshaft assembly from the vehicle.
3. Secure the halfshaft in a vise with protective jaw covers.
4. Using a suitable tool, pry up the locking tabs of the inner CV-boot bands. Remove the bands with pliers.
5. Slide the boot back to expose the tripod CV-joint. Mark the shaft and the CV-joint housing to ensure correct assembly.
6. Remove the retainer ring from the CV-joint housing and remove the CV-joint housing from the halfshaft.
7. Mark the tripod bearing and the shaft to ensure correct assembly. Using snapring pliers, remove the tripod snapring.
8. Using a soft-faced mallet, gently tap the tripod bearing from the shaft.
9. Wrap the shaft splines with tape to protect the CV-boot if the boot is to be reused.
10. Slide the inner CV-joint boot off the shaft. If the outer CV-joint boot is to be replaced, continue with the procedure.
11. On 1.9L right side halfshafts, pry up the rubber damper retaining band locking clip using a suitable tool. Remove the retaining band using pliers and remove the rubber damper from the shaft.
12. Using a suitable tool, pry up the outer CV-boot band locking tabs. Remove the bands with pliers.

13. Slide the outer CV-boot off the shaft.

NOTE: When replacing a damaged boot, check the grease for contamination by rubbing it between 2 fingers. Any gritty feeling indicates a contaminated CV-joint. A contaminated inner CV-joint must be completely disassembled, cleaned and inspected. The outer CV-joint is not serviceable and should be replaced as an assembly, if necessary. If the grease is not contaminated and the CV-joint has been operating satisfactorily, replace only the boot and add the required lubricant.

To install:
14. Cover the halfshaft splines with tape and install the outer CV-joint boot.

NOTE: The outer and inner CV-joint boots are different. Failure to correctly install the boot on the proper end of the halfshaft could lead to premature boot and/or CV-joint wear.

15. Fill the outer CV-joint housing with the proper type and amount of lubricant.
16. Position the CV-boot. Make sure the boot is fully seated in the shaft grooves and the CV-joint housing.
17. Insert a suitable tool between the boot and the CV-joint housing to allow trapped air to escape.
18. Position new bands on the outer CV-joint boot.

NOTE: Always use new bands. The bands should be mounted in the direction opposite the for-

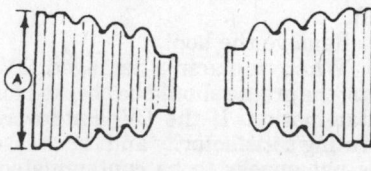

INNER CV BOOT   OUTER CV BOOT

Inner and outer CV-joint boots — 1991–93 Escort

CV-BOOT SPECIFICATIONS — 1991–93 ESCORT

	1.9L Engine		1.8L Engine	
	Right Side	Left Side	Right Side	Left Side
Ⓐ	84.0 mm (3.31 in)	90.0 mm (3.54 in)	89.9 mm (3.54 in)	
Ⓑ	89.0 mm (3.50 in)		85.2 mm (3.35 in)	

ward revolving direction of the halfshaft.

19. Wrap the bands around the boot in a clockwise direction, pull them tight with pliers and bend the locking tabs to secure the bands in position.

20. Work the CV-joint through it's full range of travel at various angles. The CV-joint should flex, extend and compress smoothly.

21. On 1.9L right side halfshafts, position the rubber damper on the halfshaft. Position a new band on the damper. Pull the band tight with pliers and fold it back. Lock the end of the band by bending the locking clip.

22. Position the inner CV-joint boot on the halfshaft.

23. Align the marks on the tripod bearing and the halfshaft. Install the tripod bearing on the halfshaft. If necessary, using a soft-faced mallet, tap the bearing into place.

24. Install the snapring.

25. Fill the inner CV-joint housing with the proper type and amount of lubricant. Coat the tripod bearing with the same lubricant.

26. Position the inner CV-joint housing over the tripod bearing, making sure to align the alignment marks. Install the retainer ring in the CV-joint housing.

27. Slide the inner CV-boot in place. Make sure the boot is fully seated in the shaft grooves and in the housing.

28. Insert a small prybar between the boot and the CV-joint housing to allow trapped air to escape.

29. Position new bands on the inner CV-joint boot.

NOTE: Always use new bands. The bands should be mounted in the direction opposite the forward revolving direction of the halfshaft.

30. Wrap the bands around the boot in a clockwise direction, pull them tight with pliers and bend the locking tabs to secure the bands in position.

31. Work the CV-joint through it's full range of travel at various angles. The CV-joint should flex, extend and compress smoothly.

32. Measure the length of the assembled halfshaft. If the length is not as specified, check the CV-joints for freedom of movement to ensure that it was assembled correctly. Repair or replace any components as necessary.

Driveshaft and U-Joints

REMOVAL & INSTALLATION

Tempo and Topaz With All Wheel Drive

1. Raise the vehicle and support safely.

2. To maintain the driveshaft balance, mark the U-joints so they may be installed in their original position.

3. Remove the front U-joint retaining bolts and straps.

4. Support the driveshaft near the center bearing. Remove the driveshaft center bearing retaining bolts.

5. Slide the driveshaft toward the rear of the vehicle to disengage from the transfer case.

6. Remove the rear U-joint bolts and straps retaining the driveshaft, from the torque tube yoke flange.

7. Slide the driveshaft toward the front of the vehicle to disengage. Do not allow the splined shafts to contact with excessive force.

8. Remove the center bearing retaining bolts. Remove the driveshaft and retain the bearing cups with tape, if necessary.

9. Inspect the U-joint assemblies

for wear and or damage, and replace if necessary.

To install:

10. Install the driveshaft at the rear torque yoke flange. Ensure that the U-joint is in its original position.

11. Install the U-joint retaining bolts and caps. Torque them to 15–17 ft. lbs. (21–23 Nm). Position the front U-joint. Install the U-joint retaining caps and bolts. Torque them to 15–17 ft. lbs. (21–23 Nm).

12. Install the center bearing and retaining bolts. Torque to 23–30 ft. lbs. (31–41 Nm). Do not drop the assembled driveshafts as the impact may cause damage to the U-joint bearing cups.

Front Wheel Hub, Knuckle and Bearings

REMOVAL & INSTALLATION

Except 1991–93 Escort

1. Remove wheel cover/hub cover from wheel and tire assembly and loosen wheel nuts.

2. Remove hub nut retainer and washer by applying sufficient torque to overcome the prevailing torque of the nut. The hub nut must be discarded after removal.

3. Raise and safely support the vehicle. Remove wheel and tire assembly.

4. Remove brake caliper by loosening caliper locating pins and rotating caliper off rotor starting from lower

CV-BOOT LUBRICANT SPECIFICATIONS – 1991–93 ESCORT

Halfshaft Assemblies	1.9L Engine		1.8L Engine	
	Right Side	Left Side	Right Side	Left Side
Differential Side	220 g (7.77 oz) Lt. Yellow	140 g (4.94 oz) Yellow	145 g (5.12 oz) Yellow	
Wheel Side	140 g (4.94 oz) Black		90 g (3.18 oz) Black	

HALFSHAFT LENGTH SPECIFICATIONS – 1991–93 ESCORT

Item	Model	1.8L Engine	1.9L Engine
Halfshaft			
Length of joint (between center of joint)	Right side	631.2 mm (24.85 in)	918.7 mm (36.16 in)
	Left side	621.7 mm (24.48 in)	640.7 mm (25.22 in)
Shaft diameter	Right side	23.0 mm (0.91 in)	
	Left side	23.0 mm (0.91 in)	

end of caliper and lifting upward. Do not remove caliper pins from caliper assembly. Lift caliper off rotor and hang it free of rotor. Do not allow caliper assembly to hang from brake hose. Support caliper assembly with a length of wire.

5. Remove rotor from hub by pulling it off hub bolts. If rotor is difficult to remove from hub, strike rotor sharply between studs with a rubber or plastic hammer. If rotor will not pull off, apply rust penetrator to inboard and outboard rotor hub mating surfaces. Install a 3 jaw puller and remove rotor by pulling on rotor outside diameter and pushing on hub center.

6. If excessive force is required for removal, check rotor for lateral runout. Lateral runout must be checked with wheel nuts clamping hat section of rotor.

7. Remove rotor splash shield.

8. Disconnect lower control arm and tie rod from knuckle (leave strut attached).

9. Loosen the 2 strut top mount-to-apron nuts.

10. Install a suitable hub removal tool and remove hub/bearing/knuckle assembly by pushing out CV-joint outer shaft until it is free of assembly.

11. Support knuckle with a length of wire, remove strut bolt and slide hub/knuckle assembly off strut.

12. Carefully remove support wire and transfer hub/bearing/knuckle assembly to bench.

13. Install front hub puller D80L-1002–L and shaft protector D80L-625–1 or equivalents, with jaws of puller on the knuckle bosses and remove hub.

NOTE: Ensure the shaft protector is centered, clears the bearing inside diameter and rests on the end face of the hub journal.

14. Remove snapring which retains bearing knuckle assembly and discard.

15. Using a hydraulic press, place a suitable front bearing spacer step side up on press plate and position knuckle on spacer with outboard side up. Install bearing removal tool on bearing inner race and press bearing out of knuckle.

16. Discard bearing.

17. Remove halfshaft.

18. Place halfshaft in vise. Remove bearing dust seal by uniformly tapping on outer edge with a light-duty hammer and a small prybar. Discard dust seal.

To install:

19. Place halfshaft in vise. Install a new dust seal using a suitable seal installer. Seal flange must face outboard.

20. Install halfshaft.

21. On bench, remove all foreign material from knuckle bearing bore and hub bearing journal to ensure correct seating of new bearing.

NOTE: If hub bearing journal is scored or damaged, replace hub. Do not attempt to service. The front wheel bearings are of a cartridge design and are pregreased, sealed and require no scheduled maintenance. The bearings are preset and cannot be adjusted. If a bearing is disassembled for any reason, it must be replaced as a unit. No individual service seals, rollers or races are available.

22. Place suitable bearing spacer step side down on hydraulic press plate and position knuckle on spacer with outboard side down. Position a new bearing in inboard side of knuckle. Install a suitable front bearing installer on bearing outer race face with undercut side facing bearing and press bearing into knuckle. Ensure that bearing seats completely against shoulder of knuckle bore.

NOTE: Ensure proper positioning of bearing installer during installation to prevent bearing damage.

23. Install a new snapring in knuckle groove using snapring pliers.

24. Place suitable front bearing spacer on arbor press plate and position hub on tool with lugs facing downward. Position knuckle assembly on hub barrel with outboard side down. Place a suitable front bearing installer on inner race of bearing and press down on tool until bearing is fully seated onto hub. Make sure hub rotates freely in knuckle after installation.

25. Suspend hub/knuckle/bearing assembly on vehicle with wire and attach strut loosely to knuckle. Lubricate CV-joint stub shaft splines with SAE 30 weight motor oil and insert shaft into hub splines as far as possible using hand pressure only. Check that spline are properly engaged.

26. On all except 1991–93 Tempo and Topaz, install suitable front hub installer and wheel bolt adapter to hub and stub shaft. Tighten hub installer tool to 120 ft. lbs. (162 Nm) to ensure that hub is fully seated. Remove tool and install washer and new hub nut retainer. Tighten hub nut retainer finger-tight.

27. On 1991–92 Tempo and Topaz, install washer and new hub nut. Rotate nut clockwise to seat CV-joint. Tighten hub nut to 188–236 ft. lbs. (255–320 Nm). Do not tighten with impact gun and do not move vehicle before retainer is tightened.

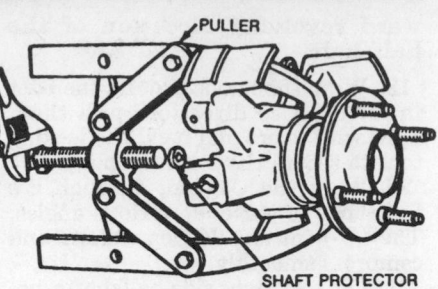

Removing the front hub—except 1991–93 Escort

28. Complete installation of front suspension components.

29. Install disc brake rotor to hub assembly.

30. Install disc brake caliper over rotor.

31. Ensure outer brake shoe spring end is seated under upper arm of knuckle.

32. Install wheel and tire assembly, tightening wheel nuts finger-tight.

33. Lower vehicle and block wheels to prevent vehicle from rolling.

34. Tighten wheel nuts to 85–105 ft. lbs. (115–142 Nm).

35. On all except 1991–93 Tempo and Topaz, manually thread hub nut retainer assembly on constant velocity output shaft as far as possible using a 30mm or 1³/₁₆ in. socket, tighten retainer assembly to 180–200 ft. lbs. (245–270 Nm). Do not use power or impact tools to tighten the hub nut. Do not move the vehicle before retainer is tightened.

NOTE: During tightening, an audible click sound will indicate proper ratchet function of the hub nut retainer. As the hub nut retainer tightens, ensure that one of the 3 locking tabs is in the slot of the CV-joint shaft. If the hub nut retainer is damaged, or more than 1 locking tab is broken, replace the hub nut retainer.

36. Install wheelcover or hub cover and lower vehicle completely to ground.

37. Remove wheel blocks.

1991–93 Escort

1. Raise and safely support the vehicle.

2. Remove the front wheel and tire assembly, brake caliper and rotor.

3. Remove the nut securing the halfshaft to the hub.

4. Remove the outer tie rod end at the steering knuckle.

5. Remove the nuts and bolts and separate the shock/strut assembly from the steering knuckle.

6. Remove the nut and bolt and separate the lower ball joint from the steering knuckle.

7. Remove the front hub/steering knuckle assembly from the halfshaft.

8. Remove the oil seal from the rear of the hub/steering knuckle assembly.

9. Position the hub/steering knuckle assembly on a hydraulic press and press the front hub out of the steering knuckle using a suitable removal tool.

NOTE: If the bearing inner race remains on the hub, use a grinder to grind a section of the bearing inner race until only 0.020 in. (0.5mm) remains. Remove the inner race with a suitable chisel.

10. Remove the E-clip from the steering knuckle.

11. Position the steering knuckle onto a hydraulic press and, using an appropriate bearing remover, press the bearing out of the steering knuckle.

NOTE: If the dust cover is removed, it must be replaced.

12. Scribe a mark in the dust cover and steering knuckle. Using a suitable chisel, remove the dust cover.

To install:

13. Scribe a mark on the new dust cover in the same position as on the previous mark. Align the marks on the steering knuckle to the mark on the dust cover and, using a suitable tool, press the dust cover onto the steering knuckle.

14. Position the steering knuckle onto a press and press the bearing into the steering knuckle, using a suitable bearing installer. Apply threadlocking compound to the wheel bearing outer race, prior to installation.

15. Install the E-clip.

16. Position the hub onto the knuckle and press the hub into the bearing and the steering knuckle, using a suitable installation tool.

17. Using an appropriate seal installer, install a new oil seal onto the inboard side of the steering knuckle. Make sure the oil seal mounts flush with the steering knuckle.

18. Install the hub/steering knuckle assembly onto the ball joint and install the nut and bolt. Tighten to 32–43 ft. lbs. (43–59 Nm). Apply Loctite® to the nut and bolt threads prior to installation.

19. Install the outer tie rod.

20. Install the steering knuckle to the shock/strut assembly. Tighten the nuts and bolts to 69–93 ft. lbs. (93–127 Nm).

21. Install a new locknut securing the halfshaft to the front hub. Tighten the locknut to 174–235 ft. lbs. (235–319 Nm). Stake the locknut to prevent it from loosening.

22. Install the brake rotor, caliper and wheel and tire assembly.

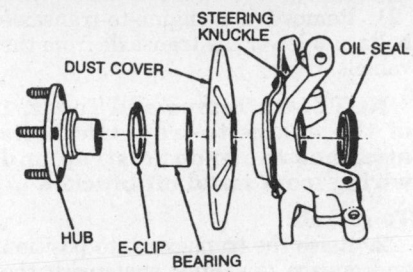

Front hub, knuckle and bearing assembly—1991–93 Escort

23. Lower the vehicle.

Axle Housing

REMOVAL & INSTALLATION

Tempo and Topaz With All Wheel Drive

1. Disconnect the negative battery cable.

2. Raise and safely support the vehicle.

NOTE: Anytime a U-joint retaining bolt is removed, Loctite® or equivalent, must be applied to the retaining bolts prior to installation.

3. Position a hoist or jack under rear axle housing.

4. Remove muffler and exhaust system from catalytic converter back.

5. Remove rear U-joint retaining bolts and straps retaining driveshaft, from torque tube yoke flange. Remove driveshaft center bearing bolts. Disengage driveshaft from axle yoke and position driveshaft off to 1 side.

6. Remove 4 retaining bolts from torque tube support bracket. Remove damper.

7. Disconnect axle vent hose clip form body.

8. Remove axle retaining bolt from left side differential support bracket.

9. Remove axle retaining bolt from center differential support bracket.

10. Lower axle assembly and remove inboard U-joint retaining bolts and straps from each halfshaft. Remove and wire halfshaft assemblies aside.

11. Remove rear axle assembly.

To install:

12. Position rear axle assembly under vehicle. Raise axle far enough for U-joint and halfshaft assemblies to be installed.

13. Position each inboard U-joint to rear axle. Install U-joint straps and retaining bolts. Using a T-30 Torx® bit, tighten bolts to 15–17 ft. lbs. (21–23 Nm).

14. Raise into position being careful not to trap or pinch axle vent hose. Install bolts attaching differential hous-

ing to left side and center differential support bracket. Tighten to 70–80 ft. lbs. (95–108 Nm).

15. Attach axle vent hose clip to body.

16. Position torque tube and mounting bracket and damper to crossmember. Install 4 attaching bolts. Tighten to 28–35 ft. lbs. (38–47 Nm). Install driveshaft and retaining bolts to torque tube yoke flange. Using a T-30 Torx® bit, tighten to 15–17 ft. lbs. (21–23 Nm).

17. Install exhaust from catalytic converter back.

18. Check lubricant level in axle.

19. Lower vehicle.

MANUAL TRANSAXLE

For further information on transmission/transaxles, please refer to "Chilton's Guide to Transmission Repair".

Transaxle Assembly

REMOVAL & INSTALLATION

1989–90 Escort and Tempo/Topaz With 2.3L Engine

1. Disconnect the negative battery cable. Wedge a 7 in. wooden block under the clutch pedal to hold the pedal up slightly beyond its normal position. Grasp the clutch cable, pull it forward and disconnect it from the clutch release shaft assembly. Remove the clutch casing from the rib on the top surface of the transaxle case.

2. Remove the upper 2 transaxle-to-engine bolts. Remove the air cleaner on Tempo and Topaz or the air management valve bracket-to-transaxle upper bolt on Escort.

3. Raise and safely support the vehicle.

4. On Tempo and Topaz, remove the front stabilizer bar-to-control arm nut and washer, on the driver's side and discard the nut. Remove both front stabilizer bar mounting brackets and discard the bolts.

5. Remove the lower control arm ball joint-to-steering knuckle nut/bolt and discard the nut/bolt; repeat this procedure on the opposite side.

6. Using a large prybar, pry the lower control arm from the steering knuckle; repeat this procedure on the opposite side.

NOTE: Be careful not to dam-

age or cut the ball joint boot and do not contact the lower arm.

7. Using a large prybar, pry the left-side inboard CV-joint assembly from the transaxle.

NOTE: Plug the seal opening (both sides), with transaxle plugs T81P-1177-B or equivalent, to prevent lubricant leakage.

8. Grasp the left-hand steering knuckle and swing it and the halfshaft outward from the transaxle; this will disconnect the inboard CV-joint from the transaxle.

NOTE: If the CV-joint assembly cannot be pried from the transaxle, insert a differential rotator tool through the left-side and tap the joint out; the tool can be used from either side of transaxle.

9. Using mechanics wire, support the halfshaft in a near level position to prevent damage to the assembly during the remaining operations; repeat this procedure on the opposite side.

10. Disengage the locking tabs and remove the backup light switch connector from the transaxle backup light switch.

11. On Tempo and Topaz, remove the starter studs-to-engine roll restrictor bracket nuts and the engine roll restrictor. Remove the starter stud bolts.

12. On Escort, remove the starter bolts.

13. Remove the shift mechanism-to-shift shaft nut/bolt, the control selector indicator switch arm and the shift shaft.

14. Remove the shift mechanism stabilizer bar-to-transaxle bolt, control selector indicator switch and bracket assembly.

15. Using a crowfoot wrench, remove the speedometer cable from the transaxle.

16. On Tempo and Topaz, remove both oil pan-to-clutch housing bolts. On Escort, remove 2 stiffener brace retaining bolts.

17. Using a floor jack and a transaxle support, position it under the transaxle and secure the transaxle to it.

18. On Tempo and Topaz, remove the both left-hand rear No. 4 insulator-to-body bracket nuts and the left-hand front No. 1 insulator-to-body bracket bolts.

19. On Escort, remove both rear mount-to-floorpan bolts, loosen the nut at the bottom of the front mount and remove the front mount-to-transaxle bolts.

20. Lower the floor jack, until the transaxle clears the rear insulator. Support the engine by placing wood under the oil pan.

21. Remove the engine-to-transaxle bolts and lower the transaxle from the vehicle.

NOTE: On Tempo and Topaz, 1 of the engine-to-transaxle bolts attaches the ground strap and wiring loom stand off bracket.

To install:

22. Raise the transaxle into position and engage the input shaft with the clutch plate. Install the lower engine-to-transaxle bolts and torque to 28-31 ft. lbs. (38-42 Nm).

NOTE: Never attempt to start the engine prior to installing the CV-joints or differential side gear for dislocation and/or damage may occur.

23. On Escort, install the front mount-to-transaxle bolts and torque to 25-35 ft. lbs. (34-47 Nm); also, tighten the nut on the bottom of the front transaxle mount.

24. On Tempo, tighten the left front No. 1 insulator bolts to 25-35 ft. lbs. (34-47 Nm) and the left rear No. 4 insulator bolts to 35-50 ft. lbs. (47-68 Nm).

25. On Escort install the air management valve-to-transaxle upper bolt, finger-tight and the bottom bracket bolt to 28-31 ft. lbs. (38-42 Nm).

26. On Escort, install both rear mount-to-floorpan brace bolts to 40-51 ft. lbs. (55-70 Nm).

27. Remove the floor jack and adapter.

28. Using a crowfoot wrench, install the speedometer cable; be careful not to cross-thread the cable nut.

29. On Tempo and Topaz, install the oil pan-to-transaxle bolts and tighten to 28-38 ft. lbs. (38-51 Nm). On Escort, install the 2 stiffener brace bolts and tighten to 15-21 ft. lbs. (21-28 Nm).

30. Install the shifter stabilizer bar/control selector indicator switch-to-transaxle bolt and torque to 23-35 ft. lbs. (31-47 Nm).

31. Install the shift mechanism-to-shift shaft, the switch actuator bracket clamp and torque the bolt to 7-10 ft. lbs. (9-13 Nm); be sure to shift the transaxle into **4th** for 4-speed or **5th** for 5-speed and align the actuator.

32. On Escort, innstall the starter bolts and tighten to 30-40 ft. lbs. (41-54 Nm). On Tempo and Topaz, install the starter stud bolts and tighten to 30-40 ft. lbs. (41-54 Nm) and install the engine roll restrictor and the attaching nuts. Tighten the attaching nuts to 14-20 ft. lbs. (19-27 Nm).

33. Install the backup light switch connector to the transaxle switch.

34. Install the new circlip onto both inner joints of the halfshafts, insert the inner CV-joints into the transaxle

and fully seat them; lightly, pry outward to confirm that the retaining rings are seated.

NOTE: When installing the halfshafts, be careful not to tear the oil seals.

35. Connect the lower ball joint to the steering knuckle, insert a new pinch bolt and torque the new nut to 37-44 ft. lbs. (50-60 Nm); be careful not to damage the boot.

36. Refill the transaxle and lower the vehicle.

37. On Escort, install the upper air management valve bracket-to-transaxle bolt and torque to 28-31 ft. lbs. (38-42 Nm). On Tempo and Topaz, install the air cleaner.

38. Install the both upper transaxle-to-engine bolts and torque to 28-31 ft. lbs. (38-42 Nm).

39. Connect the clutch cable to the clutch release shaft assembly and remove the wooden block from under the clutch pedal. Connect the negative battery cable.

NOTE: Prior to starting the engine, set the hand brake and pump the clutch pedal several times to ensure proper clutch adjustment.

1991-93 Escort

1. Disconnect the battery cables and remove the battery and the battery tray.

2. Remove the air hose and the resonance chamber.

3. Disconnect the speedometer cable at the transaxle.

4. Remove the retaining clip, then disconnect the slave cylinder line from the slave cylinder hose and plug the hose.

5. Disconnect the ground strap from the transaxle.

6. Remove the tie wrap and disconnect the 3 electrical connectors located above the transaxle. Remove the electrical connector support bracket.

7. Mount engine support bar D88L-6000-A or equivalent, and attach it to the engine hangers.

8. Remove the 3 nuts from the upper transaxle mount. Loosen the mount pivot nut and rotate the mount out of position. Remove the 3 bolts and the upper transaxle mount bracket.

9. Remove the 2 upper transaxle-to-engine bolts.

10. Raise and safely support the vehicle.

11. Remove the front wheel and tire assemblies.

12. Remove the inner fender splash shields.

13. Drain the transaxle fluid and install the drain plug.

14. Remove the halfshafts. Install 2 transaxle plugs T88C–7025–AH or equivalent, between the differential side gears.

NOTE: Failure to install the transaxle plugs may cause the differential side gears to become improperly positioned. If the gears become misaligned, the differential will have to be removed from the transaxle to align them.

15. Remove the plenum support bracket and remove the starter.

16. Remove the nut and the extension bar and the bolt and nut and shift control rod from the transaxle.

17. Remove both lower splash shields.

18. Remove the 2 transaxle mount-to-crossmember nuts and remove the lower crossmember and the front transaxle mount.

19. Position and secure a suitable jack under the transaxle.

20. Remove the 5 lower engine-to-transaxle bolts and lower the transaxle out of the vehicle.

To install:

21. Apply a thin coating of suitable grease to the spline of the input shaft.

22. Place the transaxle onto a suitable jack. Make sure the transaxle is secure.

23. Raise the transaxle into position on the engine.

24. Install the 5 lower engine-to-transaxle bolts and tighten to 27–38 ft. lbs. (37–52 Nm).

25. Install the front transaxle mount and tubing bracket. Tighten the bolts to 12–17 ft. lbs. (16–23 Nm).

26. Install the lower crossmember. Tighten the nuts and bolts to 47–66 ft. lbs. (64–89 Nm).

27. Install the 2 transaxle mount-to-crossmember nuts and tighten to 27–38 ft. lbs. (37–52 Nm).

28. Install both lower splash shields.

29. Install the shift control rod bolt and nut and tighten to 23–34 ft. lbs. (31–46 Nm).

30. Install the extension bar nut and tighten to 12–17 ft. lbs. (16–23 Nm).

31. Install the starter and the plenum support bracket.

32. Remove the transaxle plugs and install the halfshafts.

33. Install the inner fender splash shields.

34. Install the wheel and tire assemblies. Tighten the lug nuts to 65–87 ft. lbs. (88–118 Nm).

35. Lower the vehicle.

36. Install the 2 upper engine-to-transaxle bolts and tighten to 47–66 ft. lbs. (64–89 Nm).

37. Install the upper transaxle mount bracket and tighten the 3 bolts to 47–66 ft. lbs. (64–89 Nm). Rotate the mount into position and tighten

the pivot nut. Install and tighten the 3 upper mount nuts to 47–66 ft. lbs. (64–89 Nm).

38. Remove the engine support bar.

39. Install the electrical connector support bracket. Connect the 3 electrical connectors and secure with the tie wrap.

40. Connect the ground strap to the transaxle.

41. Connect the slave cylinder line to the slave cylinder hose and install the retaining clip.

42. Add the proper type and amount of fluid to the transaxle.

43. Connect the speedometer cable.

44. Install the air hose and the resonance chamber.

45. Install the battery tray and the battery. Connect the battery cables.

46. Check for fluid leaks and proper operation.

Tempo/Topaz With 3.0L Engine

1. Prop the clutch pedal to keep it from moving toward the floor when the clutch cable is disconnected.

2. Disconnect the negative battery cable.

3. Disconnect the mass air flow sensor and air charge temperature sensor connectors at the air cleaner.

4. Remove the air cleaner retaining bolt, loosen the outlet tube at the throttle body and remove the air cleaner assembly.

5. Remove the retaining bolts and remove the coil bracket assembly from the left cylinder head. Position the assembly aside.

6. Install engine lifting bracket tools T70P–6000 or equivalent, on the rear of the left cylinder head.

7. Disconnect and remove the back-up light switch.

8. Disconnect the clutch cable from the clutch release lever.

9. Remove the nut attaching the starter cable bracket to the left front transaxle support.

10. Remove the 2 top left-hand front transaxle mount-to-engine bolts.

11. Remove the nuts attaching the power steering line bracket to the engine.

12. Remove the top 4 transaxle-to-engine bolts.

13. Disconnect the vehicle speed sensor connector from the speed sensor.

14. Remove the speedometer cable from the speed sensor. Do not remove the clip retaining the cable to the speed sensor.

15. Install 3 bar engine support tool D88L–6000–A or equivalent, and connect the J-hook to the engine lifting bracket.

16. Loosen, but do not remove, the 2 Torx® head bolts attaching the right engine mounts to the right frame rail.

17. Raise and safely support the vehicle.

18. Remove the front wheel and tire assemblies.

19. Remove and discard both lower steering knuckle ball joint pinch bolts. Using a small prybar, slightly spread the knuckle pinch joint and separate each ball joint from the steering knuckle. A drift punch may be used to remove the bolt. Be careful not to damage the ball joint boot seal.

NOTE: Make sure the steering column is in the unlocked position. Do not use a hammer to separate the ball joint from the knuckle.

20. Remove the cotter pins and the nuts from the tie-rod ends. Use a suitable tool to disconnect the tie-rod ends from the steering knuckles.

21. Use a suitable prybar to disengage the CV-joints from the transaxle. Install transaxle plugs T81P–1177–B or equivalent, to prevent transaxle fluid from leaking from the transaxle.

22. Remove the nuts attaching the halfshafts to the hubs and remove the halfshafts.

23. Remove the bolt attaching the shift lever linkage to the transaxle shift rod and position the linkage aside.

24. Remove the bolt attaching the stabilizer rod to the transaxle and position the stabilizer rod aside.

25. Disconnect the neutral sensing switch connector.

26. Remove the starter support bracket and the starter.

27. Loosen the a front retaining bolt from each side on the engine-to-transaxle support bracket.

28. Remove the 2 rear retaining bolts on the engine-to-transaxle bracket and remove the 2 bracket-to-transaxle bolts.

29. From the right wheel well, loosen, but do not remove, 2 right engine mount retaining nuts.

30. Remove the lower retaining bolt from the left front transaxle mount. Loosen the through bolt and pivot the mount up away from the transaxle.

31. Remove the 2 retaining nuts from the rear transaxle mount.

32. Carefully lower the engine/transaxle assembly using the engine support fixture until the crankshaft damper just contacts the right frame rail.

NOTE: Do not let the weight of the engine rest on the crankshaft damper or the damper and crankshaft thrust bearings may be damaged.

33. Position a transaxle jack under the transaxle and install safety chains. Lower the transaxle.

34. Remove the 2 remaining transaxle-to-engine bolts.

35. Remove the transaxle from the vehicle. After clearing the clutch assembly, rotate the transaxle clutch housing toward the front of the vehicle to clear the suspension stabilizer bar.

NOTE: Do not move the vehicle with the wheels on the ground with the transaxle removed.

To install:

36. Position the transaxle on the transaxle jack with safety chains.

37. Raise the transaxle into position. Rotate the transaxle clutch housing to the front of the engine compartment to allow the rear of the transaxle to clear the suspension stabilizer bar.

38. Align the transaxle input shaft with the clutch splines and locating pin on the engine and seat the transaxle against the engine.

39. Install 2 transaxle-to-engine bolts.

40. Using the engine support fixture, raise the engine/transaxle assembly into position. Position the engine-to-transaxle support bracket to the transaxle and install but do not tighten the 2 bolts, 1 on each side.

41. Position the engine-to-transaxle support bracket to the transaxle and install but do not tighten the 2 bolts, 1 on each side.

42. Install 2 rear engine support bracket-to-engine bolts, 1 on each side.

43. Tighten the support bracket-to-engine bolts.

44. From the right wheel well, tighten the 2 right engine mount nuts to 73–97 ft. lbs. (98–132 Nm).

45. Install the lower left front engine mount-to-engine bolt and tighten to 26–33 ft. lbs. (34–46 Nm). Tighten the transaxle mount through bolt.

46. Install 2 left rear engine mount-to-body bracket nuts and tighten to 73–97 ft. lbs. (98–132 Nm).

47. Remove the transaxle jack.

48. Install the starter and the starter bracket.

49. Connect the neutral sensing switch connector.

50. Install the transaxle stabilizer bar and tighten the bolt.

51. Position the shift linkage on the shift rod and install the bolt, washer and nut.

52. Position the halfshafts in the vehicle and insert the outer CV-joints through the hub assemblies. Install the retaining nuts and tighten to 180–200 ft. lbs. (244–271 Nm).

53. Remove the plugs from the transaxle that were installed during the removal procedure.

54. Install new clips on the inner CV-joint stub axles. Install the halfshafts into the transaxle. Pull on the CV-joints to make sure they are fully seated in the transaxle.

55. Install the ball joints into the steering knuckles using new bolts. Tighten the bolts to 38–45 ft. lbs. (52–60 Nm).

56. Check the transaxle fluid level and add fluid, if necessary.

57. Lower the vehicle. Remove the engine support and lifting eye.

58. Position the coil bracket and install the retaining bolts.

59. Install the speedometer cable into the speed sensor. Pull on the cable to make sure it is fully seated in the sensor. Connect the electrical connector to the speed sensor.

60. Connect the clutch cable to the clutch release lever.

61. Coat the threads of the backup light switch with pipe sealant and install the switch. Tighten to 12–15 ft. lbs. (16–20 Nm).

62. Install the 4 upper transaxle-to-engine bolts and tighten to 25–34 ft. lbs. (34–47 Nm).

63. Position the power steering line bracket to the upper transaxle-to-engine stud bolts and install the 2 nuts.

64. Install the 2 bolts in the left front transaxle mount.

65. Position the starter cable bracket and install the attaching nut.

66. Install the air cleaner and outlet tube.

67. Connect the mass air flow sensor and air charge temperature sensor connectors at the air cleaner.

68. Tighten the top 2 right mount-to-body Torx® bolts to 40–52 ft. lbs. (54–71 Nm).

69. Connect the negative battery cable.

70. Remove the prop from the clutch pedal. Road test the vehicle.

CLUTCH

Clutch Assembly

REMOVAL & INSTALLATION

1. Disconnect the negative battery cable. Raise and safely support the vehicle. Remove the transaxle.

2. If the clutch assembly is to be reused, matchmark the pressure plate and the flywheel so they can be assembled in the same position.

3. Loosen the pressure plate-to-flywheel bolts 1 turn at a time, in sequence, until spring tension is relieved to prevent pressure plate cover distortion.

4. Support the pressure plate and remove the bolts. Remove the pressure plate and clutch disc from the flywheel.

5. Inspect the flywheel, clutch disc, pressure plate, release bearing, pilot bearing and the clutch fork for wear; replace parts, as required.

NOTE: If the flywheel shows any signs of overheating (blue discoloration) or if it is badly grooved or scored, it should be refaced or replaced.

To install:

6. If removed, install a new pilot bearing using a suitable installation tool.

7. If removed, install the flywheel. Make sure the flywheel and crankshaft flange mating surfaces are clean. Tighten the flywheel bolts to 71–76 ft. lbs. (96–103 Nm) on 1.8L engine, 54–67 ft. lbs. (73–91 Nm) on 1.9L engine, 54–64 ft. lbs. (73–86 Nm) on 2.3L engine or 59 ft. lbs. (80 Nm) on 3.0L engine.

8. Clean the pressure plate and flywheel surfaces thoroughly. Position the clutch disc and pressure plate into the installed position and support them with a dummy shaft or clutch aligning tool. If the clutch assembly is being reused, align the matchmarks that were made during the removal procedure.

9. Install the pressure plate-to-flywheel bolts. Tighten them gradually in a criss-cross pattern to 12–24 ft. lbs. (17–32 Nm) on all except 1991–93 Escort, where the torque should be 13–20 ft. lbs. (18–26 Nm). Remove the alignment tool.

10. If the release bearing was removed, lubricate the release fork where it contacts the bearing and install the bearing in the fork.

11. Install the transaxle assembly. Lower the vehicle and connect the negative battery cable.

PEDAL HEIGHT/FREE PLAY ADJUSTMENT

Except 1991–93 Escort

The pedal height and free-play are controlled by a self-adjusting feature.

1991–93 Escort

PEDAL HEIGHT

To determine if the pedal height requires adjustment, measure the distance from the bulkhead to the upper center of the pedal pad. The distance should be 7.72–8.03 in. (196–204mm). If adjustment is necessary, proceed as follows:

1. Disconnect the clutch switch electrical connector.

2. Loosen the clutch switch locknut.

3. Turn the clutch switch until the correct height is achieved.

4. Tighten the locknut to 10–13 ft. lbs. (14–18 Nm).

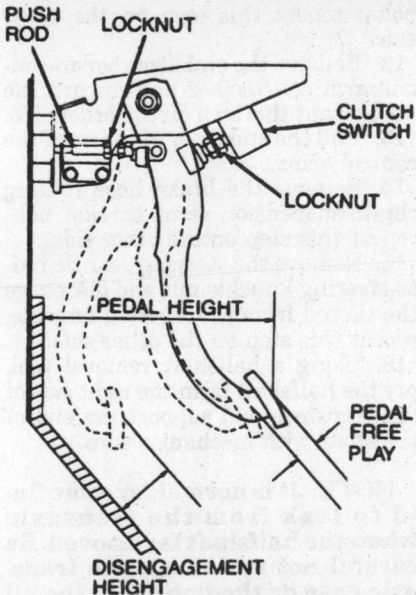

Pedal height/pedal free-play adjustment—1991–93 Escort

5. Measure the pedal free-play.
6. Connect the electrical connector.

PEDAL FREE-PLAY

To determine if the pedal free-play requires adjustment, depress the clutch pedal by hand until clutch resistance is felt. Measure the distance between the upper pedal height and where the resistance is felt. Free-play should be 0.20–0.51 in. (5–13mm). If an adjustment is necessary, proceed as follows:
1. Loosen the pushrod locknut.
2. Turn the pushrod until the pedal free-play is within specification.
3. Check that the disengagement height is correct when the pedal is fully depressed. Minimum disengagement height is 1.6 in. (41mm).
4. Tighten the pushrod locknut to 9–12 ft. lbs. (12–17 Nm).

Clutch Cable

ADJUSTMENT

Tempo, Topaz and 1989–90 Escort

The clutch control system is self-adjusting. After proper installation of the cable, adjustment is completed by pulling the clutch pedal to its upmost position.

REMOVAL & INSTALLATION

Tempo, Topaz and 1989–90 Escort

NOTE: Whenever the clutch cable is disconnected for any reason, such as transaxle or clutch removal, clutch pedal components or clutch cable replacement, it is imperative that the proper method for installing the clutch cable be followed.

1. Disconnect the negative battery cable.
2. Prop up the clutch pedal to lift the pawl free of the quadrant which is part of the self-adjuster mechanism.
3. Remove the air cleaner to gain access to the clutch cable.
4. Using a pair of pliers, grasp the extended tip of the clutch cable, pull it forward and disconnect it from the clutch bearing lever.

NOTE: Do not grasp the wire strand portion of the inner cable since it may cut the wires and cause cable failure.

5. Remove the clutch casing from the insulator which is located on the rib on the top of the transaxle case.
6. On the Tempo or Topaz, remove the panel from above the clutch pedal pad.
7. Remove the rear screw and move the clutch shield away from the brake pedal support bracket. Loosen the front retaining screw, located near the toe board, rotate the shield aside and snug the screw to retain the shield.
8. With the clutch pedal raised to release the pawl, rotate the gear quadrant forward, unhook the clutch cable and allow the quadrant to swing rearward; do not allow the quadrant to snap back.
9. Pull the cable through the recess between the clutch pedal and the gear quadrant and from the insulator on the pedal assembly.
10. Remove the cable from the engine compartment.
To install:
11. Lift the clutch pedal to disengage the adjusting mechanism. This must be done during cable installation as failure to do so will result in damage to the self-adjuster mechanism.
12. Insert the clutch cable through the dash panel and the dash panel grommet.

NOTE: Be sure the clutch cable is routed under the brake lines and not trapped at the spring tower by the brake lines. If equipped with power steering, route the cable inboard of the power steering hose.

13. Push the clutch cable through the insulator on the stop bracket and through the recess between the pedal and the gear quadrant.
14. Lift the clutch pedal to release the pawl, rotate the gear quadrant forward and hook the cable into the gear quadrant.

15. Install the clutch shield on the brake pedal support bracket.
16. On the Tempo or Topaz, install the panel above the clutch pedal.
17. Using a piece of wire, cord or tape, secure the pedal in the upmost position.
18. Insert the clutch cable through the insulator and connect the cable to the clutch release lever in the engine compartment.
19. Remove the device used to temporarily secure the pedal against its stop.
20. Adjust the clutch by depressing the clutch pedal several times. Install the air cleaner and connect the negative battery cable.

Clutch Master Cylinder

REMOVAL & INSTALLATION

1991–93 Escort

1. Disconnect the battery cables and remove the battery and battery tray.
2. Disconnect the clutch pipe from the master cylinder using a suitable line wrench.
3. Disengage the clamp and remove the master cylinder hose from the clutch master cylinder. Prevent excess fluid loss by plugging the hose.
4. Remove the external mounting nut.
5. Remove the internal mounting nut and remove the master cylinder.
To install:
6. Align the pushrod and install the clutch master cylinder.
7. Install the external and internal mounting nuts and tighten to 14–19 ft. lbs. (19–25 Nm).
8. Connect the clutch pipe and tighten the nut to 10–16 ft. lbs. (13–22 Nm).
9. Install the hose and the clamp to the master cylinder.
10. Install the battery and battery tray.
11. Bleed the air from the system.
12. Test the system and make sure there is no leakage.
13. Connect the negative battery cable.

Clutch Slave Cylinder

ADJUSTMENT

1991–93 Escort

The clutch slave cylinder is not adjustable. The only adjustments necessary on the clutch control system are pedal height and pedal free-play.

REMOVAL & INSTALLATION

1991–93 Escort

1. Disconnect the pressure line. Plug the line to prevent leaking.
2. Remove the attaching bolts and remove the slave cylinder.

To install:

3. Install the slave cylinder.
4. Install the attaching bolts and tighten to 12–17 ft. lbs. (16–23 Nm).
5. Connect the pressure line and tighten the nut to 10–16 ft. lbs. (13–22 Nm).
6. Bleed the air from the system.
7. Press on the clutch pedal and make sure there is no leakage.

Hydraulic Clutch System Bleeding

NOTE: The fluid level in the reservoir must be maintained at the ¾ level or higher during air bleeding.

1. Remove the bleeder cap from the slave cylinder and attach a vinyl hose to the bleeder screw.
2. Place the other end of the hose in a container.
3. Slowly pump the clutch pedal several times.
4. With the clutch pedal depressed, loosen the bleeder screw to release the fluid and air.
5. Tighten the bleeder screw.
6. Repeat the last 3 steps until no air bubbles appear in the fluid.

AUTOMATIC TRANSAXLE

For further information on transmission/transaxles, please refer to "Chilton's Guide to Transmission Repair".

Transaxle Assembly

REMOVAL & INSTALLATION

Except 1991–93 Escort

1. Disconnect the negative battery cable.

NOTE: Due to automatic transaxle case configuration, on all except the 3.0L engine, the right-side halfshaft assembly must be removed first. The differential rotator tool T81P–4026–A or equivalent, is then inserted into the transaxle to drive the left-side inboard CV-joint assembly from the transaxle.

2. Remove the air cleaner assembly.
3. Disconnect the electrical harness connector from the neutral safety switch.
4. Disconnect the throttle valve linkage, throttle cable if equipped with 3.0L engine, and the manual lever cable from their levers.

NOTE: Failure to disconnect the linkage or cable and allowing the transaxle to hang, will fracture the throttle valve cam shaft joint, which is located under the transaxle cover.

5. To prevent contamination, cover the timing window in the converter housing. If equipped, remove the bolts retaining the thermactor hoses.
6. If equipped, remove the ground strap, located above the upper engine mount, and the coil and bracket assembly.

NOTE: If equipped with 3.0L engine, be careful not to damage the TV cable while accessing the upper retaining bolts.

7. Remove both transaxle-to-engine upper bolts; the bolts are located below and on both sides of the distributor. Install 3 bar engine support D88L–6000–A or equivalent.
8. Raise and safely support the vehicle. Remove the front wheel and tire assemblies.
9. Remove the nut from the control arm-to-steering knuckle attaching bolt, at the ball joint. Using a hammer and a punch, drive the bolt from the steering knuckle; repeat this step on the other side. Discard the nut and bolt.

NOTE: Be careful not to damage or cut ball joint boot. The prybar must not contact lower arm.

10. Using a prybar, disengage the control arm from the steering knuckle; repeat this step on the other side.

NOTE: Do not hammer on the knuckle to remove the ball joints. The plastic shield installed behind the rotor contains a molded pocket into which the lower control arm ball joint fits. When disengaging the control arm from the knuckle, clearance for the ball joint can be provided by bending the shield back toward the rotor. Failure to provide clearance for the ball joint can result in damage to the shield.

11. Remove the stabilizer bar bracket-to-frame rail bolts and discard the bolts; repeat this step on the other side.
12. Remove the stabilizer bar-to-control arm nut/washer and discard the nut; repeat this step on the other side.
13. Pull the stabilizer bar from of the control arms.
14. Remove the brake hose routing clip-to-suspension strut bracket bolt; repeat this step on the other side.
15. Remove the steering gear tie rod-to-steering knuckle nut and disengage the tie rod from the steering knuckle; repeat this step on the other side.
16. Using a halfshaft removal tool, pry the halfshaft from the right side of the transaxle and support the end of the shaft with mechanics wire.

NOTE: It is normal for some fluid to leak from the transaxle when the halfshaft is removed. Be careful not to damage the transaxle case or the bottom of the oil pan flange when prying the halfshaft out.

17. Using differential rotator tool T81P–4026–A or equivalent, drive the left-side halfshaft from the differential side gear.
18. Pull the halfshaft from the transaxle and support the end of the shaft with mechanics wire.

NOTE: Do not allow the shaft to hang unsupported, as damage to the outboard CV-joint may result.

19. Install transaxle plugs T81P–1177–B or equivalent, into the differential seals.
20. Remove the starter support bracket, if equipped. Disconnect the starter cable. Remove the starter bolts and the starter. If equipped, remove the hose and bracket bolts on the starter and a bolt at the converter and disconnect the hoses.
21. If equipped, remove the transaxle support bracket. Remove the dust cover from the torque converter housing.
22. Remove the torque converter-to-flywheel nuts by turning the crankshaft pulley bolt to bring the nuts into position.
23. Position a suitable transmission jack under the transaxle and remove the rear support bracket nuts.
24. Remove the left front insulator-to-body bracket nuts, the bracket-to-body bolts and the bracket.
25. Disconnect the transaxle cooler lines.
26. Remove the manual lever bracket-to-transaxle case bolts.
27. Support the engine. Make sure the transaxle is supported and remove the remaining transaxle-to-engine bolts.
28. Make sure the torque converter studs will be clear the flywheel. Insert

a prybar between the flywheel and the converter, then, pry the transaxle and converter away from the engine. When the converter studs are clear of the flywheel, lower the transaxle about 2–3 in. (51–76mm).

29. Disconnect the speedometer cable and lower the transaxle.

NOTE: When moving the transaxle away from the engine, watch the No. 1 insulator. If it contacts the body before the converter studs clear the flywheel, remove the insulator.

To install:

30. Raise the transaxle and align it with the engine and flywheel. Install the No. 1 insulator, if removed. Torque the transaxle-to-engine bolts to 25–33 ft. lbs. (34–45 Nm) on the 1.9L and 2.3L engines or 34–47 ft. lbs. (46–63 Nm) on the 3.0L engine. Tighten the torque converter-to-flywheel bolts to 23–39 ft. lbs. (31–53 Nm).

31. Install the manual lever bracket-to-transaxle case bolts and connect the transaxle cooler lines.

32. Install the left front insulator-to-body bracket nuts and torque the nuts to 40–50 ft. lbs. (55–70 Nm). Install the bracket-to-body and torque the bolts to 55–70 ft. lbs. (75–90 Nm).

33. Install the transaxle support bracket and the dust cover to the torque converter housing.

34. If equipped, install the hose and bracket bolts on the starter and a bolt to the converter and connect the hoses. Install the starter and the support bracket; torque the starter-to-engine bolts to 30–40 ft. lbs. (41–54 Nm). Connect the starter cable.

35. Remove the seal plugs from the differential seals and install the halfshaft by performing the following procedures:

   a. Prior to installing the halfshaft in the transaxle, install a new circlip onto the CV-joint stub.

   b. Install the halfshaft in the transaxle by carefully aligning the CV-joint splines with the differential side gears. Be sure to push the CV-joint into the differential until the circlip is felt to seat in the differential side gear. Use care to prevent damage to the differential oil seal.

   c. Attach the lower ball joint to the steering knuckle, taking care not to damage or cut the ball joint boot. Insert a new pinch bolt and a new nut. While holding the bolt with a 2nd wrench, torque the nut to 40–54 ft. lbs. (54–74 Nm).

36. Engage the tie rod with the steering knuckle and torque the nut to 23–35 ft. lbs. (31–47 Nm).

37. Install the brake hose routing clip-to-suspension strut bracket and torque the bolt to 8 ft. lbs. (11 Nm).

38. Install the stabilizer bar to control arm and using a new nut, torque it to 98–125 ft. lbs. (133–169 Nm).

39. Install the stabilizer bar bracket-to-frame rail bolts and using new bolts, torque them to 60–70 ft. lbs. (81–95 Nm).

40. Install the wheel and tire assemblies and lower the vehicle. Install the upper transaxle-to-engine bolts and torque to 25–33 ft. lbs. (34–45 Nm) on 1.9L and 2.3L engines or 34–47 ft. lbs. (46–63 Nm) on 3.0L engine.

41. If equipped, install the ground strap, located above the upper engine mount, and the coil and bracket assembly.

42. If equipped, install the bolts retaining the thermactor hoses. Uncover the timing window in the converter housing.

43. Connect the throttle valve linkage or cable and the manual lever cable to their levers.

44. Connect the electrical harness connector from the neutral safety switch.

45. Install the air cleaner assembly.

46. Connect the negative battery cable and road test the vehicle.

1991–93 Escort

1. Disconnect the battery cables and remove the battery and battery tray.

2. Disconnect the wiring harness retaining clip from the battery tray.

3. Remove the air cleaner assembly.

4. Disconnect the shift control cable from the manual lever.

5. Disconnect the speedometer cable from the transaxle by unsnapping the cable at the speedometer driven gear.

6. Disconnect the transaxle electronic control electrical connectors and separate the harness from the transaxle clips.

7. Remove the manual lever position switch wiring brackets and disconnect the ground cables from the top of the transaxle.

8. Remove the starter.

9. Disconnect the manual lever position switch wiring connectors.

10. Install engine support D88L-6000-A or equivalent, to support the engine.

11. Disconnect the kickdown cable at the throttle cam.

12. Place a suitable drain pan under the transaxle and disconnect the transaxle cooler lines at the transaxle.

13. Remove the upper transaxle mount bolts, the mount and the upper transaxle housing bolts.

14. Disconnect the oxygen sensor electrical connector, the transaxle vent hose, and the electrical connector at the vehicle speed sensor.

15. Raise and safely support the vehicle.

16. Remove the front wheel and tire assemblies.

17. Using a suitable hammer and a flat punch, straighten the detent in the halfshaft nut.

18. Remove the nuts securing the halfshafts to the steering knuckles and remove the nuts and bolts securing the lower ball joints to the steering knuckles. Separate the lower ball joints from the steering knuckles.

19. Disconnect the halfshaft midbearing bracket from the back of the engine.

20. Remove the halfshafts from both steering knuckles.

21. Remove the 3 engine/transaxle lower splash shields and the torque converter inspection plate. Remove the nuts securing the torque converter to the flexplate.

22. Remove the bolts securing the lower transaxle to the engine oil pan. Disconnect the lower crossmember from the chassis and the transaxle mounts.

23. Remove the driver's side and then the passenger's side halfshafts. Install 2 transaxle plugs T88C-7025-AH or equivalent into the differential side gears.

NOTE: Failure to install the transaxle plugs may cause the differential side gears to become improperly positioned. If the gears become misaligned, the differential will have to be removed from the transaxle to align them.

24. Position a drain pan and remove the drainplug from the transaxle. Drain the fluid from the differential cavity. Remove the transaxle pan and drain the transaxle fluid, then install the pan and drainplug.

25. Position a suitable transmission jack under the transaxle. Secure the transaxle to the jack.

26. Remove the lower bolts securing the transaxle to the engine and carefully lower the transaxle out of the vehicle.

To install:

NOTE: A pin is used for securing the throttle cam in a fixed position on new and rebuilt transaxles. This pin must be removed to allow proper transaxle operation. If the pin is not removed, the throttle lever will remain in a fixed position. After removing the pin, apply sealant to the bolt from the previous transaxle. Install the bolt and tighten to 69–95 inch lbs. (8–11 Nm).

27. Secure the transaxle on the transmission jack.

28. Raise the transaxle into position and install the lower transaxle-to-engine bolts. Tighten the bolts to 41–59 ft. lbs. (55–80 Nm).

29. Position the torque converter to the flexplate and install the nuts. Tighten the nuts to 25–36 ft. lbs. (34–49 Nm). Install the torque converter inspection plate.

30. Remove the 2 transaxle plugs and install the halfshafts.

31. Connect the crossmember to the transaxle mounts and the chassis. Tighten the crossmember-to-transaxle mount nuts to 27–38 ft. lbs. (37–52 Nm). Tighten the crossmember-to-chassis nuts and bolts to 47–66 ft. lbs. (64–89 Nm).

32. Install the lower transaxle-to-engine oil pan bolts and tighten to 27–38 ft. lbs. (37–52 Nm). Install the engine/transaxle splash shields and the starter.

33. Position the lower ball joints into the steering knuckles and secure with the nuts and bolts. Tighten the nuts and bolts to 32–43 ft. lbs. (43–59 Nm).

34. Position the tie rod ends into steering knuckles and install the nuts. Tighten to 31–42 ft. lbs. (42–57 Nm).

35. Install the wheel and tire assemblies. Tighten the lugs to 65–88 ft. lbs. (88–118 Nm).

36. Lower the vehicle.

37. Install the transaxle-to-engine bolts and tighten to 41–59 ft. lbs. (55–80 Nm).

38. Install the upper transaxle mount and tighten the nuts to 49–69 ft. lbs. (67–93 Nm).

39. Connect the transaxle vent hose, the electrical connector at the speed sensor, the speedometer cable and the oxygen sensor connector.

40. Connect the transaxle cooler lines and connect the kickdown cable at the throttle body.

41. Remove the engine support.

42. Connect the ground wires to the transaxle and connect the manual lever position switch bracket and wiring connectors.

43. Connect the shift control cable to the cable bracket and to the selector lever. Tighten the selector lever attaching locknut to 33–47 ft. lbs. (44–64 Nm).

NOTE: Do not use any type of power wrench to tighten the locknut. Damage to the transaxle may result.

44. Install the battery tray and battery. Connect the wiring harness retaining clip to the battery tray.

45. Install the air cleaner assembly.

46. Connect the battery cables.

47. Add the proper type and quantity of transaxle fluid.

48. Check the transaxle for leaks and for proper operation.

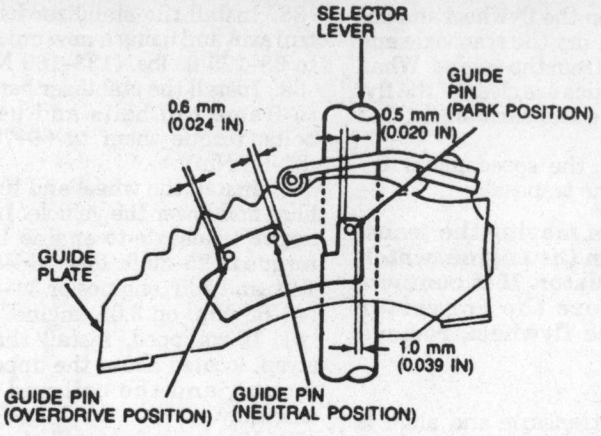

Shift control cable adjustment clearances — 1991–93 Escort

SHIFT LINKAGE ADJUSTMENT

Except 1991–93 Escort

1. Place the gear shift selector into **D**. The shift lever must be in the **D** position during linkage adjustment.

2. Working at the transaxle, loosen the transaxle manual lever-to-control cable nut.

3. Make sure the transaxle lever is in the **D** position, 2nd detent from the most rearward position.

4. Torque the retaining nut to 10–15 ft. lbs. (14–20 Nm).

5. Make sure all gears engage correctly and the vehicle will only start in **P** or **N**.

1991–93 Escort

1. Move the gear selector lever to **P**.

2. Disconnect the negative battery cable. This will deactivate the shift-lock system.

3. Remove the screw securing the gear selector knob to the gear selector lever. Remove the knob.

4. Remove the shift console as follows:

   a. Remove the rear seat ash tray and position both front seats to the rear-most position.

   b. Remove the 2 front retaining screws from the parking brake console and recline both front seats.

   c. Remove the 2 rear retaining screws from the parking brake console.

   d. With the parking brake engaged, remove the parking brake console.

   e. Remove the 2 front retaining screws from the shift console and remove the console.

5. Remove the position indicator mounting screws and disconnect the illumination bulb from the position indicator.

6. Disconnect the shift-lock servo and park range switch electrical connectors.

7. Remove the position indicator.

NOTE: Make sure the detent spring roller is in the P detent.

8. Loosen the shift control cable bracket mounting bolts.

9. Push the gear selector lever against the **P** range and hold it.

10. Tighten the shift control cable bracket mounting bolts to 69–95 inch lbs. (8–11 Nm).

11. Lightly press the gear selector pushrod and make sure the guide plate and guide pin clearances are within specifications.

12. Check that the guide plate and guide pin clearances are within the appropriate specifications when the selector lever is shifted to **N** and **OD**. If the clearances are not as specified, readjust the shift control cable.

13. Make sure the gear selector operates properly.

14. Connect the illumination bulb to the position indicator.

15. Connect the shift-lock servo and park range switch electrical connectors.

16. Install the position indicator and secure it with the mounting screws.

17. Install the shift console by reversing the removal procedure.

18. Position the gear selector knob onto the gear selector lever and secure the knob with the screw.

19. Connect the negative battery cable.

THROTTLE LINKAGE ADJUSTMENT

1989–90 1.9L Engine

1. Set the parking brake and place the transaxle shift lever into **P**.

2. Loosen the sliding trunnion block bolt, located on the throttle valve

control rod assembly, a minimum of 1 turn.

3. Make sure the trunnion block slides freely on the control rod.

4. Using a jumper wire, connect it between the STI connector and the signal return ground on the self-test connector.

5. Turn the ignition switch to the **RUN** position but do not start the engine. The Idle Speed Control (ISC) plunger should retract; wait until the plunger is fully retracted, about 10 seconds.

6. Turn the ignition switch **OFF** and remove the jumper wire.

7. Using light force, pull the throttle valve rod upward to ensure the control lever is against the internal stop.

8. Allow the trunnion to slide on the rod to it's normal position.

9. Without relaxing the pressure on the throttle valve control lever, tighten the trunnion block bolt.

2.3L Engine

1. Disconnect the negative battery cable.

2. Remove the splash shield from the cable retainer bracket.

3. Loosen the trunnion bolt on the throttle valve rod.

4. Install plastic clip using TV linkage adjustment tool T91P–7000–A or equivalent, to bottom of throttle valve rod; be sure the clip keeps the rod from telescoping.

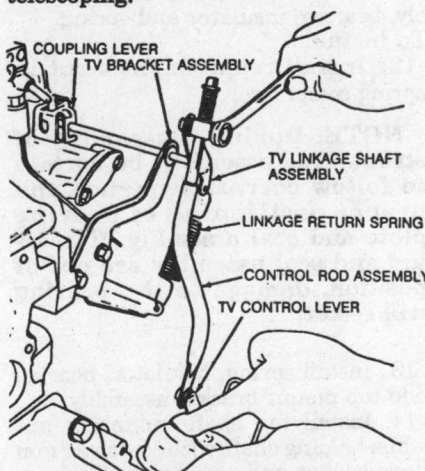

Throttle valve linkage adjustment— 1989–90 1.9L Engine

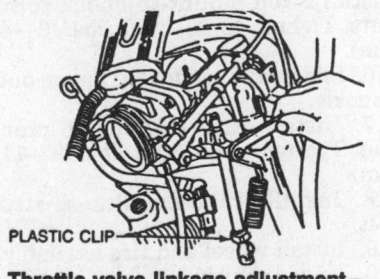

Throttle valve linkage adjustment— 2.3L Engine

5. Be sure the return spring is connected between the throttle valve rod and the retaining bracket to hold the transaxle throttle valve lever at it's idle position.

6. Make sure the throttle lever is resting on the throttle return control screw.

7. Tighten the throttle valve rod trunnion bolt and remove the plastic clip.

8. Install the splash shield. Connect the negative battery cable and check the vehicle's operation.

3.0L Engine

1. Remove the splash shield from the cable retainer bracket.

2. Unsnap the white adjuster locking clip at the cable retainer bracket.

3. Hold the transaxle lever in the idle position against the idle stop.

4. Make sure the throttle lever adjusting screw is resting against the idle stop.

5. Snap the white adjuster locking clip into the lock position.

6. Install the splash shield.

7. Check the linkage for proper operation.

TRANSFER CASE

Transfer Case Assembly

REMOVAL & INSTALLATION

1. Disconnect the negative battery cable.

2. Raise and safely support the vehicle.

3. Loosen the 2 rear engine mount bolts far enough to gain access to the transfer cup plug. Using a light hammer and a dull chisel, remove the cup plug from the transfer case and drain the oil.

4. Remove the vacuum line retaining bracket bolt.

5. Remove the driveshaft front retaining bolts and caps; disengage the front of the driveshaft from the drive yoke.

6. If the transfer case is to be disassembled, check the backlash through the cup plug opening before removal in order to reset to existing backlash at installation. The backlash should be as follows:

1989 vehicles except transaxle models PMA–BX through PMA–BX10 — 0.012–0.024 in. (0.30–0.60mm) on a 3 in. (76mm) radius.

1990–91 vehicles except transaxle

models PMA–BX through PMA–BX10 — 0.012–0.047 in. (0.30–1.20mm).

Vehicles with transaxle models PMA–BX through PMA–BX10 — 0.031–0.066 in. (0.78–1.68mm).

7. Remove the vacuum motor shield bolts and the shield.

8. Remove the vacuum lines from the vacuum servo.

9. Remove the transfer case-to-transaxle bolts; note and record the length and locations of the bolts.

10. Remove the the transfer case from the vehicle.

To install:

11. Position new maximum thickness gasket 7A191–H onto the transfer case. For transaxle models PMA–BX through PMA–BX 10, install a 7A191–J gasket.

12. Position the transfer case to the transaxle.

13. Install the transfer case bolts in the proper positions and torque the bolts, in sequence, to 15–19 ft. lbs. (21–25 Nm) for 1989 vehicles or 12–15 ft. lbs. (16–20 Nm) for 1990–91 vehicles.

14. Install backlash measuring gauge T87P–4020–B or equivalent, through the cup plug opening into the input gear. Tighten the wing nut on the end of the backlash tool.

15. Make sure the transaxle is in **P**. Remove 1 bolt from the transfer case. Install a rod on the transaxle panrail and secure a suitable dial indicator to the rod. Rotate both front wheels together until the park gear is wedged tight against the park pawl. Maintain the load on the park gear, park pawl and wheels while reading the backlash. Position the indicator foot on the end of the backlash measuring gauge. Push the backlash measuring gauge upward and zero the dial indicator.

16. Pushing down on the backlash measuring gauge, measure the back-

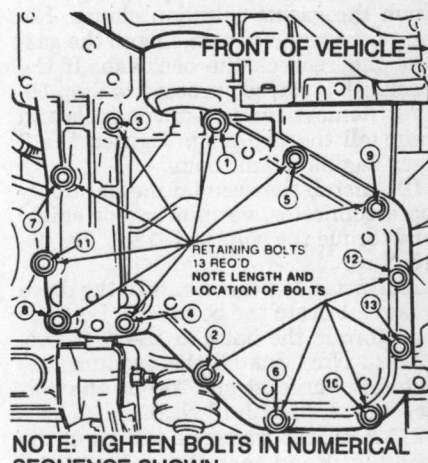

NOTE: TIGHTEN BOLTS IN NUMERICAL SEQUENCE SHOWN

Transfer case bolt torque sequence

TRANSFER CASE GASKET SELECTION CHART— 1989 VEHICLES, EXCEPT TRANSAXLE MODEL PMA– BX THROUGH PMA–BX 10

Measurement Obtained	Select Gasket Required
0.30-0.50mm (.012-.020 inch)	7A191-H
0.51-0.62mm (.021-.024 inch)	7A191-G
0.63-0.76mm (.025-.030 inch)	7A191-F
0.77-0.90mm (.031-.035 inch)	7A191-E
0.91-1.06mm (.036-.042 inch)	7A191-D
1.07-1.21mm (.043-.048 inch)	7A191-C
1.22-1.38mm (.049-.054 inch)	7A191-B
1.39-1.62mm (.055-.064 inch)	7A191-A

TRANSFER CASE GASKET SELECTION CHART— 1990–91 VEHICLES, EXCEPT TRANSAXLE MODEL PMA– BX THROUGH PMA–BX 10

Measurement Obtained	Select Gasket Required
0.30-1.20mm (.012-.047 inch)	7A191-H
1.21-1.36mm (.048-.053 inch)	7A191-G
1.37-1.52mm (.054-.060 inch)	7A191-F
1.53mm (.061 inch or greater)	7A191-E

TRANSFER CASE GASKET SELECTION CHART— TRANSAXLE MODEL PMA–BX THROUGH PMA–BX 10

Measurement Obtained	Select Gasket Required
0.78-1.68mm (.031-.066 inch)	7A191-J
1.68mm (.066 inch) or greater	7A191-I
0.78mm (.031 inch) or less	7A191-K

lash. The backlash should be within the range specified in Step 6.

17. If the backlash measurement is within specification, proceed to Step 18. If the measurment is not within specification, select the proper gasket from the gasket selection charts. Remove the transfer case, install the gasket and recheck the backlash. If the backlash is correct, proceed to Step 18.

18. Remove the measuring tools and reinstall the cup plug. Tighten the 2 rear engine mount bolts.

19. Install the vacuum motor supply hose connector, vacuum motor shield and torque the bolts to 7–12 ft. lbs. (9–16 Nm).

20. Install the driveshaft to the drive yoke, lubricate the bolts with Loctite® and torque the bolts to 15–17 ft. lbs. (21–23 Nm). Install the vacuum line retaining bracket and torque the bolt to 7–12 ft. lbs. (9–16 Nm).

21. Refill the transaxle and lower the vehicle. Road test the vehicle and check the performance of the transfer case.

FRONT SUSPENSION

MacPherson Strut

REMOVAL & INSTALLATION

Except 1991–93 Escort

NOTE: All vehicles are equipped with gas pressurized shock absorbers which will extend unassisted. Do not apply heat or flame to the shock strut tube during removal.

1. Loosen but do not remove, 2 top mount-to-shock tower nuts.
2. Raise and safely support the vehicle. Raise vehicle to a point where it is possible to reach the 2 top mount-to-shock tower nuts and the strut-to-knuckle pinch bolt.
3. Remove wheel and tire assembly.
4. Remove brake flex line-to-strut bolt.
5. Remove strut-to-knuckle pinch bolt.
6. Using a suitable tool, spread knuckle-to-strut pinch joint slightly.
7. Using a suitable bar, place top of bar under fender apron and pry down on knuckle until strut separates from knuckle. Be careful not to pinch brake hose.

NOTE: Do not pry against caliper or brake hose bracket.

8. Remove 2 top mount-to-shock tower nuts and remove strut from vehicle.
9. Install spring compressor in bench mount, install strut in compressor and compress spring.
10. Place deep 18mm socket on strut shaft nut. Insert an 8mm deep socket with ¼ in. drive wrench. Remove top shaft mounting nut from shaft while holding ¼ in. drive socket with a suitable extension.

NOTE: Do not attempt to remove shaft nut by turning shaft and holding nut. The nut must be turned and the shaft held to avoid possible damage to the shaft.

11. Loosen spring compressor tool and remove top mount bracket assembly, bearing, insulator and spring.
To install:
12. Install replacement strut in spring compressor.

NOTE: During reassembly of strut/spring assembly, be certain to follow correct sequence and proper positioning of bearing plate and seal assembly. If bearing and seal assembly are out of position, damage to the bearing will result.

13. Install spring, insulator, bearing and top mount bracket assembly.
14. Install top shaft mounting nut while holding shaft with ¼ drive 8mm deep socket and extension. Tighten nut to 35–50 ft. lbs. (48–68 Nm).
15. Install strut assembly in vehicle. Install 2 top mount-to-shock tower nuts. Tighten to 25–30 ft. lbs. (37–41 Nm).
16. Slide strut mounting flange onto knuckle.
17. Install strut-to-knuckle pinch bolt. Tighten to 68–80 ft. lbs. (92–110 Nm).
18. Install brake flex line-to-strut bolt.
19. Install wheel and tire assembly.
20. Lower vehicle.
21. Check alignment.

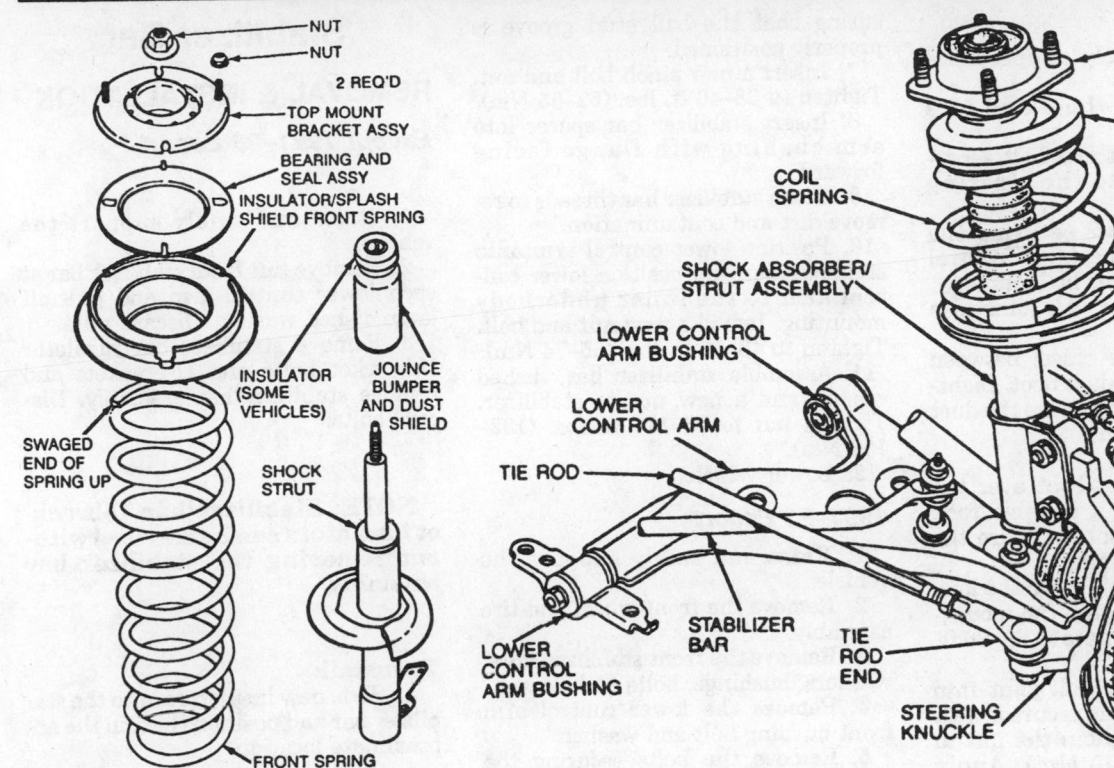

Front strut assembly—except 1991–93 Escort

Front suspension assembly—1991–93 Escort

1991–93 Escort

1. Raise and safely support the vehicle.

2. Remove the front wheel and tire assembly.

3. Remove the clip securing the flexible brake hose to the strut assembly.

4. Remove the 2 nuts and 2 bolts securing the strut assembly to the steering knuckle.

5. Remove the upper mounting block nuts and remove the strut assembly from the vehicle.

6. Remove the cap from the top of the strut assembly.

7. Secure the strut assembly mounting block in a vise. Turn the piston rod nut 1 revolution to loosen.

8. Install an appropriate spring compressor onto the strut spring and compress the spring.

9. Remove the nut, mounting block, thrust bearing, upper spring seat, rubber spring seat, coil spring and bound stopper.

To install:

10. Position the bound stopper onto the strut piston rod.

11. With the coil spring compressed, position the spring onto the strut assembly.

12. Install the rubber spring seat, upper spring seat, thrust bearing, mounting block and piston rod nut. Tighten the piston rod nut to 58–81 ft. lbs. (79–110 Nm).

13. With the nut tightened to specification, carefully remove the spring compressor from the spring while making sure the spring is properly seated in the upper and lower spring seats.

14. Install the cap.

15. Position the strut assembly into the wheel housing. Make sure the direction indicator on the mounting block faces inboard.

16. Secure the upper mounting block to the strut tower with the 4 nuts. Tighten the nuts to 22–30 ft. lbs. (29–40 Nm).

17. Attach the strut assembly to the steering knuckle and install the bolts and nuts. Tighten to 69–93 ft. lbs. (93–127 Nm).

18. Position the flexible brake hose to the strut assembly and secure it with the brake hose clip.

19. Install the front wheel and tire assembly. Tighten the lug nuts to 65–87 ft. lbs. (88–118 Nm).

20. Lower the vehicle and check the front wheel alignment.

Lower Ball Joints

INSPECTION

Except 1991–93 Escort

1. Raise and safely support the vehicle so wheels are in the full-down position.

2. Have an assistant grasp lower edge of the tire and move wheel and tire assembly in and out.

3. As wheel is being moved in and out, observe lower end of knuckle and lower control arm. Any movement indicates abnormal ball joint wear.

4. If any movement is observed, install new lower control arm assembly.

1991–93 Escort

1. Remove the lower ball joint.

2. Secure the ball joint bracket in a vise.

3. Thread the ball joint attaching nut onto the ball joint stud until the nut bottoms out on the stud.

4. Install a torque wrench onto the nut and measure the torque required to keep the stud in motion. The correct turning torque is 14–25 ft. lbs. (20–34 Nm).

5. If the turning torque is not within specification, replace the ball joint.

REMOVAL & INSTALLATION

Except 1991–93 Escort

The lower ball joint is integral to the lower control assembly and cannot be serviced individually. Any movement of the lower ball joint detected as a result of inspection requires replacement of the lower control arm assembly.

1991–93 Escort

1. Raise and safely support the vehicle.
2. Remove the wheel and tire assembly.
3. Remove the nut and bolt securing the ball joint to the steering knuckle.
4. Remove the nuts securing the lower ball joint to the lower control arm. Remove the lower ball joint.
5. Mount the lower ball joint in a vise.
6. Place a suitable chisel between the ball joint and the dust boot. Lightly tap on the chisel to separate the dust boot from the ball joint.

To install:

7. Position the dust boot over the ball joint and, using a suitable tool, press down on the tool to secure the dust boot to the ball joint.
8. Install the ball joint into the lower control arm and install the mounting nuts. Tighten the nuts to 69–86 ft. lbs. (93–117 Nm).
9. Install the lower ball joint into the steering knuckle and secure it with the nut and bolt. Tighten the nut to 32–43 ft. lbs. (43–59 Nm). Apply Loctite® to the nut and bolt threads prior to installation.
10. Install the wheel and tire assembly and lower the vehicle.

Lower Control Arms

REMOVAL & INSTALLATION

Except 1991–93 Escort

1. Raise and safely support the vehicle.
2. Remove nut from stabilizer bar end. Pull off large dished washer.
3. Remove lower control arm inner pivot nut and bolt.
4. Remove lower control arm ball joint pinch bolt. Using a suitable tool, slightly spread knuckle pinch joint and separate control arm from steering knuckle. A drift punch may be used to remove bolt.

NOTE: Do not allow the steering knuckle/halfshaft to move outward. Over extension of the tripod CV-joint could result in separation of internal parts, causing failure of the joint.

5. Remove stabilizer bar spacer from the arm bushing.

NOTE: Make sure steering column is in unlocked position. Do not use a hammer to separate ball joint from knuckle.

To install:

6. Assemble lower control arm ball joint stud to the steering knuckle, en-

suring that the ball stud groove is properly positioned.

7. Insert a new pinch bolt and nut. Tighten to 38–40 ft. lbs. (52–55 Nm).
8. Insert stabilizer bar spacer into arm bushing with flange facing forward.
9. Clean stabilizer bar threads to remove dirt and contamination.
10. Position lower control arm onto stabilizer bar and position lower control arm to the inner underbody mounting. Install a new nut and bolt. Tighten to 48–55 ft. lbs. (65–74 Nm).
11. Assemble stabilizer bar, dished washer and a new nut to stabilizer. Tighten nut to 98–115 ft. lbs. (132–156 Nm).
12. Lower vehicle.

1991–93 Escort

1. Raise and safely support the vehicle.
2. Remove the front wheel and tire assembly.
3. Remove the front stabilizer nuts, washers, bushings, bolts and sleeves.
4. Remove the lower control arm front bushing bolt and washer.
5. Remove the bolts securing the lower control arm rear bushing retaining strap.
6. Remove the nut and bolt securing the lower ball joint to the steering knuckle. Separate the steering knuckle from the lower ball joint.
7. Remove the lower control arm.
8. Remove the nut and washers from the lower control arm rear pivot bolt.
9. Remove the lower control arm rear bushing.

To install:

10. Position the lower control arm rear bushing onto the rear pivot bolt.
11. Install the washers and nut onto the lower control arm pivot bolt. Tighten the nut to 69–86 ft. lbs. (93–117 Nm).
12. Install the ball joint into the steering knuckle. Install the ball joint retaining nut and bolt and tighten the nut to 32–43 ft. lbs. (43–59 Nm). Apply Loctite® to the nut and bolt threads prior to installation.
13. Install the lower control arm rear bushing retaining strap to the lower frame. Install the bolts and tighten to 69–86 ft. lbs. (93–117 Nm).
14. Install the lower control arm front pivot bolt and washer. Tighten the nut to 69–93 ft. lbs. (93–127 Nm).
15. Install the stabilizer bolts, washers, bushings, sleeves and nuts. Tighten the stabilizer nuts so 0.67–0.75 in. (17–19mm) of thread is exposed at the end of the bolt.
16. Install the wheel and tire assembly. Tighten the lug nuts to 65–87 ft. lbs. (88–118 Nm).
17. Lower the vehicle.

Stabilizer Bar

REMOVAL & INSTALLATION

Except 1991–93 Escort

1. Raise and safely support the vehicle.
2. Remove nut from stabilizer bar at each lower control arm and pull off large dished washer. Discard nuts.
3. Remove stabilizer bar insulator U-bracket bolts and U-brackets and remove stabilizer bar assembly. Discard bolts.

NOTE: Stabilizer bar U-bracket insulators can be serviced without removing the stabilizer bar assembly.

To install:

4. Slide new insulators onto the stabilizer bar and position them in the approximate location.
5. Clean stabilizer bar threads to remove dirt and contamination.
6. Install spacers into the control arm bushings from forward side of control arm so washer end of spacer will seat against stabilizer bar machined shoulder and push mounting brackets over insulators.
7. Insert end of stabilizer bar into the lower control arms. Using new bolts, attach the stabilizer bar and the insulator U-brackets to the bracket assemblies. Hand start all 4 U-bracket bolts. Tighten all bolts halfway, then tighten bolts to 59–68 ft. lbs. (80–92 Nm) on 1989–91 Tempo/Topaz, 82–88 ft. lbs. (110–120 Nm) on 1992–93 Tempo/Topaz or 85–100 ft. lbs. (115–135 Nm) on Escort.
8. Using new nuts and the original dished washers (dished side away from bushing), attach the stabilizer bar to the lower control arm. Tighten nuts to 99–112 ft. lbs. (133–153 Nm).
9. Lower vehicle.

1991–93 Escort

1. Support the engine with engine support D88L–6000–A or equivalent.
2. Raise and safely support the vehicle.
3. Remove the front wheel and tire assemblies.
4. Remove the nuts securing the steering gear mounting brackets and position the steering gear slightly forward.
5. Remove the stabilizer bar nuts, washers, bushings, sleeves and bolts from the lower control arm.

TIGHTENING TORQUE:
A: 27–38 FT. LBS. (37–52 NM)
B: 47–66 FT. LBS. (64–89 NM)

Torque sequence and specifications for crossmember-to-frame and crossmember-to-transaxle mount bolts— 1991–93 Escort

6. Remove the rear crossmember nuts from the rear transaxle mount and the vehicle frame.
7. Loosen the front crossmember bolts and nuts from the front transaxle mount and the vehicle frame. Lower the rear end of the crossmember.
8. Remove the nuts and bolts securing the chassis frame to the vehicle frame. Lower the chassis frame.

NOTE: The engine and transaxle mounts will support the chassis frame when unbolting the chassis frame from the vehicle frame.

9. Unbolt the stabilizer bar from the chassis frame and remove the stabilizer bar from the vehicle.
To install:
10. Position the stabilizer bar into the vehicle.
11. Secure the stabilizer bar to the chassis frame with the bolts. Tighten the bolts to 32–43 ft. lbs. (43–59 Nm).
12. Install the chassis frame to the vehicle frame with the bolts and nuts. Tighten the bolts and nuts to 69–93 ft. lbs. (93–127 Nm).
13. Position the crossmember to the vehicle frame and the transaxle mounts. Tighten the bolts and nuts to the specified torque.
14. Install the stabilizer bar bolts, sleeves, bushings, washers and nuts. Tighten the stabilizer bolts so 0.67–0.75 in. (17–19mm) of thread is exposed at the end of the bolt.
15. Position the steering gear and secure it with the brackets and nuts. Tighten the nuts to 28–38 ft. lbs. (37–52 Nm).
16. Install the wheel and tire assemblies. Tighten the lug nuts to 65–87 ft. lbs. (88–118 Nm).
17. Lower the vehicle and remove the engine support.

REAR SUSPENSION

MacPherson Strut

REMOVAL & INSTALLATION

Escort

1989–90

1. Remove rear compartment access panels. On 4-door models, remove quarter trim panel.

NOTE: Do not attempt to remove shaft nut by turning shaft and holding nut. Nut must be turned and shaft held to avoid possible damage to shaft.

2. Loosen, but do not remove, top strut attaching nut using an 18mm deep socket while holding the strut rod with a ¼ drive, 8mm deep socket and suitable extension.

NOTE: If the strut is to be reused, do not grip the shaft with pliers or vise grips, as this will damage the shaft surface finish and result in severe oil leakage.

3. Raise and safely support the vehicle.
4. Remove tire and wheel assembly.

NOTE: If a frame contact lift is used, support the lower control arm with a floor jack. If a twin-post lift is used, support the body with floor jacks on lifting pads forward of the tie rod body bracket.

5. Remove stabilizer bar link from shock bracket, if equipped.
6. Remove clip retaining the brake line flexible hose to the rear shock strut and move aside.
7. Loosen and discard 2 nuts and bolts retaining strut to the spindle. Do not remove bolts at this time.
8. Remove and discard top mounting nut, washer and rubber insulator.
9. Remove and discard 2 bottom mounting bolts and remove strut from the vehicle.
To install:
10. Extend shock absorber strut to its maximum length.
11. Install a new lower washer and insulator assembly, using tire lubricant to ease insertion into the quarter panel shock tower.
12. Position upper part of shock absorber strut shaft into shock tower opening in the body and push slowly on lower part of the shock until

mounting holes are lined up with mounting holes in the spindle.
13. Install new lower mounting bolts and nuts. Do not tighten at this time.

NOTE: The heads of both bolts must be to the rear of the vehicle.

14. Place a new upper insulator and washer assembly and nut on the upper shock absorber strut shaft. Tighten nut to 35–55 ft. lbs. (48–75 Nm), using the 18mm deep socket and ¼ drive, 8mm deep socket with extension. Do not grip the shaft with pliers or vise grips.
15. Tighten 2 lower mounting bolts to 70–96 ft. lbs. (95–130 Nm).
16. Install stabilizer bar link to bracket on strut, if equipped. Tighten bolts to 40–55 ft. lbs. (55–75 Nm).
17. Install brake line flex hose and retaining clip.
18. Install wheel and tire assembly.
19. Install quarter trim and access panels, as required.

1991–93

1. Raise and safely support the vehicle.
2. Remove the wheel and tire assembly.
3. Remove the clip securing the flexible brake hose to the rear strut assembly.
4. Remove the nuts and bolts securing the rear strut assembly to the rear wheel spindle assembly.
5. On hatchback and wagon, remove the quarter lower trim panel.
6. Remove the mounting block nuts and remove the rear strut assembly from the vehicle.
7. Position the strut assembly into a vise and secure the assembly at the mounting block.
8. Remove the cap and loosen the piston rod nut 1 turn. Do not remove the piston rod nut at this time.
9. Install an appropriate coil spring compressor onto the coil spring and compress the coil spring.
10. Remove the piston rod nut, washer, retainer and mounting block.
11. Remove the coil spring.
12. Remove the bound stopper seat and stopper from the strut piston.
To install:
13. Position the strut assembly into a vise and secure.
14. Install the bound stopper seat and stopper onto the strut piston rod.
15. Install the coil spring onto the strut assembly.
16. Install the mounting block, then align the mounting block studs and the lower bracket of the strut assembly.
17. Install the retainer, washer and piston rod nut. Tighten the nut to 41–50 ft. lbs. (55–68 Nm).

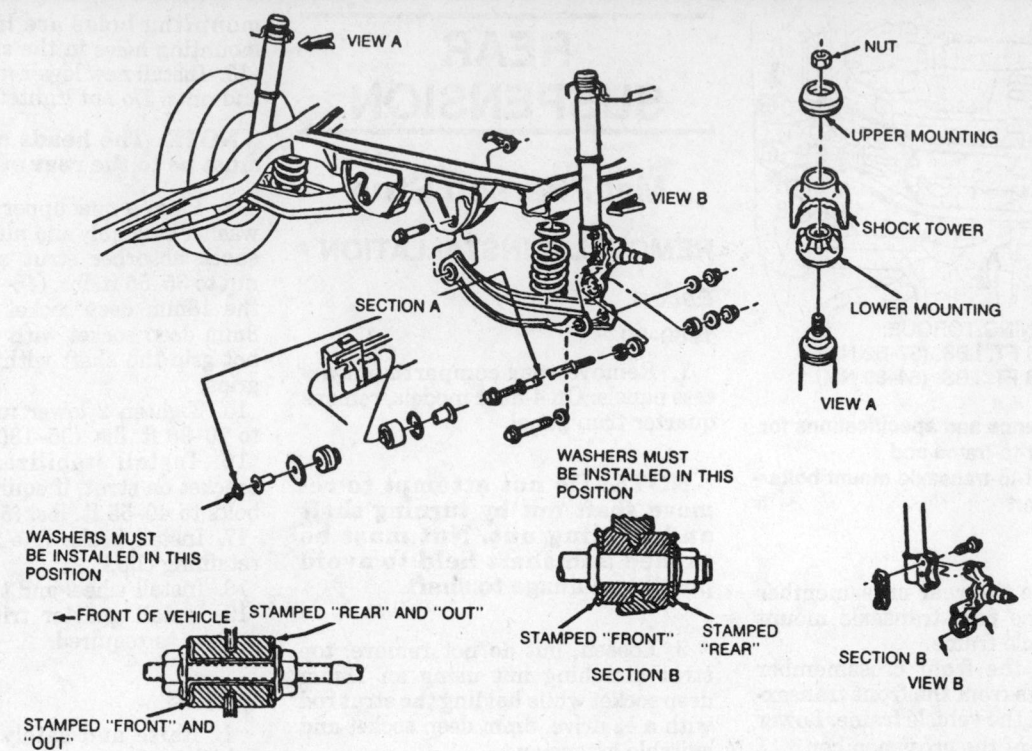

WASHERS MUST BE INSTALLED IN THIS POSITION

WASHERS MUST BE INSTALLED IN THIS POSITION

FRONT OF VEHICLE — STAMPED "REAR" AND "OUT"

STAMPED "FRONT" AND "OUT"

SECTION A

STAMPED "FRONT" STAMPED "REAR"

SECTION B

SECTION A VIEW A

VIEW B

NUT

UPPER MOUNTING

SHOCK TOWER

LOWER MOUNTING

VIEW A

SECTION B VIEW B

Rear suspension—1989–90 Escort

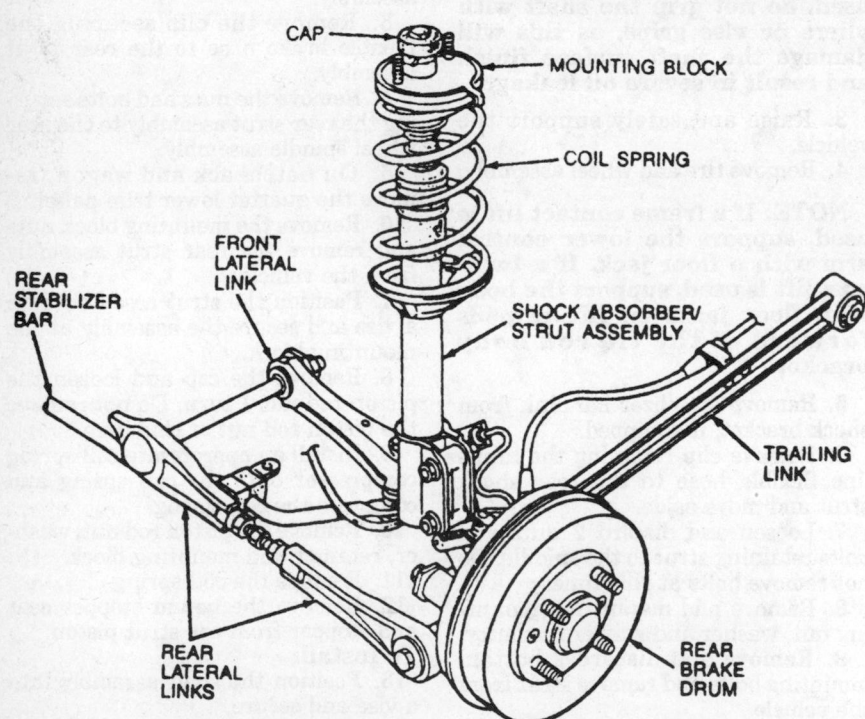

CAP

MOUNTING BLOCK

COIL SPRING

FRONT LATERAL LINK

SHOCK ABSORBER/STRUT ASSEMBLY

REAR STABILIZER BAR

TRAILING LINK

REAR LATERAL LINKS

REAR BRAKE DRUM

Rear suspension assembly—1991–93 Escort

18. Make sure the spring is properly aligned and carefully release the spring into the seats of the strut.
19. Remove the spring compressor from the coil spring and install the cap.
20. Position the strut assembly into the vehicle wheel housing.

21. Install the mounting block nuts and tighten to 22–27 ft. lbs. (29–40 Nm).
22. On hatchback and wagon, install the quarter lower trim panel.
23. Install the nuts and bolts securing the strut assembly to the rear spindle assembly. Tighten the lower strut

bolts to 69–93 ft. lbs. (93–127 Nm).
24. Install the wheel and tire assembly. Tighten the lug nuts to 65–87 ft. lbs. (88–118 Nm).
25. Check the rear alignment and lower the vehicle.

Tempo and Topaz

NOTE: All Tempo and Topaz vehicles are equipped with gas-pressurized shock absorbers which will extend unassisted. Do not apply heat or flame to the shock strut during removal.

1. Open luggage compartment and loosen but do not remove, 2 nuts retaining the upper strut mount to body.
2. Raise and safely support the vehicle. Remove the wheel and tire assembly.
3. Place a jack stand under the control arms to support the suspension.

NOTE: Care should be taken when removing the strut that the rear brake flex hose is not stretched or the steel brake tube is not bent.

4. Remove bolt attaching brake hose bracket to strut and move it aside.
5. Remove 2 bolts attaching shock strut to spindle.
6. Remove 2 upper mount-to-body nuts.
7. Remove strut from vehicle.
8. Place strut, spring and upper mount assembly in spring compressor.

CAUTION

Attempting to remove the spring from the strut without first compressing the spring with a tool designed for that purpose could cause bodily injury.

NOTE: Do not attempt to remove shaft nut by turning shaft and holding nut. Nut must be turned and shaft held to avoid possible fracture of shaft at base of hex.

9. With the spring compressed, remove strut shaft-to-mount nut and then remove spring, strut and mount from compressor tool.

To install:

10. With spring compressed, install spring, spring insulator, top mount and upper washer on strut shaft.

11. Ensure spring is properly located in upper and lower spring seats. The spring end must be within 0.39 in. (10mm) of the step in the spring seat.

12. Tighten shaft nut to 35–46 ft. lbs. (47–63 Nm). Use 18mm deep socket to turn the nut and ¼ drive 8mm deep socket to hold shaft so it will not turn while tightening nut.

13. Insert 2 upper mount studs into strut tower and hand start 2 new nuts. Do not tighten at this time.

14. Position spindle into lower strut mount and install 2 new bolts. Tighten to 85–96 ft. lbs. (115–130 Nm).

15. Install brake flex-hose bracket on the strut.

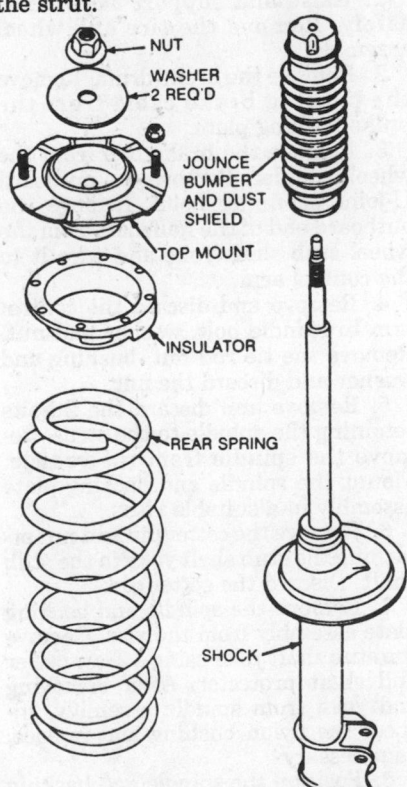

- NUT
- WASHER 2 REQ'D
- JOUNCE BUMPER AND DUST SHIELD
- TOP MOUNT
- INSULATOR
- REAR SPRING
- SHOCK

Rear strut assembly–Tempo and Topaz

16. Install wheel and tire assembly.

17. Remove jack stand and lower vehicle to the ground.

18. Tighten 2 top mount-to-body nuts to 23–29 ft. lbs. (30–40 Nm).

Coil Springs

REMOVAL & INSTALLATION

1989–90 Escort

1. Raise and safely support the vehicle.

2. Place floor jack under lower control arm. Raise lower control arm to curb position.

NOTE: If a twin-post lift is used, vehicle must be supported on jackstands place under jack pads of the underbody, forward of the tie rod bracket.

3. Remove tire and wheel assembly.

4. Remove and discard nut, bolt and washers retaining lower control arm to spindle.

5. Slowly lower control arm with floor jack until spring can be removed.

To install:

6. The spring insulator must be replaced when servicing spring.

7. Index the insulator on the spring and press insulator downward until it snaps into place. Check again to ensure insulator is properly indexed against tip of the spring.

8. Install spring in control arm. Ensure spring is properly seated in control arm spring pocket.

9. Raise control arm and spring with floor jack. position spring in pocket on underbody.

10. Using a new bolt, nut and washers, attach control arm to spindle. Install bolt with the head toward front of the vehicle. Tighten to 60–80 ft. lbs. (81–109 Nm).

11. Install tire and wheel assembly.

12. Remove floor jack and lower vehicle.

Rear Control Arms

REMOVAL & INSTALLATION

Escort

1989–90

1. Raise and safely support the vehicle.

2. Place floor jack under lower control arm. Raise lower control arm to curb position.

NOTE: If a twin-post lift is used, vehicle must be supported on jackstands placed under jack pads of the underbody forward of the tie rod bracket.

3. Remove tire and wheel assembly.

4. Remove nuts from control arm-to-body mounting and control arm-to-spindle mounting. Do not remove bolts at this time.

5. Remove and discard spindle end mounting bolt. Slowly lower control arm with floor jack until spring can be removed.

6. Remove and discard bolt from the body end and remove control arm from vehicle.

To install:

7. Attach lower control arm-to-body bracket using a new bolt and nut. Head of the bolt should face the front of the vehicle. Do not tighten at this time.

8. The spring insulator must be replaced when servicing spring.

9. Index the insulator on the spring and press insulator downward until it snaps into place. Place spring in spring pocket in lower control arm. Make sure spring is properly indexed.

10. Using a floor jack, raise lower control arm until it is in line with mounting hole in the spindle.

11. Install lower control arm to spindle using a new bolt, nut and washers. Do not tighten at this time. Bolt head should face the front of the vehicle.

12. Using the floor jack, raise lower control arm to curb height.

13. Tighten control arm-to-spindle bolt to 60–80 ft. lbs. (81–109 Nm).

14. Tighten control arm-to-body bolt to 52–74 ft. lbs. (70–100 Nm).

15. Install tire and wheel.

16. Remove floor jack and lower vehicle.

1991–93

1. Raise and safely support the vehicle.

2. Remove the wheel and tire assembly.

3. Remove the stabilizer nuts, washers, bushings, sleeves and bolts.

4. Remove the bolts securing the stabilizer bar brackets and grommets to the rear suspension crossmember.

5. Remove the stabilizer bar.

6. Remove the cap covering the front and rear lateral link pivot bolts.

7. Position a floor jack stand under the rear suspension crossmember.

8. Remove the bolts securing the rear suspension crossmember to the vehicle frame.

9. Lower the floor jack stand to allow the rear suspension crossmember to be lowered from the vehicle frame.

10. Remove the front and rear lateral link pivot nut, washer and bolt from the rear suspension crossmember.

11. Remove the front and rear lateral links from the rear suspension crossmember.

12. Remove the bolt, washers and nut securing the front and rear lateral

links to the rear wheel spindle and remove the lateral links.

13. Remove the nuts securing the parking brake cable and cable bracket to the trailing link.

14. Remove the rear trailing link bolts and washers from the vehicle frame and rear wheel spindle. Remove the rear trailing link.

To install:

15. Position the rear trailing link and install the bolts and washers. Tighten the trailing link front bolt to 46–69 ft. lbs. (63–93 Nm) and the rear bolt to 69–93 ft. lbs. (93–127 Nm).

16. Position the parking brake cable and bracket to the trailing link and secure it with the nuts.

17. Position the front and rear lateral links to the rear wheel spindle and install the washers, bolt and nut. Tighten the front and rear lateral link nut at the rear wheel spindle to 63–86 ft. lbs. (85–117 Nm).

18. Position the front and rear lateral links to the rear suspension crossmember. Tighten the front and rear lateral link nut at the rear suspension crossmember to 50–70 ft. lbs. (68–95 Nm).

19. Install the cap.

20. Raise the floor jackstand to position the rear suspension crossmember to the vehicle frame. Install and tighten the bolts. Remove the floor jackstand from under the vehicle.

21. Position the grommets onto the stabilizer bar and align the grommets to the positions painted on the bar.

22. Position the stabilizer bar to the rear suspension crossmember and secure it in place with the straps and bolts. Tighten the bolts to 32–43 ft. lbs. (43–59 Nm).

23. Install the stabilizer bolts, washers, grommets, sleeves and nuts. Tighten the stabilizer nuts so 0.64–0.72 in. (16.2–17.0mm) of thread is exposed at the end of the bolt.

24. Install the wheel and tire assembly. Tighten the lug nuts to 65–87 ft. lbs. (88–118 Nm).

25. Check the wheel alignment and lower the vehicle.

Tempo and Topaz

1. Raise and safely support the vehicle.

2. Remove and discard arm-to-spindle bolt and nut.

3. Remove and discard center retaining bolt and nut.

4. Remove arm from vehicle.

To install:

NOTE: When installing new control arms, the bushing with the 0.39 in. (10mm) hole is installed to the center of the vehicle and the bushing with the 0.48 in. (12mm) hole is installed to the

spindle. The offset on the arm must face up on the right side of the vehicle and down on the left side of the vehicle. The flange edge of the arm stamping must also face the rear of the vehicle.

5. Position arm at center of vehicle and insert new bolt and nut. Do not tighten at this time.

6. Move arm end up to spindle and insert new bolt, washer and nut. Ensure bolt engages both arms and spindle.

7. Tighten arm-to-body bolt to 30–40 ft. lbs. (40–54 Nm) on 1989–91 vehicles or 41–46 ft. lbs. (55–63 Nm) on 1992–93 vehicles.

8. Tighten arm-to-spindle nut to 60–80 ft. lbs. (81–109 Nm).

9. Lower vehicle.

Rear Wheel Bearings

REMOVAL & INSTALLATION

Except Tempo and Topaz With AWD and 1991–93 Escort

1. Raise and safely support the vehicle.

2. Remove wheel and tire assembly. Remove grease cap from hub.

3. Remove cotter pin, nut retainer, adjusting nut and flatwasher from spindle. Discard cotter pin.

4. Pull hub and drum assembly off spindle being careful not to drop outer bearing assembly.

5. Remove outer bearing assembly.

6. Using seal remover, remove and discard grease seal. Remove inner bearing assembly from hub.

7. Wipe all lubricant from spindle and inside of hub. Cover spindle with a clean cloth and vacuum all loose dust and dirt from brake assembly. Carefully remove cloth to prevent dirt from falling on spindle.

8. Clean both bearing assemblies and cups using solvent. inspect bearing assemblies and cups for excessive wear, scratches, pits or other damage. Replace all worn or damaged parts as required.

NOTE: Allow solvent to dry before repacking bearings. Do not spin-dry bearings with air pressure.

9. If cups are replaced, remove them with wheel hub cup remover D80L-927-A and bearing cup puller T77F-1102-A or equivalent.

To install:

10. If inner or outer bearing cups were removed, install replacement cups using driver handle T80T-4000-W and bearing cup replacers T77F-1202-A and T73T-1217-A or equivalent. Support drum hub on wood block

to prevent damage. Insure cups are properly seated in hub.

NOTE: Do not use cone and roller assembly to install cup as this will cause damage to bearing cup and cone and roller assembly.

11. Ensure all spindle and bearing surfaces are clean.

12. Using a bearing packer, pack bearing assemblies with a suitable wheel bearing grease. If a packer is not available, work in as much grease as possible between the rollers and the cages. Grease the cup surfaces.

13. Place inner bearing cone and roller assembly in inner cup. Apply light film of grease to lips of a new grease seal and install seal with rear hub seal replacer T81P-1249-A or equivalent. Ensure retainer flange is seated all around.

14. Apply light film of grease on spindle shaft bearing surfaces.

15. Install hub and drum assembly on spindle. Keep hub centered on spindle to prevent damage to grease seal and spindle threads.

16. Install outer bearing assembly and keyed flat washer on spindle. Install adjusting nut finger-tight. Adjust wheel bearings. Install a new cotter pin.

17. Install wheel and tire on drum.

18. Lower vehicle.

Tempo and Topaz With AWD

1. Raise and support the vehicle safely. Remove the tire and wheel assembly.

2. Remove the brake drum. Remove the parking brake cable from the brake backing plate.

3. Remove the brake line from the wheel cylinder. Remove the outboard U-joint retaining bolts. Remove the outboard end of the halfshaft from the wheel stub shaft yoke and wire it to the control arm.

4. Remove and discard the control arm to spindle bolt, washer and nut. Remove the tie rod nut, bushing and washer and discard the nut.

5. Remove and discard the 2 bolts retaining the spindle to the strut. Remove the spindle from the vehicle. Mount the spindle and backing plate assembly in a suitable vise.

6. Remove the cotter pin and nut attaching the stub shaft yoke to the stub shaft. Discard the cotter pin.

7. Remove the spindle and backing plate assembly from the vise. Remove the stub shaft yoke using a 2 jaw puller and shaft protector. After removing end yoke from spindle assembly, inspect the nylon bushing and replace, as necessary.

8. Position the spindle and backing plate assembly into a vise and remove the wheel stub shaft.

9. Remove the snapring retaining the bearing. Remove the bolts retaining the spindle to the backing plate and remove the backing plate.

10. Remove the spindle from the vise and mount it into a suitable press. With the spindle side facing upward, carefully press out the bearing from the spindle, using a driver handle and bearing cup driver. Discard the bearing after removal.

To install:

11. Mount the spindle in a press, spindle side facing down. Position a new bearing in the outboard side of the spindle and carefully press in the new bearing using a driver handle and bearing installer.

12. Remove the spindle from the press and mount it in a vise. Install the snapring retaining the bearing. Position the backing plate to the spindle and install the retaining bolts.

13. Install the wheel stub shaft. Install the stub shaft yoke and attaching nut. Torque the nut to 120–150 ft. lbs. install a new cotter pin.

14. Remove the spindle and backing plate assembly from the vise. Position the spindle onto the tie rod and then into the strut lower bracket. Insert 2 new strut-to-spindle bolts. Do not tighten at this time.

15. Install the tie rod bushing washer and new nut. Install the new control arm to spindle bolt, washers and nut. Do not tighten them at this time.

16. Install a jack stand to support the suspension at the normal curb height before tightening the fasteners.

17. Torque the spindle to strut bolts to 70–96 ft. lbs. Torque the tie rod nut to 52–74 ft. lbs. Torque the control arm to spindle nut to 60–86 ft. lbs.

18. Position the outboard end of the halfshaft to the wheel stub shaft yoke. Install the retaining caps and bolts and torque them to 15–17 ft. lbs.

19. Install the brake line to wheel cylinder. Install the parking brake cable and brake drum. Install the wheel assembly, torque the lugs nuts to 80–105 ft. lbs.

20. Lower the vehicle and bleed the brake system. Check and adjust the toe, if necessary.

1991–93 Escort

1. Raise and safely support the vehicle.

2. Remove the wheel and tire assembly.

3. Remove the brake drum or brake caliper and rotor, as necessary.

4. Remove the nut securing the rear wheel hub to the spindle and remove the hub and bearing assembly.

To install:

5. Install the rear wheel hub and bearing assembly onto the spindle.

6. Install the hub nut onto the spindle and tighten to 130–174 ft. lbs. (177–235 Nm).

7. Stake the hub nut and install the cap.

8. Install the brake drum or the brake caliper and rotor, as necessary.

9. Install the wheel and tire assembly. Tighten the lugnuts to 65–87 ft. lbs. (88–118 Nm).

10. Lower the vehicle.

ADJUSTMENT

Except Tempo and Topaz With AWD and 1991–93 Escort

1. Raise and safely support the vehicle.

2. Remove wheel cover or ornament and nut covers. Remove grease cap from hub.

3. Remove cotter pin and nut retainer. Discard cotter pin.

4. Back-off adjusting nut 1 full turn. Ensure nut turns freely on spindle threads. Correct any binding condition.

5. Tighten adjusting nut to 17–25 ft. lbs. (23–34 Nm) while rotating hub and drum assembly to seat bearings. Loosen adjusting nut ½ turn and tighten adjusting nut to 24–28 inch lbs. (2.7–3.2 Nm) using inch lb. torque wrench.

6. Position adjusting nut retainer over adjusting nut so slots in nut retainer flange are in line with cotter pin hole in spline.

7. Install a new cotter pin and bend ends around retainer flange.

8. Check hub rotation. If hub rotates freely, install grease cap. If not, check bearings for damage and replace as necessary.

9. Install wheel and tire assembly, wheel cover or ornaments, and nut covers as required.

10. Lower vehicle.

Tempo and Topaz With AWD

Bearings on 4WD vehicles are not adjustable.

1991–93 Escort

1. Raise and safely support the vehicle.

2. Remove the wheel and tire assembly.

3. Remove the brake drum or the brake caliper and rotor, as necessary.

4. Position a dial indicator to the wheel hub.

5. By hand, push and pull the wheel hub in the axial direction and measure the wheel bearing play.

6. If the wheel bearing play exceeds 0.002 in. (0.05mm), check and adjust the locknut torque or replace the wheel bearing, if necessary.

7. Install the brake drum or brake caliper and rotor, as necessary.

8. Install the wheel and tire assembly and lower the vehicle.

STEERING

Steering Wheel

——— **CAUTION** ———
On vehicles equipped with an air bag, the negative battery cable and backup power supply must be disconnected, before working on the system. Failure to do so may result in deployment of the air bag and possible personal injury.

REMOVAL & INSTALLATION

Except 1991–93 Escort

1. Make sure the wheels are in the straight-ahead position and the column is locked. Disconnect the negative battery cable.

NOTE: On most vehicles equipped with an air bag, a backup power supply is included in the system to provide air bag deployment in the event the battery or cables are damaged in an accident before the sensors can close. The power supply is a capacitor that will leak down in approximately 15 minutes after the battery is disconnected or 1 minute if the battery positive cable is grounded. If the system is equipped with a backup power supply, it must be disconnected to disarm the system.

2. On 1989–91 vehicles equipped with an air bag, perform the following procedure:

   a. Remove the 2 screws retaining the steering column opening cover to the instrument panel and remove the cover.

   b. Remove the 4 bolts retaining the bolster and remove the bolster.

   c. Disconnect the backup power supply connector.

   d. Remove the 4 nut and washer assemblies retaining the air bag assembly to the steering wheel.

   e. Disconnect the air bag electrical connector from the contact assembly connectors and remove the air bag assembly.

—————— CAUTION ——————

When carrying a live air bag, make sure the bag and trim cover are pointed away from the body. In the unlikely event of an accidental deployment, the bag will then deploy with minimal chance of injury. In addition, when placing a live air bag on a bench or other surface, always face the bag and trim cover up, away from the surface. This will reduce the motion of the module if it is accidentally deployed.

3. On 1992–93 vehicles equipped with an air bag, perform the following procedure:

a. Disconnect the positive battery cable and wait 1 minute for the backup power supply to be depleted.

b. Remove the 4 nut and washer assemblies retaining the air bag assembly to the steering wheel.

c. Disconnect the air bag electrical connector from the contact assembly connectors and remove the air bag assembly.

—————— CAUTION ——————

When carrying a live air bag, make sure the bag and trim cover are pointed away from the body. In the unlikely event of an accidental deployment, the bag will then deploy with minimal chance of injury. In addition, when placing a live air bag on a bench or other surface, always face the bag and trim cover up, away from the surface. This will reduce the motion of the module if it is accidentally deployed.

4. If not equipped with an air bag, remove the horn pad cover by removing the retaining screws from the steering wheel assembly.

NOTE: The emblem assembly is removed after the horn pad cover is removed, by pushing it out from the backside of the emblem.

5. Remove the energy absorbing foam from the wheel assembly, if equipped. Remember the energy absorbing foam must be installed when the steering wheel is assembled. Disconnect the horn pad wiring connector, if not equipped with an air bag.

6. Loosen the steering wheel retaining bolt 4–6 turns but do not remove. On air bag equipped vehicles, remove the bolt completely to remove the vibration damper, then reinstall the bolt loosely on the shaft.

7. Remove the steering wheel with a suitable puller. Do not use a knock-off type puller, because it will cause damage to the collapsible steering column. Remove the retaining bolt, grasp the rim of the steering wheel and pull the steering wheel from the upper shaft.

To install:

8. Install the steering wheel assembly on the steering column, making sure the alignment marks are correct.

9. Install a new retaining bolt. Torque the bolt to 23–33 ft. lbs. (31–45 Nm). On air bag equipped vehicles, install the vibration damper before installing the bolt.

10. If equipped with air bag, connect the air bag module wire to clockspring connector and place the module on the steering wheel with the 4 attaching nuts, torque the nuts to 35–53 inch lbs. (4–6 Nm).

11. On vehicles without air bag, connect the horn pad wiring connector and, if equipped, install the energy absorbing foam. Install the horn pad cover and torque the retaining screws to 8–10 inch lbs. (0.9–1.1 Nm).

12. On 1989–91 air bag equipped vehicles, connect the backup power supply connector and reinstall the bolster and steering column opening cover.

13. Reconnect the negative battery cable and check the steering wheel for proper operation.

1991–93 Escort

1. Disconnect the negative battery cable.

2. Remove the steering wheel cover retaining screws from the back side of the steering wheel and remove the cover.

NOTE: On 2-spoke steering wheels there are 2 retaining screws, and on 4-spoke steering wheels there are 4 retaining screws.

3. Disconnect the horn electrical connector and the cruise control electrical connector, if equipped.

4. Remove the steering wheel mounting nut or bolt and remove the steering wheel with a suitable puller. Do not attempt to remove the steering wheel by hitting the column shaft with a hammer; the column may collapse.

To install:

5. Position the steering wheel and install the mounting nut or bolt. Tighten the nut to 29–36 ft. lbs. (39–49 Nm) or the bolt to 34–46 ft. lbs. (46–63 Nm).

6. Connect the horn electrical connector and the cruise control electrical connector, if equipped.

7. Position the steering wheel cover and install the retaining screws.

8. Connect the negative battery cable.

Steering Column

REMOVAL & INSTALLATION

Except 1991–93 Escort

NOTE: On air bag equipped vehicles, whenever the steering column is separated from the steer-

ing gear for any reason, the steering column must be locked to prevent the steering wheel from being rotated, which in turn will prevent damage to the air bag clockspring.

1. Disconnect the negative battery cable.

NOTE: Before disconnecting cable on air bag equipped vehicles, ensure wheels are in straight ahead-position. Turn ignition switch to LOCK position and rotate steering wheel about 16 degrees counterclockwise until locked into position.

2. Remove steering column cover on lower portion of instrument panel (2 screws). On 1989–91 air bag equipped vehicles, remove the bolster and disconnect the backup power supply for the air bag module.

3. Remove cruise control module, if equipped (2 screws).

4. Remove lower steering column shroud (5 screws).

5. Loosen, but do not remove, 2 nuts and 2 bolts retaining steering column to support bracket and remove upper shroud.

6. Disconnect all steering column electrical connections: ignition, wash/wipe, turn signal, key warning buzzer, cruise control. On console shift automatic transaxle, remove interlock cable retaining screw and disconnect cable from steering column.

7. Loosen steering column to intermediate shaft clamp connection and remove bolt or nut.

8. Remove 2 nuts and 2 bolts retaining steering column to support bracket.

9. Pry open steering column shaft in area of clamp on each side of bolt groove with steering column locked. Open enough to disengage shafts with minimal effort. Do not use excessive force.

10. Inspect 2 steering column bracket clips for damage. If clips have been bent or excessively distorted, they must be replaced.

To install:

11. Engage lower steering shaft to intermediate shaft and hand start clamp bolt and nut.

12. Align 2 bolts on steering column support bracket assembly with outer tube mounting holes and hand start 2 nuts. Check for presence of 2 clips on outer bracket. The clips must be present to ensure adequate performance of vital parts and systems. Hand start 2 bolts through outer tube upper bracket and clip and into support bracket nuts. On console shift automatic transaxles, install interlock

cable and retaining screw. Tighten to 30–38 inch lbs. (3.3–4.3 Nm).

13. Connect all quick-connect electrical connections: turn signal, wash/wipe, key warning buzzer, ignition, cruise control and air bag clockspring connector, if equipped.

14. Install upper shroud.

15. Tighten steering column mounting nuts and bolts to 15–25 ft. lbs. (20–34 Nm).

16. On air bag equipped vehicles, unlock steering column and cycle steering wheel 1 turn left and 1 turn right to align intermediate shaft into column shaft. Power steering vehicles must have engine running.

17. Tighten steering shaft clamp nut to 20–30 ft. lbs. (27–40 Nm).

18. Install lower trim shroud with 5 screws.

19. Install cruise control module, if equipped, with 2 screws.

20. On 1989–91 air bag equipped vehicles, connect the backup power supply and install the bolster.

21. Install steering column cover on instrument panel with 2 screws.

22. Connect battery ground cable.

23. Check steering column for proper operation.

1991–93 Escort

1. Disconnect the negative battery cable.

2. Remove the steering wheel.

3. Remove the combination switch and disconnect the ignition switch electrical connector.

4. Remove the shift-lock cable mounting bracket bolt and place the bracket and cable aside.

5. Remove the 4 steering column upper mounting bracket bolts and lower the column.

6. Remove the 5 set plate mounting nuts and remove the set plate.

7. Remove the intermediate shaft-to-pinion shaft bolt.

8. Remove the 2 steering column lower mounting bracket nuts and remove the column.

To install:

9. Position the steering column and install the 2 lower mounting bracket nuts.

10. Install the intermediate shaft-to-pinion shaft bolt and tighten to 30–36 ft. lbs. (40–50 Nm).

11. Position the set plate and install the 5 mounting nuts.

12. Install the 4 steering column upper mounting bracket bolts and tighten to 80–123 inch lbs. (9–14 Nm).

13. Position the shift-lock cable mounting bracket and install the bolt. Tighten the bolt to 37–55 inch lbs. (4–6 Nm).

14. Connect the ignition switch electrical connector and install the combination switch.

15. Install the steering wheel.

16. Connect the negative battery cable and inspect the shift-lock system.

Manual Rack and Pinion

REMOVAL & INSTALLATION

Escort

1989–90

1. Disconnect the negative battery cable.

2. Turn the ignition key to the **RUN** position.

3. Remove the access trim panel from below the steering column.

4. Remove the intermediate shaft bolts at the rack and pinion input shaft and the steering column shaft.

5. Spread the slots enough to loosen the intermediate shaft at both ends. They cannot be separated at this time.

6. Raise the vehicle and support it safely.

7. Separate the tie rod ends from the steering knuckles, using a suitable tool. Turn the right wheel to the full left turn position.

8. Disconnect the speedometer cable at the transaxle on automatic transaxles only.

9. Disconnect the secondary air tube at the check valve. Disconnect the exhaust system at the manifold and remove the system.

10. Remove the gear mounting brackets and insulators. Keep separated as they are not interchangeable.

11. Turn the steering wheel full left so the tie rod will clear the shift linkage during removal.

12. Separate the gear intermediate shaft, with an assistant pulling upward on the shaft from the inside of the vehicle.

NOTE: Care should be taken during steering gear removal and installation to prevent tearing or damaging the steering gear bellows.

13. Rotate the gear forward and down to clear the input shaft through the dash panel opening.

14. With the gear in the full left turn position, move the gear through the right (passenger side) apron opening until the left tie rod clears the shift linkage and other parts so it may be lowered.

15. Lower the left side of the gear assembly and remove from the vehicle.

To install:

16. Rotate the input shaft to a full left turn stop. Position the right wheel to a full left turn.

17. Start the right side of the gear through the opening in the right apron. Move the gear in until the left tie rod clears all parts so it may be raised up to the left apron opening.

18. Raise the gear and insert the left side through the apron opening. Rotate the gear so the joint shaft enters the dash panel opening.

19. With an assistant guiding the intermediate shaft from the inside of the vehicle, insert the input shaft into the intermediate shaft coupling. Insert the intermediate shaft clamp bolts finger-tight. Do not tighten at this time.

20. Install the gear mounting insulators and brackets in their proper places. Ensure the flat in the left mounting area is parallel to the dash panel. Tighten the bracket bolts to 40–55 ft. lbs. (54–75 Nm) in the sequence as described below:

    a. Tighten the left (driver's side) upper bolt halfway.

    b. Tighten the left side lower bolt.

    c. Tighten the left side upper bolt.

    d. Tighten the right side bolts.

    e. Do not forget that the right and left side insulators and brackets are not interchangeable side to side.

21. Attach the tie rod ends to the steering knuckles. Tighten the castellated nuts to 27–32 ft. lbs. (36–43 Nm), then tighten the nuts until the slot aligns with the cotter pin hole. Insert a new cotter pin.

22. Install the exhaust system. Install the speedometer cable, if removed.

23. Tighten the gear input shaft to intermediate shaft coupling clamp bolt first. Then, tighten the upper intermediate shaft clamp bolt. Tighten both bolts to 20–37 ft. lbs. (28–50 Nm).

24. Install the access panel below the steering column. Turn the ignition key to the **OFF** position.

25. Check and adjust the toe. Tighten the tie rod end jam nuts, check for twisted bellows.

1991–93

1. Working inside the vehicle, remove the nuts securing the set plate and remove the set plate.

2. Remove the intermediate shaft-to-pinion shaft bolt from inside the vehicle.

3. Raise and safely support the vehicle.

4. Remove the front wheel and tire assemblies.

5. Remove the cotter pins and nuts securing the tie rod ends to the steering knuckles. Separate the tie rod ends from the steering knuckles using a suitable tool.

6. If equipped with manual transaxle, disconnect the extension bar.

7. Remove the nuts securing the steering gear brackets to the bulkhead. Remove the brackets.

8. Remove the steering gear from the vehicle.

To install:

9. Position the steering gear into its mounting position and install the brackets and nuts. Tighten the nuts to 27–38 ft. lbs. (37–52 Nm).

10. If equipped with a manual transaxle, connect the extension bar. Tighten the nut to 23–34 ft. lbs. (31–46 Nm).

11. Attach the tie rod ends to the steering knuckles. Install the nuts and tighten to 31–42 ft. lbs. (42–57 Nm). Install new cotter pins.

12. Install the front wheel and tire assemblies.

13. Lower the vehicle.

14. Install the intermediate shaft-to-pinion shaft bolt and tighten to 13–20 ft. lbs. (18–27 Nm).

15. Position the set plate and secure it with the nuts.

ADJUSTMENT

1989–90 Escort

The yoke clearance is not adjustable except when overhauling the steering gear assembly. Pinion bearing preload is not adjustable because of the non-adjustable bearing usage. Tie rod articulation is preset and is not adjustable. If articulation is out of specification, replace the tie rod assembly. To check tie rod articulation, proceed as follows:

1. With the tie rod end disconnected from the steering knuckle, loop a piece of wire through the hole in the tie rod end stud.

2. Insert the hook of spring scale T74P–3504–Y or equivalent, through the wire loop. Effort to move the tie rod after initial breakaway should be 0.7–5.0 lbs.

NOTE: Do not damage tie rod neck.

3. Replace ball joint/tie rod assembly if effort falls outside this range. Save the tie rod end for use on the new tie rod assembly.

1991–93 Escort

RACK PRELOAD/SUPPORT YOKE ADJUSTMENT

1. Remove the rack and pinion assembly from the vehicle and mount it in a suitable vice.

2. Loosen the locknut.

3. Tighten the adjusting bolt using yoke adjustment adapter T90P–3504–JH in the yoke plug to 8.7 inch lbs. (1 Nm), then loosen the adjusting bolt 10–40 degrees from that position.

4. Measure the pinion turning torque using pinion shaft adapting tool T86P–3504–K. The correct torque

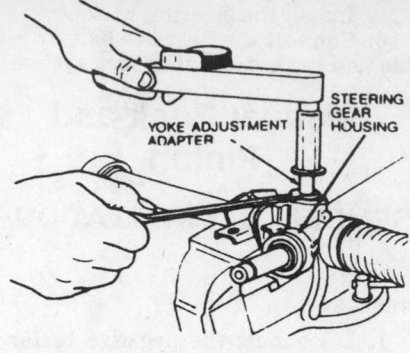

Tightening adjusting bolt on manual steering rack—1991–93 Escort

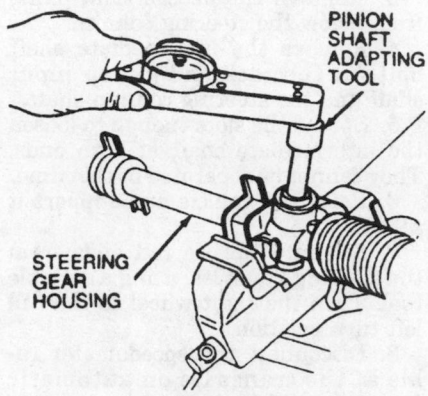

Pinion torque checking on manual steering rack—1991–93 Escort

at the neutral position ± 90 degrees should be 9–12 inch lbs. (1.0–1.3 Nm). At any other position the torque should be 14.7 inch lbs. (1.6 Nm) or less.

5. If the pinion torque is not within specification, re-adjust the adjusting bolt to achieve the correct pinion torque. Tighten the adjusting bolt locknut.

Power Rack and Pinion

REMOVAL & INSTALLATION

Except 1991–93 Escort

1. Disconnect the negative battery cable.

2. Turn the ignition key to the RUN position.

3. Remove access panel from dash below the steering column.

4. Remove screws from steering column boot at the dash panel and slide boot up intermediate shaft.

5. Remove intermediate shaft bolt at gear input shaft and loosen the bolt at the steering column shaft joint.

6. With a suitable tool, spread the slots enough to loosen intermediates shaft at both ends. The intermediate

shaft and gear input shaft cannot be separated at this time.

7. Remove the air cleaner on Escort.

8. On Escort with air conditioning, wire the air conditioner liquid line above the dash panel opening. Doing so provides clearance for gear input shaft removal and installation.

9. Separate pressure and return lines at intermediate connections on Escort or at steering gear on Tempo and Topaz and drain fluid.

10. On Tempo and Topaz, remove the pressure switch.

11. Disconnect the exhaust secondary air tube at check valve. Raise the vehicle and support it safely. Disconnect exhaust system at exhaust manifold on Escort or at intermediate connection on Tempo and Topaz and remove exhaust system.

12. Separate tie rod ends from steering knuckles.

13. Remove left tie rod end from tie rod on manual transaxle vehicles. This will allow tie rod to clear the shift linkage.

NOTE: Mark location of rod end prior to removal.

14. Disconnect speedometer cable at transaxle, if equipped with automatic transaxle. Remove the vehicle speed sensor.

15. Remove transaxle shift cable assembly at transaxle on vehicles equipped with automatic transaxle.

16. Turn steering wheel to full left turn stop for easier gear removal.

17. On Escort, remove screws holding the heater water tube to shake brace below the oil pan.

18. On Escort, remove nut from the lower of 2 bolts holding engine mount support bracket to transaxle housing. Tap bolt out as far as it will go.

19. Remove the gear mounting brackets and insulators.

20. Drape cloth towel over both apron opening edges to protect bellows during gear removal.

21. Separate gear from intermediate shaft by either pushing up on shaft with a bar from underneath the vehicle while pulling the gear down or with an assistant removing the shaft from inside the vehicle.

22. Rotate gear forward and down to clear the input shaft through the dash panel opening.

23. Make sure input shaft is in full left turn position. Move gear through the right (passenger) side apron opening until left tie rod clears left apron opening and other parts so it may be lowered. Guide the power steering hoses around the nearby components as the gear is being removed.

24. Lower the left side of the gear

and remove the gear out of the vehicle. Use care not to tear the bellows.

To install:

25. Rotate the input shaft to a full left turn stop. Position the right road wheel to a full left turn.

26. Start the right side of the gear through the opening in the right apron. Move the gear in until the left tie rod clears all parts so it may be raised up to the left apron opening.

27. Raise the gear and insert the left side through the apron opening. Move the power steering hoses into their proper position at the same time. Rotate the gear so the joint shaft enters the dash panel opening.

28. With an assistant guiding the intermediate shaft from the inside of the vehicle, insert the input shaft into the intermediate shaft coupling. Insert the intermediate shaft clamp bolts finger-tight. Do not tighten at this time.

29. Install the gear mounting insulators and brackets in their proper places. Ensure the flat in the left mounting area is parallel to the dash panel. Tighten the bracket bolts to 40–55 ft. lbs. (54–75 Nm) in the sequence as described below:

  a. Tighten the left (driver's side) upper bolt halfway.

  b. Tighten the left side lower bolt.

  c. Tighten the left side upper bolt.

  d. Tighten the right side bolts.

  e. Do not forget that the right and left side insulators and brackets are not interchangeable side to side.

30. Attach the tie rod ends to the steering knuckles. Tighten the castellated nuts to 27–32 ft. lbs. (36–43 Nm), then tighten the nuts until the slot aligns with the cotter pin hole. Insert a new cotter pin.

31. On the Escort, install the engine mount nut.

32. On the Escort, install the heater water tube to the shake brace.

33. Install the exhaust system. Install the speedometer cable, if removed. Install the vehicle speed sensor and the transaxle shift cable.

34. Connect the secondary air tube at the check valve. Connect the pressure and return lines at the intermediate connections or steering gear.

35. Install the pressure switch on Tempo and Topaz. On Escort, install the air cleaner.

36. Tighten the gear input shaft to intermediate shaft coupling clamp bolt first. Then, tighten the upper intermediate shaft clamp bolt. Tighten to 20–30 ft. lbs. (27–40 Nm).

37. Install the access panel below the steering column. Turn the ignition key to the **OFF** position.

38. Fill the system. Check and adjust the toe. Tighten the tie rod end jam nuts to 40–50 ft. lbs. (54–68 Nm), check for twisted bellows.

39. Connect negative battery cable.

1991–93 Escort

1. From inside the passenger compartment, remove the 5 set plate nuts and remove the set plate.

2. Remove the intermediate shaft-to-pinion shaft bolt.

3. Raise and safely support the vehicle.

4. Remove the front wheel and tire assemblies.

5. Remove the cotter pins and attaching nuts from the tie rod ends. Using a suitable tool, separate the tie rod ends from the steering knuckles.

6. If equipped with the 1.8L engine, remove the 2 screws from the power steering line retaining bracket and remove the bracket from the steering gear housing. If equipped with the 1.9L engine, remove the strap that holds the power steering lines to the steering gear housing and discard the strap.

7. Disconnect the high-pressure and return lines from the steering gear and plug the lines.

8. If equipped with manual transaxle, disconnect the extension bar and shift control rod from the transaxle.

9. Remove the nuts from the 2 steering gear mounting brackets.

10. Remove the splash shield from the left wheel well.

11. Remove the steering gear from the left side of the vehicle.

To install:

12. Position the steering gear in its mounting location and install the splash shield in the left wheel well.

13. Position the 2 steering gear mounting brackets and install the 2 nuts to each bracket. Tighten the nuts to 27–38 ft. lbs. (37–52 Nm).

14. If equipped with a manual transaxle, connect the extension bar and shift control rod. Tighten the extension bar nut to 23–34 ft. lbs. (31–46 Nm) and the shift control rod nut to 12–17 ft. lbs. (16–23 Nm).

15. Remove the plugs and connect the pressure and return lines to the steering gear. Tighten the flare nuts to 22–28 ft. lbs. (29–39 Nm).

16. If equipped with 1.8L engine, position the power steering line retaining bracket and install the 2 screws. If equipped with 1.9L engine, install a new strap to hold the power steering lines to the steering gear housing.

17. Position the tie rod ends in the steering knuckles and install the attaching nuts. Tighten the nuts to 31–42 ft. lbs. (42–57 Nm). Install new cotter pins.

18. Install the wheel and tire assemblies and lower the vehicle.

19. From inside the vehicle, install the intermediate shaft-to-pinion shaft bolt. Tighten the bolt to 13–20 ft. lbs. (18–27 Nm).

20. Position the set plate and install the 5 set plate nuts.

21. Fill the system with steering fluid.

ADJUSTMENT

Except 1991–93 Escort

The power rack and pinion steering gear provides for only rack yoke plug preload adjustment. This adjustment can be performed only with the gear out of the vehicle. To check rack yoke plug preload, proceed as follows:

RACK AND PINION WITH ONE-PIECE HOUSING

1. Disconnect the negative battery cable.

2. Raise and safely support the vehicle.

3. Remove power rack and pinion assembly from vehicle.

4. Clean exterior of steering gear thoroughly.

5. Mount steering gear in a suitable rack housing holding fixture.

NOTE: Do not mount gear in vise.

6. Do not remove external pressure lines, unless they are leaking or damaged. If these lines are removed, they must be replaced with new lines.

7. Drain power steering fluid by rotating unput shaft lock-to-lock twice using input shaft torque adapter T81P–3504–R or equivalent. Position adapter and wrench on input shaft.

8. Loosen yoke plug locknut with yoke locknut wrench T81P–3504–G or equivalent.

9. Loosen yoke plug using yoke plug adapter T87P–3504–G or equivalent.

10. With rack at center of travel, tighten yoke plug to 44–50 inch lbs. (5.0–5.7 Nm). Clean threads of yoke plug prior to tightening to prevent a false reading.

11. Install yoke plug adapter T87P–3504–G or equivalent. Mark location of 0 degree mark on housing. Back off adjuster so 48 degree mark lines up with 0 degree mark.

12. Place yoke locknut wrench T81P–3504–G or equivalent, on yoke plug locknut. While holding yoke plug, tighten locknut to 40–50 ft. lbs. (54–68 Nm). Do not allow yoke plug to move while tightening or preload will be affected. Check input shaft torque after tightening locknut.

13. If external pressure lines were removed, the Teflon® seal rings must be replaced. Clean out Teflon® seal shreds from housing ports prior to installation of new lines.

14. Install power rack assembly in vehicle.

15. Lower vehicle.

16. Connect negative battery cable.

RACK AND PINION WITH TWO-PIECE HOUSING

1. Disconnect the negative battery cable.

2. Raise and safely support the vehicle.

3. Remove the power rack and pinion assembly from the vehicle.

4. Clean the exterior of the gear in the yoke plug area and mount the gear in a vise, gripping it near the center of the tube. Do not over-tighten.

5. Loosen and remove the yoke plug locknut.

6. Back off the yoke plug 1 turn.

7. Tighten the yoke plug to 45 inch lbs. (5.8 Nm) using yoke plug adapter T81P-3504-U or equivalent, and an inch-pound torque wrench with a full scale reading to 100 inch lbs. maximum.

8. Scribe the gear housing in line with the 0 mark on the yoke plug adapter tool.

9. Back off the yoke plug so the second mark on the yoke plug adapter tool aligns with the scribe mark on the gear housing.

10. Hold the plug, and install and tighten the locknut to 40–50 ft. lbs. (54–68 Nm) using yoke locknut wrench T81P-3504-G or equivalent.

Power Steering Pump

REMOVAL & INSTALLATION

1989–90 Escort

1. Disconnect the negative battery cable. Remove the air cleaner, thermactor air pump and belt. Remove the reservoir filler extension and cover the hole to prevent dirt from entering.

2. If equipped with EFI and remote reservoir, remove the reservoir supply hose at the pump, drain the fluid and plug or cap the opening at the pump to prevent entry of contaminants during removal.

3. From under the vehicle, loosen 1 pump adjusting bolt. Remove 1 pump to bracket mounting bolt and disconnect the fluid return line.

4. From above the vehicle, loosen 1 adjusting bolt and the pivot bolt. Remove the drive belt and the 2 remaining pump to bracket mounting bolts.

5. Remove the pump by passing the pulley through the adjusting bracket opening. Remove the pressure hose from the pump assembly.

To install:

6. From under the vehicle, connect the pressure hose to the pump. Pass the pulley through the opening in the

adjusting bracket. Install the mounting bolts and tighten to 30–45 ft. lbs. (40–62 Nm).

7. If applicable, make sure the air pump belt is on the inner power steering pump pulley groove. Install the power steering pump belt and adjust. Tighten all bolts to 30–45 ft. lbs. (40–62 Nm).

NOTE: When adjusting belt tension, never pry on the pump or surrounding aluminum parts or brackets.

8. If not equipped with a remote reservoir, install the return line to the pump.

9. From above the vehicle, install the reservoir filler neck extension, if applicable. Install the air cleaner, if applicable.

10. Install remote reservoir supply to pump on EFI/remote vehicles.

11. Fill pump or remote reservoir with fluid and check operation.

1991–93 Escort

1.8L ENGINE

1. Disconnect the negative battery cable.

2. Loosen the power steering fluid reservoir-to-pump hose clamp and pull the hose from the reservoir. Plug the hose.

3. Remove the 2 reservoir mounting bolts and lift the reservoir from its mounting position.

4. Loosen the return hose clamp and pull the return hose from the reservoir. Plug the hose and remove the reservoir.

5. Disconnect the electrical connector from the power steering pressure switch.

6. Loosen the high-pressure line flare nut and disconnect the line from the pump. Plug the line.

7. Raise and safely support the vehicle.

8. Remove the 5 right front undercover bolts and remove the undercover.

9. Remove the belt tensioner adjustment bolt and remove the accessory drive belt from the pulley.

10. Lower the vehicle.

11. Remove the 3 pump mounting bracket bolts and remove the pump and the bracket.

12. Remove the bolt that attaches the pump to the mounting bracket.

13. Remove the nut and bolt that attaches the tensioner to the pump mounting bracket and remove the nut and bolt that attaches the tensioner to the pump.

To install:

14. Position the tensioner to the pump and install the bolt and nut.

Tighten the nut to 14–19 ft. lbs. (19–25 Nm).

15. Position the tensioner to the pump mounting bracket and install the bolt and nut. Tighten the nut to 23–34 ft. lbs. (31–46 Nm).

16. Install the bolt that attaches the pump to the mounting bracket and tighten to 27–40 ft. lbs. (36–54 Nm).

17. Position the pump and bracket and install the 3 pump mounting bracket bolts. Tighten the bolts to 27–38 ft. lbs. (37–54 Nm).

18. Raise and safely support the vehicle.

19. Position the accessory drive belt on the pulley and install the belt tensioner adjustment bolt.

20. Position the right front undercover and install the 5 bolts.

21. Lower the vehicle.

22. Unplug the high-pressure line and connect the line to the pump. Tighten the flare nut to 12–17 ft. lbs. (16–24 Nm).

23. Connect the power steering pressure switch electrical connector.

24. Unplug the return hose and connect the hose to the reservoir. Tighten the clamp.

25. Position the reservoir and install the 2 mounting bolts.

26. Unplug the reservoir-to-pump hose and connect the hose to the reservoir. Tighten the clamp.

27. Fill the system with power steering fluid and adjust the accessory drive belt tension.

1.9L ENGINE

1. Disconnect the negative battery cable and drain the cooling system.

2. Loosen the belt tensioner and remove the drive belt from the pulley. Remove the belt tensioner bolt and remove the tensioner.

3. Support the engine with a suitable floor jack.

4. Remove the engine vibration damper nut and bolt and remove the damper.

5. Remove the 2 front engine mount nuts. Loosen the engine mount pivot bolt and nut and position the engine mount aside.

6. Raise the engine to gain access to the power steering pump pulley.

7. Hold the pulley in position with a suitable tool and remove the 3 pulley mounting bolts. Remove the pulley and lower the engine.

8. Position the engine mount and install the 2 nuts.

9. Loosen the clamp and disconnect the return line from the pump. Loosen the flare nut from the high-pressure line and disconnect the line from the pump.

10. Raise and safely support the vehicle.

11. Remove the 2 passenger side splash shields.

12. If equipped, remove the 4 compressor mounting bolts and position the air conditioning compressor aside.

13. Remove the lower radiator hose.

14. Remove the 3 power steering pump mounting bolts and remove the pump.

To install:

15. Position the power steering pump and install the 3 mounting bolts. Tighten the bolts to 30–45 ft. lbs. (40–62 Nm).

16. Install the lower radiator hose.

17. If equipped, position the air conditioning compressor and install the 4 mounting bolts. Tighten the bolts to 30–40 ft. lbs. (40–55 Nm).

18. Install the 2 passenger side splash shields and lower the vehicle.

19. Connect the high-pressure line to the power steering pump and tighten the nut. Connect the return line to the pump and position the clamp.

20. Support the engine with a suitable floor jack.

21. Remove the 2 front engine mount nuts and raise the engine to gain access to the pulley.

22. Position the pulley and, holding the pulley in place with a suitable tool, install the 3 pulley mounting bolts. Tighten the bolts to 15–22 ft. lbs. (20–30 Nm).

23. Lower the engine.

24. Position the engine mount and install the 2 nuts. Tighten the engine mount pivot bolt and nut.

25. Position the engine vibration dampener and install the bolt and nut.

26. Position the belt tensioner and install the bolt loosely. Position the accessory drive belt on the pulley and tighten the tensioner mounting bolt to 30–41 ft. lbs. (40–55 Nm).

27. Fill the cooling system.

28. Add the proper type and quantity of power steering fluid.

29. Connect the negative battery cable. Check that the pump operates properly and that there are no leaks.

TEMPO and TOPAZ

1989–91 2.3L ENGINE

1. Disconnect the negative battery cable. Loosen the alternator and remove the drive belt. Pivot the alternator to it most upright position or remove the alternator.

2. Remove the radiator overflow bottle. Loosen and remove the power steering pump drive belt. Mark the pulley and pump drive hub with paint or grease pencil for location reference.

3. Remove the pulleys from the pump shaft.

4. Remove the return line from the pump. Be prepared to catch any spilled fluid in a suitable container.

5. Back off the pressure line attaching nut completely. The line will separate from the pump connection when the pump is removed.

6. Remove the pump mounting bolts and remove the pump.

To install:

7. Install the pump on the mounting bracket. Guide the pressure line into the pump outlet fitting while installing the pump.

8. Install the pressure and return lines.

9. Install 2 pulleys on the hub by aligning the previously applied marks to maintain pulley balance.

10. Install the steering pump drive belt and alternator drive belt and adjust the tension.

11. Install the radiator overflow bottle.

12. Connect the negative battery cable. Fill the pump with fluid and check operation.

1992–93 2.3L ENGINE

1. Disconnect the negative battery cable.

2. Disconnect the fluid return line at the remote reservoir and drain the power steering fluid into a suitable container.

3. Disconnect the pressure hose from the pump poutlet and drain the fluid into a suitable container.

4. Loosen the tensioner and remove the drive belt from the pump pulley.

5. Remove the 4 bolts from the pump pulley and remove the pulley.

6. Remove the 3 pump retaining bolts and remove the pump.

To install:

7. Position the pump on its bracket and install the retaining bolts.

8. Install the pulley and secure with the 4 bolts.

9. Connect the pressure line to the pump but do not overtighten the fitting. Swivel and/or endplay of the fitting is normal and does not indicate a loose fitting.

10. Connect the inlet hose to the pump and secure with the hose clamp.

11. Fill the reservoir with the proper type of fluid.

12. Connect the negative battery cable and bleed the system. Check for leaks.

3.0L ENGINE

1. Disconnect the negative battery cable.

2. Disconnect the fluid return hose from the pump inlet and drain the fluid into a suitable container.

3. Remove the pressure line from the pump outlet and drain the fluid into a suitable container.

4. Remove the plastic pulley guard.

5. Loosen the tensioner and remove the drive belt from the pulley.

6. Remove the pulley-to-pump shaft bolt and remove the pulley from the pump shaft.

7. Remove the pump-to-bracket bolts and remove the pump.

To install:

8. Install the pump onto the pump bracket and install the retaining screws. Tighten to 47–63 inch lbs. (5.2–7.2 Nm).

9. Install the pulley on the pump shaft and secure with the bolt.

10. Install the drive belt on the pulley.

11. Install the plastic pulley guard.

12. Connect the pressure line to the pump but do not overtighten the fitting. Swivel and/or endplay of the fitting is normal and does not indicate a loose fitting.

13. Connect the inlet hose to the pump and secure with the hose clamp.

14. Fill the reservoir with the proper type of fluid.

15. Connect the negative battery cable and bleed the system. Check for leaks.

BELT ADJUSTMENT

1.8L Engine

1. Raise and safely support the vehicle.

2. Loosen the power steering pump mounting bolt and nuts.

3. Adjust the belt tension by turning the pump adjusting bolt.

4. Tighten the power steering pump mounting nut near the pump adjusting bolt.

5. Check the belt tension using either a belt tension gauge or using the deflection method.

6. If using a belt tension gauge, position the gauge on the longest accessible span of belt. The tension for a new belt should be 110–132 lbs. The tension for a used belt (more than 10 minutes running time) should be 95–110 lbs.

7. If using the deflection method, apply approximately 22 lbs. pressure midway between the pulleys. The deflection on a new belt should be 0.31–0.35 in. (8–9mm). The deflection on a used belt (more than 10 minutes running time) should be 0.35–0.39 in. (9–10mm).

8. Tighten the power steering pump mounting nut, located near the adjusting bolt, to 27–38 ft. lbs. (37–52 Nm).

9. Tighten the pump mounting bolt behind the pulley to 27–40 ft. lbs. (36–54 Nm) and the remaining pump mounting nut to 23–34 ft. lbs. (31–46 Nm).

10. Lower the vehicle.

1989–90 1.9L Engine

1. From engine compartment, loos-

en pivot bolt and upper adjustment bolt.

2. Raise and safely support the vehicle. From below vehicle:

a. Loosen lower adjustment bolt.

b. Apply pressure with ½ drive breaker bar and measure the belt tension with a suitable belt tension gauge. The belt tension should be 140 ± 20 lbs. for a new belt or 110 ± 10 lbs. for a used belt.

c. Tighten lower adjustment bolt to 35 ft. lbs. (47 Nm).

3. Lower vehicle. From engine compartment, tighten pivot bolt to 50 ft. lbs. (68 Nm) and upper adjustment bolt to 35 ft. lbs. (47 Nm).

2.3L, 3.0L and 1991–93 1.9L Engines

Belt tension is maintained by an automatic belt tensioner and does not require adjustment.

SYSTEM BLEEDING

If air bubbles are present in the power steering fluid, bleed the system by performing the following:

1. Fill the reservoir to the proper level.

2. Operate the engine until the fluid reaches normal operating temperature of 165–175°F.

3. Turn the steering wheel all the way to the left then all the way to the right several times. Do not hold the steering wheel in the far left or far right position stops.

4. Check the fluid level and recheck the fluid for the presence of trapped air. If apparent that air is still in the system, fabricate or obtain a vacuum tester and purge the system as follows:

a. Remove the pump dipstick cap assembly.

b. Check and fill the pump reservoir with fluid to the **COLD FULL** mark on the dipstick.

c. Disconnect the ignition coil wire or the coil pack electrical connector if equipped with distributorless ignition, and raise the front of the vehicle and support safely.

d. Crank the engine with the starter and check the fluid level. Do not turn the steering wheel at this time.

e. Fill the pump reservoir to the **COLD FULL** mark on the dipstick. Crank the engine with the starter while cycling the steering wheel lock-to-lock. Check the fluid level.

f. Tightly insert a suitable size rubber stopper and air evacuator pump into the reservoir fill neck. Connect the ignition coil wire or coil pack electrical connector.

g. With the engine idling, apply a

15 in. Hg vacuum to the reservoir for 3 minutes. As air is purged from the system, the vacuum will drop off. Maintain the vacuum on the system as required throughout the 3 minutes.

h. Remove the vacuum source. Fill the reservoir to the **COLD FULL** mark on the dipstick.

i. With the engine idling, re-apply 15 in. Hg vacuum source to the reservoir. Slowly cycle the steering wheel to lock-to-lock stops for approximately 5 minutes. Do not hold the steering wheel on the stops during cycling. Maintain the vacuum as required.

j. Release the vacuum and disconnect the vacuum source. Add fluid, as required.

k. Start the engine and cycle the wheel slowly and check for leaks at all connections.

l. Lower the front wheels.

5. In cases of severe aeration, repeat the procedure.

Tie Rod Ends

REMOVAL & INSTALLATION

1. Remove and discard cotter pin and nut from worn tie rod end ball stud.

2. Disconnect tie rod end from spindle, using tie rod end remover tool 3290–D and adapter T81P–3504–W or equivalent.

3. Holding tie rod end with a wrench, loosen tie rod jam nut.

4. Grip tie rod hex flats with a pair of suitable locking pliers, and remove tie rod end assembly from tie rod. Note depth to which tie rod was located, using jam nut as a marker.

To install:

5. Clean tie rod threads. Apply a light coating of disc brake caliper slide grease D7AZ–19590–A or equivalent, to tie rod threads. Thread new tie rod end on tie rod to same depth as removed tie rod end. Tighten jam nut.

6. Place tie rod end stud into steering spindle.

7. Install a new nut on tie rod end stud. Tighten nut to 27–32 ft. lbs. (36–43 Nm) on all except 1991–93 Escort where the torque is 31–42 ft. lbs. (42–57 Nm), and continue tightening nut to align next castellation with cotter pin hole in stud. Install a new cotter pin.

8. Set toe to specification and tighten jam nuts to 42–50 ft. lbs. (57–68 Nm) on all except 1991–93 Escort where the torque is 25–29 ft. lbs. (34–49 Nm). Do not twist bellows.

BRAKES

Master Cylinder

REMOVAL & INSTALLATION

Except 1991–93 Escort

1. Disconnect the negative battery cable.

2. Disconnect and plug the brake lines from the primary and secondary outlet ports of the master cylinder and pressure control valves.

3. Remove the nuts attaching the master cylinder to the brake booster assembly. Disconnect the brake warning light wire.

4. Slide the master cylinder forward and upward from the vehicle.

To install:

5. Before installation, bench bleed the new master cylinder as follows:

a. Mount the new master cylinder in a suitable holding fixture. Be careful not to damage the housing.

b. Fill the master cylinder reservoir with brake fluid.

c. Using a suitable tool inserted into the booster pushrod cavity, push the master cylinder piston in slowly. Place a suitable container under the master cylinder to catch the fluid being expelled from the outlet ports.

d. Place a finger tightly over each outlet port and allow the master cylinder piston to return.

e. Repeat the procedure until clear fluid only is expelled from the master cylinder. Plug the outlet ports and remove the master cylinder from the holding fixture.

6. Position the master cylinder over the booster pushrod and booster mounting studs. Install the nuts and tighten to 13–25 ft. lbs. (18–33 Nm).

7. Remove the plugs and connect the brake lines. Tighten the fittings.

8. Make sure the master cylinder reservoir is full. Have an assistant push down on the brake pedal. When the pedal is all the way down, crack open the brake line fittings, 1 at a time, to expel any remaining air in the master cylinder and brake lines. Tighten the fittings, then have the assistant allow the brake pedal to return.

9. Repeat Step 8 until all air is expelled from the master cylinder and brake lines. Final tighten the brake line fittings to 10–18 ft. lbs. (14–24 Nm).

10. Connect the brake warning indicator connector.

11. Make sure the master cylinder reservoir is full.

12. If necessary, bleed the brake system.

13. Connect the negative battery cable. Check for fluid leaks and check for proper operation.

1991–93 Escort

1. Disconnect the battery cables and remove the battery.

2. Disconnect the low fluid level sensor electrical connector.

3. Loosen the brake line fittings and disconnect the brake lines from the master cylinder.

4. If equipped with manual transaxle, remove the clamp and pull the clutch hose from the brake/clutch fluid reservoir.

5. Cap the lines and the master cylinder ports.

6. Remove the 2 mounting nuts and remove the master cylinder assembly.

To install:

7. Adjust the piston to pushrod clearance as follows:

   a. Insert a pencil in the pushrod socket of the master cylinder. Mark the point on the pencil that is even with the end of the master cylinder with a hacksaw blade.

   b. Measure the length of the pencil to the saw mark with a ruler.

   c. Using the ruler, measure how far the master cylinder pushrod protrudes out of the booster assembly.

   d. Measure the length of the master cylinder boss with the ruler. Subtract the length of the boss from the length of the pencil. The difference in length between the master cylinder pushrod and the corrected pencil length is equal to the pushrod clearance.

   e. Adjust the pushrod length to get the correct clearance. It should be 0.025 in. (1mm) shorter than the pushrod socket.

8. Before installation, bench bleed the new master cylinder as follows:

   a. Mount the new master cylinder in a suitable holding fixture. Be careful not to damage the housing.

   b. Fill the master cylinder reservoir with brake fluid.

   c. Using a suitable tool inserted into the booster pushrod cavity, push the master cylinder piston in slowly. Place a suitable container under the master cylinder to catch the fluid being expelled from the outlet ports.

   d. Place a finger tightly over each outlet port and allow the master cylinder piston to return.

   e. Repeat the procedure until clear fluid only is expelled from the master cylinder. Plug the outlet ports and remove the master cylinder from the holding fixture.

9. Position the master cylinder over

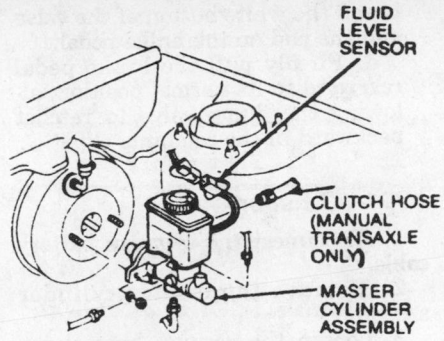

Master cylinder removal and installation—1991–93 Escort

the booster pushrod and booster mounting studs. Install the nuts and tighten to 8–12 ft. lbs. (10–16 Nm).

10. If equipped with manual transaxle, connect the clutch hose onto the brake/clutch fluid reservoir and install the clamp.

11. Remove the caps and connect the brake lines. Tighten the fittings.

12. Make sure the master cylinder reservoir is full. Have an assistant push down on the brake pedal. When the pedal is all the way down, crack open the brake line fittings, 1 at a time, to expel any remaining air in the master cylinder and brake lines. Tighten the fittings, then have the assistant allow the brake pedal to return.

13. Repeat Step 12 until all air is expelled from the master cylinder and brake lines. Tighten the brake line fittings to 10–16 ft. lbs. (13–22 Nm).

14. Connect the low fluid level sensor electrical connector.

15. Install the battery and connect the negative battery cable.

16. Make sure the master cylinder reservoir is full. Bleed the brakes, if necessary.

17. Check for brake fluid leaks and for proper brake operation.

Proportioning/ Combination Valve

REMOVAL & INSTALLATION

Except 1991–93 Escort

There are 2 pressure control valves housed in the master cylinder assembly. The valves reduce rear brake system hydraulic pressure when the pressure exceeds a preset value. The rear brake hydraulic pressure is limited in order to minimize rear wheel skidding during hard braking. Remove and install the pressure control valves as follows:

1. Disconnect the primary or secondary brake line, as necessary.

2. Loosen and remove the pressure control valve from the master cylinder housing.

To install:

3. Install the pressure control valve in the master cylinder housing port and tighten to 10–18 ft. lbs. (14–24 Nm).

4. Connect the brake line and tighten the fitting to 10–18 ft. lbs. (14–24 Nm).

5. Fill and bleed the brake system.

1991–93 Escort

1. Loosen the brake line fittings and disconnect the brake lines from the proportioning valve.

2. Remove the 2 mounting bolts and remove the valve.

To install:

3. Position the valve and install the mounting bolts. Tighten to 14–17 ft. lbs. (19–23 Nm).

4. Connect the brake lines and tighten the fittings to 10–16 ft. lbs. (13–22 Nm).

5. Properly bleed the brake system.

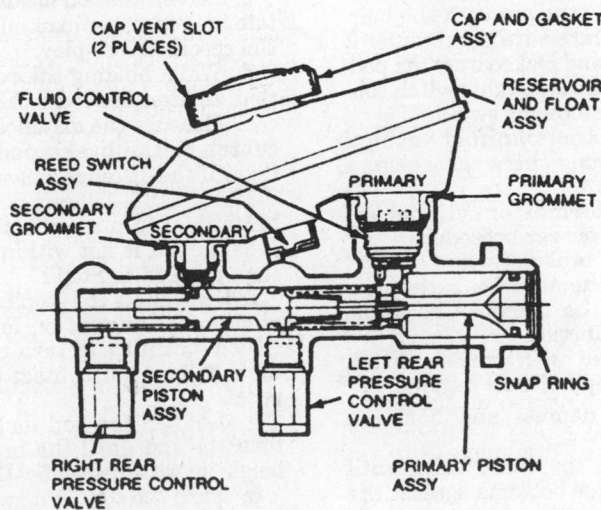

Master cylinder and pressure control valve assembly—except 1991–93 Escort

Power Brake Booster

REMOVAL & INSTALLATION

Except 1991–93 Escort

1. Disconnect the battery ground cable and remove the brake lines from the master cylinder.
2. Remove the retaining nuts and remove the master cylinder.
3. From under the instrument panel, remove the stoplight switch wiring connector from the switch. Remove the pushrod retainer and outer nylon washer from the brake pin, slide the stoplight switch along the brake pedal pin, far enough for the outer hole to clear the pin.
4. Remove the switch by sliding it upward. Remove the booster to dash panel retaining nuts. Slide the booster pushrod and pushrod bushing off the brake pedal pin.
5. Disconnect the manifold vacuum hose from the booster check valve and move the booster forward until the booster studs clear the dash panel and remove the booster.

To install:

6. Align the pedal support and support spacer inside the vehicle and place the booster in position on the dash panel. Hand-start the retaining nuts.
7. Working inside the vehicle, install the pushrod and pushrod bushing on the brake pedal pin. Tighten the booster-to-dash panel retaining nuts to 13–25 ft. lbs. (18–33 Nm).
8. Position the stoplight switch so it straddles the booster pushrod with the stoplight switch slot toward the pedal blade and the hole just clearing the pin. Slide the stoplight switch down onto the pin. Slide the assembly toward the pedal arm, being careful not to bend or deform the switch. Install the nylon washer on the pin and secure all parts to the pin with the hairpin retainer. Make sure the retainer is fully installed and locked over the pedal pin. Install the stoplight switch connector on the stoplight switch.
9. Connect the manifold vacuum hose to the booster check valve using a hose clamp.
10. Install the master cylinder according to the proper procedure.
11. Bleed the brake system.
12. Connect the negative battery cable and start the engine. Check the power brake function.
13. If equipped with cruise control, adjust the dump valve as follows:

    a. Firmly depress and hold the brake pedal.
    b. Push in the dump valve until the valve collar bottoms against the retaining clip.
    c. Place a 0.050–0.10 in. shim between the white button of the valve and the pad on the brake pedal.
    d. Firmly pull the brake pedal rearward to its normal position, allowing the dump valve to ratchet backward in the retaining clip.

1991–93 Escort

1. Disconnect the negative battery cable.
2. Remove the master cylinder assembly.
3. Loosen the vacuum hose clamp and remove the hose from the power brake booster.
4. From inside the vehicle, remove the pin and discard.
5. Remove the clevis pin.
6. Remove the 4 booster mounting nuts and remove the booster. Remove and discard the gasket.

To install:

7. Install a new gasket over the studs and position the power brake booster.
8. From inside the vehicle, install the 4 mounting nuts and tighten to 14–19 ft. lbs. (19–25 Nm).
9. Lubricate the clevis pin with white lithium grease and install. Install a new pin.
10. Position the vacuum hose to the booster and install the clamp.
11. Install the master cylinder, making sure to check the master cylinder pushrod clearance.
12. Adjust the brake pedal as follows:

    a. Press the brake pedal several times to eliminate the vacuum in the booster.
    b. Carefully press the pedal and measure the amount of free-play until resistance is felt. If the free-play is 0.16–0.28 in. (4–7mm), the pedal free-play is within specification. If the free-play is not within specification, proceed to Step c.
    c. Loosen the rod locknut and rotate the rod either in or out to obtain the specified free-play.
    d. While holding the rod in position, tighten the rod locknut.
    e. Measure the distance from the center of the brake pedal to the floor. If the distance measures 7.60–7.72 in. (193–196mm), the pedal height is within specification. If the pedal height is not within specification, proceed to Step f.
    f. Disconnect the stoplight switch electrical connector, loosen the switch locknut and turn the switch until it does not contact the brake pedal.
    g. Loosen the rod locknut and turn the rod until the brake pedal height is within specification.
    h. Turn the stoplight switch until it contacts the brake pedal, then turn it an additional ½ turn. Tighten the stoplight locknut and the rod locknut.
    i. Connect the stoplight switch electrical connector and check the operation of the stoplights and brake system.

Brake Caliper

REMOVAL & INSTALLATION

Except 1991–93 Escort

1. Disconnect the negative battery cable.
2. Raise and safely support the vehicle.
3. Remove wheel and tire assembly from rotor mounting face.
4. Disconnect flexible brake hose from caliper. Remove hollow retaining bolt that connects hose fitting to caliper. Remove hose assembly from caliper and plug hose.
5. Remove caliper locating pins using Torx® drive bit D79P–2100–T40 or equivalent.
6. Lift caliper off rotor and integral knuckle and anchor plate using rotating motion.

NOTE: Do not pry directly against plastic piston or damage to piston will occur.

To install:

7. Position caliper assembly above rotor with anti-rattle spring under upper arm of knuckle. Install caliper over rotor with rotating motion. Ensure inner shoe is properly positioned.

NOTE: Ensure correct caliper assembly is installed on correct knuckle. The caliper bleed screw should be positioned on top of caliper when assembled on vehicle.

8. Lubricate locating pins and inside of insulators with silicone grease. Install locating pins through caliper insulators and into knuckle attaching holes. The caliper locating pins must be inserted and threads started by hand.
9. Using Torx® drive bit D79P–2100–T40 or equivalent, tighten caliper locating pins to 18–25 ft. lbs. (24–34 Nm).
10. Remove plug and install brake hose on caliper with new gasket on each side of fitting outlet. Insert attaching bolt through washers and fittings. Tighten bolt to 30–40 ft. lbs. (40–54 Nm).
11. Bleed brake system. Always replace rubber bleed screw cap after bleeding.
12. Fill master cylinder as required.
13. Install wheel and tire assembly. Tighten wheel lug nuts to 80–105 ft. lbs. (109–142 Nm).

14. Connect negative battery cable.
15. Pump brake pedal prior to moving vehicle to position brake linings.
16. Road test vehicle.

1991–93 Escort
FRONT CALIPER

1. Raise and safely support the vehicle. Remove the wheel and tire assembly.
2. Remove the brake pads.
3. Clamp the brake hose and remove the brake hose attaching bolt.
4. Disconnect the brake hose from the caliper and discard the 2 copper washers.
5. Remove the 2 caliper mounting bolts and remove the caliper.

To install:

6. Position the caliper and install the 2 caliper mounting bolts. Tighten the bolts to 29–36 ft. lbs. (39–49 Nm).
7. Install 2 new copper washers to the brake hose. Position the brake hose onto the caliper and install the attaching bolt. Tighten the bolt to 16–22 ft. lbs. (22–29 Nm).
8. Remove the clamp from the brake hose.
9. Install the brake pads.
10. Bleed the brake system.
11. Install the wheel and tire assembly and lower the vehicle.

REAR CALIPER

1. Raise and safely support the vehicle. Remove the wheel and tire assembly.
2. Remove the brake pads.
3. Remove the parking brake cable bracket bolt and position the bracket aside.
4. Remove the parking brake cable from the operating lever.
5. Clamp the brake hose, remove the brake line attaching bolt and remove the 2 washers. Discard the washers.
6. Disconnect the brake line and slide the caliper off the mounting bracket.

To install:

7. Position the caliper on the mounting bracket.
8. Install 2 new washers to the brake line. Position the brake line to the caliper and install the attaching bolt. Tighten the bolt to 16–22 ft. lbs. (22–29 Nm).
9. Remove the clamp from the brake hose.
10. Attach the parking brake cable to the operating lever. Position the bracket and install the bracket bolt.
11. Install the brake pads.
12. Bleed the brake system.
13. Install the wheel and tire assembly and lower the vehicle.

Disc Brake Pads

REMOVAL & INSTALLATION

Except 1991–93 Escort

1. Remove master cylinder cap and check fluid level in reservoir. Remove brake fluid until reservoir is ½ full. Discard removed fluid.
2. Raise and safely support the vehicle.
3. Remove wheel and tire assembly.
4. Remove caliper locating pins.
5. Lift caliper assembly from integral knuckle and anchor plate and rotor using rotating motion. Do not pry directly against plastic piston or damage will occur.
6. Remove outer shoe and lining assembly.
7. Remove inner shoe and lining assembly.
8. Inspect both rotor braking surfaces. Minor scoring or buildup of lining material does not require machining or replacement of rotor. Hand-sand glaze from both rotor braking surfaces using garnet paper 100-A (medium grit) or aluminum oxide 150-J (medium).
9. Suspend caliper inside fender housing with wire. Use care not to damage caliper or stretch brake hose.

To install:

10. Use a 4 in. C-clamp and wood block 2 ¾ in. x 1 in. (70mm x 25mm) and approximately ¾ in. (19mm) thick to seat caliper hydraulic piston in its bore.

NOTE: Extra care must be taken during this procedure to prevent damage to the plastic piston. Metal or sharp objects cannot come into direct contact with the piston surface or damage will result.

11. Remove all rust buildup from inside of caliper legs where the outer shoe makes contact.
12. Install inner shoe and lining assembly in caliper piston(s). Do not bend shoe clips during installation in piston.
13. Install correct outer shoe and lining assembly. Ensure clips are properly seated.
14. Install caliper over rotor.
15. Install wheel and tire assembly. Tighten wheel nuts to 80–105 ft. lbs. (109–142 Nm).
16. Pump brake pedal prior to moving vehicle to position brake linings. Check the fluid level in the master cylinder.
17. Connect negative battery cable.
18. Road test vehicle.

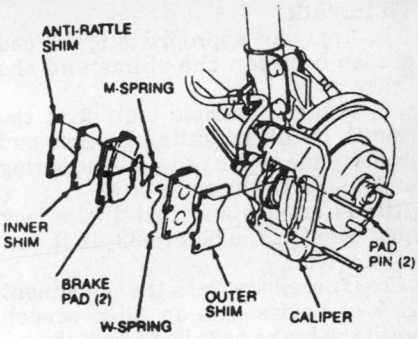

Front disc brake pad assembly— 1991–93 Escort

1991–93 Escort
FRONT DISC BRAKE PADS

1. Remove master cylinder cap and check fluid level in reservoir. Remove brake fluid until reservoir is ½ full. Discard removed fluid.
2. Raise and safely support the vehicle.
3. Remove wheel and tire assembly.
4. Remove the 2 brake pad pins and remove the M-spring and the W-spring.
5. Remove the brake pads and shims from the caliper.

To install:

6. Use a suitable tool to push the piston into the caliper bore.
7. Apply suitable grease between the shims and the brake pad guide plates and position the brake pads and shims into the caliper.
8. Install the W-spring and the M-spring. Install the 2 brake pad pins.
9. Install the wheel and tire assembly and lower the vehicle.
10. Pump brake pedal prior to moving vehicle to position brake linings. Check the fluid level in the master cylinder.
11. Road test vehicle.

REAR DISC BRAKE PADS

1. Remove master cylinder cap and check fluid level in reservoir. Remove brake fluid until reservoir is ½ full. Discard removed fluid.
2. Raise and safely support the vehicle.
3. Remove wheel and tire assembly.
4. If necessary, remove the screw plug and turn the adjustment gear counterclockwise with a hex wrench to pull the piston fully inward.
5. Remove the caliper lock bolt.
6. Using a suitable tool, pivot the caliper on its mounting bracket to access the brake pads. If the upper lock bolt requires lubrication or service, remove it and suspend the caliper with mechanics wire.
7. Remove the brake pads, shims, spring and guides.

To install:

8. Apply an appropriate brake pad grease between the shims and the brake pads.

9. Using a suitable tool, pivot the caliper on its mounting bracket and position the brake pads, shims, spring and guides to the rotor.

10. Lubricate and install the lock bolt. Tighten the bolt to 33–43 ft. lbs. (45–59 Nm).

11. If necessary, turn the adjustment gear clockwise with an Allen wrench until the brake pads just touch the rotor, then loosen the gear ⅓ of a turn. Install the screw plug and tighten to 9–12 ft. lbs. (12–16 Nm).

12. Install the wheel and tire assembly and lower the vehicle.

13. Pump brake pedal prior to moving vehicle to position brake linings. Check the fluid level in the master cylinder.

14. Road test vehicle.

Brake Rotor

REMOVAL & INSTALLATION

Except 1991–93 Escort

1. Disconnect the negative battery cable.

2. Raise and safely support the vehicle.

3. Remove wheel and tire assembly.

4. Remove caliper locating pins.

5. Lift caliper assembly from integral knuckle and anchor plate and rotor using rotating motion. Do not pry directly against plastic piston or damage will occur.

6. Position caliper aside and support it with a length of wire to avoid damaging caliper.

7. Remove rotor from hub assembly by pulling it off the hub studs. Inspect the rotor and refinish or replace, as necessary. If refinishing, check the minimum thickness specification.

To install:

8. If rotor is being replaced, remove protective coating from new rotor with carburetor degreaser. If original rotor is being installed, make sure rotor braking and mounting surfaces are clean.

9. Install rotor on hub assembly.

10. Install caliper assembly on rotor.

11. Install wheel and tire assembly. Tighten wheel nuts to 80–105 ft. lbs. (109–142 Nm).

12. Pump brake pedal prior to moving vehicle to position brake linings.

13. Connect negative battery cable.

14. Road test vehicle.

1991–93 Escort

FRONT BRAKE ROTOR

1. Raise and safely support the vehicle.

2. Remove the wheel and tire assembly.

3. Remove the 2 caliper mounting bolts.

4. Secure the caliper aside with mechanics wire.

5. Pull the rotor from the hub. Inspect the rotor and refinish or replace, as necessary. If refinishing, check the minimum thickness specification.

To install:

6. Position the rotor onto the hub.

7. Remove the mechanics wire and position the caliper.

8. Install the 2 caliper mounting bolts and tighten to 29–36 ft. lbs. (39–49 Nm).

9. Install the wheel and tire assembly and lower the vehicle.

REAR BRAKE ROTOR

1. Raise and safely support the vehicle.

2. Remove the wheel and tire assembly.

3. Remove the brake pads.

4. Remove the 2 rotor mounting screws.

5. Using a suitable tool, pivot the caliper on its mounting bracket and remove the rotor. Inspect the rotor and refinish or replace, as necessary. If refinishing, check the minimum thickness specification.

To install:

6. Using a suitable tool, pivot the caliper on its mounting bracket and position the rotor.

7. Install the 2 mounting screws.

8. Install the brake pads.

9. Install the wheel and tire assembly and lower the vehicle.

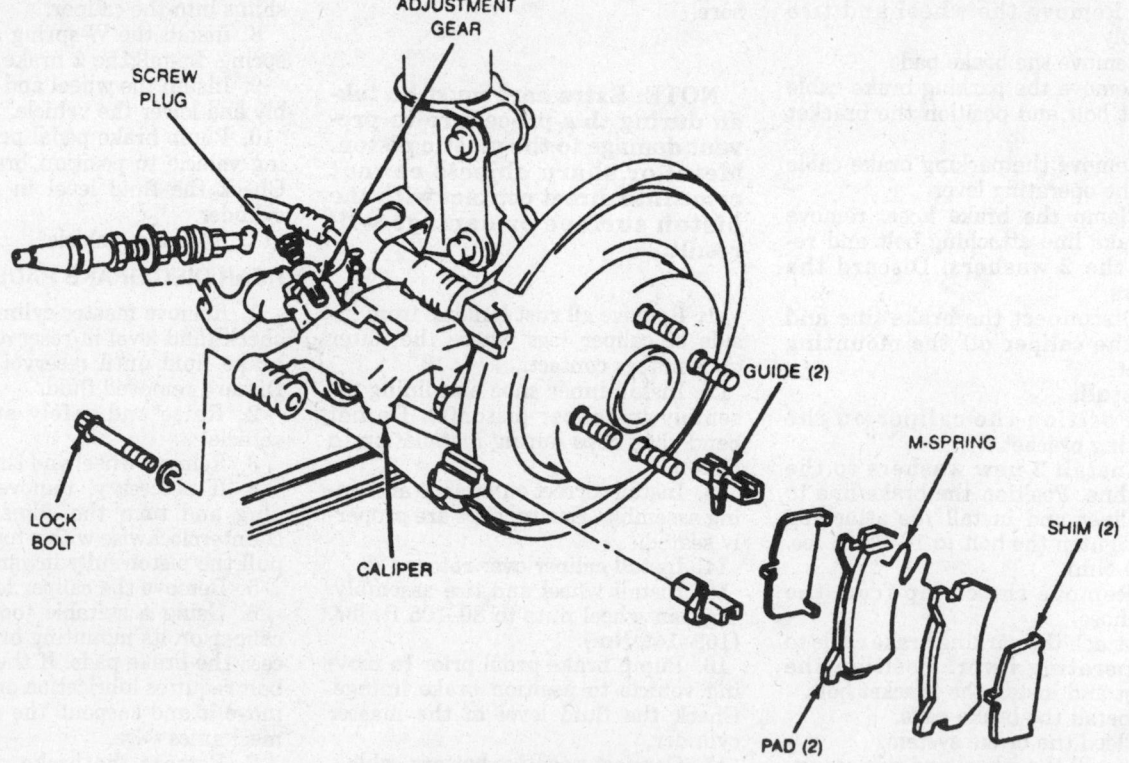

Rear disc brake pad assembly—1991–93 Escort

Brake Drums

REMOVAL & INSTALLATION

Except 1991–93 Escort and Tempo and Topaz With All Wheel Drive

1. Raise and safely support the vehicle.
2. Remove wheel and tire assembly.
3. Remove grease cap from hub. Remove cotter pin, nut lock, adjusting nut and keyed flat washer from spindle. Remove outer bearing.
4. Remove hub and drum assembly as a unit.

NOTE: If the hub/drum assembly will not come off, pry the rubber plug from the backing plate inspection hole. On vehicles with 7 in. brakes, insert a suitable tool in the hole until it contacts the adjuster assembly pivot. Apply side pressure on this pivot point to allow the adjuster quadrant to ratchet and release the brake adjustment. On vehicles with 8 in. brakes, remove the brake line-to-axle retention bracket. This will allow sufficient room for insertion of suitable tools to disengage the adjusting lever and back-off the adjusting screw.

5. Inspect the brake drum and refinish or replace, as necessary. If refinishing, check the maximum inside diameter specification.

To install:

6. Inspect and lubricate bearings, as necessary. Replace grease seal if any damage is visible.
7. Clean spindle stem and apply a thin coat of wheel bearing grease.
8. Install hub and drum assembly on spindle.
9. Install outer bearing into hub on spindle.
10. Install keyed flat washer and adjusting nut. Tighten nut finger-tight.
11. Adjust wheel bearing. Install nut retainer and a new cotter pin.
12. Install grease cap.
13. Install wheel and tire assembly. Tighten wheel nuts to 80–105 ft. lbs. (109–142 Nm).
14. Pump brake pedal prior to moving vehicle to position brake linings.
15. Connect negative battery cable.
16. Road test vehicle.

1991–93 Escort and Tempo and Topaz With All Wheel Drive

1. Raise and safely support the vehicle.
2. Remove wheel and tire assembly.
3. Remove the spring nut or attaching screws, if necessary.
4. Pull the brake drum from the hub. Inspect the drum and refinish or replace, as necessary. If refinishing, check the maximum inside diameter specification.

To install:

5. Position the brake drum on the hub.
6. Install the 2 drum attaching screws, if applicable.
7. Install the wheel and tire assembly and lower the vehicle.

Brake Shoes

REMOVAL & INSTALLATION

Except Tempo, Topaz, 1991–93 Escort and 1989–90 Escort With 8 Inch Brake Shoes

1. Raise and safely support the vehicle.
2. Remove wheel and tire assembly.
3. Remove hub and drum assembly.
4. Remove hold-down spring and pins.
5. Lift brake shoe and adjuster assembly up and away from anchor block and shoe guide. Do not damage the boots when rotating shoes off the wheel cylinder.
6. Remove the parking brake cable end from the parking brake lever to allow removal of the brake shoe and adjuster assembly.
7. Remove lower shoe-to-shoe spring from leading and trailing shoe slots.
8. Hold brake shoe/adjuster assembly and remove leading shoe-to-adjuster strut retracting spring. This can be done by rotating shoe over adjuster quadrant until spring is slack and then disconnecting spring. The leading shoe should now be free.
9. Remove trailing shoe-to-parking brake strut retracting spring by pivoting strut downward until it disengages from trailing shoe.
10. Disassemble adjuster, if necessary, by pulling quadrant away from knurled pin in strut and rotating quadrant in either direction until quadrant teeth are no longer meshed with pin. Remove spring and slide quadrant out of slot. Do not overstress spring during disassembly.
11. Remove parking brake lever from trailing shoe and lining assembly by removing horeshoe retaining clip and spring washer, and lifting lever off pin on brake shoe.

To install:

12. Apply light coating of high temperature grease at points where brake shoes contact the backing plate.
13. Apply light uniform coating of multi-purpose lubricant to strut at contact surface between strut and adjuster quadrant.

14. Install adjuster quadrant pin into slot in strut and install adjuster spring. Pivot quadrant until it meshes with knurled pin in third and fourth notch of outboard end of quadrant.
15. Assemble parking brake lever to trailing shoe. Install spring washer and new horseshoe clip. Crimp clip until lever is securely fastened.
16. Install trailing shoe-to-parking brake strut retracting spring by attaching spring to slots in each part and pivoting strut into position to tension spring. Make sure the end of the spring, with the hook that is parallel to the center line of the coils, is installed in hole in shoe web. Installed spring should be flat against shoe web and parallel to strut.
17. Install lower shoe-to-shoe retracting spring between leading and trailing shoes. The spring hook with the longest straight section fits into hole in trailing shoe.
18. Install leading shoe-to-adjuster/strut retracting spring by installing spring to both parts and pivoting leading shoe over quadrant into position to tension spring.
19. Expand shoe and strut assembly to fit over anchor plate and wheel cylinder piston inserts.
20. Attach parking brake cable to parking brake lever.
21. Install hold-down pins and springs on each shoe and lining assembly.
22. Set brake shoe diameter using a suitable brake adjusting gauge.
23. Install hub/drum and wheel and tire assemblies.
24. Adjust wheel bearings.
25. Lower vehicle and check brake operation. Adjust the parking brake.

Tempo, Topaz and 1989–90 Escort With 8 Inch Brake Shoes

1. Raise and safely support the vehicle.
2. Remove the wheel, tire, and hub and drum assembly.
3. Remove 2 shoe hold-down springs and pins.
4. Lift the brake shoes, springs and adjuster assembly off backing plate and wheel cylinder assembly. Be careful not to bend adjusting lever during assembly removal.
5. Remove the parking brake cable from the parking brake lever.
6. Remove the retracting springs from the lower brake shoe attachments and upper shoe-to-adjusting lever attachment points. This will separate the brake shoes and disengage the adjuster mechanism.
7. Remove the horseshoe retaining clip and spring washer and slide the lever off the parking brake lever pin on the trailing shoe.

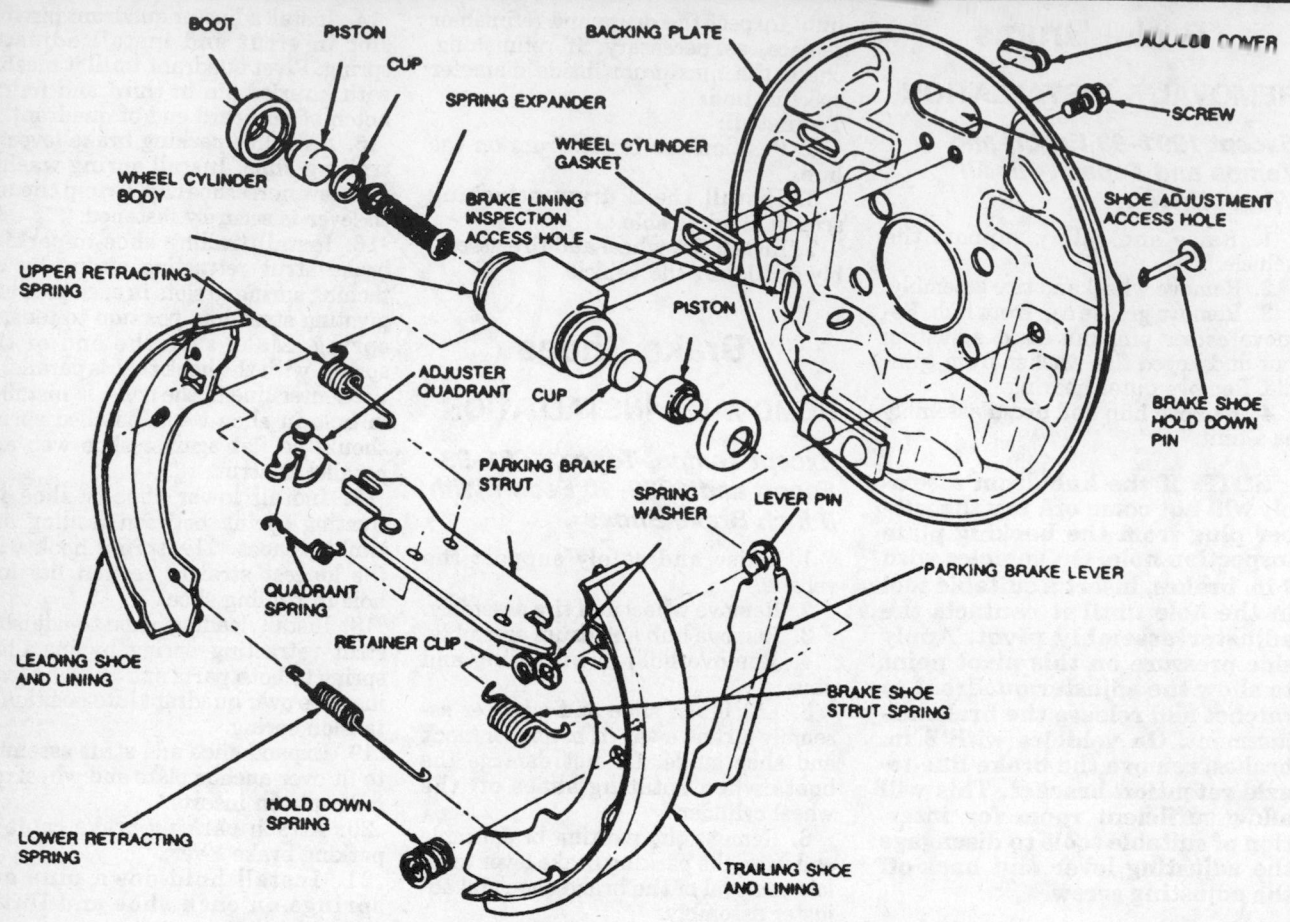

Rear brake assembly—1989–90 Escort with 7 inch brake shoes

To install:

8. Apply a light coating of high temperature grease at the points where the brake shoes contact the backing plate.

9. Apply a light coating of lubricant to the adjuster screw threads and the socket end of the adjusting screw. Install the stainless steel washer over the socket end of the adjusting screw and install the socket. Turn the adjusting screw into the adjusting pivot nut to the limit of the threads and then back-off ½ turn.

10. Assemble the parking brake lever to the trailing shoe by installing the spring washer and a new horseshoe retaining clip. Crimp the clip until it retains the lever to the shoe securely.

11. Attach the parking brake cable to the parking brake lever.

12. Attach the lower shoe retracting spring to the leading and trailing shoe assemblies and install to backing plate. It will be necessary to stretch the retracting spring as the shoes are installed downward over the anchor plate to inside of shoe retaining plate.

13. Install the adjuster screw assembly between the leading shoe slot and the slot in the trailing shoe and parking brake lever. The adjuster socket end slot must fit into the trailing shoe and parking brake lever.

NOTE: The adjuster socket blade is marked R or L for the right or left brake assemblies. The R or L adjuster blade must be installed with the letter R or L in the upright position, facing the wheel cylinder, on the correct side to ensure that the deeper of the 2 slots in the adjuster sockets fits into the parking brake lever.

14. Assemble the adjuster lever in the groove located in the parking brake lever pin and into the slot of the adjuster socket that fits into the trailing shoe web.

15. Attach the upper retracting spring to the leading shoe slot. Using a suitable spring tool, stretch the other end of the spring into the notch on the adjuster lever. If the adjuster lever does not contact the star wheel after installing the spring, it is possible that the adjuster socket is installed incorrectly.

16. Set the brake shoe diameter using a suitable brake adjusting gauge.

17. Install the hub/drum and wheel/tire assemblies and adjust the wheel bearings.

18. Lower the vehicle and check brake operation.

1991–93 Escort

1. Raise and safely support the vehicle.

2. Remove the wheel and tire assembly and remove the brake drum.

3. Remove the 2 brake shoe return springs.

4. Remove the anti-rattle spring.

5. Push and turn the 2 brake shoe hold-down clips and remove the clips.

6. Remove the leading and trailing shoes from the backing plate.

To install:

7. Use a suitable high temperature grease to lubricate the brake shoe contact points on the backing plate.

8. Position the trailing brake shoe on the backing plate and install 1 of the brake shoe hold-down clips.

9. Position the leading brake shoe on the backing plate and install the other brake shoe hold-down clip.

10. Install the anti-rattle spring.

11. Install the 2 brake shoe return springs.

12. Press the brake pedal to verify operation of the automatic brake adjuster.

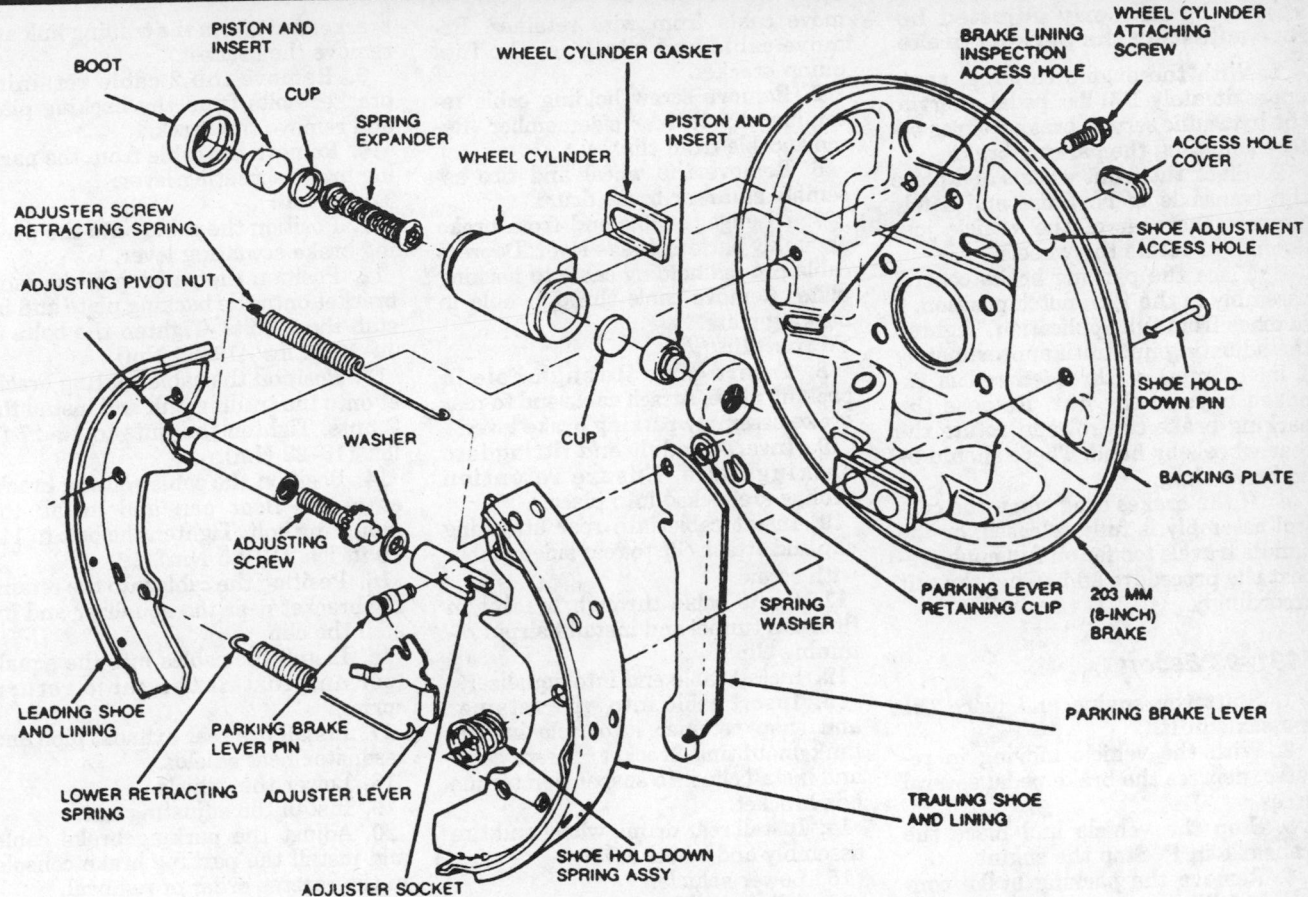

Rear brake assembly—Tempo, Topaz and 1989–90 Escort with 8 inch brake shoes

13. Install the brake drum and the wheel and tire assembly. Lower the vehicle.
14. Firmly apply the brakes 2 or 3 times to adjust the rear brakes.

Wheel Cylinder

REMOVAL & INSTALLATION

Except 1991–93 Escort

1. Raise and safely support the vehicle. Remove wheel/tire and hub/drum assemblies.
2. Remove brake shoe assembly.
3. Disconnect brake tube from wheel cylinder.
4. Remove wheel cylinder attaching bolts and remove wheel cylinder.

NOTE: Use caution to prevent brake fluid from contacting brake linings and drum braking surface. Contaminated linings must be replaced.

To install:

5. Ensure ends of hydraulic fittings are free of foreign matter before making connections.
6. Position wheel cylinder and foam seal on backing plate and finger-tighten brake tube to cylinder.

7. Secure cylinder to backing plate by installing attaching bolts. Tighten bolts to 9–13 ft. lbs. (12–18 Nm).
8. Tighten tube nut fitting.
9. Install and adjust brakes.
10. Install hub/drum and wheel assembly.
11. Bleed brake system and lower the vehicle.

1991–93 Escort

1. Raise and safely support the vehicle.
2. Remove the wheel and tire assembly and remove the brake drum.
3. Remove the upper brake shoe return spring.
4. Clamp the wheel cylinder brake hose.
5. Using a suitable flare nut wrench, loosen the wheel cylinder-to-brake line flare nut.
6. Pull the clip from the brake hose retaining bracket and remove the brake hose from the retaining bracket.
7. Remove the brake line from the wheel cylinder.
8. Remove the 2 wheel cylinder mounting bolts and remove the wheel cylinder from the backing plate.
9. Remove and discard the wheel cylinder gasket.

To install:

10. Install a new wheel cylinder gasket onto the backing plate.
11. Position the wheel cylinder onto the backing plate and install the 2 mounting bolts. Tighten the bolts to 89–115 inch lbs. (10–13 Nm).
12. Position the brake line into the wheel cylinder fitting and tighten the wheel cylinder-to-brake line flare nut to 12–16 ft. lbs. (16–22 Nm).
13. Position the brake hose into the retaining bracket and install the clip. Remove the clamp from the wheel cylinder brake hose.
14. Install the brake shoe return spring.
15. Press the brake pedal to verify the operation of the automatic brake adjuster.
16. Install the brake drum and the wheel and tire assembly.
17. Bleed the brake system and lower the vehicle.

Parking Brake Cable

ADJUSTMENT

Except 1991–93 Escort

NOTE: The rear brake shoes

should be properly adjusted before adjusting the parking brake.

1. With the engine running, apply approximately 100 lbs. pedal effort to the hydraulic service brake 3 times before adjusting the parking brake.

2. Block the front wheels and place the transaxle in **N**. Raise and safely support the rear of the vehicle just enough to rotate the wheels.

3. Place the parking brake control assembly in the 12th notch position, 2 notches from full application. Tighten the adjusting nut until approximately 1 in. (25mm) of threaded rod is exposed beyond the nut. Release the parking brake control and rotate the rear wheels by hand. There should be no brake drag.

4. If the brakes drag when the control assembly is fully released, or the handle travels too far on full apply, repeat the procedure and adjust the nut accordingly.

1991–93 Escort

1. Start the engine and place the transaxle in **R**.

2. With the vehicle moving in reverse, depress the brake pedal several times.

3. Stop the vehicle and place the transaxle in **P**. Stop the engine.

4. Remove the parking brake console as follows:

   a. Remove the rear seat ash tray.

   b. Position both front seats to the rear-most position.

   c. Remove the 2 front retaining screws from the parking brake console.

   d. Recline both front seats.

   e. Remove the 2 rear retaining screws and with the parking brake engaged, remove the parking brake console.

   f. Release the parking brake lever.

5. Turn the adjusting nut until the parking brake lever stroke is 5–7 notches when pulled with a force of 22 lbs.

6. Install the parking brake console by reversing the removal procedure.

REMOVAL & INSTALLATION

Except 1991–93 Escort

1. Place control assembly in seventh notch position and loosen adjusting nut. Completely release control assembly.

2. Raise and safely support the vehicle. Remove rear parking brake cable from equalizer.

3. Remove hairpin clip holding cable to floor pan tunnel bracket.

4. Remove wire retainer holding cable to fuel tank mounting bracket. Remove cable from wire retainer. Remove cable and clip from the fuel pump bracket.

5. Remove screw holding cable retaining clip to rear sidemember. Remove cable from clip.

6. Remove the wheel and tire assembly and rear brake drum.

7. Disengage cable end from brake assembly parking brake lever. Depress cable prongs holding cable to backing plate. Remove cable through hole in backing plate.

To install:

8. Insert cable through hole in backing plate. Attach cable end to rear brake assembly parking brake lever.

9. Insert conduit end fitting into backing plate. Ensure retention prongs are locked into place.

10. Insert cable into rear attaching clip and attach clip to rear sidemember with screw.

11. Route cable through bracket in floorpan tunnel and install hairpin retaining clip.

12. Install cable end into equalizer.

13. Insert cable into wire retainer and snap retainer into hole in fuel tank mounting bracket. Insert cable and install clip into suspension torque box bracket.

14. Install rear drum, wheel and tire assembly and wheel cover.

15. Lower vehicle.

16. Adjust parking brake.

1991–93 Escort

1. Remove the parking brake console as follows:

   a. Remove the rear seat ash tray.

   b. Position both front seats to the rear-most position.

   c. Remove the 2 front retaining screws from the parking brake console.

   d. Recline both front seats.

   e. Remove the 2 rear retaining screws and with the parking brake engaged, remove the parking brake console.

   f. Release the parking brake lever.

2. Remove the cable adjusting nut.

3. Raise and safely support the vehicle.

4. Remove the rear exhaust pipe and resonator heat shields.

5. Disconnect the equalizer return spring and remove the cables from the equalizer.

6. Remove the clip that attaches the cable to the retaining bracket located near the equalizer. Remove the cable from the bracket.

7. Remove the cable routing bracket bolt from the floorpan and remove the bracket.

8. Remove the 2 cable routing bracket nuts from the trailing link and remove the bracket.

9. Remove the 2 cable retaining bracket bolts from the backing plate and remove the bracket.

10. Remove the cable from the parking brake actuating lever.

To install:

11. Position the cable onto the parking brake actuating lever.

12. Position the parking brake cable bracket onto the backing plate and install the 2 bolts. Tighten the bolts to 14–19 ft. lbs. (19–25 Nm).

13. Position the cable routing bracket onto the trailing link and install the 2 nuts. Tighten the nuts to 12–17 ft. lbs. (16–23 Nm).

14. Position the cable routing bracket to the floor pan and install the mounting bolt. Tighten the bolt to 14–19 ft. lbs. (19–25 Nm).

15. Position the cable into the retaining bracket near the equalizer and install the clip.

16. Install the cables into the equalizer and install the cable return spring.

17. Install the rear exhaust pipe and resonator heat shields.

18. Lower the vehicle.

19. Install the adjusting nut.

20. Adjust the parking brake cable and install the parking brake console in the reverse order of removal.

Brake System Bleeding

1. Clean all the dirt from around the master cylinder filler cap.

2. Fill the reservoir with brake fluid. The reservoir must be at least ¾ full throughout the bleeding procedure.

3. If the master cylinder is known or suspected to have air in bore, it must be bled before any wheel cylinders or calipers.

4. To bleed the master cylinder, loosen 1 outlet fitting aproximately ¾ turn. Have an assistant push the brake pedal down slowly through full travel. Close the outlet fitting, then return the pedal slowly to the full released position. Wait 5 seconds, then repeat the operation until the air bubbles cease to appear.

5. Loosen the other outlet fitting approximately ¾ turn and repeat Step 4.

6. To continue to bleed the system, remove the rubber cap dust cap from the wheel cylinder bleeder fitting or caliper fitting. Check to make sure the bleeder fitting is positioned at the upper half on the front of the caliper, if not the caliper is located on the wrong side.

7. Attach a suitable length of rub-

ber hose to the fitting. Submerge the free end of the hose in a container partially filled with clean brake fluid and loosen the bleeder fitting approximately ¾ of a turn.

8. Have the assistant push brake pedal down slowly through full travel. Close the bleeder fitting, then return the pedal to the full release position. Wait 5 seconds, then repeat this operation until the air bubbles cease to appear at the submerged end of the bleeder hose.

9. When the fluid is completely free of air bubbles, properly tighten the bleeder fitting and reinstall the rubber dust cap. Repeat this process on the opposite diagonal system. Refill the master cylinder reservoir after each wheel cylinder or caliper is bled and reinstall the master cylinder cap.

NOTE: If all wheels are to be bled, proceed as follows: right rear, left front, left rear and right front.

10. When the bleeding operation is completed, the fluid level should be filled to the maximum fill level indicated on the reservoir. Always ensure the disc brake pistons are returned to their normal positions by depressing the brake pedal several times until the normal pedal travel is established. Check the pedal feel. If the pedal feels spongy, repeat the bleeding procedure.

CHASSIS ELECTRICAL

Air Bag

A driver's side air bag can be installed as optional equipment on Tempo and Topaz vehicles.

DISARMING

1989–91 Vehicles

1. Disconnect the negative battery cable.

NOTE: On most vehicles equipped with an air bag, a backup power supply is included in the system to provide air bag deployment in the event the battery or cables are damaged in an accident before the sensors can close. The power supply is a capacitor that will leak down in approximately 15 minutes after the battery is disconnected or 1 minute if the battery positive cable is grounded. If the system is equipped with a backup power supply, it must be disconnected to disarm the system.

2. Remove the 2 screws retaining the steering column opening cover to the instrument panel and remove the cover.

3. Remove the 4 bolts retaining the bolster and remove the bolster.

4. Disconnect the backup power supply connector.

5. Remove the 4 nut and washer assemblies retaining the driver air bag to the steering wheel.

6. Disconnect the driver air bag connector.

7. Attach a jumper wire to the air bag terminals on the clockspring.

8. Connect the backup power supply and negative battery cable.

1992–93 Vehicles

1. Disconnect the positive battery cable.

2. Wait 1 minute for the backup power supply to deplete its stored energy.

3. Remove the 4 nut and washer assemblies retaining the air bag to the steering wheel.

4. Disconnect the air bag electrical connector.

5. Attach air bag simulator tool 105–00008 or equivalent on the clockspring to simulate the air bag.

6. Connect the positive battery cable.

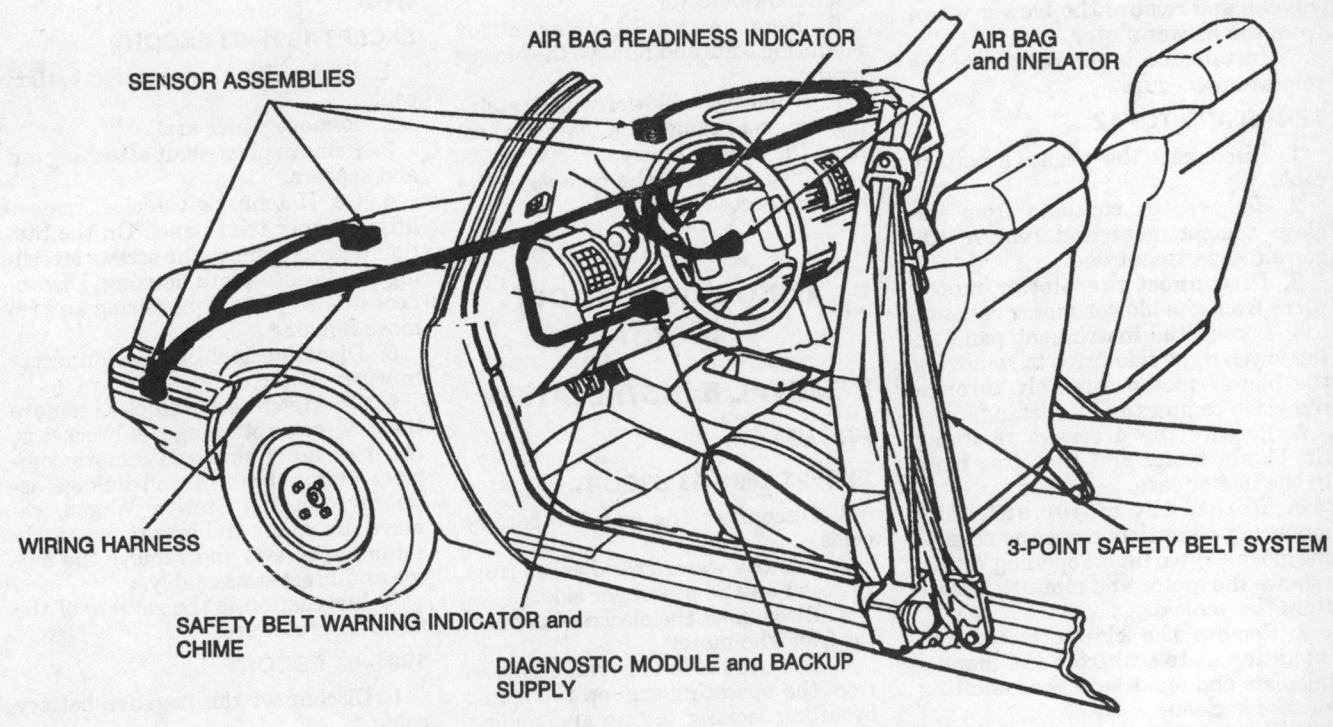

Air bag system component locations – Tempo and Topaz

Heater Blower Motor

REMOVAL & INSTALLATION

Without Air Conditioning

1989–90 ESCORT

1. Disconnect the negative battery cable.
2. Remove the glove compartment door from the instrument panel.
3. Remove the 6 screws attaching the air inlet lower duct to the blower housing and upper inlet duct and remove the lower air inlet duct.
4. Remove the pushnut from the blower wheel hub and pull the blower wheel from the blower motor shaft.
5. Remove the blower motor flange attaching screws located inside the blower housing.
6. Pull the blower motor out from the blower housing and disconnect the blower motor wires from the motor.
7. Installation is the reverse of the removal procedure.

1991–93 ESCORT

1. Disconnect the negative battery cable.
2. Remove the trim panel below the glove compartment.
3. Remove the wiring bracket and bolt.
4. Disconnect the blower motor electrical connector.
5. Remove the 3 blower motor mounting bolts and remove the blower motor.
6. Remove the blower wheel retaining clip and remove the blower wheel from the blower motor.
7. Installation is the reverse of the removal procedure.

TEMPO AND TOPAZ

1. Disconnect the negative battery cable.
2. Remove the contents from the glove compartment and remove the glove compartment door.
3. Disconnect the blower motor wires from the blower motor resistor.
4. Loosen the instrument panel at the lower right side prior to removing the blower motor assembly through the glove compartment opening.
5. Remove the 4 screws retaining the blower motor and mounting plate to the heater case.
6. Rotate the motor until the mounting plate flats clear the edge of the glove compartment opening. Then, remove the motor and mounting plate from the vehicle.
7. Remove the blower motor and mounting plate seal from the mounting plate and make sure the mounting surface is clean.
8. Remove the pushnut from the blower wheel shaft and remove the blower wheel from the motor shaft.
9. Installation is the reverse of the removal procedure. Be sure to use a new mounting plate seal.

With Air Conditioning

EXCEPT 1991–93 ESCORT

1. Disconnect the negative battery cable.
2. Remove the contents from the glove compartment and remove the glove compartment door.
3. Disconnect the blower motor wires from the blower motor resistor.
4. Loosen the instrument panel at the lower right side prior to removing the motor through the glove compartment opening.
5. Remove the blower motor and mounting plate from the evaporator case.
6. Rotate the motor until the mounting plate flat clears the edge of the glove compartment opening and remove the motor.
7. Remove the pushnut from the blower motor shaft. Then, remove the blower wheel from the motor shaft.
8. Installation is the reverse of the removal procedure.

1991–93 ESCORT

1. Disconnect the negative battery cable.
2. Remove the trim panel below the glove compartment.
3. Remove the wiring bracket and bolt.
4. Disconnect the blower motor electrical connector.
5. Remove the 3 blower motor mounting bolts and remove the blower motor.
6. Remove the blower wheel retaining clip and remove the blower wheel from the blower motor.
7. Installation is the reverse of the removal procedure.

Windshield Wiper Motor

REMOVAL & INSTALLATION

FRONT

EXCEPT 1991–93 ESCORT

1. Disconnect the negative battery cable.
2. Lift the water shield cover from the cowl on the passenger side.
3. Disconnect the electrical connector from the motor.
4. Remove the linkage retaining clip from the operating arm on the motor by lifting locking tab up and pulling clip away from pin.
5. Remove the 3 retaining bolts from the motor and bracket assembly.
6. Remove the operating arm from the motor. Unscrew the 3 bolts and separate the motor from the mounting bracket, if necessary.
7. Installation is the reverse of the removal procedure.

1991–93 ESCORT

1. Disconnect the negative battery cable.
2. Remove the wiper arm attaching nut covers, remove the attaching nuts and pull the wiper arms from the pivot shafts.
3. With the hood closed, remove the 7 screw covers.
4. Remove the 7 cowl grille retaining screws and remove the cowl grille.
5. Pry up the 4 baffle retaining clips and remove the baffle trim piece.

NOTE: Make sure the motor is in the PARK position before disconnecting the linkage.

6. Remove the wiper linkage retaining clip and disconnect the wiper linkage from the motor.
7. Disconnect the 2 motor electrical connectors.
8. Remove the 3 motor mounting bolts until they are loose from the sheet metal mounting surface. Remove the motor.
9. Installation is the reverse of the removal procedure. Tighten the 3 motor mounting bolts to 61–87 inch lbs. (7–9 Nm).

Rear

EXCEPT 1991–93 ESCORT

1. Disconnect the negative battery cable.
2. Remove wiper arm.
3. Remove pivot shaft attaching nut and spacers.
4. On Hatchback vehicles, remove liftgate inner trim panel. On the Station Wagon, remove the screws attaching the license plate housing. Disconnect license plate light wiring and remove housing.
5. Disconnect electrical connector to wiper motor.
6. On Hatchback vehicles, remove the 3 screws retaining the bracket to the door inner skin and remove complete motor, bracket and linkage assembly. On the Station Wagon, remove the motor and bracket assembly retaining screws and remove the motor and bracket assembly.
7. Installation is the reverse of the removal procedure.

1991–93 ESCORT

1. Disconnect the negative battery cable.
2. Remove the wiper arm by lifting

the wiper arm attaching nut cover, removing the attaching nut and pulling the wiper arm from the pivot shaft.

3. Remove the shaft seal from the outer bushing attaching nut.

4. Remove the outer bushing attaching nut and remove the outer bushing.

5. Remove the liftgate trim panel.

6. Disconnect the wiper motor electrical connector.

7. Remove the 3 wiper motor mounting bolts and washers and remove the wiper motor.

8. Installation is the reverse of the removal procedure. Tighten the mounting bolts to 61–87 inch lbs. (7–9 Nm) and the outer bushing attaching nut to 35–52 inch lbs. (4–6 Nm).

Windshield Wiper Switch

REMOVAL & INSTALLATION

1989–90 Escort

EXCEPT TILT STEERING WHEEL

NOTE: The switch handle is an integral part of the switch and cannot be removed separately.

1. Disconnect the negative battery cable.

2. Remove upper and lower steering column shrouds.

3. Disconnect the electrical connector.

4. Peel back the foam sight shield. Remove the 2 screws holding the switch and remove the wash/wiper switch.

5. Installation is the reverse of removal procedure.

TILT STEERING WHEEL

1. Disconnect the negative battery cable.

2. Remove the steering column shroud.

3. Peel back the side shield and disconnect the switch wiring connector.

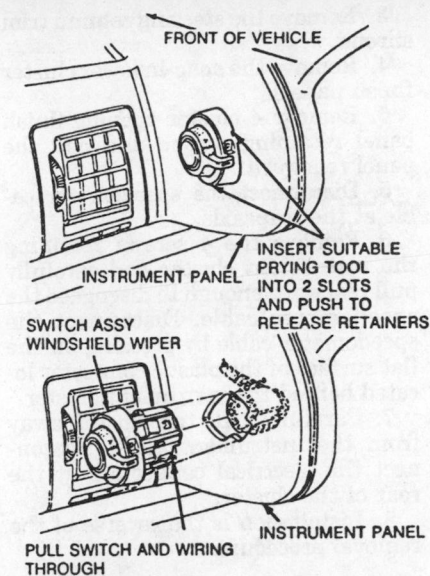

INSERT SUITABLE PRYING TOOL INTO 2 SLOTS AND PUSH TO RELEASE RETAINERS

FRONT OF VEHICLE

INSTRUMENT PANEL

SWITCH ASSY WINDSHIELD WIPER

INSTRUMENT PANEL

PULL SWITCH AND WIRING THROUGH HOLE AND DISENGAGE CONNECTOR

Wiper switch installation—Tempo and Topaz

4. Remove the screw attaching the wiring retainer to the steering column.

5. Grasp the switch handle and pull straight out to disengage the wiper switch from the turn signal switch.

6. Installation is the reverse of the removal procedure.

1991–93 Escort

Windshield wiper control is a function of the combination switch.

Tempo and Topaz

1. Disconnect the negative battery cable.

2. Insert a suitable prying tool into the small slot on top of the switch bezel. Push down on the tool to work the top of the switch bezel away from the instrument panel.

3. Insert the prying tool into the small slot on the bottom of the switch bezel. Push up on the tool to work the bottom of the switch bezel away from the instrument panel.

4. Remove the switch from the panel opening. Hold the switch and pull the wiring at the rear of the switch until the switch connector can be easily disconnected. Disconnect the connector and allow the wiring to hang from the switch mounting opening.

To install:

5. Connect the wiring connector to the new switch and route the wiring back into the mounting opening. Insert the switch into the opening so the graphics are properly aligned.

6. Push on the switch until the bezel seats against the instrument panel and the clips lock the switch into place.

7. Connect the negative battery cable.

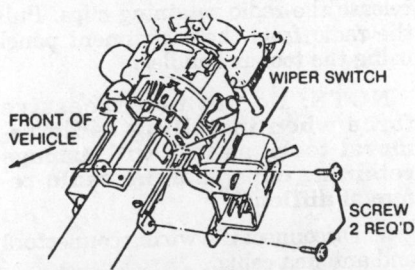

FRONT OF VEHICLE

WIPER SWITCH

SCREW 2 REQ'D

Wiper switch installation—1989–90 Escort without tilt steering wheel

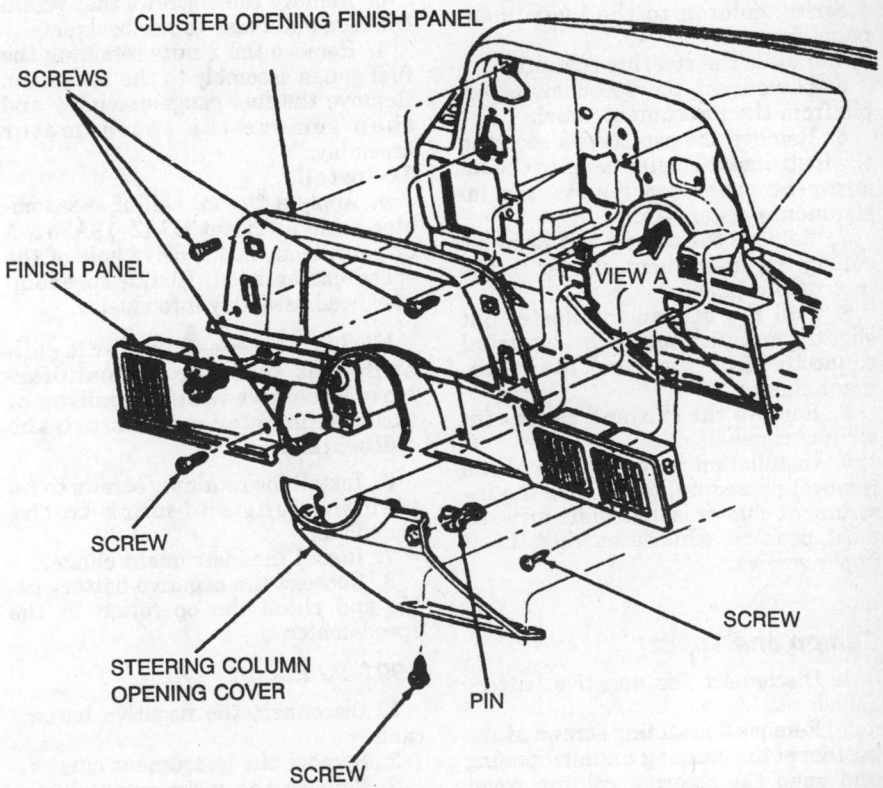

CLUSTER OPENING FINISH PANEL

SCREWS

FINISH PANEL

VIEW A

SCREW

STEERING COLUMN OPENING COVER

PIN

SCREW

SCREW

Instrument cluster panel installation—1989–90 Escort

Instrument Cluster

REMOVAL & INSTALLATION

Escort

1989–90

1. Disconnect the negative battery cable.

2. Remove the 2 retaining screws at the bottom of the steering column opening and snap the steering column cover out.

3. Remove the 10 cluster opening finish panel retainer screws and remove the finish panel.

4. Remove the 2 upper and lower screws retaining the cluster to the instrument panel.

5. Reach under the instrument panel and disconnect the speedometer cable by pressing down on the flat surface of the plastic connector (quick connect).

6. Pull the cluster away from the instrument panel. Disconnect the cluster feed plug from its receptacle in the printed circuit.

7. Installation is the reverse of the removal procedure.

1991–93

1. Disconnect the negative battery cable.

2. If equipped with a tilt column, tilt the steering wheel down.

3. If equipped with a standard column, remove the 4 bolts securing the steering column to the instrument panel frame.

4. Lower the steering column.

5. Disconnect the speedometer cable from the instrument panel.

6. Remove the cap screws securing the instrument cluster bezel to the instrument panel and remove the instrument cluster bezel.

7. Remove the screws and bolts securing the instrument cluster to the instrument panel.

8. Pull the instrument cluster out slightly and disconnect the electrical connectors from the rear of the instrument cluster.

9. Remove the cluster from the instrument panel.

10. Installation is the reverse of the removal procedure. Make sure the instrument cluster is held in its forward most position while attaching the 2 upper screws.

Tempo and Topaz

1. Disconnect the negative battery cable.

2. Remove 2 retaining screws at the bottom of the steering column opening and snap the steering column cover out.

3. Remove the steering column trim shroud.

4. Remove the snap-in lower cluster finish panels.

5. Remove 4 cluster opening finish panel retaining screws and pull the panel rearward.

5. Disconnect the speedometer cable at the transaxle.

6. Remove the 4 screws retaining the instrument cluster and carefully pull rearward enough to disengage the speedometer cable. Disconnect the speedometer cable by pressing on the flat surface of the plastic connector located behind the instrument cluster.

7. Carefully pull the cluster away from the instrument panel. Disconnect the electrical connectors at the rear of the cluster.

8. Installation is the reverse of the removal procedure.

NOTE: If gauges are being removed from the cluster assembly, do not remove the gauge pointer because the magnetic gauges cannot be recalibrated.

Speedometer

REMOVAL & INSTALLATION

Except 1991–93 Escort

1. Disconnect the negative battery cable.

2. Remove the instrument cluster.

3. Remove the 7 screws that retain the lens and mask to the backplate.

4. Remove the 2 nuts retaining the fuel gauge assembly to the backplate. Remove the fuel gauge assembly and then remove the speedometer assembly.

To install:

5. Apply a $3/16$ in. ball of speedometer cable lubricant D7AZ–19A331–A or equivalent, in the drive hole of the speedometer head. Install speedometer head assembly into cluster.

NOTE: The speedometer is calibrated at the time of manufacture. Excessive rough handling of the speedometer may disturb the calibration.

6. Install the retaining screws to retain the lens and mask to the backplate.

7. Install the instrument cluster.

8. Connect the negative battery cable and check the operation of the speedometer.

1991–93 Escort

1. Disconnect the negative battery cable.

2. Remove the instrument cluster.

3. Remove the instrument cluster lens and shroud.

4. Remove the speedometer from the instrument cluster.

5. Installation is the reverse of the removal procedure. Be careful when handling the speedometer so as not to disturb the factory calibration.

Radio

REMOVAL & INSTALLATION

Escort

1989–90

1. Disconnect the negative battery cable.

2. Remove the center instrument trim panel.

3. Remove the 4 screws retaining the radio and mounting bracket to the instrument panel.

4. Pull the radio to the front and raise the back end of the radio slightly so the rear support bracket clears the clip in the instrument panel. Pull the radio out of the instrument panel slowly.

5. Disconnect the wiring connectors and antenna cable.

6. Transfer the mounting brackets to the new radio, if necessary.

7. Installation is the reverse of the removal procedure. Tighten the retaining screws to 14–16 inch lbs. (1.5–1.9 Nm).

1991–93

1. Disconnect the negative battery cable.

2. Using radio removal tools T87P–19061–A or equivalent, pull the radio out from its mounting position so the antenna and the electrical connectors are accessible.

3. Disconnect the antenna lead and the radio electrical connectors from the radio.

4. Remove the radio.

5. Installation is the reverse of the removal procedure.

Tempo and Topaz

1. Disconnect the negative battery cable.

2. Insert radio removal tools T87P–19061–A or equivalent, into the radio face plate. Press in 1 in. (25.4mm) to release the radio retaining clips. Pull the radio from the instrument panel using the tool as handles.

NOTE: Do not use excessive force when installing radio removal tools, as this will damage retaining clips, making radio removal difficult.

3. Disconnect the wiring connectors and antenna cable.

4. Transfer the rear mounting bracket to the new radio, if necessary.

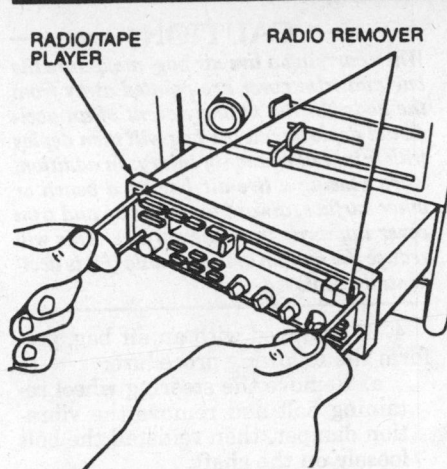

RADIO/TAPE PLAYER   RADIO REMOVER

Radio removal procedure—Tempo, Topaz and 1991–93 Escort

5. Installation is the reverse of the removal procedure.

Headlight Switch

REMOVAL & INSTALLATION

Except 1991–93 Escort

1. Disconnect the negative battery cable.

2. On vehicles without air conditioning, remove the left side air vent control cable retaining screws and let the cable hang.

3. Remove the fuse panel bracket retaining screws. Move the fuse panel assembly aside to gain access to the headlight switch.

4. Pull the headlight knob out to the **ON** position. Depress the headlight knob and shaft retainer button and remove the knob and shaft assembly from the switch.

5. Remove the headlight switch retaining bezel. Disconnect the multiple connector plug and remove the switch from the instrument panel.

To install:

6. Install the headlight switch into the instrument panel. Connect the

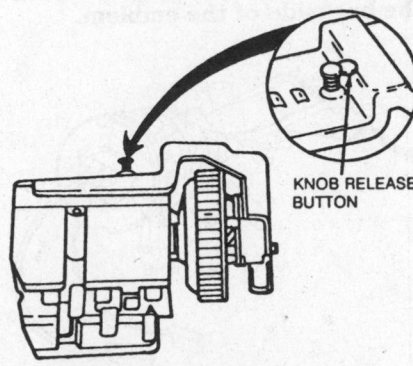

KNOB RELEASE BUTTON

Headlight switch—except 1991–93 Escort

multiple connector and install the headlight switch retaining bezel.

7. Install the knob and shaft assembly by inserting the shaft into the switch and gently pushing until the shaft locks in position.

8. Move the fuse panel back into position and install the fuse panel bracket with the 2 retaining screws.

9. On vehicles without air conditioning, install the left side air vent control cable and bracket.

10. Connect the negative battery cable.

Combination Switch

On Tempo, Topaz and 1989–90 Escort, the combination switch assembly is a multi-function switch comprising turn signal, hazard, headlight dimmer and flash-to-pass functions. The switch lever on the left side of the upper steering column controls the turn signal, headlight dimmer and flash-to-pass functions. The hazard function is controlled by the actuating knob on the lower side of the upper steering column.

On 1991–93 Escort, the combination switch assembly is a multi-function switch that controls the headlights, parking lights and taillights, the turn signals, headlight dimmer and window wipers.

REMOVAL & INSTALLATION

Except 1991–93 Escort

1. Disconnect the negative battery cable.

2. Remove the 5 column shroud screws and remove the lower column shroud.

3. Loosen the 4 steering column attaching nuts enough to allow the removal of the upper trim shroud.

4. Remove the upper shroud.

5. Remove the turn signal switch lever by pulling the lever straight out from the switch. To make removal easier, work the outer end of the lever around with a slight rotary movement before pulling it out.

6. Peel back the foam sight shield from the turn signal switch.

7. Disconnect the turn signal switch electrical connectors.

8. Remove the 2 self-tapping screws that attach the turn signal switch to the lock cylinder housing and disengage the switch from the housing.

To install:

9. Align the turn signal switch mounting holes with the corresponding holes in the lock cylinder housing and install 2 self-tapping screws until tight.

10. Apply the foam sight shield to the turn signal switch.

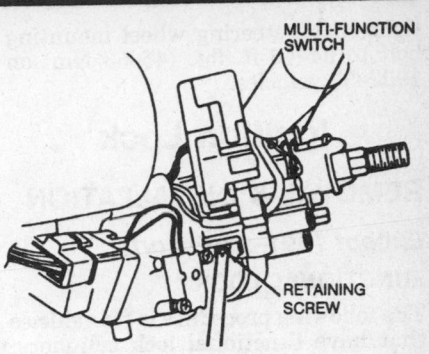

MULTI-FUNCTION SWITCH

RETAINING SCREW

Combination switch removal— 1991–93 Escort

11. Install the turn signal switch lever into the switch by aligning the key on the lever with the keyway in the switch and pushing the lever toward the switch to full engagement.

12. Install the turn signal switch electrical connectors to full engagement.

13. Install the upper steering column trim shroud.

14. Torque the steering column attaching nuts to 15–22 ft. lbs. (20–30 Nm).

15. Attach the lower steering column shroud to the upper shroud with the 5 screws.

16. Connect the negative battery cable.

17. Check the steering column and switch for proper operation.

1991–93 Escort

1. Disconnect the negative battery cable.

2. Remove the steering wheel cover retaining screws from the back side of the steering wheel and remove the cover.

3. Disconnect the horn electrical connector and the speed control electrical connectors, if equipped.

4. Remove the steering wheel mounting nut or bolt.

NOTE: Do not attempt to remove the steering wheel by hitting the column shaft with a hammer. The column may collapse.

5. Remove the steering wheel using a suitable puller.

6. Remove the 4 retaining screws from the steering column lower cover and remove the cover. Remove the upper cover.

7. Disconnect the 3 multi-function switch electrical connectors.

8. Remove the multi-function switch retaining screw, pull the electrical connectors from the retaining brackets and remove the switch.

9. Installation is the reverse of the removal procedure. Tighten the steering wheel mounting nut to 29–36 ft. lbs. (39–49 Nm) on 1991 vehicles or

tighten the steering wheel mounting bolt to 34–46 ft. lbs. (46–63 Nm) on 1992–93 vehicles.

Ignition Lock

REMOVAL & INSTALLATION

Except 1991–93 Escort
FUNCTIONAL LOCK

The following procedure is for vehicles that have functional lock cylinders. Lock cylinder keys are available for these vehicles or the lock cylinder key numbers are known and the proper key can be made.

1. Disconnect the negative battery cable.

2. If equipped with a tilt steering column, remove the upper extension shroud by unsnapping the shroud from the retaining clip at the 9 o'clock position.

3. Remove the steering column lower shroud on Escort. On Tempo and Topaz, remove the 5 attaching screws and the 2 trim shroud halves.

4. Disconnect the key warning buzzer electrical connector. With the lock cylinder key, rotate the cylinder to the **RUN** position.

5. Take a ⅛ in. diameter pin or small wire punch and push on the cylinder retaining pin. The pin is visible through a hole in the mounting surrounding the key cylinder. Push on the pin and withdraw the lock cylinder from the housing.

To install:

6. Install the lock cylinder by turning it to the **RUN** position and depressing the retaining pin. Insert the lock cylinder into the housing. Be sure the lock cylinder is fully seated and aligned in the interlocking washer before turning the key to the **OFF** position. This action will permit the cylinder retaining pin to extend into the cylinder housing hole.

7. Rotate the lock cylinder, using the lock cylinder key, to ensure correct mechanical operation in all positions.

8. Install the electrical connector for the key warning buzzer.

9. Install the lower steering column shroud or trim shroud halves.

10. Connect the negative battery cable.

11. Check for proper start in **P** or **N**. Also, make certain the start circuit cannot be actuated in the **D** and **R** positions and that the column is locked in the **LOCK** position.

NON-FUNCTIONAL LOCK

The following procedure applies to vehicles in which the ignition lock is inoperative and the lock cylinder cannot be rotated due to a lost or broken lock cylinder key, the key number is not known or the lock cylinder cap is damaged and/or broken to the extent the lock cylinder cannot be rotated.

1. Make sure the wheels are in the straight-ahead position and the column is locked. Disconnect the negative battery cable.

NOTE: On most vehicles equipped with an air bag, a backup power supply is included in the system to provide air bag deployment in the event the battery or cables are damaged in an accident before the sensors can close. The power supply is a capacitor that will leak down in approximately 15 minutes after the battery is disconnected or 1 minute if the battery positive cable is grounded. If the system is equipped with a backup power supply, it must be disconnected to disarm the system.

2. On 1989–91 vehicles equipped with an air bag, perform the following procedure:

a. Remove the 2 screws retaining the steering column opening cover to the instrument panel and remove the cover.

b. Remove the 4 bolts retaining the bolster and remove the bolster.

c. Disconnect the backup power supply connector.

d. Remove the 4 nut and washer assemblies retaining the air bag assembly to the steering wheel.

e. Disconnect the air bag electrical connector from the contact assembly connectors and remove the air bag assembly.

CAUTION

When carrying a live air bag, make sure the bag and trim cover are pointed away from the body. In the unlikely event of an accidental deployment, the bag will then deploy with minimal chance of injury. In addition, when placing a live air bag on a bench or other surface, always face the bag and trim cover up, away from the surface. This will reduce the motion of the module if it is accidentally deployed.

---

3. On 1992–93 vehicles equipped with an air bag, perform the following procedure:

a. Disconnect the positive battery cable and wait 1 minute for the backup power supply to be depleted.

b. Remove the 4 nut and washer assemblies retaining the air bag assembly to the steering wheel.

c. Disconnect the air bag electrical connector from the contact assembly connectors and remove the air bag assembly.

CAUTION

When carrying a live air bag, make sure the bag and trim cover are pointed away from the body. In the unlikely event of an accidental deployment, the bag will then deploy with minimal chance of injury. In addition, when placing a live air bag on a bench or other surface, always face the bag and trim cover up, away from the surface. This will reduce the motion of the module if it is accidentally deployed.

---

4. If equipped with an air bag, perform the following procedure:

a. Remove the steering wheel retaining bolt and remove the vibration damper, then reinstall the bolt loosely on the shaft.

b. Loosen the steering wheel on the shaft using a suitable puller.

NOTE: Do not use a knock-off type steering wheel puller or strike the retaining bolt with a hammer. This could cause damage to the steering shaft bearings.

c. Remove and discard the steering wheel retaining bolt and remove the steering wheel.

d. Remove the upper and lower shrouds.

e. Disconnect the air bag clockspring connector from the column harness.

NOTE: Before removing the air bag clockspring from the steering shaft, the clockspring must be taped to prevent the clockspring rotor from being turned accidentally and damaging the clockspring.

f. Remove the 2 screws that secure the clockspring to the retainer plate and remove the clockspring.

5. If not equipped with an air bag, perform the following procedure:

a. Remove the horn pad cover by removing 2 or 4 screws from the back of the steering wheel assembly.

NOTE: The emblem assembly is removed after the horn pad cover is removed, by pushing out from the backside of the emblem.

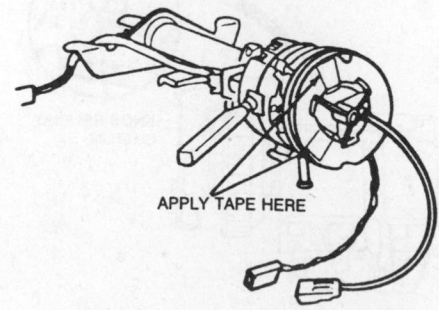

APPLY TAPE HERE

Air bag clockspring taping locations

b. Remove the energy absorbing foam from the wheel assembly, if equipped. Remember to reinstall when the steering wheel is reassembled.

c. Disconnect the horn pad wiring connector.

d. Loosen the steering wheel retaining bolt 4–6 turns. Do not remove the bolt.

e. Loosen the steering wheel on the shaft using a suitable puller.

NOTE: Do not use a knock-off type steering wheel puller or strike the retaining bolt with a hammer. This could cause damage to the steering shaft bearings.

f. Remove and discard the steering wheel retaining bolt and remove the steering wheel.

g. If equipped with a tilt column, remove the upper extension shroud by unsnapping the shroud from the retaining clip at the 9 o'clock position.

h. Remove the 2 trim shroud halves by removing the 5 retaining screws.

6. Remove the electrical connector from the key warning switch.

7. Using a ⅛ in. diameter drill bit, drill out the retaining pin, being careful not to drill deeper than ½ in. (12.7mm).

8. Place a suitable chisel at the base of the ignition lock cylinder cap and, using a suitable hammer, strike the chisel with sharp blows to break the cap away from the lock cylinder.

9. Using a ⅜ in. diameter drill bit, drill down the middle of the ignition lock key slot approximately 1¾ in. (44mm) until the lock cylinder breaks loose from the breakaway base of the lock cylinder. Remove the lock cylinder and drill shavings from the lock cylinder housing.

10. Remove the retainer, washer and steering column lock gear. Thoroughly clean all drill shavings and other foreign materials from the casting.

11. Carefully inspect the lock cylinder housing for damage. If any damage is evident, the housing must be replaced.

To install:

12. Install the ignition lock drive gear, washer and retainer.

13. Install the ignition lock cylinder and check for smooth operation.

14. Connect the electrical connector to the key warning switch.

15. If equipped with an air bag, install the clockspring, steering wheel and air bag module as follows:

a. Place the clockspring onto the steering shaft. Install the 2 retaining screws that secure the clockspring to the retainer plate. Make sure the ground wire is se-

cured with the lower retaining screw. Remove the tape that was installed during the removal procedure.

b. Connect the clockspring wire to the column harness.

c. Install the upper and lower shrouds.

d. Install the steering wheel on the steering column, making sure the alignment marks are correct. Install the vibration damper and a new retaining bolt. Tighten the bolt to 23–33 ft. lbs. (31–45 Nm).

e. Connect the air bag module wire to the clockspring connector and place the air bag module on the steering wheel. Install the 4 retaining nuts and tighten to 35–53 inch lbs. (4–6 Nm).

f. On 1989–91 vehicles, connect the backup power supply connector and install the bolster and steering column opening cover. On 1992–93 vehicles, connect the positive battery cable.

g. Connect the negative battery cable and verify the air bag indicator.

16. If not equipped with an air bag, complete the installation as follows:

a. Install the trim shroud halves.

b. Install the steering wheel assembly on the steering column making sure the alignment marks are correct. Install a new retaining bolt and tighten to 23–33 ft. lbs. (31–45 Nm).

c. Connect the horn pad wiring connector. If equipped, install the energy absorbing foam.

d. Install the horn pad cover and 2 or 4 retaining screws. Make sure the wires are not pinched. Tighten the screws to 8–10 inch lbs. (0.9–1.1 Nm).

e. Connect the negative battery cable.

1991–93 Escort

1. Disconnect the negative battery cable.

2. Remove the steering wheel cover retaining screws from the back side of the steering wheel and remove the cover.

3. Disconnect the horn electrical connector and the cruise control electrical connectors, if equipped.

4. Remove the steering wheel mounting nut or bolt.

NOTE: Do not attempt to remove the steering wheel by hitting the column shaft with a hammer. The column may collapse.

5. Remove the steering wheel using a suitable puller.

6. Remove the combination switch.

7. Disconnect the ignition switch electrical connector.

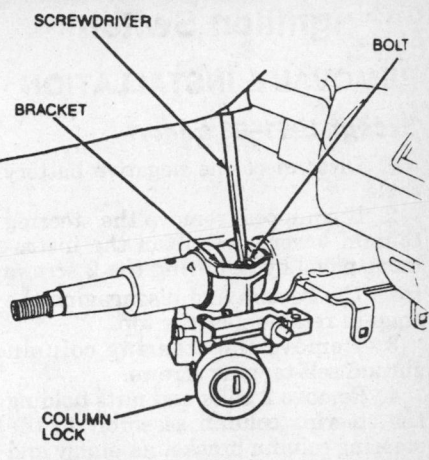

Ignition lock removal—1991–93 Escort

8. Remove the shift-lock cable mounting bracket bolt and position the bracket and cable aside.

9. Remove the 4 steering column upper mounting bracket bolts and lower the column.

10. Using a suitable hammer and chisel, make a groove in the head of each of the 2 column lock mounting bracket bolts.

11. Remove the bolts with a suitable flat bladed tool and discard the bolts.

12. Remove the steering column lock and mounting bracket.

To install:

13. Position the steering column lock and mounting bracket and install 2 new bolts, tightening them only enough to hold the column lock in position.

14. With the key in the ignition, verify the operation of the column lock. If necessary, reposition the column lock until it operates properly.

15. Tighten the mounting bracket bolts until the bolt heads break off.

16. Position the steering column and install the 4 upper mounting bracket bolts. Tighten the bolts to 80–123 inch lbs. (9–14 Nm).

17. If equipped with a tilt steering wheel, remove the upper mounting bracket retaining pin.

18. Position the shift-lock cable mounting bracket and install the bolt. Tighten to 37–55 inch lbs. (4–6 Nm).

19. Connect the ignition switch electrical connector.

20. Install the combination switch.

21. Install the steering wheel and the mounting nut or bolt. Tighten the nut on 1991 vehicles to 29–36 ft. lbs. (39–49 Nm) or the bolt on 1992–93 vehicles to 34–46 ft. lbs. (46–63 Nm).

22. Connect the horn electrical connector and the speed control electrical connectors, if equipped.

23. Position the steering wheel cover and install the retaining screws.

24. Connect the negative battery cable.

Ignition Switch

REMOVAL & INSTALLATION

Except 1991–93 Escort

1. Disconnect the negative battery cable.

2. If equipped, remove the steering column lower cover from the instrument panel by removing the 2 screws from the bottom and disengaging the snap-in retainers at the top.

3. Remove the steering column shroud self-tapping screws.

4. Remove 2 bolts and nuts holding the steering column assembly to the steering column bracket assembly and lower the steering column to the seat.

5. Remove the steering column shrouds.

6. Disconnect the electrical connector from the ignition switch.

7. Rotate ignition lock cylinder to the **RUN** position.

8. Remove 2 screws attaching the switch to the lock cylinder housing.

9. Disengage the ignition switch from the actuator pin.

To install:

10. Check to see that the actuator pin slot in the ignition switch is in the **RUN** position.

NOTE: A new switch assembly will be pre-set in the RUN position.

11. Make certain the ignition key lock cylinder is in approximately the **RUN** position to properly locate the lock actuator pin. The **RUN** position is achieved by rotating the key lock cylinder approximately 90 degrees from the **LOCK** position.

12. Install the ignition switch onto the actuator pin. It may be necessary to move the switch slightly back and fourth to align the switch mounting holes with the column lock housing threaded holes.

13. Install the new screws and tighten to 50–70 inch lbs. (5.6–7.9 Nm).

14. Connect the electrical connector to ignition switch.

15. Connect the negative battery cable.

16. Check the ignition switch for proper function including **START** and **ACC** positions. Also make certain the steering column is locked when in the **LOCK** position.

17. Position the top half of the shroud on the steering column.

18. Install the 2 bolts and nuts attaching the steering column assembly to the steering column bracket assembly. Tighten to 15–25 ft. lbs. (20–34 Nm).

19. Position lower shroud to upper shroud and install 5 self-tapping screws. Install the steering column lower cover on the instrument panel, if equipped.

1991–93 Escort

1. Disconnect the negative battery cable.

2. Remove the combination switch.

3. Disconnect the ignition switch electrical connector.

4. Remove the 3 ignition switch mounting screws and remove the ignition switch.

5. Installation is the reverse of the removal procedure. Check the switch for proper operation.

Stoplight Switch

ADJUSTMENT

1991–93 Escort

1. Measure the distance from the center of the brake pedal pad to the floor. The distance should be 7.60–7.72 in. (193–196mm). If not, proceed to Step 2.

2. Disconnect the stoplight switch electrical connector.

3. Loosen the stoplight locknut and turn the stoplight switch until it does not contact the brake pedal.

4. Loosen the rod locknut and turn the rod until the brake pedal height is within specification.

5. Turn the stoplight switch until it contacts the brake pedal, then turn it an additional ½ turn.

6. Tighten the stoplight locknut and the rod locknut.

7. Connect the stoplight switch electrical connector.

8. Check the operation of the stoplights.

REMOVAL & INSTALLATION

Except 1991–93 Escort

1. Disconnect the negative battery cable.

2. Disconnect the wire harness at the connector from the switch.

NOTE: The locking tab must be lifted before the connector can be removed.

3. Remove the hairpin retainer and white nylon washer. Slide the stoplight switch and the pushrod away from the pedal. Remove the switch by sliding the switch up/down.

NOTE: Since the switch side plate nearest the brake pedal is slotted, it is not necessary to remove the brake master cylinder pushrod black bushing and 1 white spacer washer nearest the

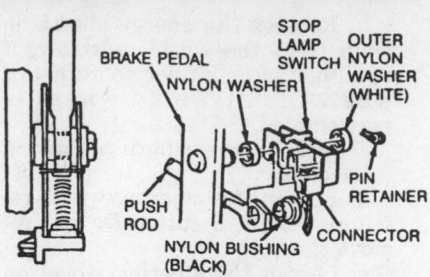

Stoplight switch installation—except 1991–93 Escort

pedal arm from the brake pedal pin.

To install:

4. Position the switch so the U-shaped side is nearest the pedal and directly over/under the pin. The black bushing must be in position in the pushrod eyelet with the washer face on the side closest to the retaining pin.

5. Slide the switch up/down, trapping the master cylinder pushrod and black bushing between the switch side plates. Push the switch and pushrod assembly firmly towards the brake pedal arm. Assemble the outside white plastic washer to the pin and install the hairpin retainer to trap the whole assembly.

NOTE: Do not substitute other types of pin retainers. Replace only with production hairpin retainer.

6. Connect the wire harness connector to the switch.

7. Connect negative battery cable.

8. Check the stoplight switch for proper operation. Stoplights should illuminate with less than 6 lbs. applied to the brake pedal at the pad.

NOTE: The stoplight switch wire harness must have sufficient length to travel with the switch during full stroke at the pedal.

1991–93 Escort

1. Disconnect the negative battery cable.

2. Disconnect the stoplight switch electrical connector.

3. Remove the stoplight switch retaining nuts and remove the stoplight switch.

4. Installation is the reverse of the removal procedure. Adjust the switch according to the proper procedure.

Clutch Switch

ADJUSTMENT

Except 1991–93 Escort

1. Remove panel above clutch pedal on Tempo and Topaz vehicles.

2. Disengage the wiring connector by flexing the retaining tab on the switch and withdrawing the connector.

3. Using a test light, check to see that the switch is open with the clutch pedal up (engaged) and closed at approximately 1 in. (25.4mm) from the clutch pedal full down position (disengaged).

4. If the switch does not operate as outlined in Step 3, check to see if the self-adjusting clip is out of position on the rod. It should be near the end of the rod.

5. If the self-adjusting clip is out of position, remove and reposition the clip approximately 1 in. (25.4mm) from the end of the rod.

6. Reset the switch by pressing the clutch pedal to the floor. Repeat Step 3. If the switch is damaged or the clips do not remain in place replace the switch.

1991–93 Escort

1. Disconnect the negative battery cable.
2. Disconnect the clutch engage electrical connector.
3. Using an ohmmeter, check the resistance between the connector terminals.
4. The ohmmeter should show continuity when the switch rod is pushed into the switch. The ohmmeter should show no continuity with the switch rod released.
5. Replace the switch if it does not perform as specified.

REMOVAL & INSTALLATION

Except 1991–93 Escort

1. Disconnect the negative battery cable.
2. Remove panel above clutch pedal on Tempo and Topaz vehicles.
3. Disconnect the switch wiring connector.
4. Remove clutch interlock attaching screw and hairpin clip and remove the switch.
To install:

NOTE: Always install the switch with the self-adjusting clip about 1 in. from the end of the rod. The clutch pedal must be fully up (clutch engaged). Otherwise, the switch may be misadjusted.

5. Insert the eyelet end of the rod over the clutch pedal pin and secure it with the hairpin clip.
6. Swing the switch around to align the hole in the mounting boss with the corresponding hole in the bracket. Attach with the screw.
7. Reset the clutch interlock switch

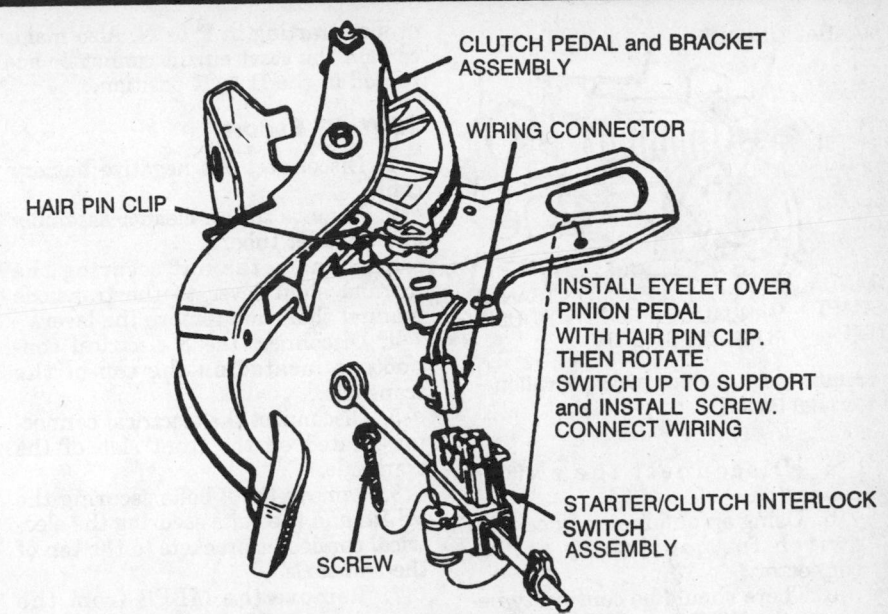

Starter/clutch interlock switch installation—except 1991–93 Escort

by pressing the clutch pedal to the floor.
8. Connect the wiring connector.
9. Install the panel above the clutch on Tempo and Topaz.
10. Connect the negative battery cable.

1991–93 Escort

1. Disconnect the negative battery cable.
2. Disconnect the electrical connector.
3. Remove the 2 retaining nuts.
4. Remove the clutch engage switch.
5. Installation is the reverse of the removal procedure.

Neutral Safety Switch

ADJUSTMENT

Except 1991–93 Escort

The mounting location of the neutral safety switch does not provide for adjustment of the switch position when installed. If the engine will not start in P or N or if it will start in R or any of the D ranges, check the control linkage adjustment and/or replace with a known good switch.

1991–93 Escort

The neutral safety switch function is performed by the Manual Lever Position Switch (MLPS). The MLPS is an adjustable switch that informs the automatic transaxle control unit of the position of the transaxle manual shaft. The MLPS will allow the vehicle to be started with the gear selector in the P or N positions when properly adjusted.

The MLPS is located externally on the transaxle housing and is positioned on the manual shaft.
1. Remove the air cleaner assembly and air inlet tube.
2. Remove the nut securing the manual shaft lever to the transaxle manual shaft.
3. Remove the lever from the manual shaft.
4. Turn the manual shaft to the neutral position.
5. Loosen the MLPS mounting bolts.
6. Align the hole of the MLPS with the hole on the manual shaft lever by inserting a 0.079 in. (2.0mm) outside diameter pin.
7. Tighten the MLPS mounting bolts to 69–95 inch lbs. (8–11 Nm). Remove the pin.
8. Check the continuity of the switch as follows:

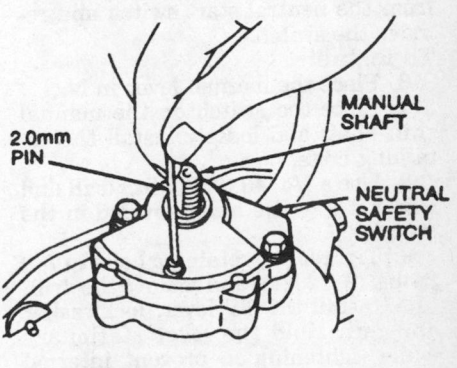

Manual lever position switch adjustment—1991–93 Escort

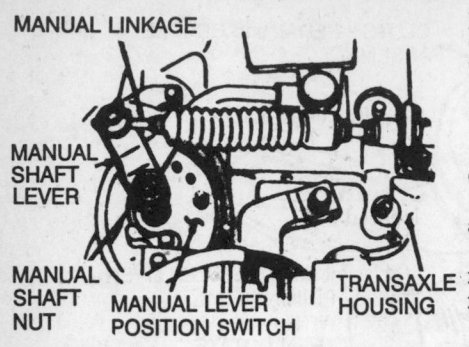

MANUAL LINKAGE

MANUAL SHAFT LEVER

MANUAL SHAFT NUT

MANUAL LEVER POSITION SWITCH

TRANSAXLE HOUSING

Manual lever position switch location—1991–93 Escort

a. Disconnect the switch connector.

b. Using an ohmmeter, check the switch for continuity at the connector.

c. There should be continuity between the **BK/BL** and **BK/R** terminals with the shift lever in the **P** or **N** position.

9. If there is no continuity, replace the MLPS.

10. Position the manual shaft lever to the manual shaft and install the nut. Tighten to 33–47 ft. lbs. (44–64 Nm).

11. Install the air cleaner assembly and air inlet tube.

REMOVAL & INSTALLATION

Except 1991–93 Escort

1. Set the parking brake.
2. Disconnect the negative battery cable.
3. Disconnect the wire connector from the neutral safety switch.
4. Remove the nut and lockwasher holding the TV lever. Hold the lever stationary while loosening to prevent internal damage.
5. Remove the 2 retaining screws from the neutral start switch and remove the switch.
To install:
6. Place the manual lever in **N**.
7. Place the switch on the manual shift shaft and loosely install the retaining bolts.
8. Use a No. 43 (0.089 in.) drill and insert it into the hole provided in the switch.
9. Tighten the retaining bolts to 7–9 ft. lbs. (9–12 Nm) and remove the drill.
10. Install the TV lever, lockwasher and nut. Hold the lever stationary while tightening to prevent internal damage. Tighten to 7.5–9.5 ft. lbs. (10–13 Nm).
11. Connect the neutral start switch connector and connect negative battery cable.
12. Check the ignition switch for

proper starting in **P** or **N**. Also make certain the start circuit cannot be actuated in the **D** or **R** position.

1991–93 Escort

1. Disconnect the negative battery cable.
2. Remove the air cleaner assembly and air inlet tube.
3. Remove the nut securing the manual shaft lever to the transaxle manual shaft and remove the lever.
4. Disconnect the 3 electrical connectors located on the top of the transaxle.
5. Disconnect the electrical connector located on the front side of the transaxle.
6. Remove the 2 bolts securing the MLPS and the bolts securing the electrical connector brackets to the top of the transaxle.
7. Remove the MLPS from the manual shaft.
To install:
8. Position the MLPS onto the manual shaft.
9. Install the bolts securing the electrical connectors to the transaxle housing.
10. Install the bolts securing the MLPS but do not tighten yet.
11. Connect the electrical connectors located on the top and on the side of the transaxle.
12. Adjust the MLPS according to the proper procedure.
13. Install the air cleaner assembly and the air inlet tube.
14. Connect the negative battery cable.

Fuses, Circuit Breakers and Relays

LOCATION

Fuses

On all vehicles, a fuse panel is located under the instrument panel to the left of the steering column. On 1991–93 Escort, a fuse block is mounted in the left-hand side of the engine compartment.

Fusible Links

Fusible links are used to prevent major wire harness damage in the event of a short circuit or an overload condition in the wiring circuits that are normally not fused, due to carrying high amperage loads or because of their locations within the wiring harness. Each fusible link is of a fixed value for a specific electrical load and should a fusible link fail, the cause of the failure must be determined and repaired prior to installing a new fusible link of the

same value. Please be advised that the color coding of replacement fusible links may vary from the production color coding that is outlined in the text that follows.

Gray 12 Gauge Wire—on 1992–93 Tempo and Topaz, there is 1 link located in the charging circuit near the starter motor relay.

Dark Green 14 Gauge Wire—on 1989–91 Tempo and Topaz and 1989–90 Escort, there is 1 link located in the charging circuit near the starter motor relay. On 1992–93 Tempo and Topaz, there is 1 link for the cooling fan relay in the wiring assembly on the starter motor relay.

Black 16 Gauge Wire—on 1989–90 Escort, there is 1 link for the rear window defogger located in the engine compartment on the starter relay. On Tempo, Topaz and 1989–90, there is 1 link for the headlight feed located in the engine compartment on the starter relay and 1 link for the ignition feed near the starter relay. On 1989–91 Tempo and Topaz, there is 1 link for the cooling fan relay located in the wiring assembly on the starter relay.

Brown 18 Gauge Wire—on Tempo and Topaz, there is 1 link used to protect the rear window defogger and the fuel door release. On 1991–93 Tempo and Topaz, there is 1 link in the charging circuit near the starter relay. On 1992–93 Tempo and Topaz, there is 1 link near the starter motor relay to protect the EEC module. On the 1989–90 Escort, there is 1 link used to protect the cooling fan motor circuit and 1 link for the EEC system power relay on the starter relay.

Dark Blue 20 Gauge Wire—on 1989–90 Escort, there are 4 links in the engine compartment near the starter for the shift indicator light module, ignition coil and distributor, passive restraint module and fuel pump relay. On 1989–91 Tempo and Topaz, there is 1 link for the fan and air conditioning clutch in the wiring assembly on the starter. On all Tempo and Topaz, there is 1 link for the air bag module in the engine compartment near the starter relay. On 1991–93 Tempo and Topaz, there is 1 link for the passive restraint module located in the engine compartment on the starter relay, 1 link for the heated oxygen sensor, 4-wheel drive and air conditioning fan controller located near the left shock tower and 1 link for the ignition coil, TFI module and ECA relay located near the left shock tower. On 1992–93 Tempo and Topaz, there is 1 link in the wiring assembly near the starter motor relay for the EEC power relay and fuel pump relay.

NOTE: Always disconnect the negative battery cable before servicing the high current fuses or serious personal injury may result.

FUSE LINK CARTRIDGE

Fuse link cartridges are used on 1991–93 Escort. Fuse link cartridges have a colored plastic housing with a clear "window" at the top. To check a fuse cartridge, look at the fuse element through the clear "window". The fuse link cartridges are located in the engine compartment fuse box. The following fuse link cartridges are listed according to their labels in the fuse box.

FUEL INJ—Pink 30 amp: to protect the electronic engine control circuit.

HEAD—Pink 30 amp: to protect the headlight circuit and the daytime running lights circuit.

MAIN—Black 80 amp for 1.8L engine or Dark Blue 100 amp for 1.9L engine: to protect all cicuits, except starter and starter solenoid circuits.

BTN—Yellow 60 amp for 1.8L engine or Green 40 amp for 1.9L engine: to protect the courtesy lights, electronic automatic transaxle, electronic engine control, exterior lights, horn, interior lights, passive restraint, power door locks, radio, shift lock and warning chime circuits.

COOLING FAN—Pink 30 amp for 1.8L engine or Green 40 amp for 1.9L engine: to protect cooling fans circuit.

Circuit Breakers

Circuit breakers are used to protect the various components of the electrical system, such as headlights and windshield wipers. The circuit breakers are located either in the control switch or mounted on or near the fuse panel.

TEMPO AND TOPAZ

Headlights and Highbeam Indicator—one 22 amp circuit breaker incorporated in the lighting switch.

Alternator Voltage Sensing Circuit—one 18 amp circuit breaker located in engine compartment wiring assembly near starter relay on 1990–91 vehicles.

HEGO, All Wheel Drive Relays, Air Conditioning Fan Controller, Fan Tester and All Wheel Drive Switch—one 20 amp circuit breaker located in the engine compartment near the starter relay on 1990–91 vehicles.

Passive Restraint Module—one 20 amp circuit breaker located in the engine compartment near the starter relay on 1990–91 vehicles.

Power Windows, Power Seats, Power Door Locks and Power Lumbar—one 20 amp circuit breaker located in the fuse panel.

Windshield Wipers—one 8.25 amp circuit breaker located in the fuse panel.

ESCORT

Headlights and High Beam Indicator—one 22 amp circuit breaker incorporated in the lighting switch, on 1989–90 vehicles.

Liftgate Wiper—one 4.5 amp circuit breaker located in the instrument panel, to the left of the radio, on 1989–90 vehicles.

Windshield Wiper and Wiper Pump Circuit—one 8.25 amp circuit breaker located in the fuse panel, on 1989–90 vehicles.

Engine Cooling Fan Motor, Without A/C—one 12 amp circuit breaker located in the fuse panel on 1990 vehicles.

Heater Blower Motor—one 30 amp circuit breaker located in the fuse panel under the dash, to the left of the steering column, on 1991–93 vehicles.

Various Relays

TEMPO AND TOPAZ

All Wheel Drive Relays—located behind the right side of the instrument panel.

Door Lock Control Relay—located below the left side of the instrument panel, near the fuse panel.

Cooling Fan Relay—located in the left front of the engine compartment.

Electronic Engine Control Power Relay—located behind the right side of the instrument panel.

Fuel Pump Relay—located behind the right side of the instrument panel.

Horn Relay—located behind the left side of the instrument panel, above the fuse panel.

Starter Relay—located on the left front fender apron in front of the strut tower.

Rear Window Defrost Relay—located behind the left side of the instrument panel, to the right of the steering column.

Shift Indicator Dimmer Relay—located behind the left side of the instrument panel, near the steering column on 1989–91 vehicles or on the right side of the brake pedal support on 1992–93 vehicles.

Window Safety Relay—located behind the left side of the instrument panel, above the fuse panel.

1989–90 ESCORT

Cooling Fan Relay—located in the left front of the engine compartment, near the left headlight.

Electronic Engine Control (EEC) Power Relay—located behind the left side of the instrument panel.

Fuel Pump Relay—located behind the left side of the instrument panel.

Horn Relay—located behind the left side of the instrument panel, to the right of the steering column.

Shift Indicator Dimmer Relay—located behind the right side of the instrument panel.

Starter Relay—located on the left side of the fender apron in front of the shock tower.

1991–93 ESCORT

Air Conditioning Relay—located on the rear of the right fender apron on 1991 vehicles or in the right rear corner of the engine compartment, on the firewall on 1992–93 vehicles.

Cooling Fan Lo and Hi Speed Relays—located on the front of the left fender apron.

Cooling Fan Relay—located on top of the left front wheel well, in the engine compartment fuse block.

Door Lock Relay—located above the left cowl on 1991 vehicles or behind the left side of the instrument panel, near the cowl on 1992–93 vehicles.

Daytime Running Lights Relay—located behind the right side of the instrument panel, near the blower motor.

Electronic Engine Control Power Relay—located behind the center of the instrument panel.

Fuel Pump Relay—located behind the center of the instrument panel.

Headlight Relay—located above the left cowl on 1991 vehicles or behind the left side of the instrument panel, near the cowl on 1992–93 vehicles.

Horn Relay—located above the left cowl on 1991 vehicles or behind the left side of the instrument panel, near the cowl on 1992–93 vehicles.

Ignition Relay—located on top of the left front wheel well, in the engine compartment fuse block.

Parking Light Relay—located behind the left side of the instrument panel.

Vane Air Flow Meter Relay—located behind the center of the instrument panel.

Wide Open Throttle Cutout Relay—located on the rear of the right fender apron on 1991 vehicles or in the right rear corner of the engine compartment, on the firewall on 1992–93 vehicles.

Computers

LOCATION

The Electronic Engine Control (EEC)

module is located behind the left side of the instrument panel on all except 1991–93 Escort. On the 1991–93 Escort, the EEC module is located behind the center of the instrument panel.

Turn Signal/Hazard Warning Flashers

LOCATION

Except 1991–93 Escort

The turn signal flasher is located on the front side of the fuse panel. The hazard flasher is located on the rear of the fuse panel behind the turn signal flasher.

1991–93 Escort

The turn signal and hazard flasher switch use the same flasher unit. The flasher unit is located with the combination switch.

Cruise Control

ADJUSTMENT

Actuator Cable

1.8L AND 1991–93 1.9L ENGINES

1. Remove the cable adjusting clip from the cable housing.
2. Pull tightly on the cable until all of the slack is taken out.
3. Install the cable adjusting clip.

2.3L AND 1989–90 1.9L ENGINES

1. With engine **OFF**, set the throttle linkage so the throttle plate is closed.
2. Remove the locking pin.
3. Pull the bead chain through the adjuster.
4. Insert the locking pin in the best hole of the adjuster to draw the bead chain tight without opening the throttle plate.

3.0L ENGINE

1. Remove the actuator cable retaining clip.
2. Pull the actuator cable through the adjuster until slight tension is felt.
3. Insert the cable retaining clip and snap into place.

Vacuum Dump Valve

1. Firmly depress the brake pedal and hold in position.
2. Push in the dump valve until the valve collar bottoms against the retaining clip.
3. Place a 0.050–0.10 in. (1.27–2.54mm) shim between the white button of the valve and the pad on the brake pedal.

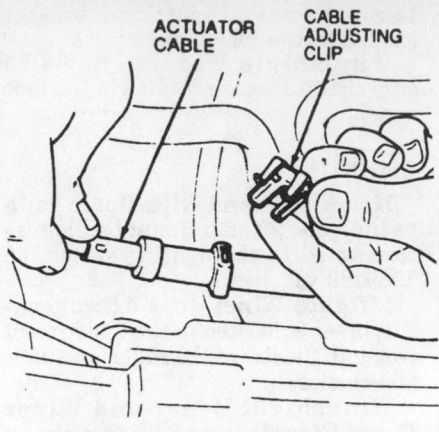

Cruise control actuator cable adjustment—1.8L and 1991–93 1.9L Engines

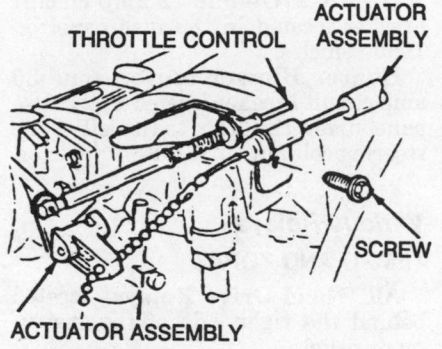

Cruise control actuator cable adjustment—2.3L and 1989–90 1.9L Engines

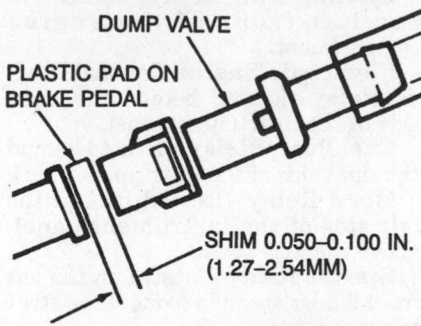

Vacuum dump valve adjustment

4. Firmly pull the brake pedal rearward to its normal position, allowing the dump valve to ratchet backwards in the retaining clip.

Clutch Switch

EXCEPT 1991–93 ESCORT

1. Prop the clutch pedal in the full-up position—pawl fully released from the sector.
2. Loosen the switch mounting screw.
3. Slide the switch forward toward the clutch pedal until the switch plunger cap is 0.030 in. (0.76mm) from contacting the switch housing. Tighten the attaching screw.
4. Remove the prop from the clutch pedal and test drive for clutch cancellation of cruise control.

1991–93 ESCORT

1. Measure the distance from the bulkhead to the upper center of the clutch pedal pad. The distance should be 7.72–8.03 in. (196–204mm). If not proceed to Step 2.
2. Disconnect the clutch switch electrical connector.
3. Loosen the switch locknut and turn the switch until the specified distance is achieved. Tighten the locknut to 10–13 ft. lbs. (14–18 Nm).
4. Push the clutch pedal down by hand until clutch resistance is felt.
5. Measure the distance between the upper pedal height and where resistance is felt. The free-play should be 0.20–0.51 in. (5–13mm). If not, proceed to Step 6.
6. Loosen the pushrod locknut and turn the pushrod until the specified free-play is achieved.
7. Check that disengagement height is correct when the pedal is fully depressed. Minimum disengagement height is 1.6 in. (41mm).
8. Tighten the pushrod locknut to 9–12 ft. lbs. (12–17mm) and connect the clutch switch electrical connector.

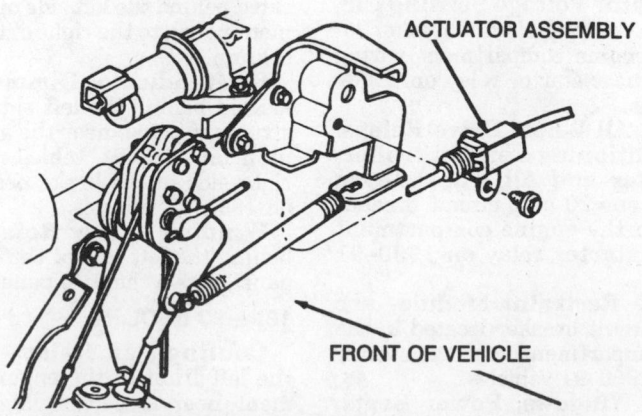

Cruise control actuator cable adjustment—3.0L Engine

Ford Motor Co.
Front Wheel Drive
FORD—FESTIVA

10

SPECIFICATIONS

VEHICLE IDENTIFICATION CHART

It is important for servicing and ordering parts to be certain of the vehicle and engine identification. The VIN (vehicle identification number) is a 20 digit number visible through the windshield on the driver's side of the dash and contains the vehicle and engine identification codes. The tenth digit indicates model year and the eighth digit indicates engine code. It can be interpreted as follows:

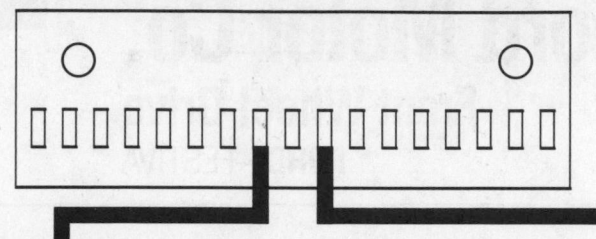

Engine Code						Model Year	
Code	Liters	Cu. In. (cc)	Cyl.	Fuel Sys.	Eng. Mfg.	Code	Year
K	1.3	81 (1319)	4	2 bbl	Kia Motors	K	1989
H	1.3	81 (1319)	4	EFI	Kia Motors	L	1990
						M	1991
						N	1992
						P	1993

EFI—Electronic Fuel Injection

ENGINE IDENTIFICATION

Year	Model	Engine Displacement Liters (cc)	Engine Series Identification (ID/VIN)	Fuel System	No. of Cylinders	Engine Type
1989	Festiva	1.3 (1319)	K	EFI	4	OHC
	Festiva	1.3 (1319)	H	EFI	4	OHC
1990	Festiva	1.3 (1319)	H	EFI	4	OHC
1991	Festiva	1.3 (1319)	H	EFI	4	OHC
1992-93	Festiva	1.3 (1319)	H	EFI	4	OHC

EFI—Electronic Fuel Injection
OHC—Overhead Cam

GENERAL ENGINE SPECIFICATIONS

Year	Engine (ID/VIN)	Engine Displacement Liters (cc)	Fuel System Type	Net Horsepower @ rpm	Net Torque @ rpm (ft. lbs.)	Bore × Stroke (in.)	Compression Ratio	Oil Pressure @ rpm ①
1989	K	1.3 (1319)	2 bbl	58 @ 5000	73 @ 3500	2.79 × 3.29	9.0:1	50–64 @ 3000
	H	1.3 (1319)	EFI	63 @ 5000	73 @ 3000	2.79 × 3.29	9.7:1	50–64 @ 3000

GENERAL ENGINE SPECIFICATIONS

Year	Engine (ID/VIN)	Engine Displacement Liters (cc)	Fuel System Type	Net Horsepower @ rpm	Net Torque @ rpm (ft. lbs.)	Bore × Stroke (in.)	Com-pression Ratio	Oil Pressure @ rpm ①
1990	H	1.3 (1319)	EFI	63 @ 5000	73 @ 3000	2.79 × 3.29	9.7:1	50–64 @ 3000
1991	H	1.3 (1319)	EFI	63 @ 5000	73 @ 3000	2.79 × 3.29	9.7:1	50–64 @ 3000
1992–93	H	1.3 (1319)	EFI	63 @ 5000	73 @ 3000	2.79 × 3.29	9.7:1	50–64 @ 3000

NOTE: Horsepower and torque are SAE net figures. They are measured at the rear of the transmission with all accessories installed and operating. Since the figures vary when a given engine is installed in different models, some are representative rather than exact.
EFI—Electronic Fuel Injection
① Hot

GASOLINE ENGINE TUNE-UP SPECIFICATIONS

Year	Engine (ID/VIN)	Engine Displacement Liters (cc)	Spark Plugs Gap (in.)	Ignition Timing (deg.) MT	Ignition Timing (deg.) AT	Fuel Pump (psi)	Idle Speed (rpm) MT	Idle Speed (rpm) AT	Valve Clearance In.	Valve Clearance Ex.
1989	K	1.3 (1319)	0.040	TDC	—	3–6	700–750	—	0.012	0.012
	H	1.3 (1319)	0.040	—	2B	64–85	—	800–900	Hyd.	Hyd.
1990	H	1.3 (1319)	0.040	10B	10B	64–85	680–720	830–870	Hyd.	Hyd.
1991	H	1.3 (1319)	0.040	10B	10B	64–85	680–720	830–870	Hyd.	Hyd.
1992	H	1.3 (1319)	0.040	10B	10B	64–85	680–720	830–870	Hyd.	Hyd.
1993	SEE UNDERHOOD SPECIFICATIONS									

NOTE: The lowest cylinder pressure should be within 75% of the highest cylinder pressure reading. For example, if the highest cylinder is 134 psi, the lowest should be 101. Engine should be at normal operating temperature with throttle valve in the wide open position.
The underhood specifications sticker often reflects tune-up specification changes in production. Sticker figures must be used if they disagree with those in this chart.
Hyd.—Hydraulic
B—Before Top Dead Center

FIRING ORDERS

NOTE: To avoid confusion, always replace spark plug wires one at a time.

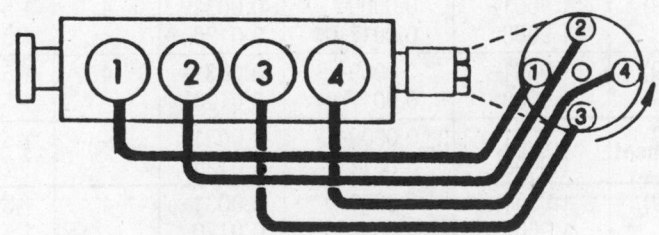

1.3L Engine
Engine Firing Order: 1–3–4–2
Distributor Rotation: Counterclockwise

CAPACITIES

Year	Model	Engine (ID/VIN)	Engine Displacement Liters (cc)	Engine Crankcase with Filter (qts.)	Transmission (pts.) 4-Spd	5-Spd	Auto.	Drive Axle (pts.)	Fuel Tank (gal.)	Cooling System (qts.)
1989	Festiva	K	1.3 (1319)	3.6	5.2	5.2	—	—	10	5.3
	Festiva	H	1.3 (1319)	3.6	—	—	11.2	—	10	5.3
1990	Festiva	H	1.3 (1319)	3.6	—	5.2	11.2	—	10	5.3
1991	Festiva	H	1.3 (1319)	3.6	—	5.2	11.2	—	10	5.3
1992–93	Festiva	H	1.3 (1319)	3.6	—	5.2	11.2	—	10	5.3

CAMSHAFT SPECIFICATIONS

All measurements given in inches.

Year	Engine (ID/VIN)	Engine Displacement Liters (cc)	Journal Diameter 1	2	3	4	5	Elevation ① In.	Ex.	Bearing Clearance	Camshaft End Play
1989	K	1.3 (1319)	1.7103–1.7112	1.7091–1.7100	1.7103–1.7112	—	—	1.4185–1.4224	1.4185–1.4224	②	0.002–0.007
	H	1.3 (1319)	1.7103–1.7112	1.7091–1.7100	1.7103–1.7112	—	—	1.4331–1.4371	1.4331–1.4371	②	0.002–0.007
1990	H	1.3 (1319)	1.7103–1.7112	1.7091–1.7100	1.7103–1.7112	—	—	1.4331–1.4371	1.4331–1.4371	②	0.002–0.007
1991	H	1.3 (1319)	1.7103–1.7112	1.7091–1.7100	1.7103–1.7112	—	—	1.4331–1.4371	1.4331–1.4371	②	0.002–0.007
1992–93	H	1.3 (1319)	1.7103–1.7112	1.7091–1.7100	1.7103–1.7112	—	—	1.4331–1.4371	1.4331–1.4371	②	0.002–0.007

① Figure shown indicates total lobe height
② Front and Rear Bearing—0.0014–0.0033 in.
　Center Bearing—0.0026–0.0045

CRANKSHAFT AND CONNECTING ROD SPECIFICATIONS

All measurements are given in inches.

Year	Engine (ID/VIN)	Engine Displacement Liters (cc)	Crankshaft Main Brg. Journal Dia.	Main Brg. Oil Clearance	Shaft End-play	Thrust on No.	Connecting Rod Journal Diameter	Oil Clearance	Side Clearance
1989	K	1.3 (1319)	1.9661–1.9668	0.0009–0.0017①	0.0031–0.0120	4	1.5724–1.5731	0.0011–0.0027	0.0043–0.0120
	H	1.3 (1319)	1.9661–1.9668	0.0009–0.0017①	0.0031–0.0120	4	1.5724–1.5731	0.0011–0.0027	0.0043–0.0120
1990	H	1.3 (1319)	1.9661–1.9668	0.0009–0.0017①	0.0031–0.0120	4	1.5724–1.7531	0.0011–0.0027	0.0043–0.0120
1991	H	1.3 (1319)	1.9661–1.9668	0.0009–0.0017①	0.0031–0.0120	4	1.5724–1.5731	0.0011–0.0027	0.0043–0.0120
1992–93	H	1.3 (1319)	1.9661–1.9668	0.0009–0.0017①	0.0031–0.0120	4	1.5724–1.5731	0.0011–0.0027	0.0043–0.0120

① Limit—0.0039 in.

VALVE SPECIFICATIONS

Year	Engine (ID/VIN)	Engine Displacement Liters (cc)	Seat Angle (deg.)	Face Angle (deg.)	Spring Test Pressure (lbs. @ in.)	Spring Installed Height (in.)	Stem-to-Guide Clearance (in.)		Stem Diameter (in.)	
							Intake	Exhaust	Intake	Exhaust
1989	K	1.3 (1319)	45	45	NA①	NA①	0.008	0.008	0.2744–0.2750	0.2742–0.2748
	H	1.3 (1319)	45	45	NA①	NA①	0.008	0.008	0.2744–0.2750	0.2742–0.2748
1990	H	1.3 (1319)	45	45	NA①	NA①	0.008	0.008	0.2744–0.2750	0.2742–0.2748
1991	H	1.3 (1319)	45	45	NA①	NA①	0.008	0.008	0.2744–0.2750	0.2742–0.2748
1992–93	H	1.3 (1319)	45	45	NA①	NA①	0.008	0.008	0.2744–0.2750	0.2742–0.2748

NA—Not available
① Check springs for free length and squareness
Free length should not be less than 1.717 in.
Maximum out-of-square is 0.059 in.

PISTON AND RING SPECIFICATIONS
All measurements are given in inches.

Year	Engine (ID/VIN)	Engine Displacement Liters (cc)	Piston Clearance	Ring Gap			Ring Side Clearance		
				Top Compression	Bottom Compression	Oil Control	Top Compression	Bottom Compression	Oil Control
1989	K	1.3 (1319)	①	0.006–0.012	0.006–0.012	0.008–0.028	0.001–0.003	0.001–0.003	snug
	H	1.3 (1319)	①	0.006–0.012	0.006–0.012	0.008–0.028	0.001–0.003	0.001–0.003	snug
1990	H	1.3 (1319)	①	0.006–0.012	0.006–0.012	0.008–0.028	0.001–0.003	0.001–0.003	snug
1991	H	1.3 (1319)	①	0.006–0.012	0.006–0.012	0.008–0.028	0.001–0.003	0.001–0.003	snug
1992–93	H	1.3 (1319)	①	0.006–0.012	0.006–0.012	0.008–0.028	0.001–0.003	0.001–0.003	snug

① Optimum—0.0015–0.0020 in.
Limit—0.006 in.

TORQUE SPECIFICATIONS
All readings in ft. lbs.

Year	Engine (ID/VIN)	Engine Displacement Liters (cc)	Cylinder Head Bolts	Main Bearing Bolts	Rod Bearing Bolts	Crankshaft Pulley Bolts	Flywheel Bolts	Manifold		Spark Plugs	Lug Nut
								Intake	Exhaust		
1989	K	1.3 (1319)	①	40–43	②	③	71–76	14–20	12–17	10–17	65–87
	H	1.3 (1319)	①	40–43	②	③	71–76	14–20	12–17	10–17	65–87
1990	H	1.3 (1319)	①	40–43	②	③	71–76	14–20	12–17	10–17	65–87
1991	H	1.3 (1319)	①	40–43	②	③	71–76	14–20	12–17	10–17	65–87
1992–93	H	1.3 (1319)	①	40–43	②	③	71–76	14–20	12–17	10–17	65–87

① Tighten in sequence in 2 steps:
Step 1—35–40 ft. lbs.
Step 2—56–60 ft. lbs.

② Tighten in 2 steps:
Step 1—11–13 ft. lbs.
Step 2—22–25 ft. lbs.

③ Pulley bolts—109–152 inch lbs.
Sprocket bolt—80–87 ft. lbs.

BRAKE SPECIFICATIONS
All measurements in inches unless noted.

| Year | Model | Master Cylinder Bore | Brake Disc | | | Brake Drum Diameter | | | Minimum Lining Thickness | |
			Original Thickness	Minimum Thickness	Maximum Runout	Original Inside Diameter	Max. Wear Limit	Maximum Machine Diameter	Front	Rear
1989	Festiva	0.75/0.59	0.050	0.43	0.003	6.69	6.75	NA	0.125	0.040
1990	Festiva	0.75/0.59	0.050	0.43	0.003	6.69	6.75	NA	0.125	0.040
1991	Festiva	0.75/0.59	0.050	0.43	0.003	6.69	6.75	NA	0.125	0.040
1992-93	Festiva	0.75/0.59	0.050	0.43	0.003	6.69	6.75	NA	0.125	0.040

NA—Not available

WHEEL ALIGNMENT

| Year | Model | Caster | | Camber | | Toe-in (in.) | Steering Axis Inclination (deg.) |
		Range (deg.)	Preferred Setting (deg.)	Range (deg.)	Preferred Setting (deg.)		
1989	Festiva	$1^5/_{16}$P–$1^{13}/_{16}$P	$1^9/_{16}$P	$1/_4$N–$1^9/_{16}$P	$1^1/_{16}$P	$1/_{32}$–$1/_4$	$14^3/_{16}$
1990	Festiva	$1^5/_{16}$P–$1^{13}/_{16}$P	$1^9/_{16}$P	$1/_4$N–$1^9/_{16}$P	$1^1/_{16}$P	$1/_{32}$–$1/_4$	$14^3/_{16}$
1991	Festiva	$1^5/_{16}$P–$1^{13}/_{16}$P	$1^9/_{16}$P	$1/_4$N–$1^9/_{16}$P	$1^1/_{16}$P	$1/_{32}$–$1/_4$	$14^3/_{16}$
1992-93	Festiva	$1^5/_{16}$P–$1^{13}/_{16}$P	$1^9/_{16}$P	$1/_4$N–$1^9/_{16}$P	$1^1/_{16}$P	$1/_{32}$–$1/_4$	$14^3/_{16}$

N—Negative
P—Positive

ENGINE MECHANICAL

NOTE: Disconnecting the negative battery cable on some vehicles may interfere with the functions of the on board computer systems and may require the computer to undergo a relearning process, once the negative battery cable is reconnected.

Engine Assembly

REMOVAL & INSTALLATION

NOTE: The engine and transaxle are removed as an assembly.

1. Properly relieve the fuel system pressure on EFI equipped vehicle.
2. Disconnect the battery cables. Remove the battery and battery tray.
3. Mark the hinge location and remove the hood.
4. Drain the radiator coolant, engine oil, transaxle fluid and, if equipped, the power steering fluid into suitable containers.
5. Properly discharge the air conditioning system, if equipped.
6. If carburetor equipped, remove the air cleaner assembly. On EFI engine, disconnect the vane airflow meter connector. Remove the vane airflow meter and hose.
7. Remove the radiator and cooling fan as an assembly.
8. Disconnect the accelerator cable from the mounting bracket and throttle lever.
9. Disconnect the speedometer cable from the transaxle.
10. Disconnect the fuel hoses. Plug or cover the hose openings to prevent dirt from entering and to avoid fuel leakage.
11. Disconnect the heater hoses and the brake booster vacuum hose.
12. On carbureted engine, disconnect the carburetor-to-chassis hoses and the wide open throttle vacuum switch connector. On EFI engine, disconnect the vacuum hose at the throttle body.
13. If equipped with automatic transaxle, disconnect the transaxle vacuum hose.
14. Tag and disconnect the carbon canister hoses and the engine harness connectors and grounds. Disconnect the distributor wiring at the coil.
15. Disconnect the power steering lines, if equipped. Disconnect the air conditioning lines and the air conditioning electrical connector, if equipped.
16. On automatic transaxles, remove the nut that connects the shift lever to the manual shaft assembly. Remove the shift cable from the transaxle. On manual transaxles, disconnect the clutch control cable from the transaxle.
17. Raise and safely support the vehicle. Remove the front wheel and tire assemblies.
18. Remove the stabilizer mounting nuts and brackets.
19. Remove the lower arm clamp bolts and nuts. Pull the lower arms downward, separating the lower arms from the knuckles.
20. Remove the halfshafts and install differential plugs T87C-7025-C or equivalent, between the differential side gears.
21. If equipped with a manual transaxle, disconnect the shift control rod and stabilizer bar from the transaxle.
22. Remove the catalytic converter inlet pipe.
23. Support the engine using 3-bar engine support D88L-6000-A or equivalent.
24. Remove the crossmember attaching bolts.
25. Remove the front and rear engine mount-to-crossmember attaching nuts and remove the crossmember.
26. Lower the vehicle.
27. Remove the attaching bolt, nut

and washer from the side mount. Remove the side mount-to-engine attaching nuts.

28. Position a suitable jack or hoist and attach it to the engine. Carefully remove the engine and transaxle as an assembly.

29. Remove the gusset plates, starter and flywheel cover.

30. If equipped with automatic transaxle, remove the torque converter bolts.

31. Remove the engine-to-transaxle bolts and separate the transaxle from the engine.

To install:

32. Mount the transaxle to the engine. Install the engine-to-transaxle bolts and tighten to 41–59 ft. lbs. (55–80 Nm).

33. If equipped with automatic transaxle, install the torque converter bolts and tighten to 26–36 ft. lbs. (34–49 Nm).

34. Install the flywheel cover and tighten the bolts to 61–87 inch lbs. (7–10 Nm). Install the starter.

35. Install the gusset plates and tighten the bolts to 27–38 ft. lbs. (37–52 Nm).

36. Position the engine and transaxle assembly in the engine compartment.

37. Install the side mount and tighten the side mount-to-engine attaching nuts to 29–40 ft. lbs. (39–54 Nm). Install the attaching bolt, washer and nut to the side mount and tighten to 29–40 ft. lbs. (39–54 Nm).

38. Raise and safely support the vehicle.

39. Position the crossmember and install the attaching bolts. Tighten the bolts to 47–66 ft. lbs. (64–89 Nm).

40. Install the front and rear engine mount-to-crossmember attaching nuts. Tighten the front nuts to 32–38 ft. lbs. (43–52 Nm) and the rear nut to 21–34 ft. lbs. (28–46 Nm).

41. Install the catalytic converter inlet pipe and tighten the nuts to 23–34 ft. lbs. (31–46 Nm).

42. If equipped with manual transaxle, install the shift control rod and stabilizer bar.

43. Remove the differential plugs and install the halfshafts. Install the lower arm ball joint to the knuckle and tighten the clamp nut and bolt to 32–40 ft. lbs. (43–54 Nm).

44. Install the stabilizer bracket and mounting nuts. Tighten the mounting nuts to 40–50 ft. lbs. (54–68 Nm).

45. Install the front wheel and tire assemblies and lower the vehicle.

46. If equipped with manual transaxle, connect the clutch cable. If equipped with automatic transaxle, install the shift lever on the manual shaft assembly and tighten the nut to 34–47 ft. lbs. (44–64 Nm). Attach the shift cable to the transaxle.

47. Connect the distributor wiring to the coil and connect all engine harness connectors and grounds.

48. If equipped with air conditioning, connect the lines and the electrical connector.

49. If equipped with automatic transaxle, connect the transaxle vacuum hose.

50. On EFI engine, connect the vacuum hose at the throttle body.

51. Connect the brake booster vacuum hose, the carbon canister hoses, the heater hoses and the fuel lines.

52. On carbureted engine, connect the carburetor-to-chassis hoses and the wide open throttle vacuum switch connector.

53. Connect the speedometer cable and connect the accelerator cable to the throttle lever and mounting bracket.

54. If equipped, connect the power steering lines.

55. Install the radiator and cooling fan.

56. On EFI engine, install the vane airflow meter and hose. Connect the vane airflow meter connector.

57. On carburetor equipped engine, install the air cleaner assembly.

58. Install the hood, aligning the marks that were made during the removal procedure.

59. Install the battery carrier and the battery. Connect the battery cables.

60. Add the proper types and quantities of engine oil, transaxle fluid and coolant.

61. If equipped, add power steering fluid to the reservoir.

62. If equipped, charge the air conditioning system.

63. Start the engine. Check for leaks and proper fluid levels. Road test.

Engine Mounts

REMOVAL & INSTALLATION

Front Mount

1. Disconnect the negative battery cable. Remove the front mount through bolt attaching nut.

2. Properly support the engine.

3. Raise and support the vehicle safely.

4. Remove the front mount to crossmember attaching nuts.

5. Raise the vehicle, as required, to gain sufficient clearance to remove the front mount. Remove the front mount from the crossmember. Note and record the position of the mount to ensure proper installation.

To install:

6. Install the engine mount onto the crossmember in the original installation position.

7. Secure the mount to the cross-

member with the attaching nuts. Torque the attaching nuts to 32–38 ft. lbs. (43–52 Nm).

8. Lower the vehicle.

9. Move the engine as necessary until the holes in the mount align with the holes in the engine bracket. Install the through bolt and attaching nut. Torque the nut to 29–40 ft. lbs. (39–54 Nm).

10. Remove the engine support.

Rear Mount

1. Disconnect the negative battery cable. Raise the vehicle and support safely.

2. Properly support the engine.

3. Remove the mount-to-crossmember attaching nut.

4. Remove the mount-to-engine attaching bolts.

5. If necessary, raise the engine to gain access to the rear mount. Remove the mount from the crossmember.

To install:

6. Position the mount onto the rear engine bracket.

7. Install the mount to engine bracket bolts. Torque the bolts to 29–40 ft. lbs. (39–54 Nm).

8. Lower the engine and mount onto the crossmember.

9. Install the attaching nut and torque to 21–34 ft. lbs. (28–46 Nm).

10. Remove the engine support.

Side Mount

1. Disconnect the negative battery cable. Properly support the engine.

2. Remove the through bolt, nut and washer.

3. Remove the bracket-to-engine attaching nuts.

4. Remove the side mount and bracket as an assembly.

To install:

5. Position the engine mount and bracket onto the engine.

6. Install the engine-to-bracket attaching nuts. Torque the nuts to 29–40 ft. lbs. (39–54 Nm).

7. Position the washer against the mount. Install the through bolt and nut. Torque the nut and bolt to 29–40 ft. lbs. (39–54 Nm).

8. Remove the engine support.

Cylinder Head

REMOVAL & INSTALLATION

1. Disconnect the negative battery cable. Drain the cooling system.

2. Position the engine at TDC on the compression stroke.

3. Remove the valve cover. Remove the timing belt cover and timing belt.

4. Remove the exhaust manifold. Remove the intake manifold.

5. Remove the spark plug wires and

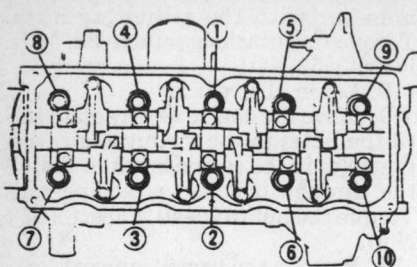

Cylinder head bolt torque sequence

spark plugs. Remove the distributor.

6. Remove the front and rear engine lift hangers. Remove the engine ground wire.

7. Remove the wiring harness connector. Remove the upper radiator hose. Remove the bypass hose and bracket.

8. Remove the cylinder head retaining bolts. Remove the cylinder head from the engine. Discard the gasket.

9. Clean all mating surfaces of dirt and old gasket material.

To install:

10. Position the cylinder head gasket on the engine block. Install the cylinder head and tighten the bolts, in sequence, in 2 equal steps. The final torque should be 56–60 ft. lbs. (75–81 Nm).

11. Connect the radiator hose, bypass hose, wiring harness connectors, engine lift hangers and engine ground wire.

12. Install the distributor, spark plugs and wires.

13. Install the intake and exhaust manifolds. Install the timing belt and cover.

14. Install the valve cover.

15. Fill the cooling system.

16. Connect the negative battery cable. Start the engine and check for leaks.

Valve Lifters

REMOVAL & INSTALLATION

All EFI engines are equipped with hydraulic lash adjusters that automatically maintain valve lash.

1. Disconnect the negative battery cable.

2. Remove the valve cover and the rocker arm shaft assemblies.

3. Remove the hydraulic lash adjuster from the rocker arm.

To install:

4. Pour engine oil into the oil reservoir in the rocker arm. Apply engine oil to the new hydraulic lash adjuster.

5. Install the hydraulic lash adjuster into the rocker arm.

NOTE: Be careful not to damage the O-ring when installing the hydraulic lash adjuster.

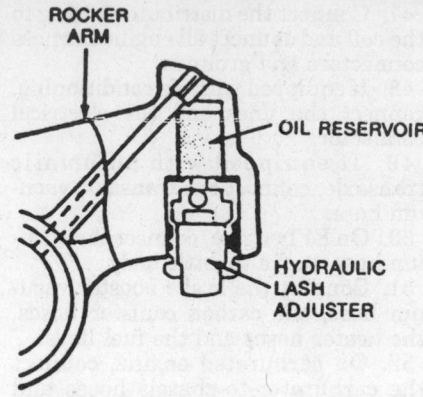

Rocker arm and hydraulic lash adjuster assembly—EFI engine

6. Install the rocker arm shaft assemblies and install the valve cover.

7. Connect the negative battery cable.

Valve Lash

ADJUSTMENT

Carbureted Engine

1. Start the engine and allow to reach normal operating temperature. Stop the engine.

2. Remove the valve cover.

3. Turn the crankshaft by hand, in the direction of normal rotation, until the piston in the No. 1 cylinder reaches TDC on the compression stroke.

4. Adjust the No. 1 and No. 2 intake valves and the No. 1 and No. 3 exhaust

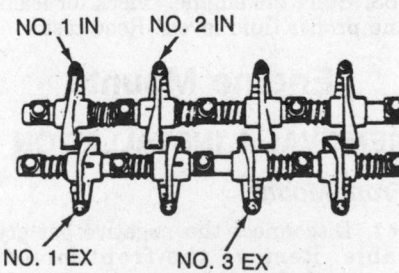

Intake and exhaust valve arrangement

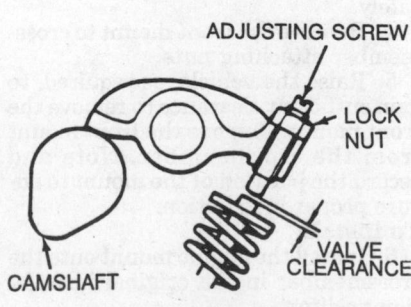

Valve lash adjustment

valves. The valve lash should be 0.012 in. (0.30mm).

5. Rotate the crankshaft 360 degrees so the No. 4 piston is at TDC on the compression stroke. Adjust the remaining valves.

6. Install the valve cover using a new gasket. Tighten the valve cover attaching bolts to 44–79 inch lbs. (5–9 Nm).

EFI Engine

Inspect hydraulic lash adjuster operation by pushing down each rocker arm by hand. If a rocker arm moves down, replace the hydraulic lash adjuster.

Rocker Arms/Shafts

REMOVAL & INSTALLATION

1. Disconnect the negative battery cable.

2. On carbureted engine, remove the air cleaner assembly. If equipped with fuel injection, remove the air hose and the resonance chamber.

3. Disconnect the accelerator cable from the throttle lever and routing bracket. Remove the PCV valve.

4. Remove the spark plug wires from the routing clips. Remove the upper timing belt cover.

5. Remove the valve cover retaining bolts. Remove the valve cover. Discard the gasket.

6. Remove the rocker arm shaft retaining bolts and remove the rocker arms/shafts assemblies from the engine. If the shafts are to be disassembled, keep all parts in order so they can be assembled in their correct positions.

To install:

7. Clean all gasket mating surfaces.

8. If disassembled, coat the rocker arms and shafts with clean engine oil and reassemble.

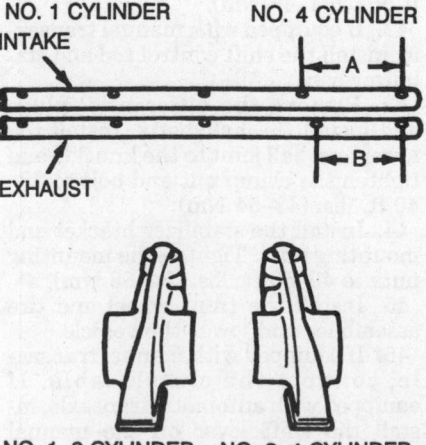

Rocker arms and shafts

9. Install the rocker arms/shafts assemblies with the shaft retaining bolts. Tighten the bolts, in sequence, to 16–21 ft. lbs. (22–28 Nm).

10. Install the valve cover with a new gasket. Tighten the valve cover retaining bolts to 44–79 inch lbs. (5–9 Nm).

11. Install the remaining components in the reverse order of removal. Check the valve lash adjustment.

Intake Manifold

REMOVAL & INSTALLATION

1. On EFI engines, relieve the fuel system pressure. Disconnect the negative battery cable and drain the cooling system.

2. Remove the air cleaner assembly, if equipped with a carburetor. If equipped with fuel injection, remove the intake manifold bracket.

3. Disconnect the accelerator cable.

4. Identify, tag and disconnect the necessary vacuum hoses and electrical connectors.

5. Disconnect the fuel line(s).

6. Support the intake manifold by hand and remove the retaining bolts. Remove the intake manifold from the cylinder head.

7. Remove the old gasket material and thoroughly clean the intake manifold and cylinder head surfaces.

To install:

8. Apply a new gasket to the cylinder head surface and hold in place.

9. Position the intake manifold onto the new gasket and install the retaining bolts. Torque the retaining bolts to 14–20 ft. lbs. (19–26 Nm) in a crisscross pattern, from the inside out.

10. Connect the vacuum hoses and electrical wiring to their respective connections. Install the accelerator cable.

11. Connect the fuel line(s).

12. Install the air cleaner assembly on carbureted engine. Install the intake manifold bracket on EFI engine and tighten to 22–34 ft. lbs. (31–46 Nm).

13. Refill the cooling system to the proper level. Connect the negative battery cable.

14. Start the engine and check for leaks.

Exhaust Manifold

REMOVAL & INSTALLATION

1. Disconnect the negative battery cable.

2. Raise and safely support the vehicle.

3. Disconnect the catalytic converter inlet pipe from the exhaust manifold.

4. If equipped, remove the pulse air tube to catalytic converter inlet pipe attaching nuts.

5. Unbolt the catalytic converter support bracket.

6. Lower the vehicle.

7. Remove the air cleaner assembly on carbureted engine. On fuel injected vehicle, remove the throttle body-to-air cleaner hose.

8. Remove the exhaust manifold heat shroud.

9. Separate the oxygen sensor wiring connector from the routing bracket and disconnect the electrical connector.

10. If equipped, unbolt the pulse air routing bracket clamp. Remove the pulse air tube and gaskets. Discard the gaskets.

11. Support the exhaust manifold by hand and remove the attaching nuts and bolts. Separate the exhaust manifold from the cylinder head and inlet pipe. Remove the inlet pipe and exhaust manifold gaskets and discard.

12. If necessary, remove the oxygen sensor. Inspect the sensor gasket for damage and replace if necessary.

To install:

13. Remove all existing gasket material from the exhaust manifold, cylinder head inlet pipe and, if equipped, the pulse air tube flange surfaces. Clean all threaded surfaces.

14. If removed, position the gasket onto the oxygen sensor and install into the exhaust manifold.

15. Apply a new gasket onto the cylinder head studs and position the exhaust manifold onto the gasket. Install the attaching nuts and bolts and torque to 12–17 ft. lbs. (16–23 Nm).

16. Install the heat shroud.

17. If equipped, install the pulse air tube and mounting bracket clamp. On fuel injected vehicle, install the air hose. On carbureted engine, install the air cleaner assembly.

18. Connect the oxygen sensor electrical connector and secure the connector in the routing bracket.

19. Raise the vehicle and support it safely.

20. Position a new gasket over the exhaust manifold studs and, if equipped, 2 new gaskets onto the pulse air tube studs.

21. Raise the catalytic converter inlet pipe into position on the exhaust manifold and pulse air tube studs and support by hand. Install the attaching nuts and torque to 23–34 ft. lbs. (31–46 Nm).

22. Install the catalytic converter inlet pipe support bracket.

23. Lower the vehicle and connect the negative battery cable.

24. Start the engine and inspect for exhaust gas leaks.

Timing Belt Front Cover

REMOVAL & INSTALLATION

1. Disconnect the negative battery cable. Remove the drive belts.

2. Remove the 3 water pump pulley attaching bolts and remove the water pump pulley.

3. Raise and safely support the vehicle.

4. Remove the right front wheel and tire assembly and the right inner fender panel.

5. Remove the 4 attaching bolts and the screws from the crankshaft pulley. Remove the spacer and outer pulley, if equipped. Remove the inner spacer, inner pulley and the baffle or guide plates, as required.

6. Remove the attaching bolts and the upper and lower covers.

To install:

7. Install the upper and lower covers. Install the attaching bolts and tighten to 69–95 inch lbs. (8–11 Nm).

8. Install the crankshaft pulley baffle with the curved lip facing outward or install the large guide plate and then the small guide plate, as required.

9. Install the inner pulley with the deep recess facing outward. Install the spacer and then the outer pulley, spacer and screws. Install the pulley bolts and tighten to 109–152 inch lbs. (12–17 Nm).

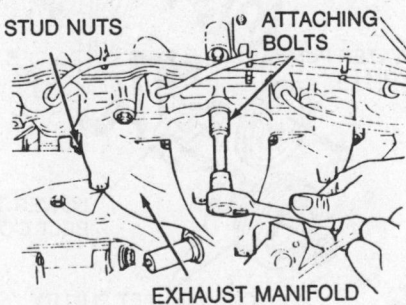

Exhaust manifold mounting bolt and nut locations

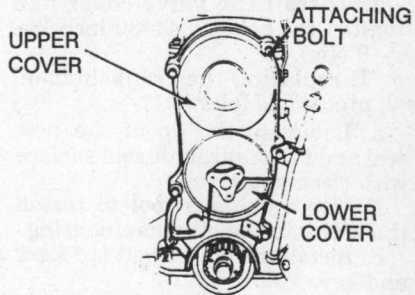

Upper and lower timing belt covers with attaching bolts

10. Install the inner fender panel and the wheel and tire assembly. Lower the vehicle.

11. Install the water pump pulley and tighten the bolts to 36–45 ft. lbs. (49–61 Nm).

12. Install the drive belts. Connect the negative battery cable.

OIL SEAL REPLACEMENT

1. Disconnect the negative battery cable.

2. Remove the timing belt covers and timing belt.

3. If replacing the crankshaft oil seal, proceed as follows:

   a. If equipped with manual transaxle, place the shift lever in 4th gear and apply the parking brake.

   b. If equipped with automatic transaxle, install flywheel holding tool T84P–6375–A or equivalent, to lock the flywheel.

   c. Remove the crankshaft sprocket attaching bolt and the sprocket and key.

   d. Use a suitable tool to pry the crankshaft seal from the oil pump housing.

4. If replacing the camshaft oil seal, proceed as follows:

   a. Remove the valve cover.

   b. Use a large open-end wrench to hold the camshaft and remove the camshaft sprocket attaching bolt.

   c. Remove the sprocket.

   d. Drive the old seal through the cylinder head. Cut the seal with side cutters and remove the seal.

To install:

5. If replacing the camshaft oil seal, proceed as follows:

   a. Clean the camshaft and cylinder head seal surface.

   b. Lubricate the seal lip and camshaft seal surface with clean engine oil.

   c. Install the seal using a seal installer.

   d. Install the camshaft sprocket and bolt.

   e. Hold the camshaft with a large open-end wrench and tighten the sprocket bolt to 36–45 ft. lbs. (49–61 Nm).

   f. Install the valve cover and tighten the bolts to 44–80 inch lbs. (5–9 Nm).

6. If replacing the crankshaft oil seal, proceed as follows:

   a. Lubricate the lip of the new seal and the crankshaft seal surface with clean engine oil.

   b. Use a suitable tool to install the seal into the oil pump housing.

   c. Install the crankshaft sprocket and key.

   d. Coat the threads of the crankshaft sprocket bolt with a non-hardening sealer. Install the bolt and tighten to 80–85 ft. lbs. (108–118 Nm).

   e. Remove the flywheel holding tool, if necessary.

7. Install the timing belt and timing belt covers.

8. Connect the negative battery cable.

Timing Belt and Tensioner

REMOVAL & INSTALLATION

1. Disconnect the negative battery cable.

2. Remove the timing belt covers. Mark the direction of rotation of the timing belt, if the belt is to be reused.

3. Remove the timing belt tensioner spring and retaining bolt. Remove the timing belt.

To install:

4. Align the camshaft and crankshaft timing marks with the marks located on the cylinder head and oil pump housing.

5. If reusing the original timing belt, install the timing belt with the mark made indicating the direction of rotation.

6. Install the timing belt tensioner spring and cover on the pulley. Position the tensioner and spring assembly on the engine and install the attaching bolt. Do not tighten the bolt at this time.

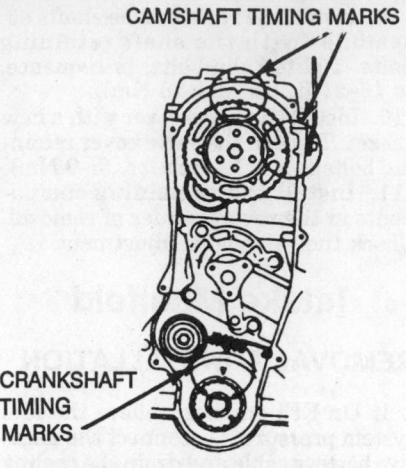

Camshaft and crankshaft timing mark alignment

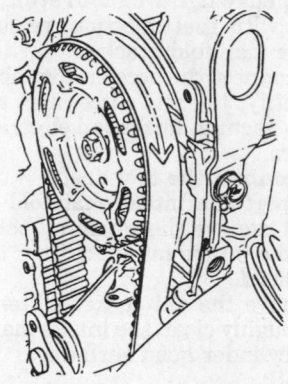

Direction of timing belt rotation

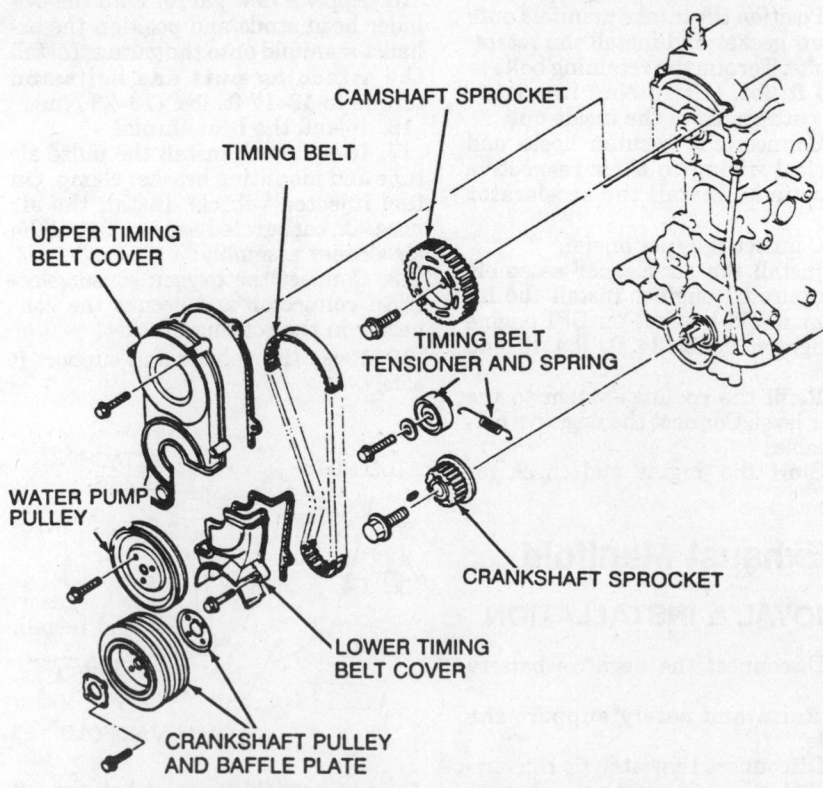

Timing belt, sprockets and related components

7. Reconnect the free end of the spring to the spring anchor. Torque the tensioner bolt to 14–19 ft. lbs. (19–26 Nm).

8. Install the timing belt covers and connect the negative battery cable.

Timing Sprockets

REMOVAL & INSTALLATION

Camshaft Sprocket

1. Disconnect the negative battery cable.

2. Remove the timing belt and timing belt tensioner.

3. Remove the valve cover.

4. With a large open-end wrench, hold the camshaft stationary and remove the camshaft sprocket retaining bolt.

5. Pull the camshaft sprocket with dowel pin from the camshaft. Take care not to lose the dowel pin.

To install:

6. Install the camshaft sprocket, dowel pin and retaining bolt.

7. Hold the camshaft stationary with the wrench and torque the retaining bolt to 36–45 ft. lbs. (49–61 Nm).

8. Install the timing belt and tensioner.

9. Install the valve cover and tighten the bolts to 44–80 inch lbs. (5–9 Nm).

10. Connect the negative battery cable.

Crankshaft Sprocket

1. Disconnect the negative battery cable.

2. Remove the timing belt and timing belt tensioner.

3. If equipped with manual transaxle, place the shift lever in 4th gear and apply the parking brake. If equipped with automatic transaxle vehicle, install flywheel holding tool T84P–6375–A or equivalent.

4. Remove the crankshaft sprocket retaining bolt.

5. Pull the crankshaft sprocket and key from the crankshaft. Make certain not to lose the key when removing the crankshaft sprocket. Replace the key if worn or damaged.

To install:

6. Position the crankshaft sprocket onto the crankshaft and align the keyways. Install the key.

7. Coat the threads of the retaining bolt with non-hardening sealer. Install the retaining bolt and torque to 80–85 ft. lbs. (108–118 Nm).

8. Remove the flywheel holding tool, if necessary.

9. Install the timing belt.

10. Connect the negative battery cable.

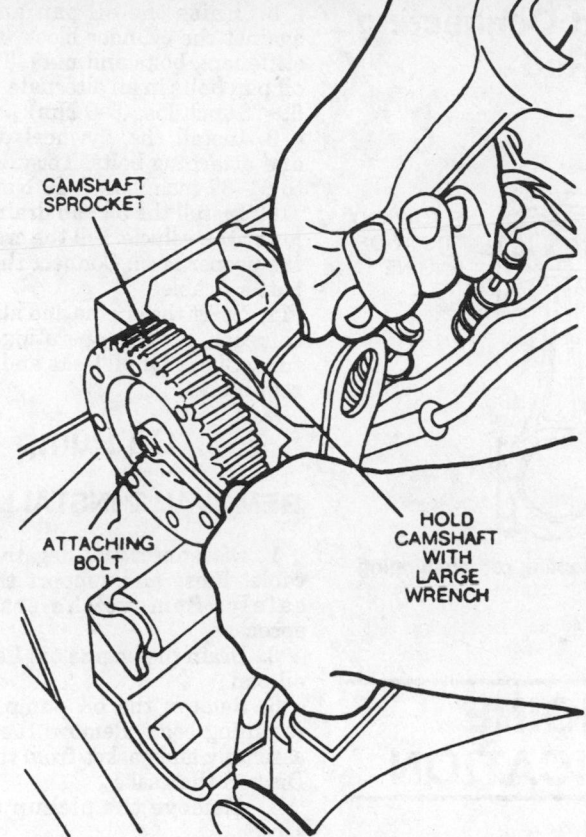

Camshaft sprocket removal

Camshaft

REMOVAL & INSTALLATION

1. Disconnect the negative battery cable. Drain the cooling system.

2. Remove the cylinder head from the engine.

3. Position the cylinder head in a suitable holding fixture. Remove the camshaft sprocket. Remove the rocker arm/shaft assemblies.

4. Remove the camshaft thrust plate and the camshaft from the cylinder head.

5. Remove the camshaft seal.

To install:

6. Lubricate the camshaft journals, lobes and bearings with clean engine oil.

7. Carefully slide the camshaft into the cylinder head, being careful not to damage the journals, lobes or bearings. Install the camshaft thrust plate.

8. Lubricate the lip of the new camshaft seal with engine oil and install, using a seal installer.

9. Install the rocker arm/shaft assemblies and tighten the mounting bolts, in sequence, to 16–21 ft. lbs. (22–28 Nm).

10. Install the camshaft sprocket. Hold the camshaft with an open-end wrench and tighten the sprocket bolt to 36–45 ft. lbs. (49–61 Nm).

11. Install the cylinder head.

12. Fill the cooling system and connect the negative battery cable.

13. Start the engine and bring to normal operating temperature. Check for leaks. Check the valve lash, if necessary.

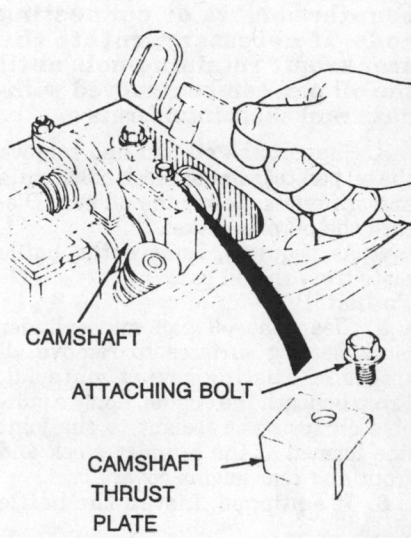

Camshaft and camshaft thrust plate

Piston and Connecting Rod

POSITIONING

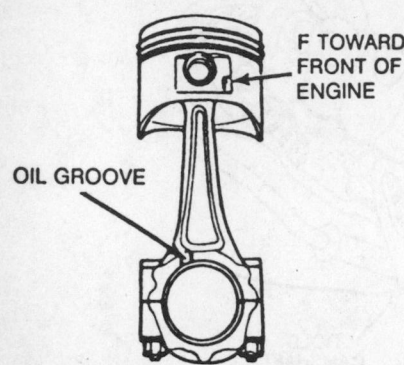

F TOWARD FRONT OF ENGINE

OIL GROOVE

Piston and connecting rod positioning

ENGINE LUBRICATION

Oil Pan

REMOVAL & INSTALLATION

1. Disconnect the negative battery cable. Raise and support the vehicle safely. Drain the engine oil.
2. Remove the flywheel dust cover retaining bolts and remove the cover.

NOTE: Depending on the position of the crankshaft, the oil pan may encounter interference during removal from the crankshaft counterweights or connecting rods. If necessary, rotate the crankshaft retaining bolt until the oil pan can be removed without crankshaft interference.

3. Support the oil pan and remove the oil pan to cylinder block bolts, nuts and stiffeners. Lower the oil pan. Discard the oil pan gasket.
4. As required, remove the baffle plate from the oil pan.
To install:
5. Clean the oil pan and cylinder block sealing surfaces to remove all traces of existing gasket material. From beneath the engine, apply a suitable oil resistant sealant to the joint line formed at the cylinder block and front and rear engine covers.
6. If equipped, install the baffle plate.
7. Apply the new rubber gasket to the oil pan.

8. Raise the oil pan and gasket against the cylinder block. Install the stiffeners, bolts and nuts. Torque the oil pan bolts in an alternate pattern to 69–78 inch lbs. (8–9 Nm).
9. Install the flywheel dust cover and attaching bolts. Torque the bolts to 61–87 inch lbs. (7–10 Nm).
10. Install the oil pan drain plug and lower the vehicle. Fill the crankcase to the proper level. Connect the negative battery cable.
11. Start the engine and allow the oil to reach normal operating temperature. Check for oil leaks and correct as required.

Oil Pump

REMOVAL & INSTALLATION

1. Disconnect the negative battery cable. Raise and support the vehicle safely. Remove the crankshaft sprocket.
2. Drain the engine oil. Remove the oil pan.
3. Remove the oil pump assembly retaining bolts. Remove the oil pump assembly and gasket from the engine. Discard the gasket.
4. Remove the pickup tube and screen.
5. Remove the screws from the oil pump cover. Remove the cover. Remove the oil pump gears.
6. Remove the front seal from the pump assembly. Remove the cotter pin, spring and relief valve from the oil pump body.
To install:
7. Clean the oil pump housing and components with a suitable solvent and allow to dry.
8. Lubricate the oil pump relief valve and install into the bore. Install the spring, retainer and cotter pin.
9. Lubricate the lip of the new crankshaft seal and install the seal into the pump, using a suitable installation tool.
10. Lubricate and install the gears in the pump body and install the pump body cover. Coat the screws with a suitable locking compound and tighten.
11. Clean the cylinder block contact surface to remove the old gasket material and sealant. Thoroughly coat both sides of the new oil pump gasket with a suitable sealant compound. Apply the gasket to the oil pump and remove any excess sealant.

NOTE: Do not allow the sealant compound to enter the oil pump discharge opening once the gasket is in place. This opening must be free and clear before the oil pump is installed onto the cylinder block.

12. Position the oil pump against the cylinder block surface and install the retaining bolts. Torque the bolts to 14–19 ft. lbs. (19–25 Nm).
13. Install a new gasket onto the oil pump inlet and bolt the pickup tube to the oil pump. Torque the bolts to 69–95 inch lbs. (8–11 Nm).
14. Install the oil pan and the crankshaft sprocket.
15. Lower the vehicle. Fill the crankcase to the proper level with engine oil. Connect the negative battery cable.
16. Start the engine and allow the oil to reach normal operating temperature. Check for leaks and correct as required.

CHECKING

1. Remove the oil pump assembly from the vehicle and disassemble. Clean all parts in solvent and allow to dry.
2. Measure the inner gear tip to outer gear clearance at the minimum clearance point. The clearance should be 0.0078 in. (0.198mm) maximum.
3. Inspect the oil pump body for scoring in the outer gear bore. A slight amount of scoring is acceptable.
4. Measure the housing-to-outer gear clearance with a feeler gauge. The clearance should be no more than 0.0087 in. (0.22mm).
5. Measure the gear endplay. Gear endplay should not exceed 0.0055 in. If the pump clearances are not within specification, replace the gears or the body. Clean the relief valve internals and inspect for nicks, burrs or binding operation. Clean the pickup tube and screen.
6. Assemble the oil pump relief valve into the bore. Install the spring, retainer and cotter pin.
7. Press or drive a new oil seal into the oil pump body bore.
8. Coat the cover attaching screws with a suitable thread locking compound and install the cover.
9. Install the oil pump assembly in the vehicle.

Rear Main Bearing Oil Seal

REMOVAL & INSTALLATION

1. Disconnect the negative battery cable.
2. Remove the transaxle from the vehicle.
3. Remove the flywheel. If necessary, remove the cover plate.
4. Remove the seal retainer. Remove the crankshaft seal.
To install:
5. Clean the sealing surface on the cover plate.

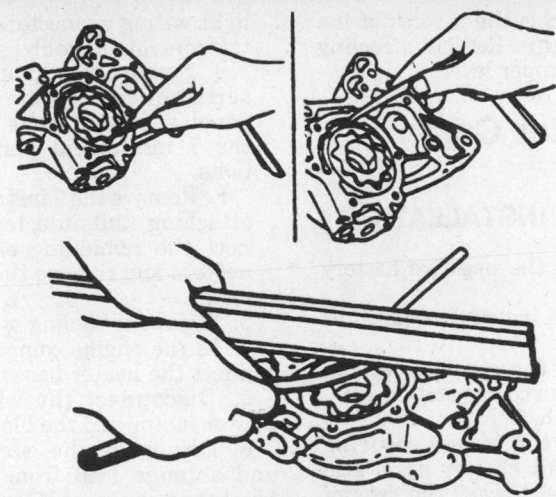

Oil pump clearance checking

6. Apply engine oil to the inside and outside of a new seal. Install the seal into the cover plate using a seal installer, with the hollow part of the seal facing the engine.

7. Install the seal retainer and tighten to 69–95 inch lbs. (8–11 Nm).

8. Trim the excess gasket material off the seal retainer gasket after installation.

9. Install the cover plate and tighten the attaching bolts to 69–95 inch lbs. (8–11 Nm).

10. Install the flywheel and tighten the bolts to 71–76 ft. lbs. (96–103 Nm).

11. Install the transaxle. Connect the negative battery cable.

ENGINE COOLING

Radiator

REMOVAL & INSTALLATION

1. Disconnect the negative battery cable.

2. Remove the radiator pressure cap from the filler neck.

— CAUTION —

Never remove the radiator cap while the engine is running or personal injury from scalding hot coolant or steam may result. If possible, wait until the engine has cooled to remove the radiator cap. If this is not possible, wrap a thick cloth around the radiator cap and turn it slowly to the first stop. Step back while the pressure is released from the cooling system. When it is certain all the pressure has been released, press down on the cap, still with the cloth, and turn and remove it.

3. Position a suitable container under the radiator and open the draincock to drain the radiator.

4. Disconnect the coolant recovery hose from the filler neck.

5. Loosen the retaining clamp and disconnect the upper radiator hose from the radiator.

6. Disconnect the cooling fan wiring harness connector. Disengage the wiring harness from the routing clamps on the cooling fan shroud.

7. Loosen the retaining clamp and disconnect the lower radiator hose.

8. Remove the 4 bolts attaching the radiator upper tank brackets to the vehicle body and remove the radiator/cooling fan assembly. Separate the fan and shroud assembly from the radiator, if necessary.

To install:

9. If removed, install the fan and shroud assembly on the radiator.

10. Lower the radiator/cooling fan assembly into the engine compartment, making sure the mounting insulators engage with their supports. Attach the radiator to the mounting brackets with the 4 bolts.

11. Connect the cooling fan wiring and position the wiring harness in the routing clips on the fan shroud.

12. Connect the coolant recovery hose and the upper and lower radiator hoses.

13. Close the radiator draincock. Connect the negative battery cable.

14. Fill and bleed the cooling system. Check for leaks.

Electric Cooling Fan

TESTING

1. Check for voltage at the cooling fan motor as follows:

a. Turn the ignition key **ON** but do not start the engine.

b. Use a voltmeter to measure the voltage at the cooling fan motor **Y** terminal.

c. If the voltage is greater than 10 volts, proceed to Step 2.

d. If the voltage is less than 10 volts, service the **Y** wire from the 20 amp cooling fan fuse to the cooling fan motor.

2. Check for operation of the cooling fan motor as follows:

a. Turn the ignition key **ON** but do not start the engine.

b. Ground the **Y/R** terminal at the cooling fan motor with a jumper wire.

c. If the cooling fan operates, proceed to Step 3.

d. If the cooling fan does not operate, service the motor side of the cooling fan harness. If the harness is okay, replace the cooling fan motor.

3. Check for power at the cooling fan relay as follows:

a. Turn the ignition key **ON** but do not start the engine.

b. Disconnect the cooling fan relay.

c. Using a voltmeter, measure the voltage at the cooling fan relay **Y/R** wire.

d. If the voltage is greater than 10 volts, proceed to Step 4.

e. If the voltage is not greater than 10 volts, service the **Y/R** wire from the cooling fan motor to the cooling fan relay, air conditioning relay and electronic control unit.

4. Check the voltage supply at the cooling fan relay as follows:

a. Turn the ignition key **ON** but do not start the engine.

b. Disconnect the cooling fan relay.

c. Using a voltmeter, measure the voltage at the cooling fan relay **BK/Y** terminal.

d. If the voltage is greater than 10 volts, proceed to Step 5.

e. If the voltage is not greater than 10 volts, service the **BK/Y** wire from the cooling fan relay to the 10 amp "METER" fuse.

5. Check the cooling fan relay as follows:

a. Make sure the ignition key is **OFF**.

b. Remove the cooling fan relay.

c. Apply battery power to the relay **A** terminal.

d. Using an ohmmeter, measure the resistance between relay **B** and **C** terminals.

e. Ground the relay **D** terminal with a jumper wire.

f. If the resistance is greater than 10,000 ohms with the **D** terminal grounded and less than 5 ohms with the **D** terminal ungrounded, proceed to Step 6.

g. If the resistance is not as specified in Step 5f, replace the cooling fan relay.

6. Check the coolant temperature switch voltage as follows:

a. Turn the ignition key **ON** but do not start the engine.

b. Disconnect the coolant temperature switch.

c. Using a voltmeter, measure the voltage at the coolant temperature switch **GN/R** terminal on 1989–90 vehicles or the **GN/Y** terminal on 1991–93 vehicles.

d. If the voltage is greater than 10 volts, proceed to Step 7.

e. If the voltage is not greater than 10 volts, service the **GN/R** wire on 1989–90 vehicles or the **GN/Y** wire on 1991–93 vehicles, that runs from the cooling fan relay to the coolant temperature switch.

7. Check the coolant temperature switch operation as follows:

a. Let the engine cool completely.

b. Remove the radiator cap.

c. Place a suitable thermometer/pyrometer probe in the radiator, under the coolant surface.

d. Using an ohmmeter, measure the resistance between the coolant temperature switch terminal and ground.

e. Start the engine. Run the engine until the coolant temperature exceeds 207°F (97°C), then shut the engine **OFF**.

f. If the switch opens at 207°F (97°C) and then closes when the coolant temperature falls below 194°F (90°C), service the cooling fan relay ground **BK** wire.

g. If the switch does not perform as specified in Step 7f, replace the cooling fan switch.

REMOVAL & INSTALLATION

1. Disconnect the negative battery cable. Partially drain the radiator to a level just below the upper radiator hose.

2. Loosen the retaining clamp and disconnect the upper radiator hose at the radiator.

3. Disconnect the cooling fan wiring harness connector and disengage the wiring harnesses from the routing clamps on the cooling fan shroud.

4. Remove the bolts attaching the top of the fan shroud to the radiator.

5. Support the fan/shroud assembly and remove the bolts attaching the bottom of the fan shroud to the radiator. Remove the fan/shroud assembly from the vehicle.

6. Remove the nut and washer and remove the fan from the motor shaft.

7. Remove the wiring harness routing strap.

8. Remove the attaching screws and remove the cooling fan motor from the fan shroud.

9. Installation is the reverse of the removal procedure. Refill the cooling system to the proper level.

Heater Core

REMOVAL & INSTALLATION

1. Disconnect the negative battery cable.

2. Remove the instrument panel as follows:

a. Remove the steering wheel, steering column covers and the combination switch.

b. Remove the screws securing the instrument cluster bezel and move the bezel toward the rear of the vehicle.

c. Disconnect the electrical connectors from the switches on the instrument cluster bezel and remove the bezel.

d. Remove the left and right heater ducts.

e. Disconnect the speedometer cable at the transaxle.

f. Remove the 4 screws securing the instrument cluster and move the cluster toward the rear of the vehicle.

g. Disconnect the instrument cluster electrical connectors and the speedometer cable from the instrument cluster. Remove the instrument cluster.

h. On 1989 vehicles, remove the spacer brace bolts under the steering column and remove the spacer brace.

i. On 1990–93 vehicles, remove the 4 shield nuts and the shield and remove the 2 shield bracket bolts and the shield bracket.

j. Remove the screws securing the glove box hinges to the glove box and remove the glove box.

k. Open the fuse panel cover, remove the fuse panel attaching screws and push the fuse panel forward. Do not remove the fuse panel.

l. If equipped with a shift lever console, remove the shift lever knob and the console attaching screws. Remove the console.

m. If equipped, remove the support bracket bolts and nut and remove the support bracket.

n. Remove the radio and disconnect the cigarette lighter connector.

o. Disconnect the cables from the mode selector, temperature control lever and recirc/fresh air lever.

p. Remove the screws securing the heater/air conditioner control assembly to the instrument panel. Pull the control assembly away from the instrument panel, disconnect the blower motor switch, air conditioning switch and illumination light wiring connectors and remove the control assembly.

q. Remove the snap-in trim inserts concealing the instrument panel attaching bolts and remove the 7 instrument panel attaching bolts.

r. Remove the 2 instrument panel attaching stud nuts, tag and disconnect the remaining electrical connectors and remove the instrument panel.

3. Drain the cooling system.

4. In the engine compartment, disconnect the heater hoses.

5. Disconnect the wiring at the blower motor and the blower resistor.

6. Disengage the wiring harness and antenna lead from the routing bracket on the front of the air distribution housing.

7. Loosen the clamp screw securing the connector duct to the air inlet housing.

8. Remove the attaching nuts at the top and bottom of the plenum, disengage the plenum from the defroster ducts and remove the plenum.

9. Disconnect the link connecting the 2 defroster doors.

10. Remove the attaching screw located just above and to the right of the blower resistor.

11. Turn the plenum around and remove the attaching screw located just to the left of the blower motor opening.

12. Remove the clips securing the 2 halves of the plenum and separate the plenum halves.

13. Remove the heater core and remove the tube insert from the heater core.

To install:

14. Install the heater core tube insert and position the heater core in the plenum.

15. Install the remaining plenum half and the plenum retaining clips.

16. Install the plenum attaching screws and connect the defroster door link.

17. Position the plenum on the dash panel. Make sure the defroster ducts and connector duct are properly seated on the plenum.

18. Install the plenum attaching nuts and tighten the connector duct clamp screw.

19. Connect the blower motor and blower resistor wiring.

20. Route the wiring harness and antenna lead through the routing bracket on the front of the plenum.

21. Install the instrument panel in the reverse order of removal.

22. Connect the heater hoses.

23. Fill the cooling system to the proper level.

24. Start the engine and allow to come to operating temperature. Check

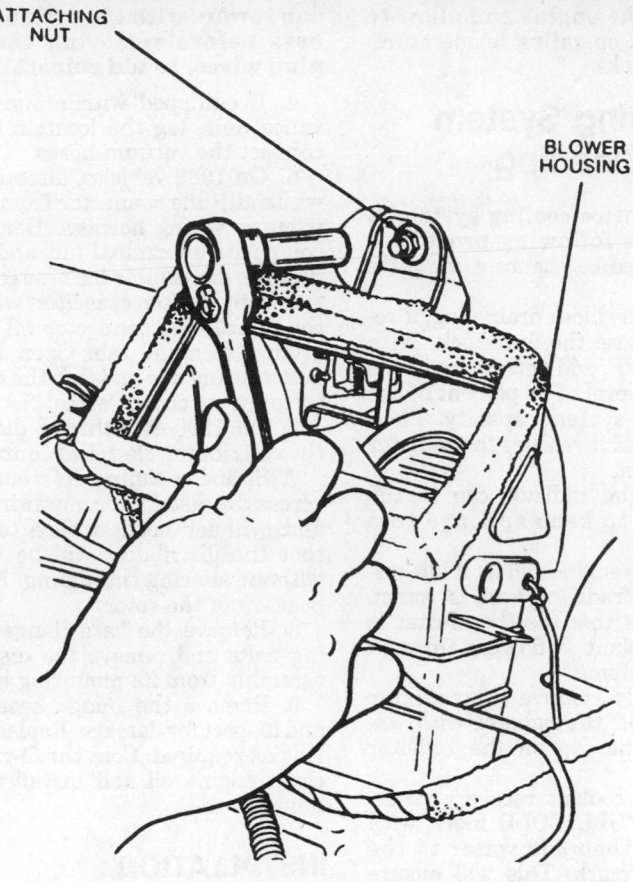

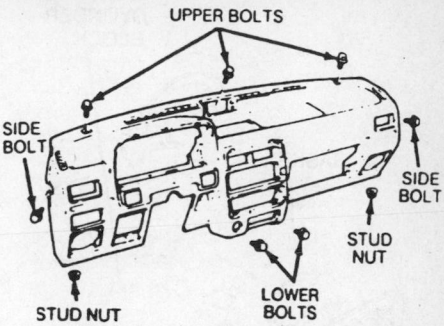

Instrument panel attaching bolts and nuts

the operation of the heating system. Check for coolant leaks.

25. Stop the engine and check the coolant level.

Water Pump

REMOVAL & INSTALLATION

1. Disconnect the negative battery cable.
2. Remove the timing belt.
3. Drain the cooling system.
4. Remove the radiator lower hose and heater return hose from the water pump inlet tube.
5. Remove the bolts attaching the inlet tube to the water pump housing. Remove the inlet tube and gasket.
6. Remove the water pump-to-cylinder block attaching bolts. Remove the water pump and gasket from the cylinder block surface.
7. Remove all existing gasket material from the cylinder block and inlet tube gasket surfaces.

To install:

8. Coat both sides of the new water pump and inlet tube gaskets with a suitable water resistant sealer. Apply the gaskets to the engine and inlet tube surfaces. Make certain the gasket holes are aligned with the bolt holes.
9. Position the water pump against the gasket. Make sure the holes in the water pump are aligned with the gasket holes and that the pump does not shift the position of the gasket.
10. Install the water pump-to-cylinder block attaching bolts and torque to 14–19 ft. lbs. (19–26 Nm). Position the inlet tube and gasket against the water pump housing and install the attaching bolts. Torque the bolts to 14–22 ft. lbs. (19–30 Nm). Tighten the inlet tube bracket nut to 27–38 ft. lbs. (37–52 Nm).
11. Connect the inlet tube hoses and install the timing belt.
12. Fill the cooling system to the proper level. Connect the negative battery cable.
13. Start the engine and allow to reach normal operating temperature. Check for coolant leaks.

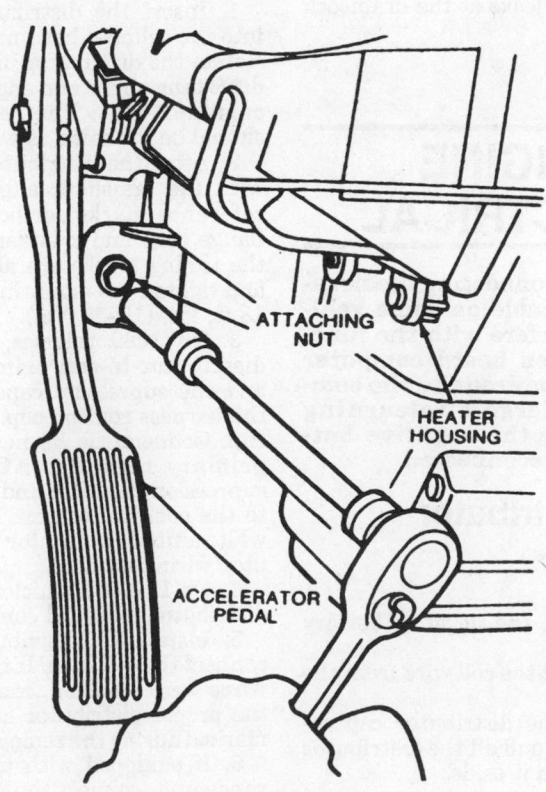

Plenum attaching nut locations

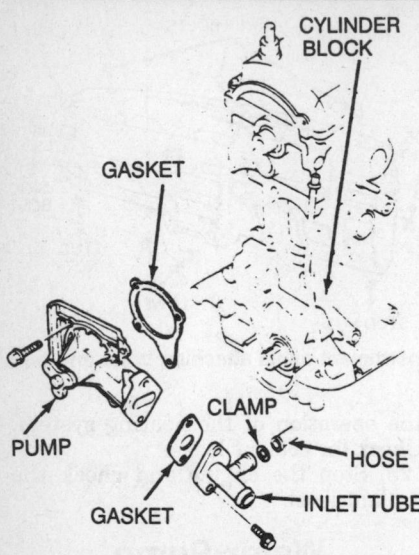

Water pump removal and installation

Thermostat

REMOVAL & INSTALLATION

1. Disconnect the negative battery cable.
2. Disconnect the cooling fan temperature switch wire.
3. Remove the radiator cap and drain the cooling system to a level below the radiator upper hose. Disconnect the radiator upper hose from the thermostat housing.
4. Remove the thermostat housing-to-cylinder head attaching bolts. Remove the thermostat housing and housing gasket. Withdraw the thermostat from the cylinder head.
5. Remove all gasket material from the thermostat housing and cylinder block surfaces.

To install:

6. Install the thermostat in the cylinder head, with the valve end first and the sub valve at the top.
7. Coat a new gasket with a suitable water resistant sealer. Apply the gasket to the cylinder block surface making sure the gasket and cylinder block holes are aligned.
8. Position the thermostat housing onto the cylinder head making sure the bolt holes are aligned and the gasket does not shift. Install the housing attaching bolts. Before tightening the bolts, ensure that the thermostat flange is properly seated against the recess of the housing. Torque the bolts to 14–19 ft. lbs. (19–26 Nm).
9. Connect the radiator upper hose to the thermostat housing. Fill the cooling system to the proper level and install the radiator cap. Connect the cooling fan temperature switch wire and the negative battery cable.

10. Start the engine and allow to reach normal operating temperature. Inspect for leaks.

Cooling System Bleeding

When the entire cooling system is drained, the following procedure should be used to ensure a complete fill.

1. Install the block drain plug, if removed and close the draincock. With the engine OFF, add anti-freeze to the radiator to a level of 50 percent of the total cooling system capacity. Then add water until it reaches the radiator filler neck seat.
2. Install the radiator cap to the first notch to keep spillage to a minimum.
3. Start the engine and let it idle until the upper radiator hose is warm. This indicates that the thermostat is open and coolant is flowing through the entire system.
4. Carefully remove the radiator cap and top off the radiator with water. Install the cap on the radiator securely.
5. Fill the coolant recovery reservoir to the FULL COLD mark with anti-freeze, then add water to the FULL HOT mark. This will ensure that a proper mixture is in the coolant recovery bottle.
6. Check for leaks at the draincock and block plug.

ENGINE ELECTRICAL

NOTE: Disconnecting the negative battery cable on some vehicles may interfere with the functions of the on board computer systems and may require the computer to undergo a relearning process, once the negative battery cable is reconnected.

Distributor

REMOVAL

1. Disconnect the negative battery cable.
2. Disconnect the coil wire from the distributor.
3. Remove the distributor cap attaching screws, pull off the distributor cap and position it aside.

NOTE: If replacing the distributor cap, mark the distributor

cap towers with the cylinder numbers before removing the spark plug wires, to aid reinstallation.

4. If equipped with a vacuum advance unit, tag the location and disconnect the vacuum hoses.
5. On 1989 vehicles, disconnect the white altitude connector from the distributor wiring harness. Remove the coil positive terminal nut and disconnect the distributor harness connector and suppression capacitor wire. Pull the distributor connector off the coil ground terminal tab. Open the harness routing clip and free the distributor primary circuit wires.
6. On 1990–93 vehicles, disconnect the distributor electrical connector.
7. Scribe a timing reference mark across the distributor mounting flange and cylinder head surface to ensure that the distributor will be installed without altering the timing. Note the position of the rotor.
8. Remove the base flange mounting bolts and remove the distributor assembly from its mounting bore.
9. Remove the flange base O-ring and inspect for damage. Replace the O-ring as required. Coat the O-ring with clean engine oil and install into the flange base.

INSTALLATION

Timing Not Disturbed

1. Insert the distributor assembly into the cylinder head mounting bore. Rotate the distributor until the offset drive tang aligns and engages with the camshaft slot. The rotor position should be the same as when removed.
2. After the distributor is engaged with the camshaft, align the timing reference marks scribed across the flange base and cylinder head. When the timing marks are aligned, install and tighten the mounting bolts to 14–18 ft. lbs. (19–25 Nm).
3. On 1989 vehicles, position the distributor-to-coil primary harness and the supression capacitor lead in the harness routing clip and close the clip. Connect the harness to the coil primary terminals. Connect the supression capacitor and battery leads to the positive terminal. Connect the white altitude connector to the distributor wiring harness.
4. On 1990–93 vehicles, connect the distributor electrical connector.
5. Install the distributor cap and connect the coil wire. If the spark plug wires were removed, connect them to the proper distributor cap towers, as marked during the removal procedure.
6. If equipped with a vacuum advance unit, connect the vacuum lines.
7. Connect the negative battery cable.

Timing Disturbed

1. If the crankshaft was rotated while the distributor was removed, the piston in No. 1 cylinder must be brought to TDC on the compression stroke.

2. Remove the No. 1 spark plug. Place a finger over the hole and rotate the crankshaft slowly in the direction of normal rotation, until engine compression is felt.

NOTE: Turn the engine only in the direction of normal rotation. Backward rotation may cause the cam belt to slip or lose teeth, altering engine timing.

3. When engine compression is felt at the spark plug hole, indicating that the piston is approaching TDC, continue to turn the crankshaft until the TDC timing mark on the pulley is aligned with the TDC mark on the engine front cover.

4. Insert the distributor assembly into the cylinder head mounting bore. Rotate the distributor until the offset drive tang aligns and engages with the camshaft slot. Install the mounting bolts, leaving them loose enough that the distributor can be moved by hand.

5. On 1989 vehicles, position the distributor-to-coil primary harness and the supression capacitor lead in the harness routing clip and close the clip. Connect the harness to the coil primary terminals. Connect the supression capacitor and battery leads to the positive terminal. Plug the vacuum advance hoses.

6. On 1990–93 vehicles, connect the distributor electrical connector.

7. Install the distributor cap and connect the coil wire. If the spark plug wires were removed, connect them to the proper distributor cap towers, as marked during the removal procedure.

8. Connect the negative battery cable. Start the engine and check and adjust the ignition timing. When the timing is set, tighten the distributor mounting bolts to 14–18 ft. lbs. (19–25 Nm).

9. On 1989 vehicles, unplug and connect the vacuum advance hoses and connect the white altitude connector at the distributor.

Ignition Timing

ADJUSTMENT

1989

1. Start the engine and allow to reach normal operating temperature.

2. Stop the engine and connect a tachometer. Start the engine and check the idle speed. Adjust the idle speed, if necessary.

3. Disconnect the vacuum hoses from the vacuum advance unit and plug the hose openings. Disconnect the white altitude connector at the distributor.

4. Turn OFF all electrical accessories.

5. Connect a timing light according to the manufacturers instructions. Start the engine.

6. With the timing light, observe the timing marks on the crankshaft pulley and timing case. The correct spark timing at idle is TDC ± 1 degree on carbureted engine or 2 degrees ± 1 degree on EFI engine.

7. If the timing is not as specified, loosen the distributor mounting bolts and rotate the distributor clockwise to advance the timing or counterclockwise to retard the timing.

8. When the timing is adjusted to specification, tighten the distributor mounting bolts.

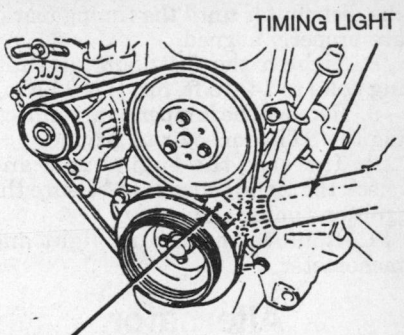

TIMING LIGHT

Ignition timing marks location—1989 vehicles

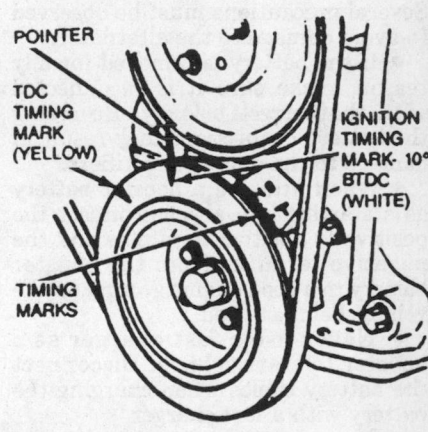

Ignition timing marks location—1990–93 vehicles

9. Stop the engine. Remove the timing light. Unplug the vacuum hoses and connect them to the vacuum advance unit. Connect the white altitude connector.

10. Start the engine and check the idle speed. Adjust the idle speed as required.

1990–93

1. Place the transaxle in **P** or **N**, then make sure the air conditioner and heater fan is **OFF**.

2. Connect an inductive timing light to the No. 1 spark plug wire. Connect a tachometer.

3. Start the engine and allow it to warm up to normal operating temperature.

4. Ground the black 1-pin STI self-test connector located near the brake master cylinder.

5. Check and adjust the idle speed, if necessary.

6. Check the base ignition timing. The white ignition timing mark on the crankshaft pulley should align with the white pointer on the timing belt cover.

7. If the white timing mark and the white pointer do not line up, loosen the distributor mounting bolts and rotate

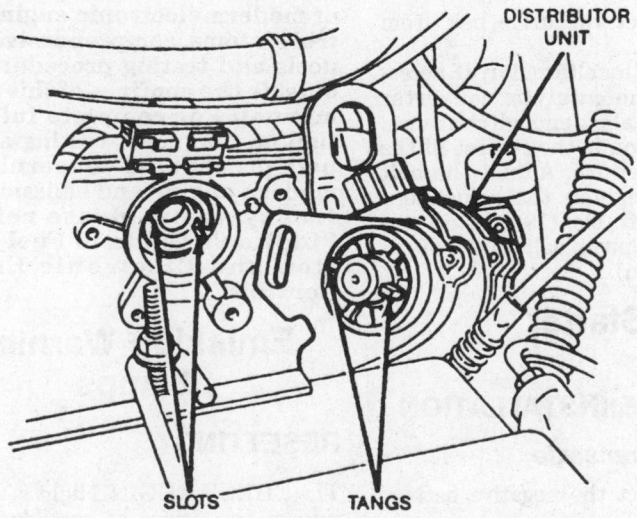

Distributor offset drive tangs and camshaft slots

the distributor until the timing marks are properly aligned.

8. Tighten the distributor mounting bolts to 14–18 ft. lbs. (19–25 Nm).

9. Remove the jumper wire connecting the STI connector to ground.

10. Increase the engine rpm and check the timing marks to be sure the ignition timing changes.

11. Remove the timing light and tachometer.

Alternator

PRECAUTIONS

Several precautions must be observed to avoid damage to the alternator.

• If the battery is removed for any reason, make sure it is reconnected with the correct polarity. Reversing the battery connections may result in damage to the one-way rectifiers.

• When utilizing a booster battery as a starting aid, always connect the positive to positive terminals and the negative terminal from the booster battery to a good engine ground on the vehicle being started.

• Never use a fast charger as a booster to start vehicle. Disconnect the battery cables when charging the battery with a fast charger.

• Never attempt to polarize the alternator.

• Do not use test lamps of more than 12 volts when checking diode continuity.

• Do not short across or ground any of the alternator terminals.

• The polarity of the battery, alternator and regulator must be matched and considered before making any electrical connections within the system.

• Never separate the alternator on an open circuit. Make sure all connections within the circuit are clean and tight.

• Disconnect the battery ground terminal when performing any service on electrical components.

• Disconnect the battery if arc welding is to be done on the vehicle.

BELT TENSION ADJUSTMENT

1. Inspect the condition of the drive belt prior to adjustment. If the inspection reveals a severely glazed, frayed, oil contaminated or cracked belt, the belt must be replaced.

2. Loosen the alternator adjustment bolt.

3. Raise the vehicle and support it safely.

4. Loosen the lower alternator mounting/pivot bolt.

5. Lower the vehicle.

6. Position a suitable prybar between the engine and the alternator. Position the bar against the alternator in an area around a case bolt. Do not pry on the stator frame.

7. Adjust the belt tension by prying on the bar. Measure the belt tension using a belt tension gauge or by using the deflection method.

8. If using a belt tension gauge, position the gauge on the longest accessible belt span. The belt tension should be 110–132 lbs. for a new belt or 95–110 lbs. for a used belt (more than 10 minutes running time).

9. If using the deflection method, apply approximately 22 lbs. of pressure to the middle of the longest accessible belt span. The deflection should be 0.31–0.35 in. (8–9mm) for a new belt or 0.35–0.39 in. (9–10mm) for a used belt (more than 10 minutes running time).

10. When the belt tension is as specified, tighten the adjustment bolt to 14–19 ft. lbs. (19–25 Nm).

11. Raise and safely support the vehicle.

12. Tighten the alternator mounting/pivot bolt to 27–46 ft. lbs. (37–52 Nm).

13. Lower the vehicle.

REMOVAL & INSTALLATION

1. Disconnect the negative battery cable.

2. If equipped, pull the rubber boot away from the **B** terminal to expose the terminal nut. Remove the nut and electrical lead from the terminal post.

3. Remove the alternator adjusting bracket bolt.

4. Disconnect the remaining electrical connector(s) from the alternator housing.

5. Raise and safely support the vehicle. Remove the alternator mounting/pivot bolt.

6. Disconnect the drive belt from the alternator.

7. Remove the alternator. If necessary, bend the catalytic converter shield brace to allow enough clearance.

8. Installation is the reverse of the removal procedure. Adjust the belt tension and tighten the adjustment bolt to 14–19 ft. lbs. (19–25 Nm) and the mounting/pivot bolt to 27–46 ft. lbs. (37–52 Nm).

Starter

REMOVAL & INSTALLATION

Automatic Transaxle

1. Disconnect the negative battery cable.

2. Remove the 2 upper starter mounting bolts.

3. Raise and safely support the vehicle.

4. Remove the 2 bolts that secure the manifold-to-cylinder block bracket, then remove the bracket.

5. Remove the bolt that secures the mounting bracket to the support bracket and remove the support bracket.

6. Remove the 2 nuts and washers that secure the mounting bracket to the starter and remove the mounting bracket.

7. Disconnect the **B** and **S** terminal connectors at the starter solenoid.

8. Remove the lower starter mounting bolt and remove the starter.

9. Installation is the reverse of the removal procedure. Tighten the starter mounting bolts to 23–34 ft. lbs. (31–46 Nm).

Manual Transaxle

1. Disconnect the negative battery cable.

2. Disconnect the **B** and **S** terminal connectors at the starter solenoid.

3. Remove the 2 bolts that secure the starter support bracket to the transaxle.

4. Remove the starter mounting bolts and remove the starter.

5. Installation is the reverse of the removal procedure. Tighten the starter mounting bolts to 23–34 ft. lbs. (31–46 Nm).

EMISSION CONTROLS

Due to the complex nature of modern electronic engine control systems, comprehensive diagnosis and testing procedures fall outside the confines of this repair manual. For complete information on diagnosis, testing and repair procedures concerning all modern engine and emission control systems, please refer to "Chilton's Guide to Fuel Injection and Electronic Engine Controls".

Emission Warning Lamps

RESETTING

The CHECK ENGINE light is used to inform the driver of possible engine malfunctions and emission system failure. The light is controlled by the

ECU. The ECU monitors engine, ignition and emission related components and signals the driver, through the CHECK ENGINE light, when the engine is running improperly or emissions are unsatisfactory. If the CHECK ENGINE light illuminates during vehicle operation, the cause of the fault or malfunction must be determined and corrected.

FUEL SYSTEM

Fuel System Service Precautions

Safety is the most important factor when performing not only fuel system maintenance but any type of maintenance. Failure to conduct maintenance and repairs in a safe manner may result in serious personal injury. Maintenance and testing of the vehicle's fuel system components can be accomplished safely and effectively by adhering to the following rules and guidelines.

• To avoid the possibility of fire and personal injury, always disconnect the negative battery cable unless the repair or test procedure requires that battery voltage be applied.

• Always relieve the fuel system pressure prior to disconnecting any fuel system component (injector, fuel rail, pressure regulator, etc.), fitting or fuel line connection. Exercise extreme caution whenever relieving fuel system pressure to avoid exposing skin, face and eyes to fuel spray. Please be advised that fuel under pressure may penetrate the skin or any part of the body that it contacts.

• Always place a shop towel or cloth around the fitting or connection prior to loosening to absorb any excess fuel. Ensure that all fuel spillage (should it occur) is quickly removed from engine surfaces. Ensure that all fuel soaked cloths or towels are deposited into a suitable waste container.

• Always keep a dry chemical (Class B) fire extinguisher near the work area.

• Do not allow fuel spray or fuel vapors to come into contact with a spark or open flame.

• Always use a backup wrench when loosening and tightening fuel line connection fittings. Always follow the proper torque specifications.

• Always replace worn fuel fitting O-rings with new. Do not substitute fuel hose or equivalent where fuel pipe is installed.

RELIEVING FUEL SYSTEM PRESSURE

EFI Engine

1. Remove the rear seat cushion.
2. Disconnect the electrical connector from the fuel pump/sending unit.
3. Start the engine and let it run until it stalls. Turn the ignition key **OFF**.
4. Reconnect the electrical lead.

Fuel Tank

REMOVAL & INSTALLATION

1. Remove the rear seat as follows:
   a. Remove the right and left front attaching bolts.
   b. Fold the rear seat forward.
   c. Remove the right and left anchor nuts on the rear side of the seat and remove the seat.
2. Remove the screw and retainers and remove the left rear quarter trim panel.
3. If EFI equipped, start the engine and disconnect the fuel pump/sending unit connector. After the engine stalls, turn the ignition key **OFF**.
4. Disconnect the negative battery cable.
5. Drain the fuel from the tank as completely as possible. This is accomplished by siphoning or pumping the fuel out through the fuel filler neck.
6. Remove the rear carpet hold-down pins using a suitable tool. Fold the carpet forward until the sending unit access plate is uncovered.
7. Remove the sending unit access plate attaching screws, lift the access plate and disconnect the sending unit wiring.
8. Disconnect the fuel supply line at the sending unit and the fuel return line from the top of the fuel tank.
9. Remove the fuel tank cover plate.
10. Disconnect the filler neck hose, overflow hose and the 2 vapor separator hoses from the fuel tank.
11. Raise and safely support the vehicle.
12. Disconnect the vapor hose from the vapor line.
13. Position a suitable jack under the fuel tank and remove the 4 attaching bolts.
14. Move the fuel tank toward the left and lower it from the vehicle.
To install:
15. Raise the fuel tank and slide it into position from the left side of the vehicle. Install the attaching bolts.
16. Connect the vapor hose to the vapor line and lower the vehicle.
17. Connect the vapor separator hoses, overflow hose and fuel filler hose to the fuel tank.
18. Connect the fuel return hose to the fitting on the top of the fuel tank and the fuel supply hose to the fitting on the fuel sending unit.
19. Add fuel to the tank and check for leaks.
20. Connect the negative battery cable and the fuel sending unit wiring. Start the engine and check for leaks. Stop the engine.
21. Install the fuel line cover plate and the fuel sender access plate.
22. Position the rear carpet and secure it in position with the retainers.
23. Install the left rear quarter panel and the rear seat.

Fuel Filter

REMOVAL & INSTALLATION

The fuel filter is located in the rear left corner of the engine compartment next to the carbon canister.

EFI Engine

1. Properly relieve the fuel system pressure.
2. Disconnect the negative battery cable.
3. Remove the clamp and line at the inlet of the fuel filter. Plug the end to prevent spillage.
4. Remove the attaching bolts from the outlet of the fuel filter.
5. Remove the fuel filter from it's brace.
To install:
6. Install the fuel filter into it's brace.
7. Install the line onto the filter outlet with the attaching bolts. Tighten the bolts to 18–25 ft. lbs. (25–34 Nm).
8. Unplug and install the supply line onto the fuel filter inlet and secure with the clamp.
9. Connect the fuel pump connector and install the rear seat cushion. Connect the negative battery cable.
10. Run the engine and check for leaks.

Carbureted Engine

1. Disconnect the negative battery cable.
2. Remove the clamp and line at the inlet of the filter. Plug the end to prevent spillage.
3. Remove the clamp and line at the filter outlet and remove the filter from it's brace.
4. Installation is the reverse of the removal procedure. Be sure to install the filter with the arrow pointing in the direction of fuel flow.

Mechanical Fuel Pump

The fuel pump is located on the firewall side of the cylinder head, near the distributor.

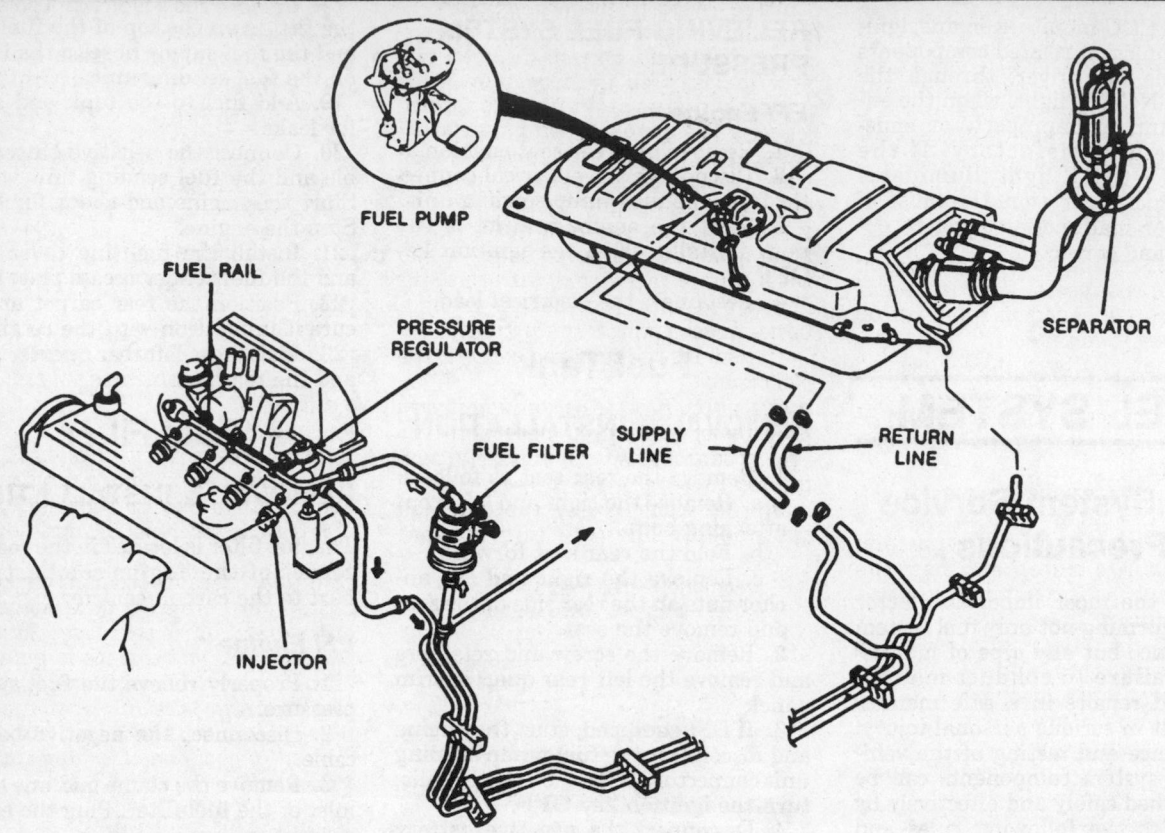

EFI engine fuel supply system

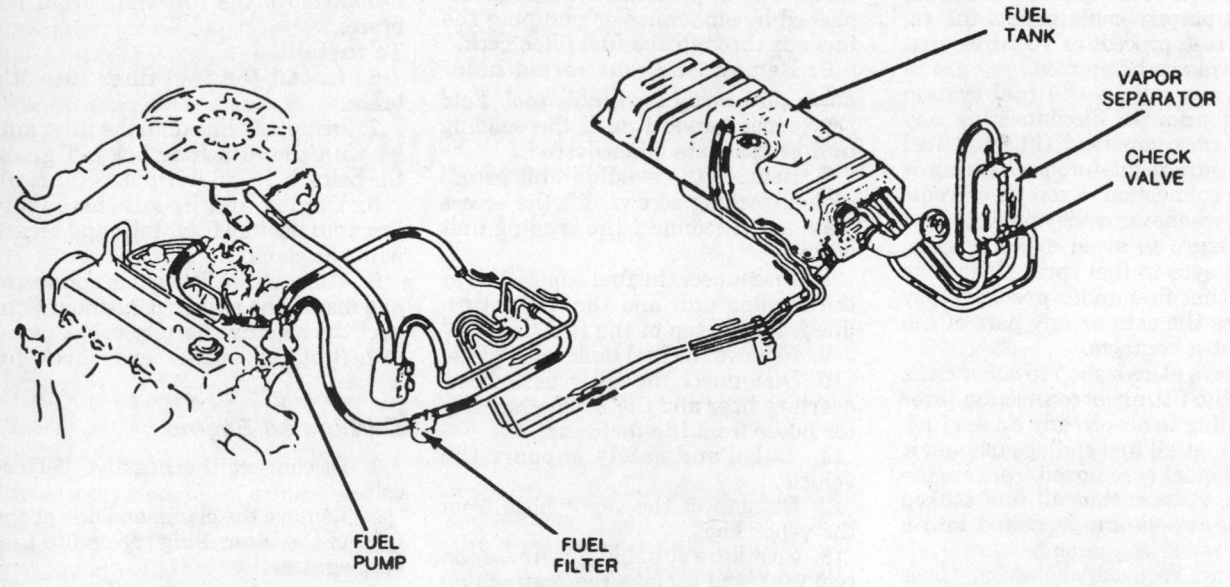

Carbureted engine fuel supply system

PRESSURE TESTING

1. Disconnect the negative battery cable.
2. Disconnect the fuel hose at the carburetor and attach a suitable fuel pressure gauge.
3. Remove the fuel return hose at the fuel pump and plug or cap the exposed port.

4. Connect the negative battery cable.
5. With the engine idling or cranking normally, check the fuel pressure. It should be 3–6 psi. If not, replace the fuel pump.
6. Remove the plug or cap at the fuel pump and connect the fuel return hose.
7. Disconnect the pressure gauge

and connect the fuel supply hose to the carburetor.
8. Start the engine and check for fuel leaks.

REMOVAL & INSTALLATION

1. Disconnect the negative battery cable.

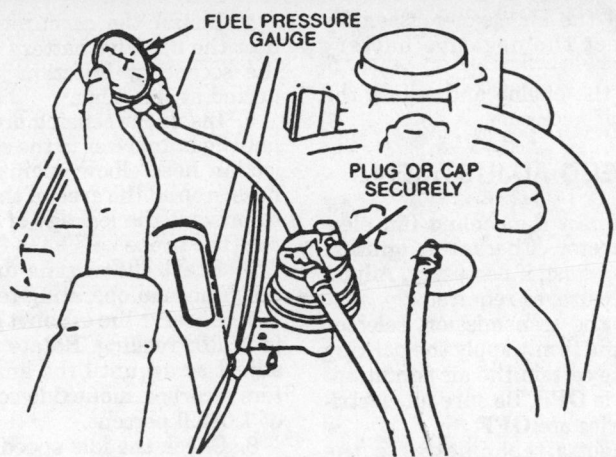

FUEL PRESSURE GAUGE

PLUG OR CAP SECURELY

Mechanical fuel pump pressure testing

2. Remove the air cleaner assembly. Identify and tag all vacuum hoses as required.

3. Tag and disconnect the fuel pump inlet, outlet and return hoses.

NOTE: The outlet line may be pressurized. Wrap a shop cloth around the line when disconnecting.

4. Loosen the fuel pump retaining bolts to allow for movement of the pump on the cylinder head mounting. Rotate the engine by hand until the pump arm is resting on the low side of the cam lobe. When the cam is properly positioned, tension on the pump will be greatly reduced.

5. Remove the pump retaining bolts.

6. Remove the pump from the mounting pad with insulator and gaskets.

7. Clean the cylinder head and insulator gasket contact surfaces.

To install:

8. Install the pump, insulator and gaskets. Install the retaining bolts and torque to 17–22 ft. lbs. (23–29 Nm).

9. Connect and secure the inlet, outlet and fuel return hoses to the fuel pump.

10. Install the air cleaner assembly and connect the vacuum lines.

11. Connect the negative battery cable. Start the engine and inspect for fuel leaks.

Electric Fuel Pump

PRESSURE TESTING

1. Properly relieve the fuel system pressure.

2. Disconnect the negative battery cable.

3. Connect a suitable fuel pressure gauge between the fuel filter outlet and the fuel rail.

4. Connect the negative battery cable.

5. Connect the **BK** and **GN/R** terminals together on the fuel pump test connector.

6. Turn the ignition key **ON** but do not start the engine.

7. The fuel pressure reading should be 64–85 psi.

8. Turn the ignition key **OFF** and remove the jumper wire from the **BK** and **GN/R** terminals.

9. Properly relieve the fuel system pressure.

10. Disconnect the negative battery cable.

11. Remove the fuel pressure tester and reconnect the fuel line and fuel rail.

12. Connect the negative battery cable. Start the engine and check for fuel leaks.

The fuel pump is located in the fuel tank as part of the sending unit assembly.

1. Properly relieve the fuel system pressure.

2. Disconnect the negative battery cable.

3. Remove the rear seat as follows:

a. Remove the right and left front attaching bolts.

b. Fold the rear seat forward.

c. Remove the right and left anchor nuts on the rear side of the seat and remove the seat.

4. Remove the rear carpet hold-down pins and fold the carpet forward until the sending unit access plate is uncovered.

5. Remove the access plate attaching screws, lift the access plate and disconnect the sending unit wiring.

6. Disconnect and plug the fuel line at the sending unit.

7. Remove the sending unit retaining screws and remove the sending unit. Discard the gasket.

8. Remove the fuel filter from the pump. Remove the fuel pump wires from the sending unit.

9. Remove the retaining clamp screw and the pump outlet hose clamp. Remove the fuel pump from the sending unit.

To install:

10. Install the fuel pump to the sending unit bracket and secure with the retaining clamp.

11. Install the pump outlet hose and secure with the clamp.

12. Connect the fuel pump wires to

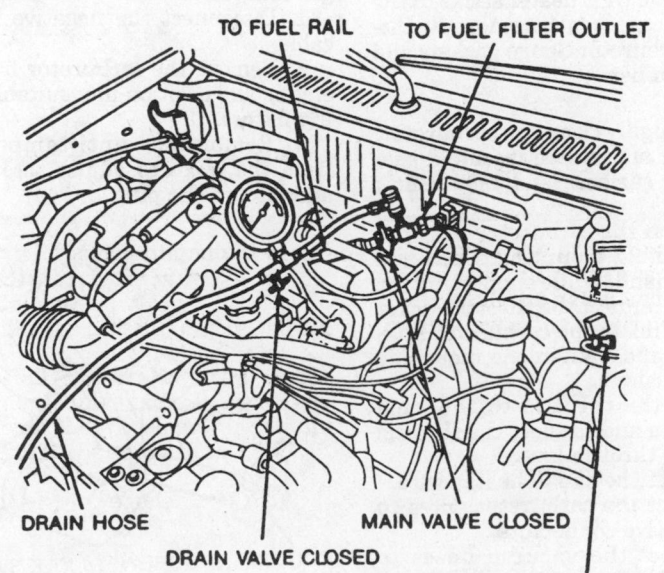

TO FUEL RAIL   TO FUEL FILTER OUTLET

DRAIN HOSE

DRAIN VALVE CLOSED

MAIN VALVE CLOSED

FUEL PUMP TEST CONNECTOR

Electric fuel pump pressure testing

the sending unit and install the fuel pump filter.

13. Position a new gasket on the fuel tank and install the sending unit with the attaching screws.

14. Connect the fuel line and the sending unit wiring.

15. Connect the negative battery cable. Start the engine and check for leaks at the fuel line connections. Stop the engine.

16. Install the access cover with the attaching screws.

17. Position the carpet and install the retaining pins.

18. Install the rear seat.

Carburetor

REMOVAL & INSTALLATION

1. Disconnect the negative battery cable.

2. Remove the air cleaner assembly.

3. Loosen the retaining clamp and disconnect the fuel supply line. Plug the hose opening to prevent contamination and the entry of foreign matter.

4. Disconnect the vacuum hoses from the carburetor. Identify each hose with its respective opening to ensure proper installation.

5. Disconnect the carburetor wiring connectors.

6. Disconnect the choke heater wire at the choke cap.

7. Move the throttle to the wide open position and disengage the throttle cable from the throttle lever.

8. Remove the carburetor retaining nuts and washers. Lift the carburetor upward from the intake manifold studs. Disconnect the throttle kicker diaphragm link from the carburetor linkage. If the EFE heater sticks to the carburetor base, gently remove it. Discard the carburetor flange gaskets and replace with new.

To install:

9. Thoroughly clean the carburetor, EFE heater and intake manifold gasket contact surfaces and install new gaskets.

10. Position the carburetor over the intake manifold mounting studs and support by hand. While supporting the carburetor, connect the throttle kicker diaphragm link to the carburetor linkage. Install and tighten the mounting nuts and washers.

11. Move the throttle to the wide open position and connect the throttle cable to the throttle lever.

12. Connect the choke heater wire.

13. Connect the carburetor wires to their respective connectors.

14. Connect the vacuum hoses to their original openings.

15. Connect the the fuel supply line and install the retaining clamp.

16. Install the air cleaner assembly and connect the negative battery cable.

17. Start the engine and adjust the idle speed, if necessary.

IDLE SPEED ADJUSTMENT

1. Disconnect the cooling fan electrical connector. Check the ignition timing and adjust, if necessary. Adjust the idle mixture, as required.

2. Place the transmission selector lever in **N** and firmly apply the parking brake. Make certain the air conditioning system is **OFF**. Be sure all electrical accessories are **OFF**.

3. Connect a tachometer to the engine.

4. Start the engine and allow to reach normal operating temperature. Make certain the choke is fully open.

5. Allow the engine to remain at idle and observe the idle speed reading. The idle speed should be 700–750 rpm.

6. If the idle speed is not within specifications, rotate the idle speed adjusting screw, located on the right side of the carburetor, as required until the correct idle speed is obtained.

7. Reconnect the cooling fan electrical connector.

IDLE MIXTURE ADJUSTMENT

Adjustment of the idle mixture screw is normally unnecessary due to the fact that the adjustment has been made at the factory. The mixture adjusting screw is sealed with an anti-tamper plug to discourage adjustment. If the adjustment is required, proceed as follows with the use of an exhaust gas analyzer.

1. Disconnect the negative battery cable.

2. Remove the carburetor from the engine and position in a suitable holding fixture.

3. Remove the anti-tamper plug from the mixture adjust screw tube and discard the plug.

4. Install the carburetor and connect the negative battery cable. Leave the secondary injection hose disconnected at this time.

5. Insert the sensing probe of an exhaust gas analyzer in the secondary injection hose elbow opening. Plug the hose around the area of the probe lead to prevent the leakage of exhaust gas past the probe.

6. Start the engine and allow to reach normal operating temperature.

7. Observe the exhaust gas analyzer indicator reading. Rotate the mixture adjust screw until the analyzer registers a carbon monoxide concentration of 1.0–2.0 percent.

8. Check the idle speed and adjust, if necessary.

9. Install a new anti-tamper plug over the mixture adjust screw and tap into position.

10. Remove the analyzer sensing probe and connect the secondary injection hose.

Fuel Injection

IDLE SPEED ADJUSTMENT

1. Disconnect the cooling fan electrical connector. Check the ignition timing and adjust if necessary.

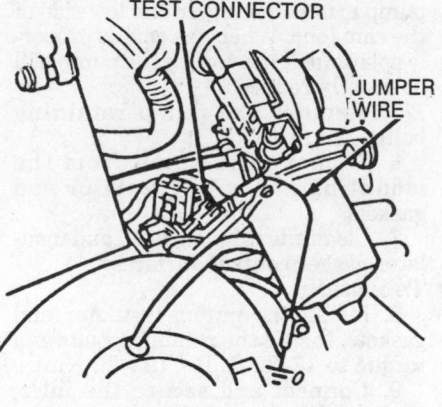

Carburetor curb idle adjustment screw location

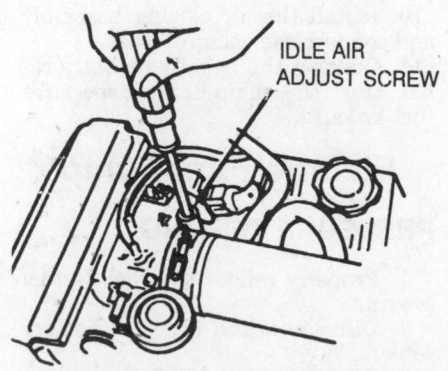

EFI engine test connector and idle air adjuster screw locations

2. Apply the parking brake. Make certain the air conditioning system is **OFF**. Be sure all lights and electrical accessories are **OFF**.

3. Connect a tachometer to the check connector (clear, pin No. 1). On 1989–90 vehicles, connect a jumper wire between the test connector (black, pin No. 1) and ground. On 1991–93 vehicles, connect a jumper wire between the black test connector (1 pin, Y/BL wire) and ground.

4. Check the idle speed on the tachometer. The idle speed should be 800–900 rpm on 1989 vehicles in **P**, 680–720 rpm on 1990–93 manual transaxle vehicles in **N** or 830–870 on 1990–93 automatic transaxle vehicles in **P**.

5. If necessary, turn the idle air adjust screw to obtain the correct idle speed.

6. After adjustment, remove the jumper wire and the tachometer.

IDLE MIXTURE ADJUSTMENT

The idle mixture screw is preset and sealed at the factory. Idle mixture cannot be adjusted.

Fuel Injector

REMOVAL & INSTALLATION

1. Properly relieve the fuel system pressure.
2. Disconnect the negative battery cable.
3. Remove the intake plenum as follows:
   a. Drain the cooling system.
   b. Disconnect the throttle cable and the air duct from the throttle body.
   c. Mark all vacuum and coolant hoses for ease of reassembly and remove the hoses from the throttle body.
   d. Disconnect the electrical connector at the throttle position sensor.
   e. Remove the intake plenum retaining bolts and/or nuts and remove the intake plenum and gasket.
4. Remove the fuel inlet and return lines from the fuel rail.
5. Remove the electrical connectors at the injectors.
6. Remove the pressure regulator.
7. Remove the attaching bolts and the fuel rail. Remove the injectors.
8. Installation is the reverse of the removal procedure. Install new O-rings on the injectors and lubricate them with gasoline, prior to installation.

DRIVE AXLE

Halfshaft

REMOVAL & INSTALLATION

1. Disconnect the negative battery cable.
2. Raise the vehicle and support it safely.
3. Drain the transaxle fluid.
4. Remove the front wheel and tire assembly. Remove the splash shields.
5. Bend back the lockwing tab on the halfshaft nut. Have an assistant apply the brakes, then loosen but do not remove, the halfshaft locknut.
6. Remove the stabilizer mounting nuts and brackets.
7. Remove the clamp bolt and nut from the lower suspension control arm. With a suitable prybar, pry the lower suspension control arm downward to disconnect the ball joint. Be careful not to tear or puncture the dust boot when disconnecting the ball joint.
8. Using a small prybar, separate the halfshaft from the transaxle.

NOTE: The halfshaft must be separated from the transaxle gradually. If the halfshaft is pulled or jerked suddenly, the oil seal may be damaged.

9. Remove and discard the halfshaft locking nut.
10. Withdraw the halfshaft from the wheel hub. Be careful not to damage the oil seal. If the halfshaft is stuck in the hub, use a suitable puller to push out the halfshaft.
11. Install differential plug tool T87C–7025–C or equivalent, to prevent the differential side gear from moving.
To install:
12. Inspect the differential and wheel hub oil seals for damage and replace, as required.
13. Remove the circlip from the inboard halfshaft spline end and replace with new. Coat the inboard and outboard halfshaft spline ends with grease.
14. Remove the differential gear holding plug.
15. Position and install the inboard end of the halfshaft into the differential side gear. Take care not to damage the differential oil seal.
16. Position and install the outboard end of the halfshaft into the wheel hub. Take care not to damage the wheel hub oil seal.
17. Install the halfshaft locknut onto the halfshaft and tighten by hand.
18. Raise the lower suspension con-

trol arm and connect the arm to the ball joint. Take care not to damage the ball joint dust boot.
19. Install the lower suspension arm clamp nut and bolt. Hold the bolt stationary and torque the nut to 32–40 ft. lbs. (43–54 Nm).
20. Have an assistant apply the brakes, then torque the outboard halfshaft locknut to 116–174 ft. lbs. (157–235 Nm). Stake the nut using a suitable tool.

NOTE: Do not stake the locking tab with a pointed tool. Make sure the locking tab is depressed at least 0.16 in. (4mm) into the locknut slot to ensure proper locking capabilty. After the lockwasher is locked into place, grasp the wheel hub and pull to ensure that the halfshaft is installed properly. Rotate the wheel hub by hand to ensure that the wheel hub turns smoothly.

21. Install the stabilizer brackets and mounting bracket nuts. Tighten the nuts to 40–50 ft. lbs. (54–68 Nm).
22. Install the splash shields and the wheel and tire assemblies. Install and tighten the transaxle drain plug.
23. Fill the transaxle with the proper grade and type fluid to specification. Lower the vehicle.

CV-Boot

REMOVAL & INSTALLATION

There are 3 different types of CV-joints used. 1989 vehicles equipped with manual transaxle are equipped with Rzeppa inboard CV-joints. All other vehicles are equipped with tripot type inboard CV-joints. All vehicles are equipped with Birfield outboard CV-joints.

The Rzeppa and tripot CV-joints can be disassembled and serviced, however the Birfield CV-joint is serviced only as an assembly with the shaft. Consequently, if outboard CV-joint boot replacement is necessary, the inboard CV-joint must first be disassembled.

Except 1989 Manual Transaxle

1. Raise and support the vehicle safely.
2. Remove the halfshaft from the vehicle. Support the assembly in a vise with protective jaws.
3. Use side cutters to cut and remove the large boot clamp from the inboard CV-joint. Roll the boot back over the shaft.
4. Check the grease for contamination by rubbing it between 2 fingers. Any gritty feeling indicates a contaminated CV-joint. A contaminated joint must be completely disassembled,

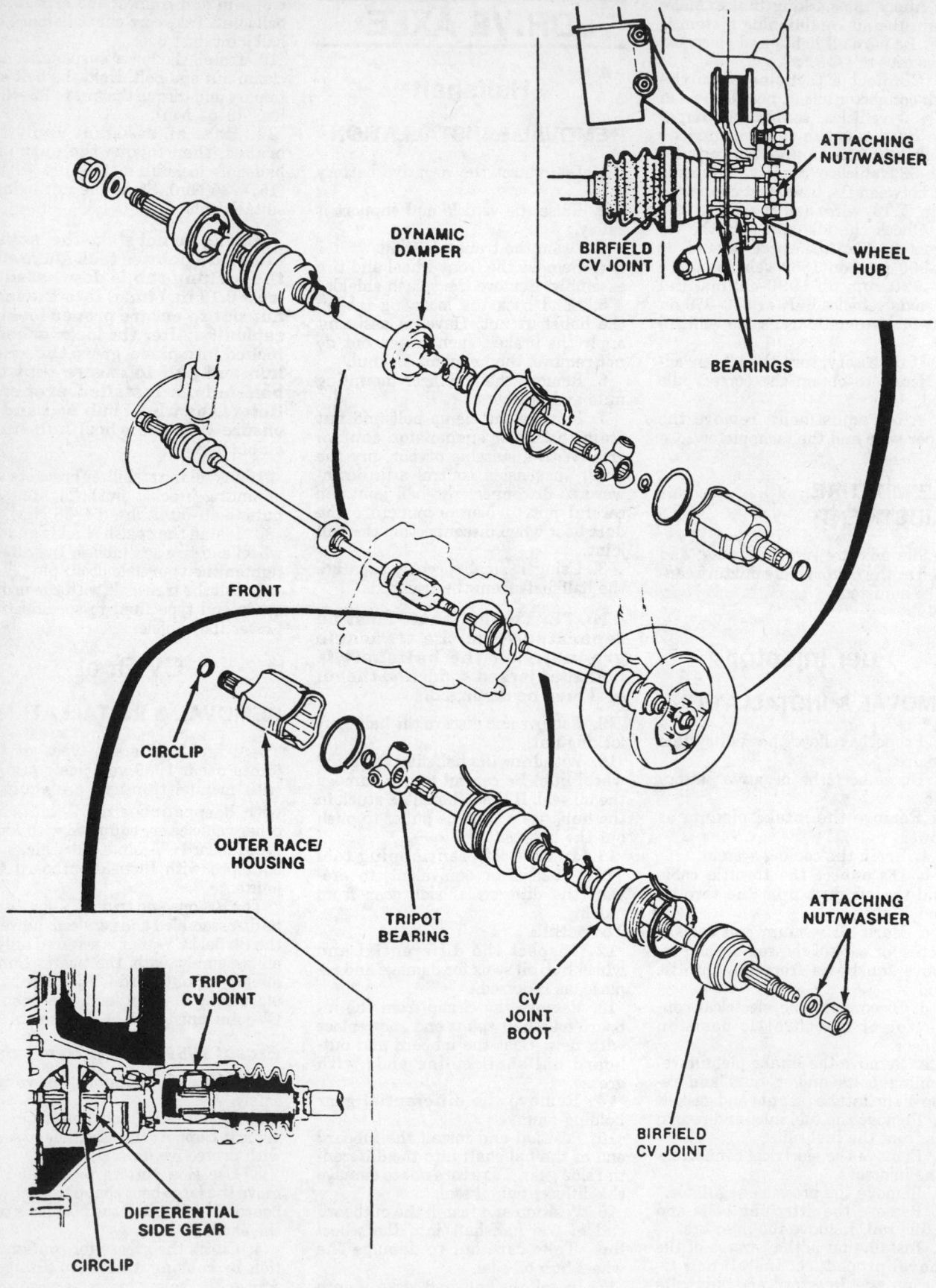

ATTACHING NUT/WASHER

DYNAMIC DAMPER

BIRFIELD CV JOINT

WHEEL HUB

BEARINGS

FRONT

CIRCLIP

OUTER RACE/ HOUSING

TRIPOT BEARING

TRIPOT CV JOINT

DIFFERENTIAL SIDE GEAR

CIRCLIP

CV JOINT BOOT

ATTACHING NUT/WASHER

BIRFIELD CV JOINT

Halfshaft assembly—except 1989 manual transaxle vehicles

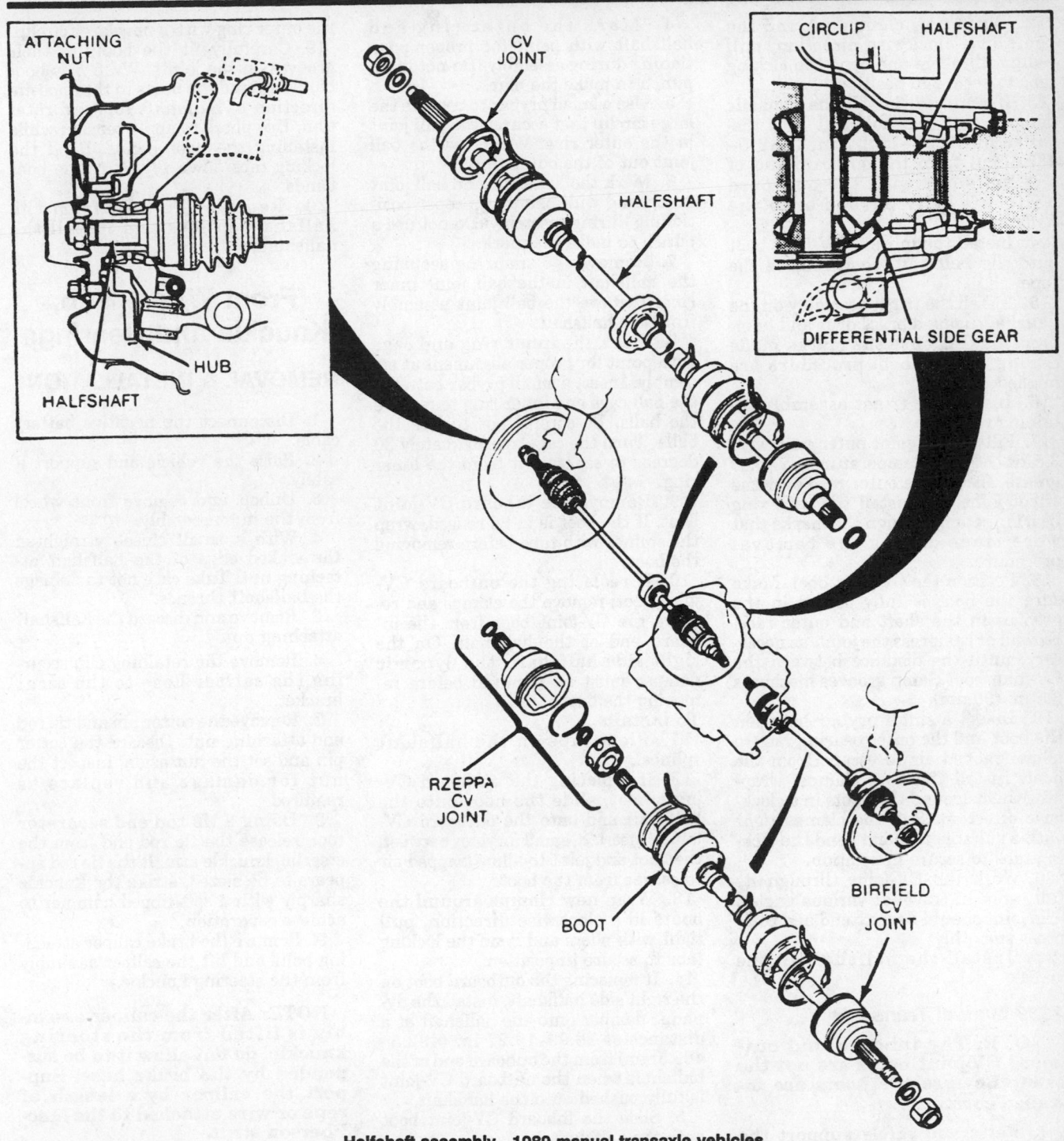

ATTACHING NUT

HALFSHAFT

HUB

CV JOINT

HALFSHAFT

CIRCLIP   HALFSHAFT

DIFFERENTIAL SIDE GEAR

RZEPPA CV JOINT

BOOT

BIRFIELD CV JOINT

Halfshaft assembly—1989 manual transaxle vehicles

cleaned and inspected. If the grease is not contaminated and the CV-joint has been operating properly, continue with boot replacement and add the required grease.

5. Remove the wire ring bearing retainer. Paint alignment marks on the outer race and tripot bearing for installation reference, then remove the outer race.

6. Paint alignment marks on the tripot bearing and shaft for assembly

reference, then remove the tripot bearing snapring. Using a brass drift and hammer, remove the tripot bearing from the shaft.

7. Remove the small clamp and the CV-joint boot from the halfshaft. If the boot is to be reused, cover the splines with tape before removing the boot.

8. If replacing the right outboard CV-joint boot, remove the dynamic damper.

9. If replacing the outboard CV-

joint boot, remove the clamps and slide the boot off of the shaft from the inboard side.

To install:

10. Cover the halfshaft splines with tape.

11. If replacing the outboard CV-joint boot, slide the boot onto the halfshaft and onto the outboard CV-joint. Insert a small prybar between the boot and joint to allow trapped air to escape from the boot.

12. Wrap new clamps around the boots in a clockwise direction, pull tight with pliers and bend the locking tabs to secure in position.

13. If removed, install the dynamic damper onto the halfshaft at a distance of 18.99–19.27 in. (482.5–489.5mm) from the outboard end of the halfshaft with the outboard halfshaft fully pushed onto the halfshaft.

14. Install the inboard CV-joint boot onto the halfshaft, then remove the tape.

15. Install the tripot assembly on the halfshaft using a brass drift and hammer, making sure the marks made during the removal procedure are aligned.

16. Install the tripot assembly retaining ring.

17. Fill the CV-joint outer race with 3.5 oz. of high temperature CV-joint grease. Install the outer race over the tripot joint and install the wire ring bearing retainer. Align the marks that were made during the removal procedure.

18. Position the CV-joint boot. Make sure the boot is fully seated in the grooves in the shaft and outer race. Extend or compress the joint, as necessary, until the distance between the CV-joint boot clamp grooves measures 3.5 in. (90mm).

19. Insert a small prybar between the boot and the outer bearing race to allow trapped air to escape from the boot. Install the boot clamps, wrapping them around the boots in a clockwise direction. Pull the clamps tight with a suitable tool and bend the locking tabs to secure in position.

20. Work the CV-joint through its full range of travel at various angles. The joint should flex, extend and compress smoothly.

21. Install the halfshaft in the vehicle.

1989 Manual Transaxle

NOTE: The inboard and outboard CV-joint boots are not the same. Be sure the boots are installed correctly.

1. Raise and safely support the vehicle.

2. Remove the halfshaft assembly and clamp it in a vise with protected jaws.

NOTE: Do not allow dust or other foreign matter to enter the halfshaft joints during disassembly and assembly.

3. Using a small prybar, pry up the locking clip of the boot bands, raise the ends of the bands with pliers and remove the bands. Slide the inboard CV-joint boot off of the inboard CV-joint.

4. Mark the outer ring and halfshaft with paint for proper positioning during assembly. Do not use a punch to make the mark.

5. Use a small prybar to remove the large circlip that secures the ball joint in the outer ring. Withdraw the ball joint out of the outer ring.

6. Mark the halfshaft and ball joint inner ring with paint for proper positioning during assembly. Do not use a punch to make the mark.

7. Remove the snapring securing the halfshaft in the ball joint inner ring. Remove the ball joint assembly from the halfshaft.

8. Mark the inner ring and cage with paint for proper alignment at assembly. Insert a small prybar between the ball cage and inner ring to remove the balls. Be careful not to lose the balls. Turn the cage approximately 30 degrees to separate it from the inner ring.

9. Remove the inboard CV-joint boot. If the boot is to be reused, wrap the splines with tape before removing the boot.

10. If replacing the outboard CV-joint boot, remove the clamps and remove the CV-joint boot from the inboard end of the halfshaft. On the right side halfshaft, the dynamic damper must be removed before removing the boot.

To install:

11. Place tape on the halfshaft splines.

12. If replacing the outboard CV-joint boot, slide the boot onto the halfshaft and onto the outboard CV-joint. Insert a small prybar between the boot and joint to allow trapped air to escape from the boot.

13. Wrap new clamps around the boots in a clockwise direction, pull tight with pliers and bend the locking tabs to secure in position.

14. If replacing the outboard boot on the right side halfshaft, install the dynamic damper onto the halfshaft at a distance of 18.99–19.27 in. (482.5–489.5mm) from the ouboard end of the halfshaft when the outboard CV-joint is fully pushed onto the halfshaft.

15. Slide the inboard CV-joint boot onto the halfshaft.

16. Observing the alignment marks made during the removal procedure, reassemble the ball cage, balls and inner ring. Apply molydenum disulfide grease to the ball joint.

17. Observing the alignment marks made during the removal procedure, replace the ball joint onto the halfshaft. Secure the ball joint onto the halfshaft with the snapring.

18. Observing the alignment marks made during the removal procedure, replace the halfshaft and ball joint into the outer ring. Secure the ball joint in the outer ring with a new large circlip.

19. Carefully fit the boots in their grooves on the joints. Wrap new boot bands around the boots in the opposite direction of halfshaft forward rotation. Use pliers to apply tension while installing the boot bands. Bend the locking tabs down to secure the boot bands.

20. Remove the tape from the halfshaft splines and install the halfshafts.

Front Wheel Hub, Knuckle and Bearings

REMOVAL & INSTALLATION

1. Disconnect the negative battery cable.

2. Raise the vehicle and support it safely.

3. Unbolt and remove front wheel from the hub assembly.

4. With a small chisel, straighten the staked edge of the halfshaft attaching nut. Take care not to damage the halfshaft threads.

5. Remove and discard the halfshaft attaching nut.

6. Remove the retaining clip securing the caliper hose to the strut bracket.

7. Remove the cotter pin and tie rod end attaching nut. Discard the cotter pin and set the nut aside. Inspect the nut for damage and replace as required.

8. Using a tie rod end separator tool, release the tie rod end from the steering knuckle arm. If the tie rod appears to be siezed, strike the knuckle sharply with a soft-tipped hammer to achieve separation.

9. Remove the brake caliper attaching bolts and lift the caliper assembly from the steering knuckle.

NOTE: After the caliper assembly is lifted from the steering knuckle, do not allow it to be suspended by the brake hose. Support the caliper by a length of rope or wire attached to the MacPherson strut.

10. Remove the clamp bolt and nut at the point where the lower control arm ball joint connects to the steering knuckle. With a medium prybar, release the lower ball joint from the steering knuckle by prying downward on the lower control arm.

11. Remove the 2 bolts that position the steering knuckle between the MacPherson strut bracket flanges.

12. Slide the knuckle/hub assembly from the end of the halfshaft. If binding occurs, tap the end of the shaft with a soft-tipped hammer. If the

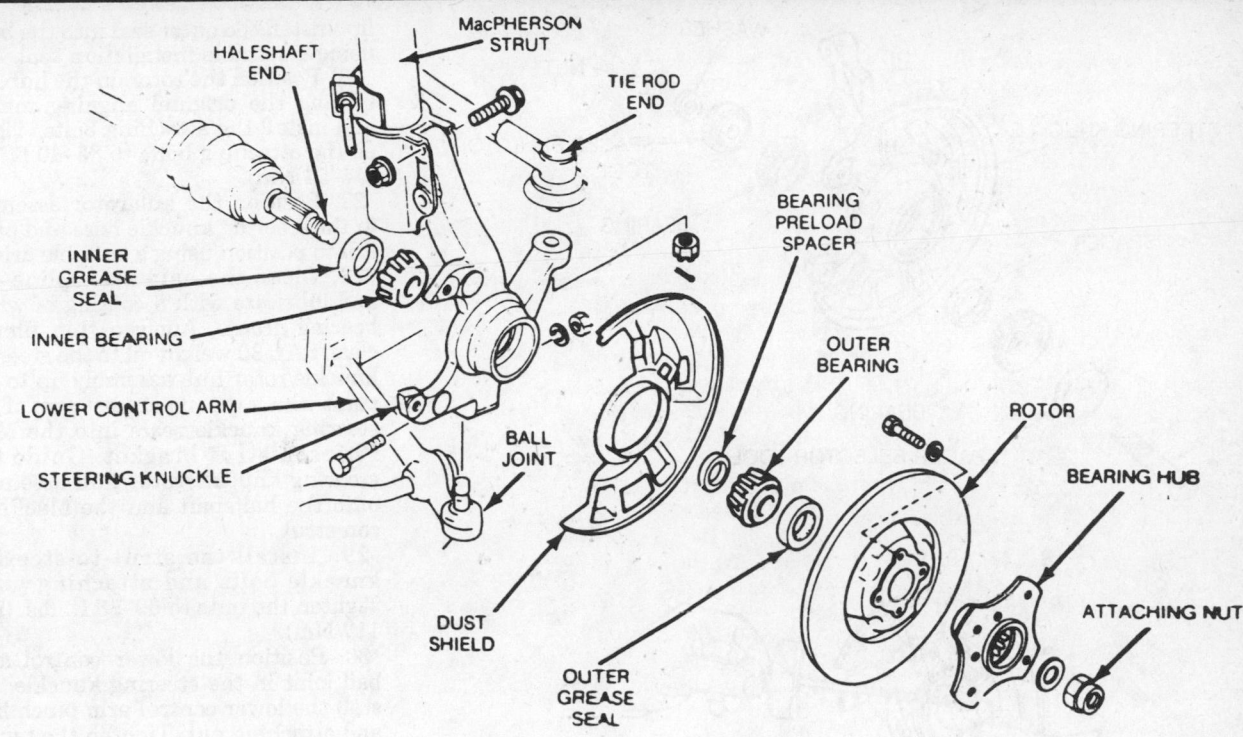

HALFSHAFT END

MacPHERSON STRUT

TIE ROD END

INNER GREASE SEAL

INNER BEARING

LOWER CONTROL ARM

STEERING KNUCKLE

BALL JOINT

DUST SHIELD

OUTER GREASE SEAL

BEARING PRELOAD SPACER

OUTER BEARING

ROTOR

BEARING HUB

ATTACHING NUT

Front wheel hub, knuckle and bearing assembly

wheel hub is rusted to the halfshaft, use either a 2 jaw puller or a hub puller to achieve separation.

13. Remove the wheel hub/rotor assembly from the steering knuckle/dust shield assembly using knuckle puller tool T87C–1104–A or equivalent.

14. Remove the bearing preload spacer from the hub.

NOTE: The spacer is preselected to yield the correct bearing preload. Save the removed spacer for use during assembly.

15. Clamp the hub/rotor assembly in a vise with protective jaw caps. Scribe aligning marks on the hub and rotor for use during assembly. Remove the attaching bolts and the rotor.

16. Remove the outer bearing from the wheel hub using a suitable bearing splitter, driver and press. Remove the outer and inner grease seals and discard. Remove the inner bearing.

17. Remove the races from the steering knuckle using a suitable puller and slide hammer. If necessary, remove the dust shield from the steering knuckle.

To install:

18. Clean and inspect all components that will be reused. Check the bearings, hub, knuckle and rotor dust shield for cracks, scoring, rusting, etc.

19. If the brake rotor dust shield was removed, install a new 1 using a suitable installation tool.

20. If the bearings or knuckle are be-

ing replaced, bearing preload must be checked as follows before assembly.

a. Install the outer bearing races in the steering knuckle using suitable tools.

b. Lubricate the bearing races and bearing with a thin film of clean engine oil. Install the bearings in the steering knuckle.

c. Install spacer selection tool T87C–1104–B or equivalent, and clamp the bolt head in a vise.

d. Tighten the center bolt in increments, to 36, 72, 108 and 145 ft. lbs. (49, 98, 147 and 196 Nm). After tightening the center bolt to a specified increment, seat the bearings by rotating the steering knuckle.

e. Remove the tool/steering knuckle from the vise. Remount the assembly in the vise, clamping it where the MacPherson strut mounts.

f. Measure the amount of torque required to rotate the spacer selector tool, using an inch pound torque wrench. The torque wrench reading must be taken just as the tool starts to rotate.

g. If the torque wrench indicates 2.2–10.4 inch lbs. (0.25–1.8 Nm), the spacer is the correct thickness. If the torque wrench indicates less than 2.2 inch lbs. (0.25 Nm), a thinner spacer must be installed. If the torque wrench indicates more than 10.4 inch lbs. (1.8 Nm), a thicker spacer must be installed.

h. Each bearing spacer has a numerical code that identifies it's thickness, stamped onto the outer diameter of the spacer. The numbers range from 1–21, with 1 being the thinnest spacer. If the number stamped on the spacer is not legible, measure the spacer with a micrometer and compare it to the spacer thickness chart to determine the number.

i. Changing the spacer thickness by 1 number, either higher or lower, will change the bearing preload by 1.7–3.5 inch lbs. (0.2–0.4 Nm).

21. If the bearings or knuckle are not being replaced, install the races in the steering knuckle using suitable tools.

22. Pack the bearings and the hub area with a suitable high temperature wheel bearing grease. Place the inner bearing into the steering knuckle bore.

23. Lubricate the lip of the new inner grease seal with the bearing grease. Form the lubricant into a strip, concentrated along the edges of the seal lip. Install the inner seal into the bore, using a suitable installation tool.

24. Place the original bearing preload spacer or the spacer selected from the bearing preload check procedure, in the steering knuckle bore. Position the bearing removed from the wheel hub in the steering knuckle bore.

25. Lubricate the lip of the new outer grease seal with the bearing grease. Form the lubricant into a strip, concentrated along the edges of the seal

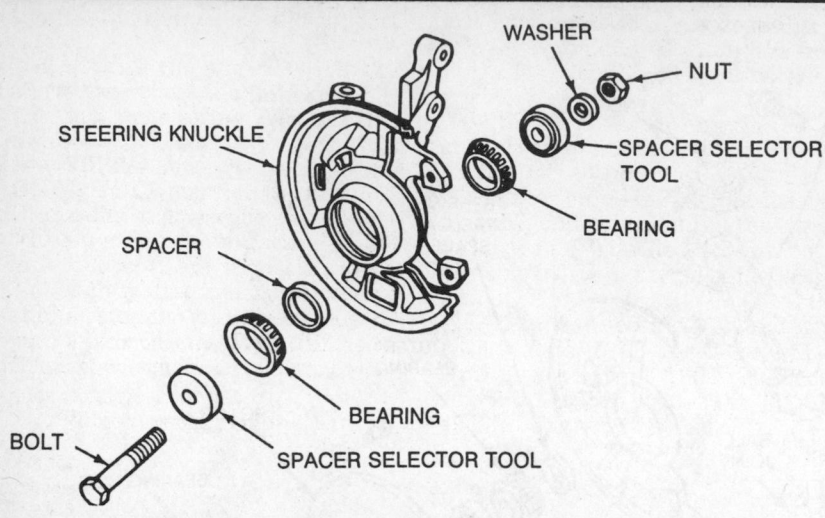

Front wheel bearing preload checking procedure

FRONT WHEEL BEARING PRELOAD SPACER THICKNESS

Stamped Mark	Thickness In. (mm)
1	0.2474 (6.285)
2	0.2490 (6.325)
3	0.2506 (6.365)
4	0.2522 (6.405)
5	0.2538 (6.445)
6	0.2554 (6.485)
7	0.2570 (6.525)
8	0.2586 (6.565)
9	0.2602 (6.605)
10	0.2618 (6.645)
11	0.2634 (6.685)
12	0.2650 (6.725)
13	0.2666 (6.765)
14	0.2682 (6.805)
15	0.2698 (6.845)
16	0.2714 (6.885)
17	0.2730 (6.925)
18	0.2746 (6.965)
19	0.2762 (7.005)
20	0.2778 (7.045)
21	0.2794 (7.085)

lip. Install the outer seal into the bore, using a suitable installation tool.

26. Position the rotor on the hub, observing the original aligning marks, and install the attaching bolts. Tighten the attaching bolts to 33–40 ft. lbs. (44–54 Nm).

27. Position the hub/rotor assembly in the steering knuckle bore and press it into position using a suitable driver.

28. Clean the halfshaft spline end and lubricate with a coating of wheel bearing grease. Apply a thin film of clean SAE 30 weight oil to the steering knuckle/rotor hub assembly up to the point where the uppermost arm of the steering knuckle seats into the MacPherson strut bracket. Guide the steering knuckle/rotor/hub assembly onto the halfshaft and the MacPherson strut.

29. Install the strut-to-steering knuckle bolts and attaching nuts. Tighten the nuts to 69–86 ft. lbs. (93–117 Nm).

30. Position the lower control arm ball joint in the steering knuckle. Install the lower control arm pinch bolt and attaching nut. Tighten the nut to 32–40 ft. lbs. (43–54 Nm).

31. Position the caliper on the steering knuckle and install the attaching bolts. Tighten the bolts to 29–36 ft. lbs. (39–49 Nm). Position the caliper hose in the strut routing bracket and install the retaining clip.

32. Install a new halfshaft attaching nut and tighten to 116–174 ft. lbs. (157–235 Nm). After installation, the wheel hub assembly must rotate freely by hand. Stake the halfshaft attaching nut into the shaft groove.

NOTE: Do not use a pointed tool to stake the nut. If the nut cracks even slightly during staking, replace it with another new one.

33. Connect the tie rod end to the steering knuckle and install the attaching nut. Tighten the attaching nut to 22–33 ft. lbs. (29–44 Nm). Install a new cotter pin through the nut and ball stud. If the openings in the nut and the hole in the ball stud are not aligned, tighten the nut slightly, just to the point of alignment. Never loosen the nut.

34. Install the wheel and tire assembly. Tighten the attaching bolts to 65–87 ft. lbs. (88–118 Nm). Lower the vehicle.

MANUAL TRANSAXLE

For further information on transmissions/transaxles, please refer to "Chilton's Guide to Transmission Repair".

Transaxle Assembly

REMOVAL & INSTALLATION

1. Disconnect the negative battery cable.
2. Disconnect the backup light switch wiring connector.
3. Disconnect the neutral switch wiring connector.
4. Loosen the clutch cable adjusting nut and disengage the cable from the release lever.
5. Remove the starter.
6. Disconnect the speedometer cable.
7. Remove the 2 bolts from the top of the clutch housing.
8. Install 3 bar engine support bar tool D88L–6000–A or equivalent. Raise and support the vehicle safely.
9. Remove the nut and bolt attaching the shift rod to the input shift rail.
10. Remove the nuts and bolts attaching the lower control arms to the steering knuckles.
11. Disengage the halfshafts from the differential side gears.
12. Install differential side gear plug tool T87C–7025–C or equivalent, to prevent the side gears from moving.
13. Remove the mounting bracket attaching bolts and the mounting brackets.
14. Remove the crossmember.
15. Position a suitable transmission jack under the transaxle and secure it with a safety chain.
16. Remove the remaining lower transaxle attaching bolts. Pull the transaxle away from the engine and lower it from the vehicle.

To install:

17. Raise the transaxle into position and seat it against the rear of the engine.
18. Install the lower transaxle attaching bolts. Torque the bolts to 47–66 ft. lbs. (64–89 Nm).
19. Install the mounting brackets and remove the transmission jack.
20. Install the crossmember and remove the differential plugs.
21. Remove and discard the old halfshaft circlips. Install new circlips and engage the halfshafts with the differential side gears.
22. Connect the lower control arms to the steering knuckles. Install the lower control arm attaching bolts and nuts.
23. Position the shift rod on the input shift rail and install the attaching bolt and nut.
24. Lower the vehicle and remove the engine support bar.
25. Install the 2 bolts at the top of

the clutch housing. Torque the bolts 47–66 ft. lbs. (64–89 Nm).
26. Install the starter.
27. Connect the clutch cable to the release lever. Connect the neutral and backup switch wiring connectors.
28. Remove the speedometer gear and sleeve assembly from the transaxle case bore. With a clean rag, wipe the assembly and reinsert the sleeve into the transaxle. Remove the sleeve and check the oil level. The oil level should be between the **F** and **L** marks on the gear sleeve. If the level is not within the normal operating range, add oil through the speedometer bore as required.
29. Install the speedometer sleeve and gear assembly and connect the speedometer cable.
30. Connect the negative battery cable.
31. Adjust the clutch pedal free-play.

CLUTCH

Clutch Assembly

REMOVAL & INSTALLATION

1. Disconnect the negative battery cable.
2. Remove the transaxle assembly.

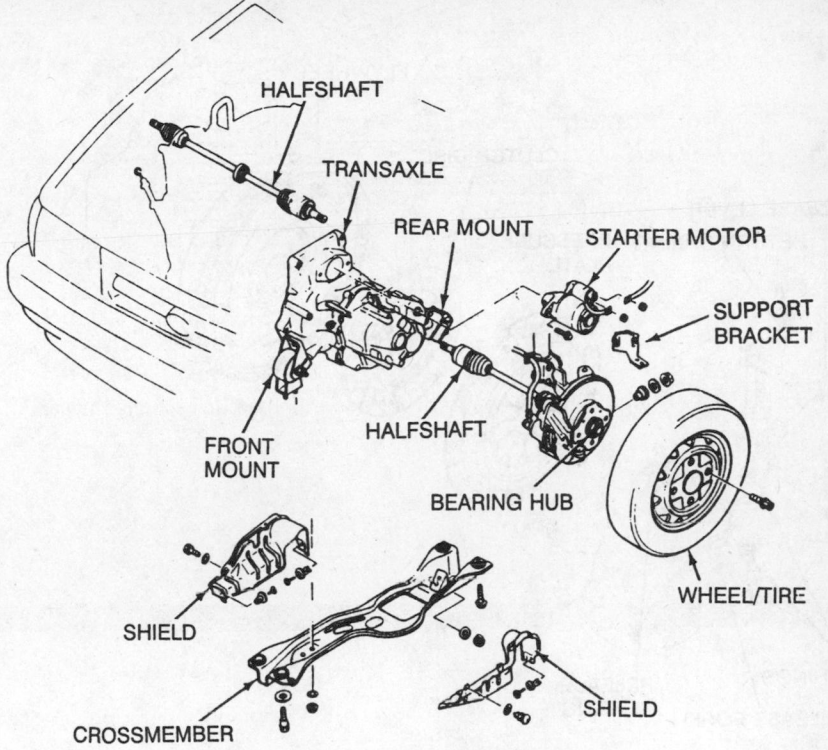

Manual transaxle removal and installation

NOTE: During the removal procedure, do not allow oil or grease to come in contact with the clutch disc facing if the disc is to be reused. Handle the disc with clean rags wrapped around the edges and do not touch the disc facing. Even a small amount of dirt or grease may cause the clutch to grab or slip.

3. If the pressure plate is to be reused, paint or scribe alignment marks on the pressure plate and flywheel for assembly reference.
4. Install an appropriate locking tool to prevent the flywheel from turning.
5. Loosen the pressure plate attaching bolts in an alternate pattern 1 turn at a time. This will relieve the pressure plate spring tension evenly and prevent distortion of the pressure plate. Remove the pressure plate and clutch disc after the bolts are removed. Replace all clutch components as required.
6. Inspect the flywheel for scoring, cracks and heat checks. Resurface or replace the flywheel, as necessary.
7. Inspect the pilot bearing for damage. Make sure the bearing turns easily. If replacement is necessary, remove the flywheel and remove the pilot bearing.

To install:

8. If necessary, install a new pilot bearing using a suitable installation

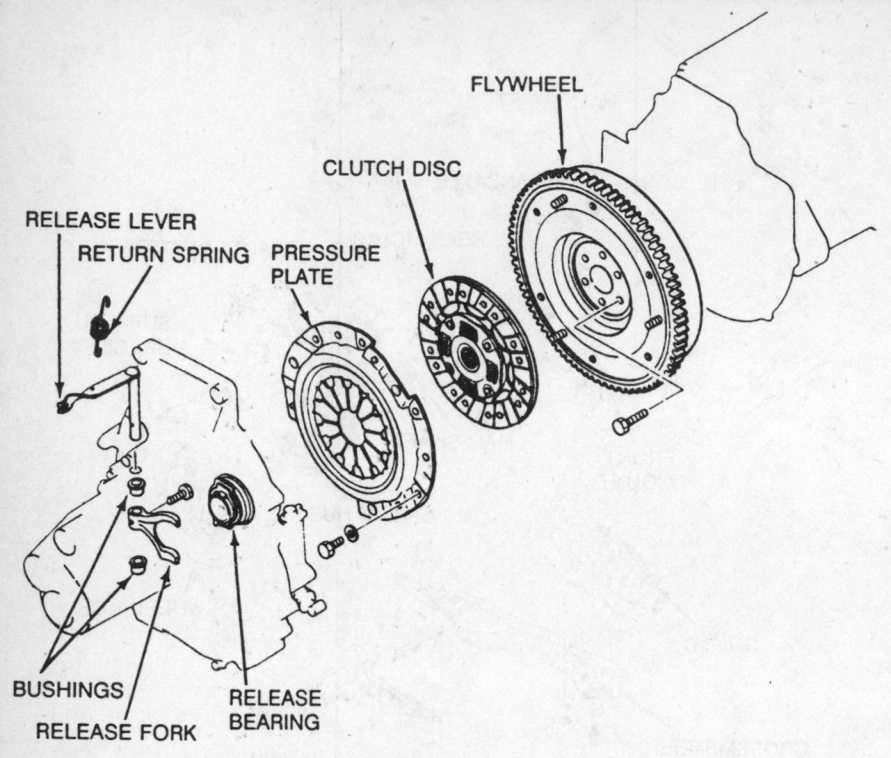

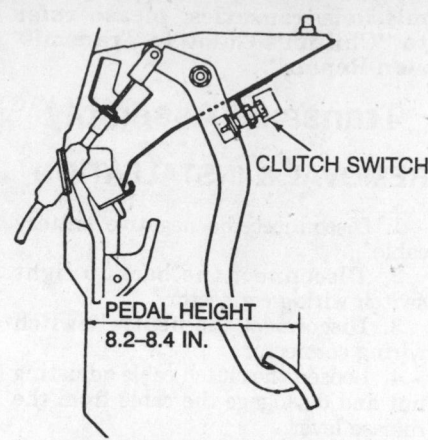

FLYWHEEL

CLUTCH DISC

RELEASE LEVER
RETURN SPRING   PRESSURE
PLATE

BUSHINGS
RELEASE FORK   RELEASE BEARING

Exploded view of the clutch assembly

CLUTCH SWITCH

PEDAL HEIGHT
8.2–8.4 IN.

Clutch pedal height adjustment

tool. Use only a driver tool that contacts the bearing outer race. A driver tool that contacts the inner race or the bearing area is unsuitable.

9. If the flywheel was removed, clean the sealant from the flywheel attaching bolts. Coat the bolt threads with a suitable sealer compound.

10. Make sure the crankshaft flange and the back of the flywheel are clean. Position the flywheel on the crankshaft and install the attaching bolts. Tighten the bolts to 71–76 ft. lbs. (96–103 Nm).

11. Position the clutch disc on the flywheel and install a clutch alignment tool to hold the disc in place.

NOTE: When installing the clutch disc, make sure the disc dampener springs are facing away from the flywheel. A new disc will be stamped FLYWHEEL to indicate the correct installation postion.

12. Align the reference marks, if present, and position the pressure plate on the flywheel and install the attaching bolts. Torque the bolts evenly, in an alternate pattern, to 13–20 ft. lbs. (18–26 Nm). The bolts must be tightened in this manner to prevent distortion of the pressure plate.

13. Remove the clutch alignment tool.

14. Clean the clutch disc splines on the input shaft with a dry rag and coat

the spline surfaces with a light film of clutch grease.

15. Install the transaxle.

16. Connect the negative battery cable.

17. Adjust the clutch pedal free-play.

PEDAL HEIGHT ADJUSTMENT

1. To eliminate the possibility that the clutch cable is affecting the pedal height, disconnect it at the transaxle release lever. Move the floor carpet and insulation out of the way of the dash panel to ensure an accurate measurement.

2. Measure the distance from the upper center of the pedal to the cowl panel. The pedal height should be from 8.2–8.4 in. (208.2–213.2mm). If the pedal height is within this range, no adjustment is necessary. If the pedal height is not within specification, inspect the clutch pedal mounting for damaged, worn or missing parts. If the mounting appears to be satisfactory, proceed as follows:

   a. Remove the air duct located under the steering column.

   b. Locate the clutch switch and loosen the attaching nuts. Thread the switch in or out until the pedal height is within specification. Tighten the attaching nuts when the correct height is obtained.

   c. Connect the clutch cable to the transaxle release lever and adjust the pedal free-play.

   d. If the pedal height changes after connecting the clutch cable, check for binding along the cable route.

   e. Install the air duct. Place the insulation and floor carpet in their original positions.

FREE-PLAY ADJUSTMENT

1. Carefully move the clutch pedal back and forth and measure the amount of travel. If the clutch pedal free-play is 0.35–0.59 in. (9–15mm), no adjustment is necessary. If the free-play is not within specification, proceed to Step 2.

2. Pull back the transaxle release lever and measure the clearance between the lever and the cable pin. Thread the adjuster in or out until the clearance between the pin and the lever is 0.06–0.10 in. (1.5–2.5mm).

3. Check the free-play at the clutch. If it is not within specification, inspect the clutch release components for a problem.

Clutch Cable

REMOVAL & INSTALLATION

1. Loosen the clutch cable adjuster nut at the transaxle release lever until the cable can be disengaged from the lever.

2. Unbolt the cable routing bracket from the transaxle housing.

3. Remove the air duct located under the steering column.

4. Remove the clip securing the cable casing to the pedal support bracket.

5. Pull upward on the cable to disengage it from the hook on the pedal.

6. If necessary, loosen the attaching

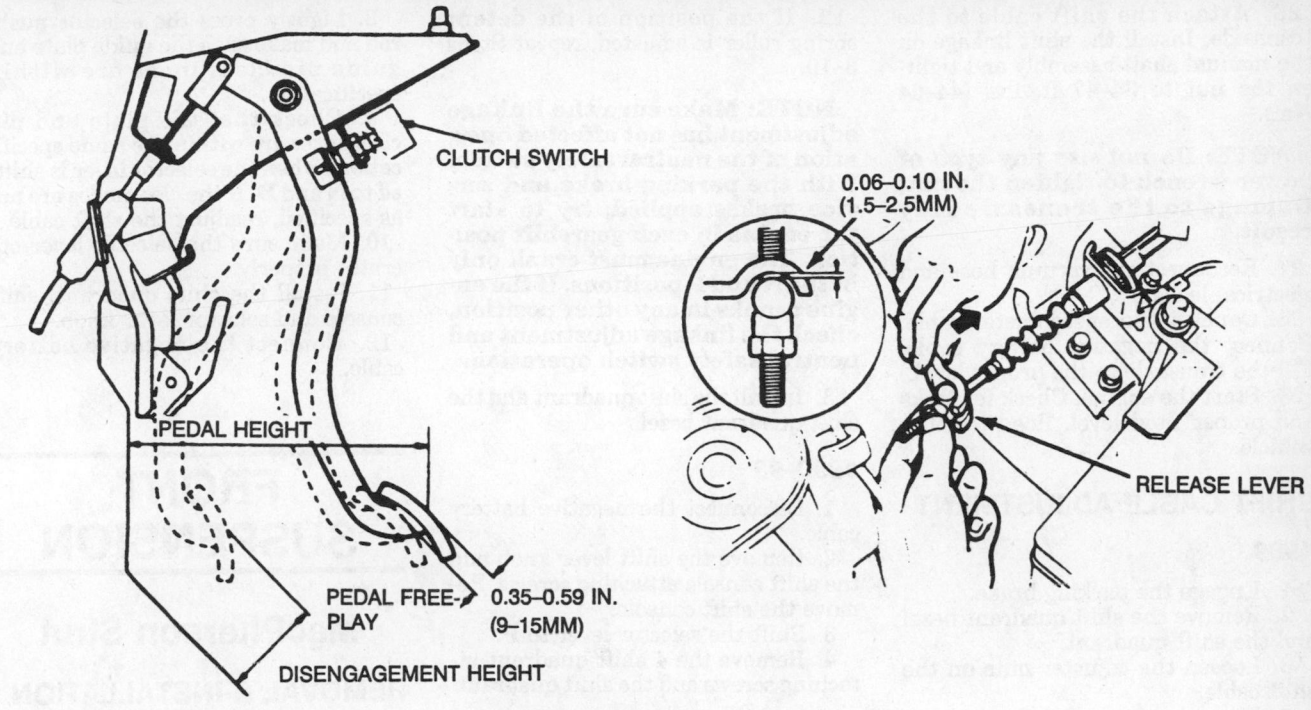

CLUTCH SWITCH

PEDAL HEIGHT

PEDAL FREE-PLAY 0.35–0.59 IN. (9–15MM)

DISENGAGEMENT HEIGHT

0.06–0.10 IN. (1.5–2.5MM)

RELEASE LEVER

Clutch pedal free-play adjustment

nut and remove the routing bracket from the cable. Withdraw the cable through the hole in the bulkhead.

To install:

7. If necessary, position the routing bracket on the cable casing and tighten the attaching nuts.

8. Install the cable. Make sure the instrument panel grommet is properly seated.

9. Pull upward on the cable and hook it over the top of the clutch pedal.

10. Install the cable casing retaining clip.

11. Install the air duct.

12. Connect the cable to the release lever. Check the clutch pedal free-play and adjust if necessary.

AUTOMATIC TRANSAXLE

For further information on transmissions/transaxles, please refer to "Chilton's Guide to Transmission Repair".

Transaxle Assembly

REMOVAL & INSTALLATION

1. Disconnect the negative battery cable. Loosen the front wheel bolts.

2. Drain the transaxle fluid. Disconnect the speedometer cable from the transaxle.

3. Disconnect the transaxle electrical connectors, which are located next to the governor.

4. Disconnect the transaxle ground wire. Disconnect the transaxle vacuum hose.

5. Remove the nut which connects the shift linkage to the manual shaft assembly.

6. Remove the shift cable from the transaxle. Support the engine using engine support bar tool D87L–6000–A or equivalent.

7. Raise and support the vehicle safely. Remove the tire and wheel assemblies.

8. Remove the left splash shield. Remove the stabilizer mounting nuts and brackets. Remove the left stabilizer body bracket.

9. Remove the lower arm clamp bolts and nuts. Pull the lower arms downward, separating the lower arms from the knuckles.

10. Remove the cotter pin and nut. Disconnect the tie rod end from the knuckle.

11. Remove the halfshafts. Install differential plug tool T87C–7025–C or equivalent, between the differential side gears.

12. Disconnect and plug the oil cooler lines. Remove the crossmember. Remove the gusset plate to transaxle bolts.

13. Remove the flywheel cover. Remove the torque converter retaining bolts. Remove the starter.

14. Properly support the transaxle assembly.

15. Remove the engine-to-transaxle retaining bolts. Carefully remove the transaxle from the vehicle.

To install:

16. Position the transaxle in the vehicle. Install the engine-to-transaxle bolts. Tighten to 41–59 ft. lbs. (55–80 Nm).

17. Install the starter. Install the torque converter bolts and tighten to 26–36 ft. lbs. (34–49 Nm).

18. Install the flywheel cover and tighten the bolts to 61–87 inch lbs. (7–10 Nm).

19. Install the crossmember and tighten the bolts to 47–66 ft. lbs. (64–89 Nm). Install the front engine mount-to-crossmember attaching nuts and tighten to 32–38 ft. lbs. (43–52 Nm). Install the rear engine mount-to-crossmember attaching nut and tighten to 21–34 ft. lbs. (28–46 Nm).

20. Install the halfshafts. Connect the oil cooler lines.

21. Connect the tie rod ends to the steering knuckles and tighten the attaching nuts to 26–30 ft. lbs. (35–40 Nm). Install new cotter pins.

22. Attach the lower arm ball joints to the knuckles. Tighten the lower arm clamp nuts and bolts to 32–40 ft. lbs. (43–54 Nm).

23. Install the stabilizer body bracket and mounting nuts. Tighten the nuts to 40–45 ft. lbs. (54–61 Nm).

24. Install the splash shield and the front wheel and tire assemblies.

25. Lower the vehicle. Remove the engine support tool.

26. Attach the shift cable to the transaxle. Install the shift linkage on the manual shaft assembly and tighten the nut to 34–47 ft. lbs. (44–64 Nm).

NOTE: Do not use any type of power wrench to tighten the nut. Damage to the transaxle may result.

27. Reconnect the vacuum hose and electrical leads.
28. Connect the speedometer cable. Connect the negative battery cable. Fill the transaxle to the proper level.
29. Start the engine. Check for leaks and proper fluid level. Road test the vehicle.

SHIFT CABLE ADJUSTMENT

1989

1. Engage the parking brake.
2. Remove the shift quadrant bezel and the shift quadrant.
3. Loosen the adjuster nuts on the shift cable.
4. Move the transaxle selector lever to the **N** position. Make sure the detent spring roller is in the **N** position.
5. Move the shift lever on the transaxle to the **N** position.
6. Tighten the lower adjusting nut by hand until it lightly contacts the T-joint, then loosen it a half turn. Tighten the upper adjuster nut to 69–95 inch lbs. (8–11 Nm).
7. Press the selector interlock button and push the selector lever toward **R** with a force of 4.4 lbs. Note the distance that the selector lever has moved. The distance of movement should be no more than 0.31 in. (8mm). Move the selector lever back to **N**.
8. Pull the selector lever toward **D** in the same way as in Step 7. Note the distance that the selector lever has moved. The distance of movement should be no more than 0.31 in. (8mm).
9. Compare the distances noted in Steps 7 and 8. If the distance recorded from **N** to **R** is larger than the distance recorded from **N** to **D**, loosen the upper adjuster nut and tighten the lower adjuster nut so the larger distance becomes smaller.
10. If the distance recorded from **N** to **D** is larger than the distance recorded from **N** to **R**, loosen the lower adjuster nut and tighten the upper adjuster nut so the larger distance becomes smaller.
11. Check the manual linkage operation. If the selector lever does not shift smoothly, set the selector lever to **P**. Loosen the attaching screws on the detent spring and roller assembly. Adjust the position of the detent spring roller.

12. If the position of the detent spring roller is adjusted, repeat Steps 3–10.

NOTE: Make sure the linkage adjustment has not affected operation of the neutral safety switch. With the parking brake and service brakes applied, try to start the engine in each gearshift position. The engine must crank only in the N and P positions. If the engine cranks in any other position, check the linkage adjustment and neutral safety switch operation.

13. Install the shift quadrant and the shift quadrant bezel.

1990–93

1. Disconnect the negative battery cable.
2. Remove the shift lever knob and the shift console attaching screws. Remove the shift console.
3. Shift the selector lever to **P**.
4. Remove the 4 shift quadrant attaching screws and the shift quadrant.

NOTE: Make sure the detent spring roller is in the P detent.

5. Loosen adjustment nuts "A" and "B" until they reach the ends of the cable thread.
6. Move the shift lever on the transaxle to the **P** position.
7. Tighten adjustment nut "A" by hand until it lightly contacts the T-joint, then tighten adjustment nut "B" to 80–97 inch lbs. (9–11 Nm).

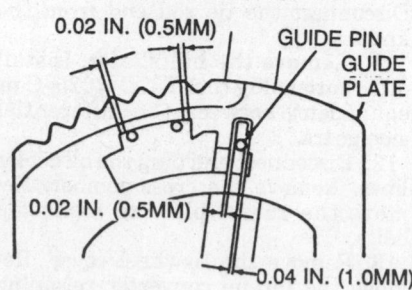

DETENT SPRING ROLLER
ADJUSTMENT NUT "A"
SHIFT CABLE   T-JOINT

Shift cable adjustment points

0.02 IN. (0.5MM)
GUIDE PIN
GUIDE PLATE
0.02 IN. (0.5MM)
0.04 IN. (1.0MM)

Guide plate and guide pin clearances—1990–93 vehicles

8. Lightly press the selector push-rod and make sure the guide plate and guide pin clearances are within specification.
9. Check that the plate and pin clearances are within the same specifications when the selector lever is shifted to **N** and **D**. If the clearances are not as specified, readjust the shift cable.
10. Make sure the selector lever operates properly.
11. Install the shift quadrant, shift console and selector lever knob.
12. Connect the negative battery cable.

FRONT SUSPENSION

MacPherson Strut

REMOVAL & INSTALLATION

1. Raise the vehicle and support it safely.
2. Remove the wheel and tire assembly.
3. Remove the brake line clip from the strut lower mounting bracket and disengage the brake line.
4. Remove the 2 nuts and bolts securing the strut lower bracket to the steering knuckle.
5. In the engine compartment, remove the 2 nuts securing the strut mounting block in the strut tower.
6. Disengage the strut lower bracket from the steering knuckle and lower the strut clear of the wheel well.
7. Attach spring compressor tool T81P–5310–A or equivalent, and compress the coil spring.
8. Pry out the mounting block cap and remove the strut upper nut and lockwasher.
9. Remove the strut mounting block and spacer plate. Remove the washer, bearing seal and bearing from the strut rod.
10. Remove the upper spring seat, seat insulator and spring. Slide the jounce bumper/shield off the strut.

NOTE: If replacing the spring, release the spring compressor progressively to prevent spring arching. Open the compressor jaws wide enough to grip the new spring in the same position and tighten the compressor screws progressively, compressing the spring until the strut can be assembled without interference.

To install:
11. Check the condition of the jounce

bumper and spring seat insulator and replace, as necessary. Make sure the bearing operates smoothly. Check the spring for uniform coil spacing, for nicks or burrs and compare the spring length with a new spring to check for excessive spring set; replace as necessary.

12. Slide the jounce bumper/shield onto the strut rod and over the body. Install the compressed spring, upper spring seat insulator and upper seat, positioning the spring ends against the steps in the seats.

13. Install the bearing, seal and plain washer on the strut rod. Install the strut mounting block with the white alignment spot on the same side of the strut as the steering knuckle mounting bracket.

14. Install the spacer plate. Install the lockwasher and nut and tighten to 40–50 ft. lbs. (54–67 Nm). Release and remove the spring compressor.

15. Place the strut assembly with spacer plate in the strut tower with the white alignment mark facing outward.

16. Install the upper mounting block stud nuts and torque to 22–27 ft. lbs. (29–36 Nm).

17. Engage the steering knuckle in the strut tower lower bracket and install the mounting bolts and nuts. Torque to 69–86 ft. lbs. (93–117 Nm).

18. Position the brake line into the strut lower mounting bracket cutout and install the retaining clip.

19. Install the wheel and tire assembly and lower the vehicle.

Lower Ball Joints

NOTE: The ball joint is an integral part of the control arm. If inspection proves the ball joint to be bad, the entire lower control arm must be replaced.

INSPECTION

Control Arm Installed

Check for ball joint wear by raising and safely supporting the vehicle until the wheel and tire assembly is clear of the floor. Support the lower control arm so there is no load on the suspension strut. Try to rock the wheel top-to-bottom; if any wobble is felt, look for movement between the control arm and steering knuckle. If the ball joint appears tight, check and adjust the wheel bearing preload, then repeat the wobble check. Any movement still present is a sign of ball joint wear. Replace the lower control arm.

Control Arm Removed

Make sure the ball joint stud swivels freely but is not loose. Grip the ball joint stud with a suitable adapter and check the stud rotating torque with a low-reading torque wrench. It should be in the range of 16–27 inch lbs. (1.8–3.1 Nm).

Lower Control Arms

REMOVAL & INSTALLATION

1. Raise and support the vehicle safely. Remove the lower control arm pivot bolt at the frame bracket.

2. Remove the ball joint clamp bolt and and nut from the steering knuckle assembly.

3. Remove the stabilizer bar bushing retaining nut from the rear of the control arm and remove the rear bushing washer and bushing.

4. Lower the control arm, prying the ball joint stud out of the steering knuckle, if necessary. Disengage and remove the control arm from the stabilizer end.

5. Inspect the control arm for deformation or cracks and check the pivot bushing for deterioration. Verify that the ball joint swivels freely but is not loose. If the control arm pivot bushing is to be replaced, remove the old bushing with C-frame tool T74P–3044–A1, bushing tool T81P–5493–B2 and receiver cup tool T88C–5493E or equivalents. Center the new bushing in the center of the control arm eye and install using the removal tools. Replace the lower control arm/ball joint assembly as required.

6. If the ball joint boot is damaged or deteriorated, pry the boot off with a small cold chisel. Install the new boot onto the ball joint using a suitable adapter such as a ¾ in. socket to properly seat the boot.

To install:

7. Position the front bushing washer and bushing onto the stabilizer end. Engage the control arm with the stabilizer.

8. Raise the control arm inner end into the pivot bracket on the frame and start the pivot bolt to hold the control arm in place. Do not completely tighten the bolt at this time.

9. Engage the control arm ball joint stud with the clamp bore in the steering knuckle and install the clamp bolt and nut.

10. Install the stabilizer rear bushing and washer onto the stabilizer end with the retaining nut. Torque the retaining nut to 47–57 ft. lbs. (64–77 Nm). Install the cotter pin.

11. Torque the pivot bolt at the control arm frame bracket to 32–40 ft. lbs. (43–54 Nm).

12. Hold the steering clamp bolt stationary and torque the clamp nut to 32–40 ft. lbs. (43–54 Nm).

13. Lower the vehicle.

Stabilizer Bar

REMOVAL & INSTALLATION

1. Raise and safely support the vehicle.

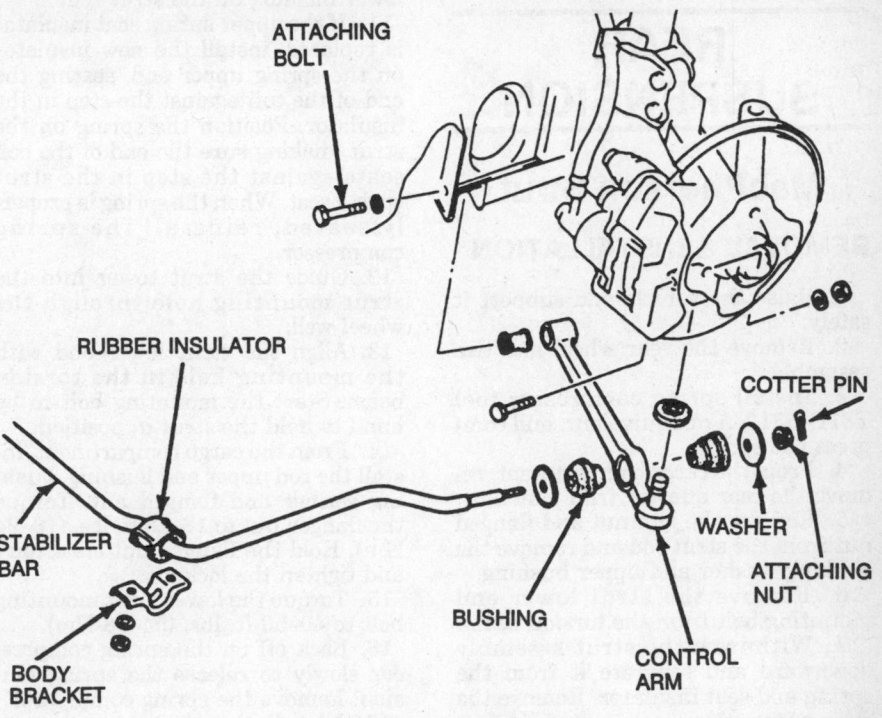

Rear suspension assembly

2. Remove the stabilizer mounting bracket nuts and mounting brackets.

3. Remove the split bushings from the stabilizer bar. Replace deteriorated or worn bushings as required.

4. Remove the stabilizer bushing nuts at the lower control arms and remove the rear washers and bushings.

5. Pull the stabilizer bar forward to disengage it from both lower control arms. Remove the bushings and washers. Replace deteriorated or worn bushings as required.

To install:

6. Install the control arm bushing washers on the ends of the stabilizer bar and install the control arm front bushings.

7. Support the stabilizer bar by hand and insert the ends of the bar into the lower control arms. Install the control arm bushings and washers with the retaining nuts. Make the retaining nuts finger-tight.

8. Install the split bushings on the the stabilizer bar cross bar with the split side forward and position them next to the white alignment marks on the bar.

9. Install the stabilizer bar mounting brackets. Torque the bracket retaining nuts to 40–50 ft. lbs. (54–68 Nm).

10. Torque the control arm bushing retaining nuts to 47–57 ft. lbs. (64–77 Nm). Install cotter pins.

11. Lower the vehicle.

REAR SUSPENSION

MacPherson Strut

REMOVAL & INSTALLATION

1. Raise the vehicle and support it safely.

2. Remove the rear wheel and tire assembly.

3. Install spring compressor tool T81P-5310-A or equivalent, and compress the spring.

4. From the cargo compartment, remove the rear quarter trim panel.

5. Remove the jam nut and flanged nut from the strut rod and remove the bushing washer and upper bushing.

6. Remove the strut lower end mounting bolt from the torsion beam.

7. Withdraw the strut assembly downward and separate it from the spring and seat insulator. Remove the spring compressor.

8. Remove the lower grommet and

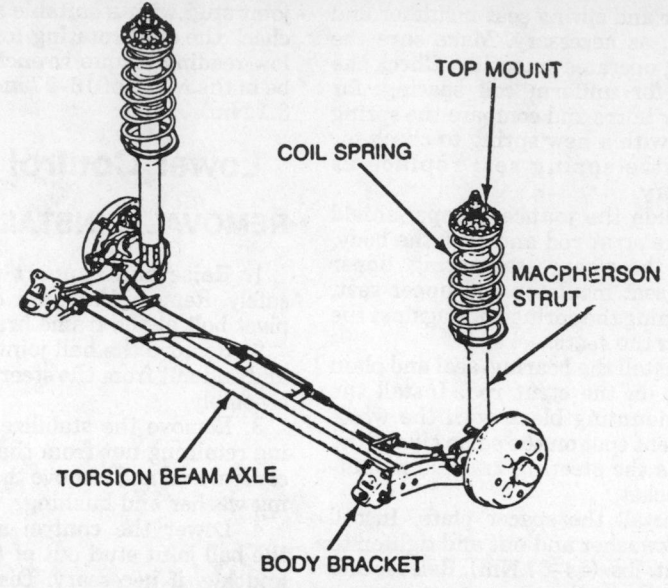

Rear strut assembly

jounce bumper seat from the strut rod. Slide the jounce bumper off the strut.

9. Inspect the material condition of the jounce bumper, spring seat insulator and strut rod bushings. Inspect the strut for leakage, endplay or erratic action. Inspect the strut lower end bushing for damage or deterioration. Replace any damaged or deteriorated components, as required.

To install:

10. Slide the jounce bumper onto the strut rod. Install the bumper seat and lower bushing on the strut rod.

11. If the upper spring seat insulator is replaced, install the new insulator on the spring upper end, seating the end of the coil against the step in the insulator. Position the spring on the strut, making sure the end of the coil seats against the step in the strut spring seat. When the spring is properly seated, reinstall the spring compressor.

12. Guide the strut tower into the strut mounting hole through the wheel well.

13. Align the strut lower end with the mounting hole in the torsion beam. Start the mounting bolt in by hand to hold the strut in position.

14. From the cargo compartment, install the rod upper end bushing, bushing washer and flanged nut. Torque the flanged nut to 12–18 ft. lbs. (16–24 Nm). Hold the flanged nut stationary and tighten the locknut.

15. Torque the lower strut mounting bolt to 40–50 ft. lbs. (54–68 Nm).

16. Back off on the spring compressor slowly to release the spring tension. Remove the spring compressor.

17. Install the rear quarter trim panel.

18. Install the wheel and tire assembly. Lower the vehicle.

Rear Wheel Bearings

REMOVAL & INSTALLATION

1. Raise the vehicle and support it safely. Make sure the parking brake is fully released.

2. Remove the wheel and tire assembly.

3. Remove the grease/dust cap.

4. On Type 1 nuts, carefully raise the staked portion of the locknut using a small cape chisel. On Type 2 nuts, remove the cotter pin and nut retaining cap.

NOTE: Some locknuts may have left hand thread. The left hand threaded locknut is located on the right side of the vehicle. Turn this locknut clockwise to loosen. The right hand threaded locknut is located on the left side of the vehicle and is turned counterclockwise to loosen.

5. Remove the locknut. Discard the Type 1 locknut or Type 2 cotter pin.

6. Pull the brake drum bearings and hub assembly away from the spindle shaft. Take care not to damage the spindle shaft threads.

7. With a small roll head prybar or equivalent, remove the bearing grease seal from the bearing hub. Discard the seal regardless of condition.

8. Remove the inner and outer bearings from the bearing hub. If the bearings are to be reused, identify and tag each bearing for installation refer-

ence. Replace worn or damaged bearings as required.

9. If the bearings are being replaced, remove the bearing races using a suitable tool.

To install:

10. If the bearings are being replaced, install the new bearing races in the hub using suitable installation tools.

11. Pack the bearings and the hub with high temperature wheel bearing grease.

12. Position the inner bearing in the hub. Install and seat a new grease seal with a suitable driving tool. Lubricate the lip of the seal with the wheel bearing grease.

13. Position the brake drum and hub assembly on the spindle. Keep the hub centered during positioning to prevent damage to the new grease seal and spindle threads.

14. Install the outer bearing, washer and locknut.

15. Adjust the bearing preload.

16. Install the grease cap, wheel and tire assembly.

17. Lower the vehicle and connect the negative battery cable.

ADJUSTMENT

1. Make sure the parking brake is fully released.

2. Raise the vehicle and support it safely. Remove the wheel and tire assembly.

3. Remove the grease cap. Rotate the brake drum to make sure there is no brake drag.

4. On Type 1 nuts, carefully raise the staked portion of the locknut using a small cape chisel. On Type 2 nuts, remove the cotter pin and nut retaining cap.

NOTE: Some locknuts may have left hand thread. The left hand threaded locknut is located on the right side of the vehicle. Turn this locknut clockwise to loosen. The right hand threaded locknut is located on the left side of the vehicle and is turned counterclockwise to loosen.

5. Remove the locknut. Discard the Type 1 locknut or Type 2 cotter pin.

6. To seat the bearings, torque the locknut to 18–22 ft. lbs. (25–29 Nm). Rotate the brake drum by hand while tightening the locknut.

7. Loosen the locknut until it can be turned by hand.

8. Before the bearing preload can be set, the amount of seal drag must be measured and added to the the required preload.

9. To measure the seal drag on Type 1 nuts, proceed as follows:

   a. Install a lug bolt and rotate the brake drum until the stud is in the 12 o'clock position.

   b. Place an inch pound torque wrench onto the bolt to measure the amount of force required to rotate the break drum.

   c. Pull the torque wrench and note and record the torque reading when rotation begins.

10. To measure the seal drag on Type 2 nuts, use a pull scale. Measure the oil seal drag by pulling on the scale until the wheel begins to turn. Record the value.

11. To determine the specified preload on Type 1 nuts, add the amount of seal drag to the required preload, which is 1.3–4.3 inch lbs. (0.15–0.49 Nm). To calculate the preload, add the seal drag value to the minimum and maximum preload specifications. For example, if the seal drag was 2.2 inch lbs. (0.25 Nm), then the minimum preload specification would be 1.3 inch lbs. (0.15 Nm) + 2.2 inch lbs. (0.25 Nm) = 3.5 inch lbs. (0.40 Nm) and the maximum preload specification would be 4.3 inch lbs. (0.49 Nm) + 2.2 inch lbs. (0.25 Nm) = 6.5 inch lbs. (0.74 Nm). Therefore, for a seal drag of 2.2 inch lbs. (0.25 Nm), the bearing preload should be within the range of 3.5–6.5 inch lbs. (0.40–0.74 Nm).

12. On Type 2 nuts, add the oil seal drag value obtained in Step 10 to the specified value of 0.6–1.9 lbs. (2.6–8.5 N). This is the standard bearing preload.

13. On Type 1 locknuts, tighten the locknut slightly. Rotate the brake drum until the nut and wheel are returned to the 12 o'clock position. Position the inch lb. torque wrench onto the nut and measure the amount of pull required to rotate the brake drum. Tighten the locknut until the torque shown on the torque wrench is within the range calculated in Step 11.

14. On Type 2 locknuts, turn the locknut slowly to adjust to the standard bearing preload, while checking with the pull scale.

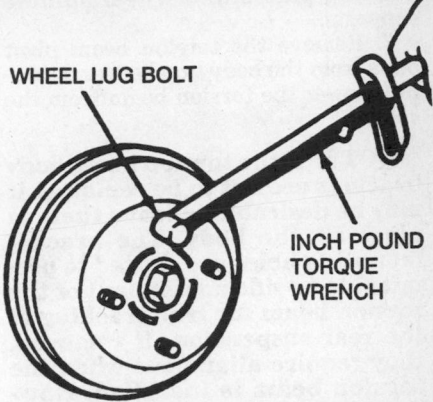

Measuring seal drag—vehicles with Type 1 locknuts

15. On Type 1 locknuts, stake the locknut in place using a cold chisel with the cutting edge rounded.

NOTE: If the nut splits or cracks after staking, it must be replaced with a new nut.

16. On Type 2 nuts, install the nut retaining cap and a new cotter pin.

17. Install the grease cap.

18. Install the wheel and tire assembly. Lower the vehicle.

Torsion Beam

REMOVAL & INSTALLATION

1. Raise and safely support the vehicle.

2. Remove the wheel and tire assemblies.

3. Remove the rear struts and disconnect the brake lines.

4. Disconnect the parking brake cable clevises at the brake backing plates.

5. Remove the parking brake equalizer and cables from the torsion beam.

6. Remove the 4 nuts from the back of each brake assembly to release the

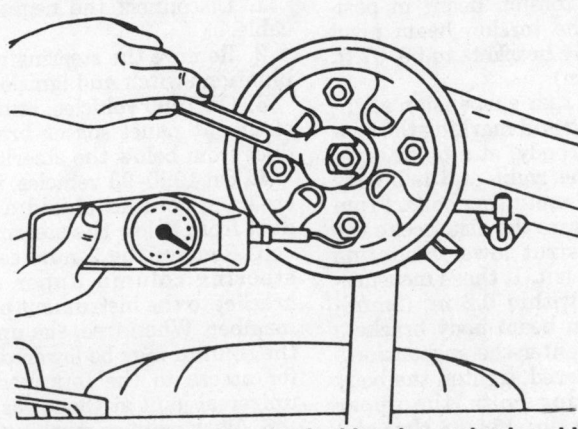

Adjusting the wheel bearings to the standard bearing preload—vehicles with Type 2 locknuts

backing plates and wheel spindle supports.

7. Remove the torsion beam pivot bolts from the body brackets and carefully lower the torsion beam from the vehicle.

NOTE: If the torsion beam body brackets are not to be replaced, it may be desirable to leave them in place on the body. The bracket mounting holes are slotted to permit side-to-side adjustment of the torsion beam for true tracking of the rear suspension. If removed, they require alignment when the torsion beam is installed. However, if the torsion beam is repaired or replaced, the alignment must be checked at assembly.

To install:

8. If removed, install the torsion beam pivot brackets on the body with flatwashers, lockwashers and 3 bolts on each side. Do not tighten the mounting bolts at this time.

9. If installing a new torsion beam, install the pivot bushings in the beam arms.

10. Install the bushing flange washers and position the beam arms in the body brackets. Align the pivot bolt holes and install the bolts but do not tighten the nuts yet.

11. Install the brake backing plates and wheel spindle support assemblies with 4 nuts each, tightening to 32–45 ft. lbs. (43–61 Nm).

12. Install the parking brake equalizer assembly on the torsion beam and connect the cable clevises to the brake levers with the clevis pins and cotter pins.

13. Connect the right and left brake lines at the routing brackets and clip in place.

14. Install the rear suspension struts.

15. Install the wheel and tire assemblies. Use a suitable jack to raise the torsion beam into normal ride height position.

16. With the torsion beam in position, tighten the torsion beam pivot bolts at the body brackets to 69–87 ft. lbs. (93–118 Nm).

17. Check the rear suspension alignment by locating and marking the center of the underbody, at a point equidistant from the right and left body bracket inboard mounting bolts. From this point, measure the distance to the centers of the strut lower mounting bolts, right and left. If these measurements are not within 0.2 in. (5mm), shift the torsion beam body brackets side-to-side to center the suspension.

18. When centered, tighten the body bracket mounting bolts, the upper bolts to 40–50 ft. lbs. (54–68 Nm) and the lower bolt to 69–87 ft. lbs. (93–118 Nm).

19. Bleed the rear brakes and lower the vehicle.

STEERING

Steering Wheel

REMOVAL & INSTALLATION

1. Disconnect the negative battery cable.

2. On 1989 vehicles, pry off the trim insert in the center of the steering wheel cover. Take care not to damage the cover.

3. On 1990–93 vehicles, remove the 2 screws from the back of the steering wheel. Disconnect the horn wire and remove the steering wheel cover.

4. Remove the steering wheel nut.

5. On 1989 vehicles, remove the attaching screws and washers located to the left and right of the steering column stud. Remove the 2 screws from the back of the steering wheel spokes. Disconnect the horn wire and remove the cover assembly.

6. Matchmark the steering wheel and steering column shaft for assembly reference. Using a steering wheel puller tool, remove the steering wheel.

7. Installation is the reverse of the removal procedure. Position the steering wheel onto the steering column shaft and align the matchmarks. Tighten the nut to 29–36 ft. lbs. (39–49 Nm).

NOTE: When installing the steering wheel, make certain the cutouts in the rear cover engage the turn signal cancelling cam.

Steering Column

REMOVAL & INSTALLATION

1. Disconnect the negative battery cable.

2. Remove the steering wheel, combination switch and ignition switch.

3. On 1989 vehicles, remove the instrument panel spacer brace and air duct from below the steering column.

4. On 1990–93 vehicles, remove the steering column shield and the air duct from below the steering column.

5. Remove the 2 nuts securing the steering column upper mounting bracket to the instrument panel crossmember. When free, the upper end of the column may be lowered as needed for access to the intermediate shaft universal joint at the lower end.

6. With paint or marking pen, make an index mark at the juncture of the steering column shaft and the inter-

mediate shaft upper universal joint to assure correct alignment during assembly. Remove the universal joint clamp screw.

7. Loosen the 2 nuts securing the steering column hinge bracket to the clutch/brake pedal support. Remove the steering column assembly by pulling to the rear, disengaging it from the universal joint. Remove the shim clips from the upper mounting bracket.

To install:

8. Install the joint clamp bolt but do not tighten it at this time as it may need to be shifted up or down on the shaft to line up with the steering column without binding.

9. Install the steering column, aligning the index marks on the column shaft and universal joint and engaging the column hinge bracket with the pedal support studs. Do not tighten the universal joint clamp bolt yet.

10. Tighten the hinge bracket nuts and raise the upper end of the column to seat under the instrument panel. Position the shim clips on the column upper bracket flanges.

11. Install the 2 steering column upper retaining nuts.

12. Turn the steering wheel lock-to-lock several times to align the universal joints, then tighten both universal joint clamp bolts.

13. Install the instrument panel brace or steering column shield, as necessary. Install the air duct.

14. Install the ignition switch, combination switch and the steering wheel.

Manual Steering Rack and Pinion

ADJUSTMENT

Only the rack preload is adjustable and only to a limited degree, since it is primarily determined by the yoke spring. Since adjustment requires removal of the steering gear, it should only be undertaken after a thorough inspection of front suspension and steering column components fails to reveal damage or binding elsewhere. If necessary, adjust the rack yoke preload as follows:

1989

1. Remove the steering rack from the vehicle.

2. Center the steering rack in a protected jaw vise, make sure there is equal left and right tie rod extension.

3. Measure the pinion operating torque with an inch lb. torque wrench and pinion torque adapter tool T87C–3504–C or equivalent. Within 90 degrees of the centered rack position, pinion torque should be 8–11.5 inch

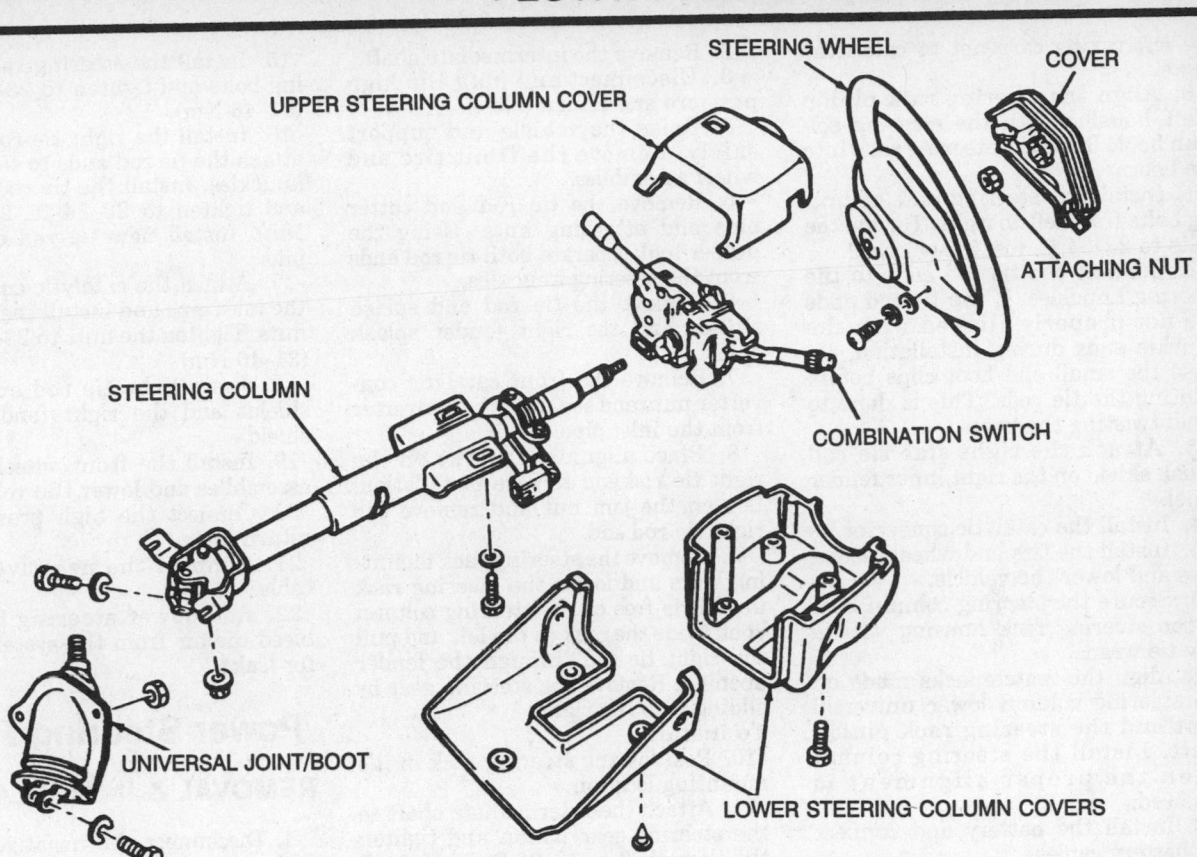

UPPER STEERING COLUMN COVER

STEERING WHEEL

COVER

ATTACHING NUT

STEERING COLUMN

COMBINATION SWITCH

UNIVERSAL JOINT/BOOT

LOWER STEERING COLUMN COVERS

Steering column assembly and related components—1990–93 vehicles, 1989 vehicles similar

lbs. (0.9–1.3 Nm). Beyond 90 degrees, left or right, pinion torque should not exceed 13.3 inch lbs. (1.5 Nm).

4. If the pinion torque is not within the specified limits, tighten or loosen the rack adjusting screw to increase or decrease the rack preload.

NOTE: Do not loosen the adjusting screw so that it no longer makes contact with the yoke spacer. Any clearance at this point will allow the rack to deflect under load, resulting in reduced tooth engagement with the pinion.

5. When the pinion operating torque is within specification, tighten the jam nut on the adjusting screw. With a suitable adapter, torque the jam nut to 7.4–11 ft. lbs. (10–15 Nm) to retain the adjustment.

6. Install the steering rack in the vehicle.

1990–93

1. Remove the steering rack from the vehicle.

2. Center the steering rack in a protected jaw vise, make sure there is equal left and right tie rod extension.

3. Remove the locknut and the yoke plug and clean the yoke plug threads.

Apply sealant to the yoke plug threads and install the yoke plug. Tighten to 78–95 inch lbs. (9–11 Nm).

4. Slowly cycle the rack back and forth through 90 percent of it's full stroke. Then center the rack so the tie rods are equally extended.

5. Loosen the yoke plug, then tighten it to 22–30 inch lbs. (2.5–3.4 Nm).

6. Use a spring scale to measure the force needed to turn the pinion 180 degrees from the rack center position.

7. Adjust the pinion to the position where the most force was needed to turn it.

8. Tighten the yoke plug to 48 inch lbs. (5.4 Nm), then back it off 5–10 degrees. Install the locknut and tighten to 29–36 ft. lbs. (39–49 Nm).

REMOVAL & INSTALLATION

1. Disconnect the negative and positive battery cables and remove the battery from the vehicle.

2. Matchmark the steering column lower universal joint and steering rack pinion for assembly reference. Remove the steering column and intermediate shaft assembly from the vehicle.

3. Cut the plastic tie wrap securing the steering column boot to the steering rack.

4. Raise the vehicle and support safely. Remove the front tire and wheel assemblies.

5. Using the proper tool, separate both tie rod ends from the steering knuckles.

6. Remove the catalytic converter.

7. Remove the plastic tie rod splash shield from the right inner fender.

8. Remove the steering rack mounting bolts and lower the steering rack until it is free of the steering column boot. Slide the rack to the right, through the inner fender tie rod opening, until the left tie rod is clear of the left inner fender, then lower the left end until the steering rack assembly can be withdrawn from the left side of the vehicle.

NOTE: While maneuvering the tie rod boots in and out of the inner fender openings, guide the steering rack assembly carefully to avoid cutting or nicking the boots.

To install:

9. From under the vehicle, insert the right side tie rod through the right inner fender tie rod opening, far enough to allow raising the left end of the assembly to enter the left inner fender opening. Shift the assembly to

the left taking care not to catch the boots.

10. Align the steering rack pinion shaft housing with the steering column boot. Raise the steering rack into the boot.

11. Install the steering rack mounting bolts from left to right. Torque the bolts to 23–34 ft. lbs. (31–46 Nm).

12. Connect the tie rod ends to the steering knuckles. If the tie rod ends are not properly aligned with the knuckle ends during installation, release the small end boot clips before rotating the tie rods. This is done to avoid twisting the boots.

13. Attach the right side tie rod splash shield on the right inner fender panel.

14. Install the catalytic converter.

15. Install the tire and wheel assemblies and lower the vehicle.

16. Secure the steering column boot to the steering rack housing with a new tie wrap.

17. Align the matchmarks made on the steering column lower universal joint and the steering rack pinion shaft. Install the steering column when the proper alignment is acheived.

18. Install the battery and connect the battery cables.

Power Steering Rack and Pinion

REMOVAL & INSTALLATION

1. Disconnect the negative battery cable.

2. Remove the intermediate shaft.

3. Disconnect and plug the high pressure and return lines.

4. Raise the vehicle and support safely. Remove the front tire and wheel assemblies.

5. Remove the tie rod end cotter pins and attaching nuts. Using the proper tool, separate both tie rod ends from the steering knuckles.

6. Remove the tie rod end splash shields and the right fender splash shield.

7. Remove the front catalytic converter nuts and separate the converter from the inlet pipe.

8. Place alignment marks on the right tie rod end to ease installation. Loosen the jam nut and remove the right tie rod end.

9. Remove the steering rack mounting bolts and lower the steering rack until it is free of the steering column boot. Slide the rack to the left and pull the right tie rod through the fender opening. Remove the steering gear by sliding it to the right.

To install:

10. Position the steering rack in it's mounting location.

11. Attach the intermediate shaft to the steering gear pinion and tighten the clamp bolt to 13–20 ft. lbs. (18–26 Nm). Guide the intermediate shaft into the steering column hole.

12. Lower the vehicle.

13. With an assistant lifting the steering gear, align the intermediate shaft with the universal joint and install the clamp bolt.

14. Raise and safely support the vehicle.

15. Install the steering rack mounting bolts and tighten to 23–34 ft. lbs. (31–46 Nm).

16. Install the right tie rod end and attach the tie rod ends to the steering knuckles. Install the tie rod end nuts and tighten to 23–34 ft. lbs. (39–44 Nm). Install new tie rod end cotter pins.

17. Attach the catalytic converter to the inlet pipe and install the attaching nuts. Tighten the nuts to 23–34 ft. lbs. (31–46 Nm).

18. Install the tie rod end splash shields and the right fender splash shield.

19. Install the front wheel and tire assemblies and lower the vehicle.

20. Connect the high pressure and return lines.

21. Connect the negative battery cable.

22. Add power steering fluid and bleed the air from the system. Check for leaks.

Power Steering Pump

REMOVAL & INSTALLATION

1. Disconnect the negative battery cable.

2. Remove the air duct and air cleaner unit.

3. Disconnect the electrical connector from the fluid pressure switch.

4. Disconnect and plug the fluid lines.

5. Remove the adjustment bolt and the locknut, washer and bracket bolt.

6. Loosen the mounting bolt and

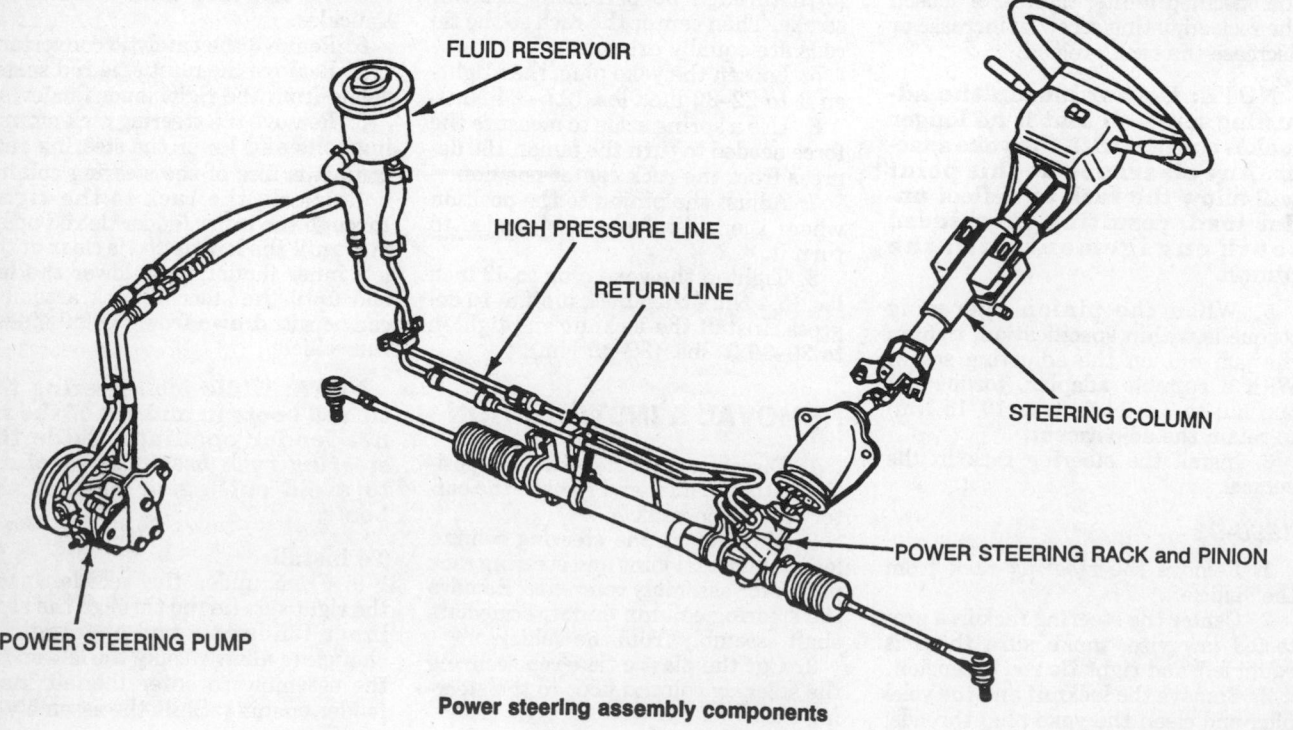

FLUID RESERVOIR

HIGH PRESSURE LINE

RETURN LINE

STEERING COLUMN

POWER STEERING RACK and PINION

POWER STEERING PUMP

Power steering assembly components

disconnect the drive belt. Remove the mounting bolt and remove the power steering pump.

7. Installation is the reverse of the removal procedure. Tighten the high pressure line nuts to 29–36 ft. lbs. (39–49 Nm). Adjust the drive belt tension.

BELT TENSION ADJUSTMENT

1. Remove the air duct and air cleaner.
2. Loosen the pump mounting bolt. Loosen the adjusting locknut.
3. Using a belt tension gauge or the deflection method, adjust the tension at the adjusing bolt.
4. If using a belt tension gauge, position the gauge in the middle of the longest accessible belt span and set new belt tension to 110–132 lbs. or used belt (more than 10 minutes of run time) tension to 95–110 lbs.
5. If using the deflection method, apply approximately 22 lbs. of pressure to the middle of the longest accessible belt span. Adjust the tension to 0.31–0.35 in. (8–9mm) for a new belt or 0.35–0.39 in. (9–10mm) for a used belt (more than 10 minutes of run time).
6. Tighten the pump mounting bolt to 27–40 ft. lbs. (36–54 Nm) and the adjustment locknut to 27–38 ft. lbs. (37–52 Nm).
7. Install the air cleaner and air duct.

SYSTEM BLEEDING

1. Add power steering fluid to the **L** mark on the reservoir cap dipstick.
2. Run the engine until it reaches normal operating temperature.
3. Turn the steering wheel lock to lock approximately 10 times.
4. Shut the engine OFF with the wheels in the straight-ahead position.
5. Check the fluid level, the level should be between the **L** and **H** marks on the reservoir cap dipstick. Repeat the procedure if needed.

Tie Rod Ends

REMOVAL & INSTALLATION

1. Raise the vehicle and support it safely.
2. Remove the wheel and tire assembly.
3. Remove the cotter pin and nut from the tie rod end stud. Discard the cotter pin. Examine the nut for damage and replace as required.
4. Separate the tie rod end from the steering knuckle using tie rod end remover tool T85M–3395–A or equivalent.

5. With paint or a suitable marker, mark the tie rod end, jam nut and tie rod to ease assembly without changing the toe-in setting.
6. Loosen the jam nut and unscrew the tie rod end counting the number of turns required for removal. Replace the tie rod end as required.

NOTE: If new tie rod ends are being installed, place the old and new ends side-by-side and place alignment marks in the new end that match as closely as possible to the marks on the old end. Please be advised that the existing jam nut may not seat in exactly the same position on the new end and the toe-in setting may have to be checked and/or readjusted as a precaution.

To install:

7. When replacing a tie rod end, install a new dust boot over the stud with a suitable adapter. A ¾ in. socket will accomplish the task simply and effectively.
8. Thread the jam nut and tie rod end onto the tie rod and align the index marks made during the removal procedure.
9. Install the tie rod end into the steering knuckle. If the tie rod is correctly aligned, the taper should seat without twisting the tie rod or boot. Torque the stud nut to 26–30 ft. lbs. (35–40 Nm) and install a new cotter pin. If the cotter pin does not align with stud bore, tighten (do not loosen) the nut until the castellations align with the pin bore.
10. Install the wheel and tire assembly. Lower the vehicle and connect the negative battery cable. Check the toe-in setting, if necessary.

BRAKES

Master Cylinder

REMOVAL & INSTALLATION

1. Disconnect the negative battery cable. Disconnect the low fluid level sensor connector.
2. Disconnect the brake lines from the master cylinder connections. Plug or cover the line openings and master cylinder ports.
3. Remove the attaching nuts and washers and separate the master cylinder from the power booster mounting studs. Clean the master cylinder and power booster contact surfaces with a clean shop towel.

To install:

4. If a new master cylinder is being installed, check the pushrod length adjustment as follows:
   a. Position master cylinder gauge T87C–2500–A or equivalent, on the end of the master cylinder, loosen the set screw and push the gauge plunger against the bottom of the primary piston.
   b. While holding the gauge in position, tighten the set screw.
   c. Invert the master cylinder gauge and place it over the brake booster pushrod.
   d. If the clearance is not zero, loosen the pushrod locknut and adjust the pushrod.

NOTE: Proper pushrod length adjustment is critical. If the pushrod is adjusted too long, the brakes will drag. If the pushrod is adjusted too short, the brake pedal will be low.

5. Before installation, bench bleed a new master cylinder as follows:
   a. Mount the new master cylinder in a suitable holding fixture. Be careful not to damage the housing.
   b. Fill the master cylinder reservoir with brake fluid.
   c. Using a suitable tool inserted into the booster pushrod cavity, push the master cylinder piston in slowly. Place a suitable container under the master cylinder to catch the fluid being expelled from the outlet ports.
   d. Place a finger tightly over each outlet port and allow the master cylinder piston to return.
   e. Repeat the procedure until clear fluid only is expelled from the master cylinder. Plug the outlet ports and remove the master cylinder from the holding fixture.
6. Position the master cylinder onto the power booster mounting studs.
7. Install the attaching washers and nuts. Torque the nuts to 7–12 ft. lbs. (10–16 Nm).
8. Connect the brake lines to master cylinder connections.
9. Make sure the master cylinder reservoir is full. Have an assistant slowly push down on the brake pedal. When the pedal is all the way down, crack open the brake line fittings, 1 at a time, to expel any remaining air in the master cylinder and brake lines. Tighten the fittings, then have the assistant allow the brake pedal to return.
10. Repeat Step 9 until all air is expelled from the master cylinder and brake lines. Tighten the brake line fittings.
11. Connect the low fluid level sensor.
12. Make sure the master cylinder

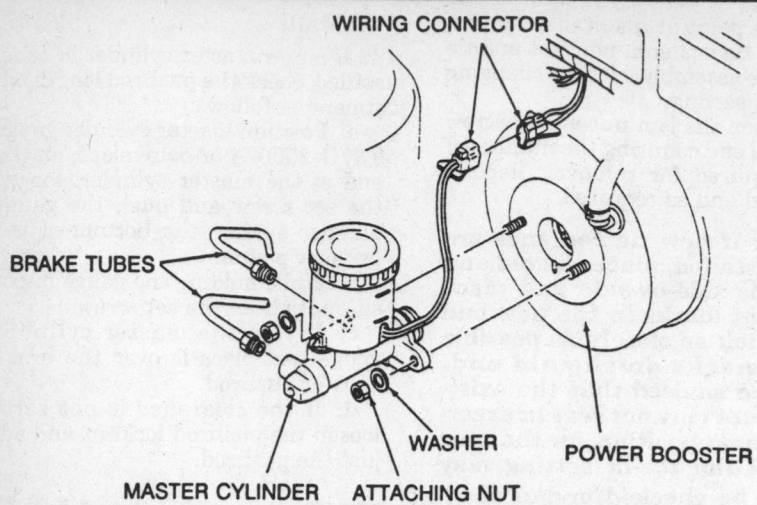

WIRING CONNECTOR

BRAKE TUBES

WASHER

MASTER CYLINDER · ATTACHING NUT · POWER BOOSTER

Master cylinder assembly

reservoir is full. If necessary, bleed the entire brake system.

13. Connect the negative battery cable.

Proportioning Valve

The proportioning valve is located in the engine compartment. It is mounted to the dash panel below and to the right of the brake booster. The valve is not repairable and must be replaced if determined to be faulty.

REMOVAL & INSTALLATION

1. Disconnect the negative battery cable. Loosen the connector nuts and disconnect the brake lines from the proportioning valve. Plug or cover the line openings to prevent the entry of dirt and grease.
2. Loosen the valve attaching bolts and remove the valve from the dash panel.
3. Installation is the reverse of the removal procedure.
4. Bleed the brake system.
5. Inspect for proper brake operation and inspect for leaks around the valve connections.

Power Brake Booster

REMOVAL & INSTALLATION

1. Disconnect the negative battery cable. Remove the master cylinder.

NOTE: It may be possible to remove the master cylinder from the booster assembly without disconnecting the brake lines from the cylinder. If possible, position the master cylinder to the side.

2. Disconnect the vacuum hose from the brake booster unit.

3. From inside the vehicle, remove and discard the cotter pin securing the clevis pin. Remove the clevis pin from the clevis.
4. Have an assistant support the power booster unit in the engine compartment.
5. From inside the vehicle, remove the 4 nuts securing the unit to the bulkhead. Remove the unit from the engine compartment.
6. Remove the gasket between the power booster unit and the bulkhead. Replace the gasket, as required.
To install:
7. Position the gasket onto the power brake booster studs and have an assistant position the unit against the bulkhead.
8. From inside the vehicle, secure the power booster to the bulkhead with the 4 retaining nuts. Torque the retaining nuts to 12–17 ft. lbs. (16–23 Nm).
9. Lubricate the clevis with a coating of white lithium grease or equivalent. From inside the vehicle, attach the clevis to the brake pedal with the clevis pin. Secure the clevis pin with a new cotter pin.
10. Connect the vacuum to the power brake booster.
11. Install the master cylinder.
12. Bleed the brake system.

Brake Caliper

REMOVAL & INSTALLATION

1. Raise and safely support the vehicle.
2. Remove the wheel and tire assembly.
3. Remove the brake pads. Remove the brake hose attaching bolt and plug the hose end. Discard the seal washers.

4. Remove the caliper attaching bolts and the anti-squeak caps.
5. Remove the caliper from the vehicle.
6. Installation is the reverse of the removal procedure.
7. Tighten the caliper mounting bolts to 29–36 ft. lbs. (39–49 Nm). Use new seal washers on the brake hose and tighten the brake hose attaching bolt to 16–22 ft. lbs. (22–29 Nm). Bleed the brake system.

Disc Brake Pads

REMOVAL & INSTALLATION

1. Remove approximately ⅓ of the brake fluid from the master cylinder. Raise and support the vehicle safely.
2. Remove the tire and wheel assembly.
3. Place a C-clamp on the caliper and tighten the clamp to move the caliper piston in the cylinder bore approximately ⅛ in. (3mm). Remove the clamp.

NOTE: Do not pry the piston away from the rotor.

4. Remove the brake pad pin retainer. Disengage the anti-rattle spring from the brake pads.
5. Remove the brake pad pins and the anti-rattle spring.
6. Remove the brake pads and shims. Do not discard the shims found behind the brake pads.
To install:
7. Push the piston back into the caliper bore.
8. Apply the grease supplied with the brake pad set to both surfaces of the inner shim and to the back of the brake pad.
9. Install the brake pads, making sure the shims are installed.
10. Install the brake pad pins, anti-rattle spring and brake pad pin retainer.
11. Install the wheel and tire assembly and lower the vehicle.
12. Apply the brake several times to seat the pads. Check the brake fluid level in the master cylinder. Add fluid as necessary.

Brake Rotor

REMOVAL & INSTALLATION

1. Disconnect the negative battery cable.
2. Raise the vehicle and support it safely.
3. Unbolt and remove front wheel from the hub assembly.
4. With a suitable tool, straighten the staked edge of the halfshaft at-

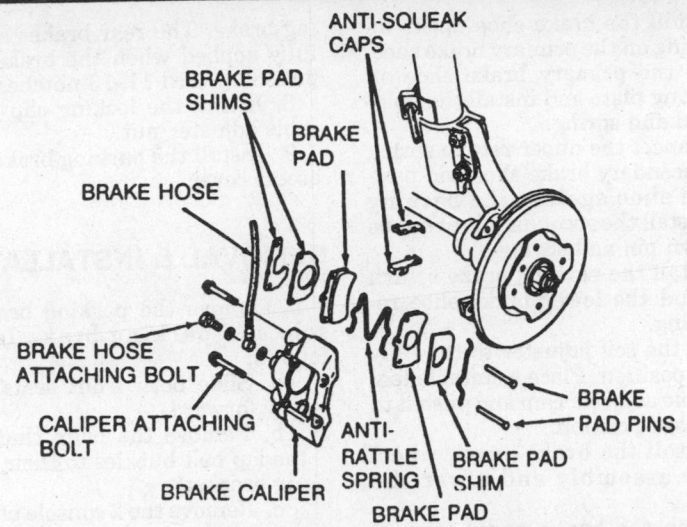

Front disc brake assembly

taching nut. Take care not to damage the halfshaft threads.

5. Remove and discard the halfshaft attaching nut.

6. Remove the retaining clip securing the caliper hose to the strut bracket.

7. Remove the cotter pin and tie rod end attaching nut. Discard the cotter pin and set the nut aside. Inspect the nut for damage and replace as required.

8. Using a tie rod end separator tool, release the tie rod end from the steering knuckle arm. If the tie rod appears to be siezed, strike the knuckle sharply with a soft-tipped hammer to acheive separation.

9. Remove the brake caliper attaching bolts. Lift the caliper assembly from the steering knuckle.

NOTE: After the caliper assembly is lifted from the steering knuckle, do not allow it to be suspended by the brake hose. Support the caliper by a length of rope or wire attached to the Mac-Pherson strut.

10. Remove the clamp bolt and nut at the point where the lower control arm ball joint connects to the steering knuckle. With a medium prybar, release the lower ball joint from the steering knuckle by prying downward on the lower control arm.

11. Remove the 2 bolts that position the steering knuckle between the Mac-Pherson strut bracket flanges.

12. Slide the knuckle/hub assembly from the end of the halfshaft. If binding occurs, tap the end of the shaft with a soft-tipped hammer. If the wheel hub is rusted to the halfshaft, use either a 2 jaw puller or a hub puller to achieve separation.

13. Remove the wheel hub/rotor assembly from the steering knuckle/dust shield assembly using puller tool T87C–1104–A or equivalent.

14. Remove the bearing preload spacer from the hub.

NOTE: The spacer is preselected to yield the correct bearing preload. Save the removed spacer for use during assembly.

15. Clamp the hub/rotor assembly in a vise with protective jaw caps. If the rotor is to be reused, scribe aligning marks on the hub and rotor for use during assembly. Remove the attaching bolts and the rotor.

To install:

16. Place the bearing preload spacer in the steering knuckle bore.

17. Position the rotor on the hub, observing the original aligning marks if the rotor is being resused and install the attaching bolts. Tighten the attaching bolts to 33–40 ft. lbs. (44–54 Nm).

18. Position the hub/rotor assembly in the steering knuckle bore and press it into position using a suitable driver.

19. Clean the halfshaft spline end and lubricate with a coating of wheel bearing grease. Apply a thin film of clean SAE 30 weight oil to the steering knuckle/rotor hub assembly up to the point where the uppermost arm of the steering knuckle seats into the Mac-Pherson strut bracket. Guide the steering knuckle/rotor/hub assembly onto the halfshaft and the Macpher-son strut.

20. Install the strut-to-steering knuckle bolts and attaching nuts. Tighten the nuts to 69–86 ft. lbs. (93–117 Nm).

21. Position the lower control arm ball joint in the steering knuckle. Install the lower control arm pinch bolt and attaching nut. Tighten the nut to 32–40 ft. lbs. (43–54 Nm).

22. Position the caliper on the steering knuckle and install the attaching bolts. Tighten the bolts to 29–36 ft. lbs. (39–49 Nm). Position the caliper hose in the strut routing bracket and install the retaining clip.

23. Install a new halfshaft attaching nut and tighten to 116–174 ft. lbs. (157–235 Nm). After installation, the wheel hub assembly must rotate freely by hand. Stake the halfshaft attaching nut into the shaft groove.

NOTE: Do not use a pointed tool to stake the nut. If the nut cracks even slightly during staking, replace it with another new one.

24. Connect the tie rod end to the steering knuckle and install the attaching nut. Tighten the attaching nut to 22–33 ft. lbs. (29–44 Nm). Install a new cotter pin through the nut and ball stud. If the openings in the nut and the hole in the ball stud are not aligned, tighten the nut slightly, just to the point of alignment. Never loosen the nut.

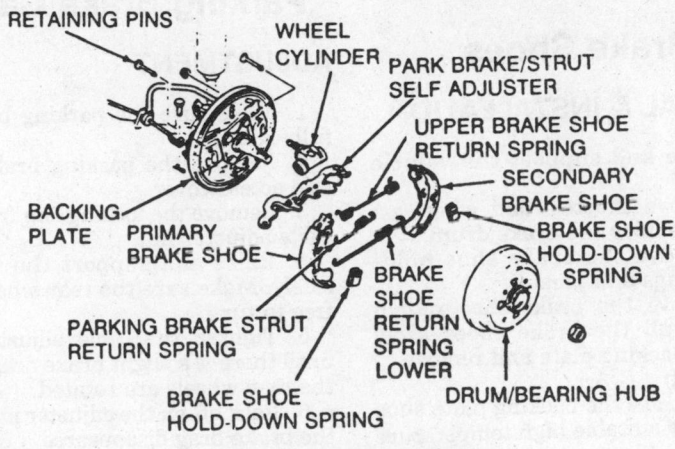

Rear drum brake assembly

25. Install the wheel and tire assembly. Tighten the attaching bolts to 65–87 ft. lbs. (88–118 Nm). Lower the vehicle.

Brake Drums

REMOVAL & INSTALLATION

1. Raise and safely support the vehicle.
2. Remove the tire and wheel assembly.
3. On Type 1 nuts, carefully raise the staked portion of the attaching nut using a small cape chisel. On Type 2 nuts, remove the cotter pin and nut retaining cap.
4. Remove the locknut. Discard Type 1 locknuts or the Type 2 cotter pin.

NOTE: Some locknuts are right and left hand thread. The left hand threaded locknut is located on the right side of the vehicle. Turn this locknut clockwise to loosen. The right hand threaded locknut is located on the left side of the vehicle and is turned counterclockwise to loosen.

5. Remove the brake drum and bearings as an assembly. Be careful not to let the outer bearing fall out of the hub during removal.

To install:
6. Make sure the bearings and the hub contain adequate lubricant.
7. Position the brake drum, bearings and hub assembly on the spindle. Keep the drum centered on the spindle to prevent damage to the grease seal and spindle threads.
8. Install the outer bearing, washer and locknut.
9. Properly adjust the wheel bearing preload.

Brake Shoes

REMOVAL & INSTALLATION

1. Raise and support the vehicle safely.
2. Remove the tire and wheel assembly. Remove the brake drum.
3. Remove the brake shoe hold-down springs and pins.
4. Remove the brake shoe return springs. Pull the brake shoes away from the backing plate and remove.
To install:
5. Lubricate the backing plate shoe pads with a suitable high temperature grease.

6. Install the brake shoe upper return spring on the primary brake shoe. Position the primary brake shoe on the backing plate and install the hold-down pin and spring.
7. Connect the upper return spring to the secondary brake shoe and position the shoe against the backing plate. Install the secondary brake shoe hold-down pin and spring.
8. Install the parking brake return spring and the lower brake shoe return spring.
9. Set the self adjuster to the fully released position. Place a suitable tool against the adjuster cam and push it to the released position.
10. Install the brake drum, wheel and tire assembly and lower the vehicle.
11. Push the brake pedal several times to set the self adjuster.

Wheel Cylinder

REMOVAL & INSTALLATION

1. Raise and support the vehicle safely.
2. Remove the rear brake shoes.
3. Disconnect the brake line from the wheel cylinder. Plug or cover the brake line opening to prevent the entry of dirt or grease.
4. Remove the 2 wheel cylinder attaching bolts and remove the wheel cylinder from the backing plate.
To install:
5. Position the wheel cylinder onto the backing plate and install the retaining bolts. Torque the retaining bolts to 7–9 ft. lbs. (10–13 Nm).
6. Connect the brake line to the wheel cylinder.
7. Install the rear brake shoes.
8. Bleed the brake system.

Parking Brake Cable

ADJUSTMENT

1. Make sure the parking brake is fully released.
2. Remove the parking brake console access cover.
3. Remove the locking clip from the cable adjuster nut.
4. Raise and support the vehicle safely. Make sure the rear wheels are free to turn.
5. Tighten the cable adjuster nut until there is a slight brake drag when the rear wheels are rotated.
6. Back off on the adjuster nut until the brake drag disappears.
7. Check the operation of the park-

ing brake. The rear brakes should be fully applied when the brake lever is pulled upward 11–16 notches.
8. Install the locking clip onto the cable adjuster nut.
9. Install the parking brake console access cover.

REMOVAL & INSTALLATION

1. Remove the parking brake console and parking brake lever as follows:
   a. Slide both front seats all the way forward.
   b. Remove the bolts that attach the lap belt buckles to their mounting brackets.
   c. Remove the 2 console attaching screws.
   d. Remove the retainer located at the front of the console.
   e. Remove the access cover and remove the parking brake console.
   f. Remove the locking clip from the cable adjuster nut and remove the cable adjuster nut.
   g. Disconnect the wiring connector from the parking brake light switch.
   h. Remove the attaching bolts and the parking brake lever.
2. Remove the attaching screws and parking brake console mounting bracket.
3. Remove the bolts attaching the lower half of the rear seat hinge to floor pan.
4. Fold the rear seat forward and remove the bolts attaching the upper half of the rear seat hinge to the floor pan.
5. Remove the rear seat.
6. Remove the rear carpet push retainers and carefully pull the carpeting forward to expose the parking brake cable guide.
7. Disconnect the parking brake cable guide by removing the attaching screws.
8. Raise and support the vehicle safely.
9. Remove the rear wheel and tire assemblies.
10. Remove the cotter pin and clevis pin attaching the parking brake cable ends to the rear brake levers.
11. Remove the routing bracket retaining clips.
12. Disengage the parking brake routing sleeves from the torsion beam routing brackets.
13. Remove the nut and bolt attaching the parking brake routing bracket to the fuel tank.
14. Remove the parking brake cable equalizer attaching bolts.
15. Withdraw the lever end of the cable through the body opening and remove from the vehicle.

To install:

16. Position the lever end of the cable through the body opening.

17. Position the cable routing bracket on the fuel tank and install the attaching bolt and nut.

18. Make sure the cable seal is properly positioned in the floor pan.

19. Position the cable equalizer and install the attaching bolts. Make sure the equalizer spacers are in position before tightening the attaching bolts.

20. Route the cable ends through the body brackets and install the retaining clips.

21. Seat the cable sleeves in the torsion beam routing brackets.

22. Attach the cable ends to the brake levers using the clevis pins and new cotter pins.

23. Install the rear wheel and tire assemblies and lower the vehicle.

24. Route the end of the cable through the park brake lever.

25. Position the cable guide and secure with the attaching screws.

26. Position the carpet and install the push retainers. Install the rear seat and torque the retaining bolts to 28–38 ft. lbs. (38–51 Nm).

27. Position the console mounting bracket and install the attaching screws.

28. Install the parking brake lever and console as follows:

  a. Position the parking brake lever and install the attaching bolts. Tighten the bolts to 12–17 ft. lbs. (16–23 Nm).

  b. Connect the wiring connector to the parking brake light switch.

  c. Install the adjuster nut and adjust the parking brake cable.

  d. Install the locking clip.

  e. Position the console over the parking brake lever.

  f. Install the access cover and the console retainer.

  g. Install the console attaching screws.

  h. Position the lap belt buckles and install the buckle-to-bracket bolts.

  i. Slide the seats to their original position.

Brake System Bleeding

When any part of the hydraulic system has been disconnected for service, air may enter the system and cause spongy pedal action. The bleeding procedure is used to remove air from the hydraulic circuits.

The brake hydraulic circuits form a split diagonal hydraulic system. The left front and right rear form 1 circuit while the right front and left rear form the other circuit. When bleeding 1 of these circuits, bleed the rear wheel first and then the front wheel at the opposite corner.

Never reuse brake fluid that has been drained from the hydraulic system or that has been allowed to stand in an open container for an extended period of time.

Bleed the brake system as follows:

1. Clean all dirt from the master cylinder filler cap. Fill the master cylinder with DOT 3 brake fluid.

NOTE: Do not allow the master cylinder to run dry during the bleeding procedure.

2. If the master cylinder is known or suspected to contain air, it must be bled before the wheel cylinders or caliper. Bleed the master cylinder as follows:

  a. Loosen the front line fitting and have an assistant push the brake pedal slowly through it's full travel.

  b. While the assistant holds the pedal down, tighten the brake line fitting. After the line fitting is tightened, the assistant may release the brake pedal.

  c. Repeat the procedure on the rear brake line.

  d. Repeat the entire process several times to make sure all air has been removed from the master cylinder.

3. Remove the bleeder screw cap from the appropriate rear wheel cylinder. Position a box end wrench on the bleeder fitting.

4. Attach a rubber hose to the bleeder fitting. The hose must fit snugly around the bleeder fitting.

5. Submerge the other end of the hose in a container partially filled with brake fluid.

6. Loosen the bleeder fitting approximately ¾ turn. Have an assistant push the brake pedal slowly through it's full travel and hold it there.

7. Close the bleeder fitting, then have the assistant release the brake pedal.

8. Repeat Steps 6 and 7 until air bubbles no longer appear at the submerged end of the bleeder hose.

9. When the fluid entering the bottle is completely free of bubbles, tighten the bleeder screw, remove the hose and install the bleeder screw cap.

10. Repeat Steps 3–9 at the front caliper located diagonally to the wheel cylinder just completed.

11. If necessary, bleed the other diagonal circuit in the same manner.

12. Check the master cylinder fluid level and add, if necessary.

13. Check the pedal feel. If the pedal is still spongy, repeat the bleeding procedure.

Heater Blower Motor

REMOVAL & INSTALLATION

1. Disconnect the negative battery cable.

2. Remove the airflow duct located below the steering column.

3. Disconnect the blower motor wiring.

4. Remove the attaching screws and the blower motor.

5. Remove the blower wheel attaching nut and remove the blower wheel and washer.

6. Installation is the reverse of the removal procedure.

Windshield Wiper Motor

REMOVAL & INSTALLATION

Front

1. Disconnect the negative battery cable. Disconnect the wiring at the wiper motor.

2. Remove the wiper motor attaching bolts.

3. Remove the access plate attaching screws and pull the plate away from the dash panel.

4. Using a suitable tool, pry the linkage pivot off the output arm. Remove the wiper motor from the vehicle.

To install:

5. Position the motor on the access plate and connect the output arm to the linkage pivot.

6. Position the mounting plate and install the attaching screws.

7. Install the wiper motor attaching bolts and tighten to 61–87 inch lbs. (7–10 Nm). Make sure the ground wire is installed with the top left attaching bolt.

8. Connect the wiper motor wiring connector and the negative battery cable. Check the wiper motor for proper operation and linkage movement.

Rear

1. Disconnect the negative battery cable.

2. Lift the attaching nut cover and remove the wiper arm attaching nut.

3. Carefully pry on the arm to disengage it from the tapered splines on the motor shaft; remove the wiper arm.

4. Remove the boot from the outer bushing attaching nut and remove the nut and bushing.

5. Remove the liftgate trim panel.

6. Peel back the wiring harness routing tape and separate the wiper motor electrical connector.

7. Remove the mounting bolts and the wiper motor. If necessary, remove the inner bushing and O-ring from the motor shaft.

To install:

8. If removed, install the O-ring and inner bushing on the motor shaft. Make sure the locating tab on the inner bushing engages the alignment tab on the brush lead cover tab.

9. Position the wiper motor and install the mounting bolts. Tighten to 6–8 ft. lbs. (8–11 Nm).

10. Connect the wiper motor electrical connector. Position the wiring harness and secure with the routing tape.

11. Install the liftgate trim panel.

12. Install the outer bushing and the attaching nut. Tighten to 2–4 ft. lbs. (3–5 Nm).

13. Install the boot onto the outer bushing attaching nut.

14. Connect the negative battery cable and turn the ignition switch ON.

15. Turn the rear wiper motor ON, allow it to cycle several times, then turn it OFF. This will locate the wiper arm shaft in the park position.

16. Turn the ignition switch OFF.

17. Install the wiper arm on the motor shaft so the tip of the wiper blade is 3.14 in. (80mm) from the edge of the liftgate window seal.

18. Install the wiper arm attaching nut and tighten to 4–7 ft. lbs. (5.0–9.5 Nm). Push the nut cover downward into position.

Windshield Wiper Switch

REMOVAL & INSTALLATION

Front

Control of the front wipers is a function of the combination switch.

Rear

1. Disconnect the negative battery cable.

2. Remove the steering column covers.

3. Remove the screws securing the instrument cluster bezel to the instrument panel and pull the bezel away from the instrument panel. Disconnect the electrical connector from the wiper switch.

4. Compress the switch lock tabs and remove it from the bezel.

5. Installation is the reverse of the removal procedure.

Instrument Cluster

REMOVAL & INSTALLATION

1. Disconnect the battery negative cable.

2. Remove the steering column covers.

3. Remove the screws securing the instrument cluster bezel to the instrument panel.

4. Pull the instrument cluster bezel away from the instrument panel.

5. If equipped with rear window defroster, disconnect the wiring from the switch.

6. If equipped with rear window wiper, disconnect the wiring from the switch.

7. Remove the screws securing the instrument cluster in the instrument panel.

8. Pull the cluster away from the instrument panel.

9. Reach behind the cluster, press the lock tab and disconnect the speedometer cable.

10. Lift the lock tab and disconnect the 2 electrical connectors from the back of the instrument cluster.

11. Remove the instrument cluster from the vehicle.

To install:

12. Position the instrument cluster in the instrument panel opening.

13. Connect the electrical connectors to the back of the instrument cluster.

14. Connect the speedometer cable.

15. Slide the instrument cluster into the instrument panel.

16. Install and tighten the instrument cluster attaching screws.

17. Position the instrument cluster bezel in the instrument panel opening. If necessary, connect the rear defogger and rear wiper switch wiring.

18. Install and tighten the instrument cluster bezel attaching screws.

19. Install the steering column covers.

20. Connect the negative battery cable.

21. Check the operation of all instruments, gauges and indicator lights.

Speedometer

REMOVAL & INSTALLATION

1. Disconnect the negative battery cable. Remove the instrument cluster from the vehicle.

2. Remove the odometer reset button, if necessary.

3. Remove the cluster illumination bar attaching screws, remove the screws attaching the illumination bar wiring to the cluster circuit board and remove the bar.

4. Press down on the lock tabs and remove the cluster lens.

5. Remove the circuit board attaching screws and remove the circuit board and gauges from the cluster housing.

6. Remove the speedometer.

7. Installation is the reverse of the removal procedure. Check the speedometer for proper operation.

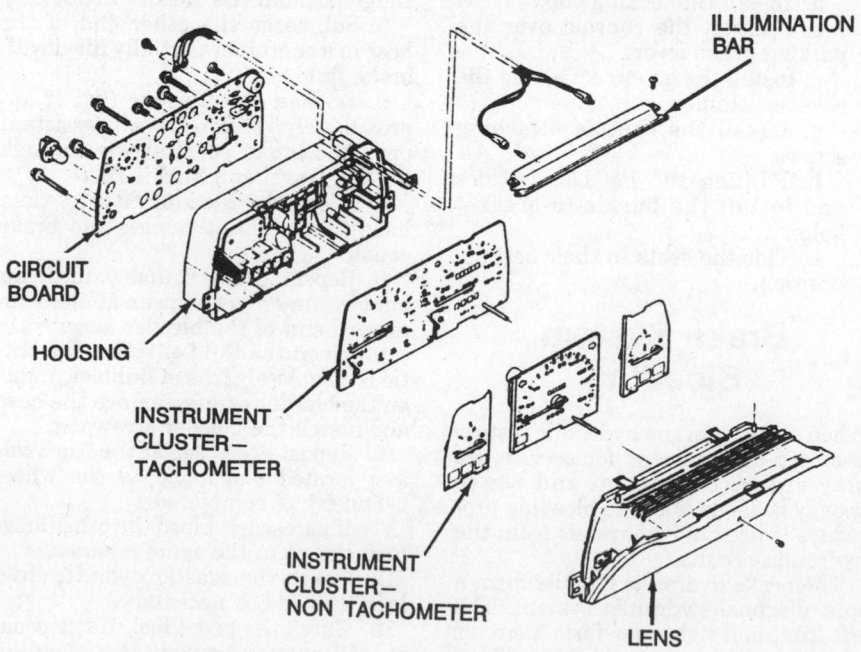

Instrument cluster exploded view—1989–90 vehicles

Labels: ILLUMINATION BAR, CIRCUIT BOARD, HOUSING, INSTRUMENT CLUSTER—TACHOMETER, INSTRUMENT CLUSTER—NON TACHOMETER, LENS

Radio

REMOVAL & INSTALLATION

1. Disconnect the negative battery cable.
2. Remove the bezel attaching screws and the trim bezel.
3. Remove the 2 screws retaining the radio in the instrument panel. Pull the radio from the instrument panel.
4. Disconnect the electrical connectors and antenna lead from the radio.
5. Remove the rubber mounting insulator from the radio ground stud. Remove the nut and the ground wire from the stud.
6. Remove the radio.
7. Installation is the reverse of the removal procedure. Check the radio for proper operation.

Combination Switch

The combination switch controls the windshield wiper, turn signal and headlight operation.

REMOVAL & INSTALLATION

1. Disconnect the negative battery cable.
2. Remove the steering wheel.
3. Remove the attaching screws from the upper half of the lower steering column cover, then remove the cover half.
4. Remove the upper steering column cover.
5. Remove the 5 clips from the lower half of the lower steering column cover.
6. Release the wiring harness clip and unplug the 4 wiring harness connectors from the rear of the combination switch. From below the steering column, loosen the band clamp securing the switch hub to the steering column jacket.
7. Pull the switch assembly off the steering column.

To install:
8. Slide the combination switch assembly onto the steering column seating the switch against the column jacket. Make certain that the switch is level, then, tighten the band clamp on the switch hub to hold the switch assembly in place.
9. Plug the 4 wiring harness connectors into the rear of the switch and clip the harness in place.
10. Position the lower half of the lower steering column cover and install the clips.
11. Install the upper steering column cover.

12. Position the upper half of the lower steering column cover and install the attaching screws.
13. Install the steering wheel. Connect the negative battery cable.

Ignition Lock

REMOVAL & INSTALLATION

1. Disconnect the negative battery cable. Remove the steering wheel, combination switch and ignition switch.
2. If necessary, remove the shift-lock cable attaching bolt and disconnect the cable from the lock housing.
3. Using slim-nose locking pliers, grip and remove the round head mounting screws securing the steering lock housing and cap to the steering column jacket. Remove the lock housing and discard the screws.

To install:
4. Position the steering lock housing onto the steering column jacket and install the mounting cap with new mounting screws. Tighten the screws enough to hold the lock in position.
5. Using the ignition key, verify that the mechanism locks and unlocks positively and without binding. If necessary, reposition the lock housing until proper operation is obtained, then tighten the mounting screws until the heads break off.
6. If necessary, install the shift-lock cable and attaching bolt. Tighten the bolt to 37–54 inch lbs. (4–6 Nm).
7. Install the ignition switch, combination switch and steering wheel. Connect the negative battery cable.

Ignition Switch

REMOVAL & INSTALLATION

1989–90

1. Disconnect the negative battery cable.
2. Remove the attaching screws from the upper half of the lower steering column cover, then remove the cover half.
3. Remove the 5 clips from the lower half of the lower steering column cover, then remove the cover half.
4. Release the ignition switch wiring harness from the harness clip.
5. Remove the retaining screw above the switch to release the switch from the steering column lock housing. Remove the switch.

To install:
6. Push the ignition switch into the steering lock housing bore and engage the switch operating tang on the lock

cylinder. If necessary, turn the lock cylinder with the ignition key until the tang aligns with the switch slot.
7. Install the retaining screw above the switch to secure the switch in the lock housing.
8. Position the switch wiring harness in the harness clip and close the clip.
9. Position the lower half of the lower steering column cover and install the clips. Position the upper half of the lower steering column cover and install the screws.
10. Connect the negative battery cable.

1991–93

1. Disconnect the negative battery cable.
2. Remove the 4 screws from the upper half of the lower steering column cover, then remove the cover half.
3. Remove the upper steering column cover.
4. Remove the 5 clips from the lower half of the lower steering column cover, then remove the cover half.
5. Remove the 4 shield nuts and the steering column shield.
6. Remove the 2 shield bracket bolts and the shield bracket.
7. Remove the air discharge duct located below the steering column.
8. Remove the steering column attaching nuts and lower the steering column mounting bracket.
9. Remove the tie strap securing the key warning buzzer switch wires to the lock cylinder housing.
10. Remove the ignition switch attaching screw and remove the switch harness from the routing clip.
11. Separate the ignition switch wiring connectors and remove the switch.

To install:
12. Position the ignition switch in the lock cylinder housing and install the attaching screw.
13. Connect the switch wiring connectors. Position the switch wiring in the routing clip and close the clip.
14. Position the key warning buzzer switch wires and secure them to the lock cylinder housing with the tie strap.
15. Raise the steering column into position and install the attaching bolts. Tighten the bolts to 23–34 ft. lbs. (31–46 Nm).
16. Install the air discharge duct.
17. Install the shield bracket and the shield with the attaching bolts and nuts.
18. Install the steering column covers.
19. Connect the negative battery cable.

Stoplight Switch

ADJUSTMENT

1. Disconnect the switch wiring connector.
2. Loosen the upper and lower attaching nuts enough to allow for rotation of the switch.
3. Connect an ohmmeter across the switch terminals.
4. Rotate the switch until the ohmmeter indicates continuity.
5. Slowly rotate the switch toward the brake pedal until the ohmmeter indicates that the switch is open (infinite resistance).
6. Rotate the switch toward the brake pedal ½ additional turn and tighten the attaching nuts to retain the adjustment.
7. Connect the switch wiring connector and check the switch for proper operation.

REMOVAL & INSTALLATION

1. Disconnect the negative battery cable. Disconnect the stoplight switch wiring connector.
2. Remove the upper attaching nut and lower the switch from the bracket.
3. Remove the lower attaching nut from the switch.
4. Installation is the reverse of the removal procedure. Adjust the switch after installation.

Clutch Switch

ADJUSTMENT

1. To eliminate the possibility that the clutch cable is affecting the pedal height, loosen the cable adjusting nut and disengage the cable pin from the transaxle release lever.
2. Move the floor carpet and insulation out of the way of the dash panel to gain sufficient room for an accurate measurement.
3. Measure the distance from the upper center of the pedal to the cowl panel. The pedal height should be 8.2–8.4 in. (208.2–213.2mm).
4. If the pedal height is within this range, no adjustment is necessary. If the pedal height is not within specification, proceed to Step 5.
5. Remove the air duct from under the instrument panel.
6. Locate the clutch switch and loosen the attaching nuts. Turn the switch in or out until the pedal height is within specification. Tighten the attaching nuts.

7. Connect the clutch cable to the transaxle release lever and adjust the pedal free-play.
8. Measure the clutch pedal height. If the pedal height has changed after connecting the clutch cable, check for binding along the cable route.
9. Install the air duct. Place the insulation and floor carpet in their original positions.

REMOVAL & INSTALLATION

1. Disconnect the negative battery cable. Move the floor carpet aside.
2. Remove the air duct located under the steering column.
3. Disconnect the clutch switch wiring connector.
4. Loosen the switch upper attaching nut and lower the switch from mounting bracket. Remove the lower attaching nut.
5. Installation is the reverse of the removal procedure. Adjust the clutch pedal height after installation.

Neutral Safety Switch

The neutral safety switch is located in the lower right side of the transaxle.

REMOVAL & INSTALLATION

1. Disconnect the negative battery cable. Raise and support the vehicle safely.
2. Disconnect the neutral safety switch electrical wires.
3. Place a drain pan under the transaxle, to catch any excess transaxle fluid.
4. Remove the neutral safety switch from its mounting.
5. Installation is the reverse of the removal procedure. Be sure to replace any lost fluid.

Fuses, Circuit Breakers and Relays

LOCATION

Fuses

The fuse panel is located in the passenger compartment, to the left of the steering column. It is concealed behind an access panel that clips into position on the instrument panel. The fuses are the cartridge type that must be removed for inspection. When making replacements, install only cartridge type fuses with the same amperage rating as the fuse that was removed.

Fusible Links

The main fuse links are located in the engine compartment on the front of the left strut tower. The main fuse link panel contains 3 fusible links—PTC on carbureted engine or EGI on EFI engine, as well as MAIN, and HEAD. The ends of the fusible links are connected to the main fuse panel through standard push-on connectors. To remove a link, grasp the insulator and pull until the connector separates from the panel. Install the new link by reversing the removal procedure.

Relays

Air Conditioning Relays—located in the left front corner of the engine compartment, left of the cooling fan. There are 3 air conditioning relays, the main relay, the wide open throttle cut-off relay and the condenser fan relay.
Cooling Fan Relay—located on the fender apron, behind the left headlight.
Daytime Running Light Relay—located on the fender apron, behind the left headlight on Canadian vehicles only.
EFE Relay—located in the passenger compartment mounted on a bracket behind the left upper corner of the instrument panel, on carbureted vehicles only.
Fuel Pump Relay—located on the left side of the instrument panel, to the left of the electronic control unit, on EFI vehicles only.
Headlight Relay—located on the fender apron, behind the left headlight.
Horn Relay—located behind left corner of instrument panel.
Main Relay—located in the left front corner of the engine compartment, attached to the fender apron.
Parking Light Relay—located in the right front corner of the engine compartment, on the fender apron.

Computers

LOCATION

The electronic control unit is located behind the instrument panel on the drivers side of the vehicle.

Flashers

LOCATION

The turn signal and hazard flashers are controlled by a single flasher unit. The flasher unit is located under the instrument panel, behind the electronic control unit.

Ford Motor Co.
Front Wheel Drive
FORD—Probe

SPECIFICATIONS

VEHICLE IDENTIFICATION CHART

It is important for servicing and ordering parts to be certain of the vehicle and engine identification. The VIN (vehicle identification number) is a 17 digit number visible through the windshield on the driver's side of the dash and contains the vehicle and engine identification codes. The tenth digit indicates model year and the eighth digit indicates engine code. It can be interpreted as follows:

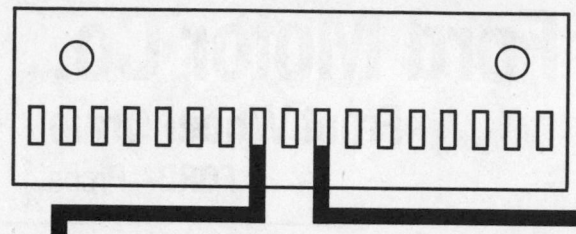

Engine Code						Model Year	
Code	Liters	Cu. In. (cc)	Cyl.	Fuel Sys.	Eng. Mfg.	Code	Year
A	2.0	122 (1993)	4	EFI	Mazda	K	1989
C	2.2	133 (2189)	4	EFI	Mazda	L	1990
L	2.2	133 (2189)	4	EFI①	Mazda	M	1991
B	2.5	153 (2501)	6	EFI	Mazda	N	1992
U	3.0	181 (2971)	6	EFI	Ford	P	1993

EFI—Electronic Fuel Injection
① Turbocharged

ENGINE IDENTIFICATION

Year	Model	Engine Displacement Liters (cc)	Engine Series (ID/VIN)	Fuel System	No. of Cylinders	Engine Type
1989	Probe GL	2.2 (2189)	C	EFI	4	OHC
	Probe LX	2.2 (2189)	C	EFI	4	OHC
	Probe GT	2.2 (2189)	L	EFI①	4	OHC
1990	Probe GL	2.2 (2189)	C	EFI	4	OHC
	Probe LX	3.0 (2971)	U	EFI	6	OHV
	Probe GT	2.2 (2189)	L	EFI①	4	OHC
1991	Probe GL	2.2 (2189)	C	EFI	4	OHC
	Probe LX	3.0 (2971)	U	EFI	6	OHV
	Probe GT	2.2 (2189)	L	EFI①	4	OHC
1992	Probe GL	2.2 (2189)	C	EFI	4	OHC
	Probe LX	3.0 (2971)	U	EFI	6	OHV
	Probe GT	2.2 (2189)	L	EFI①	4	OHC
1993	Probe	2.0 (1993)	A	EFI	4	DOHC
	Probe GT	2.5 (2501)	B	EFI	6	DOHC

DOHC—Double Overhead Camshaft
EFI—Electronic Fuel Injection
OHC—Overhead Camshaft
OHV—Overhead Valves
① Turbocharged

GENERAL ENGINE SPECIFICATIONS

Year	Engine ID/VIN	Engine Displacement Liters (cc)	Fuel System Type	Net Horsepower @ rpm	Net Torque @ rpm (ft. lbs.)	Bore × Stroke (in.)	Compression Ratio	Oil Pressure @ rpm
1989	C	2.2 (2189)	EFI	110 @ 4700	130 @ 3000	3.39 × 3.70	8.6:1	43–57 @ 3000
	L	2.2 (2189)	EFI①	145 @ 4300	190 @ 3500	3.39 × 3.70	7.8:1	43–57 @ 3000
1990	C	2.2 (2189)	EFI	110 @ 4700	130 @ 3000	3.39 × 3.70	8.6:1	43–57 @ 3000
	L	2.2 (2189)	EFI①	145 @ 4300	190 @ 3500	3.39 × 3.70	7.8:1	43–57 @ 3000
	U	3.0 (2971)	EFI	140 @ 4800	160 @ 3000	3.50 × 3.14	9.3:1	40–60 @ 2500
1991	C	2.2 (2189)	EFI	110 @ 4700	130 @ 3000	3.39 × 3.70	8.6:1	43–57 @ 3000
	L	2.2 (2189)	EFI①	145 @ 4300	190 @ 3500	3.39 × 3.70	7.8:1	43–57 @ 3000
	U	3.0 (2971)	EFI	145 @ 4800	165 @ 3400	3.50 × 3.14	9.3:1	40–60 @ 2500
1992	C	2.2 (2189)	EFI	110 @ 4700	130 @ 3000	3.39 × 3.70	8.6:1	43–57 @ 3000
	L	2.2 (2189)	EFI①	145 @ 4300	190 @ 3500	3.39 × 3.70	7.8:1	43–57 @ 3000
	U	3.0 (2971)	EFI	145 @ 4800	165 @ 3400	3.50 × 3.14	9.3:1	40–60 @ 2500
1993	A	2.0 (1993)	EFI	115 @ 5500	124 @ 3500	3.27 × 3.62	9.0:1	57–71 @ 3000
	B	2.5 (2501)	EFI	164 @ 6000	156 @ 4000	3.33 × 2.92	9.2:1	49–71 @ 3000

NOTE: Horsepower and torque are SAE net figures. They are measured at the rear of the transmission with all accessories installed and operating. Since the figures vary when a given engine is installed in different models, some are representative rather than exact.

EFI—Electronic Fuel Injection
① Turbocharged

GASOLINE ENGINE TUNE-UP SPECIFICATIONS

Year	Engine ID/VIN	Engine Displacement Liters (cc)	Spark Plugs Gap (in.)	Ignition Timing (deg.) MT	Ignition Timing (deg.) AT	Fuel Pump (psi)	Idle Speed (rpm) MT	Idle Speed (rpm) AT	Valve Clearance In.	Valve Clearance Ex.
1989	C	2.2 (2189)	0.040	6B	6B	64–85	750	750	Hyd.	Hyd.
	L	2.2 (2189)	0.040	9B	—	64–85	750	—	Hyd.	Hyd.
1990	C	2.2 (2189)	0.040	6B	6B	64–85	750	750	Hyd.	Hyd.
	L	2.2 (2189)	0.040	9B	9B	64–85	750	750	Hyd.	Hyd.
	U	3.0 (2971)	0.044	10B	10B	35–40	①	①	Hyd.	Hyd.
1991	C	2.2 (2189)	0.040	6B	6B	64–85	750	750	Hyd.	Hyd.
	L	2.2 (2189)	0.040	9B	9B	64–85	750	750	Hyd.	Hyd.
	U	3.0 (2971)	0.044	10B	10B	35–40	①	①	Hyd.	Hyd.
1992	C	2.2 (2189)	0.040	6B	6B	64–85	750	750	Hyd.	Hyd.
	L	2.2 (2189)	0.040	9B	9B	64–85	750	750	Hyd.	Hyd.
	U	3.0 (2971)	0.044	10B	10B	35–40	①	①	Hyd.	Hyd.
1993	A	2.0 (1993)	0.040	10B	12B	64–92	700	700	Hyd.	Hyd.
	B	2.5 (2501)	0.040	10B	10B	72–92	650	650	Hyd.	Hyd.

NOTE: The lowest cylinder pressure should be within 75% of the highest cylinder pressure reading. For example, if the highest cylinder is 134 psi, the lowest should be 101. Engine should be at normal operating temperature with throttle valve in the wide open position.
The underhood specifications sticker often reflects tune-up specification changes in production. Sticker figures must be used if they disagree with those in this chart.
B—Before Top Dead Center
Hyd.—Hydraulic
① Refer to Underhood Vehicle Emission
  Information label

FIRING ORDERS

NOTE: To avoid confusion, always replace spark plug wires one at a time.

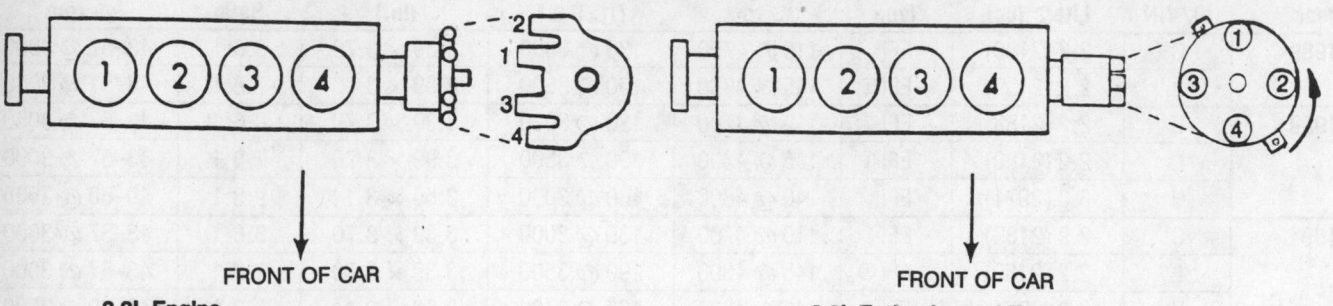

FRONT OF CAR

2.2L Engine
Engine Firing Order: 1–3–4–2
Distributor Rotation: Counterclockwise

FRONT OF CAR

2.2L Turbocharged Engine
Engine Firing Order: 1–3–4–2
Distributor Rotation: Counterclockwise

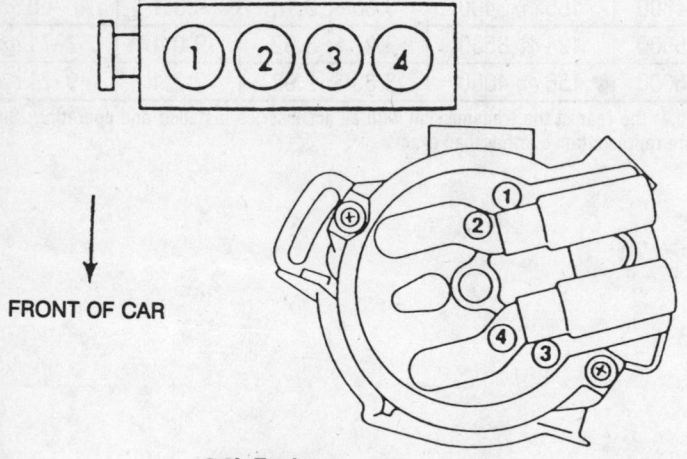

FRONT OF CAR

2.0L Engine
Engine Firing Order: 1–3–4–2
Distributor Rotation: Clockwise

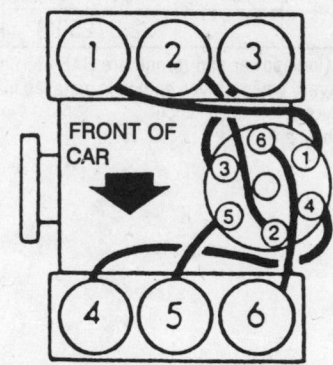

FRONT OF CAR

3.0L Engine
Engine Firing Order: 1–4–2–5–3–6
Distributor Rotation: Clockwise

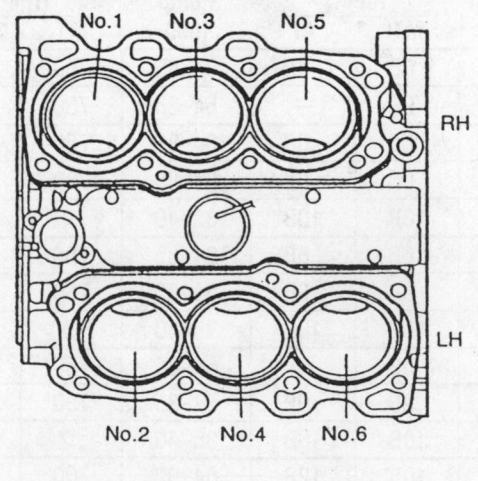

RH

LH

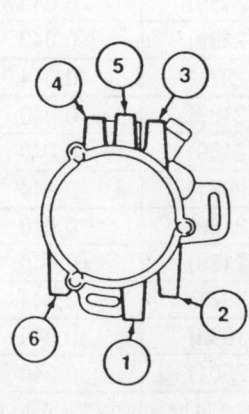

FRONT OF CAR

2.5L Engine
Engine Firing Order: 1–2–3–4–5–6
Distributor Rotation: Counterclockwise

CAPACITIES

Year	Model	Engine ID/VIN	Engine Displacement Liters (cc)	Engine Crankcase with Filter (qts.)	Transmission (pts.) 4-Spd	5-Spd	Auto.	Transfer Case (pts.)	Drive Axle Front (pts.)	Rear (pts.)	Fuel Tank (gal.)	Cooling System (qts.)
1989	Probe GL	C	2.2 (2189)	4.4	—	7.2	14.4	—	①	—	15.1	7.9
	Probe LX	C	2.2 (2189)	4.4	—	7.2	14.4	—	①	—	15.1	7.9
	Probe GT	L	2.2 (2189)	4.4	—	7.8	—	—	①	—	15.1	7.9
1990	Probe GL	C	2.2 (2189)	4.4	—	7.2	14.4	—	①	—	15.1	7.9
	Probe LX	U	3.0 (2971)	4.5	—	7.8	14.4	—	①	—	15.1	11.0
	Probe GT	L	2.2 (2189)	4.4	—	7.8	14.4	—	①	—	15.1	7.9
1991	Probe GL	C	2.2 (2189)	4.4	—	7.2	14.4	—	①	—	15.1	7.9
	Probe LX	U	3.0 (2971)	4.5	—	7.8	14.4	—	①	—	15.1	11.0
	Probe GT	L	2.2 (2189)	4.4	—	7.8	14.4	—	①	—	15.1	7.9
1992	Probe GL	C	2.2 (2189)	4.4	—	7.2	14.4	—	①	—	15.1	7.9
	Probe LX	U	3.0 (2971)	4.5	—	7.8	14.4	—	①	—	15.1	11.0
	Probe GT	L	2.2 (2189)	4.4	—	7.8	14.4	—	①	—	15.1	7.9
1993	Probe	A	2.0 (1993)	3.7	—	5.8	18.6	—	①	—	15.5	7.4
	Probe GT	B	2.5 (2501)	4.2	—	5.8	18.6	—	①	—	15.5	7.9

① Included in transaxle

CAMSHAFT SPECIFICATIONS

All measurements given in inches.

Year	Engine ID/VIN	Engine Displacement Liters (cc)	Journal Diameter 1	2	3	4	5	Elevation In.	Ex.	Bearing Clearance	Camshaft End Play
1989	C	2.2 (2189)	1.2575–1.2585	1.2563–1.2573	1.2563–1.2573	1.2563–1.2573	1.2575–1.2585	1.6200–1.6300	1.6400–1.6500	①	0.003–0.008
	L	2.2 (2189)	1.2575–1.2585	1.2563–1.2573	1.2563–1.2573	1.2563–1.2573	1.2575–1.2585	1.6200–1.6300	1.6400–1.6500	①	0.003–0.008
1990	C	2.2 (2189)	1.2575–1.2585	1.2563–1.2573	1.2563–1.2573	1.2563–1.2573	1.2575–1.2585	1.6200–1.6300	1.6400–1.6500	①	0.003–0.008
	L	2.2 (2189)	1.2575–1.2585	1.2563–1.2573	1.2563–1.2573	1.2563–1.2573	1.2575–1.2585	1.6200–1.6300	1.6400–1.6500	①	0.003–0.008
	U	3.0 (2971)	2.0074–2.0084	2.0074–2.0084	2.0074–2.0084	2.0074–2.0084	—	0.2550–0.2600	0.2550–0.2600	0.0010–0.0030	0.001–0.005
1991	C	2.2 (2189)	1.2575–1.2585	1.2563–1.2573	1.2563–1.2573	1.2563–1.2573	1.2575–1.2585	1.6200–1.6300	1.6400–1.6500	①	0.003–0.008
	L	2.2 (2189)	1.2575–1.2585	1.2563–1.2573	1.2563–1.2573	1.2563–1.2573	1.2575–1.2585	1.6200–1.6300	1.6400–1.6500	①	0.003–0.008
	U	3.0 (2971)	2.0074–2.0084	2.0074–2.0084	2.0074–2.0084	2.0074–2.0084	—	0.2550–0.2600	0.2550–0.2600	0.0010–0.0030	0.001–0.005
1992	C	2.2 (2189)	1.2575–1.2585	1.2563–1.2573	1.2563–1.2573	1.2563–1.2573	1.2575–1.2585	1.6200–1.6300	1.6400–1.6500	①	0.003–0.008
	L	2.2 (2189)	1.2575–1.2585	1.2563–1.2573	1.2563–1.2573	1.2563–1.2573	1.2575–1.2585	1.6200–1.6300	1.6400–1.6500	①	0.003–0.008
	U	3.0 (2971)	2.0074–2.0084	2.0074–2.0084	2.0074–2.0084	2.0074–2.0084	—	0.2550–0.2600	0.2550–0.2600	0.0010–0.0030	0.001–0.005
1993	A	2.0 (1993)	1.0213–1.0222	1.0213–1.0222	1.0213–1.0222	1.0213–1.0222	1.0213–1.0222	1.6859–1.6918	1.7003–1.7062	0.0014–0.0032	0.003–0.008
	B	2.5 (2501)	②	1.0201–1.0209	1.0201–1.0209	1.0201–1.0209	1.0213–1.0220	1.7067–1.7145	1.7067–1.7145	③	0.002–0.005

① No. 1 & No. 5: 0.0014–0.0033
No. 2, 3 & 4: 0.0026–0.0045

② Right head ex., left head int.: 1.0213–1.0220
Right head int., left head ex.: 1.1801–1.1811

③ No. 1 & No. 5: 0.0016–0.0032
No. 2, 3 & 4: 0.0028–0.0044

CRANKSHAFT AND CONNECTING ROD SPECIFICATIONS

All measurements are given in inches.

Year	Engine ID/VIN	Engine Displacement Liters (cc)	Crankshaft Main Brg. Journal Dia.	Crankshaft Main Brg. Oil Clearance	Crankshaft Shaft End-play	Crankshaft Thrust on No.	Connecting Rod Journal Diameter	Connecting Rod Oil Clearance	Connecting Rod Side Clearance
1989	C	2.2 (2189)	2.3597–2.3604	①	0.0031–0.0071	3	2.0055–2.0061	0.0011–0.0026	0.004–0.012
	L	2.2 (2189)	2.3597–2.3604	①	0.0031–0.0071	3	2.0055–2.0061	0.0011–0.0026	0.004–0.012
1990	C	2.2 (2189)	2.3597–2.3604	①	0.0031–0.0071	3	2.0055–2.0061	0.0011–0.0026	0.004–0.012
	L	2.2 (2189)	2.3597–2.3604	①	0.0031–0.0071	3	2.0055–2.0061	0.0011–0.0026	0.004–0.012
	U	3.0 (2971)	2.5190–2.5198	0.0005–0.0023	0.0040–0.0080	3	2.1253–2.1261	0.0009–0.0027	0.006–0.014
1991	C	2.2 (2189)	2.3597–2.3604	①	0.0031–0.0071	3	2.0055–2.0061	0.0011–0.0026	0.004–0.012
	L	2.2 (2189)	2.3597–2.3604	①	0.0031–0.0071	3	2.0055–2.0061	0.0011–0.0026	0.004–0.012
	U	3.0 (2971)	2.5190–2.5198	0.0005–0.0023	0.0040–0.0080	3	2.1253–2.1261	0.0009–0.0027	0.006–0.014
1992	C	2.2 (2189)	2.3597–2.3604	①	0.0031–0.0071	3	2.0055–2.0061	0.0011–0.0026	0.004–0.012
	L	2.2 (2189)	2.3597–2.3604	①	0.0031–0.0071	3	2.0055–2.0061	0.0011–0.0026	0.004–0.012
	U	3.0 (2971)	2.5190–2.5198	0.0005–0.0023	0.0040–0.0080	3	2.1253–2.1261	0.0009–0.0027	0.006–0.014
1993	A	2.0 (1993)	2.2020–2.2029	②	0.0031–0.0118	4	1.8872–1.8880	0.0009–0.0026	0.004–0.012
	B	2.5 (2501)	2.4382–2.4392	0.0015–0.0025	0.0032–0.0125	4	2.0841–2.0848	0.0009–0.0032	0.007–0.016

① No. 1, 2, 4 & 5: 0.0010–0.0017
 No. 3: 0.0012–0.0019
② No. 1, 2, 4 & 5: 0.0009–0.0026
 No. 3: 0.0012–0.0026

VALVE SPECIFICATIONS

Year	Engine ID/VIN	Engine Displacement Liters (cc)	Seat Angle (deg.)	Face Angle (deg.)	Spring Test Pressure (lbs. @ in.)	Spring Installed Height (in.)	Stem-to-Guide Clearance (in.) Intake	Stem-to-Guide Clearance (in.) Exhaust	Stem Diameter (in.) Intake	Stem Diameter (in.) Exhaust
1989	C	2.2 (2189)	45	45	NA①	NA①	0.0080	0.0080	0.2744–0.2750	0.2742–0.2748
	L	2.2 (2189)	45	45	NA①	NA①	0.0080	0.0080	0.2744–0.2750	0.2742–0.2748
1990	C	2.2 (2189)	45	45	NA①	NA①	0.0080	0.0080	0.2744–0.2750	0.2742–0.2748
	L	2.2 (2189)	45	45	NA①	NA①	0.0080	0.0080	0.2744–0.2750	0.2742–0.2748
	U	3.0 (2971)	45	44	180 @ 1.16	1.58	0.0010–0.0028	0.0015–0.0033	0.3126–0.3134	0.3121–0.3129

VALVE SPECIFICATIONS

Year	Engine ID/VIN	Engine Displacement Liters (cc)	Seat Angle (deg.)	Face Angle (deg.)	Spring Test Pressure (lbs. @ in.)	Spring Installed Height (in.)	Stem-to-Guide Clearance (in.)		Stem Diameter (in.)	
							Intake	Exhaust	Intake	Exhaust
1991	C	2.2 (2189)	45	45	NA①	NA①	0.0080	0.0080	0.2744–0.2750	0.2742–0.2748
	L	2.2 (2189)	45	45	NA①	NA①	0.0080	0.0080	0.2744–0.2750	0.2742–0.2748
	U	3.0 (2971)	45	44	180 @ 1.16	1.58	0.0010–0.0028	0.0015–0.0033	0.3126–0.3134	0.3121–0.3129
1992	C	2.2 (2189)	45	45	NA①	NA①	0.0080	0.0080	0.2744–0.2750	0.2742–0.2748
	L	2.2 (2189)	45	45	NA①	NA①	0.0080	0.0080	0.2744–0.2750	0.2742–0.2748
	U	3.0 (2971)	45	44	180 @ 1.16	1.58	0.0010–0.0028	0.0015–0.0033	0.3126–0.3134	0.3121–0.3129
1993	A	2.0 (1993)	45	45	NA①	NA①	0.0010–0.0024	0.0012–0.0026	0.2350–0.2356	0.2348–0.2354
	B	2.5 (2501)	45	45	NA①	NA①	0.0010–0.0023	0.0012–0.0026	0.2351–0.2356	0.2349–0.2354

NA—Not available
① Measure spring free length and out-of-square
   Maximum allowable out-of-square:
     2.0L Engine—0.061
     2.2L Engine—0.067
     2.5L Engine—0.0642
   Spring free length:
     2.0L Engine—1.732
     2.2L Engine
       Intake—1.902–1.949
       Exhaust—1.937–1.984
     2.5L Engine
       Intake—1.729
       Exhaust—1.847

PISTON AND RING SPECIFICATIONS

All measurements are given in inches.

Year	Engine ID/VIN	Engine Displacement Liters (cc)	Piston Clearance	Ring Gap			Ring Side Clearance		
				Top Compression	Bottom Compression	Oil Control	Top Compression	Bottom Compression	Oil Control
1989	C	2.2 (2189)	0.0014–0.0030	0.008–0.014	0.006–0.012	0.012–0.035	0.0010–0.0030	0.0010–0.0030	NA
	L	2.2 (2189)	0.0014–0.0030	0.008–0.014	0.006–0.012	0.008–0.028	0.0010–0.0030	0.0010–0.0030	NA
1990	C	2.2 (2189)	0.0014–0.0030	0.008–0.014	0.006–0.012	0.012–0.035	0.0010–0.0030	0.0010–0.0030	NA
	L	2.2 (2189)	0.0014–0.0030	0.008–0.014	0.006–0.012	0.008–0.028	0.0010–0.0030	0.0010–0.0030	NA
	U	3.0 (2971)	0.0014–0.0022	0.010–0.020	0.010–0.020	0.010–0.049	0.0012–0.0031	0.0012–0.0031	NA
1991	C	2.2 (2189)	0.0014–0.0030	0.008–0.014	0.006–0.012	0.012–0.035	0.0010–0.0030	0.0010–0.0030	NA
	L	2.2 (2189)	0.0014–0.0030	0.008–0.014	0.006–0.012	0.008–0.028	0.0010–0.0030	0.0010–0.0030	NA
	U	3.0 (2971)	0.0014–0.0022	0.010–0.020	0.010–0.020	0.010–0.049	0.0012–0.0031	0.0012–0.0031	NA

PISTON AND RING SPECIFICATIONS

All measurements are given in inches.

Year	Engine ID/VIN	Engine Displacement Liters (cc)	Piston Clearance	Ring Gap			Ring Side Clearance		
				Top Compression	Bottom Compression	Oil Control	Top Compression	Bottom Compression	Oil Control
1992	C	2.2 (2189)	0.0014–0.0030	0.008–0.014	0.006–0.012	0.012–0.035	0.0010–0.0030	0.0010–0.0030	NA
	L	2.2 (2189)	0.0014–0.0030	0.008–0.014	0.006–0.012	0.008–0.028	0.0010–0.0030	0.0010–0.0030	NA
	U	3.0 (2971)	0.0014–0.0022	0.010–0.020	0.010–0.020	0.010–0.049	0.0012–0.0031	0.0012–0.0031	NA
1993	A	2.0 (1993)	0.0015–0.0020	0.006–0.012	0.006–0.012	0.008–0.028	0.0014–0.0026	0.0014–0.0026	NA
	B	2.5 (2501)	0.0012–0.0022	0.006–0.0118	0.010–0.015	0.008–0.027	0.0070–0.0130	0.0070–0.0130	NA

NA—Not available

TORQUE SPECIFICATIONS

All readings in ft. lbs.

Year	Engine ID/VIN	Engine Displacement Liters (cc)	Cylinder Head Bolts	Main Bearing Bolts	Rod Bearing Bolts	Crankshaft Damper Bolts	Flywheel Bolts	Manifold		Spark Plugs	Lug Nut
								Intake	Exhaust		
1989	C	2.2 (2189)	59–64	61–65	48–51	108–116①	71–76	14–22	16–21	11–17	65–87
	L	2.2 (2189)	59–64	61–65	48–51	108–116①	71–76	14–22	16–21	11–17	65–87
1990	C	2.2 (2189)	59–64	61–65	48–51	108–116①	71–76	14–22	16–21	11–17	65–87
	L	2.2 (2189)	59–64	61–65	48–51	108–116①	71–76	14–22	16–21	11–17	65–87
	U	3.0 (2971)	②	60	25	92–122	54–64	③	15–22	7–15	65–87
1991	C	2.2 (2189)	59–64	61–65	48–51	108–116①	71–76	14–22	16–21	11–17	65–87
	L	2.2 (2189)	59–64	61–65	48–51	108–116①	71–76	14–22	16–21	11–17	65–87
	U	3.0 (2971)	④	60	25	107	54–64	③	18	7–15	65–87
1992	C	2.2 (2189)	59–64	61–65	48–51	108–116①	71–76	14–22	16–21	11–17	65–87
	L	2.2 (2189)	59–64	61–65	48–51	108–116①	71–76	14–22	16–21	11–17	65–87
	U	3.0 (2971)	④	60	25	107	54–64	③	18	7–15	65–87
1993	A	2.0 (1993)	⑤	⑥	⑥	116–123	70–75	14–19	17	11–17	65–87
	B	2.5 (2501)	⑦	⑧	⑨	116–123	45–49	14–18	14–18	11–16	65–87

① Figure given is for crankshaft sprocket bolt
② Tighten in 2 steps:
    Step 1: 33–41
    Step 2: 63–73
③ Tigthen in 2 steps:
    Step 1: 11
    Step 2: 21
④ Tighten in 4 steps:
    Step 1: 59
    Step 2: Back off all bolts 1 turn
    Step 3: 37
    Step 4: 68
⑤ Tighten in 4 steps:
    Step 1: 7–8
    Step 2: 13–16
    Step 3: Turn each bolt 90°, in sequence
    Step 4: Turn each bolt 90°, in sequence
⑥ Tighten in 2 steps:
    Step 1: 16–19
    Step 2: Turn each bolt 90°, in sequence

⑦ Tighten in 3 steps:
    Step 1: 17–19
    Step 2: Turn each bolt 90°, in sequence
    Step 3: Turn each bolt 90°, in sequence
⑧ Tighten in sequence in 3 steps:
    Step 1:
        Inner bolts: Tighten to 17–19, in 2–3 steps
        Outer bolts: Tighten to 13–15, in 2–3 steps
    Step 2:
        Inner bolts:
            Nos. 1, 2 & 3—Turn each bolt 70°
            No. 4—Turn each bolt 80°
        Outer bolts: Turn each bolt 60°
    Step 3: Repeat Step 2
⑨ Tighten in 3 steps:
    Step 1: 16–19
    Step 2: Turn each bolt 90°
    Step 3: Turn each bolt an additional 90°

BRAKE SPECIFICATIONS
All measurements in inches unless noted.

Year	Model	Master Cylinder Bore	Brake Disc Original Thickness	Brake Disc Minimum Thickness	Maximum Runout	Brake Drum Diameter Original Inside Diameter	Brake Drum Diameter Max. Wear Limit	Brake Drum Diameter Maximum Machine Diameter	Minimum Lining Thickness Front	Minimum Lining Thickness Rear
1989	Probe GL	0.875	0.940	0.860	0.004	9.0	9.060	NA	0.120	0.040
	Probe LX	0.875	0.940	0.860	0.004	9.0	9.060	NA	0.120	0.040
	Probe GT	0.875	①	②	0.004	—	—	—	0.120	0.040
1990	Probe GL	0.875	0.940	0.860	0.004	9.0	9.060	NA	0.120	0.040
	Probe LX	0.875	①	②	0.004	—	—	—	0.120	0.040
	Probe GT	0.875	①	②	0.004	—	—	—	0.120	0.040
1991	Probe GL	0.875	0.940	0.860	0.004	9.0	9.060	NA	0.120	0.040
	Probe LX	0.875	①	②	0.004	—	—	—	0.120	0.040
	Probe GT	0.875	①	②	0.004	—	—	—	0.120	0.040
1992	Probe GL	0.875	0.940	0.860	0.004	9.0	9.060	NA	0.120	0.040
	Probe LX	0.875	①	②	0.004	—	—	—	0.120	0.040
	Probe GT	0.875	①	②	0.004	—	—	—	0.120	0.040
1993	Probe	0.937	①	③	0.004	9.0	9.060	NA	0.040	0.040
	Probe GT	0.937	①	③	0.004	—	—	—	0.040	0.040

NA—Not available
① Front—0.940
　Rear—0.390
② Front—0.860
　Rear—0.315
③ Front—0.870
　Rear—0.310

WHEEL ALIGNMENT

Year	Model		Caster Range (deg.)	Caster Preferred Setting (deg.)	Camber Range (deg.)	Camber Preferred Setting (deg.)	Toe-in (in.)	Steering Axis Inclination (deg.)
1989	Probe	Front	15/32P–1 31/32P	1 7/32P	7/16N–1 1/16P	5/16P	1/8	12 25/32
		Rear	—	—	1/4N–1 1/4P	1/2P	0	—
1990	Probe	Front	11/16P–2 3/16P	1 7/16P	1N–1/2P	1/4N	1/8	12 25/32
		Rear	—	—	1 3/16N–5/16P	7/16N	1/8	—
1991	Probe	Front	15/16P–2 7/16P	1 11/16P	1N–1/2P	1/4N	1/8	12 25/32
		Rear	—	—	1 3/16N–5/16P	7/16N	1/8	—
1992	Probe	Front	15/16P–2 7/16P	1 11/16P	1N–1/2P	1/4N	1/8	12 25/32
		Rear	—	—	1 3/16N–5/16P	7/16N	1/8	—
1993	Probe	Front	2 1/4P–3 3/4P	3P	①	②	1/8	③
		Rear	—	—	1 1/8N–3/8P	5/8N	1/8	—

N—Negative
P—Positive
① 2.0L Engine: 1 7/16N–1/16P
　2.5L Engine: 1 21/32N–5/32N
② 2.0L Engine: 11/16N
　2.5L Engine: 29/32N
③ 2.0L Engine: 15 1/4
　2.5L Engine: 15 3/4

ENGINE MECHANICAL

NOTE: Disconnecting the negative battery cable on some vehicles may interfere with the functions of the on board computer systems and may require the computer to undergo a relearning process, once the negative battery cable is reconnected.

Engine Assembly

REMOVAL & INSTALLATION

2.0L Engine
AUTOMATIC TRANSAXLE

The engine is lifted from the engine compartment, leaving the transaxle in the vehicle.

1. Relieve the fuel system pressure and disconnect the battery cables. Remove the battery and battery tray.
2. Mark the position of the hood on its hinges and remove the hood.
3. Drain the cooling system and the engine oil.
4. Remove the air cleaner assembly and air ducts.
5. If equipped, remove the A/C compressor and position aside, leaving the refrigerant lines attached. Support the compressor with suitable wire.
6. Label, disconnect and plug the fuel lines at the fuel rail.
7. Label and disconnect the electrical connectors from the distributor, engine coolant temperature sensor, cooling fan temperature sensor, coolant temperature gauge sensor, throttle position sensor, air bypass valve, idle switch, fuel injectors, EGR solenoids and alternator.
8. Remove the power steering belt shield and the power steering belt. Remove the power steering hose brackets from the cylinder head cover.
9. Remove the power steering belt adjuster and disconnect the power steering pressure switch connector. Remove the power steering pump and position aside, leaving the hoses connected.
10. Loosen the alternator adjusting bolt, remove the upper mounting bolt and remove the alternator belt.
11. Remove the upper and lower radiator hoses. If equipped, disconnect the cruise control vacuum hose from the back right-hand side of the intake manifold.
12. Disconnect the vacuum line connecting the evaporative canister and the metal EGR vacuum line. If equipped, disconnect the EGR temperature sensor connector.

13. Disconnect the accelerator cable. Disconnect the power booster vacuum line from the back left-hand side of the intake manifold.
14. Disconnect the heater hoses and remove the upper starter mounting bolts. Raise and safely support the vehicle.
15. Remove the splash shields. Remove the starter and the intake manifold support bracket.
16. Remove the halfshaft support bearing mounting bolts and disconnect the oil pressure sensor connector.
17. Remove the torque converter-to-flexplate nuts. Remove the 3 engine-to-transaxle bolts and the transaxle-to-engine mounting bolts.
18. Disconnect the oxygen sensor connector. Remove and discard the exhaust pipe-to-catalytic converter nuts.
19. Remove the exhaust support bolts. Remove and discard the exhaust pipe-to-exhaust manifold nuts and remove the exhaust pipe. Support the remaining exhaust system with mechanics wire.
20. Label and disconnect the remaining alternator wiring. Remove the wiring harness bracket from the back of the alternator, remove the through bolt and remove the alternator.
21. Use a suitable holding tool to hold the crankshaft pulley and remove the pulley bolt. Remove the crankshaft pulley. Lower the engine.
22. Raise the engine slightly with a jack and remove the right-hand engine mount. Attach suitable engine lifting equipment to the lifting eyes on the engine.
23. Remove the remaining transaxle-to-engine mounting bolts and carefully remove the engine from the vehicle.
24. Remove the flexplate from the crankshaft and mount the engine on a workstand.

To install:
25. Remove the engine from the workstand. Remove the old sealant from the flexplate mounting bolts and bolt holes.
26. If reusing the flexplate bolts, apply silicone sealant to the bolt threads. Install the flexplate and loosely install the bolts.

NOTE: New flexplate mounting bolts come with sealant already on them.

27. Tighten the flex plate bolts in 2–3 steps to 75 ft. lbs. (103 Nm) in a criss-cross pattern.
28. Carefully lower the engine into the vehicle and install it to the transaxle. Install the transaxle-to-engine bolts and tighten mounting bolts **A** to 73 ft. lbs. (99 Nm).
29. Raise the engine slightly with the jack and install the right-hand engine mount. Tighten the mount through

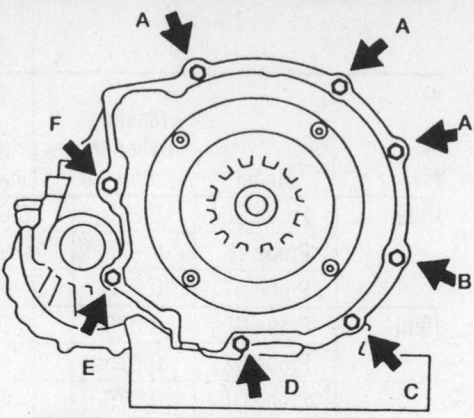
Engine and transaxle mounting bolt Identification—2.0L engine with automatic transaxle

bolt to 86 ft. lbs. (117 Nm) and mount nuts to 75 ft. lbs. (103 Nm). Remove the engine lifting equipment.
30. Raise and safely support the vehicle. Install the torque converter to the flexplate and tighten the nuts to 45 ft. lbs. (60 Nm). Rotate the flexplate, as necessary, to gain access to all of the nuts.
31. Install the remaining transaxle-to-engine mounting bolts. Tighten mounting bolt **B** to 73 ft. lbs. (99 Nm) and mounting bolt **C** to 38 ft. lbs. (51 Nm).
32. Install the engine-to-transaxle mounting bolts. Tighten mounting bolt **D** to 18 ft. lbs. (25 Nm), **E** to 38 ft. lbs. (51 Nm) and **F** to 73 ft. lbs. (99 Nm).
33. Install the alternator and loosely install the through bolt. Connect the alternator wiring and install the harness bracket to the back of the alternator.
34. Install the starter and tighten the bolts to 34 ft. lbs. (46 Nm). Install the intake manifold support bracket and tighten the bolts to 38 ft. lbs. (52 Nm).
35. Install the halfshaft support bearing bolts and tighten, in sequence, to 45 ft. lbs. (61 Nm).

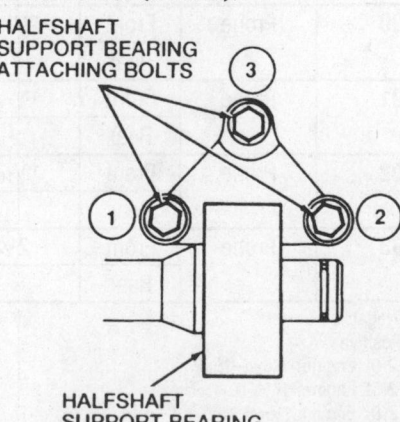
Halfshaft support bearing bolt torque sequence—2.0L Engine

36. Connect the oil pressure sensor connector. If equipped, install the A/C compressor on the mounting bracket and tighten the bolts to 26 ft. lbs. (35 Nm).

37. Install the crankshaft pulley and hold it with a suitable tool. Tighten the pulley bolt to 123 ft. lbs. (167 Nm).

38. Install the exhaust pipe to the catalytic converter and tighten the new nuts to 38 ft. lbs. (52 Nm). Attach the exhaust pipe support bracket to the engine and tighten the bolts to 38 ft. lbs. (52 Nm).

39. Install the new exhaust pipe-to-exhaust manifold nuts and tighten to 38 ft. lbs. (52 Nm). Connect the oxygen sensor connector and lower the vehicle.

40. Loosely attach the alternator to the alternator adjuster block. Install the alternator belt and adjust the tension. Tighten the alternator upper mounting bolt to 18 ft. lbs. (25 Nm).

41. Raise and safely support the vehicle. Tighten the alternator through bolt to 38 ft. lbs. (52 Nm).

42. Install the splash shields and lower the vehicle.

43. Loosely install the power steering pump through bolt and lock bolt. Connect the power steering switch connector and install the power steering belt.

44. Adjust the power steering belt tension, then tighten the through bolt to 45 ft. lbs. (61 Nm) and the lock bolt to 34 ft. lbs. (46 Nm).

45. Install the power steering pump belt shield and tighten the bolts to 86 inch lbs. (9 Nm). Install the power steering hose brackets to the cylinder head cover and tighten the bolts to 88 inch lbs. (10 Nm).

46. Connect the heater hoses. If equipped, connect the cruise control vacuum line to the back right-hand side of the intake manifold.

47. Connect the vacuum line connecting the evaporative canister to the metal EGR vacuum line. Connect the power brake booster vacuum line to the back left-hand side of the intake manifold.

48. Connect the fuel lines to the fuel rail and all remaining electrical connectors.

49. Install the accelerator cable and the radiator hoses. Install the air cleaner and air ducts.

50. Install the battery tray and battery. Connect the battery cables.

51. Install the hood, aligning the marks that were made during removal.

52. Fill the engine with the proper type and quantity of oil. Fill and bleed the cooling system.

53. Start the engine and bring to normal operating temperature. Check for leaks and proper engine operation.

MANUAL TRANSAXLE

The engine and transaxle are lifted from the engine compartment as an assembly.

1. Relieve the fuel system pressure and disconnect the battery cables. Remove the battery and battery tray.

2. Mark the position of the hood on its hinges and remove the hood.

3. Drain the cooling system and the engine oil.

4. Remove the air cleaner assembly and air ducts.

5. Remove the upper and lower radiator hoses and remove the radiator.

6. If equipped, remove the A/C compressor and position aside, leaving the refrigerant lines attached. Support the compressor with suitable wire.

7. Label, disconnect and plug the fuel lines at the fuel rail.

8. Label and disconnect the electrical connectors from the distributor, coil, engine coolant temperature sensor, coolant temperature gauge sensor, throttle position sensor, air bypass valve, fuel injectors, EGR solenoids and alternator.

9. Remove the power steering belt shield and the power steering belt. Remove the power steering hose brackets from the cylinder head cover.

10. Remove the power steering belt adjuster and disconnect the power steering pressure switch connector. Remove the power steering pump and position aside, leaving the hoses connected.

11. Loosen the alternator adjusting bolt, remove the upper mounting bolt and remove the alternator belt.

12. If equipped, disconnect the cruise control vacuum hose from the back right-hand side of the intake manifold.

13. Disconnect the vacuum line connecting the evaporative canister and the metal EGR vacuum line. If equipped, disconnect the EGR temperature sensor connector.

14. Disconnect the accelerator cable. Disconnect the power booster vacuum line from the back left-hand side of the intake manifold.

15. Disconnect the heater hoses and remove the upper starter mounting bolts. If equipped, disconnect the cruise control actuator electrical connector, remove the actuator mounting nuts and position the actuator aside.

16. Remove the ignition coil. Remove the fuel filter bracket bolts and position the filter and bracket aside.

17. Remove the ignition control module. Remove the ground wire bracket from between the transaxle and rear transaxle mount.

18. Remove the rear transaxle mount through bolt and remove the transaxle ground from the top rear of the transaxle.

19. Label and disconnect the brake on/off switch and vehicle speed sensor connectors from the rear of the transaxle.

20. Disconnect and plug the slave cylinder hydraulic line at the slave cylinder. Pull the spring clips from the slave cylinder line mounting brackets, then remove the rubber line from the metal line.

21. Label and disconnect the park/neutral position switch from the front of the transaxle. Raise and safely support the vehicle.

22. Remove the splash shields and the front wheel and tire assemblies.

23. Remove the 6 transverse member bolts and the transverse member. Remove the 6 transaxle cradle nuts and 2 bolts and remove the transaxle cradle.

24. Remove the 2 transaxle lower mount bolts and the transaxle lower mount.

25. Remove the halfshafts. Install transaxle plug tools T88C-7025-AH or equivalent, into the differential side gears.

NOTE: If the plugs are not installed, the differential side gears may become mispositioned. If the gears are mispositioned, the differential may have to be removed to reposition them.

26. Remove the intake manifold support bracket. Remove the 3 rear transaxle mount bolts and remove the rear transaxle mount.

27. Remove the starter. Label and disconnect the oil pressure sensor and oxygen sensor electrical connectors.

28. Remove and discard the exhaust pipe-to-catalytic converter nuts. Remove the exhaust support bolts. Remove and discard the exhaust pipe-to-exhaust manifold nuts and remove the exhaust pipe.

29. Remove the extension bar nut and washer, then disengage the bar from the transaxle. Remove the transaxle shift linkage through bolt and nut, then disengage the linkage from the transaxle.

30. Remove the wiring harness bracket from the rear of the alternator and remove the alternator through bolt. Label and disconnect the remaining alternator wiring and remove the alternator.

31. Hold the crankshaft pulley with a suitable tool and remove the pulley bolt. Remove the crankshaft pulley.

32. Lower the vehicle. Raise the engine slightly with a jack and remove the right-hand engine mount.

33. Attach suitable engine lifting equipment to the lifting eyes on the engine. Remove the left-hand transaxle mount nuts, bolt and through bolt and remove the mount.

34. Carefully remove the engine/transaxle assembly from the vehicle.

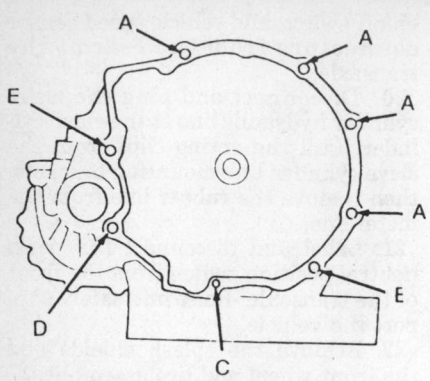

Engine and transaxle mounting bolt identification—2.0L engine with manual transaxle

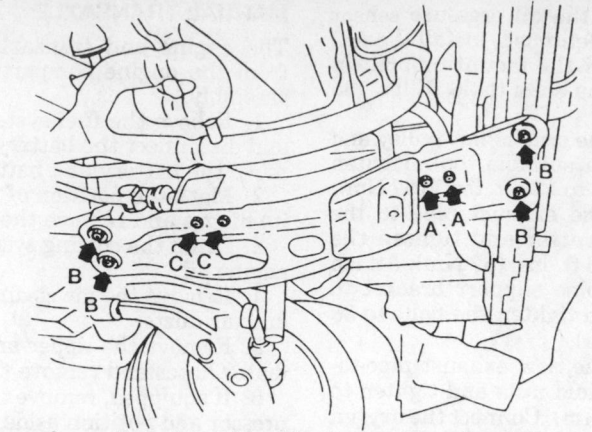

Transaxle cradle bolt/nut identification—2.0L and 2.5L Engines

35. Remove the transaxle-to-engine bolts and the engine-to-transaxle bolts. Separate the transaxle from the engine.

36. Remove the clutch assembly, flywheel and crankshaft rear cover plate. Mount the engine on a workstand.

To install:

37. Remove the engine from the workstand. Install the crankshaft rear cover plate and tighten the bolt to 88 inch lbs. (10 Nm). Install the flywheel and clutch assembly.

38. Install the transaxle on the engine. Install the transaxle-to-engine bolts. Tighten bolts **A** to 86 ft. lbs. (116 Nm), **B** to 38 ft. lbs. (51 Nm) and **C** to 18 ft. lbs. (25 Nm).

39. Install the engine-to-transaxle bolts. Tighten bolt **D** to 38 ft. lbs. (51 Nm) and bolt **E** to 86 ft. lbs. (116 Nm).

40. Lower the engine/transaxle assembly into the engine compartment.

41. Install the left-hand transaxle mount and tighten the nuts and bolt to 68 ft. lbs. (93 Nm). Tighten the mount through bolt to 86 ft. lbs. (116 Nm).

42. Raise the engine slightly with a jack and install the right-hand engine mount. Tighten the mount through bolt to 86 ft. lbs. (116 Nm) and the mount attaching nuts to 75 ft. lbs. (103 Nm). Remove the engine lifting equipment.

43. Raise and safely support the vehicle. Install the alternator and loosely install the alternator through bolt. Connect the alternator wiring and install the wiring harness bracket to the rear of the alternator.

44. Connect the extension bar to the transaxle with the washer and nut. Tighten the nut to 38 ft. lbs. (51 Nm).

45. Connect the shift linkage to the transaxle with the through bolt and nut. Tighten the through bolt to 18 ft. lbs. (25 Nm).

46. Install the exhaust pipe to the catalytic converter and tighten the new nuts to 38 ft. lbs. (52 Nm). Attach

the exhaust pipe support bracket to the engine and tighten the bolts to 38 ft. lbs. (52 Nm).

47. Install the new exhaust pipe-to-exhaust manifold nuts and tighten to 38 ft. lbs. (52 Nm). Connect the oxygen sensor and oil pressure sensor connectors.

48. Install the starter and tighten the bolts to 34 ft. lbs. (46 Nm). Install the rear transaxle mount and tighten the 3 bolts to 68 ft. lbs. (93 Nm).

49. Install the intake manifold support bracket and tighten the bolts to 38 ft. lbs. (52 Nm).

50. Remove the plugs from the differential side gears and install the halfshafts.

51. Install the transaxle lower mount and tighten the bolts to 68 ft. lbs. (93 Nm).

52. Install the transaxle cradle. Tighten bolts and nuts **B** to 68 ft. lbs. (93 Nm), nuts **A** to 77 ft. lbs. (104 Nm) and nuts **C** to 44 ft. lbs. (60 Nm).

53. Install the transverse member and tighten the 4 bolts to 96 ft. lbs. (131 Nm).

54. Install the crankshaft pulley and hold it with a suitable tool. Install the pulley bolt and tighten to 123 ft. lbs. (167 Nm). Lower the vehicle.

55. Loosely attach the alternator to the alternator adjuster block. Install the alternator belt and adjust the tension. Tighten the alternator upper mounting bolt to 18 ft. lbs. (25 Nm).

56. Raise and safely support the vehicle. Tighten the alternator through bolt to 38 ft. lbs. (52 Nm).

57. Install the splash shields and the wheel and tire assemblies. Lower the vehicle and connect the park/neutral position switch.

58. Remove the plug and install the rubber line to the clutch hydraulic metal line. Install the spring clips to the hydraulic line mounting brackets. Install the hydraulic line fitting on the slave cylinder.

59. Connect the vehicle speed sensor

and brake on/off switch electrical connectors at the rear of the transaxle.

60. Install the ground wire bracket between the transaxle and the rear transaxle mount. Install the rear transaxle mount through bolt and tighten to 68 ft. lbs. (93 Nm). Install the transaxle ground at the top rear of the transaxle.

61. Install the ignition control module. Install the fuel filter and bracket on the upper transaxle mount and tighten the bolts to 97 inch lbs. (11 Nm). Install the ignition coil.

62. If equipped, install the cruise control actuator and tighten the nuts. Connect the cruise control actuator electrical connector.

63. Install the starter mounting bolts and tighten to 34 ft. lbs. (46 Nm). Connect the heater hoses and connect the power brake booster vacuum line to the back left-hand side of the intake manifold.

64. Connect the accelerator cable. Connect the EGR temperature sensor, if equipped.

65. Connect the vacuum line between the evaporative canister and the metal EGR vacuum line. If equipped, connect the cruise control vacuum line to the back right-hand side of the intake manifold.

66. Loosely install the power steering pump through bolt and lock bolt. Connect the power steering switch connector and install the power steering belt.

67. Adjust the power steering belt tension, then tighten the through bolt to 45 ft. lbs. (61 Nm) and the lock bolt to 34 ft. lbs. (46 Nm).

68. Install the power steering pump belt shield and tighten the bolts to 86 inch lbs. (9 Nm). Install the power steering hose brackets to the cylinder head cover and tighten the bolts to 88 inch lbs. (10 Nm).

69. Connect all remaining electrical connectors.

70. Unplug and connect the fuel

lines. If equipped, install the A/C compressor and tighten the mounting bolts to 26 ft. lbs. (35 Nm).

71. Install the radiator and the radiator hoses.

72. Install the air cleaner and air ducts. Install the battery tray and battery. Connect the battery cables.

73. Install the hood, aligning the marks that were made during removal.

74. Fill the engine with the proper type and quantity of oil. Fill and bleed the cooling system. Bleed the clutch hydraulic system.

75. Start the engine and bring to normal operating temperature. Check for leaks and proper engine operation.

2.2L Engine

1. Properly relieve the fuel system pressure and disconnect the negative battery cable.

2. Mark the hood hinge-to-hood locations and remove the hood.

3. Drain the cooling system, the engine oil, power steering fluid and, if equipped, automatic transaxle fluid into suitable containers.

4. Remove the battery, the battery carrier and the fuse holder.

5. Remove the air filter assembly and ducts. Disconnect the accelerator cable, throttle valve, and the cruise control cable, if equipped.

6. Label and disconnect the electrical connectors from the electronic fuel injection system, the ignition coil, the thermostat housing sensors, the oxygen sensor, the radiator and the cooling fan assembly.

7. If equipped with an automatic transaxle, disconnect and plug the cooler lines from the radiator. Remove the radiator cooling fan assembly and the radiator.

8. If equipped with a manual transaxle, remove the clutch release cylinder and move it aside.

9. On non-turbocharged vehicles, raise and safely support the vehicle, then remove the front exhaust pipe-to-exhaust manifold nuts, the exhaust pipe-to-catalytic converter nuts and the front exhaust pipe. Lower the vehicle.

10. Properly discharge the air conditioning system and remove the air conditioning lines from the compressor. Immediately plug the lines and the compressor openings to prevent the entrance of moisture. Disconnect the electrical connector from the compressor clutch.

11. Disconnect and plug the power steering lines from the power steering pump.

12. Disconnect the ground strap from the engine.

13. Disconnect and plug the heater hoses and the fuel lines.

14. Label and disconnect the vacuum lines from the brake booster chamber, the carbon canister, the bulkhead mounted solenoids and the distributor.

15. If equipped with an automatic transaxle, label and disconnect the electrical connectors from the transaxle.

16. Disconnect the speedometer cable from the transaxle.

17. If equipped with a turbocharger, disconnect the hoses and pipe. Cover the turbocharger with a clean rag.

18. Raise and safely support the vehicle. Remove the halfshafts from the transaxle.

19. Disconnect the shift control cable, if equipped with an automatic transaxle, or disconnect the rod, if equipped with a manual transaxle, from the transaxle. Lower the vehicle.

20. Using a suitable engine lifting device, attach it to the engine and support its weight.

21. Disconnect the engine mount bolts and remove the engine/transaxle assembly from the vehicle.

22. If necessary, remove the transaxle-to-engine bolts and support the engine on an engine stand.

To install:

23. If the transaxle was removed from the engine, install it and torque the bolts to 66–86 ft. lbs. (89–117 Nm).

24. Lower the engine/transaxle assembly into the vehicle and secure the engine mount bolts.

25. Install the halfshafts.

NOTE: When installing the halfshafts, hold the shafts to prevent damage to the seals, boots and joints caused by moving the joints through angles greater than 20 degrees.

26. Depending on which transaxle the vehicle is equipped with, connect the shift control cable or rod. If equipped with a manual transaxle, install the clutch release cylinder. If equipped with an automatic transaxle, connect the electrical connectors to the transaxle.

27. Connect the speedometer cable to the transaxle and the power steering lines to the power steering pump.

28. If equipped with air conditioning, use new O-rings and connect the pressure and suction lines to the compressor. Reconnect the electrical connector to the compressor clutch.

29. Connect the engine ground strap. On non-turbocharged vehicles, install the front exhaust pipe. If equipped with a turbocharger, connect the oil pipe and hoses to the turbocharger.

30. Install the radiator and the cooling fan assembly and reconnect the electrical connectors. If equipped with

an automatic transaxle, reconnect the oil cooler lines to the radiator.

31. Connect the vacuum lines to the carbon canister, the bulkhead mounted solenoids, distributor and the brake booster.

32. Connect the heater hoses to the engine and the fuel lines to the fuel system. Connect the electrical connectors to the oxygen sensor, thermostat housing sensors, the coil and the electronic fuel injection assembly.

33. Install the accelerator cable, throttle valve cable and the cruise control cable, if equipped. Install the air filter and ducts.

34. Install the battery carrier, battery and the fuse holder. Connect the battery cables.

35. Refill the cooling system. Fill the crankcase with the proper type and quantity of engine oil. If equipped, fill the automatic transaxle with the proper type and quantity of fluid. Refill the power steering reservoir and bleed the system.

36. Start the engine, allow it to reach normal operating temperatures and check for leaks. Charge the air conditioning system.

37. Install the hood, aligning the marks that were made during the removal procedure.

2.5L Engine

AUTOMATIC TRANSAXLE

The engine and transaxle are lifted from the engine compartment as an assembly.

1. Relieve the fuel system pressure. Disconnect the battery cables and remove the battery and battery tray. Mark the position of the hood on its hinges and remove the hood.

2. Remove the air cleaner assembly and fresh air duct. Loosen the alternator belt tensioner locknut and adjuster bolt and remove the belt.

3. Raise and safely support the vehicle. Remove the front wheel and tire assemblies and the splash shields.

4. Remove the 6 transverse member bolts and remove the transverse member.

5. Disconnect the front and rear oxygen sensor connectors. Remove the exhaust pipe-to-exhaust manifold nuts.

6. Disconnect the oil pressure switch electrical connector, located at the oil filter. Remove the halfshafts.

7. Loosen the power steering belt tensioner locknut and adjuster bolt and remove the belt.

8. Remove the 3 power steering pump mounting bolts through the holes in the pump pulley. Remove the power steering hose bracket-to-power steering pump bolt and the pump rear bracket bolt. Secure the pump aside

with mechanics wire, leaving the hoses connected.

9. If equipped, remove the 4 A/C compressor mounting bolts and secure the compressor aside with mechanics wire, leaving the refrigerant lines attched. Do not let the compressor hang by the refrigerant lines.

10. Lower the vehicle and drain the cooling system.

11. Remove the radiator hoses and overflow hose. Disconnect the cooling fan electrical connectors. Disconnect and plug the transaxle cooler lines. Remove the radiator/cooling fan assembly.

12. Label and disconnect the wiring from the alternator. Remove the 2 A/C and alternator wiring harness retaining bolts, then disconnect the harness from the engine block.

13. Label and disconnect the electrical connectors from the fuel rail, vehicle speed sensor, starter, throttle position sensor, knock sensor, EGR, air bypass valve, EGR valve position sensor, neutral safety switch, engine coolant temperature sensor, cooling fan engine coolant temperature sensor, temperature gauge sending unit and crank position sensor.

14. Label and disconnect the vacuum hoses from the cruise control actuator, EGR, throttle body, power brake booster, A/C control head and fuel pressure regulator.

15. Remove the 2 heater hoses from the thermostat housing. Remove the wiring harness grounds.

16. If equipped, disconnect the cruise control actuator electrical connector. Remove the 2 nuts from the actuator bracket and position the actuator and bracket aside.

17. Disconnect the fuel supply and return lines and discard the copper crush washer. Remove the 2 fuel line retaining bolts from the fuel line bracket.

18. Disconnect the throttle cable from the throttle body. Remove the 2 nuts from the fuel filter bracket and position the filter aside, without disconnecting the fuel lines.

19. Remove the spring clip from the shift cable bracket and pull the cable from the switch. Remove the 2 bolts from the cooling fan relay bracket and position the bracket aside.

20. Raise and safely support the vehicle. Remove the front and rear transaxle mount through bolts.

21. Lower the vehicle. Attach suitable lifting equipment to the engine lifting eyes and remove any slack.

22. Remove the left-hand transaxle mount through bolt and the right-hand transaxle mount through bolt and 2 nuts. Remove the right-hand engine mount from the vehicle.

23. Carefully lift the engine/transaxle assembly from the vehicle. Separate the transaxle from the engine, if necessary.

To install:

24. If necessary, connect the engine and transaxle. Tighten the engine-to-transaxle bolts and the transaxle-to-engine bolts to 73 ft. lbs. (99 Nm).

25. Carefully lower the engine/transaxle assembly into position in the engine compartment. Install the right-hand engine mount. Tighten the through bolt to 68 ft. lbs. (93 Nm) and the nuts to 76 ft. lbs. (103 Nm).

26. Install the left-hand transaxle mount through bolt and tighten to 86 ft. lbs. (116 Nm). Remove the engine lifting equipment.

27. Raise and safely support the vehicle. Install the front and rear transaxle mount through bolts and tighten to 86 ft. lbs. (116 Nm).

28. Lower the vehicle. Align the cooling fan relay bracket and install the 2 bolts. Tighten to 88 inch lbs. (10 Nm).

29. Install the shift cable and retain with the spring clip. Align the fuel filter and install the nuts. Tighten to 88 inch lbs. (10 Nm).

30. If equipped, connect the vacuum line to the A/C control head. Connect the vacuum line to the power brake booster.

31. Connect the throttle cable and vacuum lines to the throttle body. Connect the vacuum line to the fuel pressure regulator.

32. Align the fuel line bracket and install the bolts. Tighten to 88 inch lbs. (10 Nm). Connect the fuel supply and return lines, using a new copper crush washer. Tighten the supply line to 25 ft. lbs. (34 Nm).

33. If equipped, align the cruise control actuator and install the nuts. Connect the actuator electrical connector.

34. Install the wiring harness grounds and connect the heater hoses to the thermostat housing.

35. Connect the electrical connectors for the crank position sensor, engine coolant temperature sensor, cooling fan engine coolant temperature sensor, temperature gauge sending unit, neutral safety switch, EGR valve position sensor, air bypass valve solenoid, EGR, knock sensor, throttle position sensor, starter, vehicle speed sensor and fuel rail.

36. Connect the vacuum hose to the EGR and, if equipped, cruise control actuator.

37. Align the A/C and alternator wiring harness and install the 2 bolts. Connect the 2 electrical connectors to the top of the distributor.

38. Install the radiator/cooling fan assembly and connect the cooling fan electrical connectors. Unplug and connect the transaxle oil cooler lines and install the radiator hoses.

39. Raise and safely support the vehicle. If equipped, install the A/C compressor and tighten the bolts to 38 ft. lbs. (51 Nm).

40. Align the power steering pump and install the rear bracket bolt. Tighten to 34 ft. lbs. (46 Nm). Install the power steering hose bracket bolt and tighten to 34 ft. lbs. (46 Nm).

41. Install the 3 power steering pump bolts through the pulley and tighten to 34 ft. lbs. (46 Nm). Install the power steering belt and adjust the tension.

42. Install the halfshafts. Connect the oil pressure switch electrical connector.

43. Install the exhaust pipe to the manifolds and tighten the nuts to 41 ft. lbs. (55 Nm). Connect the front and rear oxygen sensor connectors.

44. Align the transverse member and install the 6 bolts. Tighten to 93 ft. lbs. (126 Nm).

45. Install the splash shields and the wheel and tire assemblies. Lower the vehicle.

46. Install the alternator belt and adjust the tension. Make sure all electrical connectors and vacuum hose are connected.

47. Install the air cleaner assembly and fresh air duct. Install the hood, aligning the marks that were made during removal.

48. Install the battery tray and battery. Connect the battery cables.

49. Fill the cooling system. If necessary, fill the engine and transaxle with the proper types and quantities of oil.

50. Start the engine and bring to normal operating temperature. Check for leaks and proper operation. Stop the engine and check all fluid levels.

MANUAL TRANSAXLE

The engine and transaxle are lifted from the engine compartment as an assembly.

1. Relieve the fuel system pressure. Disconnect the battery cables and remove the battery and battery tray.

2. Mark the position of the hood on its hinges and remove the hood. Remove the air cleaner assembly and fresh air duct.

3. Raise and safely support the vehicle. Remove the front wheel and tire assemblies and the splash shields.

4. Remove the 6 transverse member bolts and remove the transverse member.

5. Remove the 2 bolts and 6 nuts from the transaxle cradle and remove the cradle.

6. Disconnect the front and rear oxygen sensor connectors and remove the exhaust pipe-to-exhaust manifold nuts.

7. Remove the extension bar, nut and washer, then remove the exten-

sion bar from the transaxle. Remove the transaxle shift linkage through bolt and nut, then disengage the linkage from the transaxle.

8. Disconnect the A/C and oil pressure switch electrical connectors. Disconnect and plug the hydraulic line at the slave cylinder, then remove the 2 spring clips from the line.

9. Remove the halfshafts. Remove the 3 bolts from the rear transaxle mount and remove the mount.

10. Loosen the locknut and adjuster bolt on the power steering belt tensioner and remove the belt. Remove the 3 power steering pump mounting bolts working through the pulley holes.

11. Remove the rear bracket bolt from the power steering pump and secure the pump aside with mechanics wire.

12. If equipped, remove the 4 A/C compressor mounting bolts and secure the compressor aside with mechanics wire, leaving the refrigerant lines attched. Do not let the compressor hang by the refrigerant lines.

13. Remove the power steering hose bracket from the pump. Loosen the alternator belt tensioner locknut and adjuster bolt and remove the belt.

14. Remove the radiator hoses and overflow hose. Disconnect the cooling fan electrical connectors. Remove the radiator/cooling fan assembly.

15. Label and disconnect the electrical connectors at the alternator. Remove the 2 A/C and alternator wiring harness bolts, then disconnect the harness from the engine block.

16. Label and disconnect the electrical connectors from the distributor, fuel rail, vehicle speed sensor, starter, throttle position sensor, engine coolant temperature sensor, cooling fan engine coolant temperature sensor, temperature gauge sending unit, knock sensor, crank position sensor, EGR valve, park/neutral position switch, air bypass valve solenoid, EGR valve position sensor and, if equipped, cruise control actuator.

17. Label and disconnect the vacuum hoses from the cruise control actuator, if equipped, EGR valve and fuel pressure regulator.

18. Remove the ground-to-engine bracket bolt located near the starter. If equipped, remove the 2 nuts from the cruise control actuator and position aside.

19. Remove the transaxle ground and backup light switch from the rear of the transaxle. Remove the starter-to-chassis ground.

20. Disconnect the heater hoses from the engine. Disconnect the fuel supply and return lines. Remove the 2 fuel line retaining bolts and bracket.

21. Label and disconnect the vacuum lines and the accelerator cable from the throttle body. Label and disconnect the vacuum line from the intake manifold to the A/C control head and the power brake booster vacuum hose.

22. Remove the 2 fuel filter mounting nuts and position the filter aside, leaving the fuel lines connected.

23. Attach suitable engine lifting equipment to the engine lifting eyes and take up any slack.

24. Remove both of the left-hand transaxle mount nuts and through bolt. Remove both front transaxle mount nuts and remove the 2 nuts and the through bolt from the right-hand engine mount.

25. Carefully lift the engine/transaxle assembly from the vehicle. Separate the engine and transaxle, if necessary.

To install:

26. If necessary, assemble the engine and transaxle. Tighten the engine-to-transaxle and transaxle-to-engine bolts to the proper specification.

27. Carefully lower the engine/transaxle assembly into position in the engine compartment.

28. Install the rear transaxle mount. Tighten the nuts to 68 ft. lbs. (93 Nm) and the through bolt to 86 ft. lbs. (116 Nm).

29. Install the front transaxle mount. Tighten the nuts to 75 ft. lbs. (102 Nm) and the through bolt to 86 ft. lbs. (116 Nm).

30. Install the left-hand transaxle mount. Tighten the nuts to 77 ft. lbs. (104 Nm) and the through bolt to 86 ft. lbs. (116 Nm).

31. Install the right-hand transaxle mount. Tighten the nuts to 77 ft. lbs. (104 Nm) and the through bolt to 68 ft. lbs. (93 Nm). Remove the engine lifting equipment.

32. Raise and safely support the ve-

hicle. Install the power steering pump and tighten the bolts to 34 ft. lbs. (46 Nm).

33. Tighten the power steering pump rear bracket bolt to 34 ft. lbs. (46 Nm). Install the power steering belt and adjust the tension.

34. Install the A/C compressor and tighten the bolts to 38 ft. lbs. (51 Nm). Install the alternator and A/C belt and adjust the tension.

35. Align the extension bar and tighten the nut to 33 ft. lbs. (46 Nm). Install the shift linkage and tighten the bolt to 16 ft. lbs. (22 Nm).

36. Install the halfshafts. Install the transaxle cradle. Tighten the cradle mounting bolts and nuts **B** to 68 ft. lbs. (93 Nm), nuts **A** to 77 ft. lbs. (104 Nm) and nuts **C** to 44 ft. lbs. (60 Nm).

37. Install the exhaust pipe to the exhaust manifolds and tighten the nuts to 41 ft. lbs. (55 Nm). Connect the oxygen sensor connectors.

38. Install the transverse member and tighten the bolts to 93 ft. lbs. (126 Nm). Install the splash shields and wheel and tire assemblies and lower the vehicle.

39. Install the power steering hose bracket bolt to the pump.

40. Connect the electrical connectors to the knock sensor, engine coolant temperature sensor, cooling fan engine coolant temperature sensor, temperature gauge sending unit, crank position sensor, EGR solenoids, EGR valve position sensor, vehicle speed sensor, starter, backup light switch, fuel injectors, throttle position sensor, distributor and park/neutral position switch.

41. Connect the vacuum hoses to the A/C control head, located in the right-hand rear of the engine compartment, EGR valve, fuel pressure regulator

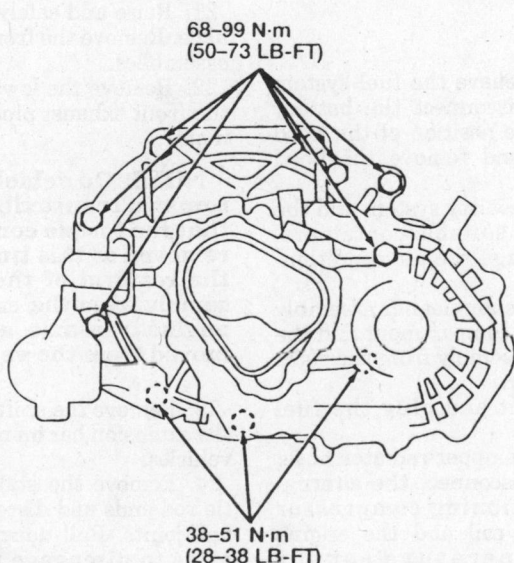

68–99 N·m
(50–73 LB-FT)

38–51 N·m
(28–38 LB-FT)

Engine and transaxle mounting bolt Identification—2.5L engine with manual transaxle

and, if equipped, cruise control actuator.

42. Install the starter-to-chassis grounds, the transaxle ground and the ground-to-engine bracket bolt.

43. Connect the heater hoses. Connect the fuel supply and return lines. Tighten the fuel line bracket bolts to 88 inch lbs. (10 Nm) and the fuel supply line to 25 ft. lbs. (34 Nm).

44. Install the fuel filter to the bracket and install the 2 nuts. Install the cruise control actuator with the nuts and connect the electrical connector.

45. Connect the vacuum lines to the throttle body and connect the accelerator cable. Connect the power brake booster vacuum hose.

46. Connect the air bypass valve, oil pressure switch, A/C compressor and alternator electrical connectors. Connect the A/C and alternator harness bracket to the engine.

47. Install the battery tray. Connect the hydraulic line to the slave cylinder and install the line bracket spring clips.

48. Install the radiator/cooling fan assembly and connect the cooling fan electrical connectors. Install the radiator hoses.

49. Install the air cleaner housing and ducts. Connect all vacuum and electrical connectors.

50. Install the battery and connect the cables. Install the hood, aligning the marks that were made during removal.

51. Fill the cooling system. If necessary, fill the engine and transaxle with the proper types and quantities of oil.

52. Bleed the air from the clutch hydraulic system.

53. Start the engine and bring to normal operating temperature. Check for leaks and proper operation. Stop the engine and check all fluid levels.

3.0L Engine

1. Properly relieve the fuel system pressure and disconnect the battery cables. Mark the position of the hood on its hinges and remove the hood assembly.

2. Drain the cooling system and the engine oil into suitable containers. Properly discharge the air conditioning system.

3. Remove the air cleaner assembly from the engine compartment and the vacuum valve assembly from the right side shock tower.

4. Disconnect and plug the fuel lines.

5. Remove the upper radiator hose.

6. Tag and disconnect the alternator, air conditioning compressor clutch, ignition coil and the engine coolant temperature sensor connectors.

7. Tag and disconnect the TFI module connector, injector wiring harness, air charge temperature sensor and the throttle position sensor.

8. Disconnect the oil pressure sending switch, ground straps at the intake manifold on both sides of the engine and the block heater, if equipped.

9. Disconnect the EGR sensor and the oil level sensor, located on the back side of the oil pan.

10. Tag and disconnect all vacuum lines, heater hoses and crankcase ventilation hoses.

11. Disconnect and plug the high pressure and return lines at the power steering pump.

12. Disconnect the air conditioning lines from the condenser and chassis, leaving the manifold lines attached to the compressor.

13. Disconnect the accelerator linkage, transmission throttle valve linkage and the cruise control cable, if equipped.

14. Remove the battery, battery tray and the fuse box assembly.

15. Disconnect and set aside the cruise control servo assembly and the transmission shift cable, if equipped with an automatic transaxle.

16. Disconnect all automatic transaxle wiring connectors and the speedometer cable on conventional (analog) cluster vehicles.

17. Disconnect the Vehicle Speed Sensor (VSS) connector on electronic cluster vehicles.

18. Disconnect and plug the cooler lines at the transaxle, if equipped with automatic transaxle.

19. Remove the clutch slave cylinder, leaving the pressure line attached, if equipped with a manual transaxle, and set it aside.

20. Remove the radiator, cooling fan and shroud.

21. Raise and safely support the vehicle. Remove the front wheel and tire assemblies.

22. Remove the lower radiator hose, the front exhaust pipe and the starter motor.

NOTE: On vehicles with an automatic transaxle, it is advised that the torque converter nuts be removed at this time to facilitate the removal of the transaxle assembly from the engine after the engine/transaxle assembly is removed from the vehicle.

23. Remove the shift control rod and the extension bar on manual transaxle vehicles.

24. Remove the stabilizer links and tie rod ends and disconnect the lower ball joints. Pull down on the control arms to disengage them from the spindle.

25. Remove the dynamic damper mounting bolts on the right halfshaft assembly.

26. Disengage both halfshafts by pulling outward on both side brake and spindle assemblies. In this procedure, the halfshaft assemblies are left in the chassis.

27. Install two T88C-7025-AH transaxle plugs or equivalent, into the differential side gears.

NOTE: Failure to install the transaxle plugs may allow the differential side gears to become misaligned, making halfshaft installation difficult or impossible, without disassembling the differential.

28. Disconnect the lower transmission mount and safely, lower the vehicle.

29. Install and position suitable engine lifting devices. Disconnect the lower front engine mount.

30. Disconnect the right side upper engine mount at the timing cover and the left side upper engine mount at the transaxle case.

31. Carefully, lift the engine and the transaxle assembly out of the vehicle.

To install:

32. Lower the engine and the transaxle assembly into the vehicle.

33. Connect and tighten the upper and lower engine mounts. Remove the engine lifting devices.

34. Remove both transaxle plugs and install the halfshafts on both sides.

35. Install the dynamic damper mounting bolts on the right side halfshaft.

36. Engage the control arms and install the lower ball joints, tie rod ends and the stabilizer links.

37. Install the shift control rod and extension bar, if equipped with a manual transaxle.

38. Replace the torque converter nuts, if equipped with an automatic transaxle.

39. Install the starter, front exhaust pipe and the lower radiator hose.

40. Replace the front tires and wheels. Safely, lower the vehicle.

41. Install the cooling fan, shroud and the radiator.

42. Install the clutch release cable with the hose attached, if equipped.

43. Reconnect the cooler lines at the transmission, if equipped.

44. Connect the Vehicle Speed Sensor (VSS) on electronic cluster vehicles.

45. Connect all automatic transmission wiring connectors and the speedometer cable on conventional (analog) cluster vehicles.

46. Install the cruise control servo

assembly and the transmission shift cable, if equipped.

47. Replace the battery, battery tray and the fuse box assembly.

48. Connect the accelerator linkage, transmission throttle valve linkage and the cruise control cable, if equipped.

49. Connect the air conditioning lines from the condenser and chassis.

50. Install the high pressure and return lines to the power steering pump.

51. Reconnect all vacuum lines, heater hoses and crankcase ventilation hoses.

52. Reconnect the EGR sensor and the oil level sensor on the back side of the oil pan.

53. Connect the oil pressure sending switch connector, the ground straps on both sides of the engine and the block heater, if equipped.

54. Reconnect the TFI module connector, injector wiring harness, air charge temperature sensor and the throttle position sensor.

55. Install the alternator, air conditioning compressor clutch, ignition coil and the engine coolant temperature sensor.

56. Connect the fuel lines and replace the upper radiator hose.

57. Install the air cleaner assembly in the engine compartment and the vacuum valve assembly on the right side shock tower.

58. Refill the cooling system. Fill the crankcase with the proper type and quantity of engine oil. If equipped, fill the automatic transaxle with the proper type and quantity of fluid.

59. Reconnect the battery cables and install the hood assembly, aligning the marks that were made during the removal procedure.

60. Start the engine and bring to normal operating temperature. Check for any leaks.

61. Recharge the air conditioning system.

Engine Mounts

REMOVAL & INSTALLATION

1. Disconnect the negative battery cable.

2. If necessary, raise and support the vehicle safely.

3. Using an engine lifting device, attach it to the engine and support it's weight.

4. Remove the engine mount-to-engine bolts/nuts, through bolt and, if necessary, the engine mount-to-chassis bolts/nuts. Remove the mount.

5. To install, reverse the removal procedure. Remove the engine lift.

Cylinder Head

REMOVAL & INSTALLATION

2.0L Engine

1. Relieve the fuel system pressure and disconnect the negative battery cable. Drain the cooling system.

2. Remove the intake manifold.

3. Remove the accessory drive belts. Remove the power steering pump bolts and secure the pump aside with mechanics wire, leaving the hoses attached.

4. Remove the alternator bracket nut and bolt and position the bracket aside. Remove the exhaust manifold.

5. Label and disconnect the spark plug wires. Remove the power steering hose brackets from the cylinder head cover.

6. Disconnect the hoses from the cylinder head cover and loosen the cover bolts in 2–3 steps, in the reverse order of the torque sequence. Remove the cylinder head cover.

7. Remove the timing belt. Label and disconnect the distributor/coil connectors, engine coolant temperature sensor connector, cooling fan coolant temperature sensor connector and temperature gauge sensor connector.

8. Remove the coolant temperature sensor housing from the cylinder head. Remove the distributor.

9. Remove the camshafts.

10. Loosen the cylinder head bolts, in 2–3 steps, in the reverse order of the torque sequence. Remove the bolts and the cylinder head.

11. Clean all gasket mating surfaces. Inspect the cylinder head for damage, cracks, and water and oil leakage. Check the head gasket surface for dis-

tortion using a straightedge and feeler gauge. Maximum allowable distortion is 0.004 in. (0.10mm).

To install:

12. Position a new cylinder head gasket on the cylinder block and install the cylinder head.

13. Install new cylinder head bolts and tighten in 2 steps, in sequence, to 16 ft. lbs. (22 Nm).

14. Paint a mark on the edge of each cylinder head bolt to use as a reference. Turn each bolt, in sequence, 90 degrees. Again, turn each bolt, in sequence, an additional 90 degrees.

15. Install the camshafts. Install the distributor and connect the distributor/coil connectors.

16. Install the timing belt.

17. Install a new cylinder head cover gasket on the cylinder head cover. Apply sealant to the cylinder head surface in the area adjacent to the front camshaft caps, then install the cover. Tighten the bolts in 2 steps, in sequence, to 69 inch lbs. (7 Nm).

18. Connect the hoses to the cylinder head cover. Connect the spark plug wires.

19. Install the exhaust manifold and the alternator bracket. Tighten the bracket nut and bolt to 19 ft. lbs. (25 Nm).

20. Install the alternator belt and adjust the tension.

21. Loosely install the power steering pump through and lock bolts. Connect the pump pressure switch connector.

22. Install the power steering pump belt and adjust the tension. Tighten the pump through bolt to 45 ft. lbs. (61 Nm) and the lock bolt to 34 ft. lbs. (46 Nm).

23. Install the power steering pump belt shield and tighten the bolts to 86

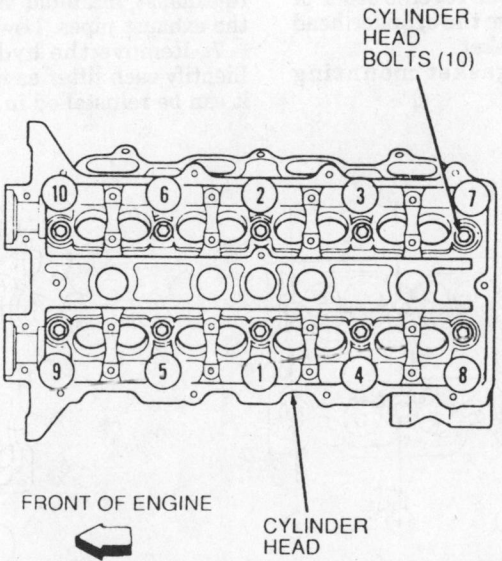

CYLINDER HEAD BOLTS (10)

FRONT OF ENGINE

CYLINDER HEAD

Cylinder head bolt torque sequence—2.0L Engine

inch lbs. (9 Nm). Install the power steering hose brackets to the cylinder head cover and tighten the bolts to 88 inch lbs. (10 Nm).

24. Install the coolant temperature sensor housing with a new gasket. Tighten the bolts to 19 ft. lbs. (25 Nm). Connect the electrical connectors at the housing.

25. Install the intake manifold.

26. Connect the negative battery cable. Fill and bleed the cooling system. Run the engine and check for proper operation.

2.2L Engine

1. Disconnect the negative battery cable. Remove the drive belts.

2. Remove the crankshaft pulley as follows:

    a. Raise and safely support the vehicle.

    b. Remove the right front wheel and tire assembly.

    c. Remove the right inner fender panel.

    d. Remove the 6 bolts, pulley and baffle plate.

    e. Lower the vehicle.

3. Remove the timing belt covers and timing belt.

4. Remove the exhaust manifold, intake manifold and the distributor.

5. Remove rocker arm cover.

6. Drain the cooling system.

7. Remove the spark plug wires and the spark plugs.

8. Tag and disconnect the electrical connectors from the thermostat housing sensors. Remove the upper radiator hose and the water bypass hose.

9. Remove the front and rear engine lifting eyes and the engine ground wire. Remove the front and rear housings and gaskets.

10. Remove the cylinder head bolts, a little at a time, in the reverse order of installation. Remove the cylinder head and discard the gasket.

11. Clean the gasket mounting surfaces.

To install:

12. Position a new cylinder head gasket on the cylinder block. Install the cylinder head and torque the bolts, in sequence, to 29–32 ft. lbs. (40–42 Nm) and then again, in sequence, to 59–64 ft. lbs. (80–86 Nm).

13. Install the front and rear housings, using new gaskets, and tighten the bolts/nuts to 14–19 ft. lbs. (19–25 Nm).

14. Install the distributor and the front and rear engine lifting eyes.

15. Install the spark plugs and spark plug wires.

16. Install the intake and exhaust manifolds.

17. Install the rocker arm cover.

18. Install the timing belt and timing covers.

18. Install the crankshaft pulley and the drive belts.

19. Fill the cooling system and connect the negative battery cable.

20. Run the engine and check for any leaks. Check the ignition timing.

2.5L Engine

1. Relieve the fuel system pressure and disconnect the negative battery cable. Drain the cooling system.

2. Remove the timing belt covers and the timing belt. Remove the intake manifold.

3. Disconnect the ventilation pipe from the left cylinder head cover, remove the bolts and remove the cylinder head covers.

4. Remove the camshafts. Remove the 3 bolts and the seal plate from the front of the engine.

5. Remove the 4 coolant elbow bolts and the coolant elbow. Raise and safely support the vehicle.

6. Disconnect the oxygen sensor connectors. Remove the exhaust pipe-to-exhaust manifold nuts and lower the exhaust pipes. Lower the vehicle.

7. Remove the hydraulic lifters. Identify each lifter as it is removed so it can be reinstalled in the same posi-

tion. If the lifters are to be reused, store them upside down in a sealed container.

8. Loosen the cylinder head bolts, in 2–3 steps, in the reverse order of the torque sequence. Remove the bolts and remove the cylinder heads.

9. Clean all gasket mating surfaces. Inspect the cylinder head for damage, cracks, and water and oil leakage. Check the head gasket surface for distortion using a straightedge and feeler gauge. Maximum allowable distortion is 0.004 in. (0.10mm).

To install:

10. If removed, install the exhaust manifolds using new gaskets. Tighten the exhaust manifold nuts and bolts to 18 ft. lbs. (25 Nm). Tighten the manifold heat shield bolts to 88 inch lbs. (10 Nm).

11. Position new head gaskets on the cylinder block. The gaskets cannot be interchanged between sides and are marked **R** and **L** for right and left side.

12. Install the cylinder heads. Apply clean engine oil to the threads of new cylinder head bolts and install. Tighten the cylinder head bolts in 2–3 steps, in sequence, to 19 ft. lbs. (26 Nm).

13. Paint a mark on the edge of each cylinder head bolt to use as a reference. Turn each bolt, in sequence, 90 degrees. Again, turn each bolt, in sequence, an additional 90 degrees.

14. Apply clean engine oil to the hydraulic lifters and install them in their original positions. Make sure they move freely in the bores.

15. Install the camshafts. Raise and safely support the vehicle.

16. Connect the exhaust pipes to the manifolds and tighten the nuts to 41 ft. lbs. (55 Nm). Connect the oxygen sensor connectors.

17. Apply selant to the cylinder head surface in the area of the front and rear camshaft caps. Install new gaskets and install the cylinder head covers. Tighten the bolts in 2 steps, in sequence, to 78 inch lbs. (8 Nm).

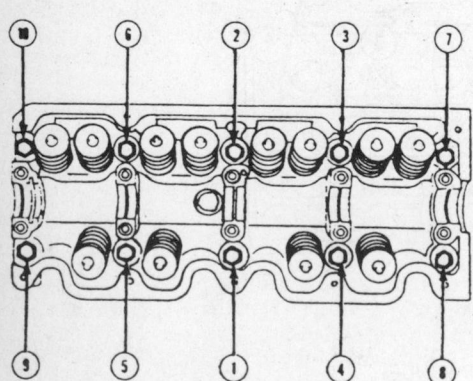

Cylinder head bolt torque sequence— 2.2L Engine

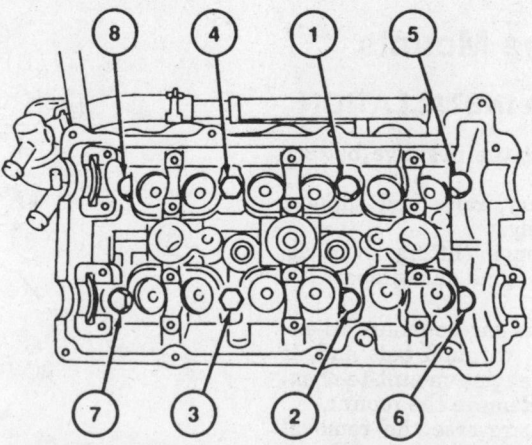

Cylinder head bolt torque sequence—2.5L Engine

18. Install the intake manifold. Install the timing belt and timing belt covers.

19. Connect the negative battery cable. Fill and bleed the cooling system. Run the engine and check for proper operation.

3.0L Engine

1. Properly relieve the fuel system pressure and disconnect the negative battery cable.

2. Drain the cooling system.

3. Remove the air cleaner hoses from the throttle body and rocker arm cover.

4. Disconnect the fuel lines from the fuel supply manifold.

5. Tag and disconnect the vacuum lines from the throttle body.

6. Tag and disconnect the air charge temperature sensor, throttle position sensor and air bypass solenoid electrical connectors.

7. Remove the EGR supply tube and the MAP sensor from the throttle body.

8. Disconnect the throttle cable and, if equipped with automatic transaxle, the throttle valve control cable from the throttle lever.

9. Remove the fuel rail bracket bolt from the throttle body, remove the 6 throttle body attaching bolts and remove the throttle body.

10. Disconnect the fuel injector harness stand-offs from the inboard rocker arm cover studs and each injector and remove from the engine.

11. Disconnect the upper radiator hose and heater hoses and move them aside.

12. Disconnect the engine coolant temperature sensor and the coolant temperature sending unit connectors.

13. Mark the distributor housing to block position, then remove the distributor cap and mark the rotor position. Remove the distributor.

14. Tag and disconnect the spark plug wires from the spark plugs and remove the wires and the distributor cap.

15. Remove the ignition coil and bracket assembly from the left cylinder head and set aside.

16. If the left cylinder head is being removed, perform the following:

   a. Remove the power steering protective shroud.

   b. Using a ½ in. drive breaker bar, rotate the automatic belt tensioner clockwise and remove the accessory drive belt.

   c. Remove the automatic belt tensioner.

   d. Remove the nut and remove the power steering pulley.

   e. Remove the air conditioning brace to the power steering support retaining bolts.

   f. Remove the 3 power steering support retaining bolts.

   g. Remove the engine oil dipstick tube attaching nut from the exhaust manifold stud. Rotate or remove the tube from the manifold.

NOTE: The power steering support bracket may be pulled away from the engine with the alternator and power steering pump intact.

17. Remove the spark plugs.

18. Remove the exhaust manifold(s), heat shield(s) and inlet pipe(s).

19. Remove the rocker arm covers.

20. Loosen the rocker arm fulcrum retaining bolts and remove the rocker arms, fulcrums and retaining bolts.

NOTE: The No. 3 intake valve pushrod must be removed to allow removal of the intake manifold, regardless of which cylinder head is being removed.

21. Remove the pushrods. Note the position of each so they may be reinstalled in their original positions.

22. Remove the intake manifold.

23. Remove the cylinder head retaining bolts and remove the cylinder head(s). Remove and discard the cylinder head gasket(s).

24. Clean all gasket mating surfaces.

To install:

25. Position new head gasket(s) on the cylinder block, using the dowel pins for alignment. Carefully position the cylinder head(s) on the block.

26. Lightly oil the threads and install the cylinder head bolts, finger-tight. On 1990 vehicles, tighten the bolts, in sequence, in 2 steps; first to 37 ft. lbs. (50 Nm), and then to 68 ft. lbs. (92 Nm). On 1991–92 vehicles, tighten the bolts, in sequence, to 59 ft. lbs. (80 Nm), then back off all bolts a minimum of 1 full turn. Retighten the bolts, in sequence, in 2 steps; first to 37 ft. lbs. (50 Nm), and then to 68 ft. lbs. (92 Nm).

27. Install the intake manifold.

28. Install the distributor, aligning the marks that were made during removal.

29. Dip each pushrod in heavy engine oil, then install in their original positions.

30. For each rocker arm, rotate the crankshaft until the lifter rests on the base circle of the camshaft lobe, before tightening the fulcrum mounting bolts. Position the rocker arms over the pushrods and tighten the fulcrum mounting bolts to 24 ft. lbs. (32 Nm). Make sure the fulcrums and pushrods are fully seated before tightening.

NOTE: If the original valve train components are being installed, a valve clearance check is

not required. If a component has been replaced, perform a valve clearance check.

31. Install the exhaust manifold(s) and tighten the retaining bolts to 18 ft. lbs. (25 Nm). Install the inlet pipe retaining nuts and tighten to 20 ft. lbs. (27 Nm).

32. Install the dipstick tube into the cylinder block. Tighten the retaining nut to 13 ft. lbs. (18 Nm).

33. Install the spark plugs and tighten to 7–15 ft. lbs. (9–20 Nm).

34. Install the rocker arm covers.

35. Install the fuel injector electrical harness to the injectors and inboard rocker arm cover studs. Connect the engine harness to the main harness and secure with the retainers.

36. Install the distributor cap and connect the spark plug wires to the spark plugs.

37. Position a new gasket and the throttle body on the lower intake manifold. Install the attaching bolts and tighten to 15–22 ft. lbs. (20–30 Nm).

38. Install the fuel rail bracket bolt on the throttle body. Connect the throttle cable and, if equipped with automatic transaxle, the throttle valve control cable to the throttle lever.

39. Install the MAP sensor and the EGR supply tube to the throttle body.

40. Connect the electrical connectors for the air charge temperature sensor, throttle position sensor and air bypass solenoid.

41. Install the ignition coil and bracket. Tighten the bolts to 35 ft. lbs. (48 Nm).

42. If the left cylinder head was removed, perform the following:

   a. Install the power steering support bracket. Tighten the 3 retaining bolts to 35 ft. lbs. (48 Nm).

   b. Install the air conditioning brace to the power steering support bracket retaining bolt. Tighten the bolt to 18 ft. lbs. (25 Nm).

   c. Install the power steering pump pulley. Tighten the retaining nut to 47 ft. lbs. (64 Nm).

   d. Install the automatic belt tensioner. Tighten the retaining bolt to 35 ft. lbs. (48 Nm). Install the accessory drive belt.

   e. Install the power steering protective shroud. Tighten the 2 retaining bolts to 7 ft. lbs. (10 Nm).

43. Connect the fuel lines to the fuel supply rail.

44. Connect the upper radiator and heater hoses. Connect the vacuum lines to their original locations.

45. Change the engine oil and filter. This is necessary because engine coolant is corrosive to all engine bearing material. Replacing the engine oil after removal of a coolant carrying component guards against later failure.

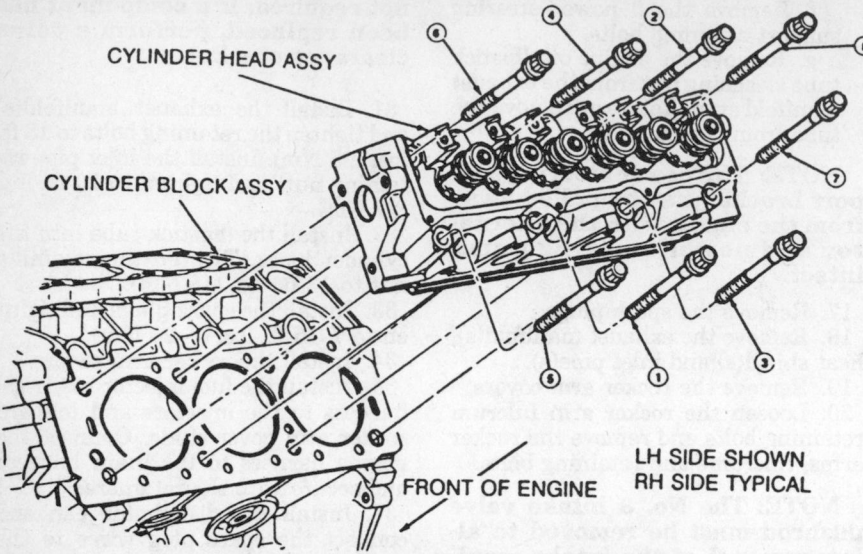

Cylinder head bolt torque sequence—3.0L Engine

46. Install the air cleaner fresh air hose to the throttle body and air cleaner. Install the closure hose to the rocker arm cover.
47. Fill the cooling system.
48. Connect the negative battery cable.
49. Start the engine and check for leaks. Check the ignition timing.

Valve Lifters

REMOVAL & INSTALLATION

2.0L and 2.5L Engines

1. Disconnect the negative battery cable.
2. Remove the cylinder head cover(s).
3. Remove the accessory drive belts, timing belt covers and timing belt.
4. Remove the camshafts.
5. Remove the hydraulic lifters. Identify each lifter as it is removed so it can be reinstalled in the same position. If the lifters are to be reused, store them upside down in a sealed container.

To install:

6. Apply clean engine oil to the lifters, then install them in their original positions.
7. Install the camshafts.
8. Install the timing belt and timing belt covers.
9. Install the accessory drive belts and adjust the tension.
10. Install the cylinder head cover(s) and connect the negative battery cable.

2.2L Engine

NOTE: The 2.2L engine is equipped with Hydraulic Lash

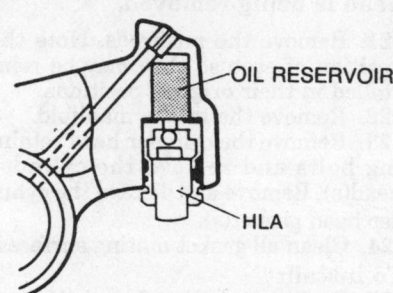

Hydraulic lash adjuster installation— 2.2L Engine

Adjusters (HLA) located in the rocker arms and directly contacting the valve stem tips.

1. Disconnect the negative battery cable.
2. Remove the rocker arm and shaft assemblies.
3. Pull the HLA out of the rocker arm by hand. If removal is difficult, pliers may be used. Do not remove the HLA unless it is absolutely necessary; it may leak oil if the O-ring is damaged.

To install:

4. Pour clean engine oil into the rocker arm reservoir. Apply clean engine oil to the HLA.
5. Carefully install the HLA into the rocker arm, being careful not to damage the O-ring.
6. Install the rocker arm/shaft assemblies and remaining components in the reverse order of removal.

3.0L Engine

NOTE: Before replacing a lifter for noisy operation, make sure the noise is not caused by improper valve-to-rocker arm clearance, worn rocker arms or pushrods.

1. Disconnect the negative battery cable.
2. Drain the cooling system.
3. Remove the rocker arm covers, and the throttle body and intake manifold assembly.
4. Loosen each rocker arm fulcrum mounting bolt to allow the rocker arm to be lifted off the pushrod and rotated to one side.
5. Remove the pushrods, marking the location of each pushrod to ensure the proper replacement in the original position.
6. Remove the lifter(s), using a magnet. Mark the location of each lifter to ensure the proper replacement in the original position.

NOTE: If the lifters are stuck in the bores due to excessive varnish or gum deposits, it may be necessary to use a hydraulic lifter puller or a claw-type tool to aid in removal. Rotate the lifter back and forth to loosen it from the gum or varnish that may have formed on the lifter.

To install:

7. Lubricate each lifter and bore with heavy engine oil and install the lifters into the bore. Install each lifter in the bore from which it was removed. If new lifters are being installed, check each one for free fit in the bore in which it is to be installed.
8. Lubricate each pushrod with the heavy engine oil and insert in their original position.
9. Place the rocker arms over the pushrods. For each rocker arm, rotate the crankshaft until the lifter rests on the base circle of the camshaft lobe, then position the fulcrums and tighten the mounting bolts to 24 ft. lbs. (32 Nm).
10. Lubricate all the rocker arm assemblies.

NOTE: Fulcrums must be fully seated in the cylinder head and the pushrods must be seated in the rocker arm sockets prior to tightening.

11. Install the throttle body and intake manifold and the rocker arm covers.
12. Connect the negative battery cable.
13. Refill the cooling system and check for leaks.

Valve Lash

CHECKING

2.0L and 2.5L Engines

The hydraulic lifters are not adjustable. When the lifters are removed from the engine, check the friction surfaces for wear or damage. Hold the lifter and try to press the plunger by hand. If the lifter is worn or damaged, or the plunger can be moved by hand, replace the lifter.

2.2L Engine

1. Warm up the engine to normal operating temperature.
2. Check the condition of the engine oil and check the oil pressure. The oil pressure should be 21–36 psi at 1000 rpm.
3. Stop the engine and remove the rocker arm cover.
4. Push down on the hydraulic lash adjuster side of the rocker arm to make sure the hydraulic lash adjuster cannot be compressed.
5. If the hydraulic lash adjuster can be compressed, it must be replaced.

3.0L Engine

This clearance check is usually only needed when the valves, valve seats and/or cylinder head gasket surface have been machined or new parts have been installed. Clearance must be checked when the lifter is completely collapsed.

1. Disconnect the negative battery cable.
2. Remove the rocker arm covers.
3. Rotate the engine until the No. 1 cylinder is at TDC of its compression stroke and check the clearance between the rocker arm and the following valves: No. 1 intake and exhaust, No. 2 exhaust, No. 3 intake, No. 4 exhaust and No. 6 intake.
4. To check the clearance, use lifter bleed down wrench T71P–6513–B or equivalent, to push down on the rocker arm and bleed the oil from the lifter.
5. Insert the appropriate thickness

feeler gauge between the rocker arm and valve stem to check the clearance.
6. Rotate the crankshaft 360 degrees and check the clearance between the rocker arm and the following valves: No. 2 intake, No. 3 exhaust, No. 4 intake, No. 5 intake and exhaust and No. 6 exhaust.
7. The clearance should be 0.09–0.19 in. (2.3–4.8mm).
8. If the clearance is less than specified, shorter pushrods are available to correct the problem. If the clearance is greater than specified, longer pushrods are available.

Rocker Arms/Shafts

REMOVAL & INSTALLATION

2.2L Engine

1. Remove the rocker arm cover.
2. Remove the rocker arm and shaft assembly mounting bolts. Start at the ends and work toward the center of the shafts, when removing the bolts.
3. If necessary, separate the rocker arms and springs from the shafts; be sure to keep the parts in order for reinstallation purposes.
4. Clean and inspect the shafts and rocker arms for wear. Measure the difference between the rocker arm shaft outside diameter and the rocker arm inside diameter; this is the oil clearance. If the oil clearance exceeds 0.004 in. (0.10mm), replace the shaft and/or the rocker arm(s).

To install:

5. If they were disassembled, coat the rocker arm shafts and rocker arms with engine oil and assemble them with the springs. When assembling and installing on the cylinder head, note the notches at the ends of the shafts; they are different on the intake

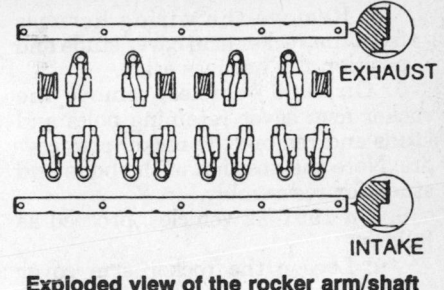

Exploded view of the rocker arm/shaft assemblies—2.2L Engines

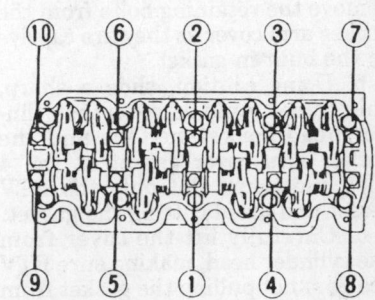

Rocker arm shaft bolt torque sequence—2.2L Engine

and exhaust side and cannot be interchanged.
6. Install the rocker arm/shaft assemblies onto the cylinder head and torque the rocker arm shaft-to-cylinder head bolts, in sequence, to 13–20 ft. lbs. (18–26 Nm), in 2 steps.
7. Install the rocker arm cover.

3.0L Engine

NOTE: The rocker arm covers on 1991–92 3.0L engines are equipped with integral (built-in) gaskets that should last the life of the car. Be sure to adhere to the instructions given in the following procedure that pertain to 1991–92 vehicles. If the integral gaskets become damaged and cannot be reused, replacement gaskets are available.

1. Disconnect the negative battery cable.
2. Tag and disconnect the spark plug wires from the spark plugs. Remove the spark plug wire separator stand-offs from the rocker arm cover studs.
3. If the left side (front) rocker arm cover is being removed, proceed as follows:
   a. Remove the wiring harness from the rocker arm cover studs and position the harness aside.
   b. Disconnect the crankcase hose from the rocker arm cover.
4. If the right side (rear) rocker arm cover is being removed, proceed as follows:
   a. Remove the air intake throttle body assembly.
   b. Remove the PCV valve.

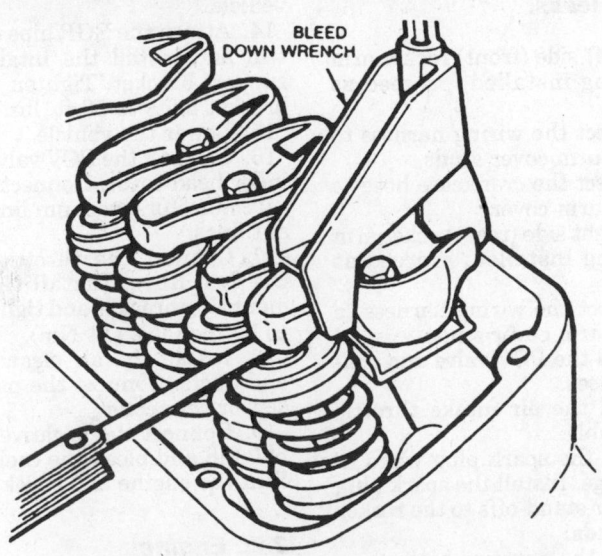

Checking collapsed lifter clearance—3.0L Engine

c. Remove the wiring harness from the rocker arm cover studs and position the harness aside.

5. On 1990 vehicles, remove the rocker arm cover retaining bolts and studs and remove the rocker arm covers. Note the position of the bolts and studs for reassembly.

6. On 1991–92 vehicles, proceed as follows:

a. Loosen the rocker arm cover retaining bolts enough to disengage them from the cylinder head. Do not remove the retaining bolts from the rocker arm cover as they are captive to the built in gasket.

b. Using caution, slide a sharp, thin bladed knife between the cylinder head gasket surface and the rocker arm cover gasket at the 4 RTV junctions. Cut only the RTV sealer and avoid cutting the gasket.

c. Carefully lift the cover from the cylinder head, making sure RTV sealer is not pulling the gasket from the cover.

7. Remove the rocker arm mounting bolts, fulcrums and rocker arms. Identify the position of the rocker arms and fulcrums so they may be reinstalled in their original positions.

8. Inspect the rocker arms, fulcrums and pushrods for wear and/or damage and replace as necessary.

To install:

9. If removed, dip each pushrod in heavy engine oil and install in it's original position. If not removed, lubricate the pushrod ends with heavy engine oil.

10. Dip each rocker arm and fulcrum in heavy engine oil and install in its original position. For each rocker arm, rotate the crankshaft until the lifter rests on the base circle of the camshaft lobe, before tightening the fulcrum mounting bolts to 24 ft. lbs. (32 Nm). Make sure the fulcrum is fully seated in the cylinder head and the pushrod is fully seated in the rocker arm socket before tightening.

NOTE: If the original valve train components are being installed, a valve clearance check is not required. If a component has been replaced, perform a valve clearance check.

11. Lightly oil all bolt and stud threads before installation. Using solvent, clean the cylinder head and rocker arm cover sealing surfaces. On 1990 vehicles, remove all old gasket material and dirt. On 1991–92 vehicles, remove all silicone sealer and dirt; do not allow solvent to come in contact with the integral rocker arm gasket.

12. If the integral gasket is no longer usable on 1991–92 vehicles, it can be replaced as follows:

a. Remove the gasket by pulling it

from the rocker arm gasket channel. Note the bolt and stud locations before removing.

b. Clean the gasket channel with a soft cloth to remove all dirt.

c. Using a suitable solvent, clean off any remaining RTV sealer.

d. Aligning the fastener holes, lay the new gasket onto the channel and install it with your finger.

e. Install a gasket to each fastener by securing the fastener head with a nut driver or socket. Seat the fastener against the cover and, at the same time, roll the gasket around the fastener collar. If installed correctly, all fasteners will be secured by the gasket and will not fall out.

f. Check the gasket for correct installation. A new gasket will lay flat to the rocker arm cover in both the channel and the fastener areas. If the gasket is installed incorrectly, there will be oil leaks.

13. On 1990 vehicles, apply a bead of silicone sealer at the cylinder head-to-intake manifold rail step (2 places per rail) and position a new gasket. Install the rocker arm cover and tighten the retaining bolts to 7–10 ft. lbs. (10–14 Nm).

14. On 1991–92 vehicles, apply a bead of silicone sealer at the cylinder head-to-intake manifold rail step (2 places per rail). Carefully position the cover on the cylinder head and install the bolts and studs. Tighten to 9 ft. lbs. (12 Nm).

NOTE: When positioning the cover to the cylinder head, use a straight down approach to align the bolt holes. Once the cover contacts the RTV sealer, any adjustment for bolt alignment can roll the gasket from the channel, causing oil leaks.

15. If the left side (front) rocker arm cover is being installed, proceed as follows:

a. Connect the wiring harness to the rocker arm cover studs.

b. Connect the crankcase hose to the rocker arm cover.

16. If the right side (rear) rocker arm cover is being installed, proceed as follows:

a. Connect the wiring harness to the rocker arm cover studs.

b. Install the PCV valve and connect the hoses.

c. Install the air intake throttle body assembly.

17. Connect the spark plug wires to the spark plugs. Install the spark plug wire separator stand-offs to the rocker arm cover studs.

18. Connect the negative battery cable. Start the engine and bring to nor-

mal operating temperature. Check for leaks.

Intake Manifold

REMOVAL & INSTALLATION

2.0L Engine

1. Relieve the fuel system pressure and disconnect the negative battery cable. Drain the cooling system.

2. Disconnect the mass air flow sensor electrical connector. Remove the air ducts and air cleaner assembly.

3. Remove the fuel line mounting bracket and disconnect the throttle cable. Disconnect and plug the fuel lines.

4. Disconnect the coolant lines from the air bypass valve and throttle body.

5. Label and disconnect the vacuum lines at the throttle body, and the vacuum lines for the brake booster and cruise control at the intake manifold.

6. Label and disconnect the electrical connectors for the throttle position sensor, EGR temperature sensor, if equipped, EGR solenoid and idle switch, if equipped with automatic transaxle.

7. Disconnect the PCV valve from the cylinder head cover.

8. Raise and safely support the vehicle.

9. Remove the intake manifold support bracket and remove the EGR pipe from the intake manifold.

10. Lower the vehicle. Remove the 5 bolts and 2 nuts and remove the intake manifold.

To install:

11. Clean all gasket mating surfaces.

12. Install the intake manifold, using a new gasket. Tighten the nuts and bolts, in sequence, to 19 ft. lbs. (25 Nm).

13. Raise and safely support the vehicle.

14. Attach the EGR pipe to the manifold and install the intake manifold support bracket. Tighten the support bracket bolts to 38 ft. lbs. (51 Nm).

15. Lower the vehicle.

16. Connect the PCV valve to the cylinder head cover. Connect the electrical connectors, vacuum lines and coolant lines.

17. Connect the throttle cable and the fuel lines. Install the fuel line mounting bracket and tighten the bolt to 97 inch lbs. (11 Nm).

18. Install the air cleaner assembly and ducts. Connect the mass air flow sensor connector.

19. Connect the negative battery cable. Fill and bleed the cooling system. Run the engine and check for leaks.

2.2L Engine

1. Properly relieve the fuel system

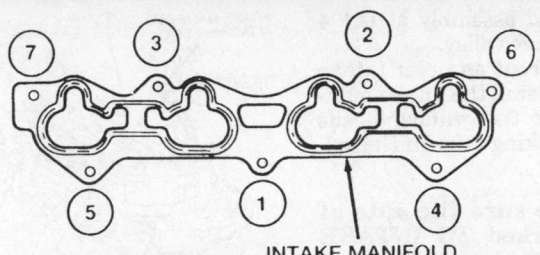

INTAKE MANIFOLD

Intake manifold bolt torque sequence—2.0L Engine

pressure and disconnect the negative battery cable.

2. Drain the cooling system.

3. From the bottom of the intake manifold, remove the water hose.

4. Disconnect the accelerator cables from the throttle body.

5. Remove the air duct from the throttle body.

6. Label and disconnect the vacuum lines and coolant hoses from the throttle body.

7. Tag and disconnect the electrical connectors from the throttle position sensor, the idle switch and the bypass air control valve.

8. Remove the engine lifting bracket mounting bolts from the throttle body and the engine block.

9. Disconnect the coolant line/EGR hose bracket from the throttle body and the throttle cable brackets from the intake plenum.

10. Remove the wire loom bracket. On non-turbocharged engines, remove the EGR back-pressure variable transducer bracket from the right-hand side of the intake plenum. On turbocharged engines, remove the vacuum pipe mounting bolts from the right-hand side of the intake plenum.

11. Remove the PCV hose from the intake plenum. Remove the nuts and bolts retaining the vacuum line assembly bracket at the rear of the intake plenum.

12. Label and disconnect the vacuum lines from the intake plenum.

13. Remove the plenum-to-intake manifold nuts and bolts, the plenum and the gasket.

14. Disconnect the electrical connectors from the fuel injectors. Carefully, bend the wire harness retainer brackets away from the wire harness and move the harness assembly away from the intake manifold.

15. Disconnect the fuel pressure and return lines at the fuel rail.

16. Disconnect the EGR pipe from the intake manifold. Label and disconnect any electrical connectors and hoses from the intake manifold.

17. Remove the intake manifold bracket-to-manifold nuts and the bracket. Remove the intake manifold-to-cylinder head nuts/bolts, the manifold and gasket.

18. If necessary, remove the fuel rail and fuel injectors from the intake manifold.

To install:

19. Clean all gasket mating surfaces.

20. Using a new gasket, position the intake manifold on the cylinder head studs and torque the nuts/bolts to 14–22 ft. lbs. (19–30 Nm).

21. Install the intake manifold bracket-to-manifold nuts and tighten to 14–22 ft. lbs. (19–30 Nm).

22. Connect the fuel lines to the fuel rail. Connect the electrical connectors to the fuel injectors.

23. Using a new gasket, install the intake plenum onto the intake manifold and torque the nuts/bolts to 14–19 ft. lbs. (19–25 Nm).

24. Connect the vacuum lines to the intake manifold. Install the retaining bolts and nuts on the vacuum line assembly bracket to the intake plenum.

25. Install the PCV hose to the intake plenum.

26. Install the wire loom bracket and the EGR variable transducer bracket or vacuum pipe bracket to the right side of the plenum.

27. Install the throttle cable bracket, engine lifting bracket mounting bolt and coolant line/EGR hose bracket to the intake plenum and throttle body.

28. Install the vacuum and coolant hoses to the throttle body.

29. Connect the throttle position sensor, idle switch and bypass air control valve connectors.

30. Install the air duct and the throttle cables to the throttle body.

31. Connect the EGR pipe and connect the water hose to the bottom of the intake manifold.

32. Connect the negative battery cable and fill the cooling system. Start the engine and check for leaks.

2.5L Engine

1. Relieve the fuel system pressure and disconnect the negative battery cable. Drain the cooling system.

2. Disconnect the vacuum hoses and electrical connectors from the air cleaner housing. Remove the air cleaner assembly.

3. Disconnect the knock sensor connector and remove the knock sensor

bracket from the intake manifold. Remove the crankshaft position sensor bracket from the right side of the intake manifold.

4. Remove the right bank (rear) spark plug wires from the spark plugs and the routing clips. Remove the Variable Resource Induction System (VRIS) solenoid connector bracket from the rear of the intake manifold.

5. Label and disconnect the necessary vacuum hoses from the rear of the intake manifold and EGR valve. Disconnect the PCV valve hose from the intake manifold, near the throttle body.

6. Label and disconnect the throttle position sensor and fuel rail electrical connectors. Disconnect the throttle cable from the throttle body and the vacuum hose from the evaporative canister.

7. Disconnect and plug the fuel supply line at the fuel rails and discard the copper crush washers. Disconnect the fuel and vacuum lines from the fuel pressure regulator.

8. Disconnect the EGR breather tube. Remove the intake manifold mounting nuts and bolts in 2–3 steps, then remove the intake manifold.

To install:

9. Clean all gasket mating surfaces.

10. Position new gaskets and install the intake manifold. Tighten the nuts and bolts in 2–3 steps to 18 ft. lbs. (25 Nm).

11. Connect the EGR breather tube and connect the fuel and vacuum lines to the fuel pressure regulator.

12. Connect the fuel supply line to the fuel rail, using new copper crush washers.

13. Connect the vacuum hoses to the evaporative canister, intake manifold, throttle body and EGR valve.

14. Connect the throttle position sensor electrical connector. Install the VRIS solenoid connector bracket.

15. Connect the spark plug wires to the spark plugs and routing clips. Install the crankshaft position sensor bracket.

16. Install the knock sensor bracket and connect the knock sensor electrical connector.

17. Install the air cleaner assembly and connect the vacuum hoses and electrical connectors to the air cleaner housing.

18. Connect the negative battery cable. Fill and bleed the cooling system. Run the engine and check for leaks.

3.0L Engine

1. Properly relieve the fuel system pressure and disconnect the negative battery cable.

2. Drain the cooling system.

3. Remove the air cleaner hoses

from the throttle body and rocker cover.

4. Disconnect the fuel lines from the fuel supply manifold. Cover the fuel line ends with clean shop rags to prevent dirt from entering.

5. Tag and disconnect the vacuum lines and electrical connectors from the throttle body.

6. Remove the plastic shield and the EGR supply tube from the throttle body.

7. Disconnect the throttle cable and, if equipped with automatic transaxle, the throttle valve control cable from the throttle lever.

8. Remove the fuel rail bracket bolt and the 6 throttle body mounting bolts. Remove the throttle body.

9. Disconnect the fuel injector harness stand-offs from the injector inboard rocker cover studs and each injector and remove from the engine.

10. Remove the brace from the fuel supply manifold and throttle body. Remove the fuel supply manifold and fuel injectors.

NOTE: The intake manifold assembly can be removed with the fuel supply manifold and fuel injectors in place.

11. Disconnect the upper radiator hose from the thermostat housing and disconnect the heater hoses.

12. Disconnect the engine coolant temperature sensor and coolant temperature sending unit connectors.

13. Tag and disconnect the spark plug wires from the spark plugs.

14. Remove the distributor cap. Mark the position of the rotor and the distributor in the engine and remove the distributor.

15. Remove the ignition coil and bracket assembly from the left side (front) cylinder head and set aside.

16. Remove the rocker arm covers.

17. Loosen the retaining bolt from the No. 3 intake valve and rotate the rocker arm fulcrum away from the valve retainer. Remove the pushrod.

18. Remove the intake manifold retaining bolts. Before attempting to remove the manifold, break the seal between the manifold and cylinder block. Place a suitable prybar between the manifold, near the thermostat, and the transaxle. Carefully pry upward to loosen the manifold.

19. Lift the intake manifold away from the engine. Place shop rags in the lifter valley to catch any dirt or gasket material. Clean all gasket mating surfaces. Be careful when scraping aluminum to prevent gouging, which may cause leak paths.

To install:

20. Lightly oil all attaching bolt and stud threads. Apply silicone sealer to the intersection of the cylinder block

and cylinder head assembly at the 4 corners of the lifter valley.

21. Install the front and rear intake manifold seals. Install the intake manifold gaskets onto the cylinder heads and insert the locking tabs on the cylinder head gaskets.

NOTE: Make sure the side of the gasket marked TO INTAKE MANIFOLD is facing away from the cylinder head.

22. Carefully lower the intake manifold into position to prevent disturbing the silicone sealer. Install bolts No. 1, 2, 3 and 4 and snug. Install the remaining bolts and tighten, in sequence, to 11 ft. lbs. (15 Nm). Then tighten, in sequence, to 21 ft. lbs. (28 Nm).

23. Install the thermostat and housing, if removed, using a new gasket. Tighten the mounting bolts to 9 ft. lbs. (12 Nm).

24. If removed, lubricate and install new O-rings on the fuel injectors and install the fuel injectors in the fuel rail, using a light twisting-pushing motion. Install the fuel rail and injectors into the intake manifold, pushing down to seat the O-rings. While holding the fuel rail assembly in place, install the 4 retaining bolts and tighten to 7 ft. lbs. (10 Nm).

25. Install the distributor assembly, aligning the housing and rotor with the marks that were made during the removal procedure.

26. Install the No. 3 cylinder intake valve pushrod. Apply oil to the pushrod and fulcrum prior to installation. Rotate the crankshaft to place the lifter on the base circle of the camshaft and tighten the rocker arm bolt to 24 ft. lbs. (32 Nm).

27. Install the rocker arm covers and connect the fuel injector electrical harness.

28. Position a new gasket and the throttle body on the intake manifold. Install the mounting bolts and tighten to 15–22 ft. lbs. (20–30 Nm).

29. Install the fuel rail bracket bolt on the throttle body and connect the throttle cable and, if equipped, the throttle valve control cable to the throttle lever.

30. Install the MAP sensor and the EGR tube to the throttle body.

31. Connect the vacuum hoses and the electrical connectors in their original positions on the throttle body. Install the plastic shield on the throttle body.

32. Install the fuel supply manifold brace. Tighten the retaining bolts to 7 ft. lbs. (10 Nm).

33. Connect the PCV hose at the PCV valve. Connect all remaining vacuum hoses.

34. Install the EGR tube and nut, if

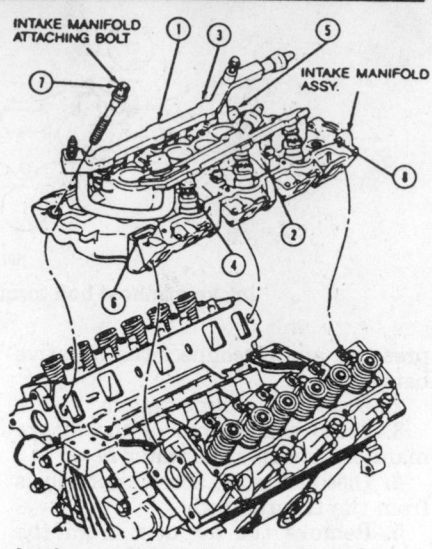

INTAKE MANIFOLD ATTACHING BOLT

INTAKE MANIFOLD ASSY.

Intake manifold bolt torque sequence— 3.0L Engine

equipped. Tighten the nuts on both ends to 37 ft. lbs. (50 Nm).

35. Connect the fuel lines to the fuel rail.

36. Install the distributor cap and connect the spark plug wires to the spark plugs. Install the wiring stand-offs to the rocker arm cover studs.

37. Install the ignition coil and bracket assembly. Tighten the mounting bolts to 35 ft. lbs. (48 Nm).

38. Connect the engine coolant temperature sensor and coolant temperature sending unit connectors.

39. Install the upper radiator and heater hoses. Fill the cooling system.

40. Change the engine oil and filter. This is necessary because engine coolant is corrosive to all engine bearing material. Replacing the engine oil after removal of a coolant carrying component guards against later failure.

41. Install the air cleaner hoses to the throttle body and rocker cover.

42. Connect the negative battery cable. Start the engine and check for coolant, oil, fuel and vacuum leaks. Check the ignition timing.

Exhaust Manifold

REMOVAL & INSTALLATION

2.0L Engine

1. Disconnect the negative battery cable.

2. Remove the 7 exhaust manifold heat shield bolts and the heat shield.

3. Disconnect the oxygen sensor electrical connector.

4. Raise and safely support the vehicle.

5. Remove and discard the exhaust pipe-to-exhaust manifold nuts. Suspend the exhaust system with wire.

6. Disconnect the EGR pipe from

the exhaust manifold and lower the vehicle.

7. Remove the 2 nuts and 8 bolts and remove the exhaust manifold. Discard the nuts.

To install:

8. Clean all gasket mating surfaces.

9. Position a new exhaust manifold gasket over the studs and install the exhaust manifold. Tighten the 8 mounting bolts to 17 ft. lbs. (23 Nm).

10. Install 2 new manifold mount nuts and tighten to 21 ft. lbs. (28 Nm). Raise and safely support the vehicle.

11. Connect the exhaust pipe to the manifold. Install new nuts and tighten to 38 ft. lbs. (52 Nm). Connect the oxygen sensor connector.

12. Connect the EGR pipe to the back of the exhaust manifold and tighten to 34 ft. lbs. (47 Nm). Lower the vehicle.

13. Install the heat shield and tighten the bolts to 88 inch lbs. (10 Nm). Connect the negative battery cable.

2.2L Engine

1. Disconnect the negative battery cable and the oxygen sensor connector.

2. Remove the turbocharger assembly, if equipped.

3. Remove the oxygen sensor from the exhaust manifold on non-turbocharged vehicles.

4. Disconnect the exhaust pipe from the exhaust manifold and remove the outer heat shield.

5. Remove the exhaust manifold-to-cylinder head bolts and the exhaust manifold, inner heat shield and gaskets.

6. Clean the mating surfaces on the exhaust manifold and the cylinder head.

To install:

7. Position the inner heat shield on the studs.

8. Install the exhaust manifold gaskets with the raised edge of the gasket facing the exhaust manifold.

9. Install the exhaust manifold and tighten the bolts to 16–21 ft. lbs. (22–28 Nm).

10. Install the outer heat shield and tighten the bolts to 14–22 ft. lbs. (19–30 Nm).

11. Install the exhaust gas oxygen sensor on non-turbocharged vehicles.

12. Install the turbocharger assembly, if equipped.

13. Connect the exhaust pipe to the exhaust manifold, using a new gasket. Tighten the bolts to 26–36 ft. lbs. (34–49 Nm).

14. Connect the exhaust gas oxygen sensor wire and connect the negative battery cable.

2.5L Engine

1. Disconnect the negative battery

cable. Raise and safely support the vehicle.

2. Disconnect the oxygen sensor connectors.

3. Remove the nuts from the front and rear exhaust pipes and lower the exhaust system. Both pipes must be disconnected, even if only one manifold is to be removed.

4. If removing the rear (right side) manifold, disconnect the EGR pipe.

5. Remove the 3 heat shield bolts and remove the heat shield.

6. Remove the 2 nuts and 5 bolts and remove the exhaust manifold.

To install:

7. Clean all gasket mating surfaces.

8. Install the exhaust manifold, using a new gasket, and tighten the nuts and bolts to 18 ft. lbs. (25 Nm).

9. Install the heat shield and tighten the bolts to 88 inch lbs. (10 Nm).

10. If installing the rear (right side) manifold, connect the EGR pipe.

11. Connect the exhaust pipes to the manifolds, using new gaskets and nuts, and tighten the nuts to 38 ft. lbs. (52 Nm).

12. Connect the oxygen sensor connectors and the negative battery cable.

3.0L Engine

LEFT SIDE (FRONT) MANIFOLD

1. Remove the oil dipstick tube, support bracket and heat shield retaining nuts. Carefully rotate the tube away from the manifold stud.

2. Raise and safely support the vehicle.

3. Remove the exhaust manifold-to-front exhaust pipe attaching nuts.

4. Lower the vehicle and remove the exhaust manifold attaching bolts and the manifold.

To install:

5. Clean all gasket mating surfaces. Lightly oil the bolt and stud threads.

6. Install the exhaust manifold on the cylinder head with the attaching bolts. Tighten the bolts to 18 ft. lbs. (25 Nm).

7. Raise and safely support the vehicle.

8. Connect the exhaust pipe to the manifold and tighten the attaching nuts to 20 ft. lbs. (27 Nm). Lower the vehicle.

9. Rotate the oil dipstick tube and bracket into position over the manifold stud. Install the heat shield and retaining nuts. Tighten the nuts to 13 ft. lbs. (18 Nm).

RIGHT SIDE (REAR) MANIFOLD

1. Raise and safely support the vehicle.

2. Remove the EGR supply tube from the exhaust manifold, if equipped. Use a back-up wrench on the lower fitting adapter.

3. Remove the heat shield retaining nuts and the manifold-to-exhaust pipe retaining nuts.

4. Remove the exhaust manifold retaining bolts and the manifold.

To install:

5. Clean all gasket mating surfaces. Lightly oil the bolt and stud threads.

6. Install the exhaust manifold on the cylinder head with the attaching bolts. Tighten the bolts to 15–22 ft. lbs. (20–30 Nm).

7. Connect the exhaust pipe to the manifold. Tighten the attaching nuts to 20 ft. lbs. (27 Nm).

8. Install the spark plug heat shield and retaining nuts. Tighten the nuts to 12–15 ft. lbs. (16–20 Nm).

9. Connect the EGR supply tube to the exhaust manifold. Tighten to 37 ft. lbs. (50 Nm). Lower the vehicle.

Timing Chain Front Cover

REMOVAL & INSTALLATION

3.0L Engine

1. Disconnect the negative battery cable.

2. Drain the cooling system.

3. Remove the 2 retaining bolts and remove the power steering protective shroud.

4. Using a suitable tool on the idler pulley tensioner, release the tension on the accessory drive belt and remove the belt. Remove the belt tensioner.

5. Raise and safely support the vehicle.

6. Remove the right front wheel and tire assembly and the plastic inner fender shield. Using a suitable tool, turn the water pump idler pulley tensioner clockwise to release the tension on the water pump belt. Remove the belt.

7. Lower the vehicle and support the engine with a floor jack.

8. If equipped with manual transaxle, remove the right engine mount from the water pump bracket.

9. Remove the 3 nuts that attach the right upper engine mount to the timing cover. Lower the floor jack carefully, allowing the engine to rest on the remaining mounts.

10. Raise and safely support the vehicle.

11. Remove the crankshaft damper bolt and flat washer. Using a suitable puller, remove the damper from the crankshaft.

12. Remove the 3 nuts and 1 bolt that attach the right side of the subframe to the body. Pull the subframe down slightly to remove the damper from the vehicle.

13. Disconnect the water pump-to-

front cover hose from the water pump connection.

NOTE: The timing cover may be removed with the water pump hose attached.

14. Drain the engine oil and remove the oil pan. Discard the oil pan gasket.

15. Remove the 4 lowest timing cover retaining bolts and lower the vehicle.

16. Support the bottom of the engine using care to prevent damage to the crankshaft and oil pump assembly. Remove the 3 nuts and 1 bolt attaching the upper engine mount to the top of the front cover.

17. Remove the 6 remaining timing cover mounting bolts. Pry the timing cover away from the cylinder block. Carefully pull the cover over the end of the crankshaft and lower it through the bottom of the engine compartment.

To install:

18. Clean all gasket material and old silicone sealer from all gasket mating surfaces. Pry the old crankshaft seal from the timing cover.

19. Lubricate the lip of a new crankshaft seal and install in the timing cover, using a seal installation tool.

20. Install a new timing cover gasket over the cylinder block dowels and install the timing cover. Install the 6 upper mounting bolts, finger-tight. Apply pipe sealant to bolt No. 5 prior to installation.

21. Raise and safely support the vehicle.

22. Install the 4 lower mounting bolts, finger-tight. Apply pipe sealant to bolt No. 2 prior to installation.

23. Tighten the timing cover bolts, in sequence, to 18 ft. lbs. (25 Nm).

24. Lower the vehicle and install the upper engine mount.

25. Raise and safely support the vehicle.

26. Install the oil pan with a new gasket. Tighten the mounting bolts to 9 ft. lbs. (12 Nm).

27. Coat the crankshaft damper sealing surface with clean engine oil. Install the damper, using a suitable tool. Install the damper bolt and flat washer and tighten to 92–122 ft. lbs. (125–165 Nm).

28. Lower the vehicle. Using a suitable floor jack, raise the engine and install the right engine mount nuts. Tighten the nuts to 55–76 ft. lbs. (74–103 Nm).

29. Install the subframe nuts and bolt. Tighten the bolt to 27–40 ft. lbs. (36–54 Nm) and the nuts to 69–97 ft. lbs. (93–132 Nm).

30. Lower the engine and remove the floor jack. If equipped with manual transaxle, install the mount to the water pump bracket.

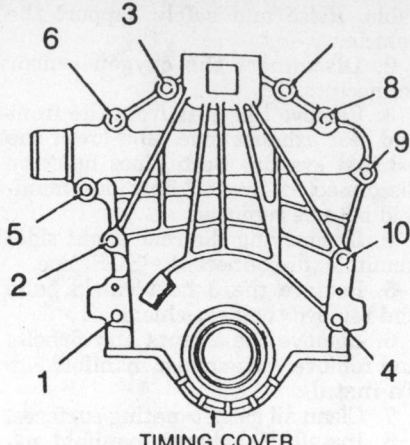

Timing chain front cover bolt torque sequence—3.0L Engine

31. Raise and safely support the vehicle. Install the water pump belt, plastic shield and the right front wheel and tire assembly.

32. Connect the hose from the timing cover to the water pump.

33. Lower the vehicle.

34. Install the accessory drive belt.

35. Install the power steering protective shroud. Tighten the retaining bolts to 7 ft. lbs. (10 Nm).

36. Fill the crankcase with the proper type and quantity of engine oil. Fill the cooling system.

37. Connect the negative battery cable, start the engine and check for leaks.

Timing Chain and Sprockets

REMOVAL & INSTALLATION

3.0L Engine

1. Disconnect the negative battery cable. Drain the cooling system and crankcase.

2. Remove the crankshaft pulley and damper. Remove the timing cover.

3. Rotate the crankshaft until the No.1 piston is at Top Dead Center (TDC) and the timing marks are aligned.

4. Remove the camshaft sprocket retaining bolt and washer.

5. Slide the sprockets and the chain forward and remove as an assembly.

6. Clean and inspect all the parts prior to installation.

To install:

7. Slide the sprockets and the chain on as an assembly with the timing marks aligned.

8. Install the camshaft retaining bolt and washer. Tighten the retaining bolt to 41–51 ft. lbs. (55–70 Nm) and lubricate the chain and sprockets with engine oil.

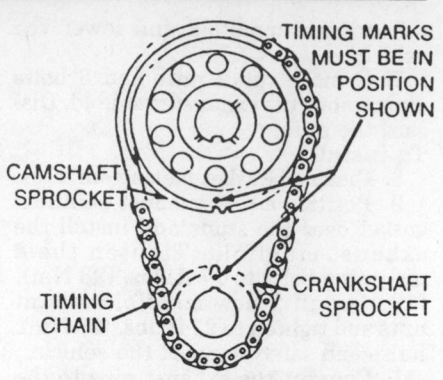

Timing mark alignment—3.0L Engine

NOTE: The camshaft retaining bolt has a drilled passage for timing chain lubrication. If damaged, do not replace with a standard bolt. Clean the oil passage with solvent prior to installation.

9. Position the timing cover gasket onto the cylinder block alignment dowels.

10. Install the timing cover onto the cylinder block, being careful not to damage the seal.

11. Install the oil pan using a new gasket.

12. Install the crankshaft damper and pulley.

13. Refill the crankcase and the cooling system. Connect the negative battery cable.

14. Start the engine and check for any leaks. Recheck the timing.

Timing Belt Front Cover

REMOVAL & INSTALLATION

2.0L Engine

1. Disconnect the negative battery cable.

2. Remove the power steering hose brackets from the cylinder head cover. Label and disconnect the spark plug wires and wire clips.

3. Disconnect the breather tube and PCV valve from the cylinder head cover. Remove the bolts, in 2 steps, in the reverse order of the torque sequence. Remove the cylinder head cover.

4. Remove the power steering belt shield. Loosen the power steering adjusting bolt, lock bolt and through bolt and remove the power steering belt.

5. Loosen the alternator adjusting bolt and upper mounting bolt. Remove the alternator belt.

6. Support the engine with engine support tool 014–00750 or equivalent. Raise the engine slightly with a jack and remove the right side engine mount.

7. Remove the timing belt upper

cover. Raise and safely support the vehicle.

8. Remove the splash shields. Using holder tool T92C–6316–AH or equivalent, hold the crankshaft pulley and remove the pulley bolt. Use a suitable puller to remove the pulley, then remove the guide plate.

9. Remove the timing belt lower cover.

To install:

10. Install the timing belt lower cover and tighten the bolts to 88 inch lbs. (10 Nm).

11. Install the guide plate, crankshaft pulley and pulley bolt. Hold the pulley with the holder tool and tighten the bolt to 123 ft. lbs. (167 Nm).

12. Install the splash shields and lower the vehicle.

13. Raise the engine slightly with the jack and install the right side engine mount. Tighten the mount through bolt to 86 ft. lbs. (116 Nm) and the mount attaching nuts to 75 ft. lbs. (103 Nm). Remove the engine support tool.

14. Install the upper timing belt cover and tighten the bolts to 88 inch lbs. (10 Nm).

15. Apply silicone sealant to the cylinder surface in the area adjacent to the front camshaft bearing caps. Apply sealant to a new gasket and install it on the cylinder head cover.

16. Install the cylinder head cover and tighten the bolts in 2 steps, in sequence, to 69 inch lbs. (7 Nm).

17. Install the power steering hose brackets and tighten the bolts to 88 inch lbs. (10 Nm). Connect the spark plug wires and wire clips. Connect the breather tube and PCV valve.

18. Install the alternator belt and adjust the tension. Tighten the upper mounting bolt to 18 ft. lbs. (25 Nm) and the lower through bolt to 38 ft. lbs. (52 Nm).

19. Install the power steering belt and adjust the tension. Tighten the through bolt to 45 ft. lbs. (61 Nm) and the lock bolt to 34 ft. lbs. (46 Nm). Install the power steering belt shield and tighten the bolts to 86 inch lbs. (9 Nm).

20. Connect the negative battery cable.

2.2L Engine

1. Disconnect the negative battery cable.

2. Loosen the air conditioning compressor and alternator adjusting and pivot bolts, rotate the compressor and alternator toward the engine and remove the drive belts.

3. Raise and safely support the vehicle.

4. Remove the right front wheel and tire assembly and the right inner fend-er panel. Remove the 6 bolts, the crankshaft pulley and baffle plate.

5. Lower the vehicle.

6. Support the engine with a floor jack. Remove the 2 nuts and dowels from the right engine mount and remove the mount.

7. Remove the 7 bolts that retain the timing belt covers and remove the covers.

To install:

8. Install the lower cover gasket and the lower cover. Tighten the bolts to 61–87 inch lbs. (7–10 Nm).

9. Install the upper cover gasket and the upper cover. Tighten the bolts to 61–87 inch lbs. (7–10 Nm).

10. Position the engine mount on the engine and install the 2 nuts and dowels. Remove the floor jack.

11. Install the crankshaft sprocket baffle with the curved outer lip facing outward. Install the crankshaft pulley with the deep recess facing out and install the 6 bolts. Tighten the bolts to 109–152 inch lbs. (12–17 Nm).

12. Install the drive belts. Adjust the belt tension and tighten the adjusting and pivot bolts.

13. Install the right inner fender panel and wheel and tire assembly. Connect the negative battery cable.

2.5L Engine

1. Disconnect the negative battery cable.

2. Label and disconnect the electrical connectors from the coolant elbow. Label and disconnect the electrical connectors from the knock sensor and crankshaft position sensor.

3. Loosen the drive belt tensioner locknuts and adjusting bolts. Remove the accessory drive belts.

4. Raise and safely support the vehicle. Remove the lower bolt from the A/C and alternator tensioner bracket.

5. Hold the crankshaft damper with holder tool T92C–6316–AH or equivalent, and remove the damper bolt. Remove the crankshaft damper.

6. Remove the timing belt cover lower bolts. Lower the vehicle.

7. Remove the A/C and alternator belt tensioner. Remove the engine oil dipstick tube.

8. Hold the water pump pulley with holder tool T92C–6312–AH or equivalent, remove the 4 bolts and the water pump pulley.

9. Remove the upper timing cover bolts and remove the timing covers.

To install:

10. Install the timing covers with the upper bolts. Tighten to 88 inch lbs. (10 Nm).

11. Install the water pump pulley and bolts. Hold the pulley with the holder tool and tighten the bolts to 88 inch lbs. (10 Nm).

12. Install the dipstick tube and the A/C and alternator belt tensioner. Raise and safely support the vehicle.

13. Install the timing belt cover lower bolts and tighten to 88 inch lbs. (10 Nm).

14. Install the crankshaft damper with the bolt. Hold the damper with the holder tool and tighten to 122 ft. lbs. (166 Nm).

15. Install the lower bolt into the A/C and alternator tensioner bracket and lower the vehicle.

16. Install the accessory drive belts and adjust the tension. Connect the electrical connectors and the negative battery cable.

OIL SEAL REPLACEMENT

1. Disconnect the negative battery cable. Remove the timing belt.

2. On 2.2L engine, proceed as follows:

   a. If equipped with manual transaxle, place the shift lever in **4TH** gear and apply the parking brake.

   b. If equipped with automatic transaxle, remove the lower flywheel cover and lock the flywheel with a suitable tool.

   c. Remove the crankshaft sprocket-to-crankshaft bolt.

3. Remove the crankshaft sprocket and key. It may be necessary to use a puller to remove the sprocket.

4. Using a small prybar, pry the oil seal from the engine block; be careful not to score the crankshaft or the seal seat.

To install:

5. Lubricate the seal lip with clean engine oil. Using a suitable oil seal installation tool, drive the new seal into the oil pump cavity. Install the seal so it is flush with the edge of the pump body on 2.0L and 2.2L engines. On 2.5L engine, install the seal so it protrudes 0.03 in. (0.7mm).

6. Install the crankshaft key and sprocket.

7. On 2.2L engine, torque the crankshaft sprocket-to-crankshaft bolt to 108–116 ft. lbs. (147–157 Nm). If necessary, remove the flywheel locking tool.

8. Install the timing belt and connect the negative battery cable.

Timing Belt and Tensioner

REMOVAL & INSTALLATION

2.0L Engine

1. Remove the timing belt covers. Temporarily reinstall the crankshaft pulley bolt.

2. Turn the crankshaft until the timing mark on the crankshaft sprock-

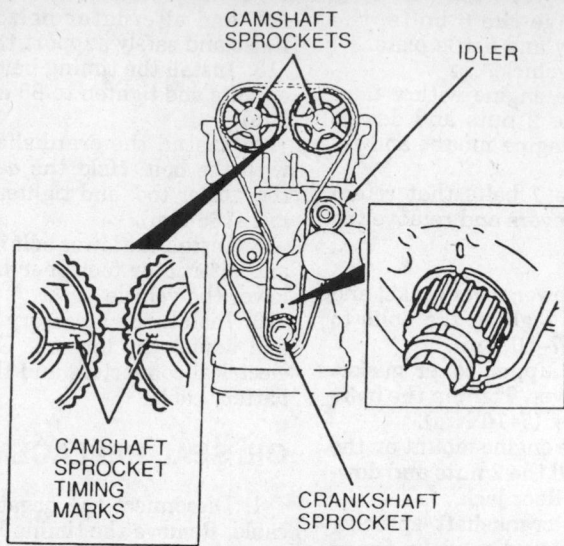

Timing belt sprocket alignment—2.0L Engine

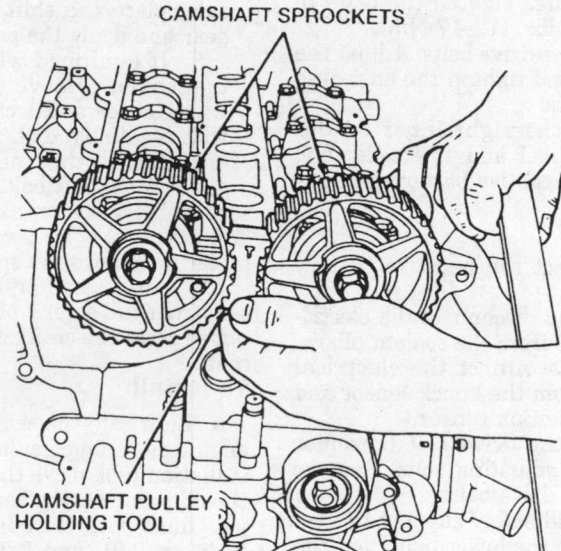

Installing the camshaft sprocket holding tool—2.0L Engine

et aligns with the timing mark on the oil pump and the camshaft sprocket timing marks, **E** and **I**, line up on the camshaft sprockets.

3. Lower the vehicle. Insert camshaft sprocket holding tool T92C–6256–AH or equivalent, between the camshaft sprockets.

4. Turn ther timing belt tensioner with an Allen wrench and remove the tensioner spring from the hook pin.

5. If the timing belt is to be reused, mark the direction of rotation on the timing belt. Remove the timing belt.

To install:

6. Make sure the timing marks on the camshaft and crankshaft sprockets are still aligned.

7. Install the timing belt. If reusing the original timing belt, make sure it is installed in the same direction of rotation.

8. Turn the tensioner clockwise with an Allen wrench and install the tensioner spring. Remove the holding tool from between the camshaft sprockets.

9. Rotate the crankshaft 2 turns in the normal direction of rotation and align the timing marks. Make sure all marks are still correctly aligned.

10. Raise and safely support the vehicle. Remove the crankshaft pulley bolt and install the timing belt covers.

2.2L Engine

1. Bring the No. 1 cylinder piston to Top Dead Center (TDC) on the compression stroke. The notch on the crankshaft damper should align with the TDC mark on the front cover.

2. Disconnect the negative battery cable.

3. Remove the drive belts, crankshaft pulley and the timing belt covers.

4. Remove the timing belt tensioner spring and retaining bolt. Remove the idler pulley retaining bolt.

5. If the timing belt is to be reused, mark the direction of rotation so it can be reinstalled in the same direction.

6. Remove the timing belt.

To install:

7. Align the camshaft and crankshaft sprockets with the marks on the cylinder head front housing and the oil pump housing.

8. Install the timing belt. If reusing the old belt, observe the direction of rotation mark made during the removal procedure.

9. Place the timing belt tensioner and spring in position. Temporarily secure the tensioner with the spring fully extended. Make sure the timing belt is installed so there is no looseness at the water pump pulley at the idler side.

10. Loosen the idler bolt. Turn the crankshaft twice in the direction of rotation; align the timing marks.

NOTE: Always turn the crankshaft in the correct direction of rotation only. If the crankshaft is turned in the opposite direction, the timing belt may lose tension and correct belt timing may be lost.

11. Check to see that the timing marks are correctly aligned. If they are not aligned, remove the timing belt and align the timing marks, then repeat Steps 8–11.

12. Tighten the tensioner bolt to 27–38 ft. lbs. (37–52 Nm).

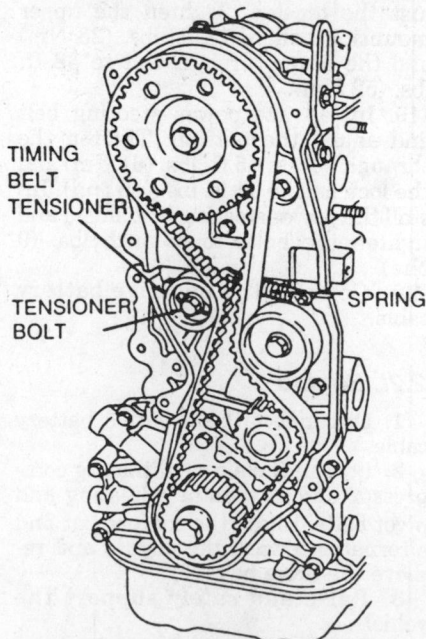

Timing belt installation—2.2L Engines

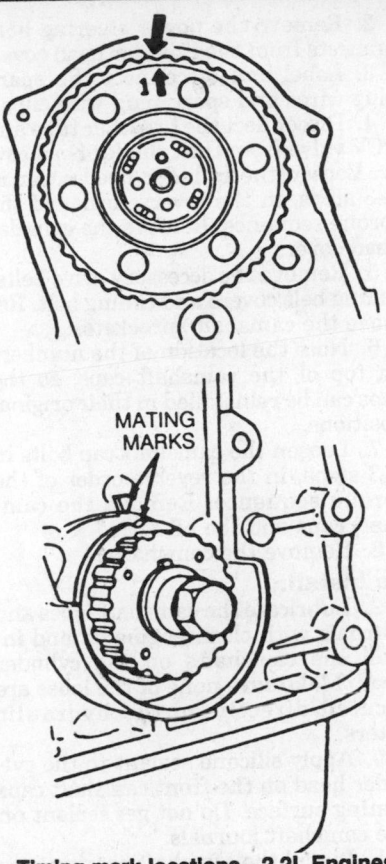

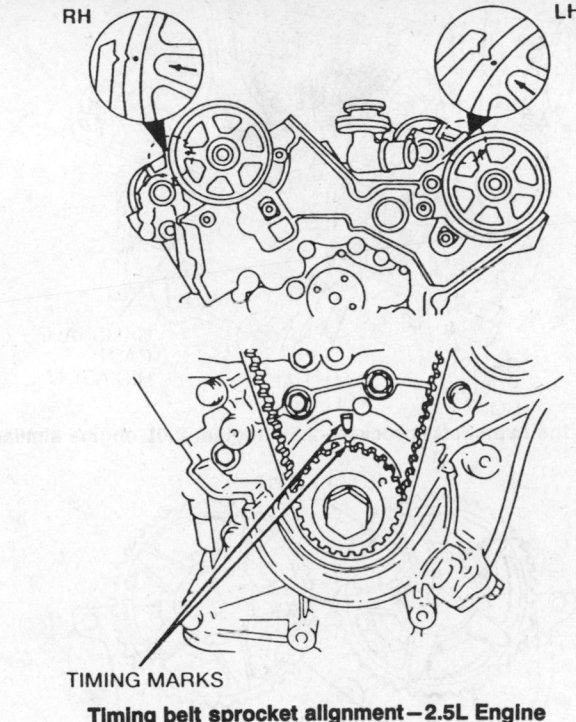

Timing belt sprocket alignment—2.5L Engine

Timing mark locations—2.2L Engines

13. Measure the belt deflection between the crankshaft and camshaft pulleys. The correct deflection should be 0.30–0.33 (7.5–8.5mm) at 22 ft. lbs. (98 Nm) of pressure. If the deflection is not correct, loosen the tensioner bolt and repeat Steps 10 and 11.

14. Install the timing belt covers, crankshaft pulley and drive belts.

15. Connect the negative battery cable.

2.5L Engine

1. Remove the timing belt covers. Temporarily reinstall the crankshaft pulley bolt.

2. Remove the nuts and through bolt from the right side engine mount and remove the mount.

3. Turn the crankshaft until the timing mark on the crankshaft sprocket aligns with the timing mark on the oil pump and the camshaft sprocket timing marks align with the marks on the cylinder head.

4. Remove the 2 bolts from the automatic tensioner, removing the lower one first.

5. If the timing belt is to be reused, mark the direction of rotation on the timing belt. Remove the timing belt.
To install:

6. Position the automatic tesnioner in a suitable press. Set a flat washer

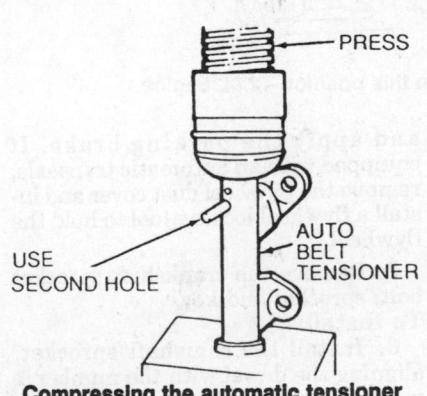

Compressing the automatic tensioner piston—2.5L Engine

under the tensioner body to prevent damage to the body plug.

7. Compress the tensioner until the hole in the piston is aligned with the 2nd hole in the tensioner case. Insert a 0.060 in. (1.6mm) diameter wire or pin through the 2nd hole to keep the piston compressed.

8. Make sure the camshaft sprocket timing marks are still aligned. Turn the crankshaft counterclockwise until the timing sprocket is offset from TDC by 1 tooth.

9. Install the timing belt. If the original belt is being reused, make sure it is installed in the same direction of rotation.

10. Turn the crankshaft clockwise, until the crankshaft sprocket timing mark is again at TDC. This should place all of the belt slack in the automatic tensioner portion of the belt.

11. Install the automatic belt tensioner and tighten the bolts to 18 ft.

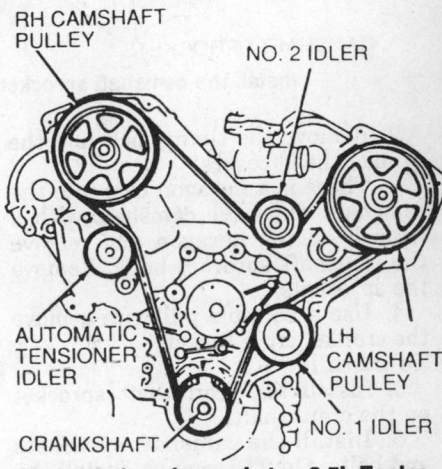

Timing belt and sprockets—2.5L Engine

lbs. (25 Nm). Remove the wire or pin from the tensioner.

12. Rotate the crankshaft 2 turns in the normal direction of rotation and align the timing marks. Make sure all marks are still correctly aligned.

13. Install the right side engine mount. Tighten the nuts to 76 ft. lbs. (103 Nm) and the through bolt to 68 ft. lbs. (93 Nm).

14. Remove the crankshaft damper bolt and install the timing belt covers.

Timing Sprockets

REMOVAL & INSTALLATION

2.0L and 2.5L Engines

1. Disconnect the negative battery cable.

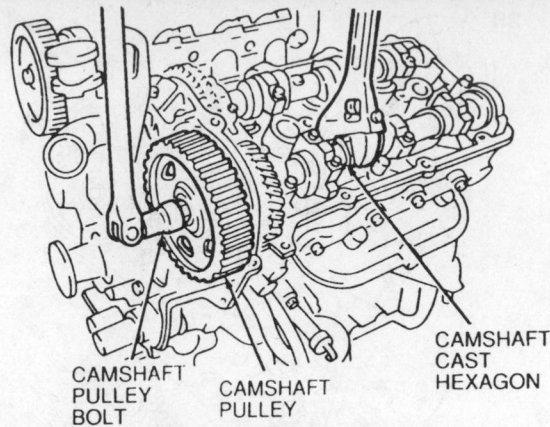

CAMSHAFT PULLEY BOLT

CAMSHAFT PULLEY

CAMSHAFT CAST HEXAGON

Removing the camshaft sprocket—2.5L engine; 2.0L engine similar

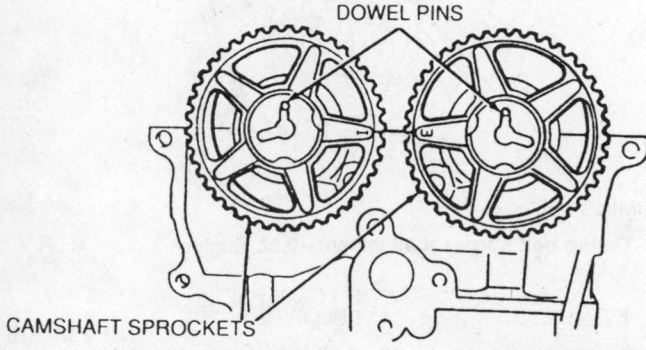

DOWEL PINS

CAMSHAFT SPROCKETS

Install the camshaft sprockets in this position—2.0L Engine

2. Remove the timing belt and the cylinder head covers.

3. There is a hexagon cast into the camshaft. Hold the camshaft with a wrench on the hexagon and remove the camshaft sprocket bolts. Remove the sprockets.

4. Use a suitable puller to remove the crankshaft sprocket.

To install:

5. Install the crankshaft sprocket on the crankshaft.

6. Install the camshaft sprockets and bolts. On 2.0L engine, install the camshaft sprockets so the **E** and **I** marks are aligned with the top of the cylinder head.

7. Hold the camshaft with the wrench on the hexagon and tighten the bolts to 45 ft. lbs. (61 Nm) on 2.0L engine or 103 ft. lbs. (140 Nm) on 2.5L engine.

8. Install the timing belt and the cylinder head covers. Connect the negative battery cable.

2.2L Engine

1. Disconnect the negative battery cable. Remove the timing belt.

2. Insert a proper tool through one of the camshaft sprocket holes to keep it from turning.

3. Remove the sprocket bolt and the sprocket from the camshaft.

4. If equipped with a manual transaxle, place the shift lever in **4th** gear

and apply the parking brake. If equipped with an automatic transaxle, remove the flywheel dust cover and install a flywheel locking tool to hold the flywheel.

5. Remove the crankshaft sprocket bolt, sprocket and key.

To install:

6. Install the camshaft sprocket, aligning the dowel with the number **1** mark.

7. Install the camshaft sprocket bolt. Hold the sprocket with a suitable tool and tighten the bolt to 35–48 ft. lbs. (47–65 Nm).

8. Install the crankshaft sprocket and key. Align the keyway with the timing mark on the oil pump housing.

9. Install the crankshaft sprocket bolt. Install the flywheel locking tool, if equipped with automatic transaxle, or place the shift lever in **4th** gear and apply the parking brake, if equipped with manual transaxle. Tighten the bolt to 108–116 ft. lbs. (147–157 Nm).

10. Install the timing belt and connect the negative battery cable.

Camshaft

REMOVAL & INSTALLATION

2.0L Engine

1. Disconnect the negative battery cable.

2. Remove the power steering hose brackets from the cylinder head cover.

3. Label and disconnect the spark plug wires and spark plug wire clips.

4. Disconnect the breather tube and PCV valve from the cylinder head cover. Loosen the cylinder head cover in 2–3 steps, in the reverse order of the torque sequence. Remove the cylinder head cover.

5. Remove the accessory drive belts, timing belt covers and timing belt. Remove the camshaft sprockets.

6. Note the location of the numbers on top of the camshaft caps, so the caps can be reinstalled in their original positions.

7. Loosen the camshaft cap bolts in 2–3 steps, in the reverse order of the torque sequence. Remove the camshaft caps and the oil seals.

8. Remove the camshafts.

To install:

9. Lubricate the camshaft lobes and journals with clean engine oil and install the camshafts on the cylinder head. Make sure none of the lobes are located directly on the hydraulic lifters.

10. Apply silicone sealant to the cylinder head on the front camshaft caps mating surface. Do not get sealant on the camshaft journals.

11. Install the camshaft bearing caps in their original locations. Install the bolts and tighten, in sequence, in 3 steps:

    Step 1: 35 inch lbs. (4 Nm)
    Step 2: 71 inch lbs. (8 Nm)
    Step 3: 126 inch lbs. (14 Nm)

12. Apply clean engine oil to the lips of new camshafts seals. Install the seals using a suitable seal installer.

13. Install the camshaft sprockets, timing belt and timing belt covers. Install the accessory drive belts and adjust the tension.

14. Apply silicone sealant to a new cylinder head cover gasket and install the gasket on the cylinder head cover.

15. Apply silicone sealant to the cylinder head in the area adjacent to the front camshaft caps.

16. Install the cylinder head cover. Tighten the bolts in 2 steps, in sequence, to 69 inch lbs. (7 Nm).

17. Install the power steering hose brackets and tighten the bolts to 88 inch lbs. (10 Nm). Connect the spark plug wires and clips.

18. Connect the nreather hose and PCV valve.

19. Connect the negative battery cable, run the engine and check for leaks.

2.2L Engine

1. Disconnect the negative battery cable. Drain the cooling system to a level below the thermostat housing.

2. Remove the timing belt covers,

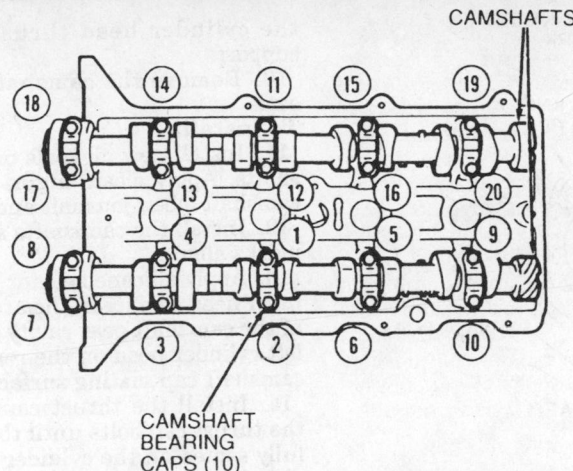

CAMSHAFTS

CAMSHAFT
BEARING
CAPS (10)

Camshaft cap bolt torque sequence—2.0L Engine

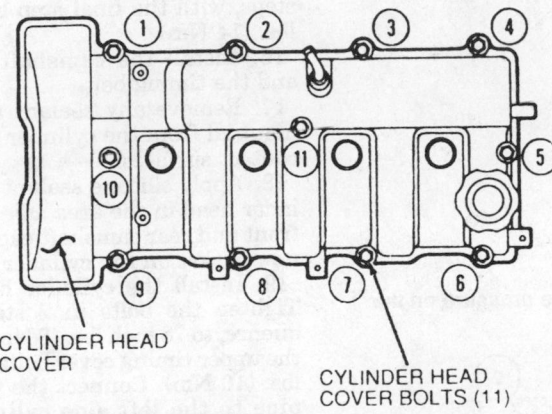

CYLINDER HEAD
COVER

CYLINDER HEAD
COVER BOLTS (11)

⬅ FRONT OF ENGINE

Cylinder head cover bolt torque sequence—2.0L Engine

the timing belt and the camshaft sprocket.

3. Disconnect the upper radiator hose and the electrical connectors from the thermostat housing.

4. Mark the position of the distributor housing and the rotor and remove the distributor.

5. Remove the rocker arm cover and the front and rear housings. If necessary, pry out the camshaft seal from the front housing.

6. Remove the rocker arm/shaft assemblies.

7. Remove the camshaft bearing caps and the camshaft.

To install:

8. Clean all gasket mating surfaces.

9. Apply a liberal amount of clean engine oil to the camshaft journals and bearings. Install the camshaft on the cylinder head with the dowel pin facing straight up.

10. Apply silicone sealant to the cylinder head area under the front and rear camshaft bearing caps. Do not let sealer come in contact with the camshaft bearings or journals.

11. Install the camshaft bearing caps

with the arrows facing the front of the engine. Install the rocker arm/shaft assemblies, making sure the notches on the end of the shafts are in the correct position. Tighten the bolts, in sequence, to 13–20 ft. lbs. (18–26 Nm) in 2 equal steps.

12. Install a new gasket and the rear housing. Tighten the bolts to 14–19 ft. lbs. (19–25 Nm).

13. If the camshaft seal was removed, lubricate the lip of a new seal and install in the front housing, using a suitable installation tool. Install a new gasket and the front housing. Tighten the bolts to 14–19 ft. lbs. (19–25 Nm).

14. Install the rocker arm cover, tightening the retaining bolts to 52–69 inch lbs. (6–8 Nm).

15. Install the distributor, aligning the marks that were made during the removal procedure.

16. Connect the electrical connectors and the upper radiator hose.

17. Install the camshaft sprocket, the timing belt and the timing belt covers.

18. Fill the cooling system, connect

the negative battery cable and start the engine. Check the ignition timing and check for leaks.

2.5L Engine

1. Disconnect the negative battery cable.

2. Remove the intake manifold. Label and disconnect the spark plug wires from the spark plugs.

3. Remove the upper timing belt cover bolts. If removing the left cylinder head cover, disconnect the ventilation pipe from the front of the left side (front) cylinder head cover.

4. Remove the bolts and the cylinder head cover.

5. Remove the timing belt and the camshaft sprockets.

6. Turn the camshafts so the knock pins are aligned with the marks on the camshaft caps. This will reduce the pressure on the hydraulic lifters.

7. Note the markings on the camshaft caps prior to removal, so they can be reinstalled in the same positions. The right hand (rear) caps are marked with numbers and the left hand (front) caps are marked with letters.

8. Loosen the front camshaft cap bolts in sequence, in 5–6 steps. Remove the front camshaft caps.

9. Remove the remaining camshaft cap bolts in the proper sequence. Remove the caps, being sure to remove the thrust caps last. Do not damage

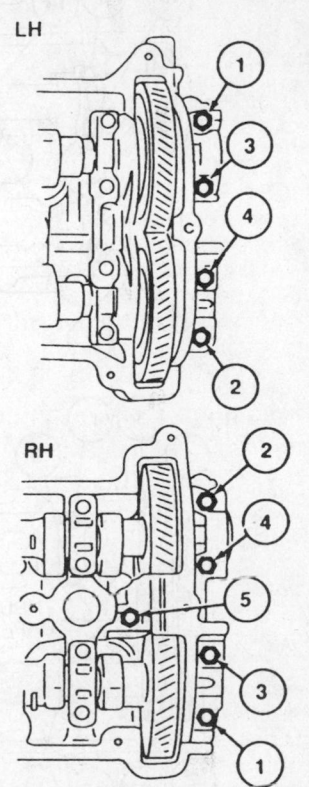

LH

RH

Front camshaft cap bolt loosening sequence—2.5L Engine

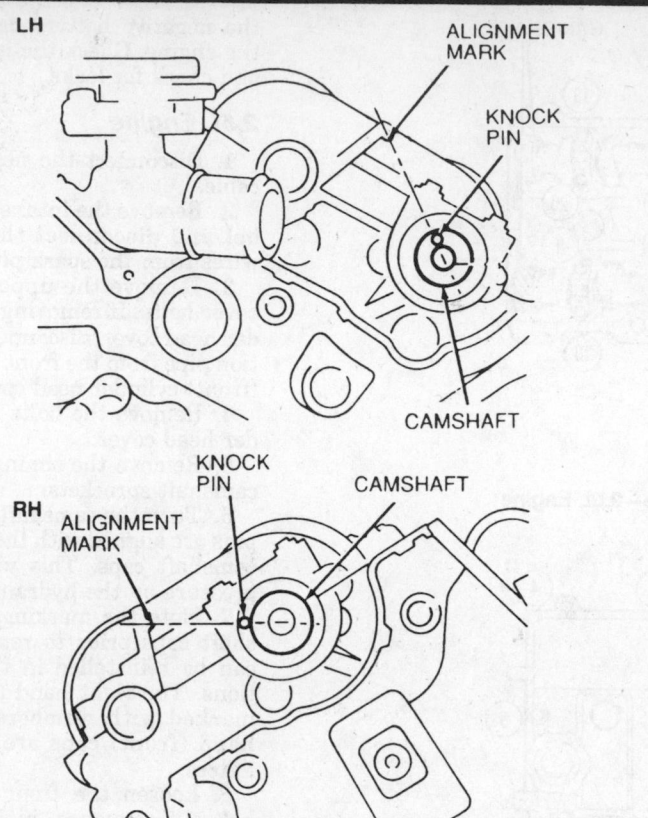

Place the camshafts in this position for removal, to reduce the pressure on the lifters—2.5L Engine

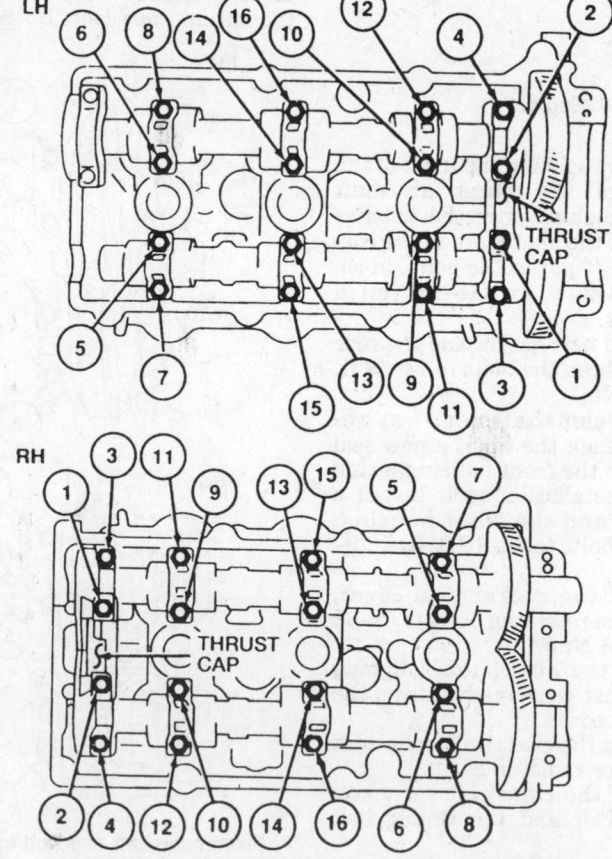

Camshaft cap bolt loosening sequence—2.5L Engine

the cylinder head thrust bearing support.

10. Remove the camshafts and oil seals.

To install:

11. Install new oil seals on the camshafts. Apply clean engine oil to the camshaft lobes, journals and supports.

12. Install the camshafts so the gear marks align.

13. Apply silicone sealant to the cylinder head surface in the area forward of the camshaft gear cavity and to the left cylinder head on the rear exhaust camshaft cap mating surface.

14. Install the thrust caps. Tighten the thrust cap bolts until the caps are fully seated on the cylinder head.

15. Install the remaining camshaft caps in their original positions. Tighten the caps, in sequence, in 5 equal steps, with the final step being 10 ft. lbs. (14 Nm).

16. Install the camshaft sprockets and the timing belt.

17. Remove any sealant and gasket material from the cylinder head cover contact surfaces.

18. Apply silicone sealant to the cylinder head in the area adjacent to the front and rear camshaft caps. Install a new gasket on the cylinder head.

19. Install the cylinder head cover. Tighten the bolts in 2 steps, in sequence, to 78 inch lbs. (8 Nm). Tighten the upper timing cover bolts to 88 inch lbs. (10 Nm). Connect the ventilation pipe to the left side cylinder head cover.

20. Install the intake manifold.

21. Connect the negative battery cable. Run the engine and check for leaks.

3.0L Engine

1. Disconnect the negative battery cable. Remove the engine assembly from the vehicle and place it on a suitable workstand.

2. Remove the timing covers, rocker arm covers and the intake manifold.

3. Remove the hydraulic lifters using a magnet and keep them in order, so they may be reinstalled in their

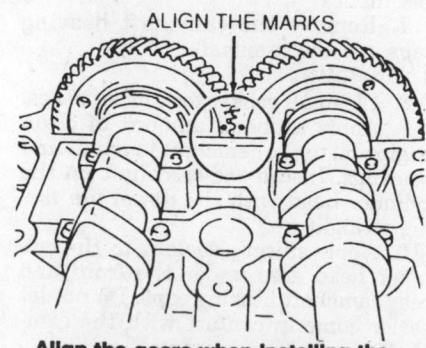

Align the gears when installing the camshafts—2.5L Engine

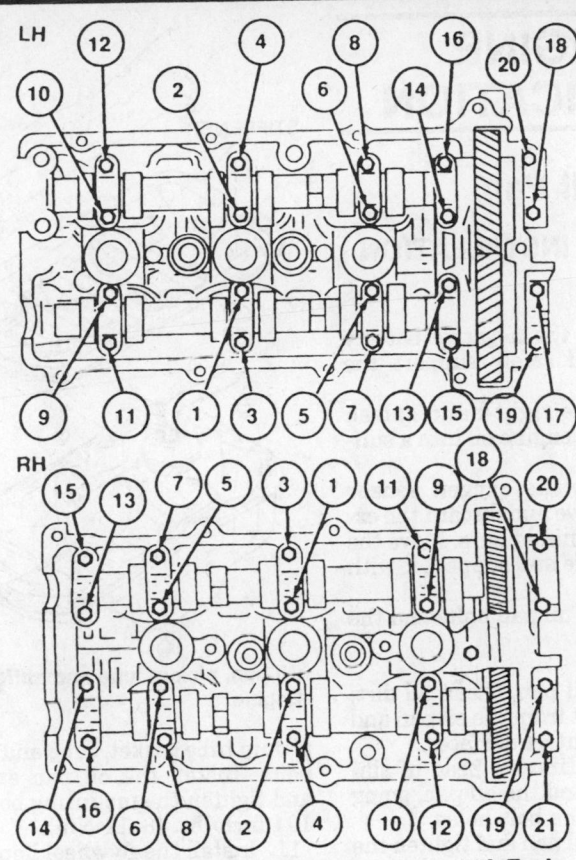

Camshaft cap bolt torque sequence—2.5L Engine

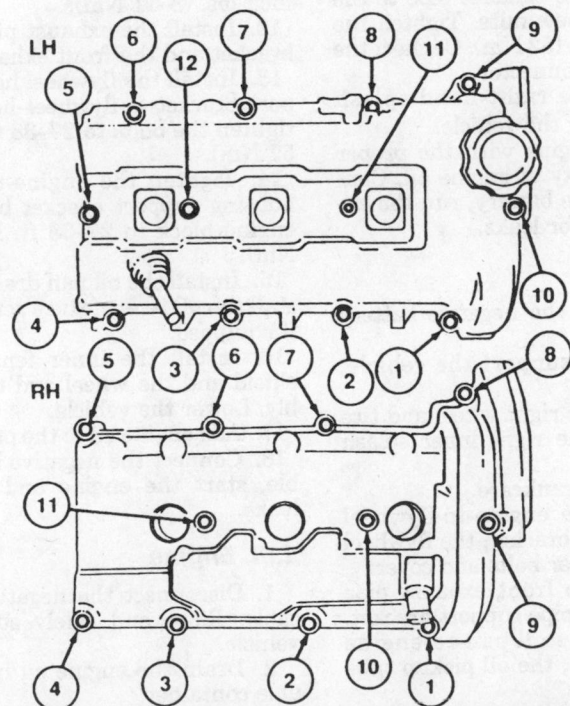

Cylinder head cover bolt torque sequence—2.5L Engine

b. Move the camshaft back and forth in the cylinder block and observe the dial indicator. If necessary, use a prybar to move the camshaft, but be careful not to damage the camshaft lobes or journals.

c. If the end-play exceeds 0.005 in. (0.127mm), replace the thrust plate.

6. Remove the camshaft thrust plate. Remove the camshaft by pulling it toward the front of the engine.

NOTE: Use caution to avoid damaging the bearings, journals and lobes.

7. Clean and inspect all parts prior to installation.

To install:

8. Lubricate the camshaft lobes and the journals with engine assembly lube. Carefully slide the camshaft through the bearings in the cylinder block.

9. Install the thrust plate and tighten the bolts to 6–8 ft. lbs. (8–12 Nm).

10. Install the timing chain and sprockets. Check the camshaft sprocket bolt for blockage of the drilled oil passages.

11. Install the timing cover and the crankshaft damper.

12. Lubricate the lifters and lifter bores with heavy engine oil and install the lifters into their original bores.

13. Install the pushrods, rocker arms, rocker covers and intake manifold.

14. Install the engine assembly and connect the negative battery cable.

15. Fill the cooling system and the crankcase. Run the engine and check for leaks.

Piston and Connecting Rod

POSITIONING

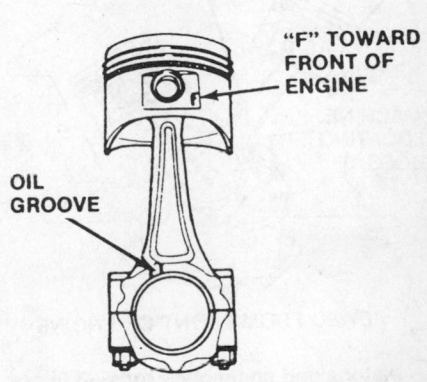

Piston and connecting rod—2.0L Engine

original positions. If the lifters are stuck in the bores, use a hydraulic lifter puller or equivalent, to remove them.

4. Remove the timing chain and sprockets.

5. Check the camshaft end-play as follows:

a. Mount a dial indicator on the front of the cylinder block and rest the indicator foot on the end of the camshaft.

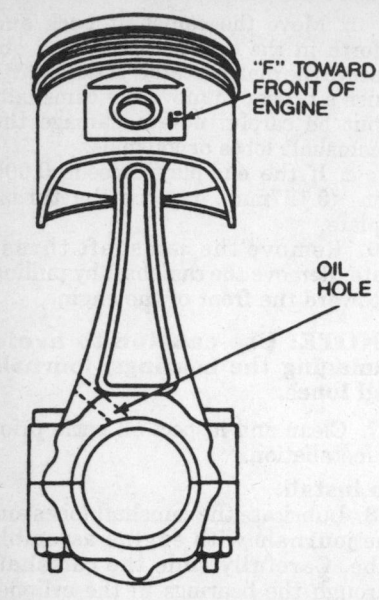

"F" TOWARD FRONT OF ENGINE

OIL HOLE

Piston and connecting rod—2.2L Engine

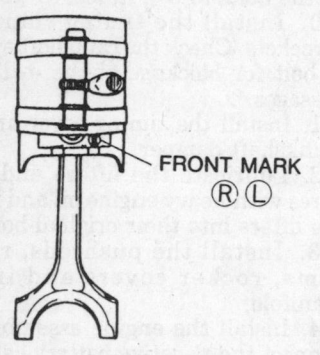

FRONT MARK
Ⓡ Ⓛ

The L mark should face front on the left bank, R mark should face front on the right bank—2.5L Engine

NOTCH ON PISTON DOME AND BUTTON ON CONNECTING ROD INDENTIFICATION MARKS MUST BE ON THE SAME SIDE

PISTON AND ROD ASSY

MACHINE LOCATING BOSS

VIEWED FROM FRONT OF ENGINE

Pistons and connecting rods—3.0L Engine

ENGINE LUBRICATION

Oil Pan

REMOVAL & INSTALLATION

2.0L Engine

1. Disconnect the negative battery cable. Raise and safely support the vehicle.
2. Remove the right-hand splash shield. Drain the engine oil into a suitable container.
3. Disconnect the oxygen sensor connector. Remove and discard the exhaust pipe-to-manifold nuts. Move the exhaust pipe aside and support it with a jack.
4. Remove the oil pan bolts and the oil pan.

To install:

5. Clean the oil pan. Clean all dirt, oil and old sealant from the oil pan and cylinder block contact surfaces.
6. Apply a continuous bead of silicone sealant around the oil pan, going on the inside of the bolt holes.
7. Install the oil pan and tighten the bolts to 19 ft. lbs. (25 Nm).
8. Connect the exhaust pipe to the manifold with new nuts. Tighten the nuts to 38 ft. lbs. (52 Nm). Connect the oxygen sensor connector.
9. Install the right-hand splash shield and lower the vehicle.
10. Fill the engine with the proper type and quantity of engine oil. Connect the negative battery, run the engine and check for leaks.

2.2L Engine

1. Disconnect the negative battery cable.
2. Raise and support the vehicle, safely.
3. Remove the right wheel and tire assembly and the right inner splash shield.
4. Drain the crankcase.
5. Remove the engine-to-flywheel housing support bracket, the flywheel housing dust cover bolts and cover.
6. Remove the front exhaust pipe and the exhaust pipe support bracket.
7. Remove the oil pan-to-engine bolts, the oil pan, the oil pickup tube and the stiffener.
8. Clean the gasket mounting surfaces.

To install:

9. Using silicone sealant, apply a continuous bead on both sides of the stiffener, along the inside of the bolt holes.
10. Install the stiffener, oil pump

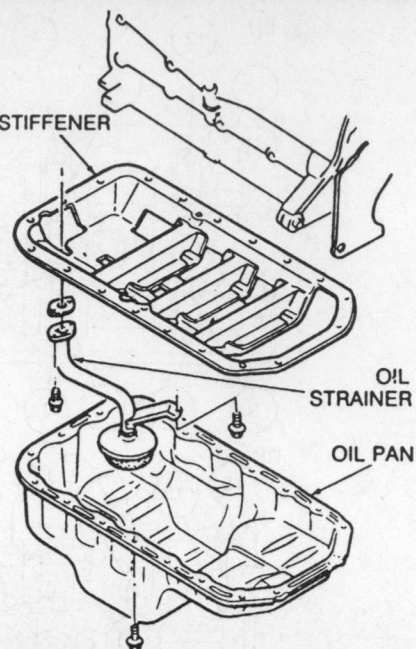

STIFFENER

OIL STRAINER

OIL PAN

Oil pan, pickup tube and stiffener—2.2L Engine

pickup tube gasket, tube and retaining bolts. Install the oil pan and gasket and tighten the mounting bolts to 69–104 inch lbs. (8–12 Nm).
11. Install the flywheel housing dust cover and tighten the bolts to 49–95 inch lbs. (8–11 Nm).
12. Install the exhaust pipe support bracket and the front exhaust pipe.
13. Install the flywheel housing support bracket-to-flywheel housing and tighten the bolts to 27–38 ft. lbs. (37–52 Nm).
14. Tighten the engine-to-flywheel housing support bracket bolts at the engine block to 27–38 ft. lbs. (37–52 Nm).
15. Install the oil pan drain plug. Install the oil temperature sending unit, if equipped.
16. Install the inner fender splash shield and the wheel and tire assembly. Lower the vehicle.
17. Add engine oil to the proper level.
18. Connect the negative battery cable, start the engine and check for leaks.

2.5L Engine

1. Disconnect the negative battery cable. Raise and safely support the vehicle.
2. Drain the engine oil into a suitable container.
3. Disconnect the oxygen sensor connectors.
4. Remove the exhaust pipe-to-manifold nuts and lower the exhaust system to gain access to the oil pan bolts.
5. Remove the oil pan bolts and the oil pan.

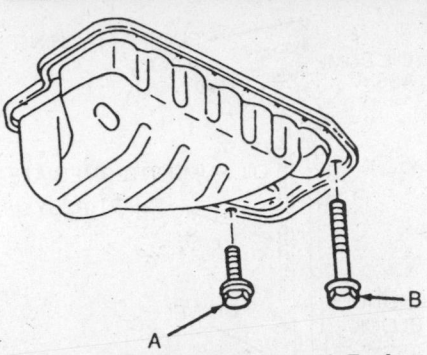

Oil pan bolt Identification—2.5L Engine

To install:

6. Clean the oil pan. Clean all dirt, oil and old sealant from the oil pan and cylinder block contact surfaces. Remove the old sealant from the threads of the oil pan bolts and the bolt holes in the block.

NOTE: Failure to remove the old sealant from the bolts and bolt holes may cause the block to crack.

7. Apply a continuous bead of silicone sealant along the inside of the bolt holes, overlapping the ends.

8. Install the oil pan. Tighten oil pan bolts **A** to 18 ft. lbs. (25 Nm) and bolts **B** 88 inch lbs. (10 Nm).

9. Connect the exhaust pipes to the manifolds with new gaskets and tighten the nuts to 41 ft. lbs. (55 Nm). Connect the oxygen sensors.

10. Lower the vehicle. Fill the engine with the proper type and quantity of engine oil. Run the engine and check for leaks.

3.0L Engine

1. Disconnect the negative battery cable. Raise and safely support the vehicle.

2. Drain the engine oil and remove the starter motor.

3. Remove the front and rear transaxle-to-engine braces.

4. Disconnect the low oil level sensor connector from the dash panel side of the oil pan.

5. Remove the exhaust inlet pipe from the manifolds and position it aside.

6. Drain the cooling system and remove the water pump.

7. Remove the water pump bracket and idler pulley tensioner.

8. Remove the mounting bolts and nut from the front end of the right crossmember.

9. Loosen, but do not remove the bolts and nut from the rear end of the right crossmember.

NOTE: Allow the crossmember to drop as low as possible to allow the removal of the oil pan. If any

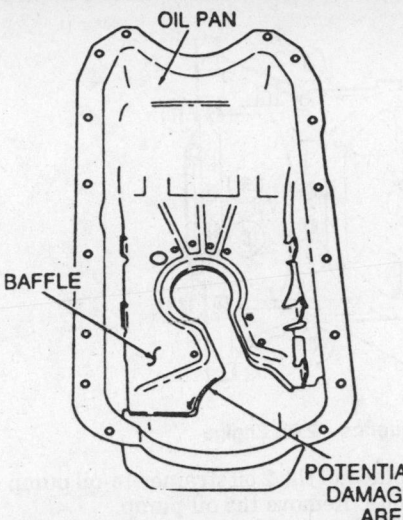

Damage to the baffle may occur in this area if the crossmember is not lowered first—3.0L Engine

attempt is made to remove the oil pan without lowering the crossmember first, damage to the baffle may occur. The oil pan must be pulled straight down without turning or prying it out.

10. Remove the oil pan mounting bolts and the oil pan.

To install:

11. Clean the oil pan and all gasket contact surfaces.

12. Apply a $\frac{1}{5}$ in. (4–5mm) bead of silicone sealer to the junction of the rear main bearing cap and the cylinder block and the junction of the front cover assembly and the cylinder block.

13. Position the oil pan gasket on the engine block and secure with gasket adhesive.

14. Place the oil pan on the cylinder block and tighten the mounting bolts to 9 ft. lbs. (12 Nm).

15. Lift the right crossmember into place and tighten all the nuts and bolts.

16. Install the water pump mounting bracket and the idler pulley tensioner.

17. Install the water pump and the exhaust inlet pipe.

18. Connect the oil level sensor and install the transaxle-to-engine braces.

19. Install the starter motor.

20. Lower the vehicle. Refill the crankcase and the cooling system.

21. Connect the negative battery cable. Run the engine and check for leaks.

Oil Pump

REMOVAL & INSTALLATION

2.0L Engine

1. Disconnect the negative battery cable.

2. Remove the timing belt and the crankshaft sprocket.

3. Remove the A/C compressor and secure it aside, leaving the refrigerant lines attached. Remove the compressor mounting bracket.

4. Remove the oil pan.

5. Remove the oil pickup tube and discard the gasket.

6. Remove the rear main seal housing-to-stiffener nuts and remove the stiffener.

7. Remove the oil pump attaching bolts and remove the oil pump.

To install:

8. Clean the oil, dirt and old sealant from all contact surfaces.

9. Apply a bead of silicone to the oil pump-to-cylinder block contact surface, going inside the bolt holes.

10. Install the oil pump and tighten the bolts to 19 ft. lbs. (25 Nm).

11. Apply a bead of silicone sealant to the perimeter of the stiffener, going inside the bolt holes.

12. Install the stiffener and the mounting bolts. Tighten the bolts in 2 steps, in sequence, to 19 ft. lbs. (25 Nm). Tighten the rear main seal housing-to-stiffener nuts to 88 inch lbs. (10 Nm).

13. Install a new gasket and the oil pump pickup tube. Tighten the mounting bolts to 88 inch lbs. (10 Nm).

14. Install the oil pan.

15. Install the A/C compressor bracket and tighten the bolts to 38 ft. lbs. (52 Nm). Install the A/C compressor and tighten the bolts to 26 ft. lbs. (35 Nm).

16. Install the remaining components in the reverse order of removal. Fill the engine with the proper type and quantity of oil. Run the engine and check for leaks.

2.2L Engine

1. Disconnect the negative battery cable. Raise and safely support the vehicle.

2. Remove the crankshaft sprocket. Drain the engine oil and remove the oil pan.

3. Remove the oil pump pickup tube-to-oil pump bolts, the tube and gasket.

4. Remove the oil pump-to-cylinder block bolts, the pump and gasket.

5. If necessary, pry the oil seal from the pump and clean the seal bore.

6. Clean the gasket mounting surfaces. Inspect the pump and gears for wear.

To install:

7. If necessary, press a new seal into the oil pump until it is flush with the edge of the pump housing and lubricate the seal lip with engine oil. Install a new O-ring into the oil pump body.

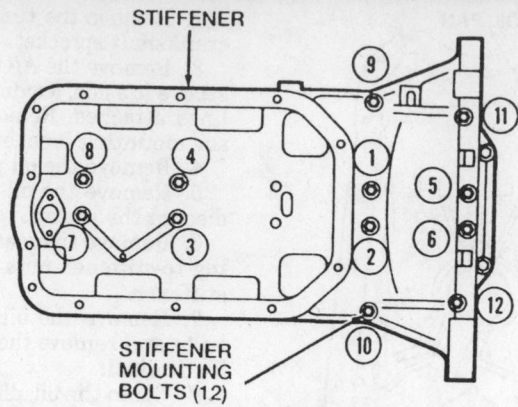

Stiffener bolt torque sequence—2.0L Engine

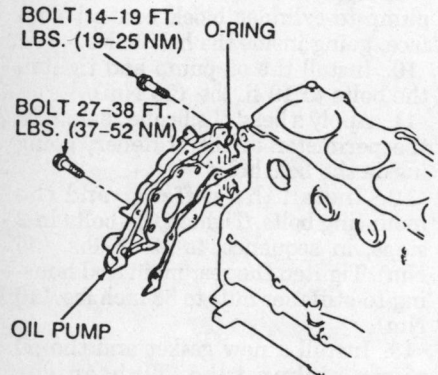

Oil pump Installation—2.2L Engine

8. Apply a continuous bead of silicone sealer to the oil pump gasket surface.

NOTE: When using sealant, do not allow the sealant to squeeze into the pump's outlet hole in the pump or cylinder block.

9. Install the oil pump to the cylinder block; be careful not to cut the oil seal lip. Tighten the 8mm oil pump-to-cylinder block bolts to 14–19 ft. lbs. (19–25 NM) and the 10mm oil pump-to-cylinder block bolts to 27–38 ft. lbs. (37–52 NM).

10. Install the oil pump pickup tube using a new gasket.

11. Install the oil pan and the crankshaft sprocket.

12. Connect the negative battery cable and refill the crankcase. Start the engine and check for leaks.

2.5L Engine

1. Remove the timing belt and the oil pan.

2. Properly discharge the refrigerant from the A/C system.

3. Remove the A/C compressor and the compressor bracket.

4. Remove the power steering pump and tensioner bolts from the engine block. Remove the pump and tensioner and position aside.

5. Remove the crankshaft sprocket.

6. Remove the 9 oil pump mounting

bolts and the 2 oil strainer-to-oil pump bolts. Remove the oil pump.

7. Remove the pump O-ring. If necessary, press the oil seal from the housing.

To install:

8. Clean the oil, dirt and old sealant from all contact surfaces.

9. If removed, press a new oil seal into the pump housing.

10. Install a new O-ring onto the oil pump. Apply a continuous bead of silicone sealant to the oil pump mating surface and install the pump.

11. Install the oil pump mounting bolts. Tighten bolts **A** and **B** to 18 ft. lbs. (25 NM).

12. Install the crankshaft sprocket and key.

13. Install the power steering pump and tensioner. Tighten the 2 power steering belt tensioner upper bolts and the power steering pump rear bracket bolt to 33 ft. lbs. (46 NM). Tighten the tensioner lower bolt to 18 ft. lbs. (25 NM).

14. Install the A/C compressor bracket and tighten the bolts to 38 ft. lbs. (51 NM). Install the A/C compressor and tighten the bolts to 38 ft. lbs. (51 NM).

15. Install the 2 oil strainer-to-oil pump bolts and tighten to 88 inch lbs. (10 NM).

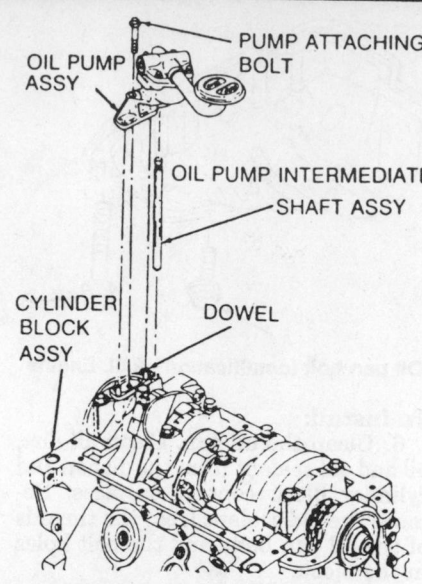

Oil pump installation—3.0L Engine

16. Install the remaining components in the reverse order of removal. Fill the engine with the proper type and quantity of oil. Run the engine and check for leaks.

17. Evacuate and charge the A/C system.

3.0L Engine

1. Disconnect the negative battery cable. Raise and support the vehicle, safely. Drain the engine oil.

2. Remove the oil pan and the oil pump mounting bolt.

3. Remove the oil pump and the intermediate shaft from the rear main bearing cap.

4. Pull the intermediate shaft out of the oil pump.

To install:

5. Insert the pump intermediate shaft into the drive hole in the pump assembly until it clicks into place.

6. Pour a small amount of clean oil into the outlet hole in the body of the oil pump.

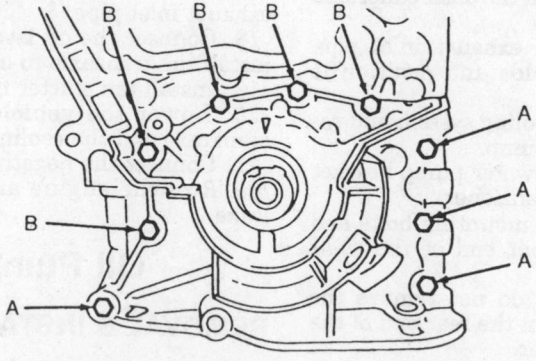

BOLT A : 40mm (1.57 IN.)
BOLT B : 25mm (0.98 IN.)

Oil pump bolt identification—2.5L Engine

7. Lift the oil pump assembly into place guiding the intermediate shaft through the hole in the rear main bearing cap. Seat the pump securely on the locating dowels.

8. Install the pump mounting bolt and tighten to 35 ft. lbs. (48 Nm).

9. Install the oil pan.

10. Lower the vehicle and refill the crankcase. Connect the negative battery cable, run the engine and check for leaks.

ENGINE COOLING

Water Pump

REMOVAL & INSTALLATION

2.0L Engine

1. Disconnect the negative battery cable. Drain the cooling system.

2. Remove the accessory drive belts.

3. Loosen the cylinder head cover bolts in 2–3 steps in the reverse of the torque sequence. Remove the cylinder head cover.

4. Raise and safely support the vehicle.

5. Remove the water pump pulley using pulley tool T92C–6312–AH or equivalent, to hold the pulley while the bolts are removed.

6. Remove the splash shields and the timing belt.

7. Remove the 5 water pump mounting bolts and remove the water pump.

To install:

8. Clean all gasket mating surfaces.

9. Install a new gasket on the water pump and install the water pump on the engine. Install the mounting bolts and tighten to 19 ft. lbs. (25 Nm).

10. Install the water pump pulley and bolts. Hold the pulley with the tool and tighten the bolts to 88 inch lbs. (10 Nm).

11. Install the timing belt.

12. Install the splash shields and tighten the bolts to 88 inch lbs. (10 Nm).

13. Lower the vehicle and install the cylinder head cover. Tighten the bolts in 2–3 steps to 69 inch lbs. (7 Nm) in the proper sequence.

14. Install the accessory drive belts and adjust the tension.

15. Connect the negative battery cable. Fill and bleed the cooling system.

16. Start the engine and bring to normal operating termperature. Check for leaks.

2.2L Engine

1. Disconnect the negative battery cable.

2. Drain the cooling system.

3. Remove the timing belt.

4. Remove the water pump-to-engine bolts, the water pump and the O-ring. Discard the O-ring.

To install:

5. Clean the mating surfaces of the water pump and the engine block.

6. Install a new O-ring onto the water pump.

7. Install the water pump and torque the bolts 14–19 ft. lbs. (19–25 Nm).

8. Install the timing belt.

9. Fill the cooling system.

10. Connect the negative battery cable, start the engine and check for leaks. Check the coolant level and add coolant, as necessary.

2.5L Engine

1. Disconnect the negative battery cable. Drain the cooling system.

2. Remove the timing belt covers and the timing belt.

3. Use pulley removal tool T92C–

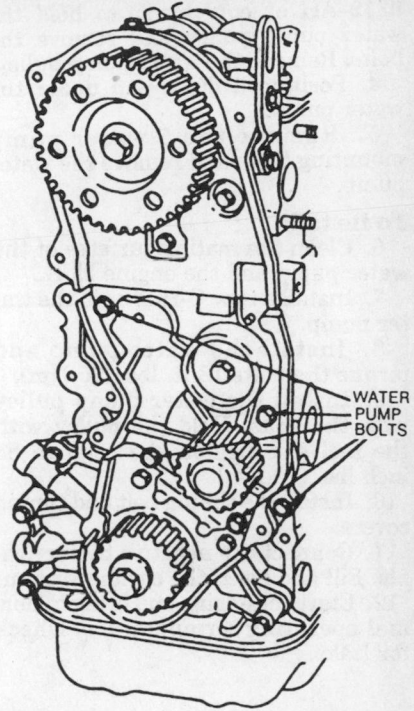

Water pump mounting bolt locations— 2.2L Engine

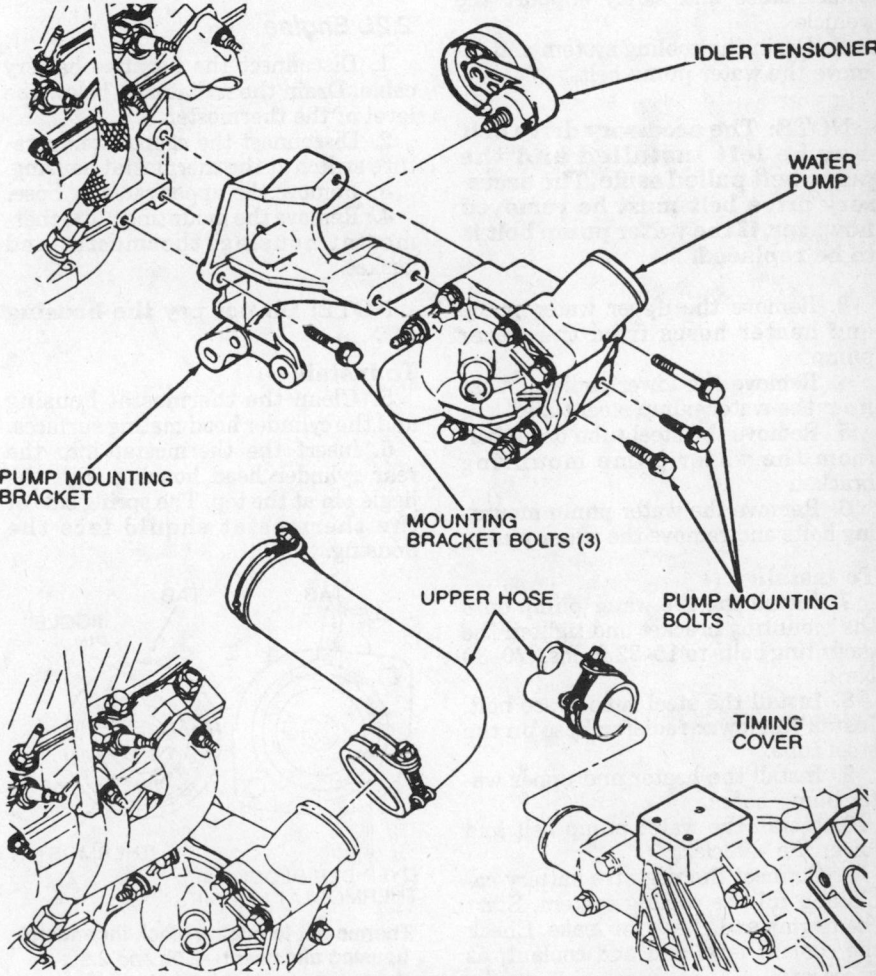

Water pump removal fond Installation—3.0L Engine

6312–AH or equivalent, to hold the water pump pulley and remove the bolts. Remove the water pump pulley.

4. Position a drain pan under the water pump.

5. Remove the 5 water pump mounting bolts and remove the water pump.

To install:

6. Clean the mating surfaces of the water pump and the engine block.

7. Install a new O-ring onto the water pump.

8. Install the water pump and torque the bolts 18 ft. lbs. (25 Nm).

9. Install the water pump pulley with the bolts. Hold the pulley with the tool and tighten the bolts to 88 inch lbs. (10 Nm).

10. Install the timing belt and timing covers.

11. Connect the negative battery cable. Fill and bleed the cooling system.

12. Start the engine and bring to normal operating termperature. Check for leaks.

3.0L Engine

1. Disconnect the negative battery cable. Raise and safely support the vehicle.

2. Drain the cooling system and remove the water pump belt.

NOTE: The accessory drive belt may be left installed and the pump belt pulled aside. The accessory drive belt must be removed however, if the water pump belt is to be replaced.

3. Remove the upper water pump and heater hoses from the water pump.

4. Remove the lower radiator hose from the water pump steel tube.

5. Remove the steel tube brace bolt from the water pump mounting bracket.

6. Remove the water pump mounting bolts and remove the water pump.

To install:

7. Install the the water pump onto the mounting bracket and tighten the mounting bolts to 15–22 ft. lbs. (20–30 Nm).

8. Install the steel tube brace bolt. Install the lower radiator hose on the steel tube.

9. Install the heater and upper water pump hoses.

10. Install the water pump belt and lower the vehicle.

11. Connect the negative battery cable and fill the cooling system. Start the engine and check for leaks. Check the coolant level and add coolant, as necessary.

Thermostat

REMOVAL & INSTALLATION

2.0L Engine

1. Disconnect the negative battery cable. Drain the cooling system.

2. Remove the lower radiator hose from the thermostat housing.

3. Remove the thermostat housing mounting bolts and remove the thermostat housing.

4. Remove the thermostat.

To install:

5. Clean the thermostat housing and engine block thermostat housing mating surfaces.

6. Install the thermostat, aligning the tab on the thermostat with the tab on the engine block thermostat housing.

7. Install the thermostat housing and tighten the bolts to 18 ft. lbs. (25 Nm).

8. Connect the lower radiator hose.

9. Connect the negative battery cable. Fill and bleed the cooling system.

10. Start the engine and bring to normal operating temperature. Check for leaks.

2.2L Engine

1. Disconnect the negative battery cable. Drain the radiator to below the level of the thermostat.

2. Disconnect the coolant temperature switch at the thermostat housing.

3. Remove the upper radiator hose.

4. Remove the mounting nuts, thermostat housing, thermostat and gasket.

NOTE: Do not pry the housing off.

To install:

5. Clean the thermostat housing and the cylinder head mating surfaces.

6. Insert the thermostat into the rear cylinder head housing with the jiggle pin at the top. The spring side of the thermostat should face the housing.

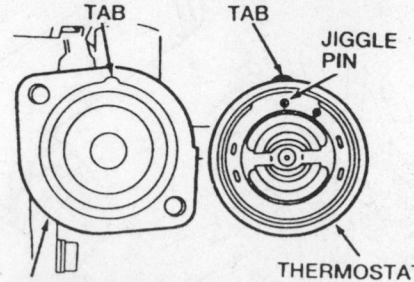

Thermostat to engine block thermostat housing alignment—2.0L and 2.5L Engines

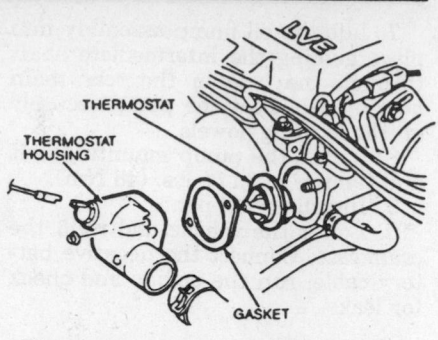

Thermostat removal and installation— 2.2L Engine

7. Install a new gasket onto the studs with the seal print side facing the rear cyinder housing.

8. Install the thermostat housing and 2 nuts. Tighten the nuts to 14–22 ft. lbs. (19–30 Nm).

9. Connect the coolant temperature switch and install the upper radiator hose.

10. Fill the cooling system. Connect the negative battery cable, start the engine and check for leaks. Check the coolant level and add coolant, as necessary.

2.5L Engine

1. Disconnect the negative battery cable. Drain the cooling system.

2. Remove the fresh air duct and air cleaner assembly.

3. Remove the lower radiator hose from the coolant inlet pipe.

4. Remove the coolant inlet pipe mounting bolt and pull the coolant inlet pipe away from the thermostat housing.

5. Remove the thermostat housing bolts and remove the thermostat housing. Discard the O-ring.

6. Remove the thermostat.

To install:

7. Clean the thermostat housing and engine block thermostat housing mating surfaces.

8. Install the thermostat, aligning the tab on the thermostat with the tab on the engine block thermostat housing.

9. Install the thermostat housing and tighten the bolts to 18 ft. lbs. (25 Nm).

10. Install a new thermostat housing O-ring and connect the coolant inlet pipe to the thermostat housing.

11. Install the coolant inlet pipe mounting bolt and tighten to 18 ft. lbs. (25 Nm).

12. Connect the lower radiator hose to the coolant inlet pipe.

13. Connect the negative battery cable. Fill and bleed the cooling system.

14. Start the engine and bring to normal operating temperature. Check for leaks.

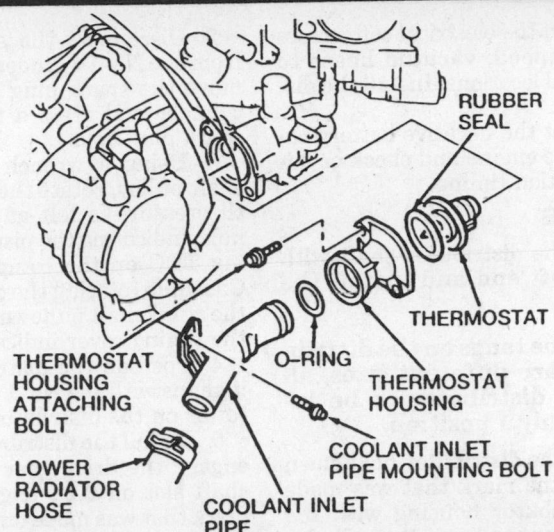

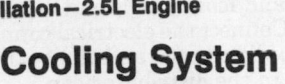

Thermostat removal and installation—2.5L Engine

3.0L Engine

1. Disconnect the negative battery cable. Drain the cooling system.
2. Remove the radiator hose from the thermostat housing.
3. Disconnect the wiring harness bracket and remove the ground wire.
4. Remove the thermostat housing mounting bolts, the thermostat housing and the thermostat.
5. Remove the gasket and discard.

To install:

6. Clean the thermostat housing and cylinder head gasket surfaces.
7. Position the thermostat in the thermostat housing, rotating in a clockwise direction to secure in place. Align the jiggle pin with the recess located near the top of the thermostat housing.
8. Position a new gasket and install the thermostat housing. Tighten the bolts to 8–10 ft. lbs. (10–14 Nm).
9. Position the harness bracket and ground wire, then install the nut.
10. Fill the cooling system. Connect the negative battery cable, start the engine and check for leaks. Check coolant level and add coolant, as necessary.

Cooling System Bleeding

When the entire cooling system is drained, the following procedure should be used to ensure a complete fill.

1. Close the drain valve. With the engine OFF, add a 50/50 mixture of water and anti-freeze to the cooling system. On 1989–92 vehicles, fill to the FULL mark on the reservoir. On 1993 vehicles with 2.0L engine, fill to the bottom of the radiator filler neck seat. On 1993 vehicles with 2.5L engine, fill to the top of the coolant elbow.
2. Install the radiator pressure cap to the first notch to keep spillage to a minimum.
3. Start the engine and let it idle until the upper radiator hose is warm. This indicates that the thermostat is open and coolant is flowing through the entire system.
4. Carefully remove the radiator pressure cap. On all except 2.5L engine, top off the radiator with the water/anti-freeze mixture. On 2.5L engine, add the coolant mixture until it

reaches the top of the coolant elbow, then stop the engine and check the coolant level in the filler port. Add coolant, if required to restore the level.

5. Install the radiator pressure cap securely.
6. Fill the coolant reservoir with the water/anti-freeze mixture to the FULL mark on the reservoir on 1989–92 vehicles. On 1993 vehicles, fill to the **F** mark on the coolant level dipstick.

ENGINE ELECTRICAL

NOTE: Disconnecting the negative battery cable on some vehicles may interfere with the functions of the on board computer systems and may require the computer to undergo a relearning process, once the negative battery cable is reconnected.

Distributor

REMOVAL

Except 2.5L Engine

1. Disconnect the negative battery cable.
2. Remove the distributor cap and position aside, leaving the spark plug wires connected. Before removing the distributor, mark the position of the No. 1 spark plug wire tower on the distributor cap.
3. On 2.0L engine, disconnect the distributor electrical connector. If equipped with automatic transaxle, disconnect the coil connector.
4. On 2.2L non-turbocharged engine, disconnect the vacuum hoses from the distributor diaphragm and the wiring harness at the coil. Tag the hoses and wires prior to removal so they can be reinstalled in their original locations.
5. On 2.2L turbocharged engine, disconnect the distributor wiring harness connector located near the distributor.
6. On 3.0L engine, disconnect the primary wiring connector from the distributor and disconnect the TFI-IV wiring harness connector at the ignition module.
7. Using a wrench on the crankshaft pulley, rotate the crankshaft to position the No. 1 piston at TDC on the compression stroke. The crankshaft pulley notch should align with the timing plate indicator and the distributor rotor should be pointing to

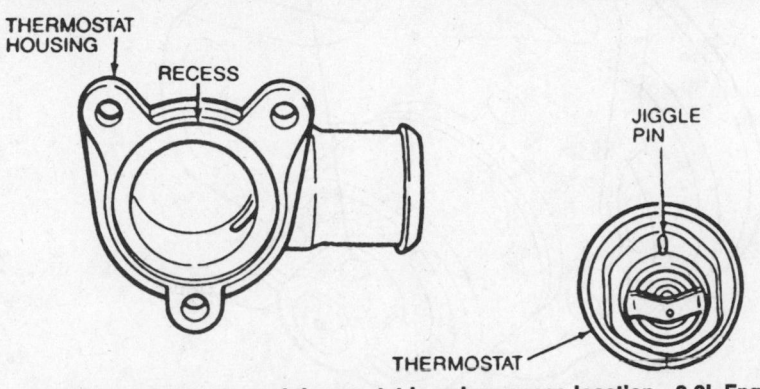

Thermostat jiggle pin and thermostat housing recess location—3.0L Engine

the No. 1 spark plug tower position on the distributor cap.

8. Using chalk or paint, mark the position of the distributor housing on the cylinder head on 2.0L and 2.2L engines, or the position of the distributor housing on the cylinder block on 3.0L engine.

9. Remove the distributor hold-down bolt(s) and remove the distributor.

10. Inspect the O-ring on the distributor housing and replace it, if it is damaged or worn.

2.5L Engine

1. Disconnect the negative battery cable.

2. Remove the 2 fresh air duct nuts and 3 bolts. Loosen the spring clamp at the front of the air cleaner assembly and slide it forward. Remove the fresh air duct.

3. Loosen the clamp on the front of the air flow meter and disconnect the air duct. Disconnect the air flow meter electrical connector at the lleft side of the air cleaner.

4. Disconnect the evaporative canister hose from the routing clip on the front of the air cleaner. Remove the fuel pressure regulator control solenoid from the air cleaner and position aside.

5. Remove the nuts and bolt and remove the air cleaner assembly.

6. Tag and disconnect the spark plug wires from the distributor cap. Disconnect the electrical connectors from the top of the distributor.

7. Using chalk or paint, mark the position of the distributor housing on the cylinder head. Remove the distributor hold-down bolts and remove the distributor.

INSTALLATION

Timing Not Disturbed

EXCEPT 2.5L ENGINE

1. Using clean engine oil, lubricate the distributor O-ring.

2. Install the distributor. Make sure the distributor rotor aligns with the No. 1 spark plug tower position on the distributor cap and the distributor housing mark aligns with the cylinder head or cylinder block mark.

NOTE: On 2.0L engine, there are existing marks on the distributor shaft and housing, which when aligned, indicate the No. 1 spark plug wire tower position. On 2.2L engine, make sure the distributor drive gear engages with the slot in the camshaft.

3. Install and loosely tighten the distributor hold-down bolt(s).

4. Connect the electrical connectors and, if equipped, vacuum hoses to their original locations. Install the distributor cap.

5. Connect the negative battery cable. Start the engine and check or adjust the ignition timing.

2.5L ENGINE

1. Align the distributor shaft with the camshaft end and install the distributor.

NOTE: The tangs on the distributor shaft are different sizes, allowing the distributor to be installed in only 1 position.

2. Install the distributor hold-down bolts. Align the mark that was made on the distributor housing with the mark that was made on the cylinder head and loosely tighten the bolts.

3. Connect the electrical connectors to the distributor and the spark plug wires to the distributor cap.

4. Install the air cleaner assembly and tighten the nuts and bolt to 18 ft. lbs. (25 Nm).

5. Install the fuel pressure regulator solenoid and connect the evaporative canister hose into the routing clip.

6. Connect the air flow meter electrical connector. Connect the air duct and tighten the clamp.

7. Align the fresh air duct and install the hose to the air cleaner assembly. Loosen the spring clamp and slide it into position. Install the fresh air duct nuts and bolts and tighten to 71–88 inch lbs. (8–10 Nm).

8. Connect the negative battery cable. Start the engine and check or adjust the ignition timing.

Timing Disturbed

EXCEPT 2.5L ENGINE

1. Using clean engine oil, lubricate the distributor O-ring.

2. Disconnect the spark plug wire from the No. 1 cylinder spark plug. Remove the spark plug from the No. 1 cylinder and press a thumb over the spark plug hole.

3. Using a wrench on the crankshaft pulley, rotate the crankshaft until pressure is felt at the spark plug hole, indicating the piston is approaching TDC on the compression stroke. Continue rotating the crankshaft until the crankshaft pulley mark aligns with the timing cover indicator.

4. Position the distributor rotor so it aligns with the No. 1 spark plug wire tower on the distributor cap.

5. Install the distributor. Be sure to engage the drive gear with the camshaft slot on 2.2L engines. Align the mark that was made on the distributor housing with the mark that was made on the cylinder head or cylinder block. Loosely tighten the distributor hold-down bolts.

6. Connect the electrical connectors and, if equipped, vacuum hoses to their original locations. Install the distributor cap.

7. Install the spark plug in the No. 1 cylinder and connect the spark plug wire.

8. Connect the negative battery cable. Start the engine and check or adjust the ignition timing.

2.5L ENGINE

1. Align the distributor shaft with the camshaft end and install the distributor.

NOTE: The tangs on the distributor shaft are different sizes, allowing the distributor to be installed in only 1 position.

2. Install the distributor hold-down bolts. Align the mark that was made on the distributor housing with the mark that was made on the cylinder head and loosely tighten the bolts.

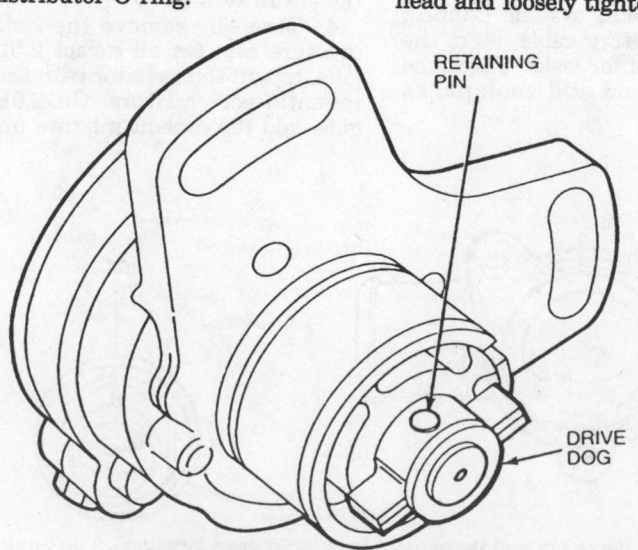

Distributor drive gear—2.2L Engine

RETAINING PIN

DRIVE DOG

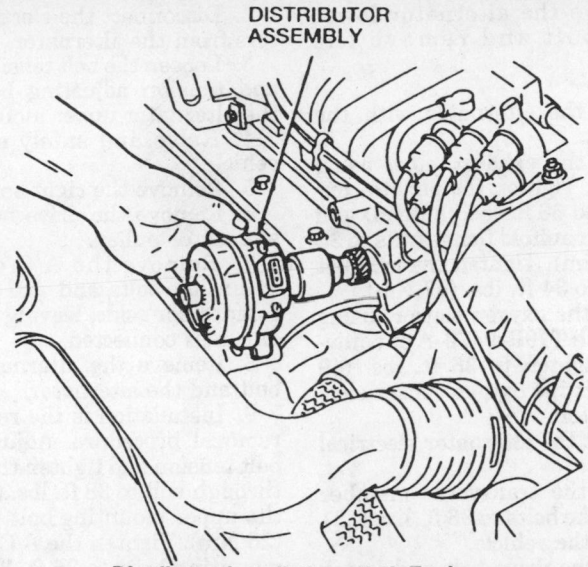

Distributor Installation—2.0L Engine

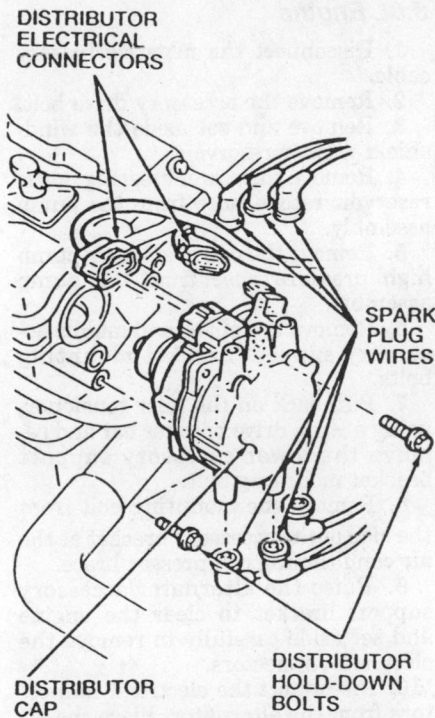

Distributor Installation—2.5L Engine

3. Connect the electrical connectors to the distributor and the spark plug wires to the distributor cap.

4. Install the air cleaner assembly and tighten the nuts and bolt to 18 ft. lbs. (25 Nm).

5. Install the fuel pressure regulator solenoid and connect the evaporative canister hose into the routing clip.

6. Connect the air flow meter electrical connector. Connect the air duct and tighten the clamp.

7. Align the fresh air duct and install the hose to the air cleaner assembly. Loosen the spring clamp and slide it into position. Install the fresh air

duct nuts and bolts and tighten to 71–88 inch lbs. (8–10 Nm).

8. Connect the negative battery cable. Start the engine and check or adjust the ignition timing.

Alternator

PRECAUTIONS

Several precautions must be observed with alternator equipped vehicles to avoid damage to the unit.

• If the battery is removed for any reason, make sure it is reconnected with the correct polarity. Reversing the battery connections may result in damage to the one-way rectifiers.

• When utilizing a booster battery as a starting aid, always connect the positive to positive terminals and the negative terminal from the booster battery to a good engine ground on the vehicle being started.

• Never use a fast charger as a booster to start vehicles.

• Disconnect the battery cables when charging the battery with a fast charger.

• Never attempt to polarize the alternator.

• Do not use test lights of more than 12 volts when checking diode continuity.

• Do not short across or ground any of the alternator terminals.

• The polarity of the battery, alternator and regulator must be matched and considered before making any electrical connections within the system.

• Never separate the alternator on an open circuit. Make sure all connections within the circuit are clean and tight.

• Disconnect the battery ground terminal when performing any service on electrical components.

• Disconnect the battery if arc welding is to be done on the vehicle.

BELT TENSION ADJUSTMENT

2.0L Engine

1. Apply approximately 22 lbs. pressure to the drive belt at a point midway between the alternator and water pump pulleys. The belt should deflect 0.26–0.27 in. (6.5–7.0mm) if it is new or 0.28–0.35 in. (7–9mm) if it is used.

NOTE: Always check the belt tension when the engine is cold or has been stopped for at least ½ hour. The alternator belt can be considered new if it has been in used on a running engine less than 5 minutes.

2. If the belt deflection is not as specified, loosen the alternator adjusting bolt and upper mounting bolt.

3. Raise and safely support the vehicle. Remove the right splash shield and loosen the alternator through bolt.

4. Lower the vehicle.

5. Turn the alternator adjusting bolt until the belt deflection is as specified in Step 1.

6. Tighten the alternator upper mounting bolt to 18 ft. lbs. (25 Nm).

7. Raise and safely support the vehicle. Tighten the alternator lower through bolt to 38 ft. lbs. (51 Nm).

8. Install the right splash shield and lower the vehicle.

2.2L Engine

1. Apply approximately 22 lbs. pressure to the alternator belt at a point midway between the crankshaft and alternator pullleys. The belt should deflect 0.24–0.31 in. (6–8mm) if it is new or 0.27–0.35 in. (7–9mm) if it is used.

NOTE: Always check the belt tension when the engine is cold or has been stopped for at least ½ hour. The alternator belt can be considered new if it has been in used on a running engine less than 5 minutes.

2. If the belt deflection is not as specified, loosen the alternator adjustment bolt and through bolt.

3. Turn the alternator adjustment bolt to adjust the belt tension.

4. After adjustment, tighten the through bolt to 38 ft. lbs. (52 Nm) and the adjusting bolt to 18 ft. lbs. (25 Nm).

2.5L Engine

1. If not equipped with A/C, apply approximately 22 lbs. pressure to the alternator drive belt at a point midway between the alternator and crankshaft pulleys. The alternator belt should deflect 0.24–0.27 in. (6–7mm) if it is new or 0.28–0.31 in. (7–8mm) if it is used.

2. If equipped with A/C, apply approximately 22 lbs. pressure to the alternator belt at a point midway between the A/C compressor and crankshaft pulleys. The belt should deflect 0.22–0.25 in. (5.5–6.5mm) if the belt is new or 0.26–0.29 in. (6.5–7.5mm) if it is used.

NOTE: Always check the belt tension when the engine is cold or has been stopped for at least ½ hour. The alternator belt can be considered new if it has been in used on a running engine less than 5 minutes.

3. If the belt deflection is not as specified, loosen the tensioner pulley locknut and turn the tenioner adjusting bolt until the belt tension is correct.

4. After adjustment, tighten the tensioner pulley locknut to 34 ft. lbs. (46 Nm).

3.0L Engine

The 3.0L engine uses an automatic tensioner to maintain proper belt tension. No adjustment is necessary.

REMOVAL & INSTALLATION

2.0L Engine

1. Disconnect the negative battery cable.
2. Remove the alternator upper mounting bolt.
3. Loosen the alternator adjusting bolt and remove the drive belt from the alternator pulley.
4. Raise and safely support the vehicle.
5. Remove the 6 bolts and remove the transverse member.
6. Disconnect the electrical connectors from the alternator.
7. Remove the front exhaust pipe as follows:
   a. Support the exhaust system at the catalytic converter with a jack.
   b. Disconnect the oxygen sensor electrical connector and remove the sensor using sensor wrench T79P–9472–A or equivalent.
   c. Remove the 3 exhaust manifold flange nuts and remove the clamp from the hold-down bracket.
   d. Remove the exhaust pipe-to-converter nuts and pry the rubber hangers from the mounting hooks. Remove the pipe.

8. Remove the alternator lower through bolt and remove the alternator.

To install:

9. Install the alternator with the through bolt.
10. Install the exhaust pipe, using new gaskets. Tighten the pipe-to-converter nuts to 66 ft. lbs. (89 Nm) and the exhaust manifold flange nuts to 38 ft. lbs. (52 Nm). Tighten the exhaust clamp nuts to 34 ft. lbs. (47 Nm).
11. Install the oxygen sensor, using sensor wrench T79P–9472–A or equivalent, and tighten to 36 ft. lbs. (49 Nm). Connect the oxygen sensor electrical connector.
12. Connect the alternator electrical connectors.
13. Install the transverse member and tighten the bolts to 96 ft. lbs. (131 Nm). Lower the vehicle.
14. Install the drive belt and upper mounting bolt. Adjust the belt tension. Tighten the lower through bolt to 38 ft. lbs. (52 Nm) and the upper mounting bolt to 10 ft. lbs. (15 Nm).
15. Connect the negative battery cable.

2.2L Engine

1. Disconnect the negative battery cable.
2. Raise and safely support the vehicle.
3. Remove the right halfshaft.
4. From the rear of the alternator, depress the lock tabs on the wiring terminals and pull the terminals straight off. Mark the location of the wires prior to removal so they can be reinstalled in their original positions.
5. Loosen the alternator adjustment and through bolts enough to allow the alternator to pivot. Remove the alternator drive belt.
6. Remove the alternator adjustment bracket, lock bolt and through bolt.
7. Hold the alternator to prevent it from falling and remove it through the space left by removing the halfshaft.

To install:

8. Position the alternator and loosely install the mounting and adjustment bolts.
9. Install the drive belt and adjust the tension. Tighten the through bolt to 38 ft. lbs. (52 Nm) and the adjusting bolt to 19 ft. lbs. (25 Nm).
10. Connect the wiring terminals at the rear of the alternator.
11. Install the right halfshaft.
12. Lower the vehicle. Connect the negative battery cable.

2.5L Engine

1. Disconnect the negative battery cable.

2. Disconnect the electrical connectors from the alternator.
3. Loosen the belt tensioner locknut and tension adjusting bolt. Remove the alternator upper mounting bolt.
4. Raise and safely support the vehicle.
5. Remove the right splash shield.
6. Remove the drive belt from the alternator pulley.
7. Remove the A/C compressor mounting bolts and and support the compressor aside, leaving the refrigerant lines connected.
8. Remove the alternator through bolt and the alternator.
9. Installation is the reverse of the removal procedure. Adjust the drive belt tension and tighten the alternator through bolt to 38 ft. lbs. (51 Nm) and the upper mounting bolt to 18 ft. lbs. (25 Nm). Tighten the A/C compressor mounting bolts to 26 ft. lbs. (35 Nm).

3.0L Engine

1. Disconnect the negative battery cable.
2. Remove the accessory drive belt.
3. Remove and set aside the windshield washer reservoir.
4. Remove the power steering pump reservoir return hose from the pump assembly.
5. Remove the power steering pump high pressure hose from the pump assembly.
6. Remove the upper and middle accessory support bracket mounting bolts.
7. Pull back on the idler tensioner, using a ½ in. drive breaker bar and remove the lower accessory support bracket mounting bolt.
8. Remove the mounting bolt from the side of the accessory bracket at the air conditioning compressor brace.
9. Raise the alternator/accessory support bracket to clear the engine and set aside carefully to remove the electrical connectors.
10. Disconnect the electrical connectors from the alternator. Place the alternator/accessory support bracket on a bench for alternator removal.
11. Remove the alternator pivot bolt and remove the mounting bolt from the back side of the alternator. Remove the alternator from the accessory support bracket.

To install:

12. Position the alternator on the accessory support bracket and install the alternator pivot bolt.
13. Install the alternator mounting bolt at the rear of the alternator.
14. Position the alternator/accessory support bracket in the engine compartment and connect the electrical connectors on the back side of the alternator.

15. Position the alternator/accessory support bracket on the engine. Install the mounting bolt through the air conditioning compressor brace into the support bracket.

16. Install the middle accessory support bracket mounting bolt.

17. Pull back on the idler tensioner, using the ½ in. drive breaker bar and install the lower accessory support bracket mounting bolt.

18. Install the upper accessory support bracket mounting bolt.

19. Connect the power steering pressure and return hoses to the pump.

20. Install the accessory drive belt.

21. Replace the windshield washer resevoir and connect the negative battery cable.

22. Fill and bleed the power steering system.

Starter

REMOVAL & INSTALLATION

2.0L Engine

1. Disconnect the negative battery cable.

2. Remove the air duct and air cleaner assembly.

3. Remove the upper starter mounting bolts.

4. Raise and safely support the vehicle.

5. Remove the intake manifold support bracket bolts and the bracket.

6. Disconnect the electrical connectors from the starter solenoid.

7. Remove the lower starter mounting bolt and remove the starter.

8. Installation is the reverse of the removal procedure. Tighten the starter mounting bolts to 34 ft. lbs. (46 Nm). The upper mounting bolts must be tightened first.

2.2L Engine

1. Disconnect the negative battery cable. Raise and support the vehicle, safely.

2. If equipped with a manual transaxle, remove the exhaust pipe bracket.

3. Remove the transaxle-to-engine bracket and intake manifold-to-engine bracket.

4. Disconnect the electrical connectors from the starter.

5. Remove the starter mounting bolts and the starter.

To install:

6. Install the starter and torque the bolts to 34 ft. lbs. (46 Nm).

7. Connect the electrical connectors to the starter.

8. Install the intake manifold-to-engine bracket and tighten the bolts to 22 ft. lbs. (30 Nm).

9. If equipped with an automatic transaxle, install the transaxle-to-engine bracket and torque the bellhousing bolt to 86 ft. lbs. (117 Nm) and the 3 other mounting bolts to 38 ft. lbs. (52 Nm).

10. If equipped with a manual transaxle, install the transaxle-to-engine bracket and connect the exhaust pipe bracket. Tighten the bracket bolts to 45 ft. lbs. (61 Nm).

11. Lower the vehicle.

12. Connect the negative battery cable and check the starter for proper operation.

2.5L Engine

1. Disconnect the negative battery cable.

2. Remove the fresh air duct and the air cleaner assembly.

3. If equipped with automatic transaxle, proceed as follows:

   a. Use a small prybar to pry the shift cable from the shift lever.

   b. Squeeze the lock tabs on the shift cable and remove the cable from the cable bracket.

   c. Label and disconnect the electrical connectors from the knock sensor, throttle position sensor, fuel rail, distributor, neutral safety switch, automatic transaxle and wiring harness.

   d. Position the wiring harness aside.

   e. Remove the 2 selector cable bracket mounting bolts and the bracket.

   f. Remove the 2 nuts and bolt from the starter bracket and remove the bracket.

4. Disconnect the electrical connectors from the starter solenoid.

5. Remove the 3 starter mounting bolts and remove the starter.

6. Installation is the reverse of the removal procedure. Tighten the starter mounting bolts to 33 ft. lbs. (46 Nm).

3.0L Engine

1. Disconnect the negative battery cable.

2. Raise and safely support the vehicle.

3. If equipped with automatic transaxle, remove the kickdown cable routing bracket from the engine block.

4. Disconnect the wire from the starter solenoid S-terminal.

NOTE: When disconnecting the plastic hard shell connector at the solenoid S-terminal, grasp the plastic connector, depress the plastic tab, and pull off the lead assembly. Do not pull on the lead wire or damage may result.

5. Remove the attaching nut from the starter solenoid B-terminal and disconnect the cable from the terminal.

6. Remove the starter mounting bolts and remove the starter.

To install:

7. Position the starter and install the mounting bolts. Tighten the bolts to 20 ft. lbs. (27 Nm).

8. Connect the cable to the starter solenoid B-terminal and install the attaching nut. Tighten the nut to 120 inch lbs. (13.5 Nm).

9. Connect the wire to the starter solenoid S-terminal.

10. If necessary, install the kickdown cable routing bracket to the engine block.

11. Lower the vehicle. Connect the negative battery cable and check the starter for proper operation.

EMISSION CONTROLS

Due to the complex nature of modern electronic engine control systems, comprehensive diagnosis and testing procedures fall outside the confines of this repair manual. For complete information on diagnosis, testing and repair procedures concerning all modern engine and emission control systems, please refer to "Chilton's Guide to Fuel Injection and Electronic Engine Controls".

Emission Warning Lamps

All vehicles are equipped with a **CHECK ENGINE** light. This light

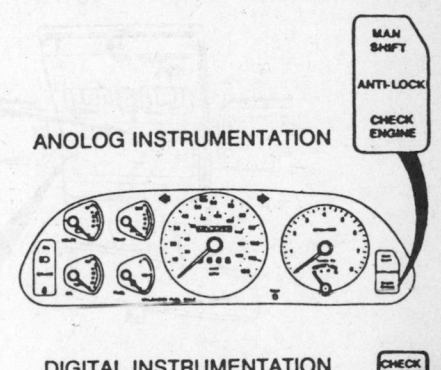

ANOLOG INSTRUMENTATION

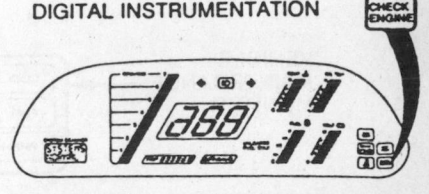

DIGITAL INSTRUMENTATION

Check engine light location—1989–92

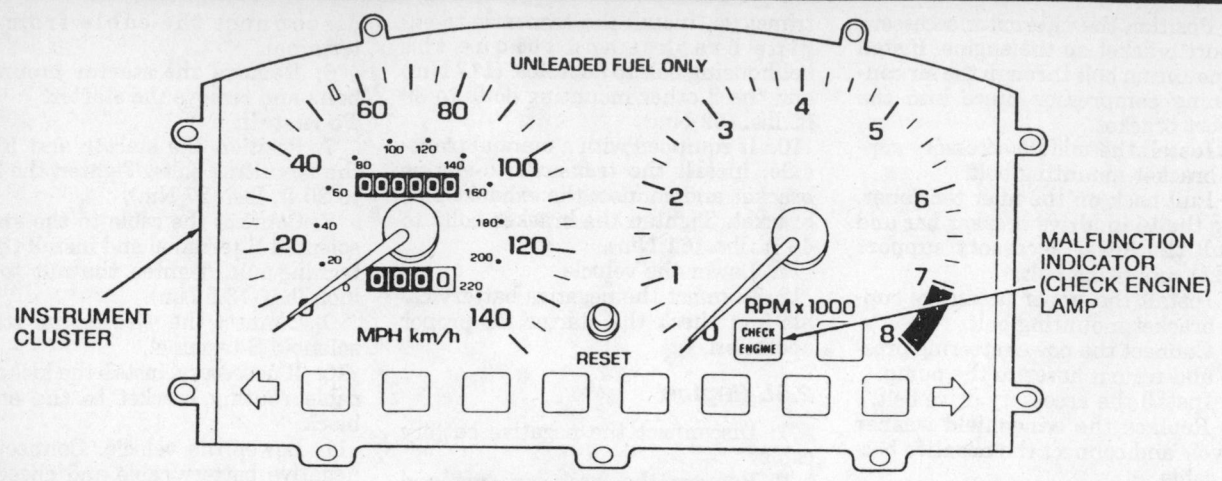

Check engine light location—1993

should come ON briefly when the ignition key is turned **ON** but should turn OFF when the engine is started. If the light stays ON after the engine is started or if it comes ON at any time during engine operation, a problem in the electronic engine control system is indicated.

On 1989–92 vehicles, there are also 2 different service interval reminder systems, the Vehicle Maintenance Monitor or System Scanner. The Vehicle Maintenance Monitor is available only on vehicles with an analog instrument cluster. It will indicate a service interval check on a module located on the front center portion of the headliner, just above the rear view mirror. The System Scanner is found on vehicles with electronic instrument clusters. It will indicate a service interval check on a display, located in the lower left corner of the instrument cluster.

RESETTING

To reset the service interval light on

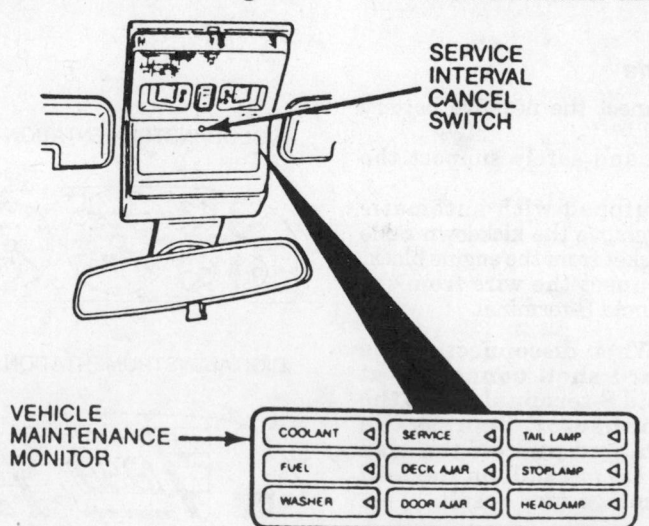

Vehicle Maintenance Monitor service interval cancel switch location

vehicles equipped with the Vehicle Maintenance Monitor, insert a small pointed instrument into the service interval cancel switch. Depress the switch once.

To cancel the service check message on the System Scanner, press the **SERV** button on the keyboard, located to the right of the instrument cluster, and hold until 3 tones are sounded.

FUEL SYSTEM

Fuel System Service Precautions

Safety is the most important factor when performing not only fuel system maintenance but any type of maintenance. Failure to conduct maintenance and repairs in a safe manner may result in serious personal injury or death. Maintenance and testing of

the vehicle's fuel system components can be accomplished safely and effectively by adhering to the following rules and guidelines.

• To avoid the possibility of fire and personal injury, always disconnect the negative battery cable unless the repair or test procedure requires that battery voltage be applied.

• Always relieve the fuel system pressure prior to disconnecting any fuel system component (injector, fuel rail, pressure regulator, etc.), fitting or fuel line connection. Exercise extreme caution whenever relieving fuel system pressure to avoid exposing skin, face and eyes to fuel spray. Please be advised that fuel under pressure may penetrate the skin or any part of the body that it contacts.

• Always place a shop towel or cloth around the fitting or connection prior to loosening to absorb any excess fuel due to spillage. Ensure that all fuel spillage, should it occur, is quickly removed from engine surfaces. Ensure that all fuel soaked cloths or towels are deposited into a suitable waste container.

• Always keep a dry chemical (Class B) fire extinguisher near the work area.

• Do not allow fuel spray or fuel vapors to come into contact with a spark or open flame.

• Always use a backup wrench when loosening and tightening fuel line connection fittings. This will prevent unnecessary stress and torsion to fuel line piping. Always follow the proper torque specifications.

• Always replace worn fuel fitting O-rings with new. Do not substitute fuel hose or equivalent where fuel pipe is installed.

RELIEVING FUEL SYSTEM PRESSURE

1. Start the engine.

2. On 1989–92 vehicles, remove the fuel pump relay from the relay box, located under the left side of the instrument panel. On 1993 vehicles, remove the fuel pump relay from the main fuse box, located in the engine compartment next to the battery.

3. After the engine stalls, turn the ignition switch **OFF** and reinstall the fuel pump relay.

Fuel Line Couplings

REMOVAL & INSTALLATION

Vehicles equipped with the 3.0L engine use several methods to connect the fuel lines and fuel system components. Two of these methods, the hairpin clip push connect fitting and the spring lock coupling, require certain procedures to disconnect and connect.

Hairpin Clip Push Connect Fitting

1. Inspect the visible internal portion of the fitting for dirt accumulation. If more than a light coating of dust is present, clean the fitting before disassembly.

2. Some adhesion between the seals in the fitting and the tubing will occur with time. To separate, twist the fitting on the tube, then push and pull the fitting until it moves freely on the tube.

3. Remove the hairpin clip from the fitting by first bending and breaking the shipping tab. Next, spread the 2 clip legs by hand about ⅛ in. each to disengage the body and push the legs into the fitting. Lightly pull the triangular end of the clip and work it clear of the tube and fitting.

NOTE: Do not use hand tools to complete this operation.

4. Grasp the fitting and pull in an axial direction to remove the fitting from the tube. Be careful on 90 degree elbow connectors, as excessive side loading could break the connector body.

5. After disassembly, inspect and clean the tube end sealing surfaces. The tube end should be free of scratches and corrosion that could provide leak paths. Inspect the inside of the fitting for any internal parts such as O-rings and spacers that may have been dislodged from the fitting. Replace any damaged connector.

To connect:

6. Install a new connector if damage was found. Insert a new clip into any 2 adjacent openings with the triangular portion pointing away from the fitting opening. Install the clip until the legs of the clip are locked on the outside of the body. Piloting with an index finger is necessary.

7. Before installing the fitting on the tube, wipe the tube end with a clean cloth. Inspect the inside of the fitting to make sure it is free of dirt and/or obstructions.

8. Apply a light coating of engine oil to the tube end. Align the fitting and tube axially and push the fitting onto the tube end. When the fitting is engaged, a definite click will be heard. Pull on the fitting to make sure it is fully engaged.

Spring Lock Coupling

The spring lock coupling is a fuel line coupling held together by a garter spring inside a circular cage. When the coupling is connected together, the flared end of the female fitting slips behind the garter spring inside the cage of the male fitting. The garter spring and cage then prevent the flared end of the female fitting from pulling out of the cage. As an additional locking feature, most vehicles have a horseshoe shaped retaining clip that improves the retaining reliability of the spring lock coupling.

Fuel Filter

REMOVAL & INSTALLATION

1. Relieve the fuel system pressure.
2. Disconnect the fuel lines from both ends of the fuel filter. Plug the lines to prevent leakage.
3. On 1989–92 vehicles, loosen the bolt and nut and remove the in-line fuel filter from its mounting bracket. On 1993 vehicles, remove the mounting nuts and remove the filter from the mounting bracket.
4. Installation is the reverse of the removal procedure. Check for any fuel leaks.

Electric Fuel Pump

PRESSURE TESTING

1. Relieve the pressure in the fuel system, then disconnect the negative battery cable.
2. Install a suitable fuel pressure gauge between the fuel filter and the fuel rail.

3. On 2.0L and 2.5L engines, connect a jumper wire between the **F/P** and **GND** terminals on the data link connector, located next to the battery. On 2.2L engines, connect a jumper wire between the **BK** and **LG** terminals of the fuel pump test connector. On the 3.0L engine, ground the fuel pump lead of the self-test connector through a jumper wire at the **FP** lead.

4. Connect the negative battery cable, turn the ignition key **ON** and check the fuel pump pressure. The pressure should be 64–92 psi. on the 2.0L engine, 64–85 psi. on the 2.2L engines, 72–92 psi. on the 2.5L engine or 35–40 psi. on the 3.0L engine.

5. If there is no fuel pressure, remove the fuel tank cap and try to hear if the fuel pump is operating. If the pump sounds like it's running, check for a restriction in the fuel line. If the pump is not running, check for power to the pump and check the pump motor ground. If there is no power to the pump, check all electrical connections and check the fuel pump relay.

6. If fuel pressure is low, check for a restriction in the fuel line or clogged fuel filters.

7. Remove the jumper wire, relieve the fuel system pressure and disconnect the negative battery cable.

8. Remove the fuel pressure gauge and reconnect the fuel line.

9. Connect the negative battery cable.

REMOVAL & INSTALLATION

The fuel pump is mounted on the fuel sending unit assembly in the fuel tank.

1989–92

1. Relieve the fuel pressure and disconnect the negative battery cable.
2. Depress the clips on each end of the rear seat cushion and remove the cushion.
3. Disconnect the electrical connector from the fuel pump/sending unit.
4. Remove the attaching screws from the fuel pump/sending unit access cover and remove the cover.
5. Disconnect the fuel supply and return hoses from the fuel pump/sending unit.
6. Remove the attaching screws and the fuel pump/sending unit from the fuel tank.

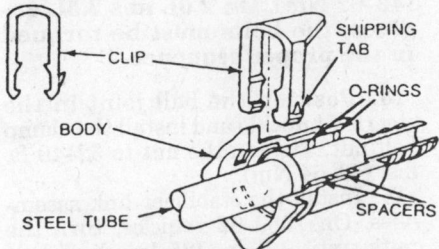

Hairpin clip push connect fitting— vehicles with 3.0L Engine

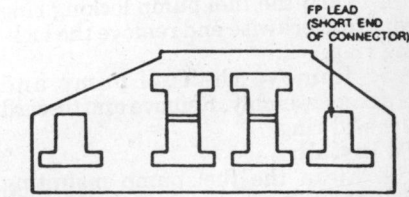

Self-test connector terminal locations— 3.0L Engine

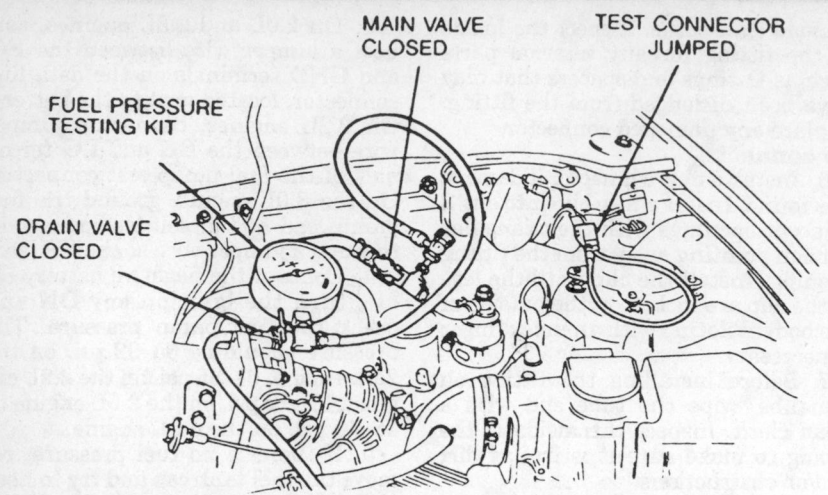

FUEL PRESSURE
TESTING KIT

MAIN VALVE
CLOSED

TEST CONNECTOR
JUMPED

DRAIN VALVE
CLOSED

Fuel pump pressure testing—2.2L Engines

7. Disconnect the sending unit electrical connector, remove the sending unit attaching nuts and remove the sending unit from the fuel pump assembly.

To install:

8. Attach the sending unit to the fuel pump assembly and install the nuts. Connect the sending unit electrical connector.

9. Install the fuel pump/sending unit into the fuel tank and install the mounting screws.

10. Connect the fuel supply and return lines.

11. Install the access cover and the mounting screws.

12. Connect the sending unit electrical connector.

13. Position the rear seat cushion over the floor, making sure to align the retaining pins with the clips. Push down firmly until the 2 retaining pins are locked into the rear seat retaining clips.

14. Connect the negative battery cable, start the engine and check for proper system operation and for fuel leaks.

1993

1. Disconnect the negative battery cable.

2. Remove the fuel tank and place it on a bench.

3. Remove any dirt that has accumulated around the fuel pump retaining flange so it will not enter the tank during pump removal and installation.

4. Turn the fuel pump locking ring counterclockwise and remove the locking ring.

5. Remove the fuel pump and bracket assembly. Remove and discard the seal ring.

To install:

6. Clean the fuel pump mounting flange, fuel tank mounting surface and seal ring groove.

7. Apply a light coating of grease on a new seal ring to hold it in place during assembly and install in the seal ring groove.

8. Install the fuel pump and bracket assembly carefully to ensure the filter is not damaged. Make sure the locating keys are in the keyways and the seal ring remains in the groove.

9. Hold the pump assembly in place and install the locking ring finger-tight. Make sure all the locking tabs are under the tank lock ring tabs.

10. Rotate the locking ring clockwise until the ring is against the stops.

11. Install the fuel tank in the vehicle. Add a minimum of 10 gallons of fuel to the tank and check for leaks.

12. Connect the negative battery cable, start the engine and check for proper system operation and for fuel leaks.

DRIVE AXLE

Halfshaft

REMOVAL & INSTALLATION

1. Disconnect the negative battery cable. Raise and safely support the vehicle.

2. Remove the front wheel and tire assembly and the necessary inner fender splash guards.

3. Remove the stabilizer link assembly from the lower control arm.

4. Using a cape chisel and a hammer, raise the staked portion of the hub nut.

5. Using an assistant to depress the brake pedal, loosen but do not remove, the hub nut.

6. Remove the lower control arm ball joint clamp bolt. Using a prybar, pry the lower control arm downward

to separate the ball joint from the steering knuckle.

NOTE: If removing the right halfshaft, remove the support bearing bracket from the cylinder block.

7. Separate the halfshaft from the transaxle by positioning a prybar between the halfshaft and transaxle case. Pry out the halfshaft while pulling out on the steering knuckle. Be careful not to damage the transaxle case, transaxle oil seal, CV-joint or CV-joint boot.

8. Remove and discard the hub nut. Pull the halfshaft out of the wheel hub.

NOTE: If the halfshaft binds in the hub splines, use a plastic hammer to tap it out or a wheel puller to press it out. Never use a metal hammer.

9. Install transaxle plugs T88C–7025–AH or equivalent, into the halfshaft openings of the transaxle case and into the differential side gears; this will keep the differential side gears from becoming mispositioned.

To install:

10. On the end of each halfshaft, install a new circlip. Start 1 end of the clip in the groove and work the clip over the stub shaft end and into the groove. This will prevent over-expanding the clip. Make sure the end gap is positioned at the top of the splines.

11. Remove the transaxle plugs and inspect the transaxle oil seals. Replace, if necessary.

12. Lubricate the halfshaft splines with a suitable grease, align the splines with the differential side gears and push the halfshaft into the differential. Make sure the retaining clip is seated in the differential side gear groove.

13. Position the halfshaft through the wheel hub and install a new attaching nut. Do not tighten the nut at this time.

NOTE: If installing the right halfshaft, install the halfshaft support bearing and tighten the mounting bolts to 31–46 ft. lbs. (42–62 Nm). On 2.0L ans 2.5L engines, the bolts must be torqued in the proper sequence.

14. Position the ball joint in the steering knuckle and install the clamp bolt/nut. Tighten the nut to 32–40 ft. lbs. (43–54 Nm).

15. Install the stabilizer link assemblies. On 1989–92 vehicles, turn the nuts until 1.0 in. (25.4mm) of bolt thread can be measured from the upper nut. When the length is reached,

2.0L

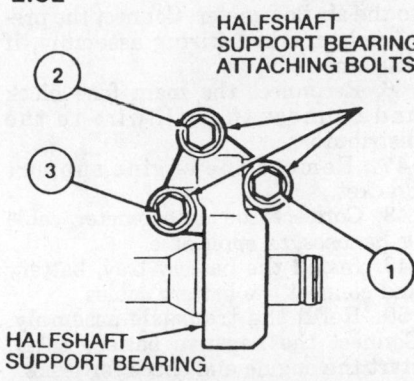

HALFSHAFT
SUPPORT BEARING
ATTACHING BOLTS

HALFSHAFT
SUPPORT BEARING

2.5L

HALFSHAFT
SUPPORT BEARING
ATTACHING BOLTS

HALFSHAFT
SUPPORT BEARING

Halfshaft support bearing bracket bolt torque sequence—1993

secure the upper nut and back off the lower nut until a torque of 12–17 ft. lbs. (16–23 Nm) is reached. On 1993 vehicles, tighten the nut to 40 ft. lbs. (54 Nm).

16. Install the splash shields.

17. Have an assistant apply the brakes and tighten the halfshaft attaching nut to 116–174 ft. lbs. (157–235 Nm) on 1989–92 vehicles or 174–235 ft. lbs. (235–319 Nm) on 1993 vehicles. Stake the nut using a suitable chisel with a rounded cutting edge.

NOTE: If the nut splits or cracks after staking, it must be replaced with a new nut.

18. Install the wheel and tire assembly.

Front Wheel Hub, Knuckle/Spindle and Bearings

REMOVAL & INSTALLATION

1. Raise and safely support the vehicle. Remove the front wheel and tire assembly.

2. Using a small cape chisel and a hammer, raise the staked portion of the hub nut.

3. Have an assistant apply the brakes and remove the hub nut. Discard the nut after removal; it must not be reused.

4. On 1989–92 vehicles, remove the stabilizer bar-to-control arm, bolt, nut, washers and bushings. On 1993 vehicles, remove the stabilizer bar link nut.

5. At the tie rod end, remove the cotter pin and nut. Using a tie rod end separator tool or equivalent, separate the tie rod end from the steering knuckle.

6. If equipped with anti-lock brakes, remove the wheel speed sensor and the sensor harness routing bracket.

7. Remove the caliper and anchor bracket and suspend the caliper assembly from the coil spring with mechanics wire.

8. Remove the brake disc rotor.

9. Remove the lower control arm ball joint clamp nut/bolt. Using a prybar, pry the lower control arm downward and separate the ball joint from the steering knuckle.

10. Remove the steering knuckle-to-strut attaching bolts and slide the steering knuckle assembly from the strut bracket.

11. Slide the steering knuckle assembly from the halfshaft and support the halfshaft with mechanics wire; be careful not to damage the seals. Should the wheel hub bind on the halfshaft, use a plastic hammer to jar it free.

NOTE: If the halfshaft splines bind in the hub, it may be necessary to use a 2-jawed wheel puller to separate them.

12. Using a prybar, pry the grease seal from the knuckle.

13. Position the steering knuckle in a suitable fixture and press the hub from the knuckle.

NOTE: If the inner race remains on the hub, grind a section of the inner race to approximately 0.020 in. (0.5mm) and use a chisel to remove it.

14. Remove the snapring from the steering knuckle.

15. Position the steering knuckle in a suitable fixture and press the bearing from the knuckle.

NOTE: Unless the disc brake dust shield is damaged, it should be left on the steering knuckle; it is pressed on and is difficult to remove without damaging.

To install:

16. Inspect the steering knuckle and hub for cracks, wear and scoring. Replace parts as necessary.

17. Position the steering knuckle in a suitable fixture and press in the wheel bearing.

18. Install the snapring.

19. Position the steering knuckle in a suitable fixture and press the hub into the steering knuckle.

20. Apply grease to the lip of a new seal and press the seal into the knuckle, using a suitable seal installer.

21. Grease the halfshaft splines. Slide the hub/steering knuckle onto the halfshaft and position it into the strut bracket. Torque the strut-to-steering knuckle nuts to 69–86 ft. lbs. (93–117 Nm).

22. Push the lower control arm ball joint into the steering knuckle and torque the clamp bolt to 32–40 ft. lbs. (43–54 Nm).

23. Install the brake rotor.

24. Install the caliper anchor bracket-to-steering knuckle bolts and torque to 58–72 ft. lbs. (78–98 Nm).

25. Have an assistant apply the brakes. Install a new hub nut and torque the nut to 116–174 ft. lbs. (157–235 Nm) on 1989–92 vehicles or 174–235 ft. lbs. (235–319 Nm) on 1993 vehicles. Stake the hub nut, using a chisel with a rounded cutting edge.

26. Connect the tie rod end to the steering knuckle, torque the nut to 22–33 ft. lbs. (29–44 Nm) and install a new cotter pin.

NOTE: Should the slots of the nut not align with the cotter pin hole, tighten the nut to align them; never loosen it.

27. On 1989–92 vehicles, connect the stabilizer bar to the lower control arm and tighten the nut until 0.79 in. (20mm) of the bolt threads are exposed beyond the nut.

28. On 1993 vehicles, connect the stabilizer bar to the link and tighten the nut to 40 ft. lbs. (54 Nm).

29. Install the wheel and tire assembly and torque the lug nuts to 65–87 ft. lbs. (88–118 Nm).

MANUAL TRANSAXLE

For further information on transmission/transaxles, please refer to "Chilton's Guide to Transmission Repair".

Transaxle Assembly

REMOVAL & INSTALLATION

1989–92

1. Disconnect the battery cables,

negative cable first. Remove the battery and the battery tray.

2. Disconnect the main fuse block and disconnect the coil wire from the distributor. Disconnect and mark the wiring assembly, as necessary.

3. Disconnect the electrical connector from the air flow meter and remove the air cleaner assembly.

4. On 2.2L non-turbocharged engine, remove the resonance chamber and bracket. On 2.2L turbocharged engine, remove the throttle body-to-intercooler air hose and the air cleaner-to-turbocharger air hose.

5. Disconnect the speedometer cable (analog cluster) or cluster harness (electronic cluster).

6. If equipped with the 3.0L engine, drain the engine coolant and close the drain valve. Remove the upper radiator hose.

7. Disconnect both ground wires from the transaxle. Raise and safely support the vehicle.

8. Remove the front wheel and tire assemblies and the splash shields. Drain the transaxle.

9. Remove the slave cylinder and move it aside.

10. Remove the tie rod ends-to-steering knuckle cotter pins and nuts. Disconnect the tie rod ends from the steering knuckle.

11. Remove the stabilizer link assemblies from the lower control arm.

12. Remove the lower control ball joint-to-steering knuckle nut/bolt. Using a prybar, pry the lower control arm downward to separate the ball joint from the steering knuckle.

13. Remove the right-hand joint shaft bracket.

14. Position a prybar between the halfshaft and transaxle case; pry the halfshafts from the transaxle and suspend them on a wire.

15. Install 2 transaxle plugs, T88C–7025–AH or equivalent, between the differential side gears to keep the gears from becoming mispositioned.

16. Remove the gusset plate-to-transaxle bolts on 2.2L engine. Disconnect the extension bar and shift control rod.

17. Remove the front exhaust pipe on the 3.0L engine.

18. Remove the flywheel inspection plate on the 2.2L engine.

19. Remove the starter motor and the access brackets.

20. Attach engine support bar D87L–6000–A or equivalent to the engine and support its weight.

21. Remove the center transaxle mount and bracket, the left transaxle mount and the right transaxle mount-to-frame nut and bolt.

22. Remove the crossmember and the left-hand side lower arm as an assembly.

23. Attach and secure a suitable jack to the transaxle.

24. Remove the transaxle-to-engine bolts, lower the transaxle and remove it from the vehicle.

To install:

25. Apply a small amount of grease to the input shaft splines.

26. Raise and position the transaxle. Install the transaxle-to-engine bolts and torque to 66–86 ft. lbs. (89–117 Nm).

27. Install the center transaxle mount and bracket and torque the bolts to 27–40 ft. lbs. (36–54 Nm) and the nuts to 47–66 ft. lbs. (64–89 Nm).

NOTE: Do not install the nut that braces the throttle air inlet hose bracket.

28. Install the left transaxle mount and torque the left transaxle-to-mount bolts on the 2.2L non-turbocharged engine to 27–38 ft. lbs. (37–52 Nm) or on the 2.2L turbocharged engine and 3.0L engine to 49–69 ft. lbs. (67–93 Nm). Torque the mount-to-bracket nut and bolt to 49–69 ft. lbs. (67–93 Nm).

29. Install the crossmember and the left side lower arm as an assembly. Tighten the bolts to 27–40 ft. lbs. (36–54 Nm) and the nuts to 55–69 ft. lbs. (75–93 Nm).

30. Install the right transaxle mount bolt and nut and tighten to 63–86 ft. lbs. (85–117 Nm).

31. Install the starter motor and access brackets.

32. Install the flywheel inspection cover on 2.2L engine. Tighten the bolts to 69–95 inch lbs. (8–11 Nm).

33. Connect the extension rod and control rod. Install the front exhaust pipe on 3.0L engine.

34. Install the slave cylinder and tighten the bolts to 14–19 ft. lbs. (19–26 Nm).

35. Install the gusset plate-to-transaxle bolts on the 2.2L engine and tighten to 27–38 ft. lbs. (37–52 Nm).

36. On the end of each halfshaft, install a new circlip. This must be done whenever halfshafts are serviced.

37. Remove the transaxle plugs and install the halfshaft until the clips snap into place. Attach the lower arm ball joints to the knuckles.

38. Install and torque the tie rod end-to-steering knuckle nut to 22–33 ft. lbs. (29–44 Nm) and install a new cotter pin. Tighten the lower control arm ball joint-to-steering knuckle nut and bolt to 32–40 ft. lbs. (43–54 Nm).

39. Install the stabilizer link assembly-to-lower control arm. Turn the upper nuts (on each assembly) until 0.79 in. (20mm) of bolt thread can be measured above the nuts.

40. Install the splash shields and the front wheel and tire assemblies;

torque the lug nuts to 65–87 ft. lbs. (88–118 Nm). Lower the vehicle.

41. Connect the ground wires to the transaxle case and tighten to 69–95 inch lbs. (8–11 Nm).

42. On the 2.2L non-turbocharged engine, install the resonance chamber and bracket; torque to 69–95 inch lbs. (8–11 Nm). On turbocharged engines, install the throttle body-to-intercooler air hose and torque the bracket-to-mount nut to 47–66 ft. lbs. (64–89 Nm).

43. On 3.0L engine, install the upper radiator hose and fill the cooling system.

44. Install the air cleaner assembly and tighten to 69–95 inch lbs. (8–11 Nm).

45. Connect the electrical connector to the air flow meter. Connect the previously marked wiring assembly, if disconnected.

46. Reconnect the main fuse block and connect the coil wire to the distributor.

47. Remove the engine support bracket.

48. Connect the speedometer cable or harness, as applicable.

49. Install the battery tray, battery and connect the battery cables.

50. Refill the transaxle assembly. Connect the negative battery cable, start the engine and check for leaks.

1993

1. Remove the fresh air duct and air cleaner assembly. Disconnect the battery cables and remove the battery and battery tray.

2. Remove the transaxle ground straps. Label and disconnect the vehicle speed sensor connector at the top right-hand rear corner of the transaxle.

3. Label and disconnect the park/neutral position switch electrical connector from the lower front of the transaxle. Label and disconnect the backup light switch electrical connector from the rear of the transaxle.

4. Disconnect the 2 spring clips from the clutch slave cylinder hydraulic line and remove the slave cylinder mounting bolts. Position the slave cylinder aside, without disconnecting the hydraulic line.

5. Support the engine with engine support tool 014–00750 or equivalent.

6. Remove the upper transaxle-to-engine mounting bolts and the upper starter bolts. Remove the fuel filter mounting nuts and position the filter aside, without disconnecting the fuel lines.

7. Remove the 2 nuts and the through bolt from the left side transaxle mount. Raise and safely support the vehicle.

8. If equipped with 2.0L engine, remove the intake manifold support bracket.

9. Disconnect the wiring from the starter, remove the lower starter bolt and remove the starter.

10. Remove the drain plug and drain the transaxle fluid into a suitable container. Discard the drain plug washer.

11. Remove the front wheel and tire assemblies. Unstake the halfshaft attaching nuts. Have an assistant apply the brakes to keep the hubs from turning, then remove the nuts and discard them.

12. Remove the lower splash shields. Remove the 6 transverse member bolts and the transverse member.

13. Remove the lower ball joint pinch bolt and nut from the left side knuckle. Pry the lower ball control arm down to separate the ball joint from the knuckle. Be careful not to damage the ball joint dust boot.

14. Pull the hub/knuckle assembly outward to separate it from the halfshaft. If the halfshaft is stuck in the hub, push it out using a suitable puller.

15. Position a prybar between the transaxle case and inner CV-joint. Pry the left halfshaft from the transaxle case. Install transaxle plug tool T88C–7025–AH or equivalent, to keep the differential side gear from becoming mispositioned.

16. If equipped with anti-lock brakes, remove the clips from the wheel speed sensor and the wheel speed sensor mounting nuts from the sensor harness mount on the left side of the vehicle.

17. If equipped with 2.5L engine, disconnect the oxygen sensor connectors. Remove and discard the exhaust pipe-to-manifold nuts. Lower the exhaust system enough to gain access to the right side halfshaft support bearing.

18. Remove the 3 right halfshaft support bearing bolts. If equipped with anti-lock brakes, remove the clips from the wheel speed sensor and the wheel speed sensor mounting nuts from the sensor harness mount on the right side of the vehicle.

19. Remove the lower ball joint pinch bolt and nut from the right side knuckle. Pry the lower ball control arm down to separate the ball joint from the knuckle. Be careful not to damage the ball joint dust boot.

20. Pull the hub/knuckle assembly outward to separate it from the halfshaft. If the halfshaft is stuck in the hub, push it out using a suitable puller.

21. Pull the right halfshaft from the transaxle case. Install transaxle plug tool T88C–7025–AH or equivalent, to keep the differential side gear from becoming mispositioned.

22. Remove the 6 nuts and 2 bolts from the transaxle cradle and remove the cradle.

23. Disconnect the shift linkage and extension bar from the transaxle.

24. Remove the 3 rear transaxle mount-to-transaxle bolts. Support the transaxle with a jack.

25. Remove the 3 rear transaxle mount bolts and the rear transaxle mount. Remove the lower transaxle-to-engine mounting bolts.

26. Separate the transaxle from the engine and lower it from the vehicle.

To install:

27. Apply a thin coating of molybdenum grease to the input shaft splines. Raise the transaxle into position and align it with the engine.

28. Connect the transaxle to the engine and loosely install the lower transaxle-to-engine bolts. Remove the transmission jack.

29. Install the 2 nuts and through bolt into the left transaxle mount. Tighten the nuts to 44 ft. lbs. (60 Nm) and the through bolt to 86 ft. lbs. (116 Nm).

30. Install the rear transaxle mount with the 3 bolts. Tighten the bolts to 68 ft. lbs. (93 Nm).

31. Connect the extension bar and shift linkage to the transaxle. Tighten the extension bar nut to 38 ft. lbs. (51 Nm) and the shift linkage nut to 18 ft. lbs. (25 Nm).

32. Install the transaxle cradle and tighten the bolts and nuts to specification.

33. Remove the transaxle plug from the right side and install the right halfshaft. Pull out on the right hub/knuckle assembly and install the halfshaft into the hub.

34. Pry the lower control arm down and insert the lower ball joint stud into

the knuckle. Install the pinch bolt and nut and tighten to 41 ft. lbs. (56 Nm).

35. If equipped with anti-lock brakes, install the wheel speed sensor harness mounting nuts and tighten to 88 inch lbs. (10 Nm). Install the sensor harness clips.

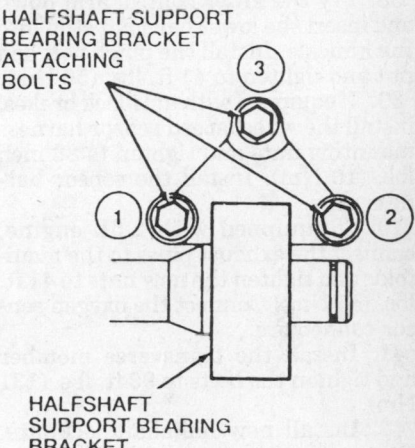

2.0L

HALFSHAFT SUPPORT BEARING BRACKET ATTACHING BOLTS

HALFSHAFT SUPPORT BEARING BRACKET

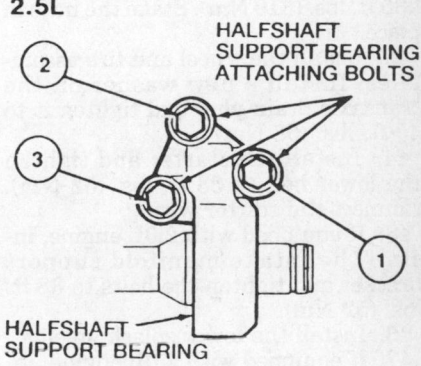

2.5L

HALFSHAFT SUPPORT BEARING ATTACHING BOLTS

HALFSHAFT SUPPORT BEARING

Transaxle cradle torque specifications—1993

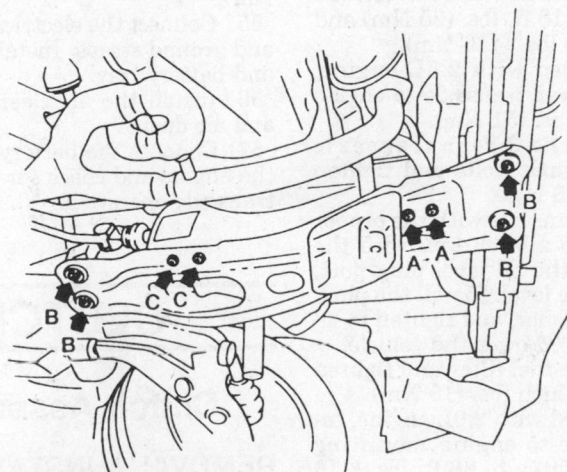

TIGHTENING TORQUE
A: 75 – 104 N·m (55 – 77 LB-FT)
B: 67 – 93 N·m (50 – 68 LB-FT)
C: 44 – 60 N·m (32 – 44 LB-FT)

Rear main bearing oil seal–3.0L Engine

36. Install the 3 halfshaft support bearing bracket bolts. Tighten the bolts, in sequence, to 45 ft. lbs. (61 Nm).

37. Remove the transaxle plug from the left side and install the left halfshaft. Pull out on the left hub/knuckle assembly and install the halfshaft into the hub.

38. Pry the lower control arm down and insert the lower ball joint stud into the knuckle. Install the pinch bolt and nut and tighten to 41 ft. lbs. (56 Nm).

39. If equipped with anti-lock brakes, install the wheel speed sensor harness mounting nuts and tighten to 88 inch lbs. (10 Nm). Install the sensor harness clips.

40. If equipped with 2.5L engine, connect the exhaust pipes to the manifolds and tighten the new nuts to 41 ft. lbs. (55 Nm). Connect the oxygen sensor connectors.

41. Install the transverse member and tighten the bolts to 96 ft. lbs. (131 Nm).

42. Install new halfshaft locknuts. Have an assistant apply the brakes to lock the hubs, then tighten the nuts to 235 ft. lbs. (319 Nm). Stake the nuts in place.

43. Install the wheel and tire assemblies. Install a new washer on the transaxle drain plug and tighten it to 43 ft. lbs. (58 Nm).

44. Install the starter and tighten the lower bolt to 38 ft. lbs. (52 Nm). Connect the starter wiring.

45. If equipped with 2.0L engine, install the intake manifold support bracket and tighten the bolts to 38 ft. lbs. (52 Nm).

46. Install the lower splash shields.

47. If equipped with 2.0L engine, install the transaxle-to-engine and engine-to-transaxle bolts B, C, D and E. Tighten bolts B and D to 38 ft. lbs. (51 Nm), bolt C to 18 ft. lbs. (25 Nm) and bolt E to 86 ft. lbs. (116 Nm).

48. If equipped with 2.5L engine, tighten the lower transaxle-to-engine bolts to 38 ft. lbs. (51 Nm).

49. Install the 3 rear transaxle mount-to-transaxle bolts and tighten to 68 ft. lbs. (93 Nm).

50. Fill the transaxle with the proper type of fluid to a level even with the lower edge of the oil level plug port, with the vehicle level. Install the plug, using a new washer, and tighten to 43 ft. lbs. (58 Nm). Lower the vehicle.

51. Install the fuel filter and tighten the nuts to 88 inch lbs. (10 Nm).

52. If equipped with 2.0L engine, install transaxle-to-engine mounting bolts A and tighten to 86 ft. lbs. (116 Nm). If equipped with 2.5L engine, install the upper transaxle-to-engine bolts to 73 ft. lbs. (99 Nm).

53. Install the upper starter bolts and tighten to 38 ft. lbs. (51 Nm). Remove the engine support tool.

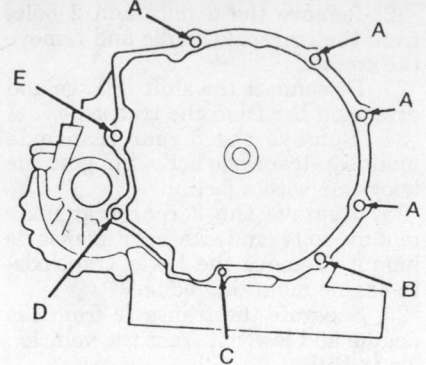

Transaxle mounting bolt identification— 2.0L engine with manual transaxle

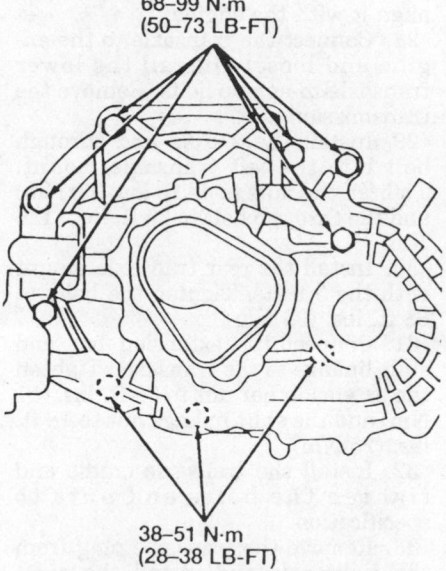

68–99 N·m
(50–73 LB-FT)

38–51 N·m
(28–38 LB-FT)

Transaxle mounting bolt torque specifications—1993 2.5L Engine

54. Install the clutch slave cylinder and tighten the bolts to 16 ft. lbs. (22 Nm).

55. Connect the electrical connectors and ground straps. Install the battery and battery tray.

56. Install the air cleaner assembly and air duct.

57. Connect the battery cables. Run the engine and check for leaks. Check transaxle operation.

CLUTCH

Clutch Assembly

REMOVAL & INSTALLATION

1. Disconnect the negative battery cable. Raise and safely support the vehicle.

2. Remove the transaxle assembly.

3. Position a suitable clutch alignment tool through the pressure plate, clutch disc and into the pilot bearing; this will keep the assembly from dropping when the bolts are removed.

4. Install flywheel holding tool T74P-6375-A or equivalent, to keep the flywheel from turning. Remove the pressure plate-to-flywheel bolts, a little at a time, evenly, to relieve the spring pressure.

5. Remove the pressure plate, clutch disc and alignment tool.

6. Inspect the pressure plate and clutch disc for wear and/or damage and replace, as necessary.

7. Inspect the pilot bearing for excessive wear or scoring. Remove it, using a suitable puller, only if replacement is necessary.

8. Inspect the flywheel for scoring, cracks, worn or broken teeth, or other damage. Remove the flywheel if machining or replacement is necessary. Use care when removing the last bolt to prevent dropping the flywheel.

9. Remove the release bearing and fork. Inspect them for wear or damage and replace, as necessary

To install:

10. Apply molybdenum grease to the release bearing where it contacts the release fork. Apply molybdenum grease to the release fork at the pivot point and to the area where it contacts the release bearing.

11. Install the release fork and bearing.

12. If removed, install the flywheel. Make sure the crankshaft flange and flywheel mating surfaces are clean. On 1993 vehicles, remove the old sealant from the flywheel bolts and apply stud and bearing mount sealant to them. If the old sealant cannot be removed, replace the bolts.

13. Install the flywheel holding tool. Tighten the flywheel bolts, in sequence, to 75 ft. lbs. (102 Nm) on 2.0L and 2.2L engines, 49 ft. lbs. (67 Nm) on 2.5L engines or 54–64 ft. lbs. (73–87 Nm) on the 3.0L engine.

14. If removed, install a new pilot bearing using a suitable installation

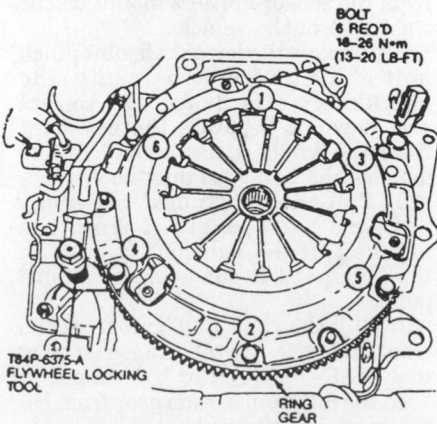

BOLT
6 REQ'D
18–26 N·m
(13–20 LB-FT)

T84P-6375-A
FLYWHEEL LOCKING
TOOL

RING
GEAR

Pressure plate bolt torque sequence

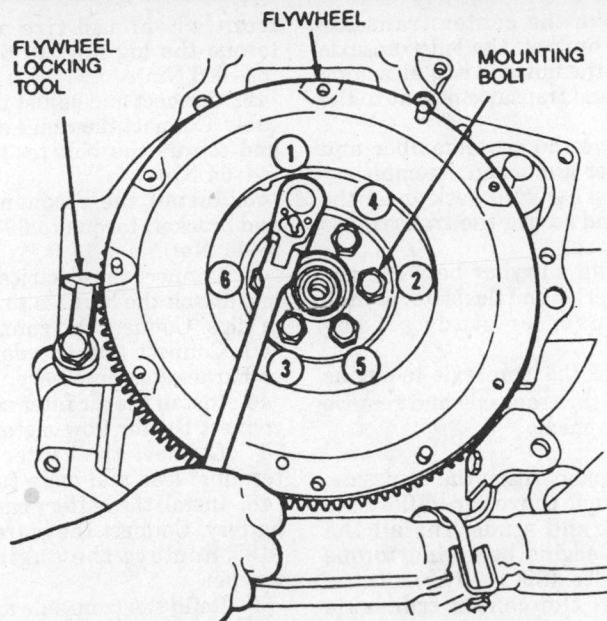

Flywheel bolt torque sequence—2.2L and 3.0L Engines

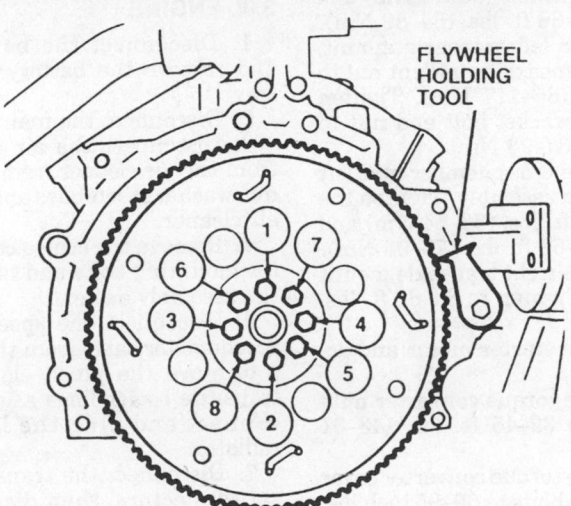

Flywheel bolt torque sequence—2.0L and 2.5L Engines

tool. When installed, the pilot bearing should be 0.150–0.165 in. (3.8–4.2mm) below the surface of the crankshaft flange on 1989–92 vehicles or 0–0.016 in. (0–0.4mm) below the surface of the crankshaft flange on 1993 vehicles.

15. Apply a small amount of molybdenum grease to the clutch disc and input shaft splines. Do not let grease get on the clutch face.

16. Install the clutch disc and alignment tool with the clutch spring plate side of the disc toward the transaxle.

17. Install the pressure plate to the flywheel. Install the pressure plate-to-flywheel bolts and torque, evenly, a little at a time, to 18 ft. lbs. (26 Nm) in the proper sequence.

18. Install the transaxle assembly and lower the vehicle.

19. Connect the negative battery cable. Check for proper clutch operation.

Clutch Master Cylinder

REMOVAL & INSTALLATION

1. Disconnect the negative battery cable. On 1989–92 vehicles, remove the ABS relay box, if equipped.

2. On 1993 vehicles, disconnect and plug the hose from the brake fluid reservoir.

3. Disconnect the hydraulic line at the master cylinder, using a tubing wrench.

4. Working inside the vehicle, remove the upper master cylinder retaining nut. Remove the other nut from the engine compartment.

5. Remove the clutch master cylinder.

To install:

6. Remove all the old gasket materi-al from the master cylinder and firewall and install a new gasket.

7. Install the clutch master cylinder and tighten the mounting nuts to 14–19 ft. lbs. (19–26 Nm).

8. Connect the hydraulic line and tighten the nut securely.

9. On 1993 vehicles, unplug and connect the hose to the brake fluid reservoir.

10. Install the ABS relay box, if equipped.

11. Bleed the air from the clutch hydraulic system, connect the negative battery cable and road test the vehicle.

Clutch Slave Cylinder

REMOVAL & INSTALLATION

1. Disconnect the negative battery cable.

2. Disconnect the hydraulic line at the slave cylinder using a tubing wrench. Plug the line to prevent leakage.

3. Remove the slave cylinder mounting bolts and remove the slave cylinder.

To install:

4. Install the slave cylinder and tighten the mounting bolts to 12–16 ft. lbs. (16–22 Nm).

5. Connect the hydraulic line and tighten the nut to 10–15 ft. lbs. (13–21 Nm).

6. Connect the negative battery cable.

7. Bleed the air from the clutch hydraulic system and road test the vehicle.

Hydraulic Clutch System Bleeding

NOTE: The fluid reservoir must be maintained at the ¾ level or higher during air bleeding.

1. Remove the bleeder cap from the slave cylinder and attach a vinyl hose to the bleeder screw.

2. Place the other end of the hose in a clear container partially filled with brake fluid.

3. Have an assistant slowly pump the clutch pedal several times.

4. With the clutch pedal depressed, loosen the bleeder screw to release the fluid and air.

5. Tighten the bleeder screw. Repeat this procedure until there are no air bubbles in the fluid in the container.

AUTOMATIC TRANSAXLE

For further information on transmission/transaxles, please refer to "Chilton's Guide to Transmission Repair".

Transaxle Assembly

REMOVAL & INSTALLATION

1989–92

2.2L ENGINE

1. Disconnect the battery cables (negative cable first). Remove the battery and the battery tray.
2. Disconnect the main fuse block and disconnect the coil wire from the distributor.
3. Disconnect the electrical connector from the air flow meter and remove the air cleaner assembly.
4. Remove the resonance chamber and bracket.
5. Disconnect the speedometer cable (analog cluster) or harness (electronic cluster).
6. Disconnect the transaxle electrical connectors and separate the harness from the transaxle clips.
7. Disconnect both ground wires, the range selector cable and the kickdown cable from the transaxle. Raise and safely support the vehicle.
8. Remove the front wheel and tire assemblies and the splash shields. Drain the transaxle fluid.
9. Disconnect and plug the oil cooler hoses from the transaxle. Insert plugs to prevent fluid leakage.
10. Remove the tie rod ends-to-steering knuckle cotter pins and nuts. Disconnect the tie rod ends from the steering knuckle.
11. Remove the stabilizer link assemblies from the lower control arm.
12. Remove the lower control ball joint-to-steering knuckle nut/bolt. Using a prybar, pry the lower control arm downward to separate the ball joint from the steering knuckle.
13. Remove the right-hand halfshaft bracket.
14. Position a prybar between the halfshaft and transaxle case; pry the halfshafts from the transaxle.
15. Install 2 transaxle plugs, T88C–7025–AH or equivalent, into the halfshaft openings of the transaxle case; this will keep the differential side gears from becoming mispositioned.
16. Remove the gusset plate-to-transaxle bolts.
17. Remove the torque converter-to-transaxle cover, the starter and the access brackets.
18. Using paint or chalk, matchmark the torque converter-to-flexplate position and remove the mounting nuts.
19. Mount engine support bar D87L–6000–A or equivalent, to the engine and support its weight.

20. Remove the center transaxle mount and bracket, the left transaxle mount and the nut and bolt attaching the right-hand transaxle mount to the frame.
21. Remove the crossmember and the left lower arm as an assembly.
22. Position a suitable jack under the transaxle and secure the transaxle to the jack.
23. Position a prybar between the torque converter and flexplate; pry the torque converter studs off the flexplate.
24. Remove the transaxle-to-engine bolts, lower the transaxle and remove it from the vehicle.

To install:
25. Raise and position the transaxle, align the torque converter-to-flexplate matchmark and studs. Install the transaxle-to-engine bolts and torque to 66–86 ft. lbs. (89–117 Nm).
26. Install the center transaxle mount and bracket and torque the bolts to 27–40 ft. lbs. (36–54 Nm) and the nuts to 47–66 ft. lbs. (64–89 Nm).
27. Install the left transaxle mount. Tighten the transaxle-to-mount nut to 63–86 ft. lbs. (85–117 Nm). Tighten the mount-to-bracket bolt and nut to 49–69 ft. lbs. (67–93 Nm).
28. Install the crossmember and left lower arm as an assembly. Tighten the bolts to 27–40 ft. lbs. (36–54 Nm) and the nuts to 55–69 ft. lbs. (75–93 Nm).
29. Install the right transaxle mount bolt and nut. Tighten to 63–86 ft. lbs. (85–117 Nm).
30. Install the starter motor and access brackets.
31. Install the torque converter nuts and tighten to 32–45 ft. lbs. (43–61 Nm).
32. Install the torque converter cover and tighten the bolts to 69–95 inch lbs. (8–11 Nm).
33. Install the gusset plate-to-tranaxle bolts and tighten to 27–38 ft. lbs. (37–52 Nm).
34. On the end of each halfshaft, install a new circlip.
35. Remove the transaxle plugs and install the halfshaft until the circlips snap into place.
36. Attach the lower ball joints to the steering knuckle.
37. Install the tie rods and tighten to 22–33 ft. lbs. (29–44 Nm). Install new cotter pins.
38. Install the bolts and nuts to the lower arm ball joints and tighten to 32–40 ft. lbs. (43–54 Nm).
39. Install the stabilizer link assembly-to-lower control arm. Turn the upper nuts (on each assembly) until 0.79 inch (20mm) of bolt thread can be measured above the nuts.
40. Install the oil cooler hoses to the transaxle.
41. Install the splash shields and the

front wheel and tire assemblies; torque the lug nuts to 65–87 ft. lbs. (88–118 Nm).
42. Connect and adjust the kickdown cable. Connect the range selector cable and torque the bolt to 33–47 ft. lbs. (44–64 Nm).
43. Install the resonance chamber and bracket; torque to 69–95 inch lbs. (8–11 Nm).
44. Connect the electrical connectors and attach the harness to the transaxle clips. Connect the gound wires.
45. Connect the speedometer cable or harness, as necessary.
46. Install the air filter assembly and connect the air flow meter connector
47. Connect the center distributor terminal lead and main fuse block.
48. Install the battery carrier and the battery. Connect the battery cables.
49. Remove the engine support bracket.
50. Refill the transaxle and check for leaks and proper operation.

3.0L ENGINE

1. Disconnect the battery cables and remove the battery and battery tray.
2. Disconnect the main fuse block.
3. Disconnect the air cleaner hose from the air cleaner, remove the bolt/nut/washer assemblies and remove the air cleaner.
4. Remove the cruise control actuator mounting bolts and nut and move the assembly aside.
5. Disconnect the speed sensor or speedometer cable from the transaxle.
6. Move the pinch clamps on the transaxle cooler lines aside, then disconnect and plug the lines at the radiator.
7. Disconnect the transaxle electrical connectors, then disconnect the harness from the routing brackets.
8. Disconnect the shift cable from the transaxle and routing bracket. Remove the transaxle wiring harness bracket and disconnect the 2 ground straps from the transaxle.
9. Disconnect the kickdown cable from the cable bracket and the throttle cam.
10. Install engine support bar D88L–6000–A or equivalent to support the engine and transaxle. Remove all accessible transaxle-to-engine bolts from the top of the engine compartment and remove the transaxle upper mount nuts.
11. Raise and safely support the vehicle.
12. Remove the front wheel and tire assemblies and the inner fender splash shields. Drain the transaxle fluid.
13. Disconnect the stabilizer links from the lower control arms and the bolts/nuts from the ball joints. Separate the ball joints from the steering

knuckles by prying downward on the lower control arm while pushing inward on the rotor.

14. Remove the mounting bolts from the right halfshaft dynamic damper. Remove the halfshafts by inserting a prybar between the shaft and transaxle case and prying out.

15. Install transaxle plugs T88C–7025–AH or equivalent, in the transaxle to prevent the differential side gears from moving out of position.

16. Remove the starter and bracket and the transaxle support bracket.

17. Remove the torque converter inspection plate. Matchmark the converter and the flexplate and remove the attaching nuts. Use a prybar to move the converter away from the flexplate, disengaging the converter studs.

18. Position a transmission jack under the transaxle. Remove the rear lower mount bolts and the front lower mount through-bolt. Remove the left front crossmember and lower control arm as an assembly.

19. Remove the remaining transaxle-to-engine bolts and lower the transaxle from the vehicle.

To install:

20. Raise the transaxle into position, aligning the matchmark and the torque converter studs with the flexplate. Install the transaxle-to-engine lower bolts and tighten to 66–86 ft. lbs. (89–117 Nm).

21. Install the left front crossmember and lower control arm assembly. Tighten the bolts to 27–40 ft. lbs. (36–54 Nm) and the nut to 55–69 ft. lbs. (75–93 Nm).

22. Install the front lower mount through bolt and tighten to 66–86 ft. lbs. (85–117 Nm). Install the rear lower mount bolts and tighten to 49–69 ft. lbs. (67–93 Nm).

23. Install the torque converter attaching nuts and tighten to 32–45 ft. lbs. (43–61 Nm). Install the inspection plate and mounting bolt.

24. Install the transaxle support bracket and the starter motor and bracket.

25. Install a new circlip on the end of each halfshaft. Remove the transaxle plugs and install the halfshaft, making sure the clips lock in place.

26. Install the mounting bolts to the right halfshaft dynamic damper. Tighten to 31–46 ft. lbs. (42–62 Nm).

27. Attach the ball joints to the steering knuckles. Install the bolts and nuts and tighten to 27–40 ft. lbs. (36–54 Nm).

28. Install the stabilizer link assemblies. Turn the nuts until 0.79 in. (20mm) of bolt thread can be measured from the upper nut.

29. Install the splash guards and the wheel and tire assemblies. Tighten the lug nuts to 65–87 ft. lbs. (88–118 Nm). Lower the vehicle.

30. Install the upper mount nuts and tighten to 47–66 ft. lbs. (64–89 Nm). Install the remaining transaxle-to-engine bolts and tighten to 66–86 ft. lbs. (89–117 Nm).

31. Remove the engine support bar.

32. Connect the kickdown cable to the throttle cam and the cable bracket. Tighten the adjusting nuts.

33. Connect the ground straps and install the wiring harness bracket.

34. Connect the shift cable to the routing bracket and the transaxle. Install the attaching nut and tighten to 33–47 ft. lbs. (44–64 Nm).

35. Connect the transaxle electrical connectors, then connect the harness routing brackets to the transaxle.

36. Unplug the transaxle cooler lines and connect them to the radiator. Install the pinch clamps.

37. Connect the speed sensor or speedometer cable to the transaxle.

38. Position the cruise control actuator and install the mounting bolts and nut.

39. Position the air cleaner assembly and install the bolt/nut/washer assemblies. Connect the air cleaner hose and install the clamp.

40. Connect the main fuse block.

41. Install the battery tray and battery. Connect the battery cables.

42. Refill the transaxle and check for leaks and proper operation. Adjust the kickdown cable.

1993

1. Disconnect the battery cables and remove the battery and battery tray.

2. Remove the air cleaner assembly.

3. Pry the shift cable from the transaxle manual lever. Remove the cable bracket lock tab retainer, press in on the lock tabs and pull the cable through the bracket.

4. Disconnect the neutral safety switch connector. Disconnect the oxygen sensor connector(s) and disconnect the transaxle electrical connector.

5. Remove the wiring harness bracket from the cable bracket. If equipped with 2.5L engine, remove the starter.

6. Disconnect the vehicle speed sensor connector. Remove the ground wire bracket and the ground wire.

7. Remove the harness support bracket to the engine block, located at the rear transaxle mount.

8. Disconnect and plug the oil cooler lines. Remove the 4 transaxle-to-engine mounting bolts.

9. Support the engine with engine support tool 014–00750 or equivalent. Remove the 2 left side transaxle mount nuts and bolt and the mount through bolt.

10. Remove the 2 fuel filter bracket nuts from the left transaxle mount. Position the filter and bracket, aside, without disconnecting the fuel lines.

11. Remove the left side transaxle mount. Disconnect the pulse signal generator connector.

12. Raise and safely support the vehicle. Remove the front wheel and tire assemblies and the splash shields.

13. Remove the 6 transverse member bolts and the transverse member. Remove the 6 transaxle cradle nuts and 2 bolts and remove the transaxle cradle.

14. Remove the 2 transaxle lower mount bolts and remove the lower mount.

15. Remove the halfshafts.

16. If equipped with 2.0L engine, remove the intake manifold support bracket and the starter.

17. Disconnect the transaxle vent hose and the dipstick tube.

18. If equipped with 2.0L engine, remove the seal rubber located next the starter opening. Use a small prybar to hold the flexplate and reach through the opening to remove the torque converter nuts.

19. If equipped with 2.5L engine, remove the 3 inspection cover bolts. Use a small prybar to hold the flexplate and remove the torque converter nuts.

20. Support the transaxle with a jack. Secure the transaxle to the jack to keep it from falling.

21. Remove the engine-to-transaxle and transaxle-to-engine bolts. Remove the 3 rear transaxle mount bolts.

22. Use a small prybar to separate the transaxle from the engine. Slightly tilt the transaxle and engine to ease removal.

23. Remove the transaxle from the engine and lower the transaxle from the vehicle.

To install:

24. Raise the transaxle into position. Align the torque converter studs with the flexplate.

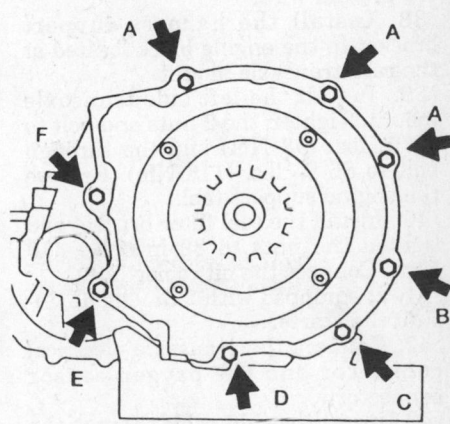

Transaxle mounting bolt identification— 2.0L engine with automatic transaxle

25. If equipped with 2.0L engine, install the transaxle-to-engine and engine-to-transaxle bolts. Tighten bolt **B** to 73 ft. lbs. (99 Nm), bolt **C** to 38 ft. lbs. (51 Nm), bolt **D** to 18 ft. lbs. (25 Nm), bolt **E** to 38 ft. lbs. (51 Nm) and bolt **F** to 73 ft. lbs. (99 Nm).

26. If equipped with 2.5L engine, install the engine-to-transaxle bolts and tighten to 73 ft. lbs. (99 Nm).

27. Install the 3 rear transaxle mount bolts and tighten to 68 ft. lbs. (93 Nm). Install the torque converter-to-flexplate nuts and tighten to 45 ft. lbs. (60 Nm).

28. On 2.0L engine, install the seal rubber. On 2.5L engine, install the inspection cover.

29. If equipped with 2.0L engine, install the intake manifold support bracket. Tighten the bolts to 38 ft. lbs. (52 Nm). Install the starter.

30. Connect the transaxle vent hose and install the dipstick tube. Tighten the dipstick tube mounting bolts to 88 inch lbs. (10 Nm).

31. Install the halfshafts.

32. Install the transaxle lower mount and tighten the bolts to 68 ft. lbs. (93 Nm). Remove the transaxle jack.

33. Install the transaxle cradle. Tighten the cradle-to-body bolts and nuts to 68 ft. lbs. (93 Nm). Tighten the cradle-to-front mount nuts to 77 ft. lbs. (104 Nm) and the cradle-to-rear mount nuts to 44 ft. lbs. (60 Nm).

34. Install the transverse member and tighten the bolts to 96 ft. lbs. (131 Nm).

35. Install the splash shields and the wheel and tire assemblies. Lower the vehicle.

36. If equipped with 2.0L engine, install transaxle-to-engine bolts **A** and tighten to 73 ft. lbs. (99 Nm). If equipped with 2.5L engine, install the upper transaxle-to-engine bolts and tighten to 73 ft. lbs. (99 Nm).

37. Connect the vehicle speed sensor and pulse signal generator connectors. Install the ground wire bracket and the ground wire.

38. Install the harness support bracket to the engine block located at the rear transaxle mount.

39. Install the left side transaxle mount. Tighten the 2 nuts and bolt to 68 ft. lbs. (93 Nm) and the through bolt to 86 ft. lbs. (116 Nm). Remove the engine support tool.

40. Install the fuel filter bracket and tighten the nuts to 88 inch lbs. (10 Nm). Connect the oil cooler lines.

41. If equipped with 2.5L engine, install the starter.

42. Connect the transaxle electrical connector and the oxygen sensor connector(s).

43. Insert the shift cable through the cable bracket and pull the cable until the lock tabs engage. Install the lock tab retainer. Connect the shift cable to the manual lever arm.

44. Connect the neutral safety switch connector. Snap the wiring harness bracket on the cable bracket.

45. Install the air cleaner assembly. Install the battery tray and battery. Connect the battery cables.

46. Fill the transaxle with the proper type and quantity of fluid. Run the engine and check for leaks. Road test and check for proper transaxle operation.

FRONT SUSPENSION

MacPherson Strut

REMOVAL & INSTALLATION

1. Raise and support the vehicle safely.

2. Remove the wheel and tire assembly.

3. On 1989–92 vehicles, remove the rubber cap from the strut mounting block. If equipped, disconnect the programmed ride control module connector.

4. At the inside of the strut mounting block and chassis strut tower, place an alignment mark.

5. On 1989–92 vehicles, if equipped, remove the programmed ride control actuator.

6. If equipped with anti-lock brakes, disconnect the electrical harness and remove the bracket.

7. Remove the brake caliper-to-steering knuckle bolts and suspend the caliper with mechanics wire; do not disconnect the pressure hose.

8. Remove the U-clip from the brake line hose and slide it out of the strut bracket.

9. Remove the strut-to-steering knuckle bolts.

10. On 1989–92 vehicles, remove the vane airflow meter assembly and the ignition coil bracket.

11. Remove the strut-to-chassis nuts and remove the strut from the vehicle.

12. Place the strut assembly in a suitable holding fixture. Loosen, but do not remove the shock nut. Compress the spring with a suitable compressor tool, then remove the shock nut. Gradually release the spring compressor.

13. Remove the programmed ride control module bracket, if equipped, strut mounting block, spring seat, dust boot, bump stopper and the coil spring from the strut assembly.

To install:

14. Install the coil spring, bump stopper, dust boot and the upper spring seat on the strut assembly.

15. Install the strut mounting block and the programmed ride control module bracket, if equipped, making sure the notch on the mounting block is 180 degrees from the knuckle mounting bracket on the strut.

16. Compress the spring with the compressor tool and install the shock nut. Tighten the nut to 47–69 ft. lbs. (64–84 Nm) on 1989–92 vehicles or 66–86 ft. lbs. (89–117 Nm) on 1993 vehicles. Gradually release the compressor tool and remove from the strut assembly.

17. Install the strut in the shock tower. Align the strut-to-chassis matchmark and torque the strut-to-chassis nuts to 34–46 ft. lbs. (46–63 Nm).

18. On 1989–92 vehicles, install the vane airflow meter assembly and the ignition coil bracket.

19. On 1989–92 vehicles, if equipped, install the programmed ride control module and the connector.

20. On 1989–92 vehicles, install the rubber cap on the strut tower.

21. Align the strut to the steering knuckle and torque the nuts/bolts to 69–86 ft. lbs. (93–117 Nm).

22. Install the brake caliper and the brake hose in its bracket. If equipped with anti-lock brakes, install the bracket and harness.

23. Install the wheel and tire assembly. Tighten the lug nuts to 65–87 ft. lbs. (88–118 Nm). Lower the vehicle.

Lower Ball Joints

INSPECTION

Raise and safely support the vehicle until the front wheel is clear of the floor. Try to rock the wheel up and down. If any play is felt, have an assistant rock the wheel while observing the lower ball joint. If any movement is seen between the steering knuckle and control arm, the ball joint is bad. If not, any wheel play indicates wheel bearing wear.

REMOVAL & INSTALLATION

The lower ball joint is an integral part of the lower control arm and cannot be serviced separately. If the lower ball joint is defective, the entire lower control arm must be replaced.

Lower Control Arms

REMOVAL & INSTALLATION

1. Raise and safely support the ve-

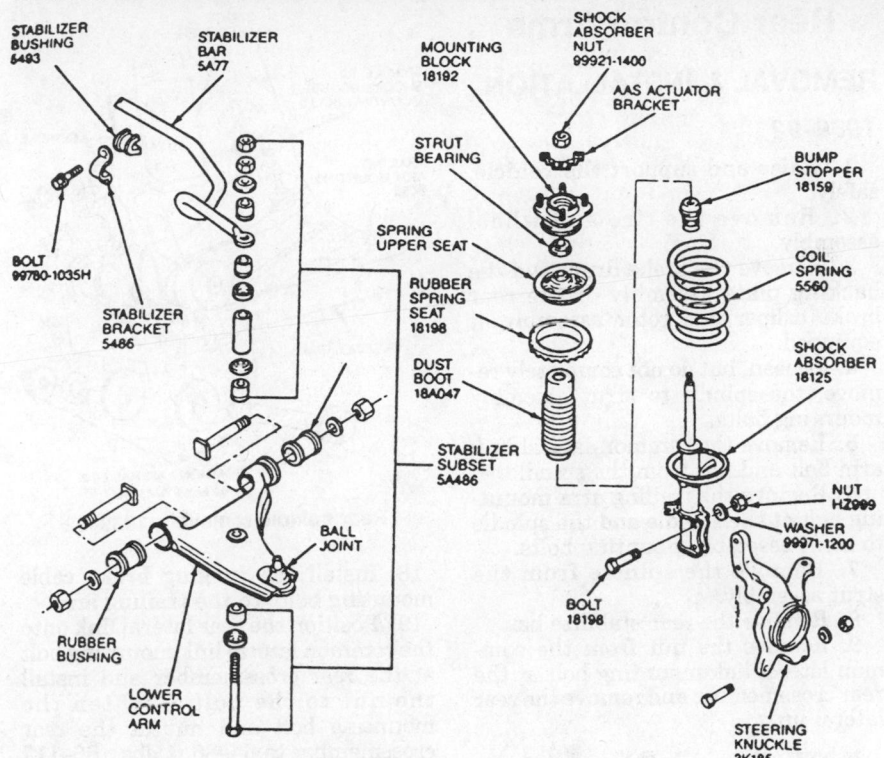

Front suspension components—1989–92

hicle. Remove the wheel and tire assembly.

2. Remove the brake caliper and support it with mechanics wire from the coil spring.

3. On 1989–92 vehicles, remove the stabilizer link assembly from the lower control arm. On 1993 vehicles, remove the stabilizer control link-to-control arm nut.

4. Remove the ball-joint clamp bolt from the steering knuckle. Using a prybar, pry downward to separate the ball joint from the steering knuckle.

5. On 1989–92 vehicles, if equipped, remove the harmonic damper from the chassis sub-frame; the damper is located on the left side of the vehicle.

6. Remove the lower control arm-to-chassis mounting bolts and nuts and remove the lower control arm.
To install:

7. Install the control arm and tighten the mounting bolts to 69–93 ft. lbs. (93–127 Nm) on 1989–92 vehicles. On 1993 vehicles, install the lower control arm rear bushing bolts and tighten to 69–96 ft. lbs. (93–131 Nm), then install the lower control arm front bushing bolt and tighten to 58–78 ft. lbs. (78–106 Nm).

8. On 1989–92 vehicles, install the harmonic damper, if equipped.

9. Install the ball joint stud into the steering knuckle and tighten the clamp bolt to 32–40 ft. lbs. (43–54 Nm).

10. On 1989–92 vehicles, install the stabilizer bar link assembly. Tighten

the nut until 0.79 in. (20mm) of thread remains above the nut.

11. On 1993 vehicles, install the stabilizer control link-to-lower control arm nut and tighten to 40 ft. lbs. (54 Nm).

12. Install the brake caliper.

13. Install the wheel and tire assembly. Tighten the lug nuts to 65–87 ft. lbs. (88–118 Nm). Lower the vehicle.

REAR SUSPENSION

MacPherson Strut

REMOVAL & INSTALLATION

1989–92

1. Raise and support the vehicle, safely. Remove the wheel and tire assembly.

2. Remove the upper trunk side garnish and lower trunk side trim to gain access to the strut assembly.

3. If equipped with programmed ride control, disconnect the programmed ride control module connector and removed the module.

4. If equipped with anti-lock brakes, remove the anti-lock brake harness and remove the bracket.

5. If equipped with drum brakes, re-

move the drum and backing plate assembly. If equipped with rear disc brakes, remove the rear disc brake caliper and rotor assembly.

6. Remove the brake line U-clip from the strut housing.

7. Loosen, but do not completely remove, the trailing arm bolt. Remove the spindle-to-strut bolts.

8. From inside the vehicle, remove the strut-to-chassis nuts. Remove the strut assembly.

9. Mount the strut assembly in a suitable vice and loosen, but do not completely remove the shock absorber nut.

10. Remove the strut assembly from the vice and compress the spring, using spring compressor 086–00029 or equivalent.

11. Remove the shock absorber nut.

12. Gradually release the spring compressor. Be careful not to strip the threads on the shock absorber as the spring expands.

13. Remove the strut mounting block, upper rubber spring seat, dust boot, bump stopper and the coil spring from the shock absorber.
To install:

14. Install the coil spring, bump stopper, dust boot and the upper spring seat on the shock absorber.

15. Install the strut mounting block. The mounting block will not seat on the shock absorber unless the notches on the block line up with those on the shock absorber.

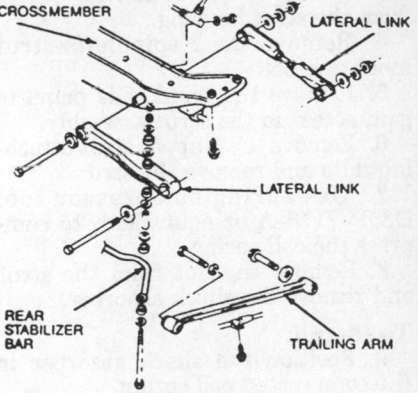

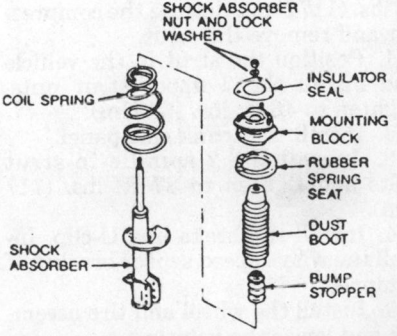

Rear suspension components—1989–92

16. Compress the spring with the compressor tool and install the shock absorber nut. Tighten the nut to 47–69 ft. lbs. (64–84 Nm).

17. Gradually release the compressor tool and remove from the strut assembly.

18. Position the strut into the strut tower and torque the strut-to-chassis nuts to 34–46 ft. lbs. (46–63 Nm).

19. If equipped with programmed ride control, install the module and reconnect the connector.

20. Install the lower trunk side trim and the upper trunk side garnish.

21. Install the spindle-to-strut mounting bolts and tighten to 69–86 ft. lbs. (93–117 Nm). Tighten the trailing arm mounting bolt to 64–86 ft. lbs. (86–117 Nm).

22. Install the brake drum and backing plate or the caliper and rotor assembly, as applicable. Install the brake line U-clip onto the strut.

23. If equipped, install the ABS brake harness and bracket.

24. Install the wheel and tire assembly and tighten the lug nuts to 65–87 ft. lbs. (88–118 Nm). Lower the vehicle.

1993

1. Raise and safely support the vehicle. Remove the rear wheel and tire assembly.

2. If equipped with anti-lock brakes, remove the speed sensor routing bracket.

3. Remove the brake line U-clip from the strut housing.

4. Remove the 2 spindle-to-strut mounting bolts.

5. Remove the trunk side panel to gain access to the strut assembly.

6. Remove the 3 upper strut attaching nuts and remove the strut.

7. Use spring compressor tool D85P–7178–A or equivalent, to compress the coil spring.

8. Remove the nut from the strut and remove the shock absorber.

To install:

9. Position the shock absorber in the compressed coil spring.

10. Install the nut and tighten to 87 ft. lbs. (117 Nm). Release the compressor and remove the strut.

11. Position the strut in the vehicle and install the 3 upper strut nuts. Tighten to 46 ft. lbs. (63 Nm).

12. Install the trunk side panel.

13. Install the 2 spindle-to-strut bolts and tighten to 87 ft. lbs. (117 Nm).

14. Install the brake line U-clip. Install the wheel speed sensor bracket, if equipped.

15. Install the wheel and tire assembly and lower the vehicle.

Rear Control Arms

REMOVAL & INSTALLATION

1989–92

1. Raise and support the vehicle, safely.

2. Remove the tire and wheel assembly.

3. Remove the brake drum and the backing plate assembly or the rear brake caliper and rotor assembly, if equipped.

4. Loosen, but do not completely remove, the spindle to strut assembly mounting bolts.

5. Remove the common lateral link arm bolt and nut from the spindle.

6. Remove the trailing arm mounting bolt at the spindle and the spindle to strut assembly mounting bolts.

7. Remove the spindle from the strut assembly.

8. Remove the rear stabilize bar.

9. Remove the nut from the common lateral link mounting bolt at the rear crossmember and remove the rear lateral link.

NOTE: Because of lack of clearance between the fuel tank and the common lateral link mounting bolt, the bolt and the front lateral link cannot be removed at this time.

10. Remove the parking brake mounting bolts from the trailing arm assembly.

11. Remove the trailing arm mounting bolt and the trailing arm.

12. Remove the exhaust mounting bolts and the brake line retaining bracket from the rear crossmember. Remove the mounting bolts from the end of the crossmember.

13. Remove the rear crossmember and front lateral link as an assembly. Remove the common lateral link mounting bolt from the rear crossmember and remove the front lateral link from the crossmember.

To install:

14. Position the front lateral link on the crossmember and install the common lateral link mounting bolt.

15. Install the crossmember into the vehicle and install the mounting bolts, exhaust mounting bolts and the brake line retaining bracket bolt to the crossmember.

16. Tighten the crossmember mounting bolts to 27–40 ft. lbs. (36–54 Nm) and the brake line retaining bracket bolt to 13–20 ft. lbs. (18–26 Nm).

17. Position the trailing arm into the body mounting bracket and tighten the mounting bolt to 49–69 ft. lbs. (63–93 Nm).

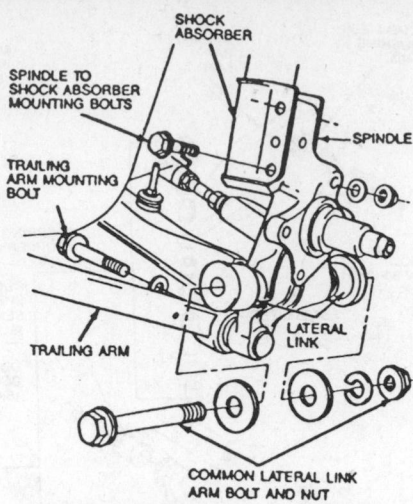

Rear spindle removal—1989–92

18. Install the parking brake cable mounting bolts to the trailing arm.

19. Position the rear lateral link onto the common lateral link mounting bolt at the rear crossmember and install the nut to the bolt. Tighten the mounting bolt and nut at the rear crossmember to 64–86 ft. lbs. (86–117 Nm).

20. Install the rear stabilizer bar assembly.

21. Place the spindle onto the strut assembly mounting bracket and tighten the mounting bolts to 69–86 ft. lbs. (93–117 Nm).

22. Install the common lateral link arm bolt and nut through the spindle and tighten to 64–86 ft. lbs. (86–117 Nm).

23. Install the trailing arm mounting bolt and tighten to 64–86 ft. lbs. (86–117 Nm).

24. Install the brake drum and backing plate assembly or the brake caliper and rotor assembly, as applicable.

25. Install the wheel and tire assembly and tighten the lug nuts to 65–87 ft. lbs. (88–118 Nm). Lower the vehicle.

1993

TRAILING ARM

1. Raise and safely support the vehicle.

2. Remove the parking brake cable bracket from the trailing arm.

3. Remove the trailing arm-to-spindle and trailing arm-to-frame bolts and remove the trailing arm.

4. Installation is the reverse of the removal procedure. Tighten the trailing arm mounting bolts to 86 ft. lbs. (117 Nm).

FRONT LATERAL LINK

1. Raise and safely support the vehicle.

2. Remove the spindle through bolt.

3. Position a jack under the rear crossmember.

4. Remove the 4 rear crossmember-to-frame bolts and lower the crossmember enough to gain access to the front lateral link to crossmember bolt.

5. Remove the access hole cap.

6. Remove the front lateral link-to-rear crossmember bolt and remove the front lateral link.

7. Installation is the reverse of the removal procedure. Tighten the spindle through bolt and front lateral link-to-rear crossmember bolt to 86 ft. lbs. (117 Nm). Tighten the rear crossmember-to-frame bolts to 40 ft. lbs. (54 Nm).

REAR LATERAL LINK

1. Raise and safely support the vehicle.

2. Remove the spindle through bolt.

3. Remove the stabilizer control link.

4. Paint an alignment mark on the cam plate and crossmember for assembly reference. Remove the adjusting cam bolt and remove the rear lateral link.

5. Installation is the reverse of the removal procedure. Tighten the spindle through bolt to 86 ft. lbs. (117 Nm). Align the marks made during removal and tighten the adjusting cam bolt to 86 ft. lbs. (117 Nm). Tighten the stabilizer link nuts to 40 ft. lbs. (54 Nm).

REAR CROSSMEMBER

1. Raise and safely support the vehicle.

2. Remove the spindle through bolt.

3. Remove the stabilizer bar.

4. Remove the rear lateral link.

5. Remove the 4 rear crossmember-to-frame bolts and remove the rear crossmember.

6. Remove the front lateral link.

7. Installation is the reverse of the removal procedure. Tighten the rear crossmember-to-frame bolts to 40 ft. lbs. (54 Nm) and the spindle through bolt to 86 ft. lbs. (117 Nm). Tighten the stabilizer control link and stabilizer bracket nuts and bolts to 40 ft. lbs. (54 Nm).

Rear Wheel Bearings

REMOVAL & INSTALLATION

1989–92

1. Raise and support the vehicle, safely.

2. Remove the wheel and tire assembly and the grease cap.

3. Using a cape chisel and a hammer, raise the staked portion of the hub nut.

4. Remove and discard the hub nut.

5. Remove the brake drum or disc brake rotor assembly from the spindle.

6. Using a small prybar, pry the grease seal from the brake drum or rotor and discard it.

7. Remove the snapring. Using a shop press, press the wheel bearing from the brake drum or rotor.

To install:

8. Using a shop press, press the new wheel bearing into the brake drum or rotor until it seats and install the snapring.

9. Lubricate the new seal lip with grease and install the seal, using a suitable installation tool.

10. Position the brake drum or rotor onto the wheel spindle.

11. Install a new locknut and tighten to 73–131 ft. lbs. (98–178 Nm).

12. Using a dull cold chisel, stake the locknut.

NOTE: If the nut splits or cracks after staking, it must be replaced with a new nut.

13. Install the grease cap and the wheel and tire assembly. Tighten the lug nuts to 65–87 ft. lbs. (88–118 Nm). Lower the vehicle.

1993

NOTE: On 1993 vehicles, the bearing cannot be disassembled from the hub.

1. Raise and safely support the vehicle. Remove the wheel and tire assembly.

2. Unstake the locknut. Have an assistant apply the brakes to lock the hub, then remove the locknut. Discard the nut; it must not be reused.

3. Remove the brake drum or, if equipped, rear disc brake caliper and rotor.

4. Remove the hub/bearing assembly.

5. Installation is the reverse of the removal procedure. Tighten a new locknut to 174 ft. lbs. (235 Nm), then stake the nut in place using a dull bladed chisel.

ADJUSTMENT

1. Raise and safely support the vehicle. Make sure the parking brake is fully released.

2. Remove the wheel and tire assembly.

3. On 1993 vehicles, install the lug nuts to hold the drum or rotor in place.

4. Rotate the drum or rotor to make sure there is no brake drag.

5. Position a suitable dial indicator with the indicator foot resting on the dust cap.

6. Check the wheel bearing end-play. End-play should not exceed 0.008 in. (0.2mm) on 1989–92 vehicles or 0.002 in. (0.05mm) on 1993 vehicles.

7. If the end-play exceeds specification, replace the wheel bearing or hub/bearing assembly, as required.

STEERING

Steering Wheel

REMOVAL & INSTALLATION

1989–92

1. Disconnect the negative battery cable.

2. Remove the steering wheel horn pad by removing the mounting screws from the rear of the steering wheel. Disconnect the wiring from the horn pad.

3. Remove the steering wheel mounting nut. Place matchmarks on the steering wheel and the shaft for installation alignment.

4. Use a steering wheel puller and remove the steering wheel.

NOTE: Do not subject the steering shaft to severe impact in the axial direction when removing or installing the steering wheel.

To install:

5. Align the matchmarks and place the steering wheel on the steering column shaft.

6. Install the steering wheel mounting nut and tighten to 29–36 ft. lbs. (39–49 Nm).

7. Connect the horn wire and install the horn pad. Connect the negative battery cable.

1993

NOTE: Always wear safety glasses when servicing an air bag vehicle and when handling an air bag.

1. Center the front wheels in the straight-ahead position.

2. Disconnect the negative battery cable and wait 1 minute for the air bag backup power supply energy to be depleted.

3. Remove the air bag module retaining bolts and lift the module from the steering wheel.

4. Label and disconnect the electrical connectors and remove the air bag module.

———— CAUTION ————

When carrying a live air bag, make sure the bag and trim cover are pointed away from the body. In the unlikely event of an accidental deployment, the bag will then deploy with minimal chance of personal injury. When placing a live air bag on a bench or other surface, always face the bag and trim cover up, away from the surface. This will reduce the motion of the module if it is accidentally deployed.

5. Make an alignment mark on the steering wheel and steering shaft for assembly reference.

6. Remove the steering wheel nut.

7. Remove the steering wheel using a suitable puller. Route the wire harness through the steering wheel as the wheel is lifted from the shaft.

NOTE: Do not try to remove the steering wheel by hitting the steering shaft with a hammer. The steering shaft will collapse, causing the steering wheel to bind.

8. Apply 2 strips of tape across the clockspring and housing to prevent accidental rotation.

To install:

9. If the clockspring has been accidentally rotated, the clockspring alignment must be adjusted, proceed as follows:

   a. Make sure the wheels are in the straight-ahead position.

   b. Turn the clockspring clockwise until it stops. Do not apply excessive force.

   c. Rotate the clockspring counterclockwise 2¾ turns.

   d. Align the marks on the clockspring with the marks on the outer housing.

10. Make sure the wheels are in the straight-ahead position.

11. Remove the tape strips from the clockspring and housing.

12. Route the wire harness through the steering wheel opening and position the steering wheel on the shaft. Align the marks made during removal.

13. Install the steering wheel nut and tighten to 36 ft. lbs. (49 Nm).

14. Connect the electrical connectors to the air bag module, position the module and install the attaching bolts. Tighten the bolts to 54 inch lbs. (6 Nm).

15. Connect the negative battery cable.

Power Steering Pump

REMOVAL & INSTALLATION

2.0L Engine

1. Disconnect the negative battery cable.

2. Remove the 2 power steering pump belt shield bolts.

3. Remove the lock and adjusting bolts. Remove the power steering belt.

4. Insert a small prybar through a hole in the power steering pump pulley to hold it in place. Loosen the pulley nut and remove the pulley.

5. Remove the 2 supply line manifold bolts and remove the high pressure line banjo bolt.

6. Disconnect the pump pressure switch and remove the pump through bolt. Remove the power steering pump.

To install:

7. Position the power steering pump and loosely install the through bolt.

8. Install the high pressure line banjo bolt, using new washers, and tighten to 33 ft. lbs. (44 Nm).

9. Connect the supply line manifold and tighten the bolts to 13 ft. lbs. (18 Nm).

10. Install the power steering pump pulley and the retaining nut. Insert a small prybar through a hole in the pulley to hold it in place and torque the nut to 43 ft. lbs. (59 Nm).

11. Install the power steering belt and the lock and adjusting bolts. Adjust the belt tension.

12. Install the 2 power steering pump belt shield bolts and connect the negative battery cable. Fill the power steering system with the proper fluid and bleed the air from the system.

2.2L Engine

1. Disconnect the negative battery cable.

2. At the right fender, remove the inner fender splash shield.

3. Loosen the power steering pump and remove the drive belt.

4. Disconnect and plug the pressure and return hoses from the pump

5. Remove the pump-to-bracket bolts and the pump; if necessary, remove the drive pulley from the pump.

To install:

6. Position the pump on the bracket and torque the bolts to 27–34 ft. lbs. (31–46 Nm).

7. Connect the pressure and return hoses to the pump.

8. Install the drive belt. Refill the power steering reservoir. Connect the negative battery cable, start the engine and bleed the system.

2.5L Engine

1. Disconnect the negative battery cable.

2. Remove the high pressure line hold-down bracket bolt and the high pressure line banjo bolt.

3. Raise and safely support the vehicle. Remove the passenger side front tire and wheel assembly and the splash shield.

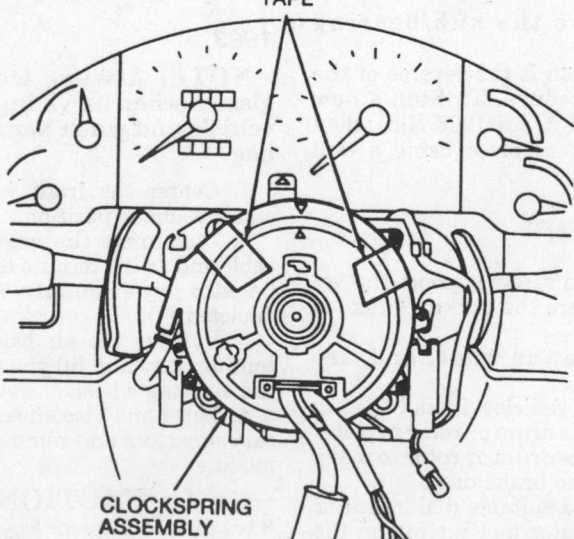

TAPE

CLOCKSPRING ASSEMBLY

Apply tape to the clockspring and housing to keep the clockspring from rotating—1993

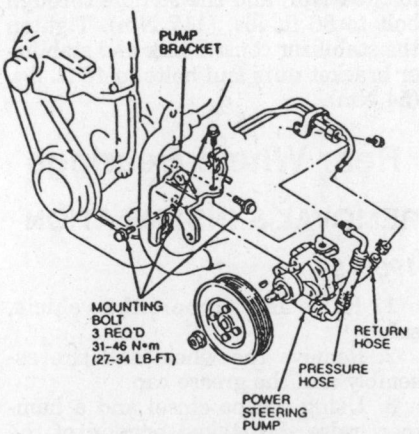

PUMP BRACKET

MOUNTING BOLT 3 REQ'D 31–46 N·m (27–34 LB-FT)

RETURN HOSE

PRESSURE HOSE

POWER STEERING PUMP

Power steering pump removal and installation—2.2L Engine

4. Loosen the adjusting bolt and remove the power steering pump belt.

5. Insert a small prybar through a hole in the power steering pump pulley to hold it in place. Loosen the pulley nut and remove the pulley.

6. Remove the 2 supply line manifold bolts and remove the high pressure line hold-down bracket nut.

7. Disconnect the power steering pump pressure switch.

8. Remove the 4 power steering pump bracket-to-engine bolts and the power steering pump.

To install:

9. Position the power steering pump and install the pump bracket-to-engine bolts. Tighten to 34 ft. lbs. (46 Nm). Connect the pressure switch connector.

10. Install the high pressure line bracket nut and tighten to 86 inch lbs. (9 Nm). Install the supply line manifold bolts and tighten to 13 ft. lbs. (18 Nm).

11. Install the power steering pump pulley and the retaining nut. Insert a small prybar through a hole in the pulley to hold it in place and torque the nut to 43 ft. lbs. (59 Nm).

12. Install the power steering pump belt and adjust the tension.

13. Install the splash shield and the front wheel and tire assembly. Lower the vehicle.

14. Install the high pressure line banjo bolt, using new washers, and tighten to 33 ft. lbs. (44 Nm).

15. Install the high pressure line hold-down bracket bolt and tighten to 86 ft. lbs. (9 Nm).

16. Connect the negative battery cable. Fill the power steering system with the proper fluid and bleed the air from the system.

3.0L Engine

1. Disconnect the negative battery cable.

2. Remove the washer reservoir and place aside.

3. Remove the plastic shield and the accessory drive belt.

4. Remove the drive pulley from the pump.

5. Disconnect and plug both power steering hoses at the pump.

6. Remove the pump mounting bolts and lift the pump from the accessory support bracket.

To install:

7. Position the pump on the accessory support bracket.

8. Install the pump mounting bolts and tighten to 15–22 ft. lbs. (20–30 Nm).

9. Install the drive pulley and replace both power steering hoses.

10. Install the drive belt and the plastic shield. Install the washer reservoir

and connect the negative battery cable.

11. Fill the pump reservoir and bleed the system.

SYSTEM BLEEDING

1. Raise and support the vehicle, safely.

2. Disconnect the coil wire. Refill the power steering pump reservoir to the specified level.

3. Crank the engine. Check and refill the reservoir.

4. Crank the engine and rotate the steering wheel from lock-to-lock.

NOTE: The front wheels must be off the ground during lock-to-lock rotation of the steering wheel.

5. Check and refill the power steering pump reservoir.

6. Connect the coil wire, start the engine and allow it to run for several minutes.

7. Rotate the steering wheel from lock-to-lock several times, until the air bubbles are eliminated from the fluid.

8. Turn the engine **OFF**. Check and/or refill the reservoir.

9. Disconnect the negative battery cable, depress the brake pedal for at least 5 seconds and reconnect the negative battery cable.

Tie Rod Ends

REMOVAL & INSTALLATION

1. Raise and safely support the vehicle. Remove the wheel and tire assembly.

2. Remove the cotter pin and the nut from the tie rod end stud.

3. Separate the tie rod end from the steering knuckle using separator tool T85M–3395–A or equivalent. If the tie rod end does not separate easily, give the steering knuckle a sharp blow with a brass hammer or drift to shock the taper.

4. Paint or mark an alignment stripe on the tie rod end, jam nut, and tie rod.

5. Loosen the jam nut and remove the tie rod end.

To install:

6. Thread the jam nut and tie rod end onto the tie rod.

7. Align the marks made during removal and tighten the jam nut to 51–72 ft. lbs. (69–98 Nm).

8. Install the tie rod end in the steering knuckle. Install the nut and tighten to 22–33 ft. lbs. (29–44 Nm).

9. Install a new cotter pin. If the slots in the nut do not align with the hole in the tie rod end stud, tighten the nut for proper alignment; never loosen the nut.

10. Install the wheel and tire assembly and lower the vehicle. Check the front end alignment.

BRAKES

Master Cylinder

REMOVAL & INSTALLATION

1. Disconnect the negative battery cable. On 1993 vehicles, remove the cruise control actuator from its bracket.

2. Disconnect the electrical connector from the fluid level sensor.

3. Disconnect the brake lines from the master cylinder. On 1993 vehicles, with manual transaxle, disconnect and plug the reservoir hose for the clutch master cylinder.

4. Cap the brake lines and the master cylinder ports.

5. Remove the mounting nuts and remove the master cylinder.

To adjust:

6. On all except 1992–93 vehicles with anti-lock brakes and 1993 vehicles with automatic transaxle, adjust the master cylinder pushrod as follows:

a. Install adjustment gauge T87C–2500–A or equivalent on the end of the master cylinder.

b. Loosen the set screw and push the gauge plunger against the bottom of the primary piston. While holding the gauge in position, tighten the set screw.

c. Apply 19.7 in. Hg of vacuum to the booster using a hand vacuum pump.

d. Invert gauge T87C–2500–A or equivalent onto the booster.

e. Check the clearance between the end of the gauge and the master cylinder pushrod. There should be no clearance between the gauge and the pushrod.

f. If adjustment is necessary, loosen the pushrod locknut and adjust the clearance.

7. On 1992–93 vehicles with anti-lock brakes and 1993 vehicles with automatic transaxle, adjust the master cylinder pushrod as follows:

a. Loosen the brass holding screw on master cylinder gauge T92C–2500–A or equivalent and retract the gauge rod. Attach the gauge to the booster and tighten the retaining nuts to 87–140 inch lbs. (10–16 Nm).

b. Start the engine and let it idle for approximately 15 seconds.

c. Push lightly on the end of the

gauge rod until it just contacts the power brake pushrod. Tighten the brass holding screw to secure the gauge rod in place.

   d. Remove the master cylinder gauge from the booster and turn the engine **OFF**.

NOTE: Be very careful not to disturb the gauge rod setting when removing the gauge from the booster. If the setting is changed during removal, a faulty measurement will be recorded and may cause unnecessary pushrod adjustment.

   e. Using a depth gauge, measure and record the height of the master cylinder gauge rod. This measurement will be called "D1".

   f. Loosen the master cylinder gauge brass holding screw and place the gauge on the master cylinder.

   g. Push lightly on the end of the gauge rod, until it just bottoms in the master cylinder piston. Tighten the brass screw.

   h. Remove the master cylinder gauge from the master cylinder.

NOTE: Be very careful not to disturb the gauge rod setting when removing the gauge from the master cylinder. If the setting is changed during removal, a faulty measurement will be recorded and may cause unnecessary pushrod adjustment.

   i. Using a depth gauge, measure and record the height of the gauge rod. This measurement will be called "D2".

   j. Subtract D1 from D2. Adjust the power brake pushrod nut to lengthen or shorten the booster pushrod the amount equal to the difference between D1 and D2. If measurement D1 is larger than D2, the pushrod must be lengthened. If measurement D2 is larger than D1, the pushrod must be shortened.

To install:

8. Position the master cylinder on the power brake booster studs.

9. Install the master cylinder mounting nuts and tighten to 8–12 ft. lbs. (10–16 Nm).

10. Connect short lengths of brake line to the master cylinder that point back into the reservoir. Position the ends of the lines so they will be submerged in brake fluid.

11. Fill the master cylinder reservoir with DOT-3 brake fluid and cover the reservoir with a shop towel. Slowly pump the brake pedal until clear fluid comes out of both temporary brake lines.

12. Remove the temporary brake lines and connect the brake lines to the master cylinder. Tighten the brake line nuts to 10–16 ft. lbs. (13–22 Nm).

If the lines are connected with banjo bolts, use new washers and tighten the banjo bolts to 16–22 ft. lbs. (22–29 Nm).

13. Connect the clutch master cylinder supply hose, if equipped.

14. Connect the fluid level sensor electrical connector.

15. Fill the master cylinder reservoir to the proper level and bleed the brake system.

Brake Caliper

REMOVAL & INSTALLATION

Front

1. Raise and safely support the vehicle.

2. Remove the wheel and tire assembly.

3. Remove the banjo bolt attaching the brake hose to the caliper, and discard the 2 sealing washers. Plug the hose to prevent fluid leakage.

4. Remove the caliper mounting bolt and pivot the caliper upward and off the brake pads.

5. Slide the caliper from the guide pin and remove from the vehicle.

To install:

6. Remove the guide pin bushing dust boots and push out the caliper guide pin bushing.

7. Lubricate the guide pin bushings with high temperature grease and install them in the caliper. Install the guide pin bushing dust boots.

8. Slide the caliper onto the guide pin and pivot the caliper down onto the brake pads. To provide the necessary clearance, it may be necessary to pull slightly outward on the caliper.

9. Install the caliper mounting bolt and tighten to 23–30 ft. lbs. (31–41 Nm) on 1989–92 vehicles or 33–36 ft. lbs. (44–49 Nm) on 1993 vehicles.

10. Install 2 new copper washers and the banjo bolt on the brake hose banjo fitting.

11. Position the brake hose on the caliper and install the banjo bolt. Tighten the bolt to 16–22 ft. lbs. (22–29 Nm).

12. Bleed the brakes.

13. Install the wheel and tire assembly and tighten the lug nuts to 65–87 ft. lbs. (80–118 Nm). Lower the vehicle.

Rear

1. Raise and safely support the vehicle. Remove the wheel and tire assembly.

2. On 1993 vehicles, remove the parking brake cable retaining clip.

3. Loosen the parking brake cable housing adjustment nut. Remove the cable housing from the bracket and the parking brake lever.

4. Remove the banjo bolt mounting the brake hose to the caliper.

5. Remove and discard the copper washers from the banjo fitting.

6. Remove the caliper mounting bolt.

7. Pivot the caliper off the brake pads and slide the caliper off the guide pin.

To install:

8. Lubricate the guide pin bushings with high temperature grease. Install the caliper onto the guide pin and pivot the caliper over the brake pads. Tighten the mounting bolt to 12–17 ft. lbs. (16–24 Nm) On 1989–92 vehicles or 25–29 ft. lbs. (34–39 Nm) on 1993 vehicles.

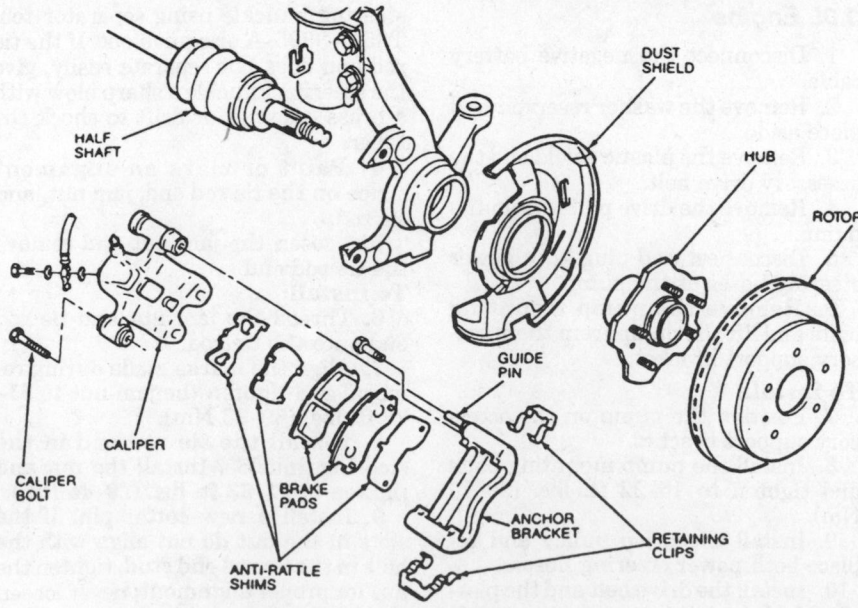

DUST SHIELD

HUB

ROTOR

HALF SHAFT

GUIDE PIN

CALIPER

CALIPER BOLT

BRAKE PADS

ANCHOR BRACKET

RETAINING CLIPS

ANTI-RATTLE SHIMS

Front disc brake assembly—1989–92

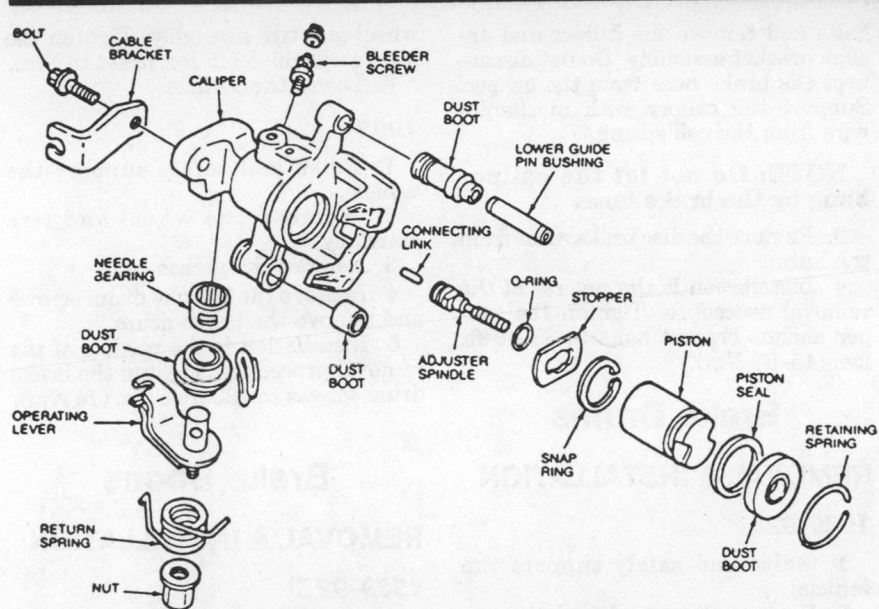

Exploded view of the rear disc brake caliper assembly

9. Install new copper washers and the banjo bolt mounting the brake hose to the caliper. Tighten the banjo bolt to 16–20 ft. lbs. (22–26 Nm).

10. Position the parking brake cable into the parking brake lever and bracket. Install the retaining clip, if equipped.

11. Adjust the parking brake cable so there is no clearance between the cable end and the parking brake lever. Tighten the parking brake cable locknut.

12. Bleed the brakes.

13. Install the wheel and tire assembly and lower the vehicle.

Disc Brake Pads

REMOVAL & INSTALLATION

Front

1. Remove approximately ⅔ of the brake fluid from the master cylinder reservoir.

2. Raise and safely support the vehicle.

3. Remove the wheel and tire assembly.

4. If necessary, clean the brake assembly with brake cleaner and allow to dry.

5. Remove the caliper mounting bolt. Pivot the caliper upward on the fixed guide pin and secure it out of the way.

WARNING: Do not allow the caliper to hang by the brake hose.

6. On 1993 vehicles, remove the 2 anti-rattle springs.

7. Remove the shims. Tag the shims so they can be reinstalled in their original position.

8. Remove the brake pads and retaining clips from the caliper anchor.

9. Inspect the disc brake rotor and machine or replace, as necessary.

To install:

10. Install the retaining clips.

11. Install the brake pads into the caliper anchor. The pad with the wear indicator is the inboard pad.

12. Install the shims in their original position.

13. Compress the caliper piston into its bore using pliers or another suitable tool.

14. Pivot the caliper down over the brake pads. On 1993 vehicles, install the anti-rattle springs. Install the caliper mounting bolt and tighten the bolt to 23–30 ft. lbs. (31–34 Nm) on 1989–92 vehicles or 33–36 ft. lbs. (44–49 Nm) on 1993 vehicles.

15. Install the wheel and tire assembly. Tighten the lug nuts to 65–87 ft. lbs. (80–118 Nm).

16. Lower the vehicle. Pump the brake pedal several times to position the caliper piston.

17. Check the fluid level in the master cylinder reservoir.

Rear

1. Remove approximately ⅔ of the brake fluid from the master cylinder reservoir.

2. Raise and support the vehicle, safely.

3. Remove the wheel and tire assembly. On 1993 vehicles, remove the parking brake cable retaining clip.

4. Loosen the parking brake cable housing adjusting nut. Remove the cable housing from the bracket and the parking brake lever.

5. On 1993 vehicles, insert an Allen wrench into the back of the caliper and turn the manual adjustment gear counterclockwise, to pull the caliper piston inward. Turn the gear until it stops.

6. Remove the caliper mounting bolt and pivot the caliper to clear the brake pads. Remove the caliper and suspend it with mechanics wire from the rear strut.

7. Remove the anti-rattle spring from the disc brake pads. Remove the disc brake pads, the shims and retaining clips.

NOTE: If the brake pads and shims are to be reused, they must be installed in their original positions.

To install:

8. Install the retaining clips. Position the shims on the disc brake pads and install the pads into the caliper anchor bracket.

9. Install the V-spring onto the disc brake pads.

10. On 1989–92 vehicles, use brake piston turning tool T75P–2588–B or equivalent, to rotate the caliper piston clockwise and screw the piston fully into the bore.

11. Lubricate the guide pin bushings with high temperature grease and install the caliper onto the guide pin. Pivot the caliper over the disc brake pads.

12. Install the caliper mounting bolt and tighten to 12–17 ft. lbs. (16–24 Nm) on 1989–92 vehicles or 25–29 ft. lbs. (34–39 Nm) on 1993 vehicles.

13. Install the parking brake cable into the parking brake lever and bracket. On 1993 vehicles, install the parking brake cable retaining clip.

14. Adjust the cable so there is no clearance between the cable end and the parking brake lever. Tighten the parking brake cable locknut.

15. On 1993 vehicles, turn the caliper manual adjustment gear clockwise with an Allen wrench until the brake pads just touch the rotor, then back off ⅓ turn.

16. Install the wheel and tire assembly and lower the vehicle.

17. Pump the brake pedal several times to position the caliper piston. Check the fluid level in the master cylinder reservoir and add clean brake fluid, if necessary.

Brake Rotor

REMOVAL & INSTALLATION

Front

1. Raise and safely support the vehicle.

2. Remove the wheel and tire assembly.

3. Remove the caliper anchor bracket bolts and remove the anchor bracket and caliper as an assembly. Support the caliper assembly from the coil spring with mechanics wire or string; do not disconnect the brake hose.

NOTE: Do not let the caliper assembly hang by the brake hose.

4. Remove the disc brake rotor. Handle the rotor with care, to prevent nicking or scratching the rotor surface.

To install:

5. Attach the disc brake rotor to the hub.

6. Install the caliper anchor bracket and tighten the bolts to 58–72 ft. lbs. (78–98 Nm).

7. Install the wheel and tire assembly. Tighten the lug nuts to 65–87 ft. lbs. (80–118 Nm).

8. Lower the vehicle. Apply the brake pedal several times to make sure the caliper piston is positioned.

Rear

1989–92

1. Raise and safely support the vehicle.

2. Remove the wheel and tire assembly.

3. Remove the 2 anchor bracket bolts and remove the caliper and anchor bracket assembly. Do not disconnect the brake hose from the caliper. Support the caliper with mechanics wire from the coil spring.

NOTE: Do not let the caliper hang by the brake hose.

4. Remove the grease cap. Unstake the wheel bearing nut, using a cape chisel. Remove the nut and washer and discard the nut.

5. Remove the disc brake rotor.

To install:

6. Install the rotor/hub assembly on the spindle.

7. Install the washer and a new nut. Tighten the nut to 73–131 ft. lbs. (98–178 Nm).

8. Stake the nut using a chisel with a rounded cutting edge. If the nut splits or cracks after staking, it must be replaced with a new nut.

9. Install the grease cap.

10. Install the caliper and anchor bracket assembly. Tighten the anchor bracket bolts to 33–49 ft. lbs. (45–67 Nm).

11. Install the wheel and tire assembly. Tighten the lug nuts to 65–87 ft. lbs. (80–118 Nm). Lower the vehicle.

1993

1. Raise and safely support the vehicle. Remove the wheel and tire assembly.

2. Remove the 2 anchor bracket bolts and remove the caliper and anchor bracket assembly. Do not disconnect the brake hose from the caliper. Support the caliper with mechanics wire from the coil spring.

NOTE: Do not let the caliper hang by the brake hose.

3. Remove the disc brake rotor from the hub.

4. Installation is the reverse of the removal procedure. Tighten the caliper anchor bracket bolts to 33–49 ft. lbs. (45–67 Nm).

Brake Drums

REMOVAL & INSTALLATION

1989–92

1. Raise and safely support the vehicle.

2. Remove the wheel and tire assembly and remove the grease cap.

3. Carefully raise the staked portion of the attaching nut using a suitable chisel.

4. Remove and discard the hub nut. Remove the brake drum/bearing assembly.

To install:

5. Position the brake drum/bearing assembly on the spindle and install a new locknut. Tighten the locknut to 73–131 ft. lbs. (98–178 Nm).

6. Stake the attaching nut using a suitable chisel with a rounded cutting edge.

NOTE: If the nut splits or cracks after staking, it must be replaced with a new nut.

7. Install the grease cap and the wheel and tire assembly. Tighten the lug nuts to 65–87 ft. lbs. (88–118 Nm).

8. Lower the vehicle.

1993

1. Raise and safely support the vehicle.

2. Remove the wheel and tire assembly.

3. Remove the grease cap.

4. Remove the 2 brake drum screws and remove the brake drum.

5. Installation is the reverse of the removal procedure. Tighten the brake drum screws to 123 inch lbs. (14 Nm).

Brake Shoes

REMOVAL & INSTALLATION

1989–92

1. Raise and safely support the vehicle.

2. Remove the wheel and tire assembly and the brake drum. Clean the brake assembly using brake cleaner.

3. Remove the brake shoe return springs and anti-rattle spring.

4. Remove the brake shoe hold-down springs. Push the hold-down spring inward using a small prybar, and twist the hold-down pin using needle-nose pliers until the head of the pin aligns with the slot in the spring. Release the spring and pin.

5. Remove the front and rear brake shoes from the parking brake strut.

NOTE: Unless they are broken or worn, leave the parking brake strut, adjuster mechanism and the adjuster spring in place.

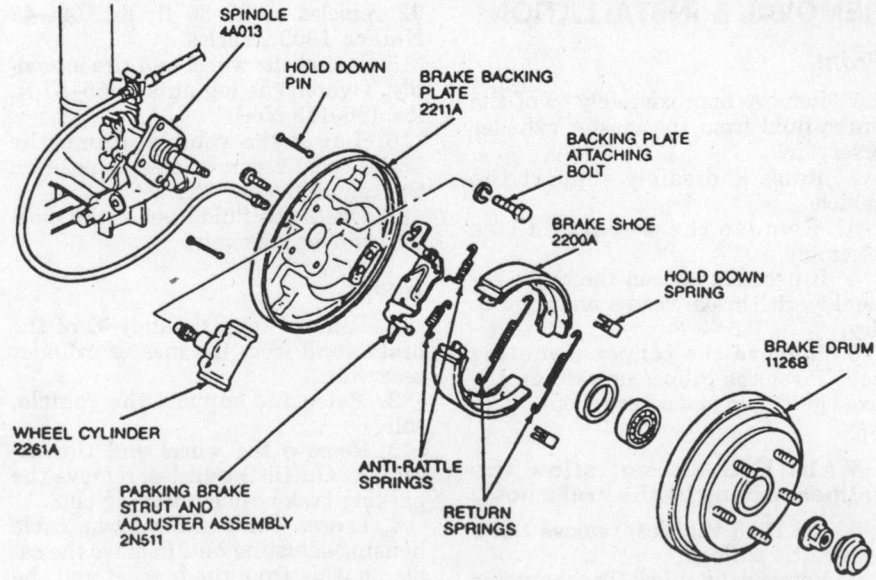

Rear drum brake assembly—1989–92

To install:

6. Inspect the anti-rattle and return springs for separated or twisted coils, twisted, bent or damaged shanks or discoloration. Discoloration indicates brake overheating; overheated springs lose some of their tension and should be replaced.

7. Using high temperature grease, lubricate the 6 shoe contact pads and the adjuster mechanism.

NOTE: If new shoes are being installed, the brake drums should always be resurfaced. This removes glazing, ensures an equal friction surface from side-to-side, and corrects out of round and bell mouth conditions.

8. Position the rear brake shoe in the parking brake strut and install the rear hold-down pin and spring.

9. Position the front brake shoe against the parking brake strut and backing plate and install the hold-down pin and spring.

10. Install the brake shoe return springs.

11. Insert a small prybar between the knurled quadrant and the parking brake strut; twist the prybar until the quadrant just touches the backing plate.

12. Install the brake drum, and wheel and tire assembly. Lower the vehicle.

13. Firmly apply the brakes 2–3 times to adjust the rear brakes.

1993

1. Raise and safely support the vehicle.

2. Unstake the hub locknut. Have an assistant apply the brakes to lock the hub, then remove the locknut.

3. Remove the brake drum and the hub.

4. Remove the brake shoe hold-down springs. Push the hold-down spring inward using a small prybar, and twist the hold-down pin using needle-nose pliers until the head of the pin aligns with the slot in the spring. Release the spring and pin.

5. Remove the parking brake cable from the parking brake anchor plate.

6. Remove the brake shoe return springs and remove the brake shoes.

To install:

7. Using high temperature grease, lubricate the 6 shoe contact pads and the anchor plate.

NOTE: If new shoes are being installed, the brake drums should always be resurfaced. This removes glazing, ensures an equal friction surface from side-to-side, and corrects out of round and bell mouth conditions.

8. Position the rear brake shoe in the parking brake strut and install the rear hold-down pin and spring.

9. Position the front brake shoe against the parking brake strut and backing plate and install the hold-down pin and spring.

10. Install the brake shoe return springs. Connect the parking brake cable.

11. Measure the drum inside diameter using gauge tool D81L–1103–A or equivalent. Insert a small prybar into the knurled quadrant of the parking brake strut and adjust the brake shoes to the same measurement as the brake drum.

12. Install the hub and the brake drum. Install a new locknut and tighten to 130–174 ft. lbs. (177–235 Nm). Stake the locknut using a dull bladed chisel.

13. The brake shoes should just touch the brake drum when properly adjusted.

14. Install the wheel and tire assembly and lower the vehicle.

Brake System Bleeding

SYSTEM PRIMING

When a new master cylinder has been installed, or the brake system emptied or partially emptied, fluid may not flow from the bleeder screws during normal bleeding. It may be necessary to prime the system using the following procedure:

1. Disconnect the brake lines from the master cylinder.

2. Install short brake lines in the master cylinder ports and position them that they point back into the reservoir and the ends of the lines are submerged in brake fluid.

3. Fill the reservoir with clean DOT-3 brake fluid and cover the reservoir with a shop towel.

4. Slowly pump the brake pedal until clear, bubble-free fluid comes out of both temporary brake lines.

NOTE: Do not allow brake fluid to spill on the vehicle's finish; it will remove the paint. In case of a spill, flush the area with water.

5. Remove the short brake lines and reconnect the vehicle brake lines to the master cylinder.

6. Bleed each brake line at the master cylinder as follows:

a. Have an assistant slowly pump the brake pedal 10 times and then hold firm pressure on the pedal.

b. Position a shop towel under the rear most brake line fitting. Open the fitting with a tubing wrench until a stream of brake fluid comes out. Have the assistant maintain pressure on the brake pedal until the brake line fitting is tightened.

c. Repeat Steps a and b until clear, bubble-free fluid comes out from around the tubing fitting.

d. Repeat the operation on the front brake line fitting.

7. If any of the brake lines, calipers, or wheel cylinders have been removed, it may be helpful to prime the system by gravity bleeding. This should be done after the master cylinder is primed and bled. To prime the system:

a. Fill the master cylinder with clean DOT-3 brake fluid.

b. Loosen both wheel cylinder bleeder screws, if equipped, and leave them open until clear brake fluid flows out. Frequently check the master cylinder reservoir to make sure it does not run dry.

c. Tighten the wheel cylinder bleeder screws.

d. One at a time, loosen the caliper bleeder screws and leave them open until clear fluid flows out. Frequently check the master cylinder reservoir to make sure it does not run dry.

e. Tighten the bleeder screws.

8. After the master cylinder has been primed, the lines bled at the master cylinder, and the brake system primed, proceed with normal brake system bleeding.

MANUAL BLEEDING

1. Clean all dirt from the master cylinder filler cap.

2. If the master cylinder is known or suspected of having air in the bore, it must be bled before any of the wheel cylinders and/or calipers are bled. Use the System Priming procedure.

3. Bleed the wheel cylinders and/or calipers as follows:

a. Begin at the rear bleeder screw.

NOTE: The brake system is diagonally split. If bleeding is begun at the right rear wheel, bleed the left front caliper next, followed by the left rear and right front. If bleeding is begun at the left rear wheel, bleed the right front caliper next, followed by the right rear and left front.

b. Attach a drain hose to the bleeder screw. The end of the hose should fit snugly around the end of the bleeder screw.

c. Place the other end of the hose in a container partially filled with clean brake fluid.

d. Have an assistant slowly pump the brake pedal 5–10 times and maintain pressure on the pedal after the last stroke.

e. Loosen the bleeder screw approximately ¾ turn. Make sure your assistant keeps constant pressure on the pedal until the pedal drops all the way down and the bleeder screw is closed again. If the pedal pressure is released, air will be drawn back into the system.

f. Tighten the bleeder screw.

g. Repeat this operation until the fluid is clear and air bubbles no longer appear in the container.

h. Repeat these steps at the other wheel cylinder and calipers.

NOTE: Never reuse the brake fluid expelled from the bleeder screws during the bleeding operation.

4. After the bleeding procedure is completed, make sure the fluid level is correct in the master cylinder reservoir.

Anti-Lock Brake System Service

PRECAUTIONS

Failure to observe the following precautions may result in system damage or personal injury.

• Before servicing any high pressure component, be sure to discharge the hydraulic pressure from the system.

• Do not allow the brake fluid to contact any of the electrical connectors.

• Use care when opening the bleeder screws due to the high system pressure from the accumulator.

RELIEVING ANTI-LOCK BRAKE SYSTEM PRESSURE

1. Turn the ignition key **OFF**.
2. Pump the brake pedal a minimum of 20 times until an increase in pedal force is clearly felt.

Hydraulic Actuation Unit

REMOVAL & INSTALLATION

1989–91

1. Disconnect the negative battery cable.
2. Remove the fuel filter and air filter assemblies.
3. Remove the coil and disconnect the wiring harness from the bottom of the coil and the fuel filter mounting bracket.

4. Remove the coil and fuel filter mounting bracket. Disconnect the 3 electrical connectors.
5. Remove the banjo bolts and copper washers from the brake lines at the hydraulic actuation unit. Disconnect the brake lines between the master cylinder and the hydraulic actuation unit.

NOTE: Note the routing of the brake lines to ensure proper installation.

6. Remove the routing clip from the brake lines. Using a 6 in. (153mm) extension and a 6-point, 10mm crowfoot wrench, disconnect the 4 brake lines at the hydraulic actuation unit.

NOTE: Note the location of each brake line to ensure proper installation.

7. Remove the mounting nuts, lockwashers and washers. Lift the hydraulic actuation unit from the mounting bracket and remove the mounting bushings from the actuation assembly. If necessary, remove the mounting bracket.

To install:

8. Install the mounting bracket, bushings and the hydraulic actuation unit. Tighten the mounting nuts to 14–19 ft. lbs. (19–25 Nm).
9. Connect the 3 electrical connectors, making sure the connectors lock in place.
10. Using a 6 in. (153mm) extension and a 6-point, 10mm crowfoot wrench, install 4 brake lines to the actuation assembly. Tighten to 10–16 ft. lbs. (13–22 Nm).
11. Position the 2 brake lines between the actuation assembly and the master cylinder. Install the banjo bolts with new copper washers and tighten the banjo bolts to 16–22 ft. lbs. (22–29 Nm).
12. Install the coil and fuel filter mounting bracket. Tighten the nuts to 34–46 ft. lbs. (56–63 Nm). Connect the wire harness to the bottom of the coil and fuel filter mounting bracket.
13. Install the coil, air filter and fuel filter assemblies.
14. Fill and bleed the brake system. Connect the negative battery cable.

1992

1. Disconnect the negative battery cable.
2. Remove the air cleaner assembly.
3. Disconnect the electrical connectors at the ignition coil.
4. Remove the 2 mounting nuts at the coil and module bracket and remove the coil and module bracket.
5. Remove the 4 mounting nuts at the fuel filter bracket and move the filter and bracket aside.

6. Disconnect the 2 electrical connectors leading to the hydraulic actuation unit.
7. Disconnect the brake lines from the hydraulic actuation unit. Remove the brake lines necessary for actuation unit removal.
8. Remove the mounting nuts and remove the hydraulic actuation unit.

To install:

9. Install the hydraulic actuation unit and tighten the nuts to 14–19 ft. lbs. (19–25 Nm).
10. Connect the brake lines and tighten to 10–16 ft. lbs. (13–22 Nm).
11. Connect the electrical connectors leading to the actuation unit.
12. Position the fuel filter and bracket and tighten the mounting nuts.
13. Install the ignition coil and module bracket. Tighten the mounting nuts.
14. Connect the electrical connectors at the ignition coil.
15. Install the air cleaner assembly.
16. Fill and bleed the brake system. Connect the negative battery cable.

1993

1. Disconnect the negative battery cable.
2. Slide the evaporative canister out of its bracket and position it aside.
3. Remove the cruise control vacuum actuator from its bracket, if equipped.
4. Disconnect the 2 electrical connectors at the hydraulic actuation assembly.
5. Loosen the 3 hydraulic assembly mounting nuts and remove the front-left brake line bolt.

NOTE: Note the routing of the brake lines to ensure proper installation.

6. Remove the brake line fittings from the actuation assembly using a tubing wrench.
7. Remove the 3 mounting nuts and washers and remove the hydraulic actuation assembly.
8. Installation is the reverse of the removal procedure. Tighten the brake lines to 16 ft. lbs. (22 Nm). Bleed the brake system.

CHASSIS ELECTRICAL

Air Bag

DISARMING

1. Disconnect the negative battery cable.

2. Wait 1 minute for the backup power supply in the diagnostic monitor to deplete its stored energy.

3. Remove the 4 bolts retaining the air bag to the steering wheel.

4. Disconnect the air bag/horn electrical connector. Disconnect the cruise control switch electrical connector, if equipped.

5. Remove the air bag module from the steering wheel.

── **CAUTION** ──

When carrying a live air bag, make sure the bag and trim cover are pointed away from the body. In the unlikely event of an accidental deployment, the bag will then deploy with minimal chance of injury. When placing a live air bag on a bench or other surface, always face the bag and trim cover up, away from the surface. This will reduce the motion of the module if it is accidently deployed.

Heater Blower Motor

REMOVAL & INSTALLATION

1989–92

1. Disconnect the negative battery cable.

2. Remove the sound deadening panel from the passenger side.

3. Remove the glove box assembly and the brace.

4. Remove the cooling hose from the blower motor assembly.

5. Disconnect the electrical connector from the blower motor.

6. Remove the 3 blower motor-to-blower motor housing screws and blower motor.

7. If necessary, remove the blower wheel-to-blower motor clip and the wheel.

8. To install, reverse the removal procedure and check the blower motor operation.

1993

1. Disconnect the negative battery cable.

2. Remove the 2 hush panel screws and disconnect the courtesy light electrical connector. Remove the hush panel.

3. Disconnect the blower motor electrical connector and remove the 3 blower motor retaining screws. Remove the blower motor.

4. If necessary, remove the clip from the motor shaft and remove the blower wheel from the motor.

5. Installation is the reverse of the removal procedure.

Windshield Wiper Motor

REMOVAL & INSTALLATION

FRONT

1989–92

1. Disconnect the negative battery cable.

2. Unscrew the retaining nut and remove the wiper arm and blade assemblies.

3. Disconnect the hose from the washer jet nozzle.

4. Remove the lower cowl moulding and wiper linkage cover.

5. Pull the wiper linkage off the wiper motor output arm.

6. Disconnect the electrical connectors from the wiper motor.

7. Remove the wiper motor mounting bolts and remove the motor from the vehicle.

8. Installation is the reverse of the removal procedure. Install the wiper arm and blade assemblies so the tip of the wiper blade is 0.79–1.18 in. (20–30mm) from the bottom of the windshield. Tighten the wiper arm retaining nut to 10 ft. lbs. (14 Nm).

1993

1. Disconnect the negative battery cable.

2. Remove the wiper arm cover cap and attaching nut and remove the wiper arm and blade assemblies.

3. Remove the lower windshield moulding.

4. Use a smalll prybar to pry the wiper linkage from the wiper motor ouput arm.

5. Remove the wiring harness bracket from the wiper motor mounting bracket.

6. Remove the 4 wiper motor mounting bracket bolts.

7. Disconnect the wiper motor ground and electrical connector and remove the wiper motor.

8. Installation is the reverse of the removal procedure. Tighten the wiper motor bolts to 87 inch lbs. (9 Nm). Install the wiper arm and bllade assembllies so the tips of the blades are 1.12–1.28 in. (28–32mm) from the top of the cowl grille. Tighten the wiper arm nuts to 121 inch lbs. (15 Nm).

Rear

1989–92

1. Disconnect the negative battery cable.

2. Lift the cover and remove the wiper arm and blade assembly retaining nut. Remove the wiper arm and blade assembly.

3. Remove the boot, nut and mount from the wiper motor pivot.

4. Remove the liftgate interior trim panel.

5. Disconnect the electrical connector from the wiper motor.

6. Remove the wiper motor mounting bolts and remove the wiper motor.

7. Installation is the reverse of the removal procedure. Install the wiper arm and blade assembly so the tip of the wiper blade is 0.79–1.18 in. (20–30mm) from the bottom of the rear window.

1993

1. Disconnect the negative battery cable.

2. Lift the wiper arm nut cover and remove the nut. Remove the wiper arm and blade assembly.

3. Remove the cover and remove the wiper motor shaft support nut.

4. Remove the liftgate lower trim.

5. Disconnect the wiper motor electrical connector.

6. Remove the 3 wiper motor mounting bolts and disconnect the ground wire. Remove the wiper motor.

7. Installation is the reverse of the removal procedure. Tighten the wiper motor mounting bolts to 87 inch lbs. (9 Nm) and the shaft support nut to 52 inch lbs. (5 Nm). Installl the wiper arm and blade assembly so the tip of the wiper blade is 1.0–1.6 in. (25–40mm) from the shaded glass area. Tighten the wiper arm nut to 87 inch lbs. (9 Nm).

Windshield Wiper Switch

REMOVAL & INSTALLATION

Front

1989–92

1. Disconnect the negative battery cable.

2. Remove the instrument cluster module as follows:

   a. Remove the steering wheel.

   b. Remove the 2 column cover screws and remove the cover.

   c. Remove the 9 cluster module mounting screws.

   d. Carefully pull the cluster module outward and disconnect the 7 electrical connectors from the cover.

   e. Remove the ignition switch illumination bulb and remove the cluster module.

3. Gently pull the washer/interval rate control switch knob and wiper control switch knob from the windshield wiper switch.

4. From the rear of the instrument cluster module cover, remove the

windshield wiper switch housing screws and the switch.

5. Installation is the reverse of the removal procedure. Check windshield wiper switch operation.

1993

Windshield wiper control is a function of the combination switch.

Rear

1989–92

1. Disconnect the negative battery cable.

2. Remove the instrument cluster module as follows:

    a. Remove the steering wheel.

    b. Remove the 2 column cover screws and remove the cover.

    c. Remove the 9 cluster module mounting screws.

    d. Carefully pull the cluster module outward and disconnect the 7 electrical connectors from the cover.

    e. Remove the ignition switch illumination bulb and remove the cluster module.

3. Gently pull the front washer/interval rate control switch knob and the front wiper control switch knob from the windshield wiper switch.

4. From the rear of the instrument cluster module cover, remove the windshield wiper switch housing screws and the switch.

5. Remove the rear wiper/washer switch-to-instrument cluster module cover screws.

6. Remove the control switch button by releasing the tangs. Remove the rear wiper/washer switch.

7. Installation is the reverse of the removal procedure. Check the windshield wiper/washer switch and the rear wiper/washer switch operation.

1993

1. Disconnect the negative battery cable.

2. Remove the floor console as follows:

    a. Remove the armrest.

    b. If equipped with manual transaxle, unscrew the shifter knob. If equipped with automatic transaxle, remove the emergency override key switch cover.

    c. Apply the parking brake.

    d. Gently pull up on the upper half of the floor console to separate it from the lower half.

    e. Disconnect the cigar lighter electrical connectors.

    f. Remove the ashtray light bulb from the upper half of the console.

3. Remove the 2 control console bezel screws and move the bezel away from the instrument panel to gain access to the wiper switch electrical connector.

4. Disconnect the wiper switch electrical connector. Squeeze the switch tabs and remove the switch from the control console bezel.

5. Installation is the reverse of the removal procedure.

Instrument Cluster

REMOVAL & INSTALLATION

1989–92

1. Disconnect the negative battery cable.

2. Remove the instrument cluster module as follows:

    a. Remove the steering wheel.

    b. Remove the 2 column cover screws and remove the cover.

    c. Remove the 9 cluster module mounting screws.

    d. Carefully pull the cluster module outward and disconnect the 7 electrical connectors from the cover.

    e. Remove the ignition switch illumination bulb and remove the cluster module.

3. Loosen the 2 cover hinge screws and remove the 6 upper cluster cover screws. Remove the cover.

NOTE: During removal, be careful not to rip the rubber seal that joins the upper and lower portions of the cluster cover panels.

4. Remove the lower cluster cover panel and remove the 4 cluster mounting screws.

5. Disconnect the electrical connectors from the back of the cluster. If equipped with analog instrument cluster, disconnect the speedometer cable.

6. Remove the cluster from the vehicle.

7. Installation is the reverse of the removal procedure.

1993

1. Disconnect the negative battery cable.

2. Loosen the hood release handle mounting nut and remove the lower instrument panel cover screw.

3. Turn the courtesy light bulb ¼ turn counterclockwise and pull it straight out from the lower instrument panel cover. Remove the lower instrument panel cover.

4. Remove the 5 instrument cluster bezel screws and disconnect the resistor panel light dimmer switch electrical connector. Remove the instrument cluster bezel.

5. Remove the 2 upper steering column mounting bolts and lower the steering column.

6. Remove the 4 instrument cluster screws and pull the cluster out to gain access to the electrical connectors at the rear of the cluster.

7. Disconnect the 2 electrical connectors and remove the instrument cluster.

8. Installation is the reverse of the removal procedure.

Headlight Switch

REMOVAL & INSTALLATION

1989–92

1. Disconnect the negative battery cable. Remove the turn signal switch.

2. Gently pull the rotary knob from the headlight switch.

3. From the rear of the instrument cluster module cover, remove the rotary switch housing screws and the switch.

4. Installation is the reverse of the removal procedure. Check headlight switch operation.

1993

Headlight operation control is a function of the combination switch.

Fuses, Circuit Breakers and Relays

LOCATION

Fuses

The main fuse block is located in the left side of the engine compartment near the battery. The interior fuse block is located above the left side kick panel on 1989–92 vehicles or behind the left side kick panel on 1993 vehicles.

Circuit Breakers

A bimetal circuit breaker, used to protect the rear window defroster circuit, is located in the joint box, which is just above the interior fuse panel on 1989–92 vehicles.

Relays

1989–92

The main relay box is located in the engine compartment on the upper left side of the firewall (bulkhead). There is also a relay box located inside the vehicle under the left side of the instrument panel.

1993

Several main relays are located within the main fuse block. These include the starter relay, main relay, fuel pump relay, parking light/turn signal relay, horn relay, daytime running light relay, A/C relay, headlight relay and fog light relay.

Ford Motor Co.
Front Wheel Drive
FORD—Taurus **LINCOLN**—Continental
MERCURY—Sable

SPECIFICATIONS
VEHICLE IDENTIFICATION CHART

It is important for servicing and ordering parts to be certain of the vehicle and engine identification. The VIN (vehicle identification number) is a 17 digit number visible through the windshield on the driver's side of the dash and contains the vehicle and engine identification codes. The tenth digit indicates model year and the eighth digit indicates engine code. It can be interpreted as follows:

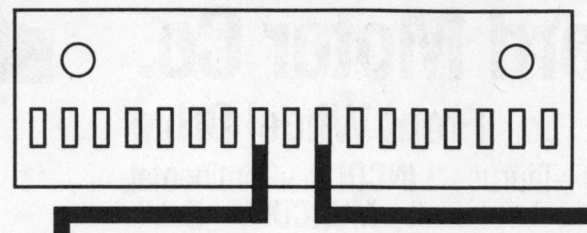

Engine Code

Code	Liters	Cu. In. (cc)	Cyl.	Fuel Sys.	Eng. Mfg.
D	2.5	154 (2524)	4	①	Ford
U	3.0	181 (2971)	6	②	Ford
Y	3.0	182 (2980)	6	SEFI	Yamaha
4	3.8	232 (3801)	6	SEFI	Ford

Model Year

Code	Year
K	1989
L	1990
M	1991
N	1992
P	1993

SEFI—Sequential Electronic Fuel Injection
① 1989–90 Central Fuel Injection
   1991 Sequential Electronic Fuel Injection
② 1989–90 Electronic Fuel Injection
   1991–93 Sequential Electronic Fuel Injection

ENGINE IDENTIFICATION

Year	Model	Engine Displacement Liters (cc)	Engine Series (ID/VIN)	Fuel System	No. of Cylinders	Engine Type
1989	Taurus	2.5 (2524)	D	CFI	4	OHV
	Taurus	3.0 (2971)	U	EFI	6	OHV
	Taurus SHO	3.0 (2980)	Y	SEFI	6	DOHC
	Taurus	3.8 (3801)	4	SEFI	6	OHV
	Sable	3.0 (2971)	U	EFI	6	OHV
	Sable	3.8 (3801)	4	SEFI	6	OHV
	Continental	3.8 (3801)	4	SEFI	6	OHV
1990	Taurus	2.5 (2524)	D	CFI	4	OHV
	Taurus	3.0 (2971)	U	EFI	6	OHV
	Taurus SHO	3.0 (2980)	Y	SEFI	6	DOHC
	Taurus	3.8 (3801)	4	SEFI	6	OHV
	Sable	3.0 (2971)	U	EFI	6	OHV
	Sable	3.8 (3801)	4	SEFI	6	OHV
	Continental	3.8 (3801)	4	SEFI	6	OHV
1991	Taurus	2.5 (2524)	D	SEFI	4	OHV
	Taurus	3.0 (2971)	U	SEFI	6	OHV
	Taurus SHO	3.0 (2980)	Y	SEFI	6	DOHC
	Taurus	3.8 (3801)	4	SEFI	6	OHV
	Sable	3.0 (2971)	U	SEFI	6	OHV
	Sable	3.8 (3801)	4	SEFI	6	OHV
	Continental	3.8 (3801)	4	SEFI	6	OHV

ENGINE IDENTIFICATION

Year	Model	Engine Displacement Liters (cc)	Engine Series (ID/VIN)	Fuel System	No. of Cylinders	Engine Type
1992-93	Taurus	3.0 (2971)	U	SEFI	6	OHV
	Taurus SHO	3.0 (2980)	Y	SEFI	6	DOHC
	Taurus	3.8 (3801)	4	SEFI	6	OHV
	Sable	3.0 (2971)	U	SEFI	6	OHV
	Sable	3.8 (3801)	4	SEFI	6	OHV
	Continental	3.8 (3801)	4	SEFI	6	OHV

CFI—Central Fuel Injection
EFI—Electronic Fuel Injection
SEFI—Sequential Electronic Fuel Injection
OHV—Overhead Valves
DOHC—Dual Overhead Cam

GENERAL ENGINE SPECIFICATIONS

Year	Engine ID/VIN	Engine Displacement Liters (cc)	Fuel System Type	Net Horsepower @ rpm	Net Torque @ rpm (ft. lbs.)	Bore × Stroke (in.)	Compression Ratio	Oil Pressure @ rpm ①
1989	D	2.5 (2524)	CFI	90 @ 4400	130 @ 2600	3.68 × 3.62	9.0:1	55–70 @ 2000
	U	3.0 (2971)	EFI	140 @ 4800	160 @ 3000	3.50 × 3.14	9.3:1	40–60 @ 2500
	Y	3.0 (2980)	SEFI	220 @ 6000	200 @ 4800	3.50 × 3.15	9.8:1	12.8 @ 800
	4	3.8 (3801)	SEFI	140 @ 3800	215 @ 2400	3.81 × 3.39	9.0:1	40–60 @ 2500
1990	D	2.5 (2524)	CFI	90 @ 4400	130 @ 2600	3.68 × 3.62	9.0:1	55–70 @ 2000
	U	3.0 (2971)	EFI	140 @ 4800	160 @ 3000	3.50 × 3.14	9.3:1	40–60 @ 2500
	Y	3.0 (2980)	SEFI	220 @ 6200	200 @ 4800	3.50 × 3.15	9.8:1	12.8 @ 800
	4	3.8 (3801)	SEFI	140 @ 3800	215 @ 2200	3.81 × 3.39	9.0:1	40–60 @ 2500
1991	D	2.5 (2524)	SEFI	105 @ 4400	140 @ 2400	3.68 × 3.62	9.0:1	55–70 @ 2000
	U	3.0 (2971)	SEFI	140 @ 4800	160 @ 3000	3.50 × 3.14	9.3:1	40–60 @ 2500
	Y	3.0 (2980)	SEFI	220 @ 6200	200 @ 4800	3.50 × 3.15	9.8:1	12.8 @ 800
	4	3.8 (3801)	SEFI	②	③	3.81 × 3.39	9.0:1	40–60 @ 2500
1992-93	U	3.0 (2971)	SEFI	140 @ 4800	160 @ 3000	3.50 × 3.14	9.3:1	40–60 @ 2500
	Y	3.0 (2980)	SEFI	220 @ 6200	200 @ 4800	3.50 × 3.15	9.8:1	12.8 @ 800
	4	3.8 (3801)	SEFI	②	③	3.81 × 3.39	9.0:1	40–60 @ 2500

NOTE: Horsepower and torque are SAE net figures. They are measured at the rear of the transmission with all accessories installed and operating. Since the figures vary when a given engine is installed in different models, some are representative rather than exact.

CFI—Central Fuel Injection
EFI—Electronic Fuel Injection
SEFI—Sequential Electronic Fuel Injection
① Engine at normal operating temperature
② Except Continental and Taurus Police—
    140 @ 3800
    Continental and Taurus Police
      1991—155 @ 4000
      1992-93—160 @ 4400
③ Except Continental and Taurus Police—
    215 @ 2400
    Continental and Taurus Police
      1991—220 @ 2200
      1992-93—225 @ 3000

GASOLINE ENGINE TUNE-UP SPECIFICATIONS

Year	Engine ID/VIN	Engine Displacement Liters (cc)	Spark Plugs Gap (in.)	Ignition Timing (deg.)		Fuel Pump (psi)	Idle Speed (rpm)		Valve Clearance	
				MT	AT		MT	AT	In.	Ex.
1989	D	2.5 (2524)	0.044	—	10B	13–17	—	675–725	Hyd.	Hyd.
	U	3.0 (2971)	0.044	—	10B	35–45	—	①	Hyd.	Hyd.
	Y	3.0 (2980)	0.044	10B	—	30–45	760–830	—	0.006–0.010	0.010–0.014
	4	3.8 (3801)	0.054	—	10B	35–45	—	①	Hyd.	Hyd.
1990	D	2.5 (2524)	0.044	—	10B	13–17	—	675–725	Hyd.	Hyd.
	U	3.0 (2971)	0.044	—	10B	35–40	—	①	Hyd.	Hyd.
	Y	3.0 (2980)	0.044	10B	—	30–45	①	—	0.006–0.010	0.010–0.014
	4	3.8 (3801)	0.054	—	10B	35–40	—	①	Hyd.	Hyd.
1991	D	2.5 (2524)	0.044	—	①	50–60	—	①	Hyd.	Hyd.
	U	3.0 (2971)	0.044	—	10B	35–40	—	①	Hyd.	Hyd.
	Y	3.0 (2980)	0.044	10B	—	30–45	①	—	0.006–0.010	0.010–0.014
	4	3.8 (3801)	0.054	—	10B	35–40	—	①	Hyd.	Hyd.
1992	U	3.0 (2971)	0.044	—	10B	35–40	—	①	Hyd.	Hyd.
	Y	3.0 (2980)	0.044	10B	—	30–45	①	—	0.006–0.010	0.010–0.014
	4	3.8 (3801)	0.054	—	10B	35–40	—	①	Hyd.	Hyd.
1993	SEE UNDERHOOD SPECIFICATIONS STICKER									

NOTE: The lowest cylinder pressure should be within 75% of the highest cylinder pressure reading. For example, if the highest cylinder is 134 psi, the lowest should be 101. Engine should be at normal operating temperature with throttle valve in the wide open position.
The underhood specifications sticker often reflects tune-up specification changes in production. Sticker figures must be used if they disagree with those in this chart.
Hyd.—Hydraulic
B—Before Top Dead Center
① Refer to the Vehicle Emission Control
  information label

FIRING ORDERS

NOTE: To avoid confusion, always replace spark plug wires one at a time.

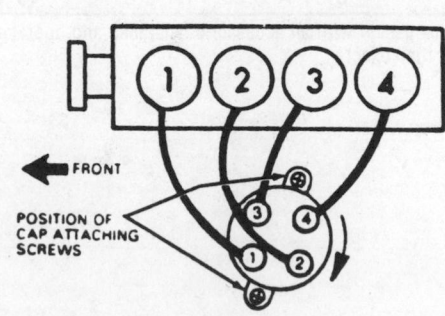

2.5L Engine
Engine Firing Order: 1–3–4–2
Distributor Rotation: Clockwise

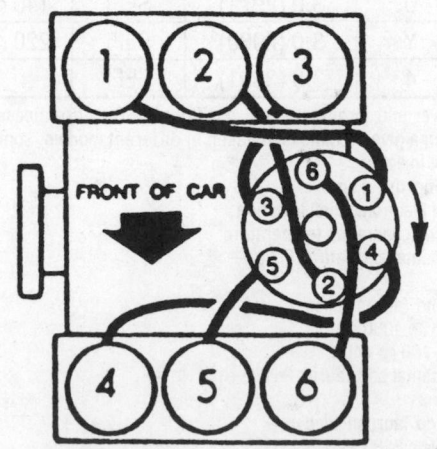

3.0L Engine
Engine Firing Order: 1–4–2–5–3–6
Distributor Rotation: Clockwise

FIRING ORDERS

NOTE: To avoid confusion, always replace spark plug wires one at a time.

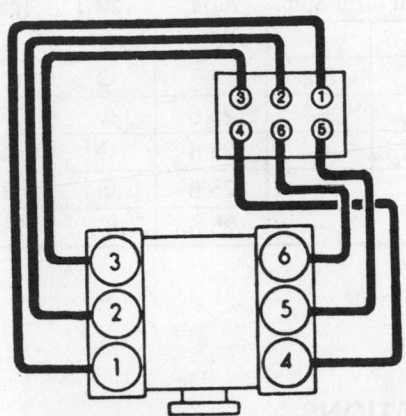

3.0L SHO Engine
Engine Firing Order: 1–4–2–5–3–6
Distributorless Ignition System

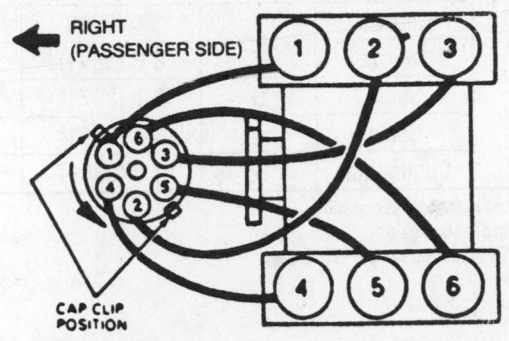

3.8L Engine
Engine Firing Order: 1–4–2–5–3–6
Distributor Rotation: Counterclockwise

CAPACITIES

Year	Model	Engine ID/VIN	Engine Displacement Liters (cc)	Engine Crankcase with Filter	Transmission (pts.) 4-Spd	5-Spd	Auto.	Drive Axle Front (pts.)	Fuel Tank (gal.)	Cooling System (qts.)
1989	Taurus	D	2.5 (2524)	5.0	—	—	16.8	①	②	8.3
	Taurus	U	3.0 (2971)	4.5	—	—	25.6	①	②	③
	Taurus	Y	3.0 (2980)	5.0	—	6.2	—	①	18.6	11.6
	Taurus	4	3.8 (3801)	4.5	—	—	25.6	①	②	12.1
	Sable	U	3.0 (2971)	4.5	—	—	25.6	①	②	③
	Sable	4	3.8 (3801)	4.5	—	—	25.6	①	②	12.1
	Continental	4	3.8 (3801)	4.5	—	—	25.6	①	18.6	11.1
1990	Taurus	D	2.5 (2524)	5.0	—	—	16.8	①	②	8.3
	Taurus	U	3.0 (2971)	4.5	—	—	25.6	①	②	③
	Taurus	Y	3.0 (2980)	5.0	—	6.2	—	①	18.6	11.6
	Taurus	4	3.8 (3801)	4.5	—	—	25.6	①	②	12.1
	Sable	U	3.0 (2971)	4.5	—	—	25.6	①	②	③
	Sable	4	3.8 (3801)	4.5	—	—	25.6	①	②	12.1
	Continental	4	3.8 (3801)	4.5	—	—	25.6	①	18.6	11.1
1991	Taurus	D	2.5 (2524)	5.0	—	—	25.6	①	②	8.3
	Taurus	U	3.0 (2971)	4.5	—	—	25.6	①	②	③
	Taurus	Y	3.0 (2980)	5.0	—	6.2	—	①	18.6	11.6
	Taurus	4	3.8 (3801)	4.5	—	—	25.6	①	②	12.1
	Sable	U	3.0 (2971)	4.5	—	—	25.6	①	②	③
	Sable	4	3.8 (3801)	4.5	—	—	25.6	①	②	12.1
	Continental	4	3.8 (3801)	4.5	—	—	25.6	①	18.6	11.1

CAPACITIES

Year	Model	Engine ID/VIN	Engine Displacement Liters (cc)	Engine Crankcase with Filter	Transmission (pts.) 4-Spd	5-Spd	Auto.	Drive Axle Front (pts.)	Fuel Tank (gal.)	Cooling System (qts.)
1992-93	Taurus	U	3.0 (2971)	4.5	—	—	25.6	①	②	③
	Taurus	Y	3.0 (2980)	5.0	—	6.2	—	①	18.6	11.6
	Taurus	4	3.8 (3801)	4.5	—	—	25.6	①	②	12.1
	Sable	U	3.0 (2971)	4.5	—	—	25.6	①	②	③
	Sable	4	3.8 (3801)	4.5	—	—	25.6	①	②	12.1
	Continental	4	3.8 (3801)	4.5	—	—	25.6	①	18.4	11.1

① Included in transaxle capacity
② Standard—16.0 gals.
  Optional extended range—18.6 gals.
③ Sedan—11.0 qts.
  Wagon—11.8 qts.

CAMSHAFT SPECIFICATIONS

All measurements given in inches.

Year	Engine ID/VIN	Engine Displacement Liters (cc)	Journal Diameter 1	2	3	4	5	Elevation In.	Ex.	Bearing Clearance	Camshaft End Play
1989	D	2.5 (2524)	2.0060–2.0090	2.0060–2.0090	2.0060–2.0090	2.0060–2.0090	2.0060–2.0090	0.244–0.249	0.234–0.239	0.0010–0.0030	0.009
	U	3.0 (2971)	2.0074–2.0084	2.0074–2.0084	2.0074–2.0084	2.0074–2.0084	—	0.255–0.260	0.255–0.260	0.0010–0.0030	0.001–0.005
	Y	3.0 (2980)	1.2189–1.2195	1.2189–1.2195	1.2189–1.2195	1.2189–1.2195	1.2189–1.2195	0.335	0.315	0.0010–0.0026	0.012
	4	3.8 (3801)	2.0505–2.0515	2.0505–2.0515	2.0505–2.0515	2.0505–2.0515	—	0.240–0.245	0.254–0.259	0.0010–0.0030	①
1990	D	2.5 (2524)	2.0060–2.0090	2.0060–2.0090	2.0060–2.0090	2.0060–2.0090	2.0060–2.0090	0.244–0.249	0.234–0.239	0.0010–0.0030	0.009
	U	3.0 (2971)	2.0074–2.0084	2.0074–2.0084	2.0074–2.0084	2.0074–2.0084	—	0.255–0.260	0.255–0.260	0.0010–0.0030	0.001–0.005
	Y	3.0 (2980)	1.2189–1.2195	1.2189–1.2195	1.2189–1.2195	1.2189–1.2195	1.2189–1.2195	0.335	0.315	0.0010–0.0026	0.012
	4	3.8 (3801)	2.0505–2.0515	2.0505–2.0515	2.0505–2.0515	2.0505–2.0515	—	0.240–0.245	0.254–0.259	0.0010–0.0030	①
1991	D	2.5 (2524)	2.0060–2.0090	2.0060–2.0090	2.0060–2.0090	2.0060–2.0090	2.0060–2.0090	0.244–0.249	0.234–0.239	0.0010–0.0030	0.009
	U	3.0 (2971)	2.0074–2.0084	2.0074–2.0084	2.0074–2.0084	2.0074–2.0084	—	0.255–0.260	0.255–0.260	0.0010–0.0030	0.001–0.005
	Y	3.0 (2980)	1.2189–1.2195	1.2189–1.2195	1.2189–1.2195	1.2189–1.2195	1.2189–1.2195	0.335	0.315	0.0010–0.0026	0.012
	4	3.8 (3801)	2.0505–2.0515	2.0505–2.0515	2.0505–2.0515	2.0505–2.0515	—	0.240–0.245	0.254–0.259	0.0010–0.0030	0.001–0.006
1992-93	U	3.0 (2971)	2.0074–2.0084	2.0074–2.0084	2.0074–2.0084	2.0074–2.0084	—	0.255–0.260	0.255–0.260	0.0010–0.0030	0.001–0.005
	Y	3.0 (2980)	1.2189–1.2195	1.2189–1.2195	1.2189–1.2195	1.2189–1.2195	1.2189–1.2195	0.335	0.315	0.0010–0.0026	0.012
	4	3.8 (3801)	2.0505–2.0515	2.0505–2.0515	2.0505–2.0515	2.0505–2.0515	—	0.240–0.245	0.254–0.259	0.0010–0.0030	0.001–0.006

① The camshaft is restrained by a spring; there is no endplay.

CRANKSHAFT AND CONNECTING ROD SPECIFICATIONS

All measurements are given in inches.

Year	Engine ID/VIN	Engine Displacement Liters (cc)	Crankshaft Main Brg. Journal Dia.	Crankshaft Main Brg. Oil Clearance	Crankshaft Shaft End-play	Thrust on No.	Connecting Rod Journal Diameter	Connecting Rod Oil Clearance	Connecting Rod Side Clearance
1989	D	2.5 (2524)	2.2489–2.2490	0.0008–0.0024	0.004–0.008	3	2.1232–2.1240	0.0008–0.0024	0.0035–0.0140
	U	3.0 (2971)	2.5190–2.5198	0.0005–0.0023	0.004–0.008	3	2.1253–2.1261	0.0009–0.0027	0.0060–0.0140
	Y	3.0 (2980)	2.5187–2.5197	0.0011–0.0031	0.001–0.008	3	2.0463–2.0472	0.0009–0.0031	0.0063–0.0138
	4	3.8 (3801)	2.5190–2.5198	0.0005–0.0023	0.004–0.008	3	2.3103–2.3111	0.0009–0.0027	0.0047–0.0140
1990	D	2.5 (2524)	2.2489–2.2490	0.0008–0.0024	0.004–0.008	3	2.1232–2.1240	0.0008–0.0024	0.0035–0.0140
	U	3.0 (2971)	2.5190–2.5198	0.0005–0.0023	0.004–0.008	3	2.1253–2.1261	0.0009–0.0027	0.0060–0.0140
	Y	3.0 (2980)	2.5187–2.5197	0.0011–0.0031	0.001–0.008	3	2.0463–2.0472	0.0009–0.0031	0.0063–0.0138
	4	3.8 (3801)	2.5190–2.5198	0.0005–0.0023	0.004–0.008	3	2.3103–2.3111	0.0009–0.0027	0.0047–0.0140
1991	D	2.5 (2524)	2.2489–2.2490	0.0008–0.0024	0.004–0.008	3	2.1232–2.1240	0.0008–0.0024	0.0035–0.0140
	U	3.0 (2971)	2.5190–2.5198	0.0005–0.0023	0.004–0.008	3	2.1253–2.1261	0.0009–0.0027	0.0060–0.0140
	Y	3.0 (2980)	2.5187–2.5197	0.0011–0.0031	0.001–0.008	3	2.0463–2.0472	0.0009–0.0031	0.0063–0.0138
	4	3.8 (3801)	2.5190–2.5198	0.0005–0.0023	0.004–0.008	3	2.3103–2.3111	0.0009–0.0027	0.0047–0.0140
1992–93	U	3.0 (2971)	2.5190–2.5198	0.0005–0.0023	0.004–0.008	3	2.1253–2.1261	0.0009–0.0027	0.0060–0.0140
	Y	3.0 (2980)	2.5187–2.5197	0.0011–0.0031	0.001–0.008	3	2.0463–2.0472	0.0009–0.0031	0.0063–0.0138
	4	3.8 (3801)	2.5190–2.5198	0.0005–0.0023	0.004–0.008	3	2.3103–2.3111	0.0009–0.0027	0.0047–0.0140

VALVE SPECIFICATIONS

Year	Engine ID/VIN	Engine Displacement Liters (cc)	Seat Angle (deg.)	Face Angle (deg.)	Spring Test Pressure (lbs. @ in.)	Spring Installed Height (in.)	Stem-to-Guide Clearance (in.) Intake	Stem-to-Guide Clearance (in.) Exhaust	Stem Diameter (in.) Intake	Stem Diameter (in.) Exhaust
1989	D	2.5 (2524)	44–45	44–45	174–190 @ 1.11	1.49	0.0018	0.0023	0.3415–0.3422	0.3411–0.3418
	U	3.0 (2971)	45	44	180 @ 1.16	1.58	0.0010–0.0028	0.0015–0.0033	0.3126–0.3134	0.3121–0.3129
	Y	3.0 (2980)	45	45.5	120.8 @ 1.19	1.52	0.0010–0.0023	0.0012–0.0025	0.2346–0.2352	0.2344–0.2350
	4	3.8 (3801)	44.5	45.8	220 @ 1.18	1.65	0.0010–0.0028	0.0015–0.0033	0.3415–0.3423	0.3410–0.3418

VALVE SPECIFICATIONS

Year	Engine ID/VIN	Engine Displacement Liters (cc)	Seat Angle (deg.)	Face Angle (deg.)	Spring Test Pressure (lbs. @ in.)	Spring Installed Height (in.)	Stem-to-Guide Clearance (in.)		Stem Diameter (in.)	
							Intake	Exhaust	Intake	Exhaust
1990	D	2.5 (2524)	44–45	44–45	174–190 @ 1.11	1.49	0.0018	0.0023	0.3415–0.3422	0.3411–0.3418
	U	3.0 (2971)	45	44	180 @ 1.16	1.58	0.0010–0.0028	0.0015–0.0033	0.3126–0.3134	0.3121–0.3129
	Y	3.0 (2980)	45	45.5	120.8 @ 1.19	1.52	0.0010–0.0023	0.0012–0.0025	0.2346–0.2352	0.2344–0.2350
	4	3.8 (3801)	44.5	45.8	220 @ 1.18	1.65	0.0010–0.0028	0.0015–0.0033	0.3415–0.3423	0.3410–0.3418
1991	D	2.5 (2524)	44–45	44–45	174–190 @ 1.11	1.49	0.0018	0.0023	0.3415–0.3422	0.3411–0.3418
	U	3.0 (2971)	45	44	180 @ 1.16	1.58	0.0010–0.0028	0.0015–0.0033	0.3126–0.3134	0.3121–0.3129
	Y	3.0 (2980)	45	45.5	120.8 @ 1.19	1.52	0.0010–0.0023	0.0012–0.0025	0.2346–0.2352	0.2344–0.2350
	4	3.8 (3801)	44.5	45.8	220 @ 1.18	1.65	0.0010–0.0028	0.0015–0.0033	0.3415–0.3423	0.3410–0.3418
1992–93	U	3.0 (2971)	45	44	180 @ 1.16	1.58	0.0010–0.0028	0.0015–0.0033	0.3126–0.3134	0.3121–0.3129
	Y	3.0 (2980)	45	45.5	120.8 @ 1.19	1.52	0.0010–0.0023	0.0012–0.0025	0.2346–0.2352	0.2344–0.2350
	4	3.8 (3801)	44.5	45.8	220 @ 1.18	1.65	0.0010–0.0028	0.0015–0.0033	0.3415–0.3423	0.3410–0.3418

PISTON AND RING SPECIFICATIONS

All measurements are given in inches.

Year	Engine ID/VIN	Engine Displacement Liters (cc)	Piston Clearance	Ring Gap			Ring Side Clearance		
				Top Compression	Bottom Compression	Oil Control	Top Compression	Bottom Compression	Oil Control
1989	D	2.5 (2524)	0.0012–0.0022	0.008–0.016	0.008–0.016	0.015–0.055	0.0020–0.0040	0.0020–0.0040	Snug
	U	3.0 (2971)	0.0014–0.0022	0.010–0.020	0.010–0.020	0.010–0.049	0.0012–0.0031	0.0012–0.0031	Snug
	Y	3.0 (2980)	0.0012–0.0020	0.012–0.018	0.012–0.018	0.008–0.020	0.0008–0.0024	0.0006–0.0022	0.0024–0.0059
	4	3.8 (3801)	0.0014–0.0032	0.011–0.022	0.010–0.020	0.015–0.058	0.0016–0.0034	0.0016–0.0034	Snug
1990	D	2.5 (2524)	0.0012–0.0022	0.008–0.016	0.008–0.016	0.015–0.055	0.0020–0.0040	0.0020–0.0040	Snug
	U	3.0 (2971)	0.0014–0.0022	0.010–0.020	0.010–0.020	0.010–0.049	0.0012–0.0031	0.0012–0.0031	Snug
	Y	3.0 (2980)	0.0012–0.0020	0.012–0.018	0.012–0.018	0.008–0.020	0.0008–0.0024	0.0006–0.0022	0.0024–0.0059
	4	3.8 (3801)	0.0014–0.0032	0.011–0.022	0.010–0.020	0.015–0.058	0.0016–0.0034	0.0016–0.0034	Snug

PISTON AND RING SPECIFICATIONS

All measurements are given in inches.

Year	Engine ID/VIN	Engine Displacement Liters (cc)	Piston Clearance	Ring Gap			Ring Side Clearance		
				Top Compression	Bottom Compression	Oil Control	Top Compression	Bottom Compression	Oil Control
1991	D	2.5 (2524)	0.0011–0.0022	0.008–0.016	0.008–0.016	0.015–0.055	0.0020–0.0040	0.0020–0.0040	Snug
	U	3.0 (2971)	0.0014–0.0022	0.010–0.020	0.010–0.020	0.010–0.049	0.0012–0.0031	0.0012–0.0031	Snug
	Y	3.0 (2980)	0.0012–0.0020	0.012–0.018	0.012–0.018	0.008–0.020	0.0008–0.0024	0.0006–0.0022	0.0024–0.0059
	4	3.8 (3801)	0.0014–0.0032	0.011–0.022	0.010–0.020	0.015–0.058	0.0016–0.0034	0.0016–0.0034	Snug
1992–93	U	3.0 (2971)	0.0014–0.0022	0.010–0.020	0.010–0.020	0.010–0.049	0.0012–0.0031	0.0012–0.0031	Snug
	Y	3.0 (2980)	0.0012–0.0020	0.012–0.018	0.012–0.018	0.008–0.020	0.0008–0.0024	0.0006–0.0022	0.0024–0.0059
	4	3.8 (3801)	0.0014–0.0032	0.011–0.022	0.010–0.020	0.015–0.058	0.0016–0.0034	0.0016–0.0034	Snug

TORQUE SPECIFICATIONS

All readings in ft. lbs.

Year	Engine ID/VIN	Engine Displacement Liters (cc)	Cylinder Head Bolts	Main Bearing Bolts	Rod Bearing Bolts	Crankshaft Damper Bolts	Flywheel Bolts	Manifold		Spark Plugs	Lug Nut
								Intake	Exhaust		
1989	D	2.5 (2524)	①	52–66	21–26	140–170	54–64	15–23	②	6–10	85–105
	U	3.0 (2971)	③	63–69	26	141–169	54–64	④	19	5–11	85–105
	Y	3.0 (2980)	⑤	⑥	⑦	113–126	⑧	11–17	26–38	17–19	85–105
	4	3.8 (3801)	⑨	65–81	31–36	93–121	54–64	⑩	15–22	5–11	85–105
1990	D	2.5 (2524)	①	52–66	21–26	140–170	54–64	15–23	②	6–10	85–105
	U	3.0 (2971)	③	63–69	26	107	59	⑪	19	5–11	85–105
	Y	3.0 (2980)	⑤	⑥	⑦	113–126	⑧	11–17	26–38	17–19	85–105
	4	3.8 (3801)	⑨	65–81	31–36	103–132	54–64	⑩	15–22	5–11	85–105
1991	D	2.5 (2524)	①	52–66	21–26	140–170	54–64	15–22	②	6–10	85–105
	U	3.0 (2971)	③	55–63	26	107	59	⑪	19	5–11	85–105
	Y	3.0 (2980)	⑤	⑥	⑦	113–126	⑧	11–17	26–38	17–19	85–105
	4	3.8 (3801)	⑫	65–81	31–36	103–132	54–64	⑩	15–22	5–11	85–105
1992–93	U	3.0 (2971)	③	58–63	26	93–121	59	15–22	15–22	5–11	85–105
	Y	3.0 (2980)	⑤	⑥	⑦	113–126	⑧	11–16	26–38	17–19	85–105
	4	3.8 (3801)	⑫	65–81	31–36	103–132	54–64	⑬	15–22	5–11	85–105

① Tighten in 2 steps:
  Step 1: 52–59 ft. lbs.
  Step 2: 70–76 ft. lbs.
② Tighten in 2 steps:
  Step 1: 5–7 ft. lbs.
  Step 2: 20–30 ft. lbs.
③ Tighten in 2 steps:
  Step 1: 37 ft. lbs.
  Step 2: 68 ft. lbs.
④ Tighten in 3 steps:
  Step 1: 11 ft. lbs.
  Step 2: 18 ft. lbs.
  Step 3: 24 ft.lbs.

⑤ Tighten in 2 steps:
  Step 1: 37–50 ft. lbs.
  Step 2: 62–68 ft. lbs.
⑥ Tighten in 2 steps:
  Step 1: 37–50 ft. lbs.
  Step 2: 58–64 ft. lbs.
⑦ Tighten in 2 steps:
  Step 1: 22–26 ft. lbs.
  Step 2: 33–36 ft. lbs.
⑧ Tighten in 2 steps:
  Step 1: 29–43 ft. lbs.
  Step 2: 51–58 ft. lbs.

⑨ Tighten in 6 steps:
  Step 1: 37 ft. lbs.
  Step 2: 45 ft. lbs.
  Step 3: 52 ft. lbs.
  Step 4: 59 ft. lbs.
  Step 5: Back off all bolts 2–3 turns
  Step 6: Repeat steps 1–4
⑩ Tighten in 3 steps:
  Step 1: 7 ft. lbs.
  Step 2: 15 ft. lbs.
  Step 3: 24 ft. lbs.
⑪ Tighten in 2 steps:
  Step 1: 11 ft. lbs.
  Step 2: 21 ft. lbs.

⑫ Tighten in 7 steps:
  Step 1: 37 ft. lbs.
  Step 2: 45 ft. lbs.
  Step 3: 52 ft. lbs.
  Step 4: 59 ft. lbs.
  Step 5: In sequence, loosen all bolts 2–3 turns
  Step 6: Tighten long bolts to 11–18 ft. lbs., then an additional 85–105 degrees
  Step 7: Tighten short bolts to 11–18 ft. lbs., then an additional 65–85 degrees
⑬ Tighten in 2 steps:
  Step 1: 8 ft. lbs.
  Step 2: 11 ft. lbs.

BRAKE SPECIFICATIONS
All measurements in inches unless noted

Year	Model	Master Cylinder Bore	Brake Disc Original Thickness	Brake Disc Minimum Thickness	Brake Disc Maximum Runout	Brake Drum Diameter Original Inside Diameter	Brake Drum Diameter Max. Wear Limit	Brake Drum Diameter Maximum Machine Diameter	Minimum Lining Thickness Front	Minimum Lining Thickness Rear
1989	Taurus	0.940	1.024	0.974	0.003	①	NA	②	0.125	0.030
	Taurus SHO	1.000	1.020	0.974	③	—	—	—	0.125	0.123
	Sable	0.940	1.024	0.974	0.003	①	NA	②	0.125	0.030
	Continental	0.940	1.020	0.970	0.002	—	—	—	0.125	0.123
1990	Taurus	0.940	④	⑤	③	①	NA	②	0.125	⑥
	Taurus SHO	1.000	④	⑤	③	—	—	—	0.125	0.123
	Sable	0.940	④	⑤	③	①	NA	②	0.125	⑥
	Continental	1.000	1.020	0.970	0.002	—	—	—	0.125	0.123
1991	Taurus	0.940	④	⑤	③	①	NA	②	0.125	⑥
	Taurus SHO	1.000	④	⑤	③	—	—	—	0.125	0.123
	Sable	0.940	④	⑤	③	①	NA	②	0.125	⑥
	Continental	1.000	④	⑤	⑦	—	—	—	0.125	0.123
1992-93	Taurus	1.000	④	⑤	③	①	NA	②	0.125	⑥
	Taurus SHO	1.000	④	⑤	③	—	—	—	0.125	0.123
	Sable	1.000	④	⑤	③	①	NA	②	0.125	⑥
	Continental	1.000	④	⑤	0.003	—	—	—	0.125	0.123

NA—Not available
① Sedan—8.85 in. Wagon—9.84 in.
② Sedan—8.91 in. Wagon—9.90 in.
③ Front—0.003 Rear—0.002
④ Front—1.024 Rear—0.940
⑤ Front—0.974 Rear—0.900
⑥ With disc brakes—0.123 With drum brakes—0.030
⑦ Front—0.002 Rear—0.003

WHEEL ALIGNMENT

Year	Model		Caster Range (deg.)	Caster Preferred Setting (deg.)	Camber Range (deg.)	Camber Preferred Setting (deg.)	Toe (in.)	Steering Axis Inclination (deg.)
1989	Taurus	Front	①	②	③	④	$^7/_{32}$N–$^1/_{32}$P	15½
		Rear	—	—	1$^5/_8$N–$^7/_{32}$N	$^{15}/_{16}$N	$^1/_{16}$N–$^3/_{16}$P	—
	Sable	Front	2$^{11}/_{16}$P–5$^{11}/_{16}$P	3$^{11}/_{16}$P	③	④	$^7/_{32}$N–$^1/_{32}$P	15½
		Rear	—	—	1$^5/_8$N–$^7/_{32}$N	$^{15}/_{16}$N	$^1/_{16}$N–$^3/_{16}$P	—
	Continental	Front	3$^5/_8$P–5$^1/_8$P	4$^3/_8$P	1$^{11}/_{16}$N–$^1/_2$N	1$^1/_8$N	$^7/_{32}$N–$^1/_{32}$P	15½
		Rear	—	—	2N–$^5/_8$N	$^{15}/_{16}$N	$^1/_{32}$N–$^7/_{32}$P	—
1990	Taurus	Front	⑤	⑥	⑦	⑧	$^7/_{32}$N–$^1/_{32}$P	15½
		Rear	—	—	1$^5/_8$N–$^7/_{32}$N	$^{15}/_{16}$N	$^1/_{16}$N–$^3/_{16}$P	—
	Sable	Front	⑨	⑩	⑪	⑫	$^7/_{32}$N–$^1/_{32}$P	15½
		Rear	—	—	1$^5/_8$N–$^7/_{32}$N	$^{15}/_{16}$N	$^1/_{16}$N–$^3/_{16}$P	—
	Continental	Front	3$^5/_8$P–5$^1/_8$P	4$^3/_8$P	1$^{11}/_{16}$N–$^1/_2$N	1$^1/_8$N	$^7/_{32}$N–$^1/_{32}$P	15½
		Rear	—	—	2N–$^5/_8$N	$^{15}/_{16}$N	$^1/_{32}$N–$^7/_{32}$P	—
1991	Taurus	Front	⑬	⑭	⑦	⑧	$^7/_{32}$N–$^1/_{32}$P	15½
		Rear	—	—	1$^5/_8$N–$^7/_{32}$N	$^{15}/_{16}$N	$^1/_{16}$N–$^3/_{16}$P	—
	Sable	Front	⑮	⑯	⑪	⑫	$^7/_{32}$N–$^1/_{32}$P	15½
		Rear	—	—	1$^5/_8$N–$^7/_{32}$N	$^{15}/_{16}$N	$^1/_{16}$N–$^3/_{16}$P	—
	Continental	Front	3$^5/_8$P–5$^1/_8$P	4$^3/_8$P	1$^{11}/_{16}$N–$^1/_2$N	1$^1/_8$N	$^7/_{32}$N–$^1/_{32}$P	15½
		Rear	—	—	2N–$^5/_8$N	$^{15}/_{16}$N	$^1/_{32}$N–$^7/_{32}$P	—

WHEEL ALIGNMENT

Year	Model		Caster Range (deg.)	Caster Preferred Setting (deg.)	Camber Range (deg.)	Camber Preferred Setting (deg.)	Toe (in.)	Steering Axis Inclination (deg.)
1992-93	Taurus	Front	⑬	⑭	⑦	⑧	7/32N–1/32P	15½
		Rear	—	—	1 5/8N–7/32N	15/16N	1/16N–3/16P	—
	Sable	Front	⑮	⑯	⑪	⑫	7/32N–1/32P	15½
		Rear	—	—	1 5/8N–7/32N	15/16N	1/16N–3/16P	—
	Continental	Front	3 5/8P–5 1/8P	4 3/8P	1 11/16N–1/2N	1 1/8N	7/32N–1/32P	15½
		Rear	—	—	2N–5/8N	15/16N	1/32N–7/32P	—

① Sedan—2 13/16P–5 13/16P
   Wagon—2 11/16P–5 11/16P
② Sedan—3 13/16P
   Wagon—3 11/16P
③ Sedan—1 1/8N–1/8P
   Wagon—1 7/16N–1/8P
④ Sedan—1/2N
   Wagon—7/8N
⑤ Sedan—2 13/16P–5 13/16P
   Wagon—2 5/8P–5 5/8P
⑥ Sedan—3 13/16P
   Wagon—3 5/8P

⑦ Sedan—1 1/8N–1/8P
   Wagon—1 1/16N–3/16P
⑧ Sedan—1/2N
   Wagon—7/16N
⑨ Sedan—2 11/16P–5 11/16P
   Wagon—2 5/8P–5 5/8P
⑩ Sedan—3 11/16P
   Wagon—3 5/8P
⑪ Sedan—1 1/8N–1/8P
   Wagon—1 1/16N–3/16P

⑫ Sedan—1/2N
   Wagon—7/16N
⑬ Sedan—2 13/16P–4 13/16P
   Wagon—2 5/8P–4 5/8P
⑭ Sedan—3 13/16P
   Wagon—3 5/8P
⑮ Sedan—2 11/16P–4 11/16P
   Wagon—2 5/8P–4 5/8P
⑯ Sedan—3 11/16P
   Wagon—3 5/8P

ENGINE MECHANICAL

NOTE: Disconnecting the negative battery cable on some vehicles may interfere with the functions of the on board computer systems and may require the computer to undergo a relearning process, once the negative battery cable is reconnected.

Engine Assembly

REMOVAL & INSTALLATION

2.5L Engine

1. Disconnect the negative battery cable and relieve the fuel system pressure.

2. Remove the transaxle timing window cover and rotate the engine until the flywheeel timing marker is aligned with the timing pointer.

3. Place a reference mark on the crankshaft pulley at the 12 o'clock position (TDC) then rotate the crankshaft pulley mark to the 6 o'clock postion (BDC).

4. Mark the position of the hood hinges and remove the hood.

5. Remove the air cleaner assembly and drain the cooling system.

6. Disconnect the upper radiator hose at the engine.

7. Identify, tag and disconnect all electrical wiring and vacuum hoses as required.

8. Disconnect the crankcase ventilation hose at the valve cover and intake manifold.

9. Disconnect the fuel lines and heater hoses.

10. Disconnect the engine ground wire.

11. Disconnect the accelerator and throttle valve control cables at the throttle body.

12. Properly discharge the air conditioning system and remove the suction and discharge lines from the compressor, if equipped.

13. Remove the drive belt and water pump pulley.

14. Remove the air cleaner-to-canister hose.

15. Raise the vehicle and support safely.

16. Drain the engine oil and remove the oil filter.

17. Disconnect the starter cable and remove the starter.

18. Remove the converter nuts and align the previously made reference mark as close to the 6 o'clock (BDC) position as possible with the converter stud visible.

NOTE: The flywheel timing marker must be in the 6 o'clock (BDC) position for proper engine removal and installation.

19. Remove the engine insulator nuts.

20. Disconnect the exhaust pipe from the manifold.

21. Disconnect the canister and halfshaft brackets from the engine.

22. Remove the lower engine-to-transaxle retaining bolts.

23. Disconnect the lower radiator hose.

24. Lower the vehicle and position a floor jack under the transaxle.

25. Disconnect the power steering lines from the pump.

26. Install engine lifting eyes tool D81L–6001–D or equivalent and engine support tool T88L–6000–A or equivalent.

27. Connect suitable lifting equipment to support the engine and remove the upper engine-to-transaxle retaining bolts.

28. Remove the engine from the vehicle and support on a suitable holding fixture.

To install:

29. Make sure the timing marker is in the 6 o'clock (BDC) position.

30. Remove the engine from the stand and position it in the vehicle. Remove the lifting equipment.

31. Install the upper engine-to-transaxle bolts and tighten to 26–34 ft. lbs. (34–47 Nm). Use a floor jack under the transaxle to aid alignment.

32. Connect the power steering lines to the pump.

33. Raise the vehicle and support it safely.

34. Connect the lower radiator hose to the tube.

35. Install the lower engine-to-transaxle attaching bolts and tighten to 26–34 ft. lbs. (34–47 Nm).

36. Connect the halfshaft bracket to the engine and the exhaust pipe to the manifold.

37. Install the engine insulator nuts and tighten to 40–55 ft. lbs. (54–75 Nm).

38. Position the marks on the crankshaft pulley as close to 6 o'clock position (BDC) as possible and install the converter nuts. Tighten the nuts to 20–33 ft. lbs. (27–46 Nm).

39. Install the starter and connect the starter cable.

40. Install the oil filter and make sure the oil drain plug is tight.

41. Lower the vehicle.

42. Install the air cleaner-to-canister hose and the water pump pulley and drive belt.

43. Connect the air conditioning lines to the compressor, if equipped.

44. Connect the accelerator cable and throttle valve control cable at the throttle body.

45. Connect the negative battery cable at the engine and connect the heater hoses and fuel lines.

46. Connect the crankcase ventilation hose at the valve cover and the intake manifold.

47. Connect the engine control sensor wiring assembly and vacuum lines.

48. Connect the upper radiator hose at the engine and install the air cleaner assembly.

49. Connect the negative battery cable.

50. Rotate the engine until the flywheel timing marker is aligned with the timing pointer. Install the timing window cover.

51. Make sure the electrical connector is connected at the inertia switch.

52. Fill the cooling system with the proper amount and type of coolant and fill the crankcase with the proper engine oil to the required level.

53. Install the hood.

54. Charge the air conditioning system, if equipped.

55. Check all fluid levels and start the vehicle. Check for leaks.

3.0L Engine

1. Disconnect the battery cables and drain the cooling system. Mark the position of the hood on the hinges and remove the hood.

2. Evacuate the air conditioning system safely and properly. Relieve the fuel system pressure. Remove the air cleaner assembly. Remove the battery and the battery tray.

3. Remove the integrated relay controller, cooling fan and radiator with fan shroud. Remove the engine bounce damper bracket on the shock tower.

4. Remove the evaporative emission line, upper radiator hose, starter brace and lower radiator hose.

5. Remove the exhaust pipes from both exhaust manifolds. Remove and plug the power steering pump lines.

6. Remove the fuel lines and remove and tag all necessary vacuum lines.

7. Disconnect the ground strap, heater lines, accelerator cable linkage, throttle valve linkage and cruise control cable.

8. Disconnect and label the following wiring connectors; alternator, air conditioning clutch, oxygen sensor, ignition coil, radio frequency supressor, cooling fan voltage resistor, engine coolant temperature sensor, coolant temperature sending switch, Thick film ignition module, injector wiring harness, ISC motor wire, throttle position sensor, oil pressure sending switch, ground wire, block heater, if equipped, knock sensor, EGR sensor and oil level sensor.

9. Raise the vehicle and support it safely. Remove the engine mount bolts and engine mounts. Remove the transaxle to engine mounting bolts and transaxle brace assembly.

10. Lower the vehicle. Install a suitable engine lifting plate onto the engine and use a suitable engine hoist to remove the engine from the vehicle. Remove the main wiring harness from the engine.

To install:

11. Install the main wiring harness on the engine. Position the engine in the vehicle and remove the engine lifting plate.

12. Raise the vehicle and support it safely. Install the engine mounts and bolts and tighten to 40–55 ft. lbs. (54–75 Nm). Install the transaxle brace assembly and tighten the bolts to 40–55 ft. lbs. (54–75 Nm).

13. Connect all wiring connectors according to their labels.

14. Connect the ground strap, heater lines, accelerator cable linkage, throttle valve linkage and speed control cables.

15. Connect the power steering pump lines.

16. Connect the exhaust pipes to the exhaust manifolds.

17. Connect the fuel lines and vacuum lines.

18. Install the evaporative emission line, upper radiator hose, starter brace and lower radiator hose.

19. Install the integrated relay controller, cooling fan and radiator with fan shroud. Install the engine bounce damper bracket on the shock tower.

20. Install the battery tray and the battery.

21. Install the air cleaner assembly and charge the air conditioning system.

22. Fill the cooling system with the proper type and quantity of coolant. Fill the crankcase with the correct type of motor oil to the required level.

23. Install the hood.

24. Connect the negative battery cable. Start the engine and check for leaks.

3.0L SHO Engine

1. Disconnect the battery cables and remove the battery and battery tray.

2. Drain the cooling system and relieve the fuel system pressure.

3. Disconnect the wiring connector retaining the under hood light, if equipped. Mark the position of the hood hinges and remove the hood.

4. Remove the oil level indicator.

5. Disconnect the alternator and voltage regulator wiring assembly.

6. Remove the radiator upper sight shield.

7. Discharge the air conditioning system.

8. Remove the radiator coolant recovery reservoir assembly.

9. Remove the integrated relay controller, air cleaner hose assembly, upper radiator hose, electric fan and shroud assembly.

10. Remove the lower radiator hose and the radiator.

11. Disconnect the fuel inlet and return hose.

12. Remove the Barometric Air Pressure (BAP) sensor.

13. Remove the engine vibration damper and bracket assembly from the right side of the engine.

14. Remove the engine to damper bracket.

15. Remove the retaining bolt from the power steering reservoir and place the reservoir aside. Disconnect the hose to the power steering cooler at the pump.

16. Disconnect the throttle linkage and disconnect and tag the vacuum hoses.

17. Disconnect the heater hoses at the heater core.

18. Disconnect the electrical connectors from the harness on the rear of the engine.

19. Loosen the belt tensioner pulleys and remove the air conditioning compressor/alternator belt and the steering pump belt. Remove the lower tensioner pulley.

20. Disconnect the cycling switch on the top of the suction accumulator/drier.

21. Disconnect the air conditioning line at the dash panel and remove the accumulator and bracket assembly.

22. Remove the alternator assembly.

23. Disconnect the air conditioning discharge hose and remove the air conditioning compressor and bracket assembly.

24. Raise the vehicle and support it safely.

25. Place a drain pan under the oil pan. Drain the motor oil and remove the filter element.

26. Remove the wheel and tire as-

semblies. Disconnect the oil level sensor switch.

27. Disconnect the right lower ball joint, tie rod end and stabilizer bar.

28. Disconnect the center support bearing bracket and right-hand CV-joint from the transaxle.

29. Disconnect the oxygen sensor assembly and the 4 exhaust catalyst to engine retaining bolts.

30. Remove the starter motor assembly.

31. Remove the lower transaxle to engine retaining bolts.

32. Remove the engine mount to sub-frame nuts.

33. Remove the crankshaft pulley assembly.

34. Lower the vehicle and remove the upper transaxle to engine retaining bolts.

35. Install engine lifting bracket D89L–6001–A or equivalent.

36. Position a floor jack under the transaxle.

37. Position suitable engine lifting equipment, raise the transaxle assembly slightly and remove the engine from the vehicle.

To install:

38. Position the engine assembly in the vehicle.

39. Install the upper transaxle to engine bolts and remove the floor jack and engine lifting equipment. Remove the engine lifting eyes.

40. Raise the vehicle and support it safely.

41. Install the crankshaft pulley assembly. Tighten the retaining bolt to 113–126 ft. lbs. (152–172 Nm).

42. Install the engine mount to sub-frame nuts and the lower transaxle to engine retaining bolts. Tighten the bolts to 25–35 ft. lbs. (34–47 Nm).

43. Install the starter motor assembly.

44. Install the 4 exhaust catalyst to engine retaining nuts and tighten them to 19–34 ft. lbs. (27–47 Nm). Apply anti-seize compound to the threads, then install the oxygen sensor assembly. Tighten to 27–33 ft. lbs. (37–45 Nm).

45. Connect the center support bearing bracket and install the right-hand CV-joint.

46. Connect the right lower ball joint, tie rod end and stabilizer bar.

47. Connect the oil level sensor and install the wheel and tire assemblies.

48. Install the oil filter. Install the oil drain plug and tighten to 15–24 ft. lbs. (20–33 Nm).

49. Lower the vehicle.

50. Install the air conditioning compressor and bracket assembly, tighten to 27–40 ft. lbs. (36–55 Nm) and connect the air conditioning discharge hose.

51. Install the alternator assembly and tighten to 36–53 ft. lbs. (48–72 Nm).

52. Install the accumulator and bracket assembly and connect the cycling switch to the top of the accumulator.

53. Install the lower belt tensioner. Install the power steering and air conditioning compressor/alternator belts and tighten the tensioner pulleys.

54. Connect the electrical connectors from the harness on the rear of the engine.

55. Connect the heater hoses, vacuum hoses and throttle linkage.

56. Connect the hose from the power steering cooler at the pump and install the power steering reservoir.

57. Install the damper bracket to the engine and install the engine vibration damper and bracket assembly to the right side of the engine.

58. Install the BAP sensor.

59. Connect the fuel inlet and return hoses.

60. Install the radiator assembly and the lower radiator hose.

61. Install the electric fan and shroud assembly, upper radiator hose, air cleaner hose, integrated relay controller, radiator coolant recovery reservoir and radiator upper sight shield.

62. Connect the alternator and voltage regulator wiring.

63. Install the oil level indicator tube.

64. Install the hood and connect the under hood light wiring, if equipped.

65. Install the battery tray and the battery.

66. Connect the battery cables.

67. Fill the cooling system with the proper type and quantity of coolant and fill the crankcase with the proper type of motor oil to the required level.

68. Drain, evacuate, pressure test and recharge the air conditioning system.

69. Start the engine and check for leaks.

3.8L Engine

TAURUS AND SABLE

1. Drain the cooling system and disconnect the negative battery cable. Properly relieve the fuel system pressure.

2. Disconnect the underhood light wiring connector. Mark position of hood hinges and remove hood.

3. Remove the oil level indicator tube.

4. Disconnect alternator to voltage regulator wiring assembly.

5. Remove the radiator upper sight shield. Remove the engine cooling fan motor relay retaining bolts and position cooling fan motor relay aside.

6. Remove the air cleaner assembly.

7. Disconnect the radiator electric fan and motor assembly. Remove fan shroud.

8. Remove upper radiator hose.

9. Disconnect the transaxle oil cooler inlet and outlet tubes and cover the openings to prevent the entry of dirt and grease. Disconnect the heater hoses.

10. Disconnect the power steering pressure hose assembly.

11. Disconnect the air conditioner compressor clutch wire assembly. Discharge the air conditioning system and disconnect the compressor-to-condenser line.

12. Remove the radiator coolant recovery reservoir assembly. Remove the wiring shield.

13. Remove accelerator cable mounting bracket.

14. Disconnect fuel inlet and return lines.

15. Disconnect power steering pump pressure and return tube brackets.

16. Disconnect the engine control sensor wiring assembly.

17. Identify, tag and disconnect all necessary vacuum hoses.

18. Disconnect the ground wire assembly. Remove the duct assembly.

19. Disconnect one end of the throttle control valve cable. Disconnect the bulkhead electrical connector and transaxle pressure switches.

20. Remove transaxle support assembly retaining bolts and remove transaxle and support assembly from vehicle.

21. Raise the vehicle and support safely. Remove the wheel and tire assemblies. Drain the engine oil and remove the filter.

22. Disconnect the oxygen sensor assembly.

23. Loosen and remove drive belt assembly. Remove the crankshaft pulley and drive belt tensioner assemblies.

24. Remove the starter motor assembly. Remove the catalytic converter housing assembly and remove the converter and inlet pipe assembly.

25. Remove the left and right front engine mount retaining nuts.

26. Remove the converter-to-flywheel nuts.

27. Disconnect the oil level indicator sensor. Remove crankshaft pulley assembly.

28. Disconnect the lower radiator hose.

29. Remove the engine-to-transaxle bolts and partially lower engine. Remove the wheel and tire assemblies.

30. Remove the water pump pulley retaining bolts and the water pump pulley.

31. Remove the distributor cap and position aside. Remove distributor rotor.

32. Remove the exhaust manifold bolt lock retaining bolts. Remove the thermactor air pump retaining bolts and the thermactor air pump, if equipped.

33. Disconnect the oil pressure engine unit gauge assembly.

34. Install engine lifting eyes D81L-60001-D or equivalent, and connect suitable lifting equipment to the lifting eyes.

35. Position a suitable jack under the transaxle and raise the transaxle a small amount.

36. Remove the engine from the vehicle and position in a suitable holding fixture.

To install:

NOTE: Lightly oil all bolt and stud threads before installation except those specifying special sealant.

37. Remove the engine assembly from the work stand and position it in the vehicle.

38. Install the engine to transaxle bolts and remove the jack from under the transaxle and the engine lifting equipment. Remove the engine lifting eyes.

39. Tighten the engine to transaxle bolts to 41–50 ft. lbs. (55–68 Nm).

40. Connect the oil pressure engine unit gauge assembly.

41. Install the air conditioning compressor and tighten the retaining bolts to 30–45 ft. lbs. (41–61 Nm). Connect the compressor to condenser discharge line and the compressor clutch wire assembly.

42. Connect the heater hoses, vacuum hoses and the fuel inlet hose and return line hose.

43. Connect the engine control module wiring assembly.

44. Connect the transaxle oil cooler inlet and outlet tubes.

45. Install the radiator assembly.

46. Partially raise the vehicle and support it safely.

47. Install the converter to flywheel bolts and tighten to 20–34 ft. lbs. (27–46 Nm).

48. Install the left and right transaxle and engine mount retaining nuts and install the converter housing cover.

49. Install the starter motor.

50. Connect the lower radiator hose.

51. Install the drive belt tensioner assembly and the crankshaft pulley assembly. Tighten the crankshaft pulley retaining bolts to 20–28 ft. lbs. (26–38 Nm).

52. Install the catalytic converter assembly and connect the heated exhaust gas oxygen sensor.

53. Install the oil filter and connect the oil level indicator sensor.

54. Lower the vehicle.

55. Position the thermactor air supply pump, if equipped, and install the retaining bolts.

56. Connect the vacuum pump and install the exhaust air supply pump pulley assembly.

57. Install the wiring shield.

58. Install the distributor cap and rotor.

59. Install the radiator coolant recovery reservoir assembly, upper radiator hose and water pump pulley.

60. Connect the alternator-to-voltage regulator wiring assembly and the engine control module wiring assembly.

61. Connect the wiring asembly ground.

62. Install the accelerator cable mounting bracket.

63. Connect the power steering pressure hose assembly and the power steering line.

64. Install the fan shroud.

65. Connect the radiator electric motor assembly and install the engine cooling fan motor relay assembly.

66. Install the drive belts.

67. Position and install the transaxle support assembly.

68. Install the radiator upper sight shield.

69. Raise the vehicle and support it safely. Install the wheel and tire assemblies.

70. Install the hood and connect the negative battery cable.

71. Fill the cooling system with the proper type and quantity of coolant and fill the crankcase with the proper type of motor oil to the required level.

72. Drain, evacuate, pressure test and recharge the air conditioning system.

73. Start the engine and check for leaks.

CONTINENTAL

1. Disconnect the negative battery cable.

2. Relieve the fuel system pressure, drain the cooling system and properly discharge the air conditioning system.

3. Tag and disconnect the alternator-to-voltage regulator, electric cooling fan, transaxle pressure switch, air conditioning compressor clutch, electronic engine control and ground wiring.

4. Disconnect the heater hoses, power steering hoses and brackets, air conditioning discharge hose, transaxle oil cooler tubes and fuel lines.

5. Tag and disconnect the vacuum lines. Disconnect the throttle cable at the throttle valve.

6. Remove the electric cooling fan and motor assembly. Remove the fan shroud.

7. Remove the engine oil dipstick

and the radiator sight shield. Remove the integrated controller relay and position aside.

8. Remove the air cleaner assembly.

9. Disconnect the upper radiator hose and remove the coolant recovery reservoir. Remove the wiring shield.

10. Remove the air suspension compressor and position aside. Remove the accelerator cable mounting bracket.

11. Remove the transaxle support assembly. Remove the air conditioning compressor.

12. Raise and safely support the vehicle.

13. Drain the engine oil and remove the oil filter. Disconnect the oxygen sensor.

14. Release the tension at the drive belts. Remove the crankshaft pulley and drive belt tensioner.

15. Remove the starter. Remove the catalytic converter housing cover and remove the converter and inlet pipe assembly from the engine.

16. Remove the nuts at the transaxle and engine mounts. Remove the torque converter-to-flywheel nuts.

17. Disconnect the oil level indicator sensor and the lower radiator hose.

18. Loosen the engine-to-transaxle bolts, leaving them loosely installed.

19. Partially lower the vehicle and remove the front wheel and tire assemblies.

20. Remove the drive belts and the water pump pulley. Remove the radiator assembly.

21. Remove the distributor cap and position aside. Remove the distributor rotor.

22. Remove the exhaust manifold lock bolts and the thermactor air pump, if equipped. Disconnect the oil pressure sending unit.

23. Install suitable engine lifting equipment and position a transmission jack. Completely remove the engine-to-transaxle bolts.

24. Raise the transaxle assembly using the jack and lift the engine from the vehicle.

To install:

25. Position the engine assembly in the vehicle and align the engine-to-transaxle bolt bores. Install the engine-to-transaxle bolts that are accessible but do not tighten at this time.

26. Remove the transmission jack and the engine lifting equipment.

27. Install the oil pressure sending unit. Install the air conditioning compressor and tighten the retaining bolts to 30–45 ft. lbs. (41–61 Nm).

28. Connect the air conditioning compressor discharge hose and the clutch wiring to the compressor.

29. Connect the heater hoses and the fuel lines. Connect the vacuum hoses and routing clips.

30. Connect the transaxle oil cooler lines and the transaxle pressure switch wiring.

31. Install the radiator assembly. Raise and safely support the vehicle.

32. Install the remaining transaxle-to-engine bolts. Tighten all the bolts to 40–50 ft. lbs. (55–68 Nm).

33. Install the torque converter-to-flywheel bolts and tighten to 20–34 ft. lbs. (27–46 Nm). Install the converter housing cover.

34. Install the transaxle mount retaining nuts and tighten to 50–70 ft. lbs. (68–95 Nm).

35. Install the starter and the lower radiator hose.

36. Install the drive belt tensioner assembly and the crankshaft pulley assembly. Tighten the crankshaft pulley retaining bolts to 20–28 ft. lbs. (26–38 Nm).

37. Install the catalytic converter and inlet pipe assembly. Connect the oxygen sensor.

38. Install the oil filter and the oil drain plug. Connect the low oil level sensor.

39. Partially lower the vehicle.

40. Install the thermactor air pump, if equipped, and tighten the mounting bolts to 30–40 ft. lbs. (40–55 Nm). Install the vacuum hose at the pump and the air pump pulley.

41. Install the wiring shield. Install the distributor rotor and cap and connect the distributor wiring.

42. Install the coolant recovery reservoir and connect the top radiator hose.

43. Install the air suspension compressor and connect the wiring. Install the water pump pulley.

44. Connect the alternator to voltage regulator wiring, the electronic engine control wiring and the ground wires.

45. Connect the power steering hoses and the throttle cable at the throttle valve. Install the accelerator cable mounting bracket.

46. Install the fan shroud and connect the fan wiring. Install the cooling fan relay and position the drive belts.

47. Install the transaxle support assembly and the upper radiator sight shield. Partially raise the vehicle.

48. Install the exhaust air supply pump valve and hose assembly. Install the drive belts. Partially lower the vehicle.

49. Install the integrated controller relay and the engine oil dipstick. Install the front wheel and tire assemblies and tighten the lug nuts to 85–105 ft. lbs. (115–142 Nm).

50. Lower the vehicle. Install the hood, aligning the marks that were made during the removal procedure.

51. Install the air cleaner assembly and connect the negative battery cable.

52. Fill the engine with the proper type and quantity of engine oil and coolant. Leak test, evacuate and charge the air conditioning system. Observe all safety precautions.

53. Start the engine and check for leaks.

Engine Mounts

REMOVAL & INSTALLATION

2.5L and 3.0L Engines

RIGHT REAR ENGINE INSULATOR (NO. 3)

1. Disconnect the negative battery cable. Raise and support the vehicle safely.

2. Place a suitable jack and a block of wood the engine block.

3. Remove the nut attaching the right front and rear insulators to the frame.

4. Raise the engine with the jack until enough of a load is taken off of the insulator.

5. Remove the insulator retaining bolts and remove the insulator from the engine support bracket.

6. Installation is the reverse of the removal procedure. Tighten the insulator to engine support bracket to 40–55 ft. lbs. (54–75 Nm). Tighten the nut attaching the right, front and rear insulators to frame to 55–75 ft. lbs. (75–102 Nm).

LEFT ENGINE INSULATOR AND SUPPORT ASSEMBLY

1. Disconnect the negative battery cable. Raise and support the vehicle safely. Remove the wheel and tire assembly.

2. Place a suitable jack and a block of wood under the transaxle and support the transaxle.

3. Remove the nuts attaching the insulator to the support assembly. Remove the through bolts attaching the insulator to the frame.

4. Raise the transaxle with the jack enough to relieve the weight on the insulator.

5. Remove the bolts attaching the support assembly to the transaxle. Remove the insulator and/or transaxle support assembly.

6. Installation is the reverse of the removal procedure. Tighten the support assembly retaining bolts to 40–55 ft. lbs. (54–75 Nm). Tighten the insulator-to-frame bolts to 60–86 ft. lbs. (81–116 Nm). Tighten the insulator to support assembly nuts to 55–75 ft. lbs. (74–102 Nm).

RIGHT FRONT ENGINE INSULATOR (NO. 2)

1. Disconnect the negative battery

cable. Remove the lower damper nut or bolt from the right side of the engine. Raise and support the vehicle safely.

2. Place a jack and a block of wood under the engine block.

3. Remove the nuts attaching the right front and rear insulators to the frame.

4. Raise the engine with the jack until enough of a load is taken off of the insulator.

5. Remove the bolt(s) and the insulator from the engine bracket.

6. Installation is the reverse of the removal procedure. Tighten the insulator-to-engine bracket bolt(s) to 40–55 ft. lbs. (54–75 Nm) on 2.5L engine or 71–95 ft. lbs. (90–130 Nm) on 3.0L engine. Tighten the nut attaching the right front and right rear insulators to frame to 55–75 ft. lbs. (75–102 Nm).

3.0L SHO Engine

RIGHT FRONT (NO. 2) AND RIGHT REAR (NO. 3)

1. Remove the lower damper bolt from the right side of the engine.

2. Raise the vehicle and support it safely.

3. Place a jack and a wood block in a suitable place under the engine.

4. Remove the roll damper to engine retaining nuts and remove the roll damper.

5. Raise the engine enough to unload the insulator.

6. Remove the 2 through bolts and remove the insulators from the engine bracket.

7. Installation is the reverse of the removal procedure. Tighten the insulator-to-engine bracket bolts to 40–55 ft. lbs. (54–75 Nm). Tighten the insulator to frame nuts to 50–70 ft. lbs. (68–95 Nm). Tighten the roll damper retaining nuts to 40–55 ft. lbs. (54–75 Nm). Tighten the engine damper to engine bolt to 40–55 ft. lbs. (54–75 Nm).

LEFT ENGINE INSULATOR AND SUPPORT ASSEMBLY

1. Remove the bolt retaining the roll damper to the lower damper bracket and place the damper shaft aside.

2. Remove the backup light switch and the energy management bracket.

3. Raise the vehicle and support it with jackstands under the vehicle body, allowing the sub-frame to hang.

4. Remove the left tire and wheel assembly.

5. Place a jack and wood block under the transaxle.

6. Remove the nuts retaining the lower damper bracket to engine mount and the bolts retaining the insulator to the transaxle and sub-frame.

7. Raise the transaxle with the jack enough to unload the insulator.

8. Remove the insulator and lower damper bracket.

9. Installation is the reverse of the removal procedure. Tighten the damper bracket to insulator nuts to 40–55 ft. lbs. (54–75 Nm). Tighten the insulator to transaxle bolts to 70–95 ft. lbs. (95–130 Nm). Tighten the insulator to frame bolts to 60–85 ft. lbs. (81–116 Nm). Tighten the damper to damper bracket bolt to 40–55 ft. lbs. (54–75 Nm).

3.8L Engine

RIGHT FRONT ENGINE INSULATOR – 1989–91 VEHICLES

1. Disconnect the negative battery cable. Remove the air conditioning compressor-to-engine mounting bracket mounting bolts and position the compressor to the side. Do not discharge the air conditioning system.

2. Raise the vehicle and support safely.

3. Remove nut attaching engine mount to air conditioning compressor bracket.

4. Temporarily attach the air conditioning compressor to the mounting bracket with the 2 lower bolts.

5. Position a jack and wood block in a convenient location under the engine block.

6. Remove the upper and lower nuts attaching the right front and right rear insulators to the frame.

7. Raise the engine with the jack enough to relieve the load on the insulator.

8. Remove insulator assembly. Remove heat shield from insulator.

9. Installation is the reverse of the removal procedure. Tighten the upper insulator stud retaining nut to 40–55 ft. lbs. (54–75 Nm) and the lower retaining nut to 50–70 ft. lbs. (68–95 Nm).

RIGHT FRONT ENGINE INSULATOR – 1992–93 VEHICLES

1. Remove the mount upper retaining nut through the engine compartment using a long extension and an 18mm swivel socket.

2. Install 3 bar engine support D88L–6000–A or equivalent.

3. Raise and safely support the vehicle.

4. Loosen the right rear and right front lower mount retaining nuts.

5. Lower the vehicle.

6. Raise the engine approximately 1 in. using the engine support tool.

7. Raise and safely support the vehicle. Remove the engine mount.

8. Installation is the reverse of the removal procedure. Tighten the lower mount retaining nuts to 51–70 ft. lbs.

(68–95 Nm). Tighten the upper mount retaining nut to 40–55 ft. lbs. (54–75 Nm).

RIGHT REAR ENGINE INSULATOR (NO. 3)

1. Disconnect the negative battery cable and raise and support the vehicle safely.

2. Remove the nuts retaining the right front and right rear engine mounts to the frame.

3. Lower the vehicle.

4. Use 3 bar engine support tool D88L–6000–A or equivalent to support the engine. Raise the engine about 1 in.

5. Loosen the retaining nut on the right rear (No. 3) mount and heat shield assembly.

6. Raise and support the vehicle safely.

7. Remove the insulator retaining nut and the insulator and heat shield assembly.

8. Installation is the reverse of the removal procedure. Tighten the top retaining nut on the insulator to 40–55 ft. lbs. (54–75 Nm). Tighten the retaining nuts on the right front and right rear engine mounts to 51–70 ft. lbs. (68–95 Nm).

LEFT ENGINE MOUNT AND SUPPORT ASSEMBLY

1. Raise the vehicle and support it safely.

2. Remove the tire and wheel assembly.

3. Place a jack and wood block under the transaxle and support the transaxle.

4. Remove the 2 bolts retaining the vertical restrictor assembly, if equipped.

5. Remove the nut retaining the transaxle mount to the support assembly.

6. Remove the 2 through bolts retaining the transaxle mount to the frame.

7. Raise the transaxle with the jack enough to unload the mount.

8. Remove the bolts retaining the support assembly to the transaxle and remove the mount and/or transaxle support assembly.

9. Installation is the reverse of the removal procedure. Tighten the support assembly to transaxle bolts to 35 ft. lbs. (48 Nm) on 1989–91 vehicles or 40–55 ft. lbs. (54–75 Nm) on 1992–93 vehicles. Tighten the mount to frame bolts to 60–86 ft. lbs. (81–116 Nm). Tighten the transaxle mount to support nut to 55–75 ft. lbs. (74–102 Nm). If equipped, tighten the 2 bolts retaining the vertical restrictor assembly to 40–55 ft. lbs. (54–75 Nm).

Cylinder Head

REMOVAL & INSTALLATION

2.5L Engine

1. Disconnect the negative battery cable. Drain the cooling system.

2. Remove the air cleaner assembly. Properly relieve the fuel system pressure.

3. On 1989–90 vehicles, disconnect the heater hose at the fitting located under the intake manifold. On 1991 vehicles, disconnect the heater hose at the heater inlet tube and disconnect the adapter hose at the water outlet connector.

4. Disconnect the upper radiator hose at the cylinder head and the electric cooling fan switch at the plastic connector.

5. Disconnect distributor cap and spark plug wire and remove as an assembly.

6. Remove spark plugs, if necessary.

7. Disconnect and tag required vacuum hoses. Disconnect the accessory drive belts.

8. Remove dipstick. Disconnect the choke cap wire.

9. Remove rocker cover retaining bolts and remove cover. Disconnect the EGR tube at the EGR valve.

10. Remove the rocker arm fulcrum bolts, the fulcrums, rocker arms and pushrods. Identify the location of each so they may be reinstalled in their original positions.

11. Disconnect the fuel supply and return lines at the rubber connections. Disconnect the accelerator cable and speed control cable, if equipped.

12. Raise the vehicle and support it safely. Disconnect the exhaust system at the exhaust pipe, hose and tube. Lower the vehicle.

13. Remove the cylinder head bolts. Remove the cylinder head and gasket with the exhaust manifold and intake manifold.

To install:

14. Clean all gasket material from the mating surface of the cylinder head and block. Position the cylinder head gasket on the cylinder block, using a suitable sealer to retain the gasket.

15. Before installing the cylinder head, thread 2 cylinder head alignment studs through the head bolt holes in the gasket and into the block at opposite corners of the block.

16. Install the cylinder head and cylinder head bolts. Run down several head bolts and remove the 2 guide bolts. Replace them with the remaining head bolts. Torque the cylinder head bolts in 2 steps, first to 52–59 ft. lbs. (70–80 Nm) and then to 70–76 ft. lbs. (95–103 Nm).

17. Raise and support the vehicle safely. Connect the exhaust system at the exhaust pipe and hose to metal tube.

18. Lower the vehicle. Install the thermactor pump drive belt, if equipped. Connect the accelerator cable and speed control cable, if equipped.

19. Connect the fuel supply and return lines. Connect the choke cap wire, if equipped.

20. Install the pushrods, rocker arms, fulcrums and fulcrum bolts in their original positions. Install the rocker arm cover.

21. Connect the EGR tube at the EGR valve. Install the distributor cap and spark plug wires as an assembly. Install the spark plugs, if removed.

22. Connect all accessory drive belts.

23. Connect the required vacuum hoses. Install the air cleaner assembly. Connect the electric cooling fan switch at the connector.

24. Connect the upper radiator hose and the heater hose. Fill the cooling system. Connect the negative battery cable.

25. Start the engine and check for leaks. After the engine has reached normal operating temperature, check and if necessary add coolant.

3.0L Except SHO Engine

1. Disconnect the negative battery cable. Properly relieve the fuel system pressure. Drain the cooling system. Remove the air cleaner assembly.

2. Loosen the accessory drive belt idler pulley, remove the drive belt.

3. If the left cylinder head is being removed, perform the following:

  a. Disconnect the alternator electrical connectors.

  b. Rotate the tensioner clockwise and remove the accessory drive belt.

  c. Remove the automatic belt tensioner assembly.

  d. Remove the alternator.

  e. Remove the power steering mounting bracket retaining bolts. Leave the hoses connected and place the pump aside in a position to prevent fluid from leaking out.

  f. Remove the engine oil dipstick tube from the exhaust manifold.

4. If the right head is being removed, perform the following:

  a. Remove the alternator belt tensioner bracket.

  b. Remove the heater supply tube retaining brackets from the exhaust manifold.

  c. Remove the vehicle speed sensor cable retaining bolt and the EGR vacuum regulator sensor and bracket.

5. Remove the exhaust manifolds from both heads. Remove the PCV and

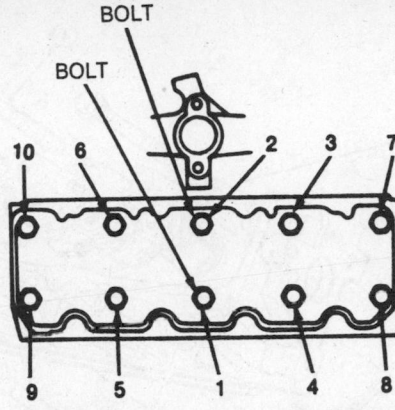

Cylinder head bolt torque sequence— 2.5L engine

the rocker arm covers. Loosen the rocker arm fulcrum attaching bolts enough to allow the rocker arm to be lifted off the pushrod and rotated to one side.

NOTE: Regardless of the cylinder head being removed, the No. 3 cylinder intake valve pushrod must be removed to allow removal of the intake manifold.

6. Remove the pushrods. Be sure to identify and label the position of each pushrod. The pushrods should be installed in their original position during reassembly.

7. Remove the intake manifold.

8. Remove the cylinder head attaching bolts and remove the cylinder heads from the engine. Remove and discard the old cylinder head gaskets.

To install:

9. Lightly oil all bolt and stud bolt threads before installation. Clean the cylinder head, intake manifold, rocker arm cover and cylinder head gasket contact surfaces. If the cylinder head was removed for a cylinder head gasket replacement, check the flatness of the cylinder head and block gasket surfaces.

NOTE: If the flat surface of the cylinder head is warped, do not plane or grind off more than 0.010 in. If the head is machined past its resurface limit, the head will have to be replaced with a new one.

10. Position new head gaskets on the cylinder block using the dowels in the engine block for alignment. If the dowels are damaged, they must be replaced.

11. Position the cylinder head on the cylinder block. Tighten the cylinder head attaching bolts in 2 steps following the proper torque sequence. The first step is 37 ft. lbs. (50 Nm) and the second step is 68 ft. lbs. (92 Nm).

NOTE: When cylinder head attaching bolts have been tightened using the above procedure, it is not necessary to retighten the bolts after extended engine operation. The bolts can be rechecked for tightness if desired.

12. Install the intake manifold. Connect the coolant temperature sending unit connectors.

13. Dip each pushrod end in oil conditioner or heavy engine oil. Install the pushrods in their original position.

14. Before installation, coat the valve tips, rocker arm and fulcrum contact areas with Lubriplate® or equivalent.

15. Rotate the engine until the lifter is on the base circle of the cam (valve closed).

16. Install the rocker arm and components and torque the rocker arm fulcrum bolts to 24 ft. lbs. (32 Nm). Be sure the lifter is on the base circle of the cam for each rocker arm as it is installed.

NOTE: The fulcrums must be fully seated in the cylinder head and the pushrods must be seated in the rocker arm sockets prior to the final tightening.

17. Install the exhaust manifolds and oil dipstick tube. Install the remaining components by reversing the removal procedure.

18. Start the engine and check for leaks.

19. Check and if necessary, adjust the transaxle throttle linkage and cruise control. Install the air cleaner outlet tube duct.

3.0L SHO Engine

1. Disconnect the negative battery cable.

2. Drain the cooling system. Properly relieve the fuel system pressure.

3. Remove the air cleaner outlet tube.

4. Remove the intake manifold.

5. Loosen the accessory drive belt idlers and remove the drive belts.

6. Remove the upper timing belt cover.

7. Remove the left idler pulley and bracket assembly.

8. Raise the vehicle and support it safely.

9. Remove the right wheel and inner fender splash shield.

10. Remove the crankshaft damper pulley.

11. Remove the lower timing belt cover.

12. Align both camshaft pulley timing marks with the index marks on the upper belt cover.

13. Release the tension on the belt by loosening the tensioner nut and rotat-

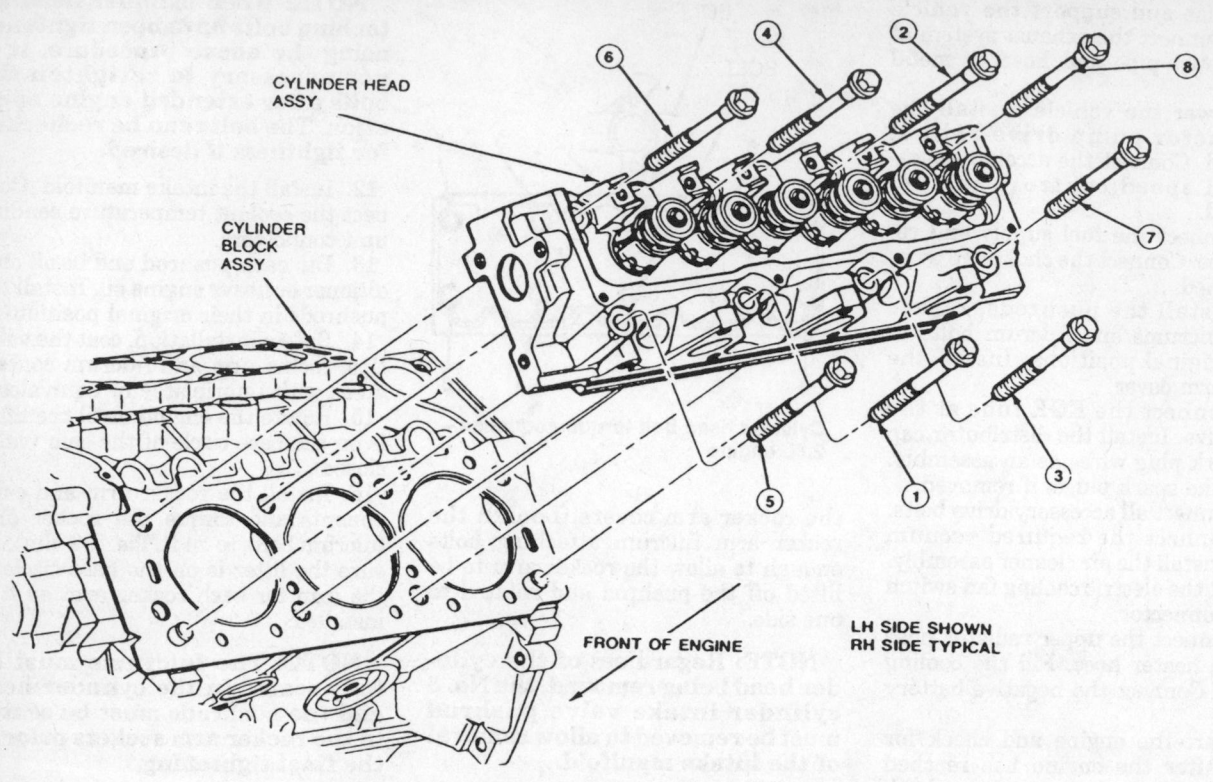

CYLINDER HEAD ASSY

CYLINDER BLOCK ASSY

FRONT OF ENGINE

LH SIDE SHOWN
RH SIDE TYPICAL

Cylinder head bolt torque sequence—3.0L engine

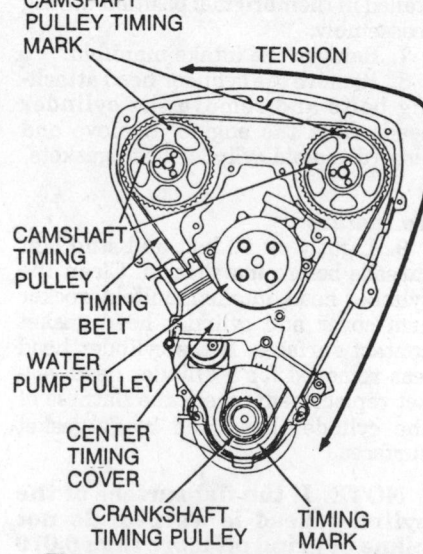

CAMSHAFT PULLEY TIMING MARK

TENSION

CAMSHAFT TIMING PULLEY

TIMING BELT

WATER PUMP PULLEY

CENTER TIMING COVER

CRANKSHAFT TIMING PULLEY

TIMING MARK

Timing mark alignment—3.0L SHO engine

ing the tensioner with a hex head wrench. When tension is released, tighten the nut. This will hold the tensioner in place. Lower the vehicle until the wheels touch but keep the vehicle supported.

14. Disconnect the crankshaft sensor wiring assembly.

15. Remove the center cover assembly.

16. Remove the timing belt noting the location of the letters **KOA** on the belt. The belt must be installed in the same direction.

17. Remove the cylinder head covers.

18. Remove the camshaft timing sprockets.

19. Remove the upper rear and the center rear timing belt covers.

20. If the left cylinder head is being removed, remove the DIS coil bracket and the oil dipstick tube. If the right cylinder head is being removed, remove the coolant outlet hose.

21. Remove the exhaust manifold on the left cylinder head. On the right cylinder head the exhaust manifold must be removed with the head.

22. Remove the cylinder head to block retaining bolts.

23. Remove the cylinder head.

To install:

NOTE: Lightly oil all bolt and stud bolt threads before installation except those specifying special sealant.

24. Clean the cylinder head and engine block mating surfaces of all gasket material.

25. Position the cylinder head and gasket on the engine block and align with the dowel pins.

26. Install the cylinder head bolts and tighten, in sequence, in 2 steps; the first to 37–50 ft. lbs. (49–69 Nm) and finally to 62–68 ft. lbs. (83–93 Nm).

27. If installing the left cylinder head, install the exhaust manifold, DIS coil bracket and oil dipstick tube. If installing the right cylinder head, install the coolant outlet hose and connect the exhaust catalyst.

28. Install the upper rear and center rear timing belt covers.

29. Install the camshaft sprockets in the timed position.

30. Install the cylinder head covers.

31. Install and adjust the timing belt.

32. Install the center timing belt cover.

33. Connect the crankshaft sensor wiring assembly and install the lower timing belt cover.

34. Raise the vehicle and support it safely.

35. Install the inner fender splash shield and the right wheel and tire assembly.

36. Install the left idler pulley and bracket.

37. Install the upper timing belt cover.

38. Install the accessory drive belts.

39. Install the intake manifold.

40. Install the air cleaner oulet tube.

41. Connect the negative battery cable.

42. Fill the engine cooling system with the proper type and quantity of coolant.

43. Start the engine and check for coolant, fuel or oil leaks.

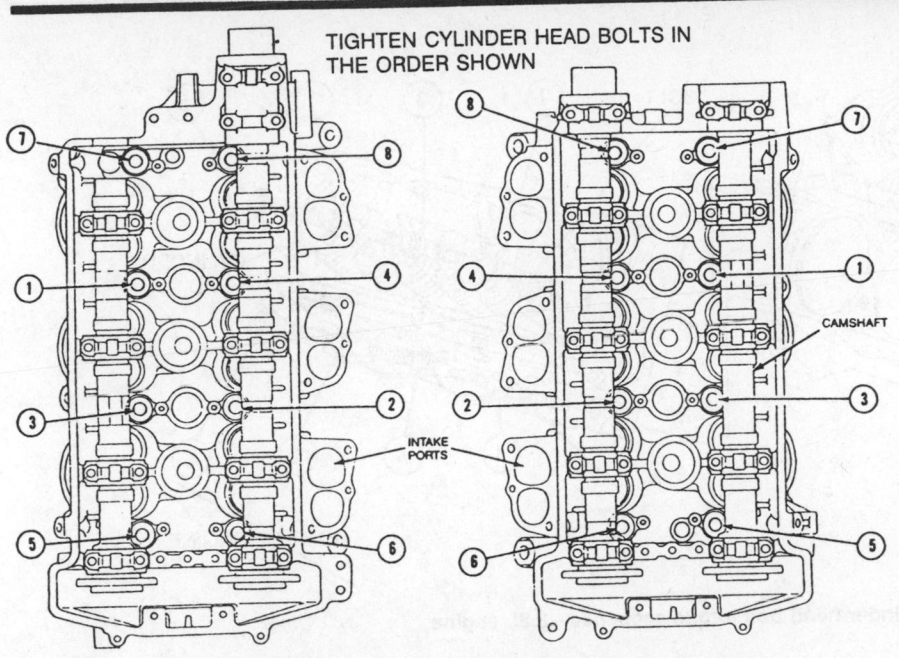

TIGHTEN CYLINDER HEAD BOLTS IN THE ORDER SHOWN

Cylinder head bolt torque sequence—3.0L SHO engine

3.8L Engine

1. Drain the cooling system and disconnect the negative battery cable.
2. Properly relieve the fuel system pressure. Remove the air cleaner assembly including air intake duct and heat tube.
3. Loosen the accessory drive belt idler and remove the drive belt.
4. If the right head is being removed, proceed to Step 5. If the left cylinder head is being removed, perform the following:
    a. Remove the oil fill cap.
    b. Remove the power steering pump. Leave the hoses connected and place the pump/bracket assembly aside in a position to prevent fluid from leaking out.
    c. If equipped with air conditioning, remove mounting bracket attaching bolts. Leaving the hoses connected, position the compressor aside.
    d. Remove the alternator and bracket.
5. If the right cylinder head is being removed, perform the following:
    a. Disconnect the thermactor air control valve or bypass valve hose assembly at the air pump.
    b. Disconnect the thermactor tube support bracket from the rear of cylinder head, if equipped.
    c. Remove accessory drive idler.
    d. Remove the thermactor pump pulley and thermactor pump, if equipped.
    e. Remove the PCV valve.
6. Remove the upper intake manifold.
7. Remove the valve rocker arm cover attaching screws.

8. Remove the injector fuel rail assembly.
9. Remove the lower intake manifold and the exhaust manifold(s).
10. Loosen the rocker arm fulcrum attaching bolts enough to allow rocker arm to be lifted off the pushrod and rotate to one side. Remove the pushrods. Identify and label the position of each pushrod. Pushrods should be installed in their original position during assembly.
11. Remove the cylinder head attaching bolts and discard. Do not reuse the old bolts.
12. Remove the cylinder head(s). Remove and discard old cylinder head gasket(s).

To install:

13. Lightly oil all bolt threads before installation.
14. Clean cylinder head, intake manifold, valve rocker arm cover and cylinder head gasket contact surfaces. If cylinder head was removed for a cylinder head gasket replacement, check flatness of cylinder head and block gasket surfaces.
15. Position the new head gasket(s) onto cylinder block using dowels for alignment. Position cylinder head(s) onto block.
16. On 1989–90 vehicles, apply a thin coating of pipe sealant with Teflon® to the threads of the short cylinder head bolts, nearest to the exhaust manifold. Do not apply sealant to the long bolts. Install the cylinder head bolts.

NOTE: Always use new cylinder head bolts to ensure a leak-tight assembly. Torque retention with used bolts can vary, which may re-sult in coolant or compression leakage at the cylinder head mating surface area.

17. Tighten the cylinder head attaching bolts, in sequence, to the following specifications:
    Step 1–37 ft. lbs. (50 Nm)
    Step 2–45 ft. lbs. (60 Nm)
    Step 3–52 ft. lbs. (70 Nm)
    Step 4–59 ft. lbs. (80 Nm)
18. Retighten the cylinder head bolts 1 at a time in the following manner:
    a. Long cylinder head bolts: Loosen the bolts and back them out 2–3 turns. Retighten to 11–18 ft. lbs. (15–25 Nm). Then tighten the bolt an additional 85–105 degrees and go to the next bolt in sequence.
    b. Short cylinder head bolts: Loosen the bolts and back them out 2–3 turns. Retighten to 11–18 ft. lbs. (15–25 Nm). Then tighten the bolt an additional 65–85 degrees.

NOTE: When cylinder head attaching bolts have been tightened using the above procedure, it is not necessary to retighten bolts after extended engine operation. However, bolts can be checked for tightness if desired.

19. Dip each pushrod end in oil conditioner or heavy engine oil. Install pushrods in their original position.
20. For each valve, rotate crankshaft until the lifter rests on the heel (base circle) of the camshaft lobe. Torque the fulcrum attaching bolts to 43 inch lbs. maximum.
21. Lubricate all rocker arm assemblies with oil conditioner or heavy engine oil.
22. Tighten the fulcrum bolts a second time to 19–25 ft. lbs. (25–35 Nm). For final tightening, camshaft may be in any position.

NOTE: If original valve train components are being installed, a valve clearance check is not required. If a component has been replaced, perform a valve clearance check.

23. Install the exhaust manifold(s), lower intake manifold and injector fuel rail assembly.
24. Position the cover(s) and new gasket on cylinder head and install attaching bolts. Note location of spark plug wire routing clip stud bolts. Tighten attaching bolts to 80–106 inch lbs. (9–12 Nm).
25. Install the upper intake manifold and connect the secondary wires to the spark plugs.
26. If the left cylinder head is being installed, perform the following: install oil fill cap, compressor mounting and support brackets, power steering

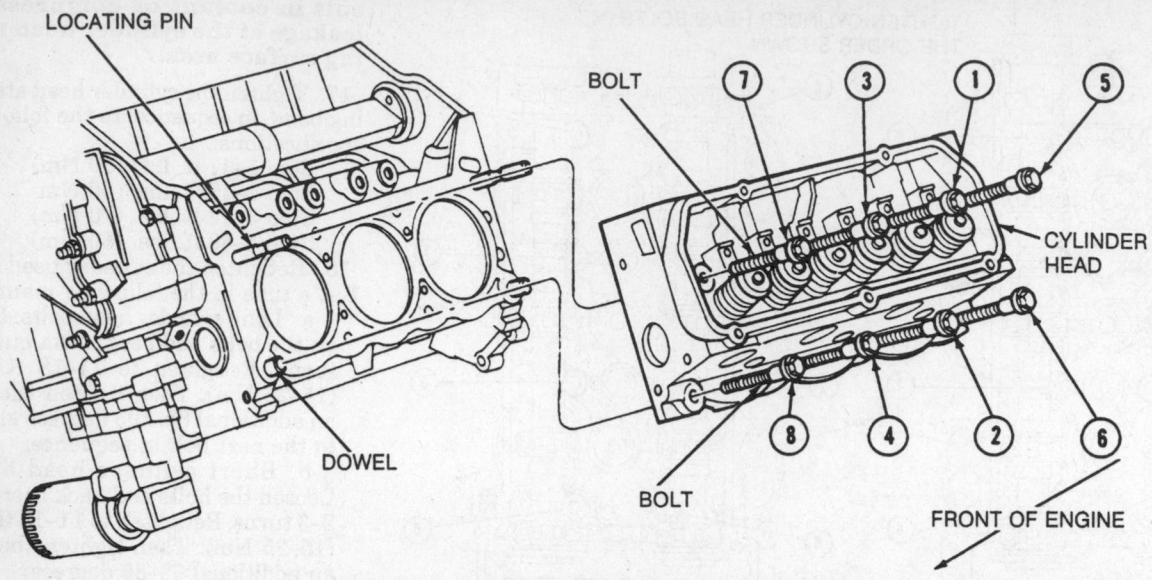

Cylinder head bolt torque sequence—3.8L engine

pump mounting and support brackets and the alternator/support bracket.

27. If the right cylinder head is being installed, perform the following: install the PCV valve, alternator bracket, thermactor pump and pump pulley, accessory drive idler, thermactor air control valve or air bypass valve hose.

28. Install the accessory drive belt. Attach the thermactor tube(s) support bracket to the rear of the cylinder head. Tighten the attaching bolts to 30–40 ft. lbs. (40–55 Nm).

29. Connect the negative battery cable and fill the cooling system.

30. Start the engine and check for leaks.

31. Check and, if necessary, adjust curb idle speed.

32. Install the air cleaner assembly including air intake duct and heat tube.

Valve Lifters
REMOVAL & INSTALLATION

2.5L Engine

1. Disconnect the negative battery cable. Remove the cylinder head.

2. Using a magnet, remove the lifters. Identify, tag and place the lifters in a rack so they can be installed in the original positions.

3. If the lifters are stuck in their bores by excessive varnish or gum, it may be necessary to use a hydraulic lifter puller tool to remove the lifters. Rotate the lifters back and forth to loosen any gum and varnish which may have formed. Keep the assemblies intact until the are to be cleaned.

4. Install the lifters through the pushrod openings with a magnet.

5. Install the cylinder head and related parts.

3.0L Engine

1. Disconnect the negative battery cable.

2. Drain the cooling system and relieve the fuel system pressure.

3. Disconnect the fuel lines from the fuel supply manifold and remove the throttle body.

4. Disconnect the spark plug wires from the spark plugs. Remove the ignition wire/separator assembly from the rocker cover retaining studs.

5. Mark the position of the distributor housing and rotor and remove the distributor.

6. Remove the rocker arm covers. Loosen the No. 3 intake valve rocker arm retaining bolt to allow the rocker arm to be rotated to 1 side. Remove the pushrod.

7. Remove the intake manifold assembly.

8. Loosen the rocker arm fulcrum retaining bolt enough to allow the rocker arm to be lifted off the pushrod and rotated to 1 side.

9. Remove the pushrod(s). If more than 1 is removed, identify each pushrod's location. The pushrods should be installed in their original position during reassembly.

10. If equipped with roller lifters, loosen the 2 roller lifter guide plate retaining bolts and remove the guide plate retainer assembly from the lifter valley. Remove the lifter guide plate(s) from the lifters by lifting straight up.

11. Remove the lifter(s) using a magnet, or grasp the lifter and pull in line with the bore.

NOTE: If the lifter(s) are stuck in the bore(s) due to excessive varnish or gum deposits, it may be necessary to use a claw-type tool to aid removal. Rotate the lifter back and forth to loosen it from the gum or varnish that may have formed on the lifter.

To install:

12. Clean all gasket mating surfaces. Place a rag in the lifter valley to catch any stray gasket material.

13. Lubricate each lifter and bore with heavy engine oil. Install the lifter in the bore, checking for free fit.

14. If equipped with roller lifters, align the lifter flats and install the lifter guide plate. Install the plate with the word UP and/or button visible. Install the guide plate retainer assembly over the guide plates. Retainer orientation is not important. Loosely install the retaining bolts, then tighten to 8–10 ft. lbs. (10–14 Nm).

15. Install the intake manifold and the distributor.

16. Dip each pushrod end in oil conditioner and install in it's original position.

17. For each valve, rotate the crankshaft until the lifter rests on the base circle of the camshaft lobe. Position the rocker arms over the pushrod and valve. Tighten the retaining bolt to 8 ft. lbs. (11 Nm) to initially seat the fulcrum into the cylinder head and onto the pushrod. Final tighten the bolt to 24 ft. lbs. (32 Nm).

18. Install the rocker arm covers.

19. Install the throttle body and connect the fuel lines to the fuel supply manifold. Install the safety clips.

20. Install the coolant hoses. Fill and bleed the cooling system. Drain and change the crankcase oil.

21. Connect the air cleaner hoses to the throttle body and rocker cover.

22. Connect the negative battery cable, start the engine and check for leaks. Check the ignition timing.

3.8L Engine

1. Disconnect the negative battery cable. Disconnect the secondary ignition wires at the spark plugs.

2. Remove the plug wire routing clips from mounting studs on the rocker arm cover attaching bolts. Lay plug wires with routing clips toward the front of engine.

3. Remove the upper intake manifold, rocker arm covers and lower intake manifold.

4. Sufficiently loosen each rocker arm fulcrum attaching bolt to allow the rocker arm to be lifted off the pushrod and rotated to one side.

5. Remove the pushrods. The location of each pushrod should be identified and labeled. When engine is assembled, each pushrod should be installed in its original position.

6. Remove the 2 lifter guide plate retainers and 6 guide plates.

7. Remove the lifters using a magnet. The location of each lifter should be identified and labeled. When engine is assembled, each lifter should be installed in its original position.

NOTE: If lifters are stuck in bores due to excessive varnish or gum deposits, it may be necessary to use a hydraulic lifter puller tool to aid removal. When using a remover tool, rotate lifter back and forth to loosen it from gum or varnish that may have formed on the lifter.

To install:

8. Lightly oil all bolt and stud threads before installation. Using solvent, clean the cylinder head and valve rocker arm cover sealing surfaces.

9. Lubricate each lifter and bore with oil conditioner or heavy engine oil.

10. Install each lifter in bore from which it was removed. If a new tappet(s) is being installed, check new lifter for a free fit in bore.

11. Align the flats on the sides of the lifters and install the 6 guide plates between the adjacent lifters. Make sure the word UP and/or button is showing. Install the 3 guide plate retainers and tighten the 4 bolts to 6–10 ft. lbs. (8–14 Nm).

12. Dip each pushrod end in oil conditioner or heavy engine oil. Install pushrods in their original positions.

13. For each valve, rotate crankshaft until lifter rests onto heel (base circle) of camshaft lobe. Position rocker arms over pushrods and install the fulcrums. Initially tighten the fulcrum attaching bolts to 44 inch lbs. maximum.

14. Lubricate all rocker arm assemblies with suitable heavy engine oil.

15. Finally tighten the fulcrum bolts to 19–25 ft. lbs. (25–35 Nm). For the final tightening, the camshaft may be in any position.

NOTE: Fulcrums must be fully seated in the cylinder head and pushrods must be seated in rocker arm sockets prior to the final tightening.

16. Complete the installation of the lower intake manifold, valve rocker arm covers and the upper intake manifold by reversing the removal procedure.

17. Install the plug wire routing clips and connect wires to the spark plugs.

18. Start the engine and check for oil or coolant leaks.

Valve Lash

Checking

The valve stem-to-rocker arm clearance for all engines except the 3.0L SHO should be within specification with the valve lifter completely collapsed. With the crankshaft in the designated positions, install lifter bleed down wrench T71P–6513–B or equivalent, on the rocker arm. Slowly apply pressure to the lifter until the plunger is completely collapsed, then use a feeler gauge to determine the rocker arm to valve lifter clearance.

2.5L Engine

1. Set the No. 1 piston on TDC on the compression stroke. The timing marks on the camshaft and crankshaft gears will be together. Check the clearance in No. 1 intake, No. 1 exhaust, No. 2 intake and No. 3 exhaust valves.

2. Rotate the crankshaft 1 complete turn, 180 degrees for the camshaft gear. Check the clearance in No. 2 exhaust, No. 3 intake, No. 4 intake and No. 4 exhaust.

3. The clearance between the rocker arm and the valve stem tip should be 0.072–0.174 in. (1.80–4.34mm) with the lifter on the base circle of the cam.

3.0L and 3.8L Engines, Except SHO

1. Rotate the engine until the No. 1 cylinder is at TDC of its compression stroke and check the clearance between the rocker arm and the following valves.

    a. No. 1 intake and No. 1 exhaust
    b. No. 3 intake and No. 2 exhaust
    c. No. 6 intake and No. 4 exhaust

2. Rotate the crankshaft 360 degrees and check the clearance between the rocker arm and the following valves.

    a. No. 2 intake and No. 3 exhaust
    b. No. 4 intake and No. 5 exhaust
    c. No. 5 intake and No. 6 exhaust

3. The clearance should be 0.09–0.19 in. (2.25–4.79mm).

3.0L SHO Engine

1. Remove the valve cover.

2. Remove the intake manifold assembly.

3. Insert a feeler gauge under the cam lobe at a 90 degree angle to the

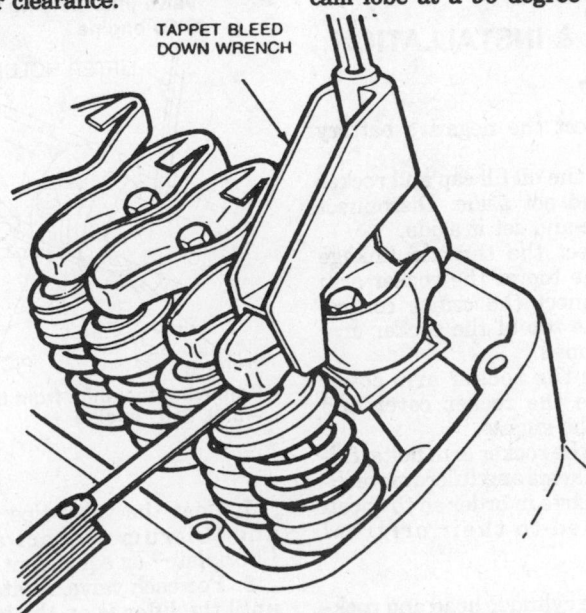

TAPPET BLEED DOWN WRENCH

Checking valve stem-to-rocker arm clearance—except 3.0L SHO engine

camshaft. Clearance for the intake valves should be 0.006–0.010 in. (0.15–0.25mm). Clearance for the exhaust valves should be 0.010–0.014 in. (0.25–0.35mm).

NOTE: The cam lobes must be directed 90 degrees or more away from the valve lifters.

ADJUSTMENT

3.0L SHO Engine

1. Disconnect the negative battery cable.
2. Remove the valve cover.
3. Remove the intake manifold assembly.
4. Install lifter compressor tool T89P-6500-A or equivalent, under the camshaft next to the lobe and rotate it downward to depress the valve lifter.
5. Install valve lifter holding tool T89P-6500-B or equivalent, and remove the compressor tool.
6. Using pick tool T71P-19703-C or equivalent, lift the adjusting shim and remove the shim with a magnet.
7. Determine the size of the shim by the numbers on the bottom face of the shim or by measuring with a micrometer. Install the replacement that will permit the specified clearance.
8. Install the replacement shim with the numbers down. Make sure the shim is properly seated.
9. Release the lifter holder tool by installing the compressor tool.
10. Repeat the procedure for each valve by rotating the crankshaft as necessary.

Rocker Arms

REMOVAL & INSTALLATION

2.5L Engine

1. Disconnect the negative battery cable.
2. Remove the oil fill cap and rocker arm filter and set aside. Disconnect the PCV hose and set it aside.
3. Disconnect the throttle linkage cable from the top of the rocker arm cover. Disconnect the cruise control cable from the top of the rocker arm cover, if equipped.
4. Remove the rocker arm cover bolts. Remove the rocker cover and gasket from the engine.
5. Remove the rocker arm bolts, fulcrums, rocker arms and fulcrum washers. Keep all parts in order so they can be reinstalled to their original position.
To install:
6. Clean the cylinder head and rocker arm cover mating surfaces.

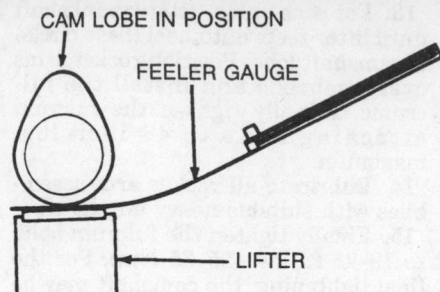

Checking valve clearance on the 3.0L SHO engine

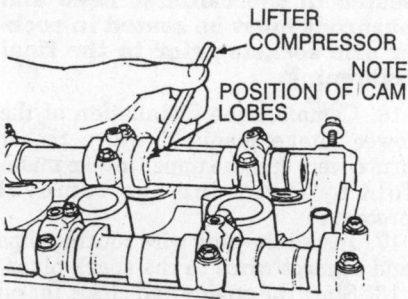

Valve lifter compressor tool—3.0L SHO engine

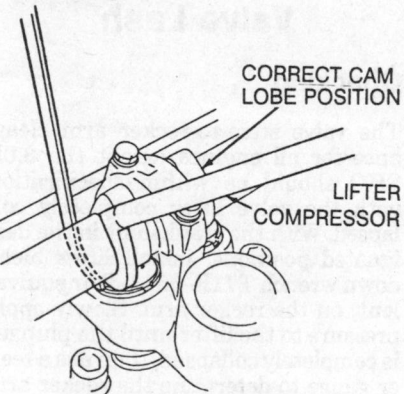

Valve lifter holding tool—3.0L SHO engine

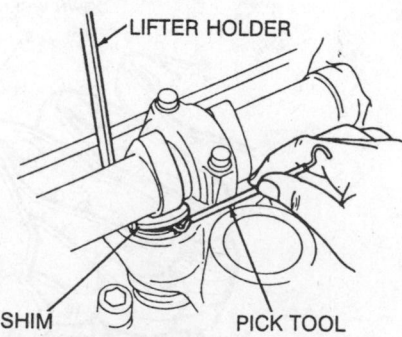

Removing the shim from the valve lifter —3.0L SHO engine

7. Coat the valve tips, rocker arm and fulcrum contact areas with Lubriplate® or equivalent.
8. For each valve, rotate the engine until the lifter is on the base circle of the cam (valve closed).

9. Install the rocker arm and components and tighten the rocker arm bolts in 2 steps, the first to 6–8 ft. lbs. (8–12 Nm) and the second torque to 20–26 ft. lbs. (28–35 Nm). Be sure the lifter is on the base circle of the cam for each rocker arm as it is installed. For the final tightening, the camshaft may be in any position. Check the valve lash.
10. Install a new rocker arm cover gasket, using suitable sealer, unless the cover is equipped with a moulded-in gasket, in which case no sealer should be used.

NOTE: If the moulded-in gasket is damaged by cuts and/or nicks less than ⅛ in. long in a maximum of 2 places, the damaged area can be filled in with RTV sealant. If the nicks or cuts are longer than ⅛ in. or there are more than 3 of any size, the entire rocker arm cover should be replaced.

11. Install the rocker arm cover and tighten the bolts to 6–8 ft. lbs. (8–12 Nm).

NOTE: On 1991 vehicles, apply 1 drop of threadlocking compound to the bolts if they are being reused. New bolts have preapplied adhesive. Failure to do so may result in an oil leak.

12. Install the throttle cable(s), PCV hose and oil filler cap. Connect the negative battery cable.

3.0L Engine

1. Disconnect the negative battery cable. Disconnect and tag the spark plug wires.
2. Remove the ignition wire/separator assembly from the rocker arm attaching bolt studs. If the left rocker arm cover is being removed, remove the oil fill cap, disconnect the air cleaner closure system hose and remove the fuel injector harness from the inboard rocker arm cover studs.
3. If the right rocker arm cover is being removed, remove the throttle body as follows:
   a. Tag and disconnect the vacuum hoses at the vacuum tree.
   b. Loosen the EGR tube nuts, if equipped, at the EGR valve and exhaust manifold fitting. Remove or rotate the tube aside.
   c. Remove the PCV hose from the tube under the throttle body.
   d. Remove the air cleaner duct hose and the idle speed control solenoid shield.
   e. Disconnect the throttle and TV cables from the throttle body linkage.
   f. Tag and disconnect the electrical connectors from the air charge

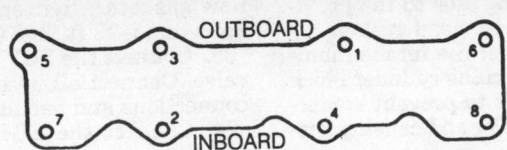

Rocker arm cover bolt torque sequence—1991-92 3.0L engine

temperature sensor, idle speed control solenoid and throttle position sensor.

g. Remove the alternator brace.

h. Remove the throttle body retaining bolts and remove the throttle body. Note the location of the bolts so they can reinstalled in their original positions.

4. If removing the right rocker arm cover, remove the PCV valve, loosen the lower EGR tube, if equipped, retaining nut and rotate the tube aside, and move the fuel injection harness aside.

5. Remove the rocker arm cover attaching screws and the covers and gaskets from the vehicle.

6. Remove the rocker arm bolts, fulcrums, rocker arms and fulcrum washers. Keep all parts in order so they can be reinstalled to their original position.

To install:

7. Coat the valve tips, rocker arm and fulcrum contact areas with Lubriplate® or equivalent. Lightly oil all the bolt and stud threads before installation.

8. Rotate the engine until the lifter is on the base circle of the cam (valve closed).

9. Install the rocker arm and components and torque the rocker arm fulcrum bolts in 2 steps: the first to 8 ft. lbs. (11 Nm) and the final to 24 ft. lbs. (32 Nm). Be sure the lifter is on the base circle of the cam for each rocker arm as it is installed.

10. Clean the cylinder head and rocker arm cover sealing surfaces of all dirt and old sealer. If not equipped with integral gaskets, make sure all old gasket material is removed.

11. Apply a bead of silicone sealant at the cylinder head to intake manifold rail step. If not equipped with integral gaskets, install a new rocker arm cover gasket.

12. Install the rocker arm cover and the bolts and studs. Tighten to 9 ft. lbs. (12 Nm). On 1991-93 vehicles, tighten the cover in the proper sequence.

13. Install the remaining components in the reverse order of their removal.

3.8L Engine

1. Disconnect the negative battery cable.

2. Tag and disconnect the spark plug wires from the spark plugs.

3. If the left cover is being removed, remove the oil fill cap.

4. If the right cover is being removed, position the air cleaner assembly aside and remove the PCV valve.

5. Remove the rocker arm cover mounting bolts and remove the rocker arm cover.

6. Remove the rocker arm bolt, fulcrum and rocker arm. Keep all parts in order so they can be reinstalled in their original positions.

To install:

7. Coat the valve tips, rocker arm and fulcrum contact areas with Lubriplate® or equivalent. Install the rocker arm, fulcrum and rocker arm bolt.

8. Rotate the crankshaft until the lifter rests on the base circle of the camshaft lobe, then tighten the rocker arm bolt. Tighten in 2 steps, first to 44 inch lbs. (5 Nm) and finally to 19-25 ft. lbs. (25-35 Nm).

9. Clean the rocker arm cover and cylinder head mating surfaces of old gasket material and dirt.

10. Position a new gasket onto the cylinder head. Install the rocker arm cover and the mounting bolts. Note the location of the spark plug wire routing clip stud bolts. Tighten the bolts to 80-106 inch lbs. (9-12 Nm).

11. Install the remaining components in the reverse order of their removal.

Intake Manifold

REMOVAL & INSTALLATION

2.5L Engine

1. Disconnect the negative battery cable. Properly relieve the fuel system pressure.

2. Drain the cooling system.

3. Remove accelerator cable and the cruise control cable, if equipped.

4. Remove air cleaner assembly and heat stove tube at heat shield.

5. Tag and disconnect the required vacuum lines and electrical connections.

6. On 1989-90 vehicles, disconnect the thermactor check valve hose at the tube assembly and remove the bracket to EGR valve attaching nuts.

7. Disconnect the fuel supply and return lines.

8. On 1989-90 vehicles, disconnect the water inlet tube at the intake manifold. On 1991 vehicles, remove the exhaust manifold heat shroud assembly.

9. Disconnect EGR tube at EGR valve.

10. Remove the intake manifold retaining bolts. Remove the intake manifold. Remove the gasket and clean the gasket contact surfaces.

To install:

11. Install intake manifold with gasket and retaining bolts.

12. Tighten the retaining bolts to 15-22 ft. lbs. (20-30 Nm) in the proper sequence.

13. On 1989-90 vehicles, connect water inlet tube at intake manifold, connect thermactor check valve hose at tube assembly and install bracket to EGR valve attaching nuts.

14. Connect EGR tube to EGR valve.

15. Connect the fuel supply and return lines.

16. Install vacuum lines and connect electrical connectors.

17. On 1991 vehicles, install the heat shroud.

18. Install air cleaner assembly and heat stove tube.

19. Install accelerator cable and cruise control cable, if equipped.

20. Connect negative battery cable and fill the cooling system.

21. Start engine and check for leaks.

3.0L Except SHO Engine

1. Disconnect the negative battery cable and drain the engine cooling system. Relieve the fuel system pressure.

2. Loosen the hose clamp attaching the flex hose to the throttle body. Remove the air cleaner flex hose.

3. Identify, tag and disconnect and all vacuum connections to the throttle body.

4. Loosen the lower EGR tube nut and rotate the tube away from the

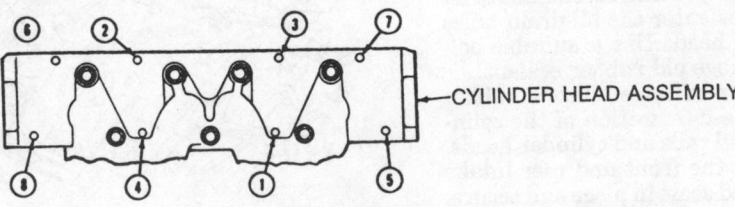

CYLINDER HEAD ASSEMBLY

Intake manifold bolt torque sequence—2.5L engine

valve. Disconnect the throttle and TV cable from the throttle linkage.

5. Disconnect the throttle position sensor, air charge temperature sensor and idle speed control electrical connectors.

6. Disconnect the PCV hose and disconnect the alternator support brace. Remove the throttle body retaining bolts and the throttle body.

7. Disconnect the fuel lines. Remove the fuel injection wiring harness from the engine.

8. Disconnect and tag the spark plug wires and remove the rocker arm covers.

9. Disconnect the upper radiator hose and heater hoses. Mark the position of the distributor housing and rotor and remove the distributor assembly.

10. Disconnect the engine coolant temperature sensor and temperature sending unit connector. Loosen the intake valve rocker arm retaining bolt from cylinder No. 3 and rotate the rocker arm from the pushrod and away from the valve stem. Remove the pushrod.

11. Remove the intake manifold attaching bolts. Use a suitable prybar to loosen the intake manifold. Pry upward using the area between the thermostat and transaxle as a leverage point. Remove the manifold and old gaskets and seals.

NOTE: The manifold assembly can be removed with the fuel supply manifold and injectors in place.

To install:

NOTE: Lightly oil all the attaching bolts and stud threads before installation. When using a silcone rubber sealer, assembly must occur within 15 minutes after the sealer has been applied. After this time, the sealer may start to set-up and its sealing quality may be reduced. In high temperature/humidty conditions, the sealant will start to set up in approximately 5 minutes.

12. Clean the gasket mating surfaces of the intake manifold and cylinder head. Lay a shop rag in the lifter valley to catch any gasket material. After scraping, carefully lift the cloth from the lifter valley, being careful not to let any particles enter the oil drain holes or cylinder head. Use a suitable solvent to remove old rubber sealant.

13. Apply a suitable silicone rubber sealer to the intersection of the cylinder block end rails and cylinder heads.

14. Install the front and rear intake manifold end seals in place and secure. Install the intake manifold gaskets,

aligning the locking tabs to the provisions on the cylinder head gaskets.

15. Carefully lower the intake manifold into position on the cylinder block and cylinder heads to prevent smearing the silicone sealer and causing gasket voids.

16. Install the retaining bolts and tighten the bolts, in sequence, to 11 ft. lbs. (15 Nm), then retorque to 21 ft. lbs. (28 Nm).

17. Install the fuel supply manifold and injectors, if removed. Apply lubricant to the injector holes in the intake manifold and fuel supply manifold prior to injector installation. Install the fuel supply manifold retaining bolts and tighten to 7 ft. lbs. (10 Nm).

18. Install the thermostat housing and a new gasket, if removed. Tighten the retaining bolts to 9 ft. lbs. (12 Nm).

19. Install the distributor assembly, aligning the marks that were made during the removal procedure.

20. Install the No. 3 cylinder intake valve pushrod. Apply Lubriplate® or equivalent to the pushrod and valve stem prior to installation. Position the lifter on the base circle of the camshaft and tighten the rocker arm bolt in 2 steps, first to 8 ft. lbs. (11 Nm) and then to 24 ft. lbs. (32 Nm).

21. Install the rocker arm covers. Install the fuel injector harness and attach to the injectors.

22. Install the throttle body with

new gaskets. Tighten the retaining bolts to 15–22 ft. lbs. (20–30 Nm).

23. Connect the PCV line at the PCV valve. Connect all necessary electrical connections and vacuum lines.

24. Connect the EGR tube and the fuel lines.

25. Install the coil and bracket. Install the upper radiator and heater hose.

26. Install and connect the air cleaner assembly and outlet tube. Fill the cooling system.

27. Reconnect the negative battery cable, start the engine and check for coolant, fuel and oil leaks.

28. Check and if necessary, adjust the engine idle speed, transaxle throttle linkage and speed control.

3.0L SHO Engine

1. Disconnect the negative battery cable. Properly relieve the fuel system pressure.

2. Partially drain the engine cooling system.

3. Tag and disconnect all electrical connectors and vacuum lines from the intake assembly.

4. Remove the air cleaner tube.

5. Disconnect the coolant lines and cables from the throttle body.

6. Remove the bolts retaining the upper intake brackets.

7. Loosen the lower bolts and remove the brackets.

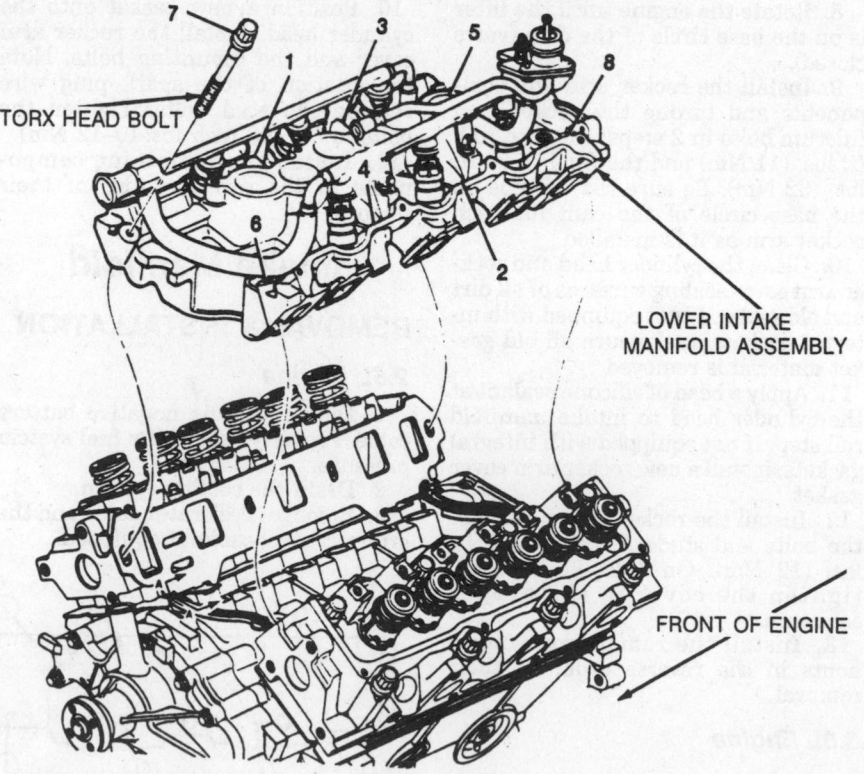

Intake manifold bolt torque sequence—3.0L engine

8. Remove the bolts retaining the intake to the cylinder heads.

9. Remove the intake assembly and the gaskets.

10. Installation is the reverse of the removal procedure.

11. Lightly oil the attaching bolts and stud threads before installation.

NOTE: The intake gasket is reuseable.

12. Install the retaining bolts and tighten to 11–16 ft. lbs. (15–23 Nm).

3.8L Engine

1. Disconnect the negative battery cable. Drain the cooling system.

2. Properly relieve the fuel system pressure. Remove the air cleaner assembly including air intake duct and heat tube.

3. Disconnect the accelerator cable at throttle body assembly. Disconnect cruise control cable, if equipped.

4. Disconnect the transaxle linkage at the upper intake manifold.

5. Remove the attaching bolts from accelerator cable mounting bracket and position cables aside.

6. Disconnect the thermactor air supply hose at the check valve, if equipped.

7. Disconnect the flexible fuel lines from steel lines over rocker arm cover.

8. Disconnect the fuel lines at injector fuel rail assembly.

9. Disconnect the radiator hose at thermostat housing connection.

10. Disconnect the coolant bypass hose at manifold connection.

11. Disconnect the heater tube at the intake manifold. Remove the heater tube support bracket attaching nut. Remove the heater hose at rear of heater tube. Loosen hose clamp at heater elbow and remove heater tube with hose attached. Remove heater tube with fuel lines attached and set the assembly aside.

12. Disconnect vacuum lines at fuel rail assembly and intake manifold.

13. Identify, tag and disconnect all necessary electrical connectors.

14. If equipped with air conditioning, remove the compressor support bracket.

15. Disconnect the PCV lines. One is located on upper intake manifold. The second is located at the left rocker cover and the lower intake stud.

16. Remove the throttle body assembly and remove the EGR valve assembly from the upper manifold.

17. Remove the attaching nut and remove wiring retainer bracket located at the left front of the intake manifold and set aside with the spark plug wires.

18. Remove the upper intake mani-

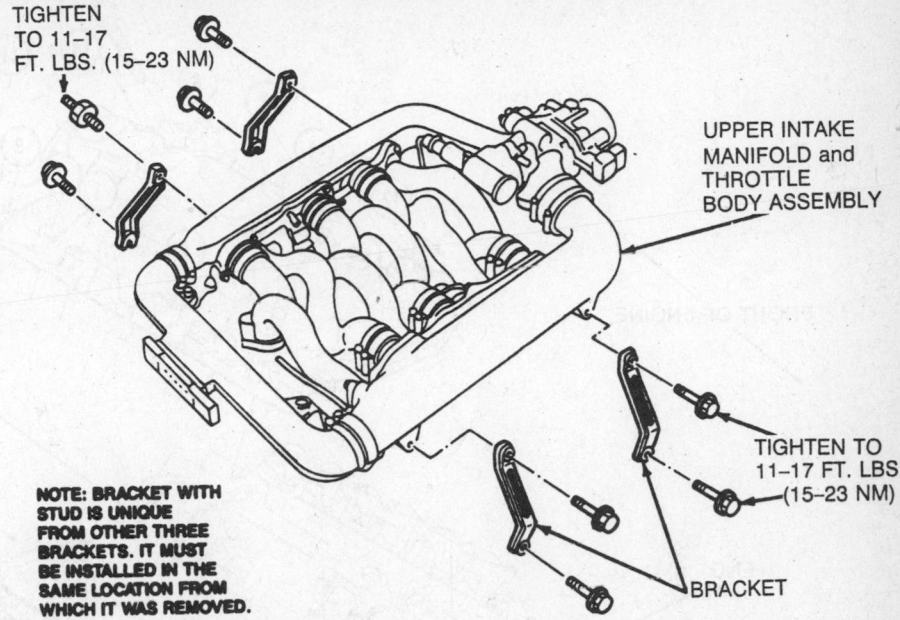

TIGHTEN TO 11–17 FT. LBS. (15–23 NM)

UPPER INTAKE MANIFOLD and THROTTLE BODY ASSEMBLY

TIGHTEN TO 11–17 FT. LBS. (15–23 NM)

BRACKET

NOTE: BRACKET WITH STUD IS UNIQUE FROM OTHER THREE BRACKETS. IT MUST BE INSTALLED IN THE SAME LOCATION FROM WHICH IT WAS REMOVED.

Intake manifold removal and installation—3.0L SHO engine

fold attaching bolts/studs. Remove the upper intake manifold.

19. Remove the injectors with fuel rail assembly.

20. Remove the heater water outlet hose.

21. Remove the lower intake manifold attaching bolts/stud and remove the lower intake manifold. Remove the manifold side gaskets and end seals. Discard and replace with new.

NOTE: The manifold is sealed at each end with RTV-type sealer. To break the seal, it may be necessary to pry on the front of the manifold with a small or medium prybar. If it is necessary to pry on the manifold, use care to prevent damage to the machined surfaces.

To install:

22. Lightly oil all attaching bolt and stud threads before installation.

NOTE: When using silicone rubber sealer, assembly must occur within 15 minutes after sealer application. After this time, the sealer may start to set-up and its sealing effectiveness may be reduced. The lower intake manifold, cylinder head and cylinder block mating surfaces should be clean and free of old gasketing material. Use a suitable solvent to clean these surfaces.

23. Apply a bead of contact adhesive to each cylinder head mating surface. Press the new intake manifold gaskets into place, using locating pins as necessary to aid in assembly alignment.

24. Apply a ⅛ in. bead of silicone sealer at each corner where the cylinder head joins the cylinder block.

25. Install the front and rear intake manifold end seals.

26. Carefully lower the intake manifold into position on cylinder block and cylinder heads. Use locating pins as necessary to guide the manifold.

27. Install the retaining bolts and stud bolts in their original locations. On 1989–91 vehicles, torque the retaining bolts, in sequence, in 3 steps; first tighten to 8 ft. lbs. (11 Nm), then to 15 ft. lbs. (20 Nm) and finally to 24 ft. lbs. (32 Nm). On 1992–93 vehicles, torque the retaining bolts, in sequence, in 2 steps; first tighten to 8 ft. lbs. (11 Nm) and then to 11 ft. lbs. (15 Nm).

28. Connect the rear PCV line to upper intake tube. Install the front PCV tube so the mounting bracket sits over the lower intake stud.

29. Install the injectors and fuel rail assembly. Tighten the screws to 6–8 ft. lbs. (8–11 Nm).

30. Position the upper intake gasket and manifold on top of the lower intake. Use locating pins to secure position of gasket between manifolds.

31. Install bolts and studs in their original locations. Tighten the 4 center bolts, then tighten the end bolts, to 8 ft. lbs. (11 Nm). Repeat the tightening procedure 2 more times in the same manner, increasing the torque first to 15 ft. lbs. (20 Nm) and finally to 24 ft. lbs. (32 Nm).

32. Install the EGR valve assembly on the manifold. Tighten the attaching nuts to 15–22 ft. lbs. (20–30 Nm).

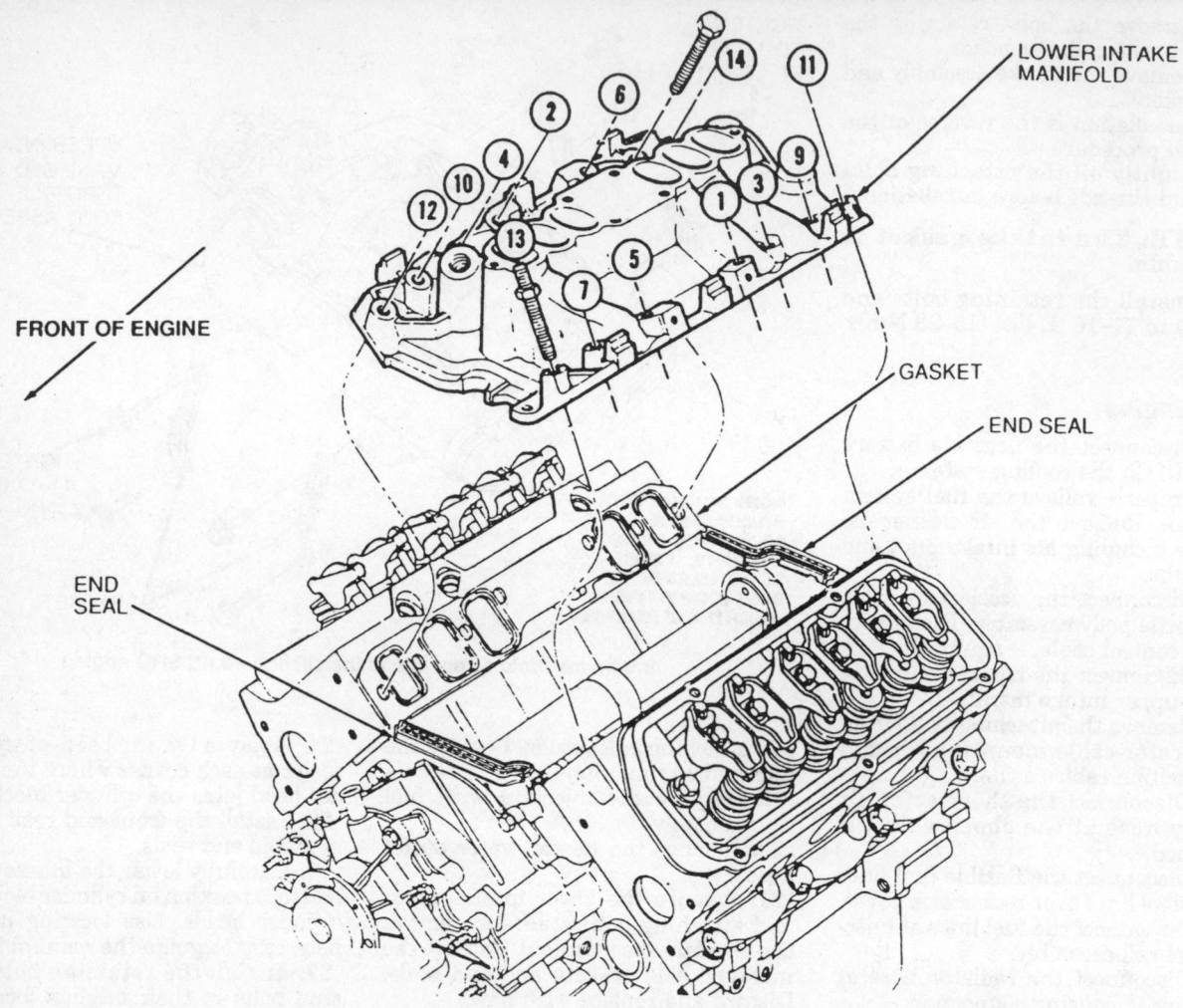

LOWER INTAKE MANIFOLD

FRONT OF ENGINE

GASKET

END SEAL

END SEAL

Lower intake manifold bolt torque sequence—3.8L engine

33. Install the throttle body. Cross-tighten the retaining nuts to 15–22 ft. lbs. (20–30 Nm).

34. Connect the rear PCV line at PCV valve and upper intake manifold connections. If equipped with air conditioning, install the compressor support bracket. Tighten attaching fasteners to 15–22 ft. lbs. (20–30 Nm).

35. Connect all electrical connectors and vacuum hoses.

36. Connect the heater tube hose to the heater elbow. Position the heater tube support bracket and tighten attaching nut to 15–22 ft. lbs. (20–30 Nm). Connect the heater hose to the rear of the heater tube and tighten hose clamp.

37. Connect coolant bypass and upper radiator hoses and secure with hose clamps.

38. Connect the fuel line(s) at injector fuel rail assembly and connect the flexible fuel lines to steel lines.

39. Position the accelerator cable mounting bracket and install and tighten attaching bolts to 15–22 ft. lbs. (20–30 Nm).

40. Connect the cruise control cable, if equipped. Connect the transaxle linkage at upper intake manifold.

41. Fill the cooling system to the proper level.

42. Start the engine and check for coolant or fuel leaks.

43. Check and, if necessary, adjust engine idle speed, transaxle throttle linkage and cruise control.

44. Install the air cleaner assembly and air intake duct.

Exhaust Manifold

REMOVAL & INSTALLATION

2.5L Engine

1. Disconnect the negative battery cable.

2. Drain the cooling system.

3. Remove the accelerator cable and the cruise control cable, if equipped.

4. Remove air cleaner assembly and heat stove tube at heat shield.

5. Identify, tag and disconnect all

necessary vacuum lines and electrical connections.

6. Disconnect the exhaust pipe-to-exhaust manifold retaining nuts.

7. Remove exhaust manifold heat shroud. Disconnect the oxygen sensor wire at the connector.

8. Disconnect the fuel supply and return lines.

9. On 1989–90 vehicles, disconnect the thermactor check valve hose at tube assembly, remove bracket-to-EGR valve attaching nuts and disconnect water inlet tube at intake manifold.

10. Disconnect EGR tube from the EGR valve.

11. Remove the intake manifold.

12. Remove the exhaust manifold retaining nuts. Remove the exhaust manifold from the vehicle.

To install:

13. Position exhaust manifold to the cylinder head using guide bolts in holes 2 and 3.

14. Install the remaining attaching bolts.

15. Tighten the attaching bolts until snug, then remove guide bolts and install attaching bolts in holes 2 and 3.

16. Tighten all exhaust manifold bolts to specification using the following tightening procedure: torque retaining bolts, in sequence, to 5–7 ft. lbs. (7–10 Nm), then retorque, in sequence, to 20–30 ft. lbs. (27–41 Nm).

17. Install the intake manifold gasket and bolts. Tighten the intake manifold retaining bolts to 15–22 ft. lbs. (20–30 Nm).

18. On 1989–90 vehicles, connect the water inlet tube at intake manifold, connect thermactor check valve hose at tube assembly and install bracket to EGR valve attaching nuts.

19. Connect the oxygen sensor wire.

20. Connect the EGR tube to EGR valve.

21. Install exhaust manifold studs.

22. Connect exhaust pipe to exhaust manifold.

23. Install vacuum lines and electrical connectors.

24. Install air cleaner assembly and heat stove tube.

25. Install accelerator cable and cruise control cable, if equipped.

26. Connect the negative battery cable.

27. Fill the cooling system.

28. Start engine and check for leaks.

3.0L Engine

LEFT SIDE

1. Disconnect the negative battery cable. Remove the oil level indicator support bracket retaining nut.

2. Remove the electrical harness connected to the dipstick support bracket, if necessary. Remove the dipstick and tube.

3. On 1989 vehicles, remove the power steering pump pressure and return hoses.

4. Raise and safely support the vehicle. Remove the manifold-to-exhaust pipe retaining nuts.

5. Lower the vehicle. Remove the exhaust manifold attaching bolts and the manifold.

6. Installation is the reverse of the removal procedure. Clean all mating surfaces and lightly oil all bolt and stud threads prior to installation. Tighten the exhaust manifold retaining bolts to 19 ft. lbs. (25 Nm) and tighten the exhaust pipe attaching nuts to 30 ft. lbs. (41 Nm).

RIGHT SIDE

1. Disconnect the negative battery cable.

2. Remove the heater hose support bracket and disconnect and plug the heater hoses, if necessary.

3. Disconnect the pressure feedback hose from the EGR tube. Remove the

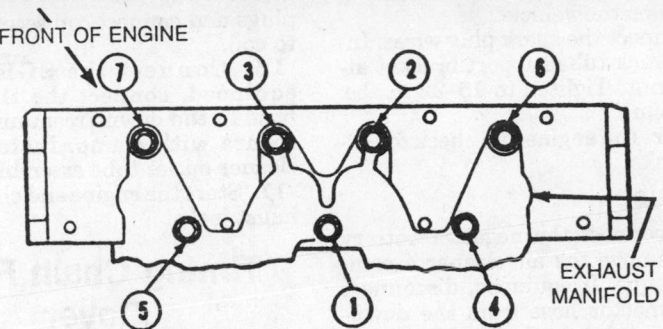

FRONT OF ENGINE

EXHAUST MANIFOLD

Exhaust manifold bolt torque sequence—2.5L engine

EGR tube from the exhaust manifold. Use a back-up wrench on the lower adapter.

4. Remove the coolant bypass tube, if necessary.

5. Raise the vehicle and support it safely. Remove the manifold-to-exhaust pipe attaching nuts and remove the pipe from the manifold.

6. Lower the vehicle. Remove the exhaust manifold attaching bolts and remove the exhaust manifold from the vehicle.

7. Installation is the reverse of the removal procedure. Clean all mating surfaces and lightly oil all bolt and stud threads prior to installation. Tighten the exhaust manifold retaining bolts to 19 ft. lbs. (25 Nm) and tighten the exhaust pipe attaching nuts to 30 ft. lbs. (41 Nm). Tighten the EGR tube to the exhaust manifold to 31 ft. lbs. (42 Nm).

3.0L SHO Engine

LEFT SIDE

1. Disconnect the negative battery cable.

2. Remove the oil level indicator tube support bracket.

3. Remove the power steering pump pressure and return hoses.

4. Remove the manifold to exhaust pipe attaching nuts.

5. Remove the heat shield retaining bolts.

6. Remove the exhaust manifold retaining nuts and manifold.

7. Installation is the reverse of the removal procedure. Clean all mating surfaces and lightly oil all bolt and stud threads before installation. Tighten the manifold retaining nuts to 26–38 ft. lbs. (35–52 Nm), the heat shield retaining bolts to 11–16 ft. lbs. (15–23 Nm) and the exhaust pipe to manifold nuts to 16–24 ft. lbs. (21–32 Nm).

RIGHT SIDE

1. Disconnect the negative battery cable.

2. Remove the right cylinder head.

3. Remove the heat shield retaining bolts.

4. Remove the exhaust manifold retaining nuts and manifold.

5. Installation is the reverse of the removal procedure. Clean all mating surfaces and lightly oil all bolt and stud threads prior to installation. Tighten the manifold retaining nuts to 26–38 ft. lbs. (35–52 Nm). Tighten the heat shield retaining bolts to 11–16 ft. lbs. (15–23 Nm).

3.8L Engine

LEFT SIDE

1. Disconnect the negative battery cable. Remove the oil level dipstick tube support bracket.

2. Tag and disconnect the spark plug wires.

3. Raise the vehicle and support safely.

4. Remove the manifold-to-exhaust pipe attaching nuts.

5. Lower the vehicle.

6. Remove the exhaust manifold retaining bolts and remove the manifold from vehicle.

To install:

7. Lightly oil all bolt and stud threads before installation. Clean the mating surfaces on the exhaust manifold, cylinder head and exhaust pipe.

8. Position the exhaust manifold on the cylinder head. Install the lower front bolt hole on No. 5 cylinder as a pilot bolt.

9. Install the remaining manifold retaining bolts. Tighten the bolts 15–22 ft. lbs. (20–30 Nm).

NOTE: A slight warpage in the exhaust manifold may cause a misalignment between the bolt holes in the head and the manifold. Elongate the holes in the exhaust manifold as necessary to correct the misalignment, if apparent. Do not elongate the pilot hole, the lower front bolt on No. 5 cylinder.

10. Raise the vehicle and support safely.

11. Connect the exhaust pipe to the manifold. Tighten the attaching nuts to 16–24 ft. lbs. (21–32 Nm).

12. Lower the vehicle.

13. Connect the spark plug wires. Install dipstick tube support bracket attaching nut. Tighten to 15–22 ft. lbs. (20–30 Nm).

14. Start the engine and check for exhaust leaks.

RIGHT SIDE

1. Disconnect the negative battery cable. Remove the air cleaner assembly and tube. If equipped, disconnect the thermactor hose from the downstream air tube check valve.

2. Tag and disconnect the coil secondary wire from coil and the wires from spark plugs. Remove the spark plugs.

3. Disconnect the EGR tube.

4. Raise the vehicle and support safely.

5. Remove the transaxle dipstick tube. If necessary, remove the thermactor air tube by cutting the tube clamp at the underbody catalyst fitting with a suitable cutting tool.

6. Remove the manifold-to-exhaust pipe attaching nuts.

7. Lower the vehicle.

8. Remove the exhaust manifold retaining bolts and the exhaust manifold.

To install:

9. Lightly oil all bolt and stud threads before installation. Clean the mating surfaces on exhaust manifold cylinder head and exhaust pipe.

10. Position the inner half of the heat shroud, if equipped, gasket and exhaust manifold on cylinder head. Start 2 attaching bolts to align the manifold with the cylinder head. Install the remaining retaining bolts and tighten to 15–22 ft. lbs. (20–30 Nm).

NOTE: A slight warpage in the exhaust manifold may cause a misalignment between the bolt holes in the head and the manifold. Elongate the holes in the exhaust manifold as necessary to correct the misalignment, if apparent. Do not elongate the pilot hole, the lower rear bolt on No. 2 cylinder.

11. Raise the vehicle and support safely.

12. Connect the exhaust pipe to manifold. Tighten the attaching nuts to 16–24 ft. lbs. (21–32 Nm). If necessary, position the thermactor hose to the downstream air tube and clamp tube to the underbody catalyst fitting.

13. Install the transaxle dipstick tube and lower vehicle.

14. Install the outer heat shroud, if equipped, and tighten the retaining screws to 50–70 inch lbs. (5–8 Nm).

15. Install the spark plugs. Connect the wires to their respective spark

plugs and connect coil secondary wire to coil.

16. Connect the EGR tube. If equipped, connect the thermactor hose to the downstream air tube and secure with clamp. Install the air cleaner outlet tube assembly.

17. Start the engine and check for exhaust leaks.

Timing Chain Front Cover

REMOVAL & INSTALLATION

2.5L Engine

1. Disconnect the negative battery cable.

2. Remove the engine and transaxle assembly from the vehicle and position in a suitable holding fixture. Remove the dipstick.

3. Remove accessory drive pulley, if equipped. Remove the crankshaft pulley attaching bolt and washer and remove pulley.

4. Remove front cover attaching bolts from front cover. Pry the top of the front cover away from the block.

5. Remove the oil pan.

6. Clean all dirt and old gasket material from all mating surfaces.

To install:

7. Clean and inspect all parts before installation. Clean the oil pan, cylinder block and front cover of gasket material and dirt. Remove the front cover oil seal.

NOTE: The front cover oil seal must be removed whenever the front cover is removed from the engine, in order to use the front cover alignment tool.

8. Apply oil resistant sealer to a new front cover gasket and position gasket into front cover.

9. Position the front cover on the engine.

10. Position front cover alignment tool T84P–6019–C or equivalent, onto the end of the crankshaft, ensuring the crank key is aligned with the keyway in the tool. Bolt the front cover to the engine and tighten the bolts to 6–9 ft. lbs. (10–12 Nm). Remove the front cover alignment tool.

11. Install a new front cover oil seal using a suitable seal installer. Lubricate the hub of the crankshaft pulley with polyethylene grease to prevent damage to the seal during installation and initial engine start. Install crankshaft pulley.

12. Install the oil pan.

13. Install the accessory drive pulley, if equipped.

14. Install crankshaft pulley attaching bolt and washer. Tighten to 140–170 ft. lbs. (190–230 Nm).

15. Install the engine and transaxle assembly in the vehicle. Connect the negative battery cable.

3.0L Engine

1. Disconnect the negative battery cable.

2. Loosen the 4 water pump pulley bolts while the water pump drive belt is in place.

3. Loosen the alternator belt-adjuster jackscrew to provide enough slack in the alternator drive belt for removal.

4. Using a ½ in. drive breaker bar, rotate the automatic belt tensioner to remove the water pump drive belt. Remove the automatic belt tensioner bolt and nuts.

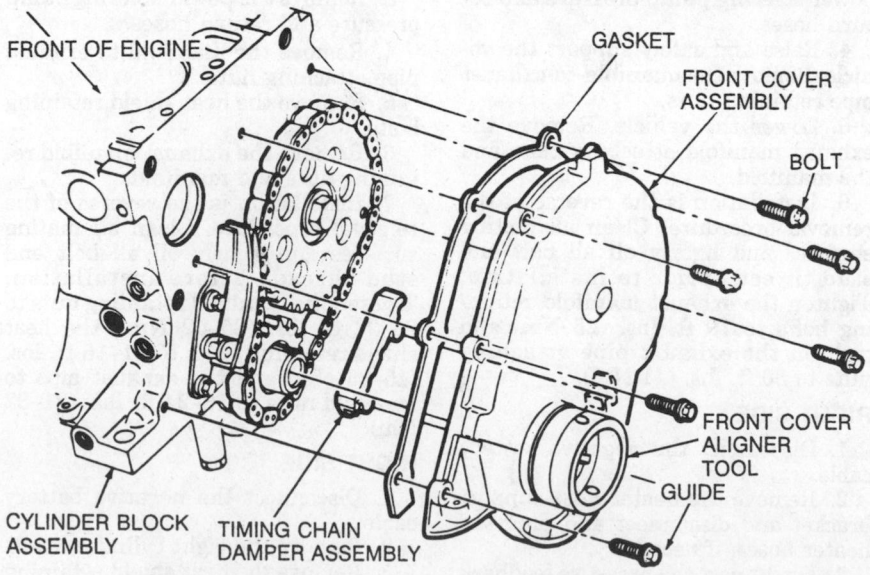

Timing chain front cover removal and installation—2.5L engine

5. Drain the cooling system.

6. Remove the lower radiator hose and the heater hose from the water pump.

7. Remove the crankshaft pulley and damper.

8. Drain and remove the oil pan.

9. Remove the retaining bolts from the timing cover to the block and remove the timing cover.

NOTE: The timing cover and water pump may be removed as an assembly by not removing bolts 11–15.

To install:

10. Lightly oil all bolt and stud threads except those specifying special sealant.

11. Clean all old gasket material and sealer from the timing cover, oil pan and cylinder block.

12. Inspect the timing cover seal for wear or damage and replace if necessary.

13. Align a new timing cover gasket over the cylinder block dowels.

14. Install the timing cover/water pump assembly onto the cylinder block with the water pump pulley loosely attached to the water pump hub.

15. Apply pipe sealant to bolt numbers 1, 2 and 3 and hand start them along with the rest of the cover retaining bolts. Tighten bolts 1–10 to 19 ft. lbs. (25 Nm) and 11–15 to 7 ft. lbs. (10 Nm).

16. Install the oil pan and tighten the retaining bolts to 9 ft. lbs. (12 Nm).

17. Hand tighten the water pump pulley retaining bolts.

18. Install the crankshaft damper and pulley. Torque the damper bolt to 107 ft. lbs. (145 Nm) and the 4 pulley bolts to 37 ft. lbs. (50 Nm).

19. Install the automatic belt tensioner. Tighten the 2 retaining nuts and bolt to 35 ft. lbs. (48 Nm).

20. Install the water pump and accessory drive belts. Torque the water pump pulley retaining bolts to 16 ft. lbs. (21 Nm).

21. Install the lower radiator hose and the heater hose and tighten the clamps.

22. Fill the crankcase with the correct amount and type of engine oil. Connect the negative battery cable. Fill and bleed the cooling system.

23. Start the engine and check for coolant and oil leaks.

3.8L Engine

1. Disconnect the negative battery cable. Drain the cooling system and crankcase.

2. Remove the air cleaner assembly and air intake duct.

3. Loosen the accessory drive belt

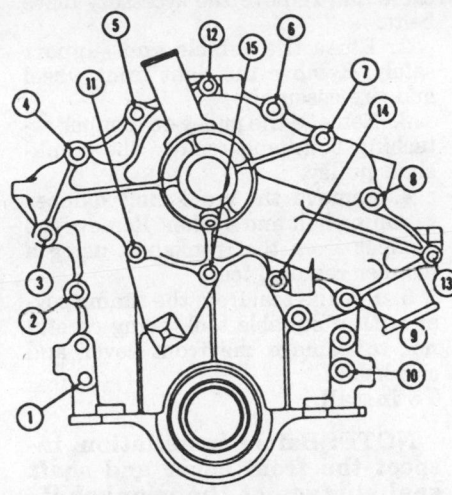

Water pump and front cover bolt Identification—3.0L engine

idler. Remove the drive belt and water pump pulley.

4. Remove the power steering pump mounting bracket attaching bolts. Leaving the hoses connected, place the pump/bracket assembly in a position that will prevent the loss of power steering fluid.

5. If equipped with air conditioning, remove the compressor front support bracket. Leave the compressor in place.

6. Disconnect coolant bypass and heater hoses at the water pump. Disconnect radiator upper hose at thermostat housing.

7. Disconnect the coil wire from distributor cap and remove cap with the spark plug wires attached. Remove the distributor retaining clamp and lift distributor out of the front cover.

8. Raise the vehicle and support safely.

9. Remove the crankshaft damper and pulley.

NOTE: If the crankshaft pulley and vibration damper have to be separated, mark the damper and pulley so they may be reassembled in the same relative position. This is important as the damper and pulley are initially balanced as a unit. If the crankshaft damper is being replaced, check if the original damper has balance pins installed. If so, new balance pins (E0SZ-6A328-A or equivalent) must be installed on the new damper in the same position as the original damper. The crankshaft pulley must also be installed in the original installation position.

10. Remove the oil filter, disconnect the radiator lower hose at the water pump and remove the oil pan.

NOTE: The front cover cannot be removed without lowering the oil pan.

11. Lower the vehicle.

12. Remove the front cover attaching bolts.

NOTE: Do not overlook the cover attaching bolt located behind the oil filter adapter. The front cover will break if pried upon if all attaching bolts are not removed.

13. Remove the ignition timing indicator.

14. Remove the front cover and water pump as an assembly. Remove the cover gasket and discard.

NOTE: The front cover houses the oil pump. If a new front cover is to be installed, remove the water pump and oil pump from the old front cover.

To install:

15. Lightly oil all bolt and stud threads before installation. Clean all gasket surfaces on the front cover, cylinder block and fuel pump. If reusing the front cover, replace crankshaft front oil seal.

16. If a new front cover is to be installed, complete the following:

a. Install the oil pump gears.

b. Clean the water pump gasket surface. Position a new water pump gasket on the front cover and install the water pump. Install the pump attaching bolts and tighten to 15–22 ft. lbs.

17. Install the distributor drive gear.

18. Lubricate the crankshaft front oil seal with clean engine oil.

19. Position a new cover gasket on the cylinder block and install the front cover/water pump assembly using dowels for proper alignment. A suitable contact adhesive is recommended to hold the gasket in position while the front cover is installed.

20. Position the ignition timing indicator.

21. Install the front cover attaching bolts. Apply Loctite® or equivalent, to the threads of the bolt installed below the oil filter housing prior to installation. This bolt is to be installed and tightened last. Tighten all bolts to 15–22 ft. lbs. (20–30 Nm).

22. Raise the vehicle and support safely.

23. Install the oil pan. Connect the radiator lower hose. Install a new oil filter.

24. Coat the crankshaft damper sealing surface with clean engine oil. Apply a small amount of silicone sealant to the crankshaft keyway.

25. Position the crankshaft pulley key in the crankshaft keyway.

26. Install the damper with damper washer and attaching bolt. Tighten the bolt to 104–132 ft. lbs. (140–180 Nm).

27. Install the crankshaft pulley and tighten the attaching bolts 19–28 ft. lbs. (26–28 Nm).

28. Lower the vehicle.

29. Connect the coolant bypass hose.

30. Rotate the crankshaft, as necessary, to position piston No. 1 at TDC on the compression stroke. Install the distributor with rotor pointing at No. 1 distributor cap tower. Install the distributor cap and coil wire.

31. Connect the radiator upper hose at thermostat housing.

32. Connect the heater hose.

33. If equipped with air conditioning, install compressor and mounting brackets.

34. Install the power steering pump and mounting brackets.

35. Position the accessory drive belt over the pulleys.

36. Install the water pump pulley. Position the accessory drive belt over water pump pulley and tighten the belt.

37. Connect the negative battery cable. Fill the crankcase and cooling system to the proper level.

38. Start the engine and check for leaks.

39. Check the ignition timing and curb idle speed; adjust as required.

40. Install the air cleaner assembly and air intake duct.

Front Cover Oil Seal

REPLACEMENT

2.5L Engine

NOTE: The removal and installation of the front cover oil seal on these engines can only be accomplished with the engine removed from the vehicle.

1. Remove the engine from the vehicle and position in a suitable holding fixture.

2. Remove the bolt and washer at the crankshaft pulley.

3. Remove the crankshaft pulley.

4. Remove the front cover oil seal, using a suitable puller or prybar.

5. Coat a new seal with grease. Install the seal, driving it in until it is fully seated. Check the seal after installation to be sure the spring is properly positioned in the seal.

6. Install the crankshaft pulley, attaching bolt and washer. Tighten the crankshaft pulley bolt to 140–170 ft. lbs. (190–230 Nm).

3.0L Engine

1. Disconnect the negative battery

cable and remove the accessory drive belts.

2. Raise the vehicle and support safely. Remove the right front wheel and tire assembly.

3. Remove the pulley-to-damper attaching bolts and remove the crankshaft pulley.

4. Remove the crankshaft damper retaining bolt and washer. Remove the damper from the crankshaft using a damper removal tool.

5. Pry the seal from the timing cover with a suitable tool, being careful not to damage the front cover and crankshaft.

To install:

NOTE: Before installation, inspect the front cover and shaft seal surface of the crankshaft damper for damage, nicks, burrs or other roughness which may cause the new seal to fail. Service or replace components as necessary.

6. Lubricate the seal lip with clean engine oil and install the seal using a seal installer tool.

7. Coat the crankshaft damper sealing surface with clean engine oil. Apply RTV to the keyway of the damper prior to installation. Install the damper using a damper installation tool. Install the damper retaining bolt and washer. Tighten to 107 ft. lbs. (145 Nm).

8. Position the crankshaft pulley and install the attaching bolts. Tighten the attaching bolts to 37 ft. lbs. (50 Nm).

9. Install the right front wheel and tire assembly and lower the vehicle.

10. Position the drive belt over the crankshaft pulley. Check the drive belt for proper routing and engagement in the pulleys.

11. Reconnect the negative battery cable, start the engine and check for oil leaks.

3.8L Engine

1. Disconnect the negative battery cable.

2. Loosen the accessory drive belt idler.

3. Raise the vehicle and support safely.

4. Disengage the accessory drive belt and remove crankshaft pulley.

5. Remove the crankshaft damper using a suitable puller.

6. Remove the seal from the front cover with a suitable prying tool. Use care to prevent damage to front cover and crankshaft.

To install:

NOTE: Inspect the front cover and crankshaft damper for damage, nicks, burrs or other rough-

ness which may cause the seal to fail. Service or replace components as necessary.

7. Lubricate the seal lip with clean engine oil and install the seal using a suitable seal installer.

8. Lubricate the seal surface on the damper with clean engine oil. Install the damper using a suitable installation tool. Install the damper attaching bolt and tighten to 103–132 ft. lbs. (140–180 Nm).

9. Position the crankshaft pulley and install the retaining bolts. Tighten to 19–28 ft. lbs. (26–38 Nm).

10. Position accessory drive belt over crankshaft pulley.

11. Lower the vehicle.

12. Check accessory drive belt for proper routing and engagement in the pulleys. Adjust the drive belt tension.

13. Connect the negative battery cable. Start the engine and check for leaks.

Timing Chain and Sprockets

REMOVAL & INSTALLATION

2.5L Engine

1. Remove the engine and transaxle from the vehicle as an assembly and position in a suitable holding fixture. Remove the dipstick.

2. Remove accessory drive pulley, if equipped. Remove the crankshaft pulley attaching bolt and washer and remove pulley.

3. Remove front cover attaching bolts from front cover. Pry the top of the front cover away from the block.

4. Clean any gasket material from the surfaces.

5. Check timing chain deflection as follows:

   a. Rotate the crankshaft in a counterclockwise direction to take up slack on the left side of the chain.

   b. Establish a reference point on the engine block and measure from this point to the chain.

   c. Rotate the crankshaft in the opposite direction to take up slack on the right side of the chain. Force the left side of the chain out by hand and measure the distance between the reference point and chain. The deflection is the difference between the 2 measurements and must not exceed ½ in.

6. Check the sprockets for excessive wear. If the timing chain and sprockets are worn, replace with new.

7. Check timing chain tensioner blade for wear and replace, as necessary.

8. Turn engine over until the timing marks are aligned. Remove cam-

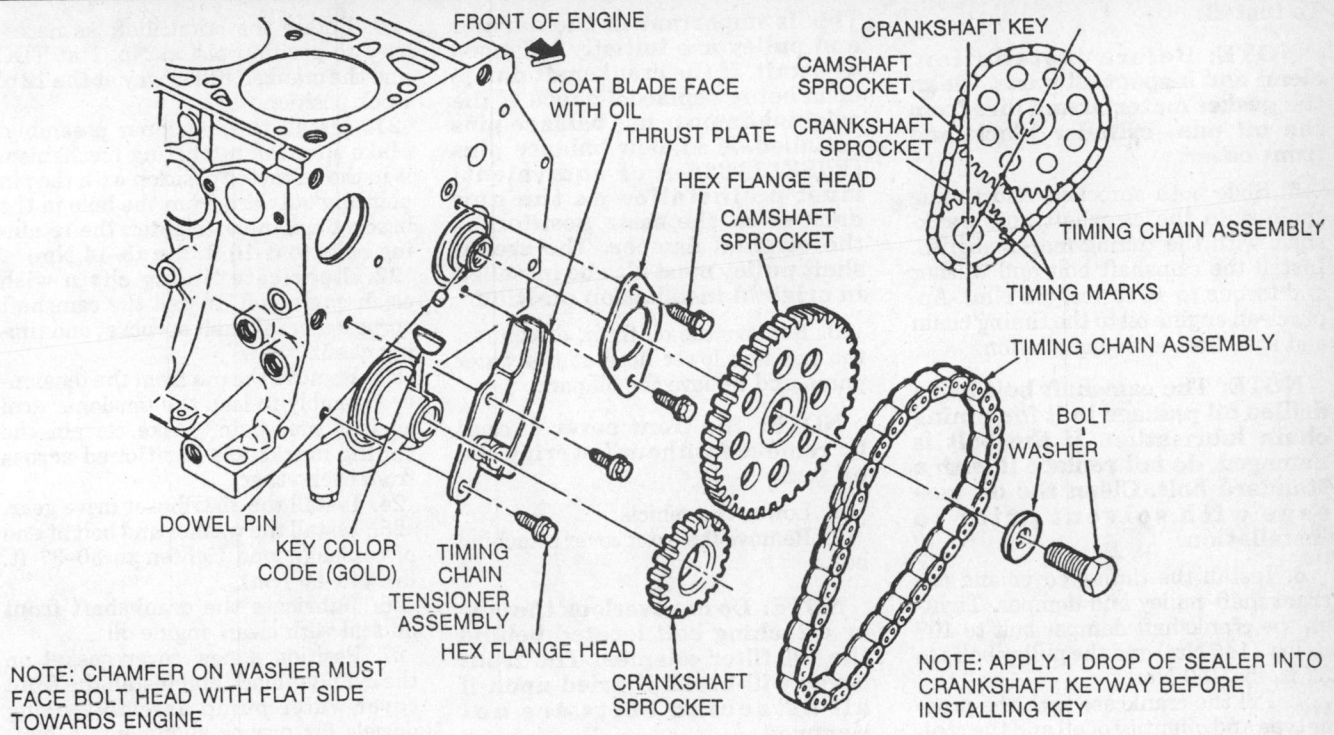

Timing chain and sprockets installation—2.5L engine

NOTE: CHAMFER ON WASHER MUST FACE BOLT HEAD WITH FLAT SIDE TOWARDS ENGINE

NOTE: APPLY 1 DROP OF SEALER INTO CRANKSHAFT KEYWAY BEFORE INSTALLING KEY

shaft sprocket attaching bolt and washer. Slide both sprockets and timing chain forward and remove as an assembly.

9. If equipped, check timing chain vibration damper for excessive wear. Replace if necessary; the damper is located inside the front cover.

10. Remove the oil pan.

To install:

11. Clean and inspect all parts before installation. Clean the oil pan, cylinder block and front cover of gasket material and dirt. Remove the front cover oil seal.

NOTE: The front cover oil seal must be removed whenever the front cover is removed from the engine, in order to use the front cover alignment tool.

12. Slide both sprockets and timing chain onto the camshaft and crankshaft with timing marks aligned. Install camshaft bolt and washer and tighten to 41–56 ft. lbs. (55–75 Nm). Oil timing chain, sprockets and tensioner after installation with clean engine oil.

13. Apply oil resistant sealer to a new front cover gasket and position gasket into front cover.

14. Position the front cover on the engine.

15. Position front cover alignment tool T84P–6019–C or equivalent, onto the end of the crankshaft, ensuring the crank key is aligned with the keyway in the tool. Bolt the front cover to

the engine and tighten the bolts to 6–9 ft. lbs. (8–12 Nm). Remove the front cover alignment tool.

16. Install a new front cover oil seal using a suitable seal installer. Lubricate the hub of the crankshaft pulley with multi-purpose grease to prevent damage to the seal during installation and initial engine start. Install crankshaft pulley.

17. Install the oil pan.

18. Install the accessory drive pulley, if equipped.

19. Install crankshaft pulley attaching bolt and washer. Tighten to 140–170 ft. lbs. (190–230 Nm).

20. Remove engine from work stand and install in vehicle.

3.0L Engine

1. Check timing chain deflection as follows:

a. Remove the left rocker arm cover.

b. Loosen the No. 5 exhaust rocker arm and rotate to 1 side. Install a dial indicator on the end of the pushrod.

c. Turn the crankshaft clockwise until the No. 1 piston is at TDC on the compression stroke. The damper timing mark should point to TDC on the timing degree indicator. The slack should now be taken up on the right side of the chain. Zero the dial indicator.

d. Slowly turn the crankshaft counterclockwise until the slightest movement is seen on the dial indica-

tor. Stop and observe the damper timing mark for number of degrees of travel from TDC.

e. If the reading on the timing degree indicator exceeds 6 degrees, replace the timing chain and sprockets.

2. Disconnect the negative battery cable. Drain the cooling system and crankcase. Remove the crankshaft pulley and front cover assemblies.

3. Rotate the crankshaft until the No. 1 piston is at the TDC on its compression stroke and the timing marks are aligned.

4. Remove the camshaft sprocket attaching bolt and washer. Slide both sprockets and timing chain forward and remove as an assembly.

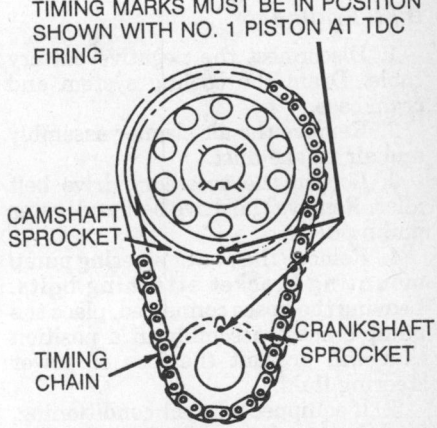

TIMING MARKS MUST BE IN POSITION SHOWN WITH NO. 1 PISTON AT TDC FIRING

Timing sprocket alignment—3.0L engine

To install:

NOTE: Before installation, clean and inspect all parts. Clean the gasket material and dirt from the oil pan, cylinder block and front cover.

5. Slide both sprockets and timing chain onto the camshaft and crankshaft with the timing marks aligned. Install the camshaft bolt and washer and torque to 46 ft. lbs. (63 Nm). Apply clean engine oil to the timing chain and sprockets after installation.

NOTE: The camshaft bolt has a drilled oil passage in it for timing chain lubrication. If the bolt is damaged, do not replace it with a standard bolt. Clean the oil passage with solvent prior to installation.

6. Install the timing cover and the crankshaft pulley and damper. Tighten the crankshaft damper bolt to 107 ft. lbs. (145 Nm) and the pulley bolts to 37 ft. lbs. (50 Nm).
7. Fill the crankcase with the proper type and quantity of oil and the cooling system with coolant. Connect the negative battery cable.

3.8L Engine

1. Disconnect the negative battery cable. Drain the cooling system and crankcase.
2. Remove the air cleaner assembly and air intake duct.
3. Loosen the accessory drive belt idler. Remove the drive belt and water pump pulley.
4. Remove the power steering pump mounting bracket attaching bolts. Leaving the hoses connected, place the pump/bracket assembly in a position that will prevent the loss of power steering fluid.
5. If equipped with air conditioning, remove the compressor front support bracket. Leave the compressor in place.
6. Disconnect coolant bypass and heater hoses at the water pump. Disconnect radiator upper hose at thermostat housing.
7. Disconnect the coil wire from distributor cap and remove cap with the spark plug wires attached. Remove the distributor retaining clamp and lift distributor out of the front cover.
8. Raise the vehicle and support safely.
9. Remove the crankshaft damper and pulley.

NOTE: If the crankshaft pulley and vibration damper have to be separated, mark the damper and pulley so they may be reassembled in the same relative position.

This is important as the damper and pulley are initially balanced as a unit. If the crankshaft damper is being replaced, check if the original damper has balance pins installed. If so, new balance pins (E0SZ–6A328–A or equivalent) must be installed on the new damper in the same position as the original damper. The crankshaft pulley must also be installed in original installation position.

10. Remove the oil filter, disconnect the radiator lower hose at the water pump and remove the oil pan.

NOTE: The front cover cannot be removed without lowering the oil pan.

11. Lower the vehicle.
12. Remove the front cover attaching bolts.

NOTE: Do not overlook the cover attaching bolt located behind the oil filter adapter. The front cover will break if pried upon if all attaching bolts are not removed.

13. Remove the ignition timing indicator.
14. Remove the front cover and water pump as an assembly. Remove the cover gasket and discard.
15. Remove the camshaft bolt and washer from end of the camshaft. Remove the distributor drive gear.
16. Remove the camshaft sprocket, crankshaft sprocket and timing chain. If the crankshaft sprocket is difficult to remove, pry it off using a pair of small prybars positioned on both sides of the sprocket.
17. Pull back on the chain tensioner ratcheting mechanism and install a pin through the hole in the bracket to relieve tension. Remove the 3 bolts and the chain tensioner assembly.

NOTE: The front cover houses the oil pump. If a new front cover is to be installed, remove the water pump and oil pump from the old front cover.

To install:
18. Lightly oil all bolt and stud threads before installation. Clean all gasket surfaces on the front cover, cylinder block and fuel pump. If reusing the front cover, replace crankshaft front oil seal.
19. If a new front cover is to be installed, complete the following:
   a. Install the oil pump gears.
   b. Clean the water pump gasket surface. Position a new water pump gasket on the front cover and install water pump. Install the pump attaching bolts and tighten to 15–22 ft. lbs.

20. Rotate the crankshaft as necessary to position piston No. 1 at TDC and the crankshaft keyway at the 12 o'clock position.
21. Install the tensioner assembly. Make sure the ratcheting mechanism is in the retracted position with the pin pointing outward from the hole in the bracket assembly. Tighten the retaining bolts to 6–10 ft. lbs. (8–14 Nm).
22. Lubricate timing chain with clean engine oil. Install the camshaft sprocket, crankshaft sprocket and timing chain.
23. Remove the pin from the tensioner assembly to load the tensioner arm against the chain. Make certain the timing marks are positioned across from each other.
24. Install the distributor drive gear.
25. Install the washer and bolt at end of camshaft and tighten to 30–37 ft. lbs. (40–50 Nm).
26. Lubricate the crankshaft front oil seal with clean engine oil.
27. Position a new cover gasket on the cylinder block and install the front cover/water pump assembly using dowels for proper alignment. A suitable contact adhesive is recommended to hold the gasket in position while the front cover is installed.
28. Position the ignition timing indicator.
29. Install the front cover attaching bolts. Apply Loctite® or equivalent, to the threads of the bolt installed below the oil filter housing prior to installation. This bolt is to be installed and tightened last. Tighten all bolts to 15–22 ft. lbs. (20–30 Nm).
30. Raise the vehicle and support safely.
31. Install the oil pan. Connect the radiator lower hose. Install a new oil filter.
32. Coat the crankshaft damper sealing surface with clean engine oil. Apply a small amount of silicone sealant to the crankshaft keyway.
33. Position the crankshaft pulley key in the crankshaft keyway.
34. Install the damper with damper washer and attaching bolt. Tighten the bolt to 104–132 ft. lbs. (140–180 Nm).
35. Install the crankshaft pulley and tighten the attaching bolts 19–28 ft. lbs. (26–28 Nm).
36. Lower the vehicle.
37. Connect the coolant bypass hose.
38. Install the distributor with rotor pointing at No. 1 distributor cap tower. Install the distributor cap and coil wire.
39. Connect the radiator upper hose at thermostat housing.
40. Connect the heater hose.
41. If equipped with air conditioning, install compressor and mounting brackets.

42. Install the power steering pump and mounting brackets.

43. Position the accessory drive belt over the pulleys.

44. Install the water pump pulley. Position the accessory drive belt over water pump pulley and tighten the belt.

45. Connect battery ground cable. Fill the crankcase and cooling system to the proper level.

46. Start the engine and check for leaks.

47. Check the ignition timing and curb idle speed; adjust as required.

48. Install the air cleaner assembly and air intake duct.

Timing Belt Front Cover

REMOVAL & INSTALLATION

3.0L SHO Engine

NOTE: The front cover on the 3.0L SHO engine is made up of 3 sections.

1. Disconnect the battery cables and remove the battery. Remove the right-hand engine roll damper.

2. Disconnect the wiring to the ignition module. Remove the intake manifold crossover tube bolts, loosen the crossover tube clamps and remove the crossover tube.

3. Loosen the alternator/air conditioner belt tensioner pulley and relieve the tension on the belt by backing out the adjustment screw. Remove the belt.

4. Loosen the water pump/power steering belt tensioner pulley and relieve the tension on the belt by backing out the adjustment screw. Remove the belt.

5. Remove the alternator/air conditioner belt tensioner pulley and bracket assembly. Remove the water pump/power steering belt tensioner pulley only.

6. Remove the upper timing belt cover.

7. Disconnect the crankshaft sensor connectors.

8. Raise and safely support the vehicle. Remove the right front wheel and tire assembly.

9. Loosen the fender splash shield and move aside. Remove the crankshaft damper using a suitable puller.

10. Remove the center and lower timing belt covers.

11. Installation is the reverse of the removal procedure. Tighten the timing belt cover retaining bolts to 60–90 inch lbs. (7–11 Nm) and the crankshaft damper bolt to 113–126 ft. lbs. (152–172 Nm).

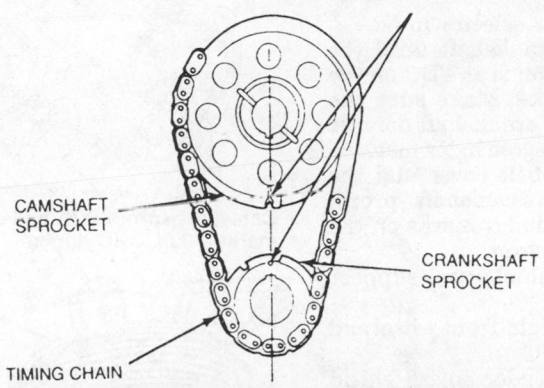

POSITIONING OF TIMING MARKS AND KEYWAYS IN CAMSHAFT AND CRANKSHAFT SPROCKETS MUST BE IN LINE AS SHOWN WITH NO. 1 PISTON AT TOP DEAD CENTER FIRING.

CAMSHAFT SPROCKET

CRANKSHAFT SPROCKET

TIMING CHAIN

Timing sprocket alignment—3.8L engine

OIL SEAL REPLACEMENT

3.0L SHO Engine

CRANKSHAFT SEAL

1. Loosen the accessory drive belts.

2. Raise the vehicle and support it safely.

3. Remove the right front wheel.

4. Remove the damper attaching bolt and the accessory drive belts from the crankshaft damper.

5. Using a suitable puller, remove the crankshaft damper from the crankshaft.

6. Remove the timing belt.

7. Remove the crankshaft timing gear using a suitable puller.

NOTE: Be careful not to damage the crankshaft sensor or shutter.

8. Remove the crankshaft front oil seal using a suitable puller.

To install:

9. Inspect the front cover and shaft seal surface of the crankshaft damper for damage, nicks, burrs or other roughness which may cause the new seal to fail. Repair or replace as necessary.

10. Using suitable tools, install a new crankshaft front oil seal and the crankshaft timing gear.

11. Install the timing belt.

12. Install the crankshaft damper using a suitable tool. Tighten the damper attaching bolt to 113–126 ft. lbs. (152–172 Nm).

13. Install the accessory drive belts.

14. Lower the vehicle.

15. Start the engine and check for oil leaks.

CAMSHAFT SEAL

1. Remove the timing belt covers and timing belt.

2. Remove the camshaft sprocket(s). Note the location of the dowel pin(s).

3. Remove the camshaft seal using a suitable puller.

To install:

4. Clean and inspect the seal surface area.

5. Apply silicone rubber or equivalent, to the seal outer diameter and seal seating surface.

6. Install the camshaft seal using a suitable seal installer.

7. Install the camshaft sprocket(s). Tighten the retaining bolt to 15–18 ft. lbs. (21–25 Nm).

8. Install the timing belt and timing belt covers.

Timing Belt and Tensioner

REMOVAL & INSTALLATION

3.0L SHO Engine

1. Disconnect the battery cables.

2. Remove the battery.

3. Remove the right-hand engine roll damper.

4. Disconnect the wiring to the ignition module.

5. Remove the intake manifold crossover tube bolts. Loosen the intake manifold tube hose clamps. Remove the intake manifold crossover tube.

6. Loosen the alternator/air conditioning belt tensioner pulley and relieve the tension on the belt by backing out the adjustment screw. Remove the alternator/air conditioning belt.

7. Loosen the water pump/power steering belt tensioner pulley and relieve the tension on the belt by backing out the adjustment screw. Remove the water pump/power steering belt.

8. Remove the alternator/air conditioning belt tensioner pulley and bracket assembly.

9. Remove the water pump/power steering belt tensioner pulley only.

10. Remove the upper timing belt cover.

11. Disconnect the crankshaft sensor connectors.

12. Place the gear selector in **N**.

13. Rotate the crankshaft until the No. 1 cylinder piston is at TDC on the compression stroke. Make sure the white mark on the crankshaft damper aligns with the **0** degree index mark on the lower timing belt cover and the marks on the intake camshaft sprockets align with the index marks on the metal timing belt cover.

14. Raise the vehicle and support safely.

15. Remove the right front wheel and tire assembly.

16. Loosen the fender splash shield and place it aside.

17. Using a suitable puller, remove the crankshaft damper.

18. Remove the lower timing belt cover.

19. Remove the center timing belt cover and disconnect the crankshaft sensor wire and grommet from the slot in the cover and the stud on the water pump.

20. Loosen the timing belt tensioner, rotate the pulley 180 degrees clockwise and tighten the tensioner nut to hold the pulley in the unload position.

21. Lower the vehicle and remove the timing belt.

To install:

NOTE: **Before installing the timing belt, inspect it for cracks, wear or other damage and replace, if necessary. Do not allow the timing belt to come into contact with gasoline, oil, water, coolant or steam. Do not twist or turn the belt inside out.**

22. Make sure the engine is at TDC on the No. 1 cylinder. Check that the camshaft sprocket marks line up with the index marks on the upper steel belt cover and that the crankshaft sprocket aligns with the index mark on the oil pump housing.

NOTE: **The timing belt has 3 yellow lines. Each line aligns with the index marks.**

23. Install the timing belt over the crankshaft and camshaft sprockets. The lettering on the belt **KOA** should be readable from the rear of the engine; top of the lettering to the front of the engine. Make sure the yellow lines are aligned with the index marks on the sprockets.

24. Release the tensioner locknut and leave the nut loose.

25. Raise the vehicle and support safely.

26. Install the center timing belt cover. Make sure the crankshaft sensor

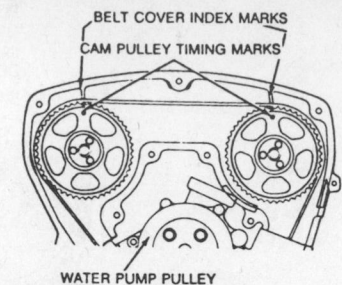

Camshaft sprocket to belt cover index marks—3.0L SHO engine

Crankshaft damper to lower timing cover index mark alignment—3.0L SHO engine

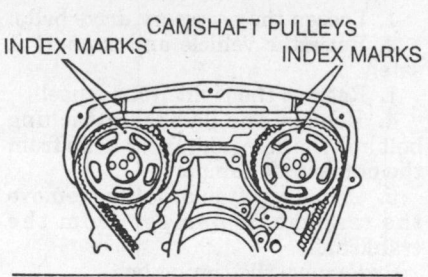

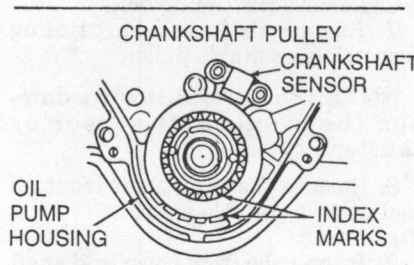

Timing belt index marks—3.0L SHO engine

wiring and grommet are installed and routed properly. Tighten the mounting bolts to 60–90 inch lbs. (7–11 Nm).

27. Install the lower timing belt cover. Tighten the bolts to 60–90 inch lbs. (7–11 Nm).

28. Using a suitable tool, install the crankshaft damper. Tighten the damper attaching bolt to 113–126 ft. lbs. (152–172 Nm).

29. Rotate the crankshaft 2 revolutions in the clockwise direction until the yellow mark on the damper aligns with the **0** degree mark on the lower timing belt cover.

30. Remove the plastic door in the lower timing belt cover. Tighten the tensioner locknut to 25–37 ft. lbs. (33–51 Nm) and install the plastic door.

31. Rotate the crankshaft 60 degrees more in the clockwise direction until

the white mark on the damper aligns with the **0** degree mark on the lower timing belt cover.

32. Lower the vehicle.

33. Make sure the index marks on the camshaft sprockets align with the marks on the rear metal timing belt cover.

34. Route the crankshaft sensor wiring and connect with the engine wiring harness.

35. Install the upper timing belt cover. Tighten the bolts to 60–90 inch lbs. (7–11 Nm).

36. Install the water pump/power steering tensioner pulley. Tighten the nut to 11–17 ft. lbs. (15–23 Nm).

37. Install the alternator/air conditioning tensioner pulley and bracket assembly. Tighten the bolts to 11–17 ft. lbs. (15–23 Nm).

38. Install the water pump/power steering and alternator/air conditioning belts and set the tension. Tighten the idler pulley nut to 25–36 ft. lbs. (34–50 Nm).

39. Install the intake manifold crossover tube. Tighten the bolts to 11–17 ft. lbs. (15–23 Nm).

40. Install the engine roll damper and the battery.

41. Connect the battery cables.

42. Raise the vehicle and support safely.

43. Install the splash shield and the right front wheel and tire assembly.

44. Lower the vehicle.

Timing Sprockets

REMOVAL & INSTALLATION

3.0L SHO Engine

1. Disconnect the negative battery cable.

2. Remove the timing belt.

3. Remove the camshaft and crankshaft timing belt sprockets. Note the location of the dowel pins when removing the camshaft sprockets.

4. Install in the reverse order of removal. Tighten the camshaft timing belt sprocket bolts to 15–18 ft. lbs. (21–25 Nm) and the crankshaft sprocket bolt to 113–126 ft. lbs. (152–172 Nm).

Camshaft

REMOVAL & INSTALLATION

2.5L Engine

1. Drain the cooling system and the crankcase. Relieve the fuel system pressure.

2. Remove the engine from the vehicle and position in a suitable holding fixture. Remove the engine oil dipstick.

3. Remove necessary drive belts and pulleys.

4. Remove cylinder head.

5. Using a magnet, remove the hydraulic lifters and label them so they can be installed in their original positions. If the lifters are stuck in the bores by excessive varnish, etc., use a suitable claw-type puller to remove them.

6. Loosen and remove the drive belt, fan and pulley and crankshaft pulley.

7. Remove the oil pan.

8. Remove the cylinder front cover and gasket.

9. Check the camshaft endplay as follows:

a. Push the camshaft toward the rear of the engine and install a dial indicator tool, so the indicator point is on the camshaft sprocket attaching screw.

b. Zero the dial indicator. Position a small prybar or equivalent, between the camshaft sprocket or gear and block.

c. Pull the camshaft forward and release it. Compare the dial indicator reading with the camshaft endplay specification of 0.009 in.

d. If the camshaft endplay is over the amount specified, replace the thrust plate.

10. Remove the timing chain, sprockets and timing chain tensioner. Remove the distributor.

11. Remove camshaft thrust plate. Carefully remove the camshaft by pulling it toward the front of the engine. Use caution to avoid damaging bearings, journals and lobes.

To install:

12. Clean and inspect all parts before installation.

13. Lubricate camshaft lobes and journals with heavy engine oil. Carefully slide the camshaft through the bearings in the cylinder block.

14. Install the thrust plate. Tighten attaching bolts to 6–9 ft. lbs. (8–12 Nm).

15. Install the timing chain, sprockets and timing chain tensioner.

16. Install the cylinder front cover and crankshaft pulley.

17. Clean the oil pump inlet tube screen, oil pan and cylinder block gasket surfaces. Prime oil pump by filling the inlet opening with oil and rotate the pump shaft until oil emerges from the outlet tube. Install oil pump, oil pump inlet tube screen and oil pan.

18. Install the accessory drive belts and pulleys.

19. Lubricate the lifters and lifter bores with heavy engine oil. Install the lifters into their original bores.

20. Install cylinder head.

21. Install the engine assembly.

22. Position No. 1 piston at TDC af-

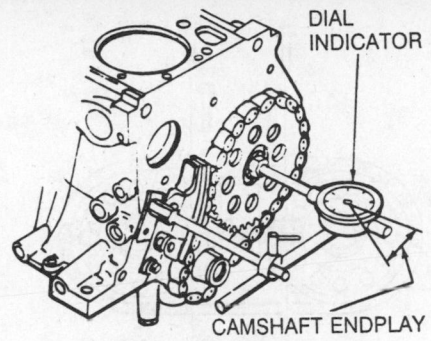

Checking camshaft endplay

ter the compression stroke. Position distributor in the block with the rotor at the No. 1 firing position. Install distributor retaining clamp.

23. Connect engine temperature sending unit wire. Connect coil primary wire. Install distributor cap. Connect spark plug wires and the coil high tension lead.

24. Fill the cooling system and crankcase to the proper levels. Connect the negative battery cable.

25. Start the engine. Check and adjust ignition timing. Check for leaks.

3.0L Except SHO Engine

1. Drain the cooling system and crankcase. Relieve the fuel system pressure.

2. Remove the engine from the vehicle and position in a suitable holding fixture.

3. Remove the accessory drive components from the front of the engine.

4. Remove the throttle body and the fuel injector harness. Remove the distributor assembly.

5. Remove and tag the spark plug wires and rocker arm covers. Loosen the rocker arm fulcrum nuts and position the rocker arms to the side. Remove the pushrods and label them so they may be installed in their original positions.

6. Remove the intake manifold.

7. Remove the lifter guide plates. Using a suitable magnet or lifter removal tool, remove the hydraulic lifters and keep them in order so they can be installed in their original positions. If the lifters are stuck in the bores by excessive varnish use a hydraulic lifter puller to remove the lifters.

8. Remove the crankshaft pulley and damper using a suitable removal tool. Remove the oil pan assembly.

9. Remove the front cover assembly. Align the timing marks on the camshaft and crankshaft gears. Check the camshaft endplay as follows:

a. Push the camshaft toward the rear of the engine and install a dial indicator tool, so the indicator point

is on the camshaft sprocket attaching screw.

b. Zero the dial indicator. Position a small prybar or equivalent, between the camshaft sprocket or gear and block.

c. Pull the camshaft forward and release it. Compare the dial indicator reading with the camshaft endplay service limit specification of 0.005 in.

d. If the camshaft endplay is over the amount specified, replace the thrust plate.

10. Remove the timing chain and sprockets.

11. Remove the camshaft thrust plate. Carefully remove the camshaft by pulling it toward the front of the engine. Remove it slowly to avoid damaging the bearings, journals and lobes.

To install:

12. Clean and inspect all parts before installation.

13. Lubricate camshaft lobes and journals with heavy engine oil. Carefully insert the camshaft through the bearings in the cylinder block.

14. Install the thrust plate. Tighten the retaining bolts to 7 ft. lbs. (10 Nm).

15. Install the timing chain and sprockets. Check the camshaft sprocket bolt for blockage of drilled oil passages prior to installation and clean, if necessary.

16. Install the front timing cover and crankshaft damper and pulley.

17. Lubricate the lifters and lifter bores with a heavy engine oil. Install the lifters into their original bores. Install the lifter guide plates, making sure the word **UP** and/or button is visible. Tighten the guide plate retainer bolts to 9 ft. lbs. (12 Nm).

18. Install the intake manifold assembly and the distributor.

19. Lubricate the pushrods and rocker arms with heavy engine oil. Install the pushrods and rocker arms into their original positions. Rotate the crankshaft to set each lifter on its base circle, then tighten the rocker arm bolt. Tighten the rocker arm bolts to 24 ft. lbs. (32 Nm).

20. Install the oil pan and the rocker covers.

21. Install the fuel injector harness and the throttle body. Connect the spark plug wires to the spark plugs.

22. Install the accessory drive components and install the engine assembly.

23. Connect the negative battery cable. Start the engine and check for leaks. Check and adjust the ignition timing.

3.0L SHO Engine

1. Disconnect the negative battery cable. Properly relieve the fuel system pressure.

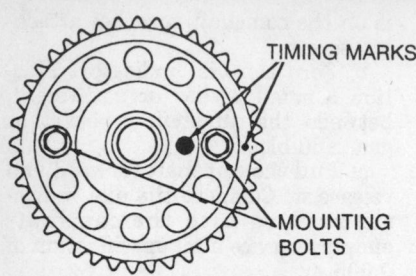

Timing chain sprocket and camshaft alignment—3.0L SHO engine

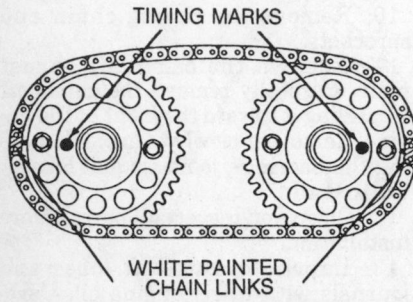

Aligning the timing chain with the timing marks—3.0L SHO engine

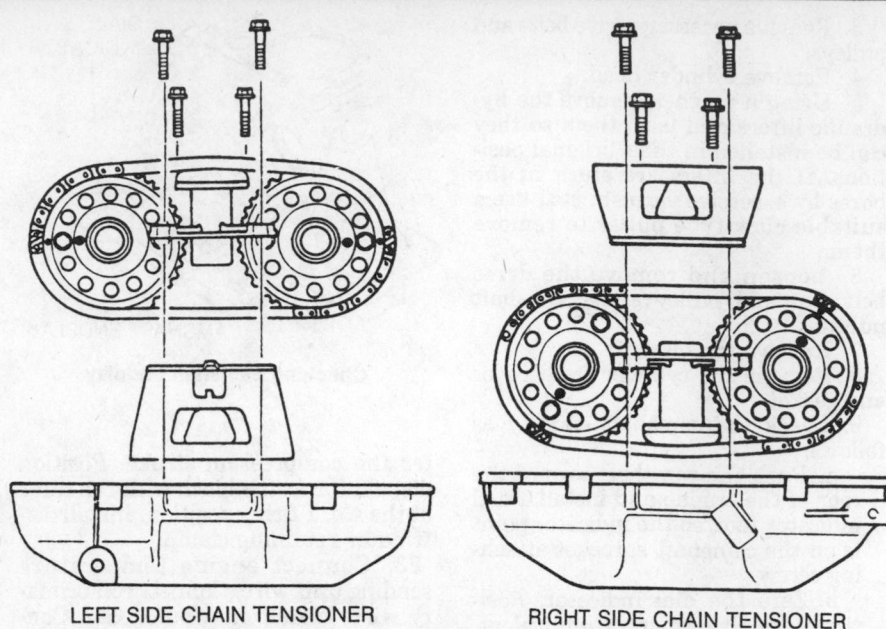

LEFT SIDE CHAIN TENSIONER · RIGHT SIDE CHAIN TENSIONER

Chain tensioner installation—3.0L SHO engine

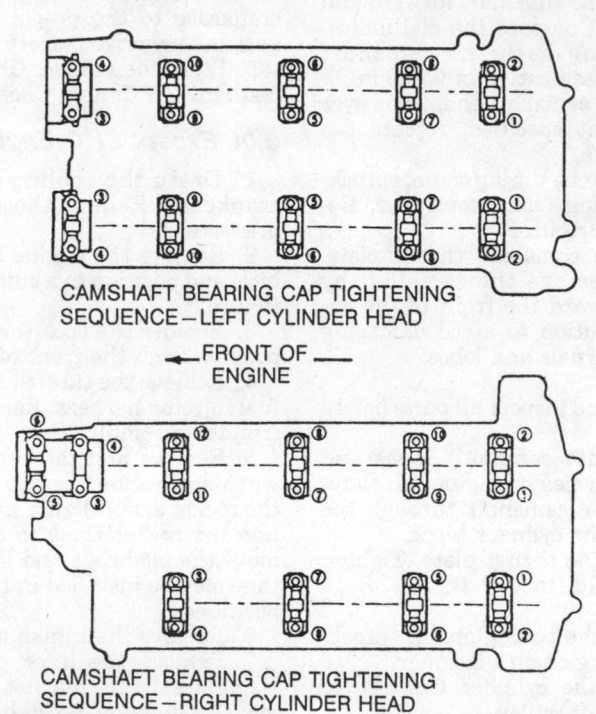

CAMSHAFT BEARING CAP TIGHTENING SEQUENCE—LEFT CYLINDER HEAD

←— FRONT OF ENGINE

CAMSHAFT BEARING CAP TIGHTENING SEQUENCE—RIGHT CYLINDER HEAD

Camshaft bearing cap tightening sequence—3.0L SHO engine

2. Set the engine on TDC on No. 1 cylinder.

3. Remove the intake manifold assembly.

4. Remove the timing cover and belt.

5. Remove the cylinder head covers.

6. Remove the camshaft sprockets, noting the location of the dowel pins.

7. Remove the upper rear timing belt cover.

8. Uniformly loosen the camshaft bearing caps.

NOTE: If the camshaft bearing caps are not uniformly loosened, camshaft damage may result.

9. Remove the bearing caps and note their positions for installation.

10. Remove the camshaft chain tensioner mounting bolts.

11. Remove the camshafts together with the chain and tensioner.

12. Remove and discard the camshaft oil seal.

13. Remove the chain sprocket from the camshaft.

To install:

14. Align the timing marks on the chain sprockets with the camshaft and install the sprockets. Tighten the bolts to 10–13 ft. lbs. (14–18 Nm).

15. Install the chain over the camshaft sprockets. Align the white painted link with the timing mark on the sprocket.

16. Rotate the camshafts approximately 60 degrees counterclockwise. Set the chain tensioner between the sprockets and install the camshafts on the cylinder head.

NOTE: The left and right chain tensioners are not interchangeable.

17. Apply a thin coat of engine oil to the camshaft journals and install bearing caps No. 2 through No. 5 and loosely install the bolts. Install the bearing caps in their original location.

NOTE: The arrows on the bearing caps point to the front of the engine when installed.

18. Apply silicone sealer to outer diameter of the new camshaft seal and the seal seating area on the cylinder head. Install the camshaft seal.

19. Apply silicone sealer to the No. 1 bearing cap and install the bearing cap.

20. Tighten the bearing caps, in sequence, in 2 steps. First tighten to 71–106 inch lbs. (8–12 Nm) and then to 12–16 ft. lbs. (16–22 Nm).

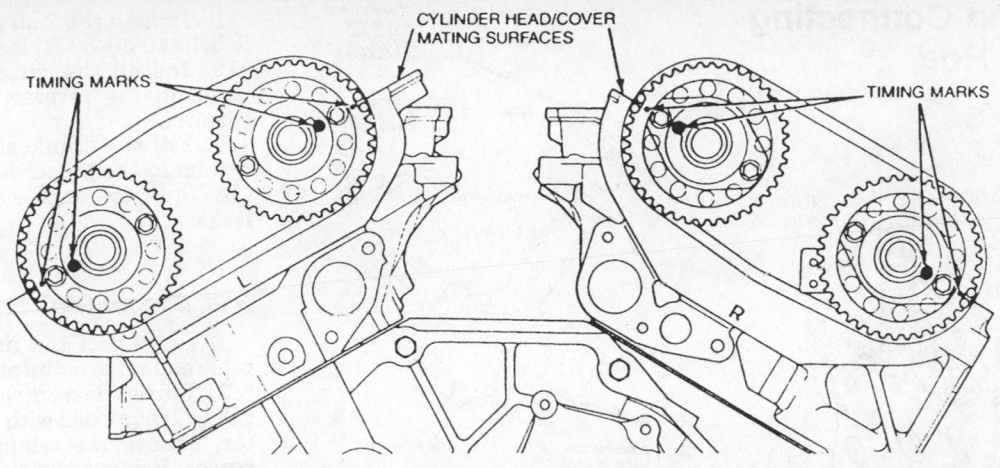

Camshaft sprocket timing mark to cylinder head cover mating surface alignment— 3.0L SHO engine

NOTE: For left camshaft installation, apply pressure to the chain tensioner to avoid damage to the bearing caps.

21. Install the chain tensioner and tighten the bolts to 11–14 ft. lbs. (15–19 Nm). Rotate the camshafts 60 degrees clockwise and check for proper alignment of the timing marks. Marks on the camshaft sprockets should align with the cylinder head cover mating surface.

22. Install the camshaft positioning tool T89P–6256–C or equivalent, on the camshafts to check for correct positioning. The flats on the tool should align with the flats on the camshaft. If the tool does not fit and/or timing marks will not line up, repeat the procedure from Step 14.

23. Install the timing belt rear cover and tighten the bolts to 70 inch lbs. (8.8 Nm).

24. Install the camshaft sprockets and tighten the bolts to 15–18 ft. lbs. (21–25 Nm).

25. Install the timing belt and cover.

26. Install the cylinder head covers and tighten the bolts to 8–11 ft. lbs. (10–16 Nm).

27. Install the intake manifold assembly.

3.8L Engine

1. Disconnect the negative battery cable.

2. Properly relieve the fuel system pressure.

3. Drain the cooling system and crankcase.

4. Remove the engine from the vehicle and position in a suitable holding fixture. Remove the intake manifold.

5. Remove the rocker arm covers, rocker arms, pushrods and lifters.

6. Remove the rocker arm covers, rocker arms, pushrods and lifters.

7. Remove the oil pan.

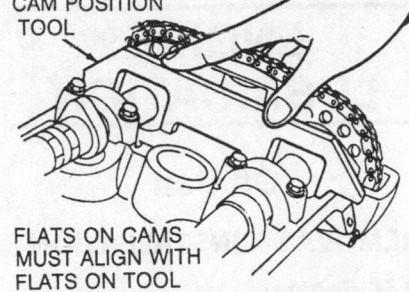

Camshaft positioning tool—3.0L SHO engine

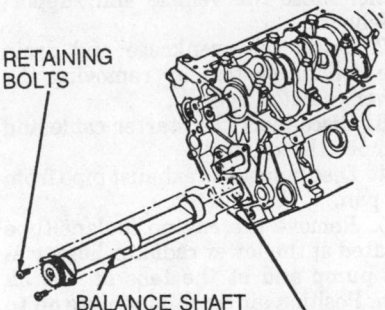

Balancer shaft—3.8L engine

8. Remove the front cover and timing chain.

9. Remove the thrust plate. Remove the camshaft through the front of the engine, being careful not to damage bearing surfaces.

To install:

10. Lightly oil all attaching bolts and stud threads before installation. Lubricate the cam lobes, thrust plate and bearing surfaces with a suitable heavy engine oil.

11. Install the camshaft being careful not to damage bearing surfaces

while sliding into position. Install the thrust plate and tighten the bolts to 6–10 ft. lbs. (8–14 Nm).

12. Install the front cover and timing chain.

13. Install the oil pan.

14. Install the lifters.

15. Install the upper and lower intake manifolds.

16. Install the engine assembly.

17. Fill the cooling system and crankcase to the proper level and connect the negative battery cable.

18. Start the engine. Check and adjust the ignition timing and engine idle speed as necessary. Check for leaks.

Balance Shaft

REMOVAL & INSTALLATION

3.8L Engine

1. Remove the engine from the vehicle.

2. Remove the intake manifolds.

3. Remove the oil pan.

4. Remove the front cover and timing chain and camshaft sprocket.

5. Remove the balance shaft drive gear and spacer.

6. Remove the balance shaft gear, thrust plate and shaft assembly.

To install:

7. Thoroughly coat the balance shaft bearings in the block with engine oil.

8. Install the balance shaft gear.

9. Install the balance shaft, thrust plate and gear and tighten the retaining bolts to 6–10 ft. lbs. (8–14 Nm).

10. Install the timing chain and camshaft sprocket.

11. Install the oil pan.

12. Install the timing cover.

13. Install the intake manifolds.

14. Install the engine in the vehicle.

Piston and Connecting Rod

POSITIONING

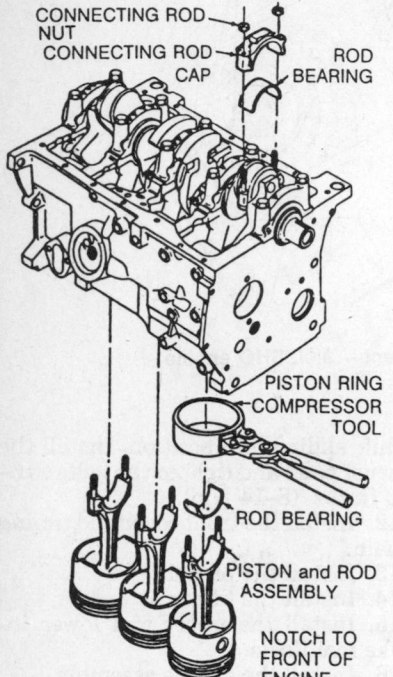

Piston and connecting rod assembly— 2.5L engine

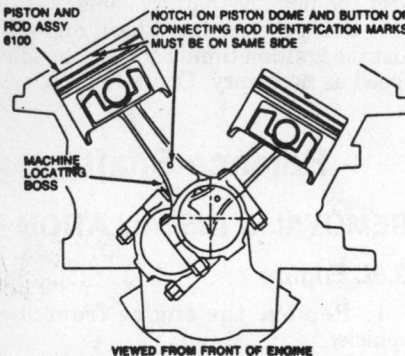

Piston and connecting rod assembly— 3.0L engine

NOTE:
DOME AND BUTTON IDENTIFICATION MUST BE ON SAME SIDE AND TOWARDS FRONT OF ENGINE (AS SHOWN)

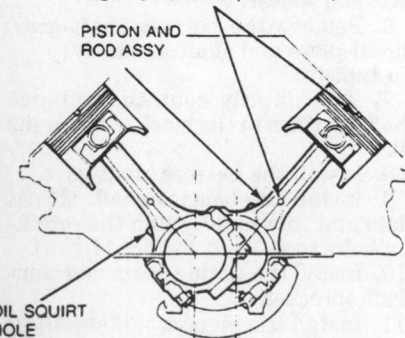

Piston and connecting rod assembly— 3.8L engine

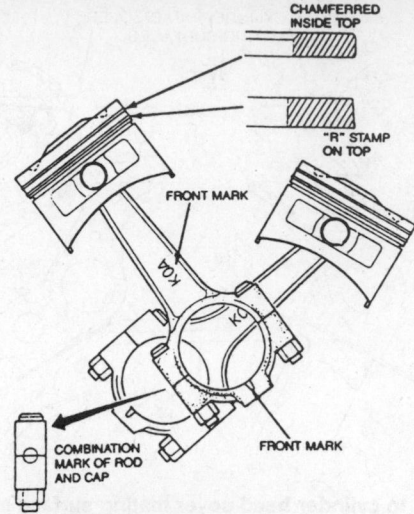

Piston and connecting rod assembly— 3.0L SHO engine

ENGINE LUBRICATION

Oil Pan

REMOVAL & INSTALLATION

2.5L Engine

1. Disconnect the negative battery cable. Raise the vehicle and support safely.
2. Drain the crankcase and drain the cooling system by removing the lower radiator hose.
3. Disconnect the starter cable and remove the starter.
4. Disconnect the exhaust pipe from oil pan.
5. Remove the engine coolant tube located at the lower radiator hose, water pump and at the tabs on the oil pan. Position air conditioner line off to the side. Remove the retaining bolts and remove the oil pan.

To install:
6. Clean both mating surfaces of oil pan and cylinder block making certain all traces of RTV sealant are removed.
7. Remove and clean oil pump pick-up tube and screen assembly. After cleaning, install tube and screen assembly.
8. Fill the oil pan groove with RTV sealer; the bead should be approximately ⅛ in. above the surface of the pan rail. Immediately (within 5 minutes) install the oil pan.
9. Install and tighten the 2 oil pan-to-transaxle bolts to 30–39 ft. lbs. (40–50 Nm) to align the pan with the transaxle then back off ½ turn.
10. Tighten the pan flange bolts to 6–9 ft. lbs. (8–12 Nm).

11. Tighten the 2 oil pan-to-transaxle bolts to 30–39 ft. lbs. (40–50 Nm).
12. Install the remaining components in the reverse order of their removal.
13. Fill the crankcase and cooling system to the proper level.
14. Start the engine and inspect for leaks.

3.0L Except SHO Engine

1. Disconnect the negative battery cable and remove the oil level dipstick.
2. Raise the vehicle and support safely. If equipped with a low level sensor, remove the retainer clip at the sensor. Remove the electrical connector from the sensor.
3. Drain the crankcase. Remove the starter motor and disconnect the electrical connector from the oxygen sensor.
4. Remove the catalyst and pipe assembly. Remove the lower engine/flywheel dust cover from the torque converter housing.
5. Remove the oil pan attaching bolts and slowly remove the oil pan from the engine block. Remove the oil pan gasket.

To install:
6. Clean the gasket surfaces on the cylinder block and oil pan. Apply a ¼ in. bead of silicone sealer to the junction of the rear main bearing cap and cylinder block junction of the front cover assembly and cylinder block.

NOTE: When using a silicone sealer, the assembly process should occur within 15 minutes after the sealer has been applied. After this time, the sealer may start to set-up and its sealing effectiveness may be affected.

7. Position the oil pan gasket over the oil pan and secure the gasket with a suitable sealer contact adhesive.
8. Position the oil pan on the engine block. Install the oil pan attaching bolts and tighten the bolts to 8–10 ft. lbs. (10–14 Nm). Back off all bolts and retighten.
9. Install the lower engine/flywheel dust cover to the torque converter housing. Install the catalyst and pipe assembly. Connect the oxygen sensor connector.
10. Install the starter motor. Install the low oil level sensor connector to the sensor and install the retainer clip. Lower the vehicle and replace the oil level dipstick.
11. Connect the negative battery cable. Fill the crankcase. Start the engine and check for oil and exhaust leaks.

3.0L SHO Engine

1. Disconnect the negative battery cable.
2. Remove the oil level dipstick.
3. Remove the accessory drive belts.
4. Remove the timing belt.
5. Raise the vehicle and support it safely.
6. If equipped with a low oil level sensor, remove the retainer clip and the electrical connector from the sensor.
7. Drain the engine oil.
8. Remove the starter motor.
9. Disconnect the oxygen sensors.
10. Remove the catalyst and pipe assembly.
11. Remove the lower flywheel dust cover from the converter housing.
12. Remove the oil pan attaching bolts and the oil pan.
To install:
13. Clean the gasket surfaces of the cylinder block and the oil pan.
14. Position the oil pan gasket on the oil pan and secure with silicone sealer.
15. Position the oil pan and tighten the retaining bolts to 11–16 ft. lbs. (15–23 Nm).
16. Install the lower engine/flywheel dust cover to the converter housing.
17. Install the catalyst and pipe assembly and connect the oxygen sensors.
18. Install the starter and connect the low oil level sensor connector to the sensor. Install the retainer clip.
19. Lower the vehicle and install the accessory drive belts.
20. Replace the oil level dipstick and connect the negative battery cable.
21. Fill the crankcase with the proper type and quantity of oil. Start the vehicle and check for leaks.

3.8L Engine

1. Disconnect the negative battery cable.
2. Raise the vehicle and support safely.
3. Drain the crankcase and remove the oil filter element.
4. Remove the catalytic converter assembly, starter motor and converter housing cover.
5. Remove the retaining bolts and remove the oil pan.
To install:
6. Clean the gasket surfaces on cylinder block, oil pan and oil pickup tube.
7. Trial fit oil pan to cylinder block. Ensure enough clearance has been provided to allow oil pan to be installed without sealant being scraped off when pan is positioned under engine.
8. Apply a bead of silicone sealer to the oil pan flange. Also apply a bead of sealer to the front cover/cylinder block

joint and fill the grooves on both sides of the rear main seal cap.

NOTE: When using silicone rubber sealer, assembly must occur within 15 minutes after sealer application. After this time, the sealer may start to harden and its sealing effectiveness may be reduced.

9. Install the oil pan and secure to the block with the attaching screws. Tighten the screws to 7–9 ft. lbs. (9–12 Nm).
10. Install a new oil filter element. Install the torque converter housing cover and starter motor.
11. Install the catalytic converter assembly and lower the vehicle.
12. Fill the crankcase and connect the negative battery cable.
13. Start the engine and check for leaks.

Oil Pump

REMOVAL & INSTALLATION

2.5L Engine

1. Remove the oil pan.
2. Remove oil pump attaching bolts and remove oil pump and intermediate driveshaft.
To install:
3. Prime oil pump by filling inlet port with engine oil. Rotate pump shaft until oil flows from outlet port.
4. If screen and cover assembly have been removed, replace gasket. Clean screen and reinstall screen and cover assembly. Tighten attaching bolts to 15–22 ft. lbs. (20–30 Nm).
5. Position intermediate driveshaft into distributor socket.
6. Insert intermediate driveshaft into oil pump. Install pump and shaft as an assembly.

NOTE: Do not attempt to force the pump into position if it will not seat. The shaft hex may be mis-aligned with the distributor shaft. To align, remove the oil pump and rotate the intermediate driveshaft into a new position.

7. Tighten the oil pump attaching bolts to 15–22 ft. lbs. (20–30 Nm).
8. Install the oil pan.
9. Fill the crankcase. Start engine and check for leaks.

3.0L Except SHO Engine

1. Remove the oil pan.
2. Remove the oil pump attaching bolts. Lift the oil pump off the engine and withdraw the oil pump driveshaft.
To install:
3. Prime the oil pump by filling either the inlet or the outlet port with

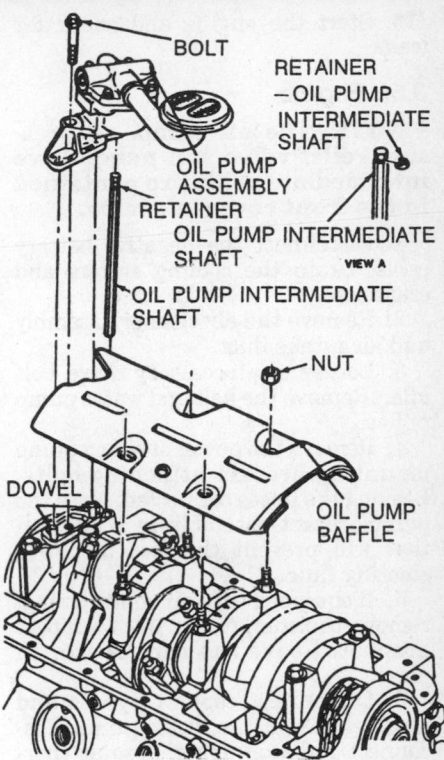

Oil pump installation—3.0L engine

engine oil. Rotate the pump shaft to distribute the oil within the oil pump body cavity.
4. Insert the oil pump intermediate shaft assembly into the hex drive hole in the oil pump assembly until the retainer "clicks" into place. Place the oil pump in the proper position and install the retaining bolt.
5. Torque the oil pump retaining bolt to 35 ft. lbs. (48 Nm).
6. Install the oil pan with new gasket.
7. Fill the crankcase. Start engine and check for leaks.

3.0L SHO Engine

1. Remove the oil pan.
2. Remove the crankshaft timing belt sprocket.
3. Remove the sump to oil pump bolts.
4. Remove the oil pump to block bolts and remove the pump.
To install:
5. Align the oil pump on the crankshaft and install the oil pump retaining bolts. Tighten the bolts to 11–17 ft. lbs. (15–23 Nm).
6. Install the oil sump to oil pump retaining bolts and tighten to 6–8 ft. lbs. (7–11 Nm).
7. Install the crankshaft timing belt sprocket.
8. Install the oil pan with a new gasket.
9. Fill the crankcase with the proper type and quantity of oil.

10. Start the engine and check for leaks.

3.8L Engine

NOTE: **The oil pump, oil pressure relief valve and pump drive intermediate shaft are contained in the front cover assembly.**

1. Disconnect the negative battery cable. Drain the cooling system and crankcase.

2. Remove the air cleaner assembly and air intake duct.

3. Loosen the accessory drive belt idler. Remove the belt and water pump pulley.

4. Remove the power steering pump mounting bracket attaching bolts. Leaving the hoses connected, place the pump/bracket assembly in a position that will prevent the loss of power steering fluid.

5. If equipped with air conditioning, remove the compressor front support bracket. Leave the compressor in place.

6. Disconnect coolant bypass and heater hoses at the water pump. Disconnect radiator upper hose at thermostat housing.

7. Disconnect the coil wire from distributor cap and remove cap with secondary wires attached. Remove the distributor hold-down clamp and lift distributor out of the front cover.

8. Raise the vehicle and support safely.

9. Remove the crankshaft damper and pulley.

NOTE: **If the crankshaft pulley and vibration damper have to be separated, mark the damper and pulley so they may be reassembled in the same relative position. This is important as the damper and pulley are initially balanced as a unit. If the crankshaft damper is being replaced, check if the original damper has balance pins installed. If so, new balance pins (E0SZ–6A328–A or equivalent) must be installed on the new damper in the same position as the original damper. The crankshaft pulley must also be installed in original installation position.**

10. Remove the oil filter, disconnect the radiator lower hose at the water pump and remove the oil pan.

11. Lower the vehicle.

12. Remove the front cover.

NOTE: **Do not overlook the cover attaching bolt located behind the oil filter adapter. The front cover will break if pried upon if all attaching bolts are not removed.**

13. Remove the oil pump cover attaching bolts and remove the cover. Lift the pump gears off the front cover pocket. Remove the cover gasket and replace with new.

To install:

14. Clean the front cover oil pump gasket contact surface. Place a straightedge across the oil pump cover mounting surface and check for wear or warpage using a feeler gauge. If the surface is out of flat by more than 0.0016 in. (0.04mm), replace the cover.

15. Lightly pack the gear pocket with petroleum jelly or coat all pump gear surfaces with oil conditioner.

16. Install the gears in the pocket. Make certain the petroleum jelly fills the gap between the gears and the pocket.

NOTE: **Failure to properly coat the oil pump gears may result in failure of the pump to prime when the engine is started.**

17. Position the oil pump cover gasket and install the oil pump cover. Tighten the oil pump cover retaining bolts to 18–22 ft. lbs. (25–30 Nm).

18. Clean the gasket surfaces of the front cover and cylinder block.

19. Position a new gasket and the front cover on the cylinder block.

20. Install the front cover attaching bolts. Apply Loctite® or equivalent, to the threads of the bolt installed below the oil filter housing prior to installation. This bolt is to be installed and tightened last. Tighten all bolts to 15–22 ft. lbs. (20–30 Nm).

21. Raise the vehicle and support safely.

22. Install the oil pan. Connect the radiator lower hose. Install a new oil filter.

23. Coat the crankshaft damper sealing surface with clean engine oil.

24. Position the crankshaft pulley key in the crankshaft keyway.

25. Install the damper with damper washer and attaching bolt. Tighten the bolt to 104–132 ft. lbs. (140–180 Nm).

26. Install the crankshaft pulley and tighten the attaching bolts 19–28 ft. lbs. (26–28 Nm).

27. Lower the vehicle.

28. Connect the coolant bypass hose.

29. Rotate the crankshaft, as necessary, to bring the piston in No. 1 cylinder to TDC on the compression stroke. Install the distributor with rotor pointing at No. 1 distributor cap tower. Install the distributor cap and coil wire.

30. Connect the radiator upper hose at thermostat housing.

31. Connect the heater hose.

32. If equipped with air conditioning, install compressor and mounting brackets.

33. Install the power steering pump and mounting brackets.

34. Position the accessory drive belt over the pulleys.

35. Install the water pump pulley. Position the accessory drive belt over water pump pulley and tighten the belt.

36. Connect battery ground cable. Fill the crankcase and cooling system to the proper level.

37. Start the engine and check for leaks.

38. Check the ignition timing and curb idle speed, adjust as required.

39. Install the air cleaner assembly and air intake duct.

CHECKING

2.5L and 3.0L Engines

1. Remove the oil pump from the vehicle. Disassemble the pump, clean the parts in a suitable solvent and allow to dry.

2. Inspect the inside of the pump housing for damage or excessive wear.

3. Check the mating surface for wear. Minor scuff marks are normal but if the cover, gears or housing are excessively worn, scored or grooved, replace the pump.

4. Inspect the rotor for nicks, burrs, or score marks. Remove minor imperfections with an oil stone.

5. Measure the inner-to-outer rotor tip clearance. The clearance must not exceed 0.012 in. (0.30mm) with a feeler gauge inserted ½ in. minimum with the rotors removed from the pump housing.

6. With the rotor assembly installed in the housing, place a straight edge across the rotor assembly and housing. Measure the clearance (rotor endplay) between the the inner and outer rotors. The clearance is 0.005 in. (0.13mm) maximum.

7. Check the relief valve spring tension. It should be 15.2–17.2 lbs. at 1.2 in. on 2.5L engine or 9.1–10.1 lbs. at 1.11 in. on 3.0L engine. If the spring is worn or damaged, replace the pump. Check the relief valve piston for freedom of movement in the bore.

3.0L SHO Engine

1. Remove the oil pump from the vehicle. Disassemble the pump, clean the parts in a suitable solvent and allow to dry.

2. Inspect the inside of the pump housing for damage or excessive wear.

3. Check the mating surface for wear. Minor scuff marks are normal but if the cover, gears or housing are excessively worn, scored or grooved, replace the pump.

4. Check the inner rotor tip-to-outer rotor tip clearance using a feeler

gauge. The clearance must not exceed 0.0024–0.0071 in. (0.06–0.18mm) with the feeler gauge inserted ½ in. (12.7mm) minimum and the rotors removed from the pump housing.

5. With the rotor assembly installed in the pump housing, place a straight-edge over the rotor assembly and the housing. Measure the clearance (rotor endplay) between the straight-edge and the rotor and outer race. The clearance should be 0.0012–0.0035 in. (0.03–0.09mm).

6. Check the relief valve spring tension. It should be 34.5 lbs. per inch. If the spring is worn or damaged, replace the pump. Check the relief valve piston for freedom of movement in the bore.

3.8L Engine
PUMP GEAR END CLEARANCE

1. Inspect the pump cover mating surface on the front cover and pump body. Visually inspect the O-ring for any cuts and/or nicks and replace, if necessary. Remove any burrs or nicks.

2. Measure the thickness of the gear using a micrometer. The gear should measure 1.19–1.20 in. (30.455–30.480mm) thick.

3. If the gear is less than the specified minimum thickness, replace the gear. If the gear thickness is within specification, it may be necessary to replace the pump body. If the gear thickness is within the specified limits, proceed to Step 4.

4. Measure the depth of the gear pocket in the oil pump body. The depth should be 1.200–1.202 in. (30.49–30.54mm).

5. If the depth is more than 1.202 in. (30.54mm), replace the oil pump body.

PUMP GEAR SIDE CLEARANCE

1. Measure the side clearance by inserting a feeler gauge between the gear tooth and the side wall of the gear pocket.

2. The clearance should be a maximum of 0.005 in. (0.13mm) and the gears should be free to turn. If the clearance is greater than 0.005 in. (0.13mm), proceed to Step 3.

3. Measure the diameter of the gear using a micrometer. The gear should be 1.505–1.509 in. (38.252–38.332mm) wide.

4. If the gear is less than 1.505 in. (38.252mm) in diameter, replace the gear and measure the clearance as in Step 1. If the diameter of the gear is within the specified limits, go to Step 5.

5. Measure the diameter of the gear pocket in the front cover. The diameter should be 1.504–1.507 in. (38.22–38.30mm). If the diameter is less than

1.504 in. (38.22mm), replace the front cover and measure the clearance as in Step 1.

Rear Main Bearing Oil Seal

REMOVAL & INSTALLATION

1. Disconnect the negative battery cable.
2. Raise the vehicle and support it safely. Remove the transaxle.
3. Remove flywheel. Remove the cover plate, if necessary.
4. With a suitable tool, remove the oil seal.

NOTE: Use caution to avoid damaging the oil seal surface.

To install:

5. Inspect the crankshaft seal area for any damage which may cause the seal to leak. If damage is evident, service or replace the crankshaft as necessary.
6. Coat the crankshaft seal area and the seal lip with engine oil.
7. Using a seal installer tool, install the seal. Tighten the 2 bolts of the seal installer tool evenly so the seal is straight and seats without misalignment.
8. Install the flywheel. Tighten attaching bolts to 54–64 ft. lbs. (73–87 Nm) on all except the 3.0L SHO engine. On the 3.0L SHO engine, tighten the bolts in 2 steps, first to 29–43 ft. lbs. (39–50 Nm) and then to 51–58 ft. lbs. (69–78 Nm).
9. Install rear cover plate, if necessary.
10. Install the transaxle and connect the negative battery cable.

LUBRICATE SEAL and SEAL MATING SURFACE WITH OIL — FRONT OF ENGINE

CYLINDER BLOCK

REAR MAIN INSTALLER

SEAL (INSTALL WITH SPRING SIDE TOWARD ENGINE)

NOTE: REAR FACE OF SEAL MUST BE WITHIN 0.005 IN. (0.127MM) OF THE REAR FACE OF THE BLOCK

Rear main oil seal installation—3.8L engine

ENGINE COOLING

Radiator

REMOVAL & INSTALLATION

———— **CAUTION** ————

Never remove the radiator cap while the engine is running or personal injury from scalding hot coolant or steam may result. If possible, wait until the engine has cooled to remove the radiator cap. If this is not possible, wrap a thick cloth around the radiator cap and turn it slowly to the first stop. Step back while the pressure is released from the cooling system. When it is certain all the pressure has been released, press down on the cap, still with the cloth, and turn and remove it.

1. Disconnect the negative battery cable.
2. Drain the cooling system by removing the radiator cap and opening the draincock located at the lower rear corner of the radiator inlet tank.
3. Remove the rubber overflow tube from the coolant recovery bottle and detach it from the radiator. On Taurus SHO, disconnect the tube from the radiator and remove the recovery bottle.
4. Remove 2 upper shroud retaining screws and lift the shroud out of the lower retaining clips.
5. Disconnect the electric cooling fan motor wires and remove the fan and shroud assembly.
6. Loosen the upper and lower hose clamps at the radiator and remove the hoses from the radiator connectors.
7. If equipped with an automatic transaxle, disconnect the transmission oil cooling lines from the radiator fittings using disconnect tool T82L–9500–AH or equivalent.
8. If equipped with 3.0L or 3.0L SHO engine, remove 2 radiator upper retaining screws. If equipped with the 3.8L engine, remove 2 hex nuts from the right radiator support bracket and 2 screws from the left radiator support bracket and remove the brackets.
9. Tilt the radiator rearward approximately 1 in. and lift it directly upward, clear of the radiator support.
10. Remove the radiator lower support rubber pads, if pad replacement is necessary.

To install:

11. Position the radiator lower support rubber pads to the lower support, if removed.
12. Position the radiator into the engine compartment and to the radiator support. Insert the moulded pins at

the bottom of each tank through the slotted holes in the lower support rubber pads.

13. Make sure the plastic pads on the bottom of the radiator tanks are resting on the rubber pads. Install 2 upper retaining bolts to attach the radiator to the radiator support. Tighten the bolts to 46–60 inch lbs. (5–7 Nm). If equipped with the 3.8L engine, tighten the bolts to 13–20 ft. lbs. (17–27 Nm).

14. If equipped with the 3.8L engine, fasten the left radiator support bracket to the radiator support with 2 screws. Tighten the screws to 8.7–17.7 ft. lbs. (11.8–24 Nm). Attach the right support bracket to the radiator support with 2 hex nuts. Tighten the nuts to 8.7–17.7 ft. lbs. (11.8–24 Nm).

15. Attach the radiator upper and lower hoses to the radiator. Position the hose on the radiator connector so the index arrow on the hose is in line with the mark on the connector. Tighten the clamps to 20–30 inch lbs. (2.3–3.4 Nm) if equipped with the 2.5L or 3.0L engine. If equipped with the 3.8L or 3.0L SHO engines, install constant tension hose clamps between the alignment marks on the hoses.

16. If equipped with automatic transaxle, connect the transmission cooler lines using oil resistant pipe sealer.

17. Install the fan and shroud assembly by connecting the fan motor wiring and positioning the assembly on the lower retainer clips. Attach the top of the shroud to the radiator with 2 screw, nut and washer assemblies. Tighten to 35 inch lbs. (4 Nm).

18. Attach the rubber overflow tube to the radiator filler neck overflow nipple and coolant recovery bottle. On Taurus SHO, install the coolant recovery bottle and connect the overflow hose.

19. Refill the cooling system. If the coolant is being replaced, refill with a 50/50 mixture of water and antifreeze. Connect the negative battery cable. Operate the engine for 15 minutes and check for leaks. Check the coolant level and add, as required.

Electric Cooling Fan

TESTING

1. Disconnect the wiring connector from the fan motor.
2. Connect a jumper wire from the positive terminal of the battery to one of the terminals in the cooling fan electrical connector.
3. Ground the other connector terminal.
4. If the cooling fan does not function, it must be replaced.
5. If the cooling fan functions but

does not run during normal engine operation, check the cooling fan temperature sensor and the integrated relay control assembly.

REMOVAL & INSTALLATION

1. Disconnect the negative battery cable.
2. Remove the radiator sight shield.
3. Disconnect the electrical connector and remove the integrated relay control assembly located on the radiator support.
4. Disconnect the fan electrical connector.
5. If necessary, remove the air bag crash sensor.
6. Unbolt the fan/shroud assembly from the radiator and remove.
7. Remove the retainer and the fan from the motor shaft and unbolt the fan motor from the shroud.
8. Installation is the reverse of the removal procedure.

Heater Core

REMOVAL & INSTALLATION

Without Air Conditioning
TAURUS AND SABLE

1. Disconnect the negative battery cable.
2. Remove the instrument panel on 1989 vehicles as follows:
   a. Remove the 4 screws retaining the steering column opening cover and remove the cover.
   b. Remove the sound insulator under the glove compartment by removing the 2 push nuts securing the insulator to the studs on the climate control case.
   c. Remove the steering column trim shrouds and disconnect all electrical connections from the steering column switches.
   d. Remove the 4 screws at the steering column bracket to remove the steering column.
   e. Remove the screws retaining the lower left and radio finish panels and remove the panels by snapping out.
   f. Remove the cluster opening finish panel retaining screws. On Taurus remove 1 jam nut behind the headlight switch and 1 screw behind the clock or clock cover. Remove the finish panel by rocking the upper edge toward the driver.
   g. Disconnect the speedometer cable by reaching up under the instrument panel and pressing on the flat surface of the plastic connector. The panel can be removed with the cluster installed.

   h. Release the glove compartment assembly by depressing the side of the glove compartment bin and swinging the door/bin down.
   i. Using the steering column, cluster and glove compartment openings and by reaching under the instrument panel, tag and disconnect all electrical connections, vacuum hoses, heater control cables and the radio antenna cable.
   j. Disconnect all underhood electrical connectors of the main wire loom. Disengage the rubber grommet from the dash panel and push the wire and connectors into the instrument panel area.
   k. Remove the right and left speaker opening covers by snapping out.
   l. Remove the 2 lower instrument panel-to-cowl side retaining screws from the right and left side. Remove the 1 instrument panel brace retaining screw from under the radio area. On Sable, remove the defroster grille by snapping out.
   m. Remove the 3 instrument panel upper retaining screws and remove the instrument panel.
3. Remove the instrument panel on 1990–91 vehicles as follows:
   a. Position the front wheels in the straight-ahead position.
   b. Remove the ignition lock cylinder and, if equipped, remove the tilt lever.
   c. Remove the steering column trim shrouds. Disconnect all electrical connections from the steering column switches.
   d. Remove the 4 bolts and opening cover and the 2 bolts and reinforcement from under the steering column.
   e. Disengage the insulator retainer and remove the insulator. Remove the 4 nuts and reinforcement from under the steering column.

NOTE: Do not rotate the steering column shaft.

   f. Remove the 4 nuts retaining the steering column to the instrument panel, disconnect the shift indicator cable and lower the column on the front seat. Install the lock cylinder to make sure the steering column shaft does not turn.
   g. Remove 1 bolt at the steering column opening attaching the instrument panel to the brace. Remove 1 instrument panel brace retaining bolt from under the radio area.
   h. Remove the sound insulator under the glove compartment by removing the 2 push nuts that secure the insulator to the studs on the climate control case.

i. Disconnect the wires of the main wire loom in the engine compartment. Disengage the rubber grommet from the dash panel, then feed the wiring through the hole in the dash panel into the passenger compartment.

j. Remove the right and left cowl side trim panels. Disconnect the wires from the instrument panel at the right and left cowl sides.

k. Remove 1 screw each from the left and right side retaining the instrument panel. Pull up to unsnap the right and left speaker opening covers and remove.

l. Release the glove compartment assembly by depressing the side of the glove compartment bin and swinging the door/bin down.

m. Using the steering column and glove compartment openings and by reaching under the instrument panel, tag and disconnect all electrical connections, vacuum hoses, heater control cables, speedometer cable and radio antenna cable.

n. Close the glove compartment door, support the panel and remove the 3 screws attaching the top of the instrument panel to the cowl top and disconnect any remaining wires. Remove the panel from the vehicle.

4. Remove the instrument panel on 1992–93 vehicles as follows:

a. Position the front wheels in the straight-ahead position and apply the parking brake.

b. Remove the ignition lock cylinder.

c. If equipped, tilt the column to the full down position and remove the tilt lever.

d. Remove the 4 bolts and opening cover from under the steering column. Remove the steering column trim shrouds.

e. Disconnect the electrical connectors from the combination switch and remove the switch.

f. Pull the gear shift lever to the full down position.

g. Remove the cluster opening finish panel retaining screws. Pull the panel toward the driver to unsnap the snap-in retainers and disconnect the wiring from the switches, clock and warning lights.

h. Remove the 2 bolts and reinforcement from under the steering column. Disengage the insulator retainer and remove the insulator.

i. Remove the 4 nuts and absorber assembly from under the steering column.

NOTE: Do not rotate the steering column shaft.

j. Disconnect the parking brake release cable and wiring connector from the parking brake and ignition switch wiring connector.

k. Remove the 4 nuts retaining the steering column to the support, disconnect the shift position indicator cable if equipped with column shift and lower the column on the front seat. Cover the front seat to protect from damage.

l. Install the lock cylinder to make sure the steering column shaft does not turn.

m. Remove the 4 retaining screws from the cluster, disconnect the wiring and remove.

n. Remove the 1 bolt at the steering column opening attaching the instrument panel to the brace. Remove the 1 instrument panel brace retaining bolt from under the radio area.

o. Remove the sound insulator under the glove compartment by removing the 2 pushnuts that secure the insulator to the studs on the climate control case.

p. Remove the 3 screws attaching the glove compartment assembly to the instrument panel and remove the door assembly.

q. Remove the air cleaner, battery and battery tray. Disconnect the main wire loom in the engine compartment. Disengage the rubber grommet from the dash panel, then feed the wiring through the hole in the dash panel into the passenger compartment.

r. Remove the right and left cowl side trim panels. Disconnect the wires from the instrument panel at the right and left cowl sides.

s. Support the panel and remove the 3 screws attaching the top of the panel to the cowl top and disconnect any remaining wires. remove the instrument panel and lay it on the front seat.

5. Drain the coolant from the radiator.

6. Disconnect and plug the heater hoses at the heater core. Plug the heater core tubes.

7. Disconnect the vacuum supply hose from the in-line vacuum check valve in the engine compartment. Remove the screw holding the instrument panel shake brace to the heater case and remove the shake brace.

8. Remove the floor register and rear floor ducts from the bottom of the heater case. Remove the 3 nuts attaching the heater case to the dash panel in the engine compartment.

9. Remove the 2 screws attaching the brackets to the cowl top panel. Pull the heater case assembly away from the dash panel and remove from the vehicle.

10. Remove the vacuum source line from the heater core tube seal and re-

move the seal from the heater core tubes.

11. Remove the 4 heater core access cover attaching screws and remove the access cover from the heater case. Lift the heater core and seals from the heater case.

To install:

12. Transfer the 3 foam core seals to the new heater core. Install the heater core and seals into the heater case.

13. Position the heater case access cover on the case and install the 4 screws.

14. Install the seal on the heater core tubes and install the vacuum source line through the seal.

15. Position the heater case assembly to the dash panel and cowl top panel at the air inlet opening. Install the 2 screws to attach the support brackets to the cowl top panel.

16. Install the 3 nuts in the engine compartment to attach the heater case to the dash panel. Install the floor register and rear floor ducts on the bottom of the heater case.

17. Install the instrument panel shake brace and screw to the heater case. Install the instrument panel by reversing the removal procedure.

18. Connect the heater hoses to the heater core. Connect the black vacuum supply hose to the vacuum check valve in the engine compartment.

19. Fill the radiator and bleed the cooling system.

20. Connect the negative battery cable and check the system for proper operation.

With Air Conditioning

NOTE: It is necessary to remove the evaporator case in order to remove the heater core. Whenever an evaporator case is removed, it will be necessary to replace the suction accumulator/drier.

TAURUS AND SABLE

1. Disconnect the negative battery cable.

2. Remove the instrument panel on 1989 vehicles as follows:

a. Remove the 4 screws retaining the steering column opening cover and remove the cover.

b. Remove the sound insulator under the glove compartment by removing the 2 push nuts securing the insulator to the studs on the climate control case.

c. Remove the steering column trim shrouds and disconnect all electrical connections from the steering column switches.

d. Remove the 4 screws at the steering column bracket to remove the steering column.

e. Remove the screws retaining the lower left and radio finish panels and remove the panels by snapping out.

f. Remove the cluster opening finish panel retaining screws. On Taurus remove 1 jam nut behind the headlight switch and 1 screw behind the clock or clock cover. Remove the finish panel by rocking the upper edge toward the driver.

g. Disconnect the speedometer cable by reaching up under the instrument panel and pressing on the flat surface of the plastic connector. The panel can be removed with the cluster installed.

h. Release the glove compartment assembly by depressing the side of the glove compartment bin and swinging the door/bin down.

i. Using the steering column, cluster and glove compartment openings and by reaching under the instrument panel, tag and disconnect all electrical connections, vacuum hoses, heater/air conditioner control cables and the radio antenna cable.

j. Disconnect all underhood electrical connectors of the main wire loom. Disengage the rubber grommet from the dash panel and push the wire and connectors into the instrument panel area.

k. Remove the right and left speaker opening covers by snapping out.

l. Remove the 2 lower instrument panel-to-cowl side retaining screws from the right and left side. Remove the 1 instrument panel brace retaining screw from under the radio area. On Sable, remove the defroster grille by snapping out.

m. Remove the 3 instrument panel upper retaining screws and remove the instrument panel.

3. Remove the instrument panel on 1990–91 vehicles as follows:

a. Position the front wheels in the straight-ahead position.

b. Remove the ignition lock cylinder and, if equipped, remove the tilt lever.

c. Remove the steering column trim shrouds. Disconnect all electrical connections from the steering column switches.

d. Remove the 4 bolts and opening cover and the 2 bolts and reinforcement from under the steering column.

e. Disengage the insulator retainer and remove the insulator. Remove the 4 nuts and reinforcement from under the steering column.

NOTE: Do not rotate the steering column shaft.

f. Remove the 4 nuts retaining the steering column to the instrument panel, disconnect the shift indicator cable and lower the column on the front seat. Install the lock cylinder to make sure the steering column shaft does not turn.

g. Remove 1 bolt at the steering column opening attaching the instrument panel to the brace. Remove 1 instrument panel brace retaining bolt from under the radio area.

h. Remove the sound insulator under the glove compartment by removing the 2 push nuts that secure the insulator to the studs on the climate control case.

i. Disconnect the wires of the main wire loom in the engine compartment. Disengage the rubber grommet from the dash panel, then feed the wiring through the hole in the dash panel into the passenger compartment.

j. Remove the right and left cowl side trim panels. Disconnect the wires from the instrument panel at the right and left cowl sides.

k. Remove 1 screw each from the left and right side retaining the instrument panel. Pull up to unsnap the right and left speaker opening covers and remove.

l. Release the glove compartment assembly by depressing the side of the glove compartment bin and swinging the door/bin down.

m. Using the steering column and glove compartment openings and by reaching under the instrument panel, tag and disconnect all electrical connections, vacuum hoses, heater/air conditioner control cables, speedometer cable and radio antenna cable.

n. Close the glove compartment door, support the panel and remove the 3 screws attaching the top of the instrument panel to the cowl top and disconnect any remaining wires. Remove the panel from the vehicle.

4. Remove the instrument panel on 1992–93 vehicles as follows:

a. Position the front wheels in the straight-ahead position and apply the parking brake.

b. Remove the ignition lock cylinder.

c. If equipped, tilt the column to the full down position and remove the tilt lever.

d. Remove the 4 bolts and opening cover from under the steering column. Remove the steering column trim shrouds.

e. Disconnect the electrical connectors from the combination switch and remove the switch.

f. Pull the gear shift lever to the full down position.

g. Remove the cluster opening finish panel retaining screws. Pull the panel toward the driver to unsnap the snap-in retainers and disconnect the wiring from the switches, clock and warning lights.

h. Remove the 2 bolts and reinforcement from under the steering column. Disengage the insulator retainer and remove the insulator.

i. Remove the 4 nuts and absorber assembly from under the steering column.

NOTE: Do not rotate the steering column shaft.

j. Disconnect the parking brake release cable and wiring connector from the parking brake and ignition switch wiring connector.

k. Remove the 4 nuts retaining the steering column to the support, disconnect the shift position indicator cable if equipped with column shift and lower the column on the front seat. Cover the front seat to protect from damage.

l. Install the lock cylinder to make sure the steering column shaft does not turn.

m. Remove the 4 retaining screws from the cluster, disconnect the wiring and remove.

n. Remove the 1 bolt at the steering column opening attaching the instrument panel to the brace. Remove the 1 instrument panel brace retaining bolt from under the radio area.

o. Remove the sound insulator under the glove compartment by removing the 2 pushnuts that secure the insulator to the studs on the climate control case.

p. Remove the 3 screws attaching the glove compartment assembly to the instrument panel and remove the door assembly.

q. Remove the air cleaner, battery and battery tray. Disconnect the main wire loom in the engine compartment. Disengage the rubber grommet from the dash panel, then feed the wiring through the hole in the dash panel into the passenger compartment.

r. Remove the right and left cowl side trim panels. Disconnect the wires from the instrument panel at the right and left cowl sides.

s. Support the panel and remove the 3 screws attaching the top of the panel to the cowl top and disconnect any remaining wires. remove the instrument panel and lay it on the front seat.

5. Drain the coolant from the radiator. Properly discharge the air conditioning system.

6. Disconnect and plug the heater hoses at the heater core. Plug the heater core tubes.

7. Disconnect the vacuum supply hose from the in-line vacuum check valve in the engine compartment.

8. Disconnect the air conditioning lines from the evaporator core at the dash panel. Cap the lines and the core to prevent entrance of dirt and moisture.

9. Remove the screw holding the instrument panel shake brace to the evaporator case and remove the shake brace.

10. Remove the 2 screws attaching the floor register and rear seat duct to the bottom of the evaporator case. Remove the 3 nuts attaching the evaporator case to the dash panel in the engine compartment.

11. Remove the 2 screws attaching the support brackets to the cowl top panel. Carefully pull the evaporator assembly away from the dash panel and remove the evaporator case from the vehicle.

12. Remove the vacuum source line from the heater core tube seal and remove the seal from the heater core tubes.

13. If equipped with automatic temperature control, remove the 3 screws attaching the blend door actuator to the evaporator case and remove the actuator.

14. Remove the 4 heater core access cover attaching screws and remove the access cover and seal from the evaporator case. Lift the heater core and seals from the evaporator case.

To install:

15. Transfer the seal to the new heater core. Install the heater core into the evaporator case.

16. Position the heater core access cover on the evaporator case and install the 4 attaching screws. If equipped with automatic temperature control, position the blend door actuator to the blend door shaft and install the 3 attaching screws.

17. Install the seal on the heater core tubes and install the vacuum source line through the seal.

18. Position the evaporator case assembly to the dash panel and cowl top panel at the air inlet opening. Install the 2 screws attaching the support brackets to the cowl top panel.

19. Install the 3 nuts in the engine compartment attaching the evaporator case to the dash panel. Install the floor register and rear seat duct to the evaporator case and tighten the 2 attaching screws.

20. Install the instrument panel shake brace and screw to the evaporator case. Install the instrument panel in the reverse order of removal.

21. Connect the air conditioning lines to the evaporator core and the heater hoses to the heater core.

22. Connect the black vacuum supply hose to the vacuum check valve in the engine compartment.

23. Fill and bleed the cooling system. Connect the negative battery cable.

24. Leak test, evacuate and charge the air conditioning system. Observe all safety precautions.

25. Check the system for proper operation.

CONTINENTAL

1. Disconnect both battery cables. On 1992–93 vehicles, wait 1 minute for the backup power supply in the air bag diagnostic monitor to deplete its stored energy.

2. Remove the instrument panel as follows:

a. Open the glove compartment door and depress the sides inward. Lower the glove compartment assembly toward the floor. On 1990–91 vehicles, disconnect the air bag backup power supply located to the right of the glove compartment opening.

NOTE: The backup power supply allows air bag deployment if the battery or battery cables are damaged in an accident before the crash sensors close. The power supply is a capacitor that will leak down in approximately 15 minutes after the battery is disconnected or in 1 minute if the battery positive cable is grounded. The backup power supply must be disconnected before any air bag related service is performed.

b. Remove the 4 nut and washer assemblies retaining the driver air bag module to the steering wheel. Disconnect the driver air bag module connector and attach a jumper wire to the air bag terminals on the clockspring. Remove the air bag from the vehicle.

c. Disconnect the passenger air bag connector. On 1989–91 vehicles, attach a jumper wire to the air bag terminals on the wiring harness side of the passenger air bag module connector. On 1992–93 vehicles, attach air bag simulator tool 105–00008 or equivalent, to the vehicle harness connector. Remove the 4 bolts/screws attaching the passenger air bag module to the instrument panel and remove the air bag from the vehicle.

—— CAUTION ——

When carrying a live air bag module, make sure the bag and trim cover are pointed away from the body. In the unlikely event of an accidental deployment, the bag will then deploy with minimal chance of injury. In addition, when placing a live air bag module on a bench or other surface, always face the bag and trim cover up, away from the surface. This will reduce the motion of the module if it is accidentally deployed.

d. Remove the right finish moulding by pulling upward to unsnap the 6 clips. Disconnect the wiring. Remove the left finish moulding by pulling upward to unsnap the 2 clips.

e. Remove the right and left lower insulators. Remove the screws retaining the lower instrument panel steering column cover and remove the cover. Remove the 4 screws retaining the lower instrument panel steering column reinforcement and remove the reinforcement.

f. If equipped, remove the 4 retaining nuts and the absorber assembly. Remove the 3 screws retaining the upper steering column shroud and remove. Remove the tilt wheel lever.

g. Remove the lock cylinder by pushing a small Allen wrench into the groove located under the lock cylinder. Place the key into the ignition and gently wiggle to work the cylinder free.

h. Remove the lower steering column shroud by pulling out. Remove the bolt retaining the shift indicator cable to the steering column. Remove the steering wheel. Disconnect all electrical connectors.

i. Disconnect the hood and brake release cables. Remove the 4 nuts retaining the steering column and lower the column. Remove the screw(s) at the steering column opening retaining the instrument panel to the brake pedal support.

j. Remove the 2 screws under the ash tray that hold the instrument panel to the air conditioning plenum case. Remove the headlight switch knob.

k. Remove the 5 screws from the cluster opening finish panel and remove the panel. Remove the 4 screws retaining the air conditioning control. Disconnect the electrical connectors and 1 vacuum connector.

l. Remove the 4 screws retaining the cluster and disconnect the electrical connectors. Remove the 3 screws to remove the glove compartment assembly.

m. Remove the 2 screws from the instrument panel to cowl top brace and 1 screw from the passenger air bag support bracket. Remove both speaker grilles by snapping out to release. Remove the 2 screws seated in the plastic push clips and remove the center defrost grille.

n. Working under the hood, disconnect all electrical connectors of the main wire loom. Disengage the rubber grommet from the dash panel and feed the wiring and connectors through the hole into the instrument panel area.

o. Remove the 3 screws (2 located on the sill plate) at both right and left cowl trim panels and remove the panels. Disconnect the wiring at the right and left cowl side panels.

p. Remove the lower 2 screws from the instrument panel, 1 at each end. Remove the 3 upper instrument panel retaining screws and carefully lower the instrument panel.

q. Disconnect the remaining electrical and vacuum connectors and remove the instrument panel.

3. Drain the coolant from the radiator and properly discharge the refrigerant from the air conditioning system.

4. Disconnect and plug the heater hoses at the heater core. Plug the heater core tubes. Disconnect the vacuum supply hose from the in-line vacuum check valve in the engine compartment.

5. Disconnect the air conditioner lines from the evaporator core at the dash panel. Cap the lines and the core to prevent the entrance of dirt and moisture.

6. Remove the screw holding the instrument panel shake brace to the evaporator case. Remove the shake brace. Remove the 2 screws attaching the floor register to the evaporator case.

7. Disconnect the vacuum line, electrical connections and aspirator hose from the evaporator case.

8. Remove the 3 nuts retaining the evaporator case to the dash panel in the engine compartment. Remove the 2 screws retaining the support brackets to the cowl top panel.

9. Carefully pull the evaporator case assembly away from the dash panel and remove from the vehicle.

10. Remove the vacuum source line from the heater core tube seal. Remove the seal from the heater core tubes.

11. Remove the 3 screws attaching the blend door actuator to the evaporator case and remove the actuator.

12. Remove the 4 heater core access cover retaining screws and remove the access cover and seal from the evaporator case. Lift the heater core and seals from the evaporator case.

To install:

13. Transfer 3 foam core seals to the new heater core. Install the heater core in the evaporator case.

14. Position the heater core access cover on the evaporator case and install the 4 retaining screws.

15. Position the blend door actuator to the blend door shaft. Install the 3 retaining screws.

16. Install the seal on the heater core tubes. Install the vacuum source line through the seal.

17. Position the evaporator case assembly against the dash panel and cowl top panel at the air inlet opening. Install the 2 screws retaining the support brackets to the cowl top panel.

18. Install the 3 nuts in the engine compartment retaining the evaporator case to the dash panel. Install the floor register to the evaporator case and tighten the 2 retaining screws.

19. Connect the vacuum line, electrical connections and aspirator hose at the evaporator case. Install the instrument panel shake brace.

20. Install the instrument panel in the reverse order of removal.

21. Connect the air conditioner lines at the evaporator core and the heater hoses at the heater core. Connect the black vacuum supply hose to the vacuum check valve in the engine compartment.

22. Fill and bleed the cooling system. Connect the negative battery cable.

23. Leak test, evacuate and charge the air conditioning system. Observe all safety precautions.

24. Check the system for proper operation.

Water Pump

REMOVAL & INSTALLATION

2.5L Engine

1. Disconnect the negative battery cable.

2. Remove the radiator cap and position a drain pan under the bottom radiator hose.

3. Raise and support the vehicle safely. Remove the lower radiator hose from the radiator and drain the coolant into the drain pan.

4. Remove the water pump inlet tube. Loosen the belt tensioner by inserting a ½ in. flex handle in the square hole of the tensioner and rotate the tensioner counterclockwise and remove the belt from the pulleys.

5. Disconnect the heater hose from the water pump. Remove the water pump retaining bolts and remove the pump from the engine.

6. Installation is the reverse of the removal procedure. Torque the water pump-to-engine block retaining bolts to 15–23 ft. lbs. (20–30 Nm).

7. Refill the cooling system to the proper level. Start the engine and allow to reach normal operating temperature and check for leaks.

3.0L Engine Except SHO

1. Disconnect the negative battery

cable and place a drain pan under the radiator drain cock.

2. Remove the radiator cap, open the drain cock on the radiator and drain the cooling system.

3. Loosen the 4 water pump pulley retaining bolts while the accessory drive belts are still tight.

4. Loosen the alternator belt adjuster jack screw to provide enough clearance for removal of the alternator belt.

5. Using a ½ in. breaker bar, rotate the automatic tensioner down and to the left. Remove the power steering/air conditioner belt.

6. Remove the 2 nuts and 1 bolt retaining the automatic tensioner to the engine.

7. Disconnect and remove the lower radiator and heater hose from the water pump.

8. Remove the water pump to engine retaining bolts and lift the water pump and pulley up and out of the vehicle.

To install:

9. Clean the gasket surfaces on the water pump and front cover.

10. Install the water pump with the pulley loosely positioned on the hub, using a new gasket.

11. Install and tighten the retaining bolts. Tighten bolts 3–9 to 15–22 ft. lbs. (20–30 Nm) and bolts 11–15 to 71–106 inch lbs. (8–12 Nm). Apply pipe sealant to bolt No. 3 prior to installation.

12. Hand tighten the water pump pulley retaining bolts.

13. Install the automatic belt tensioner assembly. Tighten the 2 retaining nuts and bolt to 35 ft. lbs. (48 Nm).

14. Install the alternator and power steering belts. Final tighten the water pump pulley retaining bolts to 16 ft. lbs. (21 Nm).

15. Install the lower radiator and heater hoses. Fill and bleed the cooling system with the appropriate quantity and coolant type.

16. Connect the negative battery cable. Start the engine and check for leaks.

3.0L SHO Engine

1. Disconnect the battery cables and remove the battery and the battery tray.

2. Drain the cooling system and remove the accessory drive belts.

3. Remove the bolts retaining the air conditioning and alternator idler pulley and bracket assembly.

4. Disconnect the electrical connector from the ignition module and ground strap.

5. Loosen the clamps on the upper intake connector tube, remove the retaining bolts and remove the connector tube.

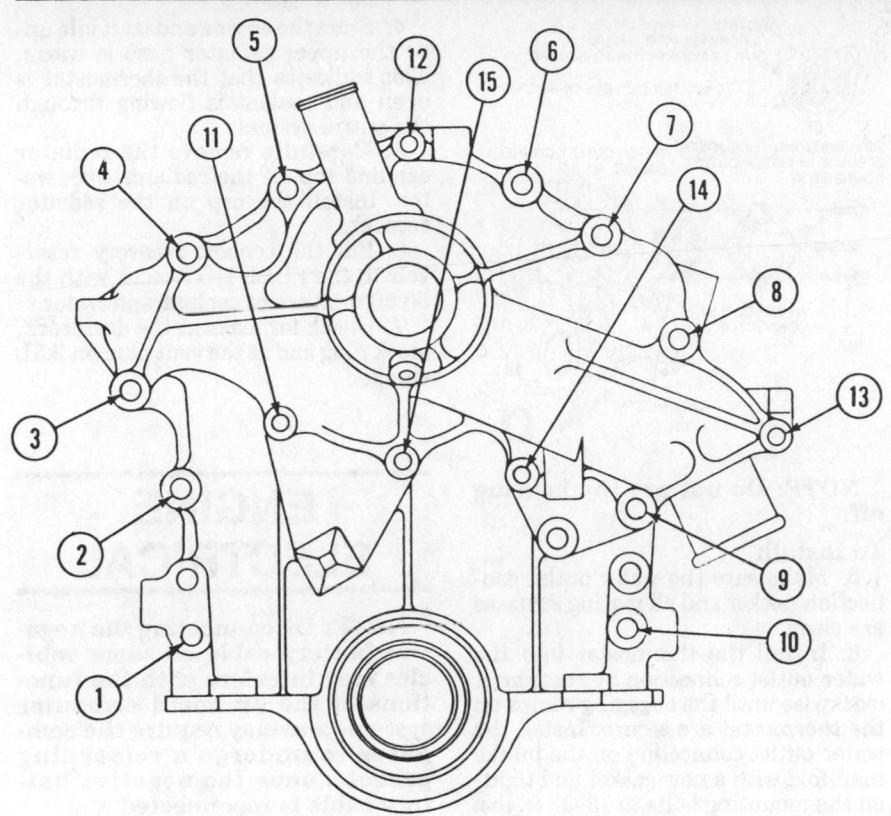

Water pump bolt identification—3.0L engine

6. Raise and safely support the vehicle. Remove the right wheel and tire assembly.

7. Remove the splash shield.

8. Remove the upper timing belt cover, crankshaft pulley and lower timing belt cover.

9. Remove the bolts from the center timing belt cover and position it aside.

10. Remove the water pump attaching bolts and remove the water pump.

11. To install, reverse the removal procedure. Tighten the water pump bolts to 12–16 ft. lbs. (15–23 Nm). Tighten the crankshaft pulley bolt to 113–126 ft. lbs. (152–172 Nm).

3.8L Engine

1. Disconnect the negative battery cable. Drain the cooling system.

2. Support the engine using engine support bar D88L–6000–A or equivalent. Remove the lower nut on both right engine mounts. Raise the engine.

3. Loosen the accessory drive belt idler. Remove the drive belt and water pump pulley.

4. Remove the air suspension pump.

5. Remove the power steering pump mounting bracket attaching bolts. Leaving hoses connected, place pump/bracket assembly aside in a position to prevent fluid from leaking out.

6. If equipped with air conditioning, remove the compressor front support bracket. Leave the compressor in place.

7. Disconnect coolant bypass and heater hoses at the water pump.

8. Remove the water pump-to-engine block attaching bolts and remove the pump from the vehicle. Discard the gasket and replace with new.

To install:

9. Lightly oil all bolt and stud threads before installation except those that require sealant. Thoroughly clean the water pump and front cover gasket contact surfaces.

10. Apply a coating of contact adhesive to both surfaces of the new gasket. Position a new gasket on water pump sealing surface.

11. Position water pump on the front cover and install attaching bolts.

12. Tighten the attaching bolts to 15–22 ft. lbs. (20–30 Nm).

13. Connect the cooling bypass hose, heater hose and radiator lower hose to water pump and tighten the clamps.

14. If equipped with air conditioning, install compressor front support bracket.

15. Position the power steering pump and mounting bracket and install the retaining bolts.

16. Position the accessory drive belt over the pulleys.

17. Lower the engine.

18. Install and tighten the lower

right engine mount nuts. Remove the engine support bar.

19. Fill cooling system to the proper level.

20. Start engine and check for coolant leaks.

Thermostat

REMOVAL & INSTALLATION

2.5L Engine

1. Disconnect the negative battery cable.

2. Position a suitable drain pan below the radiator. Remove the radiator cap and open the draincock. Drain the radiator to a corresponding level below the water outlet connection. Close the draincock.

3. Remove the vent plug from the water outlet connection.

4. Loosen the top hose clamp at the radiator, remove the water outlet connection retaining bolts, lift clear of the engine and remove the thermostat by pulling it out of the water outlet connection.

NOTE: Do not pry the housing off.

To install:

5. Make sure the water outlet connection and cylinder head mating surfaces are clean and free from gasket material. Make sure the water outlet connection pocket and air vent passage are clean and free from rust. Clean the vent plug and gasket.

6. Place the thermostat in position, fully inserted to compress the gasket and pressed into the water outlet connection to secure. Install the water outlet connection to the cylinder head using a new gasket. Tighten the bolts to 12–18 ft. lbs. (16–24 Nm). Position the top hose to the radiator and tighten the clamps.

7. Refill the cooling system. Connect the negative battery cable. Start the engine and check for leaks. Check the coolant level and add as required.

3.0L Engine

1. Disconnect the negative battery cable.

2. Place a suitable drain pan under the radiator.

3. Remove the radiator cap and open the draincock. Drain the cooling system.

4. Remove the upper radiator hose from the thermostat housing.

5. Remove the 3 retaining bolts from the thermostat housing.

6. Remove the housing and the thermostat as an assembly.

To install:

7. Make sure all sealing surfaces are free of old gasket material.

8. Install the thermostat into the housing and rotate clockwise to lock in. Make sure the jiggle valve is in the up position.

9. Position a new gasket onto the housing using the bolts as a holding device. Install the thermostat assembly and tighten the bolts to 9 ft. lbs. (12 Nm).

10. Install the upper radiator hose and tighten the clamp.

11. Fill and bleed the cooling system. Connect the negative battery cable, start the engine and check for coolant leaks. Check the coolant level and add as required.

3.0L SHO Engine

1. Disconnect the negative battery cable.

2. Place a suitable drain pan below the radiator. Remove the radiator cap and open the draincock. Partially drain the cooling system and then close the draincock.

3. Remove the air cleaner tube.

4. Disconnect the hose from the water outlet tube.

5. Remove the 2 retaining nuts and remove the water outlet tube.

6. Remove the thermostat and seal from the water outlet housing.

To install:

7. Install the seal around the outer rim of the thermostat and install the thermostat into the water outlet housing. Align the jiggle valve of the thermostat with the upper bolt on the water outlet housing.

8. Install the water outlet tube. Tighten the 2 retaining nuts to 5–8 ft. lbs. (7–11 Nm).

9. Install the air cleaner tube.

10. Refill the cooling system. Connect the negative battery cable. Start the engine and check for leaks. Check the coolant level and add as necessary.

3.8L Engine

1. Disconnect the negative battery cable.

2. Place a suitable drain pan below the radiator.

3. Remove the radiator cap and open the draincock. Drain the radiator to a level below the water outlet connection and then close the draincock.

4. Loosen the top hose clamp at the radiator, remove the water outlet connection retaining bolts and lift the water outlet clear of the engine. Remove the thermostat by rotating it counterclockwise in the water outlet connection until the thermostat becomes free to remove.

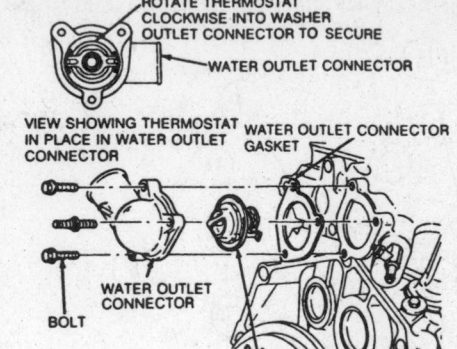

NOTE: Do not pry the housing off.

To install:

5. Make sure the water outlet connection pocket and all mating surfaces are clean.

6. Install the thermostat into the water outlet connection by rotating it clockwise until the engaging ramps on the thermostat are secure. Install the water outlet connection on the intake manifold with a new gasket and tighten the mounting bolts to 15–22 ft. lbs. (20–30 Nm). Position the top hose to the radiator and tighten the clamps.

7. Refill the cooling system. Connect the negative battery cable. Start the engine and check for leaks. Check the coolant level and add as required.

Cooling System Bleeding

When the entire cooling system is drained, the following procedure should be used to ensure a complete fill.

1. Install the block drain plug, if removed and close the draincock. With the engine off, add a 50/50 mixture of coolant and water to the radiator to a level just below the filler neck seat.

NOTE: On 2.5L engine, remove the vent plug on the water connection outlet. The vent plug must be removed before the radiator is filled or the engine may not fill completely. Do not turn the plastic cap under the vent plug or the gasket may be damaged. Do not try to add coolant through the vent plug hole. Install the vent plug after filling the radiator and before starting the engine.

2. Place the heater temperature selector in the maximum heat position.

3. Install the radiator cap to the first notch to keep spillage to a minimum.

4. Start the engine and let it idle until the upper radiator hose is warm. This indicates that the thermostat is open and coolant is flowing through the entire system.

5. Carefully remove the radiator cap and top off the radiator with water. Install the cap on the radiator securely.

6. Fill the coolant recovery reservoir to the FULL HOT mark with the 50/50 mixture of coolant and water.

7. Check for leaks at the draincock, block plug and at the vent plug on 2.5L engine.

ENGINE ELECTRICAL

NOTE: Disconnecting the negative battery cable on some vehicles may interfere with the functions of the on board computer systems and may require the computer to undergo a relearning process, once the negative battery cable is reconnected.

Distributor

REMOVAL

1. Disconnect the negative battery cable.

2. Disconnect the wiring connector from the distributor.

3. Mark the position of the No. 1 cylinder wire tower on the distributor base.

4. Remove distributor cap and position it and the attached wires aside.

5. Mark the position of the rotor in relation to the distributor housing and mark the position of the distributor housing on the engine.

6. Remove the distributor hold-down bolt and clamp and remove the distributor.

7. Use a clean shop towel to cover the distributor opening in the engine to prevent the entry of dirt or foreign material.

INSTALLATION

NOTE: Before installation, inspect the distributor O-ring and drive gear for wear and/or damage. Rotate the distributor shaft to make sure it moves freely, without binding.

Timing Not Disturbed

1. Install the distributor, aligning the distributor housing and rotor with

the marks that were made during the removal procedure.

2. Install the distributor hold-down bolt and clamp. Only snug the bolt at this time.

3. Connect the distributor to the wiring harness.

4. Install the distributor cap. Make sure the ignition wires are securely connected to the distributor cap and spark plugs. Tighten the distributor cap screws to 18–23 inch lbs. (2.0–2.6 Nm).

5. Check the ignition timing and adjust, if necessary.

6. Tighten the distributor hold-down bolt to 17–25 ft. lbs. (23–34 Nm) on the 2.5L engine, 14–21 ft. lbs. (19–28 Nm) on the 3.0L engine or 20–29 ft. lbs. (27–40 Nm) on the 3.8L engine.

7. Recheck the ignition timing after tightening the hold-down bolt.

Timing Disturbed

1. Disconnect the spark plug wire from the No. 1 cylinder spark plug and remove the spark plug.

2. Place a finger over the spark plug hole. Rotate the engine clockwise until compression is felt at the spark plug hole.

3. Align the timing pointer with the TDC mark on the crankshaft damper.

4. Rotate the distributor shaft so the rotor tip is pointing to the distributor cap No. 1 spark plug tower position.

5. Install the distributor, aligning the marks that were made on the distributor housing and engine.

6. Install the distributor hold-down bolt and clamp. Only snug the bolt at this time.

7. Connect the distributor to the wiring harness and install the distributor cap. Tighten the distributor cap hold-down screws to 18–23 inch lbs. (2.0–2.6 Nm).

8. Install the No. 1 cylinder spark plug and connect the spark plug wire.

9. Check and adjust the ignition timing.

10. Tighten the distributor hold-down bolt to 17–25 ft. lbs. (23–34 Nm) on the 2.5L engine, 14–21 ft. lbs. (19–28 Nm) on the 3.0L engine or 20–29 ft. lbs. (27–40 Nm) on the 3.8L engine.

11. Recheck the ignition timing and adjust if necessary.

Distributorless Ignition System

The 3.0L SHO engine is equipped with a Distributorless Ignition System (DIS) which consists of the following components:

    Crankshaft timing sensor
    Camshaft sensor

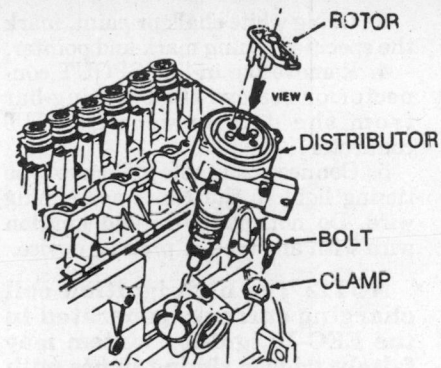

Distributor Installation – 2.5L engine

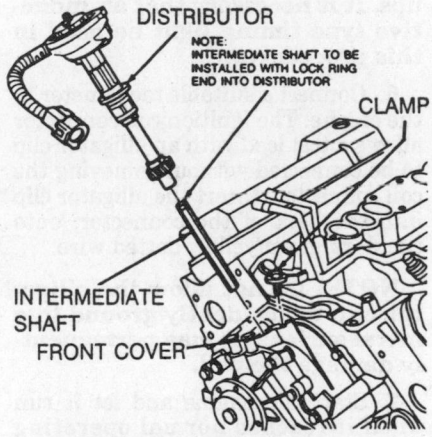

Distributor Installation – 3.8L engine

    DIS ignition module
    Ignition coil pack
    The spark angle portion of the EEC-IV module

REMOVAL & INSTALLATION

Crankshaft Timing Sensor

1. Disconnect the negative battery cable.

2. Loosen the tensioner pulleys for the air conditioning compressor and power steering pump belts. Remove the belts from the crankshaft pulley.

3. Disconnect the DIS module and remove the intake manifold crossover tube.

4. Remove the upper timing belt cover.

5. Disconnect the sensor wiring harness at the connector and route the wiring harness through the belt cover.

6. Raise the vehicle and support it safely.

7. Remove the right front wheel and tire assembly.

8. Remove the crankshaft pulley using universal puller T67L–3600–A or equivalent.

9. Remove the center and lower timing belt covers.

10. Rotate the crankshaft by hand, to position the metal vane of the shutter outside of the sensor air gap.

11. Remove the crankshaft sensor mounting screws and remove the sensor.

To install:

12. Route the sensor wiring harness through the belt cover. Install the sensor assembly on the mounting pad and install but do not tighten, the retaining screws.

13. Use a 0.03 in. (0.8mm) feeler gauge to set the clearance between the crankshaft sensor assembly and 1 vane on the crankshaft timing pulley and vane assembly. Tighten the screws to 22–31 inch lbs. (2.5–3.5 Nm).

NOTE: This is a critical torque. Overtightening can cause damage to the timing sensor.

14. Install the lower timing belt cover. Install the crankshaft pulley using a suitable tool. Tighten the pulley bolt to 112–127 ft. lbs. (152–172 Nm).

15. Install the center timing belt cover.

16. Install the right front wheel and tire assembly. Lower the vehicle.

17. Route and connect the sensor wiring harness.

18. Install the upper timing belt cover.

19. Install the intake manifold crossover tube and connect the DIS module.

20. Install the air conditioning and power steering belts and adjust them to the proper tension.

21. Connect the negative battery cable.

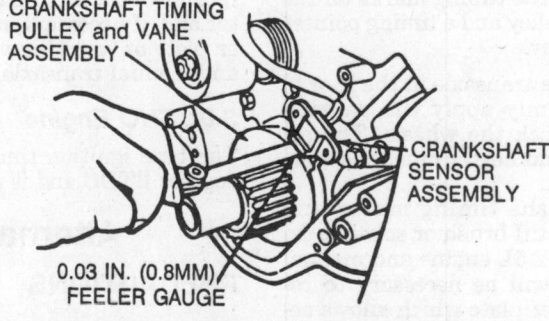

Adjusting crankshaft sensor-to-vane clearance

Camshaft Sensor Assembly

1. Disconnect the negative battery cable.
2. Remove the engine torque strut.
3. Remove the power steering belt and the pump pulley.
4. Disconnect the camshaft sensor wiring connector.
5. Remove the mounting bolts and remove the sensor.
6. To install, reverse the removal procedure. Tighten the mounting bolts to 22–31 inch lbs. (2.5–3.5 Nm).

DIS Ignition Module

1. Disconnect the negative battery cable.
2. Disconnect the wiring connectors at the module.
3. Remove the module mounting bolts and remove the module from the upper intake manifold.
4. To install, reverse the removal procedure. Apply a uniform coating of silicone dielectric compound to the mounting surface of the DIS module before it is installed. Tighten the mounting bolts to 22–31 inch lbs. (2.5–3.5 Nm).

Ignition Coil Pack

1. Disconnect the negative battery cable.
2. Remove the cover from the coil pack and disconnect the electrical connector.
3. Remove the spark plug wires by squeezing the locking tabs to release the coil boot retainers.
4. Remove the coil pack mounting screws and remove the coil pack.
5. To install, reverse the removal procedure. Tighten the mounting screws to 40–62 inch lbs. (4.5–7 Nm).

Ignition Timing

ADJUSTMENT

Except 3.0L SHO Engine

The timing marks on the 2.5L engine are visible through a hole in the top of the transaxle case. The 3.0L and 3.8L engines have the timing marks on the crankshaft pulley and a timing pointer near the pulley.

1. Place the transaxle in the **P** or **N** position. Firmly apply the parking brake and block the wheels. The air conditioner and heater must be in the **OFF** position.
2. Locate the timing marks and clean with a stiff brush or solvent. On vehicles with 2.5L engine and manual transaxle, it will be necessary to remove the cover plate which allows access to to the timing marks.

3. Using white chalk or paint, mark the specified timing mark and pointer.
4. Remove the in-line SPOUT connector or remove the shorting bar from the double wire SPOUT connector.
5. Connect a suitable inductive type timing light to the No. 1 spark plug wire. Do not, puncture and ignition wire with any type of probing device.

NOTE: The high ignition coil charging currents generated in the EEC–IV ignition system may falsely trigger timing lights with capacitive or direct connect pickups. It is necessary that an inductive type timing light be used in this procedure.

6. Connect a suitable tachometer to the engine. The ignition coil connector allows a test lead with an alligator clip to be connected without removing the coil connector. Insert the alligator clip into the back of the connector, onto the dark green/yellow dotted wire.

NOTE: Do not allow the alligator clip to accidently ground to a metal surface. It may permanently damage the coil.

7. Start the engine and let it run until it reaches normal operating temperature.

NOTE: Only use the ignition key to start the vehicle. Do not use a remote starter, as disconnecting the start wire at the starter relay will cause the TFI module to revert to start mode timing, after the vehicle is started. Reconnecting the start wire after the vehicle is running will not correct the timing.

8. Check the engine idle speed and adjust as necessary. When the idle speed is correct, aim the timing light at the timing marks. If the marks are not aligned, loosen the distributor clamp bolt slightly. Rotate the distributor body until the marks are aligned.
9. Tighten the distributor clamp bolt and recheck the ignition timing. Readjust the idle speed. Shut the engine OFF, remove all test equipment, reconnect the in-line SPOUT connector and, if necessary, reinstall the cover plate on vehicles with 2.5L engine and manual transaxle.

3.0L SHO Engine

The base ignition timing is set at 10 degrees BTDC and is not adjustable.

Alternator

PRECAUTIONS

Several precautions must be observed

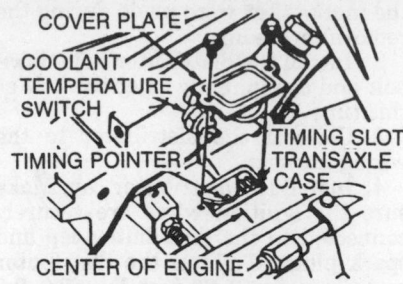

Timing marks location—2.5L engine with manual transaxle

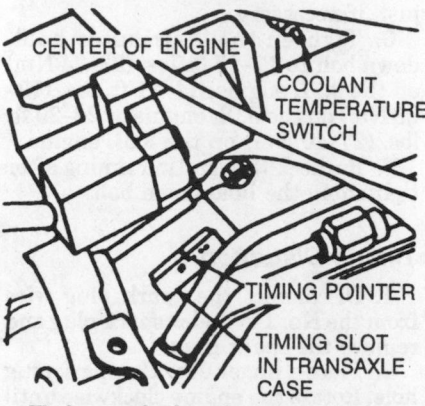

Timing marks location—2.5L engine with automatic transaxle

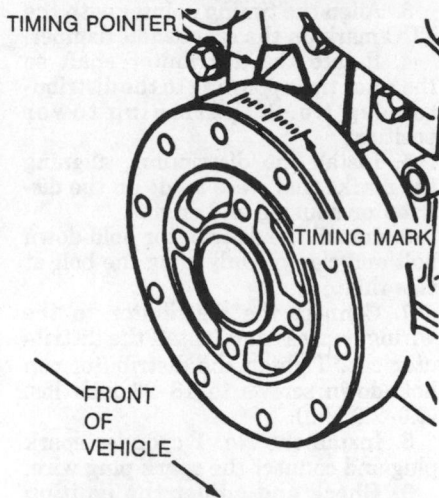

Timing marks location—3.0L engine

with alternator equipped vehicles to avoid damage to the unit.

• If the battery is removed for any reason, make sure it is reconnected with the correct polarity. Reversing the battery connections may result in damage to the one-way rectifiers.

• When utilizing a booster battery as a starting aid, always connect the positive to positive terminals and the negative terminal from the booster battery to a good engine ground on the vehicle being started.

• Never use a fast charger as a booster to start vehicles.

• Disconnect the battery cables

when charging the battery with a fast charger.

- Never attempt to polarize the alternator.
- Do not use test lights of more than 12 volts when checking diode continuity.
- Do not short across or ground any of the alternator terminals.
- The polarity of the battery, alternator and regulator must be matched and considered before making any electrical connections within the system.
- Never separate the alternator on an open circuit. Make sure all connections within the circuit are clean and tight.
- Disconnect the battery ground terminal when performing any service on electrical components.
- Disconnect the battery if arc welding is to be done on the vehicle.

BELT TENSION ADJUSTMENT

2.5L and 3.8L Engines

The V-ribbed belts used on these engines, utilize an automatic belt tensioner which maintains the proper belt tension for the life of the belt. The automatic belt tensioner has a belt wear indicator mark and **MIN** and **MAX** marks. If the indicator mark is not between the **MIN** and **MAX** marks, the belt is worn or an incorrect belt is installed.

3.0L Engine

1. Disconnect the negative battery cable.
2. Loosen the alternator adjustment and pivot bolts.
3. Apply tension to the belt using the adjusting screw.
4. Using a belt tension gauge, set the belt to the proper tension. The tension, on 1989–91 vehicles, should be 150 lbs. for a new belt or 120 lbs. for a used belt. On 1992–93 vehicles, the tension should be 200 lbs. for a new belt or 150 lbs. for a used belt.
5. When the belt is properly tensioned, tighten the alternator adjustment bolt to 27 ft. lbs. (37 Nm).
6. Remove the tension gauge and run the engine for 5 minutes.
7. With the engine **OFF** and the belt tension gauge in place, check that the adjusting screw is in contact with the bracket before loosening the alternator adjustment bolt. Rotate the adjustment screw until the belt is tensioned to 120 lbs on 1989–91 vehicles or 150 lbs. on 1992–93 vehicles.
8. Tighten the alternator adjustment bolt to 27 ft. lbs. (37 Nm) and the pivot bolt to 43 ft. lbs. (58 Nm).

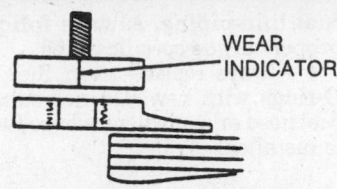

Automatic tensioner drive belt wear indicator

3.0L SHO Engine

1. Disconnect the negative battery cable.
2. Loosen the idler pulley nut.
3. Turn the adjusting bolt until the belt is adjusted to specification.
4. Position a belt tension gauge midway between the pulleys on the longest accessible belt span. The belt tension should be 220–265 lbs. for a new belt or 148–192 lbs. for a used belt.

NOTE: Turning the wrench to the right tightens the belt adjustment and turning the wrench to the left loosens the belt tension.

5. Tighten the idler pulley nut to 25–37 ft. lbs. (34–50 Nm) and check the belt tension.

REMOVAL & INSTALLATION

Except 3.0L SHO Engine

1. Disconnect the negative battery cable.
2. Tag and disconnect the wire harness from the alternator.
3. If equipped with an automatic belt tensioner, rotate the tensioner counterclockwise and remove the drive belt from the pulley.
4. If not equipped with an automatic tensioner, loosen the alternator pivot bolt and remove the adjustment arm bolt from the alternator. Remove the alternator belt from the pulley.
5. Remove the alternator mounting bolts or the pivot bolt, as required, and remove the alternator.
6. Installation is the reverse of the removal procedure. Adjust the belt tension, if not equipped with an automatic belt tensioner.

3.0L SHO Engine

1. Disconnect the battery cables and remove the battery and battery tray.
2. Tag and disconnect the wire harness from the alternator.
3. Loosen the belt tensioner and remove the alternator belt from the pulley.
4. Remove the mounting bolts and the alternator.
5. Installation is the reverse of the removal procedure. Tighten the front mounting bolt to 36–53 ft. lbs. (48–72

Nm) and the rear mounting bolts to 25–37 ft. lbs. (34–50 Nm). Adjust the belt tension.

Voltage Regulator

ADJUSTMENT

The electronic voltage regulator is calibrated and preset by the manufacturer. No adjustment is required or possible.

REMOVAL & INSTALLATION

1. Disconnect the negative battery cable.
2. Disconnect the electrical connectors from the wiring harness.
3. Remove the regulator mounting screws and the regulator.
4. Installation is the reverse of the removal procedure.
5. Connect the negative battery cable. Test the system for proper voltage regulation.

Starter

REMOVAL & INSTALLATION

1. Disconnect the negative battery cable.
2. Raise and support the vehicle safely.
3. Disconnect the wiring connection(s) at the starter.
4. Remove the cable support and ground cable connection from the upper starter stud bolt, if necessary.
5. If equipped, remove the starter brace from the cylinder block and the starter.
6. Remove the starter-to-bell housing bolts and remove the starter.
7. Installation is the reverse of the removal procedure.

EMISSION CONTROLS

Due to the complex nature of modern electronic engine control systems, comprehensive diagnosis and testing procedures fall outside the confines of this repair manual. For complete information on diagnosis, testing and repair procedures concerning all modern engine and emission control systems, please refer to "Chilton's Guide to Fuel Injection and Electronic Engine Controls".

Emission Warning Lamps

These vehicles have a "Check Engine" light that will light when there is a fault in the engine control system. This light cannot be reset without diagnosing the fault in the system. When the system has been diagnosed and the problem corrected, the light will go out.

FUEL SYSTEM

Fuel System Service Precautions

Safety is the most important factor when performing not only fuel system maintenance but any type of maintenance. Failure to conduct maintenance and repairs in a safe manner may result in serious personal injury or death. Maintenance and testing of the vehicle's fuel system components can be accomplished safely and effectively by adhering to the following rules and guidelines.

• To avoid the possibility of fire and personal injury, always disconnect the negative battery cable unless the repair or test procedure requires that battery voltage be applied.

• Always relieve the fuel system pressure prior to disconnecting any fuel system component (injector, fuel rail, pressure regulator, etc.), fitting or fuel line connection. Exercise extreme caution whenever relieving fuel system pressure to avoid exposing skin, face and eyes to fuel spray. Please be advised that fuel under pressure may penetrate the skin or any part of the body that it contacts.

• Always place a shop towel or cloth around the fitting or connection prior to loosening to absorb any excess fuel due to spillage. Ensure that all fuel spillage (should it occur) is quickly removed from engine surfaces. Ensure that all fuel soaked cloths or towels are deposited into a suitable waste container.

• Always keep a dry chemical (Class B) fire extinguisher near the work area.

• Do not allow fuel spray or fuel vapors to come into contact with a spark or open flame.

• Always use a backup wrench when loosening and tightening fuel line connection fittings. This will prevent unnecessary stress and torsion to fuel line piping. Always follow the proper torque specifications.

• Always replace worn fuel fitting O-rings with new. Do not substitute fuel hose or equivalent where fuel pipe is installed.

RELIEVING FUEL SYSTEM PRESSURE

Except 2.5L CFI Engine

The pressure in the fuel system must be released before attempting to disconnect any fuel lines. A special valve is incorporated in the fuel rail assembly for the purpose of relieving the pressure in the fuel system.

1. Remove the fuel tank cap.
2. Remove the cap from the pressure relief Schrader valve on the fuel rail.
3. Attach pressure gauge tool T80L-9974-A or equivalent, to the fuel pressure relief valve.
4. Release the pressure from the system into a suitable container.
5. Remove the pressure gauge and install the cap on the pressure relief valve. Install the fuel tank cap.

2.5L CFI Engine

1. Disconnect the electrical connector to the inertia switch, located on the left side of the luggage compartment.
2. Crank the engine for 15 seconds to relieve the system pressure.
3. Connect the inertia switch.

Fuel Line Couplings

REMOVAL & INSTALLATION

There are several methods used to connect the fuel lines and fuel system components. The hairpin clip push connect fitting and the spring lock coupling each require a different procedure to disconnect and connect.

Hairpin Clip Push Connect Fitting

1. Inspect the internal portion of the fitting for dirt accumulation. If more than a light coating of dust is present, clean the fitting before disassembly.
2. Remove the hairpin clip from the fitting by first bending the shipping tab downward so it will clear the body. This is done, using hands only, by spreading the 2 clip legs about ⅛ in. (3.2mm) each to disengage the body and pushing the legs into the fitting. Complete removal is accomplished by lightly pulling from the triangular end of the clip and working it clear of the tube and fitting.

NOTE: Do not use any tools when disconnecting the clip.

3. Grasp the fitting and hose assembly and pull in an axial direction to remove the fitting from the steel tube. Adhesion between sealing surfaces may occur. A slight twist of the fitting may be required to break this adhesion for easier removal.

NOTE: On 90 degree elbow connectors, excessive side loading could break the connector body.

4. When the fitting is removed from the tube end, inspect the clip to make sure it has not been damaged. If damaged, replace the clip. If undamaged, immediately install the clip to prevent loss or damage. To install the clip, insert the clip into any 2 adjacent openings with the triangular portion pointing away from the fitting opening. Install the clip to fully engage the body—legs of the hairpin clip locked on the outside of the body. Piloting with an index finger is necessary.

To install:

5. Before installing the fitting on the tube, wipe the tube end with a clean cloth. Inspect the inside of the fitting to make sure it is free of dirt and/or obstructions. Apply a light coat of engine oil to the tube end for ease of assembly.

6. To install the fitting onto the tube, align the fitting and tube axial and push the fitting onto the tube end. When the fitting is engaged, a definite click will be heard. Pull on the fitting to make sure it is fully engaged.

Spring Lock Coupling

The spring lock coupling is a fuel line coupling held together by a garter spring inside a circular cage. When the coupling is connected together, the flared end of the female fitting slips behind the garter spring inside the cage of the male fitting. The garter spring and cage then prevent the flared end of the female fitting from pulling out of the cage. As an additional locking feature, most vehicles have a horseshoe shaped retaining clip that improves the retaining reliability of the spring lock coupling.

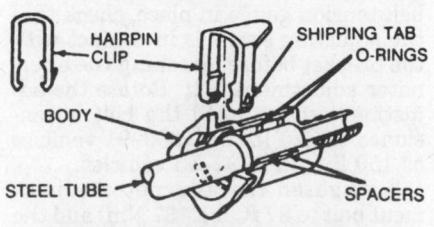

Hairpin clip push connect fitting

Fuel Filter

REMOVAL & INSTALLATION

1. Disconnect the negative battery cable. Relieve the fuel system pressure.
2. Remove the push connect fittings at both ends of the fuel filter.
3. Remove the filter from the mounting bracket by loosening the worm gear mounting clamp enough to allow the filter to pass through.
To install:
4. Install the filter in the mounting bracket, ensuring that the flow direction arrow is pointing forward. Locate the fuel filter against the tab at the lower end of the bracket.
5. Install the push connect fittings at both ends of the fuel filter.
6. Tighten the worm gear mounting clamp to 15–25 inch lbs. (1.7–2.8 Nm).
7. Start the engine and check for leaks.

Electric Fuel Pump

PRESSURE TESTING

1. Properly relieve the fuel system pressure.
2. Ground the fuel pump lead of the self-test connector through a jumper wire at the FP lead.
3. Connect a suitable fuel pressure tester to the fuel pump outlet.
4. Turn the ignition key **ON** to operate the fuel pump. Do not start the engine.
5. The fuel pressure should be 13–17 psi on 1989–90 2.5L CFI engine, 50–60 psi on 1991 2.5L EFI engine, 30–45 psi on 3.0L SHO engine or 35–40 psi on 3.0L and 3.8L engines.

REMOVAL & INSTALLATION

1. Disconnect the negative battery cable.
2. Relieve the fuel system pressure.
3. Remove the fuel tank from the vehicle and place it on a work bench. Remove any dirt from around the fuel pump attaching flange.
4. Turn the fuel pump locking ring counterclockwise and remove the lock ring.
5. Remove the fuel pump from the fuel tank and discard the flange gasket.
To install:
6. Clean the fuel pump mounting flange and fuel tank mounting surface and seal ring groove.
7. Put a light coating of grease on the new seal gasket to hold it in place during assembly and install it in the fuel ring groove.

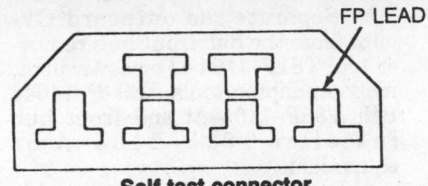

Self test connector

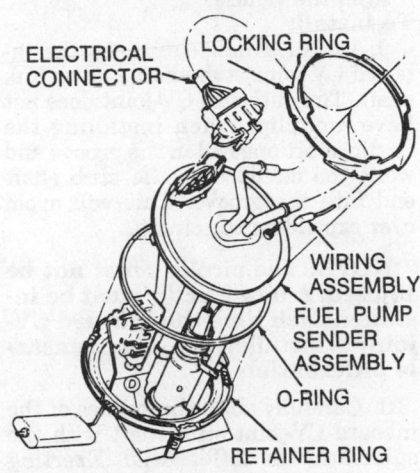

Electric fuel pump assembly

8. Install the fuel pump and sender assembly. Make sure the locating keys are in the keyways and the seal gasket remains in place.
9. Hold the assembly in place and install the lock ring making sure all locking tabs are under the tank lock ring tabs. Tighten the lock ring by turning it clockwise until it is up against the stops.
10. Install the fuel tank.
11. Fill the tank with a minimum of 10 gallons of fuel and check for leaks.
12. Turn the ignition switch to the **ON** position 5–10 times, leaving it on for 3 seconds at a time, until the system is pressurized. Check for leaks at the fittings.
13. Start the engine and recheck for leaks.

DRIVE AXLE

Halfshaft

When removing both the left and right halfshafts on vehicles equipped with manual transaxle or 3-speed automatic transaxle, install transaxle plug tools T81P–1177–B or equivalent, to prevent dislocation of the differential side gears. Should the gears become misaligned, the differential will have to be removed from the transaxle to realign the side gears.

NOTE: Due to the 3-speed automatic transaxle case configuration, the right halfshaft assembly must be removed first. Differential Rotator T81P-4026-A or equivalent, is then inserted into the transaxle to drive the left inboard CV-joint assembly from the transaxle. If only the left halfshaft assembly is to be removed for service, remove the right halfshaft assembly from the transaxle first. After removal, support it with a length of wire, then drive the left halfshaft assembly from the transaxle.

REMOVAL & INSTALLATION

1. Disconnect the negative battery cable. Remove the wheel cover/hub cover from the wheel and tire assembly and loosen the wheel nuts.
2. Raise the vehicle and support safely. Remove the wheel and tire assembly. Remove the hub nut and washer and discard the hub nut.
3. Remove the nut from the ball joint to steering knuckle attaching bolts. Drive the bolt out of the steering knuckle using a punch and hammer. Discard the bolt and nut after removal.
4. If equipped with anti-lock brakes, remove the anti-lock brake sensor and position aside. If equipped with air suspension, remove the height sensor bracket retaining bolt and wire sensor bracket to inner fender. Position the sensor link aside.
5. Separate the ball joint from the steering knuckle using a suitable prybar. Position the end of the prybar outside of the bushing pocket to avoid damage to the bushing. Use care to prevent damage to the ball joint boot. Remove the stabilizer bar link at the stabilizer bar.

NOTE: The remaining removal procedures differ according to transaxle application: manual transaxle, 4-speed automatic overdrive (AXOD) transaxle or 3-speed automatic (ATX/FLC) transaxle.

6. If equipped with AXOD transaxle and removing the right or left halfshaft, or if equipped with manual transaxle and removing the left halfshaft, proceed as follows:
   a. Install the CV-joint puller tool T86P-3514-A1 or equivalent, between CV-joint and transaxle case. Turn the steering hub and/or wire strut assembly aside.
   b. Screw extension tool T86P-3514-A2 or equivalent, into the CV-joint puller and hand tighten. Screw an impact slide hammer onto the ex-

tension and remove the CV-joint from the transaxle.

c. Support the end of the shaft by suspending it from a convenient underbody component with a piece of wire. Do not allow the shaft to hang unsupported; damage to the outboard CV-joint may occur.

d. Separate the outboard CV-joint from the hub using front hub remover tool T81P–1104–C or equivalent, metric adapter tools T83–P–1104–BH, T86P–1104–Al and front hub installer T81P–1104–A or equivalent.

e. Remove the halfshaft assembly from the vehicle.

7. If equipped with ATX/FLC or manual transaxle and removing the right halfshaft, proceed as follows:

a. Remove the bolts attaching the bearing support to the bracket. Slide the link shaft out of the transaxle. Support the end of the shaft by suspending it from a convenient underbody component with a piece of wire. Do not allow the shaft to hang unsupported, damage to the outboard CV-joint may occur.

b. Separate the outboard CV-joint from the hub using front hub remover tool T81P–1104–C or equivalent, metric adapter tools T83–P–1104–BH, T86P–1104–Al and front hub installer T81P–1104–A or equivalent.

NOTE: Never use a hammer to separate the outboard CV-joint stub shaft from the hub. Damage to the CV-joint threads and internal components may result. The right side link shaft and halfshaft assembly is removed as a complete unit.

8. If equipped with ATX/FLC transaxle and removing the left halfshaft, proceed as follows:

NOTE: Due to the automatic transaxle case configuration, the right halfshaft assembly must be removed first. Differential rotator tool T81P–4026–A or equivalent, is then inserted into the transaxle to drive the left inboard CV-joint assembly from the transaxle. If only the left halfshaft assembly is to be removed for service, remove the right halfshaft assembly from the transaxle first. After removal, support it with a length of wire, then drive the left halfshaft assembly from the transaxle.

a. Support the end of the shaft by suspending it from a convenient underbody component with a piece of wire. Do not allow the shaft to hang unsupported as damage to the outboard CV-joint may occur.

b. Separate the outboard CV-joint from the hub front hub remover tool T81P–1104–C or equivalent, metric adapter tools T83–P–1104–BH, T86P–1104–Al and front hub installer T81P–1104–A or equivalent.

c. Remove the halfshaft assembly from the vehicle.

To install:

9. Install a new circlip on the inboard CV-joint stub shaft and/or link shaft. The outboard CV-joint does not have a circlip. When installing the circlip, start one end in the groove and work the circlip over the stub shaft end into the groove. This will avoid over expanding the circlip.

NOTE: The circlip must not be re-used. A new circlip must be installed each time the inboard CV-joint is installed into the transaxle differential.

10. Carefully align the splines of the inboard CV-joint stub shaft with the splines in the differential. Exerting some force, push the CV-joint into the differential until the circlip is felt to seat in the differential side gear. Use care to prevent damage to the differential oil seal. If equipped, torque the link shaft bearing retaining bolts to 16–23 ft. lbs. (21–32 Nm).

NOTE: A non-metallic mallet may be used to aid in seating the circlip into the differential side gear groove. If a mallet is necessary, tap only on the outboard CV-joint stub shaft.

11. Carefully align the splines of the outboard CV-joint stub shaft with the splines in the hub and push the shaft into the hub as far as possible.

12. Temporarily fasten the rotor to the hub with washers and 2 wheel lug nuts. Insert a steel rod into the rotor and rotate clockwise to contact the knuckle to prevent the rotor from turning during the CV-joint installation.

13. Install the hub nut washer and a new hub nut. Manually thread the retainer onto the CV-joint as far as possible.

14. Connect the control arm to the steering knuckle and install a new nut and bolt. Tighten the nut to 40–55 ft. lbs. (54–74 Nm).

15. Install the anti-lockbrake sensor and/or the ride height sensor bracket, if equipped.

16. Connect the stabilizer link to the stabilizer bar. Tighten to 35–48 ft. lbs. (47–65 Nm).

17. Tighten the hub retainer nut to 180–200 ft. lbs. (245–270 Nm). Remove the steel rod.

18. Install the wheel and tire assembly and lower the vehicle. Tighten the wheel nuts to 80–105 ft. lbs. (108–144 Nm). Fill the transaxle to the proper level with the specified fluid.

Front Wheel Hub, Knuckle and Bearings

REMOVAL & INSTALLATION

1. Remove the wheelcover/hub cover and loosen the wheel nuts.

2. Remove the hub nut retainer and washer by applying sufficient torque to the nut to overcome the prevailing torque feature of the crimp in the nut collar. Do not use an impact-type tool to remove the hub nut retainer. The hub nut retainer is not reusable and must be discarded after removal.

3. Raise the vehicle and support it safely. Remove the wheel and tire assembly.

4. Remove the brake caliper by loosening the caliper locating pins and rotating the caliper off of the rotor, starting from the lower end of the caliper and lifting upwards. Do not remove the caliper pins from the caliper assembly. Once the caliper is free of the rotor, support it with a length of wire. Do not allow the caliper to hang from the brake hose.

5. Remove the rotor from the hub by pulling it off of the hub bolts. If the rotor is difficult to remove, strike it sharply between the studs with a rubber or plastic hammer. If the rotor will not pull off, apply a suitable rust penetrator to the inboard and outboard rotor hub mating surfaces. Install a suitable 3-jaw puller and remove the rotor by pulling on the rotor outside diameter and pushing on the hub center. If excessive force is required to remove the rotor, check it for lateral runout prior to installation. Lateral runout must be checked with the nuts clamping the stamped hat section of the rotor.

6. Remove the rotor splash shield.

7. Disconnect the lower control arm and tie rod from the knuckle but leave the strut attached. Loosen the 2 strut top mount-to-apron nuts.

8. Install hub remover/installer adapter T81P–1104–A with front hub remover/installer T81P–1104–C and wheel bolt adapters T83P–1104–BH1 and 2 stud adapter T86P–1104–A1 or equivalent, and remove the hub, bearing and knuckle assembly by pushing out the CV-joint outer shaft until it is free of the assembly.

9. Support the knuckle with a length of wire, remove the strut bolt and slide the hub/bearing/knuckle assembly off of the strut. Remove the

support wire and carry the hub/bearing/knuckle assembly to a bench.

10. Install front hub puller D80L-1002-L and shaft protector D80L-625-1 or equivalent, with the jaws of the puller on the knuckle bosses. Make sure the shaft protector is centered, clears the bearing inside diameter and rests on the end face of the hub journal. Remove the hub.

11. Remove the snapring that retains the bearing in the knuckle assembly and discard.

12. Using a suitable hydraulic press, place front bearing spacer T86P-1104-A2 or equivalent, on the press plate with the step side facing up and position the knuckle with the outboard side up on the spacer. Install front bearing remover T83P-1104-AH2 or equivalent, centered on the bearing inner race and press the bearing out of the knuckle. Discard the bearing.

To install:

13. Remove all foreign material from the knuckle bearing bore and hub bearing journal to ensure correct seating of the new bearing.

NOTE: If the hub bearing journal is scored or damaged it must be replaced. The front wheel bearings are pregreased and sealed and require no scheduled maintenance. The bearings are preset and cannot be adjusted. If a bearing is disassembled for any reason, it must be replaced as a unit, as individual service seals, rollers and races are not available.

14. Place front bearing spacer T86P-1104-A2 or equivalent, with the step side down on the hydraulic press plate and position the knuckle with the outboard side down on the spacer. Position a new bearing in the inboard side of the knuckle. Install bearing installer T86P-1104-A3 or equivalent, with the undercut side facing the bearing, on the bearing outer race and press the bearing into the knuckle. Make sure the bearing seats completely against the shoulder of the knuckle bore.

NOTE: Bearing installer T86P-1104-A3 or equivalent, must be positioned as indicated above to prevent bearing damage during installation.

15. Install a new snapring (part of the bearing kit) in the knuckle groove.

16. Place front bearing spacer T86P-1104-A2 or equivalent, on the press plate and position the hub on the tool with the lugs facing downward. Position the knuckle assembly with the outboard side down on the hub barrel. Place bearing remover T83P-1104-AH2 or equivalent, flat side down, cen-

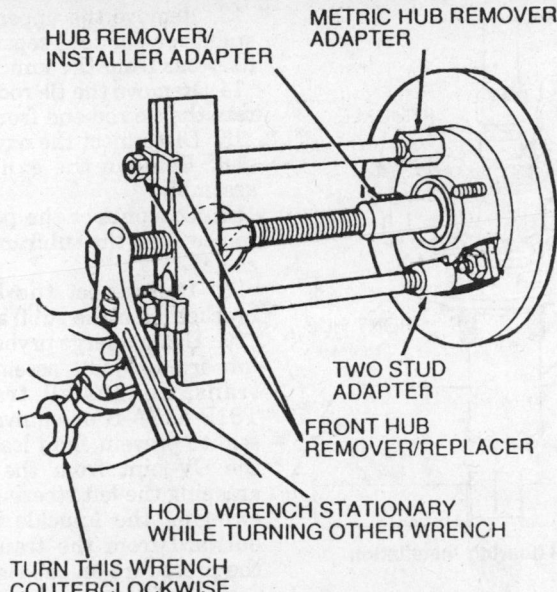

Separating the hub from the outer CV-joint

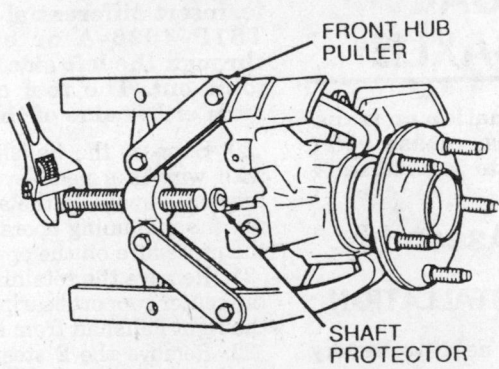

Removing the hub from the knuckle

tered on the inner race of the bearing and press down on the tool until the bearing is fully seated onto the hub. Make sure the hub rotates freely in the knuckle after installation.

17. Prior to hub/bearing/knuckle installation, replace the bearing dust seal on the outboard CV-joint with a new seal from the bearing kit. Make sure the seal flange faces outboard toward the bearing. Use drive tube T83T-3132-A1 and front bearing dust seal installer T86P-1104-A4 or equivalent.

18. Suspend the hub/bearing/knuckle assembly on the vehicle with wire and attach the strut loosely to the knuckle. Lubricate the CV-joint stub shaft with SAE 30 weight motor oil and insert the shaft into the hub splines as far as possible using hand pressure only. Make sure the splines are properly engaged.

19. Temporarily fasten the rotor to the hub with washers and 2 wheel lug nuts. Insert a steel rod or other suitable tool into the rotor diameter and

rotate clockwise to contact the knuckle.

20. Install the hub nut washer and a new hub nut retainer. Rotate the nut clockwise to seat the CV-joint. Tighten the nut to 180–200 ft. lbs. (245–270 Nm). Remove the steel rod, washers and lug nuts.

NOTE: Do not use power or impact-type tools to tighten the hub nut.

21. Install the remainder of the front suspension components and the rotor splash shield.

22. Install the disc brake rotor and caliper. Make sure the outer brake pad spring hook is seated under the upper arm of the knuckle.

23. Install the wheel and tire assembly and tighten the wheel lug nuts finger tight.

24. Lower the vehicle. Tighten the wheel lug nuts to 85–105 ft. lbs. (115–142 Nm). Install the wheelcover/hub cover.

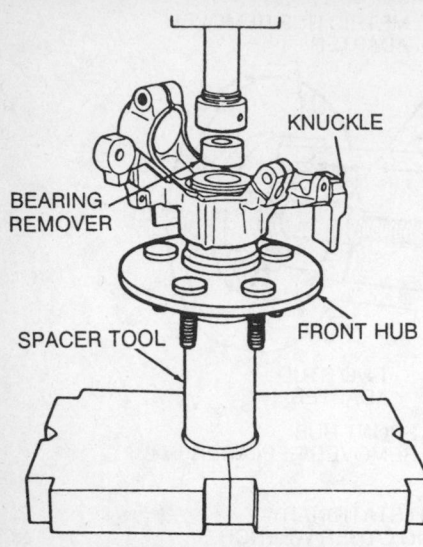

Front wheel bearing Installation

KNUCKLE

BEARING REMOVER

SPACER TOOL

FRONT HUB

MANUAL TRANSAXLE

For further information on transmission/transaxles, please refer to "Chilton's Guide to Transmission Repair".

Transaxle Assembly

REMOVAL & INSTALLATION

1. Disconnect the negative battery cable.
2. Wedge a 7 in. block of wood under the clutch pedal to hold the pedal up beyond it's normal position.
3. Remove the air cleaner hose.
4. Grasp the clutch cable and pull it forward, disconnecting it from the clutch release shaft assembly.
5. Disconnect the clutch cable casing from the rib on top of the transaxle case.
6. Install engine lifting eyes.
7. Tie up the wiring harness and power steering cooler hoses.
8. Disconnect the speedometer cable and speed sensor wire.
9. Support the engine using engine support bar 014-00750 or equivalent.
10. Raise the vehicle and support it safely. Remove the wheel and tire assemblies.
11. Remove the nut and bolt retaining the lower control arm ball joint to the steering knuckle assembly. Discard the removed nut and bolt. Repeat the procedure on the opposite side.
12. Using a suitable tool, pry the lower control arm away from the knuckle.

NOTE: Be careful not to damage or cut the ball joint boot.

13. Remove the upper nut from the stabilizer bar and separate the stabilizer bar from the knuckle.
14. Remove the tie rod nut and separate the tie rod end from the knuckle.
15. Disconnect the oxygen sensor.
16. Remove the exhaust catalyst assembly.
17. Disconnect the power steering cooler from the subframe and place it aside.
18. Disconnect the battery cable bracket from the subframe.
19. Using a large prybar, pry the left inboard CV-joint assembly from the transaxle. Install transaxle plug T81P-1177-B or equivalent into the seal to prevent fluid leakage. Remove the CV-joint from the transaxle by grasping the left steering knuckle and swinging the knuckle and halfshaft outward from the transaxle. Repeat the procedure on the right side.

NOTE: If the CV-joint assembly cannot be pried from the transaxle, insert differential rotator tool T81P-4026-A or equivalent, through the left side and tap the joint out. The tool can be used from either side of the transaxle.

20. Support the halfshaft assembly with wire in a near level position to prevent damage to the assembly during the remaining operations. Repeat the procedure on the opposite side.
21. Remove the retaining bolts from the center support bearing and remove the right halfshaft from the transaxle.
22. Remove the 2 steering gear retaining nuts from the sub-frame. Support the steering gear by wiring up the tie rod ends to the coil springs.
23. Remove the transaxle to engine retaining bolts.
24. On 1989-91 vehicles, disconnect the 2 shift cables from the transaxle. On 1992-93 vehicles, remove the shift mechanism stabilizer bar-to-transaxle retaining bolt, shift rod-to-shift shaft retaining nut and bolt and remove the rods from the transaxle.
25. Remove the engine mount bolts.
26. Position jacks under the body mount positions and remove the 4 bolts, lower the sub-frame and position it aside.
27. Remove the starter motor assembly.
28. Remove the left engine vibration dampener lower bracket.
29. Remove the backup light switch connector from the transaxle backup light switch, located on top of the transaxle and remove the backup light switch.
30. Position a suitable support jack under the transaxle.
31. Lower the transaxle, remove it from the engine and lower it from the vehicle.

To install:

32. Raise the transaxle into position. Engage the input shaft spline into the clutch disc and work the transaxle onto the dowel sleeves. Make sure the transaxle assembly is flush with the rear face of the engine before installation of the retaining bolts.
33. Install the engine to transaxle retaining bolts. Tighten to 28-31 ft. lbs. (38-42 Nm).
34. Install the backup light switch and tighten to 12-15 ft. lbs. (16-20 Nm). Connect the electrical connector.
35. Install the starter motor. Tighten the retaining bolts to 30-40 ft. lbs. (41-54 Nm).
36. Using jacks, position the subframe and raise it into position. Install the 4 bolts and tighten to 65-85 ft. lbs. (90-115 Nm).
37. Install the left vibration dampener lower bracket.
38. Install the engine mount bolts and tighten to 40-55 ft. lbs. (54-75 Nm).
39. On 1989-91 vehicles, connect the shift cables to the transaxle. On 1992-93 vehicles, connect the stabilizer and shift rod to the transaxle. Tighten the stabilizer bolt to 35-46 ft. lbs. (47-63 Nm). Tighten the shift rod clamp bolt and nut to 80-106 inch lbs. (9-12 Nm).
40. Install the engine to transaxle bolts and tighten to 28-31 ft. lbs. (38-42 Nm).
41. Install the steering gear retaining nuts and tighten to 85-100 ft. lbs. (115-135 Nm).
42. Install the center support bearing retaining bolts and tighten to 85-100 ft. lbs. (115-135 Nm).
43. Install the right halfshaft into the transaxle.
44. Install the left inboard CV-joint assembly into the transaxle.
45. Connect the battery cable bracket to the sub-frame.
46. Connect the power steering cooler to the subframe.
47. Install the exhaust catalyst retaining bolts and tighten to 25-34 ft. lbs. (34-47 Nm).
48. Connect the oxygen sensor.
49. Install the tie rod in the knuckle and the tie rod retaining nut. Tighten to 35-47 ft. lbs. (47-64 Nm).
50. Position the stabilizer bar to the knuckle and install the nut.
51. Install the lower control arm ball joint to steering knuckle assembly. Install and tighten a new retaining nut and bolt to 37-44 ft. lbs. (50-60 Nm).
52. Install the wheel and tire assemblies.
53. Check the transaxle fluid level.
54. Lower the vehicle.
55. Remove the engine support tool.
56. Install the speedometer cable. Connect the speedometer cable and speed sensor wire.

57. Remove the engine lifting eyes.
58. Connect the clutch cable to the transaxle.
59. Install the air cleaner hose and remove the wood block from the clutch pedal.
60. Connect the negative battery cable and check the transaxle for fluid leaks.

CLUTCH

Clutch Assembly

REMOVAL & INSTALLATION

1. Disconnect the negative battery cable. Raise the vehicle and support it safely. Remove the transaxle.
2. If the pressure plate is to be reused, mark the pressure plate and the flywheel so they can be assembled in the same position.
3. Loosen the attaching bolts 1 turn at a time, in sequence, until spring tension is relieved to prevent pressure plate cover distortion.
4. Support the pressure plate and remove the bolts. Remove the pressure plate and clutch disc from the flywheel.
5. Inspect the flywheel, clutch disc, pressure plate, release bearing and the release fork for wear. Replace parts as required. If the flywheel shows any signs of overheating (blue discoloration) or if it is badly grooved or scored, it should be refaced or replaced.

To install:

6. Install the flywheel, if removed. Tighten attaching bolts in 2 steps, first to 29–43 ft. lbs. (39–50 Nm) and then to 51–58 ft. lbs. (69–78 Nm).
7. Clean the pressure plate and flywheel surfaces thoroughly. Place the clutch disc and pressure plate into the installed position. The clutch disc must be installed so the flatter side is toward the flywheel. Align the marks made during the removal procedure if components are being reused. Support the clutch disc and pressure plate with a suitable dummy shaft or clutch aligning tool.
8. Install the pressure plate-to-flywheel bolts. Tighten them gradually in a criss-cross pattern to 12–24 ft. lbs. (17–32 Nm). Remove the alignment tool.
9. If the release bearing was removed, apply a light film of grease to the outer surface of the transaxle bearing retainer and the tips of the release lever where they contact the bearing. Fill the bearing groove with

grease. Slide the bearing onto the bearing retainer and attach to the release lever with the retaining pin.
10. Install the transaxle and connect the negative battery cable.

PEDAL HEIGHT/FREE-PLAY ADJUSTMENT

The clutch control system is self-adjusting during normal operation. There is no provision for pedal height/free-play adjustment.

AUTOMATIC TRANSAXLE

For further information on transmission/transaxles, please refer to "Chilton's Guide to Transmission Repair".

Transaxle Assembly

REMOVAL & INSTALLATION

1989–90

EXCEPT 2.5L ENGINE

1. Disconnect the negative battery cable. Raise and support the vehicle safely. Remove the air cleaner assembly.
2. Remove the bolt retaining the shift cable and bracket assembly to the transaxle.

NOTE: Hold the bracket with a prybar in the slot to prevent the bracket from moving.

3. Remove the shift cable bracket bolts, nut and bracket from the transaxle. Disconnect the electrical connector from the neutral safety switch.
4. Disconnect the electrical bulkhead connector from the rear of the transaxle. Remove the dipstick. If equipped with 3.8L engine, remove the throttle valve cable cover. Unsnap the throttle valve cable from the throttle body lever. Remove the throttle valve cable from the transaxle case.
5. Carefully pull up on the throttle valve cable and disconnect the throttle valve cable from the TV link.

NOTE: Pulling to hard may bend the internal TV bracket.

6. Install engine lifting brackets.
7. Disconnect the power steering pump pressure and return line bracket.
8. Remove the torque converter housing bolts from the top of the transaxle.

9. Install engine support tool D87L–6000–A or equivalent.
10. Raise the vehicle and support it safely. Remove both front wheel and tire assemblies. Remove the left-hand outer tie rod end.
11. On Continental, remove the suspension height sensor and disconnect the brake line support brackets.
12. Remove the lower ball joint pinch bolts. Disconnect the lower ball joints from each spindle. Remove stabilizer bar bolts.
13. Remove the nuts securing the steering gear to the sub-frame.
14. If equipped with 3.8L engine, disconnect the oxygen sensor electrical connection and remove the exhaust pipe, catalytic converter assembly and mounting bracket.
15. Remove the two 15mm bolts from the transaxle mount. Remove the four 15mm bolts from the left engine support and remove the bracket.
16. Support the sub-frame with suitable jacks.
17. Remove the steering gear from the sub-frame and secure to the rear of the engine compartment. Remove the sub-frame to body bolts and lower the sub-frame.
18. Remove the dust cover and the starter assembly.
19. Rotate the engine by the crankshaft pulley bolt to align the torque converter bolts with the starter drive hole. Remove the torque converter-to-flywheel retaining nuts.
20. Remove the transaxle cooler line retaining clips. Disconnect the transaxle cooler lines.
21. Remove the engine to transaxle retaining bolts.
22. Remove the speedometer sensor heat shield.
23. Remove the vehicle speed sensor from the transaxle.

NOTE: Vehicles with electronic instrument clusters do not use a speedometer cable.

24. Position a suitable transmission jack. Remove the halfshafts.
25. Remove the last 2 torque converter housing bolts.
26. Seperate the transaxle from the engine and carefully lower the transaxle from the vehicle.

To install:

27. Installation is the reverse of the removal procedure. During installation be sure to observe the following:
   a. Clean the transaxle oil cooler lines.
   b. Install new circlips on the inboard CV-joint stub shafts.
   c. Carefully install the halfshafts in the transaxle by aligning the splines of the CV-joint with the splines of the differential.

d. Attach the lower ball joint to the steering knuckle with a new nut and pinch bolt. Tighten to 40–55 ft. lbs. (54–74 Nm).

e. When installing the transaxle to the engine, verify that the converter-to-transaxle engagement is maintained. Prevent the converter from moving forward and disengaging during installation.

f. Adjust the TV and manual linkages. Check the transaxle fluid level.

g. Tighten the following bolts to the torque specifications listed:

Transaxle-to-engine bolts: 41–50 ft. lbs. (55–68 Nm)

Control arm-to-knuckle bolts: 40–55 ft. lbs. (54–74 Nm)

Stabilizer U-clamp-to-bracket bolts: 60–70 ft. lbs. (81–95 Nm)

Tie rod-to-knuckle nut: 23–35 ft. lbs. (31–47 Nm)

Starter-to-transaxle bolts: 30–40 ft. lbs. (41–54 Nm)

Converter-to-flywheel bolts: 23–39 ft. lbs. (31–53 Nm)

Insulator-to-bracket bolts: 55–70 ft. lbs. (75–90 Nm)

2.5L ENGINE

1. Disconnect the negative battery cable and remove the air cleaner assembly.

2. Position the engine control wiring harness away from the transaxle converter housing.

3. Disconnect the TV linkage and manual lever cable at the respective levers.

NOTE: Failure to disconnect the linkage during transaxle removal and allowing the transaxle to hang will damage the throttle valve cam shaft joint, which is located under the transaxle cover.

4. Remove the power steering hose brackets.

5. Remove the upper transaxle-to-engine attaching bolts.

6. Install suitable engine lifting brackets to the right and left areas of the cylinder head and attach with bolts. Install 2 suitable engine support bars.

NOTE: An engine support bar may be fabricated from a length of 4×4 wood cut to 57 in.

7. Place 1 of the engine support bars across the vehicle in front of each engine shock tower. Place another support bar across the vehicle approximately between the alternator and valve cover. Attach chains from the support bars to the engine lifting brackets. Raise the vehicle and support safely. Remove the wheel and tire assemblies.

8. Remove the catalytic converter

inlet pipe and disconnect the exhaust air hose assembly.

9. Remove each tie rod end from it's spindle. Separate the lower ball joints from the struts and remove the lower control arm from each spindle.

10. Disconnect the stabilizer bar by removing the retaining nuts.

11. Disconnect and remove the rack and pinion and auxiliary cooler from the sub-frame. Position the rack and pinion away from the sub-frame and secure with wire.

12. Remove the right front axle support and bearing assembly retaining bolts.

13. Remove the halfshaft and link shaft assembly out of the right side of the transaxle.

14. Disengage the left halfshaft from the differential side gear. Pull the halfshaft from the transaxle.

NOTE: Support and secure the halfshaft from an underbody component with a length of wire. Do not allow the halfshafts to hang unsupported.

15. Install transaxle differential plugs T81P–1177–B or equivalent.

16. Remove the front support insulator and position the left front splash shield aside.

17. Properly support the sub-frame and lower the vehicle onto the sub-frame support. Remove the sub-frame and disconnect the neutral start switch wire assembly.

18. Raise the vehicle after the sub-frame is removed. Disconnect the speedometer cable.

19. Disconnect and remove the shift cable from the transaxle.

20. Disconnect the oil cooler lines and remove the starter.

21. Remove the dust cover from the torque converter housing and remove the torque converter-to-flywheel housing nuts.

22. Position a suitable transaxle jack under the transaxle.

23. Remove the remaining transaxle-to-engine attaching bolts.

NOTE: Before the transaxle can be lowered from the vehicle, the torque converter studs must be clear of the flywheel. Insert a prybar between the flywheel and converter and carefully guide the transaxle and converter away from the engine.

24. Lower the transaxle from the engine.

To install:

25. Installation is the reverse of the removal procedure. During installation be sure to observe the following:

a. Clean the transaxle oil cooler lines.

b. Install new circlips on the inboard CV-joint stub shafts.

c. Carefully install the halfshafts in the transaxle by aligning the splines of the CV-joint with the splines of the differential.

d. Attach the lower ball joint to the steering knuckle with a new nut and bolt. Tighten the nut to 40–55 ft. lbs. (54–74 Nm). Do not tighten the bolt.

e. When installing the transaxle to the engine, verify that the converter-to-transaxle engagement is maintained. Prevent the converter from moving forward and disengaging during installation.

f. Adjust the TV and manual linkages. Check the transaxle fluid level.

g. Tighten the following bolts to the torque specifications listed:

Transaxle-to-engine bolts: 25–33 ft. lbs. (34–45 Nm)

Control arm-to-knuckle bolts: 40–55 ft. lbs. (54–74 Nm)

Stabilizer U-clamp-to-bracket bolts: 60–70 ft. lbs. (81–95 Nm)

Tie rod-to-knuckle nut: 23–35 ft. lbs. (31–47 Nm)

Starter-to-transaxle bolts: 30–40 ft. lbs. (41–54 Nm)

Converter-to-flywheel bolts: 23–39 ft. lbs. (31–53 Nm)

Insulator-to-bracket bolts: 55–70 ft. lbs. (75–90 Nm)

1991–93

1. Disconnect the battery cables and remove the battery and battery tray.

2. Remove the air cleaner assembly, hoses and tubes.

3. Disconnect the electrical connectors from the engine and remove the bolt retaining the main wiring harness bracket.

4. Remove the shift lever. Remove the EGR bracket and throttle body bracket retaining bolts and install engine lifting eyes.

5. Secure the wiring harness aside and remove the radiator sight shield. Position engine support tool D88L–6000–D or equivalent.

6. If equipped with air suspension, turn the air suspension switch located in the luggage compartment to the OFF position.

7. Remove the dipstick and disconnect the power steering line bracket. Remove the 4 torque converter housing bolts from the top of the transaxle.

8. Raise and safely support the vehicle. Remove the front wheel and tire assemblies.

9. Disconnect the left-hand outer tie rod end. Remove the suspension height sensor, if equipped. Disconnect the brake line support brackets.

10. Remove the retaining bolts from

the front stabilizer bar assembly. Remove the ball joint pinch bolts and disconnect the right and left lower arm assemblies from the knuckles.

11. Remove the steering gear retaining nuts from the sub-frame. Disconnect the oxygen sensors and remove the exhaust pipe, catalytic converter assembly and mounting bracket.

12. Remove 2 bolts from the transaxle mount and the 4 bolts from the left engine support. Remove the support.

13. Support the sub-frame with suitable jacks. Remove the steering gear from the sub-frame and secure to the rear of the engine compartment. Remove the sub-frame-to-body bolts and lower the sub-frame.

14. Remove the starter and the dust cover.

15. Rotate the engine at the crankshaft pulley to align the torque converter bolts with the starter drive hole. Remove the 4 torque converter-to-flywheel retaining nuts.

16. Disconnect the transaxle cooler lines. Remove the engine-to-transaxle retaining bolts.

17. Remove the speedometer sensor heat shield. Remove the vehicle speed sensor from the transaxle.

NOTE: Vehicles with electronic instrument clusters do not use a speedometer cable.

18. Position a suitable transaxle jack. Remove the halfshafts.

19. Remove the last 2 torque converter housing bolts, carefully separate the transaxle from the engine and lower out of the vehicle.

20. Installation is the reverse of the removal procedure. During installation be sure to observe the following:

   a. Clean the transaxle oil cooler lines.

   b. Install new circlips on the inboard CV-joint stub shafts.

   c. Carefully install the halfshafts in the transaxle by aligning the splines of the CV-joint with the splines of the differential.

   d. Attach the lower ball joint to the steering knuckle with a new nut and bolt. Tighten the nut to 40–53 ft. lbs. (53–72 Nm).

   e. When installing the transaxle to the engine, verify that the converter-to-transaxle engagement is maintained. Prevent the converter from moving forward and disengaging during installation.

   f. Adjust the TV and manual linkages. Check the transaxle fluid level.

   g. Tighten the following bolts to the torque specifications listed:

     Transaxle-to-engine bolts: 41–50 ft. lbs. (55–68 Nm)

     Control arm-to-knuckle bolts: 40–53 ft. lbs. (53–72 Nm)

     Stabilizer U-clamp-to-bracket bolts: 60–70 ft. lbs. (81–95 Nm)

     Tie rod-to-knuckle nut: 23–35 ft. lbs. (31–47 Nm)

     Starter-to-transaxle bolts: 30–40 ft. lbs. (41–54 Nm)

     Converter-to-flywheel bolts: 23–39 ft. lbs. (31–53 Nm)

     Insulator-to-bracket bolts: 55–70 ft. lbs. (75–90 Nm)

FRONT SUSPENSION

MacPherson Strut

REMOVAL & INSTALLATION

Taurus and Sable

1. Place the ignition switch in the **OFF** position and the steering column in the **UNLOCKED** position.

2. Remove the hub nut. Loosen the 3 top mount-to-shock tower nuts; do not remove the nuts at this time.

3. Raise and support the vehicle safely.

NOTE: When raising the vehicle, do not lift by the lower control arms.

4. Remove the tire and wheel assembly. Remove the brake caliper, supporting it on a wire. Remove the rotor.

5. At the tie rod end, remove the cotter pin and the castle nut. Discard the cotter pin and nut and replace with new.

6. Using tie rod end remover tool 3290–D and the tie rod remover adapter tool T81P–3504–W or equivalents, separate the tie rod from the steering knuckle.

7. Remove the stabilizer bar link nut and the link from the strut.

8. Remove the lower arm-to-steering knuckle pinch bolt and nut; it may be necessary to use a drift punch to remove the bolt. Using a suitable tool, spread the knuckle-to-lower arm pinch joint and remove the lower arm from the steering knuckle. Discard the pinch nut/bolt and replace with new.

9. Remove the halfshaft from the hub and support it on a wire.

NOTE: When removing the halfshaft, do not allow it to move outward as the internal parts of the tripod CV-joint could separate, causing failure of the joint.

10. Remove the strut-to-steering knuckle pinch bolt. Using a small prybar, spread the pinch bolt joint and separate the strut from the steering knuckle. Remove the steering knuckle/hub assembly from the strut.

11. Remove the 3 top mount-to-shock tower nuts and the strut assembly from the vehicle.

12. Compress the coil spring using a suitable spring compressor. Use a 10mm box end wrench to hold the top of the strut shaft while removing the nut with a 21mm 6-point crow foot wrench and ratchet.

13. Loosen the spring compressor, then remove the top mount bracket assembly, bearing plate assembly and spring.

To install:

14. Install the spring compressor. Install the spring, bearing plate assembly, lower washer and top mount bracket assembly.

15. Compress the spring. Install the upper washer and nut on the shock strut shaft. Tighten the nut with the 21mm 6-point crow foot wrnch and ratchet while holding the shaft with the 10mm box end wrench.

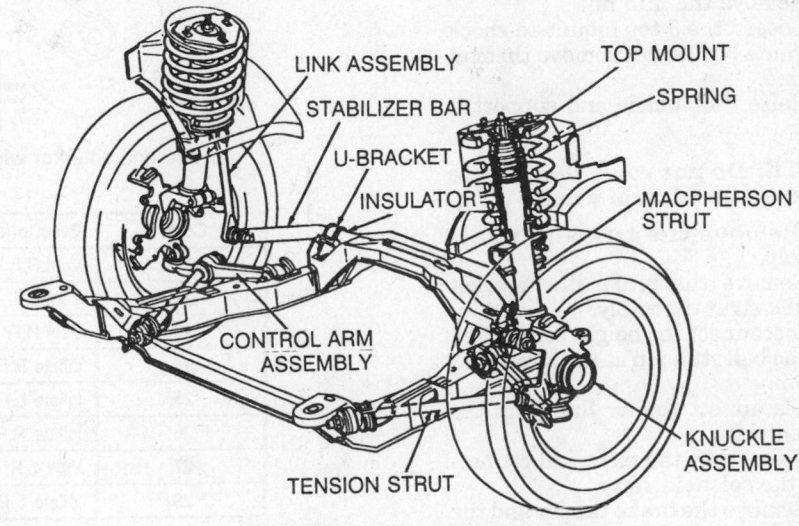

Front suspension—Taurus and Sable

16. Install the strut assembly and the 3 top mount-to-shock tower nuts.

17. Install the steering knuckle and hub assembly to the strut.

18. Install a new strut-to-steering knuckle pinch bolt. Tighten the bolt to 73–97 ft. lbs. (98–132 Nm).

19. Install the halfshaft into the hub.

20. Install the lower arm to the steering knuckle and install a new pinch bolt and nut. Tighten to 40–53 ft. lbs. (54–72 Nm).

21. Install the stabilizer link to the strut and install a new stabilizer bar link nut. Tighten to 57–75 ft. lbs. (77–101 Nm).

22. Install the tie rod end onto the knuckle using a new castle nut. Tighten the castle nut to 23–35 ft. lbs. (31–47 Nm). Retain the castle nut with a new cotter pin.

23. Install the disc brake rotor, caliper and tire and wheel assembly.

24. Tighten the 3 top mount-to-shock tower nuts to 23–29 ft. lbs. (30–40 Nm).

25. Lower the vehicle and tighten the hub nut to 170–202 ft. lbs. (230–275 Nm).

26. Depress the brake pedal several times before moving the vehicle. Check the front end alignment.

Continental

1. Turn OFF the air suspension switch, located in the left side of the luggage compartment.

2. Place the ignition switch in the OFF position and the steering column in the UNLOCKED position.

3. Remove the plastic cover from the shock tower to gain access to the upper mounting nuts and dual damping actuator.

4. Remove the actuator retaining screws. Remove the actuator and place it aside.

5. Remove the hub nut.

6. Loosen the 3 top mount-to-shock tower nuts but do not remove them at this time.

7. Raise the vehicle and support it safely.

NOTE: Do not raise the vehicle by the lower control arms.

8. Remove the tire and wheel assembly.

9. Remove the brake line bracket from the strut assembly.

10. Disconnect the height sensor link from the ball stud pin at the lower control arm.

11. Disconnect the air line from the solenoid valve.

12. Disconnect the electrical connector at the solenoid valve.

13. Remove the brake caliper and the disc brake rotor. Support the caliper with wire; do not let the caliper hang by the brake hose.

14. Remove the cotter pin and castle nut from the tie rod end. Discard the cotter pin and castle nut.

15. Using tie rod end remover TOOL–3290–D and tie rod end remover adapter T81P–3504–W or equivalent, remove the tie rod from the knuckle.

16. Remove the stabilizer bar link nut and the link from the strut.

17. Remove and discard the lower arm-to-steering knuckle pinch bolt and nut. A suitable drift punch may be used to remove the bolt. Using a small prybar, slightly spread the knuckle-to-lower arm pinch joint and remove the lower arm from the steering knuckle.

18. Remove the halfshaft from the hub.

NOTE: When removing the halfshaft, do not allow the halfshaft to move outward. This could result in seperation of the internal parts of the tripod CV-joint, causing failure of the joint.

19. Remove the strut-to-steering knuckle pinch bolt. Using a small prybar, slightly spread the knuckle-to-strut pinch joint to remove the strut from the steering knuckle.

20. Remove the 3 top mount-to-shock tower nuts and remove the strut from the vehicle.

To install:

21. Install the strut with the 3 top mount-to-shock tower nuts and leave the nuts loose.

22. Install the steering knuckle and hub assembly to the strut. Install a new strut-to-steering knuckle pinch bolt. Tighten the bolt to 73–97 ft. lbs. (98–132 Nm).

23. Install the halfshaft into the hub.

24. Install the lower arm to the steering knuckle and install a new pinch bolt and nut. Tighten to 40–53 ft. lbs. (54–72 Nm).

25. Install the stabilizer bar link to the strut and install a new stabilizer bar link nut. Tighten to 57–75 ft. lbs. (77–101 Nm).

26. Install the tie rod end onto the knuckle using a new castle nut. Before tightening the nut, make sure the steering wheel and wheels are in the straight-ahead position. Tighten the castle nut to 23–35 ft. lbs. (31–47 Nm). Install a new cotter pin in the castle nut.

27. Install the brake caliper and rotor.

28. Connect the electrical connector and the air line to the solenoid valve and position them properly.

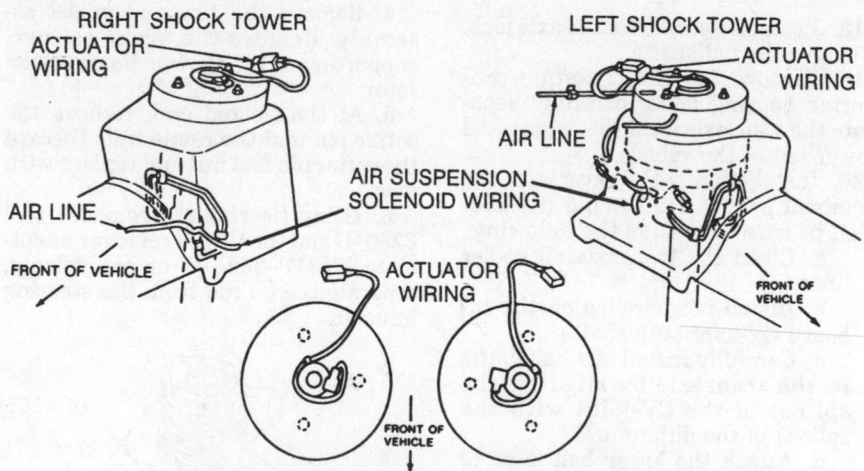

Air line and actuator wiring positioning—Continental

Code	Description
21	Vent R.F.
22	Vent L.F.
23	Vent R.R.
24	Inflate R.F.
25	Inflate L.F.
26	Inflate R.R.
27	Vent L.R.
28	Inflate L.R.

Air suspension spring fill codes—Continental

29. Install the height sensor link on the ball stud pin on the control arm.

30. Install the brake line bracket to the strut assembly.

31. Install the wheel and tire assembly.

32. Tighten the 3 top mount-to-shock tower nuts to 20–30 ft. lbs. (27–40 Nm).

33. Install the dual damping actuator and the plastic shock tower cover. Correctly position the actuator wiring.

34. Refill the air spring prior to fully lowering the vehicle. The refill procedure is as follows:

   a. Place the air suspension service switch in the **ON** position.

   b. Turn the ignition switch **OFF**.

   c. Connect a battery charger to reduce battery drain.

   d. Open the access door in the left-hand luggage compartment trim panel to plug the SUPER STAR II tester or equivalent, into the air suspension diagnostics wiring harness connector.

   e. The tester button should be in the **HOLD** (up) position.

   f. With the brake pedal depressed hard, turn the ignition switch to the **RUN** position.

   g. Move the tester button to the **TEST** (down) position.

   h. The air suspension control module will now start sending out the spring fill selection codes to be displayed on the tester. These codes will be displayed in a scrolling manner.

   i. Select the desired spring fill operation by releasing the tester button when the desired code is displayed. Select either Code 24 or Code 25 to inflate either the right front or left front air spring. As long as the tester button is released the inflation will continue. To stop inflation, move the tester button back down to the **TEST** position. The spring fill codes will again be displayed.

NOTE: Do not apply a load to the suspension until after the air spring has been inflated at least 60 seconds.

   j. To exit the spring fill mode, turn the ignition switch to the **OFF** position and unplug the tester.

35. Lower the vehicle and tighten the hub nut to 170–202 lbs. (230–275 Nm).

36. Turn on the air suspension.

37. Depress the brake pedal several times before moving the vehicle. Check the front end alignment.

Lower Ball Joints

INSPECTION

1. On Continental, turn **OFF** the air suspension switch, located in the left side of the luggage compartment.

2. Raise the vehicle and safely support it so the wheels fall to the full-down position.

3. Have an assistant grasp the lower edge of the tire and move the wheel and tire assembly in and out.

4. Observe the lower end of the knuckle and the lower control arm as the wheel is being moved in and out. Any movement indicates abnormal ball joint wear.

5. If there is any movement, install a new lower control arm assembly.

6. Lower the vehicle. On Continental, turn **ON** the air suspension.

REMOVAL & INSTALLATION

Ball joints are integral parts of the lower control arms. If an inspection reveals an unsatisfactory ball joint, the entire lower control arm assembly must be replaced.

Lower Control Arms

REMOVAL & INSTALLATION

1. On Continental, turn **OFF** the air suspension switch, located in the left side of the luggage compartment.

2. Raise and support the front of the vehicle safely. Remove the wheel and tire assembly. Position the steering column in the unlocked position.

3. Disconnect the height sensor link from the ball stud pin on Continental.

4. Remove the tension strut-to-control arm nut and the dished washer. Discard the nut.

5. Remove and discard the lower control ball joint pinch bolt. Using a small prybar, spread the pinch joint and separate the control arm from the steering knuckle. A drift punch may be used to remove the bolt.

NOTE: When separating the control arm from the steering knuckle, do not use a hammer. Be careful not to damage the ball joint boot seal.

6. Remove and discard the control arm-to-frame nut/bolt, then the control arm from the frame and the tension strut.

NOTE: Do not allow the halfshaft to move outward or the tripod CV-joint internal parts could separate, causing failure of the joint.

7. To install, use a new tension strut nut, ball joint pinch nut/bolt and lower control arm inner pivot bolt nut and reverse the removal procedures. Tighten the bolts to the following torque specifications:

   Control arm-to-frame 73–97 ft. lbs. (98–132 Nm)

   Control arm-to-steering knuckle 40–53 ft. lbs. (54–72 Nm)

   Tension strut-to-control arm 73–97 ft. lbs. (98–132 Nm)

   Wheel lug nuts 80–105 ft. lbs. (109–142 Nm)

8. Check the front end alignment.

REAR SUSPENSION

Shock Absorbers

REMOVAL & INSTALLATION

Taurus/Sable Wagon

1. Raise and support the vehicle safely.

2. Remove the wheel and tire assembly.

3. Position a jack stand under the lower suspension arm. Remove the 2 nuts retaining the shock absorber to the lower suspension arm.

4. From inside the vehicle, remove the rear compartment access panels.

5. Remove and discard the top shock absorber attaching nut using a crow's foot wrench and ratchet while holding the shock absorber shaft stationary with an open end wrench.

NOTE: If the shock absorber is to be reused, do not grip the shaft with pliers or vise grips. Gripping the shaft in this manner will damage the shaft surface finish and will result in severe oil leakage.

6. Remove the rubber insulator from the shock and the shock from the vehicle.

NOTE: The shocks are gas filled. It will require an effort to collapse the shock in order to remove it from the lower arm.

To install:

7. Install a new washer and insulator on the upper shock absorber rod.

8. Maneuver the upper part of the shock absorber into the shock tower opening in the body. Push slowly on the lower part of the shock absorber until the mounting studs are aligned with the mounting holes in the lower suspension arm.

9. Install new lower attaching nuts but do not tighten at this time.

10. Install a new insulator, washer and nut on top of the shock absorber. Torque the nut to 19–25 ft. lbs. (26–34 Nm.).

11. Install the rear compartment access panel.

12. Torque the 2 lower attaching nuts to 15–19 ft. lbs. (19–26 Nm).

13. Install the wheel and tire assembly. Remove the safety stand supporting the lower suspension arm and lower the vehicle.

MacPherson Strut

REMOVAL & INSTALLATION

Taurus/Sable Sedan

1. Raise and support the rear of the vehicle safely. Remove the wheel and tire.

NOTE: Do not raise or support the vehicle using the tension struts.

2. Raise the luggage compartment lid and loosen but do not remove, the upper strut-to-body nuts.

3. Remove the brake differential control valve-to-control arm bolt. Using a wire, secure the control arm to the body to ensure proper support leaving at least 6 in. clearance to aid in the strut removal.

4. Remove the brake hose-to-strut bracket clip and move the hose aside.

5. If equipped, remove the stabilizer bar U-bracket from the vehicle.

6. If equipped, remove the stabilizer bar-to-stabilizer link nut, washer and insulator, then separate the stabilizer bar from the link.

NOTE: When removing the strut, be sure the rear brake flex hose is not stretched or the steel brake tube is not bent.

7. Remove the tension strut-to-spindle nut, washer and insulator. Move the spindle rearward to separate it from the tension strut.

8. Remove the shock strut-to-spindle pinch bolt. If necessary, use a medium prybar, spread the strut-to-spindle pinch joint to remove the strut. Discard the bolt and replace it.

9. Lower the jackstand and separate the shock strut from the spindle.

10. Support the shock strut, then loosen the top strut-to-body nuts completely and remove the strut from the vehicle.

11. Remove the nut, washer and insulator attaching link to strut and remove link. Mark the location of the insulator to top mount, then compress the spring, using a suitable spring compressor.

12. Use a 10mm box end wrench to hold the top of the strut shaft while removing the nut with a 21mm 6-point crow foot wrench and ratchet. Loosen the spring compressor, then remove the top mount bracket assembly, spring insulator and spring.

To install:

13. Using the spring compressor, install the spring, spring insulator, bottom washer, if equipped, top mount, upper washer and nut on the strut shaft. Make sure the spring is properly located in the upper and lower spring seats and the mount washers are positioned correctly.

14. Tighten the rod nut to 35–50 ft. lbs. (48–68 Nm). Use a 21mm crow foot wrench to turn the nut and a 10mm box end wrench to hold the shaft. Do not use pliers or vise grips on the strut rod.

15. Position the stabilizer bar link in the strut bracket. Install the insulator, washer and nut and tighten to 5–7 ft. lbs. (7–9.5 Nm).

16. Insert the 3 upper mount studs into the strut tower in the apron and hand start 3 new nuts. Do not tighten the nuts at this time.

17. Partially raise the vehicle.

18. Install the strut into the spindle pinch joint. Install a new pinch bolt into the spindle and through the strut bracket. Tighten the bolt to 50–70 ft. lbs. (68–95 Nm).

19. Move the spindle rearward and install the tension strut into the spindle. Install the insulator, washer and nut on the tension strut. Tighten the nut to 35–50 ft. lbs. (48–68 Nm).

20. Position the link into the stabilizer bar. Install the insulator, washer and nut on the link. Tighten to 5–7 ft. lbs. (7–9.5 Nm).

21. Position the stabilizer bar U-bracket on the body. Install the bolt and tighten to 25–37 ft. lbs. (34–50 Nm).

22. Install the brake hose to the strut bracket.

23. Install the brake control differential valve on the control arm and remove the retaining wire.

24. Install the top mount-to-body nuts and tighten to 19–26 ft. lbs. (26–35 Nm).

25. Install the wheel and tire assembly and lower the vehicle.

Continental

1. Turn OFF the air suspension switch located in the luggage compartment.

2. From inside the luggage compartment, disconnect the electrical connector from the dual dampening actuator.

3. Loosen but do not remove the 3 nuts retaining the strut to the upper body.

4. Raise and support the vehicle safely. Remove the wheel and tire assembly.

NOTE: Do not raise the vehicle by the tension strut.

5. Disconect the air line and electrical connector from the solenoid valve.

6. Remove the brake hose retainer at the strut bracket.

7. Disconnect the parking brake cable from the brake caliper. Remove all the wire retainers and parking brake cable retainers from the lower suspension arm.

8. Disconnect the height sensor link from the ball stud pin on the lower arm.

9. Remove the caliper assembly from the spindle and position it off to the side with a piece of wire. Do not kink or place a load on the brake hose.

10. Bleed the air spring by performing the following:

a. Remove the solenoid clip.

b. Rotate the solenoid counterclockwise to the first stop.

c. Slowly pull the solenoid straight out to the second stop and bleed the air from the system.

——— CAUTION ———

Do not fully release the solenoid until the air is fully bled from the spring or personal injury may result.

d. After the air is fully bled from the system, rotate the solenoid to the third stop and remove the solenoid from the housing.

11. Mark the position of the notch on the toe adjustment cam.

12. Remove the torsion spring clamp from the spindle-to-strut bolt.

13. Remove the nut from the inboard bushing on the suspension arm.

14. Install torsion spring remover tool T88P–5310–A or equivalent, on the suspension arm. Pry up on the tool and arm using a ¾ in. drive ratchet to relieve the pressure on the pivot bolt. An assistant may be required to pull outboard on the spindle simultaneously to fully relieve the tension on the bolt. Remove the bolt and lower arm. Repeat this procedure for the opposite arm.

15. Remove the torsion spring from the arms.

16. Remove the stabilizer U-bracket from the body.

17. Remove the nut, washer and insulator attaching the stabilizer bar to the link. Separate the stabilizer bar from the link.

18. Remove the nut, washer and insulator retaining the tension strut to the spindle. Move the spindle rearward enough to separate it from the tension strut.

19. Remove and discard the strut-to-

spindle pinch bolt. With a suitable prybar, spread the strut-to-spindle pinch joint as required to assist in removing the bolt.

20. Separate the spindle from the strut. Remove the spindle as an assembly with the arms attached.

21. From inside the luggage compartment area, support the shock strut by hand and remove and discard the 3 upper mount-to-body nuts. Care should be taken not to drop the strut when removing the upper nuts. Guide the electric actuator wire through the opening to prevent snagging and damage while removing the strut assembly.

To install:

22. Install the solenoid valve on the air spring.

23. Guide the electric actuator wire through the opening and install the strut assembly. Install 3 new upper mount nuts.

24. Install the spindle and arms to the strut. Install a new strut-to-spindle pinch bolt. Do not tighten the bolt until the control arms are attached to the body and the cams are centered.

25. Position the tension strut to the spindle. Install the insulator, washer and nut retaining the tension strut to the spindle. Tighten the nut to 35–50 ft. lbs. (48–68 Nm).

26. Install the stabilizer bar to the link. Install the insulator, washer and retaining nut. Tighten the nut to 5–7 ft. lbs. (7–9.5 Nm).

27. Install the stabilizer U-bracket to the body. Tighten the bolt to 25–37 ft. lbs. (34–50 Nm).

28. Install the torsion spring to the arms.

29. Position the inboard bushing using torsion spring remover T88P-5310–A or equivalent, and install the bolt. An assistant may be required to pull outboard on the spindle to align the bushing so the bolt can be inserted. Repeat the procedure for the opposite lower arm.

30. Install the nut to the inboard bushing on the suspension arm but do not tighten at this time.

31. Tighten the spindle-to-strut bolt to 51–70 ft. lbs. (68–95 Nm).

32. Set the toe adjustment cam to the alignment mark.

33. Remove the wire from the caliper and install the caliper to the spindle.

34. Connect the height sensor link to the ball stud pin on the lower arm.

35. Install the torsion spring clamp and secure.

36. Install all wire retainers and parking brake cable retainers to the lower suspension arm.

37. Connect the parking brake cable to the brake caliper and install the brake hose retainer at the strut bracket.

38. Connect the air line and the electrical connector to the solenoid valve.

39. Install the wheel and tire assembly and partially lower the vehicle.

40. Tighten the 3 nuts retaining the strut to the upper body to 19–26 ft. lbs. (26–35 Nm).

41. From inside the luggage compartment, connect the electrical connector for the dual dampening actuator.

42. Turn on the air suspension switch and fill the air spring as follows:

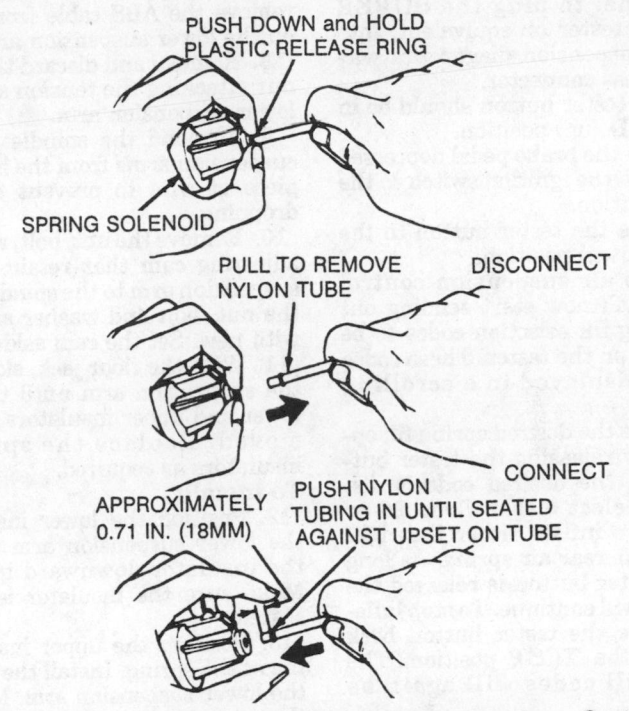

Air suspension air line connect and disconnect procedure—Continental

Code	Description
21	Vent R.F.
22	Vent L.F.
23	Vent R.R.
24	Inflate R.F.
25	Inflate L.F.
26	Inflate R.R.
27	Vent L.R.
28	Inflate L.R.

Air suspension spring fill codes—Continental

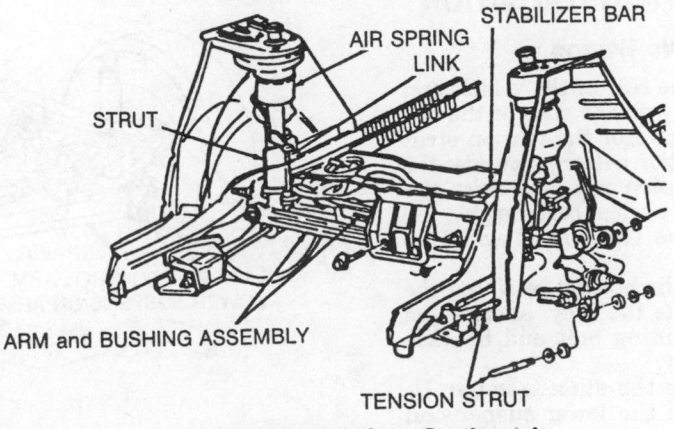

Rear suspension—Continental

a. Place the air suspension service switch in the ON position.

b. Turn the ignition switch OFF.

c. Connect a battery charger to reduce battery drain.

d. Open the access door in the left-hand luggage compartment trim panel to plug the SUPER STAR II tester or equivalent, into the air suspension diagnostics wiring harness connector.

e. The tester button should be in the HOLD (up) position.

f. With the brake pedal depressed hard, turn the ignition switch to the RUN position.

g. Move the tester button to the TEST (down) position.

h. The air suspension control module will now start sending out the spring fill selection codes to be displayed on the tester. These codes will be displayed in a scrolling manner.

i. Select the desired spring fill operation by releasing the tester button when the desired code is displayed. Select either Code 26 or Code 28 to inflate either the right rear or left rear air spring. As long as the tester button is released the inflation will continue. To stop inflation, move the tester button back down to the TEST position. The spring fill codes will again be displayed.

NOTE: Do not apply a load to the suspension until after the air spring has been inflated at least 60 seconds.

j. To exit the spring fill mode, turn the ignition switch to the OFF position and unplug the tester.

43. Lower the vehicle all of the way. Check the toe setting and adjust if necessary.

44. Tighten the inboard bushing nut to 45–65 ft. lbs. (61–88 Nm).

Coil Springs

REMOVAL & INSTALLATION

Taurus/Sable Wagon

1. Raise the rear of the vehicle and support safely on the pads of the underbody forward of the tension strut bracket. Position a floor jack under the lower suspension arm and raise the lower arm to normal curb height.

2. Remove the wheel and tire assembly.

3. Locate the bracket retaining the flexible hose to the body. Remove the bracket retaining bolt and bracket from the body.

4. Remove the stabilizer bar U-bracket from the lower suspension arm.

5. Remove and discard the nuts attaching the shock absorber to the lower suspension arm.

6. Disconnect and remove the parking brake cable and clip from the lower suspension arm.

7. If equipped with rear disc brakes, remove the ABS cable from the clips on the lower suspension arm.

8. Remove and discard the bolt and nut attaching the tension strut to the lower suspension arm.

9. Suspend the spindle and upper suspension arms from the body with a piece of wire to prevent them from dropping.

10. Remove the nut, bolt, washer and adjusting cam that retain the lower suspension arm to the spindle. Discard the nut, bolt and washer and replace with new. Set the cam aside.

11. With the floor jack, slowly lower the suspension arm until the spring, lower and upper insulators can be removed. Replace the spring and insulators as required.

To install:

12. Position the lower insulator on the lower suspension arm and press the insulator downward into place. Make sure the insulator is properly seated.

13. Position the upper insulator on top of the spring. Install the spring on the lower suspension arm. Make sure the spring is properly seated.

14. With the floor jack, slowly raise the suspension arm. Guide the upper spring insulator onto the upper spring underbody seat.

15. Position the spindle in the lower suspension arm with a new bolt, nut washer, and the existing cam. Install the bolt with the head of the bolt toward the front of the vehicle. Do not tighten the bolt at this time.

16. Remove the wire supporting the spindle and suspension arms.

17. Install the tension strut in the lower suspension arm using a new nut and bolt; do not tighten at this time.

18. Attach the parking brake cable and clip to the lower suspension arm.

19. If equipped with rear disc brakes, install the ABS cable into the clips on the lower suspension arm.

20. Position the shock absorber on the lower suspension arm and install 2 new nuts. Torque the nuts to 15–19 ft. lbs. (19–26 Nm).

21. Attach the stabilizer bar and U-bracket to the lower suspension arm using a new bolt. Torque the bolt to 23–30 ft. lbs. (30–40 Nm).

22. Attach the flexible brake hose to the body and tighten the bolt to 8–12 ft. lbs. (11–16 Nm).

23. With the floor jack, raise the lower suspension to normal curb height. Torque the lower suspension arm-to-spindle nut to 40–52 ft. lbs. (54–71 Nm). Torque the bolt that attaches the tension strut to the body bracket to 40–52 ft. lbs. (54–71 Nm).

24. Install the wheel and tire assembly. Remove the floor jack and lower the vehicle.

25. Check the rear wheel alignment and adjust if necessary.

Rear Control Arms

REMOVAL & INSTALLATION

Taurus/Sable Sedan

1. Raise the vehicle and support it safely. Do not raise the vehicle by the tension strut.

2. Disconnect the brake proportioning valve from the left side front arm.

3. Disconnect the parking brake cable from the front arms.

4. Remove and discard the arm-to-spindle bolt, washer and nut.

5. Remove and discard the arm-to-body bolt and nut.

6. Remove the arm from the vehicle.

To install:

NOTE: When installing new control arms, the offset on all arms must face up. The arms are

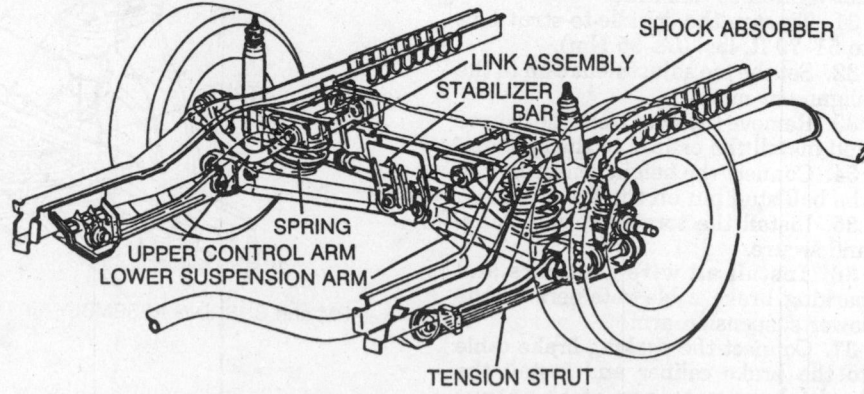

Rear suspension—Taurus and Sable wagon

SHOCK ABSORBER
LINK ASSEMBLY
STABILIZER BAR
SPRING
UPPER CONTROL ARM
LOWER SUSPENSION ARM
TENSION STRUT

stamped "bottom" on the lower edge. The flange edge of the right side rear arm stamping must face the front of the vehicle. The other 3 must face the rear of the vehicle. The rear control arms have 2 adjustment cams that fit inside the bushings at the arm-to-body attachment. The cam is installed from the rear on the left arm and from the front on the right arm.

7. Position the arm and cam where required, at the center of the vehicle. Insert a new bolt and nut but do not tighten at this time.

8. Move the arm end up to the spindle and insert a new bolt, washer and nut. Tighten the nut to 44–59 ft. lbs. (60–80 Nm).

9. Tighten the arm-to-body nut to 50–67 ft. lbs. (68–92 Nm).

10. Attach the parking brake cable to the front arms and the brake proportioning valve to the left side front arm.

11. Lower the vehicle and check the alignment.

Continental

1. Turn **OFF** the air suspension switch located in the luggage compartment.

2. Raise and support the vehicle safely.

3. Remove all wire retainers and parking brake cable retainers from the lower suspension arm.

4. Disconnect the height sensor link from the ball stud pin on the lower arm.

5. Mark the position of the notch on the toe adjustment cam.

6. Remove the torsion spring retaining clamp at the spindle.

7. Remove the nut from the inboard bushing on the suspension arm.

8. Install torsion spring remover T88P-5310-A or equivalent, on the arm. Using a ¾ in. ratchet, pry up on the tool and arm to relieve the pressure on the pivot bolt. An assistant may also be required to pull outward on the spindle at the same time to fully relieve the tension on the bolt. Remove the bolt and lower the arm.

9. Remove the nut retaining the torsion spring to the arm and seperate the spring from the arm.

10. Remove the outboard attaching bolt at the spindle.

11. Repeat the removal procedure for the other arm.

To install:

NOTE: When installing new control arms, the offset must face up. The arms are stamped "bottom" on the lower edge. The rear control arms have adjustment cams that fit inside the bushings at the arm-to-body attachment.

The cams are installed from the front of both arms.

12. Loosely attach the arm(s) at the spindle. Attach the torsion spring(s) to the arm(s).

13. Position the inboard bushing using torsion spring remover T88P-5310-A or equivalent, and install the bolt. It may be required to have an assistant pull outward on the spindle to align the bushing so the bolt can be inserted. Repeat this step for the opposite side.

14. Set the toe adjustment cam to the alignment mark for rear arm only.

15. Connect the height sensor link to the ball stud pin on the lower arm for right front only.

16. Install all wire retainers and parking brake cable retainers to the lower suspension arm.

17. Lower the vehicle and then turn **ON** the air suspension switch.

18. With the vehicle suspension at curb height, tighten the control arm-to-spindle bolt to 44–59 ft. lbs. (60–80 Nm) and the control arm-to-body bolt to 50–68 ft. lbs. (68–92 Nm).

19. Check the rear toe setting.

Taurus/Sable Wagon

UPPER ARMS

1. Raise the vehicle and support it with wood blocks on jackstands so the suspension is at normal curb height.

2. Remove the wheel and tire assembly.

3. Remove the brake line flexible hose bracket from the body.

4. Loosen, but do not remove the nuts attaching the spindle to the upper and lower suspension arms.

5. Remove and discard the nuts and bolts attaching the front and rear upper suspension arms to the body brackets. Make sure the spindle does not fall outward.

6. Carefully tilt the top of the spindle outward, letting it pivot on the lower suspension arm attaching bolt until the ends of the upper suspension arms are clear of the body bracket. Support the spindle with wire in this position.

7. Remove and discard the nut attaching the upper suspension arms to the spindle and remove the arms from the vehicle.

To install:

8. Install the upper suspension arms on the spindle and install a new nut but do not tighten the nut at this time.

9. Position the upper suspension arm ends to the body bracket and install new nuts and bolts. Tighten to 73–97 ft. lbs. (95–129 Nm). Remove the wire from the spindle.

10. Tighten the nut attaching the upper suspension arms to the spindle to 150–190 ft. lbs. (204–257 Nm). Tight-

en the nut attaching the lower suspension arm to the spindle to 40–52 ft. lbs. (54–71 Nm).

11. Install the brake line bracket to the body.

12. Install the wheel and tire assembly, remove the jackstand and wood block and lower the vehicle.

13. Check the rear wheel alignment.

LOWER ARM

1. Raise and support the vehicle safely on the lifting pads on the underbody forward of the tension strut body bracket.

2. Remove the wheel and tire assembly.

3. Place a floor jack under the lower suspension arm.

4. Remove the bracket retaining the flexible brake hose to the body.

5. Remove the stabilizer bar U-bracket from the lower suspension arm.

6. Remove and discard the nuts attaching the shock absorber to the lower suspension arm.

7. Remove the parking brake cable and clip from the lower suspension arm.

8. Remove and discard the bolt and nut attaching the tension strut to the lower suspension arm.

9. Support the spindle and upper suspension arms by wiring them to the body, to prevent them from dropping down.

10. Remove the nut, bolt, washer and adjusting cam retaining the lower suspension arm to the spindle. Discard the nut, bolt and washer.

11. Lower the suspension arm with the floor jack until the spring can be removed.

12. Remove and discard the bolt and nut attaching the lower suspension arm to the center body bracket and remove the arm.

To install:

13. Position the lower suspension arm-to-center body bracket and install but do not tighten a new bolt and nut with the bolt head toward the front of the vehicle.

14. Position the lower insulator on the lower suspension arm and press the insulator downward into place. Make sure the insulator is properly seated.

15. Position the upper insulator on top of the spring. Install the spring on the lower suspension arm, making sure the spring is properly seated.

16. Raise the suspension arm with the floor jack and guide the upper spring insulator onto the upper spring seat on the underbody.

17. Position the spindle in the lower suspension arm and install, but do not tighten, a new bolt, nut, washer and

the existing cam, with the bolt head toward the front of the vehicle.

18. Remove the wire from the spindle and suspension arms.

19. Install the tension strut in the lower suspension arm using a new bolt and nut but do not tighten at this time.

20. Install the parking brake cable and clip to the lower suspension arm.

21. Position the shock absorber on the lower suspension arm and install 2 new nuts. Tighten the nuts to 15–19 ft. lbs. (19–26 Nm).

22. Install the stabilizer bar and U-bracket to the lower suspension arm using a new bolt. Tighten the bolt to 23–30 ft. lbs. (30–40 Nm).

23. Install the flexible brake hose bracket to the body. Tighten the bolt to 8–12 ft. lbs. (11–16 Nm).

24. Using the floor jack, raise the lower suspension arm to normal curb height. Tighten the following to 40–52 ft. lbs. (54–71 Nm):

Lower suspension arm-to-body bracket nut

Lower suspension arm-to-spindle nut

Tension strut-to-body bracket bolt

25. Install the wheel and tire assembly and lower the vehicle.

26. Check the rear wheel alignment.

Rear Wheel Bearings

REMOVAL & INSTALLATION

Drum Brakes

1989

1. Raise the vehicle and support it safely. Remove the wheel from the hub and drum.

2. Remove the grease cap from the hub. Remove the cotter pin, nut retainer, adjusting nut and keyed flat washer from the spindle. Discard the cotter pin.

3. Pull the hub and drum assembly off the spindle. Remove the outer bearing assembly.

4. Using seal remover tool 1175–AC or equivalent, remove and discard the grease seal. Remove the inner bearing assembly from the hub.

5. Wipe all lubricant from the spindle and inside of the hub. Cover the spindle with a clean cloth and vacuum all loose dust and dirt from the brake assembly. Carefully remove the cloth to prevent dirt from falling on the spindle.

6. Clean both bearing assemblies and cups using a suitable solvent. Inspect the bearing assemblies and cups for excessive wear, scratches, pits or other damage and replace as necessary.

7. If the cups are to be replaced, remove them with impact slide hammer T50T–100–A and bearing cup puller T77F–1102–A or equivalent.

To install:

8. If the inner and outer bearing cups were removed, install the replacement cups using driver handle T80T–4000–W and bearing cup replacers T73T–1217–A and T77F–1217–B or equivalent. Support the drum hub on a block of wood to prevent damage. Make sure the cups are properly seated in the hub.

NOTE: Do not use the roller bearing assembly to install the cups. This will result in damage to the bearing cup and the roller bearing assembly.

9. Make sure all of the spindle and bearing surfaces are clean.

10. Using a bearing packer, pack the bearing assemblies with a suitable wheel bearing grease. If a packer is not available, work in as much grease as possible between the rollers and cages. Grease the cup surfaces.

NOTE: Allow all of the cleaning solvent to dry before repacking the bearings. Do not spin-dry the bearings with air pressure.

11. Install the inner bearing assembly in the inner cup. Apply a light film of grease to the lips of a new grease seal and install the seal with rear hub seal replacer T56T–4676–B or equivalent. Make sure the retainer flange is seated all around.

12. Apply a light film of grease on the spindle shaft bearing surfaces. Install the hub and drum assembly on the spindle. Keep the hub centered on the spindle to prevent damage to the grease seal and spindle threads.

13. Install the outer bearing assembly and the keyed flatwasher on the spindle. Install the adjusting nut and adjust the wheel bearings. Install a new cotter pin. Install the grease cap.

14. Install the wheel and tire assembly and lower the vehicle.

1990–93

1. Raise the vehicle and support it safely.

2. Remove the wheel and tire assembly.

3. Remove the 2 pushnuts retaining the drum to the hub and remove the drum.

4. Remove the grease cap from the bearing and hub assembly and discard it.

5. Remove the hub retaining nut and remove the bearing and hub assembly from the spindle.

6. Install in the reverse order of removal. Use tool T89P–19623–FH or equivalent, to install the new grease cap. Tap on the tool to make sure the grease cap is fully seated. Tighten the hub retaining nut to 188–254 ft. lbs. (255–345 Nm).

Disc Brakes

1989

1. Raise the vehicle and support it

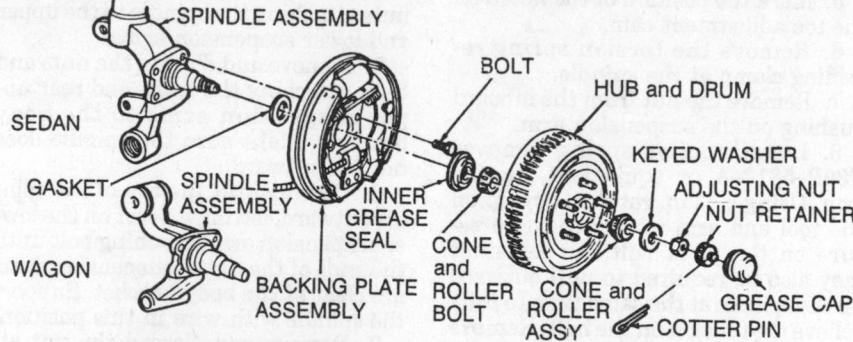

Rear wheel hub and bearing assembly—1989 vehicles with drum brakes

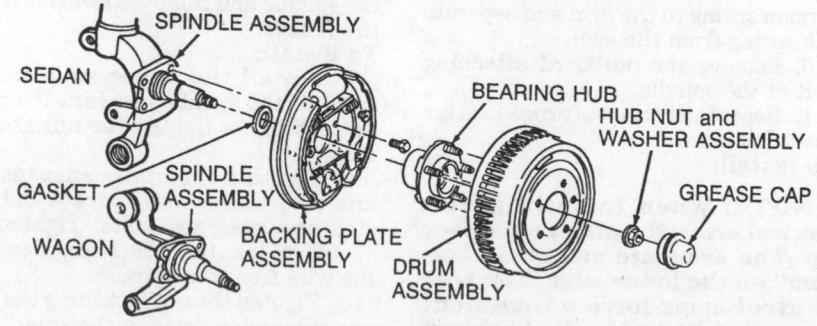

Rear wheel hub and bearing assembly—1990–93 vehicles with drum brakes

safely. Remove the tire and wheel assembly from the hub.

2. Remove the brake caliper by removing the 2 bolts that attach the caliper support to the cast iron brake adapter. Do not remove the caliper pins from the caliper assembly. Lift the caliper off of the rotor and support it with a length of wire. Do not allow the caliper assembly to hang from the brake hose.

3. Remove the 2 push-on nuts, if equipped. Remove the rotor from the hub by pulling it off the hub bolts. If the rotor is difficult to remove, strike the rotor sharply between the studs with a rubber or plastic hammer.

4. Remove the grease cap from the hub. Remove the cotter pin, nut retainer, adjusting nut and keyed flat washer from the spindle. Discard the cotter pin.

5. Pull the hub assembly off of the spindle. Remove the outer bearing assembly.

6. Using seal remover tool 1175–AC or equivalent, remove and discard the grease seal. Remove the inner bearing assembly from the hub.

7. Wipe all of the lubricant from the spindle and inside of the hub. Cover the spindle with a clean cloth and vacuum all of the loose dust and dirt from the brake assembly. Carefully remove the cloth to prevent dirt from falling on the spindle.

8. Clean both bearing assemblies and cups using a suitable solvent. Inspect the bearing assemblies and cups for excessive wear, scratches, pits or other damage and replace as necessary.

9. If the cups are being replaced, remove them with impact slide hammer tool T50T–100–A and bearing cup puller tool T77F–1102–A or equivalent.

To install:

10. If the inner and outer bearing cups were removed, install the replacement cups using driver handle tool T80T–4000–W and bearing cup replacer tools T73F–1217–A and T77F–1217–B or equivalent. Support the hub on a block of wood to prevent damage. Make sure the cups are properly seated in the hub.

NOTE: Do not use the roller bearing assembly to install the cups. This will result in damage to the bearing cup and the roller bearing assembly.

11. Make sure all of the spindle and bearing surfaces are clean.

12. Pack the bearing assemblies with a suitable wheel bearing grease using a bearing packer. If a packer is not available, work in as much grease as possible between the rollers and the cages. Grease the cup surfaces.

NOTE: Allow all of the cleaning solvent to dry before repacking the bearings. Do not spin-dry the bearings with air pressure.

13. Place the inner bearing cone and roller assembly in the inner cup. Apply a light film of grease to the lips of a new grease seal and install the seal with rear hub seal replacer tool T56T–4676–B or equivalent. Make sure the retainer flange is seated all around.

14. Apply a light film of grease on the spindle shaft bearing and grease seal surfaces. Install the hub assembly on the spindle. Keep the hub centered on the spindle to prevent damage to the grease seal and spindle threads.

15. Install the outer bearing assembly and keyed flat washer on the spindle. Install the adjusting nut and adjust the wheel bearings. Install a new cotter pin. Install the grease cap.

16. Install the disc brake rotor to the hub assembly. Install the disc brake caliper over the rotor.

17. Install the wheel and tire assembly and lower the vehicle.

1990–93

1. Raise the vehicle and support it safely.

2. Remove the wheel and tire assembly.

3. Remove the caliper assembly from the brake adapter. Support the caliper assembly with a length of wire; do not let it hang by the brake hose.

4. Remove the push on nuts that retain the rotor to the hub and remove the rotor.

5. Remove the grease cap from the bearing and hub assembly and discard the grease cap.

6. Remove the bearing and hub assembly retaining nut and remove the bearing and hub assembly from the spindle.

7. Install in the reverse order of removal. Install a new grease cap using tool T89P–19623–FH or equivalent. Tap on the tool until the grease cap is fully seated. Tighten the hub retaining nut to 188–254 ft. lbs. (255–345 Nm).

STEERING

Steering Wheel

— CAUTION —

If equipped with an air bag, the air bag must be disarmed before working on the system. Failure to do so may result in deployment of the air bag and possible personal injury. Always wear safety glasses when servicing an air bag vehicle and when handling an air bag.

REMOVAL & INSTALLATION

1989 Taurus and Sable

1. Disconnect the negative battery cable.

2. Remove the steering wheel horn pad cover by removing 2 screws from the back of the steering wheel. If equipped with cruise control, disconnect the connector from the slip ring terminal.

3. Remove and discard the steering wheel retaining bolt.

4. Remove the steering wheel from the upper shaft by grasping the rim of the steering wheel and pulling off. A steering wheel puller is not required.

To install:

5. Position the steering wheel on the end of the shaft. Align the mark on the steering wheel with the mark on the shaft to ensure the straight-ahead steering wheel position corresponds to the straight-ahead position of the front wheels.

NOTE: The combination switch lever must be in the middle position before installing the steering wheel or damage to the switch cam may result.

6. Install a new steering wheel retaining bolt and tighten to 23–33 ft. lbs. (31–45 Nm).

7. If equipped with cruise control, connect the connector to the slip ring terminal. Install the steering wheel horn pad cover with the 2 screws. Tighten to 5–10 inch lbs. (0.5–1.1 Nm).

8. Connect the negative battery cable.

1989–90 Continental

1. Center the front wheels to the straight-ahead position. Disconnect the negative battery cable. On 1990 vehicles, lower the glove compartment past it's stops and disconnect the air bag backup power supply (blue box, 1 connector).

2. Remove the lower instrument panel cover.

3. Remove the steering column lock cylinder and the tilt release lever.

4. Remove the lower steering column shroud.

5. Disconnect the contact assembly at the body wire harness and remove the contact assembly ground wire screw located at the lock cylinder housing.

6. Remove the 4 air bag module retaining nuts and remove the air bag module from the steering wheel. Disconnect the contact as an assembly at the module.

— CAUTION —

When carrying a live air bag, make sure the bag and trim cover are pointed away from the body. In the unlikely event of an accidental deployment, the bag will then deploy with minimal chance of injury. In addition, when placing a live ai bag on a bench or other surface, always face the bag and trim cover up, away from the surface. This will reduce the motion of the module if it is accidentally deployed.

7. Remove and discard the steering wheel attaching bolt.

8. Remove the steering wheel and contact assembly. Make sure the contact assembly is locked in the straight-ahead position. Do not allow the contact assembly to rotate out of position.

To install:

9. Install the steering wheel and contact assembly onto the steering column. Make sure the drive pin on the speed control/horn brush assembly engages in the drive socket on the contact assembly housing.

10. Install a new steering wheel bolt and tighten to 23–33 ft. lbs. (31–45 Nm).

11. Install the ground wire and retaining screw.

12. Connect the contact assembly wire harness and connect the contact assembly at the module.

13. Install the module to the steering wheel and tighten the retaining nuts.

14. Install the lower steering column shroud, lock cylinder, tilt release lever and the lower instrument panel cover.

15. On 1990 vehicles, connect the air bag backup power supply. Connect the negative battery cable and check the steering column for proper operation.

1990–93 Taurus and Sable and 1991–93 Continental

1. Center the front wheels in the straight-ahead position. Disconnect the negative battery cable.

2. On 1990–91 vehicles, lower the glove compartment past it's stops and disconnect the air bag backup power supply. On 1992–93 vehicles, disconnect the positive battery cable and wait 1 minute for the backup power supply in the diagnostic monitor to deplete its stored energy.

3. Remove the 4 air bag module retaining nuts and lift the module from the wheel. Disconnect the air bag wire harness from the air bag module and remove the module from the wheel.

— CAUTION —

When carrying a live air bag, make sure the bag and trim cover are pointed away from the body. In the unlikely event of an accidental deployment, the bag will then deploy with minimal chance of injury. In addition, when placing a live air bag on a bench or

other surface, always face the bag and trim cover up, away from the surface. This will reduce the motion of the module if it is accidentally deployed.

4. Disconnect the cruise control wire harness from the steering wheel. Remove and discard the steering wheel retaining bolt.

5. Install a suitable steering wheel puller and remove the steering wheel. Route the contact assembly wire harness through the steering wheel as the wheel is lifted off the shaft.

To install:

6. Make sure the vehicle's front wheels are in the straight-ahead position.

7. Route the contact assembly wire harness through the steering wheel opening at the 3 o'clock position and install the steering wheel on the shaft. The steering wheel and shaft alignment marks should be aligned. Make sure the air bag contact wire is not pinched.

8. Install a new steering wheel retaining bolt and tighten to 23–33 ft. lbs. (31–48 Nm).

9. Connect the cruise control wire harness to the wheel and snap the connector assembly into the steering wheel clip. Make sure the wiring does not get trapped between the steering wheel and contact assembly.

10. Connect the air bag wire harness to the air bag module and install the module to the steering wheel. Tighten the module retaining nuts to 36–47 inch lbs. (4.0–5.4 Nm).

11. Connect the air bag backup power supply and the battery cable(s). Verify the air bag warning indicator.

Power Rack and Pinion

REMOVAL & INSTALLATION

Integral Power Rack and Pinion—Taurus and Sable, Except 1990–93 Taurus LX and Sable with 3.8L Engine

1. Disconnect the negative battery cable. Working from inside the vehicle, remove the nuts retaining the steering shaft weather boot to the dash panel.

2. Remove the bolts retaining the intermediate shaft to the steering column shaft. Set the weather boot aside.

3. Remove the pinch bolt at the steering gear input shaft and remove the intermediate shaft. Raise the vehicle and support safely.

4. Remove the left front wheel and tire assembly. Remove the heat shield. Cut the bundling strap retaining the lines to the gear.

5. Remove the tie rod ends from the spindles. Place a drain pan under the vehicle and remove the hydraulic pressure and return lines from the steering gear.

NOTE: The pressure and return lines are on the front of the housing. Do not confuse them with the transfer lines on the side of the valve.

6. Remove the nuts from the gear mounting bolts. The bolts are pressed into the gear housing and should not be removed during gear removal.

7. Push the weather boot end into the vehicle and lift the gear out of the mounting holes. Rotate the gear so the input shaft will pass between the brake booster and the floor pan. Carefully start working the steering gear out through the left fender apron opening.

8. Rotate the input shaft so it clears the left fender apron opening and complete the removal of the steering gear. If the steering gear seems to be stuck, check the right tie rod to ensure the stud is not caught on anything.

To install:

9. Install new plastic seals on the hydraulic line fittings.

10. Insert the steering gear through the left fender apron. Rotate the input shaft forward to completely clear the fender apron opening.

11. To allow the gear to pass between the brake booster and the floorpan, rotate the input shaft rearward. Align the steering gear bolts to the bolt holes. Install the mounting nuts and torque them to 85–100 ft. lbs. (115–135 Nm). Lower the vehicle.

12. From inside the engine compartment, install the hydraulic pressure and return lines. Tighten the pressure line to 20–25 ft. lbs. (28–33Nm) and the return line to 15–20 ft. lbs. (20–28 Nm). Swivel movement of the lines is normal when the fittings are properly tightened.

13. Raise the vehicle and support safely. Secure the pressure and return lines to the transfer tube with the bundle strap. Install the heat shield.

14. Install the tie rod ends to spindles. Torque the castle nuts to 35 ft. lbs. (48 Nm). If necessary, torque the nuts a little bit more to align the slot in the nut for the cotter pin. Install the cotter pin.

15. Install the left front wheel and tire assembly and lower the vehicle. Working from inside the vehicle, pull the weather boot end out of the vehicle and install it over the valve housing. Install the intermediate shaft to the steering gear input shaft. Install the the inner weather boot to the floor pan.

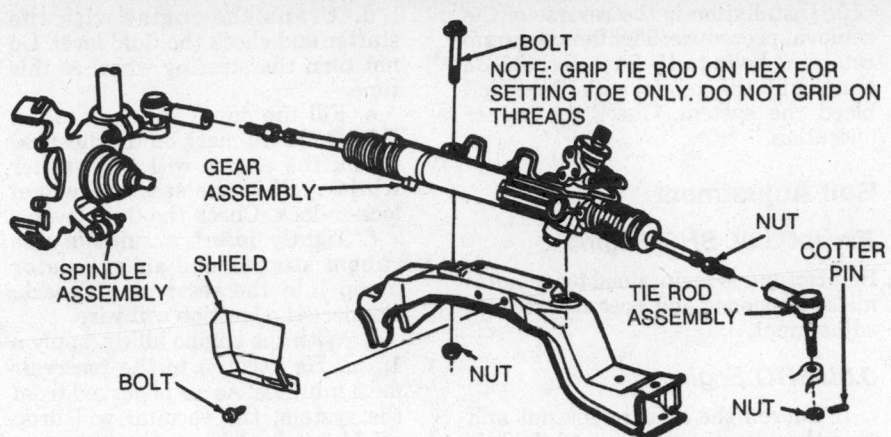

Integral power rack and pinion—Taurus and Sable, except Taurus LX and Sable with 3.8L engine

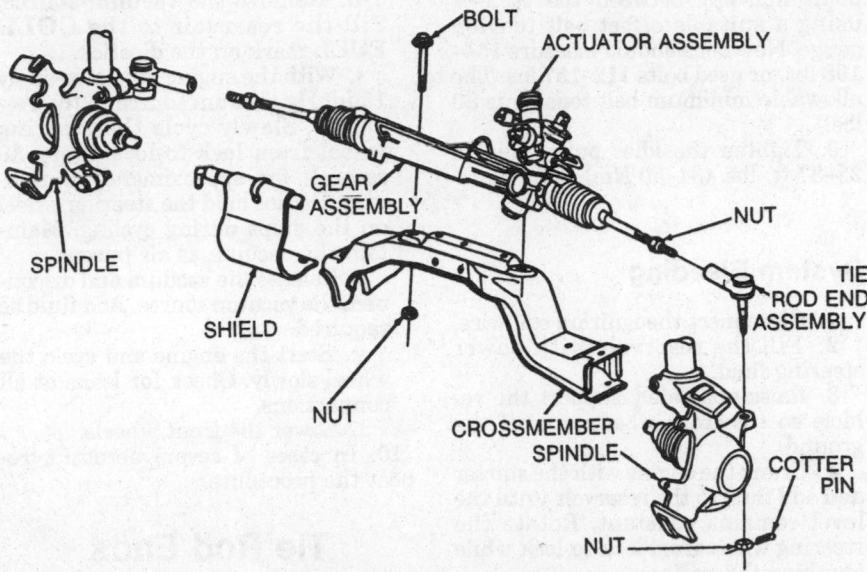

VAPS power rack and pinion

16. Install the intermediate shaft to the steering column shaft. Fill the power steering system.

17. Check the system for leaks and proper operation. Adjust the toe setting as necessary.

Variable Assist Power Steering (VAPS) System—Continental and 1990–93 Taurus LX and Sable with 3.8L Engine

The Variable Assist Power Steering (VAPS) system used on these vehicles consists of a micro-processor based module, a power rack and pinion steering gear, an actuator valve assembly, hose assemblies and a high efficiency power steering pump.

1. Disconnect the negative battery cable. Remove the primary steering column boot attachments.

2. Remove the intermediate shaft retaining bolts and remove the intermediate shaft.

3. From inside the passenger compartment, remove the secondary steering column boot.

4. Raise the vehicle and support safely. Remove the front wheel and tire assemblies. Support the vehicle under the rear edge of the sub-frame.

5. Remove the tie rod cotter pins and nuts. Remove the tie rod ends from the spindle.

6. Remove the tie rod ends from the shaft. Mark the position of the jam nut to maintain the alignment.

7. Remove the nuts from the gear-to-sub-frame attaching bolts.

8. Remove both height sensor attachments on Continental.

9. Remove the rear sub-frame-to-body attaching bolts.

10. Remove the exhaust pipe-to-catalytic converter attachment.

11. Lower the vehicle carefully until the subframe separates from the body; approximately 4 in.

12. Remove the heat shield band and fold the shield down.

13. Disconnect the VAPS electrical connector from the actuator assembly.

14. Rotate the gear to clear the bolts from the sub-frame and pull to the left to facilitate line fitting removal.

15. Position a drain pan under the vehicle and remove the line fittings. Remove the O-rings from the fitting connections and replace with new.

16. Remove the left sway bar link.

17. Remove the steering gear assembly through the left wheel well.

To install:

18. Install new O-rings into the line fittings.

19. Place the gear attachment bolts in the gear housing.

20. Install the steering gear assembly through the left wheel well.

21. Connect and tighten the line fittings to the steering gear assembly.

22. Connect the VAPS electrical connector.

23. Position the steering gear into the sub-frame.

24. Install the tie rod ends onto the shaft.

25. Install the heat shield band.

26. Attach the tie rod ends onto the spindle. Install the nuts and secure with new cotter pins.

27. Attach the sway bar link.

28. Raise the vehicle until the sub-frame contacts the body. Install the sub-frame attaching bolts.

29. Install the gear-to-sub-frame nuts and torque to 85–100 ft. lbs. (115–135 Nm).

30. Attach the exhaust pipe to the catalytic converter.

31. Attach the height sensors on Continental, install the wheel and tire assemblies and lower the vehicle.

32. Fill the power steering system.

33. Install the secondary steering column boot and attach the intermediate shaft to the steering gear. Tighten the bolt to 30–38 ft. lbs. (41–51 Nm).

34. Install the primary steering column boot and attach the intermediate shaft to the steering column.

35. Bleed the system and align the front end.

Power Steering Pump

REMOVAL & INSTALLATION

2.5L and 3.8L Engines

1. Disconnect the negative battery cable. Using the ½ in. drive hole provided in the tensioner, rotate the tensioner pulley clockwise and remove the belt from the alternator and power steering pulley.

2. Position a drain pan under the power steering pump from under-

neath the vehicle. Disconnect the hydraulic pressure and return lines.

3. Remove the pulley from the pump shaft using hub puller T69L-10300-B or equivalent. Remove the bolts retaining pump to bracket and remove the power steering pump.

4. Installation is the reverse of the removal procedure. Fill the pump with fluid and bleed the system. Check the system for proper operation.

NOTE: To install the power steering pump pulley, use steering pump pulley replacer T65P-3A733-C or equivalent. When using this tool, the small diameter threads must be fully engaged in the pump shaft before pressing on the pulley. Hold the head screw and turn the nut to install the pulley. Install the pulley face flush with the pump shaft within ± 0.100 in. (0.25mm).

3.0L Engine, Except SHO

1. Disconnect the negative battery cable. Loosen the idler pulley and remove the power steering belt.

2. Remove the radiator overflow bottle in order to gain access to the 3 screws attaching the pulleys to the pulley hub.

3. Matchmark both pulley to hub positions.

4. Remove the pulleys from the pulley hub.

5. Remove the return line from the pump. Be prepared to catch any spilled fluid in a suitable container.

6. Back off the pressure line attaching nut completely. The line will separate from the pump connection when the pump is removed.

7. Remove the pump mounting bolts and remove the pump.

8. Installation is the reverse of the removal procedure. Fill the pump with fluid and bleed the system. Check for proper operation.

3.0L SHO Engine

1. Disconnect the negative battery cable.

2. Remove the engine damper strut.

3. Remove the power steering belt.

4. Raise and support the vehicle safely.

5. Remove the right front wheel and tire assembly.

6. Position a jack under the engine and remove the right rear engine mount.

7. Remove the power steering pump pulley.

8. Place a drain pan under the pump and remove the pressure and return lines from the pump.

9. Remove the 4 pump retaining bolts and remove the pump.

10. Installation is the reverse of the removal procedure. Tighten the pump retaining bolts to 15–24 ft. lbs. (20–33 Nm). Fill the pump with fluid and bleed the system. Check for proper operation.

Belt Adjustment

Except 3.0L SHO Engine

Belt tension is maintained by an automatic tensioner and does not require adjustment.

3.0L SHO Engine

1. Loosen the idler pulley nut and turn the adjusting screw until the belt is adjusted.

2. Measure the belt tension at a point mid-way between the pulleys, using a suitable offset belt tension gauge. New belts should measure 154–198 lbs. or used belts 112–157 lbs. The allowable minimum belt tension is 80 lbs.

3. Tighten the idler pulley nut to 25–37 ft. lbs. (34–50 Nm).

System Bleeding

1. Disconnect the ignirion coil wire.

2. Fill the reservoir with power steering fluid.

3. Raise and safely support the vehicle so the front wheels are off the ground.

4. Crank the engine with the starter and add fluid to the reservoir until the level remains constant. Rotate the steering wheel from lock-to-lock while cranking the engine.

NOTE: The front wheels must be off the floor during lock-to-lock rotation of the steering wheel.

5. Check the fluid level and add, as necessary.

6. Connect the ignition coil wire and lower the front wheels.

7. Start the engine and let it run for several minutes. Rotate the steering wheel from lock-to-lock.

8. Turn the engine off and check the fluid level. Add fluid, if necessary.

9. Check the fluid for the presence of trapped air. If apparent that air is still in the system, fabricate or obtain a vacuum tester and purge the system as follows:

a. Remove the pump dipstick cap assembly.

b. Check and fill the pump reservoir with fluid to the COLD FULL mark on the dipstick.

c. Disconnect the ignition coil wire. Raise the front of the vehicle and support safely.

d. Crank the engine with the starter and check the fluid level. Do not turn the steering wheel at this time.

e. Fill the pump reservoir to the COLD FULL mark on the dipstick. Crank the engine with the starter while cycling the steering wheel lock-to-lock. Check the fluid level.

f. Tightly insert a suitable size rubber stopper and air evacuator pump into the reservoir fill neck. Connect the ignition coil wire.

g. With the engine idling, apply a 15 in. Hg vacuum to the reservoir for 3 minutes. As air is purged from the system, the vacuum will drop off. Maintain the vacuum on the system as required throughout the 3 minutes.

h. Remove the vacuum source. Fill the reservoir to the COLD FULL mark on the dipstick.

i. With the engine idling, re-apply 15 in. Hg vacuum source to the reservoir. Slowly cycle the steering wheel from lock-to-lock every 30 seconds for approximately 5 minutes. Do not hold the steering wheel on the stops during cycling. Maintain the vacuum as air purges.

j. Release the vacuum and disconnect the vacuum source. Add fluid as required.

k. Start the engine and cycle the wheel slowly. Check for leaks at all connections.

l. Lower the front wheels.

10. In cases of severe aeration, repeat the procedure.

Tie Rod Ends

REMOVAL & INSTALLATION

1. Remove and discard the cotter pin and nut from the worn tie rod end ball stud.

2. Disconnect the tie rod end from the steering spindle, using tie rod remover tool 3290-D or equivalent.

3. Hold the tie rod end with a wrench and loosen the tie rod jam nut.

4. Note the depth to which the tie rod was located using the jam nut as a marker, then grip the tie rod with a pair of suitable pliers and remove the tie rod end assembly from the tie rod.

To install:

5. Clean the tie rod threads. Thread the new tie rod end into the tie rod to the same depth as the removed tie rod end.

6. Place the tie rod end stud into the steering spindle. Make sure the front wheels are pointed straight-ahead before connecting the stud to the spindle.

7. Install a new nut on the tie rod end stud. Tighten the nut to 35 ft. lbs. (48 Nm) and continue tightening until

the next castellation on the nut is aligned with the cotter pin hole in the stud. Install a new cotter pin.

8. Set the toe to specification. Tighten the jam nut to 35–50 ft. lbs. (47–68 Nm).

BRAKES

Master Cylinder

REMOVAL & INSTALLATION

NOTE: The master cylinder on 1989 Continental is part of the anti-lock brake hydraulic actuation unit and cannot be removed separately.

1. Disconnect the negative battery cable. If equipped with anti-lock brakes, depress the brake pedal several times to exhaust all vacuum in the system.

2. Disconnect the brake lines from the primary and secondary outlet ports of the master cylinder and, if equipped, pressure control valves.

3. Remove the nuts attaching the master cylinder to the brake booster assembly. Disconnect the brake warning light wire. If equipped with anti-lock brakes, disconnect the Hydraulic Control Unit (HCU) supply hose at the master cylinder and secure in a position to prevent loss of brake fluid.

4. Slide the master cylinder forward and upward from the vehicle.

To install:

5. Before installation, bench bleed the new master cylinder as follows:

   a. Mount the new master cylinder in a holding fixture. Be careful not to damage the housing.

   b. Fill the master cylinder reservoir with brake fluid.

   c. Using a suitable tool inserted into the booster pushrod cavity, push the master cylinder piston in slowly. Place a suitable container under the master cylinder to catch the fluid being expelled from the outlet ports.

   d. Place a finger tightly over each outlet port and allow the master cylinder piston to return.

   e. Repeat the procedure until clear fluid only is expelled from the master cylinder. Plug the outlet ports and remove the master cylinder from the holding fixture.

6. Install a new seal in the groove in the master cylinder mounting face on vehicles equipped with anti-lock brakes.

7. Position the master cylinder over the booster pushrod and onto the 2 studs on the booster. Install the nuts

and tighten to 13–25 ft. lbs. (18–34 Nm).

8. Attach the brake fluid lines to the master cylinder. If equipped with anti-lock brakes, install the HCU supply hose to the master cylinder.

9. Install the brake warning light wire.

10. Bleed the system. Operate the brakes several times, then check for external hydraulic leaks.

Proportioning Valve

REMOVAL & INSTALLATION

Taurus and Sable

The valve for the sedan is mounted to the floorpan near the left rear wheel. The valves for the station wagon are screwed into the master cylinder.

SEDAN

1. Raise the vehicle and support it safely.

2. Disconnect the brake lines from the valve assembly and note their position.

3. Remove the screw retaining the valve bracket to the lower suspension arm. Remove the 2 screws retaining the valve bracket to the underbody and remove the assembly.

NOTE: The service replacement valve will have a red plastic gauge clip on the valve and must not be removed until it is installed on the vehicle.

To install:

4. Make sure the rear suspension is in the full rebound position.

5. Make sure the red plastic gauge clip is in position on the valve and that the operating rod lower adjustment screw is loose.

6. Position the valve lower mounting bracket to the lower suspension arm. Install 1 retaining screw. Make sure the valve adjuster is resting on the lower bracket and install the set screw.

7. Connect the brake lines in the same position as removed. Bleed the rear brakes.

8. Remove the red plastic gauge clip and lower the vehicle.

WAGON

1. Disconnect the primary or secondary brake line from the master cylinder, as necessary.

2. Loosen and remove the valve from the master cylinder housing.

3. Installation is the reverse of the removal procedure. Fill and bleed the brake system.

Continental

The proportioning valve is contained

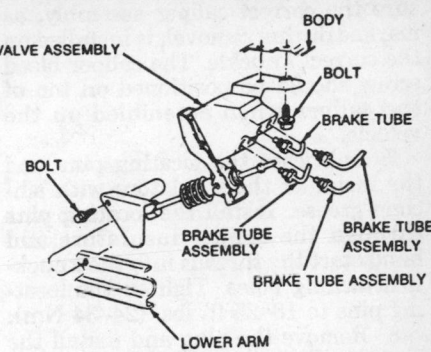

Brake pressure control valve—Taurus and Sable sedan

in the pressure control valve assembly along with a pressure switch. The control valve is located on a bracket below the hydraulic actuation unit on 1989 vehicles or the master cylinder on 1990–93 vehicles.

1. Disconnect the negative battery cable.

2. Disconnect the electrical connector from the pressure switch.

3. Disconnect the brake lines from the valve assembly.

4. Remove the retaining screw and remove the valve assembly.

5. Installation is the reverse of the removal procedure.

Brake Caliper

REMOVAL & INSTALLATION

Front

1. Raise and support the vehicle safely.

2. Remove the wheel and tire assembly. Mark the caliper to ensure that it is reinstalled on the correct knuckle.

3. Disconnect the flexible brake hose from the caliper. Remove the hollow retaining bolt that connects the hose fitting to the caliper. Remove the hose assembly from the caliper and plug the hose.

4. Remove the caliper locating pins.

5. Lift the caliper off of the rotor, integral knuckle and anchor plate using a rotating motion.

NOTE: Do not pry directly against the plastic piston or damage to the piston will result.

To install:

6. Retract the piston fully in the piston bore. Position the caliper assembly above the rotor with the anti-rattle spring under the upper arm of the knuckle. Install the caliper over the rotor with a rotating motion. Make sure the inner and outer shoes are properly positioned and the outer anti-rattle spring is properly positioned. Make

sure the correct caliper assembly, as marked during removal, is installed on the correct knuckle. The caliper bleed screw should be positioned on top of the caliper when assembled on the vehicle.

7. Lubricate the locating pins and the inside of the insulators with silicone grease. Install the locating pins through the caliper insulators and hand start the threads into the knuckle attaching holes. Tighten the locating pins to 18–25 ft. lbs. (24–34 Nm).

8. Remove the plug and install the brake hose on the caliper with a new copper washer on each side of the fitting outlet. Insert the attaching bolt through the washers and fittings and tighten to 30–45 ft. lbs. (40–60 Nm).

9. Bleed the brake system, filling the master cylinder as required.

10. Install the wheel and lower the vehicle. Pump the brake pedal prior to moving the vehicle to position the brake linings.

Rear

1. Raise and support the vehicle safely.

2. Remove the wheel and tire assembly.

3. Remove the brake flex hose from the caliper assembly.

4. Remove the retaining clip from the parking brake at the caliper. Disengage the parking brake cable end from the lever arm.

5. Hold the slider pin hex-heads with an open-end wrench and remove the pinch bolts. Lift the caliper assembly away from the anchor plate. Remove the slider pins and boots from the anchor plate.

To install:

6. Apply silicone dielectric compound to the inside of the slider pin boots and to the slider pins.

7. Position the slider pins and boots in the anchor plate. Position the caliper assembly on the anchor plate. Make sure the brake pads are installed correctly.

8. Remove the residue from the pinch bolt threads and apply 1 drop of threadlock and sealer. Install the pinch bolts and tighten to 23–26 ft. lbs. (31–35 Nm) while holding the slider pins with an open-end wrench.

9. Attach the cable end to the parking brake lever. Install the cable retaining clip on the caliper assembly.

10. Using new washers, connect the brake flex hose to the caliper. Tighten the retaining bolt to 8–11 ft. lbs. (11–16 Nm).

11. Bleed the brake system, filling the master cylinder as required.

12. Install the wheel and lower the vehicle. Pump the brake pedal prior to moving the vehicle to position the brake pads.

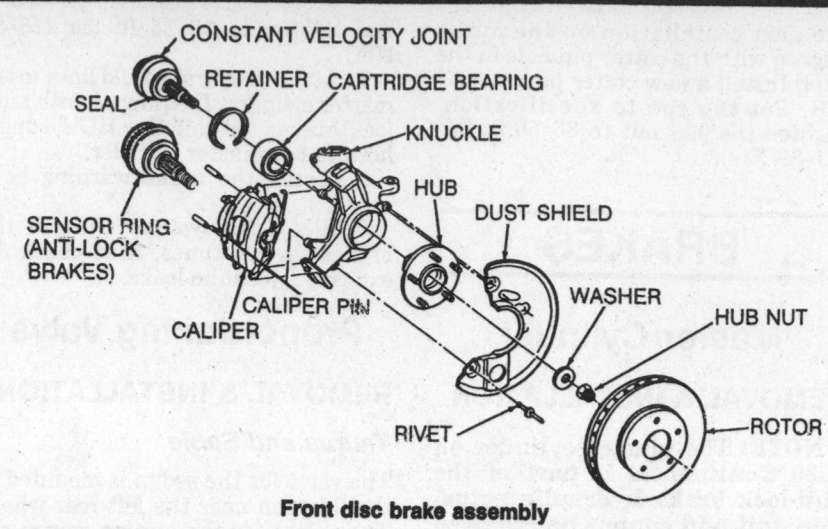

Front disc brake assembly

Disc Brake Pads

REMOVAL & INSTALLATION

Front

1. Remove the master cylinder cap and check the fluid level in the reservoir. Remove the brake fluid until the reservoir is half full. Discard the removed fluid.

2. Raise the vehicle and support it safely. Remove the wheel and tire assembly.

3. Remove the caliper locating pins. Lift the caliper assembly from the integral knuckle and anchor plate and rotor using a rotating motion. Suspend the caliper inside the fender housing with wire. Do not allow the caliper to hang from the brake hose.

NOTE: Do not pry directly against the plastic piston or damage will result.

4. Remove the inner and outer brake pads. Inspect the rotor braking surfaces for scoring and machine as necessary. Refer to the mimimum rotor thickness specification when machining. If machining is not necessary, hand sand the glaze from the braking surfaces with medium grit sand paper.

To install:

5. Use a 4 in. C-clamp and a wood block 2¾ in. × 1 in. × ¾ in. thick to seat the caliper piston in its bore. This must be done to provide clearance for the caliper assembly with the new brake pads to fit over the rotor during installation. Care must be taken during this procedure to prevent damage to the plastic piston. Do not allow metal or sharp objects to come into direct contact with the piston surface or damage will result.

6. Remove all rust buildup from the inside of the caliper legs. Install the inner pad in the caliper piston. Do not

bend the pad clips during installation in the piston or distortion and rattles can occur. Install the outer pad. Make sure the clips are properly seated.

7. Install the caliper over the rotor and install the wheel. Lower the vehicle.

8. Pump the brake pedal prior to moving the vehicle to position the brake linings. Refill the master cylinder.

Rear

1. Remove the master cylinder cap and check the fluid level in the reservoir. Remove the brake fluid until the reservoir is half full. Discard the removed fluid.

2. Raise the vehicle and support it safely.

3. Remove the wheel and tire assembly.

4. Remove the screw retaining the brake hose bracket to the shock absorber bracket. Remove the retaining clip from the parking brake cable at the caliper. Remove the cable end from the parking brake lever.

5. Hold the slider pin hex-heads with an open-end wrench. Remove the upper pinch bolt. Rotate the caliper away from the rotor.

6. Remove the brake pads.

To install:

7. Using caliper piston turning tool T87P–2588–A or equivalent, rotate the piston clockwise until it is fully seated. Make sure 1 of the 2 slots in the piston face is positioned so it will engage the nib on the brake pad.

8. Install the brake pads in the anchor plate. Rotate the caliper assembly over the rotor into position on the anchor plate. Make sure the brake pads are installed correctly.

9. Remove the residue from the pinch bolt threads and apply 1 drop of threadlock and sealer. Install and tighten the pinch bolts to 23–26 ft. lbs.

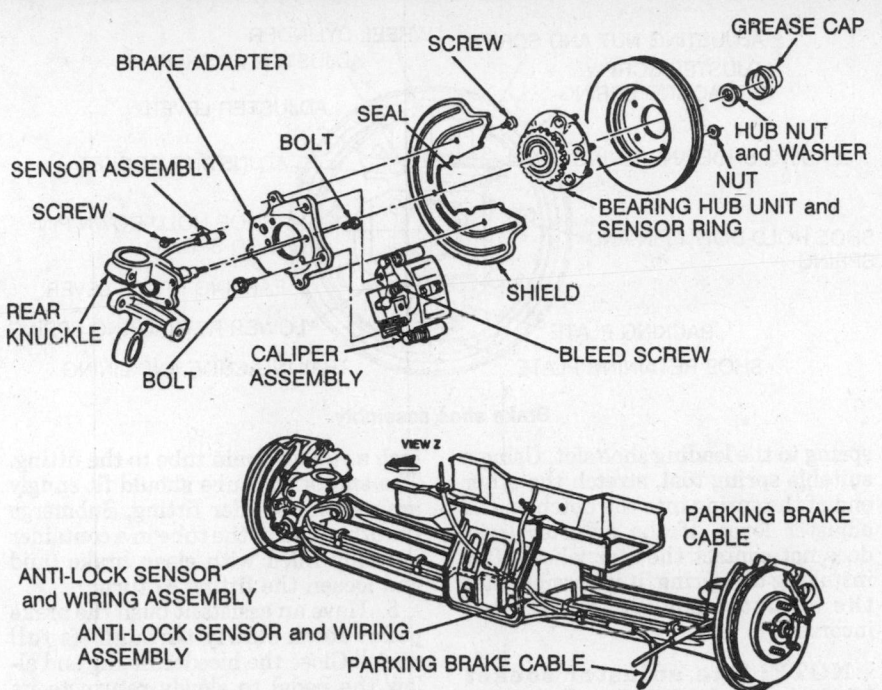

Rear disc brake assembly

(31–35 Nm) while holding the slider pins with an open-end wrench.

10. Attach the cable end to the parking brake lever. Install the cable retaining clip on the caliper assembly. Position the brake flex hose and bracket assembly to the shock absorber bracket and install the retaining screw. Tighten the screw to 8–11 ft. lbs. (11–16 Nm).

11. Install the wheel and tire assembly and lower the vehicle. Pump the brake pedal prior to moving the vehicle to position the brake linings. Refill the master cylinder.

Brake Rotor

REMOVAL & INSTALLATION

Front

1. Raise the vehicle and support it safely.
2. Remove the wheel and tire assembly.
3. Remove the caliper assembly from the rotor. Position the caliper aside and support it with a length of wire. Do not allow the caliper to hang by the brake hose.
4. Remove the rotor from the hub assembly by pulling it off the hub studs. If additional force is required to remove the rotor, apply rust penetrator on the front and rear rotor/hub mating surfaces and then strike the rotor between the studs with a plastic hammer. If this does not work, attach a 3-jaw puller and remove the rotor.

NOTE: If excessive force must be used to remove the rotor, it should be checked for lateral runout before installation.

5. Check the rotor for scoring and/or other wear. Machine or replace, as necessary. If machining, observe the minimum thickness specification.
6. Install the rotor in the reverse order of removal.

Rear

1. Raise the vehicle and support it safely.
2. Remove the wheel and tire assembly.
3. Remove the caliper assembly from the rotor and support it with a length of wire. Do not let the caliper hang from the brake line.
4. Remove the 2 rotor retaining nuts and remove the rotor from the hub.
5. Check the rotor for scoring and/or other wear. Machine or replace, as necessary. If machining, observe the minimum thickness specification.
6. Install the rotor in the reverse order of removal.

Brake Drums

REMOVAL & INSTALLATION

1989

1. Raise and safely support the vehicle.
2. Remove the wheelcover and nut covers, as required. Remove the wheel and tire assembly.
3. Remove the grease cap from the hub. Remove the cotter pin, nut lock, adjusting nut and keyed flatwasher from the spindle. Remove the outer bearing and discard the cotter pin.
4. Remove the hub/drum assembly as a unit. Be careful not to damage the grease seal and inner bearing during removal.

NOTE: If the drum will not come off, pry the rubber plug from the backing plate inspection hole. Remove the brake line-to-axle retention bracket. This will allow sufficient room to insert suitable brake tools through the inspection hole to disengage the adjusting lever and back off the adjusting screw.

5. Inspect the drum for scoring and/or other wear. Machine or replace, as necessary. If machining, observe the maximum permissible drum diameter specification.

To install:

6. Inspect and lubricate the bearings, as necessary. Replace the grease seal if any damage is visible.
7. Clean the spindle stem and apply a thin coat of wheel bearing grease.
8. Install the hub and drum assembly on the spindle. Install the outer bearing, keyed flat washer and adjusting nut. Tighten the nut finger-tight.
9. Adjust the wheel bearings. Install the nut retainer and a new cotter pin. Install the grease cap.
10. Install the wheel and tire assembly. Install the wheel cover and nut covers, as required. Lower the vehicle.

1990–93

1. Raise the vehicle and support it safely.
2. Remove the wheel cover and nut covers, as required.
3. Remove the lugnuts and the wheel and tire assembly.
4. Remove the 2 drum retaining nuts and the drum.

NOTE: If the drum will not come off, pry the rubber plug from the backing plate inspection hole. Remove the brake line-to-axle retention bracket. This will allow sufficient room to insert suitable brake tools through the inspection hole to disengage the adjusting lever and back off the adjusting screw.

5. Inspect the drum for scoring and/or other wear. Machine or replace, as necessary. If machining, observe the maximum permissible drum diameter specification.

6. Installation is the reverse of the removal procedure.

Brake Shoes

REMOVAL & INSTALLATION

1. Raise the vehicle and support it safely.
2. Remove the wheel and tire assembly and the brake drum.
3. Remove the 2 shoe hold-down springs and pins.
4. Lift the brake shoes, springs and adjuster assembly off the backing plate and wheel cylinder assembly. When removing the assembly, be careful not to bend the adjusting lever.
5. Remove the parking brake cable from the parking brake lever.
6. Remove the retracting springs from the lower brake attachments and upper shoe-to-adjusting lever attachment points. This will seperate the brake shoes and disengage the adjuster mechanism.
7. Remove the horse shoe retaining clip and spring washer and slide the lever off the parking brake lever pin on the trailing shoe.

To install:

8. Apply a light coating of disc brake caliper slide grease at the points where the brake shoes contact the backing plate.
9. Apply a thin coat of lubricant to the adjuster screw threads and socket end of the adjusting screw. Install the stainless steel washer over the socket end of the adjusting screw and install the socket. Turn the adjusting screw into the adjusting pivot nut to the limit of the threads and then back off ½ turn.
10. Assemble the parking brake lever to the trailing shoe by installing the spring washer and a new horse shoe retaining clip. Crimp the clip until it retains the lever to the shoe securely.
11. Attach the parking brake cable to the parking brake lever.
12. Attach the lower shoe retracting spring to the leading and trailing shoe and install to the backing plate. It will be necessary to stretch the retracting spring as the shoes are installed downward over the anchor plate to the inside of the shoe retaining plate.
13. Install the adjuster screw assembly between the leading shoe slot and the slot in the trailing shoe and parking brake lever. The adjuster socket end slot must fit into the trailing shoe and parking brake lever.
14. Assemble the adjuster lever in the groove located in the parking brake lever pin and into the slot of the adjuster socket that fits into the trailing shoe web.
15. Attach the upper retracting

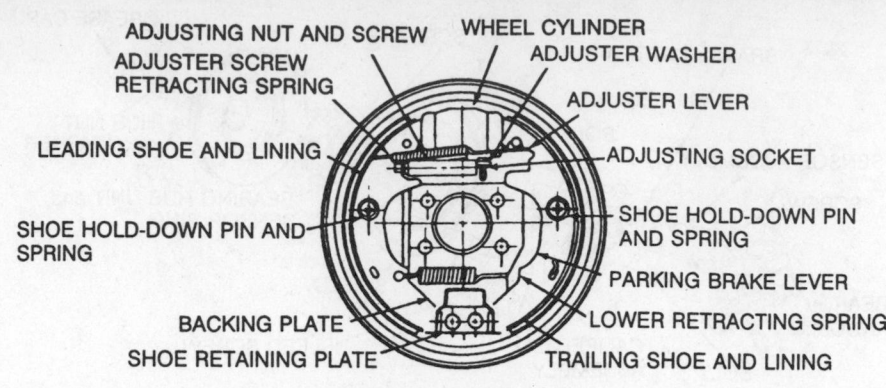

Brake shoe assembly

spring to the leading shoe slot. Using a suitable spring tool, stretch the other end of the spring into the notch on the adjuster lever. If the adjuster lever does not contact the star wheel after installing the spring, it is possible that the adjuster socket is installed incorrectly.

NOTE: The adjuster socket blade is marked R for the right-hand or L for the left-hand brake assemblies. The R or L adjuster blade must be installed with the letter R or L in the upright position, facing the wheel cylinder, on the correct side to ensure that the deeper of the 2 slots in the adjuster sockets fits into the parking brake lever.

16. Adjust the brake shoes.
17. Install the brake drum and wheel and tire assembly. Lower the vehicle.

Brake System Bleeding

Without Anti-Lock Brakes

1. Clean all dirt from the master cylinder filler cap.
2. If the master cylinder is known or suspected to have air in the bore, it must be bled before any of the wheel cylinders or calipers. To bleed the master cylinder, loosen the upper secondary left front outlet fitting approximately ¾ turn. Have an assistant depress the brake pedal slowly through it's full travel. Close the outlet fitting and let the pedal return slowly to the fully released position. Wait 5 seconds and then repeat the operation until all air bubbles disappear.
3. Repeat Step 2 with the right-hand front outlet fitting.
4. Continue to bleed the brake system by removing the rubber dust cap from the wheel cylinder bleeder fitting or caliper fitting at the right-hand rear of the vehicle. Place a suitable box wrench on the bleeder fitting and at-

tach a rubber drain tube to the fitting. The end of the tube should fit snugly around the bleeder fitting. Submerge the other end of the tube in a container partially filled with clean brake fluid and loosen the fitting ¾ turn.
5. Have an assistant push the brake pedal down slowly through its full travel. Close the bleeder fitting and allow the pedal to slowly return to its full release position. Wait 5 seconds and repeat the procedure until no bubbles appear at the submerged end of the bleeder tube. Secure the bleeder fitting and remove the bleeder tube. Install the rubber dust cap on the bleeder fitting.
6. Repeat the procedure in Steps 4 and 5 in the following sequence: left front, left rear and right front. Refill the master cylinder reservoir after each wheel cylinder or caliper has been bled and install the master cylinder cover and gasket. When brake bleeding is completed, the fluid level should be filled to the maximum level indicated on the reservoir.
7. Always make sure the disc brake pistons are returned to their normal positions by depressing the brake pedal several times until normal pedal travel is established. If the pedal feels spongy, repeat the bleeding procedure.

With Anti-Lock Brakes—Except 1989 Continental

The anti-lock brake system must be bled in 2 steps.

1. The master cylinder and hydraulic control unit must be bled using the Rotunda Anti-Lock Brake Breakout Box/Bleeding Adapter tool No. T90P-50–ALA or equivalent. If this procedure is not followed, air will be trapped in the hydraulic control unit which will eventually lead to a spongy brake pedal. To bleed the master cylinder and the hydraulic control unit, disconnect the 55-pin plug from the electronic control unit and install the Anti-Lock Brake Breakout Box/Bleeding Adapter to the wire harness 55-pin plug.

a. Place the Bleed/Harness switch in the **BLEED** position.

b. Turn the ignition to the **ON** position. At this point the red off light should come ON.

c. Push the motor button on the adapter down to start the pump motor. The red OFF light will turn OFF and the green ON light will turn ON. The pump motor will run for 60 seconds after the motor button is pushed. If the pump motor is to be turned off for any reason before the 60 seconds has elapsed, push the abort button to turn the pump motor off.

d. After 20 seconds of pump motor operation, push and hold the valve button down. Hold the valve button down for 20 seconds and then release it.

e. The pump motor will continue to run for an additional 20 seconds after the valve button is released.

2. The brake lines can now be bled in the normal fashion. Bleed the brake system by removing the rubber dust cap from the caliper fitting at the right-hand rear of the vehicle. Place a suitable box wrench on the bleeder fitting and attach a rubber drain tube to the fitting. The end of the tube should fit snugly around the bleeder fitting. Submerge the other end of the tube in a container partially filled with clean brake fluid and loosen the fitting ¾ turn.

3. Have an assistant push the brake pedal down slowly through it's full travel. Close the bleeder fitting and allow the pedal to slowly return to it's full release position. Wait 5 seconds and repeat the procedure until no bubbles appear at the submerged end of the bleeder tube. Secure the bleeder fitting and remove the bleeder tube. Install the rubber dust cap on the bleeder fitting.

4. Repeat the bleeding procedure at the left front, left rear and right front in that order. Refill the master cylinder reservoir after each caliper has been bled and install the master cylinder and gasket. When brake bleeding is completed, the fluid level should be filled to the maximum level indicated on the reservoir.

5. Always make sure the disc brake pistons are returned to their normal positions by depressing the brake pedal several times until normal pedal travel is established. If the pedal feels spongy, repeat the bleeding procedure.

With Anti-Lock Brakes—1989 Continental

The front brakes can be bled in the same manner as a vehicle without anti-lock brakes or they can be bled with a pressure bleeder. The rear brakes must be bled with a pressure bleeder or with a fully charged accumulator.

PRESSURE BLEEDING

1. Clean all dirt from the reservoir filler cap area. Attach a suitable pressure bleeder to the reservoir cap opening.

2. Maintain 35 psi pressure on the system through the pressure bleeder.

3. Remove the dust cap from the right front caliper bleeder fitting. Attach a rubber drain tube to the fitting, making sure the tube fits snugly.

4. With the ignition switch in the **OFF** position and the brake pedal in the fully released position, open the bleeder fitting for 10 seconds at a time until an air-free stream of brake fluid flow is observed.

5. Repeat the procedure at the left front, right rear and left rear calipers, in that order.

6. Place the ignition switch in the **RUN** position and pump the brake pedal several times to complete the bleeding procedure and to fully charge the accumulator.

7. Turn the ignition switch to the **OFF** position and remove the pressure bleeder. Siphon off the excess fluid in the reservoir to adjust the level to the **MAX** mark with a fully charged accumulator.

REAR BRAKE BLEEDING WITH A FULLY CHARGED ACCUMULATOR

1. Remove the dust cap from the right rear caliper bleeder fitting. Attach a rubber drain tube to the fitting, making sure the tube fits snugly.

2. Turn the ignition switch to the **RUN** position. This will turn on the electric pump to charge the accumulator, as required.

3. Have an assistant hold the brake pedal in the applied position. Open the bleeder fitting for 10 seconds at a time until an air-free stream of brake fluid flow is observed.

― **CAUTION** ―

To prevent possible injury, care must be used when opening the bleeder screws due to the high pressures available from a fully charged accumulator.

4. Repeat the procedure at the left rear caliper.

5. Pump the brake pedal several times to complete the bleeding procedure.

6. Adjust the fluid level in the reservoir to the MAX mark with a fully charged accumulator.

NOTE: If the pump motor is allowed to run continuously for approximately 20 minutes, a thermal safety switch inside the motor may shut the motor off to prevent it from overheating. If that happens, a 2–10 minute cool down period is typically required before normal operation can resume.

Anti-Lock Brake System Service

PRECAUTION

Failure to observe the following precautions may result in system damage.

● Before servicing any high pressure component, be sure to discharge the hydraulic pressure from the system.

● Do not allow the brake fluid to contact any of the electrical connectors.

● Use care when opening the bleeder screws due to the high pressures available from the accumulator.

RELIEVING ANTI-LOCK BRAKE SYSTEM PRESSURE

Before servicing any components which contain high pressure, it is mandatory that the hydraulic pressure in the system be discharged. To discharge the system, turn the ignition **OFF** and pump the brake pedal a minimum of 20 times until an increase in pedal force is clearly felt.

Hydraulic Control Unit (HCU)

REMOVAL & INSTALLATION

Except 1989 Continental

1. On all vehicles, except Taurus SHO, disconnect the battery cables and remove the battery from the vehicle. Remove the battery tray. Remove the 3 plastic push pins holding the acid shield to the HCU mounting bracket and remove the acid shield. On Taurus

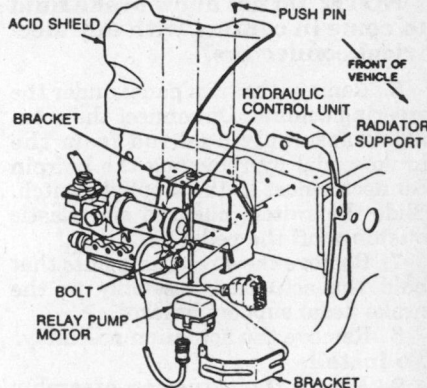

Anti-lock brake hydraulic control unit—except 1989 Continental

SHO, it is only necessary to disconnect the negative battery cable and remove the electronic control unit and it's mounting bracket from the top of the HCU mounting bracket.

2. Disconnect the 19-pin connector from the HCU to the wiring harness and disconnect the 4-pin connector from the HCU to the pump motor relay.

3. Remove the 2 lines from the inlet ports and the 4 lines from the outlet ports of the HCU. Plug each port to prevent brake fluid from spilling onto the paint and wiring.

4. Remove the 3 nuts retaining the HCU assembly to the mounting bracket and remove the assembly from the vehicle. The nut on the front of the HCU also retains the relay mounting bracket.

5. Install in the reverse order of removal. Tighten the 3 retaining nuts to 12–18 ft. lbs. (16–24 Nm) and the brake lines to 10–18 ft. lbs. (14–24 Nm). Bleed the brake system and check for fluid leaks.

1989 Continental

The hydraulic actuation assembly contains all the anti-lock brake hydraulic components: master cylinder and fluid reservoir, hydraulic pump motor and accumulator and solenoid valve block assembly.

1. Discharge the hydraulic pressure in the system.

2. Disconnect the negative battery cable.

3. Remove the air cleaner housing and duct assembly.

4. Tag and disconnect the electrical connectors from the fluid level indicator, main valve, solenoid valve block, pressure warning switch, hydraulic pump motor and ground connector from the master cylinder portion of the assembly.

5. Disconnect the 3 brake line fittings. Immediately plug each port to prevent fluid loss and contamination.

NOTE: Do not allow brake fluid to come in contact with any electrical connectors.

6. Remove the trim panel under the steering column. Disconnect the actuation assembly pushrod from the brake pedal by removing the hairpin connector next to the stoplight switch. Slide the switch, pushrod and plastic bushings off the pedal pin.

7. Remove the 4 retaining nuts that hold the actuation assembly to the brake pedal support bracket.

8. Remove the actuation assembly.
To install:

9. Mount the actuation assembly with the rubber boot and foam gasket to the engine side of the dash panel

with the 4 mounting studs and push-rod inserted in the proper holes.

10. Working in the passenger compartment, loosely start 4 retaining locknuts attaching the actuation assembly to the pedal support bracket.

11. Connect the pushrod to the brake pedal pin by sliding the flanged plastic bushing, pushrod and washer onto the brake pedal pin. Position the stoplight switch so the slot on the switch bracket straddles the pushrod on the brake pedal pin, with the hole on the opposite leg of the switch bracket just clearing the pin. Slide the switch onto the pedal pin until it bottoms. Install the outer nylon bushing and secure the assembly with the hairpin retainer.

12. Tighten the 4 locknuts to 13–25 ft. lbs. (18–34 Nm).

13. From the engine compartment, connect the brake tubes and tighten the locknuts to 13–25 ft. lbs. (18–34 Nm). Connect the electrical connectors and install the air cleaner and duct assembly.

14. Connect the negative battery cable and bleed the brake system.

Electronic Control Unit (ECU)

REMOVAL & INSTALLATION

Taurus and Sable

The ECU is located on the front right side of the engine compartment next to the washer bottle, except on Taurus SHO. On Taurus SHO it is mounted on the left side on top of the HCU mounting bracket.

1. Disconnect the negative battery cable.

2. Disconnect the 55-pin connector from the ECU. Unlock the connector by completely pulling up the lever. Move the top of the connector away from the ECU until all terminals are clear, then pull the connector up out of the slots in the ECU.

3. Remove the screws attaching the ECU and remove the ECU.

4. Install in the reverse order of removal. Connect the 55-pin connector by installing the bottom part of the connector into the slots in the ECU and pushing the top portion of the connector into the ECU. Then pull the locking lever completely down to ensure proper installation. Tighten the retaining screws to 15–20 inch lbs. (1.7–2.3 Nm).

Continental

1. Disconnect the negative battery cable.

2. Remove the trim panel in the luggage compartment (behind the back seat) to gain access to the ECU.

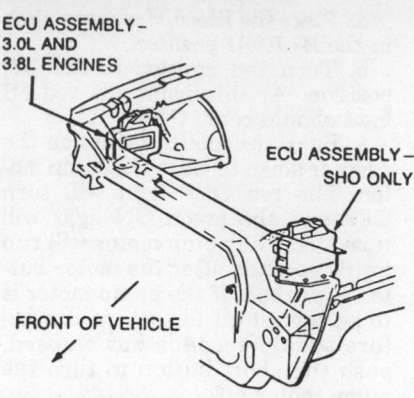

Anti-lock brake system electronic control unit location—Taurus and Sable

3. Disconnect the connector from the ECU.

4. Remove the screws attaching the ECU to the panel and remove the ECU.

5. Installation is the reverse of the removal procedure. Tighten the retaining screws to 15–20 inch lbs. (1.7–2.3 Nm).

CHASSIS ELECTRICAL

Air Bag

DISARMING

1989–91

1. Disconnect the negative battery cable.

2. On 1990–91 vehicles, open the glove compartment and lower it past its stops. Disconnect the backup power supply located to the right of the glove compartment opening.

NOTE: The backup power supply allows air bag deployment if the battery or battery cables are damaged in an accident before the crash sensors close. The power supply is a capacitor that will leak down in approximately 15 minutes after the battery is disconnected or in 1 minute if the battery positive cable is grounded. The backup power supply must be disconnected before any air bag related service is performed.

3. Remove the 4 nut and washer assemblies retaining the driver air bag module to the steering wheel.

4. Disconnect the driver air bag module connector and attach a jumper

wire to the air bag terminals on the clockspring.

5. If equipped with a passenger air bag, disconnect the passenger air bag connector, located behind the glove compartment. Attach a jumper wire to the air bag terminals on the wiring harness side of the passenger air bag module connector.

1992–93

1. Disconnect the positive battery cable.

2. Wait 1 minute for the backup power supply in the diagnostic monitor to deplete its stored energy.

3. Remove the 4 nuts attaching the air bag module to the steering wheel. Disconnect the air bag connector and connect air bag simulator tool 105–00008 or equivalent, to the vehicle harness connector.

NOTE: If equipped with optional passenger side air bag, both driver and passenger air bag modules must be disconnected.

4. On Taurus/Sable, if equipped with a passenger air bag, proceed as follows:

  a. Remove the right-hand and left-hand finish panels.

  b. Remove the instrument panel finish panel retaining spear clips.

  c. Open the glove compartment, press the side inward and lower the glove compartment to the floor.

  d. Working through the glove compartment opening, remove the 2 lower air bag module retaining bolts.

  e. Remove the 4 remaining air bag module retaining screws from the side of the air bag cover.

  f. Disconnect the electrial connector from the left side of the air bag and remove the air bag module.

––––––––– CAUTION –––––––––

When carrying a live air bag, make sure the bag and trim cover are pointed away from the body. In the unlikely event of an accidental deployment, the bag will then deploy with minimal chance of injury. In addition, when placing a live air bag on a bench or other surface, always face the bag and trim cover up, away from the surface. This will reduce the motion of the unit if it is accidentally deployed.

g. Connect air bag simulator tool 105–00008 or equivalent, to the vehicle harness connector.

5. On Continental, if equipped with passenger side air bag, proceed as follows:

  a. Open the glove compartment and rotate all the way down, past the stops.

  b. Disconnect the air bag connector and connect air bag simulator

tool 105–00008 or equivalent, to the vehicle harness connector.

6. Connect the positive battery cable.

Heater Blower Motor

REMOVAL & INSTALLATION

1. Disconnect the negative battery cable.

2. Open the glove compartment door, release the door retainers and lower the door.

3. Remove the screw attaching the recirculation duct support bracket to the instrument panel cowl.

4. If equipped with automatic temperature control, remove the nut holding the electrical connector bracket to the recirculation duct. Release the 3 connectors from the bracket and remove the bracket.

5. Remove the vacuum connection to the recirculation door vacuum motor. If equipped, disconnect the 2 aspirator hoses from the muffler.

6. Remove the screws attaching the recirculation duct to the heater or evaporator assembly.

7. Remove the recirculation duct from the heater or evaporator assembly, lowering the duct from between the instrument panel and the heater or evaporator case.

8. Disconnect the blower motor electrical lead. Remove the blower motor wheel pushnut and remove the blower motor wheel.

9. Remove the blower motor mounting plate screws and remove the blower motor from the case.

10. Installation is the reverse of removal procedure.

Windshield Wiper Motor

REMOVAL & INSTALLATION

Front

1. Disconnect the negative battery cable.

2. Disconnect the power lead from the motor.

3. Remove the left wiper arm by first applying downward pressure on the wiper arm head, while holding the wiper arm. Lift the arm to the highest position and using finger pressure only, grasp the slide latch tab and slide the latch out from under the arm head. Remove the arm and blade assembly.

4. On Continental and 1991–93 Taurus and Sable, lift the water shield cover from the cowl on the passenger side. Remove the left cowl screen on 1989–90 Taurus and Sable.

5. Remove the linkage retaining clip from the operating arm on the motor by lifting the locking tab up and pulling the clip away from the pin.

6. Remove the attaching screws from the motor and bracket assembly and remove.

7. Installation is the reverse of the removal procedure.

Rear – Station Wagon

1. Disconnect the negative battery cable.

2. Raise the wiper arm and blade assembly away from the glass and insert a 0.062 in. (1.6mm) pin in the holes in the retainer arm. Let the arm move toward the glass to relieve the arm spring tension and lift the arm off the pivot shaft.

3. Remove the pivot shaft retaining nut and spacers.

4. Disconnect the electrical connector to the wiper motor.

5. Remove the nut retaining the motor to the handle and remove the motor.

6. Installation is the reverse of the removal procedure.

Windshield Wiper Switch

REMOVAL & INSTALLATION

Front

The front wiper switch is a function of the combination switch.

Rear – Station Wagon

1989

1. Disconnect the negative battery cable.

2. Remove the 4 cluster opening finish panel retaining screws. Remove the finish panel by rocking the upper edge toward the driver.

3. Disconnect the wiring connector from the rear wiper switch.

4. Remove the wiper switch from the instrument panel. On Sable, the switch is retained with 2 screws.

5. Installation is the reverse of the removal procedure.

1990–93

1. Disconnect the negative battery cable.

2. Remove the cluster opening finish panel as follows:

  a. Engage the parking brake.

  b. Remove the ignition lock cylinder.

  c. If equipped with a tilt column, tilt the column to the full down position and remove the tilt lever.

  d. Remove the 4 bolts and the

opening cover from under the steering column.

e. Remove the steering column trim shrouds. Disconnect all electrical connections from the combination switch.

f. Remove the 2 screws retaining the combination switch and remove the switch.

g. Pull the gear shift lever to the full down position.

h. Remove the cluster opening finish panel retaining screws and, if necessary, the light switch knob and retaining nut.

i. Remove the finish panel by pulling it toward the driver to unsnap the snap-in retainers and disconnect the wiring from the switches, clock and warning lights.

3. Remove the wiper switch from the cluster opening finish panel.

To install:

4. Push the rear wiper switch into the cluster finish panel until it snaps into place.

5. Install the cluster opening finish panel in the reverse order of removal.

6. Connect the negative battery cable.

Headlight Switch

REMOVAL & INSTALLATION

1989

TAURUS

1. Disconnect the negative battery cable.

2. Pull off the headlight switch knob.

3. Remove the bezel retaining nut and remove the bezel.

4. Remove the instrument cluster finish panel.

5. Remove the 2 screws retaining the headlight switch, pull the switch out of the instrument panel and disconnect the electrical connector.

6. Installation is the reverse of the removal procedure.

SABLE

1. Disconnect the negative battery cable.

2. Remove the lower left finish panel.

3. Remove the 2 screws retaining the headlight switch to the finish panel, disconnect the electrical connector and remove the switch.

4. Installation is the reverse of the removal procedure.

1990–93 Taurus and Sable

1. Disconnect the negative battery cable.

2. Pull off the headlight switch knob and remove the retaining nut.

3. Remove the instrument cluster finish panel as follows:

a. Apply the parking brake.

b. Remove the ignition lock cylinder.

c. If equipped with a tilt column, tilt the column to the most downward position and remove the tilt lever.

d. Remove the 4 bolts and opening cover from under the steering column.

e. Remove the steering column trim shrouds. Disconnect all electrical connections from the steering column combination switch.

f. Remove the 2 screws retaining the combination switch and remove the switch.

g. Pull the gear shift lever to the full down position.

h. Remove the cluster opening finish panel retaining screws. Remove the finish panel by pulling it toward the driver to unsnap the snap-in retainers and disconnect the wiring from the switches, clock and warning lights.

4. Remove the 2 screws retaining the headlight switch, pull the switch out of the instrument panel and disconnect the electrical connector.

5. Installation is the reverse of the removal procedure.

Continental

1. Disconnect the negative battery cable.

2. Gently pull off the headlight switch knob.

3. Snap out the right and left mouldings, remove the 5 cluster opening finish panel retaining screws and the panel.

4. Remove the 2 screws retaining the headlight switch to the finish panel, disconnect the electrical connector and remove the switch.

5. Installation is the reverse of the removal procedure.

Combination Switch

The combination switch incorporates the turn signal, headlight dimmer, headlight flash-to-pass, hazard warning, cornering lights and windshield washer/wiper functions.

REMOVAL & INSTALLATION

1. Disconnect the negative battery cable. If equipped with a tilt steering column, set the tilt column to its lowest position and remove the tilt lever.

2. Remove the ignition lock cylinder. Remove the steering column shroud screws and remove the upper and lower shrouds.

3. Remove the self tapping screws attaching the switch to the steering column and disengage the switch from the steering column casting.

4. Remove the wiring harness retainer, if equipped and disconnect the electrical connectors.

To install:

5. Connect the electrical connectors. Install the wiring harness retainer, if equipped.

6. Align the turn signal switch mounting holes with the corresponding holes in the steering column and install self-tapping screws. Torque the screws to 17–26 inch lbs. (2–3 Nm).

7. Install the upper and lower steering column shroud and shroud retaining screws, torque the screws to 6–10 inch lbs. (0.7–1.1 Nm).

8. Install the ignition lock cylinder. Attach the tilt lever, if removed.

9. Connect the negative battery cable. Check the switch and the steering column for proper operation.

Ignition Lock Cylinder

REMOVAL & INSTALLATION

Functional Lock

The following procedure applies to vehicles that have functional lock cylinders. Lock cylinder keys are available for these vehicles or the lock cylinder key numbers are known and the proper key can be made.

1. Disconnect the negative battery cable.

2. Turn the lock cylinder key to the **RUN** position.

3. Using an ⅛ in. diameter wire pin or a small drift, depress the lock cylinder retaining pin through the access hole, while pulling out on the lock cylinder to remove it from the column.

To install:

4. Install the lock cylinder by turning it to the **RUN** position and depressing the retaining pin. Insert the lock cylinder into its housing. Make sure the cylinder is fully seated and aligned in the interlocking washer before turning the key to the **OFF** position. This will permit the cylinder retaining pin to extend into the cylinder housing hole.

5. Rotate the lock cylinder using the lock cylinder key, to ensure correct mechanical operation in all positions.

6. Connect the negative battery cable.

Non-Functional Lock

The following procedure applies to vehicles in which the ignition lock is inoperative and the lock cylinder cannot be rotated due to a lost or broken lock cylinder key, unknown key number or a lock cylinder cap that has been damaged and/or broken to the extent that the lock cylinder cannot be rotated.

1989–90

1. Disconnect the negative battery cable.
2. Remove the steering wheel.
3. Remove the 2 trim shroud halves by removing the 3 attaching screws.
4. Remove the electrical connector from the key warning switch.
5. Using an ⅛ in. diameter drill, drill out the retaining pin, being careful not to drill deeper than ½ in.
6. Place a suitable chisel at the base of the ignition lock cylinder cap and using a suitable hammer, strike the chisel with sharp blows to break the cap away from the lock cylinder.
7. Using a ⅜ in. diameter drill, drill down the middle of the ignition key slot approximately 1¾ in. until the lock cylinder breaks loose from the breakaway base of the lock cylinder. Remove the lock cylinder and drill shavings from the lock cylinder housing.
8. Remove the retainer, washer, ignition switch and actuator. Thoroughly clean all the drill shavings from the casting.
9. Inspect the lock cylinder housing for damage from the removal operation.

To install:

10. Replace the lock cylinder housing if it was damaged.
11. Install the actuator and ignition switch.
12. Install the trim and electrical parts.
13. Install a new ignition lock cylinder.
14. Install the steering wheel.
15. Connect the negative battery cable.
16. Check the lock cylinder operation.

1991–93

1. Disconnect the negative battery cable.
2. Remove the steering wheel.
3. Using channel lock or vise grip pliers, twist the lock cylinder cap until it separates from the lock cylinder.
4. Using a ⅜ in. diameter drill bit, drill down the middle of the ignition lock key slot approximately 1¾ in. (44mm) until the lock cylinder breaks loose from the breakaway base of the lock cylinder. Remove the lock cylinder and drill shavings from the lock cylinder housing.
5. Remove the retainer, washer, ignition switch and actuator. Thoroughly clean all drill shavings and other foreign materials from the casting.
6. Inspect the lock cylinder housing for damage from the removal opera-

tion. If the housing is damaged, it must be replaced.

To install:

7. Replace the lock cylinder housing, if damaged.
8. Install the actuator and ignition switch.
9. Install the trim and electrical parts.
10. Install the ignition lock cylinder.
11. Install the steering wheel.
12. Check the lock cylinder operation.

Ignition Switch

REMOVAL & INSTALLATION

1989 Taurus and Sable

1. Disconnect the negative battery cable.
2. Turn the ignition lock cylinder to the **RUN** position and depress the lock cylinder retaining pin through the access hole in the shroud with a ⅛ diameter punch.
3. Remove the lock cylinder. If equipped with tilt columns, remove the tilt release lever.
4. Remove the instrument panel lower cover and the steering column shroud.
5. Remove the 4 nuts attaching the steering column to the support bracket and lower the column.
6. Disconnect the ignition switch electrical connector.
7. Remove the lock actuator cover plate. The lock actuator assembly will slide freely out of the lock cylinder housing when the ignition switch is removed.
8. Remove the ignition switch and cover.

To install:

9. Make sure the ignition switch is in the **RUN** position by rotating the driveshaft fully clockwise to the **START** position and release.
10. Install the lock actuator assembly to a depth of 0.46–0.52 in. (11.75–13.25mm) from the bottom of the actuator assembly to the bottom of the lock cylinder housing.
11. While holding the actuator assembly at the proper depth, install the ignition switch. Install the ignition switch cover and tighten the retaining bolts to 30–48 inch lbs. (3.4–5.4 Nm).
12. Install the lock cylinder. Rotate the ignition lock cylinder to the **LOCK** position and measure the depth of the actuator assembly as in Step 10. The actuator assembly must be 0.92–1.00 in. (23.5–25.5mm) inside the lock cylinder housing. If the depth measured does not meet specification, the actuator assembly must be removed and installed again.
13. Install the lock actuator cover

plate and tighten the bolts to 30–48 inch lbs. (3.4–5.4 Nm).
14. Install the ignition switch electrical connector.
15. Connect the negative battery cable. Check the ignition switch for proper function in all positions, including **START** and **ACC**.
16. Check the column function as follows:

   a. With the column shift lever in the **P** position or with the floor shift key release button depressed and with the ignition lock cylinder in the **LOCK** position, make certain the steering column locks.

   b. Position the column shift lever in the **D** position or the floor shift key release button fully extended and rotate the cylinder lock to the **RUN** position. Continue to rotate the cylinder toward the **LOCK** position until it stops. In this position, make certain the engine and all electrical accessories are **OFF** and that the steering shaft does not lock.

   c. Turn the radio power button **ON**. Rotate the cylinder counterclockwise to the **ACC** position to verify that the radio is energized.

   d. Place the shift lever in **P** and rotate the cylinder clockwise to the **START** position to verify that the starter energizes.

17. Remove the ignition lock cylinder.
18. Align the steering column mounting holes with the support bracket, center the steering column in the instrument panel opening and install the 4 nuts. Tighten the nuts to 15–25 ft. lbs. (20–34 Nm).
19. Install the column trim shrouds and the instrument panel lower cover. Install the tilt release lever, if equipped.
20. Install the ignition lock cylinder.

1989–90 Continental

1. Disconnect the negative battery cable.
2. Rotate the ignition lock cylinder to the **RUN** position and depress the lock cylinder retaining pin through the access hole in the shroud with a ⅛ in. drift punch or wire pin. Push on the pin and pull out on the lock cylinder.
3. Remove the lock cylinder.
4. If equipped with tilt steering columns, remove the tilt release lever by removing the Allen head cap screw that holds the tilt lever to the steering column.
5. Remove the lower steering column/instrument panel cover by removing the 4 Torx® head sheet metal screws.
6. Remove the steering column shroud.

7. Remove the bolts and nuts that attach the steering column to the support bracket and lower the column.

8. Remove the 3 screws from the diverter plate and remove it from the column.

9. Disconnect the ignition switch electrical connector.

10. Remove the ignition switch and cover by removing the 2 tamper-resistant Torx® head bolts.

To install:

11. Make sure the ignition switch is in the **RUN** position by rotating the switch fully clockwise to the **START** position and releasing.

12. Install the ignition switch and cover. Torque the cover retaining screws to 30–48 inch lbs. (3.4–5.4 Nm).

13. Install the ignition switch electrical connector.

14. Position the diverter plate on the column and secure it with 3 screws. Tighten to 30–48 inch lbs. (3.4–5.4 Nm).

15. Align the steering column mounting holes with the support bracket, center the steering column in the instrument panel opening and install the 4 nuts. Tighten to 15–25 ft. lbs. (20–34 Nm).

16. Install the 3 self-tapping screws and install the column trim shrouds. Tighten to 6–10 inch lbs. (0.7–1.1 Nm).

17. Install the instrument panel lower cover.

18. On tilt columns, install the tilt release lever. Tighten the retaining screw to 6.5–8.5 ft. lbs. (9–11 Nm). Check the column tilt travel through it's entire range to make sure there is no interference between the column and the instrument panel.

19. Connect the negative battery cable.

20. Check the column function as follows:

a. With the column shift lever in the **P** position and with the ignition lock cylinder in the **LOCK** position, make certain the steering column locks.

b. Position the column shift lever in the **D** position and rotate the cylinder lock to the **RUN** position. Continue to rotate the cylinder toward the **LOCK** position until it stops. In this position, make certain the engine and all electrical accessories are **OFF** and that the steering shaft does not lock.

c. Turn the radio power button **ON**. Rotate the cylinder counterclockwise to the **ACC** position to verify that the radio is energized.

d. Place the shift lever in **P** and rotate the cylinder clockwise to the **START** position to verify that the starter energizes.

1990–93 Taurus and Sable and 1991–93 Continental

1. Disconnect the negative battery cable.

2. Remove the steering column shroud by removing the self-tapping screws. Remove the tilt lever, if equipped.

3. Remove the instrument panel lower steering column cover.

4. Disconnect the ignition switch electrical connector.

5. Turn the ignition key lock cylinder to the **RUN** position.

6. Remove the 2 screws attaching the ignition switch and disengage the switch from the actuator.

To install:

7. Adjust the ignition switch by sliding the carrier to the switch **RUN** position. A new replacement switch assembly will already be set in the **RUN** position.

8. Make sure the ignition key lock cylinder is in the **RUN** position. The **RUN** position is achieved by rotating the key lock cylinder approximately 90 degrees from the lock position.

9. Install the ignition switch into the actuator. It may be necessary to move the switch slightly back and forth to align the switch mounting holes with the column lock housing threaded holes.

10. Install the attaching screws and tighten to 50–69 inch lbs. (5.6–7.9 Nm).

11. Connect the electrical connector to the ignition switch.

12. Connect the negative battery cable.

13. Check the ignition switch for proper function, including **START** and **ACC** positions. Make sure the column is locked with the switch in the **LOCK** position.

14. Install the instrument panel lower steering column cover, the steering column trim shrouds and the tilt lever, if equipped.

Fuses, Circuit Breakers and Relays

LOCATION

Fuses

All vehicles have a fuse panel located under the left side of the instrument panel. In addition, Continental and 1992–93 Taurus/Sable are equipped with a high-current fuse panel located in the engine compartment on the left fender apron.

Circuit Breakers

Circuit breakers protect electrical circuits by interrupting the current flow. A circuit breaker conducts current through an arm made of 2 types of metal bonded together. If the arm starts to carry too much current, it heats up. As 1 metal expands faster than the other the arm bends, opening the contacts and interupting the current flow.

Ford Motor Co.
Front Wheel Drive
MERCURY—Capri

SPECIFICATIONS

VEHICLE IDENTIFICATION CHART

It is important for servicing and ordering parts to be certain of the vehicle and engine identification. The VIN (vehicle identification number) is a 17 digit number visible through the windshield on the driver's side of the dash and contains the vehicle and engine identification codes. The tenth digit indicates model year and the eighth digit indicates engine code. It can be interpreted as follows:

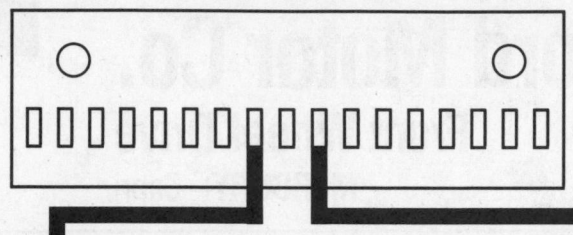

Engine Code

Code	Liters	Cu. In. (cc)	Cyl.	Fuel Sys.	Eng. Mfg.
Z	1.6	98 (1597)	4	EFI	Mazda
6	1.6	98 (1597)	4	EFI Turbo	Mazda

EFI—Electronic Fuel Injection

Model Year

Code	Year
M	1991
N	1992
P	1993

ENGINE IDENTIFICATION

Year	Model	Engine Displacement Liters (cc)	Engine Series Identification (ID/VIN)	Fuel System	No. of Cylinders	Engine Type
1991	Capri	1.6 (1597)	Z	EFI	4	DOHC
	Capri	1.6 (1597)	6	EFI Turbo	4	DOHC
1992–93	Capri	1.6 (1597)	Z	EFI	4	DOHC
	Capri	1.6 (1597)	6	EFI Turbo	4	DOHC

DOHC—Dual Overhead Cam Engine
EFI—Electronic Fuel Injection

GENERAL ENGINE SPECIFICATIONS

Year	Engine (ID/VIN)	Engine Displacement Liters (cc)	Fuel System Type	Net Horsepower @ rpm	Net Torque @ rpm (ft. lbs.)	Bore × Stroke (in.)	Compression Ratio	Oil Pressure @ rpm
1991	Z	1.6 (1597)	EFI	100 @ 5750	95 @ 5500	3.07 × 3.29	9.4:1	50-64 @ 3000
	6	1.6 (1597)	EFI	132 @ 6000	136 @ 3000	3.07 × 3.29	7.9:1	50-64 @ 3000
1992–93	Z	1.6 (1597)	EFI	100 @ 5750	95 @ 5500	3.07 × 3.29	9.4:1	43–48 @ 3000
	6	1.6 (1597)	EFI	132 @ 6000	136 @ 3000	3.07 × 3.29	7.9:1	43–48 @ 3000

NOTE: Horsepower and torque are SAE net figures. They are measured at the rear of the transmission with all accessories installed and operating. Since the figures vary when a given engine is installed in different models, some are representative rather than exact.
EFI—Electronic Fuel Injection

ENGINE TUNE-UP SPECIFICATIONS

Year	Engine (ID/VIN)	Engine Displacement Liters (cc)	Spark Plugs Gap (in.)	Ignition Timing (deg.)		Fuel Pump (psi)	Idle Speed (rpm)		Valve Clearance	
				MT	AT		MT	AT	In.	Ex.
1991	Z	1.6 (1597)	0.040	1–3 BTDC	1–3 BTDC	64–85	800–900	800–900	Hyd.	Hyd.
	6	1.6 (1597)	0.040	11–13 BTDC	—	64–85	800–900	800–900	Hyd.	Hyd.
1992	Z	1.6 (1597)	0.040	1–3 BTDC	1–3 BTDC	64-85	800–900	800–900	Hyd.	Hyd.
	6	1.6 (1597)	0.040	11–13 BTDC	—	64–85	800–900	800–900	Hyd.	Hyd.
1993	SEE UNDERHOOD SPECIFICATIONS									

NOTE: The lowest cylinder pressure should be within 75% of the highest cylinder pressure reading. For example, if the highest cylinder is 134 psi, the lowest should be 101. Engine should be at normal operating temperature with throttle valve in the wide open position.
The underhood specifications sticker often reflects tune-up specification changes in production. Sticker figures must be used if they disagree with those in this chart.
Hyd.—Hydraulic

FIRING ORDERS

NOTE: To avoid confusion, always replace spark plug wires one at a time.

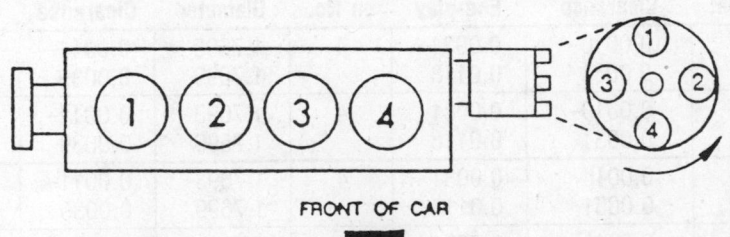

1.6L Normally Aspirated Engine
Engine Firing Order: 1–3–4–2
Distributor Rotation: Counterclockwise

FRONT OF CAR

1.6L Turbocharged Engine
Engine Firing Order: 1–3–4–2
Distributor Rotation: Counterclockwise

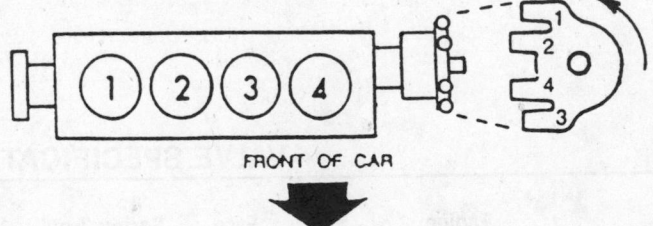

FRONT OF CAR

CAPACITIES

Year	Model	Engine (ID/VIN)	Engine Displacement Liters (cc)	Engine Crankcase with Filter (qts.)	Transmission (pts.)			Drive Axle (pts.)	Fuel Tank (gals.)	Cooling System (qts.)
					4-Spd	5-Spd	Auto.			
1991	Capri	Z	1.6 (1597)	3.8	—	6.8	12	—	11.1	5.3
	Capri	6	1.6 (1597)	3.8	—	6.8	—	—	11.1	6.3
1992-93	Capri	Z	1.6 (1597)	3.5	—	6.8	12	—	11.1	5.3
	Capri	6	1.6 (1597)	3.7	—	6.8	—	—	11.1	6.3

CAMSHAFT SPECIFICATIONS

All measurements given in inches.

Year	Engine (ID/VIN)	Engine Displacement Liters (cc)	Journal Diameter 1	2	3	4	5	Elevation In.	Ex.	Bearing Clearance	Camshaft End Play
1991	Z	1.6 (1597)	1.0213–1.0222	1.0213–1.0222	1.0213–1.0222	1.0213–1.0222	1.0213–1.0222	1.6019–1.6098	1.6019–1.6098	0.0014–0.0032	0.0028–0.0075
	6	1.6 (1597)	1.0213–1.0222	1.0213–1.0222	1.0213–1.0222	1.0213–1.0222	1.0213–1.0222	1.6019–1.6098	1.6019–1.6098	0.0014–0.0032	0.0028–0.0075
1992–93	Z	1.6 (1597)	1.0213–1.0222	1.0213–1.0222	1.0213–1.0222	1.0213–1.0222	1.0213–1.0222	1.6019–1.6098	1.6019–1.6098	0.0014–0.0032	0.0028–0.0075
	6	1.6 (1597)	1.0213–1.0222	1.0213–1.0222	1.0213–1.0222	1.0213–1.0222	1.0213–1.0222	1.6019–1.6098	1.6019–1.6098	0.0014–0.0032	0.0028–0.0075

CRANKSHAFT AND CONNECTING ROD SPECIFICATIONS

All measurements are given in inches.

Year	Engine (ID/VIN)	Engine Displacement Liters (cc)	Crankshaft Main Brg. Journal Dia.	Main Brg. Oil Clearance	Shaft End-play	Thrust on No.	Connecting Rod Journal Diameter	Oil Clearance	Side Clearance
1991	Z	1.6 (1597)	1.9661–1.9668	0.0010–0.0031	0.0031–0.0118	4	1.7693–1.7699	0.0011–0.0039	0.0043–0.0120
	6	1.6 (1597)	1.9661–1.9668	0.0010–0.0031	0.0031–0.0118	4	1.7693–1.7699	0.0011–0.0039	0.0043–0.0120
1992–93	Z	1.6 (1597)	1.9661–1.9668	0.0010–0.0031	0.0031–0.0118	4	1.7693–1.7699	0.0011–0.0039	0.0043–0.0120
	6	1.6 (1597)	1.9661–1.9668	0.0010–0.0031	0.0031–0.0118	4	1.7693–1.7699	0.0011–0.0039	0.0043–0.0120

VALVE SPECIFICATIONS

Year	Engine (ID/VIN)	Engine Displacement Liters (cc)	Seat Angle (deg.)	Face Angle (deg.)	Spring Test Pressure (lbs. @ in.)	Spring Installed Height (in.)	Stem-to-Guide Clearance (in.) Intake	Exhaust	Stem Diameter (in.) Intake	Exhaust
1991	Z	1.6 (1597)	45	45	NA ①	1.54	0.0010–0.0024	0.0012–0.0026	0.2350–0.2356	0.2348–0.2354
	6	1.6 (1597)	45	45	NA ①	1.54	0.0010–0.0024	0.0012–0.0026	0.2350–0.2356	0.2348–0.2354
1992–93	Z	1.6 (1597)	45	45	NA ①	1.54	0.0010–0.0024	0.0012–0.0026	0.2350–0.2356	0.2348–0.2354
	6	1.6 (1597)	45	45	NA ①	1.54	0.0010–0.0024	0.0012–0.0026	0.2350–0.2356	0.2348–0.2354

NA—Not available
① Check spring free length and for out-of-square
   Free length—1.803–1.858 in.
   Maximum out-of-square—0.063

PISTON AND RING SPECIFICATIONS

All measurements are given in inches.

Year	Engine (ID/VIN)	Engine Displacement Liters (cc)	Piston Clearance	Ring Gap			Ring Side Clearance		
				Top Compression	Bottom Compression	Oil Control	Top Compression	Bottom Compression	Oil Control
1991	Z	1.6 (1597)	0.0010–0.0026	0.008–0.015	0.006–0.011	0.008–0.028	0.0012–0.0026	0.0012–0.0026	0.0012–0.0026
	6	1.6 (1597)	0.0010–0.0026	0.008–0.015	0.006–0.011	0.008–0.028	0.0012–0.0026	0.0012–0.0026	0.0012–0.0026
1992–93	Z	1.6 (1597)	0.0010–0.0026	0.008–0.015	0.006–0.011	0.008–0.028	0.0012–0.0026	0.0012–0.0026	0.0012–0.0026
	6	1.6 (1597)	0.0010–0.0026	0.008–0.015	0.006–0.011	0.008–0.028	0.0012–0.0026	0.0012–0.0026	0.0012–0.0026

TORQUE SPECIFICATIONS

All readings in ft. lbs.

Year	Engine (ID/VIN)	Engine Displacement Liters (cc)	Cylinder Head Bolts	Main Bearing Bolts	Rod Bearing Bolts	Crankshaft Pulley Bolts	Flywheel Bolts	Manifold		Spark Plugs	Lug Nut
								Intake	Exhaust		
1991	Z	1.6 (1597)	①	40–43	35–38	80–87	71–76	14–19	29–42	11–17	67–88
	6	1.6 (1597)	①	40–43	35–38	80–87	71–76	14–19	29–42	11–17	67–88
1992–93	Z	1.6 (1597)	①	40–43	35–38	80–87	71–76	14–19	29–42	11–17	67–88
	6	1.6 (1597)	①	40–43	35–38	80–87	71–76	14–19	29–42	11–17	67–88

① Tighten in sequence in 2 steps:
Step 1—14–25 ft. lbs.
Step 2—56–60 ft. lbs.

BRAKE SPECIFICATIONS

All measurements in inches unless noted.

Year	Model	Master Cylinder Bore	Brake Disc			Brake Drum Diameter			Minimum Lining Thickness	
			Original Thickness	Minimum Thickness	Maximum Runout	Original Inside Diameter	Max. Wear Limit	Maximum Machine Diameter	Front	Rear
1991	Capri	0.811	①	②	0.004	—	—	—	0.120	0.120
1992–93	Capri	0.811	①	②	0.004	—	—	—	0.120	0.120

① Front—0.710 in.
Rear—0.390 in.
② Front—0.630 in.
Rear—0.350 in.

WHEEL ALIGNMENT

Year	Model		Caster		Camber		Toe-in (in.)	Steering Axis Inclination (deg.)
			Range (deg.)	Preferred Setting (deg.)	Range (deg.)	Preferred Setting (deg.)		
1991	Capri	Front	27/32P–2 11/32P	1 19/32P	1/16P–1 9/16P	13/16P	1/32N–7/32P	12 11/32
		Rear	—	—	1 3/16N–1 1/32P	0	0–3/16P	—
1992–93	Capri	Front	27/32P–2 11/32P	1 19/32P	1/16P–1 9/16P	13/16P	1/32N–7/32P	12 11/32
		Rear	—	—	1 3/16N–1 1/32P	0	0–3/16P	—

N—Negative
P—Positive

ENGINE MECHANICAL

NOTE: Disconnecting the negative battery cable on some vehicles may interfere with the functions of the on board computer systems and may require the computer to undergo a relearning process, once the negative battery cable is reconnected.

Engine Assembly

REMOVAL & INSTALLATION

1. Relieve the fuel system pressure. Drain the cooling system and discharge the air conditioning system, if equipped.
2. Disconnect the battery cables. Remove the battery, battery tray and battery tray support bracket. Release the wiring harness retaining straps from the battery support tray.
3. Disconnect the windshield washer supply hose between the washer fluid reservoir and the hood. Mark the hood hinge locations and remove the hood.
4. Disconnect the intake air tube and the wiring to the ignition coil and vane air flow meter. Remove the air cleaner/vane air flow meter assembly and remove the air cleaner support brackets.
5. Disconnect the intercooler hoses from the turbocharger, if equipped. Remove the radiator.
6. Disconnect the accelerator cable and remove the retaining bracket from the cylinder head cover. Position the cable aside.
7. Disconnect and plug the fuel lines at the fuel filter and pressure regulator. Disconnect the power brake booster manifold vacuum hose from the manifold.
8. Disconnect the heater hoses at the heater core tubes. Label and remove the vacuum hoses located at the throttle body.
9. If equipped with manual transaxle and turbocharger, disconnect the clutch cable and remove the support bracket and cable from the transaxle. On normally aspirated vehicles, disconnect the clutch slave cylinder hydraulic line.
10. If equipped with automatic transaxle, remove the transaxle cooler lines.
11. Tag and disconnect the following electrical connectors:
   a. Starter wiring at starter. Remove harness from locating strap on bracket.
   b. Alternator wiring.
   c. Wiring from engine coolant sensors located on rear of engine block.
   d. Ground connection at bracket on thermostat cover.
   e. Oxygen sensor wire, main wiring harness connector, throttle position sensor connector and knock sensor connector.
   f. Distributor and transaxle wiring.
   g. Ground wire and strap at front of engine. Reinstall lifting eye.
12. Remove the engine oil dipstick and dipstick retaining clip.
13. Remove the power steering pump from the bracket. Remove the power steering pump mounting bracket and position the pump aside, with the hoses connected.
14. Remove the upper air conditioner compressor retaining bolts, if equipped.
15. Raise and safely support the vehicle. Drain the engine oil.
16. If equipped, remove the lower air conditioner compressor mounting bolts and position the compressor aside. Do not let the compressor hang by the hoses; tie up with mechanics wire.
17. Remove the front wheel and tire assemblies. Remove the front ball joint to steering knuckle retaining bolts.
18. Remove the splash guards. Drain the transaxle oil and remove the halfshafts from the differential.
19. Remove the front exhaust pipe bracket located on the lower side of the engine. Disconnect the front exhaust pipe from the exhaust manifold or turbocharger, if equipped.
20. Remove the frame support bar to engine support bolt. Loosen the right control arm bolt and pivot the support bar downward.
21. Disengage the rubber exhaust hangers located directly behind the catalytic converter. Allow the exhaust system to hang down 6 in. and support with mechanics wire.
22. Unbolt the transaxle shift linkage and stabilizer bar at the transaxle. Remove the nuts from the front and rear engine mounts and lower the vehicle.
23. Attach suitable engine lifting equipment to the lift eyes located on the sides of the cylinder head.
24. Support the engine with the lifting equipment and remove the right engine mount through bolt. Raise the engine off the mounts and slightly pivot the engine/transaxle assembly.
25. Disconnect the oil pressure sensor and route the starter/alternator wiring harness from the engine.
26. Carefully lift the engine/transaxle assembly. Turn the assembly while raising to clear the brake master cylinder, shift linkage universal joint, radi-ator support and air conditioning lines, if equipped.
27. Remove the intake manifold support bracket. Remove the gusset plate(s), if equipped. Remove the starter.
28. Remove the transaxle to engine retaining bolts. Tag the bolts to make sure they are installed in their correct locations for installation.
29. Separate the engine from the transaxle. If equipped with manual transaxle, remove the pressure plate, clutch disc and flywheel. If equipped with automatic transaxle, remove the flywheel.
30. Install the engine on a workstand.

To install:

31. Remove the engine from the workstand. Install the end plate and tighten the retaining screw to 69–95 inch lbs. (8–11 Nm).
32. If equipped with manual transaxle, proceed as follows:
   a. Install the flywheel. Apply thread sealer to the flywheel bolts and tighten to 71–76 ft. lbs. (96–103 Nm).
   b. Position the clutch disc using an alignment tool.
   c. Install the pressure plate and tighten the retaining bolts to 14–19 ft. lbs. (18–26 Nm).
33. If equipped with automatic transaxle, install the flywheel. Tighten the retaining bolts to 71–76 ft. lbs. (96–103 Nm).
34. Install the intermediate axle shaft and bearing, if equipped. Tighten the bearing mount retaining bolts to 27–38 ft. lbs. (37–52 Nm).
35. If equipped with manual transaxle, proceed as follows:
   a. Position the transaxle to the engine and install the retaining bolts.
   b. Tighten bolts **A** to 66–86 ft. lbs. (89–117 Nm).
   c. Tighten bolts **B** to 29–38 ft. lbs. (37–52 Nm).
36. If equipped with automatic transaxle, proceed as follows:
   a. Position the transaxle to the

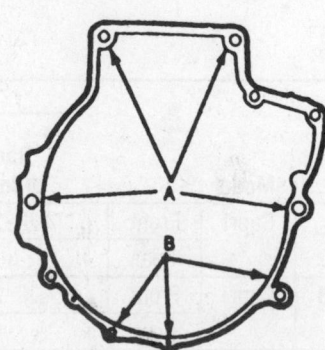

Transaxle-to-engine bolt identification

engine and install the retaining bolts.

b. Tighten bolts **A** to 41–59 ft. lbs. (55–80 Nm).

c. Align the torque converter and flywheel. Install the retaining bolts and tighten to 25–36 ft. lbs. (34–49 Nm).

d. Install the cover plate. Tighten retaining bolts **B** to 61–87 inch lbs. (7–10 Nm).

e. Install the gusset plate(s), if removed. Tighten the retaining bolts on the engine to 28–38 ft. lbs. (37–52 Nm). Tighten the bolts to the transaxle to 41–59 ft. lbs. (55–80 Nm).

37. Install the starter. Tighten the retaining bolts to 23–34 ft. lbs. (31–46 Nm).

38. Install the intake manifold support bracket. Loosely install all bolts first. Tighten the upper bolts and then the lower bolts to 22–34 ft. lbs. (31–46 Nm).

39. Install the starter bracket to manifold support bolt. Tighten to 14–19 ft. lbs. (19–25 Nm). If equipped, install the turbocharger inlet tube.

40. Lower the engine/transaxle assembly into the vehicle. Before the engine contacts the mounts, route the starter, alternator and oil pressure sensor wiring and connect the oil pressure sensor.

41. Lower the engine until the front mount seats on the crossmember. Install the through bolt on the right engine mount but do not tighten.

42. Remove the engine lifting equipment and raise and safely support the vehicle.

43. Align the rear engine mount to the crossmember and install the retaining nuts to the front and rear engine mounts. On 1991 vehicles, tighten the nuts to 47–66 ft. lbs. (64–89 Nm). On 1992–93 vehicles, tighten the front mount nuts to 47–66 ft. lbs. (64–89 Nm) and the rear mount nut to 24–34 ft. lbs. (32–47 Nm).

44. If equipped with manual transaxle, connect the shift coupling and stabilizer. Tighten the linkage retaining nut to 12–17 ft. lbs. (16–22 Nm) and the stabilizer to 23–34 ft. lbs. (31–46 Nm).

45. If equipped with automatic transaxle, connect the shift linkage and oil cooler lines. Tighten the linkage retaining bolt to 69–95 inch lbs. (8–11 Nm). Tighten the shift cable pivot nut to 33–47 ft. lbs. (44–64 Nm). Tighten the oil cooler hose clamps.

46. Connect the front exhaust pipe to the manifold or turbocharger. Install the exhaust pipe to support bracket and tighten the retaining bolts to 32–45 ft. lbs. (43–61 Nm). Tighten the manifold or turbocharger nuts to 29–42 ft. lbs. (39–57 Nm). Attach the rubber exhaust hangers.

47. Position the cross brace. Tighten the retaining nut and bolt to 26–37 ft. lbs. (35–50 Nm). Tighten the right A-arm front bolt to 47–66 ft. lbs. (64–89 Nm) on 1991 vehicles or 72–86 ft. lbs. (97–117 Nm) on 1992–93 vehicles.

48. Install the drive axles to the transaxle. Install the ball joint retaining bolts and tighten to 32–40 ft. lbs. (43–54 Nm).

49. Mount the air conditioning compressor to the engine, if equipped. Tighten the lower retaining bolts to 30–40 ft. lbs. (39–54 Nm).

50. Install the splash guards and the wheel and tire assemblies. Lower the vehicle.

51. Install the upper air conditioning compressor retaining bolts, if equipped. Tighten to 30–40 ft. lbs. (39–54 Nm).

52. Tighten the right engine mount through bolt to 33–48 ft. lbs. (45–65 Nm). Connect the alternator wiring.

53. Position the power steering pump bracket on the stud. Install the power steering pump bracket retaining bolts and nut and tighten to 35–48 ft. lbs. (47–66 Nm).

54. Install the power steering pump and belt. Tighten the adjustment nut to 27–38 ft. lbs. (37–52 Nm). Tighten the pivot bolt to 23–34 ft. lbs. (31–46 Nm).

55. Install the engine oil dipstick and the dipstick retaining clip. Install the ground strap and ground wire to the cylinder head.

56. If equipped with manual transaxle and turbocharger, install the clutch cable. If normally aspirated, connect the clutch hydraulic line.

57. Connect the transaxle and engine electrical connectors. Connect the fuel lines to the fuel filter and pressure regulator.

58. Install the intake air tube to the throttle body. If equipped, install the turbocharger intercooler hoses.

59. Install the air cleaner brackets. Install the air cleaner with the vane air flow meter attached. Install the intake air tube and connect the coil and vane air flow meter connectors.

60. Connect the coolant, crankcase and air bypass hoses. Install the vacuum hoses in their correct locations, as noted during removal.

61. Connect the accelerator cable and install the retaining bracket. Install the power brake booster hose.

62. Remove the speedometer cable from the transaxle. Fill the transaxle with the proper type and quantity of fluid. Install the speedometer cable. Connect the speedometer cable connector.

63. Fill the crankcase with the proper type and quantity of engine oil.

64. Install the radiator/fan assembly. Tighten the bracket retaining bolts to 69–95 inch lbs. (8–11 Nm). Connect the coolant hoses and fan electrical connector. Fill the cooling system with the proper type and quantity of coolant.

65. Install the hood, aligning the marks that were made during removal. Tighten the bolts to 14–21 ft. lbs. (20–28 Nm). Connect the washer hose.

66. Install the battery tray support. Install the battery tray, battery and battery hold-down. Connect the battery cables.

67. Start the engine and check for proper operation and for leaks. If equipped, evacuate and charge the air conditioning system.

68. Road test the vehicle and check for proper clutch and/or transaxle operation.

Engine Mounts

REMOVAL & INSTALLATION

Right Side Mount

1. Support the engine assembly with a floor jack.
2. Remove the mount to engine bracket retaining nuts.
3. Remove the through bolt.
4. Remove the bracket to body retaining bolts.

To install:

5. Position the bracket to the body. Tighten the smaller bolts to 14–21 ft. lbs. (20–28 Nm). Tighten the larger bolt to 49–67 ft. lbs. (67–91 Nm).
6. Install the engine mount to the engine bracket. Tighten the nuts to 44–63 ft. lbs. (60–85 Nm).
7. Install the through bolt and tighten to 33–48 ft. lbs. (45–65 Nm).
8. Remove the floor jack.

Front Mount

1. Support the engine with engine support fixture D88L–6000–A or equivalent. Raise and safely support the vehicle.
2. Remove the engine mount retaining nuts from the crossmember.
3. Remove the engine mount retaining bolts from the transaxle. Remove the through bolt, if required.

To install:

4. Position the engine mount to the transaxle. Install the retaining bolts and tighten to 27–38 ft. lbs. (37–52 Nm).
5. Apply 2 drops of threadlocking compound to the studs and install the engine mount to crossmember retaining nuts. Tighten to 47–65 ft. lbs. (64–89 Nm).
6. Install the through bolt, if removed. Tighten to 33–47 ft. lbs. (45–65 Nm) on 1991 vehicles or 48–65 ft. lbs. (64–89 Nm) on 1992–93 vehicles.

7. Lower the vehicle and remove the engine support fixture.

Rear Mount

1. Support the engine with engine support fixture D88L-6000-A or equivalent. Raise and safely support the vehicle.

2. Remove the front and rear engine mount to crossmember retaining nuts. Remove the crossmember brace retaining bolts.

3. Remove the left A-arm retaining bolt. Remove the engine support crossmember retaining nuts and bolts.

4. Remove the rear engine mount retaining bolts.

To install:

5. Install the rear engine mount. Tighten the retaining nut to 26-36 ft. lbs. (35-50 Nm).

6. Install the crossmember. Apply 2 drops of threadlocking compound and tighten the retaining bolts to 47-66 ft.

lbs. (64-89 Nm). Tighten the rear engine retaining nut to 47-66 ft. lbs. (64-89 Nm).

7. Install the crossmember brace retaining bolts.

8. Install the left A-arm retaining bolt. Tighten to 47-66 ft. lbs. (64-89 Nm).

9. Install the front and rear engine mount to crossmember retaining nuts. Tighten to 47-66 ft. lbs. (64-89 Nm).

10. Lower the vehicle and remove the engine support fixture.

Cylinder Head

REMOVAL & INSTALLATION

1. Relieve the fuel system pressure and drain the cooling system. Disconnect the negative battery cable.

2. Remove the intake air tube from the throttle body and disconnect the air bypass hoses.

3. Tag and disconnect the spark plug wires and retainers. Remove the intake air tube from the air cleaner assembly.

4. Disconnect the coolant hose from the thermostat cover. Tag and disconnect the vacuum hoses and coolant hoses from the throttle body and intake manifold.

5. Disconnect the throttle cable and remove the retaining brackets and cable. Disconnect the fuel lines at the fuel filter and pressure regulator.

6. Disconnect the main harness connector. Disconnect the oxygen sensor connector and remove the ground connection retaining screw at the bracket.

7. If equipped, disconnect the intercooler tubes from the turbocharger.

8. Remove the ground wire and strap retaining bolts at the front sides of the cylinder head. Remove the timing belt covers and timing belt.

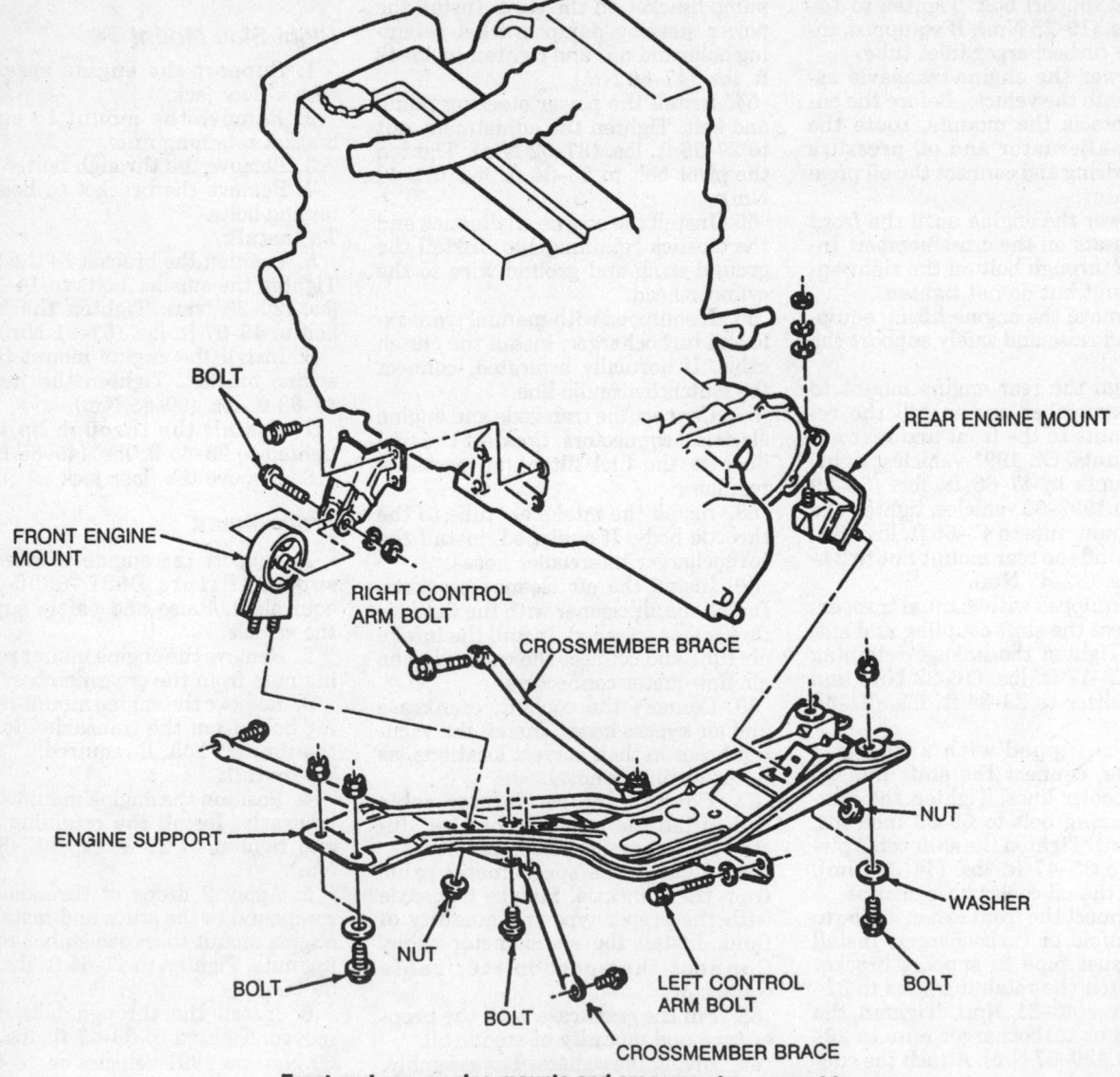

BOLT

FRONT ENGINE MOUNT

RIGHT CONTROL ARM BOLT

CROSSMEMBER BRACE

ENGINE SUPPORT

NUT

BOLT

BOLT

LEFT CONTROL ARM BOLT

CROSSMEMBER BRACE

REAR ENGINE MOUNT

NUT

WASHER

BOLT

Front and rear engine mounts and crossmember assembly

9. On turbocharged vehicle, remove the exhaust manifold and turbocharger as an assembly. On normally aspirated vehicle, disconnect the front exhaust pipe from the exhaust manifold.

10. Remove the intake manifold support upper retaining bolts. Remove the cylinder head cover.

11. Remove the cylinder head bolts and remove the cylinder head and manifold(s) as an assembly.

12. Separate the manifold(s) from the cylinder head, if required.

13. Clean all gasket mating surfaces. Inspect the cylinder head for cracks and inspect the gasket surfaces for burrs and nicks.

14. Measure the cylinder head flatness using a straight-edge and feeler gauge. If the cylinder head flatness exceeds 0.006 in. (0.15mm), machine the cylinder head surface.

NOTE: The maximum machine limit is 0.008 in. (0.20mm).

15. Measure the intake and exhaust manifold contact flatness with a straight-edge and feeler gauge. If distortion exceeds 0.006 in. (0.15mm), machine the surface or replace the cylinder head.

To install:

16. Install the exhaust manifold with new gaskets. Be sure to use the 2-piece gasket with the heavy gasket installed first. Tighten the retaining nuts to 29–42 ft. lbs. (39–57 Nm).

17. Install the intake manifold to the cylinder using a new gasket. Make sure the coolant passage openings in the gasket align with the manifold and cylinder head. Tighten the retaining nuts and bolts to 14–19 ft. lbs. (19–25 Nm).

18. Position a new head gasket on the block and carefully set the cylinder head on the block.

19. Lightly lubricate the threads of the cylinder head bolts with oil and install. Tighten the bolts, in sequence, in 2 steps, first to 14–25 ft. lbs. (20–34 Nm) and then to 56–60 ft. lbs. (76–81 Nm).

20. Install the intake manifold support upper retaining bolts and tighten to 22–39 ft. lbs. (31–46 Nm). Install the timing belt and covers.

21. Install the cylinder head cover. Tighten the retaining bolts to 69–95 inch lbs. (8–11 Nm).

22. Connect the front exhaust pipe to the exhaust manifold on the normally aspirated engine. Tighten the retaining nuts to 23–34 ft. lbs. (31–46 Nm). Install the exhaust manifold and turbocharger assembly on turbocharged engines.

23. Install the ground wire and strap to the cylinder head with the retaining bolts. Connect the intercooler tubes, if equipped.

Cylinder head bolt torque sequence

24. Connect the oxygen sensor connector and install the ground wires to the bracket on the cylinder head with the retaining screw.

25. Connect the main engine harness connector. Connect the fuel lines to the fuel filter and pressure regulator.

26. Install the throttle cable and retaining brackets. Install the coolant hoses and vacuum lines to the intake manifold and throttle body.

27. Install the coolant hose to the thermostat cover. install the intake air tube to the air cleaner.

28. Install the spark plug wires and retainers. Install the intake air tube to the throttle body and connect the air bypass hoses.

29. Fill the cooling system and connect the negative battery cable. Start the engine and check for leaks.

Valve Lifters

REMOVAL & INSTALLATION

1. Disconnect the negative battery cable.

2. Remove the camshafts.

3. Remove the lifters. If the lifters are to be reused, keep them in order so they can be reinstalled in the same locations.

4. Installation is the reverse of the removal procedure. Coat the lifters with clean engine oil prior to installation.

Intake Manifold

REMOVAL & INSTALLATION

1. Relieve the fuel system pressure and drain the cooling system.

2. Disconnect the negative battery cable.

3. Disconnect the intercooler tube and/or air intake tube. Disconnect the air bypass hoses.

4. Disconnect the main engine harness electrical connection and the throttle position sensor connector.

5. Tag and disconnect the vacuum hoses from the throttle body. Discon-

nect the fuel lines from the fuel filter and pressure regulator.

6. Disconnect the throttle cable and disconnect the hoses from the air bypass valve. Remove the air bypass valve retaining nut and bolt.

7. Remove the intake manifold retaining bolts and nuts from the support bracket and cylinder head. Remove the intake manifold and throttle body assembly.

To install:

8. Clean all gasket mating surfaces.

9. Install the new intake manifold gasket. Make sure the coolant passage openings align with the openings in the cylinder head and manifold.

10. Install the intake manifold. Tighten the retaining nut and bolts to 14–19 ft. lbs. (19–25 Nm). Tighten the support bracket retaining bolts to 23–34 ft. lbs. (31–46 Nm).

11. Install the air bypass valve and connect the air hoses. Connect the throttle cable.

12. Connect the fuel lines to the fuel filter and pressure regulator. Connect the main engine harness connector and throttle position sensor connector.

13. Connect the vacuum lines to the throttle body. Install the air intake tube. Connect the intercooler tube, if equipped.

14. Fill the cooling system and connect the negative battery cable. Start the engine and check for leaks.

Exhaust Manifold

REMOVAL & INSTALLATION

Normally Aspirated Engine

1. Disconnect the negative battery cable.

2. Remove the air intake tube.

3. Remove the front exhaust pipe to exhaust manifold retaining nuts.

4. Remove the exhaust support bracket, if equipped.

5. Remove the heat shield and diconnect the oxygen sensor electrical connector.

6. Remove the exhaust manifold.

To install:

7. Clean the gasket mating surfaces.

8. Install the exhaust manifold gaskets. The heavier gasket is installed first.

9. Install the exhaust manifold. Tighten the retaining nuts to 29–42 ft. lbs. (39–57 Nm).

10. Connect the oxygen sensor electrical connector and install the manifold heat shield. Install the air intake tube.

11. Connect the front exhaust pipe to the exhaust manifold. Tighten the retaining nuts to 23–34 ft. lbs. (31–46 Nm).

12. Install the exhaust support bracket, if removed. Tighten the engine mount bolt to 49–67 ft. lbs. (67–91 Nm).

13. Connect the negative battery cable. Start the engine and check for leaks.

Turbocharged Engine

1. Disconnect the negative battery cable.

2. Remove the exhaust manifold and turbocharger assembly.

3. Separate the exhaust manifold from the turbocharger.

To install:

4. Clean the gasket mating surfaces.

5. Install the manifold to the turbocharger assembly with a new gasket. Tighten the retaining nuts to 20–24 ft. lbs. (27–33 Nm).

6. Install the exhaust manifold and turbocharger assembly.

Turbocharger

REMOVAL & INSTALLATION

1. Disconnect the negative battery cable and drain the cooling system.

2. Remove the throttle body air intake tube. Disconnect the intercooler hose from the turbocharger and position both intercooler hoses out of the way.

3. Remove the oxygen sensor connector from its retaining clip and disconnect the oxygen sensor.

4. Remove the 3 bolts retaining the lower heat shield to the turbocharger and remove the lower heat shield.

5. Remove the 2 bolts retaining the upper heat shield to the exhaust manifold and remove the upper heat shield.

NOTE: Feed the oxygen sensor wire and guide through the upper heat shield.

6. Remove the 3 bolts retaining the side heat shield to the turbocharger and remove the side heat shield.

NOTE: It will be necessary to remove the power steering pump and mounting bracket to access the lower left exhaust manifold retaining nut and to remove the exhaust manifold from the studs.

7. Remove the power steering pump belt. Remove the power steering pump through bolt and remove the nut and bolt from the adjuster. Pull the pump from the mounting bracket and position out of the way.

8. Disconnect the lower radiator hose from the water pump.

9. Position the power steering pump to access the mounting bracket retaining bolts and nut. Remove the 2 bolts and 1 nut retaining the mounting bracket to the engine and remove the bracket.

10. Remove the 2 screws retaining the air cleaner duct tube, loosen the clamp at the turbocharger and position the duct tube out of the way.

11. Disconnect the coolant return hose at the turbocharger. Remove the bolt and brass sealing washers retaining the oil supply line at the engine block.

12. Raise and safely support the vehicle.

13. Remove the 3 retaining nuts and washers from the exhaust pipe flange. Remove the 2 bolts retaining the exhaust hanger to the engine block.

14. Slide off the 2 rubber exhaust hangers at the catalyst. Pull downward on the exhaust pipe and to the left side of the vehicle.

15. Disconnect the oil return hose and the coolant return hose at the turbocharger. Remove the 2 retaining bolts from the turbocharger support bracket.

16. Remove the 2 bolts retaining the coolant bypass tube outlet to the water pump. Lower the vehicle.

17. Loosen the retaining clamp bolt on the coolant bypass tube at the rear of the cylinder head. Remove the 11 retaining nuts from the exhaust manifold.

18. Pull the coolant bypass tube bracket from the exhaust stud and position the tube out of the way.

19. Grasp the exhaust manifold, pull off the studs and move the assembly slightly to the right side of the engine compartment to clear the cooling fan and remove from the vehicle.

20. Working on a bench, remove the 4 nuts retaining the turbocharger to the exhaust manifold, separate the assembly and discard the gasket.

To install:

21. Clean all gasket mating surfaces. Add 25cc of oil in the oil passage of the turbocharger.

22. Position a new gasket on the exhaust manifold and install the turbocharger onto the studs. Install the 4 retaining nuts and tighten to 20–24 ft. lbs. (27–33 Nm).

NOTE: Use only the proper nuts to mount the turbocharger to the exhaust manifold.

23. Remove the oil supply line from the turbocharger. Position a new exhaust gasket on the cylinder head.

24. Carefully position the turbocharger assembly in the engine compartment and slide the exhaust manifold onto the studs. Position the heater coolant bypass tube bracket onto the exhaust stud.

25. Install 11 retaining nuts on the exhaust manifold and tighten to 29–42 ft. lbs. (39–57 Nm). Tighten the coolant bypass tube retaining clamp bolt securely, then raise and safely support the vehicle.

26. Position a new gasket and install 2 retaining bolts on the coolant bypass tube outlet. Tighten the bolts to 14–19 ft. lbs. (19–25 Nm).

27. Install 2 retaining bolts into the turbocharger support bracket. Tighten the bolts to 32–45 ft. lbs. (43–61 Nm).

28. Connect the coolant return and oil return hoses.

29. Position the exhaust pipe onto the turbocharger and start the nuts and washers. Install the 2 retaining bolts on the exhaust hanger at the engine.

30. Slide on 2 rubber exhaust hangers at the catalyst. Tighten the exhaust pipe retaining nuts to 18–24 ft. lbs. (24–32 Nm). Lower the vehicle.

31. Install the retaining bolt and brass washers on the oil supply line and carefully position the oil line into the vehicle. Hand-start the bolt into the engine block. Connect the oil line to the turbocharger and finger-tighten. Tighten the oil line bolt to 104–156 inch lbs. (12–18 Nm).

NOTE: Make sure 1 brass washer is on each side of the oil line fitting.

32. Tighten the oil supply line on the turbocharger to 12–17 ft. lbs. (16–24 Nm). Connect the coolant supply hose.

33. Position the air cleaner duct tube on the turbocharger and tighten the clamp. Install the 2 screws retaining the air cleaner duct tube.

34. Position the power steering pump bracket on the engine and install the 2 retaining bolts and 1 retaining nut. Tighten to 35–48 ft. lbs. (47–66 Nm).

35. Position the power steering pump on the mounting bracket and install the through bolt and adjuster.

36. Connect the lower radiator hose and install the power steering belt.

37. Position the side heat shield and install the 3 retaining bolts finger-tight. Position the upper heat shield and install the 2 retaining bolts finger-tight.

NOTE: Feed the oxygen sensor wire through the upper heat shield. Install the wire retainer under the left bolt.

38. Position the lower heat shield and install the 3 retaining bolts finger-tight. Tighten all heat shield retaining bolts to 14–19 ft. lbs. (19–25 Nm).

39. Connect the oxygen sensor and install the connector into its retaining clip. Position the intercooler hose on the turbocharger and secure with the clamp.

40. Install the throttle body air intake tube. Fill the cooling system and connect the negative battery cable.

41. If the turbocharger was replaced, proceed as follows:

    a. Disconnect the ignition coil.

    b. Crank the engine for 20 seconds.

    c. Connect the ignition coil.

    d. Start the engine and run at idle for 30 seconds.

    e. Check for leaks.

Timing Belt Front Cover

REMOVAL & INSTALLATION

1. Disconnect the negative battery cable. Raise and safely support the vehicle.

2. Remove the right front wheel and tire assembly and remove the right splash guard. Lower the vehicle.

3. Remove the alternator and power steering belts. Remove the oil dipstick and the water pump pulley.

4. Remove the crankshaft pulley, damper and baffle plate.

5. Remove the upper, center and lower timing belt covers.

6. Installation is the reverse of the removal procedure. Tighten the timing belt cover retaining bolts to 71–97 inch lbs. (8–11 Nm). Tighten the baffle and damper retaining screws and the crankshaft pulley retaining bolts to 109–152 inch lbs. (12–17 Nm). Tighten the water pump pulley retaining bolts to 71–97 inch lbs. (8–11 Nm).

OIL SEAL REPLACEMENT

1. Disconnect the negative battery cable.

2. Remove the timing belt.

3. Remove the crankshaft timing sprocket.

4. Remove the camshaft sprockets. Hold the camshafts with a wrench to remove the sprocket retaining bolts.

5. Remove the camshaft seal plate.

6. Remove the camshaft and crankshaft seals using a seal removal tool.

To install:

7. Lubricate the seal lips with clean engine oil.

8. Install the seals using a seal installer.

9. Install the camshaft seal plate. Tighten the retaining screws to 71–97 inch lbs. (8–11 Nm).

10. Install the crankshaft timing belt sprocket. Tighten the retaining bolt to 80–87 ft. lbs. (108–118 Nm).

11. Install the camshaft sprockets. Tighten the retaining bolts to 36–45 ft. lbs. (49–61 Nm).

12. Install the timing belt.

13. Connect the negative battery cable.

Timing Belt and Tensioner

REMOVAL & INSTALLATION

1. Disconnect the negative battery cable. Raise and safely support the vehicle.

2. Remove the right front wheel and tire assembly and remove the right splash guard. Lower the vehicle.

3. Remove the spark plugs. Set the engine position to TDC on the No. 1 cylinder.

4. Remove the alternator and power steering belts. Remove the oil dipstick and the water pump pulley.

5. Remove the crankshaft pulley, damper and baffle plate.

6. Remove the upper, center and lower timing belt covers.

7. Remove the timing belt tension spring and loosen the timing belt tension pulley.

8. Support the engine with a floor jack and remove the right engine mount.

9. Mark the timing belt rotation direction and remove the timing belt.

10. Inspect the timing belt and timing sprockets for wear and/or damage and replace as necessary.

11. Check the free length of the timing belt tension spring. It should be 2.315 in. (58.8mm). Replace if out of specification.

To install:

12. Make sure the timing marks are properly positioned on the camshafts and crankshaft. The intake camshaft should have the letter **I** aligned with the arrow on the belt cover. The exhaust camshaft should have the letter **E** aligned with the arrow on the belt cover.

13. The crankshaft key should align with the arrow.

14. Tighten the tension pulley with the tension spring fully extended.

15. Install the timing belt. Keep tension on the opposite side of the tensioner as tight as possible. Make sure the rotation mark on the belt is correct.

16. Turn the crankshaft 2 full turns. Check the alignment marks. If any mark is not aligned, remove the timing belt and reset the timing.

17. Loosen the tension pulley retaining bolt to allow the tension spring to tighten the belt.

18. Tighten the tension pulley retaining bolt to 27–38 ft. lbs. (37–52 Nm). Rotate the engine 2 full turns. Make sure the timing marks are aligned.

19. Measure the timing belt tension between the camshaft pulleys. Belt deflection should be 0.33–0.45 in. (8.5–11.5mm). If incorrect, loosen the ten-

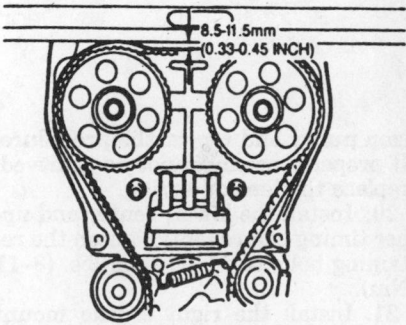

Measuring timing belt tension

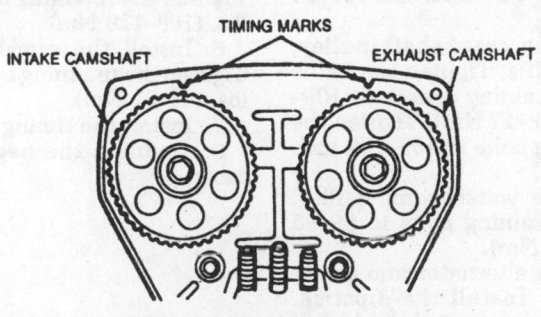

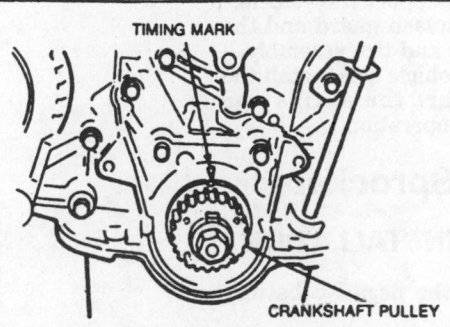

Timing belt sprocket alignment

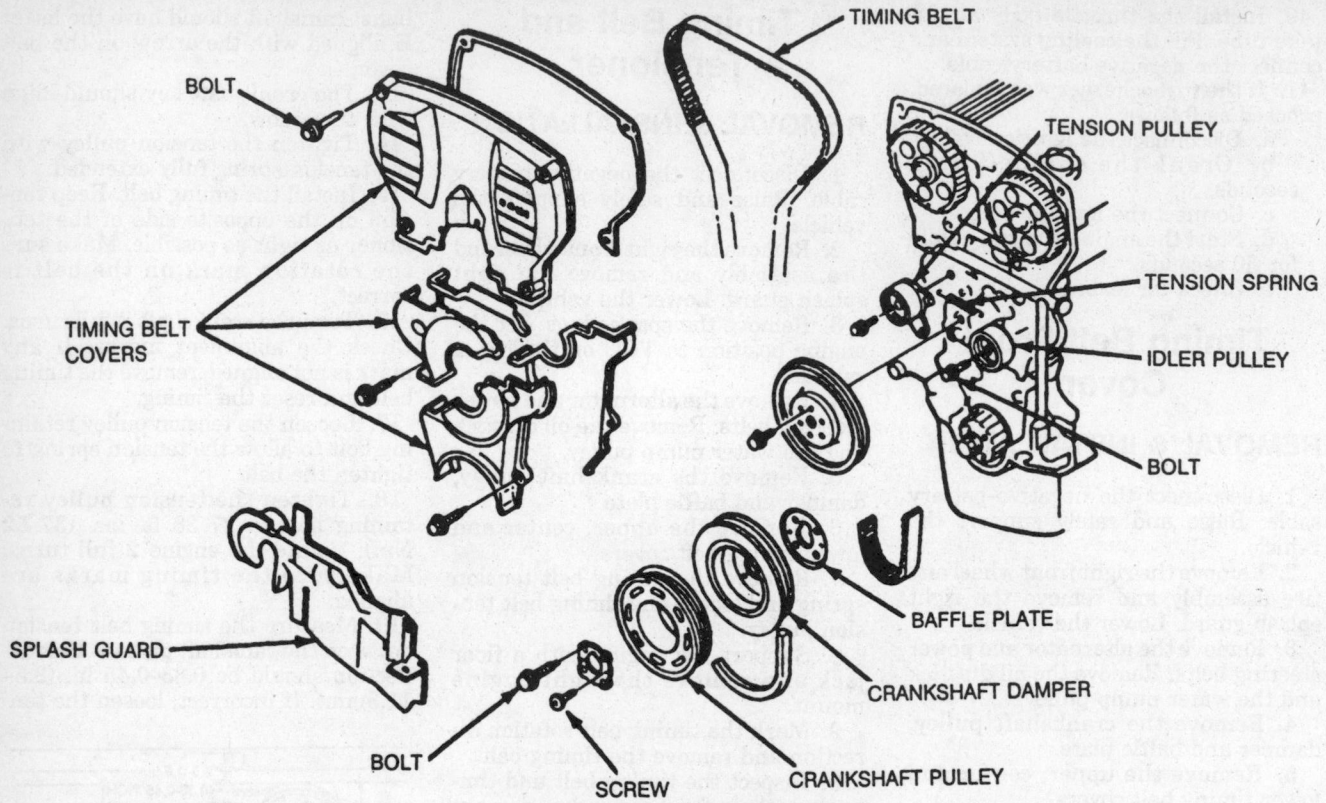

Timing belt and front covers installation

sion pulley and repeat the procedure. If proper tension cannot be achieved, replace the tension spring.

20. Install the lower, center and upper timing belt covers. Tighten the retaining bolts to 71–97 inch lbs. (8–11 Nm).

21. Install the right engine mount and lower the engine. Tighten the retaining nuts to 44–63 ft. lbs. (60–85 Nm).

22. Install the crankshaft pulley, damper and baffle. Tighten the baffle and damper retaining screws to 109–152 inch lbs. (12–17 Nm). Tighten the pulley retaining bolts to 109–152 inch lbs. (12–17 Nm).

23. Install the water pump pulley. Tighten the retaining bolts to 69–95 inch lbs. (8–11 Nm).

24. Install the alternator and power steering belts. Install the dipstick. Raise and safely support the vehicle.

25. Install the splash guard and the right front wheel and tire assembly.

26. Lower the vehicle and install the spark plugs. Start the engine and check for proper operation.

Timing Sprockets

REMOVAL & INSTALLATION

1. Disconnect the negative battery cable.
2. Remove the timing belt.

3. Remove the camshaft sprocket bolts and remove the camshaft sprockets. Hold the camshafts with a wrench to remove the retaining bolts.

4. Remove the crankshaft sprocket bolt and remove the crankshaft sprocket.

To install:

5. Install the crankshaft sprocket. Tighten the retaining bolt to 80–87 ft. lbs. (108–118 Nm).

6. Install the camshaft sprockets. Tighten the retaining bolts to 36–45 ft. lbs. (49–61 Nm).

7. Install the timing belt.

8. Connect the negative battery cable.

Camshaft

REMOVAL & INSTALLATION

1. Disconnect the negative battery cable.

2. Disconnect the air bypass hoses and remove the intake air tube.

3. Disconnect the throttle cable and remove the retaining brackets.

4. Remove the cylinder head cover and remove the timing belt.

5. Remove the camshaft sprockets. Hold the camshafts with a wrench to remove the sprocket retaining bolts.

6. Remove the seal plate. Remove

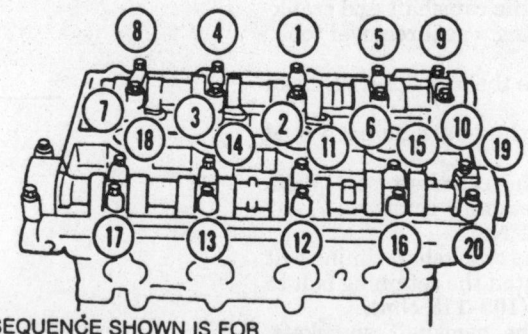

SEQUENCE SHOWN IS FOR INSTALLATION OF BOTH CAMSHAFTS. FOLLOW 1–10 SEQUENCE IF ONLY 1 CAMSHAFT IS BEING INSTALLED

Camshaft bearing cap bolt torque sequence

the camshaft seals using a seal removal tool.

7. If removing the intake camshaft, remove the distributor.

8. Note the numerical and directional markings on the camshaft bearing caps for installation. Remove the bearing cap retaining bolts alternately and gradually so as not to overstress the camshaft.

9. Remove the camshaft.

To install:

10. Lubricate the camshaft bearings and camshaft lobes and journals with clean engine oil.

11. Position the camshafts in the cylinder head. Make sure all the lifters are in place. Install the intake camshaft with the **I** straight up and the exhaust camshaft with the **E** straight up.

12. Install the bearing caps according to the numbers and arrows. The arrows point to the front of the engine. Tighten the retaining bolts, in sequence, to 100–126 inch lbs. (11–14 Nm).

13. Install the distributor, if removed.

14. Install the camshaft seals using a seal installer. Install the seal plate and tighten the retaining screws to 71–97 inch lbs. (8–11 Nm).

15. Install the camshaft sprockets. Tighten the retaining bolts to 36–45 ft. lbs. (49–61 Nm).

16. Install the timing belt. Install the cylinder head cover and tighten the retaining bolts to 71–97 inch lbs. (8–11 Nm).

17. Install the throttle cable and retaining brackets. Install the intake air tube and connect the air bypass hoses.

18. Connect the negative battery cable, start the engine and check for proper operation.

Piston and Connecting Rod

POSITIONING

Piston positioning—notch on piston faces front of engine

ENGINE LUBRICATION

Oil Pan

REMOVAL & INSTALLATION

1. Raise and safely support the vehicle. Position a drain pan under the oil pan and drain the engine oil.

2. Remove the frame brace retaining bolt. Loosen the right A-arm front bolt and pivot brace downward.

3. Disconnect the front exhaust pipe from the exhaust manifold or turbocharger. Remove the front exhaust pipe bracket retaining bolts.

4. Loosen the rubber exhaust hangers at the catalyst. Allow the exhaust to hang supported by mechanic's wire.

5. Disconnect the turbocharger oil return hose, if required.

6. Remove the oil pan retaining bolts. Carefully pry the oil pan loose from the cylinder block.

NOTE: Do not force a prying tool between the cylinder block and oil pan.

7. Remove the front and rear oil pan seals.

To install:

8. Clean the oil pan and the oil pan and cylinder block gasket surfaces.

9. Apply gasket sealant to new front and rear oil pan seals. Install the seals to the cylinder block.

10. Apply gasket sealant to the oil pan gasket surface and install the oil pan. Tighten the retaining bolts to 71–97 inch lbs. (8–11 Nm).

11. Connect the turbocharger oil return hose, if required.

12. Install the rubber exhaust hanger to the brackets.

13. Install a new gasket and connect the front exhaust pipe to the exhaust

manifold or turbocharger. Tighten the retaining nuts to 23–34 ft. lbs. (31–46 Nm) on normally aspirated vehicles or 18–23 ft. lbs. (24–32 Nm) on turbocharged vehicles.

14. Install the front exhaust pipe bracket. Tighten the retaining bolts to 34 ft. lbs. (46 Nm).

15. Pivot the frame brace into position. Tighten the retaining bolt to crossmember to 26–37 ft. lbs. (35–50 Nm). Tighten the right A-arm front retaining bolt to 47–66 ft. lbs. (64–89 Nm) on 1991 vehicles or 72–86 ft. lbs. (97–117 Nm) on 1992–93 vehicles.

16. Lower the vehicle and fill the engine with the proper type and quantity of oil. Start the engine and check for leaks.

Oil Pump

REMOVAL & INSTALLATION

1. Disconnect the negative battery cable.

2. Remove the timing belt and the oil pan.

3. Remove the crankshaft timing belt sprocket.

4. Remove the oil screen/pickup tube assembly.

5. Remove the oil pump retaining bolts and remove the oil pump.

To install:

6. Clean all gasket mating surfaces.

7. Install the oil pump, using a new gasket. Install the retaining bolts and tighten to 14–19 ft. lbs. (19–25 Nm).

8. Install the oil screen/pickup tube assembly with a new gasket. Tighten the retaining bolts to 71–97 inch lbs. (8–11 Nm).

9. Install the crankshaft timing belt sprocket. Tighten the retaining bolt to 80–87 ft. lbs. (108–118 Nm).

10. Install the oil pan and the timing belt.

11. Connect the negative battery cable.

CHECKING

1. Remove the oil pump.

2. Remove the oil pump cover and the outer and inner rotors.

3. Remove the cotter pin and remove the pressure piston, cap and spring.

4. Remove the oil seal, if necessary.

5. Thoroughly clean all parts.

6. Inspect the pressure spring for weakness or breakage. Check the free length. The spring should measure 1.791 in. (45.5mm). Replace the spring, if required.

7. Measure the inner to outer rotor clearance. If the measurement exceeds 0.0079 in. (0.20mm), replace the rotors or the oil pump.

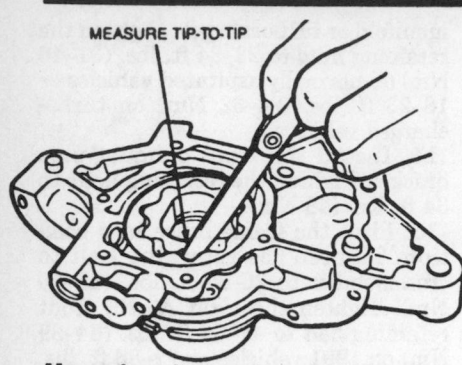

Measuring oil pump inner to outer rotor clearance

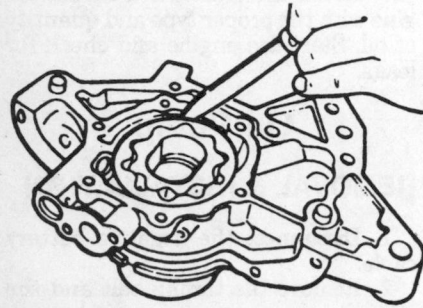

Measuring oil pump outer rotor to pump body clearance

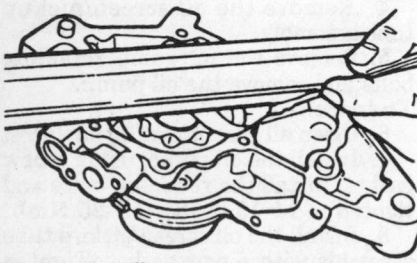

Measuring oil pump rotor to pump cover clearance

8. Measure the outer rotor to pump body clearance. If the measurement exceeds 0.0087 in. (0.22mm), replace the rotors or the oil pump.

9. Measure the rotor to pump cover clearance using a straight-edge. If the measurement exceeds 0.0055 in. (0.14mm), replace the rotors or the oil pump.

10. Install the oil seal, if removed. Press in until flush with the pump body.

11. Install the pressure piston, cap and spring with a new cotter pin. Install the inner and outer rotors.

12. Install the oil pump cover. Tighten the screws to 14–19 ft. lbs. (19–25 Nm).

Rear Main Bearing Oil Seal

REMOVAL & INSTALLATION

1. Remove the transaxle.

2. Remove the pressure plate and disc, if required.

3. Remove the flywheel.

4. Remove the seal using a seal removal tool.

To install:

5. Lubricate the seal lip with clean engine oil.

6. Install the seal using a seal installer.

7. Install the flywheel. Apply thread sealer to the flywheel retaining bolts and tighten to 71–76 ft. lbs. (96–103 Nm).

8. Install the clutch assembly, if required.

9. Install the transaxle.

ENGINE COOLING

Radiator

REMOVAL & INSTALLATION

— CAUTION —

Never remove the radiator cap while the engine is running or personal injury from scalding hot coolant or steam may result. If possible, wait until the engine has cooled to remove the radiator cap. If this is not possible, wrap a thick cloth around the radiator cap and turn it slowly to the first stop. Step back while the pressure is released from the cooling system. When it is certain all the pressure has been released, press down on the cap, still with the cloth, and turn and remove it.

1. Disconnect the negative battery cable. Disconnect the cooling fan wiring harness connector.

2. Remove the radiator pressure cap. If the cooling system is hot and pressurized, be sure to wrap a cloth around the cap and slowly turn it to the first stop, to release the pressure.

3. Place a drain pan under the radiator and open the drain valve at the bottom left of the radiator. Drain the cooling system.

4. Disconnect the radiator hoses from the radiator. Disconnect the overflow tube from the filler neck.

5. Disengage the wiring harness from the routing clips attached to the cooling fan shroud.

6. If equipped with an automatic transaxle, disconnect and plug the cooler lines.

7. Remove the 6 bolts retaining the radiator upper tank brackets to the radiator core support. Remove the radiator and cooling fan assembly.

8. Remove the 4 fan shroud retaining bolts and remove the fan and shroud assembly.

To install:

9. Place the fan and shroud assembly against the rear of the radiator and secure with the 4 bolts. Tighten to 23–33 ft. lbs. (31–46 Nm).

10. Make sure the radiator insulators are positioned on the radiator supports. Position the radiator, making sure the lower tank engages the insulators.

11. Install the 6 radiator retaining bolts through the top tank mounting brackets into the core support. Make sure the insulators are aligned and tighten the bolts securely.

12. If equipped, unplug and connect the automatic transaxle oil cooler lines.

13. Secure the wiring harness in the routing clips.

14. Connect the radiator hoses to the radiator. Connect the overflow tube to the filler neck.

15. Close the drain valve and fill the cooling system. Install the pressure cap.

16. Connect the cooling fan harness connector and the negative battery cable.

17. Start the engine and bring to normal operating termperature. Check for leaks. Check the coolant level.

Electric Cooling Fan

TESTING

1. Locate the cooling fan motor connector.

2. Ground the Y/GN wire at the connector.

3. If the cooling fan motor does not run, it must be replaced.

REMOVAL & INSTALLATION

1. Disconnect the negative battery cable.

2. Disengage the fan wiring harness from the routing clamps. Separate the cooling fan wiring connector.

3. Remove the 4 screws retaining the fan shroud to the radiator and remove the fan and shroud.

4. Remove the retaining nut and washer and remove the fan from the motor shaft.

5. Remove the 3 retaining screws and washers and separate the fan motor from the shroud.

To install:

6. Position the cooling fan on the shroud and install the 3 retaining screws and washers. Tighten to 3–4 ft. lbs. (4–6 Nm).

7. Install the fan on the motor shaft and install the retaining washer and nut.

8. Position the fan and shroud and install the 4 retaining screws. Tighten to 23–34 ft. lbs. (31–46 Nm).

9. Connect the cooling fan wiring and secure in place using the routing clamps. Connect the negative battery cable.

Heater Core

REMOVAL & INSTALLATION

1. Disconnect the negative battery cable and drain the cooling system.
2. Remove the floor console as follows:

a. Slide the front seats completely forward and remove the screws retaining the rear of the console.

b. Slide the front seat completely rearward and remove the screws retaining the rear console to the front console.

c. Raise the parking lever as far as it will go, raise the rear of the console and pull backwards to remove.

d. Disconnect the wiring harness from the mirror switch and headlight motor switch.

e. If equipped with an automatic transaxle, loosen the jam nut and unscrew the shift handle.

f. Raise the ash tray, disconnect the wiring beneath it and remove the center carpet panels. Remove the brackets, if necessary.

g. If equipped with a manual transaxle, remove the screws retaining the manual shift lever boot to the bottom of the front console. Remove the screws and front console leaving the shift knob and boot on the shift lever. Unscrew the shift knob with the boot and remove from the shift lever, if necessary.

h. If equipped with an automatic transaxle, remove the screws and the shift quadrant. Disconnect the shift quadrant light connector.

3. Remove the instrument panel as follows:

a. Remove the left and right lower cowl trim panels.

b. Remove the storage compartment, heater/radio bezel, trim covers and instrument cluster bezel.

c. Remove the instrument cluster and the steering column.

d. Loosen the nut retaining the hood release cable to the lower instrument panel and position the cable aside.

e. Remove the radio and the heater control panel.

f. Tag and remove all wiring harness retainers and connectors from the instrument panel.

g. Remove the 3 screws, lockwashers and plain washers located near the base of the windshield. Remove the 2 bolts and washers from each side of the instrument panel. An access panel is provided for the upper bolts.

h. Remove the 2 screws and lockwashers retaining the instrument panel to the center floor bracket. Remove the 2 screws retaining the instrument panel to the steering column support.

i. With the help of an assistant, gently slide the instrument panel outward. Disconnect the ducts and wiring during removal.

4. Disconnect and plug the heater hoses at the extension tubes.
5. Remove the plastic rivets and both defroster hoses. Remove the main air duct connecting the heater case to the blower case or air conditioning unit, if equipped.
6. Roll back the carpet to gain access to the lower duct and lower mounting bolts. It may be necessary to remove the carpet fasteners.
7. Disconnect the lower duct for the rear seat supply from the heater case.
8. Remove the cable ends from the heater case, if still connected and remove the wiring harness.
9. Remove the 2 lower bolts, 2 upper nuts and 1 center retaining nut from the blower case and remove the heater case.
10. Remove the 3 screws attaching the heater core cover to the heater case and remove the cover. Remove the screws securing the tube braces.
11. Loosen the clamps and remove the extension tubes from the heater core. Remove the O-ring from the outlet tube.
12. Remove the heater core by pulling it straight out. Remove the extension tubes and grommets, if necessary.

To install:
13. Install the grommets and extension tubes, if removed. Make sure the grommets are flush with the engine compartment wall.
14. Install the heater core into the heater case and install a new O-ring onto the outlet extension tube. Connect the extension tubes to the heater core and tighten the clamps.
15. Secure the extension tube braces with the screws and install the heater core cover with the 3 screws.
16. Position the heater case onto the mounting studs and guide the extension tubes through the dash panel. Make sure the grommets are sealed around the extension tubes.
17. Install 2 upper nuts, 1 center retaining nut and 2 lower bolts. Tighten all fasteners to 5–7 ft. lbs. (7–10 Nm).
18. Install the lower duct onto the heater case. Reposition the carpet and install the fasteners, if removed.
19. Attach the wiring harness and connect the defroster hoses and main air duct to the heater case. Install the plastic retaining rivets.
20. Connect the heater hoses and tighten the clamps to 36–53 inch lbs. (4–6 Nm).
21. Install the instrument panel by reversing the removal procedure. Connect the control cable to the heater case.
22. Install the floor console by reversing the removal procedure.
23. Fill the cooling system and connect the negative battery cable. Operate the heater and check for leaks.

Water Pump

REMOVAL & INSTALLATION

1. Disconnect the negative battery cable and drain the cooling system.
2. Remove the timing belt, timing belt tensioner and idler pulleys.
3. Remove the engine oil dipstick bracket retaining bolt.
4. Remove the power steering pump from the retaining bracket, leaving the hoses connected. Remove the power steering pump bracket and position the pump aside.
5. Remove the water pump outlet. Remove the water pump retaining bolts and the water pump.

NOTE: Raise the engine slightly with a floor jack, if required, to gain clearance for removal.

To install:
6. Clean all gasket mating surfaces. Transfer the rubber belt cover seal to the new water pump, if required.
7. Position the water pump with a new gasket. Install the retaining bolts and tighten to 14–19 ft. lbs. (19–25 Nm).
8. Install the pump outlet with a new gasket and O-ring. Tighten the retaining bolts to 14–19 ft. lbs. (19–25 Nm).
9. Install the oil dipstick retaining bolt.
10. Install the timing belt tensioner

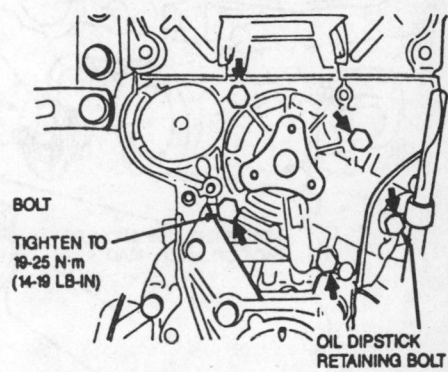

BOLT

TIGHTEN TO 19-25 N·m (14-19 LB-IN)

OIL DIPSTICK RETAINING BOLT

Water pump retaining bolt locations

and idler pulleys. Tighten the idler bolt only to 27–38 ft. lbs. (37–52 Nm).

11. Install the power steering pump bracket. Tighten the nut and bolts to 35–48 ft. lbs. (47–66 Nm).

12. Install the power steering pump and the timing belt.

13. Fill the cooling system. Start the engine and check for leaks.

Thermostat

REMOVAL & INSTALLATION

1. Disconnect the negative battery cable. Disconnect the wire from the engine cooling fan switch on the thermostat housing.

2. Remove the radiator pressure cap. If the cooling system is hot and pressurized, be sure to wrap a cloth around the cap and slowly turn it to the first stop, to release the pressure.

3. Partially drain the cooling system. Disconnect the upper radiator hose from the thermostat housing.

4. Remove the bolts retaining the thermostat housing to the cylinder head and remove the housing. Remove the thermostat and gasket.

To install:

5. Clean all gasket mating surfaces.

6. Install the thermostat in the head, valve end first, with the jiggle valve at the top.

7. Coat a new housing gasket with water resistant sealer and position it on the cylinder head with the bolt holes correctly aligned.

NOTE: The painted side of the gasket must face the thermostat.

8. Carefully position the thermostat housing to align the bolt holes without shifting the gasket and install

the 2 retaining bolts. Tighten to 14–19 ft. lbs. (19–25 Nm).

9. Connect the upper radiator hose to the thermostat housing and install the hose clamp.

10. Fill the cooling system and install the pressure cap.

11. Connect the wire from the engine cooling fan to the switch on the thermostat housing. Connect the negative battery cable.

12. Start the engine and bring to normal operating temperature. Check for leaks.

Cooling System Bleeding

When the entire cooling system is drained, the following procedure should be used to ensure a complete fill.

1. Install the block drain plug, if removed and close the draincock. With the engine off, add anti-freeze to the radiator to a level of 50 percent of the total cooling system capacity. Then add water until it reaches the radiator filler neck seat.

2. Install the radiator cap to the first notch to keep spillage to a minimum.

3. Start the engine and let it idle until the upper radiator hose is warm. This indicates that the thermostat is open and coolant is flowing through the entire system.

4. Carefully remove the radiator cap and top off the radiator with water. Install the cap on the radiator securely.

5. Fill the coolant recovery reservoir with a water/anti-freeze mixture to the FULL mark.

6. Check for leaks at the draincock and block plug, if removed.

ENGINE ELECTRICAL

NOTE: Disconnecting the negative battery cable on some vehicles may interfere with the functions of the on board computer systems and may require the computer to undergo a relearning process, once the negative battery cable is reconnected.

Distributor

REMOVAL

1. Disconnect the negative battery cable.

2. Disconnect the vacuum hose from the vacuum control unit and disconnect the electrical connectors.

3. Disconnect the coil wire from the distributor cap, remove the 2 retaining screws from the distributor cap and position aside.

4. Mark the position of the distributor housing on the cylinder head and note the position of the rotor.

5. Remove the distributor holddown bolts and remove the distributor. Inspect the O-ring and replace if damaged or worn.

INSTALLATION

NOTE: The drive tang of the distributor is off-set so as to allow only 1 installation position.

Timing Not Disturbed

1. Set the rotor to the position noted during removal. Lubricate the O-ring seal with engine oil.

2. Install the distributor on the rear of the cylinder head and align the marks made during removal.

3. Install the 2 distributor holddown bolts. Install the distributor cap and tighten the 2 retaining screws.

4. Connect the coil wire to the distributor cap, the electrical connectors and the vacuum hoses to the vacuum control unit.

5. Connect the negative battery cable and start the engine. Check the ignition timing and adjust, as necessary.

Timing Disturbed

1. Disconnect the ignition wire from the No. 1 cylinder spark plug and remove the spark plug.

2. Place a finger over the spark plug hole and turn the crankshaft, in the direction of normal rotation, until compression is felt. Continue turning the crankshaft until the TDC mark on the

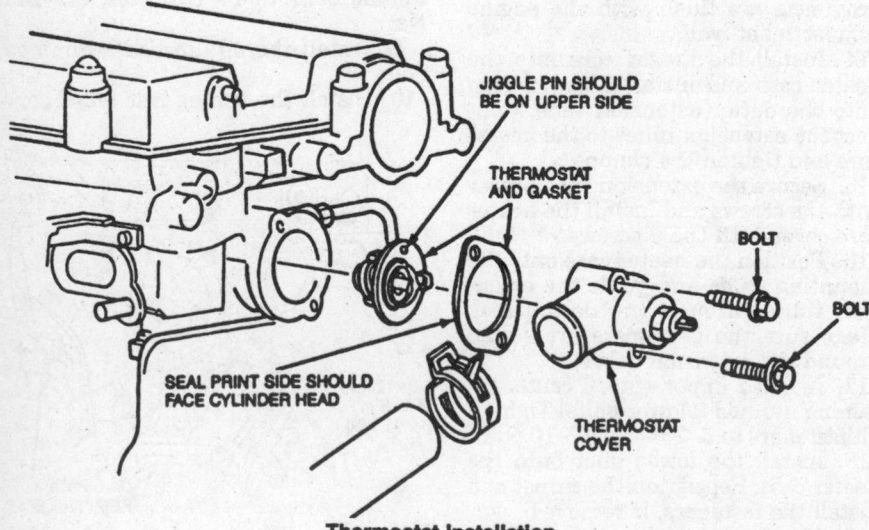

JIGGLE PIN SHOULD BE ON UPPER SIDE

THERMOSTAT AND GASKET

BOLT

BOLT

SEAL PRINT SIDE SHOULD FACE CYLINDER HEAD

THERMOSTAT COVER

Thermostat Installation

timing belt front cover is aligned with the mark on the crankshaft damper.

3. Set the rotor to point in the direction of the No. 1 ignition wire tower on the distributor cap. Lubricate the O-ring seal with engine oil.

4. Install the distributor on the rear of the cylinder head and install the 2 distributor hold-down bolts. Tighten the bolts snug only, to allow distributor movement for timing purposes.

5. Install the distributor cap and tighten the 2 retaining screws. Connect the coil wire.

6. Connect the electrical connectors and the vacuum hoses. Install the No. 1 cylinder spark plug and connect the ignition wire.

7. Connect the negative battery cable. Start the engine and check or adjust the ignition timing.

8. Tighten the distributor hold-down bolts after timing has been set.

Ignition Timing

ADJUSTMENT

1. Connect a tachometer and timing light according to the manufacturers instructions.

2. Disconnect and plug the vacuum hoses from the vacuum diaphragm. Ground the Self Test Input (STI) connector located in the right rear of the engine compartment.

3. Start the engine and bring to normal operating temperature. Turn all electrical loads **OFF**.

4. Check the idle speed. It should be 850 ± 50 rpm; adjust as necessary.

5. Aim the timing light at the timing marks located on the front timing belt cover and crankshaft damper. The timing should be 2 ± 1 degrees BTDC on normally aspirated engines or 12 ± 1 degrees BTDC on turbocharged engines.

6. If adjustment, is necessary, loosen the distributor hold-down bolts and turn the distributor until the timing marks are aligned.

7. Tighten the distributor hold-down bolts and recheck the timing.

8. Turn the engine **OFF**, remove the jumper wire from the STI connec-

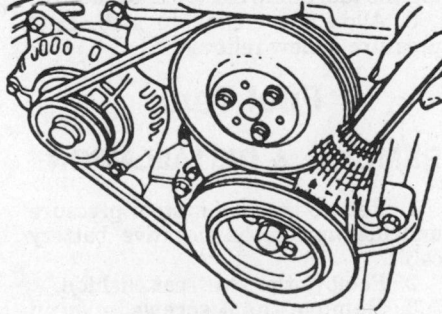

Timing mark location

tor and unplug and reconnect the distributor vacuum hoses. Remove all test equipment.

Alternator

PRECAUTIONS

Several precautions must be observed with alternator equipped vehicles to avoid damage to the unit.

- If the battery is removed for any reason, make sure it is reconnected with the correct polarity. Reversing the battery connections may result in damage to the one-way rectifiers.
- When utilizing a booster battery as a starting aid, always connect the positive to positive terminals and the negative terminal from the booster battery to a good engine ground on the vehicle being started.
- **Never use a fast charger as a booster to start vehicles.**
- **Disconnect the battery cables when charging the battery with a fast charger.**
- **Never attempt to polarize the alternator.**
- **Do not use test lights of more than 12 volts when checking diode continuity.**
- **Do not short across or ground any of the alternator terminals.**
- **The polarity of the battery, alternator and regulator must be matched and considered before making any electrical connections within the system.**
- **Never separate the alternator on an open circuit. Make sure all connections within the circuit are clean and tight.**
- **Disconnect the battery ground terminal when performing any service on electrical components.**
- **Disconnect the battery if arc welding is to be done on the vehicle.**

BELT TENSION ADJUSTMENT

1. Inspect the condition of the alternator drive belt and replace, if necessary.

2. Loosen the adjusting bar bolt and mounting bolt at the alternator.

3. Adjust the belt tension, using the deflection method or using a belt tension gauge. Check the deflection or position the gauge at the center of the longest accessible belt span.

4. Pry on the alternator with a prybar to adjust the belt tension.

NOTE: Do not pry against the stator frame. Position the prybar against a stronger point, such as the area around a case bolt.

5. A new belt, with no running time

should have 0.31–0.35 in. (8–9mm) deflection with approximately 22 lbs. pressure applied or 110–132 lbs. tension, using a gauge.

6. A used belt, with more than 10 minutes running time, should have 0.35–0.39 in. (9–10mm) deflection with approximately 22 lbs. pressure applied or 110–132 lbs. tension, using a gauge.

7. Tighten the adjusting bar bolt to 14–19 ft. lbs. (19–26 Nm) and the mounting bolt to 29–38 ft. lbs. (37–52 Nm).

REMOVAL & INSTALLATION

1991

1. Disconnect the negative battery cable.

2. Remove the alternator drive belt and the upper adjusting bolt.

3. Remove the connector from the B+ terminal by removing the retaining nut.

4. Raise and safely support the vehicle. Disconnect the voltage regulator connector.

5. On normally aspirated vehicles, proceed as follows:

 a. Remove the right wheel and tire assembly.

 b. Remove the right ball joint clamp bolt.

 c. Separate the knuckle from the ball joint.

 d. Pull the halfshaft out of the transaxle and position above the oil seal. Be careful not to damage the seal.

6. Remove the retaining nuts and separate the catalytic converter from the front exhaust pipe. Disconnect the 2 rubber exhaust hangers and lower the exhaust assembly. Support the exhaust assembly with wire out of the way.

7. Remove the alternator through bolt. Carefully move the alternator to the left side of the vehicle and remove it between the transaxle and catalytic converter.

To install:

8. Install the alternator and the through bolt. Connect the voltage regulator connector.

9. Connect the catalytic converter to the front exhaust pipe and tighten the nuts. Connect the rubber exhaust hangers.

10. On normally aspirated vehicle, proceed as follows:

 a. Install a new circlip on the halfshaft.

 b. Position the halfshaft into the transaxle and align the splines.

 c. Push forward on the knuckle assembly until the halfshaft is fully seated in the transaxle.

 d. Position the ball joint into the

knuckle assembly. Install the ball joint clamp bolt and tighten to 32–40 ft. lbs. (43–54 Nm).

e. Install the right wheel and tire assembly.

11. Lower the vehicle. Connect the **B+** terminal and install the retaining nut.

12. Install the upper adjusting bolt and the alternator drive belt. Adjust the belt tension.

13. Connect the negative battery cable.

1992–93

1. Disconnect the negative battery cable.

2. Remove the nut and eyelet connector from the **B** terminal.

3. Disconnect the electrical connector.

4. Remove the adjustment bolt from the top of the alternator.

5. Remove the pivot bolt from the bottom of the alternator and remove the alternator.

6. Installation is the reverse of the removal procedure. Adjust the belt tension.

Starter

REMOVAL & INSTALLATION

1. Disconnect the negative battery cable.

2. Disconnect the starter wires and remove the starter upper retaining bolts.

3. Remove the intake manifold support bracket upper retaining bolts. Raise and safely support the vehicle.

4. Remove the starter support bracket to intake manifold support bracket retaining bolt.

5. Remove the intake manifold support bracket lower retaining bolts and remove the starter lower retaining bolt.

NOTE: Loosen the rubber exhaust hangers, if required.

6. Remove the starter. Remove the support bracket from the starter, if required.

To install:

7. Install the support bracket to the starter, if removed. Tighten the retaining nuts to 54–70 inch lbs. (6–8 Nm).

8. Position the starter and loosely install the lower retaining bolt.

9. Position the intake manifold support bracket and loosely install the lower retaining bolts.

10. Install the starter support bracket to manifold support bracket retaining bolt. Tighten to 14–19 ft. lbs. (19–25 Nm).

11. Tighten the lower starter bolt to 23–30 ft. lbs. (31–41 Nm). Lower the vehicle.

12. Install the starter upper retaining bolts and tighten to 23–30 ft. lbs. (31–41 Nm). Make sure the starter wire support bracket is secured with the rear upper starter bolt.

13. Install the intake manifold support bracket upper retaining bolts and tighten the upper and lower bolts to 23–34 ft. lbs. (31–46 Nm).

14. Connect the starter wires. Tighten the **B** terminal retaining nut to 71–106 inch lbs. (8–12 Nm). Connect the negative battery cable.

EMISSION CONTROLS

Due to the complex nature of modern electronic engine control systems, comprehensive diagnosis and testing procedures fall outside the confines of this repair manual. For complete information on diagnosis, testing and repair procedures concerning all modern engine and emission control systems, please refer to "Chilton's Guide to Fuel Injection and Electronic Engine Controls".

Emission Warning Lamps

RESETTING

The vehicle is equipped with a "CHECK ENGINE" warning light located on the instrument cluster. The light should come ON briefly when the ignition key is turned **ON** but should turn OFF when the engine starts. If the light does not come ON when the ignition key is turned **ON** or if it comes ON and stays ON when the engine is running, there is a malfunction in the electronic engine control system. After the malfunction has been remedied, using the proper procedures, the "CHECK ENGINE" light will go out.

FUEL SYSTEM

Fuel System Service Precaution

Safety is the most important factor when performing not only fuel system maintenance but any type of maintenance. Failure to conduct maintenance and repairs in a safe manner may result in serious personal injury or death. Maintenance and testing of the vehicle's fuel system components can be accomplished safely and effectively by adhering to the following rules and guidelines.

● To avoid the possibility of fire and personal injury, always disconnect the negative battery cable unless the repair or test procedure requires that battery voltage be applied.

● Always relieve the fuel system pressure prior to disconnecting any fuel system component (injector, fuel rail, pressure regulator, etc.), fitting or fuel line connection. Exercise extreme caution whenever relieving fuel system pressure to avoid exposing skin, face and eyes to fuel spray. Please be advised that fuel under pressure may penetrate the skin or any part of the body that it contacts.

● Always place a shop towel or cloth around the fitting or connection prior to loosening to absorb any excess fuel due to spillage. Ensure that all fuel spillage (should it occur) is quickly removed from engine surfaces. Ensure that all fuel soaked cloths or towels are deposited into a suitable waste container.

● Always keep a dry chemical (Class B) fire extinguisher near the work area.

● Do not allow fuel spray or fuel vapors to come into contact with a spark or open flame.

● Always use a backup wrench when loosening and tightening fuel line connection fittings. This will prevent unnecessary stress and torsion to fuel line piping. Always follow the proper torque specifications.

● Always replace worn fuel fitting O-rings with new. Do not substitute fuel hose where fuel pipe is installed.

RELIEVING FUEL SYSTEM PRESSURE

1. Remove the rear seat cushion.
2. Run the engine while disconnecting the fuel pump electrical connector.
3. Allow the engine to stall. Fuel pressure is now relieved.

Fuel Tank

REMOVAL & INSTALLATION

1. Relieve the fuel system pressure and disconnect the negative battery cable.
2. Remove the rear seat cushion.
3. Remove the 4 screws, ground wires and fuel pump access cover. Pull

the fuel pump wiring harness through the access cover.

4. Loosen and pull back the hose clamps. Remove and plug the supply and return hoses.

5. Raise and safely support the vehicle.

6. Position a suitable container under the fuel tank. Remove the fuel tank drain plug and carefully drain the fuel into the container.

7. Remove the 2 hose clamps and hoses at the filler neck.

8. Support the fuel tank and remove the 4 retaining bolts. Lower the fuel tank enough to gain access to the vapor line.

9. Remove the clamp and the vapor line. Remove the fuel tank.

To install:

10. Position the fuel tank and install the vapor line with the clamp.

11. Install the fuel tank with the 4 retaining bolts.

12. Install the filler neck hoses and tighten the clamps. Install the fuel tank drain plug.

13. Lower the vehicle and connect the supply and return hoses with the clamps.

14. Pull the wiring harness through the access cover. Install the access cov-

er with the 4 screws. Make sure the ground wires are secured.

15. Connect the fuel pump connectors and install the rear seat cushion.

16. Add fuel to the tank. Connect the negative battery cable, start the engine and check for leaks.

Fuel Filter

REMOVAL & INSTALLATION

1. Relieve the fuel system pressure and disconnect the negative battery cable.

2. Remove the clamp and supply line from the bottom of the filter. Plug the supply line.

3. Remove the clamp and outlet line from the top of the filter. Remove the fuel filter from the bracket.

4. Installation is the reverse of the removal procedure. Start the engine and check for leaks.

Electric Fuel Pump

PRESSURE TESTING

1. Relieve the fuel system pressure.

2. Install a fuel pressure tester in the fuel line between the fuel filter and the fuel rail.

3. Connect a jumper wire between the **GN/W** terminal and the **BK** of the black 2-pin fuel pump test connector.

4. Turn the ignition key to **RUN**, to operate the fuel pump.

5. The fuel pressure should be 64–85 psi.

REMOVAL & INSTALLATION

1. Relieve the fuel system pressure and disconnect the negative battery cable.

2. Disconnect the fuel pump ground wire from the access cover and remove the cover.

3. Remove and plug the supply and return lines. Remove the fuel pump/sending unit retaining bolts.

4. Remove the fuel pump/sending unit and gasket from the fuel tank. Cover the opening of the tank to prevent dirt from entering.

5. Remove the 2 fuel pump wires from the sending unit. Remove the retaining clamp screw and remove the clamp.

6. Remove the rubber retaining

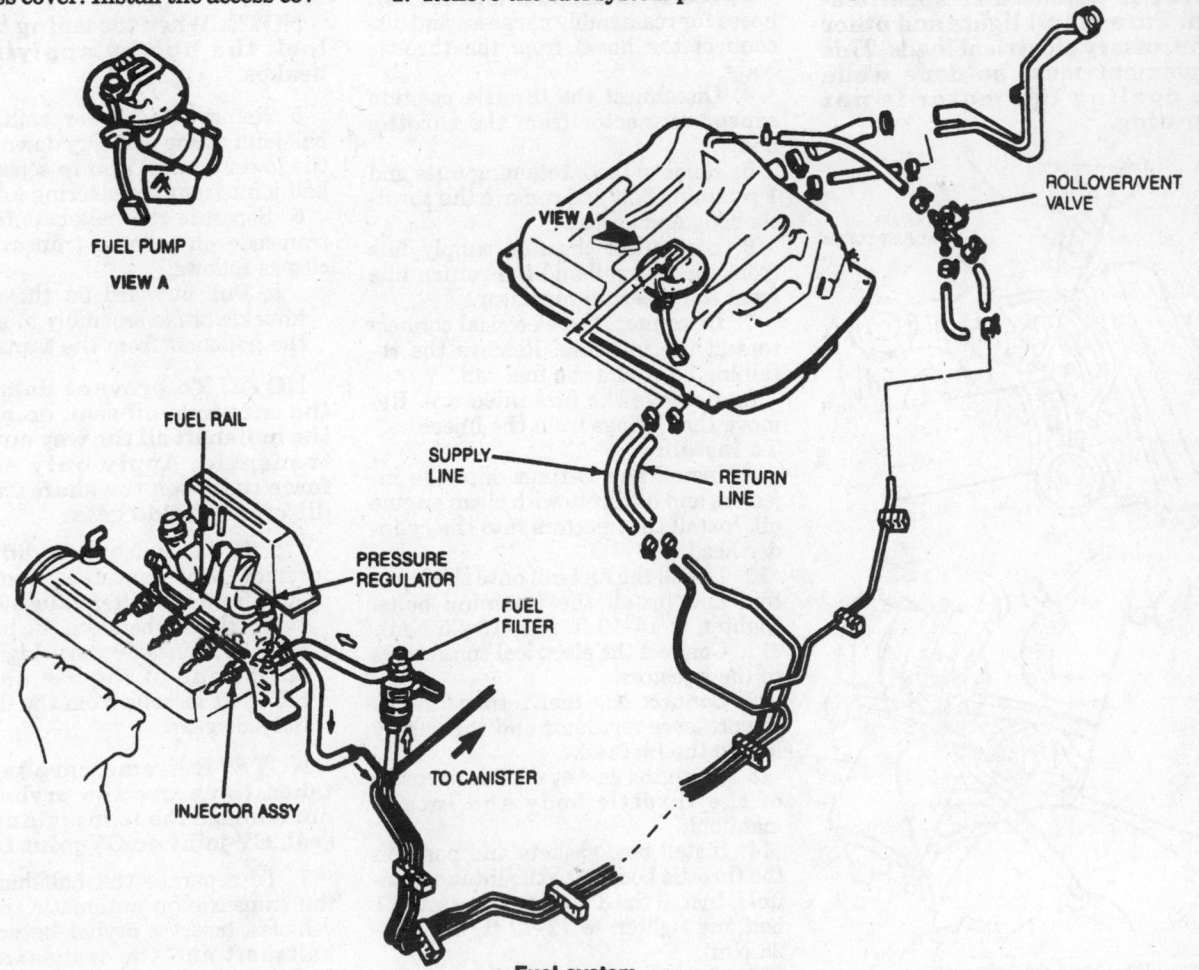

FUEL PUMP

VIEW A

FUEL RAIL

PRESSURE REGULATOR

FUEL FILTER

TO CANISTER

INJECTOR ASSY

VIEW A

SUPPLY LINE

RETURN LINE

ROLLOVER/VENT VALVE

Fuel system

band and remove the fuel pump from the sending unit.

To install:

7. Install the fuel pump to the sending unit bracket and secure with the retaining clamp.

8. Install the rubber retaining band and connect the fuel pump wires to the sending unit.

9. Position a new gasket onto the fuel tank and install the fuel pump/sending unit with the retaining bolts.

10. Unplug and connect the supply and return lines and secure with the clamps.

11. Install the access cover and connect the fuel pump connector and ground wire.

12. Connect the negative battery cable, start the engine and check for leaks. Check the operation of the fuel gauge.

13. Install the rear seat cushion.

Fuel Injection

IDLE SPEED ADJUSTMENT

NOTE: Before adjusting the idle speed, make sure the ignition timing is adjusted to specification. Turn off all lights and other unnecessary electrical loads. This adjustment must be done while the cooling fan motor is not operating.

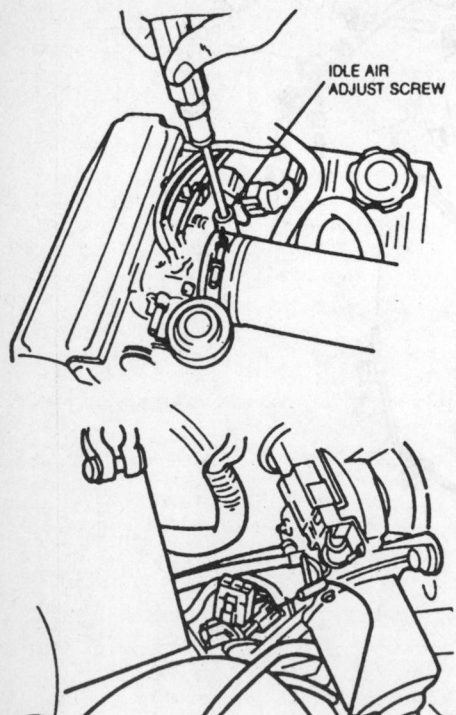

IDLE AIR ADJUST SCREW

Idle speed adjustment

1. Warm the engine to normal operating temperature.

2. Attach a suitable tachometer to the test connector (white: pin 1).

3. Check the idle speed on the tachometer. Connect a jumper wire between the test connector (green: pin 1) and ground and turn the air adjustment screw to obtain the correect idle speed of 800–900 rpm.

4. Remove the jumper wire and the tachometer.

IDLE MIXTURE ADJUSTMENT

The idle mixture screw is preset and sealed at the factory. The idle mixture cannot be adjusted.

Fuel Injector

REMOVAL & INSTALLATION

1. Relieve the fuel system pressure and disconnect the negative battery cable. Partially drain the cooling system.

2. Remove the air duct and the accelerator cable from the throttle body.

3. Mark all vacuum and coolant hoses for reassembly purposes and disconnect the hoses from the throttle body.

4. Disconnect the throttle position sensor connector from the throttle body.

5. Remove the 3 retaining nuts and 1 retaining bolt and remove the throttle body and gaskets.

6. Disconnect the fuel supply line from the fuel rail and the return line from the pressure regulator.

7. Disconnect the electrical connectors at the injectors. Remove the retaining bolts and the fuel rail.

8. Remove the fuel injectors. Remove the O-rings from the injectors.

To install:

9. Install new O-rings onto the injectors and lubricate with clean engine oil. Install the injectors into the cylinder head.

10. Install the fuel rail onto the injectors and install the retaining bolts. Tighten to 14–19 ft. lbs. (19–25 Nm).

11. Connect the electrical connectors to the injectors.

12. Connect the fuel return line to the pressure regulator and the supply line to the fuel rail.

13. Clean the gasket mating surfaces of the throttle body and intake manifold.

14. Install new gaskets and position the throttle body onto the intake manifold. Install the 3 retaining nuts and 1 bolt and tighten to 12–17 ft. lbs. (16–23 Nm).

15. Connect the throttle position sensor connector. Connect all vacuum and coolant hoses to the throttle body at the locations noted during removal.

16. Install the accelerator cable and the air duct. Fill the cooling system.

17. Connect the negative battery cable, start the engine and check for leaks.

DRIVE AXLE

Halfshaft

REMOVAL & INSTALLATION

1. Raise and safely support the vehicle. Remove the wheel and tire assemblies.

2. Remove the necessary engine compartment underbody covers.

3. Remove the stabilizer bar to control arm attaching nuts, bolt, washers and bushings.

4. Carefully raise the staked portion of the halfshaft attaching nut using a small cape chisel. Loosen, but do not remove, the halfshaft attaching nut.

NOTE: When loosening the nut, lock the hub by applying the brakes.

5. Remove the lower control arm ball joint clamp bolt. Pry downward on the lower control arm to separate the ball joint from the steering knuckle.

6. Separate the halfshaft from the transaxle on manual transaxle vehicles as follows:

a. Pull outward on the steering knuckle/brake assembly to separate the halfshaft from the transaxle.

NOTE: To prevent damage to the transaxle oil seal, do not pull the halfshaft all the way out of the transaxle. Apply only enough force to loosen the shaft from the differential side gear.

b. If the halfshaft is difficult to remove, a prybar can be used to loosen it from the differential side gear. Insert the bar between the halfshaft and the transaxle case. Lightly tap on the end of the bar until the halfshaft loosens from the differential side gear.

NOTE: Extreme care must be taken to ensure the prybar does not damage the transaxle case, oil seal, CV-joint or CV-joint boot.

7. To separate the halfshaft from the transaxle on automatic transaxle vehicles, insert a prybar between the halfshaft and the transaxle case. Lightly tap on the end of the bar until

the halfshaft loosens from the differential side gear.

NOTE: Extreme care must be taken to ensure the prybar does not damage the transaxle case, oil seal, CV-joint or CV-joint boot.

8. Remove the halfshaft attaching nut and washer and discard the nut. Pull the halfshaft out of the wheel hub.

NOTE: If the wheel hub binds on the halfshaft splines, it can be loosened using a jaw type puller. Never use a hammer to separate the halfshaft from the wheel hub—damage to the CV-joint internal components will result.

9. Support the halfshaft and slide it out of the transaxle. Use care to prevent damage to the transaxle oil seal.
10. Install differential plugs T87C–7025–C or equivalent, to prevent oil leakage.

To install:
11. Install a new circlip on the inboard CV-joint stub shaft. To install the circlip, start 1 end in the groove and work the circlip over the stub shaft end and into the groove. This will avoid over-expanding the circlip.

NOTE: The original circlip must not be used.

12. Make sure the dynamic damper, if equipped, is positioned properly.
13. Inspect the transaxle oil seal. If it shows any signs of wear or damage that may cause a leak, replace the seal.
14. Remove the differential plugs. Make sure the circlip gap is positioned at the top of the halfshaft splines and lightly lubricate the splines with grease.
15. Carefully align the CV-joint splines with the differential side gear splines and push the halfshaft into the differential.

NOTE: When it seats properly, the circlip can be felt as it snaps into the differential side gear groove.

16. Position the halfshaft through the wheel hub and install a new attaching nut. Do not tighten the nut at this time.
17. Install the lower control arm ball joint through the steering knuckle. Install the pinch bolt and attaching nut and tighten the nut to 32–40 ft. lbs. (43–54 Nm).
18. Position the stabilizer bar and install the attaching bolt, nuts, washers and bushings. Tighten the nut until 7/16 in. (10.8mm) of the bolt threads extend beyond the nut.
19. Install the removed underbody covers.

20. Install a new halfshaft attaching nut and tighten to 116–174 ft. lbs. (157–235 Nm). Stake the nut using a cold chisel with the cutting edge rounded.

NOTE: If the nut splits or cracks after staking, it must be replaced with a new nut.

21. Install the wheel and tire assemblies and lower the vehicle.

CV-Boot

REMOVAL & INSTALLATION

NOTE: Three types of CV-joints are used. Manual transaxle vehicles are equipped with Rzeppa or double offset inboard CV-joints. Automatic transaxle vehicles are equipped with tripot inboard CV-joints. All outboard CV-joints are the Birfield type. The Birfield outboard CV-joint cannot be disassembled. If the outboard CV-joint boot is to be replaced, it will be necessary to remove the inboard CV-joint.

Manual Transaxle

1. Remove the halfshaft from the vehicle and clamp it in a vise equipped with jaw caps, to prevent damage to the machined surfaces. Do not allow the vise to contact the boot or its clamps.
2. Remove the large boot clamp from the inboard CV-joint, using side cutters. After removing the clamp, roll the boot back over the shaft.

NOTE: Check the grease for contamination by rubbing it between 2 fingers. Any gritty feeling indicates a contaminated CV-joint, in which case the entire CV-joint must be disassembled, cleaned and inspected. If the grease is not contaminated and the CV-joint has been operating satisfactorily, continue with the boot replacement procedure and add the required lubricant.

3. Paint alignment marks on the outer race and shaft for assembly reference. Remove the wire ring bearing retainer and remove the outer race.
4. Paint alignment marks on the inner race and shaft for assembly reference. Remove the inner race snapring from the end of the halfshaft and remove the inner race, cage and ball bearings from the shaft as an assembly.

NOTE: Use care to prevent damage to the bearing surfaces and cage.

5. If only the boot is being replaced,

go to Step 6. If it is necessary to disassemble the CV-joint further, proceed as follows:
   a. Pry the ball bearing out of the bearing cage using a small prybar with blunted edges. Mark the inner race and the bearing cage for proper assembly.
   b. Rotate the inner race to align the bearing lands with the windows in the bearing cage. Remove the inner race through the larger end of the cage.
6. Remove the small clamp and remove the inner boot from the halfshaft. If the boot is to be reused, wrap the shaft splines with tape before removing.
7. If the outer CV-joint boot is to be replaced, remove the clamps and slide the boot off the shaft from the inboard side.

To install:
8. If the outboard boot was removed, slide the boot onto the shaft from the inboard side. Wrap tape on the splines before installing to protect the boot.
9. Install the inboard boot and remove the tape from the shaft.
10. Lubricate the inner race, bearing cage and ball bearings with high temperature CV-joint grease.
11. Position the inner race in the bearing cage and align the matchmarks.

NOTE: Install the race with the chamfered splines facing the large end of the cage.

12. Install the ball bearings in the bearing cage. The balls can be pressed into the cage windows with the heel of the hand.
13. Install the inner race, cage and balls on the halfshaft as an assembly. Make sure the chamfer on the bearing cage faces the snapring and the paint marks made during removal line up. Install the inner race snapring.
14. Lubricate the outer race with 1.4–2.1 oz. (40–60 grams) of high temperature CV-joint grease. Install the outer race and add another 0.7–1.0 oz. (20–30 grams) of high temperature CV-joint grease to the outer race. Install the wire ring bearing retainer.
15. Position the CV-joint boot(s). Make sure the boot is fully seated in the grooves in the shaft and outer race.
16. Extend or compress the inner CV-joint as necessary until the distance between the boot clamp grooves measures 3.5 in. (90mm). Do not allow this dimension to change until the boot clamps are installed.
17. Insert a small prybar with rounded edges between the boot and the outer bearing race to allow trapped air to

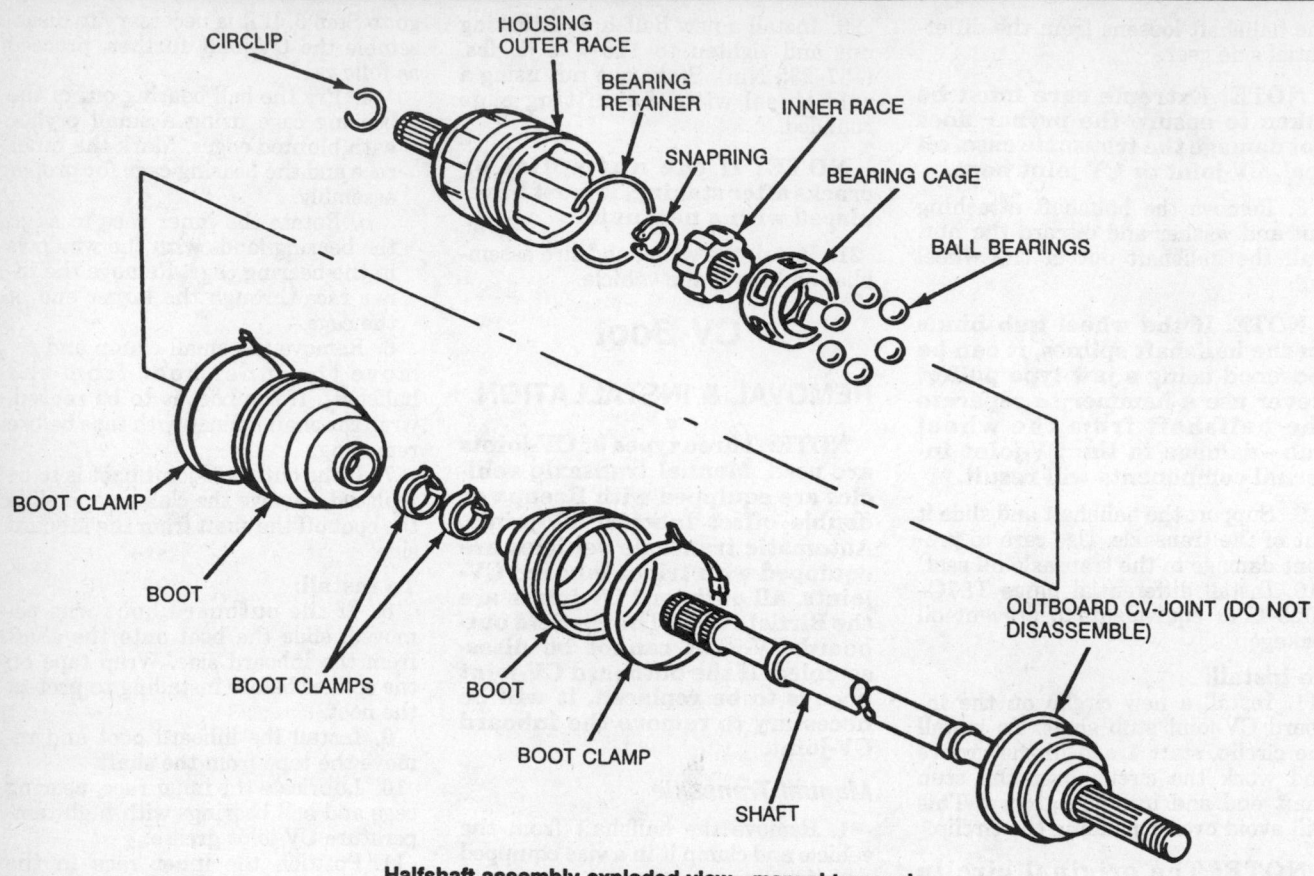

Halfshaft assembly exploded view—manual transaxle

escape from the boot. Install new boot clamps.

18. Wrap the clamps around the boots in a clockwise direction, pull tight with pliers and bend the locking tabs to secure in position.

19. Work the CV-joint through its full range of travel at various angles. The joint should flex, extend and compress smoothly.

20. Install the halfshaft into the vehicle.

Automatic Transaxle

1. Remove the halfshaft from the vehicle and clamp it in a vise equipped with jaw caps, to prevent damage to the machined surfaces. Do not allow the vise to contact the boot or its clamps.

2. Remove the large boot clamp from the inboard CV-joint, using side cutters. After removing the clamp, roll the boot back over the shaft.

NOTE: Check the grease for contamination by rubbing it between 2 fingers. Any gritty feeling indicates a contaminated CV-joint, in which case the entire CV-joint must be disassembled, cleaned and inspected. If the grease is not contaminated and

the CV-joint has been operating satisfactorily, continue with the boot replacement procedure and add the required lubricant.

3. Paint alignment marks on the outer race and shaft for assembly reference. Remove the wire ring bearing retainer and remove the outer race.

4. Paint alignment marks on the tripot bearing and shaft for assembly reference. Remove the tripot bearing snapring and, using a brass drift and hammer, remove the tripot bearing from the shaft.

5. Remove the small clamp and remove the inner boot from the halfshaft. If the boot is to be reused, wrap the shaft splines with tape before removing.

6. If the outer CV-joint boot is to be replaced, remove the clamps and slide the boot off the shaft from the inboard side.

To install:

7. If the outboard boot was removed, slide the boot onto the shaft from the inboard side. Wrap tape on the splines before installing to protect the boot.

8. Install the inboard boot and remove the tape from the shaft.

9. Install the tripot assembly on the

halfshaft. Tap the assembly onto the shaft using a hammer and brass drift. Install the tripot assembly retaining ring.

10. Fill the CV-joint outer race with 3.5 oz. (100 grams) of high temperature CV-joint grease. Install the outer race over the tripot joint and install the wire ring bearing retainer.

11. Position the CV-joint boot(s). Make sure the boot is fully seated in the grooves in the shaft and outer race.

12. Extend or compress the inner CV-joint as necessary until the distance between the boot clamp grooves measures 3.5 in. (90mm). Do not allow this dimension to change until the boot clamps are installed.

13. Insert a small prybar with rounded edges between the boot and the outer bearing race to allow trapped air to escape from the boot. Install new boot clamps.

14. Wrap the clamps around the boots in a clockwise direction, pull tight with pliers and bend the locking tabs to secure in position.

15. Work the CV-joint through its full range of travel at various angles. The joint should flex, extend and compress smoothly.

16. Install the halfshaft into the vehicle.

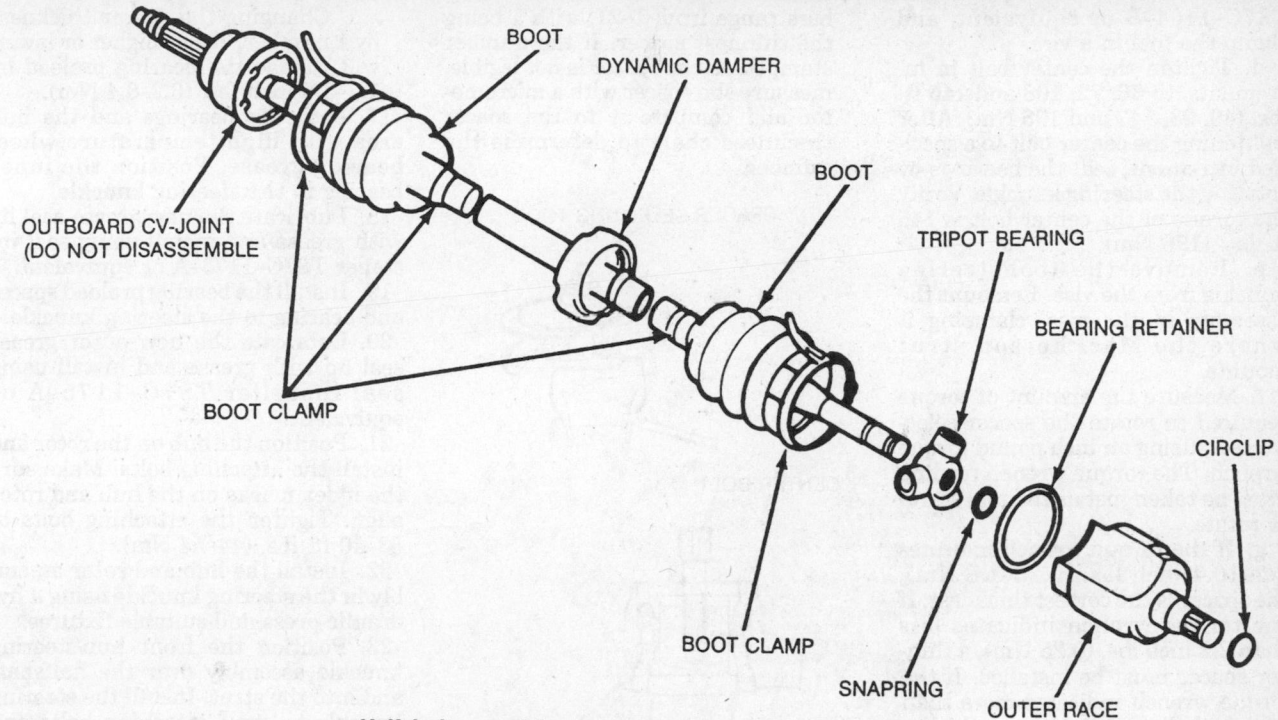

BOOT

DYNAMIC DAMPER

BOOT

OUTBOARD CV-JOINT
(DO NOT DISASSEMBLE

TRIPOT BEARING

BEARING RETAINER

CIRCLIP

BOOT CLAMP

BOOT CLAMP

SNAPRING

OUTER RACE

Halfshaft assembly exploded view—automatic transaxle

Front Wheel Hub, Knuckle and Bearings

REMOVAL & INSTALLATION

1. Raise and safely support the vehicle. Remove the front wheel and tire assembly.

2. Carefully raise the staked portion of the halfshaft attaching nut using a small cape chisel. Remove the halfshaft attaching nut and washer and discard the nut.

NOTE: When loosening the nut, lock the hub by applying the brakes.

3. Remove the stabilizer bar to control arm attaching bolt, nut, washers and bushings.

4. Remove the cotter pin and tie rod end attaching nut. Separate the tie rod end from the steering knuckle arm using a suitable tool. If the tie rod end does not separate easily, give the steering knuckle a sharp blow with a soft faced hammer to shock the taper.

5. Remove the U-shaped retaining clip from the center section of the caliper flex hose. Remove the disc brake pads and the caliper. Suspend the caliper from the strut spring; do not allow it to hang from the brake hose.

6. Remove the lower control arm ball joint clamp bolt and nut. Pry downward on the lower control arm to separate the ball joint from the steering knuckle.

7. Remove the steering knuckle to strut attaching bolts. Slide the hub/steering knuckle assembly out of its bracket in the strut and off the end of the halfshaft. Use care to prevent damage to the grease seals.

NOTE: If the hub binds on the halfshaft splines, it can be loosened by lightly tapping with a plastic faced hammer on the end of the halfshaft. Never use a metal faced hammer as damage to the CV-joint internal components will result. If the halfshaft splines become rusted to the hub, a jaw type puller must be used to separate them.

8. Remove the hub and rotor assembly from the steering knuckle using knuckle puller T87C–1104–A or equivalent. Remove the bearing preload spacer from the hub and rotor assembly.

NOTE: The spacer located between the bearings determines bearing preload. It must not be discarded.

9. Paint aligning marks on the hub and rotor assembly so they can be assembled in the same position. Remove the attaching bolts and separate the rotor from the hub. It may be helpful to mount the rotor in a soft jawed vise.

10. Remove the bearing from the wheel hub using bearing puller attachment D84L–1123–A and puller D80L–927–A or equivalent. A bearing splitter

and a large vibration damper puller can also be used. A spacer block will have to be used over the hub. A socket may also have to be used to finish pulling the bearing off the hub.

11. Remove the outer grease seal from the hub. Remove the inner grease seal from the steering knuckle using a small prybar.

12. Remove the bearing from the steering knuckle. Unless it has been damaged, the disc brake dust shield should be left on the steering knuckle.

13. If the bearings are to be replaced, remove the old bearing races using a brass drift and a hammer.

To install:

14. Clean and inspect all components that will be reused. Check the hub, knuckle and rotor dust shield for cracks, scoring, rusting, etc.

15. If the brake rotor dust shield was removed, install a new 1 using dust shield replacer tool T87C–1175–B or equivalent.

16. If the original bearings and knuckle are being reused, proceed to Step 17. If the bearings or knuckle are being replaced, bearing preload must be checked as follows before assembly.

  a. Install the outer bearing races in the steering knuckle using bearing cup replacer tool D79P–1202–A or equivalent.

  b. Lubricate the bearing races and bearing with a thin film of clean engine oil. Install the bearings and preload spacer in the steering knuckle.

  c. Install spacer selection tool

T87C–1104–B or equivalent, and clamp the tool in a vise.

d. Tighten the center bolt in increments, to 36, 72, 108 and 145 ft. lbs. (49, 98, 147 and 196 Nm). After tightening the center bolt to a specified increment, seat the bearings by rotating the steering knuckle. Verify the torque of the center bolt is 145 ft. lbs. (196 Nm).

e. Remove the tool/steering knuckle from the vise. Remount the assembly in the vise, clamping it where the MacPherson strut mounts.

f. Measure the amount of torque required to rotate the spacer selector tool, using an inch pound torque wrench. The torque wrench reading must be taken just as the tool starts to rotate.

g. If the torque wrench indicates 2.2–10.4 inch lbs. (0.25–1.8 Nm), the spacer is the correct thickness. If the torque wrench indicates less than 2.2 inch lbs. (0.25 Nm), a thinner spacer must be installed. If the torque wrench indicates more than 10.4 inch lbs. (1.8 Nm), a thicker spacer must be installed.

h. Each bearing spacer has a numerical code that identifies it's thickness, stamped onto the outer diameter of the spacer. The numbers range from 1–21, with 1 being the thinnest spacer. If the number stamped on the spacer is not legible, measure the spacer with a micrometer and compare it to the spacer thickness chart to determine the number.

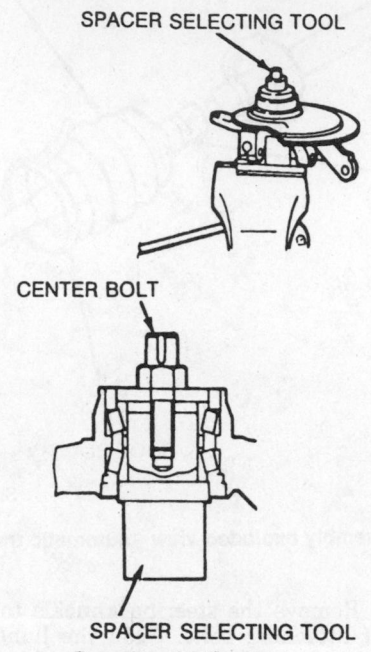

SPACER SELECTING TOOL

CENTER BOLT

SPACER SELECTING TOOL
Spacer selecting tool

i. Changing the spacer thickness by 1 number, either higher or lower, will change the bearing preload by 1.7–3.5 inch lbs. (0.2–0.4 Nm).

17. Pack the bearings and the hub area with high temperature wheel bearing grease. Position the inner bearing in the steering knuckle.

18. Lubricate the new grease seal lip with grease and install using seal installer T87C–1175–A or equivalent.

19. Install the bearing preload spacer and bearing in the steering knuckle.

20. Lubricate the new outer grease seal lip with grease and install using seal installer T87C–1175–A or equivalent.

21. Position the hub on the rotor and install the attaching bolts. Make sure the index marks on the hub and rotor align. Tighten the attaching bolts to 33–40 ft. lbs. (44–54 Nm).

22. Install the hub and rotor assembly in the steering knuckle using a hydraulic press and suitable fixtures.

23. Position the front hub/steering knuckle assembly over the halfshaft and into the strut. Install the steering knuckle to strut attaching bolts and nuts. Tighten the attaching nuts to 69–86 ft. lbs. (93–117 Nm).

24. Position the lower control arm ball joint through the steering knuckle and install the clamp bolt and nut. Tighten the clamp bolt to 32–40 ft. lbs. (43–54 Nm).

25. Position the brake caliper over the rotor and install the attaching bolts. Tighten to 29–36 ft. lbs. (39–49 Nm). Install the U-clip on the caliper flex line.

26. Install a new halfshaft attaching nut. Tighten to 116–174 ft. lbs. (157–235 Nm). Stake the halfshaft using a cold chisel with the cutting edge rounded.

NOTE: If the nut splits or cracks after staking, it must be replaced with a new nut.

27. Connect the tie rod to the steering knuckle arm and install the attaching nut. Tighten to 22–33 ft. lbs. (29–44 Nm) and install a new cotter pin.

NOTE: If the slots in the nut do not align with the hole in the ball joint stud, tighten the nut for proper alignment. Never loosen the nut.

28. Position the stabilizer bar and install the stabilizer link assembly including the attaching bolt, nut, washers, sleeve and rubber bushings. Tighten the attaching nut until 0.43 in. (10.8mm) of the bolt threads extend beyond the nut.

29. Install the wheel and tire assembly and lower the vehicle.

BEARING SPACER THICKNESS CHART

Stamped mark	Thickness
1	6.285 mm (0.2474 in)
2	6.325 mm (0.2490 in)
3	6.365 mm (0.2506 in)
4	6.405 mm (0.2522 in)
5	6.445 mm (0.2538 in)
6	6.485 mm (0.2554 in)
7	6.525 mm (0.2570 in)
8	6.565 mm (0.2586 in)
9	6.605 mm (0.2602 in)
10	6.645 mm (0.2618 in)
11	6.685 mm (0.2634 in)
12	6.725 mm (0.2650 in)
13	6.765 mm (0.2666 in)
14	6.805 mm (0.2682 in)
15	6.845 mm (0.2698 in)
16	6.885 mm (0.2714 in)
17	6.925 mm (0.2730 in)
18	6.965 mm (0.2746 in)
19	7.005 mm (0.2762 in)
20	7.045 mm (0.2778 in)
21	7.085 mm (0.2794 in)

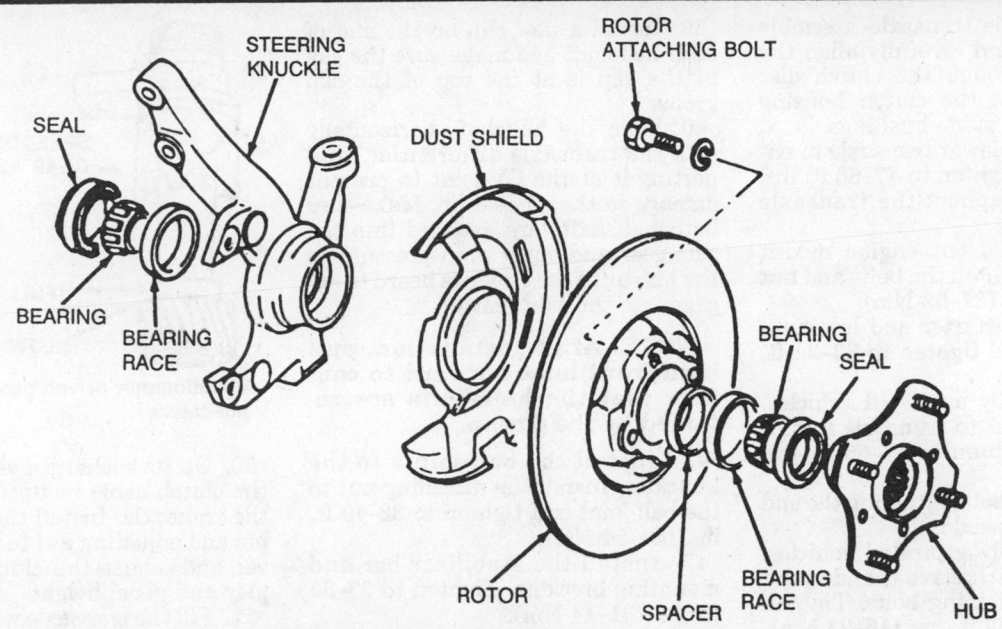

Front wheel hub, knuckle and bearings—exploded view

MANUAL TRANSAXLE

For further information on transmission/transaxles, please refer to "Chilton's Guide to Transmission Repair".

Transaxle Assembly

REMOVAL & INSTALLATION

NOTE: It is necessary to support the engine from the sling hook provided at the rear of the engine using engine support bar D88L–6000–A or equivalent.

1. Disconnect the battery cables and remove the battery. Remove the air cleaner assembly.
2. Loosen the lug nuts on both front wheels.
3. Disconnect the speedometer cable from the transaxle.
4. On normally aspirated vehicles, remove the clutch slave hydraulic line retaining bracket and nut.
5. On turbocharged vehicles, remove the clutch cable from the release lever by removing the adjusting nut and pin.
6. On turbocharged vehicles, remove the intake air bypass valve mounting nut and remove the clutch cable mounting bracket from the transaxle.
7. On normally aspirated vehicles, remove the 2 bolts retaining the ground wire and engine harness

bracket to the transaxle. Pull the harness out of the routing clip.
8. On turbocharged vehicles, remove the ground wire retaining bolt and ground wire and remove the coolant pipe bracket and wire harness clip.
9. Disconnect the connectors for the neutral switch and the backup light switch. Disconnect the body ground connector.
10. Install the engine support bar. Remove the 2 upper transaxle to engine retaining bolts and 2 upper starter retaining bolts.
11. Raise and safely support the vehicle. Remove both front wheel and tire assemblies and remove the underbody splash covers, if equipped.
12. Position a drain pan under the transaxle. Remove the transaxle drain plug and drain the fluid.
13. Remove the front stabilizer bar.
14. Remove the ball joint clamp bolts, pull the lower arms downward and separate the lower arms from the knuckles. Be careful not to damage the ball joint dust boots.
15. Remove the inner left fender splash panel, if necessary.
16. Separate both halfshafts by pulling the front hub outward as follows:
    a. Withdraw the halfshafts horizontally from the transaxle to prevent damage to the oil lip seals. Apply even pressure and increase gradually.
    b. Hold the halfshafts during removal to prevent damage to the boots and joints.
    c. Suspend the halfshafts in a horizontal position using mechanics wire.
17. Remove the 2 front crossmember

braces. Remove the crossmember brace to control arm support bolts. Remove the left control arm through bolt.
18. Remove the exhaust hanger from the crossmember. Remove the remaining crossmember bolts, beginning with the front mount bolts, followed by the rear mount bolt, then the bolt next to the rear mount and finally, the bolt next to the front mount.
19. Remove the bolt and nut attaching the shift control rod to the transaxle and slide the control rod out of the way.
20. Remove the nut or bolt from the shift extension bar mounting bracket and slide the extension bar off the bracket.
21. On normally aspirated vehicles, remove the 2 bolts retaining the clutch slave cylinder and set the wire aside.
22. Remove the lower bolts retaining the starter to the transaxle housing and remove the starter. Remove the bolts attaching the end plate to the transaxle.
23. On normally aspirated vehicles, remove the nut and washer retaining the support bracket to the exhaust manifold. Remove the gusset to transaxle retaining bolt.
24. Lower the engine slightly with the support bar. Support the transaxle with a suitable jack.
25. Remove the front engine mount and bracket from the transaxle. Remove the bolts attaching the transaxle to the engine and remove the transaxle.
To install:
26. Apply a thin coating of lubricant to the spline of the input shaft.

27. Position the transaxle assembly in the vehicle and carefully align the input shaft through the clutch disc spline and align the clutch housing onto the engine guide bushings.

28. Install the lower transaxle to engine bolts and tighten to 47–66 ft. lbs. (63–89 Nm). Support the transaxle with a jack.

29. Install the front engine mount and bracket. Tighten the bolts and nut to 27–38 ft. lbs. (37–52 Nm).

30. Install the starter and lower retaining bolts and tighten to 23–34 ft. lbs. (31–46 Nm).

31. On normally aspirated vehicles, install the gusset to transaxle retaining bolt and tighten to 47–66 ft. lbs. (63–89 Nm).

32. Install the bolts retaining the end plate to the transaxle.

33. On normally aspirated vehicles, position the clutch slave cylinder and install the 2 retaining bolts. Tighten the bolts to 12–17 ft. lbs. (16–23 Nm).

34. Slide the extension bar onto the mounting stud. Install and tighten the retaining nut or bolt to 23–34 ft. lbs. (31–46 Nm).

35. Install the control rod to the transaxle and install the nut and bolt. Tighten to 12–17 ft. lbs. (16–23 Nm).

36. Install the crossmember to the vehicle. Install the nuts and bolts to the crossmember and tighten in numerical sequence to the specified torque.

37. Install the crossmember brace to control arm support bolts. Tighten to 69–86 ft. lbs. (93–117 Nm). Install the left control arm through bolt and tighten to 69–86 ft. lbs. (93–117 Nm).

38. Install the front crossmember braces. Tighten the bolts to 23–34 ft. lbs. (31–46 Nm). Install the exhaust hanger to the crossmember.

NOTE: On turbocharged vehicles, install the intermediate shaft and support bearing assembly.

39. Install a new clip on the end of each halfshaft and make sure the gap in the clip is at the top of the clip groove.

40. Slide the halfshaft horizontally into the transaxle differential, supporting it at the CV-joint to prevent damage to the oil seal lip. Make sure both halfshafts are engaged into the side gear and apply even pressure to the hub until the circlip is heard to engage into the side gear.

NOTE: After installation, pull both front hubs outward to confirm that the halfshafts are retained by the circlip.

41. Install the ball joints to the knuckles. Install the attaching nut to the ball joint and tighten to 32–40 ft. lbs. (43–54 Nm).

42. Install the stabilizer bar and mounting brackets. Tighten to 23–33 ft. lbs. (31–44 Nm).

43. Assemble the front stabilizer link by inserting the bolt through the bushings, washers and the spacer. Install the nuts and tighten to 9–13 ft. lbs. (12–18 Nm). Tighten the nuts further, as necessary, until the threads exposed on the stabilizer link bolt past the nut are 0.43 in. (10.8mm) in length. Lock the nuts against each other.

44. Install the underbody and left fender splash panels, on normally aspirated vehicles.

45. Install the wheel and tire assemblies and lower the vehicle.

46. Install the 2 upper transaxle to engine bolts and tighten to 47–66 ft. lbs. (64–89 Nm). Install the 2 upper starter mounting bolts and tighten to 23–34 ft. lbs. (31–46 Nm).

47. Remove the engine support bar.

48. Connect the body ground connector and connect the neutral and back-up light switch connectors.

49. Connect the wire harness clip. Install the ground wire and the retaining bolt(s).

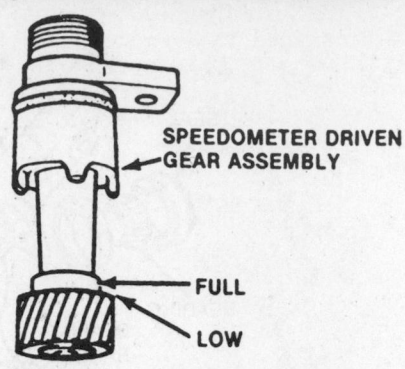

SPEEDOMETER DRIVEN GEAR ASSEMBLY

FULL

LOW

Speedometer driven gear fluid level indicators

50. On turbocharged vehicles, install the clutch cable mounting bracket to the transaxle. Install the clutch cable pin and adjusting nut to the release lever and adjust the clutch pedal free play and pedal height.

51. Fill the transaxle with the proper type and quantity of fluid as follows:

a. Remove the speedometer driven gear retaining bolt and lift the driven gear assembly from the transaxle housing. If necessary, use a small prybar to pry between the driven gear retaining flange and the housing.

b. Place a funnel into the speedometer driven gear mounting hole and add fluid to the level indicated on the speedometer driven gear.

c. Install the driven gear into the transaxle and the retaining bolt. Tighten to 69–104 inch lbs. (7.8–12.0 Nm).

d. Connect the speedometer cable and position the dust cover.

52. Install the air cleaner and the battery. Connect the battery cables.

53. Check for leaks and proper operation.

CLUTCH

Clutch Assembly

REMOVAL & INSTALLATION

1. Remove the transaxle.

2. Install flywheel locking tool T74P-6375-A or equivalent, in a transaxle mounting hole on the engine and engage the tooth of the locking tool into the flywheel ring gear. Install a clutch alignment tool into the splines of the clutch disc and the pilot bearing.

3. Remove the bolts attaching the pressure plate to the flywheel and remove the pressure plate assembly. Remove the clutch disc and the clutch alignment tool.

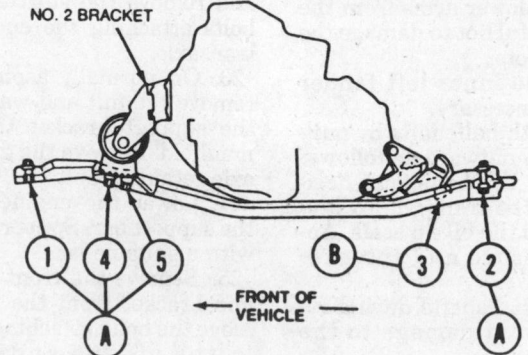

NO. 2 BRACKET

FRONT OF VEHICLE

A: TIGHTEN TO 64-89 N·m (47-66 LB-FT)
B: TIGHTEN TO 28-46 N·m (20-34 LB-FT)

Crossmember bolt tightening sequence and specifications

4. With the flywheel locking tool still engaged, remove the flywheel mounting bolts and the flywheel.

5. Inspect the pilot bearing for excessive wear or scoring and replace if necessary, using a suitable drift and hammer.

NOTE: Do not remove the pilot bearing if it is not necessary.

6. Remove the return spring from the release bearing lever and transaxle case. Remove the release bearing from the transaxle input shaft.

7. Remove the bolt attaching the release fork to the release lever. Slide the release lever shaft out through the top of the transaxle case approximately 3 in. Remove the release fork and setkey from the release lever shaft. Remove the release lever from the transaxle.

8. Inspect the pressure plate surface for scoring, cracks or discoloration. Check the diaphragm spring fingers for discoloration, scoring, broken or bent segments and spring ends that are higher or lower than the rest.

9. Check the clutch disc lining for contamination and wear. Measure the depth to the rivet heads with a vernier caliper. The minimum allowable rivet clearance is 0.012 in. (0.3mm). Check for loose clutch lining rivets.

10. Check clutch disc run-out using a dial indicator. Lateral run-out should not be more than 0.027 in. (0.7mm). Vertical run-out should not be more than 0.039 in. (1.0mm). Check for wear or rust on the splines.

11. Check the clutch release bearing by turning the bearing in both directions and check for binding or abnormal noise. Check for worn or damaged release bearing fork contact surfaces. Check the sliding condition of the bearing. Install the bearing on the transaxle input shaft and check for smooth movement.

NOTE: The clutch release bearing is a sealed bearing and must not be immersed in any type of cleaning fluid.

12. Check the flywheel for surface marks, scoring or discoloration. Machine if necessary, however, do not exceed a machining cut of 0.020 in. (0.5mm). Check for damaged or worn ring gear teeth.

To install:

13. If removed, install the pilot bearing in the flywheel with a suitable drift and a hammer.

14. Install the flywheel to the crankshaft with the beveled ring gear facing the engine. Install the flywheel locking tool.

15. Clean the old sealant from the threads of the flywheel bolts. Apply

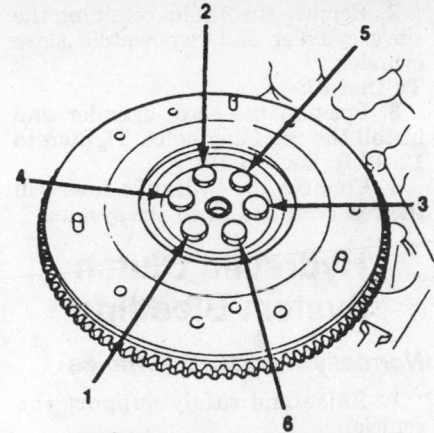

Flywheel bolt torque sequence

stud and bearing mount sealant to the threads and install the flywheel bolts. Tighten, in sequence, to 71–75 ft. lbs. (96–103 Nm).

16. Check the flywheel run-out with a dial indicator. The run-out limit is 0.008 in. (0.2mm). If the run-out exceeds the limit, the flywheel must be machined.

17. Install the release lever through the transaxle case and align the groove in the lever shaft and the groove in the release fork with the set key.

18. Align the release fork mounting bolt hole with the hole in the release lever shaft. Apply a coating of stud and bearing mount sealant to the bolt and install. Tighten to 5.8–8.0 ft. lbs. (7.8–10.8 Nm).

19. Apply lubricant to the release bearing and install the release bearing on the clutch release fork. Install the clutch release lever return spring to the transaxle case and release lever arm.

20. Clean the splines on the clutch disc and the transaxle input shaft and apply a small amount of lubricant to the clutch disc and input shaft splines. Be careful not to get grease on the clutch face.

21. Install the clutch disc with the clutch alignment tool. Install the disc with the spring plate to the transaxle side.

22. Install the pressure plate and mounting bolts. Tighten the bolts evenly in a diagonal sequence to 13–20 ft. lbs. (18–26 Nm). Use the flywheel locking tool to hold the flywheel while tightening the bolts.

23. Remove the flywheel locking tool and the clutch alignment tool.

24. Install the transaxle. Adjust the clutch pedal height and free-play.

PEDAL HEIGHT/FREE-PLAY ADJUSTMENT

Pedal Height

With the clutch pedal at the top of its

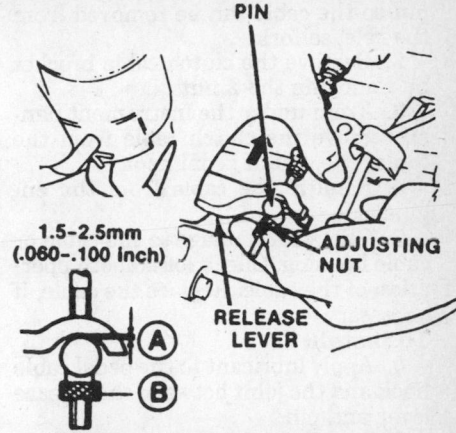

Clutch pedal free-play adjustment— turbocharged vehicles

travel, measure the distance from the upper center of the pedal pad to the dash panel. The distance should be 8.4–8.6 in. (214–219mm) on turbocharged vehicles or 9.02–9.22 in. (229–234mm) on normally aspirated vehicles. If adjustment is necessary, proceed as follows:

1. Loosen the locknut located on the clutch pedal.

2. Turn the stop bolt to obtain the correct pedal height.

3. Tighten the locknut.

Pedal Free-Play

Depress the clutch pedal lightly by hand until all free-play is removed and measure the free-play distance. The distance should be 0.350–0.590 in. (9–15mm) on turbocharged vehicles or 0.02–1.2 in. (0.6–3.0mm) on normally aspirated vehicles. If adjustment is necessary, proceed as follows:

TURBOCHARGED VEHICLES

1. Depress the clutch release lever and pull the pin away from the lever.

2. Adjust clearance **A** to 0.06–0.100 in. (1.5–2.5mm) by turning adjusting nut **B**.

3. After adjustment, make sure when the clutch is disengaged, the pedal height is 8.4–8.6 in. (214–219mm).

NORMALLY ASPIRATED VEHICLES

1. Loosen the locknut.

2. Turn the pushrod adjusting nut in the direction required to achieve the required clearance.

3. Tighten the locknut to 9–12 ft. lbs. (12–17 Nm). Make sure the pedal height is 9.02–9.22 in. (229–234mm).

Clutch Cable

REMOVAL & INSTALLATION

Turbocharged Vehicles

1. Remove the adjusting nut and

pin so the cable can be removed from the release fork.

2. Remove the clutch cable bracket by removing the 2 nuts.

3. From under the instrument panel, remove the clutch cable from the top of the clutch pedal hook.

4. Remove the cable from the engine side.

5. Check for damage to the cable or cable housing. Check for smooth operation of the cable. Replace the cable, if necessary.

To install:

6. Apply lubricant to the pedal cable hook and the joint between the release lever and pin.

7. Install the cable through the engine side.

8. From under the instrument panel, connect the clutch cable over the top of the clutch pedal hook.

9. Install the clutch cable bracket to the dash panel. Install the 2 attaching nuts and tighten to 12–17 ft. lbs. (16–23 Nm).

10. Install the end of the cable through the slot in the release fork. Install the pin so it rests in the groove of the release lever and attach the adjusting nut to the cable.

11. Adjust the pedal free-play.

Clutch Master Cylinder

REMOVAL & INSTALLATION

Normally Aspirated Vehicles

1. Disconnect the battery cables and remove the battery.

2. Remove the windshield wiper motor.

3. Disconnect the hydraulic line fitting at the retaining bracket on the transaxle case and drain the fluid. Reconnect the fitting after draining.

4. Disconnect the hydraulic line from the master cylinder. Remove the master cylinder retaining nuts and remove the master cylinder.

To install:

5. Position the master cylinder to the dash panel. Make sure the clutch pedal pushrod aligns properly.

6. Install the retaining nuts and tighten to 14–19 ft. lbs. (19–26 Nm).

7. Connect the hydraulic line to the master cylinder. Fill the reservoir and bleed the system.

8. Install the wiper motor and the battery. Connect the battery cables.

Clutch Slave Cylinder

REMOVAL & INSTALLATION

Normally Aspirated Vehicles

1. Disconnect and plug the hydraulic line.

2. Remove the 2 bolts retaining the slave cylinder and remove the slave cylinder.

To install:

3. Position the slave cylinder and install the retaining bolts. Tighten to 12–17 ft. lbs. (16–23).

4. Connect the hydraulic line. Fill the reservoir and bleed the system.

Hydraulic Clutch System Bleeding

Normally Aspirated Vehicles

1. Raise and safely support the vehicle.

2. Attach a hose to the bleeder valve on the clutch slave cylinder.

3. Open the bleeder valve ½ turn and watch for air bubbles in the brake fluid at the open end of the hose.

NOTE: Keep the reservoir full of fluid while bleeding.

4. Close the bleeder valve when the bubbling stops.

5. Depress the clutch pedal to the floor and hold.

6. Open the bleed valve ¼ turn and push the clutch pedal down as far as it will go. Close the valve, then release the pedal.

7. Fill the fluid reservoir. Check the clutch for proper operation.

AUTOMATIC TRANSAXLE

For further information on transmission/transaxles, please refer to "Chilton's Guide to Transmission Repair".

Transaxle Assembly

REMOVAL & INSTALLATION

1. Disconnect the battery cables and remove the battery. Remove the air cleaner assembly.

2. Disconnect the speedometer cable at the cable connector.

3. Make sure the transaxle is in the P position and remove the shift cable retaining nut from the neutral safety switch. Remove the shift cable retaining bolts.

4. Disconnect the kickdown cable from the throttle body housing. Route the cable out of the straps for removal with the transaxle.

5. Disconnect the electrical connectors from the transaxle. Remove the dipstick tube bracket retaining bolt and ground wire.

6. Remove the starter upper retaining bolts and remove the upper intake manifold support retaining bolts.

7. Remove the heater bypass tube bracket and remove the transaxle to engine upper retaining bolts.

8. Install engine support bar D88L–6000–A or equivalent. Raise and safely support the vehicle.

9. Place a drain pan under the transaxle and drain the transaxle fluid.

10. Remove the intake manifold support lower retaining bolts. Disconnect the starter electrical connectors and remove the starter.

11. Remove the front wheel and tire assemblies. Remove the front caliper brake hose retaining clips from the strut bracket.

12. Remove the ball joint pinch bolts and separate the ball joints from the control arms. Remove the splash shields.

13. Remove the front retaining bolt from both control arms. Remove the frame brace to crossmember retaining bolt.

14. Remove the front and rear transaxle mount to crossmember retaining nuts. Remove the crossmember braces.

15. Remove the shift cable retaining screw from the crossmember and remove the crossmember.

16. Remove the left halfshaft. Disconnect the right halfshaft and install differential plugs T88C–7025–AH or equivalent.

NOTE: Failure to install differential plugs may result in misalignment of the differential side gears.

17. Remove the gusset plate retaining bolts from the transaxle. Loosen the gusset plate retaining bolts on the engine.

18. Remove the torque converter cover plate and remove the exhaust manifold support bracket.

19. Remove the front and rear transaxle mounts and lower the vhicle.

20. Lower, but do not remove the engine/transaxle assembly with the support bar. Raise and safely support the vehicle.

21. Remove the torque converter to driveplate retaining nuts. Position a transaxle jack under the transaxle and secure with safety chains.

22. Remove the transaxle to engine lower retaining bolts and remove the transaxle from the vehicle.

To install:

23. Raise the transaxle and position to the engine.

NOTE: Raise the transaxle slowly and ensure the dipstick tube clears the battery tray. Align

the converter studs to the driveplate.

24. Install the transaxle to engine lower retaining bolts. Tighten to 47 ft. lbs. (63 Nm).

25. Install the torque converter-to-driveplate retaining nuts and tighten to 32 ft. lbs. (43 Nm).

26. Remove the transaxle jack and lower the vehicle.

27. Raise the engine/transaxle assembly into position with the support fixture.

NOTE: Use care in raising the engine/transaxle so as not to damage the air conditioning, if equipped or other engine compartment components.

28. Raise and safely support the vehicle. Install the front and rear mounts to the transaxle and tighten the retaining bolts to 27–38 ft. lbs. (37–52 Nm).

29. Install the exhaust manifold support. Tighten the transaxle mount bolt to 49–67 ft. lbs. (67–91 Nm). Tighten the manifold nut to 23–34 ft. lbs. (31–46 Nm).

30. Install the torque converter cover plate. Tighten the retaining bolts to 71–97 inch lbs. (8–11 Nm).

31. Align the gusset plates and install the retaining bolts. Tighten to 45 ft. lbs. (61 Nm).

32. Position the crossmember to the transaxle mounts. Align the rear transaxle mount stud first and loosely install the retaining nut. Align the front transaxle mount studs and loosely install the retaining nuts.

33. Install the crossmember retaining bolts and tighten to 27–39 ft. lbs. (36–54 Nm). Tighten the front and rear transaxle mount retaining nuts to 20–34 ft. lbs. (28–46 Nm).

34. Install new circlips to the inner CV-joint shafts. Install the halfshafts and new retaining nuts. Tighten the nuts to 116–174 ft. lbs. (157–235 Nm). Ensure the axles are fully seated by grasping the shafts and pulling outward.

35. Position the shift cable and install the shift cable lower retaining bolt. Tighten to 69–95 inch lbs. (8–11 Nm).

36. Install the crossmember braces and tighten the retaining bolts to 27–39 ft. lbs. (36–54 Nm).

37. Install the frame brace and tighten the crossmember bolt to 27–39 ft. lbs. (36–54 Nm).

38. Install the control arm front retaining bolts and tighten to 69–86 ft. lbs. (93–117 Nm).

39. Install the ball joint pinch bolts and tighten to 32–40 ft. lbs. (43–54 Nm).

40. Install the brake hose retaining clips and the splash shields.

41. Install the starter and the lower retaining bolts. Connect the starter electrical connectors.

42. Install the intake manifold support bracket and loosely install the lower retaining bolts.

43. Install the wheel and tire assemblies and lower the vehicle.

44. Install the transaxle to engine upper retaining bolts. Tighten to 47 ft. lbs. (63 Nm). Remove the engine support fixture.

45. Install the heater bypass tube bracket. Install the intake manifold support upper bolts and tighten all the retaining bolts to 22–34 ft. lbs. (31–46 Nm).

46. Install the starter upper retaining bolts. Tighten to 22–34 ft. lbs. (31–46 Nm).

47. Position the ground wire and install the dipstick tube retaining bolt. Tighten to 69–95 inch lbs. (8–11 Nm).

48. Route the shift cable and connect to the neutral safety switch. Tighten the cable retaining bolts to 71–97 inch lbs. (8–11 Nm). Tighten the safety switch nut to 71–97 inch lbs. (8–11 Nm).

49. Route and install the kickdown cable to the throttle housing. Connect the transaxle electrical connectors.

50. Connect the speedometer cable and install the air cleaner assembly.

51. Install the battery and connect the battery cables. Fill the transaxle with the proper type and quantity of fluid.

52. Start the engine and check for proper operation. Check for leaks.

SHIFT CONTROL CABLE ADJUSTMENT

1. Position the gear selector lever in the **N** position.

2. Remove the spring clip and pin attaching the shift cable trunnion to the transaxle shift lever.

3. Rotate the transaxle shift lever fully counterclockwise. This is the **P** position.

4. Rotate the transaxle shift lever clockwise 2 detents. This is the **N** position. As the lever is rotated, position it between the ends of the shift cable trunnion.

5. If the holes in the shift lever align with the holes in the trunnion, the cable is properly adjusted. If the holes do not align, proceed to the next step.

6. Remove the console shift quadrant as follows:

   a. Slide the front seats completely forward and remove the screws retaining the rear of the rear console.

   b. Slide the front seat completely rearward and remove the screws retaining the rear console to the front console.

   c. Raise the parking brake lever as far as it will go. Raise the rear of the rear console and pull backwards to remove.

   d. Loosen the jam nut and unscrew the shift handle. Raise the ash tray and disconnect the wiring beneath it.

   e. Remove the center carpet panels. Remove the brackets, if necessary.

   f. Remove the screws and the shift quadrant. Disconnect the shift quadrant light connector.

7. Loosen the adjuster nuts on the shift cable.

8. Position the gear selector lever in the **P** position and inspect the position of the detent spring roller. If the spring roller is centered in the **P** detent, proceed to Step 12. If the spring roller is not centered in the **P** detent, proceed to the next step.

9. Loosen the attaching screws and move the detent spring forward or backward to center it in the **P** detent.

10. Position the quadrant and install the attaching screws. Position the selector lever in the **N** position.

11. Thread the adjuster nuts up or down the cable until the holes in the transaxle shift lever and the shift cable trunnion are aligned.

12. Tighten the adjuster nut to 71–97 inch lbs. (8–11 Nm).

13. Check the alignment of the holes in the transaxle shift lever and cable trunnion to make sure the adjustment was not disturbed while tightening the nuts.

14. Install the transaxle shift lever to shift cable attaching pin and retaining clip.

15. With the gear selector lever in the **N** position, press in on the shift interlock button and carefully push the lever forward while an assistant observes the transaxle shift lever. When the transaxle shift lever begins to move, note the amount the shift lever has moved.

16. With the gear selector lever in the **N** position, press in on the shift interlock button and carefully pull the lever rearward while an assistant observes the transaxle shift lever. When the transaxle shift lever begins to move, note the amount the shift lever has moved.

17. If the forward movement and the rearward movement of the gear selector lever are not equal, turn the adjuster nuts a slight amount until they become equal.

18. Tighten the adjuster nut to 71–97 inch lbs. (8–11 Nm).

NOTE: Make sure the linkage adjustment has not affected the operation of the neutral safety switch. With the parking brake and service brakes applied, try to start the engine in each gearshift

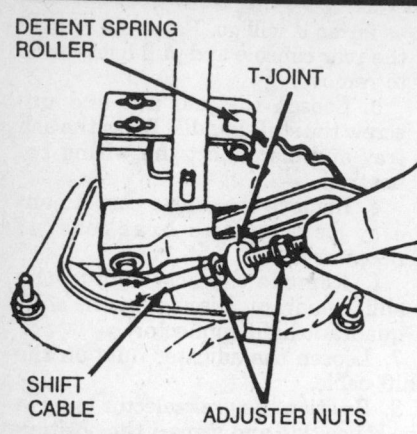

Shift control cable adjustment

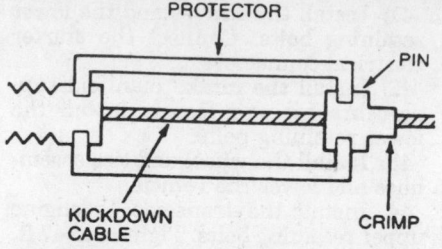

Crimp the pin with the protector installed when installing a new kickdown cable

position. The engine must crank only in N and P positions. If the engine cranks in any of the other gear selector lever positions, check the linkage adjustment and neutral safety switch operation.

19. Install the console in the reverse order of removal.

KICKDOWN CABLE ADJUSTMENT

1991

1. Remove the splash shield next to the left front tire.
2. Remove the square head plug marked **L** from the transaxle and install transmission test adapter D87C–77000–A and pressure gauge T57L–77820–A or equivalent.
3. Turn the kickdown cable locknuts to the furthest point from the throttle cam, loosen the cable all the way.
4. Shift the transaxle into **P** and warm up the engine.

NOTE: The idle speed should be 700–800 rpm.

5. Turn the locknuts toward the throttle cam until the line pressure begins to exceed 63–66 psi.
6. Turn the locknuts away from the throttle cam until a line pressure of 63–66 psi is reached.
7. Tighten the locknuts and turn OFF the engine.
8. Install the square head plug and tighten to 43–87 inch lbs. (5–10 Nm).
9. When installing a new kickdown cable, fully open the throttle valve, then crimp the pin with the protector installed. Remove the protector.

1992–93

1. Shift the transaxle to **P** and apply the parking brake. Start the engine and bring to operating temperature. The idle speed should be approximately 850 rpm.

2. Inspect the mirror cable for slack.
3. If there is any slack, adjust the outer cable adjusting nuts to remove any slack from the inner cable.
4. When installing a new kickdown cable, fully open the throttle valve, then crimp the pin with the protector installed. Remove the protector.

FRONT SUSPENSION

MacPherson Strut

REMOVAL & INSTALLATION

1. Raise and safely support the vehicle. Remove the wheel and tire assembly.
2. Remove the brake caliper and suspend it with mechanics wire; do not allow the caliper to hang from the brake hose.
3. Paint a white aligning mark on the inside of the strut mounting block. Loosen and remove the steering knuckle to strut attaching bolts and nuts.
4. Remove the U-clip from the brake line hose and slide it out of its bracket on the strut.
5. Remove the strut mount nuts from the strut tower and remove the strut from the vehicle.
6. Compress the spring with a suitable spring compressor and remove the strut rod nut. Gradually release the spring compressor.
7. Remove the mounting block, upper spring seat, bump stopper, coil spring and lower spring seat from the strut.
To install:
8. Install the lower spring seat, coil spring, bump stopper, upper spring seat and mounting block on the strut.
9. Compress the spring with the spring compressor and install the strut rod nut. Tighten to 22–27 ft. lbs. (29–36 Nm). Gradually release the spring compressor.

10. Install the strut assembly in the strut tower. Install the 4 strut attaching nuts and tighten to 17–22 ft. lbs. (23–29 Nm).

NOTE: Make sure the white aligning mark faces the center of the vehicle.

11. Install the steering knuckle to the strut and install the attaching bolts and nuts. Tighten the steering knuckle-to-strut attaching bolts to 69–86 ft. lbs. (93–117 Nm).
12. Install the brake caliper and brake hose in the bracket.
13. Install the wheel and tire assembly and lower the vehicle.

Lower Ball Joints

INSPECTION

1. Raise and safely support the vehicle.
2. Try to rock the wheel in a vertical plane. If any play is felt, have an assistant rock the wheel while observing the ball joint.
3. If any movement is detectable between the steering knuckle and control arm, the ball joint should be replaced.

REMOVAL & INSTALLATION

1. Raise and safely support the vehicle. Remove the wheel and tire assembly.
2. Remove the ball joint clamp bolt from the steering knuckle.
3. Using a small prybar, pull down on the lower control arm to separate it from the steering knuckle.
4. Remove the 2 ball joint retaining nuts from the control arm. Using a small prybar, pry the ball joint off the control arm.
To install:
5. Install the ball joint to the control arm. Tighten the bolts to 69–86 ft. lbs. (93–117 Nm).
6. Raise the lower arm and install the ball joint stud in the spindle. Install the ball joint clamp bolt and tighten to 32–40 ft. lbs. (43–54 Nm).
7. Install the wheel and tire assembly and lower the vehicle.

Lower Control Arms

REMOVAL & INSTALLATION

1. Raise and safely support the vehicle. Remove the wheel and tire assembly.
2. Disconnect the stabilizer bar from the control arm.
3. Remove the ball joint clamp bolt.
4. Remove the control arm front re-

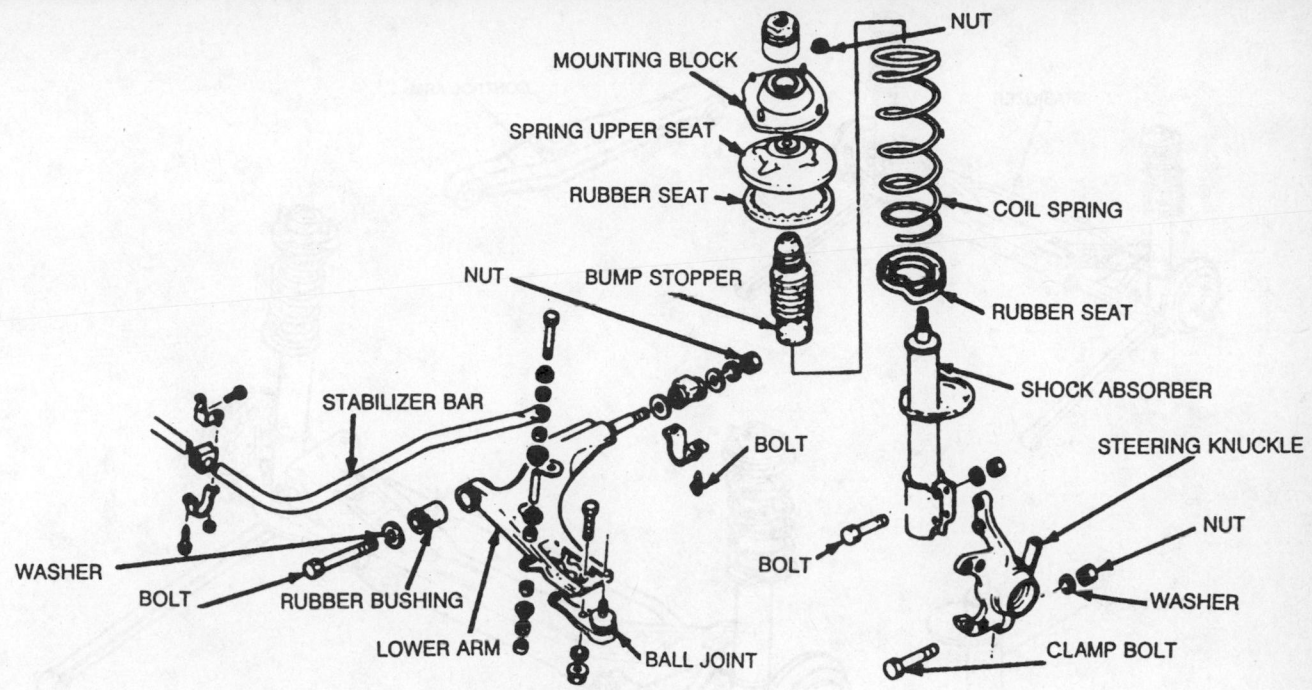

Front suspension assembly—exploded view

taining bolt and the control arm rear bracket and retaining bolts.

5. Remove the control arm.

To install:

6. Position the control arm and loosely install the front retaining bolt.

7. Install the control arm rear retaining bracket and bolts. Tighten the bolts to 44–54 ft. lbs. (59–74 Nm).

8. Tighten the front retaining bolt to 69–86 ft. lbs. (93–117 Nm).

9. Install the ball joint to the steering knuckle. Tighten the clamp bolt to 32–40 ft. lbs. (43–54 Nm).

10. Install the wheel and tire assembly and lower the vehicle.

Stabilizer Bar

REMOVAL & INSTALLATION

1. Raise and safely support the vehicle. Remove the wheel and tire assembly.

2. Remove the stabilizer bar to control arm attaching bolt, nut, washers and bushings.

3. Remove the stabilizer bar bracket bolts and remove the brackets and the stabilizer bar.

To install:

4. Install the stabilizer bar with the brackets and bracket bolts. Tighten the bolts securely.

5. Install the stabilizer link assembly including the attaching bolt, nut, washers, sleeve and rubber bushings. Tighten the attaching nut until 0.43 in. (10.8mm) of the bolt threads extend beyond the nut.

6. Install the wheel and tire assembly and lower the vehicle.

REAR SUSPENSION

MacPherson Strut

REMOVAL & INSTALLATION

1. Raise and safely support the vehicle. Remove the wheel and tire assembly.

2. Remove the rear disc brake caliper and rotor assembly.

3. Loosen the trailing arm bolt and the spindle to strut attaching bolts.

4. Remove the trailing arm attaching bolts and spindle attaching bolts.

5. Paint a white index mark on the strut rubber mounting bracket. Remove the strut attaching nuts from inside the vehicle and remove the strut assembly.

6. Compress the spring using a suitable spring compressor.

7. Remove the strut rod nut while the spring is compressed and remove the rubber mounting bracket, spring upper seat, lower seat and the rubber spring seat.

8. Slowly release the spring and remove the spring compressor. Remove the coil spring, dust boot and rebound bumpers.

To install:

9. Install the rebound bumpers and dust boot on the strut.

10. Compress and install the coil spring on the strut. Lubricate the strut rod.

11. Install the rubber seat, spring upper seat with rubber mounting bracket and strut rod nut on the strut. Tighten to 40–50 ft. lbs. (55–68 Nm).

12. Release the spring compressor and install the strut into the strut tower.

13. Install the spindle to strut mounting bolts. Tighten the bolts to 69–86 ft. lbs. (93–117 Nm). Final tightening must be done with the suspension loaded.

14. Install the rear brake assembly. Install the wheel and tire assembly and lower the vehicle.

Rear Control Arms

REMOVAL & INSTALLATION

1. Raise and safely support the vehicle. Remove the wheel and tire assembly.

2. Remove the rear disc brake caliper and rotor assembly.

3. Paint an aligning mark on each control arm and control arm bushing. Paint an aligning mark on each side of the trailing arm and crossmember.

4. Remove the stabilizer link assembly. Loosen and remove the stabilizer bar, bushings and the stabilizer.

5. Loosen both inner and outer low-

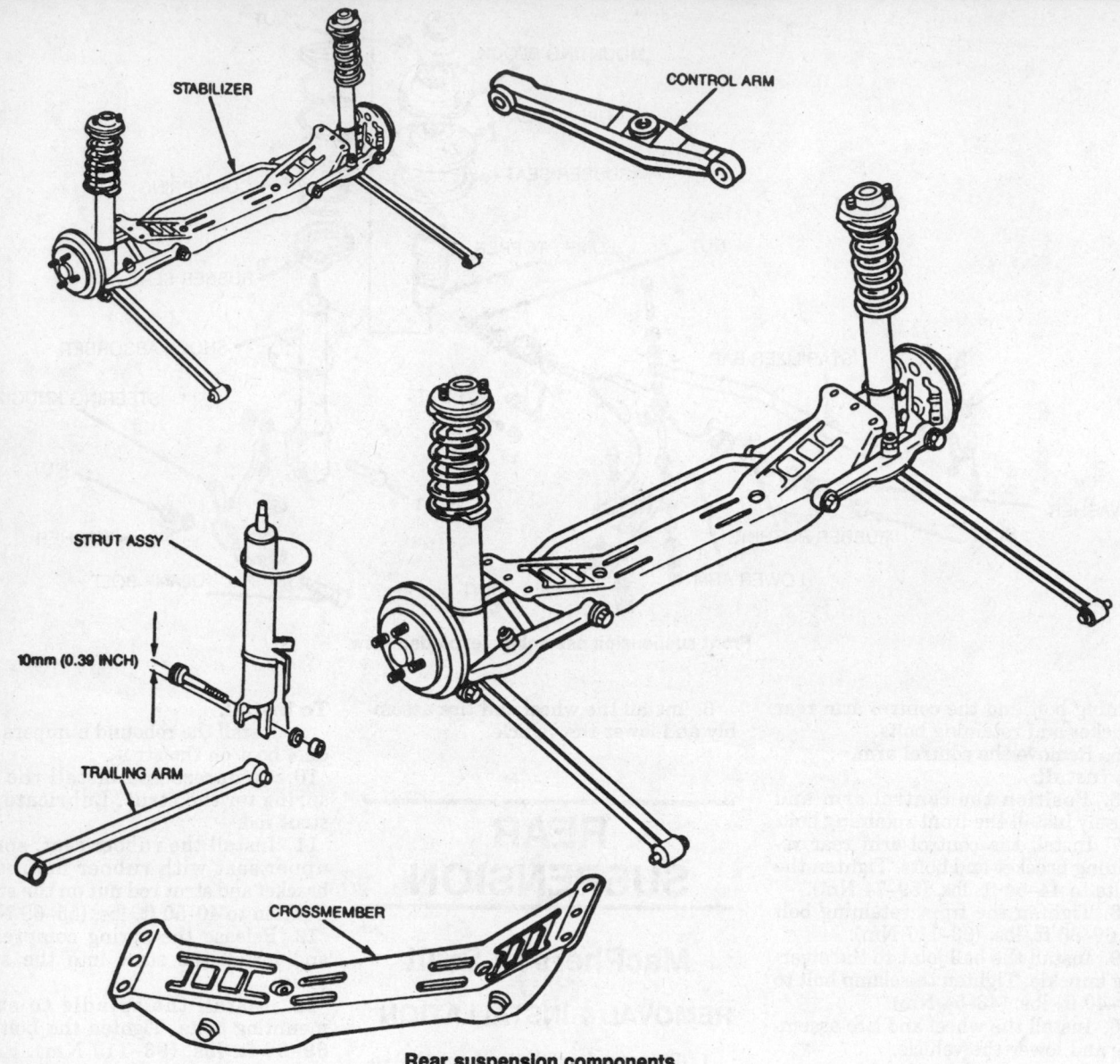

STABILIZER

CONTROL ARM

STRUT ASSY

10mm (0.39 INCH)

TRAILING ARM

CROSSMEMBER

Rear suspension components

er control arm bolts. Loosen the spindle to strut attaching bolts.

6. Remove the parking brake attaching bolt from the rear trailing assembly.

7. Loosen the trailing arm to strut attaching bolts.

8. When all control arm and trailing arm bolts are loosened, remove all the bolts and remove both the control arms and the trailing arm.

To install:

9. Mount the control arm and trailing arm on the rear crossmember and hand-tighten the bolts. Make sure the left and right arms are in the correct position.

10. Connect both control arms with the outer control arm bolt but do not install the spindle yet. Raise both control arms so the painted stripes align and tighten the rear control arm bolts.

11. Install the spindle in the strut. Tighten the spindle to strut attaching bolts to 69–86 ft. lbs. (93–117 Nm).

12. Install and tighten the control arm to spindle attaching bolt to 45–55 ft. lbs. (60–75 Nm).

13. Tighten the inner control arm bolt to 69–86 ft. lbs. (93–117 Nm).

14. Loosely install the rear stabilizer bar in the stabilizer bushing. Make sure the alignment stripe painted on the stabilizer bar aligns with the bushings. Do not fully tighten the bracket bolts yet.

15. Install the stabilizer link assembly. Tighten the stabilizer bushing bracket bolts to 32–39 ft. lbs. (45–55 Nm). Tighten the stabilizer link bolt until 0.310 in. (18mm) of thread extends beyond the nut. Final tightening must be done with the suspension loaded.

16. Install the rear brake assembly.

Install the wheel and tire assembly and lower the vehicle.

Rear Wheel Bearings

REMOVAL & INSTALLATION

1. Raise and safely support the vehicle. Remove the wheel and tire assembly.

2. Remove the 2 guide pin bolts from the caliper and lift the caliper clear of the disc with the inner cable and flexible hose attached. Tie the caliper to the strut spring.

3. Remove the grease cap. Carefully raise the staked portion of the locknut using a small cape chisel. Remove and discard the locknut.

NOTE: The locknuts are threaded left and right. The left hand threaded locknut is on the

right side of the vehicle. **Turn this locknut clockwise to loosen. The right hand threaded locknut is turned counterclockwise to loosen.**

4. Remove the washer and outer bearing from the bearing hub. Remove the brake rotor/bearing hub assembly.

5. Remove the bearing grease seal using a small prybar. Discard the seal.

6. Remove the inner bearing from the bearing hub.

NOTE: If the bearings are to be reused, they should be tagged so they can be reinstalled in their original positions.

7. If the bearings are to be replaced, remove the bearing races using a brass drift.

8. Clean the bearings with solvent and wipe out all the old grease from inside the hub.

To install:

9. If the bearing races were removed, install new ones using a brass drift.

10. Pack the bearings and the hub area with high temperature wheel bearing grease. Position the inner bearing in the hub.

11. Lubricate the lip of a new grease seal with grease. Install the seal using a seal installer.

12. Position the brake rotor/bearing hub assembly on the spindle.

NOTE: Keep the hub centered on the spindle to prevent damage to the grease seal and spindle threads.

13. Install the outer bearing, washer and a new locknut. Properly adjust the bearing preload.

14. Install the grease cap and the brake caliper. Install the wheel and tire assembly and lower the vehicle.

ADJUSTMENT

A staked attaching nut and a flat washer are used to hold the bearings and hub in position on the spindle shaft. The attaching nuts are left and right hand thread. The left hand threaded nut, located on the right side of the vehicle, must be turned counterclockwise to tighten and the right hand threaded nut, located on the left side of the vehicle, must be turned clockwise to tighten.

1. Make sure the parking brake is fully released.

2. Raise the vehicle and support it safely. Remove the wheel and tire assembly.

3. Remove the grease cap. Rotate the brake rotor to make sure there is

no brake drag. If the brakes drag, press on the inner brake pad to push the caliper piston back slightly.

4. With a small cape chisel, carefully raise the staked portion of the locknut.

5. Remove the locknut and discard. Install a new locknut.

6. To seat the bearings, torque the locknut to 18–22 ft. lbs. (25–29 Nm). Rotate the brake rotor by hand while tightening the locknut.

7. Loosen the locknut until it can be turned by hand.

8. Before the bearing preload can be set, the amount of seal drag must be measured and added to the the required preload. To measure the seal drag proceed as follows:

a. Install the proper size nut onto a wheel stud and rotate the brake rotor until the stud is in the 12 o'clock position.

b. Place an inch pound torque wrench onto the nut to measure the amount of force required to rotate the brake rotor.

c. Pull the torque wrench and note and record the torque reading when rotation begins. This value will be used to calculate the bearing preload range.

9. The required preload range, without seal drag, is 1.3–4.3 inch lbs. (0.15–0.49 Nm). To calculate the preload, add the seal drag value obtained in Step 8c to the minimum and maximum preload specifications. For example, if the seal drag was 2.2 inch lbs. (0.25 Nm), then the minimum preload specification would be 1.3 inch lbs. (0.15 Nm) + 2.2 inch lbs. (0.25 Nm) = 3.5 inch lbs. (0.40 Nm) and the maximum preload specification would be 4.3 inch lbs. (0.49 Nm) + 2.2 inch lbs. (0.25 Nm) = 6.5 inch lbs. (0.74 Nm). Therefore, for a seal drag of 2.2 inch lbs. (0.25 Nm), the bearing preload should be within the range of 3.5–6.5 inch lbs. (0.40–0.74 Nm).

10. After the preload range is determined, tighten the locknut slightly.

11. Rotate the brake rotor until the nut and wheel are returned to the 12 o'clock position. Position the inch lb. torque wrench onto the nut and measure the amount of pull required to rotate the brake rotor. Tighten the locknut until the torque shown on the torque wrench is within the range that was calculated in Step 9.

12. Using a cold chisel with the cutting edge rounded, stake the locknut in place.

NOTE: If the nut splits or cracks after staking, it must be replaced with a new nut.

13. Install the grease cap.

14. Install the wheel and tire assembly. Lower the vehicle.

STEERING

Steering Wheel

REMOVAL & INSTALLATION

NOTE: If the steering wheel is not centered, check the toe adjustment. Do not attempt to center the steering wheel by removing it and changing its position on the steering shaft.

1. Disconnect the negative battery cable.

2. Lower the glove compartment door fully by depressing the stops.

3. Disconnect the electrical connector from the battery backup, which is a blue rectangular box on the outer left side of the glove compartment and attached to the instrument panel.

NOTE: The backup power supply provides air bag firing circuit power if the battery or battery cables are damaged or cut very early in an accident before the sensors can close. The battery backup contains a capacitor that takes approximately 15 minutes to discharge after the battery is disconnected.

4. Remove the 4 nuts from the back of the steering wheel and remove the air bag module. Disconnect the air bag module connector.

— **CAUTION** —
When carrying a live air bag, make sure the bag and trim cover are pointed away from the body. In the unlikely event of an accidental deployment, the bag will then deploy with minimal chance of injury. In addition, when placing a live air bag on a bench or other surface, always face the bag and trim cover up, away from the surface. This will reduce the motion of the unit if it is accidentally deployed.

5. Loosen the steering wheel retaining bolt 4–6 turns.

NOTE: Do not use a knock-off type steering wheel puller or strike the steering wheel or shaft with a hammer. A sudden impact could damage the bearing or start to collapse the steering column.

6. Position a steering wheel puller and tighten the bolt on the puller until the steering wheel is loose.

7. Remove the steering wheel puller, steering wheel retaining bolt and the steering wheel.

NOTE: Be careful when removing the steering wheel so as not to damage the clockspring or air bag module connector.

To install:

8. Install the steering wheel onto the shaft, making sure to align the index marks on the wheel and shaft end.

9. Install a new steering wheel retaining bolt and tighten to 23–33 ft. lbs. (31–45 Nm).

10. Connect the air bag module connector and install the air bag module. Tighten the 4 retaining nuts to 18–35 inch lbs. (2–4 Nm).

11. Connect the electrical connector to the battery backup and connect the negative battery cable.

12. Check the steering column for proper operation.

Steering Column

REMOVAL & INSTALLATION

1. Position the steering wheel in the straight-ahead position. Remove the ignition key and rotate the steering wheel slightly until it locks.

2. Disconnect the negative battery cable.

3. Lower the glove compartment door fully by depressing the stops.

4. Disconnect the electrical connector from the battery backup, which is a blue rectangular box on the outer left side of the glove compartment and attached to the instrument panel.

NOTE: The backup power supply provides air bag firing circuit power if the battery or battery cables are damaged or cut very early in an accident before the sensors can close. The battery backup contains a capacitor that takes approximately 15 minutes to discharge after the battery is disconnected.

5. Remove the 4 nuts from the back of the steering wheel and remove the air bag module. Disconnect the air bag module connector.

—— CAUTION ——

When carrying a live air bag, make sure the bag and trim cover are pointed away from the body. In the unlikely event of an accidental deployment, the bag will then deploy with minimal chance of injury. In addition, when placing a live air bag on a bench or other surface, always face the bag and trim cover up, away from the surface. This will reduce the motion of the unit if it is accidentally deployed.

6. Remove the steering column access panel and trim cover.

7. Remove the defroster duct connecting hose and remove the steering column lower shroud.

8. Loosen the steering column lower retaining nuts and remove the steering cloumn upper retaining bolts.

9. With the steering column resting on the instrument panel brace, remove the ignition lock shield and ignition switch retaining screw. The ignition switch will remove with the shield.

10. Disconnect the electrical connectors from the turn signal and hazard switch. Disconnect the harness connectors from the air bag module, key warning, windshield wiper switch and slip ring assembly.

11. Remove the steering shaft universal joint pinch bolt. Carefully pull the steering column out of the instrument panel to avoid damage to any wiring or components.

To install:

12. Carefully guide the column assembly into the instrument panel. Make sure the curl strap is installed correctly and the retaining clips are tight.

13. Connect the harness connectors for the air bag module, key warning, wiper switch and slip ring assembly. Connect the connectors to the turn signal switch and hazard switch.

14. Install the ignition switch and lock shield. Tighten the retaining bolts and nut to 11–14 ft. lbs. (15–19 Nm).

15. Connect the steering shaft universal joint and install the pinch bolt. Do not tighten the pinch bolt at this time.

16. Make sure the curl strap is in place with the retaining clips and install the upper column retaining bolts. Do not tighten the bolts at this time.

17. Tighten the lower column retaining nuts to 14–19 ft. lbs. (19–25 Nm). Tighten the upper bolts to 17–22 ft. lbs. (23–31 Nm). Tighten the universal joint pinch bolt to 14–19 ft. lbs. (19–25 Nm).

18. Install the defroster duct connecting hose, lower column shroud and access panel and trim cover.

19. Connect the air bag module connector and install the air bag module. Tighten the 4 retaining nuts to 18–35 inch lbs. (2–4 Nm).

20. Connect the electrical connector to the battery backup and connect the negative battery cable.

21. Check the steering column for proper operation.

Power Rack and Pinion

ADJUSTMENT

Rack Yoke Preload

NOTE: Readjusting the rack yoke preload will seldom cure hard steering or poor steering wheel return following a turn. First, check for damage that would be caused by an impact with a curb. Then, check for tight universal joints in the steering column and for tight or binding suspension parts.

1. Remove the steering rack from the vehicle.

2. Measure the pinion torque using an inch pound torque wrench and pinion adapter T87C–3504–C or equivalent. The torque should be 6–13 inch lbs. (0.6–1.5 Nm).

3. If the pinion torque is not within specification, readjust the pinion torque by tightening or loosening the adjusting plug.

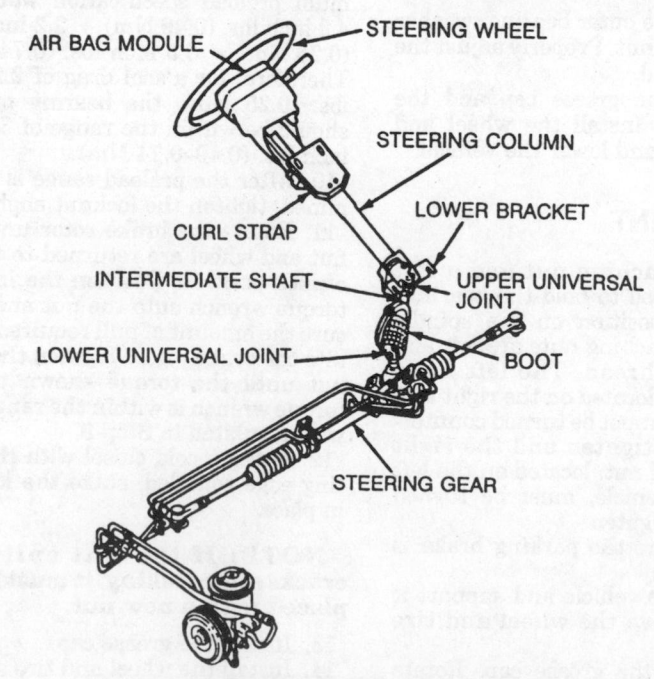

AIR BAG MODULE — STEERING WHEEL — STEERING COLUMN — LOWER BRACKET — CURL STRAP — INTERMEDIATE SHAFT — UPPER UNIVERSAL JOINT — LOWER UNIVERSAL JOINT — BOOT — STEERING GEAR

Steering system components

REMOVAL & INSTALLATION

1. Disconnect the battery cables and remove the battery.
2. Raise and safely support the vehicle. Remove the front wheel and tire assemblies.
3. Separate both tie rod ends from their steering knuckles. Remove the plastic dust shield from the right side lower inner fender.
4. Lower the vehicle, but do not allow anything but the rear wheels to touch the ground.
5. Using a pair of diagonal cutters, cut the plastic wire tie clamping the steering column dust boot to the steering gear.
6. Pull back the dust boot and have an assistant turn the steering column shaft until the clamp bolt is accessible, then lock the steering column.
7. Pull back the dust boot and paint an aligning mark on the steering column pinion shaft and the intermediate shaft lower universal joint.
8. Remove the clamp bolt from the intermediate shaft lower universal joint.
9. Using a 17mm crowfoot line wrench, loosen and remove the power steering gear return hose.
10. Using a 14mm socket, loosen and remove the banjo bolt from the power steering gear pressure hose. Discard the 2 copper washers.
11. Position the hoses aside and remove the steering gear attaching bolts.
12. Lower the steering gear until the steering shaft is clear of the intermediate shaft universal joint.
13. Carefully slide the steering gear out of the right side fender well through the tie rod opening.

To install:

14. Slide the steering gear into position through the right side lower inner fender well opening. Position the pinion shaft so it is just below the intermediate shaft universal joint.
15. Lower the vehicle enough to allow access under it. Raise the steering gear from under the vehicle and slide into position.
16. Have an assistant guide the pinion shaft into the intermediate shaft lower universal joint while at the same time making sure the alignment marks line up.
17. Install the attaching bolts through the steering gear mounting bracket and into the dash panel. Tighten to 23–34 ft. lbs. (32–47 Nm).
18. Install the clamp bolt in the intermediate shaft lower universal joint and tighten securely.
19. Attach the hoses from the power steering pump to the steering gear. Install new copper washers on the pressure line banjo fitting.
20. Connect the tie rod ends to the steering knuckle. Fill the reservoir with fluid.
21. Install the battery and connect the battery cables. Install the wheel and tire assemblies.
22. Bleed the hydraulic lines by starting the vehicle and slowly turning the steering wheel back and forth, lock to lock. Check the fluid level often.
23. Check for leaks and add fluid, as necessary.
24. Install the plastic dust shield on the right side lower inner fender. Lower the vehicle.

Power Steering Pump

REMOVAL & INSTALLATION

1. Disconnect the negative battery cable.
2. Remove the right-hand radiator support and brace. Remove the pump drive belt.
3. Disconnect the intercooler outlet hose at the throttle inlet, if equipped, and position out of the way.
4. Remove the ground wire from the engine lifting eye and remove the wire from the pressure switch.
5. Place a drain pan below the power steering pump. Remove the inlet and return hoses from the pump and plug.
6. Remove the adjusting screw, nut and block from the bracket. Remove the pivot bolt.
7. Position the pump below the pump bracket in the engine compartment. Remove the pump bracket retaining nut, bolts and pump bracket. Remove the pump.

To install:

8. Position the power steering pump in the engine compartment below the pump bracket mounting stud.
9. Install the power steering pump bracket. Tighten the retaining bolts and nut to 27–38 ft. lbs. (37–52 Nm).
10. Install the pump on the pump bracket and install the pivot bolt finger-tight.
11. Install the adjusting screw block, nut and screw finger-tight. Install the drive belt, adjust the tension and tighten the bolts.
12. Connect the pressure switch wire and install the ground wire onto the engine lifting eye bracket.
13. Install the pressure and return hoses. Connect the intercooler outlet hose, if equipped.
14. Install the right-hand radiator support and brace. Fill the pump reservoir with fluid and bleed the system.

BELT ADJUSTMENT

1. Inspect the condition of the power steering pump drive belt and replace, if necessary.
2. Loosen the locknut and adjuster bolt at the pump.
3. Adjust the belt tension, using the deflection method or using a belt tension gauge. Check the deflection or position the gauge at the center of the longest accessible belt span.
4. Tighten or loosen the adjusting bolt to adjust the belt tension.
5. New or used belts should have 0.31–0.35 in. (8–9mm) deflection with approximately 22 lbs. pressure applied or 110–132 lbs. tension, using a gauge.
6. Tighten the locknut to 32–45 ft. lbs. (43–61 Nm).

SYSTEM BLEEDING

1. Disconnect the coil wire. Raise and safely support the front of the vehicle.
2. Fill the pump reservoir with the proper type of fluid.
3. Crank the engine with the starter. Add fluid until the level remains constant.
4. While cranking the engine, rotate the steering wheel from stop to stop.

NOTE: The front wheels must be off the ground during stop-to-stop rotation of the steering wheel.

5. Check the fluid level and add, if necessary. Connect the coil wire.
6. Start the engine and allow it to run for several minutes.
7. Rotate the steering wheel from far left to far right several times.
8. Turn OFF the engine and check the fluid level. Add fluid if necessary.
9. Lower the vehicle.

Tie Rod Ends

REMOVAL & INSTALLATION

1. Disconnect the negative battery cable. Remove the front wheel and tire assembly.
2. Remove the cotter pin and tie rod end attaching nut.
3. Separate the tie rod end from the steering knuckle using tie rod end separator tool T85M-3395-A or equivalent. If the tie rod end does not separate easily, give the steering knuckle a sharp blow with a brass hammer or drift.
4. Paint an aligning stripe on the tie rod end, jam nut and tie rod. Loosen the jam nut and remove the tie rod end.

To install:

5. Thread the jam nut and tie rod end onto the tie rod. Align the index mark on the tie rod end, jam nut and tie rod. Tighten the jam nut.

6. Install the tie rod end into the steering knuckle. Tighten the attaching nut to 26–29 ft. lbs. (35–40 Nm).

NOTE: If the slots in the nut do not align with the hole in the ball joint stud, tighten the nut for proper alignment. Never loosen the nut.

7. Install a new cotter pin. Install the wheel and tire assembly and lower the vehicle. Check the toe adjustment.

BRAKES

Master Cylinder

REMOVAL & INSTALLATION

NOTE: Pump the brake pedal several times to exhaust any vacuum in the booster.

1. Disconnect the brake lines from the master cylinder. Cap the lines and master cylinder ports.
2. Remove the vacuum valve from the booster and disconnect the pressure warning switch connector.
3. Remove the 2 nuts and lockwashers retaining the master cylinder to the brake booster. Remove the master cylinder from the booster.

NOTE: It may be necessary to insert a small prybar between the booster and the master cylinder to free the master cylinder.

To install:
4. Position the master cylinder onto the booster assembly studs. Install the 2 lockwashers and nuts and tighten to 8–11 ft. lbs. (10–16 Nm).
5. Install short brake lines in the master cylinder ports and position them so they point back into the reservoir and the ends of the lines are submerged in brake fluid.
6. Fill the reservoir with brake fluid and cover the reservoir with a shop towel.
7. Pump the brakes until clear, bubble-free fluid comes out of both brake lines. If any brake fluid spills on the paint, wash it off immediately with water.
8. Remove the short brake lines and connect the vehicle brake lines to the master cylinder. Bleed each brake line at the master cylinder using the following procedure:
  a. Have an assistant pump the brake pedal 10 times and then hold firm pressure on the pedal.
  b. Crack the rear most brake line fitting with a tubing wrench until a stream of brake fluid comes out. Have the assistant maintain pressure on the brake pedal until the brake line fitting is tightened again.
  c. Repeat this operation until clear, bubble free fluid comes out from around the brake line fitting.
  d. Repeat this bleeding operation at the front brake line fitting.
9. Install the vacuum valve to the booster and connect the pressure warning switch connector.
10. Make sure the reservoir is filled to the proper level. Bleed the brake system, if necessary.
11. Check and if necessary, adjust the stoplight switch.

Proportioning Valve

REMOVAL & INSTALLATION

The proportioning valves are an integral part of the master cylinder. The master cylinder must be removed and disassembled to gain access to the proportioning valves.

1. Remove the master cylinder and drain the brake fluid from the reservoir into a container. Mount the master cylinder in a soft-jawed vise.
2. Remove the proportioning valve end plugs. Use care as the end plugs are under spring tension.
3. Remove the internal and external O-rings from the valve end plugs. Remove the valve springs and plungers

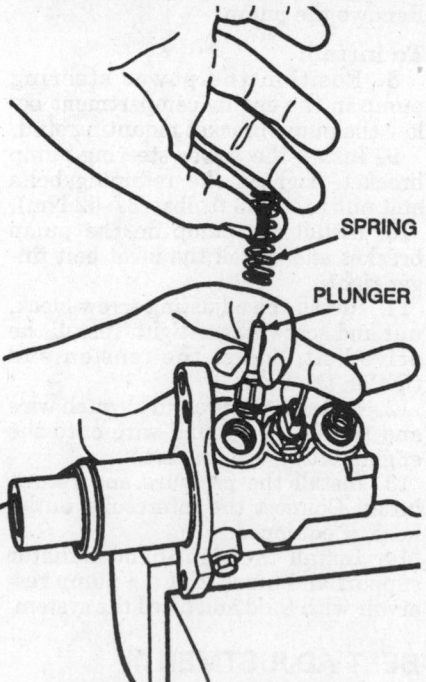

and remove the valve seals from the plungers.

To install:
4. Install a new valve seal onto the valve plungers with the serrations on the seal face away from the plungers.
5. Install new internal and external O-rings on the proportioning valve end plugs.
6. Lubricate the plunger seals with brake fluid. Install the valve springs over the plungers and position the valves into the cylinder bores.
7. Install the proportioning valve end plugs and tighten to 17–20 ft. lbs. (23–27 Nm).
8. Install the master cylinder.

Power Brake Booster

REMOVAL & INSTALLATION

NOTE: Pump the brake pedal several times to exhaust any vacuum in the booster.

1. Disconnect the battery cables and remove the battery. Remove the master cylinder.
2. Remove the rubber hose connecting the intake manifold to the power brake booster.
3. Working under the instrument panel, remove the spring clip in the brake pedal clevis pin.
4. Remove the brake pedal clevis pin and the brake pedal pushrod from the brake pedal.
5. Remove the 4 retaining nuts that hold the booster to the dash panel. Remove the booster.

To install:
6. Have an assistant position the power brake booster on the dash panel so the 4 retaining studs protrude through the dash panel into the passenger compartment.
7. Working under the instrument panel, install the 4 retaining nuts. Tighten to 14–19 ft. lbs. (19–26 Nm).
8. Apply multi-purpose grease to the clevis pin and install it through the brake pedal pushrod and the brake pedal. Install the clevis pin spring clip in the clevis pin.
9. From under the hood, install the rubber hose connecting the power brake booster to the intake manifold. Make sure the hose is installed correctly.
10. Install the master cylinder. Install the battery and connect the battery cables.

Brake Caliper

REMOVAL & INSTALLATION

Front

1. Raise and safely support the ve-

SPRING

PLUNGER

Proportioning valve installation

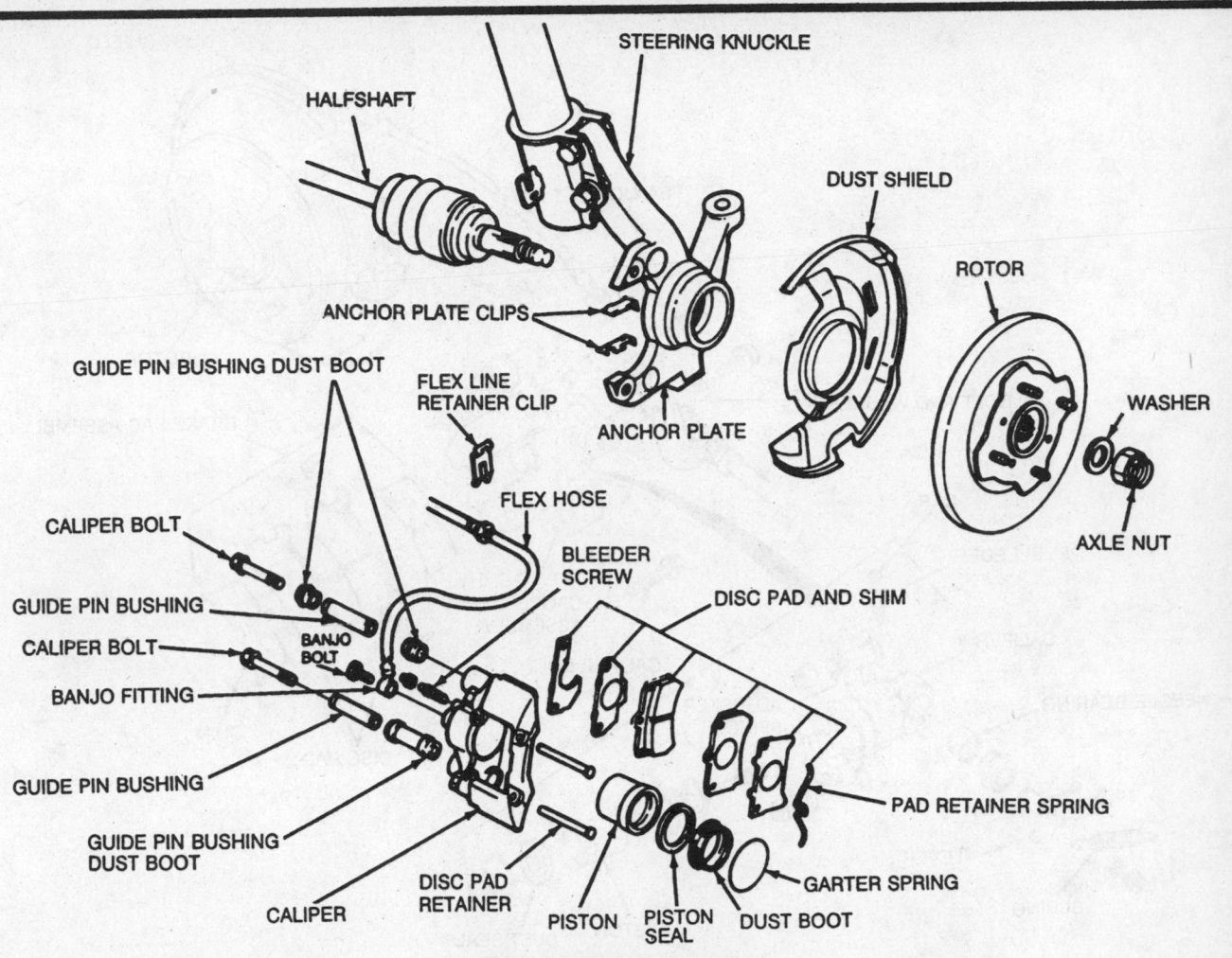

Front disc brake assembly

Labels on diagram:
HALFSHAFT — STEERING KNUCKLE — DUST SHIELD — ROTOR — WASHER — AXLE NUT — ANCHOR PLATE CLIPS — ANCHOR PLATE — GUIDE PIN BUSHING DUST BOOT — FLEX LINE RETAINER CLIP — FLEX HOSE — BLEEDER SCREW — DISC PAD AND SHIM — CALIPER BOLT — GUIDE PIN BUSHING — CALIPER BOLT — BANJO BOLT — BANJO FITTING — GUIDE PIN BUSHING — GUIDE PIN BUSHING DUST BOOT — CALIPER — DISC PAD RETAINER — PISTON — PISTON SEAL — DUST BOOT — GARTER SPRING — PAD RETAINER SPRING

hicle. Remove the front wheel and tire assembly.

2. Remove the disc brake pads.

3. Remove the banjo bolt attaching the brake flex hose to the caliper. Remove and discard the 2 copper washers.

4. Remove the caliper retaining bolts and lift the caliper off of the rotor.

To install:

5. Before installing the caliper, remove the guide pin bushing dust boots and push out the caliper guide pin bushings.

6. Lubricate the guide pin bushings with disc brake caliper slide grease and install them in the caliper. Install the guide pin bushing dust boots.

7. Position the caliper over the rotor.

NOTE: To provide the necessary clearance, it may be necessary to pull outward slightly on the caliper bushings.

8. Install the caliper retaining bolts and tighten to 29–36 ft. lbs. (39–49 Nm).

9. Install 2 new copper washers and the banjo bolt on the flex hose banjo fitting. Position the flex hose on the caliper and install the banjo bolt. Tighten to 17–21 ft. lbs. (22–29 Nm).

10. Install the brake pads and shims. Bleed the front brakes and install the wheel and tire assembly.

11. Lower the vehicle.

Rear

1. Raise and safely support the vehicle. Remove the rear wheel and tire assembly.

2. Remove the disc brake pads.

3. Remove the attaching clip from the brake flex hose.

4. Remove the banjo bolt attaching the brake flex hose to the caliper. Remove and discard the 2 copper washers.

5. Remove the lower caliper attaching bolt.

6. Using a cold chisel, remove the upper caliper guide pin dust cap to gain access to the Allen head on the guide pin. Using an Allen wrench, remove the upper caliper guide pin.

7. Lift the caliper off the rotor.

To install:

8. Install the disc brake pads and shims.

9. Before installing the caliper, remove the upper guide pin and the lower guide pin bushing. Remove the guide pin and guide pin bushing dust boots.

10. Lubricate the upper guide pin and lower guide pin bushing with disc brake caliper slide grease. Install the guide pin and guide pin bushing dust boots.

11. Position the caliper over the rotor. To provide the necessary clearance, it may be necessary to rotate the piston into the caliper.

12. Tighten the upper guide pin with an Allen wrench and install the dust cap with a plastic hammer.

13. Install the lower caliper attaching bolt through the caliper guide pin bushing. Tighten to 29–36 ft. lbs. (39–49 Nm).

14. Install 2 new copper washers and the banjo bolt on the flex hose fitting. Position the flex hose on the caliper and install the banjo bolt. Tighten the bolt to 17–21 ft. lbs. (22–29 Nm).

15. Bleed the brakes and install the

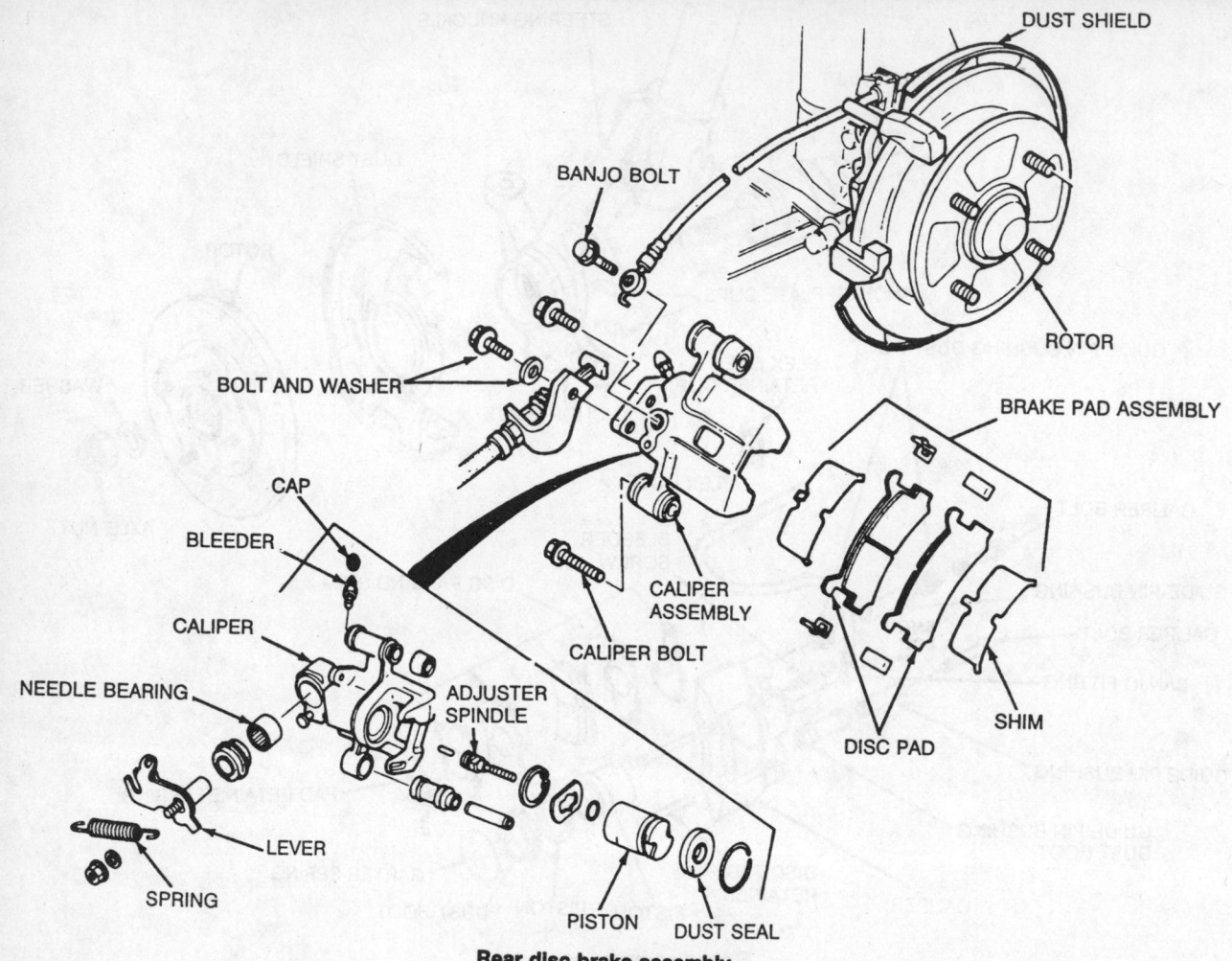

DUST SHIELD

BANJO BOLT

BOLT AND WASHER

ROTOR

CAP

BLEEDER

CALIPER

NEEDLE BEARING

ADJUSTER SPINDLE

CALIPER ASSEMBLY

CALIPER BOLT

BRAKE PAD ASSEMBLY

SHIM

DISC PAD

LEVER

SPRING

PISTON   DUST SEAL

Rear disc brake assembly

wheel and tire assembly. Lower the vehicle.

Disc Brake Pads

REMOVAL & INSTALLATION

Front

1. Remove approximately ⅔ of the brake fluid from the master cylinder.
2. Raise and safely support the vehicle. Remove the front wheel and tire assembly.
3. Using needle-nose pliers, remove the pad retainer spring that locks in the disc pad retainer pins.
4. Remove the disc pad retainer pins using a hammer and pin punch.
5. Using a small prybar, pry the caliper outboard and remove the outboard brake pad and shim. Tag the shims so they can be installed in their original position.
6. Push the caliper inboard with 1 hand and remove the inboard brake shoe and shims with the other hand. Be careful to prevent damage to the caliper piston dust boot.

7. Remove the anchor plate clips from the caliper anchor plate. Attach tape to the anchor plate clips and label **TOP** and **BOTTOM**.
8. Inspect the disc brake rotor for scoring or wear. Replace or machine, as necessary. If machining, observe the minimum thickness specification.
To install:
9. If removed, install the disc brake rotor and the caliper.
10. Install the anchor plate clips. If they are not installed in their original locations, the locating tabs may contact the rotor.
11. Push the caliper inboard and install the inboard brake pad and shims. Make sure the spring tabs on the back of the brake pad are properly aligned and fully seated in the caliper piston.
12. Pry the caliper outboard. Install the outboard brake pad and shim.
13. Install the brake pad retaining pins and install the retaining spring.
14. Install the wheel and tire assembly and lower the vehicle.
15. Pump the brake pedal several times to seat the brake pads. Check the fluid level in the master cylinder and add, if necessary.

Rear

1. Remove approximately ⅔ of the brake fluid from the master cylinder.
2. Raise and safely support the vehicle. Remove the rear wheel and tire assembly.
3. Using needle-nose pliers, remove the parking brake return springs at the back of the caliper.
4. Loosen the parking brake cable housing adjusting nut. Remove the cable housing from the bracket on the rear lower control arm.
5. Loosen the attaching bolt connecting the parking brake cable bracket to the rear caliper. Remove the parking brake cable from the rear caliper.
6. Loosen the lower caliper bolt. Pivot the caliper upward on the upper caliper guide pin.
7. Remove the disc pad retaining spring and remove the disc pads and shims.
8. Remove the anchor plate clips from the caliper anchor plate. Attach tape to the anchor plate clips and label **TOP** and **BOTTOM**.
9. Inspect the disc brake rotor for

scoring or wear. Replace or machine, as necessary. If machining, observe the minimum thickness specification.

To install:

10. If removed, install the disc brake rotor.

11. Install the anchor plate clips. If they are not installed in their original locations, the locating tabs may contact the rotor. Lubricate the anchor plate clips with disc brake caliper slide grease.

12. Install the shims on the backs of the pads and install in the anchor plate. Install the disc pad retaining spring.

13. Pivot the caliper down over the pads. If necessary, use a suitable tool to rotate the caliper piston into the caliper bore, to provide clearance. Install the lower caliper bolt and tighten to 29–36 ft. lbs. (39–49 Nm).

14. Install the parking brake cable in the caliper parking brake lever. Position the cable bracket against the rear caliper and install the cable attaching bolt.

15. Install the wheel and tire assembly.

16. Pump the brake pedal several times to seat the brake pads. Check the fluid level in the master cylinder and add, if necessary.

17. With the wheels off the ground, spin each wheel several times to make sure the calipers are not frozen and the parking brake is not adjusted too tight.

Brake Rotor

REMOVAL & INSTALLATION

Front

1. Raise and safely support the vehicle. Remove the front wheel and tire assembly.

2. Carefully raise the staked portion of the halfshaft attaching nut using a small cape chisel. Remove the halfshaft attaching nut and washer and discard the nut.

NOTE: When loosening the nut, lock the hub by applying the brakes.

3. Remove the stabilizer bar to control arm attaching bolt, nut, washers and bushings.

4. Remove the cotter pin and tie rod end attaching nut. Separate the tie rod end from the steering knuckle arm using a suitable tool. If the tie rod end does not separate easily, give the steering knuckle a sharp blow with a soft faced hammer to shock the taper.

5. Remove the U-shaped retaining clip from the center section of the caliper flex hose. Remove the disc brake pads and the caliper. Suspend the cali-

per from the strut spring; do not allow it to hang from the brake hose.

6. Remove the lower control arm ball joint clamp bolt and nut. Pry downward on the lower control arm to separate the ball joint from the steering knuckle.

7. Remove the steering knuckle to strut attaching bolts. Slide the hub/steering knuckle assembly out of its bracket in the strut and off the end of the halfshaft. Use care to prevent damage to the grease seals.

NOTE: If the hub binds on the halfshaft splines, it can be loosened bylightly tapping with a plastic faced hammer on the end of the halfshaft. Never use a metal faced hammer as damage to the CV-joint internal components will result. If the halfshaft splines become rusted to the hub, a jaw type puller must be used to separate them.

8. Remove the hub and rotor assembly from the steering knuckle using knuckle puller T87C–1104–A or equivalent.

9. If the rotor is to be reused, paint aligning marks on the hub and rotor assembly so they can be assembled in the same position. Remove the attaching bolts and separate the rotor from the hub. It may be helpful to mount the rotor in a soft jawed vise.

10. Inspect the rotor for scoring and wear. Replace or machine as necessary. If machining, observe the minimum thickness specification.

To install:

11. Position the hub on the rotor and install the attaching bolts. Make sure the index marks on the hub and rotor align. Tighten the attaching bolts to 33–40 ft. lbs. (44–54 Nm).

12. Install the hub and rotor assembly in the steering knuckle using a hydraulic press and suitable fixtures.

13. Position the front hub/steering knuckle assembly over the halfshaft and into the strut. Install the steering knuckle to strut attaching bolts and nuts. Tighten the attaching nuts to 69–86 ft. lbs. (93–117 Nm).

14. Position the lower control arm ball joint through the steering knuckle and install the clamp bolt and nut. Tighten the clamp bolt to 32–40 ft. lbs. (43–54 Nm).

15. Position the brake caliper over the rotor and install the attaching bolts. Tighten to 29–36 ft. lbs. (39–49 Nm). Install the U-clip on the caliper flex line.

16. Install a new halfshaft attaching nut. Tighten to 116–174 ft. lbs. (157–235 Nm). Stake the halfshaft using a cold chisel with the cutting edge rounded.

NOTE: If the nut splits or

cracks after staking, it must be replaced with a new nut.

17. Connect the tie rod to the steering knuckle arm and install the attaching nut. Tighten to 22–33 ft. lbs. (29–44 Nm) and install a new cotter pin.

NOTE: If the slots in the nut do not align with the hole in the ball joint stud, tighten the nut for proper alignment. Never loosen the nut.

18. Position the stabilizer bar and install the stabilizer link assembly including the attaching bolt, nut, washers, sleeve and rubber bushings. Tighten the attaching nut until 0.43 in. (10.8mm) of the bolt threads extend beyond the nut.

19. Install the wheel and tire assembly and lower the vehicle.

Rear

1. Raise and safely support the vehicle. Remove the rear wheel and tire assembly.

2. Remove the grease cap. Carefully raise the staked portion of the spindle nut using a small cape chisel. Remove the spindle nut and washer and discard the nut.

NOTE: The locknuts are threaded left and right. The left hand threaded locknut is on the right side of the vehicle. Turn this locknut clockwise to loosen. The right hand threaded locknut is turned counterclockwise to loosen.

3. Remove the disc brake pads and caliper from the anchor plate. Support the caliper with mechanics wire hung from the spring; do not let the caliper hang from the brake hose.

4. Remove the rotor and inspect for scoring and wear. Replace or machine as necessary. If machining, observe the minimum thickness specification.

To install:

5. Install the rotor on the spindle. Properly adjust the bearing preload.

6. Install the caliper and brake pads.

7. Install the wheel and tire assembly and lower the vehicle.

Parking Brake Cable

ADJUSTMENT

1. Remove the rear console as follows:

a. Slide the front seats completely forward and remove the screws retaining the rear of the rear console.

b. Slide the front seat completely rearward and remove the screws retaining the rear console to the front console.

c. Raise the parking brake lever as far as it will go. Raise the rear of the rear console and pull backwards to remove.

d. Release the parking brake lever.

2. Loosen the locknut.

3. Loosen or tighten the adjusting nut so the parking brake begins to apply when the lever is pulled up 5 notches and is fully set at 7–11 notches.

4. Using spring scale tool T74P–3504–Y or equivalent, check the force required to apply the parking brake. A properly operating system will require 44 lbs. of force to fully apply the parking brakes.

5. Tighten the locknut against the adjusting nut.

6. Make sure the brakes do not drag when the parking brake lever is released. Make sure the brake warning light illuminates when the parking brake lever is raised.

7. Install the rear console by reversing the removal procedure.

REMOVAL & INSTALLATION

1. Raise and safely support the vehicle. Remove the rear wheel and tire assemblies.

2. Using a pair of needle-nose pliers, remove the parking brake return springs at the back of each caliper.

3. Loosen the parking brake cable housing adjusting nut. Loosen the attaching bolt connecting the parking brake cable bracket to the rear caliper.

4. Remove the parking brake cable from both calipers. Remove the cable housing clamps from the rear suspension trailing arms.

5. Remove the cable housing clamp from the trailing arm support bracket. With a small prybar, gently ease the plastic cable bushings out of the brackets.

6. Disconnect the parking brake return spring from the equalizer. Remove each cable from the equalizer.

To install:

7. Install the 2 cable ends in the parking brake equalizer. Install the 2 plastic cable guides into the brackets using a plastic hammer.

8. Install the threaded ends of the cable housings into the brackets and install the adjuster nuts. Tighten to 12–16 ft. lbs. (16–23 Nm).

9. Install the parking brake cable in the caliper parking brake lever. Position the cable bracket against the rear caliper and install the cable attaching bolt. Tighten to 28–36 ft. lbs. (37–49 Nm).

10. Install the parking brake return springs at the back of each caliper.

11. Install the cable housing support

clamps and install the equalizer return spring.

12. Adjust the parking brake.

Brake System Bleeding

1. Clean all dirt from the master cylinder filler cap.

2. If the master cylinder is known or suspected of having air in the bore, it must be bled before any of the calipers. Bleed the master cylinder as follows:

a. Using a tubing wrench, remove the brake lines from the master cylinder.

b. Install short brake lines in the master cylinder and position them so they point back into the reservoir and the ends of the lines are submerged in brake fluid.

c. Fill the reservoir with brake fluid and cover the reservoir with a shop towel.

d. Pump the brakes until clear, bubble-free fluid comes out of both brake lines. If any brake fluid spills on the paint, wash it off immediately with water.

e. Remove the short brake lines and connect the vehicle brake lines to the master cylinder.

f. Have an assistant pump the brake pedal 10 times and then hold firm pressure on the pedal.

g. Crack the rear most brake line fitting with a tubing wrench until a stream of brake fluid comes out. Have the assistant maintain pressure on the brake pedal until the brake line fitting is tightened again.

h. Repeat this operation until clear, bubble free fluid comes out from around the brake line fitting.

i. Repeat this bleeding operation at the front brake line fitting.

3. To bleed the calipers, proceed as follows:

a. Begin at the right rear bleeder screw.

b. Attach a rubber drain hose to the bleeder screw. The end of the tube should fit snugly around the end of the bleeder screw.

c. Place the free end of the hose in a container partially filled with clean brake fluid.

d. Have an assistant apply and maintain pressure on the brake pedal.

e. Loosen the bleeder screw approximately ¾ turn. It is very important the helper maintain constant pressure on the pedal until the pedal drops all the way down and the bleeder screw is closed again. If the pedal pressure is released, air will be drawn back into the system.

f. Tighten the bleeder screw and release the brake pedal.

g. Repeat this operation until the fluid is clear and no more air bubbles appear at the submerged end of the hose.

h. Repeat these steps at the other calipers in the following order: left rear, then right front, then left front. Maintain proper fluid level in the reservoir at all times.

4. Top up the brake fluid when bleeding is complete. Never reuse brake fluid.

CHASSIS ELECTRICAL

Air Bag

DISARMING

1. Disconnect the negative battery cable.

2. Lower the glove compartment door fully by depressing the stops.

3. Disconnect the electrical connector from the battery backup, which is a blue rectangular box on the outer left side of the glove compartment and attached to the instrument panel.

NOTE: The backup power supply provides air bag firing circuit power if the battery or battery cables are damaged or cut very early in an accident before the sensors can close. The battery backup contains a capacitor that takes approximately 15 minutes to discharge after the battery is disconnected.

4. Remove the 4 nut and washer assemblies securing the air bag to the steering wheel. Disconnect the air bag connector from the clockspring.

— **CAUTION** —
When carrying a live air bag, make sure the bag and trim cover are pointed away from the body. In the unlikely event of an accidental deployment, the bag will then deploy with minimal chance of injury. In addition, when placing a live air bag on a bench or other surface, always face the bag and trim cover up, away from the surface. This will reduce the motion of the unit if it is accidentally deployed.

5. Attach a jumper wire to the air bag terminals on the clockspring.

6. Connect the negative battery cable and the battery backup.

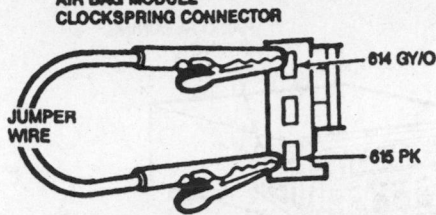

Jumper wire attached to air bag terminals on clockspring

Heater Blower Motor

REMOVAL & INSTALLATION

1. Disconnect the negative battery cable. Disconnect the electrical connector at the blower motor.

2. Remove the 3 screws retaining the motor and cover to the blower case. Remove the cover, cooling tube and blower motor.

3. Remove the nut retaining the blower wheel to the blower motor and remove the blower wheel. Remove the gasket from the blower motor.

To install:

4. Position the gasket onto the blower motor. Install the blower wheel and the attaching nut.

5. Position the blower motor, cooling tube and cover into the blower case. Install the mounting screws.

6. Connect the electrical connector to the blower motor and connect the negative battery cable.

7. Check blower motor operation.

Windshield Wiper Motor

REMOVAL & INSTALLATION

1. Disconnect the negative battery cable.

NOTE: Disconnect the linkage from the motor at the ball socket, not by removing the nut and linkage arm from the motor. This will eliminate the need to retime the motor/linkage.

2. Gently pry the linkage off the ball socket at the motor.

3. Disconnect the electrical connector from the motor.

4. Remove the 4 mounting bolts and rubber insulators securing the motor to the dash panel.

To install:

5. Position the motor and install the 4 mounting bolts and rubber

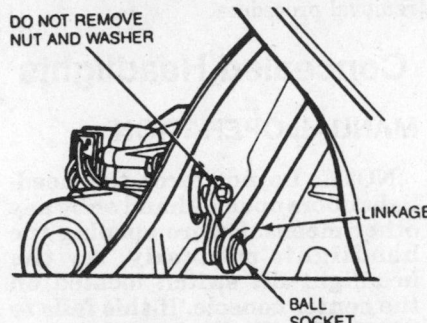

Windshield wiper motor removal procedure

insulators. Tighten to 5–7 ft. lbs. (7–10 Nm).

6. Connect the electrical connector to the motor.

7. Snap the linkage onto the ball socket.

8. Connect the negative battery cable and check the wipers for proper operation.

Instrument Cluster

REMOVAL & INSTALLATION

1. Disconnect the negative battery cable.

2. Remove the instrument cluster bezel as follows:

   a. Pull out the storage compartment. Remove the 2 upper screws, 2 lower screws and heater/radio bezel.

   b. Remove the trim covers located on both sides of the steering column by pulling outward.

   c. Remove the retaining screws and carefully pull the instrument cluster bezel partially away from the instrument panel.

   d. Disconnect the electrical connectors from the clock and the switches in the bezel.

3. Disconnect the speedometer cable at the transaxle.

4. Remove the screws and slide the instrument cluster outward.

5. Press the lock tab and release the speedometer cable from the instrument cluster.

6. Remove the connectors from the rear of the instrument cluster and remove the cluster.

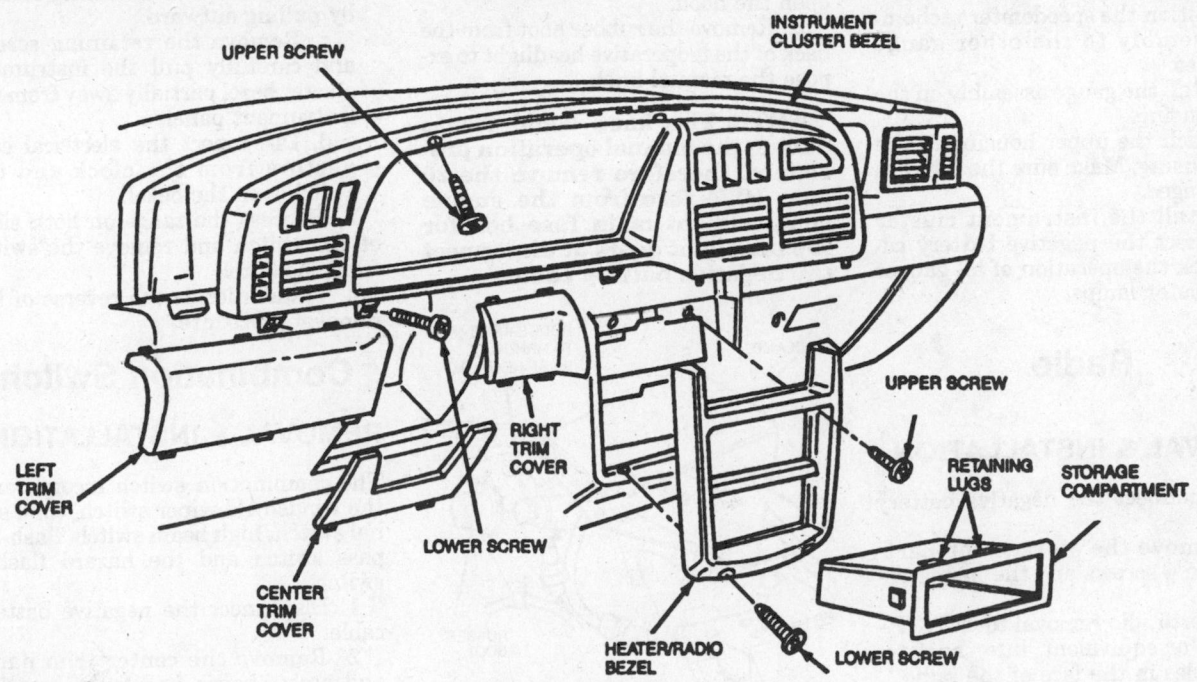

Instrument cluster bezel removal

To install:

NOTE: Before connecting the speedometer cable to the instrument cluster, apply a $^3/_{16}$ in. ball of silicone damping grease D7A7–19A331–A or equivalent, in the drive hole of the speedometer head.

7. Apply the grease and connect the speedometer cable and electrical connectors to the instrument cluster. Make sure the speedometer lock tab is fully engaged.

8. Slide the cluster into place and install the screws retaining the cluster to the instrument panel. Tighten the screws to 27–35 inch lbs. (3–4 Nm).

9. Connect the speedometer cable at the transaxle.

10. Install the instrument cluster bezel by reversing the removal procedure. Connect the negative battery cable.

Speedometer

REMOVAL & INSTALLATION

1. Disconnect the negative battery cable.

2. Remove the instrument cluster.

3. Release the tabs and separate the upper housing from the lower housing.

4. Remove the screws from the back of the instrument cluster and carefully remove the gauge assembly.

5. Separate the speedometer/tachometer gauge assembly from the other gauge assemblies.

To install:

6. Position the speedomter/tachometer assembly to the other gauge assemblies.

7. Install the gauge assembly on the lower housing.

8. Attach the upper housing to the lower housing. Make sure the tabs are fully engaged.

9. Install the instrument cluster and connect the negative battery cable. Check the operation of all gauges and indicator lamps.

Radio

REMOVAL & INSTALLATION

1. Disconnect the negative battery cable.

2. Remove the storage compartment, the 4 screws and the heater/radio bezel.

3. Insert radio removal tools T87P–19061–A or equivalent, into the 4 removal holes in the face of the radio.

4. Slide the radio rearward and dis-

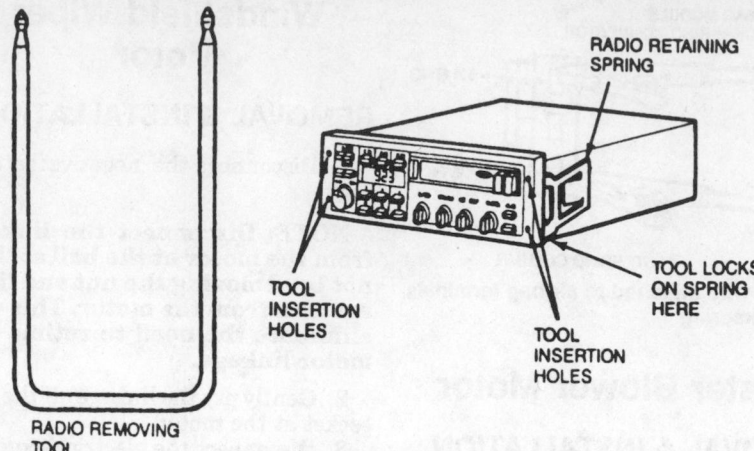

Radio removal procedure

connect the electrical connectors and antenna cable.

5. Remove the radio rear support retaining nut and support.

6. Installation is the reverse of the removal procedure.

Concealed Headlights

MANUAL OPERATION

NOTE: Do not force the headlight doors open by hand or by any other means. Before opening the headlights manually, try the headlight lift switch located on the center console. If this fails to lift the headlights, use the manual operation procedure.

1. Turn OFF the headlights and open the hood.

2. Remove the rubber boot from the back of the inoperative headlight to expose the manual knob.

NOTE: The knob could rotate during the manual operation procedure, therefore remove the 20 amp HLM fuse from the engine compartment main fuse box for the headlight doors or disconnect the negative battery cable.

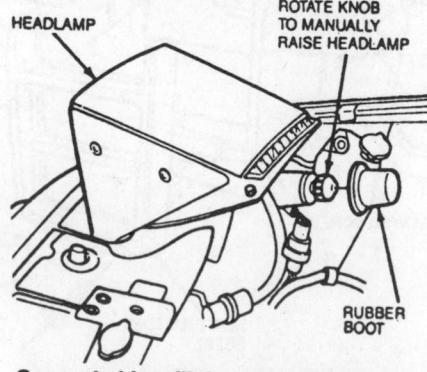

Concealed headlights manual operation

3. Turn the knob in either direction to open the headlight. Continue rotating the knob until the headlight is fully open.

4. Install the rubber boot. Install the fuse or connect the negative battery cable.

Headlight Switch

REMOVAL & INSTALLATION

1. Disconnect the negative battery cable.

2. Remove the instrument cluster bezel as follows:

   a. Pull out the storage compartment. Remove the 2 upper screws, 2 lower screws and heater/radio bezel.

   b. Remove the trim covers located on both sides of the steering column by pulling outward.

   c. Remove the retaining screws and carefully pull the instrument cluster bezel partially away from the instrument panel.

   d. Disconnect the electrical connectors from the clock and the switches in the bezel.

3. Depress the tangs on both sides of the switch and remove the switch from the bezel.

4. Installation is the reverse of the removal procedure.

Combination Switch

REMOVAL & INSTALLATION

The combination switch incorporates the windshield wiper switch, turn signal switch, high beam switch, flash-to-pass switch and the hazard flasher switch.

1. Disconnect the negative battery cable.

2. Remove the center trim panel and access cover under the steering column.

3. Remove the lower steering column shroud.

4. Remove the steering column upper retaining bolts and allow the column to rest on the instrument panel brace.

NOTE: Make sure no wires are pinched when lowering the column.

5. Remove the 2 switch retaining screws and remove the switch.

6. Grasp the switch and lever firmly and pull the lever out of the switch. Disconnect the electrical connectors from the switch.

To install:

7. Align the key with the slot and install the lever in the switch assembly.

8. Connect the electrical connectors to the switch.

9. Position the switch on the steering column and install the retaining screws.

10. Make sure the column support bracket is in position. Raise the column into position and install the retaining bolts. Tighten to 17–23 ft. lbs. (23–31 Nm).

11. Install the lower column shroud. Install the access cover and trim panel.

12. Connect the negative battery cable. Check the switch for proper operation.

Ignition Lock

REMOVAL & INSTALLATION

Functional Lock

1. Disconnect the negative battery cable.

2. Remove the lower steering column shroud.

3. With the ignition key installed, rotate the ignition lock tumbler while pushing the release pin with an ⅛ in. drift.

4. Remove the tumbler assembly by pulling it out of the housing.

To install:

5. Install the ignition lock tumbler assembly with the ignition key installed. Make sure the tumbler is fully seated.

6. Install the lower column shroud.

7. Connect the negative battery cable and check for proper operation.

Non-Functional Lock

The following procedure applies to vehicles in which the ignition lock is inoperative and the lock cylinder cannot be rotated due to a lost or broken lock cylinder key, the key number is not known or the lock cylinder cap is damaged and/or broken to the extent that the lock cylinder cannot be rotated.

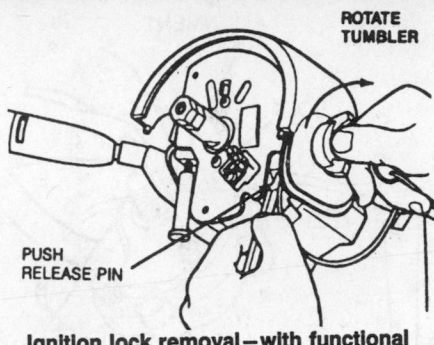

ROTATE TUMBLER

PUSH RELEASE PIN

Ignition lock removal—with functional lock

1. Disconnect the negative battery cable.

2. Remove the lower steering column shroud.

3. Using a ⅛ in. drill, drill out the retaining pin, being cautious not to drill deeper than ½ in.

4. Place a chisel at the base of the ignition lock cylinder cap and using a hammer, strike the chisel with sharp blows to break the cap away from the lock cylinder.

5. Using a ⅜ in. diameter drill, drill out the middle of the ignition lock key slot approximately 1¾ in. until the lock cylinder breaks loose from the breakaway base of the lock cylinder. Remove the lock cylinder and drill shavings from the lock cylinder housing.

6. Remove the snapring washer and steering column lock gear. Thoroughly clean all drill shavings and other foreign materials from the casting.

7. Carefully inspect the lock cylinder housing for damage. If any damage is apparent, the housing must be replaced.

To install:

8. Install the steering column lock gear and the snapring.

9. Install the ignition lock tumbler assembly with the ignition key installed. Make sure the tumbler is fully seated.

10. Install the lower column shroud.

11. Connect the negative battery cable and check for proper operation.

Ignition Switch

REMOVAL & INSTALLATION

1. Disconnect the negative battery cable.

2. Remove the lower steering column shroud. Remove the center access panel and trim cover under the steering column.

3. Remove the left side defroster connector tube.

4. Remove the steering column upper retaining bolts and allow the column to rest on the instrument panel brace.

NOTE: Make sure no wiring is pinched beneath the steering column when lowered.

5. Remove the ignition lock tumbler.

6. Remove the upper column cover and column lock shield.

7. Disconnect the ignition switch connector, remove the switch retaining screws and remove the switch.

To install:

8. Position the ignition switch to the column lock assembly. Make sure the actuator pin of the lock assembly fits into the slot in the ignition switch.

9. Install the switch retaining screws and tighten to 62–76 inch lbs. (7–9 Nm). Connect the switch electrical connector.

10. Install the column lock shield. Tighten the screws and nut to 14–18 ft. lbs. (19–25 Nm).

11. Install the upper column shroud and lock tumbler assembly. Make sure the tumbler snaps in place.

12. Raise the column and install the upper retaining bolts. Tighten to 17–23 ft. lbs. (23–31 Nm).

13. Install the defroster connector tube and the column lower shroud.

14. Install the access panel and trim cover. Connect the negative battery cable and check for proper operation.

Stoplight Switch

ADJUSTMENT

Check the distance from the brake pedal to the stoplight switch screw. The distance should be 0.078 in. (2mm). If necessary, adjust as follows:

1. Disconnect the negative battery cable. Disconnect the connector to the stoplight switch.

2. Loosen the locknut.

3. Adjust the distance by rotating the stoplight switch. Rotate the switch until the distance is within specification.

4. Tighten the locknut and connect the electrical connector.

5. Connect the negative battery cable. Check the operation of the stoplight switch and rear lights.

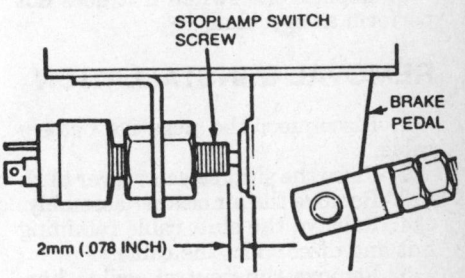

STOPLAMP SWITCH SCREW

BRAKE PEDAL

2mm (.078 INCH)

WITH PEDAL STOPPED WITHIN THE BOOSTER

Stoplight switch adjustment

REMOVAL & INSTALLATION

1. Disconnect the negative battery cable. Disconnect the connector to the stoplight switch.
2. Remove the nut securing the stoplight switch and remove the switch.
3. Installation is the reverse of the removal procedure. Adjust the switch.

Clutch Switch

ADJUSTMENT

1. Disconnect the negative battery cable.
2. Unplug the switch connector from the main wiring harness.
3. Connect an ohmmeter to the 2 terminals in the switch connector.
4. The ohmmeter should show continuity when the switch rod is pushed into the switch and no continuity with the switch rod released.
5. Replace the clutch switch if it does not perform as specified.

REMOVAL & INSTALLATION

1. Disconnect the negative battery cable.
2. Disconnect the electrical connector.
3. Remove the switch retaining nuts and remove the switch from the pedal bracket.
4. Installation is the reverse of the removal procedure.

Neutral Safety Switch

ADJUSTMENT

1. Disconnect the negative battery cable.
2. Unplug the switch connector from the main wiring harness.
3. Connect an ohmmeter between terminals **A** and **B** of the switch connector.
4. With the transmission shift selector lever in the **P** and **N** positions, there should be continuity between terminals **A** and **B**.
5. Replace the switch if it does not perform as specified.

REMOVAL & INSTALLATION

1. Disconnect the negative battery cable.
2. Place the shift selector lever in **N**.
3. Remove the air cleaner assembly.
4. Remove the shift cable retaining nut and disconnect the cable.
5. Remove the neutral switch harness from the metal retainers, cut the

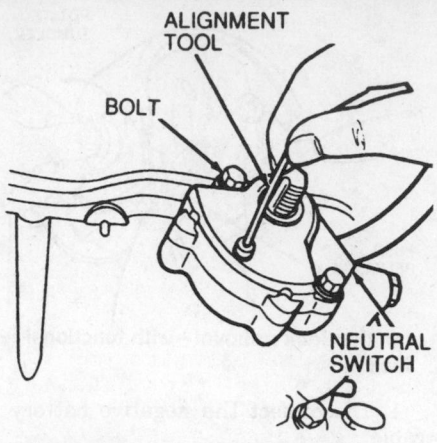

Neutral safety switch removal and installation

tapes and separate the harness from the sheathing.
6. Disconnect the electrical connectors.
7. Remove the retaining bolts and remove the switch.
To install:
8. Make sure the switch and shaft are in **N**. Install the switch.
9. Loosely install the retaining bolts. Remove the cover, screw and align the internal hole with the cover screw hole. Hold the alignment by inserting a 0.079 in. (2mm) pin through the holes.
10. Tighten the switch retaining screws to 71–97 inch lbs. (8–11 Nm).
11. Remove the pin, install the screw and tighten to 3–6 inch lbs. (0.4–0.7 Nm).
12. Route the harness into the sheathing and secure in the metal retainers. Connect the electrical connectors.
13. Install the shift cable and tighten the retaining nut to 33–47 ft. lbs. (44–64 Nm).
14. Install the air cleaner assembly.
15. Connect the negative battery cable. Check the switch for proper operation.

Fuses, Circuit Breakers and Relays

LOCATION

Fuses

The vehicle is equipped with 2 fuse panels. The main fuse panel protects the high current circuits and is located on the driver's side of the engine compartment. The interior fuse panel protects the lower current circuits and is located under the left side of the instrument panel.

Circuit Breakers

A 30 amp circuit breaker, used to protect the blower motor circuit, is attached to the interior fuse panel.

Relays

NOTE: A relay block is located just above the interior fuse panel.

Audio System Relay—located behind the lower left corner of the instrument panel.
Condenser Fan Relay—located at the left rear corner of the engine compartment, at the bulkhead.
Cooling Fan Relay—located at the left front of the engine compartment.
Foglight Relay—located at the left rear of the engine compartment, at the bulkhead.
Fuel Pump Relay—located below the center of the instrument panel, under the ECA.
Horn Relay—located at the left front of the engine compartment.
Ignition Key Relays—located behind the lower left side of the instrument panel.
Ignition Relay—located behind the lower left side of the instrument panel, at the joint box.
Main Relay—located at left front corner of engine compartment.

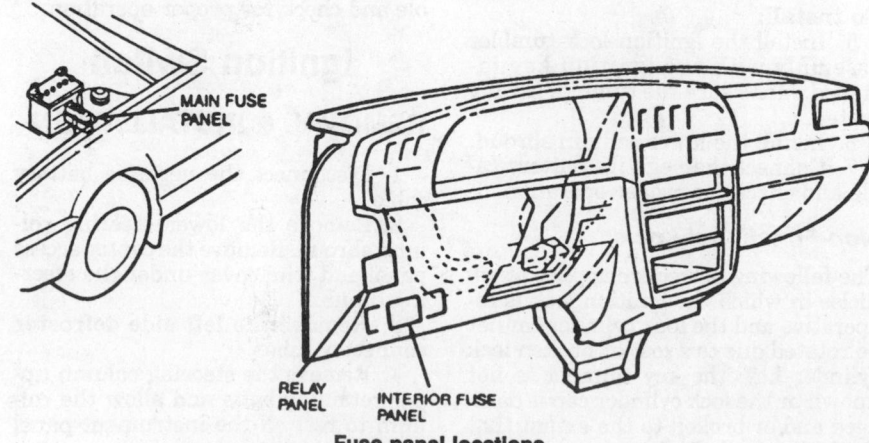

Fuse panel locations

Ford Motor Co.
Front Wheel Drive
MERCURY—Tracer

SPECIFICATIONS

VEHICLE IDENTIFICATION CHART

It is important for servicing and ordering parts to be certain of the vehicle and engine identification. The VIN (vehicle identification number) is a 17 digit number visible through the windshield on the driver's side of the dash and contains the vehicle and engine identification codes. The tenth digit indicates model year and the eighth digit indicates engine code. It can be interpreted as follows:

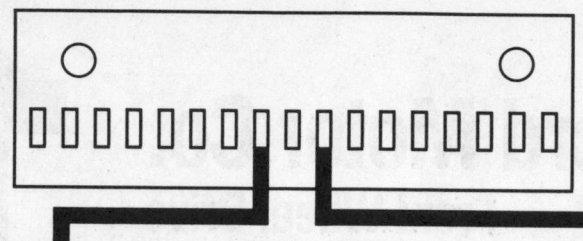

Engine Code

Code	Liters	Cu. In. (cc)	Cyl.	Fuel Sys.	Eng. Mfg.
5	1.6	98 (1597)	4	EFI	Ford
8	1.8	112 (1844)	4	EFI	Mazda
J	1.9	114 (1859)	4	EFI	Ford

EFI—Electronic Fuel Injection

Model Year

Code	Year
K	1989
L	1990
M	1991
N	1992
P	1993

ENGINE IDENTIFICATION

Year	Model	Engine Displacement Liters (cc)	Engine Series (ID/VIN)	Fuel System	No. of Cylinders	Engine Type
1989	Tracer	1.6 (1597)	5	EFI	4	OHC
1990	Tracer	1.6 (1597)	5	EFI	4	OHC
1991	Tracer	1.8 (1844)	8	EFI	4	DOHC
	Tracer	1.9 (1859)	J	EFI	4	OHC
1992-93	Tracer	1.8 (1844)	8	EFI	4	DOHC
	Tracer	1.9 (1859)	J	EFI	4	OHC

EFI—Electronic Fuel Injection
OHC—Overhead Camshaft
DOHC—Double Overhead Camshaft

GENERAL ENGINE SPECIFICATIONS

Year	Engine ID/VIN	Engine Displacement Liters (cc)	Fuel System Type	Net Horsepower @ rpm	Net Torque @ rpm (ft. lbs.)	Bore × Stroke (in.)	Compression Ratio	Oil Pressure @ rpm
1989	5	1.6 (1597)	EFI	82 @ 5000	92 @ 2500	3.07 × 3.29	9.3:1	50–64 @ 3000 ①
1990	5	1.6 (1597)	EFI	82 @ 5000	92 @ 2500	3.07 × 3.29	9.3:1	50–64 @ 3000 ①
1991	8	1.8 (1844)	EFI	127 @ 6500	114 @ 4500	3.27 × 3.35	9.0:1	43–57 @ 3000 ①
	J	1.9 (1859)	EFI	88 @ 4400	108 @ 3800	3.23 × 3.46	9.0:1	35–65 @ 2000 ①
1992-93	8	1.8 (1844)	EFI	127 @ 6500	114 @ 4500	3.27 × 3.35	9.0:1	43–57 @ 3000 ①
	J	1.9 (1859)	EFI	88 @ 4400	108 @ 3800	3.23 × 3.46	9.0:1	35–65 @ 2000 ①

NOTE: Horsepower and torque are SAE net figures. They are measured at the rear of the transmission with all accessories installed and operating. Since the figures vary when a given engine is installed in different models, some are representative rather than exact.
EFI—Electronic Fuel Injection
① Oil at normal operating temperature

GASOLINE ENGINE TUNE-UP SPECIFICATIONS

Year	Engine ID/VIN	Engine Displacement Liters (cc)	Spark Plugs Gap (in.)	Ignition Timing (deg.)		Fuel Pump (psi)	Idle Speed (rpm)		Valve Clearance	
				MT	AT		MT	AT	In.	Ex.
1989	5	1.6 (1597)	0.041	2B ①	2B ①	64–85 ②	800–900	800–900	0.012 ④	0.012 ④
1990	5	1.6 (1597)	0.041	2B ①	2B ①	64–85 ②	800–900	800–900	0.012 ④	0.012 ④
1991	8	1.8 (1844)	0.041	10B	10B	64–85 ②	700–800	700–800	Hyd.	Hyd.
	J	1.9 (1859)	0.054	10B	10B	35–40 ②	③	③	Hyd.	Hyd.
1992	8	1.8 (1844)	0.041	10B	10B	64–85 ②	700–800	700–800	Hyd.	Hyd.
	J	1.9 (1859)	0.054	10B	10B	35–40 ②	③	③	Hyd.	Hyd.
1993	SEE UNDERHOOD SPECIFICATIONS STICKER									

NOTE: The lowest cylinder pressure should be within 75% of the highest cylinder pressure reading. For example, if the highest cylinder is 134 psi, the lowest should be 101. Engine should be at normal operating temperature with throttle valve in the wide open position.
The underhood specifications sticker often reflects tune-up specification changes in production. Sticker figures must be used if they disagree with those in this chart.
B—Before Top Dead Center
Hyd.—Hydraulic
① Vacuum hoses disconnected and plugged
② Key on, engine off
③ Refer to Vehicle Emission Control information label
④ Engine warm

FIRING ORDERS

NOTE: To avoid confusion, always replace spark plug wires one at a time.

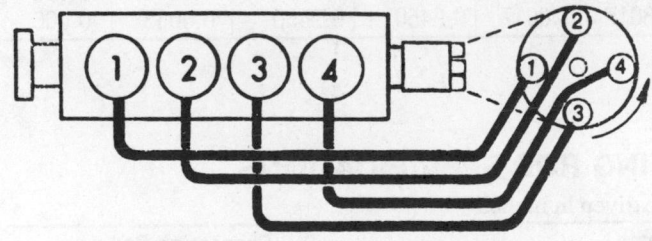

1.6L Engine
Engine Firing Order: 1–3–4–2
Distributor Rotation: Counterclockwise

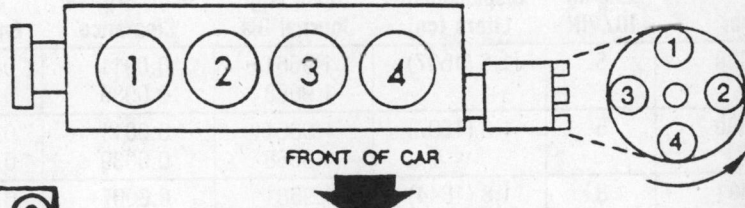

1.8L Engine
Engine Firing Order: 1–3–4–2
Distributor Rotation: Counterclockwise

1.9L Engine
Engine Firing Order: 1–3–4–2
Distributorless Ignition System

CAPACITIES

Year	Model	Engine ID/VIN	Engine Displacement Liters (cc)	Engine Crankcase with Filter (qts.)	Transmission (pts.) 4-Spd	Transmission (pts.) 5-Spd	Transmission (pts.) Auto.	Transfer case (pts.)	Drive Axle Front (pts.)	Drive Axle Rear (pts.)	Fuel Tank (gal.)	Cooling System (qts.)
1989	Tracer	5	1.6 (1597)	3.6	—	6.8	12	—	①	—	12.7	②
1990	Tracer	5	1.6 (1597)	3.6	—	6.8	12	—	①	—	12.7	②
1991	Tracer	8	1.8 (1844)	4.0	—	7.2	13.4	—	①	—	13.2	②
	Tracer	J	1.9 (1859)	4.0	—	5.6	13.4	—	①	—	11.9	②
1992–93	Tracer	8	1.8 (1844)	4.0	—	7.2	13.4	—	①	—	13.2	②
	Tracer	J	1.9 (1859)	4.0	—	5.6	13.4	—	①	—	11.9	②

① Included in transaxle capacity
② Manual transaxle—5.3 qts.
  Automatic transaxle—6.3 qts.

CAMSHAFT SPECIFICATIONS
All measurements given in inches.

Year	Engine ID/VIN	Engine Displacement Liters (cc)	Journal Diameter 1	Journal Diameter 2	Journal Diameter 3	Journal Diameter 4	Journal Diameter 5	Elevation In.	Elevation Ex.	Bearing Clearance	Camshaft End Play
1989	5	1.6 (1597)	1.7103–1.7112	1.6870–1.7091	1.7103–1.7112	—	—	1.4329–1.4437①	1.4329–1.4437①	②	0.002–0.008
1990	5	1.6 (1597)	1.7103–1.7112	1.6870–1.7091	1.7103–1.7112	—	—	1.4329–1.4437①	1.4329–1.4437①	②	0.002–0.008
1991	8	1.8 (1844)	1.0213–1.0222	1.0213–1.0222	1.0213–1.0222	1.0213–1.0222	1.0213–1.0222	1.7281–1.7360①	1.7480–1.7560①	0.0014–0.0032	0.003–0.007
	J	1.9 (1859)	1.8007–1.8017	1.8007–1.8017	1.8007–1.8017	1.8007–1.8017	1.8007–1.8017	0.2350–0.2400	0.2350–0.2400	0.0013–0.0033	0.002–0.006
1992–93	8	1.8 (1844)	1.0213–1.0222	1.0213–1.0222	1.0213–1.0222	1.0213–1.0222	1.0213–1.0222	1.7281–1.7360①	1.7480–1.7560①	0.0014–0.0032	0.003–0.007
	J	1.9 (1859)	1.8007–1.8017	1.8007–1.8017	1.8007–1.8017	1.8007–1.8017	1.8007–1.8017	0.2400–0.2450	0.2400–0.2450	0.0013–0.0033	0.002–0.006

① Specification is for total lobe height
② No. 1 and No. 3—0.0014–0.0059
  No. 2—0.0026–0.0059

CRANKSHAFT AND CONNECTING ROD SPECIFICATIONS
All measurements are given in inches.

Year	Engine ID/VIN	Engine Displacement Liters (cc)	Crankshaft Main Brg. Journal Dia.	Crankshaft Main Brg. Oil Clearance	Crankshaft Shaft End-play	Crankshaft Thrust on No.	Connecting Rod Journal Diameter	Connecting Rod Oil Clearance	Connecting Rod Side Clearance
1989	5	1.6 (1597)	1.9661–1.9668	0.0011–0.0039	0.003–0.012	4	1.7693–1.7699	0.0009–0.0039	0.012
1990	5	1.6 (1597)	1.9661–1.9668	0.0011–0.0039	0.003–0.012	4	1.7693–1.7699	0.0009–0.0039	0.012
1991	8	1.8 (1844)	1.9661–1.9668	0.0007–0.0014	0.003–0.012	4	1.7692–1.7699	0.0011–0.0027	0.004–0.012
	J	1.9 (1859)	2.2827–2.2835	①	0.004–0.008	3	1.7279–1.7287	0.0008–0.0026	0.004–0.014
1992–93	8	1.8 (1844)	1.9661–1.9668	0.0007–0.0014	0.003–0.012	4	1.7692–1.7699	0.0011–0.0027	0.004–0.012
	J	1.9 (1859)	2.2827–2.2835	①	0.004–0.008	3	1.7279–1.7287	0.0008–0.0026	0.004–0.014

① Without cylinder head—0.0018–0.0034
  With cylinder head—0.0011–0.0027

VALVE SPECIFICATIONS

Year	Engine ID/VIN	Engine Displacement Liters (cc)	Seat Angle (deg.)	Face Angle (deg.)	Spring Test Pressure (lbs. @ in.)	Spring Installed Height (in.)	Stem-to-Guide Clearance (in.) Intake	Stem-to-Guide Clearance (in.) Exhaust	Stem Diameter (in.) Intake	Stem Diameter (in.) Exhaust
1989	5	1.6 (1597)	45	45	NA①	NA①	0.0080②	0.0080②	0.2744–0.2750	0.2742–0.2748
1990	5	1.6 (1597)	45	45	NA①	NA①	0.0080②	0.0080②	0.2744–0.2750	0.2742–0.2748
1991	8	1.8 (1844)	45	45	NA③	NA③	0.0010–0.0024	0.0012–0.0026	0.2350–0.2356	0.2348–0.2354
	J	1.9 (1859)	45	45.6	200 @ 1.09	1.44–1.48	0.0008–0.0027	0.0018–0.0037	0.3159–0.3167	0.3149–0.3156
1992–93	8	1.8 (1844)	45	45	NA③	NA③	0.0010–0.0024	0.0012–0.0026	0.2350–0.2356	0.2348–0.2354
	J	1.9 (1859)	45	45.6	200 @ 1.09	1.44–1.48	0.0008–0.0027	0.0018–0.0037	0.3159–0.3167	0.3149–0.3156

NA—Not available
① Check spring free length and out of square.
    Free length: 1.665–1.720 in.
    Maximum allowable out of square: 0.059 in.

② Service limit
③ Check spring free length and out of square.
    Free length: 1.555–1.821 in.
    Maximum allowable out of square: 0.059 in.

PISTON AND RING SPECIFICATIONS

All measurements are given in inches.

Year	Engine ID/VIN	Engine Displacement liter (cc)	Piston Clearance	Ring Gap Top Compression	Ring Gap Bottom Compression	Ring Gap Oil Control	Ring Side Clearance Top Compression	Ring Side Clearance Bottom Compression	Ring Side Clearance Oil Control
1989	5	1.6 (1597)	0.0060①	0.006–0.012	0.006–0.012	0.008–0.028	0.0010–0.0030	0.0010–0.0030	SNUG
1990	5	1.6 (1597)	0.0060①	0.006–0.012	0.006–0.012	0.008–0.028	0.0010–0.0030	0.0010–0.0030	SNUG
1991	8	1.8 (1844)	0.0015–0.0020	0.006–0.012	0.006–0.012	0.008–0.028	0.0012–0.0028	0.0012–0.0028	SNUG
	J	1.9 (1859)	0.0016–0.0024	0.010–0.020	0.010–0.020	0.016–0.055	0.0015–0.0032	0.0015–0.0032	SNUG
1992–93	8	1.8 (1844)	0.0015–0.0020	0.006–0.012	0.006–0.012	0.008–0.028	0.0012–0.0028	0.0012–0.0028	SNUG
	J	1.9 (1850)	0.0016–0.0024	0.010–0.020	0.010–0.020	0.016–0.055	0.0015–0.0032	0.0015–0.0032	SNUG

① Maximum allowable

TORQUE SPECIFICATIONS

All readings in ft. lbs.

Year	Engine ID/VIN	Engine Displacement Liter (cc)	Cylinder Head Bolts	Main Bearing Bolts	Rod Bearing Bolts	Crankshaft Damper Bolts	Flywheel Bolts	Manifold Intake	Manifold Exhaust	Spark Plugs	Lug Nut
1989	5	1.6 (1597)	56–60	40–43	37–41	①	71–76	14–19	12–17	11–17	65–87
1990	5	1.6 (1597)	56–60	40–43	37–41	①	71–76	14–19	12–17	11–17	65–87
1991	8	1.8 (1844)	56–60	40–43	35–37	②	71–76	14–19	28–34	11–17	65–87
	J	1.9 (1859)	③	67–80	26–30	81–96	54–64	12–15	16–19	8–15	65–87
1992–93	8	1.8 (1844)	56–60	40–43	35–37	②	71–76	14–19	28–34	11–17	65–87
	J	1.9 (1859)	③	67–80	26–30	81–96	54–64	12–15	16–19	8–15	65–87

① Pulley bolts 36–45 ft. lbs.
    Sprocket bolt 80–94 ft. lbs.

② Pulley bolts 109–152 inch lbs.
    Sprocket bolt 80–87 ft. lbs.

③ Tighten in sequence to 44 ft. lbs.
    Loosen 2 turns

Retighten in sequence to 44 ft. lbs.
Turn all bolts, in sequence, 90 degrees
Turn all bolts, in sequence, an additional 90 degrees

BRAKE SPECIFICATIONS

All measurements in inches unless noted

Year	Model	Master Cylinder Bore	Brake Disc Original Thickness	Brake Disc Minimum Thickness	Maximum Runout	Brake Drum Diameter Original Inside Diameter	Brake Drum Diameter Max. Wear Limit	Brake Drum Diameter Maximum Machine Diameter	Minimum Lining Thickness Front	Minimum Lining Thickness Rear
1989	Tracer	0.875	①	②	0.003	7.870	7.910	NA	0.120	0.040
1990	Tracer	0.875	①	②	0.003	7.870	7.910	NA	0.120	0.040
1991	Tracer	0.875	③	④	0.004	9.000	9.040	NA	0.080	0.040
1992–93	Tracer	0.875	③	④	0.004	9.000	9.040	NA	0.080	0.040

NA—Not available
① Front 0.710
   Rear 0.390
② Front 0.630
   Rear 0.350
③ Front 0.870
   Rear 0.350
④ Front 0.790
   Rear 0.280

WHEEL ALIGNMENT

Year	Model		Caster Range (deg.)	Caster Preferred Setting (deg.)	Camber Range (deg.)	Camber Preferred Setting (deg.)	Toe-in (in.)	Steering Axis Inclination (deg.)
1989	Tracer	Front	$^{27}/_{32}$P–2$^{11}/_{32}$P	1$^{19}/_{32}$P	$^{1}/_{16}$P–1$^{9}/_{16}$P	$^{13}/_{16}$P	$^{5}/_{64}$	12$^{11}/_{32}$
		Rear	—	—	$^{3}/_{4}$N–$^{3}/_{4}$P	0	$^{5}/_{64}$	
1990	Tracer	Front	$^{27}/_{32}$P–2$^{11}/_{32}$P	1$^{19}/_{32}$P	$^{1}/_{16}$P–1$^{9}/_{16}$P	$^{13}/_{16}$P	$^{5}/_{64}$	12$^{11}/_{32}$
		Rear	—	—	$^{3}/_{4}$N–$^{3}/_{4}$P	0	$^{5}/_{64}$	
1991	Tracer	Front	1P–2$^{7}/_{8}$P	1$^{15}/_{16}$P	$^{27}/_{32}$N–1$^{1}/_{16}$P	$^{3}/_{32}$N	$^{3}/_{32}$	23$^{13}/_{16}$
		Rear	—	—	1$^{3}/_{32}$N–$^{7}/_{16}$P	$^{11}/_{32}$N	$^{3}/_{32}$	
1992–93	Tracer	Front	1P–2$^{7}/_{8}$P	1$^{15}/_{16}$P	$^{27}/_{32}$N–1$^{1}/_{16}$P	$^{3}/_{32}$N	$^{3}/_{32}$	23$^{13}/_{16}$
		Rear	—	—	1$^{3}/_{32}$N–$^{7}/_{16}$P	$^{11}/_{32}$N	$^{3}/_{32}$	

N—Negative
P—Positive

ENGINE MECHANICAL

NOTE: Disconnecting the negative battery cable on some vehicles may interfere with the functions of the on board computer systems and may require the computer to undergo a relearning process, once the negative battery cable is reconnected.

Engine Assembly

REMOVAL & INSTALLATION

1.6L Engine

1. Using a scratch awl, matchmark the hood hinges to the hood. Remove the hood-to-hinge bolts and the hood.

2. Properly relieve the fuel system pressure.

3. Disconnect the cables from the battery; negative cable first. Remove the battery-to-vehicle bolts and the tray.

4. Place a drain pan under the radiator. Remove the cooling system expansion tank cap, open the drain cock and drain the cooling system.

5. Drain the engine crankcase and the transaxle; discard the fluids.

6. Remove the air cleaner assembly and the dipstick.

7. Disconnect the electrical connector from the fan. Remove the fan shroud-to-radiator bolts, the fan and the shroud.

8. Disconnect the accelerator cable, the speedometer cable and the cruise control cable, if equipped.

9. Disconnect and plug the fuel lines.

10. Disconnect the heater hoses and the radiator hoses from the engine.

11. From the power brake booster, disconnect the vacuum hose.

12. Disconnect the carbon canister hoses.

13. Disconnect the engine ground wire and the electrical harness connectors which will interfere with the engine removal.

14. Remove the exhaust pipe-to-exhaust manifold bolts and separate the pipe from the manifold.

15. If equipped with air conditioning, remove the compressor from the engine bracket and move it aside; do not disconnect the hoses.

16. If equipped with power steering, remove the pump from the engine bracket and move it aside; do not disconnect pressure hoses.

17. If equipped with a manual transaxle, disconnect the clutch control cable. Disconnect the shift control cable (automatic) or rod (manual).

18. Raise and support the vehicle safely.

19. Remove the engine splash shield-

to-vehicle bolts and the shield. Remove the inner fender panel.

20. Remove the halfshafts from the vehicle.

21. Using a vertical lifting device, attach it to the engine and support its weight.

22. Remove the engine mount bolts and lift the engine/transaxle assembly from the vehicle. After removal, separate the engine from the transaxle.

To install:

23. Lower the engine/transaxle assembly into the vehicle.

24. Install the engine mount bolts.

25. Connect the halfshafts to the transaxle. Install the lower engine splash shield and the inner fender panel.

26. Connect the shift control cable or rod. On manual transaxle equipped vehicles, connect the clutch cable.

27. Connect the exhaust system components to the manifold. Lower the vehicle.

28. Install the air conditioning compressor and/or power steering pump, if equipped.

29. Reconnect all hoses and wires. Install the fan and fan shroud.

30. Install the remaining components in the reverse order of removal.

31. Refill the cooling system, the crankcase and the transaxle. Connect the battery. Install the hood.

32. Start the engine, allow it to reach normal operating temperature and check for leaks.

1.8L Engine

WITH AUTOMATIC TRANSAXLE

The 1.8L engine equipped with an automatic transaxle can be removed without removing the transaxle from the vehicle. The engine can be split from the transaxle and lifted out of the engine compartment.

1. Disconnect the negative battery cable.

2. Mark the position of the hood hinges and remove the hood.

3. If equipped with air conditioning, properly discharge the system.

4. Drain the cooling system.

5. Remove the air duct connecting the throttle body and resonance chamber.

6. Disconnect the power brake vacuum supply hose from the power booster.

7. If equipped with speed control, disconnect the necessary vacuum hoses from the intake plenum.

8. Disconnect the electrical connectors from the power steering pump, water thermoswitch, temperature sending unit, oil pressure switch, fuel injector wiring harness, exhaust gas oxygen sensor, throttle position sensor and distributor.

NOTE: Mark the position of the connectors prior to removal to ease reinstallation.

9. Disconnect all engine ground straps.

10. Disconnect the ignition coil high-tension lead from the distributor.

11. Disconnect the accelerator and kickdown cables from the throttle cam.

12. Remove the accelerator and kickdown cable bracket from the intake plenum and set the assembly aside.

13. Disconnect the heater core inlet and outlet hoses at the bulkhead.

14. Relieve the fuel system pressure.

15. Remove the necessary fuel line clips and disconnect the fuel pressure and return lines.

16. Remove the upper radiator hose.

17. Disconnect the electrical connectors from the cooling fan and the radiator thermoswitch.

18. Remove the starter motor.

19. Raise and safely support the vehicle.

20. Remove the right upper and both left and right lower splash shields.

21. Remove the radiator lower hose.

22. Disconnect the 2 transaxle cooling lines from the radiator and plug the lines.

23. Remove the air conditioner line routing bracket from the radiator and position the line aside.

24. Remove the halfshaft bearing support.

25. Remove the inspection plate from the oil pan, place a wrench on the crankshaft pulley, and rotate the crankshaft to gain access to the torque converter nuts. Remove the nuts.

26. Remove the power steering and air conditioner drive belt.

27. Remove the crankshaft pulley.

28. Remove the exhaust flex-pipe and mounting flange assembly from the exhaust manifold.

29. If equipped with air conditioning, remove the compressor.

30. Remove the power steering pump and bracket assembly with the hoses still connected. Suspend the pump with wire, aside of the work area.

31. Remove all accessible transaxle-to-engine bolts from the engine block.

32. Lower the vehicle.

33. Remove the radiator mounting brackets and the resonance duct.

34. Remove the radiator, fan and shroud assembly from the vehicle.

35. Remove the vacuum chamber canister located next to the intake plenum.

36. Remove the pressure regulator and bracket assembly and set it aside.

37. Remove the shutter valve actuator and bracket assembly and set it aside.

38. Remove the alternator and water

pump drive belt and remove the alternator.

39. Install a suitable engine removal sling onto the engine lifting brackets. Place a suitable engine hoist into position and support the engine.

40. Remove the oil pan-to-transaxle attaching bolts and the remaining transaxle-to-engine bolts from the engine block.

41. Remove the engine vibration dampener.

42. Remove the engine mount and the transaxle-to-engine upper right-hand bolt.

43. Carefully separate the engine from the transaxle, then remove the engine from the vehicle.

44. Install the engine onto an engine stand.

To install:

45. Install an engine removal sling onto the engine lifting brackets.

46. Place an engine hoist into position and install the engine sling. Remove the engine from the engine stand and lower it into the engine compartment.

47. Install the transaxle-to-engine upper right bolt and tighten to 41–59 ft. lbs. (55–80 Nm).

NOTE: Make sure the torque converter studs are properly seated in the flexplate mounting holes.

48. Install the engine mount. Tighten the bolt and nuts to 49–69 ft. lbs. (67–93 Nm).

50. Install the engine vibration dampener. Tighten the bolt and nuts to 41–50 ft. lbs. (55–80 Nm).

51. Remove the engine sling from the lifting brackets and remove the engine hoist.

52. Install the remaining transaxle-to-engine bolts and tighten to 41–59 ft. lbs. (55–80 Nm).

53. Install the alternator and the alternator and water pump drive belt.

54. Install the shutter valve actuator and bracket assembly.

55. Install the pressure regulator and bracket assembly.

56. Install the vacuum chamber canister located next to the intake plenum.

57. Place the power steering pump and bracket assembly into its mounting position.

58. Place the radiator, fan and shroud assembly into its mounting position.

59. Install the radiator mounting brackets along with the resonance duct. Tighten the mounting bolts to 69–95 inch lbs. (7.8–11.0 Nm).

60. Connect the cooling fan and radiator thermoswitch electrical connectors.

61. Raise and safely support the vehicle.

62. Install the oil pan-to-transaxle attaching bolts and tighten to 27–38 ft. lbs. (37–52 Nm).

63. Install the power steering pump and bracket assembly. Tighten the bolts to 27–38 ft. lbs. (37–52 Nm).

64. Install the lower radiator hose and clamps.

65. Connect the 2 transaxle cooling lines to the radiator.

66. If equipped, install the air conditioning compressor.

67. Install the air conditioning hose routing bracket to the radiator, if equipped. Tighten the bracket attaching nuts to 56–82 inch lbs. (6.4–9.3 Nm).

68. Install the crankshaft pulley and tighten the bolts to 109–152 inch lbs. (12–17 Nm).

69. Place a wrench on the crankshaft pulley and rotate the crankshaft to gain access to the torque converter studs. Install the torque converter nuts and tighten to 25–36 ft. lbs. (34–49 Nm). Install the transaxle inspection plate.

70. Install the power steering and air conditioning, if equipped, drive belt.

71. Install the halfshaft bearing support and tighten the bolts to 31–46 ft. lbs. (42–62 Nm).

72. Install the starter motor.

73. Connect the heater core inlet and outlet hoses at the bulkhead.

74. Install the exhaust flex-pipe, with a new gasket, to the exhaust manifold. Tighten the pipe-to-converter attaching nuts to 23–34 ft. lbs. (31–46 Nm).

75. Install the right and left lower splash shields and the right upper splash shield. Tighten the bolts to 69–95 inch lbs. (7.8–11.0 Nm).

76. Lower the vehicle.

77. Install the upper radiator hose and clamps.

78. Unplug the fuel pressure and return lines and connect them to the fuel rail. Install the necessary fuel line clips.

79. Install the accelerator and kickdown cable bracket onto the intake plenum. Tighten the bolts to 69–95 inch lbs. (7.8–11.0 Nm). Install the accelerator and kickdown cables onto the throttle cam.

80. Connect the power brake vacuum supply hose to the vacuum booster.

81. If equipped, connect the cruise control vacuum hoses to the intake plenum.

82. Connect all engine ground straps.

83. Connect all remaining electrical connectors to their original locations, as marked during the removal procedure.

84. Connect the ignition coil high-tension lead into the distributor.

85. Install the air duct between the throttle body and resonance chamber assembly.

86. Fill the cooling system. Fill the crankcase with the proper type and quantity of engine oil.

87. If equipped, recharge the air conditioning system according to the proper procedure.

88. Install the hood, aligning the marks that were made during the removal procedure.

89. Connect the negative battery cable.

90. Start the engine and check for leaks. Stop the engine and check the fluid levels.

With Manual Transaxle

The 1.8L engine equipped with manual transaxle requires the engine and transaxle to be removed as an assembly. Lift the assembly out of the engine compartment.

1. Disconnect the negative battery cable.

2. Mark the position of the hood on the hinges and remove the hood.

3. If equipped with air conditioning, properly discharge the system.

4. Drain the cooling system and the engine oil.

5. Remove the resonance duct and the air cleaner assembly.

6. Remove the battery and the battery tray.

7. Disconnect the accelerator cable from the throttle cam and remove the accelerator cable bracket from the intake plenum.

8. Remove the upper radiator hose and disconnect the radiator overflow hose from the radiator filler neck.

9. Disconnect the radiator thermoswitch and cooling fan electrical connectors.

10. Remove the attaching nuts to the radiator mounting brackets and remove the brackets.

11. Disconnect the alternator, oil pressure switch, throttle position sensor, idle speed control, manual lever position switch, fuel injector wiring harness, backup light switch, water thermoswitch, oxygen sensor, power steering pump and distributor electrical connectors.

NOTE: Mark the position of the connectors prior to removal to ease reinstallation.

12. Disconnect all engine ground straps.

13. Disconnect the ignition coil high-tension lead from the distributor.

14. Properly relieve the fuel system pressure.

15. Disconnect the fuel pressure and return lines.

16. Disconnect the heater core inlet and outlet, power brake vacuum supply, purge control vacuum and, if equipped, cruise control vacuum hoses.

NOTE: Mark the position of the hoses prior to removal to ease reinstallation.

17. Raise and safely support the vehicle.

18. Remove the right upper and lower splash shields.

19. Remove the clutch slave cylinder pipe bracket from the transaxle with the hose still connected. Position the slave cylinder aside.

NOTE: Be careful not to damage the pipe or the hose.

20. Disconnect the shift control rod and the extension bar from the transaxle.

21. Remove the battery duct.

22. Remove the radiator lower hose.

23. Remove the power steering and, if equipped, air conditioning compressor drive belt.

24. Remove the power steering pump and bracket assembly with the hoses still connected. Suspend the pump with wire aside of the work area.

25. Remove the air conditioning hose routing bracket, if equipped, from the transaxle crossmember and position the air conditioning hose aside.

26. If equipped, remove the air conditioning compressor with the hoses still connected. Suspend the compressor with wire aside of the work area.

27. Disconnect the speedometer cable from the transaxle.

28. Remove the exhaust pipe front mounting flange and support bracket from the exhaust manifold.

29. Mark the location and disconnect the wires from the starter motor.

30. Remove the stabilizer bar.

31. Remove the tie rod ends from the steering knuckles.

32. Remove the halfshafts from the transaxle.

33. Remove the transaxle front and rear mount attaching nuts from the crossmember.

34. Lower the vehicle.

35. Remove the radiator, fan and shroud assembly from the vehicle.

36. Install a suitable engine removal sling onto the engine lifting brackets.

37. Place a suitable engine hoist into position and support the engine.

38. Remove the engine vibration dampener.

39. Remove the engine mount, transaxle upper mount and the transaxle support bracket.

40. Remove the engine and transaxle assembly.
41. Remove the intake plenum support bracket.
42. Remove the starter motor.
43. Remove the transaxle front mount.
44. Remove all oil pan-to-transaxle bolts and transaxle-to-engine attaching bolts from the engine block and separate the transaxle from the engine.
45. Remove the clutch assembly from the engine.
46. Install the engine onto an engine stand.

To install:

47. Install an engine removal sling onto the engine lifting brackets. Place an engine hoist into position and install the engine sling.
48. Remove the engine from the engine stand and lower the engine with the hoist still supporting it.
49. Install the clutch assembly.
50. Install the transaxle onto the engine.
51. Install the transaxle-to-engine bolts and tighten to 47–66 ft. lbs. (64–89 Nm).
52. Install the oil pan-to-transaxle attaching bolts and tighten to 27–38 ft. lbs. (37–52 Nm).
53. Position the transaxle front mount onto the transaxle and install the attaching bolts. Tighten the bolts to 27–38 ft. lbs. (37–52 Nm).
54. Position the starter motor into the transaxle housing and install the mounting bolts. Tighten the bolts to 27–38 ft. lbs. (37–52 Nm).
55. Install the intake plenum support bracket. Tighten the bolts to 27–38 ft. lbs. (37–52 Nm) and the nut to 14–19 ft. lbs. (19–25 Nm).
56. Using the engine hoist, position the engine and transaxle assembly into the engine compartment and align the engine mounting points with the engine mount and the mounting holes in the transaxle crossmember.
57. Install the attaching nuts to the transaxle front and rear mounts and the transaxle crossmember.
58. Position the engine mount into the vehicle.
59. Install the engine mount through-bolt and nut. Tighten them to 49–69 ft. lbs. (67–93 Nm).
60. Install the engine mount-to-engine attaching nuts. Tighten the nuts to 54–76 ft. lbs. (74–103 Nm).
61. Install the engine mount vibration dampener and attaching bolt and nut. Tighten the bolt and nut to 41–59 ft. lbs. (55–80 Nm).
62. Place the clutch slave cylinder and pipe assembly into its proper mounting position.
63. Install the transaxle support bracket and attaching bolts. Tighten the bolts to 41–59 ft. lbs. (55–80 Nm).
64. Install the transaxle upper mount and install the attaching bolts. Tighten the bolts to 32–45 ft. lbs. (43–61 Nm).
65. Install the transaxle upper mount attaching nuts. Tighten the nuts to 49–69 ft. lbs. (67–93 Nm).
66. Place the radiator, fan and shroud assembly into its mounting position.
67. Install the radiator mounting brackets and tighten the nuts to 69–95 inch lbs. (7.8–11.0 Nm).
68. Install the upper radiator hose and connect the expansion reservoir overflow tube to the radiator filler neck.
69. Connect the cooling fan and radiator thermoswitch electrical connectors.
70. Raise and safely support the vehicle.
71. Install the lower radiator hose.
72. Install the halfshafts.
73. Install the tie rod ends into the steering knuckle.
74. Install the stabilizer bar.
75. Connect the wires to the starter motor according to their positions as marked during the removal procedure.
76. Install the exhaust front mounting flange to the exhaust manifold while making sure to install a new gasket. Tighten the flange-to-manifold attaching nuts to 23–34 ft. lbs. (31–46 Nm).
77. Install the exhaust pipe support bracket. Tighten the bracket attaching bolts to 27–38 ft. lbs. (37–52 Nm).
78. Install the speedometer cable into the transaxle.
79. If equipped, install the air conditioning compressor. Tighten the mounting bolts to 15–22 ft. lbs. (20–30 Nm).
80. Install the air conditioning routing bracket, if equipped, to the transaxle crossmember. Tighten the bolt to 56–82 inch lbs. (6.4–9.3 Nm).
81. Install the power steering pump and bracket assembly. Tighten the pump mounting bolts to 27–38 ft. lbs. (37–52 Nm).
82. Install the power steering and air conditioning, if equipped, drive belt.
83. Install the battery duct and tighten the attaching bolts to 69–95 inch lbs. (7.8–11.0 Nm).
84. Install the extension bar to the transaxle and tighten the attaching nut to 23–34 ft. lbs. (31–46 Nm).
85. Connect the shift control rod to the transaxle and tighten the attaching nut to 12–17 ft. lbs. (16–23 Nm).
86. Install the clutch slave cylinder attaching bolts and tighten to 12–17 ft. lbs. (16–23 Nm).
87. Position the slave cylinder pipe and install the routing bracket and attaching bolt. Tighten the bolt to 12–17 ft. lbs. (16–23 Nm).
88. Install the right upper and lower splash shields. Tighten the bolts to 69–95 inch lbs. (7.8–11.0 Nm).
89. Lower the vehicle.
90. Connect the heater core and vacuum hoses according to their original positions as marked during the removal procedure.
91. Connect the fuel pressure and return lines.
92. Connect the ignition coil high tension lead into the distributor.
93. Connect all engine ground straps.
94. Connect all remaining electrical connectors according to the locations marked during the removal procedure.
95. Install the accelerator cable bracket to the intake plenum and connect the accelerator cable to the throttle cam.
96. Install the battery tray and the battery.
97. Install the air cleaner assembly and the resonance duct.
98. Fill the cooling system. Fill the engine with the proper type and quantity of oil.
99. If equipped, recharge the air conditioning system.
100. Install the hood, aligning the marks that were made during the removal procedure.
101. Connect the negative battery cable.
102. Start the engine and check for leaks. Stop the engine and check the fluid levels.

1.9L Engine

WITH AUTOMATIC TRANSAXLE

On automatic transaxle vehicles, the 1.9L engine assembly is removed without the transaxle attached. The engine is lifted from the engine compartment with the transaxle assembly remaining in the vehicle, attached to the mounts.

1. Mark the position of the hood on the hinges and remove the hood.
2. Disconnect the negative battery cable.
3. Drain the cooling system and the engine oil.
4. Remove the air intake duct.
5. Remove the crankcase ventilation hose from the valve cover and the vacuum hose from the bottom side of the throttle body.
6. Disconnect the power brake booster supply hose.
7. Disconnect the following electrical connectors:
   a. Fuel charging harness, located at the right shock tower.
   b. Alternator harness, from the back side of the alternator.
   c. Oxygen sensor.

d. Ignition coil.

e. Radio suppressor, mounted on the coil bracket.

f. Coolant temperature sensor, cooling fan sensor and temperature gauge sending unit, mounted on a common water tube near the thermostat housing.

g. Radiator cooling fan.

NOTE: Mark the position of the electrical connectors prior to removal to aid reinstallation.

8. Remove the idle air bypass valve.

9. Remove the ground strap from the stud on the left side of the cylinder head near the ignition coil.

10. Disconnect the accelerator cable and the transaxle kickdown cable from the throttle lever. Remove the cable bracket from the intake manifold and position aside.

11. Disconnect both heater hoses at the engine compartment bulkhead.

12. Properly relieve the fuel system pressure and disconnect the fuel supply and return hoses at the fuel supply manifold.

13. Remove the upper radiator hose.

14. Raise and safely support the vehicle.

15. Remove the right side and the right and left front splash shields.

16. Remove the lower radiator hose from the radiator.

17. Position a drain pan under the radiator and remove the lower transaxle oil cooler line.

18. Remove the 2 oil cooler line retaining bracket bolts from the bottom of the radiator.

19. Remove the radiator fan shroud lower mounting bolts.

20. Lower the vehicle.

21. Remove the radiator fan shroud upper mounting bolts and remove the fan and shroud assembly from the vehicle.

22. Remove the upper transaxle oil cooler line from the radiator and remove the radiator from the vehicle.

23. If equipped with air conditioning, properly discharge the system.

24. Disconnect the air conditioning suction line at the suction accumulator/drier. Plug or cap the openings to prevent the entrance of dirt and moisture.

25. Remove the accessory drive belt.

26. Remove the power steering return hose from the pump reservoir and the high-pressure hose from the power steering pump.

27. Remove the power steering and air conditioner line retainer bracket bolts from the alternator bracket. Position the hoses aside.

28. Remove the accessory drive belt automatic tensioner assembly.

29. Raise and safely support the vehicle.

30. Remove the drive belt idler pulley.

31. If equipped, remove the 4 air conditioning compressor mounting bolts. Remove the compressor assembly with the lines attached and position aside. Safety wire the compressor to the vehicle sub-frame.

32. Remove the catalytic converter inlet pipe.

33. Remove the transaxle kickdown cable support bracket from the back side of the engine block. Position the cable and the bracket aside.

34. Disconnect the oil pressure switch.

35. Disconnect the relay wire and the positive battery cable from the starter.

36. Remove the flywheel inspection shield.

37. Remove the 4 torque converter attaching nuts.

38. Remove the crankshaft dampener.

39. Remove the 5 engine-to-transaxle bolts.

40. Lower the vehicle.

41. Remove the 3 starter motor mounting bolts and remove the starter out of the top of the engine compartment.

42. Remove the 2 transaxle-to-engine mounting bolts.

43. Connect an engine removal sling to engine lifting brackets. Position an engine hoist and support the engine.

44. Remove the right engine mount dampener and mount assembly.

45. With the engine assembly supported by the engine hoist, carefully separate the assembly from the transaxle.

46. Lift the engine assembly out of the vehicle.

47. Install the engine onto an engine stand.

To install:

48. Attach the engine removal sling to the engine lifting brackets and remove the engine from the stand with the engine hoist.

49. Carefully lower the engine into the vehicle and join the engine to the transaxle. Make sure the torque converter studs correctly engage the flywheel and the alignment dowels engage the transaxle housing.

50. Install the 2 transaxle-to-engine bolts but do not fully tighten them at this time.

51. Install the right engine mount insulator and dampener.

52. Position the engine hoist aside and remove the sling from the engine lifting brackets.

53. Raise and safely support the vehicle.

54. Install the 5 engine-to-transaxle bolts but do not fully tighten them at this time.

55. Install the crankshaft dampener and tighten the attaching bolt to 81–96 ft. lbs. (110–130 Nm).

56. Install the 4 torque converter attaching nuts and tighten to 25–36 ft. lbs. (34–49 Nm). Install the flywheel inspection plate.

57. Connect the oil pressure switch.

58. Install the kickdown cable support bracket.

59. If equipped, position the air conditioning compressor on the bracket and install the 4 mounting bolts. Tighten the bolts to 15–22 ft. lbs. (20–30 Nm).

60. Install the catalytic converter inlet pipe.

61. Lower the vehicle.

62. From above, position the starter motor and install the 3 mounting bolts. Connect the positive battery cable and the relay wire to the starter.

63. Tighten the 2 transaxle-to-engine bolts to 40–59 ft. lbs. (55–80 Nm).

64. Install the power steering high-pressure hose on the pump.

65. Install the accessory drive belt idler pulley and automatic tensioner.

66. Install the power steering return hose on the pump reservoir.

67. Install the power steering hose retainer bracket on the alternator bracket.

68. Install the accessory drive belt.

69. If equipped, connect the air conditioner suction line to the accumulator.

70. Install the radiator assembly.

71. Connect the upper transaxle oil cooler line at the radiator.

72. Position the cooling fan and shroud assembly and install the upper mounting bolts.

73. Raise and safely support the vehicle.

74. Install the lower shroud bolts and connect the lower transaxle oil cooler line.

75. Install the oil cooler line retaining bracket bolts.

76. Install the lower radiator hose.

77. Tighten the 5 engine-to-transaxle bolts to 27–38 ft. lbs. (37–52 Nm).

78. Install the left and right front splash shields and the right side splash shield.

79. Lower the vehicle.

80. Install the upper radiator hose.

81. Connect both heater hoses at the engine compartment bulkhead.

82. Install the accelerator cable bracket and attach the accelerator and kickdown cables to the throttle lever.

83. Install the idle air bypass valve.

84. Install the ground strap on the stud at the front left side of the cylinder head, near the ignition coil.

85. Connect the remaining electrical connectors according to the positions marked during the removal procedure.

86. Connect the fuel supply and re-

turn lines. Be sure to install the fuel line safety clips.

87. Connect the power brake supply hose, the vacuum hose on the bottom side of the throttle body, and the crankcase ventilation hose to the valve cover.

88. Install the air intake duct.

89. Connect the negative battery cable.

90. Fill the cooling system. Fill the crankcase with the proper type and quantity of engine oil.

91. Install the hood, aligning the marks that were made during the removal procedure.

92. Start the engine and check for leaks. Stop the engine and check the fluid levels.

93. If equipped, evacuate and recharge the air conditioning system according to the proper procedure.

WITH MANUAL TRANSAXLE

On manual transaxle vehicles, the 1.9L engine assembly is removed with the transaxle attached. The engine is lifted out of the engine compartment.

1. Mark the position of the hood on the hinges and remove the hood.

2. Disconnect the battery cables and remove the battery and the battery tray.

3. Drain the cooling system and the engine oil.

4. Remove the air cleaner.

5. Disconnect the crankcase ventilation hose from the valve cover and the vacuum hose from the bottom side of the throttle body.

6. Remove the power brake supply hose.

7. Disconnect the following electrical connectors:

　　a. Fuel charging harness, located at the right shock tower.

　　b. Alternator harness, from the back side of the alternator.

　　c. Oxygen sensor.

　　d. Ignition coil.

　　e. Radio suppressor, mounted on the coil bracket.

　　f. Coolant temperature sensor, cooling fan sensor and temperature gauge sending unit, mounted on a common water tube near the thermostat housing.

　　g. Radiator cooling fan.

NOTE: Mark the position of the electrical connectors prior to removal to aid reinstallation.

8. Remove the idle air bypass valve.

9. Remove the ground strap from the stud on the left side of the cylinder head near the ignition coil.

10. Disconnect the accelerator cable from the throttle lever. Remove the cable bracket from the intake manifold and position aside.

11. Disconnect both heater hoses at the engine compartment bulkhead.

12. Properly relieve the fuel system pressure and disconnect the fuel supply and return hoses at the fuel supply manifold.

13. Remove the upper radiator hose.

14. If equipped, properly discharge the air conditioning system and disconnect the suction line at the accumulator.

15. Remove the accessory drive belt and the automatic tensioner and idler pulley.

16. Disconnect the power steering return hose from the pump reservoir and the high pressure hose from the pump.

17. Remove the power steering hose and air conditioning line retainer brackets from the alternator bracket.

18. Raise and safely support the vehicle.

19. Remove the right and left side and front splash shields.

20. Disconnect the lower radiator hose from the radiator and remove the radiator fan shroud lower mounting bolts.

21. If equipped, remove the 4 air conditioning compressor mounting bolts. Remove the compressor assembly with the lines attached and position aside. Safety wire the compressor to the vehicle sub-frame.

22. Remove the catalytic converter inlet pipe.

23. Disconnect the oil pressure switch.

24. Disconnect the relay wire and the positive battery cable at the starter.

25. Remove the transaxle extension bar and shift control rod.

26. Remove the crankshaft dampener.

27. Remove the front wheel and tire assemblies.

28. Remove both halfshaft assemblies.

29. Install suitable transaxle plugs into the differential side gears.

NOTE: Failure to install the transaxle plugs may allow the differential side gears to move out of position. Should the gears become misaligned, the differential will have to be removed from the transaxle to align the gears.

30. Disconnect the speedometer cable and the neutral switch on the transaxle.

31. Remove the clutch slave cylinder and line as an assembly from the transaxle and set it aside.

32. Remove the transaxle front and rear mount bolts.

33. Lower the vehicle.

34. Remove the radiator fan shroud upper mounting bolts and remove the fan shroud assembly from the vehicle.

35. Connect an engine removal sling to the engine lifting brackets. Connect the sling to an engine hoist, position the hoist and support the engine.

36. Remove the right engine mount dampener and mount assembly.

37. Remove the transaxle upper mount.

38. Lift the engine and transaxle assembly out of the vehicle and set it down on the floor.

To install:

39. Carefully lower the engine and transaxle assembly into the vehicle with the engine hoist.

40. Position the transaxle on its mounts and install the transaxle upper mount.

41. Install the right engine mount and mount damper.

42. Remove the engine removal sling and the hoist.

43. Position the fan shroud assembly and install the upper mounting bolts.

44. Raise and safely support the vehicle.

45. Install the front and rear transaxle mount bolts.

46. Install the clutch slave cylinder and line assembly.

47. Connect the neutral switch and the speedometer cable.

48. Remove the transaxle plugs and install the halfshaft assemblies.

49. Install the crankshaft dampener and tighten the bolt to 81–96 ft. lbs. (110–130 Nm).

50. Install the transaxle extension bar and shift control rod.

51. Connect the relay wire and the positive battery cable to the starter.

52. Connect the oil pressure switch.

53. Install the catalytic converter inlet pipe.

54. If equipped, position the air conditioning compressor on its bracket and install the 4 mounting bolts.

55. Install the radiator fan shroud lower mounting bolts and install the lower radiator hose.

56. Install the left and right side and front splash shields.

57. Lower the vehicle.

58. Install the power steering hoses and install the power steering hose and air conditioner line retainer brackets.

59. Install the accessory drive belt idler pulley and automatic tensioner and install the accessory drive belt.

60. If equipped, connect the air conditioner suction line.

61. Install the upper radiator hose.

62. Connect the fuel supply and return hoses to the fuel supply manifold.

63. Connect both heater hoses.

64. Install the accelerator cable bracket on the intake manifold and connect the cable to the throttle lever.

65. Install the ground strap on the

stud at the front left side of the cylinder head.

66. Install the idle air bypass valve.
67. Connect the remaining electrical connectors according to the positions marked during the removal procedure.
68. Connect the power brake supply hose, the crankcase ventilation hose and the vacuum line at the bottom of the throttle body.
69. Install the air cleaner assembly.
70. Install the battery tray and the battery. Connect the battery cables.
71. Fill the cooling system. Fill the crankcase with the proper type and quantity of oil.
72. Install the hood, aligning the marks that were made during the removal procedure.
73. Start the engine and check for leaks. Stop the engine and check the fluid levels.
74. If equipped, evacuate and recharge the air conditioning system according to the proper procedure.

Engine Mounts

REMOVAL & INSTALLATION

1. Disconnect the negative battery cable.
2. Raise and support the vehicle safely.
3. Drain the cooling system and disconnect the upper and lower radiator hoses, as necessary.
4. Position a jack with a block of wood, under the engine.
5. Remove the engine-to-mount bolts and the mount-to-frame bolts.
6. Relieve the pressure from the mount by jacking the engine until the mount can be removed. Remove the mount.
7. Installation is the reverse order of the removal procedure.
8. Fill the cooling system to correct level. Connect the negative battery cable.

Cylinder Head

REMOVAL & INSTALLATION

1.6L Engine

1. Disconnect the negative battery cable.
2. Remove the timing belt and rocker arm cover.
3. Remove the exhaust and intake manifolds.
4. Drain the cooling system.
5. Remove the spark plug wires and the spark plugs.
6. Remove the distributor-to-cylinder head bolts and the distributor from the engine.
7. Remove the engine lifting eyes.

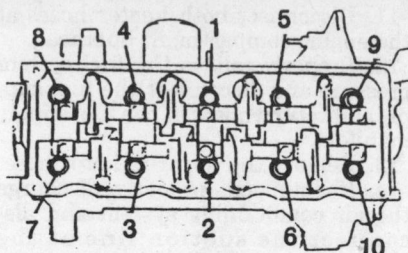

Cylinder head bolt torque sequence—1.6L engine

Disconnect the ground wire from the engine.

8. Disconnect the electrical harness connectors which may interfere with the cylinder head removal.
9. Remove the upper radiator hose, the water bypass hose and bracket.
10. Remove the cylinder head-to-engine bolts and the cylinder head.
11. Clean the gasket mating surfaces. Check the cylinder head for cracks or other damage. Check the head gasket surface for warpage using a straightedge and feeler gauge. The head must be flat within 0.006 in. (0.15mm) over the entire head area.
To install:
12. Position the cylinder head gasket on the engine block and install the cylinder head.
13. Lightly oil the threads of the cylinder head bolts with oil and install them into the head. Tighten the cylinder head bolts in sequence to 50–60 ft. lbs. (75–81 Nm) in 2 equal steps.
14. Install the water bypass hose and bracket and upper radiator hose.
15. Reconnect the wire harness connectors.
16. Install the front and rear engine lifting eyes to the cylinder head and the engine ground wire.
17. Install the distributor, spark plugs and spark plug wires.
18. Install the intake and exhaust manifolds. Torque the intake manfold-to-cylinder head bolts to 14–19 ft. lbs. (19–25 Nm) and the exhaust manifold-to-cylinder head bolts to 12–17 ft. lbs. (16–23 Nm).
19. Install the rocker arm cover, timing belt and timing belt cover.
20. Install the water pump pulley and drive belts.
21. Fill the cooling system to the correct level.
22. The remainder of the installation is the reverse order of the removal procedure.
23. Connect the negative battery cable.
24. Start the engine, allow it to reach normal operating temperature and check for leaks.

1.8L Engine

1. Properly relieve the fuel system pressure.

2. Disconnect the negative battery cable.
3. Drain the cooling system.
4. Remove the bolts from the timing belt upper and middle covers. Remove the covers and gaskets.
5. Rotate the crankshaft by hand in the direction of normal engine rotation and align the timing marks located on the camshaft pulleys and seal plate.
6. Loosen the timing belt tensioner lock bolt and temporarily secure the tensioner spring in the fully extended position.
7. Remove the timing belt from the camshaft pulleys and secure it aside to prevent damage during the removal and installation of the cylinder head.

NOTE: Do not allow the timing belt to become contaminated by oil or grease. Mark the direction of rotation on the timing belt prior to removal so it can be reinstalled in the same direction.

8. Tag and disconnect the vacuum hoses from the cylinder head cover.
9. Tag and disconnect the spark plug wires from the spark plugs and position the wires aside.
10. Remove the cylinder head cover and gasket.
11. Remove the air duct from the resonance chamber and throttle body.
12. Disconnect the accelerator cable and, if equipped with automatic transaxle, the kickdown cable from the throttle cam. Remove the cable bracket from the intake plenum.
13. Tag and disconnect all vacuum lines from the intake plenum.
14. Tag and disconnect all necessary electrical connectors from the cylinder head, exhaust manifold, intake plenum, and throttle body. Disconnect the ground straps.
15. Remove the upper radiator hose.
16. Remove the transaxle-to-engine block upper-right bolt.
17. Disconnect the fuel pressure and return lines and plug the lines.
18. Disconnect the ignition coil high-tension lead from the distributor.
19. Tag and disconnect the necessary hoses connected to the cylinder head and intake plenum.
20. Remove the 2 bolts from the transaxle vent tube routing brackets.
21. Raise and safely support the vehicle.
22. Remove the bolt from the water pump-to-cylinder head hose bracket.
23. Remove the exhaust front mounting flange and exhaust pipe support bracket from the exhaust manifold.
24. Remove the intake plenum support bracket.
25. Lower the vehicle.

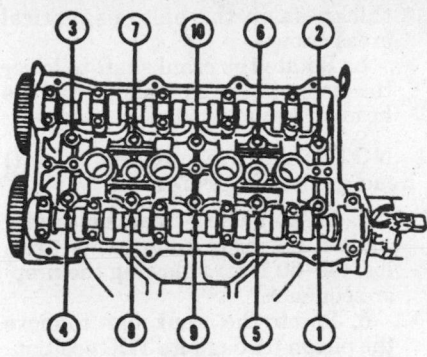

Cylinder head bolt removal sequence—1.8L engine

26. Remove the cylinder head bolts in the proper sequence.

27. Remove the cylinder head assembly, with the intake plenum and exhaust manifold attached, from the vehicle.

28. Remove the intake plenum and exhaust manifold.

29. Inspect the cylinder head for damage, cracks, and leakage of water and oil. Measure the cylinder head for warpage in 6 directions. The maximum distortion allowable is 0.004 in. (0.10mm).

30. If the cylinder head distortion exceeds specification, machine the cylinder head surface. The cylinder head must be replaced if the cylinder head height is not within 5.268–5.276 in. (133.8–134.0mm).

31. Inspect the manifold contact surface distortion in 4 directions. The maximum distortion allowable is 0.006 in. (0.15mm). If the distortion exceeds specification, machine the manifold contact surface or replace the cylinder head, as necessary.

To install:

32. Remove all dirt, oil and old gasket material from all gasket contact surfaces.

33. Install the intake plenum and exhaust manifold.

34. Install a new head gasket onto the top of the engine block, using the dowel pins for reference.

35. Place the cylinder head into its mounting position on top of the engine block.

36. Lubricate the cylinder head bolts with engine oil and install them finger-tight. Tighten the bolts in the proper sequence to 56–60 ft. lbs. (76–81 Nm).

37. Install the 2 bolts to the transaxle vent tube routing brackets.

38. Connect the heater hoses to the cylinder head and install the clamps.

39. Connect the ignition coil high-tension lead to the distributor.

40. Connect the fuel pressure and return lines to the fuel supply manifold and install the safety clips.

41. Install the transaxle-to-engine block upper-right bolt. If equipped with manual transaxle, tighten the bolt to 47–66 ft. lbs. (64–89 Nm). If equipped with automatic transaxle, tighten the bolt to 41–59 ft. lbs. (55–80 Nm).

42. Install the upper radiator hose and clamps.

43. Connect the ground straps and connect the electrical connectors that were disconnected at the cylinder head, exhaust manifold, intake plenum, and throttle body.

44. Connect the vacuum lines to the intake plenum.

45. Install the accelerator and kickdown cable bracket onto the intake plenum and tighten the bolts to 69–95 inch lbs. (7.8–11.0 Nm). Connect the cable(s) to the throttle cam.

46. Install the cylinder head cover and gasket, then connect the hose running from the plenum to the cylinder head cover. Tighten the cover bolts to 43–78 inch lbs. (4.9–8.8 Nm).

47. Install the air duct to the resonance chamber and throttle body and tighten the clamps. Connect the hose going from the air duct to the cylinder head cover.

48. Install and connect the spark plug wires.

49. Raise and safely support the vehicle.

50. Install the intake plenum support bracket. Tighten the bolts to 27–38 ft. lbs. (37–52 Nm) and the nut to 14–19 ft. lbs. (19–25 Nm).

51. Install the bolt to the water pump-to-cylinder head hose bracket.

52. Install the exhaust front mounting flange with a new gasket to the exhaust manifold. Tighten the flange-to-manifold attaching nuts to 23–34 ft. lbs. (31–46 Nm).

53. Install the exhaust pipe support bracket. Tighten the bracket attaching bolts to 27–38 ft. lbs. (37–52 Nm).

54. Make sure the yellow ignition timing mark on the crankshaft pulley is aligned with the TDC mark on the timing belt cover.

55. Lower the vehicle.

56. Make sure the timing marks on the camshaft pulleys and seal plate are aligned. Install the timing belt, in the original direction of rotation, so there is no looseness at the idler pulley side or between the 2 camshaft pulleys.

NOTE: Do not turn the crankshaft counterclockwise.

57. Turn the crankshaft 2 turns clockwise by hand and verify that the yellow ignition timing mark on the crankshaft pulley is aligned with the timing mark on the timing belt cover. Verify that the timing marks on the camshaft pulley and seal plate are aligned.

NOTE: If the timing marks are not aligned, remove the timing belt and repeat the procedure beginning with Step 54.

58. Turn the crankshaft $1\frac{5}{6}$ turns clockwise by hand and align the 4th tooth to the right of the I and E timing marks on the camshaft pulleys with the seal plate alignment marks.

59. Loosen the timing belt tensioner lock bolt and apply tension to the timing belt. Tighten the tensioner lock bolt to 27–38 ft. lbs. (37–52 Nm).

60. Turn the crankshaft $2\frac{1}{6}$ turns clockwise and verify that the timing marks on the camshaft pulleys and the seal plate are aligned.

61. Install new gaskets onto the timing belt upper and middle covers and install the covers. Tighten the mounting bolts to 69–95 inch lbs. (8–11 Nm).

62. Fill the cooling system.

63. Connect the negative battery cable.

64. Start the engine and check for leaks.

1.9L Engine

1. Properly relieve the fuel system pressure.

2. Disconnect the negative battery cable.

3. Drain the cooling system.

4. Remove the air intake duct.

5. Remove the crankcase breather hose from the rocker arm cover and the vacuum hose from the bottom of the throttle body.

6. Remove the power brake supply hose.

7. Disconnect the electrical connectors at the following:

   a. Fuel charging harness.
   b. Alternator harness.
   c. Crank angle sensor.
   d. Oxygen sensor.
   e. Ignition coil.
   f. Radio suppressor.
   g. Coolant temperature sensor, cooling fan sensor and temperature sending unit.

NOTE: Tag the connectors prior to removal to aid reinstallation.

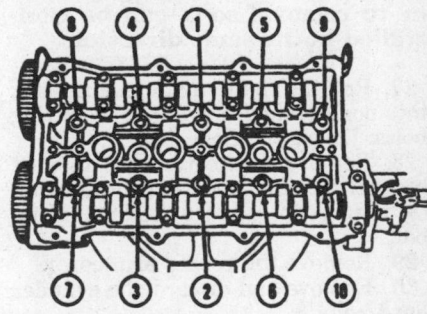

Cylinder head bolt torque sequence—1.8L engine

8. Remove the ground strap from the stud on the left side of the cylinder head.

9. Disconnect the accelerator and the transaxle kickdown cables from the throttle lever and remove the cable bracket from the intake manifold.

10. Disconnect the heater hose containing the coolant temperature switches at the bulkhead.

11. Remove the upper radiator hose.

12. Disconnect the fuel supply and return lines.

13. Remove the oil level indicator tube mounting nut from the cylinder head stud.

14. Remove the power steering hose and the air conditioner line retainer bracket bolts from the alternator bracket.

15. Remove the accessory drive belt, alternator and the drive belt automatic tensioner.

16. Raise and safely support the vehicle.

17. Remove the right side splash shield and remove the crankshaft dampener.

18. Remove the catalytic converter inlet pipe.

19. Remove the starter wiring harness from the retaining clip below the intake manifold.

20. Set the engine No. 1 cylinder on TDC.

21. Lower the vehicle.

22. Support the engine with a floor jack.

23. Remove the right engine mount dampener and the right engine mount retaining bolts from the mount bracket on the engine. Loosen the right engine mount thru-bolt and roll the mount back aside.

24. Remove the timing belt cover.

25. Loosen the belt tensioner attaching bolt and pry the tensioner as far toward the rear of the engine as possible. Tighten the attaching bolt while in this position.

26. Remove the timing belt.

NOTE: Do not allow the timing belt to become contaminated by oil or grease. Mark the direction of rotation on the timing belt prior to removal so it can be reinstalled in the same direction.

27. Roll the right engine mount back into position and install the mounting bolts. Lower the floor jack.

28. Remove the heater hose support bracket retaining bolt and the alternator bracket-to-cylinder head mounting bolt.

29. Remove the rocker arm cover.

30. Remove and discard the cylinder head bolts.

31. Remove the cylinder head with the exhaust and intake manifolds at-

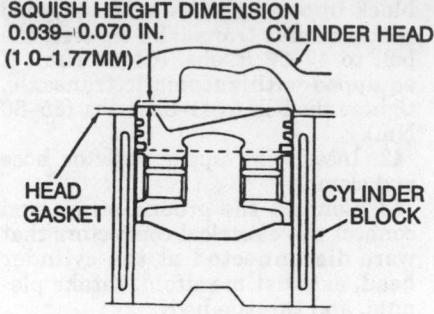

SQUISH HEIGHT DIMENSION 0.039–0.070 IN. (1.0–1.77MM)

CYLINDER HEAD

HEAD GASKET

CYLINDER BLOCK

Piston squish height dimension location—1.9L engine

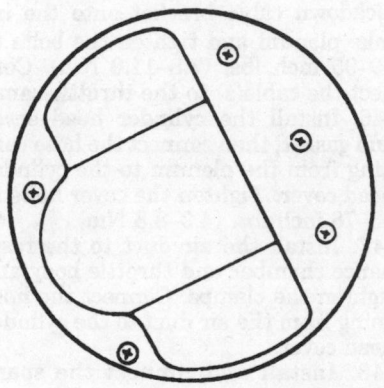

Lead solder placement positions

tached. Discard the cylinder head gasket.

NOTE: Do not lay the cylinder head flat. Damage to the spark plugs, valves or gasket surfaces may result.

To install:

32. Clean all gasket material from the mating surfaces on the cylinder head and block and clean out the head bolt holes in the block.

33. Before final installation of the cylinder head to the engine, check the piston squish height as follows:

NOTE: Squish height is the clearance of the piston dome to the combustion chamber at piston TDC. No cylinder block deck machining or use of replacement crankshaft, piston or connecting rod causing the assembled squish height to be over or under tolerance specification, is permitted. If no parts other than the head gasket are replaced, the squish height should be within specification. If parts other than the head gasket are replaced, check the squish height. If the squish height is out of specification, replace the parts again and recheck the squish height.

a. Place a small amount of soft lead solder or shot of an appropriate

thickness on the piston spherical areas shown.

b. Rotate the crankshaft to lower the piston in the bore and install the head gasket and cylinder head.

NOTE: A compressed (used) head gasket is preferred.

c. Install used head bolts and tighten the head bolts to 30–44 ft. lbs. (40–60 Nm) following the proper sequence.

d. Rotate the crankshaft to move the piston through its TDC position.

e. Remove the cylinder head and measure the thickness of the compressed solder to determine squish height at TDC. The solder should be 0.039–0.070 in. (1.0–1.77mm) for all engines.

34. Install the dowels in the cylinder block, if removed. Check the dowel height, it should be 0.41–0.46 in. (10.40–11.75mm) above the surface of the block. A dowel that is too long will not allow the cylinder head to sit properly.

35. Position the cylinder head gasket on the cylinder block.

36. Install the cylinder head and install new bolts and washers in the following order:

a. Apply a light coat of engine oil to the threads of the new cylinder head bolts and install the new bolts into the head.

b. Torque the cylinder head bolts in sequence to 44 ft. lbs. (60 Nm).

c. Loosen the cylinder head bolts approximately 2 turns and then torque again to 44 ft. lbs. (60 Nm) using the same torque sequence.

d. After setting the torque again, turn the head bolts 90 degrees in sequence and to complete the head bolt installation, turn the head bolts an additional 90 degrees in the same torque sequence.

NOTE: The cylinder head attaching bolts cannot be tightened to the specified torque more than once and must therefore be replaced when installing a cylinder head.

37. Install the rocker arm cover and the alternator bracket-to-cylinder head bolt.

38. Support the engine with a floor jack.

39. Remove the right engine mount-to-mount bracket bolts. Roll the mount aside.

40. Make sure cylinder No. 1 is at TDC.

41. Install the timing belt and the timing belt cover.

42. Roll the right engine mount into place and install the 2 mounting bolts and the mount dampener. Remove the floor jack.

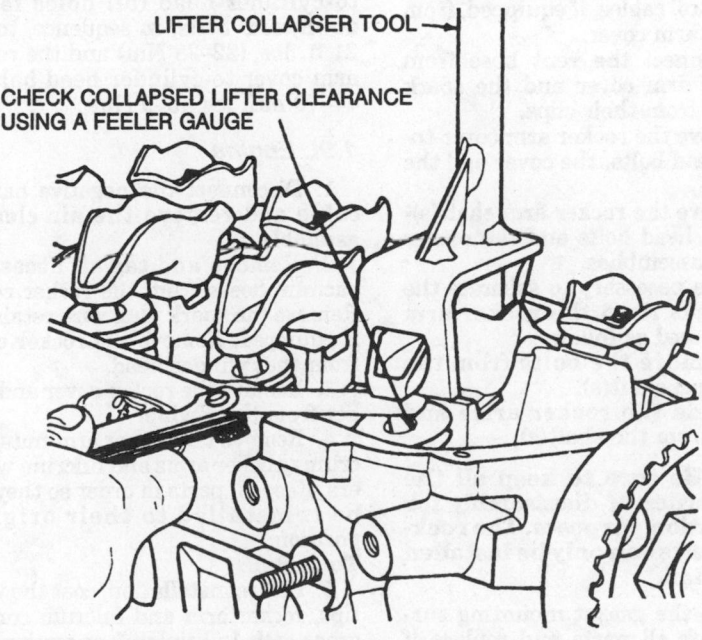

```
    9    3    1    5    7
    ◯    ◯    ◯    ◯    ◯   INTAKE

    ◯    ◯    ◯    ◯    ◯   EXHAUST
    8    6    2    4   10
```

Cylinder head bolt torque sequence—1.9L engine

43. Raise and safely support the vehicle.
44. Install the crankshaft dampener.
45. Install the starter wiring harness on the retaining clip below the intake manifold.
46. Install the catalytic converter inlet pipe and the right side splash shield.
47. Lower the vehicle.
48. Install the alternator and the accessory drive belt automatic tensioner. Install the accessory drive belt.
49. Install both the power steering hose and air conditioner line retainer bracket bolts. Install the oil level indicator tube retainer bolt.
50. Connect the fuel supply and return lines.
51. Install the upper radiator hose and connect the heater hose at the engine compartment bulkhead. Install the heater hose support bracket retaining bolt.
52. Install the accelerator cable bracket on the intake manifold and connect the accelerator and kickdown cables to the throttle lever.
53. Install the ground strap at the left side of the cylinder head.
54. Connect all remaining electrical connectors according to their positions marked during the removal procedure.
55. Connect the power brake supply hose, crankcase breather hose and the vacuum line at the bottom of the throttle body.
56. Install the air intake duct.
57. Connect the negative battery cable.
58. Fill and bleed the cooling system.
59. Start the engine and check for leaks. Stop the engine and check the coolant level.

Valve Lifters

REMOVAL & INSTALLATION

1.8L Engine

NOTE: Hydraulic lash adjusters are used on the 1.8L engine between the valve stem and the camshaft to reduce noise and to provide maintenance-free valve clearance.

1. Disconnect the negative battery cable.
2. Remove the camshafts according to the proper procedure.
3. Mark the hydraulic lash adjusters and the cylinder head with alignment marks so the hydraulic lash adjusters can be installed in their original mounting positions.
4. Remove the hydraulic lash adjusters from the cylinder head.

To install:

5. Apply clean engine oil to the hydraulic lash adjuster friction surfaces.
6. If the hydraulic lash adjusters are being reused, install them in the positions from which they were removed.
7. Make sure the hydraulic lash adjusters move smoothly in their bores.
8. Install the camshafts.
9. Connect the negative battery cable.

1.9L Engine

1. Disconnect the negative battery cable.
2. Remove air cleaner assembly. Remove valve cover and gasket.
3. Remove rocker arms, lifter guides, lifter retainers and lifters.

NOTE: Always return lifters to the original bores unless they are being replaced.

To install:

4. Lubricate each lifter bore with engine oil.
5. Install the lifters with the plunger upward and position guide flats of lifters to be parallel with centerline of camshaft. If equipped, color orientation dots on lifters should be opposite the oil feed holes in cylinder head.
6. Install the lifter guide plates over the lifter guide flats with notch toward exhaust side.
7. Lubricate lifter plunger cap and valve tip with engine oil.
8. Install lifter guide plates retainers into rocker arm fulcrum slots, in both intake and exhaust side. On 1991 vehicles, the notch to be with exhaust valve lifter. On 1992–93 vehicles, the tab should be located on the intake seal fulcrum slot.
9. Install 4 rocker arms in lifter position No's 3, 6, 7 and 8.
10. Lubricate rocker arm surface that will contact fulcrum surface with engine oil.
11. Install 4 fulcrums. Fulcrums must be fully seated in slots of cylinder head.
12. Install 4 bolts. Tighten to 17–22 ft. lbs. (23–30 Nm).
13. Rotate the engine until the camshaft sprocket keyway is in the 6 o'clock position.
14. Repeat steps 9–12 in lifter position No's 1, 2, 4 and 5.
15. Install valve cover and gasket. Install air cleaner assembly.
16. Connect negative battery cable.

Valve Lash

ADJUSTMENT

Collapsed Lifter Clearance

1.9L ENGINE

1. Connect an auxiliary starter switch in the starting circuit. Crank

LIFTER COLLAPSER TOOL →

CHECK COLLAPSED LIFTER CLEARANCE USING A FEELER GAUGE

Collapsed lifter clearance checking—1.9L engine

the engine with the ignition switch **OFF** until the No. 1 piston is on TDC of the compression stroke.

2. With the crankshaft in position, place hydraulic lifter compressor tool T81P–6500–A or equivalent, on the rocker arm. Slowly apply pressure to bleed down the lifter until it completely bottoms. Hold the lifter in this position and check the available clearance between the rocker arm and the valve stem tip with a feeler gauge. The feeler gauge width must not exceed ⅜ in., in order to fit between the rails on the rocker arm.

3. The clearance should be 0–4.5mm, 2.2mm nominal.

4. If the clearance is not within specifications, check the fulcrum, lifter, camshaft lobe and valve tip for wear.

5. With the No. 1 piston on TDC at the end of the compression stroke check the following valves: No. 1 intake, No. 1 exhaust, No. 2 intake.

6. Rotate the crankshaft 180 degrees and check the following valves: No. 3 intake, No. 3 exhaust.

7. Rotate the crankshaft another 180 degrees TDC and check the following valves: No. 4 intake, No. 4 exhaust, No. 2 exhaust.

Rocker Arms/Shafts

REMOVAL & INSTALLATION

1.6L Engine

1. Disconnect the negative battery cable. Remove the upper timing belt front cover.

2. Remove the air duct.

3. Remove the accelerator and cruise control cables, if equipped, from the rocker arm cover.

4. Disconnect the vent hose from the rocker arm cover and the spark plug wires from their clips.

5. Remove the rocker arm cover-to-cylinder head bolts, the cover and the gasket.

6. Remove the rocker arm shaft(s)-to-cylinder head bolts and the rocker arm shaft assemblies.

7. If it is necessary to separate the rocker arms from the rocker arm shafts, proceed as follows:
   a. Remove the bolts from the rocker arm shaft(s).
   b. Slide the rocker arms and springs from the shaft(s).

NOTE: Be sure to keep all the parts in order of disassembly for reinstallation purposes. The rocker arm shafts can only be installed in 1 position.

8. Clean the gasket mounting surfaces. Check all parts and replace if worn or damaged.

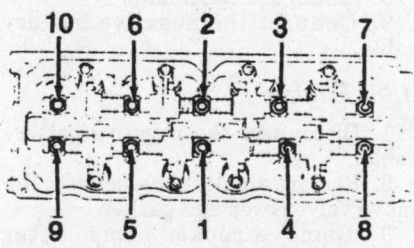

Rocker arms and shafts positioning— 1.6L engine

Rocker arm shaft torque sequence— 1.6L engine

NOTE: To prevent damage to the O-ring on the hydraulic lash adjuster of the rocker arm, do not tamper with it unless replacement is necessary.

To install:

9. To install, use new gasket or sealant and reverse the removal procedure. Torque the rocker arm shaft(s)-to-cylinder head (oil holes facing downward) bolts, in sequence, to 16–21 ft. lbs. (22–28 Nm) and the rocker arm cover-to-cylinder head bolts to 44–79 inch lbs. (5–9 Nm).

1.9L Engine

1. Disconnect the negative battery cable and remove the air cleaner assembly.

2. Remove and tag all necessary vacuum hoses from the rocker cover. Remove the spark plug wire retainers, if equipped. Remove the rocker cover from the cylinder head.

3. Remove the rocker cover and gasket from the engine.

4. Remove the rocker arm nuts, fulcrums, rocker arms and fulcrum washers. Keep all parts in order so they can be reinstalled to their original position.

To install:

5. Before installation, coat the valve tips, rocker arm and fulcrum contact areas with Lubriplate® or equivalent.

6. Rotate the engine until the lifter

is on the base circle of the cam (valve closed).

NOTE: Be sure to turn the engine only in the normal rotation. Backward rotation will cause the camshaft belt to slip or lose teeth, altering the valve timing and causing serious engine damage.

7. Install the rocker arm and components and torque the rocker arm bolts to 17–22 ft. lbs. (23–30 Nm). Be sure the lifter is on the base circle of the cam for each rocker arm as it is installed.

8. Install a new gasket and the rocker arm cover. Install the 3 retaining bolts and tighten to 4–9 ft. lbs. (5–12 Nm).

NOTE: Do not use any type of sealer with the rocker arm cover silicone gasket.

9. Connect all vacuum hoses and install the spark plug wire retainers, if equipped. Connect the negative battery cable.

Intake Manifold

REMOVAL & INSTALLATION

1.6L Engine

1. Disconnect the negative battery cable.

2. Drain the cooling system.

3. Disconnect the accelerator cable and remove the air duct from the throttle body.

4. Label and disconnect all of the necessary wiring and hoses which may interfere with the intake manifold removal.

5. Remove the throttle body and the intake plenum.

6. Remove the intake manifold-to-cylinder head bolts, the intake manifold and the gasket.

7. Clean the gasket mounting surfaces. Clean and inspect all parts for damage and/or wear; replace if necessary.

8. To install, use new gaskets and reverse the removal procedures. Torque the intake manifold-to-cylinder head bolts to 14–19 ft. lbs. (19–25 Nm). Refill the cooling system. Start the engine, allow it to reach normal operating temperature and check for leaks.

1.8L Engine

1. Properly relieve the fuel system pressure.

2. Disconnect the negative battery cable.

3. Tag and disconnect the necessary vacuum hoses from the intake manifold and plenum.

4. Remove the vacuum chamber canister from the intake plenum.

5. Disconnect the idle speed control and bypass air hoses from the intake plenum.

6. Disconnect the accelerator cable and, if equipped with automatic transaxle, the kickdown cable from the throttle cam. Remove the cable bracket from the intake plenum.

7. Tag and disconnect the throttle body electrical connectors.

8. Disconnect the fuel pressure and return line spring lock couplings.

9. Disconnect the PCV hose from the intake plenum and cylinder head cover.

10. Disconnect the fuel pressure regulator vacuum hose and the fuel injector wiring harness electrical connectors.

11. Remove the fuel rail mounting bolts and remove the fuel rail.

12. Remove the 2 bolts from the transaxle vent tube and remove the vent tube from the intake plenum.

13. Remove the intake manifold upper mounting nuts.

14. Raise and safely support the vehicle.

15. Remove the intake plenum support bracket and the intake manifold lower mounting nuts.

16. Lower the vehicle.

17. Remove the intake manifold, intake plenum and throttle body as an assembly from the vehicle.

18. Remove the intake manifold gasket.

19. If necessary, separate the intake plenum and throttle body from the intake manifold.

20. Clean all gasket mating surfaces.

To install:

21. If necessary, install the throttle body and intake plenum onto the intake manifold.

22. Install the intake manifold gasket.

23. Install the intake manifold, intake plenum and throttle body assembly onto the intake manifold mounting studs.

24. Install the mounting nuts and tighten to 14–19 ft. lbs. (19–25 Nm) in the proper sequence.

25. Raise and safely support the vehicle.

26. Install the intake plenum support bracket and tighten the bolts to specification.

27. Lower the vehicle.

28. Place the fuel rail into position and install the mounting bolts. Tighten the bolts to 14–19 ft. lbs. (19–25 Nm).

29. Connect the fuel injector wiring harness electrical connectors and connect the vacuum hose to the pressure regulator.

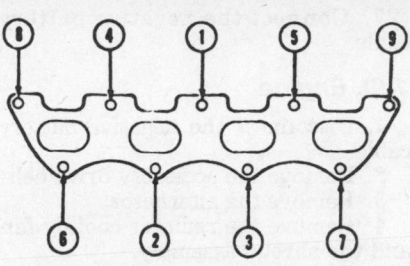

Intake manifold torque sequence— 1.8L engine

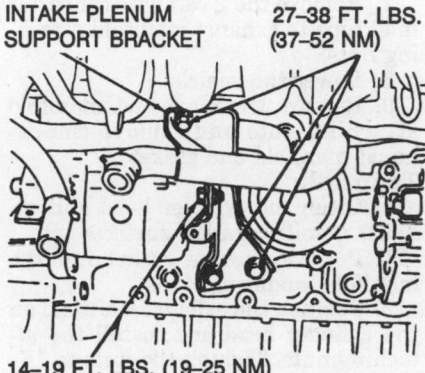

INTAKE PLENUM   27–38 FT. LBS.
SUPPORT BRACKET   (37–52 NM)

14–19 FT. LBS. (19–25 NM)

Intake plenum support bracket torque specifications—1.8L engine

30. Connect the PCV hose to the intake plenum and cylinder head cover.

31. Connect the fuel pressure and return line spring lock couplings.

32. Install the transaxle vent tube and vacuum chamber canister.

33. Connect the electrical connectors to the throttle body and the necessary vacuum hoses to the intake plenum and throttle body.

34. Connect the idle speed control and bypass air hoses to the intake plenum.

35. Install the cable bracket onto the intake plenum and connect the accelerator and, if equipped, kickdown cables to the throttle cam.

36. Install the inlet air duct that connects to the throttle body and the resonance chamber.

37. Connect the negative battery cable.

1.9L Engine

1. Properly relieve the fuel system pressure.

2. Disconnect the negative battery cable.

3. Partially drain the cooling system.

4. Remove the air intake tube.

5. Disconnect the fuel injector harness from the engine control harness at the right shock tower.

6. Disconnect the crankshaft position sensor.

7. Disconnect the fuel supply and return lines.

8. Remove the accelerator cable and, if equipped with automatic transaxle, kickdown cable from the throttle lever. Remove the cable bracket from the intake manifold and position the cables aside.

9. Remove the power brake supply hose, PCV line and the vacuum line from the bottom of the throttle body.

10. Remove the 7 attaching nuts from the intake manifold studs, slide the manifold assembly off the studs and remove it from the cylinder head. Remove and discard the intake manifold gasket.

To install:

11. Clean and inspect the mounting faces of the intake manifold and cylinder head. Both surfaces must be clean and flat.

12. Clean and oil the manifold studs and position a new gasket over them.

13. Install the intake manifold and the attaching nuts. Tighten the nuts to 12–15 ft. lbs. (16–20 Nm).

14. Install the vacuum line on the bottom of the throttle body, the power brake supply hose and the PCV line.

15. Install the accelerator cable bracket and connect the accelerator cable and, if equipped, kickdown cable on the throttle lever.

16. Connect the crankshaft position sensor electrical connector.

17. Connect the fuel supply and return lines. Install the fuel line retaining clips.

18. Connect the 2 fuel injector harness connectors to the engine control harness at the right shock tower.

19. Install the air intake tube.

20. Refill the cooling system.

21. Connect the negative battery cable.

22. Start the engine and bring to normal operating temperature. Check for leaks. Stop the engine and check the coolant level.

Exhaust Manifold

REMOVAL & INSTALLATION

1.6L Engine

1. Disconnect the negative battery cable.

2. Disconnect the electrical connector from the oxygen sensor.

3. Remove the exhaust insulators-to-exhaust manifold bolts and the insulators.

4. Remove the exhaust pipe-to-exhaust manifold nuts and separate the exhaust pipe from the manifold.

5. Remove the exhaust manifold-to-cylinder head bolts, the manifold and the gasket.

6. Clean the gasket mounting sur-

faces. Inspect all parts for damage and replace, if necessary.

7. To install, use new gaskets and reverse the removal procedures. Torque the exhaust manifold-to-cylinder head bolts to 12–17 ft. lbs. (16–23 Nm) and the exhaust pipe-to-exhaust manifold bolts and nuts to 23–34 ft. lbs. (31–46 Nm).

8. Start the engine and check for exhaust leaks.

1.8L Engine

1. Disconnect the negative battery cable.

2. Remove the resonance duct.

3. Partially drain the cooling system and disconnect the upper radiator hose.

4. Remove the cooling fan.

5. Raise and safely support the vehicle.

6. Remove the exhaust pipe from the exhaust manifold and remove the gasket.

7. Remove the 2 bolts from the exhaust pipe support bracket.

8. Remove the left lower splash shield.

9. Lower the vehicle.

10. Disconnect the oxygen sensor electrical connector.

11. Remove the exhaust manifold heat shield mounting bolts and remove the shield.

12. Remove the exhaust manifold mounting nuts and remove the assembly.

13. Remove all gasket material from the cylinder head and exhaust manifold.

To install:

14. Install a new gasket onto the exhaust manifold mounting studs.

15. Place the exhaust manifold onto the mounting studs and install the manifold mounting nuts. Tighten the nuts to 28–34 ft. lbs. (38–46 Nm).

16. Place the heat shield into its mounting position and install the shield mounting bolts. Tighten the bolts to 69–95 inch lbs. (7.8–11.0 Nm).

17. Connect the oxygen sensor electrical connector.

18. Install the cooling fan.

19. Connect the upper radiator hose.

20. Install the resonance duct.

21. Raise and safely support the vehicle.

22. Install the exhaust pipe support bracket.

23. Install a new gasket and install the exhaust pipe to the exhaust manifold. Tighten the attaching nuts to 23–34 ft. lbs. (31–46 Nm).

24. Install the left lower splash shield and tighten the bolts to 69–95 inch lbs. (7.8–11.0 Nm).

25. Lower the vehicle.

26. Refill the cooling system.

27. Connect the negative battery cable.

1.9L Engine

1. Disconnect the negative battery cable.

2. Remove the accessory drive belt.

3. Remove the alternator.

4. Remove the radiator cooling fan and the shroud assembly.

5. Remove the exhaust manifold heat shield.

6. Raise and safely support the vehicle.

7. Remove the 2 catalytic converter inlet pipe-to-exhaust manifold attaching nuts.

8. Lower the vehicle.

9. Remove the 8 exhaust manifold attaching nuts and remove the exhaust manifold and gasket.

To install:

10. Clean the cylinder head and exhaust manifold gasket surfaces.

11. Position the new gasket onto the manifold mounting studs.

12. Position the exhaust manifold on the cylinder head and install the attaching nuts. Tighten the nuts to 16–19 ft. lbs. (21–26 Nm).

13. Raise and safely support the vehicle.

14. Install the catalytic converter inlet pipe-to-exhaust manifold attaching nuts.

15. Lower the vehicle.

16. Install the exhaust manifold heat shield.

17. Install the radiator cooling fan and shroud assembly.

18. Install the alternator and the accessory drive belt.

19. Connect the negative battery cable.

Timing Belt Front Cover

REMOVAL & INSTALLATION

1.6L Engine

1. Disconnect the negative battery cable.

2. Remove the drive belt(s) from the front of the engine.

3. Remove the right inner fender panel.

4. Remove the water pump pulley-to-water pump bolts and the pulley.

5. Remove the crankshaft pulley-to-crankshaft bolts, outer spacer, outer pulley, inner spacer, inner pulley and baffle.

6. Remove the upper/lower front cover-to-engine bolts and the covers.

7. Clean the gasket mounting surfaces.

8. To install, use a new gasket and reverse the removal procedures.

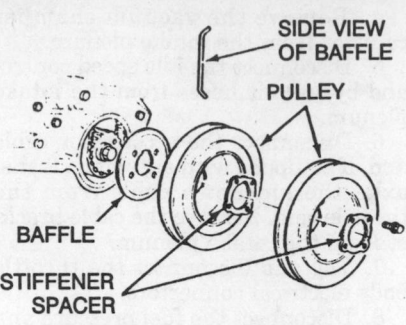

Crankshaft pulley assembly— 1.6L engine

Torque the front cover-to-engine bolts to 69–95 inch lbs. (8–11 Nm), the crankshaft pulley-to-crankshaft bolts to 36–45 ft. lbs. (49–61 Nm) and the water pump pulley-to-water pump bolts to 36–45 ft. lbs. (49–61 Nm).

1.8L Engine

1. Disconnect the negative battery cable.

2. Remove the timing belt upper cover and gasket.

3. Loosen the water pump pulley bolts.

4. Remove the alternator and water pump accessory drive belt.

5. Remove the water pump pulley bolts and remove the pulley.

6. Raise and safely support the vehicle.

7. Remove the right wheel and tire assembly.

8. Remove the right upper and lower splash shields.

9. Remove the air conditioning, if equipped, and power steering accessory drive belt.

10. Remove the crankshaft pulley, crankshaft pulley guide plate and timing belt outer and inner guide plates.

11. Remove the timing belt middle and lower covers along with the gaskets.

To install:

12. Install the timing belt middle and lower covers along with the gaskets.

13. Install the timing belt inner and outer guide plates, the crankshaft pulley and the crankshaft pulley guide plate. Tighten the bolts to 109–152 inch lbs. (12–17 Nm).

14. Install the air conditioning, if equipped, and power steering accessory drive belt.

15. Install the splash shields and tighten the bolts to 69–95 inch lbs. (7.8–11.0 Nm).

16. Install the water pump pulley and tighten the bolts to 69–95 inch lbs. (7.8–11.0 Nm).

17. Install the alternator and water pump accessory drive belt.

18. Install the right wheel and tire assembly and lower the vehicle.

19. Install the timing belt upper cover and gasket. Tighten the bolts to 69–95 inch lbs. (7.8–11.0 Nm).
20. Connect the negative battery cable.

1.9L Engine

1. Disconnect the negative battery cable.
2. Remove the accessory drive belt.
3. Remove the drive belt automatic tensioner, if equipped.
4. Remove the timing cover retaining nuts.
5. Installation is the reverse of the removal procedure. Tighten the retaining nuts to 3–5 ft. lbs. (5–7 Nm).

OIL SEAL REPLACEMENT

1.6L Engine

1. Disconnect the negative battery cable. Remove the timing belt.
2. If replacing the crankshaft seal, remove the crankshaft sprocket-to-crankshaft bolt, the sprocket and Woodruff® key.
3. If replacing the camshaft seal, remove the camshaft sprocket bolt, camshaft sprocket and dowel pin.
4. Using a small prybar, pry the oil seal from the oil pump housing and/or cylinder head.

To install:

4. Using a clean shop cloth, clean the oil seal bore(s).
5. Lubricate the new oil seal(s) with clean engine oil.
6. Using a suitable seal installer, press the oil seal into the oil pump bore and/or cylinder head.
7. If the crankshaft seal was replaced, install the crankshaft sprocket and tighten the bolt to 80–94 ft. lbs. (108–128 Nm).
8. If the camshaft seal was replaced, install the camshaft sprocket, dowel pin and retaining bolt. Tighten the bolt to 36–45 ft. lbs. (49–61 Nm).
9. Install the timing belt and remaining components in the reverse order of removal.
10. Connect the negative battery cable, start the engine and check for oil leaks.

1.8L Engine

1. Disconnect the negative battery cable.
2. Remove the timing belt.
3. Remove the crankshaft oil seal as follows:
   a. Remove the crankshaft sprocket locking bolt and remove the crankshaft sprocket. If necessary, use a suitable puller.
   b. Remove the Woodruff® key.
   c. If necessary, cut the lip of the crankshaft oil seal to ease removal.

d. Use a suitable prying tool to remove the crankshaft oil seal.
4. Remove the camshaft oil seal(s) as follows:
   a. Tag and disconnect the vacuum hoses at the cylinder head cover.
   b. Disconnect the ignition wires from the spark plugs and position aside.
   c. Remove the cylinder head cover mounting bolts and remove the cover.
   d. Hold the camshaft with a wrench and remove the camshaft sprocket lock bolt. Remove the camshaft sprocket.
   e. Remove the seal plate mounting bolts and remove the seal plate.
   f. Remove the camshaft seal using a suitable tool.

To install:

5. Install the new crankshaft oil seal as follows:
   a. Lubricate the lip of the new crankshaft oil seal with clean engine oil.
   b. Using a suitable installation tool, install the seal evenly until it is flush with the edge of the oil pump body.
   c. Install the crankshaft sprocket onto the shaft, making sure to match the alignment grooves.
   d. Install the Woodruff® key with the tapered end facing the oil pump.
   e. Install the crankshaft sprocket locking bolt. Tighten the locking bolt to 80–87 ft. lbs. (108–118 Nm).
6. Install the new camshaft oil seal(s) as follows:
   a. Apply a small amount of clean engine oil to the lip of a new camshaft oil seal.
   b. Install the seal, using a suitable seal installer.
   c. Install the seal plate and tighten the mounting bolts to 69–95 inch lbs. (7.8–11.0 Nm).
   d. Install the camshaft sprocket with the timing mark aligned with the timing mark on the seal plate.
   e. Hold the camshaft with a wrench and install the lock bolt. Tighten to 36–45 ft. lbs. (49–61 Nm).
   f. Install the cylinder head cover with a new gasket. Tighten the cylinder head cover bolts to 43–78 inch lbs. (4.9–8.8 Nm).
   g. Connect the ignition wires and the vacuum hoses.
7. Install the timing belt.
8. Connect the negative battery cable.

1.9L Engine

1. Disconnect the negative battery cable.
2. Remove the accessory drive belt.
3. Raise and safely support the vehicle.

4. Remove the right side splash shield.
5. Remove the flywheel inspection shield.
6. Use a suitable tool to hold the flywheel in place.
7. Remove the crankshaft bolt and washer and remove the crankshaft dampener.
8. Remove the timing belt.
9. Remove the crankshaft sprocket and belt guide and/or camshaft sprocket.
10. Using a suitable seal remover, remove the crankshaft and/or camshaft seal.

To install:

11. Lubricate the lip of the new seal with clean engine oil.
12. Install the new seal using a suitable installation tool.
13. Install the belt guide and crankshaft sprocket and/or camshaft sprocket. Tighten the camshaft sprocket bolt to 71–84 ft. lbs. (95–115 Nm).
14. Install the timing belt.
15. Position the crankshaft dampener on the crankshaft. Install the attaching bolt and washer and tighten to 81–96 ft. lbs. (110–130 Nm).
16. Remove the flywheel holding tool and install the inspection shield.
17. Install the right splash shield and lower the vehicle.
18. Install the accessory drive belt.
19. Connect the negative battery cable.
20. Start the engine and check for leaks.

Timing Belt and Tensioner

ADJUSTMENT

1.8L Engine

1. Disconnect the negative battery cable.
2. Remove the timing belt upper and middle covers and gaskets.
3. Place a wrench onto the crankshaft sprocket and rotate the crankshaft clockwise so the timing marks located on the camshaft sprocket and the seal plate are aligned.
4. Rotate the crankshaft clockwise 2 complete revolutions and align the timing marks on the camshaft sprockets and seal plate.
5. Make sure the yellow ignition timing mark on the crankshaft sprocket is aligned with the TDC mark on the timing belt cover.
6. Measure the timing belt deflection by applying 22 lbs. of pressure on the belt, at a point between the camshaft sprockets. The timing belt deflection should be 0.35–0.45 in. (9.0–11.5mm).

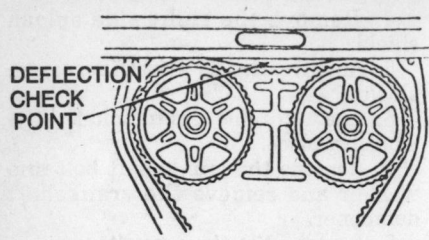

Timing belt deflection checking point—1.8L engine

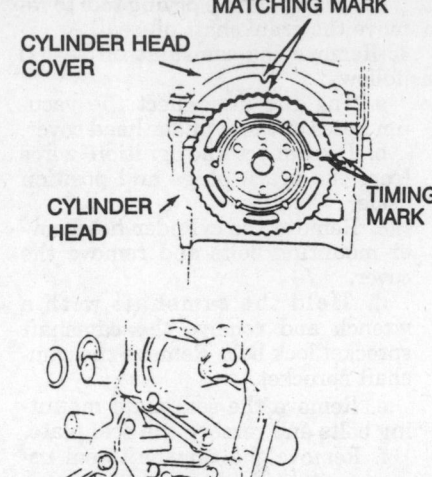

Timing sprocket alignment marks—1.6L engine

7. If the deflection is not within specification, loosen the tensioner lock bolt. Using a suitable prying tool to move the tensioner, tighten or loosen the belt, as required, so the deflection will meet specification. Tighten the tensioner lock bolt to 27–38 ft. lbs. (37–52 Nm) and recheck the timing belt deflection beginning with Step 3.

8. If the timing belt will not meet specification, it must be replaced.

9. Install new gaskets onto the timing belt covers and install. Tighten the bolts to 69–95 inch lbs. (7.8–11.0 Nm).

1.6L and 1.9L ENGINES

Timing belt adjustment is not necessary on these engines. If there is a problem with timing belt tension, the tensioner assembly must be replaced.

REMOVAL & INSTALLATION

1.6L Engine

1. Disconnect the negative battery cable.
2. Remove the timing belt covers.
3. Remove the timing belt tensioner spring and retaining bolt.
4. If the timing belt is to be reused, mark the rotation direction on belt so it can be reinstalled in the same direction.
5. Remove the timing belt.
To install:
6. Inspect the timing belt, tensioner and sprockets for signs of wear and replace, as necessary.
7. Align the marks on the camshaft and crankshaft sprockets with the cylinder head and oil pump alignment marks.
8. If reusing the timing belt, install it in the direction of the rotation mark.
9. Install the timing belt tensioner and spring. Install the spring on its anchor and hand tighten the tensioner bolt.
10. Rotate the crankshaft 2 complete revolutions and realign the timing marks. Reaffirm that the timing marks are aligned; if not, repeat the alignment procedure.
11. Torque the tensioner bolt to 14–19 ft. lbs. (19–25 Nm) and check the timing belt deflection between the crankshaft and camshaft sprockets.

The timing belt deflection should be 0.35–0.39 in. (9–10mm) at 22 lbs. pressure. If the deflection is not correct, repeat Steps 10 and 11.

12. Install the remaining components in the reverse order of their removal.

1.8L Engine

1. Disconnect the negative battery cable.
2. Remove the timing belt covers.
3. Rotate the crankshaft and align the timing marks located on the camshaft sprockets and the seal plate.
4. If the timing belt is to be reused, mark an arrow on the belt to indicate its rotational direction for installation reference.
5. Loosen the timing belt tensioner lock bolt and remove the timing belt.
To install:
6. Temporarily secure the timing belt tensioner in the far left position with the spring fully extended, then tighten the lock bolt.
7. Make sure the timing marks on the timing belt sprocket and the engine block are aligned.
8. Make sure the timing marks on the camshaft sprockets and the seal plate are aligned.
9. Install the timing belt.
10. Loosen the tensioner lock bolt. Using a prybar, position the timing belt tensioner so the timing belt is taut, then tighten the tensioner lock bolt.
11. Turn the crankshaft 2 turns clockwise and align the timing belt sprocket mark with the mark on the engine block.
12. Make sure the camshaft sprocket

marks are aligned with the seal plate marks.

NOTE: If the timing marks are not aligned, remove the belt and repeat the procedure.

13. Turn the crankshaft 1⁵⁄₆ turns clockwise and align the timing belt sprocket mark with the tension set mark, at approximately the 10 o'clock position.
14. Apply tension to the timing belt tensioner and install the tensioner lock bolt. Tighten the bolt to 27–38 ft. lbs. (37–52 Nm).
15. Turn the crankshaft 2¹⁄₆ turns clockwise and make sure the timing marks are aligned.
16. Measure the timing belt deflection by applying 22 lbs. of pressure on the belt between the camshaft sprockets. The timing belt deflection should be 0.35–0.45 in. (9.0–11.5mm). If nec-

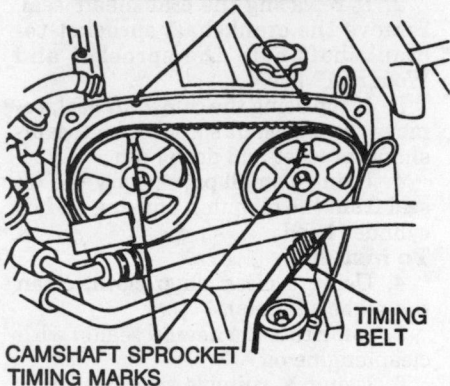
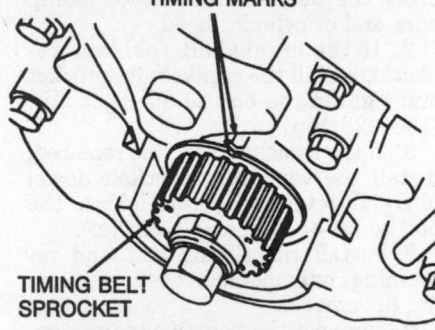

Timing sprocket alignment marks—1.8L engine

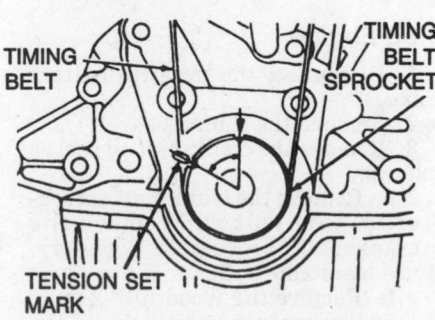

Tension set mark location—1.8L engine

essary, adjust the timing belt deflection.

17. Turn the crankshaft 2 turns clockwise and make sure the timing marks are aligned.

NOTE: If the timing marks are not aligned, repeat the procedure beginning at Step 9.

18. Install the timing belt covers and the remaining components according to the proper procedure.

19. Connect the negative battery cable.

1.9L Engine

1. Disconnect the negative battery cable.

2. Remove the accessory drive belt automatic tensioner and the accessory drive belt.

3. Remove the timing belt cover.

4. Align the timing mark on the camshaft sprocket with the timing mark on the cylinder head.

5. Confirm that the timing mark on the crankshaft sprocket is aligned with the timing mark on the oil pump housing.

6. Loosen the belt tensioner attaching bolt, pry the tensioner away from the timing belt and retighten the bolt.

7. Remove the spark plugs.

8. Raise and safely support the vehicle.

9. Remove the right side splash shield.

10. Remove the flywheel inspection shield.

11. Use a suitable tool to hold the flywheel in place.

12. Remove the crankshaft damper bolt and washer and remove the damper.

13. Remove the timing belt.

NOTE: With the timing belt removed and the No. 1 piston at TDC, Do not rotate the camshaft. If the camshaft must be rotated, align the crankshaft damper 90 degrees BTDC.

To install:

14. Install the timing belt over the sprockets in a counterclockwise direction starting at the crankshaft. Keep the belt span from the crankshaft to the camshaft tight while installing over the remaining sprocket.

15. Loosen the belt tensioner attaching bolt, allowing the tensioner to snap against the belt.

16. Rotate the crankshaft clockwise 2 complete revolutions, stopping at TDC. This will allow the tensioner spring to load the timing belt.

NOTE: Do not turn the engine counterclockwise to align the timing marks. Do not rotate the

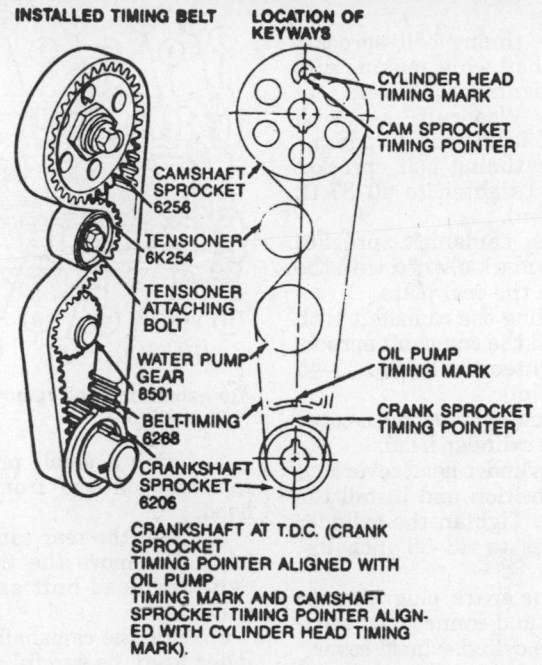

INSTALLED TIMING BELT   LOCATION OF KEYWAYS

CYLINDER HEAD TIMING MARK

CAM SPROCKET TIMING POINTER

CAMSHAFT SPROCKET 6256

TENSIONER 6K254

TENSIONER ATTACHING BOLT

WATER PUMP GEAR 8501

BELT-TIMING 6268

CRANKSHAFT SPROCKET 6206

OIL PUMP TIMING MARK

CRANK SPROCKET TIMING POINTER

CRANKSHAFT AT T.D.C. (CRANK SPROCKET TIMING POINTER ALIGNED WITH OIL PUMP TIMING MARK AND CAMSHAFT SPROCKET TIMING POINTER ALIGNED WITH CYLINDER HEAD TIMING MARK).

Timing belt and sprocket alignment position – 1.9L engine

crankshaft with the spark plugs installed.

17. Recheck the camshaft and crankshaft timing marks for alignment, to make sure the timing belt has not skipped a tooth during rotation. Repeat the procedure if the timing marks are not aligned.

18. Tighten the tensioner attaching bolt to 17–22 ft. lbs. (23–30 Nm).

19. Install the crankshaft dampener and the bolt and washer. Tighten the bolt to 81–96 ft. lbs. (110–130 Nm).

20. Install the flywheel inspection shield.

21. Install the splash shield and lower the vehicle.

22. Install the spark plugs.

23. Install the timing belt cover.

24. Install the accessory drive belt automatic tensioner and the accessory drive belt.

25. Connect the negative battery cable.

Timing Sprockets

REMOVAL & INSTALLATION

1.6L Engine

1. Disconnect the negative battery cable.

2. Remove the timing belt.

3. Insert a small prybar into a camshaft sprocket slot to keep the sprocket from turning. Remove the sprocket retaining bolt, sprocket and dowel pin.

4. If equipped with manual transaxle, place the shift lever in 4th gear and apply the parking brake. If equipped

with automatic transaxle, remove the flywheel dust cover and hold the flywheel with a suitable tool.

5. Remove the crankshaft sprocket bolt, sprocket and key.

To install:

6. Install the crankshaft sprocket and key. Install the sprocket bolt and tighten to 80–94 ft. lbs. (108–128 Nm). Remove the flywheel holding tool and replace the dust cover, if necessary.

7. Install the camshaft sprocket, dowel pin and bolt. Tighten the bolt to 36–45 ft. lbs. (49–61 Nm).

9. Install the timing belt and remaining components in the reverse order of removal.

1.8L Engine

1. Disconnect the negative battery cable.

2. Remove the timing belt according to the proper procedure.

3. Disconnect the vacuum hoses from the cylinder head cover.

4. Disconnect the spark plug wires from the spark plugs and position the wires aside.

5. Remove the cylinder head cover mounting bolts and remove the cover and gasket.

6. While holding the camshaft with a wrench, remove the camshaft sprocket lock bolt. Remove the camshaft sprocket.

7. Remove the timing belt crankshaft sprocket locking bolt.

8. Remove the timing belt sprocket. If necessary, use a suitable puller.

9. Remove the Woodruff® key from the crankshaft.

To install:

10. Install the timing belt sprocket onto the crankshaft while making sure to match the alignment grooves.

11. Install the Woodruff® key with the tapered end facing the oil pump.

12. Install the timing belt sprocket locking bolt and tighten to 80–87 ft. lbs. (108–118 Nm).

13. Install the camshaft sprocket with the timing mark aligned with the timing mark on the seal plate.

14. While holding the camshaft with a wrench, install the camshaft sprocket lock bolt. Tighten the bolt to 36–45 ft. lbs. (49–61 Nm).

15. Install a new cylinder head cover gasket onto the cylinder head.

16. Place the cylinder head cover into its mounting position and install the mounting bolts. Tighten the cylinder head cover bolts to 43–78 inch lbs. (4.9–8.8 Nm).

17. Connect the spark plug wires to the spark plugs and connect the vacuum hoses to the cylinder head cover.

18. Install the timing belt and timing belt covers according to the proper procedure.

1.9L Engine

1. Disconnect the negative battery cable.

2. Remove the timing belt cover and timing belt.

NOTE: With the timing belt removed and pistons at TDC, do not rotate the engine. If the camshaft must be rotated, align the crankshaft sprocket to 90 degrees BTDC.

3. Remove the camshaft sprocket attaching bolt and washer and camshaft sprocket.

4. Remove the crankshaft sprocket.

To install:

5. Install the camshaft sprocket and attaching bolt and washer. Tighten to 71–84 ft. lbs. (95–115 Nm).

6. Install the crankshaft sprocket.

7. Install the timing belt and cover.

8. Connect the negative battery cable.

Camshaft

REMOVAL & INSTALLATION

1.6L Engine

1. Disconnect the negative battery cable.

2. Remove the cylinder head from the vehicle and place in a suitable holding fixture.

3. Using a prybar to prevent the camshaft from turning, remove the camshaft sprocket-to-camshaft bolt and the sprocket.

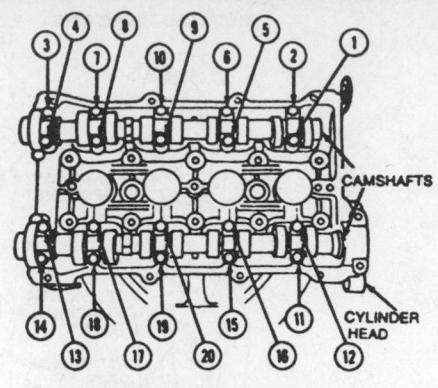

Camshaft cap bolt removal sequence— 1.8L engine

4. Using a small prybar, pry the camshaft oil seal from the cylinder head.

5. From the rear camshaft bearing journal, remove the thrust plate-to-cylinder head bolt and the thrust plate.

6. Slide the camshaft from the cylinder head; be careful not to damage the journals and/or the lobes.

To install:

7. Clean all gasket mounting surfaces. Clean and inspect all parts for damage and/or wear and replace, as necessary.

8. Lubricate the camshaft journals and lobes with clean engine oil and carefully slide the camshaft into the cylinder head.

9. Install the thrust plate and tighten the bolt to 6–9 ft. lbs. (8–12 Nm).

10. Lubricate the lip of a new camshaft seal and install into the cylinder head, using a suitable seal installer.

11. Install the camshaft sprocket and tighten the bolt to 36–45 ft. lbs. (49–61 Nm).

12. Install the cylinder head.

13. Refill the cooling system. Start the engine, allow it to reach normal operating temperature and check for leaks. Check the ignition timing.

1.8L Engine

1. Disconnect the negative battery cable.

2. Remove the distributor assembly.

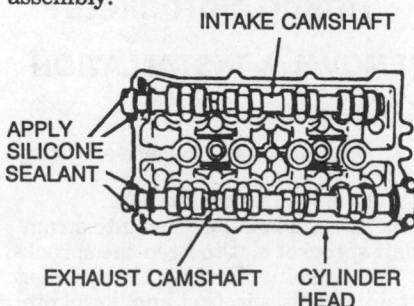

Sealant application locations—1.8L engine

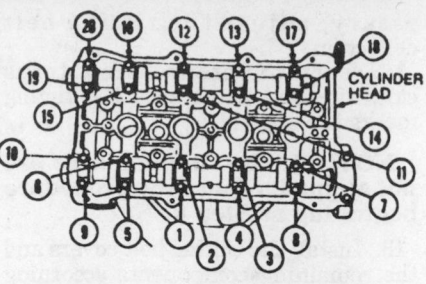

Camshaft cap bolt torque sequence— 1.8L engine

3. Remove the camshaft sprockets.

4. Remove the seal plate mounting bolts and remove the seal plate.

5. Loosen the camshaft cap bolts in the correct sequence.

6. Remove the camshaft caps and note their mounting locations for installation reference.

NOTE: The camshaft caps are numbered and have arrow marks for installation and direction reference.

7. Remove the camshaft and camshaft oil seal.

To install:

8. Apply clean engine oil to the camshaft journals and bearings.

9. Place the camshaft into its mounting position.

NOTE: The exhaust camshaft has a groove which must be installed into the distributor drive gear.

10. Apply silicone sealant to the required areas.

11. Install the camshaft caps according to the cap numbers and arrow marks.

12. Install the camshaft cap bolts and tighten them in the proper sequence to 100–126 inch lbs. (11.3–14.2 Nm).

13. Apply a small amount of clean engine oil to the lip of a new camshaft oil seal. Using a suitable installation tool, install the new seal.

14. Place the seal plate into its mounting position and install the mounting bolts. Tighten the bolts to 69–95 inch lbs. (7.8–11.0 Nm).

15. Install the camshaft sprockets and the distributor assembly.

16. Connect the negative battery cable.

1.9L Engine

1. Disconnect the negative battery cable.

2. Remove the air cleaner or air intake duct.

3. Remove the accessory drive belts and crankshaft damper.

4. Remove the timing belt cover and rocker arm cover.

5. Set the engine No. 1 cylinder at TDC prior to removing timing belt.

NOTE: Make sure the crankshaft is positioned at TDC and do not turn the crankshaft until the timing belt is installed.

6. Remove rocker arms and lifters as follows:
   a. Remove hex flange bolts.
   b. Remove fulcrums.
   c. Remove rocker arms.
   d. Remove lifter guide retainers.
   e. Remove lifters guides.
   f. Remove lifters.
7. Remove the ignition coil assembly.
8. Remove timing belt.
9. Remove the camshaft sprocket and key.
10. Remove the camshaft thrust plate.
11. Remove the cup plug from the back of the cylinder head.
12. Remove the camshaft through the back of the head toward the transaxle.
13. Replace camshaft seal.
To install:
14. Thoroughly coat the camshaft bearing journals, cam lobe surfaces and thrust plate groove with a suitable lubricant.
15. Install the camshaft through the rear of the cylinder head. Rotate the camshaft during installation, being careful to prevent bearing damage.

NOTE: Before installing the camshaft, apply a thin film of lubricant to the lip of the camshaft seal.

16. Install the camshaft thrust plate. Tighten attaching bolts to 6–9 ft. lbs. (8–13 Nm).
17. Align and install the cam sprocket over the cam key. Install attaching washer and bolt. While holding camshaft stationary, tighten the bolt to 71–84 ft. lbs. (95–115 Nm).
18. Install the cup plug using sealer. Use the sealer sparingly, as excess sealer may clog the oil holes in the camshaft.
19. Install the timing belt.
20. Install the timing belt cover.
21. Install the rocker arm assembly as follows:

NOTE: Lubricate all the parts with a heavy engine oil before installation.

   a. Install the lifters.
   b. Install the lifter guides.
   c. Install the lifter retainers.
   d. Install the rocker arms.
   e. Install the fulcrums.
   f. Install the rocker arm bolts. Tighten to 17–22 ft. lbs. (23–30 Nm).
22. Install the ignition coil assembly.

23. Install new rocker arm cover gasket, if required.

NOTE: Make sure the surfaces on the cylinder head and rocker arm cover are clean and free of sealant material.

24. Install the rocker arm cover and attaching bolts and tighten to 4–9 ft. lbs. (5–12 Nm).
25. Install the air intake duct or the air cleaner assembly.
26. Connect negative battery cable.

Piston and Connecting Rod

POSITIONING

NOTE: On 1.8L engine, the piston and rod assembly must be positioned in the engine block with the F mark facing the front of the engine.

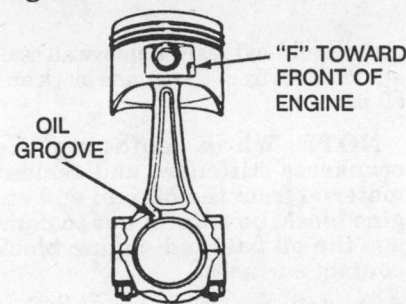

"F" TOWARD FRONT OF ENGINE

OIL GROOVE

Piston and connecting rod positioning— 1.6L engine

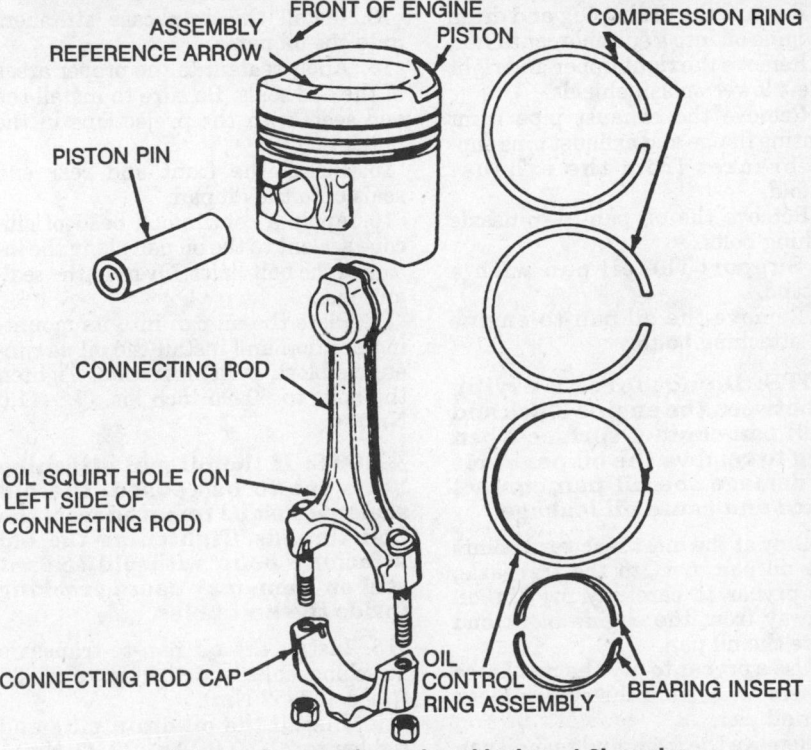

ASSEMBLY REFERENCE ARROW

FRONT OF ENGINE

PISTON

COMPRESSION RING

PISTON PIN

CONNECTING ROD

OIL SQUIRT HOLE (ON LEFT SIDE OF CONNECTING ROD)

CONNECTING ROD CAP

OIL CONTROL RING ASSEMBLY

BEARING INSERT

Piston and connecting rod positioning—1.9L engine

ENGINE LUBRICATION

Oil Pan

REMOVAL & INSTALLATION

1.6L Engine

1. Disconnect the negative battery cable.
2. Raise and support the vehicle safely.
3. Remove the under engine splash shields and the right front inner fender panel.
4. Place a drain pan under the engine, remove the oil pan plug and drain the crankcase.
5. Remove the flywheel-to-engine support housing bracket and the dust cover from the flywheel housing.
6. Remove the oil pan-to-engine nuts, bolts and stiffeners. Remove the oil pan.

NOTE: If might be necessary to rotate the crankshaft to clear the oil pan.

To install:
7. Clean the gasket mounting surfaces.
8. Apply oil resistant sealer across the joint line of the cylinder block and the front and rear engine covers. Install a new pan gasket, the oil pan and

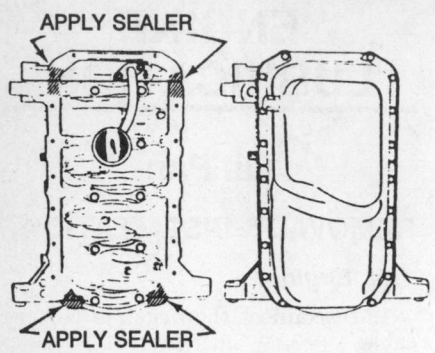

APPLY SEALER

APPLY SEALER

Sealant application locations—1.6L engine

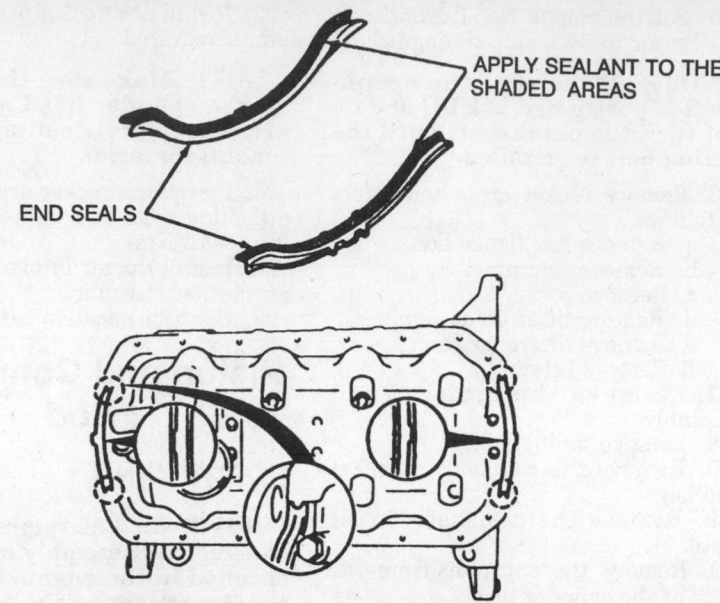

APPLY SEALANT TO THE SHADED AREAS

END SEALS

Sealant application areas—1.8L engine

stiffeners and tighten the bolts and nuts to 69–78 inch lbs. (8–9 Nm).

9. Install the dust cover and tighten the bolts to 13–20 ft. lbs. (18–26 Nm).

10. Install the engine-to-flywheel housing support bracket. Tighten the bolts to 69–86 ft. lbs. (93–117 Nm).

11. Install the oil pan drain plug and tighten.

12. Install the splash shields and inner fender panel.

13. Lower the vehicle and add the proper type and quantity of engine oil.

14. Connect the negative battery cable, start the engine and check for leaks.

1.8L Engine

1. Disconnect the negative battery cable. Remove the oil filler cap.

2. Raise and safely support the vehicle.

3. Remove the drain plug and drain the engine oil into a suitable container.

4. Remove the right upper and right and left lower splash shields.

5. Remove the exhaust pipe front mounting flange and exhaust pipe support bracket from the exhaust manifold.

6. Remove the oil pan-to-transaxle attaching bolts.

7. Support the oil pan with a jackstand.

8. Remove the oil pan-to-engine block attaching bolts.

NOTE: Do not force a prying tool between the engine block and the oil pan contact surface when trying to remove the oil pan. This may damage the oil pan contact surface and cause oil leakage.

9. Only at the most rearward points of the oil pan, next to the transaxle, use a prybar to carefully pry the oil pan away from the engine block and remove the oil pan.

10. Use a prybar to pry the crankcase stiffeners away from the engine block and/or oil pan.

11. Remove the front and rear oil pan gaskets and end seals. Remove all sealant material from the engine block and oil pan.

NOTE: When removing the crankcase stiffeners and sealant material from the oil pan and engine block, be careful not to damage the oil pan and engine block contact surfaces.

To install:

12. Apply a bead of silicone sealant to the crankcase stiffeners along the inside of the bolt holes.

13. Install the crankcase stiffeners onto the oil pan.

14. Apply sealant to the proper areas of the end seals. Be sure to install the end seals with the projections in the notches.

15. Install the front and rear end seals onto the oil pan.

16. Apply a continuous bead of silicone sealant to the oil pan along the inside of the bolt holes. Overlap the sealant ends.

17. Place the oil pan into its mounting position and install the oil pan-to-engine block attaching bolts. Tighten the bolts to 69–95 inch lbs. (7.8–11.0 Nm).

NOTE: If the oil pan attaching bolts are to be reused, the old sealant must be removed from the bolt threads. Tightening the old attaching bolts with old sealant still on them may cause cracking inside the bolt holes.

18. Install the oil pan-to-transaxle attaching bolts and tighten to 27–38 ft. lbs. (37–52 Nm).

19. Install the oil drain plug and tighten to 22–30 ft. lbs. (29–41 Nm).

20. Install the exhaust front mounting flange to the exhaust manifold using a new gasket. Tighten the mounting flange-to-exhaust manifold attaching nuts to 23–34 ft. lbs. (31–46 Nm).

21. Install the exhaust pipe support bracket and tighten the bolts to 27–38 ft. lbs. (37–52 Nm).

22. Install the splash shields. Tighten the bolts to 69–95 inch lbs. (7.8–11.0 Nm).

23. Lower the vehicle.

24. Fill the crankcase with the proper type and quantity of engine oil. Install the filler cap.

25. Connect the negative battery cable.

1.9L Engine

1. Disconnect the negative battery cable.

2. Raise the vehicle and support safely.

3. Drain the crankcase.

4. Remove the 2 oil pan-to-transaxle bolts.

5. Disconnect the exhaust inlet pipe at the manifold and converter. Remove pipe.

6. Remove oil pan retaining bolts and oil pan.

7. Remove oil pan gasket and discard.

To install:

8. Clean the oil pan gasket surface and the mating surface on the cylinder block. Wipe the oil pan rail with a solvent-soaked cloth to remove oil traces.

9. Remove and clean the oil pump pick up tube and screen assembly. Install tube and screen assembly using a new gasket.

10. Apply a bead of silicone rubber sealer at the corner of the block and at

BOLT TIGHTENING SEQUENCE
OIL PAN ASSEMBLY

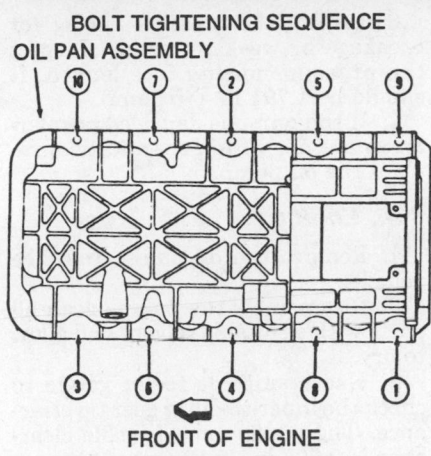

FRONT OF ENGINE

Oil pan bolt torque sequence—1.9L engine

the seating point of the oil pump and the rear seal retainer joint.

11. Install the gasket in oil pan ensuring press fit tabs are fully engaged in oil pan gasket channel.

12. Install the oil pan and the attaching bolts. Tighten the bolts lightly until the 2 oil pan-to-transmission bolts can be installed.

NOTE: If the oil pan is installed on the engine outside of the vehicle, a transaxle case, or equivalent fixture must be bolted to the block to line the oil pan up, flush with the rear face of the block.

13. Tighten the 2 pan-to-transaxle bolts to 30–40 ft. lbs. (40–54 Nm), then loosen ½ turn.

14. Tighten the oil pan flange-to-cylinder block bolts to 15–22 ft. lbs. (20–30 Nm) in the proper sequence. Retighten the 2 oil pan-to-transaxle bolts to 30–40 ft. lbs. (40–55 Nm).

15. Install the transaxle inspection plate.

16. Install the exhaust inlet pipe. Lower the vehicle and fill the crankcase with the proper type and quantity of engine oil.

17. Connect negative battery cable.

18. Start the engine and check for oil leaks.

Oil Pump

REMOVAL & INSTALLATION

1.6L Engine

1. Disconnect the negative battery cable.

2. Remove the timing belt and the oil pan.

3. Remove the crankshaft sprocket-to-crankshaft bolt and the sprocket.

4. Remove the oil pan.

5. Remove the oil pump-to-engine bolts and the oil pump.

6. Remove the oil pump pickup tube/screen assembly.

To install:

7. Clean the gasket mounting surfaces.

8. Install the pickup tube/screen assembly to the pump using a new gasket.

9. Apply a thin film of sealer to both sides of a new gasket and install the gasket and oil pump onto the cylinder block. Do not allow sealer to squeeze into the pump outlet hole in the pump or cylinder block.

10. Tighten the pump mounting bolts to 14–19 ft. lbs. (19–25 Nm).

11. Install the remaining components in the reverse order of removal.

12. Refill the crankcase with the proper type and quantity of engine oil. Start the engine and check for leaks.

1.8L Engine

1. Disconnect the negative battery cable.

2. Remove the timing belt and crankshaft sprocket.

3. Remove the oil pan.

4. Remove the oil strainer mounting bolts and remove the oil strainer and gasket.

5. If equipped, remove the air conditioning compressor mounting bolts and position the compressor so it is free from the work area.

6. Remove the air conditioning compressor mounting bracket.

7. Remove the mounting bolt from the engine oil dipstick tube bracket

and remove the alternator lower mounting bolt.

8. Remove all oil pump mounting bolts and remove the oil pump. Remove all gasket material from the oil pump.

To install:

9. Install a new gasket onto the oil pump.

10. Place the oil pump into its mounting position and install the pump mounting bolts. Tighten the bolts to 14–19 ft. lbs. (19–25 Nm).

11. Place the dipstick tube bracket bolt into its mounting position and install the mounting bolt.

12. Install the alternator lower mounting bolt and tighten to 27–38 ft. lbs. (37–52 Nm).

13. Install a new gasket onto the oil strainer, place the strainer into its mounting position and install the mounting bolts. Tighten to 69–95 inch lbs. (7.8–11.0 Nm).

14. Install the oil pan.

15. If equipped, place the air conditioning compressor bracket into its mounting position and install the mounting bolts. Tighten the bolts to 30–40 ft. lbs. (40–55 Nm).

16. If equipped, install the air conditioning compressor into its mounting position and install the mounting bolts. Tighten to 15–22 ft. lbs. (20–30 Nm).

17. Install the crankshaft sprocket and timing belt.

18. Connect the negative battery cable.

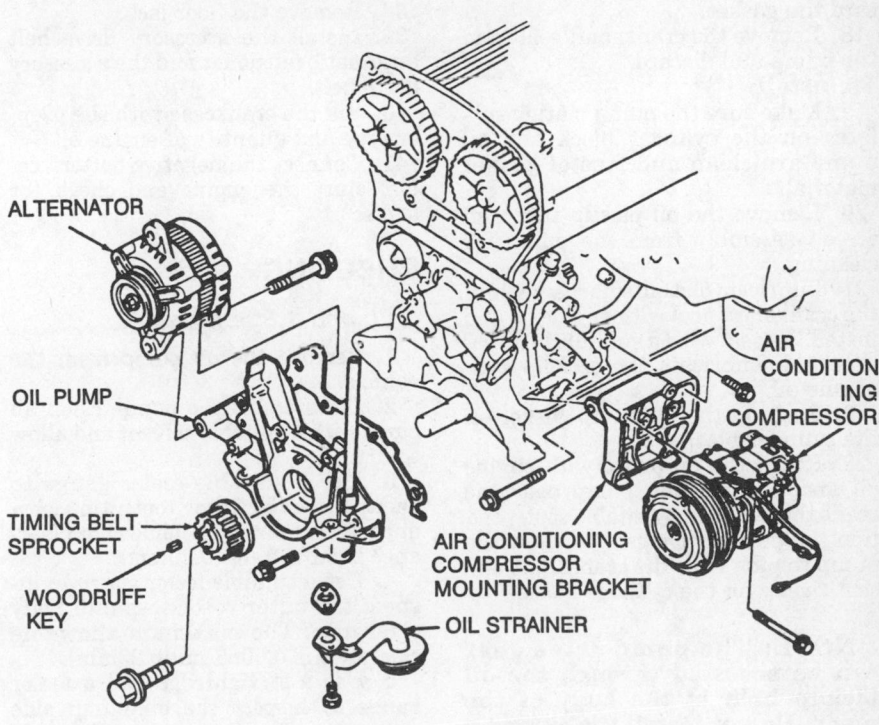

ALTERNATOR

OIL PUMP

TIMING BELT SPROCKET

WOODRUFF KEY

AIR CONDITIONING COMPRESSOR

AIR CONDITIONING COMPRESSOR MOUNTING BRACKET

OIL STRAINER

Oil pump removal and installation—1.8L engine

1.9L Engine

1. Disconnect the negative battery cable.
2. Remove the accessory drive belt and the automatic tensioner.
3. Support the engine with a floor jack.
4. Remove the right engine mount dampener and remove the right engine mount bolts from the mount bracket.
5. Loosen the mount thru-bolt and roll the mount aside.
6. Remove the timing belt cover.
7. Make sure the No. 1 cylinder is at TDC.
8. Roll the engine mount back into place and install the 2 mount bolts. Remove the floor jack.
9. Loosen the belt tensioner attaching bolt and pry the tensioner to the rear of the engine. Tighten the attaching bolt.
10. Raise and safely support the vehicle.
11. Remove the right side splash shield.
12. Remove the catalytic converter inlet pipe.
13. Drain and remove the oil pan. Remove the oil filter.
14. Remove the crankshaft damper and the timing belt.
15. Remove the crankshaft sprocket and the timing belt guide from the crankshaft.
16. Disconnect the crank angle sensor.
17. Remove the 6 oil pump-to-engine bolts and remove the oil pump assembly from the engine. Remove and discard the gasket.
18. Remove the crankshaft seal from the pump and discard.

To install:
19. Make sure the pump mating surfaces on the cylinder block and oil pump are clean and free of gasket material.
20. Remove the oil pickup tube and screen assembly from the pump for cleaning.
21. Lubricate the outside diameter of the crankshaft seal with engine oil and install the seal with a suitable installation tool. Lubricate the seal lip with engine oil.
22. Position the oil pump gasket on the cylinder block.
23. Prime the oil pump with engine oil and position the pump over the crankshaft. Using a suitable tool, position the pump drive gear to allow the pump to pilot over the crankshaft and seat firmly on the cylinder block.

NOTE: The pump drive gear can be accessed through the oil pickup hole in the body of the pump. Do not install the oil pump pickup tube and screen until the pump has been correctly installed on the cylinder block.

24. Install the 6 oil pump bolts and tighten to 8–12 ft. lbs. (11–16 Nm).

NOTE: When the oil pump bolts are tightened, the gasket must not be below the cylinder block sealing surface.

25. Install the pickup tube and screen assembly on the oil pump using a new gasket. Tighten the attaching screws to 7–9 ft. lbs. (10–13 Nm).
26. Install the timing belt guide over the end of the crankshaft and install the crankshaft sprocket.
27. Make sure the No. 1 cylinder is at TDC.
28. Position the timing belt over the sprockets.
29. Connect the crank angle sensor.
30. Install the oil pan and the crankshaft damper.
31. Install the catalytic converter inlet pipe.
32. Install the splash shield and lower the vehicle.
33. Install the timing belt according to the proper procedure. Tighten the tensioner attaching bolt to 17–22 ft. lbs. (23–30 Nm).
34. Support the engine with a floor jack.
35. Remove the right engine mount bolts and roll the mount back.
36. Install the timing belt cover.
37. Roll the engine mount back into place and install the attaching bolts. Tighten the mount thru-bolt and install the mount damper.
38. Remove the floor jack.
39. Install the accessory drive belt automatic tensioner and the accessory drive belt.
40. Fill the crankcase with the proper type and quantity of engine oil.
41. Connect the negative battery cable, start the engine and check for leaks.

CHECKING

1.6L and 1.8L Engines

1. Remove the oil pump from the vehicle.
2. Disassemble the pump, clean all parts with a suitable solvent and allow to dry.
3. Use a suitable feeler gauge to check the outer rotor tooth tip clearance. The maximum allowable clearance is 0.0079 in. (0.20mm).
4. Use a suitable feeler gauge to inspect the outer rotor-to-pump body clearance. The maximum allowable clearance is 0.0087 in. (0.22mm).
5. Use a straightedge and a feeler gauge to inspect the oil pump side clearance. The maximum allowable side clearance is 0.0055 in. (0.14mm).

6. Inspect the pressure spring for breakage or weak retraction. Inspect the pressure spring free length; it should be 1.791 in. (45.5mm).
7. If the pump is damaged or tolerances are not within specification, replace the oil pump.

1.9L Engine

1. Remove the oil pump from the vehicle.
2. Disassemble the pump, clean all parts with a suitable solvent and allow to dry.
3. Use a suitable feeler gauge to check the inner-to-outer gear tip clearance. The maximum allowable clearance is 0.007 in. (0.18mm).
4. Use a suitable feeler gauge to inspect the outer gear-to-housing clearance. The maximum allowable clearance is 0.0063 in. (0.161mm).
5. Use a straightedge and a feeler gauge to inspect the inner and outer gear-to-cover clearance (endplay). The maximum allowable clearance is 0.0035 in. (0.089mm).
6. Inspect the relief valve spring for breakage or weak retraction. The spring tension should be 9.3–10.3 lbs. at 1.11 in. (41.4–45.8 N at 28.1mm).
7. If the pump is damaged or tolerances are not within specification, replace the oil pump.

Rear Main Bearing Oil Seal

REMOVAL & INSTALLATION

1.6L Engine

1. Disconnect the negative battery cable. Raise and support the vehicle safely.
2. Remove the transaxle.
3. If equipped with a manual transaxle, remove the clutch disc and pressure plate assembly.
4. Remove the flywheel-to-crankshaft bolts and the flywheel.
5. If necessary, remove the rear engine plate-to-engine bolts and the plate.
6. Remove the rear oil seal retainer bolts and the retainer.
7. Press the oil seal from the rear oil seal retainer.

To install:
8. Clean the gasket mounting surfaces. Using a clean shop cloth, clean the oil seal bore.
9. Lubricate a new oil seal with clean engine oil and press it into the retainer.
10. Install the seal retainer with a new gasket and tighten the bolts to 69–95 inch lbs. (8–11 Nm). Trim excess gasket material from the retainer after installation.

11. Install the rear engine plate and tighten the bolts to 69–95 inch lbs. (8–11 Nm).

12. Install the flywheel. Tighten the flywheel bolts to 71–76 ft. lbs. (96–103 Nm).

1.8L Engine

1. Disconnect the negative battery cable.

2. Remove the transaxle assembly.

3. If equipped with manual transaxle, remove the clutch disc and pressure plate assembly. Remove the flywheel.

4. If necessary, remove the rear cover mounting bolts and remove the rear cover.

5. Using a suitable prybar, remove the crankshaft rear oil seal. Be careful not to damage the crankshaft seal surface or seal housing.

To install:

6. If removed, install the rear cover and attaching bolts. Tighten the bolts to 69–95 inch lbs. (7.8–11.0 Nm).

7. Lubricate the lip of a new seal and install, using a suitable installation tool.

8. Install the flywheel. Tighten the flywheel bolts to 71–76 ft. lbs. (96–103 Nm).

9. Install the transaxle. Connect the negative battery cable.

1.9L Engine

1. Disconnect the negative battery cable.

2. Raise the vehicle and support it safely. Remove the transaxle.

3. Remove flywheel and the engine cover plate.

4. With a suitable tool, remove the oil seal.

NOTE: Use caution to avoid damaging the oil seal surface.

To install:

5. Inspect the crankshaft seal area for any damage which may cause the seal to leak. If damage is evident, service or replace the crankshaft, as necessary.

6. Coat the crankshaft seal area and the seal lip with engine oil.

7. Using a suitable seal installer tool, install the seal.

8. Install the engine cover plate and the flywheel. Tighten the flywheel attaching bolts to 54–64 ft. lbs. (73–87 Nm).

9. Install the transaxle assembly.

10. Connect the negative battery cable, start the engine and check for leaks.

ENGINE COOLING

Radiator

REMOVAL & INSTALLATION

1989–90

1. Disconnect the negative battery cable.

2. Disconnect the cooling fan wiring harness connector.

3. Remove the radiator cap from the filler neck.

—————— **CAUTION** ——————

Never remove the radiator cap while the engine is running or personal injury from scalding hot coolant or steam may result. If possible, wait until the engine has cooled to remove the radiator cap. If this is not possible, wrap a thick cloth around the radiator cap and turn it slowly to the first stop. Step back while the pressure is released from the cooling system. When it is certain all the pressure has been released, press down on the cap, still with the cloth, and turn and remove it.

4. Position a fluid catch pan under the radiator. Open the drain valve and drain the cooling system.

5. Disconnect the radiator hoses and the overflow tube from the radiator.

6. Disengage the wiring harness from the routing clips on the cooling fan shroud and disconnect the coolant temperature sensor wires from the lower tank.

7. If equipped with automatic transaxle, disconnect and plug the oil cooler lines.

8. Remove the 4 radiator upper tank bracket-to-core support bolts.

9. Remove the radiator/cooling fan assembly. If necessary, remove the bolts and remove the fan/shroud assembly from the radiator.

To install:

10. If removed, install the fan/shroud assembly on the radiator and secure with the bolts.

11. Lower the radiator into position, making sure the mounting insulators engage the lower tank. Attach the radiator to the core support with the 4 bolts, making sure the insulators are aligned.

12. If equipped, connect the transaxle oil cooler lines.

13. Secure the wiring harness in the routing clips and connect the coolant temperature sensor wires.

14. Connect the radiator hoses and the overflow tube.

15. Close the drain valve. Connect the negative battery cable. Fill the cooling system and connect the cooling fan harness connector.

16. Start the engine and allow to reach normal operating temperature. Inspect for coolant leaks and correct as required.

1991–93

1. Disconnect the negative battery cable. Remove the radiator cap.

—————— **CAUTION** ——————

Never remove the radiator cap while the engine is running or personal injury from scalding hot coolant or steam may result. If possible, wait until the engine has cooled to remove the radiator cap. If this is not possible, wrap a thick cloth around the radiator cap and turn it slowly to the first stop. Step back while the pressure is released from the cooling system. When it is certain all the pressure has been released, press down on the cap, still with the cloth, and turn and remove it.

2. Position a suitable container under the radiator and open the draincock to drain the radiator.

3. Raise and safely support the vehicle.

4. Remove the right side and front splash shields and remove the lower radiator hose.

5. If equipped with automatic transaxle, remove the lower oil cooler line from the radiator. Remove the oil cooler line brackets from the bottom of the radiator.

6. Lower the vehicle.

7. If equipped with automatic transaxle and air conditioning, remove the seal located between the radiator and fan shroud.

8. If equipped with automatic transaxle, remove the upper oil cooler line from the radiator.

9. If equipped with 1.8L engine, remove the resonance duct from the radiator isomounts.

10. Disconnect the cooling fan motor electrical connector and the cooling fan thermoswitch electrical connector.

11. Remove the 3 fan shroud attaching bolts and remove the shroud assembly by pulling it straight up.

12. Remove the upper radiator hose and the 2 upper radiator isomounts. Remove the radiator by lifting it straight up.

To install:

13. Make sure the radiator lower isomounts are installed over the bolts on the radiator support.

14. Position the radiator to the radiator support, making sure the radiator lower brackets are positioned properly on the lower isomounts.

15. Install the radiator upper isomounts, making sure the radiator

locating pegs are positioned correctly. Install the upper radiator hose.

16. Lower the cooling fan shroud assembly into place and install the 3 shroud attaching bolts.

17. Connect the cooling fan motor electrical connector and thermoswitch electrical connector.

18. If equipped with 1.8L engine, install the resonance duct on the radiator isomounts.

19. Install the upper oil cooler line on the radiator.

20. If equipped with automatic transaxle and air conditioning, install the seal between the radiator and fan shroud.

21. Raise and safely support the vehicle. If equipped with automatic transaxle, install the lower oil cooler line on the radiator.

22. Install the lower radiator hose and install the right side and front splash shields.

23. Lower the vehicle and fill the cooling system.

24. Connect the negative battery cable, start the engine and check for coolant leaks.

Electric Cooling Fan

TESTING

1989–90

1. Disconnect the wiring connector from the fan motor.

2. Connect a jumper wire from the positive terminal of the battery to one of the terminals in the cooling fan electrical connector.

3. Ground the other connector terminal.

4. If the cooling fan does not function, it must be replaced.

5. If the cooling fan functions but does not run during normal engine operation, check the cooling fan temperature sensor and the cooling fan relay.

1991–93

1. Make sure the ignition key is **OFF**.

2. Apply 12 volts to the **Y** wire at the cooling fan motor on all except 1.8L engine vehicles equipped with 4EAT automatic transaxle or 1.9L engine vehicles equipped with air conditioning. Replace the motor, if it does not run.

3. On 1.8L engine vehicles equipped with 4EAT automatic transaxle or 1.9L engine vehicles equipped with air conditioning, apply 12 volts to the **BL** wire on the 1.8L engine or the **LG/Y** wire on the 1.9L engine at the cooling fan motor. Replace the motor if it does not run.

REMOVAL & INSTALLATION

1989–90

1. Disconnect the negative battery cable.

2. Disconnect the fan wiring harness from the routing clamps.

3. Disconnect the electrical connector from the cooling fan.

4. Remove the fan shroud-to-radiator screws and the shroud/fan assembly from the vehicle.

5. Remove the nut and washer and remove the fan from the motor shaft. Remove the screws and remove the motor from the shroud.

6. Installation is the reverse of the removal procedure.

1991–93

1. Disconnect the negative battery cable.

2. On 1.8L engine equipped vehicles, remove the resonance duct from the radiator isomounts.

3. Disconnect the cooling fan motor electrical connector.

4. Remove the 3 shroud attaching bolts and remove the cooling fan shroud assembly by pulling it straight up.

5. Working on a bench, remove the cooling fan retainer clip. Remove the cooling fan from the motor shaft.

6. Unclip the cooling fan motor electrical harness retainers and remove the harness from the retainers.

7. Remove the cooling fan motor attaching screws and remove the cooling fan motor from the shroud assembly.
To install:

8. Position the cooling fan motor on the shroud assembly and install the attaching screws.

9. Position the cooling fan motor electrical harness in the harness retainers and clip the retainers shut.

10. Install the cooling fan on the cooling motor shaft and install the retainer clip.

11. Carefully lower the cooling fan shroud assembly into place and install the attaching bolts. Connect the cooling fan motor electrical connector.

12. If equipped with 1.8L engine, install the resonance duct on the radiator isomounts.

13. Connect the negative battery cable.

Heater Core

REMOVAL & INSTALLATION

1989–90

1. Disconnect the negative battery cable.

2. Remove the instrument panel as follows:

a. From under the instrument panel, remove both sound deadening panels and the lap duct register panel.

b. From the blower motor case and heater case, disconnect the 3 air door control cables.

c. From behind the instrument cluster, depress the speedometer lock tab and pull the speedometer cable from the cluster.

d. From behind the instrument cluster, depress the lock tab (located in the center of the connector) of the 3 electrical harness connectors and pull the connectors from the cluster.

e. From under the steering column, remove the lap duct brace-to-instrument panel screws, the brace, the lap duct and the driver's demister tube.

f. Remove the lower cover-to-steering column screws and the lower cover.

g. Remove the steering column-to-instrument panel bolts and lower the steering column.

h. Remove the glove box-to-instrument panel screws and the glove box.

i. Remove the hood release-to-instrument panel nut and move the release cable aside.

j. Remove the center floor console-to-chassis screws and the cover.

k. From below the radio, remove the lower trim panel-to-instrument panel screws and the lower panel.

l. Using a small prybar, pry the instrument panel mounting bolt covers from the perimeter of the instrument panel. Remove the instrument panel mounting bolts and nuts. Lift and pull the panel out slightly.

m. Disconnect the electrical connector from the blower motor assembly.

n. From the rear of the radio, disconnect the antenna cable.

o. From the left corner of the instrument panel, disconnect the 3 instrument panel harness connectors and remove the instrument panel.

3. Drain the cooling system.

4. Disconnect and plug the heater hoses at the heater case.

5. Remove the defroster tubes-to-heater case push pins and the defroster tubes from the heater case. Remove the main air duct-to-heater case push pin and the main air duct.

6. Remove the 2 push pins and 1 screw attaching the lower carpet panel under the heater case.

7. From the heater case, disconnect the electrical harness braces and remove the lower brace screws and brace.

8. Remove the heater case mounting nuts and bolts. Remove the lower

duct-to-heater case push pins and lower duct. Remove the heater case by pulling it straight out, being careful not to damage the extension tubes.

9. Remove the heater core cover-to-heater case screws and the cover. Remove the tube braces and pull the heater core straight out.

10. Remove the outlet extension tube clip and tube. Loosen the inlet extension tube clamp and remove the extension tube.

To install:

11. Install a new O-ring onto the outlet extension tube, position the tube into the heater core tube and install the clip.

12. Install the inlet extension tube to the heater core inlet and tighten the clamps.

13. Slide the heater core into the heater case and install the tube braces and the heater core cover.

14. Install the heater case onto the mounting studs, being careful not to damage the heater core extension tubes. Install the mounting nuts and bolts.

15. Install the lower duct to the heater case with the 2 push pins and install the lower brace with the 3 attaching screws.

16. Reroute and connect all wiring harness braces to the heater case. Install the lower carpet panel with the screw and 2 push pins.

17. Install the defroster tube and the main air duct with the push pins.

18. Make sure the rubber grommets for the extension tubes are still in place on the engine side of the bulkhead. Uncap the extension tubes and connect the heater hoses. Tighten the clamps.

19. Install the instrument panel in the reverse order of removal.

20. Fill the cooling system, connect the negative battery cable, start the engine and check for coolant leaks and proper heater system operation.

1991–93

1. Disconnect the negative battery cable and drain the cooling system.

2. Disconnect the heater hoses at the bulkhead.

3. Remove the instrument panel as follows:

   a. Remove the 4 bolts securing the steering column to the instrument panel frame. Lower the steering column.

   b. Disconnect the speedometer cable from the instrument panel.

   c. Remove the cap screws securing the instrument cluster bezel to the instrument panel and remove the instrument cluster bezel.

   d. Remove the screws and bolts securing the instrument cluster to

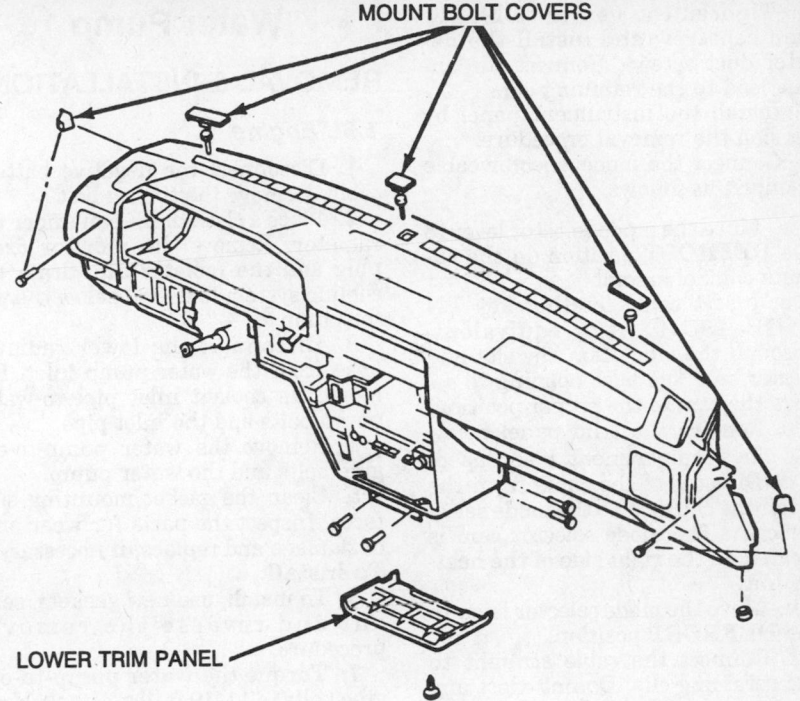

MOUNT BOLT COVERS

LOWER TRIM PANEL

Instrument panel mount bolt cover locations—1989–90 vehicles

the instrument panel. Pull the instrument cluster out slightly and disconnect the electrical connectors from the rear of the instrument cluster.

   e. Remove the instrument cluster from the instrument panel.

   f. Detach the hood release cable from the left lower dash trim panel. Carefully pry out both dash side panels.

   g. Remove the 4 retaining screws and the left lower dash trim panel. Disconnect all necessary electrical connectors.

   h. Remove the 2 hinge-to-instrument panel retaining screws and remove the glove compartment.

   i. Remove the climate control assembly and the ash tray.

   j. Remove the 7 accessory console retaining screws. Disconnect the radio antenna, radio wire connectors and cigarette lighter connector.

   k. Remove the retaining screws and the right lower dash trim panel. Disconnect the 3 amplifier wire connectors.

   l. Remove the 4 bolts attaching the instrument panel frame to the floor pan. Remove the bolts from both of the lower instrument panel mounts.

   m. Remove the 2 bolts from both of the upper instrument panel mounts. Remove the retaining screw and the defroster duct bezel.

   n. Remove the 3 mounting bolts that attach the upper instrument panel to the cowl.

   o. Pull the instrument panel slightly away from its mounting position and make sure all electrical connectors are disconnected.

   p. Remove the instrument panel from the vehicle.

NOTE: Use care to prevent any damage to the instrument panel or the surrounding interior trim.

4. Disconnect the mode selector and temperature control cables from the cams and retaining clips.

5. Remove the necessary defroster duct screws and loosen the capscrew that secures the heater-to-blower clamp.

6. Remove the 3 heater unit mounting nuts and disconnect the antenna lead from the retaining clip. Remove the heater unit.

7. Remove the insulator and the 4 brace capscrews. Remove the brace.

8. Remove the heater core from the heater unit.

To install:

9. Install the heater core into the heater unit and install the brace.

10. Install the brace capscrews and the insulator.

NOTE: If a new heater unit is being installed, save the keys that are found on the new unit for mode selector and temperature control cable adjustment.

11. Position the heater unit and attach the defroster and floor ducting. Install the heater unit mounting nuts.

12. Tighten the heater-to-blower clamp capscrew and install the defroster duct screws. Connect the antenna lead to the retaining clip.

13. Install the instrument panel by reversing the removal procedure.

14. Connect the mode selector cable and adjust as follows:

a. Move the mode selector lever to the **DEFROST** position on the climate control assembly.

b. Insert cable locating key PN E7GH–18C408–A or equivalent, through the mode cam key slot and heater case key boss opening to secure the cam in the proper position.

c. Remove the trim panel below the glove compartment, if equipped.

d. Disconnect the cable from the retaining clip next to the mode selector cam. The mode selector cam is located on the right side of the heater unit.

e. Move the mode selector lever to the **DEFROST** position.

f. Connect the cable straight to the retaining clip. Do not exert any force on the cam during cable installation.

g. Remove the cable locating key.

h. Install the trim panel, if equipped.

i. Make sure the mode selector lever moves its full stroke. If after performing the adjustment, air bleeds through the panel vents when in the **FLOOR, MIX** or **DEFROST** position, lengthen the adjustment rod 1–2 turns.

15. Connect the temperature control cable and adjust as follows:

a. Move the temperature control lever to the **COLD** position on the climate control assembly.

b. To secure the cam in the proper position, insert cable locating key PN E7GH–18G408–A or equivalent, through the cam key slot to the heater case key boss opening.

c. Disconnect the cable from the retaining clip next to the temperature control cam. The temperature control cam is located on the left side of the heater unit.

d. Connect the cable to the retaining clip.

e. Remove the cable locating key.

f. Make sure the temperature control lever moves its full stroke.

16. Connect the heater hoses at the bulkhead.

17. Fill the cooling system and connect the negative battery cable. Start the engine and check for leaks. Check the coolant level and fill as necessary.

Water Pump

REMOVAL & INSTALLATION

1.6L Engine

1. Disconnect the negative battery cable. Remove the timing belt.

2. Place a clean drain pan under the radiator. Remove the radiator drain plug and the radiator cap; drain the cooling system to a level below the water pump.

3. Disconnect the lower radiator hose from the water pump inlet. Remove the coolant inlet pipe-to-water pump bolts and the inlet pipe.

4. Remove the water pump-to-engine bolts and the water pump.

5. Clean the gasket mounting surfaces. Inspect the parts for wear and/or damage and replace, if necessary.

To install:

6. To install, use new gaskets, sealant and reverse the removal procedure.

7. Torque the water pump-to-engine bolts to 14–19 ft. lbs. (19–25 Nm), the water inlet pipe-to-water pump bolts to 14–19 ft. lbs. (19–25 Nm) and the water pump pulley-to-water pump bolts to 11–13 ft. lbs. (15–18 Nm).

8. Refill the cooling system. Start the engine, allow it to reach normal operating temperature and check for leaks.

1.8L Engine

1. Disconnect the negative battery cable.

2. Drain the cooling system.

3. Remove the timing belt according to the proper procedure.

4. Raise and safely support the vehicle.

5. Remove the engine oil dipstick tube bracket bolt from the water pump.

6. Remove the 2 bolts and the gasket from the water inlet pipe.

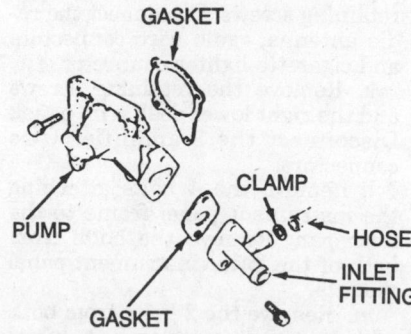

Water pump assembly – 1.6L engine

7. Remove all but the uppermost water pump mounting bolt.

8. Lower the vehicle.

9. Remove the remaining bolt and the water pump assembly.

10. If it is being reused, remove all gasket material from the water pump. Remove all gasket material from the engine block.

To install:

11. Install a new gasket onto the water pump.

12. Place the water pump into its mounting position, then install the uppermost bolt.

13. Raise and safely support the vehicle.

14. Install the remaining water pump mounting bolts and tighten all bolts to 14–19 ft. lbs. (19–25 Nm).

15. Install a new gasket onto the water inlet pipe.

16. Install the 2 bolts from the water inlet pipe to the water pump and tighten to 14–19 ft. lbs. (19–25 Nm).

17. Install the bolt to the engine oil dipstick tube bracket.

18. Lower the vehicle.

19. Install the timing belt.

20. Fill the cooling system.

21. Connect the negative battery cable.

22. Start the engine and allow to come to operating temperature. Check for coolant leaks. Check the coolant level and add coolant, as necessary.

1.9L Engine

1. Disconnect the negative battery cable.

2. Drain the cooling system.

3. Remove the accessory drive belt and its automatic tensioner.

4. Remove the timing belt cover and the timing belt.

5. Raise and safely support the vehicle.

6. Remove the lower radiator hose and remove the heater hose from the water pump.

7. Lower the vehicle.

8. Support the engine with a floor jack.

9. Remove the right engine mount attaching bolts and roll the engine mount aside.

10. Remove the water pump attaching bolts.

11. Using the floor jack, raise the engine enough to provide clearance for removing the water pump.

12. Remove the water pump and the gasket from the engine through the top of the engine compartment.

To install:

13. Make sure the mating surfaces of the cylinder block and water pump are clean and free of gasket material.

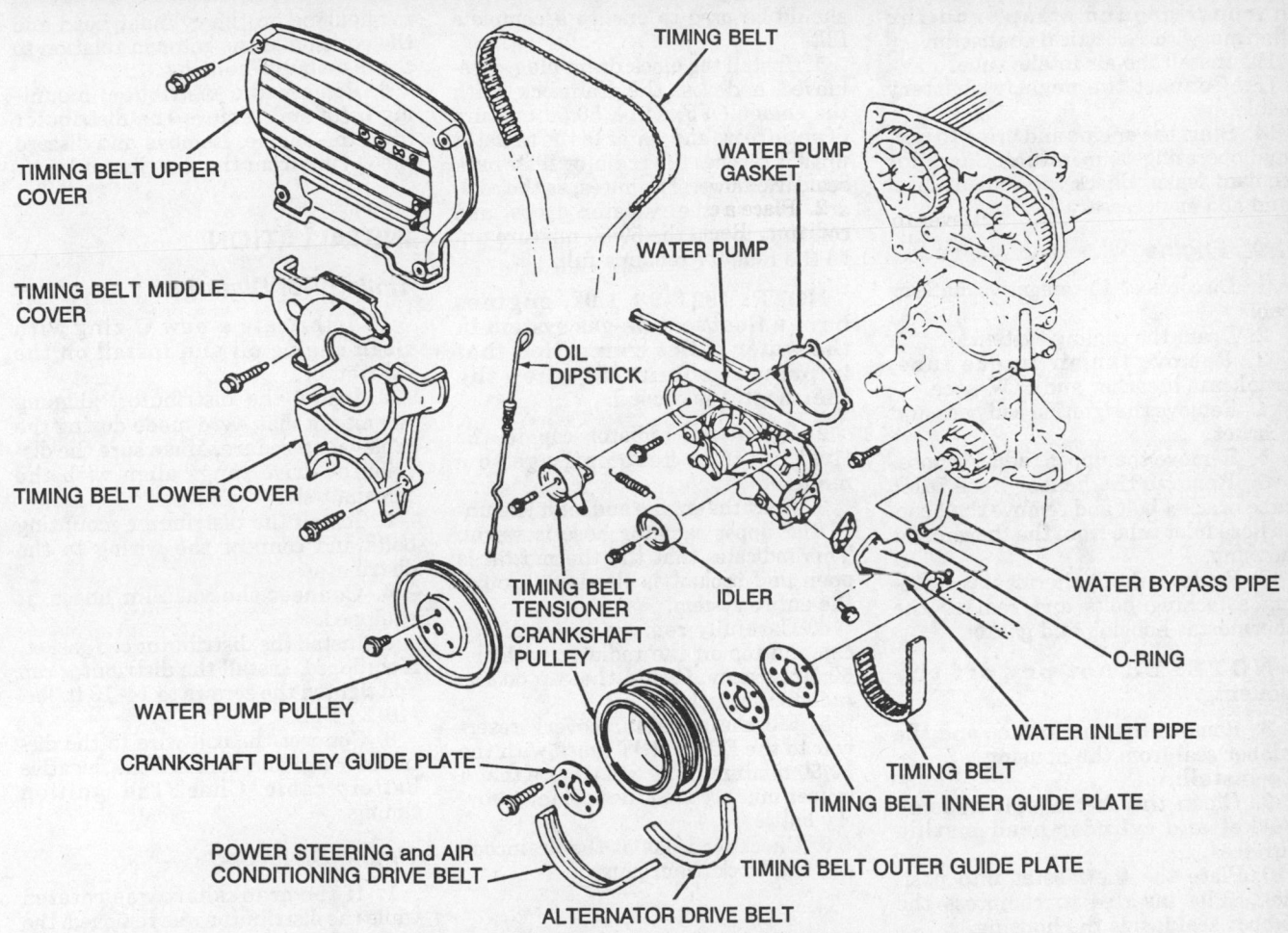

TIMING BELT

TIMING BELT UPPER COVER

WATER PUMP GASKET

WATER PUMP

TIMING BELT MIDDLE COVER

OIL DIPSTICK

TIMING BELT LOWER COVER

WATER BYPASS PIPE

TIMING BELT TENSIONER

IDLER

CRANKSHAFT PULLEY

O-RING

WATER PUMP PULLEY

WATER INLET PIPE

CRANKSHAFT PULLEY GUIDE PLATE

TIMING BELT

TIMING BELT INNER GUIDE PLATE

POWER STEERING and AIR CONDITIONING DRIVE BELT

TIMING BELT OUTER GUIDE PLATE

ALTERNATOR DRIVE BELT

Water pump removal and Installation—1.8L engine

14. If the water pump is to be replaced, transfer the timing belt tensioner components to the new water pump.

15. With the engine supported and raised with a floor jack, place the water pump and the gasket on the cylinder block and install the 4 attaching bolts. Tighten the bolts to 15–22 ft. lbs. (20–30 Nm).

16. Install the timing belt and cover.

17. Roll the right engine mount into position and install the mount bolts. Remove the floor jack.

18. Raise and safely support the vehicle.

19. Install the lower radiator hose and install the heater hose on the pump.

20. Install the crankshaft dampener and the splash shield.

21. Lower the vehicle.

22. Install the accessory drive belt automatic tensioner and the accessory drive belt.

23. Connect the negative battery cable.

24. Refill the cooling system.

25. Start the engine and allow to come to normal operating temperature. Check for coolant leaks. Check the coolant level and add as necessary.

Thermostat

REMOVAL & INSTALLATION

1.6L Engine

1. Disconnect the negative battery cable.

2. Disconnect the electrical lead from the cooling fan switch.

3. Drain the cooling system to a level below the thermostat housing.

4. Disconnect the upper radiator hose from the housing.

5. Remove the thermostat housing bolts and remove the thermostat housing and thermostat.

6. Clean the cylinder head and thermostat housing mating surfaces.

7. Installation is the reverse of the removal procedure. Torque the housing bolts to 14–22 ft. lbs. (19–30 Nm).

1.8L Engine

1. Disconnect the negative battery cable.

2. Drain the cooling system.

3. Remove the air intake tube.

4. Disconnect the water thermoswitch connector, the engine wiring harness ground strap from the connector above the housing, and the exhaust gas oxygen sensor electrical connector.

5. Remove the upper radiator hose from the housing.

6. Remove the thermostat housing attaching bolt and nut and remove the housing. Remove the gasket and the thermostat.

To install:

7. Clean the thermostat housing and cylinder head gasket surfaces.

8. Position the thermostat, gasket and housing on the cylinder head.

9. Install the attaching bolt and nut and tighten to 14–19 ft. lbs. (19–26 Nm).

10. Install the upper radiator hose.

11. Connect the oxygen sensor electrical connector, the engine wiring

harness ground strap, and the thermoswitch electrical connector.

12. Install the air intake tube.

13. Connect the negative battery cable.

14. Start the engine and bring to normal operating temperature. Check for coolant leaks. Check the coolant level and add as necessary.

1.9L Engine

1. Disconnect the negative battery cable.

2. Drain the cooling system.

3. Remove the air intake tube, crankcase breather and PCV hose.

4. Remove the ignition coil pack and bracket.

5. Remove the upper radiator hose.

6. Remove the heater hose inlet tube bracket bolt and remove the heater hose inlet tube from the thermostat housing.

7. Remove the 3 thermostat housing attaching bolts and remove the thermostat housing and gasket.

NOTE: Do not pry off the housing.

8. Remove the thermostat and the rubber seal from the housing.

To install:

9. Clean the thermostat housing pocket and cylinder head mating surfaces.

10. Place the thermostat into position, fully inserted to compress the rubber seal inside the housing.

NOTE: Make sure the thermostat tabs engage properly into the housing slots.

11. Position the thermostat housing and gasket on the cylinder head.

12. Install the 3 attaching bolts and tighten to 6.0–8.5 ft. lbs. (8.0–11.5 Nm).

13. Install the heater hose inlet pipe and the heater hose inlet pipe bracket bolt.

14. Install the upper radiator hose.

15. Install the ignition coil and bracket.

16. Install the crankcase breather, PCV hoses and the air intake tube.

17. Connect the negative battery cable.

18. Refill the cooling system.

19. Start the engine and bring to normal operating temperature. Check for coolant leaks. Check the coolant level and add as necessary.

Cooling System Bleeding

When the entire cooling system is drained, the following procedure should be used to ensure a complete fill.

1. Install the block drain plug, if removed, and close the draincock. With the engine OFF, add a 50/50 mixture of anti-freeze and water to the radiator until it reaches the radiator filler neck seat. Wait several minutes, as the coolant level in the radiator drops, and continue to add the 50/50 mixture until the radaitor remains full.

NOTE: 1991–93 1.9L engines have a float/seat de-gas system in the water outlet connection that improves coolant fill when the thermostat is closed.

2. Install the radiator cap to the first notch to keep spillage to a minimum.

3. Start the engine and let it idle until the upper radiator hose is warm. This indicates that the thermostat is open and coolant is flowing through the entire system.

4. Carefully remove the radiator cap and top off the radiator with the 50/50 mixture. Install the cap on the radiator securely.

5. Fill the coolant recovery reservoir to the FULL HOT mark with the 50/50 mixture. This will ensure that a proper mixture is in the coolant recovery bottle.

6. Check for leaks at the draincock and the block drain plug.

ENGINE ELECTRICAL

NOTE: Disconnecting the negative battery cable on some vehicles may interfere with the functions of the on board computer systems and may require the computer to undergo a relearning process, once the negative battery cable is reconnected.

Distributor

REMOVAL

1. Disconnect the negative battery cable.

2. Disconnect the coil wire, remove the distributor cap screws and move the cap aside, leaving the spark plug wires attached. Remove the cap gasket, if equipped.

3. Tag and disconnect the vacuum hoses from the vacuum advance diaphragm, if equipped.

4. Disconnect the electrical connector(s) from the distributor.

5. Mark the position of the distributor housing on the cylinder head and the position of the rotor in relation to the distributor housing.

6. Remove the distributor mounting bolts and remove the distributor from the engine. Remove and discard the O-ring from the distributor.

INSTALLATION

Timing Not Disturbed

1. Lubricate a new O-ring with clean engine oil and install on the distributor.

2. Install the distributor, aligning the marks that were made during the removal procedure. Make sure the distributor drive tangs align with the camshaft slot.

3. Install the distributor mounting bolts and connect the wiring to the distributor.

4. Connect the vacuum hoses, if equipped.

5. Install the distributor cap gasket, if equipped. Install the distributor cap and tighten the screws to 14–19 ft. lbs. (19–25 Nm).

6. Connect the coil wire to the distributor cap and connect the negative battery cable. Check the ignition timing.

Timing Disturbed

1. If the crankshaft was rotated while the distributor was removed, the piston in No. 1 cylinder must be brought to TDC on the compression stroke.

2. Remove the No. 1 spark plug. Place a finger over the hole and rotate the crankshaft slowly in the direction of normal rotation, until engine compression is felt.

NOTE: Turn the engine only in the direction of normal rotation. Backward rotation may cause the cam belt to slip or lose teeth, altering engine timing.

3. When engine compression is felt at the spark plug hole, indicating that the piston is approaching TDC, continue to turn the crankshaft until the timing mark on the pulley is aligned with the 0 mark on the engine front cover.

4. Turn the distributor shaft until the rotor aligns with the No. 1 spark plug wire on the distributor cap.

5. Place the distributor in the cylinder head, seating the distributor drive tangs in the camshaft slot and aligning the distributor housing-to-cylinder head marks.

6. Install the distributor mounting bolts and tighten them so the distributor can just barely be moved.

7. Install the distributor cap and

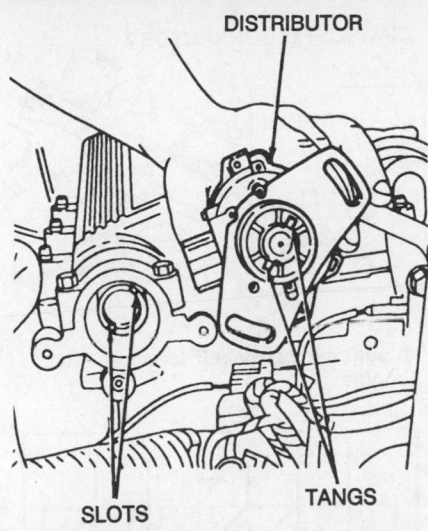

Distributor drive tang and camshaft slot locations

No. 1 cylinder spark plug. Connect all wiring.

8. Check and adjust the ignition timing.

9. After timing has been set, tighten the distributor mounting bolts to 14–19 ft. lbs. (19–25 Nm).

Distributorless Ignition System

The 1.9L engine is equipped with a Distributorless Ignition System (DIS). The DIS consists of the following components: crankshaft sensor, ignition module, ignition coil pack, the spark angle portion of the ECU and the related wiring.

The crankshaft sensor is a variable reluctance-type sensor triggered by a 36-minus-1 tooth trigger wheel configuration pressed onto the rear of the crankshaft dampener. The signal generated by this sensor is called a Variable Reluctance Sensor (VRS) signal. The VRS signal provides engine position and rpm information to the ignition module.

The ignition module is a micro-processor that receives input from the crankshaft sensor in regards to engine position and engine speed and input from the ECU pertaining to spark advance. The ignition module uses this information to direct which coil to fire and to calculate the turn ON and turn OFF times of the coils required to achieve the correct dwell and spark advance.

The ignition coil pack contains 2 separate ignition coils. Each ignition coil fires 2 cylinders simultaneously. When 1 cylinder is firing on the compression stroke, the other is firing on the exhaust stroke. During the next engine revolution, the reverse occurs. The spark plug fired on the exhaust stroke uses very little of the ignition coil's stored energy; the majority of the energy is used by the spark plug on the compression stroke. Since these 2 spark plugs are connected in series, the firing voltage of 1 plug will be negative with respect to ground, while the voltage of the other will be positive with respect to ground.

REMOVAL & INSTALLATION

Crankshaft Sensor

1. Disconnect the negative battery cable.

2. Raise and safely support the vehicle.

3. Remove the right side splash shield.

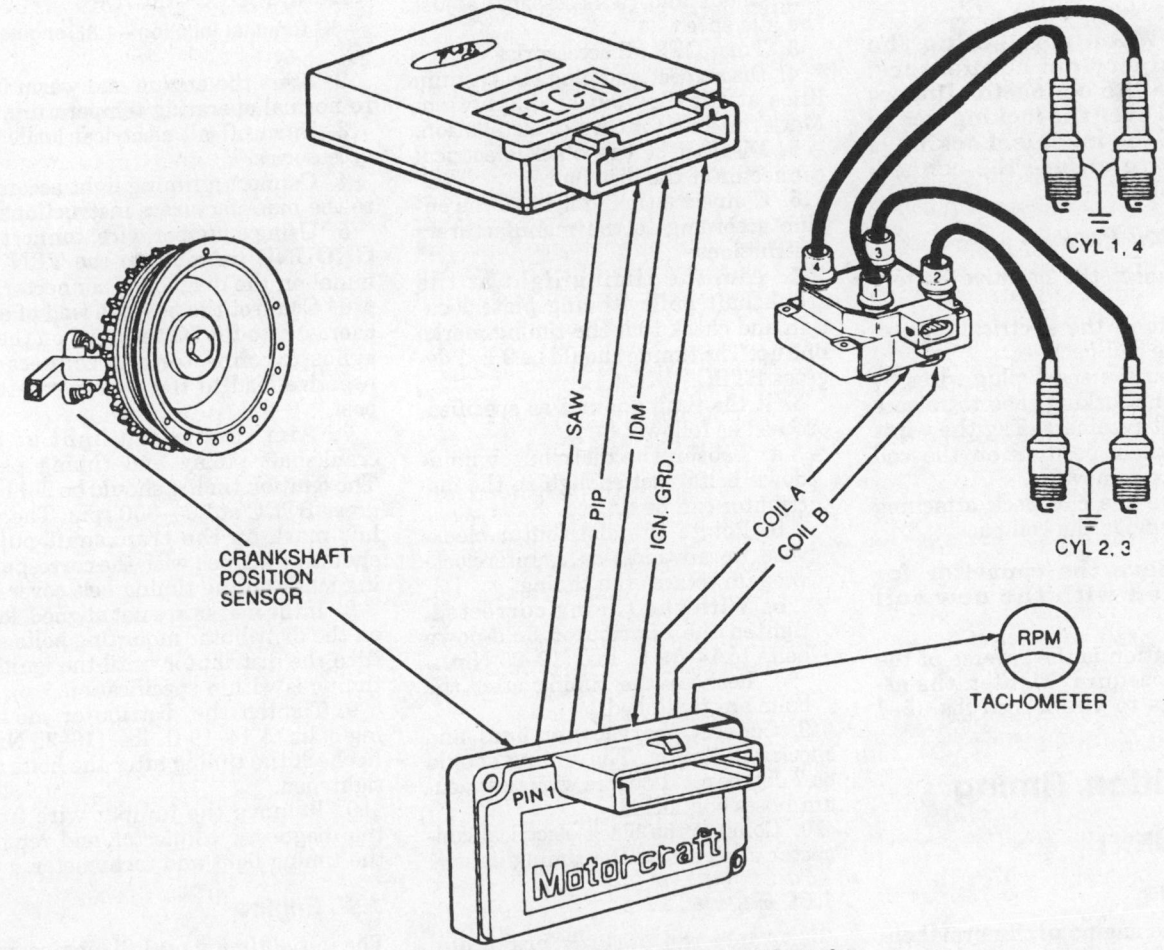

Distributorless ignition system—1.9L engine

4. Disconnect the sensor electrical connector from the wiring harness.

5. Remove the crankshaft sensor mounting screws and remove the sensor.

6. Installation is the reverse of the removal procedure. Tighten the sensor attaching screws to 40–61 inch lbs. (5–7 Nm).

Ignition Module

NOTE: The ignition module is located on the left side of the engine compartment, in front of the left strut tower.

1. Disconnect the negative battery cable.

2. Remove the 3 module sub-bracket attaching nuts.

3. Gently pull the sub-bracket and module assembly straight up and disconnect the module electrical harness.

4. Remove the 2 module attaching screws from the sub-bracket. Remove the ignition module from the sub-bracket.

5. Installation is the reverse of the removal procedure. Tighten the module attaching screws to 24–35 inch lbs. (3–4 Nm). Tighten the sub-bracket attaching nuts to 62–88 inch lbs. (7–10 Nm).

NOTE: When connecting the module electrical connectors, make sure the connector fingers are locked over the locking wedge feature of the module. Locking is important to ensure the connection is sealed.

Ignition Coil Pack

1. Disconnect the negative battery cable.

2. Disconnect the electrical connector from the coil pack.

3. Remove the spark plug wires by squeezing the locking tabs to release the coil boot retainers. Tag the wires and mark their position on the coil pack prior to removal.

4. Remove the coil pack attaching bolts and remove the coil pack.

NOTE: Save the capacitor for installation with the new coil pack.

5. Installation is the reverse of the removal procedure. Tighten the attaching bolts to 40–62 inch lbs. (5–7 Nm).

Ignition Timing

ADJUSTMENT

1.6L Engine

1. Run the engine until normal operating temperature is reached.

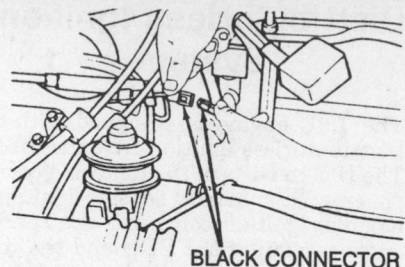

Black distributor connector location— 1.6L engine

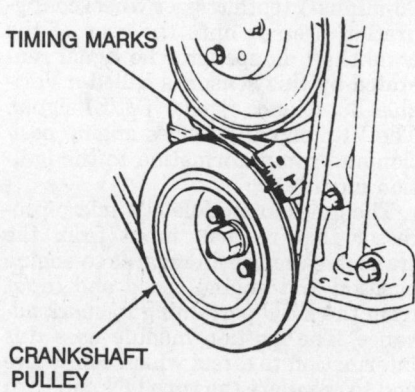

Ignition timing marks location

2. Check and, if necessary, adjust the idle speed.

3. Turn OFF all accessories.

4. Disconnect and plug the vacuum lines at the distributor diaphragm. Mark the lines for correct installation.

5. Disconnect the black electrical connector at the distributor.

6. Connect a timing light to the engine according to the manufacturers instructions.

7. Aim the timing light at the crankshaft pulley/timing plate location and check that the timing marks line up. The timing should be 2 ± 1 degrees BTDC.

8. If the timing is not as specified, proceed as follows:

    a. Loosen the distributor hold-down bolts, just enough so the distributor can be turned.

    b. Rotate the distributor clockwise (to advance) or counterclockwise (to retard) the timing.

    c. With the timing corrected, tighten the distributor hold-down bolts to 14–19 ft. lbs. (19–25 Nm).

    d. Recheck the timing after the bolts are tightened.

9. Connect the vacuum lines and check the timing. The timing should be 7 degrees ± 1 degree with the vacuum hoses connected.

10. Connect the black electrical connector and remove the timing light.

1.8L Engine

1. Apply the parking brake and make sure the vehicle is in **N** or **P**.

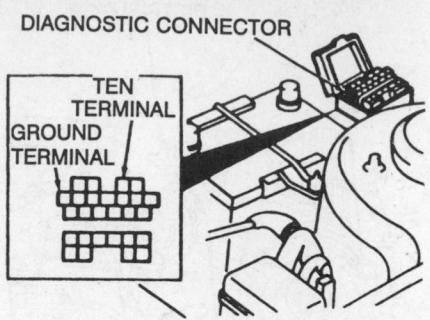

Diagnostic connector location—1.8L engine

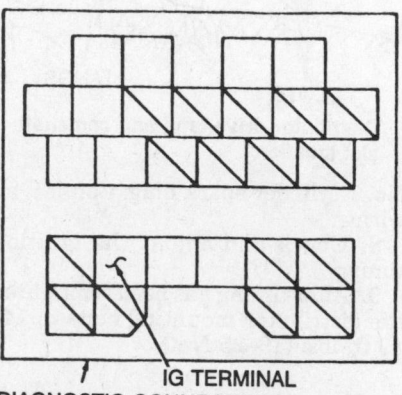

IG terminal location—1.8L engine

2. Start the engine and warm it up to normal operating temperature.

3. Turn off all electrical loads and accessories.

4. Connect a timing light according to the manufacturers instructions.

5. Using a jumper wire, connect the **GROUND** terminal to the **TEN** terminal on the diagnostic connector.

6. Connect the positive lead of a tachometer to the **IG** terminal on the diagnostic connector and connect the negative lead to the negative battery post.

7. Aim the timing light at the crankshaft pullay and timing plate. The ignition timing should be 9–11 degrees BTDC at 700–800 rpm. The yellow mark on the crankshaft pulley should be aligned with the corresponding mark on the timing belt cover.

8. If the marks are not aligned, loosen the distributor mounting bolts and turn the distributor until the ignition timing is within specification.

9. Tighten the distributor mounting bolts to 14–19 ft. lbs. (19–25 Nm). Recheck the timing after the bolts are tightened.

10. Remove the jumper wire from the diagnostic connector and remove the timing light and tachometer.

1.9L Engine

The initial timing on 1.9L engine with distributorless ignition system is fixed at 10 degrees ± 2 degrees and is not adjustable.

Alternator

PRECAUTIONS

Several precautions must be observed with alternator equipped vehicles to avoid damage to the unit.

- If the battery is removed for any reason, make sure it is reconnected with the correct polarity. Reversing the battery connections may result in damage to the one-way rectifiers.
- When utilizing a booster battery as a starting aid, always connect the positive to positive terminals and the negative terminal from the booster battery to a good engine ground on the vehicle being started.
- Never use a fast charger as a booster to start vehicles.
- Disconnect the battery cables when charging the battery with a fast charger.
- Never attempt to polarize the alternator.
- Do not use test lights of more than 12 volts when checking diode continuity.
- Do not short across or ground any of the alternator terminals.
- The polarity of the battery, alternator and regulator must be matched and considered before making any electrical connections within the system.
- Never separate the alternator on an open circuit. Make sure all connections within the circuit are clean and tight.
- Disconnect the battery ground terminal when performing any service on electrical components.
- Disconnect the battery if arc welding is to be done on the vehicle.

BELT TENSION ADJUSTMENT

1.6L and 1.8L Engines

1. Loosen the alternator adjusting bolt.
2. Raise and safely support the vehicle.
3. Loosen the alternator mounting bolt.

NOTE: Do not pry against the stator frame. Position the prybar against a stronger point, such as the area around a case bolt.

4. Position a belt tension gauge midway between the pulleys on the longest accessible belt span and tighten the belt. Adjust the tension to 85.8–103.4 lbs. for a new belt or 68.2–85.8 lbs. for a used belt.

5. If a belt tension gauge is not available, apply moderate pressure to a point midway between the pulleys on the longest accessible belt span. Adjust the tension to 0.31–0.35 in. (8–9mm) deflection for a new belt or 0.35–0.39 in. (9–10mm) deflection for a used belt.
6. Tighten the alternator adjusting bolt to 14–19 ft. lbs. (19–25 Nm).
7. Tighten the alternator mounting bolt to 27–38 ft. lbs. (37–52 Nm).
8. Lower the vehicle.

1.9L Engine

An automatic tensioner maintains correct belt tension during operation. No adjustment is necessary.

REMOVAL & INSTALLATION

1.6L Engine

1. Disconnect the negative battery cable.
2. Label and disconnect each alternator wiring connector.
3. Remove the alternator-to-adjusting bracket bolt. Loosen the alternator through bolt and allow it to pivot. Shift the alternator toward the block and remove the drive belt.
4. Remove the through bolt and the alternator.
5. To install, reverse the removal procedure. Adjust the drive belt and torque the alternator through bolt to 27–38 ft. lbs. (32–52 Nm) and the adjusting bracket bolt to 14–19 ft. lbs. (19–26 Nm).

1.8L Engine

1. Disconnect the negative battery cable.
2. Remove the nut securing the wiring connector to the alternator.
3. Remove the field terminal wiring connector.
4. Remove the upper mounting bolt securing the alternator to the alternator bracket.
5. Loosen the lower alternator mounting bolt and pivot the alternator forward.
6. Remove the alternator belt from the pulley and position the belt aside.
7. Raise and safely support the vehicle.
8. Remove the lower splash shield located under the accessory belts.
9. Remove the alternator lower mounting bolt and remove the alternator from the vehicle.
To install:
10. Position the alternator into the vehicle and install the lower mounting bolt.
11. Install the lower splash shield.
12. Lower the vehicle.
13. Position the alternator belt onto

the pulley and adjust the belt according to the proper procedure.
14. Tighten the upper mounting bolt to 14–19 ft. lbs. (19–25 Nm) and the lower mounting bolt to 27–38 ft. lbs. (37–52 Nm).
15. Install the field terminal wiring connector.
16. Position the wiring connector to the alternator and secure it with the nut.
17. Connect the negative battery cable.

1.9L Engine

1. Disconnect the negative battery cable.
2. Remove the accessory drive belt.
3. Remove the nut securing the wiring connector to the alternator.
4. Remove the 2 snap-in type wiring connectors at the alternator.
5. Remove the air conditioning hose bracket from the alternator bracket and position it aside.
6. Remove the alternator mounting bolts.
7. Remove the bolts securing the power steering reservoir and position it aside.
8. Remove the alternator from it's bracket.
To install:
9. Position the alternator onto its bracket.
10. Position the power steering reservoir and secure it with the bolts.
11. Install the alternator upper mounting bolt and tighten to 14–22 ft. lbs. (20–30 Nm). Install the alternator lower mounting bolt and tighten to 29–40 ft. lbs. (40–55 Nm).
12. Position the air conditioning hose bracket onto the alternator bracket and secure it with the bolts.
13. Install the 2 snap-in type wiring connectors into the alternator.
14. Position the wiring connector onto the alternator and secure it with the nut.
15. Install the accessory drive belt.
16. Connect the negative battery cable.

Starter

REMOVAL & INSTALLATION

1.6L Engine

1. Disconnect the negative battery cable.
2. Disconnect the electrical connectors from the starter terminals.
3. Remove the starter-to-engine support bracket.
4. Remove the starter-to-transaxle bolts and remove the starter from the vehicle.
5. To install, reverse the removal

procedure. Torque the starter-to-engine bolts to 23–30 ft. lbs. (31–41 Nm) and the support bracket nuts and thru bolt to 54–71 inch lbs. (6–8 Nm).

1.8L Engine

1. Disconnect the negative battery cable.
2. Remove the air duct that connects to the throttle body and resonance chamber.
3. Remove the starter motor upper mounting bolts.
4. Raise and safely support the vehicle.
5. Remove the intake plenum support bracket mounting bolts and remove the bracket.
6. Disconnect the S terminal connector from the starter solenoid.

NOTE: When disconnecting the plastic hard shell connector at the solenoid S terminal, grasp the plastic connector, depress the plastic tab and pull off the lead assembly. Do not pull on the lead wire or damage may result.

7. Remove the B terminal attaching nut and disconnect the cable from the terminal.
8. Remove the starter motor lower mounting bolt and remove the starter motor.
To install:
9. Place the starter motor into its mounting position and install the lower mounting bolt. Tighten the bolt to 15–20 ft. lbs. (20.3–27.0 Nm).
10. Connect the cable to the starter solenoid B terminal and install the attaching nut to the terminal. Tighten the nut to 80–120 inch lbs. (9.0–13.5 Nm).
11. Connect the electrical connector to the starter solenoid S terminal.
12. Install the intake plenum support bracket and tighten the attaching bolts to 27–38 ft. lbs. (37–52 Nm) and the attaching nut to 14–19 ft. lbs. (19–25 Nm).
13. Lower the vehicle.
14. Install the starter motor upper mounting bolts and tighten to 15–20 ft. lbs. (20.3–27.0 Nm).
15. Install the air duct that connects to the throttle body and resonance chamber.
16. Connect the negative battery cable.

1.9L Engine

1. Disconnect the negative battery cable.
2. If equipped with an automatic transaxle, remove the kickdown cable routing bracket from the engine block.
3. Disconnect the wire from the starter solenoid S terminal.

NOTE: When disconnecting the plastic hard shell connector at the solenoid S terminal, grasp the plastic connector, depress the plastic tab and pull off the lead assembly. Do not pull on the lead wire or damage may result.

4. Remove the attaching nut from the starter solenoid B terminal and disconnect the cable from the terminal.
5. Remove the starter motor mounting bolts and remove the starter motor.
To install:
6. Place the starter motor into its mounting position and install the mounting bolts. Tighten the bolts to 15–20 ft. lbs. (20.3–27.0 Nm).
7. Connect the cable to the starter solenoid B terminal and install the attaching nut. Tighten the nut to 80–120 inch lbs. (9–13.5 Nm).
8. Connect the wire to the starter solenoid S terminal.
9. If equipped with an automatic transaxle, install the kickdown cable routing bracket to the engine block.
10. Connect the negative battery cable.

EMISSION CONTROLS

Due to the complex nature of modern electronic engine control systems, comprehensive diagnosis and testing procedures fall outside the confines of this repair manual. For complete information on diagnosis, testing and repair procedures concerning all modern engine and emission control systems, please refer to "Chilton's Guide to Fuel Injection and Electronic Engine Controls".

Emission Warning Lamps

RESETTING

These vehicles have a "CHECK ENGINE" or "SERVICE ENGINE SOON" light that will light when there is a fault in the engine control system. Depending upon the system or sensor involved, the light may go out if the fault is intermittent. However, the fault code will remain stored in the ECU until the system is serviced and the ECU memory cleared. When a fault is detected in certain systems or sensors, the light will remain lit until the system is serviced. When the system has been diagnosed, the problem corrected and the ECU memory cleared, the light will go out.

FUEL SYSTEM

Fuel System Service Precautions

Safety is the most important factor when performing not only fuel system maintenance but any type of maintenance. Failure to conduct maintenance and repairs in a safe manner may result in serious personal injury or death. Maintenance and testing of the vehicle's fuel system components can be accomplished safely and effectively by adhering to the following rules and guidelines.

• To avoid the possibility of fire and personal injury, always disconnect the negative battery cable unless the repair or test procedure requires that battery voltage be applied.

• Always relieve the fuel system pressure prior to disconnecting any fuel system component (injector, fuel rail, pressure regulator, etc.), fitting or fuel line connection. Exercise extreme caution whenever relieving fuel system pressure to avoid exposing skin, face and eyes to fuel spray. Please be advised that fuel under pressure may penetrate the skin or any part of the body that it contacts.

• Always place a shop towel or cloth around the fitting or connection prior to loosening to absorb any excess fuel due to spillage. Ensure that all fuel spillage (should it occur) is quickly removed from engine surfaces. Ensure that all fuel soaked cloths or towels are deposited into a waste container.

• Always keep a dry chemical (Class B) fire extinguisher near the work area.

• Do not allow fuel spray or fuel vapors to come into contact with a spark or open flame.

• Always use a backup wrench when loosening and tightening fuel line connection fittings. This will prevent unnecessary stress and torsion to fuel line piping. Always follow the proper torque specifications.

• Always replace worn fuel fitting O-rings with new. Do not substitute fuel hose or equivalent where fuel pipe is installed.

SPRING LOCK COUPLING PROCEDURE

TO DISCONNECT COUPLING	TO CONNECT COUPLING

CAUTION — RELIEVE FUEL PRESSURE BEFORE DISCONNECTING COUPLING

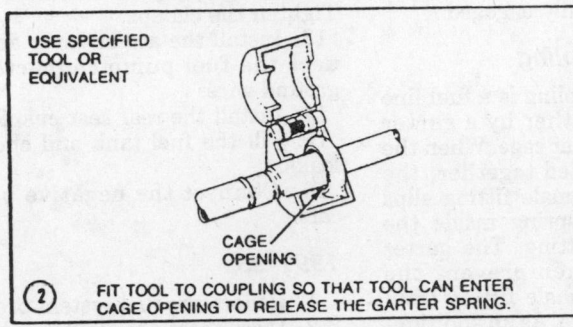

CLIP

① REMOVE CLIP FROM COUPLING

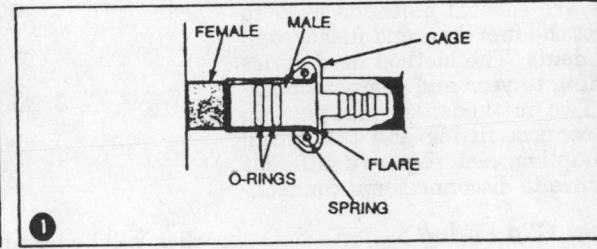

FEMALE   MALE   CAGE

O-RINGS   FLARE   SPRING

❶

USE SPECIFIED TOOL OR EQUIVALENT

CAGE OPENING

② FIT TOOL TO COUPLING SO THAT TOOL CAN ENTER CAGE OPENING TO RELEASE THE GARTER SPRING.

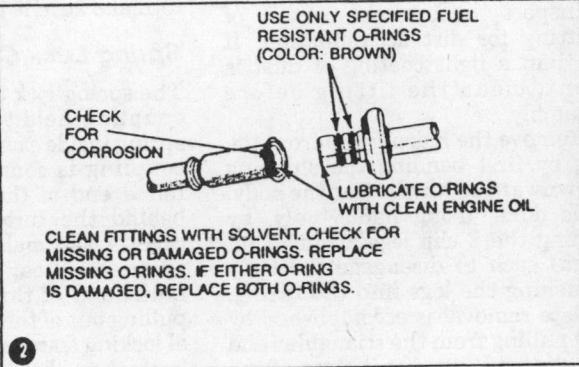

USE ONLY SPECIFIED FUEL RESISTANT O-RINGS (COLOR: BROWN)

CHECK FOR CORROSION

LUBRICATE O-RINGS WITH CLEAN ENGINE OIL

CLEAN FITTINGS WITH SOLVENT. CHECK FOR MISSING OR DAMAGED O-RINGS. REPLACE MISSING O-RINGS. IF EITHER O-RING IS DAMAGED, REPLACE BOTH O-RINGS.

❷

PUSH TOOL INTO CAGE OPENING

NOTE: SPECIFIED TOOL WILL FIT AROUND RUBBER COVERED FUEL LINE.

③ PUSH THE TOOL INTO THE CAGE OPENING TO RELEASE THE FEMALE FITTING FROM THE GARTER SPRING

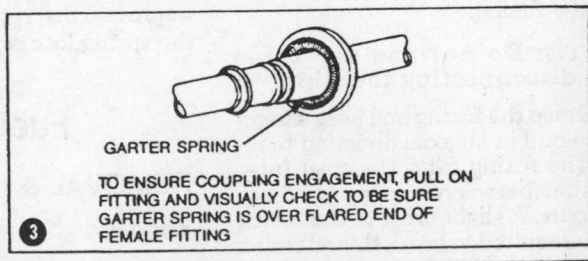

GARTER SPRING

TO ENSURE COUPLING ENGAGEMENT, PULL ON FITTING AND VISUALLY CHECK TO BE SURE GARTER SPRING IS OVER FLARED END OF FEMALE FITTING

❸

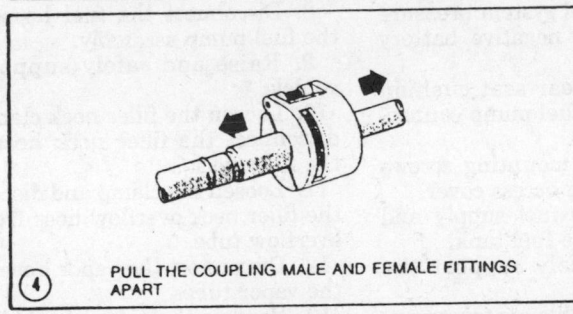

④ PULL THE COUPLING MALE AND FEMALE FITTINGS APART

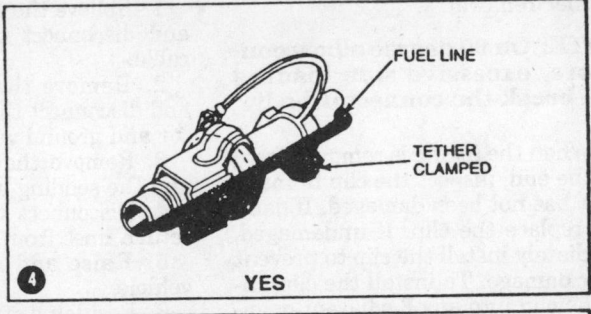

FUEL LINE

TETHER CLAMPED

❹ YES

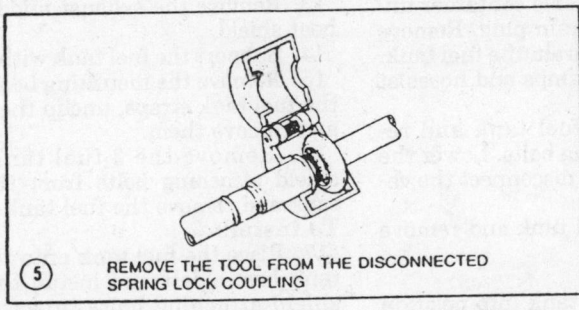

⑤ REMOVE THE TOOL FROM THE DISCONNECTED SPRING LOCK COUPLING

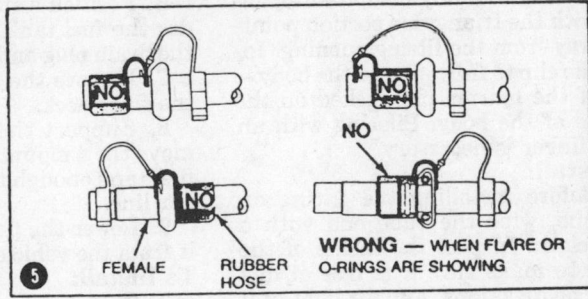

NO   NO

NO

NO

FEMALE   RUBBER HOSE

WRONG — WHEN FLARE OR O-RINGS ARE SHOWING

❺

RELIEVING FUEL SYSTEM PRESSURE

1. Start the engine.

2. Remove the rear seat cushion and disconnect the fuel pump electrical connectors.

3. Wait for the engine to stall, then turn **OFF** the ignition switch.

4. Connect the fuel pump electrical connectors and install the rear seat cushion.

Fuel Line Couplings

REMOVAL & INSTALLATION

There are several methods used to connect the fuel lines and fuel system components. The method used varies according to year and engine application. Two methods, the hairpin clip push connect fitting and the spring lock coupling, each require a different procedure to disconnect and connect.

Hairpin Clip Fitting

1. Inspect the internal portion of the fitting for dirt accumulation. If more than a light coating of dust is present, clean the fitting before disassembly.
2. Remove the hairpin clip from the fitting by first bending the shipping tab downward so it will clear the body. This is done, using hands only, by spreading the 2 clip legs about ⅛ in. (3.2mm) each to disengage the body and pushing the legs into the fitting. Complete removal is accomplished by lightly pulling from the triangular end of the clip and working it clear of the tube and fitting.

NOTE: Do not use any tools when disconnecting the clip.

3. Grasp the fitting and hose assembly and pull in an axial direction to remove the fitting from the steel tube. Adhesion between sealing surfaces may occur. A slight twist of the fitting may be required to break this adhesion for easier removal.

NOTE: On 90 degree elbow connectors, excessive side loading could break the connector body.

4. When the fitting is removed from the tube end, inspect the clip to make sure it has not been damaged. If damaged, replace the clip. If undamaged, immediately install the clip to prevent loss or damage. To install the clip, insert the clip into any 2 adjacent openings with the triangular portion pointing away from the fitting opening. Install the clip to fully engage the body—legs of the hairpin clip locked on the outside of the body. Piloting with an index finger is necessary.

To install:
5. Before installing the fitting on the tube, wipe the tube end with a clean cloth. Inspect the inside of the fitting to make sure it is free of dirt and/or obstructions. Apply a light coat of engine oil to the tube end for ease of assembly.
6. To install the fitting onto the tube, align the fitting and tube axial and push the fitting onto the tube end. When the fitting is engaged, a definite

click will be heard. Pull on the fitting to make sure it is fully engaged.

Spring Lock Coupling

The spring lock coupling is a fuel line coupling held together by a garter spring inside a circular cage. When the coupling is connected together, the flared end of the female fitting slips behind the garter spring inside the cage of the male fitting. The garter spring and cage then prevent the flared end of the female fitting from pulling out of the cage. As an additional locking feature, most vehicles have a horseshoe shaped retaining clip that improves the retaining reliability of the spring lock coupling.

Fuel Tank

REMOVAL & INSTALLATION

1989–90

1. Relieve the fuel system pressure and disconnect the negative battery cable.
2. Remove the rear seat cushion and disconnect the fuel pump connector and ground wire.
3. Remove the 4 mounting screws and the sending unit access cover.
4. Disconnect the fuel supply and return lines from the fuel tank.
5. Raise and safely support the vehicle.
6. Position a suitable container under the fuel tank drain plug. Remove the drain plug and drain the fuel tank.
7. Remove the clamps and hoses at the filler neck.
8. Support the fuel tank and remove the 4 mounting bolts. Lower the fuel tank enough to disconnect the vapor line.
9. Lower the fuel tank and remove it from the vehicle.

To install:
10. Raise the fuel tank into position and connect the vapor line. Install the tank with the 4 mounting bolts.
11. Install the filler neck hoses and tighten the clamps. Install the drain plug.
12. Lower the vehicle and connect

the fuel supply and return lines. Tighten the clamps.
13. Install the access cover and connect the fuel pump connector and ground wire.
14. Install the rear seat cushion.
15. Fill the fuel tank and check for leaks.
16. Connect the negative battery cable.

1991–93

1. Relieve the fuel system pressure.
2. Disconnect the negative battery cable.
3. Completely drain the fuel tank by siphoning or pumping out the fuel through the fuel filler hose.
4. Remove the rear seat cushion.
5. Remove the ground strap retaining screw and the 3 remaining fuel pump assembly cover screws.
6. Remove the fuel pump assembly cover.
7. Remove the clips from the fuel hoses.
8. Disconnect the fuel hoses from the fuel pump assembly.
9. Raise and safely support vehicle.
10. Loosen the filler neck clamp and disconnect the filler neck hose from the filler neck.
11. Loosen the clamp and disconnect the filler neck overflow hose from the overflow tube.
12. Disconnect the vapor hoses from the vapor tubes.
13. Remove the exhaust middle pipe heat shield.
14. Support the fuel tank with a jack.
15. Remove the mounting bolts from the fuel tank straps, unclip the straps and remove them.
16. Remove the 3 fuel tank heat shield attaching bolts from the fuel tank and remove the fuel tank.

To install:
17. Place the fuel tank onto the fuel tank heat shield and install the heat shield attaching bolts into the fuel tank.
18. Clip the fuel tank straps into their mounting positions.
19. Install the fuel tank strap mounting bolts and tighten to 27–38 ft. lbs. (37–52 Nm).

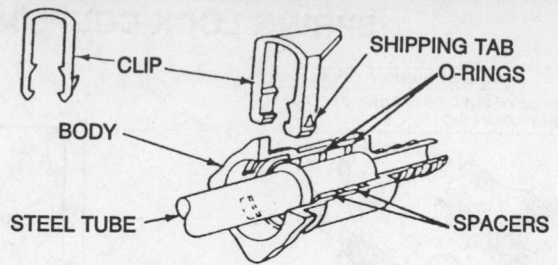

Hairpin clip push connect fitting

20. Remove the support jack from under the fuel tank.

21. Install the exhaust middle pipe heat shield.

22. Connect the vapor hoses to the vapor tubes.

23. Connect the filler neck hose to the filler neck and install the attaching clamp.

24. Connect the filler neck overflow hose to the overflow tube and install the attaching clamp.

25. Lower the vehicle.

26. Connect the fuel hoses to the fuel pump assembly.

27. Install the clips onto the fuel hoses.

28. Position the fuel pump assembly cover and ground strap and install the retaining screws.

29. Connect the fuel pump assembly electrical connector.

30. Install the rear seat cushion.

31. Replace the fuel that was drained from the tank during the removal procedure. Check for leaks.

32. Connect the negative battery cable.

33. Turn the ignition switch **ON** to run the fuel pump and pressurize the system. Check for fuel leaks.

Fuel Filter

REMOVAL & INSTALLATION

1. Properly relieve the fuel system pressure.

2. Disconnect the negative battery cable.

3. Position a suitable container below the fuel filter to collect any excess fuel that may leak from the filter and lines.

4. Remove the retaining clip or loosen the clamp from the fuel filter upper hose.

5. Disconnect the upper hose from the fuel filter and drain any excess fuel into the container. Plug the hose.

6. Loosen the fuel filter mounting clamp.

7. Raise and safely support the vehicle, if necessary.

8. Remove the retaining clip or the bolt and washers from the fuel filter lower hose.

9. Disconnect the lower hose from the fuel filter and drain any excess fuel into the container. Plug the hose.

10. Lower the vehicle.

11. Remove the fuel filter.

To install:

12. Position the fuel filter and tighten the fuel filter mounting clamp.

13. Connect the filter upper hose to the filter and install the upper hose retaining clip or tighten the clamp.

14. Raise and safely support the vehicle.

15. Connect the filter lower hose to the filter and install the lower hose retaining clip or a bolt and 2 new washers. If equipped, tighten the bolt to 18–25 ft. lbs. (25–34 Nm).

16. Lower the vehicle.

17. Connect the negative battery cable.

18. Start the engine and check for leaks.

Electric Fuel Pump

The electric fuel pump is located in the fuel tank, on the fuel sending unit.

PRESSURE TESTING

1.6L Engine

1. Relieve the fuel system pressure. Connect a fuel gauge in line with the fuel filter and the fuel rail.

2. Jumper the fuel pump check connector, so the pump will run with the key in the **ON** position.

3. Turn the ignition key **ON**, but do not start the engine.

4. Observe the pressure reading; it should be above 60 psi. If the fuel pressure is below 60 psi, check the system for restrictions. Replace the pump as needed.

5. Relieve the fuel system pressure pressure and remove the fuel pressure gauge.

1.8L Engine

1. Make sure the ignition key is in the **OFF** position.

2. Properly relieve the fuel system pressure.

3. Install a fuel pressure tester in the fuel line between the fuel filter and the fuel rail.

4. Jump the fuel pump test connector terminals together, terminal **LG** and terminal **BK** at the Self-Test connector.

5. Turn the ignition key to **RUN**, to operate the fuel pump, and observe the fuel pressure.

6. The fuel pressure should be 64–85 psi.

7. Turn the ignition key **OFF** and remove the jumper wire.

8. Properly relieve the fuel system pressure and remove the pressure tester.

1.9L Engine

1. Make sure the ignition key is in the **OFF** position.

2. Properly relieve the fuel system pressure.

3. Disconnect the fuel pump output line and connect a suitable pressure tester.

4. Ground the fuel pump lead of the

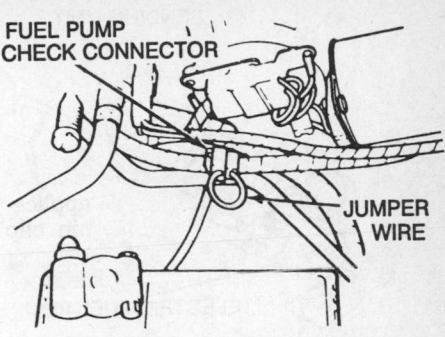

Fuel pump check connector location— 1.6L engine

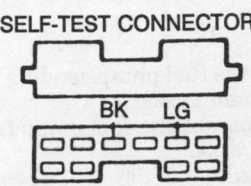

Self-test connector terminal locations— 1.8L engine

Self-Test connector through a jumper wire at the **FP** lead.

5. Turn the ignition key **ON**, to operate the fuel pump, and observe the fuel pressure.

6. The fuel pressure should be 35–40 psi.

7. Turn the ignition key **OFF** and remove the jumper wire.

8. Properly relieve the fuel system pressure and remove the pressure tester.

9. Reconnect the fuel line.

REMOVAL & INSTALLATION

1. Relieve the fuel system pressure and disconnect the negative battery cable.

2. Disconnect the ground wire and remove the fuel pump access cover.

3. Disconnect and plug the fuel supply and return lines.

4. On 1989–90 vehicles, remove the mounting bolts and remove the fuel pump/sending unit assembly and gasket from the fuel tank.

5. On 1991–93 vehicles, remove the spanner nut using a suitable tool and

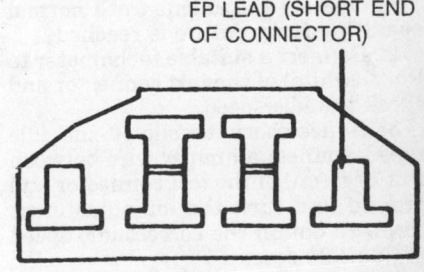

Self-test connector—1.9L engine

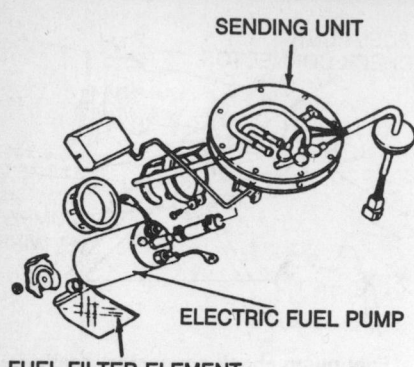

Electric fuel pump assembly—1989–90 vehicles.

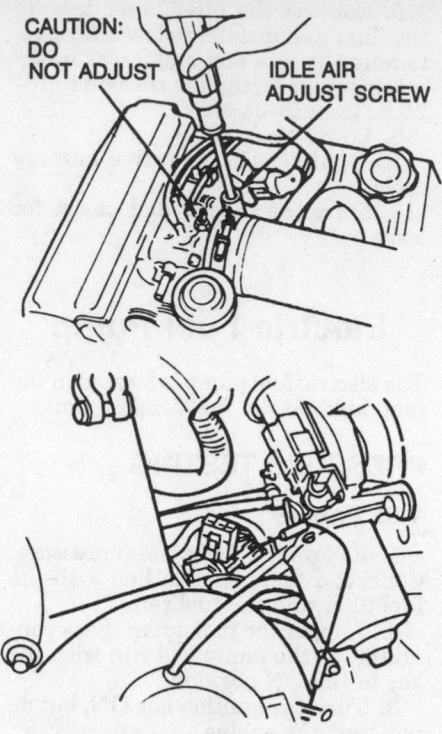

idle speed adjustment procedure—1.6L engine

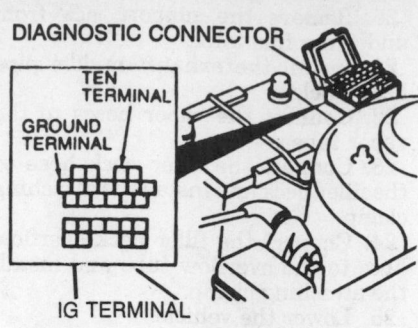

Diagnostic connector location—1.8L engine

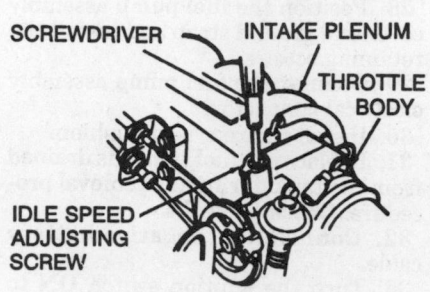

idle speed adjusting screw location—1.8L engine

remove the fuel pump/sending unit assembly and gasket.

6. Separate the fuel pump from the sending unit.

To install:

7. Install the fuel pump onto the sending unit.

8. On 1989–90 vehicles, position a new gasket onto the fuel tank and install the fuel pump/sending unit assembly with the mounting bolts.

9. On 1991–93 vehicles, install a new gasket and the fuel pump/sending unit assembly. Install the spanner nut.

10. Unplug and connect the fuel supply and return lines.

11. Install the fuel pump access cover and connect the ground wire and fuel pump electrical connector.

12. Connect the negative battery cable, start the engine and check for fuel leaks.

13. Install the rear seat cushion.

Fuel Injection

IDLE SPEED ADJUSTMENT

1.6L Engine

NOTE: Before adjusting idle speed, check ignition timing and adjust, if necessary. Turn off all lights and unnecessary electrical loads. Adjust idle speed while cooling fan motor is not operating.

1. Operate the engine until normal operating temperature is reached.

2. Connect a suitable tachometer to Pin 1 (white) of the test connector and check the idle speed.

3. If necessary to adjust the idle speed, connect a jumper wire between Pin 1 (green) of the test connector and ground and turn the air adjustment screw to obtain the correct idle speed of 800–900 rpm.

NOTE: Do not turn the adjust-

ment screw located to the right of the idle adjustment screw, for it will affect driveability and may damage the throttle body.

4. After adjustment, remove the jumper wire and the test equipment.

1.8L Engine

1. Apply the parking brake and make sure the vehicle is in **N** or **P**.

2. Start the engine and warm it up to normal operating temperature.

3. Turn off all electrical loads and accessories.

4. Using a jumper wire, connect the **GROUND** terminal to the **TEN** terminal on the diagnosis connector.

5. Connect the positive lead of a tachometer to the **IG** terminal on the diagnosis connector and the tachometer negative lead to the negative battery terminal.

6. Check the vehicle idle speed when the electric cooling fan is not operating. The idle speed should be 700–800 rpm.

NOTE: When the parking brake is not applied, the idle speed for automatic transaxle vehicles sold in Canada is approximately 800 rpm.

7. If the idle speed is not within specification, adjust the idle speed by turning the idle speed adjusting screw until the idle speed is within specification.

8. Remove the jumper wire from the diagnosis connector and remove the tachometer.

1.9L Engine

1991

1. Place the transaxle in **P** or **N** and apply the parking brake. Make sure the heater and all engine accessories are OFF.

2. Start the engine and bring to normal operating temperature. Check and, if necessary, adjust the ignition timing.

3. Turn the engine **OFF** and disconnect the negative battery cable. Leave the cable disconnected for 5 minutes, then reconnect it.

4. Start the engine and let stabilize for 2 minutes, then rev the engine and let it return to idle. Lightly rev the engine and release the accelerator; let the engine idle.

5. Check the engine idle speed specification on the emission control information label. Connect a tachometer to the engine according to the manufacturers instructions and check the engine idle speed, with the electric cooling fan OFF. If the engine does not idle properly, proceed to Step 6.

6. Stop the engine and disconnect the idle speed control air bypass solenoid.

7. Start the engine and run it at 2000 rpm for 60 seconds.

8. After the engine returns to idle,

check the idle speed. It should be 600 ± 150 rpm.

9. If the idle rpm is incorrect, turn the plate stop screw until the idle speed is within specification.

10. Turn the engine **OFF** and reconnect the idle speed control-air bypass solenoid. Verify the throttle is not stuck in the bore and the linkage is not preventing the throttle from closing.

11. Start the engine and let it stabilize for 2 minutes, then rev the engine and let it return to idle; lightly depress and release the accelerator and let the engine idle. Check idle speed.

1992–93

The idle speed on 1992–93 vehicles with the 1.9L engine is not adjustable. If the idle speed is incorrect, check for low battery and charging system, idle speed control device contamination, throttle bore contamination, fuel contamination, improper fuel octane rating, low engine operating temperature, low coolant level or leaking cooling system, clogged PCV system, faulty clutch or transmission, brakes not releasing, ignition system fault, exhaust system or EGR fault, or vacuum leaks.

IDLE MIXTURE ADJUSTMENT

Idle mixture is controlled by the Electronic Control Unit and is not adjustable.

Fuel Injector

REMOVAL & INSTALLATION

1.6L Engine

1. Relieve the fuel system pressure and disconnect the negative battery cable.
2. Drain the cooling system.
3. Disconnect the accelerator cable and remove the air duct from the throttle body.
4. Mark all vacuum and coolant hoses for ease of reassembly and remove the hoses from the throttle body.
5. Disconnect the electrical connector from the throttle position sensor.
6. Remove the intake plenum mounting bolts and nuts and remove the plenum and gaskets. Cover the intake manifold ports to prevent dirt from entering.
7. Disconnect the fuel supply and return lines from the fuel rail.
8. Disconnect the electrical connectors from the fuel injectors and remove the pressure regulator.
9. Remove the mounting bolts and the fuel rail. Remove the fuel injectors and remove and discard the O-rings.

To install:

10. Lubricate new O-rings with gasoline and install on the injectors. Install the injectors into the cylinder head.
11. Install the fuel rail onto the injectors and install the mounting bolts. Make sure the injectors seat in the manifold and fuel rail.
12. Install the pressure regulator and connect the fuel injector electrical connectors.
13. Connect the fuel supply and return lines to the fuel rail.
14. Clean the gasket mating surfaces of the intake plenum and intake manifold.
15. Install the intake plenum with the mounting bolts and nuts, using a new gasket.
16. Connect the throttle position sensor electrical connector. Connect the vacuum lines and coolant hoses to their original positions, as noted during the removal procedure.
17. Connect the accelerator cable and install the air duct to the throttle body.
18. Fill the cooling system.
19. Connect the negative battery cable and turn the ignition switch **ON** to activate the fuel pump. Check for fuel leaks.

1.8L Engine

1. Properly relieve the fuel system pressure.
2. Disconnect the negative battery cable.
3. Disconnect the fuel pressure and return lines from the fuel rail.
4. Disconnect the PCV hose from the intake plenum and cylinder head cover.
5. Disconnect the fuel pressure regulator vacuum hose and the fuel injector wiring harness electrical connectors.
6. Remove the fuel rail mounting bolts and remove the fuel rail.
7. Remove the fuel injectors, grommets and insulators.
8. Installation is the reverse of the removal procedure. Lubricate new O-rings with clean engine oil and install them on the fuel injectors prior to installation.

1.9L Engine

1. Relieve the fuel system pressure and disconnect the negative battery cable.
2. Remove spring-lock coupling retainer clips from fuel inlet and return fittings.
3. Disconnect fuel supply and return lines.
3. Remove vacuum line from fuel pressure regulator.
4. Disconnect the fuel injector wiring harness.

5. Carefully remove connectors from individual injectors(s) as required.
6. Remove the 2 bolts securing the injector manifold assembly and remove the assembly.
7. Grasping the injector's body, pull up while gently rocking the injector from side-to-side.
8. Inspect the injector O-rings (2 per injector) for signs of deterioration. Replace as required.
9. Inspect the injector "plastic hat" (covering the injector pintle) and washer for signs of deterioration. Replace as required. If hat is missing, look for it in intake manifold.

To install:

10. Use a light grade oil to lubricate new O-rings and install 2 on each injector .
11. Install the injector(s). Use a light, twisting, pushing motion to install the injector(s).
12. Carefully seat the fuel injector manifold assembly on the injectors and secure the manifold with the attaching bolts. Tighten to 15–22 ft. lbs. (20–30 Nm).
13. Connect the vacuum line to the fuel pressure regulator.
14. Connect fuel supply and fuel return lines.
15. Reconnect spring-lock coupling retaining clips on fuel inlet and return fittings.
16. Check entire assembly for proper alignment and seating.
17. Connect the negative battery cable. With the fuel injector electrical connectors disconnected, turn the ignition switch to the **RUN** position and let the fuel pump pressurize the system. Check for fuel leaks and correct, as necessary.
18. Turn the ignition switch **OFF**.
19. Connect the fuel injector wiring harness connectors.
20. Start the engine and check for leaks.

DRIVE AXLE

Halfshaft

REMOVAL & INSTALLATION

1989–90

1. Raise and support the vehicle safely.
2. Remove the necessary splash covers from under the vehicle.
3. Remove the stabilizer bar-to-lower control arm nuts, bolt, washers and bushings.
4. Remove the wheel/tire assembly.

5. Using a cape chisel and a hammer, raise the staked portion of the hub nut.

6. Using an assistant to apply the brakes, loosen the hub nut.

7. Remove the lower control arm ball joint-to-steering knuckle clamp bolt, pull the lower control arm downward to separate the ball joint from the steering knuckle.

NOTE: When separating the ball joint, be careful not to damage the ball joint dust boot.

8. If equipped with a manual transaxle, use both hands, grasp the steering knuckle/hub assembly, apply even pressure (gradually increasing), pull both halfshafts from the transaxle. If equipped with an automatic transaxle, insert a medium prybar between the halfshaft and the transaxle (a notch is provided), pry both halfshafts from the transaxle.

NOTE: When removing the halfshafts, withdraw them completely from the transaxle (to prevent damage to the oil seal lips), do not move the CV-joints in excess of a 20 degree angle (damage to the boots and/or joint may occur) and use a wire to support the halfshaft in the horizontal position.

9. Remove the hub nut (discard it) and washer. Pull the halfshaft from the steering knuckle assembly.

NOTE: If the wheel hub binds on the halfshaft splines, use a puller tool, to press the halfshaft from the wheel hub. Never use a hammer to separate the halfshaft from the wheel hub, for damage to the CV-joint may occur.

10. Install differential plugs T87C–7025–C or equivalent, to prevent oil leakage.

To install:

11. To install the halfshaft into the transaxle, perform the following procedures:

   a. Install a new locking clip on the halfshaft spline; be sure the gap in the clip is at the top of the clip groove.

   b. Slide the halfshafts into the transaxle bore; be careful not to damage the oil seal lip.

   c. Make sure the locking clip can be felt as it snaps into the differential side gear groove.

   d. Position the halfshaft through the wheel hub and install a new attaching nut. Do not tighten the nut at this time.

   e. After installation, pull the front hub outward to confirm that the circlips are engaged.

13. Install the ball joint into the steering knuckle and install the clamp bolt and attaching nut. Tighten the nut to 32–40 ft. lbs. (43–54 Nm).

14. Install the bolt, nuts, washers and bushings connecting the stabilizer bar and lower control arm. Tighten the nut until 7/16 in. (0.8mm) of bolt threads extend beyond the nut.

15. Install the splash covers.

16. Tighten the halfshaft nut to 116–174 ft. lbs. (157–235 Nm). Stake the nut using a cold chisel with a rounded edge.

NOTE: If the nut splits or cracks after staking, it must be replaced with a new nut.

17. Install the wheel and tire assembly and lower the vehicle.

1991–93

LEFT SIDE – 1.8L AND 1.9L ENGINES, RIGHT SIDE – 1.9L ENGINE

1. Raise and safely support the vehicle.

2. Remove the wheel and tire assembly.

3. Remove the splash shield.

4. Carefully raise the staked portion of the halfshaft retaining nut using a small chisel. Remove and discard the retaining nut.

5. Remove the cotter pin and nut from the tie rod end and remove the tie rod end from the steering knuckle using a suitable removal tool.

6. Remove the lower ball joint clamp bolt. Carefully pry down on the lower control arm to separate the ball joint from the steering knuckle.

7. Pull outward on the steering knuckle/brake assembly. Carefully pull the halfshaft from the steering knuckle and position it aside.

8. Removal of the left side halfshaft requires removal of the crossmember to allow access with a prybar. If the left side halfshaft is being removed, proceed as follows:

   a. Support the transaxle with a transmission jack.

   b. Remove the 4 transaxle mount-to-crossmember attaching nuts.

   c. Remove the 2 crossmember attaching nuts at the rear of the crossmember.

   d. While supporting the rear of the crossmember, remove the 2 front mounting bolts. Remove the crossmember.

9. Position a drain pan under the transaxle.

10. Insert a prybar between the halfshaft and the transaxle case. Gently pry outward to release the halfshaft from the differential side gears. Be careful no to damage the transaxle

case, oil seal, CV-joint or CV-joint boot.

11. Remove the halfshaft.

NOTE: Install suitable plugs after removing the halfshafts to prevent the differential side gears from becoming mispositioned. Should the gears become misaligned, the differential will have to be removed from the transaxle to align the gears.

To install:

12. Position the circlip on the inner CV-joint spline so the circlip gap is at the top. Lubricate the splines lightly with suitable grease.

13. Remove the plugs that were installed in the differential side gears.

14. Position the halfshaft so the CV-joint splines are aligned with the differential side gear splines. Push the halfshaft into the differential.

NOTE: When seated properly, the circlip can be felt as it snaps into the differential side gear groove.

15. Pull outward on the steering knuckle/brake assembly and insert the halfshaft into the steering knuckle.

16. Pry downward on the control arm and position the lower ball joint in the steering knuckle.

17. For left side halfshaft installation, proceed as follows:

   a. Position the crossmember in place.

   b. Install the 2 mounting bolts and the 2 attaching nuts. Tighten the nuts and bolts to 47–66 ft. lbs. (64–89 Nm).

   c. Install the 4 transaxle mount-to-crossmember attaching nuts. Tighten the nuts to 27–38 ft. lbs. (37–52 Nm).

   d. Remove the transmission jack.

18. Install the lower ball joint clamp bolt and tighten to 32–43 ft. lbs. (43–59 Nm).

19. Install the tie rod end in the steering knuckle. Install the nut to the tie rod end and tighten to 31–42 ft. lbs. (42–57 Nm). Install a new cotter pin.

20. Install a new halfshaft retaining nut and tighten to 174–235 ft. lbs. (235–319 Nm). Stake the halfshaft retaining nut using a chisel with a rounded cutting edge.

NOTE: If the nut splits or cracks after staking, replace it with a new nut.

21. Install the splash shield.

22. Install the wheel and tire assembly and lower the vehicle.

23. Check and refill the transaxle with the proper type and quantity of fluid.

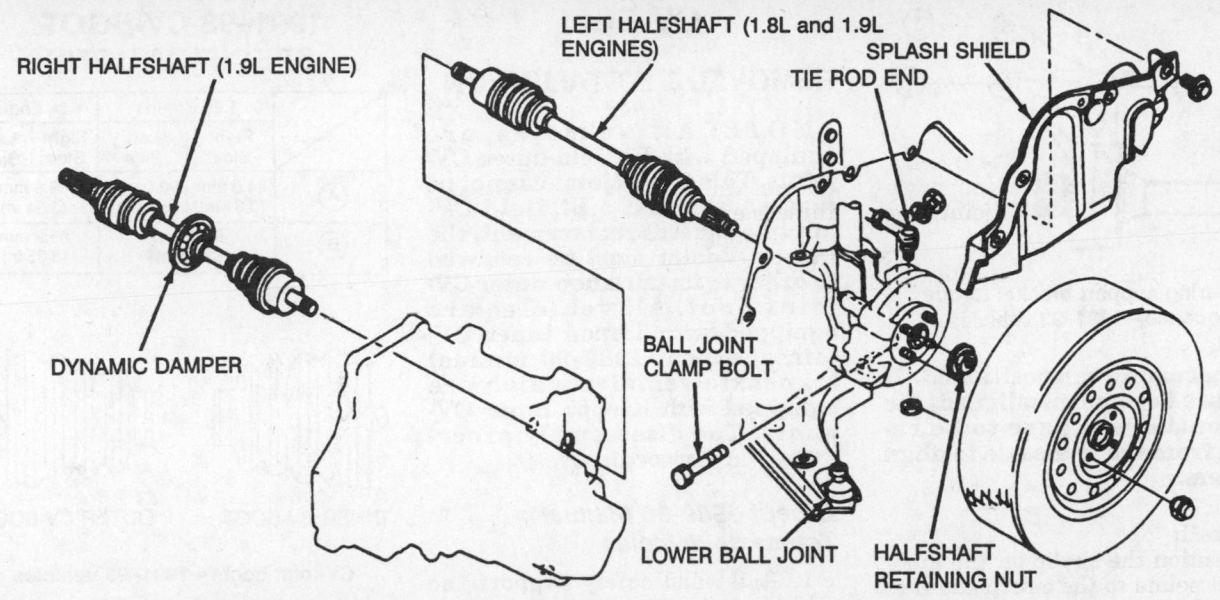

RIGHT HALFSHAFT (1.9L ENGINE)

LEFT HALFSHAFT (1.8L and 1.9L ENGINES)

SPLASH SHIELD

TIE ROD END

DYNAMIC DAMPER

BALL JOINT CLAMP BOLT

LOWER BALL JOINT

HALFSHAFT RETAINING NUT

Halfshaft removal and installation—left side, 1.8L and 1.9L engines and right side, 1.9L engine

RIGHT SIDE—1.8L ENGINE

NOTE: The right side halfshaft assembly is a 2 piece shaft with a bearing support bracket positioned between the 2 halves. The bearing support bracket is mounted on the cylinder block and must be unbolted if the entire halfshaft assembly is to be removed. If only the CV-joints/boots are to be serviced, the outboard shaft assembly may be removed, leaving the bearing support bracket mounted on the engine cylinder block.

1. Raise and safely support the vehicle.

2. Remove the right front wheel and tire assembly.

3. Remove the splash shield.

4. Carefully raise the staked portion of the halfshaft retaining nut using a suitable small chisel. Remove and discard the retaining nut.

5. Remove the cotter pin and nut from the tie rod end and remove the tie rod end from the steering knuckle using a suitable removal tool.

6. **Remove the lower ball joint clamp bolt.** Carefully pry down on the lower control arm to separate the ball joint from the steering knuckle.

7. Pull outward on the steering knuckle/brake assembly. Carefully pull the halfshaft from the steering knuckle and position it aside.

8. Position a drain pan under the transaxle.

9. Remove the 3 bearing support bracket mounting bolts.

10. Insert a prybar between the bearing support bracket and the starter bracket. Gently pry outward on the damper until the halfshaft disengages from the differential side gear.

11. Remove the halfshaft assembly. Install an appropriate differential plug in the differential side gear.

NOTE: If both halfshafts are removed, plugs must be installed to keep the differential side gears

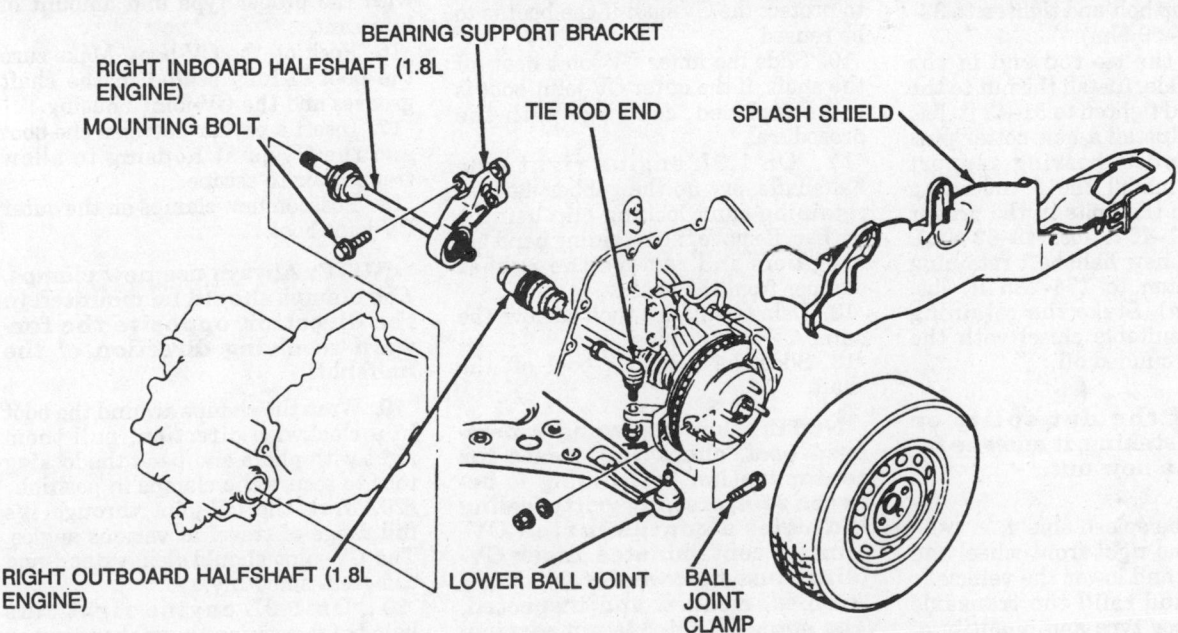

BEARING SUPPORT BRACKET

RIGHT INBOARD HALFSHAFT (1.8L ENGINE)

MOUNTING BOLT

TIE ROD END

SPLASH SHIELD

RIGHT OUTBOARD HALFSHAFT (1.8L ENGINE)

LOWER BALL JOINT

BALL JOINT CLAMP

Halfshaft removal and installation—right side, 1.8L engine

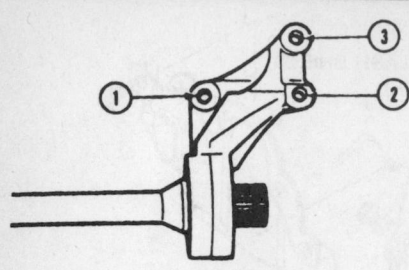

Bearing support bracket torque sequence—1991–93 vehicles

from becoming mispositioned. If the gears become misaligned, the differential will have to be removed from the transaxle to align the gears.

To install:

12. Position the circlip on the inner CV-joint spline so the circlip gap is at the top. Lubricate the splines lightly with a suitable grease.

13. Remove the differential plug from the side gear. Position the halfshaft assembly so the shaft splines are aligned with the differential side gear splines. Push the halfshaft into the differential.

NOTE: When seated properly, the circlip can be felt as it snaps into the differential side gear groove.

14. Pull outward on the steering knuckle/brake assembly and insert the halfshaft into the steering knuckle.

15. Pry downward on the control arm and position the lower ball joint in the steering knuckle. Install the lower ball joint clamp bolt and tighten to 32–43 ft. lbs. (43–59 Nm).

16. Install the tie rod end in the steering knuckle. Install the nut to the tie rod end and tighten to 31–42 ft. lbs. (42–57 Nm). Install a new cotter pin.

17. Position the bearing support bracket and install the 3 mounting bolts. Tighten the bolts in the proper sequence to 31–46 ft. lbs. (42–62 Nm).

18. Install a new halfshaft retaining nut and tighten to 174–235 ft. lbs. (235–319 Nm). Stake the retaining nut using a suitable chisel with the cutting edge rounded off.

NOTE: If the nut splits or cracks after staking, it must be replaced with a new nut.

19. Install the splash shield.
20. Install the right front wheel and tire assembly and lower the vehicle.
21. Check and refill the transaxle with the proper type and quantity of fluid.

CV-Boot

REMOVAL & INSTALLATION

NOTE: All vehicles are equipped with Birfield outer CV-joints. This type of joint cannot be disassembled. If a Birfield CV-joint boot needs replacement, the inner CV-joint must be removed in order to install a new outer CV-joint boot. All vehicles are equipped with Tripod inner CV-joints, except 1989–90 manual transaxle vehicles which are equipped with Rzeppa inner CV-joints. The disassembly procedures vary accordingly.

Except 1989–90 Manual Transaxle Vehicles

1. Raise and safely support the vehicle.
2. Remove the halfshaft assembly from the vehicle.
3. Secure the halfshaft in a vise with protective jaw covers.
4. Using a suitable tool, remove the CV-joint boot clamps.
5. Slide the boot back to expose the tripod CV-joint. Mark the shaft and the CV-joint housing to ensure correct assembly.
6. Remove the retainer ring from the CV-joint housing and remove the CV-joint housing from the halfshaft.
7. Mark the tripod bearing and the shaft to ensure correct assembly. Using snapring pliers, remove the tripod snapring.
8. Using a soft-faced mallet, gently tap the tripod bearing from the shaft.
9. Wrap the shaft splines with tape to protect the CV-boot if the boot is to be reused.
10. Slide the inner CV-joint boot off the shaft. If the outer CV-joint boot is to be replaced, continue with the procedure.
11. On 1.9L engine right side halfshafts, pry up the rubber damper retaining band locking clip using a prybar. Remove the retaining band using pliers and remove the rubber damper from the shaft.
12. Using a suitable tool, remove the outer CV-boot clamps.
13. Slide the outer CV-boot off the shaft.

NOTE: When replacing a damaged boot, check the grease for contamination by rubbing it between 2 fingers. Any gritty feeling indicates a contaminated CV-joint. A contaminated inner CV-joint must be completely disassembled, cleaned and inspected. The outer CV-joint is not serviceable and should be replaced as an

1991–93 CV-BOOT SPECIFICATIONS

	1.9L Engine		1.8L Engine	
	Right Side	Left Side	Right Side	Left Side
Ⓐ	84.0 mm (3.31 in)	90.0 mm (3.54 in)	89.9 mm (3.54 in)	
Ⓑ	89.0 mm (3.50 in)		85.2 mm (3.35 in)	

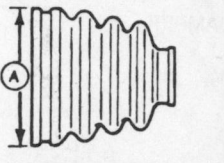 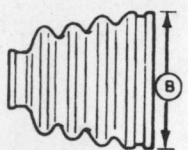

INNER CV-BOOT **OUTER CV-BOOT**

CV-joint boots—1991–93 vehicles

assembly, if necessary. If the grease is not contaminated and the CV-joint has been operating satisfactorily, replace only the boot and add the required lubricant.

To install:

14. Cover the halfshaft splines with tape and install the outer CV-joint boot.

NOTE: On 1991–93 vehicles, the outer and inner CV-joint boots are different. Failure to correctly install the boot on the proper end of the halfshaft could lead to premature boot and/or CV-joint wear.

15. Fill the outer CV-joint housing with the proper type and amount of lubricant.

16. Position the CV-boot. Make sure the boot is fully seated in the shaft grooves and the CV-joint housing.

17. Insert a prybar between the boot and the CV-joint housing to allow trapped air to escape.

18. Position new clamps on the outer CV-joint boot.

NOTE: Always use new clamps. The clamps should be mounted in the direction opposite the forward revolving direction of the halfshaft.

19. Wrap the clamps around the boot in a clockwise direction, pull them tight with pliers and bend the locking tabs to secure the clamps in position.

20. Work the CV-joint through it's full range of travel at various angles. The CV-joint should flex, extend and compress smoothly.

21. On 1.9L engine right side halfshafts, position the rubber damper on the halfshaft. Position a new band

on the damper. Pull the band tight with pliers and fold it back. Lock the end of the band by bending the locking clip.

22. Position the inner CV-joint boot on the halfshaft.

23. Align the marks on the tripod bearing and the halfshaft. Install the tripod bearing on the halfshaft. If necessary, using a soft-faced mallet, tap the bearing into place.

24. Install the snapring.

25. Fill the inner CV-joint housing with the proper type and amount of lubricant. Coat the tripod bearing with the same lubricant.

26. Position the inner CV-joint housing over the tripod bearing, making sure to align the alignment marks. Install the retainer ring in the CV-joint housing.

27. Slide the inner CV-boot in place. Make sure the boot is fully seated in the shaft grooves and in the housing. On 1989–90 vehicles, extend or compress the joint, as necessary, until the distance between the CV-joint boot clamp grooves measures 3.5 in. (90mm).

28. Insert a prybar between the boot and the CV-joint housing to allow trapped air to escape.

29. Position new clamps on the inner CV-joint boot.

NOTE: Always use new clamps. The clamps should be mounted in the direction opposite the forward revolving direction of the halfshaft.

1991–93
CV-BOOT LUBRICANT SPECIFICATIONS

Halfshaft Assemblies	1.9L Engine		1.8L Engine	
	Right Side	Left Side	Right Side	Left Side
Differential Side	220 g (7.77 oz) Lt. Yellow	140 g (4.94 oz) Yellow	145 g (5.12 oz) Yellow	
Wheel Side	140 g (4.94 oz) Black		90 g (3.18 oz) Black	

30. Wrap the clamps around the boot in a clockwise direction, pull them tight with pliers and bend the locking tabs to secure the clamps in position.

31. Work the CV-joint through it's full range of travel at various angles. The CV-joint should flex, extend and compress smoothly.

32. On 1991–93 vehicles, measure the length of the assembled halfshaft. If the length is not as specified, check the CV-joints for freedom of movement to ensure that it was assembled correctly. Repair or replace any components as necessary.

33. Install the halfshaft assembly into the vehicle.

1989–90 Manual Transaxle Vehicles

1. Raise and safely support the vehicle.

2. Remove the halfshaft assembly.

3. Secure the halfshaft in a vise with protective jaw covers.

4. Using a side cutters, remove the large boot clamp from the inner CV-joint and roll the boot back over the shaft.

NOTE: When replacing a damaged boot, check the grease for contamination by rubbing it between 2 fingers. Any gritty feeling indicates a contaminated CV-joint. A contaminated inner CV-joint must be completely disassembled, cleaned and inspected. The outer CV-joint is not serviceable and should be replaced as an assembly, if necessary. If the grease is not contaminated and the CV-joint has been operating satisfactorily, replace only the boot and add the required lubricant.

5. Mark the outer race and the shaft for assembly reference, remove the wire ring bearing retainer and remove the outer race.

6. Mark the inner race and the shaft for assembly reference and remove the snapring from the end of the halfshaft.

7. Remove the inner race, cage and ball bearings as an assembly. If the

CV-joint is good and only the boot is being replaced, go to Step 8. If the CV-joint is to be disassembled further for inspection, proceed as follows:

  a. Pry the ball bearings out of the bearing cage using a small prybar. The prybar should have blunted edges so as not to scratch the finished edges.

  b. Matchmark the inner race and bearing cage for assembly reference.

  c. Rotate the inner race to align the bearing lands with the windows in the bearing cage. Remove the inner race through the larger end of the cage.

  d. Clean the CV-joint parts (except the boot) with solvent and check for damage. If any parts are not reusable, the entire CV-joint must be replaced.

8. Remove the small clamp and remove the inner CV-boot from the halfshaft.

9. If replacing the outer CV-joint boot, remove the clamps and slide the boot along the shaft, removing it from the inner CV-joint end.

To install:

10. Cover the halfshaft splines with tape and install the outer CV-joint boot.

11. Fill the outer CV-joint housing with the proper type and amount of lubricant.

12. Position the CV-boot. Make sure the boot is fully seated in the shaft grooves and the CV-joint housing.

13. Insert a prybar between the boot and the CV-joint housing to allow trapped air to escape.

14. Position new clamps on the outer CV-joint boot.

NOTE: Always use new clamps. The clamps should be mounted in the direction opposite the forward revolving direction of the halfshaft.

15. Wrap the clamps around the boot in a clockwise direction, pull them tight with pliers and bend the locking tabs to secure the clamps in position.

16. Work the CV-joint through it's full range of travel at various angles.

1991–93 HALFSHAFT SPECIFICATIONS

Item	Model	1.8L Engine	1.9L Engine
Halfshaft			
Length of joint (between center of joint)	Right side	631.2 mm (24.85 in)	918.7 mm (36.16 in)
	Left side	621.7 mm (24.48 in)	640.7 mm (25.22 in)
Shaft diameter	Right side	23.0 mm (0.91 in)	
	Left side	23.0 mm (0.91 in)	

The CV-joint should flex, extend and compress smoothly.

17. Install the inner CV-boot.

18. Assemble the inner race, cage and balls as follows:

    a. Lubricate all parts with high temperature CV-joint grease.

    b. Position the inner race in the bearing cage and align the matchmarks. The race must be installed with the chamfered splines facing the large end of the cage.

    c. Install the ball bearings in the bearing cage. Use the heel of the hand to press the balls into the cage windows.

19. Install the inner race, cage and balls assembly on the halfshaft. Make sure the chamfer on the bearing cage faces the snapring and the marks made during removal line up. Install the snapring.

20. Lubricate the outer race with 1.4–2.1 oz. of CV-joint grease. Install the race, aligning the marks that were made at removal.

21. Add another 0.7–1.0 oz. of grease to the outer race and install the wire ring bearing retainer.

22. Position the inner CV-boot, making sure it is fully seated in the grooves in the shaft and outer race.

23. Extend or compress the CV-joint, as necessary, until the distance between the boot clamp grooves is 3.5 in. (90mm). Do not allow this distance to change until the boot clamps are installed.

24. Insert a prybar between the boot and the outer bearing race to allow trapped air to escape from the boot.

25. Install new boot clamps, wrapping them around in a clockwise direction. Pull the clamps tight with pliers and bend the locking tabs to secure.

26. Work the CV-joint through its full range of travel, at various angles. The joint should flex, extend and compress smoothly.

27. Install the halfshaft assembly into the vehicle.

Front Wheel Hub, Knuckle and Bearings

REMOVAL & INSTALLATION

1989–90

1. Raise and support the vehicle safely. Remove the wheel and tire assembly.

2. Carefully raise the staked portion of the halfshaft retaining nut. Have an assistant apply the brakes to lock the hub and remove the nut and washer. Discard the nut.

3. Remove the stabilizer bar-to-control arm attaching bolt, nut, washers and bushings.

4. Remove the cotter pin and tie rod end attaching nut. Use a suitable tool to separate the tie rod end from the steering knuckle.

5. Disconnect the U-shaped clip from the center section of the caliper hose; do not disconnect the hose from the caliper. Remove the brake caliper-to-steering knuckle bolts and support the caliper on a length of wire; do not allow the caliper to hang by the brake hose.

6. Remove the lower ball joint clamp bolt and nut. Use a prybar to pry down on the lower control arm and separate the ball joint from the steering knuckle.

7. Remove the steering knuckle-to-strut mounting bolts. Slide the hub/steering knuckle assembly out of the strut and off the end of the halfshaft. Be careful not to damage the grease seals.

NOTE: If the hub is difficult to remove from the halfshaft splines, tap the end of the halfshaft with a plastic mallet. Never use a metal hammer. If the halfshaft splines are rusted to the hub, use a suitable hub puller to separate them.

8. Use a suitable tool to press the hub and rotor assembly from the steering knuckle.

9. Remove the bearing preload spacer from the hub and rotor assembly.

NOTE: The spacer located between the bearings determines bearing preload. It must not be discarded.

10. Mark the position of the rotor on the hub. Remove the mounting bolts and remove the rotor from the hub.

11. Using a suitable puller, remove the bearing from the wheel hub. Remove the outer grease seal from the hub and pry the inner grease seal from the steering knuckle.

12. Remove the bearing from the steering knuckle. Do not remove the dust shield as it is pressed onto the knuckle and is difficult to get off without damage.

13. If the wheel bearings are to be replaced, drive the bearing races from the steering knuckle using a brass drift.

14. Inspect the hub and steering knuckle for cracks, wear, scoring or other damage and replace as necessary.

To install:

15. If the wheel bearings are to be replaced, proceed as follows:

    a. Install the new bearing races in

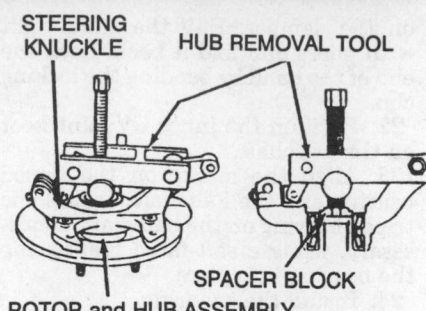

Removing the hub/rotor assembly from the steering knuckle—1989–90 vehicles

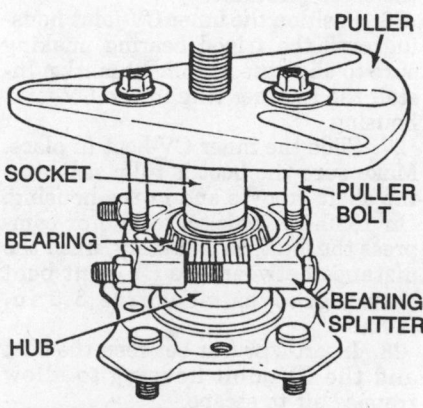

Removing the bearing from the hub—1989–90 vehicles

the steering knuckle using a bearing race driver.

    b. Install the bearing and preload spacer in the steering knuckle.

    c. Install spacer selector tool T87C–1104–B or equivalent, in the steering knuckle and clamp the tool in a vise.

    d. Tighten the center bolt in increments to 36, 72, 108 and 145 ft. lbs. (49, 98, 147 and 196 Nm). After tightening to each specified increment, seat the bearings by rotating the steering knuckle. Final torque the center bolt to 145 ft. lbs. (196 Nm).

    e. Remove the tool/steering knuckle assembly from the vise and remount in the vise, clamping where the strut mounts.

    f. Install a socket and inch pound torque wrench on the spacer selector tool and measure the amount of torque required to rotate the tool. The torque reading must be taken just as the tool starts to rotate.

    g. If the torque wrench indicates 2.21–10.44 inch lbs. (0.25–1.8 Nm), the spacer is the correct thickness. If the indication is less than 2.21 inch lbs. (0.25 Nm), a thinner spacer must be installed. If the indication is more than 10.44 inch lbs. (1.8 Nm), a thicker spacer must be installed.

    h. Each bearing spacer has a numerical code stamped on the outer

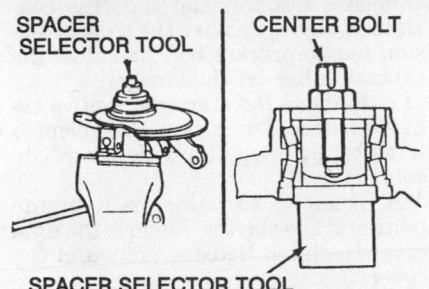

Spacer selector tool assembly—
1989–90 vehicles

WHEEL BEARING SPACER THICKNESS CHART

Stamped Mark	Thickness in. (mm)
1	0.2474 (6.285)
2	0.2490 (6.325)
3	0.2506 (6.365)
4	0.2522 (6.405)
5	0.2538 (6.445)
6	0.2554 (6.485)
7	0.2570 (6.525)
8	0.2586 (6.565)
9	0.2602 (6.605)
10	0.2618 (6.645)
11	0.2634 (6.685)
12	0.2650 (6.725)
13	0.2666 (6.765)
14	0.2682 (6.805)
15	0.2698 (6.845)
16	0.2714 (6.885)
17	0.2730 (6.925)
18	0.2746 (6.965)
19	0.2762 (7.005)
20	0.2778 (7.045)
21	0.2794 (7.085)

diameter of the spacer that corresponds to a particular thickness. If the code number is not legible, determine the spacer thickness by measuring with a micrometer.

i. Changing the bearing thickness by 1 number, either higher or lower, will change the bearing preload by 1.7–3.5 inch lbs. (0.2–0.4 Nm). After selecting a spacer, verify the bearing preload using the spacer selector tool.

16. If removed, install the dust shield on the steering knuckle using tool T87C–1175–B or equivalent.

17. Pack the bearings and the hub area with a high temperature wheel bearing grease.

18. Place the inner bearing in the steering knuckle. Lubricate the lip of a new inner grease seal and install the seal in the knuckle, using a seal installer.

19. Install the bearing preload spacer and the outer bearing in the steering knuckle. Lubricate the lip of a new outer grease seal and install the seal in the knuckle, using a seal installer.

20. Position the hub on the rotor, aligning the marks that were made during the removal procedure. Tighten the mounting bolts to 33–40 ft. lbs. (44–54 Nm).

21. Install the hub and rotor assembly in the steering knuckle using a hydraulic press and suitable fixtures.

22. Install the hub/steering knuckle assembly over the halfshaft and into the strut. Install the strut-to-steering knuckle mounting bolts and nuts and tighten to 69–86 ft. lbs. (93–97 Nm).

23. Install the lower control arm ball joint through the steering knuckle and install the clamp bolt and nut. Tighten the clamp bolt to 32–40 ft. lbs. (43–54 Nm).

24. Install the brake caliper with the mounting bolts. Tighten the bolts to 29–36 ft. lbs. (39–49 Nm). Install the U-clip on the caliper flex line.

25. Install a new halfshaft attaching nut and tighten to 116–174 ft. lbs. (157–235 Nm). Stake the nut using a chisel with a rounded cutting edge. If the nut splits or cracks after staking, it must be replaced with a new nut.

26. Connect the tie rod to the steering knuckle and install the mounting nut. Tighten the nut to 22–33 ft. lbs. (29–44 Nm) and install a new cotter pin. If the slots in the nut do not align with the hole in the ball joint stud, tighten the nut for proper alignment. Never loosen the nut.

27. Position the stabilizer bar and install the link assembly bolt, nut, washers, sleeve and rubber bushings. Tighten the nut until $7/_{16}$ in. (10.8mm) of the bolt threads extend beyond the nut.

28. Install the wheel and tire assembly and lower the vehicle.

1991–93

1. Raise and safely support the vehicle.

2. Remove the front wheel and tire assembly, brake caliper and rotor.

3. Remove the nut securing the halfshaft to the hub.

4. Remove the outer tie rod end at the steering knuckle.

5. Remove the nuts and bolts and separate the shock/strut assembly from the steering knuckle.

6. Remove the nut and bolt and separate the lower ball joint from the steering knuckle.

7. Remove the front hub/steering knuckle assembly from the halfshaft.

8. Remove the oil seal from the rear of the hub/steering knuckle assembly.

9. Position the hub/steering knuckle assembly on a hydraulic press and press the front hub out of the steering knuckle using a suitable removal tool.

NOTE: If the bearing inner race remains on the hub, use a grinder to grind a section of the bearing inner race until only 0.020 in. (0.5mm) remains. Remove the inner race with a suitable chisel.

10. Remove the E-clip from the steering knuckle.

11. Position the steering knuckle onto a hydraulic press and, using an appropriate bearing remover, press the bearing out of the steering knuckle.

NOTE: If the dust cover is removed, it must be replaced.

12. Scribe a mark in the dust cover and steering knuckle. Using a suitable chisel, remove the dust cover.

To install:

13. Scribe a mark on the new dust cover in the same position as on the

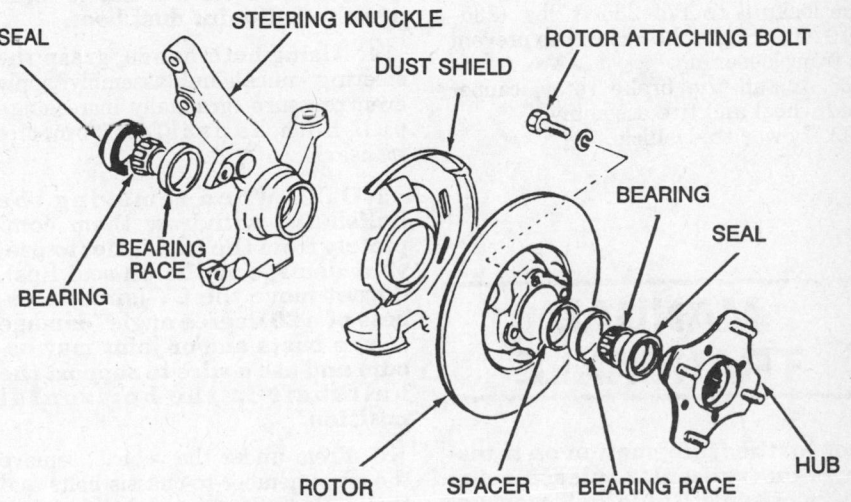

Steering knuckle/hub/wheel bearing assembly—1989–90 vehicles

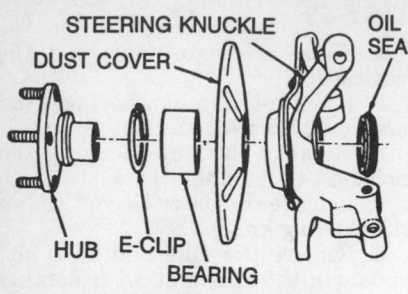

STEERING KNUCKLE OIL SEAL
DUST COVER

HUB E-CLIP BEARING

Hub/steering knuckle assembly—1991–93 vehicles

previous mark. Align the marks on the steering knuckle to the mark on the dust cover and, using a suitable tool, press the dust cover onto the steering knuckle.

14. Position the steering knuckle onto a press and press the bearing into the steering knuckle, using a suitable bearing installer. Apply threadlocking compound to the wheel bearing outer race, prior to installation.

15. Install the E-clip.

16. Position the hub onto the knuckle and press the hub into the bearing and the steering knuckle, using a suitable installation tool.

17. Using an appropriate seal installer, install a new oil seal onto the inboard side of the steering knuckle. Make sure the oil seal mounts flush with the steering knuckle.

18. Install the hub/steering knuckle assembly onto the ball joint and install the nut and bolt. Tighten to 32–43 ft. lbs. (43–59 Nm). Apply Loctite® to the nut and bolt threads prior to installation.

19. Install the outer tie rod.

20. Install the steering knuckle to the shock/strut assembly. Tighten the nuts and bolts to 69–93 ft. lbs. (93–127 Nm).

21. Install a new locknut securing the halfshaft to the front hub. Tighten the locknut to 174–235 ft. lbs. (235–319 Nm). Stake the locknut to prevent it from loosening.

22. Install the brake rotor, caliper and wheel and tire assembly.

23. Lower the vehicle.

MANUAL TRANSAXLE

For further information on transmission/transaxles, please refer to "Chilton's Guide to Transmission Repair".

Transaxle Assembly

REMOVAL & INSTALLATION

1989–90

1. Disconnect the negative battery cable.

2. Remove the air cleaner. Loosen the front wheel lug nuts.

3. From the transaxle, disconnect the speedometer cable.

4. From the clutch release lever, remove the adjusting nut, pin and the clutch cable. Remove the clutch cable bracket-to-transaxle bolts and the bracket. Remove the ground wire bolt and ground wire.

5. Remove the coolant pipe bracket bolt and the bracket.

6. Remove the secondary air pipe, the EGR pipe bracket and the electrical harness clip.

7. Disconnect the neutral switch/backup light switch coupler and the body ground connector.

8. Remove the upper 2 transaxle-to-engine bolts.

9. Using engine support bar tool D79P–6000–B or equivalent, attach it to the rear engine lifting hook and support the engine's weight.

10. Raise and support the vehicle safely.

11. Place a drain pan under the transaxle, remove the drain plug and drain the transaxle.

12. Remove the front wheel lug nuts and the wheels. Remove the engine undercover and side covers.

13. Remove the front stabilizer bar. From both sides, remove the lower control arm ball joint-to-steering knuckle nut/bolt, pull the control arm downward and separate the lower control arm from the steering knuckle.

NOTE: When separating the ball joint, be careful not to damage the ball joint dust boot.

14. Using both hands, grasp the steering knuckle/hub assembly, apply even pressure (gradually increasing), pull both halfshafts from the transaxle.

NOTE: When removing the halfshafts, withdraw them completely from the transaxle (to prevent damage to the oil seal lips), do not move the CV-joints in excess of a 20 degree angle (damage to the boots and/or joint may occur) and use a wire to support the halfshaft in the horizontal position.

15. From under the vehicle, remove the crossmember-to-chassis bolts and the crossmember.

16. Remove the shift control rod-to-

transaxle nut/bolt and slide the control rod aside. Remove the shift extension bar-to-bracket bolt and slide the extension bar off the bracket.

17. Remove the starter's positive cable-to-solenoid nut and the solenoid wire by pulling the wire from the connector.

18. Remove the starter-to-engine bolts and the starter. Remove the dust cover-to-clutch housing bolts and the cover.

19. Loosen the bracket bar hook bolt on the engine support tool to lower the transaxle. Using a floor jack, support the transaxle.

20. Remove the No. 2 engine mount-to-transaxle nut/bolt, the transaxle-to-engine bolts and lower the transaxle from the vehicle.

To install:

21. Install the transaxle by performing the following procedure:

 a. Apply a small amount of clutch grease to the input shaft spline and reverse the removal procedure.

 b. Torque the transaxle-to-engine bolts to 47–66 ft. lbs. (63–89 Nm), the No. 2 engine mount-to-transaxle nut/bolt to 27–38 ft. lbs. (37–52 Nm), the starter to engine bolts to 23–34 ft. lbs. (31–46 Nm), the extension bar-to-transaxle bracket bolt to 23–34 ft. lbs. (31–46 Nm), the control rod-to-transaxle nut/bolt to 12–17 ft. lbs. (16–22 Nm), the crossmember-to-chassis bolts to 47–66 ft. lbs. (64–89 Nm) and the rear engine mount-to-crossmember nut to 20–34 ft. lbs. (28–46 Nm).

22. To install the halfshaft into the transaxle, perform the following procedure:

 a. Install a new locking clip on the halfshaft spline; be sure the gap in the clip is at the top of the clip groove.

 b. Slide the halfshafts into the transaxle bore; be sure not to damage the oil seal lip.

 c. Push firmly on the hub assembly, making sure the circlip snaps into place.

 d. After installation, pull the front hub outward to confirm that the circlips are engaged.

23. To complete the installation, reverse the removal procedure. Torque the lower control arm ball joint-to-steering knuckle nut/bolt to 32–40 ft. lbs. (43–54 Nm), the stabilizer bar-to-chassis nuts/bolts to 23–33 ft. lbs. (31–44 Nm), stabilizer bar-to-lower control arm nuts to 9–13 ft. lbs. (12–18 Nm).

24. Fill the transaxle with the proper type and quantity of fluid. Adjust the clutch pedal free-play and pedal height.

1991–93

1. Disconnect the battery cables

and remove the battery and the battery tray.

2. Remove the air hose and the resonance chamber.

3. Disconnect the speedometer cable at the transaxle.

4. Remove the retaining clip, then disconnect the slave cylinder line from the slave cylinder hose and plug the hose.

5. Disconnect the ground strap from the transaxle.

6. Remove the tie wrap and disconnect the 3 electrical connectors located above the transaxle. Remove the electrical connector support bracket.

7. Mount engine support bar D88L-6000-A or equivalent, and attach it to the engine hangers.

8. Remove the 3 nuts from the upper transaxle mount. Loosen the mount pivot nut and rotate the mount out of position. Remove the 3 bolts and the upper transaxle mount bracket.

9. Remove the 2 upper transaxle-to-engine bolts.

10. Raise and safely support the vehicle.

11. Remove the front wheel and tire assemblies.

12. Remove the inner fender splash shields.

13. Drain the transaxle fluid and install the drain plug.

14. Remove the halfshafts. Install 2 transaxle plugs T88C-7025-AH or equivalent, between the differential side gears.

NOTE: Failure to install the transaxle plugs may cause the differential side gears to become improperly positioned. If the gears become misaligned, the differential will have to be removed from the transaxle to align them.

15. Remove the plenum support bracket and remove the starter.

16. Remove the nut and the extension bar and the bolt and nut and shift control rod from the transaxle.

17. Remove both lower splash shields.

18. Remove the 2 transaxle mount-to-crossmember nuts and remove the lower crossmember and the front transaxle mount.

19. Position and secure a jack under the transaxle.

20. Remove the 5 lower engine-to-transaxle bolts and lower the transaxle out of the vehicle.

To install:

21. Apply a thin coating of grease to the spline of the input shaft.

22. Place the transaxle onto a jack. Make sure the transaxle is secure.

23. Raise the transaxle into position on the engine.

24. Install the 5 lower engine-to-

transaxle bolts and tighten to 27–38 ft. lbs. (37–52 Nm).

25. Install the front transaxle mount and tubing bracket. Tighten the bolts to 12–17 ft. lbs. (16–23 Nm).

26. Install the lower crossmember. Tighten the nuts and bolts to 47–66 ft. lbs. (64–89 Nm).

27. Install the 2 transaxle mount-to-crossmember nuts and tighten to 27–38 ft. lbs. (37–52 Nm).

28. Install both lower splash shields.

29. Install the shift control rod bolt and nut and tighten to 23–34 ft. lbs. (31–46 Nm).

30. Install the extension bar nut and tighten to 12–17 ft. lbs. (16–23 Nm).

31. Install the starter and the plenum support bracket.

32. Remove the transaxle plugs and install the halfshafts.

33. Install the inner fender splash shields.

34. Install the wheel and tire assemblies. Tighten the lug nuts to 65–87 ft. lbs. (88–118 Nm).

35. Lower the vehicle.

36. Install the 2 upper engine-to-transaxle bolts and tighten to 47–66 ft. lbs. (64–89 Nm).

37. Install the upper transaxle mount bracket and tighten the 3 bolts to 47–66 ft. lbs. (64–89 Nm). Rotate the mount into position and tighten the pivot nut. Install and tighten the 3 upper mount nuts to 47–66 ft. lbs. (64–89 Nm).

38. Remove the engine support bar.

39. Install the electrical connector support bracket. Connect the 3 electrical connectors and secure with the tie wrap.

40. Connect the ground strap to the transaxle.

41. Connect the slave cylinder line to the slave cylinder hose and install the retaining clip.

42. Add the proper type and amount of fluid to the transaxle.

43. Connect the speedometer cable.

44. Install the air hose and the resonance chamber.

45. Install the battery tray and the battery. Connect the battery cables.

46. Check for fluid leaks and proper operation.

CLUTCH

Clutch Assembly

REMOVAL & INSTALLATION

1. Disconnect the negative battery cable. Raise and safely support the vehicle. Remove the transaxle.

2. If the clutch assembly is to be re-used, matchmark the pressure plate and the flywheel so they can be assembled in the same position.

3. Loosen the pressure plate-to-flywheel bolts 1 turn at a time, in sequence, until spring tension is relieved to prevent pressure plate cover distortion.

4. Support the pressure plate and remove the bolts. Remove the pressure plate and clutch disc from the flywheel.

5. Inspect the flywheel, clutch disc, pressure plate, release bearing, pilot bearing and the clutch fork for wear; replace parts, as required.

NOTE: If the flywheel shows any signs of overheating (blue discoloration) or if it is badly grooved or scored, it should be refaced or replaced.

To install:

6. If removed, install a new pilot bearing using a suitable installation tool.

7. If removed, install the flywheel. Make sure the flywheel and crankshaft flange mating surfaces are clean. Tighten the flywheel bolts to 71–76 ft. lbs. (96–103 Nm) on 1.6L and 1.8L engines or 54–67 ft. lbs. (73–91 Nm) on 1.9L engine.

8. Clean the pressure plate and flywheel surfaces thoroughly. Position the clutch disc and pressure plate into the installed position and support them with a dummy shaft or clutch aligning tool. If the clutch assembly is being reused, align the matchmarks that were made during the removal procedure.

9. Install the pressure plate-to-flywheel bolts. Tighten them gradually in a criss-cross pattern to 13–20 ft. lbs. (18–26 Nm). Remove the alignment tool.

10. If the release bearing was removed, lubricate the release fork where it contacts the bearing and install the bearing in the fork.

11. Install the transaxle assembly. Lower the vehicle and connect the negative battery cable.

PEDAL HEIGHT/FREE-PLAY ADJUSTMENT

Pedal Height

To determine if the pedal height requires adjustment, measure the distance from the bulkhead to the upper center of the pedal pad. The distance should be 8.4–8.6 in. (214–219mm) on 1989–90 vehicles or 7.72–8.03 in. (196–204mm) on 1991–93 vehicles. If adjustment is necessary, proceed as follows:

1989–90

1. Remove the necessary instrument panel components which block access to the clutch pedal.

2. Loosen the clutch pedal locknut.

3. Turn the stop bolt to obtain the correct pedal height of 8.4–8.6 in. (214–219mm) and tighten the locknut.

4. If components from the instrument panel were removed, reinstall them.

1991–93

1. Disconnect the clutch switch electrical connector.

2. Loosen the clutch switch locknut.

3. Turn the clutch switch until the correct height is achieved.

4. Tighten the locknut to 10–13 ft. lbs. (14–18 Nm).

5. Measure the pedal free-play.

6. Connect the electrical connector.

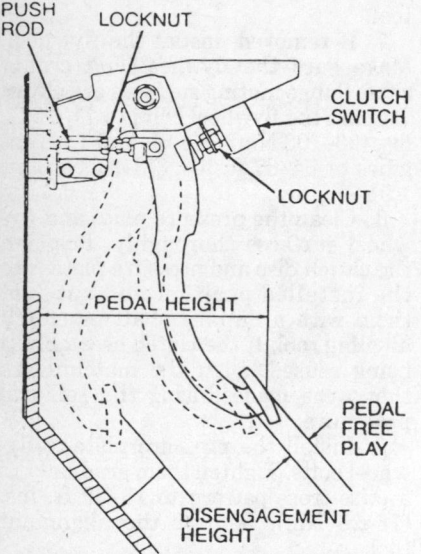

Clutch pedal height and free-play adjustments—1991–93 vehicles

Pedal Free-Play

To determine if the pedal free-play requires adjustment, depress the clutch pedal by hand until clutch resistance is felt. Measure the distance between the upper pedal height and where the resistance is felt. Free-play should be 0.35–0.59 in. (9–15mm) on 1989–90 vehicles or 0.20–0.51 in. (5–13mm) on 1991–93 vehicles. If an adjustment is necessary, proceed as follows:

1989–90

1. Depress the clutch release lever and pull the pin away from the clutch lever (at the transaxle).

2. Turn the adjusting nut (B) until the pin-to-release lever clearance (A) is 0.06–0.100 in. (1.5–2.5mm).

3. After adjustment, make sure the floor-to-upper center of pedal pad is still within specification. The disengagement height should be 3.3 in. (85mm) or more.

1991–93

1. Loosen the pushrod locknut.

2. Turn the pushrod until the pedal free-play is within specification.

3. Check that the disengagement height is correct when the pedal is fully depressed. Minimum disengagement height is 1.6 in. (41mm).

4. Tighten the pushrod locknut to 9–12 ft. lbs. (12–17 Nm).

Clutch Cable

REMOVAL & INSTALLATION

1989–90

1. At the transaxle, remove the clutch cable adjusting nut and pin; separate the cable from the release fork.

2. Remove the clutch cable bracket-to-cowl nuts and the bracket.

3. From under the instrument pan-

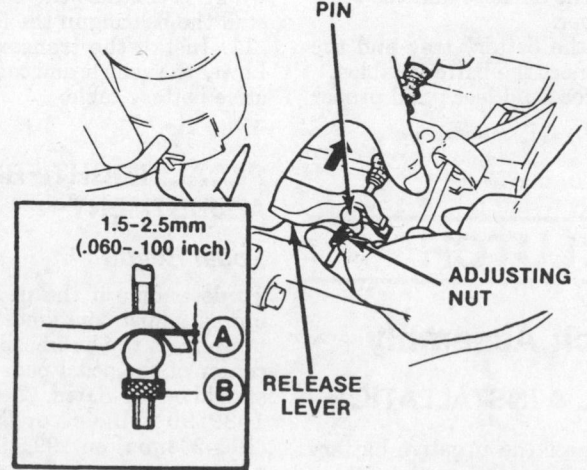

Clutch pedal free-play adjustment—1989–90 vehicles

el, separate the clutch cable from the top of the clutch pedal.

4. Pull the cable through the cowl and remove the cable assembly from the engine side.

5. Inspect the clutch cable housing for frayed wire, cracked or worn housing and the cable for smooth operation; replace the cable assembly, if necessary.

6. To install, lubricate the cable with multi-purpose grease and reverse the removal procedures. Adjust the clutch pedal free-play.

Clutch Master Cylinder

REMOVAL & INSTALLATION

1991–93

1. Disconnect the battery cables and remove the battery and battery tray.

2. Disconnect the clutch pipe from the master cylinder using a line wrench.

3. Disengage the clamp and remove the master cylinder hose from the clutch master cylinder. Prevent excess fluid loss by plugging the hose.

4. Remove the external mounting nut.

5. Remove the internal mounting nut and remove the master cylinder.

To install:

6. Align the pushrod and install the clutch master cylinder.

7. Install the external and internal mounting nuts and tighten to 14–19 ft. lbs. (19–25 Nm).

8. Connect the clutch pipe and tighten the nut to 10–16 ft. lbs. (13–22 Nm).

9. Install the hose and the clamp to the master cylinder.

10. Install the battery and battery tray.

11. Bleed the air from the system.

12. Test the system and make sure there is no leakage.

13. Connect the negative battery cable.

Clutch Slave Cylinder

ADJUSTMENT

1991–93

The clutch slave cylinder is not adjustable. The only adjustments necessary on the clutch control system are pedal height and pedal free-play.

REMOVAL & INSTALLATION

1991–93

1. Disconnect the pressure line. Plug the line to prevent leaking.

2. Remove the attaching bolts and remove the slave cylinder.

To install:

3. Install the slave cylinder.

4. Install the attaching bolts and tighten to 12–17 ft. lbs. (16–23 Nm).

5. Connect the pressure line and tighten the nut to 10–16 ft. lbs. (13–22 Nm).

6. Bleed the air from the system.

7. Press on the clutch pedal and make sure there is no leakage.

Hydraulic Clutch System Bleeding

NOTE: The fluid level in the reservoir must be maintained at the ¾ level or higher during air bleeding.

1. Remove the bleeder cap from the slave cylinder and attach a vinyl hose to the bleeder screw.

2. Place the other end of the hose in a container.

3. Slowly pump the clutch pedal several times.

4. With the clutch pedal depressed, loosen the bleeder screw to release the fluid and air.

5. Tighten the bleeder screw.

6. Repeat the last 3 steps until no air bubbles appear in the fluid.

AUTOMATIC TRANSAXLE

For further information on transmission/transaxles, please refer to "Chilton's Guide to Transmission Repair".

Transaxle Assembly

REMOVAL & INSTALLATION

1989–90

1. Disconnect the negative battery cable.

2. Remove the air cleaner. Loosen the front wheel lug nuts.

3. From the transaxle, disconnect the speedometer cable.

4. Disconnect the shift control cable-to-transaxle clip and 2 bracket bolts. Remove the ground wire from the cylinder head.

5. Remove the water pipe bracket bolt and the bracket.

6. Remove the secondary air pipe, the EGR pipe bracket and the electrical harness clip.

7. Disconnect the electrical connectors from the inhibitor switch, the neutral switch and the kickdown solenoid. Disconnect the body ground connector.

8. Remove the upper 2 transaxle-to-engine bolts.

9. Remove the vacuum hose from the vacuum diaphragm line. Disconnect and plug the oil cooler lines at the transaxle.

10. Using engine support bar tool D79P–6000–B or equivalent, attach it to the rear engine lifting hook and support the engine's weight.

11. Raise and support the vehicle safely.

12. Place a drain pan under the transaxle, remove the drain plug and drain the transaxle.

13. Remove the front wheel lug nuts and the wheels. Remove the engine undercover and side covers.

14. Remove the front stabilizer bar. From both sides, remove the lower control arm ball joint-to-steering knuckle nut/bolt, pull the control arm downward and separate the lower control arm from the steering knuckle.

NOTE: When separating the ball joint, be careful not to damage the ball joint dust boot.

15. Using a medium prybar, insert it between the halfshaft and the transaxle (a notch is provided), pry both halfshafts from the transaxle.

NOTE: When removing the halfshafts, withdraw them completely from the transaxle (to prevent damage to the oil seal lips), do not move the CV-joints in excess of a 20 degree angle (damage to the boots and/or joint may occur) and use a wire to support the halfshaft in the horizontal position.

16. From under the vehicle, remove the crossmember-to-chassis bolts and the crossmember.

17. Remove the starter's positive cable-to-solenoid nut and the solenoid wire by pulling the wire from the connector.

18. Remove the starter-to-engine bolts and the starter. Remove the dust cover bolts and the cover.

19. Matchmark the torque converter-to-flexplate location. Remove the torque converter-to-flexplate bolts and slide the torque converter back into the transaxle.

20. Loosen the bracket bar on the engine support tool to lower the transaxle. Using a floor jack, support the transaxle.

21. Remove the No. 2 engine mount-to-transaxle nut/bolt, the transaxle-to-engine bolts and lower the transaxle from the vehicle.

To install:

22. Hold the torque converter in an upright position and fill it with fluid. Install the torque converter on the transaxle input shaft. If the converter does not fit easily, remove the converter, realign the splines and refit the converter. Do not use force.

23. To make sure the converter is correctly installed, measure the clearance between the end of the converter and the end of the converter housing. The clearance should be 0.79 in. (20mm).

24. Align the mounting studs on the engine with the holes in the transaxle case and install the transaxle. Install the bolts and tighten to 47–66 ft. lbs. (64–89 Nm).

25. Raise the transaxle to the proper position and install the bolt/nut to the No. 2 engine mount. Tighten to 27–38 ft. lbs. (37–52 Nm).

26. Align the matchmarks on the converter and flexplate and install the mounting bolts. Tighten to 25–36 ft. lbs. (34–49 Nm).

27. Install the starter and tighten the mounting bolts to 23–34 ft. lbs. (31–46 Nm). Connect the solenoid wire and positive battery cable to the starter.

28. Install the crossmember. Tighten the crossmember mounting bolts to 47–66 ft. lbs. (64–89 Nm) and the rear mount bolt to 21–34 ft. lbs. (28–46 Nm).

29. Install a new clip on both halfshaft ends, with the gap at the top of the clip groove. Slide the halfshafts into the transaxle, being careful not to damage the seals. Make sure the clips engage into the side gears.

30. Install the lower ball joints into the steering knuckles. Tighten the nuts to 32–40 ft. lbs. (43–54 Nm).

31. Install the under and side covers and the wheel and tire assemblies. Lower the vehicle.

32. Install the 2 remaining upper transaxle mounting bolts and tighten to 47–66 ft. lbs. (64–89 Nm).

33. Remove the engine support bar.

34. Connect the transaxle cooler lines, the vacuum line to the vacuum diaphragm, the neutral switch connector, body ground connector, inhibitor switch and kick-down solenoid wiring.

35. Install the wire harness clip, the secondary air pipe and EGR pipe bracket, and the engine ground wire.

36. Connect the change control cable, install the mounting bracket bolts and tighten. Connect the speedometer cable and install the hold-down bolt.

37. Install the air cleaner and all remaining components.

38. Connect the negative battery cable. Fill the transaxle with the proper type and quantity of fluid. Start the engine and check for leaks.

1991–93

1. Disconnect the battery cables and remove the battery and battery tray.
2. Disconnect the wiring harness retaining clip from the battery tray.
3. Remove the air cleaner assembly.
4. Disconnect the shift control cable from the manual lever.
5. Disconnect the speedometer cable from the transaxle by unsnapping the cable at the speedometer driven gear.
6. Disconnect the transaxle electronic control electrical connectors and separate the harness from the transaxle clips.
7. Remove the manual lever position switch wiring brackets and disconnect the ground cables from the top of the transaxle.
8. Remove the starter.
9. Disconnect the manual lever position switch wiring connectors.
10. Install engine support tool D88L–6000–A or equivalent, to support the engine.
11. Disconnect the kickdown cable at the throttle cam.
12. Place a drain pan under the transaxle and disconnect the transaxle cooler lines at the transaxle.
13. Remove the upper transaxle mount bolts, the mount and the upper transaxle housing bolts.
14. Disconnect the oxygen sensor electrical connector, the transaxle vent hose, and the electrical connector at the vehicle speed sensor.
15. Raise and safely support the vehicle.
16. Remove the front wheel and tire assemblies.
17. Using a hammer and a flat punch, straighten the detent in the halfshaft nut.
18. Remove the nuts securing the halfshafts to the steering knuckles and remove the nuts and bolts securing the lower ball joints to the steering knuckles. Separate the lower ball joints from the steering knuckles.
19. Disconnect the halfshaft midbearing bracket from the back of the engine.
20. Remove the halfshafts from both steering knuckles.
21. Remove the 3 engine/transaxle lower splash shields and the torque converter inspection plate. Remove the nuts securing the torque converter to the flexplate.
22. Remove the bolts securing the lower transaxle to the engine oil pan. Disconnect the lower crossmember from the chassis and the transaxle mounts.
23. Remove the driver's side and then the passenger's side halfshafts. Install 2 transaxle plugs T88C–7025–

AH or equivalent into the differential side gears.

NOTE: Failure to install the transaxle plugs may cause the differential side gears to become improperly positioned. If the gears become misaligned, the differential will have to be removed from the transaxle to align them.

24. Position a drain pan and remove the drainplug from the transaxle. Drain the fluid from the differential cavity. Remove the transaxle pan and drain the transaxle fluid, then install the pan and drainplug.
25. Position a transmission jack under the transaxle. Secure the transaxle to the jack.
26. Remove the lower bolts securing the transaxle to the engine and carefully lower the transaxle out of the vehicle.

To install:

NOTE: A pin is used for securing the throttle cam in a fixed position on new and rebuilt transaxles. This pin must be removed to allow proper transaxle operation. If the pin is not removed, the throttle lever will remain in a fixed position. After removing the pin, apply sealant to the bolt from the previous transaxle. Install the bolt and tighten to 69–95 inch lbs. (8–11 Nm).

27. Secure the transaxle on the transmission jack.
28. Raise the transaxle into position and install the lower transaxle-to-engine bolts. Tighten the bolts to 41–59 ft. lbs. (55–80 Nm).
29. Position the torque converter to the flexplate and install the nuts. Tighten the nuts to 25–36 ft. lbs. (34–49 Nm). Install the torque converter inspection plate.
30. Remove the 2 transaxle plugs and install the halfshafts.
31. Connect the crossmember to the transaxle mounts and the chassis. Tighten the crossmember-to-transaxle mount nuts to 27–38 ft. lbs. (37–52 Nm). Tighten the crossmember-to-chassis nuts and bolts to 47–66 ft. lbs. (64–89 Nm).
32. Install the lower transaxle-to-engine oil pan bolts and tighten to 27–38 ft. lbs. (37–52 Nm). Install the engine/transaxle splash shields and the starter.
33. Position the lower ball joints into the steering knuckles and secure with the nuts and bolts. Tighten the nuts and bolts to 32–43 ft. lbs. (43–59 Nm).
34. Position the tie rod ends into the steering knuckles and install the nuts. Tighten to 31–42 ft. lbs. (42–57 Nm).
35. Install the wheel and tire assem-

blies. Tighten the lugs to 65–88 ft. lbs. (88–118 Nm).
36. Lower the vehicle.
37. Install the transaxle-to-engine bolts and tighten to 41–59 ft. lbs. (55–80 Nm).
38. Install the upper transaxle mount and tighten the nuts to 49–69 ft. lbs. (67–93 Nm).
39. Connect the transaxle vent hose, the electrical connector at the speed sensor, the speedometer cable and the oxygen sensor connector.
40. Connect the transaxle cooler lines and connect the kickdown cable at the throttle body.
41. Remove the engine support.
42. Connect the ground wires to the transaxle and connect the manual lever position switch bracket and wiring connectors.
43. Connect the shift control cable to the cable bracket and to the selector lever. Tighten the selector lever attaching locknut to 33–47 ft. lbs. (44–64 Nm).

NOTE: Do not use any type of power wrench to tighten the locknut. Damage to the transaxle may result.

44. Install the battery tray and battery. Connect the wiring harness retaining clip to the battery tray.
45. Install the air cleaner assembly.
46. Connect the battery cables.
47. Add the proper type and quantity of transaxle fluid.
48. Check the transaxle for leaks and for proper operation.

SHIFT LINKAGE ADJUSTMENT

1989–90

1. Place the gear selector lever in the **N** position.
2. At the transaxle, remove the shift cable trunnion-to-transaxle shift lever spring clip and pin.
3. Rotate the transaxle shift lever fully counterclockwise to place it in the **P** position.
4. Move the transaxle shift lever clockwise 2 detents to place it in the **N** position.

NOTE: When moving the transaxle shift lever, be sure to position it between the ends of the shift cable trunnion.

5. If the trunnion holes align with the shift lever hole, the cable is adjusted; replace the pin and spring clip. If the holes are not aligned, proceed with the remaining adjustment procedures.
6. From inside the vehicle, remove the shift quadrant bezel-to-console screws. Lift the front of the bezel to disengage it from the console and ro-

tate it to provide access to the cable adjusting nuts.

7. At the shift cable, loosen the adjusting nuts.

8. Position the gear selector lever in the **P** position and inspect the detent spring roller. If the spring is not centered, perform the following procedures:

    a. Loosen the detent spring roller screws and move the spring to center it in the **P** position.

    b. Position the shift quadrant and reinstall the screws.

9. Move the shift selector lever to the **N** position.

10. Move the shift cable adjuster nuts until the holes in the cable trunnion and transaxle shift lever are aligned. Torque the shift cable adjuster nuts to 69–95 inch lbs. (8–11 Nm).

11. Recheck the cable trunnion and transaxle shift lever holes for alignment. If aligned, install the pin and spring clip.

12. Using an assistant to watch the transaxle shift lever movement, start with the gear selector lever in the **N** position, push the shift interlock button and carefully move the shift lever forward until the transaxle shift lever begins to move; note the amount of shift selector movement.

13. With the gear selector lever in the **N** position, press in on the shift interlock button and carefully pull the lever rearward while an assistant watches the transaxle shift lever. When the transaxle lever begins to move, note the amount the shift lever has moved.

14. If the shift selector lever forward movement **a** does not equal the rearward movement **b**, turn the adjuster nuts until the movement is equal.

NOTE: Make sure the adjustment procedure does not affect the neutral safety switch operation. Apply the parking brakes and try to start the engine in the N and P positions. If the engine starts in any other gear selector lever positions, check and adjust the linkage adjustment and the neutral safety switch operation.

15. When adjustment is completed, tighten the adjuster nut to 69–95 inch lbs. (8–11 Nm). Position the shift quadrant bezel and install the attaching screws.

1991–93

1. Move the gear selector lever to **P**.

2. Disconnect the negative battery cable. This will deactivate the shift-lock system.

3. Remove the screw securing the gear selector knob to the gear selector lever. Remove the knob.

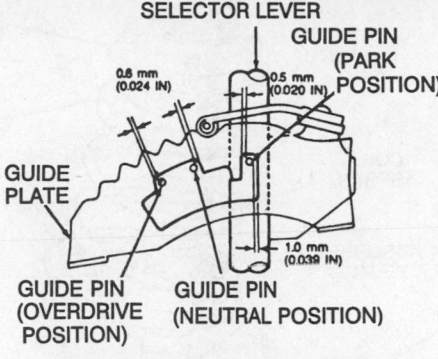

Shift control cable adjustment clearances—1991–93 vehicles

4. Remove the shift console as follows:

    a. Remove the rear seat ash tray and position both front seats to the rear-most position.

    b. Remove the 2 front retaining screws from the parking brake console and recline both front seats.

    c. Remove the 2 rear retaining screws from the parking brake console.

    d. With the parking brake engaged, remove the parking brake console.

    e. Remove the 2 front retaining screws from the shift console and remove the console.

5. Remove the position indicator mounting screws and disconnect the illumination bulb from the position indicator.

6. Disconnect the shift-lock servo and park range switch electrical connectors.

7. Remove the position indicator.

NOTE: Make sure the detent spring roller is in the P detent.

8. Loosen the shift control cable bracket mounting bolts.

9. Push the gear selector lever against the **P** range and hold it.

10. Tighten the shift control cable bracket mounting bolts to 69–95 inch lbs. (8–11 Nm).

11. Lightly press the gear selector pushrod and make sure the guide plate and guide pin clearances are within specifications.

12. Check that the guide plate and guide pin clearances are within the appropriate specifications when the selector lever is shifted to **N** and **OD**. If the clearances are not as specified, readjust the shift control cable.

13. Make sure the gear selector operates properly.

14. Connect the illumination bulb to the position indicator.

15. Connect the shift-lock servo and park range switch electrical connectors.

16. Install the position indicator and secure it with the mounting screws.

17. Install the shift console by reversing the removal procedure.

18. Position the gear selector knob onto the gear selector lever and secure the knob with the screw.

19. Connect the negative battery cable.

FRONT SUSPENSION

MacPherson Strut

REMOVAL & INSTALLATION

1. Raise and safely support the vehicle.

2. Remove the front wheel and tire assembly.

3. Remove the clip securing the flexible brake hose to the strut assembly.

4. On 1989–90 vehicles, paint a white aligning stripe on the inside of the strut mounting block.

5. Remove the 2 nuts and 2 bolts securing the strut assembly to the steering knuckle.

6. Remove the upper mounting block nuts and remove the strut assembly from the vehicle.

7. Remove the cap from the top of the strut assembly.

8. Secure the strut assembly mounting block in a vise. Turn the piston rod nut 1 revolution to loosen.

9. Install an appropriate spring compressor onto the strut spring and compress the spring.

10. Remove the nut, mounting block, thrust bearing, upper spring seat, rubber spring seat, coil spring and bound stopper.

To install:

11. Position the bound stopper onto the strut piston rod.

12. With the coil spring compressed, position the spring onto the strut assembly.

13. Install the rubber spring seat, upper spring seat, thrust bearing, mounting block and piston rod nut. Tighten the piston rod nut to 58–81 ft. lbs. (79–110 Nm).

14. With the nut tightened to specification, carefully remove the spring compressor from the spring while making sure the spring is properly seated in the upper and lower spring seats.

15. Install the cap.

16. Position the strut assembly into the wheel housing. Make sure the di-

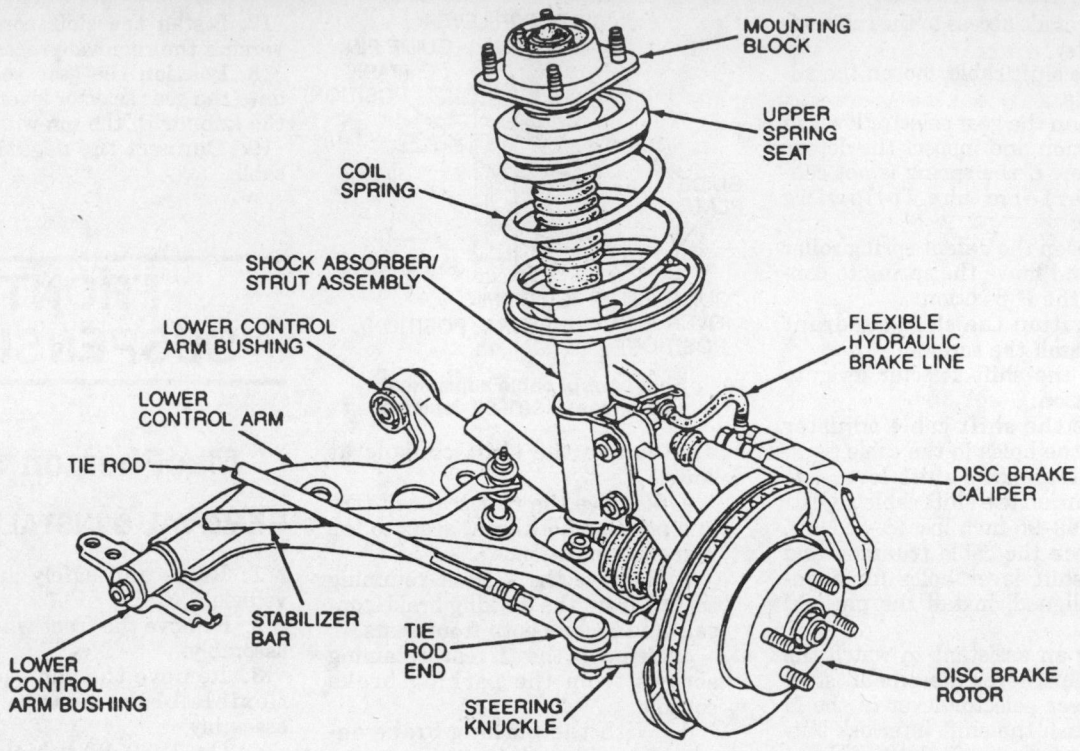

MOUNTING BLOCK

UPPER SPRING SEAT

COIL SPRING

SHOCK ABSORBER/ STRUT ASSEMBLY

LOWER CONTROL ARM BUSHING

LOWER CONTROL ARM

TIE ROD

LOWER CONTROL ARM BUSHING

STABILIZER BAR

TIE ROD END

STEERING KNUCKLE

FLEXIBLE HYDRAULIC BRAKE LINE

DISC BRAKE CALIPER

DISC BRAKE ROTOR

Front suspension assembly—1991–93 vehicles

rection indicator on the mounting block faces inboard.

17. Secure the upper mounting block to the strut tower with the nuts. Tighten the nuts to 22–30 ft. lbs. (29–40 Nm).

18. Attach the strut assembly to the steering knuckle and install the bolts and nuts. Tighten to 69–72 ft. lbs. (93–97 Nm).

19. Position the flexible brake hose to the strut assembly and secure it with the brake hose clip.

20. Install the front wheel and tire assembly.

21. Lower the vehicle and check the front wheel alignment.

Lower Ball Joints

Inspection

1989–90

1. Raise and safely support the vehicle so wheels are in the full-down position.

2. Have an assistant grasp lower edge of the tire and move wheel and tire assembly in and out.

3. As wheel is being moved in and out, observe lower end of knuckle and lower control arm. Any movement between the knuckle and control arm indicates ball joint wear.

4. If any movement is observed, install new lower ball joint.

1991–93

1. Remove the lower ball joint.

2. Secure the ball joint bracket in a vise.

3. Thread the ball joint attaching nut onto the ball joint stud until the nut bottoms out on the stud.

4. Install a torque wrench onto the nut and measure the torque required to keep the stud in motion. The correct turning torque is 14–25 ft. lbs. (20–34 Nm).

5. If the turning torque is not within specification, replace the ball joint.

REMOVAL & INSTALLATION

1989–90

1. Raise the vehicle and support it safely.

2. Rmove the wheel and tire assembly.

3. Remove the brake caliper and support it aside with mechanics wire. Do not disconnect the brake line.

4. Separate the stabilizer bar from the control arm.

5. Remove the tie rod end cotter pin and nut. Separate the tie rod from the knuckle, using the proper removal tool.

6. Remove the ball joint-to-knuckle clamp bolt and pry the lower control arm from the knuckle.

7. Remove the ball joint-to-control arm bolts and remove the ball joint.

8. Installation is the reverse of the removal procedure. Torque the ball joint-to-lower arm nuts to 69–86 ft. lbs. (93–117 Nm) and the ball joint clamp bolt to 32–40 ft. lbs. (43–54 Nm).

1991–93

1. Raise and safely support the vehicle.

2. Remove the wheel and tire assembly.

3. Remove the nut and bolt securing the ball joint to the steering knuckle.

4. Remove the nuts securing the lower ball joint to the lower control arm. Remove the lower ball joint.

5. Mount the lower ball joint in a vise.

6. Place a chisel between the ball joint and the dust boot. Lightly tap on the chisel to separate the dust boot from the ball joint.

To install:

7. Position the dust boot over the ball joint and, using a suitable tool, press down on the tool to secure the dust boot to the ball joint.

8. Install the ball joint into the lower control arm and install the mounting nuts. Tighten the nuts to 69–86 ft. lbs. (93–117 Nm).

9. Install the lower ball joint into the steering knuckle and secure it with the nut and bolt. Tighten the nut to

32–43 ft. lbs. (43–59 Nm). Apply Loctite® to the nut and bolt threads prior to installation.

10. Install the wheel and tire assembly and lower the vehicle.

Lower Control Arms

REMOVAL & INSTALLATION

1989–90

1. Raise and safely support the vehicle. Remove the wheel and tire assembly.

2. Remove the brake caliper and support it aside with mechanics wire. Do not disconnect the brake hose.

3. Remove the stabilizer link assembly.

4. Paint aligning stripes on the rear control arm bushing and mounting bracket and on the rear control arm bushing and control arm.

5. Remove the ball joint clamp bolt from the steering knuckle.

6. Loosen the lower control arm front bushing nut and rear bushing bolt.

7. Remove the lower control arm rear bushing bracket mounting bolts.

8. Remove the front bushing bracket and the rear bushing bolt.

9. Remove the lower control arm. Remove the front bushing nut and remove the bushing.

To install:

10. Install the front bushing on the lower control arm and install the nut, hand-tight.

11. Position the lower control arm on the vehicle and install the rear bushing bolt. Install the front bushing bracket.

12. Raise the lower control arm until the painted stripes align, then tighten the front bushing nut and rear bushing bolt.

13. Install the ball joint stud in the steering knuckle. Install the clamp bolt and tighten to 32–40 ft. lbs. (44–55 Nm).

14. Install the stabilizer link assembly. Tighten the nut until 0.43 in. (10.8mm) protrudes below the nut.

15. Install the brake caliper and the wheel and tire assembly. Lower the vehicle.

1991–93

1. Raise and safely support the vehicle.

2. Remove the front wheel and tire assembly.

3. Remove the front stabilizer nuts, washers, bushings, bolts and sleeves.

4. Remove the lower control arm front bushing bolt and washer.

5. Remove the bolts securing the lower control arm rear bushing retaining strap.

6. Remove the nut and bolt securing the lower ball joint to the steering knuckle. Separate the steering knuckle from the lower ball joint.

7. Remove the lower control arm.

8. Remove the nut and washers from the lower control arm rear pivot bolt.

9. Remove the lower control arm rear bushing.

To install:

10. Position the lower control arm rear bushing onto the rear pivot bolt.

11. Install the washers and nut onto the lower control arm pivot bolt. Tighten the nut to 69–86 ft. lbs. (93–117 Nm).

12. Install the ball joint into the steering knuckle. Install the ball joint retaining nut and bolt and tighten the nut to 32–43 ft. lbs. (43–59 Nm). Apply Loctite® to the nut and bolt threads prior to installation.

13. Install the lower control arm rear bushing retaining strap to the lower frame. Install the bolts and tighten to 69–86 ft. lbs. (93–117 Nm).

14. Install the lower control arm front pivot bolt and washer. Tighten the nut to 69–93 ft. lbs. (93–127 Nm).

15. Install the stabilizer bolts, washers, bushings, sleeves and nuts. Tighten the stabilizer nuts so 0.67–0.75 in. (17–19mm) of thread is exposed at the end of the bolt.

16. Install the wheel and tire assembly. Tighten the lug nuts to 65–87 ft. lbs. (88–118 Nm).

17. Lower the vehicle.

Stabilizer Bar

REMOVAL & INSTALLATION

1989–90

1. Raise and safely support the vehicle.

2. Disconnect the stabilizer links from the lower control arm.

3. Remove the stabilizer bushing bracket bolts and remove the brackets and bushings. Remove the stabilizer bar.

To install:

4. Install the stabilizer bar onto the vehicle with the bushings, brackets and bracket bolts. Install the bolts hand-tight at this time.

5. Install the stabilizer link assembly. Tighten the nut until 0.43 in. (10.8mm) protrudes below the nut.

6. Lower the vehicle. Now that the suspension is loaded, tighten the bushing bracket mounting bolts to 44–54 ft. lbs. (59–74 Nm).

1991–93

1. Support the engine with engine support tool D88L-6000-A or equivalent.

2. Raise and safely support the vehicle.

3. Remove the front wheel and tire assemblies.

4. Remove the nuts securing the steering gear mounting brackets and position the steering gear slightly forward.

5. Remove the stabilizer bar nuts, washers, bushings, sleeves and bolts from the lower control arm.

6. Remove the rear crossmember nuts from the rear transaxle mount and the vehicle frame.

7. Loosen the front crossmember bolts and nuts from the front transaxle mount and the vehicle frame. Lower the rear end of the crossmember.

8. Remove the nuts and bolts securing the chassis frame to the vehicle frame. Lower the chassis frame.

NOTE: The engine and transaxle mounts will support the chassis frame when unbolting the chassis frame from the vehicle frame.

9. Unbolt the stabilizer bar from the chassis frame and remove the stabilizer bar from the vehicle.

To install:

10. Position the stabilizer bar into the vehicle.

11. Secure the stabilizer bar to the chassis frame with the bolts. Tighten the bolts to 32–43 ft. lbs. (43–59 Nm).

12. Install the chassis frame to the vehicle frame with the bolts and nuts. Tighten the bolts and nuts to 69–93 ft. lbs. (93–127 Nm).

13. Position the crossmember to the vehicle frame and the transaxle mounts. Tighten the bolts and nuts to the specified torque.

14. Install the stabilizer bar bolts, sleeves, bushings, washers and nuts. Tighten the stabilizer bolts so 0.67–0.75 in. (17–19mm) of thread is exposed at the end of the bolt.

15. Position the steering gear and secure it with the brackets and nuts.

TIGHTENING TORQUE:
A: 27–38 FT. LBS. (37–52 NM)
B: 47–66 FT. LBS. (64–89 NM)

Crossmember mounting bolts and nuts torque specifications

Tighten the nuts to 28–38 ft. lbs. (37–52 Nm).

16. Install the wheel and tire assemblies. Tighten the lug nuts to 65–87 ft. lbs. (88–118 Nm).

17. Lower the vehicle and remove the engine support.

REAR SUSPENSION

MacPherson Strut

REMOVAL & INSTALLATION

1989–90

1. Raise and safely support the vehicle. Remove the wheel and tire assembly.

2. Remove the brake drum and backing plate or the disc brake caliper and rotor, as required.

3. Loosen the trailing arm bolt and the spindle-to-strut mounting bolts. Remove the trailing arm and spindle mounting bolts.

4. Paint a white index mark on the strut rubber mounting bracket. Remove the strut mounting nuts from inside the vehicle. Remove the strut assembly.

5. Install a coil spring compressor on the strut assembly. While the spring is compressed, remove the nut, rubber mounting bracket, spring upper seat and rubber spring seat.

6. Slowly release the coil spring and remove the spring compressor. Remove the coil spring, dust boot and rebound bumper from the strut.

To install:

7. Install the rebound bumpers and dust boot on the strut. Compress the coil spring with the spring compressor and install the spring on the strut.

8. Install the rubber seat, spring upper seat with rubber mounting bracket and the nut. Slowly release the spring compressor.

9. Install the strut assembly in the strut tower, aligning the index mark that was made during the removal procedure. Install and tighten the mounting nuts.

10. Install the spindle-to-strut mounting bolts and tighten the bolts hand-tight.

11. Install the rear brake assembly and the wheel and tire assembly. Lower the vehicle.

12. Now that the suspension is load-ed, tighten the spindle-to-strut mounting bolts to 69–86 ft. lbs. (93–117 Nm).

1991–93

1. Raise and safely support the vehicle.

2. Remove the wheel and tire assembly.

3. Remove the clip securing the flexible brake hose to the rear strut assembly.

4. Remove the nuts and bolts securing the rear strut assembly to the rear wheel spindle assembly.

5. On hatchback and wagon, remove the quarter lower trim panel.

6. Remove the mounting block nuts and remove the rear strut assembly from the vehicle.

7. Position the strut assembly into a vise and secure the assembly at the mounting block.

8. Remove the cap and loosen the piston rod nut 1 turn. Do not remove the piston rod nut at this time.

9. Install an appropriate coil spring compressor onto the coil spring and compress the coil spring.

10. Remove the piston rod nut, washer, retainer and mounting block.

11. Remove the coil spring.

12. Remove the bound stopper seat and stopper from the strut piston.

To install:

13. Position the strut assembly into a vise and secure.

14. Install the bound stopper seat and stopper onto the strut piston rod.

15. Install the coil spring onto the strut assembly.

16. Install the mounting block, then align the mounting block studs and the lower bracket of the strut assembly.

17. Install the retainer, washer and piston rod nut. Tighten the nut to 41–50 ft. lbs. (55–68 Nm).

18. Make sure the spring is properly aligned and carefully release the spring into the seats of the strut.

19. Remove the spring compressor from the coil spring and install the cap.

20. Position the strut assembly into the vehicle wheel housing.

21. Install the mounting block nuts and tighten to 22–27 ft. lbs. (29–40 Nm).

22. On hatchback and wagon, install the quarter lower trim panel.

23. Install the nuts and bolts securing the strut assembly to the rear spindle assembly. Tighten the lower strut bolts to 69–93 ft. lbs. (93–127 Nm).

24. Install the wheel and tire assembly. Tighten the lug nuts to 65–87 ft. lbs. (88–118 Nm).

25. Check the rear alignment and lower the vehicle.

Rear Control Arms

REMOVAL & INSTALLATION

1989–90

1. Raise the vehicle and support it safely.

2. Remove the wheel and tire assembly. Remove the brake drum and backing plate, if equipped with drum brakes. If equipped with disc brakes, remove the caliper and rotor.

3. Make alignment marks on the rear toe adjusting cam, on each control arm and control arm bushing, and on each side of the trailing arm and crossmember.

4. Remove the stabilizer link assembly.

5. Remove the stabilizer bar mounting bolts and remove the stabilizer bar.

6. Loosen the inner and outer trailing arm bolts, the spindle-to-strut bolts and the trailing arm-to-strut bolts. Remove the parking brake attaching bolt from the rear trailing arm assembly.

7. Remove all bolts and the control arm and the trailing arm from the vehicle.

To install:

8. Mount both control arms on the crossmember and hand-tighten the bolts.

9. Connect both control arms with the outer control arm bolt but do not install the spindle yet. Raise the control arms to align the marks made during removal, and tighten the control arm bolts. Be sure to align the marks on the control arm and alignment cam.

10. Install the spindle in the strut and tighten the bolts to 69–86 ft. lbs. (93–117 Nm). Install the control arm-to-spindle attaching bolt and tighten to 69–86 ft. lbs. (93–117 Nm).

11. Tighten the inner control arm bolt to 69–86 ft. lbs. (93–117 Nm).

12. Loosely install the stabilizer bar in the bushing, making sure the alignment mark on the bar aligns with the bushings. Do not fully tighten the bracket bolts yet.

13. Install the stabilizer link assembly.

14. Install the brake assembly and the wheel and tire assembly. Lower the vehicle.

15. Now that the suspension is load-ed, tighten the stabilizer link bolt until 0.71 in. (18mm) of thread extends beyond the nut and tighten the bushing bracket bolts to 32–40 ft. lbs. (45–55 Nm).

1991–93

1. Raise and safely support the vehicle.

2. Remove the wheel and tire assembly.

3. Remove the stabilizer nuts, washers, bushings, sleeves and bolts.

4. Remove the bolts securing the stabilizer bar brackets and grommets to the rear suspension crossmember.

5. Remove the stabilizer bar.

6. Remove the cap covering the front and rear lateral link pivot bolts.

7. Position a floor jack stand under the rear suspension crossmember.

8. Remove the bolts securing the rear suspension crossmember to the vehicle frame.

9. Lower the floor jack stand to allow the rear suspension crossmember to be lowered from the vehicle frame.

10. Remove the front and rear lateral link pivot nut, washer and bolt from the rear suspension crossmember.

11. Remove the front and rear lateral links from the rear suspension crossmember.

12. Remove the bolt, washers and nut securing the front and rear lateral links to the rear wheel spindle and remove the lateral links.

13. Remove the nuts securing the parking brake cable and cable bracket to the trailing link.

14. Remove the rear trailing link bolts and washers from the vehicle frame and rear wheel spindle. Remove the rear trailing link.

To install:

15. Position the rear trailing link and install the bolts and washers. Tighten the trailing link front bolt to 46–69 ft. lbs. (63–93 Nm) and the rear bolt to 69–93 ft. lbs. (93–127 Nm).

16. Position the parking brake cable and bracket to the trailing link and secure it with the nuts.

17. Position the front and rear lateral links to the rear wheel spindle and install the washers, bolt and nut. Tighten the front and rear lateral link nut at the rear wheel spindle to 63–86 ft. lbs. (85–117 Nm).

18. Position the front and rear lateral links to the rear suspension crossmember. Tighten the front and rear lateral link nut at the rear suspension crossmember to 50–70 ft. lbs. (68–95 Nm).

19. Install the cap.

20. Raise the floor jack stand to position the rear suspension crossmember to the vehicle frame. Install and tighten the bolts. Remove the floor jack stand from under the vehicle.

21. Position the grommets onto the stabilizer bar and align the grommets to the positions painted on the bar.

22. Position the stabilizer bar to the rear suspension crossmember and secure it in place with the straps and bolts. Tighten the bolts to 32–43 ft. lbs. (43–59 Nm).

23. Install the stabilizer bolts, wash-

ers, grommets, sleeves and nuts. Tighten the stabilizer nuts so 0.64–0.72 in. (16.2–17.0mm) of thread is exposed at the end of the bolt.

24. Install the wheel and tire assembly. Tighten the lug nuts to 65–87 ft. lbs. (88–118 Nm).

25. Check the wheel alignment and lower the vehicle.

Rear Wheel Bearings

REMOVAL & INSTALLATION

1989–90

1. Raise and support the rear of the vehicle safely.

2. Remove the wheel and tire assembly.

3. Remove the grease cup from the rear wheel hub.

4. Using a small cape chisel and a hammer, carefully raise the staked portion of the locknut. Discard the locknut.

NOTE: The locknuts are threaded left and right. The left hand threaded locknut is on the right side of the vehicle and is turned clockwise to loosen. The right hand threaded locknut is on the left side of the vehicle and is turned counterclockwise to loosen.

5. Remove the outer wheel bearing from the hub and the brake drum/bearing hub assembly.

6. Using a small prybar, pry the grease seal from the rear of the drum. Remove the inner wheel bearing from the hub.

7. If the bearings are to be replaced, remove the inner and outer bearing races using a brass drift.

To install:

8. Install the new bearing races using a brass drift.

9. Pack the bearings and the hub with high temperature grease. Install the inner bearing in the hub.

10. Lubricate the lip of a new seal with grease and install the seal in the hub using a seal installer.

11. Install the drum/bearing hub assembly. Install the outer bearing and a new locknut. Properly adjust the bearing preload.

12. Install the grease cap and the wheel and tire assembly. Lower the vehicle.

1991–93

1. Raise and safely support the vehicle.

2. Remove the wheel and tire assembly.

3. Remove the brake drum or brake caliper and rotor, as necessary.

4. Unstake the nut securing the rear wheel hub to the spindle. Remove and discard the nut. Remove the hub and bearing assembly.

To install:

5. Install the rear wheel hub and bearing assembly onto the spindle.

6. Install the hub nut onto the spindle and tighten to 130–174 ft. lbs. (177–235 Nm).

7. Stake the hub nut and install the cap.

8. Install the brake drum or the brake caliper and rotor, as necessary.

9. Install the wheel and tire assembly. Tighten the lugnuts to 65–87 ft. lbs. (88–118 Nm).

10. Lower the vehicle.

ADJUSTMENT

1989–90

1. Raise and support the vehicle safely.

2. Remove the wheel and tire assembly.

3. Remove the grease cup from the rear wheel hub.

4. Rotate the brake drum to make sure there is no brake drag.

5. Using a small cape chisel and a hammer, carefully raise the staked portion of the locknut. Discard the locknut.

NOTE: The locknuts are threaded left and right. The left hand threaded locknut is on the right side of the vehicle and is turned clockwise to loosen. The right hand threaded locknut is on the left side of the vehicle and is turned counterclockwise to loosen.

6. Install the new locknut. Seat the bearings by tightening the locknut to 18–21 ft. lbs. (25–29 Nm) while rotating the brake drum or rotor. Loosen the locknut slightly until it can be turned by hand.

7. Before bearing preload can be set, the amount of seal drag must be measured and added to the required preload. Using an inch pound torque wrench, position it (12 o'clock position) on 1 of the lug nuts and measure the torque necessary to start the wheel hub to turn.

8. The bearing preload is the seal drag plus 1.3–4.3 inch lbs. (0.15–0.49 Nm). For example, if the seal drag measures 2.2 inch lbs. (0.25 Nm), this amount must be added to the required preload:

1.3 inch lbs. + 2.2 inch lbs. = 3.5 inch lbs. minimum.

0.15 Nm + 0.25 Nm = 0.40 Nm minimum.

4.3 inch lbs. + 2.2 inch lbs. = 6.5 inch lbs. maximum.

0.49 Nm + 0.25 Nm = 0.74 Nm maximum.

9. In this example, when seal drag is added, the required bearing preload becomes 3.5–6.5 inch lbs. (0.40–0.74 Nm).

10. Tighten the wheel bearing locknut a slight amount. Place the inch pound torque wrench onto a lug nut positioned at 12 o' clock and measure the amount of pull required to rotate the brake drum.

11. Continue tightening the attaching nut until the specified amount of preload is measured with the torque wrench.

12. Stake the locknut using a cold chisel with the cutting edge rounded.

NOTE: If the nut splits or cracks after staking, it must be replaced.

13. Install the grease cap and the wheel and tire assembly. Tighten the lug nuts to 65–87 ft. lbs. (88–118 Nm).

1991–93

1. Raise and safely support the vehicle.

2. Remove the wheel and tire assembly.

3. Remove the brake drum or the brake caliper and rotor, as necessary.

4. Position a dial indicator to the wheel hub.

5. By hand, push and pull the wheel hub in the axial direction and measure the wheel bearing play.

6. If the wheel bearing play exceeds 0.002 in. (0.05mm), check and adjust the locknut torque or replace the wheel bearing, if necessary.

7. Install the brake drum or brake caliper and rotor, as necessary.

8. Install the wheel and tire assembly and lower the vehicle.

STEERING

Steering Wheel

REMOVAL & INSTALLATION

1. Disconnect the negative battery cable.

2. Remove the steering wheel cover retaining screws from the back side of the steering wheel and remove the cover.

NOTE: On 2-spoke steering wheels there are 2 retaining screws, and on 4-spoke steering wheels there are 4 retaining screws.

3. Disconnect the horn electrical connector and the cruise control electrical connector, if equipped.

4. Remove the steering wheel mounting nut or bolt. On 1989–90 vehicles, remove the steering wheel cover pad mounting bracket.

5. Paint an aligning stripe on the steering wheel and steering shaft. Remove the steering wheel with a suitable puller. Do not attempt to remove the steering wheel by hitting the column shaft with a hammer; the column may collapse.

To install:

6. Position the steering wheel on the shaft, aligning the paint marks. On 1989–90 vehicles, install the cover pad mounting bracket.

7. Install the steering wheel attaching nut or bolt. Tighten the nut to 29–36 ft. lbs. (39–49 Nm) or the bolt to 34–46 ft. lbs. (46–63 Nm).

8. Connect the horn electrical connector and the cruise control electrical connector, if equipped.

9. Position the steering wheel cover and install the retaining screws. Connect the negative battery cable.

Steering Column

REMOVAL & INSTALLATION

1989–90

1. Disconnect the negative battery cable.

2. Remove the lap duct register panel screws, the lap duct brace screws, the brace and the lap duct.

3. Remove the combination switch lower cover screws and the cover.

4. Using paint, matchmark the lower universal joint-to-intermediate shaft.

5. Remove the lower steering column nuts, the lower steering column universal joint bolt and the upper steering column bolts.

6. Lower the steering column and disconnect the electrical harness connectors from the lower steering column.

7. Remove the steering column from the vehicle.

8. To install, align the universal joint-to-intermediate shaft matchmark and reverse the removal procedures. Inspect the operation of the steering column.

1991–93

1. Disconnect the negative battery cable.

2. Remove the steering wheel.

3. Remove the combination switch and disconnect the ignition switch electrical connector.

4. Remove the shift-lock cable mounting bracket bolt and place the bracket and cable aside.

5. Remove the 4 steering column upper mounting bracket bolts and lower the column.

6. Remove the 5 set plate mounting nuts and remove the set plate.

7. Remove the intermediate shaft-to-pinion shaft bolt.

8. Remove the 2 steering column lower mounting bracket nuts and remove the column.

To install:

9. Position the steering column and install the 2 lower mounting bracket nuts.

10. Install the intermediate shaft-to-pinion shaft bolt and tighten to 30–36 ft. lbs. (40–50 Nm).

11. Position the set plate and install the 5 mounting nuts.

12. Install the 4 steering column upper mounting bracket bolts and tighten to 80–123 inch lbs. (9–14 Nm).

13. Position the shift-lock cable mounting bracket and install the bolt. Tighten the bolt to 37–55 inch lbs. (4–6 Nm).

14. Connect the ignition switch electrical connector and install the combination switch.

15. Install the steering wheel.

16. Connect the negative battery cable and inspect the shift-lock system.

Manual Rack and Pinion

ADJUSTMENT

1989–90

1. Remove the steering gear from the vehicle and place it in a vise.

2. Using an inch pound torque wrench and pinion torque adapter tool T87C–3504–C or equivalent, place the assembly on the pinion and measure the pinion turning torque; the torque should be 7.8–11.28 inch lbs. (0.9–1.3 Nm).

3. If the pinion torque is not correct, adjust by tightening or loosening the adjusting bolt. After the pinion torque is adjusted, tighten the adjusting bolt locknut to 7.2–10.8 ft. lbs. (10–15 Nm).

4. Install the steering gear and check for proper operation.

1991–93

1. Remove the rack and pinion assembly from the vehicle and mount it in a vise.

2. Loosen the locknut.

3. Tighten the adjusting bolt using yoke adjustment adapter T90P–3504–JH in the yoke plug to 8.7 inch lbs. (1 Nm), then loosen the adjusting bolt 10–40 degrees from that position.

4. Measure the pinion turning torque using pinion shaft adapting tool T86P-3504-K. The correct torque at the neutral position ± 90 degrees should be 9–12 inch lbs. (1.0–1.3 Nm). At any other position the torque should be 14.7 inch lbs. (1.6 Nm) or less.

5. If the pinion torque is not within specification, re-adjust the adjusting bolt to achieve the correct pinion torque. Tighten the adjusting bolt locknut.

REMOVAL & INSTALLATION

1989–90

1. Disconnect the terminals from the battery (negative cable first) and remove the battery from the vehicle.

2. Raise and support the vehicle safely. Remove the front wheel and tire assemblies.

3. Remove the tie rod end-to-steering knuckle cotter pins and nuts. Using a tie rod separator tool, separate the tie rod end from the steering knuckle.

4. From the right side lower inner fender, remove the plastic dust shield.

5. Using a pair of diagonal cutters, cut the steering column dust boot-to-steering gear plastic wire tie clamp. Pull the dust boot back. Have an assistant turn the steering wheel until the steering column shaft bolt is accessible and lock the steering column.

6. Using white paint, matchmark the steering gear pinion shaft-to-intermediate shaft lower universal joint.

7. Remove the steering gear pinion shaft-to-intermediate shaft lower universal joint clamp bolt.

8. Remove the steering gear-to-chassis bolts and lower the steering gear to disengage it from the intermediate shaft universal joint. Carefully slide the steering gear out through the right side fender well.

To install:

9. Slide the steering gear into position through the right side lower inner fender well opening.

10. Guide the pinion shaft into the intermediate shaft lower universal joint, aligning the marks that were made during the removal procedure. Install the steering gear mounting bolts and tighten to 23–34 ft. lbs. (32–47 Nm).

11. Install the clamp bolt in the intermediate shaft universal joint.

12. Connect the tie rod ends to the steering knuckle arms and install the nuts. Tighten the nuts to 25–29 ft. lbs. (35–40 Nm) and install new cotter pins.

NOTE: If the slots in the nut do not align the with the hole in the

ball joint stud, tighten the nut for alignment. Never loosen the nut.

13. Slide the steering column dust boot over the steering gear and install a new plastic tie strap.

14. Install the plastic dust shield and the wheel and tire assemblies. Lower the vehicle.

15. Install the battery and connect the battery cables.

1991–93

1. Working inside the vehicle, remove the nuts securing the set plate and remove the set plate.

2. Remove the intermediate shaft-to-pinion shaft bolt from inside the vehicle.

3. Raise and safely support the vehicle.

4. Remove the front wheel and tire assemblies.

5. Remove the cotter pins and nuts securing the tie rod ends to the steering knuckles. Separate the tie rod ends from the steering knuckles using a suitable tool.

6. If equipped with manual transaxle, disconnect the extension bar.

7. Remove the nuts securing the steering gear brackets to the bulkhead. Remove the brackets.

8. Remove the steering gear from the vehicle.

To install:

9. Position the steering gear into its mounting position and install the brackets and nuts. Tighten the nuts to 27–38 ft. lbs. (37–52 Nm).

10. If equipped with a manual transaxle, connect the extension bar. Tighten the nut to 23–34 ft. lbs. (31–46 Nm).

11. Attach the tie rod ends to the steering knuckles. Install the nuts and tighten to 31–42 ft. lbs. (42–57 Nm). Install new cotter pins.

12. Install the front wheel and tire assemblies.

13. Lower the vehicle.

14. Install the intermediate shaft-to-pinion shaft bolt and tighten to 13–20 ft. lbs. (18–27 Nm).

15. Position the set plate and secure it with the nuts.

Power Rack and Pinion

ADJUSTMENT

1989–90

1. Remove the power steering gear from the vehicle and place it in a vise.

2. Using an inch lb. torque wrench and pinion torque adapter tool T87C-3504-C or equivalent, place the assembly on the pinion and measure the pin-

ion turning torque; the torque should be 0.52–1.3 inch lbs. (0.6–1.5 Nm).

3. If the pinion torque is not as specified, adjust by tightening or loosening the adjusting plug.

4. Install the steering gear in the vehicle.

REMOVAL & INSTALLATION

1989–90

1. Disconnect the terminals from the battery (negative cable first) and remove the battery from the vehicle.

2. Raise and support the vehicle safely. Remove the front wheel and tire assemblies.

3. Remove the tie rod end-to-steering knuckle cotter pins and nuts. Using a tie rod separator tool, separate the tie rod end from the steering knuckle.

4. From the right side lower inner fender, remove the plastic dust shield.

5. Using a pair of diagonal cutters, cut the steering column dust boot-to-steering gear plastic wire tie clamp. Pull the dust boot back. Have an assistant turn the steering wheel until the steering column shaft bolt is accessible and lock the steering column.

6. Using white paint, matchmark the steering gear pinion shaft-to-intermediate shaft lower universal joint.

7. Remove the steering gear pinion shaft-to-intermediate shaft lower universal joint clamp bolt.

8. Using a 17mm crowsfoot tubing wrench, disconnect and plug the fluid return line from the power steering rack.

9. Using a 14mm socket, remove the banjo bolt from the pressure line at the power steering gear and discard the copper washers.

NOTE: Be sure to position the lines out of the way.

10. Remove the steering gear-to-chassis bolts and lower the steering gear to disengage it from the intermediate shaft universal joint. Carefully slide the steering gear out through the right side fender well.

To install:

11. Slide the steering gear into position through the right side lower inner fender well opening.

12. Guide the pinion shaft into the intermediate shaft lower universal joint, aligning the marks that were made during the removal procedure. Install the steering gear mounting bolts and tighten to 23–34 ft. lbs. (32–47 Nm).

13. Install the clamp bolt in the intermediate shaft universal joint.

14. Connect the tie rod ends to the steering knuckle arms and install the nuts. Tighten the nuts to 25–29 ft. lbs.

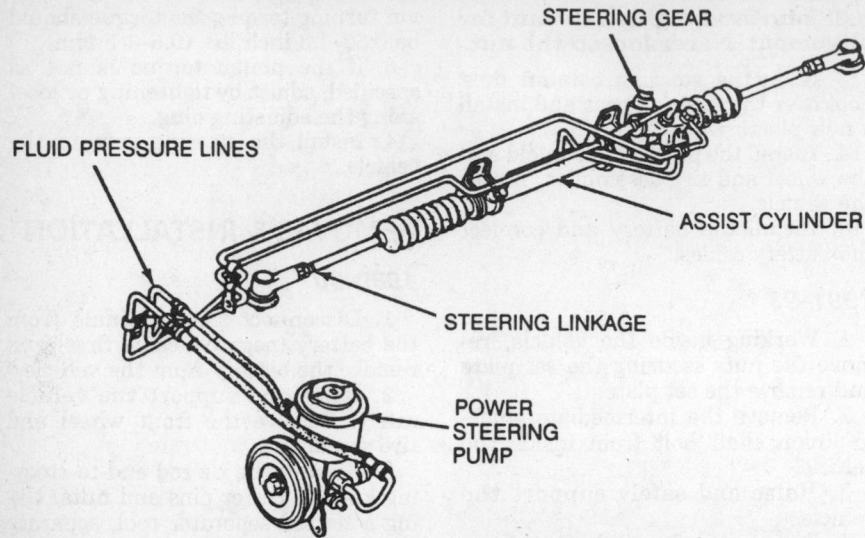

Power steering system—1989–90 vehicles

(35–40 Nm) and install new cotter pins.

NOTE: If the slots in the nut do not align the with the hole in the ball joint stud, tighten the nut for alignment. Never loosen the nut.

15. Attach the hoses from the power steering pump to the steering gear. Install new copper washers at the return line banjo fitting. Tighten the pressure hose fitting with a 17mm crowfoot tubing wrench.

16. Install the plastic dust shield and the wheel and tire assemblies. Lower the vehicle.

17. Install the battery and connect the battery cables. Fill the reservoir and bleed the hydraulic system.

18. Check for leaks.

1991–93

1. From inside the passenger compartment, remove the 5 set plate nuts and remove the set plate.

2. Remove the intermediate shaft-to-pinion shaft bolt.

3. Raise and safely support the vehicle.

4. Remove the front wheel and tire assemblies.

5. Remove the cotter pins and attaching nuts from the tie rod ends. Using a suitable tool, separate the tie rod ends from the steering knuckles.

6. If equipped with the 1.8L engine, remove the 2 screws from the power steering line retaining bracket and re-

move the bracket from the steering gear housing. If equipped with the 1.9L engine, remove the strap that holds the power steering lines to the steering gear housing and discard the strap.

7. Disconnect the high-pressure and return lines from the steering gear and plug the lines.

8. If equipped with manual transaxle, disconnect the extension bar and shift control rod from the transaxle.

9. Remove the nuts from the 2 steering gear mounting brackets.

10. Remove the splash shield from the left wheel well.

11. Remove the steering gear from the left side of the vehicle.

To install:

12. Position the steering gear in its mounting location and install the splash shield in the left wheel well.

13. Position the 2 steering gear mounting brackets and install the 2 nuts to each bracket. Tighten the nuts to 27–38 ft. lbs. (37–52 Nm).

14. If equipped with a manual transaxle, connect the extension bar and shift control rod. Tighten the extension bar nut to 23–34 ft. lbs. (31–46 Nm) and the shift control rod nut to 12–17 ft. lbs. (16–23 Nm).

15. Remove the plugs and connect the pressure and return lines to the steering gear. Tighten the flare nuts to 22–28 ft. lbs. (29–39 Nm).

16. If equipped with 1.8L engine, position the power steering line retaining bracket and install the 2 screws. If equipped with 1.9L engine, install a new strap to hold the power steering lines to the steering gear housing.

17. Position the tie rod ends in the

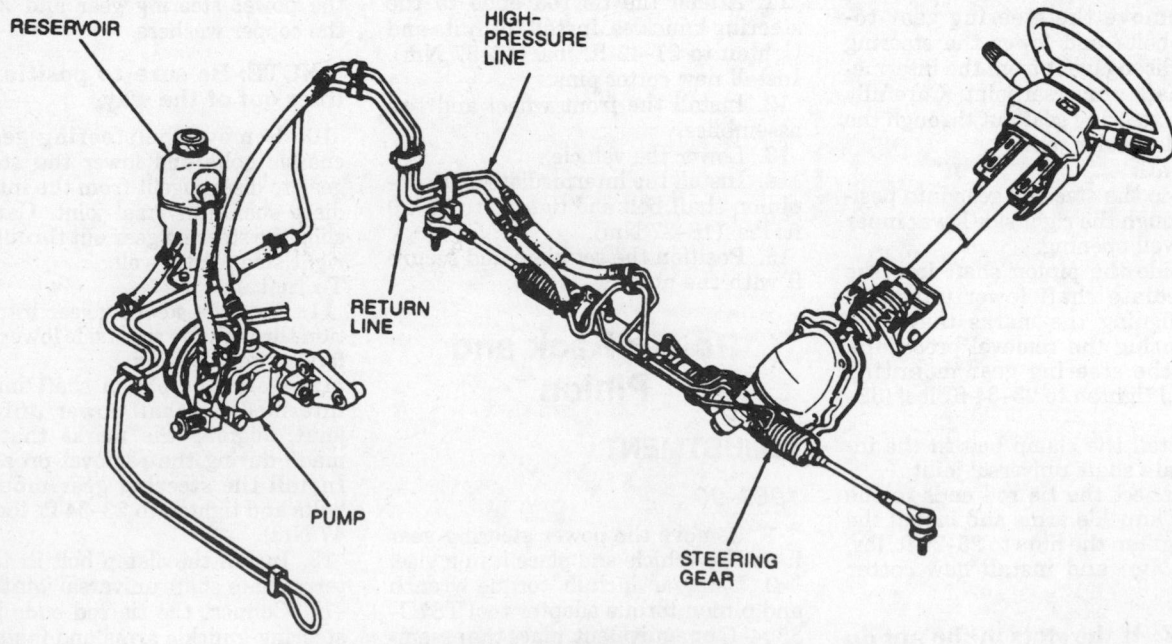

Power steering system—1991–93 vehicles with 1.8L engine

steering knuckles and install the attaching nuts. Tighten the nuts to 31–42 ft. lbs. (42–57 Nm). Install new cotter pins.

18. Install the wheel and tire assemblies and lower the vehicle.

19. From inside the vehicle, install the intermediate shaft-to-pinion shaft bolt. Tighten the bolt to 13–20 ft. lbs. (18–27 Nm).

20. Position the set plate and install the 5 set plate nuts.

21. Fill the system with steering fluid.

Power Steering Pump

REMOVAL & INSTALLATION

1.6L Engine

1. Disconnect the negative battery cable.

2. At the power steering pump, loosen the locknut and adjuster bolt. Move the pump toward the engine and remove the drive belt.

3. From the engine lifting eye, remove the ground wire.

4. Disconnect and plug the hoses from the power steering pump. Disconnect the electrical connector from the pump's pressure switch.

5. Remove the adjusting screw, nut, block, pivot bolt and pump; if necessary, remove the pump pulley.

6. To install, reverse the removal procedures. Adjust the drive belt tension. Fill the power steering pump reservoir. Bleed the power steering system.

1.8L Engine

1. Disconnect the negative battery cable.

2. Loosen the power steering fluid reservoir-to-pump hose clamp and pull the hose from the reservoir. Plug the hose.

3. Remove the 2 reservoir mounting bolts and lift the reservoir from its mounting position.

4. Loosen the return hose clamp and pull the return hose from the reservoir. Plug the hose and remove the reservoir.

5. Disconnect the electrical connector from the power steering pressure switch.

6. Loosen the high-pressure line flare nut and disconnect the line from the pump. Plug the line.

7. Raise and safely support the vehicle.

8. Remove the 5 right front undercover bolts and remove the undercover.

9. Remove the belt tensioner adjustment bolt and remove the accessory drive belt from the pulley.

10. Lower the vehicle.

11. Remove the 3 pump mounting bracket bolts and remove the pump and the bracket.

12. Remove the bolt that attaches the pump to the mounting bracket.

13. Remove the nut and bolt that attaches the tensioner to the pump mounting bracket and remove the nut and bolt that attaches the tensioner to the pump.

To install:

14. Position the tensioner to the pump and install the bolt and nut. Tighten the nut to 14–19 ft. lbs. (19–25 Nm).

15. Position the tensioner to the pump mounting bracket and install the bolt and nut. Tighten the nut to 23–34 ft. lbs. (31–46 Nm).

16. Install the bolt that attaches the pump to the mounting bracket and tighten to 27–40 ft. lbs. (36–54 Nm).

17. Position the pump and bracket and install the 3 pump mounting bracket bolts. Tighten the bolts to 27–38 ft. lbs. (37–54 Nm).

18. Raise and safely support the vehicle.

19. Position the accessory drive belt on the pulley and install the belt tensioner adjustment bolt.

20. Position the right front undercover and install the 5 bolts.

21. Lower the vehicle.

22. Unplug the high-pressure line and connect the line to the pump. Tighten the flare nut to 12–17 ft. lbs. (16–24 Nm).

23. Connect the power steering pressure switch electrical connector.

24. Unplug the return hose and connect the hose to the reservoir. Tighten the clamp.

25. Position the reservoir and install the 2 mounting bolts.

26. Unplug the reservoir-to-pump hose and connect the hose to the reservoir. Tighten the clamp.

27. Fill the system with power steering fluid and adjust the accessory drive belt tension.

1.9L Engine

1. Disconnect the negative battery cable and drain the cooling system.

2. Loosen the belt tensioner and remove the drive belt from the pulley. Remove the belt tensioner bolt and remove the tensioner.

3. Support the engine with a floor jack.

4. Remove the engine vibration damper nut and bolt and remove the damper.

5. Remove the 2 front engine mount nuts. Loosen the engine mount pivot bolt and nut and position the engine mount aside.

6. Raise the engine to gain access to the power steering pump pulley.

7. Hold the pulley in position with a suitable tool and remove the 3 pulley mounting bolts. Remove the pulley and lower the engine.

8. Position the engine mount and install the 2 nuts.

9. Loosen the clamp and disconnect the return line from the pump. Loosen the flare nut from the high-pressure line and disconnect the line from the pump.

10. Raise and safely support the vehicle.

11. Remove the 2 passenger side splash shields.

12. If equipped, remove the 4 compressor mounting bolts and position the air conditioning compressor aside.

13. Remove the lower radiator hose.

14. Remove the 3 power steering pump mounting bolts and remove the pump.

To install:

15. Position the power steering pump and install the 3 mounting bolts. Tighten the bolts to 30–45 ft. lbs. (40–62 Nm).

16. Install the lower radiator hose.

17. If equipped, position the air conditioning compressor and install the 4 mounting bolts. Tighten the bolts to 30–40 ft. lbs. (40–55 Nm).

18. Install the 2 passenger side splash shields and lower the vehicle.

19. Connect the high-pressure line to the power steering pump and tighten the nut. Connect the return line to the pump and position the clamp.

20. Support the engine with a floor jack.

21. Remove the 2 front engine mount nuts and raise the engine to gain access to the pulley.

22. Position the pulley and, holding the pulley in place with a suitable tool, install the 3 pulley mounting bolts. Tighten the bolts to 15–22 ft. lbs. (20–30 Nm).

23. Lower the engine.

24. Position the engine mount and install the 2 nuts. Tighten the engine mount pivot bolt and nut.

25. Position the engine vibration dampener and install the bolt and nut.

26. Position the belt tensioner and install the bolt loosely. Position the accessory drive belt on the pulley and tighten the tensioner mounting bolt to 30–41 ft. lbs. (40–55 Nm).

27. Fill the cooling system.

28. Add the proper type and quantity of power steering fluid.

29. Connect the negative battery cable. Check that the pump operates properly and that there are no leaks.

BELT ADJUSTMENT

1.6L Engine

1. Inspect the condition of the drive belt; replace it, if necessary.

2. Apply moderate pressure (approximately 22 lbs.) to the belt at a point midway between the power steering pump pulley and the crankshaft pulley. The drive belt deflection should be 0.31–0.35 in. (8–9mm) for a new belt or 0.35–0.39 in. (9–10mm).

NOTE: A used belt is one that has at least 10 minutes run time.

3. If adjustment is necessary, loosen the locknut and pivot bolts. Turn the adjusting bolt until the correct tension is obtained.

4. After adjustment, tighten the locknut and pivot bolts. Torque the locknut to 32–45 ft. lbs. (43–61 Nm).

1.8L Engine

1. Raise and safely support the vehicle.
2. Loosen the power steering pump mounting bolt and nuts.
3. Adjust the belt tension by turning the pump adjusting bolt.
4. Tighten the power steering pump mounting nut near the pump adjusting bolt.
5. Check the belt tension using either a belt tension gauge or using the deflection method.
6. If using a belt tension gauge, position the gauge on the longest accessible span of belt. The tension for a new belt should be 110–132 lbs. The tension for a used belt (more than 10 minutes running time) should be 95–110 lbs.
7. If using the deflection method, apply approximately 22 lbs. pressure midway between the pulleys. The deflection on a new belt should be 0.31–0.35 in. (8–9mm). The deflection on a used belt (more than 10 minutes running time) should be 0.35–0.39 in. (9–10mm).
8. Tighten the power steering pump mounting nut, located near the adjusting bolt, to 27–38 ft. lbs. (37–52 Nm).
9. Tighten the pump mounting bolt behind the pulley to 27–40 ft. lbs. (36–54 Nm) and the remaining pump mounting nut to 23–34 ft. lbs. (31–46 Nm).
10. Lower the vehicle.

1.9L Engine

Belt tension is maintained by an automatic belt tensioner and does not require adjustment.

SYSTEM BLEEDING

1. Disconnect the coil wire.
2. Fill the pump reservoir to the proper level.
3. Crank the engine with the start-er. Add fluid until the level remains constant.
4. Raise and safely support the vehicle so the front wheels are off the ground.
5. Crank the engine with the starter while rotating the steering wheel from stop-to-stop. Recheck the fluid level and add, if necessary.

NOTE: The front wheels must be off the ground during stop-to-stop rotation of the steering wheel.

6. Connect the coil wire. Start the engine and let it run for several minutes.
7. Rotate the steering wheel from far left to right several times.
8. Turn **OFF** the engine and recheck the fluid level. Add fluid, if necessary.

Tie Rod Ends

REMOVAL & INSTALLATION

1. Raise the vehicle and support it safely. Remove the wheel and tire assembly.
2. Remove the tie rod-to-steering knuckle cotter pin and nut.
3. Using tie rod separator tool T85M-3395-A or equivalent, separate the tie rod end from the knuckle. If the tie rod end does not separate easily, give the steering knuckle a sharp blow with a brass hammer or drift to shock the taper.
4. Paint an alignment mark on the tie rod end, jamb nut and tie rod.
5. Loosen the tie rod jamb nut and remove the tie rod end.
To install:
6. Install the new tie rod end into the tie rod and align the marks that were made during removal. If installing a new tie rod end, match the position of the old one as closely as possible.
7. Install the tie rod end to the steering knuckle and tighten the nut to 25–29 ft. lbs. (35–40 Nm) on 1989–90 vehicles or 31–42 ft. lbs. (42–57 Nm) on 1991–93 vehicles. Install a new cotter pin.

NOTE: If the slots in the nut do not align the with the hole in the ball joint stud, tighten the nut for alignment. Never loosen the nut.

8. Tighten the jamb nut and install the wheel and tire assembly. Lower the vehicle and check the front end alignment.

BRAKES

Master Cylinder

REMOVAL & INSTALLATION

1. On 1991–93 vehicles, disconnect the battery cables and remove the battery.
2. Disconnect the low fluid level sensor electrical connector.
3. Loosen the brake line fittings and disconnect the brake lines from the master cylinder.
4. On 1991–93 vehicles equipped with manual transaxle, remove the clamp and pull the clutch hose from the brake/clutch fluid reservoir.
5. Cap the lines and the master cylinder ports.
6. Remove the 2 mounting nuts and remove the master cylinder assembly.
To install:
7. Adjust the piston to pushrod clearance as follows:
   a. Insert a pencil in the pushrod socket of the master cylinder. Mark the point on the pencil that is even with the end of the master cylinder with a hacksaw blade.
   b. Measure the length of the pencil to the saw mark with a ruler.
   c. Using the ruler, measure how far the master cylinder pushrod protrudes out of the booster assembly.
   d. Measure the length of the master cylinder boss with the ruler. Subtract the length of the boss from the length of the pencil. The difference in length between the master cylinder pushrod and the corrected pencil length is equal to the pushrod clearance.
   e. Adjust the pushrod length to get the correct clearance. It should be 0.025 in. (1mm) shorter than the pushrod socket.
8. Position the master cylinder over the booster pushrod and booster mounting studs. Install the nuts and tighten to 8–12 ft. lbs. (10–16 Nm).
9. Connect short lengths of brake line to the master cylinder that point back into the reservoir. Fill the reservoir with brake fluid. The ends of the short lengths of brake line must be submerged in the brake fluid.
10. Place a shop towel over the top of the reservoir. Pump the brake pedal until no more air bubbles emerge from the brake lines.
11. On 1991–93 vehicles equipped with manual transaxle, connect the clutch hose onto the brake/clutch fluid reservoir and install the clamp.
12. Remove the temporary brake lines and connect the vehicle brake lines. Tighten the fittings.

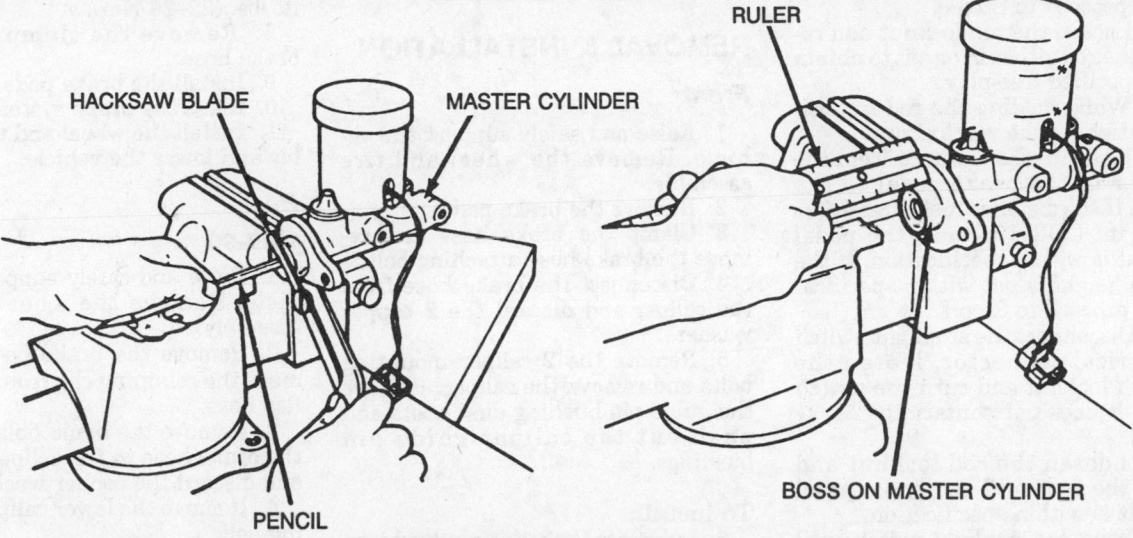

Master cylinder pushrod adjustment procedure

13. Make sure the master cylinder reservoir is full. Have an assistant push down on the brake pedal. When the pedal is all the way down, crack open the brake line fittings, 1 at a time, to expel any remaining air in the master cylinder and brake lines. Tighten the fittings, then have the assistant allow the brake pedal to return.

14. Repeat Step 13 until all air is expelled from the master cylinder and brake lines. Tighten the brake line fittings to 10–16 ft. lbs. (13–22 Nm).

15. Connect the low fluid level sensor electrical connector.

16. On 1991–93 vehicles, install the battery and connect the negative battery cable.

17. Make sure the master cylinder reservoir is full. Bleed the brakes, if necessary.

18. Check for brake fluid leaks and for proper brake operation.

Proportioning Valve

REMOVAL & INSTALLATION

1. Disconnect and plug the brake lines leading to the valve.
2. Remove the valve mounting bolts from the firewall.
3. Remove the valve.
4. Installation is the reverse of the removal procedure.
5. Bleed the brake system.

Power Brake Booster

REMOVAL & INSTALLATION

1989–90

1. Remove the cables from the battery (negative cable first) and the battery from the vehicle.

2. Remove the master cylinder.
3. Remove the vacuum hose from the brake booster.
4. From under the instrument panel, remove the spring clip and the clevis pin from the brake pedal.
5. Remove the brake booster-to-cowl nuts and the brake booster.

To install:
6. Have an assistant place the booster on the firewall so the 4 retaining studs protrude into the passenger compartment. Working under the dash, install the 4 retaining nuts.
7. Apply lithium grease to the clevis pin and install it through the brake pedal pushrod and the brake pedal. Install the clevis pin spring clip.
8. Working under the hood, connect the vacuum hose to the booster. A vacuum check valve is located in the center of the hose, so the arrow on the hose must point toward the engine.
9. Adjust the master cylinder pushrod as follows:
   a. Insert a pencil in the pushrod socket of the master cylinder. Mark the point on the pencil that is even with the end of the master cylinder with a hacksaw blade.
   b. Measure the length of the pencil to the saw mark with a ruler.
   c. Using the ruler, measure how far the master cylinder pushrod protrudes out of the booster assembly.
   d. Measure the length of the master cylinder boss with the ruler. Subtract the length of the boss from the length of the pencil. The difference in length between the master cylinder pushrod and the corrected pencil length is equal to the pushrod clearance.
   e. Adjust the pushrod length to get the correct clearance. It should

be 0.025 in. (1mm) shorter than the pushrod socket.
10. Install the master cylinder and bleed the brakes.
11. Install the battery and connect the battery cables.

1991–93

1. Disconnect the negative battery cable.
2. Remove the master cylinder assembly.
3. Loosen the vacuum hose clamp and remove the hose from the power brake booster.
4. From inside the vehicle, remove the pin and discard.
5. Remove the clevis pin.
6. Remove the 4 booster mounting nuts and remove the booster. Remove and discard the gasket.
To install:
7. Install a new gasket over the studs and position the power brake booster.
8. From inside the vehicle, install the 4 mounting nuts and tighten to 14–19 ft. lbs. (19–25 Nm).
9. Lubricate the clevis pin with white lithium grease and install. Install a new pin.
10. Position the vacuum hose to the booster and install the clamp.
11. Install the master cylinder, making sure to check the master cylinder pushrod clearance.
12. Adjust the brake pedal as follows:
   a. Press the brake pedal several times to eliminate the vacuum in the booster.
   b. Carefully press the pedal and measure the amount of free-play until resistance is felt. If the free-play is 0.16–0.28 in. (4–7mm), the pedal free-play is within specification. If

the free-play is not within specification, proceed to Step c.

c. Loosen the rod locknut and rotate the rod either in or out to obtain the specified free-play.

d. While holding the rod in position, tighten the rod locknut.

e. Measure the distance from the center of the brake pedal to the floor. If the distance measures 7.60–7.72 in. (193–196mm), the pedal height is within specification. If the pedal height is not within specification, proceed to Step f.

f. Disconnect the stoplight switch electrical connector, loosen the switch locknut and turn the switch until it does not contact the brake pedal.

g. Loosen the rod locknut and turn the rod until the brake pedal height is within specification.

h. Turn the stoplight switch until it contacts the brake pedal, then turn it an additional ½ turn. Tighten the stoplight locknut and the rod locknut.

i. Connect the stoplight switch electrical connector and check the operation of the stoplights and brake system.

Brake Caliper

REMOVAL & INSTALLATION

Front

1. Raise and safely support the vehicle. Remove the wheel and tire assembly.
2. Remove the brake pads.
3. Clamp the brake hose and remove the brake hose attaching bolt.
4. Disconnect the brake hose from the caliper and discard the 2 copper washers.
5. Remove the 2 caliper mounting bolts and remove the caliper. Remove the guide pin bushing dust boots and push out the caliper guide pin bushings.

To install:

6. Lubricate the guide pin bushings with high temperature grease and install them in the caliper with the dust boots. Position the caliper and install the 2 caliper mounting bolts. Tighten the bolts to 29–36 ft. lbs. (39–49 Nm).
7. Install 2 new copper washers to the brake hose. Position the brake hose onto the caliper and install the at-taching bolt. Tighten the bolt to 16–22 ft. lbs. (22–29 Nm).
8. Remove the clamp from the brake hose.
9. Install the brake pads.
10. Bleed the brake system.
11. Install the wheel and tire assembly and lower the vehicle.

Rear

1989–90

1. Raise and safely support the vehicle. Remove the wheel and tire assembly.
2. Remove the brake pads and remove the retaining clip from the brake flex hose.
3. Remove the banjo bolt attaching the brake hose to the caliper. Remove and discard the copper washers.
4. Remove the lower caliper mounting bolt.
5. Using a chisel, remove the upper caliper guide pin dust cap to gain access to the Allen head on the guide pin. Use an Allen head wrench to remove the upper caliper guide pin.
6. Remove the caliper from the rotor. Remove the caliper upper guide pin and the lower guide pin bushing and the dust boots.

To install:

7. Install the brake pads and shims.
8. Install the guide pin and guide pin bushing dust boots. Lubricate the upper guide pin and lower guide pin bushing with high temperature grease and install in the caliper.
9. Position the caliper over the rotor. It may be necessary to rotate the piston to provide clearance.
10. Tighten the upper guide pin with an Allen wrench and install the dust cap with a plastic hammer. Install the lower caliper mounting bolt and tighten to 29–36 ft. lbs. (39–49 Nm).
11. Install the brake hose with the banjo bolt, using new copper washers. Tighten the bolt to 16–22 ft. lbs. (22–29 Nm).
12. Bleed the brakes and install the wheel and tire assembly.

1991–93

1. Raise and safely support the vehicle. Remove the wheel and tire assembly.
2. Remove the brake pads.
3. Remove the parking brake cable bracket bolt and position the bracket aside.
4. Remove the parking brake cable from the operating lever.
5. Clamp the brake hose, remove the brake line attaching bolt and remove the 2 washers. Discard the washers.
6. Disconnect the brake line and slide the caliper off the mounting bracket.

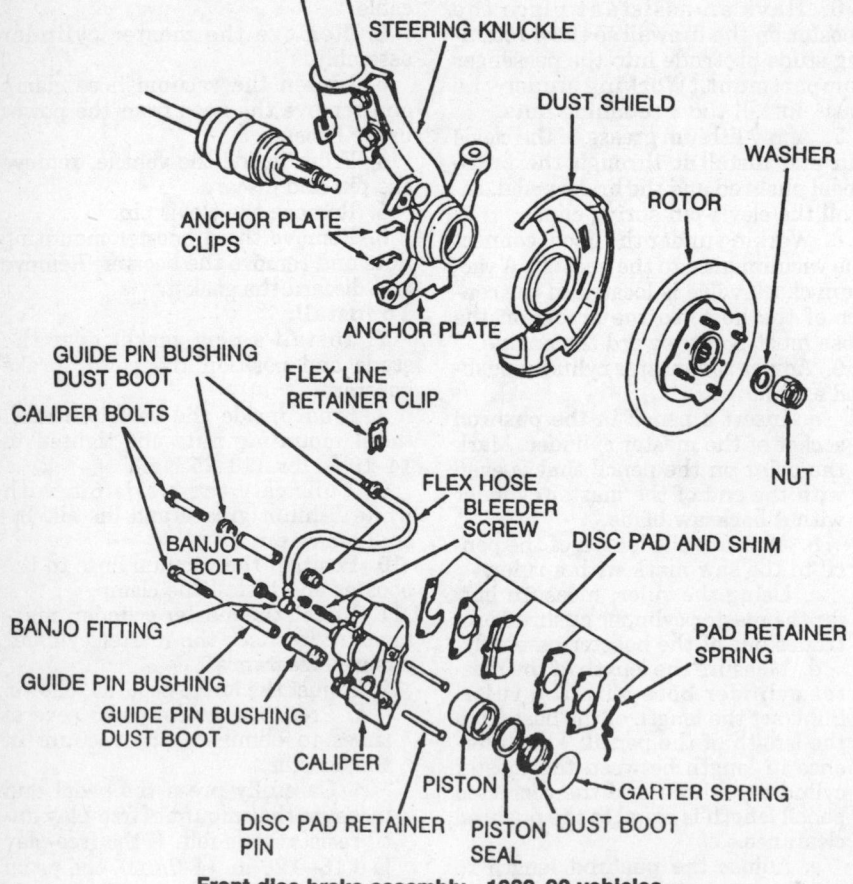

STEERING KNUCKLE

DUST SHIELD

WASHER

ROTOR

ANCHOR PLATE CLIPS

ANCHOR PLATE

GUIDE PIN BUSHING DUST BOOT

CALIPER BOLTS

FLEX LINE RETAINER CLIP

BANJO BOLT

FLEX HOSE BLEEDER SCREW

DISC PAD AND SHIM

NUT

BANJO FITTING

PAD RETAINER SPRING

GUIDE PIN BUSHING

GUIDE PIN BUSHING DUST BOOT

CALIPER

PISTON

DISC PAD RETAINER PIN

PISTON SEAL

DUST BOOT

GARTER SPRING

Front disc brake assembly–1989–90 vehicles

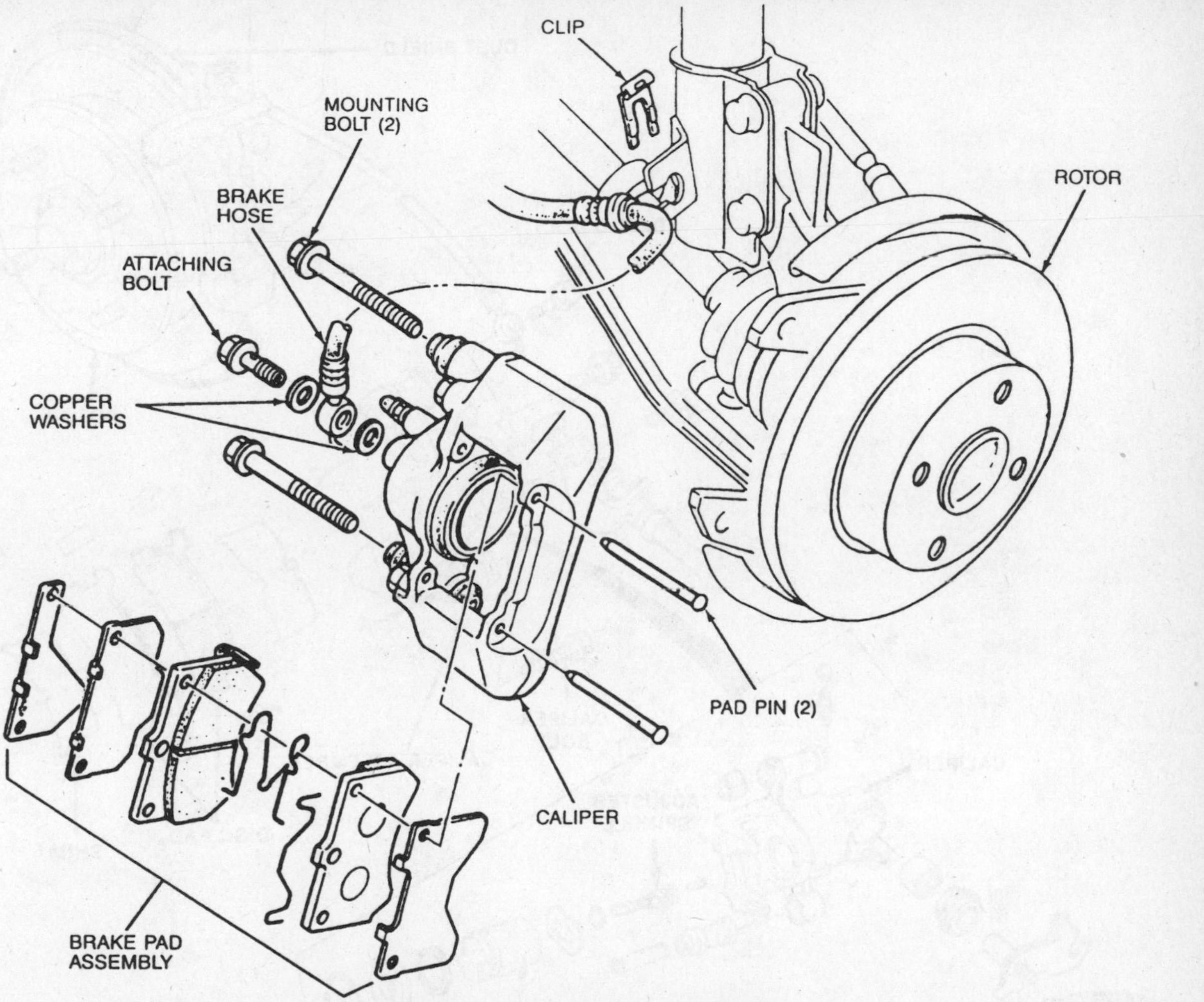

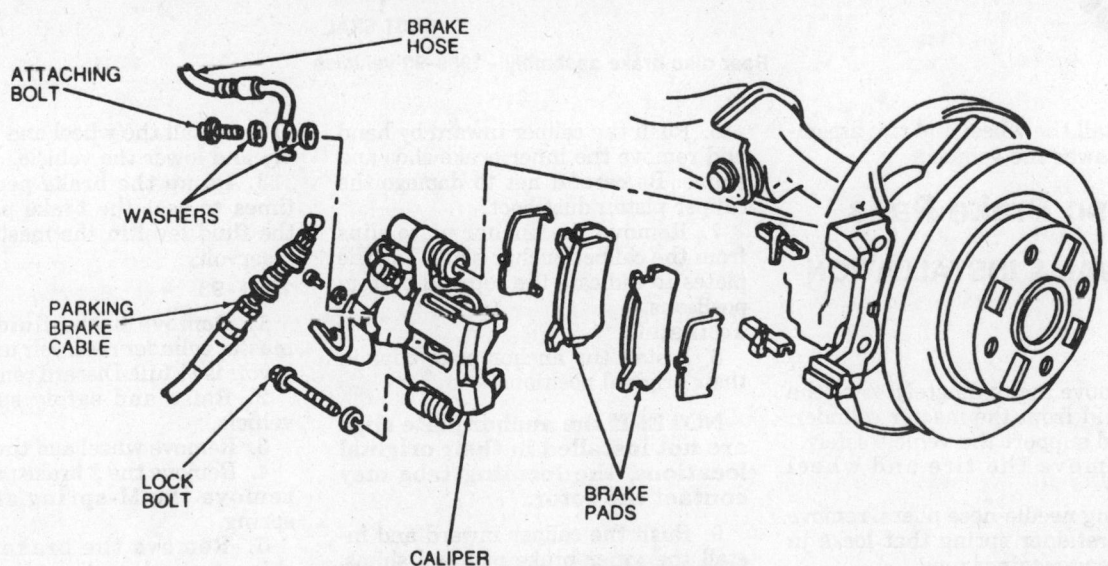

CLIP

MOUNTING
BOLT (2)

BRAKE
HOSE

ATTACHING
BOLT

ROTOR

COPPER
WASHERS

PAD PIN (2)

CALIPER

BRAKE PAD
ASSEMBLY

Front disc brake assembly—1991–93 vehicles

BRAKE
HOSE

ATTACHING
BOLT

WASHERS

PARKING
BRAKE
CABLE

LOCK
BOLT

CALIPER

BRAKE
PADS

Rear disc brake assembly—1991–93 vehicles

To install:

7. Position the caliper on the mounting bracket.

8. Install 2 new washers to the brake line. Position the brake line to the caliper and install the attaching bolt. Tighten the bolt to 16–22 ft. lbs. (22–29 Nm).

9. Remove the clamp from the brake hose.

10. Attach the parking brake cable to the operating lever. Position the bracket and install the bracket bolt.

11. Install the brake pads.

12. Bleed the brake system.

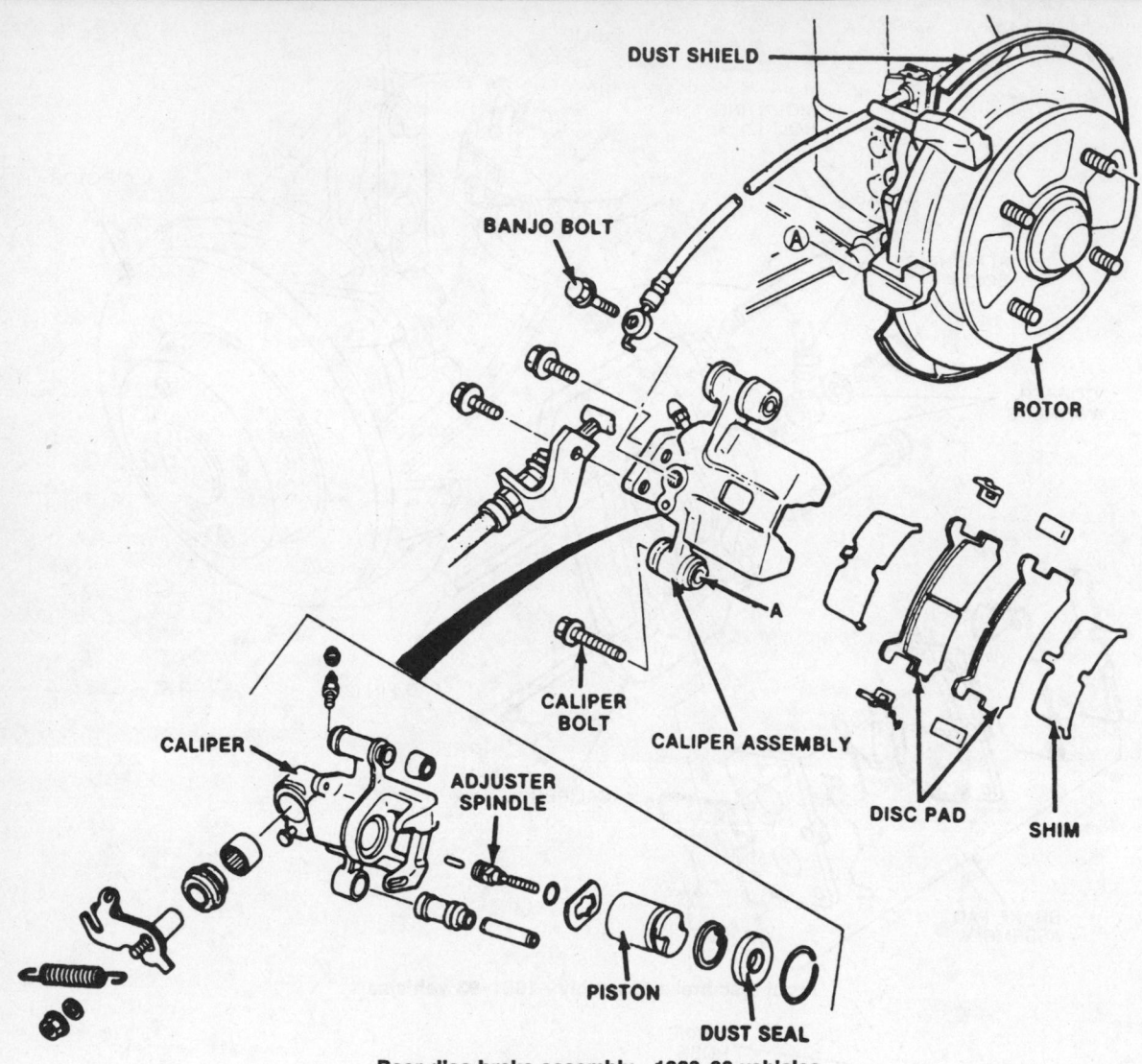

DUST SHIELD

BANJO BOLT

ROTOR

CALIPER BOLT

CALIPER ASSEMBLY

CALIPER

ADJUSTER SPINDLE

DISC PAD

SHIM

PISTON

DUST SEAL

Rear disc brake assembly — 1989–90 vehicles

13. Install the wheel and tire assembly and lower the vehicle.

Disc Brake Pads

REMOVAL & INSTALLATION

Front

1989–90

1. Remove approximately ⅔ of the brake fluid from the master cylinder. Raise and support the vehicle safely.
2. Remove the tire and wheel assembly.
3. Using needle-nose pliers, remove the pad retainer spring that locks in the disc pad retainer pins.
4. Use a hammer and a pin punch to remove the retainer pins.
5. Using a small prybar, pry the caliper outwards and remove the outer brake pad and shim. Tag the shims so they can be reinstalled in their original positions.

6. Push the caliper inward by hand and remove the inner brake shoe and shims. Be careful not to damage the caliper piston dust boot.
7. Remove the anchor plate clips from the caliper anchor plate. Tag the plates to indicate the top and bottom positions.

To install:

8. Install the anchor plate clips in their original positions.

NOTE: If the anchor plate clips are not installed in their original locations, the locating tabs may contact the rotor.

9. Push the caliper inward and install the inner brake pad and shims. Make sure the spring tabs on the back of the brake pad are properly aligned and fully seated in the caliper piston.
10. Pry the caliper outward and install the outer brake pad and shim.
11. Install the retaining pins and the spring.

12. Install the wheel and tire assembly and lower the vehicle.
13. Pump the brake pedal several times to seat the brake pads. Check the fluid level in the master cylinder reservoir.

1991–93

1. Remove brake fluid from the master cylinder reservoir until the reservoir is ½ full. Discard removed fluid.
2. Raise and safely support the vehicle.
3. Remove wheel and tire assembly.
4. Remove the 2 brake pad pins and remove the M-spring and the W-spring.
5. Remove the brake pads and shims from the caliper.

To install:

6. Use a suitable tool to push the piston into the caliper bore.
7. Apply grease between the shims and the brake pad guide plates and position the brake pads and shims into the caliper.

8. Install the W-spring and the M-spring. Install the 2 brake pad pins.

9. Install the wheel and tire assembly and lower the vehicle.

10. Pump brake pedal prior to moving vehicle to position brake linings. Check the fluid level in the master cylinder.

11. Road test vehicle.

Rear
1989–90

1. Remove approximately ⅔ of the brake fluid from the master cylinder. Raise and support the vehicle safely.

2. Remove the tire and wheel assembly.

3. Using needle-nose pliers, remove the parking brake return springs at the back of the caliper.

4. Loosen the parking brake cable housing adjusting nut and remove the cable housing from the bracket on the rear lower control arm.

5. Loosen the mounting bolt connecting the parking brake cable bracket to the caliper and remove the cable from the caliper.

6. Loosen the lower caliper bolt and pivot the caliper upward on the upper caliper guide pin.

7. Remove the disc pad retaining spring and remove the disc pads and shims.

8. Remove the anchor plate clips and label their positions, indicating top and bottom.

To install:

9. Install the anchor plate clips in their original locations. Lubricate the clips with lithium grease.

NOTE: If the anchor plate clips are not installed in their original locations, the locating tabs may contact the rotor.

10. Install the shims on the backs of the pads and install the pads in the anchor plate. Install the disc pad retaining spring.

11. Pivot the caliper down over the pads. If necessary, use a suitable tool to rotate the disc brake piston into the caliper to provide clearance. Install the lower caliper bolt.

12. Install the parking brake cable in the caliper parking brake lever. Position the cable bracket against the caliper and install the cable mounting bolt.

13. Install the wheel and tire assembly and lower the vehicle.

14. Pump the brake pedal several times to seat the brake pads. Check the fluid level in the master cylinder reservoir.

15. Raise and safely support the vehicle. Spin each wheel several times to be sure the calipers are not frozen and the parking brake is not adjusted too tight.

1991–93

1. Remove brake fluid from the master cylinder reservoir until the reservoir is ½ full. Discard removed fluid.

2. Raise and safely support the vehicle.

3. Remove wheel and tire assembly.

4. If necessary, remove the screw plug and turn the adjustment gear counterclockwise with a hex wrench to pull the piston fully inward.

5. Remove the caliper lock bolt.

6. Using a small prybar, pivot the caliper on its mounting bracket to access the brake pads. If the upper lock bolt requires lubrication or service, remove it and suspend the caliper with mechanics wire.

7. Remove the brake pads, shims, spring and guides.

To install:

8. Apply a suitable brake pad grease between the shims and the brake pads.

9. Using a small prybar, pivot the caliper on its mounting bracket and position the brake pads, shims, spring and guides to the rotor.

10. Lubricate and install the lock bolt. Tighten the bolt to 33–43 ft. lbs. (45–59 Nm).

11. If necessary, turn the adjustment gear clockwise with an Allen wrench until the brake pads just touch the rotor, then loosen the gear ⅓ of a turn. Install the screw plug and tighten to 9–12 ft. lbs. (12–16 Nm).

12. Install the wheel and tire assembly and lower the vehicle.

13. Pump brake pedal prior to moving vehicle to position brake linings. Check the fluid level in the master cylinder.

14. Road test vehicle.

Brake Rotor

REMOVAL & INSTALLATION

Front
1989–90

1. Raise and safely support the vehicle.

2. Remove the wheel and tire assembly.

3. Remove the disc brake pads and the caliper. Do not disconnect the brake hose from the caliper. Support the caliper aside with mechanics wire.

4. Using a chisel, unstake and remove the halfshaft nut and washer. Discard the nut.

5. Remove the cotter pin and nut from the tie rod end. Using a separator tool, disconnect the tie rod end from the steering knuckle.

6. Remove the clinch bolt from the lower ball joint and push the lower control arm down away from the steering knuckle. Remove the strut-to-steering knuckle bolts and remove the steering knuckle/hub/rotor assembly from the vehicle.

7. Use a suitable tool to press the rotor and hub assembly from the steering knuckle.

8. If the rotor is to be reused, mark the position of the rotor on the hub. Unbolt the rotor from the hub. If the rotor is to be machined, observe the minimum thickness specification.

To install:

9. Install the rotor on the hub, tightening the bolts to 33–40 ft. lbs. (44–54 Nm). If the rotor is being reused, be sure to align the marks made during the removal procedure.

10. Press the hub and rotor assembly into the steering knuckle.

11. Slide the hub over the halfshaft and install the steering knuckle on the strut. Install the mounting bolts and tighten to 69–86 ft. lbs. (93–117 Nm).

12. Raise the lower control arm and install the ball joint stud in the steering knuckle. Install the cinch bolt and tighten to 32–40 ft. lbs. (43–54 Nm).

13. Install the caliper and brake pads.

14. Install the washer and a new halfshaft nut. Tighten the nut to 116–174 ft. lbs. (157–235 Nm). Stake the nut using a cold chisel with a rounded cutting edge.

NOTE: If the nut splits or cracks after staking, it must be replaced with a new nut.

15. Install the wheel and tire assembly and lower the vehicle.

1991–93

1. Raise and safely support the vehicle.

2. Remove the wheel and tire assembly.

3. Remove the 2 caliper mounting bolts.

4. Secure the caliper aside with mechanics wire.

5. Pull the rotor from the hub. Inspect the rotor and refinish or replace, as necessary. If refinishing, check the minimum thickness specification.

To install:

6. Position the rotor onto the hub.

7. Remove the mechanics wire and position the caliper.

8. Install the 2 caliper mounting bolts and tighten to 29–36 ft. lbs. (39–49 Nm).

9. Install the wheel and tire assembly and lower the vehicle.

Rear
1989–90

1. Disconnect the negative battery cable.

2. Remove the wheel and tire assembly.

3. Remove the dust cap and, using a chisel, unstake and remove the wheel bearing nut and washer.

4. Remove the disc brake pads and the caliper but do not disconnect the brake hose from the caliper. Support the caliper aside with mechanics wire.

5. Remove the rotor/hub/bearing assembly.

To install:

6. Install the rotor/hub/bearing assembly on the spindle. Install a new locknut and adjust the bearing preload. Install the dust cap.

7. Install the caliper and brake pads.

8. Install the wheel and tire assembly and lower the vehicle.

1991–93

1. Raise and safely support the vehicle.

2. Remove the wheel and tire assembly.

3. Remove the brake pads.

4. Remove the 2 rotor mounting screws.

5. Using a suitable tool, pivot the caliper on its mounting bracket and remove the rotor. Inspect the rotor and refinish or replace, as necessary. If refinishing, check the minimum thickness specification.

To install:

6. Using a suitable tool, pivot the caliper on its mounting bracket and position the rotor.

7. Install the 2 mounting screws.

8. Install the brake pads.

9. Install the wheel and tire assembly and lower the vehicle.

Brake Drums

REMOVAL & INSTALLATION

1989–90

1. Raise and safely support the vehicle.

2. Remove the tire and wheel assembly.

3. Remove the grease cap from the brake drum.

4. Using a chisel, raise the staked portion of the locknut. Discard the locknut.

NOTE: The locknuts are threaded left and right. The left hand threaded locknut is on the right side of the vehicle and should be turned clockwise to loosen. The right hand threaded locknut is on the left side of the vehicle and is turned counterclockwise to loosen.

5. Remove the brake drum and bearings as an assembly.

To install:

6. Position the brake drum/bearing/hub assembly on the spindle.

7. Install a new locknut and adjust the bearing preload. Install the grease cap.

8. Install the wheel and tire assembly and lower the vehicle.

1991–93

1. Raise and safely support the vehicle.

2. Remove wheel and tire assembly.

3. Remove the spring nut or attaching screws, if necessary.

4. Pull the brake drum from the hub. Inspect the drum and refinish or replace, as necessary. If refinishing, check the maximum inside diameter specification.

To install:

5. Position the brake drum on the hub.

6. Install the 2 drum attaching screws, if applicable.

7. Install the wheel and tire assembly and lower the vehicle.

Brake Shoes

REMOVAL & INSTALLATION

1. Raise and safely support the vehicle.

2. Remove the wheel and tire assembly and remove the brake drum.

3. Remove the 2 brake shoe return springs.

4. Remove the anti-rattle spring.

5. Push and turn the 2 brake shoe hold-down clips and remove the clips.

6. Remove the leading and trailing shoes from the backing plate.

To install:

7. Use a high temperature grease to lubricate the brake shoe contact points on the backing plate.

8. Position the trailing brake shoe on the backing plate and install 1 of the brake shoe hold-down clips.

9. Position the leading brake shoe on the backing plate and install the other brake shoe hold-down clip.

10. Install the anti-rattle spring.

11. Install the 2 brake shoe return springs.

12. On 1989–90 vehicles, insert a small prybar between the knurled quadrant and the parking brake strut. Twist the prybar until the quadrant just touches the backing plate.

13. On 1991–93 vehicles, press the brake pedal to verify operation of the automatic brake adjuster.

14. Install the brake drum and the wheel and tire assembly. Lower the vehicle.

15. Firmly apply the brakes 2–3 times to adjust the rear brakes.

Wheel Cylinder

REMOVAL & INSTALLATION

1. Raise and safely support the vehicle.

2. Remove the wheel and tire assembly and remove the brake drum.

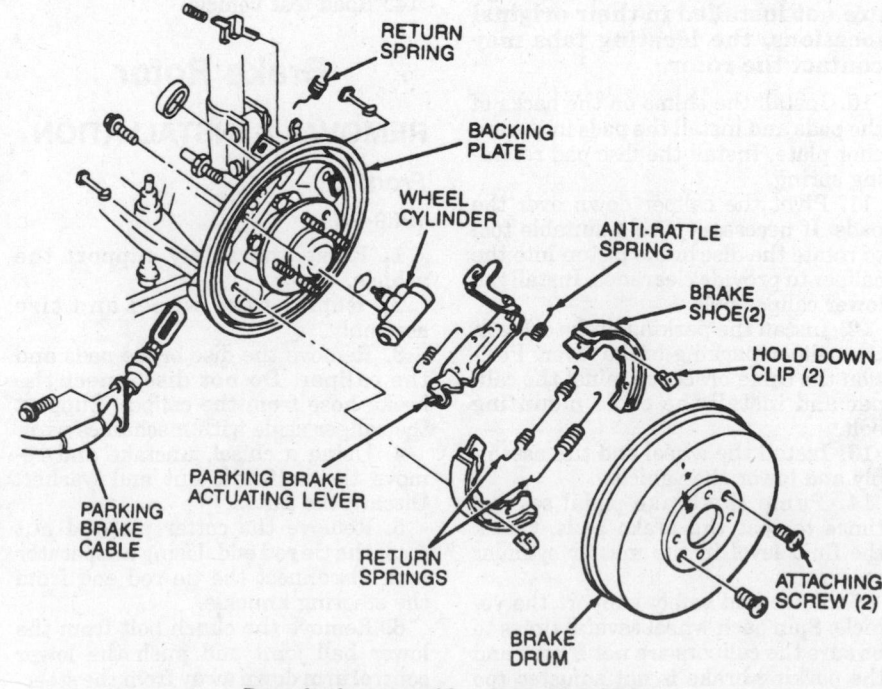

Drum brake assembly—1991-93 vehicles

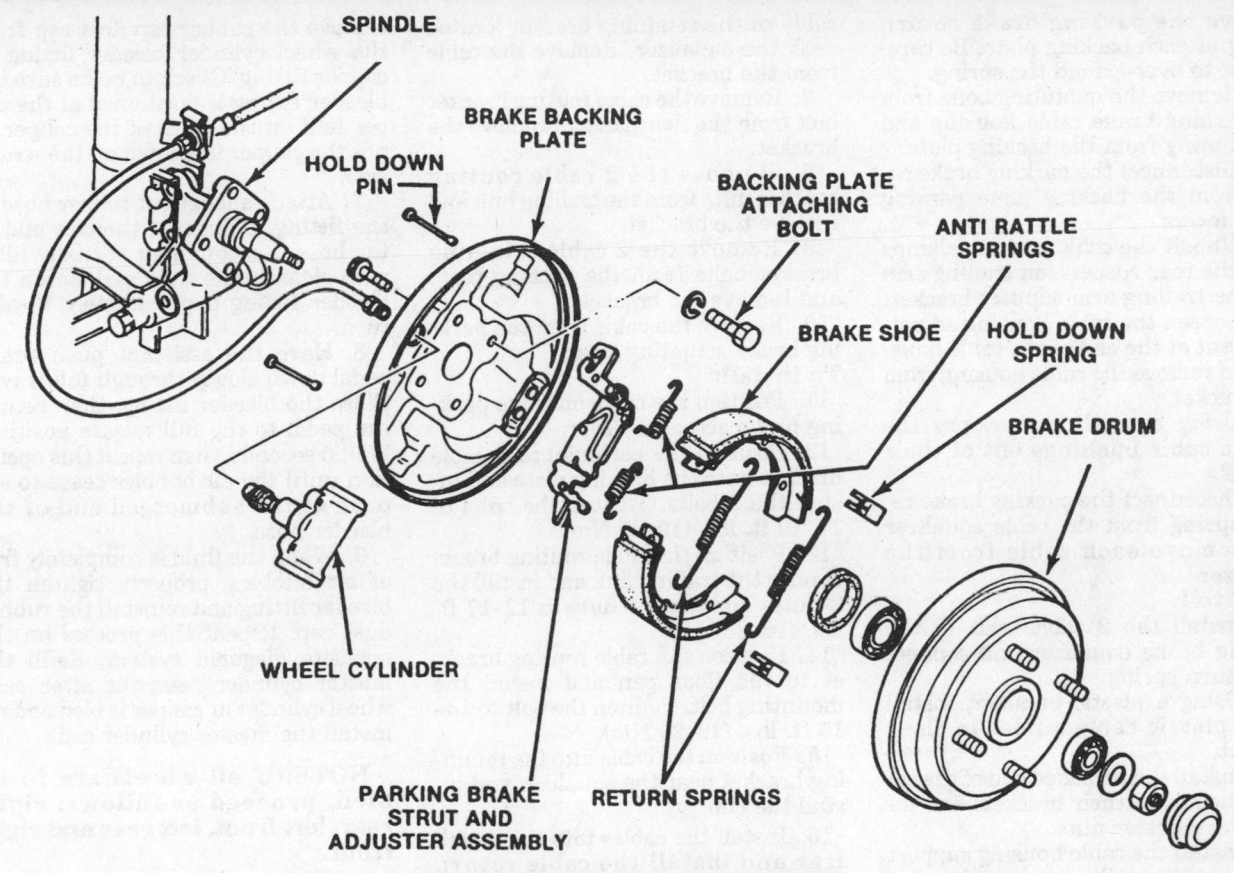

SPINDLE

BRAKE BACKING PLATE

HOLD DOWN PIN

BACKING PLATE ATTACHING BOLT

ANTI RATTLE SPRINGS

BRAKE SHOE

HOLD DOWN SPRING

BRAKE DRUM

WHEEL CYLINDER

PARKING BRAKE STRUT AND ADJUSTER ASSEMBLY

RETURN SPRINGS

Drum brake assembly—1989–90 vehicles

3. On 1989–90 vehicles, remove the brake shoes. On 1991–93 vehicles, remove the upper brake shoe return spring.

4. Clamp the wheel cylinder brake hose.

5. Using a tubing wrench, loosen the wheel cylinder-to-brake line flare nut.

6. On 1991–93 vehicles, pull the clip from the brake hose retaining bracket and remove the brake hose from the retaining bracket.

7. Remove the brake line from the wheel cylinder.

8. Remove the 2 wheel cylinder mounting bolts and remove the wheel cylinder from the backing plate.

9. On 1991–93 vehicles, remove and discard the wheel cylinder gasket.

To install:

10. On 1991–93 vehicles, install a new wheel cylinder gasket onto the backing plate.

11. Position the wheel cylinder onto the backing plate and install the 2 mounting bolts. Tighten the bolts to 89–115 inch lbs. (10–13 Nm).

12. Position the brake line into the wheel cylinder fitting and tighten the wheel cylinder-to-brake line flare nut to 12–16 ft. lbs. (16–22 Nm).

13. On 1991–93 vehicles, position the brake hose into the retaining bracket

and install the clip. Remove the clamp from the wheel cylinder brake hose.

14. On 1989–90 vehicles, install the brake shoes. On 1991–93 vehicles, install the brake shoe return spring.

15. Press the brake pedal to verify the operation of the automatic brake adjuster.

16. Install the brake drum and the wheel and tire assembly.

17. Bleed the brake system and lower the vehicle.

Parking Brake Cable

ADJUSTMENT

1989–90

1. Remove the attaching screws in the center console and remove the console.

2. Make sure the parking brake lever is fully released.

3. Tighten the adjusting nut on the left side of the lever to shorten the equalizer cable. Tighten the nut until it takes 10 notches to fully set the parking brake.

4. Install the center console.

1991–93

1. Start the engine and place the transaxle in **R**.

2. With the vehicle moving in reverse, depress the brake pedal several times.

3. Stop the vehicle and place the transaxle in **P**. Stop the engine.

4. Remove the parking brake console as follows:

a. Remove the rear seat ash tray.

b. Position both front seats to the rear-most position.

c. Remove the 2 front retaining screws from the parking brake console.

d. Recline both front seats.

e. Remove the 2 rear retaining screws and with the parking brake engaged, remove the parking brake console.

f. Release the parking brake lever.

5. Turn the adjusting nut until the parking brake lever stroke is 5–7 notches when pulled with a force of 22 lbs.

6. Install the parking brake console by reversing the removal procedure.

REMOVAL & INSTALLATION

1989–90

1. Raise and safely support the vehicle.

2. With a pair of needle-nose pliers,

remove the parking brake return spring at each backing plate. Be careful not to over-extend the spring.

3. Remove the mounting bolts from the parking brake cable housing and pull it away from the backing plate.

4. Disconnect the parking brake cables from the backing plate parking brake levers.

5. Unbolt the cable housing clamps from the rear suspension trailing arm and the trailing arm support bracket.

6. Loosen the cable housing adjustment nut at the end of the cable housing and remove the cable housing from the bracket.

7. Using a small prybar, pry the plastic cable bushings out of their brackets.

8. Disconnect the parking brake return spring from the cable equalizer and remove each cable from the equalizer.

To install:

9. Install the 2 cable ends in the parking brake equalizer and connect the return spring.

10. Using a plastic hammer, install the 2 plastic cable guides in their bracket.

11. Install the threaded end of the cable housings in their brackets and install the adjuster nuts.

12. Install the cable housing support clamps at the trailing support bracket and on each trailing arm.

13. Connect the parking brake cables to the backing plate parking brake levers.

14. Position the parking brake cable against the backing plate and install the mounting bolts.

15. Lower the vehicle and adjust the parking brake cables.

1991–93

1. Remove the parking brake console as follows:

 a. Remove the rear seat ash tray.

 b. Position both front seats to the rear-most position.

 c. Remove the 2 front retaining screws from the parking brake console.

 d. Recline both front seats.

 e. Remove the 2 rear retaining screws and with the parking brake engaged, remove the parking brake console.

 f. Release the parking brake lever.

2. Remove the cable adjusting nut.

3. Raise and safely support the vehicle.

4. Remove the rear exhaust pipe and resonator heat shields.

5. Disconnect the equalizer return spring and remove the cables from the equalizer.

6. Remove the clip that attaches the cable to the retaining bracket located near the equalizer. Remove the cable from the bracket.

7. Remove the cable routing bracket bolt from the floorpan and remove the bracket.

8. Remove the 2 cable routing bracket nuts from the trailing link and remove the bracket.

9. Remove the 2 cable retaining bracket bolts from the backing plate and remove the bracket.

10. Remove the cable from the parking brake actuating lever.

To install:

11. Position the cable onto the parking brake actuating lever.

12. Position the parking brake cable bracket onto the backing plate and install the 2 bolts. Tighten the bolts to 14–19 ft. lbs. (19–25 Nm).

13. Position the cable routing bracket onto the trailing link and install the 2 nuts. Tighten the nuts to 12–17 ft. lbs. (16–23 Nm).

14. Position the cable routing bracket to the floor pan and install the mounting bolt. Tighten the bolt to 14–19 ft. lbs. (19–25 Nm).

15. Position the cable into the retaining bracket near the equalizer and install the clip.

16. Install the cables into the equalizer and install the cable return spring.

17. Install the rear exhaust pipe and resonator heat shields.

18. Lower the vehicle.

19. Install the adjusting nut.

20. Adjust the parking brake cable and install the parking brake console in the reverse order of removal.

Brake System Bleeding

1. Clean all the dirt from around the master cylinder filler cap.

2. Fill the reservoir with brake fluid. The reservoir must be at least ¾ full throughout the bleeding procedure.

3. If the master cylinder is known or suspected to have air in bore, it must be bled before any wheel cylinders or calipers.

4. To bleed the master cylinder, loosen 1 outlet fitting aproximately ¾ turn. Have an assistant push the brake pedal down slowly through full travel. Close the outlet fitting, then return the pedal slowly to the full released position. Wait 5 seconds, then repeat the operation until the air bubbles cease to appear.

5. Loosen the other outlet fitting approximately ¾ turn and repeat Step 4.

6. To continue to bleed the system, remove the rubber cap dust cap from the wheel cylinder bleeder fitting or caliper fitting. Check to make sure the bleeder fitting is positioned at the upper half on the front of the caliper, if not the caliper is located on the wrong side.

7. Attach a length of rubber hose to the fitting. Submerge the free end of the hose in a container partially filled with clean brake fluid and loosen the bleeder fitting approximately ¾ of a turn.

8. Have the assistant push brake pedal down slowly through full travel. Close the bleeder fitting, then return the pedal to the full release position. Wait 5 seconds, then repeat this operation until the air bubbles cease to appear at the submerged end of the bleeder hose.

9. When the fluid is completely free of air bubbles, properly tighten the bleeder fitting and reinstall the rubber dust cap. Repeat this process on the opposite diagonal system. Refill the master cylinder reservoir after each wheel cylinder or caliper is bled and reinstall the master cylinder cap.

NOTE: If all wheels are to be bled, proceed as follows: right rear, left front, left rear and right front.

10. When the bleeding operation is completed, the fluid level should be filled to the maximum fill level indicated on the reservoir. Always ensure the disc brake pistons are returned to their normal positions by depressing the brake pedal several times until the normal pedal travel is established. Check the pedal feel. If the pedal feels spongy, repeat the bleeding procedure.

CHASSIS ELECTRICAL

Heater Blower Motor

REMOVAL & INSTALLATION

1989–90

1. Disconnect the negative battery cable.

2. From the passenger's side, remove the sound deadening panel.

3. Disconnect the electrical connector from the blower motor assembly.

4. Remove the blower motor-to-blower case screws, the cover, the cooling tube and the motor.

5. Remove the blower wheel-to-motor nut and pull the wheel straight off

the motor. Remove the gasket from the motor.

6. To install, reverse the removal procedure. Check the blower motor operation.

1991–93

1. Disconnect the negative battery cable.

2. Remove the trim panel below the glove compartment.

3. Remove the wiring bracket and bolt.

4. Disconnect the blower motor electrical connector.

5. Remove the 3 blower motor mounting bolts and remove the blower motor.

6. Remove the blower wheel retaining clip and remove the blower wheel from the blower motor.

7. Installation is the reverse of the removal procedure.

Windshield Wiper Motor

REMOVAL & INSTALLATION

Front

1989–90

1. Disconnect the negative battery cable.

2. From the top left side of the cowl, remove the windshield wiper motor shield-to-chassis plastic retainers and the shield.

3. From the windshield wiper motor shaft, remove the drive link nut and split washer.

4. Disconnect the electrical connector from the windshield wiper motor.

5. Remove the windshield wiper motor-to-cowl bolts, the motor and rubber insulators.

6. To install, make sure the windshield wiper motor is in the PARK position and reverse the removal procedures. Inspect the operation of the windshield wiper system.

1991–93

1. Disconnect the negative battery cable.

2. Remove the wiper arm nut covers, remove the nuts and pull the wiper arms from the wiper shaft.

3. With the hood closed, remove the 7 screw covers.

4. Remove the 7 cowl grille retaining screws and remove the cowl grille.

5. Pry up the 4 baffle retaining clips and remove the baffle trim piece.

NOTE: Make sure the motor is in the PARK position before disconnecting the linkage.

6. Remove the wiper linkage retain-ing clip and disconnect the wiper link-age from the motor.

7. Disconnect the 2 motor electrical connectors.

8. Remove the 3 motor mounting bolts until they are loose from the sheetmetal mounting surface. Remove the motor.

To install:

9. Install the motor and tighten the 3 motor mounting bolts to 61–87 inch lbs. (7–9 Nm).

10. Connect the electrical connectors and connect the wiper linkage to the motor. Install the linkage retaining clip.

11. Install the baffle trim piece and the cowl grille. Install the screw covers after tightening the retaining screws.

12. Before installing the wiper arms, turn the wiper switch ON. Let the wiper pivot shafts move 3–4 cycles, then turn the wiper switch OFF.

13. Install the wiper arms on the pivot shafts so the tips of the blades are 1.10–1.26 in. (28–32mm) from the top of the cowl grille. Tighten the nuts to 142–177 inch lbs. (16–20 Nm).

Rear

1989–90

1. Disconnect the negative battery cable.

2. Lift the cover on the wiper arm, remove the nut and remove the arm and blade assembly. Remove the luggage compartment end trim from the liftgate.

3. Remove the seal cap, nut, outer bushing, packings and inner bushings.

4. Disconnect the electrical connector and the ground wire from the windshield wiper motor.

5. Remove the windshield wiper motor-to-liftgate bolts, the motor and rubber insulators.

To install:

6. Install the wiper motor and insulators and secure with the bolts.

7. Connect the electrical lead and ground wire.

8. Install the inner bushings, packings, outer bushing, nut and seal cap.

9. Install the luggage compartment end trim on the liftgate.

10. Before installing the wiper arm, turn the wiper switch ON. Let the wiper motor shaft move 3–4 cycles, then turn the wiper switch OFF.

11. Install the wiper arm on the shaft so the end of the blade is 0.79 in. (20mm) from the bottom of the window.

1991–93

1. Disconnect the negative battery cable.

2. Remove the wiper arm by lifting the wiper arm attaching nut cover, re-moving the attaching nut and pulling the wiper arm from the pivot shaft.

3. Remove the shaft seal from the outer bushing attaching nut.

4. Remove the outer bushing attaching nut and remove the outer bushing.

5. Remove the liftgate trim panel.

6. Disconnect the wiper motor electrical connector.

7. Remove the 3 wiper motor mounting bolts and washers and remove the wiper motor.

To install:

8. Install the wiper motor with the washers and mounting bolts. Tighten the mounting bolts to 61–87 inch lbs. (7–9 Nm).

9. Connect the motor electrical lead.

10. Install the liftgate trim panel.

11. Install the outer bushing and the nut. Tighten the nut to 35–52 inch lbs. (4–6 Nm). Install the shaft seal on the nut.

12. Before installing the wiper arm, turn the wiper switch ON. Let the wiper pivot shaft move 3–4 cycles, then turn the wiper switch OFF.

13. Install the wiper arm on the shaft so the end of the blade is 0.79–0.98 in. (20–25mm) from the rear window moulding. Tighten the wiper arm attaching nut to 61–87 inch lbs. (7–10 Nm).

NOTE: If the wiper arm is slipping on the serrated pivot shaft, it can be removed, the shavings brushed away, and reinstalled several times before the wiper arm will need to be replaced.

Windshield Wiper Switch

REMOVAL & INSTALLATION

Front and rear wiper control is a function of the combination switch on all except 1989–90 station wagon vehicles, which have a separate switch to control the rear wipers.

1989–90 Station Wagon

REAR WIPER SWITCH

1. Disconnect the negative battery cable.

2. Gently pry the outer edge of the switch from the instrument panel.

3. Disconnect the electrical connector and remove the switch.

4. Installation is the reverse of the removal procedure.

Instrument Cluster

REMOVAL & INSTALLATION

1989–90

1. Disconnect the negative battery cable.
2. Remove the steering wheel.
3. Remove the instrument cluster bezel-to-instrument panel screws and bezel.
4. Remove the instrument cluster-to-instrument panel screws.
5. From under the dash, disconnect the speedometer cable from the cluster.
6. Pull the instrument cluster outward and disconnect the wiring connectors. Remove the cluster.
7. To install, reverse the removal procedure. Inspect the operation of the instruments.

1991–93

1. Disconnect the negative battery cable.
2. If equipped with a tilt column, tilt the steering wheel down.
3. If equipped with a standard column, remove the 4 bolts securing the steering column to the instrument panel frame.
4. Lower the steering column.
5. Disconnect the speedometer cable from the instrument panel.
6. Remove the cap screws securing the instrument cluster bezel to the instrument panel and remove the instrument cluster bezel.
7. Remove the screws and bolts securing the instrument cluster to the instrument panel.
8. Pull the instrument cluster out slightly and disconnect the electrical connectors from the rear of the instrument cluster.
9. Remove the cluster from the instrument panel.
10. Installation is the reverse of the removal procedure. Make sure the instrument cluster is held in its forward most position while attaching the 2 upper screws.

Speedometer

REMOVAL & INSTALLATION

1989–90

1. Disconnect the negative battery cable.
2. Remove the instrument cluster.
3. Remove the lens from the instrument cluster.
4. Remove the indicator light overlay from the instrument cluster.
5. Remove the speedometer-to-instrument cluster screws and the speedometer.

6. To install, reverse the removal procedure. Check the operation of the speedometer.

1991–93

1. Disconnect the negative battery cable.
2. Remove the instrument cluster.
3. Remove the instrument cluster lens and shroud.
4. Remove the speedometer from the instrument cluster.
5. Installation is the reverse of the removal procedure. Be careful when handling the speedometer so as not to disturb the factory calibration.

Radio

REMOVAL & INSTALLATION

1989–90

1. Disconnect the negative battery cable.
2. Remove the radio trim cover from the instrument panel.
3. Remove the radio retaining screws and pull the radio outward to gain access to the wiring.
4. Disconnect the electrical and antenna leads from the radio.
5. Installation is the reverse of the removal procedure.

1991–93

1. Disconnect the negative battery cable.
2. Using radio removal tools T87P–19061–A or equivalent, pull the radio out from its mounting position so the antenna and the electrical connectors are accessible.
3. Disconnect the antenna lead and the radio electrical connectors from the radio.
4. Remove the radio.
5. Installation is the reverse of the removal procedure.

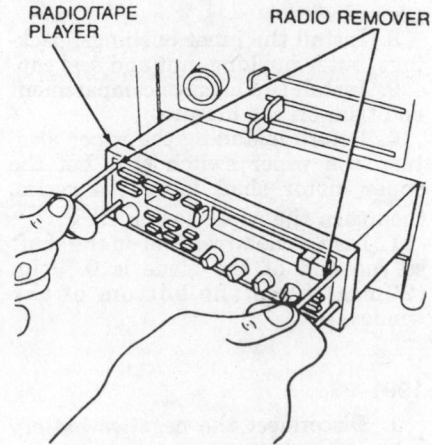

RADIO/TAPE PLAYER   RADIO REMOVER

Radio removal—1991–93 vehicles

Combination Switch

The combination switch assembly controls the turn signal, headlight, dimmer and windshield wiper switch functions.

REMOVAL & INSTALLATION

1989–90

1. Disconnect the negative battery cable and remove the steering wheel.
2. Remove the steering column covers-to-steering column screws and the covers.
3. Depress the small tang on the electrical harness clip and disconnect the clip; move the electrical harness aside.
4. Loosen the combination switch-to-steering column clamp, slide the switch slightly forward and disconnect the electrical connector from the rear of the combination switch.
5. Remove the combination switch from the steering column.
6. To install, reverse the removal procedure. Check the switch operations.

1991–93

1. Disconnect the negative battery cable.
2. Remove the steering wheel cover retaining screws from the back side of the steering wheel and remove the cover.
3. Disconnect the horn electrical connector and the speed control electrical connectors, if equipped.
4. Remove the steering wheel mounting nut or bolt.

NOTE: Do not attempt to remove the steering wheel by hitting the column shaft with a hammer. The column may collapse.

5. Remove the steering wheel using a suitable puller.
6. Remove the 4 retaining screws from the steering column lower cover

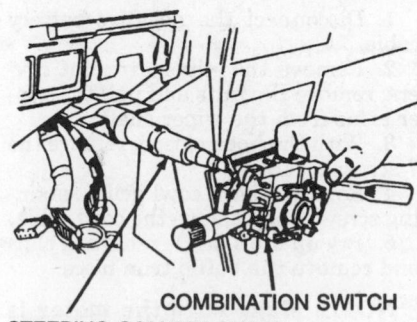

COMBINATION SWITCH
STEERING COLUMN SHAFT

Combination switch removal and installation—1989–90 vehicles

and remove the cover. Remove the upper cover.

7. Disconnect the 3 multi-function switch electrical connectors.

8. Remove the multi-function switch retaining screw, pull the electrical connectors from the retaining brackets and remove the switch.

9. Installation is the reverse of the removal procedure. Tighten the steering wheel mounting nut to 29–36 ft. lbs. (39–49 Nm) on 1991 vehicles or tighten the steering wheel mounting bolt to 34–46 ft. lbs. (46–63 Nm) on 1992–93 vehicles.

Ignition Lock

REMOVAL & INSTALLATION

1991–93

1. Disconnect the negative battery cable.

2. Remove the steering wheel cover retaining screws from the back side of the steering wheel and remove the cover.

3. Disconnect the horn electrical connector and the cruise control electrical connectors, if equipped.

4. Remove the steering wheel mounting nut or bolt.

NOTE: Do not attempt to remove the steering wheel by hitting the column shaft with a hammer. The column may collapse.

5. Remove the steering wheel using a suitable puller.

6. Remove the combination switch.

7. Disconnect the ignition switch electrical connector.

8. Remove the shift-lock cable mounting bracket bolt and position the bracket and cable aside.

9. Remove the 4 steering column upper mounting bracket bolts and lower the column.

10. Using a suitable hammer and chisel, make a groove in the head of each of the 2 column lock mounting bracket bolts.

11. Remove the bolts with a flat bladed tool and discard the bolts.

12. Remove the steering column lock and mounting bracket.

To install:

13. Position the steering column lock and mounting bracket and install 2 new bolts, tightening them only enough to hold the column lock in position.

14. With the key in the ignition, verify the operation of the column lock. If necessary, reposition the column lock until it operates properly.

15. Tighten the mounting bracket bolts until the bolt heads break off.

16. Position the steering column and install the 4 upper mounting bracket

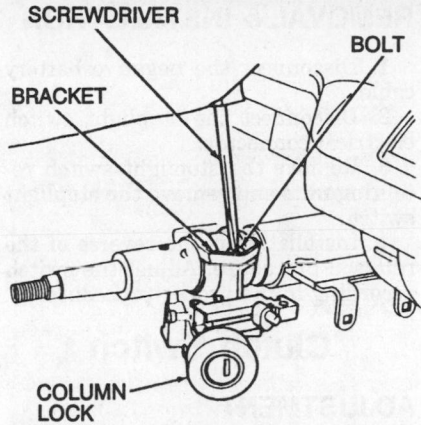

Ignition lock removal—1991–93 vehicles

SCREWDRIVER
BOLT
BRACKET
COLUMN LOCK

bolts. Tighten the bolts to 80–123 inch lbs. (9–14 Nm).

17. If equipped with a tilt steering wheel, remove the upper mounting bracket retaining pin.

18. Position the shift-lock cable mounting bracket and install the bolt. Tighten to 37–55 inch lbs. (4–6 Nm).

19. Connect the ignition switch electrical connector.

20. Install the combination switch.

21. Install the steering wheel and the mounting nut or bolt. Tighten the nut on 1991 vehicles to 29–36 ft. lbs. (39–49 Nm) or the bolt on 1992–93 vehicles to 34–46 ft. lbs. (46–63 Nm).

22. Connect the horn electrical connector and the speed control electrical connectors, if equipped.

23. Position the steering wheel cover and install the retaining screws.

24. Connect the negative battery cable.

Ignition Switch

REMOVAL & INSTALLATION

1989–90

1. Disconnect the negative battery cable.

2. Grasp the black trim ring around the ignition lock switch and pull it straight out.

3. From the driver's side, remove the sound deadening panel and the lap duct cover.

4. If equipped with air conditioning, remove the air conditioning duct assembly-to-access panel support bracket center screw, the access panel support bracket screws and the bracket.

5. From under the steering column, grasp the side window defogger duct ends, pull it outward, while twisting it slightly. From the ignition switch wiring, located under the steering column, disengage the plastic strap connector locking tang and remove the plastic strap.

6. Remove the steering column-to-instrument panel bolts and lower the column.

7. Lift the upper steering column shroud and remove it from the steering column.

8. Remove the ignition switch-to-ignition switch housing screw, grasp the ignition switch body and pull it straight outward.

9. To disengage the electrical connectors from the ignition switch, perform the following procedure:

a. Disengage the electrical connector locking tang.

b. Grasp an electrical connector in each hand and pull them straight apart.

NOTE: Be aware of the electrical connector cavity position for reassembly purposes.

10. Using a straightened paper clip, disengage the 2 key-in buzzer wires from the 4-terminal connector; the wire colors are red and red wire/orange tracer.

To install:

11. To install wires and connector, perform the following procedures:

a. Align the wire end flat sides with the grooved portion of the connector and push the wire inward until the locking tang engages wire end.

b. Push the 4-terminal connector into the housing connector until the locking tangs are in place.

c. Wrap electrical tape around the ignition switch wires.

12. Install the ignition switch-to-ignition switch housing screw and the plastic snap connector around the ignition switch wiring. Attach the connector peg to the steering column mounting bracket.

13. Install the plastic strap around the ignition switch wiring and steering column.

14. To complete the installation, reverse the removal procedure. Check the ignition switch operation.

1991–93

1. Disconnect the negative battery cable.

2. Remove the combination switch.

3. Disconnect the ignition switch electrical connector.

4. Remove the 3 ignition switch mounting screws and remove the ignition switch.

5. Installation is the reverse of the removal procedure. Check the switch for proper operation.

Stoplight Switch

ADJUSTMENT

1989-90

1. Measure the distance from the center of the brake pedal pad to the floor. The distance should be 8.62–8.82 in. (219–224mm). If not, proceed to Step 2.
2. Disconnect the stoplight switch electrical connector.
3. Loosen the switch locknut and rotate the switch until the correct pedal height is reached.
4. Tighten the locknut and connect the switch electrical connector.

1991-93

1. Measure the distance from the center of the brake pedal pad to the floor. The distance should be 7.60–7.72 in. (193–196mm). If not, proceed to Step 2.
2. Disconnect the stoplight switch electrical connector.
3. Loosen the stoplight locknut and turn the stoplight switch until it does not contact the brake pedal.
4. Loosen the rod locknut and turn the rod until the brake pedal height is within specification.
5. Turn the stoplight switch until it contacts the brake pedal, then turn it an additional ½ turn.
6. Tighten the stoplight locknut and the rod locknut.
7. Connect the stoplight switch electrical connector.
8. Check the operation of the stoplights.

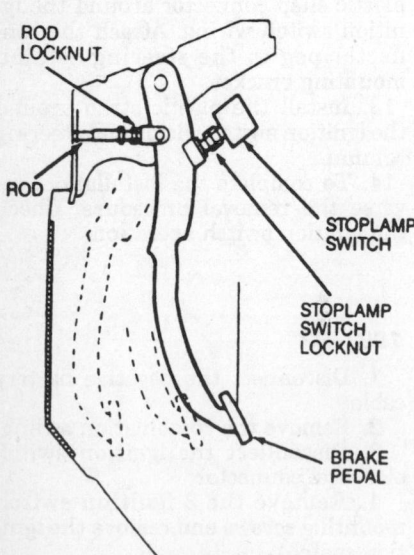

Stoplight switch adjustment—1991-93 vehicles

REMOVAL & INSTALLATION

1. Disconnect the negative battery cable.
2. Disconnect the stoplight switch electrical connector.
3. Remove the stoplight switch retaining nuts and remove the stoplight switch.
4. Installation is the reverse of the removal procedure. Adjust the switch according to the proper procedure.

Clutch Switch

ADJUSTMENT

1. Disconnect the negative battery cable.
2. Disconnect the clutch engage electrical connector.
3. Using an ohmmeter, check the resistance between the connector terminals.
4. The ohmmeter should show continuity when the switch rod is pushed into the switch. The ohmmeter should show no continuity with the switch rod released.
5. Replace the switch if it does not perform as specified.

REMOVAL & INSTALLATION

1. Disconnect the negative battery cable.
2. Disconnect the electrical connector.
3. Remove the 2 retaining nuts.
4. Remove the clutch engage switch.
5. Installation is the reverse of the removal procedure.

Neutral Safety Switch

ADJUSTMENT

1989-90

1. Disconnect the neutral safety switch connector from the main wiring harness.
2. Connect an ohmmeter between terminals A and B.
3. With the transaxle selector lever in N or P, there should be continuity between terminals A and B.
4. Replace the switch if it does not perform as specified.

1991-93

The neutral safety switch function is performed by the Manual Lever Position Switch (MLPS). The MLPS is an adjustable switch that informs the automatic transaxle control unit of the position of the transaxle manual shaft. The MLPS will allow the vehicle to be started with the gear selector in the P

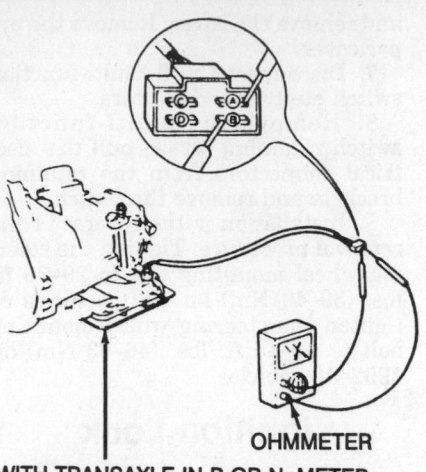

WITH TRANSAXLE IN P OR N, METER SHOULD SHOW CONTINUITY

Neutral safety switch testing—1989-90 vehicles

or N positions when properly adjusted. The MLPS is located externally on the transaxle housing and is positioned on the manual shaft.

1. Remove the air cleaner assembly and air inlet tube.
2. Remove the nut securing the manual shaft lever to the transaxle manual shaft.
3. Remove the lever from the manual shaft.
4. Turn the manual shaft to the neutral position.
5. Loosen the MLPS mounting bolts.
6. Align the hole of the MLPS with the hole on the manual shaft lever by inserting a 0.079 in. (2.0mm) outside diameter pin.
7. Tighten the MLPS mounting bolts to 69–95 inch lbs. (8–11 Nm). Remove the pin.
8. Check the continuity of the switch as follows:
   a. Disconnect the switch connector.
   b. Using an ohmmeter, check the switch for continuity at the connector.
   c. There should be continuity be-

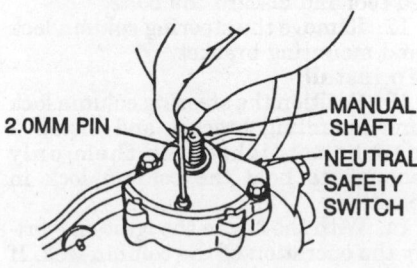

Neutral safety switch adjustment—1991-93 vehicles

tween the **BK/BL** and **BK/R** terminals with the shift lever in the **P** or **N** position.

9. If there is no continuity, replace the MLPS.

10. Position the manual shaft lever to the manual shaft and install the nut. Tighten to 33–47 ft. lbs. (44–64 Nm).

11. Install the air cleaner assembly and air inlet tube.

REMOVAL & INSTALLATION

1989–90

1. Disconnect the negative battery cable.

2. Raise and support the vehicle safely.

3. Disconnect the electrical connector from the neutral safety switch.

4. Using a wrench, remove the switch from the transaxle.

5. To install, apply sealant to the switch threads and reverse the removal procedures. Torque the neutral safety switch to 14–19 ft. lbs. (19–26 Nm).

1991–93

1. Disconnect the negative battery cable.

2. Remove the air cleaner assembly and air inlet tube.

3. Remove the nut securing the manual shaft lever to the transaxle manual shaft and remove the lever.

4. Disconnect the 3 electrical connectors located on the top of the top of the transaxle.

5. Disconnect the electrical connector located on the front side of the transaxle.

6. Remove the 2 bolts securing the MLPS and the bolts securing the electrical connector brackets to the top of the transaxle.

7. Remove the MLPS from the manual shaft.

To install:

8. Position the MLPS onto the manual shaft.

9. Install the bolts securing the electrical connectors to the transaxle housing.

10. Install the bolts securing the MLPS but do not tighten yet.

11. Connect the electrical connectors located on the top and on the side of the transaxle.

12. Adjust the MLPS according to the proper procedure.

13. Install the air cleaner assembly and the air inlet tube.

14. Connect the negative battery cable.

Fuses, Circuit Breakers and Relays

LOCATION

Fuses

All vehicles are equipped with a fuse panel mounted inside the vehicle, under the left side of the instrument panel as well as a fuse box mounted in the engine compartment.

Fuse Link Cartridge

Fuse link cartridges are used on 1991–93 vehicles. Fuse link cartridges have a colored plastic housing with a clear "window" at the top. To check a fuse cartridge, look at the fuse element through the clear "window". The fuse link cartridges are located in the engine compartment fuse box. The following fuse link cartridges are listed according to their labels in the fuse box.

Fuel Inj—Pink 30 amp: to protect the electronic engine control circuit.

Head—Pink 30 amp: to protect the headlight circuit and in Canada, the daytime running lights circuit.

Main—Black 80 amp for 1.8L engine or Dark Blue 100 amp for 1.9L engine: to protect all circuits, except starter and starter solenoid circuits.

BTN—Yellow 60 amp for 1.8L engine or Green 40 amp for 1.9L engine: to protect the courtesy lights, electronic automatic transaxle, electronic engine control, exterior lights, horn, interior lights, passive restraint, power door locks, radio, shift lock and warning chime circuits.

Cooling Fan—Pink 30 amp for 1.8L engine or Green 40 amp for 1.9L engine: to protect cooling fans circuit.

Circuit Breakers

A circuit breaker is mounted on the interior fuse panel. This breaker controls the blower motor circuit.

Various Relays

1989–90

Horn Relay—located in the engine compartment on the left inner fender.

A/C Cut-out Relay—located in the front of the left front shock tower in the engine compartment.

A/C Relay No. 1—located on the left front shock tower in the engine compartment.

A/C Relay No. 2—located on the left front shock tower in the engine compartment.

A/C Relay No. 3—located on the left front shock tower in the engine compartment.

Cooling Fan Relay—located in the left front side of the engine com-

partment, next to the coolant recovery bottle.

Door Buzzer Relay—located in the electrical equipment panel, above the fuse block.

Fuel Pump Relay—mounted under the center of the instrument panel.

1991–93

Air Conditioning Relay—located on the rear of the right fender apron on 1991 vehicles or in the right rear corner of the engine compartment, on the firewall on 1992–93 vehicles.

Cooling Fan Lo and Hi Speed Relays—located on the front of the left fender apron.

Cooling Fan Relay—located on top of the left front wheel well, in the engine compartment fuse block.

Door Lock Relay—located above the left cowl on 1991 vehicles or behind the left side of the instrument panel, near the cowl on 1992–93 vehicles.

Daytime Running Lights Relay—located behind the right side of the instrument panel, near the blower motor.

Electronic Engine Control Power Relay—located behind the center of the instrument panel.

Fuel Pump Relay—located behind the center of the instrument panel.

Headlight Relay—located above the left cowl on 1991 vehicles or behind the left side of the instrument panel, near the cowl on 1992–93 vehicles.

Horn Relay—located above the left cowl on 1991 vehicles or behind the left side of the instrument panel, near the cowl on 1992–93 vehicles.

Ignition Relay—located on top of the left front wheel well, in the engine compartment fuse block.

Parking Light Relay—located behind the left side of the instrument panel.

Vane Air Flow Meter Relay—located behind the center of the instrument panel.

Wide Open Throttle Cutout Relay—located on the rear of the right fender apron on 1991 vehicles or in the right rear corner of the engine compartment, on the firewall on 1992–93 vehicles.

Computers

LOCATION

The Electronic Control Unit (ECU) is located behind the center of the instrument panel.

Flashers

LOCATION

On 1989–90 vehicles, the turn signal/hazard flasher is located on the interior fuse panel. On 1991–93 vehicles, the flasher unit is located with the combination switch.

Cruise Control

ADJUSTMENT

Actuator Cable

1989–90

1. With the engine off, remove the clip from the actuator cable and adjust the locknut while pressing down on the cable until free-play is 0.04–0.12 in. (1–3mm).
2. Check the system operation and adjust as needed.

1991–93

1. Remove the cable adjusting clip from the cable housing.
2. Pull tightly on the cable until all of the slack is taken out.
3. Install the cable adjusting clip.

Clutch Pedal Height

1989–90

Pedal height is the distance from the cowl to the center of the clutch pedal pad.

1. Remove the necessary instrument panel components which block access to the clutch pedal.
2. Loosen the clutch pedal locknut.
3. Turn the stop bolt to obtain the correct pedal height of 8.44–8.64 in. (214.5–219.5mm). Tighten the locknut.
4. If components from the instrument panel were removed, reinstall them.

Brake Pedal Height

1989–90

Measure the distance from the center

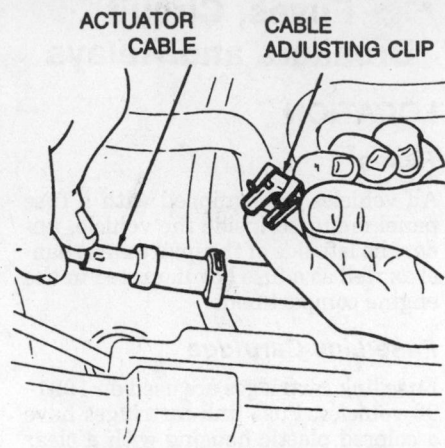

Actuator cable adjustment—1991–93 vehicles

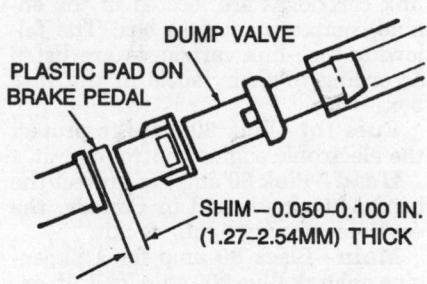

Vacuum dump valve adjustment—1991–93 vehicles

of the brake pedal to lower dash panel. Pedal height must be 8.62–8.82 in. (219–224mm). If the brake pedal height is not within these specifications, adjust as follows:

1. Disconnect the negative battery cable.
2. Adjust the pedal height by adjusting the stoplight switch.
3. Disconnect the connector on the stoplight switch.
4. Loosen the stoplight switch locknut and rotate the switch until the pedal height is 8.62–8.82 in. (219–224mm).
5. Tighten the switch locknut.

6. Connect the stoplight switch connector.
7. Connect the negative battery cable and check stoplight operation.

Vacuum Dump Valve

1991–93

1. Firmly depress the brake pedal and hold in position.
2. Push in the dump valve until the valve collar bottoms against the retaining clip.
3. Place a 0.050–0.10 in. (1.27–2.54mm) shim between the white button of the valve and the pad on the brake pedal.
4. Firmly pull the brake pedal rearward to its normal position, allowing the dump valve to ratchet backwards in the retaining clip.

Clutch Switch

1991–93

1. Measure the distance from the bulkhead to the upper center of the clutch pedal pad. The distance should be 7.72–8.03 in. (196–204mm). If not proceed to Step 2.
2. Disconnect the clutch switch electrical connector.
3. Loosen the switch locknut and turn the switch until the specified distance is achieved. Tighten the locknut to 10–13 ft. lbs. (14–18 Nm).
4. Push the clutch pedal down by hand until clutch resistance is felt.
5. Measure the distance between the upper pedal height and where resistance is felt. The free-play should be 0.20–0.51 in. (5–13mm). If not, proceed to Step 6.
6. Loosen the pushrod locknut and turn the pushrod until the specified free-play is achieved.
7. Check that disengagement height is correct when the pedal is fully depressed. Minimum disengagement height is 1.6 in. (41mm).
8. Tighten the pushrod locknut to 9–12 ft. lbs. (12–17mm) and connect the clutch switch electrical connector.

GM "B" Body
Rear Wheel Drive
Buick—Estate Wagon • Roadmaster • Roadmaster Wagon
Chevrolet—Caprice • Caprice Wagon
Oldsmobile—Custom Cruiser **Pontiac**—Safari

15

SPECIFICATIONS

VEHICLE IDENTIFICATION CHART

It is important for servicing and ordering parts to be certain of the vehicle and engine identification. The VIN (vehicle identification number) is a 17 digit number visible through the windshield on the driver's side of the dash and contains the vehicle and engine identification codes. The tenth digit indicates model year and the eighth digit indicates engine code. It can be interpreted as follows:

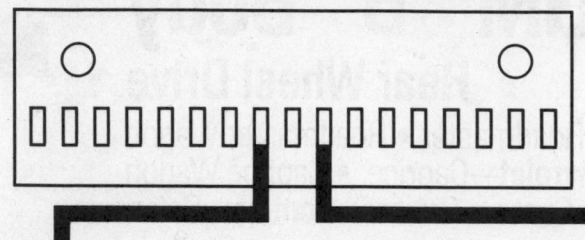

Engine Code							Model Year	
Code	Liters	Cu. In. (cc)	Cyl.	Fuel Sys.	Eng. Mfg.		Code	Year
Z	4.3	262 (4300)	6	TBI	C.P.C.		K	1989
E	5.0	305 (5011)	8	TBI	C.P.C.		L	1990
Y	5.0	305 (5011)	8	4 bbl	B.O.C.		M	1991
7	5.7	350 (5733)	8	EFI	C.P.C.		N	1992
							P	1993

B.O.C.—Buick, Oldsmobile, Cadillac
C.P.C.—Chevrolet, Pontiac, Canada
EFI—Electronic Fuel Injection
TBI—Throttle Body Injection

ENGINE IDENTIFICATION

Year	Model	Engine Displacement Liters (cc)	Engine Series (ID/VIN)	Fuel System	No. of Cylinders	Engine Type
1989	Estate Wagon	5.0 (5011)	Y	4 bbl.	8	OHV
	Caprice Sedan ①	4.3 (4300)	Z	TBI	6	OHV
	Caprice Sedan	5.0 (5011)	E	TBI	8	OHV
	Caprice Wagon	5.0 (5011)	Y	4 bbl.	8	OHV
	Caprice Sedan	5.7 (5733)	7	EFI	8	OHV
	Custom Cruiser	5.0 (5011)	Y	4 bbl.	8	OHV
	Safari	5.0 (5011)	Y	4 bbl.	8	OHV
1990	Estate Wagon	5.0 (5011)	Y	4 bbl.	8	OHV
	Caprice Sedan ①	4.3 (4300)	Z	TBI	6	OHV
	Caprice Sedan	5.0 (5011)	E	TBI	8	OHV
	Caprice Wagon	5.0 (5011)	Y	4 bbl.	8	OHV
	Caprice Sedan ②	5.7 (5733)	7	EFI	8	OHV
	Custom Cruiser	5.0 (5011)	Y	4 bbl.	8	OHV
1991	Roadmaster Sedan	5.7 (5733)	7	EFI	8	OHV
	Roadmaster Estate Wagon	5.0 (5011)	E	TBI	8	OHV
	Caprice Sedan	5.0 (5011)	E	TBI	8	OHV
	Caprice Wagon	5.0 (5011)	E	TBI	8	OHV
	Caprice Sedan ②	5.7 (5733)	7	EFI	8	OHV

ENGINE IDENTIFICATION

Year	Model	Engine Displacement Liters (cc)	Engine Series (ID/VIN)	Fuel System	No. of Cylinders	Engine Type
1991	Custom Cruiser Sedan	5.0 (5011)	E	TBI	8	OHV
	Custom Cruiser Sedan	5.7 (5733)	7	TBI	8	OHV
	Custom Cruiser Wagon	5.0 (5011)	E	EFI	8	OHV
	Custom Cruiser Wagon	5.7 (5733)	7	TBI	8	OHV
1992–93	Roadmaster Sedan	5.7 (5733)	7	EFI	8	OHV
	Roadmaster Estate Wagon	5.7 (5733)	7	EFI	8	OHV
	Caprice Sedan ③	4.3 (4300)	Z	TBi	6	OHV
	Caprice Sedan	5.0 (5011)	E	TBI	8	OHV
	Caprice Wagon	5.0 (5011)	E	TBI	8	OHV
	Caprice Wagon	5.7 (5733)	7	EFI	8	OHV
	Caprice Sedan ②	5.7 (5733)	7	EFI	8	OHV
	Custom Cruiser Sedan	5.0 (5011)	E	TBI	8	OHV
	Custom Cruiser Sedan	5.7 (5733)	7	EFI	8	OHV
	Custom Cruiser Wagon	5.0 (5011)	E	TBI	8	OHV
	Custom Cruiser Wagon	5.7 (5733)	7	EFI	8	OHV

EFI—Electronic Fuel Injection
OHV—Overhead Valves
TBI—Throttle Body Injection
① Fleet only
② Police
③ Taxi

GENERAL ENGINE SPECIFICATIONS

Year	Engine ID/VIN	Engine Displacement Liters (cc)	Fuel System Type	Net Horsepower @ rpm	Net Torque @ rpm (ft. lbs.)	Bore × Stroke (in.)	Compression Ratio	Oil Pressure @ rpm
1989	Z	4.3 (4300)	TBI	140 @ 4000	225 @ 2000	4.000 × 3.480	9.3:1	18 @ 2000
	E	5.0 (5011)	TBI	170 @ 4400	255 @ 2400	3.740 × 3.480	9.3:1	18 @ 2000
	Y	5.0 (5011)	4 bbl	148 @ 3800	250 @ 2400	3.800 × 3.385	8.0:1	40 @ 2000
	7	5.7 (5733)	TBI	195 @ 4200	295 @ 2400	4.000 × 3.500	9.8:1	18 @ 2000
1990	Z	4.3 (4300)	TBI	140 @ 4000	225 @ 2000	4.000 × 3.480	9.3:1	18 @ 2000
	E	5.0 (5011)	TBI	170 @ 4400	255 @ 2400	3.740 × 3.480	9.3:1	18 @ 2000
	Y	5.0 (5011)	4 bbl	140 @ 3200	255 @ 2000	3.800 × 3.385	8.0:1	18 @ 2000
	7	5.7 (5733)	TBI	195 @ 4200	295 @ 2400	4.000 × 3.500	9.8:1	18 @ 2000
1991	E	5.0 (5011)	TBI	170 @ 4200	255 @ 2400	3.740 × 3.480	9.3:1	18 @ 2000
	7	5.7 (5733)	TBI	195 @ 4200	295 @ 2400	4.000 × 3.500	9.8:1	18 @ 2000
1992–93	Z	4.3 (4300)	TBI	140 @ 4000	225 @ 2000	4.000 × 3.480	9.3:1	18 @ 2000
	E	5.0 (5011)	TBI	170 @ 4200	255 @ 2400	3.738 × 3.480	9.1:1	18 @ 2000
	7	5.7 (5733)	TBI	195 @ 4200	295 @ 2400	4.001 × 3.480	9.8:1	18 @ 2000

NOTE: Horsepower and torque are SAE net figures. They are measured at the rear of the transmission with all accessories installed and operating. Since the figures vary when a given engine is installed in different models, some are representative rather than exact.
EFI—Electronic Fuel Injection
TBI—Throttle Body Injection

GASOLINE ENGINE TUNE-UP SPECIFICATIONS

Year	Engine ID/VIN	Engine Displacement Liters (cc)	Spark Plug Gap (in.)	Ignition Timing (deg.)		Fuel Pump (psi)	Idle Speed (rpm)		Valve Clearance	
				MT	AT		MT	AT	In.	Ex.
1989	Z	4.3 (4300)	0.035	—	①	9–13	—	①	Hyd.	Hyd.
	E	5.0 (5011)	0.035	—	①	11	—	①	Hyd.	Hyd.
	Y	5.0 (5011)	0.060	—	①	6.0–7.5	—	①	Hyd.	Hyd.
	7	5.7 (5733)	0.035	—	①	11	—	①	Hyd.	Hyd.
1990	Z	4.3 (4300)	0.035	—	①	9–13	—	①	Hyd.	Hyd.
	E	5.0 (5011)	0.035	—	①	9–13	—	①	Hyd.	Hyd.
	Y	5.0 (5011)	0.060	—	①	6.0–7.5	—	①	Hyd.	Hyd.
	7	5.7 (5733)	0.035	—	①	9–13	—	①	Hyd.	Hyd.
1991	E	5.0 (5011)	0.035	—	①	9–13	—	①	Hyd.	Hyd.
	7	5.7 (5733)	0.035	—	①	9–13	—	①	Hyd.	Hyd.
1992	Z	4.3 (3400)	0.035	—	①	9–13	—	①	Hyd.	Hyd.
	E	5.0 (5011)	0.035	—	①	9–13	—	①	Hyd.	Hyd.
	7	5.7 (5733)	0.035	—	①	9–13	—	①	Hyd.	Hyd.
1993	SEE UNDERHOOD SPECIFICATIONS STICKER									

NOTE: The lowest cylinder pressure should be within 75% of the highest cylinder pressure reading. For example, if the highest cylinder is 134 psi, the lowest should be 101. Engine should be at normal operating temperature with throttle valve in the wide open position.
The underhood specifications sticker often reflects tune-up specification changes in production. Sticker figures must be used if they disagree with those in this chart.
Hyd.—Hydraulic
① See the Emission Control Label

FIRING ORDERS

NOTE: To avoid confusion, always replace spark plug wires one at a time.

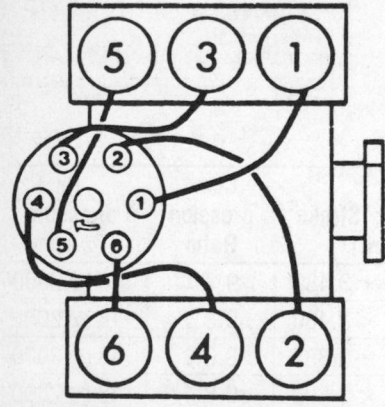

4.3L Engine
Engine Firing Order: 1–6–5–4–3–2
Distributor Rotation: Clockwise

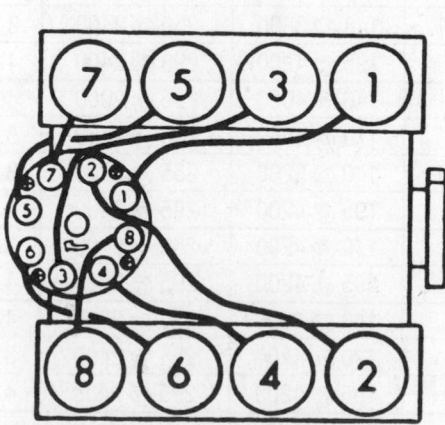

5.0L (VIN E) and 5.7L Engines
Engine Firing Order: 1–8–4–3–6–5–7–2
Distributor Rotation: Clockwise

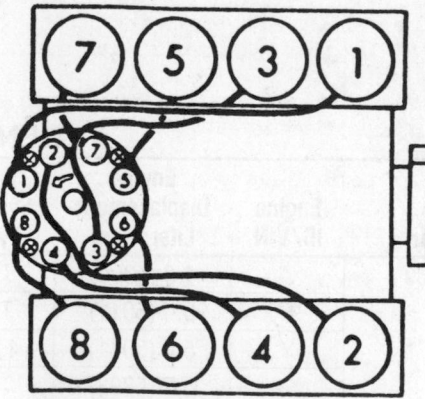

5.0L (VIN Y) Engine
Engine Firing Order: 1–8–4–3–6–5–7–2
Distributor Rotation: Counterclockwise

CAPACITIES

Year	Model	Engine ID/VIN	Engine Displacement Liters (cc)	Engine Crankcase with Filter	Transmission (pts.) 4-Spd	5-Spd	Auto.①	Drive Axle (pts.)	Fuel Tank (gal.)	Cooling System (qts.)
1989	Estate Wagon	Y	5.0 (5011)	5	—	—	7④	②	22	17.1
	Caprice Sedan	Z	4.3 (4300)	4⑧	—	—	7④	②	24.5	12.0
	Caprice Sedan	E	5.0 (5011)	5	—	—	7④	②	25	16.7
	Caprice Wagon	Y	5.0 (5011)	5	—	—	7④	②	22	17.1
	Caprice Sedan	7	5.7 (5733)	5	—	—	7④	②	25	14.9
	Custom Cruiser	Y	5.0 (5011)	5	—	—	7④	②	22	17.1
	Safari	Y	5.0 (5011)	5	—	—	7④	②	22	17.1
1990	Estate Wagon	Y	5.0 (5011)	5	—	—	7③	②	22	16.4
	Caprice Sedan⑥	Z	4.3 (4300)	4⑧	—	—	7③	②	24.5	12.0
	Caprice Sedan	E	5.0 (5011)	5	—	—	7③	②	24.5	16.7
	Caprice Wagon	Y	5.0 (5011)	5	—	—	7③	②	24.5	16.7
	Caprice Sedan⑦	7	5.7 (5733)	5	—	—	7③	②	22	14.8
	Custom Cruiser	Y	5.0 (5011)	5	—	—	7③	②	22	16.4
1991	Roadmaster Sedan	7	5.7 (5733)	5	—	—	10	②	23	14.6
	Roadmaster Estate Wagon	E	5.0 (5011)	5	—	—	10	②	23	16.7⑤
	Caprice Sedan	E	5.0 (5011)	5	—	—	10	②	23	16.7⑤
	Caprice Wagon	E	5.0 (5011)	5	—	—	10	②	23	16.7⑤
	Caprice Sedan⑦	7	5.7 (5733)	5	—	—	10	②	23	14.6
	Custom Cruiser	E	5.0 (5011)	5	—	—	10	②	23	16.7⑤
1992-93	Roadmaster Sedan	7	5.7 (5733)	5	—	—	10	②	23	16.7⑤
	Roadmaster Estate Wagon	7	5.7 (5733)	5	—	—	10	②	22	16.7⑤
	Caprice Sedan	Z	4.3 (4300)	4⑧	—	—	10	②	23	12.6⑤
	Caprice Sedan	E	5.0 (5011)	5	—	—	10	②	23	16.7⑤
	Caprice Sedan	7	5.7 (5733)	5	—	—	10	②	23	14.6⑤
	Caprice Wagon	E	5.0 (5011)	5	—	—	10	②	22	16.7⑤
	Caprice Wagon	7	5.7 (5733)	5	—	—	10	②	22	14.6⑤
	Custom Cruiser Sedan	E	5.0 (5011)	5	—	—	10	②	23	16.7⑤
	Custom Cruiser Sedan	7	5.7 (5733)	5	—	—	10	②	23	16.7⑤
	Custom Cruiser Wagon	E	5.0 (5011)	5	—	—	10	②	22	16.7⑤
	Custom Cruiser Wagon	7	5.7 (5733)	5	—	—	10	②	22	16.7⑤

① Additional transmission fluid may be required to bring level to full mark if overhauled or torque converter drained
② 7½ in. ring gear—3.5 pts.
8½ in. ring gear—4.25 pts.
8¾ in. ring gear—5.4 pts.
③ Hydra-matic 4L60-10.0 pts.
④ 700R4—10 pts.
⑤ With Heavy Duty Radiator add 0.6 qts.
⑥ Fleet only
⑦ Police
⑧ Add as necessary to bring to appropriate level.

CAMSHAFT SPECIFICATIONS

Year	Engine ID/VIN	Engine Displacement Liters (cc)	Journal Diameter 1	2	3	4	5	Elevation In.	Ex.	Clearance	End Play
1989	Z	4.3 (4300)	1.8682–1.8692	1.8682–1.8692	1.8682–1.8692	1.8682–1.8692	1.8682–1.8692	0.234	0.257	NA	0.004–0.012
	E	5.0 (5011)	1.8682–1.8692	1.8682–1.8692	1.8682–1.8692	1.8682–1.8692	1.8682–1.8692	NA	NA	NA	0.004–0.012

CAMSHAFT SPECIFICATIONS

Year	Engine ID/VIN	Engine Displacement Liters (cc)	Journal Diameter 1	2	3	4	5	Elevation In.	Ex.	Clearance	End Play
1989	Y	5.0 (5011)	2.0362	2.0360	1.9959	1.9759	1.9559	0.247	0.251	0.0038	0.006–0.022
	7	5.7 (5733)	1.8682–1.8692	1.8682–1.8692	1.8682–1.8692	1.8682–1.8692	1.8682–1.8692	0.257	0.269	NA	0.004–0.012
1990	Z	4.3 (4300)	1.8682–1.8692	1.8682–1.8692	1.8682–1.8692	1.8682–1.8692	1.8682–1.8692	0.234	0.257	NA	0.004–0.012
	E	5.0 (5011)	1.8682–1.8692	1.8682–1.8692	1.8682–1.8692	1.8682–1.8692	1.8682–1.8692	0.234	0.257	NA	0.004–0.012
	Y	5.0 (5011)	2.0362	2.0360	1.9959	1.9759	1.9559	0.247	0.251	0.0038	0.006–0.022
	7	5.7 (5733)	1.8682–1.8692	1.8682–1.8692	1.8682–1.8692	1.8682–1.8692	1.8682–1.8692	0.257	0.269	NA	0.004–0.012
1991	E	5.0 (5011)	1.8682–1.8692	1.8682–1.8692	1.8682–1.8692	1.8682–1.8692	1.8682–1.8692	0.234	0.257	NA	0.004–0.012
	7	5.7 (5733)	1.8682–1.8692	1.8682–1.8692	1.8682–1.8692	1.8682–1.8692	1.8682–1.8692	0.257	0.269	NA	0.004–0.012
1992–93	Z	4.3 (4300)	1.8682–1.8692	1.8682–1.8692	1.8682–1.8692	1.8682–1.8692	1.8682–1.8692	0.234	0.257	NA	0.001–0.009
	E	5.0 (5011)	1.8682–1.8692	1.8682–1.8692	1.8682–1.8692	1.8682–1.8692	1.8682–1.8692	0.234	0.257	NA	0.004–0.012
	7	5.7 (5733)	1.8682–1.8692	1.8682–1.8692	1.8682–1.8692	1.8682–1.8692	1.8682–1.8692	0.233	0.256	NA	0.004–0.012
	7 [1]	5.7 (5733)	1.8682–1.8692	1.8682–1.8692	1.8682–1.8692	1.8682–1.8692	1.8682–1.8692	0.257	0.269	NA	0.004–0.012

NA—Not available
[1] Police

CRANKSHAFT AND CONNECTING ROD SPECIFICATIONS

All measurements are given in inches.

Year	Engine ID/VIN	Engine Displacement Liters (cc)	Crankshaft Main Brg. Journal Dia.	Main Brg. Oil Clearance	Shaft End-play	Thrust on No.	Connecting Rod Journal Diameter	Oil Clearance	Side Clearance
1989	Z	4.3 (4300)	2.4484–2.4493①	0.0008–0.0020③	0.002–0.006	4	2.2487–2.2498	0.0013–0.0035	0.006–0.014
	E	5.0 (5011)	2.4481–2.4490④	0.0011–0.0020②	0.001–0.007	5	2.0990–2.1000	0.0013–0.0035	0.006–0.014
	Y	5.0 (5011)	2.4985–2.4995①	0.0005–0.0021③	0.003–0.013	3	2.1238–2.1248	0.0004–0.0033	0.006–0.020
	7	5.7 (5733)	2.4481–2.4990④	0.0011–0.0020②	0.001–0.007	5	2.0990–2.1000	0.0013–0.0035	0.006–0.014
1990	Z	4.3 (4300)	2.4484–2.4493①	0.0008–0.0020③	0.002–0.006	4	2.2487–2.2498	0.0013–0.0035	0.006–0.014
	E	5.0 (5011)	2.4481–2.4490④	0.0011–0.0020②	0.001–0.007	5	2.0893–2.0998	0.0013–0.0035	0.006–0.014
	Y	5.0 (5011)	2.4985–2.4995①	0.0005–0.0021③	0.003–0.013	3	2.1238–2.1248	0.0004–0.0033	0.006–0.020
	7	5.7 (5733)	2.4481–2.4990④	0.0011–0.0020②	0.001–0.007	5	2.0893–2.0998	0.0013–0.0035	0.006–0.014

CRANKSHAFT AND CONNECTING ROD SPECIFICATIONS

All measurements are given in inches.

Year	Engine ID/VIN	Engine Displacement Liters (cc)	Crankshaft				Connecting Rod		
			Main Brg. Journal Dia.	Main Brg. Oil Clearance	Shaft End-play	Thrust on No.	Journal Diameter	Oil Clearance	Side Clearance
1991	E	5.0 (5011)	2.4481–2.4490 ④	0.0011–0.0020 ②	0.001–0.007	5	2.0893–2.0998	0.0013–0.0035	0.006–0.014
	7	5.7 (5733)	2.4481–2.4490 ④	0.0011–0.0020 ②	0.001–0.007	5	2.0893–2.0998	0.0013–0.0035	0.006–0.014
1992–93	Z	4.3 (4300)	2.4485–2.4494 ⑤	0.0011–0.0023 ⑥	0.002–0.007	4	2.2487–2.2498	0.0013–0.0035	0.006–0.014
	E	5.0 (5011)	2.4481–2.4490 ④	0.0011–0.0020 ②	0.001–0.007	5	2.0893–2.0998	0.0013–0.0035	0.006–0.014
	7	5.7 (5733)	2.4481–2.4490 ④	0.0011–0.0020 ②	0.001–0.007	5	2.0893–2.0998	0.0013–0.0035	0.006–0.014

① Intermediate—2.4481–2.4490
  Rear—2.4479–2.4488
② Rear: 0.0020–0.0032

③ Intermediate—0.0011–0.0034
  Rear—0.0015–0.0031
④ Front: 2.4488–2.4493
  Rear: 2.4481–2.4488

⑤ Front: 2.4488–2.4493
  Rear: 2.4480–2.4489
⑥ Front: 0.0008–0.0020
  Rear: 0.0017–0.0032

VALVE SPECIFICATIONS

Year	Engine ID/VIN	Engine Displacement Liters (cc)	Seat Angle (deg.)	Face Angle (deg.)	Spring Test Pressure (lbs. @ in.)	Spring Installed Height (in.)	Stem-to-Guide Clearance (in.)		Stem Diameter (in.)	
							Intake	Exhaust	Intake	Exhaust
1989	Z	4.3 (4300)	46	45	194–206 @ 1.25	1.70	0.0010–0.0027	0.0010–0.0027	0.3414	0.3414
	E	5.0 (5011)	46	45	194–206 @ 1.25	1.72	0.0011–0.0027	0.0011–0.0027	NA	NA
	Y	5.0 (5011)	①	②	180–194 @ 1.27	1.72	0.0010–0.0027	0.0015–0.0032	0.3425–0.3432	0.3420–0.3427
	7	5.7 (5733)	46	45	194–206 @ 1.25	1.72	0.0011–0.0027	0.0011–0.0027	NA	NA
1990	Z	4.3 (4300)	46	45	194–206 @ 1.25	1.70	0.0010–0.0027	0.0010–0.0027	0.3414	0.3414
	E	5.0 (5011)	46	45	194–206 @ 1.25	1.70	0.0011–0.0027	0.0011–0.0027	NA	NA
	Y	5.0 (5011)	①	②	180–194 @ 1.27	1.70	0.0010–0.0027	0.0015–0.0032	0.3425–0.3432	0.3420–0.3427
	7	5.7 (5733)	46	45	194–206 @ 1.25	1.70	0.0011–0.0027	0.0011–0.0027	NA	NA
1991	E	5.0 (5011)	46	45	194–206 @ 1.25	1.70	0.0011–0.0027	0.0011–0.0027	NA	NA
	7	5.7 (5733)	46	45	194–206 @ 1.25	1.70	0.0011–0.0027	0.0011–0.0027	NA	NA
1992–93	Z	4.3 (4300)	46	45	194–206 @ 1.25	1.69–1.71	0.0011–0.0027	0.0011–0.0027	NA	NA
	E	5.0 (5011)	46	45	194–206 @ 1.25	1.70	0.0011–0.0027	0.0011–0.0027	NA	NA
	7	5.7 (5733)	46	45	194–206 @ 1.25	1.70	0.0011–0.0027	0.0011–0.0027	NA	NA

NA—Not available
① Intake—45°, Exhaust—31°
② Intake—44°, Exhaust—30°

PISTON AND RING SPECIFICATIONS

| Year | Engine ID/VIN | Engine Displacement Liters (cc) | Piston Clearance | Ring Gap | | | Ring Side Clearance | | |
				Top Compression	Bottom Compression	Oil Control	Top Compression	Bottom Compression	Oil Control
1989	Z	4.3 (4300)	0.0027	0.010–0.020	0.010–0.025	0.015–0.055	0.0012–0.0032	0.0012–0.0032	0.0020–0.0070
	E	5.0 (5011)	0.0007–0.0017	0.010–0.020	0.010–0.025	0.015–0.055	0.0012–0.0032	0.0012–0.0032	0.0020–0.0070
	Y	5.0 (5011)	0.0008–0.0018	0.009–0.019	0.009–0.019	0.015–0.055	0.0018–0.0038	0.0018–0.0038	0.0010–0.0050
	7	5.7 (5733)	0.0007–0.0017	0.010–0.020	0.010–0.025	0.015–0.055	0.0012–0.0032	0.0012–0.0032	0.0020–0.0070
1990	Z	4.3 (4300)	0.0012–0.0021	0.010–0.020	0.010–0.020	0.015–0.055	0.0012–0.0032	0.0012–0.0032	0.0020–0.0070
	E	5.0 (5011)	0.0007–0.0021	0.010–0.020	0.010–0.025	0.015–0.055	0.0012–0.0032	0.0012–0.0032	0.0020–0.0070
	Y	5.0 (5011)	0.0008–0.0018	0.009–0.019	0.009–0.019	0.015–0.055	0.0018–0.0038	0.0018–0.0038	0.0010–0.0050
	7	5.7 (5733)	0.0007–0.0021	0.010–0.020	0.010–0.025	0.015–0.055	0.0012–0.0032	0.0012–0.0032	0.0020–0.0070
1991	E	5.0 (5011)	0.0007–0.0021	0.010–0.020	0.010–0.025	0.015–0.055	0.0012–0.0032	0.0012–0.0032	0.0020–0.0070
	7	5.7 (5733)	0.0007–0.0021	0.010–0.020	0.010–0.025	0.015–0.055	0.0012–0.0032	0.0012–0.0032	0.0020–0.0070
1992–93	Z	4.3 (4300)	0.0007–0.0017	0.010–0.020	0.017–0.025	0.015–0.055	0.0014–0.0032	0.0014–0.0032	0.0014–0.0032
	E	5.0 (5011)	0.0007–0.0021	0.010–0.020	0.018–0.026	0.015–0.055	0.0012–0.0032	0.0012–0.0032	0.0020–0.0070
	7	5.7 (5733)	0.0005–0.0022	0.010–0.020	0.018–0.026	0.015–0.055	0.0012–0.0032	0.0012–0.0032	0.0020–0.0070

TORQUE SPECIFICATIONS

All readings in ft. lbs.

| Year | Engine ID/VIN | Engine Displacement Liters (cc) | Cylinder Head Bolts | Main Bearing Bolts | Rod Bearing Bolts | Crankshaft Damper Bolts | Flywheel Bolts | Manifold | | Spark Plugs | Lug [8] Nut |
								Intake	Exhaust		
1989	Z	4.3 (4300)	60–75	70–85	42–47	—	50–70	25–45	20	22	100
	E	5.0 (5011)	68	77	44	70	74	35	26	22	100
	Y	5.0 (5011)	40 [4]	[1]	18 [5]	200–310	60	40 [3]	25	25	100
	7	5.7 (5733)	68	77	44	70	74	35	26	22	100
1990	Z	4.3 (4300)	65	65	44	70 [2]	70	35	[6]	22	100 [9]
	E	5.0 (5011)	68	77	44	70 [2]	74	35	[6]	22	100 [9]
	Y	5.0 (5011)	40 [4]	[1]	18 [5]	200–310	60	40 [3]	25	25	100 [9]
	7	5.7 (5733)	68	77	44	70 [2]	74	35	[6]	22	100 [9]
1991	E	5.0 (5011)	68	77	44	70 [2]	74	35	[6]	22	100
	7	5.7 (5733)	68	77	44	70 [2]	74	35	[6]	22	100

TORQUE SPECIFICATIONS

All readings in ft. lbs.

Year	Engine ID/VIN	Engine Displacement Liters (cc)	Cylinder Head Bolts	Main Bearing Bolts	Rod Bearing Bolts	Crankshaft Damper Bolts	Flywheel Bolts	Manifold Intake	Manifold Exhaust	Spark Plugs	Lug Nut [8]
1992-93	Z	4.3 (4300)	68	77	44	70 [2]	74	35	20 [7]	11	100
	E	5.0 (5011)	68	77	44	70 [2]	74	35	20 [7]	11	100
	7	5.7 (5733)	68	77	44	70 [2]	74	35	20 [7]	11	100

[1] 80 ft. lbs. on Nos. 1-4; 120 ft. lbs. on No. 5

[2] Torque listed is for torsioner damper, crankshaft pulley is 43 ft. lbs.

[3] Dip in clean engine oil before tightening

[4] Rotate position 1, 7 & 9—120°
Rotate position 8 & 10—95°

[5] Torque in 2 steps:
1st step—18 ft.lbs.
2nd step—additional 70 degrees turn further

[6] Bolts—26 ft. lbs.
Studs—20 ft. lbs.

[7] Two inner—26 ft. lbs.

[8] Buick, wheel lug type:
$1/2 \times 20$—100 ft. lbs.
$7/16 \times 20$ steel—80 ft. lbs.
$7/16 \times 20$ aluminum—90 ft. lbs.

[9] Chevy, sedan—81 ft. lbs.
Wagon and Police—103 ft. lbs.

BRAKE SPECIFICATIONS

All measurements in inches unless noted

Year	Model	Master Cylinder Bore	Brake Disc Original Thickness	Brake Disc Minimum Thickness	Brake Disc Maximum Runout	Brake Drum Diameter Original Inside Diameter	Brake Drum Diameter Max. Wear Limit	Brake Drum Diameter Maximum Machine Diameter	Minimum Lining Thickness [1] Front	Minimum Lining Thickness [1] Rear
1989	Estate Wagon	1.125	1.043	0.980	0.004	11.00	0.090	11.060	0.030	0.030
	Caprice	1.125	1.043	0.980	0.004	11.00	0.090	11.060	0.030	0.030
	Custom Cruiser	1.125	1.043	0.980	0.004	11.00	0.090	11.060	0.030	0.030
	Safari	1.125	1.043	0.980	0.004	11.00	0.090	11.060	0.030	0.030
1990	Estate Wagon	1.125	1.043	0.980	0.004	11.00	0.090	11.060	0.030	0.030
	Caprice	1.125	1.043	0.980	0.004	11.00	0.090	11.060	0.030	0.030
	Custom Cruiser	1.125	1.043	0.980	0.004	11.00	0.090	11.060	0.030	0.030
1991	Roadmaster	1.125	1.043	0.980	0.004	11.00	0.090	11.060	0.030	0.030
	Caprice	1.125	1.043	0.980	0.004	11.00	0.090	11.060	0.030	0.030
	Custom Cruiser	1.125	1.043	0.980	0.004	11.00	0.090	11.060	0.030	0.030
1992-93	Roadmaster	1.125	1.043	0.980	0.004	11.00	0.090	11.060	0.030	0.030
	Caprice	1.125	1.043	0.980	0.004	11.00	0.090	11.060	0.030	0.030
	Custom Cruiser	1.125	1.043	0.980	0.004	11.00	0.090	11.060	0.030	0.030

[1] Replace when lining is within 0.030 in. of rivet

WHEEL ALIGNMENT

Year	Model	Caster Range (deg.)	Caster Preferred Setting (deg.)	Camber Range (deg.)	Camber Preferred Setting (deg.)	Toe-in (in.)	Steering Axis Inclination (deg.)
1989	Estate Wagon	2P-4P	3P	$0-1\frac{5}{8}$P	$\frac{13}{16}$P	$\frac{1}{32}$	$10\frac{9}{16}$
	Caprice	2P-4P	3P	$0-1\frac{5}{8}$P	$\frac{13}{16}$P	$\frac{1}{32}$	$9\frac{25}{32}$
	Custom Cruiser	2P-4P	3P	$0-1\frac{5}{8}$P	$\frac{13}{16}$P	$\frac{1}{32}$	$10\frac{19}{32}$
	Safari	2P-4P	3P	$0-1\frac{5}{8}$P	$\frac{13}{16}$P	$\frac{1}{32}$	NA
1990	Estate Wagon	2P-4P	3P	$0-1\frac{5}{8}$P	$\frac{13}{16}$P	$\frac{1}{32}$	$9\frac{3}{4}$
	Custom Cruiser	2P-4P	3P	$0-1\frac{5}{8}$P	$\frac{13}{16}$P	$\frac{1}{32}$	$9\frac{25}{32}$
	Caprice	2P-4P	3P	$0-1\frac{5}{8}$P	$\frac{13}{16}$P	$\frac{1}{32}$	$9\frac{25}{32}$

WHEEL ALIGNMENT

Year	Model	Caster Range (deg.)	Caster Preferred Setting (deg.)	Camber Range (deg.)	Camber Preferred Setting (deg.)	Toe-in (in.)	Steering Axis Inclination (deg.)
1991	Custom Cruiser	2½P–4½P	3½P	0–1⅝P	¹³/₁₆P	¹/₃₂	0
	Roadmaster	2½P–4½P	3½P	0–1⅝P	¹³/₁₆P	¹/₃₂	0
	Caprice	2½P–4½P	3½P	0–1⅝P	¹³/₁₆P	¹/₃₂	0
1992–93	Custom Cruiser	2½P–4½P	3½P	0–1⅝P	¹³/₁₆P	¹/₃₂	0
	Roadmaster	2½P–4½P	3½P	0–1⅝P	¹³/₁₆P	¹/₃₂	0
	Caprice	2½P–4½P	3½P	0–1⅝P	¹³/₁₆P	¹/₃₂	0

NA—Not available
N—Negative
P—Positive

ENGINE MECHANICAL

NOTE: Disconnecting the negative battery cable on some vehicles may interfere with the functions of the on board computer systems and may require the computer to undergo a relearning process, once the negative battery cable is reconnected.

Engine Assembly

REMOVAL & INSTALLATION
4.3L Engine

1. Relieve the fuel system pressure and disconnect the negative battery cable.
2. Remove the hood from hinges and mark for reassembly.
3. Drain coolant into a suitable container.
4. Raise and safely support vehicle.
5. Disconnect the exhaust crossover pipe at the exhaust manifolds.
6. Remove the flywheel housing cover.
7. Remove the flexplate to torque converter attaching bolts. Scribe chalk mark on the flywheel and converter for reassembly alignment.
8. Disconnect transmission oil cooler lines at the oil pan.
9. Remove right side motor mount through-bolt and loosen left side motor mount through-bolt.
10. Remove transmission to engine attaching bolts.
11. Disconnect wires at the knock sensor.
12. Disconnect the front fuel hoses from front fuel pipes.
13. Remove the lower fan shroud bolts

14. Lower the vehicle.
15. Disconnect the ECM wiring harness at the engine, and other wiring harnesses as necessary.
16. Remove the air cleaner assembly.
17. Remove the upper fan shroud.
18. Disconnect the vacuum supply hoses which supply all non-engine mounted components with engine vacuum. If equipped, the vacuum modulator, load leveler and power brake vacuum hoses should all be disconnected at the engine.
19. Disconnect accelerator and TV cables.
20. Disconnect radiator and heater hoses from engine.
21. Remove the radiator.
22. If equipped with air conditioning, disconnect compressor ground wire from the mounting bracket. Remove the electrical connector from the compressor clutch, remove the compressor to mounting bracket attaching bolts and position the compressor aside.
23. Remove power steering pump to mounting bracket bolts and position pump assembly aside.
24. Disconnect the positive battery cable and wires from the starter motor.
25. Disconnect engine to body ground strap(s) at engine.
26. Remove the AIR hose at the Catalytic converter AIR pipe and the pipe from the exhaust manifold.
27. Remove fan blade, pulleys and, if not removed already, belt(s).
28. Support the transmission.
29. Attach a safe lifting device to the engine and raise the engine enough so the remaining mounting through-bolt can be removed. Ensure the wiring harness, vacuum hoses and other parts are free and clear before lifting engine out of the vehicle.
30. Raise engine far enough to clear engine mounts, raise transmission support accordingly and alternately

until engine can be disengaged from the transmission and removed.
To install:
31. With the engine and transmission safely supported, lower engine into position and align with the transmission.
32. Install the motor mount through-bolts.
33. Install the fan blade and pulley assembly.
34. Connect the AIR hose to the catalytic converter AIR pipe and the pipe to the exhaust manifold.
35. Connect the engine ground strap(s) to the engine.
36. Connect the positive battery cable and wires to the starter motor.
37. Attach the power steering pump to mounting bracket bolts.
38. If equipped with air conditioning, connect the compressor and mounting bracket. Connect the compressor ground wire to the mounting bracket and the electrical connector to the compressor clutch.
39. Reconnect belts or serpantine belt.
40. Install radiator and connect radiator and heater hoses.
41. Connect accelerator and TV cables.
42. Reconnect vacuum hoses.
43. Install upper fan shroud.
44. Connect the air cleaner assembly.
45. Reconnect the ECM wiring harness and other engine electrical connectors.
46. Safely raise and support the vehicle.
47. Install the lower fan shroud and bolts.
48. Connect front fuel hoses to fuel pipes.
49. Connect wires to knock sensors.
50. Connect the transmission to engine attaching bolts and tighten to 35 ft. lbs. (47 Nm).

51. Connect the transmission oil cooler lines to the pan.

52. Align the flexplate to torque converter chalk marks and install the attaching bolts. Install the flywheel cover.

53. Connect the exhaust crossover pipe to the exhaust manifolds.

54. Lower vehicle. Fill cooling system and check all engine fluids

55. Align hood hinges to marks and install hood.

56. Tighten fuel filler cap and connect the negative battery cable.

57. Check fluid levels. specifications and inspect for leaks and proper operation.

5.0L and 5.7L Engines

1. Relieve the fuel system pressure and disconnect the negative battery cable.

2. Remove the hood from hinges and mark for reassembly.

3. Drain coolant into a suitable container.

4. Remove the air cleaner assembly.

5. Remove the radiator hoses and upper fan shroud.

6. Remove the radiator.

7. Remove the engine cooling fan.

8. Disconnect the heater hoses at the engine

9. Disconnect the power steering pump and air conditioning compressor brackets, if equipped, and position out of the way.

10. Disconnect the accelerator, TV, and cruise control cables.

11. Disconnect all necessary vacuum hoses.

12. Disconnect the ECM wiring harness, the engine wiring harness at the engine bulkhead, engine to bulkhead ground straps and all other wires between body and engine.

13. Set the engine on TDC and remove the distributor.

14. Remove the wiper motor, MAP sensor and battery negative to cylinder head cable.

15. Raise and support the vehicle safely.

16. Disconnect the battery positive cable and wires at the starter motor.

17. Disconnect the crossover pipe and catalytic converter as an assembly.

18. Remove the flywheel cover and torque converter to flywheel bolts.

19. Remove the engine mount through-bolts.

20. Disconnect the front fuel hoses from the front fuel pipes.

21. Disconnect the transmission converter clutch wiring at the transmission and the transmission oil cooler lines at the clip on the oil pan.

22. Disconnect the catalytic converter AIR pipe at the exhaust manifold.

23. Remove the transmission to engine bolts.

24. Lower the vehicle.

25. Support the transmission and connect a suitable lifting device to the engine.

26. Remove the engine.

To install:

27. With the engine safely supported, lower into position with the lifting device and align with the motor mounts and transmission.

28. Install motor mount through-bolts and the transmission to engine bolts. Tighten the transmission to engine bolts to 35 ft. lbs. (47 Nm).

29. Raise and support the vehicle safely.

30. Connect the catalytic converter AIR pipe to the exhaust manifold.

31. Connect the transmission converter clutch wiring to the transmission and the transmission oil cooler lines to the clip on the oil pan.

32. Connect the front fuel hoses to the front fuel pipes.

33. Install the torque converter to flywheel bolts and the flywheel housing cover.

34. Connect the crossover pipe and catalytic converter assembly.

35. Connect the battery positive cable and wires to the starter motor.

36. Lower vehicle.

37. Install the wiper motor, MAP sensor and the negative battery to cylinder head cable.

38. Set the engine on TDC and install the distributor.

39. Connect the ECM wiring harness, the engine wiring harness at the engine bulkhead, engine to bulkhead ground straps and all other wires between body and engine.

40. Connect all necessary vacuum hoses.

41. Connect the accelerator, TV and cruise control cables.

42. Connect the power steering pump and air conditioning compressor brackets, if equipped.

43. Connect the heater hoses to the engine.

44. Install the engine cooling fan.

45. Install the radiator, hoses and fan shroud.

46. Install the air cleaner assembly.

47. Install the hood, aligning the marks made during removal.

48. Connect the negative battery cable.

49. Fill the cooling system to the proper level.

50. Inspect vehicle fluid levels, specifications and verify there are no fluid leaks.

Engine Mounts

REMOVAL & INSTALLATION

1. Disconnect the negative battery cable.

2. Properly raise the engine enough to remove the weight from the engine mount.

NOTE: Do not raise or support engine with a jack under the oil pan, crankshaft pulley or any sheet metal. Because of the small clearance between the oil pan and oil pump screen, jacking against the oil pan may damage oil pickup assembly.

3. Remove the mount through-bolts.

NOTE: Verify the clearance between the rear of the engine and the firewall is sufficient enough to avoid possible damage to the distributor.

4. Raise the engine enough to remove the motor mounts and remove the mount to bracket bolts, washers and nuts. Remove the engine mounts.

To install:

5. Connect engine mount to engine or frame as necessary, insert mount bolts, nuts and washers and tighten to 47 ft. lbs. (63 Nm).

6. Lower engine into place.

7. Connect engine mount through-bolts and tighten to 47 ft. lbs. (63 Nm).

Cylinder Head

REMOVAL & INSTALLATION

1. Relieve the fuel system pressure and disconnect negative battery cable.

2. Drain cooling system into a suitable container, loosen and remove belt(s).

3. Remove the intake manifold.

4. Remove the exhaust manifold.

5. Remove the diverter valve, if equipped. If removing the left cylinder head on the 4.3L engine, remove the oil level indicator and guide tube.

6. Disconnect the power steering pump, generator, and/or air conditioning brackets, as necessary, and position aside.

7. Remove the rocker arm cover or valve cover.

8. Tag and disconnect spark plug wires from the spark plugs. Disconnect ground strap and/or negative battery cable from cylinder head as applicable.

9. Loosen cylinder head bolts gradually and in 3 passes.

10. Clean dirt from cylinder head and adjacent area to avoid getting dirt into engine.

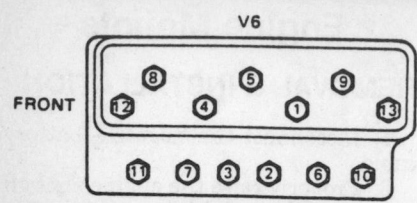

Cylinder head bolt torque sequence—4.3L engine

Cylinder head bolt torque sequence—5.0L (VIN Y) engine

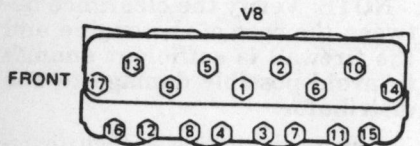

Cylinder head bolt torque sequence—5.0L and 5.7L engines (VIN E, 7)

11. If necessary, remove rocker arm assemblies and lift out pushrods.

12. Remove cylinder head.

To install:

13. Cylinder heads using a steel gasket should have both sides of the new gasket coated with a good sealer. The coating should be thin and even. Do not use sealer on composite type gaskets.

14. Place gasket over dowel pins.

15. Place cylinder head over dowel pins and gasket.

16. Coat the threads of the cylinder head bolts with sealing compound, part 1052080 or equivalent for all engines except 5.0L (VIN Y) engine. For the 5.0L (VIN Y) engine, dip the bolts in clean engine oil. Insert bolts finger-tight.

17. Following the proper torque sequence, tighten the cylinder head bolts, in 3 passes, to 68 ft. lbs. (92 Nm) for the 5.0L (VIN E) and 5.7L engines or to 65 ft. lbs. (88 Nm) for the 4.3L engine. For the 5.0L (VIN Y) engine tighten bolts to 40 ft. lbs. (54 Nm) on the first pass, then in the 2nd pass, tighten bolts 1–7 and 9 and additional 120 degrees. Finally, in a third pass, tighten bolts 8 and 10 an additional 95 degrees.

18. If removed, position pushrods and attach rocker arm assemblies.

19. Connect spark plug wires, and the body ground strap.

20. Attach rocker arm cover or valve cover.

21. Attach power steering pump, generator and/or air conditioning brackets if removed. Install the diverter valve, the oil level indicator and tube, if removed.

22. Attach the intake and exhaust manifolds.

23. Attach both ends of the negative battery to cylinder head cable.

24. Attach fuel filler cap, add coolant and inspect the engine for fluid leakage.

Valve Lifters

REMOVAL & INSTALLATION

1. Disconnect the negative battery cable.

2. Drain the coolant.

3. Remove rocker arm covers or valve covers.

4. Remove the intake manifold assembly.

5. Remove the rocker arm and pushrods. Be sure to keep them in order as they must be installed in the same bores as they were removed.

6. Remove the valve lifter retainer bolts, valve lifter retainer and the restrictor.

7. Remove the valve lifters, using the proper valve lifter removal tool. If lifters are to be reinstalled, keep them in order so that they may be installed in the same bores from which they were removed.

To install:

8. Soak the lifter assemblies with clean engine oil prior to installation. Coat the valve lifter rollers with Molykote®, prelube part 1052365 or equivalent.

9. Place valve lifters, if reinstalling, in the same location from which they were removed.

10. Install the valve lifter restrictor and lifter retainer.

11. Tighten valve lifter retainer bolts to 12 ft. lbs. (16 Nm).

12. Place pushrods in original positions and install rocker arms.

13. Install the intake manifold.

14. Install the rocker arm covers or valve covers.

15. Connect the negative battery cable and add engine coolant.

Valve Lash

ADJUSTMENT

The Chevrolet 5.0L (VIN Y) engines utilize hydraulic valve lifters, which are not adjustable. The rocker arm shaft assembly or the rockers, with pivot, are bolted to the cylinder head with a specific torque pressure, automatically positioning the lifter internal components for correct hydraulic operation. If there is excess play in the valve train, check for worn pushrods, rocker arms, valve springs and/or collapsed lifters.

The Chevrolet 4.3L, 5.0L (VIN E) and 5.7L engines do not require any routine valve lash adjustments. However, if the rocker arms are removed, the initial valve lash must be adjusted before the engine is started. Use the following procedure for Chevrolet engines.

1. Remove the rocker arm covers or valve covers.

2. Rotate the crankshaft, positioning each valve lifter on its base circle of the camshaft, remove the lash from each rocker arm and pushrod.

3. To adjust the valves, turn the engine until the mark on the vibration damper aligns with the top dead center or 0 mark on the timing tab of the front cover. At this point the engine is on the No. 1 firing position or the firing position of its opposite cylinder No. 6 on V8 engine or No. 4 on V6 engine.

NOTE: The firing cylinder may be determined by placing a finger on the No. 1 cylinder valve rocker arms as the mark on the damper comes near the 0 mark on the crankcase front cover. If the valve rocker arms moves as the mark comes up to the timing tab, the engine is on the opposite cylinder firing position, No. 6 on V8 engine or No. 4 on V6 engine and should be turned over a complete revolution to reach the No. 1 cylinder firing position.

4. With the engine in the No. 1 firing position, adjust the following valves:

    a. V8 engine—Exhaust—1, 3, 4, 8
    b. V8 engine—Intake—1, 2, 5, 7
    c. V6 engine—Exhaust—1, 5, 6
    d. V6 engine—Intake—1, 2, 3

5. Back out adjusting nut until lash is felt at the pushrod, then tighten adjusting nut until all lash is removed. This can be determined by rotating pushrod while turning adjusting nut. When play has been removed, turn adjusting nut a full additional turn clockwise, the lifter plunger will now be centered.

6. Turn the engine 1 revolution until the pointer 0 mark and the vibration damper mark are again in alignment. This is the No. 6 firing position on the V8 engine or No. 4 firing position on the V6 engine.

7. With the engine in this position, adjust the following valves:

    a. V8 engine—Exhaust—2, 5, 6, 7
    b. V8 engine—Intake—3, 4, 6, 8
    c. V6 engine—Exhaust—2, 3, 4
    d. V6 engine—Intake—4, 5, 6

8. Install the rocker arm covers or valve covers.

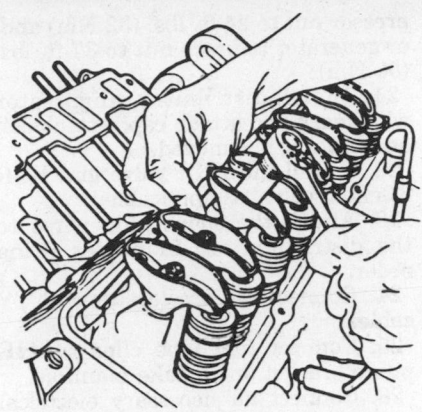

Typical valve adjustment—4.3L, 5.0L and 5.7L engines

⟵ FRONT

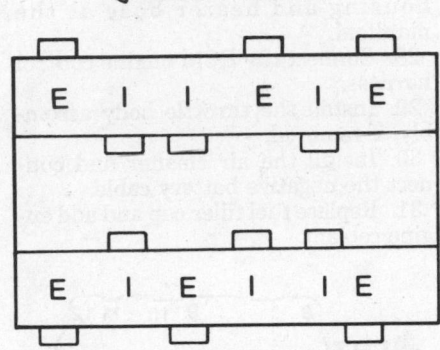

Intake and exhaust valve arrangement—4.3L engine

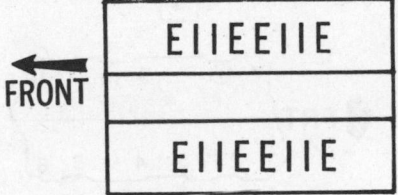

FRONT ⟵

Intake and exhaust valve arrangement—5.0L and 5.7L engines

9. Start the engine and adjust the idle speed, as required.

Rocker Arms/Shafts

REMOVAL & INSTALLATION

4.3L, 5.0L (VIN E) and 5.7L Engines

1. Disconnect the negative battery cable.

2. Remove the valve rocker covers.

3. Remove the rocker arm assembly; rocker arm nuts, rocker arm balls and rocker arms. Arrange or mark each assembly to ensure installation in original positions.

4. Remove each pushrod, if necessary, and place with the appropriate

1. Valve keys
2. Intake valve seal
3. Spring
4. Dampener rotator
5. Valve rotator
6. Exhaust valve seal
7. Identification pad
8. 22 ft. lbs.
9. Rocker arm pivot
10. Rocker arms
11. Pushrods
12. Coil spring
13. Body
14. Collar
15. Valve spring
16. Flat washer
17. Intake valve
18. Exhaust valve

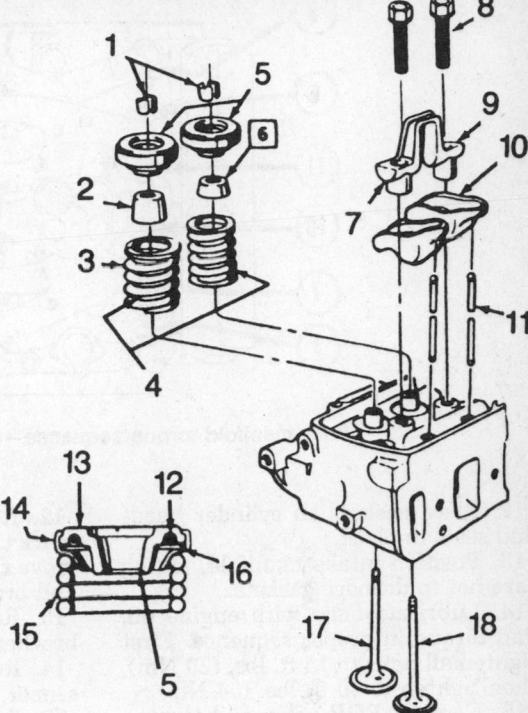

Disassembled view of the cylinder head—5.0L (VIN Y) engine

assemblies, also to ensure installation in original position.

To install:

NOTE: If new rocker arms or rocker arm balls are being installed, coat the bearing surfaces with prelube part 1052365, Molycoat® or equivalent.

5. Install the pushrods. Ensure the pushrods seat properly in the lifter socket.

6. Install the rocker arms, rocker arm balls and nuts. Tighten the rocker arm nuts until all the valve lash is eliminated.

7. Adjust the valves to proper specification.

8. Install the rocker arm covers.

9. Start the engine. Check idle speed and adjust, if necessary.

5.0L (VIN Y) Engine

1. Disconnect the negative battery cable.

2. Remove the valve covers.

3. Remove the rocker arm assemblies; rocker arm bolts, pivot and rocker arms. Indentify each rocker arm assembly to ensure installation in the original position.

To install:

4. Lubricate all wear points with 1050169 lubricant or equivalent.

5. Install the rocker arm assemblies; rocker arms, pivot and bolts.

6. Tighten bolts evenly to 22 ft. lbs. (28 Nm).

7. Install the valve covers.

8. Connect the negative battery cable and check for leaks or noise.

Intake Manifold

REMOVAL & INSTALLATION

5.0L (VIN Y) Engine

1. Disconnect the negative battery cable and drain the radiator.

2. Remove the air cleaner.

3. Disconnect hoses and pipes; upper radiator, thermostat by-pass at water pump, heater at rear of manifold, fuel, vacuum (label each hose) and AIR.

4. Disconnect the throttle and TV cables.

5. Remove generator rear brace and air conditioning rear brace.

6. Disconnect all necessary electrical leads.

7. Disconnect rear vacuum brake/idle load compensator/exhaust gas recirculation solenoid assembly and idle load compensator and bracket assembly.

8. Disconnect EGR valve.

9. Remove intake manifold bolts and manifold.

To install:

10. Clean mating surfaces and discard old gaskets.

11. Apply 1050026 sealer or equivalent, to both sides of the manifold gasket. Then apply 1052915 or equivalent RTV sealer, to the front and rear seals.

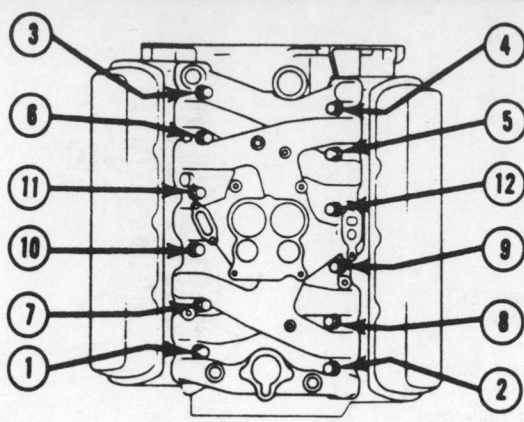

Intake manifold torque sequence—5.0 (VIN Y) engine

12. Place gaskets on cylinder heads and seals to block.

13. Position intake manifold, taking care not to dislodge gaskets.

14. Lubricate bolts with engine oil, and torque in proper sequence. First tighten all bolts to 15 ft. lbs. (20 Nm), then tighten to 40 ft. lbs. (54 Nm).

15. Connect EGR valve and tighten bolts to 20 ft. lbs. (27 Nm).

16. Connect electrical leads.

17. Connect air conditioning and generator braces.

18. Connect throttle and TV cables.

19. Connect hoses and pipes; AIR, vacuum, fuel, heater and upper radiator.

20. Install air cleaner and connect the negative battery cable.

21. Fill cooling system and inspect for leaks.

4.3L, 5.0L (VIN E) and 5.7L Engines

1. Relieve the fuel system pressure and disconnect the negative battery cable.

2. Drain the engine coolant into a suitable container and remove the air cleaner.

3. Remove the throttle body assembly, if necessary.

4. Disconnect the ECM engine control harness and lay it aside.

5. Disconnect the upper radiator hose at thermostat housing and heater hose at the manifold.

6. Remove thermostat housing and gasket, if necessary.

7. Disconnect all necessary electrical connections.

8. Disconnect fuel pipe clips at AIR pump bracket and intake manifold.

9. Disconnect accelerator and TV cables.

10. Remove the spark plug wires at the distributor cap. Mark 1 wire and location to assist in reinstallation.

11. Remove the EGR valve and EGR solenoid valve, as applicable.

12. Remove the distributor cap and mark the position of the rotor, then remove the distributor. Remove the coil and bracket as required.

13. Remove the accessory mounting brackets, as required.

14. Remove the coolant temperature sensor.

15. Remove the manifold bolts, studs and remove the intake manifold. Remove and discard the intake manifold gaskets.

To install:

16. Thoroughly clean the intake manifold and cylinder block surfaces to remove any trace of gasket material or sealant.

17. Place gasket and seals on cylinder heads and block, apply a thin bead of RTV sealer 1052289 or equivalent, to the front and rear of cylinder block. Extend the RTV bead ½ inch up each cylinder head to seal and retain gasket.

18. Install the intake manifold, manifold retaining bolts and studs taking care not to dislodge the gaskets and seals. Tighten bolts and studs in proper sequence, first to 10 ft. lbs. (14 Nm) and then to 35 ft. lbs. (47 Nm).

19. Install coolant temperature sensor.

20. Attach accessory mounting brackets, if removed. Tighten compressor brace to manifold nut to 18 ft. lbs. (24 Nm), compressor brace to com-

pressor nut to 24 ft. lbs. (32 Nm) and/or generator to brace nut to 37 ft. lbs. (50 Nm).

21. Install distributor, align rotor with mark and attach cap. Attach coil and bracket if removed.

22. Install the EGR valve and EGR solenoid valve, as applicable.

23. Attach the spark plug wires to the distributor cap in proper firing order.

24. Connect the accelerator and TV cables.

25. Connect fuel pipe clips to AIR pump bracket and intake manifold.

26. Connect all necessary electrical connections.

27. Install the thermostat housing and gasket, if removed. Connect the upper radiator hose to the thermostat housing and heater hose at the manifold.

28. Connect the ECM engine control harness.

29. Install the throttle body assembly, if removed.

30. Install the air cleaner and connect the negative battery cable.

31. Replace fuel filler cap and add engine coolant.

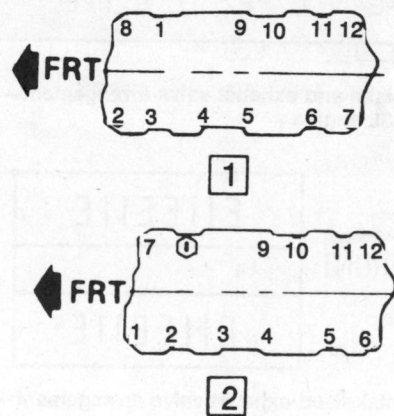

1. Initial tightening sequence
2. Final tightening sequence

Intake manifold torque sequence—4.3L engine

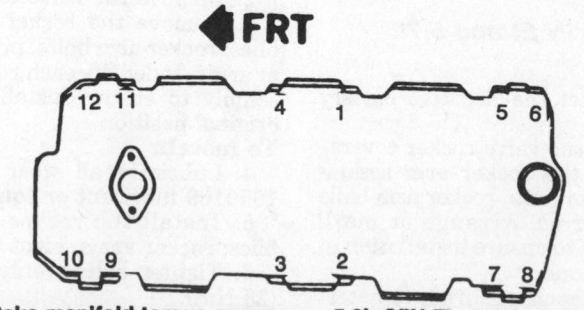

Intake manifold torque sequence—5.0L (VIN E) and 5.7L engines

32. Start the engine and inspect for leaks. Adjust timing if necessary.

Exhaust Manifold

REMOVAL & INSTALLATION

1. Disconnect the negative battery cable.
2. Raise and support vehicle safely.
3. Disconnect crossover pipe at the exhaust manifold.
4. Lower the vehicle.
5. Tag and remove spark plug wires and, if necessary, remove air cleaner.
6. Disconnect hoses, pipes, and accessory brackets, as required.
7. Remove oil level indicator and tube, if necessary and/or oxygen sensor electrical connection, if equipped.
8. Remove exhaust manifold bolts, studs, locks and washers.
9. Remove the exhaust manifold and gasket.

To install:
10. Clean mating surfaces on manifold and cylinder head.
11. Place exhaust manifold and gasket into position on cylinder head.
12. Install shields, washers, locks, studs and bolts. Tighten bolts to 25–26 ft. lbs. (34–35 Nm) and studs to 20 ft. lbs. (27 Nm).
13. Connect oxygen sensor electrical connector, if equipped and install oil level indicator tube, if removed.
14. Connect any hoses, pipes and accessory brackets which were removed.

NOTE: On fuel injected engines, it is important that fuel system pressure is relieved before disconnecting any fuel lines or connections.

15. Install air cleaner, if removed, and connect spark plug wires.
16. Raise and support vehicle safely.
17. Connect crossover pipe to the exhaust manifold and tighten nuts to 15 ft. lbs. (20 Nm).
18. Lower vehicle and connect the negative battery cable.
19. Start engine and check for leaks.

Timing Chain Front Cover

REMOVAL & INSTALLATION

5.0L (VIN Y) Engine

1. Disconnect the negative battery cable and drain the coolant.
2. Disconnect the radiator hose, heater hose and the bypass hose. Remove the fan, belts and pulley.
3. Disconnect the power steering pump bracket and, if equipped, the air conditioner compressor bracket. Position accessories and brackets aside.

4. Remove the torsional damper and crankshaft pulley.
5. Remove the front cover attaching bolts/studs and remove the cover and water pump assembly from the front of the engine.
6. Remove the dowel pins. If necessary grind a flat surface on the dowel pins to aid in removal.

To install:
7. Clean gasket mating surfaces.
8. Apply 1050026 or equivalent sealer around the coolant holes of the new cover gasket. Trim about ⅛ inch from each end of the new front pan seal and trim any excess material from the front edge of the oil pan gasket.
9. Position gasket on block and seal on front cover. Apply 1052915 or equivalent RTV sealer on the oil pan, on the seal mating surface.
10. Position front cover in place on the block, pressing to compress the oil pan seal. Guide the seal into place between the oil pan and cylinder block with a suitable small tool.
11. Apply engine oil to bolts/studs and insert 2 bolts, finger tight.
12. Install the dowel pins, chamfer ends first, through the holes in the cover.
13. Install the remaining front cover attaching bolts/studs, tighten alternately and evenly to 22 ft. lbs. (28 Nm).
14. Install the torsional damper and pulley
15. Connect the power steering pump bracket and, if equipped, the air conditioner compressor bracket.
16. Install the fan, belts and pulley. Connect the radiator hose, heater hose and the bypass hose.
17. Connect the negative battery cable and add engine coolant.

4.3L, 5.0L (VIN E) and 5.7L Engines

1. Disconnect the negative battery cable.
2. Drain the cooling system into a suitable container and remove the water pump assembly.
3. Using tool J-23523-E or equivalent, remove the torsional damper assembly.
4. Raise and safely support the vehicle. Remove the oil pan assembly.
5. Remove the engine front cover retaining bolts. Remove the front cover and discard the gasket.

To install:
6. Clean the gasket mating surfaces.
7. Coat new engine front cover gasket with sealant and place into position on the engine front cover.
8. Position cover and gasket in place and loosely install the engine front cover to block upper attaching bolts.

Tighten bolts alternately while carefully pressing downward on the engine front cover so the dowels in the block are aligned with the corresponding holes in the engine front cover. Be careful not to force the the front cover over the dowels to the point where the cover flange or dowels become distorted.
9. Install the remaining cover bolts and tighten all cover bolts alternately and evenly to 97 inch lbs. (11 Nm).
10. Install the oil pan.
11. Install the torsional damper.
12. Install the coolant pump.
13. Connect the negative battery cable and add engine coolant.

Front Cover Oil Seal

REPLACEMENT

5.0L (VIN Y) Engine

1. Disconnect the negative battery cable.
2. Remove the crankshaft pulley and torsional balancer.
3. Remove the oil seal using tool BT–6406 or J–23129 and J–1859–03 or their equivalents.

To install:
4. Coat the outside diameter of the new seal with sealer.
5. Install seal with lip facing the engine, using tool BT–6405, J–25264–A or equivalent and tighten until 0.005 inch gauge fits between front cover and tool.
6. Install crankshaft pulley and balancer.
7. Install the belts and adjust tension.
8. Reconnect the negative battery cable. Inspect cover for oil leaks.

4.3L, 5.0L (VIN E) and 5.7L Engines

1. Disconnect the negative battery cable.
2. With the torsional damper removed, remove the old seal using a suitable prying tool. Take care not to damage the front cover when removing seal.

To install:
3. Position new seal with the open end toward the inside of the engine front cover and carefully drive in the new seal with tool J–35468 or equivalent.
4. Reinstall torsional damper, connect the negative battery cable and check cover for oil leaks.

Timing Chain and Sprockets

REMOVAL & INSTALLATION

5.0L (VIN Y) Engine

1. Disconnect the negative battery cable.
2. Remove the front cover and gasket.
3. Rotate the engine until the marks on the camshaft sprocket and crankshaft sprocket are aligned with the shaft centers.
4. Remove the crankshaft oil slinger.
5. Remove the camshaft thrust button and spring.
6. Remove the fuel pump, fuel pump gasket and fuel pump eccentric.
7. Remove the camshaft sprocket and timing chain.
To install:
8. Install the camshaft timing sprocket and the timing chain with the timing marks aligned.
9. After the timing gear alignment is verified, torque the camshaft sprocket (fuel pump eccentric) bolt to 65 ft. lbs. (88 Nm).
10. Install the camshaft thrust button and spring. Install the crankshaft oil slinger.
11. Install front cover using new gasket.
12. Install fuel pump using new gasket.

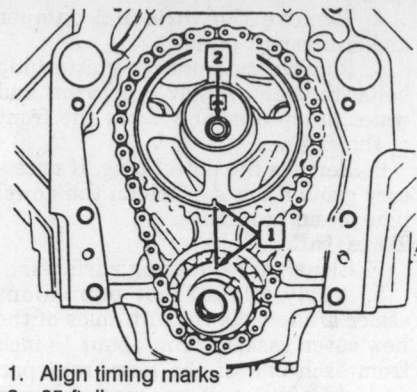

1. Align timing marks
2. 65 ft. lbs.

Timing gear alignment—5.0L (VIN Y)

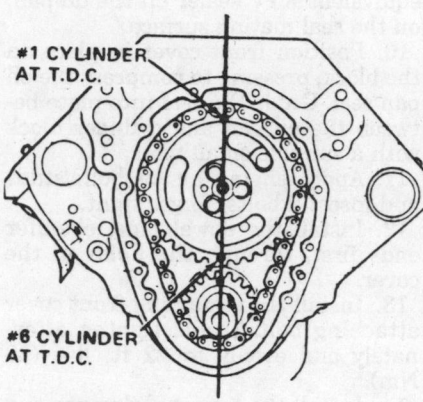

#1 CYLINDER AT T.D.C.

#6 CYLINDER AT T.D.C.

Timing gear alignment—4.3L, 5.0L (VIN E) and 5.7L engines

13. Connect the negative battery cable.

4.3L, 5.0L (VIN E) and 5.7L Engines

1. Disconnect the negative battery cable.
2. Remove the engine front cover.
3. Rotate the engine until the marks on the camshaft sprocket and crankshaft sprocket are aligned with the shaft centers.
4. Remove the camshaft sprocket retaining bolts. Remove the camshaft sprocket along with the timing chain.
To install:
5. Install the timing chain and camshaft sproket. Ensure that the timing marks on the crankshaft sprocket and the camshaft sprocket are aligned with the shaft centers.
6. Install the camshaft sprocket bolts and tighten to 21 ft. lbs. (28 Nm) Lubricate the timing chain with engine oil.
7. Install the engine front cover.
8. Connect the negative battery cable.

Timing Sprockets

The camshaft sprocket is removed during the timing chain removal procdure. The following procedures may be used if the crankshaft sprocket must also be removed.

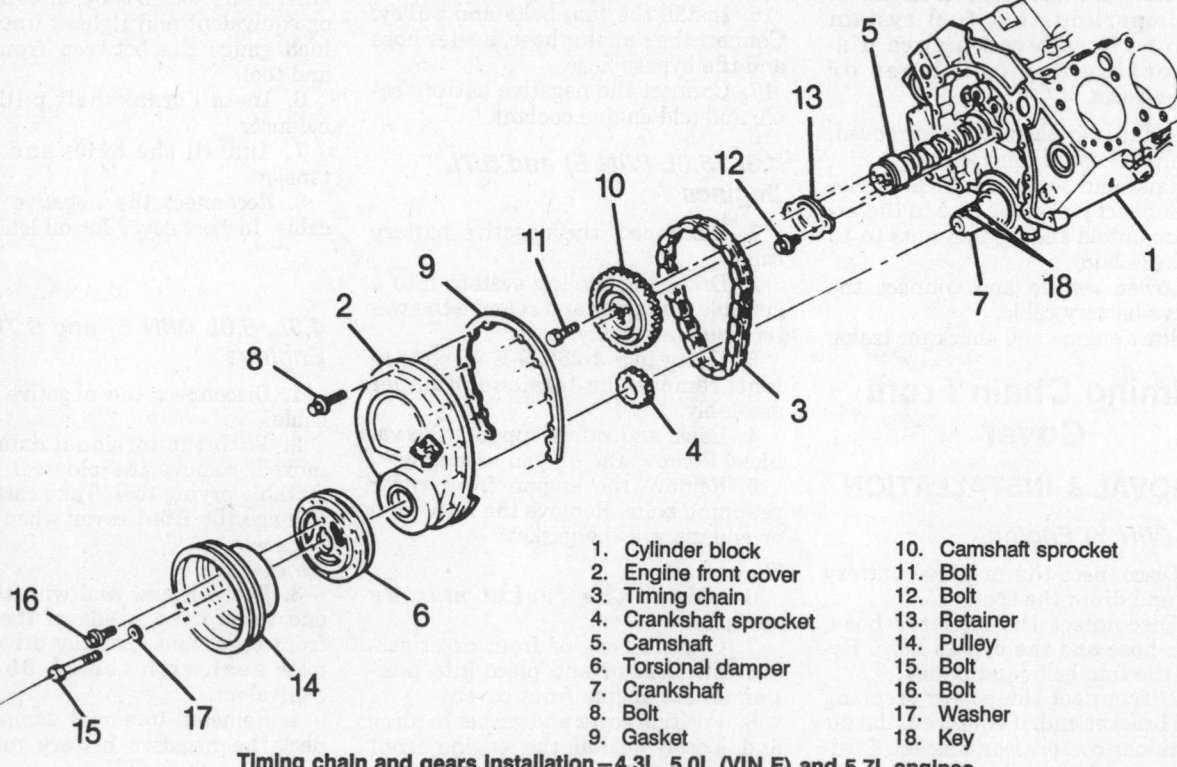

1. Cylinder block
2. Engine front cover
3. Timing chain
4. Crankshaft sprocket
5. Camshaft
6. Torsional damper
7. Crankshaft
8. Bolt
9. Gasket
10. Camshaft sprocket
11. Bolt
12. Bolt
13. Retainer
14. Pulley
15. Bolt
16. Bolt
17. Washer
18. Key

Timing chain and gears installation—4.3L, 5.0L (VIN E) and 5.7L engines

REMOVAL & INSTALLATION

5.0L (VIN Y) Engine

1. Disconnect negative battery cable.
2. Remove the timing chain and camshaft sprocket.
3. Remove the spark plugs.

NOTE: The crankshaft key has a blind keyway. The key must be removed before removing the crankshaft sprocket.

4. Remove the crankshaft key.
5. Remove the crankshaft sprocket, using removal tool BT–6812, J–25287, J–21052 or equivalent.
To install:
6. Place the timing chain on a flat surface.
7. Insert the camshaft and crankshaft timing sprockets into the timing chain with the timing marks aligned. Ensure this alignment is maintained through out the remaining procedure.
8. Place the sprockets with the timing chain into position.
9. Rotate the camshaft sprocket as required until it engages with the camshaft. With the camshaft sprocket engaged, install the fuel pump eccentric with the flat side toward the engine.
10. Install the camshaft sprocket bolt until finger-tight.
11. Rotate the crankshaft until the crankshaft sprocket and keyway are in alignment. When the keyway is aligned, tap the crankshaft key into place with a brass hammer until the key bottoms.
12. Check the timing marks are still in alignment.

NOTE: When the timing marks are aligned, the No. 6 piston is at TDC. When both timing marks are on top, the No. 1 piston is in the firing position.

13. After the timing gear alignment is verified, torque the camshaft sprocket (fuel pump eccentric) bolt to 65 ft. lbs. (88 Nm).
14. Install the camshaft thrust button and spring. Install the crankshaft oil slinger.
15. Install front cover using new gasket.
16. Install fuel pump using new gasket.
17. Install the spark plugs and connect the negative battery cable.

4.3L, 5.0L (VIN E) and 5.7L Engines

1. Disconnect the negative battery terminal.
2. Remove the timing chain and camshaft sprocket.
3. Remove the crankshaft sprocket using tool J–5825-A or equivalent.

4. Remove crankshaft key, if required.
To install:
5. Install crankshaft key, if removed.
6. Install the crankshaft sprocket using tool J-5590 or equivalent.
7. Install timing chain and camshaft.
8. Connect the negative battery.

Camshaft

REMOVAL & INSTALLATION

5.0L (VIN Y) Engine

1. Properly discharge the air conditioning system. Disconnect the negative battery cable.
2. Drain the cooling system into a suitable container.
3. Remove the upper radiator baffle.
4. Disconnect the upper radiator hose.
5. Remove the radiator assembly.
6. Remove the air cleaner assembly.
7. Disconnect the throttle cable.
8. Remove accessory brackets and drive belts. Position accessories aside with lines and connectors attached.
9. Remove AIR pump pulley.
10. Remove the fan, fan clutch and water pump pulley.
11. Disconnect the thermostat bypass hose.
12. Disconnect the electrical and vacuum connections.
13. Remove the AIR pump.
14. Remove distributor with cap and wiring intact.
15. Remove crankshaft pulley and hub.
16. Remove the fuel pump.
17. Remove engine front cover.
18. Remove both valve covers.
19. Remove intake manifold, gaskets and seals.
20. Remove rocker arms assemblies, pushrods and valve lifters.

NOTE: All parts for each assembly must be kept together and re-installed in the same location.

21. Disconnect and plug the air conditioner condenser lines.
22. Remove the condenser assembly.
23. Remove bolt securing fuel pump eccentric, remove eccentric, camshaft gear, oil slinger and timing chain.
24. Remove camshaft retaining plate and flange adapter.
25. Remove camshaft by carefully sliding it out the front of the engine.
To install:
26. Lubricate the camshaft with 1051396 or equivalent, and carefully insert into journals.
27. Install camshaft flange adapter and retaining plate.

28. Timing chain and sprockets.
29. Install fuel pump eccentric.
30. Install camshaft thrust spring and button.
31. Install the front cover and fuel pump with new gaskets.
32. Install condenser assembly and lines.
33. Install valve lifters, pushrods and rocker arm assemblies.
34. Install valve covers.
35. Install intake manifold, with new gaskets. Connect fuel lines.
36. Install crankshaft pulley and hub.
37. Install AIR pump.
38. Connect all electrical connections and vacuum hoses.
39. Connect thermostat bypass hose.
40. Install water pump pulley, fan clutch and fan.
41. Connect AIR pump pulley.
42. Install remaining accessory brackets and drive belts.
43. Connect the throttle cable.
44. Install the air cleaner assembly.
45. Install the radiator, hoses and baffle.
46. Connect the negative battery cable and add engine coolant.
47. Check for leaks and recharge air conditioning.

4.3L, 5.0L (VIN E) and 5.7L Engines

1. Disconnect the negative battery cable.
2. Remove the intake manifold
3. Remove the rocker arm assemblies and pushrods.
4. Loosen the belt tensioner and remove the serpentine belt.
5. Remove the upper fan shroud, radiator hoses, oil cooler lines and the radiator.
6. Remove the timing chain.
7. Properly discharge the air conditioning, disconnect and remove the condensor.
8. Remove the valve lifters.
9. Remove the camshaft retainer bolts and the camshaft retainer.
10. Install three 4 inch long bolts in the camshaft bolt holes and carefully pull camshaft from bearings.
To install:
11. Coat camshaft lobes and journals with prelube 1052365 or equivalent.
12. Carefully slide camshaft into the block.
13. Install the camshaft retainer and retainer bolts. Tighten bolts to 106 inch lbs. (12 Nm).
14. Install the timing chain.
15. Install new valve lifters to assure durability of the camshaft lobes and lifter rollers.
16. Install the air conditioning condenser.

17. Install the radiator, oil cooler lines and radiator hoses.

18. Install the serpentine drive belt.

19. Install the upper fan shroud.

20. Install the pushrods and rocker arm assemblies.

21. Install the intake manifold.

22. Connect the negative battery, add coolant, and adjust valves as necessary.

Piston and Connecting Rod

Positioning

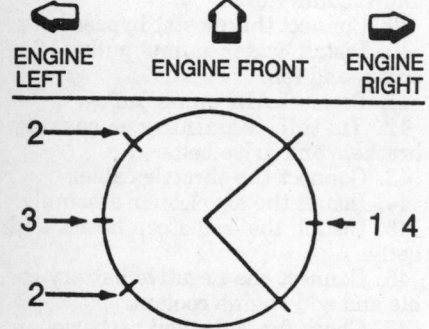

1. Oil ring spacer gap (tang in hole or slot within arc)
2. Oil ring rail gaps
3. 2nd compression ring gap
4. Top compression ring gap

Piston ring gap locations—V6 and V8 engines

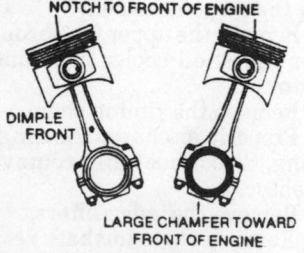

Piston assembly—5.0L (VIN E) and 5.7L engines

ENGINE LUBRICATION

Oil Pan

REMOVAL & INSTALLATION

5.0L (VIN Y) Engine

1. Disconnect negative battery cable.

2. Remove oil level indicator.

3. Remove upper fan shroud and attaching screws.

4. Raise and safely support vehicle.

5. Drain oil pan.

6. Remove flywheel cover, crossover pipe and starter.

7. Install engine support and adapter tools BT-7109, BT-7203 and BT-6501 or equivalent.

8. Disconnect engine mounts at cylinder block.

9. Carefully raise front of engine high enough and remove oil pan.

To install:

10. Clean the gasket mating surfaces and apply 1050026 or equivalent sealer to both sides of the new gasket.

11. Position gasket in place on the oil pan. Wipe front and rear seals with engine oil and position in place.

12. Apply 1052915 or equivalent RTV sealer to oil pan seals and install oil pan.

13. Install oil pan bolts, tighten to 97 inch lbs. (11 Nm), and nuts, tighten to 17 ft. lbs. (23 Nm).

14. Lower engine sufficiently to install mounts, then lower engine fully and remove bar.

15. Install the crossover pipe, starter and flywheel cover.

16. Lower vehicle and install oil level indicator.

17. Install upper fan shroud and attaching screws.

18. Fill crankcase with engine oil, connect the negative battery cable and check for leaks.

4.3L, 5.0L (VIN E) and 5.7L Engines

1. Disconnect the negative battery cable and remove the air cleaner assembly.

2. Remove the distributor cap and wires.

3. Remove the transmission and oil dipsticks.

4. Remove the upper fan shroud.

5. Raise and safely support the vehicle.

6. Drain the engine oil.

7. Disconnect the exhaust pipe at the manifolds. Remove the flywheel cover. On the 4.3L engine, disconnect the AIR pipe to converter at the exhaust manifold.

8. Disconnect the transmission fluid cooler lines at the clips on the oil pan.

9. Remove the transmission dipstick tube.

10. Remove the starter motor assembly.

11. If equipped with an oil level sensor, it must be disconnected and removed to prevent possible damage to the oil level sensor, oil pump pickup screen and pipe.

12. Disconnect the engine mount through-bolts and raise the front of the engine as far as possible.

13. Remove the oil pan attaching nuts, bolts and reinforcement.

14. Place the crankshaft timing mark to the 6 o'clock position in order to move the crankshaft out of the way, the remove the pan and discard the old gasket.

To install:

15. Clean the gasket mating surfaces. Apply a small amount of 1052914 or equivalent sealer to the front and rear cover to cylinder block junctions and continue bead 1 inch in either direction from the radius of the cavity.

16. Install the new gasket on the oil pan, and position the oil pan in place with loosely installed nuts, bolts and reinforcement.

17. Lower the engine.

18. Tighten the oil pan nuts to 17 ft. lbs. (23 Nm) and bolts to 97 inch lbs. (11 Nm).

19. Connect the engine mount through-bolts.

20. If equipped, install the oil level sensor and electrical connection.

21. Install the starter motor assembly.

22. Connect the transmission fluid cooler lines to the clips on the oil pan and install the transmission dipstick tube.

23. Install the flywheel cover. Connect the exhaust pipe to the manifolds. On the 4.3L engine, disconnect the AIR pipe to converter at the exhaust manifold.

24. Lower the vehicle.

25. Install the upper fan shroud.

26. Install the transmission and oil dipsticks.

27. Install the distributor cap and wires.

28. Install the air cleaner assembly.

29. Reconnect the battery cable, refill crankcase with proper engine oil and check engine for leaks.

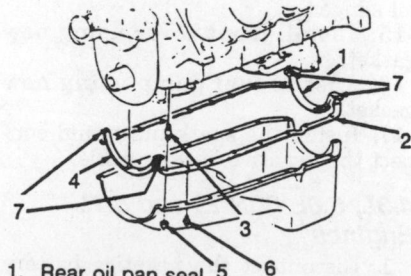

1. Rear oil pan seal
2. Side gaskets
3. Fully seat bolt
4. Front oil pan seal
5. 17 ft. lbs.
6. 10 ft. lbs.
7. Apply sealer

Oil pan and gasket—5.0L (VIN Y) engine

Oil Pump

REMOVAL & INSTALLATION

1. Disconnect the negative battery cable.
2. Remove the oil pan.
3. Remove the pump attaching bolts and remove the pump.

To install:
4. Install oil pump driveshaft with the drive tang on the distributor driveshaft.
5. Tighten the pump retaining bolts to 35 ft. lbs. (47 Nm) for 5.0L (VIN Y) engine or 77 ft. lbs. (105 Nm) for 4.3L, 5.0L (VIN E) and 5.7L engines.
6. Install oil pan.
7. Connect the negative battery cable, check engine oil level and start the engine. Watch the indicator light or oil pressure gauge to ensure immediate oil pump operation.

Rear Main Bearing Oil Seal

REMOVAL & INSTALLATION

5.0L (VIN Y) Engines

1. Remove the oil pan. Remove the oil pump, if required. Remove the rear main bearing cap.
2. Pry the lower seal out of the bearing cap with a suitable tool, being careful not to gouge the cap surface.
3. Remove the upper seal by lightly tapping on 1 end with a brass pin punch until the other end can be grasped and pulled out.
4. Clean the bearing cap, cylinder block and crankshaft mating surfaces with solvent. Inspect all these surfaces for gouges, nicks and burrs.
5. Apply a sealer, Loctite® 414, Fel-Pro Mighty Grip® or equivalent, to the seal groove.
6. Insert the seal with tool J25282-2, BT-6433 or equivalent seal installer into the grooves.
7. Cut the excess seal material flush with the surface.
8. Apply sealer to the cylinder block only where the cap mates to the surface.
9. Install the rear cap and torque the bolts to specifications. Do not use attaching bolt to draw rear cap into place, tap into place with a brass or leather mallet before inserting bolts and tightening to 120 ft. lbs. (163 Nm).
10. Install oil pump and oil pan.

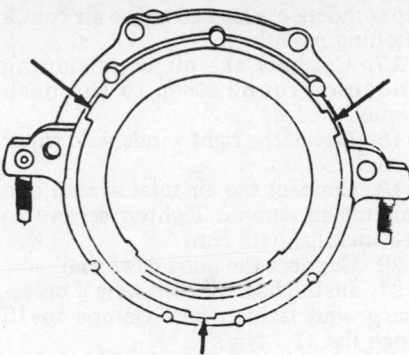

Rear main seal removal—4.3L, 5.0L (VIN E) and 5.7L engines

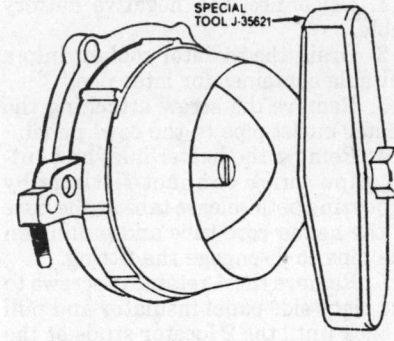

Installing rear main seal—4.3L, 5.0L (VIN E) and 5.7L engines

4.3L, 5.0L (VIN E) and 5.7L Engines

1. Remove the transmission from the vehicle.
2. Remove the flywheel.

NOTE: Care should be taken when removing the seal so as not to nick the crankshaft sealing surface.

3. Using the notches provided in the rear seal retainer, pry out the seal using a suitable tool.
To install:
4. Coat new seal entirely with clean oil.
5. Install the seal on tool J–35621 or equivalent. Thread the tool into the rear of the crankshaft seal retainer. Tighten the screws snugly, this is to insure the seal will be installed squarely over the crankshaft. Tighten the tool wing nut until it bottoms.
6. Remove the tool from the crankshaft seal retainer.
7. Install flywheel and the transmission.

ENGINE COOLING

Radiator

REMOVAL & INSTALLATION

1. Disconnect the negative battery cable.
2. Drain the radiator and remove the fan shrouds.
3. Disconnect the radiator inlet and outlet hoses.
4. Disconnect and plug the transmission fluid and/or oil cooler lines from the radiator.
5. Disconnect the low fluid sensor connector, if equipped.
6. Disconnect the coolant reservoir hose from the radiator.
7. Disconnect the heater hose, if applicable, and remove the radiator from the vehicle.
To install:
8. Position radiator in place making sure the radiator is seated on the insulators.
9. Connect the coolant recovery hose to the filler neck.
10. Connect the transmission fluid lines to the radiator and tighten to 18 ft. lbs. (24 Nm).
11. Connect the engine oil cooler lines to the radiator, if equipped, and tighten to 18 ft. lbs. (24 Nm).
12. Connect the radiator inlet and outlet hoses and clamps to the radiator.
13. Connect the heater hose and clamp to the radiator.
14. If equipped, connect the low coolant sensor.
15. Connect the upper and lower fan shrouds.
16. Connect the negative battery cable, add coolant and check system for leaks.

Heater Core

REMOVAL & INSTALLATION

Without Air Conditioning

1. Disconnect the negative battery cable and drain the engine coolant into a suitable container.
2. Disconnect the heater hoses and clamps at the heater core inlet and outlet pipes.
3. Disconnect the blower wiring.
4. Remove the blower cover housing screws and the cover housing.
5. Remove the heater core.
To install:
6. Clean sealer from the mating

flange surfaces of the heater module and blower cover housing.

7. Install heater core into the blower cover housing.

8. Apply an even ribbon of sealer completely around the flange of the blower cover housing from the edge of the rim inward to a width that covers the mounting screw holes.

9. Install the blower cover housing to the heater module with the blower cover housing screws.

10. Connect the heater hoses a the heater core inlet and outlet pipes, using new clamps and tightening them to 15 inch lbs. (1.7 Nm).

11. Connect the blower wiring.

12. Connect the negative battery cable, add engine coolant and test system for leaks.

With Air Conditioning

1989–90

1. Disconnect the negative battery cable.

2. Drain the engine coolant into a suitable container.

3. Disconnect the heater hoses and clamps at the heater core inlet and outlet pipes.

4. Pull the hood cowl seal up and off the air conditioning module flange.

5. Remove the air inlet screen attaching screws and the air inlet screen.

6. Remove the right side windshield wiper arm.

7. Remove the air conditioning module ground strap from the dash panel.

8. Disconnect all electrical connectors from components located in the air conditioning module.

9. Remove the flange mounting screws and lift the upper case straight up and off.

10. Remove the heater core and pipe seal.

To install:

11. Clean old sealer from the upper case mounting flange.

12. Fit the heater core to the mounting clip at the bottom of the air conditioning module lower case and install the core pipes seal.

13. Apply an even ribbon of sealer around flange from the edge of the rim inwards to a uniform width that covers the mounting screw holes.

14. Carefully lower the upper case into position making sure that no seals or insulators become dislodged.

15. Connect the flange mounting screws, beginning with the upper outboard flange mounting screw first, then the upper inboard screw. Continue the pattern clockwise until all screws are fastened to 27 inch lbs. (2.8 Nm).

16. Connect all electrical connectors

to components located in the air conditioning module.

17. Connect the air conditioning module ground strap to the dash panel.

18. Install the right windshield wiper arm.

19. Connect the air inlet screen and mounting screws. Tighten screws to 13 inch lbs. (1.5 Nm).

20. Connect the hood cowl seal.

21. Install heater hoses, new if necessary, and tighten new clamps to 15 inch lbs. (1.7 Nm).

22. Connect the negative battery cable.

23. Add coolant and check system for leaks.

1991–93

1. Disconnect the negative battery cable.

2. Drain the radiator coolant into a suitable container for later use.

3. Remove the screw attaching the heater outlet pipe to the cowl panel.

4. Remove the heater inlet and outlet pipe quick connect fittings by squeezing both release tabs at the base of the heater core tube and pulling on the pipe to disengage the fitting.

5. Remove the 4 retaining screws to the right side panel insulator and pull it back until the 2 locator studs at the forward edge are disengaged. Remove the panel insulator.

6. Remove the instrument panel lower reinforcement by removing the nut from the shroud panel stud and the screw from the instrument panel carrier.

7. Remove the 2 vacuum harness connectors at the lower evaporator case and position them out of the way.

8. Remove the right side trim panel by pulling it away from the pillar.

9. Remove the 7 lower evaporator case attaching screws.

10. Remove the lower evaporator housing.

11. Remove the heater core mounting straps and screws.

12. Remove the heater core by pulling it rearward and working the heater core tubes out of the seal.

To install:

13. Install heater core into position, carefully guiding the heater core tubes through the seals at the cowl panel. Connect heater core mounting straps and screws.

NOTE: If installing new heater core, transfer the quick connect tabs to the tubes of the replacement core.

14. Clean old sealer from mating surfaces of the exposed flanges.

15. Place a ribbon of new sealer on the lower evaporator case mounting flanges.

16. Guide the lower evaporator case into place, taking care to avoid wiping sealer from flanges.

17. Connect lower evaporator case with attaching screws. Begin with 2 screws mounted finger tight to hold the case in position. Install all screws and tighten evenly to compress flange.

18. Connect the vacuum harness connectors.

19. Attach the lower instrument panel reinforcement with the nut to the shroud panel and the screw to the instrument panel carrier both tightened to 89 inch lbs. (10 Nm).

20. Snap the right side pillar trim panel into place.

21. Slide the right side sound insulator into place to engage the locator studs and install the retaining screws. Tighten screws to 17 inch lbs. (1.9 Nm).

22. Connect the heater core inlet and oulet pipe quick connect fittings by aligning the tabs with the grooves in the fitting sleeve and pushing the sleeve into place on the heater core tube. Check for proper pipe installation.

23. Tighten the heater outlet pipe retaining screw to 17 inch lbs. (1.9 Nm).

24. Connect negative battery cable.

25. Refill coolant to proper level. Operate system and inspect for proper operation or leakage.

Water Pump

REMOVAL & INSTALLATION

1. Disconnect the negative battery cable.

2. Remove cooling fan as follows:

   a. Remove upper and lower fan shrouds.

   b. Remove nuts and fan clutch with cooling fan.

   c. Remove spacer if equipped, and if necessary remove bolts connecting cooling fan and clutch.

NOTE: If equipped with a clutch fan, keep the fan in an upright position during repairs to prevent the silicone fluid from leaking out.

3. Loosen and remove the serpentine belt from the coolant pump pulley and remove the pulley.

4. Drain the cooling system.

5. Unfasten the heater bypass and radiator hose from the pump, as equipped.

6. If required, remove the alternator, air conditioning compressor and/or power steering brackets.

7. Remove the bolts securing the water pump and remove the pump.

To install:

8. Clean cylinder block and coolant

pump gasket surfaces and discard old gaskets.

9. Place new gaskets on coolant pump and mounting bolts and attach coolant pump making sure gaskets remain in proper position. Tighten mounting bolts to 30 ft. lbs. (41 Nm).

10. If removed, connect the alternator, air conditioning compressor and/or power steering brackets.

11. Fasten heater bypass and radiator hose, as equipped, to the pump.

12. Attach coolant pump pulley and serpentine belt to the coolant pump.

WARNING: Inspect fan blade for bends or damage. Do not use or attempt to repair a fan blade which has been bent or damaged. It is essential that a fan blade remains in balance to prevent failure and possible injury.

13. Attach cooling fan as follows:

a. Attach cooling fan to the fan clutch, if removed, with bolts. Tighten bolts to 18 ft. lbs. (24 Nm).

b. Place spacer, if equipped, and attach fan assembly to the cooling pump. Be sure to align reference marks on the fan clutch and coolant pump hub.

c. Tighten nuts to 18 ft. lbs. (24 Nm).

d. Attach upper and lower fan shrouds and tighten screws to 53 inch lbs. (5.8 Nm).

14. Connect the negative battery cable and add coolant to engine.

15. Start engine and check for leaks.

Thermostat

REMOVAL & INSTALLATION

1. Disconnect the negative battery cable.

2. Drain the coolant from the radiator into a suitable container until the level is below the thermostat housing.

3. Remove the air cleaner assembly, if necessary, and remove the radiator inlet hose from the thermostat housing.

4. Remove the thermostat housing bolts and remove the thermostat.

5. Installation is the reverse of removal. Clean the sealing surfaces, use a new gasket and tighten the housing retaining bolts to 19–21 ft. lbs. (25–28 Nm).

Cooling System Bleeding

1. With the cooling system completely drained, begin adding a combination of ethylene glycol antifreeze and water until achieving a mixture of at least 50 percent and not exceeding 70 percent antifreeze.

2. Fill the radiator up to the lower portion of the filler neck.

3. Fill the coolant recovery reservoir to the **COLD FILL** mark and install the coolant recovery cap.

4. Start the vehicle and run the engine with the radiator cap **OFF** until normal engine operating temperature is reached.

5. With the engine idling, add coolant to the radiator until the level reaches the bottom of the filler neck.

6. Reinstall the radiator cap, ensuring the arrow on the cap is aligned with the coolant recovery hose.

7. Inspect the system for leaks.

ENGINE ELECTRICAL

NOTE: Disconnecting the negative battery cable on some vehicles may interfere with the functions of the on board computer systems and may require the computer to undergo a relearning process when the negative battery cable is reconnected.

Distributor

All vehicles use a High Energy Ignition (HEI) distributor with Electronic Spark Timing (EST). The HEI system incorporates a distributor cap, rotor, ignition module, pole piece with internal teeth and pickup coil. Vehicles use either an internally distributor mounted coil or an externally mounted ignition coil. Spark timing changes are controlled electronically by the Engine Control Module (ECM), which monitors various engine sensors, computes the desired spark timing and signals the distributor to change the timing accordingly.

REMOVAL

1. Disconnect the negative battery cable.

2. Disconnect and tag the ignition wire, tachometer wire, if equipped, and 3 terminal connector from distributor cap or externally mounted coil.

NOTE: Use care when releasing the connector locking tabs on the distributor cap.

3. Remove distributor cap with the spark plug wires attached and position it aside.

4. Disconnect the 4 terminal connector from the distributor.

5. Remove the distributor hold-down bolt and clamp. Mark the position of the rotor in relation to the engine. Pull the distributor from the engine until the rotor just stops turning counterclockwise. Again mark the position of rotor.

INSTALLATION

Timing Not Disturbed

NOTE: To ensure correct ignition timing if the engine has not been disturbed, the distributor must be installed with the rotor in the same position as when removed.

1. Align the rotor to the last mark made, tilt distributor toward the driver's side of the vehicle and slide the distributor into the engine.

2. The rotor should turn and end up at the first mark made.

3. Reconnect distributor hold-down bolt and clamp, and all connectors or wires in the reverse order of removal.

4 Check the timing when finished.

Timing Disturbed

1. Remove the No. 1 spark plug. Place a finger over the spark plug hole and slowly rotate the engine in the normal direction of rotation, until compression is felt.

2. Align the timing mark on the crankshaft pulley to the **0** on the engine timing indicator by slowly rotating the engine in the same direction.

3. Position the rotor between No. 1 and No. 8 spark plug towers on the V8 engine or the No. 1 and No. 6 spark plug towers on the V6 engine.

4. Install the distributor, distributor cap, spark plug wiring and connectors.

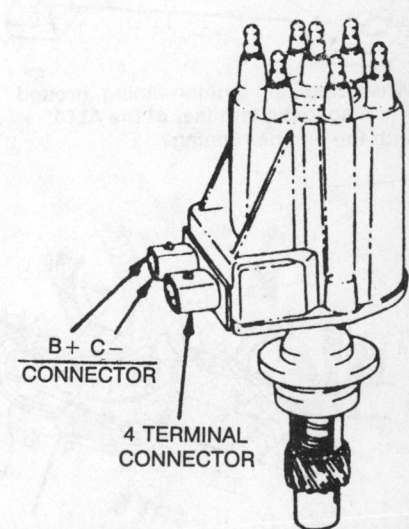

HEI distributor with externally mounted coil

5. Check the engine timing and adjust, as required.

Ignition Timing

ADJUSTMENT

NOTE: Some engines will incorporate a magnetic timing probe hole for the use with electronic timing equipment. Be sure to consult the equipment manufactures instructions for the use of this equipment.

1989–90

1. Warm the engine to operating temperature. Be sure the choke is fully open and the air conditioning is OFF.

2. With the engine running, ground the diagnostic terminal of the 12 terminal ALDL connector.

3. Connect a timing light with the pickup lead on the No. 1 plug wire and check timing at correct engine rpm as designated by the vehicle emissions information label.

4. If the timing requires adjustment, loosen the distributor and set the timing to the specifications noted on the information label.

5. Once the timing has been set and with the engine still running, disconnect the ground from the diagnostic terminal. If done before engine is shut off, no trouble codes should be set.

6. If present, any stored trouble codes may be cleared by removing the ECM fuse for 15 seconds.

1991–93

1. Warm the engine to operating temperature. Be sure the choke is fully open and the air conditioning is OFF.

2. With the engine running, disconnect the EST bypass connector located by the right front air control valve. An Engine Control Module (ECM) trouble code will set when this is done.

3. Connect the timing light with the pickup lead on the No. 1 plug wire and check timing at the correct engine rpm as designated on the vehicle emission information label.

4. If the timing requires adjustment, loosen the distributor and set the timing to the specifications noted on the information label.

5. Once the timing has been set, turn the engine OFF and reconnect the EST bypass connector.

6. Clear any stored trouble codes by interrupting power to the ECM. This can be accomplished, depending on the model, by disconnecting the ECM power feed, the ECM fuse in the fuse box or the battery cable for at least 30 seconds.

Alternator

PRECAUTIONS

Several precautions must be observed with alternator equipped vehicles to avoid damage to the unit.

- If the battery is removed for any reason, make sure it is reconnected with the correct polarity. Reversing the battery connections may result in damage to the 1-way rectifiers.
- When utilizing a booster battery as a starting aid, always connect the positive to positive terminals and the negative terminal from the booster battery to a good engine ground on the vehicle being started.
- Never use a fast charger as a booster to start vehicles.
- Disconnect the battery cables when charging the battery with a fast charger.
- Never attempt to polarize the alternator.
- Do not use test lamps of more than 12 volts when checking diode continuity.
- Never operate the alternator with the output terminal disconnected.
- Do not short across or ground any of the alternator terminals.
- The polarity of the battery, alternator and regulator must be matched and considered before making any electrical connections within the system.
- Never separate the alternator on an open circuit. Make sure all connections within the circuit are clean and tight.
- Disconnect the battery ground terminal when performing any service on electrical components.
- Disconnect the battery if arc welding is to be done on the vehicle.

BELT TENSION ADJUSTMENT

V-Belts are normally adjusted by loosening the bolts of the belt driven accessory and by moving that accessory on its pivot points until the proper tension is applied to the belt. The accessory is held in this position while the bolts are tightened. To determine proper belt tension, either a belt tension gauge will be or the deflection method can be used. Deflection is determined by pressing inward on the belt at the mid-point of the longest straight run. The belt should deflect (move inward) ⅜–½ inch Some long V-belts have idler pulleys which are used for adjusting purposes. With these systems, loosen the idler pulley and move it to take up tension on the belt.

Serpentine belts are automatically adjusted by the tensioner on the engine. If the belt is loose, check the condition of the belt and tensioner. The tensioner should place enough tension on the belt so it can only be twisted 90 degrees at it's longest run.

If belt slippage occurs, the drive belt tensioner is within its operating range, and the belt does not need replacement, check the belt tension as follows:

1. Run the engine for 10 minutes, shut OFF the engine, then using a tension gauge between any 2 pulleys, record the belt tension.

When checking Ignition timing, ground the diagnostic terminal of the ALDL with the engine running.

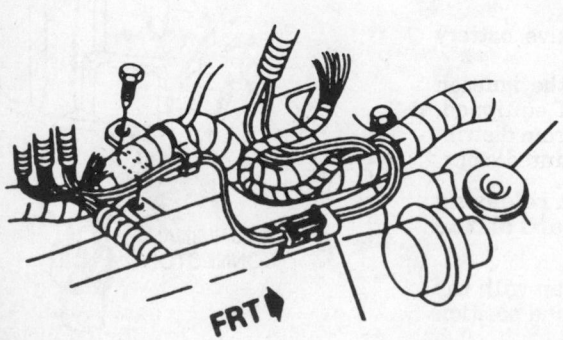

1. EST bypass connector
2. Air control valve

The EST bypass connector; located to the right of the air control valve.

2. Run the engine for 30 seconds and repeat Step 1.

3. Again run the engine for 30 seconds and repeat Step 1.

4. The belt tension is the average of the 3 readings. Serpentine belt tension should be 105–125 lbs. (467–556 Nm).

5. Replace the belt tensioner if the tension is below the minimum specification and the drive belt tensioner is within its operating range.

REMOVAL & INSTALLATION

1. Disconnect the negative battery cable.

2. Disconnect and tag the electrical connections.

3. With V-Belts, remove the bolt holding the slotted adjusting bracket to the alternator and remove the belt.

4. With serpentine belts, loosen and rotate the tensioner to release the drive belt.

5. Remove the thru-bolt(s) to release the alternator from the engine.

To install:

6. When reinstalling, reverse the removal procedure.

7. Adjust the drive belt to allow between ⅜–½ inch play on the longest run between pulleys.

8. On some vehicles, it may be necessary to loosen and rotate the fan shroud.

9. On models with air conditioning, it may be necessary to remove the compressor bracket. Do not discharge the air conditioning system.

Starter

REMOVAL & INSTALLATION

1. Disconnect the negative battery cable.

2. Safely raise and support the vehicle.

3. Remove upper support attaching bolts and the brace and wire guide tube bolt, if equipped.

4. Remove the flywheel housing cover, as required.

5. If necessary, remove the exhaust crossover pipe.

6. Remove the starter mounting bolts and lower the starter.

7. Tag and disconnect the wiring, then remove starter.

8. If equipped with dual exhaust, it may be necessary to remove the left exhaust pipe.

To install:

9. Attach left exhaust pipe, if removed in Step 8.

10. Connect starter wiring.

11. Hold starter in place and install starter mounting bolts. If shims were removed, they must be installed in

1. Nut
2. Washer
3. Bracket only on 5.7L engine
4. Bolt
5. Starter motor
6. Bolts
7. Double shim on 5.0L (VIN E, G, H) engine
8. Single shim on 5.0L (VIN E, G, H) and 5.7L engine
9. Double shim on 5.7L engine

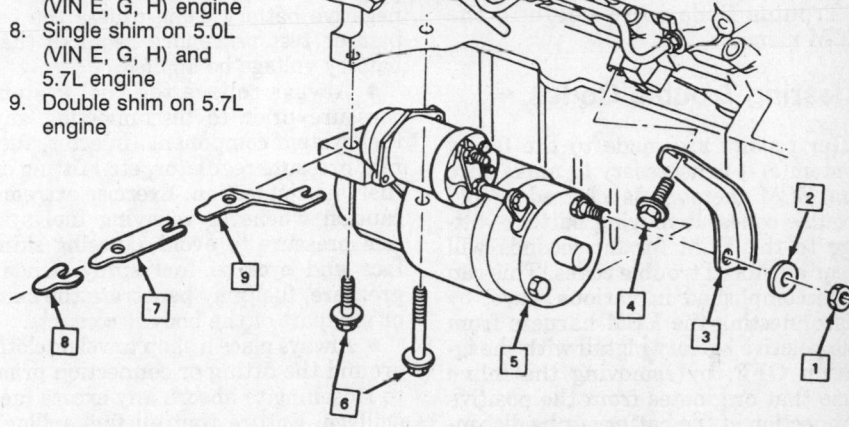

Starter mounting—1991–93 Roadmaster, Caprice and Custom Cruiser

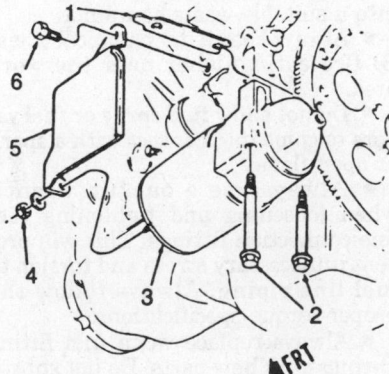

1. Shim	4. Nut – 13 ft. lbs.
2. Bolts 35 ft. lbs.	5. Shield
3. Starter assy.	6. Bolt – 20 ft. lbs.

Starter mounting—1989–90 all models

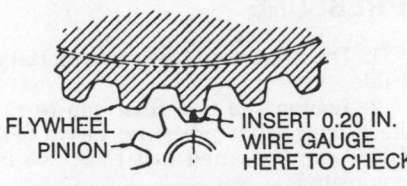

Flywheel to pinion gear clearance

their original location to assure proper drive pinion to flywheel engagement. Tighten mounting bolts to 35 ft. lbs. (37 Nm).

12. Check flywheel to pinion gear clearance.

13. If removed, attach exhaust crossover piper and flywheel housing cover.

14. Lower vehicle and connect the negative battery cable.

EMISSION CONTROLS

Due to the complex nature of modern electronic engine control systems, comprehensive diagnosis and testing procedures fall outside the confines of this repair manual. For complete information on diagnosis, testing and repair procedures concerning all modern engine and emission control systems, please refer to "Chilton's Guide to Fuel Injection and Electronic Engine Controls".

Emission Warning Lamps

RESETTING

The "Service Engine Soon" emission light located on the instrument panel and has 2 functions:

1. The light indicates to the driver when a problem has occurred and the vehicle should be taken for service as soon as reasonably possible.

2. The light is used by technicians to monitor "Trouble Codes" when the system is in the diagnostic mode.

To verify the bulb and wiring of the system is operating properly, the "Service Engine Soon" light will come ON with the key ON and the engine not running. When the engine is started, the "Service Engine Soon" light will turn OFF if the system is operating properly.

If the "Service Engine Soon" light remains ON, the self-diagnostic system has detected a problem. If the problem goes away, the light will go out in most cases after 10 seconds but a Trouble Code will remain in the ECM memory.

Clearing Trouble Codes

After repairs are made to the faulty system(s) it is necessary to make sure the ECM memory is cleared of old trouble codes. Removing battery voltage to the ECM for 30 seconds will clear all stored trouble codes. This can be accomplished in various ways; by disconnecting the ECM harness from the positive battery pigtail with the ignition **OFF**, by removing the inline fuse that originates from the positive connection of the battery or by disconnecting the ECM fuse, designated ECM or ECM/Bat, from the fuse holder.

NOTE: To prevent ECM damage, the key must be OFF when disconnecting or reconnecting power to ECM (for example battery cable, ECM pigtail, ECM fuse, jumper cables, etc.).

ECM Learning Ability

The ECM has a "learning" ability which allows it to make corrections for minor variations in the fuel system in order to improve driveability. If the battery is disconnected to clear diagnostic codes, or for repair, the "learning" process will reset and must begin again. A change may be noted in the vehicle's performance while the learning process begins. To "teach" the vehicle, make sure the vehicle is at operating temperature and drive at part throttle, with moderate acceleration and idle conditions, until normal performance returns.

FUEL SYSTEM

Fuel System Service Precautions

Safety is the most important factor when performing any type of maintenance, but this is true even more so with fuel system maintenance. Failure to conduct maintenance and repairs in a safe manner may result in serious

personal injury or even death. Maintenance and testing of the vehicle's fuel system components can be accomplished safely and effectively by adhering to the following rules and guidelines.

• To avoid the possibility of fire and personal injury, always disconnect the negative battery cable unless the repair or test procedure requires that battery voltage be applied.

• Always relieve the fuel system pressure prior to disconnecting any fuel system component (injector, fuel rail, pressure regulator, etc.) fitting or fuel line connection. Exercise extreme caution whenever relieving fuel system pressure to avoid exposing skin, face and eyes to fuel spray. Under pressure, fuel may penetrate the skin or any part of the body it contacts.

• Always place a shop towel or cloth around the fitting or connection prior to loosening to absorb any excess fuel spillage. Ensure that all fuel spillage (should it occur) is quickly removed from engine surfaces and that all fuel soaked cloths or towels are deposited into a suitable waste container.

• Always keep a dry chemical (Class B) fire extinguisher near the work area.

• Do not allow fuel spray or fuel vapors to come into contact with a spark or open flame.

• Always use a backup wrench when loosening and tightening fuel line connection fittings. This will prevent unnecessary stress and torsion to fuel line piping. Always follow the proper torque specifications.

• Always replace worn fuel fitting O-rings with new parts. Do not substitute fuel hose or equivalent where fuel pipe is installed.

RELIEVING FUEL SYSTEM PRESSURE

1. Disconnect the negative battery cable.
2. Loosen the fuel filler cap to relieve tank vapor pressure. Leave fuel filler cap loosened until service is completed.

NOTE: The internal constant bleed feature of the Model 220 TBI relieves fuel pump system pressure when the engine is turned OFF. Therefore, no further relief procedure is required.

3. Be sure to tighten fuel filler cap when maintenance or repairs are finished.

Fuel Tank

REMOVAL & INSTALLATION

1989–90

SEDAN

1. Disconnect the negative battery cable.
2. Relieve fuel system pressure, drain the fuel tank and store the fuel in a safe location.
3. Raise and support the vehicle safely.
4. Clean and disconnect fuel feed and return line quick-connect fittings at fuel level meter.
5. Clean and disconnect vapor hose connection at fuel level meter.
6. Disconnect the fuel level meter electrical connector and free it from the routing clip on the fuel tank strap.
7. With the aid of an assistant, support the fuel tank and remove the fuel tank retaining straps, nuts and bolts.
8. Remove the fuel tank and place in a safe well ventilated area.

To install:

9. With the aid of an assistant, support the fuel tank in the correct position and attach the fuel tank retaining strap, nuts and bolts. Tighten front fuel tank retaining strap bolts to 26 ft. lbs. (35 Nm) and rear tank retaining strap nuts to 97 inch lbs. (11 Nm).
10 Connect the fuel level meter electrical connector to the routing clip at the fuel tank strap and to the fuel level meter.
11. Connect vapor hose.
12. Connect fuel feed and return line quick-connect fittings to fuel level meter. Be sure to apply a few drops of clean engine oil to the male connector tube ends.
13. Lower vehicle, add fuel and install fuel filler cap.
14. Connect the negative battery cable. Turn ignition **ON** for 2 seconds, **OFF** for 10 seconds, then **ON** again and inspect the tank and lines for leaks.

WAGON

1. Disconnect the negative battery cable.
2. Drain the fuel tank and store the fuel in a safe location.
3. Remove filler neck stone shield attaching screws and shield.
4. Remove filler neck attaching screw from body bracket and remove the filler neck.
5. Raise and support the vehicle safely.
6. Disconnect fuel level meter electrical connector, free connector from routing clip at body and remove.
7. Remove ground lead from body.
8. Clean and remove fuel feed and

return pipe connecting hoses from fuel level meter.

9. Clean and remove fuel vapor hose from fuel level meter.

10. With the aid of an assistant, support the fuel tank and remove the retaining straps, nuts and bolts.

11. Remove the fuel tank and store in a safe well ventillated area.

To install:

12. With the aid of an assistant, support the fuel tank in the correct position and attach the fuel tank retaining strap, nuts and bolts. Tighten front retaining strap bolts to 26 ft. lbs. (35 Nm) and rear retaining strap nuts to 97 inch lbs. (11 Nm).

13. Connect fuel vapor, return and feed pipe hoses.

14. Connect fuel level meter electrical connector to the fuel level meter and snap electrical connector into routing clip at body.

15. Attach the ground lead to body.

16. Lower vehicle and attach filler neck to body bracket with filler neck attaching screw.

17. Attach filler neck stone shield and attaching screws.

18. Connect the negative battery cable and add fuel.

19. Start engine and inspect the tank and lines for leaks.

1991–93

1. Disconnect the negative battery cable.

2. Relieve fuel system pressure.

3. Drain the fuel tank and store the fuel in a safe location.

4. Raise and support the vehicle safely.

5. Disconnect lower fuel tank shield attaching screws and shield.

6. Clean and disconnect vapor hose at the fuel sender, vent hose at fuel filler neck vent pipe, and fuel filler tube at fuel tank.

7. Clean and disconnect fuel feed and return line quick-connect fittings at fuel sender assembly.

8. Disconnect fuel sender assembly electrical connector.

9. With the aid of an assistant, support the fuel tank and remove the fuel tank retaining straps, nuts and bolts.

10. Remove the fuel tank and place in a safe well ventilated area.

To install:

11. With the aid of an assistant, support the fuel tank in the correct position and attach the fuel tank retaining straps, nuts and bolts. Tighten front strap retaining bolts to 24 ft. lbs. (31 Nm) and rear retaining nuts to 18 ft. lbs. (24 Nm).

12. Connect fuel filler tube, vent hose, vapor hose, and clamps.

13. Connect fuel sender assembly electrical connector.

14. Attach fuel feed and return pipe quick-connect fittings. Be sure to apply a few drops of clean engine oil to the male connector tube ends.

15. Connect lower fuel tank shield and attaching screws. Tighten to 18 inch lbs. (2.0 Nm).

16. Lower vehicle, add fuel and attach filler cap.

17. Attach negative battery cable.

18. Turn the ignition **ON** for 2 seconds, **OFF** for 10 seconds, then **ON** and inspect the tank and lines for leaks.

Fuel Filter

REMOVAL & INSTALLATION

Carbureted Engine

1. Disconnect the negative battery cable.

2. Disconnect the fuel line connection at the fuel inlet filter nut on the carburetor.

3. Remove the fuel inlet filter nut from the carburetor.

4. Remove filter, filter check valve and spring.

5. Remove the gasket from the fuel inlet nut. Discard the gasket, filter check valve and filter.

To install:

6. Install the fuel filter spring first and then the fuel filter with the check valve facing out, into the carburetor opening.

7. Ensure that the filter assembly is installed with the check valve end facing the fuel inlet line. Ribs on the closed end of the filter prevent the filter from being installed incorrectly.

8. Install a new gasket onto the fuel line nut and tighten the nut into the carburetor opening.

9. Reconnect and tighten the fuel inlet line to the fuel nut.

10. Start the engine and inspect for leaks. Repair all fuel leaks immediately.

Fuel Injected Engine

The fuel injection system uses an inline filter located in the fuel feed line under the hood, attached to the frame rail or on the rear crossmember of the vehicle. There are 2 different styles of fuel lines used, the first style is the traditional metal line with fittings to secure the lines or filter and is found on 1989 vehicles. Always use a backup wrench on the fittings any time a fuel filter is removed or installed, and never replace a metal fuel line with a rubber insert. The high pressure fuel system used with all fuel injection systems requires special fuel lines to contain the pressure. Replace the O-ring at the connection and torque the fuel fitting to 22 ft. lbs. (28 Nm). The second style, found on 1990–93, is new and utilizes nylon lines and quick disconnect fittings.

WITHOUT QUICK-CONNECT FITTING

1. Disconnect the negative battery cable and relieve the fuel system pressure.

2. Disconnect the fuel lines. Use a backup wrench to hold the fuel filter connector nut stationary while disconnecting the inlet and outlet lines.

3. Remove the O-rings from the fuel line connections. Inspect the O-rings for damage and make replacements, as required.

4. Remove the fuel filter from the retainer. Discard the filter.

To install:

5. Installation is the reverse of the removal procedure. The filter has an arrow (fuel flow direction) on the side of the case to ensure proper installation.

6. Install the filter in the retainer with the arrow facing away from the fuel tank, toward the front of the engine.

7. Start the engine and inspect for leaks. Correct fuel leaks immediately.

WITH QUICK-CONNECT FITTINGS

1. Disconnect the negative battery cable and relieve fuel system pressure.

2. Remove the filter bracket attaching bolt.

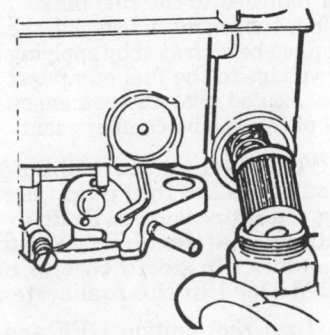

Fuel filter installation—carbureted vehicles

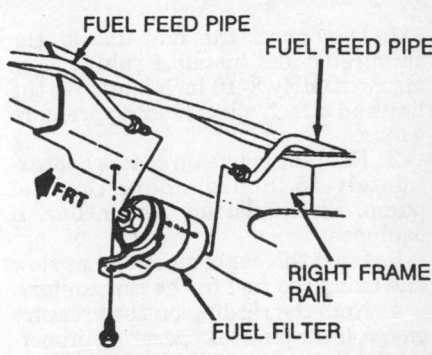

In-line fuel filter with standard fittings—fuel injected vehicles

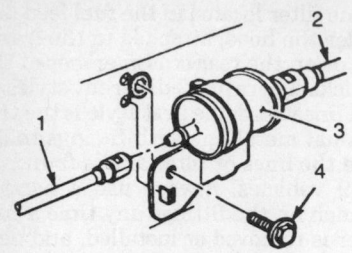

1. Fuel feed line
2. Fuel feed line
3. In-line fuel filter
4. Attaching bolt

In-line fuel filter with quick-connect fittings—fuel injected vehicles

3. While grasping the fuel filter and 1 of the fuel lines, twist the line approximately ¼ turn in each direction to loosen any dirt in the fitting and use compressed air to blow dirt out of fitting.

4. Squeeze the plastic tabs of the male connector on the fuel lines and pull connection apart.

5. Remove the fuel feed and return line body harness clips.

6. Remove the filter.

To install:

7. Position the fuel filter in original location with arrow pointing in correct direction.

8. Secure fuel filter to plastic retainers.

9. Apply a few drops of clean engine oil to both ends of fuel filter.

10. Push the fuel line connectors onto the fuel filter tubes until tabs snap into place.

11. Once installed, pull on both ends of the lines to verify they are secure.

12. Secure the filter and bracket to the frame with the attaching bolt.

13. Reconnect the battery negative cable and inspect fuel system for leaks.

Mechanical Fuel Pump

PRESSURE TESTING

1. Disconnect the fuel line at the carburetor and install a rubber hose approximately 8–10 inch long over the line and attach a low reading pressure gauge.

2. Hold the gauge up so it is approximately 16 inches. above the fuel pump. Pinch the fuel return line, if equipped.

3. Start the engine and run at slow idle using the fuel in the carburetor.

4. Note the reading on the pressure gauge, if the pump is operating properly, the pressure should be 5½–6½ psi constant.

REMOVAL & INSTALLATION

1. Disconnect the negative battery cable and loosen the fuel filler cap.

2. Clean all fuel feed and return pipe connections and surrounding areas to avoid contamination of the fuel system.

3. Disconnect the fuel feed and return hoses at the frame and cap, if necessary, to prevent leakage. Disconnect fuel feed pipe from outletside of pump.

4. Disconnect the vapor return hose, if equipped.

5. Remove the 2 mounting bolts.

6. Remove the fuel pump, pushrod, gasket and if used, the mounting plate.

To install:

7. Clean the gasket sealing surfaces.

8. Install fuel pump, pushrod, mounting plate, if used, and a new gasket with attaching bolts. Tighten bolts to 22 ft. lbs. (30 Nm).

9. Connect the vapor return hose, if equipped.

10. Connect the fuel feed pipe to the outlet side of the pump. Tighten carefully to 22 ft. lbs. (30 Nm).

11. Uncap fuel feed and return pipes, if capped, and install with clamps to connecting hoses at the frame.

12. Tighten fuel filler cap and attach the negative battery cable.

13. Start the engine and check for leaks.

Electric Fuel Pump

PRESSURE TESTING

Throttle Body Injection (TBI)

When the ignition switch is turned **ON**, the ECM will turn the in-tank fuel pump **ON**. It will remain on as long as the engine is cranking or running and the ECM is receiving ignition reference pulses. If there are no reference pulses, the ECM will shut the fuel pump **OFF** within 2 seconds after the key is turned **ON**. The pump will deliver fuel to the TBI unit at a pressure controlled by the internal regulator to approximately 9–13 psi. Excess fuel is then returned to the fuel tank.

While the engine is stopped, the fuel pump can be activated by applying battery voltage to the fuel pump test terminal located near the passenger side cowl of the engine compartment.

NOTE: Fuel pressure should be noted while the fuel pump is running. Fuel pressure will drop immediately after the fuel pump stops running due to the controlled bleed in the fuel system.

1. Turn the ignition **OFF** and relieve fuel system pressure by removing fuel filler cap.

2. Locate the engine compartment fuel feed quick-connect fitting. Uncouple the fuel supply flexible hose as follows:

  a. Grasp both ends of the fitting and twist female end ¼ turn in each direction to loosen any dirt in fitting.

  b. Wearing proper safety glasses, use compressed air to blow dirt out of the quick-connect fitting.

3. Separate the male and female leads of the connector by inserting tool into female end of the connector to release the male end.

4. Install a fuel pressure gauge between the two ends of the connector. Be sure to always lubricate the male end with a few drops of engine oil to ensure proper connection and prevent a fuel leak.

5. Apply battery voltage to the fuel pump test connector.

6. The fuel pressure should be 9–13 psi.

REMOVAL & INSTALLATION

1. Disconnect the negative battery cable and relieve the fuel system pressure.

2. Raise and support the vehicle safely.

3. Remove the fuel tank.

4. Remove the fuel tank sending unit and pump assembly as follows:

  a. On 1989 models, turn the cam lock ring counterclockwise. Lift the assembly from the fuel tank and remove the fuel pump and sending unit. Take care to prevent damage to the rubber insulator and strainer during removal.

  b. On 1990 models, use tool J-24187 or equivalent to remove the assembly retaining cam, assembly and O-ring from fuel tank. Discard the O-ring.

  c. On 1991–93 models, remove the assembly attaching nuts, retaining flag, assembly and O-ring from the tank. Discard the O-ring.

To install:

5. Install fuel sending unit in fuel tank as follows:

  a. On 1989 models, carefully insert fuel pump and sending unit into tank. Turn cam lock ring clockwise to fasten.

  b. On 1990 models, install a new O-ring on fuel tank. Use tool J-24187, or equivalent, to connect fuel meter assembly and assembly retaining cam and fuel tank.

  c. On 1991–93 models, position a new O-ring on fuel tank. Install fuel sender assembly, retaining flag, and attaching nuts to fuel tank. Tighten attaching nuts to 27 inch lbs. (3 Nm).

6. Install fuel tank.

7. Lower vehicle.

8. Turn the ignition **ON** for 2 seconds, **OFF** for 10 seconds, the **ON** and inspect the system for leaks.

Carburetor

REMOVAL & INSTALLATION

1. Disconnect the negative battery cable. Remove air cleaner.

2. Disconnect accelerator linkage.

3. Disconnect transmission detent cable.

4. Disconnect cruise control, if equipped.

5. Disconnect all necessary electrical connectors.

6. Disconnect and tag all necessary vacuum lines.

7. Disconnect fuel line at carburetor inlet and, if equipped, the choke heat pipe.

8. Remove the attaching bolts and remove carburetor.

To install:

9. Clean sealing surfaces.

10. Install carburetor on intake manifold with new gasket. Tighten bolts to 12 ft. lbs. (16 Nm). in a torque sequence beginning with 1 corner bolt, moving diagonally to the next and repeating the pattern for the remaining 2 bolts.

11. Connect the fuel line to the carburetor at the fuel inlet nut.

12. Connect the choke heat pipe if equipped.

13. Connect all vacuum lines.

14. Connect all electrical connectors

15. Connect the cruise control cable, if equipped.

16. Connect the transmission detent cable and the accelerator linkage.

17. Install the air cleaner assembly.

18. Be sure the battery cable has been disconnected long enough to clear ECM memory. If not, clear ECM memory and connect the negative battery cable.

IDLE SPEED ADJUSTMENT

On engines without Idle Speed Control (ISC) or Idle Air Control System (IACS), adjust to specifications shown on the underhood label. If no specifications are shown, no adjustment is necessary.

The Idle Speed Control (ISC) is controlled by the Electronic Control Module (ECM), which has the desired idle speed programmed in its memory. The ECM compares the actual idle speed to the desired idle speed and the plunger is moved in or out. Through the Idle Load Compensator (ILC) the ECM automatically adjusts the throttle to hold an idle rpm independent of the engine loads.

Idle Load Compensator (ILC)

The ILC is adjusted at the factory. Do not make an adjustment unless diagnosis or curb idle speed is not to specification. If this is the case, set ILC min/max and base speeds as follows:

1. Set the parking brake and block the drive wheels.

2. Prepare vehicle for adjustments—see vehicle emission information label.

3. Connect a tachometer.

4. Remove air cleaner and plug vacuum hose to Thermal Vacuum Valve (TVV).

5. Disconnect and plug vacuum hose to EGR and vacuum hose to ILC.

6. Disconnect and plug vacuum hose to canister purge port.

7. Back out idle stop screw on carburetor 3 turns.

8. Turn the air conditioning to the **OFF** position.

9. With engine running, engine warm, choke off, transmission in **D** and ILC plunger fully extended (no vacuum applied), using tool J–29607, BT–8022 or equivalent, adjust plunger to obtain 700 rpm. Jam nut on plunger must be held with wrench to prevent damage to guide tabs when tightening.

10. Measure the distance from the jam nut to the tip of the plunger, it should not exceed 1 inch. If it does, check for cause of a low idle condition.

11. Remove plug from vacuum hose, reconnect hose to ILC and observe idle speed. Idle speed should be 425–475 rpm in **D**.

12. If rpm in Step 11 is correct, proceed to Step 14. No further adjustment of the ILC is necessary.

13. If rpm in Step 10 is not correct:

   a. Stop engine and remove the ILC.

   b. With the ILC removed, remove the rubber cap from the center outlet tube.

   c. Insert a 0.090 inch ($^3/_{32}$ inch) hex key wrench, through open center tube to engage the idle speed adjusting screw inside tube. If idle speed in Step 11 was low, turn the adjusting screw counterclockwise 1 turn for every 75–100 rpm low. If idle speed was high, turn the screw clockwise 1 turn for every 75–100 rpm high. Re-install rubber cap on the center outlet.

   d. Reinstall ILC on carburetor and attach related parts such as the throttle return spring.

   e. Recheck idle speed with the transmission in **D**. If a final adjustment is required, it will be necessary to repeat Steps 13a through 13e.

   f. With the ignition switch **OFF**,

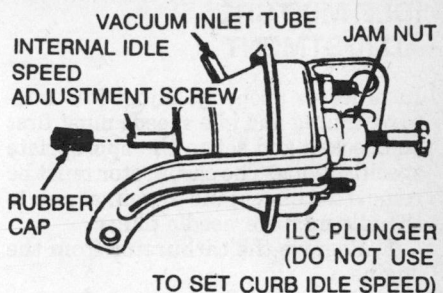

Idle load compensator–5.0L (VIN Y) engine

disconnect the power feed to the ECM for 10 seconds in order to reset the throttle position sensor value.

14. Disconnect and plug vacuum hose to ILC. Apply vacuum source, such as hand vacuum pump J–23768, BT–7517 or equivalent, to ILC vacuum inlet tube to fully retract the plunger.

15. Adjust the idle stop on the carburetor float bowl to obtain 450 rpm in **D**.

16. Place transmission in **P** and stop engine.

17. Remove plug from vacuum hose and install hose on ILC vacuum inlet tube.

18. Remove plugs and reconnect all vacuum hoses.

19. Install air cleaner and gasket.

20. Remove block from drive wheels.

Fast Idle Speed

If necessary, fast idle can be adjusted but only after the ILC min/max and base idle speeds have been set.

1. Set parking brake and block the drive wheels.

2. Prepare vehicle for adjustments—see vehicle emission control information label.

3. Connect a tachometer.

4. Remove air cleaner and plug vacuum hose to Thermal Vacuum Valve (TVV).

5. Check, and if necessary adjust the ILC min/max and base idle speeds.

6. Disconnect and plug the vacuum hose to EGR valve.

7. Place the fast idle cam follower on **LOW** step of fast idle cam.

8. With the engine warm and running, the transmission in **D** and the air conditioning **OFF** adjust fast idle adjusting screw to obtain a fast idle speed of 550 rpm.

9. Release fast idle cam, place transmission in **P** and stop engine.

10. Connect vacuum hose to EGR, install air cleaner and gasket.

11. Remove block from the drive wheels.

IDLE MIXTURE ADJUSTMENT

In order to properly adjust idle mixture, timing and idle speeds must first be checked and set to the appropriate specifications. The carburetor must be removed from engine to gain access to the idle mixture needle plugs.

1. Remove the carburetor from the engine.

2. Drain fuel from the carburetor into an appropriate container.

3. Remove the factory installed plugs from the mixture screws.

4. Using tool J–29030–B, BT–7610–B or equivalent, turn both mixture needles clockwise until lightly seated.

5. Back each mixture needle counterclockwise 3 turns.

6. Install carburetor back on engine with new flange gasket but do not connect the air cleaner or vacuum hoses at this time.

7. Run engine until it reaches normal operating temperature and connect a dwell meter to the green mixture control solenoid dwell connector.

8. With the air conditioning **OFF**, set parking brake, block rear wheels and put gear selector in **D**.

9. Adjust both mixture needles equally, in ⅛ turn increments, until dwell reading varies within the 25–35 degree range, as close to 30 degrees as possible. Allow sufficient time for the readings to stabilize between adjustments.

10. If reading is too high, turn needles clockwise. If reading is too low, turn needles counterclockwise. Install new plugs or cover mixture needle adjustment holes with RTV rubber, silicone sealant, or equivalent.

11. Reconnect all vacuum lines and the air cleaner.

12. Disconnect dwell or service tools and remove block from the drive wheels.

Fuel Injection

On the 4.3L, 5.0L and 5.7L engines, the EFI system centrally locates a single Model 220 Throttle Body Injection (TBI) unit on the intake manifold where air and fuel are distributed through two bores in the unit. Air used for combustion is controlled by two throttle valves which are connected to the accelerator pedal linkage through a throttle shaft and lever assembly. A special plate, located under the throttle valve, is used to aid in uniform mixture distribution. Fuel for combustion is supplied by 2 fuel injectors mounted on the TBI unit.

The metering tips of the fuel injectors are positioned directly above the throttle valve. Injector metering tips

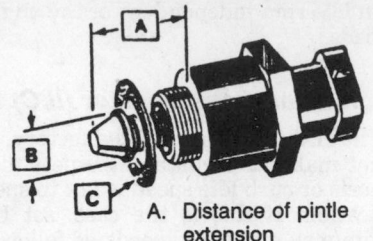

A. Distance of pintle extension
B. Diameter and shape of pintle
C. IAC valve gasket

New IAC valve pintle adjustment—fuel injected vehicles

are "pulsed" or "timed" either open or closed by an electronic output signal received from the ECM. The ECM receives inputs from various engine sensors concerning engine operating conditions, coolant temperature, exhaust gas oxygen content, etc. Information is then used to calculate the engines fuel requirements by controlling the injector pulse openings to provide an ideal fuel/air mixture ratio.

IDLE SPEED ADJUSTMENT

The idle speed and mixture are electronically controlled by the Electronic Control Module (ECM). All adjustments are preset at the factory and do not need preiodic attention. Some throttle body units are equipped with a idle stop screw to allow adjustment of the minimum idle speed if the unit is used as a replacement. The only time the idle speed should need adjustment is when the throttle body assembly has been replaced.

Fuel Injector

REMOVAL & INSTALLATION

NOTE: Exercise care when removing the fuel injectors to prevent damage to the electrical connector terminals, the injector filter and the fuel nozzle. Also, since the injectors are electrical components, they should not be immersed in any type of liquid solvent or cleaner as damage may occur.

1. Disconnect the negative battery cable and relieve the fuel system pressure.

2. Remove the air cleaner assembly and disconnect the electrical connectors from the fuel injectors by squeezing the plastic tabs and pulling straight up.

3. Remove the fuel meter cover attaching screws and assembly.

4. Remove the fuel meter outlet

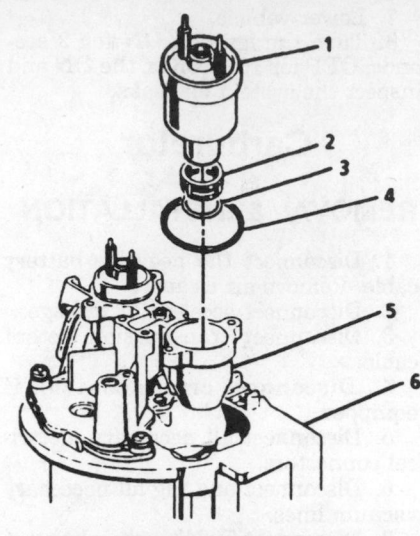

1. Fuel injector assembly
2. Fuel injector inlet filter
3. Fuel injector lower "O" ring
4. Fuel injector upper "O" ring
5. Fuel meter body assembly
6. Throttle body assembly

Fuel meter assembly—Injector and O-rings

passage gasket and pressure regulator dust seal. If, on removal of the fuel meter assembly, the fuel meter cover gasket stuck to the fuel meter body, leave it in place. If it stuck to the fuel meter cover, remove it and place it on the fuel meter body to protect the body in the next step.

5. With the cover gasket in place on the fuel meter body, carefully remove each injector and set aside.

6. Remove the lower (small) O-rings from the injector nozzles. Discard the O-rings and replace with new.

7. Remove the fuel meter cover gasket and discard.

8. Remove the upper (large) O-rings from top of each fuel injector cavity. Discard the O-rings and replace with new. Remove the steel backup washer, if equipped, from the the top of each injector cavity.

To install:

9. Inspect the fuel injector filter for evidence of dirt and contamination. If present, check for presence of dirt in fuel lines and fuel tank.

NOTE: If replacements are required, ensure that the injector is replaced with an identical part. The model 220 TBI is capable of accepting other types of injectors

but other injectors are calibrated for different flow rates.

10. Install the steel injector backup washer, if equipped, in counterbore of fuel meter body.

11. Lubricate new upper (large) O-ring with engine oil and install onto the top of the fuel meter body surface, or directly over the backup washer if equipped. Ensure the O-ring is seated properly and is flush with top of fuel meter body surface.

12. Lubricate new lower (small) O-ring with engine oil and push on nozzle end of injector until it seats against injector fuel filter.

NOTE: Backup washers and O-rings must be installed before the injectors or improper seating of large O-ring could cause fuel to leak.

13. Align the raised lug on each injector base with notch in fuel meter body cavity and install the injector. Push down with moderate pressure on injector until it is fully seated in fuel meter body. The electrical terminals of injector should be parallel with throttle shaft.

14. Install the fuel meter cover gasket.

15. Install the fuel meter cover.

16. Coat the threads of the fuel meter attaching screw with a suitable thread locking compound. Install and tighten the screws to 27 inch lbs. (3 Nm).

17. Reconnect the electrical connectors to their respective fuel injectors.

18. Tighten fuel filler cap, and reconnect the negative battery cable.

19 Turn the ignition switch **ON** for 2 seconds, **OFF** for 10 seconds, then **ON** and check for fuel leaks.

DRIVE AXLE

Driveshaft

REMOVAL & INSTALLATION

1. Raise the vehicle and support it safely.

2. Mark the relationship of the driveshaft to the differential flange.

3. Unbolt the driveshaft retaining bolts and disconnect the retaining straps. Tape the bearing caps in place to prevent losing the bearing rollers. Support the driveshaft to prevent excessive strain on the universal joint.

4. Position a suitable drain pan under the transmission end to catch any fluid that may leak out when the driveshaft is removed. Pull the shaft back

and remove it. Be careful not to damage the splines at the transmission end.

To install:

5. Lubricate spline with engine oil, 1050169 slip yoke lubricant or equivalent and slide the slip yoke into place.

6. Align the driveshaft marks, connect the retaining straps and tighten the bolts to 16 ft. lbs. (22 Nm).

7. Lower the vehicle.

Universal Joints

REMOVAL & INSTALLATION

Snapring Type

1. Raise and support the vehicle safely. Mark and remove the driveshaft.

2. Remove the snaprings from the yoke. If the snapring is difficult to remove, tap the end of the bearing cap lightly to relieve pressure from snapring.

3. Support the propeller shaft horizontally in line with the base plate of a bench vise but never clamp the driveshaft tube.

4. Place the universal joint so the lower ear of the yoke is supported on a 1⅛ inch socket. Press 1 trunnion bearing against the socket in order to press the opposite bearing from the yoke.

5. Grasp the cap and work it out, if necessary use tool J-9522-3 and J-9522-5 or equivalents.

6. Support the other side of the yoke and press the bearing cap from the yoke and as in previous steps.

7. Remove the trunnion from the driveshaft yoke.

8. Disassemble the other U-joint. Clean and check the condition of all parts. Use U-joint repair kits to replace all the wearing parts or replace with new U-joint.

To install:

9. Repack the bearings with grease and replace the trunnion dust seals after any operation that requires disassembly of the U-joint. Be sure the lubricant reservoir at the end of the trunnion is full of lubricant. Fill the reservoirs with lubricant from the bottom.

10. Insert the cross into the yoke so the trunnion seats freely in the bearing cup.

11. Install the opposite bearing cup part way. Be sure both trunnions are started straight into the bearing cups.

12. Press against opposite bearing cups, working the cross constantly to be sure it is free in the cups. If binding occurs, check the needle rollers to be sure 1 needle has not become lodged under and end of the trunnion.

13. As soon as 1 bearing retainer

groove is exposed, stop pressing and install the bearing retainer snapring.

14. Continue to press until the opposite bearing retainer can be installed. If difficulty installing the snaprings is encountered, tap the yoke with a hammer to spring the yoke ears slightly.

15. Replace the driveshaft and lower the vehicle.

Molded Retainer Type

NOTE: **Don't disassemble these joints unless replacing complete U-joint. The factory installed joints cannot be reused.**

1. Raise and support the vehicle safely and remove the driveshaft.

2. Support the driveshaft in a horizontal position in line with the base plate of a press but never clamp the driveshaft tubing in the vise. Place the U-joint so the lower ear of the shaft yoke is supported by a 1⅛ inch socket. Press the lower bearing cup of the yoke ear. This will shear the plastic retaining the lower bearing cup.

3. If the bearing cup is not completely removed, lift the cross, insert a spacer and press the cup completely out.

4. Rotate the driveshaft, shear the opposite plastic retainer, and press the other bearing cup out in the same manner.

5. Remove the cross from the yoke.

NOTE: **Production U-joints cannot be reassembled. There are no bearing retainer grooves in the cups. Discard all parts that were removed and substitute those in the overhaul kit.**

6. Remove the sheared plastic bearing retainer from the yoke. Drive a small pin or punch through the injection holes to aid in removal.

7. If the other U-joint is to be serviced, remove the bearing cups from the slip yoke.

To install:

8. Be sure the seals are installed on the service bearing cups to hold the needle bearings in place for handling. Grease the bearings, if not pregreased.

9. Install 1 bearing cup part way into 1 side of the yoke and turn this ear to the bottom.

10. Insert the cross into the yoke so the trunnion seats freely in the bearing cup.

11. Install the opposite bearing cup part way. Be sure both trunnions are started straight into the bearing cups.

12. Press against opposite bearing cups, working the cross constantly to be sure it is free in the cups. If binding occurs, check the needle rollers to be sure 1 needle has not become lodged under and end of the trunnion.

13. As soon as 1 bearing retainer

groove is exposed, stop pressing and install the bearing retainer snapring.

14. Continue to press until the opposite bearing retainer can be installed. If difficulty installing the snaprings is encountered, tap the yoke with a hammer to spring the yoke ears slightly.

15. Assemble the other half of the U-joint in the same manner.

16. Check that the cross is free in the cups. If it is too tight, tap the yoke ears again to help seat the bearing retainers.

17. Reinstall the driveshaft and lower the vehicle.

Rear Axle Shaft, Bearing and Seal

REMOVAL & INSTALLATION

1. Raise vehicle and support it safely. Remove the tire and wheel assembly. Remove the brake drum.

2. Drain the fluid. Clean all dirt from the rear carrier cover and remove. Discard the gasket.

3. Remove the pinion shaft lock bolt and the pinion gear shaft.

4. Push flanged end of axle shaft toward center of the vehicle and remove C-lock from button end of shaft.

5. Remove axle shaft from housing, being careful not to damage oil seal.

6. Remove seal from housing with a prybar behind steel case of seal, being careful not to damage housing.

7. Insert tool J-23689 or equivalent, into bore and position it behind bearing so tangs on tool engage bearing outer race. Remove bearing, using slide hammer.

To install:

8. Lubricate the new bearing with gear lubricant and install bearing so tool bottoms against shoulder in housing, using tool J-23690 or equivalent.

9. Lubricate seal lips with gear lubricant. Position seal on tool J-21128 or equivalent, and position seal into housing bore. Tap seal into place so it is flush with axle tube.

10. Insert the axle into the place while engaging the splines on the end of the shaft with the splines of the rear axle side gear. Be careful not to damage the seal.

NOTE: The 30-spline 8 ½-in. ring gear axle shaft is not interchangeable with any pre-1989 axle shaft.

11. Install the C-lock on the bottom of the axle shaft and push the shaft outward so the lock seats in the counterbore of the rear axle side gear.

12. Install the rear axle pinion gear shaft through the differential case, thrust washers and pinions, align the

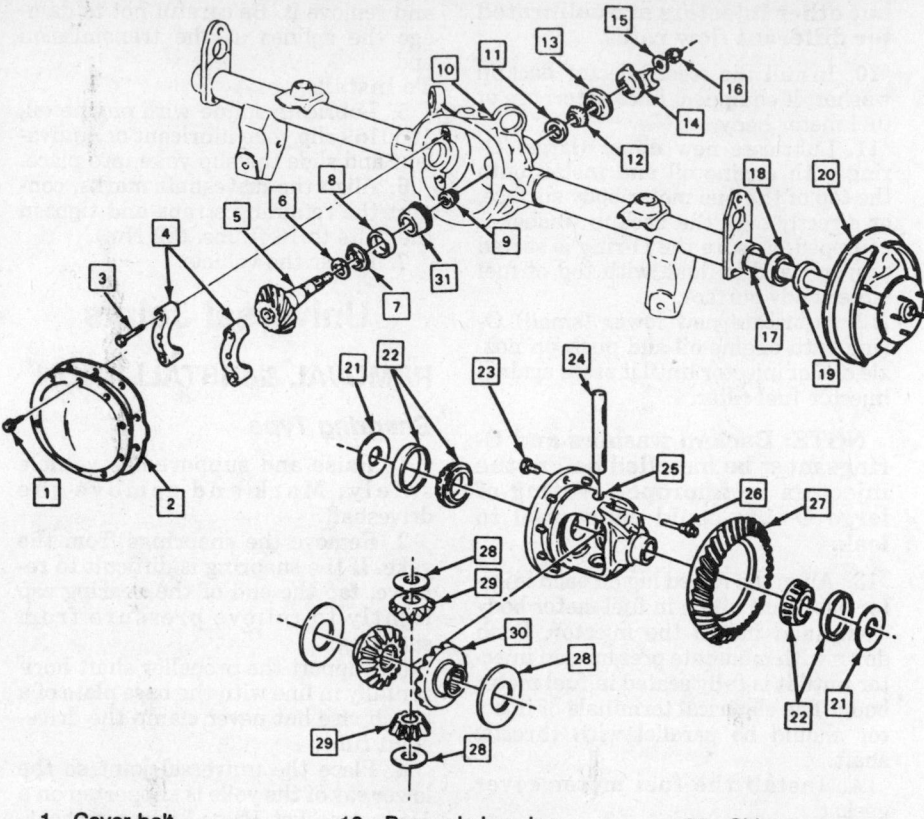

Exploded view of standard rear axle

1. Cover bolt	10. Rear axle housing	21. Shim
2. Cover gasket	11. Outer race	22. Side bearing
3. Differential bearing cap bolt	12. Front pinion bearing	23. Bolt
4. Differential bearing cap	13. Pinion yoke oil seal	24. Pinion gear shaft
5. Drive pinion	14. Pinion yoke	25. Differential case
6. Shim	15. Washer	26. Lock bolt
7. Rear pinion bearing	16. Pinion yoke nut	27. Ring gear
8. Inner race	17. Axle shaft	28. Thrust washer
9. Spacer	18. Bearing assy.	29. Pinion gear
	19. Oil seal	30. Side gear
	20. Backing plate	31. ABS sensor ring

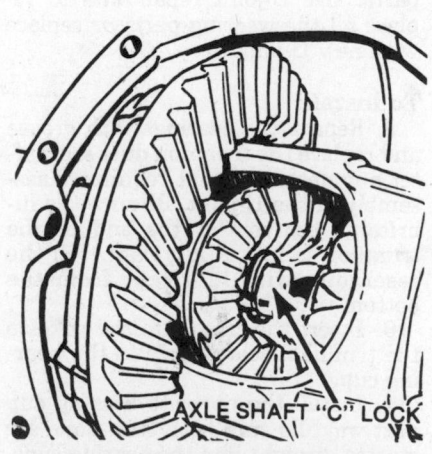

Removing and installing C-locks

hole in the shaft with the lock bolt hole. Install the lock bolt and tighten to 24 ft. lbs. (31 Nm) for 7½ inch ring gears or 20 ft. lbs. (27 Nm) for 8½ inch ring gears.

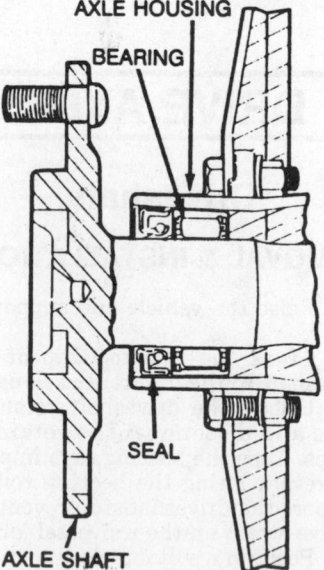

Rear axle shaft, bearing and seal—cut away view

13. Install the carrier cover and bolts using a new gasket.
14. Fill the rear assembly with the proper grade and type gear oil.
15. Install the brake drum and wheel and lower the vehicle.

Front Wheel Hub, Knuckle/Spindle and Bearings

REMOVAL & INSTALLATION

1. Disconnect the battery negative cable.
2. Raise and support the vehicle safely.
3. Disconnect the ABS wheel speed sensor, if equipped.
4. Remove the tire and wheel assembly.
5. Remove the caliper assembly.
6. Remove the dust cap, cotter pin, nut and washer from the spindle.
7. Remove the hub and rotor assembly from the spindle.
8. Remove the rotor shield and attaching bolts from the spindle.
9. Separate the tie rod from the steering knuckle.
10. Remove knuckle seal, if the knuckle is to be replaced.
11. Position a floor jack under the control arm near the spring seat and raise the jack until it just supports the lower control arm.

NOTE: In order to retain the spring and control arm in its original position, the jack must remain under the control arm during the complete removal and installation procedure.

12. Separate the ball joints from the steering knuckle.
13. Remove the steering knuckle.
To install:
14. Install the steering knuckle onto the lower ball joint stud.
15. Lower the upper control arm ball joint stud into the steering knuckle tapered hole.
16. Install the ball joint nuts, torque the upper nut to 60 ft. lbs. (82 Nm) and the lower nut to 83 ft. lbs. (112 Nm) on 1989–91 vehicles or 79 ft. lbs. (107 Nm) for 1992–93 vehicles.
17. Install the rotor splash shield and attaching bolts. Tighten bolts to 124 inch lbs. (14 Nm).
18. Install the tie rod and torque the nut to 35 ft. lbs. (47 Nm).
19. Install cotter pin in all castellated nuts.
20. Install rotor, bearings, washer and nut and adjust.
21. Install a cotter pin in wheel bearing castellated nut.
22. Install dust cap.

23. Install caliper assembly.
24. Install wheel assembly.
25. Install ABS wheel speed sensor.
26. Remove jack assembly, lower the vehicle.
27. Reconnect the negative battery cable.
28. Road test vehicle.

Pinion Seal

REMOVAL & INSTALLATION

1. Release the parking brake.
2. Raise and support the vehicle safely. It may be helpful to have the front end slightly higher than the rear to avoid fluid loss.
3. Mark and remove the driveshaft.
4. Remove the rear wheels. Rotate the rear wheels by hand to make sure there is absolutely no brake drag. If there is brake drag, remove the drums.
5. Using an inch lb. torque wrench on the pinion nut, record the force needed to rotate the pinion.
6. Mark the pinion shaft, nut and flange. Count the number of exposed threads on the pinion shaft.
7. Install a holding tool on the pinion. A very large adjustable wrench will do or if one is not available, put the drums back on, if removed, and set the parking brake as tightly as possible.
8. Remove the pinion nut and washer.
9. Slide the flange off of the pinion. A puller may be necessary.
10. Center punch the oil seal to distort it and pry the seal out, being careful to avoid scratching the bore.
To install:
11. Use a seal installer, as necessary, and position the seal in the bore and carefully drive it into place.
12. Apply seal lubricant 1050169 or equivalent to the outer diameter of the pinion yoke and to the sealing lip of the new drive pinion gear seal.
13. Carefully install the pinion yoke and push it on as far as it will go.
14. Install the pinion washer and nut on the shaft and force the pinion into place by turning the nut.

NOTE: Never hammer the yoke into place.

15. Tighten the nut until, rotating pinion occasionally until the exact number of threads previously noted appear and the marks align.
16. Measure the rotating torque of the pinion under the same circumstances as before. Compare both readings. As necessary, tighten the pinion nut in very small increments until the torque necessary to rotate the pinion is 3–5 inch lbs. (0.3–0.6 Nm) higher than the originally recorded torque.

17. Install the driveshaft and check rear fluid level.
18. Install brake drums and wheels, as necessary, and lower the vehicle.

Rear Axle Housing

REMOVAL & INSTALLATION

1889–91

1. Raise the vehicle and support it safely. Be sure the rear axle assembly is supported safely.
2. Disconnect the ABS rear axle speed sensor connector, if equipped.
3. Remove the shock absorbers from axle housing, if applicable.
4. Remove the driveshaft.
5. Remove the brake line junction block bolt at axle housing, disconnect brake lines at junction block.
6. Disconnect upper control arms from axle housing, and remove springs.
7. Remove rear wheels, drums and, if necessary, brake components.
8. Remove the axle shaft.
9. Disconnect brake lines from the axle housing clips.
10. Remove brake backing plates.
11. With a helper to stabilize the housing, disconnect the lower control arms from the axle housing.
12. Lower the rear axle housing from the hoist.
To install:
13. Raise rear axle housing into place with a hoist.
14. With a helper to stabilize the housing, install lower and upper control arms and hand tighten bolts.
15. Install brake backing plates and position brake lines under housing clips.
16. Install the axle shaft.
17. Install brake components, if removed, rear drums and wheels.
18. Install springs.
19. Connect brake lines to the junction block and the junction block to the rear axle housing.
20. Install the driveshaft.
21. Install the ABS sensor connector.
22. Install shock absorbers, where applicable.
23. Fill axle with suitable gear oil.
24. Torque upper and lower control arms with the weight of the vehicle on the axle.
25. Remove supports and lower vehicle, bleed the brake system as necessary.

1992–93

1. Raise the vehicle and support it safely. Be sure the rear axle assembly is supported safely.
2. Disconnect the ABS rear axle speed sensor connector.

3. Disconnect the automatic level sensor control link, if equipped.

4. Remove the driveshaft.

5. Remove rear wheels, drums and, if necessary, brake components.

6. Remove axle shaft.

7. Disconnect the parking brake cables. Remove the brake backing plate and rear brake pipes from the rear hose fittings. Plug brake pipes to prevent fluid loss and to protect from dirt.

8. Disconnect bolts attaching rear brake hose fitting to housing and remove hose fitting.

9. If replacing housing, remove rear brake pipes from housing.

10. With a helper, remove rear springs and disconnect upper and lower control arms.

11. Lower rear axle housing from hoist.

To install:

12. Raise rear axle housing into place with a hoist.

13. With a helper to stabilize the housing, install lower and upper control arms.

14. Install rear springs.

15. Attach rear brake pipes to housing with retaining clips or straps, if housing was replaced.

16. Connect rear brake fitting and attaching bolt to housing. Tighten bolt to 20 ft. lbs. (27 Nm).

17. Unplug and connect rear brake pipes to rear brake hose fitting. Tighten fitting to 18 ft. lbs. (24 Nm).

18. Connect parking brake cable and brake backing plate.

19. Install axle shaft.

20. Install brake components, drums and rear wheels.

21. Install the driveshaft.

22. Connect the automatic level control sensor link and the ABS rear axle speed sensor connector.

23. Fill axle housing with suitable gear oil.

24. Remove support from the housing and lower the vehicle.

25. Be sure to bleed the brake system, as required.

AUTOMATIC TRANSMISSION

For further information on transmissions/transaxles, please refer to "Chilton's Guide to Transmission Repair".

Transmission Assembly

REMOVAL & INSTALLATION

1. Disconnect the battery negative cable and remove the air cleaner.

2. Disconnect the Throttle Valve (TV) cable at the throttle lever.

3. Remove the transmission dipstick, filler tube and retaining bolt at the transmission.

4. Raise and support the vehicle safely.

5. Remove the driveshaft. If equipped, the floor pan reinforcement may require removal to free the driveshaft.

6. Disconnect the shift linkage and, if equipped, the speedometer cable, at the transmission.

7. Disconnect all electrical leads at the transmission and any clips that retain the leads to the transmission.

8. Remove the flywheel cover and bolts.

9. Mark flywheel and converter for installation reference.

10. Remove the torque converter to flywheel bolts and discard bolts.

11. Support and raise the transmission slightly. Remove the catalytic converter support bracket.

12. Remove the transmission mount-to-support nut, washer, and bolt.

13. Remove the transmission support-to-frame bolts and, if used, insulators.

14. Slide the transmission support rearward.

15. Lower the transmission to gain access to the oil cooler lines and TV cable attachments. Disconnect the lines and cap all openings, also disconnect TV cable.

16. Support the engine with a suitable tool and remove the transmission to engine bolts.

17. Install tool J–21366 or equivalent, to the converter to hold it in place.

18. Remove the transmission assembly from the vehicle.

To install:

19. Raise the transmission into place and remove tool J–21366.

20. Install the transmission to engine bolts and tighten to 35 ft. lbs. (47 Nm).

21. Install the oil cooler pipe, TV cable, fluid level tube and new seal. Tighten tube retaining bolt to 35 ft. lbs. (47 Nm).

22. Install the transmission support to frame bolts and tighten to 25 ft. lbs. (34 Nm).

23. Install the transmission mount bolts and tighten to 35 ft. lbs. (47 Nm). Install the transmission support nut,

washer if equipped, and tighten to 30 ft. lbs. (41 Nm).

24. Remove the transmission jack and install the converter to flywheel in the original position marked and finger-tighten 3 bolts, then tighten to 46 ft. lbs. (62 Nm).

25. Install the floor pan reinforcement, if removed.

26. Install the catalytic converter support bracket, converter cover and bolts and tighten to 89 inch lbs. (10 Nm).

27. Install the shift linkage, electrical leads, retaining clips, and if equipped, speedometer cable.

28. Install the driveshaft and lower the vehicle.

29. Install the TV cable at the throttle lever.

30. Install the air cleaner and the negative battery cable.

31. Adjust the shift linkage, TV cable.

32. Flush the transmission if it was not prior to installation. If already flushed, fill with transmission fluid.

SHIFT LINKAGE ADJUSTMENT

The shift control linkage should be set so the engine will only start in **P** or **N**. If adjustment is necessary proceed as follows:

1. Make sure the steering column attachment and all body bolts are secure as they may affect the shift linkage.

2. Position the steering column shift lever in **N**.

3. Raise and safely support vehicle.

4. Free the control rod and swivel.

5. Set the transmission lever to the neutral detent.

6. Hold swivel flush against the equalizer lever and finger-tighten bolt against rod. No force should be exerted in either direction on the control rod or equalizer lever while tightening bolt.

7. Tighten bolt to 21 ft. lbs. (28 Nm).

8. Lower vehicle and check that adjustment was proper.

THROTTLE VALVE (TV) CABLE ADJUSTMENT

Setting of the TV cable must be done by rotating the throttle lever at the carburetor or throttle body. Do not use the accelerator pedal to rotate the throttle lever.

1. With the engine OFF, depress and hold the reset tab at the engine end of the TV cable.

2. Move the slider until it stops against the fitting.

3. Release the rest tab.

4. Rotate the throttle lever to its full travel.

5. The slider must move (ratchet) toward the lever when the lever is rotated to its full travel position.

6. Recheck after the engine is hot and road test the vehicle.

FRONT SUSPENSION

Shock Absorbers

REMOVAL & INSTALLATION

1. Raise and support the vehicle safely.

2. Hold the shock absorber upper stem from turning and remove the upper nut, retainer and grommet.

3. Remove the 2 bolts and lock washers securing the shock to the lower control arm.

To install:

4. With the lower retainer and grommet in place over the upper stem, install the fully extended shock up through the lower control arm and spring.

5. Install the upper rubber insulator, retainer and attaching nut over the shock. Tighten the nut to 97 inch lbs. (11 Nm).

6. Install the shock lower pivot to the lower control arm with the 2 attaching bolts and tighten to 20 ft. lbs. (27 Nm).

7. Lower the vehicle.

Coil Spring

REMOVAL & INSTALLATION

1. Raise and support the vehicle safely.

2. Disconnect the ABS wheel speed sensor, if equipped, and secure aside.

3. Remove the wheel and shock absorber.

4. Remove the stabilizer linkage nut, retainer and linkage from the lower control arm.

5. Remove the steering knuckle from the tie rod end, using a suitable puller tool.

6. Install a universal spring compressor and compress the spring.

7. Support the lower control arm and remove the lower control arm to frame bolts.

8. Pivot the lower control arm rearward and remove the compressor and spring.

To install:

9. Properly position the spring onto the lower control arm, using spring compressor tool.

10. Position the control arm into the frame and install the pivot bolts but wait to lower vehicle before tightening to specification. With the front bolt installed continue from front to rear.

11. Remove the spring compressor tool, install the steering knuckle to tie rod end and tighten the nut to 35 ft. lbs. (47 Nm). Install a new cotter pin.

12. Remove the support from the lower control arm and install the stabilizer linkage and tighten the bolt/nut to 13 ft. lbs. (17 Nm).

13. Install the shock absorber. Tighten the lower attaching bolts to 20 ft. lbs. (27 Nm) and the upper attaching nut to 97 inch lbs. (11 Nm).

14. Install the ABS wheel speed sensor, if equipped.

15. Install the wheel and lower the vehicle.

16. Tighten the wheel lug nuts to 100 ft. lbs. (140 Nm) and the lower control arm nuts to 92 ft. lbs. (125 Nm).

Torsion Bars

REMOVAL & INSTALLATION

1. Raise and support the vehicle safely.

2. Disconnect each side of the torsion bar by removing the nut from the link bolt. Pull the bolt from the linkage and remove retainers, grommets and spacer.

3. Remove bracket to frame or body bolts and remove torsion bar, rubber bushings and brackets.

4. Installation is the reverse of the removal procedure.

To install:

5. Position the torsion bar with the identification forming on the right side of the vehicle and the slit in the rubber bushings facing the front of the vehicle.

6. Install the rubber insulators to stabilizer shaft and the bracket to frame bolts.

7. Install the link bolts, insulators, spacers, washers and nuts. Tighten torsion bar link bolt/nut to 13 ft. lbs. (17 Nm) and the bracket bolts to 24 ft. lbs. (33 Nm).

8. Lower the vehicle.

Upper Ball Joints

INSPECTION

1. Raise the vehicle and position floor stands under the left and right lower control arm as near as possible to each lower ball joint. There should be sufficient space between the upper control arm bumper and frame.

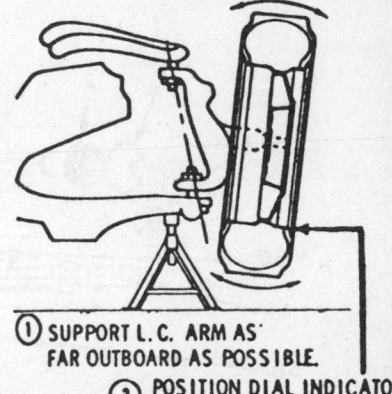

③ ROCK WHEEL IN AND OUT AT TOP AND BOTTOM

① SUPPORT L.C. ARM AS FAR OUTBOARD AS POSSIBLE.

② POSITION DIAL INDICATOR TO CHECK MOVEMENT AT THIS POINT

Upper and lower ball joint inspection

2. Position a dial indicator against the wheel rim.

3. Grasp the front wheel and push in on bottom of the tire while pulling out at the top. Read the gauge, then reverse the push-pull procedure. Horizontal deflection on the dial indicator should not exceed 0.125 inch (3.18mm).

4. If the indicator exceeds 0.125 inch (3.18mm) or if the ball stud, when disconnected from the knuckle assembly, can be twisted in its socket by hand, replace the ball joint.

Removal and Installation

1. Raise and safely support the vehicle; place floor stands under the lower control arm between the spring seats and the ball joints.

NOTE: Leave the jack under the spring seat during removal and installation, in order to compress the coil spring and relieve spring tension from the upper control arm.

2. Remove the wheel.

3. Remove the cotter pin and nut from the upper ball joint.

4. Using a ball joint splitter tool, break the stud loose and pull the stud out of the knuckle. Support the steering knuckle to prevent damage to the brake line.

5. Using a ⅛ inch diameter drill bit, drill into each of the 4 rivet heads to a depth of ¼ inch

6. Drill off the rivet heads with a ½ inch diameter bit.

7. Punch out the rivets with a suitable tool and remove the ball joint.

To install:

8. Place the new ball joint in the up-

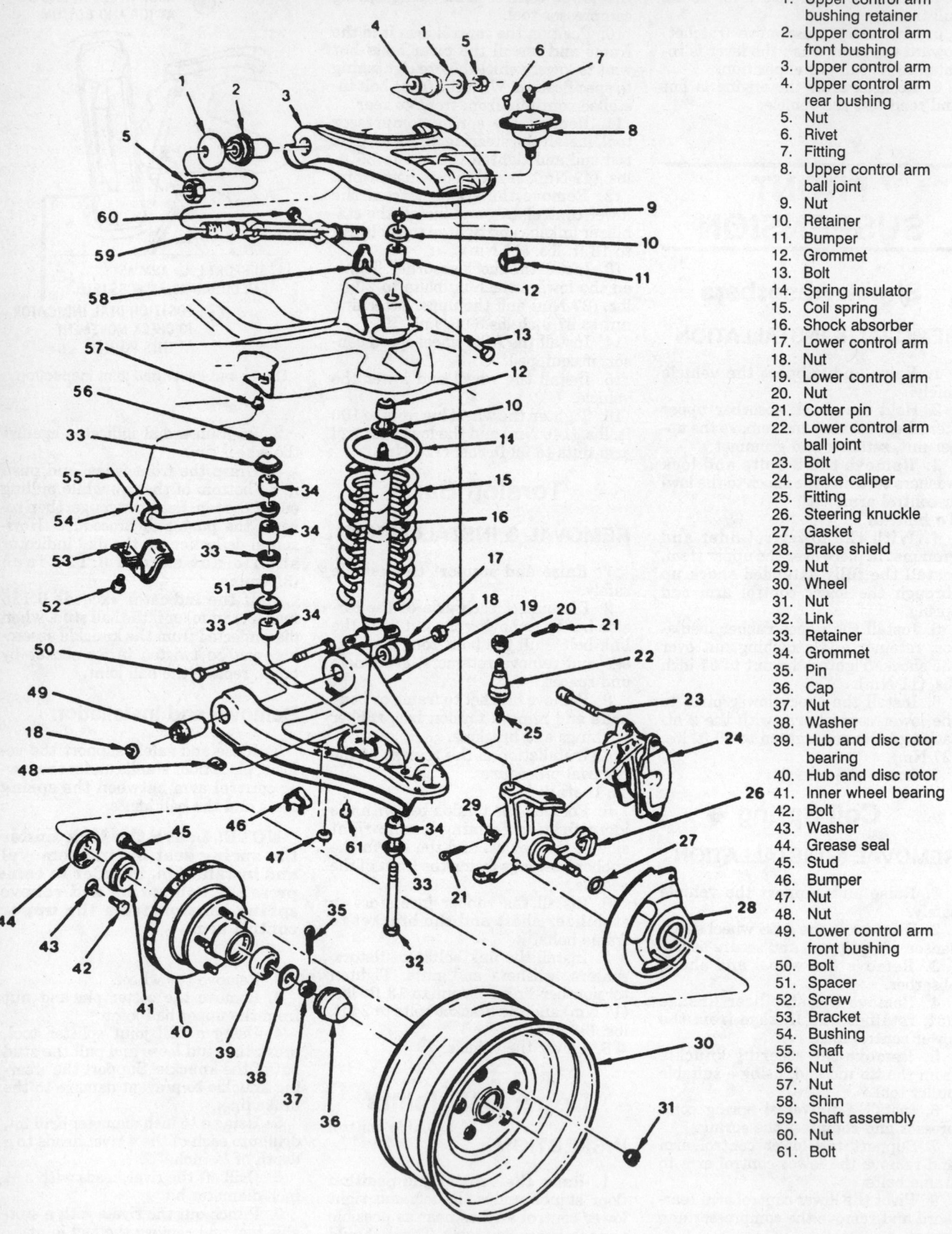

1. Upper control arm bushing retainer
2. Upper control arm front bushing
3. Upper control arm
4. Upper control arm rear bushing
5. Nut
6. Rivet
7. Fitting
8. Upper control arm ball joint
9. Nut
10. Retainer
11. Bumper
12. Grommet
13. Bolt
14. Spring insulator
15. Coil spring
16. Shock absorber
17. Lower control arm
18. Nut
19. Lower control arm
20. Nut
21. Cotter pin
22. Lower control arm ball joint
23. Bolt
24. Brake caliper
25. Fitting
26. Steering knuckle
27. Gasket
28. Brake shield
29. Nut
30. Wheel
31. Nut
32. Link
33. Retainer
34. Grommet
35. Pin
36. Cap
37. Nut
38. Washer
39. Hub and disc rotor bearing
40. Hub and disc rotor
41. Inner wheel bearing
42. Bolt
43. Washer
44. Grease seal
45. Stud
46. Bumper
47. Nut
48. Nut
49. Lower control arm front bushing
50. Bolt
51. Spacer
52. Screw
53. Bracket
54. Bushing
55. Shaft
56. Nut
57. Nut
58. Shim
59. Shaft assembly
60. Nut
61. Bolt

Front suspension components

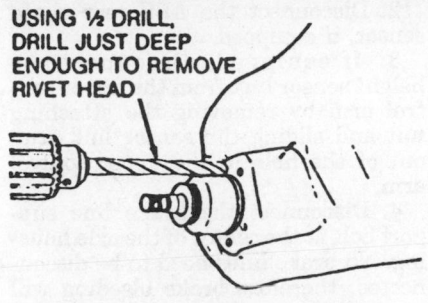

USING ½ DRILL, DRILL JUST DEEP ENOUGH TO REMOVE RIVET HEAD

Removing the upper ball joint

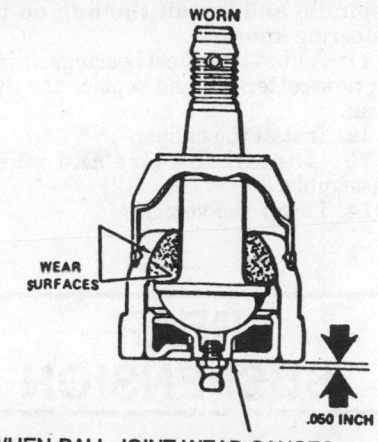

WORN

WEAR SURFACES

.050 INCH

WHEN BALL JOINT WEAR CAUSES INDICATOR TO RECEDE WITHIN THE SOCKET HOUSING, REPLACEMENT IS REQUIRED

Lower ball joint wear indicator

per control arm and secure it with 4 bolts and nuts in place of rivets. Torque the nuts to specifications.

9. Connect the ball joint to steering knuckle. Torque the nut to 60 ft. lbs. (82 Nm) and insert a new cotter pin.

NOTE: When replacing the ball joints, use only high-quality replacement parts; bolts and nuts specified to be strong enough to endure the stress. Always turn the ball stud nut to align the cotter pin hole.

10. Install the grease fitting and lubricate until grease appears at the seal.

11. Install the wheel and road test the vehicle.

Lower Ball Joints

INSPECTION

The lower ball joints contain a visual wear indicator and are checked in this fashion alone. The lower ball joint grease plug is threaded into the wear indicator protruding from the bottom of the ball joint housing. As long as the wear indicator extends out of the ball joint housing, the ball joint is not worn. If the tip of the wear indicator is parallel with or recessed into the ball joint housing, the ball joint is defective.

REMOVAL & INSTALLATION

1. Raise the vehicle and support the frame safely.
2. Remove the tire and wheel.
3. Place a floor jack or axle stand under the control arm spring seat.

NOTE: Leave the jack or axle stand under the spring seat during removal and installation, in order to keep the spring and control arm positioned.

4. Remove the cotter pin from the ball joint stud. Using a ball joint splitter tool, separate the ball joint from the steering knuckle.

5. When the stud comes loose, remove the stud nut.
6. With a small suitable tool, guide the control arm to a position where the ball joint is accessible.
7. Block the steering knuckle aside by using a block of wood between the frame and the upper control arm.
8. Remove the grease fittings.
9. Using a ball joint remover, remove the lower ball joint from the control arm.

To install:

10. Using a ball joint installer, press in a new ball joint until it bottoms on the lower control arm.

NOTE: Make sure the grease purge on the seal faces away from the brakes.

11. Assemble the suspension and torque the lower ball joint nut to 83 ft. lbs. (112 Nm) on 1989–91 vehicles or 79 ft. lbs. (107 Nm) for 1992–93 vehicles. Install the cotter pin and bend it to the side, not over the top of the nut.
12. Install the ball joint fitting and lube until grease appears at the seal.
13. Install the tire and wheel assembly.
14. Adjust wheel alingment, if necessary, and road test the vehicle.

Upper Control Arms

REMOVAL & INSTALLATION

1. If removing the left side control arm on 1991–93 vehicles, remove the air cleaner and resonator.
2. Raise and support the vehicle safely and remove the tire and wheel assembly.
3. Place a floor jack or axle stand under the lower control arm spring seat.

NOTE: Leave the floor jack or axle stand under the spring seat during removal and installation, in order to keep the spring and control arm positioned.

4. Disconnect the wheel speed sensor, if equipped with ABS.
5. Loosen the pivot shaft to frame nuts and remove alignment shims. Tape shims together and mark for installation in the original positions.
6. Remove the cotter pin and upper ball joint nut. Remove the ball joint from the steering knuckle, with suitable tool. Support the hub assembly to prevent damage to the brake line.
7. Remove the upper control arm shaft attaching nuts and remove the control arm.

To install:

8. Install the pivot shaft on the attaching bolts.
9. Install alignment shims in the same position from which they were removed and tighten upper control arm attaching nuts to 72 ft. lbs. (98 Nm).
10. Remove the temporary support from the hub and connect the ball joint to the steering knuckle. Tighten the upper nut to 60 ft. lbs. (82 Nm) and install a new cotter pin.
11. Connect the ABS wheel speed sensor, if equipped.
12. Install the tire and wheel assembly.
13. Remove the jackstands and lower the vehicle.
14. Install the air cleaner and resonator, if removed.
15. Check the wheel alignment.

Lower Control Arm

REMOVAL & INSTALLATION

1. Raise and support the vehicle safely and remove the tire and wheel assembly.
2. Remove the front coil spring and shock absorber.
3. Remove and the lower ball joint from the steering knuckle.
4. Remove the lower control arm attaching bolts and remove the assembly.

To install:

5. Install the lower ball joint stud into the steering knuckle.
6. Position spring and shock absorber in place and install the lower control arm.
7. Tighten the lower control arm bolt/nuts to 92 ft. lbs. (125 Nm), the lower ball joint stud nut to 83 ft. lbs. (112 Nm) on 1989–91 vehicles or 79 ft. lbs. (107 Nm) for 1992–93 vehicles, and the shock absorber lower attaching bolts to 20 ft. lbs. (27 Nm).

8. Install new cotter pins on all appropriate nuts.

9. Install wheel and tire assembly.

10. Lower the vehicle and check alignment.

Front Wheel Bearings

ADJUSTMENT

1. Raise the vehicle so the wheel can spin freely. Remove the wheel cover, dust cap, cotter pin and loosen the adjusting nut.

2. Tighten the adjusting nut to 12 ft. lbs. (16 Nm) while turning the wheel, this will seat the bearings and remove any burrs on the threads.

3. Back off the nut until it is just loose.

4. Finger-tighten the nut and install the cotter pin thru the retaining ring or castle nut.

NOTE: If the cotter pin cannot be installed, back off the nut until the slot aligns with the serrations on the nut. Do not back off the nut more than ¼ of a turn.

5. Once adjusted, the front wheel bearings should have 0.001–0.005 inch (0.03–0.13mm) endplay.

6. When adjusted properly reinstall the cotter pin, dust cap and wheel cover. Lower the vehicle.

REMOVAL & INSTALLATION

1. Raise and safely support the vehicle. Remove tire and wheel assembly.

2. Remove the caliper assembly and position it aside, tie it with mechanic's wire so as not to damage the break lines.

3. Remove the dust cap, spindle nut and outer roller bearing assembly.

4. Remove the hub assembly.

5. Pry the inner bearing seal from the hub, then remove the inner roller bearing assembly.

6. If necessary, remove the inner bearing outer race using tool J–29117–A or a suitable brass punch. To remove outer bearing outer race, insert tool into the hub, indexing end of drift with notches in hub and tap with a hammer.

To install:

7. Using clean solvent, clean all old grease from hub, spindle and bearings.

8. If outer races were removed, press the races into the hub using suitable press tool.

9. Pack the bearings with a high temperature wheel bearing grease and reassemble the hub. Do not mix greases.

10. Apply a thin coat of grease to the spindle and install the hub on the steering knuckle.

11. Adjust the wheel bearings, install a new cotter pin and replace the dust cap.

12. Install the caliper.

13. Install the tire and wheel assembly.

14. Lower the vehicle.

REAR SUSPENSION

Shock Absorbers

REMOVAL & INSTALLATION

1. Raise and safely support the vehicle. Be sure to support the rear axle housing.

2. Disconnect the air line, if equipped, from the shock. Turn the spring clip 90 degrees and pull gently on air line housing.

3. Remove the upper nuts and bolts from the shock absorber at the frame.

4. Using a wrench to hold the stud in place, remove the lower nut and washer from the shock at the rear axle housing. The stud must not be allowed to turn during this operation or damage may result in the bond between the bushing and stud.

5. Remove the shock.

To install:

6. Install the shock absorber and loosely connect the upper frame bolts and nuts.

7. Place the stud into the bracket on the axle housing and attach the nut and washer.

8. Holding the stud steady with a wrench, tighten to nut to 48 ft. lbs. (65 Nm). Either tighten the upper bolts at the frame to 20 ft. lbs. (27 Nm) or the nuts at the frame to 12 ft. lbs. (16 Nm), whichever is easier.

9. Connect the shock air line, if equipped.

10. Remove supports and lower the vehicle.

Coil Springs

REMOVAL & INSTALLATION

NOTE: If both control arms are to be replaced, remove and replace 1 control arm at a time to prevent the axle from rolling or slipping sideways.

1. Raise and support the vehicle safely, place an adjustable support under the axle housing.

2. Disconnect the ABS rear speed sensor, if equipped.

3. If equipped, disconnect the height sensor link from the upper control arm by removing the attaching nut and sliding the sensor link stud out of the hole in the upper control arm.

4. Disconnect the brake line support bolt at the center of the axle housing. No brake lines need to be disconnected, therefore brake bleeding will not be necessary.

5. Remove the nut and washer from the shock absorber and disconnect the shock absorber from the bracket.

6. Carefully lower the axle housing enough to remove the spring. Be careful not to stretch the brake hose.

7. Remove the spring, upper and lower insulator, as equipped.

To install:

8. Install the upper insulator, lower insulator, as equipped, and the rear spring to the bracket on the frame seat. Point the coil leg toward the left side of the vehicle, at a right angle from the centerline of the vehicle.

9. Raise the rear axle back into place with the adjustable lifting device.

10. Install the rear shock absorber to the bracket, and tighten the nut to 48 ft. lbs. (65 Nm).

11. Connect the rear brake line support bolt and tighten to 20 ft. lbs. (27 Nm).

12. Connect the height sensor link to the upper control arm, if applicable, and tighten nut to 27 inch lbs. (3 Nm).

13. Connect the ABS rear axle speed sensor, if equipped.

14. Lower vehicle and adjust the height sensor, if necessary.

Rear Control Arms

REMOVAL & INSTALLATION

UPPER ARM

NOTE: If both control arms are to be replaced, remove and replace 1 control arm at a time to prevent the axle from rolling or slipping sideways.

1. Raise and support the vehicle safely. Be sure to support the rear axle housing with a jackstand.

2. Disconnect the ABS rear axle speed sensor, if equipped.

3. If equipped, disconnect the height sensor link from the upper control arm by removing the attaching nut and sliding the sensor link stud out of the hole in the control arm.

4. Disconnect the stabilizer shaft bolts and washers from the upper control arm, for 1989–90 vehicles.

5. Remove the nut and bolt at the

rear axle housing. Disconnect the upper control arm from the housing.

6. Remove the nut and bolt at the rear frame crossmember. Remove the upper control arm from the vehicle.

To install:

7. Loosely attach the upper control arm to the rear frame crossmember using the nut and bolt.

8. Loosely attach the upper control arm to the rear axle housing using the nut and bolt.

9. For 1989–90 vehicles, loosely attach the stabilizer shaft and bolt.

10. Remove the jackstand from the rear axle and place supports under the tires. Lower the vehicle enough so the vehicle weight rests on the tires.

11. With the weight of the vehicle on the tires, tighten the bolt at the rear frame crossmember to 114 ft. lbs. (155 Nm) or the nut to 91 ft. lbs. (123 Nm). Either the nut or the bolt must be tightened, torque whichever is easiest to access.

12. With the weight of the vehicle on the tires, tighten the bolt at the rear axle housing to 80 ft. lbs. (108 Nm) or the nut to 70 ft. lbs. (95 Nm). Once again, torque whichever is easiest to access.

13. If applicable, with the weight of the vehicle on the tires, tighten the stabilizer shaft bolt to 52 ft. lbs. (70 Nm).

14. Connect the height sensor link to the upper control arm, if applicable, and tighten nut to 27 inch lbs. (3 Nm).

15. Connect the ABS rear axle speed sensor, if equipped.

16. Remove the tire supports, lower the vehicle and, if necessary, adjust the height sensor.

LOWER ARM

NOTE: If both control arms are to be replaced, remove and replace 1 control arm at a time to prevent the axle from rolling or slipping sideways.

1. Raise and support the vehicle safely. Be sure to support the rear axle housing with a jackstand.

2. Disconnect the stabilizer shaft bolts and washers, for 1991–93 vehicles.

3. Remove the nut and bolt from the bracket on the axle tube.

4. Remove the nut and bolt from the crossmember brace, if equipped, and from the bracket on the frame.

5. Remove the lower control arm from the vehicle.

To install:

6. Position the lower control arm on the vehicle.

7. Loosely install the nuts and bolts to the frame bracket, axle tube bracket and, if applicable, to the stabilizer shaft.

8. Remove the jackstand from the rear axle and place supports under the tires. Lower the vehicle enough so that the vehicle weight rests on the tires.

9. With the weight of the vehicle on the tires, tighten either the nut or the bolt, whichever is easiest to access. For 1989–90 vehicles tighten the lower control arm bolts to 122 ft. lbs. (165 Nm) or the nuts to 92 ft. lbs. (125 Nm). For 1991–93 vehicles tighten the lower control arm bolts to 74 ft. lbs. (100 Nm) or the nuts to 91 ft. lbs. (123 Nm).

10. If applicable, tighten the stabilizer bolts to 52 ft. lbs. (29 Nm).

11. Remove the tire supports and lower the vehicle.

Rear Wheel Bearings

For all rear wheel bearing removal and installation procedures, refer to Drive Axle section.

Rear Axle Assembly

For rear axle removal and installation procedures, refer to Drive Axle section.

STEERING

—— CAUTION ——

If equipped with the Supplemental Inflatable Restraint system (SIR), the system must be disabled, before working on any part of the system. Failure to do so may result in deployment of the air bag and possible personal injury.

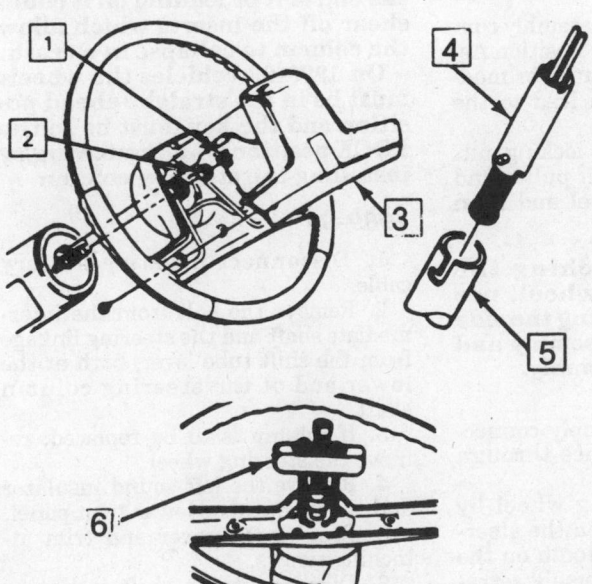

Steering wheel assembly—1989–90

Steering Wheel

REMOVAL & INSTALLATION

1989–90

NOTE: Do not pound on the steering wheel or the steering shaft. The collapsible column could be damaged enough to require replacement.

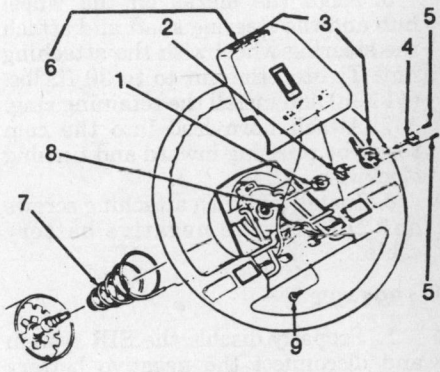

1. Steering wheel
2. Nut retainer
3. Telescoping adjuster lever
4. Steering shaft lock knob bolt
5. Steering shaft lock knob bolt positioning screw
6. Steering wheel pad
7. Horn contact spring
8. Horn lead
9. Horn pad attaching screw

Tilt and telescoping wheel assembly—1989–90

1. Retainer
2. Nut
3. Pad
4. Horn lead
5. Cam tower
6. J-1859-03

1. Disconnect the negative battery cable.

2. Remove the pad attaching screws, lift up the pad and disconnect the horn wire by pushing on the insulator and turning counterclockwise.

3. Remove the steering wheel nut and retainer.

4. Mark the steering wheel hub and shaft to assist in reinstallation.

5. Remove the steering wheel, using a puller.

To install:

6. Align the marks on the wheel hub and the steering shaft and attach the steering wheel with the attaching nut. Tighten the nut to to 30 ft. lbs. (41 Nm) and install the retaining ring.

7. Attach horn lead into the cam tower by pressing inward and turning clockwise.

8. Install pad with attaching screws and connect the negative battery cable.

1991–93

1. Properly disable the SIR system and disconnect the negative battery cable.

2. Remove the Torx® screws from the back of the steering wheel, disconnect the connector and lift up the inflator module.

— **CAUTION** —

To avoid personal injury when carrying a live inflator module, make sure the bag and trim cover are pointed away. When placing a live inflator module on a bench or other surface, always face the bag and trim cover up and away from the surface. Never carry the inflator module by the wires or connector on the underside of the module, otherwise personal injury may result if bag is deployed.

3. Disconnect the coil assembly connector and the Connector Position Assurance (CPA) from the inflator module. Disconnect the horn lead to the steering column.

4. Remove the hexagon locking nut.

5. Use a suitable wheel puller and remove the steering wheel and horn contact.

NOTE: When attaching the wheel puller to the wheel, use care to prevent threading the side screws into the coil assembly and damaging the coil assembly.

To install:

6. Route the coil assembly connector and position assurance through the steering wheel.

7. Install the steering wheel by aligning the block tooth on the steering wheel with the block tooth on the steering shaft within 1 female serration and install the locking nut.

8. Connect the horn lead to the the

1. Terminal from inflatable restraint module
2. Terminal from coil assembly
3. Connector position assurance
4. Inflator module
5. Steering wheel
6. Screw

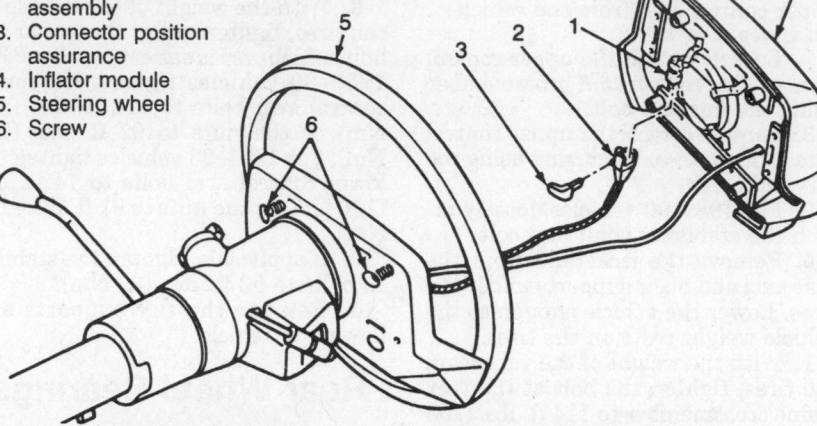

Steering wheel assembly with inflator module – 1989–90

steering column. Connect the coil assembly connector and the connector position assurance to the inflator module.

9. Center the coil assembly, if necessary.

10. Install the inflator module to the wheel and tighten the bolts to 25 inch lbs. (2.8 Nm).

11. Connect the negative battery cable and properly enable the SIR system.

Steering Column

REMOVAL & INSTALLATION

NOTE: Handle the steering column very carefully. Rapping on the end of it or leaning on it could shear off the inserts which allow the column to collapse in a crash.

On 1990–93 vehicles the wheels must be in the straight-ahead position and the key must be in the LOCK position when removing or installing the steering column

1989–90

1. Disconnect negative battery cable.

2. Remove the bolt from the intermediate shaft and the steering linkage from the shift tube lever, both at the lower end of the steering column shaft.

3. If column is to be replaced, remove the steering wheel.

4. Remove the left sound insulator and the trim cap or lower trim panel.

5. Remove the cover and trim attaching screws.

6. Disconnect the shift indicator clip from the shift bowl.

7. Remove the 2 nuts and, if used,

shims from the column upper support while holding the column in position and carefully lower the column.

8. Disconnect any necessary electrical connections.

To install:

9. Place the steering column in vehicle and connect all electrical connections.

NOTE: When installing, use only the specified hardware. Over length bolts could prevent the column from properly collapsing in a crash.

10. Carefully raise column into position and attach the column upper support nuts and washers, if applicable, finger-tight to hold the column in place.

11. Position the cover and seal to the dash panel. Install screw in the upper left hand corner of the cover and seal. Tighten scew to 53 inch lbs. (6 Nm).

12. Install upper right hand screw and tighten to same specification. Then install remaining screws to the same specification.

13. Install the intermediate shaft onto the steering column shaft.

14. Tighten the bolt and attaching nut of the intermediate shaft to 52 ft. lbs. (70 Nm) and the steering column support bracket nuts to 20 ft. lbs. (27 Nm).

15. Attach the shift indicator cable clip to the shift bowl.

16. Attach the shift linkage to shift tube lever at the lower end of the steering column. Adjust linkage as necessary.

17. Install the trim cap or lower panel and the left sound insulator.

18. Install the steering wheel, if removed.

19. Connect the negative battery cable.

1991–93

NOTE: The wheels of the vehicle must be in the straight-ahead position and the key must be in the LOCK position when removing or installing the steering column. Failure to do so will cause the coil assembly in the steering column to become off center and possibly damage the coil or deploy the SIR module.

1. Properly disable the SIR system and disconnect the negative battery cable.
2. Remove the stoplight switch.

NOTE: Failure to remove the stoplight switch may cause damage to the switch or the switch to be thrown out of adjustment.

3. Remove the steering column opening filler and driver knee bolster.
4. Remove the bolt and nut from the joint coupler attaching the intermediate shaft to the steering column.
5. Remove the capsule nuts attaching the steering column support bracket to the instrument panel carrier and carefully lower the steering column.
6. Disconnect the shift indicator cable and the shift selector rod from the steering column.
7. Disconnect all necessary electrical connectors.
8. Remove bolts attaching toe plate to the cowl.
9. If the column is being replaced, remove the steering wheel.
10. Remove the steering column from the vehicle.

To install:
11. Place steering column in vehicle.
12. Attach the toe plate to the cowl with the attaching bolts. Tighten to 58 inch lbs. (6.5 Nm)
13. Attach electrical connectors.

NOTE: If service replacement steering column is being installed, be sure to remove the anti-rotation pin.

14. Attach the shift indicator cable to the steering column.
15. Install the capsule nuts attaching the column support bracket to the instrument panel carrier and tighten to 20 ft. lbs. (27 Nm).
16. Install the bolt and nut at the joint coupling attaching the upper intermediate shaft to the steering column and tighten to 40 ft. lbs. (54 Nm).
17. Connect the shift selector rod and, if necessary, adjust linkage.
18. Install and adjust the stoplamp switch.

19. Install the driver knee boltser and the steering column opening filler.

NOTE: If service replacement steering column is being installed be sure to; remove the hexagon locking nut, remove the coil assembly shipping cover and disengage the connector from the cover.

20. Attach the steering wheel, if removed.
21. Connect the negative battery cable and enable the SIR system.

Power Steering Gear

REMOVAL & INSTALLATION

1. Disconnect the negative battery cable and lock the steering wheel in the straight-ahead position.
2. Disconnect and plug the power steering hoses from the gear assembly.
3. Raise and support the vehicle safely.
4. Disconnect the intermediate shaft from the gear and if equipped, the ABS modulator bracket.
5. Remove the pitman arm from the steering gear using tool J–29107 or equivalent.
6. Remove steering gear mounting bolts and remove the gear assembly.

To install:
7. Position the gear assembly to the frame and attach loosely with washers and bolts.
8. Adjust the flat on the gear to align as straight as possible with the flat of the intermediate shaft. Tighten the gear assembly mounting bolts to 70 ft. lbs. (95 Nm).
9. Install the pitman arm to the steering gear.
10. Install the intermediate shaft.
11. If equipped, install the ABS modulator bracket to power steering gear and tighten the nut to 18 ft. lbs. (24 Nm).
12. Lower the vehicle.
13. Connect the inlet and outlet hoses, then tighten fittings to 21 ft. lbs. (28 Nm).
14. Connect the negative battery cable and bleed the system.

Power Steering Pump

REMOVAL & INSTALLATION

1. Disconnect the negative battery cable.
2. Loosen and remove power steering pump belt or serpentine belt.
3. Remove the power steering pump pulley, if required.
4. Disconnect at the pump and cap the inlet and outlet lines.

5. Remove the bolts, nut and spacer, as applicable, from the adjuster bracket.
6. Either remove the pump assembly upward through the engine compartment, or if necessary, safely raise and support the vehicle and lower the pump assembly from the engine compartment.

To install:
7. Position pump assembly to bracket and loosely install bolts, nut and spacer, as applicable.
8. Uncap and connect the inlet and outlet hoses.
9. Install the pump pulley, if removed.
10. Install the power steering pump belt or serpentine belt. Tighten power steering nut to 30 ft. lbs. (41 Nm) and the bolts to 37 ft. lbs. (50 Nm).
11. Fill with fluid, bleed the system and adjust belt(s) to proper tension.

BELT ADJUSTMENT

V-BELT

5.0L (VIN Y) Engine

Use a belt tension gauge and adjust to 112 ft. lbs. (500 Nm) on used belts or 169 ft. lbs. (750 Nm) on new belts.

Serpentine Belt

If belt slippage occurs and the drive belt tensioner is within its operating range, check the belt tension as follows:
1. Run the engine for 10 minutes, shut OFF the engine, then using a tension gauge between any 2 pulleys, record the belt tension.
2. Run the engine for 30 seconds and repeat Step 1.
3. Again run the engine for 30 seconds and repeat Step 1.
4. The belt tension is the average of the 3 readings. Serpentine belt tension should be 105–125 lbs. (467–556 N).
5. Replace the belt tensioner if the tension is below the minimum specification and the drive belt tensioner is within its operating range.

SYSTEM BLEEDING

When the power steering system has been serviced, air must be bled from the system by using the following procedure:
1. With the front wheels off the ground, turn wheels all the way to the left and add power steering fluid to the cold mark on the level indicator.
2. Bleed the system by turning the wheels from side to side several times, without hitting stops.
3. Start engine and run at fast idle momentarily, shut engine OFF and

recheck the fluid level. If necessary add fluid to the cold mark.

4. Start engine and bleed system by turning wheels from side to side without hitting stops. Keep the fluid level at the cold mark.

5. Return the wheels to the center position and continue running the engine for a few minutes. Road test to check the operation of the steering.

6. Recheck the fluid level it should now be stabilized at the Hot level on the indicator.

Tie Rod Ends

REMOVAL & INSTALLATION

1. Raise and support the vehicle safely.

2. Remove the cotter pins from the ball studs and remove the castellated nuts.

3. Disconnect the tie rod end from the steering arm or knuckle with a tie rod joint separator.

4. Remove the inner ball stud from the intermediate rod with a puller.

5. Mark the tie rod end position before removing from the adjuster. Loosen the clamp bolts and unscrew the ends from the adjuster tubes. If a force of more than 7 ft. lbs. (10 Nm) is required to remove the ends after break away, the fasteners should be replaced.

6. Clean and inspect all parts.

To install:

7. Run the tie rod end to the position marked and tighten the adjuster clamp bolt to 14 ft. lbs. (19 Nm).

8. Insert the inner balls stud to the intermediate rod and loosely attach nut.

9. Connect outer ball stud to the steering knuckle attach nut. Tighten both nuts to 35 ft. lbs. (47 Nm).

10. After tightening castellated nuts, tighten again, just enough to align slot in nut with hole in studs. Do not back off to insert cotter pins.

11. Lower vehicle, check and adjust alingment if necessary.

BRAKES

Master Cylinder

REMOVAL & INSTALLATION

NOTE: Be sure to clean the area where the master cylinder is mounted, before beginning removal.

1. Disconnect and cap or plug hydraulic lines to prevent fluid contamination or loss.

2. Remove the attaching nuts.

3. If the combination valve bracket is mounted over the master cylinder on the power brake booster studs, pull the bracket from the studs and reposition it aside.

4. Remove the master cylinder.

To install:

5. Install the master cylinder on the power booster studs.

6. If applicable, install the combination valve bracket on the power booster studs.

7. Install the attaching nuts and tighten to 20 ft. lbs. (27 Nm) for all except 1991 vehicles or tighten to 15 ft. lbs. (21 Nm) for 1991 vehicles only.

8. Unplug hydraulic lines, attach to the master cylinder and tighten to 24 ft. lbs. (32 Nm).

9. Fill with approved brake fluid and bleed system.

Combination Valve

REMOVAL & INSTALLATION

1989–90

1. Raise and safely support vehicle.

2. Disconnect the hydraulic lines at the combination valve and plug the lines to prevent fluid contamination or loss.

3. Disconnect the electrical connector from the valve switch terminal.

4. Remove bolts attaching the combination valve to the frame and remove the valve.

To install:

5. Place the combination valve against the frame and install attaching bolts. Tighten bolts to 15 ft. lbs. (20 Nm).

6. Attach the electrical connector to the valve switch terminal.

7. Unplug and install hydraulic lines to the combination valve. Tighten fittings to 18 ft. lbs. (24 Nm).

8. Check that the hydraulic lines are at least 1 inch from the driveshaft.

9. Lower the vehicle and bleed the brake system.

1991–93

1. Disconnect the hydraulic lines at the combination valve.

2. Plug the lines to prevent fluid contamination or loss.

3. Remove the electrical wire connector from the pressure differential warning switch.

4. Remove the 2 attaching nuts from the power brake booster and remove the combination valve bracket and valve.

To install:

5. Place the combination valve and

bracket in position on the power brake booster studs.

6. Install and tighten the attaching nuts to 15 ft. lbs. (21 Nm) on 1991 vehicles or 20 ft. lbs. (27 Nm) for 1992–93 vehicles.

7. Unplug the hydraulic lines and attach them to the combination valve. Tighten fittings to 11 ft. lbs. (15 Nm) on 1991 vehicles or 24 ft. lbs. (32 Nm) on 1992–93 vehicles.

8. Connect the electrical connector and bleed the brake system.

Power Brake Booster

REMOVAL & INSTALLATION

1. Disconnect the vacuum hose from the vacuum check valve and plug the hose.

2. Remove the 2 nuts holding the master cylinder, and combination valve bracket if applicable, to the power unit. Carefully position the aside, being careful not to kink any of the hydraulic lines. It is not necessary to disconnect the brake lines.

3. Loosen the 4 nuts that hold the power unit mounted on the firewall.

4. Disconnect the retainer, outer washer, air valve pushrod assembly and inner washer, as applicable, from the brake pedal. Do not force the pushrod to the side when disconnecting.

5. Remove the 4 mounting nuts and remove the power unit.

To install:

6. Place the power unit against the firewall and loosely attach nuts.

7. Connect the inner washer, air valve pushrod assembly, outer washer, and retainer to the brake pedal.

8. Tighten the power unit attaching nuts to 15 ft. lbs. (21 Nm).

9. Install the master cylinder and, if applicable, the combination valve bracket on the power booster mounting studs. Tighten bolts to specification.

10. Unplug and connect the vacuum hose to the vacuum check valve.

Brake Caliper

REMOVAL & INSTALLATION

1. Remove ⅔ of the brake fluid from the master cylinder.

2. Raise the vehicle and support it safely.

3. Mark the relationship of the wheel to the hub for reinstallation and remove the tire and wheel assembly.

4. Position a C-clamp over the outboard shoe and lining and the caliper housing.

5. Bottom the piston into the caliper bore with the C-clamp.

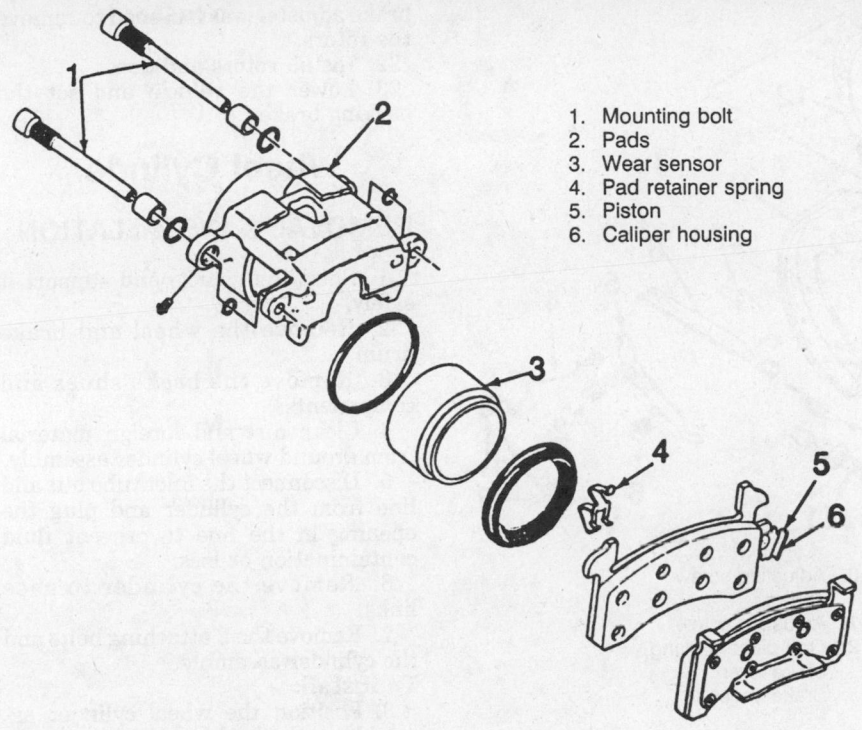

1. Mounting bolt
2. Pads
3. Wear sensor
4. Pad retainer spring
5. Piston
6. Caliper housing

Front brake caliper assembly

NOTE: If removing the caliper assembly only to access other brake parts skip Step 5. If removing the caliper entirely from the vehicle, the brake system will have to be bled.

6. Remove the bolt, copper washers and inlet fitting from the caliper housing. Plug the line to prevent fluid contamination and loss.
7. Remove the mounting bolts and the sleeves and remove the caliper from the rotor.
To install:
8. Lubricate the sleeves and bushings with silicone grease and insert sleeves into caliper housing.
9. Position the caliper assembly onto the rotor and bracket.
10. Insert mounting bolts and tighten to 38 ft. lbs. (51 Nm).
11. If removed, bolt new copper washers and the inlet fitting to the caliper housing, tighten to 32 ft. lbs. (44 Nm).
12. Align the marks on the wheel and hub and install the lug nuts.
13. Lower the vehicle.
14. Fill the master cylinder to the proper level and, if necessary, bleed the caliper.

Disc Brake Pads

REMOVAL & INSTALLATION

1. Raise the vehicle and support it safely.

2. Remove the tire and wheel assembly.
3. Remove the caliper assembly and suspend it from the front suspension using a fabricated wire hanger.
4. Remove the inner and outer brake pads from the caliper.
5. Remove the bushings and sleeves from the grooves in the caliper housing.
6. Remove the shoe retainer spring from the inboard pad.
To install:
7. Clean and then lubricate bushings and sleeves with silicone grease.
8. Install the bushings in the grooves in the caliper housing.
9. Install the shoe retainer spring on the inboard pad.
10. Install the inboard pad. Be sure to seat the shoe retainer spring in the piston.

NOTE: The wear sensor should be at the leading edge of the inboard pad during forward wheel rotation.

11. Install the outboard pad.
12. Install the caliper assembly.
13. Apply the brake pedal 3 times to seat the pads.
14. With the aid of an assistant holding pressure on the brake pedal, use a pair of channel lock pliers to clinch down the outboard shoe ears.
15. Install the front wheels on the vehicle.

Brake Rotor

REMOVAL & INSTALLATION

1. Disconnect the negative battery cable.
2. Raise and support the vehicle safely.
3. Disconnect the ABS wheel speed sensor from the steering knuckle and secure, if equipped.
4. Remove the brake caliper and position aside.
5. Remove the dust cap from the hub then remove the cotter pin, nut and washer from the spindle. Carefully remove the hub and rotor from the spindle.

To install:
6. Position hub and rotor assembly onto the spindle.
7. Place the washer and nut on the spindle. Initially torque the wheel hub spindle nut to 12 ft. lbs. while turning the wheel forward by hand. When finished with adjustment, install a new cotter pin.
8. Attach the dust cap to the hub assembly and install the ABS sensor, if equipped.
9. Install the brake caliper assembly.
10. Lower vehicle and connect the negative battery cable.

Brake Drums

REMOVAL & INSTALLATION

1. Raise and support the vehicle safely.
2. Mark the relationship of the wheel to the axle flange and remove the wheel.
3. Make sure the parking brake is released and carefully slide the rotor from the axle flange studs.
4. If there is difficulty removing the rotor, use a rubber mallet to tap gently on the outer rim of the drum and/or the inner drum diameter by the spindle. If necessary, remove the adjusting hole or knockout plate from the backing plate and back off the adjusting screw with a suitable tool.

To install:
5. Adjust the brakes as necessary.
6. Position rotor in place and slide onto mounting studs. Mount tires, aligning marks on the wheels and axle flanges.
7. Lower vehicle and set the parking brake.

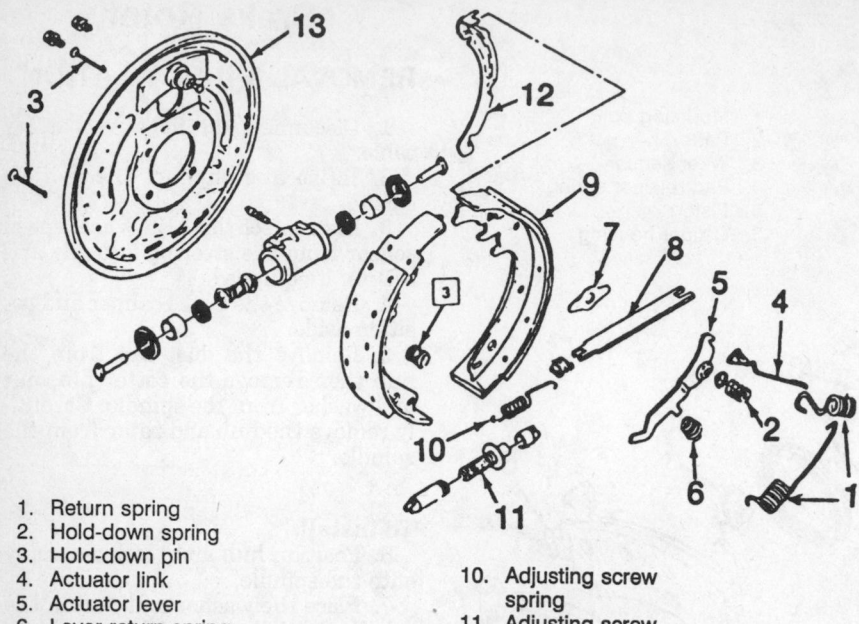

1. Return spring
2. Hold-down spring
3. Hold-down pin
4. Actuator link
5. Actuator lever
6. Lever return spring
7. Shoe guide
8. Parking brake strut
9. Brake shoes

10. Adjusting screw spring
11. Adjusting screw
12. One piece parking brake lever
13. Brake shoes

Rear drum brake assembly—standard duty

Brake Shoes

REMOVAL & INSTALLATION

1. Raise the vehicle and support it safely.

2. Remove the tire and wheel assembly.

3. Remove the brake drum. If the brake drum cannot be removed, try the following:

a. Make sure the parking brake is released.

b. Back off the parking brake cable adjustment.

c. Remove the adjusting hole knockout plate from the backing plate and back off the adjusting screw.

d. Use a rubber mallet to tap on the outer rim of the drum and around the inner drum diameter by the spindle.

4. Remove the return springs.

5. Remove the hold-down pins and springs.

6. Remove the actuator lever pivot.

7. Lift up on the actuator lever to remove the actuator link. Remove the lever, pawl if equipped, and lever return spring.

8. Remove the shoe guide and the parking brake strut and spring.

9. Remove the brake shoes from the backing plate and the parking brake cable.

10. Remove the adjusting screw as-

sembly and spring from the brake shoes.

11. Remove the parking brake lever by unhooking the lever tab from the slot in the brake shoe.

To install:

12. Clean the adjusting screw with a wire brush and then clean all components with brake cleaner or denatured alcohol.

13. Using 5450032 or equivalent, lubricate the adjusting screw threads, inside diameter of the socket and the socket face, for smooth rotation.

14. Install the parking brake lever by hooking lever tab into slot in primary or secondary shoe lining.

15. Install the adjusting screw assembly and the adjusting screw spring.

16. Connect the primary, secondary shoes and linings to the parking brake cable and the brake backing plate.

17. Install the shoe guide.

18. Install the pawl, if equipped, actuator lever and the lever return spring.

19. Connect the actuator link to the actuator pin. Install the actuator link into actuator lever while holding up on actuator lever.

20. Install the return springs with suitable tool.

21. Adjust the brake shoes. The outside diameter of both shoe and linings should be 0.050 inch (1.27mm) less than the inside diameter of the brake drum on each wheel. Be sure to adjust the parking brake cable, if the parking

brake adjuster was loosened to remove the rotors.

22. Install rotors and tires.

23. Lower the vehicle and set the parking brake.

Wheel Cylinder

REMOVAL & INSTALLATION

1. Raise the vehicle and support it safely.

2. Remove the wheel and brake drum.

3. Remove the brake shoes and components.

4. Clean dirt and foreign material from around wheel cylinder assembly.

5. Disconnect the inlet tube nut and line from the cylinder and plug the opening in the line to prevent fluid contamination or loss.

6. Remove the cylinder to shoe links.

7. Remove the 2 attaching bolts and the cylinder assembly.

To install:

8. Position the wheel cylinder assembly to the backing plate.

9. Connect the wheel cylinder attaching bolts and tighten to 13 ft. lbs. (18 Nm).

10. Install the cylinder shoe links.

11. Connect the brake rear pipe to the wheel cylinder and tighten to 18 ft. lbs. (24 Nm).

12. Install the shoes and brake components.

13. Install the rotors and wheels.

14. Lower the vehicle and bleed the brake system.

Parking Brake Cable

ADJUSTMENT

NOTE: Before attempting to adjust the parking brake, verify the rear brakes are correctly adjusted. If rear brakes are adjusted properly, the parking brake original adjustment should not have to be changed.

1. Clean and lubricate the exposed threads of the adjuster rod, to either side of the nut.

2. Apply the parking brake 3 clicks for 1989–90 vehicles or 6 clicks for 1991–93 vehicles, then raise and support the vehicle safely.

3. Tighten the adjusting nut until the rear wheels can barely be turned backward, using 2 hands, but lock up when moved forward.

4. With the parking brake disengaged the rear wheel should turn freely in either direction with no brake drag.

5. Lower the vehicle.

REMOVAL & INSTALLATION

Front

1. Raise the vehicle and support it safely.
2. Loosen equalizer enough to gain necessary cable slack.
3. Disconnect the front cable at the connector.
4. Disconnect the cable casing at frame by compressing retainer fingers and pulling outward.
5. Lower the vehicle.
6. Remove driver's side wheelhouse panel screws and panel bolts. Pull panel out to gain access to the front cable.
7. Disconnect the front cable and casing at the lever assembly, by compressing retainer fingers and pulling outward.
8. Remove the front cable and grommet from the vehicle.

To install:

9. Position front cable and grommet in vehicle.
10. Connect the front cable and casing at the lever assembly.
11. Install the wheelhouse panel bolts, tighten to 18 ft. lbs. (25 Nm), and screws, tighten to 89 inch lbs. (10 Nm).
12. Raise and safely support the vehicle.
13. Connect the cable casing at the frame and connect the cable to the connector.
14. Adjust the parking brake and lower the vehicle.

Rear

1. Raise the vehicle and support it safely.
2. Loosen the equalizer enough to gain cable slack, as necessary.
3. On the left side disconnect the cable from the connector and the equalizer. On the right side, disconnect the cable from the equalizer. Disconnect the cable and casing at the frame by compressing the retainer fingers and pulling outward. Disconnect the cable and casing from the axle housing clips.
4. Mark the relationship of the wheel to the axle flange and remove the tire and wheel assembly.
5. Remove the brake drum, the primary shoe return spring, secondary shoe hold-down spring and the parking brake strut, as necessary.
6. Compress the retainer fingers and loosen the cable and casing from the backing plate. Disconnect the cable from the parking brake lever and remove the cable.

To install:

7. Connect the cable and casing into the brake backing plate and attach to the parking brake lever.
8. Install the primary brake shoe return spring, secondary shoe hold-down spring, parking brake strut and rotor.
9. Align the wheel and axle flange marks. Install the tire and wheel assembly.
10. On the left side connect the cable to the connector and the equalizer. On the right side, connect the cable and casing to the frame and to the axle housing clips. Then connect the cable to the equalizer.
11. Adjust the parking brake and lower the vehicle.

Brake System Bleeding

The brake system must be bled when any brake line is disconnected or if it is suspected that there is air in the system.

NOTE Always prevent fluid from touching a painted surface.

1. Clean the master cylinder of excess dirt and remove the cylinder cover and the diaphragm.
2. Fill the master cylinder to the proper level. Check the fluid level periodically during the bleeding process and replenish it, as necessary. Do not allow the master cylinder to fall below ½ full.
3. If the master cylinder is suspected or known to have air in the bore, bleed it before any wheel cylinder or caliper as follows:

   a. Disconnect the forward brake line connection at the master cylinder.

   b. Allow brake fluid to fill the master cylinder bore until it begins to flow from the forward line connector port.

   c. Connect the forward brake line to the master cylinder and tighten.

   d. Have an assistant depress the brake pedal slowly, 1 full thrust at a time and hold while loosening the forward brake line connection at the master cylinder to purge the air from the bore. Tighten the connection and then have an assistant release the brake pedal slowly. Wait 15 seconds and repeat the sequence. Repeat the sequence, including the 15 second pause, until all air is removed from the bore.

   e. After all air is removed at the forward connection, repeat the above procedure for the rear connection at the master.

NOTE: Never bleed a wheel cylinder when a drum is removed.

4. Bleed the individual wheel cylinders or calipers only after all air is removed from the master cylinder.

   a. Attach the proper size box end wrench over the bleeder valve.

   b. Attach a length of clear vinyl hose to the bleeder screw of the brake to be bled. Insert the other end of the hose into a clear jar half full of clean brake fluid, so the end of the hose is beneath the level of fluid. The correct sequence for bleeding is to work from the brake farthest from the master cylinder to the 1 closest; right rear, left rear, right front, left front.

5. Have an assistant depress and release the brake pedal 1 time and hold. Loosen the bleeder valve to purge the air from the cylinder. Tighten the bleeder screw and slowly release the pedal and wait 15 seconds. Repeat the sequence, including the 15 second pause, until all air is removed.

NOTE: Make sure an assistant presses the brake pedal to the floor slowly. Rapid pumping of the brake pedal pushes the master cylinder secondary piston down the bore in a way that makes it difficult to bleed the rear side of the system.

6. Repeat this procedure at each of the wheels. Tighten the bleeder screw to 115 inch lbs. (13 Nm) when bleeding is completed. Remember to check the master cylinder level occasionally. Use only fresh fluid to refill the master cylinder, not the fluid bled from the system.
7. When the bleeding process is complete, refill the master cylinder, install its cover and diaphragm and discard the fluid bled from the brake system.

Anti-Lock Brake System Service

PRECAUTIONS

Failure to observe the following precautions may result in system damage.

• Before performing electric arc welding on the vehicle, disconnect the Electronic Brake Control Module (EBCM) and the hydraulic modulator connectors.

• When performing painting work on the vehicle, do not expose the Electronic Brake Control Module (EBCM) to temperatures in excess of 185°F (85°C) for longer than 2 hours. The system may be exposed to temperatures up to 200°F (95°C) for less than 15 minutes.

• Never disconnect or connect the Electronic Brake Control Module (EBCM) or hydraulic modulator connectors with the ignition switch ON.

• Never disassemble any component of the Anti-Lock Brake System (ABS) which is designated non-ser-

viceable; the component must be replaced as an assembly.
● When filling the master cylinder, always use Delco Supreme 11 brake fluid or equivalent, which meets DOT-3 specifications; petroleum base fluid will destroy the rubber parts.

Modulator Valve

REMOVAL & INSTALLATION

CAUTION

The modulator is not repairable and no screws on the modulator may be loosened. If the screws are loosened, it will not be possible to to get the brake circuits leak-tight and personal injury injury may result.

1. Disconnect the negative battery cable.
2. Remove the air intake duct and resonator and move the upper coolant hose aside.
3. Disconnect the canister purge line at the canister and move aside.
4. Remove the retaining screw and remove the modulator valve cover.
5. Unlock the tab and disconnect the modulator valve electrical connector.
6. Remove the nut and disconnect the ground wire from the modulator.
7. Note the hydraulic brake pipe locations then disconnect and plug the lines from the modulator to prevent fluid contamination or loss.
8. Remove the 3 nuts retaining the modulator to the bracket.
9. Remove bracket taking care to protect the vehicle from any brake fluid spillage. If replacing the modulator assembly, remove the insulators from the modulator valve.

To install:

10. If applicable, install the insulators to the modulator valve.
11. Install the modulator valve to the bracket and tighten the 3 nuts to 89 inch lbs. (10 Nm).
12. If a new modulator is being used, remove shipping plugs from the valve openings.
13. Connect the hydraulic brake pipes to their original locations in the modulator and tighten to 11 ft. lbs. (15 Nm).

CAUTION

If brake pipes are switched (inlet vs. outlet) wheel lockup will occur and personal injury may result.

14. Install the ground wire and nut to the modulator, tighten nut to 25 inch lbs. (2.8 Nm).
15. Install the modulator valve electrical connector.
16. Install the the modulator valve

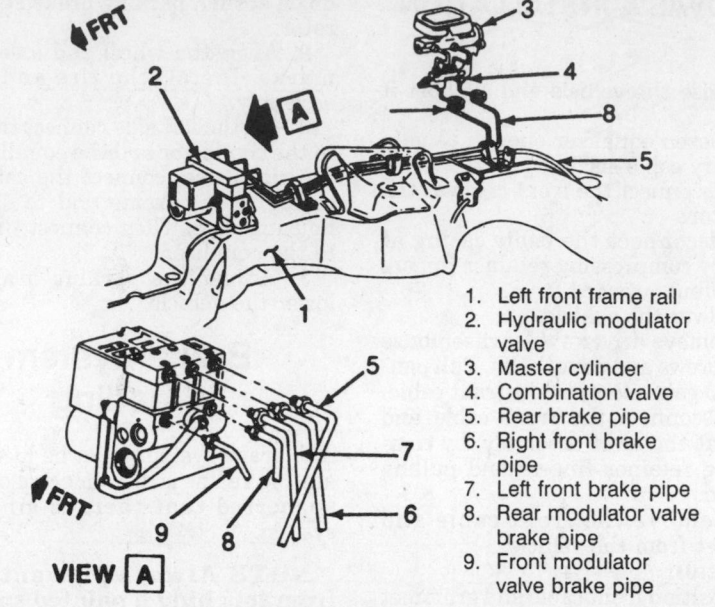

1. Left front frame rail
2. Hydraulic modulator valve
3. Master cylinder
4. Combination valve
5. Rear brake pipe
6. Right front brake pipe
7. Left front brake pipe
8. Rear modulator valve brake pipe
9. Front modulator valve brake pipe

ABS brake line routing

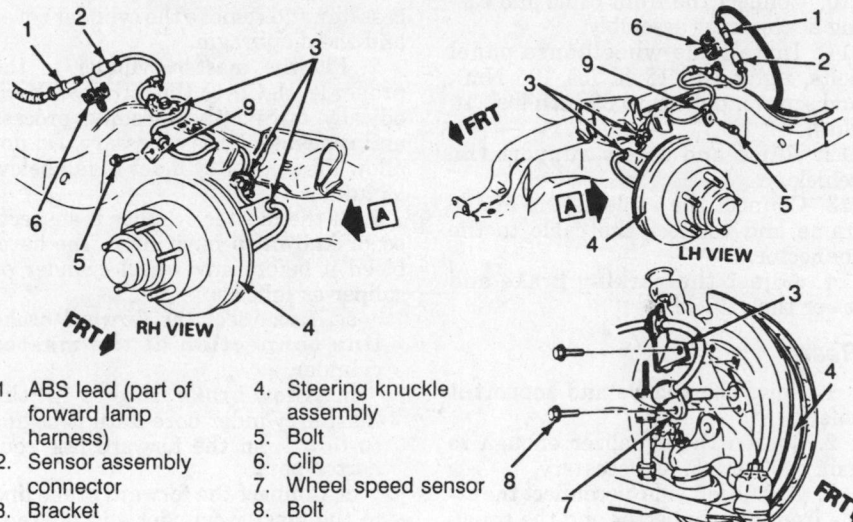

1. ABS lead (part of forward lamp harness)
2. Sensor assembly connector
3. Bracket
4. Steering knuckle assembly
5. Bolt
6. Clip
7. Wheel speed sensor
8. Bolt
9. Bracket

ABS front wheel speed sensor

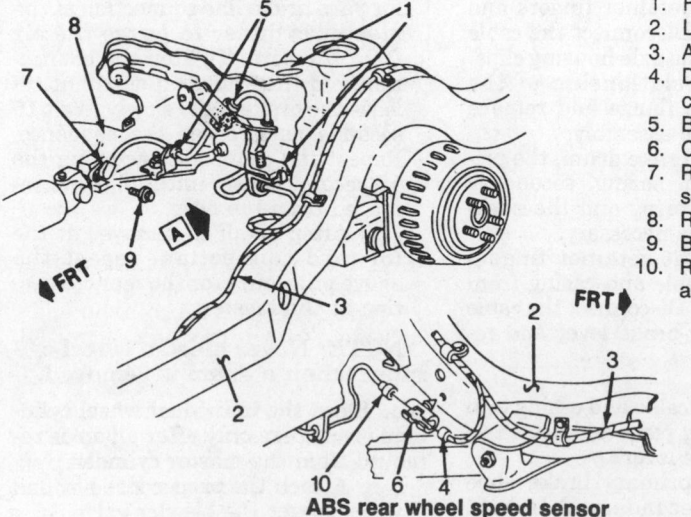

1. Frame cross bar
2. Left frame rail
3. ABS wiring harness
4. Differential sensor connector
5. Bracket
6. Clip
7. Rear axle speed sensor
8. Rear axle housing
9. Bolt
10. Rear sensor assembly connector

ABS rear wheel speed sensor

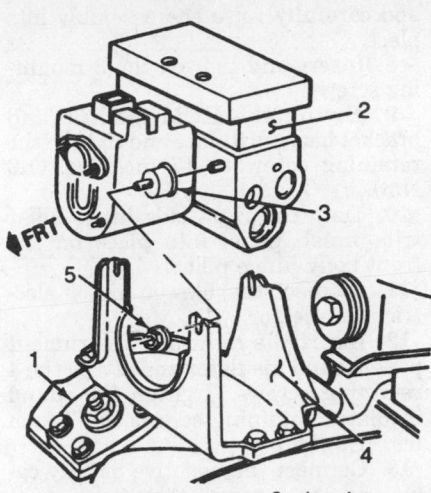

1. Steering gear
2. Hydraulic modulator valve
3. Insulator
4. Bracket
5. Nut

ABS Hydraulic modulator valve removal

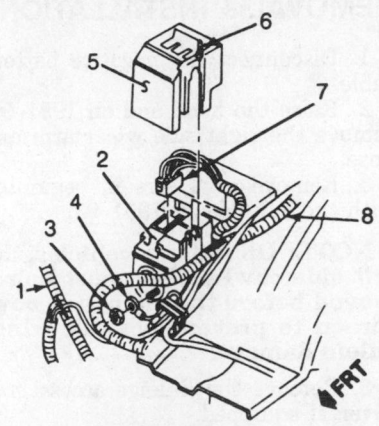

1. Forward lamp harness
2. Hydraulic modulator valve
3. Nut
4. Ground wire
5. Modulator valve cover
6. Screw
7. Modulator valve electrical connector
8. ABS wiring harness

ABS Hydraulic modulator valve electrical connections

cover with the retaining screw and tighten to 13 inch lbs. (1.5 Nm).
17. Connect the canister purge line to the canister.
18. Install the air intake duct and resonator and move the upper coolant hose into position.
19. Connect the negative battery cable.
20. Use only DOT 3 hydraulic brake fluid, fill and bleed the brake system.
21. Road test the vehicle.

Electronic Brake Control Module (EBCM)

For 1991 vehicles, the EBCM is located at the bottom of the "D" pillar on most vehicles, except for Chevrolet sedans where it is located between the deck lid hinge pillar and the wheelhouse panel. For 1992–93 vehicles, it has been relocated under the left side instrument panel, above the brake pedal, on the DERM bracket.

Front Wheel Speed Sensor

REMOVAL & INSTALLATION

1. Disconnect the negative battery cable.
2. For the right side speed sensor, unclip the connectors from the clip and separate.
3. Raise and support the vehicle safely.
4. For the left side speed sensor, with the vehicle safely supported, unclip the connectors from the clip and separate.
5. Remove the sensor wiring harness mounting bolt and bracket from the frame rail.
6. Remove the sensor retaining bolt and remove the sensor from the knuckle assembly.
To install:
7. Coat the steering knuckle with anti corrosion compound 1052856 or equivalent, at the knuckle contact point.
8. Install the wheel speed senor to the steering knuckle and tighten the sensor retaining bolt to 71 inch lbs. (8 Nm).

NOTE: Proper installation of the wheel speed sensor cables is critical to proper operation of the ABS system. Make sure the cables are installed in the retainers. Failure to do this may result in contact with moving parts and the over extension of the cables, resulting in an open circuit.

9. Connect the sensor wiring harness mounting bolt and bracket to the frame rail and tighten to 89 inch lbs. (10 Nm).
10. For the left side speed sensor, with the vehicle safely supported, attach the connectors and position them in the clip.
11. Lower the vehicle.
12. For the right side speed sensor, attach the connectors and position them in the clip.

13. Connect the negative battery cable and road test vehicle.

Rear Axle Speed Sensor

REMOVAL & INSTALLATION

1. Disconnect the negative battery cable. Raise and support the vehicle safely.
2. Disconnect the rear sensor assembly from the differential sensor connector.
3. Remove the sensor wiring harness from the retainer brackets.
4. Remove the sensor retaining bolt and remove the speed sensor from the rear axle housing.
To install:
5. Install the sensor into the rear axle housing. The sensor is a tight fit but it must be pushed in by hand. Do not hammer the sensor into position.
6. Tighten the sensor retaining bolt to 71 inch lbs. (8 Nm).
7. Insert the sensor wiring harness into the retainer brackets.
8. Connect the rear sensor assembly to the differential sensor connector.
9. Lower the vehicle.
10. Connect the negative battery cable and road test the vehicle.

NOTE: Proper installation of the wheel speed sensor cables is critical to proper operation of the ABS system. Make sure the cables are installed in the retainers. Failure to do this may result in contact with moving parts and the over extension of the cables, resulting in an open circuit.

CHASSIS ELECTRICAL

Air Bag

DISARMING

1. Align the steering wheel so the vehicle wheels are pointing in the straight-ahead position.
2. Turn the ignition switch to the **LOCK** position.
3. Remove the SIR fuse from the fuse block.
4. Disconnect the yellow 2-way SIR harness wire connector at the base of the steering column.

To enable system:

5. Turn the ignition switch to the **LOCK** position.

6. Reconnect the yellow 2-way connector at the base of the steering column.

7. Reinstall the SIR fuse.

8. Turn the ignition switch to the **RUN** position.

9. Verify the SIR indicator light flashes 7–9 times, if not, inspect system for malfunction.

Air Bag Coil Assembly

NOTE: The coil assembly must remain centered in order to avoid accidental deployment of the air bag after any repair procedures to the internals of the steering column. There are 2 different styles of coil assemblies, 1 rotates clockwise and the other rotates counterclockwise.

ADJUSTMENT

1. With the system properly disarmed, hold the coil assembly with the clear bottom up to see the coil ribbon.

2. While holding the coil assembly, depress the lock spring and rotate the hub in the direction of the arrow until it stops. The coil should now be wound up snug against the center hub.

3. Rotate the coil assembly in the opposite direction approximately 2½ turns and release the lock spring between the locking tabs in front of the arrow.

4. Install the coil assembly onto the steering shaft.

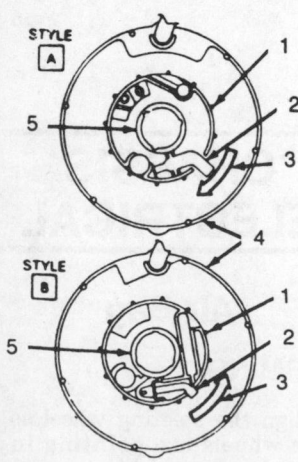

1. Locking tab
2. Spring
3. Hub direction
4. Coil housing
5. Coil hub

Centering the coil assembly

Heater Blower Motor

REMOVAL & INSTALLATION

Without Air Conditioning

1. Disconnect the negative battery cable.

2. Disconnect the blower motor wiring harness.

3. Remove the blower motor retaining screws and pull the blower motor and fan straight forward out of the heater module.

4. Installation is the reverse of removal. Clean and replace sealer as necessary.

With Air Conditioning

1989–90

1. Disconnect the negative battery cable.

2. Disconnect the blower motor wiring harness.

3. Remove the blower motor cooling tube.

4. Remove the blower motor retaining screws and lift the blower motor and fan straight up and out of the upper case of the air conditioning module.

To install:

5. Clean and replace sealer as necessary.

6. Lower blower motor into upper case of the air conditioning module and tighten motor retaining screws.

7. Connect the blower motor cooling tube.

8. Connect blower motor wiring harness.

9. Connect the negative battery cable and check for proper motor operation.

1991–93

1. Disconnect the negative battery cable.

2. Remove the 4 retaining screws and remove the right side instrument panel sound insulator.

3. Disconnect the blower motor electrical connector.

4. Remove the right side hinge pillar trim finish panel by pulling it away from the front body hinge pillar.

5. Remove the screw from the secondary ECM bracket and swing the ECM module and bracket aside to provide access to the blower motor.

6. Remove the blower mounting mounting screws, leaving the screw closest to the relay for last. Carefully lower the blower motor fan assembly and remove.

To install:

7. Align the blower motor and fan assembly, making sure the ECM module and retainer are out of the way,

and carefully raise the assembly into place.

8. Insert and tighten the 3 mounting screws.

9. Swing the ECM module and bracket back into place and tighten the retaining screw to 17 inch lbs. (1.9 Nm).

10. Snap the right side hinge pillar trim finish panel into place on the front body hinge pillar.

11. Connect the blower motor electrical connector.

12. Insert the right side instrument panel sound insulator and attach the 4 retaining screws. Tighten the sound insulator retaining screws to 17 inch lbs. (1.9 Nm).

13. Connect the negative battery cable and check motor operation.

Windshield Wiper Motor

REMOVAL & INSTALLATION

1. Disconnect the negative battery cable.

2. Raise the hood and on 1991–93, remove the right side wiper arm and hose.

3. Remove cowl screen, beginning with the left side on 1991–93.

NOTE: On 1991–93 vehicles, the left side cowl screen must be removed before the right side cowl screen to prevent possible windshield damage.

3. Remove the linkage access hole cover, if equipped.

4. Loosen the transmission drive link to crank arm retaining bolts. Remove the drive link from the motor crank arm.

5. Disconnect the electrical wiring and any remaining washer hoses from the motor assembly.

6. Remove the motor retaining screws. Remove the windshield wiper motor while guiding the crank arm through the hole.

To install:

7. Guide the wiper motor guiding crank arm through the hole.

8. Insert and tighten wiper motor attaching bolts to 80 inch lbs. (9 Nm).

9. Attach electrical connectors.

10. Place the motor in the **P** position and attach the motor crank arm to the drive link. Tighten drive link nuts to 27 inch lbs. (3 Nm).

11. Attach wiper linkage access hole cover with screws. Tighten hole cover screws to 13 inch lbs. (1.5 Nm).

12. Install right and left side cowl screens.

NOTE: On 1991–93 vehicles, the right side cowl screen must be in-

stalled before the left side cowl screen to prevent possible windshield damage.

13. Attach the right side wiper arm and hose.

14. Connect the negative battery cable and check wiper motor operation.

Windshield Wiper Switch

REMOVAL & INSTALLATION

NOTE: If equipped with an air bag, it is imperative that the disarming procedure is followed before repairs, and that the coil centering and rearming procedures are followed after repairs.

1. Disarm the air bag, if equipped, and disconnect the negative battery cable.

2. Remove the turn signal assembly.

3. Remove the SIR coil assembly from the column if necessary, as follows:

　a. Remove wiring protector.

　b. Attach a length of mechanics wire to the terminal connector to aid in reassembly.

　c. Carefully pull wire through the column.

4. Remove the lock cylinder set.

5. Remove lock housing cover screws.

6. Remove the tilt lever, if equipped and remove the lock housing cover.

7. Remove the base plate and the dimmer switch rod actuator.

8. Disconnect and remove wiper switch actuator pivot pin.

9. Disconnect wiper switch connector from vehicle wire harness and remove switch. Attach a piece of mechanic's wire to the connector to aid in reinstallation and gently pull wire harness through column.

To install:

10. Connect the wiper switch assembly to the lock housing cover assembly.

11. Attach the switch actuator pivot pin to the switch and cover.

12. Pull wiper switch wire connector through the steering column with mechanic's wire and attach to the vehicle wire harness.

13. Attach the dimmer switch rod actuator to the base plate and lubricate with lithium grease.

14. Connect base plate to lock housing cover assembly. The bottom edge of the dimmer switch rod actuator must rest on the bend in the dimmer switch rod.

15. Position lock housing cover in place and, if equipped, attach tilt lever.

16. Starting with the housing cover screw in the 12 o'clock position, then 8

1. Lock housing cover assembly
2. Dimmer switch rod actuator
3. Housing cover end base plate
4. Housing cover end cap
5. Dimmer switch rod

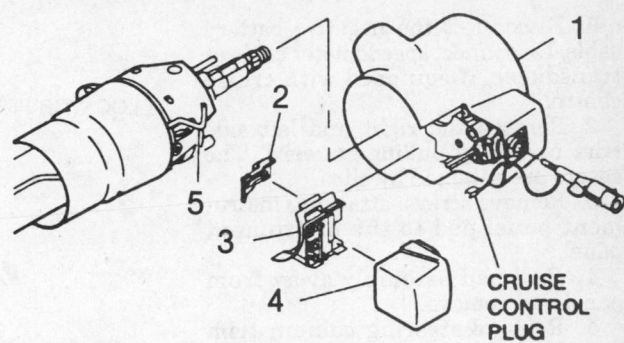

Removing lock housing cover

o'clock and finally 3 o'clock positions, tighten the screws to 80 inch lbs. (9 Nm).

17. Install the lock cylinder set.

18. Attach the SIR coil assembly, if necessary, by pulling wire connector through the steering column and reattaching the wire protector.

19. Install the turn signal assembly.

20. Be sure to center SIR coil assembly before reinstalling SIR inflator module and steering wheel.

21. Connect the negative battery cable and enable SIR system.

Instrument Cluster

REMOVAL & INSTALLATION

1989–90 Estate Wagon

1. Disconnect the negative battery cable.

2. Remove the steering column trim plate, left hand trim plate or right hand trim plate as necessary.

3. Remove the center trim plate.

4. Pull the indicator housing far enough forward to disconnect the electrical connector, bulb and socket assemblies.

5. Disconnect the speedometer cable and remove indicator housing.

NOTE: If equipped with tilt steering wheel, it may be helpful to tilt the wheel all the way down and pull the gear select lever to low, when removing the cluster.

To install:

6. Position indicator housing to the instrument panel and connect the speedometer cable.

7. Connect the electrical connector, bulb and socket assemblies.

8. Attach the center trim plate.

9. Attach the steering column trim plate, left hand trim plate, or right hand trim plate, if removed.

10. Connect the negative battery cable.

1989–90 Caprice and 1989 Safari

1. Disconnect the negative battery cable.

2. Remove the steering column trim plate screws and the trim plate.

3. Remove the left hand sound insulator, if applicable.

4. Disconnect the shift indicator cable from the steering column.

5. Remove the steering column to instrument panel screws. Lower the steering column.

NOTE: Use extreme care when lowering the steering column in order to prevent damage to column assembly.

6. Remove the screws and the snap in fasteners from the perimeter of the instrument cluster lens.

7. Reach behind the instrument panel and remove the stud nuts from the lower corner of the cluster.

8. Reach behind the instrument panel and disconnect the speedometer cable, if applicable, and wiring harness connections.

9. Remove the assembly from the vehicle.

To install:

10. Position instrument assembly to the instrument panel and connect the speedometer cable.

11. Attach the wiring harness connections.

12. Install nuts attaching 2 rear lower corner studs to the instrument panel carrier.

13. Attach cluster to carrier with screws.

14. Carefully raise the steering column and attach with screws to the instrument panel.

15. Connect the shift indicator cable to the steering column.

16. If removed, connect the left hand sound insulator.

17. Connect the steering column trim plate and screws.

18. Connect the negative battery cable.

1989–90 Custom Cruiser

1. Disconnect the negative battery cable. Disconnect speedometer cable at transducer, if equipped with cruise control.
2. Remove the right and left side trim covers by pulling outward. The covers are retained by clips.
3. Remove screws attaching instrument panel pad to the instrument panel.
4. Pull pad assembly away from panel and remove.
5. Remove steering column trim cover.
6. Disconnect shift indicator clip from steering column shift bowl.
7. Remove the steering column to instrument panel screws. Lower the steering column.

NOTE: Use extreme care when lowering the steering column in order to prevent damage to column assembly.

8. Remove screws holding instrument cluster to the instrument panel support.
9. Pull instrument cluster assembly rearward far enough to reach behind cluster and disconnect speedometer cable, if applicable, and circuit board wiring connector.
10. Remove the screws attaching center air duct to the instrument cluster assembly.
11. Remove instrument cluster.

To install:

12. Position the instrument cluster to the instrument panel and use screws to attach the center air duct to the cluster assembly.
13. Connect the speedometer cable, if applicable, and the circuit board wiring connector.
14. Use screws to attach the instrument cluster to the instrument panel support.
15. Carefully raise steering column and attach with instrument panel screws.
16. Connect shift indicator clip to steering column shift bowl. Attach steering column trim cover.
17. Attach pad assembly to panel and secure with instrument panel screws.
18. Snap right and left trim covers back into place.
19. Reconnect speedometer cable at transducer, if equipped, and connect the negative battery cable.

1991–93

NOTE: This vehicle is equipped with an air bag system, make certain to follow the recommended disarming procedures before, and arming procudures after, repairs.

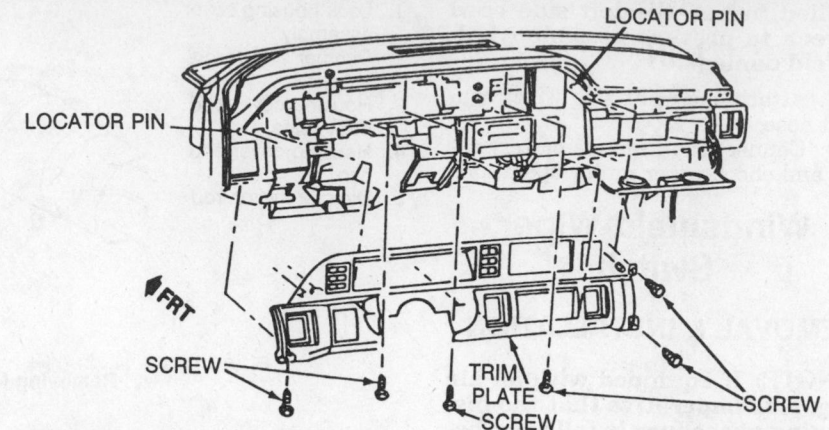

Left side trim plate assembly—1991–93 Roadmaster, Caprice and Custom Cruiser

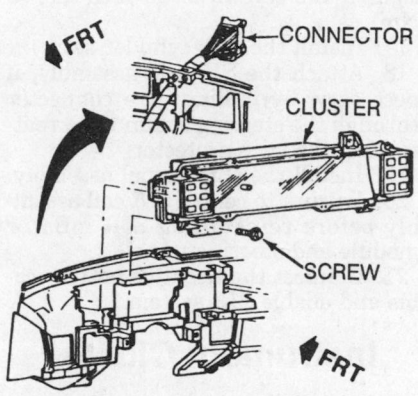

Instrument cluster assembly—1991–93 Roadmaster, Caprice and Custom Cruiser

1. Disconnect the negative battery cable.
2. Remove the left side trim plate:
   a. Remove the steering column opening filler.
   b. Open the instrument panel compartment door and unsnap the right side molding from the carrier.
   c. Loosen the capsule nuts attaching the steering column support bracket to the carrier, to the end of the threads but do not remove from the bolts. Gently lower the steering column.
   d. Remove the 6 screws attaching the trim plate to the carrier and carefully unsnap and pull away.
3. Remove the 4–5 screws attaching the cluster to the carrier.
4. Disconnect the shift indicator cable from the steering column.
5. Gently pull the cluster from the electrical connector and remove the cluster from the vehicle.

To install:

6. Position the cluster in the vehicle and gently snap onto the connector.
7. Attach the shift indicator cable to the steering column.
8. Attach cluster to the carrier with the 4–5 carrier screws and tighten to 17 inch lbs. (1.9 Nm).
9. Attach the left side trim plate and, if necessary, adjust the shift indicator as follows:
   a. Remove the steering column opening filler.
   b. The shift lever should be in the **N** gate notch.
   c. Position the guide clip on the edge of the gearshift lever bowl to centrally position the pointer on **N**. Push the guide clip onto the gearshift lever bowl.
10. Connect negative battery cable and enable the SIR system.

Speedometer

REMOVAL & INSTALLATION

NOTE: The 1991–93 Roadmaster, Caprice and the 1991–92 Custom Cruiser speedometer assemblies must be replaced as a unit or sent to an authorized repair facility. No individual parts are available for replacement.

1. Disconnect the negative battery cable.
2. Remove the instrument cluster.
3. Remove the speedometer retaining screws. Pull the assembly forward in order to disconnect the speedometer cable. To gain slack, it may be necessary to disconnect the cable at the cruise control transducer or the transmission.
4. Remove the speedometer assembly from the vehicle.

To install:

5. Position speedometer assembly in vehicle and attach the speedometer cable and retaining screws.
6. Attach instrument cluster.
7. Connect the negative battery cable.

Radio

REMOVAL & INSTALLATION

1889–90 Except Caprice

1. Disconnect the negative battery cable.
2. Remove the center trim plate.
3. Remove the attaching screws from the front of the radio or from the radio brakets as applicable.
4. Pull the radio from the instrument panel to obtain access to the electrical connections. Detach the wiring harness and the antenna lead.
5. Remove remove the radio.

To install:

6. Position radio to instrument panel and attach the wiring harness and antenna lead.
7. Slide radio and fix in place with attaching screws either to the front of the radio or to the brackets as applicable.
8. Attach the center trim plate and connect the negative battery cable.

1989–90 Caprice

1. Disconnect the negative battery cable.
2. Remove the ash tray.
3. Remove the instrument panel compartment.
4. Disconnect the air conditioning and heater cables.
5. Remove the air conditioning and radio trim plate.
6. Remove the radio and air conditioning heater control assembly.
7. Remove the screws holding the bracket to the trim plate and remove the bracket. Disconnect the radio wiring harness and antenna.
8. Remove the screws holding the radio to the bracket and remove the radio.

To install:

9. Position the radio in the bracket and attach with screws.
10. Connect the radio wiring harness and antenna. Attach the trim plate to the bracket with screws.
11. Connect the radio and air conditioning heater control assembly.
12. Connect the air conditioning and heater cables.
13. Attach the instrument panel compartment and insert the ash tray.
14. Connect the negative battery cable.

1991–93

1. Disconnect the negative battery cable.

NOTE: This vehicle is equipped with an air bag system, make certain to follow the recommended disarming procedure before, or arming procedure after, repairs.

2. Remove the left hand trim plate:
   a. Remove the steering column opening filler.
   b. Open the instrument panel compartment door and carefully unsnap the right side molding from the carrier.
   c. Loosen the capsule nuts attaching the steering column support bracket to the carrier, to the end of the threads but do not remove from the bolts. Gently lower the steering column.
   d. Remove the 6 screws attaching the trim plate to the carrier and carefully unsnap and pull away.
3. Remove the 3 screws attaching the bracket to the carrier and remove the bracket and the attached radio from the carrier.
4. Disconnect the body harness connector and the antenna lead from the radio.
5. Remove the 3 nuts attaching the bracket to the radio and if necessary remove the 3 bolts from the radio.

To install:

6. Attach the bolts to radio, if necessary, and use nuts to attach the radio to the bracket. Tighten nuts to 27 inch lbs. (3 Nm).
7. Attach the body harness and antenna connectors to the radio.
8. Use screws to attach the braket to the carrier. Tighten screws to 17 inch lbs. (1.9 Nm).
9. Attach the left hand trim plate:
   a. Attach trim plate with screws and snaps.
   b. Gently raise the steering column into place and attach with capsule nuts to the carrier.
   c. Snap the right side molding to the carrier.
   d. Attach the steering column opening filler.
10. Attach the negative battery cable and enable the SIR system.

Headlight Switch

REMOVAL & INSTALLATION

1989–90

KNOB TYPE SWITCH

1. Disconnect the negative battery cable.
2. Remove the left hand sound insulator.
3. Pull the headlight switch to the **ON** position.
4. Depending upon the switch mechanism, pull the trim knob from the switch by either reaching under the dash and depressing the switch shaft release button while pulling the knob and shaft from the light switch or by using a suitable tool and pushing the tang under the trim knob while pulling the knob from the shaft.
5. Remove the left hand trim plate, panel cover or switch cover plate as neccessary and remove the ferrule nut retaining the switch to the dash panel.
6. Disconnect the electrical connector and remove the switch.
7. Installation is the reverse of the removal procedure.

ROCKER TYPE SWITCH

1. Disconnect the negative battery cable.
2. Remove the left side sound insulator and steering column trim plate or cover, as necessary.
3. Disconnect the electrical connectors from the switch.
4. Remove the screws attaching the switch to the instrument panel and remove the switch.
5. Installation is the reverse of the removal procedure.

1991–93

1. Disconnect the negative battery cable.

NOTE: If equipped with an air bag system, make certain to fol-

1. Headlight switch indicator light (with twilight sentinel)
2. Panel light dimmer switch connector
3. Switch
4. Screw
5. Twilight sentinel switch connector
6. Headlight switch connector

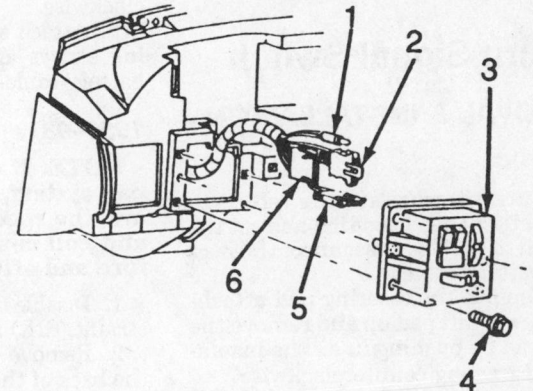

Rocker type headlight switch—1991–93 Roadmaster, Caprice and Custom Cruiser

low the recommended disarming procedure before or arming procedure after repairs.

2. Remove the left side trim plate:
   a. Remove the steering column opening filler.
   b. Open the instrument panel compartment door and unsnap the right side molding from the carrier.
   c. Loosen the capsule nuts attaching the steering column support bracket to the carrier, to the end of the threads but do not remove from the bolts. Gently lower the steering column.
   d. Remove the 6 screws attaching the trim plate to the carrier and carefully unsnap and pull away.

3. Remove the 3 screws attaching the switch to the instrument carrier and remove the switch.

To install:

4. Place switch in instrument carrier and attach with screws.

5. Attach left side trim plate.

6. Enable SIR system and connect the negative battery cable.

Dimmer Switch

REMOVAL & INSTALLATION

NOTE: If equipped with an air bag system, make certain to follow the recommended disarming procedure before, and rearming procedure after, repairs.

1. Disconnect the negative battery cable.

2. The dimmer switch is attached to the lower steering column jacket. Disconnect all electrical connections from the switch.

3. Remove the nut and screw that attach the switch to the steering column jacket and remove the switch.

4. Install the dimmer switch and depress it slightly to insert a $^3/_{32}$ inch drill. Force the switch up to remove lash, then tighten screw and nut to 4.0 ft. lbs.

Turn Signal Switch

REMOVAL & INSTALLATION

1989–90

1. Turn the wheels of the vehicle to the straight-ahead position and set the ignition to **LOCK**. Disconnect the negative battery cable.

2. Remove the steering pad attaching screws. Lift pad up and remove the horn lead by pushing in on the insulator and turning counterclockwise.

3. Remove the nut retainer and nut, and remove steering wheel with suit-

able puller. Remove the shaft lock cover.

4. Depress the shaft lock using tool J–23653 or equivalent. Remove the shaft lock retaining ring, the shaft lock and the shaft lock cover.

5. Remove the turn signal cancelling cam and spring assembly. It may be neccessary to turn the multifunction lever to the **RIGHT TURN** position. Remove the upper bearing spring, seat and inner race.

6. Rotate multifunction lever to the **RIGHT TURN** position and remove the screw and multifunction lever actuator arm.

7. Remove the wiring protector and hazard knob. Disconnect the switch wire connector at the lower end of the steering column.

8. Remove screws attaching the switch to the housing. Pull the switch out. If equipped with cruise control, the wiring harness will have to be carefully pulled up through the gearshift lever bowl of the steering column. If wires must be pulled through the column, attach a length of mechanic's wire to the connector to aid in reassembly.

To install:

9. Gently pull the wiring harness through the steering column.

10. Attach turn signal switch to the housing using screws. Tighten to 30 inch lbs. (3.4 Nm).

11. Using screw, attach the multifunction lever. Tighten screw to 20 inch lbs. (2.3 Nm).

12. Install the inner race, upper bearing seat and upper bearing spring.

13. Install the turn signal cancelling cam.

14. Using tool J–23653-B or equivalent, depress the shaft lock and install the shaft lock retaining ring.

15. Attach the shaft lock cover and steering wheel.

16. Tighten steering wheel retaining nut to 30 ft. lbs. (41 Nm) and attach nut retainer.

17. Attach the horn lead in cam tower by pushing inward and turning clockwise.

18. Attach steering pad with attaching screws and connect the negative battery cable.

1991–93

NOTE: If equipped with an air bag system, make certain to follow the recommended disarming and coil centering procedure before and after repairs.

1. Disable the Supplemental Air Restraint (SIR) air bag system.

2. Remove the Torx® screws from the back of the steering wheel, disconnect the connector and remove the inflator module.

------ **CAUTION** ------

To avoid personal injury when carrying a live inflator module, make sure the bag and trim cover are pointed away. Always face the air bag assembly up, and never carry the inflator module by the wires or connector, otherwise personal injury may result if the module should deploy.

3. Disconnect the negative battery cable.

4. Remove the locking nut and use a suitable puller to remove the steering wheel.

5. Remove the coil assembly retaining ring and allow the coil assembly to hang.

6. Remove the wave washer.

7. Remove the shaft lock bolt guard:
   a. Turn the ignition switch to the **RUN** position.
   b. Rotate shaft so the blocking tooth is at 7 o'clock and bolt guard screws are accessible through large slots on lock shaft.
   c. Loosen screws on lock bolt guard and remove.
   d. Return ignition to the **LOCK** position.

8. Remove the shaft lock retaining ring using tool J–23653-C or equivalent.

------ **CAUTION** ------

Use a ½ inch wrench to hold the shaft of tool J–23653-C or equivalent, stationary when releasing the nut. Failure to do so may cause the tool to fly off and cause personal injury.

9. Remove the shaft lock, turn signal canceling cam, upper bearing spring, upper bearing inner race seat and inner race.

10. Turn the multifunction lever to the **RIGHT TURN** position and remove the multifunction lever and hazard knob assembly.

11. Remove the retaining screw and signal switch arm.

12. Remove the wiring protector from the steering column then disconnect the switch connector.

13. Remove the screws retaining the turn signal switch to the steering column, using care not to drop the screws in the column. Attach a length of mechanic's wire to the connector to aid in reinstallation and gently pull wire harness through the steering column.

To install:

14. Using the mechanic's wire, gently pull the turn switch connector through the steering column and attach switch connector to the vehicle wire harness.

15. Install the turn switch assembly and screws. Tighten turn switch mounting screws to 30 inch lbs. (3.4 Nm).

16. Install the signal switch arm and

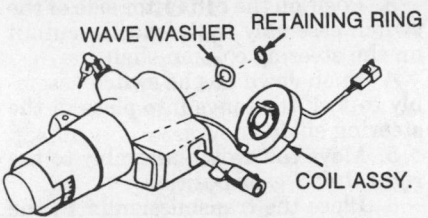

Removal of coil assembly from steering shaft—1991–92 Roadmaster, Caprice and Custom Cruiser

1. Shaft lock
2. Turn signal cancelling cam
3. Upper bearing spring
4. Upper bearing inner race seat
5. Inner race

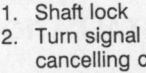

Removal of upper shaft bearing components—1991–92 Roadmaster, Caprice and Custom Cruiser

1. Multi-function lever
2. Screw
3. Hazard warning button
4. Spring
5. Hazard warning knob
6. Screw
7. Screw
8. Signal switch arm
9. Turn signal and hazard warning switch

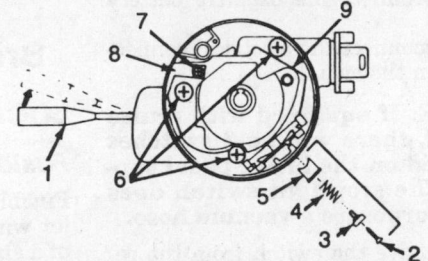

Turn signal and hazard switch removal—1991–92 Roadmaster, Caprice and Custom Cruiser

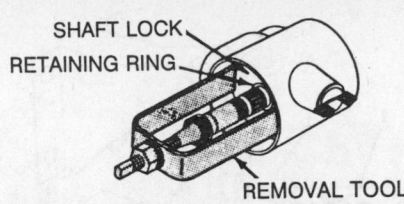

Removal of shaft lock retaining ring

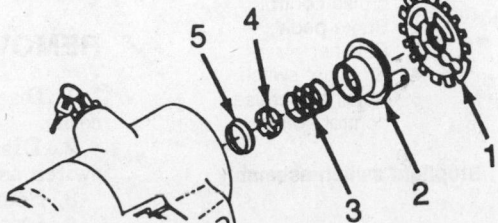

retaining screw. Tighten screw to 20 inch lbs. (2.3 Nm).

17. Install the hazard knob assembly and multifunction lever.

18. Install the inner race, upper bearing race seat and upper bearing spring.

19. Lubricate turn signal cancelling cam with synthetic grease and install cancelling cam assembly.

20. Install shaft lock and new shaft lock retaining ring using tool J-23653-C or equivalent.

21. Install shaft lock bolt guard as follows:

   a. Turn ignition switch to the **RUN** position.

   b. Rotate shaft until the block tooth is at the 7 o'clock position and bolt guard screw holes are accessible though large slots on lock shaft.

   c. Tighten screws on lock bolt guard until they bottom out, then torque to 20 inch lbs. (2.3 Nm).

22. Install the wave washer.

23. Install and center the coil assembly and retaining ring.

24. Connect wiring protector, if removed.

25. Install steering wheel, and tighten the locking nut.

26. Attach the inflator module.

27. Connect the negative battery cable and enable the SIR system.

Ignition Switch

REMOVAL & INSTALLATION

NOTE: If equipped with an air bag system, make certain to follow the recommended disarming procedure before, and rearming procedure after, repairs.

1. Disconnect the negative battery cable and disable the air bag system, if equipped.

2. Remove the column to instrument panel trim plates and attaching nuts.

3. Lower the steering column and disconnect the shift indicator cable.

4. Disconnect the ignition and dimmer switch wire connectors.

NOTE: The steering column must be supported at all times to prevent damage.

5. Remove the switch attaching screws and remove the dimmer switch followed by the ignition switch.

To install:

6. Move the key lock to the **LOCK** position.

7. Move the actuator rod hole in the switch to the **LOCK** position.

8. Install the switch with the rod in the hole. Adjust the ignition switch as follows:

   a. 1989–90—Place a $^3/_{32}$ inch drill bit in the hole on the switch to lock the switch into position. Move the switch slider to the extreme left position then move the slider 1 detent to the right **OFF LOCK** position. Remove the drill bit.

   b. 1991–93—Install the ignition switch in the **LOCK** position. Move the switch slider to the extreme right position and move the slider 1 detent to the left **LOCK** position. Depress switch mechanism slightly to insert a $^3/_{32}$ inch drill bit into ignition switch.

9. Position and reassemble the steering column in reverse of the disassembly following the proper coil centering procedure. Enable the air bag system, if equipped, as follows:

   a. Connect the yellow 2-way SIR harness connector located at the base of the steering column.

   b. Install the SIR fuse to the fuse block.

   c. Turn the ignition switch to **RUN** and verify the inflatable restraint indicator flashes 7–9 times and then turns off.

Ignition Lock Cylinder

REMOVAL & INSTALLATION

1989–90

1. Disconnect the negative battery cable.

2. Position the ignition lock cylinder in the **LOCK** position.

3. Remove the turn signal switch.

4. Remove key from lock cylinder. Remove the buzzer switch and clip.

5. Reinsert key into the lock cylinder and turn key to the **LOCK** position. Remove the lock cylinder retaining screw and the lock cylinder.

To install:

6. Match the key position upon removal of the lock cylinder. Be sure that the lock cylinder aligns the cylinder key with the keyway in the lock housing.

7. Push the lock all the way in and install the retaining screw. Tighten screw to 22 inch lbs. (2.5 Nm).

8. Install turn signal switch.

9. Connect the negative battery cable.

1991–93

NOTE: This vehicle is equipped

with an air bag system, make certain to follow the recommended disarming and coil centering procedure before and after repairs.

1. Disable the SIR system.
2. Disconnect the negative battery cable.
3. Remove the turn signal assembly.
4. Remove the SIR coil assembly from the column if necessary, as follows:
   a. Remove wiring protector.
   b. Attach a length of mechanics wire to the terminal connector to aid in reassembly.
   c. Carefully pull wire through the column.
5. Remove the key from the lock cylinder and remove the buzzer switch assembly.
6. Reinsert the key into the lock cylinder, be sure the key is in the **LOCK** position.
7. Remove the lock cylinder retaining screw.
8. Remove the lock cylinder from the steering column.
To install:
9. Reinstall the lock cylinder set with key inserted. Attach with the retaining screw tighten at the steering column to 22 inch lbs. (2.5 Nm).
10. Insert the ignition key and turn it to the **RUN** position, and install the buzzer switch retaining clip, then return the key to the **LOCK** position.
11. Gently pull turn signal switch wiring connector through the steering column and allow assembly to hang freely.
12. Gently pull the coil assembly through the steering column and allow assembly to hang freely.
13. Install the turn signal switch assembly.
14. Be sure to follow proper SIR coil centering assembly.
15. Connect the negative battery cable and enable the SIR system.

Stoplight Switch

ADJUSTMENT

1. Install the switch into the clip until the switch body is seated fully in the clip.
2. Pull the brake pedal up against internal pedal stop.
3. The switch will move in the retainer clip until the pedal assembly is against the stop.
4. Proper adjustment has been reached when no clicks are heard while pulling the pedal up and the brake lights do not remain on when pedal is released.

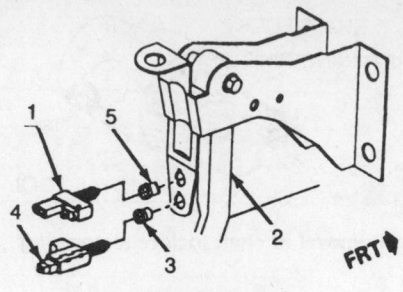

1. Release switch—cruise control
2. Brake pedal
3. Retainer
4. Stoplight switch
5. Retainer—cruise control switch

Stoplight switch assembly

Removal and Installation

1. Disconnect the negative battery cable.
2. Disconnect the electrical connection from the switch.

NOTE: If equipped with cruise control, there will be 2 switches mounted on the brake pedal support. The stoplight switch does not incorporate a vacuum hose.

3. Remove the switch from the retainer clip on the brake pedal mounting bracket.
4. Installation is the reverse of the removal procedure.

Neutral Safety Switch

All steering columns use a mechanical and electrical neutral start system. The mechanical system relies on a block which prevents starting the engine in positions other than **P** or **N**. The mechanical block is achieved by a wedge shaped finger added to the ignition switch actuator rod. The finger will only pass through the bowl plate notches when the shift lever is in the **P** and **N** positions, which then allows the lock cylinder to rotate to the **START** position.

The electrical switch permits voltage to pass to the starter when the vehicles gear selector is in **P** or **N**. The switch also permits voltage to the backup lights when the gear selector is in the **R** postion.

ADJUSTMENT

1. Block the drive wheels and place the transmission in **N**.
2. Align the actuator on the switch assembly with the hole on the shaft tube.

3. Position the connector side of the switch assembly to fit into the cutout on the steering column shaft.
4. Push down on the switch assembly to lock the tangs into place in the steering shaft.
5. Move the switch assembly to the right, **LOW** gear position.
6. Place the transmission in **P**, the switch assembly will ratchet as it adjusts itself.
7. Verify the switch is adjusted properly.

REMOVAL & INSTALLATION

1. Disconnect the negative battery cable.
2. Disconnect the wiring at the switch assembly.
3. Remove the switch assembly.
4. Installation is the reverse of the removal procedure. properly adjust the switch.

Fuses, Circuit Breakers and Relays

LOCATION

Fusible Links

Fusible links are used to prevent major wire harness damage in the event of a short circuit or an overload condition in the wiring circuits which are normally not fused. Each fusible link is of a fixed value for a specific electrical load and should a link fail, the cause of the failure must be determined and repaired prior to installing a new fusible link of the same value.

Circuit Breakers

Various circuit breakers are located under the instrument panel. In order to gain access to these components it may be necessary to first remove the under dash padding.

Fuse Panel

The fuse panel is located on the left side of the vehicle. It is under the instrument panel assembly on the left front hinge pillar. Access is gained through a removable panel on the instrument panel carrier.

Various Relays

ABS Solenoid valve relay—integrated into the brake pressure modulator located in the left side of the engine compartment left of the generator.
A/C Blower Relay—integrated into the brake pressure modulator located in the left side of the engine compartment left of the generator.
A/C Blower Relay—located in the

GM—Cadillac
Rear Wheel Drive
CADILLAC—Brougham • Fleetwood Brougham

SPECIFICATIONS

VEHICLE IDENTIFICATION CHART

It is important for servicing and ordering parts to be certain of the vehicle and engine identification. The VIN (vehicle identification number) is a 17 digit number visible through the windshield on the driver's side of the dash and contains the vehicle and engine identification codes. The tenth digit indicates model year and the eighth digit indicates engine code. It can be interpreted as follows:

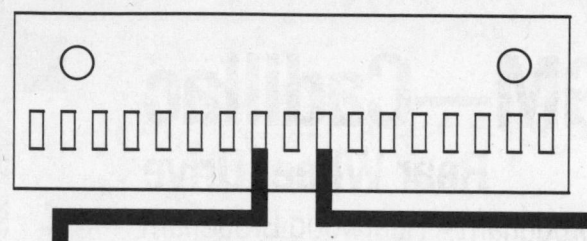

Engine Code

Code	Liters	Cu. In. (cc)	Cyl.	Fuel Sys.	Eng. Mfg.
Y	5.0	307 (5032)	8	Carburetor	B.O.C.
E	5.0	305 (5011)	8	TBI	C.P.C.
7	5.7	350 (5733)	8	TBI	C.P.C.

TBI—Throttle Body Injection
B.O.C.—Buick, Oldsmobile, Cadillac
C.P.C.—Chevrolet, Pontiac, Canada

Model Year

Code	Year
K	1989
L	1990
M	1991
N	1992
P	1993

ENGINE IDENTIFICATION

Year	Model	Engine Displacement Liters (cc)	Engine Series (ID/VIN)	Fuel System	No. of Cylinders	Engine Type
1989	Brougham	5.0 (5032)	Y	Carbureted	8	OHV
1990	Brougham	5.0 (5032)	Y	Carbureted	8	OHV
	Brougham	5.7 (5733)	7	TBI	8	OHV
1991	Brougham	5.0 (5011)	E	TBI	8	OHV
	Brougham	5.7 (5733)	7	TBI	8	OHV
1992	Brougham	5.0 (5011)	E	TBI	8	OHV
	Brougham	5.7 (5733)	7	TBI	8	OHV
1993	Fleetwood Brougham	5.7 (5733)	7	TBI	8	OHV

OHV—Overhead valves

GENERAL ENGINE SPECIFICATIONS

Year	Engine ID/VIN	Engine Displacement Liters (cc)	Fuel System Type	Net Horsepower @ rpm	Net Torque @ rpm (ft. lbs.)	Bore × Stroke (in.)	Compression Ratio	Oil Pressure @ rpm
1989	Y	5.0 (5032)	4 bbl	140 @ 3200	255 @ 2000	3.800 × 3.385	8.0:1	30–45 ①
1990	Y	5.0 (5032)	4 bbl	140 @ 3200	255 @ 2000	3.800 × 3.385	8.0:1	30–45 ①
	7	5.7 (5733)	TBI	185 @ 3800	300 @ 2400	4.000 × 3.480	9.3:1	18 ②
1991	E	5.0 (5011)	TBI	170 @ 4200	255 @ 2400	3.740 × 3.480	9.3:1	18 ②
	7	5.7 (5733)	TBI	185 @ 3800	300 @ 2400	4.000 × 3.480	9.3:1	18 ②
1992	E	5.0 (5011)	TBI	170 @ 4200	255 @ 2400	3.740 × 3.480	9.3:1	18 ②
	7	5.7 (5733)	TBI	185 @ 3800	300 @ 2400	4.000 × 3.480	9.3:1	18 ②
1993	7	5.7 (5733)	TBI	185 @ 3800	300 @ 2400	4.000 × 3.480	9.8:1	18 ②

TBI—Throttle Body Injection
① @ 1500 rpm
② @ 2000 rpm

GASOLINE ENGINE TUNE-UP SPECIFICATIONS

Year	Engine ID/VIN	Engine Displacement Liters (cc)	Spark Plugs Gap (in.)	Ignition Timing (deg.) MT	AT	Fuel Pump (psi)	Idle Speed (rpm) MT	AT	Valve Clearance In.	Ex.
1989	Y	5.0 (5032)	0.060	—	20B	6.0–7.5	—	450	Hyd.	Hyd.
1990	Y	5.0 (5032)	0.060	—	①	6.0–7.5	—	①	Hyd.	Hyd.
	7	5.7 (5733)	0.035	—	①	9.0–13.0	—	①	Hyd.	Hyd.
1991	E	5.0 (5011)	0.035	—	①	9.0–13.0	—	①	Hyd.	Hyd.
	7	5.7 (5733)	0.035	—	①	9.0–13.0	—	①	Hyd.	Hyd.
1992	E	5.0 (5011)	0.035	—	①	9.0–13.0	—	①	Hyd.	Hyd.
	7	5.7 (5733)	0.035	—	①	9.0–13.0	—	①	Hyd.	Hyd.
1993	SEE UNDERHOOD SPECIFICATIONS STICKER									

NOTE: The lowest cylinder pressure should be within 75% of the highest cylinder pressure reading. For example, if the highest cylinder is 134 psi, the lowest should be 101. Engine should be at normal operating temperature with throttle valve in the wide open position.
The underhood specifications sticker often reflects tune-up specification changes in production. Sticker figures must be used if they disagree with those in this chart.
Hyd.—Hydraulic
① Use data on underhood vehicle specification sticker

FIRING ORDERS

NOTE: To avoid confusion, always replace spark plugs and wires one at a time.

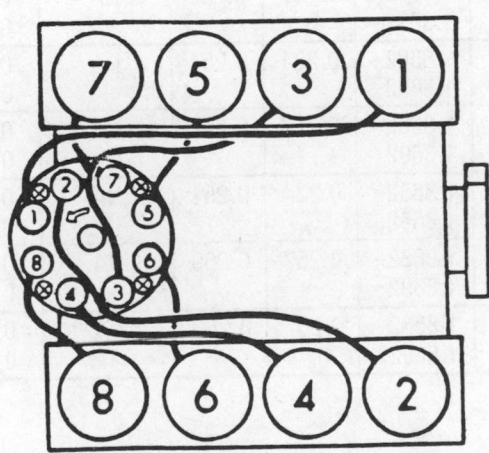

5.0L (VIN Y) Engine
Engine Firing Order: 1–8–4–3–6–5–7–2
Distributor Rotation: Counterclockwise

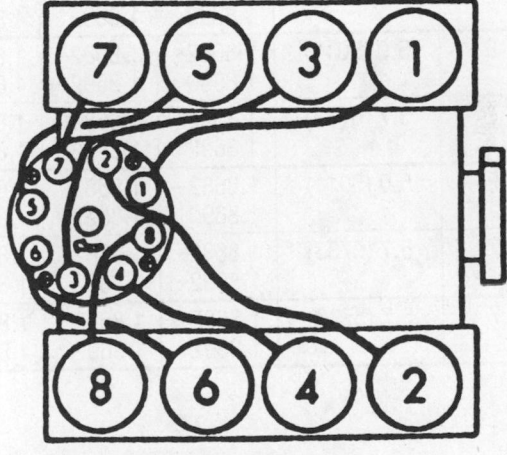

5.0L (VIN E) and 5.7L Engines
Engine Firing Order: 1–8–4–3–6–5–7–2
Distributor Rotation: Clockwise

CAPACITIES

Year	Model	Engine ID/VIN	Engine Displacement Liters (cc)	Engine Crankcase (qts.) with Filter	Transmission (pts.) 4-Spd	5-Spd	Auto.	Drive Axle (pts.)	Fuel Tank (gal.)	Cooling System (qts.)
1989	Brougham	Y	5.0 (5032)	5.0	—	—	②	④	20.7	15.2①
1990	Brougham	Y	5.0 (5032)	5.0	—	—	②	④	25.0	15.2①
	Brougham	7	5.7 (5733)	5.0	—	—	③	④	25.0	16.5
1991	Brougham	E	5.0 (5011)	5.0	—	—	⑤	④	25.0	16.7
	Brougham	7	5.7 (5733)	5.0	—	—	⑤	④	25.0	16.5

CAPACITIES

Year	Model	Engine ID/VIN	Engine Displacement Liters (cc)	Engine Crankcase (qts.) with Filter	Transmission (pts.) 4-Spd	5-Spd	Auto.	Drive Axle (pts.)	Fuel Tank (gal.)	Cooling System (qts.)
1992	Brougham	E	5.0 (5011)	5.0	—	—	⑤	④	25.0	17.6
	Brougham	7	5.7 (5733)	5.0	—	—	⑤	④	25.0	17.6
1993	Fleetwood Brougham	7	5.7 (5733)	5.0	—	—	⑤	④	25.0	17.6

All capacities shown are approximate. Add fluid as necessary to bring to proper level
① Heavy duty—15.6
② Pan 6.0, overhaul 20.0
③ Pan 9.0, overhaul 20.0
④ Fill to Flush or ¼″ (6mm) of Filler Hole
⑤ Pan 10.0, overhaul 22.4

CAMSHAFT SPECIFICATIONS

All measurements given in inches.

Year	Engine ID/VIN	Engine Displacement Liters (cc)	Journal Diameter 1	2	3	4	5	Elevation In.	Ex.	Bearing Clearance	Camshaft End Play
1989	Y	5.0 (5032)	2.0352–2.0365	2.0152–2.0166	1.9952–1.9965	1.9752–1.9765	1.9552–1.9565	0.247	0.251	0.0020–0.0058	0.006–0.022
1990	Y	5.0 (5032)	2.0352–2.0365	2.0152–2.0166	1.9952–1.9965	1.9752–1.9765	1.9552–1.9565	0.247	0.251	0.0020–0.0058	0.006–0.022
	7	5.7 (5733)	1.8682–1.8692	1.8682–1.8692	1.8682–1.8692	1.8682–1.8692	1.8682–1.8692	0.257	0.269	NA	0.004–0.012
1991	E	5.0 (5011)	1.8682–1.8690	1.8682–1.8692	1.8682–1.8692	1.8682–1.8692	1.8682–1.8692	0.234	0.251	NA	0.004–0.012
	7	5.7 (5733)	1.8682–1.8692	1.8682–1.8692	1.8682–1.8692	1.8682–1.8692	1.8682–1.8692	0.257	0.269	NA	0.004–0.012
1992	E	5.0 (5011)	1.8682–1.8690	1.8682–1.8692	1.8682–1.8692	1.8682–1.8692	1.8682–1.8692	0.234	0.251	NA	0.004–0.012
	7	5.7 (5733)	1.8682–1.8692	1.8682–1.8692	1.8682–1.8692	1.8682–1.8692	1.8682–1.8692	0.257	0.269	NA	0.004–0.012
1993	7	5.7 (5733)	1.8682–1.8692	1.8682–1.8692	1.8682–1.8692	1.8682–1.8692	1.8682–1.8692	0.257	0.269	NA	0.004–0.012

NA—Not available

CRANKSHAFT AND CONNECTING ROD SPECIFICATIONS

All measurements are given in inches.

Year	Engine ID/VIN	Engine Displacement Liters (cc)	Crankshaft Main Brg. Journal Dia.	Main Brg. Oil Clearance	Shaft Endplay	Thrust on No.	Connecting Rod Journal Diameter	Oil Clearance	Side Clearance
1989	Y	5.0 (5032)	2.4985–2.4995②	0.0005–0.0021①	0.0035–0.0135	3	2.1238–2.1248	0.0004–0.0033	0.006–0.020
1990	Y	5.0 (5032)	2.4985–2.4995②	0.0005–0.0021①	0.0035–0.0135	3	2.1238–2.1248	0.0004–0.0033	0.006–0.020
	7	5.7 (5733)	2.4481–2.4490④	0.0011–0.0020③	0.0010–0.0070	5	2.0893–2.0998	0.0013–0.0035	0.006–0.014
1991	E	5.0 (5011)	2.4481–2.4490④	0.0011–0.0020③	0.0010–0.0070	5	2.0893–2.0998	0.0013–0.0035	0.006–0.014
	7	5.7 (5733)	2.4481–2.4490④	0.0011–0.0020③	0.0010–0.0070	5	2.0893–2.0998	0.0013–0.0035	0.006–0.014

CRANKSHAFT AND CONNECTING ROD SPECIFICATIONS

All measurements are given in inches.

Year	Engine ID/VIN	Engine Displacement Liters (cc)	Crankshaft Main Brg. Journal Dia.	Crankshaft Main Brg. Oil Clearance	Crankshaft Shaft Endplay	Crankshaft Thrust on No.	Connecting Rod Journal Diameter	Connecting Rod Oil Clearance	Connecting Rod Side Clearance
1992	E	5.0 (5011)	2.4481–2.4490 ④	0.0011–0.0020 ③	0.0010–0.0070	5	2.0893–2.0998	0.0013–0.0035	0.006–0.014
	7	5.7 (5733)	2.4481–2.4490 ④	0.0011–0.0020 ③	0.0010–0.0070	5	2.0893–2.0998	0.0013–0.0035	0.006–0.014
1993	7	5.7 (5733)	2.4481–2.4490 ④	0.0011–0.0020 ③	0.0010–0.0070	5	2.0893–2.0998	0.0013–0.0035	0.006–0.014

① No. 5—0.0015–0.0031
② No. 1—2.4988–2.4998
③ No. 1—0.0008–0.0020
  No. 5—0.0017–0.0032
④ No. 1—2.4488–2.4493
  No. 5—2.4481–2.4488

VALVE SPECIFICATIONS

Year	Engine ID/VIN	Engine Displacement Liters (cc)	Seat Angle (deg.)	Face Angle (deg.)	Spring Test Pressure (lbs. @ in.)	Spring Installed Height (in.)	Stem-to-Guide Clearance (in.) Intake	Stem-to-Guide Clearance (in.) Exhaust	Stem Diameter (in.) Intake	Stem Diameter (in.) Exhaust
1989	Y	5.0 (5032)	45 ①	44 ①	180–194 @ 1.27	1 43/64	0.0010–0.0027	0.0015–0.0032	0.3425–0.3432	0.3420–0.3427
1990	Y	5.0 (5032)	45 ①	44 ①	180–194 @ 1.27	1 43/64	0.0010–0.0027	0.0015–0.0032	0.3425–0.3432	0.3420–0.3427
	7	5.7 (5733)	46	45	194–206 @ 1.25	1 23/32	0.0011–0.0027	0.0011–0.0027	NA	NA
1991	E	5.0 (5011)	46	45	194–206 @ 1.25	1 23/32	0.0011–0.0027	0.0011–0.0027	NA	NA
	7	5.7 (5733)	46	45	194–206 @ 1.25	1 23/32	0.0011–0.0027	0.0011–0.0027	NA	NA
1992	E	5.0 (5011)	46	45	194–206 @ 1.25	1 23/32	0.0011–0.0027	0.0011–0.0027	NA	NA
	7	5.7 (5733)	46	45	194–206 @ 1.25	1 23/32	0.0011–0.0027	0.0011–0.0027	NA	NA
1993	7	5.7 (5733)	46	45	194–206 @ 1.25	1 23/32	0.0011–0.0027	0.0011–0.0027	NA	NA

NA—Not available
① Exhaust Valve—31° Seat, 30° Face

PISTON AND RING SPECIFICATIONS

All measurements are given in inches.

Year	Engine ID/VIN	Engine Displacement Liters (cc)	Piston Clearance	Ring Gap Top Compression	Ring Gap Bottom Compression	Ring Gap Oil Control	Ring Side Clearance Top Compression	Ring Side Clearance Bottom Compression	Ring Side Clearance Oil Control
1989	Y	5.0 (5032)	0.0008–0.0017 ①	0.009–0.019	0.009–0.019	0.015–0.055	0.0018–0.0038	0.0018–0.0038	0.001–0.005
1990	Y	5.0 (5032)	0.0008–0.0017 ①	0.009–0.019	0.009–0.019	0.015–0.055	0.0018–0.0038	0.0018–0.0038	0.001–0.005
	7	5.7 (5733)	0.0007–0.0021	0.010–0.020	0.010–0.025	0.015–0.055	0.0012–0.0032	0.0012–0.0032	0.002–0.007

PISTON AND RING SPECIFICATIONS

All measurements are given in inches.

Year	Engine ID/VIN	Engine Displacement Liters (cc)	Piston Clearance	Ring Gap			Ring Side Clearance		
				Top Compression	Bottom Compression	Oil Control	Top Compression	Bottom Compression	Oil Control
1991	E	5.0 (5011)	0.0007–0.0021	0.010–0.020	0.010–0.025	0.015–0.055	0.0012–0.0032	0.0012–0.0032	0.002–0.007
	7	5.7 (5733)	0.0007–0.0021	0.010–0.020	0.010–0.025	0.015–0.065	0.0012–0.0032	0.0012–0.0032	0.002–0.007
1992	E	5.0 (5011)	0.0007–0.0021	0.010–0.020	0.010–0.025	0.015–0.055	0.0012–0.0032	0.0012–0.0032	0.002–0.007
	7	5.7 (5733)	0.0007–0.0021	0.010–0.020	0.010–0.025	0.015–0.065	0.0012–0.0032	0.0012–0.0032	0.002–0.007
1993	7	5.7 (5733)	0.0007–0.0021	0.010–0.020	0.010–0.025	0.015–0.065	0.0012–0.0032	0.0012–0.0032	0.002–0.007

① Clearance to bore (selective)

TORQUE SPECIFICATIONS

All readings in ft. lbs.

Year	Engine ID/VIN	Engine Displacement Liters (cc)	Cylinder Head Bolts	Main Bearing Bolts	Rod Bearing Bolts	Crankshaft Damper Bolts	Flywheel Bolts	Manifold		Spark Plugs	Lug Nut
								Intake	Exhaust		
1989	Y	5.0 (5032)	40①③	70⑤	18④	255	60	40①	25	25	100
1990	Y	5.0 (5032)	40①③	70⑤	18④	255	60	40①	25	25	100
	7	5.7 (5733)	70	75	45	70	75	35	26②	22	100
1991	E	5.0 (5011)	70	75	45	70	75	35	26②	22	100
	7	5.7 (5733)	70	75	45	70	75	35	26②	22	100
1992	E	5.0 (5011)	70	75	45	70	75	35	26②	22	100
	7	5.7 (5733)	70	75	45	70	75	35	26②	22	100
1993	7	5.7 (5733)	70	75	45	70	75	35	26②	22	100

① Dip bolt in oil before installation
② Stud 20
③ Rotate bolts 1–7 and 9—120°
   Roate bolts 8 and 10—95°
④ Rotate 70°
⑤ Rear main bearing torque 105

BRAKE SPECIFICATIONS

All measurements in inches unless noted.

Year	Model	Master Cylinder Bore	Brake Disc			Brake Drum Diameter			Minimum Lining Thickness	
			Original Thickness	Minimum① Thickness	Maximum Runout	Original Inside Diameter	Max. Wear Limit	Maximum Machine Diameter	Front	Rear
1989	Brougham	1.125	1.032	0.972	0.0005	11.00	11.09	11.06	0.030	0.030
1990	Brougham	1.125	1.032	0.972	0.0005	11.00	11.09	11.06	0.030	0.030
1991	Brougham	1.125	1.032	0.972	0.0005	11.00	11.09	11.06	0.030	0.030
1992	Brougham	1.125	1.032	0.972	0.0005	11.00	11.09	11.06	0.030	0.030
1993	Fleetwood Brougham	1.125	1.032	0.972	0.0005	11.00	11.09	11.06	0.030	0.030

① Figure given is Minimum Refinishing Thickness.
All rotors have a discard thickness cost into them. This dimension is usually smaller than the refinish dimension. Do not cut a rotor to the discard thickness.

WHEEL ALIGNMENT

Year	Model	Caster Range (deg.)	Caster Preferred Setting (deg.)	Camber Range (deg.)	Camber Preferred Setting (deg.)	Toe-in (in.)	Steering Axis Inclination (deg.)
1989	Brougham	2P–4P	3P	5/16N–5/16P	0	3/64	NA
1990	Brougham	2P–4P	3P	5/16N–5/16P	0	3/64	NA
1991	Brougham	2P–4P	3P	5/16N–5/16P	0	3/64	NA
1992	Brougham	2P–4P	3P	5/16N–5/16P	0	3/64	NA
1993	Fleetwood Brougham	2P–4P	3P	5/16N–5/16P	0	3/64	NA

NA—Not available
N—Negative
P—Positive

ENGINE MECHANICAL

NOTE: Disconnecting the negative battery cable on some vehicles may interfere with the functions of the on board computer systems and may require the computer to undergo a relearning process.

Engine Assembly

REMOVAL & INSTALLATION

5.0L (VIN Y) Engine

1. Disconnect the negative battery cable and properly relieve the fuel system pressure.
2. Drain the cooling system and remove the air cleaner assembly. Remove the hot air pipe.
3. Mark the hood position for reassembly and remove the hood.
4. Disconnect the ground cable at the inner fender panel. Disconnect the engine ground cable from the right cylinder head.
5. Remove the upper radiator support and the fan. Remove the drive belts.
6. Disconnect the radiator hoses and the automatic transmission cooler lines. Remove the radiator and the fan shroud.
7. Remove the heater and vacuum hoses. Tag all vacuum hoses for reassembly.
8. Disconnect the power steering pump and air conditioning compressor with hoses attached and position aside.
9. Disconnect the fuel hose from the fuel line. Disconnect electrical engine harness from the engine, except at the starter. Disconnect the accelerator control and transmission throttle valve cables.
10. Disconnect the AIR pipe-to-catalytic converter. Raise and support the vehicle safely.
11. Disconnect the exhaust and crossover pipes at the manifolds. Remove the torque converter cover.
12. Mark the relationship of the flywheel to the converter and remove the converter bolts. Remove the engine mount bolts or nuts.
13. Remove the starter with wires attached and support it aside, to the frame.
14. Disconnect all transmission to engine bolts, except the lower left and lower the vehicle.
15. Secure a suitable lifting device to the engine. Place a board on top of a jack and support the transmission.
16. Remove the remaining transmission to engine bolt and remove the engine.
17. Install a converter holding device to prevent damage to the torque converter.

To install:

18. Remove the converter holding device and lower the engine assembly into the engine compartment. Align the engine dowels into the transmission and position the through bolts into the engine mounts.
19. Install the lower left engine bolt, remove the engine support and the transmission jack.
20. Raise and support the vehicle safely. Install the remaining transmission to engine bolts. Tighten the bolts to 35 ft. lbs. (47 Nm).
21. Install the starter and tighten the starter to block bolts to 32 ft. lbs. (44 Nm).
22. Align the torque converter to flywheel marks made earlier. Make sure the weld nuts on the torque converter are flush with the flywheel and the torque converter has freedom of rotation. Install bolts and tighten finger-tight, then tighten to 46 ft. lbs. (63 Nm). Then retighten the first bolt.
23. Install the torque converter cover. Connect the exhaust pipes to the manifolds and lower the vehicle.
24. Install the radiator. Connect the radiator hoses and the transmission cooler lines.
25. Install the heater hoses and the vacuum hoses.
26. Install the power steering pump and the air conditioning compressor.
27. Connect the fuel hose to the fuel line. Connect the engine ground cable from the cowl to the right cylinder head and connect the ground cable to the inner fender panel.
28. Install the fan and the upper radiator support. Connect the electrical harness to the engine.
29. Connect the accelerator control and the transmission throttle valve cables.
30. Connect the AIR pipe-to-catalytic converter. Install the drive belts and adjust for proper tension.
31. Install the air cleaner assembly and the hot air pipe.
32. Align the hood with the marks made earlier and install.
33. Connect the negative battery cable, tighten the fuel filler cap and add engine coolant.
34. Check all fluids and operate engine. Check for fluid leaks.

5.0L (VIN E) and 5.7L Engines

1. Disconnect the battery cables and properly relieve fuel system pressure.
2. Mark the hood hinge outline for proper reassembly alignment and remove the hood. Remove the air cleaner assembly.
3. Drain the cooling system. Disconnect the radiator hoses. Disconnect the heater hose from the radiator. Disconnect and plug the transmission and engine oil cooler lines.

4. Remove the radiator cover and tie struts. Disconnect the fan shroud from the radiator assembly and position it aside. Remove the radiator from the vehicle.

5. Remove the serpentine drive belt. Remove the cooling fan assembly and the fan shroud from the vehicle.

6. Disconnect the heater hose at the rear of the intake manifold. Disconnect and plug the power steering hoses at the power steering gear.

7. Remove the air conditioning compressor and position it aside.

8. Disconnect the accelerator, cruise control and throttle valve cables from their mountings and position out of the way. Remove the vacuum pipe and fuel lines from the throttle body.

9. Remove the alternator assembly. Disconnect the fuel line clips at the thermostat housing and air pump. Position the fuel lines aside. As required, remove the air pump assembly.

10. Disconnect and plug all required electrical connectors. Remove the distributor cap. Remove the negative battery cable from the cylinder head.

11. Raise and support the vehicle safely. Disconnect the the crossover pipe at both manifolds.

12. Disconnect the starter electrical connectors and the positive battery cable. If necessary, remove the starter retaining bolts and remove the starter from the vehicle.

13. Remove the flywheel cover. Remove the torque converter to flywheel retaining bolts. Remove the motor mount through bolts.

14. Disconnect the transmission oil cooler lines at the clip on the oil pan. Disconnect the oil pressure, knock and oxygen sensor connectors. Remove the oil cooler hose shield.

15. Remove the ground wires from the rear of the cylinder head at both sides.

16. Remove the transmission to engine retaining bolts. Lower the vehicle.

17. Install the lifting equipment to the engine. Support the transmission properly.

18. Raise the engine slightly and pull it forward to disengage it from the transmission. Remove the engine from the vehicle.

To install:

19. Lower the engine assembly into the engine compartment; align the transmission bellhousing dowels and motor mounts.

20. Loosely install 2 transmission-to-engine bolts.

21. Remove the engine and transmission supports.

22. Raise and safely support the vehicle, install the engine mount through bolts and tighten to 70 ft. lbs. (95 Nm).

23. Route the wiring harness into its original location and reconnect the oil

pressure, knock sensor and oxygen sensor connectors.

24. Reinstall the oil cooler line bracket and heat shield.

25. Connect the ground straps to the back of the cylinder heads.

26. Install and torque all transmission-to-engine bolts to 55 ft. lbs. (75 Nm).

27. Install the starter assembly, if removed and/or reconnect the wiring. Clip the transmission cooler lines to the oil pan bracket.

28. Install the flywheel-to-torque converter bolts and torque the bolts to 45 ft. lbs. (62 Nm). Install the flywheel cover.

29. Reconnect the exhaust and exhaust hangers. Tighten the crossover pipe bolts to 15 ft. lbs. (20 Nm).

30. Lower the vehicle.

31. Install heater hose to the right rear of intake manifold. Reconnect the throttle cable brackets and cables.

32. Install the distributor cap and coil wires.

33. Install the alternator with wiring, but leave the rear brace disconnected. Connect the negative battery cable at the cylinder head.

34. Unplug and connect the power steering lines at the power steering gear.

35. Route the fuel lines and connect at the throttle body. Install the fuel line clips at the thermostat housing and the AIR pump.

36. Connect the rear alternator brace. Connect all vacuum hoses to the throttle body. Connect all electrical connections to the intake manifold and the throttle body.

37. Connect the AIR hose from the diverter valve to the converter.

38. Install the fan and fan shroud assembly.

39. Install the radiator assembly. Connect the transmission and oil cooler lines.

40. Connect the the heater hose to the radiator tank and the radiator hoses.

41. Install the radiator cover and secure the fan shroud. Install the radiator tie struts.

42. Install the air conditioning compressor and serpentine belt. Install the air cleaner assembly.

43. Fill the cooling system and connect the battery cables.

44. Check all fluid levels, start engine and inspect for leaks.

45. Align the marks made earlier and install the hood assembly.

Engine Mounts

REMOVAL & INSTALLATION

1. Disconnect the negative battery cable.

2. Remove the engine mount through bolt and nut.

3. Using a suitable lifting device, carefully raise the front of the engine far enough to remove the engine mount retaining bolts and the engine mount. Watch the clearance between the rear of the engine and the cowl panel.

4. Remove the engine mount nuts, bolts and the engine mount.

5. Installation is the reverse of the removal procedure. Tighten the engine mount bolts to 35 ft. lbs. (47 Nm) and the mount through bolts to 75 ft. lbs. (100 Nm) for 5.0L (VIN Y) engines or to 70 ft. lbs. (95 Nm) for other engines.

Cylinder Head

REMOVAL & INSTALLATION

5.0L (VIN Y) Engine

1. Disconnect the negative battery cable and properly relieve the fuel system pressure. Drain the radiator.

2. Remove the intake manifold.

3. Remove the exhaust manifolds.

4. Remove the valve covers, rocker assemblies and pushrods. Note the location of the valve train components so they can be reassembled in the proper location.

5. As required, remove the alternator, power steering pump, air pump and air conditioning compressor brackets.

6. Remove the ground cable to cowl.

7. Remove the cylinder head retaining bolts. Remove the cylinder head and discard the old gasket.

To install:

8. Place the new gaskets in position on the block. Do not use any sealing materials.

9. Position the cylinder heads on the block. Coat the cylinder head bolts with clean engine oil and allow to drain.

10. Install the cylinder head bolts and tighten in the proper sequence to 40 ft. lbs. (54 Nm). Then rotate bolts 1–7 and 9 an additional 120 degrees and rotate bolts 8 and 10 an additional 95 degrees.

11. Install the pushrods and rocker arm assemblies.

12. Install the accessory brackets, as required and connect the cowl ground cable.

13. Install the valve covers.

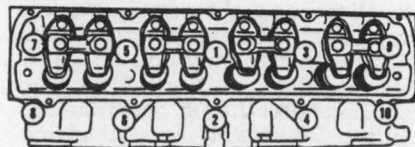

Cylinder head bolt torque sequence— 5.0L (VIN Y) Engine

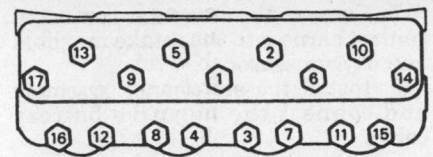

Cylinder head bolt torque sequence—
5.0L (VIN E) and 5.7L Engines

14. Install the exhaust manifolds.
15. Install the intake manifold.
16. Connect the negative battery cable, tighten the fuel filler cap and fill the cooling system. Start the engine and check for leaks.

5.0L (VIN E) and 5.7L Engines

1. Disconnect the negative battery cable and properly relieve the fuel system pressure. Drain the radiator.
2. Remove the intake manifold.
3. Remove the valve covers, rocker assemblies and pushrods. Note the location of the valve train components so they can be reassembled in the proper location.
4. Remove the exhaust manifolds.
5. Remove the diverter valve.
6. As required, remove one stud at the front of the cylinder head attaching the the alternator/power steering pump bracket and/or the air pump/air conditioning compressor bracket.
7. Remove the the cylinder head bolts. Remove the cylinder head and place on 2 blocks of wood to prevent damage. Remove and discard the old gasket.
To install:
8. Position the new cylinder head gasket in place on the block over the dowl pins with the proper side up. Do not use any sealer on a composition gasket.
9. Install the cylinder head in on the dowl pins over the gasket.
10. Coat the threads of the cylinder head bolts with sealing compound, GM part 1052080 or equivalent. Install the bolts finger-tight. The intermediate length bolts go in positions 14 and 17. Tighten the bolts with 3 passes in the proper sequence to 70 ft. lbs. (95 Nm).
11. Install the accessory brackets, as required.
12. Install the exhaust manifolds and the diverter valve.
13. Install the intake manifold.
14. Install and adjust the rocker arm and pushrod assemblies. Install the valve covers.
15. Connect the negative battery cable, tighten the fuel filler cap and fill the cooling system.

Valve Lifters

REMOVAL & INSTALLATION

1. Disconnect the negative battery cable and properly relieve the fuel system pressure. Drain the radiator.
2. Remove the intake manifold.
3. Remove the valve covers.
4. Remove the rocker arms and pushrod assemblies. Mark all valve train components, so they may be installed into there original positions.
5. Remove the lifter retainer bolts and remove the lifter retainer and restrictor. Using the proper valve lifter removal tool, remove the valve lifters. If the same lifters are to be reinstalled, position or mark the lifters so they will be installed in their original locations.
To install:
6. For the 5.0L (VIN Y) engine, prime the lifters by pumping them while they are submerged in clean engine oil. For the 5.0L (VIN E) and the 5.7L engines, coat the lifters with Molykote® or equivalent.
7. Install the lifters. If the old lifters are being reinstalled, be sure to place them in their orignial bores.
8. Install the valve lifter restrictor, the lifter retainer and the retainer bolts. Tighten the bolts to 82 inch lbs. (9 Nm) for the 5.0L (VIN Y) engine or to 12 ft. lbs. (16 Nm) for other engines.
9. Install the intake manifold.
10. Install the pushrod and rocker arm assemblies and adjust as applicable. Install the valve covers.
11. Connect the negative battery cable, tighten the fuel filler cap and fill the cooling system.

Valve Lash

ADJUSTMENT

5.0L (VIN Y) Engine

The rocker arm assembly on this engine is equipped with rocker arm pivots. The hydraulic lifters are properly positioned in their bores once the rocker arm pivots are torqued to specification, thereby eliminating the need for valve adjustment.

5.0L (VIN E) and 5.7L Engines

The valve lifters on these engines should not require periodic adjustment. Any time the rocker arms are removed valve lash must be set upon reinstallation.
1. Disconnect the negative battery cable and remove the valve covers.
2. Tighten the rocker arm nuts, as necessary, until rocker arm lash is eliminated.
3. Adjust the valves when the lifter is on the base circle of the camshaft lobe. To do this, crank or slowly turn the engine until the mark on the vibration damper lines up with the center or 0 mark on the timing tab, which is fastened to the crankcase front cover. Ensure the engine is in the No. 1 firing position.

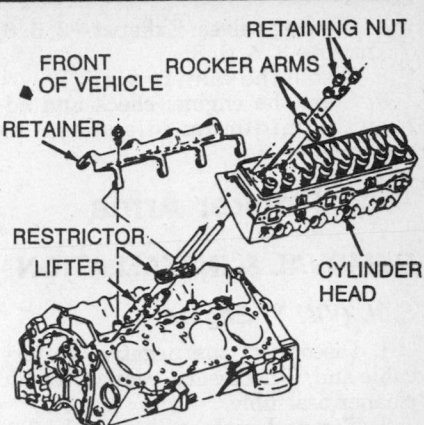

Rocker arm assembly and related components—5.0L (VIN E) and 5.7L Engines

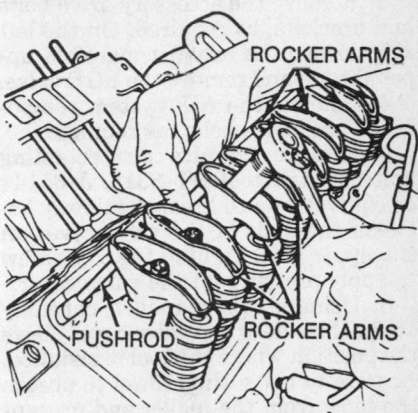

Valve adjustment procedure

NOTE: This may be determined by placing a finger on the No. 1 valve as the mark on the damper comes near the 0 mark on the crankcase front cover. If the valves move as the mark comes up to the timing tab, the engine is in the No. 6 firing position and should be turned 1 full turn to reach the No. 1 firing position.

4. With the engine in the No. 1 firing position, adjust the following valves. Exhaust—1, 3, 4, 8; Intake—1, 2, 5, 7.
5. Back out adjusting nut until lash is felt at the pushrod, then turn in adjusting nut until all lash is removed. This can be determined by rotating pushrod while turning the adjusting nut. When the pushrod stops turning, turn in the adjusting nut ¾-1¼ additional turns.
6. Crank or slowly turn the engine one revolution until the pointer, 0 mark and the vibration damper mark are again in alignment. This is the No. 6 firing position.
7. With the engine in this position, repeat the above procedure, adjusting

the following valves: Exhaust—2, 5, 6, 7; Intake—3, 4, 6, 8.

8. Install the valve covers.

9. Start the engine, check and adjust the minimum idle speed, as required.

Rocker Arms

REMOVAL & INSTALLATION

5.0L (VIN Y) Engine

1. Disconnect the negative battery cable and, if necessary, remove the air cleaner assembly.

2. Tag and remove the spark plug wires and all electrical leads or hoses preventing access to the valve cover retaining bolts.

3. Remove the accessory drive belts and brackets, as required. On the left side, loosen the exhaust manifold upper shroud and remove the EGR valve.

4. Remove the AIR system components and drive belts, as required.

5. Remove the valve cover retaining bolts. Install tool BT–8315, J–34144 or equivalent seal breaker midway between the ends of the valve cover on the upper side. Tighten the tool screw to apply pressure on the valve cover.

6. Using a rubber mallet, carefully strike the side of the valve cover above the position where the tool is installed. Be sure to use a shop towel to absorb the blow from the mallet and prevent valve cover damage.

7. Remove the valve cover from the engine. Remove the rocker arm bolts, pivots and the rocker arms.

To install:

8. Lubricate the wear points with appropriate chasis lube. Install the pivots, rocker arms and rocker arm bolts. Tighten the rocker arm bolts evenly to 22 ft. lbs. (28 Nm.)

9. Clean the valve cover and cylinder head mating surfaces. Apply a ¼ inch (6mm) bead of RTV sealant or equivalent to the valve cover and install. The RTV must be wet to the touch when the cover is installed. Install and tighten the valve cover bolts to 90 inch lbs. (10 Nm).

10. Install the AIR system components and drive belts, as required.

11. Install the EGR valve and secure the exhaust manifold upper shroud.

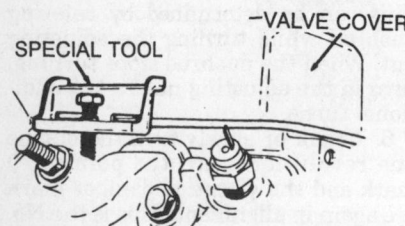

Valve cover removal tool positioning—5.0L (VIN Y) Engine

Install the accessory brackets and drive belts, as required.

12. Connect the spark plug wires and all electrical leads or hoses which were disconnected to access the valve covers.

13. Install the air cleaner assembly, if removed, and connect the negative battery cable.

5.0L (VIN E) and 5.7L Engines

1. Disconnect the negative battery cable. Remove the air cleaner assembly.

2. Disconnect the computer command control harness from the intake manifold and oxygen sensor.

3. Disconnect the power brake vacuum pipe and disconnect the AIR hose at the manifold check valve. Tag and remove the spark plug wires.

4. Disconnect the wiring harnesses from the valve covers. Remove the crankcase air inlet hose and connector.

5. Remove the EGR valve solenoid bracket. Remove the PCV valve and hose from the valve cover.

6. Relieve fuel system pressure and disconnect the fuel lines, as required. Remove the alternator rear support bracket and wire harness.

7. Remove the valve cover retaining bolts and washers. Remove the valve covers from the engine and discard the gaskets.

8. Remove the rocker arm nuts, rocker arm balls and rocker arms, marking each component to ensure they are installed in their original location.

To install:

9. If installing new rocker arms or balls, coat their bearing surfaces with Molykote® or equivalent. Install all used components in their original locations.

10. Install the rockers arms, balls and adjusting nuts. Tighten the nuts until all lash is eliminated and properly adjust the valves.

11. Thoroughly clean the cylinder head and valve cover mating surfaces. Install the new gaskets and the valve covers to the cylinder heads.

12. Install the valve cover washers and retaining bolts. Tighten the bolts to 95 inch lbs. (11 Nm).

13. If removed, connect the fuel lines and tighten the fuel filler cap. Install the alternator rear support bracket and wire harness.

14. Install the PCV valve and hose, and the air inlet hose and connector to the appropriate valve covers. Install the EGR valve solenoid bracket.

15. Connect the wiring harnesses to the valve covers and connect the spark plug wires.

16. Connect the AIR hose to the manifold check valve and connect the power brake vacuum pipe.

17. Connect the computer command control harness to the intake manifold and oxygen sensor.

18. Install the air cleaner assembly and connect the negative battery cable.

Intake Manifold

REMOVAL & INSTALLATION

5.0L (VIN Y) Engine

1. Disconnect the negative battery cable and properly relieve the fuel system pressure.

2. Remove the air cleaner assembly and drain the radiator.

3. Remove the upper radiator hose, thermostat bypass hose at the coolant pump, and heater hose at the rear of the manifold.

4. Remove and tag all vacuum lines from the intake manifold.

5. Disconnect and plug the fuel line. Remove the AIR hose. Remove the throttle cable and the detent cable.

6. Disconnect alternator rear brace, the air conditioning compressor rear brace and all necessary electrical leads.

7. Remove the computer command control solenoid assembly and the idle load compensator and bracket assembly. Remove the EGR valve.

8. As required, remove the carburetor assembly from the intake manifold.

9. Remove the intake manifold retaining bolts. Remove the intake manifold from the vehicle and discard all gaskets.

To install:

10. Clean all gasket mating surfaces. Apply a suitable RTV sealant to both sides of the manifold gasket and to the front and rear corners of the manifold seals.

11. Install the gasket to the cylinder heads and the seals to the block then position the intake manifold.

12. Lubricate the manifold bolts with clean engine oil and install. Tighten in the proper sequence to 15 ft. lbs. (20

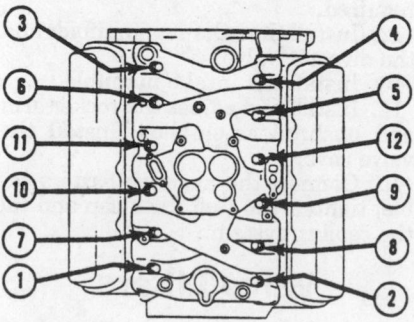

Intake manifold torque sequence—5.0L (VIN Y) Engine

Nm) on the 1st pass and to 40 ft. lbs. (54 Nm) for the 2nd pass.

13. Install carburetor, if removed, and the EGR valve.

14. Install the idle load compensator with bracket assembly and the computer command control solenoid assembly.

15. Connect all electrical leads and install the air conditioning and alternator rear braces.

16. Install and adjust as neceesary, the throttle cable and detent cable.

17. Install the AIR hose and connect the fuel line.

18. Connect all vacuum lines to the intake manifold.

19. Install the upper radiator hose, thermostat bypass hose and the heater hose.

20. Install the air cleaner assembly and connect the negative battery cable.

21. Tighten the fuel filler cap and add the proper type and amount of engine coolant.

5.0L (VIN E) and 5.7L Engines

1. Disconnect the negative battery cable and properly relieve the fuel system pressure.

2. Remove the air cleaner assembly and drain the radiator fluid into a suitable container.

3. Remove the throttle body assembly, if necessary, as follows:

a. Disconnect all electrical connectors and remove the fuel injector wiring harness.

b. Disconnect the throttle cable, transmission control cable and the cruise control cable.

c. Tag and remove all necessary vacuum hoses. Disconnect and plug the fuel feed and return lines. Discard the old fuel line O-rings.

d. Remove the TBI attaching bolts and the TBI unit. Discard the old gasket.

4. Disconnect the computer command control harness and position it aside.

5. Remove the radiator hose at the thermostat housing and the heater hose from the rear of the intake mani-

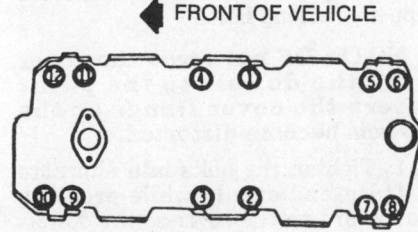

Intake manifold torque sequence—5.0L (VIN E) and 5.7L Engines

FRONT OF VEHICLE

fold. Remove the thermostat housing and gasket, if required.

6. Disconnect the power brake vacuum pipe. Disconnect the accelerator cable and throttle valve cable retaining bracket. Disconnect the fuel line clips, as required.

7. Tag and remove the spark plug wires at the distributor cap and remove the distributor cap. Mark the position of the rotor and distributor and remove the distributor assembly from the engine.

8. Remove the EGR valve and the coil.

9. Remove the coolant temperature sensor. Disconnect the air conditioning compressor brace and the alternator brace, as required.

10. Remove the intake manifold retaining bolts and studs. Remove the intake manifold from the engine. Discard the gaskets.

To install:

11. Clean the gasket and seal surfaces and position new gaskets on the cylinder heads.

12. Apply a $^3/_{16}$ inch (5mm) bead of RTV sealant, part number 1052289 or equivalent on the front and rear of the cylinder block. Extend the bead of RTV sealant $^1/_2$ inch (13mm) up each cylinder head to seal and retain the gaskets in position.

13. Install the intake manifold on the engine. Install the retaining bolts and tighten the bolts in the proper sequence to 35 ft. lbs. (47 Nm).

14. Install the compute control harness and the coolant temperature sensor.

15. Install the distributor assembly aligning the marks made earlier. Install the distributor cap and the coil.

16. Install the spark plug wires to the distributor cap. Connect the accelerator cable and throttle valve cable retaining bracket.

17. Connect the fuel line clips, as required and connect the power brake vacuum pipe.

18. Connect wires and hoses as necessary and install the EGR valve.

19. Install the thermostat housing and gasket, as required. Connect the radiator and heater hoses.

20. Connect the air conditioning compressor brace and the alternator brace.

21. If removed, install the throttle body assembly. Tighten the TBI unit retaining bolts to 16 ft. lbs. (22 Nm) and be sure to install new O-rings on the fuel lines.

22. Install the air cleaner assembly and connect the negative battery cable.

23. Fill the radiator, using the proper quantity and type coolant.

24. Check and adjust the ignition timing as necessary.

Exhaust Manifold

REMOVAL & INSTALLATION

5.0L (VIN Y) Engine

LEFT SIDE

1. Disconnect the negative battery cable and remove the air cleaner assembly.

2. Raise and support the vehicle safely. Flatten the exhaust manifold bolt lock tabs.

3. Remove the exhaust pipe from the exhaust manifold and lower the vehicle.

4. Remove the heat shield retaining bolts and remove the heat shield.

5. Loosen the lower alternator bracket bolts and move the bracket aside, as required.

6. Remove the exhaust manifold retaining bolts and remove the exhaust manifold from the engine.

To install:

7. If necessary, replace the gasket and install the exhaust manifold. Tighten the retaining bolts to 25 ft. lbs. (34 Nm).

8. Install the lower alternator bracket and the heat shield.

9. Raise and safely support the vehicle. Connect the exhaust pipe to the manifold and bend-up the lock tabs.

10. Lower the vehicle, install the air cleaner and connect the negative battery cable.

RIGHT SIDE

1. Disconnect the negative battery cable.

2. Remove the oxygen sensor lead wire.

3. Raise and support the vehicle safely. Disconnect the crossover pipe and the exhaust pipe.

4. Remove the oil filter adapter and gasket.

5. If necessary, remove the right front wheel to gain access to the exhaust manifold bolts. Flatten the exhaust manifold bolt lock tabs.

6. Remove the exhaust manifold retaining bolts and remove the exhaust manifold and gasket from the engine.

To install:

7. Install a new gasket, if necessary and install the exhaust manifold. Tighten the retaining bolts to 25 ft. lbs. (34 Nm).

8. Install the oil filter adapter, the croosover pipe and the exhaust pipe. Bend-up the lock tabs.

9. Install the right front wheel, if removed, and lower the vehicle.

10. Connect the oxygen sensor lead and connect the negative battery cable.

5.0L (VIN E) and 5.7L Engines

LEFT SIDE

1. Disconnect the negative battery cable and remove the air cleaner assembly.
2. Raise and support the vehicle safely, remove the crossover pipe and lower the vehicle.
3. Tag and remove the spark plug wires and the wire clips.
4. Disconnect the oxygen sensor connector and disconnect the AIR hose at the check valve. Loosen or remove the generator brace, as necessary.
5. Remove the exhaust manifold retaining bolts and studs. Remove the exhaust manifold and heat shield from the engine.

To install:

6. Clean the mating surfaces and position the manifold and heat shield to the cylinder head. Install the retaining bolts and studs. Tighten the bolts and studs to 25 ft. lbs. (35 Nm) and the nuts on the studs to 20 ft. lbs. (25 Nm).
7. Connect the oxygen sensor connector and connect the AIR hose to the check valve.
8. Install the spark plug wire clips and connect the spark plug wires.
9. Install and/or tighten the alternator brace.
10. Raise and safely support the vehicle, install the crossover pipe and tighten the nuts to 15 ft. lbs. (20 Nm). Lower the vehicle.
11. Install the air cleaner assembly and connect the negative battery cable.

RIGHT SIDE

1. Disconnect the negative battery cable and remove the air cleaner assembly.
2. Raise and support the vehicle safely. Disconnect the crossover pipe at both exhaust manifolds.
3. Remove the exhaust mount at the rear of the catalytic converter and remove the back two exhaust manifold retaining studs. Lower the vehicle.
4. Tag and disconnect the spark plug wires at the spark plugs.
5. Remove the diverter valve and AIR pipes.
6. Remove the air conditioning compressor brace.
7. Remove the remaining exhaust manifold bolts, studs and locks. Remove the exhaust manifold from the engine.

To install:

8. Clean the mating surface and position the exhaust manifold onto the cylinder head.
9. Install the 4 front manifold bolts and studs, including the flat washers and locks onto the 2 front bolts. Tighten the bolts and studs to 25 ft. lbs. (34

Nm) and the nuts on the studs to 20 ft. lbs. (25 Nm).
10. Install the diverter valve and AIR pipes. Install the air conditioning compressor brace and the spark plug wires.
11. Raise and support the vehicle safely. Install the 2 rear most manifold studs with flat washers and lock. Tighten the studs to 25 ft. lbs. (34 Nm).
12. Install the dipstick and AIR pipe brackets to the studs.
13. Install the crossover pipe to both manifolds and tighten the nuts to 15 ft. lbs. (20 Nm).
14. Install the exhaust mount at the rear of the catalytic converter and lower the vehicle.
15. Install the air cleaner assembly and connect the negative battery cable.

Timing Chain Front Cover

REMOVAL & INSTALLATION

5.0L (VIN Y) Engine

1. Disconnect the negative battery cable and drain the cooling system.
2. Remove the radiator and cooling system hoses.
3. Remove the accessory drive belts.
4. Remove the power steering pump with hoses attached and position aside.
5. Remove the AIR pump pulley. Remove the air conditioning compressor front bracket and position the compressor to the side.
6. Remove the fan shroud. Remove the fan assembly and fan pulley. Use hub balancer puller J-8614 or equivalent and remove the hub balancer.
7. The water pump assembly may be removed from the front cover assembly for convenience, or it may be removed as a unit with the front cover.
8. Remove the front cover retaining bolts/studs, timing indicator and front cover assembly. Discard the gasket.
9. Remove the dowel pins. It may be necessary to grind a flat surface on the dowel pins to aid in removal.

To install:

10. Clean the front cover and engine mating surfaces. Remove the front cover oil seal using an appropriate oil seal removal tool.
11. Apply a suitable sealing compound around the coolant holes of the new front cover gasket and position the gasket on the cylinder block.
12. Trim ⅛ inch (3.2mm) from each end of the oil pan seal and install the seal onto the front cover.
13. Apply a suitable sealant to the mating surface of the oil pan and in-

stall the front cover. Press down on the front cover to compress the oil seal and guide the seal into the cavity between the oil pan and cylinder block with a small suitable tool.
14. Apply engine oil to the bolts and studs. Install 2 bolts finger tight.
15. Insert the dowel pins with the tapered or chamfer ends first, through the holes in the front cover.
16. Install the timing indicator and, if removed, the water pump.
17. Install the remaining bolts and studs and tighten to specification.
18. Install the hub balancer and tighten the retaining bolt to 255 ft. lbs. (345 Nm). Install the hub pulley and tighten the bolts to 28 ft. lbs. (40 Nm).
19. Move the air conditioning compressor into position and connect the front bracket. Intsall the AIR pump pulley and the power steering pump with hoses.
20. Install the pan and pulley to the coolant pump, tighten the bolts to 20 ft. lbs. (27 Nm).
21. Install the accessory drive belts.
22. Install the radiator and hoses.
23. Connect the negative battery cable, add engine coolant and adjust belt tension as necessary.

5.0L (VIN E) and 5.7L Engines

1. Disconnect the negative battery cable and remove the serpentine drive belt.
2. Raise and support the vehicle safely.
3. Remove the vibration damper retaining bolt. Remove the crankshaft pulley bolts and the crankshaft pulley.
4. Using tool J-23523-E or equivalent harmonic balancer puller, remove the vibration damper.
5. Remove the oil pan and lower the vehicle.
6. Remove the water pump.
7. Remove the front cover retaining bolts. Remove the front cover and discard the gasket.

To install:

8. Clean the front cover and engine mating surfaces and coat the new cover gasket with gasket sealant.
9. Position the cover and the gasket over the crankshaft end.
10. Loosely install the cover to block upper retaining bolts.

NOTE: Do not force the cover over the dowels to the point where the cover flange or the dowels become distorted.

11. Tighten the bolts in a alternate pattern and evenly while pressing downward on the cover so the dowels in the block are aligned with the corresponding holes in the cover. Position the engine front cover so the dowels

enter the holes in the cover without binding.

12. Install the remaining cover bolts. Tighten all bolts alternately and evenly to 100 inch lbs. (11 Nm).

13. Install the water pump assembly.

14. Raise and support the vehicle safely and install the oil pan.

15. Coat the portion of the damper which contacts the front engine cover seal with oil and position the damper over the crankshaft key on the crankshaft.

16. Install the damper using J-23523–E or equivalent harmonic balancer installer. Be sure to thread the tool at least ½ inch into the crankshaft and pull the damper into position.

17. Install the crankshaft pulley and tighten the retaining bolts to 45 ft. lbs (60 Nm). Install the damper retaining bolt and tighten to 70 ft. lbs. (95 Nm).

18. Lower the vehicle and install the serpentine drive belt.

19. Connect the negative battery cable and add engine coolant.

Front Cover Oil Seal

REPLACEMENT

5.0L (VIN Y) Engine
COVER INSTALLED

1. Remove the crankshaft pulley and retaining bolts.

2. Remove the harmonic balancer, using the proper tools.

3. Using seal removal tool J-23129 and J-185903 remove the oil seal from the front cover.

To install:

4. Coat the outside diameter of the new seal with sealing compound and install the seal with the lip facing the engine with J-25264A or equivalent. Tighten the installation tool until a 0.005 inch gauge will just fit between the front cover and the installation tool.

5. Install the harmonic balancer with the proper tool.

6. Install the crankshaft pulley and retaining bolts.

COVER REMOVED

1. Remove the front cover from the engine.

2. Using the proper tool, remove and discard the old seal.

3. Install the engine front and tighten to specification.

4. Coat the outside diameter of the new seal with sealing compound and install the seal with the lip facing the engine using the proper installation tool.

5. Finish the engine front cover installation procedure.

5.0L (VIN E) and 5.7L Engines
COVER INSTALLED

1. Disconnect the negative battery cable and remove the serpentine drive belt.

2. Raise and support the vehicle safely.

3. Remove the vibration damper retaining bolt. Remove the crankshaft pulley bolts and the crankshaft pulley.

4. Using tool J-23523–E or equivalent harmonic balancer puller, remove the vibration damper.

5. Pry the old seal from the cover, with a small suitable tool. Care should be taken not to damage the cover.

To install:

6. Position the new seal so the open end of the seal faces toward the inside of the engine cover. Use tool J-35468 or equivalent to properly align and install the new oil seal.

7. Coat the portion of the damper which contacts the front engine cover seal with clean engine oil and position the damper over the crankshaft key on the crankshaft. Install the damper using J-23523–E or equivalent harmonic balancer installer. Be sure to thread the tool at least ½ inch into the crankshaft and pull the damper into position.

8. Install the crankshaft pulley and tighten the retaining bolts to 45 ft. lbs. (60 Nm). Install the damper retaining bolt and tighten to 70 ft. lbs. (95 Nm).

9. Lower the vehicle, install the serpentine drive belt and connect the negative battery cable.

COVER REMOVED

1. Remove the front cover from the engine.

2. Using a small suitable tool pry the old seal from the engine front cover and discard it. Be careful not to damage the cover when removing the seal.

3. Position the new seal so that the open end of the seal faces toward the inside of the engine cover. Support the rear of the engine cover at the seal area and use tool J-35468 or equivalent to properly align and install the new oil seal.

4. Install the front cover to the engine.

Timing Chain and Sprockets

REMOVAL & INSTALLATION

5.0L (VIN Y) Engine

1. Disconnect the negative battery cable.

2. Remove the engine front cover.

3. Remove the crankshaft oil slinger, camshaft thrust button and spring.

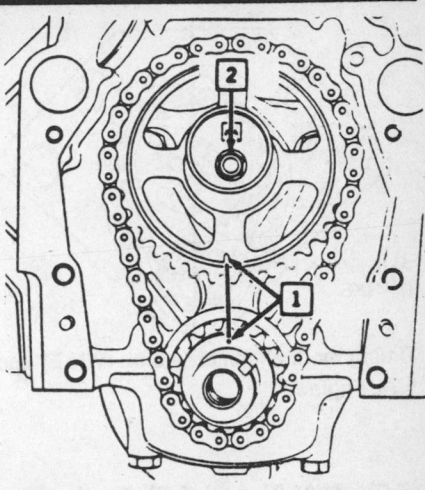

Timing mark alignment—5.0L (VIN Y) Engine

4. Remove the fuel pump, gasket and eccentric.

5. Remove the camshaft sprocket retaining bolt. Remove the camshaft sprocket and timing chain assembly.

6. Remove the crankshaft key before attempting to remove the crankshaft sprocket. Using an appropriate puller tool, remove the crankshaft sprocket.

To install:

7. Insert the camshaft sprocket and crankshaft sprocket into the timing chain, with the timing marks aligned.

8. Grasp both sprockets and the timing chain together and position them in place. Rotate the camshaft sprocket and engage it on the camshaft, while maintaining timing mark alignment.

9. Install the fuel pump eccentric, flat side toward the engine. Install the camshaft sprocket bolt finger-tight.

10. Rotate the crankshaft until the keyways are aligned. Install the crankshaft sprocket key, tap it in with a brass hammer until the key bottoms.

11. When the timing marks are in alignment, the No. 6 cylinder should be at TDC. When both timing marks are on the top, the No. 1 cylinder is at TDC of the compression stroke.

12. Install the fuel pump eccentric. Slowly and evenly draw the camshaft sprocket onto the camshaft, using the mounting bolt and torque the bolt to 65 ft. lbs. (88 Nm).

13. Install the camshaft thrust button and spring. Install the crankshaft oil slinger.

14. Install the engine front cover. When installing the front cover, be sure to trim the ends of the oil pan seal and install the seal onto the front cover.

15. Connect the negative battery cable.

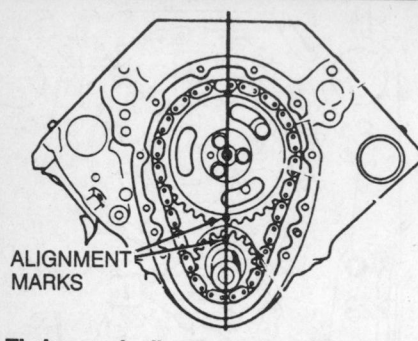

ALIGNMENT
MARKS

Timing mark alignment—5.0L (VIN E) and 5.7L Engines

5.0L (VIN E) and 5.7L Engines

1. Disconnect the negative battery cable.

2. Remove the engine front cover and water pump assembly.

3. Rotate the engine slowly until the marks on both the camshaft sprocket and crankshaft sprocket align with the shaft centers.

4. Remove the camshaft sprocket retaining bolts. Remove the camshaft sprocket along with the timing chain.

NOTE: Do not allow the crankshaft to turn after the timing chain has been removed to prevent damage to engine parts.

5. Using a crankshaft sprocket removal tool, remove the crankshaft sprocket. Remove the crankshaft sprocket key, if required.

To install:

6. Remove the old gasket from the timing cover and engine mating surfaces.

7. Install the crankshaft key, if removed and install the crankshaft sprocket onto the crankshaft using GM tool J-5590 or equivalent gear installer.

NOTE: A new timing chain must be installed any time a new crankshaft sprocket is installed.

8. Install the timing chain with the camshaft sprocket onto the camshaft.

9. Ensure the timing marks on the crankshaft sprocket and the camshaft sprocket are aligned as close together as possible and centered with the shafts.

10. Install the bolts securing the camshaft sprocket to the camshaft and torque to 21 ft. lbs. (28 Nm).

11. Lubricate the timing chain with oil and install the engine front cover assembly.

12. Reconnect the negative battery cable, check and adjust the ignition timing as necessary.

Camshaft

REMOVAL & INSTALLATION

5.0L (VIN Y) Engine

1. Disconnect the negative battery cable and properly relieve the fuel system pressure.

2. Drain the cooling system. Remove the radiator shroud assembly, lines, hoses and the radiator.

3. Remove the air cleaner and disconnect the throttle cable.

4. Remove the drive belts and the AIR pump pulley. Remove the cooling fan, fan clutch and the water pump pulley.

5. Remove the alternator assembly with bracket and position aside. Remove the power steering pump with bracket and hoses and position it to the side. Remove the compressor bracket and position the compressor aside with the hoses attached.

6. Remove the thermostat bypass hose. Label and disconnect all necessary electrical and vacuum connections.

7. Remove the air pump. Remove the distributor cap with the wiring intact.

8. Remove the crankshaft pulley and hub. Remove the fuel pump and the engine front cover.

9. Remove the valve covers and the intake manifold.

10. Remove the rocker arm assemblies, pushrods and lifters. Be sure to note the location of each component for proper installation.

11. Move the air conditioning condenser and support aside, until the camshaft has been removed, then replace them in their original position.

12. Rotate the crankshaft and align the timing marks. Remove the camshaft thrust button and spring, the fuel pump eccentric, the camshaft gear and the timing chain.

13. Remove the camshaft retaining plate and camshaft flange adapter. Carefully remove the camshaft. Do not force the camshaft as damage may occur to the bearings.

To install:

14. Lubricate the camshaft journals with a suitable lifter prelube and carefully install the camshaft.

15. Install the camshaft flange adapter and retainer plate.

16. Install the timing chain and the camshaft sprocket. Be sure that the timing marks are in proper alignment.

17. Install the fuel pump eccentric, the camshaft thrust spring and button.

18. Install the engine front cover and the fuel pump.

19. Install the crankshaft hub and pulley.

20. Install the lifters, pushrods, rocker arms and pivots in their original positions.

21. Install the valve covers and the intake manifold.

22. Install the air conditioning compressor, power steering pump and alternator.

23. Connect all necessary electrical leads. Install the AIR pump. Connect the vacuum hoses and the fuel lines.

24. Install the water pump pulley, fan and fan clutch.

25. Instrll the AIR pump pulley. Position and secure the air conditioning condenser with the lines attached.

26. Install the radiator, hoses, lines and shroud assembly.

27. Install and adjust the accessory drive belts.

28. Be sure to replace engine oil and filter before running engine.

29. Connect the negative battery cable, tighten the fuel filler cap and add engine coolant.

5.0L (VIN E) and 5.7L Engines

1. Disconnect the negative battery cable and properly relieve the fuel system pressure.

2. Drain the cooling system. and remove the intake manifold.

3. Remove the valve covers, rocker arm assemblies, pushrods and lifters. Be sure to note the location of each component for proper installation.

4. Remove the clutch fan bolts and remove the serpentine drive belt.

5. Remove the radiator tie struts at the radiator cradle. Remove the fan shroud bolts at the top and bottom of the shroud. Push the shroud back and remove the fan clutch and water pump pulley.

6. Remove the radiator hoses from the water pump and thermostat. Remove the transmission and oil cooler lines from the radiator.

7. Remove the radiator and the fan shroud.

8. Remove the timing chain and camshaft sprocket.

9. Remove the camshaft retainer and bolts.

10. Carefully pull the camshaft partially out of the engine using the bolts as a handle. Remove the bolts from the camshaft and carefully remove the camshaft from the engine. All camshaft journals are the same diameter, so care must be used in pulling the camshaft from the bearings to prevent damage.

To install:

11. When installing a new camshaft, lubricate the camshaft lobes with Molykote® or equivalent prelube, before installing the camshaft and use new lifters.

12. Lubricate the camshaft bearing journals with clean engine oil and par-

tially install the camshaft. Install three $5/16-18 \times 4$ inch bolts in the camshaft timing gear bolt holes to serve as a handle and finish inserting the camshaft.

13. Remove the installation bolts and install the camshaft retainer and retainer bolts. Tighten the bolts to 105 inch lbs. (12 Nm).

14. Install the timing chain and engine front cover.

15. Install the valve lifters.

16. Install the fan shroud, water pump pulley and fan clutch, and the radiator. Connect all radiator hoses and lines.

17. Install the serpentine drive belt and tighten the fan clutch bolts. Secure the fan shroud top and bottom bolts. Install the radiator tie struts at the radiator cradle.

18. Install the valve rocker arms and pushrods. Adjust as necessary and install the valve rocker covers.

19. Install the intake manifold and connect the negative battery cable.

20. Tighten the fuel filler cap and add engine coolant.

Piston and Connecting Rod

POSITIONING

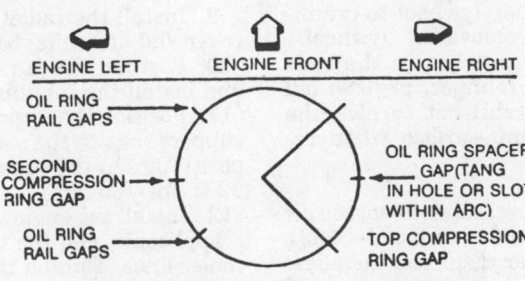

Piston positioning and identification — 5.0L (VIN Y) Engine

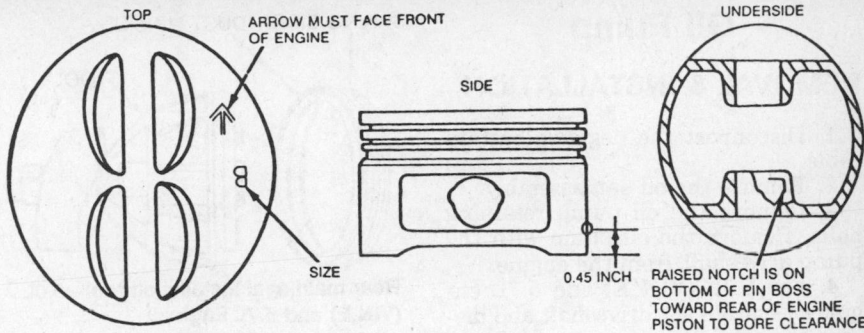

Piston positioning and Identification — 5.0L (VIN E) and 5.7L Engines

ENGINE LUBRICATION

Oil Pan

REMOVAL & INSTALLATION

1. Disconnect the negative battery cable.

2. As required remove the air cleaner assembly, the AIR pipe at the diverter valve outlet hose and/or the oil level indicator.

3. Remove the fan shroud attaching screws. Position the fan shroud backward and out of the way.

4. Raise and support the vehicle safely. If applicable, remove the bracket securing the AIR pipe to the rear of the cylinder head.

5. Drain the engine oil. Disconnect the exhaust crossover pipe and remove the flywheel cover.

6. Remove the starter assembly.

7. Using the proper jack, with a block of wood on top, place it under the crankshaft hub to support the engine. Remove both engine mount through bolts.

8. Carefully raise the front of the engine. Remove the oil pan retaining bolts, nuts and, if equipped, reinforcements.

9. Lower the oil pan enough to determine if the crankshaft throw and counterbalance are clear and remove the oil pan from the engine. If necessary turn the crankshaft slowly to create to clear the throw and weight.

To install:

10. Clean all the gasket material from the pan and the block mating surfaces.

11. For 5.0L (VIN Y) engines apply a thin amount of gasket sealer to both sides of the new gasket. Install the gasket onto the oil pan. Wipe the seals with engine oil and install the front and rear seals onto the oil pan. Apply RTV sealant to the front and rear seals and install the oil pan onto the engine. Tighten the bolts to 10 ft. lbs. (14 Nm) and the nuts to 17 ft. lbs. (24 Nm).

12. For 5.0L (VIN E) and 5.7L engines, apply a thin amount of gasket sealer only to the front cover and cylinder block junction and to the rear seal retainer and cylinder block junction. Continue the bead of sealer for 1 inch (25mm) on either side of these junctions. Install the gasket onto the oil pan and loosely install the oil pan onto the engine with the bolts, nuts and retainers.

13. Lower the engine into position. For the 5.0L (VIN E) and the 5.7L engines tighten the oil pan bolts to 100 inch lbs. (11 Nm) and the nuts to 17 ft. lbs. (23 Nm).

14. Install the engine mount through bolts and remove the engine support.

15. Install the starter assembly and, if applicable, attach the transmission oil cooler lines to the clips on the oil pan.

16. Install the flywheel cover and the exhaust crossover pipe.

17. If applicable, install the AIR pipe bracket to the rear of the cylinder head.

18. Lower the vehicle and secure the fan shroud assembly.

19. As required, install the oil level indicator, the AIR pipe at the diverter valve outlet hose and the air cleaner assembly.

20. Connect the negative battery cable and refill the engine crankcase with the proper type and amount of engine oil.

Oil Pump

REMOVAL & INSTALLATION

1. Disconnect the negative battery cable.

2. Remove the oil pan assembly.

3. Remove the oil pump retaining bolts. Remove the oil pump with the pump driveshaft from the engine.

4. For 5.0L (VIN E) and 5.7L engines, separate the driveshaft and discard the retainer.

To install:

5. For the 5.0L (VIN Y) engine, install the driveshaft extension ensuring that it is fully engaged. The end of the extension nearest the washers must be inserted into the driveshaft. Install the oil pump to the engine and tighten the retaining bolts to 35 ft. lbs. (47 Nm).

6. For the 5.0L (VIN E) and 5.7L engines, install the new retainer to the oil pump driveshaft and install the driveshaft extension to the pump. Align the slot on the end of the driveshaft extension with the drive tang on the distributor driveshaft and install the oil pump assembly. Tighten the retaining bolt to 80 ft. lbs. (105 Nm).

7. Install the oil pan assembly.

8. Remove the oil pressure sending unit and install an oil pressure gauge.

9. Connect the negative battery cable, start the engine and ensure the oil pressure is within specification.

Rear Main Bearing Oil Seal

REMOVAL & INSTALLATION

5.0L (VIN Y) Engine

NOTE: If upper seal replacement is necessary, crankshaft removal will be required. The following procedure is intended for engine-in-vehicle repair of the main bearing upper oil seal.

1. Disconnect the negative battery cable.

2. Remove the oil pan.

3. Remove the rear main bearing cap.

To install:

4. Using packing tool BT–6433, J–25282–2 or equivalent, drive both sides of the old seal gently into the groove until it is packed tight.

5. Measure the amount of the seal which was driven up on one side and add ¹⁄₁₆ inch Cut this length from the old seal that was removed from the main bearing cap.

6. Measure the amount of the seal which was driven up on the other side and add ¹⁄₁₆ inch Cut another length

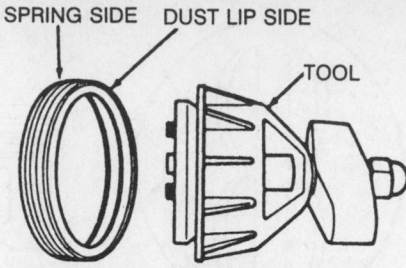

Rear main seal installation tool—5.0L (VIN E) and 5.7L Engines

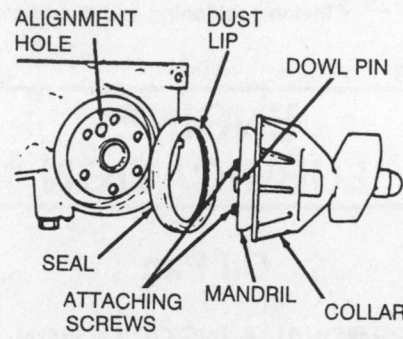

Installing one piece rear main seal—5.0L (VIN E) and 5.7L Engines

from the old seal. Use the main bearing cap as a holding fixture when cutting the seal.

7. Work these 2 pieces of the seal into the cylinder block (one piece on each side). Pack the short pieces up into the block and trim using tool BT–6436 or equivalent sharp blade. Use a small piece of shim stock between the seal and the crankshaft to protect the bearing surface while trimming.

8. Form a new rope seal in the rear main bearing cap. Place a drop of a suitable sealer on each end of the seal and cap. Install the main bearing cap. Do not use the attaching bolts to pull down the bearing cap. Tap the cap gently into place with a suitable tool.

9. Install the rear main bearing cap bolts and tighten to specification.

10. Install the oil pan and connect the negative battery cable.

5.0L (VIN E) and 5.7L Engines

1. Disconnect the negative battery cable.

2. Remove the transmission assembly.

3. Remove the flywheel-to-crankshaft bolts and remove the flywheel.

4. Using the notches in the rear crankshaft seal retainer, pry the old seal out. Be careful not to nick the crankshaft sealing surface when removing the seal.

To install:

5. Coat the new seal with engine oil and install the seal onto tool J–35621 or equivalent rear main seal installer.

6. Install the tool onto the rear of

the crankshaft and tighten the screws snugly to ensure the seal will be installed squarely over the crankshaft.

7. Install the seal onto the crankshaft and into the rear seal retainer by tightening the wing nut of the tool until it bottoms. Remove the tool from the retainer.

8. Reinstall the flywheel and tighten the attaching bolts to 75 ft. lbs. (100 Nm).

9. Install the transmission assembly.

10. Connect the negative battery cable, lower the vehicle and inspect the engine for oil leaks.

ENGINE COOLING

Radiator

REMOVAL & INSTALLATION

1. Disconnect the negative battery cable. Drain the cooling system into a suitable container.

2. Disconnect the top and bottom radiator hoses from the radiator. Remove the reservoir hose from the radiator filler neck.

3. Disconnect and plug the transmission fluid cooler lines. Disconnect and plug the oil cooler lines, if equipped.

4. Remove the bolts retaining the engine compartment support rod to the radiator core support. Loosen each anchor bolt and position the support rods aside.

5. Remove the fan shroud retaining bolts. Position the fan shroud assembly aside.

6. Remove the radiator core support cover retaining bolts. Remove the radiator core support cover.

7. Carefully lift the radiator assembly upward and out of the vehicle.

To install:

8. Lower the radiator into place making sure it is properly seated on the insulators.

9. Install the radiator core support cover and attaching bolts.

10. Position the fan shroud in place and install the retaining bolts.

11. Position the engine compartment support rods to the radiator core support. Tighten the support bar bolts to 22 ft. lbs. (30 Nm).

12. Install the engine oil cooler lines, if applicable, and the transmission oil cooler lines. Tighten the fittings to 20 ft. lbs. (27 Nm).

13. Install the top, bottom and reservoir hoses and tighten the clamps to 26 inch lbs. (3 Nm).

14. Connect the negative battery cable and refill the cooling system with the proper type and quantity of coolant mixture.

Heater Core

REMOVAL & INSTALLATION

1. Disconnect the negative battery cable and partially drain the cooling system so the coolant level falls below the heater core inlet and outlet hoses.

2. Disconnect and tag the electrical connectors from the blower motor, compressor cycling switch, power module and radio lead-in connections. Position the wiring harness aside.

3. Remove the 2 screws holding the compressor cycling switch to the module. Remove the black insulation, loosen the 2 hose clamps and carefully remove the switch. Remove the right windshield washer nozzle.

4. Remove the 3 retaining screws and the right secondary air inlet screen. Partially remove the rubber molding above the plenum (1 screw on the right side).

5. Remove the remaining screws and remove the primary inlet screen. Remove the blower motor.

6. Remove the screws securing the case cover. Remove the cover. Remove the heater hoses and clamps from the heater core outlets.

7. Remove the screw and the retainer holding the heater core to the frame at the top of the assembly.

8. With the temperature door in the **MAX/HOT** position, reach through the temperature housing and push the lower forward corner of the heater core away from the housing.

9. Rotate the core parallel to the housing. This will cause the core to snap out of the lower clamp. Remove the heater core from the assembly. The core cannot be removed in a vertical direction due to the configuration of the components.

To install:

10. If sealer was used on the case cover, be sure to completely remove the old sealer and replace before installation.

11. Install the heater core into the vehicle and push down firmly to seat the core into the bottom clip. Install the heater core to the frame with the screw and retainer.

12. Connect the heater hoses to the core outlets and secure with hose clamps.

13. Install the case cover and attaching screws. Install the blower motor.

14. Install the primary and secondary inlet screens and the rubber molding.

15. Connect the right windshield washer nozzle.

16. Install the 2 screws on the compressor cycling switch. Apply black insulation, install the 2 hose clamps and install the switch.

17. Connect the wiring harness connectors to the blower motor, compressor cycling switch, power module and the radio lead-in connections. Properly reposition the wiring harness.

18. Connect the negative battery cable and refill the cooling system.

Water Pump

REMOVAL & INSTALLATION

1. Disconnect the negative battery cable and drain the cooling system.

2. Disconnect the lower radiator hose, the bypass hose and the heater hose from the water pump, as applicable.

3. Disconnect the engine compartment support rods from the radiator core support, loosen the anchor bolt and push rods out of the way.

4. Remove the fan shroud screws and the fan shroud.

5. Disconnect the 4 nuts attaching the fan assembly to the water pump hub.

6. Pull that fan and clutch assembly forward, then up and remove from the vehicle. Remove the spacer if equipped. Support the assembly in a vertical position to prevent damage to the clutch.

7. Remove the serpentine drive belt, or all drive belts, as applicable.

8. Remove the water pump pulley.

9. Remove accessory brackets, as necessary and position the accessories aside.

10. Remove the water pump retaining bolts and remove the water pump from the engine. Discard the old pump gasket.

To install:

11. Clean the cylinder block and pump gasket mating surfaces.

12. Install a new gasket and thin bead of sealer to the water pump.

13. Install the water pump to the vehicle and secure with the mounting bolts. For 1989 vehicles, tighten the bolts to 13 ft. lbs. (18 Nm). For 1990–93 vehicles, tighten the pump-to-block bolts to 22 ft. lbs. (30 Nm) and the pump-to-front cover bolts to 10 ft. lbs. (14 Nm).

14. Install the accessory brackets with the accessories, as applicable.

15. Install all hoses and tighten the clamps to 27 inch lbs. (3 Nm).

16. Install the water pump pulley and the serpentine drive belt, if applicable. Loosely install the accessory V-belts on the 5.0L (VIN Y) engine.

17. Inspect the fan assembly and replace as necessary. Install the fan and clutch assembly, be sure to install the spacer, if equipped. Tighten the nuts to 18 ft. lbs. (24 Nm).

— CAUTION —

It is essential that the fan assembly remain in proper balance. Balance cannot be assured once a fan assembly has been bent or damaged. A fan that is not in proper balance could fail and fly apart during use creating an extremely dangerous situation.

18. Install the fan shroud and screws. Position the engine compartment support rods and tighten the bolts to 22 ft. lbs. (30 Nm).

19. For the 5.0L (VIN Y) engine, tighten all accessory drive V-belts.

20. Connect the negative battery cable and refill the cooling system with the correct mixture of antifreeze and water. Start the engine and check for leaks.

Thermostat

REMOVAL & INSTALLATION

1. Disconnect the negative battery cable. Drain the cooling system to a level below the thermostat housing.

2. Remove the radiator hose from the thermostat housing and on the 5.0L engines, remove the clamp on the coolant bypass hose.

3. Remove the thermostat housing retaining bolts. Remove the thermostat housing assembly from the engine.

4. Remove the thermostat and discard the gasket.

To install:

5. Install the thermostat into the intake manifold with the arrow or marking pointing up.

6. Install a new gasket and the thermostat housing onto the manifold. Tighten the thermostat housing bolts to 21 ft. lbs. (28 Nm).

7. Connect the radiator inlet hose and the coolant bypass hose, as applicable. Tighten the hose clamp(s) to 27 inch lbs. (3 Nm).

8. Connect the negative battery cable and refill the cooling system using the proper coolant mixture.

Cooling System Bleeding

1. With the engine **OFF** and completely cool, remove the radiator cap to relieve all pressure.

2. Position a suitable container under the vehicle. Drain the coolant by

opening the radiator drain cock located on the bottom right of the radiator, and removing the 2 block drain plugs located on either side of the engine block.

3. Dispose of used coolant properly. Close the radiator drain cock and reinstall the engine block drain plugs.

4. Fill the cooling system with water and run the engine until the thermostat opens. Repeat steps 1–4 until drained fluid is free of coolant and/or rust.

5. Tighten the engine drain plugs to 15 ft. lbs. (21 Nm) and the drain cock to 106 inch lbs. (12 Nm).

6. With the engine turned **OFF**, fill the cooling system to just below the filler neck. Use a mixture of at least 50/50 ethylene glycol antifreeze and water; but not exceeding 70 percent antifreeze.

7. Fill the coolant recovery reservoir to the **COLD FILL** mark.

8. Run the engine with the radiator cap removed until normal operating temperature is reached (radiator inlet hose becomes hot).

9. With the engine idling, add coolant to the radiator until it reaches the bottom of the filler neck.

10. Install the radiator cap, with the arrows on the cap aligned with the coolant reservoir hose.

ENGINE ELECTRICAL

NOTE: Disconnecting the negative battery cable on some vehicles may interfere with the functions of the on board computer systems and may require the computer to undergo a relearning process.

Distributor

All vehicles use a High Energy Ignition (HEI) distributor with Electronic Spark Timing (EST). The 5.0L (VIN Y) carbureted engine distributor utilizes an internal ignition coil while the 5.0L (VIN E) and 5.7L Throttle Body Injection (TBI) engines use an externally mounted ignition coil.

REMOVAL

1. Disconnect the negative battery cable. If necessary, remove the air cleaner assembly.
2. On 5.0L (VIN Y) engine, without a tool carefully disconnect the coil locking tab connectors. On the 5.0L (VIN E) and 5.7L engines, disconnect

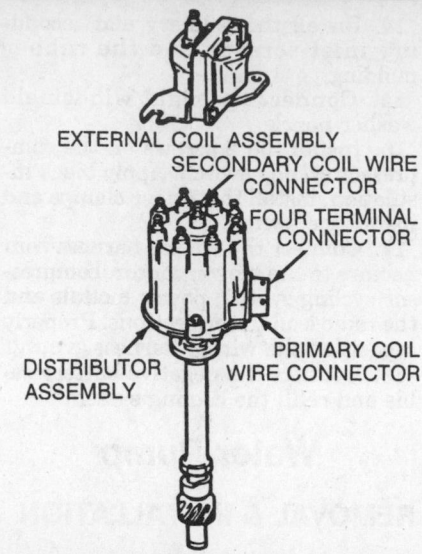

EXTERNAL COIL ASSEMBLY
SECONDARY COIL WIRE CONNECTOR
FOUR TERMINAL CONNECTOR
PRIMARY COIL WIRE CONNECTOR
DISTRIBUTOR ASSEMBLY

Distributor assembly—5.0L (VIN E) and 5.7L Engines

the wiring harness connectors at the side of the distributor cap.

3. Remove the distributor cap with spark plug wires attached and position it to the side. If necessary to remove the spark plug wires, be sure to tag all wires before disconnection.

4. On the 5.0L (VIN Y) engine, disconnect the 4 terminal ECM harness from the distributor.

5. Remove the distributor assembly retaining bolt.

6. Note and mark the position of the rotor. Pull the distributor upward until the rotor stops turning and again note and mark the position of the rotor. Remove the distributor assembly from the vehicle.

INSTALLATION

Timing Not Disturbed

1. To install the distributor, position the rotor in the last position as marked and lower the assembly into the distributor bore of the engine. On TBI vehicles, the distributor will install easier if it is tilted toward the driver's side of the vehicle and then slid into place. When the distributor rotor stops turning and the unit is seated, the rotor should be pointing to the first position marked.

2. Tighten the distributor retaining bolt.

3. Install the distributor cap. Connect all required electrical connections.

4. If removed, install the air cleaner assembly.

5. Connect the negative battery cable and check the ignition timing.

Timing Disturbed

1. If the engine has been accidently

cranked with the distributor out, remove the No. 1 spark plug. Place a finger over the No. 1 spark plug hole and crank the engine slowly until a compression build up can be felt in that cylinder.

2. Carefully align the timing mark on the crankshaft pulley to the **O** mark on the timing indicator of the engine. Turn the distributor rotor to point between the No. 1 and No. 8 spark plug towers on the distributor cap.

3. Lower the assembly into the distributor bore of the engine. When the distributor rotor stops turning and the unit is seated, the rotor should be pointing to No. 1 cylinder segment of the distributor cap.

4. Tighten the distributor retaining bolt.

5. Install the distributor cap. Install the spark plug wires. Connect all required electrical connections.

6. If removed, install the air cleaner assembly.

7. Connect the negative battery cable and check the ignition timing.

Ignition Timing

ADJUSTMENT

NOTE: Always refer to the timing specifications listed on the Emission Control Information Label.

1. Connect a timing light and a suitable tachometer to the engine. Some tachometers currently available are not compatible with the HEI ignition system. Be sure to connect the timing light to the No. 1 spark plug wire and to connect the tachometer according to the tools instructions.

2. Start the engine and operate until normal operating temperature is reached and the chock is fully opened.

3. Turn all accessories **OFF** and with the engine running, ground the

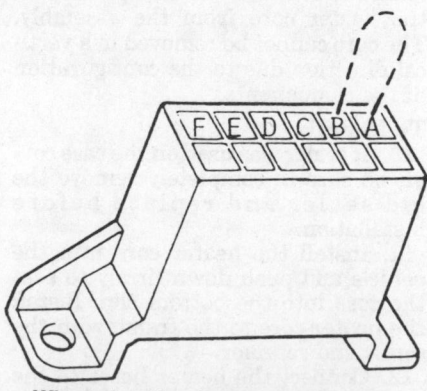

When checking ignition timing, the diagnostic terminal of the ALDL connector must be grounded with the engine running

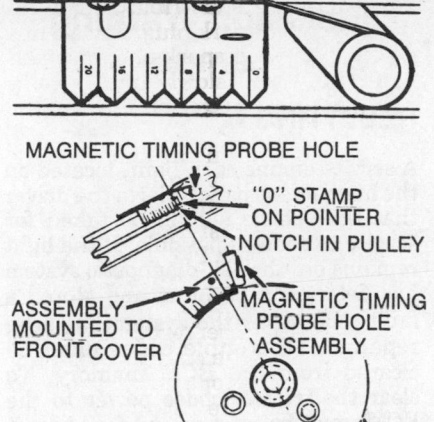

Typical timing mark location

diagnostic terminal of the ALDL connector using a jumper.

4. Check the ignition timing at the specified rpm. If the ignition timing is not within specification, loosen the distributor clamp bolt and rotate the distributor gradually until the specified timing is obtained.

5. Tighten the distributor clamp bolt making sure the distributor does not change position. Recheck the ignition timing.

6. With the engine still running, remove the jumper from the ALDL terminal.

7. Make fuel system adjustments, as required.

8. Turn the engine **OFF**. Remove the tachometer and timing light.

Alternator

PRECAUTIONS

Several precautions must be observed with alternator equipped vehicles to avoid damage to the unit.

• If the battery is removed for any reason, make sure it is reconnected with the correct polarity. Reversing the battery connections may result in damage to the 1-way rectifiers.

• When utilizing a booster battery as a starting aid, always connect the positive to positive terminals and the negative terminal from the booster battery to a good engine ground on the vehicle being started.

• Never use a fast charger as a booster to start vehicles.

• Disconnect the battery cables when charging the battery with a fast charger.

• Never attempt to polarize the alternator.

• Do not use test lights of more than 12 volts when checking diode continuity.

• Never operate the alternator with the output terminal disconnected.

• Do not short across or ground any of the alternator terminals.

• The polarity of the battery, alternator and regulator must be matched and considered before making any electrical connections within the system.

• Never separate the alternator on an open circuit. Make sure all connections within the circuit are clean and tight.

• Disconnect the battery ground terminal when performing any service on electrical components.

• Disconnect the battery if arc welding is to be done on the vehicle.

BELT TENSION ADJUSTMENT

5.0L (VIN Y) Engine

1. Using belt tension gauge J-23600 or equivalent, adjust the alternator belt as follows:

   a. If the belt is used, the correct belt tension is 112 lbs. (500 N), as indicated on the gauge.

   b. If the belt is new, the correct tension is 157 lbs. (700 N), as indicated on the gauge.

2. Adjust the air conditioning compressor and air pump belt tension as follows:

   a. If the belt is used, the correct belt tension is 112 lbs. (500 N), as indicated on the gauge.

   b. If the belt is new, the correct tension is 167 lbs. (750 N), as indicated on the gauge.

3. Adjust the power steering belt tension as follows:

   a. If the belt is used, the correct belt tension is 90 lbs. (400 N), as indicated on the gauge.

   b. If the belt is new, the correct tension is 170 lbs. (750 N), as indicated on the gauge.

5.0L (VIN E) and 5.7L Engines

NOTE: Serpentine belts are automatically adjusted by the tensioner on the engine. If the belt is loose, check the condition of the belt and tensioner. The tensioner should place enough tension on the belt so it can only be twisted 90 degrees at it's longest run.

1. Run the engine for about 10 minutes and shut the engine **OFF**.

2. Using belt tension gauge J-23600-B or equivalent, check the belt tension between 2 pulleys and record the reading.

3. Remove the gauge. Run the engine for about 30 seconds and shut the engine **OFF**.

4. Check the belt tension between

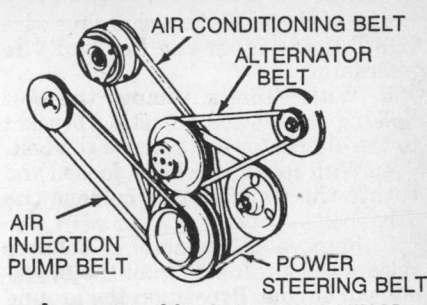

Accessory drive belts—5.0L (VIN Y) Engine

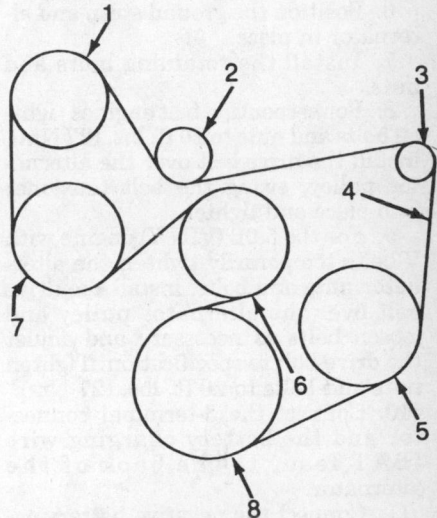

1. Air conditioning compressor belt
2. Drive belt tensioner
3. Alternator pulley
4. Serpentine drive belt
5. Power steering pump pulley
6. Water pump pulley
7. Air injection pump pulley
8. Crankshaft pulley

Accessory drive belt—5.0L (VIN E) and 5.7L Engines

the same 2 pulleys and record the reading.

5. Remove the gauge. Run the engine for about 30 seconds and shut the engine **OFF**.

6. Check the belt tension between the same 2 pulleys and record the reading.

7. Take the average of the 3 recorded readings. The belt tension should be 99–121 lbs. (440–538 N).

8. If the drive belt is not worn and the drive tensioner is operating normally but the tension is still below specification, replace the belt tensioner.

REMOVAL & INSTALLATION

1. Disconnect the negative battery cable.

2. Disconnect the 3-terminal con-

nector and the battery charging wire (BAT lead) from the back of the alternator.

3. With V-Belts, remove the bolt holding the slotted adjusting bracket to the alternator and remove the belt.

4. With serpentine belts, loosen and rotate the tensioner to release the drive belt.

5. Remove the remaining bolts to release the alternator from the brackets and engine. Reposition the ground strap and remove the alternator.

To install:

6. Position the ground strap and alternator in place.

7. Install the retaining bolts and nuts.

8. For serpentine belt engines tighten bolts and nuts to 20 ft. lbs. (27 Nm), install the drive belt over the alternator pulley, swing the belt tensioner into place and tighten.

9. For the 5.0L (VIN Y) engine with V-belts temporarily tighten the alternator nuts and bolts, install the drive belt over the alternator pulley and loosen bolts as necessary and adjust the drive belt to specification. Tighten nuts and bolts to 20 ft. lbs. (27 Nm).

10. Connect the 3-terminal connector and the battery charging wire (BAT lead) to the back of the alternator.

11. Connect the negative battery cable. Check and adjust belt tension for the serpentine drive belt, if necessary.

Starter

REMOVAL & INSTALLATION

5.0L (VIN Y) Engine

1. Disconnect the negative battery cable.

2. Raise and support the vehicle safely.

3. Remove the heat shield bolts, nuts and washers. Remove the heat shield.

4. Remove the flywheel cover attaching bolts and the flywheel cover.

5. Remove the starter motor retaining bolts and lower the starter. Remove any starter shims, if equipped.

6. Disconnect and tag the wires and the battery cable while supporting the starter. Remove the starter from the vehicle.

To install:

7. Support the starter under the vehicle and attach the wires and battery cable in their original positions.

8. Raise the starter into position and install the mounting bolts. If equipped, be sure to install shims in their original position. Tighten the bolts to 32 ft. lbs. (44 Nm).

9. Install the flywheel housing cover and attaching bolts.

10. Install the heat shield, being careful not to pinch leads between the heat shield and the engine. Tighten the heat shield bolt to 20 ft. lbs. (27 Nm) and the nut to 13 ft. lbs. (25 Nm).

11. Lower the vehicle and connect the negative battery cable.

5.0L (VIN E) and 5.7L Engines

1. Disconnect the negative battery cable.

2. Raise and support the vehicle safely.

3. Remove front support attaching bolt, nut and bracket.

4. Disconnect and tag the wiring at the solenoid.

5. Disconnect the exhaust pipe from the left manifold and loosen the pipe from the right manifold.

6. Remove the starter mounting bolts, lower the starter and, if equipped, remove the shims.

To install:

7. Position the starter in the vehicle. If shims were removed, they must be installed in their original location to assure proper drive pinion to flywheel engagement.

8. Check the pinion to flywheel clearance. A 0.020 inch (0.5 mm) gauge should just fit between the center end of a flywheel tooth and the pinion gear. Add shims, if necessary.

9. Tighten the starter mounting bolts to 35 ft. lbs. (47 Nm).

10. Connect the electrical connections to the starter solenoid and the exhaust pipes to the manifolds.

11. Install the front starter bracket. Tighten the bolt to 18 ft. lbs. (24 Nm) and the nut to 71 inch lbs. (8 Nm).

12. Lower the car and connect the negative battery cable.

EMISSION CONTROLS

Due to the complex nature of modern electronic engine control systems, comprehensive diagnosis and testing procedures fall outside the confines of this repair manual. For complete information on diagnosis, testing and repair procedures concerning all modern engine and emission control systems, please refer to "Chilton's Guide to Fuel Injection and Electronic Engine Controls".

Emission Warning Lamps

RESETTING

A service engine soon light, located on the instrument panel, alerts the driver that the vehicle should be taken for service as soon as possible. If the light remains on, the self-diagnostic system has detected a problem and stored a fault code. After the system has been repaired, all trouble codes must be cleared from the ECM memory. To clear the trouble codes power to the ECM must be interrupted for at least 30 seconds with the ignition switch turned **OFF**. This can be done in various ways depending on the vehicle. The ECM fuse may be removed from the fuse box or the ECM power feed at the positive battery terminal inline fuseholder may be disconnected. The negative battery terminal may also be disconnected, but this will affect other systems such as radio pre-sets.

FUEL SYSTEM

Fuel System Service Precautions

Safety is the most important factor when performing any type of maintenance, but even more so when performing fuel system maintenance. Failure to conduct maintenance and repairs in a safe manner may result in serious personal injury or death. Maintenance and testing of the vehicle's fuel system components can be accomplished safely and effectively by adhering to the following rules and guidelines.

• To avoid the possibility of fire and personal injury, always disconnect the negative battery cable unless the repair or test procedure requires that battery voltage be applied.

• Always relieve the fuel system pressure prior to disconnecting any fuel system component (injector, fuel rail, pressure regulator, etc.), fitting or fuel line connection. Exercise extreme caution whenever relieving fuel system pressure to avoid exposing skin, face and eyes to fuel spray. Under pressure, fuel may penetrate the skin or any part of the body that it contacts.

• Always place a shop towel or cloth around the fitting or connection prior to loosening to absorb any excess fuel due to spillage. Ensure that all fuel spillage, should it occur, is quickly removed from engine surfaces. Ensure that all fuel soaked cloths or towels are deposited into a suitable waste container.

- Always keep a dry chemical (Class B) fire extinguisher near the work area.
- Do not allow fuel spray or fuel vapors to come into contact with a spark or open flame.
- Always use a backup wrench when loosening and tightening fuel line connection fittings. This will prevent unnecessary stress and torsion to fuel line piping. Always follow the proper torque specifications.
- Always replace worn fuel fitting O-rings with new. Do not substitute fuel hose or equivalent where fuel pipe is installed.

RELIEVING FUEL SYSTEM PRESSURE

5.0L (VIN Y) Engine

1. Release the fuel vapor pressure in the fuel tank by removing the fuel tank cap.
2. Ensure the engine is cold and disconnect the negative battery cable.
3. Cover the fuel line with an absorbent shop cloth and loosen the connection slowly, using the proper tool, to release the fuel pressure gradually.

5.0L (VIN E) and 5.7L Engines

1. Release the fuel vapor pressure in the fuel tank by removing the fuel tank cap.
2. Ensure the engine is cold and disconnect the negative battery cable.
3. The internal constant bleed feature to throttle body injection relieves the fuel pump system pressure when the engine is not running. Therefore, no further action is required.

Fuel Tank

REMOVAL & INSTALLATION

5.0L (VIN Y) Engine

1. Disconnect the negative battery cable and relieve fuel system pressure.
2. Drain the fuel tank and disconnect the sending unit lead connector.
3. Raise and support the vehicle safely. To help avoid the possibility of the vehicle falling off the hoist, provide additional support at the opposite end of the vehicle from where the work is to take place.
4. Disconnect the ground lead retaining screw from the underbody. Clean the area surrounding the connections and remove the hoses from the sending unit.
5. Support the fuel tank and re-

move the fuel tank retaining straps. Lower the tank from the vehicle.
6. If necessary, remove the fuel tank sending unit retaining cam with an appropriate tool and remove the sending unit from the tank.

To install:
7. If removed, install the sending unit with a new gasket to the fuel tank.
8. Raise and support the fuel tank in position and connect the fuel tank retaining straps. Tighten the front retaining strap bolts to 25 ft. lbs. (34 Nm) and the rear strap bolts to 10 ft. lbs. (13 Nm).
9. Connect the hoses to the sending unit and tighten the clamps. Connect the ground lead to the underbody. Connect the sending unit lead connector.
10. Lower the vehicle, connect the negative battery cable and fill the fuel tank.

5.0L (VIN E) and 5.7L Engines

1. Disconnect the negative battery cable and relieve fuel system pressure.
2. Drain the fuel tank, raise and support the vehicle safely. To help avoid the possibility of the vehicle falling off the hoist, provide additional support at the opposite end of the vehicle from where the work is to take place.

NOTE: If a nylon fuel line becomes kinked and cannot be straightened or becomes otherwise damaged, it must be replaced.

3. Disconnect the quick-connect fuel pipe fittings from the fuel pump assembly as follows:
   a. Grap both ends of 1 pipe connection and twist ¼ turn in each direction to loosen dirt.
   b. While wearing safety glasses, use compressed air to blow dirt out of the fittings.
   c. Disconnect the fitting by squeezing the plastic tabs of the male connector and pulling the fitting apart.
4. Clean and disconnect the vapor hose connection at the fuel pump assembly. Disconnect the fuel pump assembly electrical connector.
5. Support the fuel tank with the aid of an assistant and remove the fuel tank retaining strap, nuts, bolts and straps. Lower the fuel tank from the vehicle.

To install:
6. Raise and support the fuel tank in position and install the retaining straps. Tighten the front retaining strap bolts to 26 ft. lbs. (35 Nm) and the rear strap nuts to 10 ft. lbs. (13 Nm).

7. Connect the vapor hose and the fuel pump assembly electrical connector.
8. Install the quick-connect fuel pipe fittings to the fuel pump assembly as follows:
   a. Apply a few drops of clean engine oil to the male ends of the fittings to ensure proper reconnection and prevent leaks.
   b. Push the connectors together until the retaining tabs/fingers snap into place.
   c. Gently pull on both ends of each connected fitting to assure the connection is secure.
9. Lower the vehicle, fill the fuel tank and connect the negative battery cable.
10. Turn the ignition switch to the **ON** position for 2 seconds, **OFF** for 5 seconds, then to the **ON** position and check for fuel leaks.

Fuel Filter

REMOVAL & INSTALLATION

5.0L (VIN Y) Engine

1. Disconnect the negative battery cable and properly relieve fuel system pressure.
2. Remove the air cleaner assembly.
3. Using the proper tools disconnect the fuel line connection from the fuel filter nut at the base of the carburetor.
4. Remove the fuel filter nut from the carburetor. Remove the fuel filter, gasket and spring.

To install:
5. Install the fuel inlet filter spring, filter and check valve assembly into the carburetor. The check valve end of the filter faces towards the fuel line. Ribs are provided on the filter element to prevent incorrect installation.
6. Install the fuel filter nut and tighten to 46 ft. lbs. (62 Nm).
7. Install the fuel line connection and tighten to 30 ft. lbs. (41 Nm).
8. Connect the negative battery cable, tighten the fuel filler cap and operate the system to check for leaks.

5.0L (VIN E) and 5.7L Engines

1. Disconnect the negative battery cable and properly relieve the fuel system pressure.
2. Raise and support the vehicle safely.
3. Grasp the fuel filter and one of the fuel line fittings. Twist the quick connect assembly about a ¼ turn in each direction to loosen any dirt within the fitting.
4. Grasp the fuel filter and the other fuel line fitting. Twist the quick connect assembly about a ¼ turn in each direction to loosen any dirt within the fitting.

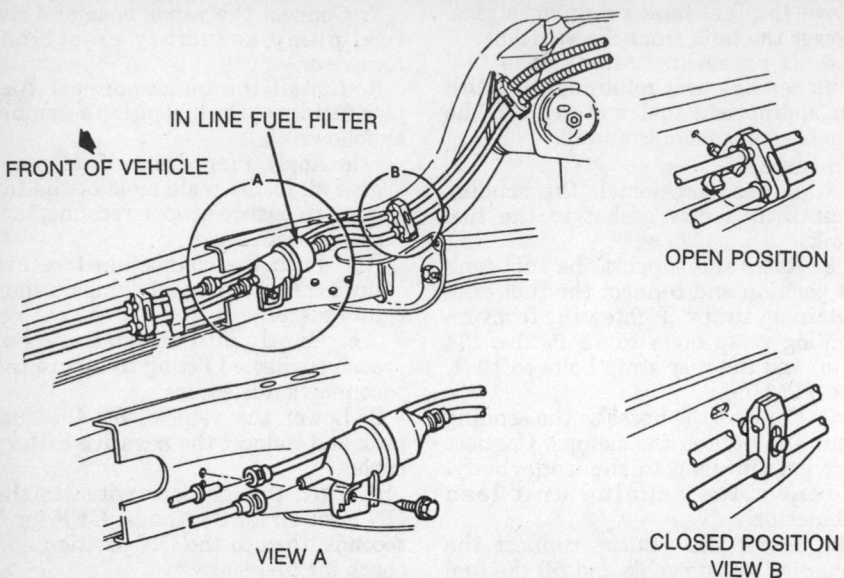

In-line fuel filter location and related lines—5.0L (VIN E) and 5.7L Engines

5. Clean the areas surrounding the fuel line fittings. If compressed air is used, be sure to wear safety glasses to prevent eye injury from flying dirt.

6. Squeeze the plastic tabs of the male connectors and pull the connections apart.

7. Remove the fuel filter bracket retaining bolt. Remove the fuel filter from its mounting.

To install:

8. Prior to installation, apply a few drops of clean engine oil to both tube ends of the filter.

NOTE: The application of clean engine oil will ensure proper reconnection and prevent a possible fuel leak. During normal operation the O-ring that is located in the connector will swell and may prevent proper reconnection if not lubricated. If the new filter is nicked, scratched or damaged during installation it must be replaced.

9. Remove the protective caps from the new filter and install the new plastic connector retainers on the filter inlet and outlet pipes, in the same manner as the old filter.

10. Install the quick connect fittings onto the filter, after applying oil, by pushing the connectors together causing the retaining tabs/fingers to snap into place.

11. Gently tug on both ends of each connection to ensure that the connection is secure.

12. Install the fuel filter into the bracket on the frame and install the attaching bolt. Tighten the bolt to 88 inch lbs. (10 Nm).

13. Connect the negative battery cable and tighten the fuel filler cap.

14. Turn the ignition switch to the **ON** position for 2 seconds, **OFF** for 5 seconds, then to the **ON** position and check for fuel leaks.

Mechanical Fuel Pump

The mechanical fuel pump was used on the 5.0L (VIN Y) carbureted engine until the engine was replaced by the 5.0L (VIN E) TBI engine in 1991.

PRESSURE TESTING

1. Disconnect the negative battery cable and properly relieve the fuel pump pressure.

2. Remove the air cleaner assembly.

3. Using the proper tools disconnect the fuel line from the fuel filter at the base of the carburetor.

4. Install a rubber hose about 8–10 inch long over the fuel line and connect a low-reading fuel pressure gauge.

5. Position the pressure gauge upward about 16 inch above the fuel pump. If equipped with a fuel return line, pinch it.

6. Start the engine and run at slow idle using the fuel in the carburetor.

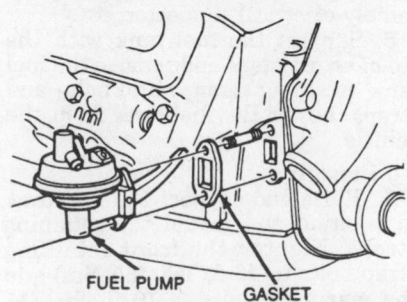

Fuel pump location—5.0L (VIN Y) Engine

7. If the fuel pump is performing properly the pressure should be 5.5–6.5 psi. If not within specification, replace the fuel pump.

REMOVAL & INSTALLATION

1. Disconnect the negative battery cable and properly relieve the fuel pump pressure.

2. Remove the air conditioning compressor drive belt.

3. If equipped with an air pump, loosen the air pump pulley bolts and remove the air pump hoses and electrical leads to the air pump. Remove the air pump pulley and the air pump from the engine.

4. Remove the compressor front bracket. Remove the fuel inlet hose from the fuel pump. Disconnect the vapor return hose, if equipped.

5. Remove the fuel outlet pipe. Remove the 2 bolts securing the fuel pump to the engine. Remove the fuel pump from the engine. Discard the gasket.

To install:

6. Install the fuel pump with a new gasket. Install the 2 securing bolts turning the alternately and evenly.

7. Connect the fuel outlet pipe by tightening the fitting securely while holding the fuel pump nut with a wrench.

8. Connect the fuel inlet pipe and, if equipped, the vapor return hose.

9. Install the air conditioning compressor with front bracket. Install and tighten the compressor drive belt.

10. If equipped with AIR, install the AIR pump. Connect the AIR hoses and the electrical leads. Install the pump pulley. Install and tighten the pump pulley drive belt.

11. Connect the negative battery cable, tighten the fuel filler cap, start the engine and check for leaks.

Electric Fuel Pump

PRESSURE TESTING

When the ignition switch is turned **ON**, the ECM will turn the in-tank fuel pump **ON**. It will remain on as long as the engine is cranking or running and the ECM is receiving ignition reference pulses. If there are no reference pulses, the ECM will shut the fuel pump **OFF** within 2 seconds after the key is turned **ON**. The pump will deliver fuel to the TBI unit at a pressure controlled by the internal regulator to approximately 9–13 psi. Excess fuel is then returned to the fuel tank.

While the engine is stopped, the fuel pump can be activated by applying battery voltage to the fuel pump test terminal located near the passenger side cowl of the engine compartment.

NOTE: The fuel pressure should be recorded while the fuel pump is operating. Fuel pump pressure will drop immediately after the fuel pump stops running due to a controlled bleed within the fuel system. The fuel pump test location is on the right side of the engine compartment.

1. Turn the ignition **OFF** and relieve fuel system pressure by removing fuel filler cap.

2. Locate the engine compartment fuel feed quick-connect fitting. Uncouple the fuel supply flexible hose as follows:

a. Grasp both ends of the fitting and twist female end ¼ turn in each direction to loosen any dirt in fitting.

b. Wearing proper safety glasses, use compressed air to blow dirt out of the quick-connect fitting.

3. Separate the male and female leads of the connector by inserting tool into female end of the connector to release the male end.

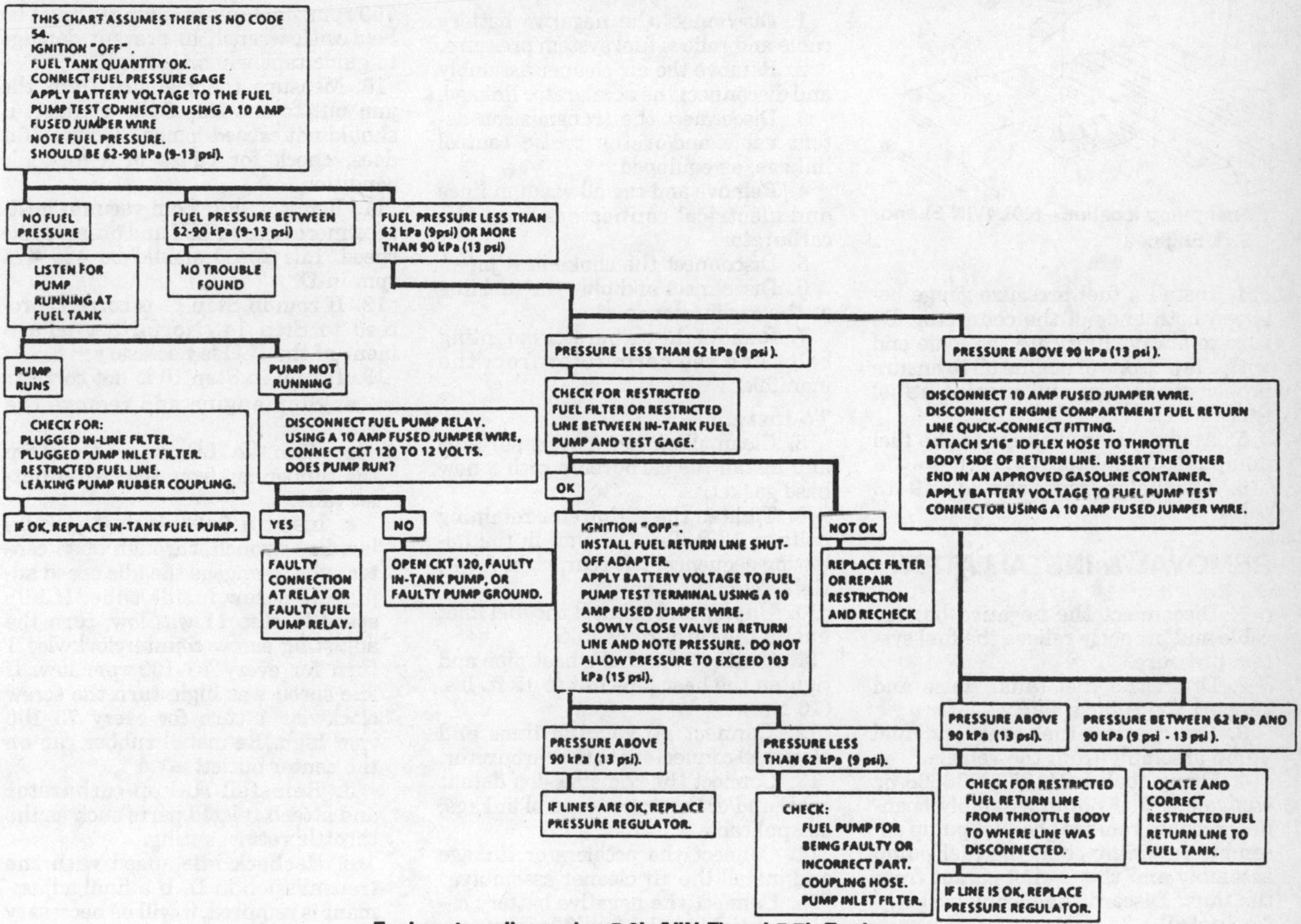

THIS CHART ASSUMES THERE IS NO CODE 54.
IGNITION "OFF".
FUEL TANK QUANTITY OK.
CONNECT FUEL PRESSURE GAGE
APPLY BATTERY VOLTAGE TO THE FUEL PUMP TEST CONNECTOR USING A 10 AMP FUSED JUMPER WIRE
NOTE FUEL PRESSURE.
SHOULD BE 62-90 kPa (9-13 psi).

NO FUEL PRESSURE

FUEL PRESSURE BETWEEN 62-90 kPa (9-13 psi)

FUEL PRESSURE LESS THAN 62 kPa (9psi) OR MORE THAN 90 kPa (13 psi)

LISTEN FOR PUMP RUNNING AT FUEL TANK

NO TROUBLE FOUND

PUMP RUNS

PUMP NOT RUNNING

CHECK FOR:
PLUGGED IN-LINE FILTER.
PLUGGED PUMP INLET FILTER.
RESTRICTED FUEL LINE.
LEAKING PUMP RUBBER COUPLING.

DISCONNECT FUEL PUMP RELAY.
USING A 10 AMP FUSED JUMPER WIRE, CONNECT CKT 120 TO 12 VOLTS.
DOES PUMP RUN?

IF OK, REPLACE IN-TANK FUEL PUMP.

YES

NO

FAULTY CONNECTION AT RELAY OR FAULTY FUEL PUMP RELAY.

OPEN CKT 120, FAULTY IN-TANK PUMP, OR FAULTY PUMP GROUND.

PRESSURE LESS THAN 62 kPa (9 psi).

CHECK FOR RESTRICTED FUEL FILTER OR RESTRICTED LINE BETWEEN IN-TANK FUEL PUMP AND TEST GAGE.

OK

IGNITION "OFF".
INSTALL FUEL RETURN LINE SHUT-OFF ADAPTER.
APPLY BATTERY VOLTAGE TO FUEL PUMP TEST TERMINAL USING A 10 AMP FUSED JUMPER WIRE.
SLOWLY CLOSE VALVE IN RETURN LINE AND NOTE PRESSURE. DO NOT ALLOW PRESSURE TO EXCEED 103 kPa (15 psi).

NOT OK

REPLACE FILTER OR REPAIR RESTRICTION AND RECHECK

PRESSURE ABOVE 90 kPa (13 psi).

IF LINES ARE OK, REPLACE PRESSURE REGULATOR.

PRESSURE LESS THAN 62 kPa (9 psi).

CHECK:
FUEL PUMP FOR BEING FAULTY OR INCORRECT PART.
COUPLING HOSE.
PUMP INLET FILTER.

PRESSURE ABOVE 90 kPa (13 psi).

DISCONNECT 10 AMP FUSED JUMPER WIRE.
DISCONNECT ENGINE COMPARTMENT FUEL RETURN LINE QUICK-CONNECT FITTING.
ATTACH 5/16" ID FLEX HOSE TO THROTTLE BODY SIDE OF RETURN LINE. INSERT THE OTHER END IN AN APPROVED GASOLINE CONTAINER.
APPLY BATTERY VOLTAGE TO FUEL PUMP TEST CONNECTOR USING A 10 AMP FUSED JUMPER WIRE.

PRESSURE ABOVE 90 kPa (13 psi).

PRESSURE BETWEEN 62 kPa AND 90 kPa (9 psi - 13 psi).

CHECK FOR RESTRICTED FUEL RETURN LINE FROM THROTTLE BODY TO WHERE LINE WAS DISCONNECTED.

LOCATE AND CORRECT RESTRICTED FUEL RETURN LINE TO FUEL TANK.

IF LINE IS OK, REPLACE PRESSURE REGULATOR.

Fuel system diagnosis—5.0L (VIN E) and 5.7L Engines

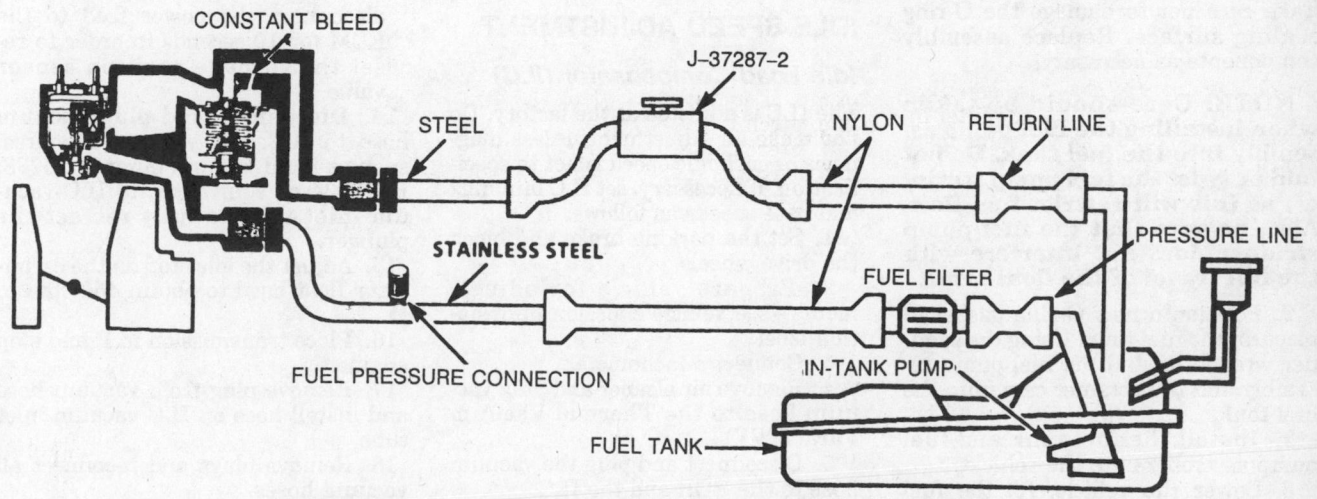

CONSTANT BLEED

J-37287-2

STEEL

NYLON

RETURN LINE

STAINLESS STEEL

FUEL PRESSURE CONNECTION

FUEL FILTER

PRESSURE LINE

IN-TANK PUMP

FUEL TANK

Fuel line pressure connector location—5.0L (VIN E) and 5.7L Engines

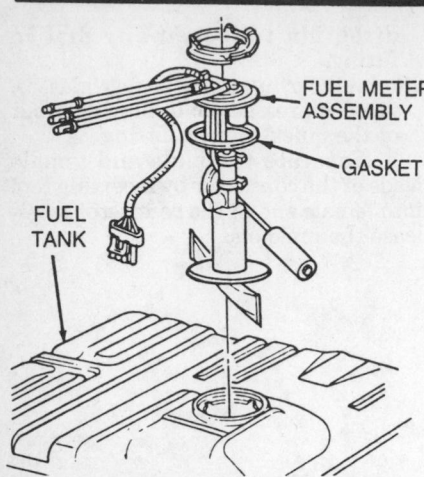

Fuel pump location—5.0L (VIN E) and 5.7L Engines

4. Install a fuel pressure gauge between both ends of the connector. Be sure to always lubricate the male end with a few drops of engine oil to ensure proper connection and prevent a fuel leak.

5. Apply battery voltage to the fuel pump test connector.

6. The fuel pressure should be 9–13 psi.

REMOVAL & INSTALLATION

1. Disconnect the negative battery cable and properly relieve the fuel system pressure.

2. Drain the fuel tank. Raise and support the vehicle safely.

3. Remove the fuel tank and fuel pump assembly from the vehicle.

4. Using tool J–24187, J–36608 or equivalent fuel pump assembly spanner wrench, remove the fuel pump assembly retaining cam, the fuel pump assembly and the O-ring gasket from the tank. Discard the O-ring gasket.

To install:

5. Clean and inspect the assembly. Take care not to damage the O-ring sealing surface. Replace assembly components as necessary.

NOTE: Care should be taken when installing the fuel pump assembly into the fuel tank. Do not fold or twist the fuel pump strainer, as this will restrict fuel flow. Also, be sure that the fuel pump strainer does not interfere with the full travel of the float arm.

6. Position a new O-ring gasket in place on the fuel tank. Using the spanner wrench, install the fuel pump assembly and the retainer cam onto the fuel tank.

7. Install the fuel tank and fuel pump assembly onto the vehicle.

8. Lower the vehicle, fill the fuel tank and connect the negative battery cable.

9. Turn the ignition switch to the **ON** position for 2 seconds, **OFF** for 5 seconds, then to the **ON** position and check for fuel leaks.

Carburetor

REMOVAL & INSTALLATION

1. Disconnect the negative battery cable and relieve fuel system pressure.

2. Remove the air cleaner assembly and disconnect the accelerator linkage.

3. Disconnect the transmission detent cable and/or the cruise control linkage, as equipped.

4. Remove and tag all vacuum lines and electrical connectors from the carburetor.

5. Disconnect the choke heat pipe.

6. Disconnect and plug the fuel line at the carburetor inlet.

7. Remove the carburetor mounting bolts and the carburetor from the manifold.

To install:

8. Clean all gasket mating surfaces and install the carburetor with a new base gasket.

9. Tighten the carburetor retaining bolts to 12 ft. lbs. (16 Nm) in the following sequence: left rear, right front, right rear, left front.

10. Unplug and connect the fuel inlet line to the carburetor inlet.

11. Connect the choke heat pipe and tighten the heat pipe nut to 12 ft. lbs. (16 Nm).

12. Connect all vacuum lines and electrical connectors to the carburetor.

13. Connect the transmission detent cable and/or the cruise control linkage, as applicable.

14. Connect the accelerator linkage and install the air cleaner assembly.

15. Connect the negative battery cable and tighten the fuel filler cap.

IDLE SPEED ADJUSTMENT

Idle Load Compensator (ILC)

The ILC is adjusted at the factory. Do not make an adjustment unless diagnosis or curb idle speed is not to specification. If necessary, set ILC min/max and base speeds as follows:

1. Set the parking brake and block the drive wheels.

2. Prepare vehicle for adjustments—see vehicle emission information label.

3. Connect a tachometer.

4. Remove air cleaner and plug vacuum hose to the Thermal Vacuum Valve (TVV).

5. Disconnect and plug the vacuum hose to the EGR and the ILC.

6. Disconnect and plug the vacuum hose to the canister purge port.

7. Back out idle stop screw on carburetor 3 turns.

8. Turn the air conditioning to the **OFF** position.

9. With engine running, engine warm, choke off, transmission in **D** and ILC plunger fully extended (no vacuum applied). Using tool J–29607, BT–8022 or equivalent ILC adjusting wrench, adjust plunger to obtain 650–750 rpm. Jam nut on plunger must be held with wrench to prevent damage to guide tabs when tightening.

10. Measure the distance from the jam nut to the tip of the plunger, it should not exceed 1 inch (25mm). If it does, check for cause of a low idle condition.

11. Remove plug from vacuum hose, reconnect hose to ILC and observe idle speed. Idle speed should be 425–475 rpm in **D**.

12. If rpm in Step 11 is correct, proceed to Step 14. No further adjustment of the ILC is necessary.

13. If rpm in Step 10 is not correct:

a. Stop engine and remove the ILC.

b. With the ILC removed, remove the rubber cap from the center outlet tube.

c. Insert a 0.090 inch ($^3/_{32}$ inch) hex key wrench, through open center tube to engage the idle speed adjusting screw inside tube. If idle speed in step 11 was low, turn the adjusting screw counterclockwise 1 turn for every 75–100 rpm low. If idle speed was high, turn the screw clockwise 1 turn for every 75–100 rpm high. Re-install rubber cap on the center outlet.

d. Reinstall ILC on carburetor and attach related parts such as the throttle return spring.

e. Recheck idle speed with the transmission in **D**. If a final adjustment is required, it will be necessary to repeat Steps 13a through 13e.

f. With the ignition switch **OFF**, disconnect the power feed to the ECM for 10 seconds in order to reset the throttle position sensor value.

14. Disconnect and plug vacuum hose to ILC. Apply vacuum source, such as hand vacuum pump J–23738, BT–8334 or equivalent, to ILC vacuum inlet tube to fully retract the plunger.

15. Adjust the idle stop on the carburetor float bowl to obtain 450 rpm in **D**.

16. Place transmission in **P** and stop engine.

17. Remove plug from vacuum hose and install hose on ILC vacuum inlet tube.

18. Remove plugs and reconnect all vacuum hoses.

19. Install air cleaner and gasket.

20. Remove block from drive wheels.

Fast Idle Speed

If necessary, fast idle can be adjusted but only after the ILC min/max and base idle speeds have been set.

1. Set parking brake and block the drive wheels.
2. Prepare vehicle for adjustments—see vehicle emission control information label.
3. Connect a tachometer.
4. Remove air cleaner and plug vacuum hose to the Thermal Vacuum Valve (TVV).
5. Check, and if necessary, adjust the ILC min/max and base idle speeds.
6. Disconnect and plug the vacuum hose to EGR valve.
7. Place the fast idle cam follower on **LOW** step of fast idle cam.
8. With the engine warm and running, the transmission in **D** and the air conditioning **OFF** adjust fast idle adjusting screw to obtain a fast idle speed of 550 rpm.
9. Release fast idle cam, place transmission in **P** and stop engine.
10. Connect vacuum hose to EGR, install air cleaner and gasket.
11. Remove block from the drive wheels.

IDLE MIXTURE ADJUSTMENT

In order to properly adjust idle mixture, timing and idle speeds must first be checked and set to the appropriate specifications. The carburetor must be removed from engine to gain access to the idle mixture needle plugs.

1. Remove the carburetor from the engine.
2. Drain fuel from the carburetor into an appropriate container.
3. Remove the factory installed plugs from the mixture screws.
4. Using tool J–29030–B, BT–7610–B or equivalent idle mixture needle socket, turn both mixture needles clockwise until lightly seated.
5. Back each mixture needle counterclockwise 3 turns.
6. Install carburetor back on engine with new flange gasket but do not connect the air cleaner or vacuum hoses at this time.
7. Run engine until it reaches normal operating temperature and connect a dwell meter to the green mixture control solenoid dwell connector.
8. With the air conditioning **OFF**, set parking brake, block rear wheels and put gear selector in **D**.
9. Adjust both mixture needles equally, in ⅛ turn increments, until dwell reading varies within the 25–35 degree range, as close to 30 degrees as possible. Allow sufficient time for the readings to stabilize between adjustments.
10. If reading is too high, turn needles clockwise. If reading is too low, turn needles counterclockwise.
11. Check and if necessary, adjust the ILC min/max and base speeds. Then recheck that the idle dwell is in the 25–35 degree range, and adjust as necessary.
12. Install new plugs or cover mixture needle adjustment holes with RTV rubber, silicone sealant, or equivalent.
13. Reconnect all vacuum lines and install the air cleaner and gasket.
14. Disconnect dwell or service tools and remove block from the drive wheels.

Fuel Injection

IDLE SPEED ADJUSTMENT

The idle speed and mixture are electronically controlled by the Electronic Control Module (ECM). All adjustments are preset at the factory and do not need periodic attention. Some replacement throttle body units are equipped with a idle stop screw to allow adjustment of the minimum idle speed. The only time the idle speed should need adjustment is when the throttle body assembly has been replaced.

1. Block the drive wheels and apply the parking brake. Remove the air cleaner assembly and/or air duct.
2. Connect a scan tool to the ALDL connector and select the field service mode. Turn the ignition **ON** and leave the engine **OFF**. Wait at least 45 seconds, this will allow the Idle Air Control (IAC) pintle to seat in the throttle body.
3. With the ignition switch in the **ON** position, the engine **OFF** and the scan tool in field service mode, disconnect the IAC valve electrical connector and the distributor set-timing connector.
4. Connect a tachometer to the engine to monitor the engine speed.
5. Place the transmission in the **P** or **N** position and start the engine.
6. Run the engine until it reaches normal operating temperature or closed loop operation as indicated by the scan tool. It may be necessary to hold the throttle open slightly in order to maintain idle.
7. The idle speed should be 450–500 rpm, be sure the throttle and, if applicable, the cruise control cables do not hold the throttle open. If not as specified, remove the idle speed stop screw plug and adjust as necessary.
8. Turn the ignition **OFF** and reconnect the IAC valve electrical connector and the distributor set-timing connector.
9. Reset the Idle Air Control (IAC) valve pintle position.
10. Connect the air cleaner assembly, check and clear all ECM trouble codes.

IAC Valve Pintle Adjustment

Idle speed is controlled by the ECM through voltage pulses sent to the Idle Air Control (IAC) motor windings. Based on the number of voltage pulses received, the motor will move the IAC pintle in or out allowing more or less air through the throttle body.

NOTE: If installing a new IAC valve measure and adjust the valve accordingly. If reinstalling a used IAC valve, do not push or pull on the pintle to adjust pintle length or damage to the IAC worm gear might occur. The valve is preset at the factory and will self adjust when the following procedure is performed.

1. On new IAC valve only, measure the distance between the tip of the pintle and the valve mounting surface. If greater than 1.10 inch (28mm), use light finger pressure to slowly retract the pintle. The force required to retract a new IAC valve will not damage the valve.
2. Install the IAC valve and gasket.
3. Connect the IAC valve wire connector.
4. Reset the IAC valve pintle position as follows:
   a. Depress the accelerator pedal slightly.
   b. Start the engine and run for 5 seconds.
   c. Turn the ignition **OFF** for 10 seconds.
   d. Restart the vehicle and check for proper idle operation.

IDLE MIXTURE ADJUSTMENT

The idle mixture is controlled by the ECM, therefore no service adjustments are necessary. The ECM will change the air/fuel ratio by controlling the fuel injectors, based on oxygen sensor and various other outputs. A 14.7:1 ratio is required for efficient catalytic converter operation.

Fuel Injector

REMOVAL & INSTALLATION

1. Disconnect the negative battery

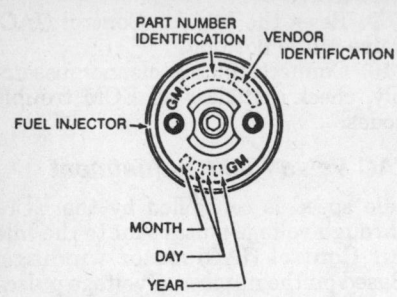

Fuel Injector Identification data

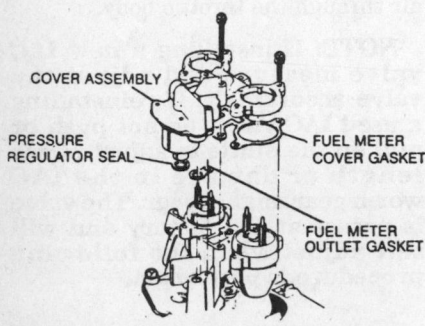

Fuel meter cover assembly and related components—5.0L (VIN E) and 5.7L Engines

cable and properly relieve the fuel system pressure.

2. Remove the air cleaner assembly and extension. Disconnect the electrical connectors to the fuel injectors.

3. Remove the fuel meter cover retaining screws. Remove the fuel meter cover assembly.

4. Remove the fuel meter outlet passage gasket and the pressure regulator dust seal.

NOTE: If the fuel meter cover gasket is stuck to the fuel meter body, leave it in place. If it is stuck to the fuel meter cover, remove it and place it on the fuel meter body.

5. With the fuel meter cover gasket in place on the fuel meter body, use a proper pry tool and fulcrum to carefully pry out the fuel injector.

6. Remove and discard the small O-ring from the nozzle end of the fuel injector.

7. Remove and discard the fuel meter cover gasket. Remove and discard the large O-ring and fuel injector washer from the top of the injector cavity.

To install:

8. Be sure to replace fuel injectors with an identical part. Injectors from other models may fit, but are calibrated for different flow rates.

NOTE: When installing the injectors, install the fuel injector washer and large O-ring before the injector, to be sure the O-ring

is properly seated. Reversing these procedures could result in a fuel leak and possible engine fire.

9. Lubricate the new upper (large) O-ring with engine oil and install. Be sure the ring is properly seated and flush with the top of the fuel meter body.

10. Lubricate the new lower (small) O-ring with engine oil and install on the end of the injector by pushing the O-ring far enough to contact the filter.

11. Install the fuel injector by aligning the raised lug on the injector base with the notch in the fuel meter body cavity. Push down on the injector until it is fully seated. The electrical terminals of the injector should be parallel with the throttle shaft.

12. Install the new pressure regulator dust seal, fuel meter outlet gasket and cover gasket.

13. Install the fuel meter cover assembly. Coat the fuel meter cover attaching screws with appropriate thread-locking compound. Install and tighten the screws to 27 inch lbs. (3.0 Nm).

14. Connect the electrical connectors to the fuel injectors and install the air cleaner assembly.

15. Connect the negative battery cable and tighten the fuel filler cap.

DRIVE AXLE

Driveshaft and U-Joints

REMOVAL & INSTALLATION

1. Raise and support the vehicle safely. Position a drain pan under the transmission.

2. Mmark the relationship of the driveshaft to the axle pinion flange so the driveshaft can be reinstalled in its original position. Remove the rear driveshaft flange capscrews.

NOTE: Never let the full weight of the driveshaft be supported only by the front universal joint.

3. Push the driveshaft forward to clear the pinion flange, then pull the driveshaft rearward to disengage the slip yoke from the transmission.

4. Plug the transmission to prevent fluid contamination or loss. If the bearing cups are loose, tape them together to prevent dropping and losing the bearing rollers.

5. Support the driveshaft horizontally in line with the base plate of a press but do not clamp the tube.

6. Place the U-joint so the lower ear of the shaft yoke is supported on a $1\frac{1}{8}$ inch socket.

7. Press the lower bearing cap out of the yoke ear by placing tool J–9522–3 or equivalent cross press, on the open horizontal bearing caps and pressing the lower bearing cap out of the yoke ear.

8. This will shear the plastic retaining ring on the lower bearing cup. If the bearing cap is not completely removed, lift tool J–9522–3 and insert tool J–9522–5 or equivalent spacer, between the bearing cap and seal and continue pressing the U-joint out of the yoke.

9. Repeat the procedure for opposite bearing cup.

10. Remove the cross from the yoke and remove the remains of the sheared plastic retainer from the ears of the yoke.

11. If the front U-joint is also being replaced, remove in the same manner.

To install:

12. When replacing U-joints always replace the entire assembly consisting of 1 pregreased spider, 4 bearing cup assemblies with seals, needle rollers, washers, grease and 4 snaprings.

13. Install 1 bearing cap part way into 1 side of the yoke. Turn this yoke ear to the bottom.

14. Using tool J–9522–3 or equivalent cross press, seat the trunnion into the bearing cup. Install the opposite bearing cap partially and ensure that both trunnions are straight and true in the bearing cups.

15. Press against the opposite bearing cups, while working the cross back and forth to ensure free movement of the trunnions in the bearings. If the trunnion is binding, one or more of the needle bearings have tipped under the end of the trunion.

16. Stop pressing when 1 bearing cap clears the retainer groove inside the yoke and install a snapring by pressing it into place. Continue to press until the opposite snapring may be pressed into place. If necessary, strike the yoke with a hammer to aid in seating the snaprings, this will spring the yoke slightly.

17. Repeat the procedure for the other half of the U-joint.

18. Remove any nicks, burrs, dirt or rust from the pinion yoke. Thoroughly clean the slip yoke with kerosene and dry with compressed air.

19. Pack slip yoke lubricant between the lips of the transmission extension housing seal. Lubricate the yoke with slip yoke lubricant and install onto the transmission output shaft.

20. Install the rear of the shaft, aligning the marks made earlier and install the capscrews. Tighten the capscrews to 16 ft. lbs. (21 Nm).

21. Remove the drainpan and lower the vehicle.

Rear Axle Shaft, Bearing and Seal

REMOVAL & INSTALLATION

1. Raise and support the vehicle safely. Remove the wheel and tire assembly. Remove the brake drum.
2. Clean any dirt from the differential cover. Loosen the cover attaching bolts, and drain the lubricant by removing the cover.
3. Remove the pinion shaft lockbolt and remove the pinion shaft.
4. Push in on the flanged end of the axle shaft and remove the C-lock from the splined end of the axle shaft.
5. Remove the axle shaft from the housing, being cautious not to damage the oil seal.
6. Use a prybar behind the steel case of the seal to remove the oil seal from the bore. Be careful not to damage the housing.
7. Insert an axle shaft bearing puller into position behind the bearing so that the tangs on the tool engage the bearing outer race. Remove the bearing using a slide hammer.

To install:

8. Lubricate the new bearing with gear lubricant. Use bearing installer tool J–23765 or equivalent, and install the bearing so the tool bottoms out against the shoulder in the housing.
9. Lubricate the lips of the seal with gear lubricant. Position the new seal on seal installer tool J–23771 or equivalent, and position the seal into the housing bore. Tap the seal into place so it is flush with the axle tube.
10. Carefully slide the axle shaft into the housing taking care that the splines do not damage the oil seal. Continue to slide the axle into position and engage the splines of the differential side gear.
11. Install the axle shaft C-lock on the splined end of the axle shaft in the differential. Push the shaft outward so the shaft lock seats in the counterbore of the differential side gear.
12. Install the pinion shaft through the differential case, thrust washers and pinions. Align the lockbolt hole and install the lock screw, tightening it to 20 ft. lbs. (27 Nm).
13. Clean the differential housing and cover mating surfaces and install the cover with a new gasket. Tighten the retaining bolts in a crosswise pattern to 22 ft. lbs. (30 Nm).
14. Fill the differential with lubricant flush with, or within ¼ inch (6 mm) of the filler hole.

15. Install the brake drum and install the tire and wheel assembly.
16. Lower the vehicle.

Pinion Seal

REMOVAL & INSTALLATION

1. Raise and support the vehicle safely.
2. Mark and remove the driveshaft from the pinion yoke. Either remove the driveshaft completely from the vehicle or suspend it from the exhaust pipe with a length of mechanic's wire. If the bearings are not retained by a strap, use a piece of tape to hold them on their journals.
3. Mark the position of the pinion yoke, pinion shaft and nut so the proper pinion bearing preload can be maintained.
4. Position a drain pan under the assembly to catch any fluid that may drain from the rear assembly. Remove the pinion yoke nut and washer. Remove the pinion yoke.
5. Remove the oil seal by driving it out of the carrier using a blunt chisel. Be careful not to damage the carrier.

To install:

6. Be sure to inspect the seal surface of the yoke for damage. Check the carrier bore and remove any burrs which might cause leaks around the outer diameter of the seal.
7. Install the new oil seal with a suitable installation tool.
8. Coat the outside diameter of the yoke and the sealing lip of the new seal with seal lubricant, part number 1050169 or equivalent.
9. Install the yoke, washer and nut. Tighten the yoke nut to the position marked previously. While holding the pinion yoke tighten the nut an additional ¹⁄₁₆ inch beyond the alignment marks.
10. Align the marks made earlier and install the driveshaft. Check and add gear lubricant to the carrier, if necessary.
11. Lower the vehicle.

Differential Carrier

REMOVAL & INSTALLATION

1. Raise and safely support the vehicle.
2. Remove the drive axles.
3. Mark the differential bearing caps **L** and **R** to make sure they will be reassembled in their original location.
4. Remove the bearing cap bolts and caps.
5. Using a suitable tool, remove the differential carrier. Be careful not to damage the gasket sealing surface when removing the unit. Place the

right and left bearing outer races of the side bearing assemblies and shims in sets with the marked differential bearings caps so they can be reinstalled in their original positions.

To install:

6. Inspect the differential carrier housing for foreign material. Check the ring and pinion for chipped teeth, excessive wear and scoring. Check the carrier bearings visually and by feel. Clean the differential housing and replace components, as necessary.
7. Lubricate all parts with rear axle lubricant and install the differential carrier. Check the carrier bearing preload and ring and pinion backlash and adjust, as necessary. Tighten the differential bearing cap bolts to 55 ft. lbs. (75 Nm).
8. Install the axles.
9. Install the gasket to the carrier cover. Install the carrier cover and tighten the carrier cover bolts in a crosswise pattern to 22 ft. lbs. (30 Nm).
10. Add rear axle lubricant to a level flush with or within ¼ inch (6 mm) of the filler hole and install the filler plug.
11. Lower the vehicle.

Axle Housing

REMOVAL & INSTALLATION

1. Raise and support the vehicle safely, Place an adjustable support under the rear axle.
2. Remove the tire and wheel assemblies and remove the brake drums.
3. Disconnect the shock absorbers from axle. Mark the driveshaft, disconnect it from the rear axle pinion flange and support the it out of the way.
4. Remove the brake line junction block bolt at the axle housing. Disconnect and plug the brake lines at the junction block. If equipped with ABS, disconnect all required electrical connectors.
5. Disconnect the upper control arms from axle housing. Lower the rear axle assembly slightly and remove the springs.
6. If necessary, remove the rear axle cover and the axle shafts, the brake lines from the axle housing clips, and the backing plates.
7. Disconnect the lower control arms from the axle housing.
8. Continue lowering the rear axle assembly and remove it from the vehicle.

To install:

9. Raise the rear axle housing sufficiently and connect the upper and lower control arms. Hand tighten the bolts.

10. If applicable, install the brake backing plates, position the brake lines under the axle housing clips, install the axle shafts and install the rear axle cover.

11. Install the springs.

12. Unplug and connect the brake lines to the junction block. Install the junction block retaining bolt.

13. Align the marks and install the driveshaft. Install the shock absorbers.

14. With the vehicle's weight resting on the axle, tighten the upper and lower control arm bolts to specification.

15. Install the brake drums, tires and wheels. Remove the support from the axle housing and lower the vehicle.

16. Bleed the hydraulic brake system.

AUTOMATIC TRANSMISSION

For further information on transmission/transaxles, please refer to "Chilton's Guide to Transmission Repair".

Transmission Assembly

REMOVAL & INSTALLATION

1. Disconnect the negative battery cable and position the selector lever in the **N** detent position.

2. Remove the air cleaner assembly. Disconnect the accelerator cable and detent cable, as required.

3. Remove the transmission dipstick retaining bolt and the dipstick tube.

4. Raise and support the vehicle safely.

5. Remove the floor pan reinforcement. Matchmark the driveshaft for reinstallation in its original position and remove the driveshaft.

6. Disconnect the shift linkage, speedometer cable or wire and all electrical connections or clips at the transmission.

7. Remove the flywheel cover retaining bolts and cover. Mark the flexplate and converter so they can be realigned in their original location. Remove the flexplate-to-converter bolts.

8. If necessary, remove the catalytic converter support bracket. Position a transmission jack under the transmission and remove the transmission mount to support bolt(s).

9. Slide the support rearward and remove the crossmember cattaching

bolts and remove the crossmember. Lower the transmission slightly on the support to gain access to the oil cooler pipes and the TV cable attachments.

10. Disconnect the transmission oil cooler pipes and the required cables. Plug all openings to prevent fluid contamination or loss.

11. Support the engine with a suitable tool and remove the transmission-to-engine bolts.

12. Install a torque converter holding tool and remove the transmission assembly from the vehicle.

To install:

13. Properly flush the transmission oil cooler and lines.

14. Raise the transmission into place and remove the torque converter holding tool.

15. Install the transmission to engine bolts and tighten to 35 ft. lbs. (47 Nm).

16. Install the transmission oil cooler pipes and required cables to the transmission.

17. Install the transmission support to the frame and tighten the bolts to 41 ft. lbs. (55 Nm). Install the support-to-mount bolt(s) and tighten to 25 ft. lbs. (34 Nm) for 5.0L (VIN Y) engines or to 35 ft. lbs. (47 Nm) for 5.0L (VIN E) and 5.7L engines. Remove the engine and transmission supports.

18. Align the marks made earlier, making sure the weld nuts on the converter are flush with the flywheel and install the converter-to-flywheel bolts. Finger-tighten 3 bolts then tighten bolts to 46 ft. lbs. (63 Nm) for the 5.0L (VIN Y) engine or to 35 ft. lbs. (47 Nm) for the 5.0L (VIN E) and 5.7L engines. When finished, retighten the first bolt tightened.

19. Install the floor pan reinforcement and the catalytic converter support bracket, as required.

20. Install the flywheel cover and bolts. Tighten the bolts to 89 inch lbs. (10 Nm). Connect the shift linkage, the speedometer cable or wire and the electrical leads and retaining clips.

21. Align the marks made earlier and install the driveshaft.

22. Lower the vehicle and install the fluid filler tube with a new seal. Install the filler tube retaining bolt and the fluid indicator.

23. Connect the TV and detent cables, as required.

24. Install the air cleaner assembly and connect the negative battery cable.

25. Adjust the shift linkage and the TV cable, as necessary.

26. Check and add transmission fluid, as necessary.

SHIFT LINKAGE ADJUSTMENT

1. With the column lever and the transmission selector lever in the **N** detent, tighten the linkage rod retaining bolt to 17–22 ft. lbs. (24–32 Nm).

2. The linkage is correctly adjusted if at final vehicle inspection with the column lever raised and centered in the **N** detent, the column lever can be lowered and will engage in the column neutral notch.

3. Adjustment is unacceptable if any rotation of the column lever is required to engage the column neutral notch.

THROTTLE VALVE CABLE ADJUSTMENT

1. Remove the air cleaner assembly.

2. Depress and hold-down the metal readjustment tab at the engine end of the throttle valve cable.

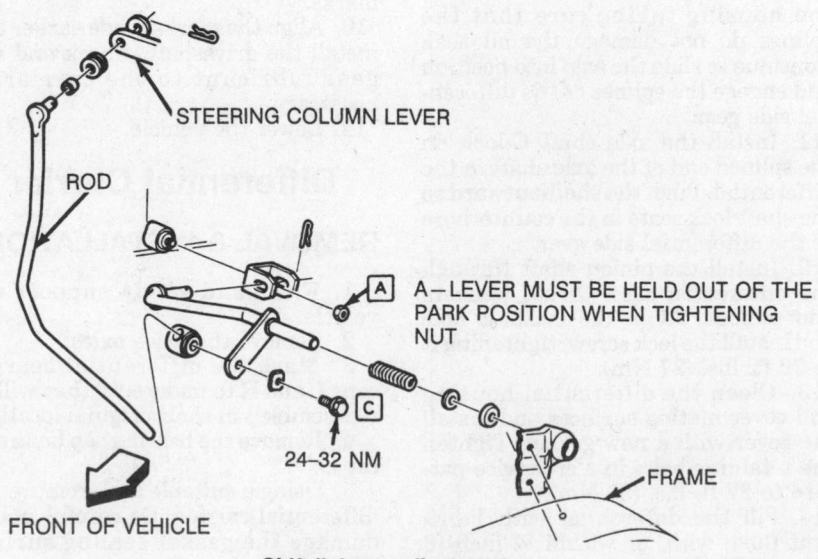

STEERING COLUMN LEVER

ROD

A—LEVER MUST BE HELD OUT OF THE PARK POSITION WHEN TIGHTENING NUT

24–32 NM

FRAME

FRONT OF VEHICLE

Shift linkage adjustment

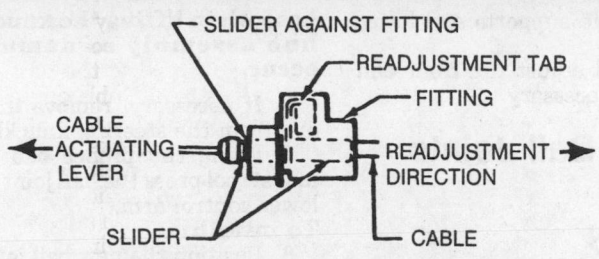

Throttle valve cable adjustment

3. Move the slider until it stops against the fitting. Release the readjustment tab.

4. Rotate the throttle lever to its full travel position.

5. The slider must ratchet toward the lever when the lever is rotated to its full travel position.

6. Check that the cable moves freely. The cable may function properly with a cold engine and not with a warm engine. Start the engine and run until normal operating temperature is reached.

7. Shut the engine **OFF** and check that the cable moves freely with a

FRONT SUSPENSION

Shock Absorbers

REMOVAL & INSTALLATION

1. Remove the top shock absorber retaining nut using a suitable socket.

2. Raise and support the vehicle safely.

NOTE: Throughout this procedure raise or lower the vehicle, as necessary to reach the components. Always support the vehicle safely.

3. Remove the 2 bottom shock absorber bolts attaching the shock absorber to the lower control arm.

4. Lower the shock absorber through the bottom of the control arm and remove the shock from the vehicle.

To install:

5. Install the retainer and grommet onto the shock and fully extend the shock absorber rod. Insert the shock up into the coil spring and guide the stem through the frame.

6. Install the grommet and retainer over the stem on top of the frame and secure with the nut. Tighten the nut to 97 inch lbs. (11 Nm). Using a suitable socket and a box wrench, tighten

the nut to end of the threads, approximately 1–⅛ inch when measured from the top of the nut to the top of the shock absorber mounting stud.

7. Position the lower shock absorber mount to the lower control arm and secure with the 2 bolts. Tighten the bolts to 20 ft. lbs. (27 Nm).

8. Lower the vehicle.

Coil Springs

REMOVAL & INSTALLATION

1. Raise and support the vehicle safely. Be sure the vehicle is supported so the lower control arms hang free.

2. Remove the lower shock absorber retaining bolts and push the shock absorber up through the control arm and into the spring.

3. Secure tool J–23028–01, or equivalent lower control arm compressor to a suitable jack. Position the tool to cradle the lower control arm inner bushings.

4. Remove the stabilizer to lower control arm attachment.

5. Raise the jack to relieve tension on the lower control arm pivot bolts. Install a safety chain around the spring and through the lower control arm as a safety precaution.

6. Remove the lower control arm rear pivot bolt first, then remove the lower control arm front pivot bolt.

7. Lower the control arm assembly from its mounting slowly. When all compression is removed from the spring, remove the spring and the safety chain.

To install:

8. Properly position the spring into the frame and lift the control arm with the tool and jack.

NOTE: The lower end of the coil must cover all or part of one inspection hole in the lower control arm. The second hole must be partly or completely uncovered.

9. Position the lower control arm into the frame and install the pivot bolts and nuts. Tighten the nuts to 92 ft. lbs. (125 Nm). The rear bolt head may be tightened instead of the nut, to 114 ft. lbs. (155 Nm).

10. Install the stabilizer shaft link and tighten the nut to 13 ft. lbs. (17 Nm).

11. Install the lower shock absorber and tighten the bolts to 20 ft. lbs. (27 Nm).

12. Lower the vehicle, check and adjust the alignment, as necessary.

Upper Ball Joints

INSPECTION

1. Raise and support the vehicle safely using jack stands positioned un-

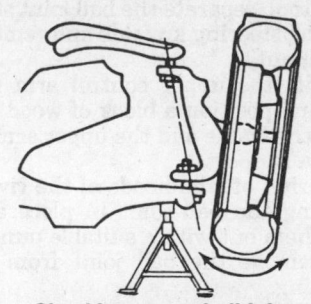

Checking upper ball joints

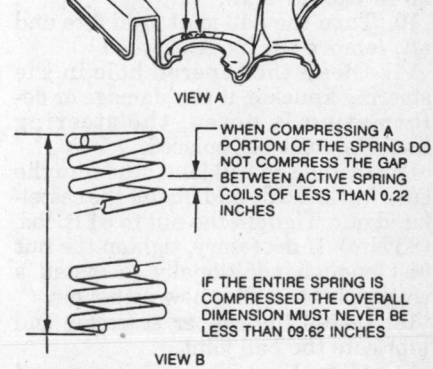

Front coil spring positioning

der the lower control arms as near as possible to each lower ball joint. The vehicle must not rock on the stands and the upper control arm bumpers must not contact the frame.

2. Position a dial indicator gauge against the wheel rim.

3. Grasp the front wheel and push in on the bottom of the tire while pulling out at the top, read and record the gauge.

4. Reverse the push pull procedure, read and record the gauge.

5. Horizontal deflection should not exceed 0.125 inch (3.18 mm). If the horizontal deflection exceeds the specification, or if the ball joint has been disconnected from the knuckle assembly and looseness is detected or the stud can be twisted in the socket, ball joint replacement is necessary.

REMOVAL & INSTALLATION

1. Raise and support the vehicle safely, making sure to support the lower control arm on the side which is being worked upon.

2. Mark and remove the tire and wheel assembly.

3. Remove the caliper and properly support it so the brake hose is not damaged.

4. Remove the cotter pin from the ball joint and loosen the locknut not more than 1 turn, do not remove it.

5. Using the proper ball joint separating tool, separate the ball joint stud from the steering knuckle and remove the locknut.

6. Lift the upper control arm upward and position a block of wood between the frame and the upper arm to act as a support.

7. Grind off the heads of the rivets retaining the ball joint in place and drive them out with a suitable punch.

8. Remove the ball joint from its mounting.
To install:
9. Install the new ball joint using the nut and bolt assemblies provided. Insert the bolts from the bottom with the nuts on top and tighten the nuts to 20 ft. lbs. (27 Nm).

10. Turn the ball joint stud fore and aft, remove the block of wood.

11. Clean the tapered hole in the steering knuckle, if any damage or deformation is noted, the steering knuckle must be replaced.

12. Install the ball joint stud into the steering knuckle and install the castellated nut. Tighten the nut to 61 ft. lbs. (83 Nm). If necessary, tighten the nut just enough additionally to install a cotter pin. Install a new cotter pin.

13. Install the caliper assembly and lubricate the ball joint.

14. Align the marks made earlier and install the tire and wheel assembly.

15. Remove the supports and lower the vehicle.

16. Check and adjust the front end alignment, as necessary.

Lower Ball Joints

INSPECTION

The vehicle must be supported by the wheel so the weight of the vehicle will properly load the ball joints. The lower ball joint is checked for wear by visual inspection. Wear is indicated by protrusion of the ½ inch (12.7mm) diameter nipple into which the grease fitting is threaded. The round nipple projects 0.050 inch (1.27mm) beyond the surface of the ball joint cover on a new ball joint. Normal wear will result in the surface of this nipple retreating slowly inward. The stud of a worn joint will be flush with or below the cover.

Stud tightness in the knuckle can be checked by shaking the wheel. Inspect for movement at the stud end and/or the check nut torque at the knuckle boss. Looseness may indicate a bent stud or damaged hole in the knuckle. Replace all worn or damaged parts.

REMOVAL & INSTALLATION

1. Raise and support the vehicle safely, make sure to support the lower control arm to prevent the spring from forcing it downward.

2. Mark and remove the tire and wheel assembly.

3. Remove the cotter pin from the lower ball joint. Loosen the locknut not more than 1 turn, do not remove the locknut.

4. Using the proper ball joint separator tool, separate the ball joint from the steering knuckle and remove the locknut.

5. Lift the upper control arm with the knuckle and hub assembly attached and position a block of wood between the frame and the upper arm to act as a support.

NOTE: Do not pull on the brake

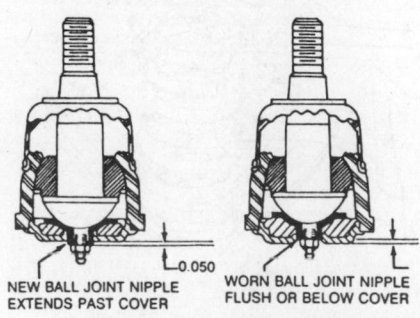

0.050

NEW BALL JOINT NIPPLE EXTENDS PAST COVER

WORN BALL JOINT NIPPLE FLUSH OR BELOW COVER

Checking lower ball joints

hose when lifting the knuckle and hub assembly as damage may occur.

6. If necessary, remove the tie rod end from the steering knuckle.

7. Using the proper ball joint removal tool press the ball joint from the lower control arm.
To install:
8. Position the new ball joint in the lower control arm and install using a suitable ball joint installation tool. Remove the block of wood.

9. Clean the tapered hole in the steering knuckle, if any damage or deformation is noted, the steering knuckle must be replaced.

10. Insert the ball joint stud into the steering knuckle and install the castellated nut. Tighten the nut to 83 ft. lbs. (113 Nm). If necessary, tighten the nut additionally to insert the new cotter pin. The maximum torque allowable is 92 ft. lbs. (125 Nm) or an additional ¹⁄₁₆ of a turn. Do not back off the nut to install the cotter pin.

11. If removed, install the tie rod end to the steering knuckle.

12. Align the marks made earlier and install the tire and wheel assembly.

13. Remove the supports and lower the vehicle.

14. Check and adjust the front end alignment, as necessary.

Upper Control Arms

REMOVAL & INSTALLATION

1. Raise and support the vehicle safely, making sure to support the lower control arm.

2. Mark and remove the tire and wheel assembly.

3. Separate the upper ball joint from the steering knuckle, using the proper tools.

4. Remove the upper control arm shaft to frame bracket nuts.

5. Tape the shims exactly in the same position they were removed and label for reinstallation.

6. Remove the upper control arm assembly from the vehicle.
To install:
7. Position the new control arm attaching bolts loosely in the frame and install the control arm cross shaft on the attaching bolts.

8. Using a free running nut, tighten both nuts until the serrated bolts are reseated. Remove the free running nuts and install the locknuts.

9. Install the shims in their original location and tighten the mounting nuts to 72 ft. lbs. (98 Nm). Tighten the nut on the thinner shim pack first for improved clamping force and torque retention.

10. Clean the tapered hole in the

steering knuckle, if any damage or deformation is noted, the steering knuckle must be replaced.

11. Install the ball joint stud into the steering knuckle and install the castellated nut. Tighten the nut to 61 ft. lbs. (83 Nm). If necessary, tighten the nut just enough additionally to install a cotter pin. Install a new cotter pin.

12. Align the marks made earlier and install the tire and wheel assemblies.

13. Remove the supports and lower the vehicle.

14. Check and adjust the front end alignment, as required.

Lower Control Arms

REMOVAL & INSTALLATION

1. Raise and support the vehicle safely, making sure the lower control arms hang freely.

2. Mark and remove the tire and wheel assembly.

3. Remove the coil spring.

4. Disconnect the lower ball joint from the steering knuckle, using the proper tools.

5. Remove the lower control arm from the vehicle.

To install:

6. Position the lower control arm to the vehicle.

7. Clean the tapered hole in the steering knuckle, if any damage or deformation is noted, the steering knuckle must be replaced.

8. Install the ball joint stud into the steering knuckle and install the castellated nut. Tighten the nut to 61 ft. lbs. (83 Nm). If necessary, tighten the nut just enough additionally to install a cotter pin. Install a new cotter pin.

9. Install the coil spring.

10. Align the marks made earlier and install the tire and wheel assembly.

11. Lower the vehicle.

12. Check and adjust the front end alignment, as necessary.

Sway Bar

REMOVAL & INSTALLATION

1. Raise and support the vehicle safely.

2. Remove the nuts, retainer and grommet from the top of each stabilizer link.

3. Remove the bolts from the mounting brackets holding the sway bar to the frame and remove the mounting brackets.

4. Remove the rubber bushings from the sway bar shaft and remove the grommets, retainers, spacers and links from the ends of the sway bar.

5. Turn the wheels of the vehicle to full stop and remove the sway bar.

To install:

6. Position the sway bar under the front frame side rails and slide the rubber bushings into place. The slit should be forward, toward the front of the vehicle. Sway bar grommets are larger than those on the shock absorbers, be sure all replacement parts are of this larger type.

7. Install the mounting brackets over the rubber bushings and secure with the attaching bolts. Tighten the bracket bolts to 24 ft. lbs. (33 Nm).

8. Install the grommets, retainers, links and spacers on the ends of the sway bar shaft. Make sure all components are properly arranged.

9. Install the grommet retainer and nut on top of the link and sway bar. Tighten the nut to 13 ft. lbs. (17 Nm).

10. Lower the vehicle.

Knuckle/Spindle Assembly

REMOVAL & INSTALLATION

1. Disconnect the negative battery cable.

2. Raise and support the vehicle safely. Be sure to support the lower control arm to keep the coil spring compressed at curb height throughout the procedure.

3. Mark and remove the tire and wheel assembly.

4. Disconnect the tie rod end from the steering knuckle.

5. Remove the brake caliper from the mounting bracket and support out of the way so the brake line does not kink or bend

6. Remove the brake rotor.

7. If equipped with ABS, disconnect the speed sensor cable from the bracket.

8. Remove the brake splash shield. If equipped, remove the wheel speed sensor.

9. Disconnect the upper and lower ball joints from the steering knuckle and remove the knuckle from the vehicle.

To install:

10. Position the steering knuckle in the vehicle and attach the upper and lower ball joints.

11. Tighten the upper nut to 61 ft. lbs. (83 Nm) and if necessary tighten just enough more to insert a new cotter pin. Tighten the lower nut to 83 ft. lbs. (113 Nm). If necessary, tighten the nut additionally to insert the new cotter pin. The maximum torque allowable for the lower nut is 92 ft. lbs. (125 Nm) or an additional $\frac{1}{16}$ of a turn. Do not back off either nut to install the cotter pins.

12. Install the brake splash shield.

13. If equipped with ABS, connect the speed sensor cable to the bracket and install the wheel speed sensor.

14. Install the brake rotor.

15. Install the tie rod end to the steering knuckle.

16. Install the brake caliper. Align the marks made earlier and install the tire and wheel assembly.

17. Adjust the wheel bearings install a new cotter pin and the dust cap.

18. Install the wheel cover, remove the supports and lower the vehicle.

19. Connect the negative battery cable and fill the master cylinder with to the proper level with clean brake fluid. Do not attempt to move the vehicle until the shoe linings are properly seated.

20. Check and adjust the alignment, as necessary.

Front Wheel Bearings

ADJUSTMENT

1. Raise and support the vehicle safely.

2. Remove the dust cap and cotter pin from the spindle nut. Be sure the hub is fully seated on the spindle.

3. To adjust, spin the wheel forward by hand, to fully seat the bearing and tighten the locknut nut to 12 ft. lbs. Stop the wheel.

4. Back off the nut until it is free and then tighten it finger-tight.

5. Insert the cotter pin. If the pin cannot be installed in this position, back off the nut slightly until the holes align. Make certain the pin fits tightly and will not interfere with the dust cap.

6. There should be 0.001–0.005 inch end-play when the wheel bearings are properly adjusted.

REMOVAL & INSTALLATION

1. Raise and support the vehicle safely. Mark and remove the tire and wheel assembly.

2. Remove the brake caliper and properly support it making sure not to damage the brake line.

3. Remove the dust cap, cotter pin, locknut and washer.

4. Remove the outer wheel bearing from the hub assembly.

5. Remove the rotor taking care not to damage the spindle threads. Remove the inner bearing grease seal, bearing assembly. Discard the old seal.

6. Inner and outer bearing cups are pressed into the hub and can be removed with a suitable tool. Insert the tool and tap alternately on opposite sides of the cup to avoid cocking the cup and damaging the rotor.

To install:

7. Thoroughly clean and inspect all parts. Use a clean solvent to remove all

traces of old grease and any dirt or contaminants. If any parts are worn or pitted, replace the complete bearing assembly.

8. Lubricate the spindle and the rotor bore with a thin film of high melting point wheel bearing grease to prevent rust.

9. Install the outer bearing cup using a suitable installing punch and arbor to press the cup into the rotor. Install the inner bearing cup in the same manner.

10. Pack the bearing with high melting point wheel bearing grease. Force grease in at the large end of the roller cage until grease protrudes from the small end.

11. Install the inner bearing into the bearing cup and install a new grease seal with a flat plate until the seal is flush with the rotor hub.

12. Install the rotor onto the spindle and place outer bearing into the bearing cup.

13. Install the washer and spindle finger-tight.

14. Install the brake caliper.

15. Align the marks made earlier and install the tire and wheel assembly.

16. Adjust the wheel bearings and install a new cotter pin, the dust cap and the wheel cover.

17. Lower the vehicle.

REAR SUSPENSION

Shock Absorbers

REMOVAL & INSTALLATION

1. Raise and support the vehicle safely. Properly support the rear axle assembly.

2. If equipped with Electronic Level Control (ELC), disconnect the air line fitting(s) at the shock absorber.

3. Remove the upper shock absorber retaining bolt and nut.

4. Hold the the lower shock absorber stem steady and remove the retaining nut.

5. Remove the shock absorber from the vehicle.

To install:

6. Place the shock absorber to the vehicle and position the upper mount cross bar so the shock angles naturally toward the lower mount.

7. Install the upper retaining bolt and nut. Tighten the bolts to 20 ft. lbs. (27 Nm).

8. Guide the shock lower stud into the mounting bracket and install the

nut and washer. While holding the stud to keep from rotating, tighten the nut to 65 ft. lbs. (88 Nm).

9. If equipped with ELC, connect the air line fitting(s). Turn the ignition ON and ground the compressor test lead with a jumper to activate the system and inflate the shocks. Do not place vehicle weight on the shocks until they have been inflated, or damage may occur.

10. Lower the vehicle.

Coil Springs

REMOVAL & INSTALLATION

1. Raise and support the vehicle safely. Place an adjustable support under the rear axle assembly.

2. Remove the shock absorbers.

3. Remove the stabilizer shaft.

NOTE: Do not lower the axle assembly to the point at which the brake hoses become taut, as damage may result.

4. Remove the bolt that secures the brake hose junction block to the top of the rear axle housing and disconnect the brake lines from the retaining clips.

5. If equipped, remove the link from the height sensor arm.

6. Raise the axle housing slightly to relieve tension from the lower control arm bolts and remove the bolts at the axle housing.

7. Mark and remove the driveshaft from the pinion yoke and support the driveshaft to the side.

8. Remove the upper control arm pivot bolts at the rear axle housing.

9. Disconnect the left side parking brake cable at the equalizer and disconnect the cable at the frame by removing the clip. Slide the cable through the hole.

10. Disconnect the cable from the clip at the center of the rear crossmember and disconnect the cable at the "C" shaped connector which is located at the left of the frame.

11. With the rear frame rails supported, lower the axle to the point where the springs can be pried out. Be careful not to stretch the brake line or cable.

12. Remove the springs from the vehicle. If the axle is allowed to wind up as it is lowered, the springs may snap from their seats causing injury or damage.

To install:

13. Tape the upper rubber insulators to the top of the springs. Position the upper end of the left rear spring coil toward the left frame side rail and the upper right end of the right spring coil toward the right frame side rail.

14. Seat the bottom of the springs on the rear axle and raise the axle, being careful to engage the axle in the upper control arms. Loosely install the nuts and pivot bolts.

15. Install the parking brake cable in clip at the center of the rear crossmember and connect the cable to the "C"shaped connector.

16. Slide the cable through the hole and connect the left parking brake cable to the equalizer and install the clips.

17. Remove support from driveshaft and install to the pinion yoke, aligning the marks made earlier.

18. Loosely install the lower control arm to the axle.

19. If equipped, install the link to the height sensor arm.

20. Install the bolt securing the brake junction block to the top of the axle housing and secure the brake lines to the clips.

21. Install the stabilizer shaft.

22. Install the shock absorbers. If equipped with Electronic Level Control (ELC), be sure to engage the system and properly inflate the shock absorbers before lowering the vehicle.

23. Check and adjust the parking brake, if necessary.

24. Remove the supports and lower the vehicle.

25. With the vehicle in the normal standing height position, tighten the upper control arm nuts to 70 ft. lbs. (95 Nm) and the lower control arm nuts to 122 ft. lbs. (165 Nm).

Upper Control Arms

REMOVAL & INSTALLATION

NOTE: If both control arms are being replaced, replace one control arm at a time to prevent the rear axle from rolling or slipping sideways.

1. Raise and support the vehicle safely. Be sure to properly support the rear axle assembly.

2. If equipped with Electronic Level Control (ELC), remove the height sensor link retaining nut and remove the height sensor link.

3. Remove the upper control arm retaining bolts.

4. Remove the upper control arm from the vehicle.

To install:

5. Install the upper control arm to the vehicle with the flanged surface of the bushing facing inboard. Loosely install the front pivot bolt and nut then loosely install the rear pivot bolt and nut into the axle bracket.

6. Lower the car and with the vehicle at normal curb height, tighten the frame nut to 122 ft. lbs. (165 Nm) and the axle nut to 70 ft. lbs. (95 Nm).

7. If equipped with ELC, raise the vehicle and install the height sensor link to the right upper control arm with the attaching nut. Inflate the system by grounding the compressor test lead with a jumper and lower the vehicle.

Lower Control Arms

REMOVAL & INSTALLATION

NOTE: If both control arms are being replaced, replace one control arm at a time to prevent the rear axle from rolling or slipping sideways.

1. Raise and support the vehicle safely. Be sure to properly support the rear axle assembly.
2. Disconnect the stabilizer arm bracket at the lower control arm.
3. Remove the front and rear lower control arm retaining nuts.
4. Raise the axle assembly slightly to relieve the tension on the lower control bolts.
5. Remove the lower control arm bolts and remove the control arm from the vehicle.
To install:
6. Slide the control arm into position. Be sure the stabilizer arm bracket holes are towards the rear of the frame. Install the front bolt form the outboard side and the rear bolt from the inboard side. Raise or lower the axle slightly, as necessary to ease bolt installation.
7. Connect the stabilizer shaft bracket to the lower control arm and tighten the bolts to 21 ft. lbs. (29 Nm).
8. Lower the car and with the vehicle at normal curb height, tighten the nuts to 122 ft. lbs. (165 Nm).

STEERING

Steering Wheel

REMOVAL & INSTALLATION

1. Disconnect the negative battery cable and turn the ignition to the **RUN** position in order to facilitate removal.
2. Remove the horn pad retaining screws. Remove the horn pad and switch.
3. Remove the horn contact wire from the plastic tower by pushing in on the wire and turning counterclockwise. The wire will spring out of the tower.
4. If applicable, remove the screws

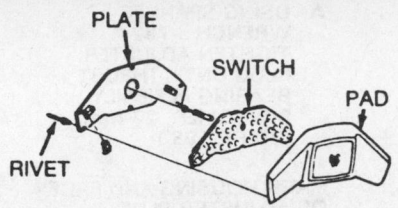

PAD AND HORN SWITCH

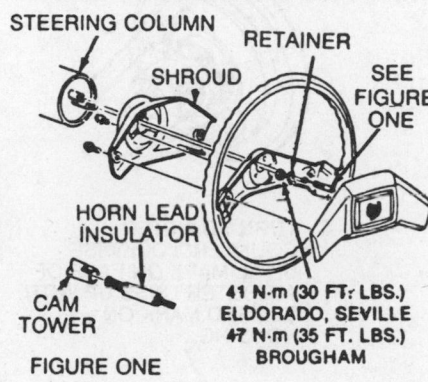

41 N·m (30 FT. LBS.) ELDORADO, SEVILLE
47 N·m (35 FT. LBS.) BROUGHAM

FIGURE ONE

TILT AND TELESCOPING COLUMN

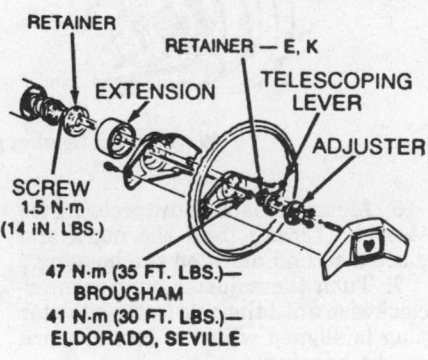

SCREW 1.5 N·m (14 IN. LBS.)

47 N·m (35 FT. LBS.)— BROUGHAM
41 N·m (30 FT. LBS.)— ELDORADO, SEVILLE

STANDARD COLUMN

Steering wheel and related components

that secure the telescope locking lever assembly to the adjuster. Unscrew and remove the adjuster from the steering shaft. Remove the telescope lever from the column.
5. Scribe an alignment mark on the steering wheel hub in line with the slash mark on the steering shaft for use during installation.
6. Loosen the locknut on the steering shaft and position it flush with the end of the shaft. Using the proper steering wheel puller, remove the wheel from its mounting on the steering shaft.
7. Remove the steering wheel removal tool, the locknut and the steering wheel from the vehicle.
To install:
8. Install the steering wheel onto

the steering column, aligning the marks made during the removal procedure. The steering wheel should in no case be driven onto the column as this could seriously damage column components.
9. Install the locknut and tighten to 35 ft. lbs. (47 Nm).
10. If applicable, install the telescope lever onto the shaft. Install the telescope adjuster screw by hand. Position the locking lever and bolts along the marks made by the bolts when they were tightened and tighten the bolts to 35 inch lbs. (4 Nm). Check operation of the tilt and telescoping column. Make sure the wheel locks securely into position when the lever is all the way to the right. Adjust the slotted locking lever bolt holes, if necessary.
11. Install the horn contact into the plastic cavity, push it against the spring and twist clockwise.
12. Install the horn pad assembly and secure it with the 2 attaching screws.
13. Turn the ignition **OFF** and connect the negative battery cable.

Steering Column

REMOVAL & INSTALLATION

1. Disconnect the negative battery cable and lock the steering column with the wheels in the straight-ahead position.
2. Disconnect the transmission shift linkage under the hood at the lower shift lever.
3. Remove the coupling nut attaching the intermediate shaft to the steering column. Separate the shaft from the column.
4. Remove the steering column lower cover and 4 retaining screws from the instrument panel, exposing the upper support bolts.
5. If necessary, remove the lower fuse cover panel by removing 2 screws and 1 wing nut and/or remove the left air conditioning outlet duct and screw.
6. Disconnect the turn signal wiring connector. If equipped with cruise control, disconnect the harness.
7. If necessary, disconnect the park neutral switch, the parking brake release hose from the column and/or the headlight dimmer switch connector from the column.
8. Remove the clip securing the shift cable to the shift bowl.
9. Loosen bolts at the steering column upper support. Do not completely remove the upper support nuts or bolts as the steering column could bend under its own weight.
10. Move the rubber carpet out of the way to gain access to the cowl insulator and cowl seal.

11. Remove the cowl insulator and cowl cover seal. Remove the bolts at the upper column bracket while supporting the column.

12. Carefully pull the steering column up and out of the vehicle. If the shaft hangs up in the upper coupling, secure the upper mounting bracket and free the coupling from the steering shaft. Remove the column assembly.

To install:

13. Carefully position the column in the vehicle, taking care not to damage and levers or switches. Install the upper mounting bracket nuts finger-tight.

14. Install the coupling nut securing the steering column to the intermediate shaft, finger-tight. Connect the transmission linkage to the lower shift lever.

15. Attach the clip securing the shift pointer to the shift bowl. Check and adjust alignment, as necessary.

16. Install the steering column cowl seal and finger-tighten.

17. Connect all electrical connections.

18. Tighten the upper column bracket nuts to 20 ft. lbs. (27 Nm), the cowl cover seal nuts and bolts to 35 inch lbs. (4 Nm) and the intermediate shaft coupling bolt to 52 ft. lbs. (71 Nm).

19. Install the cowl seal insulator and reposition the carpeting. If removed, install the left air conditioning outlet duct and the lower fuse cover panel.

20. Install the steering column lower cover.

21. Connect the negative battery cable.

Power Steering Gear

ADJUSTMENT

NOTE: Adjust the worm bearing preload first, then proceed with the pitman shaft over-center adjustment.

Worm Thrust Bearing Preload

1. Remove the steering gear.
2. Rotate the stub shaft and drain the power steering fluid into a suitable container.
3. Mount the gear in a vise and remove the adjuster plug nut.
4. Turn the adjuster plug in (clockwise) using a suitable spanner wrench until the adjuster plug and thrust bearing are firmly bottomed in the housing. Tighten the adjuster plug to 22 ft. lbs. (30 Nm).
5. Place an index mark on the housing even with 1 of the holes in the adjuster plug.

A. USING SPANNER WRENCH J-7624. TIGHTEN ADJUSTER PLUG UNTIL THRUST BEARING IS FIRMLY BOTTOMED, 27 N·m (20 FT. LBS.)

MARK HOUSING AND FACE OF ADJUSTER PLUG.

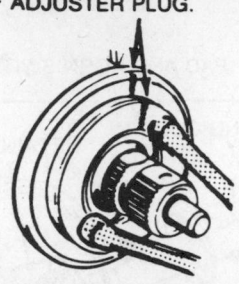

B. MEASURE BACK COUNTERCLOCKWISE 13mm (½") AND PLACE A SECOND MARK ON HOUSING.

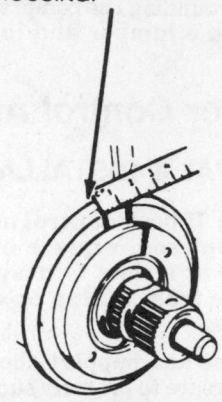

C. TURN ADJUSTER COUNTERCLOCKWISE UNTIL MARK ON FACE OF ADJUSTER LINES UP WITH SECOND MARK ON HOUSING.

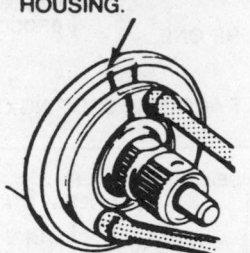

D. USING PUNCH IN NOTCH TIGHTEN LOCK NUT SECURELY. HOLD ADJUSTER PLUG TO MAINTAIN ALIGNMENT OF THE MARKS.

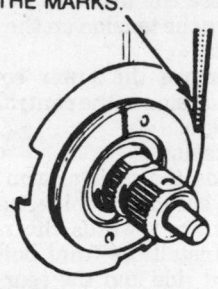

Worm thrust bearing preload adjustment

6. Measure back counterclockwise ½ inch (13mm) from the mark and place a second mark on the housing.
7. Turn the adjuster plug counterclockwise until the hole in the adjuster plug is aligned with the second mark on the housing.
8. Install the adjuster plug nut and using a suitable drift in a notch, tighten securely to 80 ft. lbs. (109 Nm). Hold the adjuster plug to maintain alignment of the marks.
9. Adjust the pitman shaft over-center if necessary. Install the steering gear.

Pitman Shaft Over-Center

1. Remove the steering gear.
2. If necessary, adjust the worm bearing preload.
3. Rotate the stub shaft and drain the power steering fluid into a suitable container and loosen the adjuster locknut.
4. Turn the pitman shaft adjuster screw counterclockwise until fully extended, then turn in (clockwise) 1 full turn.
5. Rotate the stub shaft from stop-to-stop using a 12-point socket and count the number of turns.

6. Starting at either stop, turn the stub shaft back ½ the total number of turns. This is the "Center" position of the gear. When the gear is centered, the flat on the stub shaft should face upward and be parallel with the side cover and the master spline on the pitman shaft should be in line with the adjuster screw.
7. Rotate the stub shaft 45 degrees each side of the center using a suitable torque wrench with the handle in the vertical position. The stub shaft should move smoothly and not stick or bind. Record the worm bearing preload measured on or near the center gear position, it should be in the 6–5 inch lbs. (0.7–1.7 Nm) range with the worm and ballnut installed. If the torque is outside this range, the gear assembly should be readjusted, repaired or replaced.
8. Adjust the over-center drag torque by turning the pitman shaft adjuster screw clockwise until the correct drag torque is obtained: Add 6–10 inch lbs. (0.7–1.1 Nm) of torque to the previously measured worm bearing preload torque. Tighten the adjuster locknut to 20 ft. lbs. (27 Nm), except for on 1992–93 vehicles which should

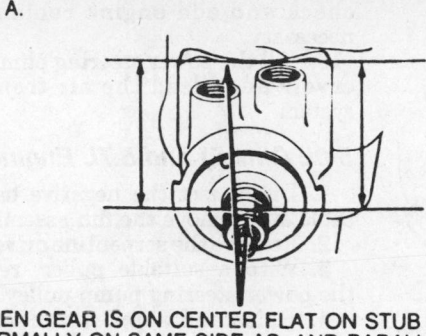

A.

WHEN GEAR IS ON CENTER FLAT ON STUB SHAFT IS NORMALLY ON SAME SIDE AS, AND PARALLEL WITH, SIDE COVER.

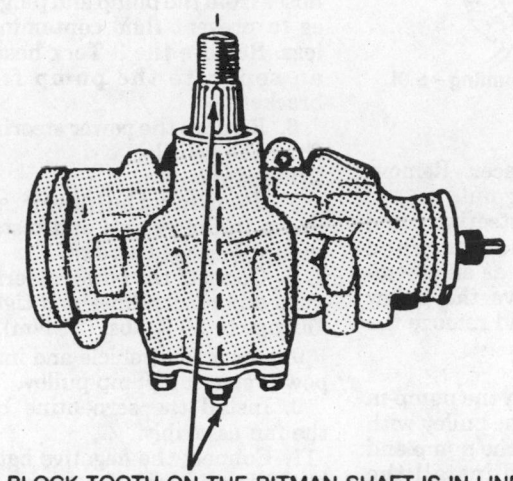

THE BLOCK TOOTH ON THE PITMAN SHAFT IS IN LINE WITH THE OVER-CENTER PRELOAD ADJUSTER.

B. BACK OFF PRELOAD ADJUSTER UNTIL IT STOPS, THEN TURN IT IN ONE FULL TURN.

WITH GEAR AT CENTER OF TRAVEL, CHECK TORQUE TO TURN STUB SHAFT (READING #1).

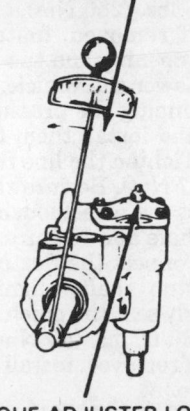

C. TURN ADJUSTER IN UNTIL TORQUE TO TURN STUB SHAFT IS 0.6 TO 1.2 N·m (6 TO 11 IN. LBS.) MORE THAN READING #1.

TORQUE ADJUSTER LOCK NUT TO 27 N·m (20 FT. LBS.)

PREVENT ADJUSTER SCREW FROM TURNING WHILE TORQUING LOCK NUT.

Pitman shaft "over-center" sector adjustment

be tightened 36 ft. lbs. (49 Nm). Prevent the adjuster screw from turning while tightening the adjuster locknut.

9. Install the steering gear.

REMOVAL & INSTALLATION

1. Position a drain pan under the steering gear.
2. If necessary, remove the air cleaner snorkle.
3. Disconnect the pressure and return lines from the steering gear assembly. Plug the opening to prevent fluid contamination or loss.
4. Remove the pinch bolt from the flex coupling and disconnect the coupling from the gear.

NOTE: Failure to disconnect the flexible coupling from the steering gear stub shaft may result in damage to the steering gear and or the intermediate shaft. This damage can cause the loss of steering control which could result in a vehicle crash and bodily injuries.

5. Raise the vehicle and support it safely.
6. Remove the pitman arm nut and washer. Remove the pitman arm from

the steering gear using a pitman arm puller tool.

7. If necessary, partially remove the wheelhouse opening and front shield to gain access to the steering gear mounting bolts.

8. Remove the retaining bolts and

washers holding the steering gear to the side rail. Lower the gear assembly from the vehicle.

To install:

9. Position the power steering gear to the frame side rail and install the bolts. Tighten the mounting bolts to

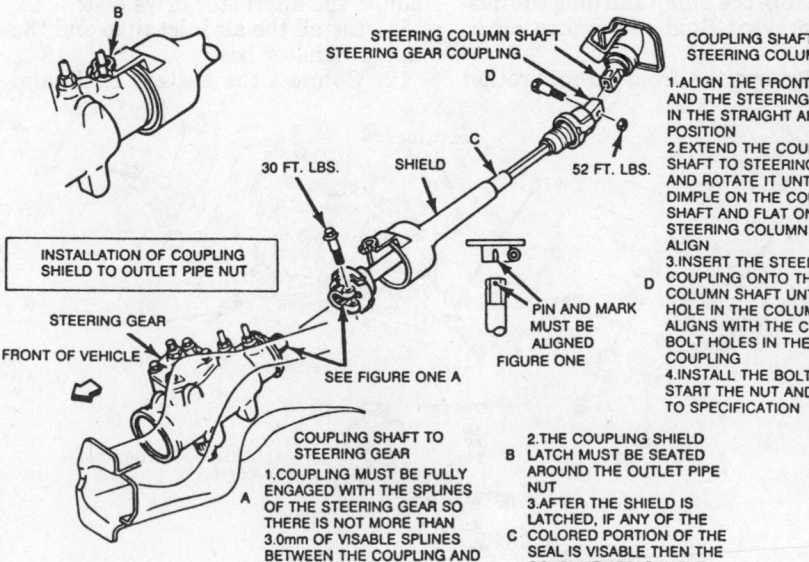

STEERING COLUMN SHAFT
STEERING GEAR COUPLING

30 FT. LBS.   SHIELD   52 FT. LBS.

INSTALLATION OF COUPLING SHIELD TO OUTLET PIPE NUT

STEERING GEAR

FRONT OF VEHICLE

SEE FIGURE ONE A

PIN AND MARK MUST BE ALIGNED FIGURE ONE

COUPLING SHAFT TO STEERING GEAR
1.COUPLING MUST BE FULLY ENGAGED WITH THE SPLINES OF THE STEERING GEAR SO THERE IS NOT MORE THAN 3.0mm OF VISABLE SPLINES BETWEEN THE COUPLING AND THE GEAR

COUPLING SHAFT TO STEERING COLUMN SHAFT
1.ALIGN THE FRONT WHEELS AND THE STEERING COLUMN IN THE STRAIGHT AHEAD POSITION
2.EXTEND THE COUPLING SHAFT TO STEERING COLUMN AND ROTATE IT UNTIL THE DIMPLE ON THE COUPLING SHAFT AND FLAT ON THE STEERING COLUMN SHAFT ALIGN
3.INSERT THE STEERING GEAR COUPLING ONTO THE COLUMN SHAFT UNTIL THE HOLE IN THE COLUMN SHAFT ALIGNS WITH THE CROSS BOLT HOLES IN THE SHAFT COUPLING
4.INSTALL THE BOLT AND START THE NUT AND TORQUE TO SPECIFICATION

2.THE COUPLING SHIELD LATCH MUST BE SEATED AROUND THE OUTLET PIPE NUT
3.AFTER THE SHIELD IS LATCHED, IF ANY OF THE COLORED PORTION OF THE SEAL IS VISABLE THEN THE COUPLING ATTACHMENT SHOULD BE REINSPECTED

Steering gear and alignment data

70 ft. lbs. (95 Nm). If the mounting threads are stripped, do not attempt repair, the housing must be replaced.

10. Connect the pitman arm to the shaft and install the lockwasher and nut. Tighten the pitman arm nut to 185 ft. lbs. (250 Nm).

11. If removed, install the wheelhouse opening and the front shield.

12. Lower the vehicle.

13. Unplug the pressure and return lines and install them to the steering gear. Tighten the line fittings to 20 ft. lbs. (27 Nm). Be sure the lines do not contact the wheelhousing or the lines may chafe and rupture.

14. Connect the flex coupling to the gear stub shaft, aligning the shaft. Properly seat the pinch bolt and tighten to 30 ft. lbs. (40 Nm).

15. If removed, install the air cleaner snorkle.

16. Fill and bleed the power steering system.

Power Steering Pump

REMOVAL & INSTALLATION

5.0L (VIN Y) Engine

1. Disconnect the negative battery cable and position a drain pan under the upper radiator hose.

2. Disconnect and relocate the air cleaner inlet tube and the upper radiator hose to gain access to the pump. Position the hose with the open end raised to prevent excessive coolant leakage.

3. Remove the alternator belt. Loosen the alternator mounting bolts, except for the long bolt and rotate the unit upward to gain access by pivoting on the long bolt.

4. Remove the pressure and return hoses from the pump and plug the hoses to prevent fluid contamination or loss.

5. Remove the front pump bracket

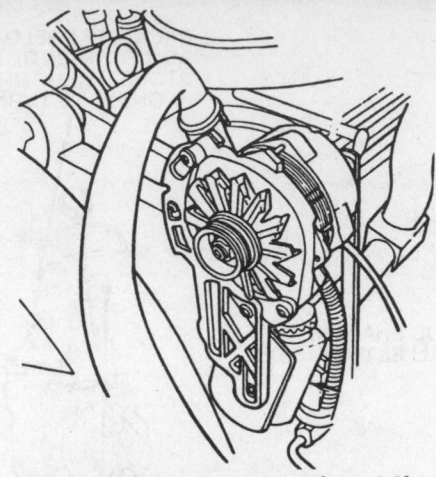

Power steering pump mounting—5.0L (VIN E) and 5.7L Engines

mounting bolts and spacer. Remove the rear pump mounting nut.

6. Remove the power steering pump drive belt. Remove the pump and bracket from the engine as an assembly. If necessary, remove the pulley with a suitable puller and remove the bracket from the pump.

To install:

7. If removed, position the pump in the bracket and install the pulley with a suitable tool. Position the pump and bracket in the car and install the mounting bolts and nuts. Tighten the bolts and nuts to specification, except for the 2 rear bolts which are used in belt adjustment.

8. Install the pressure and return hoses and tighten the fittings to 20 ft. lbs. (27 Nm).

9. Install the pump drive belt and adjust tension.

10. Reposition the alternator and install the mounting bolts. Install and adjust the alternator drive belt.

11. Install the air inlet tube and the upper radiator hose.

12. Connect the battery cable and

check and add engine coolant, as necessary.

13. Fill the power steering pump reservoir and bleed the air from the system.

5.0L (VIN E) and 5.7L Engines

1. Disconnect the negative battery cable and remove the fan assembly.

2. Remove the serpentine drive belt.

3. With a suitable puller, remove the power steering pump pulley.

4. Raise and support the vehicle safely.

5. Remove the pressure and return hoses from the pump and plug the hoses to prevent fluid contamination or loss. Remove the 3 Torx head screws an separate the pump from the bracket.

6. Remove the power steering pump from the vehicle.

To install:

7. Position the power steering pump in the vehicle and install the 3 pump torx head screws.

8. Connect the power steering pressure and return lines and tighten the fittings to 20 ft. lbs. (27 Nm).

9. Lower the vehicle and install the power steering pump pulley.

10. Install the serpentine belt and the fan assembly.

11. Connect the negative battery cable, fill and bleed the power steering system.

BELT ADJUSTMENT

5.0L (VIN Y) Engine

1. Disconnect the negative battery cable.

2. Loosen the power steering pump mounting bolts.

3. Install the belt tension gauge. Correct tension is 90 lbs. (400 N) minimum for a used belt or 170 lbs. (750 N) maximum for a new belt.

4. Adjust the belt by prying the power steering pump away from the engine.

NOTE: When adjusting the power steering pump belt be sure

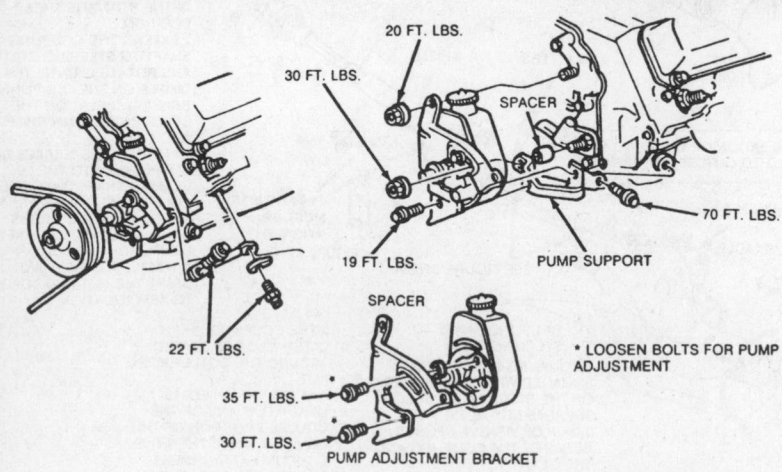

Power steering pump mounting—5.0L (VIN Y) Engine

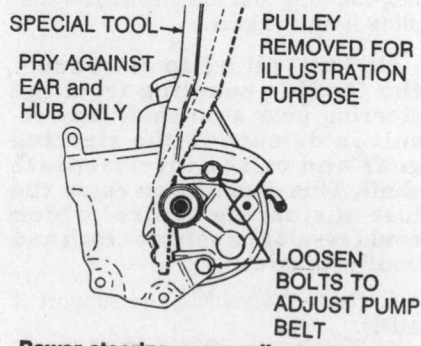

Power steering pump adjustment—5.0L (VIN Y) Engine

not to pry against the pump reservoir. Only the power steering pump bracket should be pryed against when adjusting the belt.

5. Once the belt is adjusted, tighten the power steering pump bolts to specification.

5.0L (VIN E) and 5.7L Engines

The serpentine drive belt is self adjusting within the tensioner operating limits. For a drive belt and tensioner test procedure, refer to the alternator belt adjusting section.

SYSTEM BLEEDING

1. Raise and support the vehicle safely.
2. With the wheels turned all the way to the left add power steering fluid to the **COLD** mark on the dipstick.
3. Start the engine. Check the fluid level. Add fluid as necessary to bring the level to the **COLD** mark on the dipstick.
4. Bleed the system by turning the steering wheel from side to side without hitting the stops.
5. Be sure to maintain the fluid level at the **HOT/COLD** mark on the dipstick. Fluid with air in it will have a light tan appearance. This air must be expelled from the system before normal steering action can be obtained.
6. Return the wheels to the center position. Allow the engine to run for several minutes and then turn the engine **OFF**.
7. Road test the vehicle and make sure the steering performs properly and there is no noise from the power steering pump.
8. Recheck the power steering fluid. Be sure the fluid level is at the **HOT** mark on the dipstick after the system has stabilized at its normal operating temperature.

Tie Rod Ends

REMOVAL & INSTALLATION

1. Raise and support the vehicle safely.
2. Remove the cotter pin and castellated nut from the outer tie rod end.
3. Using the proper tool disconnect the tie rod end from the steering knuckle.
4. Using the proper tool remove the inner ball stud from the intermediate rod.

NOTE: When disconnecting a linkage joint no attempt should be made to disengage the joint by driving a wedge between the joint and the retained part as seal damage may result.

5. Remove the tie rod adjuster clamp bolts. Discard the nuts and bolts if the torque necessary to remove them after breakaway exceeds 80 inch lbs. (9 Nm).
6. Unscrew the tie rod end assemblies from the adjuster tube. Count the number of turns necessary to remove the tie rod from the adjuster tube to assure reassembly in the same position.
To install:
7. Lubricate the tie rod threads with chasis lube and install into the adjuster tube. Thread the tie rod ends into the adjuster tube with an equal number of turns as was necessary to remove them.
8. Be sure the threads on the ball studs and nuts are clean and free from damage. There should be no nicks on the ball stud tapers and the seals should be free of damage. Install the ball studs into the steering knuckle and the intermediate rod.
9. Install the ball stud nuts and tighten to 35 ft. lbs. (48 Nm). If necessary continue to tighten the nut just enough to align a slot in the castellated nut with a hole in the stud. Install new cotter pins.
10. Make sure the tie rod ends are in alignment with their ball studs and the adjuster clamps are properly positioned. The clamps must be between and clear of the dimples, with the bolts underneath the adjuster rod. Tighten the adjuster tube clamp bolts to 14 ft. lbs. (19 Nm).
11. Lower the vehicle, check and adjust front end alignment, as required.

BRAKES

Master Cylinder

REMOVAL & INSTALLATION

1. Place a container under the master cylinder to catch any brake fluid leakage.
2. Disconnect the brake lines at the master cylinder. Plug the lines to prevent fluid contamination or loss.
3. Remove the nuts securing the master cylinder to the power booster.
4. Remove the master cylinder from the vehicle.
To install:
5. Position the master cylinder in the vehicle and install the attaching nuts. Tighten the nuts to 28 ft. lbs. (38 Nm).
6. Begin filling the forward chamber of the reservoir and when brake fluid appears at the outlet, unplug and connect the appropriate brake line.

Repeat for the rear chamber, unplug and connect the other brake line.
7. Tighten the brake line fittings to 12 ft. lbs. (17 Nm).
8. Remove the drain pan and bleed the hydraulic brake system, as required.

Combination Valve

For 1989 vehicles the combination valve is located on the frame side rail extension at the left side of the car. For 1990–93 vehicles, the valve is located on a bracket mounted below the master cylinder.

REMOVAL & INSTALLATION

1. Disconnect the negative battery cable. Disconnect the electrical connector from the valve assembly.
2. Disconnect plug the brake lines at the valve. Plug the lines to prevent fluid contamination or loss.
3. Remove the valve retaining bolt(s) and remove the valve from its mounting.
4. Installation is the reverse of the removal procedure. Be sure to properly bleed the hydraulic brake system.

Power Brake Booster

REMOVAL & INSTALLATION

1. Remove the master cylinder retaining nuts and position the assembly aside.
2. Disconnect the vacuum line from the vacuum check valve.
3. If necessary, remove the steering column lower cover inside the vehicle to access the brake pedal and the booster attaching nuts.
4. Disconnect the power booster pushrod from the brake pedal arm.
5. Remove the nuts that secure the power unit to the firewall and remove the power booster unit.
To install:
6. Position the booster to the firewall and install the attaching nuts. Tighten the nuts to 28 ft. lbs. (38 Nm).
7. Connect the power booster pushrod to the brake pedal.
8. Install the steering column lower cover, if removed.
9. Connect the vacuum line to the booster check valve.
10. Reposition the master cylinder onto the booster mounting studs and tighten the nuts to 28 ft. lbs. (38 Nm).

Brake Caliper

REMOVAL & INSTALLATION

1. Drain ⅔ of the brake fluid from the master cylinder assembly.

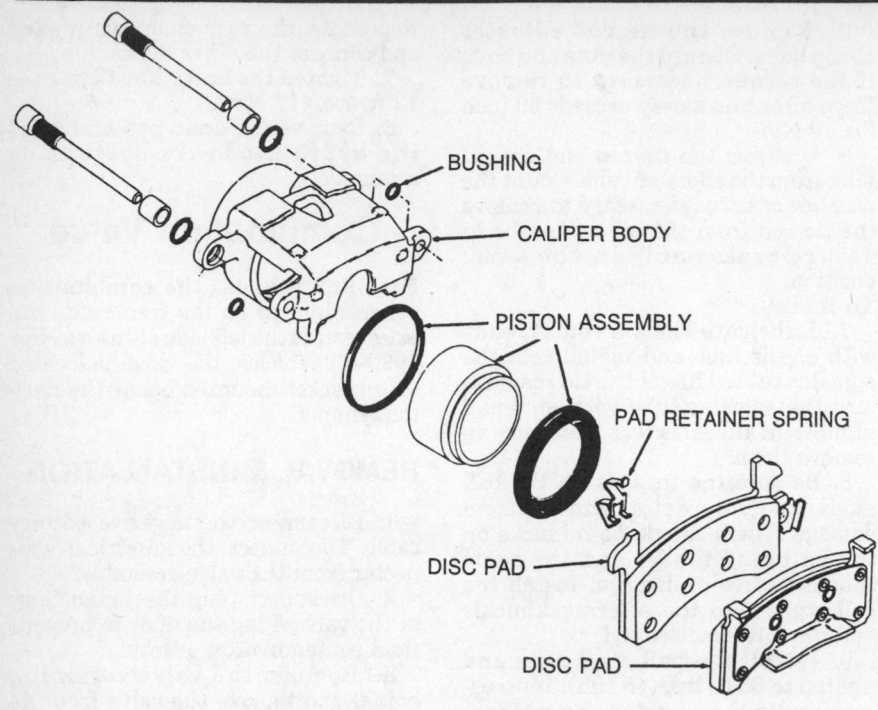

BUSHING

CALIPER BODY

PISTON ASSEMBLY

PAD RETAINER SPRING

DISC PAD

DISC PAD

Front caliper assembly

2. Raise and support the vehicle safely.

3. Mark the relationship of the wheel to the rotor and remove the tire and wheel assembly.

4. Position a C-clamp over the inboard brake shoe tab and and the inboard caliper housing, carefully compress the piston assembly back into the caliper housing.

5. Disconnect the brake line hose at the caliper and plug the line to prevent fluid loss or contamination.

6. Remove the caliper mounting bolt and sleves the remove the caliper assembly from its mounting bracket.

To install:

7. Lubricate the sleeves and bushings with silicone grease and install the sleeves into the caliper ears. Position the caliper over the rotor in the mounting bracket.

8. Install the mounting bolts and tighten to 38 ft. lbs. (51 Nm). Be sure there is 0.005–0.012 in. (0.13–0.30mm) of clearance between the top and bottom of the caliper and the bracket stops. If necessary, remove the caliper and file the end of the bracket stops.

9. Unplug and install the brake line hose to the caliper. Tighten the fitting to 33 ft. lbs. (45 Nm).

10. Algin the marks made earlier and install the tire and wheel assemblies.

11. Lower the vehicle.

12. Fill the master cylinder to the proper level with clean brake fluid and bleed the hydraulic brake system.

Disc Brake Pads

REMOVAL & INSTALLATION

1. Drain ⅔ of the brake fluid from the master cylinder assembly.

2. Raise and support the vehicle safely.

3. Mark the relationship of the wheel to the rotor and remove the tire and wheel assembly.

4. Position a C-clamp over the inboard brake shoe tab and and the inboard caliper housing, carefully compress the piston assembly back into the caliper housing.

5. Remove the caliper mounting bolt and sleves the remove the caliper assembly from its mounting bracket. Do not allow the caliper to hang by the brake line. Support the caliper from the vehicle with a hook or length of mechanic's wire.

6. Remove the outboard shoe and lining then remove the inboard shoe and lining.

7. Remove the bushings from the grooves in the mounting bolt holes.

To install:

8. Using silicone grease lubricate and install the new bushings into the grooves in the mounting bolt holes.

9. Lubricate and install the sleeves and into the mounting bolt holes.

10. Install the retainer spring to the inboard shoe and lining assembly. Install the shoe by snapping into place on the piston with the wear sensor at the

leading edge of the shoe during forward wheel rotation.

11. Install the outboard shoe and lining with the back of the shoe flat against the caliper and position the caliper over the rotor in the mounting bracket.

12. Install the mounting bolts and tighten to 38 ft. lbs. (51 Nm). Be sure there is 0.005–0.012 in. (0.13–0.30mm) of clearance between the top and bottom of the caliper and the bracket stops. If necessary, remove the caliper and file the end of the bracket stops.

13. Apply about 175 lbs. (778 N) of force to the brake pedal 3 times to seat the linings. Position a pair of channel lock pliers over the brake shoe ears and bottom edge of the caliper. While applying about 50 lbs. (222 N) of force on the brake pedal, clinch the outboard shoe ears to the caliper.

14. Align the marks made earlier and install the tire and wheel assemblies.

15. Lower the vehicle and fill the master cylinder reservoir to the proper level with clean brake fluid.

Brake Rotor

REMOVAL & INSTALLATION

1. Drain ⅔ of the brake fluid from the master cylinder assembly.

2. Raise and support the vehicle safely.

3. Mark the relationship of the wheel to the rotor and remove the tire and wheel assembly.

4. Position a C-clamp over the inboard brake shoe tab and and the inboard caliper housing, carefully compress the piston assembly back into the caliper housing.

5. Remove the caliper mounting bolt and sleves the remove the caliper assembly from its mounting bracket. Do not allow the caliper to hang by the brake line. Support the caliper from the vehicle with a hook or length of mechanic's wire.

6. Remove the wheel bearing dust cap. Remove the cotter pin, locknut, washer and outer bearing assembly.

7. Remove the rotor assembly from the spindle.

To install:

8. Postition the rotor assembly on the spindle and install the outer bearing assembly.

9. Install the washer and spindle nut finger-tight.

10. Install the brake caliper.

11. Align the marks made during removal and install the tire and wheel assembly.

12. Adjust the wheel bearings install a new cotter pin and the dust cap.

13. Install the wheel cover, lower the

vehicle and fill the master cylinder with to the proper level with clean brake fluid. Do not attempt to move the vehicle until the shoe linings are properly seated.

Brake Drums

REMOVAL & INSTALLATION

1. Raise and support the vehicle safely.
2. Mark the relationship of the wheel to the axle flange for reinstallation and remove the tire and wheel assembly.
3. Mark the relationship of the drum to the axle flange for retinstallation.
4. Ensure parking brake is released and remove the drum.
5. If necessary, tap the outer rim of the drum gently with a rubber mallet and/or back off automatic brake adjuster to aid in drum removal.
6. Installation is the reverse of the removal procedure. Be sure to align all marks made earlier.

Brake Shoes

REMOVAL & INSTALLATION

1. Raise and support the vehicle safely.
2. Mark and remove the tire and wheel assembly and the brake drum.
3. Using the proper tool, remove the return springs. Remove the hold-down springs and pins.
4. Remove the lever pivot. Lift up on the actuator lever and remove the actuator link.

5. Remove the actuator lever, pawl and lever return spring.
6. Remove the shoe guide, parking brake strut and strut spring.
7. Remove the shoe and lining assemblies, after disconnecting the parking brake cable.
7. Remove the adjusting screw assembly and spring. Unhook the parking brake lever tab from the shoe slot.
To install:
8. Replace any worn or heat stressed parts and lubricate slide points on the backing plate and the adjusting screw.
9. Install the parking brake lever tab into the shoe slot and install the adjusting screw assembly and spring.
10. Attach the parking brake cable and install the shoe and lining assemblies.
11. Spread the shoes sufficiently to install the parking brake strut and strut spring. The end of the strut without the spring engages the parking brake lever and shoe. The end with the spring engages the opposite shoe and lining.
12. Install the shoe guide, the pawl, the actuator lever and the lever return spring.
13. Install the shoe hold-down pins, the lever pivot and the hold-down springs.
14. Install the actuator link on the anchor pin, then hold the actuator lever up and install the link into the lever.
15. Install the shoe return springs and adjust brake shoes as follows:
   a. Measure the drum inside diameter using tool J–21177–A or equivalent brake shoe setting gauge.
   b. Turn the star wheel adjusting

screw and adjust the shoe and lining assembly to be 0.050 inch (1.27mm) less than the inside drum diameter for each rear wheel.
16. Align the marks made earlier and install wheel and tire assemblies.
17. Lower and roadtest the vehicle, checking for proper brake operation.

Wheel Cylinder

REMOVAL & INSTALLATION

1. Raise and support the vehicle safely.
2. Mark and remove the tire and wheel assembly and the brake drum.
3. Remove the brake shoes or components, if required.
4. Disconnect plug the brake line at the wheel cylinder and plug the line to prevent fluid contamination or loss.
5. Remove the wheel cylinder links from the wheel cylinder.
6. Remove the wheel cylinder retaining bolts and remove the wheel cylinder from its mounting.

To install:
7. Position the wheel cylinder assembly in place and install the attaching bolts. Tighten the attaching bolts to 13 ft. lbs. (18 Nm).
8. Unplug and connect the inlet tube to the wheel cylinder. Tighten the fitting to 12 ft. lbs. (17 Nm).
9. Install the brake shoes or components, if removed.
10. Align the marks made earlier and install the brake drum and the wheel and tire assembly.
11. Bleed the wheel cylinder and lower the vehicle.

1. Return spring
2. Return spring
3. Hold down spring
4. Lever pivot
5. Hold down pin
6. Actuator link
7. Actuator lever
8. Pawl
9. Lever return spring
10. Shoe guide
11. Parking brake
12. Strut spring
13. Primary shoe
14. Secondary shoe
15. Adjusting screw spring
16. Parking brake lever
17. Backing plate
18. Adjusting screw assembly
19. Anchor pin

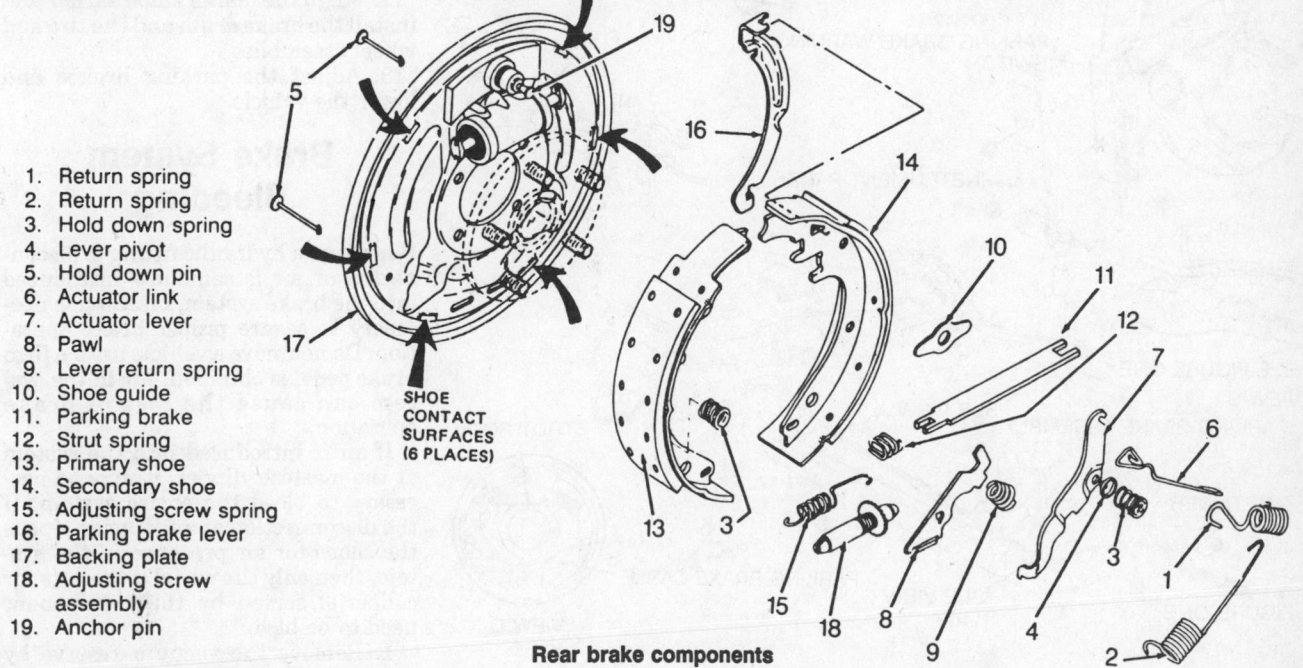

Rear brake components

Parking Brake Cable

ADJUSTMENT

1. Be sure the rear brakes are properly adjusted before adjusting the parking brake. Check the parking brake linkage for the free movement of all the cables. Lubricate or replace, as necessary.

2. Depress the parking brake pedal ¼ stroke or 3 ratchet clicks.

3. Raise and support the vehicle safely.

4. Before attempting to turn the adjusting nut, clean and lubricate the exposed threads of the adjusting rod. Then tighten the adjusting nut until the right rear wheel can just be turned rearward with 2 hands but cannot be turned forward.

5. When the parking brake is released the wheels should turn freely with no brake shoe drag.

REMOVAL & INSTALLATION

Front Cable

NOTE: As required, raise and lower the vehicle to gain access to the components. Be sure to safely support the vehicle at all times.

1. Release the parking brake.

2. Remove the equalizer nut and separate the cable stud from the equalizer.

3. Loosen the adjuster nut and disconnect the front cable from the connector. Compress the cable retainer fingers and loosen the assembly at the frame.

4. Remove the cable at the pedal assembly. Remove the cable end from the parking brake assembly clevis.

5. Pull the cable through the hole in the frame and remove it from the vehicle.

To install:

6. Insert the cable through the hole in the body. Install the cable end into the clevis in the pedal assembly and install the cable conduit at the pedal assembly.

7. Install the cable grommet into the hole in the body.

8. Insert the cable through the hole in the frame and install the cable conduit at the frame.

9. Connect the cable to the left rear cable at the "C" shaped connector. Connect the cable stud at the equalizer and install the nut.

10. Adjust the parking brakes and lower the vehicle.

Rear Cable

1. Release the parking brake, raise and support the vehicle safely.

2. Mark and remove the tire and wheel assembly and brake drum for the cable being replaced.

3. Remove the equalizer nut and the retainer. If applicable, separate the equalizer from the right rear cable stud.

4. If applicable, remove the end of the left rear cable from the cable connector and equalizer.

5. If removing the right rear cable, remove the clip retaining the cable to the axle housing. Pull the cable rearward and remove it from the bracket.

6. Remove the cable from the brake backing plate by compressing the multiple prong retainer with a suitable clamp. Remove the pawl spring and pawl lever from the actuating lever.

7. Remove the cable end from the operating lever and remove the cable from the backing plate.

To install:

8. Route the cable end through the rear of the backing plate and install to the operating lever. Install the pawl lever and pawl spring.

9. Pull on the front end of the cable from the other side of the backing plate and check for proper cable operation. The cable should not bind.

10. If installing the left cable, route the cable over the top of the left rear suspension lower control arm, insert the cable through the hole in the equalizer bracket securing it with a clip. Install the left hand cable into the "C" shaped connector.

11. If installing the right cable, route the cable out the rear exit hole on the backing plate, along the right rear axle tube, across the axle cover, over the left axle tube to the anchor hole on the left lower front control arm bracket. Install the right rear cable in the clip on the right rear spring seat and the rear axle cover at the 12 o'clock position. Connect the cable stud to the equalizer bracket.

12. Align the marks made earlier and install the brake drum and the tire and wheel assemblies.

13. Adjust the parking brakes and lower the vehicle.

Brake System Bleeding

Whenever a hydraulic fitting is disconnected or air is somehow introduced into the brake system, bleeding is necessary to assure proper brake operation. Do not move a vehicle until a firm brake pedal is obtained. Air in the system can cause the loss of brake operation.

If air is introduced into the system at the master cylinder, it may be necessary to bleed the entire system. If the disconnection of a fitting or pipe is the cause for air presence in the system, then only the wheel cylinder(s) or caliper(s) served by that component need to be bled.

1. Remove the vacuum reserve by

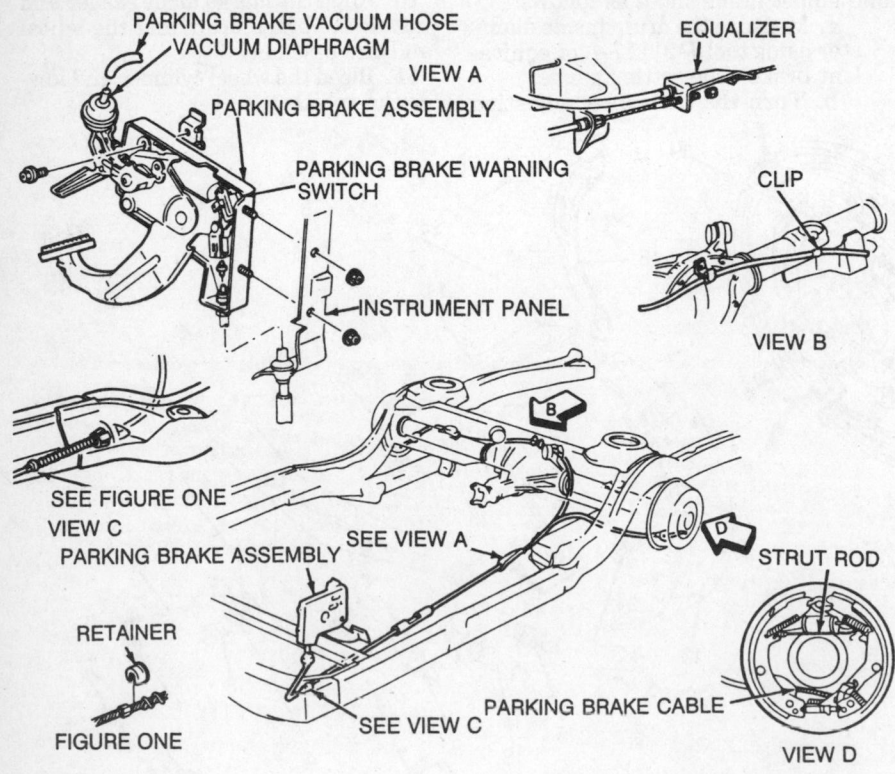

PARKING BRAKE VACUUM HOSE
VACUUM DIAPHRAGM
VIEW A
PARKING BRAKE ASSEMBLY
PARKING BRAKE WARNING SWITCH
EQUALIZER
CLIP
INSTRUMENT PANEL
VIEW B
SEE FIGURE ONE
VIEW C
PARKING BRAKE ASSEMBLY
SEE VIEW A
STRUT ROD
RETAINER
FIGURE ONE
SEE VIEW C
PARKING BRAKE CABLE
VIEW D

applying the brakes several times, with the engine **OFF**.

2. Fill the master cylinder reservoir with brake fluid and keep it at least half full of fluid at all times during the bleeding operation.

3. If the master cylinder is known or suspected to have air in the bore, bleed the unit before wheel cylinders or calipers, in the following manner:

a. Disconnect the forward brake line connection at the master cylinder.

b. Allow brake fluid to fill the master cylinder bore until it begins to flow from the forward brake line port at the master cylinder.

c. Connect the forward brake line to the master cylinder and tighten.

d. Have an assistant depress the brake pedal slowly 1 time and hold. Loosen the forward brake line connection at the master cylinder to purge air from the bore. Tighten the connection and have the assistant release the pedal slowly. Wait 15 seconds and repeat the sequence, including the 15 second pause, until all air is removed from the bore. Ensure brake fluid does not contact any painted surface.

e. Repeat the procedure at the rear master cylinder brake line connection.

f. If it is known that the calipers and wheel cylinders do not contain any air, it will not be necessary to bleed them.

4. If it is necessary to bleed all of the wheel cylinders and calipers, follow the proper sequence: Right rear, left rear, right front, left front.

5. Bleed individual wheel cylinders or calipers, only after all air is removed from the master cylinder, as follows:

a. Place a suitable bleeder wrench over the bleeder valve.

b. Attach a clear tube over the bleeder valve and allow the tube to hang, submerged in a clear container partially filled with brake fluid.

c. Have an assistant depress the brake pedal slowly 1 time and hold. Loosen the bleeder valve to purge the air from the cylinder. Tighten the bleeder screw and have the assistant slowly release the pedal. Wait 15 seconds and repeat the sequence, including the 15 second pause, until all air is removed.

d. It may be necessary to repeat the sequence 10 or more times to remove all of the air.

NOTE: Rapid pumping of the brake pedal pushes the master cylinder secondary piston down the bore in a way that makes it difficult to bleed the rear side of the system.

6. Check the brake pedal for spongi-ness and the red brake warning light for an indication of unbalanced pressure. Repeat the bleeding procedure to correct either of these conditions.

Anti-Lock Brake System Service

PRECAUTIONS

Failure to observe the following precautions may result in system damage or failure which could result in bodily injury.

● Before performing electric arc welding on the vehicle, disconnect the Electronic Brake Control Module (EBCM) and the hydraulic modulator connectors.

● When performing painting work on the vehicle, do not expose the Electronic Brake Control Module (EBCM) to temperatures in excess of 185°F (85°C) for longer than 2 hours. The system may be exposed to temperatures up to 200°F (95°C) for less than 15 minutes.

● Never disconnect or connect the Electronic Brake Control Module (EBCM) or hydraulic modulator connectors with the ignition switch **ON**.

● Never disassemble any component of the Anti-Lock Brake System (ABS) which is designated non-servicable; the component must be replaced as an assembly.

● When filling the master cylinder, always use Delco Supreme 11 brake fluid or equivalent, which meets DOT-3 specifications; petroleum base fluid will destroy the rubber parts.

RELIEVING ANTI-LOCK BRAKE SYSTEM PRESSURE

When servicing and bleeding ABS components, follow normal manual or pressure bleeding procedures. Although the ABS system has the ability to increase, decrease or hold brake line pressure, the hydraulic modulator cannot increase the pressure above that which is transmitted by the master cylinder. Special service procedures for bleeding the brake system with a hydraulic modulator are not required.

Hydraulic Modulator

REMOVAL & INSTALLATION

1. Disconnect the negative battery cable.

2. Remove the left front radiator brace and the air cleaner intake hose.

3. Remove the ABS modulator relay cover. Disconnect the modulator 12-pin connector and ground strap.

4. Disconnect all brake line connections at the modulator assembly and plug the lines to prevent fluid contamination and loss.

5. Remove the modulator mounting nuts and remove the modulator assembly from the bracket.

6. Remove the insulators from the modulator.

To install:

7. Install the insulators onto the modulator and position the modulator in the mounting bracket. Secure the modulator with the nuts and tighten to 8 ft. lbs. (11 Nm).

8. Unplug and connect all brake lines to the modulator. Tighten the fittings to 9 ft. lbs. (12 Nm).

9. Connect the modulator connector and ground strap. Install the ABS relay cover.

10. Install the air cleaner intake hose and the left front radiator brace.

11. Connect the negative battery cable and bleed the brake system.

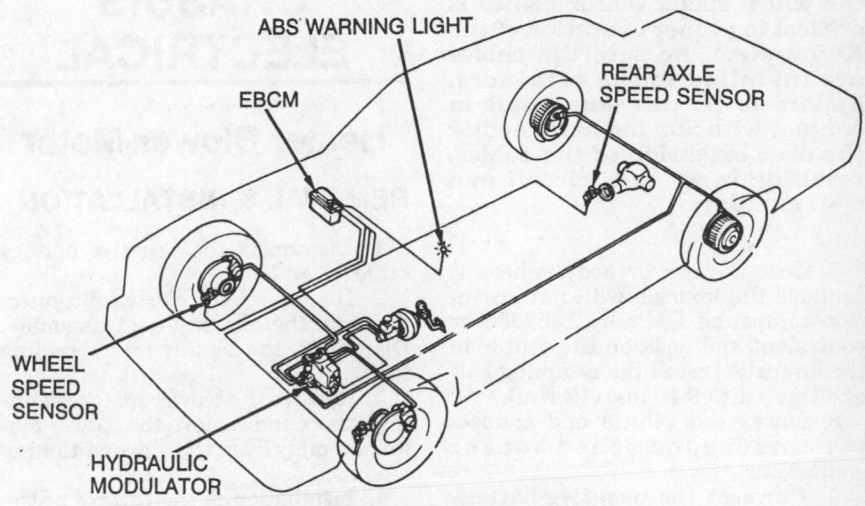

ABS braking system component layout

Electronic Brake Control Module

REMOVAL & INSTALLATION

1. Disconnect the negative battery cable.
2. Remove the passenger side close-out panel and remove the glove box liner.
3. Disconnect the EBCM wire harness connector and remove the EBCM from its retaining bracket.
4. Installation is the reverse of the removal procedure.

Front Wheel Speed Sensor

The speed sensor is non-adjustable, with the sensor gap set at the factory. It is mounted in the steering knuckle and a connector is located underhood near the fenderwell.

REMOVAL & INSTALLATION

1. Disconnect the negative battery cable.
2. Disconnect the sensor connector from under the hood near the fenderwell.
3. Raise and support the vehicle safely.
4. Remove the sensor cable from the retainers.
5. Remove the sensor mounting bolt and remove the sensor from the vehicle.

To install:
6. Route the sensor cable and install in the retainers.

NOTE: Proper installation of the wheel speed sensor cables is critical to proper operation of the ABS system. Be sure the cables are installed in the retainers. Failure to do this may result in contact with moving parts and/or the over extension of the cables, resulting in an open circuit and system failure.

7. Coat the sensor body, where it contacts the knuckle with anti-corrosion compound GM part 1052856 or equivalent and position the sensor in the knuckle. Install the retaining bolt and tighten to 9 ft. lbs. (12 Nm).
8. Lower the vehicle and connect the underhood speed sensor connector.
9. Connect the negative battery cable.

Rear Axle Speed Sensor

The rear axle speed sensor is located in the axle carrier housing. It is connected to the EBCM via a jumper harness which runs from the sensor connector to the ABS harness, under the hood, near the left fenderwell. It is non-adjustable and set at the factory.

REMOVAL & INSTALLATION

1. Disconnect the negative battery cable. Raise and support the vehicle safely.
2. Disconnect the sensor connector and remove the sensor cable from the retainer brackets.
3. Remove the sensor mounting bolt. Remove the sensor, plastic spacer and the O-ring from the vehicle.

To install:
4. Position the O-ring, plastic spacer and the sensor in the rear axle carrier housing and install the mounting bolt. Tighten the bolt to 9 ft. lbs. (12 Nm).
5. Install the rear speed sensor cable in the retainers.

NOTE: Proper installation of the wheel speed sensor cable is critical to proper operation of the ABS system. Be sure the cables are installed in the retainers. Failure to do this may result in contact with moving parts and/or the over extension of the cable, resulting in an open circuit.

6. Connect the wheel speed sensor connector and lower the vehicle.
7. Connect the negative battery cable.

CHASSIS ELECTRICAL

Heater Blower Motor

REMOVAL & INSTALLATION

1. Disconnect the negative battery cable.
2. Disconnect the electrical connector from the blower motor assembly. Disconnect the blower motor cooling tube.
3. Remove the blower motor retaining screws and remove the blower motor assembly from the air conditioning module.
4. Installation is the reverse of the removal procedure.

Windshield Wiper Motor

REMOVAL & INSTALLATION

1. Disconnect the negative battery cable.
2. Remove the cowl screen.
3. Reach through the opening and disengage the transmission drive link from the wiper crank arm by loosening the nuts.
4. Disconnect the electrical wiring and washer hoses.
5. Remove the bolts that secure the wiper/washer unit to the firewall.
6. Remove the entire assembly.

To install:
7. Be sure the wiper crank arm is in the park position and install the assembly with the attaching bolts.
8. Connect the electrical wiring and the washer hoses.
9. Reach through the opening and engage the transmission drive link to the wiper crank arm. Tighten the retaining nuts.
10. Install the cowl screen and connect the negative battery cable.

Windshield Wiper Switch

REMOVAL & INSTALLATION

1989

1. Disconnect the negative battery cable.
2. Loosen the set screw in the left climate control outlet door knob and remove the knob.
3. Remove the left climate control air outlet grille with a suitable tool.
4. Remove the 6 left trim panel attaching screws. One screw is located inside the left of the air conditioning outlet grille opening.
5. Remove the lower steering column cover and 4 attaching screws.
6. Disconnect the steering column seal from lower surface and remove the trim plate.
7. Remove the wiper switch mounting screws. Remove the switch and disconnect the electrical connector.
8. Installation is the reverse of the removal procedure.

1990–93

1. Disconnect the negative battery cable.
2. With a $\frac{1}{16}$ in Allen wrench, loosen the screw on the bottom of the left climate control outlet door knob and remove the knob.
3. Remove the lower steering column cover and the 2 retaining screws.

4. Remove the 6 retaining screws from the trim panel and remove the panel. To facilitate panel removal, depress the brake pedal and move the shift lever out of the **P** position. Remove the panel and place the shift lever back into **P**.

5. Remove the 2 retaining screws from the wiper switch.

6. Disconnect the electrical connector from the wiper switch and remove the switch from the vehicle.

To install:

7. Connect the electrical connection to the switch and position the switch in place.

8. Install the 2 switch mounting screws.

9. Position the left side trim plate and install the 6 attaching screws.

10. Install the outlet grille directional knob and secure with the attaching screw.

11. Attach the lower column cover and screws.

12. Connect the negative battery cable.

Instrument Cluster

REMOVAL & INSTALLATION

1. Disconnect the negative battery cable.

2. Remove the left side trim panel by removing the left climate control outlet knob, the lower steering column cover and the left side trim panel attaching screws. For 1989 vehicles, it will be necessary to remove the left climate control outlet grille to expose 1 of the trim panel attaching screws and it may be necessary to remove the lower steering column seal.

3. To ease removal of the trim panel, depress the brake pedal and move the shift lever from the **P** position.

4. With the shift lever in the **P** position, remove the shift indicator cable and clip from the steering column.

5. Remove the cluster assembly retaining screws. Carefully pull the cluster outward and disengage the speedometer cable, if equipped. Disconnect all electrical connections.

6. Place the shift lever in the **L** and the tilt wheel in the lower position. Remove the cluster assembly from the dash.

To install:

7. Hold the cluster near position in the housing and connect the electrical connecter and, if equipped, the speedometer cable.

8. Install the cluster with the attaching screws. Set the shift lever in the **N** position and install the indicator clip with cable to the steering column.

Adjust the clip until the pointer is in the **N** position. Move the gear selector over the entire range to be sure that full indicator travel is possible.

9. Install the left side trim plate, attaching screws, lower steering column cover and the left climate control outlet knob. For 1989 vehicles remember to install the left climate control outlet grille and the lower steering column seal.

10. Connect the negative battery cable.

Radio

The radio for 1989 vehicles is a self contained unit including the receiver, controls and tape deck. For 1990–93 vehicles, the radio consists of 2 components. The visible component is an in-dash control assembly which contains the controls, displays, the cassette deck and, if applicable, the compact disc player. A separate receiver unit is located under the dash and contains the radio components, antenna relay driver and the speaker connections.

REMOVAL & INSTALLATION

1989

1. Disconnect the negative battery cable.

2. Remove the center air conditioning outlets, using tool J–24612 or equivalent, to access the center panel retaining screws.

3. Once the outlets are removed, remove the center panel retaining screws.

4. Remove the radio assembly retaining knobs, anti-rattle springs and radio nuts as required.

5. Remove the remaining trim plate screws and remove the trim plate from the vehicle.

6. Remove the radio retaining screws and pull the radio assembly forward. Disconnect the 3 electrical connections and remove the radio assembly from the vehicle.

7. Installation is the reverse of the removal procedure.

1990–93

1. Disconnect the negative battery cable.

2. Loosen the set screws on the bottom of each air conditioning vent levers heads and remove the heads by pulling forward.

3. Remove the 2 phillips head screws from the bottom trim plate. Lower the plate out and down.

4. Remove the black screw from the top center and remove the 2 screws from the bottom ends of the radio control assembly brackets.

5. Slide the radio control assembly

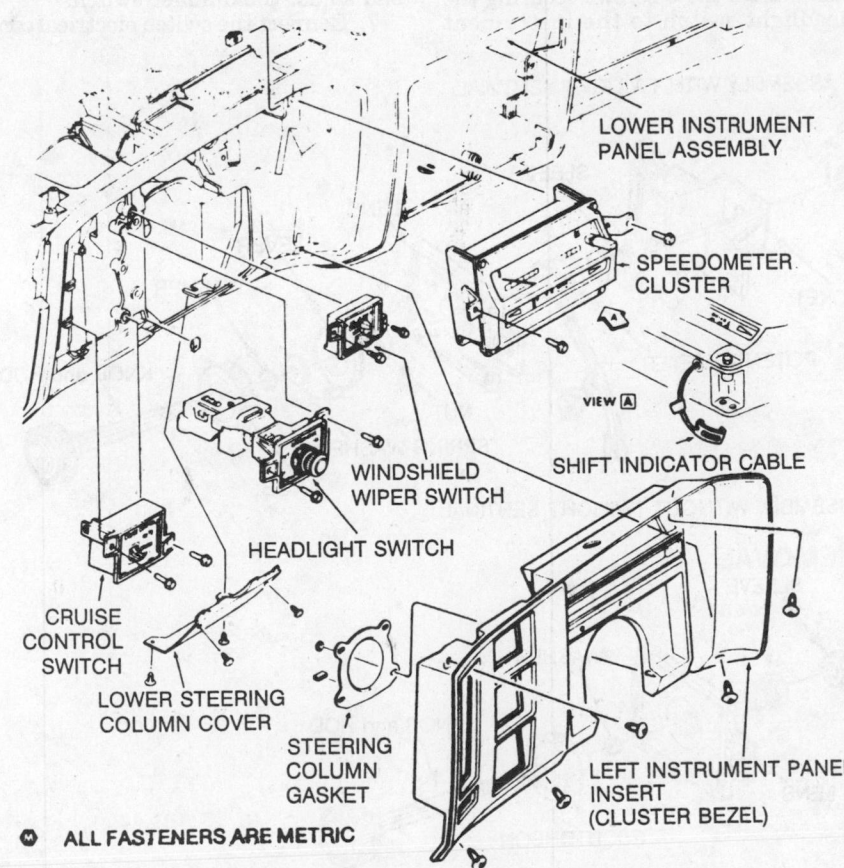

LOWER INSTRUMENT PANEL ASSEMBLY

SPEEDOMETER CLUSTER

VIEW Ⓐ

SHIFT INDICATOR CABLE

WINDSHIELD WIPER SWITCH

HEADLIGHT SWITCH

CRUISE CONTROL SWITCH

LOWER STEERING COLUMN COVER

STEERING COLUMN GASKET

LEFT INSTRUMENT PANEL INSERT (CLUSTER BEZEL)

Ⓜ **ALL FASTENERS ARE METRIC**

Instrument cluster and related components

forward, carefully maneuvering the lower bracket over the mirror switch.

6. Disconnect the electrical connectors.

7. If installing an exchange radio, remove the plastic locating pin and clip stud from the rear of the assembly and remove the brackets.

To install:

8. If removed, install the plastic locating pin, clip and stud and the mounting brackets to the new radio control assembly.

9. Connect the electrical connectors to the assembly. Install the assembly carefully into place making sure to maneuver the unit over the mirror switch and to route the harness with the connectors down and to the left of the control head.

10. Install the bracket retaining screws and reposition the center trim plate.

11. Install the trim plate retaining screws and the air conditioning vent lever heads.

12. Connect the negative battery cable.

Headlight Switch

REMOVAL & INSTALLATION

1. Disconnect the negative battery cable.

2. Remove the left side trim panel by removing the left climate control outlet knob, the lower steering column cover and the left side trim panel attaching screws. For 1989 vehicles it will be necessary to remove the left climate control outlet grille to expose 1 of the trim panel attaching screws and it may be necessary to remove the lower steering column seal.

3. Remove the screws securing the headlight switch to the instrument panel.

4. Remove the cruise control switch retaining screws, if equipped, and pull the switch forward slightly to better access the headlight switch.

5. Disconnect the 2 piece connector from the headlight switch.

6. Remove the switch rod by depressing the retaining button while pulling the switch rod from the switch. Disconnect the twilight sentinel wiring, if equipped.

7. Remove the switch by unthreading the retaining nut from the front of the lens housing.

To install:

8. Thread the switch onto the lens housing and install the rod into the switch.

9. Connect the twilight sentinal wiring, if equipped and attach the 2 piece electrical connector to the headlight switch.

10. Install the 3 screws securing the headlight switch to the instrument panel. Reposition and install the cruise control switch, if applicable.

11. Install the left side trim plate, attaching screws, lower steering column cover and the left climate control outlet knob. For 1989 vehicles remember to install the left climate control outlet grille and the lower steering column seal.

12. Connect the negative battery cable and check for proper switch function.

Dimmer Switch

REMOVAL & INSTALLATION

1. Disconnect negative battery cable and set the ignition in the **LOCK** position.

2. Remove left sound insulator and the lower column cover as necessary to access the steering column.

3. Remove 2 nuts securing steering column to upper mounting bracket.

4. Carefully lower and support the steering column.

5. Remove the 2 screws securing the ignition switch and the dimmer switch. Disconnect electrical connection and remove the dimmer switch.

To install:

6. Install the switch to the steering column with the actuator rod in place and adjust the dimmer switch.

7. Connect the switch electrical con-

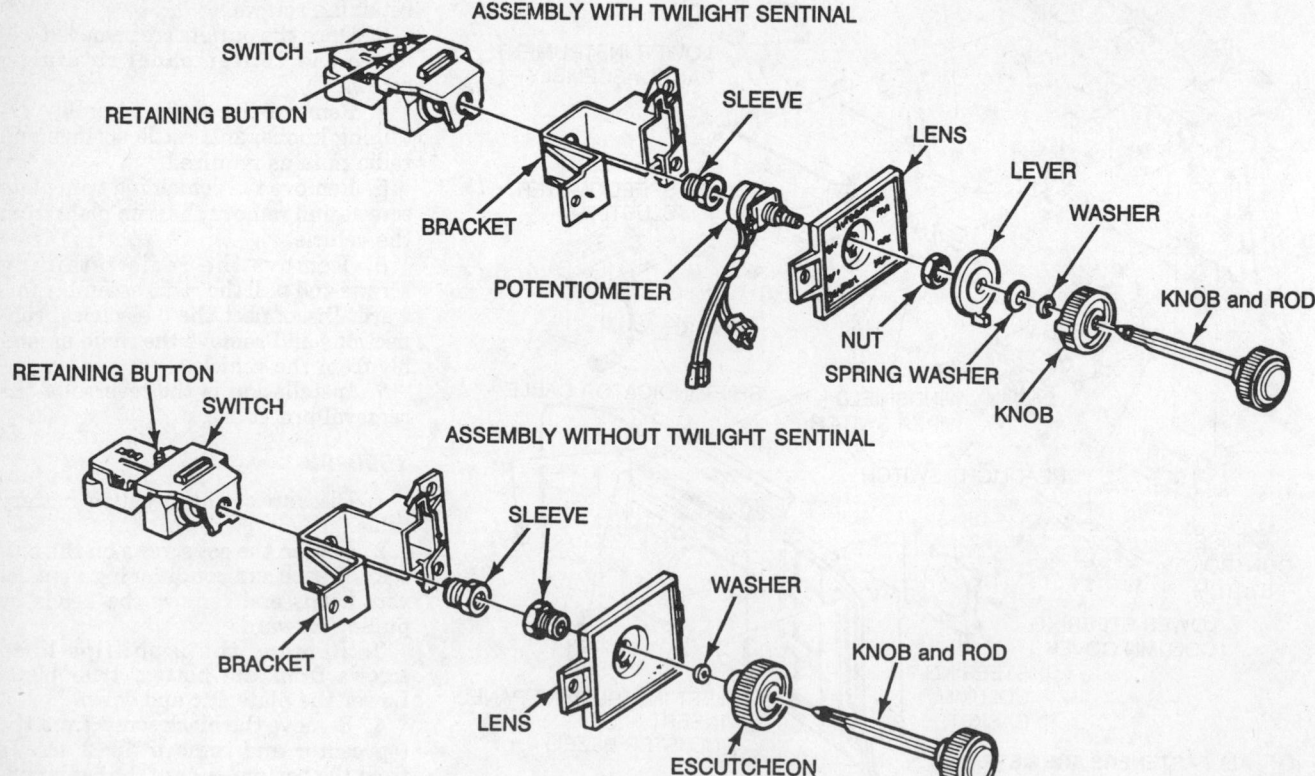

Exploded view of headlight switch assemblies

nection. Raise the steering column into position and attach the securing nuts.

8. Install the left sound insulator and the lower steering column cover as necessary.

9. Connect the negative battery cable and check switch operation.

ADJUSTMENT

1. Depress the switch slightly to insert the proper alignment tool ($^3/_{32}$ inch drill bit) through the locating hole.

2. Loosen the adjustment screws attaching the dimmer switch mounting bracket.

3. Slide the dimmer switch firmly against the actuator arm to remove all lash and tighten both adjusting screws.

Turn Signal Switch

REMOVAL & INSTALLATION

1. Disconnect the negative battery cable.

2. Remove the steering wheel.

3. Remove the ignition lock cylinder.

4. Remove the hazard switch and screw from the column.

5. Unscrew and remove the tilt column lever, if applicable.

6. Remove the turn signal lever by pulling outward and off the column.

7. Remove the lock housing cover and screws.

8. Remove the lower column cover and fuse panel cover to gain access to the switch electrical connector.

9. Disconnect the electrical harness connector and the wiring protector.

10. Remove the turn signal switch mounting screws.

11. If the switch is known to be bad, cut the wires and discard the switch. Tape the connector of the new switch to the old wires, and pull the new harness down through the steering column while removing the old wires.

12. If the original switch is to be reused, wrap tape around the connector and pull the harness up through the column. It may be helpful to attach a length of mechanic's wire to the harness connector before pulling it up through the column to assist with installation.

13. After freeing the switch wiring protector from its mounting, pull the turn signal switch straight up and remove the switch, switch harness and the connector from the column.

To install:

14. Pull the switch harness connector through the column, either with the old switch wires or the length of

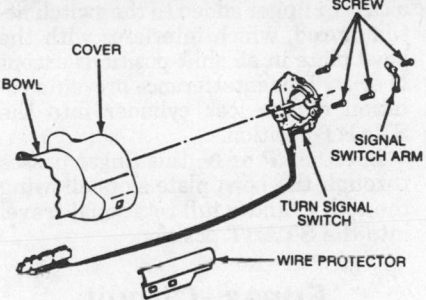

Turn signal switch assembly

mechanic's wire which was attached to the old connector during removal.

15. Install the switch and attaching screws to the column.

16. Connect the electrical harness connector and the wiring protector.

17. Install the lock housing cover and screws. Install the hazard switch to the column.

18. Install the turn signal and tilt column levers, as applicable.

19. Install the ignition lock cylinder and the steering wheel.

20. Connect the negative battery cable and check switch operation.

Ignition Lock

REMOVAL & INSTALLATION

1. Disconnect the negative battery cable.

2. Remove the steering wheel.

3. Remove the spacers, the steering shaft bumper, and the plastic retainer, as applicable.

4. Install a suitable lock plate tool onto the steering shaft. Tighten the tool to compress the lock plate and the spring. Remove the lock retainer.

5. Remove the lock plate, carrier assembly and the upper bearing spring from the upper steering shaft.

6. Insert the key into the ignition switch and turn the ignition switch to the RUN position.

7. Remove the key warning buzzer switch and retaining clip.

8. Remove the ignition cylinder retaining screw located inside the lock housing cover.

9. Remove the lock cylinder from the column.

To install:

10. Install the lock cylinder to the steering column and install the lock cylinder retaining screw.

11. Install the key warning buzzer and retaining clip, with the cylinder still in the run position.

12. Install the upper bearing spring, the carrier assembly and the lock plate, from the upper steering shaft.

13. Using a suitable lock plate tool, compress the lock plate and the spring and install the lock retainer.

14. Install the plastic retainer, the steering shaft bumper and the spacers, as applicable.

15. Install the steering wheel.

16. Connect the negative battery cable.

Ignition Switch

REMOVAL & INSTALLATION

1. Disconnect negative battery cable and set the ignition in the LOCK position.

2. Remove left sound insulator and the lower column cover as necessary to access the steering column.

3. Remove 2 nuts securing steering column to upper mounting bracket.

4. Carefully lower and support the steering column.

5. Remove the 2 screws securing the ignition switch and the dimmer switch. Disconnect electrical connection and remove the ignition switch.

To install:

6. Install the dimmer and ignition switches to the steering column and connect the ignition switch electrical connection. Adjust the dimmer switch as necessary.

7. Assemble the ignition switch on the actuator rod and adjust it to the LOCK position.

8. If equipped with a standard column, hold the switch actuating rod stationary with while moving the switch toward the bottom of the column until it reaches the end of its travel, which is the ACC position. Back off 2 detents to the right, which is the OFF/UNLOCK position, then with the key also in the OFF/UNLOCK position, tighten the switch mounting screws to 35 inch lbs.

9. If equipped with a tilt wheel, hold the switch actuating rod stationary with one hand while moving the switch toward the upper end of column until it reaches the end of its travel, which is the ACC position. Back off 1 detent and with the key in LOCK position, tighten the switch mounting screws to 35 inch lbs.

10. Raise the steering column into position and attach the securing nuts.

11. Install the left sound insulator and the lower steering column support, as necessary.

12. Connect the negative battery cable and check that the starting system will only start in the P and N positions.

Stoplight Switch

ADJUSTMENT

1. Place the stoplight switch clip in

the bore on the pedal assembly bracket.

2. With the brake pedal depressed, insert the switch well into the clip. Clicks can be heard as the threaded portion of the switch is pushed through the clip towards the brake pedal.

3. Pull the brake pedal rearward just enough to reach the normal released position. The switch will move in the clip automatically adjusting the switch. There should be free-play between the pedal and switch bodies when the pedal is pulled toward the released direction from the unapplied position.

4. When the switch is properly adjusted, no clicks should be heard and the stoplights should not remain on when the pedal is pulled upward. Nominal actuation of stop lamp contacts is at $5/16$-$11/16$ in. (7.5–17mm) of pedal travel measured at the centerline of the brake pedal pad.

5. Finish installation and verify that the stoplights operate correctly.

6. If necessary, repeat step 3 and adjust the switch within the clip to correct the adjustment.

REMOVAL & INSTALLATION

NOTE: The cruise control release switch and the stoplight switch are adjusted or replaced in the same manner.

1. Disconnect the negative battery cable. Remove the left sound insulator and the lower steering column cover, as required.

2. Disconnect the wire harness connector from the switch. Remove the switch from the clip and then remove the clip from the bracket.

To install:

3. Place the clip in its bore on the bracket.

4. With the brake pedal depressed, insert the switch into the clip and depress the switch body. Clicks can be heard as the threaded portion of the switch is pushed through the clip towards the brake pedal.

5. Adjust the switch, connect the negative battery cable and check for proper switch operation.

6. Install the left sound insulator and the lower steering column cover, as necessary.

Neutral Safety Switch

These vehicles incorporate a mechanical neutral start system. This system relies on a mechanical block, rather than the starter safety switch to prevent starting the engine in other than P or N positions.

The mechanical block is achieved by a cast in finger added to the switch actuator rod, which interferes with the bowl plate in all shift positions except N or P. This interference prevents rotation of the lock cylinder into the START position.

In either P or N, this finger passes through the bowl plate slots allowing the lock cylinder full rotational travel into the START position.

Fuses, Circuit Breakers and Relays

LOCATION

Fusible Links

Fusible links are used to prevent major wire harness damage in the event of a short circuit or an overload condition in the wiring circuits which are normally not fused, due to carrying high amperage loads or because of their locations within the wiring harness. Each fusible link is of a fixed value for a specific electrical load and should a link fail, the cause of the failure must be determined and repaired prior to installing a new fusible link of the same value.

Circuit Breakers

Various circuit breakers are located under the instrument panel. In order to gain access to these components, it may be necessary to first remove the under dash padding. Circuit breakers function by creating an open circuit if a short or overload condition occurs within the circuit which might damage other components.

Circuit breakers of 2 types can be found in these vehicles. The standard breaker is used, which will continue to cycle open and closed until the high current is removed. Also used is the Positive Temperature Coefficient (PTC) type breaker which will not reset until the circuit is manually opened by removing voltage from its terminals. The PTC breaker should reset within a few seconds after the open circuit condition is manually created.

Fuse Panel

The fuse panel is located on the left side of the vehicle. It is under the instrument panel assembly. In order to gain access to the fuse panel, it may be necessary to first remove the under dash padding.

Relays

All vehicles use a combination of the following electrical relays in order to function properly.

Air Condition Compressor Control Relay—located on the left side of the firewall in the engine compartment.

Brake Modulator Pump Motor Relay—incorporated into the electronic brake modulator located in left hand front of the engine compartment, ahead of the engine.

Brake Modulator Solenoid Relay—incorporated into the electronic brake modulator located in left hand front of the engine compartment, ahead of the engine.

Defogger Relay—located in the accessory relay panel under the left side dash panel, to the left of the fuse block.

Door Lock Relay—attached to the lower right shroud panel behind the kick panel.

Electronic Level Control Relay—located in the accessory relay panel under the left side dash panel, to the left of the fuse block.

Fuel Pump Relay—located in the accessory relay panel under the left side dash panel, to the left of the fuse block.

Horn Relay—located in the convenience center, under the left side of the dash panel, to the left of the steering column.

Moon Roof Relay—located in the center of the windshield header, to the right of the moon roof actuator assembly.

Over-Voltage Protection Relay—located on the ABS harness near the EBCM under the glove box.

Power Antenna Relay—located in the accessory relay panel under the left side of the dash panel, to the left of the fuse box.

Reverse Light Relay—located in the accessory relay panel under the left side of the dash panel, to the left of the fuse box.

Starter Interrupt Relay—located in the accessory relay panel under the left side of the dash panel, to the left of the fuse box.

Theft Deterrent Relay—located behind the left side of the instrument panel to the right of the steering column.

Wiper/Washer Park and Pulse Relays—incorporated into the wiper/washer assembly on the firewall in the engine compartment.

Computers

LOCATION

ECM

The Electronic Control Module (ECM) is located on the right side of the vehicle. It is positioned in front of the right kick panel.

GM "L" Body
Front Wheel Drive
CHEVROLET—Beretta • Corsica

SPECIFICATIONS

VEHICLE IDENTIFICATION CHART

It is important for servicing and ordering parts to be certain of the vehicle and engine identification. The VIN (vehicle identification number) is a 17 digit number visible through the windshield on the driver's side of the dash and contains the vehicle and engine identification codes. The tenth digit indicates model year and the eighth digit indicates engine code. It can be interpreted as follows:

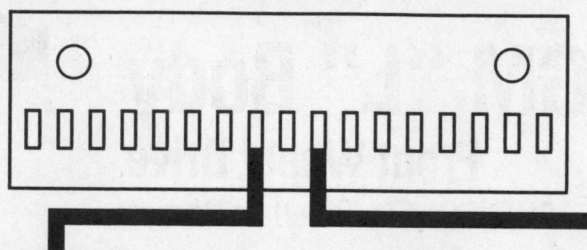

Engine Code							Model Year	
Code	Liters	Cu. In. (cc)	Cyl.	Fuel Sys.	Eng. Mfg.		Code	Year
1	2.0	121 (1983)	4	TBI	Chevrolet		K	1989
G	2.2	133 (2180)	4	TBI	Chevrolet		L	1990
A	2.3	138 (2262)	4	PFI	Chevrolet		M	1991
W	2.8	173 (2835)	6	PFI	Chevrolet		N	1992
T	3.1	191 (3130)	6	PFI	Chevrolet		P	1993
4	2.2	133 (2180)	4	PFI	Chevrolet			

PFI—Port Fuel Injection
TBI—Throttle Body Injection

ENGINE IDENTIFICATION

Year	Model	Engine Displacement Liters (cc)	Engine Series (ID/VIN)	Fuel System	No. of Cylinders	Engine Type
1989	Beretta	2.0 (1983)	1	TBI	4	OHV
	Beretta	2.8 (2835)	W	PFI	6	OHV
	Corcisa	2.0 (1983)	1	TBI	4	OHV
	Corcisa	2.8 (2835)	W	PFI	6	OHV
1990	Beretta	2.2 (2180)	G	TBI	4	OHV
	Beretta	2.3 (2262)	A	PFI	4	OHC
	Beretta	3.1 (3130)	T	PFI	6	OHV
	Corcisa	2.2 (2180)	G	TBI	4	OHV
	Corcisa	3.1 (3130)	T	PFI	6	OHV
1991	Beretta	2.2 (2180)	G	TBI	4	OHV
	Beretta	2.3 (2262)	A	PFI	4	OHC
	Beretta	3.1 (3130)	T	PFI	6	OHV
	Corcisa	2.2 (2180)	G	TBI	4	OHV
	Corcisa	3.1 (3130)	T	PFI	6	OHV
1992-93	Beretta	2.2 (2180)	4	PFI	4	OHV
	Beretta	2.3 (2262)	A	PFI	4	OHC
	Beretta	3.1 (3130)	T	PFI	6	OHV
	Corcisa	2.2 (2180)	4	PFI	4	OHV
	Corcisa	3.1 (3130)	T	PFI	6	OHV

OHC—Overhead Cam
OHV—Overhead Valves

PFI—Port Fuel Injection
TBI—Throttle Body Injection

GENERAL ENGINE SPECIFICATIONS

Year	Engine ID/VIN	Engine Displacement Liters (cc)	Fuel System Type	Net Horsepower @ rpm	Net Torque @ rpm (ft. lbs.)	Bore × Stroke (in.)	Compression Ratio	Oil Pressure @ rpm
1989	1	2.0 (1983)	TBI	90 @ 5600	108 @ 3200	3.500 × 3.150	9.0:1	67–77 @ 1200
	W	2.8 (2835)	PFI	125 @ 4500	160 @ 3600	3.500 × 2.990	8.9:1	50–65 @ 1200
1990	G	2.2 (2180)	TBI	95 @ 5200	120 @ 3200	3.500 × 3.460	9.0:1	63–77 @ 1200
	A	2.3 (2262)	PFI	180 @ 6200	160 @ 5200	3.622 × 3.460	10.0:1	30 @ 2000
	T	3.1 (3130)	PFI	135 @ 4200	180 @ 3600	3.500 × 3.310	8.8:1	50–65 @ 2400
1991	G	2.2 (2180)	TBI	95 @ 5200	120 @ 3200	3.500 × 3.460	9.0:1	63–77 @ 1200
	A	2.3 (2262)	PFI	180 @ 6200	160 @ 5200	3.622 × 3.460	10.0:1	30 @ 2000
	T	3.1 (3130)	PFI	140 @ 4200	185 @ 3200	3.500 × 3.310	8.8:1	50–65 @ 2400
1992–93	4	2.2 (2180)	PFI	110 @ 5200	130 @ 2800	3.500 × 3.460	9.0:1	63–77 @ 1200
	A	2.3 (2262)	PFI	180 @ 6200	160 @ 5200	3.622 × 3.460	10.0:1	30 @ 2000
	T	3.1 (3130)	PFI	140 @ 4200	185 @ 3200	3.500 × 3.310	8.8:1	50–65 @ 2400

NOTE: Horsepower and torque are SAE net figures. They are measured at the rear of the transmission with all accessories installed and operating. Since the figures vary when a given engine is installed in different models, some are representative rather than exact.
PFI—Port Fuel Injection
TBI—Throttle Body Injection

GASOLINE ENGINE TUNE-UP SPECIFICATIONS

Year	Engine ID/VIN	Engine Displacement Liters (cc)	Spark Plugs Gap (in.)	Ignition Timing (deg.) MT	Ignition Timing (deg.) AT	Fuel Pump (psi)	Idle Speed (rpm) MT	Idle Speed (rpm) AT	Valve Clearance In.	Valve Clearance Ex.
1989	1	2.0 (1983)	0.035	①	①	9–13	①	①	Hyd.	Hyd.
	W	2.8 (2835)	0.045	①	①	9–13	①	①	Hyd.	Hyd.
1990	G	2.2 (2180)	0.035	①	①	9–13	①	①	Hyd.	Hyd.
	A	2.3 (2262)	0.035	①	①	②	①	①	Hyd.	Hyd.
	T	3.1 (3130)	0.045	①	①	②	①	①	Hyd.	Hyd.
1991	G	2.2 (2180)	0.035	①	①	9–13	①	①	Hyd.	Hyd.
	A	2.3 (2262)	0.035	①	①	②	①	①	Hyd.	Hyd.
	T	3.1 (3130)	0.045	①	①	②	①	①	Hyd.	Hyd.
1992	4	2.2 (2180)	0.045	①	①	②	①	①	Hyd.	Hyd.
	A	2.3 (2262)	0.035	①	①	②	①	①	Hyd.	Hyd.
	T	3.1 (3130)	0.045	①	①	②	①	①	Hyd.	Hyd.
1993	SEE UNDERHOOD SPECIFICATIONS STICKER

NOTE: The lowest cylinder pressure should be within 75% of the highest cylinder pressure reading. For example, if the highest cylinder is 134 psi, the lowest should be 101. Engine should be at normal operating temperature with throttle valve in the wide open position.
The underhood specifications sticker often reflects tune-up specification changes in production. Sticker figures must be used if they disagree with those in this chart.
Hyd.—Hydraulic
① Ignition timing and idle speed is controlled by the electronic control module. No adjustments are possible
② 1—Connect fuel pressure gauge, engine at normal operating temperature
  2—Turn ignition switch on
  3—After approx. 2 seconds; pressure should read 41–47 psi and hold steady
  4—Start engine and idle; pressure should drop 3–10 psi from static pressure

FIRING ORDERS

NOTE: To avoid confusion, always replace spark plug wires 1 at a time.

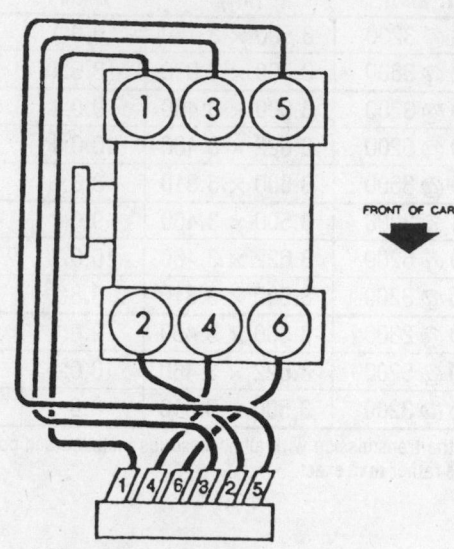

FRONT OF CAR

2.8L and 3.1L Engines
Engine Firing Order: 1–2–3–4–5–6
Distributorless Ignition System

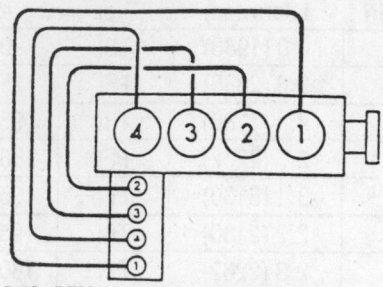

2.0L (VIN 1) and 2.2L (VIN G) Engines
Engine Firing Order: 1–3–4–2
Distributorless Ignition System

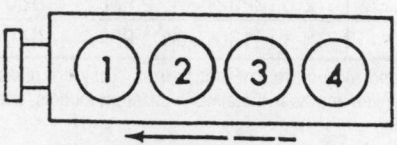

FRONT OF ENGINE

2.3L Engine
Engine Firing Order: 1–3–4–2
Distributorless Ignition System

CAPACITIES

| Year | Model | Engine ID/VIN | Engine Displacement Liters (cc) | Engine Crankcase with Filter (qts.) | Transmission (pts.) | | | Transfer case (pts.) | Drive Axle | | Fuel Tank (gal.) | Cooling System (qts.) |
					4-Spd	5-Spd	Auto.		Front (pts.)	Rear (pts.)		
1989	Beretta	1	2.0 (1983)	4.0①	NA	4.0	8.0②	—	—	—	14	14.1⑤
		W	2.8 (2835)	4.0①	NA	4.0	8.0②	—	—	—	14	⑥
	Corcisa	1	2.0 (1983)	4.0①	NA	4.0	8.0②	—	—	—	14	14.1⑤
		W	2.8 (2835)	4.0①	NA	4.0	8.0②	—	—	—	14	⑥
1990	Beretta	G	2.2 (2180)	4.0①	NA	4.0	14.0③	—	—	—	15.6	④⑦
		A	2.3 (2262)	4.0①	NA	4.0	14.0③	—	—	—	15.6	⑦
		T	3.1 (3130)	4.0①	NA	4.0	14.0③	—	—	—	15.6	⑧
	Corcisa	G	2.2 (2180)	4.0①	NA	4.0	14.0③	—	—	—	15.6	④⑦
		T	3.1 (3130)	4.0①	NA	4.0	14.0③	—	—	—	15.6	⑧
1991	Beretta	G	2.2 (2180)	4.0①	NA	4.2	14.0③	—	—	—	15.6	④⑦
		A	2.3 (2262)	4.0①	NA	4.2	14.0③	—	—	—	15.6	⑦
		T	3.1 (3130)	4.0①	NA	4.2	14.0③	—	—	—	15.6	⑧
	Corcisa	G	2.2 (2180)	4.0①	NA	4.2	14.0③	—	—	—	15.6	④⑦
		T	3.1 (3130)	4.0①	NA	4.2	14.0③	—	—	—	15.6	⑧
1992–93	Beretta	4	2.2 (2180)	4.0①	NA	4.0	8.0②	—	—	—	15.6	9.2
		A	2.3 (2262)	4.0①	NA	4.0	8.0②	—	—	—	15.6	10.3
		T	3.1 (3130)	4.0①	NA	4.0	8.0②	—	—	—	15.6	13.1
	Corcisa	4	2.2 (2180)	4.0①	NA	4.0	8.0②	—	—	—	15.6	9.2
		T	3.1 (3130)	4.0①	NA	4.0	8.0②	—	—	—	15.6	13.1

NA—Not available

① Additional oil will be required if filter is changed.

② This figure is for drain and refill. After a complete overhaul, use 12.0 pts.

③ This figure is for drain and refill, if equipped with HM-3T40, after complete overhaul, use 18.0 pts.

④ Automatic transaxle
With air conditioning—9.5 qts.
Without air conditioning—9.6 qts.

⑤ Without air conditioning—13.1 qts.

⑥ Automatic transaxle
With air conditioning—16.6 qts.
Without air conditioning—16.7 qts.

Manual transaxle
With air conditioning—16.1 qts.
Without air conditioning—16.2 qts.

⑦ Manual transaxle
With or without air conditioning—9.5 qts.

⑧ Automatic transaxle—12.4 qts.
Manual transaxle—11.8 qts.

CAMSHAFT SPECIFICATIONS

All measurements given in inches.

Year	Engine ID/VIN	Engine Displacement Liters (cc)	Journal Diameter					Elevation		Bearing Clearance	Camshaft End Play
			1	2	3	4	5	In.	Ex.		
1989	1	2.0 (1983)	1.867–1.869	1.867–1.869	1.867–1.869	1.867–1.869	1.867–1.869	0.260	0.260	0.001–0.004	NA
	W	2.8 (2835)	1.868–1.881	1.868–1.881	1.868–1.881	1.868–1.881	—	0.263	0.273	0.001–0.004	NA
1990	G	2.2 (2180)	1.867–1.869	1.867–1.869	1.867–1.869	1.867–1.869	1.867–1.869	0.259	0.259	0.001–0.004	NA
	A	2.3 (2262)	1.572–1.573	1.375–1.376	1.375–1.376	1.375–1.376	1.375–1.376	0.410	0.410	0.002–0.004	0.0010–0.0090
	T	3.1 (3130)	1.868–1.881	1.868–1.881	1.868–1.881	1.868–1.881	—	0.263	0.273	0.001–0.004	NA
1991	G	2.2 (2180)	1.867–1.869	1.867–1.869	1.867–1.869	1.867–1.869	1.867–1.869	0.259	0.259	0.001–0.004	NA
	A	2.3 (2262)	1.572–1.573	1.375–1.376	1.375–1.376	1.375–1.376	1.375–1.376	0.410	0.410	0.002–0.004	0.0010–0.0090
	T	3.1 (3130)	1.868–1.881	1.868–1.881	1.868–1.881	1.868–1.881	—	0.263	0.273	0.001–0.004	NA
1992–93	4	2.2 (2180)	1.867–1.869	1.867–1.869	1.867–1.869	1.867–1.869	1.867–1.869	0.259	0.259	0.001–0.004	NA
	A	2.3 (2262)	1.572–1.573	1.375–1.376	1.375–1.376	1.375–1.376	1.375–1.376	0.410	0.410	0.002–0.004	0.0009–0.0088
	T	3.1 (3130)	1.868–1.882	1.868–1.882	1.868–1.882	1.868–1.882	—	0.263	0.273	0.001–0.004	NA

NA—Not available

CRANKSHAFT AND CONNECTING ROD SPECIFICATIONS

All measurements are given in inches.

Year	Engine ID/VIN	Engine Displacement Liters (cc)	Crankshaft				Connecting Rod		
			Main Brg. Journal Dia.	Main Brg. Oil Clearance	Shaft End-play	Thrust on No.	Journal Diameter	Oil Clearance	Side Clearance
1989	1	2.0 (1983)	2.4945–2.4954	0.0006–0.0019	0.002–0.008	1	1.9983–1.9994	0.0010–0.0030	0.0040–0.0150
	W	2.8 (2835)	2.6473–2.6483	0.0016–0.0033	0.002–0.008	4	1.9983–1.9993	0.0010–0.0030	0.0060–0.0170
1990	G	2.2 (2180)	2.4945–2.4954	0.0006–0.0019	0.002–0.007	4	1.9983–1.9994	0.0010–0.0030	0.0040–0.0150
	A	2.3 (2262)	2.0470–2.0480	0.0005–0.0023	0.003–0.009	3	1.8887–1.8897	0.0005–0.0020	0.0059–0.0177
	T	3.1 (3130)	2.6473–2.6483	0.0012–0.0030	0.002–0.008	3	1.9983–1.9994	0.0010–0.0040	0.0140–0.0270
1991	G	2.2 (2180)	2.4945–2.4954	0.0006–0.0019	0.002–0.007	4	1.9983–1.9994	0.0010–0.0030	0.0040–0.0150
	A	2.3 (2262)	2.0470–2.0480	0.0005–0.0023	0.003–0.009	3	1.8887–1.8897	0.0005–0.0020	0.0059–0.0177
	T	3.1 (3130)	2.6473–2.6483	0.0012–0.0030	0.002–0.008	3	1.9983–1.9994	0.0010–0.0040	0.0140–0.0270

CRANKSHAFT AND CONNECTING ROD SPECIFICATIONS

All measurements are given in inches.

Year	Engine ID/VIN	Engine Displacement Liters (cc)	Crankshaft				Connecting Rod		
			Main Brg. Journal Dia.	Main Brg. Oil Clearance	Shaft End-play	Thrust on No.	Journal Diameter	Oil Clearance	Side Clearance
1992-93	4	2.2 (2180)	2.4945–2.4954	0.0006–0.0019	0.002–0.007	4	1.9983–1.9994	0.0010–0.0030	0.0040–0.0150
	A	2.3 (2262)	2.0470–2.0480	0.0005–0.0023	0.003–0.009	3	1.8887–1.8897	0.0005–0.0020	0.0059–0.0177
	T	3.1 (3130)	2.6473–2.6483	0.0012–0.0030	0.002–0.008	3	1.9983–1.9994	0.0010–0.0040	0.0140–0.0270

VALVE SPECIFICATIONS

Year	Engine ID/VIN	Engine Displacement Liters (cc)	Seat Angle (deg.)	Face Angle (deg.)	Spring Test Pressure (lbs. @ in.)	Spring Installed Height (in.)	Stem-to-Guide Clearance (in.)		Stem Diameter (in.)	
							Intake	Exhaust	Intake	Exhaust
1989	1	2.0 (1983)	46	45	208–222① @ 1.22	1.61②	0.0011–0.0026	0.0014–0.0030	NA	NA
	W	2.8 (2835)	46	45	215① @ 1.29	1.70②	0.0010–0.0027	0.0010–0.0027	NA	NA
1990	G	2.2 (2180)	46	45	208–222① @ 1.22	1.61②	0.0011–0.0026	0.0014–0.0030	NA	NA
	A	2.3 (2262)	45	44	193–207① @ 1.04	1.44②	0.0010–0.0027	0.0015–0.0032	0.274–0.275	0.274–0.275
	T	3.1 (3130)	46	45	90①	1.60②	0.0010–0.0027	0.0010–0.0027	NA	NA
1991	G	2.2 (2180)	46	45	208–222① @ 1.22	1.61②	0.0011–0.0026	0.0014–0.0031	NA	NA
	A	2.3 (2262)	46	45	193–207① @ 1.04	1.44②	0.0010–0.0027	0.0015–0.0032	0.274–0.275	0.274–0.275
	T	3.1 (3130)	46	45	215① @ 1.29	1.57②	0.0010–0.0027	0.0010–0.0027	NA	NA
1992-93	4	2.2 (2180)	46	45	225–233① @ 1.25	1.64②	0.0011–0.0026	0.0014–0.0031	NA	NA
	A	2.3 (2262)	46	45	193–207① @ 1.04	1.44②	0.0010–0.0027	0.0015–0.0032	0.274–0.275	0.274–0.275
	T	3.1 (3130)	46	45	215① @ 1.29	1.57②	0.0010–0.0027	0.0010–0.0027	NA	NA

NA—Not available
① With valve open
② With valve closed

PISTON AND RING SPECIFICATIONS

All measurements are given in inches.

Year	Engine ID/VIN	Engine Displacement Liters (cc)	Piston Clearance	Ring Gap			Ring Side Clearance		
				Top Compression	Bottom Compression	Oil Control	Top Compression	Bottom Compression	Oil Control
1989	1	2.0 (1983)	0.0010–0.0022	0.010–0.020	0.010–0.020	0.010–0.050	0.001–0.003	0.001–0.003	0.0080
	W	2.8 (2835)	0.0009–0.0022	0.010–0.020	0.010–0.020	0.020–0.050	0.001–0.003	0.001–0.003	0.0080

PISTON AND RING SPECIFICATIONS

All measurements are given in inches.

| Year | Engine ID/VIN | Engine Displacement Liters (cc) | Piston Clearance | Ring Gap | | | Ring Side Clearance | | |
				Top Compression	Bottom Compression	Oil Control	Top Compression	Bottom Compression	Oil Control
1990	G	2.2 (2180)	0.0007–0.0017	0.010–0.020	0.010–0.020	0.010–0.050	0.002–0.003	0.002–0.003	0.0020–0.0082
	A	2.3 (2262)	0.0007–0.0020	0.014–0.024	0.016–0.026	0.016–0.055	0.003–0.005	0.002–0.003	—
	T	3.1 (3130)	0.0009–0.0022	0.010–0.020	0.020–0.028	0.010–0.030	0.002–0.003	0.002–0.003	0.0080
1991	G	2.2 (2180)	0.0007–0.0017	0.010–0.020	0.010–0.020	0.010–0.050	0.002–0.003	0.002–0.003	0.0020–0.0082
	A	2.3 (2262)	0.0007–0.0020	0.014–0.024	0.016–0.026	0.016–0.055	0.003–0.005	0.002–0.003	—
	T	3.1 (3130)	0.0009–0.0022	0.010–0.020	0.020–0.028	0.010–0.030	0.002–0.003	0.002–0.003	0.0080
1992–93	4	2.2 (2180)	0.0007–0.0017	0.010–0.020	0.010–0.020	0.010–0.050	0.002–0.003	0.002–0.003	0.0020–0.0082
	A	2.3 (2262)	0.0007–0.0020	0.014–0.024	0.016–0.026	0.016–0.055	0.003–0.005	0.002–0.003	—
	T	3.1 (3130)	0.0009–0.0022	0.010–0.020	0.020–0.028	0.010–0.030	0.002–0.003	0.002–0.003	0.0080

TORQUE SPECIFICATIONS

All readings in ft. lbs.

| Year | Engine ID/VIN | Engine Displacement Liters (cc) | Cylinder Head Bolts | Main Bearing Bolts | Rod Bearing Bolts | Crankshaft Damper Bolts | Flywheel Bolts | Manifold | | Spark Plugs | Lug Nut |
								Intake	Exhaust		
1989	1	2.0 (1983)	62–70①	63–77	34–43	66–89	45–59②	15–22	6–13	20	100
	W	2.8 (2835)	③	63–83	34–44	67–85	45–59②	18	15–23	20	100
1990	G	2.2 (2180)	⑫	70	38	85④	52⑤	18	⑥	11	100
	A	2.3 (2262)	26⑦	15⑧	18⑨	74⑩	22⑪	18⑭	27⑮	17	100
	T	3.1 (3130)	③	73	39	66–85	45–59②	⑯	18	20	100
1991	G	2.2 (2180)	⑬	70	38	77④	52⑤	18	⑥	11	100
	A	2.3 (2262)	26⑦	15⑧	18⑨	74⑩	22⑪	18⑭	31⑮	17	100
	T	3.1 (3130)	③	73	39	76	52	⑯	18	18	100
1992–93	4	2.2 (2180)	⑬	70	38	77④	52⑤	22	⑥	11	100
	A	2.3 (2262)	26⑦	15⑧	18⑨	74⑩	22⑪	18⑭	31⑮	17	100
	T	3.1 (3130)	③	73	39	76	52	⑯	18	18	100

① Specification is for the shorter bolts. Torque the longer bolts to 73–83 ft. lbs.

② Specification is for automatic transaxle. Torque the manual transaxle bolts to 47–63 ft. lbs.

③ Cylinder head bolts should first be torqued to 33 ft. lbs. Then tighten the bolts by rotating the torque wrench an additional 90 degrees.

④ Specification is for the crankshaft center bolt. Torque the pulley to hub bolts to 37 ft. lbs.

⑤ Specification is for automatic transaxle. Torque the manual transaxle bolts to 55 ft. lbs.

⑥ Nuts to 115 inch lbs. Stubs to 89 inch lbs.

⑦ Cylinder head bolts should first be torqued in sequence to 26 ft. lbs. Then tighten the bolts by rotating the torque wrench an additional:
100 degrees for short bolts
110 degrees for long bolts.

⑧ Main bearing bolts should first be torqued to 15 ft. lbs. Then tighten the bolts by rotating the torque wrench an additional 90 degrees.

⑨ Connecting rod bolts should first be torqued to 18 ft. lbs. Then tighten the bolts by rotating the torque wrench an additional 80 degrees.

⑩ Crankshaft balancer to crankshaft bolt should first be torqued to 74 ft. lbs. Then tighten an additional 90 degrees.

⑪ Flywheel bolts should first be torqued to 22 ft. lbs. Then tighten an additional 45 degrees.

⑫ Tighten all bolts in sequence to 41 ft. lbs. Then tighten all bolts 45 degrees in sequence. Then tighten all bolts an additional 45 degrees in sequence. Then tighten the long bolts (8, 4, 1 5 & 9) an additional 20 degrees and the short bolts (7, 3, 2, 6 & 10) an additional 10 degrees.

⑬ Tighten all bolts in sequence to: long bolts (8, 4, 1, 5 & 9) to 46 ft. lbs. amd short bolts (7, 3, 2, 6 & 10) to 43 ft. lbs. Then tighten all bolts an additional 90 degrees in sequence.

⑭ Cylinder head studs—96 inch lbs.

⑮ Cylinder head studs—106 inch lbs.

⑯ Tighten all bolts to 15 ft. lbs. Then tighten all bolts to 24 ft. lbs.

BRAKE SPECIFICATIONS
All measurements in inches unless noted

Year	Model	Master Cylinder Bore	Brake Disc Original Thickness	Brake Disc Minimum Thickness	Maximum Runout	Brake Drum Diameter Original Inside Diameter	Brake Drum Diameter Max. Wear Limit	Brake Drum Diameter Maximum Machine Diameter	Minimum Lining Thickness Front	Minimum Lining Thickness Rear
1989	Beretta	0.945	0.885	0.830	0.004	7.879	7.929	7.899	3/32	3/32
	Corsica	0.945	0.885	0.830	0.004	7.879	7.929	7.899	3/32	3/32
1990	Beretta	0.875	0.885	0.830	0.004	7.879	7.929	7.899	3/32	3/32
	Corsica	0.875	0.885	0.830	0.004	7.879	7.929	7.899	3/32	3/32
1991	Beretta	0.875	0.885	0.830	0.004	7.879	7.929	7.899	3/32	3/32
	Corsica	0.875	0.885	0.830	0.004	7.879	7.929	7.899	3/32	3/32
1992–93	Beretta	0.874	0.806	0.736	0.003	7.879	7.929	7.899	3/32	3/32
	Corsica	0.874	0.806	0.736	0.003	7.879	7.929	7.899	3/32	3/32

WHEEL ALIGNMENT

Year	Model		Caster Range (deg.)	Caster Preferred Setting (deg.)	Camber Range (deg.)	Camber Preferred Setting (deg.)	Toe-in (in.)	Steering Axis Inclination (deg.)
1989	Beretta	Front	2/5P–19/10P	12/10P	0–12/10P	6/10P	0	—
		Rear	—	—	9/10N–4/10P	1/4P	5/16P	—
	Corsica	Front	2/5P–19/10P	12/10P	0–12/10P	6/10P	0	—
		Rear	—	—	8/10N–3/10P	1/4P	1/4P	—
1990	Beretta	Front	2/5P–19/10P	12/10P	0–12/10P	6/10P	0	—
		Rear	—	—	9/10N–4/10P	1/4P	5/16P	—
	Corsica	Front	2/5P–19/10P	12/10P	0–12/10P	6/10P	0	—
		Rear	—	—	8/10N–3/10P	1/4P	1/4P	—
1991	Beretta	Front	2/5P–19/10P	13/20P	②	③	①	14
		Rear	—	—	13/16N–5/16P	1/4N	1/16P	—
	Corsica	Front	2/5P–19/10P	13/20P	②	③	①	14
		Rear	—	—	7/8N–3/8P	1/4P	3/16P	—
1992–93	Beretta	Front	2/5P–19/10P	13/20P	②	③	①	14
		Rear	—	—	13/16N–5/16P	1/4N	1/16P	—
	Corsica	Front	2/5P–19/10P	13/20P	②	③	①	14
		Rear	—	—	7/8N–3/8P	1/4P	3/16P	—

N—Negative
P—Positive
① Not adjustable
② Except Beretta GTZ and Corcisa w/Sport
  Susp.: 9/16P–13/16P
  Beretta GTZ and Corsica w/Sport
  Susp.: 13/16N–7/16P
③ Except Beretta GTZ and Corcisa w/Sport
  Susp.: 1/8P
  Beretta GTZ and Corsica w/Sport
  Susp.: 13/16N

ENGINE MECHANICAL

NOTE: Disconnecting the negative battery cable on some vehicles may interfere with the functions of the on board computer systems and may require the computer to undergo a relearning process, once the negative battery cable is reconnected.

Engine Assembly

REMOVAL & INSTALLATION

2.0L and 2.3L Engines

1. Relieve the fuel system pressure. Disconnect the battery cables (negative cable first). Remove the battery from the vehicle.
2. Position a clean drain pan under the radiator, open the drain cock and drain the cooling system. Remove the air intake hose.
3. Disconnect the underhood lamp wiring and remove the hood from the vehicle.
4. Disconnect the TV and accelerator cables from the throttle body. Disconnect the ECM electrical harness connector from the engine.
5. Remove all vacuum hoses, not a part of the engine assembly, the upper/lower radiator hoses and the heater hoses from the engine.
6. Remove the heat shield from the exhaust manifold. Disconnect and label the engine wiring harness from the firewall.
7. Disconnect the windshield washer hoses and the bottle. Rotate the tensioner pulley, to reduce the belt tension and remove the serpentine drive belt.
8. Disconnect and plug the fuel hoses. Raise and safely support the vehicle.
9. Remove the right side inner fender splash shield.
10. Remove the air conditioning compressor-to-bracket bolts and move it aside, so it will not interfere with the engine removal; do not disconnect the refrigerant lines.
11. Remove the flywheel splash shield. Label and disconnect electrical wires from the starter.
12. Remove the front starter brace, the starter-to-engine bolts and the starter.
13. If equipped with an automatic transaxle, remove the torque converter-to-flywheel bolts and push the converter back into the transaxle.
14. Remove the crankshaft pulley-to-crankshaft bolt. Using a crankshaft

pulley hub remover tool, press the pulley from the crankshaft.
15. Remove the oil filter. Remove the engine-to-transaxle support bracket.
16. Disconnect the right rear engine mount.
17. Remove the exhaust pipe-to-exhaust manifold bolts, the exhaust pipe from the center hanger and loosen the muffler hanger.
18. Remove the TV and shift cable bracket. Remove both lower engine-to-transaxle bolts.
19. Lower the vehicle. From the intake manifold, remove the TV and accelerator cable bracket.
20. Remove the right front engine mount nuts. Disconnect the electrical connectors. Remove the alternator-to-bracket bolts and the alternator.
21. Remove the master cylinder-to-booster nuts, move the master cylinder and support it aside; do not disconnect the brake lines.
22. Using a vertical lifting device, install to the engine and lift it slightly.
23. Remove the right front engine mount bracket. Remove the remaining engine-to-transaxle bolts.
24. **Remove the power steering pump-to-engine bolts and move it aside; do not disconnect the high pressure hoses.**
25. Carefully lift and remove the engine from the vehicle.

To install:
26. Secure the engine on a engine suitable lifting device.
27. Support the transaxle with floor jack.
28. Carefully lower the engine into the vehicle, aligning it to the transaxle.
29. Install the engine-to-transaxle bolts. Install the right front engine mount bracket and attaching nuts.
30. Install the right rear engine mount and attaching bolts.
31. Install the engine-to-transaxle support bracket and attaching bolts.
32. Lower the transaxle jack and remove it from the vehicle.
33. Install the power steering pump and pump-to-engine attaching bolts.
34. Install the master cylinder and the master cylinder-to-booster attaching nuts.
35. Install the alternator, bracket and attaching bolts. Connect the electrical connectors to the alternator.
36. Install the TV and accelerator cable bracket.
37. Install the TV and shift cable bracket.
38. Raise and safely support the vehicle.
39. Install the exhaust pipe to the exhaust manifold and install the center hanger. Install the exhaust pipe-to-exhaust manifold attaching bolts.
40. Install the oil filter.

41. Install the crankshaft pulley on the crankshaft and install the pulley-to-crankshaft attaching bolt.
42. If equipped with an automatic transaxle, install the torque converter-to-flywheel attaching bolts.
43. Install the starter, front starter brace and the starter-to-engine attaching bolts.
44. Connect the electrical wires to the starter.
45. Install the flywheel splash shield.
46. Lower the vehicle.
47. Install the air conditioning compressor, with the refrigerant lines attached. Install the air conditioning compressor-to-bracket bolts.
48. Install the right side inner fender splash shield.
49. Connect the fuel hoses.
50. Install the windshield washer bottle and connect the washer hoses.
51. Rotate the tensioner pulley and install the serpentine drive belt.
52. Install the heat shield to the exhaust manifold. Connect the engine wiring harness to the firewall.
53. Install all vacuum hoses, the upper and lower radiator hoses and heater hoses to the engine.
54. Connect the TV and accelerator cables to the throttle body.
55. Connect the ECM electrical harness connector to the engine.
56. Install the air intake hose and install the hood.
57. Close the radiator pet cock and refill the cooling system.
58. Install the battery and secure it in place. Connect the battery cables (the negative cable first).
59. Start the engine, allow it to reach normal operating temperatures and check for leaks.

2.2L Engine

1. Disconnect the negative battery cable.
2. Relieve the fuel system pressure and drain the cooling system.
3. Disconnect the underhood lamp wiring and remove the hood from the vehicle.
4. Remove the throttle body duct and on the GTZ model, remove the rear firewall cover shield.
5. Remove the battery and the air cleaner housing.
6. Disconnect the upper radiator hose and the brake booster vacuum hose.
7. Remove the upper alternator brace and disconnect the wiring.
8. Disconnect the upper engine harness from the engine.
9. Properly discharge the A/C system and disconnect the compressor-to-condenser and accumulator lines.
10. Raise and safely support the vehicle and remove the engine splash shield.

11. Remove the exhaust system from the vehicle.

12. Disconnect the lower engine wiring.

13. Remove the flywheel inspection cover and remove the front wheels from the vehicle.

14. Remove the lower radiator hose and remove the heater hoses from the heater core.

15. Remove the brake calipers from the discs and support them.

16. Disconnect the tie rods from the struts and lower the vehicle.

17. Remove the clutch slave cylinder.

18. Disconnect the fuel lines.

19. Disconnect the transaxle linkage at the transaxle and disconnect the following cables:
   a. Accelerator cable
   b. Cruise control cable
   c. TV cable (automatic only)

20. Disconnect the transaxle cooling lines from the transaxle (automatic only).

21. Disconnect the power steering hoses from the power steering pump and raise the vehicle.

22. Remove the 4 center support bolts and align and support the engine with the dolly/support fixture.

23. Support the rear of the vehicle and remove the transaxle mount.

24. Remove the upper strut bolts and nuts.

25. Remove the right side engine mount and mount strut.

26. Remove the 4 front and the 4 rear suspension support bolts.

27. Install wire to the front suspension support bolt holes to prevent axle separation.

28. Raise the vehicle and remove the engine and transaxle assembly on the dolly.

To install:

29. Lower the vehicle and raise the engine and transaxle assembly into place.

30. Install the suspension support bolts.

31. Install the transaxle mount, the right engine mount and the engine mount strut. Do not tighten until all 3 are installed.

32. Connect the following:
   a. Power steering hoses
   b. Accelerator cable
   c. Cruise control cable
   d. TV cable
   e. Transaxle cooling lines
   f. Transaxle linkage
   g. Fuel lines

33. Install the clutch slave cylinder and raise the vehicle.

34. Install the tie rods and brake calipers.

35. Connect the heater hoses and lower radiator hoses.

36. Install the A/C compressor to the vehicle.

37. Install the flywheel inspection cover and engine splash shield.

38. Install the front wheels and lower the vehicle.

39. Connect the upper engine wiring and install the A/C condenser and accumulator lines.

40. Connect the brake booster vacuum hose.

41. Install the alternator top brace and connect the wiring.

42. Connect the upper radiator hose and install the upper strut bolts and nuts.

43. Raise the vehicle and connect the lower engine wiring.

44. Install the exhaust system to the vehicle and lower the vehicle.

45. Install the throttle body and the air cleaner. Properly charge the A/C system.

46. Check and adjust the wheel alignment if necessary.

47. Install the hood to the vehicle and connect the hood lamp wiring.

48. Install the rear firewall shield/cover (GTZ only).

49. Install the battery and connect the cables.

2.8L and 3.1L Engines

1. Relieve the fuel pressure. Disconnect the battery cables (negative cable first). Remove the battery from the vehicle.

2. Remove the air cleaner, the air inlet hose and the mass air flow sensor.

3. Position a clean drain pan under the radiator, open the drain cock and drain the cooling system. Remove the exhaust manifold crossover assembly bolts and separate the assembly from the exhaust manifolds.

4. Remove the serpentine belt tensioner and the drive belt. Remove the power steering pump-to-bracket bolts and support the pump aside.

5. Disconnect the radiator hose from the engine.

6. Disconnect the TV and accelerator cables from the throttle valve bracket on the plenum.

7. Disconnect the electrical connectors. Remove the alternator-to-bracket bolts and the alternator. Label and disconnect the electrical wiring harness from the engine.

8. Disconnect and plug the fuel hoses. Remove the coolant overflow and bypass hoses from the engine.

9. From the charcoal canister, disconnect the purge hose. Label and disconnect all the necessary vacuum hoses.

10. Using a engine holding fixture tool, support the engine.

11. Raise and safely support the vehicle.

12. Remove the right inner fender splash shield. Remove the crankshaft pulley-to-crankshaft bolt. Using a wheel puller, press the crankshaft pulley from the crankshaft.

13. Remove the flywheel cover. Label and disconnect the starter wires. Remove the starter-to-engine bolts and the starter.

14. Disconnect the wires from the oil pressure sending unit.

15. Remove the air conditioning compressor-to-bracket bolts and the bracket-to-engine bolts. Support the compressor so it will not interfere with the engine; do not disconnect the refrigerant lines.

16. Disconnect the exhaust pipe from the rear of the exhaust manifold.

17. If equipped with an automatic transaxle, remove the torque converter-to-flywheel bolts and push the converter into the transaxle.

18. Remove the front and rear engine mount bolts along with the mount brackets.

19. Remove the intermediate shaft bracket from the engine.

20. Disconnect the shifter cable from the transaxle.

21. Remove the lower engine-to-transaxle bolts and lower the vehicle.

22. Disconnect the heater hoses from the engine.

23. Using an vertical engine lift, install it to the engine and lift it slightly. Remove the engine holding fixture. Using a floor jack, support the transaxle.

24. Remove the upper engine-to-transaxle bolts. Remove the front engine mount bolts and transaxle mounting bracket.

25. Remove the engine from the vehicle.

To install:

26. Secure the engine on a engine suitable lifting device.

27. Carefully lower the engine into the vehicle, aligning it to the transaxle.

28. Install the upper engine-to-transaxle bolts. Tighten bolts to 55 ft. lbs. (75 Nm).

29. Install the transaxle mount bracket and front engine mount attaching bolts. Tighten the bolts to 65 ft. lbs. (88 Nm).

30. Using a floor jack, support the transaxle and remove the engine lifting device from the engine.

31. Install the lower engine-to-transaxle.

32. Connect the heater hoses to the engine.

33. Connect the shifter cable to the transaxle.

34. Install the intermediate shaft bracket to the engine.

35. Install the front and rear engine mount bolts along with the mount brackets.

36. Lower the jack and remove it from the transaxle.

37. Raise the vehicle and support it safely.

38. If equipped with an automatic transaxle, install the torque converter-to-flywheel bolts.

39. Install the flywheel cover and attaching bolts.

40. Connect the exhaust pipe to the the exhaust manifold and install the attaching bolts.

41. Lower the vehicle.

42. Position the air conditioning compressor, with the lines attached, in place and install the compressor-to-bracket bolts.

43. Install the compressor bracket-to-engine bolts.

44. Connect the wires to the oil pressure sending unit.

45. Connect the starter wires. Position the starter in place and install the starter-to-engine bolts.

46. Install the crankshaft pulley and install the pulley-to-crankshaft bolt. Install the right inner fender splash shield.

47. Connect the purge hose to the charcoal canister. Connect all the necessary vacuum hoses.

48. Connect the coolant overflow and bypass hoses to the engine.

49. Connect the fuel delivery hoses to the engine.

50. Position the alternator in place and install the alternator-to-bracket mmbolts. Connect the electrical connectors to the alternator.

51. Connect all electrical wiring harnesses to the engine.

52. Connect the TV and accelerator cables to the throttle valve bracket on the plenum.

53. Connect the radiator hoses to the engine.

54. Install the serpentine belt tensioner and the drive belt.

55. Position the power steering pump in place and install the power steering pump-to-bracket bolts.

56. Connect the crossover pipe to the exhaust manifold and install the attaching bolts.

57. Install the air cleaner, air inlet hose and the mass air flow sensor.

58. Close the radiator cock and refill the cooling system.

59. Install the battery and secure it in place. Connect the battery cables (the negative cable last).

60. Start the engine, allow it to reach normal operating temperatures and check for leaks.

Engine Mounts

REMOVAL & INSTALLATION

Front

1. Disconnect the negative battery cable.

2. Install an engine holding fixture tool and support the engine.

3. Remove the upper mount-to-body bracket bolts.

4. Remove the engine mount-to-engine mount bracket bolts.

5. Raise and safely support the vehicle.

6. Remove the right side inner fender shield.

7. Remove the lower engine mount-to-body bracket bolt.

8. Remove the engine mount.

To install:

9. Install the lower engine mount and the mount-to-body bracket bolt. Tighten to 50 ft. lbs. (68 Nm).

10. Install the engine mount through bolts. Tighten to 35 ft. lbs. (47 Nm).

11. Install the left side inner fender shield.

12. Lower the vehicle.

13. Install the upper engine mount-to-body bracket bolt. Tighten to 50 ft. lbs. (68 Nm).

14. Remove the engine holding fixture tool.

15. Lower the vehicle.

16. Connect the negative battery cable.

Rear

1. Disconnect the negative battery cable.

2. Install an engine holding fixture tool and support the engine.

3. Raise and safely support the vehicle.

4. Remove the engine mount nuts/bolts and the engine mount.

To install:

5. Install the engine mount and the engine mount nuts/bolts. Tighten the mounting bolts to 50 ft. lbs. (68 Nm) and nuts to 18 ft. lbs. (24 Nm).

6. Lower the vehicle.

7. Remove the engine holding fixture.

8. Connect the negative battery cable.

Cylinder Head

REMOVAL & INSTALLATION

2.0L Engine

1. Relieve the fuel pressure and disconnect the negative battery cable.

2. Drain the cooling system. Remove the TBI cover.

3. Raise and safely support the vehicle.

4. Disconnect the exhaust pipe-to-exhaust manifold bolts and separate the exhaust pipe from the manifold.

5. Lower the vehicle. Disconnect the heater hose from the intake manifold.

6. Disconnect the TV and accelerator cable bracket.

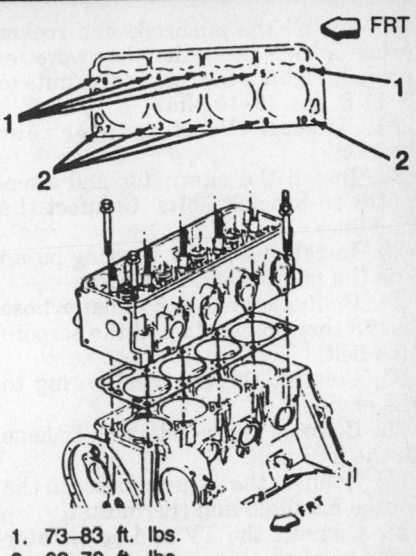

1. 73–83 ft. lbs.
2. 62–70 ft. lbs.

Cylinder head bolt torque sequence— 2.0L and 2.2L engines

7. Label and disconnect the vacuum hoses from the intake manifold and thermostat.

8. Disconnect the accelerator linkage from the TBI unit.

9. Label and disconnect the electrical wiring from the engine.

10. Disconnect the upper radiator hose from the thermostat. Remove the serpentine belt.

11. Remove the power steering pump-to-bracket bolts and support the pump aside; do not disconnect the high pressure hoses from the pump.

12. Disconnect and plug the fuel lines. Remove the alternator-to-bracket bolts and the alternator. Position it aside, with electrical connectors attached.

13. Remove the alternator rear brace.

14. Remove the rocker arm cover-to-cylinder head bolts and the cover. Remove the rocker arm bolts, the rocker arms and pushrods; be sure to keep valve train components in the order that they were removed.

15. Starting with the outer bolts, remove the cylinder head-to-engine bolts.

To install:

16. Clean and inspect the gasket mounting surfaces. Make sure the threads on the cylinder head bolts and in the block are clean.

17. Position the cylinder head gasket in place on the engine block dowel pins.

18. Install the cylinder head and tighten the head bolts hand tight.

19. Following the torquing sequence, tighten the head bolts in 3 steps to 73–83 ft. lbs. (99–113 Nm) on the intake side and 62–70 ft. lbs. (84–95 Nm) on the exhaust side.

20. Install the pushrods and rocker arms in the same order they were removed. Tighten the rocker arm nuts to 7–11 ft. lbs. (9–15 Nm).

21. Install the alternator rear bracket.

22. Install the alternator and alternator-to-bracket bolts. Connect the fuel lines.

23. Install the power steering pump and the pump-to-bracket bolts.

24. Connect the upper radiator hose to the thermostat. Install the serpentine belt.

25. Connect the electrical wiring to the engine.

26. Connect the accelerator linkage to the TBI unit.

27. Connect the vacuum hoses to the intake manifold and thermostat.

28. Connect the TV and accelerator cable bracket.

29. Connect the heater hose to the intake manifold.

30. Raise and safely support the vehicle.

31. Connect the exhaust pipe and install the pipe-to-exhaust manifold bolts.

32. Lower the vehicle.

33. Connect the negative battery cable.

34. Fill cooling system and check for leaks. Start the engine and allow to come to normal operating temperature. Recheck for leaks. Top-up coolant.

2.2L Engine

1. Relieve the fuel system pressure and disconnect the negative battery cable.

2. Remove the air inlet duct and properly drain the coolant from the cooling system.

3. Disconnect the vacuum lines and electrical connections. Disconnect the accelerator linkage.

4. Remove the coolant reservoir and the serpentine belt.

5. Remove the alternator and the power steering pump.

6. Remove the belt tensioner and the secondary ignition wires.

7. Disconnect the following:
   a. Canister purge line (below the manifold)
   b. Upper radiator hose
   c. Throttle body cables from the bracket
   d. Coolant inlet hose
   e. Fuel lines

8. Remove the intake manifold brace and the valve cover.

9. Remove the rocker arms and pushrods. Keep in order for easier installation.

10. Remove the secondary ignition cable bracket and the engine lift bracket.

11. Remove the exhaust pipe and the head bolts.

12. If equipped with an automatic transaxle, remove the trans fluid level indicator bracket.

13. Remove the cylinder head from the vehicle.

NOTE: Clean all gasket surfaces with plastic or wood scraper. Do not use any sealing material.

To install:

14. Install the cylinder head gasket over the dowel pins and carefully install the head onto the pins and the gasket.

15. Install the cylinder head bolts finger tight and then following the proper sequence tighten the long bolts to 46 ft. lbs. (63 Nm) and the short bolts to 43 ft. lbs. (58 Nm).

16. Tighten all bolts an additional 90 degrees in sequence.

17. Install the throttle body cables and the trans fluid level indicator bracket bolt.

18. Install the engine lift bracket and the secondary ignition cable bracket.

19. Install the rocker arms and the pushrods and install the valve cover.

20. Connect the vacuum lines, fuel lines and electrical connectors.

21. Connect the coolant inlet hose and install the intake manifold brace.

22. Install the upper radiator hose and connect the secondary ignition wires.

23. Install the belt tensioner and the power steering pump.

24. Install the alternator and the serpentine drive belt.

25. Install the coolant reservoir and the air cleaner assembly.

26. Raise the vehicle and connect the exhaust pipe.

27. Lower the vehicle and refill the coolant to the proper level.

28. Inspect for leaks and connect the negative battery cable.

2.3L Engine

1. Relieve the fuel system pressure. Disconnect the negative battery cable. Drain the engine coolant into a clean container for reuse.

2. Disconnect heater inlet and throttle body heater hoses from water outlet. Disconnect upper radiator hose from water outlet.

3. Remove exhaust manifold.

4. Remove intake and exhaust camshaft housings.

5. Remove oil cap and dipstick. Pull oil fill tube upward to unseat from block.

6. Disconnect and tag injector harness electrical connector.

7. Disconnect throttle body to air cleaner duct. Remove throttle cable and bracket and position aside.

8. Remove throttle body from intake manifold with electrical harness, hoses, cable attached and position aside.

9. Disconnect and tag MAP sensor vacuum hose from intake manifold.

10. Remove intake manifold bracket to block bolt.

11. Disconnect and tag 2 coolant sensor connections.

12. Remove cylinder head to block bolts.

NOTE: When removing cylinder head to block bolts follow reverse of tighten sequence.

13. Remove cylinder head and gasket.

NOTE: Clean all gasket surfaces with plastic or wood scraper. Do not use any sealing material.

To install:

14. Install the cylinder head gasket to the cylinder block and carefully position the cylinder head in place.

15. Coat the head bolt threads with clean engine oil and allow the oil to drain off before installing.

16. Tighten the cylinder head bolts in sequence in 2 steps as follows:
   Step 1: in sequence, tighten the long and short cylinder head to block bolts—26 ft. lbs. (35 Nm).
   Step 2: in sequence, tighten the short bolts—80 degree turn and the long bolts—90 degree turn.

17. Install the intake manifold-to-block bracket bolt and bracket.

18. Connect the MAP sensor vacuum hose to the intake manifold.

19. Install the throttle body on the intake manifold with electrical harness, hoses and cable attached.

20. Connect the throttle body-to-air cleaner duct. Install the throttle cable and bracket.

21. Connect the injector harness electrical connector.

22. Connect the 2 coolant sensor connections.

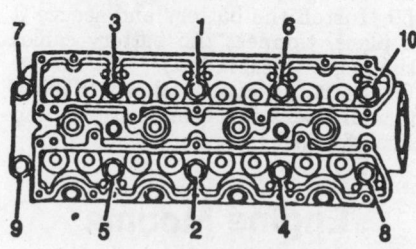

Cylinder head bolt torque sequence—2.3L engine (1989–91)

FRONT OF ENGINE

USE THE TIGHTENING PROCEDURE
DETAILED IN THE TEXT

BOLTS 1 THROUGH 6 - 35 N•m (26 LBS. FT.)
BOLT 7 AND 8 - 20 N•m (15 LBS. FT.)
BOLTS 9 AND 10 - 30 N•m (22 LBS. FT.)

Cylinder head torque sequence–2.3L engine (1992–93)

HEAD TORQUE SEQUENCE

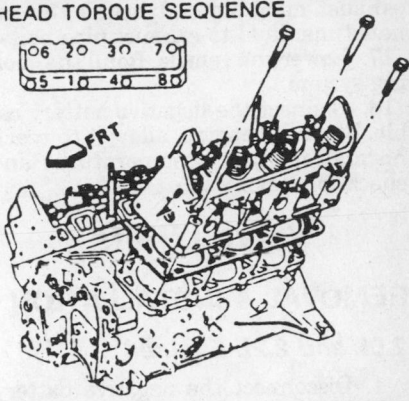

Cylinder head bolt torque sequence—
2.8L and 3.1L engines

23. Install the oil cap and dipstick. Install the oil fill tube into the block.

24. Install the exhaust and intake camshaft housings.

25. Install the exhaust manifold.

26. Connect the heater inlet and throttle body heater hoses to the water outlet. Connect the upper radiator hose to the water outlet.

27. Fill the cooling system and connect the negative battery cable.

28. Start the engine, allow it to reach operating temperature and check for leaks.

2.8L and 3.1L Engines

LEFT SIDE

1. Relieve the fuel pressure.

2. Disconnect the negative battery cable and remove the air cleaner assembly.

3. Place a drain pan under the radiator and drain the cooling system.

4. Remove the rocker cover attaching bolts and remove rocker cover.

5. Remove the intake manifold-to-cylinder head bolts and the remove the intake manifold.

6. Remove the fuel plenum and fuel rail assembles.

7. Disconnect the exhaust crossover from the right exhaust manifold.

8. Disconnect the oil level indicator tube bracket.

9. Loosen the rocker arms nuts, turn the rocker arms and remove the pushrods.

NOTE: **Be sure to keep the parts in order for installation purposes.**

10. Remove the cylinder head-to-engine bolts; start with the outer bolts and work toward the center. Remove the cylinder head with the exhaust manifold.

To install:

11. Clean the gasket mounting surfaces. Inspect the surfaces of the cylinder head, block and intake manifold damage and/or warpage. Clean the threaded holes in the block and the cylinder head bolt threads.

12. Using new gaskets, align the new cylinder head gasket over the dowels on the block with the note **This Side Up** facing the cylinder head.

13. Install the cylinder head and exhaust manifold crossover assembly on the engine.

14. Coat the cylinder head bolt threads with engine oil and install the hand tight.

15. Using the proper torque sequence, tighten the bolts to 33 ft. lbs. (45 Nm). After all bolts are torqued to 33 ft. lbs. (45 Nm), rotate the torque wrench another 90 degrees or ¼ turn. This will apply the correct torque to the bolts.

16. Install the pushrods in the same order that they were removed. Tighten the rocker arm nuts to 14–20 ft. lbs. (19–27 Nm).

17. Install the intake manifold using a new gasket and following the correct sequence, tighten the bolts to 24 ft. lbs. (33 Nm) and nuts to 18 ft. lbs. (24 Nm).

18. Install the fuel plenum and fuel rail. Tighten the plenum bolts to 16 ft. lbs. (22 Nm).

19. Connect the exhaust crossover to the right exhaust manifold.

20. Connect the oil level indicator tube bracket.

21. Refill the cooling system. Connect the negative battery cable.

22. Operate the engine until normal operating temperatures are reached and check for leaks.

RIGHT SIDE

1. Relieve the fuel pressure. Disconnect the negative battery cable. Drain the cooling system and remove the air cleaner.

2. Raise and safely support the vehicle. Remove the exhaust manifold-to-exhaust pipe bolts and separate the pipe from the manifold.

3. Lower the vehicle. Remove the exhaust manifold-to-cylinder head bolts and exhaust manifold.

4. Remove the rocker arm cover. Remove the intake manifold-to-cylinder head bolts and the intake manifold.

5. Loosen the rocker arms nuts, turn the rocker arms and remove the pushrods.

NOTE: **Be sure to keep the components in order for reassembly purposes.**

6. Remove the cylinder head-to-engine bolts, starting with the outer bolts, working towards the center of the head.

7. Lift the cylinder head from the engine.

To install:

8. Clean the gasket mounting surfaces. Inspect the parts for damage and/or warpage; if necessary, machine or replace the parts.

9. Clean the engine block's threaded holes and the cylinder head bolt threads.

10. Using new gaskets, reverse the removal procedures. Using sealant, coat the cylinder head bolts and install the bolts hand tight.

11. Using the torquing sequence, tighten the bolts to 33 ft. lbs. (45 Nm). After all bolts are torqued to 33 ft. lbs. (45 Nm), rotate the torque wrench another 90 degrees or ¼ turn; this will apply the correct torque to the bolts.

12. Install the pushrods in the same order as they were removed. Tighten the rocker arm nuts to 14–20 ft. lbs. (19–27 Nm).

13. Follow the torquing sequence, use a new gasket and install the intake manifold.

14. Install the exhaust manifold and exhaust manifold-to-cylinder head bolts.

15. Raise the vehicle and support it safely.

16. Connect the exhaust pipe to the

exhaust manifold and install the exhaust manifold-to-exhaust pipe bolts.

17. Lower the vehicle. Refill the cooling system.

18. Connect the negative battery cable. Start the engine, allow it to reach normal operating temperatures and check for leaks.

Valve Lifters

REMOVAL & INSTALLATION

2.0L and 2.2L Engines

1. Disconnect the negative battery cable. Remove the rocker arm cover.

2. Loosen the rocker arms nuts enough to move the rocker arms aside and remove the pushrods.

3. Using a valve lifter remover tool, remove the lifters from the engine.

To install:

4. Using Molykote® or equivalent, coat the base of the new lifters. Using a valve lifter remover tool, install the lifters into the engine.

5. Install the pushrods and reposition the rocker arms. Tighten the rocker arm nuts to 7–11 ft. lbs. (9–15 Nm) for the 2.0L engine or to 22 ft. lbs. (30 Nm) for the 2.2L engine.

6. Install the rocker arm cover. Tighten the rocker arm cover bolts to 8 ft. lbs. (11 Nm).

7. Connect the negative battery cable.

2.3L Engine

The valve train consists of 2 chain driven overhead camshafts with direct acting lifters, therefore, camshaft removal is necessary in order to gain access to the lifters. Once the camshafts are removed from their mountings the valve lifters can be removed from their bores.

2.8L and 3.1L Engines

1. Disconnect the negative battery cable.

2. Drain the cooling system.

3. Remove the rocker arm covers and intake manifold.

4. Loosen the rocker arm nuts enough to move the rocker arms aside and remove the pushrods.

5. Remove the lifters from the engine.

To install:

6. Using Molykote® or equivalent, coat the base of the new lifters and install them into the engine.

7. Install the pushrods and the reposition the rocker arms. Tighten the rocker arm nuts to 18 ft. lbs. (25 Nm).

8. Install the rocker arm covers.

9. Install the intake manifold. Tighten the intake manifold-to-cylinder head bolts to 20 ft. lbs. (27 Nm).

10. Connect the negative battery cable.

Valve Lash

ADJUSTMENT

Hydraulic valve lifters are used in the 2.0L, 2.2L, 2.8L and 3.1L engines and are not adjustable. If valve system noise is present, check the torque on the rocker arm nuts. The correct torque is 7–11 ft. lbs. (9–15 Nm) for 2.0L and 2.2L engines or 14–20 ft. lbs. (19–27 Nm) for 2.8L and 3.1L engines. If noise is still present, check the condition of the camshaft, lifters, rocker arms, pushrods and valves.

On the 2.3L engine, direct acting hydraulic valve lifters are used. The valve lifter body includes a harden iron contact foot bonded to a steel shell. These lifters are not serviceable or adjustable.

Rocker Arms

REMOVAL & INSTALLATION

2.0L and 2.2L Engines

1. Disconnect the negative battery cable. Remove the air hose from the TBI unit and the air cleaner.

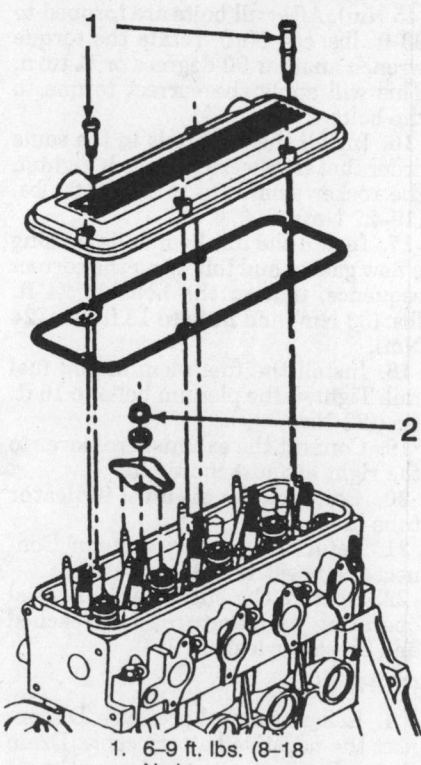

1. 6–9 ft. lbs. (8–18 Nm)
2. 11–18 ft. lbs. (15–25 Nm)

Rocker arm and cover installation—2.0L and 2.3L engines

2. Remove the intake manifold-to-rocker cover hose.

3. Remove the rocker arm cover bolts and the cover.

4. Remove the rocker arm nuts and the rocker arms.

NOTE: Be sure to keep the components in order for installation purposes.

To install:

5. Install the rocker arms and rocker arm nuts. Tighten to 7–11 ft. lbs. (9–15 Nm) on the 2.0L engine or to 22 ft. lbs. (30 Nm) on the 2.2L engine.

6. Install the rocker arm cover.

7. Connect the intake manifold-to-rocker cover.

8. Connect the hose to the TBI unit and air cleaner.

9. Connect the negative battery cable.

2.3L Engine

The valve train consists of 2 chain driven overhead camshafts with direct acting lifters.

2.8L and 3.1L Engines

Left Side

1. Disconnect the negative battery cable. Disconnect the bracket tube from the rocker cover.

2. Remove the spark plug wire cover. Drain the cooling system and remove the heater hose from the filler neck.

3. Remove the rocker arm cover-to-cylinder head bolts and the rocker cover.

NOTE: If the rocker arm cover will not lift off the cylinder head easily, strike the end with the palm of the hand or a rubber mallet.

4. Remove the rocker arm nuts and the rocker arms; be sure to keep the components in order for installation purposes.

To install:

5. Clean the gasket mounting surfaces.

6. Install the rocker arms and rocker arm nuts. Tighten to 14–20 ft. lbs. (19–27 Nm).

7. Install the rocker cover.

8. Install the spark plug wire cover.

9. Connect the negative battery cable.

10. Fill cooling system and check for leaks. Start the engine and allow to come to normal operating temperature. Recheck for leaks. Top-up coolant.

RIGHT SIDE

1. Disconnect the negative battery cable. Disconnect the brake booster vacuum line from the bracket.

2. Disconnect the cable bracket from the plenum.

3. Disconnect the vacuum line bracket from the cable bracket.

4. Disconnect the lines from the alternator brace stud.

5. Remove the rear alternator brace and the serpentine drive belt.

6. Remove the alternator and support it aside.

7. Remove the PCV valve.

8. Loosen the alternator bracket.

9. Disconnect the spark plug wires from the spark plugs. Remove the rocker cover-to-cylinder head bolts and the rocker cover.

NOTE: If the rocker arm cover will not lift off the cylinder head easily, strike the end with the palm of the hand or a rubber mallet.

10. Remove the rocker arm nuts and the rocker arms; be sure to keep the components in order for installation purposes.

To install:

11. Clean the gasket mounting surfaces.

12. Install the rocker arm and rocker arm nuts. Tighten the rocker arm nuts to 14–20 ft. lbs. (19–27 Nm).

13. Install the rocker cover and the rocker cover-to-cylinder head bolts. Connect the spark plug wires to the spark plugs.

14. Tighten the alternator bracket.

15. Install the PCV valve.

16. Install the alternator.

17. Install the rear alternator brace and the serpentine drive belt.

18. Connect the lines to the alternator brace stud.

19. Connect the vacuum line bracket to the cable bracket.

20. Connect the cable bracket to the plenum.

21. Connect the brake booster vacuum line to the bracket.

22. Connect the negative battery cable.

Intake Manifold

REMOVAL & INSTALLATION

2.0L and 2.2L Engines

1. Disconnect the negative battery cable. Relieve the fuel pressure. Remove the TBI cover and if necessary, remove the air cleaner.

2. Drain the cooling system. Label and disconnect the vacuum lines and electrical connectors from the intake manifold.

3. Disconnect and plug the fuel line.

4. Disconnect the TBI linkage. Remove the throttle body-to-intake manifold bolts and the throttle body.

5. Remove the serpentine drive belt. Remove the power steering pump-to-bracket bolts and support the pump aside; do not disconnect the pressure hoses.

6. Raise and safely support the vehicle.

7. Disconnect the TV cable, accelerator cable and brackets.

8. Disconnect the heater hose from the bottom of the intake manifold. Lower the vehicle.

9. Remove the intake manifold-to-cylinder head nuts/bolts and the manifold.

To install:

10. Clean the gasket mounting surfaces. Install new intake manifold gaskets.

11. Install the intake manifold and the intake manifold-to-cylinder head nuts/bolts. Tighten the intake manifold-to-cylinder heads bolts, in the proper sequence to 15–22 ft. lbs. (20–30 Nm).

12. Raise and safely support the vehicle.

13. Connect the heater hose to the bottom of the intake manifold.

14. Connect the TV cable, accelerator cable and brackets.

15. Lower the vehicle.

16. Install the serpentine drive belt. Install the power steering pump-to-bracket bolts and support the pump aside; do not disconnect the pressure hoses.

17. Install the throttle body-to-intake manifold bolts and the throttle body. Connect the TBI linkage.

18. Connect the fuel line.

19. Connect the vacuum lines and electrical connectors to the intake manifold.

20. Install the TBI cover and the air cleaner assembly, if removed.

21. Connect the negative battery cable.

22. Fill cooling system and check for leaks. Start the engine and allow to come to normal operating temperature. Recheck for leaks. Top-up coolant.

2.3L Engine

1. Disconnect the negative battery cable.

2. Drain the coolant to the proper level.

3. Disconnect the following:
   a. Vacuum hose from the MAP sensor
   b. Electrical connector from the MAP sensor

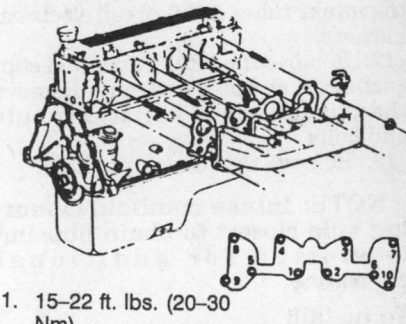

1. 15–22 ft. lbs. (20–30 Nm)

Intake manifold bolt torque sequence— 2.0L and 2.2L (VIN G) engines

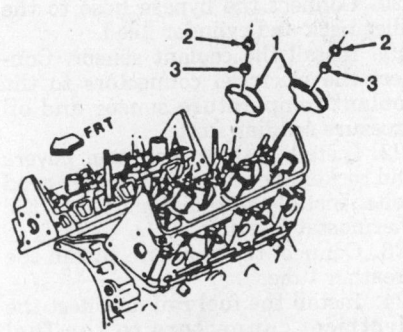

1. Rocker arms
2. 14–20 ft. lbs. (20–27 Nm)
3. Ball

Rocker arm installation—2.3L engine

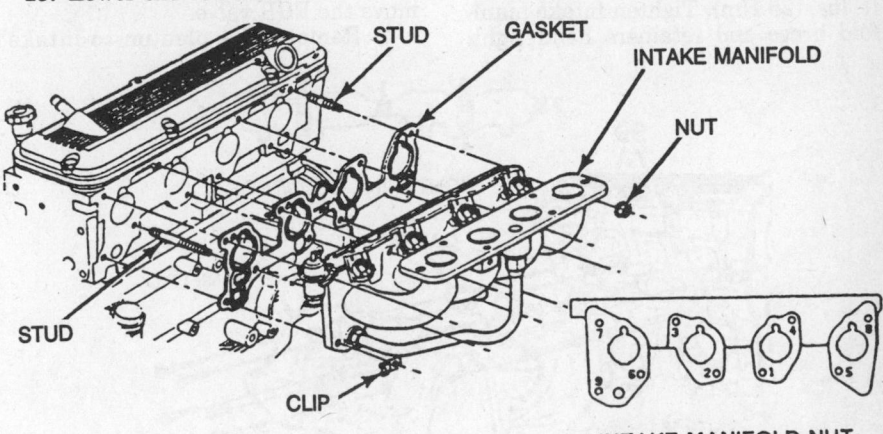

STUD

GASKET

INTAKE MANIFOLD

NUT

STUD

CLIP

INTAKE MANIFOLD NUT TIGHTENING SEQUENCE

Intake manifold installation—2.2L engine (VIN 4)

c. Electrical connector from the MAT sensor

d. Electrical connector from the purge solenoid

e. Fuel injector harness connectors

4. Disconnect the vacuum hoses from the intake manifold and the hose at the fuel regulator and purge solenoid to canister.

5. Disconnect the throttle body to the air cleaner duct and the vent tube to the air cleaner duct.

6. Remove the throttle cable bracket and remove the power brake vacuum hose, including the retaining bracket to power steering bracket and position it to the side.

7. Disconnect the coolant lines from the throttle body and remove the oil/air separator bolts and hoses. Leave the hoses attached to the separator, disconnect from the oil fill, chain housing and the intake manifold. Remove as an assembly.

8. Remove the oil fill cap and oil level indicator stick.

9. Pull the oil tube fill upward to unseat from block and remove.

10. Disconnect the injector harness connector.

11. Remove the fill tube out top, rotating as necessary to gain clearance for the oil/air separator nipple between the intake tubes and fuel rail electrical harness.

12. Remove the intake manifold support bracket bolts and nut. Remove the intake manifold attaching nuts and bolts.

13. Remove the intake manifold.

NOTE: Intake manifold mounting hole closest to chain housing is slotted for additional clearance.

To install:

14. Install the intake manifold and gasket. Tightening the intake manifold bolts/nuts in sequence and to 18 ft. lbs. (25 Nm). Tighten intake manifold brace and retainers hand tight.

Tighten to specifications in the following sequence:

a. Nut to stud bolt—18 ft. lbs. (25 Nm).

b. Bolt to intake manifold—40 ft. lbs. (55 Nm).

c. Bolt to cylinder block—40 ft. lbs. (55 Nm).

15. Lubricate a new oil fill tube ring seal with engine oil. Install the tube between No. 1 and 2 intake tubes. Rotate as necessary to gain clearance for oil/air separator nipple on fill tube.

16. Locate the oil fill tube in its cylinder block opening. Align the fill tube so it is approximately in its installed position. Place the palm of the hand over the oil fill opening and press straight down to seat fill tube and seal into cylinder block.

17. Install oil/air separator assembly, it may be necessary to lubricate the hoses for ease of assembly.

18. Install throttle body to intake manifold using a new gasket.

19. Connect the injector harness connector.

20. Install the oil fill cap and oil level indicator stick.

21. Install the power brake vacuum hose.

22. Install the throttle cable bracket.

23. Connect the throttle body to air cleaner duct.

24. Install the coolant recovery tank, vacuum hose and electrical connector to the MAP sensor and to the MAT sensor.

25. Connect the negative battery cable.

2.8L Engine

1. Disconnect the negative battery cable. Relieve the fuel pressure. Drain the cooling system.

2. Disconnect the TV and accelerator cables from the plenum.

3. Remove the throttle body-to-plenum bolts and the throttle body. Remove the EGR valve.

4. Remove the plenum-to-intake

manifold bolts and the plenum. Disconnect and plug the fuel lines and return pipes at the fuel rail.

5. Remove the serpentine drive belt. Remove the power steering pump-to-bracket bolts and support the pump aside; do not disconnect the pressure hoses.

6. Remove the alternator-to-bracket bolts and support the alternator aside.

7. Loosen the alternator bracket. From the throttle body, disconnect the idle air vacuum hose.

8. Label and disconnect the electrical connectors from the fuel injectors. Remove the fuel rail.

9. Remove the breather tube. Disconnect the runners.

10. Remove both rocker arm cover-to-cylinder head bolts and the covers. Remove the radiator hose from the thermostat housing.

11. Label and disconnect the electrical connectors from the coolant temperature sensor and oil pressure sending unit. Remove the coolant sensor.

12. Remove the bypass hose from the filler neck and cylinder head.

13. Remove the intake manifold-to-cylinder head bolts and the manifold.

14. Loosen the rocker arm nuts, turn them 90 degrees and remove the pushrods; be sure to keep the components in order for installation purposes.

To install:

15. Clean all gasket mounting surfaces.

16. Place a $\frac{3}{16}$ in. bead of RTV sealant on the ridges where the manifold contacts the block.

17. Install a new intake manifold gasket.

18. Install the pushrod. Ensure proper seat in the lifter. Tighten the rocker arm nuts to 18 ft. lbs. (25 Nm).

19. Install the intake manifold and intake manifold bolts. Tighten the intake manifold-to-cylinder head bolts, following the torquing sequence, to 15 ft. lbs. (20 Nm) and retighten to 24 ft. lbs. (33 Nm).

20. Connect the bypass hose to the filler neck and cylinder head.

21. Install the coolant sensor. Connect the electrical connectors to the coolant temperature sensor and oil pressure sending unit.

22. Install both rocker arm covers and rocker arm cover-to-cylinder head bolts. Install the radiator hose to the thermostat housing.

23. Connect the runners. Install the breather tube.

24. Install the fuel rail. Connect the electrical connectors to the fuel injectors.

25. Install the alternator and the alternator-to-bracket bolts.

26. Connect the idle air vacuum hose to the throttle body.

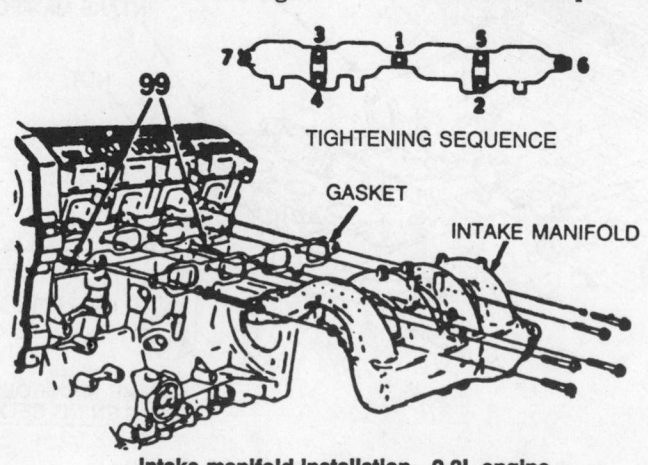

TIGHTENING SEQUENCE

GASKET

INTAKE MANIFOLD

Intake manifold installation—2.3L engine

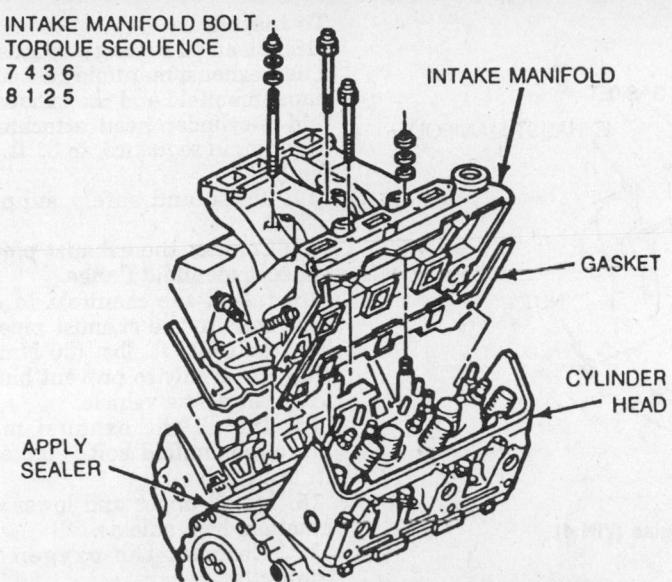

INTAKE MANIFOLD BOLT : TORQUE SEQUENCE
7 4 3 6
8 1 2 5

INTAKE MANIFOLD

GASKET

CYLINDER HEAD

APPLY SEALER

Intake manifold installation—2.8L and 3.1L engines

27. Install the power steering pump-to-bracket bolts. Install the serpentine drive belt.

28. Install the plenum and the plenum-to-intake manifold bolts. Connect the fuel lines and return pipes at the fuel rail.

29. Install the throttle body-to-plenum bolts and the throttle body. Install the EGR valve.

30. Connect the TV and accelerator cables to the plenum.

31. Connect the negative battery cable.

32. Fill cooling system and check for leaks. Start the engine and allow to come to normal operating temperature. Recheck for leaks. Top-up coolant.

3.1L Engine

1. Disconnect the negative battery cable. Relieve the fuel pressure and remove the air cleaner assembly. Drain the cooling system.

2. Disconnect the cables at the throttle body.

3. Disconnect the brake vacuum pipe at the plenum. Remove the cable bracket from the plenum.

4. Disconnect the throttle body at the plenum and remove the EGR valve from the plenum. Disconnect the harness at the plenum and remove the plenum assembly.

5. Disconnect the fuel lines at the fuel rail. Remove the serpentine drive belt. Remove the power steering pump-to-bracket bolts and support the pump aside; do not disconnect the pressure hoses.

6. Remove the alternator-to-bracket bolts and support the alternator aside.

7. Loosen the alternator bracket.

From the throttle body, disconnect the idle air vacuum hose.

8. Label and disconnect the electrical connectors from the fuel injectors. Remove the fuel rail.

9. Remove the plug wires at the intake.

10. Remove both rocker arm cover-to-cylinder head bolts and the covers. Remove the radiator hose from the thermostat housing.

11. Label and disconnect the electrical connectors from the coolant temperature sensor and oil pressure sending unit. Remove the coolant sensor.

12. Remove the bypass hose from the filler neck and cylinder head.

13. Remove the intake manifold-to-cylinder head bolts and the manifold.

14. Loosen the rocker arm nuts, turn them 90 degrees and remove the pushrods; be sure to keep the components in order for installation purposes.

To install:

15. Clean all gasket mounting surfaces.

16. Place a $3/16$ in. bead of RTV sealant on the ridges where the manifold contacts the block.

17. Install a new intake manifold gasket.

18. Install the pushrod. Ensure proper seat in the lifter. Tighten the rocker arm nuts to 18 ft. lbs. (25 Nm).

19. Install the intake manifold and intake manifold bolts. Tighten the intake manifold-to-cylinder head bolts, following the torquing sequence, to 15 ft. lbs. (20 Nm) and retighten to 24 ft. lbs. (33 Nm).

20. Connect the bypass hose to the filler neck and cylinder head.

21. Install the coolant sensor. Connect the electrical connectors to the coolant temperature sensor and oil pressure sending unit.

22. Install both rocker arm covers and rocker arm cover-to-cylinder head bolts. Install the radiator hose to the thermostat housing.

23. Connect the runners. Install the breather tube.

24. Install the fuel rail. Connect the electrical connectors to the fuel injectors.

25. Install the alternator and the alternator-to-bracket bolts.

26. Connect the idle air vacuum hose to the throttle body.

27. Install the power steering pump-to-bracket bolts. Install the serpentine drive belt.

28. Install the plenum and the plenum-to-intake manifold bolts. Connect the fuel lines and return pipes at the fuel rail.

29. Install the throttle body-to-plenum bolts and the throttle body. Install the EGR valve.

30. Connect the cables to the plenum.

31. Connect the negative battery cable.

32. Fill cooling system and check for leaks. Start the engine and allow to come to normal operating temperature. Recheck for leaks. Top-up coolant.

Exhaust Manifold

REMOVAL & INSTALLATION

2.0L and 2.2L Engines

1. Disconnect the negative battery cable.

2. Disconnect the oxygen sensor wire.

3. Remove the serpentine belt.

4. Remove the alternator-to-bracket bolts and position the alternator aside with the wires attached.

5. Raise and safely support the vehicle.

6. Disconnect the exhaust pipe-to-exhaust manifold bolts and lower the vehicle.

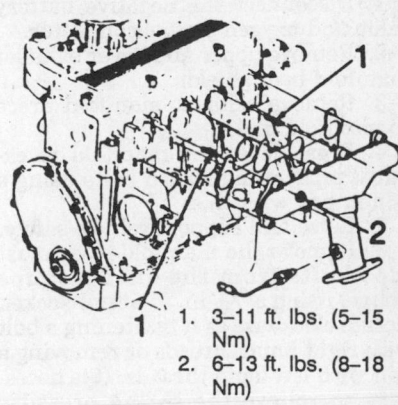

1. 3–11 ft. lbs. (5–15 Nm)
2. 6–13 ft. lbs. (8–18 Nm)

Exhaust manifold installation—2.0L and 2.2L (VIN G) engines

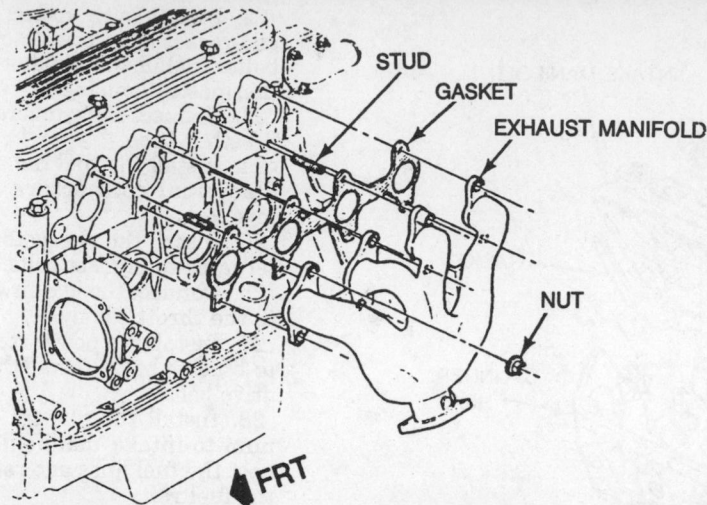

Exhaust manifold installation–2.2L engine (VIN 4)

7. Remove the oil fill tube and remove the exhaust manifold-to-cylinder head bolts.

8. Remove the exhaust manifold from the exhaust pipe flange and the manifold from the vehicle.

To install:

9. Clean the gasket mounting surfaces.

10. Using new gaskets, install the exhaust manifold and connect to the exhaust pipe flange. Tighten the exhaust manifold-to-cylinder head nuts to 3–11 ft. lbs. (4–15) Nm and bolts to 6–13 ft. lbs. (8–18 Nm).

11. Raise and safely support the vehicle.

12. Install the exhaust pipe-to-exhaust manifold bolts and lower the vehicle.

13. Install the alternator and the alternator-to-bracket bolts.

14. Install the serpentine belt.

15. Install the oil fill tube and connect the oxygen sensor wire.

16. Connect the negative battery cable.

2.3L Engine

1. Disconnect the negative battery cable and oxygen sensor connector.

2. Remove upper and lower exhaust manifold heat shields.

3. Remove exhaust manifold brace to manifold bolt.

4. Break loose the manifold to exhaust pipe spring loaded bolts using a 13mm box wrench.

5. Raise and support vehicle safely.

6. Remove the manifold-to-exhaust pipe bolts from the exhaust pipe flange, using a 7/32 in. (5.5mm) socket. Rotate clockwise as if tightening a bolt with right hand threads or removing a bolt with left hand threads. It is necessary to relieve the spring pressure from 1 bolt prior to removing the second bolt. If the spring pressure is not

relieved, it will cause the exhaust pipe to twist and bind the bolt as it is removed. Relieve the spring pressure by:

a. Thread 1 bolt out 4 turns.

b. Move to the other bolt and turn it all the way out of the exhaust pipe flange.

c. Return to the first bolt and rotate it the rest of the way out of the exhaust pipe flange.

7. Pull down and back on the exhaust pipe to disengage it from the exhaust manifold bolts.

8. Lower vehicle.

9. Remove exhaust manifold to cylinder head attaching nuts and remove exhaust manifold.

To install:

10. Clean all sealing surfaces. Install a new exhaust manifold gasket, the exhaust manifold and the exhaust manifold-to-cylinder head attaching nuts. Tighten, in sequence, to 31 ft. lbs. (42 Nm).

11. Raise and safely support the vehicle.

12. Connect the exhaust pipe to the exhaust manifold flange.

13. Install the manifold to exhaust pipe bolts to the exhaust pipe flange. Tighten to 22 ft. lbs. (30 Nm). Turn the nuts evenly to prevent binding.

14. Lower the vehicle.

15. Install the exhaust manifold brace-to-manifold bolt. Tighten to 19 ft. lbs. (26 Nm).

16. Install upper and lower exhaust manifold heat shields.

17. Connect the oxygen sensor connector.

18. Connect the negative battery cable.

2.8L and 3.1L Engines

LEFT SIDE

1. Disconnect the negative battery cable. Drain the cooling system.

2. Remove the air cleaner, air inlet hose and the mass air flow sensor.

3. Remove the coolant bypass pipe and coolant fan. Remove the manifold heat shield.

4. Disconnect the exhaust manifold crossover assembly at the right manifold.

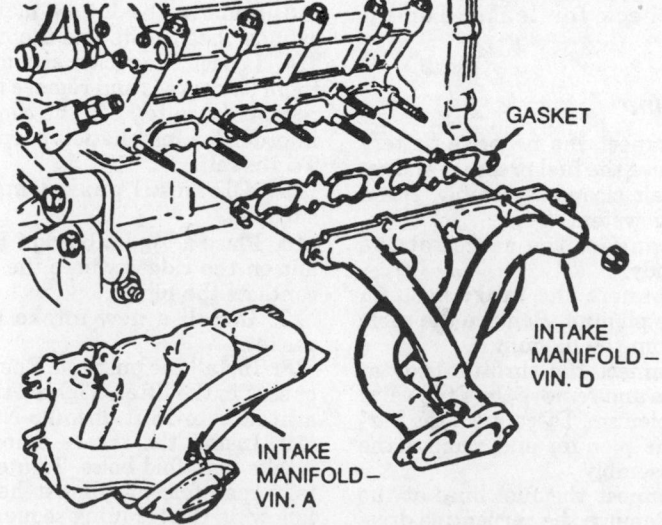

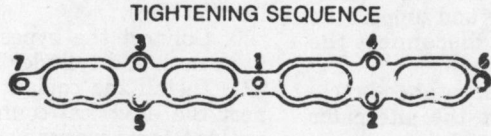

Exhaust manifold installation–2.3L engine

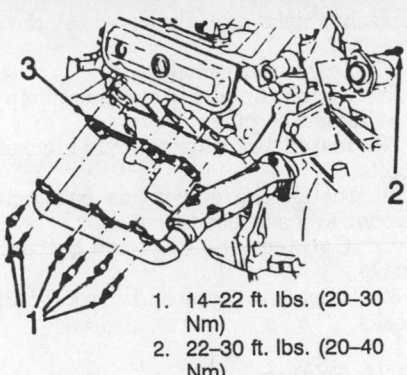

1. 14–22 ft. lbs. (20–30 Nm)
2. 22–30 ft. lbs. (20–40 Nm)
3. Gasket

Left side exhaust manifold installation—2.8L and 3.1L engines

5. Remove the exhaust manifold-to-cylinder head attaching bolts.
6. Remove the exhaust manifold with the crossover assembly.

To install:

7. Clean the gasket mounting surfaces.
8. Install the exhaust manifold with the crossover assembly. Tighten the exhaust manifold-to-cylinder head bolts to 19 ft. lbs. (26 Nm).
9. Connect the exhaust manifold crossover assembly to the right manifold.
10. Install the coolant bypass pipe. Install the manifold heat shield.
11. Install the mass air flow sensor, air inlet hose and air cleaner.
12. Connect the negative battery cable.
13. Fill cooling system and check for leaks. Start the engine and allow to come to normal operating temperature. Check for exhaust leaks and re-check for coolant leaks. Top-up coolant.

RIGHT SIDE

1. Remove the air cleaner assembly and disconnect the negative battery cable.
2. Raise and safely support the vehicle.
3. Remove the heat shield.
4. Remove the exhaust pipe-to-exhaust manifold bolts and the crossover pipe-to-exhaust manifold bolts.
5. Remove the EGR pipe-to-exhaust manifold bolts and the pipe.
6. Remove the accelerator cables and TV cables. Disconnect the oxygen sensor wire.
7. Remove the exhaust manifold-to-cylinder head bolts and the exhaust manifold from the vehicle.

To install:

8. Clean the gasket mounting surfaces.
9. Install the exhaust manifold and exhaust manifold-to-cylinder head bolts. Tighten the exhaust manifold-to-cylinder head bolts to 19 ft. lbs. (26

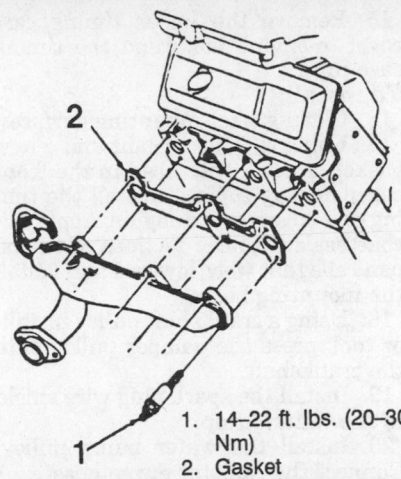

1. 14–22 ft. lbs. (20–30 Nm)
2. Gasket

Right side exhaust manifold installation—2.8L and 3.1L engines

Nm) and the crossover pipe bolts to 25 ft. lbs. (34 Nm).
10. Connect the oxygen sensor wire.
11. Install the EGR pipe and the EGR pipe-to-exhaust manifold bolts.
12. Install the exhaust pipe-to-exhaust manifold bolts and the crossover pipe-to-exhaust manifold bolts.
13. Install the heat shield.
14. Lower the vehicle.
15. Connect the negative battery cable. Start the engine and check for leaks.

Timing Chain Front Cover

REMOVAL & INSTALLATION

2.0L and 2.2L Engines

1. Disconnect the negative battery cable.
2. Raise and safely support the vehicle.
3. Drain the engine oil and remove the oil pan.
4. Lower the vehicle.
5. Remove the serpentine belt and the belt tensioner.
6. Remove the crankshaft pulley attaching bolt. Using a crankshaft pulley puller tool, remove the crankshaft pulley.
7. Remove the timing case cover bolts. Tap the cover with a rubber mallet and remove the cover.

To install:

8. Clean gasket mounting surfaces.
9. Using new gaskets, install the timing case cover over the dowels on the block and reverse the removal procedures. Tighten the timing case cover-to-engine bolts to 97 inch lbs. (11 Nm).
10. Using a crankshaft pulley installer tool, press the pulley onto the crankshaft. Tighten the crankshaft

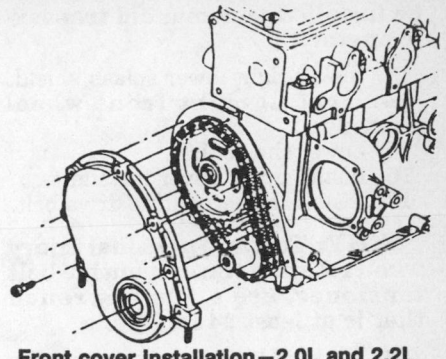

Front cover installation—2.0L and 2.2L engines

pulley bolt to 66–88 ft. lbs. (89–119 Nm).
11. Install the belt tensioner and serpentine belt.
12. Raise and safely support the vehicle.
13. Install the oil pan.
14. Lower the vehicle.
15. Fill the crankcase with oil to specification.
16. Connect the negative battery cable.
17. Start the engine and check for leaks.
18. Stop the engine, allow to stand for several minutes and check oil level.

2.3L Engine

1. Disconnect the negative battery cable from the battery. Remove coolant recovery reservoir.
2. Remove the serpentine drive belt.

NOTE: To avoid personal injury when rotating the serpentine belt tensioner, use a 13mm wrench that is at least 24 inch long.

3. Remove upper cover fasteners.
4. Raise and safely support the vehicle.
5. Remove right front wheel assembly.
6. Remove right lower splash shield.
7. Remove crankshaft balancer assembly.
8. Remove lower cover fasteners and lower vehicle.
9. Remove the front cover.

To install:

10. Install the front cover using new gaskets. Tighten to 106 inch lbs. (12 Nm).
11. Raise and safely support the vehicle. Install the remaining front cover bolts. Tighten to 106 inch lbs. (12 Nm).
12. Install crankshaft balancer assembly. Tighten the attaching bolt and washer for balancer assembly to 74 ft. lbs. (100 Nm).

NOTE: The automatic transaxle crankshaft balancer must not

be installed on a manual transaxle engine.

13. Install right lower splash shield.
14. Install right front wheel assembly.
15. Lower the vehicle.
16. Install upper cover fasteners.
17. Install the serpentine drive belt.

NOTE: To avoid personal injury when rotating the serpentine belt tensioner, use a 13mm wrench that is at least 24 inch long.

18. Install coolant recovery reservoir.
19. Connect the negative battery cable.

2.8L Engine

1. Disconnect the negative battery cable. Drain the cooling system.
2. Remove the serpentine belt and the belt tensioner.
3. Remove the alternator-to-bracket bolts and with the wires attached to the alternator, position it aside.
4. Remove the power steering pump-to-bracket bolts and support it aside; do not disconnect the pressure hoses.
5. Raise and safely support the vehicle.
6. Remove the right side inner fender splash shield and the flywheel dust cover.
7. Using a crankshaft pulley puller tool, remove the crankshaft damper.
8. Label and disconnect the starter wires and remove the starter.
9. Loosen the front 5 oil pan bolts, on both sides, enough to lower the oil pan ½ in.
10. Lower the vehicle. Disconnect the radiator hose from the water pump.
11. Disconnect the heater coolant hose from the cooling system filler pipe.
12. Remove the bypass and overflow hoses.
13. Remove the water pump pulley. Disconnect the canister purge hose.
14. Remove the spark plug wire shield from the water pump.

15. Remove the upper timing case cover-to-engine bolts and the timing case cover.

To install:
16. Clean gasket mounting surfaces.
17. Using silicone sealant and a new gasket, apply a thin bead to the front cover mating surface, install the timing case cover on the engine. Apply silicone sealant to the sections of the oil pan rails that were lowered and install the mounting bolts.
18. Using a crankshaft pulley installer tool, press the damper pulley onto the crankshaft.
19. Install the spark plug wire shield to the water pump.
20. Install the water pump pulley. Connect the canister purge hose.
21. Install the bypass and overflow hoses.
22. Connect the heater coolant hose to the cooling system filler pipe.
23. Raise and safely support the vehicle. Connect the radiator hose to the water pump.
24. Raise the oil pan into position and tighten the front 5 oil pan bolts.
25. Install the starter and connect the starter wires.
26. Install the right side inner fender

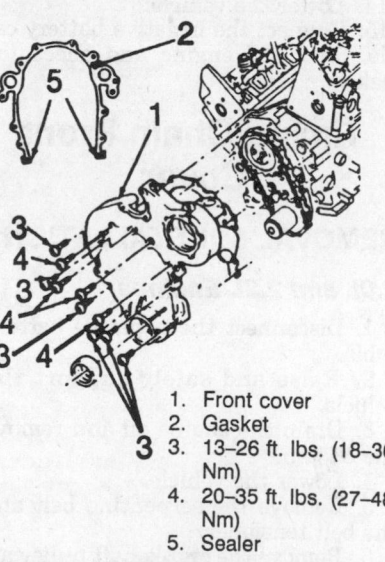

1. Front cover
2. Gasket
3. 13–26 ft. lbs. (18–36 Nm)
4. 20–35 ft. lbs. (27–48 Nm)
5. Sealer

Front cover Installation—2.8L and 3.1L engines

splash shield and the flywheel dust cover.
27. Lower the vehicle.
28. Install the power steering pump-to-bracket bolts.
29. Install the alternator-to-bracket bolts.
30. Install the serpentine belt tensioner and serpentine belt.
31. Connect the negative battery cable.
32. Start the engine and check for oil leaks.

3.1L Engine

1. Disconnect the negative battery cable. Drain the cooling system.
2. Remove the coolant reservoir.
3. Remove the serpentine belt and the belt tensioner.
4. Remove the power steering pump-to-bracket bolts and support it aside; do not disconnect the pressure hoses.
5. Raise and safely support the vehicle.
6. Remove the right side inner fender splash shield and the flywheel dust cover.
7. Using a crankshaft pulley puller tool, remove the crankshaft damper.
8. Remove the serpentine belt idler pulley.
9. Remove the oil pan and remove the lower cover bolts.
10. Lower the vehicle. Disconnect the radiator hose from the water pump.
11. Disconnect the bypass pipe at the front cover.
12. Disconnect the canister purge hose.
13. Remove the upper timing chain cover-to-engine bolts and the timing cover.

To install:
14. Clean gasket mounting surfaces.
15. Using silicone sealant and a new gasket, apply a thin bead to the front cover mating surface, install the timing case cover to the engine.
16. Raise and safely support the vehicle and install the oil pan.
17. Install the lower cover bolts.
18. Install the serpentine belt pulley and the crankshaft balancer.
19. Install the flywheel cover and the inner splash shield.
20. Lower the vehicle and connect the water pump hose, the bypass pipe and the canister purge hose.
21. Install the power steering pump.
22. Install the drive belt tensioner and install the serpentine belt to the vehicle.
23. Install the coolant reservoir. Fill the cooling system and connect the negative battery cable.
24. Start the engine and inspect for leaks.

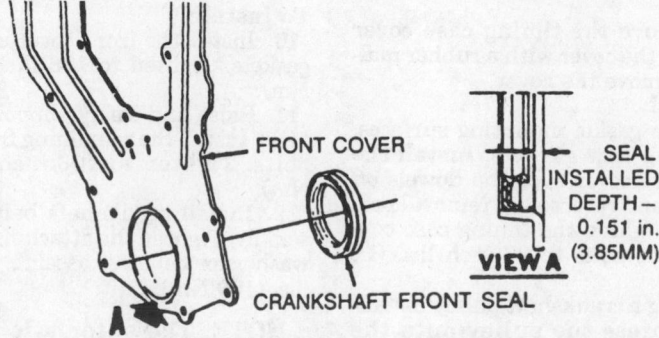

FRONT COVER

CRANKSHAFT FRONT SEAL

SEAL INSTALLED DEPTH— 0.151 in. (3.85MM)

VIEW A

Front cover Installation—2.3L engine

Front Cover Oil Seal

REPLACEMENT

2.0L and 2.2L Engines

1. Disconnect the negative battery cable. Remove the serpentine belt.
2. Raise and safely support the vehicle. Remove the right front wheel and tire assembly.
3. Remove the inner fender splash shield.
4. Remove the crankshaft pulley bolt.
5. Using a crankshaft pulley puller tool, remove the crankshaft pulley.
6. Using a small prybar, pry the oil seal from the front cover.

NOTE: Use care not to damage the seal seat or the crankshaft while removing or installing the seal. Inspect the sealing surface of the crankshaft for grooves or other wear.

To install:

7. Using an oil seal centering tool, drive the new seal into the cover with the lip facing towards the engine.
8. Install a crankshaft pulley installer tool, onto the crankshaft pulley and press the pulley onto the crankshaft. Install the pulley bolt and tighten to 66–88 ft. lbs. (89–119 Nm).
9. Remove the inner fender splash shield.
10. Remove the right front wheel and tire assembly.
11. Lower the vehicle.
12. Install the serpentine belt.
13. Connect the negative battery cable.

2.3L Engine

1. Disconnect the negative battery cable from the battery. Remove coolant recovery reservoir.
2. Remove the serpentine drive belt.

NOTE: To avoid personal injury when rotating the serpentine belt tensioner, use a 13mm wrench that is at least 24 in. long.

3. Remove upper cover attaching bolts.
4. Raise vehicle and support it safely.
5. Remove right front wheel assembly.
6. Remove right lower splash shield.
7. Remove crankshaft balancer assembly.
8. Remove lower cover attaching bolts and lower the vehicle.
9. Remove the front cover.

To install:

10. Install the front cover. Tighten the front cover attaching bolts to 106 inch lbs. (12 Nm).
11. Raise and safely support the vehicle.
12. Install lower cover attaching bolts.
13. Install crankshaft balancer assembly. Tighten attaching bolt and washer for balancer assembly to 74 ft. lbs. (100 Nm).

NOTE: The automatic transaxle crankshaft balancer must not be installed on a manual transaxle engine.

14. Install right lower splash shield.
15. Install right front wheel assembly.
16. Lower the vehicle.
17. Install upper cover attaching bolts.
18. Install the serpentine drive belt.

NOTE: To avoid personal injury when rotating the serpentine belt tensioner, use a 13mm wrench that is at least 24 in. long.

19. Install coolant recovery reservoir.
20. Connect the negative battery cable.

2.8L Engine

1. Disconnect the negative battery cable. Remove the serpentine belt.
2. Raise and safely support the vehicle. Remove the right side inner fender splash shield.
3. Remove the damper attaching bolt.
4. Using a crankshaft pulley puller tool, press the damper pulley from the crankshaft.
5. Using a small prybar, pry out the seal in the front cover.

NOTE: Use care not to damage the seal seat or the crankshaft while removing or installing the seal. Inspect the crankshaft seal surface for signs of grooves or wear.

To install:

6. Using a seal installer tool, drive the new seal in the cover with the lip facing towards the engine.
7. Using a crankshaft pulley installer tool, press the crankshaft pulley onto the crankshaft. Tighten the damper bolt to 67–85 ft. lbs. (90–115 Nm).
8. Install the right side inner fender splash shield. Lower the vehicle.
9. Install the serpentine belt.
10. Connect the negative battery cable.

3.1L Engine

1. Disconnect the negative battery cable. Remove the serpentine belt.
2. Raise and safely support the vehicle. Remove the right front wheel and remove the right side inner fender splash shield.
3. Remove the damper attaching bolt.
4. Using a crankshaft pulley puller tool, press the damper pulley from the crankshaft.
5. Remove the key from the keyway.
6. Using a small prybar, pry out the seal in the front cover.

NOTE: Use care not to damage the seal seat or the crankshaft while removing or installing the seal. Inspect the crankshaft seal surface for signs of grooves or wear.

To install:

7. Using a seal installer tool, drive the new seal in the cover with the lip facing towards the engine.
8. Install the key to the keyway.
9. Using a crankshaft pulley installer tool, press the crankshaft pulley onto the crankshaft. Tighten the damper bolt to 67–85 ft. lbs. (90–115 Nm).
10. Install the right side inner fender splash shield and the right front wheel. Lower the vehicle.
11. Install the serpentine belt.
12. Connect the negative battery cable.

Timing Chain and Sprockets

REMOVAL & INSTALLATION

2.0L and 2.2L Engines

1. Disconnect the negative battery cable. Remove the timing case cover.

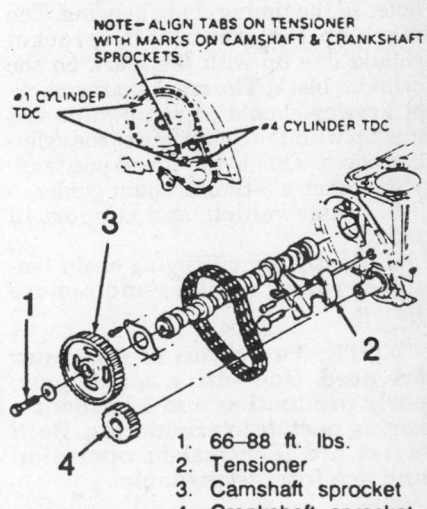

NOTE— ALIGN TABS ON TENSIONER WITH MARKS ON CAMSHAFT & CRANKSHAFT SPROCKETS.

#1 CYLINDER TDC   #4 CYLINDER TDC

1. 66–88 ft. lbs.
2. Tensioner
3. Camshaft sprocket
4. Crankshaft sprocket

Timing chain and sprockets installation— 2.0L and 2.2L engines

2. Rotate the crankshaft to until the marks on the crankshaft and camshaft sprockets are aligned.

3. Remove the timing chain tensioner upper bolt.

4. Loosen the timing chain tensioner nut as far as possible but do not remove the nut.

5. Remove the timing chain and camshaft sprocket.

6. Using a gear puller, remove the crankshaft sprocket.

To install:

7. Before installing the camshaft sprocket, lubricate the thrust side with Molykote® or equivalent. Using a sprocket installer tool, install the crankshaft sprocket.

8. Align the camshaft sprocket mark with the crankshaft sprocket marks. Install the timing chain and camshaft sprocket.

9. Press the camshaft sprocket onto the camshaft using the camshaft sprocket bolt. Tighten the camshaft sprocket bolt to 66–88 ft. lbs. (89–119 Nm).

10. Align the tabs on the tensioner with the marks on the camshaft and crankshaft sprockets and tighten the tensioner.

11. Install the timing case cover.

12. Connect the negative battery cable.

2.3L Engine

NOTE: Prior to removing the timing chain, review the entire procedure.

1. Disconnect the negative battery cable.

2. Remove front engine cover and crankshaft oil slinger.

3. Rotate the crankshaft clockwise, as viewed from front of engine/normal rotation until the camshaft sprockets' timing dowel pin holes line up with the holes in the timing chain housing. The mark on the crankshaft sprocket should line up with the mark on the cylinder block. The crankshaft sprocket keyway should point upwards and line up with the centerline of the cylinder bores. This is the timed position.

4. Remove 3 timing chain guides.

5. Raise vehicle and support in safely.

6. Gently pry off timing chain tensioner spring retainer and remove spring.

NOTE: Two styles of tensioner are used. One with a spring post, early production and 1 without a spring post, late production. Both styles are identical in operation and are interchangeable.

7. Remove timing chain tensioner shoe retainer.

8. Make sure all the slack in the timing chain is above the tensioner assembly; remove the chain tensioner shoe. The timing chain must be disengaged from the wear grooves in the tensioner shoe in order to remove the shoe. Slide a prybar under the timing chain while pulling shoe outward.

9. If difficulty is encountered removing chain tensioner shoe, proceed as follows:

a. Lower the vehicle.

b. Hold the intake camshaft sprocket with a holding tool and remove the sprocket bolt and washer.

c. Remove the washer from the bolt and re-thread the bolt back into the camshaft by hand, the bolt provides a surface to push against.

d. Remove intake camshaft sprocket using a 3-jaw puller in the 3 relief holes in the sprocket. Do not attempt to pry the sprocket off the camshaft or damage to the sprocket or chain housing could occur.

10. Remove tensioner assembly attaching bolts and tensioner.

--- **CAUTION** ---
Tensioner piston is spring loaded and could fly out causing personal injury.

11. Remove chain housing to block stud, timing chain tensioner shoe pivot.

12. Remove timing chain.

NOTE: Failure to follow this procedure could result in severe engine damage.

To install:

13. Tighten intake camshaft sprocket attaching bolt and washer, to specification while holding sprocket in place.

14. Install a special tool through holes in camshaft sprockets into holes in timing chain housing, this positions the camshafts for correct timing.

15. If the camshafts are out of position and must be rotated more than 1/8 turn in order to install the alignment dowel pins, perform the following:

a. The crankshaft must be rotated 90 degrees clockwise off TDC in order to give the valves adequate clearance to open.

b. Once the camshafts are in position and the dowels installed, rotate the crankshaft counterclockwise back to top dead center. Do not rotate the crankshaft clockwise to TDC, valve or piston damage could occur.

16. Install timing chain over exhaust camshaft sprocket, around idler sprocket and around crankshaft sprocket.

17. Remove the alignment dowel pin from the intake camshaft. Using a dowel pin remover tool rotate the intake camshaft sprocket counterclockwise enough to slide the timing chain over the intake camshaft sprocket. Release the camshaft sprocket wrench. The length of chain between the 2 camshaft sprockets will tighten. If properly timed, the intake camshaft

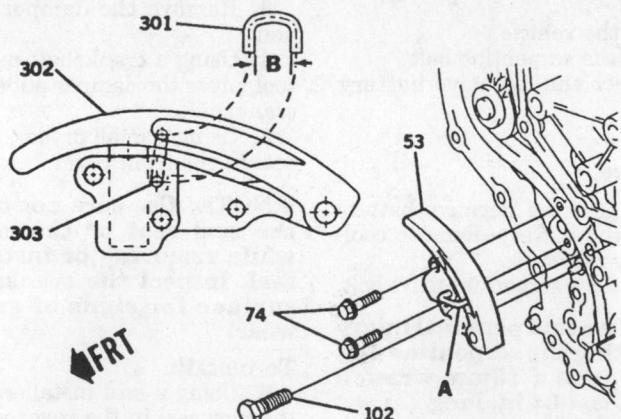

A. AFTER INSTALLATION, REMOVE ANTI-RELEASE
   FROM TENSIONER ASSEMBLY TO RELEASE TENSIONER
B. 13 MM (1/2 INCH)

53. TIMING CHAIN TENSIONER AND SHOE ASSEMBLY

74. BOLTS, 10 N•m (84 LBS. IN.)

120. BOLT - 26 N•m (19 LBS. FT.)

301. ANTI-RELEASE KEEPER - FABRICATE FROM
     HEAVY GAGE WIRE OR STEEL ROD
302. BLADE
303. RESET ACCESS HOLE

Timing chain tensioner–2.3L engine (1992–93)

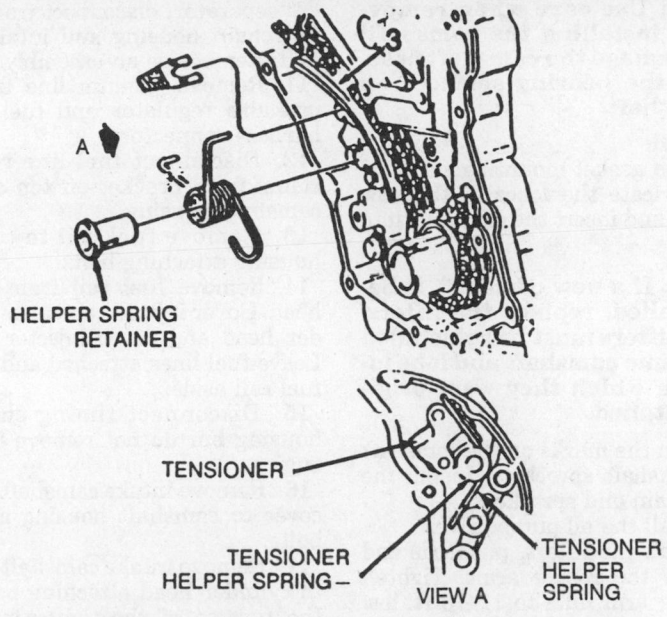

Installing the timing chain tensioner—1989–91 2.3L engine

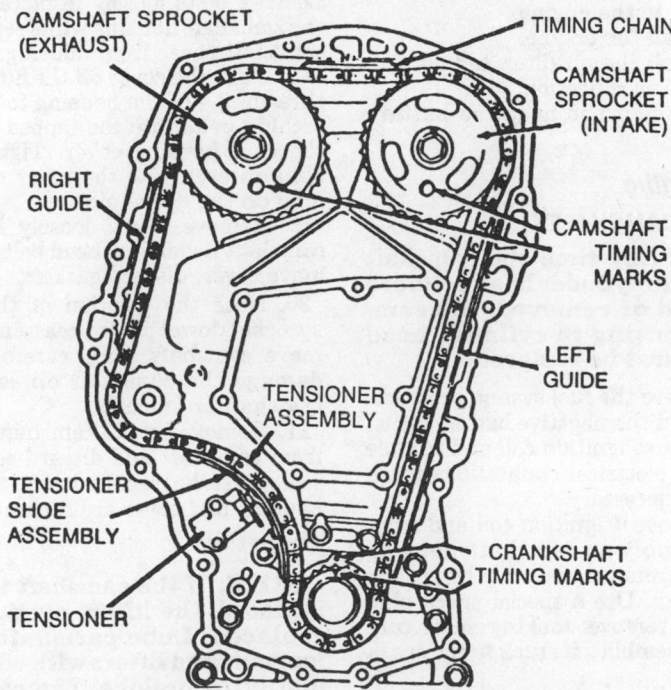

Timing chain installation—2.3L engine

alignment dowel pin should slide in easily. If the dowel pin does not fully index, the camshafts are not timed correctly and the procedure must be repeated.

18. Leave the alignment dowel pins installed.

19. With slack removed from chain between intake camshaft sprocket and crankshaft sprocket, the timing marks on the crankshaft and the cylinder block should be aligned. If marks are not aligned, move the chain 1 tooth forward or rearward, remove slack and recheck marks.

20. Tighten chain housing to block stud, timing chain tensioner shoe pivot. Stud is installed under the timing chain. Tighten to 19 ft. lbs. (26 Nm).

21. Reload timing chain tensioner assembly to its zero position as follows:

a. Assemble restraint cylinder, spring and nylon plug into plunger. Index slot in restraint cylinder with peg in plunger. While rotating the restraint cylinder clockwise, push the restraint cylinder into the plunger until it bottoms. Keep rotating the restraint cylinder clockwise but allow the spring to push it out of the plunger. The pin in the plunger will lock the restraint in the loaded position.

b. Install a special plunger installer tool into plunger assembly.

c. Install plunger assembly into tensioner body with the long end toward the crankshaft when installed.

22. Install tensioner assembly to chain housing. Recheck plunger assembly installation. It is correctly installed when the long end is toward the crankshaft.

23. Install and tighten timing chain tensioner bolts and tighten to 10 ft. lbs. (14 Nm).

24. Install tensioner shoe and tensioner shoe retainer.

25. Remove the special tool from the plunger and squeeze plunger assembly into tensioner body to unload the plunger assembly.

26. Lower vehicle enough to reach and remove the alignment dowel pins. Rotate crankshaft clockwise 2 full rotations. Align crankshaft timing mark with mark on cylinder block and reinstall alignment dowel pins. Alignment dowel pins will slide in easily if engine is timed correctly.

NOTE: If the engine is not correctly timed, severe engine damage could occur.

27. Install 3 timing chain guides and crankshaft oil slinger.

28. Install engine front cover.

29. Connect the negative battery cable. Start engine and check for oil leaks.

2.8L and 3.1L Engines

1. Disconnect the negative battery cable. Remove the front cover.

2. Rotate the crankshaft to position the No. 1 piston at TDC with the crankshaft and camshaft sprockets aligned.

NOTE: When the camshaft and crankshaft marks are aligned, the No. 4 piston is on the TDC of its compression stroke.

3. Remove the camshaft sprocket bolts, the sprocket and the timing chain.

4. Remove the crankshaft sprocket.

To install:

5. Before installing the sprockets, apply Molykote® or equivalent, to the thrust face of the sprocket(s).

6. Install the sprocket on the crankshaft.

7. Hold the camshaft sprocket with the chain hanging down. Align the

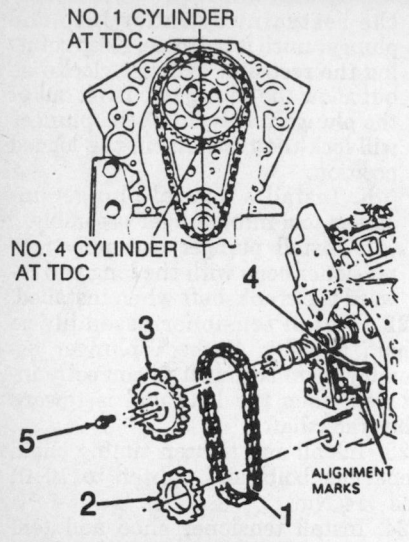

NO. 1 CYLINDER AT TDC

NO. 4 CYLINDER AT TDC

NOTE—ALIGN TIMING MARKS ON CAM & CRANK SPROCKETS USING ALIGNMENT MARKS ON DAMPER STAMPING OR CAST ALIGNMENT MARKS ON CYL & CASE.

1. Timing chain
2. Crankshaft sprocket
3. Camshaft sprocket
4. Damper
5. 15–20 ft. lbs.

Timing chain and sprockets installation— 2.8L and 3.1L engines

marks on the camshaft and crankshaft sprockets.

8. Align the dowel in the camshaft with the sprocket. Install the sprocket and timing chain using a camshaft bolt to pull the sprocket into position.

9. Tighten the camshaft bolts to 15–20 ft. lbs. (20–27 Nm).

10. Lubricate the new timing chain with clean engine oil.

11. Install the front cover.

12. Connect the negative battery cable. Start the engine and check for leaks.

Camshaft

REMOVAL & INSTALLATION

2.0L and 2.2L Engines

1. Relieve the fuel pressure. Disconnect the negative battery cable. Remove the engine and attach it to an engine stand.

2. Remove the timing chain and sprocket from the engine.

3. Drain the engine oil and remove the oil filter.

4. Remove the rocker cover. Loosen the rocker arms and turn the rocker arms 90 degrees. Remove the pushrods and lifters; note the position of the valve train components for reassembly purposes.

5. Remove the oil pump drive.

6. Remove the camshaft thrust plate-to-engine bolts and carefully pull the camshaft from the engine.

NOTE: Use care when removing and installing the camshaft; do not damage the camshaft bearings or the bearing surfaces on the camshaft.

To install:

7. Clean gasket mounting surfaces.

8. Lubricate the lobes of the new camshaft and insert the camshaft into the engine.

NOTE: If a new camshaft is being installed, replace the lifters. Reused lifters must be reinstalled on the same camshaft and lobe location in which they were originally installed.

9. Align the marks on the camshaft and crankshaft sprockets. Install the timing chain and sprocket.

10. Install the oil pump drive.

11. Install the lifters, pushrods and reposition the rocker arms. Tighten the rocker arm nuts to 11–18 ft. lbs. (15–24 Nm).

12. Install the rocker covers.

13. Install the timing chain and sprockets to the engine.

14. Install the engine.

15. Install the oil filter and add engine oil to specification.

16. Connect the negative battery cable.

2.3L Engine

INTAKE CAMSHAFT

NOTE: Any time the camshaft housing to cylinder head bolts are loosened or removed, the camshaft housing to cylinder head gasket must be replaced.

1. Relieve the fuel system pressure. Disconnect the negative battery cable.

2. Remove ignition coil and module assembly electrical connections mark or tag, if necessary.

3. Remove 4 ignition coil and module assembly to camshaft housing bolts and remove assembly by pulling straight up. Use a special spark plug boot wire remover tool to remove connector assemblies if stuck to the spark plugs.

4. Remove the idle speed power steering pressure switch connector.

5. Loosen 3 power steering pump pivot bolts and remove drive belt.

6. Disconnect the 2 rear power steering pump bracket to transaxle bolts.

7. Remove the front power steering pump bracket to cylinder block bolt.

8. Disconnect the power steering pump assembly and position aside.

9. Using special tools remove power steering pump drive pulley from intake camshaft.

10. Remove oil/air separator bolts and hoses. Leave the hoses attached to

the separator, disconnect from the oil fill, chain housing and intake manifold. Remove as an assembly.

11. Remove vacuum line from fuel pressure regulator and fuel injector harness connector.

12. Disconnect fuel line retaining clamp from bracket on top of intake camshaft housing.

13. Remove fuel rail to camshaft housing attaching bolts.

14. Remove fuel rail from cylinder head. Cover injector openings in cylinder head and cover injector nozzles. Leave fuel lines attached and position fuel rail aside.

15. Disconnect timing chain and housing but do not remove from the engine.

16. Remove intake camshaft housing cover to camshaft housing attaching bolts.

17. Remove intake camshaft housing to cylinder head attaching bolts. Use the reverse of the tightening procedure when loosening camshaft housing to cylinder head attaching bolts. Leave 2 bolts loosely in place to hold the camshaft housing while separating camshaft cover from housing.

18. Push the cover off the housing by threading 4 of the housing to head attaching bolts into the tapped holes in the cam housing cover. Tighten the bolts in evenly so the cover does not bind on the dowel pins.

19. Remove the 2 loosely installed camshaft housing to head bolts and remove cover, discard gaskets.

20. Note the position of the chain sprocket dowel pin for reassembly. Remove camshaft being careful not to damage the camshaft oil seal from camshaft or journals.

21. Remove intake camshaft oil seal from camshaft and discard seal. This seal must be replaced any time the housing and cover are separated.

To install:

NOTE: If the camshaft is being replaced, the lifters must also be replaced. Lube camshaft lobes, journals and lifters with camshaft and lifter prelube. The camshaft lobes and journals must be adequately lubricated or engine damage could occur upon start up.

22. Install camshaft in same position as when removed. The timing chain sprocket dowel pin should be straight up and line up with the centerline of the lifter bores.

23. Install new camshaft housing to camshaft housing cover seals into cover. Do not use sealer.

NOTE: Cam housing to cover seals are all different.

24. Apply locking type sealer to cam-

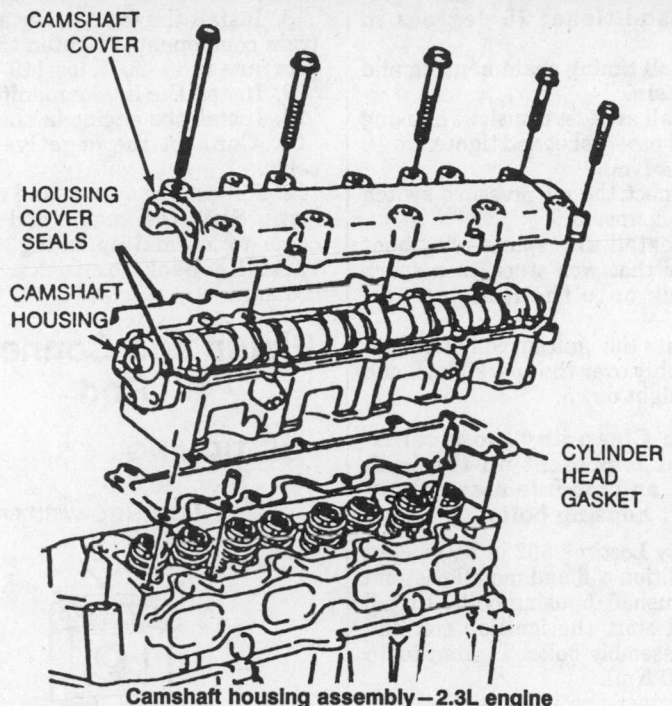

Camshaft housing assembly — 2.3L engine

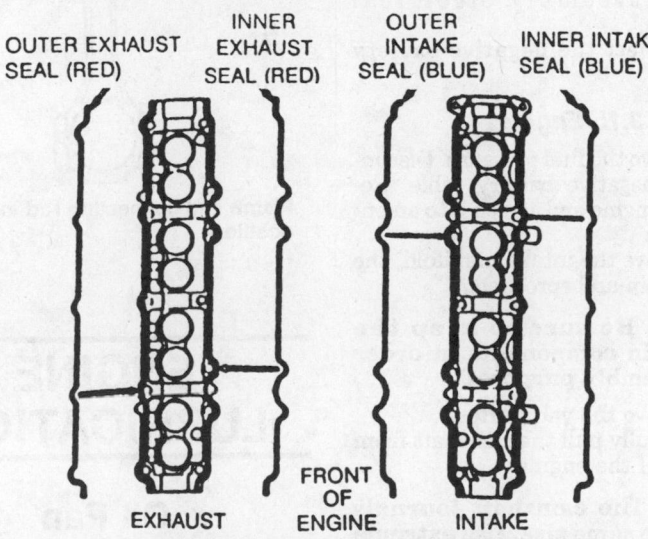

OUTER EXHAUST SEAL (RED)   INNER EXHAUST SEAL (RED)   OUTER INTAKE SEAL (BLUE)   INNER INTAKE SEAL (BLUE)

EXHAUST   FRONT OF ENGINE   INTAKE

Camshaft cover seals — 2.3L engine

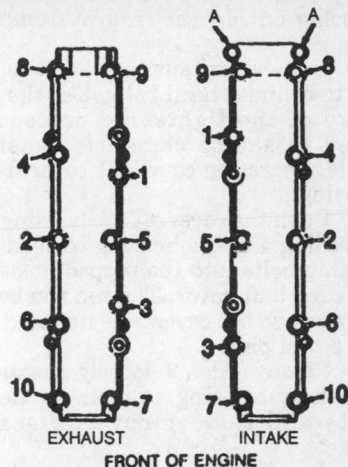

EXHAUST   INTAKE

FRONT OF ENGINE

A. 16 ft. lbs. (15 Nm), rotate and additional 25 degrees

Camshaft housing bolt torque sequence — 2.3L engine

shaft housing and cover attaching bolt threads.

25. Install bolts and tighten to 11 ft. lbs. (15 Nm). Rotate the bolts an additional 75 degrees in sequence.

NOTE: Tighten the 2 rear bolts that hold fuel pipe to camshaft housing to 11 ft. lbs. (15 Nm), then rotate the bolts an additional 25 degrees.

26. Install timing chain housing and timing chain.
27. Uncover fuel injectors and install new fuel injector ring seals lubed with engine oil.
28. Install fuel rail to cylinder head.
29. Install fuel rail to camshaft housing attaching bolts.

30. Connect fuel line retaining clamp to bracket on top of intake camshaft housing.
31. Install vacuum line to fuel pressure regulator and fuel injector harness connector.
32. Install oil/air separator bolts and hoses.
33. Install power steering pump drive pulley to intake camshaft.
34. Install the power steering pump assembly.
35. Install the front power steering pump bracket to cylinder block bolt.
36. Connect the 2 rear power steering pump bracket to transaxle bolts.
37. Tighten the 3 power steering pump pivot bolts and install serpentine belt.

38. Connect the idle speed power steering pressure switch connector.
39. Install ignition module assembly and the 4 ignition coil and module assembly to camshaft housing bolts.

NOTE: Clean any loose lubricant that is present on the ignition coil and module assembly to camshaft housing bolts. Apply Loctite® 592 or equivalent onto the ignition coil and module assembly to camshaft housing bolts. Install the bolts and tighten to 13 ft. lbs. (18 Nm).

40. Connect ignition coil and module assembly electrical connectors.
41. Connect the negative battery cable.

EXHAUST CAMSHAFT

NOTE: Any time the camshaft housing to cylinder head bolts are loosened or removed the camshaft housing to cylinder head gasket must be replaced.

1. Relieve the fuel system pressure. Disconnect the negative battery cable.
2. Remove electrical connection from ignition coil and module assembly.
3. Remove 4 ignition coil and module assembly to camshaft housing bolts and remove assembly by pulling straight up. Use a special tool to remove connector assembly if stuck to the spark plugs.
4. Remove electrical connection from oil pressure switch.
5. Remove transaxle fluid level indicator tube assembly from exhaust camshaft cover and position aside.
6. Remove exhaust camshaft cover and gasket.
7. Disconnect timing chain and

housing but do not remove from the engine.

8. Remove exhaust camshaft housing to cylinder head bolts. Use the reverse of the tightening procedure when loosening camshaft housing while separating camshaft cover from housing.

9. Push the cover off the housing by threading 4 of the housing to head attaching bolts into the tapped holes in the camshaft cover. Tighten the bolts in evenly so the cover does not bind on the dowel pins.

10. Remove the 2 loosely installed camshaft housing to cylinder head bolts and remove cover, discard gaskets.

11. Loosely reinstall 1 camshaft housing to cylinder head bolt to hold the camshaft housing in place during camshaft and lifter removal.

12. Note the position of the chain sprocket dowel pin for reassembly. Remove camshaft being careful not to damage the camshaft or journals.

13. If removing the camshaft housing, remove the valve lifters. Keep the lifters in order so they can be reinstalled in the same location.

14. Remove the camshaft housing and gasket.

To install:

15. Install the camshaft housing and gasket.

16. Loosely install one camshaft housing-to-cylinder head bolt to hold the housing in place.

NOTE: Used lifters must be returned to their original position in the camshaft. If the camshaft is being replaced, the lifters must also be replaced. Lube camshaft lobe, journals and lifters with camshaft and lifter prelube. The camshaft lobes and journals must be adequately lubricated or engine damage could occur upon start up.

17. Install the lifters into the lifter bores.

18. Install camshaft in same position as when removed. The timing chain sprocket dowel pin should be straight up and line up with the centerline of the lifter bores.

19. Install new camshaft housing-to-camshaft housing cover seals into cover, no sealer is needed.

NOTE. Cam housing to cover seals are all different.

20. Remove the bolt holding the housing in place. Apply locking type sealer to camshaft housing and cover attaching bolt threads.

21. Install camshaft housing cover to camshaft housing.

22. Install bolts and tighten in sequence to 11 ft. lbs. (15 Nm), then ro-

tate an additional 75 degrees in sequence.

23. Install timing chain housing and timing chain.

24. Install exhaust camshaft housing cover and new gasket and tighten to 10 ft. lbs. (14 Nm).

25. Connect the oil pressure switch electrical connector.

26. Reinstall any spark plug boot connector that was stuck to a spark plug back onto the ignition coil assembly.

27. Locate the ignition coil and module assembly over the spark plugs and push straight down.

NOTE: Clean any loose lubricant that is present on the ignition coil and module assembly to camshaft housing bolts.

28. Apply Loctite® 592 or equivalent to the ignition coil and module assembly to camshaft housing bolts. Install and hand start the ignition coil and module assembly bolts. Tighten to 15 ft. lbs. (20 Nm).

29. Connect the ignition coil and module assembly electrical connectors.

30. Connect the negative battery cable.

2.8L and 3.1L Engines

1. Relieve the fuel pressure. Disconnect the negative battery cable. Remove the engine and attach it to an engine stand.

2. Remove the intake manifold, the timing chain and sprockets.

NOTE: Be sure to keep the valve train components in order for reassembly purposes.

3. Remove the valve lifters.

4. Carefully pull the camshaft from the front of the engine.

NOTE: The camshaft journals are all the same size. Use extreme care when removing or installing the camshaft not to damage the camshaft bearings or the bearing journals of the camshaft.

To install:

5. Clean gasket mounting surfaces.

6. If installing a new camshaft, lubricate the camshaft lobes and insert the camshaft in the engine.

NOTE: If a new camshaft is being used, replace all of the lifters. Used lifters can only be used on the camshaft that they were originally installed with; provided they are installed in the exact same position they were removed.

7. Align the camshaft and crankshaft sprocket marks. Install the timing chain and sprocket.

8. Install the front cover and valve train components. Tighten the rocker arm nuts to 14–20 ft. lbs. (19–27 Nm).

9. Install the intake manifold.

10. Install the engine in the vehicle.

11. Connect the negative battery cable.

12. Fill cooling system and check for leaks. Start the engine and allow to come to normal operating temperature. Recheck for leaks. Top-up coolant.

Piston and Connecting Rod

POSITIONING

NOTCH TOWARD FRONT OF ENGINE

Piston and connecting rod installation position

ENGINE LUBRICATION

Oil Pan

REMOVAL & INSTALLATION

2.0L and 2.2L Engines

1. Disconnect the negative battery cable. Remove the exhaust pipe shield.

2. Raise and safely support the vehicle. Drain the engine oil.

3. Disconnect the starter brace from the block. Label and disconnect the starter wires. Remove the starter.

4. Remove the flywheel dust cover.

5. Remove the right support bolts and lower the support for clearance to remove the oil pan. If equipped with an automatic transaxle, remove the oil filter and extension.

6. Remove the oil pan-to-engine bolts and nuts. Remove the oil pan.

To install:

7. Clean gasket mounting surfaces.

8. Install a new gasket. Apply a small bead of RTV sealant to the oil pan-to-engine block sealing surface. Apply a thin layer of RTV sealant on the ends of the oil pan rear seal.

9. Install the oil pan and attaching bolts. Tighten the oil pan-to-engine bolts to 6 ft. lbs. (8 Nm).

10. If removed, install the oil filter and extension.

11. Install the starter. Connect the electrical connectors. Install the starter brace to the block.

12. Install the flywheel cover and lower the vehicle.

13. Connect the negative battery cable.

14. Refill the engine with the clean engine oil. Start the engine and check for leaks.

2.3L Engine

1. Disconnect the negative battery cable.

2. Raise and support the vehicle safely.

3. Drain the oil and the cooling system.

4. Remove the flywheel inspection cover and remove the right front wheel.

5. Remove the splash shield-to-suspension support bolt.

6. Release tension from the serpentine drive belt. Remove the engine mount strut and strut bracket.

7. Remove the A/C compressor from the bracket and support it out of the way.

8. Remove the radiator and air conditioning outlet pipes from the suspension supports.

9. Remove the exhaust manifold brace.

10. Remove the oil pan to flywheel cover bolt and nut and remove the flywheel cover stud.

11. Remove the radiator outlet pipe from the lower radiator hose and from the oil pan.

12. Disconnect the oil level sensor wire, if equipped.

13. Remove the oil pan bolts. Remove the oil pan from the engine.
To install:

14. Install the oil pan to the engine. Install the oil pan bolts. Tighten the chain housing and carrier seal bolts to 106 inch lbs. (12 Nm). Tighten the oil pan-to-block bolts to 17 ft. lbs. (23 Nm).

15. Install the spacer and install the stud.

16. Install the oil pan-to-transaxle nut and tighten to 41 ft. lbs. (56 Nm).

17. Connect the oil level sensor wire.

18. Connect the radiator outlet pipes and the air conditioning pipes.

19. Install the exhaust manifold brace.

20. Install the engine mount strut

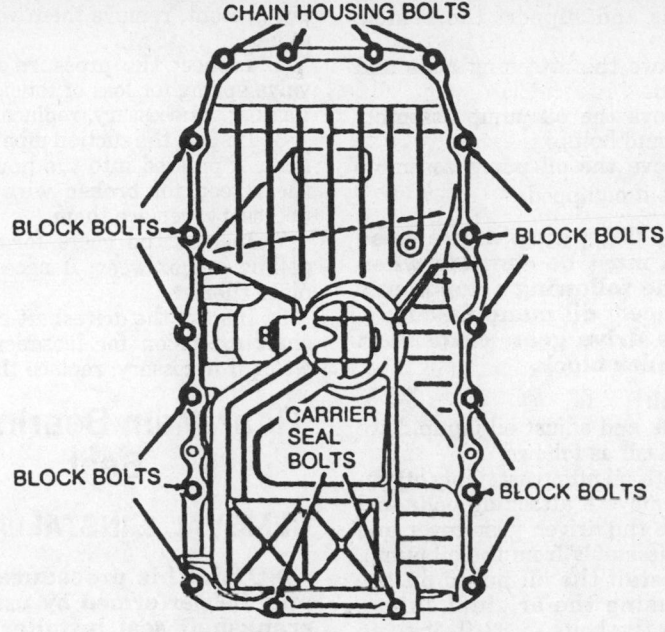

Oil pan installation—2.3L engine

bracket and install the A/C compressor. Install the engine mount strut.

21. Apply tension to the serpentine drive belt and install the right splash shield.

22. Install the right front wheel and the flywheel cover. Lower the vehicle.

23. Fill the crankcase with oil to specification and fill the cooling system.

24. Connect the negative battery cable. Start the engine and check for leaks.

25. Turn the engine OFF and allow to stand. Check oil level, add as necessary.

2.8L and 3.1L Engines

1. Disconnect the negative battery cable.

2. Raise and safely support the vehicle. Drain the engine oil.

3. Remove the flywheel dust cover and the oil filter.

4. Label and disconnect the starter wires. Remove the starter.

5. Remove the oil pan-to-engine nuts/bolts and the oil pan.
To install:

6. Clean gasket mounting surfaces.

7. Install a new gasket. Install the oil pan and attaching bolts. Tighten the oil pan nuts to 6–9 ft. lbs. (8–12 Nm) or bolts to 15–22 ft. lbs. (20–30 Nm).

8. Install the starter. Connect the electrical connectors.

9. Install the flywheel dust cover.

10. Install a new oil filter.

11. Lower the vehicle.

12. Fill the crankcase with oil to specification.

13. Connect the negative battery ca-

ble. Start the engine and check for leaks.

14. Turn the engine OFF and allow to stand. Check oil level, add as necessary.

Oil Pump

REMOVAL & INSTALLATION

Except 2.3L Engine

1. Disconnect the negative battery cable. Raise and safely support the vehicle. Drain the engine oil.

2. Remove the oil pan-to-engine bolts and the oil pan.

3. Remove the oil pump-to-rear main bearing cap bolt, the oil pump and extension shaft.
To install:

4. Install the extension shaft, oil pump and pump-to-rear main cap bolt. Tighten the oil pump-to-bearing cap bolt to 25–38 ft. lbs. (34–52 Nm) and the upper oil pump drive bolt to 14–22 ft. lbs. (19–30 Nm), on the 2.0L and 2.2L engines or to 25–38 ft. lbs. (34–52 Nm) on the 2.8L and 3.1L engines.

5. Install the oil pan and attaching bolts.

6. Lower the vehicle.

7. Fill the crankcase with oil to specification.

8. Connect the negative battery cable. Start the engine and check oil pressure and check for leaks.

9. Turn the engine OFF and allow to stand. Check oil level, add as necessary.

2.3L Engine

1. Disconnect the negative battery cable.

2. Raise and support the vehicle safely.

3. Remove the attaching bolts and the oil pan.

4. Remove the oil pump assembly retainers and bolts.

5. Remove the oil pump assembly and shims if equipped.

NOTE: Oil pump drive gear backlash must be checked when any of the following components are replaced: oil pump assembly, oil pump drive gear, crankshaft and cylinder block.

To install:

6. Check and adjust oil pump drive gear backlash as follows:

a. With oil pump assembly off engine, remove 3 attaching bolts and separate the driven gear cover and screen assembly from the oil pump.

b. Install the oil pump on the block using the original shims. Tighten the bolts to 33 ft. lbs. (45 Nm).

c. Install the dial indicator assembly to measure backlash between oil pump to drive gear.

d. Record oil pump drive to driven gear backlash correct backlash clearance is 0.0091–0.0201 in. (0.23–0.51mm). When taking measurement crankshaft cannot move.

e. Remove oil pump from block reinstall driven gear cover and screen assembly to pump and tighten to 106 inch lbs. (12 Nm).

f. Reinstall the pump assembly on block. Tighten oil pump-to-block bolts 33 ft. lbs. (45 Nm).

7. Install the oil pump assembly, including shims if removed.

8. Tighten oil pump to block bolts to 33 ft. lbs. (45 Nm).

9. Install the oil pan and attaching bolts.

10. Lower the vehicle.

11. Fill the crankcase with oil to specification.

12. Connect the negative battery cable. Start the engine and check oil pressure and check for leaks.

13. Turn the engine OFF and allow to stand. Check oil level, add as necessary.

CHECKING

1. If foreign matter is present, determine it's source.

2. Check the pump cover and housing for cracks, scoring and/or damage; if necessary, replace the housings.

3. Inspect the idler gear shaft for looseness in the housing; if necessary, replace the pump or timing chain, depending on the model.

4. Inspect the pressure regulator valve for scoring or sticking; if burrs

are present, remove them with an oil stone.

5. Inspect the pressure regulator valve spring for loss of tension or distortion; if necessary, replace it.

6. Inspect the suction pipe for looseness, if pressed into the housing and the screen for broken wire mesh; if necessary, replace them.

7. Inspect the gears for chipping, galling and/or wear; if necessary, replace them.

8. Inspect the driveshaft and driveshaft extension for looseness and/or wear; if necessary, replace them.

Rear Main Bearing Oil Seal

REMOVAL & INSTALLATION

NOTE: This procedure should only be performed by using rear crankshaft seal installer tool J–34686 for 2.0L (VIN 1), 2.2L, 2.8L or 3.1L engines or J–36005 for the 2.3L engine or equivalent.

1. Disconnect the negative battery cable. Remove the transaxle.

2. If equipped with a manual transaxle, matchmark and remove the clutch/flywheel assembly. If equipped with an automatic transaxle, remove the flywheel.

3. Using a small prybar, pry the rear main seal from the engine.

NOTE: Use care when removing or installing the seal to avoid damage to the crankshaft sealing surface. If equipped with a manual transaxle, inspect the condition of the clutch to insure that the clutch was not damaged by oil loss from the rear main seal.

To install:

4. To install the rear main oil seal, perform the following procedures:

a. Lubricate the seal bore and seal surface with engine oil.

b. Using a seal installation tool, press the new rear oil seal into the engine. The seal must fit squarely against the back of the tool.

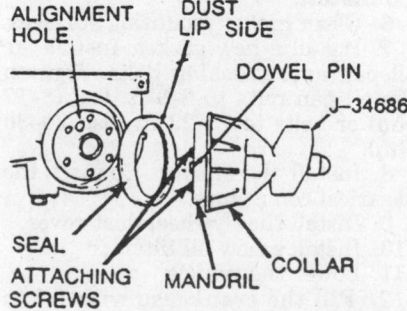

Rear main bearing oil seal installation

c. Align the dowel pin of the tool with the dowel pin in the crankshaft and tighten the attaching screws on the tool to 2–5 ft. lbs. (3–7 Nm).

d. Tighten the T-handle of the tool to push the seal into the seal bore.

e. Loosen the T-handle. Remove the attaching screws and tool.

f. Check the seal to make sure it is seated squarely in the bore.

5. Install the flywheel. Tighten the flywheel-to-crankshaft bolts to 45–59 ft. lbs. (61–80 Nm) for automatic transaxles or to 47–63 ft. lbs. (64–85 Nm) for manual transaxles.

6. Lower the vehicle and connect the negative battery cable.

7. Start the engine and check for leaks.

ENGINE COOLING

Radiator

REMOVAL & INSTALLATION

—— **CAUTION** ——

Before attempting any work on the cooling system, allow the engine to first cool sufficiently. To avoid personal injury, do not remove the radiator cap while the engine is at or above normal operation temperature.

1. Disconnect the negative battery cable. Remove the battery on 3.1L engine.

2. Remove the air cleaner assembly.

3. Drain the engine coolant into a clean container for reuse.

4. Disconnect the electrical connection from the electric fan.

5. Remove the fan-to-chassis mounting bolts and remove the fan assembly.

6. Disconnect the radiator upper and lower hoses at the radiator end.

7. If equipped with an automatic transaxle, disconnect the transaxle cooler lines and plug.

8. If equipped with A/C, disconnect the condenser line retaining clip.

9. Remove the upper radiator mounting bolts.

10. Remove the condenser-to-radiator mounting bolts.

11. Carefully lift the radiator out.

To install:

12. Install the radiator in the vehicle.

13. Install the condenser-to-radiator mounting bolts.

14. Install the upper radiator mounting bolts.

15. Tighten the radiator mounting bolts to 90 inch lbs. (10 Nm).

16. If equipped with an automatic transaxle, connect the transaxle cooler lines.

17. Connect the radiator upper and lower hoses at the radiator end.

18. Install the fan assembly and the fan-to-chassis mounting bolts.

19. Connect the electrical connection to the electric fan.

20. Connect the negative battery cable. Install the battery to the 3.1L engine.

21. Fill cooling system and check for leaks. Start the engine and allow to come to normal operating temperature. Recheck for leaks. Top-up coolant.

22. Install the air cleaner assembly.

Electric Cooling Fan

TESTING

Coolant Temperature Switch

The coolant temperature switch is located at the left side of the engine on the coolant outlet on 2.0L and 2.2L engines. On the left rear of side of the engine on the 2.3L engine or on the top left side of the engine on 2.8L and 3.1L engines.

1. Drain the cooling system to a level below the coolant temperature switch.

2. Disconnect the electrical connector and remove the switch.

3. Using an ohmmeter, connect it's leads to the switch and submerge the tip of the switch in a container of water.

4. Heat the water to at least 230°F (108°C); the switch should close and cause the ohmmeter to show conductivity.

5. Allow the switch to cool to at least 220°F (101°C); the switch should open and cause the ohmmeter to show no conductivity.

6. If the switch does respond accordingly, replace it.

Coolant Fan Pressure Switch

If equipped with air conditioning, the coolant fan pressure switch is located on the refrigerant line at the front, right side of the engine compartment.

When the air conditioning switch is turned **ON** and the low pressure switch is CLOSED, the cooling fan will turn ON.

Electric Fan Relay

The electric fan relay is located at the center, front of the dash on the relay block.

The ECM reads the sensor information and sends an electrical impulse to

the relay's primary circuit causing the cooling fan to turn ON.

REMOVAL & INSTALLATION

1. Disconnect the negative battery cable.

2. Disconnect the electrical wiring harness from the cooling fan frame.

3. Remove the fan assembly from the radiator support.

To install:

4. Install the fan assembly to the radiator support. Tighten the fan assembly-to-radiator support bolts to 7 ft. lbs. (10 Nm).

5. Connect the cooling fan electrical connector.

6. Connect the negative battery cable.

Heater Core

REMOVAL & INSTALLATION

1989–90

WITHOUT AIR CONDITIONING

1. Disconnect the negative battery cable. Drain the engine coolant into a clean container for reuse.

2. Disconnect the heater hoses from the heater core.

3. Remove the right and left sound insulators and the steering column trim cover.

4. Remove the heater air outlet deflector.

5. Remove the heater core cover, the heater core and retaining straps.

To install:

6. Install the heater core cover, the heater core and retaining straps.

7. Install the heater air outlet deflector.

8. Install the right and left sound insulators and the steering column trim cover.

9. Connect the heater hoses to the heater core.

10. Connect the negative battery cable.

11. Fill cooling system and check for leaks. Start the engine and allow to come to normal operating temperature. Recheck for leaks. Top-up coolant.

WITH AIR CONDITIONING

1. Disconnect the negative battery cable. Drain the engine coolant into a clean container for reuse.

2. Raise and safely support the vehicle.

3. Remove the drain tube from the heater case and the heater hoses from the heater core. Lower the vehicle.

4. Remove the right and left side sound insulators and the steering column trim cover.

5. Remove the heater air outlet deflector and the glove box.

6. Remove the heater core cover, the heater core and retaining straps.

To install:

7. Install the heater core cover, the heater core and retaining straps.

8. Install the heater air outlet deflector and the glove box.

9. Install the right and left side sound insulators and the steering column trim cover.

10. Raise and safely support the vehicle. Connect the heater hoses to the heater core and connect the drain tube to the heater case.

11. Lower the vehicle.

12. Connect the negative battery cable.

13. Fill cooling system and check for leaks. Start the engine and allow to come to normal operating temperature. Recheck for leaks. Top-up coolant.

1991

1. Disable the SIR system and disconnect the negative battery cable.

2. Remove the instrument panel assembly.

3. Remove the heater floor outlet screws and turn the outlet clockwise and to the right to release.

4. Drain the engine coolant into a clean container for reuse.

5. Raise and safely support the vehicle.

6. Disconnect the heater hoses from the heater core and drain the tube elbow from the heater core cover.

7. Lower the vehicle and remove the heater core cover screws and the heater core cover.

8. Remove the heater core screws and clamps and remove the heater core from the vehicle.

To install:

9. Position the heater core in place and install the core straps and screws. Tighten the screws to 12 inch lbs. (1.4 Nm)

10. Install the heater core cover and screws.

11. Install the floor outlet and screws.

12. Install the instrument panel assembly.

13. Raise and safely support the vehicle.

14. Connect the heater hoses to the heater core and lower the vehicle.

15. Fill the cooling system with coolant and connect the negative battery cable.

16. Enable the SIR system.

1992–93

1. Disable the SIR system.

2. Disconnect the negative battery cable and remove the radio from the vehicle.

3. Gaining access through the radio opening, release the heater core cover clips.

4. Remove the heater floor outlet screws and turn the outlet clockwise and to the right to release.

5. Drain the engine coolant into a clean container for reuse.

6. Raise and safely support the vehicle.

7. Disconnect the heater hoses from the heater core and drain the tube elbow from the heater core cover.

8. Lower the vehicle and remove the heater core cover screws and the heater core cover.

9. Remove the heater core screws and clamps and remove the heater core from the vehicle.

To install:

10. Position the heater core in place and install the core straps and screws. Tighten the screws to 12 inch lbs. (1.4 Nm).

11. Install the heater core cover and screws.

12. Reach through the radio opening and position the heater core cover under the clips.

13. Install the radio.

14. Install the floor outlet and screws.

15. Raise and safely support the vehicle.

16. Connect the heater hoses to the heater core and lower the vehicle.

17. Fill the cooling system with coolant and connect the negative battery cable.

18. Enable the SIR system.

Water Pump

REMOVAL & INSTALLATION

Except 2.3L Engine

1. Disconnect the negative battery cable.

2. Drain the engine coolant into a clean container for reuse.

3. Remove the serpentine drive belt.

4. If equipped with the 2.0L engine, remove the alternator and bracket with wires attached and position it aside.

5. If equipped with the 3.1L engine, remove the radiator hoses and heater hoses.

6. Remove the water pump pulley bolts and the pulley.

7. Remove the water pump-to-engine bolts and the pump.

To install:

8. Clean the gasket mounting surfaces.

9. Install the water pump and the water pump attaching bolts. Tighten the water pump-to-engine bolts to 14–22 ft. lbs. (19–30 Nm) on the 2.0L and 2.2L engines or to 6–9 ft. lbs. (8–12 Nm) on the 2.8L and 3.1L engines.

10. Install the water pump pulley and attaching bolts.

11. If equipped with the 3.1L engine, install the radiator hoses and heater hoses.

12. If equipped with the 2.0L engine, install the alternator and bracket.

13. Install the serpentine drive belt.

14. Connect the negative battery cable.

15. Fill cooling system and check for leaks. Start the engine and allow to come to normal operating temperature. Recheck for leaks. Top-up coolant.

2.3L Engine

1. Disconnect the negative battery cable.

2. Drain the engine coolant into a clean container for reuse.

NOTE: Remove the heater hose from the thermostat housing for additional draining.

3. Disconnect the oxygen sensor connector.

4. Remove the upper and lower exhaust manifold heat shield attaching bolts and remove the shields.

5. Remove the exhaust manifold brace-to-manifold attaching bolt.

6. Using a 13mm box wrench, loosen the exhaust pipe-to-manifold spring bolts from the engine compartment.

7. Raise and safely support the vehicle.

8. Remove the bolts from the exhaust flange using a $^7/_{32}$ in. (5.5mm) socket an 1 bolt rotate clockwise first.

NOTE: Rotating the bolt clockwise is necessary to relieve the spring pressure from 1st bolt prior to removing the 2nd bolt otherwise the exhaust pipe will twist and bind the bolt as it is removed.

9. Thread the bolt with least pressure on it out 4 turns.

10. Move the other bolt and turn it all the way out of the exhaust pipe flange.

11. Return to the 1st bolt and rotate it the rest of the way out.

12. Pull the exhaust pipe back from the exhaust manifold.

13. Remove the radiator outlet pipe from the oil pan and transaxle.

14. Remove the exhaust manifold brace.

15. Pull down on the radiator outlet pipe to disengage it from the water pump.

16. Lower the vehicle.

17. Remove the exhaust manifold-to-cylinder head attaching nuts.

18. Remove the exhaust manifold, seals and gaskets.

19. Remove the water pump cover-to-engine attaching bolts.

20. Remove the water pump-to-timing chain housing attaching nuts.

21. Remove the water pump and cover assembly from the engine.

22. Remove the water pump cover-to-radiator pump assembly.

To install:

NOTE: Before installing the water pump it is important to first read over the entire procedure. Pay special attention to the tightening sequence, to avoid part damage and to insure proper sealing.

23. Clean all mating surfaces throughly and use new gaskets.

24. Position the water pump cover to the radiator pump assembly and install the attaching bolts. Do not tighten.

25. Lubricate the splines of the radiator pump drive with the an approved chassis grease and install the pump and cover assembly.

26. Install the pump cover-to-engine attaching bolts. Do not tighten.

27. Install the timing chain housing nuts. Do not tighten.

28. Lubricate the O-ring on the radiator outlet pipe with a solution of antifreeze and slide the pipe into the radiator pump cover. Install the attaching bolts. Do not tighten.

29. Tighten the bolts and nuts in following order:

 a. Pump assembly-to-timing chain housing nuts—19 ft. lbs. (26 Nm).

 b. Water pump-to-pump cover assembly—106 inch lbs. (12 Nm).

 c. Water Pump cover-to-engine (tighten the bottom bolt first)—19 ft. lbs. (26 Nm).

 d. Radiator outlet pipe assembly-to-pump cover—125 ft. lbs. (14 Nm).

30. Install the exhaust manifold with new gaskets.

31. Install the exhaust manifold-to-cylinder head attaching nuts. Tighten the attaching nuts in sequence to 22 ft. lbs. (30 Nm).

32. Raise and safely support the vehicle.

33. Seat the exhaust manifold bolts into the exhaust pipe flange.

34. Using a $^7/_{32}$ in. (5.5mm) socket start both bolts. Rotate the bolts counterclockwise.

35. Turn both bolts in evenly to avoid cocking the exhaust pipe and binding the bolts. Turn the bolts in until fully seated.

36. Install the radiator outlet pipe to the transaxle and to the oil pan and install the exhaust manifold brace.

37. Lower the vehicle.

38. Install the exhaust manifold brace-to-manifold attaching bolt.

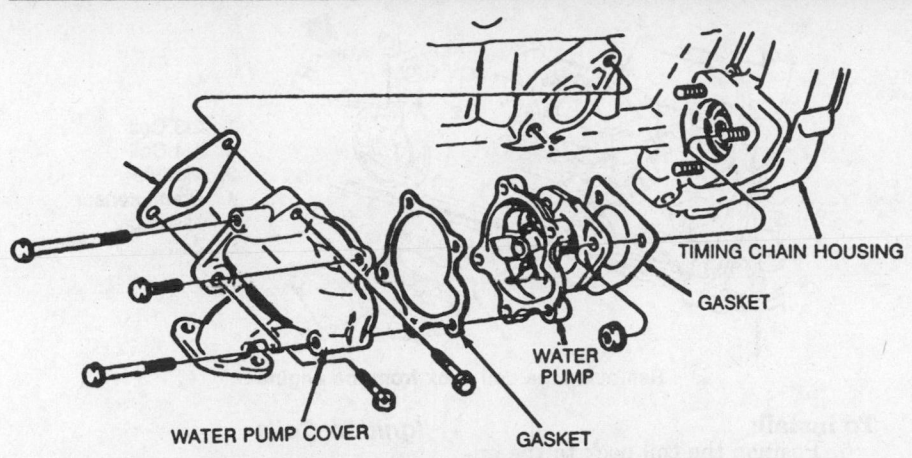

Water pump removal and installation—2.3L engine

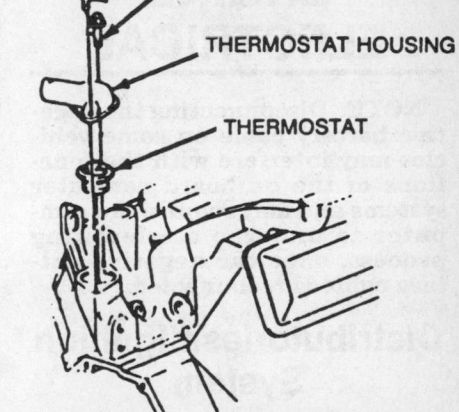

Thermostat removal and installation—
2.3L engine

39. Using a 13mm wrench, tighten the exhaust pipe-to-manifold nuts to 22 ft. lbs. (30 Nm).

40. Install the lower heat shields.

41. Connect the oxygen connector to the oxygen sensor.

42. Connect the negative battery cable.

43. Fill cooling system and check for leaks. Start the engine and allow to come to normal operating temperature. Recheck for leaks. Top-up coolant.

Thermostat

REMOVAL & INSTALLATION

1. Disconnect the negative battery cable.

2. Remove the air cleaner assembly.

3. Drain the engine coolant level below the thermostat housing.

4. Remove the upper radiator hose from the thermostat water outlet and position it to the side.

5. On the 2.3L engine, remove the heater and throttle body coolant hoses from the thermostat housing and disconnect the electrical connector from the coolant temperature sensor.

6. Remove the thermostat attaching bolts.

7. Remove the thermostat housing gasket and thermostat.

To install:

8. Throughly clean the mating surfaces of the engine and thermostat.

9. Install the new thermostat, gasket and housing, being careful not to allow the thermostat to slip out of position.

10. Install the attaching bolts and tighten to 6–9 ft. lbs. (8–12 Nm) for 2.0L and 2.2L engines, 15–22 ft. lbs. (20–30 Nm) for the 2.8L and 3.1L engines or 19 ft. lbs. (26 Nm) for the 2.3L engine.

11. On 2.3L engine, connect the heater and throttle body coolant hoses the thermostat housing and connect the coolant temperature sensor connector.

12. Connect the upper radiator hose

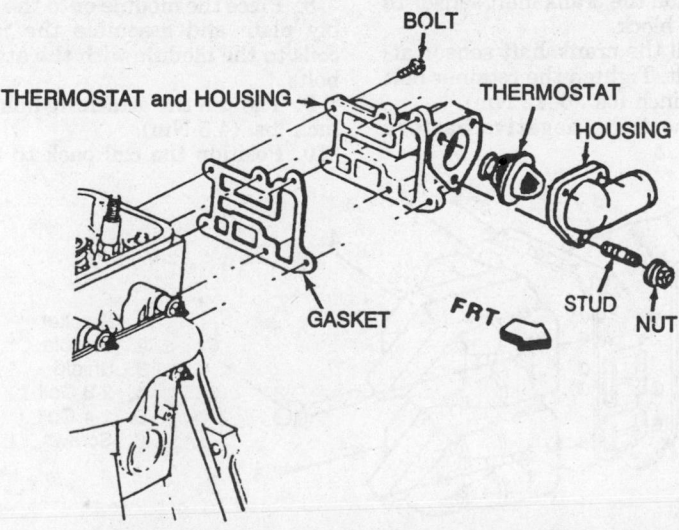

Thermostat removal and installation–2.2L engine (VIN 4)

[Figure: Thermostat removal and installation — 2.8L and 3.1L engines, labeled APPLY SEALER, THERMOSTAT HOUSING, THERMOSTAT]

Thermostat removal and installation—
2.8L and 3.1L engines

to the thermostat housing water outlet.

13. Refill and bleed the cooling system. Start the engine, allow it to reach normal operating temperature and check for leaks.

14. Allow time for the thermostat to open, recheck the coolant level and top up, as required.

Cooling System Bleeding

After working on the cooling system, even to replace the thermostat, the system must be bled. Air trapped in the system will prevent proper coolant circulation and leave the system coolant level low, causing a risk of overheating.

1. To bleed the system, start with the system cool, the radiator cap off and the radiator filled to about an inch below the filler neck.

2. Start the engine and run it at slightly above normal idle speed. This will insure adequate circulation. If air bubbles appear and the coolant level drops, fill the system with a mixture of

anti-freeze and water to bring the level back to the proper level.

3. Run the engine this way until the thermostat opens. When this happens, the coolant will move abruptly across the top of the radiator and the temperature of the upper radiator tank and upper radiator hose will rise suddenly.

4. At this point, air is often expelled and the level may drop quite a bit. Keep refilling the system until the level is near the top of the radiator and remains constant.

5. If the vehicle has an overflow tank, fill the radiator up to the top of the filler neck and check the coolant the level in the overflow tank.

ENGINE ELECTRICAL

NOTE: Disconnecting the negative battery cable on some vehicles may interfere with the functions of the on board computer systems and may require the computer to undergo a relearning process, once the negative battery cable is reconnected.

Distributorless Ignition System

REMOVAL & INSTALLATION

Coil Pack

1. Disconnect the negative battery cable.

2. Disconnect the electrical connectors from the coil pack.

3. Mark the spark plug wires for correct installation and remove them from each coil.

4. Remove the coil pack-to-engine bolts and remove the coil pack from the engine.

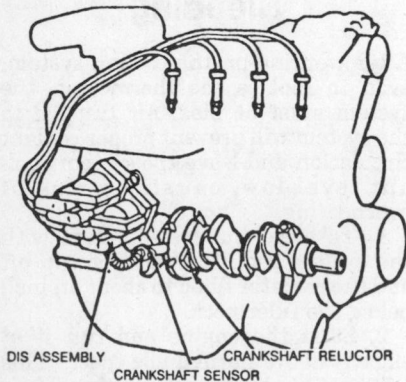

View of the Direct Ignition System (DIS) 2.0L, 2.2L, 2.8L and 3.1L engines

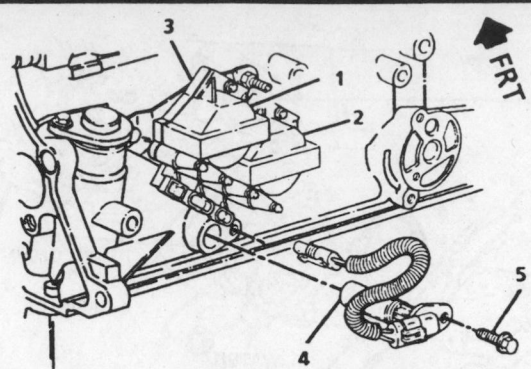

Removing the coil pack from the engine

1. 2-3 Coil
2. 1-4 Coil
3. Module
4. Crank sensor assembly
5. Bolt

To install:

5. Position the coil pack to the engine block and install the attaching bolts. Tighten the attaching bolts to 15–21 ft. lbs. (20–30 Nm).

6. Connect the spark plug wires to their respective positions, marked during removal, on the ignition coils.

7. Connect the electrical connectors to the coil pack.

8. Connect the negative battery cable.

9. Start the engine and test the engine performance.

Crankshaft Sensor

1. Disconnect the negative battery cable.

2. Disconnect the sensor harness connector at the ignition module.

3. Remove the crankshaft sensor attaching bolt and remove the sensor from the engine.

NOTE: Prior to installing the crankshaft sensor, inspect the O-ring for wear, cracks or signs of leakage. Replace it, if necessary. If it is necessary to replace the seal, lubricate it with engine oil prior to installation.

To install:

4. Position the crankshaft sensor to the engine block.

5. Install the crankshaft sensor attaching bolt. Tighten the retainer bolt to 53–107 inch lbs. (6–12 Nm).

6. Connect the negative battery cable.

Ignition Coils

1. Disconnect the negative battery cable.

2. Remove the ignition coil attaching bolts.

3. Remove the coil from the module.

To install:

4. Position the ignition coil to the module and install the attaching bolts.

5. Tighten the ignition coil attaching bolts to 40 inch lbs. (4.5 Nm). Connect the negative battery cable.

6. Start the engine and check performance.

Ignition Module

1. Disconnect the negative battery cable.

2. Disconnect the electrical connectors from the coil pack.

3. Mark the spark plug wires for correct installation and remove them from each ignition coil.

4. Remove the bolts attaching the coil pack to the engine block.

5. Remove the coil pack from the engine.

6. Remove the ignition coils from the ignition module.

7. Remove the ignition module from the assembly plate.

To install:

8. Place the module onto the assembly plate and assemble the ignition coils to the module with the attaching bolts.

9. Tighten the attaching bolts to 40 inch lbs. (4.5 Nm).

10. Position the coil pack to the en-

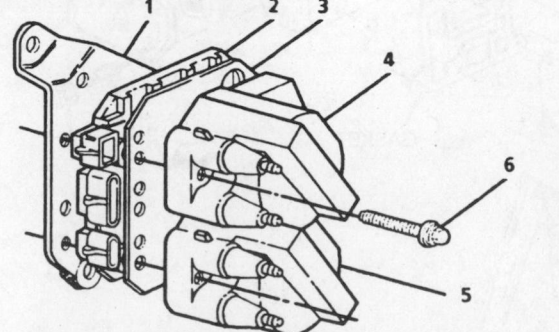

1. Bracket
2. Module
3. Shield
4. 2-3 Coil
5. 1-4 Coil
6. Screws

Removing the ignition coils and module from the assembly plate

gine block and install the attaching bolts. Tighten the attaching bolts to 15–21 ft. lbs. (20–30 Nm).

11. Connect the spark plug wires to the ignition coils (marked during removal).

12. Connect the electrical connectors to the coil pack.

13. Connect the spark plug wires and electrical connectors to their respective places.

14. Connect the negative battery cable.

15. Start the engine and check performance.

INTEGRATED DIRECT IGNITION SYSTEM

REMOVAL & INSTALLATION

Ignition Assembly

1. Disconnect the negative battery cable.

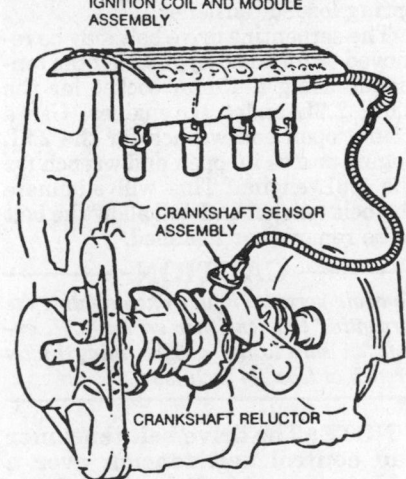

View of the Integrated Direct Ignition System (IDIS) 2.3L engine

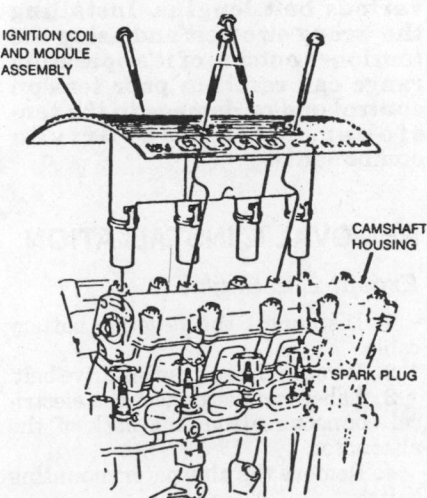

Removing the IDIS ignition assembly from the engine

2. Disconnect the harness connector from the coil and module assembly.

3. Remove the ignition assembly-to-camshaft housing attaching bolts.

4. Carefully remove the ignition assembly from the engine.

NOTE: If the spark plug boots present a problem coming off, it may be necessary to use a special removal tool, first twisting and pulling upward on the retainers.

To install:

5. Install the spark plug boots and retainers on the ignition assembly housing secondary terminals.

NOTE: If the boots and retainers are not in place on the housing secondary terminals prior to installing the ignition assembly, damage to the ignition system may result.

6. Position the ignition assembly to the engine while carefully aligning the boots to the spark plug terminals.

7. Coat the ignition assembly-to-camshaft housing attaching bolts with an approved lubricant and install them into the housing.

8. Tighten the attaching bolts to 19 ft. lbs. (26 Nm).

9. Connect the harness connector to the ignition coil module assembly.

10. Connect the negative battery cable.

11. Start the engine and check the engine performance.

Crankshaft Sensor

1. Disconnect the negative battery cable.

2. Disconnect the harness connector at the crankshaft sensor.

3. Remove the sensor attaching bolt.

4. Remove the crankshaft sensor from the engine.

5. Inspect the sensor O-ring for wear, cracks or signs of leakage. Replace it, if necessary.

To install:

6. Lubricate the O-ring with engine oil and install it on the sensor.

7. Position the sensor to the engine block and install the attaching bolt. Tighten the attaching bolt to 88 inch lbs. (10 Nm).

8. Connect the sensor harness connector.

9. Connect the negative battery cable.

10. Start the engine and test engine performance.

Ignition Coil

1. Disconnect the negative battery cable.

2. Disconnect the harness connector from the coil and module assembly.

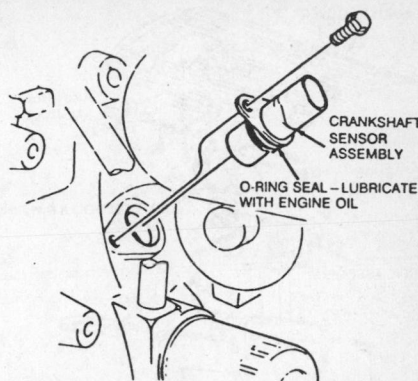

Removing crankshaft sensor from the engine

3. Remove the ignition assembly-to-camshaft housing attaching bolts.

4. Carefully remove the ignition assembly from the engine.

NOTE: If the spark plug boots present a problem coming off, it may be necessary to use a special removal tool, first twisting and pulling upward on the retainers.

5. Remove the ignition coil housing-to-cover bolts.

6. Remove the cover from the coil housing.

7. Disconnect the ignition coil harness connectors from the coil pack assembly.

8. Carefully lift the coil pack out and remove the contacts and seals from the housing.

To install:

9. Install new coil seals into the coil housing.

10. Install the coil contacts to the coil housing and retain with petroleum jelly.

11. Place the coil pack into the housing and connect the harness connectors.

12. Assemble the cover to the coil housing and install the attaching bolts. Tighten the attaching bolts to 35 inch lbs. (4 Nm).

13. Install the spark plug boots and retainers on the ignition assembly housing secondary terminals.

NOTE: If the boots and retainers are not in place on the housing secondary terminals prior to installing the ignition assembly, damage to the ignition system may result.

14. Position the ignition assembly to the engine while carefully aligning the boots to the spark plug terminals.

15. Coat the ignition assembly-to-camshaft housing attaching bolts with an approved lubricant and install them into the housing.

16. Tighten the attaching bolts to 19 ft. lbs. (26 Nm).

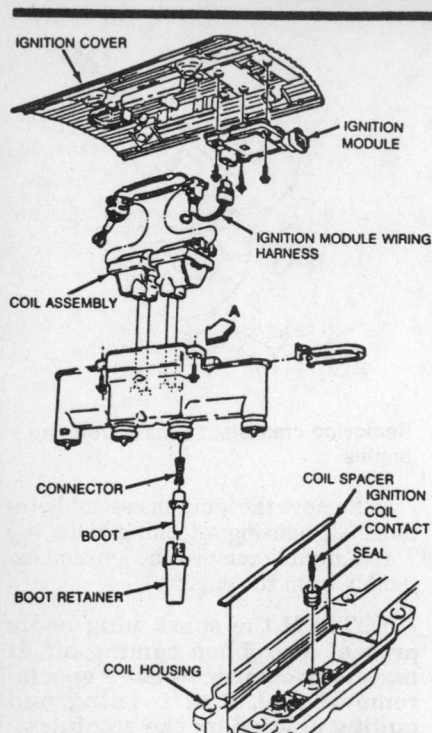

IGNITION COVER

IGNITION MODULE

IGNITION MODULE WIRING HARNESS

COIL ASSEMBLY

CONNECTOR

BOOT

BOOT RETAINER

COIL HOUSING

COIL SPACER
IGNITION COIL CONTACT

SEAL

VIEW A

Exploded view of the IDIS Ignition assembly

17. Connect the harness connector to the ignition coil module assembly.

18. Connect the negative battery cable.

19. Start the engine and test the engine performance.

Ignition Module

1. Disconnect the negative battery cable.

2. Disconnect the harness connector from the coil and module assembly.

3. Remove the ignition assembly-to-camshaft housing attaching bolts.

4. Carefully remove the ignition assembly from the engine.

NOTE: If the spark plug boots present a problem coming off, it may be necessary to use a special removal tool, first twisting and pulling upward on the retainers.

5. Remove the ignition coil housing-to-cover bolts.

6. Remove the cover from the coil housing.

7. Disconnect the coil harness connector from the module.

8. Remove the screws attaching the module to the ignition assembly cover.

NOTE: If the same module is going to be replaced, take care not to remove the grease from the module or coil. If a new module is to be installed, a package of silicone grease will be included with it. This grease aids in preventing the module from overheating.

To install:

9. Place the module on the ignition cover and install the attaching bolts. Tighten the attaching bolts to 35 inch lbs. (4 Nm).

10. Connect the coil harness connector to the module.

11. Assemble the module cover to the coil housing and install the attaching bolts. Tighten the attaching bolts to 35 inch lbs. (4 Nm).

12. Install the spark plug boots and retainers on the ignition assembly housing secondary terminals.

NOTE: If the boots and retainers are not in place on the housing secondary terminals prior to installing the ignition assembly, damage to the ignition system may result.

13. Position the ignition assembly to the engine while carefully aligning the boots to the spark plug terminals.

14. Coat the ignition assembly-to-camshaft housing attaching bolts with an approved lubricant and install them into the housing.

15. Tighten the attaching bolts to 19 ft. lbs. (26 Nm).

16. Connect the harness connector to the ignition coil module assembly.

17. Connect the negative battery cable.

18. Start the engine and test the engine performance.

Ignition Timing

ADJUSTMENT

Ignition timing is controlled by the Electronic Control Module (ECM). No adjustments are possible.

Alternator

PRECAUTIONS

Several precautions must be observed with alternator equipped vehicles to avoid damage to the unit.

• If the battery is removed for any reason, make sure it is reconnected with the correct polarity. Reversing the battery connections may result in damage to the one-way rectifiers.

• When utilizing a booster battery as a starting aid, always connect the positive to positive terminals and the negative terminal from the booster battery to a good engine ground on the vehicle being started.

• Never use a fast charger as a booster to start vehicles.

• Disconnect the battery cables when charging the battery with a fast charger.

• Never attempt to polarize the alternator.

• When checking diode continuity, ensure the tester does not exceed 12 volts.

• Do not short across or ground any of the alternator terminals.

• The polarity of the battery, alternator and regulator must be matched and considered before making any electrical connections within the system.

• Never separate the alternator on an open circuit. Make sure all connections within the circuit are clean and tight.

• Disconnect the battery ground terminal when performing any service on electrical components.

• Disconnect the battery if arc welding is to be done on the vehicle.

BELT TENSION ADJUSTMENT

A single (serpentine) belt is used to drive all engine mounted components. Drive belt tension is maintained by a spring loaded tensioner.

The serpentine drive belt may be removed or installed by rotating the tensioner using a 15mm socket for the 2.0L, 2.2L and 3.1L engines. Use a 13mm open end wrench for the 2.3L engine or a ¾ in. open end wrench for the 2.8L engine. This will eliminate the belt tension and will allow the belt to be removed or installed.

——— CAUTION ———

To avoid personal injury when rotating the serpentine belt tensioner on the 2.3L engine, be sure to use a tight fitting 13mm wrench at least 24 inch long.

NOTE: The drive belt tensioner can control belt tension over a wide range of belt lengths; however, there are limits to the tensioner's ability to compensate for various belt lengths. Installing the wrong size belt and using the tensioner outside of it's operating range can result in poor tension control and/or damage to the tensioner, belt and driven components.

REMOVAL & INSTALLATION

Except 2.3L Engine

1. Disconnect the negative battery cable.

2. Remove the serpentine drive belt.

3. Label and disconnect the electrical connectors from the back of the alternator.

4. Remove the alternator mounting bolts.

5. Remove the alternator-to-bracket bolts and the alternator.

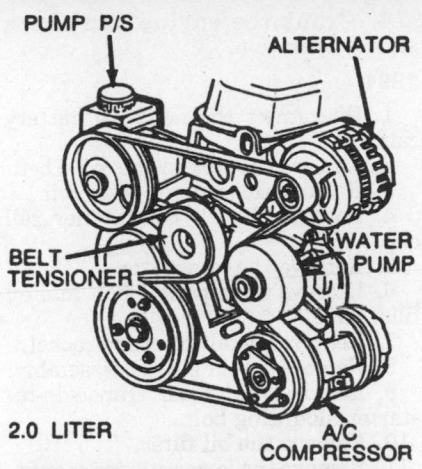

2.0 LITER

View of the drive belt routing—2.0L and 2.2L engines

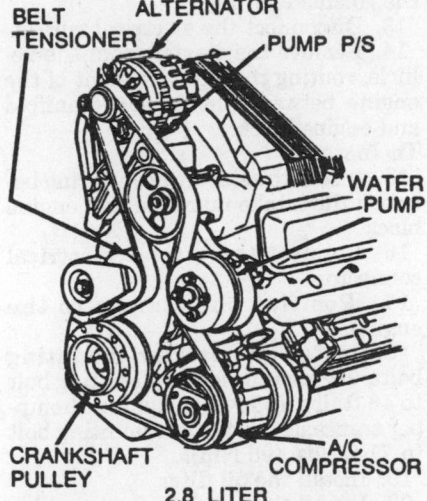

2.8 LITER

View of the drive belt routing—2.8L and 3.1L engines

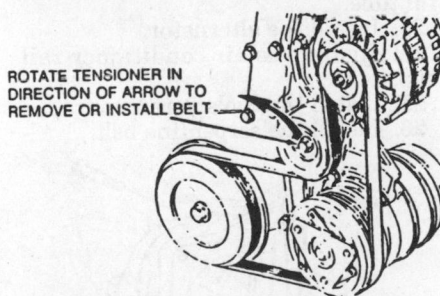

ROTATE TENSIONER IN DIRECTION OF ARROW TO REMOVE OR INSTALL BELT

View of the drive belt routing—2.3L engine

To install:

6. Position the alternator to the the mounting bracket and install the attaching bolts.
7. Connect the alternator electrical connectors to the rear of the alternator.
8. Install the serpentine drive belt.
9. Connect the negative battery cable.
10. Start the engine and perform a charging system test.

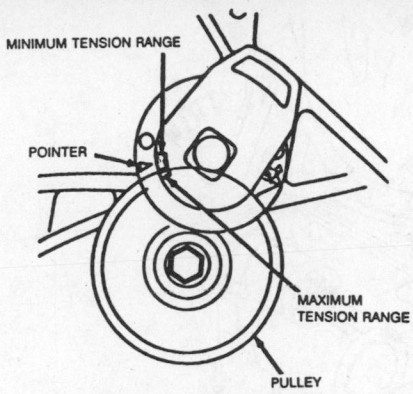

Tensioner operating range

2.3L Engine

1. Disconnect the negative battery cable.
2. Remove the serpentine drive belt.

— **CAUTION** —

To avoid personal injury when rotating the serpentine belt tensioner, be sure to use a tight fitting 13mm wrench at least 24 inch long.

3. Remove the coolant and washer reservoir attaching screws.
4. Disconnect the washer pump electrical connector and position the reservoir to the side.
5. Remove the air conditioner line rail clip.
6. Disconnect the 2 vacuum lines at the front of the engine and remove vacuum harness attaching bracket, as required.
7. Disconnect and tag electrical connections from injector harness and alternator.
8. Remove the rear alternator mounting bolts.
9. Remove the front alternator mounting bolt and engine harness clip.
10. Carefully remove the alternator from between the mounting bracket and the air conditioning and condenser hose.

NOTE: Extreme care must be taken when removing or installing the alternator as not to damage the air conditioner compressor and condenser hoses.

To install:

11. Place the alternator between the air conditioner compressor and condenser hoses and install it on the bracket.
12. Install the rear mounting bolt. Tighten the mounting bolt to 19 ft. lbs. (26 Nm).
13. Install the front mounting bolts. Tighten the upper mounting bolt to 37 ft. lbs. (50 Nm) and the lower mounting bolt to 19 ft. lbs. (26 Nm).
14. Install the serpentine drive belt.

— **CAUTION** —

To avoid personal injury when rotating the serpentine belt tensioner, be sure to use a tight fitting 13mm wrench at least 24 in. long.

15. Install the air conditioner rail clip.
16. Connect the washer pump electrical connector.
17. Install the coolant and washer pump reservoir.
18. Connect the electrical connections for the alternator and injector harness.
19. If removed, install the vacuum harness attaching bracket and connect the vacuum lines at the front of the engine.
20. Connect the negative battery cable.
21. Start the engine and perform a charging system test.

Starter

REMOVAL & INSTALLATION

2.2L Engine (VIN G and 4)

1. Disconnect the negative battery cable.
2. Raise and safely support the vehicle.
3. Disconnect the starter motor wiring.
4. Remove the wiring clamp at the support bracket.
5. Remove the 1 bolt between the support bracket and the engine.
6. Remove the 2 bolts from the starter motor and remove the starter with the shims (if used).

To install:

7. Install the shims (if used) and the starter motor. Install the 2 bolts and tighten to 32 ft. lbs. (43 Nm).
8. Install the support bracket bolt and tighten to 24 ft. lbs. (32 Nm).
9. Install the wiring clamp to the support bracket and tighten the bolt to 106 inch lbs. (12 Nm).
10. Connect the starter motor wiring and lower the vehicle.
11. Connect the negative battery cable.

3.1L Engine (VIN T)

1. Disconnect the negative battery cable.
2. Raise and safely support the vehicle.
3. Remove the starter motor to engine bolts.
4. Lower the starter and disconnect the starter leads while supporting the starter.
5. Remove the starter from the vehicle.

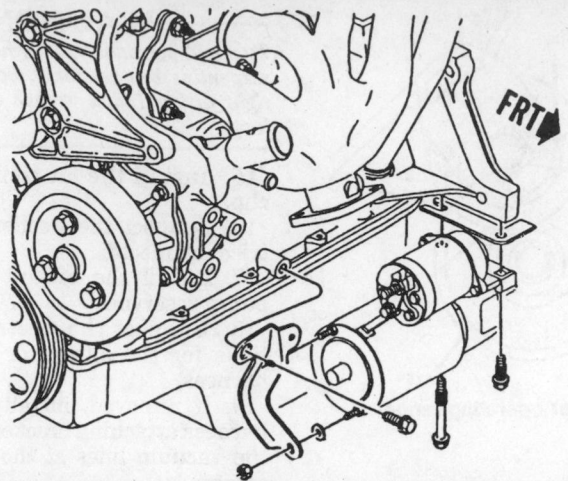

Starter removal and Installation–2.2L (VIN G and 4) engine

To install:

6. Install the starter to the vehicle and connect the electrical leads while supporting the starter.

7. Install the starter motor mounting bolts and tighten to 32 ft. lbs. (43 Nm).

8. Lower the vehicle and connect the negative battery cable.

2.0L and 2.8L Engines

1. Disconnect the negative battery cable.

2. Remove the air cleaner assembly, as required.

3. Raise and safely support the vehicle.

NOTE: If equipped with an oil cooler, remove the oil filter and position the hose next to the starter to the side.

4. Remove the air conditioning compressor brace attaching nuts and remove the brace from the engine, as required.

5. Remove flywheel inspection cover bolts and remove the inspection cover, as required.

6. Remove the starter attaching bolts.

7. Carefully lower the starter and remove the shims. Note the number and position of any shims.

8. Disconnect the electrical wiring connections at the starter.

To install:

9. Connect the electrical connections to the starter.

10. Position the shims in place and install the starter and mounting bolts. Tighten the bolts to 32 ft. lbs. (43 Nm).

NOTE: If equipped with an oil cooler, position the cooler hose next to the starter motor and install the oil filter.

11. If removed, install the flywheel inspection cover and attaching bolts.

12. If removed, install the air conditioning compressor brace and attaching nuts.

13. Lower vehicle and connect the negative battery cable.

14. If removed, install the air cleaner assembly.

15. Crank the engine and check the starter operation.

2.3L Engine

1990

1. Disconnect the negative battery cable.

2. Disconnect the electrical connector from the cooling fan.

3. Remove the cooling fan mounting bolts and remove the fan assembly.

4. Remove the intake manifold-to-engine brace bolts and remove the the brace from the engine.

5. Remove the starter mounting bolts.

6. Carefully lift the starter away from the engine with the solenoid harness attached to it.

7. When the starter is clear, disconnect the solenoid harness connections and lift the starter up and out toward the front of the vehicle.

To install:

8. Connect the solenoid harness connections to the starter, while supporting the starter toward the mounting position.

9. Rotate the starter so the solenoid faces the engine at a slight angle to clear the bottom of the intake manifold.

10. Install the starter to the engine and install the mounting bolts. Tighten the bolts to 32 ft. lbs. (43 Nm).

11. Install the intake manifold-to-engine brace and the attaching bolts.

12. Install the cooling fan and attaching bolts. Tighten bolts to 89 inch lbs. (10 Nm).

13. Connect the negative battery cable.

14. Crank the engine and check starter operation.

1991

1. Disconnect the negative battery cable.

2. Remove the serpentine drive belt.

3. Remove the coolant reservoir.

4. Remove the air conditioner rail clip.

5. Remove the alternator.

6. Remove the dipstick, bolt and oil filler tube.

7. Remove the alternator bracket.

8. Remove the air cleaner assembly.

9. Remove the upper transaxle-to-starter mounting bolt.

10. Remove the oil filter.

11. Remove the lower starter mounting bolt.

12. Position the starter for access to the solenoid wiring.

13. Disconnect the electrical wiring.

14. Remove the starter from the vehicle, routing through the front of the engine between the intake manifold and engine block.

To install:

15. Install the starter by lowering between the intake manifold and engine block.

16. Connect the starter electrical connectors.

17. Position the starter to the engine.

18. Install the starter mounting bolts. Tighten the lower mounting bolt to 46 ft. lbs. (63 Nm). Tighten the upper transaxle-to-starter mounting bolt to 71 ft. lbs. (96 Nm).

19. Install the oil filter.

20. Install the air cleaner assembly.

21. Install the alternator bracket.

22. Install the dipstick, bolt and oil fill tube.

23. Install the alternator.

24. Install the air conditioner rail clip.

25. Install the coolant reservoir.

26. Install the serpentine belt.

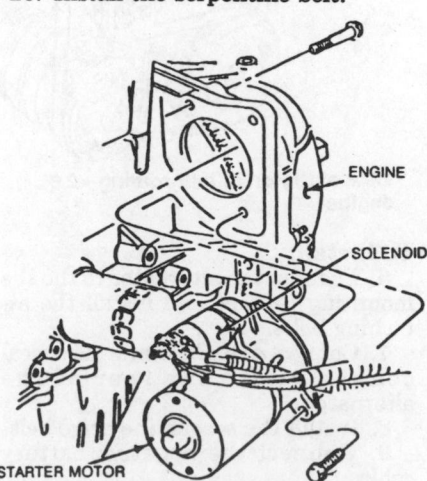

Starter removal and Installation—2.3L (VIN A), 2.8L and 3.1L engines

27. Connect the negative battery cable.

28. Refill the engine oil as necessary and check for leaks.

1992–93

1. Disconnect the negative battery cable.

2. If necessary, remove the air induction tubing.

3. Raise and safely support the vehicle. Remove the oil filter.

4. Remove the starter mounting bolts.

5. Position starter aside to gain access to the wiring. Disconnect the starter wiring.

6. Remove the starter from the vehicle.

To install:

7. Connect the wiring to the starter and position the starter to the engine.

8. Install the upper and lower mounting bolts and tighten to 74 ft. lbs. (100 Nm).

9. Install the oil filter and connect the air induction tubing, if disconnected.

10. Lower the vehicle.

11. Connect the negative battery cable, refill the engine with oil and check for leaks.

EMISSION CONTROLS

Due to the complex nature of modern electronic engine control systems, comprehensive diagnosis and testing procedures fall outside the confines of this repair manual. For complete information on diagnosis, testing and repair procedures concerning all modern engine and emission control systems, please refer to "Chilton's Guide to Fuel Injection and Electronic Engine Controls".

Emission Warning Lamps

RESETTING

When the ECM finds a problem, the Service Engine Soon light will turn ON and a trouble code will be recorded in the ECM memory. If the problem is intermittent, the Service Engine Soon light will light go out after 10 seconds, when the fault goes away. However, the trouble code will stay in the ECM memory until the battery voltage to the ECM is removed. Removing the battery voltage for 10 seconds will clear all stored trouble codes. This is done by disconnecting the ECM harness from the positive battery pigtail for 30 seconds with the ignition **OFF** or by disconnecting the ECM fuse, designated ECM or ECM/BAT, from the fuse holder.

NOTE: To prevent ECM damage, the ignition switch must be OFF when disconnecting or reconnecting power to ECM (for example battery cable, ECM pigtail, ECM fuse, jumper cables, etc.).

FUEL SYSTEM

Fuel System Service Precautions

Safety is the most important factor when performing not only fuel system maintenance but any type of maintenance. Failure to conduct maintenance and repairs in a safe manner may result in serious personal injury or death. Maintenance and testing of the vehicle's fuel system components can be accomplished safely and effectively by adhering to the following rules and guidelines.

● To avoid the possibility of fire and personal injury, always disconnect the negative battery cable unless the repair or test procedure requires that battery voltage be applied.

● Always relieve the fuel system pressure prior to disconnecting any fuel system component (injector, fuel rail, pressure regulator, etc.), fitting or fuel line connection. Exercise extreme caution whenever relieving fuel system pressure to avoid exposing skin, face and eyes to fuel spray. Please be advised that fuel under pressure may penetrate the skin or any part of the body that it contacts.

● Always place a shop towel or cloth around the fitting or connection prior to loosening to absorb any excess fuel due to spillage. Ensure that all fuel spillage (should it occur) is quickly removed from engine surfaces. Ensure that all fuel soaked cloths or towels are deposited into a suitable waste container.

● Always keep a dry chemical (Class B) fire extinguisher near the work area.

● Do not allow fuel spray or fuel vapors to come into contact with a spark or open flame.

● Always use a backup wrench when loosening and tightening fuel line connection fittings. This will prevent unnecessary torsional stress to fuel line piping. Always follow the proper torque specifications.

● Always replace worn fuel fitting O-rings with new. Do not substitute fuel hose or equivalent where fuel pipe is installed.

RELIEVING FUEL SYSTEM PRESSURE

Throttle Body Injection

1. Disconnect the negative battery cable.

2. Remove the fuel filler cap to relieve tank vapor pressure.

3. Wrap a shop towel around the fuel line fitting.

4. Open the fuel line and absorb any excess fuel remaining in the line.

5. When the line fitting is reconnected, use a new O-ring.

Port Fuel Injection

EXCEPT 2.3L ENGINE

1. Disconnect the negative battery cable.

2. Remove the fuel filler cap to relieve tank vapor pressure.

3. Connect a fuel gauge to the fuel pressure test fitting.

NOTE: Be sure to wrap a shop cloth around the fuel line fitting when connecting the fuel gauge tool to the fuel pressure connector.

4. Place the bleeder hose and shop cloth in an approved fuel container. Open the pressure valve to bleed the fuel pressure from the system.

5. After the fuel pressure is bled, retighten the fuel pressure valve.

2.3L ENGINE

1. Loosen the fuel filler cap to relieve the tank pressure.

2. Raise and safely support the vehicle.

3. Disconnect the fuel pump electrical connector.

4. Lower the vehicle.

5. Start the engine and run until the fuel supply remaining in the fuel lines is consumed. Engage the starter for 3.0 seconds to assure relief of any remaining pressure.

6. Raise and safely support the vehicle.

7. Connect the fuel pump electrical connector.

8. Lower the vehicle.

9. Disconnect the negative battery cable to avoid possible fuel discharge if an accidental attempt is made to start the engine.

Fuel Filter

REMOVAL & INSTALLATION

An inline fuel filter is used on all engines. It is located on a frame crossmember near the rear of the vehicle.

Threaded Fuel Line Fitting

1. Relieve the fuel system pressure.
2. Raise and safely support the vehicle.
3. Using a backup wrench, remove the fuel line fittings from the fuel filter.
4. Remove the fuel filter-to-crossmember screws and the filter from the vehicle.

To install:

5. Install the fuel filter and the attaching screws.
6. Replace the fuel filter O-rings.
7. Connect the fuel lines. Using a backup wrench, tighten the fuel line fittings to 22 ft. lbs. (30 Nm).
8. Lower the vehicle.
9. Connect the negative battery cable.

Quick-Connect Fitting

1. Disconnect the negative battery cable.
2. Relieve the fuel system pressure.
3. Raise and safely support the vehicle.
4. Remove the fuel filter attaching screw.

NOTE: If the nylon fuel feed or return connecting lines become kinked and cannot be straightened, they must be replaced.

5. Grasp the filter and 1 nylon fuel connecting line fitting. Twist the quick-connect fitting ¼ turn in each direction to loosen any dirt within the fitting. Repeat for the other nylon fuel connecting line fitting.
6. Using compressed air, blow out any accumulated dirt from the quick-connect fittings at both ends of the fuel filter.
7. Squeeze the plastic tabs of the male end connector and pull connection apart. Repeat for the other fitting.
8. Remove the fuel filter.

To install:

9. Apply a few drops of clean engine oil to the male tube ends of the filter.
10. Remove the protective caps from the new filter.
11. Install new plastic connector retainers on the filter inlet and outlet tubes.
12. Push the connectors together to cause the retaining tabs/fingers to snap into place.
13. Once installed, pull on both ends of each connection to ensure they are secure.

14. Place the fuel filter into position and install the attaching screw.
15. Tighten the fuel filler cap.
16. Connect the negative battery cable.

Electric Fuel Pump

PRESSURE TESTING

TBI System

1. Disconnect the negative battery cable. Relieve the fuel system pressure.
2. Remove the air cleaner and plug the thermal vacuum port on the throttle body.
3. Disconnect the quick-connect fuel supply fitting and install a fuel line adapter and fuel pressure gauge tool between the fittings.

NOTE: Before connecting the quick-connect fitting, use air pressure to blow any dirt from the fitting that would otherwise enter and contaminate the fuel system.

4. Connect the negative battery cable. Start the engine and read the fuel pressure on the gauge, it should be 9–13 psi.
5. Turn the ignition **OFF**, relieve the fuel system pressure and remove the fuel pressure gauge.
6. When connecting the quick-connect fittings, apply a few drops of clean engine oil to the male tube ends. Make sure the connections are tight.
7. Remove the plug from the thermac vacuum port at the throttle body and install the air cleaner.
8. Connect the negative battery cable. Start the engine and check for fuel leaks.

PFI System

1. Relieve the fuel system pressure.
2. Using a fuel pressure gauge tool, connect it to the fuel pressure connection fitting on the fuel rail.
3. Using a clean shop cloth, wrap it around the fitting to catch any fuel leakage when connecting the gauge.
4. Turn the ignition **ON** and read the fuel pressure on the gauge, it should be 37–43 psi.
5. Start the engine and again note the fuel pressure on the gauge.
6. With the engine idling, the fuel pressure should be 33–40 psi. This idle pressure will vary somewhat depending on barometric pressure but it should be lower.
7. Relieve the fuel system pressure and disconnect the gauge.

REMOVAL & INSTALLATION

The fuel pump is located in the fuel

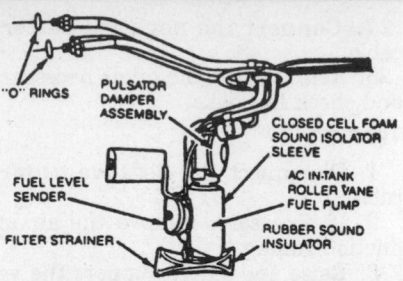

Fuel pump and sending unit assemblies

tank. Removal and installation procedures require the fuel tank to be removed from the vehicle.

CAUTION

The fuel system pressure must be relieved before attempting any service procedures. Use caution to avoid the risk of fire by disposing of any fuel and fuel soaked rags properly.

1. Relieve the fuel pressure.
2. Disconnect the negative battery cable.
3. Using a siphon hose and pump, drain the fuel from the fuel tank.
4. Raise and safely support the vehicle.
5. Support the fuel tank and disconnect the retaining straps.
6. Lower the tank enough to disconnect the sending unit wire, the hoses and the ground strap. Remove the fuel tank from the vehicle.
7. Using a locking cam tool, remove the sending unit retaining cam from the fuel tank.
8. Remove the fuel pump and sending unit assembly from the tank. Remove and discard the O-ring gasket.

To install:

9. Install a new O-ring and gasket. Carefully install the fuel pump and sending unit assembly into the fuel tank.
10. Install the retaining cam and lock and secure the sending unit in place to the fuel tank.
11. Raise the tank in position to connect the sending unit wire, the hoses and the ground strap. Install the tank retaining straps and secure the tank in place.
12. Lower the vehicle and refill the tank with fuel.
13. Connect the negative battery cable. Turn the ignition switch to the **ON** position, to restore system pressure.
14. Start the engine and check for fuel leaks.

Fuel Injection

Throttle Body Injection (TBI)

The 2.0L and 2.2L (VIN G) engines are equipped with Throttle Body Injection (TBI).

This injection system uses a single throttle body injection unit (model 700 TBI). It is located on the intake manifold where the carburetor is normally mounted. The TBI unit is computer controlled and supplies the correct amount of fuel during all engine operating conditions. In the TBI system, a single fuel injector mounted at the top of the throttle body, sprays fuel through the throttle valve and into the intake manifold. The activating signal for the injector originates with the electronic control module ECM, which monitors engine temperature, throttle position, vehicle speed and several other engine related conditions. A fuel pressure regulator inside the throttle body maintains fuel pressure at 9–13 psi and routes unused fuel back to the fuel tank through a fuel return line.

Port Fuel Injection (PFI)

This system uses Bosch fuel injectors, 1 at each intake port. The injectors are mounted on a fuel rail and are activated by a signal from the Electronic Control Module (ECM). The injector is a solenoid operated valve which remains open depending on the width of the electronic pulses, length of the signal from the ECM; the longer the open time, the more fuel is injected. In this manner, the air/fuel mixture can be precisely controlled for maximum performance with minimum emissions. A pressure regulator maintains 28–36 psi in the fuel line to the injectors and the excess fuel is fed back to the tank.

IDLE SPEED AND IDLE MIXTURE ADJUSTMENT

Idle speed and mixture are controlled by the Electronic Control Module (ECM). No adjustments are possible.

Fuel Injector

REMOVAL & INSTALLATION

2.0L and 2.2L (VIN G) Engines

1. Relieve the fuel system pressure.
2. Remove the air cleaner. Disconnect the negative battery cable from the battery.
3. Disconnect the electrical connector from the fuel injector.
4. Remove the injector retainer-to-throttle body screw and the retainer.
5. Using a small prybar and a fulcrum, carefully lift the injector until it is free from the fuel meter body.
6. Remove the O-rings form the nozzle end of the injector.
7. Inspect the fuel injector filter for dirt and/or contamination.
To install:
8. Lubricate the O-rings with automatic transmission fluid and place them on the fuel injector.
9. Push the fuel injector straight into the fuel meter body, apply thread locking compound on the fuel injector retainer screw and install.
10. Connect the electrical connector to the fuel injector.
11. Install the air cleaner. Connect the negative battery cable.
12. Turn the ignition switch to the ON position, to restore system pressure. Start the engine and check for fuel leaks.

2.2L (VIN 4), 2.3L, 2.8L and 3.1L Engines

1. Relieve the fuel system pressure.
2. Disconnect the negative battery cable.
3. Disconnect the fuel line from the fuel rail.
4. Remove the fuel rail-to-intake manifold bolts and the fuel rail assembly from the intake manifold.

NOTE: When removing the fuel rail, the fuel injectors will pull straight out of the intake manifold.

5. Remove the fuel injector-to-fuel rail retaining clips and the injectors from the fuel rail.
To install:
6. Replace the O-rings on the fuel injectors.
7. Install the injectors to the fuel rail and fuel injector-to-fuel rail retaining clips.
8. Install the fuel rail assembly to the intake manifold and the fuel rail-to-intake manifold bolts.
9. Connect the fuel line to the fuel rail.
10. Connect the negative battery cable.

DRIVE AXLE

Halfshaft

REMOVAL & INSTALLATION

If equipped with an automatic transaxle, the inner joint on the right side halfshaft uses a male spline that locks into the transaxle gears. The left side halfshaft uses a female spline that is installed over the stub shaft on the transaxle.

An intermediate shaft is installed between the transaxle and the right halfshaft.

Except Intermediate Shaft

1. With the weight of the vehicle on the tires, loosen the hub nut.

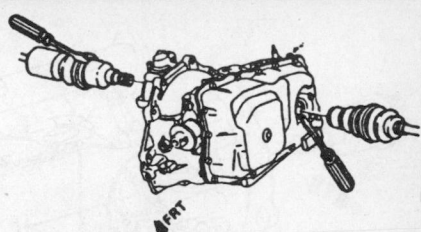

Removing the halfshafts from the transaxle

2. Raise and safely support the vehicle.
3. Remove the hub nut.
4. Install boot protectors on the boots.
5. Remove the brake caliper with the line attached and support it (on a wire) aside; do not allow the caliper to hang from the line.
6. Remove the brake rotor and caliper mounting bracket.
7. Remove the strut to steering knuckle bolts. Pull the steering knuckle out of the strut bracket.
8. Using a halfshaft removal tool and an extension, remove the halfshafts from the transaxle and support them safely.
9. Using a spindle remover tool, remove the halfshaft from the hub and bearing.
To install:
10. Loosely place the halfshaft on the transaxle and in the hub and bearing.
11. Properly position the steering knuckle to the strut bracket and install the bolt. Tighten the bolts to 133 ft. lbs. (181 Nm).
12. Install the brake rotor, caliper bracket and caliper. Place a holding device in the rotor to prevent it from turning.
13. Install the hub nut and washer. Tighten the nut to 71 ft. lbs. (96 Nm).
14. Seat the halfshafts into the transaxle using a prybar on the groove on the inner retainer.
15. Verify that the shafts are seated by grasping the CV-joint and pulling outwards; do not grasp the shaft. If the snapring is seated, the halfshaft will remain in place.
16. Remove the boot protectors.
17. Lower the vehicle.
18. When the vehicle is lowered with the weight on the wheels, tighten the hub nut to 191 ft. lbs. (259 Nm).

Intermediate Shaft

1. Raise and safely support the vehicle. Remove the front right wheel and tire assembly.
2. Drain the transaxle.
3. Using a modified boot protector, place it over the outer boot.
4. Remove the stabilizer bar from the right control arm.
5. Remove the right ball joint-to-steering knuckle cotter pin and nut.

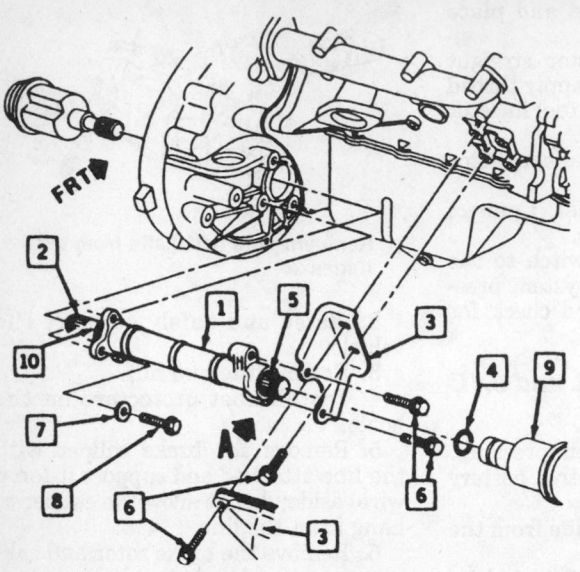
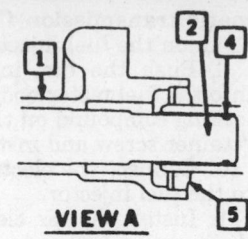

VIEW A

1. Intermediate shaft
2. Intermediate shaft
3. Bracket
4. Axle shaft retaining ring
5. Lip seal
6. Bolt–37 ft. lbs. (50 Nm)
7. Washer
8. Bolt–18 ft. lbs.
9. Right drive axle
10. O-ring seal

Exploded view of the intermediate shaft assembly

Using a ball joint remover tool, separate the ball joint from the steering knuckle.

6. Pull the steering knuckle outward and separate the halfshaft from the intermediate shaft.

7. Remove the intermediate shaft housing-to-bracket bolts and the lower bracket-to-engine bolt. Loosen the upper bracket-to-engine bolt and swing the bracket aside.

8. Remove the intermediate shaft housing-to-transaxle bolts, disengage the housing from the transaxle and remove the intermediate shaft assembly.

To install:

9. Lubricate the intermediate shaft splines with grease and install the intermediate shaft. Tighten the intermediate shaft housing-to-transaxle bolts to 18 ft. lbs. (25 Nm), the intermediate shaft housing-to-bracket bolts to 37 ft. lbs. (50 Nm) and the bracket-to-engine bolts to 37 ft. lbs. (50 Nm).

10. Install the intermediate shaft housing-to-bracket bolts and the lower bracket-to-engine bolt.

11. Connect the halfshaft to the intermediate shaft.

12. Connect the ball joint to the steering knuckle. Install the ball joint-to-steering knuckle nut and cotter pin.

13. Install the stabilizer bar to the right control arm.

14. Remove the boot protector.

15. Install the right front tire and wheel assembly.

16. Lower the vehicle.

17. Refill the transaxle.

18. Start the engine and allow to come to normal operating temperature. Check the automatic transaxle fluid level. Top-up as necessary.

CV-Boot

REMOVAL & INSTALLATION

Inner

1. Remove the halfshaft.
2. Cut the seal retaining clamps.
3. Using a pair of snapring pliers, remove the retaining ring from the shaft and remove the spider assembly.
4. Remove the old boot from the shaft.

To install:

5. Using solvent, clean the splines of the shaft and repack the joint.
6. Install the inner boot clamp first and the new boot second.
7. Push the CV-joint assembly onto the shaft until the retaining ring is seated on the shaft.
8. Slide the boot onto the joint. Install both the inner and outer clamps.
9. Install the halfshaft.

Outer

1. Remove the halfshaft from the vehicle.
2. Cut off the boot retaining clamps and discard them. Remove the old boot.
3. If equipped with a deflector ring, use a brass drift and carefully tap it off.
4. Using a pair of snapring pliers, spread the retaining ring inside the outer CV-joint and tap the joint off the halfshaft.

To install:

5. Using solvent, clean the splines of the halfshaft and the CV-joint and repack the joint. Install a new retaining ring inside the joint.

6. Install the inner boot clamp first, the new boot second.

7. Push the joint assembly onto the halfshaft until the ring is seated on the shaft.

8. Slide the boot onto the joint and install the clamps on both the inner and outer part of the boot.

9. Install the halfshaft.

Front Wheel Hub, Knuckle and Bearings

REMOVAL & INSTALLATION

The hub and bearing are replaced as an assembly only.

1. With the vehicle weight on the tires, loosen the hub nut.

2. Raise and safely support the vehicle. Remove the wheel and tire assembly.

3. Install a boot cover over the outer CV-joint boot.

4. Remove the hub nut. Remove the brake caliper and support it aside (on a wire); do not allow the caliper to hang on the brake line.

5. Remove the hub and bearing mounting bolts.

6. Remove the brake rotor splash shield.

7. Using a hub puller tool, press the hub and bearing from the halfshaft.

8. Disconnect the stabilizer link from the lower control arm.

9. Remove the cotter pin and the ball joint-to-knuckle attaching nut.

10. Disconnect the ball joint from the steering knuckle, using a ball joint separator tool.

11. Remove the halfshaft from the knuckle and support it aside.

12. Matchmark the strut in relationship to the knuckle, for alignment purposes and remove the strut-to-knuckle attaching nuts.

13. Remove the knuckle from the strut.

14. Using a brass drift, remove the inner knuckle seal.

To install:

15. Clean and inspect the steering knuckle bore and the bearing mating surfaces.

16. Using a seal driver tool, install it into the steering knuckle; be sure to lubricate the new seal and the bearing with a high temperature wheel bearing grease.

17. Connect the ball joint to the knuckle and install the ball joint-to-knuckle attaching nut, hand tight.

18. Position the knuckle to the strut and install the attaching bolts. Align the matchmarks and tighten the attaching bolts to 129 ft. lbs. (175 Nm). Tighten the ball joint-to-knuckle attaching nut to 55 ft. lbs (75 Nm).

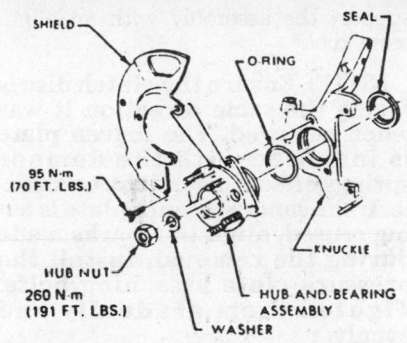

Exploded view of the hub, knuckle and bearing

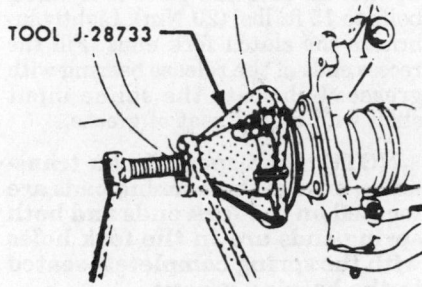

Removing halfshaft from steering knuckle bearing

19. Install a new O-ring between the bearing and knuckle assembly.

20. Install the splash shield, hub/bearing assembly, to the knuckle and install the attaching bolts. Tighten the attaching bolts to 67 ft. lbs. (90 Nm).

21. Remove the boot cover from the outer CV-joint boot and slide the halfshaft into the knuckle assembly.

22. Install the hub washer and attaching nut, (use and new nut) on the halfshaft. Tighten the attaching nut to 71 ft. lbs. (100 Nm).

23. Connect the stabilizer link to the lower control arm.

24. Install the brake rotor, caliper and the wheel/tire assembly.

25. Lower the vehicle and tighten the hub nut to 191 ft. lbs. (259 Nm).

MANUAL TRANSAXLE

For further information on transmission/transaxles, please refer to "Chilton's Guide to Transmission Repair".

Transaxle Assembly

REMOVAL & INSTALLATION

NOTE: Before performing any maintenance that requires the removal of the slave cylinder, transaxle or clutch housing, the clutch master cylinder pushrod must first be disconnected from the clutch pedal. Failure to disconnect the pushrod will result in permanent damage to the slave cylinder if the clutch pedal is depressed with the slave cylinder disconnected.

Muncie

5TM40/NVT550

1. Disconnect the negative battery cable and remove the battery.

2. Using an engine support fixture tool and an adapter, install them on the engine and raise the engine enough to take the engine weight off the engine mounts.

3. Remove the left side sound insulator.

4. Disconnect the clutch master cylinder pushrod from the clutch pedal.

5. Remove the air cleaner and duct assembly.

6. Disconnect the clutch slave cylinder-to-transaxle support bolts and position the cylinder aside.

7. Remove the transaxle-to-mount through bolt.

8. Raise and safely support the vehicle.

9. Remove both exhaust crossover bolts at the right side manifold.

10. Lower the vehicle. Remove the left side exhaust manifold.

11. Disconnect the transaxle mounting bracket.

12. Disconnect the shifter cables.

13. Remove the upper transaxle-to-engine bolts.

14. Raise and safely support the vehicle.

15. Remove the left front wheel and tire assembly and the left side inner splash shield.

16. Remove the transaxle strut and bracket.

17. Place a drain pan under the transaxle, remove the drain plug and drain the fluid from the transaxle.

18. Remove the clutch housing cover bolts.

19. Disconnect the speedometer wire.

20. From the left suspension support and control arm, disconnect the stabilizer shaft.

21. Remove the left suspension support mounting bolts and move the support aside.

22. Disconnect both halfshafts from the transaxle and remove the left halfshaft from the vehicle.

23. Using a transmission jack, attach it to and support the transaxle.

24. Remove the remaining transaxle-to-engine bolts.

25. Slide the transaxle away from the engine, lower it and remove the right side halfshaft.

To install:

26. Raise the vehicle and support it safely.

27. Support the transaxle assembly on a transaxle jack.

28. Raise the transaxle in position and guide the right halfshaft into the bore of the transaxle.

NOTE: The right halfshaft cannot be readily installed after the transaxle is connected to engine.

29. Install the transaxle to engine and install the mounting bolts. Tighten the bolts to 60 ft. lbs. (81 Nm).

30. Install the left halfshaft into its bore and seat both halfshafts to the transaxle securely.

31. Install the suspension support-to-body bolts.

32. Install the stabilizer shaft-to-suspension support and install the control arm.

33. Install the speedometer wire connector.

34. Install the clutch housing cover bolts.

35. Install the strut bracket to transaxle and install the strut.

36. Install the inner splash shield.

37. Tire and wheel assembly and lower the vehicle.

38. Install the upper transaxle-to-engine bolts.

39. Connect the shift cables.

40. Install left side exhaust manifold.

41. Raise vehicle and support it safely.

42. Install both exhaust crossover bolts at the right side manifold.

43. Lower the vehicle.

44. Install the transaxle-to-mount thru bolt.

45. Install the clutch slave cylinder to the support bracket.

46. Install the air cleaner and air intake duct assembly.

47. Remove engine support fixture.

48. Install the clutch master cylinder pushrod to clutch pedal.

49. Install the left sound insulator.

50. Refill the transaxle and check for leaks.

51. Connect the negative battery cable.

Isuzu

1. Disconnect the negative battery cable.

2. Using an engine support fixture tool and an adapter, install them on the engine and raise the engine enough to take the engine weight off the engine mounts.

3. Remove the left side sound insulator.

4. Disconnect the clutch master cylinder pushrod from the clutch pedal.

5. Disconnect the clutch slave cylinder-to-transaxle support bolts and position the cylinder aside.

6. Remove the wiring harness from the transaxle mount bracket and the shift wire electrical connector.

7. Remove the transaxle-to-mount bolts and the transaxle mount bracket-to-chassis nuts/bolts.

8. Disconnect the shift cables and remove the retaining clamp from the transaxle. Remove the ground cables from the transaxle mounting studs.

9. Raise and safely support the vehicle.

10. Remove the front wheel and tire assemblies and the left side inner splash shield.

11. Remove the transaxle front strut and bracket.

12. Remove the clutch housing cover bolts. Disconnect the speedometer wire connector.

13. From the left suspension support and control arm, disconnect the stabilizer shaft.

14. Remove the left suspension support mounting bolts and move the support aside.

15. Disconnect both halfshafts from the transaxle and remove the left halfshaft from the vehicle.

16. Place a drain pan under the transaxle, remove the drain plug and drain the fluid from the transaxle.

17. Using a transmission jack, attach it to and support the transaxle.

18. Remove the transaxle-to-engine bolts.

19. Slide the transaxle away from the engine, lower it and remove the right side halfshaft.

To install:

20. Raise the vehicle and support it safely.

21. Support the transaxle assembly on a transaxle jack.

22. Raise the transaxle in position and guide the right halfshaft into the bore of the transaxle.

NOTE: The right halfshaft cannot be readily installed after the transaxle is connected to engine.

23. Install the transaxle to engine and install the mounting bolts. Tighten the bolts to 60 ft. lbs. (81 Nm).

24. Install the left halfshaft into its bore and seat both halfshafts to the transaxle securely.

25. Install the suspension support-to-body bolts.

26. Install the stabilizer shaft-to-suspension support and install the control arm.

27. Install the speedometer wire connector.

28. Install the clutch housing cover bolts.

29. Install the front strut bracket to transaxle and install the front strut.

30. Install the inner splash shield.

31. Install the tire and wheel assembly and lower the vehicle.

32. Install the ground cables at the mounting studs.

33. Install the electrical connections for the shift light.

34. Install the slave cylinder to the transaxle bracket aligning the pushrod into the pocket of the clutch release lever. Install the attaching nuts and tighten evenly to prevent damage to the cylinder.

35. Install the transaxle mount bracket.

36. Install the transaxle mount to the side frame and install the attaching bolts.

37. Connect the wire harness at the mount bracket.

38. Remove the engine support.

39. Install the shift cables.

40. Refill the transaxle and check for leaks.

41. Connect the negative battery cable.

LINKAGE ADJUSTMENT

No adjustments are possible on the manual transaxle shifting cables or linkage. If the transaxle is not engaging completely, check for stretched cables or broken shifter components or a faulty transaxle.

CLUTCH

Clutch Assembly
REMOVAL & INSTALLATION

1. Raise and safely support the vehicle. Disconnect the negative battery cable.

2. Remove the left side sound insulator panel.

3. Disconnect the clutch master cylinder pushrod from the clutch pedal.

4. Remove the transaxle.

5. Using paint or chalk, matchmark the pressure plate and flywheel assembly to insure proper balance during reassembly.

6. Loosen the pressure plate-to-flywheel bolts, 1 turn at a time, until the spring pressure is released.

7. Support the pressure plate and remove the bolts.

8. Remove the pressure plate and disc assembly; be sure to note the flywheel side of the clutch disc.

9. Clean and inspect the clutch assembly, flywheel, release bearing, clutch fork and pivot shaft for signs of wear. Replace any necessary parts.

To install:

10. Position the clutch disc and pressure plate in the appropriate position, support the assembly with an alignment tool.

NOTE: Ensure the clutch disc is facing the same direction it was when removed. The driven plate is installed with the damper springs offset toward the transaxle. If the same pressure plate is being reused, align the marks made during the removal, install the pressure plate attaching bolts. Tighten them gradually and evenly.

11. Remove the alignment tool and tighten the pressure plate-to-flywheel bolts to 15 ft. lbs. (20 Nm). Lightly lubricate the clutch fork ends. Fill the recess ends of the release bearing with grease. Lubricate the spline input shaft with a light coat of grease.

NOTE: On 5-speed Isuzu transaxles, ensure the bearing pads are located on the fork ends and both spring ends are in the fork holes with the spring completely seated in the bearing groove.

12. Install the transaxle in the vehicle.

NOTE: The clutch lever must not be moved towards the flywheel until the transaxle is bolted to the engine. Damage to the transaxle, release bearing and clutch fork could occur if this is not followed.

13. Connect the clutch master cylinder pushrod to the clutch pedal.

14. Install the left side sound insulator.

15. Connect the negative battery cable.

PEDAL HEIGHT/FREE-PLAY ADJUSTMENT

Push the clutch pedal all the way to the floor; the distance of travel should be 6.4 ± 0.5 in. (163 ± 13mm). If the measurement is not correct check the following areas:

   Clutch pedal assembly distorted
   Incorrect clutch master cylinder pushrod length
   Dash mat under the neutral start switch
   Mislocated neutral start switch

Clutch Master and Slave Cylinder

A hydraulic clutch mechanism is used on all clutch equipped vehicles. This mechanism uses a clutch master cylinder with a remote reservoir and a slave cylinder connected to the master cylinder. Whenever the system is disconnected for repair or replacement, the clutch system must be bled to insure proper operation.

REMOVAL & INSTALLATION

The clutch master and slave cylinders are removed from the vehicle as an assembly. After installation the clutch hydraulic system must be bled.

1. Disconnect the negative battery cable.

2. From inside the vehicle, remove the left side sound insulator.

NOTE: If equipped with a 2.8L or 3.1L engine, remove the air cleaner, the mass air flow sensor and the air intake duct as an assembly.

3. Disconnect the clutch master cylinder pushrod from the clutch master cylinder.

4. From the front of the dash, remove the trim cover.

5. Remove the clutch master cylinder-to-clutch pedal bracket nuts and the remote reservoir-to-chassis screws.

6. Remove the slave cylinder-to-transaxle nuts and the slave cylinder.

7. Remove the hydraulic system (as a unit) from the vehicle.

To install:

8. Install the slave cylinder-to-transaxle support, align the pushrod to the clutch fork outer lever pocket. Tighten the slave cylinder-to-transaxle support nuts to 14–20 ft. lbs. (19–27 Nm).

NOTE: If installing a new clutch hydraulic system, do not break the pushrod plastic retainer; the straps will break on the first pedal application.

9. Install the master cylinder-to-clutch pedal bracket. Tighten the nuts evenly, to prevent damaging the master cylinder, to 15–20 ft. lbs. (20–27 Nm). Remove the pedal restrictor from the pushrod. Lubricate the pushrod bushing on the clutch pedal; if the bushing is cracked or worn, replace it.

10. If equipped with cruise control, check the switch adjustment at the clutch pedal bracket.

NOTE: When adjusting the cruise control switch, do not exert more than 20 lbs. of upward force on the clutch pedal pad for damage to the master cylinder pushrod retaining rod can result.

11. Depress the clutch pedal several times to break the plastic retaining straps; do not remove the plastic button from the end of the pushrod.

NOTE: If equipped with a 2.8L or 3.1L engine, install the air cleaner, the mass air flow sensor and the air intake duct as an assembly.

12. Install the left side sound insulator.

13. Connect the negative battery cable.

14. If necessary, bleed the clutch hydraulic system.

Hydraulic Clutch System Bleeding

PROCEDURE

1989

1. Remove any dirt or grease around the reservoir cap so dirt cannot enter the system.

NOTICE: PEDAL RESTRICTOR SHOULL NOT BE REMOVED FROM THE REPLACEMENT SYSTEM UNTIL AFTER THE SLAVE CYLINDER HAS BEEN ATTACHED TO THE TRANSAXLE SUPPORT

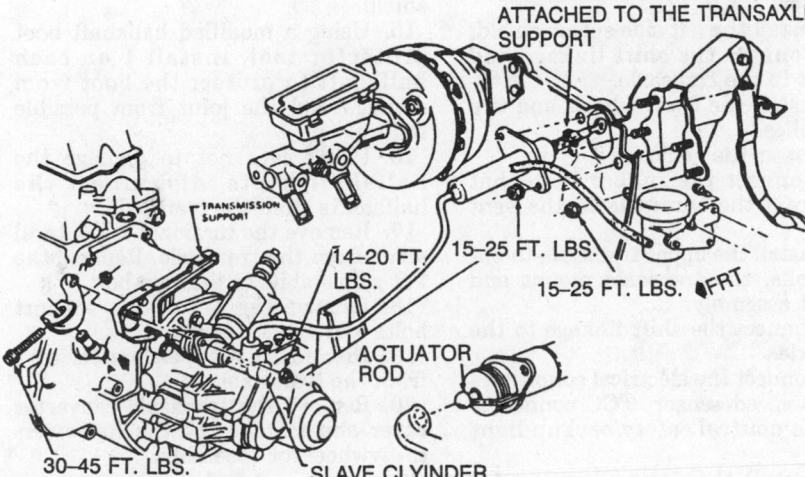

2. Fill the reservoir with an approved DOT 3 brake fluid.

3. Loosen but do not remove, the bleeder screw on the slave cylinder.

4. Fluid will now flow from the master cylinder to the slave cylinder.

NOTE: It is important that the reservoir remain filled throughout the procedure.

5. Air bubbles should now appear at the bleeder screw.

6. Continue this procedure until a steady stream of fluid without any air bubbles is present.

7. Tighten the bleeder screw. Check the fluid level in the reservoir and refill to the proper mark.

8. The system is now fully bled. Check the clutch operation by starting the engine, pushing the clutch pedal to the floor and placing the transmission in reverse.

9. If any grinding of the gears is noted, repeat the procedure.

NOTE: Never under any circumstances reuse fluid that has been in the system. The fluid may be contaminated with dirt and moisture.

1990–93

1. Disconnect the slave cylinder from the transaxle.

2. Loosen the master cylinder mounting attaching nuts. Do not remove the master cylinder.

3. Remove any dirt or grease around the reservoir cap so dirt cannot enter the system. Fill the reservoir with an approved DOT 3 brake fluid.

4. Depress the hydraulic actuator cylinder pushrod approximately 0.787 in. (20.0mm) into the slave cylinder bore and hold.

5. install the diaphragm and cap on the reservoir while holding the slave cylinder pushrod.

6. Release the slave cylinder pushrod.

7. Hold the slave cylinder vertically with the pushrod end facing the ground.

NOTE: The slave cylinder should be lower than the master cylinder.

8. Press the pushrod into the slave cylinder bore with short 0.390 in. (10.0mm) strokes.

9. Observe the reservoir for air bubbles. Continue until air bubbles no longer enter the reservoir.

10. Connect the slave cylinder to the transaxle.

11. Tighten the master cylinder attaching nuts.

12. Top-up the clutch master cylinder reservoir.

13. To test the system, start the en-

gine and push the clutch pedal to the floor. Wait 10 seconds and select reverse gear. There should be no gear clash. If clash is present, air may still be present in the system. Repeat bleeding procedure.

AUTOMATIC TRANSAXLE

For further information on transmission/transaxles, please refer to "Chilton's Guide to Transmission Repair".

Transaxle Assembly

REMOVAL & INSTALLATION

2.0L, 2.2L and 2.3L Engines

1. Disconnect the negative battery cable. Remove the air cleaner and air intake assembly.
2. Disconnect the TV cable from the throttle lever and the transaxle.
3. Remove the fluid level indicator and the filler tube.
4. Using an engine support fixture tool and an adapter, install them onto the engine.
5. Remove the wiring harness-to-transaxle nut.
6. Label and disconnect the electrical connectors for the speed sensor, TCC connector and the neutral safety/backup light switch.
7. Disconnect the shift linkage from the transaxle.
8. Remove the upper transaxle-to-engine bolts, the transaxle mount and bracket assembly.
9. Disconnect the rubber hose that runs from the transaxle to the vent pipe.
10. Raise and safely support the vehicle.
11. Remove the front wheels and tire assemblies.
12. Disconnect the shift linkage and bracket from the transaxle.
13. Remove the left side splash shield.
14. Using a modified halfshaft boot protector tool, install 1 on each halfshaft to protect the boot from damage and the joint from possible failure.
15. Using care not to damage the halfshaft boots, disconnect the halfshafts from the transaxle.
16. Remove the transaxle strut. Remove the left side stabilizer link pin bolt and bushing clamp nuts from the support.
17. Remove the left frame support bolts and move it aside.

18. Disconnect the speedometer wire from the transaxle.
19. Remove the transaxle converter cover and matchmark the torque converter-to-flywheel for reassembly.
20. Disconnect and plug the transaxle cooler pipes.
21. Remove the transaxle-to-engine support.
22. Using a transmission jack, position and secure the jack to the transaxle. Remove the remaining transaxle-to-engine bolts.
23. Making sure the torque converter does not fall out, remove the transaxle from the vehicle.

NOTE: The transaxle cooler and lines should be flushed any time the transaxle is removed for overhaul or replacing the pump, case or converter.

To install:

24. Put a small amount of grease on the pilot hub of the converter and make sure the converter is properly engaged with the pump.
25. Raise the transaxle to the engine while guiding the right side halfshaft into the transaxle.
26. Install the lower transaxle mounting bolts and remove the jack.
27. Align the converter with the matchmarks on the flywheel and install the bolts hand tight.
28. Tighten the converter bolts to 46 ft. lbs. (62 Nm); retighten the first bolt after the others.
29. Connect the transaxle cooler pipes.
30. Connect the speedometer wire to the transaxle.
31. Install the left frame support bolts.
32. Install the left side stabilizer link pin bolt and bushing clamp nuts to the support. Install the transaxle strut.
33. Connect the halfshafts to the transaxle.
34. Remove the halfshaft boot protector.
35. Install the left side splash shield.
36. Connect the shift linkage and bracket to the transaxle.
37. Install the front wheels and tire assemblies.
38. Lower the vehicle.
39. Connect the rubber hose that runs from the transaxle to the vent pipe.
40. Install the upper transaxle-to-engine bolts, the transaxle mount and bracket assembly.
41. Connect the shift linkage to the transaxle.
42. Connect the electrical connectors for the speed sensor, TCC connector and the neutral safety/backup light switch.
43. Install the wiring harness-to-transaxle nut.

44. Remove the engine support fixture tool and an adapter.
45. Install the fluid level indicator and the filler tube.
46. Connect the TV cable to the throttle lever and the transaxle.
47. Install the air cleaner and air intake assembly.
48. Connect the negative battery cable. Check the fluid level when finished.

2.8L and 3.1L Engines

1. Disconnect the negative battery cable. Remove the air cleaner, bracket, Mass Air Flow (MAF) sensor and air tube as an assembly.
2. Disconnect the exhaust crossover from the right side manifold and remove the left side exhaust manifold. Raise and support the manifold/crossover assembly.
3. Disconnect the TV cable from the throttle lever and the transaxle.
4. Remove the vent hose and the shift cable from the transaxle.
5. Remove the fluid level indicator and the filler tube.
6. Using an engine support fixture tool and an adapter, install them on the engine.
7. Remove the wiring harness-to-transaxle nut.
8. Label and disconnect the wires for the speed sensor, TCC connector and the neutral safety/backup light switch.
9. Remove the upper transaxle-to-engine bolts.
10. Remove the transaxle-to-mount through bolt, the transaxle mount bracket and the mount.
11. Raise and safely support the vehicle.
12. Remove the front wheel and tire assemblies.
13. Disconnect the shift cable bracket from the transaxle.
14. Remove the left side splash shield.
15. Using a modified halfshaft boot protector tool, install 1 on each halfshaft to protect the boot from damage and the joint from possible failure.
16. Using care not to damage the halfshaft boots, disconnect the halfshafts from the transaxle.
17. Remove the torsional and lateral strut from the transaxle. Remove the left side stabilizer link pin bolt.
18. Remove the left frame support bolts and move it aside.
19. Disconnect the speedometer wire from the transaxle.
20. Remove the transaxle converter cover and matchmark the converter-to-flywheel for assembly.
21. Disconnect and plug the transaxle cooler pipes.

22. Remove the transaxle-to-engine support.

23. Using a transmission jack, position and secure it to the transaxle. Remove the remaining transaxle-to-engine bolts.

24. Make sure the torque converter does not fall out and remove the transaxle from the vehicle.

NOTE: The transaxle cooler and lines should be flushed any time the transaxle is removed for overhaul, to replace the pump, case or converter.

To install:

25. Put a small amount of grease on the pilot hub of the converter and make sure the converter is properly engaged with the pump.

26. Raise the transaxle to the engine while guiding the right side halfshaft into the transaxle.

27. Install the lower transaxle mounting bolts and Install the jack.

28. Align the converter with the matchmarks on the flywheel and install the bolts hand tight.

29. Tighten the converter bolts to 46 ft. lbs. (62 Nm); retighten the first bolt after the others.

30. Connect the transaxle cooler pipes.

31. Connect the speedometer wire to the transaxle.

32. Install the left frame support bolts.

33. Install the left side stabilizer link pin bolt. Install the torsional and lateral strut to the transaxle.

34. Connect the halfshafts to the transaxle.

35. Remove the boot protectors.

36. Install the left side splash shield.

37. Connect the shift cable bracket to the transaxle.

38. Install the front wheel and tire assemblies.

39. Lower the vehicle.

40. Install the transaxle-to-mount through bolt, the transaxle mount bracket and the mount.

41. Install the upper transaxle-to-engine bolts.

42. Connect the wires for the speed sensor, TCC connector and the neutral safety/backup light switch.

43. Install the wiring harness-to-transaxle nut.

44. Remove the engine support fixture tool.

45. Install the fluid level indicator and the filler tube.

46. Install the vent hose and the shift cable to the transaxle.

47. Connect the TV cable to the throttle lever and the transaxle.

48. Install the left side exhaust manifold. Connect the exhaust crossover to the right side manifold.

49. Install the air cleaner, bracket, Mass Air Flow (MAF) sensor and air tube as an assembly.

50. Connect the negative battery cable. Check the fluid level when finished.

FRONT SUSPENSION

MacPherson Strut

REMOVAL & INSTALLATION

1. Disconnect the upper strut-to-body attaching bolts.

2. Raise and safely support the vehicle. Allow the suspension to hang free. Remove the wheel assembly. Install a halfshaft boot protector.

3. Remove the cotter pin and tie rod attaching nut. Using a tie rod separator tool, separate the tie rod from the strut.

4. Support the steering knuckle to prevent tension from being applied to the brake line.

5. Matchmark the strut in relationship to the knuckle and remove both strut-to-knuckle attaching bolts. Remove the strut assembly from the vehicle.

To install:

6. Installation is the reverse of the removal procedures. When installing the mounting bolts be sure to place the flats of the bolts in the horizontal position.

7. Tighten the strut-to-knuckle bolts to 129 ft. lbs. (175 Nm) and the upper strut-to-body attaching bolts to 18 ft. lbs. (25 Nm).

8. Lower the vehicle. Check and adjust the alignment as required.

Lower Ball Joints

INSPECTION

1. Raise and safely support the vehicle; be sure the weight of the vehicle does not rest on the lower control arm assemblies.

2. With the ball joint installed to the steering knuckle, grasp the top and bottom of the wheel, then move the wheel using an in and out shaking motion. Observe any movement between the steering knuckle and the control arm. If movement exists, replace the ball joint.

REMOVAL & INSTALLATION

1. Raise and safely support the vehicle and remove the wheel assembly.

2. If no countersink is found on the lower side of the rivets, carefully locate the center of the rivet body and mark it using a punch.

3. Properly drill out the rivets of the ball joint assembly. Using a ball joint separator tool, separate the ball joint from the steering knuckle.

4. Disconnect the stabilizer bar from the lower control arm. Remove the ball joint from the vehicle.

To install:

5. Installation is the reverse of the removal procedures.

6. Attach the ball joint the lower control arm with the attaching bolts and nuts. Tighten the attaching bolts and nuts to 50 ft. lbs. (68 Nm).

7. Lower the vehicle. Check and align the front end as required.

Lower Control Arms

REMOVAL & INSTALLATION

1. Raise and safely support the vehicle and remove the wheel assembly.

2. Disconnect the stabilizer bar from the lower control arm assembly. Using a ball joint separator tool, separate the ball joint from the steering knuckle.

3. Remove the lower control arm attaching bolts and remove the lower control arm from the vehicle.

To install:

4. Installation is the reverse of the removal procedures. Tighten the lower control arm bolts to 63 ft. lbs. (85 Nm). Tighten the ball joint-to-knuckle attaching nut to 55 ft. lbs. (75 Nm). Check and align the front end as required.

Sway Bar

REMOVAL & INSTALLATION

1. Open the hood and install an engine support tool. Raise and safely support the vehicle; allow the suspension to hang free. Remove the left front wheel assembly.

2. Disconnect the stabilizer link bolts and nuts from the control arms. Disconnect the stabilizer shaft from the support assemblies.

3. Loosen the front bolts and remove the bolts from the rear and center of the support assemblies, allowing the supports to be lowered enough to remove the stabilizer bar assembly. Remove the assembly from the vehicle.

To install:

4. Installation is the reverse of the removal procedures. Loosely assemble all components while insuring that the stabilizer bar is centered, side-to-side. Tighten the stabilizer bar support as-

semblies to 14 ft. lbs. (19 Nm). Tighten the stabilizer link bolts and nuts 14 ft. lbs. (19 Nm).

5. Lower the vehicle.

REAR SUSPENSION

Shock Absorbers

REMOVAL & INSTALLATION

1. Open the trunk and remove the shock absorber trim cover, if equipped. Remove the upper shock absorber attaching bolt. Remove each shock absorber separately when both assemblies are being replaced.
2. Raise and safely support the vehicle and the rear axle assembly.
3. Remove the lower shock attaching bolts. Remove the shock absorber from the vehicle.

To install:

4. Installation is the reverse of the removal procedures. Tighten the lower shock attaching bolt to 35 ft. lbs. (48 Nm) and the upper shock attaching bolt to 22 ft. lbs. (30 Nm).

Coil Springs

REMOVAL & INSTALLATION

1. Raise and safely support the vehicle under the rear control arms. Support the rear axle assembly with and jack.
2. Remove the wheel assembly. Remove the right and left brake line bracket attaching screws from the body and allow the brake line to hang free.
3. Remove the shock absorber lower attaching bolts. Lower the rear axle assembly to remove the coil springs. Do not allow the axle assembly to hang unsupported in this position.

To install:

4. Installation is the reverse of the removal procedures. Before installing the coil springs it is necessary to install the insulators to the body using adhesive.
5. Position the spring and insulator in the spring seat and raise the axle. The upper ends of the coil must be positioned properly in the seat of the body.
6. Tighten the shock absorber lower attaching bolts to 21 ft. lbs. (28 Nm).
7. Install the wheel assemblies and lower the vehicle.

Stabilizer Bar

REMOVAL & INSTALLATION

1. Raise and safely support the vehicle.
2. Remove the nuts and bolts at both axle and control arm attachments.
3. Remove the bracket. Remove the insulator and the stabilizer bar assembly assembly.

To install:

4. Installation is the reverse of the removal procedures. Tighten the bracket-to-axle bolts to 13 ft. lbs. (18 Nm) and the bracket-to-control arm bolts to 16 ft. lbs. (22 Nm).

Rear Wheel Bearings

REMOVAL & INSTALLATION

The rear wheel hub and bearing are replaced as an assembly only.

1. Raise and safely support the vehicle.
2. Remove the wheel and tire assembly and the brake drum.
3. Remove the hub/bearing assembly-to-rear axle nuts/bolts.

NOTE: The top mounting bolt will not clear the brake shoe when removing the hub and bearing. The hub and bearing must be partially removed while the top bolt is being turned out.

To install:

4. To install, insert and turn the top bolt in while installing the hub and bearing. Install the attaching bolts.
5. Tighten the hub/bearing assembly-to-rear axle nuts/bolts to 38 ft. lbs. (52 Nm).
6. Install the brake drum and wheel and tire assembly.

Rear Axle Assembly

REMOVAL & INSTALLATION

1. Raise and safely support the vehicle under the rear control arms. Support the rear axle assembly with and jack.

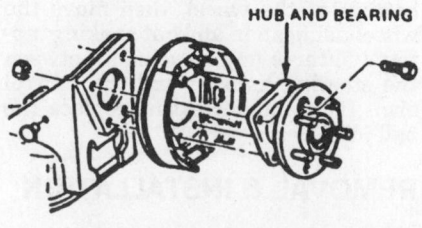

Rear wheel hub and bearing mounting

2. Remove the wheel assembly. Remove the right and left brake line bracket attaching screws from the body and allow the brake line to hang free.
3. Remove the stabilizer bar brackets. Remove the insulator and the stabilizer bar assembly.
4. Remove the shock absorber lower attaching bolts. Lower the rear axle assembly to remove the coil springs. Do not allow the axle assembly to hang in this position.
5. Remove the control arm attaching bolts from the underbody bracket and lower the axle.
6. Remove the hub attaching bolts an remove the hub, bearing and backing plate assembly.

NOTE: Be careful not to drop the hub/bearing assembly, damage to the bearing could result.

To install:

7. Install the backing plate and hub/bearing assembly to the rear axle assembly. Install the attaching bolts and nuts and tighten to 38 ft. lbs. (52 Nm).
8. Install the stabilizer bar to the rear axle assembly and install the attaching nuts and bolts. Tighten the bracket-to-axle bolts to 13 ft. lbs. (18 Nm) and the bracket-to-control arm bolts to 16 ft. lbs. (22 Nm).
9. Secure the axle assembly on a transmission jack and raise it into position.
10. Install the control arms to the underbody bracket and install the mounting nuts and bolts. Do not tighten the bolts at this time. The bolts must be tightened at curb height.

NOTE: The control arm mounting bolts must be install from the inboard side.

11. Connect the brake line connections and install the brake cable to the rear axle assembly.
12. Position the springs and insulators in the spring seat and raise the axle. The upper ends of the coil must be positioned properly in the seat of the body.
13. Connect the shock absorber at the lower end and install attaching bolt. Tighten the attaching bolt to 35 ft. lbs. (48 Nm).
14. Connect the parking brake to the guide hook. Adjust the cable as required.
15. Bleed the brake system and refill the reservoir. Adjust the brakes as required.
16. Lower the axle to curb height and tighten the axle-to-body mounting bolts. Tighten the bolts to 66 ft. lbs. (90 Nm).
17. Install the wheel assemblies and lower the vehicle. Tighten the lug nuts to 100 ft. lbs. (140 Nm).

STEERING

Steering Wheel

REMOVAL & INSTALLATION

1. Disconnect the negative battery cable.
2. If equipped with SIR, disable the system and remove the inflator module.
3. Without SIR, remove the horn cover-to-steering wheel screws.
4. Disconnect the horn electrical connector from the steering wheel and remove the horn contact.
5. Remove the steering wheel-to-column retainer, nut, washer.
6. Mark the steering wheel alignment with the steering shaft for installation purposes.
7. Using a steering wheel puller, press the steering wheel from the steering column.

NOTE: Under no circumstances should the steering wheel or shaft be hammered on. Sharp blows to the steering column could loosen the plastic injections which maintain column rigidity.

To install:
8. If equipped with SIR, feed the coil assembly connector through the steering wheel.
9. Align the matchmarks made during removal and install the steering wheel.
10. Align the steering wheel with the turn signal cancelling cam assembly.
11. Install the hexagon locking nut. Tighten the steering wheel nut to 31 ft. lbs. (42 Nm).
12. If equipped with SIR, install the inflator module and enable the system.
13. Connect the negative battery cable.

Steering Column

REMOVAL & INSTALLATION

1. Disconnect the negative battery cable.
2. Remove the left side sound insulator.
3. Disconnect the combination switch electrical connector.
4. If equipped, disable the SIR system.
5. Disconnect the ignition and dimmer switch connectors and if equipped, disconnect the cruise switch terminal connection.
6. Remove the steering column support bracket bolts.

7. Remove the flange and coupling pinch bolt.
8. Remove the upper and lower steering column support bolts.
9. Disconnect the dimmer switch and turn signal switch electrical connectors.
10. If equipped with park lock, remove the park lock cable from the ignition switch.

NOTE: If equipped with park lock, the park lock cable must be disconnected by pressing the locking tab at the ignition switch inhibitor before removing the column from the vehicle.

11. Remove the steering column assembly from the vehicle.

To install:
12. Position the steering column in the vehicle.
13. Connect the park lock cable to the ignition switch.
14. Connect the electrical connectors.
15. Position the steering column into the flange and coupling assembly.
16. Install the lower steering column support bolts. Tighten to 21 ft. lbs. (28 Nm).
17. Install the steering column support bracket-to-steering column bolts. Tighten to 22 ft. lbs. (30 Nm).
18. Install the upper steering column support bolts. Tighten to 21 ft. lbs. (28 Nm).
19. Install the flange coupling pinch bolt. Tighten to 30 ft. lbs. (41 Nm).
20. Connect the hazard/turn signal switch electrical connectors.
21. If equipped, connect the cruise control electrical connector.
22. If equipped, enable the SIR system.
23. Install the left side sound insulator.
24. Connect the negative battery cable.

Power Steering Rack

ADJUSTMENT

1. Disconnect the negative battery cable. Raise and safely support the vehicle.
2. With the front tires off the ground, loosen the locknut on the bottom of the steering rack.
3. Turn the adjuster plug clockwise until it bottoms out in the housing.
4. Turn the adjuster plug in the opposite direction 50–70 degrees.
5. While holding the adjuster plug, tighten the locknut to 50 ft. lbs. (68 Nm).

NOTE: If the adjuster plug is not held, damage to the pinion

teeth on the steering rack may occur.

6. Check to make sure the steering wheel returns to center.

REMOVAL & INSTALLATION

1. Disconnect the negative battery cable. From inside the vehicle, remove the left side lower sound insulator.
2. Remove the upper steering shaft-to-steering rack coupling pinch bolt.
3. Place a drain pan under the steering gear and disconnect the pressure lines from the steering gear.
4. Raise and safely support the vehicle.
5. Remove both front wheel and tire assemblies.
6. Using a ball joint remover, disconnect the tie rod ends from the steering knuckles.
7. Lower the vehicle.
8. Remove both steering gear-to-chassis clamps.
9. Slide the steering gear forward and remove the lower steering shaft-to-steering rack coupling pinch bolt.
10. From the firewall, disconnect the coupling and seal from the steering gear.
11. Raise and safely support the vehicle.
12. Through the left wheel opening, remove the steering gear with the tie rods.

To install:
13. Installation is the reverse of the removal procedures. Lower the vehicle.
14. Tighten the steering gear-to-chassis clamp bolts to 28 ft. lbs. (38 Nm), the tie rod nut to 44 ft. lbs. (60 Nm) and the fluid lines to 18 ft. lbs. (24 Nm).
15. Refill power steering pump reservoir and bleed the power steering system. Connect the negative battery cable.
16. Check and adjust the front end alignment as required.

Power Steering Pump

REMOVAL & INSTALLATION

1. Disconnect the negative battery cable.
2. Remove the pressure and return hoses from the pump and drain the system into a suitable container.
3. Cap the fittings at the pump.
4. Remove the serpentine belt.
5. Locate the pump attaching bolts through the pulley and remove the bolts.
6. Remove the pump assembly.
To install:
7. Installation is the reverse of the removal procedures.

8. Tighten the power steering pump bolts to 20 ft. lbs. (27 Nm).

9. Refill power steering pump reservoir and bleed the system.

10. Connect the negative battery cable.

BELT ADJUSTMENT

1. Install a belt tension gauge on the power steering belt.

2. Loosen pump adjustment bolts.

3. Tighten the front bracket-to-engine bolt A to 9 inch lbs. (1 Nm).

4. Set the belt tension by turning adjustment stud.

NOTE: The adjustment bolts are all tighten to different torque specifications. Tighten each bolt as follows:

5. Tighten adjustment bolts A to 67 ft. lbs. (91 Nm), bolts B to 19 ft. lbs. (26 Nm) and bolts C to 40 ft. lbs. (54 Nm).

6. Start engine and run it for a minimum of 2 minutes. Re-adjust the belt tension.

SYSTEM BLEEDING

NOTE: Automatic transmission fluid is not compatible with the seals and hoses of the power steering system. Under no circumstances should automatic transmission be used in place of power steering fluid in this system.

1. With the engine turned **OFF**, turn the wheels all the way to the left.

2. Fill the reservoir with power steering fluid until the level is at the **COLD** mark on the reservoir.

3. Start and operate the engine at fast idle for 15 seconds. Turn the engine **OFF**.

4. Recheck the fluid level and fill it to the **COLD** mark.

5. Start the engine and bleed the system by turning the wheels in both directions slowly to the stops.

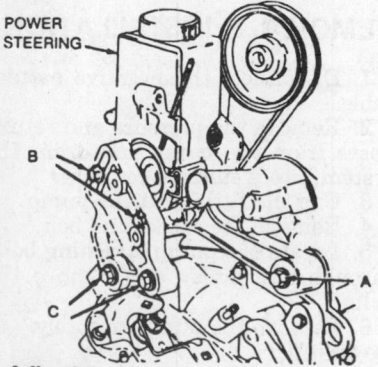

POWER STEERING

Adjusting the power steering belt tension—2.3L engine

6. Stop the engine and check the fluid. Fluid that still has air in it will be a light tan color.

7. Repeat this procedure until all air is removed from the system.

BRAKES

Master Cylinder

REMOVAL & INSTALLATION

1989–91

1. Disconnect the negative battery cable and the electrical connector from the fluid level sensor.

2. Disconnect and plug the 4 brake lines on the master cylinder.

3. Remove the master cylinder-to-power booster nuts and the master cylinder with the reservoir attached.

To install:

4. Bench bleed the new master cylinder and reverse the removal procedures. Tighten the master cylinder-to-power booster nuts to 20 ft. lbs. (27 Nm) and the brake lines-to-master cylinder to 13 ft. lbs. (18 Nm).

5. Connect the fluid level electrical sensor wires. Refill the reservoir with an approved DOT 3 brake fluid and bleed the brake system. Connect the negative battery cable.

1992–93

1. Disconnect the electrical connector from the fluid level sensor and the connectors from both solenoids.

2. Disconnect the 3 pin and 6 pin motor pack electrical connectors

3. Disconnect the brake lines from the master cylinder and from the modulator assembly. Plug the lines.

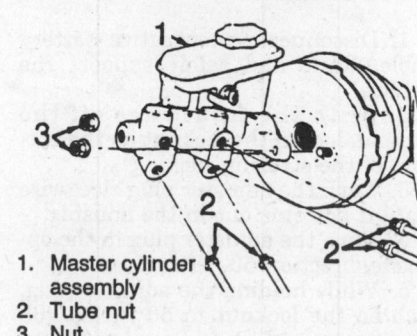

1. Master cylinder assembly
2. Tube nut
3. Nut

Master cylinder Installation—1989–91 vehicles

4. Remove the master cylinder mounting nuts and remove the master cylinder and modulator assembly.

To install:

5. Install the master cylinder and modulator assembly to the vehicle and install the mounting nuts. Tighten the mounting nuts to 20 ft. lbs. (27 Nm).

6. Connect the brake lines to the master cylinder and the modulator. Tighten the nuts to 15 ft. lbs. (20 Nm).

7. Connect the electrical connectors.

8. Fill the master cylinder with brake fluid to the proper level and bleed the brake system as necessary.

BENCH BLEEDING

This procedure is used to bench bleed the master cylinder.

1. Refill the master cylinder reservoir.

2. Push the plunger several times to force fluid into the piston.

3. Continue pumping the plunger until the fluid is free of the air bubbles.

4. Plug the outlet ports and install the master cylinder.

Proportioning Valve

REMOVAL & INSTALLATION

NOTE: It is necessary to remove the master cylinder in order to remove the proportioning valve. Bleed the brake system when finished.

1. Disconnect the negative battery cable.

2. Remove the master cylinder from the vehicle.

3. Remove the proportioning valve cap on the master cylinder.

4. Remove and discard the O-rings.

5. Remove the springs, the proportioning valve pistons and the seals from the valves.

6. Inspect the valves for corrosion or abnormal wear, replace as required.

7. Clean all parts in denatured alcohol or an equivalent. Dry all parts with air before reassembling.

To install:

8. Assemble the springs, proportioning valve pistons and the seals on the valves.

9. Install new O-ring seals.

10. Install the proportioning valve cap on the master cylinder.

11. Tighten the caps to 20 ft. lbs. (27 Nm). Refill the reservoir and bleed the brake system.

12. Install the master cylider to the vehicle and connect the negative battery cable.

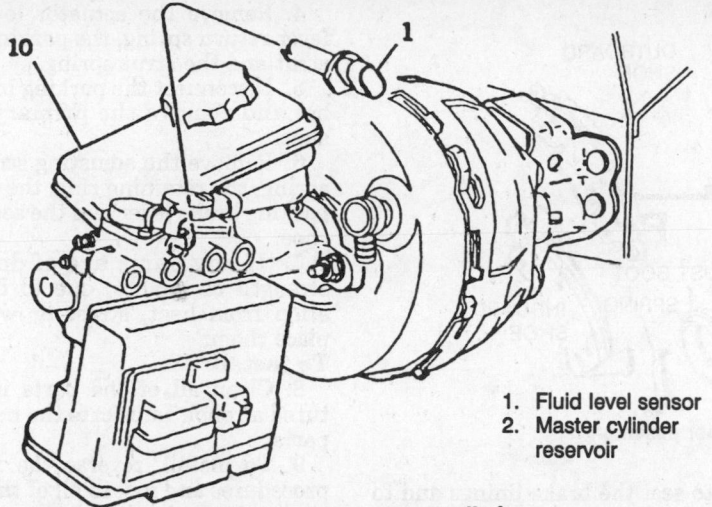

1. Fluid level sensor
2. Master cylinder reservoir

1992–93 vehicle master cylinder

1 Master cylinder
2 Proportioning valve cap
3 O-ring
4 Spring
5 Proportioning valve piston
6 Proportioning valve seal

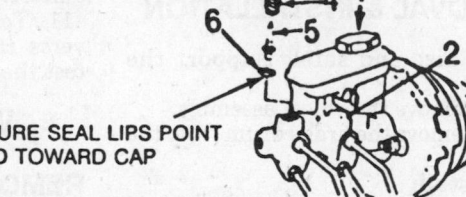

MAKE SURE SEAL LIPS POINT
UPWARD TOWARD CAP

Proportioning valve Installation

Power Brake Booster

REMOVAL & INSTALLATION

1. Disconnect the negative battery cable. Remove the master cylinder.

NOTE: Place the master cylinder in an upright position to prevent fluid loss.

2. Remove the lower-left trim panel inside the vehicle and disconnect the brake pedal-to-booster pushrod from the brake pedal.
3. Disconnect the vacuum line from the booster.
4. Remove the brake booster mounting nuts and the booster.

To install:

5. Installation is the reverse of the removal procedures. Tighten the master cylinder-to-power booster to 20 ft. lbs. (27 Nm) and the power booster mounting nuts to 20 ft. lbs. (27 Nm).
6. Bleed the brake system. Connect the negative battery cable.

Brake Caliper

REMOVAL & INSTALLATION

1. Disconnect the negative battery cable.

2. Remove half of the brake fluid from the master cylinder.
3. Raise and support the vehicle safely and remove the wheel assembly.

NOTE: Remove the brake hose attaching bolt, only if the caliper is going to be overhauled or replaced.

4. Position a large C-clamp over the caliper with the screw end against the outboard brake pad. Tighten the clamp until the caliper piston is pushed out enough to bottom the piston.
5. Remove the C-clamp. Remove the caliper guide pins and lift the caliper off the rotor.
6. Support the caliper so there is no strain on the brake hose.
7. Press the inboard pad outward and remove it from the caliper.
8. Remove and discard the O-ring bushings and steel sleeves, new parts are to be installed.
9. Check the condition of the rotor. If rotor measurements exceed manufacturer's specifications or has mild scoring, machine the rotor.

To install:

10. Lubricate and install the O-ring bushings. Install the sleeves by pressing them through the O-rings until the sleeve end on the pad side is flush with caliper ear.

11. Position the inboard pads so the pad contacts the piston and the support spring ends. The inboard and outboard pads are similar but not interchangeable.
12. Press down on the ears at the top of the inboard pad until the pad lies flat and the spring ends are just inside the lower edge of the pad.
13. Position the outboard pad with the ears toward the positioning pin holes and the tab on the inner edge of the pad resting in the notch in the edge of the caliper. Bend the ears to provide a slight interference fit in the caliper.
14. Press the outboard pad tightly into position and clinch the ears of the outboard pad over the outboard caliper half.
15. Position the caliper over the rotor.
16. Install the caliper over the rotor.
17. Install the caliper mounting bolts and tighten to 38 ft. lbs. (51 Nm).
18. If the brake hose attaching nut was disconnected, reconnect it and tighten to 33 ft. lbs. (45 Nm).
19. Install the wheel assembly and lower the vehicle.
20. Fill the master cylinder with brake fluid and bleed the system.
21. Connect the negative battery cable.

Disc Brake Pads

REMOVAL & INSTALLATION

1. Raise and safely support the front of the vehicle. Remove the wheel assembly; reinstall 2 lug nuts to retain the rotor to the axle hub.
2. Using a siphon, remove $\frac{2}{3}$ of the brake fluid from the master cylinder.
3. Using a pair of large adjustable pliers, position the jaws over the inboard pad tab and the inboard caliper housing. Squeeze the pliers to bottom the piston in the caliper housing.
4. Remove the caliper-to-bracket boots, bolt coverings, the bolts and sleeve assemblies.
5. Remove the caliper from the rotor. Using a wire, suspend the caliper from the strut.
6. Remove the outboard pad, the inboard pad and the bushing from the mounting bolt hole groves.

To install:

7. Using silicone grease, lubricate the new mounting bolt bushings and install them in the holes.
8. Install the retainer spring onto the inboard pad and the pad into the caliper by snapring the retaining spring into the piston; the inboard pad must lay flat against the piston.

NOTE: On some models, the retaining spring is already staked to the inboard pad.

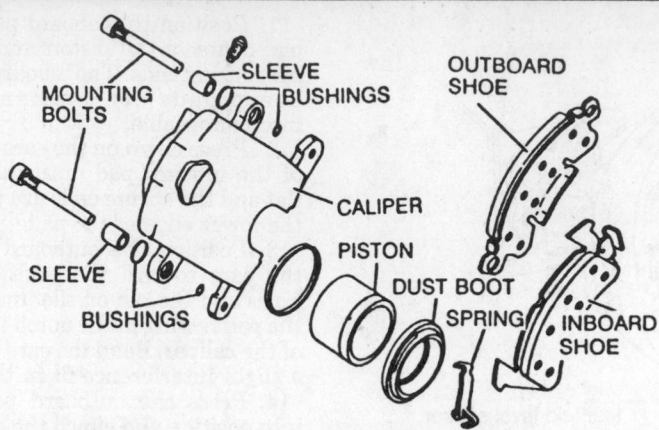

MOUNTING BOLTS — SLEEVE BUSHINGS — OUTBOARD SHOE — CALIPER — PISTON — DUST BOOT — SPRING — INBOARD SHOE — SLEEVE BUSHINGS

Exploded view of the brake caliper assembly

9. Install the outboard pad with the wear sensor at the leading edge of the forward wheel rotating; the pad must lay flat against the caliper.

10. Position the caliper assembly over the rotor in the mounting bracket. Tighten the caliper-to-bracket bolts to 38 ft. lbs. (51 Nm).

11. Using a small prybar, position it between the outboard pad and the rotor hub to hold the pad in position. Have an assistant, apply approximately 50 lbs. pressure on the brake pedal.

12. While the assistant is applying pressure, position a ball peen hammer on the outboard pad tab and tap it with another hammer to drive the tab downward to a 45 degree angle to lock the pad into position.

13. Remove the 2 rotor-to-wheel hub nuts and install the wheel.

14. Lower the vehicle. Refill the master cylinder reservoir and road test the vehicle.

Brake Rotor

REMOVAL & INSTALLATION

1. Raise and safely support the vehicle. Remove wheel assembly.

2. Remove caliper attaching bolts and remove the caliper. Using a wire suspend the caliper from the strut.

3. Remove the rotor by sliding it off the hub assembly.
To install:

4. Slide the rotor onto the hub assembly and install 2 lug nuts to hold it in place.

5. Install the brake pads into the caliper and place the caliper assembly over the rotor.

6. Install the caliper mounting bolts and tighten to 38 ft. lbs. (51 Nm).

7. Remove the lug nuts from the caliper and install the wheel assembly.

8. Lower the vehicle.

9. Fill the master cylinder with brake fluid.

10. Depress the brake pedal 3-4

times to seat the brake linings and to restore pressure in the system.

Brake Drums

REMOVAL & INSTALLATION

1. Raise and safely support the vehicle.

2. Remove the wheel assembly.

3. Remove the brake drum from the spindle.
To install:

4. Using a brake adjusting tool, adjust the brake shoe to 0.50 in. (1.27mm) less than the brake drum diameter. Install the brake drum to the axle.

5. Install the wheel assembly and lower the vehicle.

Brake Shoes

REMOVAL & INSTALLATION

1. Raise and safely support the vehicle. Remove the wheel assembly.

2. If the brake drum is difficult to remove, perform the following procedures:

a. Make sure the parking brake is released.

b. Back off the parking brake cable adjustment.

c. Remove the adjusting hole knockout plate and back off the adjusting screw.

NOTE: On some drum designs, the knockout plate must be drilled out using a $7/16$ in. (11mm) drill bit. A rubber adjusting hole cover is available for installation purposes.

d. Using a rubber mallet, tap the drum from the spindle.

3. Remove the return springs, the hold-down springs and the lever pivot. While lifting up on the actuator lever, remove the actuator link.

4. Remove the actuator lever, the lever return spring, the parking brake strut and the strut spring.

5. Disconnect the parking brake cable and remove the primary brake shoe.

6. Remove the adjusting screw, the spring, the retaining ring, the pin, the parking brake lever and the secondary shoe.

7. If any parts are of doubtful strength or quality, due to discoloration from heat, stress or wear, replace them.
To install:

8. Clean all of the parts in denatured alcohol. Lubricate the necessary parts.

9. To install, reverse the removal procedures and install all of the parts, except the brake drum.

10. Using a brake adjusting tool, adjust the brake shoe to 0.50 in. (1.27mm) less than the brake drum diameter. Install the brake drum.

11. To complete the installation, reverse the removal procedures. Road test the vehicle.

Wheel Cylinder

REMOVAL & INSTALLATION

1. Raise and safely support the vehicle. Remove the wheel assembly and brake drum Remove the brake shoes and attaching hardware.

2. Clean any dirt from around the wheel cylinder.

3. Disconnect and plug the brake line from the wheel cylinder.

4. Remove the wheel cylinder-to-backing plate bolt and lockwasher.

5. Remove the wheel cylinder.
To install:

6. Apply a liquid gasket to the shoulder of the wheel cylinder that faces the backing plate and reverse the removal procedures. Tighten the wheel cylinder-to-backing plate bolt to 15 ft. lbs. (20 Nm) and the brake line-to-wheel cylinder to 12 ft. lbs. (17 Nm).

7. Bleed the brake system. Lower the vehicle and check the brake operation.

Parking Brake Cable

ADJUSTMENT

1989–91

1. Apply and release the parking brake lever (10 clicks) at least 6 times. Apply the parking brake lever 4 clicks.

2. Raise and safely support the vehicle.

3. Locate the access hole in the backing plate and adjust the parking

brake cable until a ⅛ in. drill bit can be inserted between the the brake shoe webbing and the parking brake lever.

4. Check to make sure a ¼ in. drill bit will not fit in the same position.

5. Release the parking brake and check to see if both wheels turn freely by hand.

6. Lower the vehicle.

1992–93

1. Apply and release the parking brake lever (10 clicks) at least 6 times. Apply the parking brake lever 5 clicks or if floor mounted parking brake, apply pedal 2 clicks.

2. Raise and safely support the vehicle.

3. Locate the access hole in the backing plate and adjust the parking brake cable until the right rear wheel can be turned rearward but is locked when attempting to turn forward.

4. Release the parking brake and check to see if both wheels turn freely by hand.

5. Lower the vehicle.

REMOVAL & INSTALLATION

Front Cable

1989–91

1. Raise and safely support the vehicle.

2. Loosen but do not remove the equalizer nut to remove the cable.

3. Disconnect the cable from the equalizer and right side cable.

4. Remove the hand grip from the parking brake lever inside the vehicle.

5. Remove the console.

6. Disconnect the cable from the parking brake lever.

7. Remove the nut holding the cable to the floor.

8. Remove the exhaust hanger bracket mounting nuts.

9. Remove the catalytic converter shield.

10. Remove the cable.

11. To install, Lubricate the cable and reverse the removal procedures. Adjust the parking brake.

1992–93

1. Raise and safely support the vehicle.

2. Loosen but do not remove the equalizer nut.

3. Remove the console.

4. Disconnect the parking brake cable from the lever.

5. Remove the cable retaining nut that secures the cable to the floor panel.

6. Loosen the catalytic converter shield and disconnect the brake cable from the body.

7. Disconnect the cable from the equalizer, from the guides and from the underbody clips.

To install:

8. Connect the cable to the equalizer, to the guides and secure with the underbody clips.

9. Connect the the cable to the underbody and tighten the catalytic converter shield.

10. Install the cable retaining nut that secures the cable to the floor panel.

11. Connect the cable to the lever.

12. Install the console and adjust the cable as necessary.

13. Lower the vehicle.

Rear Cable

1989–91

1. Raise and safely support the vehicle.

2. Loosen the equalizer nut until the cable tension is released.

3. Disconnect the right side cable button from the connector.

4. Disconnect the conduit end of the cable from the bracket on the axle.

5. Remove the wheel/tire assembly and the brake drum.

6. Disconnect the cable from the parking brake lever attached to the brake shoes.

7. Remove the conduit end from the brake shoe backing plate.

8. To install, lubricate the cable and reverse the removal procedures. Adjust the parking brake.

1992–93

1. Raise and safely support the vehicle.

2. Loosen the equalizer nut until the cable tension is released.

3. Remove the tire/wheel assembly and the brake drum.

4. Place a screwdriver between the brake shoe and the top part of the brake adjuster bracket.

5. Release the top adjuster bracket by pushing the bracket to the front.

6. Remove the following:

   a. Hold-down spring
   b. Actuator lever
   c. Lever return spring
   d. Adjuster screw spring
   e. Top rear brake shoe return spring

7. Disconnect the parking brake cable from the parking brake lever.

8. Disconnect the conduit fitting from the backing plate while depressing the retaining tangs.

9. Remove the cable end button from the right side connector.

10. Disconnect the conduit fitting from the axle bracket while depressing the retaining tangs.

To install:

11. Connect the conduit fitting to the axle bracket.

12. Connect the cable end button to the connector on the right side.

13. Connect the conduit fitting to the backing plate.

14. Install the parking brake cable to the parking brake lever.

15. Install the top rear brake shoe return spring and the adjuster screw spring.

16. Install the lever return spring, the actuator lever and the rear hold-down spring.

17. Install the top adjuster bracket rod.

18. Install the brake drum and the tire/wheel.

19. Adjust the brake cable as necessary and lower the vehicle.

Brake System Bleeding

PROCEDURE

1. Clean the bleeder screw at each wheel.

2. Attach a small rubber hose to the bleed screw and place the end in a clear container of fresh brake fluid.

3. Fill the master cylinder reservoir with fresh brake fluid. The master cylinder reservoir level should be checked

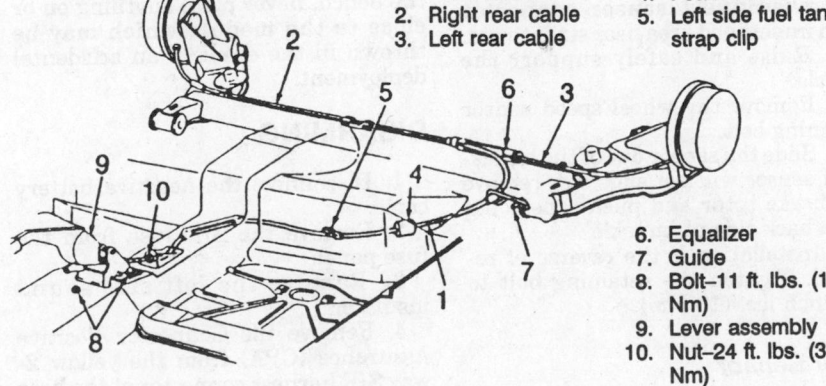

1. Front cable
2. Right rear cable
3. Left rear cable
4. Foam sleeve
5. Left side fuel tank strap clip
6. Equalizer
7. Guide
8. Bolt–11 ft. lbs. (15 Nm)
9. Lever assembly
10. Nut–24 ft. lbs. (33 Nm)

Parking brake cables–Beretta

and filled often during the bleeding procedure.

4. Have an assistant slowly pump the brake pedal and hold the pressure.

5. Open the bleeder screw about ¼ turn. The pedal should fall to the floor as air and fluid are pushed out. Close the bleeder screw while the assistant holds the pedal to the floor. Slowly release the pedal and wait 15 seconds. Repeat the process until no more air bubbles are forced from the system when the brake pedal is applied. It may be necessary to repeat this 10 or more times to get all of the air from the system.

6. Repeat this procedure on the remaining wheel cylinders and calipers. Make sure the master cylinder does not run out of brake fluid.

NOTE: Wait 15 seconds between each bleeding and do not pump the pedal rapidly. Rapid pumping of the brake pedal pushes the master cylinder secondary piston down the bore in a manner that makes it difficult to bleed the system.

7. Check the brake pedal for sponginess and the brake warning light for an indication of unbalanced pressure. Repeat the entire bleeding procedure to correct either of these conditions. Check the fluid level when finished.

Anti-Lock Brake System Service

PRECAUTIONS

Failure to observe the following precautions may result in system damage.

• Before performing electric arc welding on the vehicle, disconnect the Electronic Brake Control Module (EBCM) and the hydraulic modulator connectors.

• When performing painting work on the vehicle, do not expose the Electronic Brake Control Module (EBCM) to temperatures in excess of 185°F (85°C) for longer than 2 hrs. The system may be exposed to temperatures up to 200°F (95°C) for less than 15 min.

• Never disconnect or connect the Electronic Brake Control Module (EBCM) or hydraulic modulator connectors with the ignition switch ON.

• Never disassemble any component of the Anti-Lock Brake System (ABS) which is designated non-serviceable; the component must be replaced as an assembly.

• When filling the master cylinder, always use Delco Supreme 11 brake fluid or equivalent, which meets DOT-3 specifications; petroleum base fluid will destroy the rubber parts.

The anti-lock brake system that is utilized on the Beretta and the Corsica is the GM ABS VI® system. The system consists of a motor pack assembly which is connected directly to the master cylinder and vacuum booster unit and individual wheel speed sensors.

ABS Motor Pack Assembly

REMOVAL & INSTALLATION

1. Disconnect the negative battery cable.
2. Remove the master cylinder assembly from the vehicle.
3. Remove the 6 attaching Torx® bolts and remove the motor pack assembly.
4. Installation is the reverse of removal. Tighten the Torx® bolts to 27 inch lbs. (3 Nm).

ABS Hydraulic Modulator Assembly

REMOVAL & INSTALLATION

1. Disconnect the negative battery cable.
2. Remove the master cylinder assembly from the vehicle.
3. Remove the 6 attaching Torx® bolts and remove the motor pack assembly.
4. Remove the 2 modulator-to-master cylinder through bolts and separate the modulator from the master cylinder.
5. Installation is the reverse of removal. Tighten the 2 thru bolts to 12 ft. lbs. (16 Nm) and the Torx® bolts to 27 inch lbs. (3 Nm).

Wheel Speed Sensor

REMOVAL & INSTALLATION

Front Sensor

1. Disconnect sensor connector from underhood area near strut tower.
2. Raise and safely support the vehicle.
3. Remove the wheel speed sensor retaining bolt.
4. Slide the sensor out of the knuckle. If sensor will not slide out, remove the brake rotor and push sensor out from back side of knuckle.
5. Installation is the reverse of removal. Tighten the retaining bolt to 106 inch lbs. (12 Nm).

Rear Sensor

1. Raise and safely support the vehicle.

2. Remove the rear wheel and tire assembly.
3. Remove the rear brake drum and disconnect the sensor electrical connector.
4. Remove the bolts and nuts that attach the rear wheel bearing and speed sensor and remove the assemblies.
5. Installation is the reverse of the removal. Tighten the bolts to 38 ft. lbs. (52 Nm).

CHASSIS ELECTRICAL

Air Bag
—— CAUTION ——

Some vehicles are equipped with the Supplemental Inflatable Restraint (SIR) or air bag system. The SIR system must be disabled before performing service on or around SIR system components, steering column, instrument panel components, wiring and sensors. Failure to follow safety and disabling procedures could result in accidental air bag deployment, possible personal injury and unnecessary SIR system repairs.

PRECAUTIONS

Several precautions must be observed when handling the inflator module to avoid accidental deployment and possible personal injury.

• Never carry the inflator module by the wires or connector on the underside of the module.

• When carrying a live inflator module, hold securely with both hands, and ensure that the bag and trim cover are pointed away.

• Place the inflator module on a bench or other surface with the bag and trim cover facing up.

• When the inflator module is on the bench, never place anything on or close to the module which may be thrown in the event of an accidental deployment.

DISARMING

1. Disconnect the negative battery cable.
2. Remove the SIR fuse from the fuse panel.
3. Remove the left side sound insulator.
4. Remove the Connector Positive Assurance (CPA) from the yellow 2-way SIR harness connector at the base of the steering column and separate the connector.

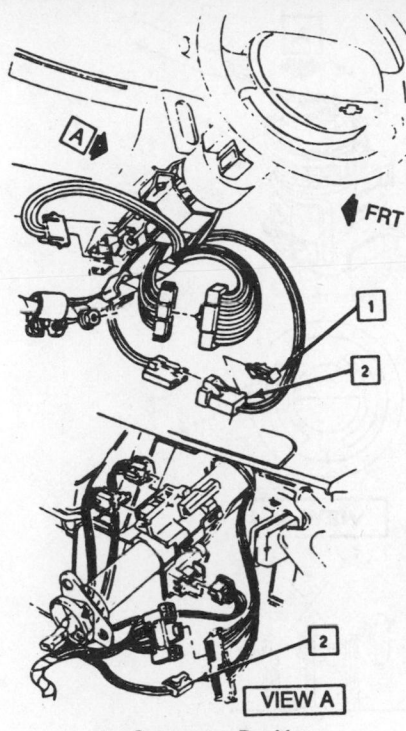

1. Connector Positive Assurance (CPA)
2. Yellow 2-way SIR harness connector

Location of yellow 2-way SIR harness connector

ARMING

1. Turn the ignition switch to the **OFF** position.
2. Connect the yellow 2-way SIR connector at the base of the steering column and insert the Connect Positive Assurance (CPA).
3. Install the left side sound insulator.
4. Install the SIR fuse in the fuse panel.
5. Connect the negative battery cable.

REMOVAL & INSTALLATION

Inflator Module

1. Disconnect the negative battery cable.
2. Disarm the SIR system.

NOTE: Rotate the steering wheel so the access holes on the back of the steering wheel are at the 12 and 6 o'clock positions. This will allow tool access and reduce the possibility of marring the steering column cover.

3. Remove the 4 screws from the back of the inflator module.
4. Remove the inflator module from the steering wheel.
5. Remove the Connector Positive

Assurance (CPA) from the inflator module electrical connector and disconnect the connector.

To install:

6. Connect the coil assembly connector. Install the CPA into the connector.

NOTE: Ensure that no wires at the back of the inflator module are pinched when aligning the inflator module to the steering wheel.

7. Install the inflator module and the 4 attaching bolts.
8. Arm the SIR system.
9. Connect the negative battery cable.

CENTERING THE COIL ASSEMBLY

In the event the coil becomes uncentered, perform the following:

1. With the steering wheel removed, remove the coil assembly from the steering column.
2. Hold the coil assembly with the clear bottom up in order to see the coil ribbon.
3. There are 2 styles of coils: one rotates clockwise and the other rotates counterclockwise.
4. While holding the coil assembly, depress the spring lock to rotate the hub in the direction of the arrow until it stops. The coil ribbon should be wound up snug against the center hub.
5. Rotate the coil hub in the opposite direction approximately 2½ turns.
6. Release the spring lock between the locking tabs adjacent to the arrow.

Heater Blower Motor

REMOVAL & INSTALLATION

1. Disconnect the negative battery cable.
2. Disconnect the electrical connections from the blower motor and resistor.
3. Remove the plastic water shield from the right side of the cowl, if equipped.
4. If equipped with the 3.1L engine, it may be necessary to remove the alternator.
5. Remove the blower motor cooling hose.
6. Remove the blower attaching screws and pull the blower motor from the cowl.
7. Remove the fan attaching nut and the fan from the motor.

To install:

8. Install the fan on the new blower motor with the opening facing away

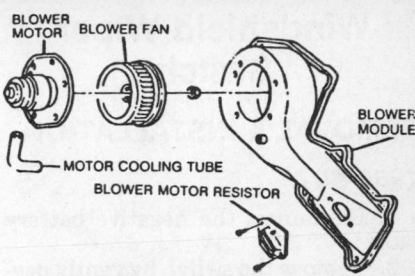

Removal and Installation of the blower motor assembly

from the motor and install the attaching nut.
9. Position the blower motor assembly to the cowl and install the attaching screws.
10. Install the blower motor cooling hose.
11. If equipped with the 3.1L engine, install the alternator, if removed.
12. Install the plastic water shield on the right side of the cowl, if equipped.
13. Connect the electrical connections to the blower motor and resistor.
14. Connect the negative battery cable.

Windshield Wiper Motor

REMOVAL & INSTALLATION

1. Disconnect the negative battery cable.
2. Remove the left and right side wiper arms.
3. Loosen the drive link adjusting screws and disconnect the wiper motor drive link from the crank arm.
4. Disconnect the electrical connectors and washer hoses.
5. Remove the wiper motor-to-chassis bolts and the wiper motor by guiding the crank arm through the hole.
6. Remove the crank arm from the motor.

To install:

7. Install the crank arm on the new wiper motor shaft and install the attaching nut.
8. Install the wiper motor while guiding the crank arm through cowl opening.
9. Install the wiper motor to the chassis and install the attaching bolts.
10. Connect the blower motor electrical connectors to the wiper harness connectors and connect the washer hoses.
11. Connect the wiper arm drive link to the crank arm.
12. Install the top vent screen shroud in place to the cowl area.
13. Install the left and right wiper arms.
14. Connect the negative battery cable.

Windshield Wiper Switch

REMOVAL & INSTALLATION

1989–90

1. Disconnect the negative battery cable.
2. Remove the switch by gently prying behind the switch.
3. Disconnect the electrical connectors.
4. Remove the switch assembly.

To install:

5. Connect the electrical connectors to the new switch and press it into the instrument panel to the same depth as the old switch.
6. Reconnect the negative battery cable and check the wiper operation.

1991–93

1. Disconnect the negative battery cable.
2. Remove the instrument cluster bezel.
3. Squeeze the small knob at the side and pull straight out.
4. Insert a small flat blade into the slots adjacent to the center of the inner knob to disengage the knob from the switch.
5. Remove the screws attaching the switch to the bezel.
6. Remove the switch.

To install:

7. Install the switch to the bezel. Install the attaching screws.
8. Position the inner knob on the switch. Ensure the tabs are lined up with the slots and press to secure the knob.
9. Position the outer knob on the switch and align the D-shaped hole in the knob to the shaft on the switch and press to secure the knob.
10. Install the instrument cluster bezel.
11. Connect the negative battery cable.

Instrument Cluster Bezel

REMOVAL & INSTALLATION

1991–93

1. Disconnect the negative battery cable.
2. Remove the bezel-to-instrument panel screws.
3. Pull the bezel to the rear to disengage the retaining clips.
4. Disconnect the headlight and windshield wiper switch electrical connectors.
5. If removing the switches, remove

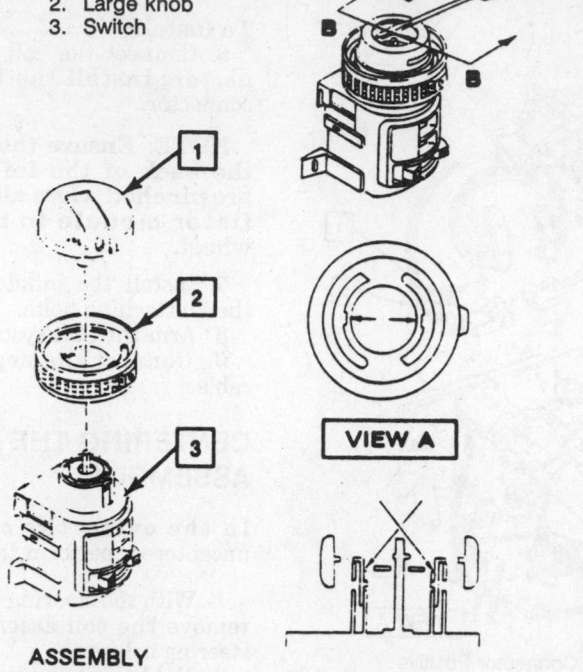

1. Small knob
2. Large knob
3. Switch

VIEW A

SECTION B–B

ASSEMBLY SEQUENCE

Headlight and windshield wiper switch assembly sequence—1991–93

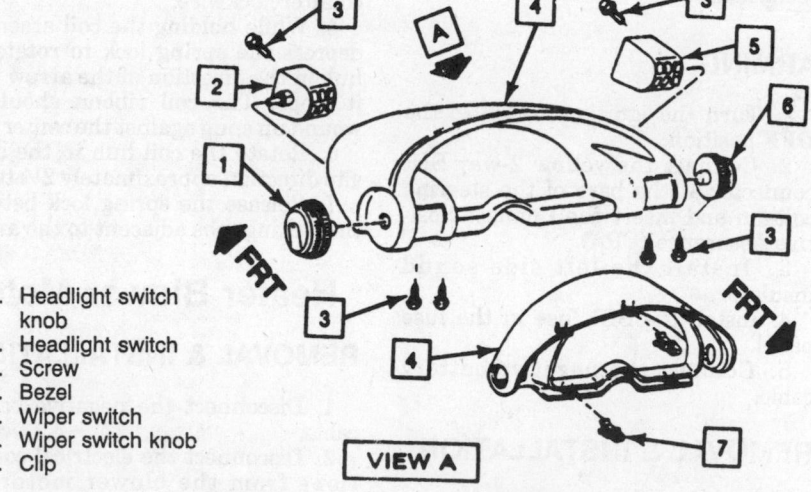

1. Headlight switch knob
2. Headlight switch
3. Screw
4. Bezel
5. Wiper switch
6. Wiper switch knob
7. Clip

VIEW A

Instrument cluster bezel—1991–93

the screws attaching the switches to the bezel.
6. Remove the clips, as required.

To install:

7. If removed, install the clips to the bezel.
8. If removed, install the headlight and windshield wiper switches to the bezel and install the attaching screws.
9. Install the switch knobs.
10. Connect the electrical connectors.
11. Position the bezel and press in to engage the retaining clips.

12. Install the instrument panel-to-bezel screws.
13. Connect the negative battery cable.

Instrument Cluster

REMOVAL & INSTALLATION

The speedometer and gauge cluster are replaced as an assembly.

NOTE: Whenever working on any electronic equipment, make

sure to have a clean, static free environment in which to work. Always cover the work surface with a mat that is grounded and static free. Static electricity from walking across the floor or sliding across a car seat is enough to damage any equipment.

1989–90

1. Disconnect the negative battery cable.

2. Remove the left side sound insulator attaching screws and remove the insulator from the lower dash and cowl.

3. Remove the 2 screws from the top of the trim cover. Remove the trim cover.

4. Remove the 2 bolts from the upper part of the column and bolt(s) from the lower part of the column. Lower and support the column to prevent tension on the flex joint.

5. Remove the instrument cluster trim panel attaching hardware. Pull the trim panel rearward.

6. Disconnect the electrical connectors.

7. Remove the trim panel.

8. Remove the 4 screws attaching instrument cluster.

9. Pull the cluster rearward to disconnect the electrical connectors.

10. Remove the instrument cluster.

To install:

11. Position the instrument cluster close to the wiring harness and connect to the harness. Ensure the cluster connectors plug in securely to the connectors in the cluster carrier.

12. Slide the instrument cluster into position and install the mounting screws.

13. Position the instrument cluster trim panel close to the wiring harness and connect the electrical connectors. Install the cluster trim panel and attaching hardware.

14. Raise the steering wheel into position and install the bolt(s) at the bottom part of the column and 2 bolts at the top of the column.

15. Install the trim cover and 2 attaching screws.

16. Install the left side sound insulator.

17. Connect the negative battery cable.

1991–93

1. Disconnect the negative battery cable.

2. Remove the instrument cluster bezel.

3. Remove the instrument cluster-to-instrument panel attaching screws.

4. Remove the instrument cluster. The electrical connector will release as the cluster is removed.

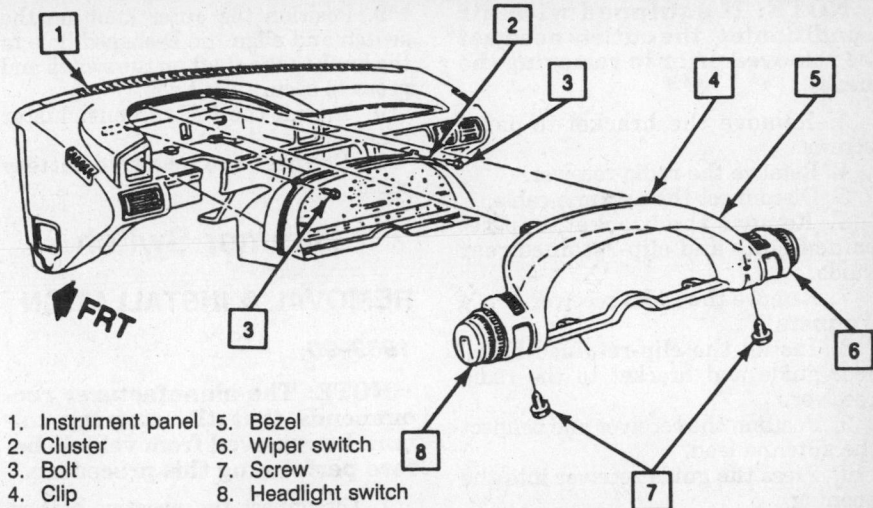

1. Instrument panel
2. Cluster
3. Bolt
4. Clip
5. Bezel
6. Wiper switch
7. Screw
8. Headlight switch

Instrument cluster Installation—1991–93

To install:

5. Carefully, install the instrument cluster. The electrical connector will align and engage as the cluster is pushed into position.

6. Install the instrument cluster bezel.

7. Connect the negative battery cable.

Radio

REMOVAL & INSTALLATION

1989–90

The radio is part of the accessory center, which also includes the heater and air conditioning controls.

1. Disconnect the negative battery cable.

2. Remove left side sound insulator attaching screws and remove the insulator from the lower dash.

3. On the Beretta, remove the lower trim panel screws and pull the trim panel out to release the taps at the top and remove the trim panel.

4. On Corsica, the trim panel has no attaching screws. Carefully pull the trim panel out and release it from the retaining taps and remove the trim panel.

5. Remove the accessory center attaching screws from the top and from the bottom.

6. Pull the accessory center away from the carrier.

7. On vehicles with air conditioning, remove the electrical and vacuum harness from the back of the heater and air conditioning control assembly.

8. On vehicles without air conditioning, remove the cables from the control module.

9. Disconnect the antenna connec-

tion and unplug a label the attaching electrical connections.

10. Pull the accessory center assembly from the dash.

11. Place the assembly on a clean working area.

12. Remove all controls knobs by pulling off.

13. Remove the screws attaching the trim plate to the radio. Separate the radio from the trim plate.

To install:

14. Assemble the radio to the trim plate and accessory center. Install the attaching screws.

15. Install the knobs by pushing in place.

16. Position the accessory center assembly to the dash and connect the electrical harness connections.

17. On vehicles with air conditioning, connect the electrical and vacuum harnesses at the rear of the heater and air conditioning control assembly.

18. On vehicles without air conditioning, connect the control cables to the control module.

19. Connect the antenna lead to the radio.

20. Slide the accessory center into place in the dash. Install the attaching screws at top and bottom.

21. Install the trim panel in place.

22. Install the left side sound insulator to lower dash and cowl and install the attaching screws.

23. Connect the negative battery cable.

1991–93

1. Disconnect the negative battery cable.

2. Remove the accessory center bezel by inserting a flat blade tool to separate the bezel from the panel and disengage the clips. Remove the bezel.

NOTE: If equipped with air conditioning, the outlets need not be removed prior to removing the bezel.

3. Remove the bracket-to-panel screws.
4. Remove the radio receiver.
5. Disconnect the antenna cable.
6. Remove the bracket, clip-retained bolts and clip-retained rear guide.
7. Remove the radio receiver.

To install:
8. Install the clip-retained bolts, rear guide and bracket to the radio receiver.
9. Position the receiver and connect the antenna lead.
10. Press the guide receiver into the opening.

NOTE: Ensure the rear guide is engaged into the slot in the instrument panel.

11. Install the attaching screws.
12. Place the trim bezel into position, align the clips to the holes in the panel and press in to secure.
13. Connect the negative battery cable.

Headlight Switch

REMOVAL & INSTALLATION

1989–90

1. Disconnect the negative battery cable.
2. Remove the switch by gently prying behind the switch.
3. Disconnect and label the wiring.

To install:
4. Connect the wires to the new switch and press it into the instrument panel.
5. Connect the negative battery cable and test the switch operation.

1991–93

1. Disconnect the negative battery cable.
2. Remove the instrument cluster bezel.
3. Squeeze the small knob at the side and pull straight out.
4. Insert a small flat blade into the slots adjacent to the center of the inner knob to disengage the knob from the switch.
5. Remove the screws attaching the switch to the bezel.
6. Remove the switch.

To install:
7. Install the switch to the bezel. Install the attaching screws.
8. Position the inner knob on the switch. Ensure the tabs are lined up with the slots and press to secure the knob.

9. Position the outer knob on the switch and align the D-shaped hole in the knob to the shaft on the switch and press to secure the knob.
10. Install the instrument cluster bezel.
11. Connect the negative battery cable.

Dimmer Switch

REMOVAL & INSTALLATION

1989–90

NOTE: The manufacturer recommends that the steering column be removed from vehicle before performing this procedure.

1. Disconnect the negative battery cable.
2. Place the ignition switch in the **OFF-LOCK** position.
3. Remove the steering column and place in a suitable holding fixture.
4. Remove the dimmer switch nut, bolt and disconnect the dimmer switch from the actuator rod.
5. Remove the switch.

To install:
6. Make sure the ignition lock cylinder is in the **OFF-LOCK** position.
7. Insert the dimmer switch actuator rod into the hole in the dimmer switch.

NOTE: Should the actuator rod become disengaged from the rod cap, upon installation the tab on the rod must engage the wide slot in the rod cap and snap into place.

8. Position the dimmer switch in place on the stud and install the retainer nut and screw. Do not tighten.
9. Adjust the dimmer switch by inserting a $3/32$ in. drill bit or a 2.34mm diameter gauge pin into the adjustment hole in the dimmer switch. Push the switch against the actuator rod to remove all the lash.
10. Tighten the nut and screw to 35 inch lbs. (4 Nm).
11. Remove the adjustment tool from the dimmer switch.
12. Install the steering column in the vehicle.
13. Connect the negative battery cable.

1991–93

1. Disconnect the negative battery cable.
2. Disable the Supplemental Inflatable Restraint (SIR) system.
3. Place the ignition switch in the **OFF-LOCK** position.
4. Remove the left side sound insulator panel.
5. Remove the bolts from the lower steering column support.

6. Remove the flange and coupling pinch bolt.
7. Remove the upper and lower bolts from the upper steering column support.
8. Disconnect the dimmer and ignition switch electrical connectors.
9. Lower the steering column.
10. Remove the hexagonal nut and bolt/screw attaching the dimmer switch.
11. Disengage the dimmer switch actuator from the switch and remove the switch.

To install:
12. Ensure the ignition switch is in the **OFF-LOCK** position.
13. Engage the dimmer switch actuator rod in the dimmer switch and position the dimmer switch on the mounting stud.
14. Install the nut and bolt/screw. Do not tighten.
15. Adjust the dimmer switch by inserting a $3/32$ in. drill bit or a 2.34mm diameter gauge pin into the adjustment hole in the dimmer switch. Push the switch against the actuator rod to remove all the lash.
16. Tighten the nut and screw to 35 inch lbs. (4 Nm).
17. Remove the adjustment tool from the dimmer switch.
18. Support the steering column and install the column into the flange and coupling assembly.
19. Connect the dimmer and ignition switch electrical connectors.
20. Raise the column into position and loosely install the lower bolts to the upper steering column support bracket.
21. Install the lower steering column support bracket bolts. Tighten to 22 ft. lbs. (30 Nm).
22. Install the upper bolts to the upper steering column support bracket. Tighten the upper and lower bolts to 21 ft. lbs. (28 Nm).
23. Install the flange and coupling assembly pinch bolt. Tighten to 30 ft. lbs. (41 Nm).
24. Install the right side sound insulator panel.
25. Enable the SIR system.
26. Connect the negative battery cable.

Turn Signal Switch

REMOVAL & INSTALLATION

1989–90

NOTE: A special terminal remover tool is required to remove the terminals from the connector on the turn signal switch.

1. Disconnect the negative battery cable. Remove the steering wheel.

2. Remove the turn signal canceling cam assembly from the steering shaft.

3. Remove the hazard warning knob-to-steering column screw and the knob.

4. Disconnect the dimmer switch actuator rod.

NOTE: Before removing the turn signal assembly, position the turn signal lever so the turn signal assembly-to-steering column screws can all be removed.

5. Remove the column housing cover-to-column housing bowl screw and the cover.

NOTE: If equipped with cruise control, disconnect the cruise control electrical connector.

6. Remove the turn signal lever attaching screw and the lever.

7. Using a terminal remover tool, disconnect and label the wires F and G on the connector at the buzzer switch assembly from the turn signal switch electrical harness connector.

8. Remove the turn signal switch-to-steering column screws and the switch.

To install:

9. Position the turn signal switch into the steering column and install the switch-to-steering column screws. Tighten the screws to 35 inch lbs. (4 Nm).

10. Connect wires F and G of the buzzer switch assembly, to the turn signal switch harness connector.

11. Install the dimmer actuator assembly.

12. Install the turn signal lever and attaching screw to the pivot assembly. Tighten the attaching screw to 18 inch lbs. (2 Nm).

13. Install the actuator pivot assembly and screw. Tighten to 20 inch lbs. (2.3 Nm).

NOTE: If equipped with cruise control, connect the cruise control electrical connector.

14. Install the column housing cover and attaching screw. Tighten the attaching screw to 35 inch lbs. (4 Nm).

15. Install the hazard warning knob and attaching screw. Tighten to 7 inch lbs. (0.8 Nm).

16. Install the turn signal canceling cam assembly over the steering shaft. Install the steering wheel and attaching nut. Tighten the nut to 30 ft. lbs. (41 Nm).

17. Connect the negative battery cable. Check the switch operation.

1991–93

1. Disconnect the negative battery cable.

2. Disable the SIR system.

3. Remove the steering wheel.

4. Remove the coil assembly retaining ring.

5. Lift the coil assembly from the end of the steering shaft and allow coil to hang freely.

6. Remove the wave washer.

7. If equipped with a standard column, remove the spacer shaft lock.

8. Remove the shaft lock retaining ring using tool J–23653–C or equivalent, to compress the shaft lock.

9. Pry off the retaining ring.

10. Remove the shaft lock.

11. Remove the turn signal cancelling cam assembly.

12. Remove the upper bearing spring.

13. Position the turn signal lever to the right turn position.

14. Remove the multi-function lever by performing the following:

a. Ensure the lever is in the center or **OFF** position.

b. If equipped with cruise control, disconnect the cruise control connector from the steering column assembly.

c. Pull the lever straight out of the turn signal switch.

15. Remove the hazard knob assembly.

16. Remove the screw and signal switch arm. If equipped with tilt column and cruise control, allow the switch arm to hang freely.

17. Remove the turn signal switch screws. Allow the switch to hang freely.

18. Disconnect the turn signal/hazard switch assembly terminal from the instrument panel harness.

19. If equipped with tilt column, disconnect the buzzer switch assembly terminals from the turn signal/hazard assembly connector. Remove the tan/black wire lead from cavity E and the light green wire from the cavity F.

20. Remove the upper steering column bolts.

21. Remove the wiring protector.

22. Connect a length of wire to the turn signal/hazard assembly terminal connector to aid in reassembly.

23. Gently pull the wire harness through the steering column housing shroud, steering column housing and lock assembly cover.

24. Disconnect the wire from the connector.

To install:

25. Connect the wire to the turn signal/hazard switch assembly connector.

26. Gently pull the connector through the steering column housing shroud, steering column housing and lock assembly cover.

27. Remove the wire.

28. Install the wiring protector.

29. If disconnected, connect the buzzer switch terminals to the turn signal/hazard switch assembly connec-

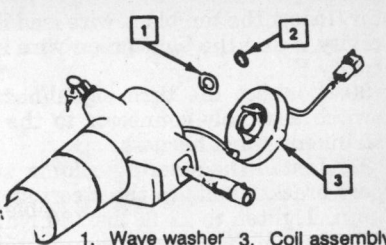

1. Wave washer   3. Coil assembly
2. Retaining ring

SIR coil assembly installation

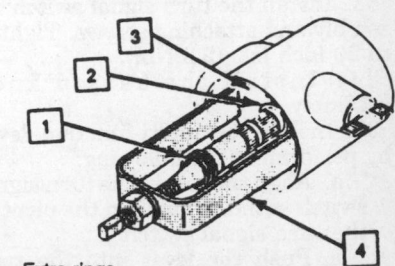

1. Extra rings
2. Retaining ring
3. Shaft lock
4. Shaft lock retaining ring compressor

Shaft lock retaining ring removal—SIR steering column

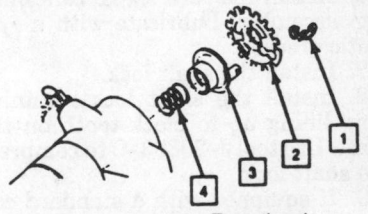

1. Shaft lock spacer   3. Turn signal cancelling cam
2. Shaft lock
4. Upper bearing spring

Lock plate steering column

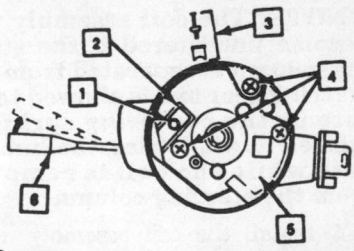

1. Screw
2. Signal switch arm
3. Hazard knob assembly
4. Screw
5. Turn signal/hazard switch assembly
6. Multi-function turn signal lever

Upper SIR steering column component locations—tilt column shown

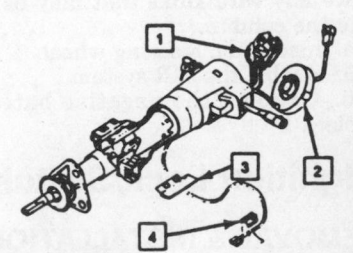

1. Turn signal/hazard switch assembly
2. Coil assembly
3. Wiring protector
4. Connector shroud

SIR steering column assembly

tor. Insert the tan/black wire lead into cavity E and the light green wire into cavity F.

30. Connect the turn signal/hazard switch assembly connector to the instrument panel harness.

31. Install the steering column support bracket bolts to the steering column. Tighten to 22 ft. lbs. (30 Nm).

32. Install the steering column upper support bolts. Tighten to 20 ft. lbs. (28 Nm).

33. Install the turn signal switch assembly and attaching screws. Tighten to 20 inch lbs. (2.3 Nm).

34. Install the hazard knob assembly.

35. Install the multi-function lever by performing the following:

   a. Align the tab on the turn signal switch with the notch in the pivot of the turn signal switch.

   b. Push the lever into the turn signal switch.

   c. If equipped with cruise control, connect the connector to the steering column assembly.

36. Install the turn signal cancelling cam assembly. Lubricate with a synthetic grease.

37. Install the shaft lock.

38. Install the shaft lock retaining ring, lining up to block tooth on the shaft. Use tool J–23653–C to compress the shaft lock.

39. If equipped with a standard column, install the spacer shaft lock.

40. Install the wave washer.

41. Ensure the coil assembly is centered.

NOTE: The coil assembly will become uncentered if the steering column is separated from the steering gear and is allowed to rotate or the centering spring is pushed down, letting the hub rotate while the coil is removed from the steering column.

42. Install the coil assembly using the horn tower on the cancelling cam assembly inner ring and projections on the outer ring for alignment.

43. Install the coil assembly retaining ring. The ring must be firmly seated in the groove on the shaft. Gently pull the lower coil assembly wire to remove any wire kinks that may be inside the column.

44. Install the steering wheel.

45. Enable the SIR system.

46. Connect the negative battery cable.

Ignition Lock/Switch

REMOVAL & INSTALLATION

1989–90

The manufacturer recommends the

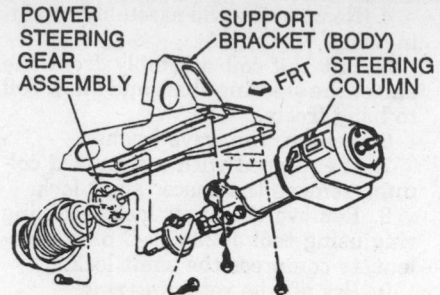

POWER STEERING GEAR ASSEMBLY   SUPPORT BRACKET (BODY)   FRT   STEERING COLUMN

Steering column mounting

steering column be removed from the vehicle prior to ignition lock removal and installation.

Standard Steering Column

1. Disconnect the negative battery cable. Remove the left side sound insulator panel.

2. Remove the steering column-to-support screws and lower the steering column.

3. Disconnect the dimmer and turn signal switch connectors.

4. Remove the wiring harness-to-firewall nuts and steering column.

5. If equipped with a park lock cable, insert a small prybar into the ignition switch inhibitor switch access hole, depress the locking tab and disconnect the park lock cable from the inhibitor switch.

6. Remove the steering column-to-steering gear bolt and the steering column from the vehicle.

7. Remove the combination switch.

8. Place the lock cylinder in the **RUN** position.

9. Remove the steering shaft assembly and turn signal switch housing as an assembly.

10. Using a terminal remover tool, disconnect and label the wires F and G on the connector at the buzzer switch assembly from the turn signal switch electrical harness connector.

11. Place the lock cylinder in the **RUN** position and remove the buzzer switch.

12. Place the lock cylinder in the **ACC** position. Remove the lock cylinder attaching screw and the lock cylinder.

13. Remove the dimmer switch nut/bolt, the dimmer switch and actuator rod.

14. Remove the dimmer switch mounting stud, the mounting nut was mounted to it.

15. Remove the ignition switch-to-steering column screws and the ignition switch.

16. Remove the lock bolt screws and the lock bolt.

17. Remove the switch actuator rack and ignition switch.

18. Remove the steering shaft lock and spring.

To install:

19. To install the lock bolt, lubricate it with lithium grease and install the lock bolt, spring and retaining plate.

20. Lubricate the teeth on the switch actuator rack. Install the rack and the ignition switch through the opening in the steering bolt until it rests on the retaining plate.

21. Install the steering column lock cylinder set by holding the barrel of the lock cylinder, insert the key and turn it to the ACC position.

22. Install the lock set in the steering column while holding the rack against the lock plate.

23. Install the lock attaching screw and tighten the screw to 27 inch lbs. (3 Nm). Insert the key in the lock cylinder and turn the lock cylinder to the **START** position and the rack will extend.

24. Center the slotted holes on the ignition switch mounting plate and install the ignition switch mounting screw and nut.

25. Install the dimmer switch and actuator rod into the center slot on the switch mounting plate. Tighten the dimmer switch stud to 35 inch lbs. (4 Nm).

26. Install the buzzer switch and turn the lock cylinder to the **RUN** position. Push the switch in until it is bottomed out with the plastic tab that covers the lock attaching screw.

27. Install the steering shaft and turn signal housing as an assembly.

28. Install the turn signal switch. Tighten the turn signal switch housing screws to 88 inch lbs. (10 Nm), the turn signal switch screws to 35 inch lbs. (4 Nm) and the steering wheel locknut to 30 ft. lbs. (41 Nm).

29. To complete the installation, reverse the removal procedures.

TILT STEERING COLUMN

1. Disconnect the negative battery cable. Tilt the column up as far as it will go and remove the left side lower trim panel.

2. Remove the steering column-to-support screws and lower the steering column.

3. Disconnect the dimmer switch and turn signal switch connectors.

4. Remove the wiring harness-to-firewall nuts and steering column.

5. If equipped with a park lock cable, insert a small prybar into the ignition switch inhibitor switch access hole, depress the locking tab and disconnect the park lock cable from the inhibitor switch.

6. Remove the steering column-to-steering gear bolt and the steering column from the vehicle.

7. Remove the combination switch.

8. Using a flat type pry blade, position it in the square opening of the

spring retainer, push downward to the left, to release the spring retainer. Remove the wheel tilt spring.

9. Remove the spring retainer, the tilt spring and the tilt spring guide.

10. Remove the shoe pin retaining cap. Using a pivot pin removal tool, remove both pivot pins.

11. Place the lock cylinder in the **RUN** position.

12. Pull the shoe release lever and release the steering column housing.

13. Remove the column housing, the steering shaft assembly and turn signal switch housing as an assembly.

14. Using a terminal remover tool, disconnect and label the wires F and G on the connector at the buzzer switch assembly from the turn signal switch electrical harness connector.

15. Place the lock cylinder in the **RUN** position and remove the buzzer switch.

16. Place the lock cylinder in the **ACC** position. Remove the lock cylinder attaching screw and the lock cylinder.

17. Remove the dimmer switch nut/bolt, the dimmer switch and actuator rod.

18. Remove the dimmer switch mounting stud, the mounting nut was mounted to it.

19. Remove the ignition switch-to-steering column screws and the ignition switch.

20. Remove the lock bolt screws and the lock bolt.

21. Remove the switch actuator rack and ignition switch.

22. Remove the steering shaft lock and spring.

To install:

23. To install the lock bolt, lubricate it with lithium grease and install the lock bolt, spring and retaining plate.

24. Lubricate the teeth on the switch actuator rack. Install the rack and the ignition switch through the opening in the steering bolt until it rests on the retaining plate.

25. Install the steering column lock cylinder set by holding the barrel of the lock cylinder, insert the key and turn the key to the **ACC** position.

26. Install the lock set in the steering column while holding the rack against the lock plate.

27. Install the lock attaching screw and tighten the screw to 27 inch lbs. (3 Nm). Insert the key in the lock cylinder. Turn the lock cylinder to the **START** position and the rack will extend.

28. Center the slotted holes on the ignition switch mounting plate. Install the ignition switch mounting screw and nut.

29. Install the dimmer switch and actuator rod into the center slot on the switch mounting plate. Tighten the

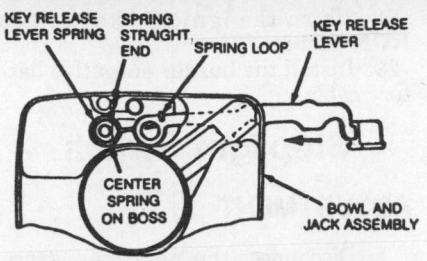

Key release lever spring installation position

dimmer switch stud to 35 inch lbs. (4 Nm).

30. Install the buzzer switch and turn the lock cylinder to the **RUN** position. Push the switch in until it is bottomed out with the plastic tab that covers the lock attaching screw.

31. Install the steering shaft and turn signal housing as an assembly.

32. Install the turn signal switch. Tighten the turn signal switch housing screws to 88 inch lbs. (10 Nm), the turn signal switch screws to 35 inch lbs. (4 Nm) and the steering wheel locknut to 30 ft. lbs. (41 Nm).

33. Connect the negative battery cable.

1991–93

IGNITION SWITCH

1. Disconnect the negative battery cable.

2. Disable the SIR system.

3. Place the ignition switch in the **OFF-LOCK** position.

4. Remove the left side sound insulator panel.

5. Remove the bolts from the lower steering column support.

6. Remove the flange and coupling pinch bolt.

7. Remove the upper and lower bolts from the upper steering column support.

8. Disconnect the dimmer and ignition switch electrical connectors.

9. Lower the steering column.

10. Remove the hexagonal nut and bolt/screw attaching the dimmer switch.

11. Disengage the dimmer switch actuator from the switch and remove the switch.

12. Remove the ignition switch stud.

13. Disconnect the ignition switch actuator rod.

14. Disconnect the park lock cable from the ignition switch.

15. Remove the ignition switch.

To install:

16. Ensure the ignition switch is in the **OFF-LOCK** position.

17. Adjust the ignition switch by performing the following:

a. Place the ignition switch slider in the far left position and move

back 1 detent to the right of the **OFF-LOCK** position.

b. Insert a ³⁄₃₂ in. drill bit or a 2.34mm diameter gauge pin into the adjustment hole in the ignition switch to hold the switch slider in the proper position during installation.

18. Connect the park lock switch to the ignition switch.

19. Connect the ignition switch actuator rod.

20. Install the ignition switch mounting stud. Tighten to 35 inch lbs. (4 Nm).

21. Remove the adjustment tool from the ignition switch.

22. Engage the dimmer switch actuator rod in the dimmer switch and position the dimmer switch on the mounting stud.

23. Install the nut and bolt/screw. Do not tighten.

24. Adjust the dimmer switch by inserting a ³⁄₃₂ in. drill bit or a 2.34mm diameter gauge pin into the adjustment hole in the dimmer switch. Push the switch against the actuator rod to remove all the lash.

25. Tighten the nut and screw to 35 inch lbs. (4 Nm).

26. Remove the adjustment tool from the dimmer switch.

27. Support the steering column and install the column into the flange and coupling assembly.

28. Connect the dimmer and ignition switch electrical connectors.

29. Raise the column into position and loosely install the lower bolts to the upper steering column support bracket.

30. Install the lower steering column support bracket bolts. Tighten to 22 ft. lbs. (30 Nm).

31. Install the upper bolts to the upper steering column support bracket. Tighten the upper and lower bolts to 21 ft. lbs. (28 Nm).

32. Install the flange and coupling assembly pinch bolt. Tighten to 30 ft. lbs. (41 Nm).

33. Install the right side sound insulator panel.

34. Enable the SIR system.

35. Connect the negative battery cable.

LOCK CYLINDER

1. Disconnect the negative battery cable.

2. Disable the SIR system.

3. Remove the steering wheel.

4. Remove the coil assembly retaining ring.

5. Lift the coil assembly from the end of the steering shaft and allow coil to hang freely.

6. Remove the wave washer.

7. If equipped with a standard column, remove the spacer shaft lock.

8. Remove the shaft lock retaining ring using tool J–23653–C or equivalent, to compress the shaft lock.

9. Pry off the retaining ring.

10. Remove the shaft lock.

11. Remove the turn signal cancelling cam assembly.

12. Remove the upper bearing spring.

13. Position the turn signal lever to the right turn position.

14. Remove the multi-function lever by performing the following:

    a. Ensure the lever is in the center or **OFF** position.

    b. If equipped with cruise control, disconnect the cruise control connector from the steering column assembly.

    c. Pull the lever straight out of the turn signal switch.

15. Remove the hazard knob assembly.

16. Remove the screw and signal switch arm. If equipped with tilt column and cruise control, allow the switch arm to hang freely.

17. Remove the turn signal switch screws. Allow the switch to hang freely.

18. Disconnect the turn signal/hazard switch assembly terminal from the instrument panel harness.

19. If equipped with tilt column, disconnect the buzzer switch assembly terminals from the turn signal/hazard assembly connector. Remove the tan/black wire lead from cavity E and the light green wire from the cavity F.

20. Remove the upper steering column bolts.

21. Remove the wiring protector.

22. Connect a length of wire to the turn signal/hazard assembly terminal connector to aid in reassembly.

23. Gently pull the wire harness through the steering column housing shroud, steering column housing and lock assembly cover.

24. Disconnect the wire from the connector.

25. Ensure the lock cylinder is in the **LOCK** position. Remove the lock cylinder attaching screw.

26. Remove the lock cylinder.

To install:

27. Install the lock cylinder and attaching screw. Tighten to 40 inch lbs. (4 Nm).

28. Turn the ignition key to the **RUN** position.

29. Install the buzzer snegative battery cable.

Stoplight Switch

ADJUSTMENT

1. Disconnect the negative battery cable.

2. Remove the lower, left trim panel and locate the stoplight switch on the brake pedal support.

3. Disconnect the electrical connector from the switch and remove the switch by twisting it out of the tubular retaining clip.

4. Pull back on the brake pedal and push the switch through the retaining clip noting the clicks; repeat this procedure until no more clicks can be heard.

5. Connect the electrical connector to the switch.

6. Connect the negative battery cable and check the switch operation.

REMOVAL & INSTALLATION

1. Disconnect the negative battery cable.

2. Remove the lower, left trim panel. Locate the stoplight switch on the brake pedal support.

3. Disconnect the electrical connector from the switch and remove the switch by twisting it out of the tubular retaining clip.

To install:

4. Using a new retaining clip, install the switch and connect the electrical connector.

5. To adjust the switch, pull back on the brake pedal, push the switch through the retaining clip noting the clicks; repeat this procedure until no more clicks can be heard.

6. Connect the negative battery cable and check the switch operation.

Fuses, Circuit Breakers and Relays

Location

Fuse Panel

The fuse panel is located on the left side of the instrument panel assembly. In order to gain access to the fuse panel, it is necessary to first remove the lower trim panel.

Fusible Links

Fusible links—A and E are located rear of the engine compartment, at the battery junction box.

Fusible links—B, C and D are located at the front section of the engine at the starter solenoid.

Fusible link—F is located on the left side of the engine compartment, near the battery.

Circuit Breakers

Circuit breakers No. 12 and No. 15 are located in fuse block.

Various Relays

The coolant fan, air conditioning compressor, air conditioning high blower speed and fuel pump relays are all located in the engine compartment mounted to the center of the firewall on the relay bracket.

Computers

LOCATION

The electronic control module is located on the right side of the vehicle. It is positioned up behind the glove box. In order to gain access to the electronic control module, remove the right side trim panel and/or glove box assembly.

Flashers

LOCATION

Turn Signal Flasher

The turn signal flasher is located behind the lower left side of the instrument panel on the steering column.

Hazard Warning Flasher

The hazard flasher is located behind the lower left side of the instrument panel on the steering column.

SPECIFICATIONS
VEHICLE IDENTIFICATION CHART

It is important for servicing and ordering parts to be certain of the vehicle and engine identification. The VIN (vehicle identification number) is a 17 digit number visible through the windshield on the driver's side of the dash and contains the vehicle and engine identification codes. The tenth digit indicates model year and the eighth digit indicates engine code. It can be interpreted as follows:

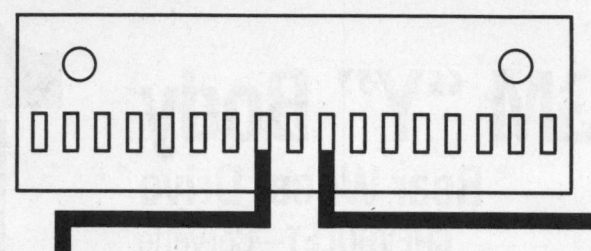

Engine Code

Code	Liters	Cu. In. (cc)	Cyl.	Fuel Sys.	Eng. Mfg.
8	5.7	350 (5733)	8	PFI	Chevrolet
P	5.7	350 (5733)	8	PFI	Chevrolet
J	5.7	350 (5727)	8	PFI	Chevrolet

PFI—Port Fuel Injection

Model Year

Code	Year
K	1989
L	1990
M	1991
N	1992
P	1993

ENGINE IDENTIFICATION

Year	Model	Engine Displacement Liters (cc)	Engine Series (ID/VIN)	Fuel System	No. of Cylinders	Engine Type
1989	Corvette	5.7 (5733)	8	PFI	8	OHV
1990	Corvette	5.7 (5733)	8	PFI	8	OHV
	Corvette ZR-1	5.7 (5727)	J	PFI	8	DOHC
1991	Corvette	5.7 (5733)	8	PFI	8	OHV
	Corvette ZR-1	5.7 (5727)	J	PFI	8	DOHC
1992-93	Corvette	5.7 (5733)	P	PFI	8	OHV
	Corvette ZR-1	5.7 (5727)	J	PFI	8	DOHC

DOHV—Dual Overhead Valves
OHV—Overhead Valves
PFI—Port Fuel Injection

GENERAL ENGINE SPECIFICATIONS

Year	Engine ID/VIN	Engine Displacement Liters (cc)	Fuel System Type	Net Horsepower @ rpm	Net Torque @ rpm (ft. lbs.)	Bore × Stroke (in.)	Compression Ratio	Oil Pressure @ rpm ①
1989	8	5.7 (5733)	PFI	245 @ 4300	340 @ 3200	4.000 × 3.480	9.5:1	18 @ 2000
1990	8	5.7 (5733)	PFI	245 @ 4000	340 @ 3200	4.000 × 3.480	10.25:1	18 @ 2000
	J	5.7 (5727)	PFI	375 @ 5800	370 @ 4500	3.897 × 3.661	11:1	40 @ 2000
1991	8	5.7 (5733)	PFI	245 @ 4000	340 @ 3200	4.000 × 3.480	10.25:1	18 @ 2000
	J	5.7 (5727)	PFI	375 @ 5800	370 @ 4800	3.897 × 3.661	11:1	40 @ 2000
1992-93	P	5.7 (5733)	PFI	300 @ 5000	330 @ 4000	4.000 × 3.480	10.25:1	18 @ 2000
	J	5.7 (5727)	PFI	375 @ 5800	370 @ 4800	3.897 × 3.661	11:1	40 @ 2000

NOTE: Horsepower and torque are SAE net figures. They are measured at the rear of the transmission with all accessories installed and operating. Since the figures vary when a given engine is installed in different models, some are representative rather than exact.
PFI—Port Fuel Injection
① Measurement is the minimum with the engine HOT

GASOLINE ENGINE TUNE-UP SPECIFICATIONS

Year	Engine ID/VIN	Engine Displacement Liters (cc)	Spark Plugs Gap (in.)	Ignition Timing (deg.) MT	AT	Fuel Pump (psi)	Idle Speed (rpm) MT	AT	Valve Clearance In.	Ex.
1989	8	5.7 (5733)	0.035	①	①	34–47	①	①	Hyd.	Hyd.
1990	8	5.7 (5733)	0.035	①	①	34–47	①	①	Hyd.	Hyd.
	J	5.7 (5727)	0.035	①	①	48–55	①	①	Hyd.	Hyd.
1991	8	5.7 (5733)	0.035	①	①	34–47	①	①	Hyd.	Hyd.
	J	5.7 (5727)	0.035	①	①	48–55	①	①	Hyd.	Hyd.
1992	P	5.7 (5733)	0.050	①	①	41–47	①	①	Hyd.	Hyd.
	J	5.7 (5727)	0.035	①	①	48–55	①	①	Hyd.	Hyd.
1993	SEE UNDERHOOD SPECIFICATIONS STICKER									

NOTE: The lowest cylilder pressure should be within 75% of the highest cylinder pressure reading. For example, if the highest cylinder is 134 psi, the lowest should be 101. Engine should be at normal operating temperature with throttle valve in the wide open position.
The underhood specifications sticker often reflects tune-up specification changes in production. Sticker figures must be used if they disagree with those in this chart.
Hyd.—Hydraulic
① Refer to Vehicle Emission Control Information label for ignition timing and idle specifications. If no specifications are shown, no adjustment is required.

FIRING ORDERS

NOTE: To avoid confusion, always replace spark plug wires one at a time.

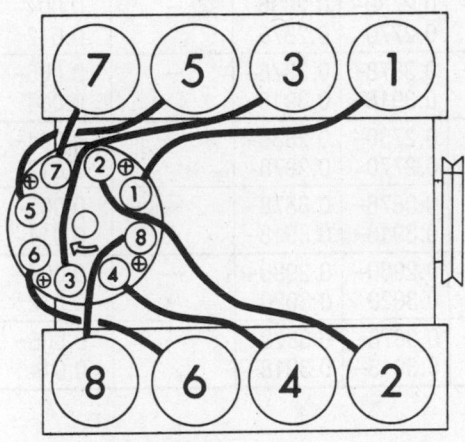

5.7L (VIN 8) Engine
Engine Firing Order: 1–8–4–3–6–5–7–2
Distributor Rotation: Clockwise

5.7L (VIN J) Engine
Engine Firing Order: 1–8–4–3–6–5–7–2
Distributorless Ignition System

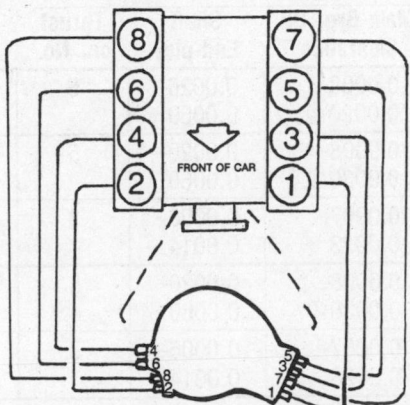

5.7L (VIN P) Engine
Engine Firing Order: 1–8–4–3–6–5–7–2
Distributor Rotates with Camshaft

CAPACITIES

Year	Model	Engine ID/VIN	Engine Displacement Liters (cc)	Engine Crankcase (qts.) without Filter	Transmission (pts.)			Drive Axle (pts.)	Fuel Tank (gal.)	Cooling System (qts.)
					4-Spd	5-Spd	Auto.			
1989	Corvette	8	5.7 (5733)	4.0	—	②	10	3.75①	20	14.5
1990	Corvette	8	5.7 (5733)	4.0	—	②	10	3.75①	20	14.5
	Corvette ZR-1	J	5.7 (5727)	7.6	—	②	—	3.75①	20	16.7
1991	Corvette	8	5.7 (5733)	4.0	—	②	10	①	20	14.5
	Corvette ZR-1	J	5.7 (5727)	7.6	—	②	—	①	20	16.7
1992–93	Corvette	P	5.7 (5733)	4.0	—	②	10	①	20	9.6
	Corvette ZR-1	J	5.7 (5727)	7.6	—	②	—	①	20	14.7

① Fluid level should be no lower than a ¼"
  (6mm) below filler plug opening.
② ZF 6 speed transmission—4.4 pts.

CAMSHAFT SPECIFICATIONS

All measurements given in inches.

Year	Engine ID/VIN	Engine Displacement Liters (cc)	Journal Diameter					Elevation		Bearing Clearance	Camshaft End Play
			1	2	3	4	5	In.	Ex.		
1989	8	5.7 (5733)	1.8682–1.8692	1.8682–1.8692	1.8682–1.8692	1.8682–1.8692	1.8682–1.8692	0.2713–0.2753	0.2800–0.2840	—	0.004–0.012
1990	8	5.7 (5733)	1.8682–1.8692	1.8682–1.8692	1.8682–1.8692	1.8682–1.8692	1.8682–1.8692	0.2730–0.2770	0.2836–0.2876	—	0.004–0.012
	J	5.7 (5727)	1.1400–1.1410	1.1400–1.1410	1.1400–1.1410	1.1400–1.1410	1.1400–1.1410	0.3878–0.3918–	0.3878–0.3918–		0.006–0.014
1991	8	5.7 (5733)	1.8682–1.8692	1.8682–1.8692	1.8682–1.8692	1.8682–1.8692	1.8682–1.8692	0.2730–0.2770	0.2836–0.2876	—	0.004–0.012
	J	5.7 (5727)	1.1400–1.1410	1.1400–1.1410	1.1400–1.1410	1.1400–1.1410	1.1400–1.1410	0.3878–0.3918–	0.3878–0.3918–	—	0.006–0.014
1992–93	P	5.7 (5733)	1.8682–1.8692	1.8682–1.8692	1.8682–1.8692	1.8682–1.8692	1.8682–1.8692	0.2980–0.3020	0.2980–0.3020	—	0.004–0.012
	J	5.7 (5727)	1.1400–1.1410	1.1400–1.1410	1.1400–1.1410	1.1400–1.1410	1.1400–1.1410	0.3878–0.3918–	0.3878–0.3918–	—	0.006–0.014

CRANKSHAFT AND CONNECTING ROD SPECIFICATIONS

All measurements are given in inches.

Year	Engine ID/VIN	Engine Displacement Liters (cc)	Crankshaft				Connecting Rod		
			Main Brg. Journal Dia.	Main Brg. Oil Clearance	Shaft End-play	Thrust on. No.	Journal Diameter	Oil Clearance	Side Clearance
1989	8	5.7 (5733)	2.4484–2.4493①	0.0008–0.0020②	0.0020–0.0060	5	2.0988–2.0998	0.0013–0.0035	0.006–0.014
1990	8	5.7 (5733)	2.4484–2.4493①	0.0008–0.0030④	0.0020–0.0060	5	2.0988–2.0998	0.0035③	0.006–0.014
	J	5.7 (5727)	2.7550–2.7560	0.0007–0.0023	0.0006–0.0014	3	2.0993–2.1000	0.0007–0.0027	0.008–0.028
1991	8	5.7 (5733)	2.4484–2.4493①	0.0008–0.0030④	0.0020–0.0060	5	2.0988–2.0998	0.0035③	0.006–0.014
	J	5.7 (5727)	2.7550–2.7560	0.0007–0.0023	0.0006–0.0014	3	2.0993–2.1000	0.0007–0.0027	0.008–0.028

CRANKSHAFT AND CONNECTING ROD SPECIFICATIONS

All measurements are given in inches.

| Year | Engine ID/VIN | Engine Displacement Liters (cc) | Crankshaft | | | | Connecting Rod | | |
			Main Brg. Journal Dia.	Main Brg. Oil Clearance	Shaft End-play	Thrust on. No.	Journal Diameter	Oil Clearance	Side Clearance
1992–93	P	5.7 (5733)	2.4484–2.4493 ①	0.0008–0.0020 ⑤	0.0020–0.0070	5	2.0893–2.0998	0.0013–0.0035	0.006–0.014
	J	5.7 (5727)	2.7550–2.7560	0.0007–0.0023	0.0006–0.0014	3	2.0993–2.1000	0.0007–0.0027	0.008–0.028

① Specification applies to the No. 1 bearing.
　Nos. 2, 3, 4—2.4481–2.4490
　VIN 8 No. 5—2.4479–2.4488
　VIN P No. 5—2.4481–2.4488
② Specification applies to the No. 1 bearing.

Nos 2, 3, 4—0.0011–0.0023
No. 5—0.0017–0.0032
Specifications shown apply to new components
③ Maximum clearance
④ Specification applies to the No. 1 bearing.

Nos 2, 3, 4—0.0011–0.0033
No. 5—0.0017–0.0042
⑤ Specification applies to the No. 1 bearing
　Nos. 2, 3, 4—0.0011–0.0020
　No. 5—0.0017–0.0032

VALVE SPECIFICATIONS

| Year | Engine ID/VIN | Engine Displacement Liters (cc) | Seat Angle (deg.) | Face Angle (deg.) | Spring Test Pressure (lbs. @ in.) | Spring Installed Height (in.) | Stem-to-Guide Clearance (in.) | | Stem Diameter (in.) | |
							Intake	Exhaust	Intake	Exhaust
1989	8	5.7 (5733)	46	45	194–206 @ 1.25 ①	1.72 ②	0.0010–0.0027	0.0010–0.0027	0.3410–0.3417	0.3410–0.3417
1990	8	5.7 (5733)	46	45	194–206 @ 1.25	1.72	0.0010–0.0037	0.0010–0.0047	—	—
	J	5.7 (5727)	44	45	146.8–166.4 @ 0.95 ④	1.34 ③	0.0012–0.0026	0.0014–0.0030	—	—
1991	8	5.7 (5733)	46	45	194–206 @ 1.25	1.72	0.0010–0.0037	0.0010–0.0047	—	—
	J	5.7 (5727)	44	45	146.8–166.4 @ 0.95 ④	1.34 ③	0.0012–0.0026	0.0014–0.0030	—	—
1992–93	P	5.7 (5733)	46	45	252–272 @ 1.305	1.78	0.0011–0.0027	0.0011–0.0027	—	—
	J	5.7 (5727)	44	45	146.8–166.4 @ 0.95 ④	1.34 ③	0.0012–0.0026	0.0014–0.0030	—	—

① Exhaust valve—1.16
② Exhaust—1.59
③ Inner spring—1.18 in.
④ Inner spring—75.5–81.8 lb. @ 0.79 in.

PISTON AND RING SPECIFICATIONS

All measurements are given in inches.

| Year | Engine ID/VIN | Engine Displacement Liters (cc) | Piston Clearance | Ring Gap | | | Ring Side Clearance | | |
				Top Compression	Bottom Compression	Oil Control	Top Compression	Bottom Compression	Oil Control
1989	8	5.7 (5733)	0.0007–0.0021 ①	0.010–0.020	0.013–0.017	0.010–0.030	0.0012–0.0029	0.0012–0.0029	0.0012–0.0029
1990	8	5.7 (5733)	②	0.010–0.030	0.013–0.027	0.010–0.040	0.0012–0.0039	0.0012–0.0039	0.0012–0.0039
	J	5.7 (5727)	—	0.016–0.026	0.031–0.039	0.012–0.024	0.0020–0.0030	0.0020–0.0030	0.0010–0.0020

PISTON AND RING SPECIFICATIONS

All measurements are given in inches.

Year	Engine ID/VIN	Engine Displacement Liters (cc)	Piston Clearance	Ring Gap			Ring Side Clearance		
				Top Compression	Bottom Compression	Oil Control	Top Compression	Bottom Compression	Oil Control
1991	8	5.7 (5733)	②	0.010–0.030	0.013–0.027	0.010–0.040	0.0012–0.0039	0.0012–0.0039	0.0012–0.0039
	J	5.7 (5727)	—	0.016–0.026	0.031–0.039	0.012–0.024	0.0020–0.0030	0.0020–0.0030	0.0010–0.0020
1992–93	P	5.7 (5733)	0.0007–0.0021②	0.010–0.020	0.018–0.026	0.010–0.030	0.0012–0.0032	0.0012–0.0032	0.0020–0.0070
	J	5.7 (5727)	—	0.016–0.026	0.031–0.039	0.012–0.024	0.0020–0.0030	0.0020–0.0030	0.0010–0.0020

① 0.0025 maximum
② 0.0027 maximum

TORQUE SPECIFICATIONS

All readings in ft. lbs.

Year	Engine ID/VIN	Engine Displacement Liters (cc)	Cylinder Head Bolts	Main Bearing Bolts	Rod Bearing Bolts	Crankshaft Damper Bolts	Flywheel Bolts	Manifold		Spark Plugs	Lug Nut
								Intake	Exhaust		
1989	8	5.7 (5733)	67	80	45	60	74	35	19	22	100
1990	8	5.7 (5733)	67	80	45	70	74	35②	19	22	100
	J	5.7 (5727)	③	⑤	22⑥	148	74	④	22①	15	100
1991	8	5.7 (5733)	67	80	45	70	74	35②	19	22	100
	J	5.7 (5727)	③	⑤	22⑥	148	74	④	22①	19	100
1992–93	P	5.7 (5733)	65	68⑦	47	60	74	35⑧	26	11	100
	J	5.7 (5727)	③	⑤	22⑥	148	74	④	22⑨	15	100

① Manifold studs only, all others; 11 ft. lbs.
② All except Nos. 1 and 4; 1 and 4, 45 ft. lbs.
③ Torque bolts in 3 steps: 1st at 45 ft. lbs.; 2nd at 74 ft. lbs.; and final at 118 ft. lbs.
④ Injector Housing Bolts & Fuel Rail Bolts; 20 ft. lbs.
⑤ Torque bolts on No. 1, 3 and 5 to 30 ft. lbs. (40 Nm) plus 45–50° turn
Torque bolts on No. 2 and 4 to 15 ft. lbs. (20 Nm), plus 77.5–82.5° turn
⑥ Plus 80–85° turn
⑦ Inboard bolts on 4-bolt cap—78 ft. lbs.
⑧ Tighten in 2 passes. 1st pass torque to 71 inch lbs.
⑨ Studs only, tigthen bolts to 18 ft. lbs.

BRAKE SPECIFICATIONS

All measurements in inches unless noted

Year	Model	Master Cylinder Bore	Brake Disc			Brake Drum Diameter			Minimum Lining Thickness	
			Original Thickness	Minimum Thickness ①	Maximum Runout	Original Inside Diameter	Max. Wear Limit	Maximum Machine Diameter	Front	Rear
1989	Corvette	—	0.795②	0.744③	0.006	—	—	—	0.062	0.062
1990	Corvette	—	0.795④	0.744③	0.006	—	—	—	0.062	0.062
1991	Corvette	—	0.795④	0.744③	0.006	—	—	—	0.062	0.062
1992–93	Corvette	—	0.795④	0.744③	0.006	—	—	—	0.062	0.062

① All rotors have a discard dimension cast into them. This is a wear, not refinish, dimension. Only cut rotors to the minimum thickness specification listed here.
② Heavy duty—1.100
③ Heavy duty—1.059
④ Heavy duty—1.110

WHEEL ALIGNMENT

Year	Model		Caster Range (deg.)	Caster Preferred Setting (deg.)	Camber Range (deg.)	Camber Preferred Setting (deg.)	Toe-in (deg.)	Axis Inclination (deg.)
1989	Corvette	Front	$5^5/_{16}P$–$6^5/_{16}P$	$5^{13}/_{16}P$	0–1P	$\frac{1}{2}P$	$^3/_{32}N$–$^3/_{32}P$	—
		Rear	—	—	$^5/_{16}N$–$^{11}/_{16}P$	0	0	—
1990	Corvette	Front	$5\frac{1}{2}P$–$6\frac{1}{2}P$	6P	0–1P	$\frac{1}{2}P$	$^3/_{32}N$–$^3/_{32}P$	—
		Rear	—	—	$\frac{1}{2}N$–$\frac{1}{2}P$	0	0	—
1991	Corvette	Front	$5\frac{1}{2}P$–$6\frac{1}{2}P$	6P	0–1P	$\frac{1}{2}P$	$^3/_{32}N$–$^3/_{32}P$	—
		Rear	—	—	$\frac{1}{2}N$–$\frac{1}{2}P$	0	0	—
1992–93	Corvette	Front	$5\frac{1}{2}P$–$6\frac{1}{2}P$	6P	0–1P	$\frac{1}{2}P$	$^3/_{32}N$–$^3/_{32}P$	—
		Rear	—	—	$\frac{1}{2}N$–$\frac{1}{2}P$	0	0	—

N—Negative
P—Positive

ENGINE MECHANICAL

NOTE: Disconnecting the negative battery cable on some vehicles may interfere with the functions of the on board computer systems and may require the computer to undergo a relearning process.

Engine Assembly

REMOVAL & INSTALLATION

5.7L (VIN 8) Engine

1. Mark the relationship between each hood hinge and the hood, then remove the hood.
2. Disconnect the negative battery cable and properly relieve fuel system pressure.
3. Drain the coolant into a suitable container.
4. Disconnect the throttle, transmission and cruise control cables at the engine, as equipped.
5. Remove the plenum extension. Disconnect the spark plug wires from the plugs. Remove the wires and distributor cap as an assembly.
6. Remove the distributor from the engine, noting the position of the rotor before and after removal. Remove the EGR Pipe from the intake and exhaust manifold, if required.
7. Remove the cowl screen and the nut from the wiper motor arm, if required.
8. Disconnect the wiper motor wires and remove the wiper motor cover. Remove the wiper motor, if required.
9. Disconnect the oil pressure switches, if required. Remove the air intake duct.
10. Disconnect the brake booster vacuum hose.
11. Disconnect the canister hose at the PCV pipe.
12. Disconnect all necessary wiring and vacuum hoses from the engine.
13. Disconnect manifold vapor hose, if equipped.
14. Disconnect the heater hoses at the pipe.
15. Disconnect the upper radiator hose at the thermostat housing.
16. Remove the coolant pump damper and remove the serpentine belt and coolant pump pulley.
17. Remove the AIR control valve with the bracket attached at the air conditioning compressor.
18. Disconnect and plug the fuel lines at the rail.
19. Disconnect the catalytic converter AIR pipe, if necessary.
20. Remove the air conditioning accumulator clamp bolt and, if required, remove the right side wheelhouse lower center panel.
21. Remove the air conditioning compressor braces.
22. Remove the air compressor and accumulator from the brackets and set aside.
23. Disconnect the fuel lines at the block.
24. Disconnect the lower radiator hose and the heater hose from the water pump.
25. Disconnect heater hose from the oil cooler pipe and, if necessary, remove the belt tensioner.
26. Remove the alternator and the AIR pump with brackets.
27. Remove the power steering pump with reservoir and wire it aside.
28. Remove the water pump pulley and the crankshaft pulley.
29. Raise and safely support the vehicle.
30. Disconnect the wires harness connection at the oxygen sensor, the Electronic Spark Control (ESC) system harness, and the temperature sensors.
31. Remove the temperature sensor wire retainer at the block.
32. Disconnect the ground wires at the engine.
33. Disconnect the AIR pipe at the manifold and, if equipped, disconnect the transmission oil cooler lines at the transmission.
34. Remove the starter and flywheel cover.
35. Disconnect the exhaust system crossover pipe at the manifolds and at the converter hanger.
36. Drain the engine oil into a suitable container.
37. Remove the oil filter.
38. Remove the oil cooler adapter and lines at the block.
39. Disconnect the clutch assembly and manual transmission, if equipped.
40. Remove the engine mount through bolt nuts.
41. Remove the transmission to engine bolts and remove the torque converter to flywheel bolts, if equipped with an automatic transmission.
42. Lower the vehicle.
43. Support the transmission with a transmission jack.
44. Install a suitable lifting device and remove the motor mount through bolts.
45. Remove the engine from the vehicle.

To install:
46. Using a suitable lifting device, lower the engine into the vehicle.
47. Install the engine mount through bolts and remove the lifting device, then raise and support vehicle safely.
48. Support the transmission with a suitable jack.
49. Install the engine mount through

bolt nuts and tighten to 40 ft. lbs. (54 Nm).

50. Install the engine to transmission attaching bolts and install the torque converter to flywheel bolts, if equipped with an automatic transmission.

51. If equipped with a manual transmission, install the clutch assembly and the transmission.

52. Install the oil cooler adapter and oil filter, the starter and the flywheel cover.

53. Install the exhaust system.

54. Connect the oil cooler line at the oil pan and, if equipped, the transmission cooler lines at the flywheel cover.

55. Connect the catalytic converter AIR pipe to the manifold.

56. Connect the ground wire to the engine block.

57. Connect the temperature sensors, oxygen sensor, ESC electrical connectors and any remaining under vehicle electrical connectors.

58. Lower vehicle, then install the crankshaft pulley and water pump and pulley.

59. Install the power steering pump, then the power steering pump reservoir at the fan shroud.

60. Install the AIR pump and the alternator with brackets.

61. Connect fuel lines to the engine, then install the accumulator.

62. If removed, install the belt tensioner, then install the air conditioning compressor and brackets.

63. Install the catalytic converter AIR pipe. If removed, install the wheelhouse lower center panel , then the AIR control valve.

64. Unplug and connect the fuel lines to the fuel rail.

65. Install the serpentine belt, the coolant pump damper and then the radiator and heater hoses.

66. Connect the injector wire harness at the intake.

67. Connect all vacuum hoses and wires connectors previously removed.

68. Connect the canister hose to the PCV, the brake booster hose and/or the cruise control and air conditioning vacuum connector, as applicable.

69. Install the wiper motor and cowl screen, if removed. Install the air intake duct and the oil pressure sender switch, as applicable.

70. Align the marks and install the distributor, then install the cap and wires.

71. Install the plenum extension then connect the throttle, transmission and cruise control cables, as applicable.

72. Fill crankcase with oil, connect the negative battery cable and tighten the fuel filler cap.

73. Properly fill the engine cooling system and check for leaks.

74. Align the marks made earlier and install the hood.

5.7L (VIN P) Engine

1. Mark the relationship between each hood hinge and the hood, then remove the hood.

2. Disconnect the negative battery cable and properly relieve fuel system pressure.

3. Drain the coolant into a suitable container.

4. Remove the air intake duct.

5. Disconnect the electrical harness and vacuum connections from the top of the engine.

6. Disconnect the upper radiator and lower radiator and the heater hose from the pump and remove the throttle body coolant hose.

7. Remove the power steering pump and support aside.

8. Remove the alternator and support aside.

9. Remove the left, wheel well center panel. Remove the serpentine drive belt.

10. Remove the air conditioning compressor from the bracket and position aside.

11. Remove the electrical connector and the cover from the wiper motor.

12. Disconnect the AIR diverter valve hose.

13. Disconnect and plug the fuel lines at the fuel rail.

14. Remove the hoses from the power steering fluid reservoir.

15. Disconnect the accelerator cable from the throttle body.

16. Raise and safely support the vehicle.

17. Remove the starter motor.

18. Remove the left and right catalytic converters, then remove the exhaust pipe and muffler assembly.

19. Remove the transmission.

20. If equipped with a manual transmission, remove the clutch cover and plate, then remove the flywheel.

21. Remove the ground leads from the rear of the engine, then disconnect the electrical connectors from the oil level, knock, oil and coolant temperature sensors.

22. Remove the nuts from the engine mount studs, then lower the vehicle.

23. Install a suitable lifting device and carefully remove the engine from the vehicle.

To install:

24. Lower the engine into position in the vehicle.

25. Remove the lifting device from the engine, raise and safely support the vehicle.

26. Install the nuts on the engine mount studs.

27. Connect the sensor electrical connectors and then connect the ground leads to the rear of the engine.

28. If equipped with a manual transmission, install the flywheel, then install the clutch cover and plate.

29. Install the transmission.

30. Install the right and left catalytic converters, then install the exhaust pipe and muffler assembly.

31. Install the starter and lower the vehicle.

32. Connect the accelerator cable to the throttle body and install the hose to the power steering reservoir.

33. Unplug and connect the fuel lines to the fuel rail.

34. Connect the AIR diverter valve hose.

35. Install the electrical connector and cover to the wiper motor.

36. Install the air conditioning compressor.

37. Install the serpentine drive belt, then install the left wheel well center panel.

38. Install the alternator and the power steering pump.

39. Install the throttle body coolant hose. Connect the heater and radiator hoses.

40. Connect the electrical harness and all vacuum connections to the top of the engine.

41. Install the air intake duct and properly fill the engine cooling system.

42. Check all fluid levels, connect the negative battery cable and tighten the fuel filler cap.

43. Reset the CHANGE OIL indicator and adjust the ASR control cables, as necessary

44. Start the engine and check for leaks and bleed the power steering system.

5.7L (VIN J) Engine

1. Mark the relationship between each hood hinge and the hood, then remove the hood.

2. Disconnect the battery negative cable and properly relieve fuel system pressure.

3. Raise and support the vehicle safely.

4. Drain engine coolant into a suitable container and drain the engine oil.

5. Remove the complete exhaust system and remove the driveshaft.

6. Position a suitable transmission support stand under transmission and remove the transmission support beam.

7. Remove transmission from the vehicle.

8. Remove the clutch actuator cylinder, left side converter shield, clutch housing cover, then the clutch cover and disc.

9. Install a suitable engine lift hook to rear of engine.

10. Remove the AIR tube center section from the AIR hose and oil pan.

11. Disconnect oxygen sensor electrical connectors.

12. Remove the power steering lower hose from the oil cooler.

13. Remove the negative battery cable from the cylinder case.

14. Remove the nuts attaching the engine mounts to the driveline and the frame and lower the vehicle.

15. Remove the air cleaner assembly and air duct.

16. Disconnect the engine oil cooler lines from the oil filter housing.

17. Raise the rear of the engine.

18. Disconnect the fuel lines from the fuel rail.

19. Remove the evaporator housing panel and the resistor.

20. Remove the bolts attaching the right bulkhead connector.

21. Remove the engine right side wiring harness.

22. Remove the instrument panel right lower sound insulator panel.

23. Disconnect the bulkhead wiring harness connectors from under the dash.

24. Remove the air bleed hose from the plenum.

25. Remove the radiator upper and lower hoses, then disconnect the power steering pump vacuum lines.

26. Properly discharge the air conditioning system.

27. Remove the air conditioning suction and discharge line flange from the compressor, then remove the air conditioning compressor to accumulator line from the accumulator.

28. Remove the air conditioning accumulator and position aside.

29. Remove the air conditioning accumulator bracket from the vehicle.

30. Disconnect and plug the power steering pressure line at the power steering gear.

31. Disconnect the throttle body linkage shield, then remove the throttle body cable to plenum retainers.

32. Disconnect the accelerator and cruise control cables from the throttle body.

33. Install a suitable engine lift hook to front of the engine.

34. Remove the ECM from the ECM bracket, then disconnect ECM harness connectors.

35. Remove the left front fender attaching bolts, shims and seal. Remove the left fender.

36. Remove the positive cable from the battery, battery hold-down clamp, and then remove the battery from the vehicle.

37. Disconnect the engine left side bulkhead block electrical connector.

38. Disconnect the engine wiring harness fusible links at the junction block.

39. Disconnect the engine harness connectors from the following:
Secondary injector modules
Positive battery cable at junction block
Differential pressure switch vacuum and electrical connectors
Air conditioning cutout relay
Air conditioning high blower relay
Transmission shift solenoid relay
Fuel pump fuse
Forward light link connector
Positive battery lead
Air conditioning blower resistor
Air conditioning pressure sensors
Air conditioning cooling fan switch
Windshield washer pump
Low coolant sensor
Blower motor
ESC knock sensor
ESC knock sensor relay

40. Disconnect hoses from the vacuum pump, then disconnect the front and rear vacuum connections.

41. Reposition engine harness aside and remove the braided ground strap from the left side frame rail.

42. Reposition the positive battery cable aside and remove the left side plenum panel screen.

43. Disconnect the brake booster vacuum hose.

44. Remove the windshield wiper motor from the vehicle.

45. Remove the MAP sensor and the MAP sensor bracket from the plenum.

46. Disconnect the AIR hose from the left exhaust manifold.

47. Install a suitable lifting device and remove the engine from the vehicle.

48. Transfer the following parts to the new engine, as necessary:
Oil level indicator tube
The exhaust manifolds
The converter heat shields
The wire pack heat shields
Engine mounts

To install:

49. Install the engine mounts to the drivetrain and to the frame, finger-tighten only.

50. Using a suitable lifting device, position the engine into the vehicle.

51. Install the engine mount/bracket bolts, then remove the the lifting device and lifting brackets.

52. Connect the AIR hose to the left exhaust manifold.

53. Install the MAP sensor and bracket to the plenum.

54. Install the wiper motor.

55. Install the left side plenum panel screen.

56. Route the left side wiring harness into position, then install the braided ground strap to the frame rail.

57. Connect the left side bulkhead block connector.

58. Connect the engine harness fusible links and relays.

59. Install the battery and hold-down clamps.

60. Connect the battery positive cable to the battery, then install the left front fender.

61. Install the ECM to the ECM bracket, then connect the ECM electrical connector.

62. Connect power brake booster vacuum hose to the plenum.

63. Connect the cruise control and throttle cables to the throttle body. Install the cable shield, then install cable retainers to the plenum.

64. Install the power steering pressure line to the power steering gear.

65. Connect the engine oil cooler lines to the engine.

66. Install the accumulator bracket and then install the accumulator.

67. Connect the air conditioning lines.

68. Attach the vacuum lines to the power steering pump.

69. Connect the radiator upper and lower hoses.

70. Connect the air bleed hose to the plenum.

71. Connect the bulkhead wire connector to the bulkhead.

72. Connect the evaporator housing panel resistor electrical connector.

73. Install the hose onto the vacuum pump, then connect the front and rear vacuum connections.

74. Connect the engine harness connectors to the following:

Air conditioning blower resistor
Air conditioning pressure sensor
Air conditioning cooling fan
Windshield washer pump
Low coolant sensor
Blower motor
ESC knock sensor
ESC knock sensor relay
Differential pressure switch

75. Connect the fuel lines to the fuel rail.

76. Install the engine right side wiring harness under the dash.

77. Install the instrument panel right sound insulator panel.

78. Raise and safely support the vehicle, then tighten the engine/bracket bolts and nuts to 40 ft. lbs. (54 Nm).

79. Install the power steering hose to power steering oil cooler.

80. Install the oxygen sensor wire connectors.

81. Connect the AIR tube center section to the AIR hose and oil pan.

82. Connect the negative battery cable to the engine, suitably support the engine and remove the engine rear lift hook.

83. Install the clutch cover and disc, the housing to the cylinder block and the housing cover.

84. Install the left side converter shield to the housing, then position the actuator cylinder and install the retaining nuts.

85. Install the transmission and support beam.

86. Install the driveshaft.

87. Install the complete exhaust system.

88. Lower the vehicle and add the proper type and amount of engine oil.

89. Tighten the fuel filler cap and connect the negative battery cable.

90. Properly fill the engine cooling system and check for leaks.

91. Recharge the air conditioning system.

Engine Mounts

REMOVAL & INSTALLATION

5.7L (VIN 8) Engine

1. Disconnect the negative battery cable.

2. Remove the air intake duct from the air cleaner assembly.

3. Raise and support the vehicle safely.

4. When removing the right engine mount, remove the Electronic Spark Control (ESC) sensor shield.

5. Remove the engine mount through bolts and nuts.

6. Raise engine slightly for sufficient clearance, then remove engine mount bolts and engine mount from the engine block.

To install:

7. Install the engine mount to the block and tighten the bolts to 41 ft. lbs. (56 Nm).

8. Lower the engine into place.

9. Install the engine mount through bolts and nuts. Tighten the nuts to 40 ft. lbs. (54 Nm).

10. If removed, install the ESC sensor shield.

11. Lower the vehicle and install the air intake duct.

12. Connect the negative battery cable.

5.7L (VIN P) Engine

1. Disconnect the negative battery cable.

2. Raise and support the vehicle safely.

3. Remove the engine mount nuts from both sides.

4. Disconnect the catalytic converters from the exhaust manifolds and reposition.

5. Raise the engine with a suitable device, sufficiently for the mount studs to clear the crossmembers.

6. Remove the engine mount through bolt and nut.

7. Remove the engine mounts, heat shield, and if necessary, spacers.

8. Remove the engine bracket bolts and remove the bracket.

To install:

9. Install the engine bracket and bolts. Tighten the bolts to 41 ft. lbs. (56 Nm).

10. Install the engine mounts, heat shield and spacers.

11. Install the engine mount through bolt and nut.

12. Lower the engine and tighten the nuts to 40 ft. lbs. (54 Nm) and the through bolt to 77 ft. lbs. (105 Nm).

13. Install the catalytic converters and nuts to the exhaust manifolds. Tighten the nuts to 15 ft. lbs. (21 Nm).

14. Lower the vehicle and connect the negative battery cable.

5.7L (VIN J) Engine

1. Disconnect the battery negative cable.

2. Remove the exhaust manifolds.

3. Remove the nuts attaching the engine mounts to the drivetrain and frame.

4. Using a suitable tool, safely raise and support the engine sufficiently to remove the engine mounts.

5. Remove the engine mount/bracket nuts and bolts from the brackets.

6. Remove the engine mounts and heat shields from the vehicle.

7. Remove the bolts attaching the brackets to the cylinder case and remove the brackets from the vehicle.

To install:

8. Install the engine mount brackets to the cylinder case and install the retaining bolts. Tighten the bolts to 38 ft. lbs. (52 Nm).

9. Install the engine mounts and heat shields onto the vehicle with the engine mount/bracket bolts and nuts. Tighten the nuts to 40 ft. lbs. (54 Nm).

10. Lower the engine back into position and install the nut retaining the mount to the drivetrain and frame. Tighten the nut to 40 ft. lbs. (54 Nm).

11. Install the exhaust manifolds.

12. Connect the negative battery cable.

Cylinder Head

REMOVAL & INSTALLATION

5.7L (VIN 8) Engine

RIGHT SIDE

1. Disconnect the negative battery cable and properly relieve the fuel system pressure.

2. Remove the intake manifold.

3. Remove the right exhaust manifold.

4. Remove the air conditioning compressor mounting bracket attaching bolts, then the mounting bracket and position aside.

5. Remove the rocker arm and pushrod assemblies.

6. Remove the cylinder head bolts, washers and the cylinder head.

To install:

7. Thoroughly clean the cylinder head and cylinder case mating surfaces. Make sure both surfaces are free of any foreign matter, nicks or scratches. The threads in both the bolts holes and on the bolts must be clean and free of old sealer.

8. Position the new gasket in place on the cylinder case and install the head. Coat the bolts with 1052080 or equivalent sealer and install. Tighten the bolts in the proper sequence to 67 ft. lbs. (91 Nm).

9. Install the rocker arm and pushrod assemblies.

10. Install the air conditioning compressor with bracket.

11. Install the right exhaust manifold.

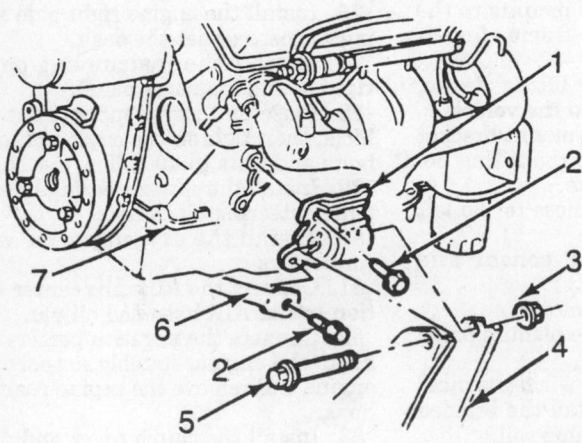

1. Engine mount
2. Bolt
3. Engine mount nut
4. Frame
5. Engine mount bolt
6. Support brace
7. Engine block

Engine mount removal—5.7L (VIN 8) Engine

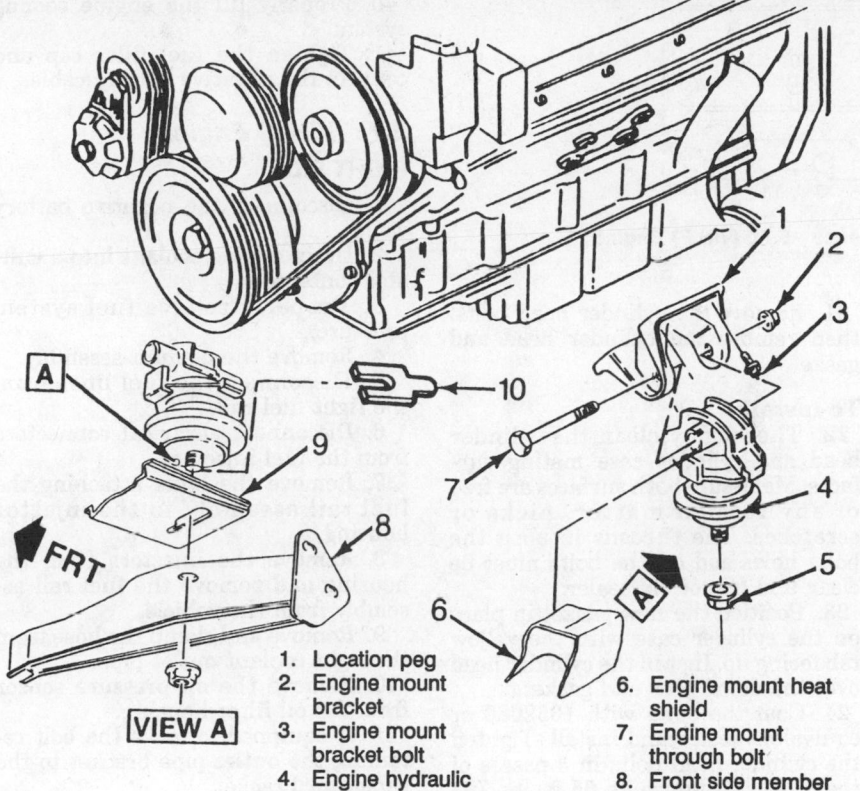

1. Location peg
2. Engine mount bracket
3. Engine mount bracket bolt
4. Engine hydraulic mount
5. Engine mount nut
6. Engine mount heat shield
7. Engine mount through bolt
8. Front side member
9. Frame
10. Engine mount spacer

VIEW A

Engine mount removal—5.7L (VIN J) Engine

12. Install the intake manifold.
13. Connect the negative battery cable and inspect the engine for leaks.

LEFT SIDE

1. Disconnect the negative battery cable and properly relieve fuel system pressure.
2. Remove the left exhaust manifold.
3. Remove the alternator.
4. Remove the 2 bolts and 1 nut attaching the AIR pump bracket to the head. Position pump and bracket assembly aside.
5. Remove the bolts attaching the power steering pump bracket to the cylinder head.
6. Remove the rocker arm and pushrod assemblies.
7. Remove the cylinder head bolts, washers and the cylinder head.

To install:

8. Thoroughly clean the cylinder head and cylinder case mating surfaces. Make sure both surfaces are free of any foreign matter, nicks or scratches. The threads in both the bolts holes and on the bolts must be clean and free of old sealer.
9. Position the new gasket in place on the cylinder case and install the head. Coat the bolts with 1052080 or equivalent sealer and install. Tighten

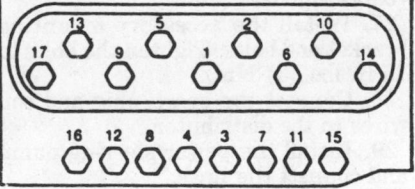

Cylinder head bolt torque sequence— 5.7L (VIN 8) Engine

the bolts in the proper sequence to 67 ft. lbs. (91 Nm).
10. Install the rocker arm and pushrod assemblies.
11. Install the bolts securing the power steering pump to the cylinder head.
12. Install the 2 bolts and 1 nut securing the AIR pump bracket to the cylinder head.
13. Install the alternator.
14. Install the left exhaust manifold.
15. Install the intake manifold.
16. Connect the negative battery cable and check for leaks.

5.7L (VIN P) Engine

RIGHT SIDE

1. Disconnect the negative battery cable and properly relieve the fuel system pressure.

2. Raise and support the vehicle safely.
3. Disconnect the catalytic converter and drain the engine cooling system.
4. Lower the vehicle.
5. Remove the lower radiator and heater hose from the coolant pump.
6. Disconnect the power steering pump reservoir from the cylinder head and reposition aside.
7. Remove the coil and bracket.
8. Remove the intake manifold.
9. Remove the spark plug wires from the clips and the front wire bracket.
10. Remove the oil level indicator tube.
11. Disconnect the spark plug wires from the plugs and remove the spark plugs.
12. Remove the right exhaust manifold.
13. Using a backup wrench on the pipe fitting, disconnect the left rear vent pipe from the left cylinder head.
14. Remove the right valve rocker cover and remove the rocker arm and pushrod assemblies.
15. Remove the cylinder head bolts.
16. Remove the cylinder head, gasket and the rear vent pipe.
17. If necessary, remove the rear vent pipe from the cylinder head.

To install:

18. Thoroughly clean the cylinder head and cylinder case mating surfaces. Make sure both surfaces are free of any foreign matter, nicks or scratches. The threads in both the bolts holes and on the bolts must be clean and free of old sealer.
19. If removed, install the rear vent pipe to the cylinder head, finger-tight.
20. Position the new gasket in place on the cylinder case with the yellow tab facing up. Install the cylinder head over the dowel pins and gasket.
21. Coat the bolts with 1052080 or equivalent sealer and install. Tighten the cylinder head bolts in 3 passes of the proper sequence, to 65 ft. lbs. (88 Nm).
22. Install the rocker arm and pushrod assemblies.
23. Install the valve rocker cover and tighten the bolts to 90 inch lbs. (10 Nm).
24. Connect the rear vent pipe to the left cylinder head and torque the vent pipe to both cylinder heads. Using a backup wrench, tighten the rear vent pipe to 30 ft. lbs. (41 Nm).
25. Install the right exhaust manifold.
26. Install the spark plugs and tighten to 11 ft. lbs. (15 Nm).
27. Connect the spark plug wires to the plugs, install the oil level indicator tube and connect the spark plug wires

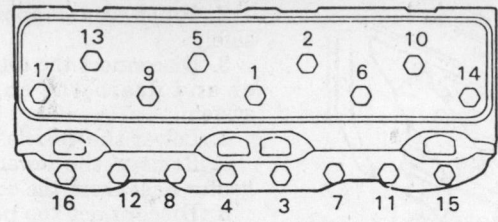

◀ FRT

Cylinder head bolt torque sequence – 5.7L (VIN P) Engine

to the front wire bracket and the wire clips.

28. Install the intake manifold.

29. Install the coil and bracket.

30. Install the power steering pump reservoir.

31. Install the lower radiator and heater hose to the coolant pump.

32. Raise and safely support the vehicle.

33. Connect the catalytic converter and lower the vehicle.

34. Properly fill the cooling system.

35. Tighten the fuel filler cap and connect the negative battery cable.

LEFT SIDE

1. Disconnect the negative battery cable and properly relieve the fuel system pressure.

2. Raise and support the vehicle safely.

3. Disconnect the catalytic converter and drain the engine cooling system.

4. Lower the vehicle.

5. Remove the upper radiator hose.

6. Remove the serpentine drive belt.

7. Remove the intake manifold.

8. Remove the left wheel well center panel.

9. Disconnect the air conditioning compressor from the bracket and position aside. Remove the compressor and alternator brace.

10. Remove the spark plug wire bracket, disconnect the wires from the spark plugs and remove the spark plugs.

11. Remove the left exhaust manifold.

12. Remove the remaining alternator brace and remove the alternator.

13. Disconnect the AIR diverter valve hose.

14. Remove the left valve rocker cover.

15. Remove the drive belt idler pulley and the drive belt tensioner.

16. Remove the power steering lines from the pump and remove the pump.

17. Remove the spark plug and coil wires from the distributor.

18. Remove the accessory mounting bracket.

19. Remove the rocker arm and pushrod assemblies.

20. Disconnect the rear vent pipe from the cylinder head.

21. Remove the cylinder head bolts, then remove the cylinder head and gasket.

To install:

22. Thoroughly clean the cylinder head and cylinder case mating surfaces. Make sure both surfaces are free of any foreign matter, nicks or scratches. The threads in both the bolts holes and on the bolts must be clean and free of old sealer.

23. Position the new gasket in place on the cylinder case with the yellow tab facing up. Install the cylinder head over the dowel pins and gasket.

24. Coat the bolts with 1052080 or equivalent sealer and install. Tighten the cylinder head bolts in 3 passes of the proper sequence, to 65 ft. lbs. (88 Nm).

25. Connect the rear vent pipe to the cylinder head and tighten to 30 ft. lbs. (41 Nm).

26. Install the rocker arm and pushrod assemblies.

27. Install the accessory mounting bracket and bolts. Tighten the bolts to 25 ft. lbs. (34 Nm).

28. Connect the spark plug and coil wires to the distributor.

29. Install the power steering pump and connect the lines.

30. Install the drive belt tensioner and the idler pulley. Tighten the tensioner and pulley bolts to 24 ft. lbs. (33 Nm).

31. Install the left valve rocker cover and bolts. Tighten the bolts to 90 inch lbs. (10 Nm).

32. Connect the AIR diverter valve hose and install the alternator lower brace.

33. Install the left exhaust manifold.

34. Install the spark plugs and tighten to 11 ft. lbs. (15 Nm). Connect the spark plug wires to the plugs and insert the wires into the brackets.

35. Install the air conditioning compressor and alternator brace, then install the compressor.

36. Install the left wheel well center panel.

37. Install the intake manifold.

38. Install the serpentine drive belt and the upper radiator hose.

39. Raise and safely support the vehicle, connect the catalytic converter and lower the vehicle.

40. Properly fill the engine cooling system.

41. Tighten the fuel filler cap and connect the negative battery cable.

5.7L (VIN J) Engine

RIGHT SIDE

1. Disconnect the negative battery cable.

2. Drain engine coolant into a suitable container.

3. Properly relieve fuel system pressure.

4. Remove the plenum assembly.

5. Disconnect the fuel lines from the right fuel rail.

6. Disconnect electrical connectors from the fuel injectors.

7. Remove the bolts attaching the fuel rail assembly to the injector housing.

8. Remove the injectors from the housing and remove the fuel rail assembly from the vehicle.

9. Remove and clamp the hose from the right coolant outlet pipe.

10. Remove the oil pressure sensor from the oil filter housing.

11. If equipped, remove the bolt retaining the outlet pipe bracket to the generator bracket.

12. Remove the screws attaching the outlet pipe to the injector housing, then remove the outlet pipe and gasket.

13. Remove PCV grommet and the ventilation hose from the injector housing.

14. Remove the bolt attaching the alternator rear support bracket to the alternator.

15. Remove the bolt attaching the alternator rear support bracket and right side ventilation pipe to the injector housing.

16. Remove the ventilation pipe and bracket from the vehicle.

17. Remove the bolts attaching the injector housing to the cylinder head.

18. Remove the injector housing and gasket from the vehicle.

19. Remove the right bank camshafts and valve lifters.

20. Remove the alternator assembly.

21. Disconnect the right exhaust manifold from the cylinder head. It is not necessary to completely remove the exhaust manifold from the vehicle for cylinder head removal.

22. Remove the fuel filter heat shield, if necessary.

23. Remove the vacuum hose from secondary port throttle valve actuator.

24. Remove the access plug from the right cylinder head.

25. Remove the bolt attaching the right secondary timing chain guide.

26. Remove cylinder head bolts and remove the cylinder head and gasket from the vehicle.

To install:

27. Thoroughly clean the cylinder head and cylinder case mating surfaces. Make sure both surfaces are free of any foreign matter, nicks or scratches. The threads in both the bolts holes and on the bolts must be clean and free of old sealer.

NOTE: Cylinder head gaskets are not interchangeable between cylinder banks.

28. Install the cylinder head locating dowels into block, if loosened or removed, then position the new gasket in place on the cylinder case.
29. Install the cylinder head over the dowels. Coat bolt threads and washers with clean engine oil and insert.
30. Tighten the cylinder head bolts in sequence as follows:

   1st pass–45 ft. lbs. (60 Nm)
   2nd pass–74 ft. lbs. (100 Nm)
   3rd pass–118 ft. lbs. (160 Nm)

31. Apply Loctite® 262 to the fixed guide bolt threads, install the bolt and tighten to 19 ft. lbs. (26 Nm).
32. Install the access plug into the cylinder head and torque to 15 ft. lbs. (20 Nm).
33. Connect the vacuum hose to the actuator.
34. Raise and support vehicle, drain the engine oil and lower the vehicle.
35. Install the fuel filter heat shield, if removed.
36. Install the exhaust manifold.
37. Install the alternator.
38. Install valve lifters and camshafts.
39. Clean the injector housing and cylinder head sealing surfaces. Install the new gasket, the housing, generator rear bracket, right ventilation pipe and bolts. Be sure the spark plug wire harness retainer is secured by the injector housing rear bolt and tighten the housing bolts to 19 ft. lbs. (26 Nm).
40. Install the ventilation hose and clamp, then install the PCV grommet into the injector housing.
41. Install a new coolant outlet gasket, outlet and screws. Tighten the screws to 89 inch lbs. (10 Nm).
42. Connect the hose and clamp to the right coolant outlet pipe.
43. Install new fuel injector O-rings and install the fuel rail assembly to the injector housing. Tighten the bolts to 19 ft. lbs. (26 Nm).
44. Connect the fuel injector electrical connections.
45. Connect the fuel lines to the right fuel rail.
46. Install the plenum assembly.
47. Fill the engine crankcase with the proper type and amount of engine oil.
48. Tighten the fuel filler cap and properly refill the cooling system.

49. Connect the negative battery cable.

LEFT SIDE

1. Disconnect the negative battery cable.
2. Drain engine coolant into a suitable container.
3. Properly relieve fuel system pressure.
4. Remove the plenum assembly.
5. Disconnect fuel lines from the fuel rail.
6. Disconnect electrical connectors from the injectors.
7. Remove the bolts attaching the fuel rail assembly to the injector housing.
8. Remove the injectors from the housing and the fuel rail assembly from the vehicle.
9. Remove the hose from left coolant outlet pipe.
10. Remove the bolt attaching the outlet pipe bracket to the power steering pump bracket, if equipped.
11. Remove screws attaching the outlet pipe to the injector housing, then remove the outlet pipe and gasket from the vehicle.
12. Remove PCV grommet from injector housing.
13. Disconnect the ventilation hose from injector housing.
14. Disconnect the coolant temperature sensor and cooling fan switch electrical connectors.
15. Remove bolts attaching the injector housing to the cylinder head, then remove the injector housing and gasket from vehicle.
16. Remove the vacuum hose from the secondary port throttle valve actuator.
17. Remove the power brake booster assembly.
18. Remove the left bank valve lifters and camshafts.
19. Remove the AIR control valve hoses, then disconnect the electrical connector.

20. Remove the camshaft position sensor.
21. Disconnect the left exhaust manifold from the cylinder head. It is not necessary to completely remove the exhaust manifold from the vehicle for cylinder head removal.
22. Remove the access plug from the left cylinder head.
23. Remove the bolt attaching the left secondary timing chain guide.
24. Remove the cylinder head bolts. Remove the cylinder head and gasket from the vehicle.

To install:

25. Thoroughly clean the cylinder head and cylinder case mating surfaces. Make sure both surfaces are free of any foreign matter, nicks or scratches. The threads in both the bolts holes and on the bolts must be clean and free of old sealer.

NOTE: Cylinder head gaskets are not interchangeable between cylinder banks.

26. Install the cylinder head locating dowels into block, if loosened or removed, then position the new gasket in place on the cylinder case.
27. Install the cylinder head over the dowels. Coat bolt threads and washers with clean engine oil and insert.
28. Tighten the cylinder head bolts in sequence as follows:

   1st pass–45 ft. lbs. (60 Nm)
   2nd pass–74 ft. lbs. (100 Nm)
   3rd pass–118 ft. lbs. (160 Nm)

29. Apply Loctite® 262 to the fixed guide bolt threads, install the bolt and tighten to 19 ft. lbs. (26 Nm).
30. Install the access plug into the cylinder head and torque to 15 ft. lbs. (20 Nm).
31. Connect the vacuum hose to the actuator.
32. Raise and support vehicle, drain the engine oil and lower the vehicle.
33. Install the exhaust manifold.
34. Install the camshaft position sensor.

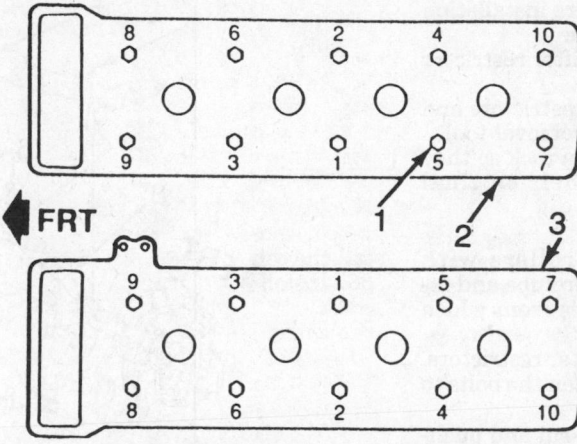

1. Cylinder head bolt
2. Right cylinder head
3. Left cylinder head

Cylinder head bolt torque sequence–5.7L (VIN J) Engine

35. Connect the AIR control valve hoses and electrical connector.

36. Install the valve lifters and camshafts.

37. Install the new housing gasket, housing and bolts. Be sure the spark plug wiring harness retainer is secured by the rear housing bolt. Tighten the bolts to 19 ft. lbs. (26 Nm).

38. Install the ventilations hose and the PCV grommet.

39. Connect the electrical connectors to the coolant temperature sensor and to the cooling fan switch.

40. Install a new coolant outlet pipe gasket, the outlet and screws. Tighten the screws to 89 inch lbs. (10 Nm).

41. Connect the hose to the left coolant outlet pipe.

42. Install new fuel injector O-rings and install the fuel rail assembly to the injector housing and tighten the bolts to 19 ft. lbs. (26 Nm).

43. Engage the fuel injector electrical connectors.

44. Connect the fuel lines to the fuel rail.

45. Install the plenum assembly.

46. Fill the engine crankcase with the proper type and amount of engine oil.

47. Tighten the fuel filler cap and properly refill the cooling system.

48. Connect the negative battery cable.

Valve Lifters

REMOVAL & INSTALLATION

5.7L (VIN 8 and VIN P) Engines

1. Disconnect the negative battery cable and properly relieve fuel system pressure.

2. Drain the engine cooling system into a suitable container.

3. Remove the intake manifold assembly.

4. Remove the valve rocker covers.

5. Remove the rocker arms and pushrod assemblies. Be sure to keep all parts in order to assure installation in their original location.

6. Remove the valve lifter restrictor retainer and bolts.

7. Remove the valve restrictors and lifters using a suitable removal tool.

8. Place the lifters in a rack so they may be installed in their original bores.

To install:

9. Coat the lifter rollers with 1052365 or equivalent prelube and install into the same bores from which they were removed.

10. Install the valve lifter restrictors, retainer and bolts. Tighten the bolts to 15 ft. lbs. (20 Nm).

11. Install the rocker arm and pushrod assemblies.

12. Install the valve rocker covers.

13. Install the intake manifold.

14. Tighten the fuel filler cap and connect the negative battery cable.

15. Properly fill the engine cooling system.

5.7L (VIN J) Engine

1. Disconnect the negative battery cable.

2. Remove the camshaft covers.

3. Remove the camshafts.

4. Remove lifters from bores.

NOTE: If lifters are to be reused, be sure to retain them in proper order so each lifter can be reinstalled in its original bore.

5. Installation is the reverse of the removal procedure. Lubricate lifter bores with engine oil.

6. Lifters should be replaced as sets with a camshaft. If new lifters are being used, be sure to pre-oil them.

Valve Lash

ADJUSTMENT

5.7L (VIN J and VIN P) Engines

NOTE: The 5.7L (VIN 8 and VIN P) engines utilize hydraulic lifters which normally require very little maintenance or adjustment. These components are simple in design and are best maintained through regular, scheduled engine oil changes. If the engine is running well and no audible clicking sounds are heard from the valve train, do not attempt to remove or disassemble the valve lifters.

1. Disconnect the negative battery cable.

2. Remove the valve rocker covers.

3. Tighten the rocker arm nuts until all lash is eliminated.

4. Adjust the valves when the lifter is on the base circle of the camshaft lobe. Slowly turn or crank the engine until the mark on the vibration damper aligns with the 0 mark on the timing chain cover and the engine is in the No. 1 firing position.

NOTE: The No. 1 firing position may be determined by placing a finger over the No. 1 spark plug hole as the mark on the damper comes near the 0 mark on the crankcase front cover. If both the intake and exhaust valves are closed as the mark comes up to the timing tab, the engine is in the No. 1 firing position.

If either valve opens as the timing mark approaches 0, the engine is in No. 6 firing position and should be turned over one full revolution in order to reach the No. 1 firing position.

5. With the engine in the No. 1 firing position, adjust the following valves:

    a. Exhaust—1, 3, 4, 8

    b. Intake—1, 2, 5, 7

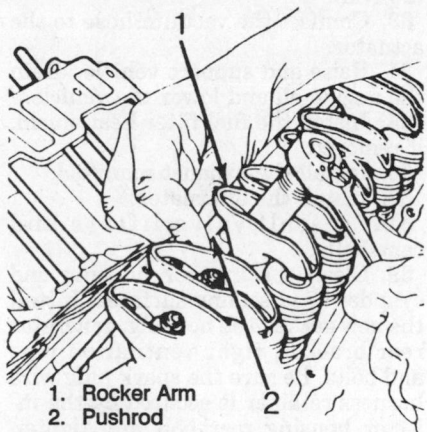

1. Rocker Arm
2. Pushrod

Valve adjusting—5.7L (VIN 8 and VIN P) Engines

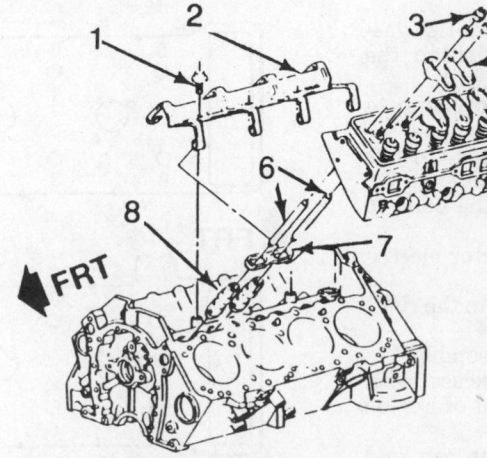

1. Retainer bolt
2. Valve lifter restrictor retainer
3. Valve rocker arm adjustment nut
4. Rocker arm ball
5. Valve rocker arm
6. Pushrod
7. Valve lifter guide
8. Lifter

Rocker arms and pushrod assembly—5.7L (VIN 8 and VIN P) Engines

6. Back out the adjusting nut until lash is felt at the pushrod then turn in adjusting nut until all lash is removed. This can be determined by rotating pushrod while turning adjusting nut. When play has been removed, the pushrod will not turn. Then, tighten the adjusting nut a full additional turn.

7. Slowly turn or crank the engine 1 revolution until the **0** mark and the vibration damper mark are again in alignment. This is the No. 6 firing position.

8. With the engine in this position, adjust the following valves:

   a. Exhaust—2, 5, 6, 7

   b. Intake—3, 4, 6, 8

9. Install the valve rocker arm covers.

10. Connect the battery negative cable.

5.7L (VIN J) Engine

This engine is equipped with hydraulic lifters which maintain zero lash between the camshaft lobes and the valve stem. The lifter is non-adjustable and upon failure, must be replaced.

Rocker Arms

REMOVAL & INSTALLATION

5.7L (VIN 8) Engine

1. Disconnect the negative battery cable.

2. Remove the right valve rocker cover as follows:

   a. Drain the engine coolant into a suitable container.

   b. Remove the EGR pipe assembly.

   c. Remove the crankcase vent pipe.

   d. Disconnect the spark plug wires from the plugs and retainers, and position the wires aside.

   e. Remove the injector harness retaining nuts and position the harness aside.

   f. Remove the plenum bend hose, the heater core to plenum coolant hose and the AIR hoses at the control valve.

   g. Remove the bolts securing the air conditioning compressor and position the compressor aside.

   h. Remove the valve rocker cover bolts, cover and gasket. Replace the gasket as required.

3. Remove the left rocker arm cover as follows:

   a. Remove the PCV valve.

   b. Remove the injector harness retaining nuts and position the harness aside.

   c. Disconnect the spark plug

wires from the plugs and retainers, and position the wires aside.

   d. Remove the serpentine drive belt from the AIR pump pulley.

   e. Remove the AIR pump pulley and loosen the AIR pump lower mounting bolt.

   f. Remove the valve rocker cover bolts, cover and gasket. Replace the gasket as required.

4. Remove the rocker arm nuts, rocker arm balls, rocker arms and pushrods. Mark or place the assemblies in a rack to assure installation in their original locations.

To install:

5. Coat the bearing surfaces of new rocker arms and/or rocker arm balls with 3755008 or equivalent pre-lube, prior to installation.

6. Install the pushrods making certain they seat in the lifter sockets.

7. Install the rocker arms, rocker arm balls and rocker arm nuts in their original positions.

8. Tighten the rocker arm nuts until all lash is eliminated.

9. Adjust the valves.

10. Thoroughly clean the gasket mating surfaces and install the valve rocker arm covers in the reverse order of removal. Tighten the valve rocker cover bolts to 80 inch lbs. (9 Nm) for 1989 vehicles or to 90 inch lbs. (10 Nm) for 1990–91 vehicles.

11. Connect the battery negative cable.

12. Properly fill the engine cooling system and inspect for leaks.

5.7L (VIN P) Engine

1. Disconnect the negative battery cable.

2. Remove the right valve rocker cover as follows:

   a. Remove the fuel rail cover and the fuel rail bolts.

   b. Disconnect the fuel pressure regulator vacuum hose.

   c. Remove the fuel injector and rail assembly from the manifold and reposition.

   d. Remove the fuel rail cover studs and position the wiring harness aside.

   e. Remove the AIR pipe and check valve from the intake and exhaust manifolds.

   f. Disconnect the crankcase vent hose.

   g. Remove the valve rocker cover bolts, cover and gasket. Replace the gasket as necessary.

3. Remove the left rocker arm cover as follows:

   a. Remove the alternator brace and bolts.

   b. Remove the remaining alternator bolts and position the alternator aside.

   c. Disconnect the AIR diverter valve hose from the check valve.

   d. Remove the fuel rail cover.

   e. Remove the fuel rail cover studs and position the wiring harness aside.

   f. Remove the valve rocker cover bolts, cover and gasket. Replace the gasket as necessary.

4. Remove the rocker arm nuts, rocker arm balls, rocker arms and pushrods. Mark or place the assemblies in a rack to assure installation in their original locations.

To install:

5. Coat the bearing surfaces of the

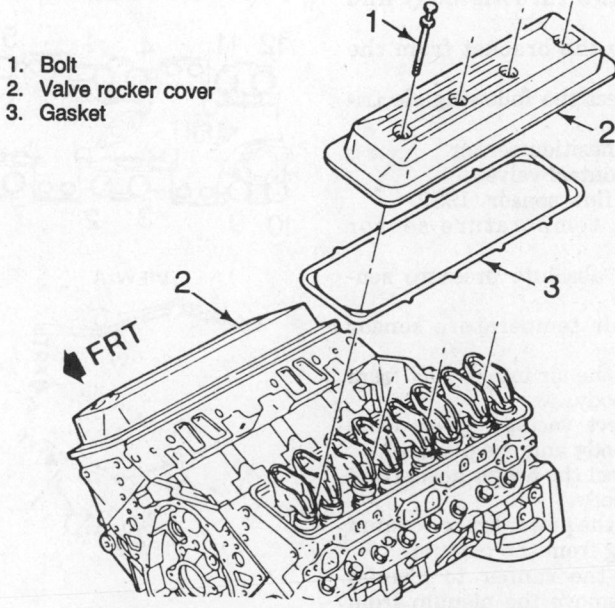

1. Bolt
2. Valve rocker cover
3. Gasket

Valve cover installation—5.7L (VIN P) Engine

rocker arms and rocker arm balls with 1052365 or equivalent pre-lube, prior to installation.

6. Install the pushrods making certain they seat in the lifter sockets.

7. Install the rocker arms, rocker arm balls and rocker arm nuts in their original positions.

8. Tighten the rocker arm nuts until all lash is eliminated.

9. Adjust the valves.

10. Thoroughly clean the gasket mating surfaces and install the valve rocker arm covers in the reverse order of removal. Tighten the valve rocker cover bolts to 90 inch lbs. (10 Nm).

11. Properly fill the engine cooling system.

12. Connect the battery negative cable, start the engine and inspect for leaks.

5.7L (VIN J) Engine

This engine utilizes an overhead cam design, thus eliminating the need for any rocker arm assembly. This design improves and smoothens engine operation.

Intake Manifold

REMOVAL & INSTALLATION

5.7L (VIN 8) Engine

1. Disconnect the negative battery cable.

2. Properly relieve system fuel pressure.

3. Drain engine coolant into a suitable container.

4. Disconnect the throttle and cruise control cables from the throttle body and cable bracket.

5. If equipped, disconnect the TV cable from the throttle body and bracket.

6. Remove the bracket from the plenum.

7. Disconnect the following electrical connectors:
Throttle position sensor
Idle air control valve
Mass air flow sensor (1989)
Coolant temperature sensor (1990–91)
Manifold absolute pressure sensor (1990–91)
Intake air temperature sensor (1990–91)

8. Remove the air intake duct from the throttle body.

9. Disconnect vacuum hoses from the throttle body and the plenum.

10. Disconnect the heater hoses from the throttle body.

11. Remove the power brake vacuum booster fitting from the plenum.

12. Remove the runner to plenum bolts, then remove the plenum from the vehicle.

13. On 1990–91 vehicles, remove the vacuum harness from the EGR solenoid.

14. On 1990–91 vehicles, remove the EGR solenoid assembly from the coolant outlet, then the EGR valve from the intake manifold.

15. Remove the injector harness attaching nuts, then disconnect the injector harness connectors.

16. Remove the runner to manifold attaching bolts, then remove the runners.

17. Disconnect the fuel lines.

18. Remove the fuel rail and injector assembly.

19. Remove the distributor.

20. Remove the radiator upper hose, then the AIR pump brace.

21. Remove the EGR valve pipe and position aside.

22. Remove the PCV valve hose from the manifold.

23. Remove the crankcase vent tube from the manifold.

24. Remove the intake manifold attaching bolts, then the intake manifold and gaskets.

To install:

25. Thoroughly clean the cylinder block, intake manifold and cylinder head surfaces with the proper cleaning compound to remove any traces of gasket material and RTV sealant. Any material left on these surfaces will cause installation interference and improper sealing.

26. Install the new manifold gaskets on the cylinder head with the coolant passage restrictor in gaskets positioned at the rear of the engine. Locate the gasket tabs and bend the tabs so

they are flush with the front face of the cylinder head.

27. After the tabs are bent into place, apply a $^3/_{16}$ inch (5mm) bead of RTV onto the front and rear cylinder case ridges.

28. Apply Loctite®, 1052624, 1052080 or equivalent sealant to the threads of the intake manifold retaining bolts.

29. With the sealant on the cylinder case wet to the touch, install the intake manifold and bolts. Tighten the intake manifold retaining bolts in sequence to 35 ft. lbs. (47 Nm), except positions 1 and 4. Torque positions 1 and 4 to 45 ft. lbs. (61 Nm).

30. Install the crankcase vent tube, the PCV hose to manifold and the EGR valve pipe.

31. Install the AIR pump brace, then connect the radiator upper hose.

32. Install the distributor.

33. Install the fuel rail and injector assemblies.

34. Connect the fuel lines and the injector harness electrical connectors.

35. Install the runners, gaskets and the runner to manifold bolts. Tighten the bolts to 18 ft. lbs. (25 Nm) for 1989 vehicles or to 25 ft. lbs. (34 Nm) for 1990–91 vehicles.

36. Position the injector harness and install the nuts. Tighten to 90 inch lbs. (10 Nm).

37. For 1990–91 vehicles, install the EGR valve and tighten the bolt to 12 ft. lbs. (16 Nm), then install the EGR solenoid assembly to the coolant outlet and tighten the bolt to 25 ft. lbs. (34 Nm). Install the vacuum harness to the EGR solenoid.

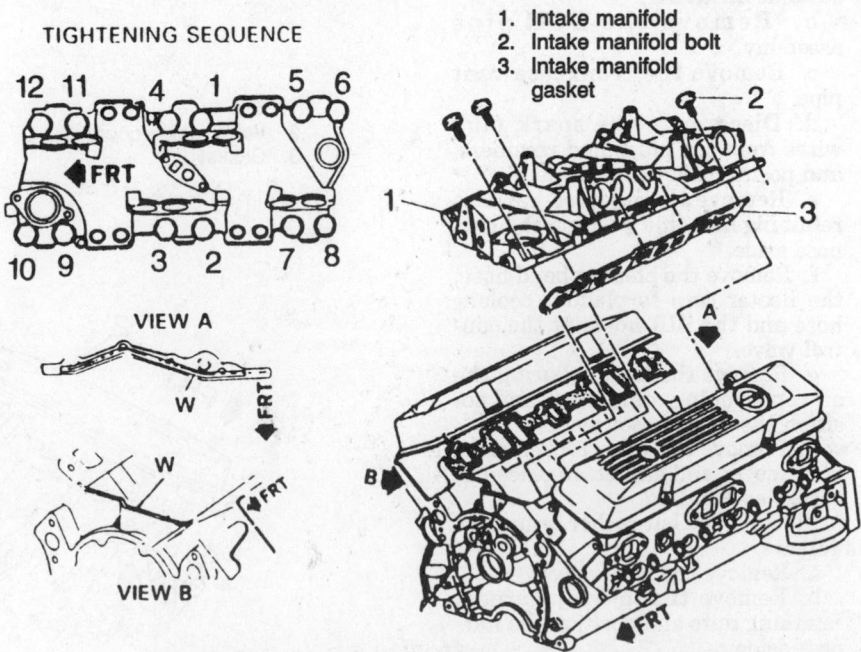

TIGHTENING SEQUENCE

VIEW A

VIEW B

1. Intake manifold
2. Intake manifold bolt
3. Intake manifold gasket

Intake manifold bolt torque sequence—5.7L (VIN 8) Engine

38. Install the plenum and the runner to plenum bolts. Tighten the bolts to 18 ft. lbs. (25 Nm) for 1989 vehicles or to 25 ft. lbs. (34 Nm) for 1990–91 vehicles.

39. Install the power brake vacuum fitting to the plenum and tighten to 108 inch lbs. (12 Nm).

40. Connect the heater hoses, the vacuum hoses and the air intake duct.

41. Connect the electrical connectors to the various sensors disconnected during manifold removal.

42. Install the cable bracket to the plenum and connect the throttle, TV and cruise control cables, as applicable.

43. Tighten the fuel filler cap and connect the negative battery cable.

44. Properly fill the engine cooling system and check for leaks.

5.7L (VIN P) Engine

1. Disconnect the negative battery cable.

2. Drain engine coolant into a suitable container.

3. Remove the fuel rail covers.

4. Remove the throttle body air duct.

5. Disconnect the wiring harness connectors from the fuel injectors and position the harnesses aside.

6. Remove the accelerator cable bracket and cables from the throttle body.

7. Disconnect the AIR diverter valve hoses.

8. Remove the electrical ground strap from the intake manifold.

9. Remove the fuel rail bolts and disconnect the fuel pressure regulator vacuum hose.

10. Carefully remove the fuel rail and injector assembly and position aside.

11. Disconnect the vacuum and crankcase vent hoses.

12. Remove the EGR solenoid bracket and the fuel vapor canister purge solenoid bracket.

13. Remove the EGR valve.

14. Remove the AIR pipe from the intake and the right exhaust manifold.

15. Remove the alternator brace.

16. Disconnect the coolant hoses from the throttle body.

17. Remove the throttle body bolts, the throttle body and gasket.

18. Remove the intake manifold bolts and studs.

19. Remove the intake manifold and gaskets.

To install:

20. Thoroughly clean the intake manifold bolts and studs. Inspect and clean all gasket mating surfaces.

21. Apply a $^3/_{16}$ inch (5mm) bead of RTV sealer to the front and rear of the cylinder block. Extend the bead ½ inch

(13mm) up each cylinder head to seal and retain the gaskets.

22. Position the new gaskets and install the intake manifold.

23. Install the manifold bolts and studs and tighten using 2 passes in the proper sequence. First, tighten the bolts/studs to 71 inch lbs. (8 Nm), then tighten them to 35 ft. lbs. (48 Nm).

24. Install the throttle body, gasket and retaining bolts. Tighten the throttle body bolts to 19 ft. lbs. (26 Nm).

25. Connect the coolant hoses to the throttle body.

26. Install the alternator brace.

27. Install the accelerator cables and bracket. Tighten the bracket bolts to 90 inch lbs. (10 Nm).

28. Install the AIR pipe. Tighten the manifold fitting and the bracket to cylinder head bolt to 25 ft. lbs. (34 Nm) and tighten the flange bolts to the intake manifold to 19 ft. lbs. (26 Nm).

29. Install the EGR valve, then EGR solenoid and bracket. Tighten valve bolts to 16 ft. lbs. (22 Nm) and the bracket nut to 25 ft. lbs. (34 Nm).

30. Install the fuel vapor canister purge solenoid bracket and tighten the nut to 25 ft. lbs. (34 Nm).

31. Connect the vacuum and crankcase vent hoses.

32. Install the fuel injector and fuel rail assembly to the intake manifold, connect the fuel pressure regulator vacuum hose and install the fuel rail bolts. Tighten the bolts to 15 ft. lbs. (20 Nm).

33. Connect the electrical ground strap to the intake manifold.

34. Connect the AIR diverter valve hoses.

35. Position the left and right wiring harnesses and engage the harnesses to the fuel injectors.

36. Install the throttle body air duct.

37. Install the fuel rail covers.

38. Properly fill the engine cooling system.

39. Connect the negative battery cable and adjust the accelerator and cruise control cables, as necessary.

Injector Housing and Plenum Assembly

REMOVAL & INSTALLATION

5.7L (VIN J) Engine

1. Disconnect the negative battery cable and properly relieve fuel system pressure.

2. Drain the cooling system into a suitable container.

3. Remove the air intake duct.

4. Remove the throttle cable cover and attaching hardware.

5. Remove the throttle and cruise control cables from the throttle body. Remove the cable hold down clamp and set the cables aside.

6. Disconnect the electrical connectors from the IAC, TPS and the IAT sensors.

7. Disconnect the coolant air bleed hose from the plenum.

8. Remove the power brake booster hose and fuel pressure regulator vacuum hose from the plenum.

9. Remove the left and right vacuum hoses at the mid-plenum.

10. Remove the MAP sensor.

11. Remove the bolts securing the fuel feed and return lines.

12. Disconnect the fuel lines and discard the O-rings.

13. Remove the plenum assembly attaching bolts.

14. Remove the PCV dual hose fitting from the plenum.

15. Remove the canister hose from the plenum.

16. Lift the front of the plenum assembly and disconnect the following:

   a. Left and right fresh air hoses from the throttle body extension.

   b. Canister vacuum signal hose from the throttle body extension.

   c. Electrical connector from the ignition module.

17. Remove the plenum assembly and discard the gaskets.

18. Cover the intake ports to prevent

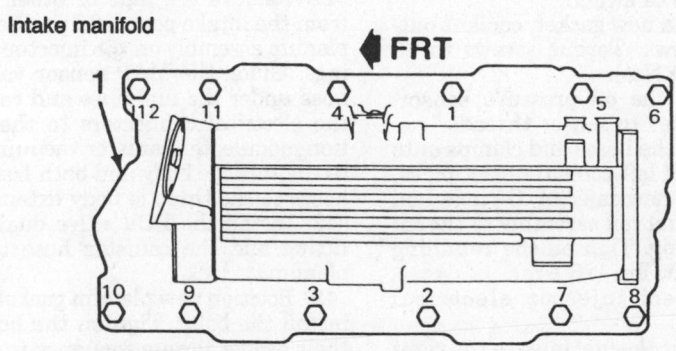

1. Intake manifold

Intake manifold bolt torque sequence—5.7L (VIN P) Engine

dirt or other contaminants from entering.

19. Disconnect the fuel lines at the right fuel rail.

20. Disconnect the electrical connectors from the fuel injectors.

21. Remove the bolts attaching the fuel rail assembly to the injector housing.

22. Remove the injectors from the housing and the fuel rail assembly from the vehicle.

23. Disconnect the hoses from the left and right coolant outlet pipes.

24. Remove the oil pressure sensor from the oil filter housing.

25. Remove the bolt attaching the outlet pipe to the injector housing. Remove the outlet pipe and gasket from the vehicle.

26. Remove the PCV grommet from the injector housing.

27. Remove the clamp and ventilation hose from the injector housing.

28. Remove the bolt attaching the alternator rear support bracket to the alternator.

29. Remove the bolt attaching the alternator rear support bracket and right side ventilation pipe to the injector housing.

30. Remove the ventilation pipe and bracket from the vehicle.

31. Disconnect the electrical connectors from the coolant temperature sensor and the cooling fan switch.

32. Remove the injector housings attaching bolts. Remove the injector housings and gaskets from the vehicle.

To install:

33. Thoroughly clean all gasket mating surfaces and position the new housing gaskets.

34. Install injector housings, alternator bracket, right ventilation pipe and bolts. Be sure the spark plug wire harness retainer is secured by the injector housing rear bolt and tighten the bolts to 19 ft. lbs. (26 Nm).

35. Install the remaining ventilation hose.

34. Install PCV grommet into the injector housing.

35. Engage the electrical connectors to the coolant temperature sensor and the cooling fan switch.

36. Install a new gasket, coolant outlet and screws. Torque screws to 89 inch lbs. (10 Nm).

36. Install the oil pressure sensor. Apply Loctite® to sensor threads.

37. Install the hoses and clamps onto the right and left coolant outlet pipes.

38. Install new injector O-rings and install the fuel rail assembly to the injector housing. Tighten the retaining bolts to 19 ft. lbs. (26 Nm).

39. Connect injector electrical connectors.

40. Connect the fuel lines to the right fuel rail.

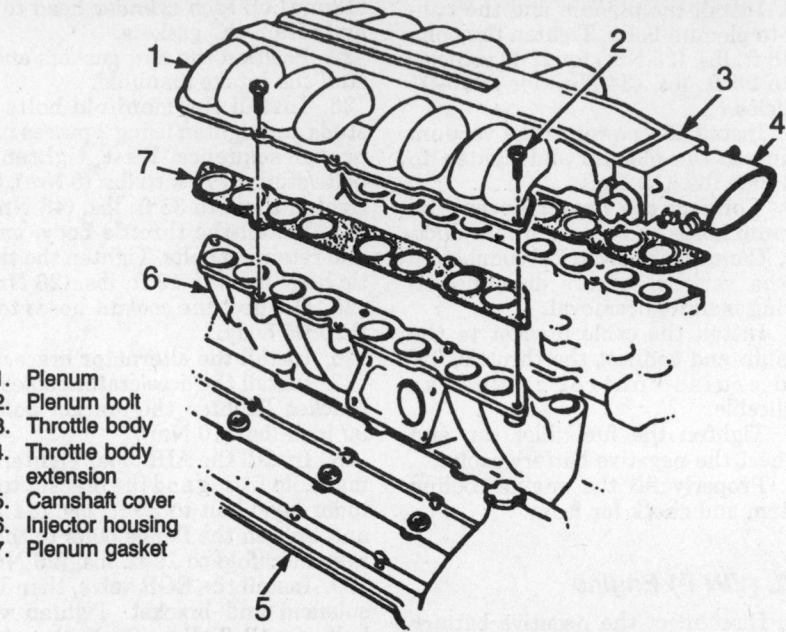

1. Plenum
2. Plenum bolt
3. Throttle body
4. Throttle body extension
5. Camshaft cover
6. Injector housing
7. Plenum gasket

Injector housing and plenum assembly—5.7L (VIN J) Engine

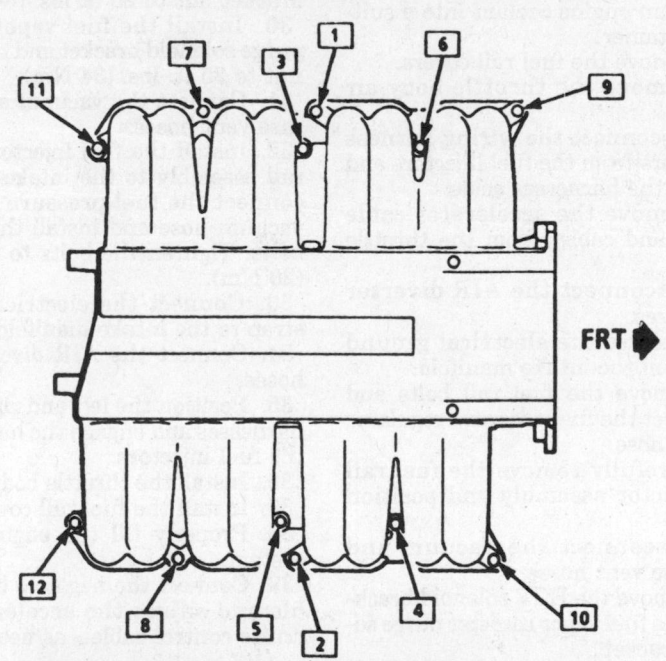

Plenum assembly torque sequence—5.7L (VIN J) Engine

41. Remove the tape or other cover from the intake ports and position the plenum assembly on the injector housings. Guide the MAP sensor vacuum hose under the fuel lines and connect the electrical connectors to the ignition module, the canister vacuum hose to the throttle body and both fresh air hoses to the throttle body extension.

42. Install the PCV valve dual hose fitting and the canister hose to the plenum.

43. Position new plenum gaskets and install the bolts. Tighten the bolts in their proper torque sequence to 20 ft. lbs. (26 Nm).

44. Reconnect the fuel feed return lines and install the fuel line retaining bolts to 13 ft. lbs. (18 Nm).

45. Install the MAP sensor.

46. Connect the left and right vacuum hoses, the fuel pressure regulator vacuum hose to the plenum and connect the coolant air bleed hose.

47. Connect the power brake booster vacuum hose to the plenum.

48. Connect the electrical connectors to the TPS, IAC and IAT sensors.

49. Connect the throttle and cruise control cables to the throttle. Make sure the cables do not hold the throttle open, adjust if necessary.

50. Install the cable hold-down clamp, the cable shield and attaching hardware.

51. Install the air intake duct, tighten the fuel filler cap and connect the negative battery terminal.

52. Properly refill the engine cooling system.

Exhaust Manifold

REMOVAL & INSTALLATION

5.7L (VIN 8) Engine
RIGHT SIDE

1. Disconnect the negative battery cable.

2. Remove the EGR valve pipe and set aside.

3. Remove the air conditioning compressor brace.

4. Remove the oil level indicator and guide tube.

5. Remove the AIR check valve at the manifold.

6. Disconnect the electrical connector from the temperature sending.

7. Disconnect the spark plug wires from the plugs and retainers, then set the wires aside.

8. Remove the spark plugs.

9. Raise and support the vehicle safely.

10. Disconnect the AIR pipe clamp at the manifold.

11. Disconnect the exhaust crossover pipe at the manifold.

12. Lower the vehicle.

13. Support the exhaust manifold and remove the retaining bolts.

14. Remove the exhaust manifold from the vehicle.

To install:

15. Thoroughly clean the manifold and cylinder head gasket mating surfaces.

16. Install the gaskets, exhaust manifold and bolts. Torque bolts to 19 ft. lbs. (26 Nm).

17. Raise and support the vehicle safely.

18. Install front crossover pipe to manifold flange nuts. Torque nuts to 15 ft. lbs. (21 Nm).

19. Install to AIR pipe clamp to the manifold.

20. Lower the vehicle.

21. Install spark plugs, wires and retainers.

22. Connect the temperature sensor electrical connector.

23. Install the AIR check valve to manifold.

24. Install the oil level indicator and guide tube.

25. Install the air conditioning compressor brace.

26. Install the EGR valve pipe.

27. Connect the negative battery ca-

ble, start the engine and check for leaks.

LEFT SIDE

1. Disconnect the negative battery cable.

2. Disconnect the AIR hose at the exhaust check valve.

3. Disconnect the rear alternator brace from the manifold.

4. Remove the spark plug wires from the plugs, then from the wire retainers and position aside.

5. Remove the spark plugs.

6. Raise and support the vehicle safely.

7. Disconnect the front crossover pipe to manifold flange nuts.

8. Lower the vehicle.

9. Support the manifold and remove the retaining bolts.

10. Remove the exhaust manifold from the vehicle.

To install:

11. Thoroughly clean the manifold and cylinder head gasket mating surfaces.

12. Install the gaskets, exhaust manifold and bolts. Torque bolts to 19 ft. lbs. (26 Nm).

13. Raise and support the vehicle safely.

14. Install front crossover pipe to manifold flange nuts. Torque nuts to 15 ft. lbs. (21 Nm).

15. Install to AIR pipe clamp to the manifold.

16. Lower the vehicle.

17. Install the spark plugs, spark plug wires and retainers.

18. Connect the alternator brace to the manifold.

19. Connect the AIR hose to the check valve.

20. Connect the negative battery cable, start engine and check for leaks.

5.7L (VIN P) Engine
RIGHT SIDE

1. Disconnect the negative battery cable.

2. Raise and support the vehicle safely. Disconnect the catalytic converter from the exhaust manifold and lower the vehicle.

3. Remove the fuel rail covers and disconnect the wiring harness connectors from the fuel injectors.

4. Remove the vacuum hose from the fuel pressure regulator.

5. Remove the fuel rail bolts and the remove the fuel injector/rail assembly from the intake manifold.

6. Disconnect the spark plug wires from the plugs, wire clips and supports. Remove the spark plugs.

7. Remove the front spark plug bracket and bolt.

8. Remove the oil level indicator and guide tube.

9. Remove the AIR pipe, gasket and check valve as an assembly from the intake and exhaust manifolds and cylinder head.

10. Remove the exhaust manifold studs and bolts.

11. Remove the heat shields, exhaust manifold and gaskets.

To install:

12. Thoroughly clean the manifold and cylinder head gasket mating surfaces.

13. Install the exhaust manifold gasket, manifold and heat shields.

14. Install the exhaust manifold studs and bolts. Tighten to 26 ft. lbs. (35 Nm).

15. Install the AIR pipe, gasket and check valve with the retaining bolts. Tighten the AIR pipe fitting to manifold and the bracket bolt to 25 ft. lbs. (34 Nm) and tighten the pipe flange bolts to 19 ft. lbs. (26 Nm).

16. Apply 1052080 or equivalent sealer to the oil level indicator quide tube ½ inch (13mm) below the head. Install the level indicator and guide tube into the block.

17. Install the front spark plug bracket and bolt. Tighten to 105 inch lbs. (12 Nm).

18. Install the spark plugs and tighten to 11 ft. lbs. (15 Nm).

19. Install the spark plug wires and clips.

20. Install the fuel injectors and fuel rail to the intake manifold. Tighten the fuel rail bolts to 15 ft. lbs. (20 Nm).

21. Connect the fuel pressure regulator vacuum hose.

22. Connect the wiring harness connectors to the fuel injectors.

23. Install the fuel rail covers.

24. Raise and support the vehicle safely. Connect the catalytic converter and nuts to the exhaust manifold.

25. Tighten catalytic converter nuts to 15 ft. lbs. (21 Nm) and lower the vehicle.

26. Connect the negative battery cable.

LEFT SIDE

1. Disconnect the negative battery cable.

2. Raise and support the vehicle safely. Disconnect the catalytic converter from the exhaust manifold and lower the vehicle.

3. Remove the air intake duct and the serpentine drive belt.

4. Remove the left wheel well center panel.

5. Disconnect the air conditioning compressor/alternator top brace, then diconnect the compressor and position aside.

6. Remove the AIR pipe, check valve and hose as an assembly from the exhaust manifold.

7. Remove the spark plug wires

from the plugs and the clips from the supports, then position the wires aside.

8. Remove the accessory braces.

9. Remove the spark plug wire supports and the spark plugs.

10. Remove the exhaust manifold studs and bolts.

11. Remove the heat shields, exhaust manifold and gasket.

To install:

12. Thoroughly clean the manifold and cylinder head gasket mating surfaces.

13. Install the exhaust manifold gasket, manifold and heat shields.

14. Install the exhaust manifold studs and bolts. Tighten to 26 ft. lbs. (35 Nm).

15. Install the spark plugs and tighten to 11 ft. lbs. (15 Nm).

16. Install the spark plug wire supports and tighten to 105 inch lbs. (12 Nm).

17. Install the accessory braces to the manifold.

18. Connect the spark plug wires and clips.

19. Install the AIR pipe, check valve and hose assembly. Tighten the AIR pipe fitting to manifold and the bracket bolt to 25 ft. lbs. (34 Nm).

20. Install the air conditioning compressor and the compressor/alternator top brace.

21. Install the left wheel well center panel.

22. Install the serpentine drive belt and the air intake duct.

23. Raise and support the vehicle safely and install the catalytic converter to the manifold.

24. Tighten the converter nuts to 15 ft. lbs. (21 Nm) and lower the vehicle.

25. Connect the negative battery cable.

5.7L (VIN J) Engine
RIGHT SIDE

1. Disconnect the negative battery cable, then raise and support the vehicle safely.

2. Remove the wheel house lower rear and center panels.

3. For vehicles up until early 1992, remove the center stud nut.

4. For late 1992 and later vehicles, remove the manifold outer heat shields.

5. Disconnect the exhaust system assembly from the catalytic converter.

6. If equipped, remove the engine block heat shield.

7. For late 1992 and later vehicles, disconnect the catalytic converter from the manifold.

8. Disconnect the oxygen sensor electrical connector. To gain access to the connector, it may be necessary to perform the following steps:

a. Remove the bolts located at the right front of the oil pan, attaching the ignition timing sensor/oxygen sensor connector bracket.

b. Slide the connector bracket assembly to the rear.

9. For early 1992 vehicles, or as applicable, remove the catalytic converter heat shields.

10. Remove the rear exhaust manifold bolts, spacers and nut.

11. Lower the vehicle.

12. Disconnect the AIR check valve and hose from the manifold.

13. Remove the oil level indicator and guide tube from the vehicle.

14. Remove the remaining exhaust manifold attaching bolts and spacers.

15. Remove the exhaust manifold and gasket from the vehicle.

To install:

16. Thoroughly clean the manifold and cylinder head gasket mating surfaces.

17. Install the gasket and manifold to the engine using the front and center manifold bolts and spacers.

18. Install the oil level indicator and guide tube, then tighten the manifold bolts to 11 ft. lbs. (15 Nm) for 1990–91 vehicles or to 18 ft. lbs. (24 Nm) for 1992–93 vehicles.

19. Install the AIR check valve and hose.

20. Raise and safely support the vehicle.

21. Install the rear manifold bolts, spacers and nut. Tighten the bolts and nut to 18 ft. lbs. (24 Nm).

22. For early 1992 vehicles, or as applicable, install the catalytic converter heat shields.

23. Install the oxygen sensor connector.

24. For late 1992 and later vehicles, connect the catalytic converter and bolts to the manifold. Tighten the bolts to 17 ft. lbs. (23 Nm).

25. Install the engine block heat shield.

26. Connect the exhaust system assembly.

27. For late 1992 and later vehicles, install the manifold outer heat shields.

28. For vehicles up until early 1992, install the center stud nut and tighten to 11 ft. lbs. (15 Nm) for 1990–91 vehicles or to 18 ft. lbs. (24 Nm) for 1992 vehicles.

29. Install the wheelhouse lower rear and center panels.

30. Lower the vehicle and connect the negative battery cable.

LEFT SIDE

1. Disconnect the negative battery cable, then raise and support the vehicle safely.

2. Remove the wheelhouse lower rear and center panels.

3. Disconnect the exhaust assembly from the catalytic converter.

4. As applicable, remove the left floor pan heat shield and remove the heat shield from the frame and/or remove the engine block heat shield.

5. Disconnect the converter oxygen sensor electrical connector.

6. For vehicles up until early 1992, remove the screws attaching the converter heat shields, then remove the heat shield from the vehicle.

7. Disconnect the AIR check valves, hoses and pipes from the manifold.

8. For late 1992 and later vehicles, remove the manifold outer heat shield and remove the catalytic converter from the exhaust manifold.

9. Remove the exhaust manifold bolts, spacers and nut.

10. If applicable, remove the center stud nut.

11. Remove the manifold and gasket from the vehicle.

To install:

12. Thoroughly clean the manifold and cylinder head gasket mating surfaces.

13. Install the gasket and manifold to the engine.

14. Install the manifold bolts, spacer, nut, and if applicable, center stud nut. Tighten the bolts and nut(s) to 11 ft. lbs. (15 Nm) for 1990–91 vehicles or to 18 ft. lbs. (24 Nm) for 1992–93 vehicles.

15. For late 1992 and later vehicles, install the catalytic converter and bolts to the manifold. Tighten to 17 ft. lbs. (23 Nm) and install the manifold outer heat shield.

16. Install the AIR check valve, hoses and pipe.

17. For vehicles up until early 1992, install the converter heat shields.

18. Install the oxygen sensor connector.

19. If applicable, install the engine block heat shield and the left side heat shield to the frame and floor pan.

20. Install the exhaust system assembly to the catalytic converter.

21. Install the wheelhouse lower rear and center panels.

22. Lower the vehicle and connect the negative battery cable.

Timing Chain Front Cover
REMOVAL & INSTALLATION
5.7L (VIN 8) Engine

1. Disconnect the negative battery cable and properly relieve fuel system pressure.

2. Drain the engine coolant and remove the serpentine drive belt.

3. Remove the coolant pump damper.

4. Remove the crankshaft pulley.

5. Remove the power steering gear line.

6. Install tool J–23523 or equivalent harmonic balancer tool, onto the vibration damper assembly. Remove the vibration damper from the face of the crankcase front cover.

NOTE: The use of pullers, such as the universal claw type, that pull on the outside of the hub may damage the torsional damper. The outside ring of the damper is bonded to the hub with rubber. The use of the improper type puller may destroy this bond.

7. Raise and safely support the vehicle.

8. Drain the engine oil and remove the oil pan.

9. Lower the vehicle. Remove the AIR control valve, pipe and silencer as an assembly.

10. On 1989 vehicles, remove the AIR pump pulley, then remove the air pump retaining bolts and the air pump.

11. Disconnect the fuel inlet and return pipes.

12. Remove the air conditioner compressor mounting bracket.

13. Remove the water pump.

14. Remove the front timing cover retaining screws, then remove the front cover and discard the gasket.

To install:

15. Thoroughly clean the gasket mating surfaces on the cylinder block and front cover. Inspect the front cover for damage and distortion. Replace the front cover and/or the oil seal, as necessary.

16. With a suitable cutting tool, remove any excess gasket material that may be protruding at the oil pan to engine block surface.

17. Coat the new cover gasket with a suitable sealing compound and apply the gasket onto the front cover sealing surface.

18. Position the front cover and gasket onto the cylinder block surface so the dowels enter the holes in the cover without binding. Hold in place and install the cover retaining screws finger-tight.

19. Tighten the retaining screws evenly in an alternate pattern. While tightening the retaining screws, readjust the position of the front cover, as required, to ensure the cylinder block locating dowels are evenly aligned with the holes in the cover. Do not force the cover over the locating dowels.

20. When the front cover is properly in place, torque the retaining screws to 80 inch lbs. (9 Nm) on 1989 vehicles or 98 inch lbs. (11 Nm) on 1990–91 vehicles.

21. Install the water pump.

22. Install the compressor mounting bracket.

23. Connect the AIR hose to the right exhaust manifold and connect the fuel lines.

24. Connect the electrical connector to the compressor.

25. Install the AIR pump and pulley, if removed.

26. Install the AIR control valve, and/or the control valve, check valve pipe and silencer assembly.

27. Raise and support the vehicle safely.

28. Apply an even coating of GM sealant 1052080 or equivalent, about 1 inch in either direction at the front cover and cylinder block junctions. Also apply sealant where the rear retainer meets the case and install the oil pan gasket and oil pan.

29. Lower the vehicle.

30. Coat the vibration damper seal contact area with clean engine oil and place the damper in position over the crankshaft Woodruff key.

31. Install the appropriate threaded end of vibration damper tool J–23523 or equivalent, into the crankshaft. Be sure at least 0.5 inch (13mm) of thread engagement is obtained. Complete tool assembly and pull the damper into position.

32. Remove the tool from the crankshaft and install the crankshaft pulley.

33. For 1989 vehicles, install and tighten the damper bolt to 60 ft. lbs. (81 Nm). Then tighten the center pulley bolt to 70 ft. lbs. (95 Nm) and the outer bolts to 32 ft. lbs. (43 Nm).

34. For 1990–91 vehicles, tighten the crankshaft pulley bolts to 32 ft. lbs. (43 Nm) and then tighten the damper retaining bolt to 70 ft. lbs. (95 Nm).

35. Install the power steering gear cylinder line.

36. Install the water pump damper.

37. Install the serpentine drive belt and properly fill the engine crankcase with oil.

38. Tighten the fuel filler cap and connect the negative battery cable.

39. Properly fill the engine cooling system and check for leaks.

5.7L (VIN P) Engine

1. Disconnect the negative battery cable.

2. Drain the engine oil and engine coolant into suitable containers.

3. Remove the throttle body air intake duct.

4. Remove the serpentine drive belt.

5. Remove the water pump assembly.

6. Remove the torsional damper and the distributor.

7. Remove the oil pan assembly.

8. Remove the engine front cover bolts.

9. Remove the engine front cover and gasket.

To install:

10. Thoroughly clean the engine front cover and cylinder block gasket mating surfaces. Inspect the engine front cover and seals for damage, replace as necessary.

11. Using J–39087 or equivalent gear shaft front cover seal protector, install the gasket and front cover into position over the coolant pump drive shaft and the guide pins.

12. Install the engine front cover bolts and tighten to 100 inch lbs. (11 Nm).

13. Install the oil pan and gasket.

14. Install the distributor and the torsional damper.

1. Bolt
2. Washer
3. Pulley
4. Torsional damper
5. Front cover seal
6. Timing chain cover
7. Timing chain cover gasket

8. Engine block
9. Camshaft
10. Keys
11. Crankshaft
12. Camshaft retainer

13. Timing chain
14. Camshaft sprocket
15. Crankshaft sprocket
16. Pin

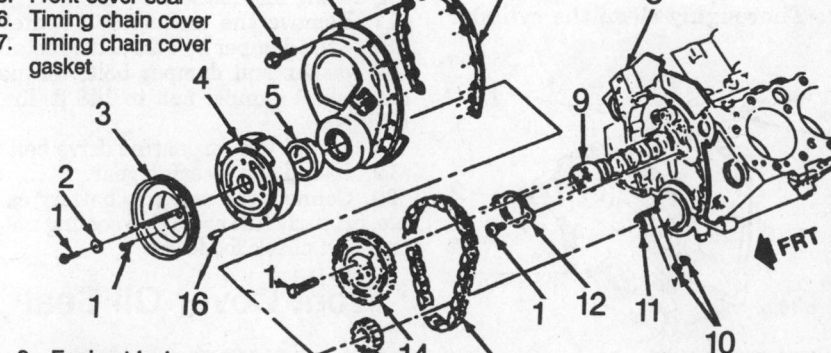

Timing chain, camshaft and front cover assembly—5.7L (VIN 8) Engine

15. Install the water pump.

16. Install the serpentine drive belt and the throttle body air duct.

17. Properly fill the engine crankcase with oil.

18. Tighten the fuel filler cap and properly fill the engine cooling system.

19. Connect the negative battery cable, operate the engine and check for leaks.

5.7L (VIN J) Engine

1. Disconnect the negative battery cable and drain the engine coolant into a suitable container.

2. Remove the water pump assembly.

3. Remove the air conditioning compressor as follows:

   a. Properly discharge the air conditioning system.

   b. Remove the throttle body.

   c. Remove the serpentine drive belt.

   d. Remove the engine oil temperature sensor.

   e. Remove the alternator.

   f. Remove the refrigerant hose from the A/C compressor, the immediately cap or plug the open lines.

   g. Remove the compressor mounting bolts and electrical connection.

   h. Remove the compressor from the vehicle.

4. Remove the steering gear.

5. Remove the bolt and washer attaching the torsional damper to the crankshaft.

6. Using tool J–24420–C or equivalent torsional damper puller, remove the torsional damper and drift key from the crankshaft.

7. Remove the front cover attaching bolts and, if equipped, nuts.

8. Remove the front cover and gasket from the vehicle. If necessary, remove the old seal from the front cover using J–29077-A or equivalent oil seal remover.

To install:

9. Thoroughly clean the cylinder

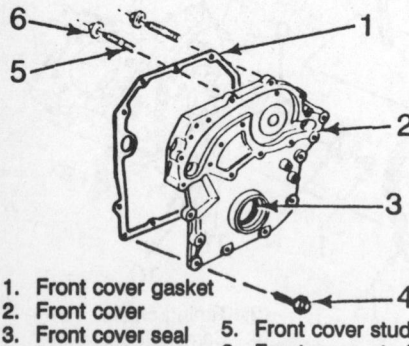

1. Front cover gasket
2. Front cover
3. Front cover seal
4. Front cover bolt
5. Front cover stud
6. Front cover stud nut

Front timing cover assembly–5.7L (VIN J) Engine

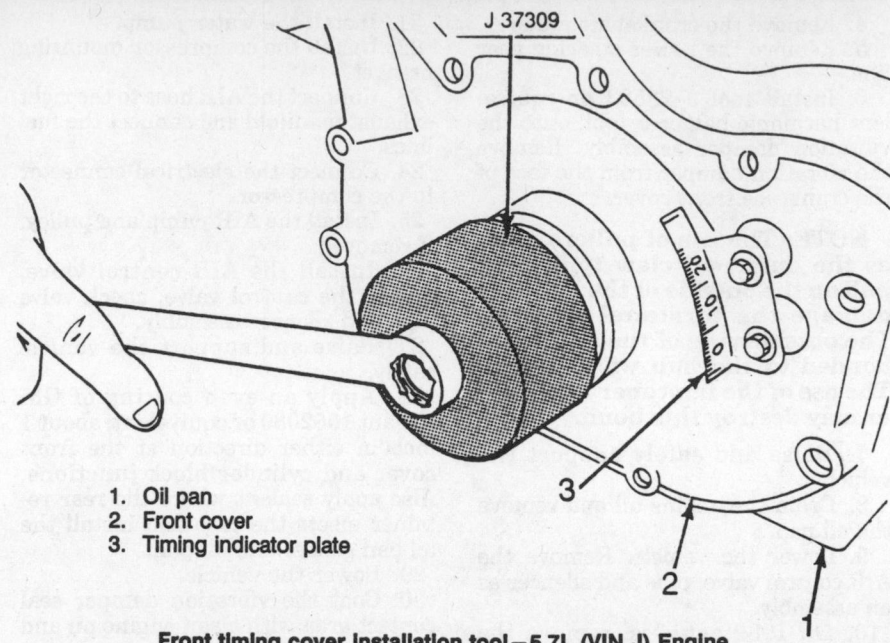

1. Oil pan
2. Front cover
3. Timing indicator plate

Front timing cover Installation tool–5.7L (VIN J) Engine

case, front cover and water pump sealing surfaces.

10. Apply Loctite® 262 to studs and Loctite® 565 to the bolt threads.

11. Install a new cover gasket and the cover, nuts and bolts.

12. Install a new front cover oil seal using J-37309 or equivalent front cover seal installer.

13. Tighten the front cover attaching bolts to 19 inch lbs. (26 Nm) and the stud nuts to 21 ft. lbs. (28 Nm).

14. Install the water pump assembly.

15. Install the air conditioning compressor in the reverse order of the removal procedure. Replace the refrigerant line seal washers and coat the new washers with 525 refrigerant oil prior to assembly. When installed, properly evacuate and charge the A/C system.

16. Install the key to the crankshaft and install the torsional damper using J-38463 or equivalent torsional damper installer. Check for proper key seating during installation.

17. Remove the tool apply Loctite® 262 to the damper bolt threads. Install the washer and damper bolt, torque crankshaft damper bolt to 148 ft. lbs. (200 Nm).

18. Install the serpentine drive belt.

19. Install the steering gear.

20. Connect the negative battery cable, properly fill the engine cooling system and check for leaks.

Front Cover Oil Seal

REPLACEMENT

5.7L (VIN 8) Engine

FRONT COVER REMOVED

1. Tap the old seal out of the front

cover from the rear, using an appropriate tool and being careful not to damage the cover.

2. Discard the old oil seal.

3. With a clean rag, ensure the front cover sealing surfaces are free from dirt and grease.

4. Support the rear of the front cover and position the new seal so the open end of the seal is toward the the inside of the front cover.

5. With tool J–35468 or equivalent seal installer, drive the new seal into the front cover. Visually inspect the seal to ensure it is seated evenly in the front cover.

FRONT COVER INSTALLED

1. Disconnect the negative battery cable.

2. Remove the serpentine drive belt.

3. Remove the water pump damper.

4. Remove the crankshaft pulley.

5. Remove the power steering gear cylinder line.

6. Install tool J–23523 or equivalent harmonic balancer tool, onto the vibration damper assembly. Remove the vibration damper from the face of the crankcase front cover.

NOTE: The use of pullers, such as the universal claw type, that pull on the outside of the hub may damage the torsional damper. The outside ring of the damper is bonded to the hub with rubber. The use of the improper type puller may destroy this bond.

7. Using the appropriate tool, pry the old seal from the front cover. Exercise caution when removing the seal to prevent damaging the front cover and crankshaft surfaces.

8. Discard the old oil seal.

9. With a clean rag, ensure the front cover sealing surfaces are free from dirt and grease.

10. With tool J-35468 or equivalent, drive the new seal into the front cover with the open end of the seal facing the inside of the cover. Visually inspect the seal to ensure it is seated evenly in the front cover.

11. Coat the vibration damper seal contact area with clean engine oil and place the damper in position over the crankshaft Woodruff key.

12. Install the appropriate threaded end of vibration damper tool J-23523 or equivalent, into the crankshaft. Be sure at least 0.5 inch (13 mm) of thread engagement is obtained. Complete tool assembly and pull the damper into position.

13. Remove the tool from the crankshaft and install the crankshaft pulley.

14. For 1989 vehicles, install and tighten the damper bolt to 60 ft. lbs. (81 Nm). Then tighten the center pulley bolt to 70 ft. lbs. (95 Nm) and the outer bolts to 32 ft. lbs. (43 Nm).

15. For 1990–91 vehicles, tighten the crankshaft pulley bolts to 32 ft. lbs. (43 Nm) and then tighten the damper retaining bolt to 70 ft. lbs. (95 Nm).

16. Install the power steering gear cylinder line.

17. Install the water pump damper.

18. Install the serpentine drive belt and connect the negative battery cable.

5.7L (VIN P) Engine

1. Disconnect the battery negative cable.

2. Remove the engine front cover.

3. Using a suitable tool, remove the crankshaft, distributor shaft and/or water pump driven gear shaft seals, as necessary.

4. As applicable; use tool J-35468 or equivalent aligner and installer, to intall the crankshaft seal, tool J-39090 or equivalent driveshaft seal installer, to install the distributor shaft seal and/or tool J-39088 or equivalent driven gear shaft seal installer, to install the water pump shaft seal.

5. Install the engine front cover.

6. Connect the negative battery cable.

5.7L (VIN J) Engine

1. Disconnect the battery negative cable.

2. Remove the timing chain front cover assembly.

3. Remove the seal from the front cover using tool J-29077-A or equivalent seal remover.

4. Thoroughly clean the cylinder case, front cover and water pump sealing surfaces.

5. Apply Loctite® 262 to studs and Loctite® 565 to the bolt threads.

6. Install a new cover gasket and the cover, nuts and bolts.

7. Install the new seal coated with engine oil using tool J–37309 or equivalent.

NOTE: Do not remove seal installing tool J–37309, until the front cover bolts are torqued.

8. Tighten the front cover attaching bolts to 19 inch lbs. (26 Nm) and the stud nuts to 21 ft. lbs. (28 Nm).

9. Complete the front cover installation procedure and connect the negative battery cable.

Timing Chain and Sprockets

REMOVAL & INSTALLATION

5.7L (VIN 8) Engine

1. Disconnect the negative battery cable.

2. Remove the timing chain front cover.

3. Rotate the crankshaft and align the timing marks.

4. Remove the camshaft sprocket mounting bolts.

5. Remove the camshaft gear and the timing chain.

6. Remove the damper key from the crankshaft and using a suitable puller, carefully remove the crankshaft sprocket.

To install:

7. Inspect the keyway surface for excessive wear or rounding and the crankshaft and camshaft sprocket for chipped, missing and cracked teeth. Replace all damaged parts.

8. Install the crankshaft timing sprocket Woodruff key.

9. Install the crankshaft sprocket using a suitable installation tool.

10. Place the camshaft sprocket on the dowel and temporarily secure with a finger-tight bolt. Align the timing marks on the 2 timing chain sprockets by slightly rotating the camshaft or crankshaft as necessary, then remove the camshaft sprocket.

11. Install the timing chain and camshaft sprocket assembly with the timing marks aligned.

12. Install the camshaft sprocket bolts and tighten to 20 ft. lbs. (27 Nm).

13. Lubricate the timing chain and sprockets with clean engine oil.

14. Install the timing chain front cover.

15. Connect the negative battery cable.

5.7L (VIN P) Engine

1. Disconnect the negative battery cable.

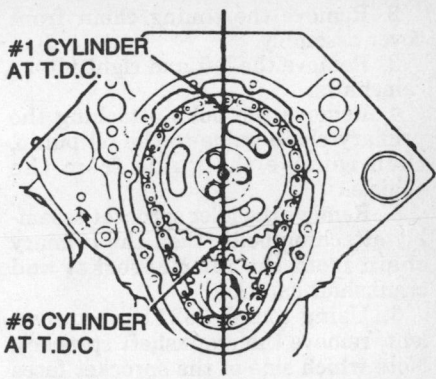

Timing mark alignment—5.7L (VIN 8 and VIN P) Engines

2. Remove the timing chain front cover.

3. Rotate the crankshaft until the timing marks on the timing chain sprockets are aligned.

4. Remove the camshaft sprocket bolts.

5. Remove the camshaft sprocket and timing chain.

NOTE: Do not turn the crankshaft after the timing chain has been removed to prevent piston or valve damage.

6. Remove the water pump driven gear bolts, then remove the gear using J-39243 or equivalent gear assembly remover.

7. Remove the crankshaft sprocket using J-5825-A or equivalent crankshaft remover.

8. If necessary, remove the crankshaft key.

To install:

9. If removed, install the crankshaft key.

10. Install the crankshaft sprocket using a suitable installation tool.

11. Install the water pump driven gear with a suitable tool. Install the gear bolts and tighten to 105 inch lbs. (12 Nm).

12. Align the timing marks and install the camshaft sprocket and timing chain. The gears must mesh or damage to the thrust plate retainer could occur.

13. Install the camshaft sprocket bolts and tighten to 21 ft. lbs. (28 Nm).

14. Install a new ring to the water pump driven gear shaft using a suitable tool.

15. Install the timing chain front cover and connect the negative battery cable.

5.7L (VIN J) Engine

PRIMARY TIMING CHAIN AND CRANKSHAFT SPROCKET

1. Disconnect battery negative cable.

2. Remove the timing chain front cover assembly.

3. Remove the left and right intake camshafts.

4. Remove the bolts attaching the primary chain guide to the oil pump, then remove the guide from the vehicle.

5. Remove the idler sprocket assembly attaching bolts, then the primary chain from the idler sprocket and crankshaft sprocket.

6. Using tool J–38211 or equivalent, remove the crankshaft sprocket. Note which side of the sprocket faces forward for installation purposes.

7. Remove the key and oil pump seal seat from the crankshaft.

To install:

8. Inspect the primary chain guide for excessive wear. Wear groove should not exceed a depth of 0.040 inch (1.0mm). If necessary, replace wear strip.

9. Inspect the primary chain and sprocket for wear or damage. If abnormal wear or damage is present on the sprocket, chain or crankshaft sprocket, all 3 must be replaced as an assembly.

10. Install oil pump seal seat and key onto the crankshaft.

11. Install the crankshaft sprocket using J–38132 or equivalent installer. Make sure sprocket is installed with same side to the front as noted during removal, this should be the wide shoulder.

12. Engage the primary chain onto the idler and crankshaft sprockets.

13. Apply Loctite® 262 to the idler sprocket assembly bolts and tighten to 19 ft. lbs. (26 Nm).

14. Apply Loctite® 262 to the primary chain guide bolts. Install the guide and bolts. Push the guide so the slack is removed from the chain and tighten the bolts to 89 inch lbs. (10 Nm).

NOTE: When installing guide, do not use any leverage tools, finger pressure is sufficient.

15. Install the left and right intake camshafts.

16. Install the timing chain front cover.

17. Connect the negative battery cable.

SECONDARY TIMING CHAINS AND IDLER SPROCKET ASSEMBLY

1. Disconnect battery negative cable.

2. Remove the camshafts.

3. Remove the primary timing chain and crankshaft sprocket.

4. Disengage the left and right secondary chains from the idler sprocket.

5. Remove the idler sprocket assembly.

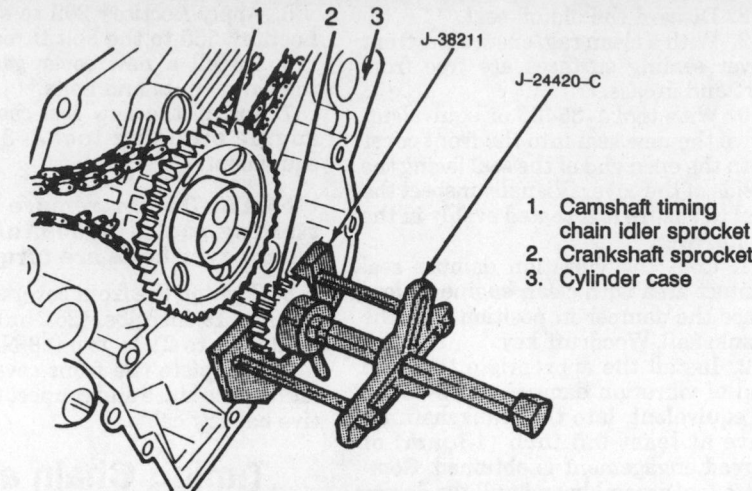

1. Camshaft timing chain idler sprocket
2. Crankshaft sprocket
3. Cylinder case

Crankshaft sprocket removal—5.7L (VIN J) Engine

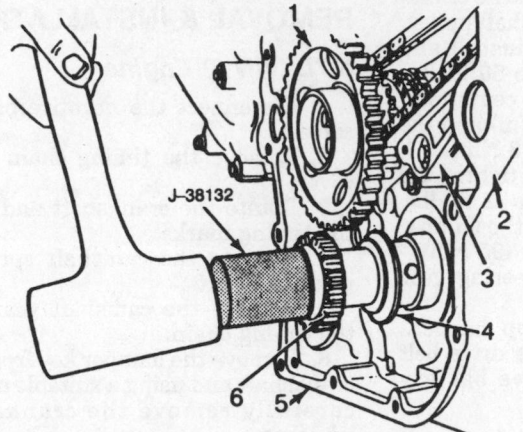

1. Camshaft timing chain idler sprocket
2. Cylinder case
3. Camshaft secondary timing chain fixed left side guide
4. Oil pump seal seat
5. Crankcase
6. Crankshaft sprocket

Crankshaft sprocket installation—5.7L (VIN J) Engine

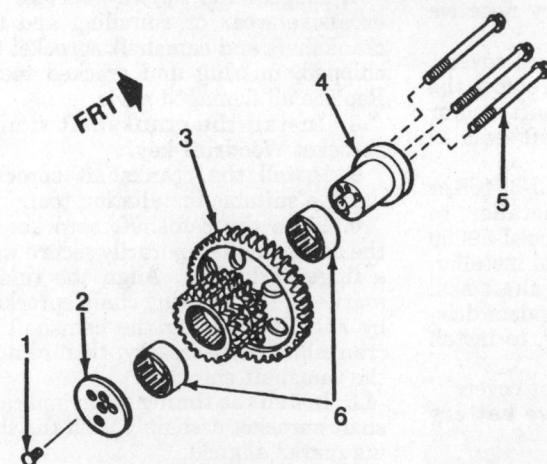

1. Camshaft idler sprocket assembly screw
2. Camshaft timing chain idler sprocket washer
3. Camshaft timing chain idler sprocket
4. Camshaft timing chain idler sprocket shaft
5. Camshaft idler sprocket bolt
6. Camshaft idler sprocket bolt
7. Camshaft timing chain idler sprocket bearing

Timing chain idler sprocket assembly—5.7L (VIN J) Engine

6. Remove the left and right secondary chains from the vehicle.

To install:

7. Inspect chains and sprockets for abnormal wear or damage. If abnormal wear or damage is present on either the secondary timing chain, cam sprockets or idler sprockets, the entire assembly must be replaced.

8. Inspect the idler sprocket shaft bearings for wear or damage. If necessary, replace idler sprocket shaft bearings as follows:

a. Using tool J–37328 or equivalent, remove bearings from idler sprocket.

b. When installing bearings, ensure the manufacture's name and

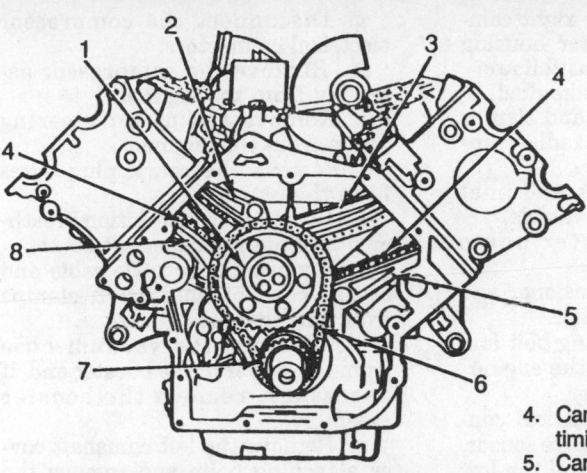

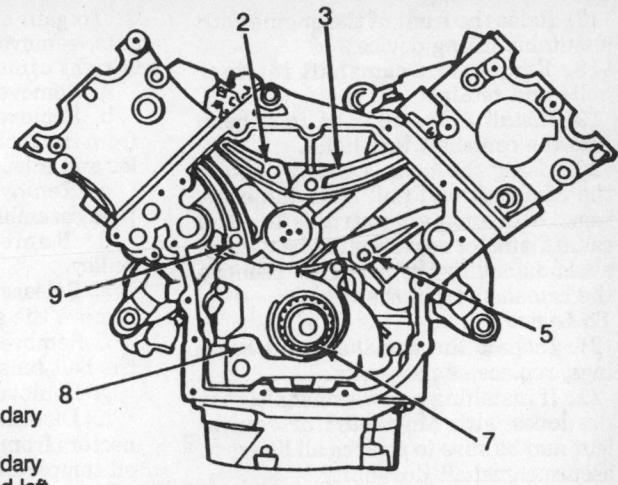

1. Camshaft timing chain idler sprocket assembly
2. Camshaft secondary timing chain fixed right side guide
3. Camshaft secondary timing chain pivot left side guide
4. Camshaft secondary timing chain
5. Camshaft secondary timing chain fixed left side guide
6. Camshaft primary timing chain
7. Crankshaft sprocket
8. Oil pump
9. Camshaft timing chain pivot right side guide

Primary and secondary timing assembly—5.7L (VIN J) Engine

part No. are visible from either end of the sprocket assembly.

c. Using a suitable press, press in bearings until bearings are flush with idler sprocket. Apply minimum pressure to obtain a fit 0.0–1.3mm below the surface.

9. Install the shorter (inner) secondary chain through the right head and install J-38099 or equivalent timing chain retaining tool.

10. Locate the right chain onto the rear idler sprocket.

11. Install the longer (outer) secondary chain through the left head and install J-38099 or equivalent timing chain retaining tool.

12. Locate the left chain onto the middle idler sprocket.

13. Install the primary timing chain.

14. Install the camshafts.

15. Connect the negative battery cable.

Camshaft

REMOVAL & INSTALLATION

5.7L (VIN 8) Engine

1. Disconnect the negative battery cable and properly relieve fuel system pressure.

2. Drain the engine cooling system and properly discharge the air conditioning system.

3. Remove the radiator.

4. Reposition the accumulator assembly and/or the fan assembly as necessary, and remove the condenser.

5. Align the timing marks on the crankshaft pulley and timing chain cover to the **TDC** position or 0 mark. Mark and remove the distributor assembly.

6. Remove the intake manifold assembly.

7. Remove the valve rockers arm assemblies.

8. Remove the valve lifters.

9. Remove the timing chain front cover and the timing chain.

10. Remove the camshaft retainer bolts and retainer.

11. Carefully pull the camshaft from the block. Be sure to rotate and support the camshaft as it is drawn from the block. If necessary, temporarily reinstall the camshaft gear to help rotate the camshaft.

To install:

12. Using a micrometer, check the camshaft bearing journals for an out-of-round condition. If journals exceed 0.001 in. out-of-round, the camshaft should be replaced.

13. Inspect the camshaft bearings for wear or damage. Replace as necessary.

NOTE: When installing a new camshaft, coat camshaft lobes and distributor gear with Molykote®, 12345501 or equivalent pre-lube.

14. Lubricate the camshaft journals with clean engine oil and install the camshaft into the block.

15. Install the timing chain and the timing chain front cover.

16. Install the valve lifters. If installing a new camshaft, install new lifters.

17. Install the rocker arm assemblies.

18. Install the intake manifold and the distributor assembly.

19. Install the air conditioning condenser and secure the accumulator assembly and/or the fan assembly, as applicable.

20. Install the radiator assembly.

21. If a new camshaft was installed, change the engine oil and filter.

22. Tighten the fuel filler cap and connect the negative battery cable.

23. Properly fill the engine cooling system and check for leaks.

24. Properly evacuate and recharge the air conditioning system.

5.7L (VIN P) Engine

1. Disconnect battery negative cable and remove the air cleaner assembly.

2. Remove the timing chain front cover.

3. Remove the intake manifold.

4. Remove the retaining bolt and lift the oil pump driveshaft assembly from the rear of the lifter valley.

5. Remove the rocker arm and pushrod assemblies.

6. Remove the valve lifters.

7. Remove the high fill reservoir from the radiator.

8. Remove the relay bracket from the left side of the radiator support.

9. Remove the AIR pump intake duct and bolts, then reposition the AIR pump.

10. Remove the retaining nuts and screws, then remove the radiator support.

11. Remove the radiator.

12. Raise and support the vehicle safely.

13. Disconnect the cooling fan electrical connectors.

14. Remove the lower fan shroud bolts and lower the vehicle.

15. Remove the fan shroud and fan assembly.

16. Disconnect the A/C condenser line bracket at the front crossmember.

17. Raise the front of the engine with a suitable lifting device.
18. Remove the camshaft retainer bolts and retainer.
19. Install 3 $^{5}/_{16}$–18 × 4 inch bolts into the camshaft bolt holes.
20. Using the bolts, carefully rotate the camshaft and pull from the bearings. All camshaft journals are the same diameter so care must be used to avoid damaging the bearings. Remove the camshaft from the vehicle.

To install:
21. Inspect the camshaft and bearings, replace as necessary.
22. If installing a new camshaft, coat the lobes with Molykote® or equivalent and be sure to replace all lifters to assure camshaft durability.
23. Lubricate all camshaft journals with clean engine oil and carefully insert the camshaft into the engine block.
24. Install the camshaft retainer and tighten the bolts to 105 inch lbs. (12 Nm).
25. Lower the front of the engine and connect the A/C condenser line bracket to the front crossmember.
26. Install the fan and shroud assembly.
27. Raise and support the vehicle safely, then install the lower fan shroud bolts.
28. Connect the cooling fan electrical connections and lower the vehicle.
29. Install the radiator, upper radiator support, nuts and screws.
30. Install the AIR pump, bolts and intake duct.
31. Install the relay bracket to the left side of the radiator support and the high fill reservoir to the radiator.
32. Install the valve lifters.
33. Install the camshaft sprocket.
34. Install the valve rocker arm and pushrod assemblies.
35. Install the oil pump driveshaft assembly and bolt. Tighten the bolt to 13 ft. lbs. (18 Nm).
36. Install the intake manifold.
37. Install the timing chain front cover.
38. Install the air cleaner assembly and connect the negative battery cable.

5.7L (VIN J) Engine

The VIN J engine utilizes 4 overhead camshafts. Certain shafts will have identifying bands between the first journal and lobe to distinguish between the right and left, intake and exhaust camshafts. The right intake has 1 flat band. The right exhaust has 1 raised band. The left intake has 1 flat and 1 raised band. The left exhaust has 2 raised bands.
1. Disconnect battery negative cable and drain the engine coolant into a suitable container.

2. To gain access to the right camshafts, remove the oil filter housing and right camshaft cover as follows:
   a. Remove the air intake duct.
   b. Remove the hoses and clamps from the coolant outlets, radiator inlet and inlet pipe.
   c. Remove the hoses and inlet pipe assembly from the vehicle.
   d. Remove the water pump pulley.
   e. Release the belt tensioner and remove the serpentine belt.
   f. Remove the retaining bolt and the belt tensioner from the engine.
   g. Remove the oil filter.
   h. Disconnect the electrical connectors from the oil pressure sensor, oil temperature sensor and the low oil pressure switch.
   i. Remove the oil pressure sensor from the oil filter housing.
   j. Remove the alternator bracket from the oil filter housing.
   k. Disconnect and plug the oil cooler lines from the filter housing.
   l. Remove the oil filter housing mounting bolts and remove the assembly.

NOTE: If equipped with a 1 piece front cover/oil filter housing gasket, cut the old gasket along the front cover.

   m. Remove spark plug wires from plugs.
   n. Disconnect the electrical connector from the blower motor resistor block.
   o. Remove the screws attaching the evaporator housing quarter panel, then remove the panel.
   p. Remove the bolts attaching the coolant outlet pipe bracket to the alternator bracket and the pipe to the injector housing, then position aside.
   q. Remove the bolt attaching the fresh air pipe bracket to the injector housing.
   r. Remove the camshaft cover attaching bolts and the camshaft cover.
3. To gain access to the left camshafts, remove the air conditioning compressor and left valve cover as follows:
   a. Properly discharge the air conditioning system.
   b. Remove the throttle body assembly and the serpentine drive belt.
   c. Remove the engine oil temperature sensor.
   d. Remove the alternator assembly.
   e. Disconnect and plug the refrigerant hose from the rear of the compressor.
   f. Remove the compressor mounting bolts.

   g. Disconnect the compressor electrical connectors.
   h. Remove the compressor assembly from the engine.
   i. Remove the power steering pump from the engine.
   j. Remove the spark plug wires from the plugs.
   k. Remove the ventilation breather pipe from the camshaft cover.
   l. Remove the throttle cable and cruise control hold-down clamps from the plenum.
   m. Remove the vacuum hose from the power brake booster and, if necessary, remove the booster assembly.
   n. Remove the left camshaft cover attaching bolts and remove the cover.
4. Raise and support the vehicle safely.
5. Disconnect the electrical connector from the crankshaft ignition timing sensor.
6. Remove the ignition timing sensor from the cylinder case.
7. Install crankshaft timing slot locator tool J–38098 or equivalent, into the ignition timing sensor opening. Make sure the tool head is fully seated with the indicating pin inserted in deep notch of the crankshaft timing disc.
8. Lower vehicle.
9. Remove the bolts attaching the secondary timing chain tensioner housing to the cylinder head, then remove the O-ring and tensioner from the cylinder case.
10. Remove the bolts and washers attaching the camshaft to the sprockets.

NOTE: Install a wrench on the rear camshaft hex when removing the sprocket bolts, to prevent the camshafts from exerting force on the crankshaft timing slot locator tool J–38098.

11. Remove the camshaft timing plates and pins.
12. Remove the camshaft retainers and thrust washers.
13. Remove the camshafts and sprockets from the vehicle. Install timing chain retainers J–38099 or equivalent, to retain secondary chain loops.
14. Remove lifters from bores and inspect. Make sure any lifters, to be reused, are retained in proper order so each one can be returned to its original bore.

To install:
15. Inspect the camshaft bearing journals for wear or damage.
16. Inspect the camshaft bearing surfaces in the cylinder head and camshaft cover for wear or damage.

NOTE: The camshaft cover and cylinder head must be replaced as

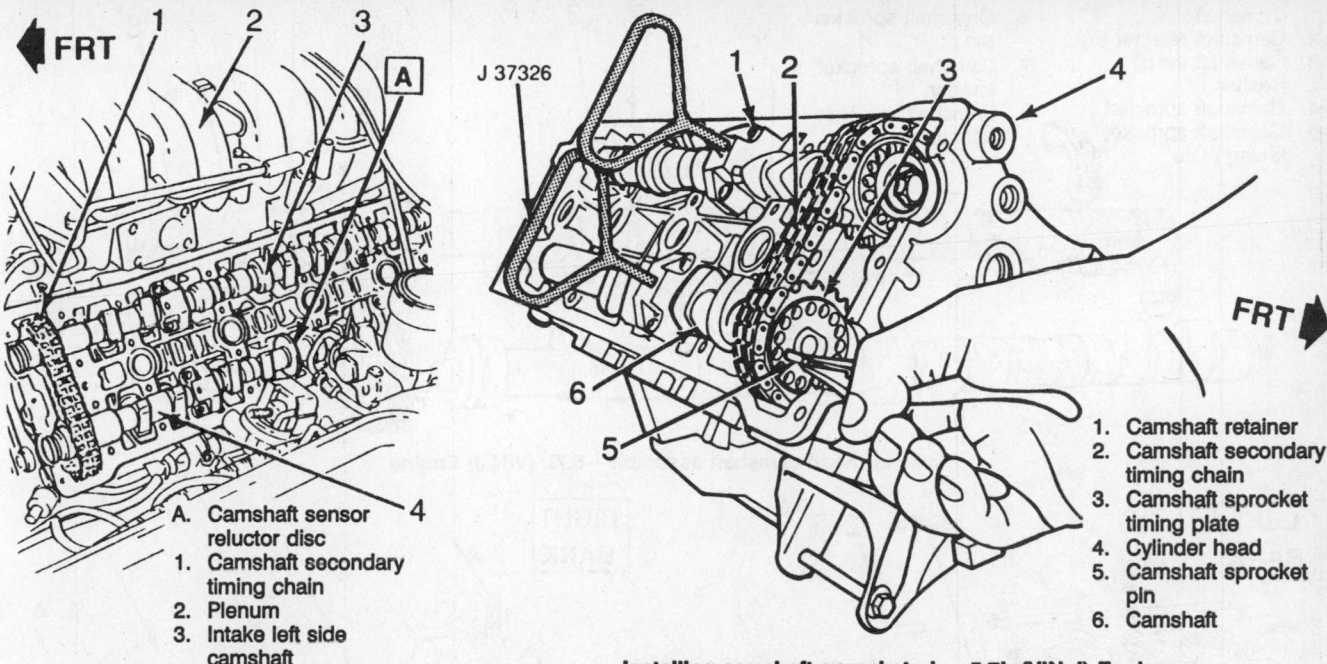

FRT

A

J 37326

FRT

A. Camshaft sensor
   reluctor disc
1. Camshaft secondary
   timing chain
2. Plenum
3. Intake left side
   camshaft
4. Exhaust left side
   camshaft

1. Camshaft retainer
2. Camshaft secondary
   timing chain
3. Camshaft sprocket
   timing plate
4. Cylinder head
5. Camshaft sprocket
   pin
6. Camshaft

**Camshaft assembly–left cylinder
pictured–5.7L (VIN J) Engine**

Installing camshaft sprocket pin–5.7L (VIN J) Engine

**a set if excessive wear or damage
to the bearing surfaces is found.**

17. Lubricate lifters and bores with
clean engine oil, then install lifters
into bores. If a camshaft is replaced,
new lifters must also be used.

18. Install the camshaft sprocket
onto the secondary timing chain, while
removing the timing chain retainers
J–38099.

19. Slide the camshaft into the
sprocket, noting the position of the
alignment hole for timing pin tool in-

stallation. Position the camshaft in
the neutral position, no valves opened.

20. Lubricate camshaft journals,
lobes, thrust washers and retainers
with clean engine oil.

21. Install the camshaft thrust washers, retainers and bolts. Torque bolts
to 89 inch lbs. (10 Nm).

22. Repeat steps 15–21 for the remaining camshafts.

23. Install timing pins J–37326 into
camshaft retainers and indexing holes
in camshafts. Camshafts can be rotated using the cast hex at the camshaft
rear.

24. Install camshaft secondary chain
pre-tensioner J–37305 or equivalent.

Hand tighten to remove slack from the
timing chain.

25. Install timing plates, pins and
washers. If no holes line up on the timing plate, reverse the plate.

26. Install new bolts finger-tight.
New camshaft bolts should be used
each time the camshaft is removed.

27. Apply Loctite® 262 on the camshaft sprocket bolts, install the bolts
and tighten to 18 ft. lbs. (25 Nm) and
turn 80–85 degrees using torque angle
meter J–36660 or equivalent. A backup wrench should be used on the rear
camshaft hex.

28. Remove timing pins J–37326.

29. Remove the secondary timing

4   J 38098

KNOB IS FULLY SEATED WHEN DEEP
NOTCH IS LOCATED

1. Cylinder head
2. Cylinder case
3. Crankcase
4. Oil pan

KNOB IS
UNSEATED WHEN
PIN IS NOT IN
DEEP NOTCH

4   J 38098

FRT

Crankshaft timing slot locator tool–5.7L (VIN J) Engine

1. Camshaft
2. Camshaft retainer
3. Camshaft thrust washer
4. Camshaft sprocket
5. Camshaft sprocket timing plate
6. Camshaft sprocket pin
7. Camshaft sprocket washer
8. Camshaft sprocket washer

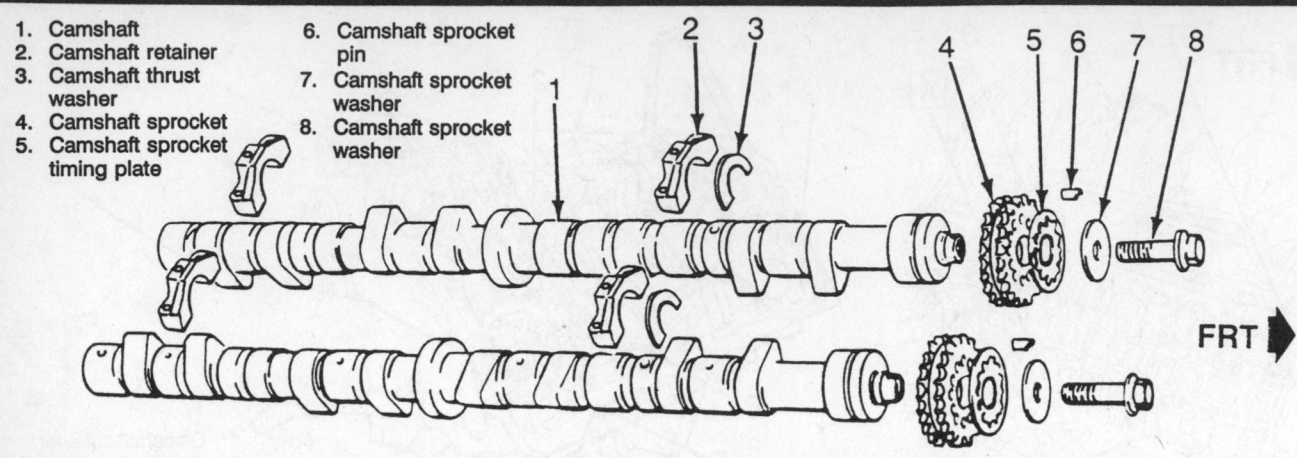

Cylinder head camshaft assembly—5.7L (VIN J) Engine

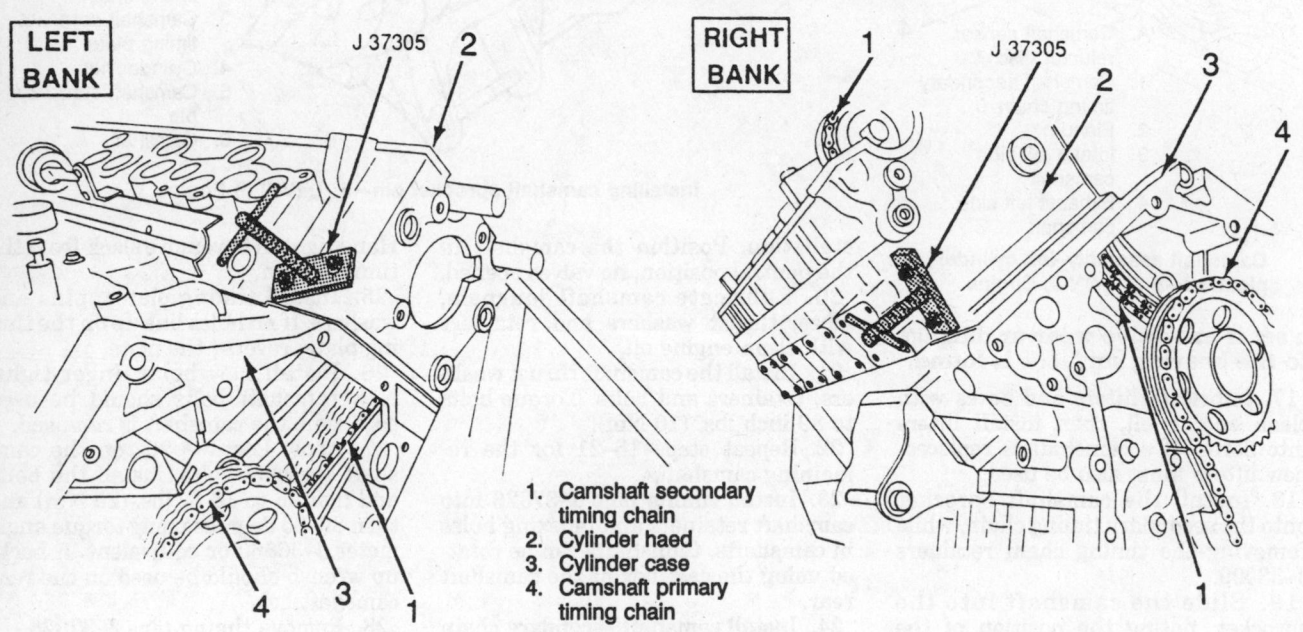

1. Camshaft secondary timing chain
2. Cylinder haed
3. Cylinder case
4. Camshaft primary timing chain

Camshaft chain pretensioner tool—5.7L (VIN J) Engine

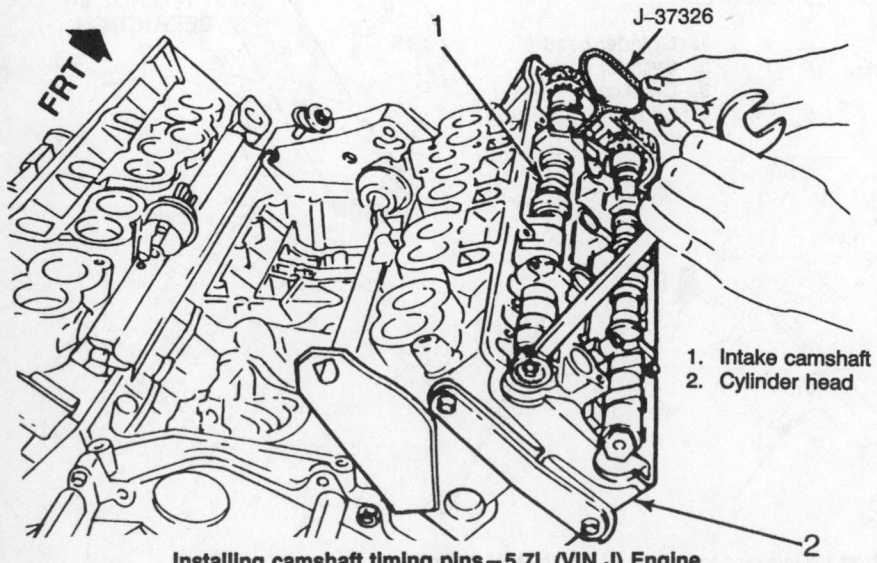

1. Intake camshaft
2. Cylinder head

Installing camshaft timing pins—5.7L (VIN J) Engine

chain pre-tensioner tool and install the new secondary timing chain tensioner, housing, new O-ring and bolts. Lubricate tensioner with engine oil.

30. Ensure that oil hole in tensioner piston be installed in a vertical position and that the fork on the end of the tensioner is properly engaged onto the chain guide. After installing, use a blunt punch to release the plunger.

31. Torque chain tensioner bolts to 89 inch lbs. (10 Nm).

32. Raise and support the vehicle safely.

33. Remove crankshaft timing slot locator J-38098 from the cylinder case.

34. Install the ignition timing sensor into the cylinder case and tighten the bolts to 71 inch lbs. (8 Nm).

35. Connect timing sensor electrical connector and lower the vehicle.

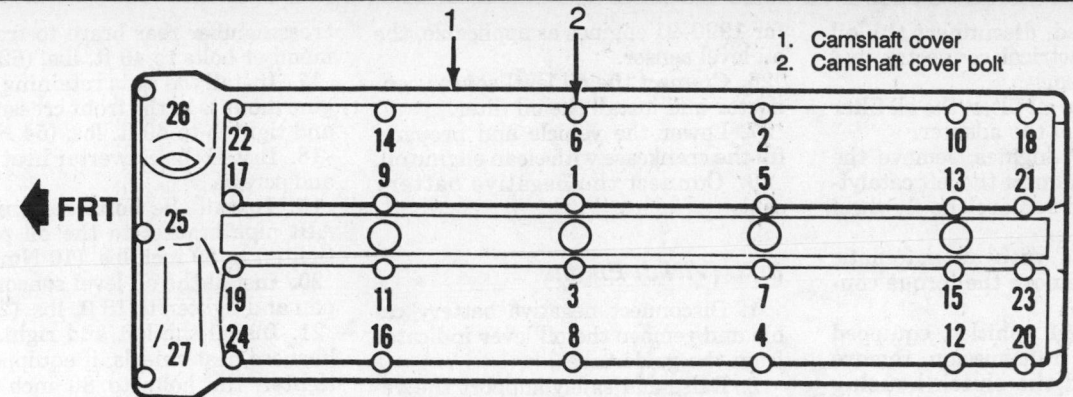

1. Camshaft cover
2. Camshaft cover bolt

Valve cover torque sequence—5.7L (VIN J) Engine

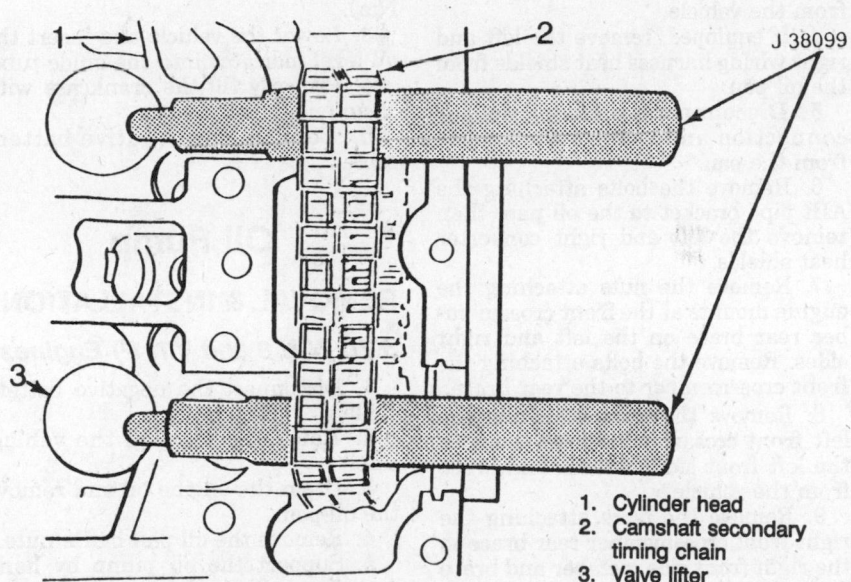

J 38099

1. Cylinder head
2. Camshaft secondary timing chain
3. Valve lifter

Secondary timing chain retainers—5.7L (VIN J) Engine

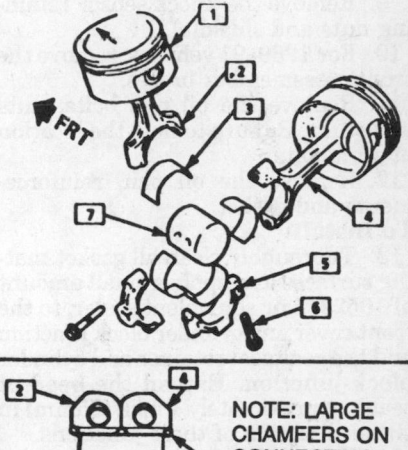

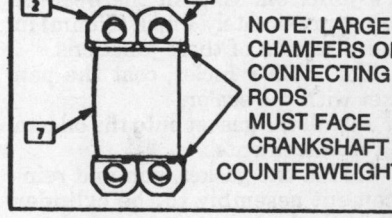

NOTE: LARGE CHAMFERS ON CONNECTING RODS MUST FACE CRANKSHAFT COUNTERWEIGHTS

1. Piston
2. LH Connecting rod
3. Connecting rod bearing
4. RH connecting rod
5. Connecting rod bearing cap
6. Connecting rod bearing cap bolt
7. Crankshaft

Piston assembly—1990–93 Engines

36. Apply Permabond® A136 to the camshaft covers and Loctite® 565 to the end plugs. Install the end plugs and new spark plug bore O-rings in place prior to cover installation.

37. Install the camshaft covers in the reverse order of removal. Tighten the M8 bolts to 15 ft. lbs. (20 Nm), repeat 3 times. Tighten the M6 screws to 89 inch lbs. (10 Nm). Also, be sure to install a new coolant outlet cover gasket and tighten the cover screws to 89 inch lbs. (10 Nm).

38. For the right bank camshafts, install oil filter housing assembly.

39. For the left bank camshafts, install the air conditioning compressor assembly.

40. Reconnect the battery negative cable and properly fill the engine cooling system.

Piston and Connecting Rod

POSITIONING

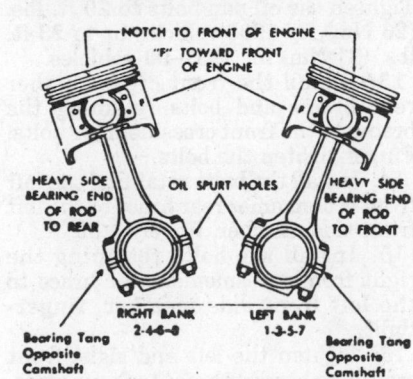

NOTCH TO FRONT OF ENGINE
"F" TOWARD FRONT OF ENGINE

HEAVY SIDE BEARING END OF ROD TO REAR

OIL SPURT HOLES

HEAVY SIDE BEARING END OF ROD TO FRONT

RIGHT BANK 2-4-6-8

LEFT BANK 1-3-5-7

Bearing Tang Opposite Camshaft

Bearing Tang Opposite Camshaft

Piston assembly—1989 5.7L (VIN 8) Engine

ENGINE LUBRICATION

Oil Pan

REMOVAL & INSTALLATION

5.7L (VIN 8 and VIN P) Engines

1. Disconnect the negative battery cable.
2. Raise and safely support the vehicle, then drain the engine oil.

3. If equipped, disconnect the oil level sensor electrical connector and remove the sensor.

4. Remove the oil filter, the oil filter adapter bolts and the adapter.

5. On VIN P engines, remove the starter and disconnect the left catalytic converter and remove the flywheel cover.

6. If equipped with an automatic transmission, remove the torque converter cover.

7. For 1989–91 vehicles, equipped with a manual transmission, remove the starter and the clutch housing cover.

8. For 1989–91 vehicles, disconnect the oil cooler pipe at the oil pan.

9. Remove the knock sensor retaining nuts and shield(s).

10. For 1989–91 vehicles, remove the front crossmember braces.

11. Remove the oil pan bolts, nuts and studs. Be sure to note the location of stud bolts.

12. Remove the oil pan, reinforcements and gasket.

To install:

13. Thoroughly clean all gasket mating surfaces and apply a small amount of 1052914 or equivalent sealer, to the front cover and cylinder block junction and the rear seal retainer and cylinder block junction. Extend the bead of sealer approximately 1 inch (25mm) in either direction of these junctions.

14. For 1989 vehicles, coat the pan gasket with the sealer.

15. Install the gasket onto the oil pan and reinforcements.

16. Install the gasket, pan and reinforcement assembly to the cylinder block with the bolts, studs and nuts.

17. For 1989 vehicles, tighten the bolts to 16 ft. lbs. (22 Nm). For 1990–91 vehicles, tighten the left and right front 2 pan bolts and the rear pan nuts to 16 ft. lbs (22 Nm), then the remaining bolts to 8 ft. lbs (11 Nm). For 1992–93 vehicles, tighten the corner bolts or stud and nuts to 17 ft. lbs. (23 Nm) and the remainder of the bolts and studs to 8 ft. lbs. (11 Nm).

18. For 1989–91 vehicles, install the front crossmember brace.

19. For VIN P engines, install the oil level sensor and tighten to 16 ft. lbs. (22 Nm).

20. Install the knock sensor shield(s).

21. For 1989–91 vehicles, connect the oil cooler line to the oil pan.

22. If applicable, install the clutch housing cover.

23. For 1989–91 vehicles, install the starter and, if required, the torque converter cover.

24. For VIN P engines, install the flywheel cover, connect the left catalytic converter and install the starter.

25. Install the oil filter adapter and, for 1990–91 engines as applicable, the oil level sensor.

26. Connect the oil level sensor connector and install the oil filter.

27. Lower the vehicle and properly fill the crankcase with clean engine oil.

28. Connect the negative battery cable.

5.7L (VIN J) Engine

1. Disconnect negative battery cable and remove the oil lever indicator from the guide tube.

2. Raise and safely support the vehicle, then drain the engine oil.

3. Remove the clutch housing cover attaching bolts, then remove the cover from the vehicle.

4. If equipped, remove the left and right wiring harness heat shields from the oil pan.

5. Disconnect the low oil sensor connection and remove the sensor from the pan.

6. Remove the bolts attaching the AIR pipe bracket to the oil pan, then remove the left and right converter heat shields.

7. Remove the nuts attaching the engine mounts at the front crossmember rear brace on the left and right sides. Remove the bolts attaching the front crossmember to the rear brace.

8. Remove the bolts attaching the left front crossmember rear brace to the left front side member and brace from the vehicle.

9. Remove the bolts attaching the right front crossmember rear brace to the right front side member and brace from the vehicle.

10. Remove the bolts attaching the oil pan and crankcase. Remove the oil pan and gasket from the vehicle.

To install:

11. Apply Loctite® 242 to the oil pan screw threads.

12. Install the oil pan and new gasket to the engine crankcase. Tighten the oil pan front screws to 89 inch lbs. (10 Nm) for 1990 vehicles or to 106 inch lbs. (12 Nm) for 1991–93 vehicles. Tighten the oil pan bolts to 20 ft. lbs. (26 Nm) for 1990 vehicles or to 23 ft. lbs. (31 Nm) for 1991–93 vehicles.

13. Install the front crossmember rear braces and bolts retaining the braces to the front crossmember bolts. Finger-tighten the bolts.

14. Install the bolts retaining the left front crossmemer rear brace to the left front side member, finger-tight.

15. Install the bolts retaining the right front crossmemer rear brace to the left front side member, finger-tight.

16. Tighten the left and right front crossmember rear brace to front crossmember bolts to 59 ft. lbs. (80 Nm), then tighten the left and right front crossmember rear brace to front side member bolts to 46 ft. lbs. (62 Nm).

17. Install the nuts retaining the engine mounts to the front crossmember and tighten to 40 ft. lbs. (54 Nm).

18. Install the converter heat shields and screws.

19. Install the bolts retaining the AIR pipe bracket to the oil pan and tighten to 89 inch lbs. (10 Nm).

20. Install the oil level sensor in the pan and tighten to 18 ft. lbs. (25 Nm).

21. Install the left and right wiring harness heat shields, if equipped, and tighten the bolts to 80 inch lbs. (9 Nm).

22. Install the clutch housing cover and tighten the bolts to 80 inch lbs. (9 Nm).

23. Lower the vehicle and insert the oil level indicator into the guide tube.

24. Properly fill the crankcase with clean engine oil.

25. Connect the negative battery cable.

Oil Pump

REMOVAL & INSTALLATION

5.7L (VIN 8 and VIN P) Engines

1. Disconnect the negative battery cable.

2. Raise and support the vehicle safely.

3. Drain the engine oil and remove the oil pan.

4. Remove the oil pan baffle nuts.

5. Support the oil pump by hand and remove the bolt attaching the oil pump to the main bearing cap.

6. Carefully remove the baffle, if equipped, and remove the oil pump assembly.

To install:

NOTE: The oil pump pickup should be submerged in oil and the pump primed prior to installation. Failure to prime the pump may result in oil pump failure or internal engine damage.

7. Install the oil pump assembly, aligning the slot on the top of the extension shaft with the drive tang on the lower end of the distributor driveshaft.

8. Install the oil pan baffle, if equipped, and install the main bearing cap bolt. Tighten the bolt to 80 ft. lbs. (108 Nm) for 1989 vehicles or to 65 ft. lbs. (88 Nm) for 1990–93 vehicles. Tighten the baffle nuts to 25 ft. lbs. (34 Nm).

9. Install the oil pan and lower the vehicle.

10. Properly fill the engine crankcase with clean engine oil and connect the negative battery cable.

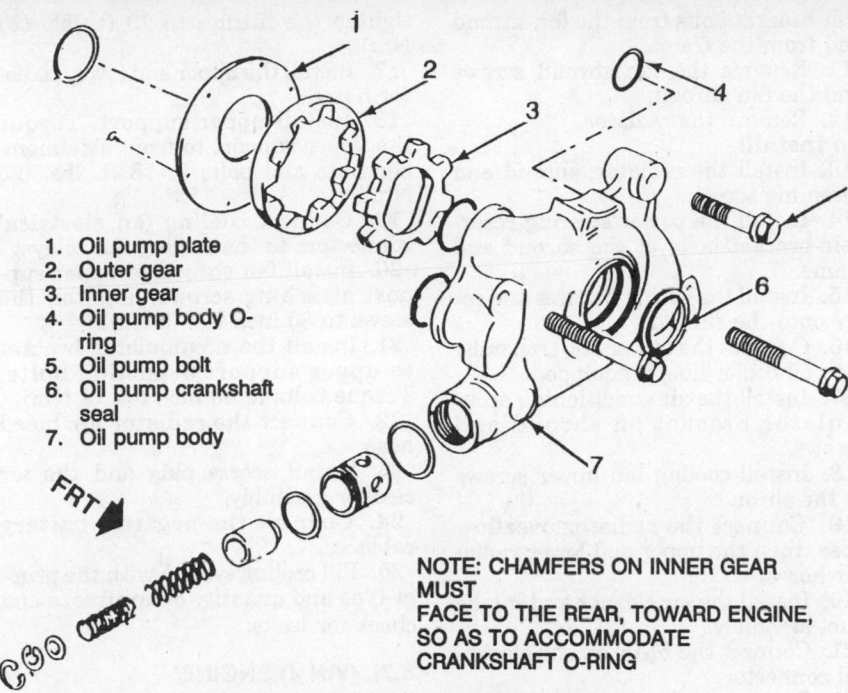

1. Oil pump plate
2. Outer gear
3. Inner gear
4. Oil pump body O-ring
5. Oil pump bolt
6. Oil pump crankshaft seal
7. Oil pump body

NOTE: CHAMFERS ON INNER GEAR MUST
FACE TO THE REAR, TOWARD ENGINE,
SO AS TO ACCOMMODATE
CRANKSHAFT O-RING

Oil pump assembly—5.7L (VIN J) Engine

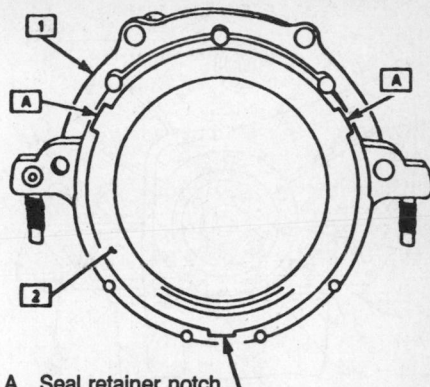

A. Seal retainer notch
1. Rear seal retainer
2. Crankshaft rear seal

**Rear crankshaft seal removal points—
5.7L (VIN 8 and VIN P) Engines**

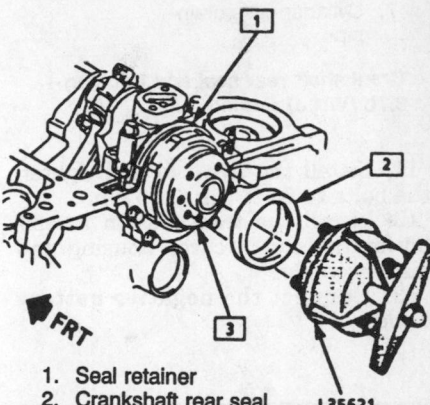

1. Seal retainer
2. Crankshaft rear seal
3. Crankshaft

J 35621

**Rear crankshaft seal installation—
5.7L (VIN 8 and VIN P) Engines**

5.7L (VIN J) Engine

1. Disconnect battery negative cable.
2. Remove the primary timing chain and crankshaft sprocket.
3. Remove bolts attaching the oil pump to the cylinder case, then remove the oil pump from the vehicle.
4. Remove O-rings from crankshaft and, if applicable, the oil pump.

To install:

5. Install new O-rings onto the crankshaft and oil pump, as applicable.
6. Apply Loctite® 262 to the oil pump bolts and install them finger-tight.

NOTE: Make sure the 2 flats of the pump drive gear are aligned with the 2 flats on the crankshaft. Do not force pump onto crankshaft.

7. Using oil pump aligning tool J–38135 or equivalent pump aligner/seal installer, align oil pump on the crankshaft. Tighten the oil pump bolts to 19 ft. lbs. (26 Nm).
8. Install a new oil pump shaft seal using tools J–38135 and J–38463 or equivalent seal installers.

NOTE: Install a new oil pump shaft seal whenever the pump is removed from the vehicle.

9. Install the primary timing chain and crankshaft sprocket.
10. Connect the negative battery cable.

Rear Main Bearing Oil Seal

REMOVAL & INSTALLATION

5.7L (VIN 8 and VIN P) Engines

1. Disconnect the negative battery cable.
2. Raise the vehicle and support it safely.
3. Remove the transmission assembly or the clutch cover and disc assembly.
4. Remove the flywheel bolts and remove the flywheel from the vehicle.
5. Using the notches provided in the seal retainer, pry the old seal out using a small suitable too. Be careful not to nick the crankshaft sealing surface when removing the seal.

To install:

6. Entirely lubricate the inside and outside of a new seal with engine oil.
7. Install the seal on tool J–35621 or equivalent rear main seal installer.
8. Thread the screws of the tool into the rear of the crankshaft and tighten the screws snugly to assure proper seal alignment and installation.
9. Tighten the tool wingnut until it bottoms and then remove the tool.
10. Install the flywheel and tighten the bolts to 74 ft. lbs. (100 Nm).
12. Install the transmission assembly or the clutch cover and disc assembly.
13. Lower the vehicle and connect the negative battery cable.

NOTE: Whenever the seal re-

tainer is removed, a new gasket and rear main seal must be installed.

5.7L (VIN J) Engine

1. Disconnect battery negative cable.
2. Remove transmission or the clutch cover and disc assembly.
3. Remove the flywheel bolts and flywheel.
4. Remove the screws attaching the crankshaft rear main oil seal/housing assembly to the cylinder case.
5. Remove the seal/housing assembly from the engine.
6. Remove the seal from the housing.

To install:

7. Lubricate the seal lip with engine oil.
8. Install seal into housing using crankshaft rear seal tool J–37312 or equivalent.
9. Seal should be installed 1.0–1.5mm below the housing surface.
10. Install the housing and tighten the bolts to 89 inch lbs. (10 Nm).

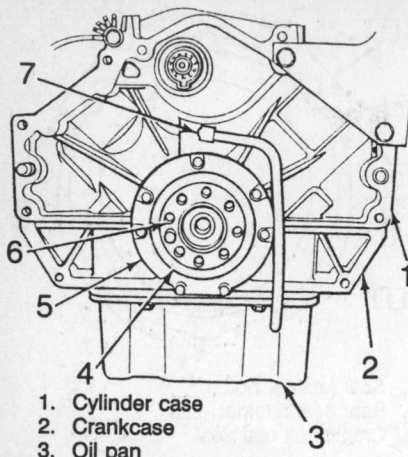

1. Cylinder case
2. Crankcase
3. Oil pan
4. Crankcase rear seal
5. Rear oil seal housing
6. Crankshaft
7. Cylinder case drain
   pipe

Crankshaft rear seal and housing—5.7L (VIN J) Engine

11. Install the flywheel and tighten the bolts to 74 ft. lbs. (100 Nm).
12. Install the transmission assembly or the clutch cover housing and disc assembly.
13. Connect the negative battery cable.

ENGINE COOLING

Radiator

REMOVAL & INSTALLATION

1989

1. Disconnect battery negative cable.
2. Drain the cooling system into a suitable container.
3. Remove air cleaner and intake duct assembly, then disconnect MAF electrical connector.
4. Remove the upper and lower radiator hoses.
5. Disconnect the radiator overflow hose at the radiator.
6. Remove the engine cooling fan upper screws at the shroud.
7. Remove the air conditioning accumulator bracket at the shroud and position aside.
8. Disconnect and plug the transmission oil cooler line, if equipped.
9. Disconnect the cooling fan wires and relay from the fan shroud and frame.
10. Remove the power steering reser-

voir bracket bolts from the fan shroud and from the frame.
11. Remove the fan shroud screws and the fan shroud.
12. Remove the radiator.
To install:
13. Install the radiator, shroud and retaining screws.
14. Install the power steering reservoir bracket bolts at the shroud and frame.
15. Install the wiring harness and relay onto the shroud.
16. Connect the automatic transmission oil cooler line, if equipped.
17. Install the air conditioning accumulator bracket on shroud and screws.
18. Install cooling fan upper screws at the shroud.
19. Connect the radiator overflow hose, then the upper and lower radiator hoses.
20. Install the air cleaner and intake duct assembly.
21. Connect the MAF sensor electrical connector.
22. Reconnect the negative battery cable.
23. Fill cooling system with the proper type and quantity of antifreeze. Start and check the cooling system for leaks.

1990–93

5.7L (VIN 8 and VIN P) ENGINES

1. Disconnect battery negative cable.
2. Drain the engine coolant into a suitable container.
3. Remove the air cleaner assembly.
4. Disconnect the electrical connectors from the cooling fan relays.
5. Remove the bolts attaching the accumulator bracket to the radiator upper support.
6. Remove the fan shroud to upper support attaching bolts.
7. Remove the rubber access plug from the top of the radiator.
8. Remove the radiator air bleed hose.
9. Remove the nuts and bolts attaching the upper support to the front side member.
10. Remove the screws attaching the upper support to the lower support.
11. Remove upper support.
12. Remove the radiator upper and lower hose clamps, then the hoses.
13. Disconnect and plug the transmission oil cooler lines from the radiator, if equipped.
14. Remove the radiator from the vehicle.
To install:
15. Install the radiator.
16. Connect transmission cooler lines to the radiator, if equipped, and

tighten the fittings to 20 ft. lbs. (27 Nm).
17. Install the upper and lower radiator hoses.
18. Install upper support. Torque the upper support to front side member nuts and bolts to 18 ft. lbs. (25 Nm).
19. Connect cooling fan electrical connectors to the cooling fan relays.
20. Install fan shroud to upper support attaching screws. Tighten the scews to 80 inch lbs. (9 Nm).
21. Install the accumulator bracket to upper support attaching bolts. Torque bolts to 80 inch lbs. (9 Nm).
22. Connect the radiator air bleed hose.
23. Install access plug and the air cleaner assembly.
24. Connect the negative battery cable.
25. Fill cooling system with the proper type and quantity of antifreeze and check for leaks.

5.7L (VIN J) ENGINE

1. Disconnect battery negative cable.
2. Drain the engine coolant into a suitable container.
3. Remove the air cleaner assembly and remove the radiator upper air deflector.
4. Disconnect the electrical connectors from the cooling fan relays.
5. Remove the bolts attaching the accumulator bracket to the radiator upper support.
6. Remove the fan shroud to upper support attaching bolts.
7. Remove the rubber access plug from the top of the radiator.
8. Remove the radiator air bleed hose.
9. Remove the nuts and bolts attaching the upper support to the front side member.
10. Remove the bolt retaining oil cooler lines to the oil cooler.
11. Remove the seal retainers and seal from the oil cooler and air conditioning line.
12. Remove the air pump assembly.
13. Remove the air pump bracket at the rear and loosen the front bolt.
14. Remove the air pump intake duct.
15. Remove the screws attaching the upper support to the lower support and Remove upper support from the vehicle.
16. Remove the radiator upper and lower hoses and clamps.
17. Remove the radiator from the vehicle.
To install:
18. Install the radiator.
19. Install the upper and lower radiator hoses.
20. Install upper support. Torque

the upper support to front side member nuts and bolts to 18 ft. lbs. (25 Nm).

21. Install the air pump intake duct, retaining brackets and the air pump assembly.

22. Connect the cooling fan relay electrical connectors.

23. Install fan shroud to upper support attaching screws. Tighten the screws to 80 inch lbs. (9 Nm).

24. Install the accumulator bracket to upper support attaching bolts. Torque the bolts to 80 inch lbs. (9 Nm).

25. Install the seal retainers and seal onto the oil cooler and air conditioning line.

26. Install the bolt retaining the oil cooler lines to the oil cooler. Tighten the bolt to 89 inch lbs. (10 Nm).

27. Connect the radiator air bleed hose.

28. Install the rubber access plug on the radiator support, the upper air deflector and the air cleaner assembly.

29. Connect the negative battery cable.

30. Fill cooling system with the proper type and quantity of antifreeze and check for leaks.

Electric Cooling Fans

REMOVAL & INSTALLATION

1989

ENGINE COOLING FAN

1. Disconnect the negative battery cable.

2. Remove the air cleaner and the intake air duct assembly.

3. Disconnect the MAF sensor and cooling fan electrical connector.

4. Remove fan assembly upper screws.

5. Raise and support the vehicle safely.

6. Remove cooling fan lower mounting screws.

7. Lower the vehicle and remove engine cooling fan.

To install:

8. Install the fan assembly and the upper mounting screws. Tighten the screws to 20 ft. lbs. (27 Nm).

9. Engage the electrical connector to the fan motor.

10. Install the air cleaner and intake duct assembly.

11. Connect the MAF sensor electrical connector.

12. Raise and support the vehicle safely and install the lower fan assembly screws.

13. Tighten the screws to 20 ft. lbs. (27 Nm) and lower the vehicle.

14. Connect the negative battery cable.

AUXILIARY COOLING FAN

1. Disconnect the negative battery cable.

2. Remove the air cleaner assembly.

3. Disconnect the electrical connector and feed the grommet and harness through the baffle.

4. Remove the upper fan screws.

5. Raise and support the vehicle safely.

6. Remove the lower fan screw and remove the fan assembly.

To install:

7. Install the fan assembly and lower screw. Tighten the lower screw to 20 ft. lbs. (27 Nm).

8. Feed the harness and grommet through the baffle and lower the vehicle.

9. Install the fan upper screws and tighten to 20 ft. lbs. (27 Nm).

10. Engage the electrical connector and install the air cleaner assembly.

11. Connect the negative battery cable.

1990–93

5.7L (VIN 8 and VIN P) ENGINES

Although this procedure is for both the primary and auxiliary fans, the primary fan does not need to be removed if only the auxiliary fan requires service.

1. Disconnect battery negative cable and remove the air intake duct assembly.

2. For VIN 8 engine, remove the power steering pump reservoir bracket to front crossmember bolts and position the pump aside.

3. Disconnect the electrical connector from the primary cooling fan.

4. For VIN 8 engine, remove the bolts attaching the fan motor to the motor support.

5. Remove the screws attaching the fan assembly to the fan shroud.

6. For VIN 8 engine, remove the end cap from the power steering pump pulley.

7. Remove the primary fan assembly from the vehicle.

8. Remove the auxiliary fan upper right mounting bolt.

9. Raise and safely support the vehicle.

10. Disconnect the auxiliary cooling fan electrical connector from the fan motor.

11. Remove remaining auxiliary cooling fan mounting bolts and remove the auxiliary cooling fan from the vehicle.

To install:

12. Install the auxiliary cooling fan assembly and tighten the retaining bolts to 89 inch lbs. (10 Nm).

13. Connect the auxiliary fan electrical connector and lower the vehicle.

14. Install the remaining bolt attaching the upper right of the fan assembly to the fan shroud.

15. Install the primary fan assembly and tighten the bolts to 89 inch lbs. (10 Nm).

16. For VIN 8 engine, install the fan motor retaining screws and tighten to 89 inch lbs. (10 Nm), the install the power steering pump bracket to the front crossmember bolts.

17. Engage the electrical connector to the fan motor.

18. For VIN 8 engine, install the end cap on the power steering pump pulley.

19. Install the air intake duct and connect the negative battery cable.

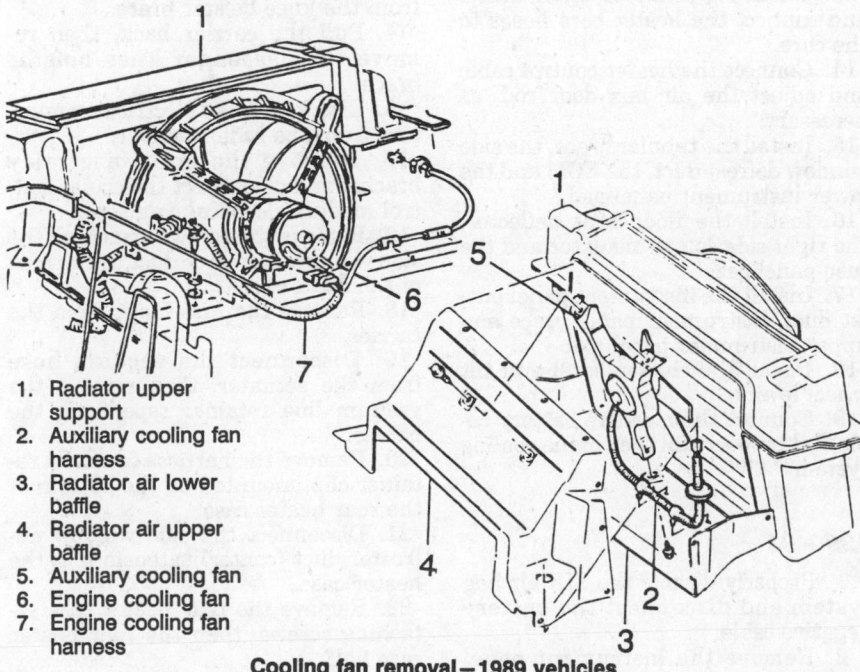

1. Radiator upper support
2. Auxiliary cooling fan harness
3. Radiator air lower baffle
4. Radiator air upper baffle
5. Auxiliary cooling fan
6. Engine cooling fan
7. Engine cooling fan harness

Cooling fan removal–1989 vehicles

5.7L (VIN J) ENGINES

1. Disconnect the negative battery cable.
2. Drain the engine coolant into a suitable container.
3. Remove the air intake duct.
4. Remove the hoses and clamps from the coolant outlets, the radiator inlet and the bypass inlet pipe.
5. Remove the hose and inlet pipe assembly from the vehicle.
6. Disconnect the electrical connector from the fan motor.
7. Remove the screws retaining the fan motor to the motor support and remove the bolt retaining the air conditioning discharge line clamp to the crossmember.
8. Remove the bolts retaining the fan assembly to the fan shroud, remove the end cap from the power steering pump pulley and remove the primary fan assembly from the vehicle.
9. Remove the bolt retaining the upper right of the auxiliary fan assembly to the fan shroud.
10. Raise and support the vehicle safely.
11. Disconnect the electrical connector from the auxiliary fan motor.
12. Remove the bolts retaining the fan assembly to the fan shroud and remove the assembly from the vehicle.

To install:
13. Install the auxiliary fan assembly to the vehicle and tighten the fan-to-fan shroud bolts to 89 inch lbs. (10 Nm).
14. Engage the electrical connector to the auxiliary fan motor and lower the vehicle.
15. Install the upper right bolt retaining the assembly to the fan shroud.
16. Install the primary fan assembly and tighten the bolts to 89 inch lbs. (10 Nm).
17. Install the screws retaining the motor to the motor support and tighten the bolts to 89 inch lbs. (10 Nm).
18. Engage the electrical connector to the primary fan motor.
19. Install the bolt retaining the air conditioning discharge line clamp to the crossmember and install the end cap to the power steering pump pulley.
20. Install the hose and inlet pipe assembly. Connect the hoses and clamps to the coolant outlets, the radiator inlet and the bypass inlet pipe.
21. Install the air intake duct and connect the negative battery cable.
22. Fill the cooling system with the proper type and amount of coolant and check the system for leaks.

Heater Core

REMOVAL & INSTALLATION

1989

1. Disconnect the negative battery cable.
2. Drain the cooling system into a suitable container.
3. Remove the instrument cluster bezel including the tilt wheel lever sufficiently to access the 8 instrument panel upper pad screws, including 2 located from the defrost duct. Remove the screws and the upper instrument panel pad.
4. Remove the instrument panel brace and the panel outlet duct.
5. Remove the fuse panel bezel, the right sound insulator panel and the floor heat deflector.
6. Remove the instrument panel lower right hand pad, the ECM and the side window defroster duct.
7. Remove the tubular brace by loosening the upper bolts, removing the bottom bolts and rotating the brace rearward.
8. Disconnect the heater control cable.
9. Disconnect the heater hoses from the heater core.
10. Remove the heater core case screws and separate the case.
11. Remove the core retainers and remove the heater core.

To install:
12. Install the heater core and retainers. Install the heater core case, making sure to position the air mix door rod through the heater core prior to assembly.
13. Check for sealer or other debris and connect the heater core hoses to the core.
14. Connect the heater control cable and adjust the air mix door rod, as necessary.
15. Install the tubular brace, the side window defrost duct, the ECM and the lower instrument panel pad.
16. Install the floor heat deflector, the right side sound insulator and the fuse panel bezel.
17. Install the instrument panel outlet duct, instrument panel brace and upper instrument panel pad.
18. Install the cluster bezel and tilt wheel lever.
19. Connect the negative battery cable and properly fill the engine cooling system.

1990–93

1. Properly disable the SIR air bag system and disconnect the battery negative cable.
2. Remove the instrument panel upper trim pad as follows:

a. Remove the lower right trim panel.
b. Remove the fuse box cover and side trim panel.
c. Remove the glove compartment.
d. Remove the right outer air outlet and center air outlet.
e. Remove the console trim plate and accessory trim plate.
f. Remove the windshield defroster grill.
g. Remove the left outer air outlet.
h. Remove the dash pad retaining bolts/screws and remove the pad by pulling rearward and upward.
3. Drain the engine coolant into a suitable container.
4. Disconnect the in-vehicle temperature sensor aspirator hose.
5. Disconnect the in-vehicle temperature sensor electrical connector.
6. Remove the floor heat deflector attaching screws, right side knee bolster brace and the the floor heat deflector.
7. Disconnect the relays from the multi-use relay bracket.
8. Loosen the nuts attaching the wiring harness retainer to the radio receiver, then slide the wiring harness retainer from the receiver.
9. Remove the harnesses from the wiring harness retainer, then remove the wiring harness retainer.
10. Remove the carrier nuts from the right side pillar.
11. Remove the multi-use relay bracket.
12. Remove the passenger knee bolster brace attachments.
13. Unclip the side window defroster duct clip, then remove the duct hose from the knee bolster brace.
14. Pull the carrier back, then remove the passenger knee bolster brace.
15. Disconnect the electrical connectors from the radio receiver.
16. Remove the multi-use relay bracket and disconnect the cruise control module electrical connector.
17. Remove the screws attaching the side window defroster duct to the rear of the heater case.
18. Remove the fuse block from the carrier.
19. Disconnect the vacuum hose from the actuator, then remove the vacuum line retainer tape from the heater.
20. Remove the harness from the retainer clip, mounted on the bottom of the rear heater case.
21. Disconnect the side window defroster duct (center) extension, in the heater case.
22. Remove the rear heater case attaching screws, then the rear heater case half.
23. Remove the high fill reservoir.

24. Disconnect the heater hoses from the heater core.

25. Remove the heater core from the case.

To install:

26. Install heater core into the case.

27. Connect the heater hoses to the heater core. Install high fill reservoir, then the rear heater case.

28. Install the side window defroster duct extension.

29. Install harnesses to the retainer clip on the bottom rear of the heater case.

30. Install vacuum line and tape onto retainer.

31. Connect vacuum hose to the actuator.

32. Install fuse block to carrier.

33. Install side window defroster duct screws to the rear of the heater case.

34. Connect the radio receiver and cruise control module electrical connectors.

35. Install multi-use relay bracket, the knee bolster brace and attacments.

36. Install carrier to pillar attachment, then the wiring harness retainer, harness retainer to the radio receiver and the relays to the multi-use relay bracket.

37. Install floor heat deflector, the right side knee bolster brace and then the floor heat deflector screws.

38. Connect the in-vehicle temperature sensor electrical connectors and the aspirator hose.

39. Install upper instrument pad assembly in the reverse order of removal.

40. Connect the negative battery cable and enable the SIR sysyem.

41. Properly fill the engine cooling system and check for leaks.

Water Pump

REMOVAL & INSTALLATION

5.7L (VIN 8) Engine

1. Disconnect the negative battery cable.

2. Remove the air cleaner and air intake duct assembly.

3. For 1989 vehicles, disconnect the MAF sensor electrical connector.

4. Drain the cooling system into a suitable container.

5. Using a ½ breaker bar, rotate the tensioner to loosen and remove the serpentine belt.

6. Remove the water pump damper and pulley.

7. Remove the air conditioner compressor mounting bolts.

8. Remove the AIR pump mounting bolts.

9. Remove the cover from the AIR control valve.

10. Remove the upper hose from the AIR control valve.

11. Remove the electrical connector at the control valve.

12. Remove the air pipe and control valve retaining nut. Position the assembly aside.

13. Remove the heater hose at the pump.

14. Remove the belt tensioner bolt.

15. Properly relieve the fuel system pressure from the fuel rails and disconnect the fuel lines.

16. Remove the air pump bracket retaining bolts.

17. Remove the nut retaining the air pump brace.

18. Remove the radiator lower hose.

19. Remove the air conditioner compressor bracket mounting bolts.

20. Remove the AIR pipe retaining bracket bolt.

21. Remove the water pump mounting bolts and stud nuts. Remove the water pump from the engine.

To install:

22. If replacing the water pump, transfer the heater hose fitting to the new pump.

23. Thoroughly clean the water pump and engine block mating surfaces.

24. Secure the water pump to the engine block with a new gasket and torque the nuts and bolts to 30 ft. lbs. (40 Nm).

25. Install the AIR pipe retaining bracket bolt.

26. Install the air conditioner compressor bracket mounting bolts.

27. Install the radiator lower hose.

28. Install the air pump bracket retaining bolts.

29. Connect the fuel lines.

30. Install the belt tensioner bolt.

31. Install the heater hose at the pump.

32. Install the air pipe and control valve retaining nut.

33. Connect the electrical connector to the control valve.

34. Install the upper hose and the cover onto the AIR control valve.

35. Install the AIR pump mounting bolts and the AIR pump brace nut. Tighten the pump brace nut to 25 ft. lbs. (33 Nm).

36. Install the air conditioner compressor mounting bolts.

37. Install the water pump damper and pulley, tighten the retaining bolts to 22 ft. lbs. (29 Nm).

38. Using a ½ inch breaker bar to retract the tensioner, install the serpentine belt.

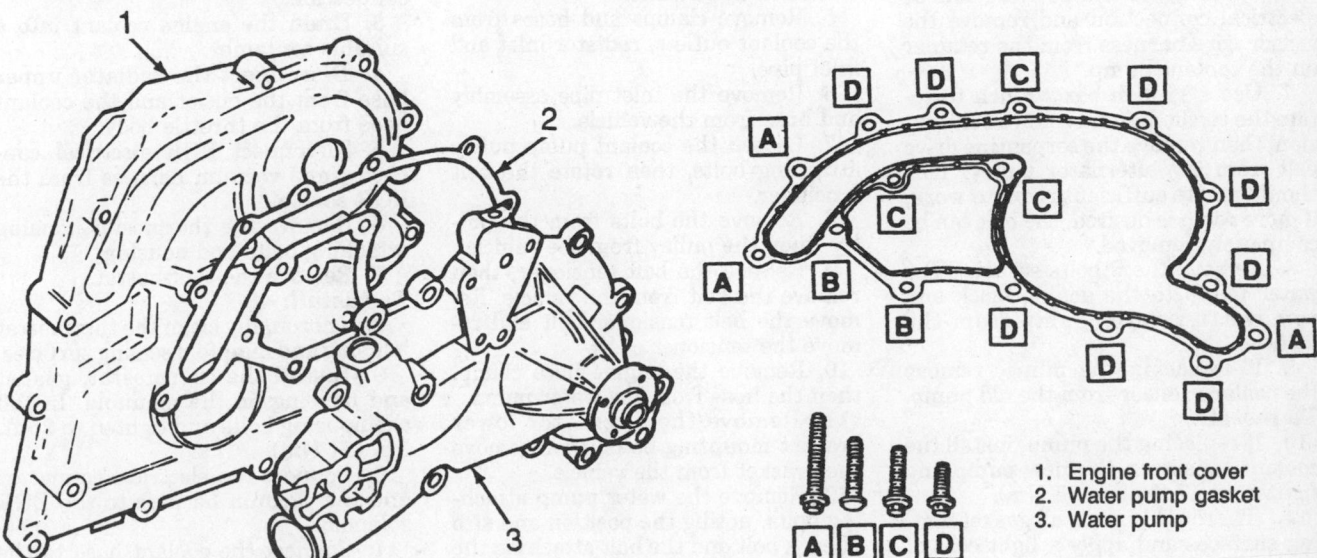

1. Engine front cover
2. Water pump gasket
3. Water pump

Water pump assembly—5.7L (VIN J) Engine

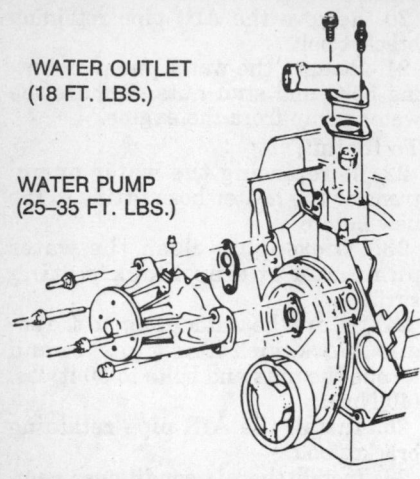

WATER OUTLET
(18 FT. LBS.)

WATER PUMP
(25–35 FT. LBS.)

Water pump assembly—5.7L (VIN 8) Engine

39. Install the air cleaner and air intake duct assembly.

40. For 1989 vehicles, install the MAF sensor electrical connector.

41. Connect the negative battery cable.

42. Properly fill the engine cooling system and check for leaks.

5.7L (VIN P) Engine

1. Disconnect the negative battery cable.

2. Disconnect the IAT electrical connection.

3. Remove the air cleaner and air intake duct assembly.

4. Drain the cooling system into a suitable container and remove the knock sensors.

5. Remove the upper and lower radiator hoses and the heater hose from the water pump.

6. Disconnect the coolant sensor electrical connection and remove the sensor wire harness from the retainer on the coolant pump.

7. Use a ⅝ inch box wrench to rotate the tensioner and relieve belt tension, then remove the serpentine drive belt from the alternator pulley. This should create sufficient room to work, if more room is desired, the belt can be completely removed.

8. Remove the 6 bolts securing the water pump to the engine block and remove the water pump from the vehicle.

9. If replacing the pump, remove the coolant sensor from the old pump.

To install:

10. If replacing the pump, install the coolant sensor on the new pump and tighten to 17 ft. lbs. (23 Nm).

11. Thoroughly clean all gasket mating surfaces and apply a light coat of grease to the seals and splines before assembling the coupling to the water pump. The white band on the coupling

should be positioned towards the engine.

12. Install the new gaskets with the tabs up, the coolant pump with the drive coupling and the mounting bolts. Tighten the bolts to 30 ft. lbs. (41 Nm).

13. Install the serpentine drive belt.

14. Connect the coolant sensor wire harness to the retainer and engage the sensor electrical connection.

15. Connect the heater hose and the upper and lower radiator hoses to the water pump.

16. Open the bleed valves on the thermostat housing and the throttle body. Fill the cooling system through the radiator surge tank until a solid stream of coolant comes out of the bleeds.

17. Close all bleeds and continue to fill the surge tank until the coolant is level at the base of the surge tank neck.

18. Install the radiator pressure cap and check the coolant recovery reservoir for the proper level of coolant, add as necessary.

19. Install the air cleaner and intake duct assembly.

20. Connect the IAT electrical connection and clean any excess coolant from the engine compartment.

21. Connect the negative battery cable, start the engine and check for leaks.

5.7L (VIN J) Engine

1. Disconnect the negative battery cable.

2. Drain engine coolant into a suitable container.

3. Disconnect the air intake duct.

4. Remove the screws attaching the throttle body extension to the throttle body, then remove the throttle body extension and gasket.

5. Remove clamps and hoses from the coolant outlets, radiator inlet and inlet pipe.

6. Remove the inlet pipe assembly and hose from the vehicle.

7. Loosen the coolant pump pulley attaching bolts, then rotate the belt tensioner.

8. Remove the bolts from the pulley, then the pulley from the vehicle.

9. Release the belt tensioner, then remove the belt from the vehicle. Remove the belt tensioner bolt and remove the tensioner.

10. Remove the engine hose clamp, then the hose from the water pump.

11. Remove the alternator lower bracket mounting bolts, then remove the bracket from the vehicle.

12. Remove the water pump attaching bolts, noting the position and size of each bolt and the bolt attaching the air conditioning compressor to the water pump. Remove the water pump from the vehicle.

To install:

13. Thoroughly clean the pump and front cover sealing surfaces.

14. Install the water pump, new gasket and bolts, finger-tight only.

15. Install bolt attaching air conditioning compressor to pump.

16. Torque air conditioning compressor bolt and water pump attaching bolts to 20 ft. lbs. (26 Nm).

17. Install engine hoses and clamps.

18. Install alternator bolts. Apply Loctite® 565 to bolt threads. Torque alternator mounting bolts to 39 ft. lbs. (52 Nm) and bracket bolts to 20 ft. lbs. (26 Nm).

19. Install the belt tensioner. Torque belt tensioner bolt to 45 ft. lbs. (60 Nm).

20. Install the serpentine belt, rotate the tensioner and install the water pump pulley. Torque water pump pulley bolts to 89 inch lbs. (10 Nm).

21. Install the hose and inlet pipe assembly.

22. Install throttle body extension and gasket. Torque bolts to 53 inch lbs. (6 Nm).

23. Install air intake duct and connect the negative battery cable.

24. Refill the cooling system with the proper type and quantity of antifreeze and inspect the system for leaks.

Thermostat

REMOVAL & INSTALLATION

5.7L (VIN 8) Engine

1. Disconnect the negative battery cable.

2. Remove the air cleaner and intake duct assembly and, if equipped, disconnect the MAF sensor electrical connection.

3. Drain the engine coolant into a suitable container.

4. Disconnect the radiator upper hose from the outlet and the coolant hose from the throttle body.

5. Disconnect EGR electrical connector and vacuum harness from the EGR solenoid.

6. Remove the thermostat housing attaching bolts and housing.

7. Remove the thermostat.

To install:

8. Thoroughly clean the thermostat housing and manifold sealing surfaces.

9. Install the thermostat, gasket and housing on the manifold. Install the housing bolts and tighten to 25 ft. lbs. (34 Nm).

10. Connect the electrical connector and the vacuum harness to the EGR solenoid.

11. Connect the coolant hose to the throttle body and the radiator upper hose to the outlet.

12. Install the air cleaner and intake

duct assembly and, if equipped, connect the MAF sensor electrical connection.

13. Connect the negative battery cable and properly fill the engine cooling system.

5.7L (VIN P) Engine

1. Disconnect the negative battery cable.

2. Disconnect the IAT electrical connection.

3. Remove the air cleaner and intake duct assembly.

4. Drain the cooling system into a suitable container.

5. Disconnect the radiator hose from the thermostat housing inlet of the water pump.

6. Remove the thermostat housing bolts and housing.

7. Remove the thermostat and seal.

To install:

8. Thoroughly clean the thermostat housing and water pump sealing surfaces.

9. Install the thermostat, seal with the taper up and the housing with bolts to the water pump. Tighten the bolts to 8 ft. lbs. (10 Nm).

10. Connect the radiator hose to the thermostat inlet on the water pump.

11. Open the bleed valves on the thermostat housing and the throttle body. Fill the cooling system through the radiator surge tank until a solid stream of coolant comes out of the bleeds.

12. Close all bleeds and continue to fill the surge tank until the coolant is level at the base of the surge tank neck.

13. Install the pressure cap and check the coolant recovery reservoir for the proper level of coolant, add as necessary.

14. Install the air cleaner and intake duct assembly.

15. Connect the IAT electrical connection and clean any excess coolant from the engine compartment.

16. Connect the negative battery cable, start the engine and check for leaks.

5.7L (VIN J) Engine

1. Disconnect the negative battery cable.

2. Drain the engine coolant into a suitable container.

NOTE: A large amount of engine coolant will remain in the VIN J engine after coolant has drained through the radiator draincock. Much of this coolant will drain from the thermostat housing when the 2-piece housing is separated.

3. Raise and safely support the vehicle.

4. Remove the bolts attaching the thermostat housing sections.

5. Loosen the bolts attaching the housing assembly bracket to the front side member.

6. Remove the thermostat and seal from the housing.

To install:

7. Thoroughly clean all gasket mating surfaces.

8. Install the thermostat, seal and housing. Be sure the seal is installed with the taper towards the radiator and remains seated in housing groove when assembling the housing sections.

9. Tighten the thermostat housing and bracket bolts to 18 ft. lbs. (25 Nm).

10. Lower the vehicle and connect the negative battery cable.

11. Properly fill the cooling system and check for leaks.

Cooling System

BLEEDING

If flushing is required, do not use a chemical flush. Drain and fill the cooling system with clean water until the water drained from the system in this procedure is clear.

If a flush is performed, when filling the engine with coolant begin by adding 100 percent ethylene glycol in the amount of 8.2 qts. for 5.7L (VIN 8 and VIN P) engines or 6.9 qts of for 5.7L (VIN J) engine. Then complete the filling procedure with clean water.

5.7 (VIN 8 and VIN J) Engines

1. With the cooling system completely drained, the engine **OFF** and radiator drain plug closed, begin adding antifreeze. Use a combination of 50 percent ethylene glycol antifreeze and 50 percent water for system refills.

2. Slowly fill the cooling system through the opening in the high fill surge tank until the level is even with the base of the fill neck. Also, be sure the coolant recovery reservoir is filled to the **COLD** mark.

3. Run the engine with the pressure cap removed until normal operating temperature is reached and the upper radiator hose becomes hot.

NOTE: The coolant temperature gauge must be monitored during the running of the engine and at no time should the engine temperature be allowed to reach the 260°F mark or the engine HOT light be allowed to come ON. If this should occur, the engine should be turned OFF immediately and allowed to cool down to

80°F (27°C) before continuing with the bleeding process.

4. With the engine idling, add coolant until the level reaches the bottom of the high fill reservoir filler neck.

5. Install the pressure cap, making sure the arrows line up with the overflow tube.

6. Check that the coolant recovery reservoir is now at the **HOT** level, and add coolant as necessary.

5.7 (VIN P) Engines

1. With the cooling system completely drained, the engine **OFF** and radiator drain plug closed, open the bleed valves on the thermostat housing and the throttle body.

2. Begin adding antifreeze. Use a combination of 50 percent ethylene glycol antifreeze and 50 percent water for system refills. Fill the cooling system through the radiator surge tank until a solid stream of coolant comes out of the bleeds.

3. Close all bleeds and continue to fill the surge tank until the coolant is level at the base of the surge tank neck.

4. Install the pressure cap and check the coolant recovery reservoir for the proper level of coolant, add as necessary.

5. Install the air cleaner and intake duct assembly.

6. Connect the IAT electrical connection and clean any excess coolant from the engine compartment.

7. Connect the negative battery cable, start the engine and check for leaks.

ENGINE ELECTRICAL

NOTE: Disconnecting the negative battery cable on some vehicles may interfere with the functions of the on board computer system and may require the computer to undergo a relearning process when the negative battery cable is reconnected.

Distributor

While the 5.7L (VIN 8) engine uses a top engine mounted distributor assembly, the 5.7 (VIN P) introduced for 1992 utilizes a front engine mounted distributor assembly.

REMOVAL

5.7 (VIN 8) Engine

NOTE: When making compression checks, the ignition system can be disabled by disconnecting the ignition switch feed wire and the 4-terminal ECM harness.

1. Disconnect the negative battery cable.
2. Remove the intake manifold plenum extension.
3. Disconnect the battery feed wire and tachometer wire from the distributor cap.
4. Remove the distributor cap and retaining screws. Position the cap off to the side.
5. Disconnect the 4-terminal ECM wire connector from the distributor. Tag and remove any remaining electrical connections, if necessary.
6. Remove the distributor hold-down bolt and clamp.
7. Note the position of the rotor to the distributor housing. Then pull the distributor assembly up from the engine until the rotor stops turning and again note the position of the rotor.

5.7 (VIN P) Engine

NOTE: The ignition system may be disabled for compression checks by removing the "INJ 1" fuse from the fuse block.

1. Disconnect the negative battery cable and the Intake Air Temperature (IAT) sensor harness connector.
2. Remove the air intake duct and the serpentine drive belt.
3. Drain the engine coolant into a suitable container and remove the coolant hoses from the water pump assembly.
4. Disconnect the ECM coolant sensor connector and remove the water pump assembly.
5. Remove the crankshaft torsional damper as follows:
    a. Raise and safely support the vehicle or lower the vehicle, as necessary.
    b. Position a suitable drain pan and remove the power steering fluid cooler.
    c. Remove the motor mount nuts and carefully raise the engine enough to gain tool access to the damper.
    d. Remove the torsional damper bolts and remove the damper from the hub.
6. Remove the belt tensioner from the engine.
7. Disconnect the spark plug wires from the distributor. Be sure to twist each boot ½ turn and pull only on the boot to remove each wire.

8. Disconnect the 4-terminal ECM connector from the distributor.
9. Remove the distributor mounting bolts and pull the distributor forward until it the drive shaft disengages from the engine. Mark the top of the shaft for alignment during reassembly.

INSTALLATION

Timing Not Disturbed

NOTE: To ensure correct ignition timing the distributor must be installed with the rotor in the same position as it was removed.

5.7L (VIN 8) ENGINE

1. Install the distributor into engine, positioning the marks made on the rotor and housing.
2. Install distributor hold-down clamp and bolt and hand tighten.
3. Connect the 4-terminal ECM wire connector to distributor, then install the distributor cap.
4. Connect the coil connector, the ignition switch battery feed wire and tachometer wire to the distributor cap.
5. Install the wiring harness retainer and the spark plug wires, if removed.
6. Connect the battery negative cable, check and adjust the ignition timing. Tighten the hold-down clamp bolt to 25 ft. lbs. (34 Nm).
7. Install the intake manifold plenum extension and again, check the ignition timing.

5.7L (VIN P) ENGINE

1. With the mark made on the distributor shaft earlier on top, install the distributor to the engine. Tighten the distributor bolts to 8 ft. lbs. (11 Nm).
2. Connect the ECM connector and the spark plug wires to the distributor.
3. Install the belt tensioner.
4. Install the torsional damper as follows:
    a. Raise and support the vehicle safely or lower the vehicle, as necessary.
    b. Position the damper to the hub and install the damper bolts. Tighten the bolts to 60 ft. lbs. (81 Nm).
    c. Lower the engine and install the power steering fluid cooler.
    d. Install the motor mount nuts and tighten to 40 ft. lbs. (54 Nm).
5. Install the water pump assembly, the ECM coolant temperature sensor and the coolant hoses.
6. Install the serpentine drive belt and the air intake duct.
7. Connect the IAT sensor connector.
8. Connect the negative battery cable, fill the engine to the proper level

with coolant and bleed the power steering system, as necessary.

Timing Disturbed

5.7L (VIN 8) ENGINE

1. If the engine has been cranked with the distributor out, remove the No. 1 spark plug.
2. Verify the transmission is N or P. Place a finger over the spark plug hole and crank the engine slowly until compression is felt.
3. Align the timing mark on the pulley to 0 on the engine timing indicator. Position the rotor between the No. 1 and No. 8 spark plug towers.
4. The distributor can now be correctly installed in the engine.
5. Install distributor hold-down clamp and bolt and hand tighten.
6. Connect the 4-terminal ECM wire connector to distributor, then install the distributor cap.
7. Connect the coil connector, the ignition switch battery feed wire and tachometer wire to the distributor cap.
8. Install the wiring harness retainer and the spark plug wires, if removed.
9. Connect the battery negative cable, check and adjust the ignition timing. Tighten the hold-down clamp bolt to 25 ft. lbs. (34 Nm).
10. Install the intake manifold plenum extension and again, check the ignition timing.

Distributorless Ignition System

REMOVAL & INSTALLATION

Crankshaft Sensor

1. Disconnect the battery negative cable.
2. Raise and safely support vehicle.
3. Disconnect crankshaft sensor electrical connector.
4. Remove the crankshaft sensor mounting bolt, crankshaft sensor and sensor shim, if applicable.
To install:
5. Coat crankshaft sensor O-ring with engine oil.
6. Install the sensor shim, sensor and mounting bolt, as applicable. Torque the crankshaft sensor bolt to 71 inch lbs. (8 Nm).
7. Connect the sensor electrical connector.
8. Lower the vehicle and connect the battery negative cable.

Ignition Module

NOTE: Before removing the ignition module, refer to the manufacture's instructions provided

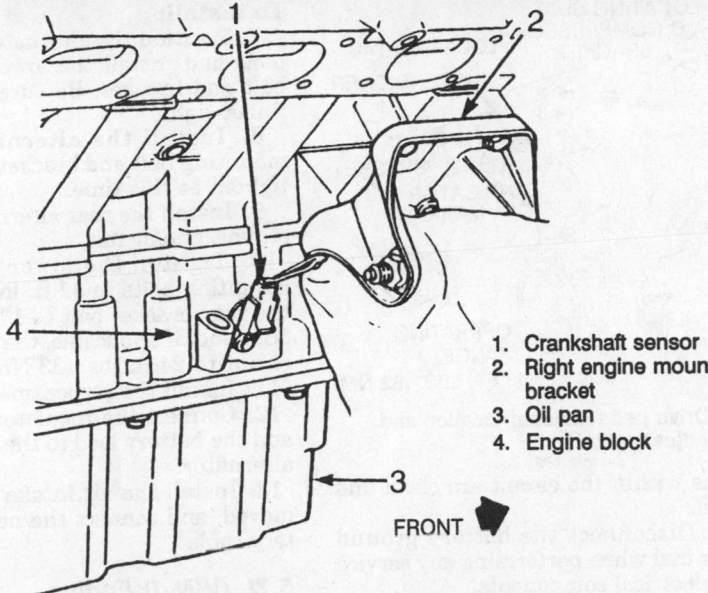

1. Crankshaft sensor
2. Right engine mount bracket
3. Oil pan
4. Engine block

FRONT ◄

Crankshaft sensor location—5.7L (VIN J) Engine

1. Timing indicator
2. Timing mark

Ignition timing mark—5.7L (VIN 8) Engine

with the replacement ignition module.

1. Disconnect the battery negative cable.
2. Remove the intake plenum assembly. The ignition module is mounted on the bottom of the plenum.
3. Disconnect the electrical connectors from the ignition module.
4. Remove the mounting bolts, then the ignition module.

To install:

5. Apply a suitable dielectric grease to the back of the ignition module. Install the module and tighten the 4 mounting bolts to 89 inch lbs. (10 Nm).
6. Engage the electrical connectors.
7. Install the intake plenum assembly.
8. Connect the negative battery cable.

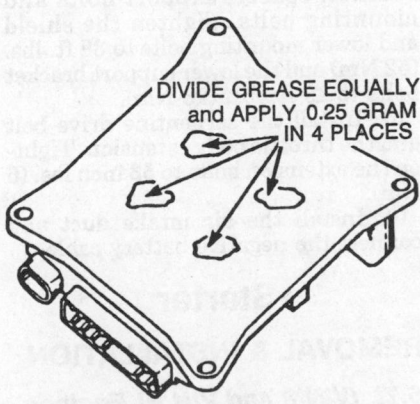

DIVIDE GREASE EQUALLY and APPLY 0.25 GRAM IN 4 PLACES

Ignition module dielectric grease application—5.7L (VIN J) Engine

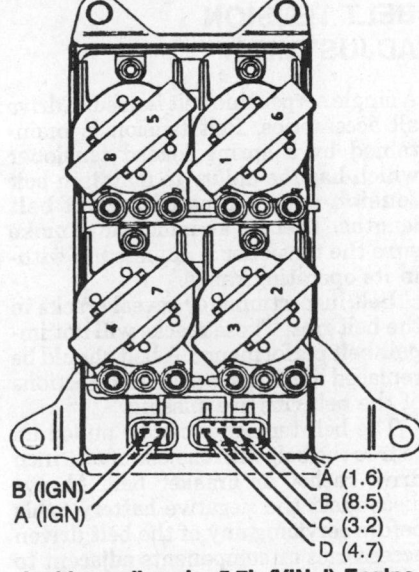

B (IGN)
A (IGN)

A (1.6)
B (8.5)
C (3.2)
D (4.7)

Ignition coil pack—5.7L (VIN J) Engine

Ignition Coil Pack

1. Disconnect the battery negative cable.
2. Remove the intake plenum assembly.
3. Tag and disconnect the spark plug wires from the ignition coil pack.
4. Remove the 2 mounting bolts and the ignition coil pack.
5. Installation is the reverse of the removal procedure.
6. Torque mounting bolts to 40 inch lbs. (4.5 Nm).

Ignition Housing

1. Disconnect battery negative cable.
2. Remove intake plenum assembly.

3. Tag and disconnect the electrical connectors and spark plug wires.
4. Remove the 4 ignition housing bracket mounting bolts.
5. Remove the ignition coil mounting bolts. Note the position of each coil and remove the coils from the ignition housing. Remove the ignition housing from the bracket.

To install:

6. Install the ignition housing on the bracket and install the 4 seals packaged with the housing.
7. Install the coils in their proper position on the housing and tighten the coil retaining bolts to 40 inch lbs. (4.5 Nm).
8. Install the ignition housing bracket to the engine and tighten the bracket bolts as follows: M6–16 bolts to 89 inch lbs.; M8–20 bolts to 19 ft. lbs.
9. Connect the electrical connector and the spark plug wires.
10. Install the intake plenum assembly.
11. Connect the negative battery cable.

Ignition Timing

The 5.7L (VIN 8) engine is the only engine on which a timing adjustment is possible. The use of an inductive pickup timing light is recommended.

On the 5.7L (VIN 8) Engine, the base timing is manually adjusted and the ECM has the ability to modify the ignition timing. If detonation is detected, the ECM retards the spark advance for about 20 seconds through the Electronic Spark Control (ESC).

For the 5.7L (VIN J and VIN P) engines the base timing is preset at the factory, no adjustment is possible. Timing advance and retard are accomplished through the ECM with the EST and the Electronic Spark Control (ESC).

ADJUSTMENT

5.7L (VIN 8) Engine

1. Refer to and follow all instructions on the vehicle emissions control information label.

2. Turn the ignition **OFF** and connect a timing light to the No. 1 spark plug. Use a jumper lead between the wire and the plug or an inductive type pickup. Connect the timing light power leads according to the manufacture's instructions.

3. Disconnect the ECM harness connector at the distributor.

4. Start the engine and warm to normal operating temperature. Aim the light at the timing mark and not the engine timing. If an adjustment is necessary, loosen the distributor holddown bolt and rotate the distributor accordingly.

5. If adjusted, retighten the holddown clamp bolt to 25 ft. lbs. (34 Nm) and recheck the ignition timing.

6. Turn the ignition **OFF** and reconnect the No 1. spark plug wire, if disconnected. Connect the ECM harness connector.

Alternator

PRECAUTIONS

Several precautions must be observed with alternator equipped vehicles to avoid damage to the unit.

• If the battery is removed for any reason, make sure it is reconnected with the correct polarity. Reversing the battery connections may result in damage to the 1-way rectifiers.

• When utilizing a booster battery as a starting aid, always connect the positive to positive terminals and the negative terminal from the booster battery to a good engine ground on the vehicle being started.

• Never use a fast charger as a booster to start vehicles.

• Disconnect the battery cables when charging the battery with a fast charger.

• Never attempt to polarize the alternator.

• Do not use test lights of more than 12 volts when checking diode continuity.

• Never operate the alternator with the output terminal disconnected.

• Do not short across or ground any of the alternator terminals.

• The polarity of the battery, alternator and regulator must be matched and considered before making any electrical connections within the system.

• Never separate the alternator on an open circuit. Make sure all connec-

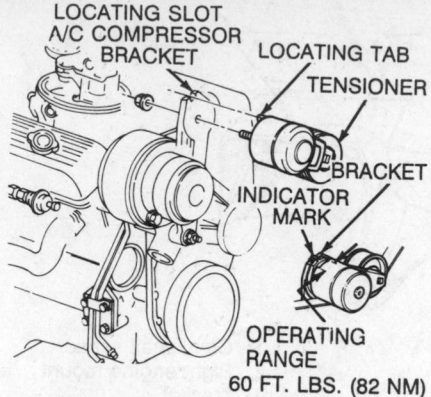

Drive belt tensioner location and adjustments

tions within the circuit are clean and tight.

• Disconnect the battery ground terminal when performing any service on electrical components.

• Disconnect the battery if arc welding is to be done on the vehicle.

BELT TENSION ADJUSTMENT

A single serpentine belt is used to drive all accessories. Belt tension is maintained by a spring loaded tensioner which has the ability to maintain belt tension over a broad range of belt lengths. There is an indicator to make sure the tensioner is adjusted to within its operating range.

Belt inspection may reveal cracks in the belt ribs. These cracks will not impair belt performance. A belt should be replaced if belt slip occurs or if sections of the belt ribs are missing.

The belt tensioner can be pulled up to free the belt with the use of a ½ inch drive rachet or breaker bar. Always disconnect the negative battery cable before servicing any of the belt driven accessories or components adjacent to the belt.

REMOVAL & INSTALLATION

5.7L (VIN 8 and VIN P) Engines

1. Disconnect the negative battery cable.

2. Remove the air intake duct, if necessary.

3. Disconnect the regulator connector and the battery lead from the back of the alternator.

4. Use a ½ breaker bar to rotate the tensioner and remove the serpentine drive belt.

5. Remove the rear alternator mounting bolt, nut and bracket.

6. Remove the alternator mounting bolts. Remove the upper or lower brackets, as necessary and remove the alternator from the vehicle.

To install:

7. Position the alternator in the vehicle and install the lower mounting bolt and bracket. Be sure the bolt is finger-tight.

8. Install the alternator upper mounting bolt and bracket, but do not tighten at this time.

9. Install the rear alternator bracket, bolt and/or nut.

10. Tighten the lower and upper mounting bolts to 37 ft. lbs. (50 Nm), the rear bracket bolt to 17 ft. lbs. (23 Nm) and, if applicable, the rear bracket nut to 24 ft. lbs. (33 Nm).

11. Install the serpentine drive belt.

12. Connect the regulator connector and the battery lead to the back of the alternator.

13. Install the air intake duct, if removed, and connect the negative battery cable.

5.7L (VIN J) Engine

1. Disconnect the negative battery cable.

2. Remove the air intake duct and the throttle body extension.

3. Remove the serpentine drive belt.

4. Remove the alternator lower mounting bolt, noting the length for reinstallation.

5. Remove the lower support bracket bolts and shield.

6. Remove the upper support bolts and shield.

7. Disconnect the oil sender electrical connection and remove the sender.

8. Disconnect the alternator electrical connections and remove the alternator.

To install:

9. Engage the electrical connections to the alternator and position the alternator in the vehicle.

10. Install the oil sender and electrical connections.

11. Apply Loctite® 565 to all generator mounting bolt threads.

12. Install the upper support shield and bolts, then the lower support bracket, spacer, support bolts and mounting bolts. Tighten the shield and lower mounting bolts to 38 ft. lbs. (52 Nm) and the lower support bracket bolts to 19 ft. lbs. (26 Nm).

13. Install the serpentine drive belt and the throttle body extension. Tighten the extension bolts to 53 inch lbs. (6 Nm).

14. Install the air intake duct and connect the negative battery cable.

Starter

REMOVAL & INSTALLATION

5.7L (VIN 8 and VIN P) Engines

1. Disconnect the negative battery cable.

2. Raise and support the vehicle safely.

3. Disconnect the wiring from the starter solenoid. Tag the wiring positions to avoid improper connections during installation.

4. Loosen the 2 starter mounting bolts, support the starter and remove the bolts. Lower the starter from the vehicle and remove shims, if equipped.

To install:

5. Position the shims and starter into the vehicle and insert the mounting bolts. Tighten the bolts to 34 ft. lbs. (47 Nm) and replace sealer.

6. Check that flywheel to pinion clearance is 0.020 inch (0.5mm) and add or subtract shims, if necessary.

7. Connect the start wiring.

8. Lower vehicle and connect the battery negative cable.

5.7L (VIN J) Engine

1. Disconnect battery negative cable.

2. Remove the intake plenum assembly.

3. Remove the coil pack assembly.

4. Raise and support the vehicle safely.

5. Disconnect the wiring from the starter solenoid. Tag the wiring positions to avoid improper connections during installation.

6. Remove the 2 starter mounting bolts, then remove the starter from the vehicle.

To install:

7. Coat the threads of the starter mounting bolts with Loctite® 262.

8. Position the starter in the vehicle and install the mounting bolts. Tighten the starter mounting bolts to 38 ft. lbs. (52 Nm).

9. Connect the starter wiring and lower the vehicle.

10. Install the coil pack assembly.

11. Install the intake plenum assembly.

12. Connect the negative battery cable.

EMISSION CONTROLS

Due to the complex nature of modern electronic engine control systems, comprehensive diagnosis and testing procedures fall outside the confines of this repair manual. For complete information on diagnosis, testing and repair procedures concerning all modern engine and emission control systems, please refer to "Chilton's Guide to Fuel Injection and Electronic Engine Controls".

Emission Warning Lamps

The "Service Engine Soon" emission light located on the instrument panel has 3 functions:

1. The light indicates to the driver that a problem has occurred and the vehicle should be taken for service as soon as reasonably possible.

2. The light is used by technicians to monitor "Trouble Codes" when the system is in the diagnostic mode.

3. The light indicates "Open Loop" or "Closed Loop" operation.

To verify the bulb and wiring of the system is operating properly, the "Service Engine Soon" light will come ON with the key **ON** and the engine not running. When the engine is started, the "Service Engine Soon" light will turn OFF if the system is operating properly.

If the "Service Engine Soon" light remains ON, the self-diagnostic system has detected a problem. Should the problem disappear, the light will go out in most cases in about 10 seconds, but a Trouble Code will remain in the ECM memory.

RESETTING

After repairs are made to the faulty system(s) it is necessary to make sure the ECM memory is cleared of old trouble codes. Removing battery voltage to the ECM for 30 seconds will clear all stored trouble codes. This can be accomplished in various ways; by disconnecting the ECM power feed from the positive battery pigtail with the ignition **OFF**, by removing the inline fuse that originates from the positive connection of the battery, or by disconnecting the ECM fuse from the fuse block.

NOTE: To prevent ECM damage, the key must be OFF when disconnecting or reconnecting power to ECM (for example battery cable, ECM pigtail, ECM fuse, jumper cables, etc.).

If the negative battery terminal is disconnected, other onboard memory data, such as pre-set radio tuning will be lost. For this reason, it may be more desirable to clear codes by removing power only from the ECM.

FUEL SYSTEM

Fuel System Service Precautions

Safety is the most important factor when performing any type of maintenance, but even more so when performing fuel system maintenance. Failure to conduct maintenance and repairs in a safe manner may result in personal injury or death. Maintenance and testing of the vehicle's fuel system components can be accomplished safely and effectively by adhering to the following rules and guidelines.

● To avoid the possibility of fire and personal injury, always disconnect the negative battery cable unless the repair or test procedure requires that battery voltage remain connected.

● Always relieve the fuel system pressure prior to disconnecting any fuel system component (injector, fuel rail, pressure regulator, etc.), fitting or fuel line connection. Exercise extreme caution whenever relieving fuel system pressure to avoid exposing skin, face and eyes to fuel spray. Under pressure, fuel may penetrate the skin or any part of the body that it contacts.

● Always place a shop towel or cloth around a fitting or connection prior to loosening, to absorb any excess fuel due to spillage. Ensure that all fuel spillage (should it occur) is quickly removed from engine surfaces. Ensure that all fuel soaked cloths or towels are deposited into a suitable waste container.

● Always keep a dry chemical (Class B) fire extinguisher near the work area.

● Do not allow fuel spray or fuel vapors to come into contact with a spark or open flame.

● Always use a backup wrench when loosing and tightening fuel line connection fittings. This will prevent unnecessary stress and torsion to fuel line piping. Always follow the proper torque specifications.

● Always replace worn fuel fitting O-rings with new. Do not substitute fuel hose or equivalent, where fuel pipe is installed.

RELIEVING FUEL SYSTEM PRESSURE

1. Disconnect the negative battery cable.

2. Loosen the fuel filler cap to relieve the tank pressure.

3. Wrap a shop towel around the fuel pressure valve fitting to catch any fuel spray and connect a fuel gauge J–

34730–1 or equivalent, to the fuel pressure valve.

4. Install the bleed hose into a suitable container, then open the valve to bleed the fuel system pressure.

5. Close the valve and disconnect the fuel gauge. Drain any remaining fuel from the gauge into the bleed container.

Fuel Tank

REMOVAL & INSTALLATION

NOTE: Ensure an approved dry chemical (Class B) fire extinguisher is near the work area. For safety, additional vehicle supports should be added to the end of the vehicle opposite the work area to keep the vehicle stable on the lift.

1. Disconnect the negative battery cable and properly relieve fuel system pressure.

2. Drain the fuel tank into an approved container.

3. Remove the fuel door bezel and filler cap.

4. Lift the filler neck housing and disconnect the the drain hose from the nipple.

5. Reinstall the filler cap to prevent dirt from entering and remove the filler neck housing.

6. Disconnect the fuel sender electrical connector at the tank.

7. Thoroughly clean the surrounding areas to prevent fuel system contamination, then disconnect the fuel hoses from the sender assembly.

8. Remove the license plate and all rear lamps to provide access, then remove the carriage bolts securing the fascia to the impact bar.

9. Raise and safely support the vehicle.

10. Remove the spare tire and tire carrier from the frame.

11. With the aid of an assistant, remove the mufflers as an assembly from the converter.

12. Remove the canister splash shield, if equipped, and both rear inner fender braces at the frame.

13. Remove both rear wheel house liner panels.

14. Remove the antenna ground strap and clip at the antenna base and frame.

15. Disconnect the fuel vapor pipes from the canister or the bottom of the tank. Remove that canister, if equipped.

16. Remove both fuel tank cables from the stabilizer shaft supports.

17. Remove the bumper to energy absorbing pad bottom attaching screws.

18. Remove the marker lamps and spare tire light.

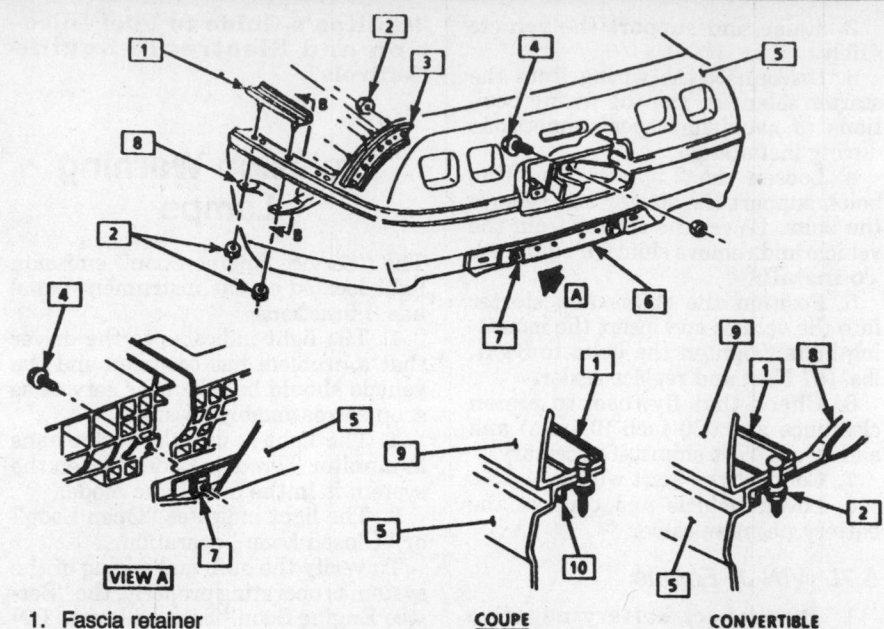

1. Fascia retainer
2. Nut
3. LH Fascia outer retainer
4. Bolt
5. Rear bumper fascia
6. Fascia lower reinforcement
7. J–Nut
8. LH Fascia support
9. Upper rear body panel
10. LH Fascia upper retainer

VIEW A   **COUPE**   **CONVERTIBLE**

Rear fascia assembly

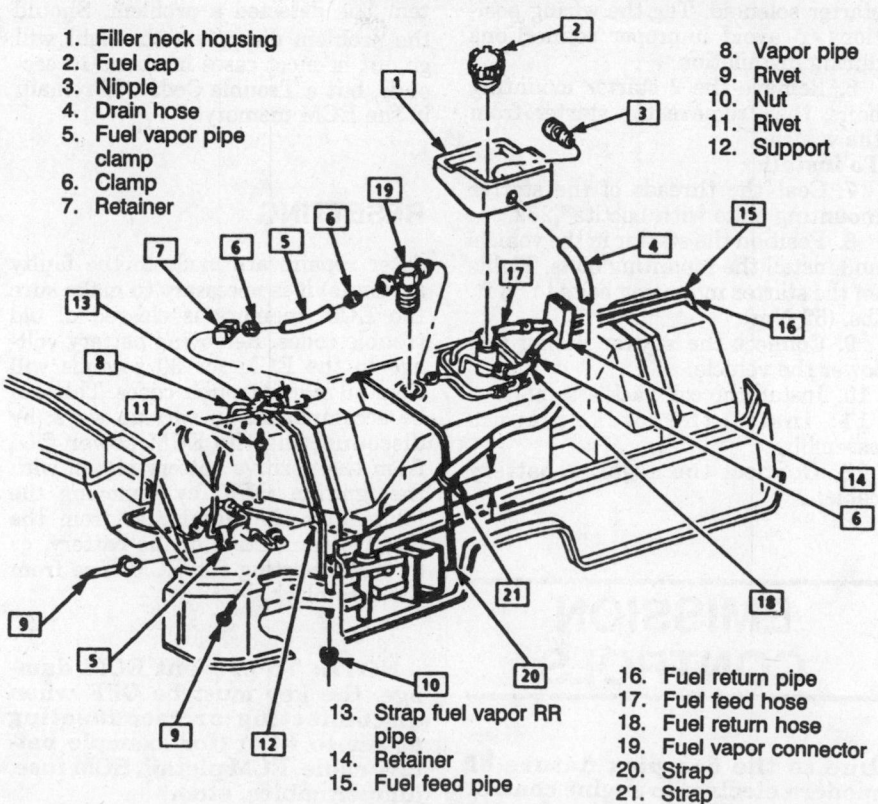

1. Filler neck housing
2. Fuel cap
3. Nipple
4. Drain hose
5. Fuel vapor pipe clamp
6. Clamp
7. Retainer
8. Vapor pipe
9. Rivet
10. Nut
11. Rivet
12. Support
13. Strap fuel vapor RR pipe
14. Retainer
15. Fuel feed pipe
16. Fuel return pipe
17. Fuel feed hose
18. Fuel return hose
19. Fuel vapor connector
20. Strap
21. Strap

Fuel tank assembly

19. Remove the nuts attaching each side fascia to the horizontal body retainer. Then remove the nuts securing each side of the vertical body retainer to the fascia.

20. For 1989–91 vehicles, safely support the rear frame section and with the help of an assistant, remove the rear subframe to main frame bolts. Pull the frame and fuel tank assembly

to the rear, pushing the the cover outward and letting the frame assembly down to clear the cover. Place the fuel tank and frame assembly in a suitable work area and remove the fuel tank.

21. For 1992–93 vehicles, remove 6 impact bar bolts and loosen the front 2 bolts, 1 on each side. With the aid of an assistant, support the impact bar, and remove the front bar bolts. Remove the impact bar and fuel tank assembly and remove the fuel tank.

22. If the tank is being replaced, transfer the cables, vapor connections and hoses, fuel sender assembly, and/or fuel connector, as required and applicable.

To install:

23. For 1989–91 vehicles, install the fuel tank into the rear subframe assembly and secure with retaining straps. Torque the strap bolts to 11 ft. lbs. (15 Nm) and the strap nuts to 40 inch lbs. (4.5 Nm). Install the rear subframe and fuel tank assembly to the main frame with the mounting bolts.

24. For 1992–92 vehicles, install the fuel tank to the impact bar assembly and tighten the strap bolts to 11 ft. lbs. (15 Nm) and the strap nuts to 40 inch lbs. (4.5 Nm). Install the impact bar assembly and tighten the bolts to 37 ft. lbs. (50 Nm).

25. Install rear and side fascia to body retainer with attaching nuts. Tighten the nuts to 53 inch lbs. (6 Nm).

26. Install the marker lights and the spare tire light sockets.

27. Attach screws from bottom of bumper to energy absorber pad.

28. Reattach fuel tank cables. Tighten the cable attaching nuts to 15 ft. lbs. (20 Nm) for 1989–91 vehicles or the stablizer shaft nuts to 18 ft. lbs. (25 Nm) for 1992–93 vehicles.

29. Install the carriage bolts securing the fascia to the impact bar, then install the antenna ground strap and clip.

30. Install both inner fender panels, then the braces to the frame.

31. Connect the vapor hose to the canister or the bottom of the tank and, if equipped, install the canister splash shield.

32. With the aid of an assistant, install the muffler assembly to the converter.

33. Install the spare tire and carrier to the frame.

34. Lower the vehicle and install all rear lamps.

35. Install the license plate.

36. Connect all lines and electrical connections to the fuel sender assembly.

37. Refill the fuel tank, tighten the fuel filler cap and connect the negative battery cable.

38. Turn the ignition **ON** for 2 seconds, **OFF** for 10 seconds, then **ON** again and inspect the system for leaks.

39. Install the drain hose, seal and fuel filler door bezel.

Fuel Filter

REMOVAL & INSTALLATION

1. Disconnect the battery negative cable and properly relieve the fuel system pressure.

2. Raise and safely support the vehicle.

3. If equipped, remove the fuel filter shield attaching screws and remove the filter shield.

4. Clean the filter connections and surrounding areas to prevent fuel system contamination, disconnect the fuel pipes from the filter and drain any remaining fuel into a suitable container.

5. Remove the fuel filter attaching screw and remove the filter from the vehicle.

To install:

6. Loosely install the fuel filter to the rail with the attaching screw.

7. Inspect the fuel line O-rings and replace as necessary. Connect the fuel lines to the fuel filter and tighten to 22 ft. lbs. (30 Nm) for 1989–91 vehicles or to 20 ft. lbs. (27 Nm) for 1992–93 vehicles. Use a backup wrench to prevent the filter from turning.

8. Tighten the fuel filter attaching screw to 53 inch lbs. (6 Nm).

9. If equipped, install the fuel filter shield and attaching screws.

10. Lower the vehicle, tighten the fuel filler cap and connect the negative battery cable.

11. Turn the ignition **ON** for 2 seconds, **OFF** for 10 seconds, then **ON** again and inspect the system for leaks.

Electric Fuel Pump

PRESSURE TESTING

1. Properly relieve fuel system pressure.

2. With ignition **OFF**, install fuel pressure gauge J–34730–1 or equivalent, to the fuel rail pressure connection.

3. For the 5.7L (VIN J) engine, test the primary fuel pump by removing the secondary fuel pump fuse (FP2) or test the secondary fuel pump by removing the primary fuel pump fuse (FP1).

4. Turn the ignition switch **ON**, but with the engine not running. The fuel pump will operate for 2 seconds and then turn **OFF**.

5. Fuel pressure should be 34–47 psi, if equipped with the 5.7L (VIN 8) engine, 41–47 psi, if equipped with the 5.7L (VIN P) engine or 48–55 psi, if equipped with the 5.7L (VIN J) engine.

6. The pressure should hold steady when the pump stops, with little or no pressure drop.

7. Start the engine and the pressure should drop approximately 3–10 psi.

REMOVAL & INSTALLATION

1989

NOTE: The fuel pump is part of the fuel sender assembly mounted inside the fuel tank.

1. Disconnect the negative battery cable and properly relieve the fuel system pressure.

2. Remove the fuel tank assembly from the vehicle.

3. Remove the fuel sending unit assembly by turning the cam lock ring counter clockwise and lifting the assembly from the tank.

4. Remove the fuel pump from the assembly by pulling the pump up into the attaching hose or pulsator while pulling outward, away from the bottom support. Take care to prevent damage to the rubber insulator and strainer.

5. After the pump is clear of the bottom support, pull the pump out of the rubber connector or pulsator.

To install:

6. Push the pump into the attaching hose and position in the fuel sender assembly.

7. Using a new gasket, install the fuel sender assembly into the fuel tank. Do not fold or twist the strainer when installing the sending unit, as this could cause fuel restriction. Also, be sure the strainer does not block full travel of the float arm.

8. Install the cam lock over the assembly and lock by turning clockwise.

9. Install the fuel tank.

10. Tighten the fuel filler cap and connect the negative battery cable.

11. Turn the ignition **ON** for 2 seconds, **OFF** for 10 seconds, then **ON** again and inspect the system for leaks.

1990–93

NOTE: Vehicles equipped with the 5.7L (VIN J) engine use 2 fuel pumps which are not serviced separately, therefore if one fuel pump is not operational, the fuel sender assembly with both pumps must be replaced as a unit.

1. Disconnect the negative battery cable.

2. Properly relieve the fuel system pressure and drain the fuel tank.

3. Remove the filler door bezel attaching screws, then the filler door bezel.

4. Lift the fuel tank filler neck housing and disconnect the drain hose from the nipple. Remove filler neck housing.

5. Clean the area around all fuel fittings to prevent system contamination, then disconnect and plug the fuel pipes and fuel vapor pipe.

6. Disconnect the sending unit electrical connector, remove the attaching bolts and remove the sending unit assembly from the vehicle.

7. If equipped with the 5.7L (VIN J) engine, replace fuel sender assembly.

8. If equipped with the 5.7L (VIN 8 or VIN P) engines, proceed as follows:

 a. Note the position of the fuel strainer on the pump.

 b. Support the pump with one hand and grasp the strainer with the other. Turn the strainer in one direction, pull the strainer off the pump and discard it.

 c. Diconnnect the fuel pump electrical connection.

 d. Place the fuel sender assembly upside down on a flat bench.

 e. Pull the fuel pump downward to remove it from the mounting bracket, then tilt the pump outward and remove it from the pulsator.

To install:

9. If equipped with the 5.7L (VIN 8 or VIN P) engine, install the pump to the sending assembly as follows:

 a. Assemble the rear bumper and insulator onto the fuel pump.

 b. Position the fuel sender assembly upside down on a flat bench and install the fuel pump between the fuel pulse dampener and mounting bracket.

 c. Install the pump electrical connector.

 d. Install the new fuel strainer into the same position as noted during disassembly.

10. Position a new gasket on the fuel tank with the notch facing forward in the right hand corner of the fuel tank.

11. Carefully fold the strainer to allow it to fit through the opening in the tank. Make sure the strainer unfolds in the tank and lower the fuel sender assembly into position.

12. Install the fuel sender assembly attaching screws and tighten alternately and evenly to 45 inch lbs. (5 Nm).

13. Engage the fuel sender assembly electrical connector.

14. Connect all sender assembly fuel and vapor hoses.

15. Connect the fuel drain hose to the nipple on the rubber filler neck housing, then position the housing around the fuel tank filler neck.

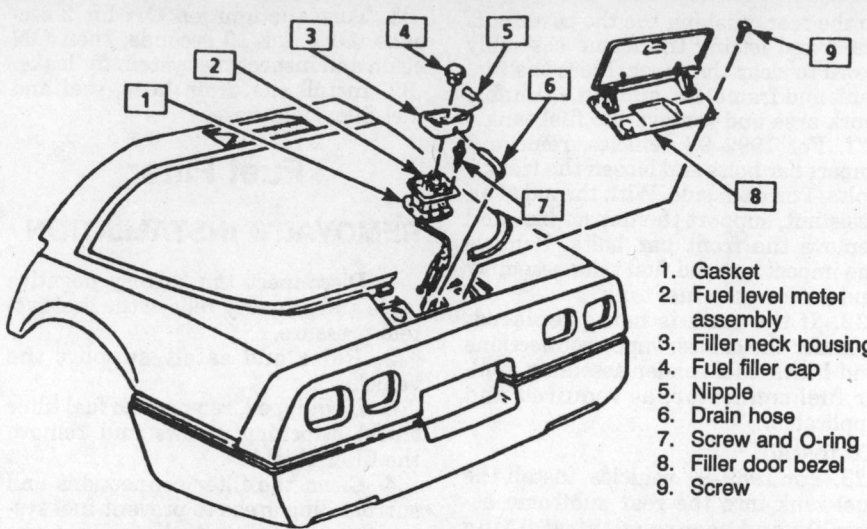

1. Gasket
2. Fuel level meter assembly
3. Filler neck housing
4. Fuel filler cap
5. Nipple
6. Drain hose
7. Screw and O-ring
8. Filler door bezel
9. Screw

Fuel sender and pump assembly removal—1990–93 vehicles

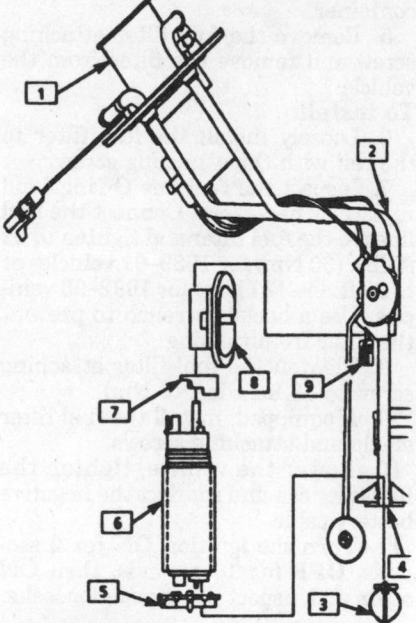

1. Fuel level meter
2. Inlet tube
3. Fuel pump filter
4. Mounting bracket
5. Rubber insulator
6. Fuel pump
7. Rubber bumper
8. Pulsator
9. Electrical connector

Fuel pump and sender assembly—1990–93 5.7L (VIN 8 and VIN P) Engines

16. Install the filler door bezel with the attaching screws.

17. Add fuel, tighten the filler cap and connect the negative battery cable.

18. Turn the ignition **ON** for 2 seconds, **OFF** for 10 seconds, then **ON** again and inspect the system for leaks.

Fuel Injection

IDLE SPEED ADJUSTMENT

Idle speed is controlled by the ECM through the Idle Air Control (IAC) valve pintle position. The ECM is programmed to determine the correct pintle position based on various inputs, therefore idle speed is not adjustable.

When installing a new IAC valve, measure the distance between the tip of the valve pintle and the mounting flange. The distance should be no more than 1.10 inch (28mm). If the distance is greater, adjust the valve pintle by applying finger pressure to retract the pintle. Do not push the pintle of a used IAC valve, as this may damage the valve.

If the negative battery cable is disconnected and reconnected with the engine running or if the IAC valve is replaced, the idle speed may be wrong. If this is the case the IAC valve may be reset as follows:

1. Depress the accelerator pedal slightly.

2. Start the engine and run for 5 seconds.

3. Turn the ignition **OFF** for 10 seconds.

4. Restart the vehicle and check for proper idle operation.

Fuel Injector

REMOVAL & INSTALLATION

5.7L (VIN 8) Engine

1. Disconnect the negative battery cable and properly relieve fuel system pressure.

2. Drain the cooling system suffi-

ciently to remove the lower coolant hose at the throttle body.

3. Remove the throttle, transmission and cruise control cables, then remove the cable retaining bracket.

4. Remove the throttle body air intake duct.

5. Remove the vacuum hoses at the intake assembly, the lower throttle body coolant hose and the AIR hoses from the air management valve.

6. Remove the throttle body attaching bolts and the throttle body.

7. Disconnect the TPS and IAC electrical connectors and the fuel injector electrical connectors. Remove the harness attaching nuts and remove the harnesses.

8. Remove the left intake runner to plenum and runner to manifold bolts, then remove the PCV valve and hose.

9. Remove the right intake runner to plenum and runner to manifold bolts, then remove the EGR solenoid.

10. Remove the right manifold to runner bolt. Remove the plenum and the right runner and discard the gaskets.

11. Remove the left side manifold to runner bolt. Remove the left runner and discard the gaskets.

12. Using a backup wrench, disconnect the fuel feed and return lines. Discard the old O-rings.

13. Remove the fuel tube bracket bolt.

14. Remove the pressure regulator vacuum line.

15. Remove the fuel rail attaching bolts and carefully remove the fuel rail assembly.

16. Rotate the injector lock ring to the release positition.

17. Remove the injector.

NOTE: When replacing single injectors, always replace with the identical part number. Intermixed injectors will result in an excessive rough idle and increased emissions.

To install:

18. Lubricate new injector O-ring seals with clean engine oil and install the seals onto the injector.

19. Install a new retainer clip onto the injector.

20. Install injector into fuel rail socket with injector electrical connector facing outward.

21. Rotate the injector clip to the **LOCK** position.

22. Install the fuel rail assembly into the intake manifold.

23. Install the fuel rail attaching bolts and the fuel tube bracket bolt. Tighten the rail bolts to 15 ft. lbs. (20 Nm) and the tube bracket bolt to 25 ft. lbs. (34 Nm).

24. Rotate the injectors as necessary to avoid stretching the wire harness

and install the inejctor electrical connections.

25. Install the vacuum line to the pressure regulator.

26. Install the new O-rings on the fuel feed and return lines and connect the lines. Tighten the line fittings to 20 ft. lbs. (27 Nm). Use a backup wrench to support the fuel rail tube fittings.

27. Temporarily connect the battery cable and turn the ignition switch **ON** for 2 seconds, then to the **OFF** position for 10 seconds. Repeat the procedure once again, then disconnect the battery negative cable and inspect the fuel system for leaks.

28. Install new gaskets on the runners and the intake manifold. Install the left side runners and finger-tighten the runner to manifold bolts.

29. Install the left manifold to runner bolt and tighten to 25 ft. lbs. (34 Nm).

30. Install the right runners and finger-tighten the runner to manifold bolts and the manifold to runner bolt.

31. Install the intake plenum and the runner to plenum bolts.

32. Tighten the runner to manifold bolts, beginning at the center and working outwards, to 18 ft. lbs. (25 Nm) for 1989 vehicles or to 25 ft. lbs. (34 Nm) for 1990–91 vehicles. Tighten the right manifold to runner bolt to 18 ft. lbs. (25 Nm) for 1989 vehicles or to 25 ft. lbs. (34 Nm) for 1990–91 vehicles. Tighten the runner to plenum bolts, beginning at the center and working outwards, to 18 ft. lbs. (25 Nm) for 1989 vehicles or to 25 ft. lbs. (34 Nm) for 1990–91 vehicles.

33. Install the EGR solenoid, the PCV valve and hose.

34. Connect the power brake vacuum line to the plenum fitting and tighten line nut to 108 inch lbs. (12.2 Nm).

35. Install the injector harness attaching nuts. Connect the TPS and IAC electrical connections.

36. Install the throttle body with at-

taching bolts and tighten the bolts to 18 ft. lbs. (24 Nm).

37. Connect the AIR hoses to the management valve, the lower coolant hose to the throttle body, and any remaining vacuum hoses.

38. Install the throttle body intake air duct. Install the throttle cable bracket, connect the throttle TV and cruise control cables.

39. Tighten the fuel filler cap and connect the negative battery cable.

40. Properly refill the engine cooling system.

5.7L (VIN P) Engine

1. Disconnect the negative battery cable and properly relieve fuel system pressure.

2. Remove the fuel rail cover.

3. Disconnect the quick-connect fittings at the fuel rail feed and return pipes as follows:

   a. Grasp both ends of a connection and twist ¼ turn in each direction to loosen any dirt. Repeat for other fitting.

   b. While wearing safety glasses, use compressed air to blow out dirt from the fittings.

   c. Insert a proper fuel line separator tool, into the female connector, then push inward to release the male connector and repeat for the other fitting.

4. Disconnect the vacuum line at the pressure regulator.

5. Disconnect the injector electrical connectors.

6. Remove the fuel rail attaching bolts and carefully remove the fuel rail assembly.

7. Rotate the injector retaining clip to the release position and remove the injector from the fuel rail assembly.

8. Remove and discard the O-ring seals from either side of the injector.

9. Remove and discard the injector retaining clip.

To install:

10. Lubricate the new injector O-rings with clean engine oil and install onto the injector.

NOTE: Always replace injectors using an identical part number as inscribed in the old injector.

11. Connect a new retainer clip onto the fuel injector and install the injector to the fuel rail assembly. Rotate the injector retaining clip to the lock position.

12. Install the fuel rail assembly to the intake manifold. Tighten the attaching bolts to 15 ft. lbs. (20 Nm).

13. Rotate the fuel injectors as necessary to avoid stretching the wire harnesses and connect the injector electrical connections.

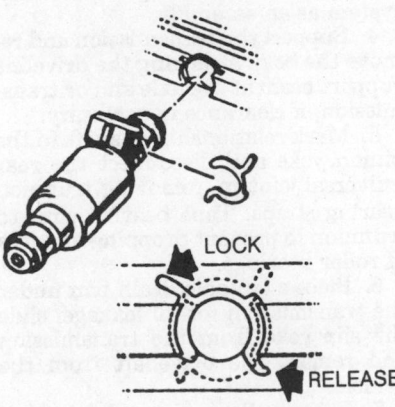

Fuel Injector removal—5.7L (VIN 8) Engine

14. Connect the vacuum line to the pressure regulator.

15. Apply a few drops of clean engine oil to the male ends of the fuel line quick-connect fittings. Connect the fittings by pushing the connectors together until the retaining tabs snap into place. Pull gently on both sides of each fitting to be sure the connection is secure.

16. Tighten the fuel filler cap and connect the negative battery cable.

17. Turn the ignition **ON** for 2 seconds, **OFF** for 10 seconds, then **ON** again and inspect the system for leaks.

5.7L (VIN J) Engine

1. Disconnect the negative battery cable and properly relieve fuel system pressure.

2. Drain the cooling system into a suitable container.

3. Remove the plenum assembly.

4. Disconnect the fuel injector wire connectors.

5. Remove the bolts securing the fuel rail to the injector housing.

6. Carefully remove the fuel rails making sure not to damage the injector connector terminals or spray tips. Remove the spacers, if equipped. Note the position of vacuum hoses around the fuel rail before removing the rail.

7. Remove the injector retaining clip, then remove the injector.

8. Remove and discard the injector O-ring seals.

To install:

9. Lubricate new injector O-rings with engine oil and install the injector with retaining clip onto fuel rail. Make sure the injector wire connection is facing outward and push the injector onto the rail enough to engage the clip with the machined slots on the rail socket.

NOTE: Each injector is calibrated for a specific flow rate and must be replaced with an indentical part number.

10. Install the fuel rail into the injector housing, routing the vacuum lines in their previous positions around the rails.

11. Be sure the spacers, if equipped, are positioned under the rail mounting brackets.

12. Install the fuel rail bolts and tighten to 20 ft. lbs. (26 Nm).

13. Engage the injector electrical connectors, turning the injectors if necessary to avoid stretching the wire harnesses.

14. Install new O-rings to the fuel feed and return pipes.

15. Temporarily connect the fuel feed and return lines with the retaining bolts tightened to 13 ft. lbs. (18 Nm). Temporarily connect the nega-

Fuel Injector removal—5.7L (VIN J) Engine

tive battery cable and turn the ignition switch **ON** for 2 seconds, then **OFF** for 10 seconds. Repeat the procedure once again, then disconnect the battery negative cable and inspect the fuel system for leaks.

16. Relieve fuel system pressure and disconnect the fuel feed and return lines.

17. Install the plenum assembly.

18. Tighten the fuel filler cap and connect the negative battery terminal.

19. Properly refill the engine cooling system.

DRIVE AXLE

Driveshaft and U-Joints

REMOVAL & INSTALLATION

1. Raise and support the vehicle safely.

2. Remove the upper and lower underbody braces, if equipped.

3. Remove the complete exhaust system as an assembly.

4. Support the transmission and remove the bolts attaching the driveline support beam at the axle and/or transmission, if clearance is necessary.

5. Mark relationship of shaft to the pinion yoke and disconnect the rear universal joint by removing trunnion bearing straps. Tape bearing cups to trunnion to prevent dropping and loss of roller bearings.

6. Place a suitable drain pan under the transmission for oil leakage, slide the slip yoke from the transmission and remove the drivehaft from the vehicle.

7. Remove the universal joints, if necessary, as follows:

   a. Remove the snapring. If it does

not readily come out, tap the end of the bearing cap lightly to relieve pressure against the ring.

   b. Place the drive shaft horizontally in line with the base plate of a press, but do not clamp the tube.

   c. Support the lower ear of the universal joint with a 1⅛ inch socket.

   d. Press the lower bearing cap out from the yoke by pushing on the upper bearing cap.

   e. Rotate the driveshaft, then remove the the opposite bearing cap.

   f. Remove the universal joint from the yoke.

To install:

8. If removed, install U-joints, as follows:

   a. Install one bearing cap partially into 1 side of the yoke, then turn this side to the bottom.

   b. Install the joint into the yoke so the trunnion seats freely in the bearing cap.

   c. Install the opposite bearing cap partially into the yoke, verifying the trunnions are straight and true in the bearing caps.

   d. Press against the opposite bearing caps, while verifying the joint is not binding and turns freely. If the joint begins to bind, there is probably a needle bearing out of place.

   e. When 1 bearing cap snapring retainer groove clears the inside of the yoke, stop pressing and install a snapring into place.

   f. Continue to press the opposite side until a snapring can be inserted. If difficulty is encountered, strike the yoke firmly with a hammer to slightly spring the yoke ears.

   g. Assemble the other half of the joint in the same manner.

9. Slide the driveshaft slip yoke into the transmission extension.

10. Align the marks made during removal and and install the rear of the driveshaft to the pinion yoke. If no marks were made or the driveshaft is being replaced, align the black paint dot on the driveshaft as close to 180 degrees opposite the yellow paint dot on the axle pinion yoke.

11. Install the propeller shaft retainers and bolts. Tighten the bolts to 18 ft. lbs. (24 Nm).

12. If removed, install and align driveline support beam as follows:

   a. To ensure proper alignment of the driveline, a clearance of 1.53–2.00 in. (39–51mm) must be maintained between the top of the beam to the underbody and a clearance of 0.86–1.34 in. (22–34mm) from the passenger side of the beam to the side wall.

   b. Take the measurements direct-

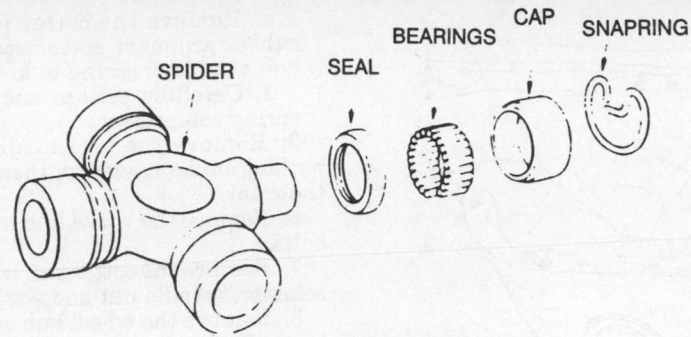

SPIDER SEAL BEARINGS CAP SNAPRING

Universal joint assembly

ly above and to the right of the driveshaft yoke.

c. Apply sealer to the support sealing surfaces at the transmission extension and the differential carrier.

d. Install the washers, bolts and nuts then tighten the bolts at the carrier to 59 ft. lbs. (80 Nm) and the transmission bolts to 37 ft. lbs. (50 Nm).

e. Remove the transmission support.

13. Install the exhaust system assembly.

14. Install the upper and lower underbody braces, if equipped.

15. Lower the vehicle.

Rear Axle Shaft, Bearing and Seal

REMOVAL & INSTALLATION

1. Raise and support the vehicle safely.

NOTE: Do not support the vehicle by means of the differential or the transverse leaf springs.

2. Remove the rear leaf spring from the knuckle as follows:

a. Remove 1 rear wheel assembly.

b. Install tool J–33432, or equivalent transverse leaf compressor, onto the rear transverse spring and compress the spring.

c. Remove the cotter pin, nut, rubber grommets and bolt attaching spring to knuckle.

d. Carefully release and remove spring compressor.

3. Remove the cotter pin, axle tie rod nut and washer from the tie rod outer socket at knuckle. Using a suitable linkage puller, disconnect the outer tie rod from the knuckle.

4. Disconnect the spindle rod bracket at the differential carrier.

5. Separate the spindle support rod from the mounting bracket at the carrier.

6. Remove the axle shaft universal

joint straps at the spindle and yoke shaft ends.

7. Push out on the knuckle assembly and remove the axle shaft.

8. If necessary, remove rear axle yoke, oil seal and bearing as follows:

a. If equipped, remove the upper and lower underbody braces.

b. Disconnect the crossover pipe or remove the exhaust assembly, as required.

c. Support the rear differential, then remove the differential carrier outer support bolts.

d. Remove the carrier cover and drain the gear oil into a suitable container.

e. Remove the snapring from the axle shaft yoke and remove the yoke.

f. If only replacing the seal, pry the axle shaft yoke seal out using a

suitable tool. Be careful not to damage the yoke shaft bearing assembly.

g. If the seal cannot be removed in this manner or the bearing assembly is to be replaced as well, remove the differential assembly.

h. Using tools J–34171 for the 7.875 inch axle or J–35509 for the 8.5 inch axle, and driver handle J–8592 or equivalents and a hammer, remove the seal and bearing assembly. Discard the seal and bearing.

To install:

9. If removed, install a new rear axle shaft bearing and seal as follows:

a. Clean the seal bore.

b. Install a new rear axle bearing assembly. Use tools J–26938 for the 7.875 inch axle or J–35511 for the 8.5 inch axle with driver handle J–8592 or equivalents and a hammer.

c. Lubricate bearings with a suitable hypoid lubricate.

d. Apply a light coat of hypoid lubricant on the lip of the axle shaft seal.

e. Install axle shaft seal using tools J–26938 for 7.875 in. axle or J–35511 for 8.5 in. axle and driver J–8592 or equivalents.

f. If removed, install the differential assembly.

g. Install the axle yoke shaft and snapring into the differential carrier.

h. If a new yoke shaft is installed, yoke shaft end play should be

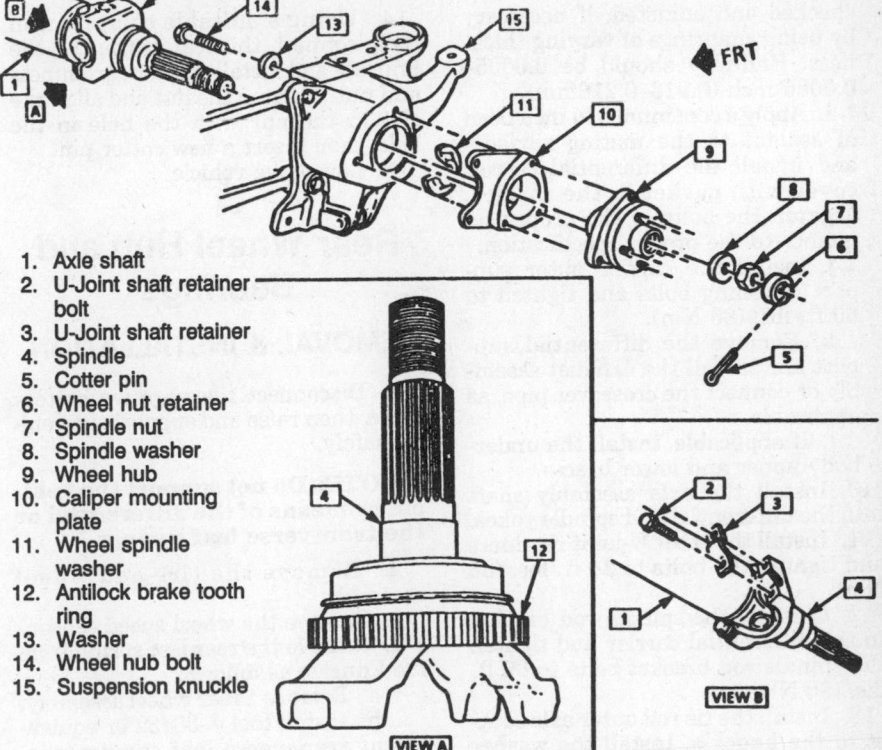

1. Axle shaft
2. U-Joint shaft retainer bolt
3. U-Joint shaft retainer
4. Spindle
5. Cotter pin
6. Wheel nut retainer
7. Spindle nut
8. Spindle washer
9. Wheel hub
10. Caliper mounting plate
11. Wheel spindle washer
12. Antilock brake tooth ring
13. Washer
14. Wheel hub bolt
15. Suspension knuckle

Rear wheel hub, bearing and spindle assembly

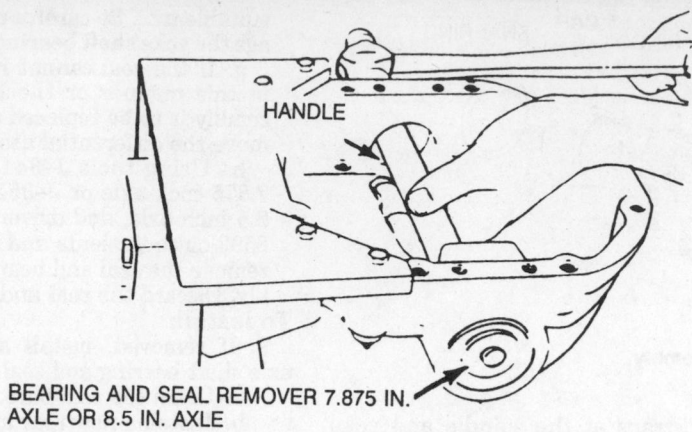

BEARING AND SEAL REMOVER 7.875 IN.
AXLE OR 8.5 IN. AXLE

Removing axle shaft seal and bearing from differential housing

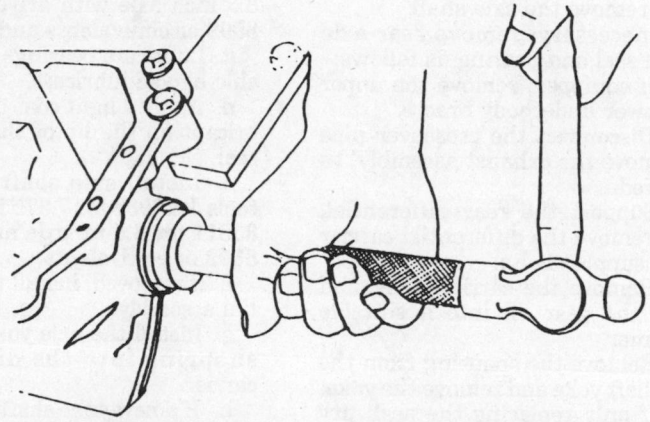

Installing axle seal shaft into differential housing

checked and adjusted, if necessary by using snaprings of varying thickness. End-play should be 0.0005–0.0085 inch (0.013–0.216mm).

i. Apply a continuous ¼ inch bead of sealant to the mating surfaces and install the differential carrier cover with gasket to the carrier. Tighten the bolts in the proper sequence to the proper specification.

j. Install the carrier outer support retaining bolts and tighten to 60 ft. lbs. (80 Nm).

k. Remove the differential support and install the exhaust assembly or connect the crossover pipe, as applicable.

l. If applicable, install the underbody upper and lower braces.

10. Install the axle assembly shaft into the differential and spindle yokes.

11. Install the shaft U-joint retainers and tighten the bolts to 26 ft. lbs. (35 Nm).

12. Connect the spindle rod bracket to the differential carrier and tighten the spindle rod bracket bolts to 60 ft. lbs. (80 Nm).

13. Install the tie rod outer axle socket to the knuckle. Install the washer and nut, tighten the end nut to 33 ft. lbs. (45 Nm) and replace the cotter pin.

14. Using a suitable compression tool, connect the leaf spring to the knuckle and install the bolt, grommets and nut. Tighten the nut and align the slot in the nut with the hole in the bolt, then insert a new cotter pin.

15. Lower the vehicle.

Rear Wheel Hub and Bearings

REMOVAL & INSTALLATION

1. Disconnect the negative battery cable, then raise and support the vehicle safely.

NOTE: Do not support the vehicle by means of the differential or the transverse leaf springs.

2. Remove the tire and wheel assembly.

3. Remove the wheel speed sensor.

4. Remove the rear leaf spring from the knuckle as follows:

a. Remove 1 rear wheel assembly.

b. Install tool J–33432 or equivalent transverse leaf compressor, onto the rear transverse spring and compress the spring.

c. Remove the cotter pin, nut, rubber grommet and/or spacer and bolt attaching spring to knuckle.

d. Carefully release and remove spring compressor.

5. Remove the brake caliper and parking brake assembly, then remove the rotor.

6. Remove the wheel hub mounting bolts.

7. Remove the cotter pin, wheel nut retainer, spindle nut and washer.

8. Remove the wheel hub and bearing, caliper mounting plate and wheel spindle washer from the vehicle.

To install:

9. Inspect the wheel hub and bearing seal, replace if necessary. Also inspect the wheel spindle washer and replace, if necessary.

10. Install the wheel hub and bearing, caliper mounting plate and the wheel spindle washer. The flat of the washer should firmly seat against the shoulder of the wheel spindle. The lip of the washer should face the the wheel spindle splines.

11. Install the wheel hub mounting bolts and tighten to 66 ft. lbs. (90 Nm).

12. Install the washer hub mounting bolts and tighten the spindle nut to 164 ft. lbs. (223 Nm). The vehicle should not rest on the tires or move until the spindle nut is tightened.

13. Install the wheel retainer and a new cotter pin.

14. Install the brake rotor and the caliper and parking brake assembly.

15. Install the wheel speed sensor, then install the wheel and tire assembly.

16. Lower the vehicle and connect the negative battery cable.

Rear Wheel Axle Shaft Spindle

REMOVAL & INSTALLATION

1. Disconnect the negative battery cable, then raise and support the vehicle safely.

NOTE: Do not support the vehicle by means of the differential or the transverse leaf springs.

2. Remove the tire and wheel assembly.

3. Remove the wheel speed sensor.

4. Remove the cotter pin, wheel nut retainer, spindle nut and washer.

5. Remove the axle shaft.

6. Remove the wheel spindle from the wheel hub and bearing.

7. Remove the wheel spindle washer from the spindle.

To install:

8. Inspect the spindle washer and replace, if necessary. Install the spin-

dle washer onto the wheel spindle with the flat portion seated firmly against the shoulder of the spindle. The lip of the washer should face the spindle splines.

9. Install the spindle through the wheel hub and bearing.

10. Install the axle shaft.

11. Install the washer and spindle nut, tighten the nut to 164 ft. lbs. (223 Nm). The vehicle should not move or rest on the tires until the nut is tightened.

12. Install the wheel speed sensor.

13. Install the tire and wheel assembly.

14. Lower the vehicle and connect the negative battery cable.

Pinion Seal

REMOVAL & INSTALLATION

1. Raise and safely support the vehicle. Remove the upper and lower underbody braces, if equipped.

2. Disconnect the crossover pipe or remove the exhaust system assembly, as required.

3. Remove the driveline support beam and driveshaft.

4. Using a suitable tool to hold the yoke, remove the pinion nut and yoke.

5. Inspect the yoke seal area for wear, replace the yoke if necessary.

6. Carefully pry the pinion yoke seal from the differential housing using a suitable tool. Be careful not to damage the pinion threads.

To install:

7. Clean the seal bore of the differential carrier.

8. Use J-34163 for the 7.875 inch rear, J-35503 for the 8.5 inch rear or equivalent pinion seal installation tool and install the new seal into the carrier bore.

9. Install the pinion yoke and nut using a suitable tool to hold the pinion yoke. Tighten the pinion nut to 200 ft. lbs. (271 Nm) if equipped with an au-

tomatic transmission or 250 ft. lbs. (339 Nm) if equipped with a manual transmission.

10. Install the driveshaft and the driveline support beam.

11. Install the exhaust assembly or crossover pipe, as applicable.

12. Install the upper and lower underbody braces, if equipped.

13. Check and fill the differential, as necessary.

14. Lower the vehicle.

Differential Carrier

REMOVAL & INSTALLATION

1. Disconnect the negative battery cable.

2. Raise and support the vehicle safely.

3. Remove the rear axle assembly.

4. Remove the differential cover and drain the gear oil into a suitable container, then mount the assembly in a suitable support.

5. Remove the snaprings from each axle shaft yoke in the differential carrier. Mark each snapring to indicate which side it was removed from. The snaprings come in several different sizes.

6. Remove the axle shaft yokes.

7. Remove the differential bearing caps and note the matched letters stamped on the caps and carrier.

8. Mount the carrier housing spreader tools J-24385-01 and J-24385-20 or equivalents, to the carrier housing and install a dial indicator set.

9. Measure the carrier spread using the dial indicator mounted to the assembly.

10. Spread the case, but do not exceed 0.010 inch (0.25mm) of spread.

11. Use 2 suitable prybars to pry the carrier assembly from the case. Be sure to avoid damage to any machined surfaces and tag the bearing cups to indicate from which side they were removed.

12. Remove the spreader after the assembly has been removed.

To install:

13. With carrier and housing spreader mounted to carrier, spread the carrier, not exceeding 0.010 in. (0.25mm) of spread then remove the dial set.

14. Lubricate and assemble the bearing cups to the differential bearing.

15. Install the differential assembly into the carrier and properly seat the differential assembly into the cross bore of the carrier.

16. Install the bearing caps and bolts, ensure the letters stamped on the caps and carrier assembly coincide in both the direction and letter.

17. Tighten the cap bolts to 45 ft. lbs. (60 Nm) for the 7.875 inch axle or to 63 ft. lbs. (85 Nm) for the 8.5 inch axle.

18. Measure the ring gear backlash at 3 equally spaced points:

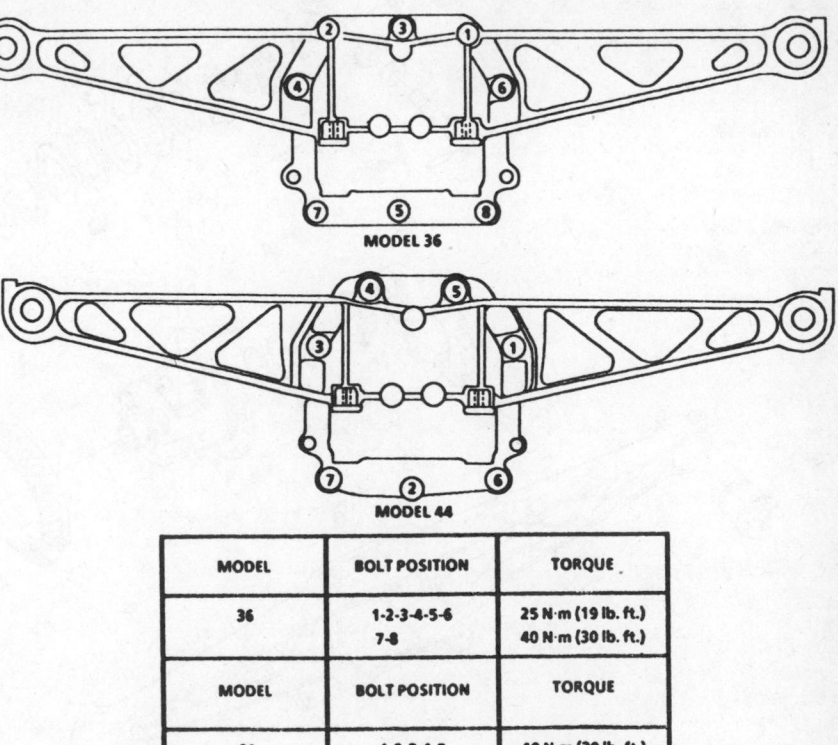

MODEL 36

MODEL 44

MODEL	BOLT POSITION	TORQUE
36	1-2-3-4-5-6	25 N·m (19 lb. ft.)
	7-8	40 N·m (30 lb. ft.)
MODEL	BOLT POSITION	TORQUE
44	1-2-3-4-5	40 N·m (30 lb. ft.)
	6-7	47 N·m (35 lb. ft.)

1. Pinion flange remover, tool J-8614-01
2. Propeller shaft yoke
3. Pinion flange shoulder bolts

Removal and Installation of differential pinion yoke

Differential carrier cover torque specification and sequence

a. Backlash tolerance is 0.006–0.009 in. (0.15–0.23mm) and cannot vary more than 0.0010–0.0015 in. (0.03–0.04mm).

b. High backlash is corrected by moving some shims opposite side of the case to the ring gear side, thus moving the ring gear closer to the pinion.

c. Low backlash is corrected by moving shims from the ring gear side of the case to the opposite side, thus moving the ring gear away from the pinion.

19. Install axle shaft yokes and snaprings, ensuring snaprings are installed on the side they were removed from.

20. Apply a continuous ¼ inch bead of 1052914 or equivalent sealant, to the mating surfaces and install the carrier cover with gasket onto the carrier. Tighten the bolts in sequence to specification.

21. Install the carrier assembly into vehicle.

22. Lower the vehicle and connect the negative battery cable.

Axle Housing

There are 2 differential assemblies used, a Dana model 36 with a 7.875 inch ring gear used on vehicles equipped with an automatic transmission and a Dana model 44 with a 8.5

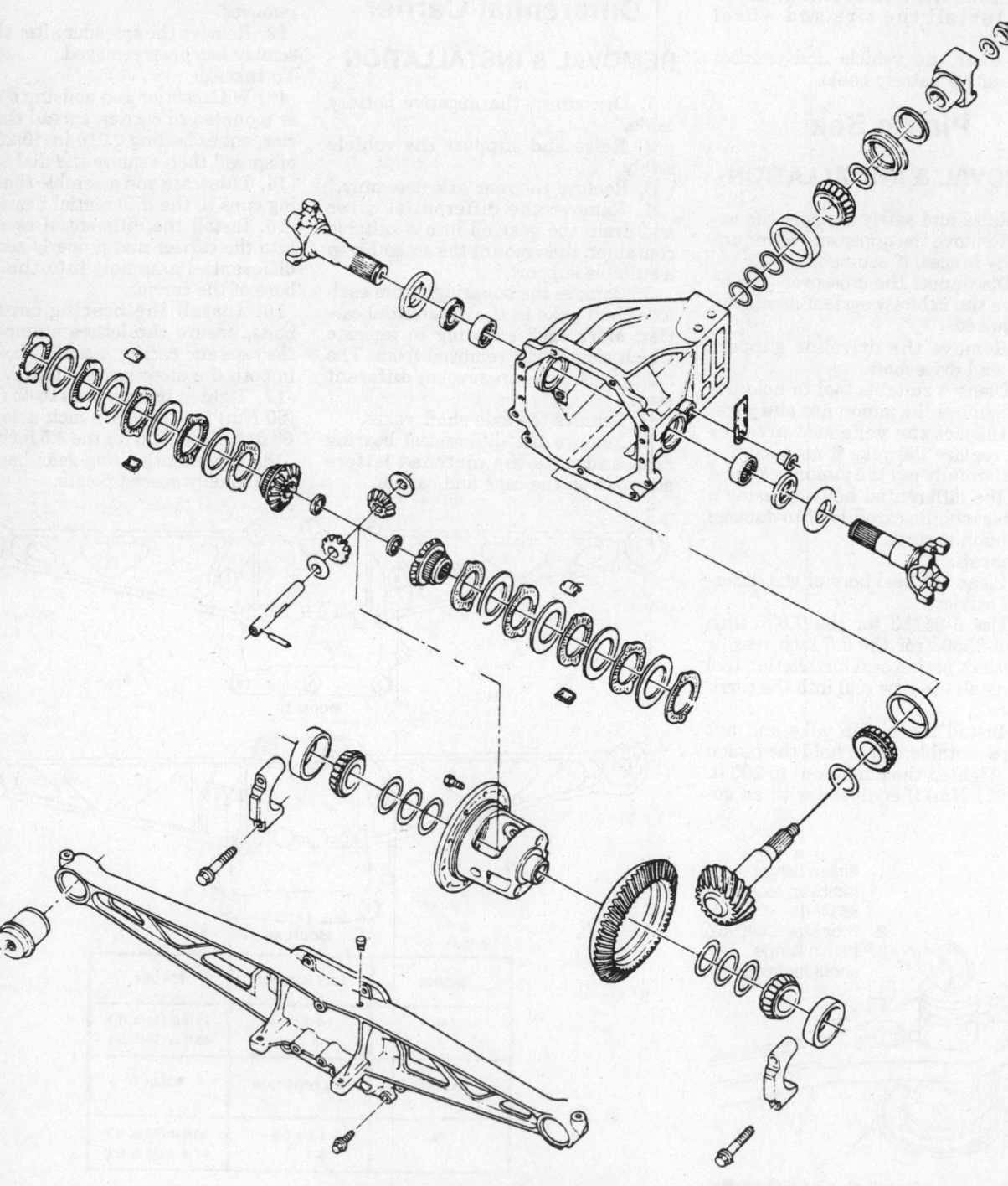

Exploded view of rear axle assembly

inch ring gear used on vehicles equipped with a manual transmission.

REMOVAL & INSTALLATION

1. Raise and safely support the vehicle.
2. Remove the spare tire, then remove tire cover by removing support hooks.
3. Remove the upper and lower underbody braces, if equipped.
4. Remove the complete exhaust system as an assembly.
5. Remove the transverse leaf springs from vehicle.
6. Remove exhaust hangers, if necessary.
7. Remove the spindle support rod, bolts and mounting bracket from the carrier.
8. Remove both tie rod ends from knuckles.
9. Remove the axle universal joint straps from differential inside yokes.
10. Support the axle shaft and push the wheel and tire assembly outward to disengage joints from differential yokes.
11. Scribe alignment marks on driveshaft and pinion yoke for installation.
12. Remove the driveshaft U-joint straps from the pinion flange and push the driveshaft forward into the transmission, then support the shaft from the driveline support beam.
13. Support the rear axle assembly with a suitable jack on which it can be lowered and install a support under the transmission.
14. Remove the carrier cover attaching bolts at the frame brackets.
15. Remove the drive line support beam attaching bolts at the rear axle rear axle housing.
16. Remove the rear axle assembly from the vehicle.

To install:

17. Raise the rear axle assembly into position on the vehicle.
18. Apply 9636067 or equivalent sealant to the driveline support and the differential carrier, then install the driveline support bolts at the front of the carrier cover.
19. To ensure proper alignment of the driveline, a clearance of 1.53–2.00 in. (39–51mm) must be maintained between the top of the beam to the underbody and a clearance of 0.86–1.34 in. (22–34mm) from the passenger side of the beam to the side wall. Take the measurements directly above and to the right of the driveshaft yoke and adjust if necessary, then tighten the bolts to 59 ft. lbs. (80 Nm).
20. Install the differential carrier cover retaining bolts at the frame brackets and tighten to 23 ft. lbs. (31 Nm) for the 7.875 inch axle or to 35 ft. lbs. (48 Nm) for the 8.5 inch axle.

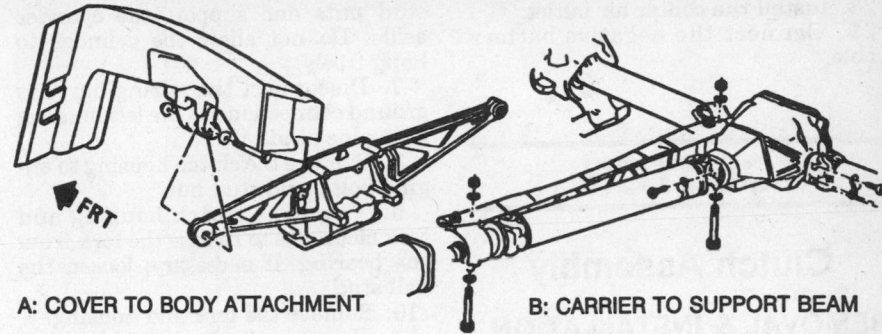

A: COVER TO BODY ATTACHMENT   **B: CARRIER TO SUPPORT BEAM**

Differential carrier cover attachments

21. Align the marks on driveshaft and yoke, and install the driveshaft. Tighten the U-joint strap bolts to 18 ft. lbs. (24 Nm).
22. Install wheel axle shaft joints into the yokes.
23. Install rear axle shaft universal joint retainers onto the yoke shafts and tighten the retainers to 26 ft. lbs. (35 Nm).
24. Install tie rod ends into knuckle. Install the washers and nuts, then tighten the tie rod nut to 33 ft. lbs. (45 Nm) to align slot in nut with hole in stud. Install a new cotter pin.
25. Install the spindle support rod mounting bracket onto the carrier and tighten the bolts to 60 ft. lbs. (80 Nm).
26. Install the transverse leaf spring.
27. If removed, install the exhaust system hangers and nuts, tighten the nuts to 13 ft. lbs. (17 Nm).
28. Install the exhaust system assembly.
29. If equipped, install the upper and lower underbody braces.
30. Install the spare tire cover and spare tire.
31. Fill the rear axle with a suitable lubricant.
32. Adjust the rear suspension, as necessary, then lower the vehicle.

MANUAL TRANSMISSION

For further information on transmission/transaxles, please refer to "Chilton's Guide to Transmission Repair".

Transmission Assembly

REMOVAL & INSTALLATION

1. Disconnect the negative battery cable.

2. Remove the center air outlet.
3. Remove the console and accessory trim plates.
4. Remove the control lever button.
5. Remove the shift lever knob assembly.
6. Remove the center console trim plate.
7. Remove the shift lever snapring.
8. Remove the shifter retainer nuts.
9. Raise and safely support the vehicle.
10. Remove the complete exhaust assembly.
11. Remove the driveshaft.
12. Support the transmission with a suitable jack.
13. Remove the driveline support beam.
14. Remove the electrical connectors from the speed sensor, backup light switch and shift solenoid.
15. Remove the transmission to clutch housing attaching bolts.
16. Remove the transmission assembly from the vehicle.

To install:

17. Install transmission assembly into the vehicle.
18. Install and torque the transmission to clutch housing bolts to 37 ft. lbs. (50 Nm).
19. Connect the speed sensor, backup light switch and shift solenoid.
20. Install the driveline support beam.
21. Tighten the driveline support beam to differential bolts to 60 ft. lbs. (80 Nm) and the driveline support beam to transmission bolts to 37 ft. lbs. (50 Nm).
22. Install the driveshaft assembly.
23. Remove the transmission support jack.
24. Check transmission oil level and add if necessary.

NOTE: In a horizontal position, the transmission should be filled to the point of overflow.

25. Install the exhaust system.
26. Lower the vehicle.
27. Install the shifter and console assembly.

28. Install the center air outlet.
29. Connect the negative battery cable.

CLUTCH

Clutch Assembly

REMOVAL & INSTALLATION

1989

1. Disconnect the negative battery cable, then raise and support the vehicle safely.
2. Remove the starter from the vehicle.
3. Remove the clutch housing cover bolts and cover.
4. Remove the exhaust assembly.
5. Remove the transmission assembly.
6. Remove the clutch slave cylinder

stud nuts and support the cylinder aside. Do not allow the cylinder to hang freely.
7. Disconnect the wiring harness ground connections at the left housing to engine stud.
8. Remove the clutch housing to engine bolts, and stud nut.
9. Twist the clutch housing and fork clockwise to release the fork from the bearing. If necessary, loosen the ball stud.
10. Remove the fork and housing.
11. Remove the ball stud locking screw, stud and fork.
12. Mark the alignment of the clutch cover assembly to the flywheel, then remove the assembly to flywheel bolts. Bolts should be loosened evenly, 1 turn at a time until spring pressure is properly released or damage may occur to the flywheel and cover assembly.
13. Remove the cover assembly and clutch disc.
To install:
14. Install the clutch cover assembly

and disc with a universal clutch disc alignment arbor in place.
15. Make sure the marks made earlier are in alignment and install the cover assembly to flywheel bolts. Tighten the bolts in the proper sequence, 1 turn at a time, until spring pressure is properly attained and the bolts are tightened to 30 ft. lbs. (41 Nm).
16. Install the ball stud, fork, and ball stud locking screw.
17. Position the clutch housing to the engine while pushing the fork as far forward as possible, then twist the housing and fork clockwise to engage the fork on the release bearing.
18. Make sure the housing is correctly positioned on the engine dowel pins. Tighten the housing to engine bolts and stud nut to 37 ft. lbs. (50 Nm).
19. Connect the wiring harness ground connections to the left housing to engine stud.
20. Install the clutch slave cylinder and tighten the nuts to 19 ft. lbs. (25 Nm).

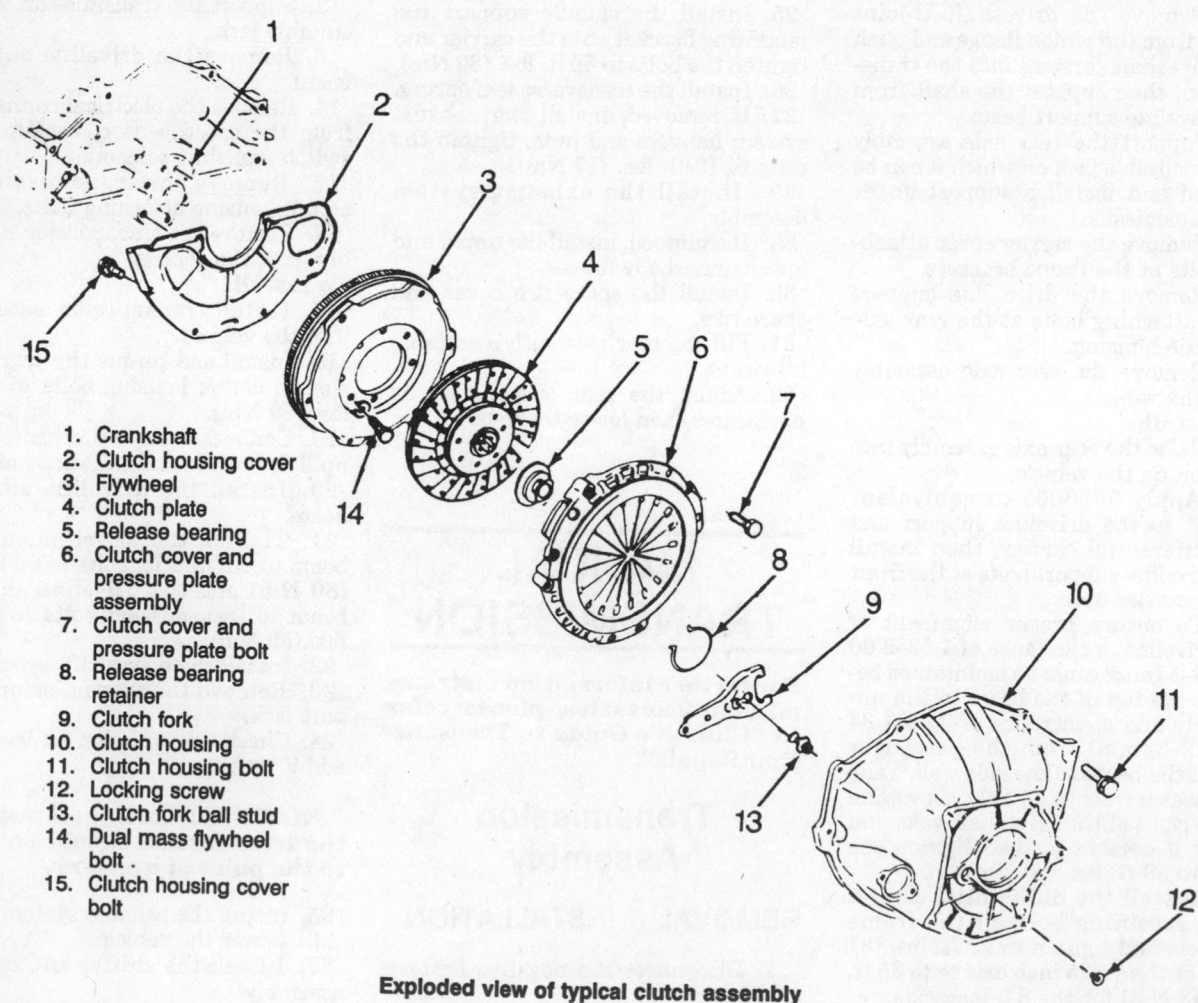

1. Crankshaft
2. Clutch housing cover
3. Flywheel
4. Clutch plate
5. Release bearing
6. Clutch cover and pressure plate assembly
7. Clutch cover and pressure plate bolt
8. Release bearing retainer
9. Clutch fork
10. Clutch housing
11. Clutch housing bolt
12. Locking screw
13. Clutch fork ball stud
14. Dual mass flywheel bolt .
15. Clutch housing cover bolt

Exploded view of typical clutch assembly

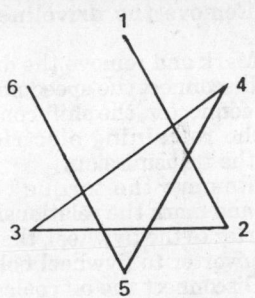

Clutch cover assembly tightening sequence

21. Install the transmission assembly.
22. Install the exhaust assembly.
23. Install the clutch housing cover and bolts, tighten the bolts to 80 inch lbs. (9 Nm).
24. Install the starter.
25. Lower the vehicle and connect the negative battery cable.

1990–93

1. Disconnect the negative battery cable, then raise and support the vehicle safely.
2. Remove the complete exhaust system.
3. Remove the transmission assembly.
4. Disconnect the ground wire connected to the clutch housing left side, if equipped.
5. Remove the nuts attaching the clutch slave cylinder to the housing and support the cylinder to the side. Do not allow the cylinder to hang freely.
6. Remove the starter assembly, for 5.7L (VIN 8 and VIN P) engines only.
7. Remove the left side converter shield, for 5.7L (VIN J) engine only.
8. Remove the clutch housing cover.
9. Remove the bolts retaining the housing to the engine block and, for the 5.7L (VIN J) engine, the right side converter heat shield.
10. Align the fork onto the 2 flats of the release bearing and push the fork away from the bearing with a twisting motion. Remove the clutch housing and, for 5.7L (VIN P) engines, the aluminum spacers.

NOTE: Excessive clutch wear may require removal of the ball stud locking screw and loosening of the ball stud to disengage the fork and housing.

11. Mark the alignment of the clutch cover and flywheel for installation.
12. Loosen the clutch cover bolts evenly, 1 turn at a time until spring pressure is released. Failure to properly release spring pressure may result in damage to the clutch cover assembly and the flywheel.

13. Remove the clutch plate and disc assembly.

To install:

14. Inspect flywheel, clutch plate and disc for heat stress, cracks or worn parts and replace as necessary.
15. Install the clutch assembly using a suitable alignment tool.
16. Make sure the marks made earlier are in alignment and install the cover assembly to flywheel bolts. Tighten the bolts in the proper sequence, 1 turn at a time, until spring pressure is properly attained and the bolts are tightened to 30 ft. lbs. (41 Nm).
17. Position the clutch housing to the engine block and engage the fork onto the release bearing. If equipped, be sure the aluminum spacer is in position.
18. Verify the housing is properly positioned on the 2 engine dowel pins and, for the 5.7L (VIN J) engine, that the right converter heat shield is installed.
19. Tighten the clutch housing bolts to 37 ft. lbs. (50 Nm), the ball stud to 33 ft. lbs. (45 Nm) and the ball stud locking screw to 20 ft. lbs. (27 Nm), as applicable.
20. Connect the ground harness connection to the housing cover, if equipped.
21. Install the housing cover and tighten the bolts to 80 inch lbs. (9 Nm).
22. Install the left heat shield, if removed and tighten the shield to housing cover retaining nut to 12 inch lbs. (1.4 Nm).
23. Install the clutch slave cylinder and tighten the retaining nuts to 19 ft. lbs. (25 Nm).
24. Install the transmission assembly.
25. Install the starter assembly, if removed.
26. Install the exhaust system and lower the vehicle.
27. Connect the battery negative cable and check clutch operation.

Clutch Master Cylinder

REMOVAL & INSTALLATION

1. Disconnect the negative battery cable.
2. Remove the hush panel from under the dash.
3. Disconnect the pushrod retaining clip and pushrod at the clutch pedal.
4. Disconnect and plug the hydraulic line at the clutch master cylinder.
5. Remove the clutch master cylinder retaining bolts at the front of the dash.
6. Remove the clutch master cylinder from the vehicle.

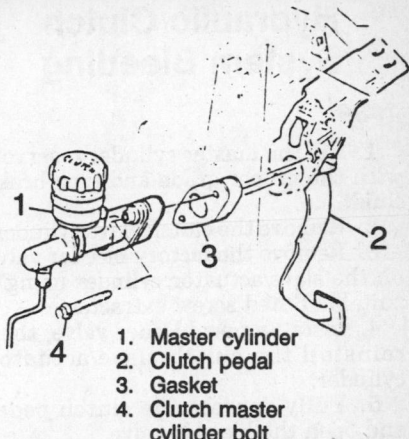

1. Master cylinder
2. Clutch pedal
3. Gasket
4. Clutch master cylinder bolt

Clutch master cylinder assembly

To install:

7. Install the master cylinder into the vehicle and tighten the mounting bolts to 12 ft. lbs. (17 Nm).
8. Unplug and connect the hydraulic fitting to the master cylinder and tighten to 13 ft. lbs. (18 Nm).
9. Connect the pushrod to the pedal and install the retaining clip.
10. Install the under dash hush panel.
11. Bleed the system, as required.
12. Connect battery negative cable.

Clutch Slave/Actuator Cylinder

REMOVAL & INSTALLATION

1. Disconnect the negative battery cable.
2. Raise and support the vehicle safely.
3. Remove the actuator cylinder stud nuts.
4. Note the position of the hydraulic line and disconnect the line from the retaining clip.
5. Remove the actuator and pushrod assembly from the clutch housing.
6. Disconnect and plug the hydraulic line at the actuator cylinder.

To install:

7. Unplug and connect the hydraulic line to the actuator cylinder. Tighten the fitting to 13 ft. lbs. (18 Nm).
8. Install the pushrod and actuator assembly. Tighten the stud nuts to 19 ft. lbs. (25 Nm).
9. Place the hydraulic line in its original position in the retaining clip.
10. Bleed the system, as required.
11. Connect the negative battery cable.

Hydraulic Clutch System Bleeding

1989

1. Fill the master cylinder reservoir with the proper grade and type brake fluid.
2. Remove the clutch slave cylinder.
3. Remove the factory bleeder valve on the slave/actuator cylinder using a suitable fluted screw extractor.
4. Install a new bleeder valve, then reinstall the clutch slave/actuator cylinder.
5. Fully depress the clutch pedal and open the bleeder valve.
6. Close the bleeder valve and release the clutch pedal.
7. Repeat the steps 5 and 6 until all air is expelled from the system, check the fluid reservoir and refill as required to prevent air from being drawn into the system.
8. Tighten the bleeder screw to 13 ft. lbs. (18 Nm).

1990–93

1. Disconnect the negtaive battery cable and remove the ECM from the mounting bracket to access the master cylinder for filling. Fill the master cylinder reservoir with the proper grade and type of fresh brake fluid or hydraulic clutch fluid.
2. Prior to bleeding the actuator, most of the air can be removed as follows:
   a. Remove the master cylinder cap and moisture barrier.
   b. Install the master cylinder cap.
   c. Lightly stroke the clutch pedal to release trapped air through the master cylinder.
   d. Remove the master cylinder cap and install the moisture barrier.
   e. Install the master cylinder cap.
3. Raise and support the vehicle safely.
4. Remove the actuator cylinder attaching stud nuts.
5. Remove the pushrod and actuator cylinder from the clutch housing and the hydraulic line from the retaining clip.
6. Lower cylinder for access and disconnect the hydraulic hose fitting from the actuator cylinder.
7. Remove the bleed screw dust cap.
8. Remove the factory bleed screw from the actuator cylinder using a fluted screw extractor, then install a new bleed screw.
9. Connect hydraulic hose fitting to the actuator.
10. Fully depress the clutch pedal and open the bleeder screw.
11. Close the bleed screw and release the clutch pedal.
12. Repeat Steps 10 and 11 until all the air is expelled from the system. Check the fluid reservoir and replenish, as required during the procedure.
13. For 1990–91 vehicles, torque bleeder screw until screw breaks. This is required for body clearance. Screw should break at approximately 10–14 ft. lbs. (14–19 Nm), then install the dust cap on the bleeder screw.
14. For 1992–93 vehicles, tighten the bleeder screw and install the dust cap.
15. Install the hydraulic line into the retaining clip, position the actuator cylinder and tighten the stud nuts to 19 ft. lbs. (25 Nm).
16. Lower the vehicle.
17. Install the ECM and connect the negative battery cable.

AUTOMATIC TRANSMISSION

For further information on transmission/transaxles, please refer to "Chilton's Guide to Transmission Repair".

Transmission Assembly

REMOVAL & INSTALLATION

1. Disconnect the negative battery cable and remove the transmission fluid level indicator.
2. Disconnect the TV cable at the throttle lever.
3. Raise and support the vehicle safely.
4. Remove the upper and lower underbody braces, if equipped.
5. Remove the complete exhaust system.
6. Support the transmission with a suitable jack.

7. Remove the driveline support beam.
8. Mark and remove the driveshaft.
9. Disconnect the speedometer electrical connector, the shift control cable and the remaining electrical leads from the transmission.
10. Remove the torque converter cover and mark the relationship of the converter to the flywheel, then remove the converter to flywheel bolts.
11. Disconnect the oil cooler pipes at the transmission.
12. Disconnect the TV cable at the transmission.
13. Remove the transmission to engine mounting bolts and fasten the torque converter to the transmission with a suitable tool or wire.
14. Carefully move the transmission rearward, downward and out from under the vehicle. If interference is encountered with cables, cooler lines, etc., remove the component(s) before finally lowering the transmission.

To install:

15. Properly flush the transmission oil cooler lines using J-35944 or equivalent transmission cooler and line flushing tool.
16. Install a suitable tool to hold the torque converter in place.
17. Support the transmission with a suitable jack, then raise the transmission into position and remove the torque converter holding tool.
18. Install and tighten the transmission to engine bolts to 35 ft. lbs. (47 Nm).
19. Connect the TV cable and the oil cooler pipes to the transmission.
20. Align the marks made during removal and start the torque converter to flywheel bolts by hand. Tighten the bolts to 46 ft. lbs. (62 Nm).
21. Install converter cover and torque screws to 89 inch lbs. (10 Nm).
22. Connect the electrical connectors to the transmission.
23. Connect the shift control cable.

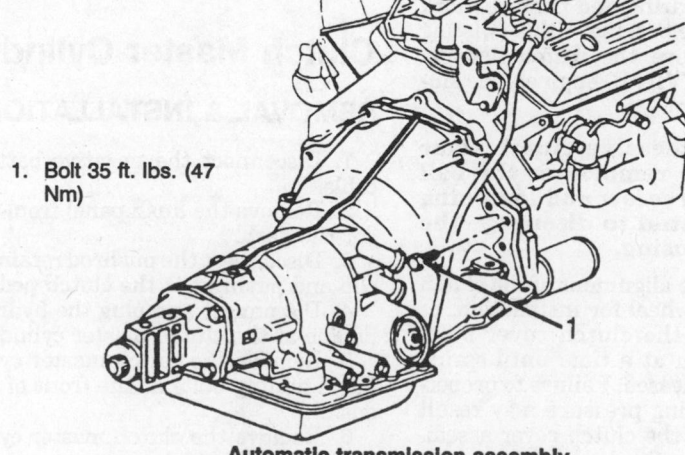

1. Bolt 35 ft. lbs. (47 Nm)

Automatic transmission assembly

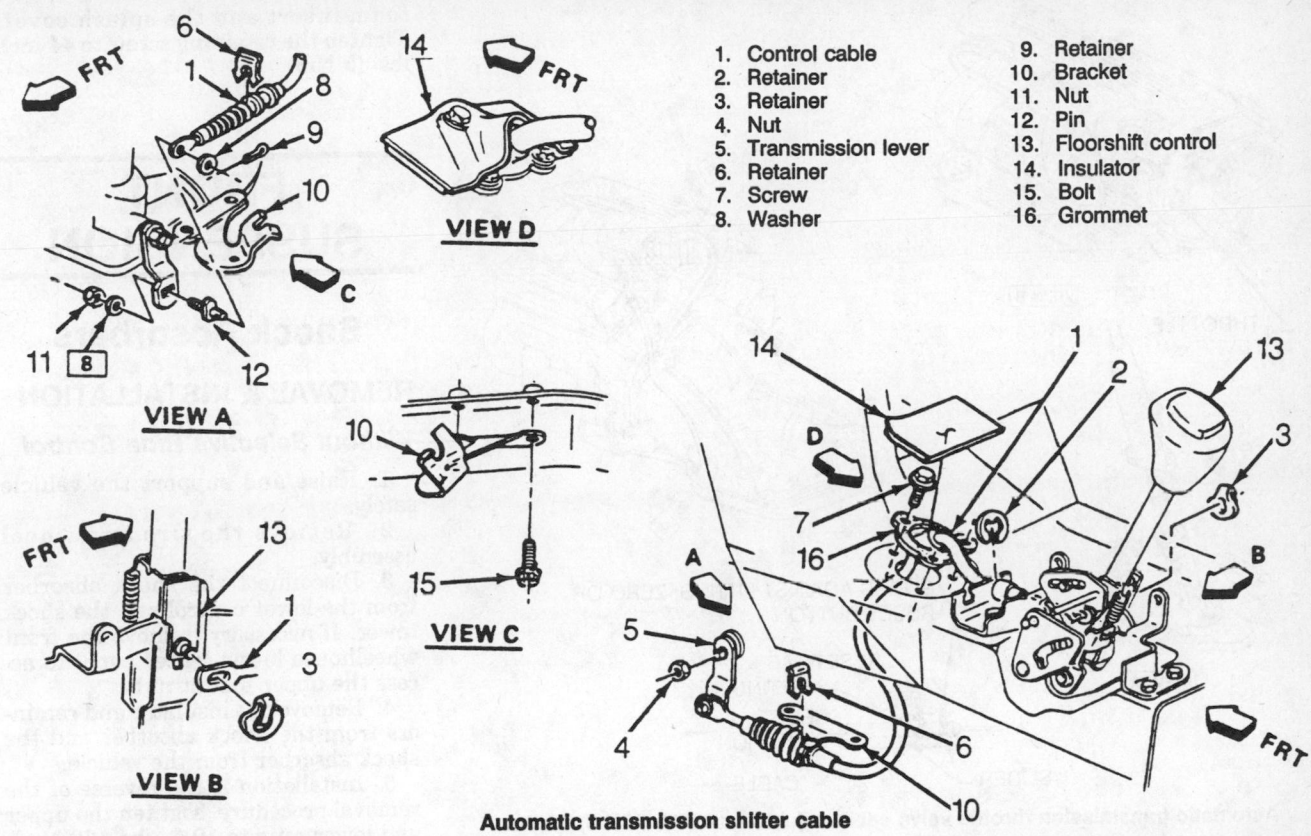

1. Control cable
2. Retainer
3. Retainer
4. Nut
5. Transmission lever
6. Retainer
7. Screw
8. Washer
9. Retainer
10. Bracket
11. Nut
12. Pin
13. Floorshift control
14. Insulator
15. Bolt
16. Grommet

Automatic transmission shifter cable

24. Connect the speedometer electrical connector.

25. Align the marks made earlier and install the driveshaft, then the driveline support beam.

26. Install the exhaust system and the underbody braces.

27. Lower the vehicle and install the oil level indicator.

28. Connect the TV cable to the throttle lever.

29. Connect the negative battery cable.

30. Check and add the proper type and amount of transmission fluid.

SHIFT LINKAGE ADJUSTMENT

1. Disconnect the negative battery cable.

2. Place the control lever in the **N** position.

3. Raise and support the vehicle safely.

4. Loosen the cable attachment at the shift lever.

5. Rotate the shift lever clockwise to **P** detent and then back to **N**.

6. Tighten the cable attachment to 15 ft. lbs. (20 Nm).

NOTE: The lever must be held out of the P position when tightening the nut.

7. Lower the vehicle.

8. Check the cable adjustment by rotating the control lever through the detents.

9. Connect the battery negative cable.

THROTTLE LINKAGE ADJUSTMENT

5.7L (VIN 8) Engine

1. If the cable slider is not in the **0** or fully reset position, adjustment is necessary.

2. Rotate the throttle idler lever to the wide open throttle stop position.

3. Slider must move toward the lever, when the lever is rotated to the wide open throttle stop position.

4. Release the lever.

5. Check TV cable operation. If readjustment is necessary, proceed as follows:

   a. Depress and hold the metal reset tab.

   b. Move the slider back through fitting in the direction away from the throttle idler lever, until the slider stops against fitting.

   c. Release the reset tab.

   d. Repeat the procedure until proper adjustment is obtained.

5.7L (VIN P) Engine

1. Remove the adjuster assembly splash cover retaining screw.

2. Remove the adjuster assembly splash cover and foam insert.

3. Remove the cable cam cover.

4. Release the lock tab on the transmission TV cable to allow the sheath to extend to full length.

5. Depress the reset tab on the throttle body and accelerator pedal cables and fully extend the cable sheaths.

6. Disconnect the cruise control cable from the cruise servo.

7. Insert a ⅛ inch drill bit into the adjuster assembly alignment hole. Make sure the bit does not contact the adjuster assembly gear or improper adjustment may occur.

8. Turn the cams approximately ⅛ turn by hand and hold in this position.

9. Insert a ¼ inch drive torque wrench with extension into the square hole on the cruise control cam or through the cruise control cam into the accelerator pedal, as applicable.

10. Turn the torque wrench clockwise several clicks of the adjusters until obtaining a torque of 71 inch. lbs. (8 Nm). Hold the torque wrench at this setting and lock the transmission TV cable to its adjusted position.

11. Remove the torque wrench and fully depress the accelerator pedal to automatically adjust the cable.

12. Remove the ⅛ inch drill bit.

13. Adjust the cruise control cable, as applicable.

14. Check for proper adjustment. Us-

foam insert and the splash cover. Tighten the retaining screw to 44 inch lbs. (5 Nm).

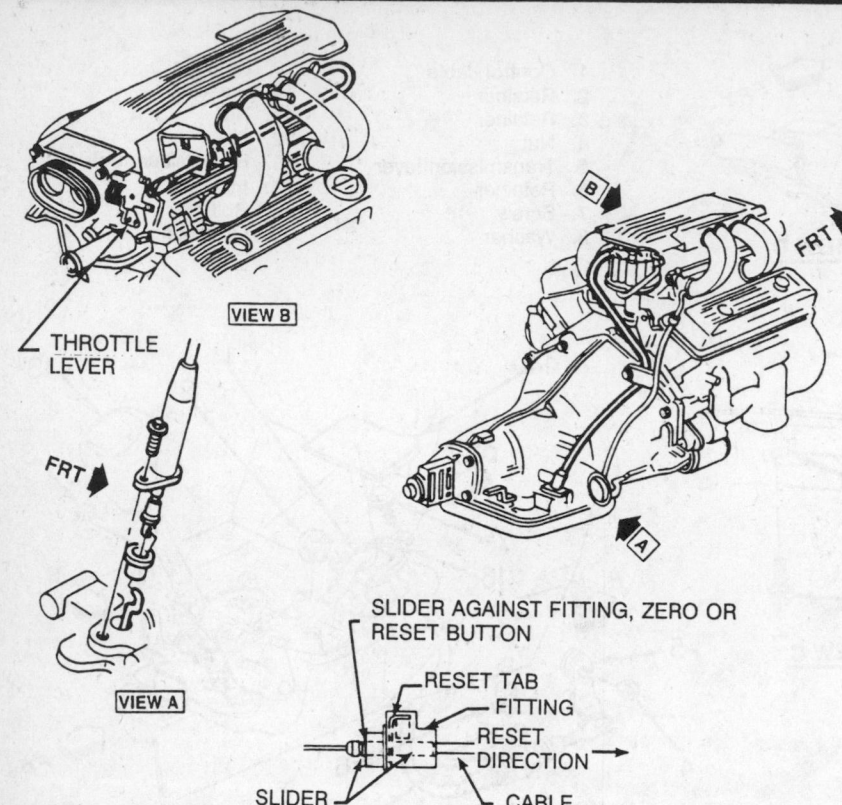

VIEW B

THROTTLE LEVER

FRT

VIEW A

SLIDER AGAINST FITTING, ZERO OR RESET BUTTON

RESET TAB
FITTING
RESET DIRECTION
SLIDER
CABLE

Automatic transmission throttle valve cable adjustment—5.7L (VIN 8) Engine

ing a suitable diagnostic tool such as the Tech 1 with a Brake System Cartridge, depress the accelerator pedal fully and check that the throttle open-

ing is at 100 percent. Release the pedal and verify the throttle opening is 0 percent.

15. Install the cable cam cover, the

FRONT SUSPENSION

Shock Absorbers

REMOVAL & INSTALLATION

Without Selective Ride Control

1. Raise and support the vehicle safely.
2. Remove the tire and wheel assembly.
3. Disconnect the shock absorber from the lower control and the shock tower. If necessary, remove the front wheelhouse lower center panel to access the upper mount nut.
4. Remove the insulator and retainers from the shock absorber and the shock absorber from the vehicle.
5. Installation is the reverse of the removal procedure. Tighten the upper and lower nuts to 19 ft. lbs. (26 Nm).

With Selective Ride Control

1. Disconnect the negative battery cable.
2. Raise and safely support vehicle,

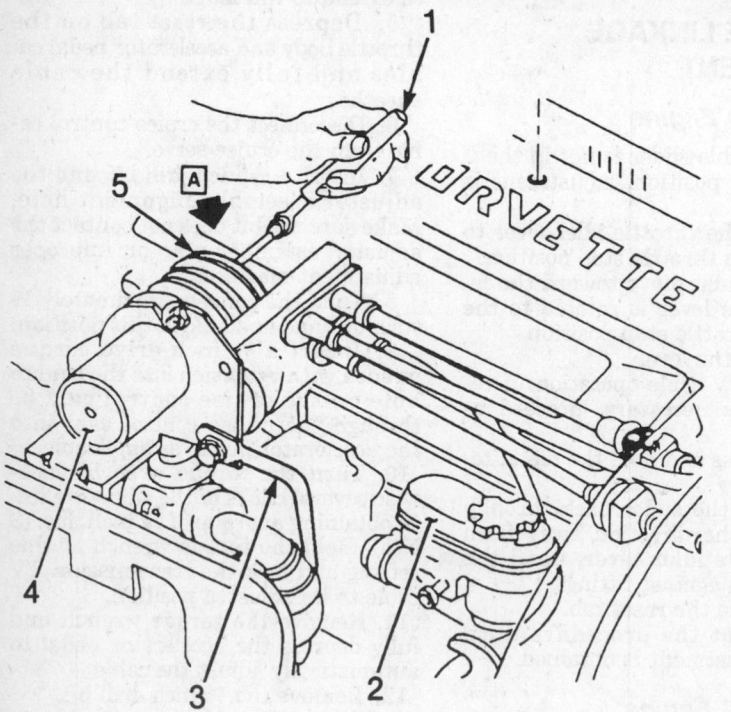

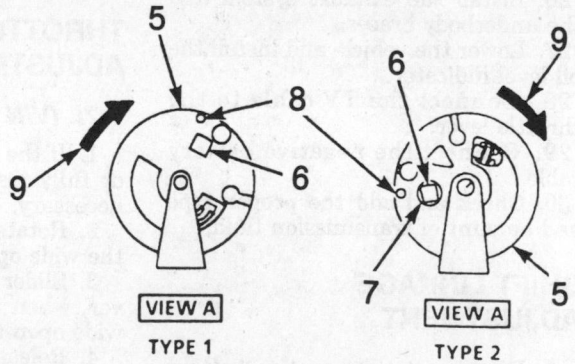

VIEW A TYPE 1

VIEW A TYPE 2

VIN P ADJUSTMENT ROUTINE SHOWN
VIN J ADJUSTMENT SIMILAR

1. Torque wrench
2. Master cylinder
3. Support rod
4. DC motor
5. Cruise control cam
6. ¼ inch drive adjustment hole
7. Clearance hole
8. Insert ⅛ inch drill bit here
9. Direction of adjustment rotation

Throttle and transmission TV cable adjustment—5.7L (VIN P) Engine

then remove the tire and wheel assembly.

3. Safely support the lower control arm with a suitable jack.

4. Remove the actuator retaining clip, then remove the actuator from the cup retainer. Note the position of the actuator electrical leads for installation purposes.

5. Remove the shock absorber upper mounting nut.

6. Remove the cup retainer, then the upper insulator retainer and insulator.

7. Remove the shock absorber lower mounting bolts, nuts, then compress the shock absorber and remove it from the vehicle. If necessary, remove the lower insulator from the shock.

To install:

8. If removed, install the lower insulator to the shock absorber, compress the shock and install into the vehicle.

9. Install the shock absorber lower mounting nuts and bolts, then tighten the bolts to 19 ft. lbs. (26 Nm).

10. Install the upper insulator and retainer, then install the cup assembly retainer.

11. Install the upper mounting nut and tighten the 31 ft. lbs. (42 Nm). The selector gear should be at least 0.178 inch (4.5mm) above the top of the cup assembly retainer.

12. Install and properly seat the actuator retaining clip onto the cup assembly retainer. Make sure the ends of the actuator clip protrude outward from the retainer.

13. Install the actuator onto the cup assembly retainer with the electrical leads in the same position as noted earlier. Verify that there is at least 0.315 inch (8mm) of clearance between the front wheelhouse lower center panel and the actuator electrical leads.

NOTE: Very little effort is required to snap the actuator onto the retainer, do not force it into position.

14. Remove the jack stand, then install the tire and wheel assembly.

15. Lower the vehicle and connect the negative battery cable.

Transverse Spring

REMOVAL & INSTALLATION

1. Raise and support the vehicle safely. Position the supports so the front suspension hangs freely.

2. Remove both front tire and wheel assemblies.

NOTE: Do not use corrosive cleaning agents, engine degreasers or solvents near the fiberglass front spring, or extensive damage

could occur to the spring assembly.

3. Disconnect both shock absorbers from the lower control arms, then disconnect the stabilizer shaft links from both lower control arms.

4. For 1989–90 vehicles, remove the ABS speed sensor brackets from the knuckles. For 1991–93 vehicles, disconnect the wheel speed sensor electrical connectors, then remove the speed sensor wire from the bracket.

5. Remove the spring protectors.

6. Compress the front leaf springs using tool J–33432 and adapters J–33432-88 or a suitable equivalent tool, then compress the spring.

7. Disconnect the lower control arms from the steering knuckles by separating the ball joints from the knuckle bore.

8. Remove the spring retainer nuts and retainers, then carefully release the spring compression and remove the tools.

9. With the aid of an assistant, pull both lower control arms downward to release the spring ends from the lower control arms.

10. Remove the spring and retainer shims from the vehicle. Use care not to scratch or damage the spring and note the number, types and positions of the shims.

To install:

11. Lubricate the spring pads with an appropriate lubricant.

12. Carefully install the retainer shims and the spring. Use care not to scratch the spring and to use the correct number and type of shims.

13. With the aid of an assistant, pull both lower control arms downward while seating the spring ends into the lower control arms.

14. Using the J–33432 and J–33432-88 or equivalents, compress the spring.

15. Install the retainers and hand-tighten the retainer nuts. Install both lower control arm ball joints into the

steering knuckles. The ball joints must be positioned so the cotter pins can be inserted from the rear to the front of the vehicle.

16. Install both lower control arm ball stud washers and nuts. Tighten the lower control arm ball stud nuts to 50 ft. lbs. (68 Nm). Tighten the nut additionally as necessary to insert the cotter pin but do not exceed 88 ft. lbs. (120 Nm).

17. Install the cotter pins from the rear to the front of the vehicle.

18. Release and remove the spring compression tool.

19. Install both spring protectors and tighten the bolts to 18 ft. lbs. (25 Nm).

20. Install the wheel speed sensor connector, cable and/or bracket, as applicable.

21. Properly install the stabilizer shaft links, bolts and nuts to the lower control arm and hand-tighten the nuts.

22. Connect both shock absorbers to the lower control arms and tighten the lower mounting nuts to 19 ft. lbs. (26 Nm).

23. Use suitable jack stands to hold the suspension at proper trim height and tighten the spring retainer nuts to 46 ft. lbs. (63 Nm) and the stabilizer shaft link nuts to 33 ft. lbs. (45 Nm).

24. Remove the jack stand supports, then install the tire and wheel assemblies.

25. Lower the vehicle, check and adjust the front end alignment, as necessary.

Upper Ball Joints

INSPECTION

1. Raise and safely support the vehicle with jackstands under the left and right lower control arms, as far outboard and nearest to the ball joint as possible.

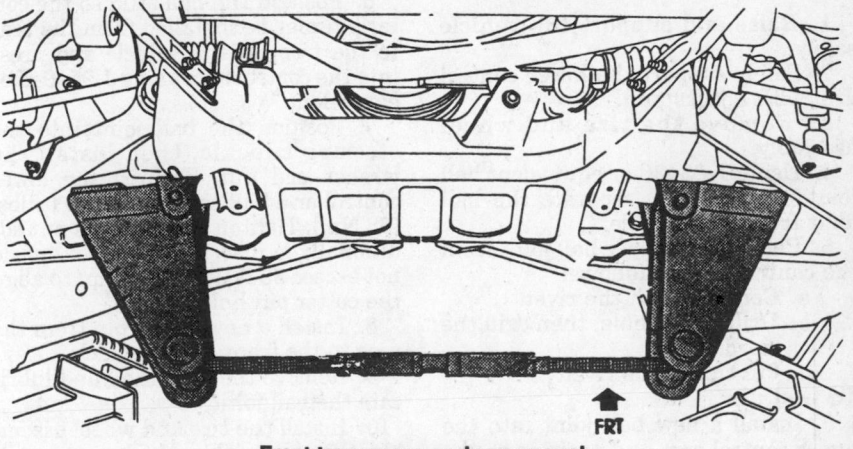

Front transverse spring removal

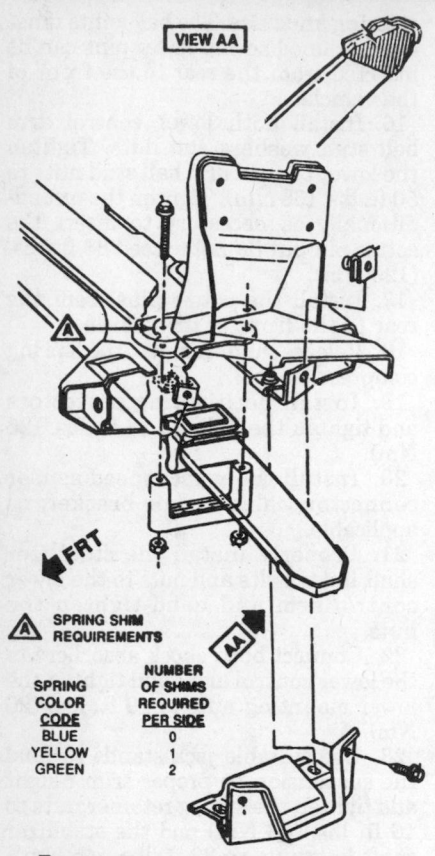

VIEW AA

FRT

⚠ SPRING SHIM REQUIREMENTS

SPRING COLOR CODE	NUMBER OF SHIMS REQUIRED PER SIDE
BLUE	0
YELLOW	1
GREEN	2

Front transverse spring and shim installation

2. Make sure the vehicle is stable and does not rock on the stands.
3. Position a dial indicator against the wheel rim.
4. Grasp the front tire and push in on the bottom while pulling out at the top. Read the dial indicator, then reverse the push-pull procedure.
5. Horizontal deflection on the dial indicator must not exceed 0.125 in. (3.18mm).
6. If specifications are not as indicated, replace the ball joint.

REMOVAL & INSTALLATION

1. Raise and support the vehicle safely.
2. Safely support the lower control arm with a jackstand.
3. Remove the tire and wheel assembly.
4. Using J–33436 or equivalent ball joint removal tool, separate the ball joint from the knuckle.
5. Remove the upper ball joint from the control arm as follows:
   a. Center punch the rivet.
   b. Drill a pilot hole, then drill the rivet head.
   c. Punch out the rivet.
To install:
6. Install a new ball joint into the upper control arm and position so the

cotter pin can be installed from the rear to the front of the vehicle.
7. Install and tighten the mounting nuts to 19 ft. lbs. (25 Nm) for 1989–90 vehicles, or to 13 ft. lbs. (18 Nm) for 1991–93 vehicles.
8. Position the ball stud into the steering knuckle, then install the upper ball joint stud washer and nut. Tighten the upper control arm ball stud nut to 33 ft. lbs. (45 Nm). Tighten the nut additionally as necessary to insert the cotter pin but do not exceed 63 ft. lbs. (85 Nm).
9. Install a new cotter pin from the rear to the front of the vehicle.
10. Remove the jackstand and lubricate the ball joint.
11. Install the tire and wheel assembly, then lower the vehicle.

Lower Ball Joints

INSPECTION

1. With the weight of the vehicle properly loading the ball joints, check the wear indicators on the lower ball joints.
2. The wear indicator should protrude 0.050 in. (1.27mm) when new.
3. When the wear indicator shoulder retreats below the surface, the ball joint must be replaced.

REMOVAL & INSTALLATION

1. Raise and support the vehicle safely.
2. Safely support the lower control arm with a jackstand.
3. Remove the tire and wheel assembly.
4. Using J–33436 or equivalent ball joint removal tool, separate the ball joint from the knuckle.
5. Press the upper ball joint from the control arm using tool J–9519–E or an equivalent removal tool.
To install:
6. Position the ball stud so the cotter pin may be installed from the rear to the front of the vehicle and press into the control arm using J–9519-E or equivalent.
7. Position the ball joint into the steering knuckle, then install the washer and nut. Tighten the lower control arm ball stud nut to 50 ft. lbs. (68 Nm). Tighten the ball stud nut additionally to insert a cotter pin but do not exceed 88 ft. lbs. (120 Nm) to align the cotter pin holes.
8. Install a new cotter pin from the rear to the front of the vehicle.
9. Remove the jackstand and lubricate the ball joint.
10. Install the tire and wheel assembly, then lower the vehicle.

Upper Control Arms

REMOVAL & INSTALLATION

1. Disconnect the negative battery cable, then raise and support the vehicle safely.
2. Remove the tire and wheel assembly.
3. Remove the front wheelhouse panel seal and lower center panel.
4. Remove the shock absorber actuator wire connector, if equipped.
5. Support the lower control arm with a jackstand.
6. For 1990 vehicles disconnect the ABS speed sensor cable bracket from the knuckle and set aside. For 1991–93 vehicles, disconnect the speed sensor electrical connector and remove the cable from the bracket.
7. Use tool J–33436 or equivalent and disconnect the upper ball joint from the knuckle.
8. Remove the upper control arm attaching bolts, shims and nuts, noting the position of the shims for reinstallation purposes. Remove the control arm.
To install:
9. Position the bolts through the frame, then install the upper control arm and shims. Place the shims in the locations noted during removal. Install and tighten the control arm nuts to 37 ft. lbs. (50 Nm).
10. Connect the ball joint to the knuckle and install the nut and washer. Properly tighten the nut and install a new cotter pin.
11. Connect the ABS speed sensor bracket, cable and/or electrical connection, as applicable.
12. Connect the shock absorber electrical actuator connection, if equipped.
13. Remove the jackstand and install the front wheelhouse lower center panel and seal.
14. Install the tire and wheel assembly.
15. Lower the vehicle and connect the negative battery cable.
16. Check and adjust the front end alignment, as necessary.

Lower Control Arms

REMOVAL & INSTALLATION

1. Disconnect the negative battery cable, then raise and support the vehicle safely.
2. Remove the tire and wheel assembly, then remove both spring protectors.
3. Using tool J–33432 and adapters J–33432–88 or equivalent, compress the spring.
4. Support the lower control arm with a jackstand.

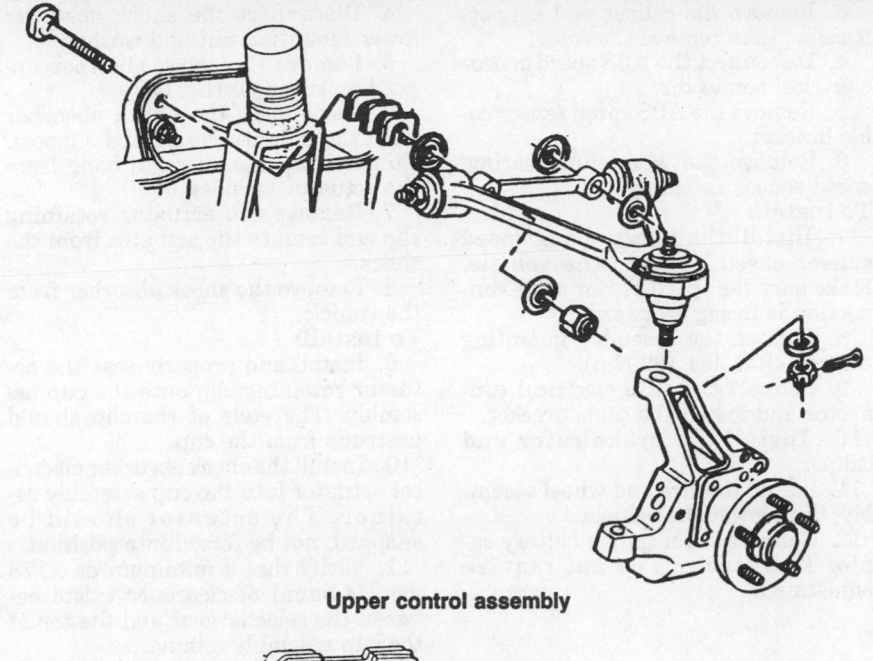

Upper control assembly

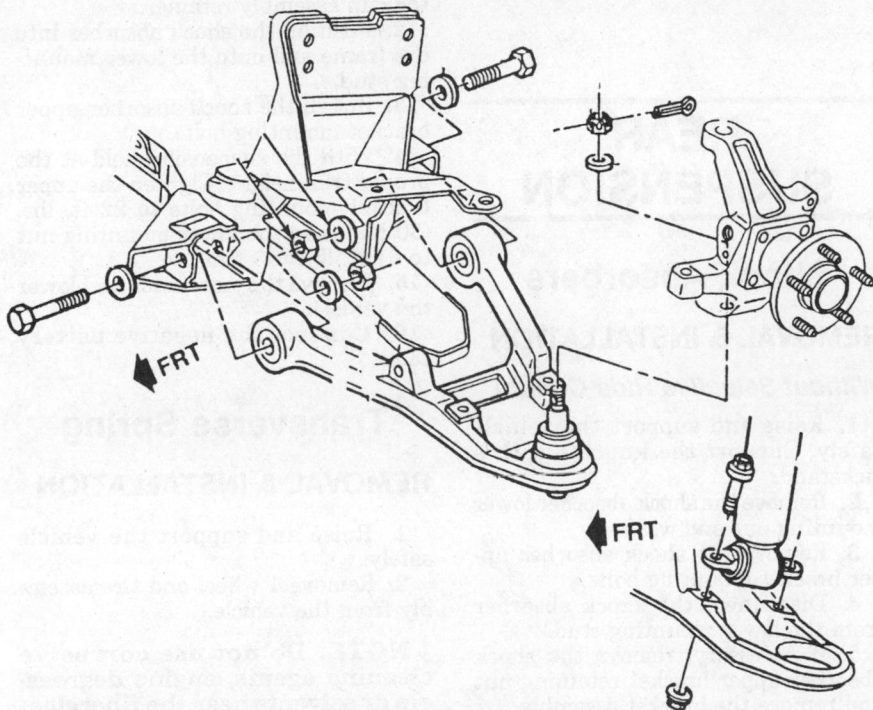

Lower control assembly

13. For 1992–93 vehicles, install the engine support bracket.

14. Install the lower ball joint stud into the steering knuckle. Properly tgithen the nut and install a new cotter pin.

15. Connect the ABS speed sensor bracket, cable and/or electrical connection, as applicable.

16. Connect the stabililzer shaft link to the lower control arm but hand-tighten the nuts only.

17. Remove the spring compression tool and adapters.

18. Hold the suspension at the proper trim height using jackstands and tighten the stabilizer link nuts to 35 ft. lbs. (48 Nm) and the lower control arm bolts to 82 ft. lbs. (112 Nm).

19. Connect the shock absorber to the lower control arm and tighten the nuts to 19 ft. lbs. (26 Nm).

20. Remove the jackstands and install both spring protectors. Tighten the bolts to 18 ft. lbs. (25 Nm).

21. Install the tire and wheel assembly.

22. Lower the vehicle and connect the negative battery cable.

Stabilizer Shaft

REMOVAL & INSTALLATION

1. Raise and support vehicle safely, then remove the tire and wheel assemblies.

2. Support the lower control arms using jackstands.

3. Remove the stabilizer shaft insulator clamp bolts and brackets from the frame.

4. Remove the stabilizer shaft to links attaching bolts.

5. Remove the stabilizer shaft from the vehicle.

6. Installation is the reverse of the removal procedure.

7. Install the shaft link bolts and nuts facing the same positions as they were removed. With the suspension held at the proper trim height, tighten the stabilizer shaft link nuts to 35 ft. lbs. (48 Nm) and the insulator clamp bolts to 40 ft. lbs. (54 Nm).

Streering Knuckle

REMOVAL & INSTALLATION

1. Disconnect the negative battery cable, then raise and support the vehicle safely.

2. Remove the tire and wheel assembly.

3. Remove the brake caliper and rotor.

4. Disconnect the ABS speed sensor electrical connection and remove the cable bracket.

5. Disconnect the shock absorber from the lower control arm, then disconnect the front stabililzer shaft link from the lower control arm.

6. For 1990 vehicles disconnect the ABS speed sensor cable bracket from the knuckle and set aside. For 1991–93 vehicles, disconnect the speed sensor electrical connector and remove the cable from the bracket.

7. Using tool J–33436 or equivalent, disconnect the lower ball joint from the knuckle.

8. For 1992–93 vehicles, remove the engine support bracket.

9. Remove nuts, washers and bolts attaching the lower control arm to the frame.

10. Remove the jackstand and the lower control arm.

To install:

11. Install the lower control arm, bolts, washers and nuts.

12. Support the lower control arm with a jackstand.

5. For 1989–90 vehicles remove the speed sensor, then remove the wheel hub.

6. For 1991–93 vehicles remove the wheel hub/speed sensor assembly.

7. Support the lower control arm with a jackstand.

8. Separate the upper and lower ball joints from the steering knuckle using J-33436 or equivalent ball joint remover tool.

9. Remove the tie rod ball stud from the steering knuckle using, J-6627-A or equivalent steering linkage puller.

10. Remove the knuckle from the vehicle.

To install:

11. Position the knuckle and install the tie rod ball stud, positioned so the cotter pin can be installed from the rear to the front of the vehicle. Properly tighten the stud nut and install a new cotter pin.

12. Install the upper and lower ball joints to the steering knuckle. Properly tighten the stud nuts and install new cotter pins.

13. Remove the jack stand.

14. Install the wheel hub or the wheel hub/speed sensor assembly, as applicable.

15. For 1989–90 vehicles, install the ABS speed sensor.

16. Install the ABS speed sensor bracket and connect the electrical connection.

17. Install the rotor and caliper.

18. Install the tire and wheel assembly.

19. Lower the vehicle and connect the negative battery cable.

Front Wheel Hub and Bearing Assembly

REMOVAL & INSTALLATION

1989–90

1. Raise and support the vehicle safely.

2. Remove the tire and wheel assembly.

3. Remove the caliper and support it aside, then remove the rotor.

4. Remove the hub and bearing assembly.

5. Installation is the reverse of the removal procedure.

6. Tighten the hub assembly nuts to 46 ft. lbs. (62 Nm). The bearings do not require adjustment.

1991–93

1. Disconnect the negative battery cable, then raise and support the vehicle safely.

2. Remove the tire and wheel assembly.

3. Remove the caliper and support it aside, then remove the rotor.

4. Disconnect the ABS speed sensor electrical connector.

5. Remove the ABS speed sensor cable bracket.

6. Remove the wheel hub/bearing/speed sensor assembly.

To install:

7. Install the hub/bearing/speed sensor assembly onto the vehicle. Make sure the speed sensor cable connection is facing rearward.

8. Tighten the assembly mounting nuts to 46 ft. lbs. (62 Nm).

9. Connect the ABS electrical connector and install the cable bracket.

10. Install the brake rotor and caliper.

11. Install the tire and wheel assembly, then lower the vehicle.

12. Connect the negative battery cable. The bearings do not require adjustment.

REAR SUSPENSION

Shock Absorbers

REMOVAL & INSTALLATION

Without Selective Ride Control

1. Raise and support the vehicle safely. Support the knuckle with a jackstand.

2. Remove the shock absorber lower mounting nut and washer.

3. Remove the shock absorber upper bracket mounting bolts.

4. Disconnect the shock absorber from the lower mounting stud.

5. If necessary, remove the shock absorber upper bracket retaining nut and remove the bracket assembly.

6. Installation is the reverse of the removal procedure.

7. Tighten the upper bracket retaining nut, if removed, to 19 ft. lbs. (26 Nm). With the suspension at proper trim height, tighten the upper bracket mounting bolts to 22 ft. lbs. (30 Nm) and the lower mounting nut to 61 ft. lbs. (83 Nm).

With Selective Ride Control

1. Disconnect the negative battery cable.

2. Raise and support the vehicle safely.

3. Support the rear knuckle with a jackstand.

4. Disconnect the shock absorber lower mounting nut and washer.

5. Remove the shock absorber upper bracket mounting bolts.

6. Disconnect the shock absorber from the mounting stud and support. Do not allow the shock to hang from the actuator harness.

7. Remove the actuator retaining clip and remove the actuator from the shock.

8. Remove the shock absorber from the vehicle.

To install:

9. Install and properly seat the actuator retaining clip onto the cup assembly. The ends of the clip should protrude from the cup.

10. Install the shock absorber electrical actuator into the cup assembly retainer. The actuator should be snapped, not be forced into position.

11. Verify that a minimum of 0.178 inch (4.5mm) of clearance exists between the selector gear and the top of the cup assembly retainer.

12. Position the shock absorber into the frame and onto the lower mounting stud.

13. Install the shock absorber upper bracket mounting bolts.

14. With the suspension held at the proper trim height. Tighten the upper bracket mounting bolts to 22 ft. lbs. (30 Nm) and the lower mounting nut to 61 ft. lbs. (83 Nm).

15. Remove the jackstands and lower the vehicle.

16. Connect the negative battery cable.

Transverse Spring

REMOVAL & INSTALLATION

1. Raise and support the vehicle safely.

2. Remove 1 wheel and tire assembly from the vehicle.

NOTE: Do not use corrosive cleaning agents, engine degreasers or solvents near the fiberglass rear spring or extensive damage could occur to the spring assembly.

3. Install tool J-33432 or equivalent spring compressor, onto the rear transverse spring, then compress the spring.

4. Remove the cotter pins, retaining nuts, insulators and spring bolts attaching the spring to the knuckles.

5. Carefully release and remove the spring compression tool.

6. Remove the rear spring anchor plate bolts, then the anchor plate, spacers and insulator from the vehicle. Note the spacer positioning for reinstallation purposes.

7. Remove the transverse spring from the vehicle.

To install:

8. Position the spring in the vehicle. Take care not to scratch the spring during installation.

9. Position the spacers as noted during removal, then install the insualtors and anchor plates onto the differential carrier.

10. Install the anchor plate bolts and tighten to 37 ft. lbs. (50 Nm).

11. Install the spring compression tool and compress the spring.

12. Position the spring to the knuckles and install the spring bolts, insulators and nuts. Tighten the nuts until slot in nut aligns with hole in bolt and install a new cotter pin.

13. Carefully release and remove the spring compression tool.

14. Install the tire and wheel assembly.

15. Remove the jackstands and lower the vehicle.

Rear Control Arms

REMOVAL & INSTALLATION

1. Raise and support the vehicle safely.

2. For 1989 vehicles, disconnect the spring at the knuckle.

3. Remove the control arm nut, bolt and washers at the knuckle.

4. Remove control arm nut and bolt at the body bracket.

5. Remove the control arm from the vehicle.

6. Installation is the reverse of the removal procedure.

7. With the suspension held at the proper trim height, tighten the body bracket bolt to 63 ft. lbs. (85 Nm) and the nut at the knuckle to 140 ft. lbs. (190 Nm).

Spindle/Support Rod

REMOVAL & INSTALLATION

1. Raise and support vehicle safely.

2. Scribe alignment marks on the wheel spindle/support rod adjustment bolt and the spindle/support rod bracket so they can be installed in the same position.

3. Remove the adjustment bolt, cam and nut, then separate the spindle/support rod from the bracket.

4. Remove the spindle/support bolt, washer and nut at the knuckle, then remove the spindle/support rod from the vehicle.

5. Installation is the reverse of the removal procedure. Be sure to align the marks made during removal.

6. With the suspension held at the proper trim height, tighten the spin-

dle/support rod to knuckle nut to 107 ft. lbs. (145 Nm), then tighten the spindle/support rod adjustment nut to 186 ft. lbs. (253 Nm).

7. Check and adjust the rear suspension alignment, as necessary.

STEERING

Steering Wheel

NOTE: 1990-93 vehicles are equipped with a Supplemental Inflatable Restraint system, make certain to follow the recommended disarming procedure before and the coil centering and SIR enabling procedures, after repairs.

REMOVAL & INSTALLATION

1989

1. Disconnect the battery negative cable.

2. Remove the horn cap from the steering wheel by pulling rearward, then disconnect the horn button wire.

3. Remove the telescope lever attaching screws and the shaft lock knob screw, then remove the telescope adjustment lever.

4. Remove the steering wheel nut retainer, then the steering wheel nut.

NOTE: Before removing steering wheel, scribe marks on steering wheel hub and steering wheel shaft for installation purposes.

5. Using suitable steering wheel puller, remove the steering wheel from the vehicle.

6. If necessary, remove the horn contact spring.

To install:

7. Install the horn contact spring, if removed.

8. Align the marks made earlier and position the steering wheel.

9. Install the wheel nut and tighten to 30 ft. lbs. (40 Nm). Install the wheel nut retainer.

10. Install the telescoping adjustment lever through the slot in the top of the steering wheel, then install the shaft lock screw. Tighten the screw to 30 inch lbs. (2.8 Nm).

11. Position the adjustment lever as far to the right as possible while aligning the screw holes. Install the telescoping lever screws and tighten to 40 inch lbs. (3.3 Nm).

12. Connect the horn button wire and install the horn cap to the steering wheel.

13. Connect the negative battery cable.

1990–93

1. Properly disable the SIR system and disconnect the negative battery cable.

2. Remove screws from the back of the steering wheel attaching the inflator module.

3. Remove the inflator module from the steering wheel.

4. Disconnect the Connector Pin Assurance (CPA) and the SIR electrical connector at the inflator module.

5. Remove the steering wheel attaching nut and the horn connector. Mark the relationship of the steering wheel to the column splines for installation purposes.

NOTE: To avoid damaging the SIR coil, do not use any steering wheel puller other than those recommended.

6. Using steering wheel puller tool J–1859–03 and puller screws J–38720, remove the steering wheel. If the steering wheel does not come off easily, proceed as follows:

   a. With the puller installed and the side screws threaded to the

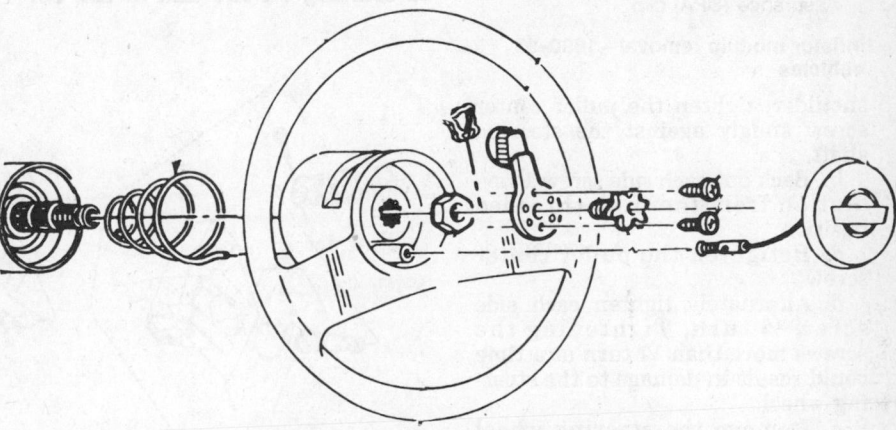

Steering wheel assembly–1989 vehicles

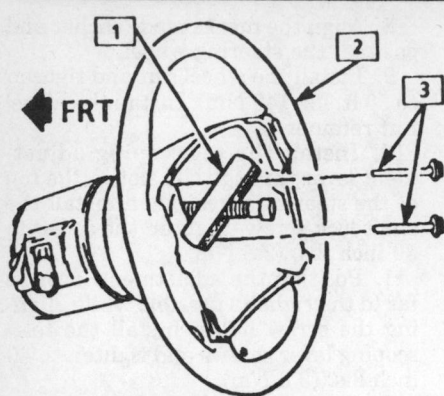

1. Steering wheel puller
2. Steering wheel
3. Puller side screws

Steering wheel removal—1990–93 vehicles

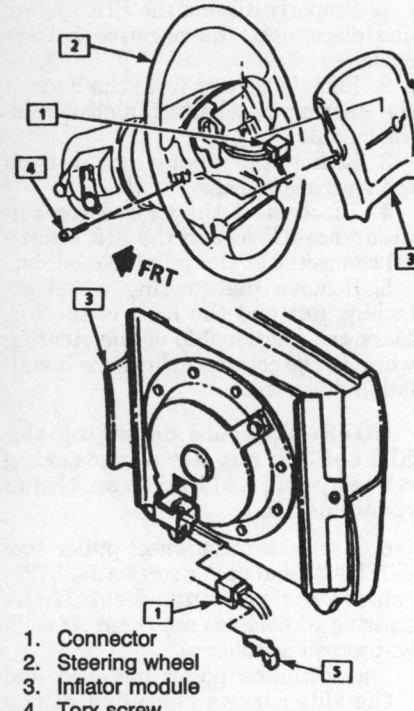

1. Connector
2. Steering wheel
3. Inflator module
4. Torx screw
5. Connector Pin Assurance (CPA) clip

Inflator module removal—1990–93 vehicles

shoulder, tighten the puller center screw snugly against the steering shaft.

b. Back out each side screw 1 revolution from the fully threaded position.

c. Retighten the puller center screw.

d. Alternately tighten each side screw ¼ turn. Tightening the screws more than ¼ turn at a time could result in damage to the steering wheel.

e. Remove the steering wheel from the vehicle.

To install:

7. Connect the horn connector, then install the steering wheel to the column aligning the marks made earlier.

8. Install a new steering wheel retaining nut and tighten the new nut to 30 ft. lbs. (41 Nm).

9. Connect the SIR coil electrical connector to the inflator module and install the CPA.

10. Position the inflator module onto the steering wheel and install new module retaining screws. Tighten the new screws to 87 inch lbs. (9.7 Nm).

11. Connect the negative battery cable and properly enable the SIR system.

Steering Column

REMOVAL & INSTALLATION

1989

1. Position the wheels in the straight-ahead position and turn the ignition switch to the **LOCK** position. Make sure the switch remains locked throughout the procedure or internal components of the steering column may be damaged.

2. Disconnect the negative battery cable.

3. Remove the steering wheel.

4. Remove the upper intermediate shaft bolt and separate the coupling from the lower end of steering column.

5. Remove the left side instrument panel sound insulator and lower trim pad.

6. Disconnect the park lock cable from the backdrive pin and bracket, then disconnect all electrical connectors from the column assembly.

7. Remove the nuts securing the lower support plate to the floor.

8. Remove the bolts securing the bracket to the instrument panel.

NOTE: Handle the steering column very carefully. Hammering or leaning on the end of the col-

umn could shear off the plastic type inserts which allow the column to collapse in a collision.

9. Remove the steering column assembly from the vehicle.

To install:

10. Position the steering column assembly in the vehicle and lower the steering shaft assembly into the U-joint of the intermediate shaft.

11. Loosely attach the steering column to the studs on the lower support plate.

12. Loosely attach the steering column to the instrument panel reinforcement assembly with the capsule bolts.

13. Tighten the bolts to 20 ft. lbs. (27 Nm), the nuts to 10 ft. lbs. (14 Nm) and the intermediate shaft upper bolt to 44 ft. lbs. (60 Nm).

14. Connect the steering column electrical connectors.

15. Attach the park lock cable to the cable backdrive and bracket.

16. Install the instrument panel sound insulator.

17. Connect the negative battery cable.

NOTE: These vehicles are equipped with an air bag system, make certain that the SIR system is disabled before, and properly enabled after repairs.

Also ensure the steering wheel and the front wheels of the vehicle are locked in the straight-ahead position before disconnecting the intermediate shaft.

Failure to follow these procedures may cause improper alignment of some internal components and result in damage to the SIR coil assembly.

1990–93

1. Properly disable the SIR sytem.

2. Disconnect battery negative cable.

3. Verify the steering wheel and vehicle wheels are straight-ahead and

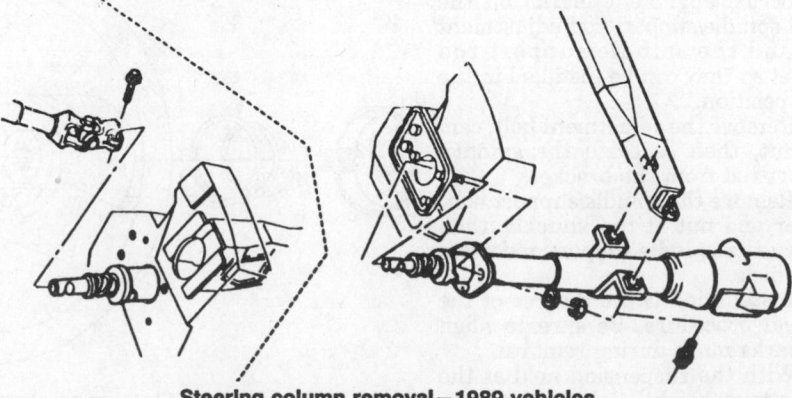

Steering column removal—1989 vehicles

the ignition key is in the **LOCKED** position, then remove the steering wheel.

4. Remove the intermediate shaft upper bolt.

5. Disconnect the ALDL connector and the light from the sound insulator, then remove the sound insulator, if required.

6. Remove the driver's side knee bolster.

7. Remove the tilt lever.

8. Remove the nuts from the lower support plate and the capsule bolts from the reinforcement assembly. For vehicles equipped with automatic transmission, the bolts must also be removed from the upper support plate and cable backdrive assembly.

9. Disconnect the electrical connectors from the steering column.

10. Disconnect the steering column to lower support bracket.

11. Remove the acclerator pedal bracket nuts.

12. Remove the steering column assembly from the vehicle.

To install:

13. Inspect the steering column to lower cowl gasket for tears. If damaged, the gasket must be replaced tears could allow carbon monoxide into the vehicle resulting in possible serious injuries or death.

14. Position steering column assembly into the vehicle and insert the lower steering shaft assembly into the U-joint of the intermediate shaft. Loosely install the shaft upper bolt.

15. Loosely attach the steering column and upper support plate to the instrument panel reinforcement assembly with the capsule bolts, and on automatic transmission vehicles, with the cable backdrive.

16. Loosely attach the steering column nuts to the support plate studs.

17. Tighten the intermediate shaft bolt to 26 ft. lbs. (34 Nm).

18. Tighten the lower support plate nuts to 10 ft. lbs. (14 Nm) and then tighten the capsule to reinforcement bolts to 20 ft. lbs. (27 Nm). The lower support plate nuts must be tightened first to prevent damage to the column assembly.

19. Connect all electrical connectors to the steering column, except the SIR connector.

20. Install the driver's side knee bolster.

21. Install the sound insulator and connect the ALDL connector and lamp, if removed.

22. Connect the sound insulator bracket to the column lower support.

23. Install the accelerator pedal bracket nuts and tighten to 71 inch lbs. (8 Nm).

24. Install the steering wheel and the inflator module assembly.

25. Connect the negative battery ca-

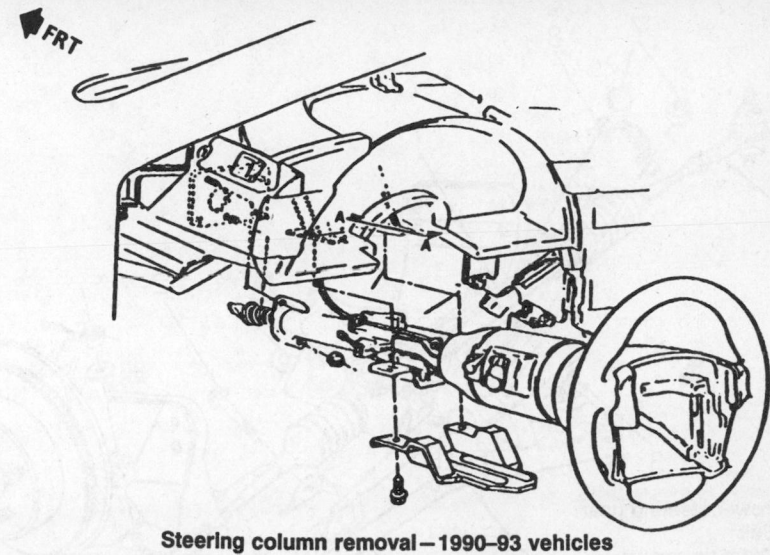

Steering column removal – 1990–93 vehicles

ble and properly enable the SIR system.

Power Rack and Pinion

ADJUSTMENT

Rack Bearing Preload

1. Raise and safely support the vehicle so the front wheels are raised and the steering wheel is centered.

2. Loosen the adjuster plug locknut.

3. Turn adjuster plug clockwise until it bottoms, then back off 50–70 degrees.

4. Keep the adjuster plug from turning and tighten the locknut to 50 ft. lbs. (70 Nm).

5. Inspect the steering wheel returnability to center after adjustment.

REMOVAL & INSTALLATION

1. Disconnect the negative battery cable and position a drain pan under the vehicle to catch fluid.

2. Remove the power steering gear inlet hose assembly from the steering gear.

3. Remove the power steering gear outlet hose assembly from the steering gear.

NOTE: If equipped with a power steering fluid cooling pipe, disconnect fluid cooling pipe outlet hose from the fluid cooling pipe.

4. Remove the steering gear coupling shield.

5. Remove the intermediate shaft from the power steering gear and lower steering shaft, and position aside.

6. Raise and support the vehicle safely.

7. Remove the front tire and wheel assemblies.

8. Remove both outer tie rods from the knuckles using a suitable puller.

9. Remove the power steering cooler assembly, if necessary.

10. Remove the stabilizer shaft.

11. Remove the steering gear to frame attaching clamp nuts, then the bolts and clamp from the vehicle.

12. Remove the power steering gear attaching attaching nuts and bolts.

13. Remove the power steering gear from the vehicle.

14. Remove the outer tie rods from the power steering gear, if necessary.

15. Remove rack and pinion boots, if necessary.

16. Remove the inner tie rods if necessary.

To install:

17. Install tie rods, if removed.

18. Install the rack and pinion boots, if removed.

19. Connect the cooling pipe, if removed.

20. Install the power steering gear, nuts and bolts. Torque nuts to 30 ft. lbs. (40 Nm). Torque the steering gear clamp nuts to 18 ft. lbs. (25 Nm).

21. Install the stabilizer shaft and, if removed, the power steering cooler assembly.

22. Install both outer tie rods to the steering knuckle.

23. Install tire and wheel assemblies and lower the vehicle.

24. Install the intermediate shaft and the steering gear coupling shield.

25. Install the power steering gear outlet hose assembly to the power steering gear. Tighten fitting to 21 ft. lbs. (28 Nm).

26. Install the power steering gear inlet hose assembly to the power steering gear. Tighten the fitting to 21 ft. lbs. (28 Nm).

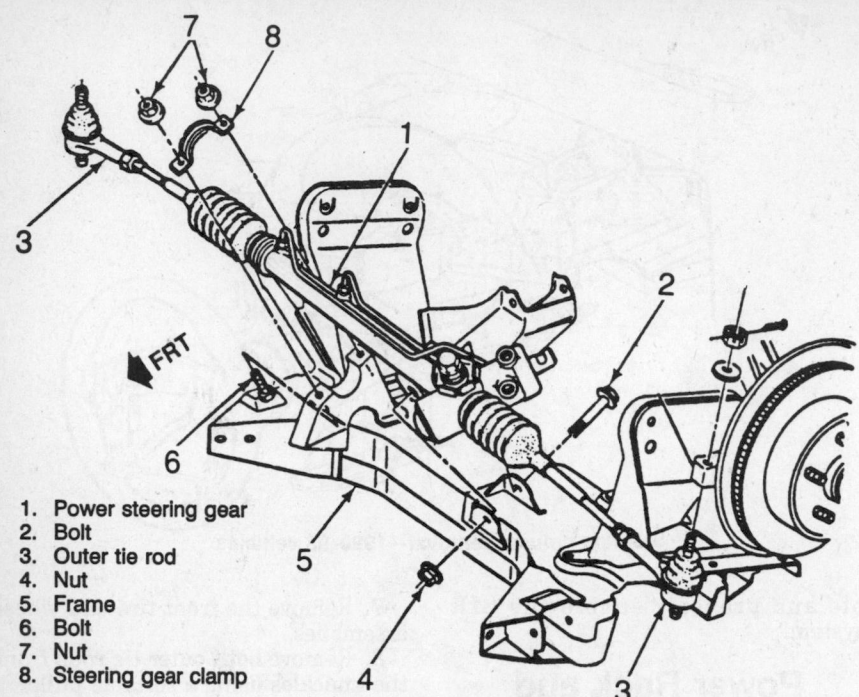

1. Power steering gear
2. Bolt
3. Outer tie rod
4. Nut
5. Frame
6. Bolt
7. Nut
8. Steering gear clamp

Typical power rack and pinion assembly

27. Remove the drain and fill the power steering reservoir.

28. Connect the negative battery cable, bleed the system and check for proper operation.

Power Steering Pump

REMOVAL & INSTALLATION

5.7L (VIN 8) Engine

1. Disconnect the negative battery cable and place a drain pan under the vehicle to catch fluid.

2. Remove the serpentine drive belt.

3. Remove the water pump damper, if equipped with an automatic transmission.

4. Remove the power steering pump reservoir bracket bolts and reposition the barcket and hoses for pulley clearance.

5. Remove the power steering pump pulley dust cap and the remove the pulley with J-25034-B or equivalent puller.

6. Disconnect the power steering gear inlet hose assembly from the power steering pump.

7. Disconnect the power steering reservoir hose and clamp from the power steering pump.

8. Remove the bolt attaching the power steering pump rear bracket to power steering pump rear bracket.

9. Remove the engine mount bolt, then the power steering pump rear brace.

10. Remove the power steering pump

attaching bolts and remove the pump with the support bracket.

To install:

11. Position the power steering pump and the support bracket to the alternator/power steering bracket. Install the bolts and tighten to 18 ft. lbs. (25 Nm).

12. Install the power steering pump

securing the power steering pump rear bracket to the power steering pump, if removed, to 18 ft. lbs. (25 Nm).

13. Install the reservoir hose and clamp to the pump and tighten the hose clamp screw to 22 inch lbs. (2.5 Nm).

14. Connect the inlet hose to the power steering pump and tighten the fitting to 21 ft. lbs. (28 Nm).

15. Using a suitable installation tool, install the power steering pump pulley so the pump shaft is flush with the hub of the pulley.

16. Install the hub dust cap to the pulley.

17. Position the reservoir bracket and hoses, install the bolts and tighten to 89 inch lbs. (10 Nm).

18. Install the water pump damper, if applicable.

19. Install the serpentine drive belt.

20. Connect the negative battery cable and remove the drain pan.

21. Refill the power steering pump reservoir and properly bleed the system.

5.7L (VIN P) Engine

1. Disconnect the negative battery cable and place a drain pan under the vehicle to catch fluid.

2. Remove serpentine drive belt.

3. Remove the power steering pump pulley hub cap and remove the pulley using J-25034-B or equivalent pump pulley puller.

4. Disconnect the inlet hose assembly from the pump.

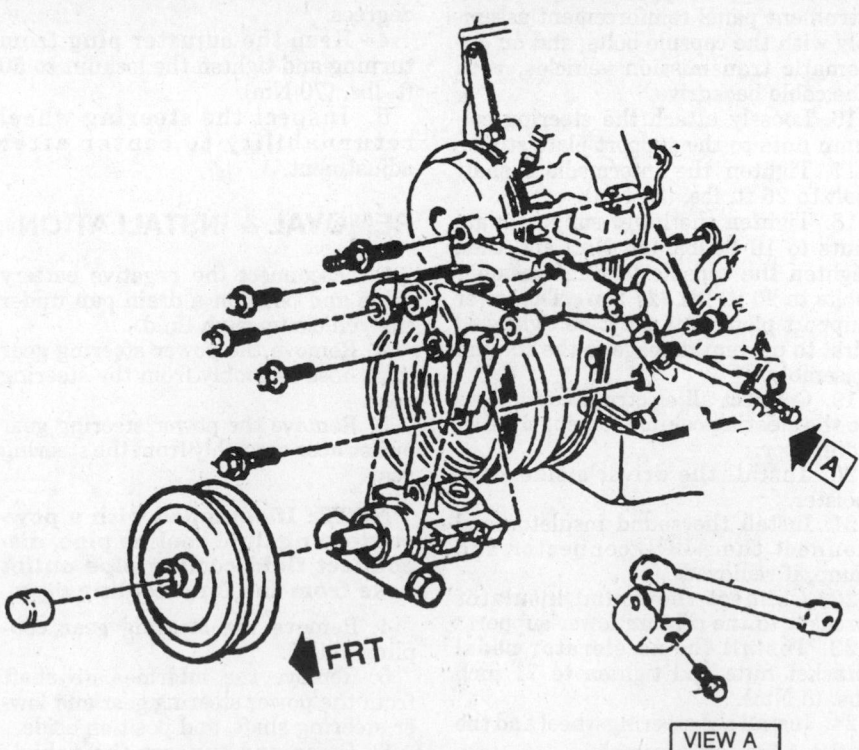

VIEW A

Power steering pump assembly—5.7L (VIN 8) Engine

5. Disconnect the reservoir hose and clamp from the pump.

6. Remove the power steering pump mounting bolts.

7. Remove the power steering pump and front bracket.

To install:

8. Install the power steering pump and front bracket with the mounting bolts. Tighten the bolts to 18 ft. lbs. (25 Nm).

9. Connect the power steering pump reservoir hose and clamp to the pump. Tighten the clamp to 22 inch lbs. (2.5 Nm).

10. Connect the power steering gear inlet hose assembly to the power steering pump and tighten the fitting to 21 ft. lbs. (28 Nm).

11. Using J-25033-B or an equivalent installation tool, install the power steering pump pulley so the front of the pulley hub is flush with the front of the pump shaft.

12. Install the hub cap to the pulley.

13. Install the serpentine drive belt.

14. Connect the negative battery cable and remove the drain pan.

15. Refill the power steering reservoir and properly bleed the system.

5.7L (VIN J) Engine

1. Disconnect the negative battery cable and remove the air intake duct.

2. Drain the engine cooling system into a suitable container.

3. Drain and appropriately discard the power steering fluid.

4. Disconnect the vacuum hose retainer from the pump reservoir, then remove the vacuum hoses and set aside.

5. Remove the left coolant outlet housing and hose.

6. Remove the serpentine drive belt.

7. Remove the power steering pump bracket to cylinder head bolts.

8. Remove the pump bracket to air conditioning compressor bolt.

9. Remove the cooler assembly outlet hose from the reservoir.

10. Disconnect the power steering gear inlet pipe from the power steering pump.

11. Remove the power steering pump assembly from the vehicle.

12. If necessary, remove the pump pulley using tool J-25033-B or equivalent puller. Remove the reservoir hose from the pump. Remove the power steering pump to mounting bracket bolts and remove the pump from the bracket.

To install:

13. If removed, position the power steering pump to the bracket, apply Loctite® 565 to the pump to bracket mounting bolts and install. Tighten the bolts to 19 ft. lbs. (26 Nm). Connect the pump reservoir hose to the

pump and tighten the clamp screw to 22 inch lbs. (2.5 Nm).

14. If removed, install the power steering pump pulley using a suitable installation tool.

15. Position the pump assembly onto the engine.

16. Connect the gear inlet pipe to the pump and tighten the fitting to 21 ft. lbs. (28 Nm).

17. Install the cooler assembly outlet hose to the reservoir and tighten the hose clamp screw to 22 inch lbs. (2.5 Nm).

18. Install the A/C compressor to power steering pump bracket bolt and tighten to 19 ft. lbs. (26 Nm).

19. Apply Loctite® 565 to the pump bracket to cylinder head bolt, install and tighten the bolt to 19 ft. lbs. (26 Nm).

20. Install the serpentine drive belt.

21. Install the left coolant outlet cover and hose.

22. Install the vacuum hoses and connect the retainer to the power steering pump reservoir. Tighten the screws to 13 inch lbs. (1.5 Nm).

23. Install the air intake duct and connect the negative battery cable.

24. Refill the power steering reservoir.

25. Properly fill the engine cooling system.

26. Bleed the power steering system.

SYSTEM BLEEDING

1. With the engine **OFF** and wheels off the ground, turn the steering wheel all the way to the left. Add power steering fluid to the **COLD** mark on the fluid level indicator.

2. Bleed the system by turning the wheels from side-to-side without reaching the stop at either end.

3. Start the engine. With engine idling, recheck the fluid level. If necessary add fluid to bring the fluid up to the **COLD** mark.

4. Return the wheels to the center position. Lower the front wheels to the ground.

5. Road test the vehicle to ensure the steering functions normal and free from noise.

6. Check for fluid leakage. Ensure that fluid level is at the **HOT** mark after system is stabilized at its normal operating temperature.

Tie Rod Ends

REMOVAL & INSTALLATION

1. Disconnect battery ground cable.

2. Raise and support the vehicle safely, then remove the front wheel assembly.

3. Remove the tie rod cotter pin and

hex slotted nut from the tie rod assembly.

4. Loosen tie rod jam nut.

5. Using tool J-24319-01 or equivalent linkage puller, remove the tie rod from the steering knuckle.

6. Remove the tie rod from the steering rack assembly.

To install:

7. Install the tie rod to the steering rack assembly, but do not tighten the jam nut.

8. Install the tie rod to the steering knuckle and install the hex slotted nut to the tie rod stud.

9. Tighten the hex nut to 35 ft. lbs. (47 Nm), then tighten additionally to insert the cotter pin. Do not exceed a total torque of 52 ft. lbs. (70 Nm) and do not back off the original torque to insert a new cotter pin.

10. Adjust the toe by turning the inner tie rod, making sure the rack and pinion boot is not twisted or puckered during toe adjustment.

11. Tighten the jam nut against the tie rod to 50 ft. lbs. (68 Nm).

BRAKES

Master Cylinder

REMOVAL & INSTALLATION

1. Disconnect the negative battery cable.

2. Disconnect the electrical connector from the warning switch and, if

1. Master cylinder body
2. Proportioning valve
3. Ground spring
4. O-Ring seal
5. End plug

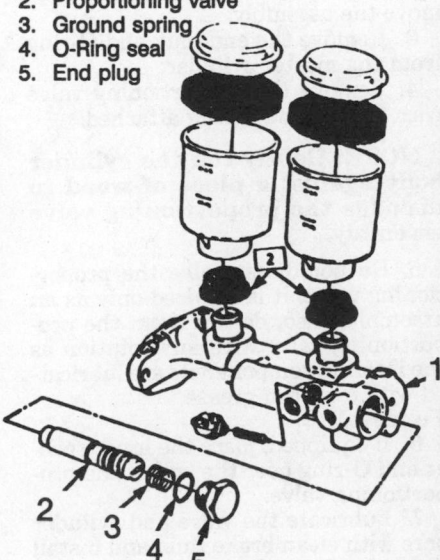

Master cylinder and proportioning valve—1989–91 vehicles

equipped, the fluid level warning switch assemblies.

3. Disconnect the hydraulic brake lines at the master cylinder. Plug the lines to prevent fluid contamination or loss.

4. If equipped, disconnect the master cylinder prime pipe from the reservoir.

5. Remove the retaining nuts holding the cylinder to the brake booster assembly.

6. Reposition the battery cable and cruise control cable, if necessary.

7. Remove the master cylinder assembly.

To install:

8. Position the master cylinder assembly to the power booster assembly.

9. Connect the battery cable and cruise control cable clip, if removed.

10. Install the master cylinder retaining nuts and tighten to 13 ft. lbs. (18 Nm).

11. Connect the hydraulic brake lines to the master cylinder and tighten the fittings to 13 ft. lbs. (18 Nm).

12. If equipped, connect the master cylinder prime pipe.

13. Connect the electrical connections to the warning switch assemblies, as required.

14. Fill the master cylinder and properly bleed the hydraulic brake system.

15. Connect the negative battery cable.

Proportioning Valve

REMOVAL & INSTALLATION

1. Disconnect the negative battery cable.

2. Disconnect the warning switch assembly electrical connector and remove the assembly.

3. Remove the end plug and O-ring from the master cylinder.

4. Remove the proportioning valve with the ground spring attached.

NOTE: Gently tap the cylinder body against a piece of wood to dislodge the proportioning valve assembly.

5. Do not disassemble the proportioning valve, it is serviced only as an assembly. Also, do not clean the proportioning valve with any solution as the internal componenets are lubricated with a special grease.

To install:

6. If equipped, place the inner spacer and O-ring over the end of the proportioning valve.

7. Lubricate the valve and cylinder bore with clean brake fluid and install the valve into the master cylinder. Bottom the valve into the bore.

8. Install a new O-ring over the end

plug and place the spring on the valve, then install the end plug.

9. Tighten the proportioning valve end plug to 18 ft. lbs. (25 Nm).

10. Install the warning switch assembly, but hand tighten only.

11. Connect the warning switch electrical connector.

12. Properly bleed the hydraulic brake system and connect the negative battery cable.

Power Brake Booster

REMOVAL & INSTALLATION

1989

1. Disconnect the negative battery cable.

2. Remove the master cylinder from the booster assembly and reposition. If necessary remove the cylinder from the vehicle.

3. Disconnect the vacuum hose from the vacuum check valve.

4. Remove the pushrod end of the valve assembly from the brake pedal by removing the retaining clip.

5. Remove the brake booster attaching nuts, then remove the power booster assembly from the vehicle.

6. Installation is the reverse of the removal procedure.

7. Torque power booster attaching bolts to 15 ft. lbs. (21 Nm).

8. Connect the negative battery cable.

9. If the master cylinder was removed entirely from the vehicle, bleed the hydraulic brake system.

1990–93

1. Disconnect the negative battery cable.

2. Remove the ECM, then the ECM housing bracket attaching bolt.

3. Remove the cruise control cable from the cruise control servo and the servo mounting bracket.

4. Disconnect the pressure differen-

tial sensor electrical connector and the vacuum hose.

5. Disconnect the master cylinder warning switch electrical connector, then remove the nuts attaching the master cylinder to the power booster assembly.

6. Position the master cylinder, cruise control cable and the battery cable aside.

7. Remove the power booster vacuum check valve from the power booster assembly.

8. Remove the instrument panel left sound insulator.

9. Remove the input pushrod assembly retaining ring and washer from the brake pedal.

10. Remove the power booster assembly attaching nuts and washers, then remove the power booster with seals and the ECM bracket attached.

To install:

11. Install the seals, ECM bracket and power booster assembly to the brake pedal bracket. Have an assistant engage the pushrod assembly onto the brake pedal while installing the booster.

12. Install the booster assembly retaining nuts and tighten to 15 ft. lbs. (21 Nm).

13. Install the washer and retaining clip to the brake pedal, then install the left sound insulator.

14. Connect the vacuum check valve to the power booster assembly.

15. Position the master cylinder, cruise control cable bracket and the battery cable clip and install the retaining nuts. Tighten the nuts to 13 ft. lbs. (18 Nm).

16. Connect the master cylinder warning switch electrical connector.

17. Connect the pressure differential sensor electrical connection and vacuum hose.

18. Connect the cruise control cable to the servo and the mounting bracket.

19. Install the ECM housing bracket bolt and tighten to 18 ft. lbs. (25 Nm).

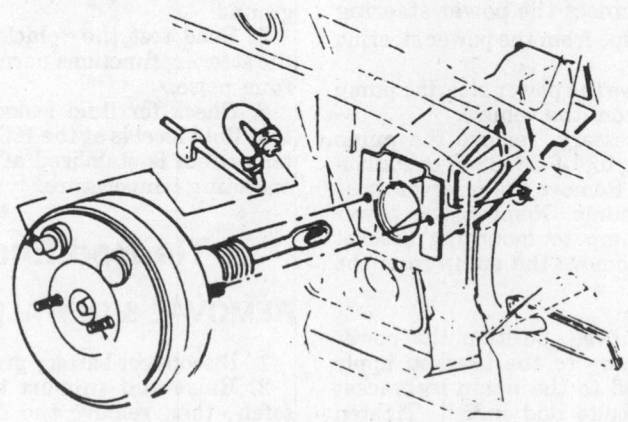

Power brake booster assembly—1989 vehicles

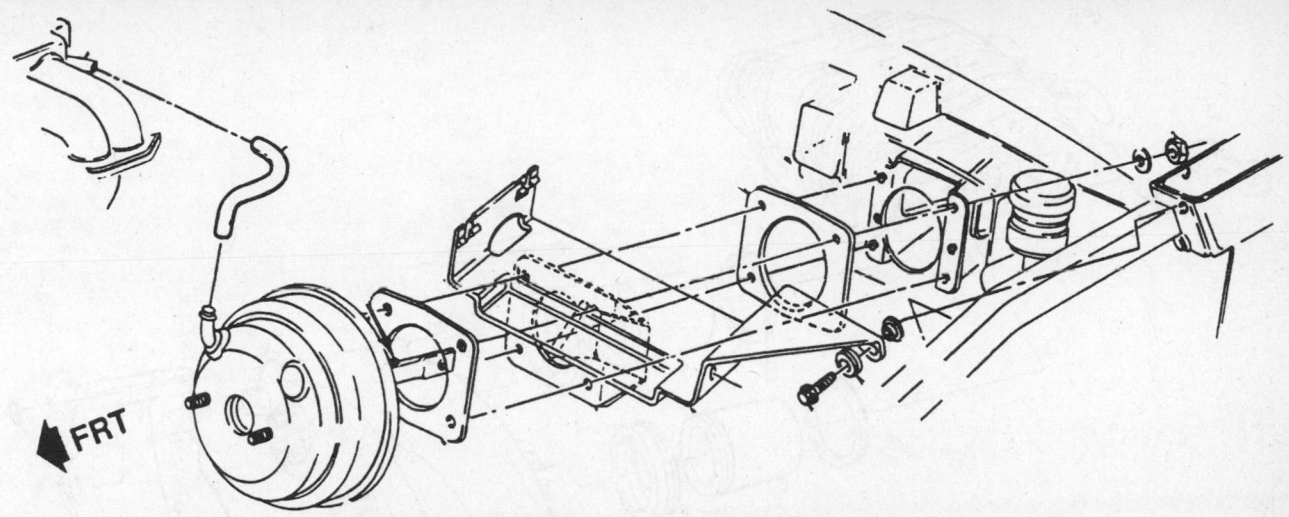

Typical power brake booster assembly—1990–93 vehicles

20. Install the ECM.
21. Connect the negative battery cable.

Brake Caliper

REMOVAL & INSTALLATION

Front

1. Disconnect the negative battery cable and remove ⅔ of the brake fluid from the master cylinder reservoir.
2. Raise and support the vehicle safely.
3. Mark the relationship between the wheel and axle flange, then remove the tire and wheel assembly.
4. Install 2 wheel nuts to retain the brake rotor.
5. With a suitable tool, depress the caliper pistons into the caliper bores to provide clearance between the pads and the rotor.
6. If the caliper is being completely removed from the vehicle for service, disconnect the brake line fitting at the caliper by removing the bolt, 2 gaskets and then the brake hose inlet fitting. Plug all openings to prevent fluid contamination or loss.

NOTE: Do not allow the fluid to come into contact with the transverse spring as damage to the spring may occur.

7. Remove the circlip and the retainer pin, then the caliper housing from the rotor and the caliper mounting bracket. Remove the caliper from the vehicle or if the brake line is still attached, support the caliper from the control arm with a suitable hook or length of mechanic's wire.
To install:
8. Install the caliper over the brake rotor and into the caliper mounting bracket. Make sure the shoe lining

guiding surfaces are correctly seated in the bracket.

NOTE: There are 2 sets of retainer pins in most repair kits. One set is for base calipers and the other is for heavy duty calipers. Make certain that the correct retainer pins are installed.

9. Compress the bias springs by applying pressure to the mounting bracket, then install the new retainer pin and circlip.
10. If removed, connect the brake hose inlet fitting, 2 new gaskets and the inlet fitting bolt. Tighten the bolt to 30 ft. lbs. (40 Nm).
11. If the inlet fitting was removed, properly bleed the hydraulic brake system.
12. Remove the wheel nuts retaining the rotor, align the marks made earlier and install the tire and wheel assembly.
13. Lower the vehicle and check the brake fluid., add as necessary.
14. Connect the negative battery cable, start the engine and pump the brake pedal slowly and firmly 3 times to seat the shoe and lining assemblies.

Rear

1. Disengage the parking brake automatic adjuster as follows:
  a. Remove the drivers seat cushion.
  b. Remove the parking brake lever cover and screws.
  c. Using a suitable tool, disengage and hold the drive pawl from the drive sector.
  d. Insert a nail or drift through the hole in the anchor plate to retain the drive pawl in the disengaged position.
  e. Move the parking brake lever until it aligns with the lock pawl.

  f. Depress the button on the lever and move the lever to the down position.
  g. Verify the anchor plate is against the stud on the parking brake lever, if not as specified, repeat the procedure.
2. Remove ⅔ of the brake fluid from the master cylinder reservoir.
3. Raise and support the vehicle safely.
4. Mark the relationship between the wheel and axle flange, then remove the tire and wheel assembly.
5. Install 2 wheel nuts to retain the brake rotor.
6. Disconnect the brake line fitting at the caliper by removing the bolt, 2 gaskets and the brake hose inlet fitting. Plug all openings to prevent fluid contamination or loss.

NOTE: Do not remove the lever return spring unless the parking brake cable automatic adjuster has been properly disabled.

7. Remove the lever return spring. If the coils are opened, discard.
8. Disconnect the brake cable from the lever and bracket.
9. Remove the 2 guide pins bolts and discard.
10. Remove the caliper housing from the brake rotor and caliper mounting bracket.
To install:
11. Inspect the guide pins for free movement and replace the pins or boots if damaged or corroded.
12. Install the caliper over the brake rotor and into the mounting bracket.
13. Install 2 new guide pin bolts. Tighten the upper bolt to 26 ft. lbs. (35 Nm) and the lower bolt to 16 ft. lbs. (22 Nm).
14. Install the cable to the bracket and parking brake lever, then install the lever return spring.

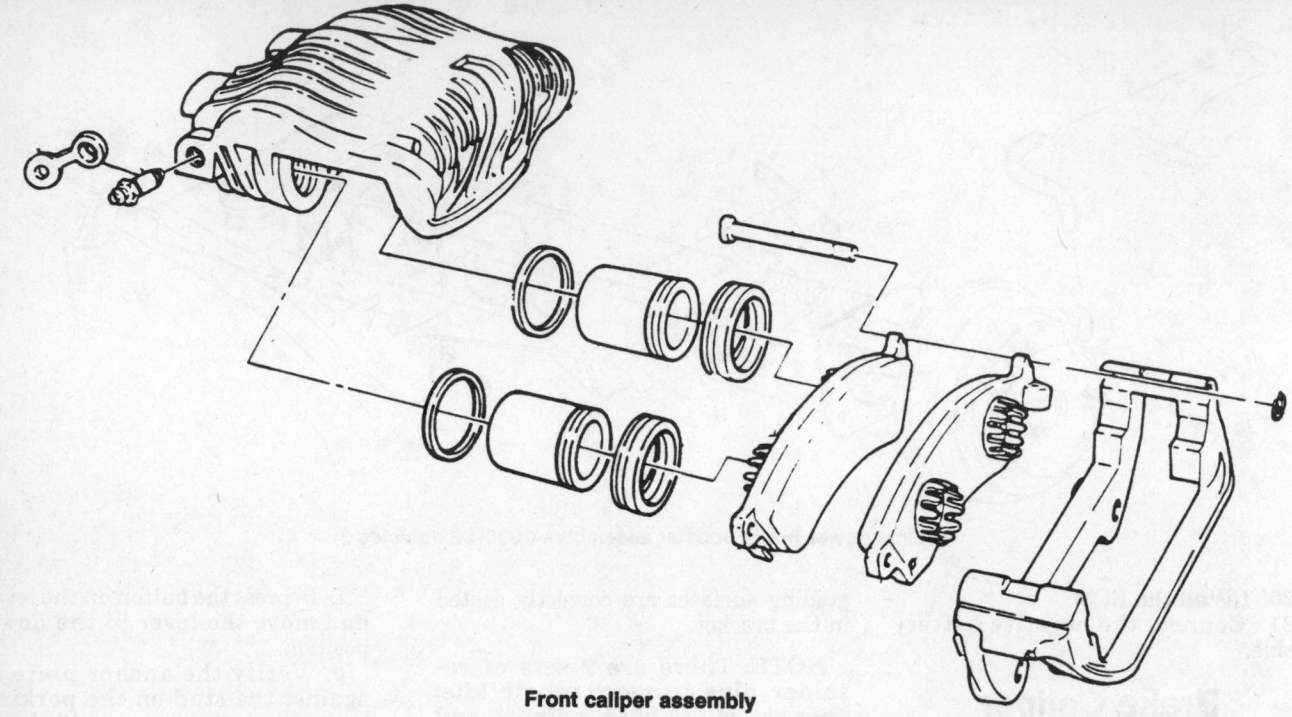

Front caliper assembly

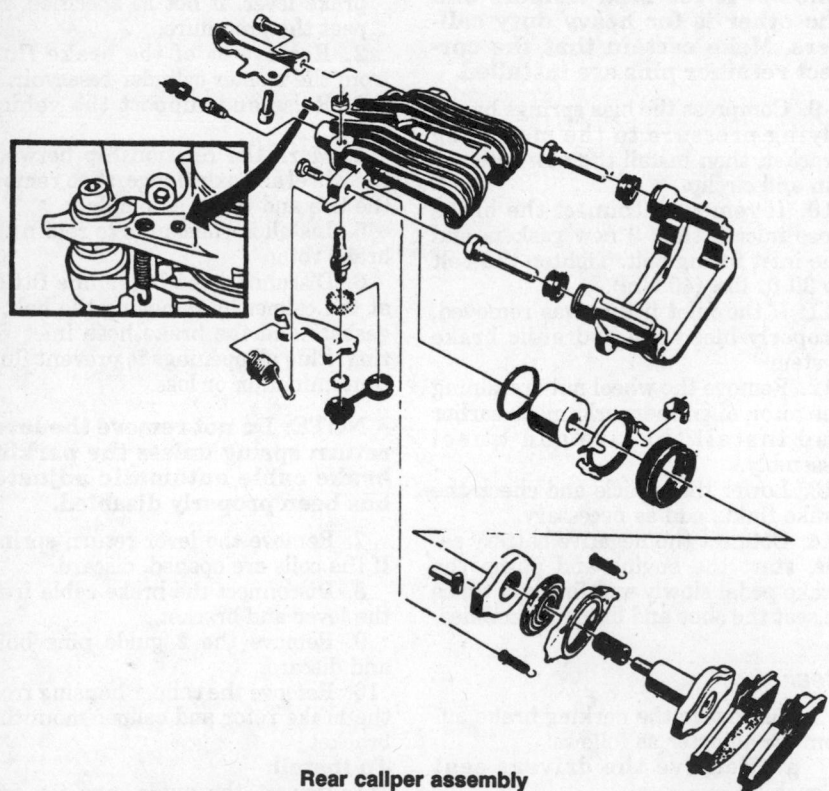

Rear caliper assembly

15. Connect the brake line fitting, 2 new gaskets and the inlet fitting bolt. Tighten the bolt to 30 ft. lbs. (40 Nm).
16. Properly bleed the hydraulic brake system.
17. Enable the parking brake automatic adjuster in the reverse order of the disable procedure and make sure the levers are against the stops on the caliper housing.

18. Remove the 2 nuts securing the rotor to the hub, align the marks made earlier and install the tire and wheel assembly.
19. Lower the vehicle and check the brake fluid level.
20. Connect the negative battery cable, start the engine and pump the brake pedal slowly and firmly 3 times to seat the shoe and lining assemblies.

Disc Brake Pads

REMOVAL & INSTALLATION

Front

1. Disconnect the negative battery cable.
2. Remove the caliper from the mounting bracket but do not disconnect the brake hose and inlet fitting assembly.
3. Suspend the caliper from the upper control arm with wire to avoid damage to the brake hose.
4. Remove the pad and lining assemblies from the caliper.

To install:

5. Clean all residue from the pad and lining assembly guiding surfaces on the caliper housing and the mounting bracket.
6. Install the outboard pad with the insulator to the caliper housing and the inboard pad with the wear sensor into the caliper pistons. Press the pads firmly until they are they are fully seated.
7. Remove the support and install the caliper to the moutning bracket.
8. Connect the negative battery cable.

Rear

1. Disconnect the negative battery cable and remove ⅔ of the brake fluid from the master cylinder reservoirs.
2. Raise and support the vehicle safely.
3. Mark the relationship between the wheel to the axle flange.
4. Remove the tire and wheel as-

sembly. Install 2 wheel nuts to retain the brake rotor.

5. Depress the caliper pistons into the caliper bores to provide clearance between the pads and the rotor.

6. Remove the caliper upper guide pin bolt and discard, then rotate the caliper on the lower guide pin to access the pad linings. Be careful not to strain the cable conduit or the hoses.

7. Remove the pads from the caliper.

To install:

8. Install the outboard pad with the insulator to the caliper housing and the inboard pad with the wear sensor nearest the caliper pistons. The wear sensor must be in the trailing position during forward wheel rotation. Press the pads firmly until they are they are fully seated.

9. Rotate the caliper housing into position and install a new upper guide pin bolt. Tighten the bolt to 26 ft. lbs. (35 Nm).

10. Remove the wheel nuts securing the rotor to the hub and install the tire and wheel assembly.

11. Lower the vehicle and fill the master cylinder to the proper level with clean brake fluid.

12. Connect the negative battery cable, start the engine and pump the brake pedal slowly and firmly 3 times to seat the shoe and lining assemblies.

Brake Rotor

REMOVAL & INSTALLATION

Front and Rear

1. Disconnect battery negative cable.

2. Remove the caliper assembly.

3. Remove the rotor from the vehicle.

4. Installation is the reverse of removal.

Parking Brake Cable

ADJUSTMENT

1. To disable the automatic parking brake adjuster, proceed as follows:

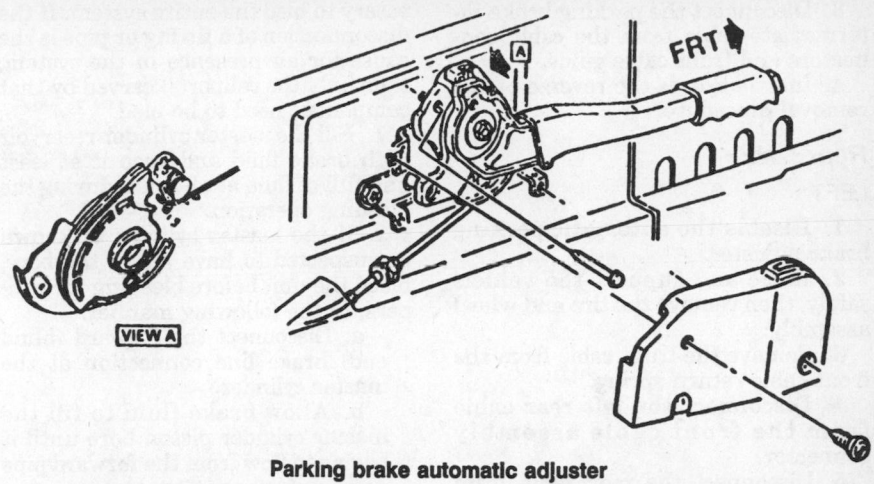

Parking brake automatic adjuster

a. Remove the driver's seat cushion.

b. Remove the parking brake lever cover and screws.

c. Using a suitable tool, disengage and hold the drive pawl from the drive sector.

d. Insert a nail or drift through the hole in the anchor plate to retain the drive pawl in the disengaged position.

e. Move the parking brake lever until it aligns with the lock pawl.

f. Depress the button on the lever and move the lever to the down position.

g. Verify the anchor plate is against the stud on the parking brake lever, if not as specified, repeat the procedure.

2. To enable the automatic parking brake adjuster, proceed as follows:

a. Remove the nail or drift pin from the anchor plate.

b. Apply and release the parking brake 3 times.

c. Pull up on the parking brake lever. Proper adjustment will result in the lever moving 3–5 ratchet clicks with a force of 61 lbs. (270 N).

d. Release the parking brake, there should be no rear brake drag and no gap between the caliper housings and caliper parking brake levers. It may be necessary to remove the tire and wheel assemblies to see the caliper housings and levers.

e. Install the wheel and tire assembly.

f. Install the parking brake lever cover and screws.

g. Install the driver's seat cushion.

REMOVAL & INSTALLATION

Front Cable

1. Remove the driver's seat cushion and frame assembly.

2. Properly disable the parking brake automatic adjuster.

3. Raise the vehicle and support it safely.

4. Disconnect the front cable from the front cable connector.

5. Disconnect the front cable from the front cable return spring.

6. Disconnect the left rear cable from the parking brake front cable assembly connector.

7. Remove the front cable attaching clip bolt and clip.

8. Lower the vehicle and remove the front cable from the automatic adjuster.

9. Remove the front cable attaching nut and washer.

10. Remove the front cable from the vehicle.

To install:

11. Install the front cable to the vehicle, then attach the front cable washer and nut. Tighten the nut 24 ft. lbs. (33 Nm).

12. Connect the front cable to the automatic adjuster.

13. Raise and safely support the vehicle.

14. Install the front cable clip and bolt. Tighten the bolt to 8 ft. lbs. (11 Nm).

15. Connect the parking brake left rear cable to the front cable assembly connector.

16. Connect the parking brake front cable to the front cable return spring and then to the parking brake cable connector.

17. Lower the vehicle.

18. Properly enable the automatic brake adjsuter.

19. Install the driver's seat cushion and frame assembly.

Intermediate Cable

1. Disable the parking brake automatic adjuster.

2. Raise the vehicle and support it safely.

3. Disconnect the parking brake intermediate cable from the cable connectors and front cable guide.

4. Installation is the reverse of the removal procedure.

Rear Cable

LEFT

1. Disable the automatic parking brake adjuster.

2. Raise and support the vehicle safely, then remove the tire and wheel assembly.

3. Remove the front cable from the front cable return spring.

4. Disconnect the left rear cable from the front cable assembly connector.

5. Disconnect the rear cable from the left rear cable bracket.

6. Disconnect the left rear cable from the caliper mounting bracket and lever.

To install:

7. Install the left rear cable to the caliper lever and mounting bracket. Be sure the boot on the end of the cable is attached to the conduit end fitting.

8. Installation is the reverse of the removal procedure.

9. Be sure to properly enable the parking brake automatic adjuster.

RIGHT

1. Disable the parking brake automatic adjuster.

2. Raise the vehicle and support it safely, then remove the tire and wheel assembly.

3. Disconnect the right rear cable from the intermediate cable.

4. Disconnect the right rear cable from the right rear cable bracket.

5. Disconnect the right rear cable from the caliper mounting bracket and lever.

To install:

6. Install the right rear cable to the caliper lever and mounting bracket. Be sure the boot on the end of the cable is attached to the conduit end fitting.

7. Installation is the reverse of the removal procedure.

8. Be sure to properly enable the parking brake automatic adjuster.

Brake System Bleeding

Whenever a hydraulic fitting is disconnected or air is somehow introduced into the brake system, bleeding is necessary to assure proper brake operation. Do not move a vehicle until a firm brake pedal is obtained. Air in the system can cause the loss of brake operation.

If air is introduced into the system at the master cylinder, it may be necessary to bled the entire system. If the disconnection of a fitting or pipe is the cause for air presence in the system, then only the caliper(s) served by that component need to be bled.

1. Fill the master cylinder reservoir with brake fluid and keep it at least half full of fluid at all times during the bleeding operation.

2. If the master cylinder is known or suspected to have air in the bore, bleed the unit before bleeding the calipers, in the following manner:

a. Disconnect the forward (blind end) brake line connection at the master cylinder.

b. Allow brake fluid to fill the master cylinder piston bore until it begins to flow from the forward pipe connector port at the master cylinder.

c. Connect the forward brake line to the master cylinder and tighten.

d. Have an assistant depress the brake pedal slowly 1 time and hold. Loosen the forward brake line connection at the master cylinder to purge air from the bore. Tighten the connection and have the assistant release the pedal slowly. Wait 15 seconds and repeat the sequence, including the 15 second pause, until all air is removed from the bore. Make sure brake fluid does not contact any painted surface.

e. Repeat the procedure at the rear master cylinder brake line connection.

f. If it is known that the calipers do not contain any air, it will not be necessary to bleed them.

3. If it is necessary to bleed all of the calipers, follow the proper sequence: right rear, left rear, right front, left front.

4. After all air is removed from the master cylinder, bleed the individual calipers as follows:

a. Place a suitable bleeder wrench over the bleeder valve.

b. Attach a clear tube over the bleeder valve and allow the tube to hang, submerged in a clear container partially filled with brake fluid.

c. Have an assistant depress the brake pedal slowly 1 time and hold. Loosen the bleeder valve to purge the air from the cylinder. Tighten the bleeder screw and have the assistant slowly release the pedal. Wait 15 seconds and repeat the sequence, including the 15 second pause, until all air is removed.

d. It may be necessary to repeat the sequence 10 or more times to remove all of the air.

NOTE: Rapid pumping of the brake pedal pushes the master cylinder secondary piston down the bore in a way that makes it difficult to bleed the system.

6. Check the brake pedal for sponginess and the red brake warning light for an indication of unbalanced pressure. Repeat the bleeding procedure to correct either of these conditions.

Anti-Lock Brake System Service

PRECAUTIONS

Failure to observe the following precautions may result in system damage.

• Before performing electric arc welding on the vehicle, disconnect the Electronic Brake Control Module (EBCM) and the hydraulic modulator connectors.

• When performing painting work on the vehicle, do not expose the Electronic Brake Control Module (EBCM) to temperatures in excess of 185°F (85°C) for longer than 2 hrs. The system may be exposed to temperatures up to 200°F (95°C) for less than 15 min.

• Always note the routing, position, mounting and location of all system components. Speed sensor wiring, routing and retention is especially important to help prevent false signals due to electrical noise picked up by the wiring.

• Never disconnect or connect the Electronic Brake Control Module (EBCM) or hydraulic modulator connectors with the ignition switch ON.

• Never disassemble any component of the Anti-Lock Brake System (ABS) which is designated non-servicable; the component must be replaced as an assembly.

• When filling the master cylinder, always use Delco Supreme 11 brake fluid or equivalent, which meets DOT-3 specifications; petroleum base fluid will destroy the rubber parts.

Modulator Valve

REMOVAL & INSTALLATION

1989–91

1. Disconnect the negative battery cable.

2. Remove the storage tray and insulation.

3. Disconnect the ABS wiring harness.

4. Disconnect the modualtor ground wire from the body wiring harness.

5. Note the brake pipe locations for reinstallation purposes, then disconnect the pipes from the modulator valve. Plug the pipes to prevent fluid contamination or loss.

6. Carefully remove the modulator valve from the storage compartment.

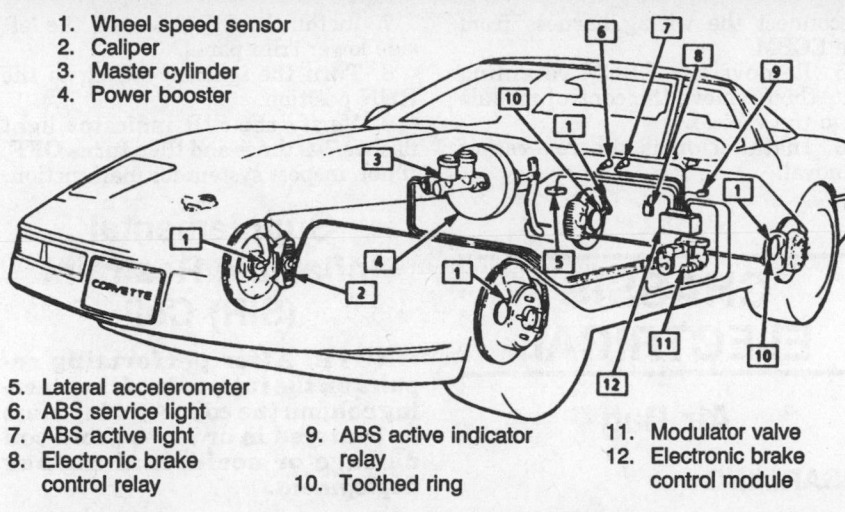

1. Wheel speed sensor
2. Caliper
3. Master cylinder
4. Power booster

5. Lateral accelerometer
6. ABS service light
7. ABS active light
8. Electronic brake control relay

9. ABS active indicator relay
10. Toothed ring

11. Modulator valve
12. Electronic brake control module

Antilock brake system components

Be sure to protect the vehicle interior from possible brake fluid spillage. Clean any brake fluid from the bottom of the storage compartment.

7. If the modulator is being replaced, remove the ground wire and insualtors.

To install:

8. If removed, install the ground wire and insulators.
9. Install the modulator valve to the bracket and tighten the attaching nuts to 86 inch lbs. (10 Nm).
10. Unplug the brake pipes and connect to the modulator in their original positions as noted earlier. Tighten the fittings to 13 ft. lbs. (18 Nm).
11. Connect the modulator ground wire to the body wiring harness.
12. Connect the ABS wiring harness.
13. Connect the negative battery cable.
14. Properly fill the master cylinder and bleed the hydraulic brake system.
15. Install the insulation and storage tray.
16. Check for proper system operation.

1992–93

1. Disconnect the negative battery cable.
2. Remove the storage campartment door and frame, then remove the sound insulator pad.
3. Disconnect the wire harness with selective ride control module, if equipped.
4. Release the retaining clip and remove the wiring harness connector from the Electronic Brake Control Module (EBCM), them remove the EBCM from the vehicle.
5. Disconnect the brake lines from the modulator valve and note the location for reinstallation purposes. Plug the lines to prevent fluid contamination or loss.

6. Raise and support the vehicle safely, remove the modulator valve bracket to underbody cover attaching bolts, then lower the vehicle.
7. Remove the modulator valve assembly.

To install:

8. If the modulator valve is being replaced, transfer the ground wire, valve bracket and relays to the new valve.
9. Install the modulator valve assembly.
10. Raise and support the vehicle safely, then install the modulator valve bracket to underbody cover attaching bolts.
11. Tighten the bolts to 86 inch lbs. (10 Nm), then lower the vehicle.
12. Unplug and install the brake lines in their original locations, then tighten the fittings to 13 ft. lbs. (18 Nm).

NOTE: It is extremely important that all brake lines are correctly attached or wheel lock up could occur causing personal injury to the vehicle operator.

13. Install the EBCM.
14. Connect the wiring harness with selective ride control module, if equipped.
15. Connect the negative battery cable and properly bleed the hydraulic brake system.
16. Install the sound insulator pad, the rear storage compartment door and frame assembly.
17. Check for proper system operation.

Lateral Accelerometer

REMOVAL & INSTALLATION

1. Disconnect the negative battery cable.

2. Remove the console and accessory trim plates.
3. Remove the radio assembly.
4. Push on the spring to release and disconnect the ABS/ASR wiring harness connector from the lateral accelerometer.
5. Remove the lateral accelerometer attaching screws from the carrier assembly and remove the accelerometer from the vehicle.
6. Installation is the reverse of removal.

Wheel Speed Sensor

The front wheel speed sensors for 1991–93 vehicles are part of the wheel hub assembly and cannot be replaced separately. Replace 1989–90 front wheel speed sensors and all rear speed sensors as follows.

REMOVAL & INSTALLATION

1. Disconnect the negative battery cable.
2. Raise and support the vehicle safely.
3. Remove the tire and wheel assembly.
4. Disconnect the sensor wiring harness from the ABS wiring harness connector. Unclip the connectors from the bracket and separate.
5. If replacing a rear sensor, remove the bracket and bolt from the knuckle.
6. Remove sensor wiring harness with the grommets from the bracket. Note the position of the grommets and the harness routing for installation purposes.
7. Remove the wheel speed sensor attaching bolt, then remove the speed sensor from the knuckle.

To install:

8. Clean all sealant from the sensor and the sensor mounting in the knuckle.
9. Apply 12345489 or equivalent anti-corrosion sealer, to the speed sensor and install the sensor into the knuckle. The sensor is a tight fit and must be installed by hand. Do not hammer the sensor into position.
10. Install the sensor retaining bolt and tighten to 86 inch lbs. (10 Nm).
11. Install the sensor wiring harness with grommets into the brackets, make sure the grommets and routing is the same as what was noted during removal.
12. Install the bracket and bolt to knuckle, tighten the bolt to 86 inch lbs. (10 Nm).
13. Connect the sensor wiring harness connector to the wiring harness connector. Make sure the connection is tight, then snap the connectors into the bracket.

14. Install the tire and wheel assembly, then lower the vehicle.

15. Connect the negative battery cable and check for proper system operation.

Electronic Brake Control Module

REMOVAL & INSTALLATION

1989–91

1. Disconnect the negative battery cable.

2. Remove the storage tray and insulator.

3. Release the retaining clip and disconnect the electrical connector from the control module.

4. Remove the module relay from the brackets.

5. Remove the control module attaching bolts, then remove the control module from the vehicle.

6. Installation is the reverse of removal.

1992–93

1. Disconnect the negative battery cable.

2. For coupes, open the left rear storage compartment. For convertibles, remove the storage compartment frame and covers.

3. Remove the sound insulator pad.

4. Release the retaining clips and

disconnect the wiring harness from the ECBM.

5. Remove the EBCM retaining nut, then remove the control module from the vehicle.

6. Installation is the reverse of removal.

CHASSIS ELECTRICAL

Air Bag

DISARMING

1. Turn the steering wheel to align the wheels in the straight-ahead position.

2. Turn the ignition switch to the **LOCK** position.

3. Remove the AIR BAG fuse from the fuse block.

4. Remove the left side lower trim panel and disconnect the yellow 2-way SIR harness wire connector and the Connector Position Assurance (CPA) at the base of the steering column.

To enable system:

5. Turn the ignition switch to the **LOCK** position.

6. Connect the yellow 2-way connector and the CPA at the base of the steering column.

7. Install the SIR fuse and the left side lower trim panel.

8. Turn the ignition switch to the **RUN** position.

9. Verify the SIR indicator light flashes 7–9 times and then turns **OFF**. If not, inspect system for malfunction.

Supplemental Inflatable Restraint (SIR) Coil

NOTE: After performing repairs on the internals of the steering column the coil assembly must be centered in order to avoid coil damage or accidental air bag deployment.

ADJUSTMENT

1. Hold the coil assembly with the clear bottom up to see the coil ribbon.

2. While holding the coil assembly, depress the spring lock and rotate the hub in the direction of the arrow until it stops. The coil ribbon should now be wound up snug against the center hub.

3. Rotate the coil assembly in the opposite direction approximately 2½ turns and release the lock spring between the locking tabs in front of the arrow.

4. Install the coil assembly onto the steering shaft.

Heater Blower Motor

REMOVAL & INSTALLATION

1. Disconnect the negative battery cable.

2. Remove the front wheel house rear panel and seal.

3. Disconnect the motor electrical connectors.

4. Remove the blower motor cooling tube.

5. Remove the motor and fan.

6. Installation is the reverse of the removal procedure.

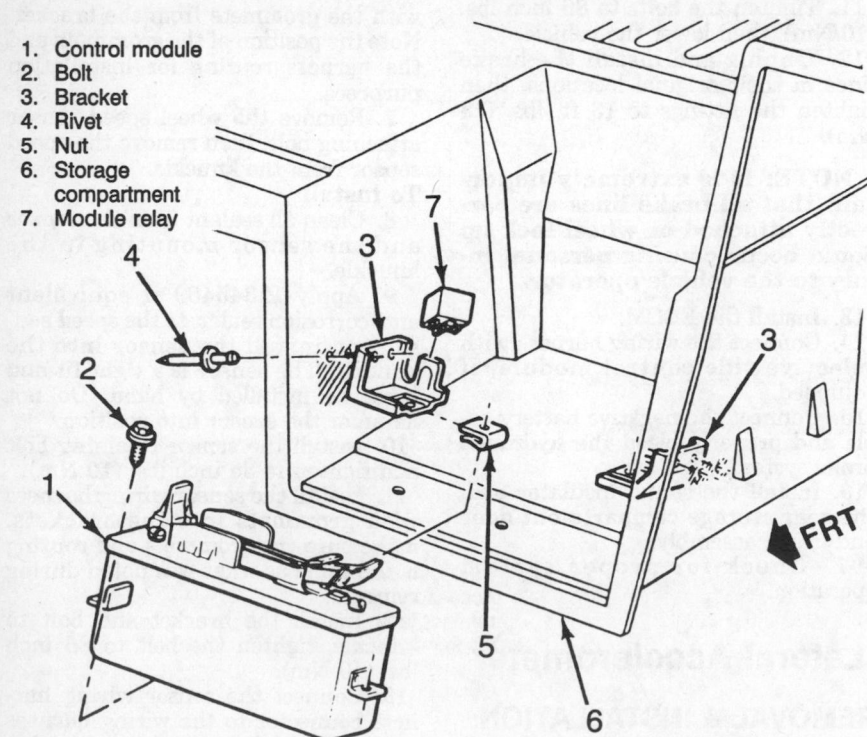

1. Control module
2. Bolt
3. Bracket
4. Rivet
5. Nut
6. Storage compartment
7. Module relay

Antilock electronic brake control module—1989–91 vehicles

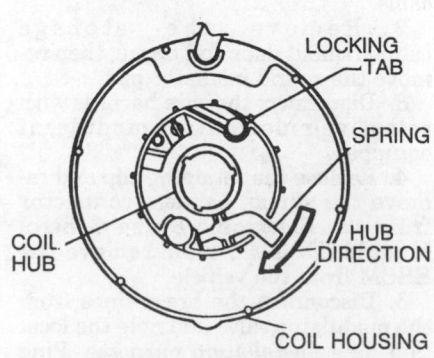

LOCKING TAB

SPRING

HUB DIRECTION

COIL HUB

COIL HOUSING

Centering the SIR coil assembly

Windshield Wiper Motor

REMOVAL & INSTALLATION

1989–90 5.7L (VIN 8) Engine

1. Raise the hood.
2. Remove the wiper arms.
3. Remove the left plenum screen.
4. Turn ignition **ON** and activate wiper motor with the switch. Allow motor crank arm to rotate to the 4–5 o'clock position as viewed from passenger compartment. Stop the crank arm in this position by turning the ignition switch **OFF**.
5. Disconnect the battery negative cable.
6. Disconnect upper motor electrical connectors.
7. Remove the nuts securing the motor crank arm to the transmission link sockets and the motor mounting bolts.
8. With crank arm in position described in Step 4, motor may now be removed from vehicle. Disconnect the lower electrical connectors from the motor as removal gives access.

To install:
9. Connect the lower electrical connections to the wiper motor.
10. Install the wiper motor by guiding the crank arm through the hole in the plenum panel. Install the motor mounting bolts and tighten to 27 inch lbs. (3 Nm).
11. Connect the motor upper electrical connectors.
12. Install the nuts holding the motor crank arm in the wiper transmission link sockets. Tighten the nuts to 27 inch lbs. (3 Nm).
13. Install the left side plenum screen and the wiper arms. Adjust the wiper arms, if necessary.
14. Connect the negative battery cable.

Except 1989–90 5.7L (VIN 8) Engine

1. Disconnect the negative battery cable.
2. Disconnect the motor park switch and the PC-board electrical connectors.
3. Remove the left side plenum screen.
4. Remove the wiper transmission nuts and sockets.
5. Disconnect the vacuum booster supply hose at the plenum, if equipped.
6. Disconnect the wiper mounting bolts.
7. Disconnect any remaining motor electrical connectors while removing wiper motor assembly.

To install:
8. Connect the wiper motor electrical connector.
9. Install the wiper motor and gasket by guiding the crank arm through the hole in the plenum panel and positioning it over the transmission.
10. Install the motor mounting bolts and tighten to 27 inch lbs. (3 Nm).
11. If applicable, connect the vacuum hose.
12. Install the transmission link sockets and nuts. Tighten the nuts to 27 inch lbs. (3 Nm).
13. Install the left plenum screen and connect the motor upper electrical connectors.
14. Reconnect the battery negative cable and check motor operation.

Windshield Wiper Switch

REMOVAL & INSTALLATION

1989

1. Disconnect the negative battery cable.
2. Remove the drivers door armrest, filler and the accessory trim plate.
3. Disconnect the electrical connections from the switch.

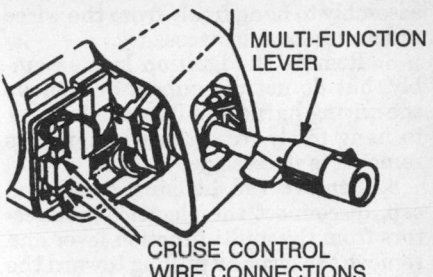

Multi-function lever removal— 1990–93 vehicles

4. Remove the switch from the panel.
5. Installation is the reverse of the removal procedure.

1990–93

NOTE: The vehicle is equipped with a SIR air bag system, it is imperative that the disarming procedure is followed before repairs, and that the coil centering and rearming procedures are followed after repairs.

1. Disarm the SIR and disconnect the negative battery cable.
2. Remove the turn signal assembly, but do not disconnect or remove the wiring harness. Allow the switch

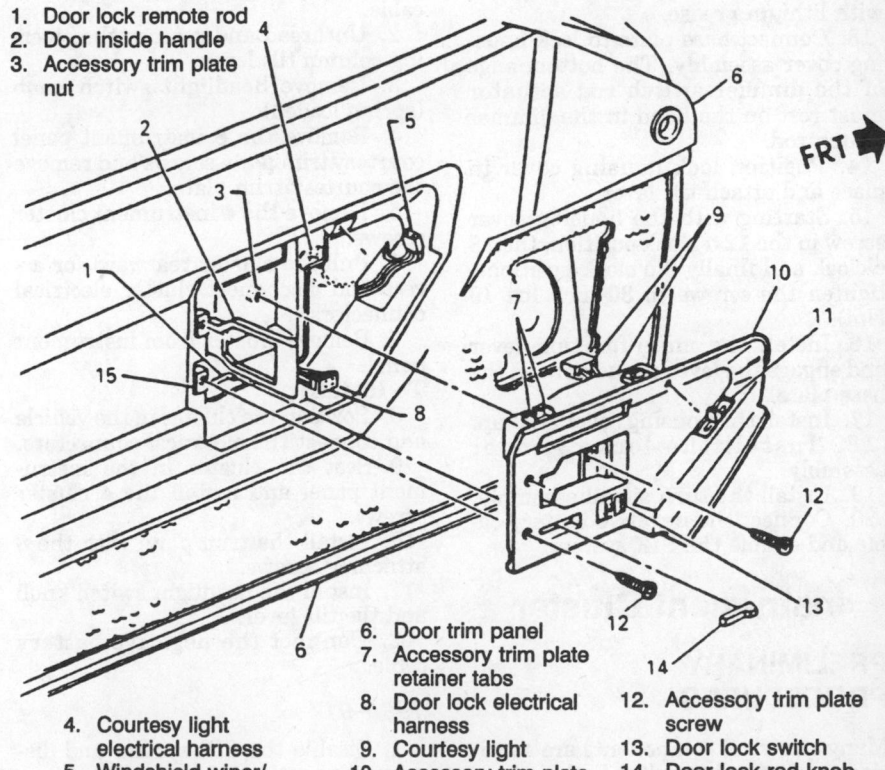

1. Door lock remote rod
2. Door inside handle
3. Accessory trim plate nut

4. Courtesy light electrical harness
5. Windshield wiper/ washer electrical harness

6. Door trim panel
7. Accessory trim plate retainer tabs
8. Door lock electrical harness
9. Courtesy light
10. Accessory trim plate
11. Windshield/wiper washer switch

12. Accessory trim plate screw
13. Door lock switch
14. Door lock rod knob
15. Accessory trim plate U-nut

Windshield wiper switch removal—1989 vehicles

assembly to hang freely from the wires unless removal is necessary.

3. Remove the ignition lock assembly, but do not disconnect or remove the wiring harness. Allow the lock set to hang freely from the wires, unless removal is necessary.

4. Remove the housing cover end cap, disconnect the electrical connectors from the multi-function lever and remove the lever by pulling toward the driver's door.

5. Remove the housing cover screws, unthread and remove the tilt lever from the column assembly.

6. Remove the lock housing cover assembly.

7. Remove the base plate, the dimmer switch rod actuator and the wiper switch actuator pivot pin.

8. Disconnect wiper switch connector from vehicle wire harness and remove switch. Attach a piece of mechanic's wire to the connector to aid in reinstallation and gently pull the wire harness through the column.

To install:

9. Connect the wiper switch assembly to the lock housing cover assembly.

10. Attach the switch actuator pivot pin to the switch and cover.

11. Pull wiper switch wire connector through the steering column with mechanic's wire and attach to the vehicle wire harness.

12. Attach the dimmer switch rod actuator to the base plate and lubricate with lithium grease.

13. Connect base plate to lock housing cover assembly. The bottom edge of the dimmer switch rod actuator must rest on the bend in the dimmer switch rod.

14. Position lock housing cover in place and attach tilt lever.

15. Starting with the housing cover screw in the 12 o'clock position, then 8 o'clock and finally 3 o'clock positions, tighten the screws to 80 inch lbs. (9 Nm).

16. Install the multi-function lever and engage the lever connectors on the base plate.

17. Install the housing cover end cap.

18. Install the lock cylinder assembly.

19. Install the turn signal assembly.

20. Connect the negative battery cable and enable the SIR system.

Instrument Cluster

PRELIMINARY PROCEDURES

Many electrical components are sensitive to static electricity discharge; in order to avoid damaging any components certain precautions should be taken:

1. To discharge personal static electricity, touch a ground point on the vehicle.

2. Personal static discharge should be performed any time you walk across the shop, slide across the seat or sit down and get up.

3. Do not touch any electric terminals on components or connectors with your fingers or any tool.

4. Always touch the component packaging to a ground before removing the component.

5. Components which may be damaged by electrostatic discharge are:

    a. The antilock brake system controller.

    b. The chime module.

    c. The cruise control module.

    d. The distributorless ignition system module.

    e. The electronic digital instrument clusters.

    f. The electronic control module and attributing parts.

    g. The low tire pressure warning system module.

    h. The radio assembly.

    i. The theft deterrent modules.

    j. The electronic automatic air conditioning assembly.

REMOVAL & INSTALLATION

1989

1. Disconnect the negative battery cable.

2. Unthread and remove the steering column tilt lever.

3. Remove headlight switch knob (spring loaded).

4. Remove the 8 instrument panel courtesy trim plate screws and remove the courtesy trim plate.

5. Remove the 4 instrument cluster screws.

6. Pull the cluster rearward for access and disconnect cluster electrical connectors.

7. Remove cluster from instrument panel.

To install:

8. Position the cluster in the vehicle and connect the electrical connectors.

9. Seat the cluster in the instrument panel and install the 4 cluster screws.

10. Install the trim plate with the 8 attaching screws.

11. Install the headlight switch knob and the tilt lever.

12. Connect the negative battery cable.

1990–91

1. Disable the SIR system and disconnect negative battery cable.

2. Remove shifter button, snapring and shift knob.

3. Remove center console trim plate

attaching screws, disconnect electrical connectors from trim plate, then remove trim plate.

4. Remove the center air outlet. Remove the accessory trim plate attaching screws and clips.

5. Remove the lower trim panel screws and retainers. Carefully disconnect the courtesy light instrument panel harness connector assembly. Remove the ALDL connector assembly screw.

6. Remove the knee bolster screws and the steering column tilt lever assembly.

7. Remove the steering column from the support bolts, then lower the steering column for access and support the column.

8. Remove the cluster bezel attaching screws and the cluster screws, disconnect the instrument panel cluster electrical connector and remove the instrument panel cluster.

To install:

9. Connect the electrical connector and install the cluster to the instrument panel.

10. Install the cluster bezel assembly to instrument panel screws and tighten to 29 inch lbs. (3.3 Nm).

11. Install the steering column to the support bolts and the tilt lever to the steering column.

12. Install the knee bolster.

13. Connect the courtesy lamp instrument panel harness connector and the ALDL connector screw. Install the lower trim panel.

14. Install the accessory trim plate to the instrument panel.

15. Connect the instrument panel harness to the trim plate and install the plate to the instrument panel.

16. Install the shifter knob, snapring and shifter button to the shift rod.

17. Connect negative battery cable and enable the SIR system.

1992–93

1. Remove the knee bolster and the lower trim panel.

2. Disable the SIR system and disconnect the negative battery cable.

3. Remove the steering column support bolts and carefully lower the steering column.

4. Remove the cluster bezel screws and the bezel.

5. If necessary, remove the lens screws and the lens.

6. Remove the cluster mounting bolts/screws, disconnect the electrical connectors and remove the cluster.

To install:

7. Install the lens to the cluster, if removed.

8. Position the cluster and engage the electrical connectors. Tighten the cluster bolts/screws to 16 inch lbs. (1.8 Nm).

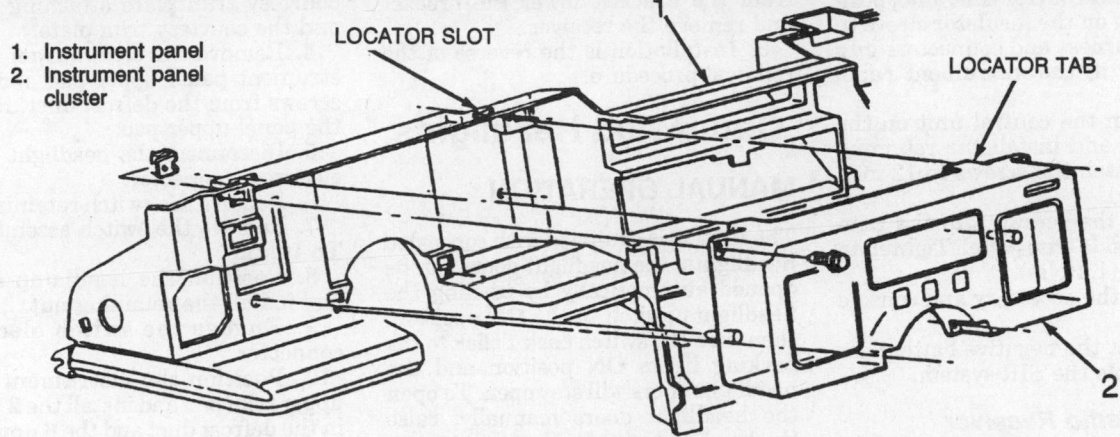

1. Instrument panel
2. Instrument panel cluster

LOCATOR SLOT

LOCATOR TAB

Instrument panel cluster—1989 vehicles

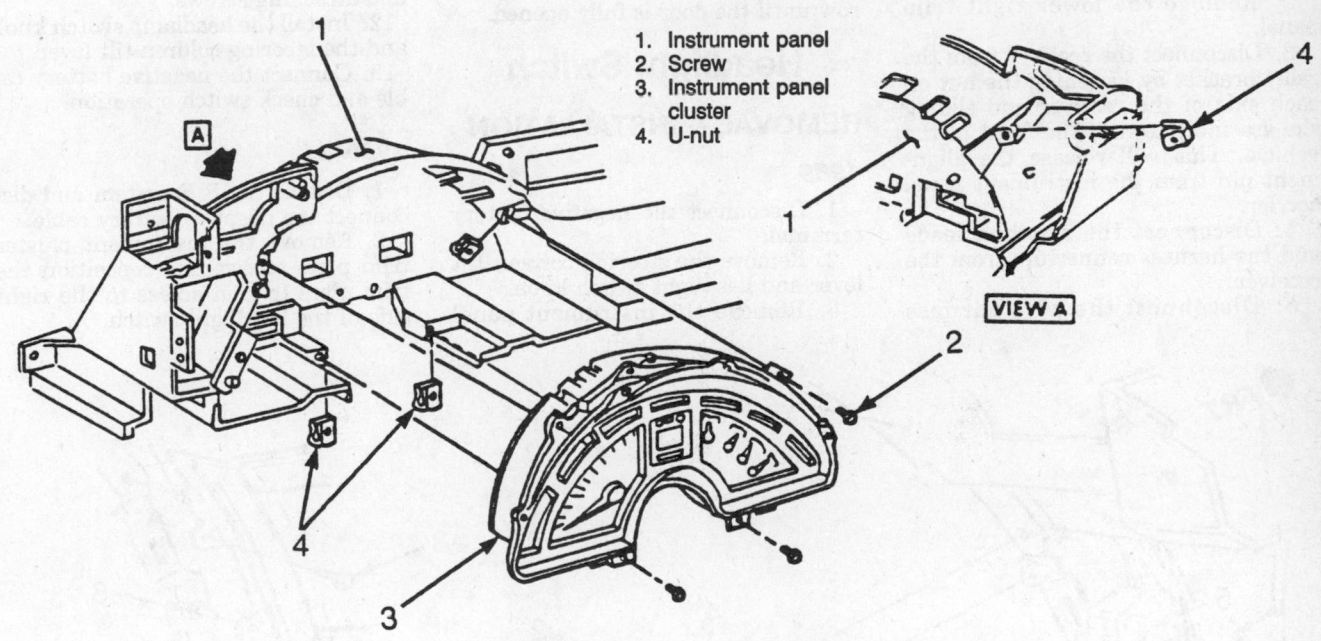

1. Instrument panel
2. Screw
3. Instrument panel cluster
4. U-nut

VIEW A

Instrument panel cluster—1990–93 vehicles

9. Install the bezel and tighten the screws to 29 inch lbs. (3.3 Nm).

10. Raise the steering column and tighten the supporting bolts to 20 ft. lbs. (27 Nm).

11. Connect the negative battery cable and enable the SIR system.

12. Install the knee bolster and the lower trim panel.

Radio

The 1989 Corvette utilizes a single in-dash radio assembly. For the 1990–93 Corvettes the radio consists of 2 separate units. The control assembly is mounted in the dash for direct operation while a remote receiver, containing the various AM/FM circuitry, is located under the dash.

REMOVAL & INSTALLATION

1989 Radio Assembly

1. Disconnect the negative battery cable.

2. Remove the instrument panel trim plates as necessary.

3. Remove the 4 radio attaching screws and carefully pull the radio outwards.

4. Disconnect the electrical connectors and the antenna lead from radio.

5. Remove the radio from the vehicle.

6. Installation is the reverse of the removal procedure.

1990–93 Radio Control Unit

1. Disable the SIR system and disconnect the negative battery cable.

2. Remove the console and accessory trim plates, as necessary to access the control unit.

3. Remove the screws from the right side trim panel to the instrument panel carrier and from the right of the driver information center securing the instrument panel upper trim pad to the carrier.

4. Reposition the trim pad and trim panel to access the right side control unit mounting screw.

5. Remove the screws from the control unit. Pull the unit outward and disconnect the electrical connectors. Remove the unit from the vehicle.

To install:

6. Connect the instrument panel harness connectors to the control unit and slide the insulator sleeve toward the connector.

7. Slide the control unit into position pushing on the insulator sleeve to guide the harness and connectors into the opening in the instrument panel carrier.

8. Position the control unit on the locator pins and install the retaining screws. Tighten the screws to 12 inch lbs. (1.4 Nm).

9. Install the screws into the trim pad and the side trim panel. Tighten to 12 inch lbs. (1.4 Nm).

10. Install the accessory and console trim plates.

11. Connect the negative battery cable and enable the SIR system.

1990–93 Radio Receiver

1. Disable the SIR system and disconnect the negative battery cable.

2. Remove the lower right trim panel.

3. Disconnect the receiver from the relay bracket by loosening the nut on each side of the receiver and sliding the assembly toward the front of the vehicle. This will release the alignment pin from the instrument panel carrier.

4. Disconnect the antenna leads and the harness connectors from the receiver.

5. Disconnect the wire harness from the bracket, lower the bracket and remove the receiver.

6. Installation is the reverse of the removal procedure.

Concealed Headlights

MANUAL OPERATION

The vehicle is equipped with concealed headlights, the headlight doors can be opened automatically by turning the headlights switch to the **ON** position, then turn the switch back 1 click to the parking lights **ON** position and the headlight doors will stay open. To open the headlight doors manually, raise the hood and turn the headlight manual control knob, located on the headlamp door, in the direction of the arrow until the door is fully opened.

Headlight Switch

REMOVAL & INSTALLATION

1989

1. Disconnect the negative battery terminal.

2. Remove the steering column tilt lever and headlight switch knob.

3. Remove the instrument panel courtesy trim plate attaching screws and the courtesy trim plate.

4. Remove the screws from the instrument panel upper pad and the 2 screws from the defrost duct. Remove the panel upper pad.

5. Disconnect the headlight switch electrical connector.

6. Remove the switch retaining nut.

7. Remove the switch assembly.

To install:

8. Position the headlamp switch and install the retaining nut.

9. Engage the switch electrical connector.

10. Position the instrument panel upper trim pad and install the 2 screws in the defrost duct and the 6 upper pad screws.

11. Install the courtesy trim plate and attaching screws.

12. Install the headlamp switch knob and the steering column tilt lever.

13. Connect the negative battery cable and check switch operation.

1990–93

1. Disable the SIR system and disconnect the negative battery cable.

2. Remove the instrument cluster trim plate screws and reposition the trim plate to gain access to the right side of the headlight switch.

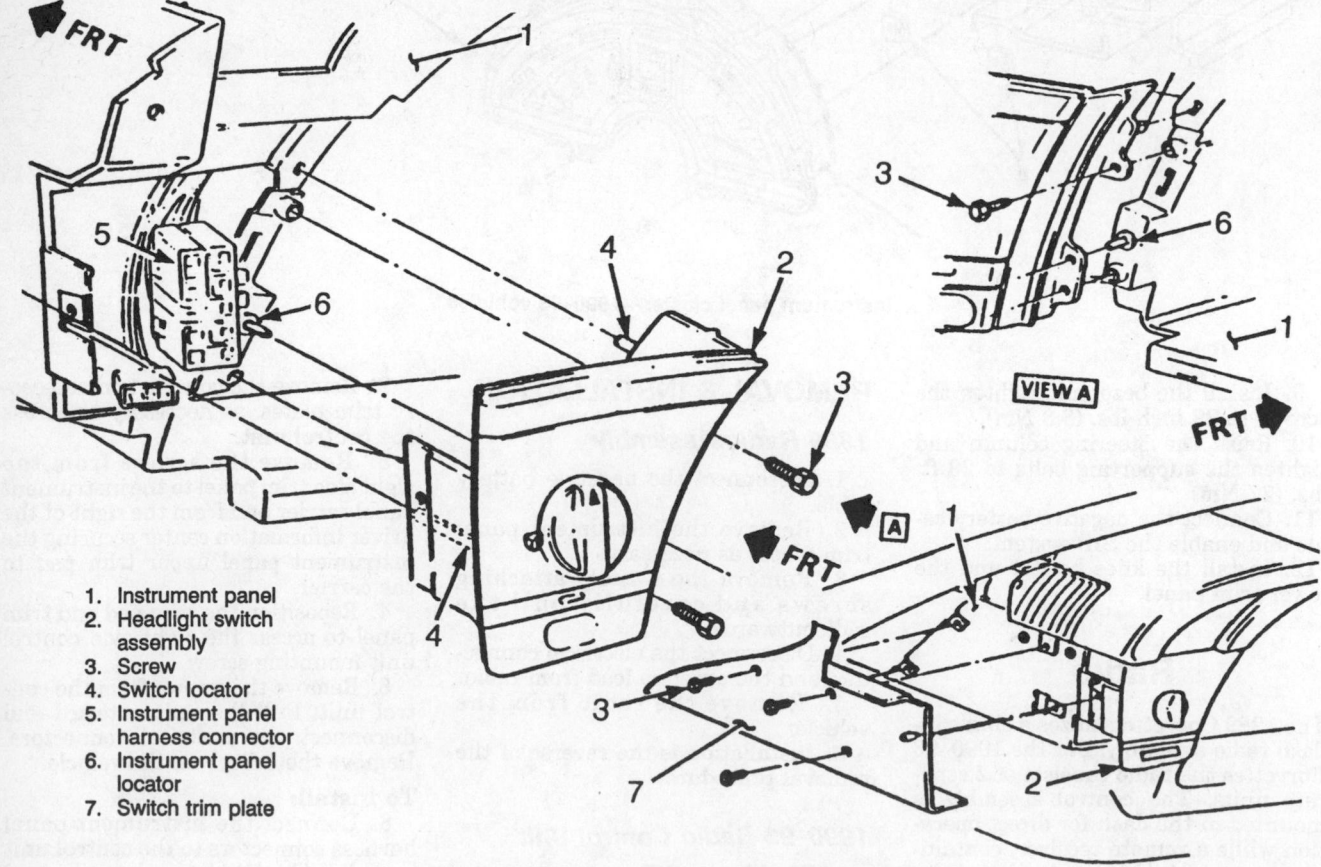

1. Instrument panel
2. Headlight switch assembly
3. Screw
4. Switch locator
5. Instrument panel harness connector
6. Instrument panel locator
7. Switch trim plate

Headlight switch assembly–1990–93 vehicles

3. Remove headlight switch attaching screws and disconnect electrical connectors.

4. Remove the headlight switch.

5. Installation is the reverse of the removal procedure. Be sure to connect the negative battery cable and properly enable the SIR system.

Dimmer Switch

REMOVAL & INSTALLATION

1. Properly disable the SIR system, if equipped and disconnect the negative battery cable.

2. Remove the instrument panel lower trim plate.

3. Remove the steering column mounting bolts, lower and properly support the column.

4. Remove the washer head screw and nut securing the switch to the column.

5. Remove the horn ground strap attached to the dimmer/ignition switch mounting stud, if equipped.

6. Remove the cable bracket, if equipped.

7. Disengage the switch assembly from the actuator rod, disconnect the wire connector and remove the switch assembly.

To install:

8. Position the dimmer switch and, if equipped, the cable bracket, onto the steering column. Install the nut and screw finger-tight.

9. Connect the horn ground strap and switch wire connector.

10. Insert a $^3/_{32}$ inch drill bit in the switch hole to limit travel.

11. Push against dimmer switch to remove all free-play.

12. Tighten the switch nut and screw to 35 inch lbs. (4.0 Nm).

13. Remove the drill bit.

14. Raise the steering column and install the mounting bolts.

15. Install the instrument panel lower trim plate.

16. Connect the negative battery cable and, if equipped, enable the SIR system.

Turn Signal Switch

REMOVAL & INSTALLATION

1989

1. Disconnect the negative battery cable.

2. Remove the steering wheel.

3. Remove the steering column left side lower trim cover. Disconnect the turn signal harness at the base of the steering column.

4. Remove the spacers and snapring retainer.

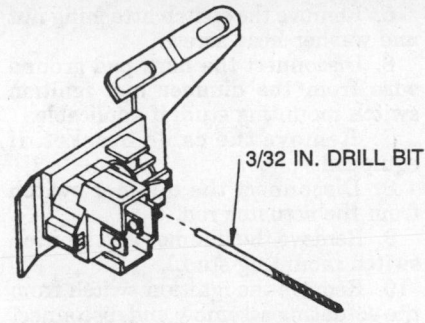

3/32 IN. DRILL BIT

Typical dimmer switch adjustment

5. Install the lock plate compressing tool over the steering shaft and remove the lock plate retainer.

6. Remove the tool and lift out the lock plate and the horn contact carrier. Remove the the upper bearing spring, upper bearing seat and the inner race.

7. Position the turn signal switch to the right and remove the switch actuator pivot and switch screws.

8. Remove the switch wiring from the protective jacket.

9. Remove the turn signal lever and hazard knob.

10. Attach a length of mechanic's wire to the wiring harness to assist in installation. Remove the switch by pulling it straight up while guiding the wiring harness out of the housing and pulling the mechanic's wire through the column.

To install:

11. Pull the replacement switch harness connector down through the housing and under the mounting bracket with the mechanic's wire.

12. Install the harness cover and clip the connector to the column.

13. Install the switch mounting screws and tighten to 27 inch lbs. (3 Nm). Install the turn signal lever and the flasher knob and tighten the pivot assembly bolt to 18 inch lbs. (2 Nm).

14. Install the inner race, upper bearing seat, upper bearing spring, the shaft lock and the horn contact carrier assembly.

15. Position the lock plate tool and compress the plate sufficiently to install the shaft lock retainer.

16. Remove the tool and install the plastic snapring retainer and spacers.

17. Install the lower dash trim cover and the steering wheel.

18. Connect the negative battery cable.

1990–93

NOTE: The vehicle is equipped with a SIR air bag system, it is imperative that the disarming procedure is followed before repairs, and that the coil centering and rearming procedures are followed after repairs.

1. Properly disable the SIR system. Place the ignition switch to the **LOCK** position to prevent uncentering of the coil assembly.

2. Disconnect the negative battery cable.

3. Properly remove and store the inflator module and the steering wheel.

4. Remove the coil assembly retaining ring. Remove the coil assembly and allow it to hang freely.

NOTE: The coil assembly will become uncentered if the steering column is separated from the steering gear and allowed to rotate or the center spring of the coil assembly is pushed down, letting the hub rotate while the coil is removed from the steering column. In the event this should occur, follow the recommended procedure for recentering of the coil in order to avoid accidental deployment of the air bag or damage to the internal components of the steering column.

5. Remove the wave washer.

6. Remove the shaft lock retaining ring using tool J23653-C or equivalent shaft lock compressor. Discard the old ring.

7. Remove the shaft lock, turn signal cancelling cam and upper bearing assembly.

8. Move the multi-function lever to the **RIGHT TURN** position. Remove the column housing cover end cap by pulling toward the vehicle front. Disconnect the electrical harness connector and remove the turn signal lever by pulling toward the driver door.

9. Remove the hazard knob retaining screw and assembly.

10. Remove the turn signal switch arm and screws.

11. Remove the turn signal switch screws.

12. Remove the column lower trim and disconnect the switch harness connector.

13. Disconnect the switch connector from the bulkhead connector. Remove the wiring protector from the steering column. For 1992–93 vehicles, remove the horn pad ground wiring assembly from slot "D" of the switch connector.

14. Attach a length of mechanic's wire to the switch harness to aid in reinstallation and gently pull the assembly up through the housing.

15. Remove the switch and harness from the vehicle, leaving the wire in the column.

To install:

16. Using the mechanic's wire, pull the switch harness through the column and connect to the bulkhead connector. For 1992–93 vehicles, connect the horn pad ground wiring assembly

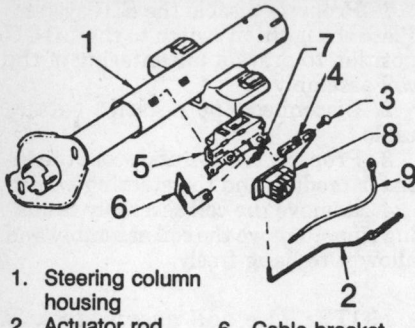

1. Steering column housing
2. Actuator rod
3. Screw
4. Nut
5. Ignition switch
6. Cable bracket
7. Stud
8. Dimmer switch
9. Horn pad ground

Ignition and dimmer switch assembly

to slot "D" of the turn signal switch connector.

17. Reconnect the harness wiring protector and lower trim panel.

18. Install the turn signal switch assembly and the attaching screws. Tighten the screws to 30 inch lbs. (3.4 Nm).

19. Install the switch arm and mounting screws. Tighten the screws to 20 inch lbs. (2.3 Nm).

20. Install the hazard knob assembly and the multi-function lever.

21. Install the inner race, the upper bearing race seat, and the upper bearing spring.

22. Lubricate with synthetic grease and install the turn signal cancelling cam.

23. Position the shaft lock. Install the a new shaft lock retaining ring using tool J23653-C or equivelent. Be sure the ring is firmly seated in the groove of the shaft.

24. Install the wave washer.

25. Install the coil assembly, making sure it is properly centered.

26. Install the steering wheel and the inflator module.

27. Connect the negative battery cable and enable the SIR system.

Ignition Switch

REMOVAL & INSTALLATION

1. Disable the SIR system, if equipped and disconnect the negative battery terminal.

2. Remove the column to instrument panel trim plates and attaching nuts.

3. Loosen the steering column mounting bolts.

4. Carefully lower the steering column assembly.

NOTE: Be sure the steering column is supported at all times in order to prevent damage to the column.

5. Remove the switch attaching nut and washer head screw.

6. Disconnect the horn pad ground wire from the dimmer and ignition switch mounting stud, if applicable.

7. Remove the cable bracket, if equipped.

8. Disconnect the dimmer switch from the actuator rod.

9. Remove the dimmer and ignition switch mounting stud.

10. Remove the ignition switch from the actuating assembly and disconnect the the switch wire connector.

To install:

11. Verify that the key cylinder is in the **LOCK** position.

12. Move the actuator rod hole in the switch to the **LOCK** position. New switches will be pinned in this position and the pin must be removed after installation or switch damage may result.

13. Install the switch with the rod in the hole and adjust as necessary. To verify the switch is in the lock position, move the switch slider to the extreme right position and then move the slider 1 detent to the left.

14. Install the switch mounting stud and tighten to 35 inch lbs. (4.0 Nm).

15. Install the dimmer switch assembly to the actuator rod.

16. If equipped, install the cable bracket and the horn pad ground wire.

17. Install and finger-tighten the washer head screw and the hex nut.

18. Adjust the dimmer switch and tighten the screw and nut to 35 inch lbs. (4.0 Nm).

19. Connect the ignition switch connector and raise the steering column into position. Install the mounting supports and the trim plates.

20. Connect the negative battery cable and, if equipped, enable the SIR system.

Ignition Lock

REMOVAL & INSTALLATION

1989

1. Disconnect the negative battery cable.

2. Remove turn signal switch assembly, but do not disconnect or pull the wire harness through the column. Allow the switch assembly to hang freely from the wires.

3. Remove the key from the lock cylinder.

4. Remove the buzzer switch and clip.

5. Reinsert the key into the lock cylinder. Be sure the key is in the **LOCK** position.

6. Remove the lock retaining screw.

7. Disconnect the PASS Key wire harness connector at the base of the steering column.

8. Attach a piece of string or mechanic's wire to the wire connector to aid in installation and carefully pull the connector up through the column.

9. Remove the lock cylinder set.

To install:

10. Using the length of string or mechanic's wire, pull PASS Key wire down through the column in the original position. Connect the PASS Key wire harness.

11. Install the lock cylinder set and secure with the retaining screw. Tighten the screw to 27 inch lbs. (3 Nm).

12. Turn the key to the **RUN** position and install the key buzzer switch and clip. Return the key to the **LOCK** position.

13. Install the turn signal switch assembly.

14. Connect the negative battery cable.

1990–93

NOTE: The vehicle is equipped with a SIR air bag system, it is imperative that the disarming procedure is followed before repairs, and that the coil centering and rearming procedures are followed after repairs.

1. Disable the SIR system and disconnect the negative battery cable.

2. Remove turn signal switch assembly, but do not disconnect or pull the wire harness through the column. Allow the switch assembly to hang freely from the wires.

3. If necessary, remove the coil assembly as follows:

a. Disconnect the coil terminal connector from the vehicle harness.

b. Remove wiring protector.

c. Attach a length of mechanic's wire to the terminal connector to aid in reassembly.

d. Carefully pull wire through the column.

4. Remove the key from the lock cylinder.

5. Remove the buzzer switch and clip.

6. Reinsert the key into the lock cylinder, be sure the key is in the **LOCK** position.

7. Remove the lock retaining screw.

8. Disconnect the Pass Key wire harness connector at the base of the steering column. Remove the wiring protector, if not removed already.

9. Attach a piece of string or mechanic's wire to the wire connector to aid in reassembly, disconnect the retaining clip from the housing cover and pull the wire up through the column.

10. Remove the lock cylinder.

To install:

11. Using the length of string or the mechanic's wire, pull the PASS Key wire harness down through the column into the original position and engage the connector.

12. Install the lock cylinder set. Snap the wire retaining clip into the hole in the housing.

13. Install the lock cylinder retaining screw and tighten to 22 inch lbs. (2.5 Nm).

14. Remove the key from the lock cylinder set and install the key buzzer switch and clip.

15. Insert the key back into the lock cylinder and make sure it is in the **LOCK** position.

16. If removed, pull the turn signal switch wiring connector and/or the coil wiring connector through the steering column, connect the harnesses and install the wiring protector.

17. Install the turn signal switch assembly.

18. Connect the negative battery cable and enable the SIR system.

Stoplight Switch

ADJUSTMENT

While depressing the brake pedal, insert the switch into the retainer until seated. Pull the brake pedal rearward against the pedal stop with a force of 42 lbs. (187 N) until the clicking sounds are not heard. The Switch will move in the retainer providing proper adjustment. Release the brake pedal and repeat, to ensure that no clicking sounds are heard. Check for proper stop lamp operation.

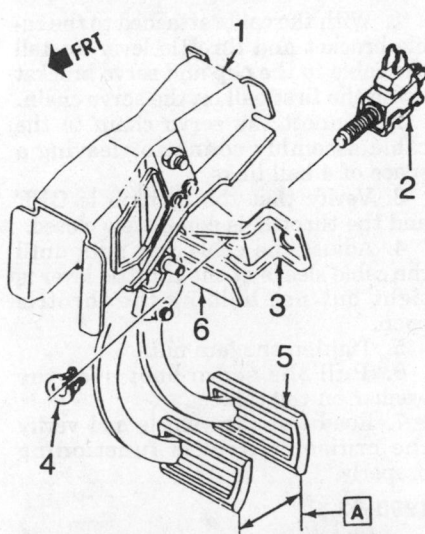

1. Normal travel
2. Brake pedal bracket
3. Stoplight switch
4. Retainer
5. Brake pedal
6. Actuator

Stoplight switch assembly

REMOVAL & INSTALLATION

1. Disconnect the battery negative cable. Remove the lower trim panel.

2. Disconnect the electrical connector from the switch.

3. Remove the retainer and the switch from the vehicle.

4. Installation is the reverse of the reverse of the removal procedure.

5. Adjust the stoplight switch and check for proper operation.

Clutch Switch

REMOVAL & INSTALLATION

1. Disconnect the negative battery cable.

2. Remove the sound insulator panel from under the dash.

3. Remove the clip retainer from the actuating rod at the clutch pedal.

4. Remove the bolt, switch and rod from the clutch bracket.

5. Disconnect the wire connector form the switch and remove the switch assembly.

To install:

6. Connect the electrical connector to the switch.

7. Place a new switch in position with the actuating rod in line with the hole in the clutch pedal and install the bolt.

8. Insert the rod into the bracket and secure with the retainer.

9. Install the sound insulator panel under the dash.

10. Connect the negative battery cable and check for proper switch operation.

Neutral Safety Switch

ADJUSTMENT

1. Disconnect battery negative cable.

2. Remove the switch assembly.

3. Position the shift control lever in **N**.

4. Align tang on switch with the tang slot on the shift control.

5. Loosely assemble the the mounting nuts to the case.

6. Rotate the switch until the service adjustment hole aligns with the tang hole. Insert the gage pin $\frac{3}{32}$ inch (2.34mm) into the service adjustment hole and rotate switch until pin drops to a depth of $\frac{19}{32}$ inch (15mm).

7. Tighten the nuts to 26 inch lbs. (3 Nm) and install the gauge pin.

8. Connect negative battery cable and verify the engine only starts in **P** or **N**.

9. Install the console and shifter knob assembly.

REMOVAL & INSTALLATION

1. Disconnect negative battery cable.

2. Remove the shifter knob assembly.

3. Remove the console assembly.

4. Remove the neutral switch mounting bolts.

5. Remove the switch and the gauge pin.

To install:

6. Position shifter lever in the **N** position.

7. Insert carrier tang on the switch in the slot on the shifter.

8. If installing a new switch, install the mounting nuts and move the shift control lever out of the **N** position to shear the factory installed plastic retaining pin.

NOTE: If installing a new switch and the holes do not align with shifter control, check that the shifter control lever is in N. Do not rotate the switch as this will shear the retaining pin. If a new switch was rotated and the pin was already broken, switch adjustment must be performed.

9. If installing an old switch or a new switch with a sheared retaining pin, perform switch adjustment.

10. Tighten switch mounting bolts to 26 inch lbs. (3 Nm).

11. Connect the negative battery cable and check that engine starts only in the **P** or **N** positions. If engine starts in any other position, readjust neutral switch.

12. Install console and shifter knob assembly.

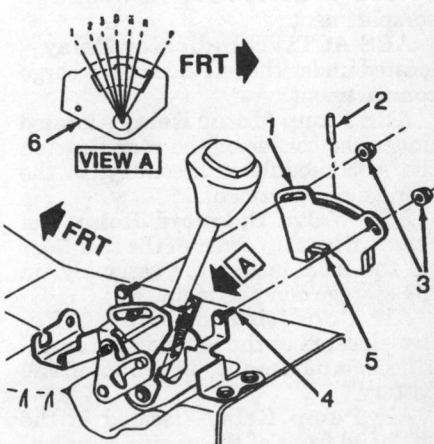

1. Neutral start switch
2. Gauge pin
3. Nut
4. Mounting stud
5. Carrier tang
6. Detent plate

Neutral safety switch

Fuses, Circuit Breakers and Relays

LOCATION

Fusible Links

Fusible links are located in various positions, including at the jump start junction block. Fusible links, which are normally not fused, are used to prevent wire harness damage in the event of a short circuit or an overload condition. Each fusible link is of a fixed value for a specific electrical load. Should a link fail, the cause of the failure must be determined and repaired prior to installing a new fusible link of the same value.

Circuit Breakers

There are 3 different style circuit breakers used. A standard heat activated circuit breaker is used which will cycle open and closed until the overload condition is corrected. There is a mechanical type breaker and a solid state design called a Positive Temperature Coefficient (PTC) circuit breaker, both will not reset until the current source is removed for a few seconds. Various circuit breakers are located throughout the vehicle and the fuse block.

Fuse Block

The main fuse block assembly is located behind the far right side of the instrument panel. The 2 auxiliary fuse blocks are found below the right of the instrument panel, next to the radio receiver box.

Relays

ABS Control Module Relay (1989–90)—located under the corner of the rear floor, in storage compartment.
ABS ACTIVE Indicator Relay—located under the left side of the cargo compartment.
ABS Pump Motor Relay—located under the corner of the rear floor on the ABS modulator assembly, in storage compartment.
ABS Valve Solenoid Relay—located under the corner of the rear floor on the ABS modulator assembly, in the storage compartment.
Air Conditioning Clutch Relay—located in the left side of the engine compartment, in front of the battery.
Air Pump Relay—located in the left hand front of the engine compartment, on top of the air pump.
Amplifier Relay—located behind the left side of the instrument panel, to the right of the instrument cluster.

Blower Relays (High and Low)—located in the left side of the engine compartment, on the wheelhouse.
Cruise Control Cut-Off Relay—located below the instrument panel, left of the steering column.
Deck Lid Release Relay—located on the right front of the cargo compartment.
Delayed Accessory Bus (DAB) Relay—located below the left side of the instrument panel.
Dome Lamp Relay—located on the multi-use relay bracket to the bottom right side of the instrument panel.
Engine Cooling Fan Relays (Primary and Secondary)—located in the front of the engine compartment on the left side of the radiator shroud.
Fuel Pump Relay (1989)—located to the right of the master cylinder.
Fuel Pump Relays (1990–92)—located below right side of the instrument panel, left of the glove compartment on the multi-use relay bracket. The 5.7L (VIN J) engine uses a second relay located below the left side of the instrument panel.
Fog Lamp Relay—located on the multi-use relay bracket to the bottom right side of the instrument panel.
Hatch Release Relay—located in the rear of the cargo compartment, on the end panel.
Horn Relay—located on the multi-use relay bracket to the bottom right of the instrument panel.
Power Antenna Relay (1989 Coupe)—located in the left side rear of cargo compartment, on the end panel.
Power Antenna Relay (Convertible and 1990–93 Coupe)—located on the left side of the cargo compartment above the rear of the wheel house.
Rear Defogger Relay—located on the multi-use relay bracket to the bottom right of the instrument panel.
Secondary Injector Relays (VIN J)—located rear of the left hand front wheelhouse, in front of the battery and behind the battery near the left hand door hinges.
Starter Enable Relay—located below the left side of the instrument panel, left of the steering column.
Shift-Up Relay—located in the left hand middle of the engine compartment, near the frame rail.

Computers

LOCATION

Electronic Brake Control Module (EBCM)—located under the left corner of cargo compartment, behind the driver's seat.

Central Control Module (CCM, 1990–93)—located behind the middle of the instrument panel.
Diagnostic Energy Reserve (DERM) Module—located in the middle of the instrument panel, in front of and below the CCM.
Electronic Control Module (ECM) 1989—located behind the right side of the dash.
Electronic Control Module (ECM) 1990–92—located in the engine compartment, above the battery.
Electronic Spark Control Module (1989–90)—located on the right side of air conditioning heater blower housing.
Select Ride Control Module (SRCM)—located rear of the cargo compartment, under the cargo deck.

Flashers

LOCATION

Turn Signal (1989)—located behind the right side of the dash panel, near the fuse panel.
Turn Signal (1990–93)—located below left side of instrument panel, to the left of the steering column.
Hazard Flasher—located near the radio on the right side of the instrument panel.

Cruise Control

ADJUSTMENT

Servo Linkage

1989

1. With the cable attached to the cable bracket and throttle lever, install the cable to the clip and servo bracket using the first ball on the servo chain.
2. Connect the servo chain to the cable assembly connector leaving a space of 4 ball links.
3. Verify that the ignition is **OFF** and the throttle is completely closed.
4. Adjust the cable jam nuts until the cable sleeve at the throttle lever is tight but not holding the throttle open.
5. Tighten the jam nuts.
6. Pull the servo boot over the washer on the cable.
7. Road test the vehicle and verify the cruise control is functioning properly.

1990–93

1. With the cruise control cable installed into servo bracket.
2. Pull servo assembly end of cable toward servo without moving the throttle lever.

GM "T" Body
Front Wheel Drive
PONTIAC—LeMans

SPECIFICATIONS

VEHICLE IDENTIFICATION CHART

It is important for servicing and ordering parts to be certain of the vehicle and engine identification. The VIN (vehicle identification number) is a 17 digit number visible through the windshield on the driver's side of the dash and contains the vehicle and engine identification codes. The tenth digit indicates model year and the eighth digit indicates engine code. It can be interpreted as follows:

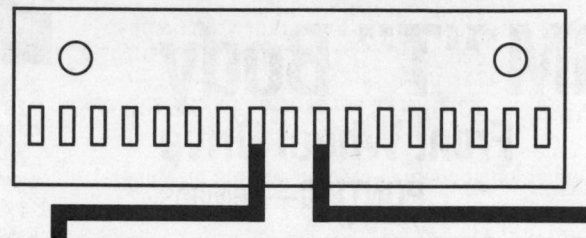

Engine Code						Model Year	
Code	Liters	Cu. In. (cc)	Cyl.	Fuel Sys.	Eng. Mfg.	Code	Year
6	1.6	98 (1598)	4	TBI	GM	K	1989
K	2.0	121 (1998)	4	TBI	GM	L	1990
TBI—Throttle body injection						M	1991
						N	1992
						P	1993

ENGINE IDENTIFICATION

Year	Model	Engine Displacement Liters (cc)	Engine Series (ID/VIN)	Fuel System	No. of Cylinders	Engine Type
1989	Lemans	1.6 (1598)	6	TBI	4	OHC
	Lemans	2.0 (1998)	K	TBI	4	OHC
1990	Lemans	1.6 (1598)	6	TBI	4	OHC
	Lemans	2.0 (1998)	K	TBI	4	OHC
1991	Lemans	1.6 (1598)	6	TBI	4	OHC
	Lemans	2.0 (1998)	K	TBI	4	OHC
1992-93	Lemans	1.6 (1598)	6	TBI	4	OHC

OHC—Overhead cam
TBI—Throttle Body Injection

GENERAL ENGINE SPECIFICATIONS

Year	Engine ID/VIN	Engine Displacement Liters (cc)	Fuel System Type	Net Horsepower @ rpm	Net Torque @ rpm (ft. lbs.)	Bore × Stroke (in.)	Compression Ratio	Oil Pressure @ rpm
1989	6	1.6 (1598)	TBI	74 @ 5600	88 @ 3400	3.11 × 3.21	8.5:1	55 @ 2000
	K	2.0 (1998)	TBI	96 @ 4800	118 @ 3600	3.39 × 3.39	8.8:1	55 @ 2000
1990	6	1.6 (1598)	TBI	74 @ 5600	90 @ 2800	3.11 × 3.21	8.5:1	55 @ 2000
	K	2.0 (1998)	TBI	96 @ 4800	118 @ 3600	3.39 × 3.39	8.8:1	55 @ 2000
1991	6	1.6 (1598)	TBI	74 @ 5600	90 @ 2800	3.11 × 3.21	8.5:1	55 @ 2000
	K	2.0 (1998)	TBI	96 @ 4800	118 @ 3600	3.39 × 3.39	8.8:1	55 @ 2000
1992-93	6	1.6 (1598)	TBI	74 @ 5600	90 @ 2800	3.11 × 3.21	8.5:1	55 @ 2000

TBI—Throttle body injection

ENGINE TUNE-UP SPECIFICATIONS

Year	Engine ID/VIN	Engine Displacement Liters (cc)	Spark Plugs Gap (in.)	Ignition Timing (deg.) MT	Ignition Timing (deg.) AT	Fuel Pump (psi)	Idle Speed (rpm) MT	Idle Speed (rpm) AT	Valve Clearance In.	Valve Clearance Ex.
1989	6	1.6 (1598)	0.060	①	①	18–27	600	500	Hyd.	Hyd.
	K	2.0 (1998)	0.060	①	①	18–27	600	600	Hyd.	Hyd.
1990	6	1.6 (1598)	0.045	①	①	18–27	600	500	Hyd.	Hyd.
	K	2.0 (1998)	0.045	①	①	18–27	600	600	Hyd.	Hyd.
1991	6	1.6 (1598)	0.045	①	①	18–27	600	500	Hyd.	Hyd.
	K	2.0 (1998)	0.045	①	①	18–27	600	600	Hyd.	Hyd.
1992	6	1.6 (1598)	0.045	①	①	18–27	600	500	Hyd.	Hyd.
1993	SEE UNDERHOOD SPECIFICATIONS STICKER									

NOTE: The lowest cylinder pressure should be within 75% of the highest cylinder pressure reading. For example, if the highest cylinder is 134 psi, the lowest should be 101. Engine should be at normal operating temperature with throttle valve in the wide open position.
The underhood specifications sticker often reflects tune-up specification changes in production. Sticker figures must be used if they disagree with those in this chart.
Hyd.—Hydraulic
① See underhood specifications sticker.

FIRING ORDERS

NOTE: To avoid confusion, always replace spark plug wires one at a time.

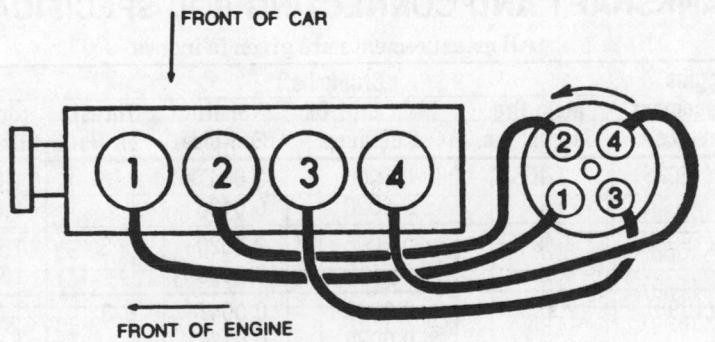

1.6L and 2.0L Engines
Engine Firing Order: 1–3–4–2
Distributor Rotation: Counterclockwise

CAPACITIES

Year	Model	Engine ID/VIN	Engine Displacement Liters (cc)	Engine Crankcase with Filter (qts.)	Transmission (pts.) 4-Spd.	Transmission (pts.) 5-Spd.	Transmission (pts.) Auto.	Drive Axle (pts.)	Fuel Tank (gal.)	Cooling System (qts.)
1989	Lemans	6	1.6 (1598)	4.0	3.5	3.5	8 ①	—	13.0	8.1
	Lemans	K	2.0 (1998)	4.0	3.5	4.5	8 ①	—	13.0	8.1
1990	Lemans	6	1.6 (1598)	4.0	3.5	3.5	8 ①	—	13.0	8.1
	Lemans	K	2.0 (1998)	4.0	3.5	4.5	8 ①	—	13.0	8.1
1991	Lemans	6	1.6 (1598)	4.0	3.4	3.4	8 ①	—	13.0	8.1
	Lemans	K	2.0 (1998)	4.0	3.4	4.4	8 ①	—	13.0	8.1
1992–93	Lemans	6	1.6 (1598)	4.0	3.4	3.4	8 ①	—	13.0	8.1

① Overhaul—12 pts.

CAMSHAFT SPECIFICATIONS

All measurements given in inches.

Year	Engine ID/VIN	Engine Displacement Liters (cc)	Journal Diameter					Elevation		Bearing Clearance	Camshaft End Play
			1	2	3	4	5	In.	Ex.		
1989	6	1.6 (1598)	1.552–1.553	1.562–1.563	1.572–1.573	1.582–1.583	1.592–1.593	0.221	0.241	0.0018–0.0035	0.0016–0.0064
	K	2.0 (1998)	1.867–1.869	1.867–1.869	1.867–1.869	1.867–1.869	1.867–1.869	0.259	0.259	0.0010–0.0039	0.0016–0.0063
1990	6	1.6 (1598)	1.552–1.553	1.562–1.563	1.572–1.573	1.582–1.583	1.592–1.593	0.220	0.241	0.0018–0.0035	0.0035–0.0083
	K	2.0 (1998)	1.670–1.671	1.671–1.672	1.691–1.692	1.701–1.702	1.710–1.711	0.237	0.252	0.0011–0.0035	0.0016–0.0063
1991	6	1.6 (1598)	1.552–1.553	1.562–1.563	1.572–1.573	1.582–1.583	1.592–1.593	0.220	0.241	0.0018–0.0035	0.0035–0.0083
	K	2.0 (1998)	1.670–1.671	1.671–1.672	1.691–1.692	1.701–1.702	1.710–1.711	0.237	0.252	0.0011–0.0035	0.0016–0.0063
1992–93	6	1.6 (1598)	1.552–1.553	1.562–1.563	1.572–1.573	1.582–1.583	1.592–1.593	0.220	0.241	0.0018–0.0035	0.0035–0.0083

CRANKSHAFT AND CONNECTING ROD SPECIFICATIONS

All measurements are given in inches.

Year	Engine ID/VIN	Engine Displacement Liters (cc)	Crankshaft				Connecting Rod		
			Main Brg. Journal Dia.	Main Brg. Oil Clearance	Shaft End-play	Thrust on No.	Journal Diameter	Oil Clearance	Side Clearance
1989	6	1.6 (1598)	2.1653	0.0006–0.0020	0.0047–0.0138	3	1.6918–1.6920	0.0007–0.0025	0.0027–0.0095
	K	2.0 (1998)	2.4945–2.4954	0.0006–0.0019	0.0020–0.0070	3	1.9983–1.9994	0.0010–0.0031	0.0039–0.0149
1990	6	1.6 (1598)	2.1653	0.0006–0.0020	0.0047–0.0138	3	1.6918–1.6920	0.0007–0.0025	0.0028–0.0095
	K	2.0 (1998)	2.2828–2.2833	0.0006–0.0016	0.0028–0.0118	3	1.9279–1.9287	0.0007–0.0025	0.0028–0.0095
1991	6	1.6 (1598)	2.1700	0.0006–0.0020	0.0047–0.0138	3	1.6918–1.6920	0.0018–0.0035	0.0028–0.0095
	K	2.0 (1998)	2.2828–2.2833	0.0006–0.0016	0.0028–0.0118	3	1.9279–1.9287	0.0007–0.0025	0.0028–0.0095
1992–93	6	1.6 (1598)	2.1700	0.0006–0.0020	0.0047–0.0138	3	1.6918–1.6920	0.0018–0.0035	0.0028–0.0095

VALVE SPECIFICATIONS

Year	Engine ID/VIN	Engine Displacement Liters (cc)	Seat Angle (deg.)	Face Angle (deg.)	Spring Test Pressure (lbs. @ in.)	Spring Installed Height (in.)	Stem-to-Guide Clearance (in.)		Stem Diameter (in.)	
							Intake	Exhaust	Intake	Exhaust
1989	6	1.6 (1598)	45	46	139 @ 0.85	1.24	0.0008–0.0020	0.0016–0.0028	0.275	0.275
	K	2.0 (1998)	45	46	208–222 @ 1.22	1.61	0.0011–0.0026	0.0014–0.0030	0.275	0.276

VALVE SPECIFICATIONS

Year	Engine ID/VIN	Engine Displacement Liters (cc)	Seat Angle (deg.)	Face Angle (deg.)	Spring Test Pressure (lbs. @ in.)	Spring Installed Height (in.)	Stem-to-Guide Clearance (in.)		Stem Diameter (in.)	
							Intake	Exhaust	Intake	Exhaust
1990	6	1.6 (1598)	46	46	140 @ 0.85	1.24	0.0008–0.0020	0.0016–0.0028	0.276	0.275
	K	2.0 (1998)	45	46	165–197 @ 1.043	1.48	0.0006–0.0017	0.0012–0.0024	0.276	0.275
1991	6	1.6 (1598)	46	46	140 @ 0.85	1.24	0.0008–0.0020	0.0016–0.0028	0.276	0.275
	K	2.0 (1998)	45	46	165–197 @ 1.043	1.48	0.0006–0.0017	0.0012–0.0024	0.276	0.275
1992–93	6	1.6 (1598)	46	46	140 @ 0.85	1.24	0.0008–0.0020	0.0016–0.0028	0.276	0.275

PISTON AND RING SPECIFICATIONS

All measurements are given in inches.

Year	Engine ID/VIN	Engine Displacement Liters (cc)	Piston Clearance	Ring Gap			Ring Side Clearance		
				Top Compression	Bottom Compression	Oil Control	Top Compression	Bottom Compression	Oil Control
1989	6	1.6 (1598)	0.0008	0.012–0.020	0.012–0.020	0.016–0.055	0.0024–0.0036	0.0019–0.0032	NA
	K	2.0 (1998)	0.0010–0.0022	0.010–0.020	0.010–0.020	0.010–0.050	0.0019–0.0027	0.0019–0.0027	0.0019–0.0082
1990	6	1.6 (1598)	0.0008	0.012–0.020	0.012–0.020	0.016–0.055	0.0024–0.0036	0.0019–0.0032	NA
	K	2.0 (1998)	0.0004–0.0012	0.010–0.018	0.012–0.020	0.010–0.050	0.0024–0.0036	0.0019–0.0032	0.0019–0.0082
1991	6	1.6 (1598)	0.0008	0.012–0.020	0.012–0.020	NA	0.0024–0.0036	0.0019–0.0032	NA
	K	2.0 (1998)	0.0004–0.0012	0.010–0.018	0.012–0.020	0.010–0.050	0.0024–0.0036	0.0019–0.0032	0.0019–0.0082
1992–93	6	1.6 (1598)	0.0008	0.012–0.020	0.012–0.020	NA	0.0024–0.0036	0.0019–0.0032	NA

NA—Not available

TORQUE SPECIFICATIONS

All readings in ft. lbs.

Year	Engine ID/VIN	Engine Displacement Liters (cc)	Cylinder Head Bolts	Main Bearing Bolts	Rod Bearing Bolts	Crankshaft Damper Bolts	Flywheel Bolts	Manifold		Spark⑦ Plugs	Lug Nuts
								Intake	Exhaust		
1989	6	1.6 (1598)	18①	36②	18③	40	25④	16	16	15	66
	K	2.0 (1998)	18①	70	38	20	⑤	16	16	18	66
1990	6	1.6 (1598)	18①	44⑥	18③	41	25④	16	10	15	66
	K	2.0 (1998)	18①	44⑥	26④	13	⑤	16	10	15	66
1991	6	1.6 (1598)	18①	37②	18③	41	26④	16	16	15	65
	K	2.0 (1998)	18①	44⑥	26④	13	⑤	16	10	15	65
1992–93	6	1.6 (1598)	18①	37②	18③	41	26④	16	16	15	65

① Cold—plus 2 turns of 60 degrees each and 1 turn of 30 degrees
② Plus a 45–60 degree turn
③ Plus a 30 degree turn
④ Plus a 30–45 degree turn
⑤ Automatic—52 ft. lbs.
  Manual—55 ft. lbs.
⑥ Plus a 40–50 degree turn
⑦ Only replace spark plugs with the cylinder head cold.

BRAKE SPECIFICATIONS

All measurements in inches unless noted.

| Year | Model | Master Cylinder Bore | Brake Disc | | | Brake Drum Diameter | | | Minimum Lining Thickness | |
			Original Thickness	Minimum Thickness	Maximum Runout	Original Inside Diameter	Max. Wear Limit	Maximum Machine Diameter	Front	rear
1989	Lemans	0.813	0.50	0.42 ①	0.004	7.87	7.90	7.90	0.28 ③	0.02 ④
1990	Lemans	0.874	0.50	0.42 ①	0.004	7.87	7.90	7.90	0.28 ③	0.02 ④
1991	Lemans	0.874	0.50	0.42 ①	0.004	7.87	7.90	7.90	0.28 ③	0.02 ④
1992–93	Lemans	0.874	0.94	0.86 ②	0.004	7.87	7.90	7.90	0.28 ③	0.02 ④

① Specification is minimum refinish thickness.
  Discard rotor at 0.38 in.
② Specification is minimum refinish thickness.
  Discard rotor at 0.83 in.
③ Shoe and lining together
④ Above any rivet head

WHEEL ALIGNMENT

| Year | Model | | Caster | | Camber | | Toe-in (in.) | Steering Axis Inclination (deg.) |
			Range (deg.)	Preferred Setting (deg.)	Range (deg.)	Preferred Setting (deg.)		
1989	Lemans	Front	¾P–2¾P	NA	1N–½P	NA	0	—
		Rear	—	—	1N	NA	NA	—
1990	Lemans	Front	¾P–2¾P	NA	1N–½P	NA	0	—
		Rear	—	—	1N	NA	NA	—
1991	Lemans	Front	¾P–2¾P	NA	1N–½P	NA	0	—
		Rear	—	—	1N	NA	NA	—
1992–93	Lemans	Front	¾P–2¾P	NA	1¼N–¼P	NA	0	—
		Rear	—	—	1N–0	NA	NA	—

NA—Not adjustable
N—Negative
P—Positive

GM "A" Body
Front Wheel Drive
BUICK—Century **CHEVROLET**—Celebrity
OLDSMOBILE—Cutlass **PONTIAC**—6000

SPECIFICATIONS

VEHICLE IDENTIFICATION CHART

It is important for servicing and ordering parts to be certain of the vehicle and engine identification. The VIN (vehicle identification number) is a 17 digit number visible through the windshield on the driver's side of the dash and contains the vehicle and engine identification codes. The tenth digit indicates model year and the eighth digit indicates engine code. It can be interpreted as follows:

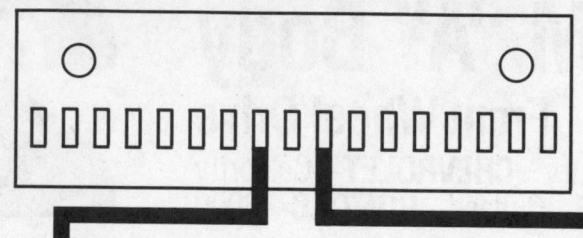

		Engine Code			
Code	Liters	Cu. In. (cc)	Cyl.	Fuel Sys.	Eng. Mfg.
R	2.5	151 (2475)	4	TBI	CPC
W	2.8	173 (2835)	6	PFI	CPC
T	3.1	192 (3147)	6	PFI	CPC
N	3.3	204 (3344)	6	PFI	BOC

Model Year	
Code	Year
K	1989
L	1990
M	1991
N	1992
P	1993

TBI—Throttle Body Injection
PFI—Port Fuel Injection
CPC—Chevrolet Pontiac Canada
BOC—Buick Oldsmobile Cadillac

ENGINE IDENTIFICATION

Year	Model	Engine Displacement Liters (cc)	Engine Series (ID/VIN)	Fuel System	No. of Cylinders	Engine Type
1989	Celebrity	2.5 (2475)	LR8/R	TBI	4	OHV
	Celebrity	2.8 (2835)	LB6/W	PFI	6	OHV
	Century	2.5 (2475)	LR8/R	TBI	4	OHV
	Century	2.8 (2835)	LB6/W	PFI	6	OHV
	Century	3.3 (3344)	LG7/N	PFI	6	OHV
	Cutlass ①	2.5 (2475)	LR8/R	TBI	4	OHV
	Cutlass ①	2.8 (2835)	LB6/W	PFI	6	OHV
	Cutlass ①	3.3 (3344)	LG7/N	PFI	6	OHV
	6000	2.5 (2475)	LR8/R	TBI	4	OHV
	6000	2.8 (2835)	LB6/W	PFI	6	OHV
	6000	3.1 (3147)	LH0/T	PFI	6	OHV
1990	Celebrity	2.5 (2475)	LR8/R	TBI	4	OHV
	Celebrity	3.1 (3147)	LH0/T	PFI	6	OHV
	Century	2.5 (2475)	LR8/R	TBI	4	OHV
	Century	3.3 (3344)	LG7/N	PFI	6	OHV
	Cutlass ①	2.5 (2475)	LR8/R	TBI	4	OHV
	Cutlass ①	3.3 (3344)	LG7/N	PFI	6	OHV
	6000	2.5 (2475)	LR8/R	TBI	4	OHV
	6000	3.1 (3147)	LH0/T	PFI	6	OHV

ENGINE IDENTIFICATION

Year	Model	Engine Displacement Liters (cc)	Engine Series (ID/VIN)	Fuel System	No. of Cylinders	Engine Type
1991	Century	2.5 (2475)	LR8/R	TBI	4	OHV
	Century	3.3 (3344)	LG7/N	PFI	6	OHV
	Cutlass ①	2.5 (2475)	LR8/R	TBI	4	OHV
	Cutlass ①	3.3 (3344)	LG7/N	PFI	6	OHV
	6000	2.5 (2475)	LR8/R	TBI	4	OHV
	6000	3.1 (3147)	LH0/T	PFI	6	OHV
1992–93	Century	2.5 (2475)	LR8/R	TBI	4	OHV
	Century	3.3 (3344)	LG7/N	PFI	6	OHV
	Cutlass ①	2.5 (2475)	LR8/R	TBI	4	OHV
	Cutlass ①	3.3 (3344)	LG7/N	PFI	6	OHV

TBI—Throttle Body Injection
PFI—Port Fuel Injection
OHV—Overhead Valves
① Ciera and Cruiser

GENERAL ENGINE SPECIFICATIONS

Year	Engine ID/VIN	Engine Displacement Liters (cc)	Fuel System Type	Net Horsepower @ rpm	Net Torque @ rpm (ft. lbs.)	Bore × Stroke (in.)	Compression Ratio	Oil Pressure @ rpm
1989	LR8/R	2.5 (2475)	TBI	92 @ 4000	134 @ 2800	4.000 × 3.000	8.3:1	37.5 @ 2000
	LB6/W	2.8 (2835)	PFI	130 @ 4800	155 @ 3600	3.503 × 2.992	8.9:1	50–65 @ 1200
	LH0/T	3.1 (3147)	PFI	120 @ 4200	175 @ 2200	3.503 × 3.312	8.8:1	50–65 @ 2400
	LG7/N	3.3 (3344)	PFI	160 @ 5200	185 @ 2000	3.700 × 3.160	9.0:1	45 @ 2000
1990	LR8/R	2.5 (2475)	TBI	92 @ 4400	134 @ 2800	4.000 × 3.000	8.3:1	37.5 @ 2000
	LH0/T	3.1 (3147)	PFI	120 @ 4200	175 @ 2200	3.503 × 3.312	8.8:1	50–65 @ 2400
	LG7/N	3.3 (3344)	PFI	160 @ 5200	185 @ 2000	3.700 × 3.160	9.0:1	45 @ 2000
1991	LR8/R	2.5 (2475)	TBI	110 @ 5200	135 @ 3200	4.000 × 3.000	8.3:1	26 @ 800
	LH0/T	3.1 (3147)	PFI	140 @ 4400	185 @ 3200	3.503 × 3.312	8.8:1	15 @ 1100
	LG7/N	3.3 (3344)	PFI	160 @ 5200	185 @ 2000	3.700 × 3.160	9.0:1	60 @ 1850
1992–93	LR8/R	2.5 (2475)	TBI	110 @ 5200	135 @ 3200	4.000 × 3.000	8.3:1	26 @ 800
	LG7/N	3.3 (3344)	PFI	160 @ 5200	185 @ 2000	3.700 × 3.160	9.0:1	60 @ 1850

NOTE: Horsepower and torque are SAE net figures. They are measured at the rear of the transmission with all accessories installed and operating. Since the figures vary when a given engine is installed in different models, some are representative rather than exact.
TBI—Throttle Body Injection
PFI—Port Fuel Injection

GASOLINE ENGINE TUNE-UP SPECIFICATIONS

Year	Engine ID/VIN	Engine Displacement Liters (cc)	Spark Plugs Gap (in.)	Ignition Timing (deg.) MT	Ignition Timing (deg.) AT	Fuel Pump (psi)	Idle Speed (rpm) MT	Idle Speed (rpm) AT	Valve Clearance In.	Valve Clearance Ex.
1989	LR8/R	2.5 (2475)	0.060	①	①	6.0–7.0	①	①	Hyd.	Hyd.
	LB6/W	2.8 (2835)	0.045	①	①	40.0–46.0	①	①	Hyd.	Hyd.
	LH0/T	3.1 (3147)	0.045	①	①	34.0–47.0	①	①	Hyd.	Hyd.
	LG7/N	3.3 (3344)	0.060	①	①	37.0–43.0	①	①	Hyd.	Hyd.

GASOLINE ENGINE TUNE-UP SPECIFICATIONS

Year	Engine ID/VIN	Engine Displacement Liters (cc)	Spark Plugs Gap (in.)	Ignition Timing (deg.)		Fuel Pump (psi)	Idle Speed (rpm)		Valve Clearance	
				MT	AT		MT	AT	In.	Ex.
1990	LR8/R	2.5 (2475)	0.060	①	①	6.0–7.0	①	①	Hyd.	Hyd.
	LH0/T	3.1 (3147)	0.045	①	①	34.0–47.0	①	①	Hyd.	Hyd.
	LG7/N	3.3 (3344)	0.060	①	①	37.0–43.0	①	①	Hyd.	Hyd.
1991	LR8/R	2.5 (2475)	0.060	①	①	9.0–13.0	①	①	Hyd.	Hyd.
	LH0/T	3.1 (3147)	0.045	①	①	40.5–47.0	①	①	Hyd.	Hyd.
	LG7/N	3.3 (3344)	0.060	①	①	41.0–47.0	①	①	Hyd.	Hyd.
1992	LR8/R	2.5 (2475)	0.060	①	①	9.0–13.0	①	①	Hyd.	Hyd.
	LG7/N	3.3 (3344)	0.060	①	①	41.0–47.0	①	①	Hyd.	Hyd.
1993			SEE UNDERHOOD SPECIFICATIONS STICKER							

NOTE: The lowest cylinder pressure should be within 75% of the highest cylinder pressure reading. For example, if the highest cylinder is 134 psi, the lowest should be 101. Engine should be at normal operating temperature with throttle valve in the wide open position.
The underhood specifications sticker often reflects tune-up specification changes in production. Sticker figures must be used if they disagree with those in this chart.
Hyd.—Hydraulic
① Refer to underhood specifications sticker

FIRING ORDERS

NOTE: To avoid confusion, always replace spark plug wires one at a time.

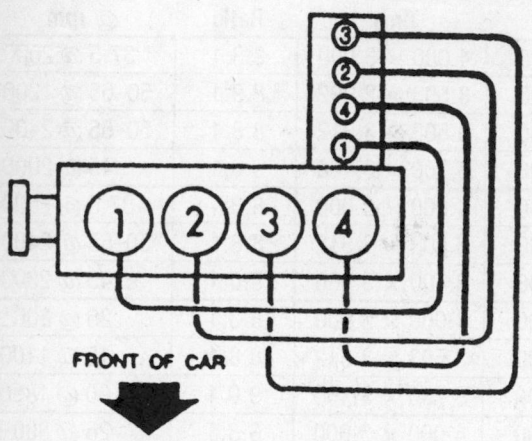

2.5L Engine
Engine Firing Order: 1–3–4–2
Distributorless Ignition System

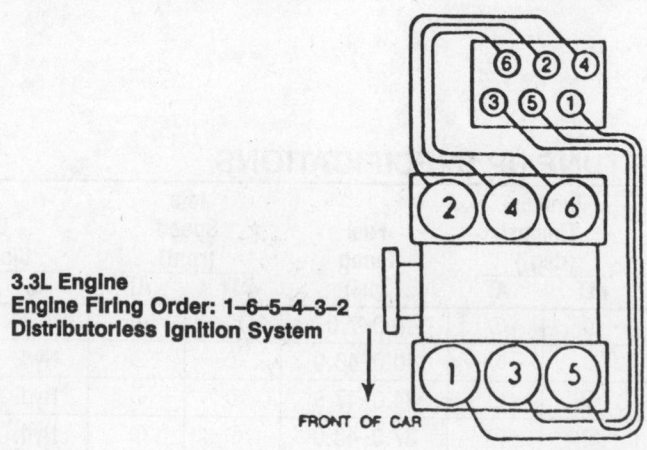

3.3L Engine
Engine Firing Order: 1–6–5–4–3–2
Distributorless Ignition System

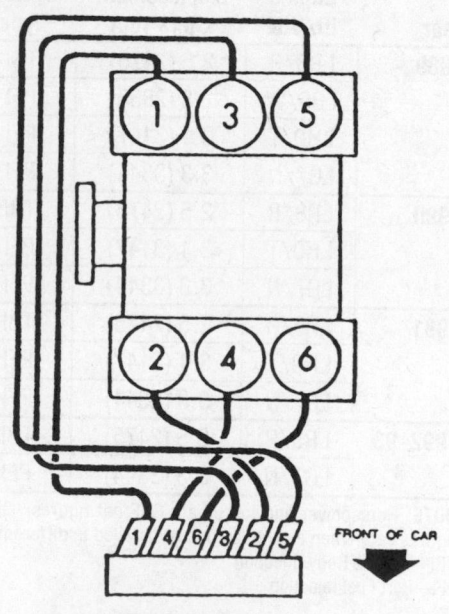

2.8L and 3.1L Engines
Engine Firing Order: 1–2–3–4–5–6
Distributorless Ignition System

CAPACITIES

Year	Model	Engine ID/VIN	Engine Displacement Liters (cc)	Engine Crankcase with Filter	Transmission (pts.) 4-Spd	5-Spd	Auto.	Transfer case (pts.)	Drive Axle Front (pts.)	Rear (pts.)	Fuel Tank (gal.)	Cooling System (qts.)
1989	Celebrity	LR8/R	2.5 (2475)	4.0	—	—	①	—	—	—	15.7	9.7②
	Celebrity	LB6/W	2.8 (2835)	4.0	—	—	①	—	—	—	15.7	13.2
	Century	LR8/R	2.5 (2475)	4.0	—	—	①	—	—	—	15.7	9.7②
	Century	LB6/W	2.8 (2835)	4.0	—	—	①	—	—	—	15.7	13.2
	Century	LG7/N	3.3 (3344)	4.0	—	—	①	—	—	—	15.7	12.0③
	Cutlass ⑤	LR8/R	2.5 (2475)	4.0	—	—	①	—	—	—	15.7	9.7②
	Cutlass ⑤	LB6/W	2.8 (2835)	4.0	—	—	①	—	—	—	15.7	13.2
	Cutlass ⑤	LG7/N	3.3 (3344)	4.0	—	—	①	—	—	—	15.7	12.0③
	6000	LR8/R	2.5 (2475)	4.0	—	—	①	—	—	—	15.7	9.7②
	6000	LB6/W	2.8 (2835)	4.0	—	—	①	—	—	—	15.7	13.2
	6000	LH0/T	3.1 (3147)	4.0	—	—	①	—	—	—	15.7	12.6
1990	Celebrity	LR8/R	2.5 (2475)	4.0	—	—	①	—	—	—	15.7	9.7②
	Celebrity	LH0/T	3.1 (3147)	4.0	—	—	①	—	—	—	15.7	12.8
	Century	LR8/R	2.5 (2475)	4.0	—	—	①	—	—	—	15.7	9.7②
	Century	LG7/N	3.3 (3344)	4.0	—	—	①	—	—	—	15.7	12.0③
	Cutlass ⑤	LR8/R	2.5 (2475)	4.0	—	—	①	—	—	—	15.7	9.7②
	Cutlass ⑤	LG7/N	3.3 (3344)	4.0	—	—	①	—	—	—	15.7	12.9④
	6000	LR8/R	2.5 (2475)	4.0	—	—	①	—	—	—	15.7	9.7②
	6000	LH0/T	3.1 (3147)	4.0	—	—	①	—	—	—	15.7	12.6
1991	Century	LR8/R	2.5 (2475)	4.0	—	—	①	—	—	—	15.7	9.7②
	Century	LG7/N	3.3 (3344)	4.0	—	—	①	—	—	—	15.7	12.9④
	Cutlass ⑤	LR8/R	2.5 (2475)	4.0	—	—	①	—	—	—	15.7	9.7②
	Cutlass ⑤	LG7/N	3.3 (3344)	4.0	—	—	①	—	—	—	15.7	12.9④
	6000	LR8/R	2.5 (2475)	4.0	—	—	①	—	—	—	15.7	9.7②
	6000	LH0/T	3.1 (3147)	4.0	—	—	①	—	—	—	15.7	12.6
1992-93	Century	LR8/R	2.5 (2475)	4.0	—	—	①	—	—	—	15.7	9.7②
	Century	LG7/N	3.3 (3344)	4.0	—	—	①	—	—	—	15.7	12.9④
	Cutlass ⑤	LR8/R	2.5 (2475)	4.0	—	—	①	—	—	—	15.7	9.7②
	Cutlass ⑤	LG7/N	3.3 (3344)	4.0	—	—	①	—	—	—	15.7	12.9④

① 125C—8 pts.
  Overhaul—12 pts.
  440.T4—13 pts.
  Overhaul—20 pts.
② Air Cond.—9.9 pts.
③ Air Cond.—12.7 pts.
④ Air Cond. & Heavy Duty Radiator—13.2 qts.
⑤ Ciera and Cruiser

CAMSHAFT SPECIFICATIONS

All measurements given in inches.

Year	Engine ID/VIN	Engine Displacement Liters (cc)	Journal Diameter 1	2	3	4	5	Elevation In.	Ex.	Bearing Clearance	Camshaft End Play
1989	LR8/R	2.5 (2475)	1.8690	1.8690	1.8690	—	—	0.232	0.232	0.0007–0.0027	0.0015–0.0050
	LB6/W	2.8 (2835)	1.8678–1.8815	1.8678–1.8815	1.8678–1.8815	1.8678–1.8815	—	0.262	0.273	0.0010–0.0040	NA
	LH0/T	3.1 (3147)	1.8678–1.8815	1.8678–1.8815	1.8678–1.8815	1.8678–1.8815	—	0.263	0.273	0.0010–0.0040	NA
	LG7/N	3.3 (3344)	1.7850–1.7860	1.7850–1.7860	1.7850–1.7860	1.7850–1.7860	—	0.250	0.255	0.0005–0.0035	NA

CAMSHAFT SPECIFICATIONS

All measurements given in inches.

Year	Engine ID/VIN	Engine Displacement Liters (cc)	Journal Diameter					Elevation		Bearing Clearance	Camshaft End Play
			1	2	3	4	5	In.	Ex.		
1990	LR8/R	2.5 (2475)	1.8690	1.8690	1.8690	—	—	0.248	0.248	0.0007–0.0027	0.0015–0.0050
	LH0/T	3.1 (3147)	1.8678–1.8815	1.8678–1.8815	1.8678–1.8815	1.8678–1.8815	—	0.263	0.273	0.0010–0.0040	NA
	LG7/N	3.3 (3344)	1.7850–1.7860	1.7850–1.7860	1.7850–1.7860	1.7850–1.7860	—	0.250	0.255	0.0005–0.0035	NA
1991	LR8/R	2.5 (2475)	1.8690	1.8690	1.8690	—	—	0.248	0.248	0.0007–0.0027	0.0015–0.0050
	LH0/T	3.1 (3147)	1.8677–1.8815	1.8677–1.8815	1.8677–1.8815	1.8677–1.8815	—	0.263	0.273	0.0010–0.0040	NA
	LG7/N	3.3 (3344)	1.7850–1.7860	1.7850–1.7860	1.7850–1.7860	1.7850–1.7860	—	0.250	0.255	0.0005–0.0035	NA
1992-93	LR8/R	2.5 (2475)	1.8690	1.8690	1.8690	—	—	0.248	0.248	0.0007–0.0027	0.0015–0.0050
	LG7/N	3.3 (3344)	1.7848–1.7862	1.7848–1.7862	1.7848–1.7862	1.7848–1.7862	—	0.250	0.255	0.0016–0.0044	NA

NA—Not available

CRANKSHAFT AND CONNECTING ROD SPECIFICATIONS

All measurements are given in inches.

Year	Engine ID/VIN	Engine Displacement Liters (cc)	Crankshaft				Connecting Rod		
			Main Brg. Journal Dia.	Main Brg. Oil Clearance	Shaft End-play	Thrust on No.	Journal Diameter	Oil Clearance	Side Clearance
1989	LR8/R	2.5 (2475)	2.3000	0.0005–0.0022	0.003–0.008	5	1.9995–2.0005	0.0005–0.0026	0.006–0.022
	LB6/W	2.6 (2835)	2.6473–2.6483	0.0016–0.0033	0.002–0.008	3	1.9983–1.9993	0.0013–0.0026	0.006–0.017
	LH0/T	3.1 (3147)	2.6473–2.6483	0.0012–0.0027	0.002–0.008	3	1.9983–1.9994	0.0013–0.0031	0.014–0.027
	LG7/N	3.3 (3344)	2.4988–2.4998	0.0003–0.0018	0.003–0.011	3	2.2487–2.2499	0.0003–0.0026	0.003–0.015
1990	LR8/R	2.5 (2475)	2.3000	0.0005–0.0022	0.003–0.008	5	1.9995–2.0005	0.0005–0.0026	0.006–0.022
	LH0/T	3.1 (3147)	2.6473–2.6483	0.0012–0.0027	0.002–0.008	3	1.9983–1.9994	0.0013–0.0031	0.014–0.027
	LG7/N	3.3 (3344)	2.4988–2.4998	0.0003–0.0018	0.003–0.011	3	2.2487–2.2499	0.0003–0.0026	0.003–0.015
1991	LR8/R	2.5 (2475)	2.3000	0.0005–0.0022	0.005–0.010	5	2.0000	0.0005–0.0030	0.006–0.024
	LH0/T	3.1 (3147)	2.6473–2.6483	0.0012–0.0030	0.002–0.008	3	1.9983–1.9994	0.0011–0.0034	0.014–0.027
	LG7/N	3.3 (3344)	2.4988–2.4998	0.0003–0.0018	0.003–0.011	3	2.2487–2.2499	0.0003–0.0026	0.003–0.015
1992-93	LR8/R	2.5 (2475)	2.3000	0.0005–0.0022	0.005–0.010	5	2.0000	0.0005–0.0030	0.006–0.024
	LG7/N	3.3 (3344)	2.4988–2.4998	0.0008–0.0022	0.003–0.011	3	2.2487–2.2499	0.0008–0.0022	0.003–0.015

VALVE SPECIFICATIONS

Year	Engine ID/VIN	Engine Displacement Liters (cc)	Seat Angle (deg.)	Face Angle (deg.)	Spring Test Pressure (lbs. @ in.)	Spring Installed Height (in.)	Stem-to-Guide Clearance (in.)		Stem Diameter (in.)	
							Intake	Exhaust	Intake	Exhaust
1989	LR8/R	2.5 (2475)	46	46	176 @ 1.254	1.440	0.0010–0.0028	0.0013–0.0041	0.3130–0.3140	0.3120–0.3130
	LB6/W	2.8 (2835)	46	45	215 @ 1.291	1.727	0.0010–0.0027	0.0010–0.0027	0.3412–0.3416	0.3412–0.3416
	LH0/T	3.1 (3147)	46	45	215 @ 1.291	1.575	0.0010–0.0027	0.0010–0.0027	NA	NA
	LG7/N	3.3 (3344)	45	45	215 @ 1.291	1.701	0.0010–0.0027	0.0010–0.0027	NA	NA
1990	LR8/R	2.5 (2475)	46	46	176 @ 1.254	1.440	0.0010–0.0028	0.0013–0.0041	NA	NA
	LH0/T	3.1 (3147)	46	45	215 @ 1.291	1.575	0.0010–0.0027	0.0010–0.0027	NA	NA
	LG7/N	3.3 (3344)	45	45	215 @ 1.291	1.701	0.0010–0.0027	0.0010–0.0027	NA	NA
1991	LR8/R	2.5 (2475)	46	45	173 @ 1.240	1.680	0.0010–0.0028	0.0013–0.0041	NA	NA
	LH0/T	3.1 (3147)	46	45	215 @ 1.291	1.575	0.0010–0.0027	0.0010–0.0027	NA	NA
	LG7/N	3.3 (3344)	45	45	210 @ 1.315	1.690–1.720	0.0015–0.0035	0.0015–0.0032	NA	NA
1992–93	LR8/R	2.5 (2475)	46	45	173 @ 1.240	1.680	0.0010–0.0028	0.0013–0.0041	NA	NA
	LG7/N	3.3 (3344)	45	45	210 @ 1.315	1.690–1.720	0.0015–0.0035	0.0015–0.0035	NA	NA

PISTON AND RING SPECIFICATIONS

All measurements are given in inches.

Year	Engine ID/VIN	Engine Displacement Liters (cc)	Piston Clearance	Ring Gap			Ring Side Clearance		
				Top Compression	Bottom Compression	Oil Control	Top Compression	Bottom Compression	Oil Control
1989	LR8/R	2.5 (2475)	0.0014–0.0022 ①	0.010–0.020	0.010–0.020	0.020–0.060	0.0020–0.0030	0.0010–0.0030	0.0150–0.0550
	LB6/W	2.8 (2835)	0.0020–0.0028	0.010–0.020	0.010–0.020	0.020–0.055	0.0010–0.0030	0.0010–0.0030	0.0050–0.0080
	LH0/T	3.1 (3147)	0.0022–0.0028	0.010–0.020	0.010–0.020	0.010–0.050	0.0020–0.0040	0.0020–0.0040	0.0080 ②
	LG7/N	3.3 (3344)	0.0004–0.0022 ③	0.010–0.025	0.010–0.025	0.010–0.040	0.0010–0.0030	0.0010–0.0030	0.0010–0.0080
1990	LR8/R	2.5 (2475)	0.0014–0.0022 ①	0.010–0.020	0.010–0.020	0.020–0.060	0.0020–0.0030	0.0010–0.0030	0.0150–0.0550
	LH0/T	2.8 (2835)	0.0022–0.0028	0.010–0.020	0.010–0.020	0.010–0.050	0.0020–0.0040	0.0020–0.0040	0.0080 ②
	LG7/N	3.3 (3344)	0.0004–0.0022 ③	0.010–0.025	0.010–0.025	0.010–0.040	0.0010–0.0030	0.0010–0.0030	0.0010–0.0080

PISTON AND RING SPECIFICATIONS

All measurements are given in inches.

Year	Engine ID/VIN	Engine Displacement Liters (cc)	Piston Clearance	Ring Gap			Ring Side Clearance		
				Top Compression	Bottom Compression	Oil Control	Top Compression	Bottom Compression	Oil Control
1991	LR8/R	2.5 (2475)	0.0014–0.0022 ①	0.010–0.020	0.010–0.020	0.020–0.060	0.0020–0.0030	0.0010–0.0030	0.0150–0.0550
	LH0/T	2.8 (2835)	0.0009–0.0022	0.010–0.020	0.010–0.028	0.010–0.030	0.0020–0.0035	0.0020–0.0035	0.0080 ②
	LG7/N	3.3 (3344)	0.0004–0.0022 ③	0.010–0.025	0.010–0.025	0.010–0.040	0.0013–0.0031	0.0013–0.0031	0.0011–0.0081
1992–93	LR8/R	2.5 (2475)	0.0014–0.0022 ①	0.010–0.020	0.010–0.020	0.020–0.060	0.0020–0.0030	0.0010–0.0030	0.0150–0.0550
	LG7/N	3.3 (3344)	0.0004–0.0022 ③	0.010–0.025	0.010–0.025	0.015–0.055	0.0013–0.0031	0.0013–0.0031	0.0011–0.0081

① Measured ⅛ in. down from piston top.
② Maximum clearance
③ 44 mm from top of piston

TORQUE SPECIFICATIONS

All readings in ft. lbs.

Year	Engine ID/VIN	Engine Displacement Liters (cc)	Cylinder Head Bolts	Main Bearing Bolts	Rod Bearing Bolts	Crankshaft Damper Bolts	Flywheel Bolts	Manifold		Spark Plugs	Lug Nut
								Intake	Exhaust		
1989	LR8/R	2.5 (2475)	①	70	32	162	55	25	③	15	100
	LB6/W	2.8 (2835)	②	73	39	76	52	⑨	15–23	10–25	100
	LH0/T	3.1 (3147)	②	73	34–40	76	52	⑨	19	10–25	100
	LG7/N	3.3 (3344)	⑥	⑦	⑧	219	④	88 ⑤	41	20	100
1990	LR8/R	2.5 (2475)	①	65	29	162	55	25	③	15	100
	LH0/T	3.1 (3147)	②	73	39	76	52	⑨	19	10–25	100
	LG7/N	3.3 (3344)	⑥	⑦	⑧	219	④	88 ⑤	41	20	100
1991	LR8/R	2.5 (2475)	①	65	29	162	55	25	③	20	100
	LH0/T	3.1 (3147)	②	73	39	76	52	⑨	19	18	100
	LG7/N	3.3 (3344)	⑥	⑦	⑧	219	④	89 ⑤	41	20	100
1992–93	LR8/R	2.5 (2475)	①	65	29	162	55	25	③	20	103
	LG7/N	3.3 (3344)	⑥	⑦	⑧	219	④	89 ⑤	41	20	103

① Step 1: All bolts to 18 ft. lbs.
  Step 2: Except position "1 or 9" to 26 ft. lbs.
  Step 3: Retorque position "1 or 9" to 18 ft. lbs.
  Step 4: All bolts +90° turn
② Step 1: 33 ft. lbs.
  Step 2: +90° turn
③ Inner bolts: 37 ft. lbs.
  Outer bolts: 28 ft. lbs.
④ Step 1: 89 inch lbs.
  Step 2: +90° turn
⑤ Inch lbs.
⑥ Step 1: 35 ft. lbs.
  Step 2: +130° turn
  Step 3: +30° turn on 4 center bolts only
⑦ Step 1: 26 ft. lbs.
  Step 2: +45° turn
⑧ Step 1: 20 ft. lbs.
  Step 2: +50° turn
⑨ Manifold-to-cylinder head: 24 ft. lbs.
  Manifold-to-plenum: 16 ft. lbs.

BRAKE SPECIFICATIONS
All measurements in inches unless noted

Year	Model	Master Cylinder Bore	Brake Disc			Brake Drum Diameter			Minimum Lining Thickness	
			Original Thickness	Minimum Thickness	Maximum Runout	Original Inside Diameter	Max. Wear Limit	Maximum Machine Diameter	Front	Rear
1989	Celebrity	0.874②	0.885⑧	0.830	0.004	8.863	0.057	8.920⑦	0.030	①
	Century	0.874②	0.885⑧	0.830	0.004	8.863	0.057	8.920⑦	0.030	①
	Cutlass⑥	0.874②	0.885⑧	0.830	0.004	8.863	0.057	8.920⑦	0.030	①
	6000	0.874②	0.885⑧	0.830	0.004	8.863	0.057	8.920⑦	0.030	①
1990	Celebrity	0.874②	0.885⑧	0.830③④	0.004⑤	8.863	0.057	8.920⑦	0.030	0.030
	Century	0.874②	0.885⑧	0.830③	0.004	8.863	0.057	8.920⑦	0.030	0.030
	Cutlass⑥	0.874②	0.885⑧	0.830③	0.004	8.863	0.057	8.920⑦	0.030	0.030
	6000	0.874②	0.885⑧	0.830③④	0.004⑤	8.863	0.057	8.920⑦	0.030	0.030
1991	Century	0.874②	0.885⑧	0.830③④	0.004	8.863	0.057	8.920⑦	0.030	0.030
	Cutlass⑥	0.874②	0.885⑧	0.830③	0.004	8.863	0.057	8.920⑦	0.030	0.030
	6000	0.874②	0.885⑧	0.830③	0.004⑤	8.863	0.057	8.920⑦	0.030	0.030
1992-93	Century	0.874②	0.885⑧	0.830③	0.004	8.863	0.057	8.920⑦	0.030	0.030
	Cutlass⑥	0.874②	0.885⑧	0.830③	0.004	8.863	0.057	8.920⑦	0.030	0.030

① 0.030 in. over rivet head; if bonded, 0.062 in. over shoe
② Medium and heavy duty—0.944
③ Medium & heavy duty—0.972
④ Rear disc—0.756
⑤ Rear disc—0.003
⑥ Ciera and Cutlass
⑦ Wagon—8.877
⑧ Medium & heavy duty—1.043

WHEEL ALIGNMENT

Year	Model	Caster		Camber		Toe-in (in.)	Steering Axis Inclination (deg.)
		Range (deg.)	Preferred Setting (deg.)	Range (deg.)	Preferred Setting (deg.)		
1989	Celebrity	23/32P-2 23/32	1 23/32P	1/2N-1/2P	0	3/32N-3/32P	NA
	Century	3/4P-2 3/4P	1 3/4P	1/2N-1/2P	0	3/32N-3/32P	NA
	Cutlass①	1 5/16P-2 5/16P	1 13/16P	3/16P-1 3/16P	11/16P	3/32N-3/32P	NA
	6000	11/16P-2 11/16P	1 11/16P	1/2N-1/2P	0	3/32N-3/32P	NA
1990	Celebrity	11/16P-2 11/16	1 11/16P	1/2N-1/2P	0	3/32N-3/32P	NA
	Century	3/4P-2 3/4P	1 3/4P	1/2N-1/2P	0	3/32N-3/32P	NA
	Cutlass①	1 1/2P-2 1/2P	2P	3/16P-1 3/16P	11/16P	3/32N-3/32P	NA
	6000	11/16P-2 11/16P	1 11/16P	1/2N-1/2P	0	3/32N-3/32P	NA
1991	Celebrity	3/4P-2 3/4P	1 3/4P	1/2N-1/2P	0	3/32N-3/32P	NA
	Cutlass①	1 1/2P-2 1/2P	2P	3/16P-1 3/16P	11/16P	3/32N-3/32P	NA
	6000	11/16P-2 11/16P	1 11/16P	1/2N-1/2P	0	3/32N-3/32P	NA
1992-93	Celebrity	7/10P-1 7/10P	1 1/5P	1/2N-1/2P	0	1/5N-1/5P	NA
	Cutlass①	7/10P-1 7/10P	1 3/4P	1/2N-1/2P	0	1/5N-1/5P	NA

NA—Not available
N—Negative
P—Positive
① Ciera and Cruiser

ENGINE MECHANICAL

NOTE: Disconnecting the negative battery cable on some vehicles may interfere with the functions of the on board computer systems and may require the computer to undergo a relearning process, once the negative battery cable is reconnected.

Engine Assembly

REMOVAL & INSTALLATION

2.5L Engine

1. Relieve the fuel system pressure. Disconnect the negative battery cable.
2. Scribe reference marks at the hood supports and remove the hood. Install covers on both fenders.
3. Drain the cooling system. Remove the air cleaner assembly and ducts.
4. Disconnect engine harness connector.
5. Disconnect the vacuum, radiator and heater hose connections.
6. If equipped with air conditioning, remove the air conditioning compressor from mounting brackets and set aside. Do not discharge the air conditioning system.
7. Remove the alternator and the alternator bracket.
8. Remove the front engine strut assembly.
9. Disconnect the throttle and transaxle linkage.
10. Raise the vehicle and support it safely. Remove transaxle-to-engine bolts leaving the upper 2 bolts in place.
11. Remove front mount-to-cradle nuts.
12. Remove forward exhaust pipe.
13. Remove flywheel inspection cover and remove starter motor.
14. Remove torque converter-to-flywheel bolts.
15. Remove power steering pump and bracket with hoses attached and set aside.
16. Disconnect the fuel line.
17. Remove the 2 rear support bracket bolts.
18. Using a floor jack and a block of wood placed under the transaxle, raise engine and transaxle until engine front mount studs clear cradle.
19. Connect engine lift equipment and put tension on engine.
20. Remove the 2 remaining transaxle bolts.
21. Slide engine forward and remove from the vehicle.

To install:
22. Position the engine in the engine compartment, aligning the engine with the transaxle bellhousing.
23. With the engine supported by the lifting tool, install the 2 upper bellhousing bolts. Do not lower the engine while the jack is supporting the transaxle.
24. Remove the transaxle support jack and lower the engine onto the engine mounts. Remove the engine lift tool.
25. Install the bellhousing bolts.
26. Raise and safely support the vehicle. Install the front mount-to-cradle nuts.
27. Connect the fuel supply line at fuel filter.
28. Install the 2 rear transaxle support bracket bolts.
29. Install power steering pump and bracket.
30. Install torque converter-to-flywheel bolts.
31. Install starter motor and flywheel inspection cover.
32. Install forward exhaust pipe.
33. Lower the vehicle.
34. Install front engine strut assembly.
35. Install the alternator and the bracket.
36. If equipped with air conditioning, install the air conditioning mounting brackets and compressor.
37. Connect the heater, radiator and vacuum hoses.
38. Connect throttle and transaxle linkage.
39. Connect engine harness connector.
40. Install the air cleaner assembly and preheat tube.
41. Install the hood.
42. Connect the negative battery cable.
43. Fill cooling system and check for leaks. Start the engine and allow to come to normal operating temperature. Check for leaks.

2.8L and 3.1L Engines

1. Relieve the fuel system pressure.
2. Disconnect the negative battery cable. Scribe reference marks at the hood supports and remove the hood. Install covers on both fenders.
3. Remove the airflow tube at the air cleaner and throttle valve.
4. Drain the cooling system.
5. Disconnect vacuum hoses from all non-engine mounted components.
6. Disconnect the accelerator linkage and TV cable. Disconnect the cruise control cable, if equipped.
7. Disconnect the engine harness connector from the ECM and pull the connector through the front of dash.

Disconnect the engine harness from the junction block at the dash panel.
8. Remove the engine strut bracket from the radiator support and position aside, as required.
9. Disconnect the radiator hoses from radiator and heater hoses from engine. Disconnect and plug the transaxle cooler lines.
10. Remove the serpentine belt cover and belt.
11. On vehicles with the air conditioning compressor mounted on the upper portion of the engine, remove the AIR pump and bracket. Then, remove the air conditioning compressor from the mounting bracket and position aside.
12. If equipped, remove power steering pump from engine and set it aside.
13. Disconnect and plug the fuel lines.
14. Disconnect the EGR at the exhaust, as required.
15. Raise and safely support the vehicle.
16. On vehicles with the air conditioning compressor mounted on the lower portion of the engine, remove the air conditioning compressor from the engine. Do not discharge the air conditioning system.
17. Remove the engine front mount-to-cradle and mount-to-engine bracket retaining nuts, as required.
18. Disconnect and tag all electrical wiring at the starter. Remove the starter retaining bolts and remove the starter.
19. If equipped with automatic transaxle, remove the transaxle inspection cover and disconnect the torque converter from the flexplate.
20. Disconnect the exhaust pipe.
21. Remove the 1 transaxle-to-engine bolt from the back side of the engine.
22. Disconnect the power steering cut-off switch, if equipped.
23. Lower the vehicle.
24. Remove the exhaust crossover pipe.
25. Remove the remaining transaxle-to-engine bolts.
26. Support the transaxle by positioning a floor jack and a block of wood under the transaxle. Install an engine lift tool and remove the engine from the vehicle.

To install:
27. Position the engine in the vehicle while aligning the transaxle. Install the transaxle-to-engine bolts.
28. Position the front engine mount studs in the cradle and engine bracket.
29. Remove the engine lift tool. Raise and support the vehicle safely.
30. Install the engine mount retaining nuts.
31. If equipped, connect the power steering cut-off switch.

32. Install the 1 transaxle-to-engine bolt from the back side of the engine.

33. Connect the exhaust pipe.

34. If equipped with automatic transaxle, connect the torque converter to the flexplate and install the transaxle inspection cover.

35. Install the starter and retaining bolts. Connect the starter electrical connectors.

36. Install the engine front mount-to-cradle and mount-to-engine bracket retaining nuts.

37. On vehicles with the air conditioning compressor mounted on the lower portion of the engine, install the air conditioning compressor.

38. Lower the vehicle.

39. Connect the EGR at the exhaust, if removed.

40. Connect the fuel lines.

41. If equipped, install power steering pump.

42. On vehicles with the air conditioning compressor mounted on the upper portion of the engine, install the air conditioner compressor. Install the AIR pump and bracket.

43. Install the serpentine belt cover and belt.

44. Connect the radiator and heater hoses. Connect the transaxle cooler lines.

45. Install the engine strut bracket to the radiator support.

46. Connect the engine harness connector to the ECM.

47. Connect the accelerator linkage and TV cable. Connect the cruise control cable, if equipped.

48. Connect vacuum hoses to all non-engine mounted components.

49. Install the airflow tube at the air cleaner and throttle valve.

50. Install the hood using the reference marks made upon removal.

51. Connect the negative battery cable.

52. Fill cooling system and check for leaks. Start the engine and allow to come to normal operating temperature. Recheck for leaks. Top-up coolant.

3.3L Engine

1989–91

1. Disconnect the negative battery cable. Scribe reference marks at the hood supports and remove the hood. Install covers on both fenders.

2. Relieve the fuel system pressure.

3. Disconnect the negative battery cable and remove the air cleaner and duct assembly.

4. Drain the cooling system. Disconnect the radiator and heater hoses. Disconnect and plug the transaxle cooler lines.

5. Remove the upper engine strut and engine cooling fan.

6. Disconnect vacuum hoses from all non-engine mounted components. Disconnect all electrical connections.

7. Disconnect the fuel lines from the fuel rail.

8. Remove the cable bracket and cables from the throttle body.

9. Remove the drive belt. If equipped, remove the power steering pump and locate to the side.

10. Remove the upper transaxle-to-engine retaining bolts.

11. Raise and safely support the vehicle. Disconnect the exhaust pipe from the rear manifold.

12. Remove the air conditioning compressor and locate to the side.

13. Remove the engine mount-to-frame nuts, flywheel dust cover and flywheel-to-converter bolts.

14. Remove the lower engine-to-transaxle bolts; 1 bolt is located behind the transaxle case and engine block.

15. Lower the vehicle. Install an engine lift tool and remove the engine from the vehicle.

To install:

16. Install the engine in the engine compartment. Install the upper engine-to-transaxle bolts. Remove the engine lift tool.

17. Raise and safely support the vehicle. Connect the exhaust pipe to the rear manifold.

18. Install the lower engine-to-transaxle bolts; 1 bolt is located behind the transaxle case and engine block.

19. Install the flywheel-to-converter bolts, flywheel dust cover and engine mount-to-frame nuts.

20. Install the air conditioning compressor.

21. Lower the vehicle.

22. If equipped, install the power steering pump. Install the serpentine belt.

23. Install the cable bracket and cables to the throttle body.

24. Install the intake duct to the throttle body. Connect vacuum hoses to all non-engine mounted components. Connect all electrical connections.

25. Install the upper engine strut and engine cooling fan.

26. Connect the radiator and heater hoses. Connect the transaxle cooler lines.

27. Connect the fuel lines. Install the hood.

28. Connect the negative battery cable.

29. Fill cooling system and check for leaks. Start the engine and allow to come to normal operating temperature. Recheck for leaks. Top-up coolant.

1992–93

1. Disconnect the negative battery cable.

2. Remove the air cleaner and duct assembly.

3. Drain the coolant and disconnect the heater and radiator hoses.

4. Remove the exhaust crossover pipe.

5. Relieve the fuel pressure and disconnect the fuel lines at the quick disconnect fittings.

6. Remove the engine torque strut.

7. Remove the serpentine drive belt.

8. Disconnect the power steering pump lines from the pump.

9. Disconnect the brake vacuum booster hose from the brake booster.

10. Disconnect the TV control cables from the throttle body and bracket.

11. Remove the alternator from the vehicle.

12. Disconnect the engine electrical harness and place harness out of the way.

13. Mark and disconnect the engine vacuum hoses.

14. Disconnect the engine ground wires from the transaxle mounting bolts.

15. Remove the wiring harness retaining clips from the right side of the engine compartment.

16. Raise and safely support the vehicle.

17. Drain the engine oil. Remove both front wheels.

18. Remove the exhaust pipe from the rear manifold.

19. Remove the right engine splash shield.

20. Remove the air conditioning compressor from the brackets and set aside.

21. Remove the flywheel inspection cover and remove the starter.

22. Use a scribe and mark the relationship of the torque converter to the flywheel for reassembly.

23. Remove the flywheel to converter bolts and remove the engine mount nuts from the frame.

24. Disconnect the oil pressure sensor, knock sensor and ground connectors near the power steering pump bracket.

25. Remove the transaxle support bolts from the transaxle and remove the lower rear engine to transaxle bolt (located between transaxle case and engine block and positioned in the opposite direction).

26. Lower the vehicle and remove the transaxle to engine bolts.

27. Install an engine lifting tool and remove the engine from the vehicle.

To install:

28. Install the engine in the engine compartment. Install the upper engine-to-transaxle bolts. Remove the engine lift tool.

29. Raise and safely support the vehicle.

30. Install the lower engine-to-trans-

axle bolts; the bolt is located behind the transaxle case and engine block.

31. Install the transaxle support bracket bolts to the transaxle.

32. Connect the ground connectors and install the engine mount to frame nuts.

33. Line up the torque converter with the flywheel and install the bolts. Tighten the bolts to 46 ft. lbs. (62 Nm).

34. Install the starter and the flywheel inspection cover with bolts.

35. Install the A/C compressor to the bracket and connect the lower radiator hose.

36. Install the right engine shield and connect the exhaust pipe to the exhaust manifold.

37. Install the front wheels, fill the engine to the proper level with oil and lower the vehicle.

38. Install the right side engine wiring harness retaining clips and connect the engine ground wires to the transaxle mounting bolts.

39. Connect the engine vacuum hoses and the engine electrical harness and connectors.

40. Install the alternator and connect the TV control cables to the throttle body and the bracket.

41. Install the brake vacuum booster hose to the brake booster. Connect the power steering lines to the power steering pump.

42. Install the serpentine drive belt and the engine torque strut.

43. Connect the fuel lines and install the exhaust crossover pipe.

44. Connect the upper and lower radiator hoses and the heater hoses.

45. Install the air cleaner and duct assembly and connect the negative battery cable.

46. Fill cooling system and check for leaks. Start the engine and allow to come to normal operating temperature. Recheck for leaks. Top-up coolant.

Engine Mounts

REMOVAL & INSTALLATION

1. Disconnect the negative battery cable.

2. Raise and support the vehicle safely.

3. Using a suitable tool, support the engine and remove the engine mounting bracket nuts.

4. Raise the engine slightly until the engine mount is free from the vehicle chassis.

5. Remove the nuts holding the engine mount to the frame.

6. Remove the engine mounts and discard.

To install:

7. Install the engine mounts.

8. Install the nuts holding the engine mount to the frame.

9. Lower the engine onto the mount and install the engine mounting bracket nuts.

10. Remove the engine lift tool.

11. Connect the negative battery cable.

Cylinder Head

REMOVAL & INSTALLATION

2.5L Engine

1. Relieve the pressure in the fuel system before disconnecting any fuel line connections.

2. Disconnect the negative battery cable.

3. Raise and safely support the vehicle.

4. Disconnect the exhaust pipe and the oxygen sensor connector.

5. Lower the vehicle and disconnect the auxilary ground cable.

6. Remove the oil level indicator tube and remove the air cleaner assembly.

7. Disconnect the wiring, throttle linkage and fuel lines from the TBI assembly.

8. Disconnect the heater hoses from the intake manifold and disconnect the vacuum hoses.

9. Disconnect the electrical connectors from the cylinder head and from the intake manifold.

10. Remove the engine torque strut bolt from the upper support.

11. Remove the serpentine belt.

12. Remove the air conditioning brackets and swing the compressor aside.

13. Remove the alternator brackets and place the alternator off to the side.

14. Remove the upper power steering pump bracket and remove the radiator hoses.

15. Remove the valve cover and remove the rocker arms.

16. Remove the cylinder head bolts and remove the cylinder head from the engine.

To install:

17. Clean the cylinder head and block from any foreign matter, nicks or heavy scratches. Clean the cylinder head bolt threads and threads in the cylinder block.

18. Position the new cylinder head gasket over the dowel pins.

19. Carefully guide the cylinder head into place. Coat the cylinder head bolts with sealing compound and install finger-tight.

20. Torque the cylinder head bolts as follows:

   a. Torque the cylinder head bolts gradually to 25 ft. lbs. in the proper sequence.

   b. Torque all bolts except No. 9/I in sequence again to 22 ft. lbs. Torque No. 9/I to 29 ft. lbs.

   c. Repeat sequence. Turn all bolts, except No. 9/I, 120 degrees (2 flats). Turn No. 9/I a ¼ turn (90 degrees).

21. Install the rocker arms and rocker arm cover.

22. Install the power steering pump bracket and pump.

23. Connect the radiator hoses and engine strut rod bolt to the upper support.

24. Connect all vacuum and electrical connections to the cylinder head.

25. If equipped with air conditioning, install the compressor bracket bolts and install the compressor.

26. Install the serpentine belt.

27. If removed, install the alternator bracket-to-cylinder head bolts.

28. Connect the exhaust pipe and the oxygen sensor connector. Install the intake and exhaust manifolds.

29. Connect the throttle linkage and fuel lines.

30. Install the air cleaner and the oil level indicator tube.

31. Connect the negative battery cable.

32. Fill cooling system and check for leaks. Start the engine and allow to come to normal operating temperature. Check for leaks. Refill coolant to proper level.

2.8L and 3.1L Engines

LEFT SIDE

1. Relieve the pressure in the fuel system before disconnecting any fuel line connections. Disconnect the fuel lines.

2. Disconnect the negative battery cable. Raise and safely support the vehicle.

3. Drain the cylinder block and lower the vehicle.

4. Remove the oil level indicator tube, rocker arm cover, intake manifold and plenum, as required.

5. Remove the exhaust crossover, alternator bracket, AIR pump and brackets.

6. Disconnect and tag all electrical wiring and vacuum hoses that may interfere with the removal of the left cylinder head.

7. Loosen the rocker arm until the pushrods can be removed. Remove the pushrods. Keep the pushrods in the same order as removed.

8. Remove the cylinder head bolts. Remove the cylinder head. Do not pry on the head to loosen it.

To install:

9. Clean the cylinder head and block from any foreign matter, nicks or heavy scratches. Clean the cylinder

head bolt threads and threads in the cylinder block.

10. Position the new cylinder head gasket over the dowel pins with the words "This Side Up" facing upwards. Carefully guide the cylinder head into place.

11. Install the cylinder head bolts and tighten in sequence to 33 ft. lbs. (45 Nm). Turn an additional 90 degrees in sequence.

12. Install the pushrods. Make sure the lower ends of the pushrods are in the lifter seats. Install the rocker arm nuts and torque the nuts to 14–20 ft. lbs. (20–27 Nm).

13. Install the intake manifold.

14. Connect all electrical wiring and vacuum hoses.

15. Install the exhaust crossover, alternator and AIR pump brackets, alternator and AIR pump.

16. If removed, install the oil level indicator tube, rocker arm cover, intake manifold and plenum.

17. Connect the fuel lines.

18. Connect the negative battery cable.

19. Adjust the valve lash, as required.

RIGHT SIDE

1. Relieve the pressure in the fuel system before disconnecting any fuel line connections.

2. Disconnect the negative battery cable. Raise the vehicle and support it safely.

3. Drain the cylinder block and lower the vehicle.

4. If equipped, remove the cruise control servo bracket, the air management valve and hose and the intake manifold.

5. Remove the exhaust pipe at crossover, crossover and heat shield, as required.

6. Disconnect and tag all electrical wiring and vacuum hoses that may interfere with the removal of the right cylinder head.

7. Remove the rocker cover. Loosen the rocker arm nuts and remove the pushrods. Keep the pushrods in the order in which they were removed.

8. Remove the cylinder head bolts. Remove the cylinder head. Do not pry on the head to loosen it.

To install:

9. Clean the cylinder head and block from any foreign matter, nicks or heavy scratches. Clean the cylinder head bolt threads and threads in the cylinder block.

10. Position the new cylinder head gasket over the dowel pins with the words "This Side Up" facing upwards. Carefully guide the cylinder head into place. Install the pushrods and loosely retain with the rocker arms.

11. Install the cylinder head bolts

and tighten in sequence to 33 ft. lbs. (45 Nm). Turn an additional 90 degrees in sequence.

12. Install the pushrods. Make sure the lower ends of the pushrods are in the lifter seats. Install the rocker arm nuts and torque the nuts to 14–20 ft. lbs. (20–27 Nm).

13. Install the intake manifold.

14. Install the rocker cover.

15. Connect all electrical wiring and vacuum hoses.

16. If removed, install the crossover exhaust pipe and heat shield.

17. If equipped, install the cruise control servo bracket, the air management valve and hose.

18. Connect the negative battery cable.

19. Fill cooling system and check for leaks. Start the engine and allow to come to normal operating temperature. Recheck for leaks. Top-up coolant.

20. Adjust the valve lash, as required.

3.3L Engine

1. Relieve the pressure in the fuel system before disconnecting any fuel line connections.

2. Disconnect the negative battery cable. Raise the vehicle and support it safely.

3. Drain the cylinder block and lower the vehicle.

4. Remove the exhaust crossover and remove the intake manifold and exhaust manifold.

5. Remove the valve cover.

6. Remove the ignition module and coils as a unit.

7. Disconnect and tag all electrical wiring and vacuum hoses, as necessary.

8. If equipped with air conditioning,

1. Apply sealing compound No. 102080 or equivalent to bolts shown

2. Mounting surfaces of block assy., head assy. and both sides of gasket must be free of oil.

3. Locating pins

remove the air conditioning compressor and position to the side.

9. Remove the alternator and power steering pump and position to the side. Remove the belt tensioner assembly.

10. Remove the rocker arm assembly, guide plate and pushrods.

11. Remove the cylinder head bolts and remove the cylinder head.

To install:

12. Clean the cylinder head and block of any foreign matter, nicks or heavy scratches. Clean the cylinder head bolt threads and threads in the cylinder block.

13. Position the new cylinder head gasket on the block.

14. Carefully guide the cylinder head into place.

15. Coat the cylinder head bolts with sealing compound and install into the head. Tighten the cylinder head bolts

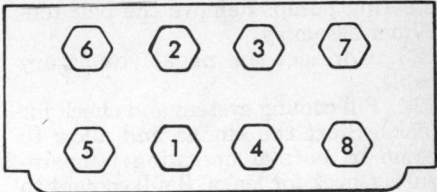

Cylinder head torque sequence—2.8L and 3.1L engines

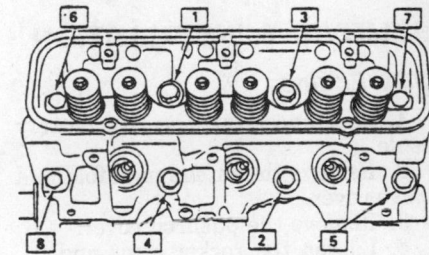

Cylinder head torque sequence—3.3L engine

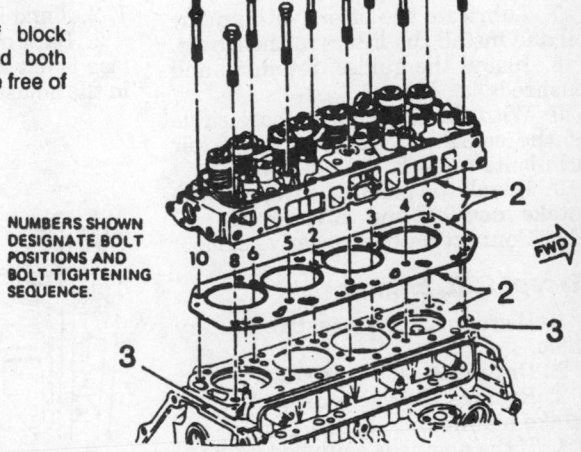

NUMBERS SHOWN DESIGNATE BOLT POSITIONS AND BOLT TIGHTENING SEQUENCE.

Cylinder head torque sequence—2.5L engine

according to the following procedure:

    a. Tighten in sequence to 35 ft. lbs. (47 Nm).

    b. Using an appropriate torque angle gauge, rotate each bolt in sequence an additional 130 degrees.

    c. Rotate the center 4 bolts an additional 30 degrees in sequence.

16. Install the pushrods, guide plate and rocker arm assembly. Tighten the rocker arm pivot bolts to 28 ft. lbs. (38 Nm).

17. Install the intake manifold and exhaust manifold.

18. Install the valve cover.

19. Remove the ignition module and coils as a unit, as required.

20. Connect all electrical wiring and vacuum hoses.

21. If equipped with air conditioning, install the air conditioning compressor.

22. Install the alternator and power steering pump. Remove the belt tensioner assembly.

23. Connect the negative battery cable.

24. Fill cooling system and check for leaks. Start the engine and allow to come to normal operating temperature. Check for leaks. Refill coolant to proper level.

Valve Lifters

REMOVAL & INSTALLATION

2.5L Engine

1. Disconnect the negative battery cable.

2. Remove the intake manifold and valve cover.

3. Remove the pushrod cover.

4. Loosen the rocker arms and rotate to clear the pushrods.

5. Remove the pushrods, retainer and guide.

6. Remove the lifters. Keep all components separated so they may be reinstalled in the same location.

To install:

7. Lubricate the lifters with engine oil and install the lifters in their bore.

8. Install the guides, retainers and pushrods.

9. With the lifter on the base circle of the camshaft, tighten the rocker arm bolts to 24 ft. lbs. (32 Nm).

10. Install the pushrod cover and the intake manifold and valve cover.

11. Connect battery negative cable.

Except 2.5L Engine

1. Disconnect the negative battery cable.

2. Drain the cooling system.

3. Remove the valve cover and the intake manifold.

4. If the engine is equipped with individual rocker arms, loosen the rocker arm adjusting nut and rotate the arm so as to clear the pushrod.

5. If the engine is equipped with a rocker shaft assembly, remove the rocker shaft retaining bolts/nuts and remove the shaft assembly.

NOTE: Be sure to keep all valve train parts in order so they may be reinstalled in their original locations and with the same mating surfaces as when removed.

6. Remove the pushrods and valve lifters using tool J-3049 or equivalent.

To install:

7. Lubricate the bearing surfaces with Molykote® or equivalent.

8. Install the lifters in their original locations.

9. With the lifter on the base circle of the camshaft, tighten the rocker arm bolts to 14–20 ft. lbs. (20–27 Nm).

10. Connect the negative battery cable.

11. Adjust the valves, as required.

Valve Lash

ADJUSTMENT

Except 2.8L Engine

Hydraulic valve lifter keep all parts of the valve train in constant contact and adjust automatically to maintain zero lash under all conditions.

2.8L Engine

Anytime the valve train has been disturbed, the valve lash must be readjusted.

1. Crank the engine until the timing mark on the damper aligns with the 0 mark on the timing scale. Both valves in the No. 1 cylinder should be closed. If the valves are moving as the timing marks align, the engine is in the No. 4 firing position. Turn the crankshaft one more revolution. With the engine in the No. 1 firing position, adjust the following valves: exhaust— 1, 2, 3 and intake—1, 5, 6.

2. Back out the adjusting nut until lash is felt at the pushrod. Then, turn in the adjusting nut until all lash is re-

moved. This can be determine by rotating the pushrod while turning the adjusting nut. When all lash has been removed, turn the adjusting nut in 1½ additional turns to center the lifter plunger.

3. Rotate the crankshaft one full revolution, until the timing mark on the damper aligns with the 0 mark on the timing scale once again. This is the No. 4 firing position. Adjust the following valves: exhaust—4, 5, 6 and intake—2, 3, 4.

Rocker Arms

REMOVAL & INSTALLATION

2.5L Engine

1. Relieve pressure in the fuel system before disconnecting any fuel lines.

2. Disconnect the negative battery cable.

3. Remove the valve cover.

4. If only the pushrod is being removed, loosen the rocker arm bolt and swing the rocker arm aside.

5. Remove the rocker arm nut and ball.

6. Lift the rocker arm off the stud, keeping rocker arms in order for installation.

To install:

7. If the pushrod was removed, install through the cylinder head and into the lifter seat.

8. Install the guide, rocker arm, ball and bolt. Tighten to 24 ft. lbs. (32 Nm).

9. Install the valve cover.

10. Connect the negative battery cable.

2.8L and 3.1L Engines

1. Relieve pressure in the fuel system before disconnecting any fuel lines.

2. Disconnect the negative battery cable. Remove the valve covers.

3. Remove the rocker arm nuts, pivot balls, rocker arms and pushrods. Keep all components separated so they may be reinstalled in the same location.

NOTE: The intake and exhaust pushrods are of different lengths.

To install:

4. Install the pushrods in their original location. Be sure they are seated in the lifter.

5. Coat the bearing surfaces of the rocker arms and pivots balls with Molykote® or equivalent.

6. If equipped with adjustable lifters, install the rocker arms and pivot balls. Loosely retain with the rocker

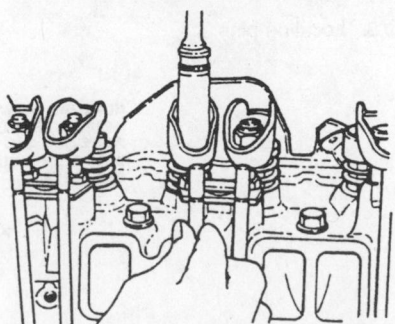

Adjusting valve lash—2.8L engine

arms nuts until the valve lash is eliminated.

7. If equipped with non-adjustable lifters, install the pushrods. Make sure the lower ends of the pushrods are in the lifter seats. Install the rocker arm nuts and torque the nuts to 14–20 ft. lbs. (20–27 Nm).

8. Install the valve cover.

9. Connect the negative battery cable.

10. Adjust valve lash, as required.

3.3L Engine

1. Relieve pressure in the fuel system before disconnecting any fuel lines. Disconnect the negative battery cable.

2. Remove the valve covers.

3. Remove the rocker arm bolts, pivots, and rocker arms assembly. Keep all components separated so they may be reinstalled in the same location.

To install:

4. Install the rocker arms, pivots and bolts. Tighten bolts to 37 ft. lbs. (51 Nm).

5. Install the valve covers.

6. Connect the negative battery cable.

Intake Manifold

REMOVAL & INSTALLATION

2.5L Engine

1. Relieve the pressure in the fuel system before disconnecting any fuel line connections.

2. Disconnect the negative battery cable.

3. Drain the coolant and disconnect the PCV hose at the TBI and at the valve cover.

4. Disconnect the fuel lines and position to the side.

5. Disconnect the vacuum hoses including the power brake booster hoses.

6. Disconnect the wiring and throttle linkage from the TBI unit.

7. Disconnect the transaxle downshift linkage bracket and if equipped with cruise control, disconnect the servo cable.

8. Disconnect the throttle and TV cable and position to the side for clearance.

9. Remove the heater hose and remove the intake manifold retaining bolts.

10. Remove the intake manifold from the vehicle.

To install:

11. Clean the cylinder head and intake manifold surfaces from any foreign matter, nicks or heavy scratches.

12. Install the intake manifold with a new gasket and tighten the retaining

bolts in sequence to the specified torque.

13. Connect the heater hose, throttle and TV cable.

14. If equipped with cruise control, connect the servo cable.

15. Install the transaxle downshift linkage bracket.

16. Connect the wiring and throttle linkage to the TBI assembly.

17. Connect the vacuum hoses and fuel lines. Connect the PCV hose at the TBI and at the valve cover.

18. Install the air cleaner and connect the negative battery cable.

19. Fill coolant to proper level and check for leaks. Start the engine and allow to come to normal operating temperature. Recheck for leaks. Check coolant level.

2.8L and 3.1L Engines

1. Relieve the pressure in the fuel system before disconnecting any fuel line connections.

2. Disconnect the negative battery cable.

3. Disconnect the accelerator and TV cable bracket at the plenum.

4. Disconnect the throttle body at the plenum.

5. Disconnect the EGR valve at the plenum.

6. Remove the plenum.

7. Disconnect the fuel inlet and return pipes at the fuel rail.

8. Remove the serpentine belt.

9. Remove the power steering pump and lay it aside.

10. Disconnect the alternator and lay it aside.

11. Loosen the alternator bracket.

12. Disconnect the idle air vacuum hose at the throttle body.

13. Disconnect the wires at the injectors.

14. Disconnect the fuel rail.

15. Remove the breather tube.

16. Remove both rocker covers.

17. Drain the cooling system.

18. Disconnect the radiator hose at the thermostat housing.

19. Disconnect the wires at the coolant sensor and the oil sending switch.

20. Remove the coolant sensor.

21. Disconnect the bypass hose at the fill neck and head.

22. Loosen the rocker arms and remove the pushrods.

23. Remove the intake manifold bolts and remove the intake manifold.

To install:

24. Place a ³⁄₁₆ in. (5mm) diameter bead GM sealer 1052917 or equivalent, on each ridge.

25. Position a new intake manifold gasket.

26. Install the pushrods and tighten the rocker arm nuts to 14–20 ft. lbs. (19–27 Nm).

27. Install the intake manifold and torque the bolts to specifications.

28. Connect the bypass hose to the filler neck and head.

29. Install the coolant sensor.

30. Connect the wires to the coolant sensor and the oil sending switch.

31. Connect the radiator hose to the thermostat housing.

32. Install both rocker covers.

33. Install the breather tube.

34. Connect the fuel rail.

35. Connect the wires to the injectors.

36. Connect the idle air vacuum hose to the throttle body.

37. Tighten the alternator bracket.

38. Connect the alternator electrical connectors.

39. Install the power steering pump.

40. Install the serpentine belt.

41. Connect the fuel inlet and return pipes to the fuel rail.

42. Install the plenum.

43. Connect the EGR valve to the plenum.

44. Connect the throttle body to the plenum.

45. Connect the accelerator and TV cable bracket to the plenum.

46. Connect the negative battery cable.

47. Fill cooling system and check for leaks. Start the engine and allow to come to normal operating temperature. Recheck for leaks. Top-up coolant.

48. Adjust the valve, as required.

3.3L Engine

1. Relieve the pressure in the fuel system before disconnecting any fuel line connections.

2. Disconnect the negative battery cable and remove the air cleaner assembly.

3. Drain the cooling system.

4. Remove the serpentine belt, alternator and braces and power steering pump braces.

5. Disconnect the rear spark plug wires and place to the side.

6. Remove the coolant bypass hose, heater pipe and upper radiator hose.

7. Remove the air inlet duct, throttle cable bracket and cables.

8. Disconnect and tag all vacuum hoses and electrical connectors, as necessary.

9. Remove the fuel rail, vapor canister purge line and heater hose from the throttle body.

10. Remove the intake manifold retaining bolts and intake manifold.

To install:

11. Clean the cylinder head and intake manifold surfaces from any foreign matter, nicks or heavy scratches.

12. Apply sealer 12345336 or equivalent, to the ends of the manifold seals.

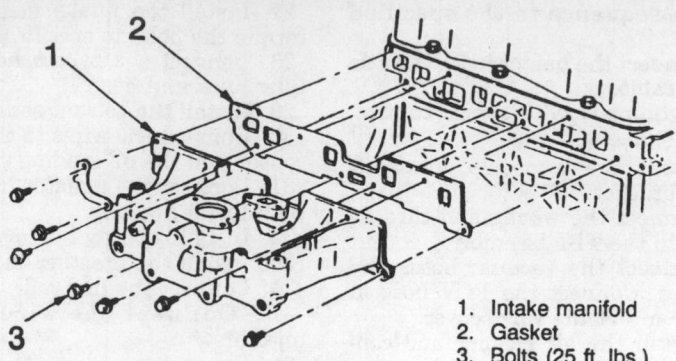

1. Intake manifold
2. Gasket
3. Bolts (25 ft. lbs.)

Intake manifold assembly—2.5L engine

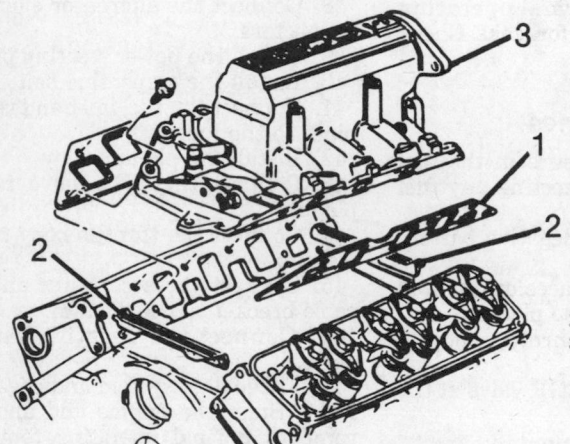

1. Intake manifold gasket
2. Intake manifold seal
3. Intake manifold

Intake manifold assembly—3.3L engine

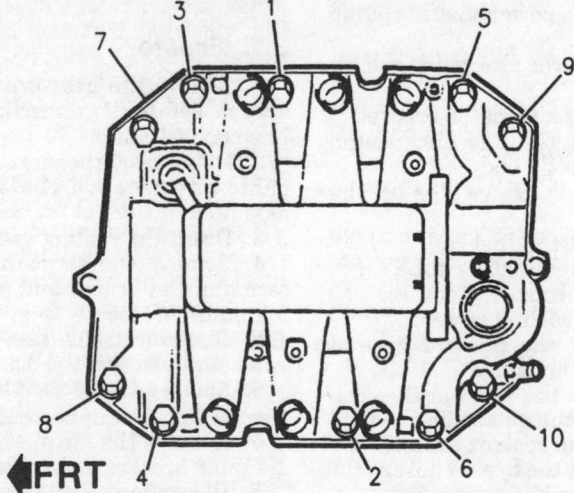

◄FRT

Intake manifold assembly—3.3L engine

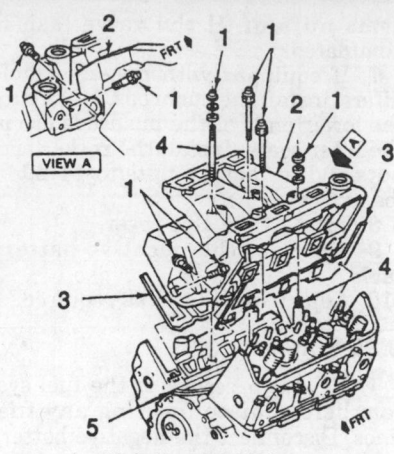

VIEW A

1. 16 ft. lbs. (22 Nm)
   Then 23 ft. lbs. (32 Nm)
   Retorque 23 ft. lbs. (32 Nm) in sequence
2. Intake manifold
3. Gasket
4. 24 ft. lbs. (33 Nm)
5. Sealer

Intake manifold assembly—2.8L and 3.1L engines

18. Install the serpentine belt, alternator and braces and power steering pump braces.
19. Connect the negative battery cable.
20. Fill cooling system and check for leaks. Start the engine and allow to come to normal operating temperature. Recheck for leaks. Top-up coolant.

Exhaust Manifold

REMOVAL & INSTALLATION

2.5L Engine

1. Disconnect the negative battery cable. Remove the air cleaner.
2. Remove the engine torque strut bolts at the cylinder head.
3. Remove the engine torque strut bracket from the cylinder head.
4. Disconnect the oxygen sensor connector and remove oil level indicator tube and nut. Move the tube aside.
5. Disconnect the exhaust pipe from the manifold.
6. Remove the manifold attaching bolts and remove the manifold.
To install:
7. Install the exhaust manifold and gasket to the cylinder head. Torque all bolts in sequence to the specified torque value.
8. Connect the exhaust pipe to the manifold.
9. Install the dipstick tube attaching bolt and the engine mount bracket to the cylinder head.
10. Connect the oxygen sensor con-

Clean the intake manifold bolts and bolt holes. Apply thread lock compound 1052624 or equivalent, to the intake manifold bolt threads before assembly.

13. Install the new gasket and intake manifold. Tighten the intake manifold bolts twice to 88 inch lbs. (10 Nm) in the proper sequence.

14. Install the fuel rail, vapor canister purge line and heater hose from the throttle body.
15. Connect all vacuum hoses and electrical connectors including the spark plug wires.
16. Install the air inlet duct, throttle cable bracket and cables.
17. Install the coolant bypass hose, heater pipe and upper radiator hose.

nector and install the torque rod bracket and torque rod.

11. Install the air cleaner, connect the negative battery cable and inspect for any exhaust leaks

2.8L and 3.1L Engines

LEFT SIDE

1. Disconnect the negative battery cable.

2. Remove the air supply plumbing from the exhaust manifold, as required.

3. Remove the coolant recovery bottle, if necessary.

4. Remove the serpentine belt cover and belt, as required.

5. Remove the air conditioning compressor and lay aside, if necessary.

6. Remove the right side torque strut, air conditioning and torque strut mounting bracket, as required.

7. Remove the heat shield, if equipped.

8. Remove the exhaust crossover pipe at the manifold.

9. Remove the exhaust manifold retaining bolts and manifold.

To install:

10. Install the exhaust manifold and retaining bolts. Tighten to 15–22 ft. lbs. (20–30).

11. Install the exhaust crossover pipe at the manifold.

12. Install the heat shield, if equipped.

13. If removed, install the right side torque strut, air conditioning and torque strut mounting bracket.

14. If removed, install the air conditioning compressor.

15. If removed, install the serpentine belt and cover.

16. If removed, install the coolant recovery bottle.

17. Install the air supply plumbing to the exhaust manifold.

18. Connect the negative battery cable.

RIGHT SIDE

1. Disconnect the negative battery cable.

2. Raise and safely support the vehicle.

3. Disconnect the exhaust pipe and lower the vehicle.

4. Remove the air cleaner assembly, breather, mass air flow sensor and heat shield.

5. Remove the crossover at the manifold.

6. Remove the accelerator and TV cables and brackets, as required.

7. Remove the exhaust manifold retaining bolts and remove the manifold.

To install:

8. Install the exhaust manifold and retaining bolts. Tighten to 15–22 ft. lbs. (20–30 Nm).

9. If removed, install the accelerator, TV cables and brackets.

10. Install the crossover at the manifold.

11. Install the air cleaner assembly, breather, mass air flow sensor and heat shield.

12. Raise and safely support the vehicle.

13. Connect the exhaust pipe and lower the vehicle.

14. Connect the negative battery cable.

1989–90 2.3L Engine

LEFT SIDE

1. Disconnect the negative battery cable.

2. Remove the air cleaner assembly. Remove the spark plug wires and the spark plugs.

3. Remove the alternator and remove the engine torque strut and mount brackets.

4. Remove the exhaust crossover pipe. Remove the oil level indicator and tube assembly.

5. Remove the engine cooling fan assembly and exhaust heat sheild.

6. Remove the manifold support bracket and remove the exhaust manifold retaining bolts and the manifold.

To install:

7. Install the exhaust manifold, bolts and studs. Tighten to 38 ft. lbs. (52 Nm).

8. Install the manifold support bracket and install the engine heat shield.

9. Install the cooling fan assembly and oil fill tube assembly.

10. Install the exhaust crossover pipe. Install the spark plugs and plug wires.

11. Install the torque strut and mount bracket.

12. Install the alternator and install the air cleaner assembly.

13. Connect the negative battery cable and inspect for exhaust leaks.

RIGHT SIDE

1. Disconnect the negative battery cable.

2. Remove the air cleaner and duct assembly.

3. Remove the sepentine belt and drain the coolant.

4. Disconnect the power steering pump brace and remove the bolts from the bracket. Position the pump out of the way.

5. Remove the spark plug wires and disconnect the oxygen sensor wire connector.

6. Remove the engine lift bracket nuts from the exhaust manifold.

7. Disconnect the coolant tube, engine lift bracket and the fuel line clamp screw from the coolant tube assembly and place to the side.

8. Remove the right bank set of spark plugs and remove the exhaust crossover tube.

9. Remove the transaxle fill tube retaining bolt and move tube out of way.

10. Raise and safely support the vehicle.

11. Disconnect the exhaust pipe from the manifold and lower the vehicle.

12. Remove the exhaust heat shield retaining nuts and pull the shield back.

13. Remove the manifold studs and remove the manifold.

To install:

14. Install the exhaust manifold and retaining bolts. Tighten to 18 ft. lbs. (26 Nm). Install the manifold heat shield.

15. Install the exhaust heat shield retaining nuts and raise and safely support the vehicle.

16. Connect the exhaust pipe to the manifold and lower the vehicle.

17. Install the transaxle fill tube retaining bolt and install the exhaust crossover pipe.

18. Install the right bank side set of spark plugs.

19. Install the coolant tube, engine lift bracket and fuel line clamp screw to the coolant tube assembly.

20. Install the spark plug wires, oxygen sensor connector.

21. Install the power steering pump and bracket.

22. Refill the ccolant and install the serpentine belt.

23. Install the air cleaner assembly and connect the negative battery cable. Inspect for exhaust leaks.

1991–92 2.3L Engine

LEFT SIDE

1. Remove the air cleaner assembly. Disconnect the negative battery cable.

2. Remove the alternator from the vehicle.

3. Remove the engine torque strut and mount brackets.

4. Mark and disconnect the spark plug wires and remove the spark plugs.

5. Remove the exhaust crossover pipe and remove the oil level indicator tube assembly.

6. Remove the engine cooling fan assembly.

7. Remove the exhaust heat shield and the manifold support bracket.

8. Remove the manifold studs and bolts and remove the manifold.

To install:

9. Install the manifold, bolts and studs.

10. Install the manifold support bracket. Install the exhaust heat shield.

11. Install the cooling fan assembly. Install the oil indicator tube assembly.

12. Install the exhaust crossover pipe. Install the spark plugs and wires.

13. Install the engine torque strut and mount bracket

14. Install the alternator and install the air cleaner assembly.

15. Connect the negative battery cable.

RIGHT SIDE

1. Disconnect the negative battery cable. Remove the air cleaner and duct assembly.

2. Remove the serpentine belt and drain the coolant.

3. Remove the power steering pump brace and bolts and move pump forward.

4. Mark and remove spark plug wires.

5. Disconnect the oxygen sensor connector and remove the engine lift bracket nuts from the exhaust manifold.

6. Remove the coolant tube, engine lift bracket and fuel line clamp screw from the coolant tube assembly and set to the side.

7. Remove the right bank of spark plugs and remove the exhaust crossover tube.

8. Remove the transaxle fill tube retaining bolt and remove tube for access.

9. Raise and safely support the vehicle.

10. Disconnect the exhaust pipe from the manifold and lower the vehicle.

11. Remove the exhaust heat shield retaining nuts and pull shield out of the way.

12. Remove the manifold studs and remove the manifold. Remove the heat shield.

To install:

13. Install the manifold, studs and heat shield assembly.

14. Raise and safely support the vehicle, connect the exhaust pipe to the manifold. Lower the vehicle.

15. Install the transaxle fill tube retaining bolt and install the exhaust crossover pipe.

16. Install the right bank of spark plugs.

17. Install the coolant tube, engine lift bracket and fuel line clamp screw.

18. Install the engine lift bracket nuts to the exhaust manifold.

19. Connect the oxygen sensor connector and connect the spark plug wires.

20. Install the power steering pump brace and pump bolts to the mounting bracket.

21. Refill the coolant to the proper level and install the serpentine belt.

22. Install the air cleaner and duct assembly. Connect the negative battery cable.

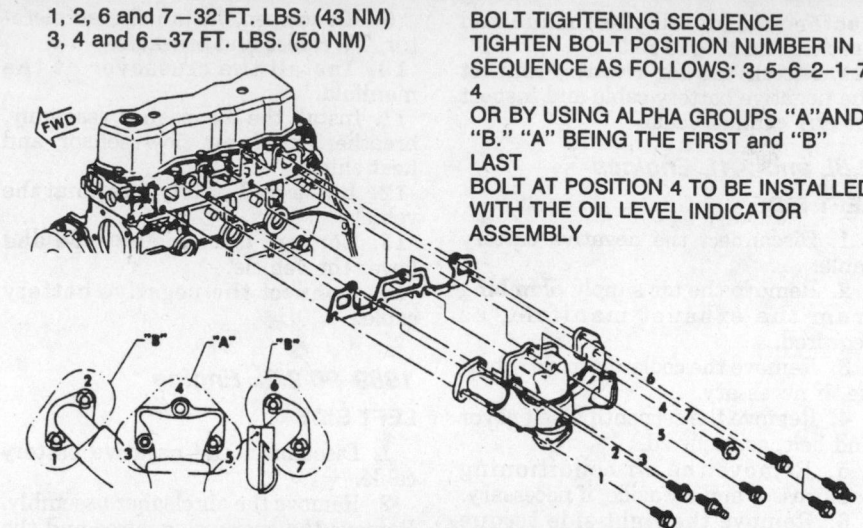

1, 2, 6 and 7—32 FT. LBS. (43 NM)
3, 4 and 6—37 FT. LBS. (50 NM)

BOLT TIGHTENING SEQUENCE
TIGHTEN BOLT POSITION NUMBER IN SEQUENCE AS FOLLOWS: 3–5–6–2–1–7–4
OR BY USING ALPHA GROUPS "A" AND "B." "A" BEING THE FIRST and "B" LAST
BOLT AT POSITION 4 TO BE INSTALLED WITH THE OIL LEVEL INDICATOR ASSEMBLY

Exhaust manifold assembly—2.5L engine

1. Studs
2. Exhaust manifold
3. Heat shield
4. Nuts

Left exhaust manifold—3.3L engine

1. Oxygen sensor
2. Studs
3. Nuts
4. Exhaust manifold heat shield
5. Exhaust manifold
6. Bolt

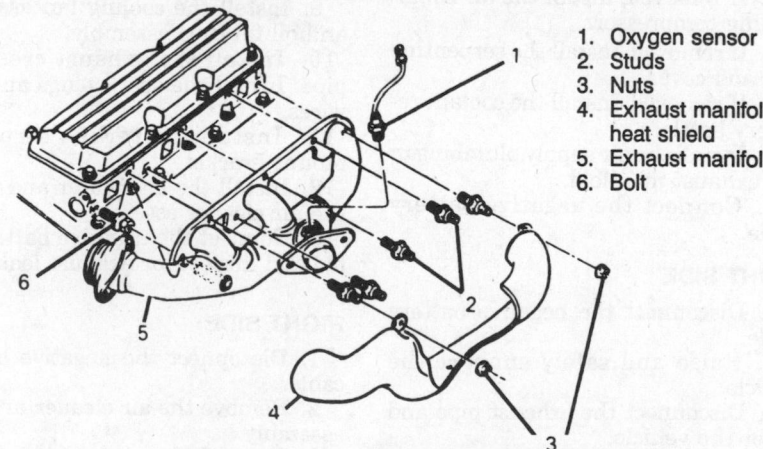

Right exhaust manifold—3.3L engine

Timing Chain Front Cover

REMOVAL & INSTALLATION

2.5L Engine
1989–90

1. Relieve the pressure in the fuel

system before disconnecting any fuel line connections.

2. Disconnect the negative battery cable.

3. Remove the serpentine belt.

4. Remove the inner fender splash shield. Remove the crankshaft pulley.

5. Remove the alternator lower bracket and support the engine with the proper tool.

6. Remove the engine mount and bracket assembly.

7. Remove the oil pan-to-front cover screws and front cover-to-block screws.

8. Pull the cover slightly forward, just enough to allow cutting of the oil pan front seal flush with the block on both sides.

9. Remove the front cover and attached portion of the pan seal.

10. Clean the gasket surfaces thoroughly.

To install:

11. Cut the tabs from the new oil pan front seal.

12. Install the seal on the front cover pressing the tips into the holes provided.

13. Coat the new gasket with sealer and position it on the front cover.

14. Apply a ⅛ in. bead of silicone sealer to the joint formed at the oil pan and stock.

15. Align the front cover seal with a centering tool and install the front cover. Tighten the screws. Install the pulley and connect the battery negative cable.

1992–93

1. Disconnect the negative battery cable.

2. Remove the drive belt tensioner.

3. Remove the upper front cover to engine bolts.

4. Raise and safely support the vehicle. Remove the right front wheel.

5. Remove the right side engine splash shield. Remove the crankshaft pulley.

6. Remove the lower front cover bolts and remove the front cover.

7. Clean the gasket surfaces thoroughly.

To install:

8. Apply a ⅛ in. bead of silicone sealer to the oil pan, engine block and front cover.

9. Align the front cover seal with a centering tool and install the front cover. Tighten the screws and bolts.

10. Install the pulley and right engine splash shield.

11. Install the right wheel and lower the vehicle.

12. Install the upper cover bolts and the drive belt tensioner.

13. Connect the battery negative cable.

2.8L and 3.1L Engines

1. Relieve the pressure in the fuel system before disconnecting any fuel line connections. Disconnect the negative battery cable.

2. Drain the cooling system.

3. Remove the serpentine belt and tensioner.

4. Remove the alternator and power steering pump. Locate and support these accessories to the side.

5. Raise and support the vehicle safely.

6. Remove the inner splash shield. Remove the torsion damper using tool J–24420–B or equivalent.

7. Remove the flywheel cover at the transaxle and starter.

8. Remove the serpentine belt idler pulley.

9. Drain the engine oil. Remove the oil pan and lower front cover bolts.

10. Lower the vehicle.

11. Remove the radiator hose at the water pump. Remove the heater hose at fill pipe.

12. Remove the bypass hose and overflow hoses. Remove the canister purge hose.

13. Remove the upper front cover retaining bolts and remove the front cover.

14. After removing the timing cover, pry oil seal from front of cover. Lubricate the seal lip and install new lip seal with lip, open side of seal, facing toward the cylinder block. Carefully drive or press seal into place.

To install:

15. Clean the mating surfaces of the front cover and cylinder block.

16. Install a new gasket. Make sure not to damage the sealing surfaces. Apply sealer 1052080 or equivalent, to the sealing surface of the front cover.

17. Position the front cover on the engine block and install the upper cover bolt.

18. Raise and safely support the vehicle. Install the oil pan and lower cover bolts.

19. Install the serpentine belt idler pulley.

20. Install the flywheel cover to the transaxle. Install the starter.

21. Install the torsion damper. Install the inner splash shield.

22. Lower the vehicle.

23. Install the bypass hose and overflow hoses. Install the canister purge hose.

24. Connect the radiator hose to the water pump. Connect the heater hose to fill pipe.

25. Install the alternator and power steering pump.

26. Install the tensioner serpentine belt.

27. Connect the negative battery cable.

3.3L Engine

1. Relieve the pressure in the fuel system before disconnecting any fuel line connections. Disconnect the negative battery cable.

2. Drain the cooling system and drain the engine oil.

3. Remove the serpentine belt.

4. Remove the heater pipes. Remove the coolant bypass hose and lower radiator hose from cover.

5. Raise and support the vehicle safely.

6. Remove the inner splash shield.

7. Remove the crankshaft balancer.

8. Disconnect all electrical connectors at the camshaft sensor, crankshaft sensor and oil pressure sender.

9. Remove the oil pan-to-front cover retaining bolts, front cover retaining bolts and remove the front cover.

To install:

10. Clean the mating surfaces of the front cover and cylinder block.

11. Install a new gasket on the cylinder block. Install the front cover. Apply sealer to the threads of the cover retaining bolts and secure the cover. Tighten the bolts to 22 ft. lbs. (30 Nm).

12. Install the oil pan-to-front cover bolts. Tighten the bolts to 88 inch lbs. (10 Nm).

13. Reconnect the camshaft sensor, crankshaft sensor and oil pressure sender electrical connectors. Adjust the crankshaft sensor using tool J–37087 or equivalent.

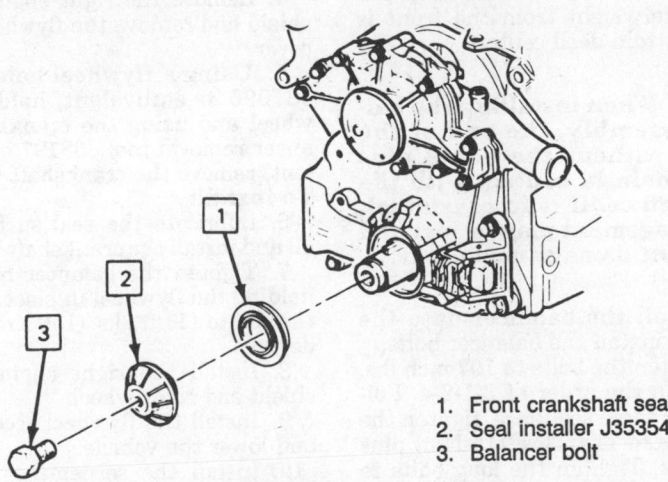

1. Front crankshaft seal
2. Seal installer J35354
3. Balancer bolt

Installing front cover oil seal

14. Install the crankshaft balancer.
15. Install the inner splash shield.
16. Lower the vehicle.
17. Install the heater pipes. Install the coolant bypass hose and lower radiator hose from cover.
18. Install the serpentine belt.
19. Connect the negative battery cable.
20. Fill cooling system and check for leaks. Start the engine and allow to come to normal operating temperature. Check for leaks. Refill coolant to proper level.

Front Cover Oil Seal

REPLACEMENT

1. Remove the harmonic crankshaft balancer.
2. Pry out the old oil seal with a screwdriver.

NOTE: Use extra caution to avoid damaging seal bore or seal contact surfaces.

3. Using oil seal installation tool (J35354 or equivalent) install the oil seal.
4. Tighten the crankshaft balancer bolt until the seal becomes seated and then remove the installation tool.
5. Install the crankshaft balancer.

Crankshaft Balancer

REMOVAL & INSTALLATION

2.5L Engine

1. Disconnect the negative battery cable and drain the engine oil.
2. Remove the oil pan.
3. Remove the crankshaft balancer retaining bolts and remove the balancer.
To install:
4. Rotate the crankshaft until the 4th counterweight from the front is exactly bottom dead center.

NOTE: When installing the balancer assembly, the end of the housing without the dowel pins must remain in contact with the block surface. If it loses contact, gear engagement may be lost and permanent damage may occur.

5. Install the balancer onto the block and install the balancer bolts.
6. Tighten the bolts to 107 inch lbs. (12 Nm) in the order of 3-1-2-4. Following the same sequence, tighten the short bolts to 11 ft. lbs. (15 Nm) plus 72 degrees. Tighten the long bolts to 11 ft. lbs. (15 Nm) plus 86 degrees.

7. Rotate the crankshaft several times and check clearance between the 4th counterweight and the balancer weights.
8. Install the oil pan and connect the negative battery cable. Refill the engine with oil and inspect for leaks.

2.8L and 3.1L Engines

1. Disconnect the negative battery cable.
2. Remove the serpentine belt, raise and safely support the vehicle.
3. Remove the right side inner fender splash shield and remove the flexplate shield.
4. Remove the balancer retaining bolt and have an assistant hold the flywheel from turning.
5. Install the torsional damper removal tool J2440B or equivalent, and turn the puller screw to remove the balancer.
To install:
6. Coat front contact seal area with engine oil.
7. Apply sealant to key and keyway and place balancer in position over key on the crankshaft.
8. Pull the balancer onto the crankshaft and install the damper installation tool J29113 or equivalent.
9. Pull the balancer into position and remove the tool.
10. Install the balancer retaining bolt and tighten to 77 ft. lbs. (105 Nm).
11. Install the flexplate shield and engine splash shield.
12. Install the serpentine belt and connect the negative battery cable.

3.3L Engine

1. Disconnect the negative battery cable.
2. Remove the serpentine belt.
3. Raise and safely support the vehicle. Remove the right front wheel.
4. Remove the right engine splash shield and remove the flywheel access cover.
5. Using a flywheel holding tool J37096 or equivalent, hold the flywheel and using the crankshaft balancer removal tool J38197 or equivalent, remove the crankshaft balancer.
To install:
6. Lubricate the seal surface with oil and install the crankshaft balancer.
7. Tighten the balancer bolt while holding the flywheel in place. Tighten the bolt to 111 ft. lbs. (150 Nm) plus 76 degrees.
8. Install the right engine splash shield and right wheel.
9. Install the flywheel access cover and lower the vehicle.
10. Install the serpentine belt and connect the negative battery cable.

Timing Chain and Sprockets

REMOVAL & INSTALLATION

2.5L Engine

1989–90

NOTE: The camshaft gear is press fitted on the camshaft. If replacement of the camshaft gear is necessary, the engine must be removed from the vehicle and the camshaft and gear removed from the engine.

1. Relieve the pressure in the fuel system before disconnecting any fuel line connections.
2. Disconnect the negative battery cable.
3. Remove the engine from the vehicle.
4. Remove the camshaft and gear assembly from the engine block.
5. Using an arbor press and adapter, remove the gear from the camshaft. Position the thrust plate to avoid damage by interference with the Woodruff® key as the gear is removed.
To install:
6. Support the camshaft at the back of the front journal in the arbor press using press plate adapters.
7. Position the spacer ring thrust plate over the end of the shaft and Woodruff® key in keyway.
8. Press the gear on the shaft with the bottom against the spacer ring. Measure the end clearance at the thrust plate. Clearance should be within 0.0015–0.0050 in. (0.0381–1.270mm).
9. If the clearance is less than 0.0015 in. (0.0381mm), replace the spacer ring.
10. If more than 0.0050 in. (1.270mm), make certain the gear is seated properly against the spacer. If the clearance is still excessive, replace the thrust plate.
11. Measure the backlash at position outside the 2 retainer plate access holes and at 2 other areas 90 degrees from these holes. If the backlash is not within specifications, replace the camshaft and crankshaft gears.
12. Lubricate the camshaft journals with a high quality engine oil supplement. Install the camshaft and gear into the engine block.
13. Rotate the camshaft and crankshaft so the timing marks on the gear teeth align. The engine is now in No. 4 cylinder firing position.
14. Install the camshaft thrust plate-to-block screws and tighten to 90 inch lbs. (10 Nm).
15. Install the engine in the vehicle.
16. Connect the negative battery cable.

1991–93

1. Disconnect the negative battery cable.
2. Remove the front cover.
3. Loosen the camshaft bolt. Align the cam and crankshaft timing marks and remove the camshaft bolt.
4. Remove the timing chain and sprocket.

To install:

5. Install the timing chain and sprocket. Align the cam and crankshaft (with engine at TDC).
6. Install the camshaft bolt and tighten to 43 ft. lbs. (58 Nm).
7. Install the front cover.

2.8L and 3.1L Engines

1. Relieve the pressure in the fuel system before disconnecting any fuel line connections. Disconnect the negative battery cable.
2. Remove the crankcase front cover.
3. Place the No. 1 piston at TDC with the marks on the camshaft and crankshaft sprockets aligned.
4. Remove the camshaft sprocket and chain.

NOTE: If the sprocket does not come off easily, a light blow with a plastic mallet on the lower edge of the sprocket should dislodge the sprocket.

5. Remove the crankshaft sprocket.

To install:

6. Install the crankshaft sprocket. Apply Molykote® or equivalent, to the sprocket thrust surface.
7. Hold the sprocket with the chain hanging down and align the marks on the camshaft and crankshaft sprockets.
8. Align the dowel in the camshaft with the dowel hole in the camshaft sprocket.
9. Draw the camshaft sprocket onto the camshaft using the mounting bolts. Tighten the camshaft sprocket mounting bolts to 18 ft. lbs. (25 Nm).
10. Lubricate the timing chain with engine oil. Install the crankcase front cover. Connect battery negative cable.

3.3L Engine

1. Relieve the pressure in the fuel system before disconnecting any fuel line connections. Disconnect the negative battery cable.
2. Remove the crankcase front cover.
3. Turn the crankshaft so the timing marks are aligned.
4. Remove the timing chain damper and camshaft sprocket bolts.
5. Remove the camshaft sprocket and chain. Remove the crankshaft sprocket.

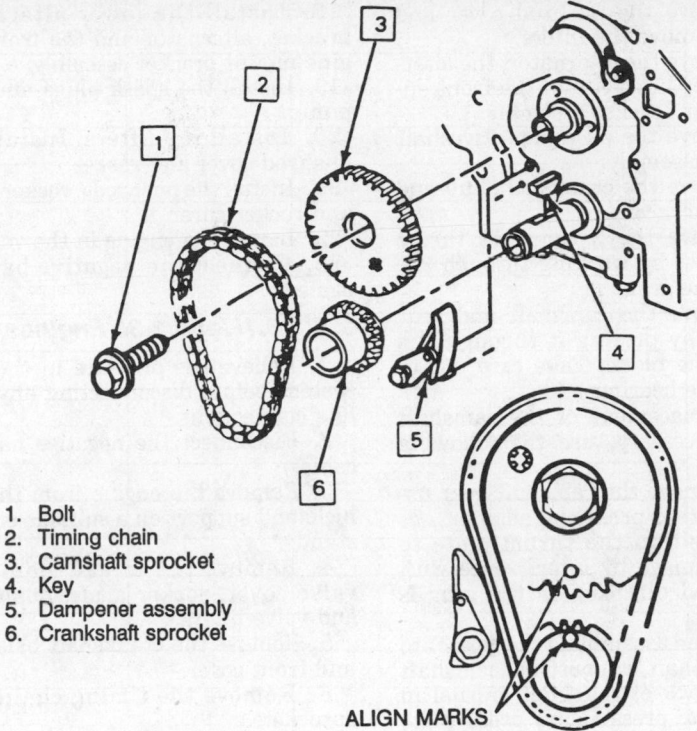

1. Bolt
2. Timing chain
3. Camshaft sprocket
4. Key
5. Dampener assembly
6. Crankshaft sprocket

ALIGN MARKS

Timing chain and sprocket assembly—3.3L engine

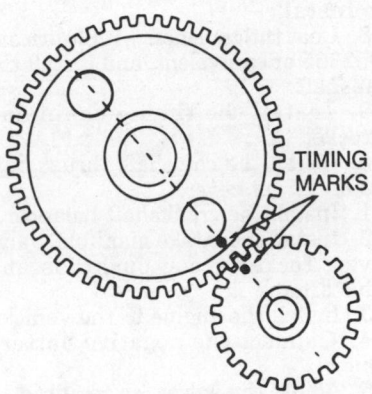

TIMING MARKS

Timing gear alignment—2.5L engine

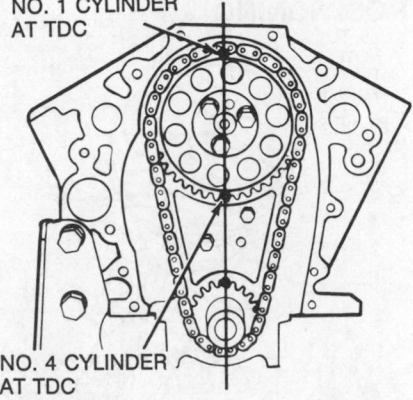

NO. 1 CYLINDER AT TDC

NO. 4 CYLINDER AT TDC

Timing gear alignment—2.8L and 3.1L engines

To install:

6. Make sure the crankshaft is positioned so No. 1 piston is at TDC on compression stroke.
7. Rotate the camshaft with the sprocket temporarily installed, so the timing mark is straight down.
8. Assembly the timing chain on the sprockets with the timing marks aligned. Install the timing chain and sprocket.
9. Install the camshaft sprocket bolts. Torque the bolts to 74 ft. lbs. (100 Nm) +105 degrees using tool J36660 or equivalent.
10. Install the timing chain damper and engine front cover. Connect battery negative cable.

Camshaft

REMOVAL & INSTALLATION

2.5L Engine

1. Relieve the pressure in the fuel system before disconnecting any fuel line connections.
2. Disconnect the negative battery cable.
3. Remove the engine from the vehicle and support on a suitable engine stand.
4. Remove the rocker cover, rocker arms and pushrods.
5. Remove the spark plugs and fuel pump.

6. Remove the pushrod cover and gasket. Remove the lifters.

7. Remove the alternator, the alternator lower bracket and the front engine mount bracket assembly.

8. Remove the oil pump driveshaft and gear assembly.

9. Remove the crankshaft hub and timing gear cover.

10. Remove the 2 camshaft thrust plate screws by working through the holes in the gear.

11. Remove the camshaft and gear assembly by pulling it through the front of the block. Take care not to damage the bearings.

12. If replacement of the camshaft gear is necessary, use the following procedure:

   a. Remove the camshaft gear using an arbor press and adapter.

   b. Position the thrust plate to avoid damage by interference with the Woodruff® key as the gear is removed.

   c. When assembling the gear onto the camshaft, support the camshaft at the back of the front journal in the arbor press using press plate adapters.

   d. Press the gear on the shaft until it bottoms against the spacer ring.

   e. Measure the end clearance of the thrust plate. End clearance should be 0.0015–0.0050 in.

   f. If clearance is less than 0.0015 in., replace the spacer ring.

   g. If clearance is more than 0.0050 in., replace the thrust plate.

To install:

13. Lubricate the camshaft journals with a high quality engine oil supplement and carefully install the camshaft and gear into the cylinder block.

14. Rotate the camshaft and crankshaft so the timing marks on the gear teeth align. The engine is now in No. 4 cylinder firing position.

15. Install the camshaft thrust plate-to-block screw. Torque the screw to 90 inch lbs. (10 Nm).

16. Install the crankshaft hub and timing gear cover.

17. Install the oil pump driveshaft and gear assembly.

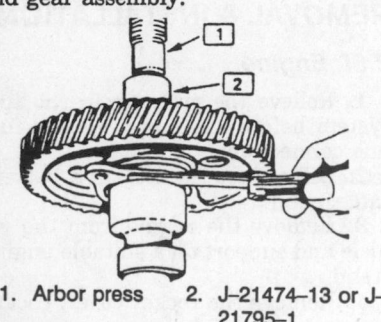

1. Arbor press   2. J–21474–13 or J–21795–1

Camshaft timing gear/thrust plate end clearance—2.5L engine

18. Install the lower alternator bracket, alternator and the front engine mount bracket assembly.

19. Install the spark plugs and fuel pump.

20. Install the lifters. Install the pushrod cover and gasket.

21. Install the pushrods, rocker arms and rocker cover.

22. Install the engine in the vehicle.

23. Connect the negative battery cable.

2.8L, 3.1L and 3.3L Engines

1. Relieve the pressure in the fuel system before disconnecting any fuel line connections.

2. Disconnect the negative battery cable.

3. Remove the engine from the vehicle and support on a suitable engine stand.

4. Remove the intake manifold, valve cover, rocker arms, pushrods and valve lifters.

5. Remove the crankshaft balancer and front cover.

6. Remove the timing chain and sprockets.

7. Carefully remove the camshaft. Avoid marring the camshaft bearing surfaces.

To install:

8. Coat the camshaft with lubricant 1052365 or equivalent, and install the camshaft.

9. Install the timing chain and sprocket.

10. Install the camshaft thrust button and front cover.

11. Install the crankshaft balancer.

12. Install the intake manifold, valve cover, rocker arms, pushrods and valve lifters.

13. Install the engine in the vehicle.

14. Connect the negative battery cable.

15. Adjust the valves, as required.

Piston and Connecting Rod

POSITIONING

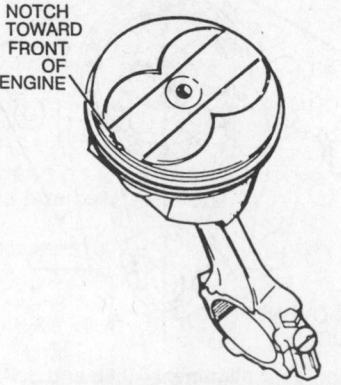

NOTCH TOWARD FRONT OF ENGINE

Piston Identification—2.8L engine

ENGINE LUBRICATION

Oil Pan

REMOVAL & INSTALLATION

2.5L Engine

1. Disconnect the negative battery cable. Remove the air cleaner and duct assembly.

2. Remove the serpentine belt. Remove the engine torque strut from the engine bracket.

3. Remove the 2 upper front air conditioning compressor bolts to the mounting bracket.

4. Raise and support the vehicle safely. Drain the oil.

5. Remove cradle-to-front engine mount nuts.

6. Disconnect exhaust pipe at manifold and at rear transaxle mount.

7. Disconnect starter and remove flywheel housing inspection cover.

8. Remove upper alternator bracket. Remove the splash shield, if equipped, in order to gain working clearance.

9. Install suitable engine support equipment and raise engine.

10. Remove lower alternator bracket and engine support bracket.

11. Remove oil pan retaining bolts and remove oil pan.

To install:

12. Thoroughly clean all gasket sealing surfaces.

13. Install rear oil pan gasket in rear main bearing cap and apply a small quantity of sealer in depressions where pan gasket engages into block.

14. Install front oil pan gasket on timing gear cover pressing tips into holes provided in cover.

15. Install side gaskets on oil pan using grease as a retainer.

16. Apply a ⅛ inch by ¼ inch long bead of sealer at split lines of front and side gaskets.

17. Install oil pan. Bolts into timing gear cover should be installed last. They are installed at an angle and holes align after rest of pan bolts are snugged up.

18. Install lower alternator bracket and engine support bracket.

19. Lower the engine and remove engine support equipment.

20. Install upper alternator bracket. If removed, install the splash shield.

21. Install flywheel housing inspection cover. Connect starter.

22. Connect exhaust pipe at manifold and at rear transaxle mount.

23. Install cradle-to-front engine mount nuts.

24. Lower the vehicle.
25. Fill the crankcase with oil.
26. Connect the negative battery cable.
27. Start the engine and check for leaks.

2.8L and 3.1L Engines

1. Disconnect the battery ground.
2. Remove the serpentine belt cover, belt and tensioner.
3. Support the engine with tool J–28467–A or equivalent, using an extra support leg.
4. Raise and safely support the vehicle.
5. Drain the oil.
6. Remove the right tire and wheel assembly. Remove the splash shield.
7. Remove the steering gear pinch bolt, as required.
8. Remove the transaxle mount retaining nuts and engine-to-frame mount retaining nuts, as required.
9. Remove the front engine horse collar bracket from the block, as required.
10. Remove the bellhousing cover and remove the starter.
11. Position a jackstand under the frame front center crossmember.
12. Loosen but do not remove the rear frame bolts.
13. Remove the front frame bolts and lower the front frame.
14. Remove the oil pan retaining bolts and remove the oil pan.

To install:

NOTE: The oil pan on some vehicles may not require a gasket. If a gasket is not required, the oil pan is installed using RTV gasket material. Make sure the sealing surfaces are free of old RTV material. Use a ⅛ inch bead of RTV material on the pan sealing flange. Torque the pan bolts to 8–10 ft. lbs.

15. Install the oil pan using a new gasket or RTV gasket material.
16. Raise the front frame and install the the front frame bolts.
17. Tighten the rear frame bolts.
18. Remove the jackstand from the front center crossmember.
19. Install the starter and bellhousing cover.
20. If removed, install the front engine horse collar bracket from the block.
21. Install the transaxle mount retaining nuts and engine to frame mount retaining nuts.
22. If removed, install the steering gear pinch bolt.
23. Install the splash shield. Install the right tire and wheel assembly.
24. Lower the vehicle.

25. Install the tensioner, serpentine belt and cover.
26. Fill the crankcase with oil.
27. Connect the negative battery cable.

3.3L Engine

1. Disconnect the negative battery cable.
2. Raise and support the vehicle safely.
3. Drain the engine oil.
4. Remove the flywheel inspection cover and remove the right front wheel.
5. Remove the engine splash shield.
6. Remove the oil filter, oil pan retaining bolts and oil pan assembly.
To install:
7. Clean the oil pan and cylinder block mating surfaces.
8. Install a new oil pan gasket to the oil pan flange.
9. Install the oil pan and torque the oil pan to cylinder block bolts to 12 ft. lbs. (16 Nm). Torque the oil pan to front cover bolts to 124 in. lbs. (14 Nm).
10. Install the oil filter and install the engine splash sheild.
11. Install the right front wheel and install the flywheel inspection cover.
12. Lower the vehicle and fill the crankcase with oil.
13. Connect the negative battery cable.

Oil Pump

REMOVAL & INSTALLATION

2.5L Engine

1. Disconnect the negative battery cable.
2. Raise and support the vehicle safely.
3. Drain the engine oil and remove the oil filter and the oil pan.
4. Remove the oil pump cover.
5. Remove the pump and screen as an assembly.
To install:
6. Remove the 4 cover attaching screws and cover from the oil pump assembly.
7. Pack the space around the oil pump gears completely full of petroleum jelly. There must be no air space left inside the pump. If the pump is not packed, it may not begin to pump oil as soon as the engine is started and engine damage may result.
8. Align the oil pump shaft to match with the oil pump drive shaft tang, then install the oil pump to the block positioning the flange over the oil pump driveshaft lower bushing. Do not use any gasket. Torque the bolts to 20 ft. lbs. (30 Nm).

9. Install the oil pan using a new gasket and seals.
10. Install the 2 flange mounting bolts and nut to the main bearing cap bolt.
11. Lower the vehicle.
12. Fill the crankcase with oil.
13. Connect the negative battery cable.

2.8L and 3.1L Engines

1. Disconnect the negative battery cable.
2. Raise and support the vehicle safely.
3. Drain the engine oil and remove the oil pan.
4. Remove the pump-to-rear main bearing cap bolt and remove the pump and extension shaft.
To install:
5. Remove the 4 cover attaching screws and cover from the oil pump assembly.
6. Pack the space around the oil pump gears completely full of petroleum jelly. There must be no air space left inside the pump. If the pump is not packed, it may not begin to pump oil as soon as the engine is started and engine damage may result.
7. Assemble the pump and extension shaft with retainer to rear main bearing cap, aligning the top end of the extension shaft with the lower end of the drive gear.
8. Install the pump-to-the rear bearing cap bolt. Tighten to 30 ft. lbs. (40 Nm).
9. Install the oil pan.
10. Lower the vehicle.
11. Fill the crankcase with oil.
12. Connect the negative battery cable.

3.3L Engine

1. Disconnect the negative battery cable.
2. Remove the front engine cover. Drain the engine oil.
3. Remove the oil filter adapter, pressure regulator valve and spring.
4. Remove the oil pump cover attaching screws and cover.
5. Remove the gears.
To install:
6. Lubricate the gears with petroleum jelly.
7. Assemble the gears in the housing.
8. Pack the gear cavity with petroleum jelly.
9. Install the oil pump cover and screws. Tighten to 97 inch lbs. (11 Nm).
10. Install the pressure regulator and spring valve.
11. Install the oil filter adapter with a new gasket. Tighten the oil filter adapter bolts to 24 ft. lbs. (33 Nm).

12. Install the front cover on the engine.

13. Fill the crankcase with oil.

14. Connect the negative battery cable.

Rear Main Bearing Oil Seal

REMOVAL & INSTALLATION

2.5L and 3.3L Engines

1. Disconnect the negative battery cable.

2. Support the engine. Remove the transaxle and flywheel.

3. Being careful not to scratch the crankshaft, pry out the old seal with an suitable pry tool.

To install:

4. Coat the new seal with clean engine oil and install it by hand or use seal installer tool J–34924 onto the crankshaft. The seal backing must be flush with the block opening.

5. Install the flywheel.

6. Install the transaxle.

7. Connect the negative battery cable.

2.8L and 3.1L Engines

1. Disconnect the negative battery cable.

2. Support the engine with tool J–28467–A or equivalent.

3. Remove the transaxle and flywheel.

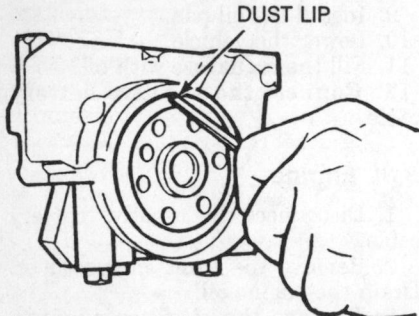

Remove rear seal—2.8L and 3.1L engines

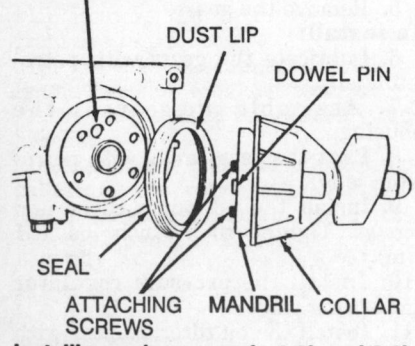

Installing main rear seal—2.8L and 3.1L engines

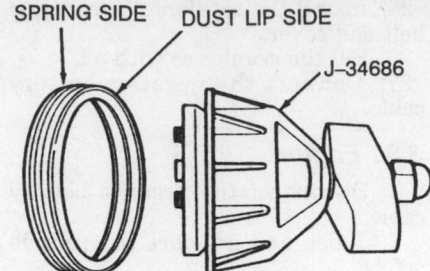

SEAL BORE TO SEAL SURFACE TO BE LUBRICATED WITH ENGINE OIL BEFORE ASSEMBLY

Rear main seal and tool—2.8L and 3.1L engines

4. Carefully remove the old seal by inserting a prying tool through the dust lip at an angle. Pry out the old seal with an suitable pry tool.

To install:

5. Coat the new seal with clean engine oil, and install it using seal installer tool J–34686 or equivalent.

6. Install the flywheel.

7. Install the transaxle.

8. Remove the engine support tool.

9. Connect the negative battery cable.

ENGINE COOLING

Radiator

REMOVAL & INSTALLATION

1. Disconnect the negative battery cable and drain the cooling system.

2. Remove the air cleaner assembly and air cleaner duct.

3. Remove the engine strut brace bolts from the upper mounting panel. Loosen the bolt to prevent damage to the bushing, then swing the strut rearward.

4. On the 2.5L engine, remove the air intake resonator mounting nut and remove the resonator.

5. Disconnect the electrical connector from the fan and remove the cooling fan attaching bolts, and then the cooling fan.

6. On the 1989 models, scribe the hood latch location on the radiator support, then remove the latch.

7. Disconnect the coolant hoses from the radiator and the coolant recovery tank hose. Disconnect the transaxle oil cooler lines.

8. Remove the radiator attaching bolts, then the radiator. If equipped with air conditioning, it may be necessary to raise the left side of the radiator so the radiator neck will clear the compressor.

To install:

9. Install the radiator and attaching bolts.

10. Connect the coolant hoses to the radiator. Connect the oil cooler lines.

11. On the 1989 models, install the hood latch observing the scribe marks made upon removal.

12. Install the cooling fan and attaching bolts.

13. Install the air intake resonator to the 2.5L engine. Connect the electrical connector to the fan.

14. Install the engine forward strut bracket to the radiator and install the air cleaner assembly.

15. Connect the negative battery cable.

16. Fill cooling system and check for leaks. Start the engine and allow to come to normal operating temperature. Recheck for leaks. Top-off coolant level.

Electric Cooling Fan

TESTING

Cooling Fan Does Not Run

1. Turn the ignition switch to the **RUN** position. Ground the diagnostic terminal **C1/21** for 2.5L engine or **C3/E8** for 2.8L, 3.1L and 3.3L engines with a fused jumper wire.

2. If the coolant fan runs, replace the ECM. If the coolant fan does not run, go to the next step.

3. Remove the connector from the coolant fan relay which is located on the left front fender. Measure the voltage from the brown wire to the ground. Turn the ignition switch to the **RUN** position.

4. If there is no voltage present, inspect the brown and white wire for an open. Repair as necessary.

5. If there is voltage, move the voltmeter to between the brown wire and the green wire for 2.5L engine or green/white wire for 2.8L, 3.1L and 3.3L engines.

6. If there is no voltage present, inspect the green or green/white wire for an open or short. Repair as necessary.

7. If there is voltage present, measure the voltage between the **A** (red) terminal and the coolant fan relay ground at the connector.

8. If there is no voltage present, inspect the red wire for an open or short. Repair as necessary.

9. If there is voltage present, connect a fused jumper between terminals **A** and **E** of the coolant fan relay connector.

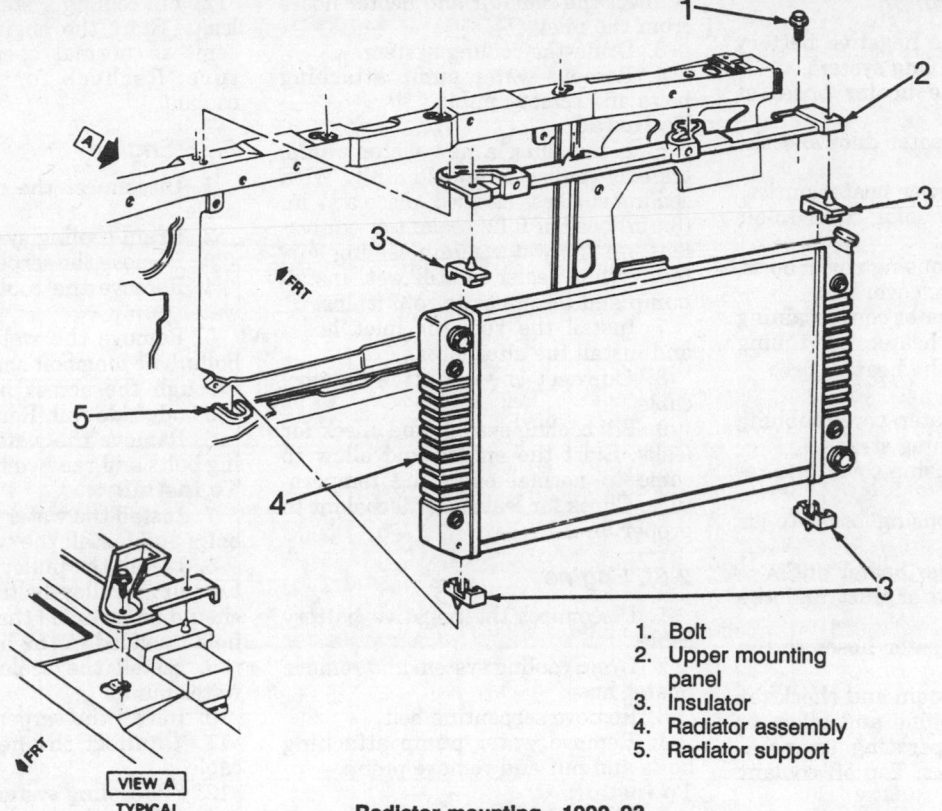

1. Bolt
2. Upper mounting panel
3. Insulator
4. Radiator assembly
5. Radiator support

VIEW A
TYPICAL

Radiator mounting—1990–93

10. If the coolant fan runs, replace the coolant fan relay. If the coolant fan does not run, go to the next step.

11. With the fused jumper still in place, remove the coolant fan connector and connect a test lamp to terminal **B** of the connector and ground.

12. If the lamp does not light, inspect the wiring for an open and repair as necessary. If the lamp lights, go to the next step.

13. Move the test lamp ground lead to terminal **A** of the coolant fan connector. If the test lamp does not light, check wire for an open and repair as necessary.

Cooling Fan Runs Continuously

IGNITION SWITCH IN RUN POSITION

1. Check for diagnostic Code 14 or 15. If either of these codes are present, replace the coolant sensor. If no code is present, go to the next step.

2. Inspect the dark green and white wire for an open and repair, as necessary. If the wire shows continuity on the 2.5L engine, replace the coolant fan relay. On all other engines, go to the next step.

3. Remove the connector from the fan temperature backup switch and turn the ignition switch to **RUN**.

4. If the coolant fan runs, replace

the coolant fan relay. If the coolant fan does not run, replace the fan temperature backup switch located between the coolant fan relay and the ECM.

IGNITION SWITCH IN OFF POSITION

1. Remove the connector from the coolant fan relay.

2. If the coolant fan runs, check for a short to battery voltage. Repair as necessary.

3. If the coolant fan stops running, replace the coolant fan relay.

REMOVAL & INSTALLATION

1. Disconnect the negative battery cable.

2. Tag and disconnect the electrical connector from the fan motor and fan frame.

3. Remove the fan frame-to-radiator support bolts.

4. Remove the fan and frame assembly from the vehicle.

To install:

5. Install the fan and frame assembly to the vehicle.

6. Install the fan frame-to-radiator support bolts.

7. Connect the electrical connector to the fan motor.

8. Connect the negative battery cable.

Heater Core

REMOVAL & INSTALLATION

Without Air Conditioning

1. Disconnect the negative battery cable. Drain the cooling system.

2. Remove the heater inlet and outlet hoses.

3. Remove the radio noise suppression strap and blow residual coolant from heater core using compressed air.

4. Remove the heater core cover retaining screws. Remove the cover.

5. Remove the heater core.

To install:

6. Install the heater core.

7. Install the heater core cover and retaining screws.

8. Install the radio noise suppression strap.

9. Install the heater inlet and outlet hoses.

10. Fill cooling system and check for leaks. Start the engine and allow to come to normal operating temperature. Check for leaks. Top off coolant level.

11. Connect the negative battery cable.

With Air Conditioning

1. Disconnect the negative battery cable. Drain the cooling system.
2. Disconnect the heater hoses at the heater core.
3. Remove the heater duct and the lower side covers.
4. Remove the lower heater outlet.
5. Remove the housing cover-to-air valve housing clips.
6. Remove the housing cover bolts. Remove the housing cover.
7. Remove the heater core retaining straps. Remove the heater core tubing retainers. Lift out the heater core.

To install:

8. Install the heater core, tubbing retainers and retaining straps.
9. Install the housing cover and retaining bolts.
10. Install the housing cover-to-air valve housing clips.
11. Install the lower heater outlet.
12. Install the heater duct and the lower side covers.
13. Connect the heater hoses to the heater core.
14. Fill cooling system and check for leaks. Start the engine and allow to come to normal operating temperature. Check for leaks. Top off coolant level.
15. Connect the negative battery cable.

Water Pump

REMOVAL & INSTALLATION

2.5L Engine

1989

1. Disconnect the negative battery cable.
2. Remove the drive belt.
3. Drain the cooling system.
4. Remove water pump attaching bolts and remove pump.

To install:

6. If installing a new water pump, transfer pulley from old unit. With sealing surfaces cleaned, place a ⅛ in. (3mm) bead of RTV sealant or equivalent, on the water pump sealing surface. While sealer is still wet, install pump and torque bolts to 6 ft. lbs.
7. Install the drive belt.
8. Connect the negative battery cable.
9. Fill cooling system and check for leaks. Start the engine and allow to come to normal operating temperature. Check for leaks. Refill coolant to proper level.

1990–93

1. Disconnect the negative battery cable.
2. Remove the alternator and dis-

connect the radiator and heater hoses from the inlet.
3. Drain the cooling system.
4. Remove water pump attaching bolts and remove pump.

To install:

6. If installing a new water pump, transfer pulley from old unit. With sealing surfaces cleaned, place a ⅛ in. (3mm) bead of RTV sealant or equivalent, on the water pump sealing surface. While sealer is still wet, install pump and torque bolts to 6 ft. lbs.
7. Install the radiator inlet hoses and install the alternator.
8. Connect the negative battery cable.
9. Fill cooling system and check for leaks. Start the engine and allow to come to normal operating temperature. Check for leaks. Refill coolant to proper level.

2.8L Engine

1. Disconnect the negative battery cable.
2. Drain cooling system and remove heater hose.
3. Remove serpentine belt.
4. Remove water pump attaching bolts and nut and remove pump.

To install:

5. Clean the sealing surfaces and place a 3/32 in. (2mm) bead of RTV sealant or equivalent on the water pump sealing surface.
6. Coat bolt threads with pipe sealant 1052080 or equivalent.
7. Install pump and torque bolts to 10 ft. lbs.
8. Connect the negative battery cable.
9. Fill cooling system and check for leaks. Start the engine and allow to come to normal operating temperature. Recheck for leaks. Top-up coolant.

3.1L Engine

1. Disconnect the negative battery cable.
2. Drain cooling system.
3. Remove the serpentine belt.
4. Remove the heater hose and radiator hose.
5. Remove the water pump cover attaching bolts and remove the cover.
6. Remove the water pump attaching bolts and remove the water pump.

To install:

7. Position the water pump on the engine and install the attaching bolts. Torque bolts to 89 inch lbs. (10 Nm).
8. Install the water pump cover and attaching bolts.
9. Install the heater hose and radiator hose.
10. Install the serpentine belt.
11. Connect the negative battery cable.

12. Fill cooling system and check for leaks. Start the engine and allow to come to normal operating temperature. Recheck for leaks. Top-up coolant.

3.3L Engine

1. Disconnect the negative battery cable.
2. Drain cooling system.
3. Remove the serpentine drive belt.
4. Remove the coolant hose at the water pump.
5. Remove the water pump pulley bolts. The long bolt should be removed through the access hole provided in the body side rail. Remove the pulley.
6. Remove the water pump attaching bolts and remove the water pump.

To install:

7. Install the water pump attaching bolts and install the water pump.
8. Install the pulley. Install the water pump pulley bolts. The long bolt should be installed through the access hole provided in the body side rail.
9. Install the coolant hose at the water pump.
10. Install the serpentine drive belt.
11. Connect the negative battery cable.
12. Fill cooling system and check for leaks. Start the engine and allow to come to normal operating temperature. Check for leaks. Refill coolant to the proper level.

Thermostat

REMOVAL & INSTALLATION

1. Disconnect the negative battery cable. Drain the cooling system.
2. If equipped with cruise control and vacuum modulator is connected to the thermostat housing, remove the

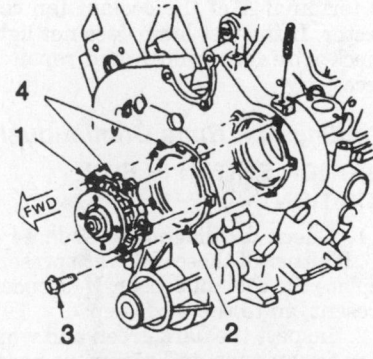

1. Water pump
2. Gasket
3. Bolt – 89 inch lbs. (10 Nm)
4. Locator – Must be vertical

Water pump mounting—2.8L and 3.1L engines

vacuum modulator from the thermostat housing.

3. On all vehicles unbolt the water outlet from the intake manifold. Remove the outlet and lift the thermostat from the the intake manifold.

To install:

4. Clean mating surfaces throughly. Apply a ⅛ inch bead of suitable RTV sealant in the groove of the water outlet.

5. Install the thermostat with the spring toward the engine. Install the water outlet. Torque bolts to 21 ft. lbs.

6 If equipped with cruise control, install the vacuum modulator to the thermostat housing.

7. Connect the negative battery cable.

8. Fill cooling system and check for leaks. Start the engine and allow it to come to normal operating temperature. Check for leaks. Fill coolant to proper level.

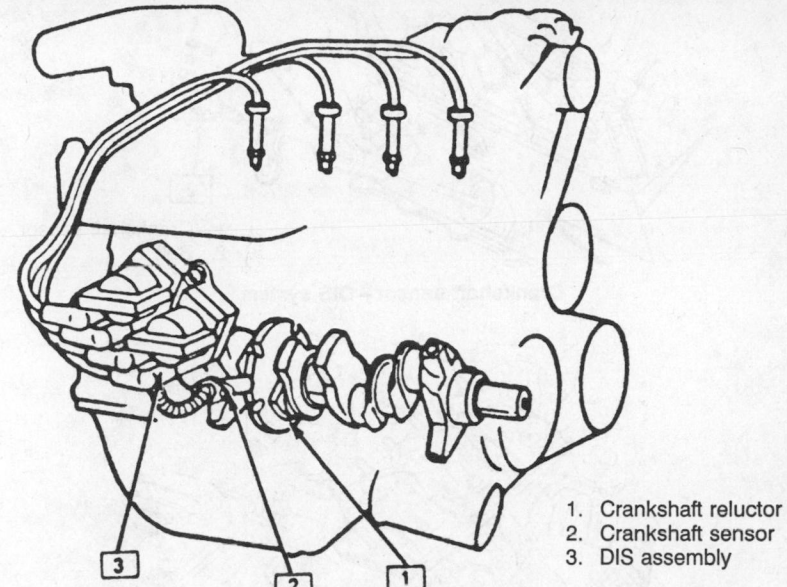

1. Crankshaft reluctor
2. Crankshaft sensor
3. DIS assembly

Direct Ignition System (DIS) components

ENGINE ELECTRICAL

NOTE: Disconnecting the negative battery cable on some vehicles may interfere with the functions of the on board computer systems and may require the computer to undergo a relearning process, once the negative battery cable is reconnected.

Direct Ignition System (DIS)

REMOVAL & INSTALLATION

2.5L, 2.8L and 3.1L Engines

DIS ASSEMBLY

1. Disconnect the negative battery cable.

2. Disconnect the DIS electrical connectors.

3. Tag and disconnect the spark plug wires.

4. Remove the DIS assembly attaching bolts.

5. Remove the DIS assembly from the engine.

To install:

6. Install the DIS assembly and attaching bolts.

7. Connect the spark plug wires.

8. Connect the DIS electrical connectors.

9. Connect the negative battery cable.

10. On 3.1L engine, perform the Idle Learn Procedure as follows:

   a. Connect the Scan tool to the ALDL.

   b. Turn the ignition switch to the **ON** position with the engine not running.

   c. In the "Misc. Test" mode, select "IAC System", then "Idle Learn".

   d. Proceed with idle learn as directed.

IGNITION COIL(S)

1. Disconnect the negative battery cable.

2. Disconnect and tag spark plug wires.

3. Remove ignition coil(s) attaching bolts, then the ignition coil from the module.

To install:

4. Install the coil(s) and attaching bolts.

5. Connect the spark plug wires.

6. Connect the negative battery cable.

7. On 3.1L engine perform the Idle Learn Procedure as follows:

   a. Connect the Scan tool to the ALDL.

   b. Turn the ignition switch to the **ON** position with the engine not running.

   c. In the "Misc. Test" mode, select "IAC System", then "Idle Learn".

   d. Proceed with idle learn as directed.

IGNITION MODULE

1. Disconnect the negative battery cable.

2. Remove the DIS assembly from the engine.

3. Remove the coils from the assembly.

4. Remove DIS module from the assembly plate.

To install:

5. Install the DIS module to the assembly plate.

6. Install the coils to the assembly.

7. Install the DIS assembly to the engine.

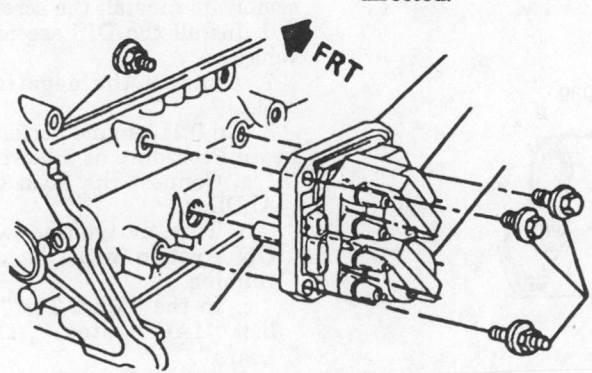

DIS coil system—2.5L engine

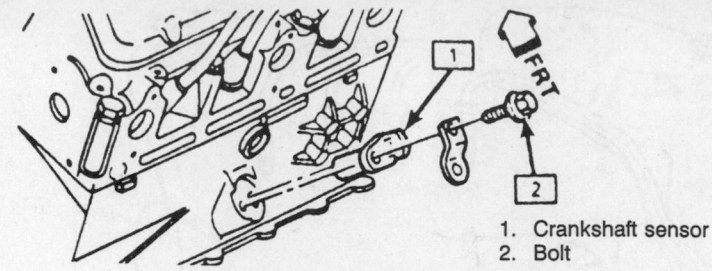

1. Crankshaft sensor
2. Bolt

Crankshaft sensor—DIS system

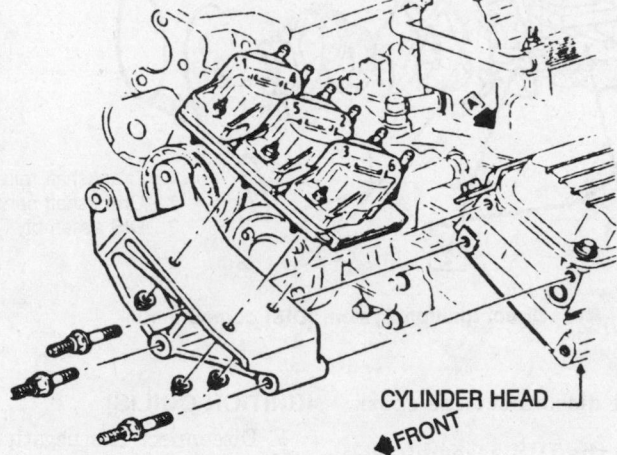

CYLINDER HEAD
FRONT

Ignition system coils and module assemblies—C³I system

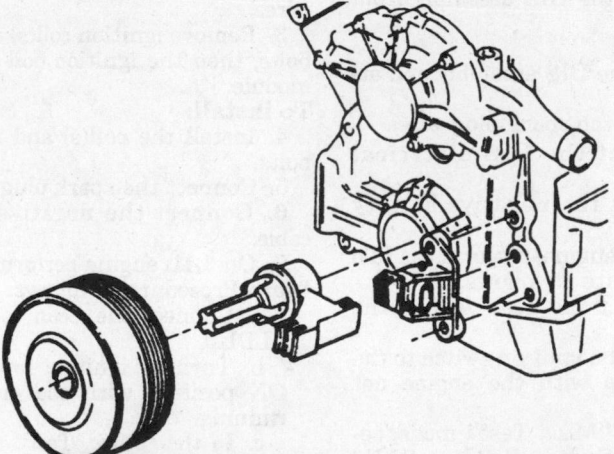

Positioning alignment tool on crankshaft—C³I system

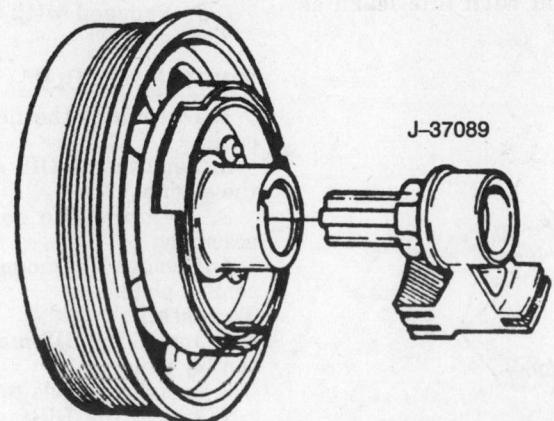

J–37089

Checking harmonic balancer vanes—C³I system

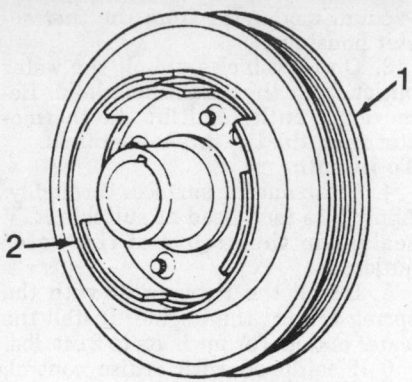

1. Harmonic balancer (crankshaft pulley)
2. Dual concentric interrupter rings

Harmonic balancer with integral concentric interrupter rings—C³I system

8. Connect the negative battery cable.
9. On 3.1L engine perform the Idle Learn Procedure as follows:
  a. Connect the Scan tool to the ALDL.
  b. Turn the ignition switch to the **ON** position with the engine not running.
  c. In the "Misc. Test" mode, select "IAC System", then "Idle Learn".
  d. Proceed with idle learn as directed.

CRANKSHAFT SENSOR

1. Disconnect the negative battery cable.
2. Remove the DIS assembly.
3. Remove the sensor screws and remove the sensor from the DIS assembly.
To install:
4. Inspect the sensor O-ring for wear, cracks or leakage. Replace as necessary. Lubricate the new O-ring with engine oil prior to installation.
5. Install the sensor to the DIS assembly and install the screws.
6. Install the DIS assembly to the vehicle.
7. Connect the negative battery cable.
8. On 3.1L engine perform the Idle Learn Procedure as follows:
  a. Connect the Scan tool to the ALDL.
  b. Turn the ignition switch to the **ON** position with the engine not running.
  c. In the "Misc. Test" mode, select "IAC System", then "Idle Learn".
  d. Proceed with idle learn as directed.

Computer Controlled Coil Ignition (C³I) System

REMOVAL & INSTALLATION

3.3L Engine
C³I MODULE

1. Disconnect the negative battery cable.
2. Disconnect the 14-way connector at the ignition module.
3. Tag and disconnect the spark plug wires at the coil assembly.
4. Remove the nuts and washers securing the C³I module assembly to the bracket.
5. Remove the 6 nuts attaching the coil assemblies to the ignition module.
To install:
6. Install the coil assemblies to the ignition module and install the 6 attaching nuts.
7. Install the nuts and washers attaching the assembly to the bracket.
8. Connect the spark plug wires.
9. Connect the 14-way connector to the module.
10. Connect the negative battery cable.

IGNITION COIL(S)

1. Disconnect the negative battery cable.
2. Tag and disconnect spark plug wires.
3. Remove ignition coil(s) attaching nuts, then the ignition coil from the module.
To install:
4. Install the coil(s) and attaching nuts.
5. Connect the spark plug wires.
6. Connect the negative battery cable.

DUAL CRANKSHAFT SENSOR

1. Disconnect battery negative cable.
2. Disconnect serpentine belt from crankshaft pulley.

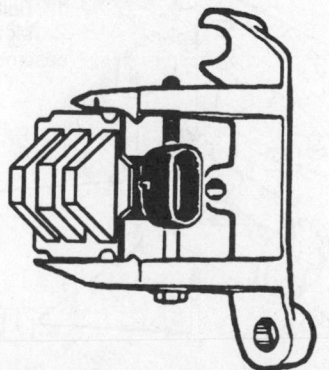

Dual crankshaft sensor—3.3L engine

3. Raise and safely support the vehicle.
4. Remove right front tire and wheel assembly, then the inner fender access cover.
5. Remove crankshaft harmonic balancer retaining bolt and crankshaft harmonic balancer.
6. Disconnect electrical connector from sensor, remove the foreign object deflector and remove the crankshaft sensor from the vehicle.
To install:
7. Loosely install the crankshaft sensor on the pedestal.
8. Position the sensor with the pedestal attached on special tool J–37089.
9. Position the tool on the crankshaft.
10. Install the bolts to hold the pedestal to the block face. Tighten to 18–26 ft. lbs. (25–35 Nm).
11. Tighten the pedestal pinch bolt to 26–44 inch lbs. (3–5 Nm).
12. Remove special tool J–37089 and install the foreign object deflector.
13. Place special tool J–37089 on the harmonic balancer and turn. If any vane of the harmonic balancer touches the tool, replace the balancer assembly.
14. Install the balancer on the crankshaft and install the crankshaft balancer bolt. Tighten to 104 ft. lbs. + 56 degrees (140 Nm + 56 degrees).
15. Install the inner fender shield.
16. Install the tire and wheel assembly. Tighten to 100 ft. lbs. (140 Nm).
17. Lower the vehicle.
18. Install the serpentine belt.
19. Connect the negative battery cable.

Ignition Timing

All vehicles are equipped with either the Direct Ignition System (DIS) or the Computer Controlled Coil Ignition (C³I) system. The systems consist of a coil pack, ignition module, crankshaft interrupter ring(s), magnetic sensor and an Electronic Control Module (ECM). Timing advance and retard are accomplished through the ECM with the Electronic Spark Timing (EST) and Electronic Spark Control (ESC) circuitry. No ignition timing adjustment is required or possible.

Alternator

Precautions

Several precautions must be observed with alternator equipped vehicles to avoid damage to the unit.

● If the battery is removed for any reason, make sure it is reconnected with the correct polarity. Reversing the battery connections may result in damage to the one-way rectifiers.

● When utilizing a booster battery as a starting aid, always connect the positive to positive terminals and the negative terminal from the booster battery to a good engine ground on the vehicle being started.

● Never use a fast charger as a booster to start vehicles.

● Disconnect the battery cables when charging the battery with a fast charger.

● Never attempt to polarize the alternator.

● Do not use test lamps of more than 12 volts when checking diode continuity.

● Do not short across or ground any of the alternator terminals.

● The polarity of the battery, alternator and regulator must be matched and considered before making any electrical connections within the system.

● Never separate the alternator on an open circuit. Make sure all connections within the circuit are clean and tight.

● Disconnect the battery ground terminal when performing any service on electrical components.

● Disconnect the battery if arc welding is to be done on the vehicle.

BELT TENSION ADJUSTMENT

Serpentine Belt

A single serpentine belt is used to drive all engine accessories. The belt tension is maintained by a spring loaded tensioner. The belt tensioner has the ability to control the belt tension over a broad range of belt lengths. However, there are limits to which the tensioner can compensate for varying lengths. If the belt tension is below the minimum specifications, replace the belt tensioner.

Check the serpentine belt tension with tool J–23600B or equivalent, belt tension gauge in the following manner:

1. Start the engine and run until operating temperature is reached.
2. Shut the engine **OFF** and place the tension gauge midway between the pulleys. Install the gauge on the longest belt span possible. If the belt is notched on the inner surface, place the middle finger of the tensioner gauge into 1 of the notches. Correct belt tension readings should be approximately:

40 lbs. (178 Nm)—2.5L Engine
70 lbs. (311 Nm)—2.8L Engine
50–70 lbs. (225–315 Nm)—3.1L Engine
67 lbs. (298 Nm)—3.3L Engine

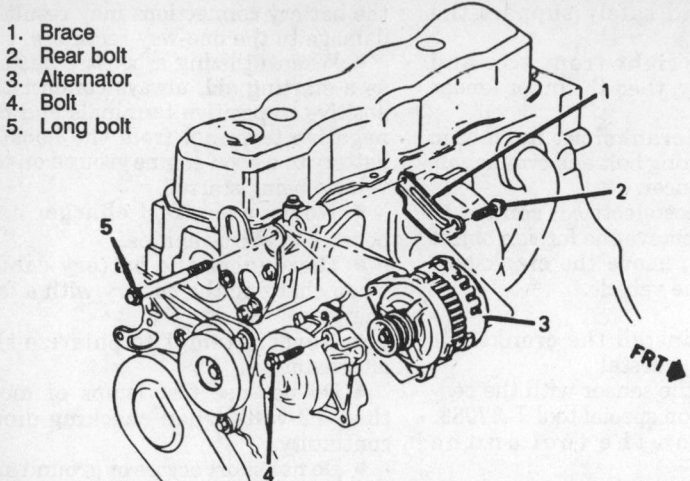

1. Brace
2. Rear bolt
3. Alternator
4. Bolt
5. Long bolt

Alternator mounting—3.3L engine

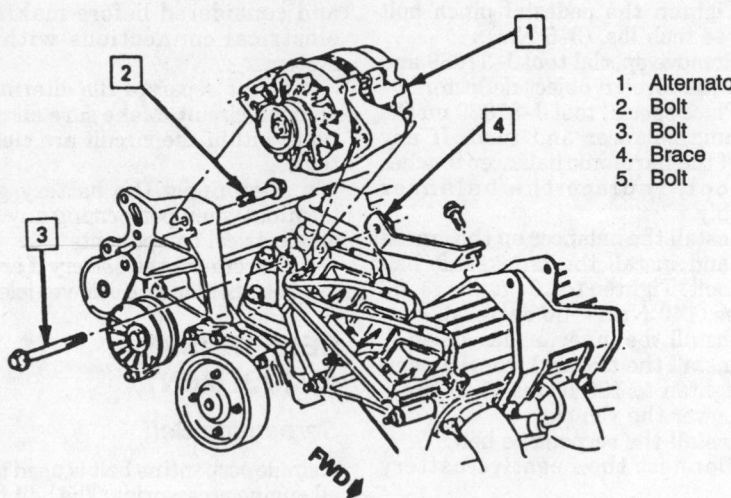

1. Alternator
2. Bolt
3. Bolt
4. Brace
5. Bolt

Alternator mounting—2.5L engine

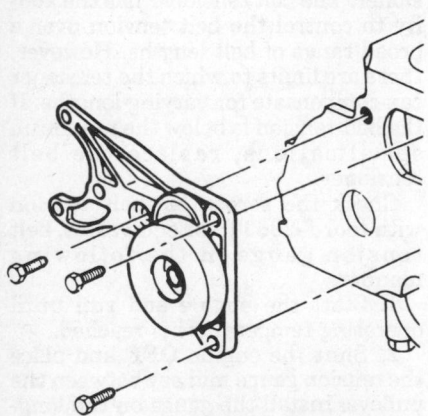

Belt tensioner installation—2.5L engine

Belt tensioner installation—3.3L engine

REMOVAL & INSTALLATION

1. Disconnect the negative battery cable.
2. Disconnect the alternator electrical connectors.
3. Remove the serpentine belt.

4. Remove the alternator front and rear attaching bolts complete with the rear brace.
5. Remove the alternator.
To install:
6. Position the alternator in the bracket.

7. Install the alternator front attaching bolts but do not tighten.
8. Install the rear attaching bolts and brace. Tighten bolts to the proper torque specs.
9. Install the serpentine belt.
10. Connect the alternator electrical connectors.
11. Connect the negative battery cable.

Starter

REMOVAL & INSTALLATION

2.5L and 2.8L Engines

1. Disconnect the negative battery cable.
2. Raise and safely support the vehicle.
3. Remove the bolts from the flywheel inspection cover and remove the cover.
4. Remove the bolts from the bracket and remove the starter bolts.
5. Disconnect the starter wiring.
6. Remove the starter and any shims.
To install:

NOTE: If replacing the starter, transfer the starter bracket to the new starter.

7. Install the starter and any shims.
8. Install the 2 starter attaching bolts.
9. On the 2.5L engine, install the bolt attaching the starter bracket to the engine.
10. Install the flywheel inspection cover and install the bolts.
11. Connect the starter wires.
12. Lower the vehicle.
13. Connect the negative battery cable.

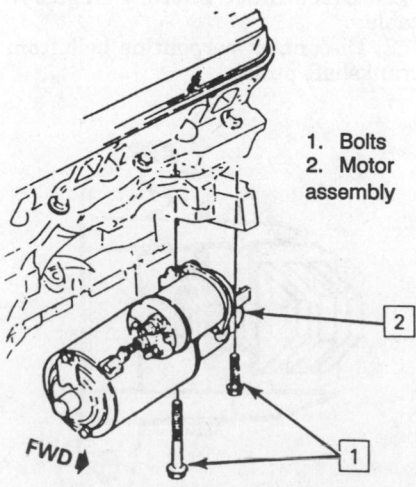

1. Bolts
2. Motor assembly

Starter mounting—3.3L engine

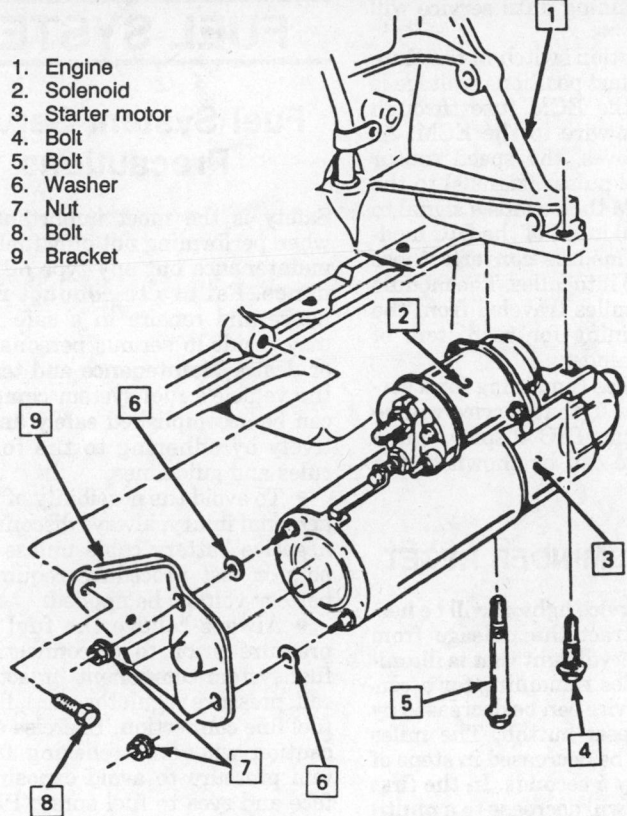

1. Engine
2. Solenoid
3. Starter motor
4. Bolt
5. Bolt
6. Washer
7. Nut
8. Bolt
9. Bracket

Starter mounting—2.5L engine

3.1L Engine

1. Disconnect the negative battery cable.
2. Raise and safely support the vehicle.
3. If equipped, remove the nut from the brace at the air conditioning compressor.
4. If equipped, remove the nuts from the starter-to-engine brace.
5. Remove the drain pan under the engine oil pan.
6. Disconnect the oil pressure sending unit electrical connector. Remove the oil pressure sending unit.
7. Remove the oil filter.
8. Remove the bolts from the flywheel inspection cover. Remove the inspection cover.
9. Remove the bolts from the starter motor.
10. Remove the starter motor and any shims.
11. Disconnect the starter motor electrical connectors.

To install:
12. Connect the starter motor electrical connectors.
13. Install the starter motor and any shims.
14. Install the starter motor attaching bolts. Tighten to 32 ft. lbs. (43 Nm).
15. Install the flywheel inspection cover and attaching bolts.

16. Install the oil filter.
17. Install the oil pressure sending unit. Connect the electrical connector.
18. Install the drain pan.
19. Install the nuts to the starter-to-engine brace.
20. Install the nut to brace at the air conditioner compressor.
21. Lower the vehicle.
22. Connect the negative battery cable.
23. Check the engine oil level, add as required.

3.3L Engine

1. Disconnect the negative battery cable.
2. Properly discharge the air conditioning system.
3. On 3.3L engine, remove the cooling fan assembly.
4. Remove the front exhaust manifold.
5. Raise and support the vehicle safely.
6. Remove the bolts from the flywheel inspection cover and remove the cover.
7. Disconnect the air conditioner condenser hose from the compressor and position aside.
8. Disconnect the starter motor electrical connectors.
9. Remove the 2 bolts attaching the starter.

10. Remove the starter and any shims.

To install:
11. Install the starter motor and any shims.
12. Install the 2 bolts attaching the starter. Tighten to 30 ft. lbs. (40 Nm).
13. Connect the starter motor electrical connectors.
14. Replace the condenser O-ring. Lubricate with refrigerant oil. Connect the air conditioner condenser hose to the compressor.
15. Install the flywheel inspection cover and attaching bolts.
16. Lower the vehicle.
17. Install the front exhaust manifold.
18. Install the cooling fan assembly.
19. Evacuate, recharge and leak test the air conditioning system.
20. Connect the negative battery cable.

EMISSION CONTROLS

Due to the complex nature of modern electronic engine control systems, comprehensive diagnosis and testing procedures fall outside the confines of this repair manual. For complete information on diagnosis, testing and repair procedures concerning all modern engine and emission control systems, please refer to "Chilton's Guide to Fuel Injection and Electronic Engine Controls".

Emission Warning Lamps

RESETTING

1989–93 Cutlass Ciera and Cutlass Cruiser

Vehicles equipped with an engine oil life index display as a part of the Driver Information System (DIS), have a display that will show when to change the engine oil.

The oil change interval is determined by the driver information system and will usually fall at or between the 2 recommended alternative intervals of 3000 miles and 7500 miles but it could be shorter than 3000 miles under some severe driving conditions. The driver information system will also signal the need for an oil change at 7500 miles or one year passed since the last oil change. If the drive information system does not indicate the need for an oil change after 7500 miles or one year if the engine oil life index display fails to appear, the oil should be changed and the driver information system serviced.

When the engine oil life index reaches 10 percent or less, the change oil light display will function as a reserve trip odometer, indicating the distance to an oil change. Until the engine oil lift index reset is performed, the driver information system will display the distance to the oil change and sound a beep when the ignition switch is turned to the **ACCESSORY** or **RUN** position the first time each day.

When the distance to the next oil change reaches 0, the driver information system will display the change oil now light. Until an engine oil life index reset is performed the the driver information system will display the change oil now light and sound a beep when the ignition switch is turned to the **ACCESSORY** or **RUN** position the first time each day.

The driver information system will not detect dusty conditions or engine malfunctions which may affect the engine oil. If driving in severe conditions exists, change the engine oil every 3000 miles or 3 months which ever comes first, unless instructed otherwise by the driver information system. The driver information center does not measure the engine oil level, it remains the owner's responsibility to check the engine oil level. After the oil has been changed, the engine oil life index light must be reset. Reset the can be accomplished as follows:

a. The engine oil life index can be reset by pressing the **RESET** and **OIL** buttons simultaneously for at least 5 seconds while on the engine oil life index display. The driver information system will reset the engine oil life index to 100 percent and display an engine oil life index of 100 percent.

b. Oil life index 100 message appears.

NOTE: The Engine Oil Life Index is stored on a non-volatile memory chip and will not reset by disconnecting the battery and or fuse.

6000

The Service Reminder section of the Driver Information Center (DIC) display shows how many miles remain until service is needed. When the reset button is pressed twice, the type of service and the number of miles remaining until the service is needed will be displayed. Each time the Reset button is pressed, another type of service and

the miles remaining until service will be displayed.

With the ignition switch in the Run, Bulb Test or Start positions, voltage is applied from the ECM fuse through the Pink/Black wire to the ECM. As the vehicle moves, the speed sensor sends electrical pulses (signals) to the ECM. The ECM then sends a signal to the speed signal input of the DIC module. The DIC module converts these pulses (signals) into miles. The module subtracts the miles traveled from the distance remaining for each item of the service reminder.

When the miles remaining for a service approaches 0, that service will be displayed on the DIC display. All 4 types of service can be shown at the same time.

SERVICE REMINDER RESET

To reset the service light, it will be necessary to subtract the mileage from the service interval light that is illuminated. The miles remaining for a certain type of service can be decreased by holding the Reset button. The miles remaining will be decreased in steps of 500 miles every 5 seconds. In the first step, the miles will decrease to a multiple of 500. For example, 2880 miles will decrease to 2500 miles. If the Reset button is held in and the miles remaining reach 0, the DIS display will show the service interval for the service selected. The service intervals are as follows:

1. Change oil — 7500 miles
2. Oil filter change — 7500 miles
3. Next filter change — 15,000 miles
4. Rotate tires — 7500 miles
5. Next tire rotation — 15,000 miles
6. Tune Up — 30,000 miles

If the Reset button is still held down, the miles will decrease in steps of 500 miles from the service interval. When the Reset button is released, the mile display shown will be the new distance until the service should be performed.

When a service distance reaches 0, the service reminder item will be displayed. If the service interval is reset within 10 miles, the display will go out immediately. If more than 10 miles passes before the service interval is reset, the item will remain displayed for another 10 miles after being reset before going out.

NOTE: On some models it may be necessary to depress the system Recall button, in order to display the service interval light on the driver information center in order to decrease the mileage from it, so as to reset the interval light.

FUEL SYSTEM

Fuel System Service Precautions

Safety is the most important factor when performing not only fuel system maintenance but any type of maintenance. Failure to conduct maintenance and repairs in a safe manner may result in serious personal injury or death. Maintenance and testing of the vehicle's fuel system components can be accomplished safely and effectively by adhering to the following rules and guidelines.

• To avoid the possibility of fire and personal injury, always disconnect the negative battery cable unless the repair or test procedure requires that battery voltage be applied.

• Always relieve the fuel system pressure prior to disconnecting any fuel system component (injector, fuel rail, pressure regulator, etc.), fitting or fuel line connection. Exercise extreme caution whenever relieving fuel system pressure to avoid exposing skin, face and eyes to fuel spray. Please be advised that fuel under pressure may penetrate the skin or any part of the body that it contacts.

• Always place a shop towel or cloth around the fitting or connection prior to loosening to absorb any excess fuel due to spillage. Ensure that all fuel spillage (should it occur) is quickly removed from engine surfaces. Ensure that all fuel soaked cloths or towels are deposited into a suitable waste container.

• Always keep a dry chemical (Class B) fire extinguisher near the work area.

• Do not allow fuel spray or fuel vapors to come into contact with a spark or open flame.

• Always use a backup wrench when loosening and tightening fuel line connection fittings. This will prevent unnecessary stress and torsion to fuel line piping. Always follow the proper torque specifications.

• Always replace worn fuel fitting O-rings with new. Do not substitute fuel hose or equivalent where fuel pipe is installed.

RELIEVING FUEL SYSTEM PRESSURE

Throttle Body Injection (TBI)

1. On a cold engine, remove the fuse marked "Fuel Pump" from the fuse block in the passenger compartment.

2. Loosen the fuel filler cap to relive the tank pressure.

3. Start the engine and run until the fuel supply remaining in the fuel lines is exhausted. When the engine stops, engage the starter again for 3.0 seconds to assure dissipation of any remaining pressure.

4. With the ignition **OFF**, replace the fuel pump fuse.

5. Disconnect the negative battery cable.

Port Fuel Injection (PFI)

1. Disconnect the negative battery cable to avoid possible fuel discharge if an accidental attempt is made to start the engine.

2. Loosen the fuel filler cap to relieve the tank pressure.

3. Connect a suitable fuel pressure gauge to the fuel pressure test fitting. Wrap a shop towel around the fitting while connecting gauge to avoid spillage.

4. Place the bleed hose in an approved container and open the valve on the pressure gauge to relieve system pressure.

5. Dispose of the discharged liquid fuel promptly.

Fuel Tank

REMOVAL & INSTALLATION

1. Disconnect the negative battery cable.

2. Relieve fuel system pressure.

3. Drain the fuel tank into an approved container.

4. Raise and safely support the vehicle.

5. Remove the filler tube and clamp.

6. Remove the fuel tank vent tube and clamp at the fuel tank.

7. Disconnect the electrical connectors.

8. Disconnect the vapor hose connector and clamp from the fuel tank.

9. Disconnect the fuel line hoses from the tank meter assembly.

10. If equipped with quick-connect fuel line fittings, perform the following:

  a. Grasp the fuel level meter feed tube and fuel feed line quick-connect fitting. Twist the quick-connect fitting ¼ turn in each direction to loosen any dirt. Repeat for the fuel return line quick-connect fitting.

  b. Squeeze the plastic tabs of the male end of the connector and pull the connection apart. Repeat for the other fitting.

11. With the aid of an assistant, support the fuel tank and remove the 2 front fuel tank retaining strap attaching bolts, 2 rear fuel tank strap attach-

ing nuts and bolts, bolt fuel tank retaining straps and remove the tank.

To install:

12. With the aid of an assistant, position and support the fuel tank. Install the 2 fuel tank retaining straps, front attaching bolts and rear attaching bolts and nuts.

13. Connect the fuel lines to the tank meter assembly.

14. If equipped with quick-connect fuel line connectors, perform the following:

  a. Apply a few drops of clean engine oil to the male connector tube ends.

  b. Push the connectors together to cause the retaining tabs/fingers to snap into place.

  c. Once installed, pull on both ends of each connection to make sure the connection is secure.

  d. Repeat for the other fittings.

15 Connect the vapor hose and clamp.

16. Connect the fuel level meter electrical connector.

17. Connect the fuel tank vent tube and clamp.

18. Connect the filler tube and clamp.

19. Lower the vehicle.

20. Add fuel to the tank and install the fuel filler cap.

21. Connect the negative battery cable.

22. Turn the ignition switch to the **ON** position for 2 seconds, then turn to the **OFF** position for 10 seconds. Turn the ignition switch back to the **ON** position and check for fuel leaks.

Fuel Filter

REMOVAL & INSTALLATION

Threaded Fitting

The filter is an in-line unit located just ahead of the TBI unit or to the left of the fuel tank.

1. Ensure the engine is cold, then unclamp and remove the fuel hose.

2. Unscrew the filter from the fuel line.

To install:

3. Place the new filter into position and connect the fuel lines.

4. Tighten the retaining clamp.

5. Start the engine and check for fuel leaks.

Quick Connect Fitting

1. Disconnect the negative battery cable.

2. Relieve the fuel system pressure.

3. Raise and safely support the vehicle.

4. Remove the filter bracket attaching screw and filter bracket.

5. Grasp the filter and 1 fuel line fitting. Twist the quick-connect fitting ¼ turn in each direction to loosen any dirt within the fitting. Repeat for the other fuel line fitting.

6. Use compressed air, blow out dirt from the quick-connect fittings at both ends of the fuel filter.

7. To disconnect the fuel line fittings, squeeze the plastic tabs of the male end of the connector and pull the

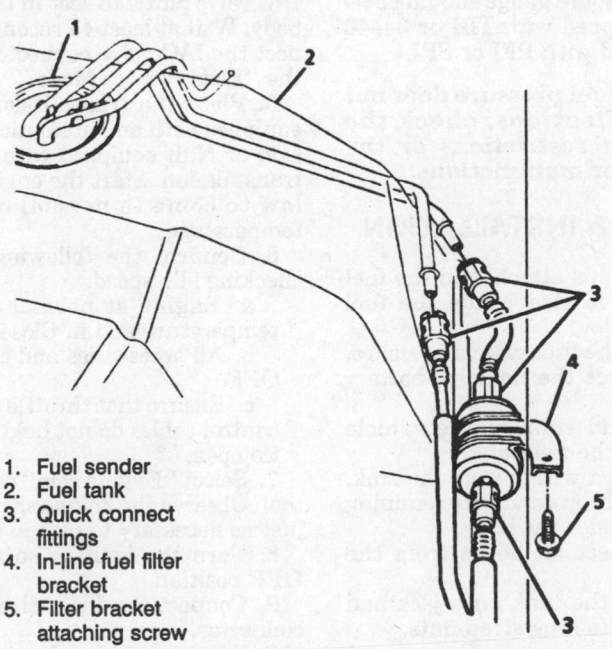

1. Fuel sender
2. Fuel tank
3. Quick connect fittings
4. In-line fuel filter bracket
5. Filter bracket attaching screw

Quick connect fitting in-line fuel filter replacement

connector apart. Repeat for the other fitting.

8. Remove the fuel filter.

To install:

9. Remove the protective caps from the new filter.

10. Install new plastic connector retainers on the filter inlet and outlet tubes. Observe the positions on the old filter and duplicate with new filter.

11. Connect the quick-connect fittings by performing the following:

    a. Apply a few drops of clean engine oil to the male tube ends of the fuel filter and fuel level meter assembly.

    b. Push the connectors together until the retaining tabs/fingers snap into place.

    c. Once installed, pull on both ends of each connector to ensure a tight connection.

12. Align the fuel filter bracket on the frame with the brake line mounting bracket and install the filter bracket attaching screw.

13. Lower the vehicle.

14. Tighten the fuel filler cap.

15. Connect the negative battery cable.

Electric Fuel Pump

PRESSURE TESTING

1. Disconnect the fuel line from the EFI unit.

2. Install a suitable pressure gauge to the fuel line.

3. Connect a jumper wire from the positive terminal on the battery to the G terminal of the ALDL.

4. Fuel pressure gauge should be 9–13 psi if equipped with TBI or 34–46 psi if equipped with PFI or SFI.

NOTE: If fuel pressure does not meet specifications, check the fuel line for restrictions or the fuel pump for malfunctions.

REMOVAL & INSTALLATION

The fuel pump is attached to the fuel sending unit located inside the fuel tank.

1. Relieve the fuel system pressure, then disconnect the negative battery cable.

2. Raise and support the vehicle safely. Drain the fuel tank.

3. Disconnect wiring from the tank, then remove the ground wire retaining screw from under the body.

4. Disconnect all hoses from the tank.

5. Support the tank on a jack and remove the retaining strap nuts.

6. Lower the tank and remove it from the vehicle.

7. Remove the fuel gauge/pump retaining ring using a suitable spanner wrench.

8. Remove the gauge unit and the pump.

To install:

9. Install the gauge unit and the pump.

10. Install the fuel gauge/pump retaining ring using a suitable spanner.

11. Raise the tank and and install it to the vehicle.

12. Support the tank on a jack stand and install the retaining strap nuts.

13. Connect the hoses to the tank.

14. Connect the electrical connectors and the ground wire, if equipped.

15. Lower the vehicle.

16. Fill the fuel tank.

17. Turn the ignition switch to the **ON** position for 2 seconds, then turn to the **OFF** position for 10 seconds. Turn the ignition switch back to the **ON** position and check for fuel leaks.

Fuel Injection

IDLE SPEED ADJUSTMENT

Throttle Body Injection (TBI)

NOTE: This procedure should be performed only after throttle body parts have been replaced.

1. Block the drive wheels and apply the parking brake.

2. Connect a Scan tool to the ALDL connector.

3. Turn the ignition switch to the **ON** position.

4. Select the "Field Service Mode" on the Scan tool. This will cause the IAC valve pintle to seat in the throttle body. Wait at least 45 seconds, disconnect the IAC valve connector and exit the "Field Service Mode."

5. Place the transmission in **P**, if equipped with an automatic transmission or **N**, if equipped with a manual transmission. Start the engine and allow to come to normal operating temperature.

6. Confirm the following prior to checking idle speed:

    a. Engine at normal operating temperature and in Closed Loop.

    b. All accessories and cooling fan OFF.

    c. Ensure that throttle and cruise control cables do not hold the throttle open.

7. Select "Engine rpm" on the Scan tool. Observe the engine speed and adjust as necessary to 600 ± 50 rpm.

8. Turn the ignition switch to the **OFF** position.

9. Connect the IAC valve electrical connector.

10. Reset the IAC valve pintle position by performing the following:

    a. Select "Engine rpm" on the Scan tool.

    b. Start the engine and hold speed above 2000 rpm. Select "Field Service Mode" for 10 seconds.

    c. Exit "Field Service Mode" and allow the engine to return to idle.

    d. Turn the ignition switch to the **OFF** position. Restart the engine and check for proper idle operation.

11. Disconnect the Scan tool.

12. Remove the block from the drive wheels.

Port Fuel Injeciton (PFI) and Sequential Fuel Injection (SFI)

1. Using an suitable tool, pierce the idle stop screw plug, located on the side of the throttle body, and remove it by prying it from the housing.

2. Using a jumper wire, ground the diagnostic lead of the IAC motor.

3. Turn the ignition ON. Do not start the engine. After 30 seconds, disconnect the IAC electrical connector. Remove the diagnostic lead ground lead and start the engine. Allow the system to go to closed loop.

4. Adjust the idle set screw to 550 rpm on automatic transaxle in **D** or 650 rpm on manual transaxle.

5. Turn the ignition OFF and reconnect the IAC motor lead.

6. Using a voltmeter, adjust the TPS to 0.55 ± 0.1 volt and secure the TPS.

7. Recheck the setting, then start the engine and check for proper idle operation.

8. Seal the idle stop screw with silicone sealer.

Fuel Injector

All fuel injectors are serviced as a complete assembly only. Since it is an electrical component, it should not be immersed in any type of cleaner.

REMOVAL & INSTALLATION

Throttle Body Injection (TBI)

1. Relieve fuel system pressure. Disconnect the negative battery cable.

2. Remove the air cleaner assembly.

3. Squeeze the 2 tabs on the injector electrical connector together and pull straight upward.

4. Remove the fuel meter cover retaining screws. The 2 front retaining screws are shorter than the 3 rear retaining screws. Remove the fuel meter cover.

5. With the fuel meter cover gasket in place, use a prying tool and carefully lift the injector until it is free from the fuel meter body.

6. Remove the small O-ring from the injector nozzle end. Carefully ro-

tate the injector fuel filter back and forth and remove the filter from the base of the injector.

7. Remove and discard the fuel meter cover gasket. Remove the large O-ring and steel backup washer from the top counterbore of the fuel meter body injector cavity.

To install:

8. Install the fuel injector nozzle filter on the nozzle end of the fuel injector, with the larger end of the filter facing the injector, so the filter covers raised rib at the base of the injector.

9. Lubricate the new small O-ring with automatic transmission fluid and push the O-ring on the nozzle end of the injector until it presses against the injector fuel filter.

10. Install the steel backup washer in the top counterbore of the fuel meter body injector cavity.

11. Lubricate the new large O-ring with automatic transmission fluid and install it directly over the backup washer. Be sure the O-ring is seated properly in the cavity and is flush with the top of the fuel meter body casting surface.

12. Install the injector into the cavity, aligning the raised lug on the injector base with cast-in notch in the fuel meter body cavity. Push down on the injector until it is fully seated in the cavity. The electrical terminals of the injector will be approximately parallel to the throttle shaft.

13. Install a new dust seal into the recess on the fuel meter body.

14. Install a new fuel outlet passage gasket on the fuel meter cover and a new cover gasket on the fuel meter body.

15. Install the fuel meter cover, making sure the pressure regulator dust seal and cover gaskets are in place; then, apply a thread locking compound to the threads on the fuel meter cover attaching screws. Install the fuel meter cover attaching screws and lock washers and torque to 28 inch lbs. (3 Nm). The 2 short screws go to the front of the injector. Connect battery negative cable.

Port Fuel Injeciton (PFI) and Sequential Fuel Injection (SFI)

NOTE: Always support the fuel rail to avoid damaging other components while removing the injectors.

1. Relieve fuel system pressure. Disconnect the negative battery cable.
2. Remove the intake manifold plenum.
3. Remove the fuel rail.
4. Remove the injector retaining clips and remove the injectors.
5. Remove the injector O-ring seals from both ends of the injector and discard.

To install:

6. Lubricate the new injector seals with clean engine oil and install on the injectors.

7. Install new injector retaining clips on the injectors. Position the open end of the clip facing the injector electrical connector.

8. Install the injectors into the fuel rail assembly. Push in far enough to engage the retainer clip with the machined slots on the injector socket.

9. Install the fuel rail assembly and intake manifold plenum.

10. Complete installation by reversing the removal procedure. Connect battery negative cable.

DRIVE AXLE

Halfshaft

REMOVAL & INSTALLATION

Front Axle

1. Raise and safely support the vehicle. Remove the wheel and tire assembly.
2. Remove the shaft nut, using tool J34826 and discard. A new shaft nut must be used for reassembly.
3. Disconnect the brake hose clip from the MacPherson strut but do not disconnect the hose from the caliper. Remove the brake caliper from the spindle and support the caliper with a length of wire. Do not allow the caliper to hang by the brake hose unsupported.
4. Remove the brake rotor and remove the lower ball joint and pinch bolt.
5. Install drive axle seal protector tool J34754 onto drive axle.
6. Remove the ball joint from the steering knuckle.
7. Remove the halfshaft from the transaxle.
8. Using spindle remover tool J-28733 or equivalent, remove the halfshaft from the hub and bearing assembly. Do not allow the halfshaft to hang unsupported. If necessary, support using a length of wire in order to prevent component damage.

To install:

9. If a new halfshaft is to be installed, a new knuckle seal should be installed first along with a boot seal protector when necessary.
10. Loosely install the halfshaft into the transaxle and steering knuckle.
11. Loosely attach the steering knuckle to the suspension strut.

12. The halfshaft is an interference fit in the steering knuckle. Press the axle into place, then install the hub nut. When the shaft begins to turn with the hub, insert a drift through the caliper into one of the cooling slots in the rotor to keep it from turning.

NOTE: On some vehicles, the hub flange has a notch in it which can be used to prevent the hub and the shaft from turning, when one of the hub bearing retainer bolts is removed, by placing a longer bolt put in its place through the notch.

13. Tighten the hub nut to 70 ft. lbs. (95 Nm) to completely seat the shaft.
14. Install the brake caliper. Tighten the caliper mounting bolts to 30 ft. lbs. (41 Nm).
15. Load the hub assembly by lowering it onto a jackstand. Align the camber cam bolt marks made during removal, install the bolt and tighten to 140 ft. lbs. (190 Nm). Tighten the upper nut to the same value.
16. Install the halfshaft all the way into the transaxle using a suitable tool inserted into the groove provided on the inner retainer. Tap the tool until the shaft seats in the transaxle. Remove the boot seal protector.
17. Connect the brake hose clip the the strut. Install the tire and wheel, lower the vehicle and tighten the hub nut to 192 ft. lbs. (261 Nm).

Rear Axle

6000 STE AWD

1. Raise and safely support the vehicle.
2. Remove the tire and wheel assembly.
3. Disconnect the parking brake cable end from the bracket.
4. Insert a suitable tool through the caliper into the rotor to prevent the rotor from turning.
5. Remove the shaft nut and washer using special tool J-34826. Discard the shaft nut.
6. Remove the anti-lock brake sensor bolt and move the sensor aside.
7. Remove the 2 brake caliper bolts and remove the caliper. Support the caliper using a length of wire.

NOTE: Do not allow the caliper to hang by the brake hose unsupported.

8. Remove the rotor from the hub and bearing assembly.
9. Install leaf spring compression tool J-33432 or equivalent.
10. Remove the 3 bolts mounting the hub and bearing to the knuckle.
11. Remove the hub and bearing assembly from the knuckle using special tool J-28733-A or equivalent.

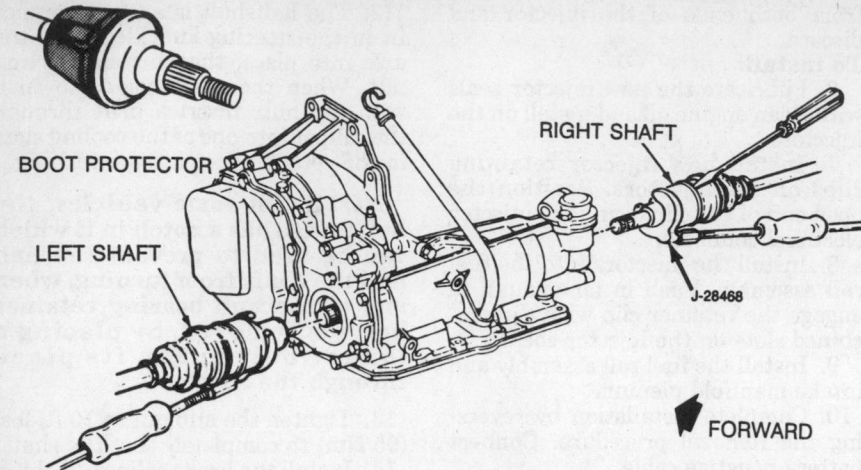

BOOT PROTECTOR

RIGHT SHAFT

LEFT SHAFT

J-28468

FORWARD

Halfshaft removal using special tools attached to slide hammers

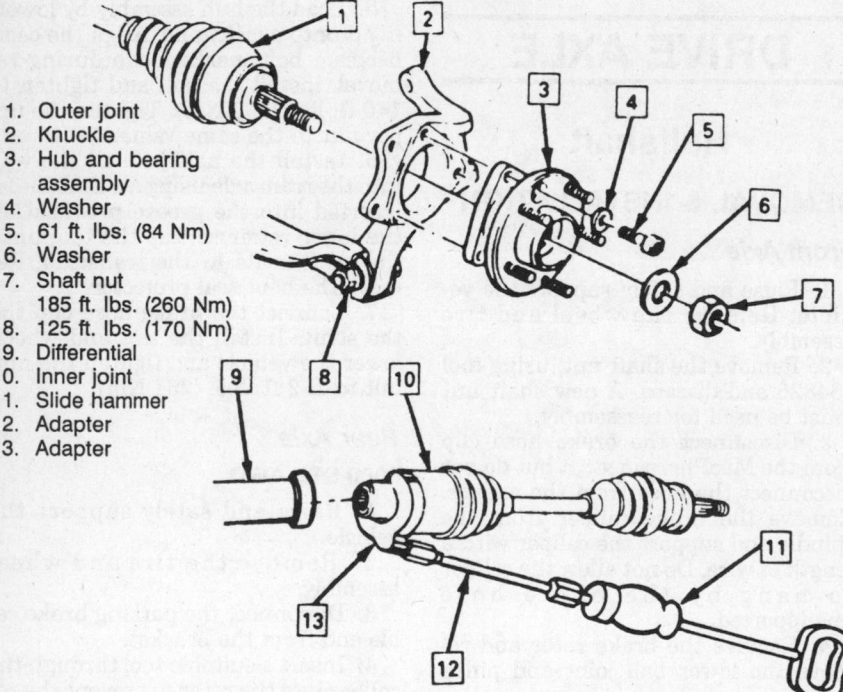

1. Outer joint
2. Knuckle
3. Hub and bearing assembly
4. Washer
5. 61 ft. lbs. (84 Nm)
6. Washer
7. Shaft nut 185 ft. lbs. (260 Nm)
8. 125 ft. lbs. (170 Nm)
9. Differential
10. Inner joint
11. Slide hammer
12. Adapter
13. Adapter

Rear drive axle removal—6000 STE AWD

12. Remove the bolts and nut plate attaching the lower strut mount to the knuckle. Scribe the position of the upper bolt prior removing.

13. Install a suitable CV-boot protector to prevent damage to the boot.

14. Swing the knuckle downward and away from the driveshaft.

15. Remove the drive axle from the differential using a suitable slide hammer.

To install:

16. Install the drive axle to the differential. Ensure positive engagement by pulling outward on the inner axle end. Grasp the housing only. Do not grasp and pull on the axle shaft.

17. Swing the knuckle up to the lower strut mount.

18. Position the nut plate and install the lower strut mount bolts to the knuckle. Align the top bolt with scribe marks before tightening the bolts. Tighten the bolts to 148 ft. lbs. (200 Nm).

19. Remove the CV boot protector.

20. Install the hub and bearing assembly to the knuckle and axle spline.

21. Install the hub and bearing attaching bolts. Tighten to 61 ft. lbs. (84 Nm).

22. Remove the leaf spring compression tool.

23. Install the rotor to hub and bearing assembly.

24. Install the brake caliper to the rotor and install the retaining bolts. Tighten the bolts to 38 ft. lbs. (51 Nm).

25. Install the anti-lock brake sensor to the knuckle and install the retaining bolt. Using a non-ferrous feeler gauge, adjust the sensor gap to 0.028 in. (0.7mm). Tighten the adjustment screw to 19 inch lbs. (2.2 Nm).

26. Connect the parking brake cable end into the bracket.

27. Install the shaft washer and new torque prevailing nut. Hold the rotor with a suitable to prevent the axle from turning while tightening. Tighten to 185 ft. lbs. (260 Nm).

28. Install the tire and wheel assembly.

29. Check the rear wheel camber. Adjust as necessary.

NOTE: If the lower strut to knuckle bolts are properly aligned with the scribe marks, no camber adjustment should be necessary.

30. Lower the vehicle.

CV-Boot

REMOVAL & INSTALLATION

Outer Boot

1. Raise and support the vehicle safely.

2. Remove the front tire and wheel assembly.

3. Remove the caliper bolts. Remove the caliper and support using a length of wire.

4. Remove the hub nut, washer and wheel bearing.

5. Using a brass drift, lightly tap around the seal retainer to loosen it. Remove the seal retainer.

6. Remove the seal retaining clamp or ring and discard.

7. Using snapring pliers, remove the race retaining ring from the halfshaft.

8. Pull the outer joint assembly and the outboard seal away from the halfshaft.

9. Flush the grease from the joint and repack with half of the grease provided. Put the remainder of the grease in the seal.

To install:

10. Assemble the inner seal retainer, outboard seal and outer seal retainer to the halfshaft. Push the joint assembly onto the shaft until the retaining ring is seated in the groove.

11. Slide the outboard seal onto the joint assembly and secure using the outer seal retainer. Using seal clamp tool J-35910 or equivalent, torque the outer clamp to 130 ft. lbs. (176 Nm) and the inner clamp to 100 ft. lbs. (136 Nm).

12. Install the wheel bearing, washer and hub nut. Tighten the hub nut to 192 ft. lbs. (260 Nm).

13. Install the caliper and caliper attaching bolts.
14. Install the front tire and wheel assembly.
15. Lower the vehicle.

Inner Boot

1. Raise and safely support the vehicle.
2. Remove the front tire and wheel assembly.
3. Remove the caliper bolts. Remove the caliper and support using a length of wire.
4. Remove the hub nut, washer and wheel bearing.
5. Remove the halfshaft. Place in a suitable holding fixture being careful not place undue pressure on the halfshaft.
6. Remove the joint assembly retaining ring. Remove the joint assembly.
7. Remove the race retaining ring and remove the seal retainer.
8. Remove the inner seal retaining clamp. Remove the inner joint seal.
9. Flush the grease from the joint and repack with half of the grease provided. Put the remainder of the grease in the seal.
To install:
10. Assemble the inner seal retainer, outboard seal and outer seal retainer to the halfshaft. Push the joint assembly onto the shaft until the retaining ring is seated in the groove.
11. Slide the outboard seal onto the joint assembly and secure using the outer seal retainer. Using seal clamp tool J–35910 or equivalent, torque the outer clamp to 130 ft. lbs. (176 Nm) and the inner clamp to 100 ft. lbs. (136 Nm).
12. Install the halfshaft assembly.
13. Install the wheel bearing, washer and hub nut. Tighten the hub nut to 192 ft. lbs. (260 Nm).
14. Install the caliper and caliper attaching bolts.
15. Install the front tire and wheel assembly.
16. Lower the vehicle.

Driveshafts

REMOVAL & INSTALLATION

6000 STE AWD
ORIGINAL DRIVESHAFT

1. Raise and safely support the vehicle.

NOTE: The relationship between the center bearing support and the floor pan must be maintained. Established at the assembly plant, the relationship has an influence on the front joint stoke capacity and remains constant for the vehicle, regardless of the driveshaft installed.

2. Scribe the transmission output shaft flange opposite the "painted" marking on the front driveshaft. The rear pinion flange must be scribed opposite the "painted" marking on the rear driveshaft. Scribe the center support mounting plate to floor pan of the vehicle.
3. Remove the 4 bolts connecting the rear driveshaft to the rear axle pinion flange.

NOTE: Do not loosen, remove or disconnect the 4 bolts adjacent to the center double cardan joint. Disturbing these fasteners may result in a vibration.

4. With the aid of an assistant, support the driveshaft while performing the following:
   a. Remove the 3 nuts retaining the center bearing support to the underbody of the vehicle.
   b. Remove the 4 bolts connecting the front driveshaft to the transaxle output shaft flange.
   c. Remove the driveshaft from the vehicle.
To install:
5. With the aid of an assistant, perform the following:
   a. Install the driveshaft to the vehicle.
   b. Align the rear driveshaft flange to the rear axle pinion flange, aligning the scribe marks.

NOTE: The center mount plate must be reinstalled at the scribed position so the front CV joint is correctly located within its travel limits.

   c. Loosely install the nuts to the center bearing support and bolts to the rear axle pinion flange. Tighten the rear driveshaft flange to the rear axle pinion flange bolts to 40 ft. lbs. (54 Nm).
   d. Install the bolts to the front driveshaft-to-transmission output flange, using the reference marks to align the front flange position and center bracket location. Tighten the center bearing support bolts using the scribed reference marks to 25 ft. lbs. (34 Nm); nuts to 20 ft. lbs. (27 Nm). Tighten the front propeller shaft-to-transmission output flange bolts to 40 ft. lbs. (54 Nm).
6. Remove the support and lower the vehicle.

NEW DRIVESHAFT

1. Raise and safely support the vehicle.

NOTE: The relationship between the center bearing support and the floor pan must be maintained. Established at the assembly plant, the relationship has an influence on the front joint stoke capacity and remains constant for the vehicle, regardless of the driveshaft installed.

2. Scribe the transmission output shaft flange opposite the "painted" marking on the front driveshaft. The rear pinion flange must be scribed opposite the "painted" marking on the rear driveshaft. Scribe the center support mounting plate to floor pan of the vehicle.
3. Remove the 4 bolts connecting the rear driveshaft to the rear axle pinion flange.

NOTE: Do not loosen, remove or disconnect the 4 bolts adjacent to the center double cardan joint. Disturbing these fasteners may result in a vibration.

4. With the aid of an assistant, support the driveshaft while performing the following:
   a. Remove the 3 nuts retaining the center bearing support to the underbody of the vehicle.
   b. Remove the 4 bolts connecting the front driveshaft to the transaxle output shaft flange.
   c. Remove the driveshaft from the vehicle.
To install:
5. Using a dial indicator, measure and mark the bolt hole corresponding to the high point of radial runout on both the transmission output flange and rear axle pinion flange.
6. Transfer the center bearing bracket from the old driveshaft to the new driveshaft assembly.
7. With the aid of an assistant, perform the following:
   a. Install the driveshaft to the vehicle.
   b. Align the point marks supplied on the flanges of the propeller shaft to the scribe marks made during removal.
   c. Loosely install the nuts to the center bearing support and bolts to the rear axle pinion flange. Tighten the rear driveshaft flange to the rear axle pinion flange bolts to 40 ft. lbs. (54 Nm).
   d. Push the propeller shaft forward until a click is heard. Temporarily install a $15/16$ in. (23mm) thick spacer between the output flange and the front driveshaft flange. Clamp in this position.
8. Install the remaining center bracket nuts. Tighten to 20 ft. lbs. (27 Nm).
9. Remove the spacer, extend the front CV-joint to meet the output flange and tighten the bolts. Tighten

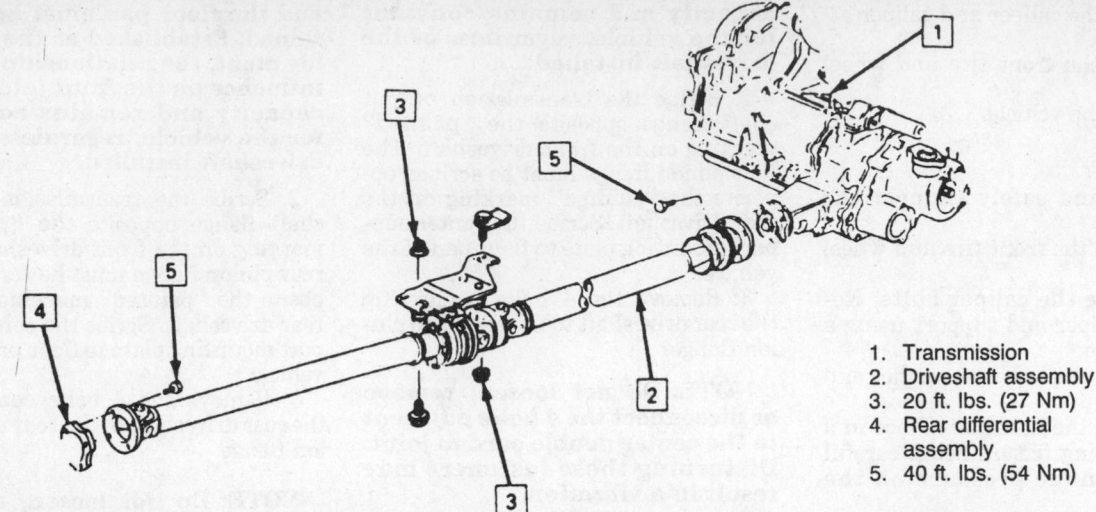

1. Transmission
2. Driveshaft assembly
3. 20 ft. lbs. (27 Nm)
4. Rear differential assembly
5. 40 ft. lbs. (54 Nm)

Driveshafts—6000 STE AWD

A. Correct CV joint plunge location
1. Driveshaft
2. Transmission output shaft flange
3. Transmission
4. Stabilizer shaft
5. Exhaust system

Verifying correct CV-joint plunge location—6000 STE AWD

the front propeller shaft-to-transmission output flange bolts to 40 ft. lbs. (54 Nm).

10. Verify correct location of the front CV-joint plunge.

11. Remove the supports. Lower the vehicle.

Front Wheel Hub, Knuckle and Bearings

REMOVAL & INSTALLATION

1. Disconnect the negative battery cable.
2. Remove the wheel cover, loosen the lug nuts. Raise and safely support the vehicle.
3. Remove the tire and wheel assembly.
4. Install boot cover tool J–28712, for a double off-set joint or tool J–33162 for a tri-pot joint.
5. Remove and discard the hub nut. A new hub nut must be used during assembly.
6. Remove the brake caliper and rotor.

7. Remove the 3 hub and bearing attaching bolts. Remove the hub.

NOTE: If the old bearing is to be reused, make matchmarks on the bolts and holes for installation purposes.

8. Attach bearing puller J–28733 or equivalent, then remove the bearing. **To install:**
9. Clean the mating surfaces of all dirt and corrosion. Check the knuckle bore and seal for damage. If a new bearing is to be installed, remove the old knuckle seal and install a new one. Grease the lips of new seal.
10. Push the bearing onto the halfshaft. Install a new washer and hub nut.
11. Tighten the hub nut on the halfshaft until the new bearing is seated. If the rotor and hub start to rotate as the hub nut is tightened, insert a drift through the caliper and into the rotor cooling fins to prevent rotation.

NOTE: Do not apply full torque to the hub nut at this time.

12. Install the brake shield, if re-

moved, and the bearing retaining bolts. Torque bolts to 63 ft. lbs. (85 Nm).

13. Install the caliper and rotor. Ensure the caliper hose is not twisted. Install caliper bolts.

14. Install the wheel assembly. Torque the lug nuts to the proper torque.

15. Connect battery negative cable.

Differential Carrier

REMOVAL & INSTALLATION

6000 STE AWD

1. Disconnect the negative battery cable.
2. Disconnect the air pressure from the Electroinic Level Control (ELC) system.
3. Raise and safely support the vehicle.
4. Drain the lubricant from the differential carrier housing.
5. Remove the tire and wheel assemblies.

NOTE: Mark the relationship of the driveshaft to the rear axle pinion flange prior to removal of the driveshaft from the rear axle pinion flange to ensure proper driveshaft alignment.

6. Disconnect the rear driveshaft at the rear axle pinion flange.
7. Remove the rear axle assembly.
8. Remove the rear axle shafts.
9. Disconnect the rear axle remote vent hose.
10. Remove the 3 bolts attaching the differential carrier assembly to the rear axle assembly.
11. Remove the differential carrier assembly from the rear axle assembly.

To install:

12. Position the differential carrier in the rear axle assembly.
13. Install the 3 differential carrier retaining bolts. Tighten to 60 ft. lbs. (82 Nm).
14. Connect the rear axle remote vent hose and clamp.
15. Install the rear axle shafts.
16. Install the rear axle assembly in the vehicle.

NOTE: The driveshaft must be installed using the reference mark made during removal of the driveshaft.

17. Connect the rear driveshaft to the rear axle pinion flange.
18. Install the tire and wheel assemblies.
19. Fill the differential carrier housing with 1.9 qts. (1.8L) of SAE 80W–90 weight gear lubricant.
20. Remove the axle assembly supporting device.
21. Lower the vehicle.
22. Connect the negative battery cable.
23. Check the rear camber and align, as necessary.

AUTOMATIC TRANSAXLE

For further information on transmission/transaxles, please refer to "Chilton's Guide to Transmission Repair".

Transaxle Assembly

REMOVAL & INSTALLATION

THM 125C

NOTE: By September 1, 1991, Hydra-matic will have changed the name designation of the THM 125C automatic transaxle. The new name designation for this transaxle will be Hydra-matic 3T40. Transaxles built between 1989–90 will serve as transitional years in which a dual system, made up of the old designation and the new designation will be in effect.

1. Disconnect the negative battery cable.
2. Remove the air cleaner and duct assembly.
3. Remove the bolt that secures the TV cable to the transaxle.
4. Disconnect the shift cable.
5. Disconnect the electrical connector at the neutral switch.
6. Remove all the engine-to-transaxle bolts except the one near the starter. The one nearest the firewall is installed from the engine side of the vehicle.
7. Loosen but do not remove the engine-to-transaxle bolt near the starter.
8. Disconnect the speedometer cable at the upper and lower coupling. If equipped with cruise control, remove the speedometer cable at the transducer.
9. Remove the retaining clip and washer from the shift linkage at the transaxle. Remove the 2 shift linkages at the transaxle. Remove the 2 shift linkage bracket bolts.
10. Disconnect and plug the cooler lines at the transaxle.
11. Install an engine holding fixture. Raise the engine enough to take its weight off the mounts.
12. Unlock the steering column. Raise and safely support the vehicle.
13. Remove the 2 nuts holding the anti-sway bar to the left lower control arm (driver's side).
14. Remove the 4 bolts attaching the covering plate over the stabilizer bar to the engine cradle on the left side of vehicle.
15. Loosen but do not remove the 4 bolts holding the stabilizer bar bracket to the right side of the engine cradle. Pull the bar downward.
16. Disconnect the front and rear transaxle mounts at the engine cradle.
17. Remove the 2 rear center crossmember bolts.
18. Remove the 3 right (passenger) side front engine cradle attaching bolts. The nuts are accessible under the splash shield next to the frame rail.
19. If equipped with V6 engine, remove the top bolt from the lower front transaxle shock absorber, as required.
20. Remove the left side front and rear cradle-to-body bolts.
21. Remove the left front wheel. Attach an halfshaft removing tool J–28468 or equivalent, to a slide hammer. Place the tool behind the halfshaft cones and pull the cones out away from the transaxle. Remove the right shaft in the same manner. Set the shafts aside. Plug the openings in the transaxle to prevent fluid leakage and the entry of dirt.
22. Swing the partial engine cradle to the left (driver) side and wire it aside outboard of the fender well.
23. Remove the 4 torque converter and starter shield bolts. Remove the 2 transaxle extension bolts from the engine-to-transaxle bracket.
24. Attach a transaxle jack to the case.
25. Use a felt pen to matchmark the torque converter and flywheel. Remove the 3 torque converter-to-flywheel bolts.
26. Remove the transaxle-to-engine bolt near the starter. Remove the transaxle by sliding it to the left, away from the engine.

To install:

27. As the transaxle is installed, slide the right halfshaft into the case. Install the cradle-to-body bolts before the stabilizer bar is installed. To aid in stabilizer bar installation, a pry hole has been provided in the engine cradle.
28. Install the 3 torque converter-to-flywheel bolts. Tighten to 46 ft. lbs. (62 Nm).
29. Install the 4 torque converter and starter shield bolts. Install the 2 transaxle extension bolts to the engine-to-transaxle bracket.
30. Swing the partial engine cradle into position and install attaching bolts.
31. Install the halfshafts. Install the left front wheel.
32. Install the left side front and rear cradle-to-body bolts.
33. If equipped with V6 engine, install the top bolt to the lower front transaxle shock absorber, as required.
34. Install the 3 right (passenger) side front engine cradle attaching bolts.
35. Install the 2 rear center crossmember bolts.
36. Disconnect the front and rear transaxle mounts at the engine cradle.
37. Tighten the 4 bolts holding the stabilizer bar bracket to the right side of the engine cradle.
38. Install the 4 bolts attaching the covering plate over the stabilizer bar to the engine cradle on the left side of vehicle.
39. Install the 2 nuts holding the anti-sway bar to the left lower control arm (driver's side).
40. Lower the vehicle.
41. Remove the engine holding fixture.
42. Connect the cooler lines to the transaxle.
43. Install the 2 shift linkage bracket bolts. Install the 2 shift linkages at the transaxle. Install the retaining clip and washer to the shift linkage on the transaxle.
44. Connect the speedometer cable at the upper and lower coupling. If equipped with cruise control, connect the speedometer cable to the transducer.
45. Tighten the engine-to-transaxle bolt near the starter.
46. Install all the engine-to-transaxle bolts except the one near the starter. The one nearest the firewall is installed from the engine side of the vehicle.
47. Install the 2 transaxle strut

bracket bolts at the transaxle, if equipped.

48. Connect the detent cable.
49. Install the air cleaner.
50. Connect the negative battery cable.

THM 440–T4

NOTE: By September 1, 1991, Hydra-matic will have changed the name designation of the THM 440–T4 automatic transaxle. The new name designation for this transaxle will be Hydra-matic 4T60. Transaxles built between 1989–90 will serve as transitional years in which a dual system, made up of the old designation and the new designation will be in effect.

1. Disconnect the negative battery cable.
2. Remove the air cleaner and disconnect the TV cable at the throttle body.
3. Disconnect the shift linkage at the transaxle.
4. Remove the engine support fixture tool J–28467 or equivalent.
5. Disconnect all electrical connectors.
6. Remove the 3 bolts from the transaxle to the engine.
7. Disconnect the vacuum line at the modulator.
8. Raise and safely support the vehicle.
9. Remove the left front wheel and tire assembly.
10. Remove the left side ball joint from the steering knuckle.
11. Disconnect the brake line bracket at the strut.

NOTE: A halfshaft seal protector tool J–34754 should be modified and installed on any halfshaft prior to service procedures on or near the halfshaft. Failure to do so could result in seal damage or joint failure.

12. Remove the halfshafts from the transaxle.
13. Disconnect the pinch bolt at the intermediate steering shaft. Failure to do so could cause damage to the steering gear.
14. Remove the frame to stabilizer bolts.
15. Remove the stabilizer bolts at the control arm.
16. Remove the left front frame assembly.
17. Disconnect the speedometer cable or wire connector from the transaxle.
18. Remove the extension housing to engine block support bracket.
19. Disconnect the cooler pipes.

20. Remove the converter cover and converter-to-flywheel bolts.
21. Remove all of the remaining transaxle-to-engine bolts except one.
22. Position a jack under the transaxle.
23. Remove the remaining transaxle-to-engine bolt and remove the transaxle.

To install:
24. Install the transaxle in the vehicle. Install the engine-to-transaxle bolt accessible from under the vehicle. Tighten to 55 ft. lbs. (75 Nm).
25. Install all of the remaining transaxle-to-engine bolts. Tighten to 55 ft. lbs. (75 Nm).
26. Remove the jack.
27. Install the converter-to-flywheel bolts and the converter cover.
28. Connect the cooler pipes.
29. Install the extension housing to engine block support bracket.
30. Connect the speedometer cable or wire connector to the transaxle.
31. Install the left front frame assembly.
32. Install the stabilizer bolts at the control arm.
33. Install the frame-to-stabilizer bolts.
34. Connect the pinch bolt at the intermediate steering shaft.
35. Install the halfshafts to the transaxle.
36. Connect the brake line bracket at the strut.
37. Install the left side ball joint to the steering knuckle.
38. Install the left front wheel and tire assembly.
39. Lower the vehicle.
40. Connect the vacuum line at the modulator.
41. Install the 3 bolts from the transaxle to the engine.
42. Connect all electrical connectors.
43. Remove the engine support tool.
44. Connect the shift linkage to the transaxle.
45. Connect the TV cable at the throttle body and adjust as necessary. Install the air cleaner.
46. Connect the negative battery cable.

SHIFT CONTROL CABLE ADJUSTMENT

1. Place the shift lever in N. To determine the N position, rotate the selector shaft clockwise from P through R to N.
2. Place the shift control assembly in N.
3. Push the tab on the cable adjuster to adjust the cable in cable mounting bracket.

PARK/LOCK CONTROL CABLE ADJUSTMENT

The shifter lever must not be able to move to any other positions with the shift lever in P and the key in the LOCK position. Also, with the key in the RUN position and the shift lever in N, ensure that the key cannot be turned to the LOCK position. If these conditions cannot be met, adjustment is necessary.

1. If the key cannot be removed in the P position, snap the connector lock button to the UP position.
2. Move the cable connector nose rearward until the key can be removed from the ignition.
3. Push the snap lock button down.

TV DETENT CABLE ADJUSTMENT

1. With the engine OFF, depress and hold-down the readjust tab at the TV cable adjuster.
2. Move the cable conduit until it stops against the fitting. Release the readjustment tab.
3. Rotate the throttle lever by hand to its full travel position. The slider must ratchet toward the lever when the lever is rotated to its full travel.

NOTE: Check that the cable moves freely. The cable may appear to function properly with the engine OFF and COLD. Recheck after the engine is HOT.

FRONT SUSPENSION

MacPherson Strut

REMOVAL & INSTALLATION

1. Loosen the wheel nuts, raise and support vehicle, then remove the wheel and tire assembly.
2. Remove the brake hose clip-to-strut bolt, if equipped. Do not disconnect the hose from the caliper. Install a halfshaft cover to protect the axle boot.
3. Mark the camber cam eccentric adjuster for assembly.
4. Remove the 2 lower strut-to-steering knuckle bolts and the 3 upper strut-to-body nuts. Remove the strut assembly.

To install:
5. Install the strut assembly. Install the 2 lower strut-to-steering knuckle

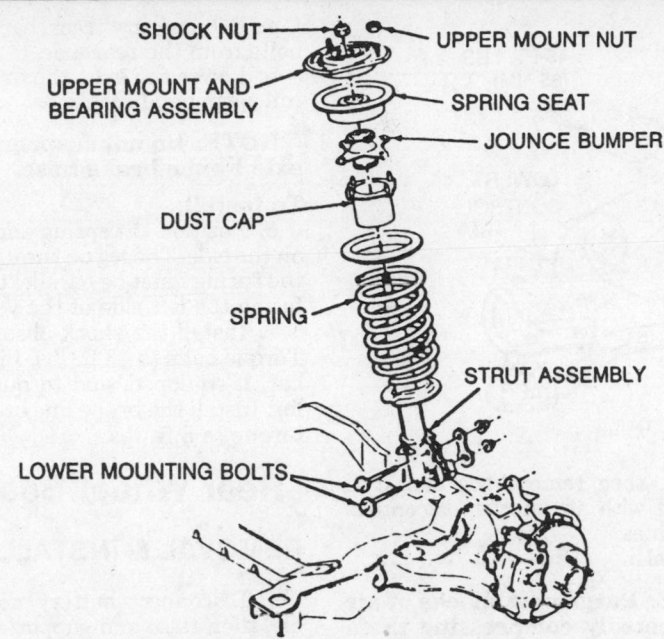

SHOCK NUT — UPPER MOUNT NUT

UPPER MOUNT AND BEARING ASSEMBLY — SPRING SEAT

JOUNCE BUMPER

DUST CAP

SPRING

STRUT ASSEMBLY

LOWER MOUNTING BOLTS

Front suspension components

bolts and 3 upper strut-to-body nuts. Realign the camber marks made upon removal.

6. Install the brake hose clip-to-strut bolt.

7. Remove the axle boot protector.

8. Install the tire and wheel assembly.

9. Lower the vehicle.

Lower Ball Joints

INSPECTION

1. Raise and support vehicle safely.

2. Grasp the wheel at the top and bottom and shake the wheel in and out.

3. If any movement is seen of the steering knuckle relative to the control arm, the ball joints are defective and must be replaced. Note that movement elsewhere may be due to loose wheel bearings or other problems; watch the knuckle-to-control arm connection.

4. If the ball stud is disconnected from the steering knuckle and any looseness is noted, often the ball joint stud can be twisted in its socket with your fingers, replace the ball joints.

REMOVAL & INSTALLATION

1. Loosen the wheel nuts, raise and support vehicle safely, then remove the tire and wheel assembly.

2. Using an 1/8 inch drill bit, drill a hole approximately 1/4 inch deep in the center of each of the 3 ball joint rivets.

3. Using a 1/2 inch drill bit, drill off the rivet heads. Drill only enough to remove the rivet head.

4. Using a hammer and punch, remove the rivets, driving them out from the bottom.

5. Loosen the ball joint pinch bolt in the steering knuckle, then remove the ball joint.

To install:

6. Install a new ball joint in the control arm. Torque new bolts to 13 ft. lbs.

7. Install the ball stud into the steering knuckle pinch bolt fitting. It should go in easily; if not, check the stud alignment. Install the pinch bolt from the rear to the front. Torque to 45 ft. lbs.

8. Install the wheel and lower the vehicle.

Lower Control Arms

REMOVAL & INSTALLATION

1. Loosen the wheel nuts, raise and support vehicle safely, then remove the tire and wheel assembly.

2. Remove the stabilizer bar from the control arm.

3. Remove the ball joint from the steering knuckle.

4. Remove the control arm mounting bolts, then the control arm from the vehicle.

To install:

5. Install the control arm into the fittings. Install the pivot bolts from the rear to the front. Torque bolts to 50 ft. lbs. (68 Nm).

6. Install the ball stud into the pinch bolt fitting. It should go in easily; if not, check the ball joint stud alignment.

7. Install the pinch bolt from the rear to the front. Torque bolts 33 ft. lbs. (45 Nm).

8. Install the stabilizer bar attachment. Torque bolts to 35 ft. lbs. (47 Nm).

9. Install the tire and wheel assembly and lower the vehicle.

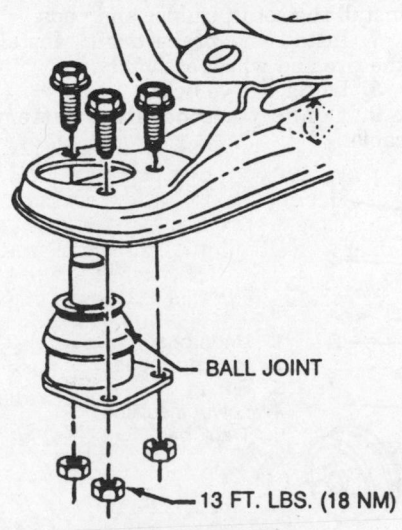

BALL JOINT

13 FT. LBS. (18 NM)

Ball joint installation

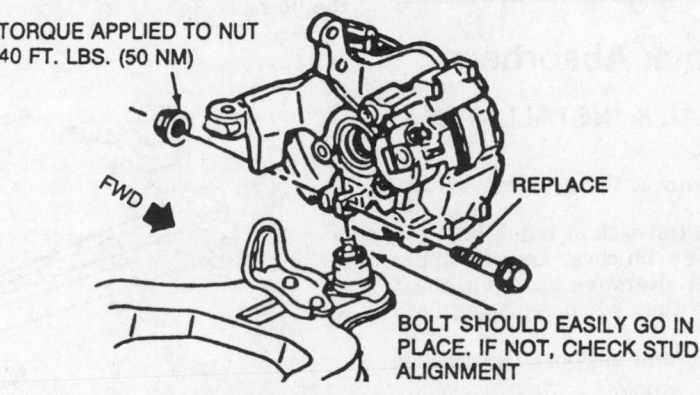

TORQUE APPLIED TO NUT 40 FT. LBS. (50 NM)

FWD

REPLACE

BOLT SHOULD EASILY GO IN PLACE. IF NOT, CHECK STUD ALIGNMENT

Ball joint stud should go in easily

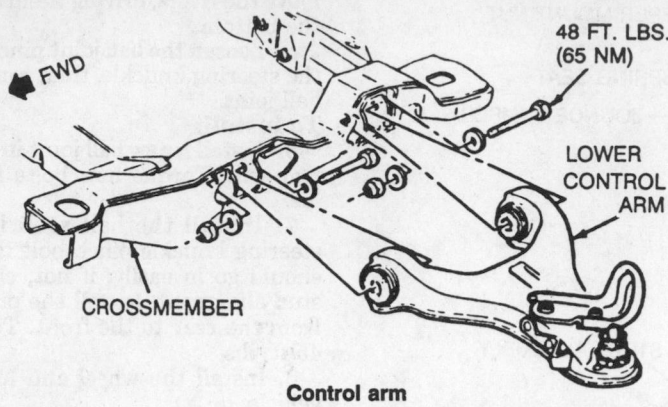

Control arm

Stabilizer Shaft

REMOVAL & INSTALLATION

1. Disconnect battery negative cable.
2. Raise and safely support the vehicle.
3. Remove the stabilizer shaft insulator clamp and insulator at the control arms. Do not remove the studs from the control arm.
4. Remove the plate from the frame at each side, then the stabilizer shaft and insulator bushings from the vehicle.

To install:

5. Install the stabilizer insulator bushings, stabilizer shaft and plate to the frame at each side. Tighten plate to frame bolts to 40 ft. lbs. (55 Nm)
6. Install the insulators at the control arms. Install the stabilizer shaft insulator clamp. Tighten insulator clamp nuts to 33 ft. lbs. (45 Nm).
7. Lower the vehicle.
8. Connect the negative battery cable.

REAR SUSPENSION

Shock Absorbers

REMOVAL & INSTALLATION

1. Disconnect the negative battery cable.
2. Open the deck or trunk lid, then remove the trim cover and the upper shock nut. Remove and replace 1 shock at a time when replacing both shocks.
3. Raise and support the vehicle safely.
4. Remove the shock lower attach-

ing bolt, then remove the shock. If equipped with air shocks, disconnect the air lines.

To install:

NOTE: Purge new shocks of air by repeatedly compressing them while inverted and extending them in their normal installed position.

5. Install the shock absorber and attaching bolts. Tighten to 43 ft. lbs. (58 Nm).
6. Lower the vehicle.
7. Install the upper shock absorber nut. Tighten the upper nut to 13 ft. lbs. (18 Nm).
8. Install the trim cover.
9. Connect the negative battery cable.

Coil Springs

REMOVAL & INSTALLATION

1. Disconnect the battery negative cable.
2. Raise and safely support the vehicle using jacks that can be raised and lowered.
3. Remove the brake hose attaching brackets (right and left), allowing the hoses to hang freely. Do not disconnect the hoses.

4. Remove the track bar attaching bolts from the rear axle.
5. Lower the axle, then remove the coil spring and insulator.

NOTE: Do not suspend the rear axle by the brake hose.

To install:

6. Position the spring and insulator on the axle. The leg on the upper coil of the spring must be parallel to the axle, facing the left side of the vehicle.
7. Install the shock absorber bolts. Torque bolts to 43 ft. lbs. Install track bar, if equipped, and torque to 33 ft. lbs. Install the brake line brackets and torque to 8 ft. lbs.

Rear Wheel Bearings

REMOVAL & INSTALLATION

1. Disconnect battery negative cable, then raise and support vehicle.
2. Remove the wheel and brake drum. Do not hammer on the brake drum as damage to the bearing may result.
3. If equipped with anti-lock brakes, remove caliper, rotor and pads.
4. On all vehicles, remove the hub and bearing assembly from the rear axle attaching bolts and remove the rear axle.

NOTE: The bolts attaching the hub and bearing assembly also support the brake assembly. When removing these bolts, support the brake assembly with a length of wire. Do not let the brake assembly hang by the brake line unsupported.

To install:

5. On all vehicles, install the rear axle and install the hub and bearing assembly attaching bolts.
6. If equipped with anti-lock brakes, install the rotor, caliper and pads.
7. Install the brake drum. Install the tire and wheel assembly.
8. Lower the vehicle.
9. Connect the negative battery cable.

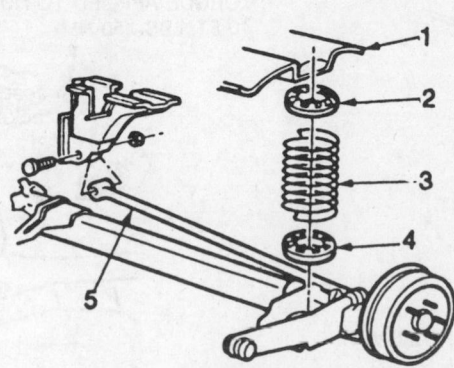

1. Underbody
2. Insulator upper
3. Spring
4. Lower insulator
5. Track bar

A-body rear suspension

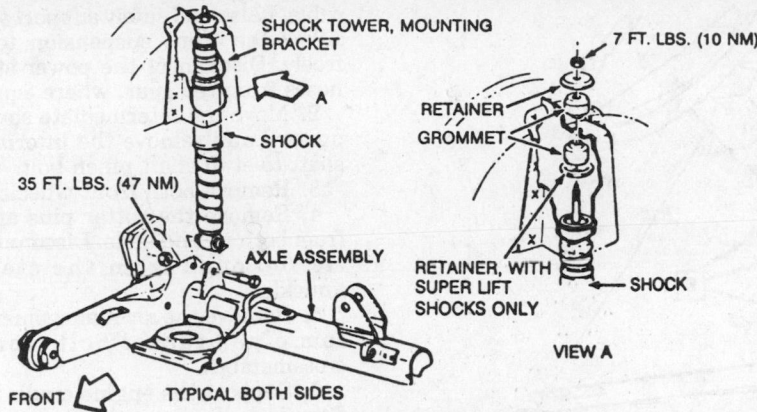

Shock absorber Installation

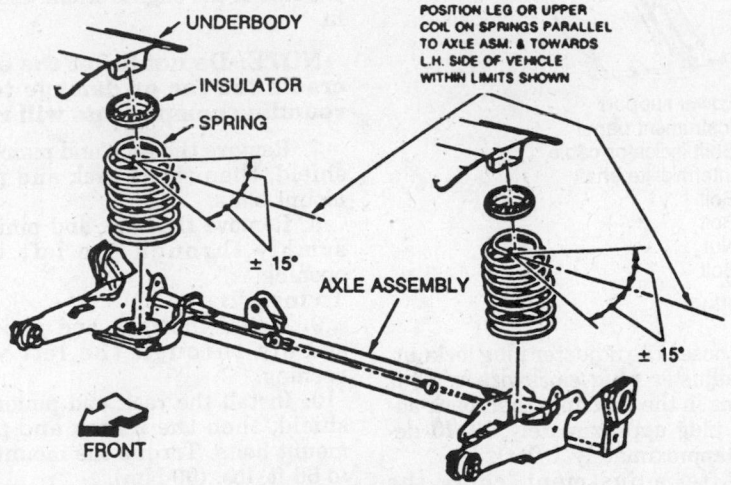

POSITION LEG OR UPPER COIL ON SPRINGS PARALLEL TO AXLE ASM. & TOWARDS L.H. SIDE OF VEHICLE WITHIN LIMITS SHOWN

Spring Installation

Rear Axle Assembly

REMOVAL & INSTALLATION

1. Raise and safely support the vehicle. Disconnect the negative battery cable.

NOTE: If removing the rear axle on a twin post lift, the axle assembly must be supported securely to prevent the possibility of the axle assembly slipping from the lift when certain fasteners are removed.

2. Remove the rear wheels. Remove the rear brake drums. Disconnect the parking brake from the rear axle.
3. If equipped with anti-lock brakes, remove the caliper, rotor and pads.
4. On all models, remove the brake brackets from the vehicle frame.
5. Remove the rear shock absorbers. Remove the track bar.
6. Disconnect the rear brake hoses.
7. Lower the axle assembly and remove the coil springs and insulators.
8. Remove the hub attaching bolts.

Remove the hub and bearing assembly.
9. Remove the control arm bracket attaching bolts. Remove the control arms. Lower the axle from the vehicle.

To install:
10. Raise the axle assembly into position. Install the control arms and control arm bracket attaching bolts.
11. Install the hub and bearing assembly. Install the hub attaching bolts.
12. Install the coil springs and insulators. Raise the axle assembly.
13. Install the shock absorbers. Install the track bar.
14. Connect the brake hoses.
15. Install the brake brackets to the vehicle frame.
16. If equipped with anti-lock brakes, install the rotor, caliper and pads.
17. Connect the parking brake to the rear axle. Install the rear brake drums. Install the rear tire and wheel assemblies.
18. Bleed the brake system and adjust the parking brake, as required.
19. Lower the vehicle. Connect the negative battery cable.

Steering Wheel

REMOVAL & INSTALLATION

NOTE: When installing the steering wheel, always make sure the turn signal lever is in the neutral position.

1. Disconnect the negative battery cable. Remove the trim retaining screws from behind the wheel. On steering wheels with a center cap, pull off the cap.
2. Lift the trim off and pull the horn wires from the turn signal cancelling cam.
3. Remove the retainer and the steering wheel nut.
4. Mark the wheel-to-shaft relationship and then remove the wheel with a puller.

To install:
5. Install the wheel on the shaft, aligning the previously made marks. Tighten the nut to 30 ft. lbs. (41 Nm).
6. Insert the horn wires into the cancelling cam.
7. Install the center trim and reconnect the battery cable.

Steering Column

NOTE: Once the steering column is removed from the vehicle, the column is extremely susceptible to damage. Dropping the column assembly on its end could collapse the steering shaft or loosen the plastic injections which maintain column rigidity. Leaning on the column assembly could cause the jacket to bend or deform. Any of the above damage could impair the column's collapsible design. If it is necessary to remove the steering wheel, use a standard wheel puller. Under no condition should the end of the shaft be hammered upon, as hammering could loosen the plastic injection which maintains column rigidity.

REMOVAL & INSTALLATION

1. Disconnect the negative battery cable. Remove the left instrument panel sound insulator and trim panel.
2. If column repairs are to be made, remove the steering wheel.
3. Remove the nuts and bolts attaching the flexible coupling to the bottom of the steering column. Remove the safety strap and bolt if equipped.
4. Remove the steering column trim

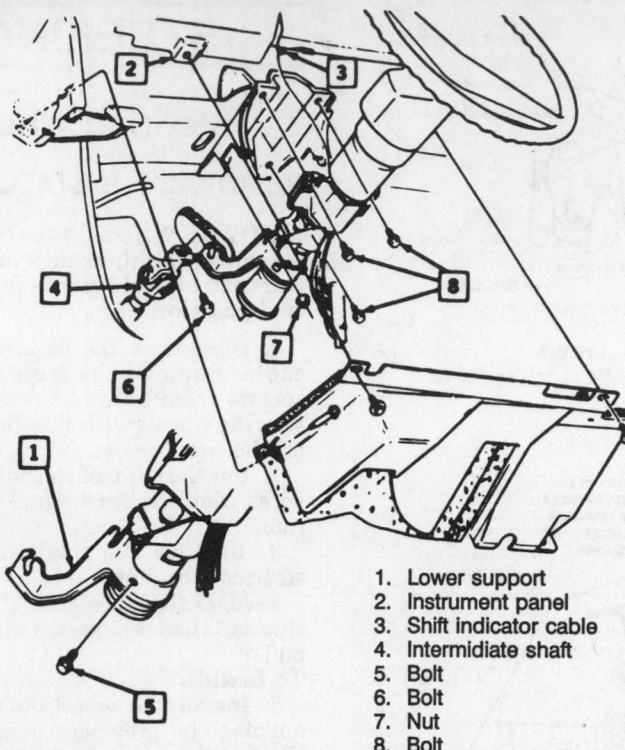

1. Lower support
2. Instrument panel
3. Shift indicator cable
4. Intermidiate shaft
5. Bolt
6. Bolt
7. Nut
8. Bolt

Steering column mounting

shrouds and column covers. Disconnect the shift indicator cable.

5. Disconnect all wiring harness connectors. Remove the dust boot mounting screws and column mounting bracket bolts.

6. Lower the column to clear the mounting bracket and carefully remove from the vehicle.

To install:

7. Install the column in the vehicle.

8. Install the column mounting bracket bolts. Install the dust boot mounting screws. Connect all wiring harness connectors.

9. Install the steering column trim shrouds and column covers. Connect the shift indicator cable.

10. Install the safety strap and bolt if equipped. Install the nuts and bolts attaching the flexible coupling to the bottom of the steering column.

11. If removed, install the steering wheel. Install the instrument panel sound insulator.

12. Connect the negative battery cable.

Power Steering Rack

BEARIGN PRELOAD ADJUSTMENT

1. Raise and safely support vehicle.

2. When adjusting, ensure front wheels are raised and the steering wheel centered.

3. Loosen the adjuster plug locknut, turn adjuster plug clockwise until it bottoms in the housing, then back adjuster plug approximately 50–70 degrees (approximately 1 flat).

4. After adjustment, check the returnabilty of the steering wheel.

REMOVAL & INSTALLATION

1. Disconnect the negative battery cable. Raise and safely support vehicle. Allow the front suspension to hang freely. Disconnect the power steering hoses from the gear, where equipped.

2. Move the intermediate shaft seal upward and remove the intermediate shaft-to-stub shaft pinch bolt.

3. Remove both front wheels.

4. Remove the cotter pins and nut from both tie rod ends. Disconnect the tie rod ends from the steering knuckles.

5. Remove the air management system pipe bracket bolt from the crossmember.

6. Support the engine cradle with a floor jack. Remove the 2 rear cradle mount bolts and, using a jack, lower the rear of the engine cradle about 4–5 in.

NOTE: Do not lower the engine cradle too far or damage to surrounding components will result.

7. Remove the rack and pinion heat shield, then the 2 rack and pinion mount bolts.

8. Remove the rack and pinion assembly through the left wheel opening.

To install:

9. Install the rack and pinion assembly through the left wheel opening.

10. Install the rack and pinion heat shield, then the 2 rack and pinion mount bolts. Torque the mount bolts to 66 ft. lbs. (90 Nm).

11. Raise the engine cradle into position and install the 2 rear cradle mount bolts.

12. Install the air management system pipe bracket bolt to the crossmember.

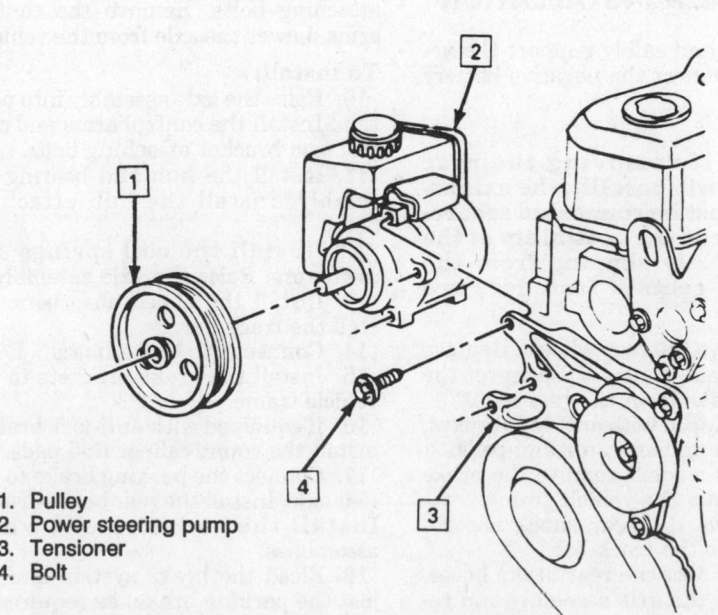

1. Pulley
2. Power steering pump
3. Tensioner
4. Bolt

Windshield wiper switch and related components—models with tilt wheel

1. Belt tensioner
2. Power steering pump
3. Bolt/screw
4. Belt tensioner brace
5. Pulley
6. Accessory drive belt
7. Bolt

Windshield wiper switch and related components—models without tilt wheel

13. Connect the tie rod ends to the steering knuckles. Install the cotter pin and nut to both tie rod ends. Tighten the tie rod end nuts to 30 ft. lbs. (41 Nm).
14. Install both front wheels.
15. Install the intermediate shaft-to-stub shaft pinch bolt. Tighten the pinch bolt to 45 ft. lbs. (61 Nm).
16. If equipped, connect the power steering hoses to the steering gear. Refill the system.
17. Lower the vehicle. Connect the negative battery cable.

Power Steering Pump

REMOVAL & INSTALLATION

2.5L Engine

1. Disconnect the negative battery cable. Raise and safely support the vehicle.
2. Remove the right front wheel and right side engine splash shield.
3. Remove the serpentine belt and siphon the fluid from the pump reservoir.
4. Disconnect the hydraulic lines/hoses from the pump.
5. Remove the radiator hose clamp bolt.
6. Remove the upper and lower bolts and nuts from the front pump bracket.
7. Remove the pump from the engine.
To install:
8. Install the pump to the engine.
9. Install the upper and lower bolts and nuts to the front pump bracket.
10. Install the radiator hose clamp bolt.
11. Connect the hydraulic lines/hoses to the pump.

12. Install serpentine belt. Refill the system.
13. Install the right side engine splash shield and right front wheel.
12. Lower the vehicle.
13. Connect the negative battery cable.
14. Bleed the system.

3.3L Engine

1. Disconnect the negative battery cable.
2. Remove the serpentine belt.
3. Remove the rear power steering pump bracket.
4. Disconnect the power steering lines at the pump.
5. Remove the power steering mounting bolts and remove the pump from the vehicle.
To install:
6. Install the pump and secure with the pump mounting bolts.
7. Torque mounting nuts to 21 ft. lbs. (29 Nm).
8. Connect the power steering lines to the power steering pump.
9. Install the rear power steering pump bracket.
10. Install the serpentine belt.
11. Connect the negative battery cable.
12. Bleed the system.

Except 2.5L and 3.3L Engines

1. Disconnect the negative battery cable at the battery. Remove air cleaner, if necessary.
2. Disconnect the blower motor wiring and remove the blower motor.
3. Remove the coolant hose from the water pump.
4. Siphon the fluid from the pump reservoir, then disconnect the lines from the pump.
5. Remove the serpentine drive belt.
6. Remove the 1 nut which attaches

the rear pump bracket to the engine bracket.
7. Remove the 2 front pump bracket-to-engine bolts, then remove the pump and bracket assembly.
To install:
8. Install the pump and bracket assembly. Install the 2 front pump bracket-to-engine bolts.
9. Install the 1 nut which attaches the rear pump bracket to the engine bracket.
10. Install the serpentine belt.
11. Connect the lines to the pump. Refill the system.
12. Install the coolant hose to the water pump.
13. Install the blower motor. Connect the blower motor wiring.
14. If removed, install the air cleaner.
15. Connect the negative battery cable.
16. Bleed the system.

BELT ADJUSTMENT

The accessories are driven by a single serpentine belt. Belt tension is controlled automatically by the spring-loaded tensioner. No adjustment is necessary.

SYSTEM BLEEDING

1. Fill the fluid reservoir.
2. Let fluid stand undisturbed for 2 minutes, then crank engine for about 2 seconds. Refill reservoir if necessary.
3. Repeat Steps 1 and 2 until fluid level remains constant after cranking the engine.
4. Raise the front of the vehicle until both wheels are off the ground, then start the engine. Increase engine speed to 1500 rpm.
5. Turn the wheels lightly against the stop to the left and right, checking the fluid level and refilling, as necessary.

Tie Rod Ends
REMOVAL & INSTALLATION

1. Loosen the jam nut on the steering rack inner tie rod.
2. Remove the tie rod end nut. Separate the tie rod end from the steering knuckle using a suitable puller.
3. Unscrew the tie rod end, counting the number of turns.
To install:
4. Screw the tie rod end onto the steering rack inner tie rod the same number of turns as counted for removal. This will give approximately correct toe.
5. Install the tie rod end into the knuckle. Install nut and torque to 40 ft. lbs. (54 Nm).

6. If the toe must be adjusted, use pliers to expand the boot clamp. Turn the inner tie rod to adjust. Replace clamp.

7. Tighten the jam nut to 59 ft. lbs. (80 Nm).

BRAKES

Master Cylinder

REMOVAL & INSTALLATION

1. Disconnect the negative battery cable. Disconnect the electrical connector from the fluid level sensor, if equipped.

2. Disconnect and plug the hydraulic lines at master cylinder.

3. Remove the master cylinder retaining nuts and lock washers.

4. Remove the master cylinder from the vehicle.

To install:

5. Install the cylinder on the booster. Install nuts and lock washers. Tighten the attaching nuts to 20 ft. lbs. (27 Nm).

6. Install hydraulic lines. Tighten to 24 ft. lbs. (32 Nm).

7. Connect the fluid level sensor electrical connector.

8. Bleed the brakes system.

Proportioner Valve

REMOVAL & INSTALLATION

1. Disconnect the negative battery cable.

NOTE: It may be necessary to remove the master cylinder reservoir to remove the proportioner valves.

2. Remove the proportioner valve caps (2).

3. Remove the proportioner O-rings and springs.

4. Carefully remove the valve pistons using needle nose pliers.

To install:

5. Lubricate the O-rings, proportioner valve seals and stems of valve pistons with silicone grease (supplied in repair kit).

6. Install the seals onto the proportioner pistons with the seal lips facing up toward the cap assembly.

7. Install the proportioner valve pistons and seals into the master cylinder body.

8. Install the springs into the master cylinder body.

9. Install new O-rings onto the proportioner valve caps and install to the master cylinder body. Torque the caps to 20 ft. lbs. (27 Nm).

10. Connect the negative battery cable.

Power Brake Booster

REMOVAL & INSTALLATION

1. Disconnect the negative battery cable.

2. Remove the master cylinder attaching nuts and remove the master cylinder from the booster.

3. Disconnect the booster vacuum hose from the vacuum check valve. Remove the nuts and lock washers that secure the booster to firewall.

4. Disconnect the booster pushrod from the brake pedal. Tilt the booster slightly and work the booster pushrod off of the pedal clevis pin without putting excessive pressure on the side pin. Remove the booster from the engine compartment.

5. Remove the booster from the vehicle.

To install:

6. Install the booster to the engine compartment.

7. Working inside the vehicle, install the nuts and lock washers that secure the booster to the firewall. Tighten the mounting nuts to 20 ft. lbs. (28 Nm). Connect the pushrod at the brake pedal.

8. Position the master cylinder on the booster and install the attaching nuts.

9. Connect vacuum hose to the vacuum check valve.

10. Connect the negative battery cable. Check operation of stop lights. Allow engine vacuum to build before applying brakes.

Brake Caliper

REMOVAL & INSTALLATION

1. Disconnect the negative battery cable.

2. Raise and safely support the vehicle. Remove the tire and wheel assembly.

3. Remove ⅔ of the brake fluid from the master cylinder.

4. Position a 12 inch adjustable pliers over the inboard brake shoe tab and the inboard caliper housing. Squeeze the pliers to compress the piston back into the caliper bore and to provide clearance between the lining and rotor.

5. If equipped with rear disc brakes, disconnect the parking brake cable and return spring from the parking brake lever, then the parking brake cable from the bracket.

6. On all models, remove the caliper mounting bolts, then lift caliper from bracket and remove the inner and outer pads with the anti-rattle springs.

7. Disconnect the hydraulic hose. Remove the caliper from the vehicle.

To install:

8. Connect the hydraulic hose.

9. On all models, install the caliper on the mounting brackets and install the mounting bolts. Install the inner and outer pads with the anti-rattle springs.

10. If equipped with rear disc brakes, connect the parking brake cable to the bracket and the cable and return spring to the parking brake lever.

11. Install the tire and wheel assembly.

12. Lower the vehicle.

13. Fill the master cylinder reservoir.

14. Connect the negative battery cable.

15. Bleed the brake system.

Disc Brake Pads

REMOVAL & INSTALLATION

1. Disconnect the negative battery cable.

2. Raise and safely support the vehicle. Remove the tire and wheel assembly.

3. Remove ⅔ of the brake fluid from the master cylinder.

4. Position a 12 inch adjustable pliers over the inboard brake shoe tab and the inboard caliper housing. Squeeze the pliers to compress the piston back into the caliper bore and to provide clearance between the lining and rotor.

5. If equipped with rear disc brakes, disconnect the parking brake cable and return spring from the parking brake lever, then the parking brake cable from the bracket.

6. On all models, remove the caliper mounting bolts, then lift caliper from bracket and remove the inner and outer pads complete with the anti-rattle springs.

To install:

7. On all models, install the caliper and mounting bolts. Install the inner and outer pads complete with the anti-rattle springs.

8. If equipped with rear disc brakes, connect the parking brake cable to the bracket and the cable and return spring to the parking brake lever.

9. Install the tire and wheel assembly.

10. Lower the vehicle.

11. Fill the master cylinder reservoir with fresh brake fluid.

12. Apply the brake pedal until the pedal is firm and steady.

13. If the pedal remains spongy and/

or sinks to the floor, bleed the brake system.

14. Top-up fluid level in the master cylinder, as necessary.

Brake Rotor

REMOVAL & INSTALLATION

1. Disconnect the negative battery cable.

2. Raise and safely support the vehicle.

3. Remove the tire and wheel assembly.

4. Remove the caliper. Support the caliper using a length of wire.

5. Remove the rotor.

To install:

6. Install the rotor.

7. Install the caliper.

8. Install the tire and wheel assembly.

9. Lower the vehicle.

10. Apply the brake pedal until the pedal is firm and steady.

11. If the pedal remains spongy and/or sinks to the floor, bleed the brake system.

12. Top-up fluid level in the master cylinder, as necessary.

13. Connect the negative battery cable.

Brake Drums

REMOVAL & INSTALLATION

1. Disconnect battery negative cable.

2. Raise and safely support the vehicle. Remove the tire and wheel assembly.

3. Remove the brake drum. If the drum is difficult to remove, make sure parking brake is released and/or remove the access plug from the backing plate and back off the adjusting screw.

To install:

4. Install the brake drum.

5. Adjust the brakes.

6. Install the tire and wheel assembly.

7. Lower the vehicle.

8. Connect the negative battery cable.

Brake Shoes

REMOVAL & INSTALLATION

1. Disconnect the negative battery cable.

2. Raise and safely support vehicle. Remove the tire and wheel assembly.

3. Remove the brake drum. If the drum is difficult to remove, remove the access plug from the backing plate and back off the adjusting screw.

4. Remove the return springs from the anchor using appropriate brake spring pliers.

5. Remove the hold-down springs and retaining pins. Remove the lever pivot, actuator link, actuator lever, actuator pivot and lever return spring, parking brake strut and strut spring.

6. Remove the brake shoes, then disconnect the parking brake cable.

7. Remove the adjusting screw assembly and spring. Note position of adjusting spring.

NOTE: Do not interchange the adjusting screws or adjusting screw springs from right to left brake assembly.

8. Remove the retaining ring, pin and parking brake lever from the secondary shoe.

To install:

9. Lubricate the shoe contact surfaces on the backing plate and adjusting screw assembly.

10. Install the parking brake lever on the secondary shoe with the pin and retaining ring.

11. Install the adjusting screw assembly and spring. The coil of the spring must not be over the star wheel.

12. Install the shoe and lining assemblies after attaching the parking brake cable.

13. Install the parking brake strut and spring by spreading the shoes apart. Ensure the strut is properly positioned. The end with the spring engages the primary shoe and the end without the spring engages the parking brake lever.

14. Install the actuator pivot, actuator lever and return spring.

15. Install the actuator link in the shoe retainer.

16. Install the link into the lever while holding up on the lever.

17. Install the hold-down pins, lever pivot and hold-down springs.

18. Install the shoe return springs.

19. Install the brake drum, wheel and tire assembly, then lower vehicle. Apply the brake pedal several times to seat the brake shoes. Check and adjust the parking brake, as required.

20. Check the master cylinder reservoir. Connect the negative battery cable.

Wheel Cylinder

REMOVAL & INSTALLATION

1. Disconnect the negative battery cable.

2. Loosen the wheel lug nuts, raise and safely support the vehicle. Remove the tire and wheel assembly. Remove the drum and brake shoes. Leave the hub and wheel bearing assembly in place.

3. Remove any dirt from around the brake line fitting, then disconnect the brake line.

4. Remove the wheel cylinder attaching bolts and remove the wheel cylinder from the backing plate.

To install:

5. Install the wheel cylinder to the backing plate and install the 2 attaching bolts. Tighten the bolts to 15 ft. lbs. (20 Nm).

6. Connect the inlet tube to the wheel cylinder. Tighten to 12 ft. lbs. (17 Nm).

7. Install the brake shoes and drum. Adjust the brakes.

8. Install the tire and wheel assembly.

9. Lower the vehicle.

10. Bleed the brake system.

11. Connect the negative battery cable.

Parking Brake Cable

ADJUSTMENT

1. Raise the rear of the vehicle and support it safely using jackstands, with both rear wheels off the ground.

2. Apply the parking brake 3 ratchet clicks from the fully released position.

3. Loosen the equalizer locknut, the tighten the adjusting nut until a light to moderate drag is felt when the rear wheels are rotate. Tighten the locknut.

4. Fully release parking brake and rotate rear wheels; no drag should be felt.

REMOVAL & INSTALLATION

Front Cable

1. Raise and safely support the vehicle.

2. Loosen the equalizer nut.

3. Disconnect the front cable from the connector and equalizer.

4. Remove the clip at the frame.

5. Remove the cable from the hanger.

6. Lower the vehicle.

7. Remove the 3 screws and 1 nut and lower the driver's side sound insulator panel.

8. Remove the carpet finish molding. Lift the carpet.

9. Remove the cable retaining clip at the lever assembly.

10. Depress the retaining tangs and remove the cable and casing from the lever assembly.

11. Remove the cable from the retaining clips.

12. Remove the grommet retainer from the floor pan.

13. Unseat the grommet and pull the cable through the floor pan.

To install:

14. Insert the cable through the floor pan and grommet.

15. Seat the grommet. Install the grommet retainer to the floor pan.

16. Fasten the cable in the retaining clips.

17. Connect the cable and casing to the lever assembly. Seat the retaining tangs.

18. Install the cable retaining clip at the lever assembly.

19. Place the carpet into position. Install the carpet finish molding.

20. Install the driver's side sound insulator panel and attaching screws and nuts.

21. Raise and safely support the vehicle.

22. Fasten the cable to the hanger.

23. Install the clip to the frame.

24. Connect the front cable to the equalizer and connector.

25. Adjust the parking brake cable.

26. Lower the vehicle.

Rear Cables

1. Raise and safely support the vehicle.

2. Loosen the equalizer nut.

3. Disconnect the cable at the equalizer and connector.

4. Remove the tire, wheel and brake drum.

5. Disconnect the cable from the parking brake lever.

6. Depress the retaining tangs on the cable. Remove the cable and casing from the backing plate.

To install:

7. Install the cable through the rear of the backing plate. Seat the retaining tangs in the backing plate.

8. Connect the cable to the parking brake lever.

9. Install the brake drum, tire and wheel.

10. Connect the cable at the equalizer and connector.

11. Adjust the parking brake cable.

12. Lower the vehicle.

Anti-Lock Brake System Service

PRECAUTIONS

Failure to observe the following precautions may result in system damage.

• Before performing electric arc welding on the vehicle, disconnect the Electronic Brake Control Module (EBCM) and the hydraulic modulator connectors.

• When performing painting work on the vehicle, do not expose the Electronic Brake Control Module (EBCM)

to temperatures in excess of 185°F (85°C) for longer than 2 hrs. The system may be exposed to temperatures up to 200°F (95°C) for less than 15 min.

• Never disconnect or connect the Electronic Brake Control Module (EBCM) or hydraulic modulator connectors with the ignition switch ON.

• Never disassemble any component of the Anti-Lock Brake System (ABS) which is designated non-serviceable; the component must be replaced as an assembly.

• When filling the master cylinder, always use Delco Supreme 11 brake fluid or equivalent, which meets DOT-3 specifications; petroleum base fluid will destroy the rubber parts.

RELIEVING ANTI-LOCK BRAKE SYSTEM PRESSURE

──────── **CAUTION** ────────

Failure to fully depressurize the accumulator before performing any repairs could result in injury, and/or damage to the system.

With the igntion switch in the **OFF** position, apply and release the brake pedal a minimum of 20 times using approximately 50 lbs. (222 N) of force on the pedal. A change in the pedal feel will occur when the accumulator is completely discharged.

Hydraulic Unit

REMOVAL & INSTALLATION

1. Depressurize the system, then disconnect the negative battery cable.

2. Disconnect the electrical connectors from the unit, then remove the fluid from the reservoir.

3. Remove the wire clip from the return hose fitting, then the return hose from the pump.

4. Remove the pressure hose attaching bolt, then the pressure hose and O-ring from the pump.

5. Remove the pump mounting bolt, then the energy unit from the hydraulic unit.

6. Disconnect the 4 brake lines from the valve block and hydraulic unit.

7. Disconnect the pushrod from the brake pedal, then push the dust boot forward off the rear half of the pushrod and unthread the 2 halfs of the pushrod.

8. Remove the hydraulic unit attaching bolts from the pushrod bracket, then the hydraulic unit from the vehicle.

To install:

9. Install the hydraulic unit to the pushrod bracket. Torque bolts to 37 ft. lbs. (50 Nm).

10. Thread the 2 halfs of pushrod together, reposition the dust boot, then install pushrod to the brake pedal. Torque bolts to 27 ft. lbs. (37 Nm).

11. Connect the 4 brake lines to the valve block and hydraulic unit. Torque brake lines to 11 ft. lbs. (15 Nm).

12. Install energy unit to hydraulic unit, then the pump mounting bolt.

13. Install the pressure hose and O-ring to the pump, then the pressure hose bolt. Torque bolt to 15 ft. lbs.

14. Install return hose to pump, then the wire clip to the return hose fitting.

15. Connect electrical connectors to hydraulic unit, then the battery negative cable.

Valve Block

REMOVAL & INSTALLATION

1. Depressurize the system.

2. Remove the hydraulic unit.

3. Remove the valve block attaching nuts and bolts, then the valve block and O-rings from the vehicle.

To install:

4. Replace the O-ring. Install the valve block and attaching nuts and bolts. Tighten the valve block bolts to 18 ft. lbs. (25 Nm).

5. Install the hydraulic unit.

6. Bleed the brake system.

Pump Motor

REMOVAL & INSTALLATION

1. Depressurize system, then disconnect the battery negative cable.

2. Remove the brake fluid from the reservoir, then disconnect the electrical connectors from the pressure switch and the pump motor.

3. Remove the hydraulic accumulator and O-ring.

4. Remove the pressure hose attaching bolt, then the pressure hose and O-ring from pump.

5. Remove the wire clip and return hose fitting, then the return hose from the pump.

6. Remove the pump attaching bolts and grommets, then the pump from the hydraulic unit.

To install:

7. Install the pump to the hydraulic unit. Install the attaching bolts and grommets. Tighten the pump mounting bolts to 71 inch lbs. (8 Nm).

8. Connect the return hose to the pump. Install the wire clip.

9. Replace the pressure hose O-ring and install the pressure hose attaching bolt. Tighten the pressure hose bolt to 15 ft. lbs. (20 Nm).

10. Replace the hydraulic accumulator O-ring and install the hydraulic ac-

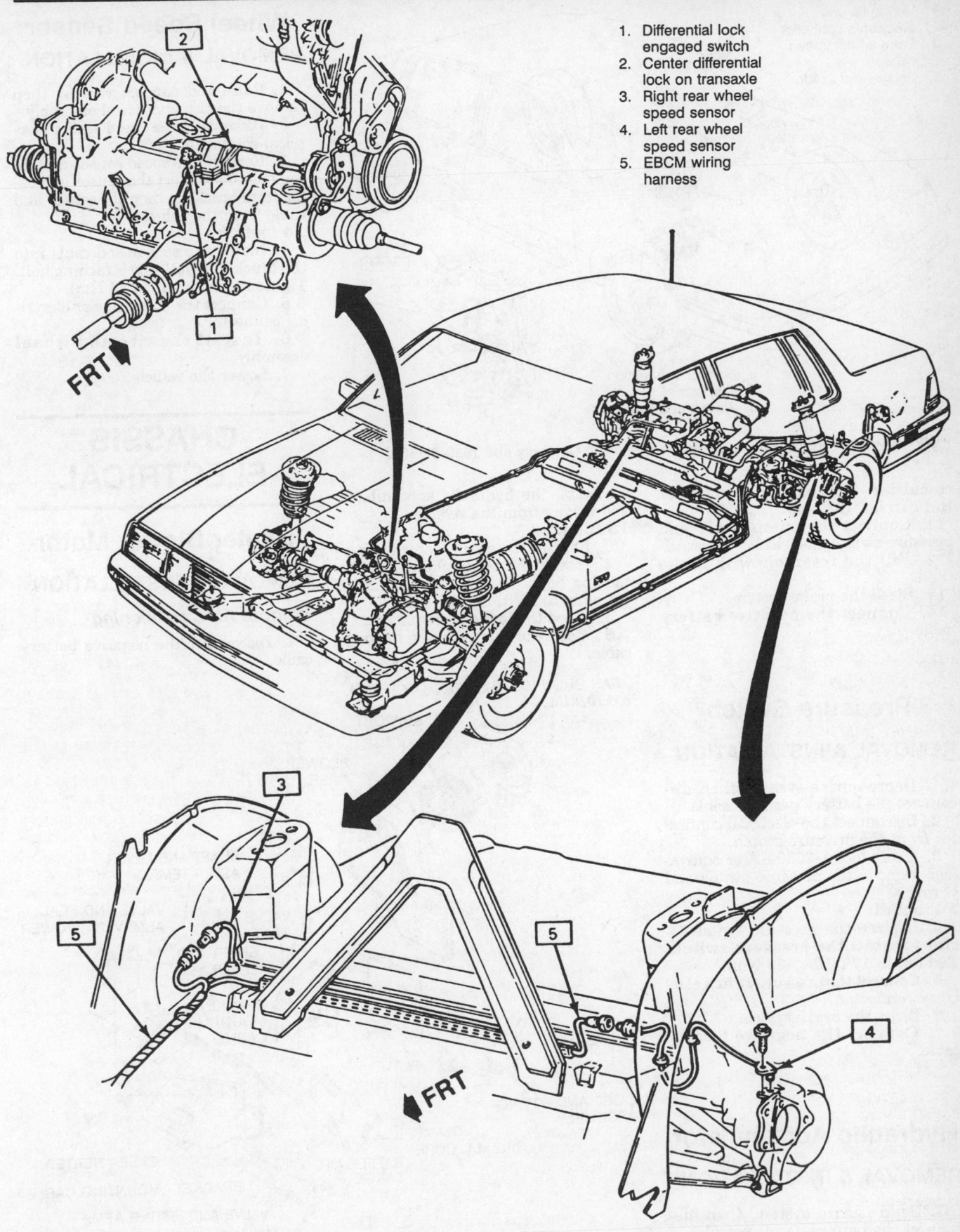

1. Differential lock engaged switch
2. Center differential lock on transaxle
3. Right rear wheel speed sensor
4. Left rear wheel speed sensor
5. EBCM wiring harness

Anti-lock brake system components—1990 Celebrity and 1990–91 6000

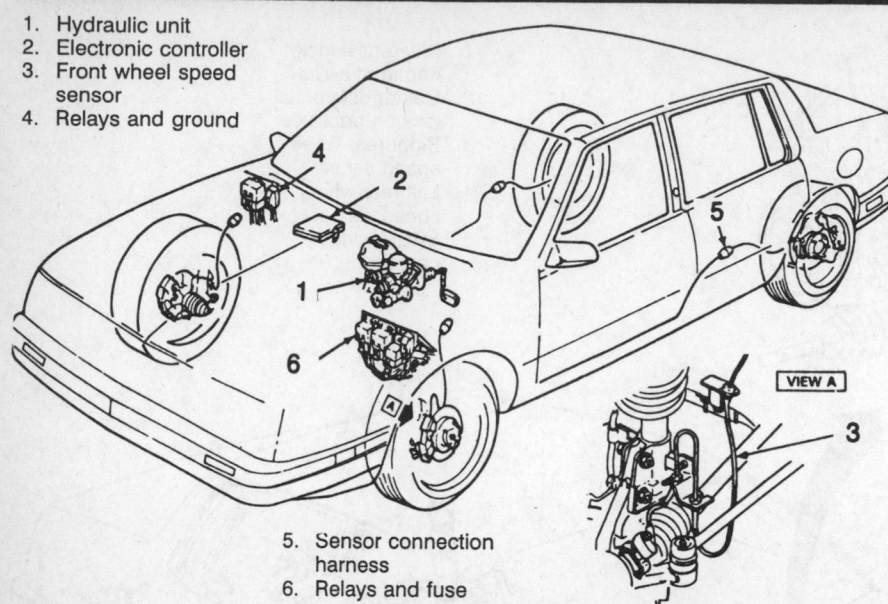

1. Hydraulic unit
2. Electronic controller
3. Front wheel speed sensor
4. Relays and ground
5. Sensor connection harness
6. Relays and fuse

Anti-Lock brake system components—1990 Celebrity and 1990–91 6000

cumulator. Tighten the accumulator to 17 ft. lbs. (23 Nm).

11. Connect the pump motor and pressure switch electrical connectors.

12. Fill the reservoir with brake fluid.

13. Bleed the brake system.

14. Connect the negative battery cable.

Pressure Switch

REMOVAL & INSTALLATION

1. Depressurize system, then disconnect the battery negative cable.

2. Disconnect the electrical connector from the pressure switch.

3. Using tool J–35804–A or equivalent, remove the pressure switch and O-ring.

To install:

4. Replace the pressure switch O-ring. Install the pressure switch. Tighten to 17 ft. lbs. (23 Nm).

5. Connect the pressure switch electrical connector.

6. Bleed the brake system.

7. Connect the negative battery cable.

Hydraulic Accumulator

REMOVAL & INSTALLATION

1. Depressurize system, then disconnect the battery negative cable.

2. Remove the hydraulic accumula-

tor bolts, the hydraulic accumulator and O-ring from the vehicle.

To install:

3. Replace the accumulator O-ring.

4. Install the accumulator and attaching bolts. Tighten the accumulator bolts to 17 ft. lbs. (23 Nm).

5. Bleed the brake system.

6. Connect the negative battery cable.

Wheel Speed Sensor

REMOVAL & INSTALLATION

1. Raise and support vehicle, then remove the tire and wheel assembly.

2. Disconnect the speed sensor electrical connector.

3. Remove the speed sensor attaching bolt, disconnect the sensor and cable from brackets, then the sensor and cable from the vehicle.

To install:

4. Install the sensor and cable into the bracket. Install the attaching bolt. Tighten to 53 inch lbs. (6 Nm).

5. Connect the speed sensor electrical connector.

6. Install the tire and wheel assembly.

7. Lower the vehicle.

CHASSIS ELECTRICAL

Heater Blower Motor

REMOVAL & INSTALLATION

Without Air Conditioning

1. Disconnect the negative battery cable.

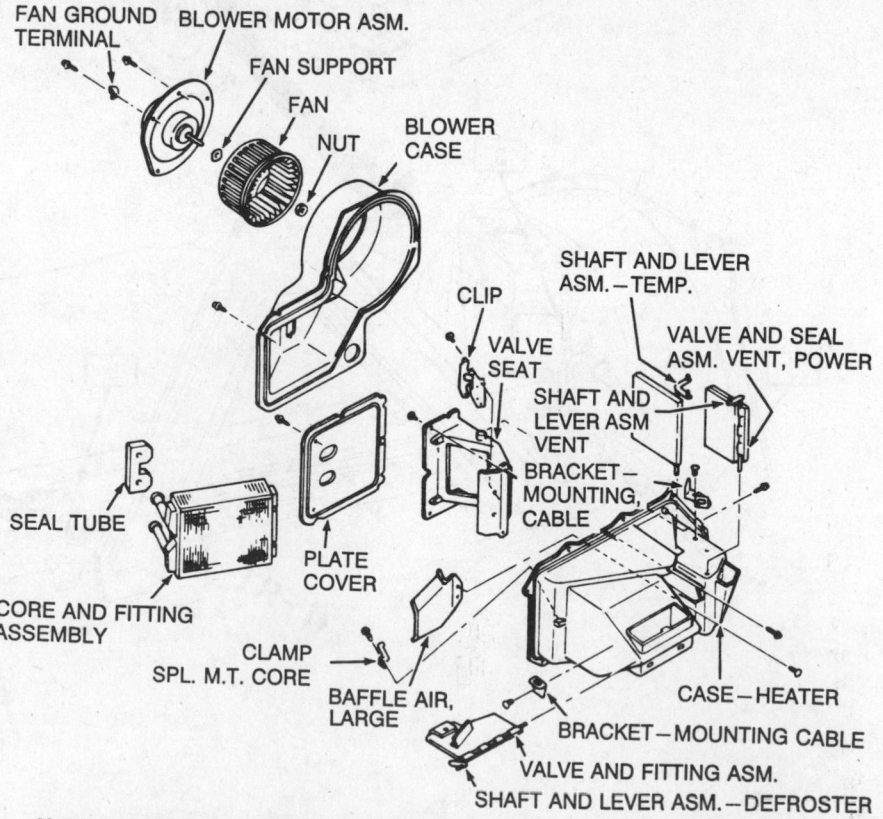

Heater core, blower motor and related components—without air conditioning

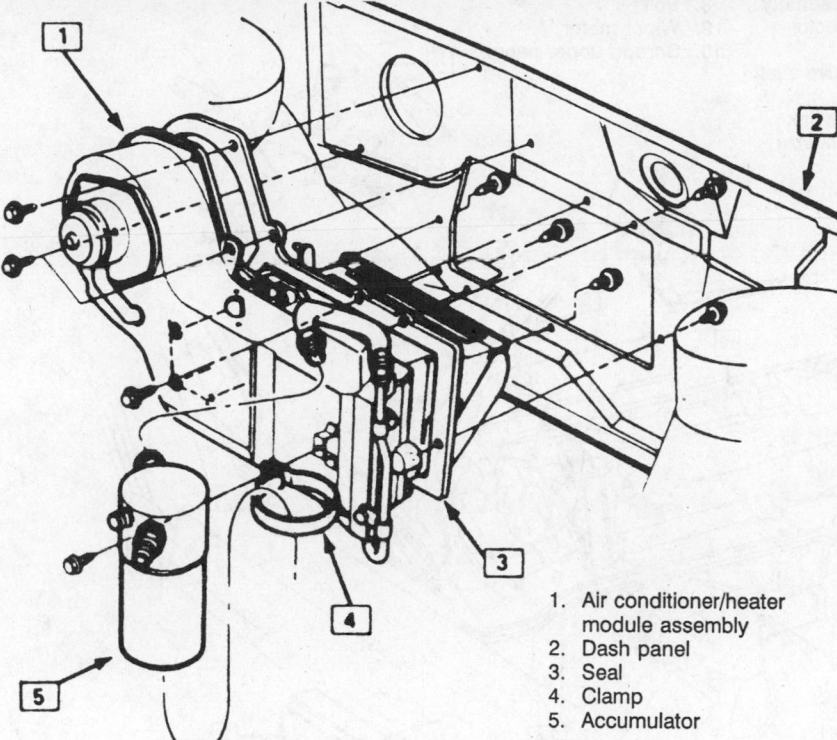

1. Air conditioner/heater module assembly
2. Dash panel
3. Seal
4. Clamp
5. Accumulator

Module assembly and accumulator—with air conditioning

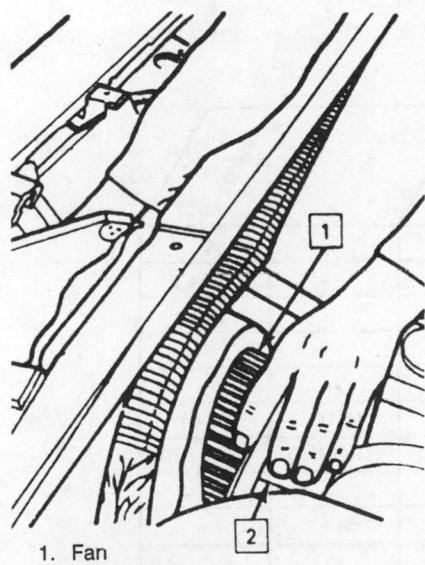

1. Fan
2. Blower motor

Blower motor removal—with air conditioning

2. Tag and disconnect the blower motor electrical leads.

3. Remove the motor retaining bolts and remove the blower motor.

4. If the blower motor is to be replaced, separate the fan from the blower motor by removing the retaining nut and sliding the fan from the shaft.

To install:

5. If the blower motor is to be replaced, install the fan to the new blower motor and install the retaining nut.

6. Install the fan in the heater module and install the retaining bolts.

7. Connect the electrical connector.

8. Connect the negative battery cable.

With Air Conditioning

1. Disconnect the negative battery cable.

2. Remove the wiper arms.

3. Remove the cowl panel.

4. Disconnect the blower motor electrical connector and vent tube for 3.3L engine only.

5. Remove the blower motor retaining screws.

6. Remove the fan retaining nut from the blower motor shaft by reaching through the plenum opening.

7. While reaching through the plenum opening, hold the fan to separate the blower motor from the fan and remove the blower motor from the air conditioner/heater module.

To install:

8. Install the blower motor to the air conditioner/heater module by reaching through the plenum opening to hold the fan and insert the blower motor shaft into the fan.

9. Install the fan retaining nut to the blower motor shaft.

10. Install the blower motor retaining screws.

11. Connect the blower motor electrical connector and the vent tube.

12. Install the cowl panel.

13. Install the wiper arms.

14. Connect the negative battery cable.

Windshield Wiper Motor

REMOVAL & INSTALLATION

1. Disconnect the negative battery cable.

2. Remove the wiper arm and blade assemblies.

3. Remove the cowl cover.

4. Disconnect the wiper arm drive link from the crank arm.

5. Disconnect the wiper motor electrical connectors.

6. Remove the wiper motor attaching bolts.

7. Remove the wiper motor, guiding the crank arm through the hole.

To install:

8. Insert the wiper motor, guiding the crank arm through the hole.

9. Install the wiper motor attaching bolts.

10. Connect the electrical connectors.

11. Connect the wiper arm drive link to the crank arm.

12. Install the cowl cover.

13. Install the wiper arms.

14. Connect the negative battery cable.

Windshield Wiper Switch

REMOVAL & INSTALLATION

1. Disconnect the negative battery cable.

2. Remove the steering wheel and turn signal switch. It may be necessary to first remove the column mounting nuts and remove the 4 bracket-to-mast jacket screws, then separate the bracket from the mast jacket to allow the connector clip on the ignition switch to be pulled from the column assembly.

3. Tag and disconnect the washer/wiper switch lower connector.

4. Remove the screws attaching the column housing to the mast jacket. Be sure to note the position of the dimmer switch actuator rod for reassembly in the same position. Remove the column housing and switch as an assembly.

NOTE: Certain tilt and travel columns are equipped with a removable plastic cover on the column housing. This provides access to the wiper switch without removing the entire column housing.

5. Turn upside down and use a drift

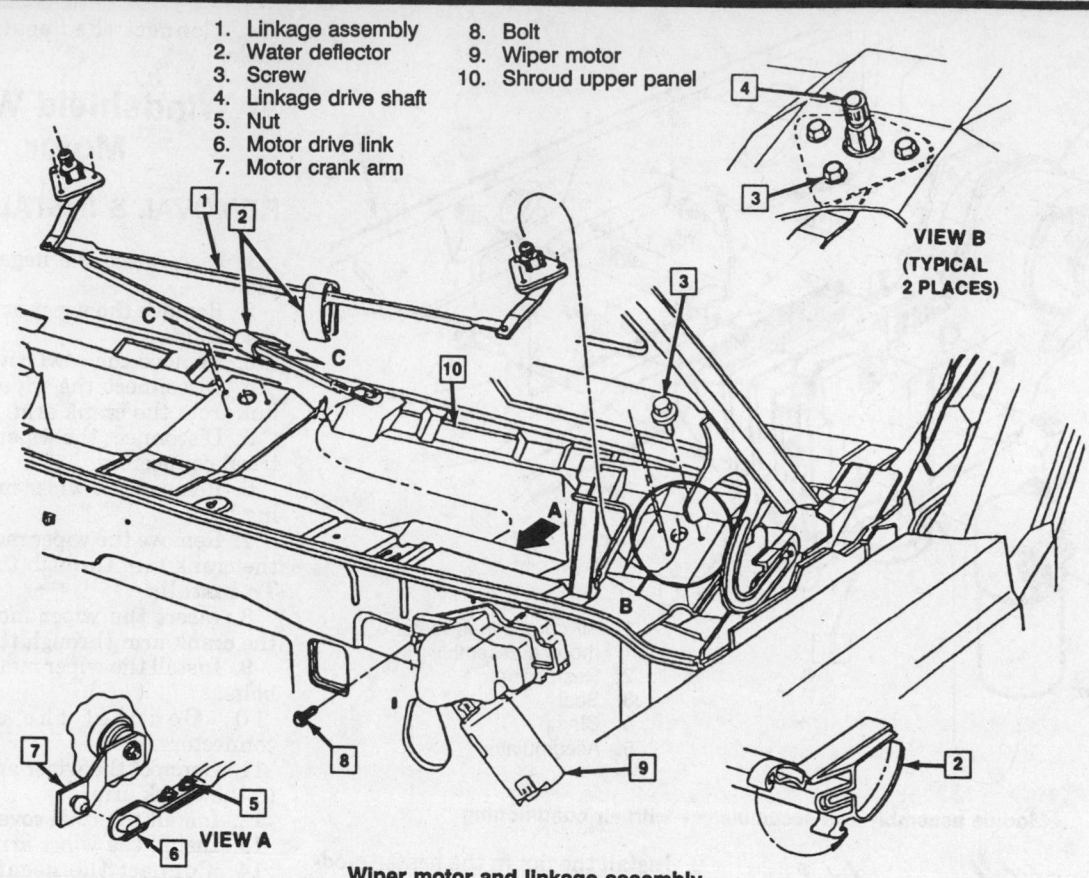

1. Linkage assembly
2. Water deflector
3. Screw
4. Linkage drive shaft
5. Nut
6. Motor drive link
7. Motor crank arm
8. Bolt
9. Wiper motor
10. Shroud upper panel

VIEW B
(TYPICAL 2 PLACES)

VIEW A

Wiper motor and linkage assembly

	SWITCH MODE / TERMINAL #	MIST	OFF	PULSE	LO	HI †	WASH
PULSE	1	C	C	C	C	C	C
	2	B(+)	—	B(+)	B(+)	—	*B(+)
	3	B(+)	B(+)	—	B(+)	—	*B(+)
	4	—	—	—	—	—	—
	5	—	—	—	—	—	—
	6	10-12V	10-12V	10-12V	10-12V	10-12V	B(+)
	7	GROUND	GROUND	GROUND	GROUND	GROUND	GROUND
	8	C	C	C	C	C	C
	9	—	—	—	—	B(+)	—
STANDARD	1			C		C	C
	2			—		B(+)	—
	3			B(+)		B(+)	—
	4			—		—	—
	5			—		—	—
	6			—		—	B(+)
	7			GROUND		GROUND	GROUND
	8			C		C	C
	9			—		B(+)	—

C = CONTINUITY   † TERMINALS #2 & #3 CONNECTED TOGETHER.   *EXCEPT ON HI.

Wiper-washer switch check chart

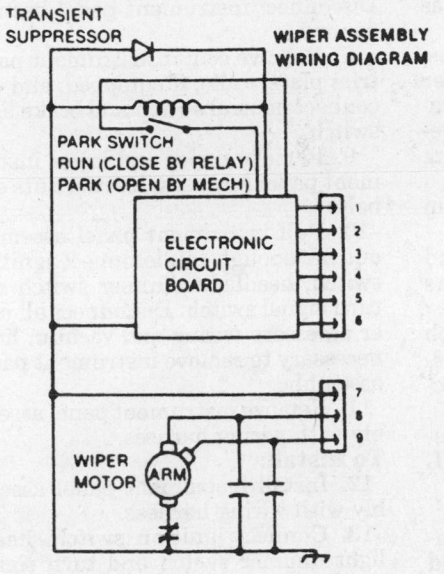

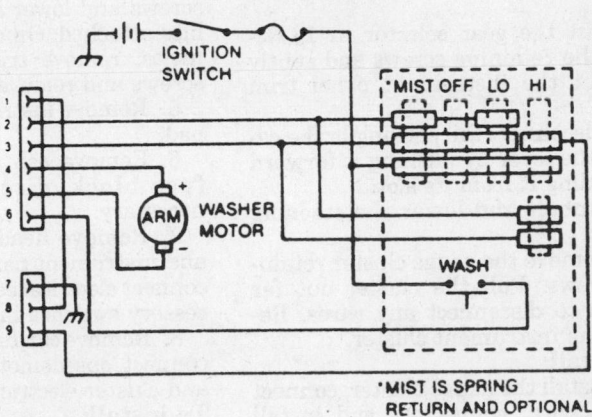

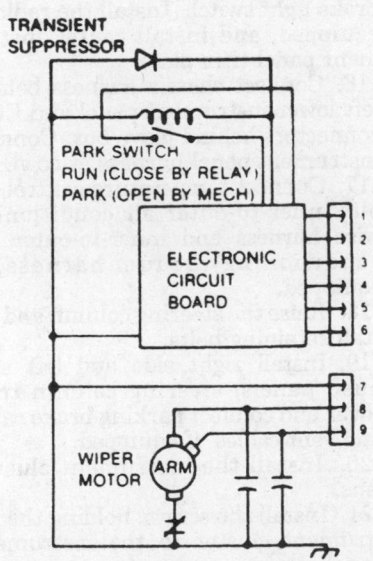

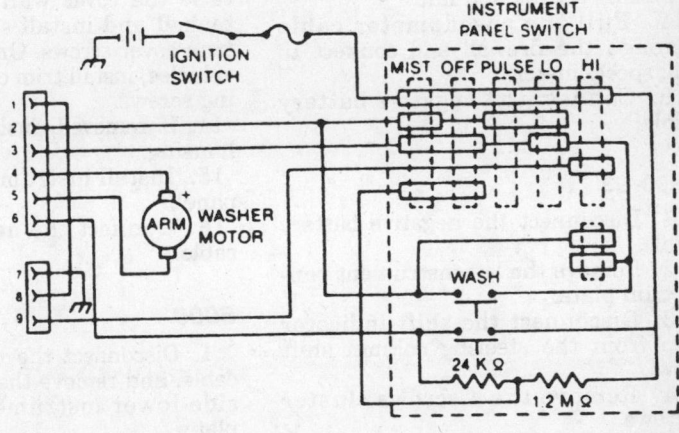

Wiper-washer wiring diagrams

to remove the pivot pin from the washer/wiper switch. Remove the switch.

To install:

6. Place the switch into position in the housing. Install the pivot pin.

7. Position the housing onto the mast jacket and attach by installing the screws. Install the dimmer switch actuator rod in the same position as noted when removed. Check switch operation.

8. Reconnect lower end of the switch assembly.

9. Install the ignition switch connector clip to the column assembly.

10. Install the mast jacket to the bracket.

11. If removed, install the column mounting nuts and the retaining bolts.

12. Install the turn signal switch and steering wheel.

13. Connect the negative battery cable.

Instrument Cluster

REMOVAL & INSTALLATION

Century

1989

1. Disconnect the negative battery cable.

2. Disconnect the speedometer cable and pull it through the firewall.

3. Remove the left side instrument panel trim plate retaining screws and nut.

4. Remove the shift indicator cable clip.

5. Remove the steering column trim plate.

6. Put the gear selector in 1. Remove the retaining screws and gently pull out the instrument panel trim plate.

7. Disconnect the parking brake cable at the lever by pushing it forward and sliding it from its slot.

8. Unbolt and lower the steering column.

9. Remove the gauge cluster retaining screws. Pull the cluster out far enough to disconnect any wires. Remove the instrument cluster.

To install:

10. Install the gauge cluster, connect the electrical connectors and install the retaining screws.

11. Position the steering column and install the retaining bolts.

12. Connect the parking brake cable at the lever.

13. Put the gear selector in **P**. Install the instrument panel trim plate.

14. Install the steering column trim plate.

15. Install the shift indicator cable clip.

16. Install the right side hush panel retaining screws and nut.

17. Pull the speedometer cable through the firewall and connect to the speedometer.

18. Connect the negative battery cable.

1990–93

1. Disconnect the negative battery cable.

2. Remove the left instrument panel trim plate.

3. Disconnect the shift indicator clip from the steering column shift bowl.

4. Remove the 4 screws cluster screws.

5. If equipped with column shift, shift the transaxle to 1.

6. Pull the cluster outward to remove from the vehicle.

To install:

7. Install the cluster to the vehicle.

8. Install the 4 screws.

9. If equipped with column shift, shift the transaxle to **P**.

10. Install the shift indicator clip and make sure the indicator lines up properly.

11. Install the left instrument panel trim plate.

Celebrity

1. Disconnect the negative battery cable.

2. Remove instrument panel hush panel.

3. Remove vent control housing, as required.

4. On non-air conditioning vehicles, remove steering column trim cover screws and lower cover with vent cables attached. On air conditioning vehicles, remove trim cover attaching screws and remove cover.

5. Remove instrument cluster trim pad.

6. Remove ash tray, retainer and fuse block, disconnect wires as necessary.

7. Remove headlight switch knob and instrument panel trim plate. Disconnect electrical connectors of any accessory switches in trim plate.

8. Remove cluster assembly and disconnect speedometer cable, **PRNDL** and cluster electrical connectors.

To install:

9. Install cluster assembly and connect speedometer cable, **PRNDL** and cluster electrical connectors.

10. Install headlight switch knob and instrument panel trim plate. Connect electrical connectors of any accessory switches in trim plate.

11. Install ash tray, retainer and fuse block, connect electrical connectors.

12. Install instrument cluster trim pad.

13. On non-air conditioned vehicles, raise the cover with vent cables attached and install steering column trim cover screws. On air conditioned vehicles, install trim cover and attaching screws.

14. If removed, install vent control housing.

15. Install instrument panel hush panel.

16. Connect the negative battery cable.

6000

1. Disconnect the negative battery cable, and remove the center and left side lower instrument panel trim plate.

2. Remove the screws holding the instrument cluster to the instrument panel carrier.

3. Remove the instrument cluster lens to gain access to the speedometer head and gauges.

4. Remove right side and left side hush panels, steering column trim cover and disconnect parking brake cable and vent cables, if equipped.

5. Remove steering column retaining bolts and drop steering column.

6. Disconnect temperature control cable, inner-to-outer air conditioning wire harness and inner-to-outer air conditioning vacuum harness, if equipped.

7. Disconnect chassis harness behind left lower instrument panel and ECM connectors behind glove box. Disconnect instrument panel harness at cowl.

8. Remove center instrument panel trim plate, radio, if equipped, and disconnect neutral switch and brake light switch.

9. Remove upper and lower instrument panel retaining screws, nuts and bolts.

10. Pull instrument panel assembly out far enough to disconnect ignition switch, headlight dimmer switch and turn signal switch. Disconnect all other accessory wiring and vacuum lines necessary to remove instrument panel assembly.

11. Remove instrument panel assembly with wiring harness.

To install:

12. Install instrument panel assembly with wiring harness.

13. Connect ignition switch, headlight dimmer switch and turn signal switch. Connect all other accessory wiring and vacuum lines.

14. Install upper and lower instrument panel retaining screws, nuts and bolts.

15. Connect neutral switch and brake light switch. Install the radio, if equipped, and install center instrument panel trim plate.

16. Connect chassis harness behind left lower instrument panel and ECM connectors behind glove box. Connect instrument panel harness at cowl.

17. Connect temperature control cable, inner-to-outer air conditioning wire harness and inner-to-outer air conditioning vacuum harness, if equipped.

18. Raise the steering column and install retaining bolts.

19. Install right side and left side hush panels, steering column trim cover and connect parking brake cable and vent cables, if equipped.

20. Install the instrument cluster lens.

21. Install the screws holding the instrument cluster to the instrument panel carrier.

22. Install the center and left side lower instrument panel trim plate.

23. Connect the negative battery cable.

Cutlass Ciera and Cutlass Cruiser

1. Disconnect the negative battery cable. Remove upper console, if equipped.

2. Remove the accessory trim plate assembly.

3. Remove the cluster trim plate assembly.

4. Remove the steering column trim trim collar and trim cover.

5. Disconnect shift indicator clip from steering column shift bowl.

6. Remove the 4 bolts securing the cluster assembly.

7. Pull cluster rearward to remove and remove unit from the vehicle.

To install:

8. Install the cluster assembly.

9. Install the 4 bolts.

10. Connect the shift indicator clip to the shift bowl.

11. Shift the indicator to make sure needle alignment is correct.

12. Install the steering column trim cover.

13. Install the cluster trim plate.

14. Install the accessory trim plate and upper console, if equipped.

15. Connect the negative battery cable.

Speedometer

REMOVAL & INSTALLATION

Century

1989

1. Disconnect the negative battery cable.

2. Remove the left side trim plate.

3. Remove the 4 screws securing the lens assembly and remove the lens.

4. Remove the 4 screws holding the speedometer and pull the speedometer outward.

5. Disconnect the speedometer cable by pushing on the clip and pulling on the cable.

6. Remove the screw holding the vehicle speed sensor optic head and remove the head.

7. Remove the speedometer from the vehicle.

To install:

8. Install the VSS optic head and install the screw.

9. Connect the speedometer cable to the speedometer.

10. Install the speedometer and secure with the 4 attaching screws.

11. Install the lens assembly and install the 4 screws.

12. Install the left trim plate and connect the negative battery cable.

1990–93

1. Disconnect the negative battery cable.

2. Remove the left side trim plate.

3. Remove the 4 speedometer lens screws and remove the speedometer lens.

4. Remove the 4 screws holding the speedometer to the instrument and remove the speedometer assembly.

To install:

5. Install the speedometer assembly and the screws holding the speedometer assembly to the instrument panel.

6. Install the speedometer lens and retaining screws.

7. Install the left side trim plate.

8. Connect the negative battery cable.

Celebrity

1. Disconnect the negative battery cable.

2. Remove the cluster trim panel.

3. Remove the cluster lens screws. Remove the cluster lens.

4. Remove the speedometer-to-cluster attaching screws. Remove the speedometer from the instrument cluster.

5. Disconnect the speedometer cable and remove the speedometer assembly.

To install:

6. Position the speedometer assembly and connect the speedometer cable.

7. Install the speedometer-to-instrument cluster and install the attaching screws.

8. Install the cluster lens and attaching screws.

9. Install the cluster trim panel.

10. Connect the negative battery cable.

Cutlass Ciera and Cutlass Cruiser

1989

1. Disconnect the negative battery cable.

2. Remove the instrument cluster assembly.

3. Remove the vehicle speed sensor bolt from the rear of the speedometer. Remove the vehicle speed sensor.

4. Remove the speedometer lens screws and remove the speedometer lens. Remove the bezel.

5. Remove the screw that holds the speedometer at the rear of the cluster.

6. Remove the front cluster screws. Remove the speedometer by gently pulling forward.

To install:

7. Install the speedometer head and install the front 2 screws.

8. Install the rear screw that holds the speedometer to the instrument cluster.

9. Install the speedometer lens and attaching screws. Install the bezel.

10. Install the vehicle speed sensor and the attaching bolt at the rear of the speedometer.

11. Install the instrument cluster assembly.

12. Connect the negative battery cable.

6000

1. Disconnect the negative battery cable.

2. Remove the center and left lower trim plates.

3. Remove the screws holding the instrument cluster assembly to the dash assembly. Remove the instrument cluster.

4. Remove the instrument cluster lens screws. Remove the instrument cluster lens.

5. Remove the screws holding the speedometer to the instrument cluster. Remove the speedometer.

6. Disconnect the speedometer cable from the rear of the speedometer.

To install:

7. Connect the speedometer cable at the rear of the speedometer.

8. Install speedometer and the screws holding the speedometer to the instrument cluster.

9. Install the instrument cluster lens and attaching screws.

10. Install the instrument cluster and the screws holding the instrument cluster assembly to the dash assembly.

11. Install the center and left lower trim plates.

12. Connect the negative battery cable.

Radio

REMOVAL & INSTALLATION

1. Disconnect battery negative cable.

2. Remove the accessory trim plate.

3. Remove the instrument cluster trim plate.

4. Remove the radio attaching bolts, then disconnect electrical connectors.

5. Remove radio from vehicle.

To install:

6. Install the radio in the vehicle.

7. Connect the electrical connectors. Install the radio attaching bolts.

8. Install the instrument cluster trim plate.

9. Install the accessory trim plate.

10. Connect the negative battery cable.

Headlight Switch

NOTE: Follow the steps below if equipped with dash mounted headlight switch. Refer to combination switch section if equipped with column mounted multi-function switch.

REMOVAL & INSTALLATION

Century

1. Disconnect the negative battery cable.

2. Remove the instrument panel trim plate.

3. Remove the left side instrument panel switch trim panel by removing the 3 screws and gently rocking the panel out.

4. Remove the 3 screws and pull the switch straight out.

To install:

5. Install the switch and the 3 attaching screws.

6. Install the left side instrument panel switch trim panel and 3 attaching screws.

7. Install the instrument panel trim plate.

8. Connect the negative battery cable.

Celebrity

1. Disconnect the negative battery cable.

2. Remove the headlight switch knob.

3. Remove the instrument panel trim pad.

4. Unbolt the switch mounting plate from the instrument panel carrier.

5. Disconnect the wiring from the switch.

6. Remove the switch.

To install:

7. Install the switch.

8. Connect the wiring to the switch.

9. Install the bolts attaching the switch mounting plate to the instrument panel carrier.

10. Install the instrument panel trim pad.

11. Install the headlight switch knob.

12. Connect the negative battery cable.

Cutlass Ciera and Cutlass Cruiser

1. Disconnect the negative battery cable.

2. Remove the left side instrument panel trim pad.

3. Unbolt the switch from the instrument panel.

4. Pull the switch rearward and remove it.

To install:

5. Install the switch and connect the electrical connectors.

6. Install the bolts attaching the switch to the instrument panel.

7. Install the left side instrument panel trim pad.

8. Connect the negative battery cable.

6000

1. Disconnect the negative battery cable.

2. Remove the steering column trim cover and headlight rod and knob by reaching behind the instrument panel and depressing the lock tab.

3. Remove the left instrument panel trim plate.

4. Unbolt and remove the switch and bracket assembly from the instrument panel.

5. Loosen the bezel and remove the switch from the bracket.

To install:

6. Install the switch to the bracket and install the bezel.

7. Install the switch and bracket assembly to the instrument panel and install the attaching bolts.

8. Install the left instrument panel trim plate.

9. Install the headlight rod and knob. Install the steering column trim cover.

10. Connect the negative battery cable.

Dimmer Switch

NOTE: Some vehicles have the dimmer switch incorporated into the combination switch. If equipped as such, refer to the combination switch section.

REMOVAL & INSTALLATION

1. Disconnect the negative battery cable.

2. Remove the steering wheel. Remove the trim cover.

3. Remove the turn signal switch assembly.

4. Remove the ignition switch stud and screw. Remove the ignition switch.

5. Remove the dimmer switch actuator rod by sliding it from the switch assembly.

6. Remove the dimmer switch bolts and remove the dimmer switch.

To install:

7. Install the dimmer switch and attaching bolts.

8. Install the dimmer switch actuator rod by sliding it into the switch assembly.

9. Adjust the dimmer switch by depressing the switch slightly and inserting a $\frac{3}{32}$ in. drill bit into the adjusting hole. Push the switch up to remove any play and tighten the dimmer switch adjusting screw.

10. Install the ignition switch, stud and screw.

11. Install the turn signal switch assembly.

12. Install the trim cover. Install the steering wheel.

13. Connect the battery negative cable.

Combination Switch

NOTE: If equipped with a dash mounted headlight switch, refer to headlight switch section.

REMOVAL & INSTALLATION

1. Disconnect the negative battery cable. Remove the steering wheel and trim cover.

2. Loosen the cover screws. Pry the cover upward and remove it from the shaft.

3. Position U-shaped lock plate compressing tool J–23653–C on the end of the steering shaft and compress the lockplate by turning the shaft nut clockwise. Pry the wire snapring from the shaft groove.

4. Remove the tool and lift the lock plate off the shaft.

5. Slip the cancelling cam, upper bearing preload spring and thrust washer off the shaft.

6. Remove the turn signal lever. Push the flasher knob in and unscrew it. Remove the button retaining screw and remove the button, spring and knob.

7. Pull the switch connector out the mast jacket and tape the upper part to facilitate switch removal. Attach a long piece of wire to the turn signal switch connector. When installing the turn signal switch, feed this wire through the column first, and then use this wire to pull the switch connector into position. If equipped with tilt-wheel, place the turn signal and shifter housing in the lowest position and remove the harness cover.

8. Remove the 3 switch mounting screws. Remove the switch by pulling it straight up while guiding the wiring harness cover through the column.

To install:

9. Install the replacement switch by working the connector and cover down through the housing and under the bracket. If equipped with tilt-wheel, work the connector down through the housing, under the bracket and install the harness cover.

10. Install the switch mounting screws and the connector on the mast jacket bracket. Install the column-to-dash trim plate.

11. Install the flasher knob and the turn signal lever.

12. With the turn signal lever in the middle position and the flasher knob out, slide the thrust washer, upper bearing preload spring and cancelling cam onto the shaft.

13. Position the lock plate on the shaft and press it down until a new snapring can be inserted in the shaft groove. Always use a new snapring when assembling.

14. Install the cover and the steering wheel. Connect the battery negative cable.

Ignition Lock

REMOVAL & INSTALLATION

1. Disconnect the negative battery cable. Place the lock in the **RUN** position. Remove the steering wheel.

2. Remove the lock plate, turn signal switch and buzzer switch.

3. Remove the screw and lock cylinder.

NOTE: Be careful not to drop the screw which could fall into the column assembly requiring complete disassembly of the column to retrieve the screw.

To install:

4. Rotate the cylinder clockwise to align cylinder key with the keyway in the housing.

5. Push the lock all the way in.

6. Install the screw. Tighten the screw to 14 inch lbs. for adjustable columns or 25 inch lbs. for standard columns. Connect battery negative cable.

Ignition Switch

REMOVAL & INSTALLATION

The switch is connected to the jacket

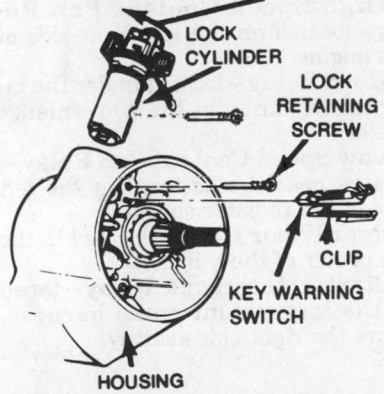

TO ASSEMBLE, ROTATE TO STOP WHILE HOLDING CYLINDER

LOCK CYLINDER

LOCK RETAINING SCREW

CLIP

KEY WARNING SWITCH

HOUSING

Mounting of the ignition lock cylinder assembly, removal of the key warning switch, is shown in the inset

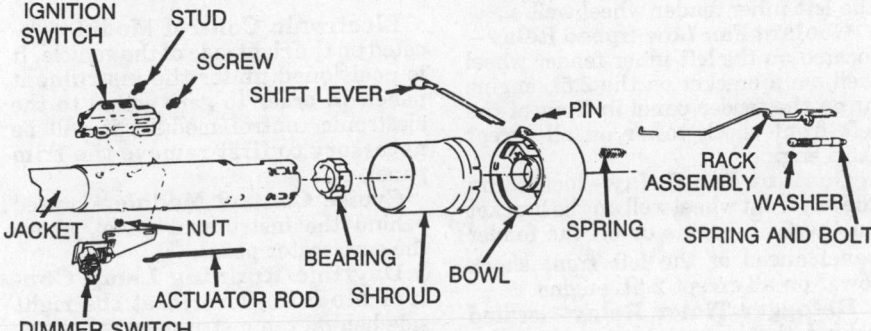

IGNITION SWITCH

STUD

SCREW

SHIFT LEVER

PIN

JACKET

NUT

BEARING

SHROUD

BOWL

SPRING

RACK ASSEMBLY

WASHER

SPRING AND BOLT

ACTUATOR ROD

DIMMER SWITCH

Installation of the ignition switch

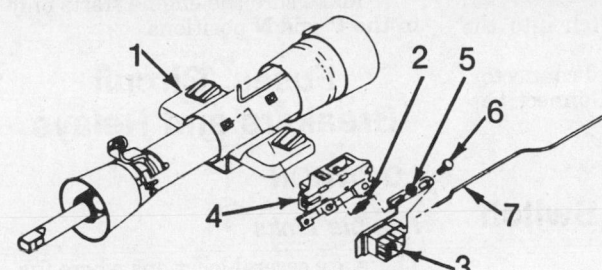

Ignition and dimmer switch removal

1. Jacket assembly
2. Dimmer and ignition switch mounting stud
3. Dimmer switch assembly
4. Ignition switch assembly
5. Nut
6. Screw
7. Dimmer switch rod

assembly of the steering column housing. The switch is actuated by a rod and rack assembly. A gear on the end of the lock cylinder engages the toothed upper end of the rod.

1. Disconnect the negative battery cable.

2. Put the ignition switch in the **OFF–LOCKED** position. Remove the steering wheel.

3. Using tool J-23653-C, depress the shaft lock and remove the shaft lock retaining ring and the shaft lock.

4. Remove the turn signal cancelling cam.

5. Remove the upper bearing spring and thrust washer.

6. Set the turn signal to the RIGHT turn setting and remove the combination switch lever.

7. Remove the screws from the actuator switch and remove the switch assembly.

8. Remove the hazard knob assembly.

9. Disconnect the turn signal switch and allow it to hang freely.

10. Remove the key from the lock cylinder set and remove the alarm assembly and clip.

11. Insert key into lock cylinder and set to **LOCK** position.

12. If equipped with cruise control, remove the housing cover end cap, unplug the connector and carefully pull through the shroud. Remove the combination switch assembly.

13. Remove the ignition switch screws and remove the switch assembly.

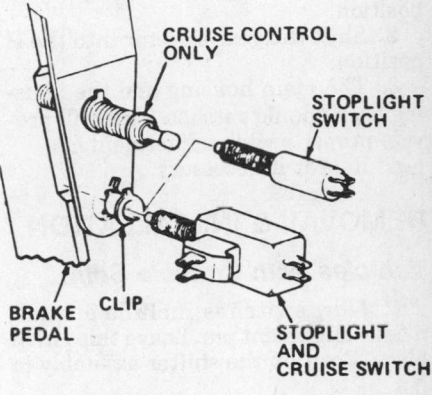

CRUISE CONTROL ONLY

STOPLIGHT SWITCH

BRAKE PEDAL

CLIP

STOPLIGHT AND CRUISE SWITCH

Stoplight switch location

To install:

14. Before installing, place the new switch in **OFF–UNLOCKED** position and make sure the lock cylinder and actuating rod are in **OFF–UN-LOCKED**, third detent from the top.

15. Install the activating rod into the switch and assemble the switch on the column. Tighten the mounting screws. Use only the specified screws since over-length screws could impair the collapsibility of the column.

16. Reinstall the steering column assembly. Connect battery negative cable.

Stoplight Switch

ADJUSTMENT

1. The switch is mounted on the brake pedal bracket.

2. To adjust, depress the pedal and push the switch through the circular retaining clip until it contacts the brake pedal, then pull the pedal up against the internal pedal stop. This places the switch in the correct position within the clip.

REMOVAL & INSTALLATION

1. Disconnect the negative battery cable. Disconnect the electrical connector to the switch.

2. Remove the switch from the brake pedal bracket.

To install:

3. Install the new switch into the bracket.

4. Connect the electrical connector.

5. Adjust the switch. Connect battery negative cable.

Neutral Safety Switch

ADJUSTMENT

1. After the switch is installed, move the housing towards the **L** gear position.

2. Shift the gear selector into the **P** position.

3. The main housing and the housing back should ratchet. This will provide proper switch adjustment.

4. Repeat if necessary.

REMOVAL & INSTALLATION

Vehicles With Console Shift

1. New switches include a small plastic alignment pin. Leave this pin in place. Position the shifter assembly in **N**.

2. Disconnect the negative battery cable. Remove the old switch and install the replacement, align the pin on the shifter with the slot in the switch and fasten with the 2 screws.

3. Move the shifter from the **N** position. This shears the plastic alignment pin and frees the switch.

4. If the switch is to be adjusted, insert a 3/32 in. drill bit or similar size pin and align the hole switch. Position switch, adjust as necessary. Remove the pin before shifting from **N**. Connect battery negative cable.

Vehicles With Column Shift

1. Disconnect the negative battery cable. Disconnect the electrical connectors from the combination backup and neutral safety switch.

2. Remove the 2 screws attaching the switch to the steering column.

3. Remove the switch.

To install:

4. Install the new switch and 2 attaching screws.

5. Adjust the switch by performing the following:

a. Position the shift lever in **N**.

b. Loosen the attaching screws. Install a 0.090 in. gauge pin into the outer hole in the switch cover.

c. Rotate the switch until the pin goes into the alignment hole in the inner plastic slide.

d. Tighten the switch-to-column attaching screws and remove the gauge pin. Torque the screws to 20 inch lbs. maximum.

6. Connect battery negative cable.

7. Make sure the engine starts only in the **P** and **N** positions.

Fuses, Circuit Breakers and Relays

LOCATION

Fusible Links

There are several locations where fusible links can be found. They are located ahead of the left side front shock tower, near the positive battery connection or at the starter solenoid near the front of the engine.

Circuit Breakers

Circuit breakers are used along with the fusible links to protect the various components of the electrical system, such as headlights, the windshield wipers and electric windows. The circuit breakers are located either in the switch or mounted on or near the lower lip of the instrument panel, to the right or left of the steering column.

Fuse Panel

The fuse panel is located on the left side of the vehicle. It is under the instrument panel assembly. In order to gain access to the fuse panel, it may be necessary to first remove the under dash padding.

Relays

EXCEPT CENTURY

Air Conditioner Compressor Relay—located on the upper right corner of the engine cowl.

Air Conditioner Delay Relay—located in the upper right corner of the engine cowl.

Air Conditioner/Heater Blower Relay—located on the plenum, on the right side of the firewall.

Altitude Advance Relay—located on the left inner fender, in front of the shock tower.

Charging System Relay—located behind the instrument panel, near the fuse block.

Constant Run Relay—located on the left inner fender wheel well.

Coolant Fan Low-Speed Relay—located on the left inner fender wheel well, on a bracket on the 2.5L engine or on the fender panel in front of the left front shock tower on all except 2.5L engine.

Coolant Fan Relay—located on the left front wheel well on the bracket on the 2.5L engine or on the fender panel ahead of the left front shock tower on all except 2.5L engine.

Defogger Timer Relay—located behind the instrument panel, under the instrument cluster.

Early Fuel Evaporation Heater Relay—located on the upper right side of the engine cowl.

Electronic Level Control Relay—located on the frame behind the left rear wheel well.

Fuel Pump Relay—located on the upper right side of the engine cowl.

High Mount Stop Light Relays—located on the left rear wheel well, in the trunk.

Horn Relay—located on the convenience center.

Low Brake Vacuum Relay—taped to the instrument panel above the fuse block.

Rear Wiper Relay—located in the top center of the tailgate.

Starter Interrupt Relay—located above the ashtray, taped to the instrument panel harness.

CENTURY

Air Conditioner Coolant Fan Relay (2.5L engine)—located on the right side of the firewall.

Blower Relay—located on the right side of the firewall.

Coolant Fan Delay Relay (SFI)—located in front of the left front shock tower, on a bracket.

Coolant Fan Relay—located in front of the left front shock tower.

Fuel Pump Relay (2.5L engine)—located in the relay bracket on the right side of the firewall.

High Speed Coolant Fan Relay—located on the left front side of the engine.

Horn Relay—located under the instrument panel, in the convenience center.

Low Speed Coolant Fan Relay—located near the battery, on the left side of the radiator shroud.

Rear Wiper Relay—located in the top center of the tailgate.

Starter Interrupt Relay—taped to the instrument panel harness, above the right side ashtray.

Computers

LOCATION

Electronic Control Module—located on the right side of the vehicle. It is positioned under the instrument panel. In order to gain access to the electronic control module, it will be necessary to first remove the trim panel.

Cruise Control Module—located behind the instrument panel, above the accelerator pedal.

Daytime Running Lamp Control Module—located at the right side behind the instrument panel.

GM "C" & "H" Body

Front Wheel Drive

Buick—Electra • LeSabre • Park Avenue
Cadillac—DeVille • Fleetwood
Oldsmobile—Delta 88 • 88 Royale • Ninety-Eight
Pontiac—Bonneville

SPECIFICATIONS

VEHICLE IDENTIFICATION CHART

It is important for servicing and ordering parts to be certain of the vehicle and engine identification. The VIN (vehicle identification number) is a 17 digit number visible through the windshield on the driver's side of the dash and contains the vehicle and engine identification codes. The tenth digit indicates model year and the eighth digit indicates engine code. It can be interpreted as follows:

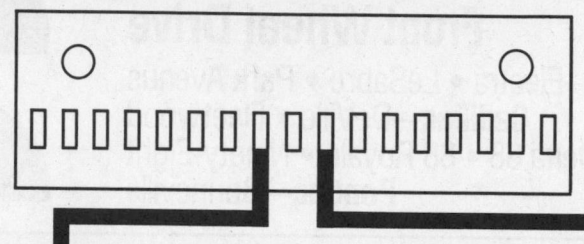

Engine Code

Code	Liters	Cu. In. (cc)	Cyl.	Fuel Sys.	Eng. Mfg.
C	3.8	231 (3786)	6	SFI	Buick
L	3.8	231 (3786)	6	PFI	Buick
5	4.5	273 (4474)	8	TBI	Cadillac
3	4.5	273 (4474)	8	PFI	Cadillac
B	4.9	300 (4894)	8	PFI	Cadillac
1	3.8	231 (3786)	6	PFI	Buick

PFI—Port Fuel Injection
SFI—Sequential Fuel Injection
TBI—Throttle Body Injection

Model Year

Code	Year
K	1989
L	1990
M	1991
N	1992
P	1993

ENGINE IDENTIFICATION

Year	Model	Engine Displacement Liters (cc)	Engine Series (ID/VIN)	Fuel System	No. of Cylinders	Engine Type
1989	DeVille	4.5 (4474)	5	TBI	8	OHV
	Fleetwood	4.5 (4474)	5	TBI	8	OHV
	Electra	3.8 (3786)	C	SFI	6	OHV
	Park Avenue	3.8 (3786)	C	SFI	6	OHV
	LeSabre	3.8 (3786)	C	SFI	6	OHV
	Ninety Eight	3.8 (3786)	C	SFI	6	OHV
	Delta 88	3.8 (3786)	C	SFI	6	OHV
	Bonneville	3.8 (3786)	C	SFI	6	OHV
1990	DeVille	4.5 (4474)	3	PFI	8	OHV
	Fleetwood	4.5 (4474)	3	PFI	8	OHV
	Electra	3.8 (3786)	C	SFI	6	OHV
	Park Avenue	3.8 (3786)	C	SFI	6	OHV
	LeSabre	3.8 (3786)	C	SFI	6	OHV
	Ninety Eight	3.8 (3786)	C	SFI	6	OHV
	Delta 88	3.8 (3786)	C	SFI	6	OHV
	Bonneville	3.8 (3786)	C	SFI	6	OHV

ENGINE IDENTIFICATION

Year	Model	Engine Displacement Liters (cc)	Engine Series (ID/VIN)	Fuel System	No. of Cylinders	Engine Type
1991	DeVille	4.9 (4894)	B	PFI	8	OHV
	Fleetwood	4.9 (4894)	B	PFI	8	OHV
	Park Avenue	3.8 (3786)	L	PFI	6	OHV
	LeSabre	3.8 (3786)	C	SFI	6	OHV
	Ninety Eight	3.8 (3786)	L	PFI	6	OHV
	88 Royale	3.8 (3786)	L	PFI	6	OHV
	Bonneville	3.8 (3786)	C	SFI	6	OHV
1992-93	DeVille	4.9 (4894)	B	PFI	8	OHV
	Fleetwood	4.9 (4894)	B	PFI	8	OHV
	Park Avenue	3.8 (3786)	L	PFI	6	OHV
	LeSabre	3.8 (3786)	L	SFI	6	OHV
	Ninety Eight	3.8 (3786)	L	PFI	6	OHV
	Ninety Eight	3.8 (3786)	1	PFI	6	OHV
	88 Royale	3.8 (3786)	L	PFI	6	OHV
	Bonneville	3.8 (3786)	L	PFI	6	OHV

PFI—Port Fuel Injection
SFI—Sequential Fuel Injection
TBI—Throttle Body Injection
OHV—Overhead Valves

GENERAL ENGINE SPECIFICATIONS

Year	Engine ID/VIN	Engine Displacement Liters (cc)	Fuel System Type	Net Horsepower @ rpm	Net Torque @ rpm (ft. lbs.)	Bore × Stroke (in.)	Compression Ratio	Oil Pressure @ rpm
1989	5	4.5 (4474)	TBI	155 @ 4000	240 @ 2800	3.622 × 3.307	9.0:1	37 @ 1500
	C	3.8 (3786)	SFI	165 @ 5200	210 @ 2000	3.800 × 3.400	8.5:1	37 @ 2400
1990	3	4.5 (4474)	PFI	180 @ 4300	245 @ 3000	3.622 × 3.307	9.5:1	37 @ 1500
	C	3.8 (3786)	SFI	165 @ 5200	210 @ 2000	3.800 × 3.400	8.5:1	40 @ 1850
1991	C	3.8 (3786)	SFI	165 @ 5200	210 @ 2000	3.800 × 3.400	8.5:1	60 @ 1850
	L	3.8 (3786)	PFI	170 @ 4800	220 @ 3200	3.800 × 3.400	8.5:1	60 @ 1850
	B	4.9 (4894)	PFI	200 @ 4100	275 @ 3000	3.623 × 3.623	9.5:1	53 @ 2000
1992-93	B	4.9 (4894)	PFI	200 @ 4100	275 @ 3000	3.623 × 3.623	9.5:1	53 @ 2000
	L	3.8 (3786)	PFI	170 @ 4800	220 @ 3200	3.800 × 3.400	8.5:1	60 @ 1850
	1	3.8 (3786)	PFI	205 @ 4400	260 @ 2600	3.800 × 3.400	8.5:1	60 @ 1850

NOTE: Horsepower and torque are SAE net figures. They are measured at the rear of the transmission with all accessories installed and operating. Since the figures vary when a given engine is installed in different models, some are representative rather than exact.
PFI—Port Fuel Injection
SFI—Sequential Fuel Injection
TBI—Throttle Body Injection

GASOLINE ENGINE TUNE-UP SPECIFICATIONS

Year	Engine ID/VIN	Engine Displacement Liters (cc)	Spark Plugs Gap (in.)	Ignition Timing (deg.) MT	Ignition Timing (deg.) AT	Fuel Pump (psi)	Idle Speed (rpm) MT	Idle Speed (rpm) AT	Valve Clearance In.	Valve Clearance Ex.
1989	5	4.5 (4474)	0.060	—	①	9-12	—	①	Hyd.	Hyd.
	C	3.8 (3786)	0.060	—	①	40-47	—	①	Hyd.	Hyd.

GASOLINE ENGINE TUNE-UP SPECIFICATIONS

Year	Engine ID/VIN	Engine Displacement Liters (cc)	Spark Plugs Gap (in.)	Ignition Timing (deg.) MT	AT	Fuel Pump (psi)	Idle Speed (rpm) MT	AT	Valve Clearance In.	Ex.
1990	3	4.5 (4474)	0.060	—	①	40–47	—	①	Hyd.	Hyd.
	C	3.8 (3786)	0.060	—	①	40–47	—	①	Hyd.	Hyd.
1991	C	3.8 (3786)	0.060	—	①	40–47	—	①	Hyd.	Hyd.
	L	3.8 (3786)	0.060	—	①	40–47	—	①	Hyd.	Hyd.
	B	4.9 (4894)	0.060	—	①	40–50	—	①	Hyd.	Hyd.
1992	1	3.8 (3786)	0.060	—	①	40–47	—	①	Hyd.	Hyd.
	L	3.8 (3786)	0.060	—	①	40–47	—	①	Hyd.	Hyd.
	B	4.9 (4894)	0.060	—	①	40–50	—	①	Hyd.	Hyd.
1993	REFER TO UNDERHOOD SPECIFICATIONS STICKER									

NOTE: The lowest cylinder pressure should be within 75% of the highest cylinder pressure reading. For example, if the highest cylinder is 134 psi, the lowest should be 101. Engine should be at normal operating temperature with throttle valve in the wide open position.
The underhood specifications sticker often reflects tune-up specification changes in production. Sticker figures must be used if they disagree with those in this chart.
① These vehicles are equipped with computerized emissions systems which have no distributor vacuum advance unit. The idle speed and ignition timing are controlled by the ECM/PCM.
Hyd.—Hydraulic

FIRING ORDERS

NOTE: To avoid confusion, always replace spark plug wires one at a time.

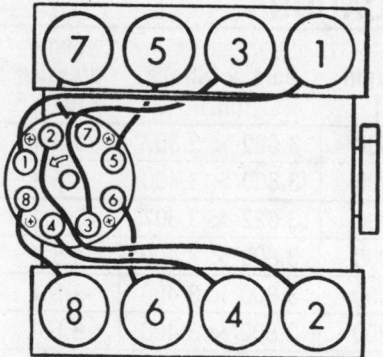

4.5L and 4.9L Engines
Engine Firing Order: 1–8–4–3–6–5–7–2
Distributor Rotation: Counterclockwise

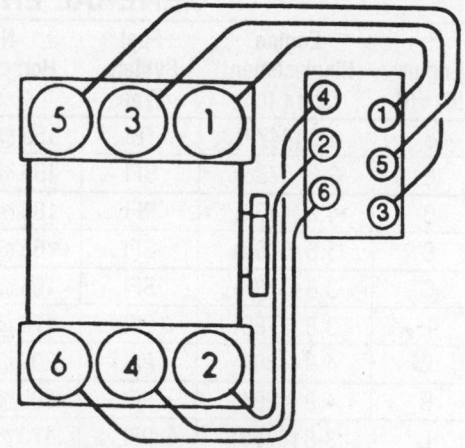

3.8L Engine VIN C and L
Engine Firing Order: 1–6–5–4–3–2
Distributorless Ignition System

CAPACITIES

Year	Model	Engine ID/VIN	Engine Displacement Liters (cc)	Engine Crankcase with Filter (qts.)	Transmission (pts.) 4-Spd	5-Spd	Auto.	Drive Axle Front (pts.)	Rear (pts.)	Fuel Tank (gal.)	Cooling System (qts.)
1989	DeVille	5	4.5 (4474)	5.5	—	—	22③	—	—	18	13.0
	Fleetwood	5	4.5 (4474)	5.5	—	—	22③	—	—	18	13.0
	Electra	C	3.8 (3786)	4.0①	—	—	22③	—	—	18	13.0
	Park Avenue	C	3.8 (3786)	4.0①	—	—	22③	—	—	18	13.0

CAPACITIES

Year	Model	Engine ID/VIN	Engine Displacement Liters (cc)	Engine Crankcase with Filter (qts.)	Transmission (pts.) 4-Spd	5-Spd	Auto.	Drive Axle Front (pts.)	Rear (pts.)	Fuel Tank (gal.)	Cooling System (qts.)
1989	LeSabre	C	3.8 (3786)	4.0①	—	—	22③	—	—	18	13.0
	Ninety Eight	C	3.8 (3786)	4.0①	—	—	22③	—	—	18	12.50
	Delta 88	C	3.8 (3786)	4.0①	—	—	22③	—	—	18	13.25
	Bonneville	C	3.8 (3786)	4.0①	—	—	22③	—	—	18	13.0
1990	DeVille	3	4.5 (4474)	5.5	—	—	22③	—	—	18	13.2
	Fleetwood	3	4.5 (4474)	5.5	—	—	22③	—	—	18	13.2
	Electra	C	3.8 (3786)	4.0①	—	—	22③	—	—	18	13.0
	Park Avenue	C	3.8 (3786)	4.0①	—	—	22③	—	—	18	13.0
	LeSabre	C	3.8 (3786)	4.0①	—	—	22③	—	—	18	13.0
	Ninety Eight	C	3.8 (3786)	4.0①	—	—	22③	—	—	18	13.0
	Delta 88	C	3.8 (3786)	4.0①	—	—	22③	—	—	18	13.0
	Bonneville	C	3.8 (3786)	4.0① ②	—	—	22③	—	—	18	13.0
1991	DeVille	B	4.9 (4894)	5.5	—	—	22③	—	—	18	13.2
	Fleetwood	B	4.9 (4894)	5.5	—	—	22③	—	—	18	13.2
	Park Avenue	L	3.8 (3786)	4.0①	—	—	22③	—	—	18	13.0
	LeSabre	C	3.8 (3786)	4.0①	—	—	22③	—	—	18	13.0
	Ninety Eight	L	3.8 (3786)	4.0①	—	—	22③	—	—	18	13.0
	88 Royale	L	3.8 (3786)	4.0①	—	—	22③	—	—	18	13.0
	Bonneville	C	3.8 (3786)	4.0① ②	—	—	22③	—	—	18	13.0
1992–93	DeVille	B	4.9 (4894)	5.5	—	—	22③	—	—	18	13.2
	Fleetwood	B	4.9 (4894)	5.5	—	—	22③	—	—	18	13.2
	Park Avenue	L	3.8 (3786)	5.0	—	—	22③	—	—	18	13.0
	Park Avenue	1	3.8 (3786)	5.0	—	—	22③	—	—	18	13.0
	LeSabre	L	3.8 (3786)	5.0	—	—	22③	—	—	18	13.0
	Ninety Eight	1	3.8 (3786)	5.0	—	—	22③	—	—	18	13.0
	Ninety Eight	L	3.8 (3786)	5.0	—	—	22③	—	—	18	13.0
	Eighty Eight	L	3.8 (3786)	5.0	—	—	22③	—	—	18	13.0
	Bonneville	L	3.8 (3786)	5.0②	—	—	22③	—	—	18	13.0

① Additional oil may be necessary to bring level to full
② SSE—5.5 qts.
③ Specification for transaxle overhaul. 12 pts for fluid and filter change.

CAMSHAFT SPECIFICATIONS

All measurements given in inches.

Year	Engine ID/VIN	Engine Displacement Liters (cc)	Journal Diameter 1	2	3	4	5	Elevation In.	Ex.	Bearing Clearance	Camshaft End Play
1989	C	3.8 (3786)	1.7850–1.7860	1.7850–1.7860	1.7850–1.7860	1.7850–1.7860	—	0.250	0.255	0.0005–0.0035	NA
	5	4.5 (4474)	2.6350–2.6360	2.6350–2.6360	2.6350–2.6360	2.6350–2.6360	2.6350–2.6360	0.384	0.396	0.0018–0.0037	NA

CAMSHAFT SPECIFICATIONS

All measurements given in inches.

Year	Engine ID/VIN	Engine Displacement Liters (cc)	Journal Diameter					Elevation		Bearing Clearance	Camshaft End Play
			1	2	3	4	5	In.	Ex.		
1990	C	3.8 (3786)	1.7850–1.7860	1.7850–1.7860	1.7850–1.7860	1.7850–1.7860	—	0.250	0.255	0.0005–0.0035	NA
	3	4.5 (4474)	2.6350–2.6360	2.6350–2.6360	2.6350–2.6360	2.6350–2.6360	2.6350–2.6360	0.384	0.396	0.0018–0.0037	NA
1991	B	4.9 (4894)	2.6350–2.6360	2.6350–2.6360	2.6350–2.6360	2.6350–2.6360	2.6350–2.6360	0.384	0.396	0.0018–0.0037	NA
	L	3.8 (3786)	1.7850–1.7860	1.7850–1.7860	1.7850–1.7860	1.7850–1.7860	—	0.250	0.255	0.0005–0.0035	NA
	C	3.8 (3786)	1.7850–1.7860	1.7850–1.7860	1.7850–1.7860	1.7850–1.7860	—	0.250	0.255	0.0005–0.0035	NA
1992–93	B	4.9 (4894)	2.6350–2.6360	2.6350–2.6360	2.6350–2.6360	2.6350–2.6360	2.6350–2.6360	0.384	0.396	0.0018–0.0037	NA
	L	3.8 (3786)	1.7850–1.7860	1.7850–1.7860	1.7850–1.7860	1.7850–1.7860	—	0.250	0.255	0.0005–0.0035	NA
	1	3.8 (3786)	1.7850–1.7860	1.7850–1.7860	1.7850–1.7860	1.7850–1.7860	—	0.250	0.255	0.0005–0.0035	NA

NA—Not available

CRANKSHAFT AND CONNECTING ROD SPECIFICATIONS

All measurements are given in inches.

Year	Engine ID/VIN	Engine Displacement Liters (cc)	Crankshaft				Connecting Rod		
			Main Brg. Journal Dia.	Main Brg. Oil Clearance	Shaft End-play	Thrust on No.	Journal Diameter	Oil Clearance	Side Clearance
1989	C	3.8 (3786)	2.4988–2.4998	0.0003–0.0018	0.003–0.011	2	2.2487–2.2499	0.0003–0.0026	0.003–0.015
	5	4.5 (4474)	2.6354–2.6364	①	0.001–0.007	3	2.0520–0.0540	0.0005–0.0028	0.008–0.020
1990	C	3.8 (3786)	2.4988–2.4998	0.0003–0.0018	0.003–0.011	2	2.2487–2.2499	0.0003–0.0026	0.003–0.015
	3	4.5 (4474)	2.6354–2.6364	①	0.001–0.007	3	2.0520–0.0540	0.0005–0.0028	0.008–0.020
1991	C	3.8 (3786)	2.4988–2.4998	0.0003–0.0018	0.003–0.011	2	2.2487–2.2499	0.0003–0.0026	0.003–0.015
	L	3.8 (3786)	2.4988–2.4998	0.0003–0.0018	0.003–0.011	2	2.2487–2.2499	0.0003–0.0026	0.003–0.015
	B	4.9 (4894)	2.6354–2.6364	①	0.001–0.008	3	2.0520–0.0530	0.0005–0.0028	0.008–0.020
1992–93	1	3.8 (3786)	2.4988–2.4998	0.0003–0.0018	0.003–0.011	2	2.2487–2.2499	0.0003–0.0026	0.003–0.015
	L	3.8 (3786)	2.4988–2.4998	0.0003–0.0018	0.003–0.011	2	2.2487–2.2499	0.0003–0.0026	0.003–0.015
	B	4.9 (4894)	2.6354–2.6364	①	0.001–0.008	3	2.0520–0.0530	0.0005–0.0028	0.008–0.020

① No. 1 bearing—0.0008–0.0031
No. 2–5 bearing—0.0016–0.0039

VALVE SPECIFICATIONS

Year	Engine ID/VIN	Engine Displacement Liters (cc)	Seat Angle (deg.)	Face Angle (deg.)	Spring Test Pressure (lbs. @ in.)	Spring Installed Height (in.)	Stem-to-Guide Clearance (in.)		Stem Diameter (in.)	
							Intake	Exhaust	Intake	Exhaust
1989	C	3.8 (3786)	45	45	200–220 @ 1.315 in.	1.690–1.750	0.0015–0.0035	0.0015–0.0032	0.3401–0.3412	0.3405–0.3412
	5	4.5 (4474)	45	44	②	NA	0.0010–0.0030	0.0010–0.0030	0.3420–0.3413	0.3401–0.3408
1990	C	3.8 (3786)	45	45	200–220 @ 1.315 in.	1.690–1.750	0.0015–0.0035	0.0015–0.0032	0.3401–0.3412	0.3405–0.3412
	3	4.5 (4474)	45	44	214–232 @ 1.35 in.	NA	0.0010–0.0030	0.0020–0.0040	0.3420–0.3413	0.3401–0.3408
1991	C	3.8 (3786)	45	45	210 @ 1.315 in.	1.690–1.720	0.0015–0.0035	0.0015–0.0035	NA	NA
	L	3.8 (3786)	45	45	210 @ 1.315 in.	1.690–1.720	0.0015–0.0035	0.0015–0.0035	NA	NA
	B	4.9 (4894)	45	45	214–232 @ 1.35 in.	NA	0.0010–0.0030	0.0020–0.0040	0.3420–0.3413	0.3401–0.3408
1992–93	B	4.9 (4894)	45	45	214–232 @ 1.35 in.	NA	0.0010–0.0030	0.0020–0.0040	0.3420–0.3413	0.3401–0.3408
	L	3.8 (3786)	45	45	210 @ 1.315 in.	1.690–1.720	0.0015–0.0035	0.0015–0.0032	NA	NA
	1	3.8 (3786)	45	45	210 @ 1.315 in.	1.690–1.720	0.0015–0.0035	0.0015–0.0032	NA	NA

NA—Not available

PISTON AND RING SPECIFICATIONS

All measurements are given in inches.

Year	Engine ID/VIN	Engine Displacement Liters (cc)	Piston Clearance	Ring Gap			Ring Side Clearance		
				Top Compression	Bottom Compression	Oil Control	Top Compression	Bottom Compression	Oil Control
1989	C	3.8 (3786)	①	0.010–0.025	0.010–0.025	0.015–0.055	0.0013–0.0031	0.0013–0.0031	0.0011–0.0081
	5	4.5 (4474)	0.0010–0.0018	0.015–0.024	0.015–0.024	0.010–0.050	0.0016–0.0037	0.0016–0.0037	None (side sealing)
1990	C	3.8 (3786)	0.0004–0.0022	0.010–0.025	0.010–0.025	0.015–0.055	0.0013–0.0031	0.0013–0.0031	0.0011–0.0081
	3	4.5 (4474)	0.0010–0.0018	0.015–0.024	0.015–0.024	0.010–0.050	0.0016–0.0037	0.0016–0.0037	None (side sealing)
1991	C	3.8 (3786)	0.0004–0.0022	0.010–0.025	0.010–0.025	0.015–0.055	0.0013–0.0031	0.0013–0.0031	0.0011–0.0081
	L	3.8 (3786)	0.0004–0.0022	0.010–0.025	0.010–0.025	0.015–0.055	0.0013–0.0031	0.0013–0.0031	0.0011–0.0081
	B	4.9 (4894)	0.0004–0.0020	0.012–0.022	0.012–0.022	0.010–0.050	0.0016–0.0037	0.0016–0.0037	None (side sealing)

PISTON AND RING SPECIFICATIONS

All measurements are given in inches.

Year	Engine ID/VIN	Engine Displacement Liters (cc)	Piston Clearance	Ring Gap			Ring Side Clearance		
				Top Compression	Bottom Compression	Oil Control	Top Compression	Bottom Compression	Oil Control
1992-93	B	4.9 (4894)	0.0004–0.0020	0.012–0.022	0.012–0.022	0.010–0.050	0.0016–0.0037	0.0016–0.0037	None (side sealing)
	L	3.8 (3786)	0.0004–0.0022	0.010–0.025	0.010–0.025	0.015–0.055	0.0013–0.0031	0.0013–0.0031	0.0011–0.0081
	1	3.8 (3786)	0.0004–0.0022	0.010–0.025	0.010–0.025	0.015–0.055	0.0013–0.0031	0.0013–0.0031	0.0011–0.0081

① Skirt Top: 0.0007–0.0027
Skirt Bottom: 0.0010–0.0045

TORQUE SPECIFICATIONS

All readings in ft. lbs.

Year	Engine ID/VIN	Engine Displacement Liters (cc)	Cylinder Head Bolts	Main Bearing Bolts	Rod Bearing Bolts	Crankshaft Damper Bolts	Flywheel Bolts	Manifold		Spark Plugs	Lug Nut
								Intake	Exhaust		
1989	C	3.8 (3786)	60⑤	90	43	219	61	88	41	20	100
	5	4.5 (4474)	①	85	24	65	70	②	18	11	100
1990	C	3.8 (3786)	35	90	43	219	61	88④	41	20	100
	3	4.5 (4474)	①	85	24	65	70	②	18	11	100
1991	C	3.8 (3786)	⑥	⑦	⑧	③	61	88④	41	20	100
	L	3.8 (3786)	⑥	⑦	⑧	③	61	88④	41	20	100
	B	4.9 (4894)	①	85	25	70	70	②	18	23	100
1992-93	B	4.9 (4894)	①	85	25	70	70	②	18	23	100
	L	3.8 (3786)	⑥	⑦	⑧	③	61	88④	41	20	100
	1	3.8 (3786)	⑥	⑦	⑧	③	61	88④	41	20	100

① Tighten in 3 steps:
1. Tighten bolts in sequence to 38 ft. lbs.
2. Tighten bolts in sequence to 68 ft. lbs.
3. Tighten bolts, 1, 3 and 4 to 90 ft. lbs.
② Tighten in 3 steps:
1. Tighten 1, 2, 3, 4 in sequence to 8 ft. lbs.
2. Tighten bolts 5 through 16 in sequence to 8 ft. lbs.
3. Retighten all bolts in sequence to 12 ft. lbs.

③ 105 ± 7 (+56° ±4)
④ Inch lbs.
⑤ 3 Step procedure: Should you reach 60 ft. lbs. at any time in step 2 or 3, stop tightening. Do not complete the balance of the 90 degree turn of this bolt.
Step 1: 25 ft. lbs.
Step 2: 90 degrees
Step 3: 90 degrees

⑥ Tighten in 3 steps:
1. Tighten bolts in sequence to 35 ft. lbs.
2. Rotate each bolt an additional 130 degrees in sequence
3. Rotate the center 4 bolts an additional 30 degrees in sequence
⑦ 26 ± 3 (+50° ±3)
⑧ 20 ± 3 (+50° ±3)

BRAKE SPECIFICATIONS

All measurements in inches unless noted

Year	Model	Master Cylinder Bore	Brake Disc			Brake Drum Diameter			Minimum Lining Thickness	
			Original Thickness	Minimum Thickness	Maximum Runout	Original Inside Diameter	Max. Wear Limit	Maximum Machine Diameter	Front	Rear
1989	DeVille	0.937	1.043	0.972	0.004	8.860	0.006	8.880	0.030	0.030
	Fleetwood	0.937	1.043	0.972	0.004	8.860	0.006	8.880	0.030	0.030
	Electra	0.937	1.043	0.972	0.004	8.860	0.006	8.880	0.030	0.030
	Park Ave.	0.937	1.043	0.972	0.004	8.860	0.006	8.880	0.030	0.030
	LeSabre	0.937	1.043	0.972	0.004	8.860	0.006	8.880	0.030	0.030

BRAKE SPECIFICATIONS

All measurements in inches unless noted

Year	Model	Master Cylinder Bore	Brake Disc Original Thickness	Brake Disc Minimum Thickness	Maximum Runout	Brake Drum Diameter Original Inside Diameter	Brake Drum Diameter Max. Wear Limit	Brake Drum Diameter Maximum Machine Diameter	Minimum Lining Thickness Front	Minimum Lining Thickness Rear
1989	Ninety Eight	0.937	1.043	0.972	0.004	8.860	0.006	8.880	0.030	0.030
	Delta 88	0.937	1.043	0.972	0.004	8.860	0.006	8.880	0.030	0.030
	Bonneville	0.937	1.043	0.972	0.004	8.860	0.006	8.880	0.030	0.030
1990	DeVille	0.937	1.043	0.972	0.004	8.860	0.006	8.880	0.030	0.030
	Fleetwood	0.937	1.043	0.972	0.004	8.860	0.006	8.880	0.030	0.030
	Electra	0.937	1.043	0.972	0.004	8.860	0.006	8.880	0.030	0.030
	Park Ave.	0.937	1.043	0.972	0.004	8.860	0.006	8.880	0.030	0.030
	LeSabre	0.937	1.043	0.972	0.004	8.860	0.006	8.880	0.030	0.030
	Ninety Eight	0.937	1.043	0.972	0.004	8.860	0.006	8.880	0.030	0.030
	Delta 88	0.937	1.043	0.972	0.004	8.860	0.006	8.880	0.030	0.030
	Bonneville	0.937	1.043	0.972	0.004	8.860	0.006	8.880	0.030	0.030
1991	DeVille	1.000	1.276	1.224	0.004	8.860	0.006	8.880	0.030	0.030
	Fleetwood	1.000	1.276	1.224	0.004	8.860	0.006	8.880	0.030	0.030
	Park Ave.	1.000	1.276	1.204	0.004	8.860	0.006	8.880	0.030	0.030
	LeSabre	1.000	1.043	0.972	0.004	8.860	0.006	8.880	0.030	0.030
	Ninety Eight	1.000	1.276	1.204	0.004	8.860	0.006	8.880	0.030	0.030
	88 Royale	1.000	1.043	0.972	0.004	8.860	0.006	8.880	0.030	0.030
	Bonneville	1.000	1.043	0.972	0.004	8.860	0.006	8.880	0.030	0.030
1992–93	DeVille	1.000	1.276	1.224	0.004	8.860	0.006	8.880	0.030	0.030
	Fleetwood	1.000	1.276	1.224	0.004	8.860	0.006	8.880	0.030	0.030
	Park Ave.	1.000	1.276	1.224	0.004	8.860	0.006	8.880	0.030	0.030
	LeSabre	1.000	1.276	1.224	0.004	8.860	0.006	8.880	0.030	0.030
	Ninety Eight	1.000	1.276	1.224	0.004	8.860	0.006	8.880	0.030	0.030
	Eighty Eight	1.000	1.276	1.224	0.004	8.860	0.006	8.880	0.030	0.030
	Bonneville	1.000	1.276	1.224	0.004	8.860	0.006	8.880	0.030	0.030

WHEEL ALIGNMENT

Year	Model	Caster Range (deg.)	Caster Preferred Setting (deg.)	Camber Range (deg.)	Camber Preferred Setting (deg.)	Toe-in (in.)	Steering Axis Inclination (deg.)
1989	DeVille	2½P–3½P	3P	①	①	0	—
	Fleetwood	2½P–3½P	3P	①	①	0	—
	Electra	2½P–3½P	3P	$^5/_{16}$N–$^{11}/_{16}$P	$^3/_{16}$P	0	—
	Park Avenue	2½P–3½P	3P	$^5/_{16}$N–$^{11}/_{16}$P	$^3/_{16}$P	0	—
	LeSabre	2½P–3½P	3P	$^5/_{16}$N–$^{11}/_{16}$P	$^3/_{16}$P	0	—
	Ninety Eight	2½P–3½P	3P	$^5/_{16}$N–$^{11}/_{16}$P	$^3/_{16}$P	0	½P
	Delta 88	2½P–3½P	3P	$^5/_{16}$N–$^{11}/_{16}$P	$^3/_{16}$P	0	½P
	Bonneville	2½P–3½P	3P	$^5/_{16}$N–$^{11}/_{16}$P	$^3/_{16}$P	0	½P

WHEEL ALIGNMENT

Year	Model	Caster Range (deg.)	Caster Preferred Setting (deg.)	Camber Range (deg.)	Camber Preferred Setting (deg.)	Toe-in (in.)	Steering Axis Inclination (deg.)
1990	DeVille	2½P–3½P	3P	①	①	0	—
	Fleetwood	2½P–3½P	3P	①	①	0	—
	Electra	2½P–3½P	3P	5/16N–11/16P	3/16P	0	—
	Park Avenue	2½P–3½P	3P	5/16N–11/16P	3/16P	0	—
	LeSabre	2½P–3½P	3P	5/16N–11/16P	3/16P	0	—
	Ninety Eight	2½P–3½P	3P	5/16N–11/16P	3/16P	0	½P
	Delta 88	2½P–3½P	3P	5/16N–11/16P	3/16P	0	½P
	Bonneville	2½P–3½P	3P	5/16N–11/16P	3/16P	0	½P
1991	DeVille	2½P–3½P	3P	①	①	0	—
	Fleetwood	2½P–3½P	3P	①	①	0	—
	Park Avenue	2½P–3½P	3P	5/16N–11/16P	3/16P	0	—
	LeSabre	2½P–3½P	3P	5/16N–11/16P	3/16P	0	—
	Ninety Eight	2½P–3½P	3P	5/16N–11/16P	3/16P	0	½P
	88 Royale	2½P–3½P	3P	5/16N–11/16P	3/16P	0	½P
	Bonneville	2½P–3½P	3P	5/16N–11/16P	3/16P	0	½P
1992–93	DeVille	2½P–3½P	3P	①	①	0	—
	Fleetwood	2½P–3½P	3P	①	①	0	—
	Park Avenue	2½P–3½P	3P	5/16N–11/16P	3/16P	0	—
	LeSabre	2½P–3½P	3P	5/16N–11/16P	3/16P	0	—
	Ninety Eight	2½P–3½P	3P	5/16N–11/16P	3/16P	0	—
	Eighty Eight	2½P–3½P	3P	5/16N–11/16P	3/16P	0	—
	Bonneville	2½P–3½P	3P	5/16N–11/16P	3/16P	0	—

N—Negative
P—Positive
① Left wheel
   Min.—1N
   Pref.—½N
   Max.—0

② Right wheel
   Min.—0
   Pref.—½P
   Max.—1P

ENGINE MECHANICAL

NOTE: Disconnecting the negative battery cable on some vehicles may interfere with the functions of the on board computer systems and may require the computer to undergo a relearning process, once the negative battery cable is reconnected.

Engine Assembly

REMOVAL & INSTALLATION

3.8L Engine

1989–91 VIN C

1. Disconnect the negative battery cable. Using a scribing tool, matchmark the hood hinges and remove the hood.

2. Label and disconnect the air flow sensor wiring. Depressurize the fuel system.

3. Remove the air intake duct. Remove the throttle cable and bracket from the throttle body. Place a clean drain pan under the radiator, open the drain cock and drain the cooling system.

4. Raise and safely support the vehicle.

5. Remove the exhaust pipe-to-exhaust manifold bolts and separate the exhaust pipe.

6. Remove the Engine mount bolts.

7. If equipped with a driveline vibration absorber, remove the bolts and disconnect the absorber.

8. Label and disconnect the electrical connectors from the starter. Remove the starter-to-engine bolts and the starter.

9. If equipped with air conditioning, remove the compressor mounting bolts and position aside. Do not discharge the system or disconnect the refrigerant lines.

10. Place a pan under the power steering gear. Disconnect the hydraulic lines and drain the fluid. Use a length of wire to hold the hoses aside.

11. Remove the lower transaxle-to-engine bolts.

NOTE: One bolt is situated between the transaxle case and the Engine block. It is installed in the opposite direction to the other bolts.

12. Remove the flywheel cover. Matchmark the flexplate-to-torque converter relationship to insure proper alignment upon installation. Remove the flexplate-to-torque converter bolts.

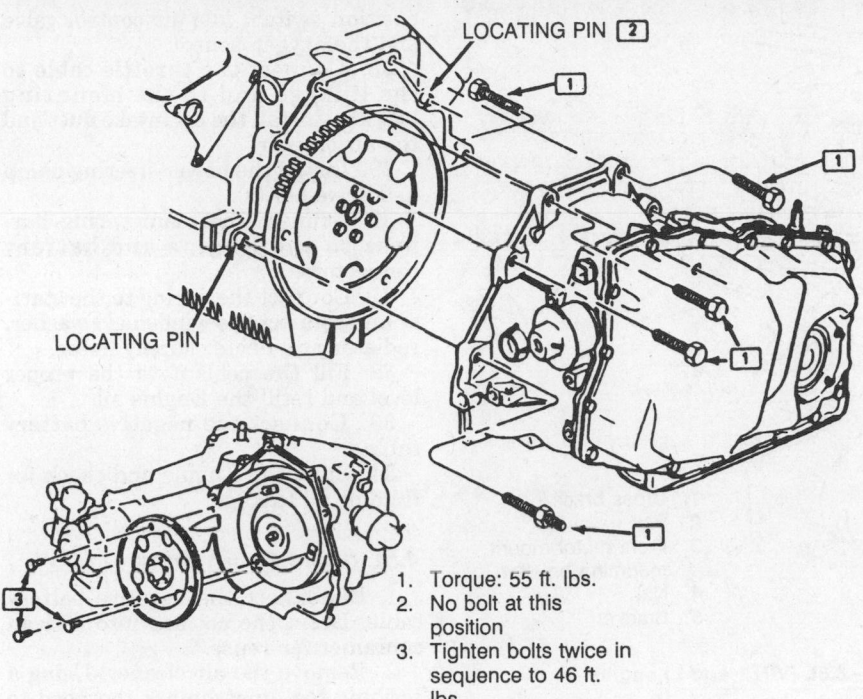

LOCATING PIN [2]

LOCATING PIN

1. Torque: 55 ft. lbs.
2. No bolt at this position
3. Tighten bolts twice in sequence to 46 ft. lbs.

Engine-to-transaxle mounting location—3.8L (VIN C) engine

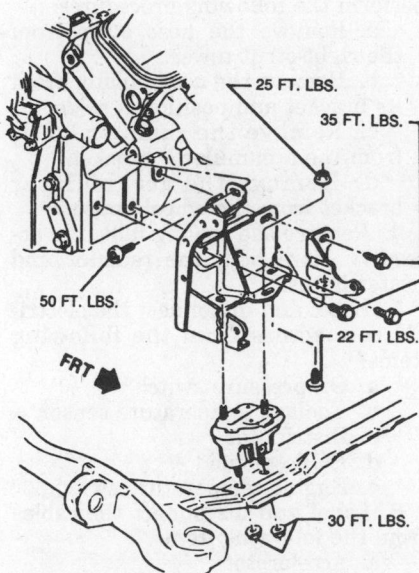

25 FT. LBS.

35 FT. LBS.

50 FT. LBS.

22 FT. LBS.

FRT

30 FT. LBS.

Engine mounting—3.8L (VIN C) engine

13. Remove the Engine support bracket-to-transaxle bolts and the bracket. Lower the vehicle.
14. Attach an Engine hoist to the Engine lift brackets and support the engine.
15. Remove the radiator and heater hoses from the Engine and position them aside.
16. Label and disconnect the hoses from the vacuum modulator and canister purge lines.

17. Label and disconnect the Engine electrical wiring harness(es) and position them out of way.
18. Remove the upper transaxle-to-engine bolts.
19. Carefully remove the Engine from the vehicle.
To install:
20. Install the Engine in the vehicle.
21. Connect and reposition the Engine electrical wiring harness, secure the bracket.
22. Connect the hoses to the vacuum modulator and the canister purge lines.
23. Install the radiator and the heater hoses.
24. Remove the Engine hoist. Raise and safely support the vehicle.
25. Replace the Engine support bracket-to-transaxle bolts.
26. Replace the upper transaxle-to-engine bolts. Install the Engine mount bolts and tighten to 70 ft. lbs. (95 Nm).
27. Install the torque converter and tighten the bolts to 46 ft. lbs. (62 Nm). Replace the flywheel cover.
28. Install the lower transaxle-to-engine bolts, tighten to 55 ft. lbs. (75 Nm).
29. Connect the power steering hydraulic lines to the power steering gear.
30. Install the air conditioning compressor, if equipped.
31. Install the starter and tighten the mounting bolts to 35 ft. lbs. (47 Nm).

32. Connect the electrical connections at the starter motor.
33. Connect the driveline vibration absorber, if equipped.
34. Install the exhaust pipe and replace the exhaust pipe-to-manifold bolts.
35. Lower the vehicle.
36. Connect the air flow sensor wiring. Install the hood assembly.
37. Connect the negative battery cable. Refill the cooling system.
38. Start the engine, allow it to reach normal operating temperatures and check for leaks.

1991–93 VIN L and 1

1. Disconnect the negative battery cable. Using a scribing tool, matchmark the hood hinges and remove the hood.
2. Depressurize the fuel system.
3. Drain the coolant and the Engine oil from the vehicle.
4. Remove the strut tower cross brace. Disconnect the windshield washer, radiator and heater supply hoses.
5. Disconnect the wiring to the starter. Disconnect the main wiring at the harness near the relay center.
6. Remove the drive belt(s). Disconnect the power steering pump and set off to the side.
7. Remove the air inlet duct and the air cleaner assembly. Disconnect the throttle cable from the linkage.
8. Disconnect the wiring harness connectors from the MAT sensor, the throttle position switch, the idle air control valve and the oxygen sensor.
9. Disconnect the ignition coil ground strap from the fender inner panel. Disconnect the fuel lines from the fuel rail and from the pressure regulator.
10. Disconnect the emission control hoses from the throttle body connections.
11. Disconnect the brake booster and heater control hoses from the vacuum connections.
12. Raise and safely support the vehicle.
13. Disconnect the exhaust pipe from the right side manifold and disconnect the vacuum lines from the cruise control and servo assembly.
14. Attach an Engine lifting device to the Engine and raise so it begins to support the engine.
15. Disconnect the air conditioner compressor and tie back away from the engine. If equipped with an Engine oil cooler, disconnect the cooler lines.
16. Remove the front Engine mount and remove the right front Engine to transaxle bracket.
17. Support the transaxle and remove the Engine to transaxle bolts.

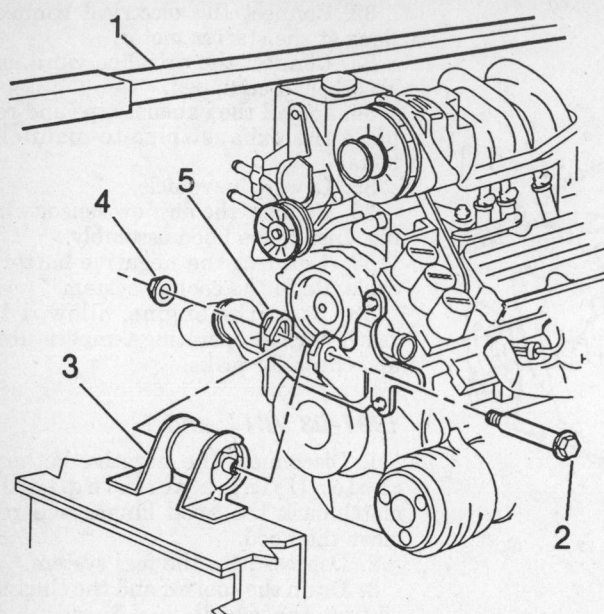

1. Cross brace
2. Bolt
3. Front motor mount mounting bracket
4. Nut
5. Bracket

Front Engine mount assembly—3.8L (VIN 1 and L) engine

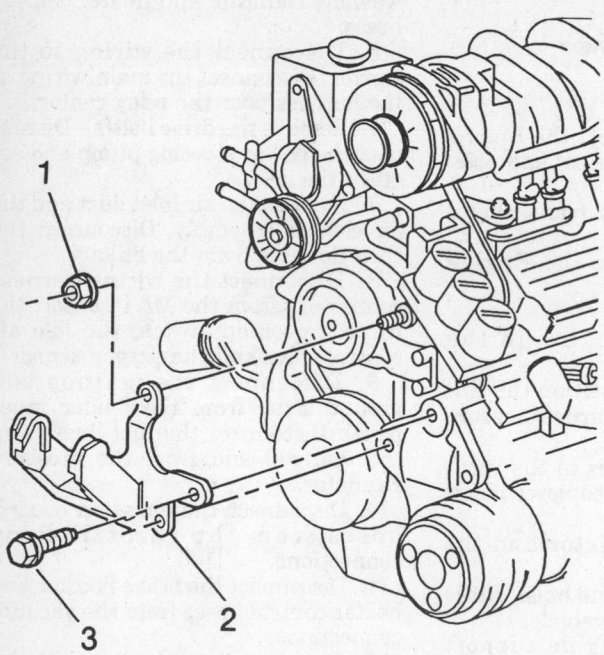

1. Nut
2. Front motor mount mounting bracket
3. Bolt

Engine mounting bracket—3.8L (VIN 1 and L) engine

Remove the flywheel cover.

18. Remove the torque converter to flywheel bolts and use a scribe to mark the proper flywheel to torque converter relationship.

19. Seperate the Engine from the transaxle and remove the Engine from the vehicle.

To install:

20. Install the Engine in the vehicle.

21. Install the Engine to transaxle bolts. Install the right front Engine to transaxle bracket.

22. Install the front Engine mount.

23. Install the torque converter to flywheel bolts, making sure flywheel and converter are aligned as before.

24. Install the flywheel cover and the oil cooler lines, if equipped.

25. Install the air conditioning compressor. Connect the cruise control and vacuum hoses at the servo.

26. Connect the exhaust pipe to the right side manifold.

27. Connect the wiring harness connectors to the MAT sensor, throttle

position switch, idle air control valve and the oxygen sensor.

28. Connect the throttle cable to the linkage and to the mounting bracket. Install the air intake duct and the air cleaner.

29. Install the power steering pump and drive belt(s).

30. Connect the main wiring harness to the Engine and battery connectors.

31. Connect the wiring to the starter and connect the windshield washer, radiator and heater supply hoses.

32. Fill the coolant to the proper level and refill the Engine oil.

33. Connect the negative battery cable.

34. Start the Engine and check for fluid or oil leakage.

4.5L and 4.9L Engines

1. Disconnect the negative battery cable. Drain the coolant into a clean container for reuse.

2. Remove the air cleaner. Using a scribing tool, matchmark the hood to the support brackets and remove the hood.

3. If equipped with air conditioning, perform the following procedures:

    a. Remove the hose strap from the right-strut tower.

    b. Remove the accumulator from its bracket and position it aside.

    c. Remove the canister hoses from the accumulator bracket.

    d. Remove the accumulator bracket from the wheel house.

4. Remove the cooling fans, the accessory drive belt, the radiator and heater hoses.

5. Label and disconnect the electrical connectors from the following items:

    a. Oil pressure switch

    b. Coolant temperature sensor

    c. Distributor

    d. EGR solenoid

    e. Engine temperature switch

6. Label and disconnect the cables from the following items:

    a. Accelerator

    b. Cruise control linkage

    c. Transaxle Throttle Valve (TV) cable

7. If equipped with cruise control, remove the diaphragm with the bracket attached and move it aside.

8. Remove the vacuum supply hose and the exhaust crossover pipe.

9. Disconnect the oil cooler lines from the oil filter adapter, the oil line cooler bracket from the transaxle and position them aside.

10. Remove the air cleaner mounting bracket.

11. Properly relieve the fuel system pressure. Disconnect the fuel lines from the throttle body. Remove the

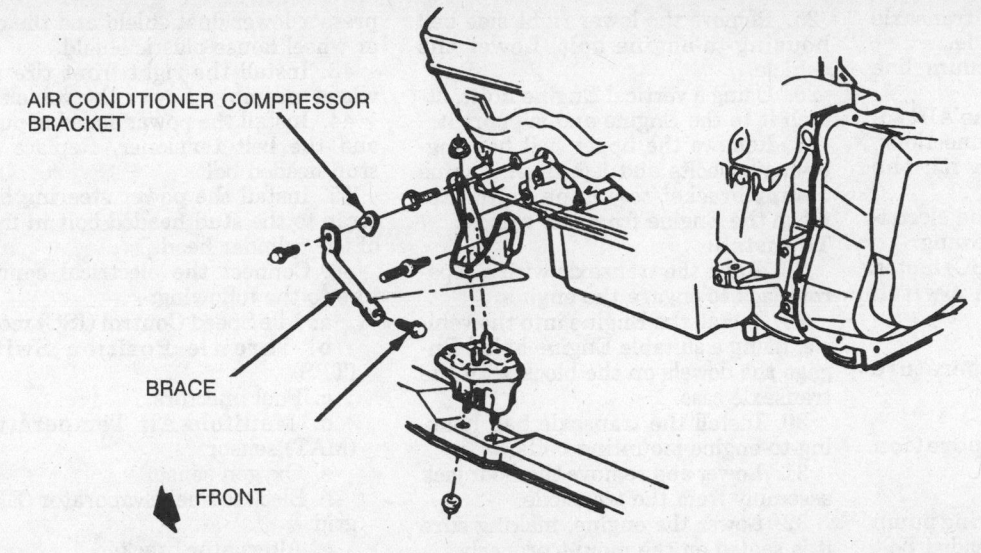

AIR CONDITIONER COMPRESSOR
BRACKET

BRACE

FRONT

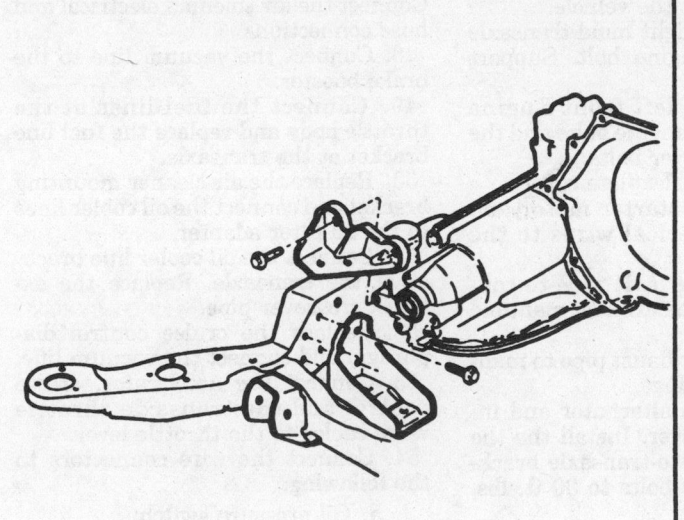

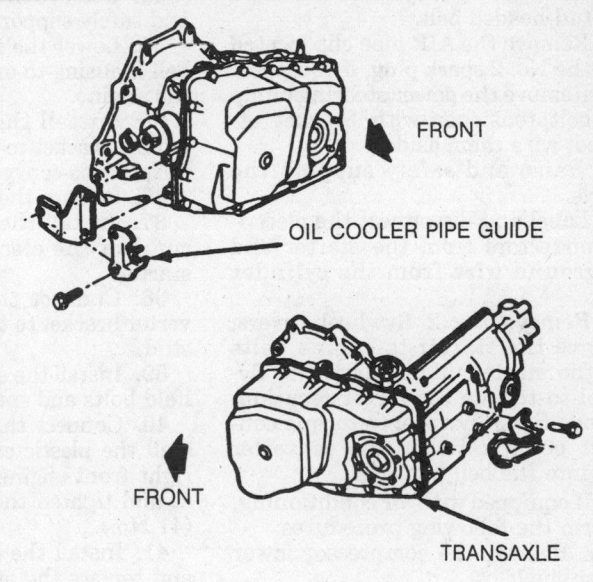

FRONT

OIL COOLER PIPE GUIDE

FRONT

TRANSAXLE

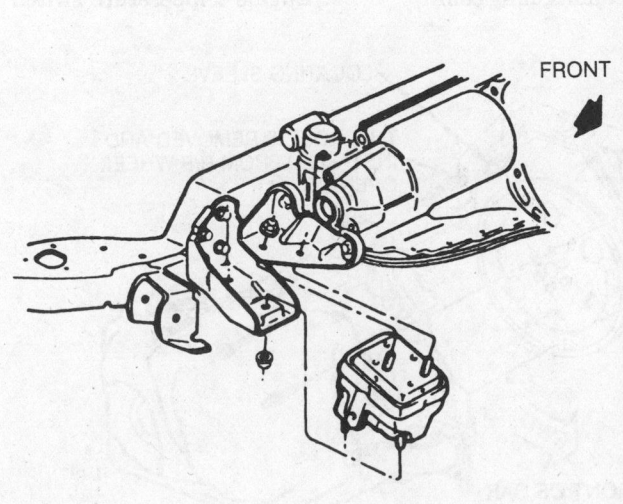

FRONT

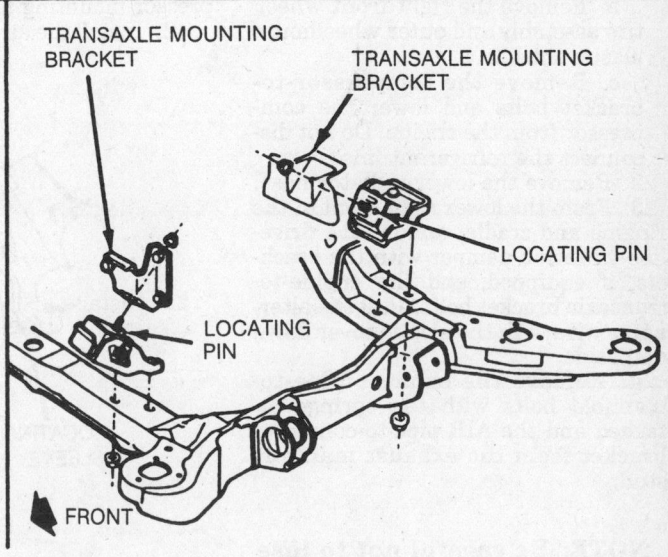

TRANSAXLE MOUNTING
BRACKET

TRANSAXLE MOUNTING
BRACKET

LOCATING PIN

LOCATING
PIN

FRONT

Engine and transmission mounts—4.5L and 4.9L engines

fuel line bracket from the transaxle and secure the fuel lines aside.

12. Remove the small vacuum line from the brake booster.

13. Label and disconnect the AIR solenoid electrical and hose connections. Remove the AIR valves with the bracket.

14. Label and disconnect the electrical connectors from the following:

   a. Idle Speed Control (ISC) motor
   b. Throttle Position Switch (TPS)
   c. Fuel injectors
   d. Manifold Air Temperature (MAT) sensor
   e. Oxygen sensor
   f. Electric Fuel Evaporation (EFE) grid
   g. Alternator bracket

15. Remove the power steering pump hose strap from the stud-headed bolt in front of the right cylinder head and the stud-headed bolt.

16. Remove the AIR pipe clip located near the No. 2 spark plug, if equipped.

17. Remove the power steering pump and belt tensioner with bracket attached; wire them aside.

18. Raise and safely support the vehicle.

19. Label and disconnect the electrical connectors from the starter and the ground wire from the cylinder block.

20. Remove the 2 flywheel covers. Remove the starter-to-engine bolts and the starter. Matchmark the flywheel-to-torque converter location. Remove the 3 flywheel-to-torque converter bolts and slide the converter back into the bell housing.

21. If equipped with air conditioning, perform the following procedures:

   a. Remove the compressor lower dust shield.
   b. Remove the right front wheel/tire assembly and outer wheelhouse plastic shield.
   c. Remove the compressor-to-bracket bolts and lower the compressor from the engine. Do not disconnect the refrigerant lines.

22. Remove the lower radiator hose.

23. From the lower right front of the Engine and cradle, remove the driveline vibration damper with the brackets, if equipped, and the engine-to-transaxle bracket bolts. Pull the alternator wire with the plastic cover down and aside.

24. Remove the exhaust pipe-to-manifold bolts with the springs attached and the AIR pipe-to-converter bracket from the exhaust manifold stud.

NOTE: Be careful not to lose the springs when detaching the exhaust pipe.

25. Remove the lower right side bell housing-to-engine bolt. Lower the vehicle.

26. Using a vertical Engine hoist, attach it to the Engine and support it.

27. Remove the upper bell housing-to-engine bolts and left front Engine mount bracket-to-engine bolts. Remove the Engine from the vehicle.

To install:

28. Raise the transaxle with a separate jack to engage the engine.

29. Install the Engine into the vehicle, using a suitable Engine hoist. Engage the dowels on the block with the transaxle case.

30. Install the transaxle bell housing-to-engine mounting bolts.

31. Lower and remove the floor jack assembly from the transaxle.

32. Lower the engine, making sure it is seated on the mount properly.

33. Remove the Engine hoist. Raise and safely support the vehicle.

34. Lower the right hand transaxle bell housing-to-engine bolt. Support the engine.

35. Install the left front Engine mount bracket-to-engine bolts and the flexplate-to-converter bolts.

36. Replace the flexplate covers.

37. Install the starter motor and connect the electrical wires to the starter.

38. Connect the AIR pipe-to-converter bracket to the exhaust manifold stud.

39. Install the exhaust pipe to manifold bolts and springs.

40. Connect the alternator and install the plastic cover. Install the the right front engine-to-transaxle bracket and tighten the bolts to 30 ft. lbs. (41 Nm).

41. Install the lower radiator hose and replace the air conditioning compressor mounting bolts.

42. Install the air conditioning com-

pressor lower dust shield and the outer wheel house plastic shield.

43. Install the right front tire and wheel assembly. Lower the vehicle.

44. Install the power steering pump and the belt tensioner. Replace the stud headed bolt.

45. Install the power steering hose strap to the stud headed bolt in front of the cylinder head.

46. Connect the electrical connectors to the following:

   a. Idle Speed Control (ISC) motor
   b. Throttle Position Switch (TPS)
   c. Fuel injectors
   d. Manifold Air Temperature (MAT) sensor
   e. Oxygen sensor
   f. Electric Fuel Evaporator (EFE) grid
   g. Alternator bracket

47. Replace the air valve and bracket. Connect the air solenoid electrical and hose connections.

48. Connect the vacuum line to the brake booster.

49. Connect the fuel lines at the throttle body and replace the fuel line bracket at the transaxle.

50. Replace the air cleaner mounting bracket and connect the oil cooler lines to the oil filter adapter.

51. Connect the oil cooler line bracket at the transaxle. Replace the exhaust crossover pipe.

52. Replace the cruise control diaphragm and connect the vacuum line.

53. Connect the accelerator, cruise control and the transaxle throttle valve cables to the throttle lever.

54. Connect the wire connectors to the following:

   a. Oil pressure switch
   b. Coolant temperature sensor
   c. Distributor
   d. EGR solenoid
   e. Engine temperature switch

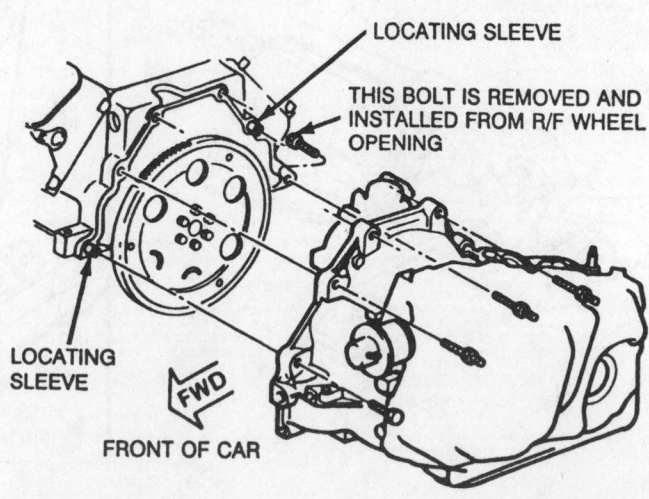

Engine-to-transaxle mounting location—4.5L and 4.9L engines

55. Replace the accessory drive belt, heater hoses and upper radiator hose.

56. Install the cooling fans and connect the air conditioning accumulator bracket.

57. Install the air conditioning accumulator and connect the wires and hoses.

58. Install the hood assembly and replace the air cleaner.

59. Refill the Engine coolant. Connect the negative battery cable.

60. Start the engine, allow it to reach normal operating temperatures and check for leaks.

Engine Mounts

REMOVAL & INSTALLATION

3.8L Engine

1. Disconnect the negative battery cable.

2. Raise and support the vehicle safely.

3. Remove the Engine mount through bolt. Using a vertical lifting device, attach it to the Engine and raise the engine.

4. Remove the Engine mount bolts and the mount.

To install:

5. Install the Engine mount and the mount bolts.

6. Lower the Engine into the Engine mount. Install the Engine mount through bolt.

7. Lower the vehicle.

8. Connect the negative battery cable.

4.5L and 4.9L Engines

RIGHT

1. Disconnect the negative battery cable and brace from the Engine bracket to the engine.

2. Remove the nuts securing the Engine bracket to the mount.

3. Raise and safely support the vehicle.

4. Support the vehicle with stands at each front frame horn.

5. Remove the nuts on the Engine mount securing to the frame.

6. Remove the nuts securing the transaxle mount to the mount.

7. Remove the nuts securing the transaxle mount to the frame bracket.

8. Raise the Engine using an Engine support tool.

9. Raise the Engine until the bracket is free of the Engine mount. Remove the stud and the bolts that secure the bracket to the block. Remove the mount and bracket by pulling forward.

10. Remove the transaxle mounting bracket from the transaxle.

11. Remove the mount assembly.

To install:

12. Position the Engine mount and bracket, in place between the transaxle and frame and secure the bracket to the transaxle with the 2 bolts and tighten to 34 ft. lbs. (46 Nm).

13. While lowering the engine, guide the motor mount into location and install the Engine mount to frame and transaxle mount to frame bracket with the 2 nuts each and tighten to 22 ft. lbs. (30 Nm).

14. Install the nuts to the Engine mount studs and the nuts to transaxle mount studs and tighten to 22 ft. lbs. (30 Nm).

15. Remove the brace from the Engine bracket to engine.

16. Remove the stands and lower the hoist. Connect the negative battery cable.

LEFT

1. Raise the vehicle and support it safely. Disconnect the negative battery cable.

2. Support the vehicle with stands at each front frame horn.

3. Remove the nut securing the mount to the transaxle bracket and nuts securing the mount to the frame.

4. Lift the Engine using Engine support tool.

5. Remove the bolts securing the bracket to the transaxle.

6. Raise the Engine assembly until the brackets are free.

7. Remove the mount and bracket by pulling it upward.

To install:

8. Position the Engine mount and bracket in place between the transaxle and frame. Tighten the bracket to 41 ft. lbs. (56 Nm) and nuts to 22 ft lbs. (30 Nm).

9. Lower the transaxle onto the mount until it is seated.

10. Install the nut securing the mount to the bracket and tighten to 22 ft. lbs. (30 Nm).

11. Connect the negative battery cable.

Cylinder Head

REMOVAL & INSTALLATION

3.8L (VIN C, L and 1) Engines

1. Disconnect the negative battery cable.

2. Remove the intake and exhaust manifolds.

3. Remove the valve covers.

4. Label and disconnect the ignition module wires, spark plug wires and alternator bracket. Remove air conditioning compressor bracket bolt.

5. Remove the power steering pump, tensioner assembly and the fuel line heat shield.

6. Remove the rocker arm assemblies, guide plate and the pushrods.

7. Remove the cylinder head bolts and remove the cylinder head.

8. Clean all gasket mating surfaces and the cylinder head bolt holes in the block.

To install:

9. Install the cylinder head gasket and head onto the block.

10. Install the cylinder head bolts and tighten as follows:

   a. Tighten the cylinder head bolts, in sequence, to 35 ft. lbs. (47 Nm).

   b. Rotate each bolt 130 degrees, in sequence.

   c. Rotate the center 4 bolts an additional 30 degrees, in sequence.

11. Install the pushrods, guide plate and the rocker arm assemblies. Tighten the rocker arm pedestal bolts to 28 ft. lbs. (38 Nm).

12. Install the intake manifold, exhaust manifold and the valve covers.

13. Replace the air conditioning compressor bracket bolt and tighten to 52 ft. lbs. (71 Nm).

14. Install the alternator support bracket and replace the igniton module and spark plug wires.

15. Install the tensioner, power steering pump and the fuel line heat shield.

16. Connect the negative battery cable. Start the Engine and check for leaks.

4.5L and 4.9L Engines

RIGHT

1. Disconnect the negative battery cable. Drain the coolant into a clean container for reuse. Properly relieve the fuel system pressure.

2. Remove the rocker arm covers and the intake manifold assembly.

3. Remove the right side exhaust manifold and disconnect the Engine lift bracket and AIR pump bracket.

4. Remove the cylinder head bolts in the reverse order of the tightening sequence. Remove the cylinder head.

5. Clean all gasket mating surfaces and the cylinder head bolt holes in the block.

To install:

6. Install the cylinder head gasket and the cylinder head.

7. Tighten the cylinder head bolts as follows:

   a. Tighten the cylinder head bolts, in sequence, to 38 ft. lbs. (50 Nm).

   b. Tighten the cylinder head bolts, in sequence, to 68 ft. lbs. (90 Nm).

   c. Tighten cylinder head bolts 1, 3 and 4 to 90 ft. lbs. (120 Nm).

8. Install the Engine lift bracket and the air pump bracket.

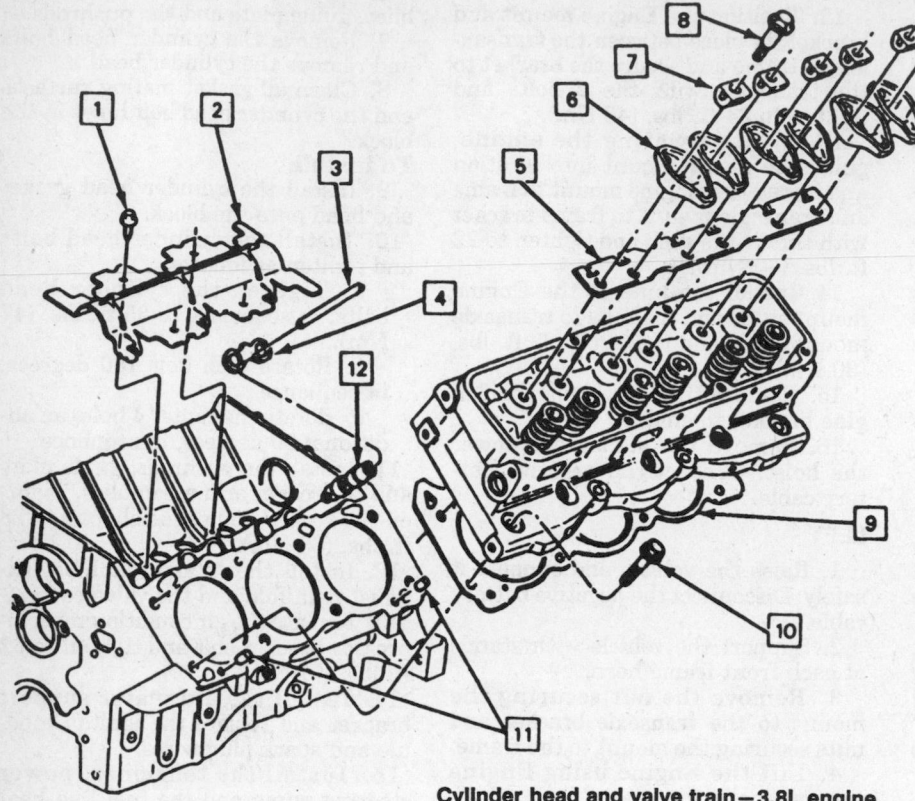

1. Bolt
2. Lifter guide retainer
3. Pushrod
4. Lifter guide
5. Pushrod guide
6. Rocker arm
7. Rocker arm pivot
8. Bolt
9. Head gasket
10. Head bolt
11. Dowel pin
12. Valve lifter

Cylinder head and valve train—3.8L engine

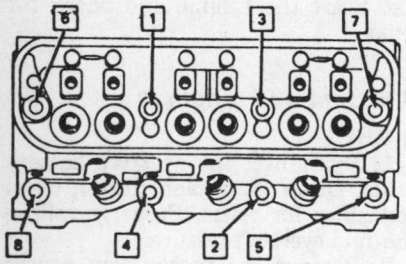

Cylinder head bolt tightening sequence—3.8L engine

9. Install the exhaust manifold, intake manifold and the rocker arm covers.
10. Refill the Engine coolant. Connect the negative battery cable.
11. Start the Engine and check for leaks.

LEFT

1. Disconnect the negative battery cable. Drain the Engine coolant.
2. Remove the rocker arm covers and the intake manifold assembly.
3. Remove the left side exhaust manifold.
4. Remove the cooling fans and the dipstick tube.
5. Remove the cylinder head mounting bolts and remove the cylinder head.

6. Clean all gasket mating surfaces and the cylinder head bolt holes in the block.
To install:
7. Install a new head gasket over the dowels on the cylinder block.
8. Install the cylinder head and tighten the bolts as follows:
   a. Tighten the cylinder head bolts, in sequence, to 38 ft. lbs. (50 Nm).
   b. Tighten the cylinder head bolts, in sequence, to 68 ft. lbs. (90 Nm).
   c. Tighten cylinder head bolts 1, 3 and 4 to 90 ft. lbs. (120 Nm).
9. Install the dipstick tube and replace the cooling fans.
10. Install the exhaust manifold, intake manifold and the rocker arm covers.
11. Refill the Engine coolant. Connect the negative battery cable.
12. Start the Engine and check for leaks.

Valve Lifters

REMOVAL & INSTALLATION

3.8L Engine

1. Disconnect the negative battery cable.

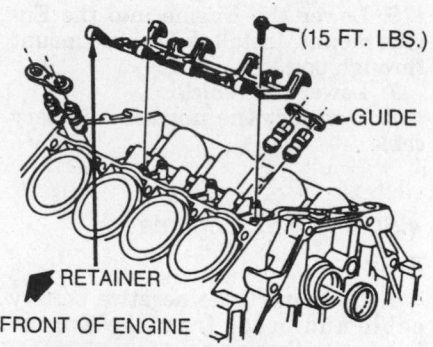

Lifter guides and retainer—4.5L and 4.9L engines

2. Remove the valve covers and the intake manifold.
3. Remove the rocker arm bolts, rocker arms and the pedestals.
4. Remove the pushrods, guide retainer bolts and the retainer.
5. Remove the lifter guides and lift out the lifters, using the proper tool.
To install:
6. Prior to installation dip the lifters in the proper prelube.
7. Install the lifters and lifter guides.
8. Install the pushrods, guide retainer bolts and the retainer.
9. Install the pedestals, rocker arms and rocker arms bolts.
10. Install the valve covers and the intake manifold.

11. Connect the negative battery cable.

4.5L and 4.9L Engines

1. Disconnect the negative battery cable.
2. Remove the valve covers and the intake manifold.
3. Remove the rockers and the pushrods.
4. Disconnect the valve guide retainer.
5. Remove the valve lifter guides and pull out the lifters, using the proper tool.

To install:

6. Prior to installation dip the lifters in the proper prelube.
7. Install the valve lifters and lifter guides.
8. Connect the valve guide retainer. Tighten the retainer bolts to 15 ft. lbs.
9. Install the rockers and the pushrods.
10. Install the valve covers and the intake manifold.
11. Connect the negative battery cable.

Rocker Arms

REMOVAL & INSTALLATION

3.8L (VIN C, L and 1) Engines
RIGHT

1. Disconnect the negative battery cable. Remove the accessory drive belt.
2. Loosen the power steering pump bolts and slide the pump forward. Disconnect the power steering bracket.
3. Disconnect the EGR pipe and remove EGR valve and adapter from the throttle body.
4. Disconnect the spark plug wires and remove the rocker arm cover bolts and cover.
5. Remove the rocker arm pedestal retaining bolts and lift out the pedestal and rocker arm assembly.

To install:

6. Install the pedestal, rocker arm assembly and rocker arm pedestal retaining bolts. Tighten the pedestal bolts to 28 ft. lbs. (38 Nm).
7. Install the rocker arm cover and bolts. Tighten to 88 inch lbs. (10 Nm). Connect the spark plug wires.
8. Install the EGR valve and adapter to the throttle body. Connect the EGR pipe.
9. Connect the power steering bracket. Slide the power steering pump into position and install the bolts.
10. Install the serpentine drive belt. Connect the negative battery cable.

LEFT

1. Disconnect the negative battery cable. Remove the accessory drive belt.
2. Remove the alternator mounting bracket bolt and bracket.
3. Disconnect the spark plug wires. Remove the valve cover bolts and the valve cover.
4. Remove the rocker arm pedestal retaining bolts and lift out the pedestal and rocker arm assembly.

To install:

5. Install the rocker arm pedestal, rocker arm assembly and retaining bolts. Tighten to 28 ft. lbs. (38 Nm).
6. Install the valve cover and bolts. Tighten to 88 inch lbs. (10 Nm). Connect the spark plug wires.
7. Install the alternator mounting bracket and bolt.
8. Connect the negative battery cable.

4.5L and 4.9L Engines
RIGHT

1. Disconnect the negative battery cable. Remove the air cleaner and the AIR management valve with bracket, move the assembly aside.
2. From the throttle body, remove the Manifold Absolute Pressure (MAP) hose.
3. Remove the right side spark plug wires and conduit.
4. Remove the fuel vapor canister pipe bracket from the valve cover stud.
5. Drain the cooling system to a level below the thermostat housing. Remove the heater hose from the thermostat housing and move it aside.
6. Remove the brake booster vacuum hose from the intake manifold.
7. Remove the rocker arm cover-to-cylinder screws, the cover and the gasket/seals. Discard them.
8. Remove the rocker arm pivot-to-rocker arm support bolts, the pivots and the rocker arms.
9. If necessary, remove the rocker arm support-to-cylinder head nuts/bolts and the support.
10. Clean the gasket mounting surfaces. Inspect the parts for wear and/or damage and replace the parts, if necessary.

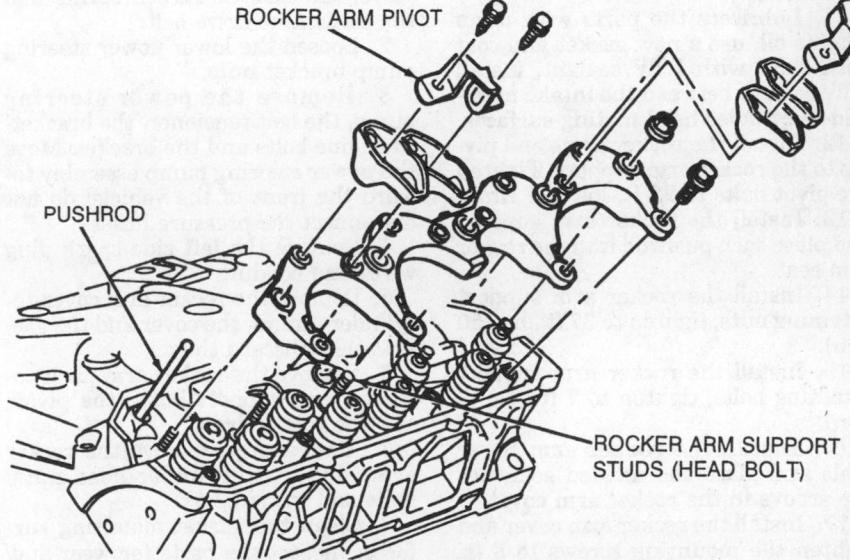

Rocker arm assembly—4.5L and 4.9L engines

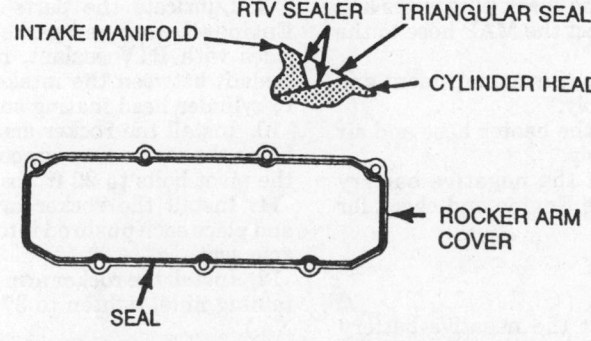

Rocker arm cover sealing—4.5L and 4.9L engines

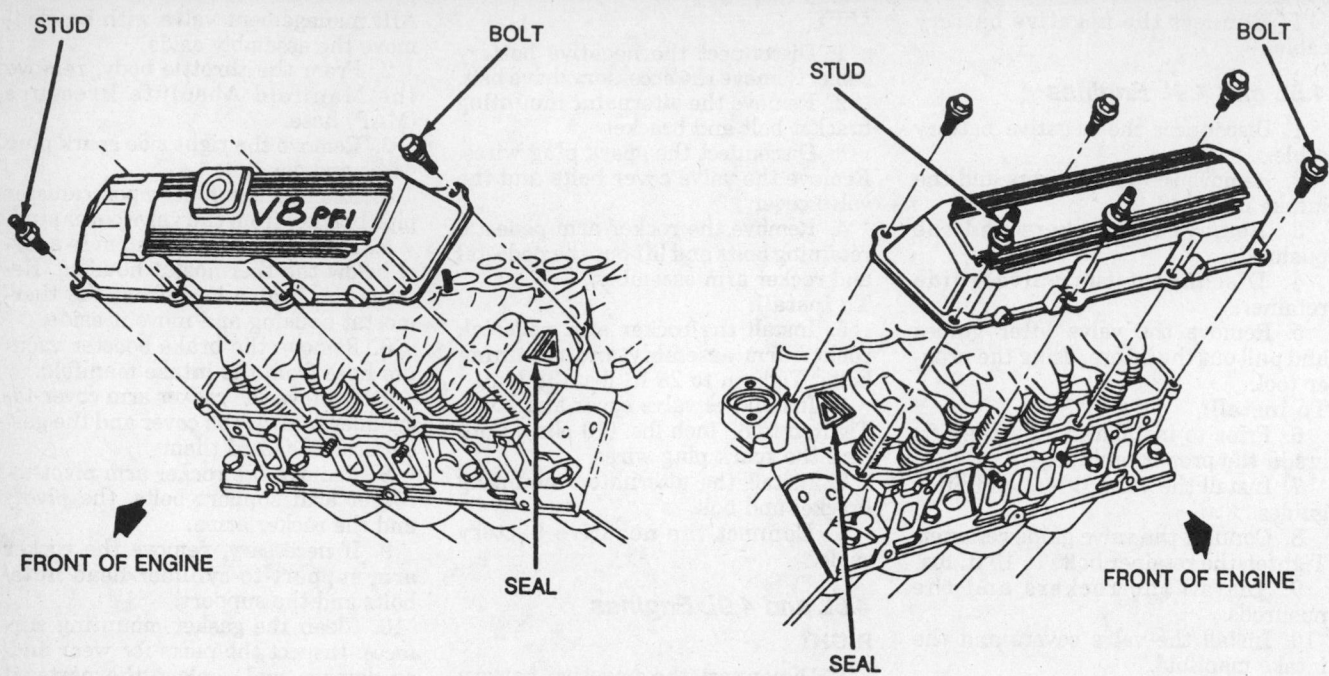

Rocker arm covers—4.5L and 4.9L engines

To install:

11. Lubricate the parts with clean Engine oil, use a new gasket and coat both sides with RTV sealant, install RTV sealant between the intake manifold-to-cylinder head mating surfaces.

12. Install the rocker arms and pivots to the rocker arm support. Tighten the pivot bolts to 22 ft. lbs. (30 Nm).

13. Install the rocker arm support and place each pushrod into the rocker arm seat.

14. Install the rocker arm support retaining nuts, tighten to 37 ft. lbs. (50 Nm).

15. Install the rocker arm support retaining bolts, tighten to 7 ft. lbs. (9 Nm).

16. Install the rocker arm cover seals and place the molded seal into the groove in the rocker arm cover.

17. Install the rocker arm cover and tighten the mounting screws to 8 ft. lbs. (11 Nm).

18. Connect the brake booster vacuum hose and the EECS pipe bracket.

19. Install the spark plug wires and conduit. Connect the MAP hose to the throttle body.

20. Install the air management and bracket assembly.

21. Replace the heater hose and air cleaner assembly.

22. Connect the negative battery cable. Start the Engine and check for leaks.

LEFT

1. Disconnect the negative battery cable. Remove the air cleaner, the PCV

valve, the throttle return spring and the serpentine drive belt.

2. Loosen the lower power steering pump bracket nuts.

3. Remove the power steering pump, the belt tensioner, the bracket-to-engine bolts and the bracket. Move the power steering pump assembly toward the front of the vehicle; do not disconnect the pressure hoses.

4. Remove the left side spark plug wires and conduit.

5. Remove the rocker arm cover-to-cylinder screws, the cover and the gasket/seals. Discard them.

6. Remove the rocker arm pivot-to-rocker arm support bolts, the pivots and the rocker arms.

7. If necessary, remove the rocker arm support-to-cylinder head nuts/bolts and the support.

8. Clean the gasket mounting surfaces. Inspect the parts for wear and/or damage and replace the parts, if necessary.

To install:

9. Lubricate the parts with clean Engine oil, use a new gasket, coat both sides with RTV sealant, install RTV sealant between the intake manifold-to-cylinder head mating surfaces.

10. Install the rocker arms and pivots to the rocker arm support. Tighten the pivot bolts to 22 ft. lbs. (30 Nm).

11. Install the rocker arm support and place each pushrod into the rocker arm seat.

12. Install the rocker arm support retaining nuts, tighten to 37 ft. lbs. (50 Nm).

13. Install the rocker arm support re-

taining bolts, tighten to 7 ft. lbs. (9 Nm).

14. Install the rocker arm cover seals and place the molded seal into the groove in the rocker arm cover.

15. Install the rocker arm cover and tighten the mounting screws to 8 ft. lbs. (11 Nm).

16. Install the spark plug wires and conduit.

17. Install the power steering pump, belt tensioner and bracket assembly. Replace the accessory drive belt.

18. Install the throttle return spring and the PCV valve.

19. Install the air cleaner and connect the negative battery cable.

20. Start the Engine and check for leaks.

Intake Manifold

REMOVAL & INSTALLATION

3.8L (VIN C) Engine

1. Relieve the fuel system pressure.

2. Disconnect the negative battery cable. Place a clean drain pan under the radiator, open the drain cock and drain the cooling system.

3. Remove the serpentine drive belt, the alternator and the bracket.

4. Remove the power steering pump, the braces and move it aside; do not disconnect the pressure lines.

5. Remove the coolant bypass hose, the heater pipe and the upper radiator hose from the intake manifold.

6. Remove the vacuum hoses and

1. Throttle body
2. Gasket
3. 20 ft. lbs.
4. Throttle body adapter
5. Gasket
6. Stud
7. Intake manifold

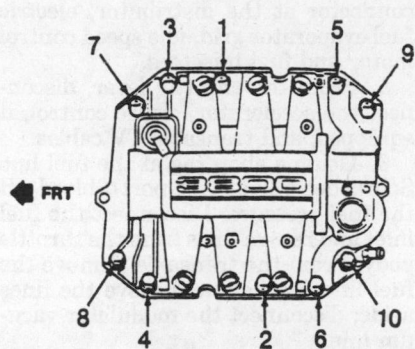

Throttle body and adapter to the intake manifold—3.8L (VIN C) engine

View of the intake manifold bolt torquing sequence—3.8L (VIN C) engine

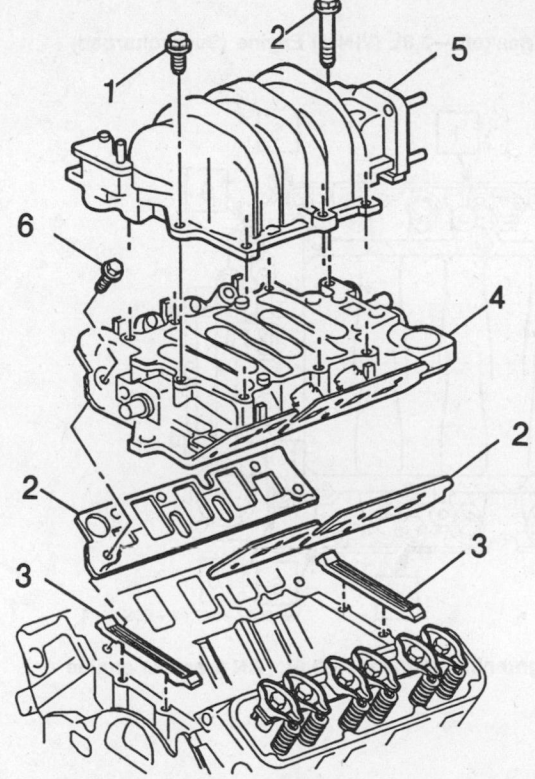

1. Upper intake manifold bolt
2. Intake manifold gasket
3. Intake manifold seal
4. Lower intake manifold
5. Upper intake manifold
6. Lower intake manifold bolt

Intake manifold and gaskets—3.8L (VIN L) Engine (Non-supercharged)

disconnect the electrical connectors from the intake manifold.

7. Remove the EGR pipe, the EGR valve and the adapter from the throttle body.

8. Remove the throttle body coolant pipe, the throttle body and the throttle body adapter.

9. Disconnect the rear spark plug wires. Remove the intake manifold-to-engine bolts and the manifold.

10. Clean the gasket mounting surfaces.

To install:

11. Install new gaskets and the proper sealant on the ends of the manifold seals.

12. Install the intake manifold and tighten the mounting bolts, in sequence, twice to 88 inch lbs. (10 Nm).

13. Connect the rear spark plug wires.

14. Install the throttle body adapter, throttle body and the throttle body coolant pipe. Tighten the bolts to 20 ft. lbs. (27 Nm).

15. Install the EGR valve and adapter. Replace the EGR pipe.

16. Connect the vacuum hoses and the electrical connections to the intake manifold.

17. Install the coolant pipe, upper radiator hose and the upper bypass hose to the intake manifold.

18. Install the power steering pump and bracket assembly.

19. Install the alternator and bracket assembly. Replace the serpentine belt.

20. Refill the cooling system and connect the negative battery cable. Start the engine, allow it to reach normal operating temperatures and check for leaks.

3.8L (VIN 1 and L) Engines

1. Disconnect the negative battery cable. Relieve the fuel system pressure.

2. Remove the fuel injector sight shield and the air intake duct.

3. Remove and tag the right side spark plug wires. Remove the fuel rail assembly.

4. Remove the exhaust crossover heat shield.

5. Remove the cable bracket to the cylinder head mounting bolt.

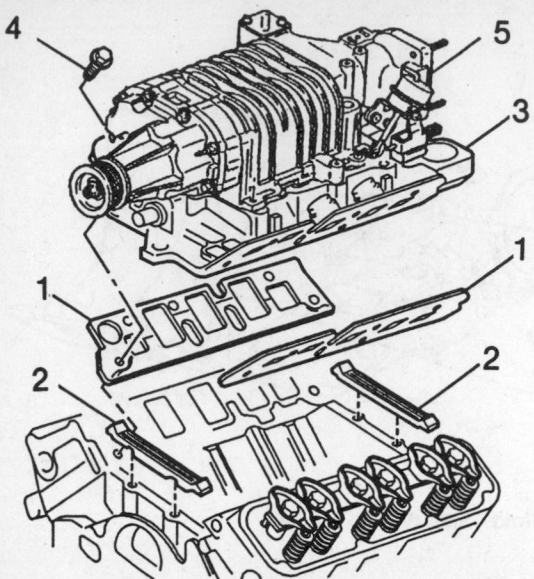

1. Intake manifold gasket
2. Intake manifold seal
3. Lower intake manifold
4. Lower intake manifold bolt
5. Supercharger

Intake manifold and gaskets—3.8L (VIN 1) Engine (Supercharged)

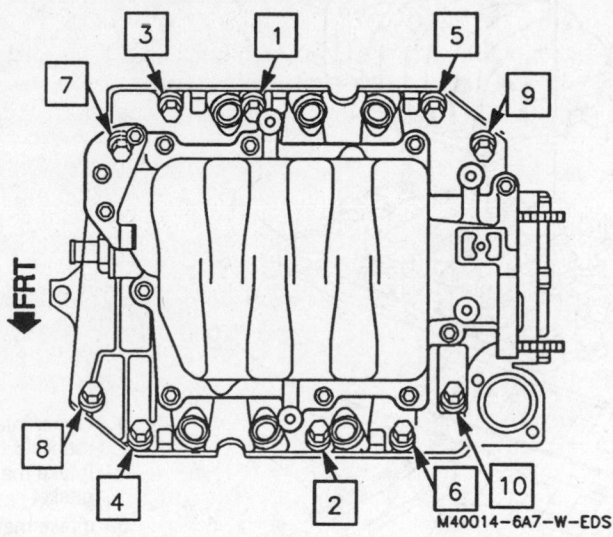

M40014-6A7-W-EDS

Intake manifold bolt tightening sequence—3.8L (VIN 1 and L) engine

6. Remove the power steering pump support bracket. Remove the alternator bracket and remove the alternator out of the way.

7. Remove the heater pipes and bypass hose.

8. Remove the intake manifold bolts and the intake manifold assembly.

NOTE: On the supercharged Engine (VIN 1), the supercharger does not have to be removed when removing the intake manifold. It may be left together as a complete assembly.

To install:

9. Install the intake manifold bolts and tighten the bolts to 88 inch lbs. (10 Nm) twice in the proper sequence.

10. Connect the bypass hose and the heater pipes.

11. Install the alternator bracket and return the alternator to it's proper position.

12. Install the power steering pump support bracket. Install the cable bracket to the cylinder head.

13. Install the exhaust crossover heat shield and the fuel rail.

14. Install the right side spark plug wires and install the fuel injector sight shield and air intake duct.

15. Connect the negative battery cable.

4.5L and 4.9L Engines

1. Disconnect the negative terminal from the battery. Drain the cooling system to a level below the intake manifold. Disconnect the upper radiator hose from the thermostat housing.

2. Remove the air cleaner and the serpentine drive belt. Label and disconnect the spark plug wires from the spark plugs.

3. Remove the upper power steering pump bracket-to-engine bolts and loosen the lower nuts.

4. Disconnect the following electrical connections and position the wiring harness aside: distributor, oil pressure switch, EGR solenoid, coolant sensor, mass airflow temperature sensor, throttle position sensor, 4-way connector at the distributor, electric fuel evaporator grid, idle speed control motor and fuel injectors.

5. From the throttle lever, disconnect the accelerator, cruise control, if equipped, and transaxle TV cables.

6. Using a shop rag at the fuel line Schraeder valve (test port), bleed off the fuel pressure. Disconnect the fuel inlet and return lines from the throttle body. From the transaxle, remove the fuel line brackets and move the lines aside; disconnect the modulator vacuum line.

7. Disconnect the heater hose from the nipple at the rear of the intake manifold.

8. From the intake manifold, remove the cruise control bracket, if equipped. Remove the vacuum line from the left rear Engine lift bracket and the throttle body.

9. Disconnect the electrical connectors from the alternator and AIR management solenoid. Remove the alternator, the idler pulley, the AIR management valve/bracket and EGR solenoid/bracket. Disconnect the hose from the MAP hose.

10. From the right cylinder head, remove the power steering pipe and the AIR pipe. Raise and safely support the vehicle.

11. Drain the Engine oil and remove the oil filter. Lower the vehicle.

12. Remove the distributor. Remove both rocker arm covers. Remove the rocker arm support with the rocker arms intact by first alternately and evenly removing the 4 bolts followed by the 5 nuts. Keep the pushrods in sequence so they may be reassembled in their original positions.

13. If equipped with air conditioning, partially remove the compressor; do not discharge the system. Remove the vacuum harness connections from the TVS at the rear of the intake manifold.

14. Remove the intake manifold

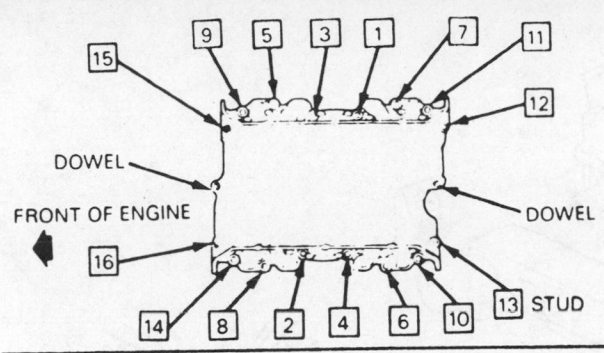

BOLT TIGHTENING SEQUENCE

1   TIGHTEN BOLTS 1, 2, 3, & 4 IN SEQUENCE TO 12.0 N·m (8 FT·LBS).

2   TIGHTEN BOLTS 5 THRU 16 IN SEQUENCE TO 12.0 N·m (8 FT·LBS).

3   RETIGHTEN ALL BOLTS IN SEQUENCE TO 16.0 N·m (12 FT·LBS).

4   REPEAT STEP 3 UNTIL TORQUE LEVEL IS MAINTAINED.

BOLT POSITION	BOLT LENGTH (MM)	BOLT POSITION	BOLT LENGTH (MM)
1	55	9	40
2	55	10	40
3	55	11	40
4	55	12	55
5	30	13	40 W'Studhead
6	30	14	40
7	30	15	55
8	30	16	40

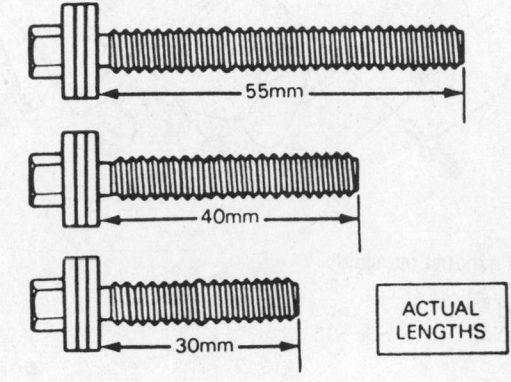

ACTUAL LENGTHS

Intake manifold bolt size and torque sequence—1989–90 4.5L and 4.9L engines

bolts and remove the 2 bolts securing the lower thermostat housing to the front cover. Remove the Engine lift brackets or bend them aside.

15. Remove the intake manifold and lower the thermostat housing as an assembly by lifting it straight up off the dowels.

16. Clean the gasket mounting surfaces.

To install:

17. Install new gaskets and apply the proper RTV sealant to the 4 corners where the end seals meet.

18. Install the intake manifold, using new gaskets.

19. Tighten the ounting bolts as follows:

   a. Torque the No. 1–4 bolts, in sequence, to 8 ft. lbs. (12 Nm).

   b. Torque the No. 5–16 bolts, in sequence, to 8 ft. lbs. (12 Nm).

   c. Retorque all bolts, in sequence, to 12 ft. lbs. (16 Nm).

   d. Repeat Step c until torque level is maintained.

20. Install the right side Engine lift brackets. Install the alternator and idler pulley mounting bracket and replace the brackets at the right cylinder head.

21. Install the pushrods and the rocker arm support assemblies.

22. Install the rocker arm covers, using new seals.

23. Replace the EGR valve and bracket assembly. Connect the MAP hose.

24. Connect the wire connectors at the ISC motor, TPS, the fuel injectors and the MAT sensor.

25. Connect the air management wires, valves and the bracket assembly.

26. Install the alternator and connect the electrical wires.

27. Install the belt tensioner, power steering pump and bracket assembly.

28. Connect the transaxle modulator vacuum line and the vacuum supply line at the throttle body.

29. Install the vacuum line bracket at the left rear Engine lift bracket.

30. Install the cruise control servo bracket and connect the fuel lines at the throttle body. Connect the fuel line brackets at the transaxle.

31. Replace the upper radiator hose.

32. Connect the transmission TV, cruise control and accelerator cables at the throttle body.

33. Install the distributor cap, wires and conduit.

34. Connect the wire connectors at the distributor, oil pressure switch, coolant sensor and the EGR solenoid.

35. Replace the heater hose at the thermostat housing.

36. Raise and support the vehicle safely. Replace the oil filter and tighten the oil drain plug.

37. Install the upper left side power steering pump bracket bolts. Replace the accessory drive belt.

38. Install the air cleaner assembly and refill the cooling system.

39. Connect the negative battery cable. Start the Engine and allow it to reach normal operating temperatures and check for leaks.

Exhaust Manifold

REMOVAL & INSTALLATION

3.8L Engine

RIGHT

1. Disconnect the negative battery cable.

2. If necessary, disconnect the Mass Air Flow (MAF) sensor, air intake duct, the crankcase ventilation pipe and the IAC connector from the throttle body.

3. Label and disconnect the wires from the spark plugs. Disconnect the oxygen sensor lead.

4. If equipped, disconnect the heater inlet pipe from the manifold stud. If equipped, remove the transaxle oil indicator tube.

5. Remove the exhaust crossover pipe-to-exhaust manifold bolts and the pipe. Disconnect the alternator bracket, if necessary.

6. Raise and support the vehicle safely. Remove the exhaust pipe-to-manifold bolts, the exhaust manifold-to-cylinder head bolts and the manifold.

7. Remove the EGR pipe from the exhaust manifold.

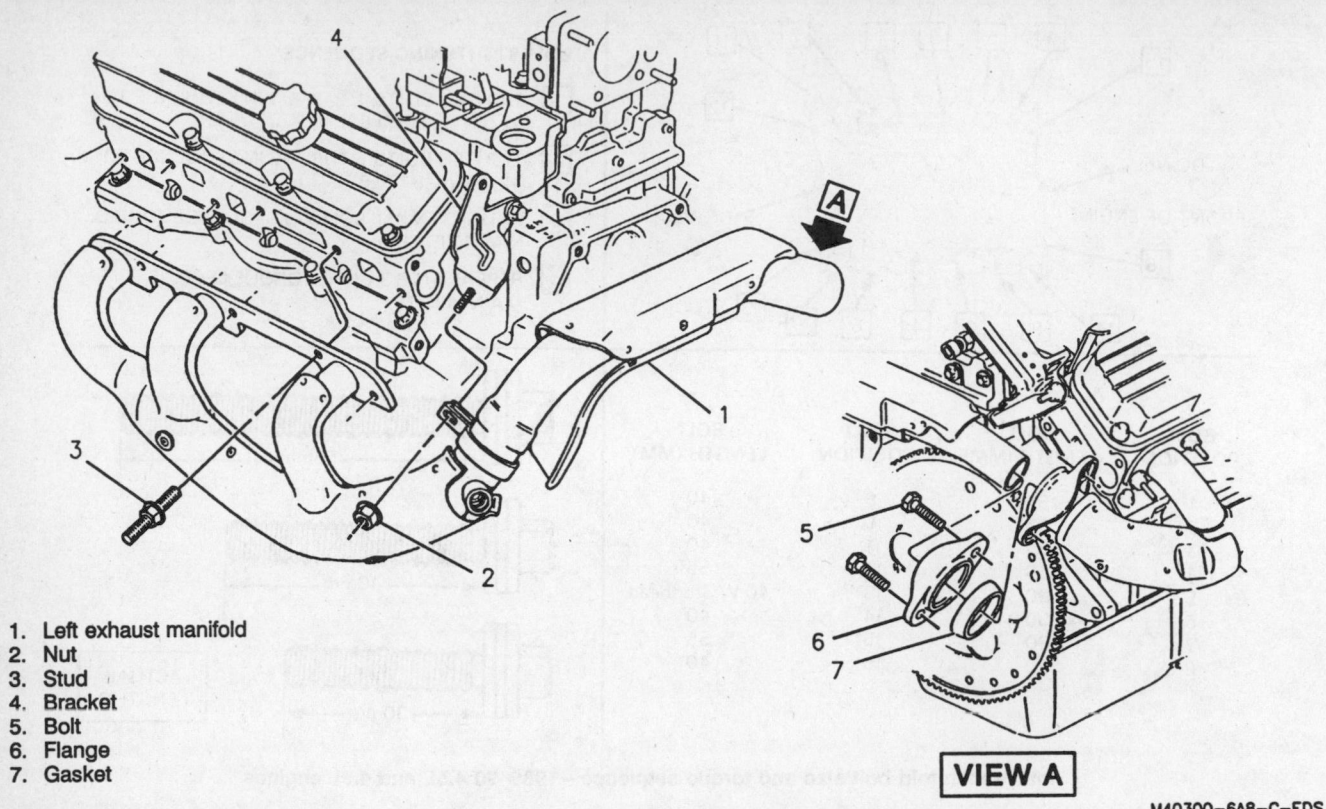

1. Left exhaust manifold
2. Nut
3. Stud
4. Bracket
5. Bolt
6. Flange
7. Gasket

VIEW A

M40300–6A8–C–EDS

Left side exhaust manifold—Supercharged 3.8L engine

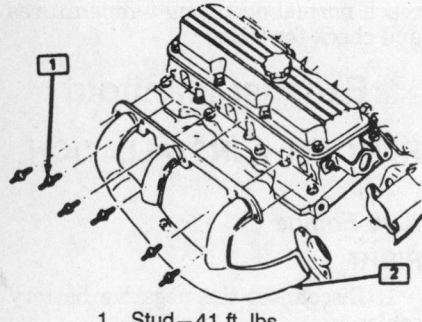

1. Stud—41 ft. lbs.
2. Left (front) exhaust manifold

Left side exhaust manifold—3.8L engine

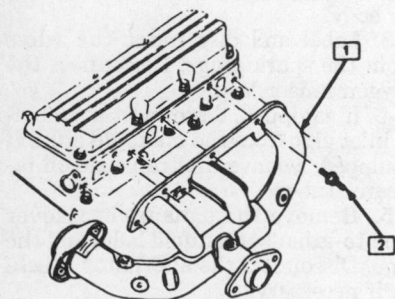

1. Right (rear) exhaust manifold
2. Stud—41 ft. lbs.

Right side exhaust manifold—3.8L engine

8. Clean the gasket mounting surfaces.

To install:

9. Replace the EGR pipe to the exhaust manifold.

10. Install the exhaust manifold, using a new gasket. Tighten the mounting studs to 37–41 ft. lbs. (50–56 Nm).

11. Lower the vehicle. Connect the alternator bracket, if necessary.

12. Install the crossover pipe and replace the exhaust manifold-to-cylinder bolts.

13. If equipped, replace the transaxle oil indicator tube. Connect the heater inlet pipe to the manifold, if equipped.

14. Connect the oxygen sensor lead and the spark plug wires.

15. If removed, connect the Mass Air Flow sensor, air intake duct, the crankcase ventilation pipe and the IAC connector from the throttle body.

16. Connect the negative battery cable. Start the Engine and check for leaks.

NON-SUPERCHARGED—LEFT

1. Disconnect the negative battery cable. If necessary, remove the Mass Air Flow sensor, air intake duct and crankcase ventilation pipe.

2. Remove the exhaust crossover pipe-to-exhaust manifold bolts. Label and disconnect the spark plug wires.

3. Remove the exhaust manifold-to-cylinder head bolts and the manifold.

NOTE: It may be necessary to remove the oil dipstick tube to provide additional clearance.

To install:

4. Clean the gasket mounting surfaces and install a new gasket.

5. Install the exhaust manifold and tighten the manifold mounting studs to 37–41 ft. lbs. (50–56 Nm).

6. Connect the spark plug wires. Install the exhaust crossover pipe-to-exhaust manifold bolts.

7. If removed, install the Mass Air Flow sensor, air intake duct and crankcase ventilation pipe.

8. Connect the negative battery cable.

9. Start the Engine and check for exhaust leaks.

SUPERCHARGED

1. Disconnect the negative battery cable.

2. Remove the 2 flange bolts and the manifold to bracket nut.

3. Remove the manifold to Engine studs and remove the manifold.

To install:

4. Clean the gasket mounting surfaces and install a new gasket.

5. Install the exhaust manifold and tighten the manifold mounting studs to 37–41 ft. lbs. (50–56 Nm).

6. Install the manifold to bracket

nut and the flange gasket. Install the flange bolts.

7. Connect the negative battery cable.

8. Start the Engine and check for exhaust leaks.

4.5L and 4.9L Engines
RIGHT

1. Disconnect the negative battery cable. Remove the air cleaner.

2. Remove the exhaust crossover pipe. Disconnect the oxygen and coolant temperature sensors.

3. Remove the catalytic converter-to-AIR pipe clip bolt. Remove the upper manifold-to-cylinder head bolts. Raise and safely support the vehicle.

4. Disconnect the converter air pipe bracket from the stud and remove the converter-to-manifold exhaust pipe.

5. Support the Engine cradle with screw jacks and remove the rear cradle bolts. Loosen the front cradle bolts and slightly lower the Engine cradle.

6. Remove the remaining exhaust manifold-to-cylinder head bolts, the AIR pipe and the manifold.

7. Clean the gasket mounting surfaces.
To install:

8. Install the exhaust manifold and replace the AIR pipe. Tighten the manifold mounting bolts to 16–18 ft. lbs.

9. Install the manifold-to-converter exhaust pipe and replace the converter air pipe bracket to the stud.

10. Raise the Engine cradle and install the rear cradle bolts. Tighten to 75 ft. lbs (102 Nm).

11. Lower the vehicle. Replace the upper manifold-to-cylinder head bolts.

12. Replace the converter air pipe to AIR pipe clip bolt.

13. Connect the coolant temperature and oxygen sensor connectors. Replace the exhaust crossover pipe.

14. Replace the air cleaner and connect the negative battery cable.

15. Start the Engine and check for leaks.

LEFT

1. Disconnect the negative battery cable. Remove the cooling fan(s) and the exhaust crossover pipe.

2. Remove the serpentine drive belt and the AIR pump pivot bolt.

3. Remove the belt tensioner and the power steering pump brace.

4. Remove the exhaust manifold-to-cylinder head bolts, the AIR pipe and the manifold.
To install:

5. Clean the gasket mounting surfaces.

6. Install the manifold, AIR pipe and exhaust manifold-to-cylinder head bolts. Tighten to 16–18 ft. lbs. (22–24 Nm).

7. Install the belt tensioner and the power steering pump brace.

8. Install the AIR pump pivot bolt and the serpentine drive belt.

9. Install both cooling fans and the exhaust crossover pipe.

10. Connect the negative battery cable.

Supercharger

REMOVAL & INSTALLATION

3.8L Engine (VIN 1)

1. Disconnect the negative battery cable.

2. Remove the accessory drive belt from the supercharger pulley.

3. Relieve the fuel pressure and remove the fuel injector sight shield.

4. Disconnect the fuel pipes from the fuel rail and vacuum hose at the pressure regulator.

5. Disconnect the electrical connectors from the fuel injectors and remove the fuel rail mounting bolts. Remove the fuel rail with the injectors intact.

6. Disconnect the electrical connectors at the IAC, TPS, MAF, EGR and boost control solenoid. Lay the wiring harness aside.

7. Remove the air intake duct and remove the EGR pipe from the supercharger.

8. Disconnect the throttle cable and the cruise control cable. Remove the cable bracket.

9. Remove the tensioner bracket to supercharger mounting stud.

10. Remove the supercharger to intake manifold bolts, remove the supercharger from the intake manifold. Remove the supercharger gasket and coolant passage O-rings.
To install:

11. Replace the oil passage O-rings and the supercharger gasket.

12. Install the supercharger and bolts. Install the tensioner bracket to the supercharger bolt. Tighten the bolts to 19 ft. lbs. (26 Nm).

13. Install the cable bracket and connect the throttle and cruise control cables.

14. Connect the EGR pipe to the supercharger and install the air intake duct.

15. Connect the electrical connectors to the IAC, TPS, MAF, EGR and boost control solenoid.

16. Install the fuel rail and bolts and tighten the bolts to 15 ft. lbs. (24 Nm).

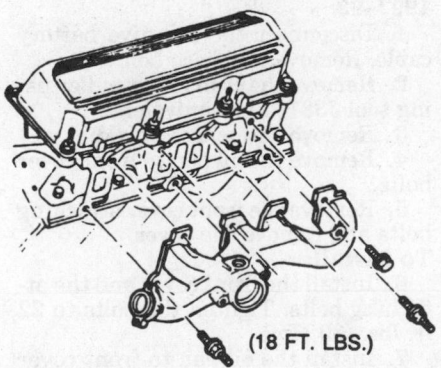

FRONT OF ENGINE

(18 FT. LBS.)

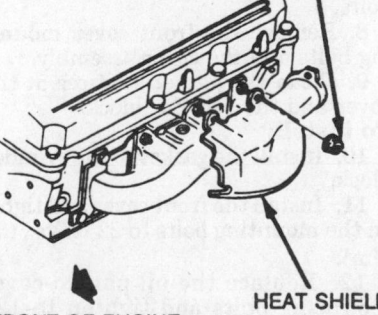

(8 FT. LBS.)

FRONT OF ENGINE

HEAT SHIELD

Exhaust manifolds—4.5L and 4.9L engines

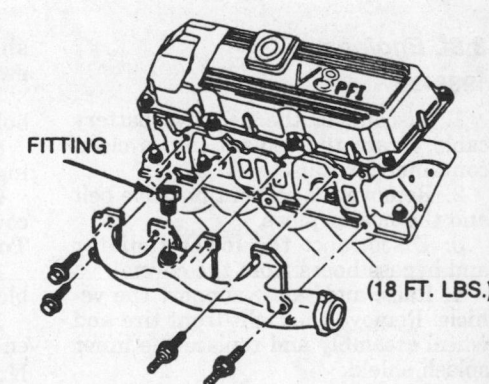

FRONT OF ENGINE

FITTING

(18 FT. LBS.)

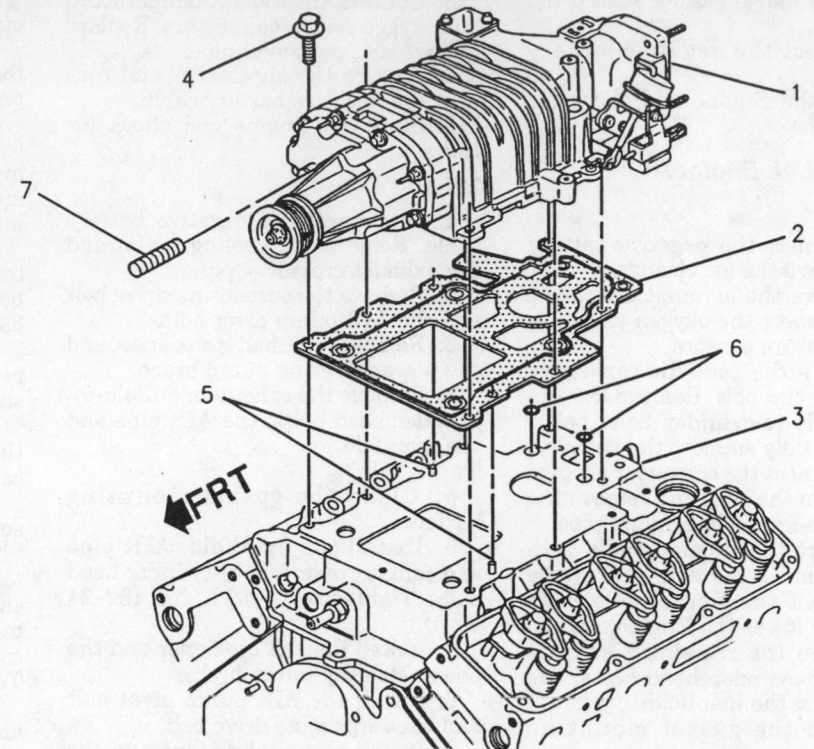

1. Supercharger
2. Gasket
3. Lower intake manifold
4. Supercharger bolts
5. Locator pins
6. Coolant passage O-rings
7. Tensioner bracket to supercharger stud

Supercharger assembly—3.8L (VIN 1) engine

17. Connect the connectors to the fuel injectors and the vacuum hoses at the pressure regulator.

18. Connect the fuel pipes to the fuel rail and install the fuel injector sight shield.

19. Install the accessory drive belt to the supercharger and connect the negative battery cable.

Timing Chain Front Cover

REMOVAL & INSTALLATION

3.8L Engines

1989–90

1. Disconnect the negative battery cable. Drain the coolant into a clean container for reuse.

2. Remove the serpentine drive belt and the heater pipes.

3. Disconnect the lower radiator and bypass hoses from the cover.

4. Raise and safely support the vehicle. Remove the right front tire and wheel assembly and replace the inner splash shield.

5. Remove the crankshaft bolt and balancer.

6. Disconnect the electrical connections at the camshaft sensor, crank-

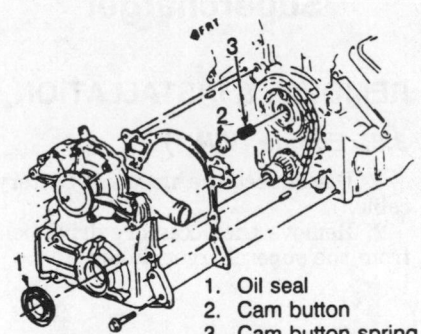

1. Oil seal
2. Cam button
3. Cam button spring

Exploded view of the front cover assembly—3.8L engine

shaft sensor and the oil pressure switch.

7. Remove the oil pan-to-front cover bolts.

8. Remove the front cover mounting bolts and the cover assembly.

9. Clean the gasket surfaces at the cover and the cylinder block.

To install:

10. Install the gasket to the cylinder block.

11. Install the front cover and tighten the mounting bolts to 22 ft. lbs. (30 Nm).

12. Replace the oil pan-to-cover mounting bolts and tighten to 124 inch lbs. (14 Nm).

13. Connect the electrical connec-

tions and replace the crankshaft balancer and tighten the bolt to 219 ft. lbs. (298 Nm).

14. Install the inner fender splash shield and the right front tire and wheel assembly.

15. Lower the vehicle. Replace the coolant bypass hose and radiator hoses.

16. Connect the heater pipes and install the drive belt.

17. Refill the cooling system and connect the negative battery cable.

18. Start the Engine and check for leaks.

1991–93

1. Disconnect the negative battery cable. Remove the drive belt.

2. Remove the crankshaft pulley using tool J38197 or equivalent.

3. Remove the sensor shield.

4. Remove the oil pan to front cover bolts.

5. Remove the front cover attaching bolts and remove the cover.

To install:

6. Install the front cover and the attaching bolts. Tighten the bolts to 22 ft. lbs. (30 Nm).

7. Install the oil pan to front cover bolts and tighten to 124 inch lbs. (14 Nm).

8. Adjust the crankshaft sensor using tool J37087 or equivalent.

9. Install the sensor shield and in-

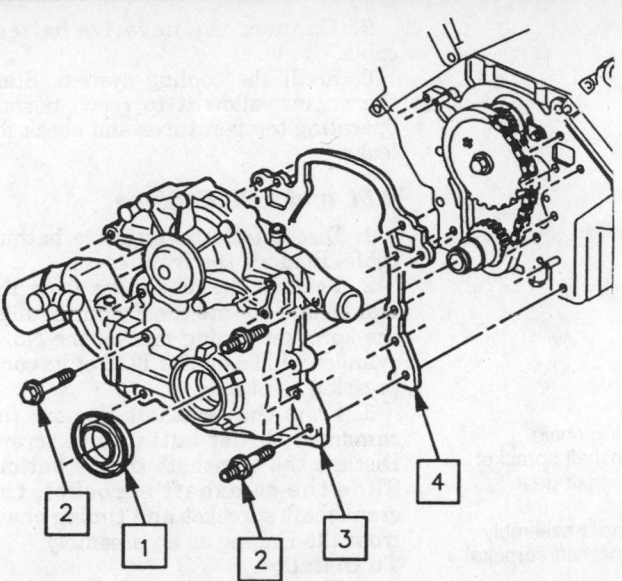

1. Oil seal
2. Bolt
3. Cover
4. Gasket

Timing chain front cover—3.8L (VIN C, L and 1) engines

stall the pulley and the bolt. Tighten the bolt to 105 ft. lbs. (140 Nm) + 56 degrees turn.

10. Install the drive belt and connect the negative battery cable.

4.5L and 4.9L Engines

1. Disconnect the negative battery cable. Remove the air cleaner.

2. Drain the coolant into a clean container for reuse.

3. Remove the right cross car brace and coolant reservoir. Remove the serpentine belt.

4. Label and disconnect the alternator wiring. Remove the alternator and the alternator bracket.

5. Remove the air conditioner accumulator from the bracket and move it aside. Do not disconnect the fittings on the accumulator.

6. Remove the water pump pulley and pump. Remove the idler pulley, as required.

7. Raise and safely support the vehicle.

8. Remove the crankshaft pulley-to-crankshaft pulley bolt. Attach a puller to the crankshaft damper/pulley; using the center bolt, press the crankshaft damper/pulley from the crankshaft.

9. Remove the front cover-to-engine bolts, the oil pan-to-front cover bolts and the front cover.

10. Clean the gasket mounting surfaces.

To install:

11. Install the timing cover and tighten the mounting bolts to 15 ft. lbs. (20 Nm).

12. Install the crankshaft damper and tighten the bolt to 18 ft. lbs. (24 Nm).

13. Lower the vehicle. Replace the water pump and pulley.

14. If removed, install the idler pulley. Install the serpentine belt.

15. Connect the alternator wiring and install the alternator and bracket.

16. Replace the air conditioner accumulator and connect the bracket.

17. Replace the air cleaner and refill the cooling system.

18. Connect the negative battery cable. Start the Engine and check for leaks.

Front Cover Oil Seal

Replacement

3.8L Engine

1. Disconnect the negative battery cable.

2. Remove the serpentine drive belt. Remove the crankshaft balancer-to-crankshaft bolt.

3. Using a small prybar, pry the oil seal from the front cover. Be careful not to damage the sealing surfaces.

To install:

4. Clean the oil seal mounting surface. Using the proper lubricant coat the outside of the seal and the crankshaft balancer.

5. Using the oil seal installation tool, drive the new seal into the front cover until it seats.

6. Install the crankshaft balancer-to-crankshaft bolts. On 1989–90 models, tighten to 219 ft. lbs. (298 Nm). On 1991–93 models tighten to 105 ft. lbs. (140 Nm) + 56 degrees turn. Install the serpentine drive belt.

7. Connect the negative battery cable.

4.5L and 4.9L Engines

1. Disconnect the negative battery cable. Remove the serpentine belt.

2. Remove the crankshaft pulley-to-crankshaft pulley bolt.

3. Attach a puller tool to the crankshaft pulley/damper. Using the center bolt, press the crankshaft pulley/damper from the crankshaft.

4. Using the oil seal removal tools, press the oil seal from the front cover. Clean the oil seal mounting surface.

To install:

5. Lubricate the new seal with Engine oil. Using a hammer and an oil seal installation tool, drive the new oil seal into the front cover until it seats.

6. Install the crankshaft pulley/damper to the crankshaft. Tighten the crankshaft pulley-to-crankshaft bolt to 18 ft. lbs. (24 Nm).

7. Install the serpentine belt.

8. Connect the negative battery cable.

Timing Chain and Sprockets

REMOVAL & INSTALLATION

3.8L Engine

1. Disconnect the negative battery cable. Remove the front cover.

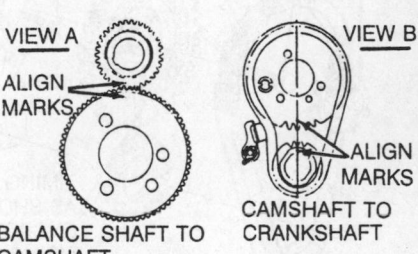

View of the timing chain, sprockets and balancer shaft alignment—3.8L engine

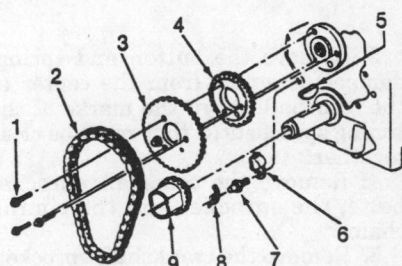

1. 27 ft. lbs.
2. Timing chain
3. Camshaft sprocket
4. Camshaft gear
5. Key
6. Damper
7. Special bolt (14 ft. lbs.)
8. Spring
9. Crankshaft sprocket

Exploded view of the timing chain, sprockets and balancer shaft sprocket—1989–90 3.8L engine

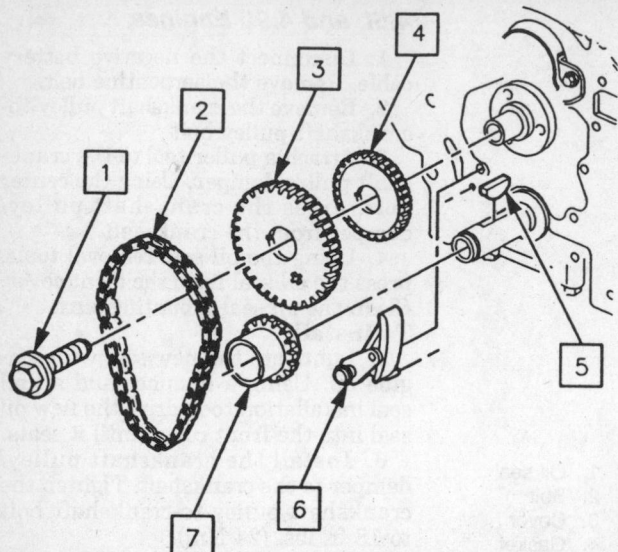

1. Bolt
2. Timing chain
3. Camshaft sprocket
4. Camshaft gear
5. Key
6. Damper assembly
7. Crankshaft sprocket

Exploded view of the timing chain and sprockets—1991–93 3.8L engine

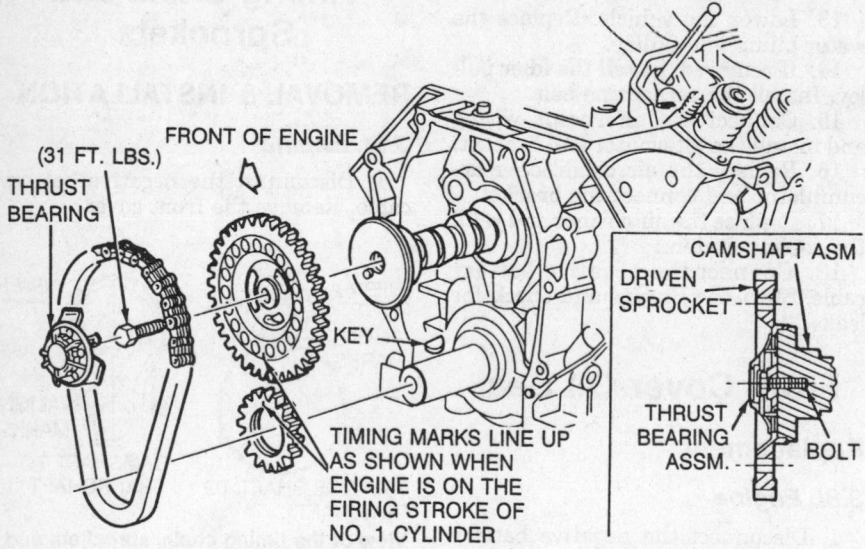

Camshaft and timing chain alignment—4.5L and 4.9L engines

2. Remove the button and spring/damper assembly from the center of the camshaft. Align the marks of the timing sprockets as they must be close together.

4. Remove the camshaft sprocket bolts, the sprocket and the timing chain.

5. Remove the crankshaft sprocket. Clean the gasket mounting surfaces.

To install:

6. Install the timing chain and sprockets by performing the following:

   a. Assemble the timing chain on the camshaft sprocket and crankshaft sprockets.

   b. Align the marks on the sprockets; they must face each other.

   c. Slide the assembly onto the camshaft and crankshaft. Install the camshaft sprocket-to-camshaft bolts. Tighten the camshaft sprocket-to-camshaft sprocket bolts to 27–28 ft. lbs. (37–38 Nm) except 1992–93 vehicles. Tighten the camshaft sprocket-to-camshaft bolts on the 1992–93 vehicles to 74 ft. lbs. (100 Nm) + 105 degrees.

NOTE: If equipped with 3.8L (VIN C or L) engines, align the camshaft sprocket mark with the balancer shaft sprocket mark.

7. Install the camshaft button and spring/damper assembly. Tighten the bolt to 14 ft. lbs. (19 Nm).

8. Replace the front cover assembly.

9. Connect the negative battery cable.

10. Refill the cooling system. Start the engine, allow it to reach normal operating temperatures and check for leaks.

4.5L and 4.9L Engines

1. Disconnect the negative battery cable. Remove the front cover.

2. Remove the oil slinger from the crankshaft. Rotate the Engine to align the sprocket timing marks; the No. 1 cylinder will be on the TDC of its compression stroke.

3. From the camshaft, remove the camshaft thrust button and screw. Discard the camshaft thrust button. Slide the camshaft sprocket, the crankshaft sprocket and timing chain from the Engine as an assembly.

To install:

4. Clean the gasket mounting surfaces. Inspect the parts for wear and/or damage; if necessary, replace the parts.

5. Install the timing chain and sprockets by performing the following:

   a. Assemble the timing chain on the camshaft sprocket and crankshaft sprockets.

   b. Align the timing marks on the sprockets; they must face each other.

   c. Align the dowel pin in the camshaft with the index hole in the sprocket.

   d. Slide the assembly onto the camshaft and crankshaft. Install the camshaft sprocket-to-camshaft bolts. Torque the camshaft sprocket-to-camshaft sprocket bolt to 37 ft. lbs. (50 Nm).

6. Install the new thrust button and install the oil slinger to the crankshaft.

7. Install the front cover. Connect the negative battery cable.

8. Refill the cooling system. Start the engine, allow it to reach normal operating temperatures and check for leaks.

Camshaft

REMOVAL & INSTALLATION

3.8L Engine

1989–90

1. Disconnect the negative battery cable. Remove the Engine assembly and position in a suitable holding fixture.

2. Remove the intake manifold, the front timing cover, timing chain and sprockets.

3. Remove the valve covers, the rocker arm shaft or rocker arm assemblies, the pushrods and the hydraulic lifters.

NOTE: Keep all valve components in order so they may be re-installed in their original positions.

4. Carefully, slide the camshaft forward, out of the bearing bores; do not damage the bearing surfaces.

To install:

5. Clean the gasket mounting surfaces. Inspect the parts for wear and/or damage, replace if necessary.

6. Lubricate the valve lifters and camshaft with multi-lube 1052365 or equivalent, and install in the original positions.

NOTE: If equipped with 3.8L (VIN C or L) engine, align the camshaft gear with the balancer shaft gear timing marks.

7. Carefully, install the camshaft in the engine.

8. Install the hydraulic lifters, pushrods, rocker arm assemblies and valve covers.

9. Install the timing chain and sprockets, front timing cover and intake manifold.

10. Install the Engine assembly in the vehicle.

11. Connect the negative battery cable.

12. Fill cooling system and check for leaks. Start the Engine and allow to come to normal operating temperature. Recheck for leaks. Top-up coolant.

1991-93

1. Disconnect the negative battery cable. Remove the Engine assembly and position in a suitable holding fixture.

2. Remove the intake manifold, the valve covers, rocker arms, pushrods and valve lifters.

3. Remove the crankshaft pulley, sensor cover, front timing cover, timing chain and sprockets.

NOTE: Keep all valve components in order so they may be re-installed in their original positions.

4. Remove the camshaft thrust plate and remove the camshaft.

To install:

5. Clean the gasket mounting surfaces. Inspect the parts for wear and/or damage, replace if necessary.

6. Lubricate the valve lifters and camshaft with multi-lube 1052365 or equivalent, and install in the original positions.

NOTE: If equipped with 3.8L (VIN C or L) engine, align the camshaft gear with the balancer shaft gear timing marks.

7. Carefully, install the camshaft in

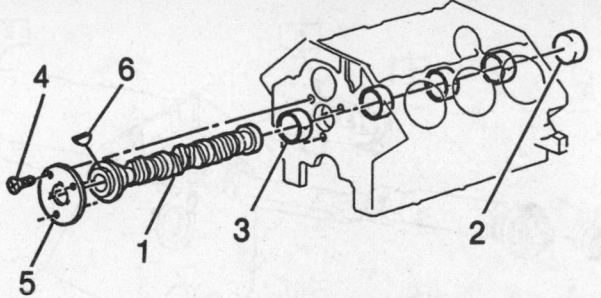

1. Camshaft
2. Plug
3. Bearings
4. Bolt
5. Plate
6. Key

Camshaft—1991–93 3.8L engine

the Engine and install the camshaft thrust plate.

8. Install the timing chain and sprockets and install the front timing cover.

9. Install the crankshaft sensor cover and crankshaft pulley.

10. Install the valve lifters, pushrods, and rocker arms.

11. Install the valve covers and install the intake manifold.

12. Install the Engine to the vehicle and connect the negative battery cable.

4.5L and 4.9L Engines

1. Disconnect the negative battery cable. Remove the Engine assembly and position in a suitable holding fixture.

2. Remove the intake manifold and the timing chain and remove the valve lifters.

NOTE: Keep all valve components in order so they may be re-installed in their original positions.

3. Carefully slide the camshaft out from the front of the engine. Be sure not to damage the camshaft bearings.

To install:

4. Clean the gasket mounting surfaces. Inspect the parts for wear and/or damage; if necessary, replace the parts.

5. Lubricate the camshaft and carefully install in the engine. Temporarily install cam sprocket to the camshaft to act as a handle.

NOTE: If a new camshaft is to be installed, new lifters and a distributor drive gear must also be installed.

6. Install the lifters, timing chain and intake manifold.

7. Install the Engine in the vehicle.

8. Connect the negative battery cable.

9. Fill cooling system and check for leaks. Start the Engine and allow to come to normal operating temperature. Recheck for leaks. Top-up coolant.

Balance Shaft

REMOVAL & INSTALLATION

3.8L Engine

1. Disconnect the negative battery cable. Remove the Engine and secure it to a workstand.

2. Remove the flywheel-to-crankshaft bolts and remove the flywheel.

3. Remove the timing chain cover-to-engine bolts and the cover.

4. Remove the camshaft sprocket-to-camshaft gear bolts, the sprocket, the timing chain and the gear.

5. To remove the balance shaft, perform the following procedures:

a. Remove the balance shaft gear-to-shaft bolt and the gear.

b. Remove the balance shaft retainer-to-engine bolts and the retainer.

c. Using the slide hammer tool, pull the balance shaft from the front of the engine.

To install:

6. If replacing the rear balance shaft bearing, perform the following:

a. Drive the rear plug from the engine.

b. Using the camshaft remover/installer tool, press the rear bearing from the rear of the engine.

c. Dip the new bearing in clean Engine oil.

d. Using the balance shaft rear bearing installer tool, press the new rear bearing into the rear of the engine.

e. Install the rear cup plug.

7. Using the balance shaft installer tool, screw it into the balance shaft and install the shaft into the engine; remove the installer tool.

8. Clean the gasket mounting surfaces. Inspect the parts for wear and/or damage; replace the parts, if necessary.

9. Install the balance shaft retainer. Torque the balance shaft retainer-to-engine bolts to 27 ft. lbs. (37 Nm).

10. Align the balance shaft gear with the camshaft gear timing marks. In-

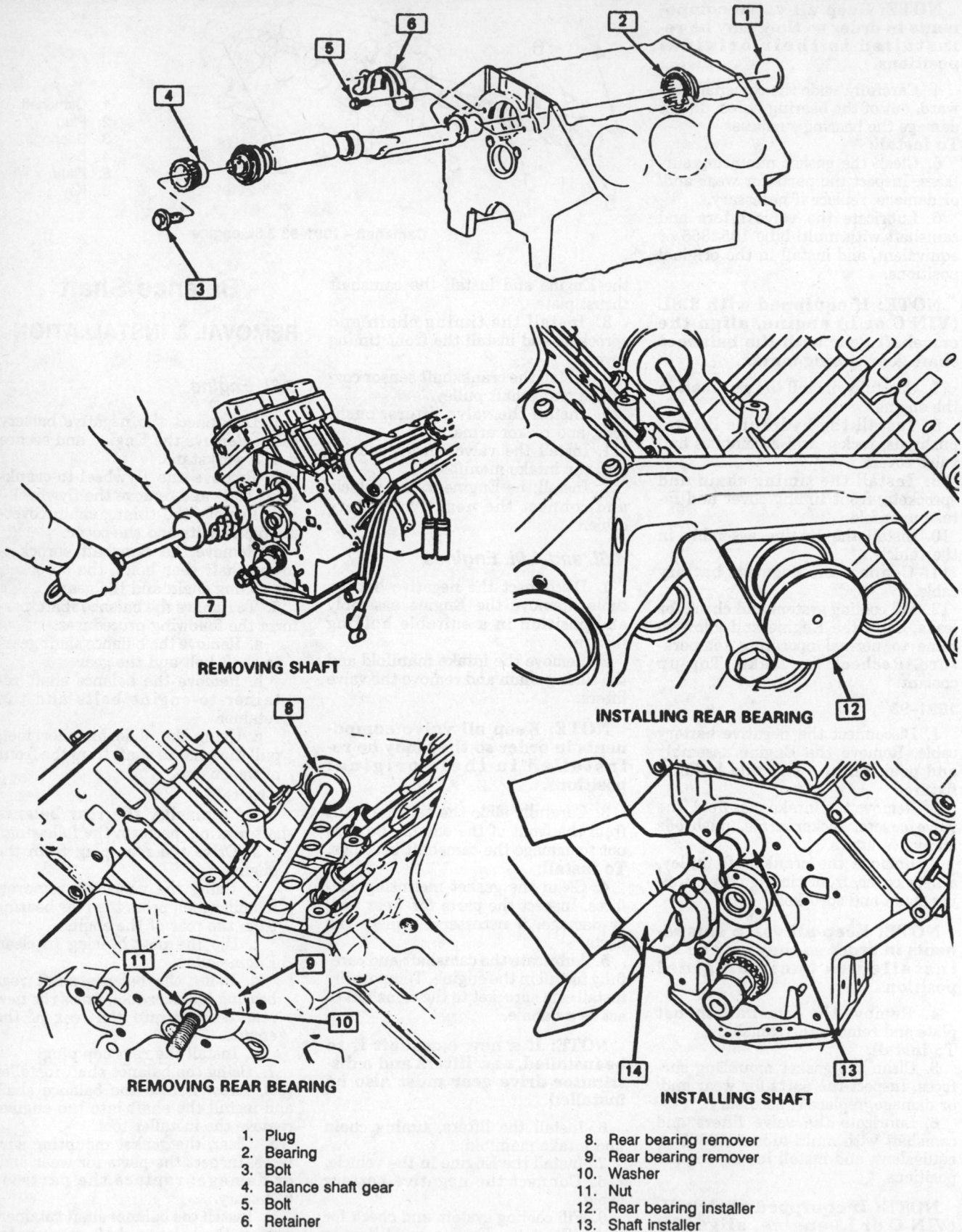

REMOVING SHAFT

INSTALLING REAR BEARING

REMOVING REAR BEARING

INSTALLING SHAFT

1. Plug
2. Bearing
3. Bolt
4. Balance shaft gear
5. Bolt
6. Retainer
7. Slide hammer
8. Rear bearing remover
9. Rear bearing remover
10. Washer
11. Nut
12. Rear bearing installer
13. Shaft installer
14. Driver handle

Balance shaft service—3.8L engine

stall the balance shaft gear onto the balance shaft. Torque the balance gear-to-balance shaft bolt to 14 ft. lbs (19 Nm), then using a torque angle meter tool, rotate another 35 degrees.

11. Align the marks on the balance shaft gear and the camshaft gear by turning the balance shaft.

12. Turn the crankshaft so the No. 1 piston is at TDC.

13. Install the timing chain and sprocket.

14. Replace the balance shaft front bearing retainer and bolts. Tighten the bolts to 61 ft. lbs.

15. Install the front timing cover and the lifter guide retainer.

16. Install the intake manifold and flywheel assembly. Tighten the flywheel bolts to 61 ft. lbs. (83 Nm).

17. Install the Engine assembly and connect the negative battery cable. Start the Engine and check for leaks.

Piston and Connecting Rod

POSITIONING

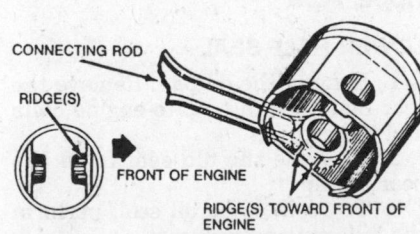

Piston installation direction—3.8L, 4.5L and 4.9L engines

1. Retainer
2. Piston
3. Connecting rod
4. Pin
5. Retainer groove

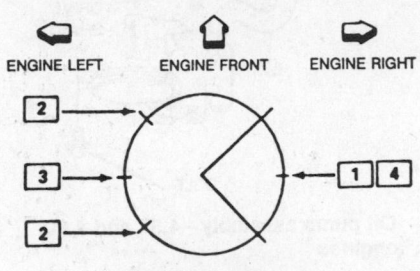

Piston, piston pin and connecting rod—Supercharged 3.8L engine

ENGINE LEFT   ENGINE FRONT   ENGINE RIGHT

1. Oil ring spacer gap (tang in hole or slot with arc)
2. Oil ring rail gaps
3. 2nd compression ring gap
4. Top compression ring gap

Piston ring gap locations—3.8L engine

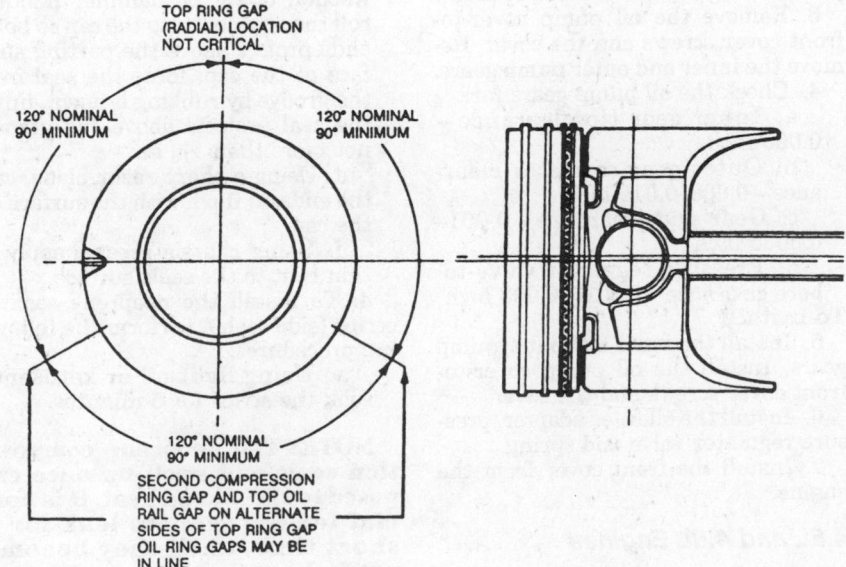

Piston ring orientation—4.5L and 4.9L engines

ENGINE LUBRICATION

Oil Pan

REMOVAL & INSTALLATION

3.8L Engine

1. Disconnect the negative battery cable. Raise and safely support the vehicle.

2. Drain the crankcase and remove the transaxle converter cover.

3. Remove the oil filter and the starter motor.

4. Remove the oil pan-to-engine bolts and the oil pan.

To install:

5. Clean the gasket mounting surfaces.

6. Install the oil pan and the oil pan-to-engine bolts. Tighten bolts according to 124 inch lbs. (14 Nm).

7. Install a new oil filter and the starter motor.

8. Install the transaxle converter cover.

9. Lower the vehicle.

10. Fill the crankcase with oil.

11. Connect the negative battery cable.

4.5L and 4.9L Engines

1. Disconnect the negative battery cable. Raise and safely support the vehicle.

2. Drain the crankcase and remove the oil filter. Remove the flywheel covers.

3. Remove the oil pan-to-engine bolts and the oil pan.

NOTE: If the pan is difficult to remove, lightly tap the edges with a plastic hammer.

To install:

4. Clean the gasket mounting surfaces.

5. Install a new oil pan gasket. Install the oil pan to the engine. Tighten the oil pan-to-engine bolts to 14 ft. lbs. (18 Nm).

6. Install the flywheel inspection cover.

7. Install a new oil filter.

8. Lower the vehicle.

9. Refill the crankcase with oil.

10. Connect the negative battery cable.

11. Start the Engine and check for leaks.

Oil Pump

REMOVAL & INSTALLATION

3.8L Engine

1. Disconnect the negative battery cable. Remove the front cover from the engine.

2. Remove the oil filter adapter, pressure regulator valve and spring.

3. Remove the oil pump cover-to-front cover screws and the cover. Remove the inner and outer pump gears.

To install:

4. Using petroleum jelly, pack the pump and assemble the gears in the housing. Tighten the oil pump cover-to-front cover screws to 97 inch lbs. (11 Nm).

5. Install the pressure regulator spring and valve. Install the oil filter adapter.

6. Install the front cover to the engine.

7. Connect the negative battery cable.

4.5L and 4.9L Engines

1. Disconnect the negative battery cable. Raise and safely support the vehicle.

2. Drain the crankcase. Remove the oil pan mounting bolts and remove the oil pan.

3. Remove the oil pump-to-engine screws/nut and the oil pump from the engine.

To install:

4. Clean the mounting surfaces. Install the pump assembly and tighten the mounting screws to 15 ft. lbs. (20 Nm) and the nut to 22 ft. lbs. (30 Nm).

5. Install a new oil pan gasket. Install the oil pan and bolts.

6. Lower the vehicle.

7. Connect the negative battery cable.

8. Refill the crankcase start the Engine and check for leaks.

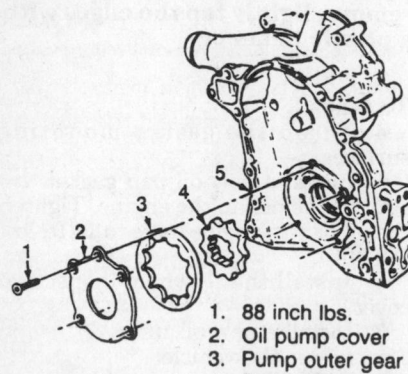

1. 88 inch lbs.
2. Oil pump cover
3. Pump outer gear
4. Pump inner gear
5. Front cover

Exploded view of the oil pump assembly—3.8L engine

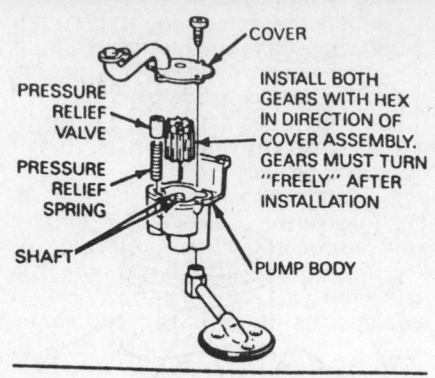

COVER

PRESSURE RELIEF VALVE

PRESSURE RELIEF SPRING

SHAFT

INSTALL BOTH GEARS WITH HEX IN DIRECTION OF COVER ASSEMBLY. GEARS MUST TURN "FREELY" AFTER INSTALLATION

PUMP BODY

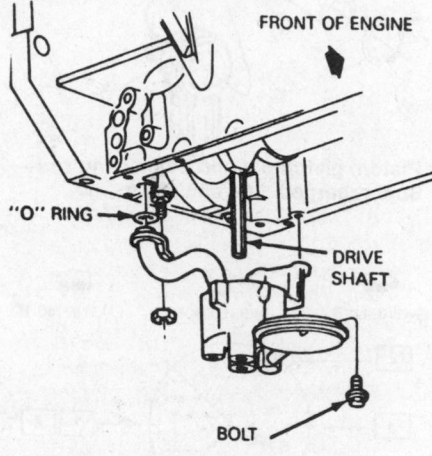

FRONT OF ENGINE

"O" RING

DRIVE SHAFT

BOLT

Oil pump assembly—4.5L and 4.9L engines

CHECKING

3.8L Engine

1. Remove the front cover from the engine.

2. Remove the oil filter adapter, pressure regulator valve and spring.

3. Remove the oil pump cover-to-front cover screws and the cover. Remove the inner and outer pump gears.

4. Check the oil pump gears for:

   a. Inner gear tip clearance—0.006 inch

   b. Outer gear diameter clearance—0.008–0.015 inch

   c. Gear end clearance—0.001–0.0035 inch

   d. Pressure regulator valve-to-bore clearance—0.0015–0.003 inch

To install:

5. Install the inner and outer pump gears. Install the oil pump cover-to-front cover screws and the cover.

6. Install the oil filter adapter, pressure regulator valve and spring.

7. Install the front cover from the engine.

4.5L and 4.9L Engines

1. Raise and support the vehicle safely.

2. Remove the oil pump assembly

and the screws mounting the pump cover to the housing.

3. Remove the oil pressure regulator spring from the bore in the housing. Check the free length of the regulator spring, should be 2.57–2.69 inches. A force of 9.3–10.5 lbs. should be required to compress the spring to 1.46 inch.

To install:

4. Assemble the oil pump.

5. Replace the O-ring at the oil pump outlet pipe.

6. Position the oil pump to the Engine block, engaging the drive rod to the distributor gear. Install the 2 screws and 1 nut. Tighten the nut to 22 ft. lbs. (30 Nm) and screws to 15 ft. lbs. (20 Nm).

7. Install the oil pan.

8. Lower the vehicle.

9. Refill the crankcase with oil.

Rear Main Bearing Oil Seal

REMOVAL & INSTALLATION

1989–90 3.8L (VIN C) Engine Rope Type

LOWER HALF-SEAL

1. Remove the oil pan. Remove the rear main bearing cap-to-engine bolts and the cap.

2. Remove the old seal from the bearing cap.

3. To replace the oil seal, perform the following procedures:

   a. Using a suitable sealant, apply it to the main bearing cap seal groove and wait for 1 minute.

   b. Using a new rope seal and a wooden dowel or hammer handle, roll the new seal into the cap so both ends project above the parting surface of the cap; force the seal into the groove by rubbing it down, until the seal projects above the groove not more than $\frac{1}{16}$ in.

   c. Using a sharp razor blade, cut the ends off flush with the surface of the cap.

   d. Using chassis grease, apply a thin coat to the seals surface.

4. To install the neoprene sealing strips (side seals), perform the following procedures:

   a. Using light oil or kerosene, soak the strips for 5 minutes.

NOTE: The neoprene composition seals will swell up once exposed to the oil and heat. It is normal for the seals to leak for a short time, until they become properly seated. The seals must not be cut to fit.

   b. Place the sealing strips in the

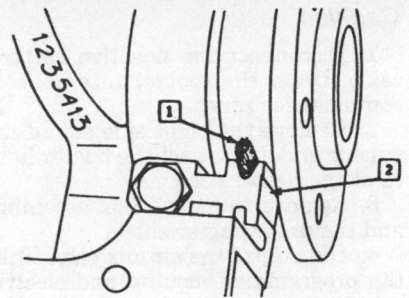

1. Short piece of rope seal
2. Guide tool installed

Installation of rope type seal—3.8L engine

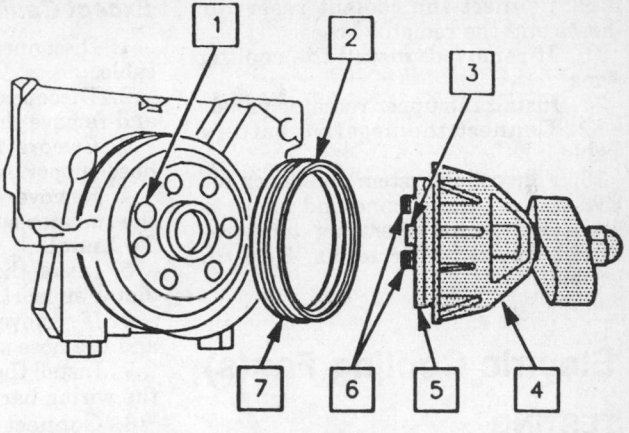

1. Alignment hole
2. Dust lip
3. Dowel pin
4. Collar
5. Mandril
6. Attaching screws
7. Seal

Installing rear main seal—1 piece lip type

grooves on the sides of the bearing cap.

5. Using sealer the proper sealer, apply it to the main bearing cap mating surface; do not apply sealer to the bolt holes.

To install:

6. Install the main bearing cap. Torque the main bearing cap-to-engine bolts to 90 ft. lbs. (122 Nm).

7. Install the oil pan.

8. Lower the vehicle.

9. Refill the crankcase.

10. The Engine must be operated at low rpm when first started, after a new seal is installed.

UPPER HALF-SEAL

1. Remove the oil pan. Remove the rear main bearing cap-to-engine bolts and the cap.

2. Using the seal packing tool, insert it against each side of the upper seal and drive the seal in until it is tight.

3. Measure the amount the seal was driven into the Engine and add about $1/16$ in. Using a razor blade, cut that amount off the old lower seal.

4. Using the seal packing tool, work the short packing pieces into the cylinder block; a small amount of oil on the seal will help the installation.

5. Repeat this process on the other side and install the lower bearing cap.

To install:

6. Install the main bearing cap. Tighten the main bearing cap-to-engine bolts to 90 ft. lbs. (122 Nm).

7. Install the oil pan.

8. Lower the vehicle.

9. Refill the crankcase.

10. The Engine must be operated at low rpm when first started, after a new seal is installed.

1991–93 3.8L (VIN C, L and 1) Engines
One-Piece Lip Type

1. Disconnect the negative battery cable.

2. Raise and safely support the vehicle.

3. Remove the transaxle.

4. Remove the flywheel.

5. Insert a suitable prying tool through the dust lip and pry the seal out by moving the handle of the tool toward the end of the crankshaft pilot. Repeat the process, as required, around the seal until it is removed.

NOTE: Use care when prying out the seal to avoid damage to the OD and chamfer of the crankshaft.

To install:

6. Apply Engine oil to the ID and OD of the new seal. Slide the new seal over the mandrel until the back of the seal bottoms squarely against the collar of the tool.

7. Align the dowel pin of the installation tool with the dowel pin in the crankshaft and attach the tool to the crankshaft by hand or by tightening the attaching screw to 60 inch lbs. (5 Nm).

8. Turn the T-handle of the tool so the collar pushes the seal into the bore. Continue turning until the collar is tight against the case. This will ensure that the seal is seated properly.

9. Loosen the T-handle of the tool until it comes to a stop. This will ensure that the collar will be in the proper position for install another new seal.

10. Remove the attaching screws.

11. Install the flywheel.

12. Install the transaxle.

13. Lower the vehicle.

14. Connect the negative battery cable.

4.5L and 4.9L Engines

1. Raise and safely support the vehicle.

2. Remove the transaxle assembly. Remove the flexplate from the crankshaft.

3. Using the proper tool J26868 or equivalent, pry out the old seal from the rear of the engine.

To install:

4. Lubricate the new seal with wheel bearing grease and install on the crankshaft with the spring facing inside the engine.

5. Press the seal into position, using the proper tool J34604 or equivalent.

NOTE: The seal should be flush with the block. It is necessary to use the proper tool because the seal must be installed square or an oil leak could result.

6. Install the flexplate to the crankshaft.

7. Install the transaxle assembly.

8. Lower the vehicle.

ENGINE COOLING

Radiator

REMOVAL & INSTALLATION

1. Disconnect the negative battery cable.

2. Drain the radiator coolant. Remove the upper radiator panel.

3. Disconnect and remove the cooling fans, as required.

4. Disconnect the coolant reservoir hoses and the radiator hoses.

5. If equipped, disconnect the Engine coolant lines from the radiator.

6. Disconnect the transaxle cooler lines. Remove the radiator.

To install:

7. Install the radiator. Connect the transaxle cooler lines.

8. If removed, connect the Engine coolant lines to the radiator.

9. Connect the coolant reservoir hoses and the radiator hoses.

10. If removed, install the cooling fans.

11. Install the upper radiator panel.

12. Connect the negative battery cable.

13. Fill cooling system and check for leaks. Start the Engine and allow to come to normal operating temperature. Recheck for leaks. Top-up coolant.

Electric Cooling Fan(s)

TESTING

1. Disconnect the electrical connector from the cooling fan.

2. Using an ammeter and jumper wires, connect the fan motor in series with the battery and ammeter. With the fan running, check the ammeter reading, it should be 3.4–5.0 amps; if not, replace the motor.

3. Reconnect the fan's electrical connector. Start the engine, allow it to reach temperatures above 194°F and confirm that the fan runs. If the fan doesn't run, replace the temperature switch.

REMOVAL & INSTALLATION

Cadillac

1. Disconnect the negative battery cable.

2. Raise and safely support the vehicle.

3. Disconnect the electrical connectors from the rear of the fan assemblies.

4. Remove the fan-to-lower radiator cradle bolts.

5. Lower the vehicle.

6. For right fan removal, remove the air conditioning accumulator to gain working clearance. Remove the air cleaner intake duct.

7. Remove the upper fan-to-radiator panel bolts and the upper radiator panel.

8. Remove the cooling fan assemblies.

To install:

9. Install the cooling fan(s). Replace the mounting bolts.

10. Replace the air cleaner intake duct.

11. Raise and safely support the vehicle.

12. Replace the fan-to-lower radiator cradle mounting bolts.

13. Connect the electrical connectors. Lower the vehicle.

14. Connect the negative battery cable.

Except Cadillac

1. Disconnect the negative battery cable.

2. Disconnect the wiring harness and remove the fan frame.

3. Remove the fan guard and the hose support, as required.

4. Remove the fan assembly from the radiator support.

To install:

5. Install the fan assembly to the radiator support.

6. If removed, install the fan guard and the hose support.

7. Install the fan frame and connect the wiring harness.

8. Connect the negative battery cable.

Heater Core

REMOVAL & INSTALLATION

Except Cadillac

1. Disconnect the negative battery cable. Drain the coolant into a clean container for reuse.

2. Remove the right side sound insulator and disconnect the heater hoses at the heater core.

3. Remove the center and lower instrument panel trim plates.

4. If equipped with electronic climate control, perform the following procedures:

   a. Disconnect the wires and the hose from the programmer.

   b. Remove the programmer linkage cover and linkage.

   c. Remove the programmer mounting bolts and the programmer.

5. Remove the heater core cover and heater core assembly.

To install:

6. Install the heater core assembly and heater core cover.

7. If equipped with electronic climate control, perform the following:

   a. Install the programmer mounting bolts and the programmer.

   b. Install the programmer linkage and linkage cover.

   c. Connect the wires and the hose to the programmer.

8. Install the center and lower instrument panel trim plates.

9. Install the right side sound insulator and disconnect the heater hoses at the heater core.

10. Connect the negative battery cable.

11. Fill cooling system and check for leaks. Start the Engine and allow to come to normal operating temperature. Recheck for leaks. Top-up coolant.

Cadillac

1. Disconnect the negative battery cable. Drain the coolant into a clean container for reuse.

2. Remove the right side sound insulator and disconnect the heater hoses at the heater core.

3. Remove the glove box assembly and the programmer shield.

4. Disconnect the air mix valve link, the programmer vacuum and electrical connectors.

5. Remove the heater core cover with the programmer attached.

6. Remove the heater core retaining screws and the heater core assembly.

7. Clean the mounting surfaces.

To install:

8. Install the heater core assembly. Replace the heater core cover with the programmer attached.

9. Connect the vacuum and electrical connections.

10. Connect the air mix valve link and adjust the air mix.

11. Install the glove box assembly and connect programmer shield.

12. Install the right side sound insulator and connect the heater hoses at the heater core.

13. Connect the negative battery cable.

14. Fill cooling system and check for leaks. Start the Engine and allow to come to normal operating temperature. Recheck for leaks. Top-up coolant.

Water Pump

REMOVAL & INSTALLATION

3.8L Engine

1. Disconnect the negative battery cable. Drain the coolant into a clean container for reuse.

2. Remove the serpentine drive belt and the coolant hoses from the water pump.

3. Remove the water pump pulley bolts and the pulley; the long bolt can be removed through the access hole in the body side rail.

4. Remove the water pump-to-engine bolts and the pump.

To install:

5. Clean the gasket mounting surfaces. Install a new gasket and pump assembly.

6. Install the water pump-to-engine mounting bolts and tighten to 29 ft. lbs. (26 Nm) for the long bolts and 97 inch lbs. (11 Nm) for the short bolts.

7. Connect the coolant hoses to the water pump and install the serpentine drive belt.

8. Connect the negative battery cable.

9. Fill cooling system and check for

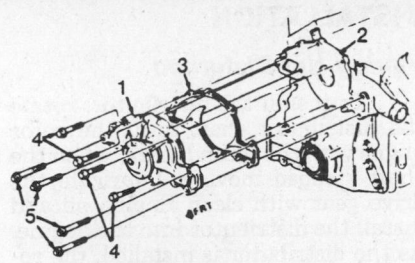

1. Water pump
2. Engine front cover assembly
3. Gasket
4. 97 inch lbs.
5. 29 ft. lbs.

Exploded view of the water pump—3.8L engine

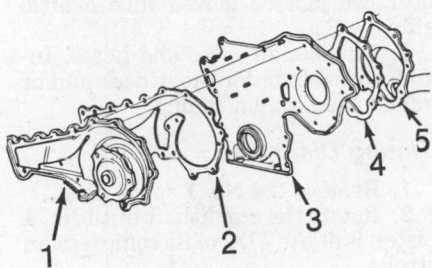

1. WATER PUMP ASSEMBLY
2. WATER PUMP GASKET
3. FRONT COVER
4. WATER PUMP INLET GASKET
5. WATER PUMP INLET

Exploded view of the water pump—4.5L and 4.9L engines

leaks. Start the Engine and allow to come to normal operating temperature. Recheck for leaks. Top-up coolant.

4.5L and 4.9L Engines

1. Disconnect the negative battery cable.
2. Drain the coolant into a clean container for reuse.
3. Remove the air conditioning accumulator from its bracket, move the bracket and accumulator aside without discharging the air conditioning system.
4. Remove the right cross brace and the serpentine drive belt.
5. Remove the water pump pulley-to-water pump bolts and the pulley.
6. Remove the water pump-to-engine bolts and the water pump.
7. Clean the gasket mounting surfaces.
To install:
8. Install a new gasket and pump the water pump pulley, do not fully tighten the screws.
9. Install the right cross brace.
10. Install the air conditioning accumulator bracket and accumulator.

11. Install the serpentine drive belt.
12. Tighten the water pump pulley bolts fully.
13. Connect the negative battery cable.
14. Fill cooling system and check for leaks. Start the Engine and allow to come to normal operating temperature. Recheck for leaks. Top-up coolant.

Thermostat

REMOVAL & INSTALLATION

1. Disconnect the negative battery cable. Drain the coolant to below the thermostat housing.
2. Remove the thermostat housing mounting screws/bolts.
3. Remove the thermostat housing and lift out the thermostat.
To install:
4. Clean the mounting surfaces and install new gasket(s) or O-ring.
5. Install the thermostat and mounting screws/bolts.

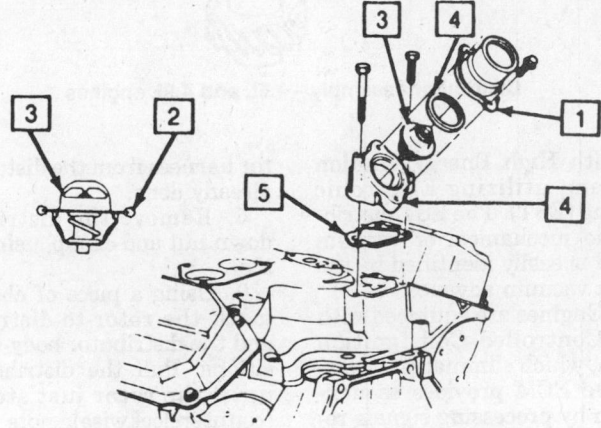

1. Upper housing
2. Gasket
3. Thermostat housing
4. Lower housing
5. Gasket

Location of thermostat—4.5L and 4.9L engines

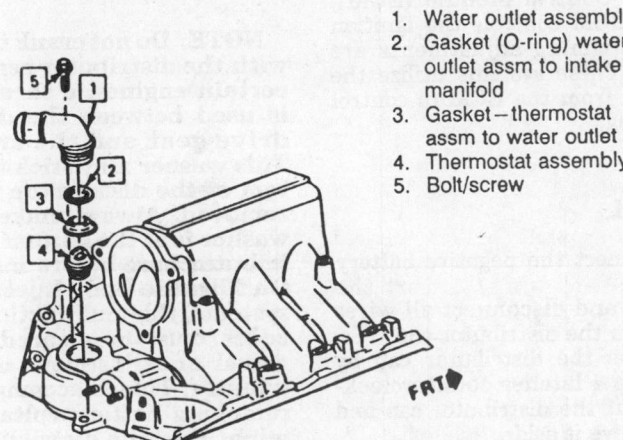

1. Water outlet assembly
2. Gasket (O-ring) water outlet assm to intake manifold
3. Gasket—thermostat assm to water outlet
4. Thermostat assembly
5. Bolt/screw

Location of thermostat—3.8L engine

6. Connect the negative battery cable.
7. Fill cooling system and check for leaks. Start the Engine and allow to come to normal operating temperature. Recheck for leaks. Top-up coolant.

ENGINE ELECTRICAL

NOTE: Disconnecting the negative battery cable on some vehicles may interfere with the functions of the on board computer systems and may require the computer to undergo a relearning process, once the negative battery cable is reconnected.

Distributor

The 4.5L and 4.9L Engines are

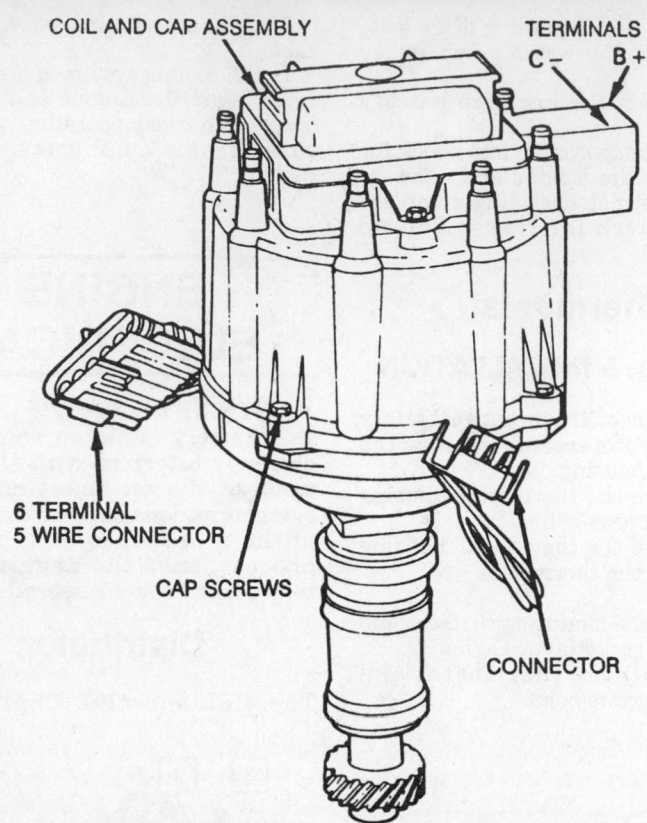

COIL AND CAP ASSEMBLY

TERMINALS
C –   B +

6 TERMINAL
5 WIRE CONNECTOR

CAP SCREWS

CONNECTOR

Distributor assembly—4.5L and 4.9L engines

equipped with High Energy Ignition (HEI) system, utilizing Electronic Spark Timing (EST). The EST distributor uses no mechanical or vacuum advance and is easily identified by the absence of a vacuum advance.

All other Engines are equipped with Computer Controlled Coil Ignition (C³I) system, which eliminates the distributor. The ECM provides sequential injection by processing signals received from the crankshaft and camshaft sensors.

The C³I system consists of the coil pack, ignition module, various hall effect sensors, interrupter rings and the Electronic Control Module (ECM). Since the ECM controls the ignition timing, no timing adjustments are necessary. These systems utilize the EST signal from the ECM to control spark timing.

REMOVAL

1. Disconnect the negative battery cable.
2. Label and disconnect all wires leading from the distributor cap.
3. Remove the distributor cap by turning the 4 latches counterclockwise. Lift off the distributor cap and carefully move it aside.
4. Disconnect the electrical connec-

tor harness from the distributor, if not already done.
5. Remove the distributor hold-down nut and clamp, using the proper tool.
6. Using a piece of chalk or paint, mark the rotor-to-distributor body and the distributor body-to-engine positions. Pull the distributor upward until the rotor just stops turning (counterclockwise); note the position of the rotor once again. Remove the distributor.

NOTE: Do not crank the Engine with the distributor removed. On certain engines, a thrust washer is used between the distributor drive gear and the crankcase. This washer may stick to the bottom of the distributor when it is removed. Always make sure the washer is at the bottom of the distributor bore before installation. On Throttle Body Injection (TBI) systems, the malfunction trouble codes must be cleared after removal or adjustment of the distributor. This is accomplished by removing battery voltage to terminal R of the distributor for 10 seconds.

INSTALLATION

Timing Not Disturbed

1. To install the distributor, rotate the distributor shaft until the rotor aligns with the second mark, when the shaft stopped moving. Lubricate the drive gear with clean Engine oil and install the distributor into the engine. As the distributor is installed, the rotor should rotate to the first alignment mark; this will ensure proper timing. If the marks do not align properly, remove the distributor and reset; be sure to install the thrust washer, if equipped.
2. Install the clamp and hold-down nut. Tighten the nut until the distributor can just be moved with a little effort.
3. Connect all wires and hoses. Install the distributor cap. Check and/or adjust the ignition timing.

Timing Disturbed

1. Remove the No. 1 spark plug.
2. Rotate the crankshaft until No. 1 piston is at the TDC of its compression stroke.

NOTE: The compression stroke can be determined by placing a thumb over the hole while slowly cranking the engine. Crank until compression is felt at the hole and continue cranking slowly until the timing mark on the crankshaft pulley aligns with the 0 degrees timing mark located on the timing chain cover.

3. Position the distributor in the block but do not, at this time, allow it to engage with the drive gear.
4. Rotate the distributor shaft until the rotor points between No. 1 and No. 8 spark plug towers and lower the distributor to engage the camshaft.

NOTE: It may be necessary to turn the rotor a small amount in either direction in order to achieve this engagement. The rotor will rotate slightly as the distributor gear engages. If installed correctly, the rotor should point toward the No. 1 spark plug terminal in the distributor cap.

5. Press down firmly on the distributor housing. This will ensure that the distributor shaft engages the oil pump shaft, thereby allowing the distributor to fully contact the Engine block.
6. Install the hold-down clamp and tighten the nut until it is snug, do not tighten.
7. Install the distributor cap, making sure the rotor points to No. 1 terminal in the cap.
8. Attach all wires and hoses.
9. Start the engine. Check and/or

adjust the ignition timing. Torque the distributor hold-down nut to 20 ft. lbs.

NOTE: Malfunction trouble codes must be cleared after removal or adjustment of the distributor. The ECM power feed must be disconnected for at least 30 seconds to clear the codes.

IGNITION MODULE

Removal & Installation

4.9L ENGINE

1. Disconnect the negative battery cable.
2. Disconnect the wires from the distributor cap and remove the distributor cap.
3. Remove the rotor.
4. Remove the module attaching screws and lift the shield and module up.
5. Disconnect the electrical leads from the module. Note the connections for installation purposes.
To install:
6. Connect the electrical leads to the module and install it along with the shield. Make sure the connections are correct.
7. Install the rotor and distributor cap and connect the spark plug and coil wires.
8. Connect the negative battery cable.

Distributorless Ignition System

REMOVAL & INSTALLATION

Crankshaft Sensor

3.8L (VIN C, L and 1) ENGINES

1. Disconnect the negative battery cable.
2. Remove the serpentine drive belt.
3. Raise the vehicle and support it safely.
4. Remove the right front tire and wheel assembly.
5. Remove the inner fender access panel.
6. Using the proper socket, remove the crankshaft balancer bolt and balancer.
7. Disconnect the sensor electrical connector.
8. Remove the sensor and pedestal from the block face.
9. Remove the sensor from the pedestal.
To install:
10. Loosely install the crankshaft sensor on the pedestal.
11. Position the sensor with the pedestal attached on the proper tool.
12. Position the special tool on the crankshaft.

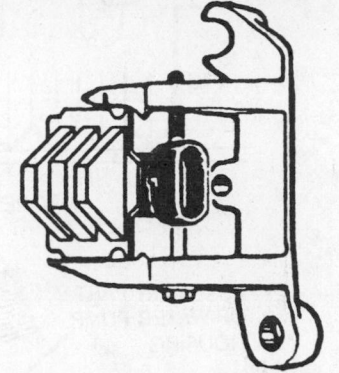

Crankshaft sensor—3.8L (VIN C) engine

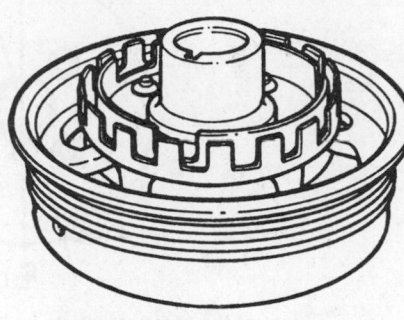

Crankshaft balancer with interrupter rings—3.8L engine

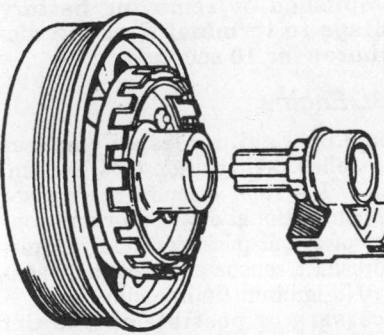

Crankshaft sensor tool to harmonic balancer—3.8L engine

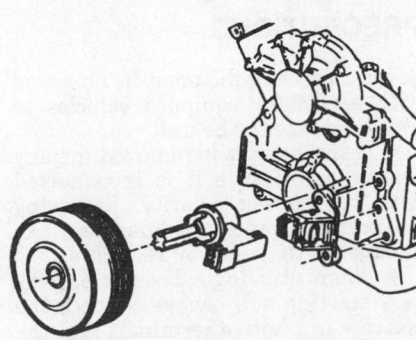

Crankshaft sensor tool to crankshaft

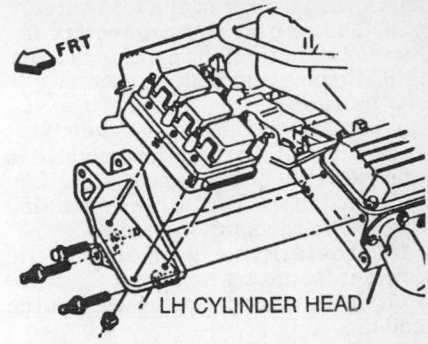

Ignition module and coil assembly—3.8L engine

13. Install the bolts to hold the pedestal to the block face and torque to 14–28 ft. lbs.
14. Torque the pedestal pinch bolt to 36–40 ft. lbs.
15. Remove the tool.
16. Place special tool on the harmonic balancer and turn. If any vane of the harmonic balancer touches the tool, replace the balancer assembly.
17. Install the balancer on the crankshaft.
18. Torque the crankshaft bolt to 110 ft. lbs. plus 76 degrees.
19. Install the inner fender access panel.
20. Install the wheel and torque the lug nuts to 100 ft. lbs.
21. Lower the vehicle and install the serpentine belt.
22. Connect the battery cable.

Ignition Coil

1. Disconnect the negative battery cable.
2. Remove the spark plug wires and the Torx screws attaching the coil to the ignition module.
3. Position the coil assembly aside and disconnect the coil to module connectors.
4. Remove the coil assembly.
To install:
5. Install the coil assembly and attaching screws.
6. Connect the electrical connectors.
7. Connect the spark plug wires.
8. Connect the negative battery cable.

Ignition Module

3.8L ENGINE

1. Disconnect the negative battery cable.
2. Remove the spark plug wires at the coil assembly.
3. Remove the ignition module bracket mounting nuts.
4. Remove the Torx screws mounting the coil to the ignition module.

Mark the position of the lead wires.

5. Disconnect the connecters between the coil and the ignition module.

6. Remove the ignition module.

To install:

7. Install the ignition module.

8. Connect the ignition module to coil electrical connectors.

9. Install the Torx screws mounting the coil to the ignition module.

10. Install the ignition module bracket mounting nuts.

11. Install the spark plug wires at the coil assembly.

12. Connect the negative battery cable.

Ignition Timing

ADJUSTMENT

4.5L and 4.9L Engines

NOTE: The 4.5L and 4.9L Engines incorporate a magnetic timing probe hole for use with special electronic timing equipment. Consult the manufacturer's instructions before using this system. The following procedure is for use with the HEI-EST distributor.

1. Connect a timing light to the No. 1 spark plug wire according to the light manufacturer's instructions; do not pierce the spark plug wire to connect the timing light.

2. Follow the instructions on the Vehicle Emission Control Information label located in the Engine compartment.

3. If equipped with an Electronic Spark Timing (EST) distributor, disconnect the 4-wire terminal plug from the distributor. Some models may require grounding the diagnostic connector located under the left side of the dash.

4. Start the Engine and allow it to run at idle speed.

5. Aim the timing light at the degree scale just over the harmonic balancer.

6. Adjust the timing by loosening the hold-down clamp and rotate the distributor until the desired ignition advance is achieved. When the correct timing marks are aligned, tighten the clamp.

7. Adjust the timing, replace and tighten the hold-down clamp. To advance the timing, rotate the distributor opposite the normal direction of rotor rotation. Retard the timing by rotating the distributor in the normal direction of rotor rotation.

NOTE: If equipped with Throttle Body Injection (TBI), the malfunction trouble codes must be

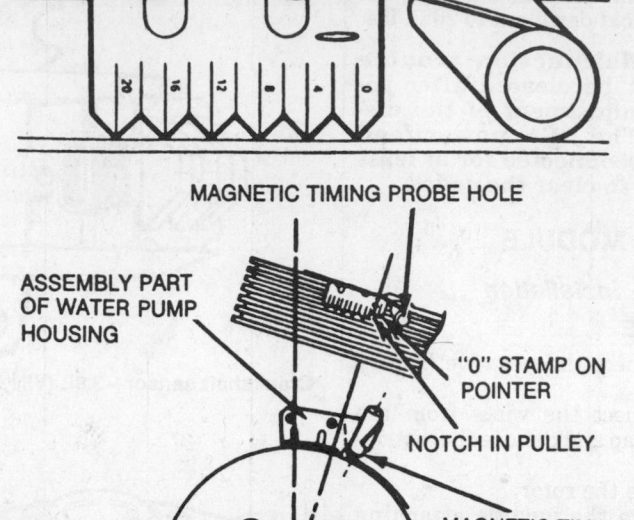

View of the magnetic timing probe hole—4.5L and 4.9L engines

cleared after removal or adjustment of the distributor. This is accomplished by removing battery voltage to terminal R of the distributor for 10 seconds.

3.8L Engine

The 3.8L Engine uses a Computer Controlled Coil Ignition (C³I) system. The C³I system components replace the conventional distributor and consists of a coil pack, ignition module, crankshaft sensor and camshaft sensor. No ignition timing adjustment is necessary or possible on the C³I system.

Alternator

PRECAUTIONS

Several precautions must be observed with alternator equipped vehicles to avoid damage to the unit.

• If the battery is removed for any reason, make sure it is reconnected with the correct polarity. Reversing the battery connections may result in damage to the one-way rectifiers.

• When utilizing a booster battery as a starting aid, always connect the positive to positive terminals and the negative terminal from the booster

battery to a good Engine ground on the vehicle being started.

• Never use a fast charger as a booster to start vehicles.

• Disconnect the battery cables when charging the battery with a fast charger.

• Never attempt to polarize the alternator.

• Do not use test lights of more than 12 volts when checking diode continuity.

• Do not short across or ground any of the alternator terminals.

• The polarity of the battery, alternator and regulator must be matched and considered before making any electrical connections within the system.

• Never separate the alternator on an open circuit. Make sure all connections within the circuit are clean and tight.

• Disconnect the battery ground terminal when performing any service on electrical components.

• Disconnect the battery if arc welding is to be done on the vehicle.

BELT TENSION ADJUSTMENT

A single serpentine belt is used to drive all Engine mounted accessories. Drive belt tension is maintained by a spring

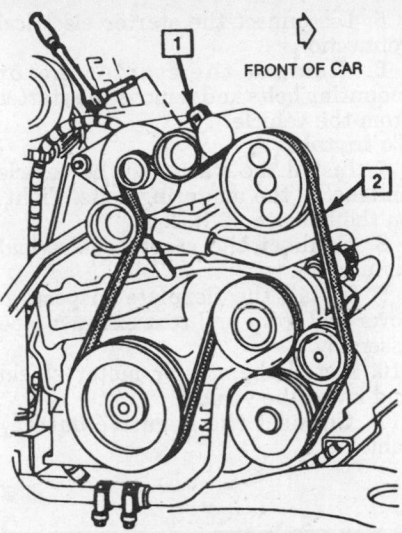

1. Drive belt tensioner
2. Serpentine drive belt

Drive belt—4.5L and 4.9L engines

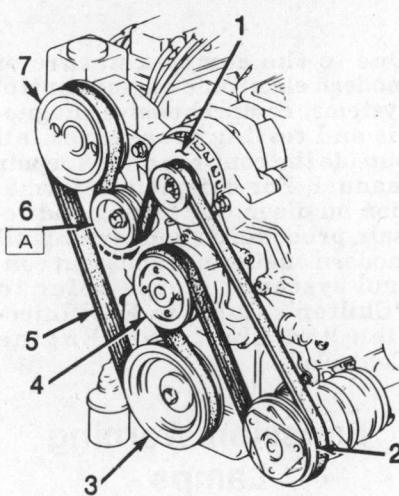

1. Generator pulley	7. P/S pump pulley
2. A/C compressor	A. Rotate the drive belt tensioner in direction of arrow in order to install or remove the drive belt
3. Crankshaft balancer	
4. Water pump pulley	
5. Serpentine belt	
6. Belt tensioner	

View of the serpentine drive belt routing—3.8L engine

loaded tensioner. A belt squeak when the Engine is started or stopped is normal and has no effect on belt durability. The drive belt tensioner can control belt tension over a broad range of belt lengths; however, there are limits to the tensioner's ability to compensate.

1. Inspect tensioner markings to see if the belt is within operating lengths. Replace belt if the belt is ex-

cessively worn or is outside of the tensioner's operating range.

2. Run Engine with the accessories **OFF** until the Engine is warmed. Turn the Engine **OFF** and read belt tension with a proper belt tension gauge or equivalent placed halfway between the alternator and the air conditioning compressor. For non-air conditioning applications read tension between the power steering pump and crankshaft pulley. Remove tool.

3. Start the engine, with accessories **OFF**, and allow the system to stabilize for 15 seconds. Turn the Engine **OFF**. Using the proper tool, apply clockwise force (tighten) to the tensioner pulley bolt. Release the force and immediately take a tension reading without disturbing belt tensioner position.

4. Apply a counterclockwise force to the tensioner pulley bolt and raise the pulley to the fully raised position. Slowly lower the pulley to engage the belt and take a tension reading without disturbing the belt tensioner position.

5. Average the 3 readings. If the average of the 3 readings is lower than the tension specified and the belt is within the tensioner's operating range, replace the belt tensioner. The drive belt tension should be 110 lbs. for 4.5L, 120 lbs. for 4.9L Engines or never below 67 lbs. for 3.8L engine. If the belt tensioner is adjusted beyond it's movable limit, replace the serpentine drive belt.

REMOVAL & INSTALLATION

3.8L Engine

1. Disconnect the negative battery cable.

2. Label and disconnect the electrical connectors from the back of the alternator.

3. If equipped, remove the brace at the back of the alternator and the fuel rail cover.

4. Rotate the tensioner counterclockwise to remove the serpentine drive belt.

5. While supporting the alternator, remove the mounting bolts and the alternator.

To install:

6. Support the alternator in position and install the alternator.

7. Install the serpentine drive belt and rotate the tensioner into position.

8. If equipped, install the brace at the back of the alternator and the fuel rail cover.

9. Connect the electrical connectors at the back of the alternator.

10. Connect the negative battery cable.

4.5L and 4.9L Engines

1. Disconnect the negative battery cable.

2. Remove the air intake assembly at the throttle body.

3. Remove the serpentine belt from the tensioner pulley.

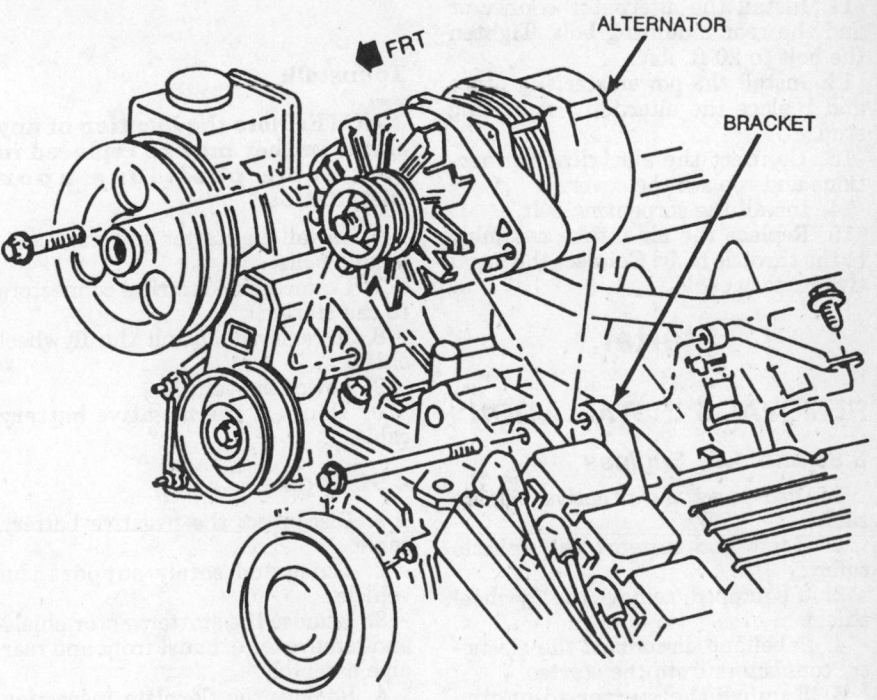

Alternator mounting location—3.8L engine

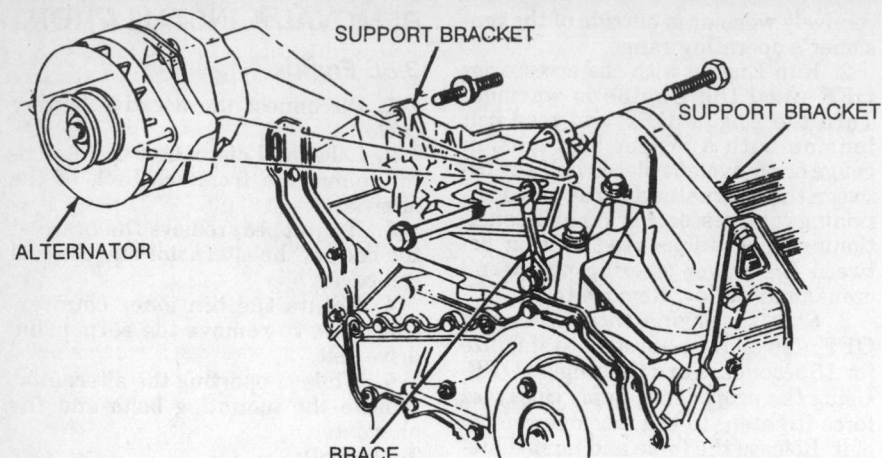

Alternator mounting location—4.5L and 4.9L engines

4. Remove the cover from the rear of the alternator and disconnect the electrical connections.

5. Disconnect the alternator mounting stud and the brace from the power steering pump.

6. Remove the rear alternator bolt and move the alternator upward and remove the connector.

7. Disconnect the heated windshield power module connection, if equipped.

8. Disconnect the front alternator bolt and remove the alternator.

To install:

9. Install the alternator and replace the front alternator bolt, tighten to 32 ft. lbs.

10. Connect the heated windshield power leads, if equipped.

11. Install the alternator connector and the rear mounting bolt. Tighten the bolt to 20 ft. lbs.

12. Install the power steering brace and replace the alternator mounting stud.

13. Connect the electrical connections and replace the cover.

14. Install the serpentine belt.

15. Replace the air intake assembly to the throttle body. Connect the negative battery cable.

Starter

REMOVAL & INSTALLATION

3.8L and 4.5L Engines

1. Disconnect the negative battery cable.

2. Raise and support the vehicle safely.

3. If equipped, remove the flywheel shield.

4. Label and disconnect the electrical connectors from the starter.

5. Remove the starter-to-engine bolts and the starter.

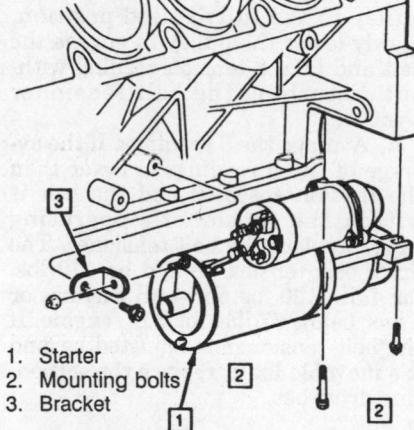

1. Starter
2. Mounting bolts
3. Bracket

Starter mounting location—4.5L and 4.9L engines

To install:

NOTE: Note the location of any shims so they may be replaced in the same positions upon installation.

6. Install the starter and starter-to-engine bolts.

7. Connect the electrical connectors to the starter.

8. If removed, install the flywheel shield.

9. Lower the vehicle.

10. Connect the negative battery cable.

4.9L Engine

1. Disconnect the negative battery cable.

2. Raise and safely support the vehicle.

3. Remove the starter motor shield and remove the exhaust front and rear pipe assembly.

4. Remove the flexplate inspection cover.

5. Disconnect the starter electrical connections.

6. Remove the starter motor mounting bolts and remove the starter from the vehicle.

To install:

7. Install the starter to the vehicle and install the mounting bolts. Tighten the bolts to 32 ft. lbs.

8. Connect the starter electrical connectors.

9. Install the flexplate inspection cover and front and rear exhaust pipe assembly.

10. Install the starter motor shield and lower the vehicle.

11. Connect the negative battery cable.

EMISSION CONTROLS

Due to the complex nature of modern electronic engine control systems, comprehensive diagnosis and testing procedures fall outside the confines of this repair manual. For complete information on diagnosis, testing and repair procedures concerning all modern engine and emission control systems, please refer to "Chilton's Guide to Fuel Injection and Electronic Engine Controls".

Emission Warning Lamps

The dash mounted "Service Soon" and "Service Now" lights are used to indicate a malfunction that the computer has detected in the vehicle's operation. The malfunctions can be related to the operating sensors or the Electronic Control Module (ECM). The service light will go out automatically if the trouble is cleared or intermittent.

The ECM, however will automatically store the trouble code until the diagnostic system is "Cleared".

CLEARING ECM TROUBLE CODES

Except Cadillac

With the ignition switch in the **OFF** position, disconnect battery voltage to the ECM for at least 30 seconds by performing 1 of the following:

1. Remove the ECM fuse from the fuse panel.
2. Disconnect the ECM pigtail.
3. Disconnect the negative battery cable.

NOTE: Disconnecting the negative battery cable should only be done as a last resort as it will also erase the memories for the digital radio, digital clock, trip odometer etc.

Cadillac

1. Turn the key to the **ON** position.
2. Simultaneously press the **OFF** and **HI** buttons on the climate control panel until E.O.O appears in the readout.
3. To clear the Body Computer Module (BCM) codes, depress the **OFF** and **LO** buttons simultaneously until F.O.O appears.
4. After E.O.O or F.O.O is displayed, .7.0 will appear. With the .7.0 displayed turn the ignition **OFF** for at least 10 seconds before re-entering the diagnostic mode.

FUEL SYSTEM

Fuel System Service Precautions

Safety is the most important factor when performing fuel system maintenance. Failure to conduct maintenance and repairs in a safe manner may result in serious personal injury or death. Maintenance and testing of the vehicle's fuel system components can be accomplished safely and effectively by adhering to the following rules and guidelines.

● To avoid the possibility of fire and personal injury, always disconnect the negative battery cable unless the repair or test procedure requires that battery voltage be applied.

● Always relieve the fuel system pressure prior to disconnecting any fuel system component (injector, fuel rail, pressure regulator, etc.), fitting or fuel line connection. Exercise extreme caution whenever relieving fuel system pressure to avoid exposing skin, face and eyes to fuel spray. Please be advised that fuel under pressure may penetrate the skin or any part of the body that it contacts.

● Always place a shop towel or cloth around the fitting or connection prior to loosening to absorb any excess fuel due to spillage. Ensure that all fuel spillage (should it occur) is quickly removed from Engine surfaces. Ensure

that all fuel soaked cloths or towels are deposited in a suitable waste container.

● Always keep a dry chemical (Class B) fire extinguisher near the work area.

● Do not allow fuel spray or fuel vapors to come into contact with a spark or open flame.

● Always use a backup wrench when loosening and tightening fuel line connection fittings. This will prevent unnecessary stress and torsion to fuel line piping. Always follow the proper torque specifications.

● Always replace worn fuel fitting O-rings with new. Do not substitute fuel hose or equivalent where fuel pipe is installed.

RELIEVING FUEL SYSTEM PRESSURE

1. Disconnect the negative battery cable.
2. Loosen the fuel filler cap to relieve the tank vapor pressure.
3. Connect a suitable fuel pressure gauge to the fuel pressure connection. Wrap a shop towel around the fitting while connecting the gauge to avoid spillage.
4. Install a bleed hose into a container and open the valve to bleed the system pressure. The system is now safe for servicing.

Fuel Tank

REMOVAL & INSTALLATION

1. Disconnect the negative battery cable. Relieve the fuel system pressure.
2. Drain all fuel from the tank into a proper container.
3. Disconnect the sender assembly wires, tank filler and the vent hoses.
4. Disconnect the fuel pipe quick connectors.
5. Have an assistant support the fuel tank and disconnect the 2 tank retaining straps.
6. Disconnect the exhaust at the rear hanger and remove the tank from the vehicle.
To install:
7. Install the fuel tank to the vehicle and install the 2 retaining straps.
8. Raise the exhaust and connect the rear hanger.
9. Connect the fuel pipe quick connectors.
10. Connect the sender wires, the tank filler and vent hoses.
11. Refill the tank with fuel and connect the negative battery cable.
12. Inspect for any fuel leakage.

Fuel Filter

REMOVAL & INSTALLATION

1. Disconnect the negative battery cable.
2. Raise and safely support the vehicle.
3. Disconnect the fuel lines from the filter.
4. Remove the filter from the vehicle.
To install:
5. Install the filter and connect the fuel lines to the filter.
6. Secure the filter and lower the vehicle.
7. Connect the negative battery cable. Start the Engine and check for leaks.

Electric Fuel Pump

PRESSURE TESTING

1. Disconnect the negative battery cable.
2. Raise and safely support the vehicle.
3. Connect a suitable fuel pressure gauge to the fuel line fitting.
4. Lower the vehicle and connect the negative battery cable. Measure the fuel pressure while cranking the engine.
5. Raise and safely support the vehicle. Remove the fuel pressure gauge.
6. Lower the vehicle.

REMOVAL & INSTALLATION

The electric fuel pump is located in the fuel tank.
1. Relieve the fuel system pressure. Disconnect the negative battery cable.
2. Drain the fuel from the tank. Raise and safely support the vehicle.
3. Support the tank and disconnect the tank retaining straps.
4. Lower the exhaust at the rear hanger.
5. Lower the tank enough to disconnect the wires, hoses and ground strap, if equipped. Remove the fuel tank.
6. Using a brass drift and a hammer, drive (turn) the cam lock ring-to-fuel tank counterclockwise and lift the assembly from the fuel tank.
7. Pull the fuel pump up into the attaching hose while pulling outward away from the bottom support. Take care to prevent damage to the rubber sound insulator and strainer during removal. Once the pump assembly is clear of the bottom support, pull it out of the rubber connector.
To install:
8. Install the pump into the fuel

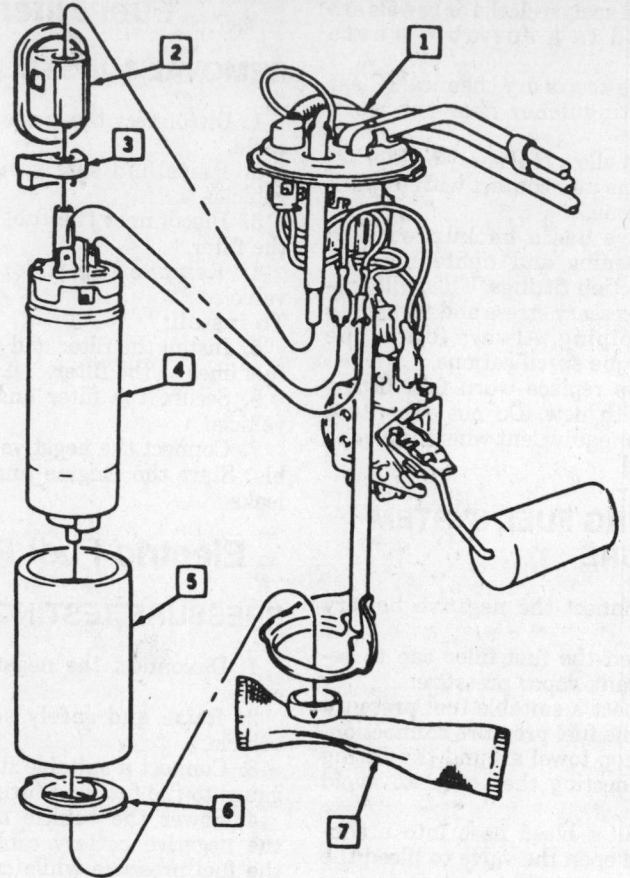

1. Fuel tank meter assembly
2. Pulsator (port injection only)
3. Bumper
4. Fuel pump
5. Sound insulator sleeve
6. Sound insulator
7. Filter

Exploded view of the fuel pump assembly

tank. Connect the fuel lines, wires and the ground strap, if equipped.

9. When installing the fuel tank, make sure all rubber sound isolators or anti-squeak spacers are replaced in their original locations.

10. Support the tank and install the tank retaining straps.

11. Lower the vehicle. Refill the fuel tank.

12. Connect the negative battery cable. Start the Engine and check for fuel leaks.

Fuel Injection

ADJUSTMENTS

Idle speed and idle mixture are controlled automatically by the Electronic Control Module (ECM) and are not adjustable.

Fuel Injector

REMOVAL & INSTALLATION

3.8L Engine

1. Properly relieve the fuel system pressure. Remove the air cleaner assembly. Disconnect the negative battery cable.

2. Label and disconnect the fuel injector electrical connectors.

3. Remove the fuel rail retaining bolts. Disconnect the fuel injector electrical connectors and the fuel supply line.

4. Remove the fuel rail.

5. Separate the injector(s) from the fuel rail.

To install:

6. Replace the fuel injector O-rings.

7. Install the injector(s) into the fuel rail.

8. Install the fuel rail.

9. Install the fuel rail retaining bolts. Connect the the fuel injector electrical connectors and the fuel supply line.

10. Install the air cleaner assembly.

11. Connect the negative battery cable.

1989 4.5L Engines

NOTE: Care must be taken when removing injectors to prevent damage to the electrical connector pins on the injector and nozzle. The injectors are serviced as a complete assembly only. Injectors are an electrical component and should not be immersed in any type of cleaner.

1. Properly relieve the fuel system pressure.

2. Disconnect the negative battery cable. Remove the air cleaner assembly.

3. Disconnect the electrical connector from the fuel injector(s) by squeezing the 2 tabs together and pulling it straight up.

4. Remove the fuel meter cover-to-throttle body screws and the cover; be sure to note the position of the 4 short screws. Allow the gasket to remain in place to prevent damage to the casting housing.

5. Using a small prybar and a ¼ in. rod, pry the fuel injector(s) from the throttle body; discard the O-rings.

To install:

6. Use new O-rings, lubricate with Dexron®II automatic transmission fluid, and install the injectors by pushing them into the sockets.

7. Install the fuel cover-to-throttle body screws, in the positions noted upon removal.

8. Connect the fuel injector electrical connectors.

9. Replace the air filter assembly and connect the negative battery cable.

10. Start the Engine and check for leaks.

1990 4.5L and 1991–93 4.9L Engines

1. Disconnect the negative battery cable.

2. Position the power steering pump aside.

3. Relieve the fuel system pressure.

4. Disconnect the vacuum lines from the pressure regulator and the base assembly.

5. Disconnect the fuel feed line from the rear of the rail assembly. Discard the O-ring.

6. Remove the fuel return line. Discard the O-ring.

7. Disconnect the electrical connec-

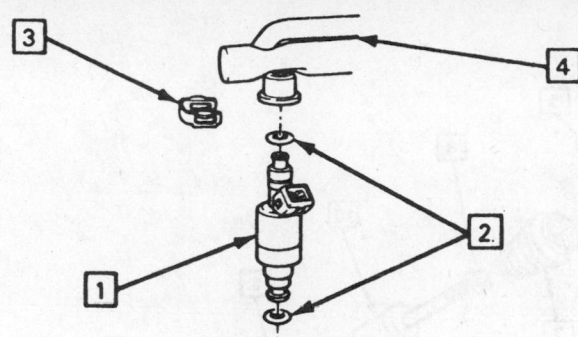

1. Injector assembly
2. Seal-O-ring injector
3. Clip-injector retainer
4. Fuel rail

Fuel Injector—1990 4.5L and 4.9L engines

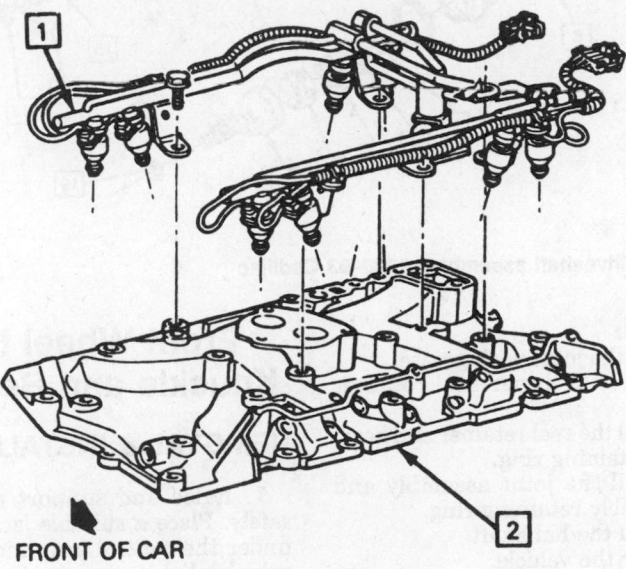

FRONT OF CAR

1. Fuel rail assembly
2. Intake manifold

Fuel rail assembly—1990 4.5L and 4.9L engines

tors at the front and the rear of the rail assembly.

8. Remove the rail support bracket mounting bolts and remove the rail assembly from the intake manifold.

9. Disconnect the electrical connector from the fuel injector by pushing in the clip while pulling the connector body away from the injector.

10. Disconnect the injector retaining clip. Discard the clip.

11. Remove the fuel injector assembly, by twisting back and forth while removing. Remove and discard the O-rings from the injectors.

To install:

12. Lubricate new O-rings and install on the injector assembly.

13. Install a new injector clip on the injector.

14. Install the fuel injector into the fuel rail socket. Push in to engage the retainer clip with the fuel rail cup.

NOTE: The electrical connectors should be facing the Engine front for injectors 1–4. The connectors should be facing the rear of the Engine for injectors 5–8.

15. Install the electrical connector to the injector assembly.

16. Install the fuel rail assembly and connect the support bracket mounting bolts.

17. Connect the electrical connectors at the front and rear of the rail assembly.

18. Install the fuel return line, using a new O-ring.

19. Connect the fuel feed line at the rear of the rail assembly, using a new O-ring.

20. Connect the vacuum lines to the base assembly and the pressure regulator.

21. Reposition the power steering pump and connect the negative battery cable.

22. Start the Engine and check for leaks.

DRIVE AXLE

Halfshaft

REMOVAL & INSTALLATION

NOTE: Use care when removing the halfshaft. Tri-pots can be damaged if the halfshaft is overextended.

1. Raise and safely support the vehicle. Remove the tire and wheel assembly.

2. Use a halfshaft boot seal protector tool and install it onto the seal.

3. Insert drift into rotor and caliper to prevent rotor from turning.

4. Remove hub nut and washer using a hub nut socket tool.

5. Remove the lower ball joint cotter pin and nut and loosen the joint using a ball joint separator tool. If removing the right halfshaft, turn the wheel to the left, if removing the left halfshaft turn the wheel to the right.

6. With a prybar between the suspension support and the lower control arm, separate the joint.

7. Pull out on the lower knuckle area and with a plastic or rubber mallet strike the end of the axle shaft to disengage the axle from the hub and bearing. The shaft nut can be partially installed to protect the threads.

8. Separate the hub and bearing assembly from the halfshaft and move the strut and knuckle assembly rearward. Remove the inner joint from the transaxle using the proper tool from the intermediate shaft, if equipped.

NOTE: If equipped with the anti-lock brake system, care must be used to prevent damage to the toothed sensor ring on the halfshaft and the wheel speed sensor on the steering knuckle.

To install:

9. Seat the halfshaft into the transaxle by placing the proper tool into the groove on the joint housing and tapping until seated.

10. Verify the halfshaft is seated into

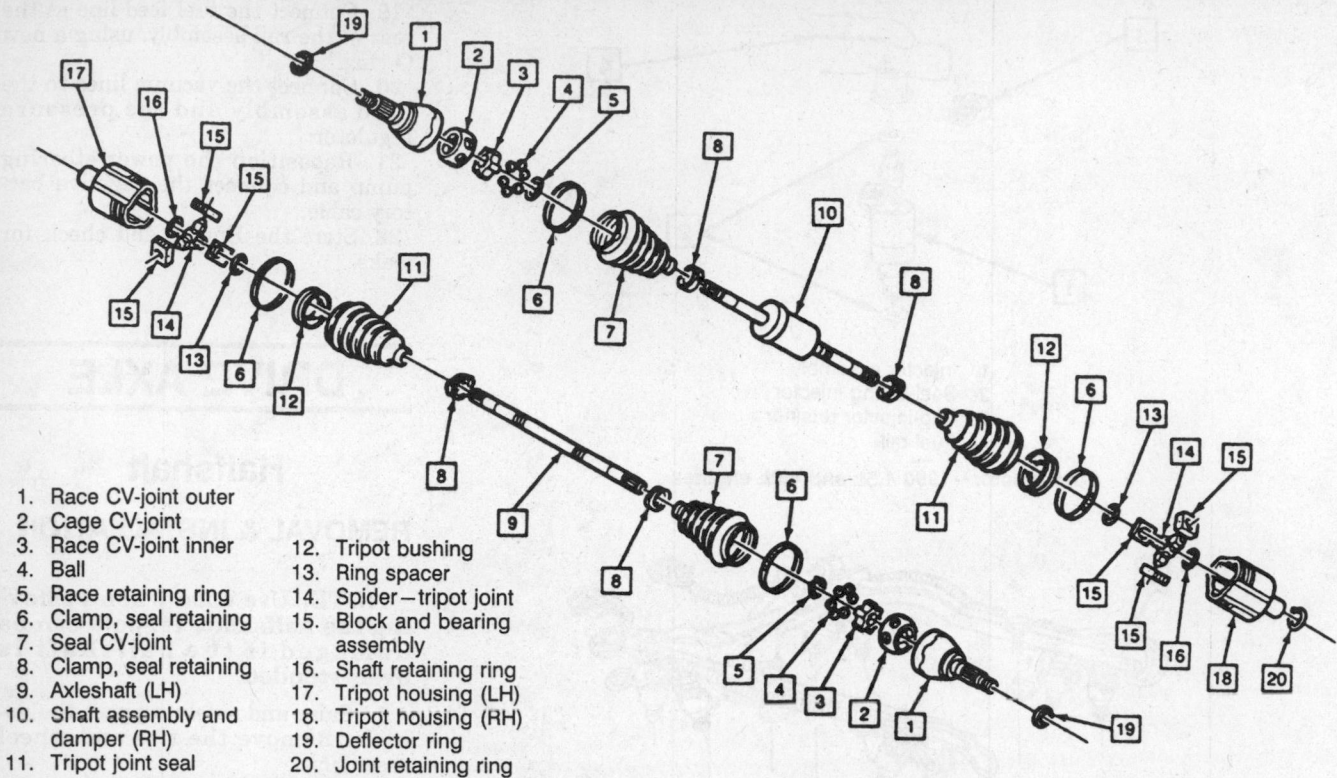

1. Race CV-joint outer
2. Cage CV-joint
3. Race CV-joint inner
4. Ball
5. Race retaining ring
6. Clamp, seal retaining
7. Seal CV-joint
8. Clamp, seal retaining
9. Axleshaft (LH)
10. Shaft assembly and damper (RH)
11. Tripot joint seal
12. Tripot bushing
13. Ring spacer
14. Spider—tripot joint
15. Block and bearing assembly
16. Shaft retaining ring
17. Tripot housing (LH)
18. Tripot housing (RH)
19. Deflector ring
20. Joint retaining ring

Exploded view of driveshaft assembly—1990–93 Cadillac

the transaxle by grasping on the housing and pulling outboard. Do not pull on the halfshaft.

11. Install the halfshaft into the hub and bearing assembly.

12. Install the lower ball joint to the knuckle. Tighten the nut to 41 ft. lbs. (56 Nm) minimum and to 50 ft. lbs. (68 Nm) maximum to install the cotter pin.

13. Install the cotter pin.

14. Install the washer and new shaft nut.

15. Insert drift into rotor and caliper to prevent rotor from turning.

16. Torque the shaft nut to 185 ft. lbs. (251 Nm).

17. Remove the boot protector.

18. Install the tire and wheel assembly. Lower the vehicle.

CV-Boot

REMOVAL & INSTALLATION

Inner Boot (Inboard)

1. Raise and support the vehicle safely. Remove the halfshaft.

2. Remove the joint assembly retaining ring and the joint assembly.

3. Remove the bearing race retaining ring and the seal retainer.

4. Remove the inner seal retainer clamp and the inner joint seal.

To install:

5. Pack the joint with grease.

6. Install the inner seal retainer clamp.

7. Install the seal retainer and bearing race retaining ring.

8. Install the joint assembly and joint assembly retaining ring.

9. Install the halfshaft.

10. Lower the vehicle.

Outer Boot (Outboard)

1. Raise and support the vehicle safely. Remove the halfshaft.

2. Using a brass drift, lightly tap around the seal retainer to loosen it. Remove the seal retainer.

3. Remove the seal retainer clamp and discard.

4. Using snapring pliers, remove the race retaining ring from the halfshaft.

5. Pull the outer joint assembly and the outboard seal away from the halfshaft.

To install:

6. Pack the joint with grease.

7. Install the outboard seal and outer joint assembly on the halfshaft.

8. Install the race retaining ring on the halfshaft.

9. Install a new seal retainer clamp.

10. Install the halfshaft.

11. Lower the vehicle.

Front Wheel Hub, Knuckle and Bearings

REMOVAL & INSTALLATION

1. Raise and support the vehicle safely. Place a suitable jacking device under the control arm and lower the vehicle slightly to rest the weight of the vehicle on the control arm.

2. Remove the tire and wheel assembly. Remove the caliper bolts, remove and support the caliper aside.

3. Remove the rotor and using the proper tool, separate the hub from the halfshaft.

4. Remove the hub and bearing retaining bolts, shield, hub and bearing assembly and the O-ring.

5. Disconnect the ball joint from the steering knuckle, using the proper tool.

6. Remove the halfshaft assembly and tap the seal from the steering knuckle. Remove the steering knuckle from the hub.

NOTE: The hub and bearing are replaced only as an assembly.

To install:

7. Install a new hub and bearing seal in the steering knuckle with the proper seal installer tool. Install the steering knuckle to the strut.

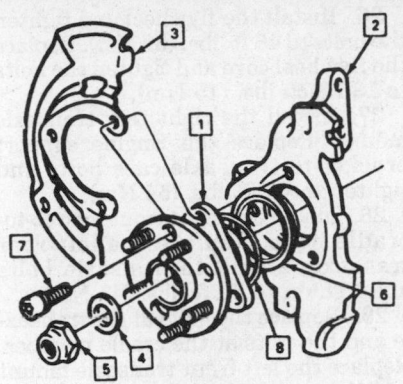

1. Hub and bearing assembly
2. Steering knuckle
3. Shield
4. Washer
5. Hub nut
6. Seal
7. Hub and bearing retaining bolt
8. O-ring

Front hub and bearing assembly

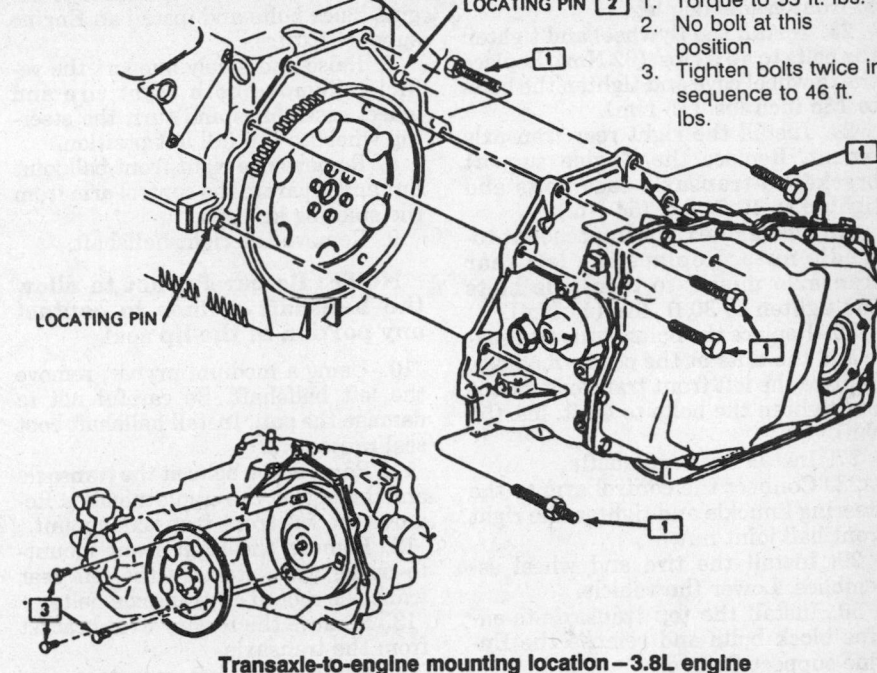

LOCATING PIN [2]
1. Torque to 55 ft. lbs.
2. No bolt at this position
3. Tighten bolts twice in sequence to 46 ft. lbs.

LOCATING PIN

Transaxle-to-engine mounting location—3.8L engine

8. Lubricate the hub and bearing with grease and install the halfshaft.

9. Connect the ball joint to the steering knuckle and insert a new O-ring around the hub and bearing assembly.

10. Install the hub and bearing assembly into the steering knuckle. Tighten the bolts to 75 ft. lbs. (101 Nm).

11. Install the rotor and caliper assembly. Tighten the caliper bolts to 38 ft. lbs. (52 Nm).

12. Install the shaft washer and nut. Tighten the nut to 180 ft. lbs. (244 Nm).

13. Install the tire and wheel assembly.

14. Lower the vehicle.

AUTOMATIC TRANSAXLE

For further information on transmission/transaxles, please refer to "Chilton's Guide to Transmission Repair".

Transaxle Assembly

REMOVAL & INSTALLATION

3.8L Engine With 4T60 Transmission

1989

1. Disconnect the negative terminal from the battery. Disconnect the wire connector at the Mass Air Flow sensor, if equipped.

2. Remove the air intake duct and the Mass Air Flow sensor as an assembly.

3. Disconnect the cruise control assembly and the the shift control linkage.

4. Label and disconnect the following:
   a. Park/Neutral switch
   b. Torque converter clutch
   c. Vehicle speed sensor and fuel pipe retainers
   d. Vacuum modulator hose at the modulator

5. Remove the top transaxle-to-engine block bolts and install an Engine support fixture.

6. Raise and safely support the vehicle. Remove both front tire and wheel assemblies and turn the steering wheel to the full left position.

7. Remove the right front ball joint nut and separate the control arm from the steering knuckle.

8. Remove the right halfshaft.

NOTE: Be careful not to allow the halfshaft splines to contact any portion of the lip seal.

9. Using a medium prybar, remove the left halfshaft. Be careful not to damage the pan. Install halfshaft boot seal protectors.

10. Remove the bolts at the transaxle and the nuts at the cradle member. Remove the left front transaxle mount.

11. Remove the right front mount-to-cradle nuts. Remove the left rear transaxle mount-to-transaxle bolts.

12. Remove the right rear transaxle mount. Remove the Engine support bracket-to-transaxle case bolts.

13. Remove the flywheel cover, matchmark the flywheel-to-torque converter and remove the flywheel-to-converter bolts.

NOTE: Be sure to matchmark the flywheel-to-converter relationship for proper alignment upon reassembly.

14. Remove the rear cradle member-to-front cradle dog leg.

15. Remove the front left cradle-to-body bolt and the front cradle dog leg-to-right cradle member bolts.

16. Install a transaxle support fixture into position.

17. Remove the cradle assembly by swinging it aside and supporting it with jackstand.

18. Disconnect and plug the oil cooler lines at the transaxle.

NOTE: One bolt located between the transaxle and the Engine block is installed in the opposite direction.

19. Remove the remaining lower transaxle-to-engine bolts and lower the transaxle from the vehicle.
To install:

20. Install the transaxle into the vehicle using the dowel pin as guide. Tighten the bolts to 55 ft. lbs. (75 Nm).

21. Connect the oil cooler lines and remove the support fixture.

22. Install the front left cradle-to-

body bolts and replace the rear cradle-to-front cradle dog leg.

23. Install the flywheel and tighten the bolts to 46 ft. lbs. (62 Nm). Replace the flywheel cove and tighten the bolts to 136 inch lbs. (15 Nm).

24. Install the right rear transaxle mount. Replace the Engine support bracket-to-transaxle case bolts and tighten to 40 ft. lbs. (54 Nm).

25. Install the right front mount-to-cradle nuts. Replace the left rear transaxle mount-to-transaxle bolts and tighten to 30 ft. lbs. (41 Nm).

26. Replace the bolts at the transaxle and the nuts at the cradle member. Replace the left front transaxle mount and tighten the bolts to 40 ft. lbs. (54 Nm).

27. Install both halfshafts.

28. Connect the control arm to the steering knuckle and tighten the right front ball joint nut.

29. Install the tire and wheel assemblies. Lower the vehicle.

30. Install the top transaxle-to-engine block bolts and remove the Engine support fixture.

31. Connect the following:
   a. Park/Neutral switch
   b. Torque converter clutch
   c. Vehicle speed sensor and fuel pipe retainers
   d. Vacuum modulator hose at the modulator

32. Connect the cruise control assembly and the the shift control linkage.

33. Replace the air intake duct and the Mass Air Flow sensor as an assembly.

34. Connect the wire connector at the Mass Air Flow sensor, if equipped.

35. Connect the negative battery cable.

3.8L Engine With 4T60/4T60E

Transmission

1990–93

1. Disconnect the negative terminal from the battery. Disconnect the wire connector at the Mass Air Flow sensor, if equipped.

2. Remove the cross brace to strut towers, if equipped. Reinstall the inboard strut nuts.

3. Remove the air intake duct.

4. Disconnect the cruise control assembly and the the shift control linkage.

5. Label and disconnect the following:
   a. Transaxle neutral start and backup lamp switch
   b. Transaxle electrical connector
   c. Vehicle speed sensor and fuel pipe retainers
   d. Vacuum modulator hose at the modulator

6. Remove the top transaxle-to-engine block bolts and install an Engine support fixture.

7. Raise and safely support the vehicle. Remove both front tire and wheel assemblies and turn the steering wheel to the full left position.

8. Remove the right front ball joint nut and separate the control arm from the steering knuckle.

9. Remove the right halfshaft.

NOTE: Be careful not to allow the halfshaft splines to contact any portion of the lip seal.

10. Using a medium prybar, remove the left halfshaft. Be careful not to damage the pan. Install halfshaft boot seal protectors.

11. Remove the bolts at the transaxle and the nuts at the cradle member. Remove the left front transaxle mount.

12. Remove the right front mount-to-cradle nuts. Remove the left rear transaxle mount-to-transaxle bolts.

13. Remove the torque strut bracket from the transaxle.

14. Remove the left rear transaxle mount. Remove the transaxle brace from the Engine bracket.

15. Remove the stabilizer shaft link to control arm bolt.

16. Remove the flywheel cover, matchmark the flywheel-to-torque converter and remove the flywheel-to-converter bolts.

NOTE: Be sure to matchmark the flywheel-to-converter relationship for proper alignment upon reassembly.

17. Remove the rear frame member-to-front cradle dog leg.

18. Remove the front left cradle-to-body bolt and the front cradle dog leg-to-right cradle member bolts.

19. Install a transaxle support fixture into position.

20. Remove the cradle assembly by swinging it aside and supporting it with jackstand.

21. Disconnect and plug the oil cooler lines at the transaxle.

NOTE: One bolt located between the transaxle and the Engine block is installed in the opposite direction.

22. Remove the remaining lower transaxle-to-engine bolts and lower the transaxle from the vehicle.

To install:

23. Install the transaxle into the vehicle using the dowel pin as guide. Tighten the bolts to 55 ft. lbs. (75 Nm).

24. Connect the oil cooler lines and remove the support fixture.

25. Install the front left cradle-to-body bolts and replace the rear cradle-to-front cradle dog leg.

26. Install the flywheel and tighten the bolts to 46 ft. lbs. (62 Nm). Replace the flywheel cove and tighten the bolts to 136 inch lbs. (15 Nm).

27. Install the right rear transaxle mount. Replace the Engine support bracket-to-transaxle case bolts and tighten to 40 ft. lbs. (54 Nm).

28. Install the right front mount-to-cradle nuts. Replace the left rear transaxle mount-to-transaxle bolts and tighten to 30 ft. lbs. (41 Nm).

29. Replace the bolts at the transaxle and the nuts at the cradle member. Replace the left front transaxle mount and tighten the bolts to 40 ft. lbs. (54 Nm).

30. Install both halfshafts.

31. Connect the control arm to the steering knuckle and tighten the right front ball joint nut.

32. Install the tire and wheel assemblies. Lower the vehicle.

33. Install the top transaxle-to-engine block bolts and remove the Engine support fixture.

34. Connect the following:
   a. Park/Neutral switch
   b. Torque converter clutch
   c. Vehicle speed sensor and fuel pipe retainers
   d. Vacuum modulator hose at the modulator

35. Connect the cruise control assembly and the the shift control linkage.

36. Replace the air intake duct and install the cross brace to strut towers, if equipped.

37. Connect the wire connector at the Mass Air Flow sensor, if equipped.

38. Connect the negative battery cable.

4.5L Engines With 440T4 Transaxle

1989–90

1. Disconnect the negative terminal from the battery. Remove the air cleaner and the TV cable.

2. Disconnect the shift linkage from the transaxle. Install an Engine support fixture and support the engine.

3. Label and disconnect the electrical connectors from the following items:
   a. Converter clutch
   b. Vehicle speed sensor
   c. Vacuum line at the modulator

4. Remove the upper bell housing-to-engine bolts and studs.

5. Raise and support the vehicle safely. Remove both front wheels.

6. From the left side of the vehicle, disconnect the lower ball joint from steering knuckle. Remove both drive axles from the transaxle.

7. Remove the stabilizer bar-to-left control arm bolt.

8. Remove the left front cradle assembly.

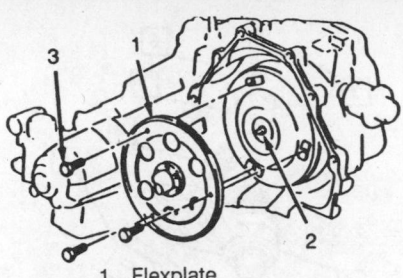

1. Flexplate
2. Torque converter
3. Bolt

Converter-to-flexplate attachments—4.5L and 4.9L engines

9. Remove the extension housing-to-engine support bracket.
10. Disconnect and plug the oil cooler lines at the transaxle case.
11. Remove the right and left transaxle mount attachments.
12. Remove the flywheel splash shield. Matchmark the torque converter-to-flywheel and remove the converter-to-flywheel bolts.
13. Remove the lower bell housing bolts.
14. Using a floor jack, position it under the transaxle and remove the last bell housing bolt.

NOTE: To reach the last bell housing bolt, use a 3 in. socket wrench extension through the right wheel arch opening.

15. Remove the transaxle assembly.
To install:
16. Install the transaxle assembly and replace the lower bell housing bolts. Tighten the bolts to 55 ft. lbs. (75 Nm).
17. Replace the converter-to-flexplate bolts and tighten to 46 ft. lbs. (62 Nm). Install the flexplate splash shield.
18. Connect the oil cooler lines at the transaxle case.
19. Install the extension housing-to-engine support bracket. Replace the left front cradle assembly.
20. Replace the stabilizer bar-to-left control arm bolt.
21. Install both halfshafts. Fully seat the halfshafts by inserting the proper tool in the groove on the joint housing and tap until the joints are seated.
22. Connect the lower ball joint to the steering knuckle and replace the left and right front transaxle mount-to-cradle attachments. Tighten the nuts to 23 ft. lbs. (31 Nm).
23. Replace both front tire and wheel assemblies. Lower the vehicle.
24. Replace the upper bell housing-to-engine bolts/studs and tighten to 55 ft. lbs. (75 Nm).
25. Connect the electrical connec-

tors to the converter clutch, vehicle speed sensor and the vacuum line to the modulator.
26. Connect the shift linkage to the transaxle. Remove the Engine support fixture tool.
27. Replace the air cleaner and the TV cable.
28. Connect the negative battery cable. Check the fluid levels and start the Engine and check for leaks.

4.5L and 4.9L Engines With 4T60E Transaxle

1991–93

1. Disconnect the negative terminal from the battery. Remove the air cleaner and the TV cable.
2. Disconnect the shift cable and remove the bracket.
3. Disconnect all of the electrical connectors between the transaxle and engine.
4. Remove the Engine harness bracket.
5. Disconnect the Engine oil cooler line, vacuum hose. Remove the fuel line bracket.
6. Remove the vacuum modulator, transaxle filler tube and mounting bracket.
7. Remove the upper bell housing-to-engine bolts and studs.
8. Install an Engine support device.
9. Raise and support the vehicle safely. Remove both front wheels.
10. Remove both side stabilizer link bolts, ball joint cotter pins and nuts. Separate both ball joints from the steering knuckles. Remove both drive axles from the hubs and then from the transaxle.
11. Remove the air conditioning splash shield, right and left wheelhouse splash shields.
12. Return the power steering return line bracket and ABS pump from the bracket.
13. Remove the flywheel splash shield. Matchmark the torque converter-to-flywheel and remove the converter-to-flywheel bolts.
14. Disconnect the power steering line and trans line.
15. Remove the right and left cradle mount bolts and the right side motor mount nuts.
16. Seperate the right front corner of the cradle from the cradle. Remove the cradle insulator bolt and remove the left cradle member.
17. Using a floor jack, position it under the transaxle and remove the bracket assembly from the transaxle mount bracket.
18. Remove the Engine to transaxle and to left side transaxle brackets.

NOTE: To reach the last bell housing bolt, use a 3 in. socket

wrench extension through the right wheel arch opening.

19. Remove the 2 lower bell housing bolts and remove the transaxle assembly.
To install:
20. Install the transaxle assembly and replace the lower bell housing bolts. Tighten the bolts to 55 ft. lbs. (75 Nm).
21. Replace the converter-to-flexplate bolts and tighten to 46 ft. lbs. (62 Nm). Install the flexplate splash shield.
22. Connect the oil cooler lines at the transaxle case.
23. Install the extension housing-to-engine support bracket. Replace the left front cradle assembly.
24. Replace both the right and left side cradle mount bolts and motor mount nuts.
25. Connect the power steering line and trans lines. Install the power steering return line bracket and ABS pump.
26. Install both drive axles. Fully seat by inserting the proper tool in the groove on the joint housing and tap until the joints are seated.
27. Connect the lower ball joint to the steering knuckle and replace the left and right front transaxle mount-to-cradle attachments. Tighten the nuts to 23 ft. lbs. (31 Nm).
28. Replace both front tire and wheel assemblies. Lower the vehicle.
29. Replace the upper bell housing-to-engine bolts/studs and tighten to 55 ft. lbs. (75 Nm).
30. Connect the electrical connectors and connect the shift linkage to the transaxle. Remove the Engine support fixture tool.
31. Replace the air cleaner and the TV cable.
32. Connect the negative battery cable. Check the fluid levels and start the Engine and check for leaks.

SHIFT LINKAGE ADJUSTMENT

1. Position the shift lever in the **N** position.
2. Raise and safely support the vehicle.
3. Push the tab on the cable adjuster to adjust the cable in the cable mounting bracket on 3.8L and 1991–93 4.5L and 4.9L engines.
4. Loosen and tighten the adjusting nut to 20 ft. lbs. (27 Nm) to adjust the cable on 1989–90 4.5L and 4.9L engines.
5. Lower the vehicle.

THROTTLE LINKAGE ADJUSTMENT

1. Stop the engine. Raise and safely support the vehicle.

NOTE: Check the throttle body for full travel prior to any adjustments.

2. Depress and hold-down the metal readjust tab at the Engine end of the TV cable.

3. Move the slider until it stops against the fitting.

4. Release the adjustment tab.

5. Rotate the throttle lever to the full travel position.

6. The slider must move toward the lever when the lever is rotated to it's full travel position.

FRONT SUSPENSION

MacPherson Strut

REMOVAL & INSTALLATION

1. Loosen the bar assembly through bolts.

2. Disconnect the 3 mounting nuts from the top of the strut assembly.

3. Raise and safely support the vehicle. Position a jackstand under the Engine cradle and lower the vehicle so the weight of the vehicle rests on the a jackstand and not the control arms.

4. Remove the tire and wheel assemblies. If equipped with ABS, disconnect the front sensor.

5. Disconnect the brake line bracket from the strut assembly. Remove the strut-to-steering knuckle bolts.

6. Remove the strut assembly from the vehicle.

To install:

7. Install the strut assembly.

8. Install the strut-to-steering knuckle bolts. Connect the brake line bracket to the strut assembly.

9. If equipped with ABS, connect the front sensor. Install the tire and wheel assemblies.

10. Remove the jackstand. Lower the vehicle.

11. Connect the mounting nuts to the top of the strut assembly.

Lower Ball Joints

INSPECTION

1. Raise and support the vehicle safely. Position a jackstand under the

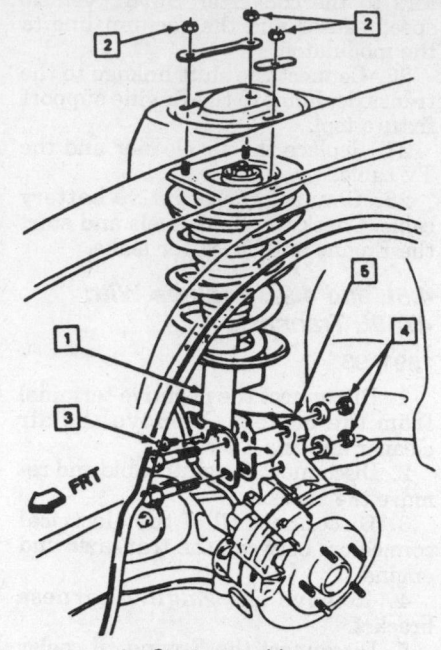

1. Strut assembly
2. Strut-to-body nuts
3. Brake line bracket bolt
4. Strut-to-steering knuckle nuts
5. Retain steering knuckle with wire once strut assembly is removed

Strut mount location

Engine cradle and lower the vehicle so the weight of the vehicle rests on the a jackstand and not the control arms.

2. Grasp the wheel at the top and the bottom and shake the wheel in and out.

3. If the is any movement of the steering knuckle in relation the control arm, the ball joints are defective and must be replaced.

REMOVAL & INSTALLATION

1. Raise and safely support the vehicle. Position a jackstand under the Engine cradle and lower the vehicle so the weight of the vehicle rests on the jackstand and not the control arms.

2. Remove the tire and wheel assembly.

3. Disconnect the ball joint from the steering knuckle, using the proper tool.

4. Drill out the rivets retaining the ball joint and loosen the stabilizer shaft bushing assembly nut.

5. Remove the ball joint from the steering knuckle and the control arm.

To install:

6. Install the ball joint to the steering knuckle and the control arm.

7. Install the 3 ball joint bolts facing

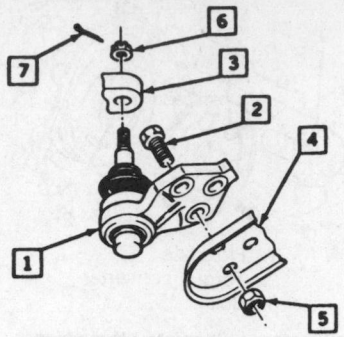

1. Ball joint
2. Ball joint mounting bolts must face down
3. Steering knuckle
4. Control arm
5. Ball joint mounting nuts
6. Ball joint-to-steering knuckle nut

Exploded view of ball joint assembly

down. Tighten nuts to 50 ft. lbs. (68 Nm). Tighten the stabilizer shaft bushing assembly nut to 13 ft. lbs. (17 Nm).

8. Connect the ball joint to the steering knuckle. Install a new cotter pin.

9. Install the tire and wheel assembly.

10. Lower the vehicle.

Lower Control Arms

REMOVAL & INSTALLATION

1. Raise and safely support the vehicle. Position a jackstand under the Engine cradle and lower the vehicle so the weight of the vehicle rests on the jackstand and not the control arms.

2. Remove the tire and wheel assembly. Disconnect the stabilizer shaft-to-control arm bolt.

3. Remove the ball joint from the steering knuckle and the control arm.

4. Remove the control arm mounting bolts and remove the control arm from the Engine cradle.

To install:

5. Install the control arm to the Engine cradle. Do not tighten the control arm bolts at this time.

6. Install the stabilizer shaft bushings and connect the ball joint to the steering knuckle.

7. Raise the vehicle so the weight of the vehicle is supported by the control arm.

NOTE: The weight of the vehicle must be supported by the control arms when tightening the control arm mounting nuts.

8. Tighten the rear control arm

mounting nut to 90 ft. lbs. (122 Nm) and the front mounting nut to 140 ft. lbs. (190 Nm).

9. Install the ball joint to the control arm and tighten the nut to 37 ft. lbs. (50 Nm).

10. Replace the tire and wheel assembly.

11. Raise the vehicle and remove the jackstand.

12. Lower the vehicle.

Sway Bar
REMOVAL & INSTALLATION

1. Raise and safely support the vehicle. Position a jackstand under the Engine cradle and lower the vehicle so the weight of the vehicle rests on the jackstand and not the control arms.

2. Remove the tire and wheel assemblies.

3. Remove the bolts connecting the stabilizer bar bushings to the control arms.

4. Remove the stabilizer bar mounting bolts. Matchmark and disconnect the tie rod ends from the steering knuckles.

5. Disconnect the exhaust pipe from the exhaust manifold and turn the passenger side strut assembly completely to the right.

6. Slide the stabilizer bar over the steering knuckle and pull down until the stabilizer bar clears the frame.

7. Remove the stabilizer bar from the vehicle.

To install:

8. Install the stabilizer bar over the steering knuckle.

9. Raise the stabilizer bar over the frame and slide into position.

10. Loosely, install the stabilizer bar mount bushings, brackets and bolts.

11. Install the tie rod ends to the steering knuckles, tighten the nuts to 52 ft. lbs. (71 Nm). Tighten the stabilizer bar mounting bolts to 37 ft. lbs. (50 Nm).

12. Connect the exhaust pipe to the exhaust manifold and tighten the bolts to 15 ft. lbs. (20 Nm).

13. Replace the tire and wheel assemblies.

14. Raise the vehicle and remove the jackstands.

15. Lower the vehicle.

REAR SUSPENSION

MacPherson Strut

REMOVAL & INSTALLATION

1. Raise and safely support the vehicle.

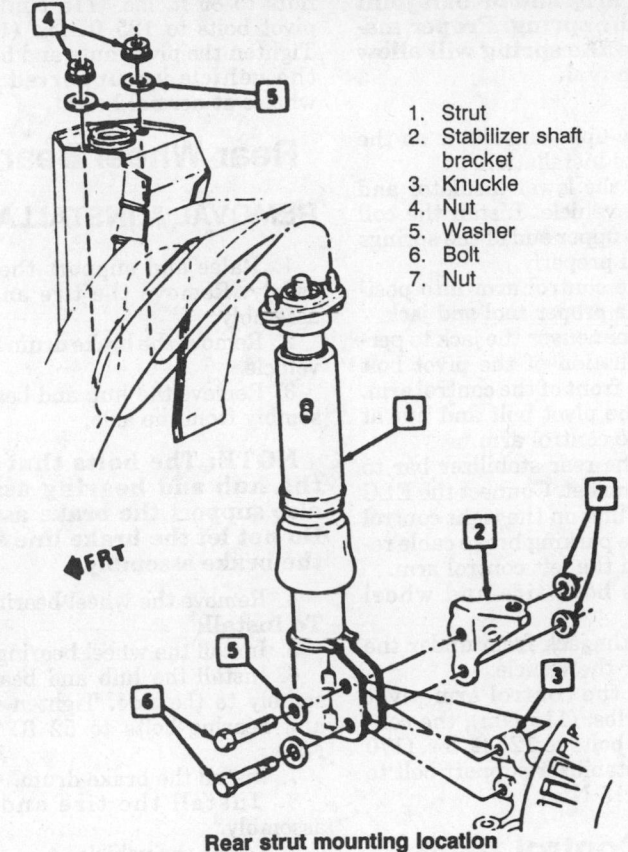

1. Strut
2. Stabilizer shaft bracket
3. Knuckle
4. Nut
5. Washer
6. Bolt
7. Nut

Rear strut mounting location

2. Remove the trunk side cover. Remove the tire and wheel assemblies.

3. Support the control arm with a suitable jack.

4. Disconnect the Electronic Level Control (ELC) air tube and separate from the strut air tube, if equipped. If equipped with Computer Command Ride (CCR), disconnect the strut electrical connector from the harness.

5. Disconnect the strut tower mounting nuts. The nuts are located inside the trunk.

6. Remove the strut anchor bolts, washers and nuts from the steering knuckle and bracket.

7. Remove the strut assembly from the vehicle.

To install:

8. Install the strut assembly and connect the upper strut mounting nuts.

9. Replace the strut anchor bolts, washer, knuckle bracket and nuts.

10. Connect the ELC tube or CCR connector if equipped.

11. Tighten the upper mount nuts to 35 ft. lbs. (47 Nm) and the strut-to-knuckle nuts to 140 ft. lbs. (190 Nm).

12. Replace the tire and wheel assemblies. Remove the jack from under the vehicle.

13. Replace the trunk side cover and lower the vehicle.

Coil Springs

REMOVAL & INSTALLATION

1. Raise and support the vehicle safely. Support the vehicle so the control arms hang free.

2. Remove both tire and wheel assemblies.

3. Disconnect the ELC height sensor on the right control arm and/or the parking brake cable retaining clip on the left control arm.

4. Place a proper tool and jack into position and remove the tension from the control arm pivot bolts.

NOTE: Place a chain around the spring and through the control arm as a safety measure.

5. Remove the pivot bolt and nut from the rear of the control arm.

6. Slowly, maneuver the jack to relieve in the front control arm pivot bolt.

7. Lower the jack to allow the control arm to pivot downward.

8. When all the compression is removed from the spring remove the safety chain, spring and the insulators.

NOTE: Do not apply force to

the control arm and/or ball joint to remove the spring. Proper maneuvering of the spring will allow for easy removal.

To install:

9. Snap the upper insulator on the spring prior to installation.

10. Position the lower insulator and spring in the vehicle. Install the coil springs so the upper end of the springs are positioned properly.

11. Raise the control arm into position, using the proper tool and jack.

12. Slowly, maneuver the jack to permit the installation of the pivot bolt and nut at the front of the control arm.

13. Install the pivot bolt and nut at the rear of the control arm.

14. Attach the rear stabilizer bar to the knuckle bracket. Connect the ELC height sensor link on the right control arm and/or the parking brake cable retaining clip on the left control arm.

15. Replace both tire and wheel assemblies.

16. Remove the jack from under the vehicle. Lower the vehicle.

17. Tighten the control arm pivot nuts to 85 ft. lbs. (115 Nm), the control arm pivot bolts to 125 ft. lbs. (170 Nm) and the stabilizer support bolt to 160 inch lbs. (18 Nm).

Rear Control Arms

REMOVAL & INSTALLATION

1. Raise and support the vehicle safely. Remove the tire and wheel assembly.

2. If equipped, disconnect the ELC height sensor on the right control arm and/or the parking brake cable retaining clip on the left control arm.

3. Disconnect the suspension adjustment link retaining nut and separate the link assembly from the control arm.

4. Remove the ball stud and the castellated nut. Turn over and install with the flat portion facing up. Do not tighten.

5. Separate the knuckle from the ball stud, using the proper tool. Remove the control arm.

To install:

6. Install the control arm. Connect the knuckle to the ball stud. Install the castellated nut.

7. Connect the link assembly to the control arm. Connect the suspension adjustment link retaining nut.

8. If equipped, connect the ELC height sensor on the right control arm and/or the parking brake cable retaining clip on the left control arm.

9. Install the tire and wheel assembly.

10. Lower the vehicle.

11. Tighten the control arm pivot

nuts to 85 ft. lbs. (115 Nm) and the pivot bolts to 125 ft. lbs. (170 Nm). Tighten the pivot nuts and bolts with the vehicle unsupported and the wheels at normal height.

Rear Wheel Bearings

REMOVAL & INSTALLATION

1. Raise and support the vehicle safely. Remove the tire and wheel assembly.

2. Remove the brake drum from the vehicle.

3. Remove the hub and bearing assembly from the axle.

NOTE: The bolts that attach the hub and bearing assembly also support the brake assembly. Do not let the brake line support the brake assembly.

4. Remove the wheel bearings.

To install:

5. Install the wheel bearings.

6. Install the hub and bearing assembly to the axle. Tighten the hub and bearing bolts to 52 ft. lbs. (71 Nm).

7. Install the brake drum.

8. Install the tire and wheel assembly.

9. Lower the vehicle.

STEERING

Steering Wheel
— CAUTION —

Some vehicles are equipped with the Supplemental Inflatable Restraint or air bag system. The air bag system must be disabled before performing service on or around the air bag, instrument panel components, wiring and sensors. Failure to follow safety and disabling procedures could result in accidental air bag deployment, possible personal injury and unnecessary air bag system repairs.

REMOVAL & INSTALLATION

Without SIR System

1. Disconnect the negative battery cable.

2. Remove the screws holding the steering pad.

3. Remove the steering pad and disconnect the horn lead.

4. Remove the retainer and nut.

5. Remove the steering wheel, using the proper tool.

To install:

6. Install the steering wheel. Tight-

en the steering shaft nut to 30 ft. lbs. (41 Nm).

7. Install the retainer and nut.

8. Connect the horn lead and install the steering pad.

9. Install the screws holding the steering pad.

10. Connect the negative battery cable.

With SIR System

1. Disconnect the negative battery cable.

2. Disable the SIR system.

3. Remove the inflator module by performing the following:

   a. Remove the inflator module attaching screws from the back of the steering wheel.

   b. Lift the inflator module from the steering wheel.

   c. Push down and twist the horn lead out of the cam tower.

   d. Remove the CPA retainer and coil assembly connector from the inflator module.

4. Remove the hexagonal steering wheel locknut.

5. Mark the steering shaft and steering wheel to ensure proper alignment during installation.

6. Remove the steering wheel, using a suitable puller.

To install:

7. Feed the SIR coil assembly lead through the slot in the steering wheel.

8. Align the mark on the steering wheel with the mark on the shaft.

9. Install the steering wheel.

10. Install the hexagonal steering wheel locknut. Tighten to 30 ft. lbs. (41 Nm).

11. Install the inflator module by performing the following:

   a. Feed the horn lead into the cam tower.

   b. Connect the coil assembly connector and CPA retainer to the inflator module.

   c. Install the inflator module to the steering wheel. Ensure that the inflator module is properly aligned with the steering wheel and that the wires behind the module are not pinched during installation.

   d. Install the inflator module attaching screws to the back of the steering wheel.

12. Enable the SIR system.

13. Connect the negative battery cable.

Steering Column
REMOVAL & INSTALLATION

Except Cadillac

1. Disconnect the negative battery cable. If equipped with SIR, disable the system.

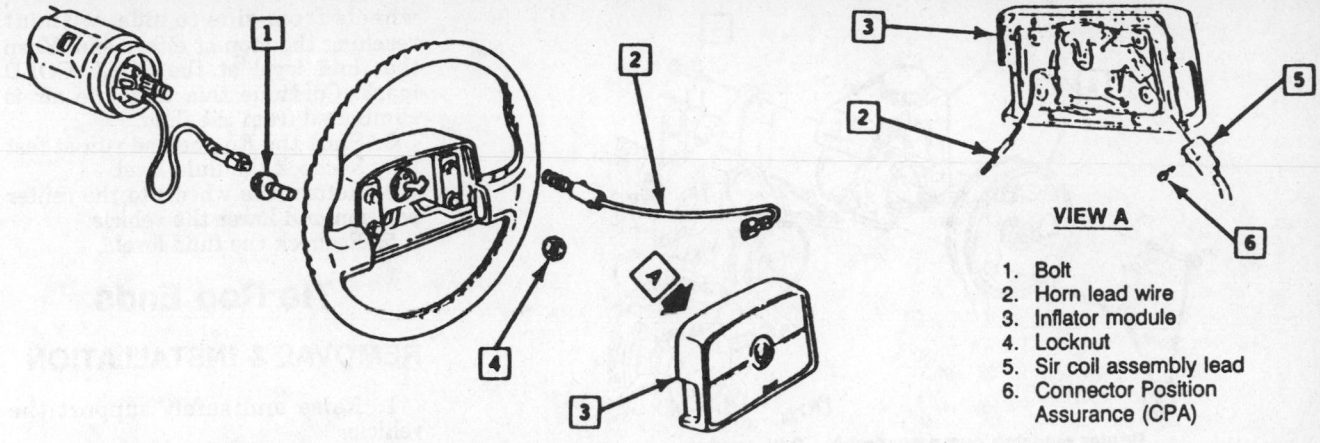

Steering wheel and inflator module—1990–93 Cadillac

VIEW A

1. Bolt
2. Horn lead wire
3. Inflator module
4. Locknut
5. Sir coil assembly lead
6. Connector Position Assurance (CPA)

2. Remove the lower instrument panel trim plates. Remove the left side sound insulator panel.

3. Remove the shift indicator cable from the shift bowl.

4. Label and disconnect the electrical connectors from the steering column. Remove the steering column-to-dash bolts.

5. Remove the steering shaft-to-intermediate shaft bolt and the steering column from the vehicle.

To install:

6. Install the steering column to the vehicle and steering shaft-to-intermediate shaft bolt.

7. Install the steering column-to-dash bolts. Connect the electrical connectors to the steering column.

8. Install the shift indicator cable to the shift bowl.

9. Install the lower instrument panel trim plates. Install the left side sound insulator panel.

10. Enable the SIR system. Connect the negative battery cable.

Cadillac

1. Disconnect the negative battery cable.

2. If equipped, disable the SIR system and remove the inflator module.

3. Remove the steering column trim plate.

4. Remove the retaining filler, the column reinforcement plate and disconnect the electrical connections. Remove the shift control cable at the actuator.

5. Remove the bolts securing the seal assembly and the bolt from the upper knuckle of the intermediate steering shaft.

6. Disconnect the lower brace assembly and the lower support bracket.

7. Remove the bolts securing the column to the upper support and remove the column assembly.

To install:

8. Install the column assembly. Install the bolts securing the column to the upper support.

9. Connect the lower brace assembly and the lower support bracket.

10. Install the bolts securing the seal assembly and the bolt to the upper knuckle of the intermediate steering shaft.

11. Install the retaining filler, the column reinforcement plate and connect the electrical connections. Install the shift control cable at the actuator.

12. Install the steering column trim plate.

13. If equipped with SIR, install the inflator module and enable the SIR system.

14. Connect the negative battery cable.

Power Steering Rack

ADJUSTMENT

Rack Bearing Preload

1. Loosen the adjuster plug locknut and turn the adjuster plug clockwise until it bottoms in the housing. Then back off 50–70 degrees which is approximately one flat.

2. Raise and support the vehicle safely to make the proper adjustments. Be sure to check the returnability of the steering wheel to the center position after the adjustment.

3. Tighten the locknut to the adjuster plug to 50 ft. lbs.

REMOVAL & INSTALLATION

1. Raise and safely support the vehicle. Allow the front suspension to hang freely. Disconnect the pressure lines from the steering gear and drain the excess fluid into a container. Be sure to plug the openings.

2. Move the intermediate shaft cover upward and remove the intermediate shaft-to-stub shaft pinch bolt. Remove both front tire and wheel assemblies.

3. Disconnect the tie rod ends from the steering knuckles. Remove the line retainer, outlet and pressure hoses.

4. Remove the rack/pinion assembly-to-chassis bolts.

5. Loosen the front Engine cradle mounting bolts and the lower the rear of the cradle about 3 inches, if necessary. Remove the rack and pinion assembly.

To install:

6. Install the rack and pinion assembly into the vehicle. Raise the front Engine cradle into position and tighten the attaching bolts.

7. Install the rack/pinion assembly-to-chassis bolts. Tighten the rack mounting bolts to 50 ft. lbs. (68 Nm).

8. Connect the tie rod ends to the steering knuckles. Tighten the tie rod end nut to 35–52 ft. lbs. (47–71 Nm). Install the line retainer, outlet and pressure hoses.

9. Install the intermediate shaft-to-stub shaft pinch bolt. Move the intermediate shaft cover upward into position. Install both front tire and wheel assemblies.

10. Refill the power steering pump reservoir.

11. Bleed the power steering system and check for leaks.

12. Lower the vehicle.

13. Check and/or adjust the front wheel alignment.

Power Steering Pump

REMOVAL & INSTALLATION

3.8L Engine

1. Disconnect the negative battery cable.

2. Remove the serpentine drive belt

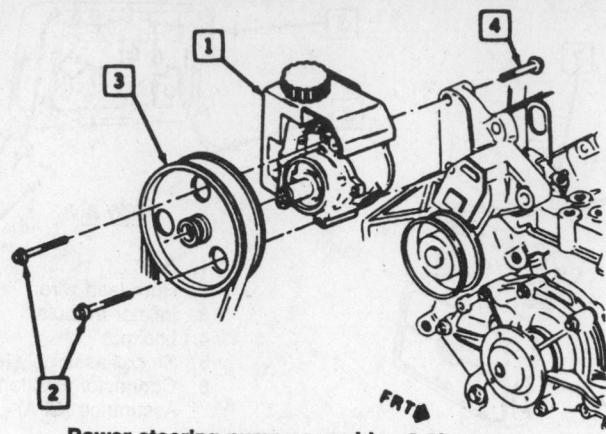

Power steering pump assembly—3.8L engine

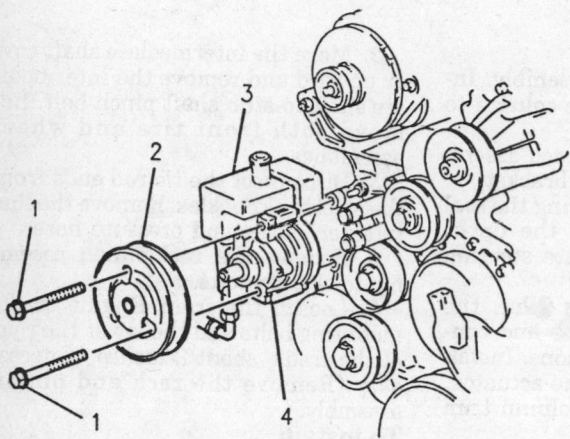

1. Bolt
2. Pulley
3. Reservoir
4. Pump

Power steering pump assembly—Supercharged 3.8L engine

and disconnect the pressure and return hoses.

3. Remove the power steering pump mounting bolts.

4. Remove the pump assembly. Transfer the pulley as necessary.

To install:

5. Install the pump assembly.

6. Remove the power steering pump mounting bolts.

7. Remove the drive belt and disconnect the pressure and return hoses.

8. Connect the negative battery cable.

9. Install the serpentine drive belt and bleed the power steering system.

4.5L and 4.9L Engines

1. Disconnect the negative battery cable.

2. Remove the serpentine drive belt and the power steering pump pulley, using the proper tool.

3. Disconnect and plug the high pressure and feed lines from the pump. Remove the belt tensioner, as required.

4. Remove the power steering pump-to-bracket bolts and the pump.

To install:

5. Install the power steering pump-to-bracket bolts and the pump. Tighten the power steering pump mounting bolts to 18 ft. lbs. (24 Nm).

6. Connect the high pressure and feed lines to the pump. If removed, install the belt tensioner.

7. Install the power steering pump pulley and the serpentine drive belt.

8. Refill the power steering pump reservoir. Bleed the power steering system.

9. Connect the negative battery cable.

BELT ADJUSTMENT

The serpentine is self adjusting within the tensioner operating limits.

SYSTEM BLEEDING

1. Raise and support the vehicle safely. Fill the fluid reservoir.

2. Bleed the system by turning the wheels from side to side, without reaching the stop at either end. Keep the fluid level at the FULL COLD mark. Continue this until the air is eliminated from the fluid.

3. Start the Engine and run at fast idle. Recheck the fluid level.

4. Return the wheels to the center position and lower the vehicle.

5. Recheck the fluid level.

Tie Rod Ends

REMOVAL & INSTALLATION

1. Raise and safely support the vehicle.

2. Remove the cotter pin and loosen the jam nut from the outer tie rod end.

3. Disconnect the outer tie rod end from the steering knuckle, using the proper tool.

4. Matchmark the threads and disconnect the outer tie rod end from the inner tie rod. Remove the tie rod end.

5. Install the tie rod end to the matchmarks on the inner tie rod.

To install:

6. Install the tie rod end to the matchmarks on the inner tie rod. Tighten the hex nut to 35–45 ft. lbs. (47–61 Nm).

7. Connect the outer tie rod end to the steering knuckle.

8. Tighten the jam nut on the outer tie rod end. Install a new cotter pin.

9. Lower the vehicle.

BRAKES

Master Cylinder

REMOVAL & INSTALLATION

1. Disconnect the negative battery cable and, if equipped, the electrical connector from the level sensor unit.

NOTE: If equipped with Antilock Brake System (ABS), ensure that the hydraulic accumulator is fully depressurized before disconnecting any hydraulic lines, hoses or fittings.

2. Disconnect and plug hydraulic lines from the master cylinder.

3. Remove the mounting bolts and the master cylinder assembly.

To install:

4. Install the master cylinder assembly and mounting bolts.

5. Connect the hydraulic lines to the master cylinder.

6. Connect the negative battery cable and, if equipped, the electrical connector to the level sensor unit.

7. Refill the master cylinder with clean brake fluid. Bleed the brake system.

Proportioning Valve

REMOVAL & INSTALLATION

1. Disconnect the negative battery cable.

NOTE: If equipped with Anti-lock Brake System (ABS), ensure that the hydraulic accumulator is fully depressurized before disconnecting any hydraulic lines, hoses or fittings.

2. Disconnect and plug the brake lines at the master cylinder on the non-ABS models. On ABS equipped models, disconnect the front brake line from the proportioner valve and plug.

3. Remove the proportioner valve and O-ring assembly.

To install:

4. Install new O-rings on the proportioner valve.

5. Install the new valve(s) into the master cylinder on non-ABS system. If equipped with ABS, install the new valve(s) to brake lines.

6. Refill the master cylinder and bleed the brake system.

7. Connect the negative battery cable.

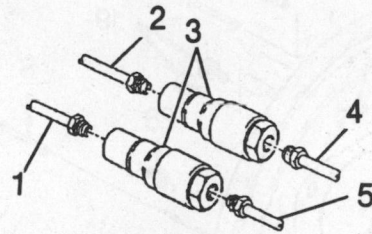

1. LR brake line
2. RR brake line
3. Brake proportioning valve
4. RH crossover pipe
5. Rear brake intermediate pipe

ABS equipped system proportioning valve

Power Brake Booster

REMOVAL & INSTALLATION

1. Disconnect the negative battery cable.

2. From inside the vehicle, detach the brake pushrod from the brake pedal.

3. Remove the master cylinder-to-power brake booster bolts and move the master cylinder aside.

4. Disconnect the vacuum hose from the power brake booster.

5. Remove the power brake booster-to-cowl nuts and the booster.

To install:

6. Install the booster and the power brake booster-to-cowl nuts.

7. Connect the vacuum hose to the power brake booster.

8. Move the master cylinder into position and install the master cylinder-to-power brake booster bolts.

9. From inside the vehicle, attach the brake pushrod to the brake pedal.

10. Connect the negative battery cable.

Brake Caliper

REMOVAL & INSTALLATION

NOTE: If equipped with Anti-lock Brake System (ABS), ensure that the hydraulic accumulator is fully depressurized before disconnecting any hydraulic lines, hoses or fittings.

1. Raise and safely support the vehicle. Remove the tire and wheel assembly.

2. Push the piston into caliper, using the proper tool, to provide clearance between the pad and the rotor.

3. Disconnect and plug the brake line and remove the mounting bolts and sleeves.

4. Remove the caliper from the rotor and the mounting bracket.

To install:

5. Install the caliper onto the rotor and mounting bracket.

6. Connect the brake line to the caliper.

7. Install the caliper mounting nuts and sleeves. Tighten the caliper mounting bolts to 38 ft. lbs. (52 Nm).

8. With the caliper mounting bolts tight, ensure that the brake line fitting is tight.

9. Install the tire and wheel assembly.

10. Lower the vehicle.

11. Check the brake fluid level in the reservoir.

12. Before starting the engine, depress the brake pedal until the pedal is firm. Bleed the brake system, as required.

13. Recheck the master cylinder fluid level.

Disc Brake Pads

REMOVAL & INSTALLATION

1. If the brake pads are to be re-

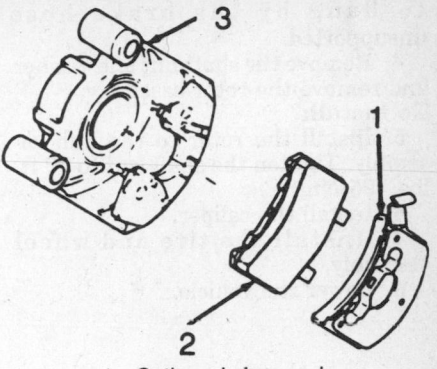

1. Outboard shoe and lining
2. Inboard shoe and lining
3. Caliper housing

Brake pad mounting

placed, use a syringe or similar tool to remove the brake fluid from the master cylinder reservoir until it is approximately ⅓–½ full.

2. Raise and safely support the vehicle. Remove the tire and wheel assembly.

3. Remove the caliper from the rotor and support the caliper out of the way.

4. Remove the brake pads from the caliper.

5. Using a C-clamp, press the piston into caliper to provide additional clearance between the pad and rotor for the new pads.

To install:

6. Install new bushings into the grooves in the mounting bolt holes. Install the inboard pad by snapping the retainer spring into the piston.

7. Install the outboard pad with the back of the pad flat against the caliper.

8. Install the caliper to the rotor. Install the caliper attaching bolts.

9. Install the tire and wheel assembly.

10. Check the brake fluid level in the master cylinder reservoir. Top-up as necessary.

11. Before starting the engine, slowly depress the brake pedal until the pedal is firm. Bleed the brake system, as required.

12. Recheck the master cylinder fluid level.

Brake Rotor

REMOVAL & INSTALLATION

1. Raise and safely support the vehicle. Remove the tire and wheel assembly.

2. Remove the caliper from the rotor. Support the caliper aside using a length of wire. Do not allow the caliper

to hang by the brake hose unsupported.

4. Remove the shaft nut and washer and remove the rotor assembly.

To install:

5. Install the rotor to the hub assembly. Tighten the shaft nut to 70 ft. lbs. (95 Nm).

6. Install the caliper.

7. Install the tire and wheel assembly.

8. Lower the vehicle.

Brake Drums

REMOVAL & INSTALLATION

1. Raise and safely support the vehicle.

2. Matchmark the wheel to the hub flange.

3. Remove the tire and wheel assembly. Matchmark the drum to the hub flange.

4. Remove the brake drum assembly. Make sure the parking brake is released.

To install:

5. Install the brake drum.

6. Install the tire and wheel assembly.

7. Lower the vehicle.

Brake Shoes

REMOVAL & INSTALLATION

1. Raise and safely support the vehicle. Remove the brake drum assembly.

2. Remove the actuator and the upper return spring with the proper tools.

3. Disconnect the spring connecting link, adjuster actuator and the hold-down washer.

4. Remove the hold-down springs and the pins. Disconnect the brake shoes from the parking brake cable.

5. Remove the brake shoe and lining assemblies.

To install:

6. Install the brake shoe and lining assemblies.

7. Connect the brake shoes to the parking brake cable. Install the brake shoe hold-down pins and springs.

8. Connect the hold-down washer, adjuster actuator and spring connecting link.

9. Install the upper return springs and actuator.

10. Install the brake drum.

11. Install the tire and wheel assembly.

12. Adjust the brakes.

13. Lower the vehicle and road test.

Wheel Cylinder

REMOVAL & INSTALLATION

1. Raise and safely support the vehicle. Remove the rear drum assembly.

2. Remove the brake shoe and lining assembly.

3. Disconnect and plug the inlet line. Remove the mounting screws and lockwashers.

4. Remove the wheel cylinder assembly.

To install:

5. Install the wheel cylinder assembly.

6. Install the mounting screws and lockwashers.

7. Install the brake shoe and lining assembly.

8. Install the brake drum.

9. Bleed the brake system. Check the brake fluid level in the master cylinder frequently while bleeding the system.

10. Lower the vehicle.

Parking Brake Cable

ADJUSTMENT

1. Adjust the rear brakes.

2. Apply and release the parking

1. Actuator spring
2. Upper shoe return spring
3. Spring connecting link
4. Adjuster actuator
5. Spring washer
6. Lower return spring
7. Hold-down spring assembly
8. Hold-down pin
9. Adjuster shoe and lining
10. Shoe and lining
11. Adjuster socket
12. Spring clip
13. Adjuster nut
14. Adjuster screw
15. Retaining ring

16. Pin
17. Spring washer
18. Park brake lever
19. Screw and lockwasher
20. Boot
21. Piston
22. Seal
23. Spring assembly
24. Bleeder valve
25. Wheel cylinder
26. Bleeder valve cap
27. Backing plate assembly
28. Access hole plug

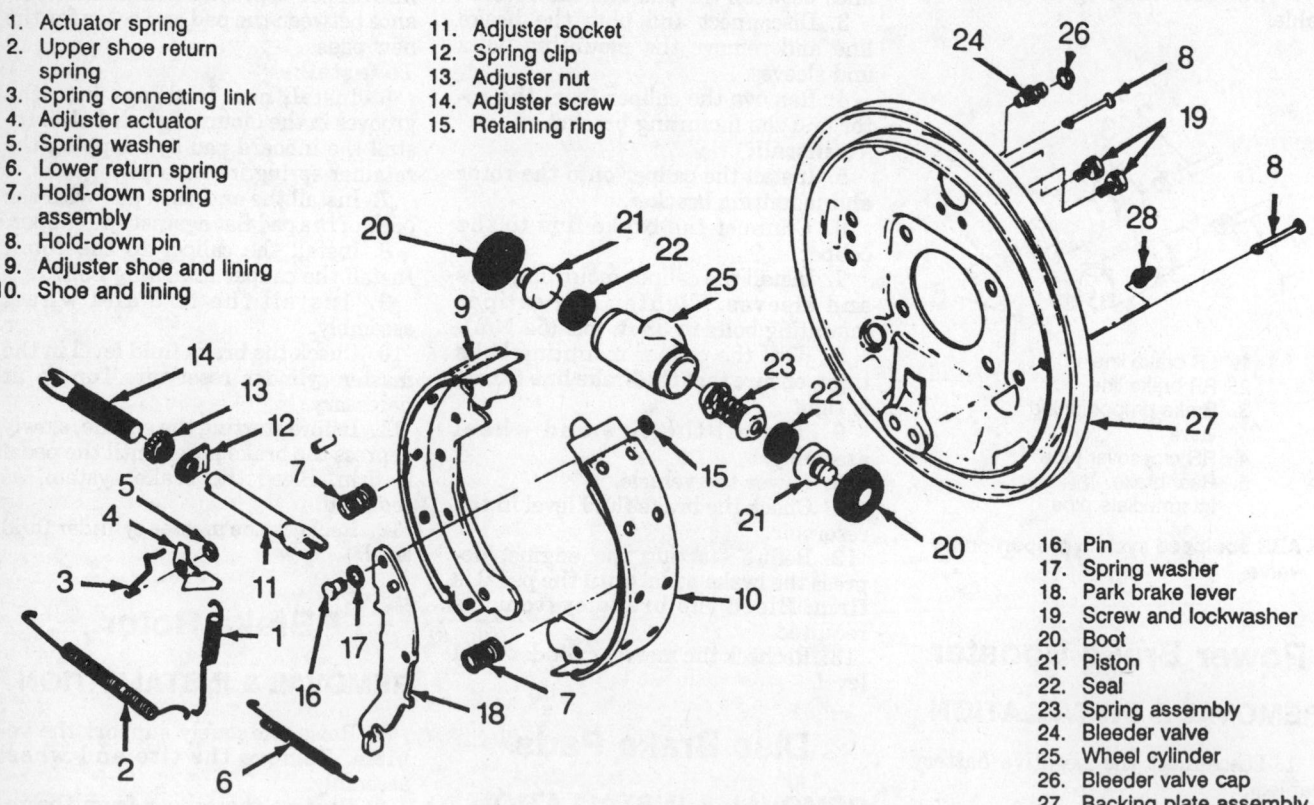

Exploded view of the rear brake assembly

brake 6 times to 10 clicks. Release the park brake pedal.

3. Raise and support the vehicle safely. Remove the access plug.

4. Adjust the park brake cable until a ⅛ drill can be inserted through the access hole into the space between the shoe web and the park brake lever.

5. Check for free wheel rotation. Replace the access plug.

6. Lower the vehicle.

REMOVAL & INSTALLATION

Front

1. Raise and safely support the vehicle.

2. Loosen the equalizer assembly at the front parking brake cable. Remove the front parking brake cable from the equalizer assembly.

3. Disconnect the cable casing retaining nut at the underbody. Remove the cable casing and cable from the control assembly.

To install:

4. Install the cable casing and cable to the control assembly. Connect the cable casing retaining nut at the underbody. Tighten the casing retaining nut to 22 ft. lbs. (30 Nm).

5. Install the front parking brake cable to the equalizer assembly. Tighten the equalizer assembly at the front parking brake cable.

6. Adjust the cable.

7. Lower the vehicle.

Intermediate

1. Raise and safely support the vehicle.

2. Disconnect the intermediate brake cable from the adjuster.

3. Remove the clip from the brake pipe retainer and cable and remove the cable from the rear equalizer.

4. Remove the cable from the bracket and from the brake pipe retainers.

To install:

5. Install the cable into the brake pipe retainers and snap the cable into the bracket.

6. Install the cable through the top support hole in the underbody.

7. Connect the left and right rear cables to the intermediate cable, utilizing the equalizer.

8. Install the clip around the cable and the brake pipe retainer and tighten the bolt to 17 inch lbs. (3 Nm).

9. Connect the cable to the adjuster and adjust the cable as necessary.

10. Lower the vehicle.

Rear

1. Raise and safely support the vehicle. Remove the tire and wheel assembly.

2. Remove the brake drum and insert the proper tool between the brake shoe and the top part of the actuator bracket.

3. Push the bracket to the front and release the top adjuster bracket rod.

4. Remove the rear hold-down spring, actuator lever and the lever return spring.

5. Disconnect the adjuster screw spring and remove the top rear brake shoe return spring.

6. Disconnect the parking brake cable from the parking brake lever.

7. Depress the conduit fitting retaining tangs and remove the conduit fitting from the backing plate.

8. Remove the left rear cable by backing off the equalizer nut and disconnecting the conduit from the under body bracket.

9. Remove the right rear cable by disconnecting the cable end button from the connector and remove the conduit fitting from the axle bracket.

To install:

10. Install the right rear cable by connecting the conduit fitting to the axle bracket and cable end button to the connector.

11. Install the left rear cable by connecting the conduit fitting to the axle bracket and the left cable to the equalizer nut. Connect the conduit fitting the underbody bracket.

12. Install the conduit fitting to the backing plate and connect the parking brake cable to the parking brake lever.

13. Install the top brake shoe return spring and the adjuster screw spring.

14. Replace the lever return spring, actuator lever and the rear hold-down spring.

15. Install the top adjuster bracket rod. Replace the brake drum assembly.

16. Install the tire and wheel assembly. Adjust the parking brake cable.

17. Lower the vehicle.

Brake System Bleeding

1. Fill the master cylinder reservoirs with brake fluid. Keep the level at least ½ full during the bleeding operation.

2. Disconnect and plug the brake lines. Fill the master cylinder until fluid begins to flow from the front pipe connector port.

3. Connect the brake lines to the master cylinder and tighten.

4. Depress the brake pedal slowly one time and hold, tighten the connection and then release the brake pedal slowly. Wait 15 seconds.

5. Repeat the sequence until all the air has been removed from the master cylinder bore.

6. After all the air has been re-moved from the front connections repeat the same procedure at the rear connections of the master cylinder.

7. Individual wheel cylinders and calipers are bled only after all the air has been removed from the master cylinder.

8. To bleed the caliper or the wheel cylinder perform the following:

a. Fill the master cylinder reservoirs with brake fluid. Keep the level at least ½ full during the bleeding operation.

b. Raise and support the vehicle safely. Attach a transparent tube over the bleeder screw.

c. Using an assistant, depress the brake pedal slowly, one time and hold.

d. Loosen the bleeder valve to purge the air from the cylinder.

e. Tighten the bleeder screw and slowly release the brake pedal. Wait 15 seconds.

f. Repeat this sequence until all the air is removed. The bleeding sequence is R/R, L/F, L/R and R/F.

g. Lower the vehicle and refill the master cylinder.

Anti-Lock Brake System Service

PRECAUTION

Failure to observe the following precautions may result in system damage.

● Before performing electric arc welding on the vehicle, disconnect the Electronic Brake Control Module (EBCM) and the hydraulic modulator connectors.

● When performing painting work on the vehicle, do not expose the Electronic Brake Control Module (EBCM) to temperatures in excess of 185°F (85°C) for longer than 2 hrs. The system may be exposed to temperatures up to 200°F (95°C) for less than 15 min.

● Never disconnect or connect the Electronic Brake Control Module (EBCM) or hydraulic modulator connectors with the ignition switch ON.

● Never disassemble any component of the Anti-Lock Brake System (ABS) which is designated non-serviceable; the component must be replaced as an assembly.

● When filling the master cylinder, always use Delco Supreme 11 brake fluid or equivalent, which meets DOT-3 specifications; petroleum base fluid will destroy the rubber parts.

RELIEVING ANTI-LOCK BRAKE SYSTEM PRESSURE

1. Disconnect the negative battery

cable. Turn the ignition to the **OFF** position.

2. Pump the brake pedal a minimum of 25 times.

3. When a definite increase in pedal effort is felt, stroke the pedal a few more times.

4. This should relieve all the hydraulic pressure from the system.

Hydraulic Unit (1989–90)

REMOVAL & INSTALLATION

1. Disconnect the negative battery cable.

2. Depressurize the hydraulic accumulator by applying and releasing the brake pedal a minimum of 20–25 times, using 50 lbs. of pedal force. A noticeable change in pedal feel will occur when the pressure is released.

3. Disconnect the electrical connectors at the hydraulic unit.

4. Remove the pump mounting bolts and move the energy unit to gain access to the brake lines.

5. Disconnect the brake lines at the valve block.

6. Remove the left and right sound insulators on Cadillac only.

7. Disconnect the pushrod from the brake pedal and push the dust boot forward past the hex on the pushrod.

8. Separate the pushrod halves by unthreading the 2 pieces.

9. From under the hood, remove the hydraulic unit-to-pushrod mounting bolts.

10. Remove the hydraulic unit from the vehicle, the front part of the push-

rod will remain locked into the hydraulic unit.

To install:

11. Install the hydraulic unit to the pushrod bracket. Tighten the support bolts to 37 ft. lbs. (50 Nm).

12. Install the pushrod halves by threading the 2 pieces together.

13. Install the pushrod to the brake pedal and reposition the dust boot.

14. Install the left and the right sound insulators on Cadillac only.

15. Connect the brake lines to the valve block and tighten to 11 ft. lbs.

16. Reposition the energy unit and replace the pump mounting bolts. Tighten to 71 inch lbs.

17. Connect the electrical connections at the hydraulic unit.

18. Connect the negative battery cable and bleed the brake system.

Pressure Modulator Valve (PMV) Assembly (1991–93)

REMOVAL & INSTALLATION

1. Disconnect the negative battery cable and remove the air cleaner assembly.

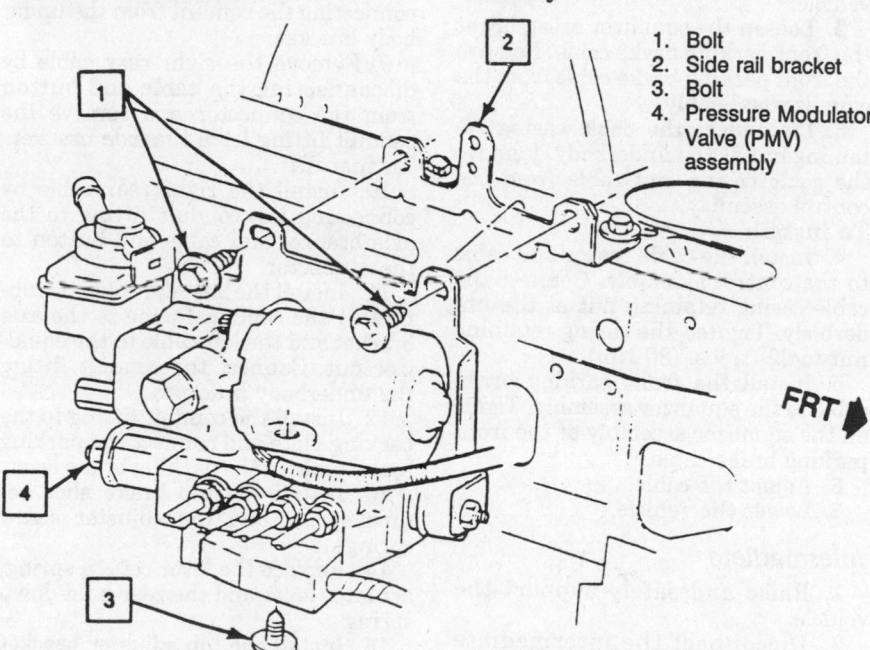

1. Bolt
2. Side rail bracket
3. Bolt
4. Pressure Modulator Valve (PMV) assembly

FRT ▶

Pressure Modulator Valve (PMV) assembly—1991–93 vehicles with ABS

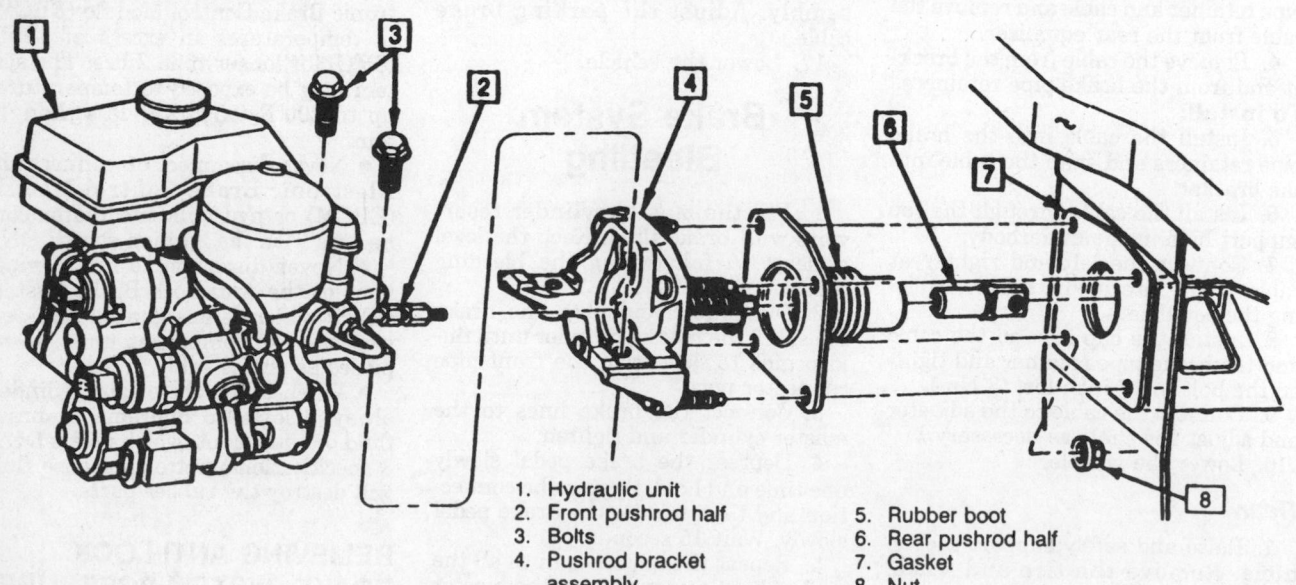

1. Hydraulic unit
2. Front pushrod half
3. Bolts
4. Pushrod bracket assembly
5. Rubber boot
6. Rear pushrod half
7. Gasket
8. Nut

Mounting of the hydraulic unit—1989–90 vehicles

2. Disconnect the PMV electrical connectors.

3. Remove the clamp on the PMV reservoir and disconnect the hose. Plug the hose to prevent loss of brake fluid.

4. Disconnect the brake lines from the PMV assembly.

5. Raise and safely support the vehicle. Remove the lower PMV assembly bolt. Lower the vehicle.

6. Remove the upper PMV assembly bolts and remove the PMV assembly from the vehicle.

To install:

7. Install the PMV assembly to the vehicle. Install the bolts and tighten the bolts to 20 ft. lbs. (27 Nm).

8. Install the lower PMV assembly bolt and tighten to 20 ft. lbs. (27 Nm).

9. Connect the brake lines to the PMV assembly and tighten to 11 ft. lbs. (15 Nm).

10. Connect the reservoir hose to the PMV reservoir and install the clamp.

11. Connect the electrical connectors to the PMV assembly.

12. Connect the negative battery cable and install the air cleaner assembly.

13. Fill the brake reservoir. Bleed the brake system.

Electronic Brake Control Module (EBCM)

REMOVAL & INSTALLATION

1. Disconnect the negative battery cable.

2. Lower the lower dash panel and disconnect the EBCM module from the bracket.

3. Disconnect the EBCM connector and remove the EBCM module.

To install:

4. Install the EBCM module and connect the EBCM electrical connector.

5. Connect the EBCM to the bracket and install the lower dash panel.

6. Connect the negative battery cable.

Wheel Speed Sensor

1989–90 VEHICLES

Removal and Installation

FRONT

1. Disconnect the negative battery cable.

2. Disconnect the sensor connector from the wiring harness.

3. Raise and safely support the vehicle. Remove the tire and wheel assembly.

4. Remove the sensor mounting screw and remove the sensor.

To install:

5. Install the sensor and sensor mounting screw.

6. Install the tire and wheel assembly. Lower the vehicle.

7. Connect the negative battery cable.

REAR

1. Disconnect the negative battery cable.

2. Disconnect the sensor connector located in the trunk.

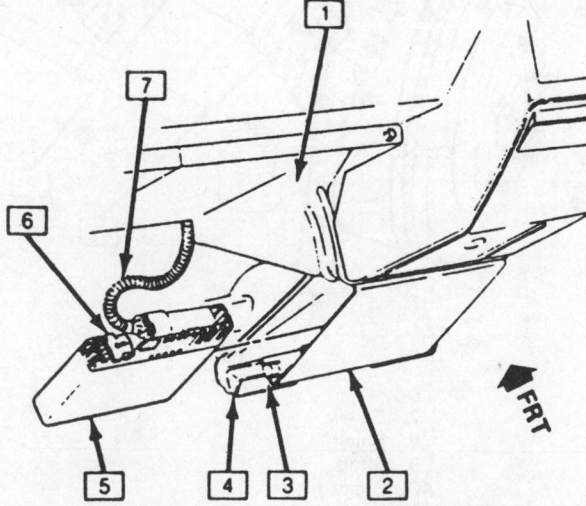

1. Right sound insulator
2. EBCM bracket
3. Locking tab
4. HVAC outlet
5. EBCM
6. Locking plate
7. EBCM harness

Location of the Electronic Brake Control Module (EBCM)—Cadillac equipped with ABS

3. Raise and safely support the vehicle. Remove the tire and wheel assembly.

4. Remove the grommet retaining screws.

5. Remove the sensor mounting bolts and remove the sensor.

To install:

6. Install the sensor and sensor mounting bolts.

7. Install the grommet retaining screws.

8. Install the tire and wheel assembly. Lower the vehicle.

9. Connect the sensor connector located in the trunk.

10. Connect the negative battery cable.

1991–93 VEHICLES

Removal and Installation

FRONT

1. Disconnect the negative battery cable.

2. Raise and safely support the vehicle. Remove the tire and wheel assembly.

3. Disconnect the wheel speed sensor electrical connector.

4. Remove the front hub and bearing assembly.

5. Pry the wheel speed sensor slinger off, using a screwdriver. Discard the old slinger.

6. Remove the sensor by gently prying the bearing assembly off.

To install:

7. Apply locking fixative to the groove in the outer diameter of the bearing hub.

8. Using tool J38764 or equivalent and a press, install the sensor.

9. Install the hub and bearing assembly and connect the sensor connector.

10. Install the tire and wheel assembly and lower the vehicle.

11. Connect the negative battery cable.

REAR

1. Disconnect the negative battery cable.

2. Raise and safely support the vehicle. Remove the tire and wheel assembly.

3. Disconnect the wheel speed sensor electrical connector.

4. Remove the rear hub and bearing assembly.

5. Remove the Torx screws and remove the sensor.

To install:

6. Install the sensor with O-ring intact.

7. Install the Torx screws and tighten to 33 inch lbs. (3.7 Nm).

8. Install the hub and bearing assembly.

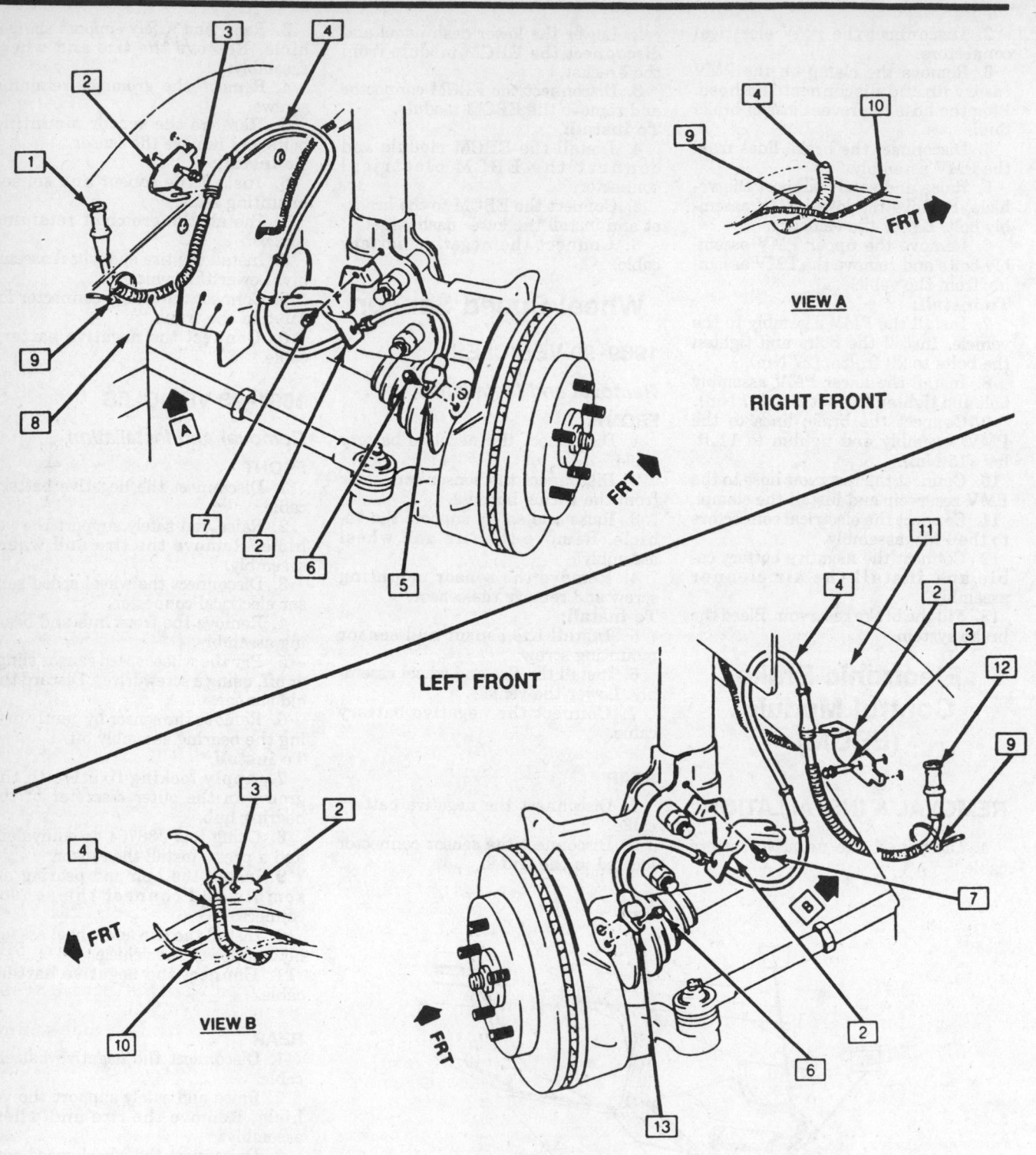

VIEW A

RIGHT FRONT

LEFT FRONT

VIEW B

FRT

1. Right wheel speed sensor connector
2. Bracket
3. Rivet
4. Wheel speed sensor lead
5. Right wheel speed sensor
6. Bolt
7. Screw
8. Shield
9. Strap
10. Brake pipe
11. Frame rail
12. Left wheel speed sensor connector
13. Left wheel speed sensor

Front wheel speed sensors—1989-90 vehicles

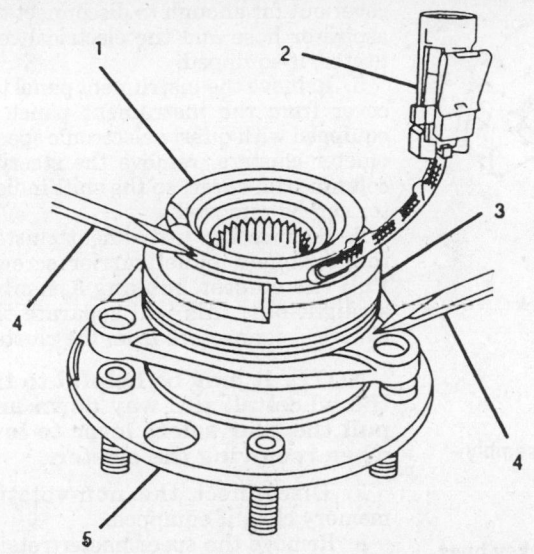

1. Wheel speed sensor slinger
2. Connector
3. Wheel speed sensor
4. Screwdriver
5. Hub and bearing assembly

Front Wheel Speed Sensor—1991–93 vehicles

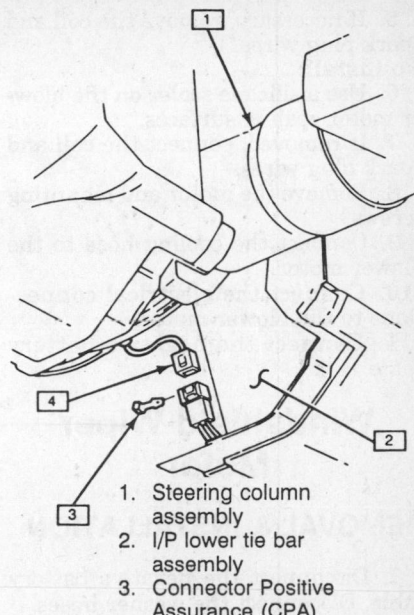

1. Steering column assembly
2. I/P lower tie bar assembly
3. Connector Positive Assurance (CPA)
4. Yellow SIR harness connector

Yellow 2-way SIR harness connector

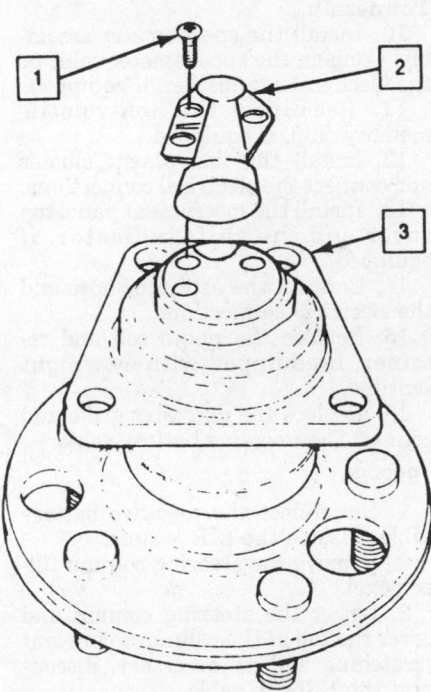

1. Screw
2. Wheel speed sensor
3. Hub

Rear Wheel Speed Sensor—1991–93 vehicles

9. Connect the wheel speed sensor electrical connector.
10. Install the tire and wheel assembly and lower the vehicle.
11. Connect the negative battery cable.

CHASSIS ELECTRICAL

Air Bag
CAUTION
Some vehicles are equipped with the Supplemental Inflatable Restraint (SIR) or air bag system. The SIR system must be disabled before performing service on or around SIR system components, steering column, instrument panel components, wiring and sensors. Failure to follow safety and disabling procedures could result in accidental air bag deployment, possible personal injury and unnecessary SIR system repairs.

PRECAUTIONS

Several precautions must be observed when handling the inflator module to avoid accidental deployment and possible personal injury.

● Never carry the inflator module by the wires or connector on the underside of the module.
● When carrying a live inflator module, hold securely with both hands, and ensure that the bag and trim cover are pointed away.
● Place the inflator module on a bench or other surface with the bag and trim cover facing up.
● With the inflator module on the bench, never place anything on or close to the module which may be thrown in the event of an accidental deployment.

DISABLING SIR SYSTEM

1. Disconnect the negative battery cable.
2. Remove the SIR fuse from the fuse panel.
3. Remove the left side sound insulator.
4. Remove the Connector Positive Assurance (CPA) from the yellow 2-way SIR harness connector at the base of the steering column and separate the connector.

ENABLING SIR SYSTEM

1. Connect the yellow 2-way SIR connector at the base of the steering column and insert the Connector Positive Assurance (CPA).
2. Install the left side sound insulator.
3. Install the SIR fuse in the fuse panel.
4. Connect the negative battery cable.

Heater Blower Motor

REMOVAL & INSTALLATION

1. Disconnect the negative battery cable.
2. Disconnect the electrical connections from the blower motor.
3. Disconnect the cooling hose from the blower motor.
4. Remove the mounting screws and the motor.

5. If necessary, remove the coil and spark plug wires.

To install:

6. Use a silicone sealer on the blower motor sealing surfaces.

7. If removed, connect the coil and spark plug wires.

8. Remove the motor and mounting screws.

9. Connect the cooling hose to the blower motor.

10. Connect the electrical connections to the blower motor.

11. Connect the negative battery cable.

Windshield Wiper Motor

REMOVAL & INSTALLATION

1. Disconnect the negative battery cable. Disconnect the washer hoses.

2. Remove the wiper arms and the air inlet screen assembly.

3. Disconnect the wiper arm drive link from the crank arm.

4. Disconnect the electrical connectors and remove the wiper motor mounting bolts.

5. Guide the crank arm through the hole in the dash and remove the motor.

To install:

6. Guide the crank arm through the hole in the dash and place the motor into position.

7. Install the wiper motor mounting bolts and connect the electrical connectors.

8. Connect the wiper arm drive link to the crank arm. Install the wiper arms and the air inlet screen assembly.

9. Connect the washer hoses and connect the negative battery cable.

Windshield Wiper Switch

REMOVAL & INSTALLATION

1. Disconnect the negative battery cable.

2. Remove the steering wheel, the cover and the lock plate assembly.

3. Remove the turn signal actuator arm, the lever and the hazard flasher button.

4. Remove the turn signal switch screws, the lower steering column trim panel and the steering column bracket bolts.

5. Disconnect the the turn signal switch and the wiper switch connectors.

6. Pull the turn signal switch rear-

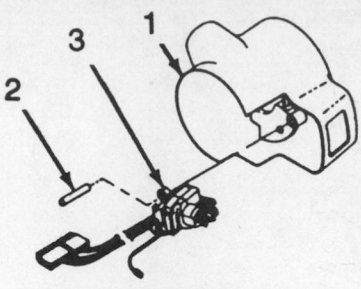

1. Cover assembly, lock housing
2. Pin, switch actuator pivot
3. Switch assembly, pivot and pulse

Windshield washer switch assembly— Cadillac

ward 6–8 inches, remove the key buzzer switch and cylinder lock assembly.

7. Remove and pull the steering column housing rearward. Remove the housing cover screw.

8. Remove the wiper switch pivot and the switch assembly.

To install:

9. Install the pivot and switch assembly.

10. Reposition and reinstall the steering column. Replace the housing cover screw.

11. Install the cylinder lock and key buzzer assembly. Reposition the turn signal switch.

12. Connect the turn signal switch and wiper switch connectors.

13. Install the steering column bracket bolts and the column trim panel.

14. Replace the turn signal switch screws.

15. Install the hazard flasher button, turn signal actuator arm and lever.

16. Install the lock plate assembly, cover and the steering wheel.

17. Connect the negative battery cable.

Instrument Cluster

REMOVAL & INSTALLATION

Except Cadillac

1989–91

1. Disconnect the negative battery cable. If equipped with SIR, disable the SIR system.

2. Remove the steering column filler panel.

2. Remove the instrument panel top cover-to-instrument panel screws.

3. If equipped with a twilight sentinel, pop up the photocell retainer and turn the photocell counterclockwise in the retainer and pull it down-and-out.

4. Slide the instrument panel top

cover out far enough to disconnect the aspirator hose and the electrical connector, if equipped.

5. Remove the instrument panel top cover from the instrument panel. If equipped with quartz electronic speedometer clusters, remove the steering column trim cover, so the shift indicator can be removed.

6. Remove the instrument cluster-to-instrument panel carrier screws. Pull the cluster housing assembly straight out; this will separate the electrical connectors from the cluster.

NOTE: It may be helpful to tilt the wheel all the way down and pull the gear select lever to low, when removing the cluster.

7. Disconnect the non-volatile memory chip, if equipped.

8. Remove the speedometer retaining screws and disconnect the speedometer cable or the electrical connection, if equipped.

9. Remove the speedometer assembly.

To install:

10. Install the speedometer assembly. Connect the speedometer cable or the electrical connection, if equipped.

11. Reconnect the non-volatile memory chip, if equipped.

12. Install the instrument cluster and connect the electrical connections.

13. Install the instrument panel top cover and the shift indicator, if equipped.

14. Connect the aspirator hose and the electrical connections.

15. Replace the photo cell and retainer, if equipped with a twilight sentinal.

16. Replace the defroster grille and connect the negative battery cable.

1992–93

1. Disconnect the negative battery cable. Disable the SIR system.

2. Remove the steering column filler panel.

3. Lower the steering column and cover the top of the column to prevent scratching and, if necessary, disconnect the PRNDL cable.

4. Remove the instrument panel trim plate by removing the screws and/or gently prying outward.

5. Remove the cluster to instrument panel screws and pull right end of cluster rearward.

6. Disconnect the cluster connector by reaching around cluster and depressing the locking tab on the connector.

7. Pull the bottom of the cluster rearward and rotate the assembly so it is facing up.

8. Remove the cluster assembly by sliding toward the center of the vehicle.

To install:

9. Install the cluster to the vehicle and rotate into the proper position.

10. Connect the cluster connector, being careful not to damage the connector.

11. Install the cluster to instrument panel screws and install the instrument panel cluster trim plate.

12. Remove the protective cover from the steering column, connect the PRNDL cable and raise the steering column to the proper position.

13. Enable the SIR system and connect the negative battery cable.

Cadillac

1. Disable the SIR system, if equipped, and disconnect the negative battery cable.

2. Remove the upper trim pad and remove the trim plate screws and the trim plate.

3. Remove the cluster mounting screws.

4. Disconnect the electrical connectors.

5. Remove the shift indicator cable clip.

6. Remove the instrument cluster.

NOTE: On a digital cluster, remove the memory chip for the season odometer before sending the unit to an authorized repair center. The printed circuit must be lifted to gain access to the memory chip.

7. Remove the lens mounting screws and the speedometer retaining screws.

8. Disconnect the speedometer cable or electrical connection, if equipped.

9. Remove the speedometer assembly.

To install:

10. Install the speedometer assembly. Connect the speedometer cable or electrical connection, if equipped.

11. Install the instrument cluster and connect the electrical connectors.

12. Install and adjust the shift indicator clip. Replace the cluster mounting screws.

13. Install the trim pad.

14. Enable the SIR system, if equipped, and connect the negative battery cable.

Radio

REMOVAL & INSTALLATION

1. Disconnect the negative battery cable.

2. Remove the radio trim plate and the mounting screws from the mounting bracket.

3. Disconnect the electrical connectors and remove the antenna lead.

4. Remove the bracket mounting nuts and the bracket.

5. Remove the radio.

To install:

6. Install the radio.

7. Install the bracket and bracket mounting nuts.

8. Connect the electrical connectors and the antenna lead.

9. Install the mounting screws to

the mounting bracket and install the radio trim plate.

10. Connect the negative battery cable.

Headlight Switch

REMOVAL & INSTALLATION

All Except 1991–93 Park Avenue

1. Disconnect the negative battery cable. Remove the steering column lower cover or the instrument panel trim plate covering the headlight switch, if equipped with a rocker-type headlight switch.

2. Disconnect the electrical harness retainer below headlight switch assembly. The switch connector is integral to the instrument panel. Pull the switch outward to disconnect it, except on Cadillac.

3. On Cadillac, depress spring loaded release button on top of headlight switch and remove switch, knob and rod assembly with the switch in the **ON** position.

4. Remove screw with ground wire at bottom of switch housing and all other mounting screws.

5. Pull assembly down and rearward, disconnect wiring harness connectors, bulb(s) and remove assembly.

To install:

6. Connect wiring harness connectors, bulb(s) and install the assembly.

7. Install the screw with ground wire at the bottom of switch housing and all other mounting screws.

8. Connect the electrical harness retainer below headlight switch assembly. Push the switch inward to connect it, except on Cadillac.

9. On Cadillac, install the switch, knob and rod assembly with the switch in the **ON** position.

10. Install the steering column lower cover or the instrument panel trim plate covering the headlight switch, if equipped with a rocker-type headlight switch.

11. Connect the negative battery cable.

1991–93 Park Avenue

1. Disconnect the negative battery cable.

2. Remove the driver's side door trim panel.

3. Remove the 2 head light switch to door panel attaching bolts and disconnect the electrical connector.

4. Remove the switch assembly.

To install:

5. Install the switch to the door panel and connect the electrical connector.

6. Remove the 2 bolts securing the switch to the door panel.

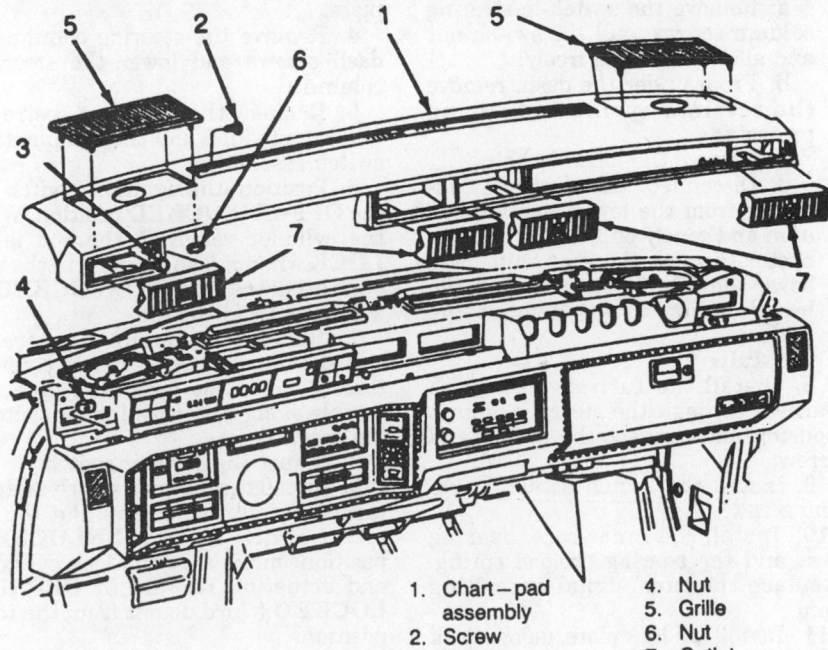

1. Chart–pad assembly	4. Nut
2. Screw	5. Grille
3. Screw	6. Nut
	7. Outlet

Upper trim panel—Cadillac

7. Install the driver's side door panel and connect the negative battery cable.

Dimmer Switch

The dimmer switch is attached to the lower portion of the steering column and is controlled by an actuator rod connected to the turn signal lever.

REMOVAL & INSTALLATION

1. Disconnect the negative battery cable.
2. Remove the left side sound insulator.
3. Lower the steering column trim plate.
4. Remove the steering column-to-dash screws and lower the steering column.
5. Position the ignition switch in the **OFF-UNLOCKED** position. With the cylinder removed, the rod is in **LOCK** when it is in the next to the uppermost detent; **OFF-UNLOCKED** is 2 detents from the top.
6. Remove the mounting screws and disconnect the electrical connectors. Remove the ignition switch assembly along with the dimmer switch.
7. To adjust the dimmer switch, perform the following procedures:
   a. Install the dimmer switch-to-steering column screws loosely.
   b. Position the switch to firmly contact the actuator rod.
   c. Tighten the screws and test the actuator smoothness in all the tilt positions, if equipped with tilt wheel.

To install:
8. Install the dimmer switch and attach the mounting screws. Put the ignition switch in **OFF-UNLOCKED** position; make sure the lock cylinder and actuating rod are in **OFF-UN-LOCKED** (third detent from the top) position.
9. Install the activating rod into the switch and assemble the switch on the column. Tighten the mounting screws.
10. Connect the electrical connections to the dimmer switch.
11. Position the steering column in place and install the column mounting screws.
12. Install the column trim plate and replace the sound insulator.
13. Connect the negative battery cable.

Turn Signal Switch

REMOVAL & INSTALLATION

1. Disconnect the negative battery cable and remove the steering wheel and the shroud.

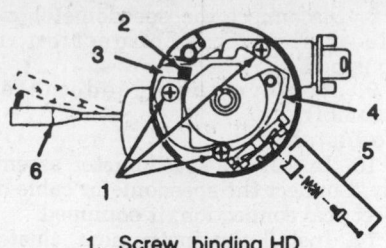

1. Screw, binding HD cross recess
2. Screw
3. Arm, signal switch
4. Switch assembly, turn signal
5. Multi-function lever
6. Hazard knob assembly

Turn signal switch

2. Remove the inflation restraint (air bag module) coil assembly-to-steering shaft lock screw (home boss) and retaining ring. Remove the coil assembly from the shaft and allow it to hang freely.
3. Using the lock plate compression tool or equivalent, position it on the end of the steering shaft and compress the lock plate by turning the shaft nut clockwise. Pry the wire snapring out of the shaft groove.
4. Remove the tool and lift the lock plate from the shaft.
5. Remove the cancelling cam, upper bearing preload spring, bearing seat and inner race from the shaft.
6. Position the turn signal switch in the right turn position. Remove the turn signal lever screw and the lever.
7. Remove the turn signal switch by performing the following:
   a. Remove the switch-to-steering column screws, pull the switch out and allow it to hang freely.
   b. From under the dash, remove the retainer spring and wiring protector.
   c. Remove the hazard knob.
   d. Disconnect the electrical connector from the lower steering column and gently pull the wiring connector through the gear shift lever bowl, the column housing and the lock housing cover. Remove the switch.

To install:
8. Install the turn signal switch harness through the steering column housing and connect the switch and screw.
9. Install the switch actuator arm and screw.
10. Install the inner race, bearing seat and the bearing preload spring. Replace the turn signal cancelling cam.
11. Install the lock plate, using a lock plate compression tool, compress the lock plate and install the shaft lock retaining ring.

12. Install the steering wheel and the shroud.
13. To install the inflation restraint coil, perform the following procedures:
   a. Install the home boss-to-steering column lock screw, allowing the hub to rotate.
   b. While holding the coil assembly (in one hand) with the steering wheel connector facing upwards, rotate the coil hub counterclockwise until it stops; the coil ribbon is now wound snug.
   c. Rotate the coil hub 2½ turns clockwise until the center lock hole is even with the notch in the coil housing.
   d. While holding the hub in position, install the lock screw into the center lock hole.
   e. Install the coil assembly using the horn tower on the inner ring cancelling cam and outer ring projections for alignment purposes.
14. Connect the negative battery cable.

Combination Switch

The combination switch is attached to the upper portion of the steering column and is part of the turn signal lever.

REMOVAL & INSTALLATION

1. Disconnect the negative terminal from the battery and disable the SIR system.
2. Remove the left side sound insulator.
3. Lower the steering column trim plate.
4. Remove the steering column-to-dash screws and lower the steering column.
5. Remove the inflation restraint (air bag module) and the combination switch assembly.
6. Position the ignition switch in the **OFF-UNLOCKED** position. With the cylinder removed, the rod is in **LOCK** when it is in the next to the uppermost detent; **OFF-UNLOCKED** is 2 detents from the top.
7. Remove the mounting screws and disconnect the electrical connectors. Remove the ignition switch assembly along with the dimmer switch.

To install:
8. Adjust the dimmer switch.
9. Install the dimmer switch and attach the mounting screws. Put the ignition switch in **OFF-UNLOCKED** position; make sure the lock cylinder and actuating rod are in **OFF-UN-LOCKED** (third detent from the top) position.
10. Install the activating rod into the switch and assemble the switch on the column. Tighten the mounting screws.

11. Connect the electrical connections at the dimmer switch.

12. Install the combination switch and replace the air bag module.

13. Position the steering column in place and install the column mounting screws.

14. Install the column trim plate and replace the sound insulator.

15. Connect the negative battery cable and enable the SIR system.

Ignition Switch

REMOVAL & INSTALLATION

1. Disconnect the negative battery cable and lower the steering column; be sure to properly support it.

2. Position the switch in the **OFF-UNLOCKED** position. With the lock cylinder removed, the rod is in **LOCK** when it is in the next to the uppermost detent; **OFF-UNLOCKED** is 2 detents from the top.

3. Remove both switch screws and the switch assembly.

To install:

4. Place the new switch in the **OFF-UNLOCKED** position. Ensure the lock cylinder and actuating rod are in **OFF-UNLOCKED** position (3rd detent from the top).

5. Install the actuating rod into the switch and assemble the switch on the column. Tighten the mounting screws.

NOTE: Use only the specified screws since over-length screws could impair the collapsibility of the column.

6. Install the steering column.

7. Connect the negative battery cable.

Ignition Lock

REMOVAL & INSTALLATION

1. Disconnect the negative battery cable and remove the turn signal switch assembly.

2. Remove the key from the lock cylinder. Remove the buzzer switch and clip.

3. Reinsert the key into the lock cylinder and turn it to the **LOCK** position.

4. Remove the cylinder lock-to-steering column screw and the lock set.

To install:

5. Install the cylinder lock and tighten the lock-to-steering column screw to 22 inch lbs.

6. Position the key in the **RUN** position and reverse the removal procedures. Tighten the turn signal switch-to-steering column screws to 30 inch

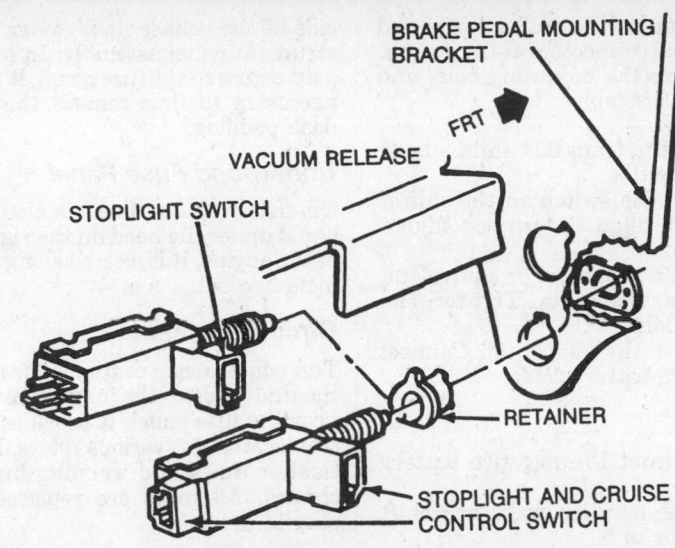

Stoplight switch location

lbs. and the turn signal lever screw to 20 inch lbs.

7. Connect the negative battery cable.

Stoplight Switch

ADJUSTMENT

1. Install the switch into the tubular clip until the switch assembly seats itself on the tubular clip.

2. Pull the brake pedal rearward against the pedal stop.

3. The switch will be moved in the tubular clip which will adjust itself properly.

4. The proper switch adjustment is achieved when no clicks are heard when the pedal is pulled upward and the brake lights stay OFF when the brake pedal is released.

REMOVAL & INSTALLATION

1. Disconnect the negative terminal from the battery. Remove the left side sound insulator if necessary.

2. Loosen the tubular clip from the stoplight switch assembly.

3. Disconnect the electrical connector from the rear of the switch assembly.

4. On 1991–93 vehicles, disconnect the vacuum hose from the switch.

5. Remove the stoplight switch from the vehicle.

To install:

6. Install the stoplight switch into the vehicle.

7. Connect the electrical connector to the rear of the switch assembly and connect the vacuum hose.

8. Tighten the tubular clip to the stoplight switch assembly.

9. Install the left side sound insula-

tor. Connect the negative battery cable.

Neutral Safety Switch

ADJUSTMENT

1. Disconnect the negative battery cable.

2. Place the transaxle shifter lever in the **N** position.

3. Loosen the switch mounting screws.

4. Rotate the switch on the shifter assembly to align the service adjustment holes.

5. Insert a gauge pin or equivalent, into the service slots. Tighten the mounting bolts.

6. Remove the gauge pin. Connect the negative battery cable.

REMOVAL & INSTALLATION

1989–90

1. Disconnect the negative battery cable.

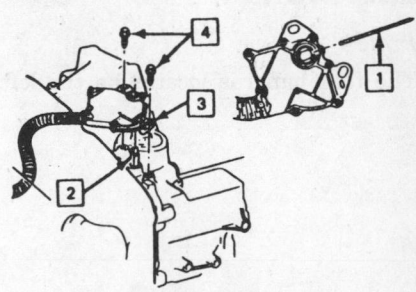

1. ³⁄₃₂ in. drill bit
2. Selector shaft
3. Neutral start and back up lamp switch
4. Bolts

Neutral safety switch adjustment

2. Disconnect the shift linkage and the electrical connectors at the switch.

3. Remove the mounting bolts and the switch assembly.

To install:

4. Place the transaxle shifter lever in the N position.

5. Rotate the switch on the shifter assembly to align the service adjustment holes.

6. Insert a gauge pin or equivalent, into the service slots. Tighten the mounting bolts.

7. Remove the gauge pin. Connect the negative battery cable.

1991–93

1. Disconnect the negative battery cable.

2. Set the parking brake and shift the indicator to **N**.

3. Remove the shifter/linkage cable nut and remove the bracket from the shaft.

4. Remove the 2 neutral safety switch bolts and disconnect the electrical connector.

5. Remove the nut on the starter that connects the cable to the neutral safety switch.

6. Remove the neutral safety switch from the vehicle.

To install:

7. Install the neutral safety switch to the vehicle.

8. Connect the electrical connectors and connect the cable to the starter.

9. Insert a gauge pin into the service slot to properly align switch.

10. Install the 2 bolts and tighten to 20 ft. lbs.

11. Remove the gauge pin and install the linkage cable bracket to the switch complete with the nut.

12. Connect the negative battery cable.

Fuses, Circuit Breakers and Relays

LOCATION

Fuses

The fuse panel is located on the left side of the vehicle. It is under the instrument panel assembly. In order to gain access to the fuse panel, it may be necessary to first remove the under dash padding.

Underhood Fuse Panel

On some vehicles there is also a fuse panel under the hood on the right side of the engine. It is located along the vehicle firewall.

Circuit Breakers

The convenience center is located on the underside of the instrument panel near the fuse panel. It provides a central location for various relays, hazard flasher units and warning buzzers/chimes. All units are replaced with plug-in modules.

Relays

The relay center is located on the right side of the instrument panel. The relay center is mounted behind the glove box assembly.

Computers

LOCATION

ECM

The electronic control module is located on the right side of the vehicle. It is positioned under the instrument panel. In order to gain access to electronic control module, it will be necessary to first remove the trim panel.

BCM

The body control module is located on the right side of the vehicle and positioned under the instrument panel. In order to gain access to body control module, it will be necessary to first remove the trim panel.

EBCM

The electronic brake control module is located on the right side of the vehicle and positioned under the right sound insulator panel. In order to gain access to electronic brake control module, it will be necessary to first remove the trim panel.

OLM

The oil life module is located on the right side of the vehicle, under the glove compartment. In order to gain access to the oil life module, the lower dash trim panel must first be removed.

HVAC Programmer

The heating and air conditioner controller (HVAC programmer) is located in the center of the vehicle below the dashboard. Access to the unit can be obtained from beneath the dashboard.

Flashers

LOCATION

The turn signal flasher unit is located behind the instrument panel near the steering column, along with the hazard flasher. It is secured in place with a plastic retainer. In order to gain access to components, it may first be necessary to remove certain under dash padding.

The hazard flasher is located on the fuse block. It is positioned on the lower right side corner of the fuse block assembly. In order to gain access to the turn signal flasher it may be necessary to first remove the under dash padding.

Cruise Control

ADJUSTMENT

1. Turn the ignition switch **OFF**.

2. Fully retract the idle speed control motor plunger.

NOTE: The throttle lever must not touch the idle speed control plunger.

3. Connect the cruise control cable to the hole in the servo blade that leaves the minimum slack.

4. Install the retainer at the servo.

GM "E", "K" & "V" Body

Front Wheel Drive

BUICK—Reatta • Riviera
CADILLAC—Allante • Eldorado • Seville
OLDSMOBILE—Toronado • Trofeo

SPECIFICATIONS

VEHICLE IDENTIFICATION CHART

It is important for servicing and ordering parts to be certain of the vehicle and engine identification. The VIN (vehicle identification number) is a 17 digit number visible through the windshield on the driver's side of the dash and contains the vehicle and engine identification codes. The tenth digit indicates model year and the eighth digit indicates engine code. It can be interpreted as follows:

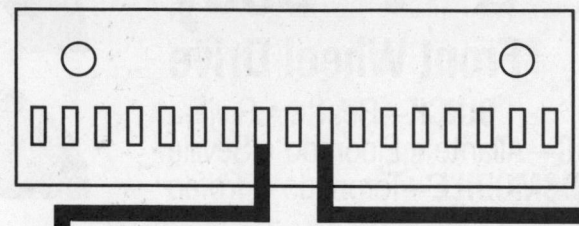

		Engine Code						Model Year	
Code	Liters	Cu. In. (cc)	Cyl.	Fuel Sys.	Eng. Mfg.		Code		Year
C	3.8	231 (3786)	6	SFI	Buick		K		1989
L	3.8	231 (3786)	6	SFI	Buick		L		1990
5	4.5	273 (4474)	8	TBI	Cadillac		M		1991
8	4.5	273 (4474)	8	SFI	Cadillac		N		1992
3	4.5	273 (4474)	8	SFI	Cadillac		P		1993
B	4.9	300 (4917)	8	SFI	Cadillac				
9	4.6	279 (4573)	8	SFI	Cadillac				

SFI—Sequential Fuel Injection
TBI—Throttle Body Injection

ENGINE IDENTIFICATION

Year	Model	Engine Displacement Liters (cc)	Engine Series (ID/VIN)	Fuel System	No. of Cylinders	Engine Type
1989	Allante	4.5 (4474)	8	SFI	8	OHV
	Eldorado	4.5 (4474)	5	TBI	8	OHV
	Reatta	3.8 (3786)	C	SFI	6	OHV
	Riviera	3.8 (3786)	C	SFI	6	OHV
	Seville	4.5 (4474)	5	TBI	8	OHV
	Toronado	3.8 (3786)	C	SFI	6	OHV
1990	Allante	4.5 (4474)	8	SFI	8	OHV
	Eldorado	4.5 (4474)	3	SFI	8	OHV
	Reatta	3.8 (3786)	C	SFI	6	OHV
	Riviera	3.8 (3786)	C	SFI	6	OHV
	Seville	4.5 (4474)	3	SFI	8	OHV
	Toronado	3.8 (3786)	C	SFI	6	OHV
	Trofeo	3.8 (3786)	C	SFI	6	OHV

ENGINE IDENTIFICATION

Year	Model	Engine Displacement Liters (cc)	Engine Series (ID/VIN)	Fuel System	No. of Cylinders	Engine Type
1991	Allante	4.5 (4474)	8	SFI	8	OHV
	Eldorado	4.9 (4917)	B	SFI	8	OHV
	Reatta	3.8 (3786)	C	SFI	6	OHV
	Riviera	3.8 (3786)	C	SFI	6	OHV
	Seville	4.9 (4917)	B	SFI	8	OHV
	Toronado	3.8 (3786)	C	SFI	6	OHV
	Trofeo	3.8 (3786)	C	SFI	6	OHV
1992–93	Allante	4.5 (4474)	8	SFI	8	OHV
	Allante	4.6 (4573)	9	SFI	8	OHV
	Eldorado	4.9 (4917)	B	SFI	8	OHV
	Riviera	3.8 (3786)	L	SFI	6	OHV
	Seville	4.9 (4917)	B	SFI	8	OHV
	Toronado	3.8 (3786)	L	SFI	6	OHV

OHV—Overhead Valve
SFI—Sequential Fuel Injection
TBI—Throttle Body Injection

GENERAL ENGINE SPECIFICATIONS

Year	Engine ID/VIN	Engine Displacement Liters (cc)	Fuel System Type	Net Horsepower @ rpm	Net Torque @ rpm (ft. lbs.)	Bore × Stroke (in.)	Compression Ratio	Oil Pressure @ rpm
1989	C	3.8 (3786)	SFI	165 @ 5200	210 @ 2000	3.800 × 3.400	8.5:1	37 @ 2400
	5	4.5 (4474)	TBI	155 @ 4200	240 @ 2800	3.620 × 3.310	9.0:1	①
	8	4.5 (4474)	SFI	200 @ 4400	270 @ 3200	3.620 × 3.310	9.0:1	①
1990	C	3.8 (3786)	SFI	165 @ 5200	210 @ 2000	3.800 × 3.400	8.5:1	37 @ 2400
	8	4.5 (4474)	SFI	200 @ 4400	230 @ 3200	3.620 × 3.310	9.0:1	①
	3	4.5 (4474)	SFI	180 @ 4000	245 @ 3000	3.620 × 3.310	9.5:1	①
1991	C	3.8 (3786)	SFI	165 @ 4800	210 @ 2000	3.800 × 3.400	8.5:1	40 @ 1850
	8	4.5 (4474)	SFI	200 @ 4400	270 @ 3200	3.620 × 3.310	9.0:1	①
	B	4.9 (4917)	SFI	200 @ 4100	275 @ 3000	3.620 × 3.620	9.5:1	53 @ 2000
1992–93	L	3.8 (3786)	SFI	170 @ 4800	220 @ 3200	3.800 × 3.400	8.5:1	60 @ 1850
	8	4.5 (4474)	SFI	200 @ 4400	270 @ 3200	3.620 × 3.310	9.0:1	①
	9	4.6 (4573)	SFI	290 @ 5600	290 @ 4400	3.660 × 3.310	10.3:1	35 @ 2000
	B	4.9 (4917)	SFI	200 @ 4100	275 @ 3000	3.620 × 3.620	9.5:1	53 @ 2000

NOTE: Horsepower and torque are SAE net figures. They are measured at the rear of the transmission with all accessories installed and operating. Since the figures vary when a given engine is installed in different models, some are representative rather than exact.
SFI—Sequential Fuel Injection
TBI—Throttle Body Injection
① 26–30 psi at 30 mph at normal operating temperature

GASOLINE ENGINE TUNE-UP SPECIFICATIONS

Year	Engine ID/VIN	Engine Displacement Liters (cc)	Spark Plugs Gap (in.)	Ignition Timing (deg.) MT	Ignition Timing (deg.) AT	Fuel Pump (psi)	Idle Speed (rpm) MT	Idle Speed (rpm) AT	Valve Clearance In.	Valve Clearance Ex.
1989	C	3.8 (3786)	0.060	—	①	31–42 ②	—	①	Hyd.	Hyd.
	5	4.5 (4474)	0.060	—	①	9–12	—	①	Hyd.	Hyd.
	8	4.5 (4474)	0.060	—	①	40–50	—	①	Hyd.	Hyd.
1990	C	3.8 (3786)	0.060	—	①	③	—	①	Hyd.	Hyd.
	8	4.5 (4474)	0.060	—	①	40–50	—	①	Hyd.	Hyd.
	3	4.5 (4474)	0.060	—	①	40–50	—	①	Hyd.	Hyd.
1991	C	3.8 (3786)	0.060	—	①	③	—	①	Hyd.	Hyd.
	8	4.5 (4474)	0.060	—	①	40–50	—	①	Hyd.	Hyd.
	B	4.9 (4917)	0.060	—	①	40–50	—	①	Hyd.	Hyd.
1992	C	3.8 (3786)	0.060	—	①	③	—	①	Hyd.	Hyd.
	8	4.5 (4474)	0.060	—	①	40–50	—	①	Hyd.	Hyd.
	B	4.9 (4917)	0.060	—	①	40–50	—	①	Hyd.	Hyd.
1993	REFER TO UNDERHOOD SPECIFICATIONS STICKER									

NOTE: The lowest cylinder pressure should be within 75% of the highest cylinder pressure reading. For example, if the highest cylinder is 134 psi, the lowest should be 101. Engine should be at normal operating temperature with throttle valve in the wide open position.
The underhood specifications sticker often reflects tune-up specification changes in production. Sticker figures must be used if they disagree with those in this chart.
Hyd.—Hydraulic
① Controlled by ECM
② Engine idling at normal operating temp.
③ 1—Connect fuel pressure gauge, engine at normal operating temperature
2—Turn ignition switch on
3—After approx. 2 seconds pressure should read 41–47 psi and hold steady
4—Start engine and idle, pressure should drop 3–10 psi from static pressure

FIRING ORDERS

NOTE: To avoid confusion, always replace spark plug wires one at a time.

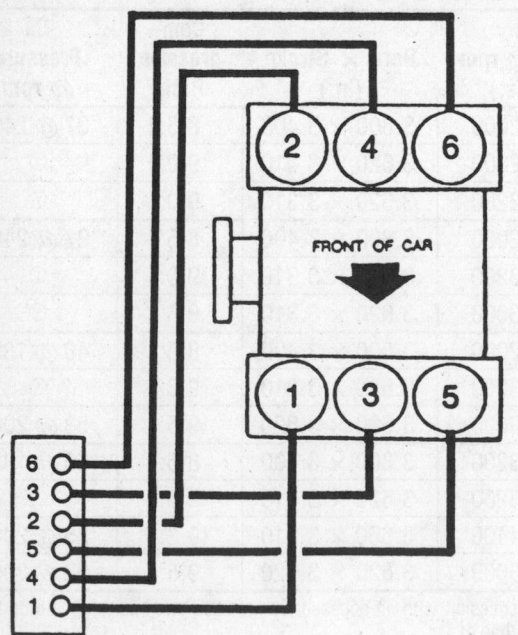

3.8L Engine VIN L
Engine Firing Order: 1–6–5–4–3–2
Distributorless Ignition System

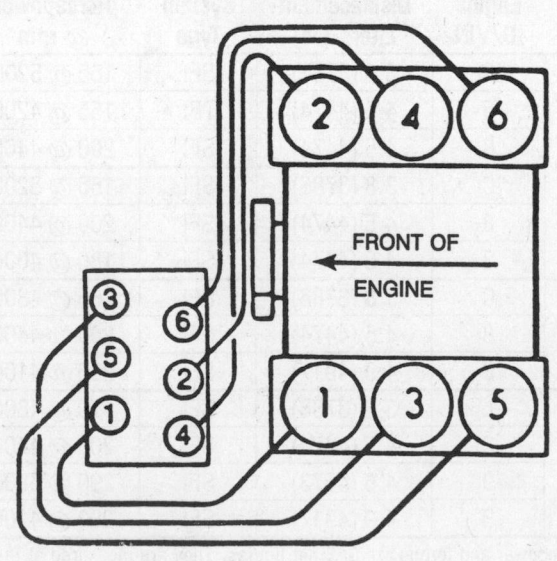

3.8L Engine VIN C
Engine Firing Order: 1–6–5–4–3–2
Distributorless Ignition System

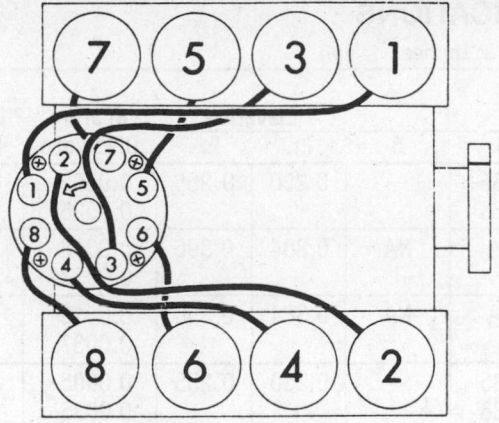

4.5L and 4.9L Engines
Engine Firing Order: 1–8–4–3–6–5–7–2
Distributor Rotation: Counterclockwise

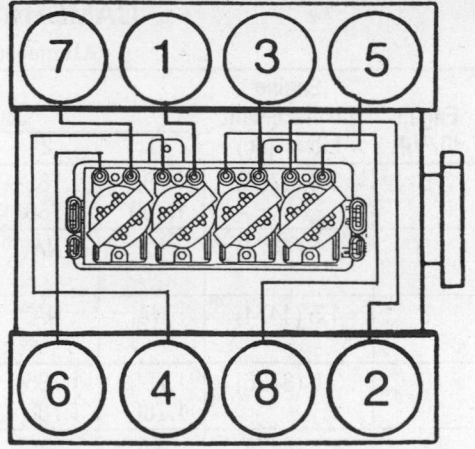

4.6L Engine VIN 9
Engine Firing Order: 1–2–7–3–4–5–6–8
Distributorless Ignition System

CAPACITIES

Year	Model	Engine ID/VIN	Engine Displacement Liters (cc)	Engine Crankcase (qts.) with Filter	Transmission (pts.) 4-Spd	5-Spd	Auto.	Transfer case (pts.)	Drive Axle Front (pts.)	Rear (pts.)	Fuel Tank (gal.)	Cooling System (qts.)
1989	Allante	5	4.5 (4474)	5.5	—	—	13	—	—	—	22	12.1
	Eldorado	5	4.5 (4474)	5.5	—	—	13	—	—	—	18.8	12
	Reatta	C	3.8 (3786)	5.0	—	—	12	—	—	—	18	13
	Riviera	C	3.8 (3786)	5.0	—	—	12	—	—	—	18	13
	Seville	5	4.5 (4474)	5.5	—	—	13	—	—	—	18.8	12.1
	Toronado	C	3.8 (3786)	5.0	—	—	12	—	—	—	18	13
1990	Allante	8	4.5 (4474)	5.5	—	—	13	—	—	—	22	12.1
	Eldorado	3	4.5 (4474)	5.5	—	—	13	—	—	—	18.8	12.1
	Reatta	C	3.8 (3786)	5.0	—	—	12	—	—	—	18	13
	Riviera	C	3.8 (3786)	5.0	—	—	12	—	—	—	18	13
	Seville	3	4.5 (4474)	5.5	—	—	13	—	—	—	18.8	12.1
	Toronado	C	3.8 (3786)	5.0	—	—	12	—	—	—	18	13
	Trofeo	C	3.8 (3786)	5.0	—	—	12	—	—	—	18	13
1991	Allante	8	4.5 (4474)	6.5	—	—	13	—	—	—	22	12.1
	Eldorado	B	4.5 (4474)	5.5	—	—	13	—	—	—	18.8	12.1
	Reatta	C	3.8 (3786)	5.0	—	—	12	—	—	—	18	13
	Riviera	C	3.8 (3786)	5.0	—	—	12	—	—	—	18	13
	Seville	B	4.9 (4917)	5.5	—	—	13	—	—	—	18.8	12.1
	Toronado	C	3.8 (3786)	5.0	—	—	12	—	—	—	18	13
	Trofeo	C	3.8 (3786)	5.0	—	—	12	—	—	—	18	13
1992–93	Allante	8	4.5 (4474)	6.5	—	—	13	—	—	—	22	12.1
	Allante	9	4.6 (4573)	7.5	—	—	13	—	—	—	22	12.5
	Eldorado	B	4.9 (4917)	5.5	—	—	13	—	—	—	18.8	12.1
	Riviera	L	3.8 (3786)	5.0	—	—	13	—	—	—	18	13
	Seville	B	4.9 (4917)	5.5	—	—	13	—	—	—	18.8	12.1
	Toronado	L	3.8 (3786)	5.0	—	—	13	—	—	—	18	13
	Trofeo	L	3.8 (3786)	5.0	—	—	13	—	—	—	18	13

CAMSHAFT SPECIFICATIONS

All measurements given in inches.

Year	Engine ID/VIN	Engine Displacement Liters (cc)	Journal Diameter 1	2	3	4	5	Elevation In.	Ex.	Bearing Clearance	Camshaft End Play
1989	C	3.8 (3786)	1.785–1.786	1.785–1.786	1.785–1.786	1.785–1.786	—	0.250	0.255	0.0005–0.0035	NA
	5	4.5 (4474)	NA	NA	NA	NA	NA	0.384	0.396	0.0018–0.0037	NA
	8	4.5 (4474)	NA	NA	NA	NA	NA	0.384	0.396	0.0018–0.0037	NA
1990	C	3.8 (3786)	1.785–1.786	1.785–1.786	1.785–1.786	1.785–1.786	—	0.250	0.255	0.0005–0.0035	NA
	8	4.5 (4474)	NA	NA	NA	NA	NA	0.384	0.396	0.0018–0.0037	NA
	3	4.5 (4474)	NA	NA	NA	NA	NA	0.384	0.396	0.0018–0.0037	NA
1991	C	3.8 (3786)	1.785–1.786	1.785–1.786	1.785–1.786	1.785–1.786	—	0.250	0.255	0.0005–0.0035	NA
	8	4.5 (4474)	NA	NA	NA	NA	NA	0.384	0.396	0.0018–0.0037	NA
	B	4.9 (4917)	NA	NA	NA	NA	NA	0.384	0.396	0.0018–0.0037	NA
1992–93	L	3.8 (3786)	1.785–1.786	1.785–1.786	1.785–1.786	1.785–1.786	—	0.250	0.255	0.0005–0.0035	NA
	8	4.5 (4474)	NA	NA	NA	NA	NA	0.384	0.396	0.0018–0.0037	NA
	9	4.6 (4573)	1.061–1.062	1.061–1.062	1.061–1.062	1.061–1.062	1.061–1.062	0.370	0.339	0.0020–0.0030	NA
	B	4.9 (4917)	NA	NA	NA	NA	NA	0.384	0.396	0.0018–0.0037	NA

NA—Not available

CRANKSHAFT AND CONNECTING ROD SPECIFICATIONS

All measurements are given in inches.

Year	Engine ID/VIN	Engine Displacement Liters (cc)	Crankshaft Main Brg. Journal Dia.	Main Brg. Oil Clearance	Shaft End-play	Thrust on No.	Connecting Rod Journal Diameter	Oil Clearance	Side Clearance
1989	C	3.8 (3786)	2.4988–2.4998	0.0018–0.0030	0.003–0.011	2	2.2487–2.2499	0.0003–0.0028	0.003–0.015
	5	4.5 (4474)	2.6350–2.6360	0.0016–0.0039 ①	0.001–0.007	3	1.9270	0.0005–0.0028	0.008–0.020
	8	4.5 (4474)	2.6350–2.6360	0.0016–0.0039 ①	0.001–0.007	3	1.9270	0.0005–0.0028	0.008–0.020
1990	C	3.8 (3786)	2.4988–2.4998	0.0018–0.0030	0.003–0.011	2	2.2487–2.2499	0.0003–0.0028	0.003–0.015
	8	4.5 (4474)	2.6350–2.6360	0.0016–0.0039 ①	0.001–0.007	3	1.9270	0.0005–0.0028	0.008–0.020
	3	4.5 (4474)	2.6350–2.6360	0.0016–0.0039 ①	0.001–0.007	3	1.9270	0.0005–0.0028	0.008–0.020

CRANKSHAFT AND CONNECTING ROD SPECIFICATIONS

All measurements are given in inches.

Year	Engine ID/VIN	Engine Displacement Liters (cc)	Crankshaft Main Brg. Journal Dia.	Crankshaft Main Brg. Oil Clearance	Crankshaft Shaft End-play	Crankshaft Thrust on No.	Connecting Rod Journal Diameter	Connecting Rod Oil Clearance	Connecting Rod Side Clearance
1991	C	3.8 (3786)	2.4988–2.4998	0.0018–0.0030	0.003–0.011	2	2.2487–2.2499	0.0003–0.0028	0.003–0.015
	8	4.5 (4474)	2.6350–2.6360	0.0016–0.0039 ①	0.001–0.007	3	1.9270–1.9280	0.0005–0.0028	0.008–0.020
	B	4.9 (4917)	2.6350–2.6360	0.0016–0.0039 ①	0.001–0.008	3	1.9270–1.9280	0.0005–0.0028	0.008–0.020
1992–93	L	3.8 (3786)	2.4988–2.4998	0.0018–0.0030	0.003–0.011	2	2.2487–2.2499	0.0003–0.0028	0.003–0.015
	8	4.5 (4474)	2.6350–2.6360	0.0016–0.0039 ①	0.001–0.007	3	1.9270–1.9280	0.0005–0.0028	0.008–0.020
	9	4.6 (4573)	2.5195–2.5205	NA	0.002–0.019	3	NA	0.0010–0.0030	0.008–0.020
	B	4.9 (4917)	2.6350–2.6360	0.0016–0.0039 ①	0.001–0.008	3	1.9270–1.9280	0.0005–0.0028	0.008–0.020

NA—Not available
① No. 1—0.0008–0.0031

VALVE SPECIFICATIONS

Year	Engine ID/VIN	Engine Displacement Liters (cc)	Seat Angle (deg.)	Face Angle (deg.)	Spring Test Pressure (lbs. @ in.)	Spring Installed Height (in.)	Stem-to-Guide Clearance (in.) Intake	Stem-to-Guide Clearance (in.) Exhaust	Stem Diameter (in.) Intake	Stem Diameter (in.) Exhaust
1989	C	3.8 (3786)	45	45	200–220 @ 1.315 ①	1.690–1.750	0.0015–0.0035	0.0015–0.0032	NA	NA
	5	4.5 (4474)	45	44	204–221 @ 1.28 ①	2.216 ②	0.0010–0.0030	0.0010–0.0030	0.3413–0.3420	0.3401–0.3408
	8	4.5 (4474)	45	44	204–221 @ 1.28 ①	2.216 ②	0.0010–0.0030	0.0010–0.0030	0.3413–0.3420	0.3401–0.3408
1990	C	3.8 (3786)	45	45	200–220 @ 1.315 ①	1.690–1.750	0.0015–0.0035	0.0015–0.0032	NA	NA
	8	4.5 (4474)	45	44	204–221 @ 1.28 ①	2.216 ②	0.0010–0.0030	0.0010–0.0030	0.3413–0.3420	0.3401–0.3408
	3	4.5 (4474)	45	44	214–232 @ 1.35 ①	2.216 ②	0.0010–0.0030	0.0010–0.0030	0.3413–0.3420	0.3401–0.3408
1991	C	3.8 (3786)	45	45	200–220 @ 1.315 ①	1.690–1.720	0.0015–0.0035	0.0015–0.0032	NA	NA
	8	4.5 (4474)	45	44	204–221 @ 1.28	2.216 ②	0.0010–0.0030	0.0020–0.0040	0.3413–0.3420	0.3401–0.3408
	B	4.9 (4917)	45	45	214–232 @ 1.35	1.949 ②	0.0010–0.0030	0.0020–0.0040	0.3413–0.3420	0.3401–0.3408
1992–93	L	3.8 (3786)	45	45	200–220 @ 1.315 ①	1.690–1.720	0.0015–0.0035	0.0015–0.0032	NA	NA
	8	4.5 (4474)	45	44	204–221 @ 1.28	2.216 ②	0.0010–0.0030	0.0020–0.0040	0.3413–0.3420	0.3401–0.3408
	9	4.6 (4573)	46	45	NA	1.190 ②	0.0010–0.0030	0.0020–0.0040	0.2331–0.2339	0.2331–0.2339
	B	4.9 (4917)	45	45	214–232 @ 1.35	1.949 ②	0.0010–0.0030	0.0020–0.0040	0.3413–0.3420	0.3401–0.3408

NA—Not available ② Free length
① Load open

PISTON AND RING SPECIFICATIONS

All measurements are given in inches.

Year	Engine ID/VIN	Engine Displacement Liters (cc)	Piston Clearance	Ring Gap Top Compression	Ring Gap Bottom Compression	Ring Gap Oil Control	Ring Side Clearance Top Compression	Ring Side Clearance Bottom Compression	Ring Side Clearance Oil Control
1989	C	3.8 (3786)	0.0004–0.0022 ①	0.010–0.025	0.010–0.025	0.015–0.055	0.0013–0.0031	0.0013–0.0031	0.0011–0.0081
	5	4.5 (4474)	0.0010–0.0018	0.015–0.024	0.015–0.024	0.010–0.050	0.0016–0.0037	0.0016–0.0037	②
	8	4.5 (4474)	0.0010–0.0018	0.015–0.024	0.015–0.024	0.010–0.050	0.0016–0.0037	0.0016–0.0037	②
1990	C	3.8 (3786)	0.0004–0.0022 ①	0.010–0.025	0.010–0.025	0.015–0.055	0.0013–0.0031	0.0013–0.0031	0.0011–0.0081
	8	4.5 (4474)	0.0010–0.0018	0.015–0.024	0.015–0.024	0.010–0.050	0.0016–0.0037	0.0016–0.0037	②
	3	4.5 (4474)	0.0010–0.0018	0.015–0.024	0.015–0.024	0.010–0.050	0.0016–0.0037	0.0016–0.0037	②
1991	C	3.8 (3786)	0.0004–0.0022 ①	0.010–0.025	0.010–0.025	0.015–0.055	0.0013–0.0031	0.0013–0.0031	0.0011–0.0081
	8	4.5 (4474)	0.0010–0.0018	0.015–0.024	0.015–0.024	0.010–0.050	0.0016–0.0037	0.0016–0.0037	②
	B	4.9 (4917)	0.0004–0.0020	0.012–0.022	0.012–0.022	0.004–0.020	0.0016–0.0037	0.0016–0.0037	②
1992–93	L	3.8 (3786)	0.0004–0.0022 ①	0.010–0.025	0.010–0.025	0.015–0.055	0.0013–0.0031	0.0013–0.0031	0.0011–0.0081
	8	4.5 (4474)	0.0010–0.0018	0.015–0.024	0.015–0.024	0.010–0.050	0.0016–0.0037	0.0016–0.0037	②
	9	4.6 (4573)	0.0004–0.0020	NA	NA	NA	NA	NA	②
	B	4.9 (4917)	0.0004–0.0020	0.012–0.022	0.012–0.022	0.004–0.020	0.0016–0.0037	0.0016–0.0037	②

① 44mm from top of piston
② None, side sealing

TORQUE SPECIFICATIONS

All readings in ft. lbs.

Year	Engine ID/VIN	Engine Displacement Liters (cc)	Cylinder Head Bolts	Main Bearing Bolts	Rod Bearing Bolts	Crankshaft Damper Bolts	Flywheel Bolts	Manifold Intake	Manifold Exhaust	Spark Plugs	Lug Nut
1989	C	3.8 (3786)	③	90	43	219⑤	61	88⑥	41	20	100
	5	4.5 (4474)	②	85	24④	18	70	⑧	18	11	100
	8	4.5 (4474)	②	85	24④	18	70	⑧	18	11	100
1990	C	3.8 (3786)	③	90	43	219⑤	61	88⑥	41	20	100
	8	4.5 (4474)	②	85	24④	18	70	⑧	18	11	100
	3	4.5 (4474)	②	85	24④	18	70	⑧	18	11	100
1991	C	3.8 (3786)	③	90	43	219⑤	61	88⑥	41	20	100
	8	4.5 (4474)	②	85	24④	18	70	⑧	18	11	100
	B	4.9 (4917)	②	85	25	70⑤	70	⑧	16	23	100

TORQUE SPECIFICATIONS

All readings in ft. lbs.

Year	Engine ID/VIN	Engine Displacement Liters (cc)	Cylinder Head Bolts	Main Bearing Bolts	Rod Bearing Bolts	Crankshaft Damper Bolts	Flywheel Bolts	Manifold		Spark Plugs	Lug Nut
								Intake	Exhaust		
1992-93	L	3.8 (3786)	③	⑨	①	⑦	61	88⑥	38	12	100
	8	4.5 (4474)	②	85	24④	18	70	⑧	18	11	100
	9	4.6 (4573)	NA	NA	NA	NA	⑩	⑪	20	11	100
	B	4.9 (4917)	②	85	25	70⑤	70	⑧	16	23	100

NA—Not available

① 20±3 ft. lbs. + 50°±3°
② Torque in sequence to 38 ft. lbs.; then torque to 68 ft. lbs.; then torque No. 1, 3 and 4 bolts to 90 ft. lbs.
③ Torque in sequence to 35 ft. lbs.; then turn each bolt 10 degrees; then rotate each bolt an add'l. 30 degrees.
④ Lubricate with engine oil

⑤ Crankshaft balancer assembly
⑥ Inch lbs.
⑦ 105±7 ft. lbs. + 56°±4°
⑧ Torque bolts 1, 2, 3 and 4 in sequence to 8 ft. lbs.; then tighten bolts 5 through 16 in sequence to 8 ft. lbs.; then retighten all bolts in sequence to 12 ft. lbs.; then retorque above step until torque level is maintained.

⑨ 26±3 ft. lbs. + 50°±3°
⑩ 11 ft. lbs. + 50°
⑪ 4 ft. lbs. + 120°

BRAKE SPECIFICATIONS

All measurements in inches unless noted.

Year	Model	Master Cylinder Bore	Brake Disc			Brake Drum Diameter			Minimum Lining Thickness	
			Original Thickness	Minimum Thickness	Maximum Runout	Original Inside Diameter	Max. Wear Limit	Maximum Machine Diameter	Front	Rear
1989	Allante	①	1.035④	0.971②	0.004③	NA	NA	NA	0.030	0.030
	Eldorado	①	1.035④	0.971②	0.004③	NA	NA	NA	0.030	0.030
	Reatta	①	1.035④	0.971②	0.004③	NA	NA	NA	0.030	0.030
	Riviera	①	1.035④	0.971②	0.004③	NA	NA	NA	0.030	0.030
	Seville	①	1.035④	0.971②	0.004③	NA	NA	NA	0.030	0.030
	Toronado	①	1.035④	0.971②	0.004③	NA	NA	NA	0.030	0.030
1990	Allante	①	1.035④	0.971②	0.004③	NA	NA	NA	0.030	0.030
	Eldorado	①	1.035④	0.971②	0.004③	NA	NA	NA	0.030	0.030
	Reatta	①	1.035④	0.971②	0.004③	NA	NA	NA	0.030	0.030
	Riviera	①	1.035④	0.971②	0.004③	NA	NA	NA	0.030	0.030
	Seville	①	1.035④	0.971②	0.004③	NA	NA	NA	0.030	0.030
	Toronado	①	1.035④	0.971②	0.004③	NA	NA	NA	0.030	0.030
	Trofeo	①	1.035④	0.971②	0.004③	NA	NA	NA	0.030	0.030
1991	Allante	1.000	1.035④	0.971②	0.004③	NA	NA	NA	0.030	0.030
	Eldorado	1.000	1.035④	0.971②	0.004③	NA	NA	NA	0.030	0.030
	Reatta	1.000	1.035④	0.971②	0.004③	NA	NA	NA	0.030	0.030
	Riviera	1.000	1.035④	0.971②	0.004③	NA	NA	NA	0.030	0.030
	Seville	1.000	1.035④	0.971②	0.004③	NA	NA	NA	0.030	0.030
	Toronado	1.000	1.035④	0.971②	0.004③	NA	NA	NA	0.030	0.030
	Trofeo	1.000	1.035④	0.971②	0.004③	NA	NA	NA	0.030	0.030
1992-93	Allante	1.000	1.260⑤⑦	1.250⑥⑧	0.002⑨	NA	NA	NA	0.030	0.030
	Eldorado	1.000	1.260⑤	1.250⑥	0.002	NA	NA	NA	0.030	0.030
	Riviera	1.000	1.260⑤	1.250⑥	0.002	NA	NA	NA	0.030	0.030
	Seville	1.000	1.260⑤	1.250⑥	0.002	NA	NA	NA	0.030	0.030
	Toronado	1.000	1.260⑤	1.250⑥	0.002	NA	NA	NA	0.030	0.030
	Trofeo	1.000	1.260⑤	1.250⑥	0.002	NA	NA	NA	0.030	0.030

① Standard—1.126 in.
 Quick Take-up—1.574 in.
 Anti-Lock—1.000 in.
② Rear—0.444 in.
③ Rear—0.003 in.
④ Rear—0.494 in.
⑤ Rear—0.433 in.
⑥ Rear—0.423 in.
⑦ 1992 Original Thickness—1.035—Front
 0.494—Rear
⑧ 1992 Minimum Thickness—0.971—Front
 0.444—Rear
⑨ 1992 Maximum Runout—0.004—Front
 0.003—Rear

WHEEL ALIGNMENT

Year	Model		Caster Range (deg.)	Caster Preferred Setting (deg.)	Camber Range (deg.)	Camber Preferred Setting (deg.)	Toe-in (in.)	Steering Axis Inclination (deg.)
1989	Allante	Front	1 13/16P-2 13/16P	2 5/16P	13/16N-13/16P	0	3/32	13 5/16
		Rear	—	—	1/2N-1/8P	3/16N	3/32	—
	Eldorado	Front	1 5/16P-3 5/16P	2 5/16P	13/16N-13/16P	0	0	13 5/16
		Rear	—	—	13/32N-3/16P	3/32N	3/32	—
	Reatta	Front	1 13/16P-3 13/16P	2 13/16P	13/16N-13/16P	0	0	NA
		Rear	—	—	0-1 5/16P	5/8P	3/32	—
	Riviera	Front	1 5/16P-3 3/16P	2 5/16P	13/16N-13/16P	0	0	NA
		Rear	—	—	0-1 5/16P	5/8P	3/32	—
	Seville	Front	1 5/16P-3 5/16P	2 5/16P	13/16N-13/16P	0	0	13 5/16
		Rear	—	—	13/32N-3/16P	3/32N	3/32	—
	Toronado	Front	1 5/16P-3 5/16P	2 5/16P	13/16N-13/16P	0	0	NA
		Rear	—	—	13/32N-7/32P	3/32N	7/64	—
	Trofeo	Front	1 5/16P-3 5/16P	2 5/16P	13/16N-13/16P	0	0	NA
		Rear	—	—	13/32N-7/32P	3/32N	7/64	—
1990	Allante	Front	1 13/16P-2 13/16P	2 5/16P	13/16N-13/16P	0	3/32	13 5/16
		Rear	—	—	1/2N-1/8P	3/16N	3/32	—
	Eldorado	Front	1 5/16P-3 5/16P	2 5/16P	13/16N-13/16P	0	0	13 5/16
		Rear	—	—	13/32N-3/16P	3/32N	3/32	—
	Reatta	Front	1 13/16P-3 13/16P	2 13/16P	13/16N-13/16P	0	0	NA
		Rear	—	—	0-1 5/16P	5/8P	3/32	—
	Riviera	Front	1 5/16P-3 3/16P	2 5/16P	13/16N-13/16P	0	0	NA
		Rear	—	—	0-1 5/16P	5/8P	3/32	—
	Seville	Front	1 5/16P-3 5/16P	2 5/16P	13/16N-13/16P	0	0	13 5/16
		Rear	—	—	13/32N-3/16P	3/32N	3/32	—
	Toronado	Front	1 5/16P-3 5/16P	2 5/16P	13/16N-13/16P	0	0	NA
		Rear	—	—	13/32N-7/32P	3/32N	7/64	—
	Trofeo	Front	1 5/16P-3 5/16P	2 5/16P	13/16N-13/16P	0	0	NA
		Rear	—	—	13/32N-7/32P	3/32N	7/64	—
1991	Allante	Front	1 13/16P-2 13/16P	2 5/16P	13/16N-13/16P	0	0	13 5/16
		Rear	—	—	13/32N-3/16P	3/32N	3/32	—
	Eldorado	Front	1 5/16P-3 5/16P	2 5/16P	13/16N-13/16P	0	0	13 5/16
		Rear	—	—	13/32N-3/16P	3/32N	3/32	—
	Reatta	Front	1 13/16P-3 13/16P	2 13/16P	13/16N-13/16P	0	3/32	13 5/16
		Rear	—	—	5/8N-3/8P	1/8N	3/32	—
	Riviera	Front	1 5/16P-3 5/16P	2 5/16P	13/16N-13/16P	0	3/32	13 5/16
		Rear	—	—	1/2N-1/2P	0	3/32	—
	Seville	Front	1 5/16P-3 5/16P	2 5/16P	13/16N-13/16P	0	0	13 5/16
		Rear	—	—	13/32N-3/16P	3/32N	3/32	—
	Toronado	Front	1 5/16P-3 5/16P	2 5/16P	13/16N-13/16P	0	3/32	13 15/16
		Rear	—	—	11/16N-5/16P	3/16N	3/32	—
	Trofeo	Front	1 5/16P-3 5/16P	2 5/16P	13/16N-13/16P	0	3/32	13 15/16
		Rear	—	—	11/16N-5/16P	3/16N	3/32	—

WHEEL ALIGNMENT

Year	Model		Caster Range (deg.)	Caster Preferred Setting (deg.)	Camber Range (deg.)	Camber Preferred Setting (deg.)	Toe-in (in.)	Steering Axis Inclination (deg.)
1992-93	Allante	Front	1¹³/₁₆P–2¹³/₁₆P	2⁵/₁₆P	¹³/₁₆N–1³/₁₆P	0	0	13⁵/₁₆
		Rear	—	—	¹³/₃₂N–³/₁₆P	³/₃₂N	³/₃₂	—
	Eldorado	Front	1³/₁₆P–3³/₁₆P	2³/₁₆P	¹³/₁₆N–1³/₁₆P	0	³/₃₂	13⁵/₁₆
		Rear	—	—	¹³/₁₆N–1³/₁₆P	0	³/₃₂	—
	Riviera	Front	1⁵/₁₆P–3⁵/₁₆P	2⁵/₁₆P	¹³/₁₆N–1³/₁₆P	0	³/₃₂	13⁵/₁₆
		Rear	—	—	¹/₂N–¹/₂P	³/₁₆N	³/₃₂	—
	Seville	Front	1³/₁₆P–3³/₁₆P	2³/₁₆P	¹³/₁₆N–1³/₁₆P	0	³/₃₂	13⁵/₁₆
		Rear	—	—	¹³/₁₆N–1³/₁₆P	0	³/₃₂	—
	Toronado	Front	1⁵/₁₆P–3⁵/₁₆P	2⁵/₁₆P	¹³/₁₆N–1³/₁₆P	0	³/₃₂	13¹⁵/₁₆
		Rear	—	—	¹¹/₁₆N–⁵/₁₆P	³/₁₆N	³/₃₂	—
	Trofeo	Front	1⁵/₁₆P–3⁵/₁₆P	2⁵/₁₆P	¹³/₁₆N–1³/₁₆P	0	³/₃₂	13¹⁵/₁₆
		Rear	—	—	¹¹/₁₆N–⁵/₁₆P	³/₁₆N	³/₃₂	—

NA—Not available
N—Negative
P—Positive

ENGINE MECHANICAL

NOTE: Disconnecting the negative battery cable on some vehicles may interfere with the functions of the on board computer systems and may require the computer to undergo a relearning process, once the negative battery cable is reconnected.

Engine Assembly

REMOVAL & INSTALLATION

Rivera, Reatta, Tornado and Trofeo

3.8L ENGINE (VIN C)

1. Matchmark the hood hinge-to-hood and remove the hood.
2. Properly relieve the fuel pressure and disconnect the fuel lines from the fuel rail.
3. Disconnect the negative battery cable. Remove the air intake duct.
4. Remove the upper engine strut. From the throttle body, remove the throttle cable bracket and the cables.
5. Raise and safely support the vehicle.
6. Drain the cooling system and the engine oil.
7. Remove the exhaust pipe from the rear exhaust manifold.
8. Using a vertical lifting device, secure it to the engine and support its weight. Remove the engine mounting bolts.
9. Disconnect the electrical connectors from the starter. Remove the starter-to-engine bolts and the starter.
10. Remove the serpentine drive belt. Remove the air conditioning compressor-to-bracket bolts and move the compressor aside; do not disconnect the pressure hoses.
11. Disconnect and plug the power steering hoses at the steering gear.
12. Remove the lower transaxle-to-engine bolts.

NOTE: One of the lower transaxle bolts is located between the transaxle case and the engine block and is installed in the opposite direction.

13. Remove the flywheel cover. Matchmark the torque converter-to-flywheel for alignment purposes. Remove the torque converter-to-flywheel bolts and slide the torque converter rearward.
14. Remove the engine support bracket-to-transaxle bolts and the bracket.
15. Lower the vehicle.
16. Disconnect the vacuum hoses from the vacuum modulator and the emission control canister. Disconnect and move aside any electrical harness connectors which may be in the way.
17. Remove the radiator and heater hoses from the engine.
18. Remove the remaining transaxle-to-engine bolts. Lift the engine assembly from the vehicle and attach it to a work stand.

To install:

19. Install engine assembly in vehicle. Install upper engine-to-transaxle bolts and tighten until snug. Do not tighten at this time.
20. Install radiator and connect heater hoses to engine.
21. Connect vacuum hoses to vacuum modulator and the emission control canister. Connect electrical harness connectors previously removed.
22. Raise and safely support the vehicle.
23. Install the engine support bracket-to-transaxle bolts and bracket.
24. Install the torque convertor-to-flywheel bolts. Tighten to 46 ft. lbs. (62 Nm). Install flywheel cover aligning marks made during removal.
25. Install lower transaxle bolts. Tighten to 55 ft. lbs. (75 Nm).

NOTE: One of the lower transaxle bolts is located between the transaxle case and the engine block; it is installed in the opposite direction.

26. Connect the power steering hoses at the steering gear.
27. Install the air conditioning compressor in the bracket and install the compressor-to-bracket bolts. Install the serpentine belt.
28. Install the starter on the engine and connect starter electrical connector.
29. Install engine mounting bolts. Tighten to 70 ft. lbs. (90 Nm). Remove lifting device.

30. Connect the exhaust pipe to the rear exhaust manifold.
31. Lower the vehicle.
32. Fill the cooling system.
33. Connect the throttle cable bracket and cables to the throttle body. Install the upper engine strut.
34. Install the air intake duct. Connect negative battery cable.
35. Connect the fuel lines to the fuel rail.
36. Install the hood at matchmarks made during removal.
37. Start the engine and check for fuel, coolant and transaxle leaks.

3.8L (VIN L) ENGINE

1. Matchmark the hood hinge-to-hood and remove the hood.
2. Properly relieve the fuel pressure and disconnect the fuel lines from the fuel rail.
3. Disconnect the negative battery cable. Darin the coolant and the engine oil.
4. Disconnect the windshield washer, radiator and heater supply hoses.
5. Disconnect the wiring to the starter and to the engine and battery connectors located near the relay center.
6. Remove the accessory drive belt. Remove the power steering pump from the brackets and set off to the side, out of the way.
7. Remove the air flow duct and air cleaner assembly.
8. Remove the throttle cable from the throttle linkage mounting bracket.
9. Disconnect the mat sensor, throttle position switch, idle air control valve and the oxygen sensor connectors.
10. Disconnect the ignition coil ground strap from the fender inner panel.
11. Disconnect the fuel feed and return pipes from the fuel rail and the fuel pressure regulator.
12. Disconnect the emission control canister hoses from the throttle body connections.
13. Disconnect the brake booster, heater control, cruise control and servo vacuum hoses.
14. Raise and safely support the vehicle.
15. Remove the exhaust pipe from the right manifold.
16. Using a vertical lifting device, secure it to the engine and support its weight.
17. Disconnect the air conditioning compressor from the mounts and secure it out of the way.
18. Remove the left front engine mount and the right front engine to transaxle bracket.
19. Remove the torque strut assembly and front engine to frame stabilizer.

20. Place a jack or other support under the transaxle and remove the engine to transaxle bolts.
21. Remove the flywheel cover. Matchmark the torque converter-to-flywheel for alignment purposes. Remove the torque converter-to-flywheel bolts and slide the torque converter rearward.
22. Disconnect and move aside any electrical harness connectors which may be in the way.
23. Lift the engine assembly from the vehicle and attach it to a work stand.

To install:
24. Install engine assembly in vehicle. Install upper engine-to-transaxle bolts.
25. Install the right front engine to transaxle bracket and left front engine mount.
26. Install the front engine to frame stabilizer.
27. Install the torque converter-to-flywheel bolts aligning marks made during removal. Tighten to 46 ft. lbs. (62 Nm). Install flywheel cover.
28. Install the air conditioner compressor and connect the cruise control vacuum hoses to the servo unit.
29. Connect the exhaust pipe to the manifold. Connect the wiring harness connectors to the mat sensor, throttle position switch, idle air control valve, and the oxygen sensor.
30. Connect the throttle cable to the linkage. Install the air flow duct and air cleaner assembly.
31. Install the power steering pump to the engine.
32. Connect the main wiring harness connectors behind the relay housing.
33. Connect the wiring to the starter. Connect the windshield washer, radiator and heater supply hoses.
34. Add ccolant and engine oil.
35. Connect the negative battery cable.
36. Install the hood at matchmarks made during removal.
37. Start the engine and check for fuel, coolant and transaxle leaks.

Allante

1989–92

1. Disconnect the negative battery cable. Properly relieve the fuel system pressure. Position a drain pan under the radiator, open the drain cock and drain the cooling system.
2. Remove the air cleaner. Matchmark the hood hinge-to-hood position and remove the hood.
3. Remove the cooling fans and the accessory drive belt.
4. Remove the upper intake manifold. Remove the upper radiator hose and disconnect the heater hose from the thermostat housing.

5. Disconnect the following electrical connectors and position aside:
   a. Oil pressure sending unit
   b. Coolant temperature sensor
   c. Distributor
   d. EGR solenoid
   e. Engine temperature switch
   f. Idle speed control
   g. Throttle position sensor
   h. Injector electrical connections
   i. MAT sensor
   j. Oxygen sensor
   k. Throttle body base warmer
   l. Alternator
   m. Ground wires at the alternator mounting bracket
6. Disconnect the accelerator, the cruise control and the transaxle throttle valve cables from the throttle lever.
7. Disconnect the cruise control diaphragm/bracket and move them aside.
8. Disconnect the transaxle oil cooler lines from the radiator. Remove the radiator.
9. Disconnect and remove the oil cooler lines from the oil filter adapter.
10. Remove the oil cooler lines-to-transaxle bracket.
11. Remove the air cleaner bracket and the oil filter adapter.
12. Disconnect the air injection tubes from the diverter valve.
13. Remove the cross brace.
14. Remove the right front heater hose and the coolant reservoir.
15. Remove the Air Injection Reactor (AIR) filter and bracket.
16. Remove the power steering line brace from the right cylinder head. Remove the pump and belt tensioner as an assembly and position them forward of the engine.
17. Properly discharge and recover the refrigerant from the air conditioning system and remove the air conditioning lines from the accumulator and condenser.
18. Disconnect supply and return fuel lines from the fuel rail. Remove the fuel line bracket from the transaxle and move the fuel lines aside.
19. Raise and safely support the vehicle.
20. Label and disconnect the electrical connectors from the starter. Disconnect any ground wires still connected to the engine.
21. Disconnect the oxygen sensor wire and remove the oxygen sensors.
22. Disconnect and remove the exhaust Y-pipe. Remove the starter-to-engine bolts and the starter.
23. Remove the torque converter covers. Matchmark the torque converter-to-flywheel and remove the flywheel-to-torque converter bolts.
24. Remove the air conditioning compressor lower dust shield, the right front tire and the outer wheel house plastic shield.
25. Remove the right rear transaxle-

to-engine mount bolt, the front engine mount nuts and the right rear transaxle mount bolts.

26. Remove the alternator. Remove the oxygen sensor wires. Remove the heater bypass bracket from the right side of the vehicle.

27. Remove the right side engine brace and lower the vehicle to the ground.

28. Remove the engine-to-transaxle bolts. The bolts are accessible from the top.

29. Connect a chain from a lifting crane down to both lift points on top of the engine and ensure it is secure. Lift the engine out of the vehicle.

To install:

30. Situate a floor jack under the transaxle and raise it slightly so it will align with the engine. Lower the engine into the engine compartment and engage the dowels that are on the engine block with the corresponding holes in the transaxle.

31. Install the upper transaxle-to-engine bolts. Lower the engine, directing it squarely onto the mounts. Remove the lifting equipment.

NOTE: Ensure that converter is properly positioned to the flexplate and engaged in the front pump of the transaxle.

32. Install 5 upper transaxle bellhousing-to-engine bolts.

33. Lower floor jack and remove from transaxle.

34. Lower engine making sure it is properly seated on mounts.

35. Remove lifting equipment. Raise and safely support the vehicle.

36. Install right side engine brace.

37. Remove engine support.

38. Install alternator and oxygen sensor wires and heater bypass bracket to right side of vehicle.

39. Install front engine mount nuts and right rear transaxle mounting bolts.

40. Connect oil level sensor at oil pan and both oxygen sensors.

41. Install right rear transaxle-to-engine mounting bolt.

42. Install outer wheel house plastic shield.

43. Install right front tire and wheel assembly.

44. Install air conditioning compressor lower dust shield.

45. Install 3 flexplate-to-converter bolts. Install flexplate cover.

46. Install starter. Install exhaust "Y" pipe.

47. Install electrical connectors at starter and ground wires to block.

48. Lower vehicle.

49. Install fuel line bracket. Install fuel lines at fuel rail.

50. Install air conditioning lines to accumulator and condenser.

51. Install power steering pump and tensioner. Install power steering line brace on right cylinder head.

52. Install AIR system air filter and bracket.

53. Install coolant reservoir. Install right front heater hose.

54. Install front right and rear cross braces.

55. Install AIR tubes on diverter valve.

56. Install oil filter adapter.

57. Install air cleaner mounting bracket.

58. Install oil cooler line bracket at transaxle. Install oil cooler lines to oil filter adapter.

59. Install radiator. Install engine oil and transaxle oil cooler lines to radiator.

60. Connect cruise control diaphragm with bracket.

61. Install the following wiring connectors:
  a. Injectors
  b. Ground wires at alternator bracket
  c. Oil pressure switch
  d. Coolant temperature sensor
  e. Distributor
  f. Engine temperature switch

62. Connect cables from throttle lever including: accelerator, cruise control and transaxle throttle valve.

63. Install accessory drive belt.

64. Install upper radiator hose and heater hose to thermostat housing.

65. Install cooling fan.

66. Install air conditioning accumulator hose brace.

67. Install vehicle hood.

68. Install air cleaner. Install engine coolant. Connect negative battery cable.

69. Evacuate, recharge and leak test the air conditioning system.

70. Start engine and check for oil, coolant and transaxle leaks.

1993

1. Disconnect the negative battery cable. Remove the air cleaner inlet duct.

2. Matchmark the hood hinge-to-hood and remove the hood.

3. Drain the coolant from the radiator.

4. Remove the left and right torque struts. Install the left front strut bolt back into the bracket.

5. Disconnect the radiator hoses at the water crossover. Remove both cooling fans from the engine.

6. Remove the serpentine accessory drive belt.

7. Disconnect the cruise control servo connections and the ISC motor electrical connector.

8. Disconnect the throttle cable from the throttle body cam. Disconnect the shift cable from the park/neu-

tral switch. Remove the cable bracket at the transaxle.

9. Remove the park/neutral switch and disconnect the power brake vacuum hose.

10. At the rear of the right head, disconnect the cylinder head temperature switch.

11. Remove the bellhousing bolts.

12. Remove the ignition coils and remove the spark plug wires.

13. Raise and safely support the vehicle.

14. Remove the oil pan-to-transmission brace. Remove the torque converter splash shield and the 4 converter-to-flywheel bolts.

15. Disconnect the oil cooler lines from the oil filter adapter.

16. Remove the A/C compressor mounting bolts and disconnect the electrical connectors. Move compressor out of way.

17. Disconnect the electrical connectors from the left side of the engine and move the harness from behind the exhaust manifold.

18. Remove the 2 nuts that secure the motor mount to the engine cradle front crossmember.

19. Remove the exhaust Y-pipe and remove the right front wheel.

20. Remove the crankcase to transmission bracket at the transmission tail shaft. Disconnect the knock sensor.

21. Remove the bolt from the transmission to the cylinder head brace at the cylinder head.

22. Lower the vehicle. Disconnect the fuel inlet and fuel return lines using special tool J37088 or equivalent.

23. Disconnect the injector harness connector and the hoses from the coolant reservoir. Remove the reservoir.

24. Disconnect the cam position sensor. Disconnect the heater hoses from the water pipes at the front of the right cylinder head.

25. Disconnect the battery cable from the junction block and remove the retainer at the cylinder head.

26. Disconnect the starter cable from the junction block.

27. Disconnect the power steering pump pressure and return lines at the pump. Return power steering line retainer from the right front of the crankcase.

28. Disconnect the rear oxygen sensor.

29. Remove the 3 screws securing the wiring harness retainer to right cam cover and position harness out of the way.

30. Connect an engine lifting device to the engine using the support hooks at left and right rear of engine. The torque strut bracket at the left front of the engine should be used as a third lifting hook.

31. Carefully remove the engine from the vehicle.

To install:

32. Lower the engine into the vehicle. Remove the lifting device.

33. Install the 4 bell housing bolts and tighten to 75 ft. lbs. (100 Nm).

34. Raise and safely support the vehicle.

35. Install 2 nuts to the motor mount at the front cradle crossmember. Do not fully tighten.

36. Install bolt to the cylinder head for transmission brace. Do not fully tighten.

37. Install the transmission to crankcase bracket with the 4 bolts. Do not fully tighten the bolts.

38. Tighten the motor mount to cradle crossmember bolts to 30 ft. lbs. (40 Nm). Tighten the transmission brace bolt and transmission to crankcase bolts to 45 ft. lbs. (60 Nm).

39. Install the right front wheel and connect the knock sensor.

40. Install the exhaust Y-pipe.

41. Install the 4 torque converter to flywheel bolts and tighten to 45 ft. lbs. (60 Nm).

42. Install the converter splash shield and install the transmission to oil pan brace. Tighten the bolt to 35 ft. lbs. (50 Nm).

43. Position the A/C compressor in place and install the mounting bolts.

44. Route the electrical harness along the left side of the engine and connect the connectors.

45. Connect the oil cooler lines to the oil filter adapter.

46. Lower the vehicle.

47. Secure the wiring harness to the right cam cover with the 3 screws.

48. Connect the rear oxygen sensor and connect the cam position sensor.

49. Connect the power steering hoses to the pump and secure the return line to the crankcase.

50. Connect the heater hoses to the water pipes.

51. Connect the starter and battery cables at the junction box. Secure battery cable with retainer.

52. Connect and install the coolant reservoir.

53. Install coils and secure with 4 screws.

54. Install the serpentine drive belt and connect the injector harness to the FIS harness.

55. Connect the fuel line connectors. Connect the cylinder head temperature switch to the rear of the right head.

56. Connect the power brake vacuum line.

57. Install the park/neutral switch and shift cable. Adjust switch if necessary.

58. Install the cruise servo and connect the ISC motor.

59. Connect the throttle cable and install both cooling fans.

60. Connect the radiator hoses to the water crossover.

61. Install the torque struts and adjust the preload to zero.

62. Connect the negative battery cable.

63. Refill the engine with coolant. Install the hood and install the air cleaner.

64. Start engine and check for oil, coolant and transaxle leaks.

Eldorado and Seville

1. Disconnect the negative battery cable. Properly relieve the fuel system pressure. Position a drain pan under the radiator, open the drain cock and drain the cooling system.

2. Remove the air cleaner. Matchmark the hood hinge-to-hood and remove the hood.

3. Remove the cooling fan and the accessory drive belt.

4. Remove the upper radiator hose and disconnect the heater hose from the thermostat housing.

5. Disconnect the following electrical connectors, if equipped and position the wires aside:
   a. Oil pressure sending unit
   b. Coolant temperature sensor
   c. Distributor
   d. EGR solenoid
   e. Engine temperature switch
   f. Idle speed control
   g. Throttle position sensor
   h. Injector electrical connections
   i. MAT sensor
   j. Oxygen sensor
   k. Throttle body base warmer
   l. Alternator
   m. Ground wires at the alternator mounting bracket

6. Disconnect the accelerator, the cruise control and the transaxle throttle valve cables from the throttle lever.

7. Disconnect the cruise control diaphragm/bracket and move them aside.

8. Disconnect the transaxle oil cooler lines from the radiator. Remove the radiator.

9. Disconnect and remove the oil cooler lines from the oil filter adapter.

10. Remove the oil cooler lines-to-transaxle bracket.

11. Remove the air cleaner bracket and the oil filter housing adapter.

12. If equipped, disconnect the air injection tubes from the diverter valve.

13. Remove the right front and right rear body braces.

14. Remove the right front heater hose and the coolant reservoir.

15. If equipped, remove the Air Injection Reactor (AIR) filter box and bracket. Remove the idler pulley for the accessory drive belt.

16. Remove the power steering line brace from the right cylinder head. Remove the pump and belt tensioner as an assembly and position them forward of the engine.

17. Properly discharge and recover the refrigerant from the air conditioning system and remove the air conditioning lines from the accumulator and condenser.

18. Disconnect supply and return fuel lines from the throttle body. Remove the fuel line bracket from the transaxle and move the fuel lines aside.

19. Remove the EGR lines and brackets. Remove the vacuum modulator line and the fuel filter; reposition them aside.

20. Raise and safely support the vehicle.

21. Remove the starter heat shield. Label and disconnect the electrical connectors from the starter. Disconnect any ground wires still connected to the engine.

22. Disconnect and remove the exhaust crossover pipe. Remove the starter-to-engine bolts and the starter.

23. Remove the torque converter covers. Matchmark the torque converter-to-flywheel and remove the flywheel-to-torque converter bolts.

24. Remove the air conditioning compressor lower dust shield, the right front tire and the outer wheel house plastic shield.

25. Remove the right rear transaxle-to-engine mount bolt and the lower engine mounting damper nut.

26. Remove the front engine mount nuts and the right rear transaxle mount nuts.

27. Remove the alternator. Remove the oxygen sensor wires. Remove the heater bypass bracket from the right side of the vehicle.

28. Remove the right side engine brace and lower the vehicle to the ground.

29. Remove the engine-to-transaxle bolts. The bolts are accessible from the top.

30. Run a chain from a lifting crane down to both lift points on top of the engine and ensure it is secure. Lift the engine out of the vehicle.

To install:

31. Situate a floor jack under the transaxle and raise it slightly so it will align with the engine. Lower the engine into the engine compartment and engage the dowels on the engine block with the corresponding holes in the transaxle.

NOTE: Ensure that converter is properly positioned to the flexplate and engaged in the front pump of transaxle.

32. Install upper 5 transaxle bellhousing-to-engine bolts.

33. Lower floor jack and remove from transaxle.

34. Lower engine making sure it is seated on the mount properly.

35. Remove lifting equipment.

36. Raise and safely support the vehicle.

37. Support the engine. Install right side engine brace. Remove engine support.

38. Install alternator and oxygen sensor wires and heater bypass bracket to right side of vehicle.

39. Install front engine mount nuts and right rear transaxle mount bolts.

40. Install lower engine damper nut.

41. Install right rear transaxle-to-engine mounting bolt.

42. Install outer wheel house plastic shield.

43. Install right front tire and wheel assembly.

44. Install air conditioner compressor lower dust shield.

45. Install 3 flexplate-to-converter bolts. Install 2 flexplate covers.

46. Install starter to engine and connect electrical connectors. Install engine ground connectors.

47. Install exhaust crossover pipe.

48. Install starter heat shield.

49. Lower vehicle.

50. Install vacuum modulator line and vacuum hose to power brake booster.

51. Install EGR lines and bracket.

52. Install fuel line bracket at transaxle. Install fuel lines at throttle body.

53. Install air conditioning lines to accumulator and condenser.

54. Install power steering pump and tensioner. Install power steering line brace on right cylinder head.

55. If equipped, install A.I.R. system air filter and bracket.

56. Install coolant reservoir. Install right front heater hose.

57. Install front right and rear cross braces.

58. If equipped, install A.I.R. tubes on diverter valve.

59. Install oil filter adapter.

60. Install air cleaner mounting bracket.

61. Install oil cooler line bracket at transaxle. Install oil cooler lines to oil filter adapter.

62. Install radiator. Install engine oil and transaxle oil cooler lines to radiator.

63. Connect cruise control diaphragm with bracket.

64. Install the following wiring connectors:

    a. ISC
    b. TPS
    c. Injectors
    d. MAT sensor
    e. Oxygen sensor
    f. Electric EFE grid

    g. Ground wires at alternator bracket
    h. Oil pressure switch
    i. Coolant temperature sensor
    j. Distributor
    k. EGR solenoid
    l. Engine temperature switch

65. Connect cables from throttle lever including: accelerator, cruise control and transaxle throttle valve.

66. Install accessory drive belt.

67. Install upper radiator hose and heater hose to thermostat housing.

68. Install cooling fan.

69. Install air conditioning accumulator hose brace.

70. Install vehicle hood.

71. Install air cleaner. Install engine coolant. Connect negative battery cable.

72. Evacuate, recharge and leak test the air conditioning system.

73. Start engine and check for oil, coolant and transaxle leaks.

Engine Mounts

REMOVAL & INSTALLATION

Rivera, Reatta, Tornado and Trofeo

1. Disconnect the negative battery cable.

2. Safely support the engine using a suitable engine holding fixture.

3. Raise and safely support the vehicle.

4. Remove the engine mount bracket nuts.

5. Raise the engine slightly.

6. Remove the engine mount retaining bolts. Remove the engine mount.

To install:

7. Install the engine mount and mount retaining bolts.

8. Lower the engine.

9. Install the engine mount bracket nuts.

10. Lower the vehicle.

11. Remove the engine holding fixture.

12. Connect the negative battery cable.

Allante — 1989–92

RIGHT SIDE ENGINE AND TRANSAXLE MOUNT

1. Disconnect the negative battery cable.

2. Raise and safely support the vehicle.

3. Remove 2 heat shield screws.

4. Remove screw from engine mount brace at engine mount bracket.

5. Loosen nut at top of brace to exhaust manifold and position brace aside.

6. Support the engine with a transaxle jack.

7. Remove 2 screws securing mount bracket to transaxle.

8. Remove 4 nuts at top and bottom of mount.

9. Raise engine with transaxle jack.

10. Remove mount.

To install:

11. Position transaxle mount and bracket in place between transaxle and frame. Secure bracket to transaxle with 2 bolts. Tighten to 50 ft. lbs. (70 Nm).

NOTE: Guide engine mount into location while lowering engine.

12. Lower engine.

13. Install mount to frame and transaxle bracket with 2 nuts each. Tighten to 30 ft. lbs. (40 Nm).

14. Install brace from bracket to engine. Tighten to 25 ft. lbs. (35 Nm).

15. Install heat shield.

16. Remove transaxle jack and lower hoist.

LEFT SIDE ENGINE MOUNT

1. Disconnect the negative battery cable.

2. Remove air cleaner assembly.

3. Remove serpentine belt.

4. Properly discharge and recover the refrigerant from the air conditioning system.

5. Lower center exhaust manifold nuts.

6. Raise and safely support the vehicle.

7. Remove right side engine compartment splash shield. Remove air conditioning splash shield.

8. Remove 2 air conditioning compressor brackets. Remove air conditioning compressor.

9. Remove engine mount bracket bolts from engine block and cradle.

10. Raise engine with transaxle jack and remove mount and bracket.

To install:

11. Place mount in vise and position mount bracket onto mount. Tighten 2 nuts to 30 ft. lbs. (40 Nm).

12. Install engine mount and bracket through right side wheel well.

13. Install engine mount bracket bolts to engine block. Tighten to 50 ft. lbs. (70 Nm).

14. Install engine mount to cradle nuts. Tighten to 30 ft. lbs. (40 Nm).

15. Install air conditioning compressor. Install 2 air conditioning compressor brackets.

16. Install air conditioning splash shield. Install right side engine compartment splash shield.

17. Lower vehicle.

18. Install lower center exhaust manifold nut.

19. Install serpentine belt.

20. Connect negative battery cable.
21. Install air cleaner assembly.
22. Evacuate, recharge and leak test the air conditioning system.

Allante — 1993

FRONT ENGINE MOUNT

1. Disconnect the negative battery cable and remove right side cooling fan.
2. Remove left side cooling fan.
3. Remove the right and left torque struts.
4. Install an engine support fixture, J28467A or equivalent. Connect only one support at left rear engine bracket.
5. Raise and safely support the vehicle.
6. Remove the 2 nuts that secure the motor mount to the engine cradle.
7. Remove the 2 bolts that secure the motor mount bracket to the crankcase.
8. Lower the vehicle.
9. Remove the 2 bolts that secure the motor mount bracket to the cylinder head. Remove the 2 nuts that secure the motor mount to the bracket.
10. Raise engine by tightening support chain. Separate mount and bracket and remove mount.

To install:
11. Position the motor mount and bracket into position at front of engine.
12. Install the 2 nuts that secure the mount to the bracket. Do not fully tighten the nuts.
13. Install the 2 bolts securing the mount bracket to the cylinder head. Do not fully tighten the bolts.
14. Lower the engine and guide the motor mount studs into the engine cradle.
15. Raise and safely support the vehicle.
16. Install the 2 bolts securing the mount bracket to the crankcase. Tighten the bolts to 25 ft. lbs. (30 Nm).
17. Install the 2 nuts securing the motor mount to the cradle and tighten to 25 ft. lbs. (30 Nm).
18. Lower the vehicle.
19. Torque the 2 mount bracket to cylinder head bolts to 25 ft. lbs. (30 Nm).
20. Remove the engine support fixture.
21. Install the 2 nuts securing the motor mount to the bracket and tighten to 25 ft. lbs. (30 Nm).
22. Tighten the 2 nuts that secure the mount to the engine cradle to 25 ft. lbs. (30 Nm).
23. Install the 2 torque struts and set to zero preload.
24. Install both cooling fans and connect the negative battery cable.

Eldorado and Seville

RIGHT SIDE ENGINE AND TRANSAXLE MOUNT

1. Disconnect the negative battery cable.
2. Remove the brace from the engine bracket to engine.
3. Remove 2 engine bracket-to-mount nuts.
4. Raise and safely support the vehicle.
5. Remove 2 nuts securing the engine mount to the frame. Remove 2 nuts securing transaxle bracket to mount. Remove 2 nuts securing the transaxle mount to the frame bracket.
6. Using the engine support tool, raise the engine.
7. Raise the engine slowly until the bracket is free from the engine and transaxle mount. Remove the bracket-to-block stud and bolts. Remove the mount and bracket by pulling forward.
8. Remove the transaxle mounting bracket from the transaxle. Remove the mount assembly.

To install:
9. Position engine mount and bracket in place between cylinder block and frame. Secure bracket to block with 1 stud and 2 bolts. Tighten to 34 ft. lbs. (46 Nm).
10. Position transaxle mount and bracket in place between transaxle and frame. Secure bracket to transaxle with 2 bolts. Tighten to 34 ft. lbs. (46 Nm).

NOTE: Guide engine mount into location while lowering engine.

11. Lower engine.
12. Install engine mount to frame and transaxle mount to frame bracket with 2 nuts. Tighten to 22 ft. lbs. (31 Nm).
13. Install 2 nuts to engine mount studs and 2 nuts to transaxle mount studs. Tighten to 22 ft. lbs. (31 Nm).
14. Remove brace from engine bracket to engine.
15. Remove stands and lower vehicle.
16. Connect negative battery cable.

LEFT SIDE ENGINE MOUNT

1. Disconnect the negative battery cable. Remove the air cleaner assembly.
2. Remove the serpentine belt. Properly discharge and recover the refrigerant from the air conditioning system.
3. Install the engine support tool.
4. Remove the lower center exhaust manifold nut and top nut of the engine damper.
5. Raise and safely support the vehicle.
6. Remove the right side engine compartment splash shield and air conditioning splash shield.
7. Remove the engine damper. Remove both air conditioning compressor brackets. Remove the air conditioning compressor.
8. Remove the water pipe bracket bolt.
9. Remove the engine mount bracket bolts from the engine block and cradle. Remove the engine mount and bracket through the right side wheel well.

To install:
10. Place mount in vice and position mount bracket onto mount. Tighten 2 nuts to 31 ft. lbs. (41 Nm).
11. Install engine mount and bracket through right wheel well.
12. Install engine mount bracket bolts to engine block. Tighten to 50 ft. lbs. (68 Nm).
13. Install engine mount to cradle nuts. Tighten bolts to 31 ft. lbs. (41 Nm).
14. Install water pipe bracket bolt.
15. Install air conditioning compressor brackets.
16. Install engine damper.
17. Install air conditioning compressor splash shield.
18. Install right side engine compartment splash shield.
19. Lower vehicle.
20. Install lower center exhaust manifold nut and top nut on engine damper.
21. Remove engine support tool.
22. Install serpentine belt.
23. Connect negative battery cable.
24. Install air cleaner assembly.
25. Evacuate, recharge and leak test the air conditioning system.

Cylinder Head

REMOVAL & INSTALLATION

3.8L Engine

1. Disconnect the negative battery cable.
2. Remove the intake and exhaust manifolds.
3. Remove the valve cover.
4. If removing the front (left) side cylinder head, perform the following:
   a. Remove the C^3I and spark plug wires.
   b. Remove the alternator bracket.
   c. Remove 1 air conditioning compressor bracket bolt.
5. If removing the rear (right) side cylinder head, perform the following:
   a. Remove the power steering pump.
   b. Remove the belt tensioner assembly.
   c. Remove fuel line heat shield.
6. Remove rocker arm assemblies, guide plate and pushrods.

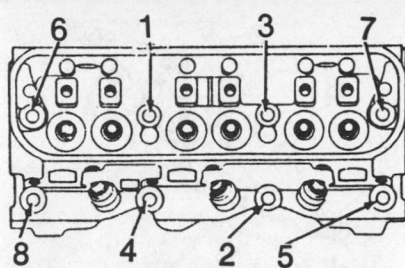

Cylinder head torque sequence—3.8L engine

7. Remove cylinder head bolts and cylinder head.

NOTE: Clean all gasket mating surfaces and cylinder head bolt holes in block.

To install:
8. Clean threads in block using an appropriate tap.
9. Install cylinder head gasket on block.
10. Apply an appropriate sealant to cylinder head bolt threads. Install cylinder head bolts.
11. Tighten cylinder head bolts using the following steps:
  a. Tighten each cylinder head bolt to 35 ft. lbs. (47 Nm) following the proper sequence.
  b. Rotate each bolt 130 degrees, in sequence, using an appropriate torque angle meter.
  c. Rotate each bolt an additional 30 degrees, in sequence, using torque angle meter.
12. Install pushrods, guide plate and rocker arm assemblies.
13. Apply an appropriate high temperature, high strength thread sealant compound to the rocker arm pedestal bolts. Tighten to 28 ft. lbs. (38 Nm).
14. Install intake manifold.
15. Install valve cover.
16. Install exhaust manifold.
17. If the front (left) side cylinder head was removed, perform the following:
  a. Install air conditioning compressor bracket bolt. Tighten to 52 ft. lbs. (80 Nm).
  b. Install alternator support bracket to cylinder head.
  c. Install alternator.
  d. Install C³I and spark plug wires.
18. If the rear (right) side cylinder head was removed, perform the following:
  a. Install belt tensioner assembly.
  b. Install power steering pump.
  c. Install fuel line heat shield.
19. Connect negative battery cable.
20. Start engine and check for coolant, oil and fuel leaks. Allow engine to come to normal operating temperature and recheck for leaks.

4.5L and 4.9L Engines
RIGHT SIDE
1. Disconnect the negative battery cable. Drain the engine coolant.
2. Remove rocker arm covers.
3. Remove the lower intake and right side exhaust manifolds.
4. Remove engine lift bracket and oil dipstick tube.
5. Reposition AIR bracket.
6. Remove 10 cylinder head bolts.
7. Remove cylinder head.

To install:

NOTE: Clean sealing surfaces of cylinder head, block and liners. Clean cylinder head bolt holes with an appropriate tap. Ensure that bolt holes are free of shavings, oil and coolant.

8. Install new head gasket over dowels on cylinder block with either side facing up.
9. Install cylinder head.
10. Apply an appropriate lubricant to the threads of the head bolts. Install cylinder head bolts finger-tight.
11. Tighten cylinder head bolts, in sequence, to 38 ft. lbs. (50 Nm).
12. Tighten cylinder head bolts, in sequence, to 68 ft. lbs. (90 Nm).
13. Tighten No. 1, 3 and 4 cylinder head bolts to 90 ft. lbs. (120 Nm).
14. Install engine lift bracket and AIR bracket.
15. Install lower intake and right side exhaust manifolds.
16. Install rocker arm covers.
17. Fill cooling system.
18. Connect negative battery cable.
19. Start engine and check for coolant, oil and fuel leaks. Allow engine to come to normal operating temperature and recheck for leaks.

LEFT SIDE

1. Disconnect the negative battery cable.
2. Drain the cooling system.
3. Remove the rocker arm covers.
4. Remove the intake manifold-to-engine bolts and intake manifold.
5. Disconnect the exhaust manifold

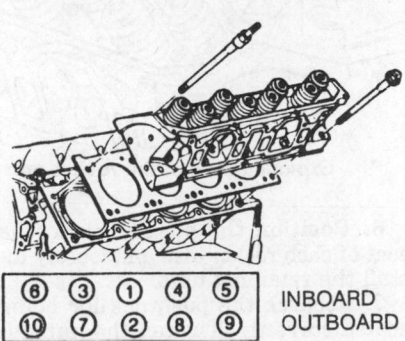

Cylinder head torque sequence—4.5L and 4.9L engines

crossover pipe, the exhaust pipe-to-exhaust manifold bolts, the exhaust manifold-to-cylinder head bolts and the exhaust manifold.
6. Remove the engine lifting bracket and the dipstick tube.
7. Remove the AIR bracket-to-engine bolts and move the bracket aside.
8. Remove the cylinder head-to-engine bolts and the cylinder head.

To install:
9. Clean the gasket mounting surfaces.
10. Install new head gasket over dowels on cylinder block with either side facing up.
11. Install cylinder head.
12. Apply a suitable lubricant to the cylinder head bolt threads.
13. Install cylinder head bolts finger-tight.
14. Tighten bolts, in sequence, to 38 ft. lbs. (50 Nm).
15. Tighten cylinder head bolts, in sequence, to 68 ft. lbs. (90 Nm).
16. Tighten No. 1, 3 and 4 cylinder head bolts to 90 ft. lbs. (120 Nm).
17. Install AIR bracket. Install dipstick tube and engine lift bracket.
18. Install exhaust manifold. Install lower intake manifold.
19. Install rocker arm covers.
20. Fill cooling system.
21. Connect negative battery cable.
22. Start engine and check for coolant, oil and fuel leaks. Allow engine to come to normal operating temperature and recheck for leaks.

Valve Lifters

REMOVAL & INSTALLATION

NOTE: When disassembling valve train components, ensure that all parts are kept in order so they can be reinstalled in their original locations and with the same mating surfaces.

1. Disconnect the negative battery cable. Remove the intake manifold.
2. Remove the rocker arm cover and discard the old gasket.
3. Remove the rocker arm assemblies. Remove the pushrods.
4. Remove the lifter guide retainer bolts and retainer.
5. Remove the lifter retainers.
6. Using the valve lifter removal tool, remove the valve lifters.

To install:
7. Clean the gasket mounting surfaces.
8. Lubricate the lifters with clean engine oil, use new gaskets and/or sealant.
9. Install the valve lifters.
10. Install the lifter guide, retainer and retainer bolts.

11. Install the pushrods. Install the rocker arm assemblies.

12. Install the rocker arm cover.

13. Install the intake manifold.

14. Connect the negative battery cable.

Valve Lash

All engines use hydraulic lifters which are non-adjustable. Hydraulic valve lifters keep all parts of the valve train in constant contact and adjust automatically to maintain 0 lash under all operating conditions.

Rocker Arms

REMOVAL & INSTALLATION

3.8L Engine

1. Disconnect the negative battery cable. Remove the rocker arm cover nuts, washers, seals, the cover and gasket, discard the gasket.

2. Remove the rocker arm pivot-to-cylinder head bolts, the pivots, the rocker arms and the pushrod guide.

NOTE: Be sure to keep the parts in order for reassembly purposes.

3. Clean the gasket mounting surfaces.

4. Install the pushrod guide, rocker arms, pivots and rocker arm pivot-to-cylinder head bolts. Tighten to 28 ft. lbs. (38 Nm).

5. Install the rocker arm cover using a new gasket.

6. Connect the negative battery cable.

4.5L and 4.9L Engines

1. Disconnect the negative battery cable. Remove the rocker arm cover.

2. Remove the rocker arm support-to-cylinder head bolts.

3. Remove the rocker arm support-to-cylinder head stud nuts.

NOTE: This method of removal is preferred as the pivot assemblies may be damaged if the pivot bolt torque is not removed evenly against the valve spring tension.

4. Place the rocker arm support in a vise and remove the rocker arm pivot-to-rocker arm support bolts.

To install:

5. Lubricate all parts with axle lube 1052271 or equivalent, and reverse the removal procedures. Tighten the rocker arm pivot-to-rocker arm support bolts to 22 ft. lbs. (30 Nm).

NOTE: The pivot bolts are self-tapping.

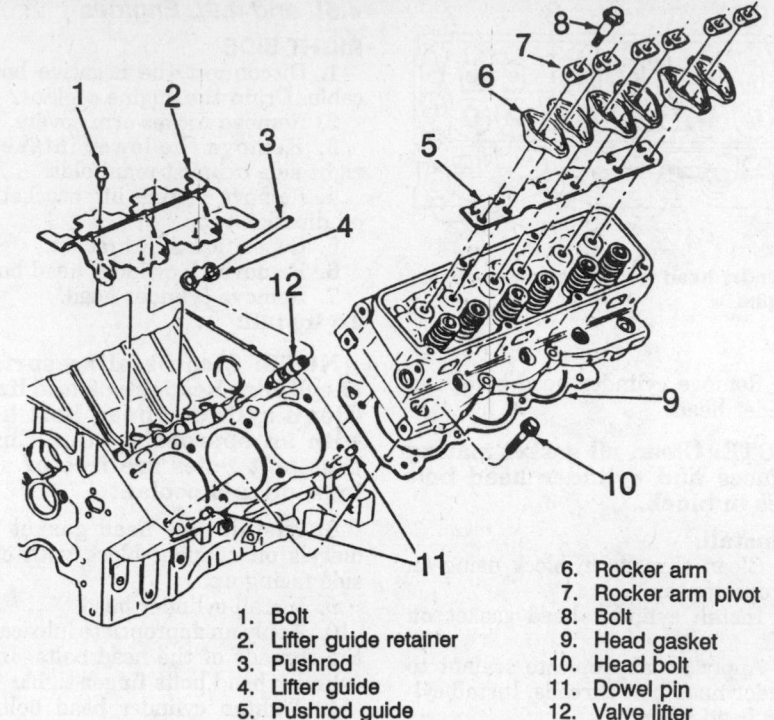

1. Bolt	6. Rocker arm
2. Lifter guide retainer	7. Rocker arm pivot
3. Pushrod	8. Bolt
4. Lifter guide	9. Head gasket
5. Pushrod guide	10. Head bolt
	11. Dowel pin
	12. Valve lifter

Exploded view of the rocker arm assembly—3.8L engine

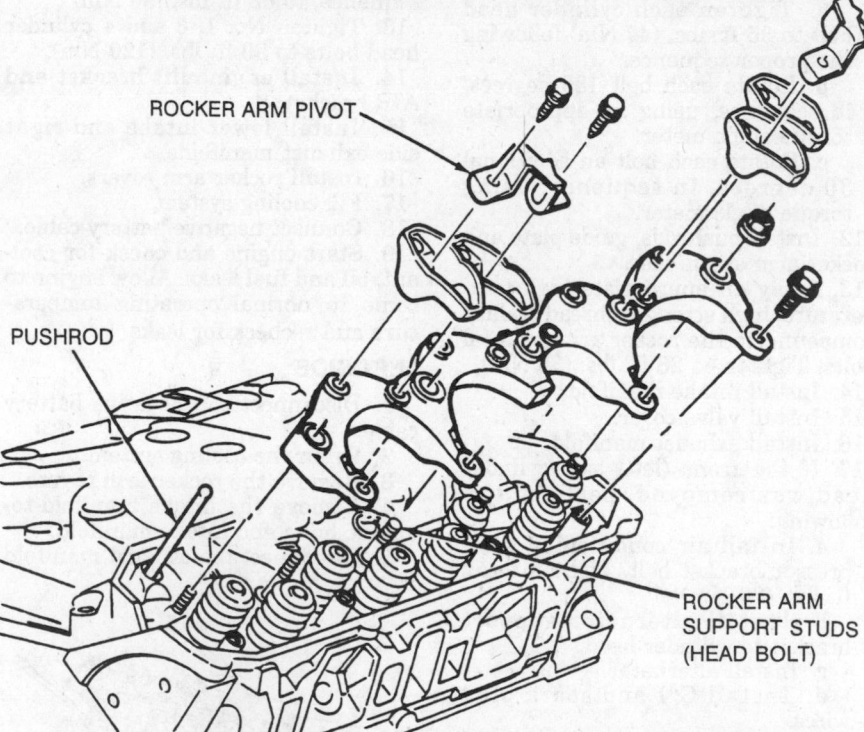

Exploded view of the rocker arm assembly—4.5L and 4.9L engines

6. Position the pushrod into the seat of each rocker arm and loosely install the retaining nuts.

7. Recheck the pushrods for being seated correctly. Tighten the nuts alternately and evenly, checking the position of the pushrods while tightening.

8. When the nuts have been seated and the pushrods are correct, tighten the rocker arm support-to-cylinder head nuts to 37 ft. lbs. (50 Nm) and the bolts to 7 ft. lbs. (10 Nm).

9. Install the rocker arm cover.

10. Connect the negative battery cable.

Intake Manifold

REMOVAL & INSTALLATION

Rivera, Reatta, Tornado and Trofeo

1989–90

1. Properly relieve the fuel system pressure.

2. Disconnect the negative battery cable. Place a clean drain pan under the radiator, open the drain cock and drain the cooling system.

3. Remove the serpentine drive belt, the alternator and bracket.

4. Remove the power steering pump, the braces and move it aside. Do not disconnect the pressure lines.

5. Remove the coolant bypass hose, the heater pipe and the upper radiator hose from the intake manifold.

6. Remove the vacuum hoses and disconnect the electrical connectors from the intake manifold.

7. Remove the EGR pipe, the EGR valve and adapter from the throttle body.

8. Remove the throttle body coolant pipe, the throttle body and the throttle body adapter.

9. Disconnect the rear spark plug wires. Remove the intake manifold-to-engine bolts and the manifold.

To install:

10. Clean the gasket mounting surfaces.

11. Using new gaskets and sealant 12345336 or equivalent, on the ends of the manifold seals, install the intake manifold. Tighten the intake manifold bolts, in sequence, to 88 inch lbs. (10 Nm).

12. Install the rear spark plug wires.

13. Install the throttle body adapter, throttle body and throttle body coolant pipe.

14. Install the EGR adapter to the throttle body, the EGR valve and the EGR pipe.

15. Install the vacuum hoses and connect the electrical connectors to the intake manifold.

16. Connect the upper radiator hose, heater pipe and coolant bypass hose to the intake manifold.

17. Install the power steering pump braces and power steering pump.

18. Install the alternator bracket and alternator. Install the serpentine drive belt.

19. Fill the cooling system.

20. Connect negative battery cable.

21. Start the engine and check for coolant, oil and fuel leaks. Allow the engine to come to normal operating temperature and recheck for leaks.

1991–93

1. Disconnect the negative battery

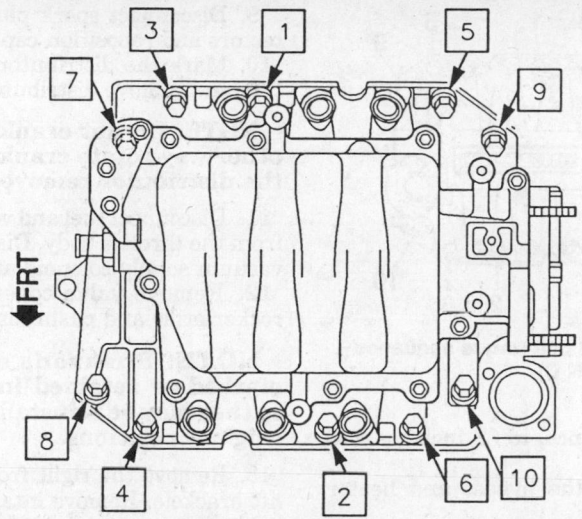

Intake manifold bolt torque sequence—3.8L engine (VIN L)

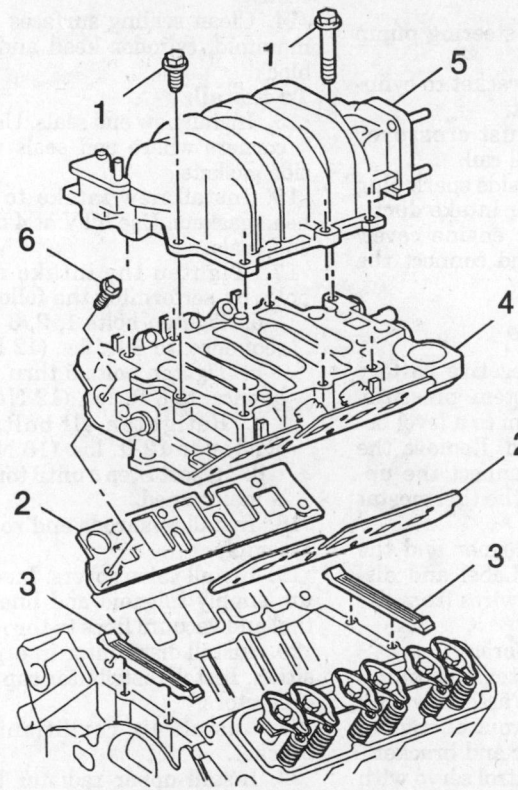

1. Upper intake manifold bolt
2. Intake manifold gasket
3. Intake manifold seal
4. Lower intake manifold
5. Upper intake manifold
6. Lower intake manifold bolt

Intake manifold assembly—3.8L engine (VIN L)

cable and remove plastic engine cover/fuel injector sight shield.

2. Remove the air intake duct. Tag and disconnect the right side spark plug wires.

3. Remove the fuel rail assembly.

4. Remove the exhaust crossover heat shield and the cable bracket to cylinder head mounting bolt.

5. Remove the power steering pump support bracket and loosen the alternator. Move alternator out of way.

6. Remove the alternator bracket.

7. Disconnect the heater pipes and bypass hose.

8. Remove the intake manifold bolts and remove the manifold from the vehicle.

To install:

9. Clean the gasket mounting surfaces.

10. Using new gaskets and sealant 12345336 or equivalent, on the ends of the manifold seals, install the intake manifold. Tighten the intake manifold

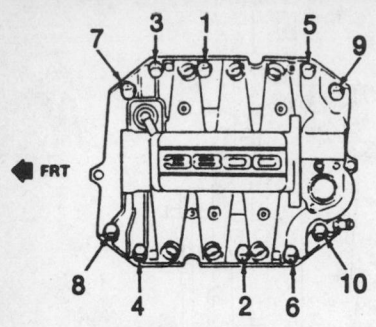

Intake manifold bolt torque sequence— 3.8L engine (VIN C)

bolts, in sequence, to 88 inch lbs. (10 Nm) twice.

11. Connect the bypass and heater hoses.

12. Install the alternator bracket and return the alternator to the proper position.

13. Install the power steering pump support bracket.

14. Install the cable bracket to cylinder head mounting bolt.

15. Install the exhaust crossover heat shield and the fuel rail.

16. Connect the right side spark plug wires and install the air intake duct.

17. Install the plastic engine cover/injector sight shield and connect the negative battery cable.

Eldorado and Seville

1. Disconnect the negative battery cable. Relieve fuel system pressure. Drain the cooling system to a level below the intake manifold. Remove the coolant reservoir. Disconnect the upper radiator hose from the thermostat housing.

2. Remove the air cleaner and the serpentine drive belt. Label and disconnect the spark plug wires from the spark plugs.

3. Remove the cross brace.

4. Remove power steering pump and tensioner bracket assembly and reposition toward the front of engine.

5. Remove alternator and bracket.

6. Remove cruise control servo with bracket and throttle valve cables and position aside.

7. Disconnect wire connections and reposition:
   a. Distributor
   b. Oil pressure switch
   c. Coolant temperature sensor
   d. EGR solenoid
   e. ISC motor
   f. Throttle position switch
   g. If equipped, electric EFE grid
   h. Injectors
   i. MAT sensor

8. If equipped, disconnect the MAP hoses. Remove upper radiator hose and heater hose. Remove air conditioning hose bracket.

9. Disconnect spark plug wire protectors and reposition cap.

10. Mark the distributor rotor position and remove distributor.

NOTE: Do not crank or in any other way rotate crankshaft with the distributor removed.

11. Disconnect fuel and vacuum lines from the throttle body. Disconnect the vacuum supply solenoid and lines.

12. Remove valve covers. Remove rocker arms and pushrods.

NOTE: Pushrods should be marked or retained in sequence so they may be reinstalled in their original positions.

13. Remove the right front and rear lift brackets. Remove intake manifold bolts and remove intake manifold, gaskets and seals. Discard gaskets and seals.

14. Clean sealing surfaces of intake manifold, cylinder head and cylinder block.

To install:

15. Install new end seals. Use RTV at 4 corners where end seals will meet side gaskets.

16. Install new intake to cylinder head gaskets. Use RTV at 4 corners of end seals.

17. Tighten the intake manifold bolts by performing the following:
   a. Tighten bolts 1, 2, 3 and 4, in sequence, to 8 ft. lbs. (12 Nm).
   b. Tighten bolts 5 thru 16, in sequence, to 8 ft. lbs. (12 Nm).
   c. Retighten all bolts, in sequence, to 12 ft. lbs. (16 Nm).
   d. Repeat Step c until torque level is maintained.

18. Install pushrods and rocker arm assembly.

19. Install valve covers. Install vacuum supply solenoid and lines. Install fuel and vacuum lines to throttle body.

20. Install distributor in original position. Install distributor cap and wire protectors.

21. Install air conditioning hose bracket.

22. Install upper radiator hose and heater hose. If equipped, connect the MAP hoses.

23. Connnect following wire connectors:
   a. Distributor
   b. Oil pressure switch
   c. Coolant temperature sensor
   d. EGR solenoid
   e. ISC motor
   f. Throttle position switch
   g. If equipped, electric EFE grid
   h. Injectors
   i. MAT sensor

24. Install cruise control servo and throttle valve cables.

25. Install alternator bracket and alternator.

26. Install power steering pump and tensioner assembly. Install power steering line brace to right side cylinder head.

27. Install serpentine drive belt. Install coolant reservoir.

28. Install cross brace.

29. Fill cooling system.

30. Install air cleaner assembly.

31. Connect negative battery cable.

32. Start engine and check for coolant, oil and fuel leaks. Allow engine to come to normal operating temperature and recheck for leaks.

Allante—1989–92
UPPER INTAKE MANIFOLD

1. Disconnect the negative battery cable.

2. Shock tower support bracket, as required.

3. Label and disconnect vacuum hoses.

4. Remove the transmission dipstick tube bolt.

5. Disconnect the MAT sensor electrical connector.

6. Remove the rear upper intake manifold support.

7. Remove the throttle body assembly from the upper intake manifold and discard the gasket.

8. Remove the throttle heater assembly and discard the gasket.

9. Remove the 4 upper intake manifold attaching nuts.

10. Remove the upper intake manifold and discard the gasket.

To install:

11. Ensure that all gasket mating surfaces are free of old gasket material.

12. Install a new upper intake-to-lower intake gasket.

13. Install the upper intake manifold and attaching nuts. Tighten to 15 ft. lbs. (20 Nm).

14. Install a new throttle heater gasket. Install the throttle heater assembly.

15. Install a new throttle body gasket. Install the throttle body to the upper intake manifold. Tighten throttle body attaching bolts to 15 ft. lbs. (20 Nm).

16. Install the rear upper intake manifold support.

17. Connect the MAT sensor electrical connector.

18. Install the transmission dipstick tube bolt.

19. Connect all vacuum lines.

20. If removed, install the shock tower support bracket.

21. Connect the negative battery cable.

LOWER INTAKE MANIFOLD

1. Disconnect the negative battery

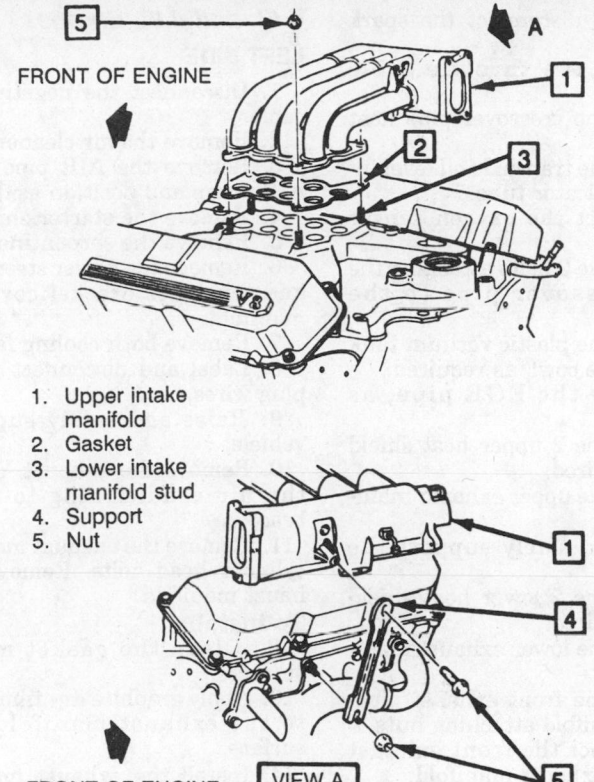

1. Upper intake manifold
2. Gasket
3. Lower intake manifold stud
4. Support
5. Nut

Upper intake manifold—4.5L engine—Allante

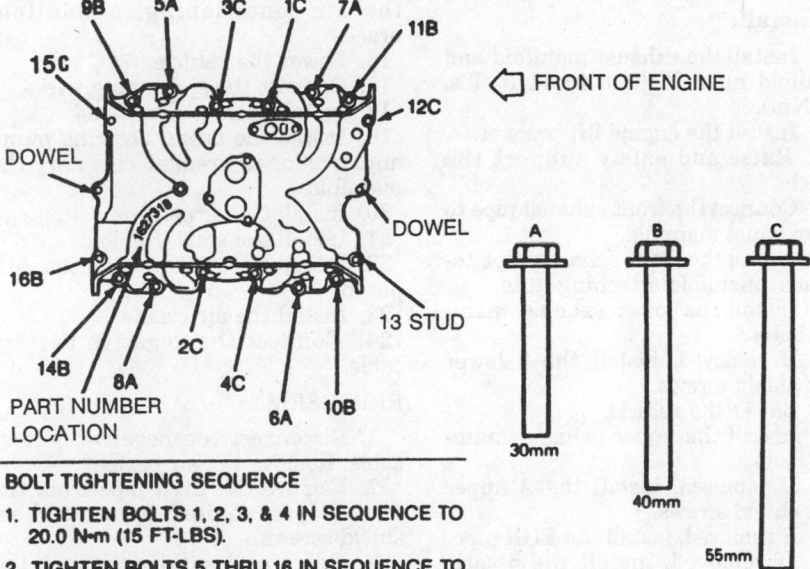

BOLT TIGHTENING SEQUENCE

1. TIGHTEN BOLTS 1, 2, 3, & 4 IN SEQUENCE TO 20.0 N·m (15 FT-LBS).
2. TIGHTEN BOLTS 5 THRU 16 IN SEQUENCE TO 30.0 N·m (22 FT-LBS).
3. RETIGHTEN ALL BOLTS IN SEQUENCE TO 30.0 N·m (22 FT-LBS).
4. REPEAT STEP 3.

Intake manifold bolt torque sequence—4.5L and 4.9L engines

cable. Relieve fuel system pressure. Drain the cooling system to a level below the lower intake manifold. Remove the coolant reservoir. Remove serpentine drive belt.

2. Remove the air cleaner assembly.

3. Label and disconnect appropriate vacuum lines.

4. Remove the upper intake manifold and fuel rails.

5. Remove the power steering line brace on the right side cylinder head.

6. Remove the power steering pump and tensioner bracket assembly and reposition toward the front of the engine.

7. Remove alternator with bracket and idler pulley.

8. Remove cruise control servo with bracket and cables. Reposition aside.

9. Disconnect wire connections as follows:
   a. Distributor
   b. Oil pressure switches
   c. Coolant temperature sensor
   d. Ground wires

10. Disconnect the upper radiator hose and 2 heater hose connections.

11. Disconnect spark plug wire protectors and reposition cap.

12. Mark distributor rotor position and remove distributor.

NOTE: Do not crank or in any other way rotate crankshaft with the distributor removed.

13. Remove valve covers. Remove rocker arms and pushrods.

NOTE: Pushrods should be marked or retained in sequence so they may be reinstalled in their original positions.

14. Remove intake manifold bolts and remove intake manifold, gaskets and seals. Discard gaskets and seals.

15. Clean sealing surfaces of intake manifold, cylinder head and cylinder block.

To install:

16. Install new end seals. Use RTV 1052915 or equivalent, at the 4 corners where end seals meet side gaskets.

17. Install new intake to cylinder head gaskets. Use RTV at 4 corners of end seals.

18. Tighten the intake manifold bolts by performing the following:
   a. Tighten bolts 1, 2, 3 and 4, in sequence, to 8 ft. lbs. (12 Nm).
   b. Tighten bolts 5 thru 16, in sequence, to 8 ft. lbs. (12 Nm).
   c. Retighten all bolts, in sequence, to 12 ft. lbs. (16 Nm).
   d. Repeat Step c until torque level is maintained.

19. Install pushrods and rocker arm assembly.

20. Install valve covers.

21. Install distributor in original position. Install distributor cap and wire protectors.

22. Install air conditioning hose bracket.

23. Install upper radiator hose and heater hose.

24. Connect following wire connectors:
   a. Distributor
   b. Oil pressure switch
   c. Coolant temperature sensor
   d. Ground wires

25. Install cruise control servo and throttle valve cables.

26. Install alternator bracket and alternator.

27. Install power steering line brace to right side cylinder head. Install power steering pump and tensioner assembly.

28. Install serpentine drive belt. Install coolant reservoir.

29. Install fuel rail assembly and upper intake manifold to the lower intake manifold.

30. Connect vacuum lines.

31. Install heater assembly and gasket.

32. Install accelerator, cruise control and throttle valve cables.

33. Fill cooling system.

34. Install air cleaner assembly.

35. Connect negative battery cable.

36. Start engine and check for coolant, oil and fuel leaks. Allow engine to come to normal operating temperature and recheck for leaks.

Exhaust Manifold

REMOVAL & INSTALLATION

3.8L Engine

LEFT SIDE

1. Disconnect the negative battery cable.

2. Remove the engine strut.

3. Remove the 2 bolts attaching the exhaust crossover pipe-to-exhaust manifold.

4. Remove the cooling fan assembly, as required.

5. Label and disconnect the spark plug wires.

6. Remove the oil dipstick tube to provide access to the manifold bolts, as required.

7. Remove the exhaust manifold-to-cylinder head bolts and the manifold.

To install:

8. Install the exhaust manifold gasket. Tighten the exhaust manifold-to-cylinder head bolts to 41 ft. lbs. (55 Nm).

9. If removed, install the oil dipstick tube.

10. Connect the spark plug wires.

11. If removed, install the cooling fan assembly.

12. Install the 2 exhaust crossover pipe-to-exhaust manifold attaching bolts. Tighten the exhaust crossover pipe-to-manifold bolts to 22 ft. lbs. (30 Nm).

13. Install the engine strut.

14. Connect the negative battery cable. Start the engine and check for exhaust leaks.

RIGHT SIDE

1. Disconnect the negative battery cable.

2. Label and disconnect the spark plug wires.

3. Remove the throttle cable bracket.

4. Remove the crossover pipe heat shield.

5. Remove the transaxle oil level indicator and indicator tube.

6. Disconnect the oxygen sensor lead.

7. Remove the 2 bolts attaching the exhaust crossover pipe to the manifold.

8. Remove the plastic vacuum tank mounted on the cowl, as required.

9. Remove the EGR pipe, as required.

10. Remove the 2 upper heat shield screws, as required.

11. Remove the upper exhaust manifold bolts.

12. Raise and safely support the vehicle.

13. Remove the 2 lower heat shield screws, as required.

14. Remove the lower exhaust manifold bolts.

15. Remove the front exhaust pipe-to-exhaust manifold attaching nuts.

16. Disconnect the front exhaust pipe from the exhaust manifold.

17. Lower the vehicle.

18. Remove the engine lift bracket.

19. Remove the exhaust manifold nuts and remove the manifold.

To install:

20. Install the exhaust manifold and manifold nuts. Tighten to 41 ft. lbs. (55 Nm).

21. Install the engine lift bracket.

22. Raise and safely support the vehicle.

23. Connect the front exhaust pipe to the exhaust manifold.

24. Install the front exhaust pipe-to-exhaust manifold attaching nuts.

25. Install the lower exhaust manifold bolts.

26. If removed, install the 2 lower heat shield screws.

27. Lower the vehicle.

28. Install the upper exhaust manifold bolts.

29. If removed, install the 2 upper heat shield screws.

30. If removed, install the EGR pipe.

31. If removed, install the plastic vacuum tank mounted on the cowl.

32. Install the 2 bolts attaching the exhaust crossover pipe to the manifold.

33. Connect the oxygen sensor lead.

34. Install the transaxle oil level indicator and indicator tube.

35. Install the crossover pipe heat shield.

36. Install the throttle cable bracket.

37. Connect the spark plug wires.

38. Connect the negative battery cable.

4.5L and 4.9L Engines

LEFT SIDE

1. Disconnect the negative battery cable.

2. Remove the air cleaner.

3. Remove the AIR pipe from the AIR pump and position aside.

4. Remove the starter shield.

5. Remove the serpentine belt.

6. Remove the power steering pump and tensioner bracket covering the manifold.

7. Remove both cooling fans.

8. Label and disconnect the spark plug wires.

9. Raise and safely support the vehicle.

10. Remove the exhaust Y-pipe and the air conditioning-to-manifold brace.

11. Remove the exhaust manifold-to-cylinder head bolts. Remove the exhaust manifold.

To install:

12. Clean the gasket mounting surfaces.

13. Apply graphite dry film lubricant to the exhaust manifold sealing surface.

14. Install the exhaust manifold to the cylinder head. Install the 7 attaching bolts and tighten to 16 ft. lbs. (20 Nm).

15. Install the exhaust Y-pipe and the air conditioning-to-manifold brace.

16. Lower the vehicle.

17. Connect the spark plug wires.

18. Install both cooling fans.

19. Install the power steering pump and tensioner bracket covering the manifold.

20. Install the serpentine belt.

21. Install the starter shield.

22. Install the AIR pipe to the AIR pump.

23. Install the air cleaner.

24. Connect the negative battery cable.

RIGHT SIDE

1. Disconnect the negative battery cable. Remove the air cleaner.

2. Remove the EGR pipe from the manifold, as required. Remove 2 heat shield screws.

3. Raise and safely support the vehicle.

4. Disconnect the Y-pipe from the manifold.

5. Remove the engine mount brace from the front of the manifold.

6. Disconnect the oxygen sensor wire. Remove heat shield.

7. Support engine cradle with screw jacks and remove rear cradle bolts on both sides. Loosen front cradle bolts. Slightly lower engine cradle.

8. Remove the exhaust manifold-to-cylinder head bolts and the manifold.

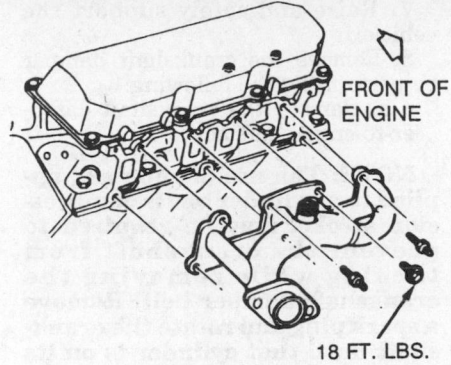

FRONT OF
ENGINE

18 FT. LBS.

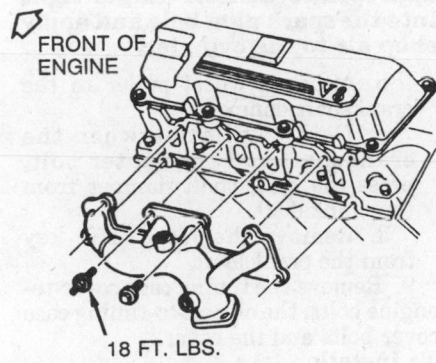

FRONT OF
ENGINE

18 FT. LBS.

**Exploded view of the exhaust manifolds—
4.5L and 4.9L engines**

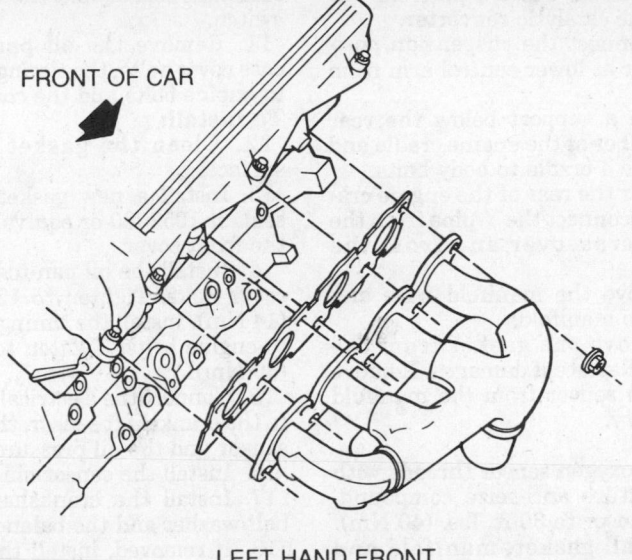

FRONT OF CAR

LEFT HAND FRONT

RIGHT HAND REAR

4.6L engine exhaust manifolds

To install:

9. Clean the gasket mounting surfaces.

10. Apply graphite dry film lubricant to the exhaust manifold sealing surface.

11. Install the exhaust manifold to the cylinder head. Install the 7 attaching bolts and tighten to 16 ft. lbs. (20 Nm).

12. Install the heat shield.

13. Connect the oxygen sensor wire.

14. Install the engine brace on the right side of the manifold.

15. Raise the engine cradle and install the rear bolts. Tighten all mounting bolts to 75 ft. lbs. (100 Nm).

16. Install the exhaust crossover pipe.

17. Lower the vehicle.

18. Install the 2 heat shield screws.

19. Install the air cleaner.

20. Connect the negative battery cable.

4.6L Engine

LEFT SIDE

1. Disconnect the negative battery cable. Remove the left side motor mount and bracket.

2. Remove the rear alternator bracket.

3. Remove the 2 bolts at the manifold outlet flange.

4. Disconnect the oxygen sensor.

5. Remove the exhaust manifold from the cylinder head and remove the manifold.

6. Remove the gasket. Remove the oxygen sensor from the manifold.

To install:

7. Install gasket to the manifold. Insert 2 screws to hold gasket in place.

8. Insert outlet pipe partially into exhaust crossover pipe to install exhaust manifold. Move manifold into position.

9. Tighten the manifold bolts to 20 ft. lbs. (25 Nm).

10. Coat the oxygen sensor threads with Hi temperature anti-seize compound and install the sensor. Tighten sensor nut to 30 ft. lbs. (40 Nm).

11. Connect the oxygen sensor connector and install the rear alternator bracket. Tighten the crankcase bolts to 40 ft. lbs. (60 Nm) and the alternator bolts to 25 ft. lbs. (30 Nm).

12. Install the motor mount and bracket.

13. Install 2 new bolts at the manifold outlet flange and tighten to 35 ft. lbs. (50 Nm).

14. Connect the negative battery cable.

RIGHT SIDE

1. Disconnect the negative battery cable.

2. Disconnect the rear oxygen sensor at the rear of the right cam cover. Disconnect the harness clip.

3. Raise and safely support the vehicle.

4. Disconnect the Y-pipe from the front of the catalytic converter.

5. Disconnect the suspension position sensor at lower control arm from both sides.

6. Place a support below the rear cross member of the engine cradle and remove the 4 cradle to body bolts.

7. Lower the rear of the engine cradle and disconnect the Y-pipe from the exhaust crossover and from the manifold.

8. Remove the manifold nuts and remove the manifold.

9. Remove the gasket from the manifold. Replace if damaged. Remove the oxygen sensor from the manifold as necessary.

To install:

10. Coat oxygen sensor threads with hi-temperature anti-seize compound. Tighten sensor to 30 ft. lbs. (40 Nm).

11. Install gasket, manifold and nuts. Tighten nuts to 25 ft. lbs. (30 Nm).

12. Install exhaust Y-pipe and install 4 new bolts. Tighten the bolts to 45 ft. lbs. (60 Nm).

13. Raise engine cradle into position and tighten the bolts to 75 ft. lbs. (100 Nm).

14. Connect the exhaust Y-pipe to the catalytic converter and tighten 2 new bolts to 35 ft. lbs. (50 Nm).

15. Connect the suspension position sensors to the lower control arms.

16. Lower the vehicle and connect the oxygen sensor. Install the harness retainer.

17. Connect the negative battery cable.

Timing Chain Front Cover

REMOVAL & INSTALLATION

3.8L Engine

1. Disconnect the negative battery cable.

2. Drain the cooling system. Remove the lower radiator hose and the coolant bypass hose from the timing case cover. Remove the heater pipes.

3. Remove the serpentine drive belt and the water pump pulley.

4. Raise and safely support the vehicle.

5. Remove right front tire and wheel assembly.

6. Remove the inner splash shield.

7. Remove the front engine-to-frame stabilizer and bracket, as required.

8. Remove the crankshaft balancer bolt/washer and the balancer.

9. Remove the sensor shield.

10. Disconnect the electrical connectors from the crankshaft sensor, the camshaft sensor and the oil pressure switch.

11. Remove the oil pan-to-timing case cover bolts, the timing case cover-to-engine bolts and the cover.

To install:

12. Clean the gasket mounting surfaces.

13. Install a new gasket and apply sealant 1052080 or equivalent. Install the front cover.

14. Install the oil pan-to-timing case cover bolts. Tighten to 124 inch lbs. (14 Nm). Install the timing case cover-to-engine bolts. Tighten to 22 ft. lbs. (30 Nm).

15. Connect the electrical connectors to the crankshaft sensor, the camshaft sensor and the oil pressure switch.

16. Install the sensor shield.

17. Install the crankshaft balancer bolt/washer and the balancer.

18. If removed, install the front engine-to-frame stabilizer and bracket.

19. Install the inner splash shield.

20. Install right front tire and wheel assembly.

21. Lower the vehicle.

22. Install the water pump pulley and serpentine drive belt.

23. Install the lower radiator hose and the coolant bypass hose to the timing case cover. Install the heater pipes.

24. Connect the negative battery cable.

25. Fill cooling system and check for leaks. Start the engine and allow to come to normal operating temperature. Recheck for leaks. Top-up coolant.

4.5L and 4.9L Engines

1. Disconnect the negative battery cable.

2. Drain the cooling system. Remove the air cleaner.

3. Remove the serpentine belt.

4. Remove the cross-car brace and coolant reservoir.

5. Remove the AIR air filter and bracket, if equipped.

6. Remove the water pump pulley bolts and the pulley. Remove the water pump from the vehicle.

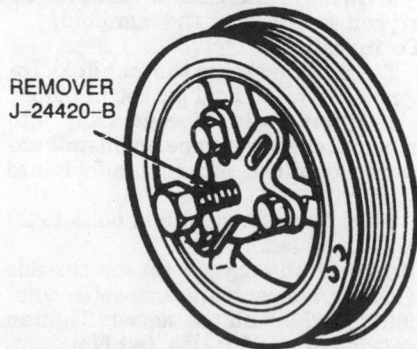

REMOVER J-24420-B

Using the wheel puller tool to remove the damper pulley—4.5L and 4.9L engines

7. Raise and safely support the vehicle.

8. Remove the crankshaft damper by performing the following:

a. Remove the crankshaft damper-to-crankshaft bolt.

NOTE: The use of shop air, applied to a cylinder on its compression stroke, may be required to prevent the crankshaft from turning while removing the crankshaft damper bolt. Remove a spark plug and rotate the crankshaft until that cylinder is on its compression stroke. Install the appropriate adapter finger-tight into the spark plug hole and apply shop air to the cylinder.

b. Attach a wheel puller to the crankshaft damper.

c. Using a pilot between the crankshaft and the center bolt, press the crankshaft damper from the crankshaft.

d. Remove the Woodruff® key from the crankshaft.

9. Remove the timing case cover-to-engine bolts, the oil pan-to-timing case cover bolts and the cover.

To install:

10. Clean the gasket mounting surfaces.

11. To avoid oil leakage, apply RTV sealer according to the following:

a. Apply a bead of RTV on the front cover lip on the oil pan sealing surface. Ensure that this bead is placed along the front cover lip behind the 2 oil pan-to-front cover bolts.

b. Apply a ¼ in. bead of RTV on the oil pan where the oil pan, block and front cover join.

c. Remove any excess RTV that is squeezed out of the sealing area.

12. Install the front cover.

13. Install the crankshaft damper by performing the following:

a. Lubricate the bore of the hub and the inside diameter of the seal with EP lubricant.

b. Install the Woodruff® key in the key slot in the crankshaft.

c. Position the damper on the crankshaft, lining up the key slot with the key.

d. Thread the installer into the end of the crankshaft. Position the thrust bearing with the inner race forward, washer next and installer nut last.

e. Install the damper on the crankshaft by tightening the installer nut.

NOTE: The use of compressed air, applied to a cylinder on its compression stroke, may be required to prevent the crankshaft from turning while installing the

crankshaft damper bolt. Remove a spark plug and rotate the crankshaft until that cylinder is on its compression stroke. Install an adapter finger-tight into the spark plug hole and apply shop air to the cylinder.

  f. Tighten nut until the hub bottoms out on the crankshaft. Tighten the nut to 60–65 ft. lbs. (80–90 Nm) to fully seat the balancer and timing gear. Remove the installer and reinstall the bolt and washer into the crankshaft. Tighten to 60–65 ft. lbs. (80–90 Nm).

  g. Exhaust the compressed air to the cylinder, remove the adapter and reinstall the spark plug.

14. Lower the vehicle.
15. Install the water pump.
16. Install the water pump pulley.
17. Install the serpentine belt.
18. Install the coolant reservoir and cross-car brace.
19. Connect the negative battery cable.
20. Fill cooling system and check for leaks. Start the engine and allow to come to normal operating temperature. Recheck for leaks. Top-up coolant.

4.6L Engine

1. Disconnect the negative battery cable.
2. Remove the serpentine belt.
3. Remove the harmonic balancer as described below:
  a. Release tension from the accessory drive belt.
  b. Raise and safely support the vehicle, remove the right front wheel.
  c. Remove the splash shields from the wheelhouse and remove the brace between the oil pan and the transmission case.
  d. Install the flywheel holder tool J39411 or equivalent and remove the balancer bolt.
  e. Support the engine cradle and remove the 3 bolts from the right side of the cradle.
  f. Disconnect the RSS sensor from the right lower control arm.
  g. Lower the engine cradle enough for clearance of puller tool.
  h. Install pilot tool J39344-2 into the end of the crankshaft.
  i. Remove the harmonic balancer using puller tool J38416 or equivalent.
4. Remove the belt tensioner and the belt idler pulley.
5. Remove the front cover bolts and remove the cover with the gasket.

To install:
6. Install the cover gasket over the dowel pins.
7. Install the front cover over the

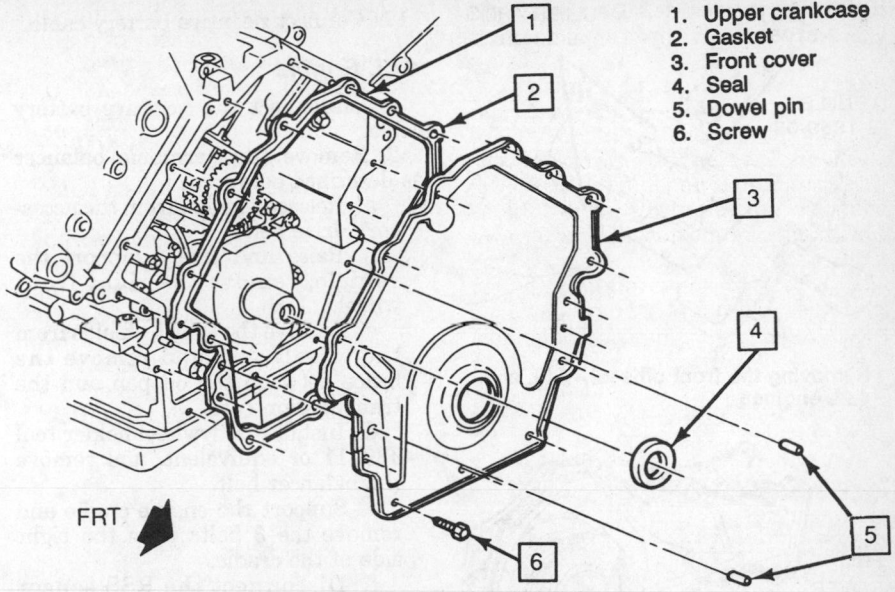

1. Upper crankcase
2. Gasket
3. Front cover
4. Seal
5. Dowel pin
6. Screw

FRT

Front cover removal—4.6L engine

dowel pins and tighten the cover screws to 7 ft. lbs. (10 Nm).
8. Install the idler pulley and the belt tensioner. Tighten both to 35 ft. lbs. (50 Nm).
9. Install the harmonic balancer as described below:
  a. Position the balancer to the crankshaft and using tool J39344 or equivalent install the balancer.
  b. Clean the balancer bolt threads and apply oil to the threads. Tighten the balancer bolt to 105 ft. lbs. (145 Nm) + 120 degrees.
  c. Raise the engine cradle into place and install the 3 bolts. Tighten the 3 bolts to 75 ft. lbs. (100 Nm).
  d. Reconnect the suspension position sensors to the lower control arms.
  e. Remove the flywheel holder tool and install the oil pan-to-trans brace. Tighten the 4 bolts to 35 ft. lbs. (50 Nm).
  f. Install the wheel house splash shields and the right front wheel.
  g. Lower the vehicle and install the accessory drive belt.
  c. Remove any excess RTV that is squeezed out of the sealing area.
10. Install the serpentine drive belt and connect the negative battery cable.

Front Cover Oil Seal

REPLACEMENT

3.8L Engine

1. Disconnect the negative battery cable.
2. Remove the serpentine drive belt.
3. Remove the crankshaft balancer-to-crankshaft bolts.

4. Using a small prybar, pry the oil seal from the timing case cover; be careful not to damage the sealing surfaces.

To install:
5. Clean the oil seal mounting surface.
6. Using GM lubricant 1050169 or equivalent, coat the outside of the seal and the crankshaft balancer.
7. Using an appropriate oil seal installation tool, press the new seal into the timing case cover until it seats.
8. Install the crankshaft balancer-to-crankshaft bolt according to the following:
  a. On 3.8L (VIN C) engine, tighten the crankshaft balancer-to-crankshaft bolt to 219 ft. lbs. (297 Nm).
  b. On 3.8L (VIN L) engine, tighten the crankshaft balancer-to-crankshaft bolt to 105 ± 7 ft. lbs. (140 ± 10 Nm) plus 56 ± 4 degrees.
9. Install the serpentine drive belt.
10. Connect the negative battery cable.

4.5L and 4.9L Engines

1. Disconnect the negative battery cable.
2. Remove the serpentine belt.
3. Raise and safely support the vehicle.
4. Remove right front tire. Remove right front air deflector.
5. Loosen and reposition the heater bypass line.
6. Remove the crankshaft pulley-to-crankshaft pulley bolt. Attach a wheel puller to the crankshaft pulley. Using a pilot between the crankshaft and the center bolt, press the crankshaft pulley from the crankshaft. Remove the Woodruff® key from the crankshaft.

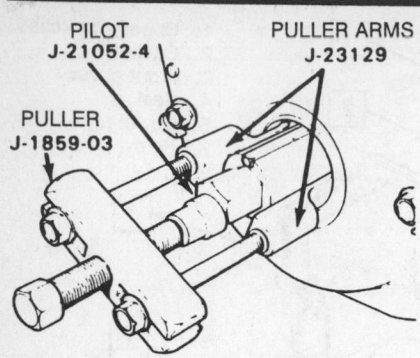

Removing the front oil seal—4.5L and 4.9L engines

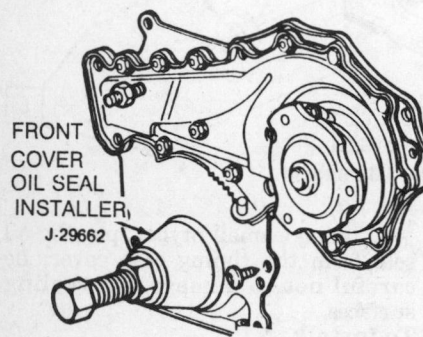

Installing the front oil seal—4.5L and 4.9L engines

7. Using a small prybar, pry the oil seal from the timing case cover, discard it.

To install:

8. Clean the oil seal mounting surface. Lubricate the new seal with engine oil.

9. Using a hammer and the oil seal installation tool, drive the new oil seal into the timing case cover until it seats.

10. Lubricate bore of hub and inside diameter of seal with EP lubricant to prevent seizure to crankshaft and provide lubrication of oil seal lip.

11. Position damper on crankshaft, lining up key slot in hub with key on crankshaft.

12. Position installer on end of crankshaft. Position thrust bearing with inner race forward, then washer and installer nut last. Install damper on crankshaft by tightening installer nut.

13. Hub will bottom out on crankshaft. Tighten installer nut to 65 ft. lbs. (90 Nm) to ensure balancer and timing gear are fully seated. Remove installer and reinstall bolt/washer in crankshaft. Tighten to 65 ft. lbs. (90 Nm).

14. Install heater bypass line.

15. Install right front air deflector. Install right front tire.

16. Install serpentine belt.

17. Connect negative battery cable.

4.6L Engine

1. Disconnect the negative battery cable.

2. Remove the harmonic balancer as described below:

   a. Release tension from the accessory drive belt.

   b. Raise and safely support the vehicle, remove the right front wheel.

   c. Remove the splash shields from the wheelhouse and remove the brace between the oil pan and the transmission case.

   d. Install the flywheel holder tool J39411 or equivalent, and remove the balancer bolt.

   e. Support the engine cradle and remove the 3 bolts from the right side of the cradle.

   f. Disconnect the RSS sensor from the right lower control arm.

   g. Lower the engine cradle enough for clearance of puller tool.

   h. Install pilot tool J39344-2 into the end of the crankshaft.

   i. Remove the harmonic balancer using puller tool J38416 or equivalent.

3. Using a small prybar, pry the oil seal out of the bore. Use caution not to damage the bore. Discard the old oil seal.

To install:

4. Clean the oil seal mounting surface. Lubricate the new seal with engine oil.

5. Install the new seal to the front cover, using seal installer tool J38818 and harmonic balancer installation tool J39344 or equivalents.

6. Install the harmonic balancer as described below:

   a. Position the balancer to the crankshaft and using tool J39344 or equivalent install the balancer.

   b. Clean the balancer bolt threads and apply oil to the threads. Tighten the balancer bolt to 105 ft. lbs. (145 Nm) + 120 degrees.

   c. Raise the engine cradle into place and install the 3 bolts. Tighten the 3 bolts to 75 ft. lbs. (100 Nm).

   d. Reconnect the suspension position sensors to the lower control arms.

   e. Remove the flywheel holder tool and install the oil pan-to-trans brace. Tighten the 4 bolts to 35 ft. lbs. (50 Nm).

   f. Install the wheel house splash shields and the right front wheel.

   g. Lower the vehicle and install the accessory drive belt.

   h. Remove any excess RTV that is squeezed out of the sealing area.

7. Connect the negative battery cable.

Timing Chain and Sprockets

REMOVAL & INSTALLATION

3.8L Engine

1. Disconnect the negative battery cable. Remove the front cover.

2. Rotate the crankshaft to align the marks of the timing sprockets.

3. Remove the button and spring or damper from the center of the camshaft.

4. Remove the camshaft sprocket bolts, the sprocket and the timing chain.

5. Remove the crankshaft sprocket and the Woodruff® key.

To install:

6. Clean the gasket mounting surfaces. Inspect the parts for wear and/or damage. Replace as required.

7. Install the timing chain and sprockets by performing the following:

   a. Ensure that the camshaft sprocket mark is aligned with the balancer shaft sprocket mark.

   b. Assemble the timing chain on the camshaft sprocket and crankshaft sprockets.

   c. Align the 0 marks on the sprockets; they must face each other.

   d. Slide the assembly onto the camshaft and crankshaft. Install the camshaft sprocket-to-camshaft bolts. Tighten the camshaft sprocket-to-camshaft sprocket bolts to 27 ft. lbs. (37 Nm) for VIN C vehicles or

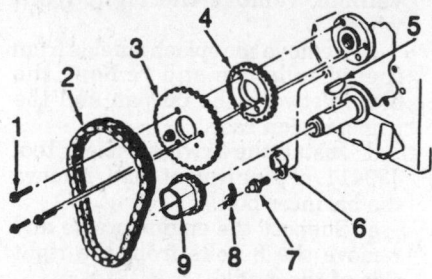

Exploded view of the timing chain assembly—3.8L engine

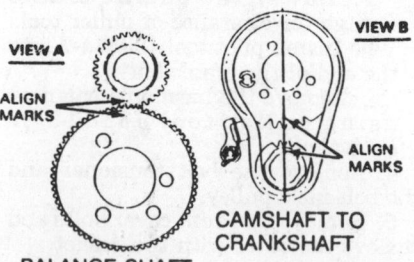

View of the timing sprocket alignment—3.8L engine

to 74 ft. lbs. (100 Nm) + 105 degrees for VIN L vehicles.

8. Using petroleum jelly, pack the oil pump.

9. Install the button and spring/camshaft damper to the center of the camshaft.

10. Install the front cover.

11. Connect the negative battery cable.

12. Fill cooling system and check for leaks. Start the engine and allow to come to normal operating temperature. Recheck for leaks. Top-up coolant.

4.5L and 4.9L Engines

1. Disconnect the negative battery cable. Drain the cooling system.

2. Remove engine front cover.

3. Remove oil slinger from crankshaft.

4. Rotate the engine until the crankshaft and camshaft timing marks are aligned.

5. Remove thrust button and screw securing camshaft sprocket to camshaft. Discard thrust button.

6. Remove camshaft and crankshaft sprockets with chain attached.

To install:

7. If timing was disturbed, rotate crankshaft until timing mark on crank sprocket is positioned straight up.

8. Install timing chain over camshaft sprocket.

9. Install cam sprocket, crank sprocket and timing chain over crankshaft, ensuring that timing marks are aligned.

10. Move camshaft until the dowel pin mates with the index hole in the sprocket.

11. Hold camshaft sprocket in position against end of camshaft and press sprocket onto camshaft by hand, being sure index pin in camshaft is aligned with index hole in sprocket.

12. Install screw securing camshaft sprocket to camshaft. Tighten to 36 ft. lbs. (48 Nm).

NOTE: It may be necessary to keep the engine from rotating while setting the torque.

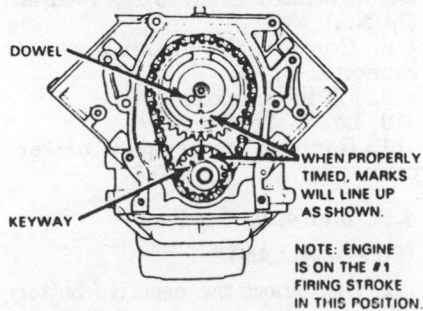

Aligning the timing marks — 4.5L and 4.9L engines

13. Install new thrust button.

14. Install oil slinger on crankshaft with smaller end of slinger against crankshaft sprocket.

15. Install engine front cover.

16. Connect negative battery cable.

Camshaft

REMOVAL & INSTALLATION

3.8L Engine

To perform this procedure on the 3.8L VIN C equipped vehicle, the engine must first be removed and attached to an engine stand.

1. Disconnect the negative battery cable.

2. Remove the intake manifold.

3. Remove the rocker arm covers, rocker arms, pushrods and lifters.

NOTE: Keep all valve train components in order so they may be reinstalled in their original positions.

4. Remove the crankshaft pulley/balancer. Remove the crankshaft sensor cover for VIN L engine.

5. Remove the front cover.

6. Remove the timing chain and sprockets.

7. Remove the camshaft thrust plate.

8. Carefully, remove the camshaft.

To install:

9. Coat the camshaft with prelube 10423565 or equivalent, prior to installation.

10. Carefully, install the thrust plate.

11. Install the timing chain and sprockets.

12. Install the front cover.

13. Install the crankshaft sensor cover.

14. Install the crankshaft pulley/balancer.

15. Install the lifters, pushrods and rocker arms in their original positions.

16. Install the rocker arm covers.

17. Install the intake manifold.

18. Connect the negative battery cable.

4.5L and 4.9L Engines

To perform this procedure, the engine must be removed from the vehicle and attached to an engine stand.

1. Disconnect the negative battery cable. Remove the intake manifold and the timing chain.

2. Remove the rocker arm covers, rocker arms, pushrods and valve lifters.

NOTE: Keep all valve train components in order so they may be reinstalled in their original positions.

3. Carefully slide the camshaft out from the front of the engine.

To install:

NOTE: If a new camshaft is to be installed, new lifters and a distributor drive gear must also be installed.

4. Lubricate the camshaft with camshaft prelube 1052365 or equivalent, on all camshaft lobes, distributor drive and driven gear teeth and bearing journals.

5. Carefully, install the camshaft into the engine.

6. Install the camshaft sprocket-to-camshaft bolt and tighten to 31 ft. lbs. (50 Nm).

7. Install the lifters, pushrods and rocker arms in their original positions. Install the rocker arm covers.

8. Install the timing chain and intake manifold.

9. Connect the negative battery cable.

Silent Shaft

REMOVAL & INSTALLATION

3.8L Engine

1. Disconnect the negative battery cable. Remove the engine and secure it to a workstand.

2. Remove the flywheel-to-crankshaft bolts and the flywheel.

3. Remove the intake manifold.

4. Remove the lifter guide retainer.

5. Remove the front cover-to-engine bolts and front cover.

6. Remove the camshaft sprocket-to-camshaft gear bolts, the sprocket, the timing chain and the gear.

7. To remove the balance shaft, perform the following:

a. Remove the balance shaft gear-to-shaft bolt and the gear.

b. Remove the balance shaft retainer-to-engine bolts and the retainer.

c. Using the slide hammer tool, pull the balance shaft from the front of the engine.

8. If replacing the rear balance shaft bearing, perform the following procedures:

a. Drive the rear plug from the engine.

b. Using the camshaft remover/installer tool, press the rear bearing from the rear of the engine.

c. Dip the new bearing in clean engine oil.

d. Using the balance shaft rear bearing installer tool, press the new rear bearing into the rear of the engine.

e. Install the rear cup plug.

To install:

9. Using the balance shaft installer

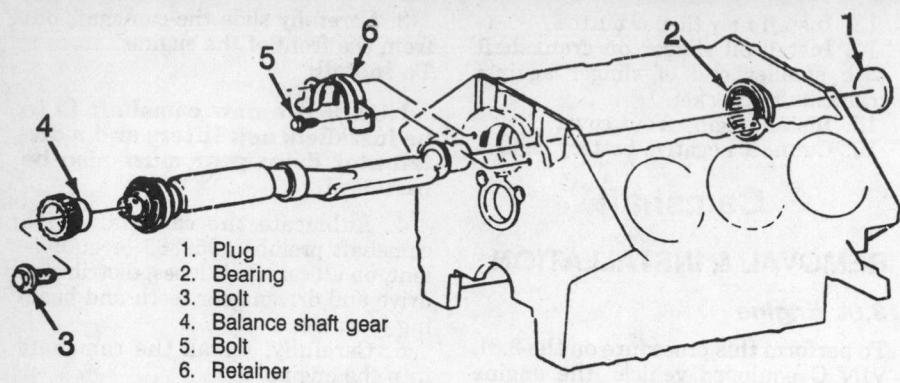

1. Plug
2. Bearing
3. Bolt
4. Balance shaft gear
5. Bolt
6. Retainer

Exploded view of the balance shaft assembly—3.8L engine

tool, screw it into the balance shaft and install the shaft into the engine. Remove the installer.

10. Turn the camshaft with the camshaft sprocket temporarily installed, so the timing mark is straight down.

11. With the camshaft sprocket and the camshaft gear removed, turn the balance shaft so the timing mark on the gear points straight down.

12. Align the marks on the balance shaft gear and camshaft gear by turning the balance shaft. Install the camshaft gear.

13. Turn the crankshaft so No. 1 piston is on TDC.

14. Install the timing chain and camshaft sprocket.

15. Install the balance shaft front bearing retainer and bolts. Tighten to 22 ft. lbs. (30 Nm).

16. Install the front cover.

17. Install the lifter guide retainer.

18. Install the intake manifold.

19. Install the flywheel. Tighten the attaching bolt to 61 ft. lbs. (82 Nm) for the VIN C engine or to 11 ft. lbs. (15 Nm) + 50 degrees for VIN L engine.

20. Install the engine and connect the negative battery cable.

Piston and Connecting Rod

POSITIONING

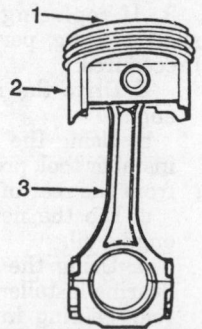

1. Notch (installed toward front of engine)
2. Piston
3. Connecting rod

View of the piston assembly using 1 notch on the piston and the oil hole on the side of the connecting rod—4.5L and 4.9L engines

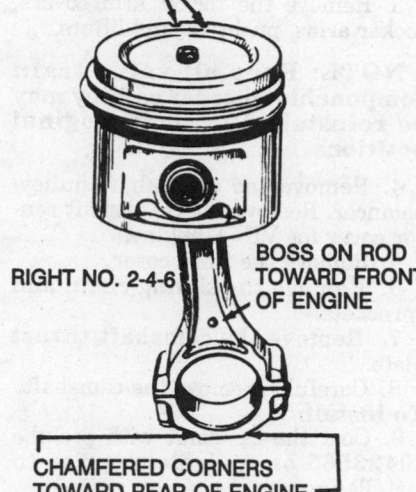

NOTCHES TOWARD FRONT OF ENGINE

RIGHT NO. 2-4-6

BOSS ON ROD TOWARD FRONT OF ENGINE

CHAMFERED CORNERS TOWARD REAR OF ENGINE

View of the right bank piston and rod positioning—3.8L engine

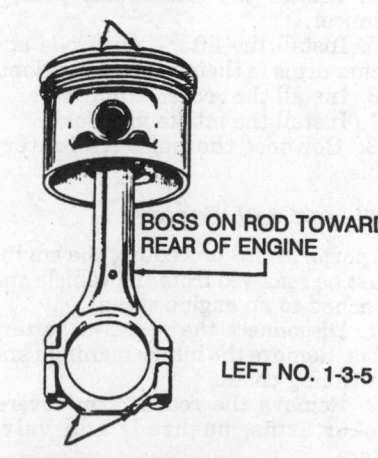

NOTCHES TOWARD FRONT OF ENGINE

BOSS ON ROD TOWARD REAR OF ENGINE

LEFT NO. 1-3-5

CHAMFERED CORNERS TOWARD FRONT OF ENGINE

View of the left bank piston and rod positioning—3.8L engine

ENGINE LUBRICATION

Oil Pan

REMOVAL & INSTALLATION

3.8L Engine

VIN C

1. Disconnect the negative battery cable.
2. Raise and safely support the vehicle.
3. Drain the crankcase.
4. Remove the torque converter cover and the oil filter.
5. Disconnect the electrical connectors from the starter. Remove the starter-to-engine bolts and the starter.
6. Remove the oil pan-to-engine bolts and the oil pan.

To install:

7. Clean the gasket mounting surfaces.
8. Install the oil pan and oil pan-to-engine bolts. Tighten to 124 inch lbs. (14 Nm).
9. Install the starter and connect the electrical connectors.
10. Install the oil filter and torque converter cover.
11. Fill the crankcase.
12. Lower the vehicle.
13. Connect the negative battery cable.

VIN L

1. Disconnect the negative battery cable.
2. Raise and safely support the vehicle.
3. Drain the crankcase.
4. Disconnect the oil level sensor connector.
5. Remove the oil pan retaining bolts and remove the oil pan.

To install:

6. Clean the gasket mounting surfaces and install a new gasket to the pan.
7. Install the oil pan and oil pan-to-engine bolts. Tighten to 124 inch lbs. (14 Nm).
8. Connect the oil level sensor connector.
9. Fill the crankcase.
10. Lower the vehicle.
11. Connect the negative battery cable.

4.5L and 4.9L Engines

1989–92 ALLANTE

1. Disconnect the negative battery cable.
2. Raise and safely support the vehicle.

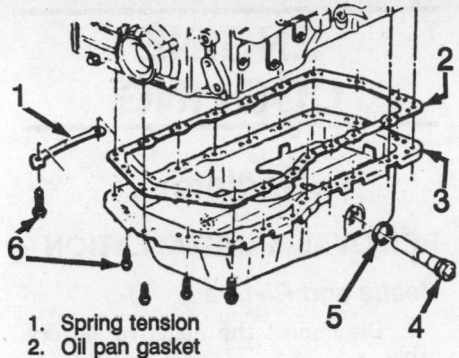

1. Spring tension
2. Oil pan gasket
3. Oil pan
4. Oil level indicator switch—40 ft. lbs.
5. Seal
6. Bolt

Exploded view of the oil pan assembly—3.8L engine

3. Drain the crankcase. Disconnect the oil level sensor, if equipped.
4. Remove the flywheel covers.
5. Remove the exhaust Y-pipe.
6. Remove the oil pan-to-engine bolts/nuts and the oil pan.

To install:

7. Clean the gasket mounting surfaces.

NOTE: Apply a ¼ in. bead of RTV at the rear main bearing cap and front cover to block joints.

8. Install the oil pan and oil pan-to-engine bolts/nuts. Tighten to 14 ft. lbs. (18 Nm).
9. Install the flywheel covers.
10. Install the exhaust Y-pipe.
11. If equipped, connect the oil level sensor.
12. Lower the vehicle.
13. Fill the crankcase.
14. Connect the negative battery cable.

ELDORADO AND SEVILLE

1. Disconnect the negative battery cable. Raise and safely support the vehicle. Drain the crankcase.
2. Remove the 2 torque converter/flywheel covers from the lower side of the transaxle.
3. Remove the exhaust crossunder pipe and reposition.
4. Remove the oil pan-to-engine bolts and the oil pan.

To install:

5. Clean the gasket mounting surfaces.

NOTE: Apply a ¼ in. bead of RTV at the rear main bearing cap and front cover to block joints.

6. Install the oil pan and oil pan-to-engine bolts. Tighten to 14 ft. lbs. (18 Nm).
7. Install the exhaust crossunder pipe.

8. Install the 2 torque converter/flywheel covers.
9. Lower the vehicle.
10. Fill the crankcase.
11. Connect the negative battery cable.

Oil Pump

REMOVAL & INSTALLATION

3.8L Engine

The oil pump is located in the bottom of the front cover. The oil pump is an integral part of the front cover with the crankshaft passing through the pump.

1. Disconnect the negative battery cable. Remove the front cover.
2. Clean the gasket mounting surfaces.
3. To inspect the pump gears, perform the following:
   a. Remove the oil pump cover-to-front cover screws and the cover.
   b. Remove the inner and outer pump gears.
   c. Using solvent, clean the gears.
   d. Inspect the gears for wear and/or damage; if necessary, replace the parts.

To install:

4. Using petroleum jelly, pack the pump and reinstall the parts. Tighten the oil pump cover-to-front cover screws to 88 inch lbs. (11 Nm) for VIN C engine or to 22 ft. lbs. (30 Nm) for VIN L engine.

NOTE: The oil pump must be primed this way or no pressure will be produced when the engine is started.

5. Install the front cover.
6. Connect the negative battery cable.
7. Check and/or refill the oil level in the crankcase. Replace the oil filter. Start the engine and check for leaks.

4.5L and 4.9L Engines

1. Disconnect the negative battery cable. Remove the oil pan.
2. Remove the oil pump-to-engine screws/nut and the oil pump from the engine.
3. To disassemble, remove the oil pump cover-to-housing screws, slide the driveshaft, drive gear and driven gear from the pump housing.
4. Remove the oil pressure regulator valve and spring from the bore in the housing assembly.
5. Inspect the oil pressure regulator valve for nicks and burrs.
6. Measure the free length of the regulator valve spring. It should be 2.57–2.69 in. (65.28–68.32mm).
7. Inspect the drive gear and driven gear for nicks and burrs.

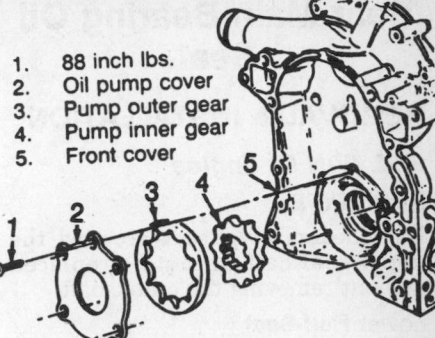

1. 88 inch lbs.
2. Oil pump cover
3. Pump outer gear
4. Pump inner gear
5. Front cover

Exploded view of the gerotor oil pump assembly—3.8L engine

To install:

8. Assemble the pump drive gear over the driveshaft so the retaining ring is inside the gear. Position the drive gear over the pump housing shaft closest to the pressure regulator bore.
9. Slide the driven gear over the remaining shaft in the pump housing, meshing the driven gear with the drive gear.
10. Install the oil pressure regulator spring and valve in the bore of the pump housing assembly.
11. Install the pump cover-to-pump housing screws to 5 ft. lbs. (7 Nm), the oil pump-to-engine screws to 15 ft. lbs. (20 Nm) and nut to 22 ft. lbs. (30 Nm).
12. Install the oil pan.
13. Connect the negative battery cable.

CHECKING

1. If foreign matter is present, determine it's source.
2. Check the pump cover and housing for cracks, scoring and/or damage; if necessary, replace the housing(s).
3. Inspect the idler gear shaft for looseness in the housing; if necessary, replace the pump or timing chain, depending on the model.
4. Inspect the pressure regulator valve for scoring or sticking; if burrs are present, remove them with an oil stone.
5. Inspect the pressure regulator valve spring for loss of tension or distortion; if necessary, replace it.
6. Inspect the suction pipe for looseness, if pressed into the housing, and the screen for broken wire mesh; if necessary, replace them.
7. Inspect the gears for chipping, galling and/or wear; if necessary, replace them.
8. If the oil pump is driveshaft driven from the distributor, inspect the driveshaft and driveshaft extension for looseness and/or wear. Replace as required.

Rear Main Bearing Oil Seal

REMOVAL & INSTALLATION

3.8L (VIN C) Engine
ROPE TYPE

If braided rope type seals are used, the upper seal half cannot be replaced without removing the crankshaft.

Lower Half-Seal

1. Disconnect the negative battery cable. Remove the oil pan.
2. Remove the rear main bearing cap-to-engine bolts and the cap.
3. Remove the old seal from the bearing cap.

To install:

4. To replace the oil seal, perform the following procedures:

   a. Using sealant GM 1052621, Loctite® 414 or equivalent, apply it to the main bearing cap seal groove and wait for 1 minute.

   b. Using a new rope seal and a wooden dowel or hammer handle, roll the new seal into the cap so both ends projecting above the parting surface of the cap; force the seal into the groove by rubbing it down, until the seal projects above the groove not more than $1/16$ in.

   c. Using a sharp razor blade, cut the ends off flush with the surface of the cap.

   d. Using chassis grease, apply a thin coat to the seals surface.

5. To install the neoprene sealing strips (side seals), perform the following procedures:

   a. Using light oil or kerosene, soak the strips for 5 minutes.

NOTE: The neoprene composition seals will swell up once exposed to the oil and heat. It is normal for the seals to leak for a short time, until they become properly seated. The seals must not be cut to fit.

   b. Place the sealing strips in the grooves on the sides of the bearing cap.

6. Using sealer GM 1052621 or equivalent, apply it to the main bearing cap mating surface; do not apply sealer to the bolt holes.

7. To complete the installation, reverse the removal procedures. Tighten the main bearing cap-to-engine bolts to 90 ft. lbs. (122 Nm). Refill the crankcase. The engine must be operated at low rpm when first started, after a new seal is installed.

Upper Half-Seal

Engine and crankshaft removal are not necessary if the following time sav-er procedure is followed. While this procedure is effective for stopping leakage from the upper half of the seal, it is not a replacement procedure.

1. Disconnect the negative battery cable. Remove the oil pan.
2. Remove the rear main bearing cap-to-engine bolts and the cap.

To install:

3. Using the seal packing tool, insert it against each side of the upper seal and drive the seal until it is tight.
4. Measure the amount the seal was driven into the engine and add about $1/16$ in. Using a razor blade, cut that amount off the old lower seal.
5. Using the seal packing tool, work the short packing pieces into the cylinder block; a small amount of oil on the seal will help the installation.
6. Repeat this process on the other side.
7. Install the main bearing cap. Tighten the main bearing cap-to-engine bolts to 90 ft. lbs. (122 Nm).
8. Install the oil pan.
9. Connect the negative battery cable.
10. Refill the crankcase. The engine must be operated at low rpm when first started, after a new seal is installed.

3.8L (VIN L), 4.5L and 4.9L Engines
LIP TYPE

NOTE: To perform this procedure, use a seal removal tool and a seal installer tool.

1. Disconnect the negative battery cable. Remove the transaxle.
2. Unbolt and remove the flexplate from the rear end of the crankshaft.
3. Using a seal removal tool, remove the old seal. Throughly clean the seal bore of any left over seal material with a clean rag.

To install:

4. Lubricate the lip of the new seal with wheel bearing grease. Position it over the crankshaft and into the seal bore with the spring facing inside the engine.
5. Using a seal installer tool, press the seal into place. The seal must be square and flush with the block to 1mm indented.
6. Install the flexplate and tighten according to the followng:

   a. On Allante and Eldorado/Seville, tighten the flexplate-to-crankshaft bolts to 70 ft. lbs. (95 Nm).

   b. On the 3.8L (VIN L) engine, tighten the flexplate-to-crankshaft bolts to 61 ft. lbs. (82 Nm).

7. Install the transaxle.
8. Connect the negative battery cable.

ENGINE COOLING

Radiator

REMOVAL & INSTALLATION

Reatta and Riviera

1. Disconnect the negative battery cable.
2. Drain coolant from radiator.
3. Remove plastic radiator support cover.
4. Remove engine-to-radiator torque strut.
5. Remove the rear cooling fan.
6. Remove coolant reservoir hose at filler neck.
7. Remove upper and lower radiator hoses from radiator.
8. Remove transaxle oil cooler lines at radiator.
9. Remove radiator top support, 3 remaining bolts with torque strut removed.
10. Remove radiator from vehicle; lift radiator straight up and out.

To install:

11. Install radiator in vehicle.
12. Install radiator top support, securing with 3 retaining bolts. Tighten to 18 ft. lbs. (25 Nm).
13. Connect oil cooler lines at radiator. Tighten to 20 ft. lbs. (27 Nm).
14. Install upper and lower radiator hoses to radiator, securing hose clamps.
15. Connect reservoir hose at filler neck, securing hose clamp.
16. Install rear cooling fan.
17. Install engine-to-radiator torque strut and 2 remaining strut/radiator support retaining bolts. Tighten radiator support retaining bolts to 18 ft. lbs. (25 Nm).
18. Install plastic radiator support cover.
19. Fill radiator with coolant.
20. Connect negative battery cable.
21. Start engine and check for leaks. Check transaxle fluid level and add, as necessary. Allow engine to come to normal operating temperature and check again for leaks.

Allante, Eldorado and Seville

1. Disconnect the negative battery cable.
2. Drain cooling system.
3. Remove the plastic radiator support cover.
4. Remove right and left cooling fans. On Eldorado and Seville remove rear cooling fan.
5. Disconnect coolant reservoir hose at filler neck.

6. Remove upper and lower radiator hoses from radiator.

7. Remove engine oil cooler lines and transaxle oil cooler lines from the radiator.

8. Remove the radiator top support.

9. Remove radiator from car, lifting radiator straight up and out.

To install:

10. Install radiator in vehicle.

11. Install radiator top support. Tighten radiator support retaining bolts to 18 ft. lbs. (25 Nm).

12. Connect transaxle oil cooler lines at radiator. Tighten to 20 ft. lbs. (27 Nm).

13. Connect oil cooler lines at radiator. Tighten to 13 ft. lbs. (18 Nm).

14. Install upper and lower radiator hoses to radiator securing hose clamps.

15. Connect coolant reservoir hose at filler neck.

16. Install cooling fan(s) and plastic radiator support cover.

17. Fill cooling system.

18. Connect negative battery cable.

19. Start engine and check for leaks. Check transaxle fluid level and add, as necessary. Allow engine to come to normal operating temperature and check again for leaks.

Toranado and Trofeo

1. Disconnect the negative battery cable.

2. Drain cooling system.

3. Remove plastic radiator support cover.

4. Remove engine-to-radiator torque strut.

5. Remove rear cooling fan.

6. Remove upper air cleaner duct and/or silencer, as necessary.

7. Remove coolant reservoir hose at filler neck.

8. Remove upper and lower radiator hoses from radiator.

9. Remove transaxle oil cooler lines.

10. Remove radiator top support, 3 remaining bolts with torque strut removed.

11. Remove radiator from vehicle, lifting straight up and out.

To install:

12. Install radiator in vehicle.

13. Install radiator top support, securing with 3 retaining bolts.

14. Connect transaxle oil cooler lines at radiator. Tighten to 20 ft. lbs. (27 Nm).

15. Connect upper and lower radiator hoses to radiator, securing with clamps.

16. Connect coolant reservoir hose at filler neck, securing with hose clamp.

17. Install rear cooling fan.

18. Install upper air cleaner duct and/or silencer, if removed.

19. Install engine-to-radiator torque strut and 2 remaining strut/radiator

support retaining bolts. Tighten to 18 ft. lbs. (25 Nm).

20. Install plastic radiator support cover.

21. Fill cooling system.

22. Connect negative battery cable.

23. Start engine and check for leaks. Check transaxle fluid level and add, as necessary. Allow engine to come to normal operating temperature and check again for leaks.

Electric Cooling Fan

TESTING

1. Check fuse or circuit breaker for power to cooling fan motor.

2. Remove connector(s) at cooling fan motor(s). Connect jumper wire and apply battery voltage to the positive terminal of the cooling fan motor.

3. Using and ohmmeter, check for continuity in cooling fan motor.

NOTE: Remove the cooling fan connector at the fan motor before performing continuity checks. Perform continuity check of the motor windings only. The cooling fan control circuit is connected electrically to the ECM through the cooling fan relay center. Ohmmeter battery voltage must not be applied to the ECM.

4. Ensure proper continuity of cooling fan motor ground circuit at chassis ground connector.

REMOVAL & INSTALLATION

Reatta and Riviera

FRONT FAN

1. Disconnect the negative battery cable.

2. Remove plastic radiator cover.

3. Remove front fan guard cover; 4 clips for Riviera. Remove front grill on Reatta.

4. Disconnect fan electrical connector.

5. Remove front cooling fan from vehicle (3 bolts).

To install:

6. Install front fan, securing with 3 bolts. Tighten to 89 inch lbs. (10 Nm).

7. Connect electrical fan connector.

8. Install front fan guard cover; 4 clips for Riviera. Install front grille on Reatta.

9. Install plastic radiator cover.

10. Connect negative battery cable.

REAR FAN

1. Disconnect the negative battery cable.

2. Remove upper engine-to-radiator support torque strut.

3. Disconnect fan electrical connector.

4. Remove 2 upper and 2 lower retaining bolts and remove fan from vehicle.

To install:

5. Install fan to vehicle, securing with 4 bolts. Tighten to 89 inch lbs. (10 Nm).

6. Connect fan electrical connector.

7. Install upper engine-to-radiator mounting bolts. Tighten to 18 ft. lbs. (25 Nm).

8. Connect negative battery cable.

1989–92 Allante

RIGHT OR LEFT FAN

1. Disconnect the negative battery cable.

2. Disconnect fan electrical connector.

3. For the left side fan, remove upper engine-to-radiator support torque strut; 4 bolts from radiator support.

4. Remove fan retaining bolts and remove fan from vehicle.

To install:

5. Install fan to vehicle. Tighten retaining bolts to 88 inch lbs. (10 Nm).

6. Connect fan electrical connector.

7. For the left side fan, install upper engine-to-radiator support torque strut. Tighten to 17 ft. lbs. (23 Nm).

8. Connect negative battery cable.

1993 Allante

RIGHT OR LEFT FAN

1. Disconnect the negative battery cable.

2. Remove the beauty panel assembly.

3. Remove the left side engine torque support strut.

4. Position upper radiator hose out of the way.

5. Disconnect the fan electrical connector.

6. Remove retaining bolts and remove fan(s).

To install:

7. Install fan(s) to vehicle. Tighten retaining bolts to 88 inch lbs. (10 Nm).

8. Connect fan electrical connector.

9. Reposition upper radiator hose and install left side engine torque strut.

10. Install beauty panel assembly and connect the negative battery cable.

Eldorado and Seville

FRONT FAN

1. Disconnect the negative battery cable.

2. Remove radiator cover panel.

3. Disconnect electrical connector.

4. Remove fan control module and bracket for 1989. Remove right headlight bracket for 1990–93.

5. On the 1989 vehicle, remove front grill.

6. Remove fan retaining bolts and remove fan from vehicle.

To install:

7. Install fan to vehicle. Tighten to 88 inch lbs. (10 Nm).

8. Connect electrical connector.

9. Install fan control module and bracket for 1989. Install right headlight for 1990–93.

10. Install front grill for 1989.

11. Install radiator cover panel.

12. Connect negative battery cable.

REAR FAN

1. Disconnect the negative battery cable.

2. Disconnect fan electrical connector.

3. On 1989 vehicles, remove air cleaner duct and air conditioning hose bracket.

4. On 1990–93 vehicles, remove upper engine-to-radiator support torque strut and oil cooler line bracket from fan.

5. Remove fan retaining bolts and remove fan from vehicle.

To install:

6. Install fan in vehicle. Tighten bolts to 97 inch lbs. (11 Nm).

7. Connect electrical connector.

8. On 1989 vehicles, connect air cleaner duct and air conditioning hose bracket.

9. On 1990–93 vehicles, connect upper engine-to-radiator support torque strut and oil cooler line bracket to fan. Tighten torque strut-to-radiator mounting bolts to 17 ft. lbs. (23 Nm).

10. Connect negative battery cable.

Toronado and Trofeo
FRONT FAN

1. Disconnect the negative battery cable.

2. Remove plastic radiator cover.

3. Remove front grill from 1989–91 vehicles.

4. Disconnect electrical connector.

5. Remove fan retaining bolts and remove fan from vehicle.

To install:

6. Install fan in vehicle. Tighten bolts to 89 inch lbs. (10 Nm).

7. Connect electrical connector.

8. Install front grill for 1989–91 vehicles.

9. Install plastic radiator cover.

10. Connect negative battery cable.

REAR FAN

1. Disconnect the negative battery cable.

2. Remove the upper engine-to-radiator support torque strut.

3. Disconnect the fan electrical connector.

4. Remove the fan attaching bolts

and remove the fan assembly from the vehicle.

To install:

5. Install the fan assembly and 4 attaching bolts. Tighten to 89 inch lbs. (10 Nm).

6. Connect the fan electrical connector.

7. Install the upper engine-to-radiator support torque strut. Tighten bolts to 18 ft. lbs. (25 Nm).

8. Connect the negative battery cable.

Heater Core

REMOVAL & INSTALLATION

Reatta and Riviera
1989

1. Disconnect the negative battery cable.

2. Drain the cooling system.

3. Remove console and instrument panel, as required.

4. Disconnect the hoses from the heater core.

5. Remove the right side sound insulator and courtesy light.

6. Remove the glove box.

7. Disconnect the air conditioning programmer the electrical and vacuum connectors. Remove the air conditioning programmer screws and the programmer.

8. Disconnect the ECM electrical connectors. Remove the ECM and bracket.

9. Disconnect the BCM electrical connectors. Remove the BCM and bracket.

10. Remove the heater core cover screws, the cover, the retaining clip, the heater core screws and the heater core.

To install:

11. Install heater core cover screws, the cover, the retaining clip, heater core screws and heater core.

12. Install BCM bracket and connect BCM electrical connectors.

13. Install ECM bracket and connect ECM electrical connectors.

14. Install air conditioner programmer and connect air conditioning programmer electrical and vacuum connectors. Check adjustment of the programmer.

15. Install glove box.

16. Install right side sound insulator and courtesy light.

17. Connect the heater core hoses.

18. Connect negative battery cable.

19. Fill cooling system.

20. Start engine and check for coolant leaks. Allow engine to come to normal operating temperature. Recheck for coolant leaks.

1990–93

1. Disconnect the negative battery cable.

2. Drain the engine coolant into a clean container for reuse.

3. If equipped, disarm the SIR system.

4. Remove console and instrument panel.

5. Remove air conditioner programmer attaching screws. Disconnect the programmer electrical connectors. Remove the programmer.

6. Disconnect the BCM electrical connectors. Remove BCM and mounting bracket.

7. Disconnect the ECM electrical connectors. Remove ECM and mounting bracket.

8. Remove heater core cover from housing.

9. Disconnect inlet and outlet heater hoses from heater core.

10. Remove 2 heater retaining screws.

11. Remove heater core from vehicle.

To install:

12. Install heater core to heater case, securing with 2 screws.

13. Connect inlet and outlet heater hoses to heater core.

14. Install heater core cover.

15. Install ECM mounting bracket and ECM. Connect the ECM electrical connectors. Install the ECM attaching screws.

16. Install BCM mounting bracket and BCM. Connect the BCM electrical connectors. Install the BCM attaching screws.

17. Install air conditioner programmer. Connect the programmer electrical connectors. Install the programmer attaching screws. Check adjustment of the programmer.

18. Install instrument panel and console.

19. If equipped, arm the SIR system.

20. Connect negative battery cable.

21. Fill cooling system and check for leaks. Start the engine and allow to come to normal operating temperature. Recheck for leaks. Top-up coolant.

Allante

1. Disconnect the negative battery cable.

2. Drain the cooling system to a level below the heater core.

3. Remove the glove box screws. Label and disconnect the electrical connectors from the glove box.

4. Remove the glove box assembly from the vehicle.

5. Remove the lower sound insulator to gain working clearance.

6. Remove the radio.

7. Remove the air conditioning programmer, the Electronic Control Module (ECM) screws and the ECM.

8. Remove the module assembly heater core cover. Disconnect the hoses from the heater core.

9. Remove the heater core screws and the heater core.

To install:

10. Install heater core in vehicle.

11. Install module assembly heater core cover. Connect hoses to the heater core.

12. Install ECM bracket, ECM and electrical connectors.

13. Install air conditioning programmer. Check adjustment of the programmer.

14. Install radio and lower sound insulator.

15. Install glove box assembly and glove box electrical connectors.

16. Fill cooling system.

17. Start engine and check for coolant leaks. Allow engine to come to normal operating temperature. Recheck for coolant leaks.

Eldorado and Seville

1. Disconnect the negative battery cable.

2. Drain the cooling system to a level below the heater core.

3. Remove the glove box screws. Label and disconnect the electrical connectors from the glove box.

4. Remove the glove box assembly from the vehicle.

5. Remove the lower sound insulator to gain working clearance.

6. Remove the air conditioner programmer, the Electronic Control Module (ECM) screws and the ECM.

7. Remove the module assembly heater core cover. Disconnect the hoses from the heater core.

8. Remove the heater core screws and the heater core.

To install:

9. Install the heater core in vehicle.

10. Connect hoses to heater core. Install module assembly heater core cover.

11. Install the air conditioner programmer and the ECM. Check adjustment of the programmer.

12. Install the lower sound insulator.

13. Install the glove box assembly to vehicle. Connect the electrical connectors to the glove box.

14. Fill cooling system.

15. Start engine and check for coolant leaks. Allow engine to come to normal operating temperature. Recheck for coolant leaks.

Toronado and Trofeo

1989

1. Disconnect the negative battery cable.

2. Drain the engine coolant into a clean container for reuse.

3. Remove the left side sound insulator. Disconnect the courtesy light.

4. Remove the right side sound insulator. Disconnect the courtesy light.

5. Remove the steering column opening filler panel screws and remove the filler panel.

6. Remove the steering column bolts. Lower the steering column and allow the steering wheel to rest on the seat.

7. Remove the windshield defroster nozzle grille. Remove the deflector housings.

8. Remove the screws attaching the top of the instrument panel that were under the deflector housings and windshield defroster nozzle grille. Remove the bolts attaching the bottom of the instrument panel.

9. Disconnect the bulkhead electrical connector.

10. Move the instrument panel rearward.

11. Remove the aspirator duct.

12. Disconnect the fuel filler door release electrical connector.

13. Disconnect the trunk lid release electrical connector.

14. Disconnect the antenna lead.

15. Remove the fuse panel attaching screws.

16. Remove the instrument panel from the vehicle. Set the panel on a clean, protected surface.

17. Disconnect the heater hoses from the heater core.

18. Remove the air conditioner programmer attaching screws. Disconnect the programmer electrical and vacuum connectors. Remove the programmer.

19. Remove the power module attaching screws. Disconnect the power module electrical connectors. Remove the power module.

20. Remove the heater core cover attaching screws. Remove the heater core.

21. Remove the heater core retaining clip. Remove the heater core attaching screws. Remove the heater core.

To install:

22. Apply strip caulk to seal the heater core to the case.

23. Install the heater core and attaching screws. Install the retaining clip.

24. Install the heater core cover and attaching screws.

25. Install the power module. Connect the electrical connectors and the power module attaching screws.

26. Install the air conditioner programmer. Connect the vacuum and electrical connectors. Install the programmer attaching screws. Check adjustment of the programmer.

27. Install the instrument panel.

28. Install the fuse panel attaching screws.

29. Connect the antenna lead.

30. Connect the trunk lid release electrical connector.

31. Connect the fuel filler door release electrical connector.

32. Install the aspirator duct.

33. Move the instrument panel forward.

34. Connect the bulkhead electrical connector.

35. Install the bolts attaching the top and bottom of the instrument panel.

36. Install the windshield defroster deflector housings. Install the nozzle grille.

37. Raise the steering column into position. Install the 4 steering column bolts.

38. Install the steering column opening filler panel. Install the filler panel attaching screws.

39. Install the right side sound insulator. Install the sound insulator attaching screws.

40. Install the left side sound insulator. Connect the courtesy light electrical connector. Install the sound insulator attaching screws.

41. Connect the negative battery cable.

42. Fill cooling system and check for leaks. Start the engine and allow to come to normal operating temperature. Recheck for leaks. Top-up coolant.

1990–92

1. Disconnect the negative battery cable.

2. Drain the engine coolant into a clean container for reuse.

3. If equipped, disarm the SIR system.

4. Remove console and instrument panel.

5. Remove air conditioner programmer attaching screws. Disconnect the programmer electrical connectors. Remove the programmer.

6. Disconnect the BCM electrical connectors. Remove BCM and mounting bracket.

7. Disconnect the ECM electrical connectors. Remove ECM and mounting bracket.

8. Remove heater core cover from housing.

9. Disconnect inlet and outlet heater hoses from heater core.

10. Remove 2 heater retaining screws.

11. Remove heater core from vehicle.

To install:

12. Install heater core to heater case, securing with 2 screws.

13. Connect inlet and outlet heater hoses to heater core.

14. Install heater core cover.

15. Install ECM mounting bracket and ECM. Connect the ECM electrical connectors. Install the ECM attaching screws.

16. Install BCM mounting bracket and BCM. Connect the BCM electrical

connectors. Install the BCM attaching screws.

17. Install air conditioner programmer. Connect the programmer electrical connectors. Install the programmer attaching screws. Check adjustment of the programmer.

18. Install instrument panel and console.

19. If equipped, arm the SIR system.

20. Connect negative battery cable.

21. Fill cooling system and check for leaks. Start the engine and allow to come to normal operating temperature. Recheck for leaks. Top-up coolant.

Air Conditioner Programmer

ADJUSTMENT

1. Remove the right side sound insulator and glove box.

2. On the temperature control panel, set the temperature for 90°F, allow 1–2 minutes for the programmer arm to travel to its maximum heat position.

3. Disconnect the threaded rod from the plastic retainer on the programmer output arm.

4. To check the air mixture valve for free travel, push the valve to the maximum air conditioning position and check for binding.

5. Place the pre-load air mixture valve in the maximum heat position; pull on the threaded rod to ensure the valve is seating. The programmer arm should be in the maximum heat position.

6. To avoid influencing the programmer arm or air mixture valve position, carefully snap the threaded rod into the plastic retainer.

7. Adjust the temperature setting to 60°F, then, check to verify the programmer arm and air mixture valve travel to the maximum air conditioning position.

Water Pump

REMOVAL & INSTALLATION

3.8L Engine

1. Disconnect the negative battery cable.

2. Position a drain pan under the radiator, open the drain cock and drain the cooling system.

3. Disconnect the hoses from the water pump.

4. Remove the serpentine drive belt.

5. Remove the water pump pulley bolts and the pulley.

NOTE: The long bolt is removed through the access hole provided in the body side rail.

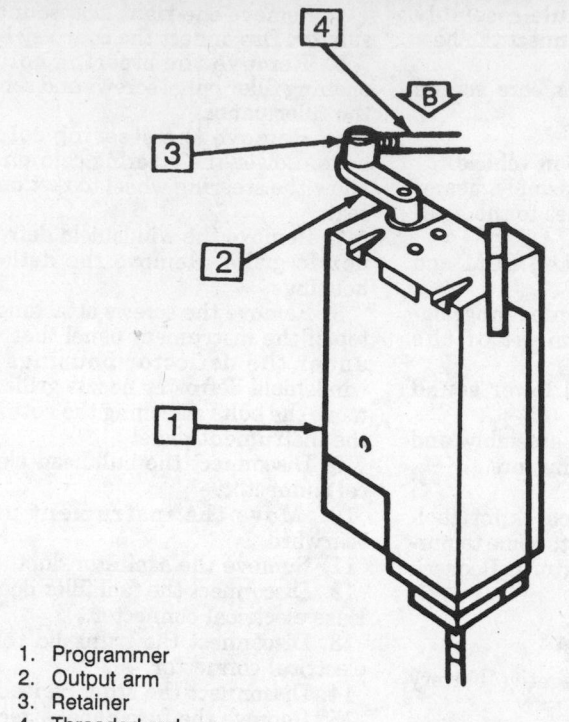

1. Programmer
2. Output arm
3. Retainer
4. Threaded rod
5. Max. air conditioning position
6. Max. heat position

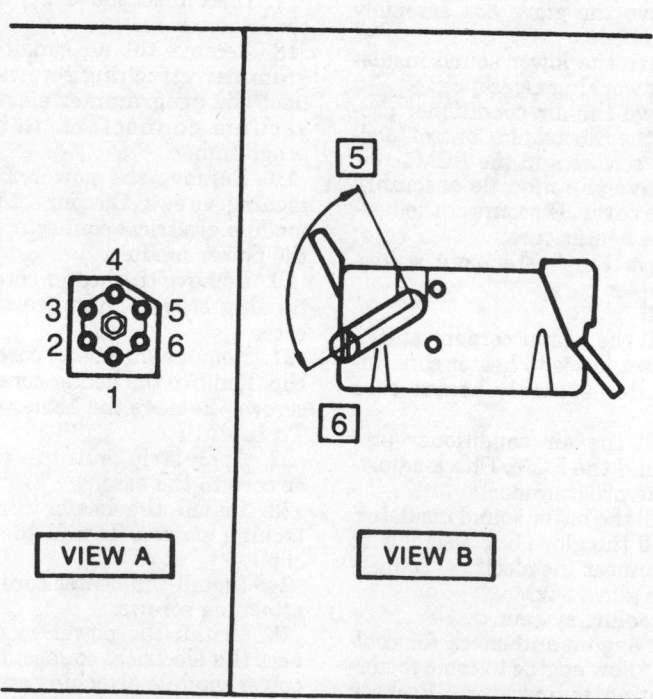

VIEW A   VIEW B

Electronic climate control programmer and linkage

6. Remove the water pump-to-engine bolts and the pump.

To install:

7. Clean the gasket mounting surfaces.

8. Install the water pump using a new gasket.

9. Tighten the water pump-to-engine long bolts to 29 ft. lbs. (39 Nm) and the short bolts to 97 inch lbs. (11 Nm).

10. Connect the hoses to the water pump.

11. Install the serpentine drive belt.

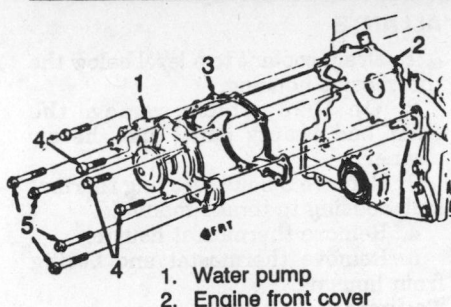

1. Water pump
2. Engine front cover assembly
3. Gasket
4. 97 inch lbs.
5. 29 ft. lbs.

Exploded view of the water pump—3.8L engine

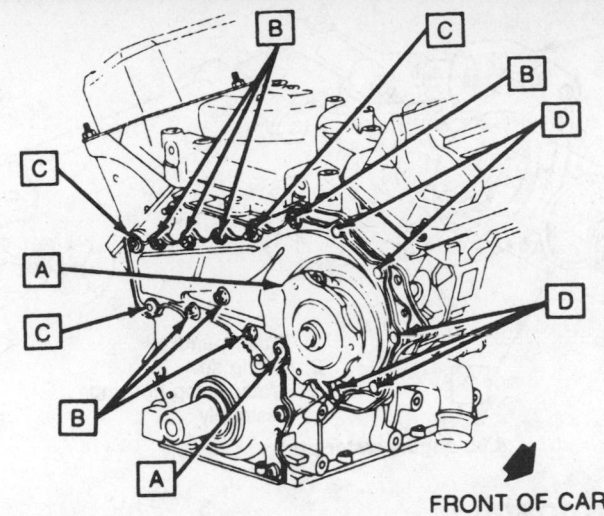

FRONT OF CAR

KEY	FASTENER TYPE	QTY.	TORQUE	
			N·m	FT. LBS.
A	TORX SCREW	2	40	30
B	NUT	7	7	5
C	HEX SCREW	3	40	30
D	HEX SCREW	5	7	5

Water pump fasteners—4.5L and 4.9L engines

12. Connect the negative battery cable.
13. Fill cooling system and check for leaks. Start the engine and allow to come to normal operating temperature. Recheck for leaks. Top-up coolant.

NOTE: Because the radiator is made of aluminum and plastic, make sure the antifreeze solution is approved for use in cooling systems with a high aluminum content. GM recommends the use of a supplement/sealant 3634621 or equivalent, specifically designed for use in aluminum engines to protect the engine from damage.

4.5L and 4.9L Engines

1. Disconnect the negative battery cable.
2. Drain the engine coolant into a clean container for reuse.
3. Remove the air filter assembly. Disconnect and remove the coolant recovery tank.
4. Disconnect and remove the cross brace.
5. Remove the water pulley bolts.
6. Remove the serpentine drive belt and the water pump pulley.
7. Remove the water pump-to-engine bolts and the pump.
To install:
8. Clean the gasket mounting surfaces.
9. Place a new gasket over the water pump studs.
10. Install the water pump. Tighten the water pump bolts as follows:
    Water pump-to-engine Torx® bolts to 30 ft. lbs. (40 Nm)
    Water pump-to-engine stud nuts to 5 ft. lbs. (7 Nm)
    Hex head bolts to 30 ft. lbs. (40 Nm)
    Remaining hex head bolts to 5 ft. lbs. (7 Nm).
11. Install the water pump pulley. Install the water pump pulley bolts finger-tight.

12. Install the serpentine drive belt.
13. Tighten the water pump pulley bolts to 22 ft. lbs. (30 Nm).
14. Install the cross brace.
15. Install the connect the coolant recovery tank. Install the air filter assembly.
16. Connect the negative battery cable.
17. Fill cooling system and check for leaks. Start the engine and allow to come to normal operating temperature. Recheck for leaks. Top-up coolant.

NOTE: Because the engine block and radiator are aluminum, make sure the antifreeze solution is approved for use in cooling systems with a high aluminum content. GM recommends the use of a supplement/sealant 3634621 or equivalent, specifically designed for use in aluminum engines to protect the engine from damage.

4.6L Engine

1. Disconnect the negative battery cable.
2. Drain the engine coolant into a clean container for reuse.
3. Remove the air cleaner assembly.
4. Remove the water pump pulley bolts.
5. Remove the water pump drive belt and the water pump pulley.

6. Remove the water pump-to-engine bolts and the pump.
To install:
7. Clean the gasket mounting surfaces.
8. Place a new gasket over the water pump studs.
9. Install the water pump and tighten the housing bolts to 5 ft. lbs. (7 Nm).
10. Install the water pump pulley. Install the water pump pulley bolts finger tight.
11. Install the drive belt.
12. Tighten the water pump pulley bolts to 22 ft. lbs. (30 Nm).
13. Install the air cleaner assembly.
14. Connect the negative battery cable.
15. Fill cooling system and check for leaks. Start the engine and allow to come to normal operating temperature. Recheck for leaks. Top-up coolant.

NOTE: Because the engine block and radiator are aluminum, make sure the antifreeze solution is approved for use in cooling systems with a high aluminum content. GM recommends the use of a supplement/sealant 3634621 or equivalent, specifically designed for use in aluminum engines to protect the engine from damage.

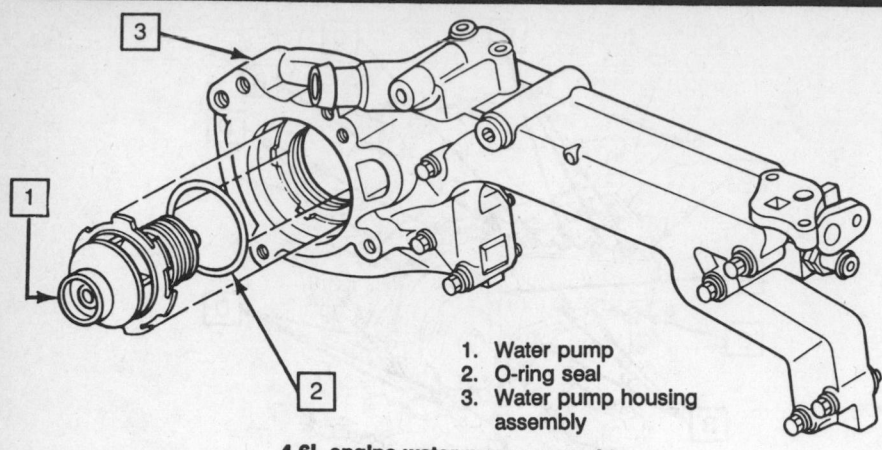

1. Water pump
2. O-ring seal
3. Water pump housing assembly

4.6L engine water pump assembly

Thermostat

REMOVAL & INSTALLATION

3.8L Engine

1. Drain the coolant until it is below the level of thermostat. Remove the thermostat housing. Observe the direction of the thermostat upon removal.
2. Remove the fuel rail cover from engine and remove thermostat housing bolt(s) and housing.

To install:

3. Replace the thermostat and O-ring ensuring the proper direction of new thermostat.
4. Install the thermostat housing and bolt(s) and tighten the bolt(s) to 10 ft. lbs. (14 Nm).
5. Refill cooling system to proper level with a 50/50 mixture of water and ethylene glycol antifreeze.
6. Start engine and check for coolant leaks. Allow engine to come to normal operating temperature. Recheck for coolant leaks.

ELDORADO and SEVILLE

1. Drain coolant to a level below the thermostat housing.
2. Remove 2 bolts securing upper thermostat housing to lower housing.
3. Remove upper thermostat housing.
4. Remove thermostat and O-ring from lower housing.

To install:

5. Install thermostat and a new O-ring to lower housing.
6. Install upper thermostat housing to lower housing. Tighten thermostat housing bolts to 20 ft. lbs. (27 Nm).
7. Refill cooling system using a 50/50 mixture of water and ethylene glycol antifreeze.
8. Start engine and check for coolant leaks. Allow engine to come to normal operating temperature. Recheck for coolant leaks.

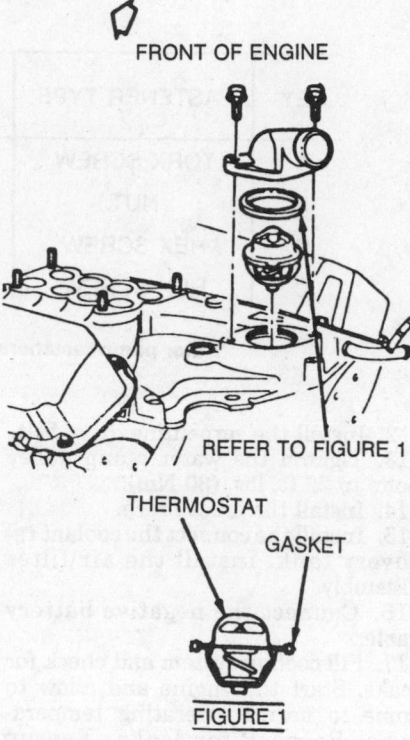

FRONT OF ENGINE

REFER TO FIGURE 1

THERMOSTAT

GASKET

FIGURE 1

Replacing thermostat—4.5L Allante

THERMOSTAT ASSEMBLY

GASKET

FIGURE 1

ALLANTE

1. Drain coolant to a level below the thermostat housing.
2. On 1993 vehicle, remove the front end beauty panel and the air cleaner.
3. Remove 2 bolts securing thermostat housing to intake manifold.
4. Remove thermostat housing.
5. Remove thermostat and O-ring from housing.

To install:

6. Install thermostat and new O-ring to housing.
7. Install thermostat housing to intake manifold. Tighten thermostat housing bolts to 18 ft. lbs. (25 Nm).
8. Refill cooling system using a 50/50 mixture of water and ethylene glycol antifreeze.
9. Install air cleaner and beauty panel, if removed.
10. Start engine and check for coolant leaks. Allow engine to come to normal operating temperature. Recheck for coolant leaks.

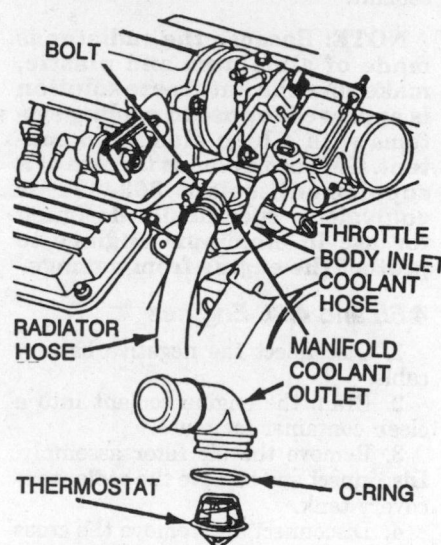

BOLT

THROTTLE BODY INLET COOLANT HOSE

RADIATOR HOSE

MANIFOLD COOLANT OUTLET

THERMOSTAT

O-RING

Replacing thermostat—3.8L Engine

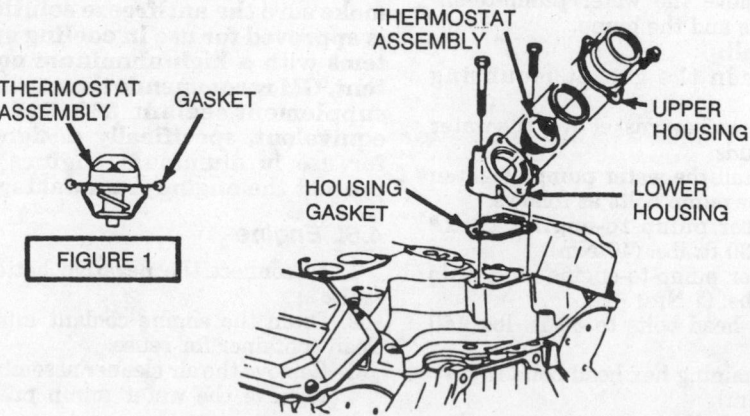

REFER TO FIGURE

THERMOSTAT ASSEMBLY

UPPER HOUSING

HOUSING GASKET

LOWER HOUSING

Replacing thermostat—Eldorado and Seville

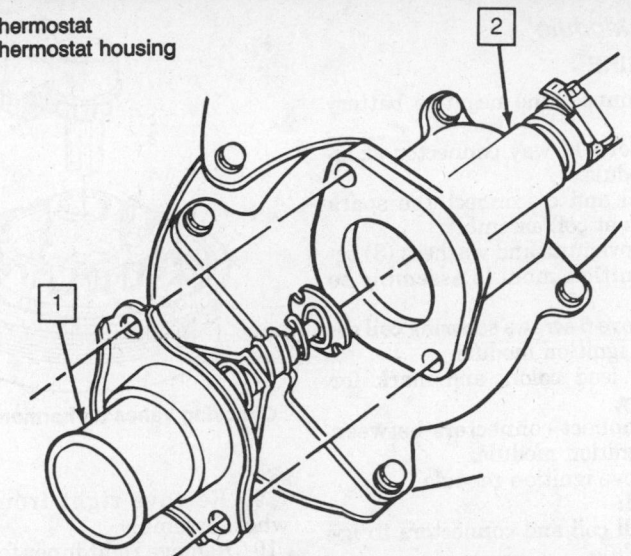

1. Thermostat
2. Thermostat housing

Replacing thermostat—4.6L engine—Allante

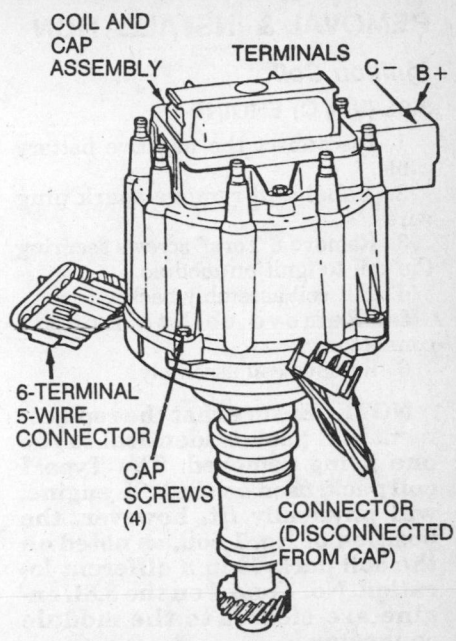

COIL AND CAP ASSEMBLY

TERMINALS C- B+

6-TERMINAL 5-WIRE CONNECTOR

CAP SCREWS (4)

CONNECTOR (DISCONNECTED FROM CAP)

EST distributor with coil-in-cap

Cooling System Bleeding

1. With the cooling system completely drained, fill the system with at least a 50/50 mixture of ethylene glycol antifreeze and water but no more than a 70/30 mixture of water to antifreeze.
2. Fill the radiator to just below the filler neck. Fill the coolant recovery reservoir to the COLD FILL mark.
3. Run the engine with the radiator cap removed until normal operating temperature is reached, with the radiator inlet hose hot.
4. With the engine idling, add coolant to the radiator until it reaches the bottom of the filler neck.
5. Position the heating system controls on maximum; allowing coolant to circulate through the heater core.
6. Check the coolant level again and add, as necessary.
7. Install the radiator cap.

ENGINE ELECTRICAL

NOTE: Disconnecting the negative battery cable on some vehicles may interfere with the functions of the on board computer systems and may require the computer to undergo a relearning process, once the negative battery cable is reconnected.

Distributor

The High Energy Ignition (HEI) distributor with Electronic Spark Timing (EST) easily identified by the presence of a 6 terminal ECM connector.

REMOVAL

1. Disconnect the negative battery cable.
2. Set No. 1 cylinder to TDC of its compression stroke.
3. Remove distributor appearance cover and retainer, if equipped.
4. Remove ignition switch battery feed wire from distributor cap. Remove coil connectors from cap.

NOTE: Do not use a prybar to release locking tabs.

5. Remove 4 bolts from distributor cap and move cap off to the side. Note the location of the cap "doghouse" upon removal and reinstall in same position.
6. Remove 6 terminal ECM harness from distributor. Matchmark the rotor-to-housing and the housing-to-engine.
7. Remove distributor clamp nut and hold-down nut. Use special tool J-29791 or equivalent, to remove hold-down nut.
8. Note the position of rotor, then pull distributor up until rotor just stops turning counterclockwise and again note position of rotor. Remove distributor.

INSTALLATION

Timing Not Disturbed

1. Insert the distributor into the engine, making sure the tip of the rotor is aligned with the alignment marks on the distributor housing and the engine.
2. Make sure the oil pump intermediate driveshaft is properly seated in the oil pump.
3. Install the distributor lock but do not tighten.
4. Connect the electrical harness connector(s) to the distributor, then, install distributor cap.
5. Start the engine and allow to come to normal operating temperature. Check and/or adjust the timing.

Timing Disturbed

1. Remove the No. 1 cylinder spark plug and place a finger over the hole. Using a wrench on the crankshaft pulley bolt, slowly turn the engine until compression is felt.
2. Align the timing marks so No. 1 cylinder is on TDC of the compression stroke.
3. Position the distributor in the engine with the rotor at No. 1 firing position. Make sure the oil pump intermediate driveshaft is properly seated in the oil pump.
4. Install the distributor retainer and lock bolt, tighten the lock bolt.
5. Reconnect the electrical harness connector(s) to the distributor and install distributor cap.
6. Start the engine and allow to come to normal operating temperature. Check and/or adjust the timing.

Distributorless Ignition System

The Computer Controlled Coil Ignition (C³I) system uses an ignition coil pack, ignition module, dual crankshaft sensor and associated wiring.

REMOVAL & INSTALLATION

Ignition Coil

3.8L (VIN C) ENGINE

1. Disconnect the negative battery cable.
2. Label and remove spark plug wires.
3. Remove 6 Torx® screws securing the coil to ignition module.
4. Tilt coil assembly back.
5. Remove coil to module connectors.
6. Remove coil assembly.

NOTE: Ensure that the replacement coil pack is identical to the one being removed. The Type I coil pack, used on the 3.8L engine, will physically fit, however, the position of No. 1 coil, as noted on the coil pack, is in a different location, No. 1 and 4 on the 3.8L engine are closest to the module connector.

To install:

7. Install coil assembly and connectors.
8. Install 6 Torx® screws and tighten to 27 inch lbs. (3 Nm).
9. Install spark plug wires.

3.8L (VIN L) ENGINE

1. Disconnect the negative battery cable.
2. Label and disconnect the spark plug wires.
3. Remove the 2 screws securing the individual coil pack to the ignition module.
4. Remove the coil assembly.

To install:

5. Install the coil assembly.
6. Install the 2 screws and tighten to 40 inch lbs. (4–5 Nm).
7. Connect the spark plug wires.
8. Connect the negative battery cable.

4.5L AND 4.9L ENGINES

1. Disconnect the negative battery cable.
2. Disconnect the battery lead wire and coil connections from the cap.
3. Remove the 2 coil cover attaching screws and remove the cover.
4. Remove the coil attaching screws and remove coil and leads from the cap.

To install:

5. Connect the coil leads to the cap.
6. Install the 4 coil attaching screws and install the coil cover and attaching screws.
7. Connect the battery feed wire and coil connection to the cap. Connect the negative battery cable.

Ignition Module

3.8L ENGINE

1. Disconnect the negative battery cable.
2. Remove 14-way connector at ignition module.
3. Label and disconnect the spark plug wires at coil assembly.
4. Remove nuts and washers (3) securing ignition module assembly to bracket.
5. Remove 6 screws securing coil assembly to ignition module.
6. Note lead colors and mark for reassembly.
7. Disconnect connectors between coil and ignition module.
8. Remove ignition module.

To install:

9. Install coil and connectors to ignition module.
10. Install 6 screws and tighten to 27 inch lbs. (3 Nm).
11. Install nuts and washers securing assembly to bracket.
12. Install plug wires.
13. Connect 14-way connector to module.
14. Connect the negative battery cable.

4.5L AND 4.9L ENGINES

1. Disconnect the negative battery cable.
2. Remove the distributor cap from the distributor and remove the rotor.
3. Remove the module attaching screws, remove the shield and lift module up.
4. Note color code on leads to module for reassembly. Disconnect the leads from the module.

To install:

5. Connect the leads to the module, observing the color coded wiring.
6. Install the module shield and module attaching screws.
7. Install the rotor and the cap.
8. Connect the negative battery cable.

Crankshaft Sensor

1. Disconnect the negative battery cable.
2. Remove nuts holding vibration damper support to ignition module bracket and vibration damper to engine bracket.
3. Remove support.
4. Remove bolts holding bracket to front of engine (2).
5. Remove nut from vibration damper to engine cradle.
6. Remove vibration damper and support assembly.
7. Remove serpentine belt from crankshaft pulley.
8. Raise and safely support the vehicle.

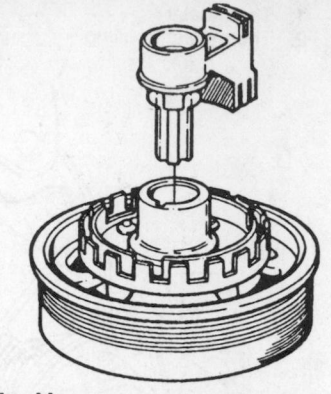

Checking vanes on harmonic balancer

9. Remove right front tire and wheel assembly.
10. Remove right inner fender access cover.
11. Remove crankshaft harmonic balancer retaining bolt using 28mm socket.
12. Remove crankshaft harmonic balancer.
13. Disconnect sensor electrical connector.
14. Remove sensor and pedestal from block face.
15. Remove sensor from pedestal.

To install:

16. Loosely install crankshaft sensor on pedestal.
17. Position sensor with pedestal attached on special tool J-37089.
18. Position special tool on crankshaft.
19. Install bolts to hold pedestal to block face. Tighten to 14–28 ft. lbs. (20–40 Nm).
20. Tighten pedestal pinch bolt to 36–40 ft. lbs. (4–4.5 Nm).
21. Remove special tool J-37089.
22. Place special tool J-37089 on harmonic balancer and turn. If any vane of the harmonic balancer touches the tool, replace the balancer assembly.
23. Install balancer on crankshaft.
24. Tighten crankshaft bolt to 200–239 ft. lbs. (270–315 Nm).
25. Install inner fender shield.
26. Install tire and wheel assembly and tighten to 100 ft. lbs. (140 Nm).
27. Connect the negative battery cable.

Ignition Timing

ADJUSTMENT

NOTE: Always consult the Vehicle Emission Control Information label in the engine compartment before adjusting timing. If the underhood sticker differs from the following procedures, follow the sticker.

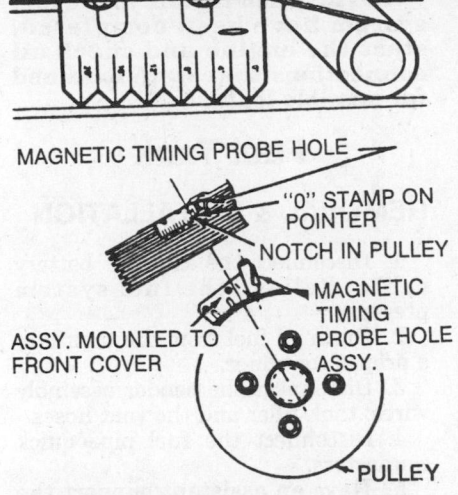

MAGNETIC TIMING PROBE HOLE

"0" STAMP ON POINTER

NOTCH IN PULLEY

MAGNETIC TIMING PROBE HOLE ASSY.

ASSY. MOUNTED TO FRONT COVER

PULLEY

View of timing marks and magnetic timing probe holder—4.5L and 4.9L engines

3.8L Engine

The 3.8L engines are equipped with a C³I ignition system which does not incorporate a distributor. Ignition timing is controlled by the ECM/PCM and is not adjustable.

4.5L AND 4.9L ENGINES

NOTE: The engine incorporates a magnetic timing probe hole for use with special electronic timing equipment. The following procedure is for use with the HEI—EST distributor.

1. Connect a timing light to the No. 1 spark plug wire according to the light manufacturer's instructions. Do not pierce the spark plug wire to connect the timing light.

2. Set the parking brake and place the transaxle in the **P** position.

NOTE: Do not attempt to time the engine if it is not operating on all cylinders, as damage to the catalytic converter may occur.

3. Connect a jumper wire between pins **A** (ground) and **B** of the Assembly Line Data Link (ALDL) connector, located near the parking brake pedal under the dash. By jumping the Assembly Line Data Link (ALDL) connector, the ECM will command the BCM to display a SET TIMING message on the Climate Control Driver Information Panel (CCDIC). The engine will now operate at base timing. The timing can now be checked with a standard timing light at 10 degrees BTDC at 900 rpm or less. Varify proper timing setting with the Vehicle Emission Control Information label.

4. Start the engine and allow to come to normal operating temperature.

5. Aim the timing light at the degree scale just over the harmonic balancer; the line on the pulley should align with the mark on the timing plate.

6. If timing adjustment is necessary, use a distributor wrench to loosen the hold-down clamp. Rotate the distributor until the desired ignition advance is achieved. When the correct timing is set, tighten the hold-down clamp nut/bolt to 20 ft. lbs. (27 Nm).

NOTE: To advance the timing, rotate the distributor opposite the normal direction of rotor rotation. Retard the timing by rotating the distributor in the normal direction of rotor rotation.

Alternator

PRECAUTIONS

Several precautions must be observed with alternator equipped vehicles to avoid damage to the unit.

● If the battery is removed for any reason, make sure it is reconnected with the correct polarity. Reversing the battery connections may result in damage to the one-way rectifiers.

● When utilizing a booster battery as a starting aid, always connect the positive to positive terminals and the negative terminal from the booster battery to a good engine ground on the vehicle being started.

● **Never use a fast charger as a booster to start vehicles.**

● **Disconnect the battery cables when charging the battery with a fast charger.**

● **Never attempt to polarize the alternator.**

● Do not use test lights of more than 12 volts when checking diode continuity.

● Do not short across or ground any of the alternator terminals.

● The polarity of the battery, alternator and regulator must be matched and considered before making any electrical connections within the system.

● Never separate the alternator on an open circuit. Make sure all connections within the circuit are clean and tight.

● Disconnect the battery ground terminal when performing any service on electrical components.

● Disconnect the battery if arc welding is to be done on the vehicle.

BELT TENSION ADJUSTMENT

All accessories are driven by a single serpentine belt. The tension is maintained automatically by a spring-loaded tensioner. Periodic adjustment is not required.

Belt tension can be checked using a suitable belt tension gauge. The tensioner should maintain approximately 110 lbs. (490 N) of tension throughout its functional travel. If the tension is below specification and the tensioner is resting on the maximum travel stop, replace the serpentine belt.

REMOVAL & INSTALLATION

1. Disconnect the negative battery cable.

2. Label and disconnect the electrical connectors from the back of the alternator.

3. Release the tension from the drive belt and remove the belt from the alternator pulley. Do not remove the belt from any other pulleys.

4. Remove the alternator-to-bracket bolts and the alternator from the vehicle. If necessary, disconnect the ABS ground strap.

To install:

5. Install alternator on vehicle.

6. Reposition drive belt on alternator pulley.

7. Install electrical connectors.

8. Connect negative battery cable.

Starter

REMOVAL & INSTALLATION

1. Disconnect the negative battery cable.

2. Raise and safely support the vehicle.

3. If equipped, remove the starter motor shield.

4. Remove the 4 flywheel inspection cover bolts, as required.

5. Disconnect the solenoid wires and battery cables.

6. Remove starter motor mounting bolts and stud.

NOTE: If the starter is mounted using shims, note their position prior to removal and ensure that they are repositioned properly upon installation.

To install:

7. Install starter motor mounting bolts and stud. Tighten to 32 ft. lbs. (43 Nm).

8. If removed, install the 4 flywheel inspection cover bolts.

9. Connect solenoid wires and battery cable to the starter.

10. If equipped, install starter motor shield.

11. Lower the vehicle.

12. Connect the negative battery cable.

EMISSION CONTROLS

Emission Warning Lamps

The dash mounted "Service Engine Soon" and "Service Vehicle Soon" lights are used to indicate a malfunction that the computer has detected in the vehicle's operation. The malfunctions can be related to the operating sensors or the Electronic Control Module (ECM). The service light will go out automatically if the trouble is cleared or intermittent.

The ECM, however will automatically store the trouble code until the diagnostic system is "Cleared".

CLEARING ECM TROUBLE CODES

Except Allante, Eldorado and Seville

With the ignition switch in the **OFF** position, disconnect battery voltage to the ECM for at least 30 seconds by performing 1 of the following:
1. Remove the ECM fuse from the fuse panel.
2. Disconnect the ECM pigtail.
3. Disconnect the negative battery cable.

NOTE: Disconnecting the negative battery cable should only be done as a last resort as it will also erase the memories for the digital radio, digital clock, trip odometer etc.

Allante, Eldorado and Seville

1. Turn the key to the **ON** position.
2. Simultaneously press the **OFF** and **HI** buttons on the climate control panel until CODES CLEAR appears in the readout.
3. To clear the Body Computer Module (BCM) codes, depress the **OFF** and **LO** buttons simultaneously until CODES CLEAR appears.

FUEL SYSTEM

Fuel System Service Precautions

Safety is the most important factor when performing not only fuel system maintenance but any type of maintenance. Failure to conduct maintenance and repairs in a safe manner may result in serious personal injury or death. Maintenance and testing of the vehicle's fuel system components can be accomplished safely and effectively by adhering to the following rules and guidelines.

- To avoid the possibility of fire and personal injury, always disconnect the negative battery cable unless the repair or test procedure requires that battery voltage be applied.
- Always relieve the fuel system pressure prior to disconnecting any fuel system component (injector, fuel rail, pressure regulator, etc.), fitting or fuel line connection. Exercise extreme caution whenever relieving fuel system pressure to avoid exposing skin, face and eyes to fuel spray. Please be advised that fuel under pressure may penetrate the skin or any part of the body that it contacts.
- Always place a shop towel or cloth around the fitting or connection prior to loosening to absorb any excess fuel due to spillage. Ensure that all fuel spillage (should it occur) is quickly removed from engine surfaces. Ensure that all fuel soaked cloths or towels are deposited into a suitable waste container.
- Always keep a dry chemical (Class B) fire extinguisher near the work area.
- Do not allow fuel spray or fuel vapors to come into contact with a spark or open flame.
- Always use a backup wrench when loosing and tightening fuel line connection fittings. This will prevent unnecessary stress and torsion to fuel line piping. Always follow the proper torque specifications.
- Always replace worn fuel fitting O-rings with new. Do not substitute fuel hose or equivalent where fuel pipe is installed.

RELIEVING FUEL SYSTEM PRESSURE

1. Disconnect the negative battery cable.
2. Loosen fuel filler cap to relieve tank vapor pressure. Do not tighten until service has been completed.
3. Connect a suitable fuel pressure gauge to fuel pressure connection on fuel rail assembly. Wrap a shop towel around fitting while connecting gauge to avoid spillage.
4. Install bleed hose into an approved container and open valve to bleed system pressure. Fuel connections are now safe for servicing.
5. Drain any fuel into an approved container.

NOTE: When repairs to the fuel system have been completed, start the engine and check all connections that were loosened for possible leaks.

Fuel Tank

REMOVAL & INSTALLATION

1. Disconnect the negative battery cable. Relieve the fuel system pressure.
2. Drain all fuel from the tank into a proper container.
3. Disconnect the sender assembly wires, tank filler and the vent hoses.
4. Disconnect the fuel pipe quick connectors.
5. Have an assistant support the fuel tank and disconnect the 2 tank retaining straps.
6. Disconnect the exhaust at the rear hanger and remove the tank from the vehicle.

To install:
7. Install the fuel tank to the vehicle and install the 2 retaining straps.
8. Raise the exhaust and connect the rear hanger.
9. Connect the fuel pipe quick connectors.
10. Connect the sender wires, the tank filler and vent hoses.
11. Refill the tank with fuel and connect the negative battery cable.
12. Inspect for any fuel leakage.

Fuel Filter

REMOVAL & INSTALLATION

1. Disconnect the negative battery cable.
2. Relieve fuel system pressure.
3. Raise and safely support the vehicle.
4. Remove bolt retaining fuel filter bracket or open fuel filter bracket release tabs, as required.
5. If equipped with quick-connect fuel fittings, perform the following procedures:
   a. Grasp filter and 1 fuel line fitting. Twist quick-connect fitting ¼ turn in each direction to loosen any dirt within fitting. Repeat for other fuel line fitting.
   b. Using compressed air, blow out dirt from quick-connect fittings at both ends of fuel filter.
   c. Remove quick-connect fittings by squeezing plastic tabs of male end connector and pull connection apart. Repeat for other fitting.
6. If equipped with threaded fuel fittings, perform the following:
   a. Using a backup wrench on fuel filter, loosen fuel line retaining nut. Repeat for other fuel line fitting.

b. Using compressed air, blow out dirt from fuel line fittings at both ends of fuel filter.

c. Back off nut completely so fuel line can be separated from filter at both ends.

7. Remove fuel filter.

To install:

NOTE: Before installing a new filter, always apply a few drops of clean engine oil to both ends of the filter. This will ensure proper reconnection and prevent a possible fuel leak.

8. Remove protective caps from new filter.

9. If equipped with quick-connect fuel fittings, perform the following:

a. Install new plastic connector retainers on filter inlet and outlet tubes.

b. Install filter in retainer noting direction of flow indicated on filter.

c. Install quick-connect fittings by pushing connectors together to cause the retaining tabs/fingers to snap into place.

NOTE: Once installed, pull on both ends of each connection to make sure connection is secure.

10. If equipped with threaded fuel fittings, install new O-ring seals, install fuel lines into the filter.

NOTE: Use backup wrench when installing fuel lines into new filter to prevent filter O-ring or fuel line damage.

11. Install fuel filter into retainer and engage bracket tabs or install retainer bracket bolt, as required.

12. Lower vehicle.

13. Tighten fuel filler cap.

14. Connect negative battery cable.

NOTE: Before cranking the engine, turn ignition switch to the ON position for 2 seconds, then turn switch OFF for 5 seconds. Again turn ignition switch to ON position and check for fuel leaks.

Electric Fuel Pump

The fuel pump is mounted in the tank and is part of the fuel tank meter assembly. The tank must be removed from the vehicle in order to service the fuel pump and fuel tank meter assembly.

PRESSURE TESTING

1. Connect a suitable fuel pressure gauge to the fuel pressure test fitting on the fuel rail assembly. Wrap a shop towel around the fuel pressure tap to absorb any fuel leakage that may occur when installing the gauge.

2. Turn ignition switch to the ON position. Check to see that pressure is within specification.

3. Turn ignition switch OFF. Pressure should not leak down with fuel pump OFF.

4. Pressure at idle should be 3–10 psi (21–69 kPa) lower than static pressure.

REMOVAL & INSTALLATION

1. Disconnect the negative battery cable.

2. Relieve fuel system pressure.

3. Remove fuel filler cap to release fuel tank vapors. Leave cap off until repairs are completed.

――――― CAUTION ―――――

Gasoline fuel vapors are extremely flammable. Ensure that fuel is stored in a container that can be properly sealed. Never store fuel in an open container. Store container in a safe place away from heat.

4. Remove fuel tank by performing the following:

a. Drain fuel from the tank into an approved container for storage.

b. Raise and safely support the vehicle.

c. Remove rear stabilizer bar at links, pivot bar downward.

d. Remove hoses and pipes from tank unit.

e. Remove hoses at tank from filler and vent pipe.

f. Disconnect tank unit harness from rear body harness.

g. Support fuel tank and disconnect 2 fuel tank retaining straps.

h. Remove tank from vehicle.

5. Remove sending unit, gasket and pump assembly by turning cam lock ring counterclockwise. Lift assembly from fuel tank and remove fuel pump from fuel tank sending unit.

6. Pull fuel pump up into attaching hose while pulling outward away from bottom support. Take care to prevent damage to rubber insulator and strainer during removal. After pump assembly is clear of bottom support, pull pump assembly out of rubber connector for removal.

To install:

7. Push fuel pump assembly into attaching hose.

8. Install fuel tank sending unit and pump assembly into tank assembly. Use new O-ring seal during reassembly.

9. Install cam lock over assembly and lock by turning clockwise.

10. Support tank and position in vehicle. Install tank straps and secure with retaining bolts. Tighten to 25 ft. lbs. (33 Nm).

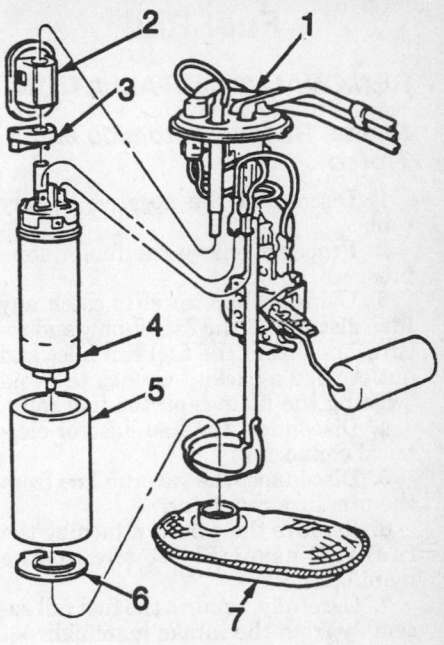

1. Fuel tank meter assembly
2. Pulsator
3. Bumper
4. Fuel pump
5. Sound isolator sleeve
6. Sound insulator
7. Filter strainer

Exploded view of the electric fuel pump/sending unit assembly

11. Connect tank unit harness to body harness.

12. Connect hoses to filler and vent pipes. Tighten clamps.

13. Connect hoses and pipes to tank unit.

14. Connect rear stabilizer bar to links. Tighten bolts to 42 ft. lbs. (58 Nm).

15. Lower vehicle.

16. Refill tank and install filler cap.

17. Connect negative battery cable.

18. Start engine and check for leaks.

Fuel Injection

IDLE SPEED ADJUSTMENT

Idle speed is automatically controlled by the ECM. Periodic adjustments are not required.

IDLE MIXTURE ADJUSTMENT

Idle mixture is automatically maintained by the ECM. Periodic adjustments are not required.

Fuel Rail

REMOVAL & INSTALLATION

Reatta, Riviera, Toronado and Trofeo

1. Disconnect the negative battery cable.
2. Properly relieve the fuel system pressure.
3. Using a shop towel to catch any fuel, disconnect the fuel supply and return lines from the fuel rail inlet and outlet. Use a backup wrench to avoid twisting the fittings on the fuel rail.
4. Disconnect the fuel injector electrical connectors.
5. Disconnect the vacuum line from the pressure regulator.
6. Remove the 4 bolts attaching the fuel rail assembly to the intake manifold.
7. Carefully, remove the fuel rail assembly from the intake manifold.

NOTE: With the fuel rail removed, cover the injector openings to prevent the entry of dirt and other contaminants.

To install:

8. Install the new injector O-rings. Lubricate lightly with engine oil.
9. Carefully, install the fuel rail to the intake manifold. Seat each injector by hand.
10. Install the 4 bolts attaching the fuel rail to the intake manifold. Tighten to 7–14 ft. lbs. (10–20 Nm).
11. Connect the fuel supply and return lines to the fuel rail.
12. Connect the fuel injector electrical connectors.
13. Connect the vacuum line to the fuel pressure regulator.
14. Connect the negative battery cable.
15. Start the engine and check for fuel leaks.

Allante, Eldorado and Seville

1. Disconnect the negative battery cable.
2. Remove the air cleaner.
3. Properly relieve the fuel system pressure.
4. Remove the power steering pump.
5. Disconnect the vacuum line from the pressure regulator and base assembly.
6. Disconnect the accelerator cable, cruise control cable and bracket.
7. Disconnect the electrical connectors from the TPS, ISC, coolant and MAT sensors.
8. Disconnect the coolant hose to the thermostat housing.

NOTE: Wrap a shop cloth around the fuel lines to collect that leaks when disconnecting the fuel lines.

9. Disconnect the fuel feed line from the rear fuel rail assembly. Discard the O-ring.
10. Disconnect the fuel return line. Discard the O-ring.
11. Disconnect the EGR vacuum lines and remove the EGR valve.
12. Remove the 5 fuel rail support bracket attaching bolts.
13. Disconnect the front and rear fuel rail electrical connectors.
14. Carefully, remove the fuel rail from the intake manifold.
15. Remove the lower O-ring seal from the injectors and discard.

To install:

16. Install new injector O-rings. Lubricate lightly with engine oil.
17. Carefully, install the fuel rail assembly to the intake manifold.
18. Install the 5 fuel rail attaching bolts. Tighten to 18 ft. lbs. (24 Nm).
19. Connect the front and rear fuel rail electrical connectors.
20. Install the EGR valve and connect the vacuum lines.
21. Install new fuel feed line O-rings. Lubricate O-rings with petroleum based grease. Connect the fuel feed line. Using a backup wrench, tighten to 22 ft. lbs. (30 Nm).
22. Install new fuel return line O-rings. Lubricate O-rings with petroleum based grease. Connect the fuel return line. Using a backup wrench, tighten to 22 ft. lbs. (30 Nm).
23. Connect the coolant hose to the thermostat housing.
24. Connect the electrical connectors to the TPS, ISC, coolant and MAT sensors.
25. Connect the accelerator cable, and cruise control cable and bracket.
26. Connect the vacuum line to the pressure regulator and base assembly.
27. Install the power steering pump.
28. Install the air cleaner.
29. Connect the negative battery cable.
30. Start the engine and check for fuel leaks.

Fuel Injector

REMOVAL & INSTALLATION

NOTE: Care must be taken when removing injectors to prevent damage to the electrical connector pins on the injector and the nozzle. The injectors are serviced as a complete assembly only. Injectors are an electrical component and should not be immersed in any type of cleaner.

Sequential Fuel Injection (SFI)

1. Disconnect the negative battery cable.
2. Properly relieve the fuel pressure.
3. Remove the fuel rail.
4. On Allante, Eldorado and Seville, disconnect the injector electrical connector by pushing in the wire connector clip while pulling the connector body away from the injector.
5. Remove the injector retainer clip from the injector.
6. Separate the injector from the fuel rail.
7. Remove the injector O-rings and discard.

To install:

8. Lubricate new injector O-rings lightly and install on the injector.
9. If supplied, install new injector clip on the injector.
10. Install the fuel injector assembly into the fuel rail socket.

NOTE: On Allante, Eldorado and Seville, the electrical connectors should be facing the front of the engine for injectors 1–4 and the rear of the engine for injectors 5–8.

11. Connect the electrical connector to the injector assembly.
12. Install the fuel rail assembly.
13. Connect the negative battery cable.
14. Start the engine and check for fuel leaks.

Throttle Body Injection (TBI)

1. Disconnect the negative battery cable. Remove the air cleaner.
2. Properly relieve the fuel system pressure.
3. Disconnect the electrical connector from the fuel injector(s) by squeezing both tabs together and pulling it straight up.
4. Remove the fuel meter cover-to-throttle body screws and the cover; be sure to note the position of the short screws. Allow the gasket to remain in place to prevent damage to the casting housing.
5. Using a small prybar and a ¼ in. rod, pry the fuel injector(s) from the throttle body; discard the O-rings.

To install:

6. Lubricate the new small O-ring with clean Dexron®II automatic transmission fluid. Push the new small O-ring onto the nozzle end of the injector pressing the ring up against the injector fuel filter.
7. Install the steel backup washer into the recess of the fuel meter body.
8. Lubricate the new large O-ring with clean Dexron®II automatic transmission fluid. Install the O-ring directly above the backup washer, pressing

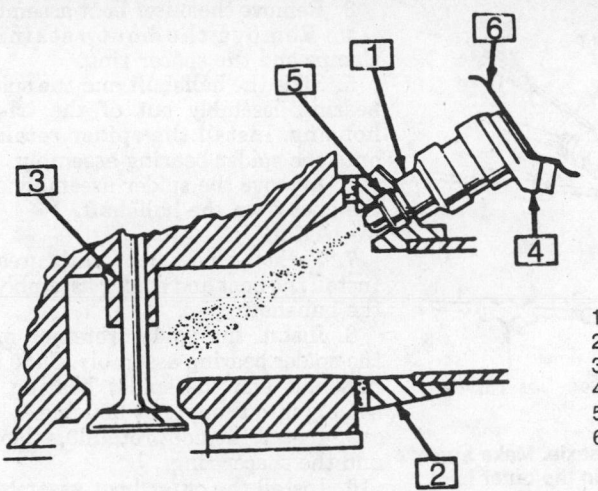

1. Fuel injector
2. Intake manifold
3. Intake valve
4. Electrical terminal
5. O-ring
6. Fuel rail

Port/sequential fuel injector installation

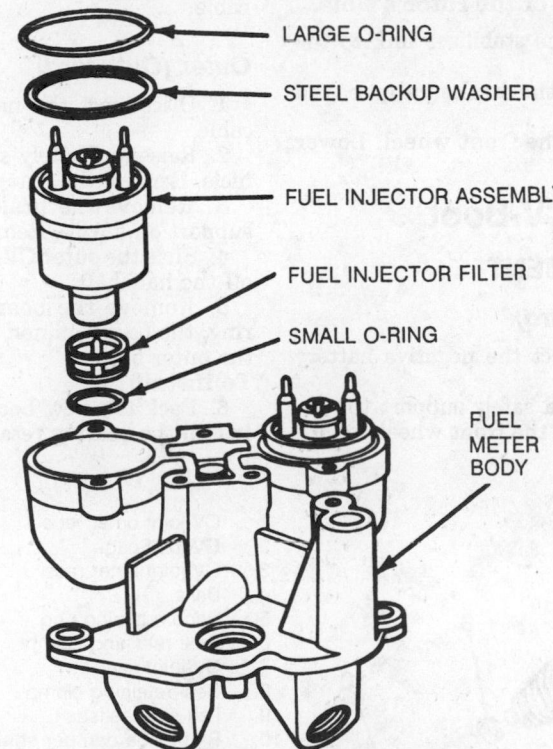

LARGE O-RING

STEEL BACKUP WASHER

FUEL INJECTOR ASSEMBLY

FUEL INJECTOR FILTER

SMALL O-RING

FUEL METER BODY

Throttle body fuel injector components

the O-ring down into the cavity recess. O-ring is located properly when it is flush with the fuel meter body casting surface.

NOTE: Do not attempt to reverse this procedure and install the backup washer and O-ring after the injector is located in the cavity. To do so will prevent the seating of the O-ring in the cavity recess which may result in a fuel leak.

9. Install the injector using a push-ing/twisting motion to center the nozzle O-ring in the bottom of the injector cavity. Align the raised lug on the injector base with the notch cast into the fuel meter body. Push down on the injector making sure it is fully seated in the cavity. The injector installation is correct with the lug seated in the notch and the electrical terminals parallel to the throttle shaft in the throttle body.

10. Install the fuel meter cover.
11. Connect the injector electrical connector.
12. Install the air cleaner.

13. Connect the negative battery cable.
14. Start the engine and check for fuel leaks.

DRIVE AXLE

Halfshaft

REMOVAL & INSTALLATION

1. Remove the hub nut and washer.
2. Raise and safely support the vehicle. Remove the front wheel.
3. Remove the brake caliper and rotor.
4. Remove the stabilizer link from the control arm.
5. Remove the tie rod end-to-steering knuckle cotter pin and nut. Using a ball joint removal tool, separate the tie rod end from the steering knuckle.
6. Remove the lower ball joint-to-steering knuckle cotter pin and nut. Using a ball joint removal tool, separate the lower ball joint from the steering knuckle.
7. Using a prybar and a wooden block, pry the halfshaft from the transaxle and suspend it on a wire.

NOTE: When removing the halfshaft, be careful not to allow the shaft to drop causing damage to the CV-joints. Do not allow the halfshaft to overextended because the Tri-Pot (S-plan) joint can disengage from the bearing blocks.

8. Using the halfshaft removal tool, press the halfshaft from the steering knuckle hub and remove it from the vehicle.

NOTE: If equipped with an anti-lock brake system, be careful not to damage the toothed sensor ring (on halfshaft) and the wheel speed sensor (on steering knuckle).

To install:
9. Install the drive axle into the transaxle. Verify that the drive axle snapring is properly seated by grasping the housing and pulling outboard.

NOTE: Do not pull on the drive axle.

10. Install the outer end of the drive axle into the hub and bearing assembly.
11. Install the lower ball joint stud to the steering knuckle.
12. Install the washer and new torque prevailing nut. Tighten to 183 ft. lbs. (245 Nm).

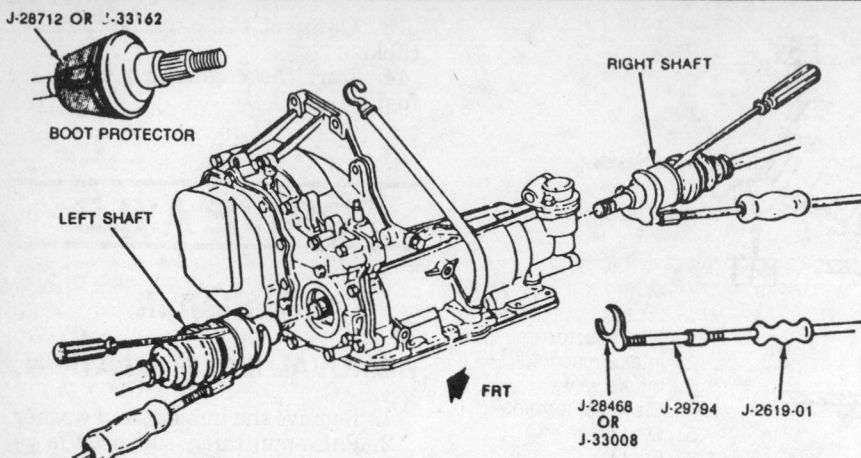

Using a prybar and special tools to pull the halfshafts from the transaxle. Make sure to support the axles at the center to avoid putting downward force on the outer joint

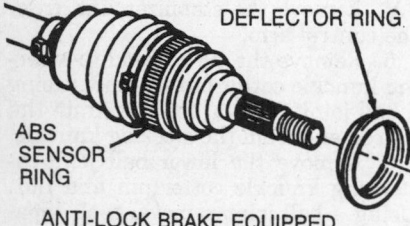

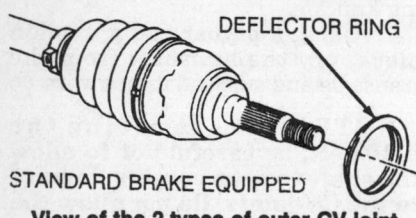

View of the 2 types of outer CV-joint assemblies and deflector rings

NOTE: To keep the halfshaft from turning, place a small drift pin into one of the rotor's slots.

13. Install the stabilizer link to the control arm.

14. Install the brake caliper and rotor.

15. Install the front wheel. Lower the vehicle

CV-Boot

REPLACEMENT

Inner (Inboard)

1. Disconnect the negative battery cable.

2. Raise and safely support the vehicle. Remove the front wheels.

3. Remove the outer boot assembly.

4. Remove the boot retaining clamps and the spacer ring.

5. Slide the halfshaft and the spider bearing assembly out of the tri-pot housing. Install the spider retainer onto the spider bearing assembly.

6. Remove the spider assembly and the boot from the halfshaft.

To install:

7. Pack the new boot with grease. Install the boot and spider assembly to the halfshaft.

8. Install the spider retainer onto the spider bearing assembly. Slide the halfshaft and the spider bearing assembly into the tri-pot housing.

9. Install the boot retaining clamps and the spacer ring.

10. Install the outer boot assembly.

11. Install the front wheels. Lower the vehicle.

12. Connect the negative battery cable.

Outer (Outboard)

1. Disconnect the negative battery cable.

2. Raise and safely support the vehicle. Remove the front wheels.

3. Remove the brake caliper and support on a wire. Remove the rotor.

4. Slide the outer CV-joint assembly off the halfshaft.

5. Remove the bearing retaining ring, the boot retainer, the clamp and the outer boot.

To install:

6. Pack the new boot with grease. Install the bearing retaining ring, the

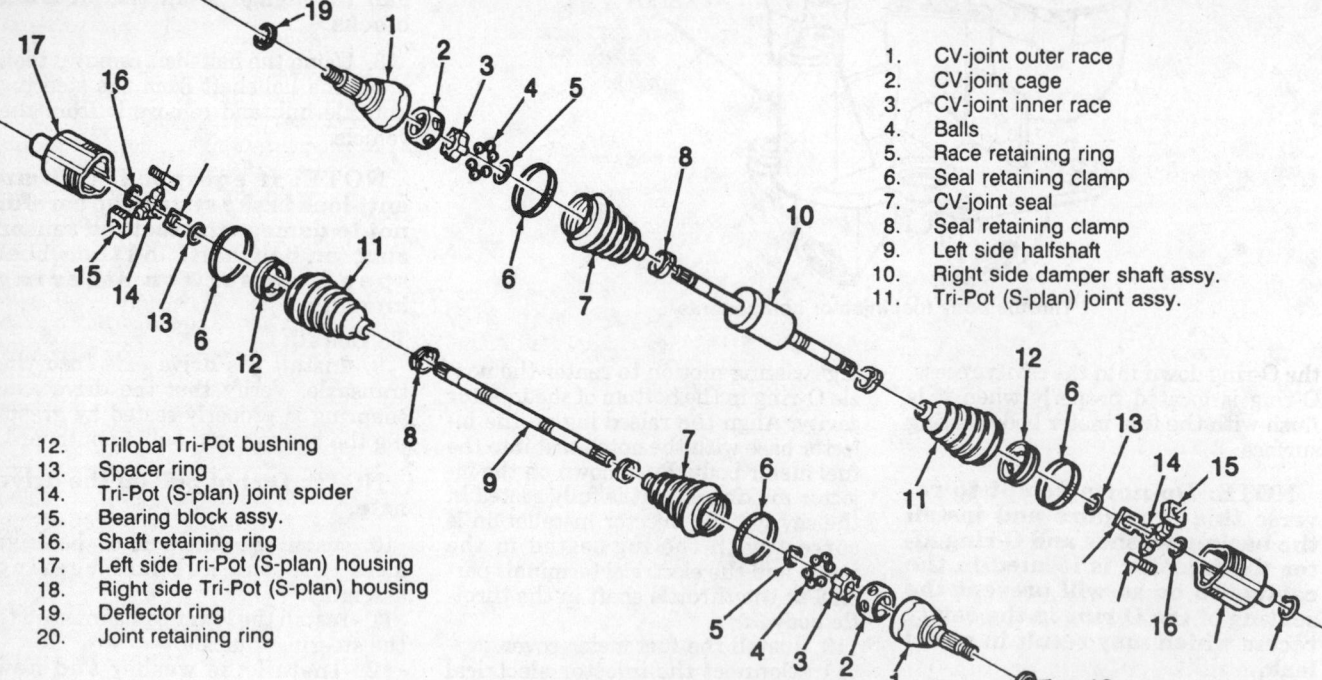

1. CV-joint outer race
2. CV-joint cage
3. CV-joint inner race
4. Balls
5. Race retaining ring
6. Seal retaining clamp
7. CV-joint seal
8. Seal retaining clamp
9. Left side halfshaft
10. Right side damper shaft assy.
11. Tri-Pot (S-plan) joint assy.

12. Trilobal Tri-Pot bushing
13. Spacer ring
14. Tri-Pot (S-plan) joint spider
15. Bearing block assy.
16. Shaft retaining ring
17. Left side Tri-Pot (S-plan) housing
18. Right side Tri-Pot (S-plan) housing
19. Deflector ring
20. Joint retaining ring

Exploded view of the halfshaft assemblies—Tri-Pot (S-plan)

boot retainer, the clamp and the outer boot.

7. Slide the outer CV-joint assembly onto the halfshaft.

8. Install the rotor. Install the brake caliper.

9. Install the front wheels.

10. Connect the negative battery cable.

Front Wheel Hub, Spindle and Bearing

NOTE: The bearings are preadjusted and require no lubrication, maintenance or adjustment. There are darkened areas on the bearing assembly which are the result of a heat treating process.

REMOVAL & INSTALLATION

1. Raise and safely support the vehicle.

2. Place jackstands under the cradle and lower the vehicle slightly so the weight of the vehicle rests on the jackstands and not on the control arms.

3. Remove the wheel assembly.

4. Insert a drift punch into the rotor and remove the hub nut/washer.

5. Remove the brake caliper, support and the rotor.

6. Using the front hub spindle remover tool, separate the halfshaft from the hub.

7. Remove the hub/bearing assembly-to-steering knuckle bolts and the hub/bearing assembly.

To install:

8. If replacing the seal, drive the seal towards the engine. Cut the seal off the halfshaft; be careful not to damage the halfshaft boot.

NOTE: If the speed sensor bracket is removed or loosened from the steering knuckle, the speed sensor gap must be adjusted. If the speed sensor is removed from the bracket, speed sensor wax must be applied to the sensor before it is reinstalled in the bracket. Failure to apply the wax will permit corrosion and may result in sensor failure.

9. To install the new grease seal, lubricate the with wheel bearing grease and using the hub seal installer tool, install the seal.

10. Install the hub/bearing assembly-to-steering knuckle bolts and the hub/bearing assembly. Tighten the hub/bearing assembly-to-steering knuckle bolts to 70 ft. lbs. (95 Nm).

11. Install the halfshaft to the hub.

12. Install the rotor and caliper.

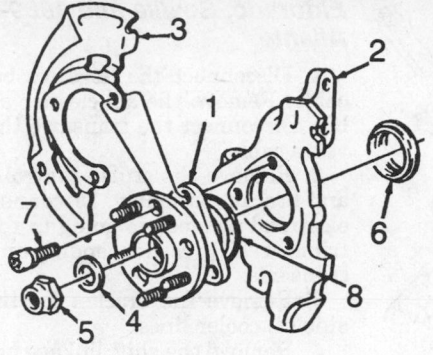

1. Hub/bearing assembly
2. Steering knuckle
3. Shield
4. Washer
5. Hub nut—180 ft. lbs.
6. Seal
7. Hub/bearing bolt—70 ft. lbs.
8. O-ring
9. Speed sensor bracket
10. Bracket bolts—19 ft. lbs.
11. Speed sensor
12. Sensor bolts—9 ft. lbs.

Exploded view of the front wheel bearing assembly

13. Install the hub nut and washer. Tighten to 183 ft. lbs. (245 Nm).

14. Install the wheel assembly.

15. Remove the jackstands and lower the vehicle.

AUTOMATIC TRANSAXLE

For further information on transmission/transaxles, please refer to "Chilton's Guide to Transmission Repair".

Transaxle Assembly

REMOVAL & INSTALLATION

Rivera, Reatta, Tornado and Trofeo

1. Disconnect the negative battery cable. Remove the air intake duct.

2. Disconnect the Throttle Valve (TV) cable from the transaxle and the throttle body. Disconnect the cruise control servo and cable.

3. Remove the exhaust pipe crossover.

4. Disconnect the shift control linkage lever from the manual shaft and the mounting bracket from the transaxle.

5. Disconnect the electrical harness connectors from the neutral start/backup light switch, the Torque Converter Clutch (TCC) and the Vehicle Speed Sensor (VSS).

6. Disconnect the hose from the vacuum modulator.

7. Remove the upper transaxle-to-engine bolts.

8. Using the engine support fixture tool, attach it to the engine, turn the wing nuts to relieve the tension on the engine cradle and mounts.

9. Turn the steering wheel to the full left position.

10. Raise and safely support the vehicle. Remove both from wheel assemblies.

11. Using the halfshaft seal protector tool, install one on each halfshaft. Remove both front ball joint-to-steering knuckle nuts and separate the control arms from the steering knuckles.

12. Using a medium prybar, pry the halfshaft from the transaxle and support it on a wire. Do not remove the halfshaft from the steering knuckle.

NOTE: When removing the halfshaft, be careful not to damage the seal lips.

13. Remove the right rear transaxle-to-frame nuts, the left rear transaxle mount-to-transaxle bolts and the right rear transaxle mount.

14. Remove the stabilizer shaft from the left control arm.

15. Remove the flywheel cover bolts and the cover.

16. Matchmark the torque converter-to-flywheel bolts for reinstallation purposes. Remove the torque converter-to-flywheel bolts and push the torque converter back into the transaxle.

17. Remove the partial frame-to-main frame bolts, the partial frame-to-body bolts and the partial frame.

18. Disconnect and plug the oil cooler tubes from the transaxle.

19. Remove the lower transaxle-to-engine bolts.

NOTE: One bolt is located between the engine and the transaxle case and is positioned in the opposite direction.

20. Lower the transaxle from the vehicle. Be careful not to damage the hoses, lines and wiring.

To install:

21. Raise transaxle into position. Install the lower transaxle bolts.

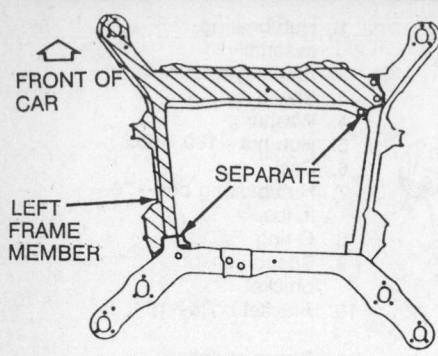

FRONT OF
CAR

SEPARATE

LEFT
FRAME
MEMBER

View of the frame separation points

NOTE: Make sure the opposite-facing bolt is reinstalled in the proper direction.

22. Unplug and connect the oil cooler tubes to the transaxle.

23. Install the partial frame. Secure with the partial frame-to-body and the partial frame-to-main frame bolts.

24. Install the torque converter observing matchmarks made on disassembly and secure with torque converter-to-flywheel bolts. Tighten to 46 ft. lbs. (62 Nm). Install flywheel cover and secure with flywheel cover bolts.

25. Install left control arm and stabilizer shaft.

26. Install right rear transaxle mount, right rear transaxle-to-frame nuts and the left rear transaxle mount-to-frame nuts.

27. Install halfshaft into transaxle.

NOTE: When installing halfshafts, be sure not to damage seals.

28. Connect the control arms to the transaxle and secure with both front ball joint-to-steering knuckle nuts.

29. Install both wheel and tire assemblies.

30. Lower the vehicle.

31. Remove engine support fixture tool.

32. Install the upper transaxle-to-engine bolts.

33. Connect vacuum modulator hose.

34. Connect electrical harness connectors to neutral start/backup light switch, Torque Converter Clutch (TCC) and the Vehicle Speed Sensor (VSS).

35. Connect shift control linkage lever to manual shaft and mounting bracket to transaxle.

36. Install exhaust crossover pipe.

37. Connect Throttle Valve (TV) cable to the transaxle and throttle body. Connect cruise control servo.

38. Install air intake duct. Connect negative battery cable.

39. Start engine and check for transaxle leaks. Refill as necessary.

Eldorado, Seville and 1989–92 Allante

1. Disconnect the negative battery cable. Remove the air cleaner assembly. Disconnect the transaxle throttle valve cable.

2. Remove the cruise control servo and bracket assembly. Disconnect the electrical connectors going to the distributor, oil pressure sending unit and transaxle.

3. Remove the bracket for the engine oil cooler lines.

4. Remove the shift linkage bracket from the transaxle and the manual shift lever from the manual shift shaft; leave the cable attached to the lever and bracket.

5. Remove the fuel line bracket and disconnect the neutral safety switch connector.

6. Remove the vacuum modulator.

7. Remove the throttle valve cable support bracket and engine oil cooler line bracket. Remove the bellhousing bolts except the left and right side bolts; note the bolt lengths and positions.

8. Remove the air injection reactor crossover pipe fitting and reposition the pipe. Remove the radiator hose bracket and transaxle mount-to-bracket nuts.

9. Install an engine support fixture, noting the positions of the hooks.

10. Raise and safely support the vehicle.

11. Remove both front wheels, the right and left stabilizer link bolts. Remove the ball joint cotter pins and nuts and press the ball joints from the steering knuckles.

12. Remove the air conditioner splash shield and the mount cover for the forward most cradle insulator.

13. Remove the hose connections from the ends of the air injection reactor pipes. Remove the vacuum hoses and the wire loom from the clips at the front of the cradle.

14. Remove the engine mount and dampener-to-cradle attachments. Remove the transaxle mount-to-cradle attachments. Remove the wire loom clip from the transaxle mount bracket and lower the vehicle.

15. Using both left side support hooks on the engine support fixture to raise the transaxle 2 in. from its normal position. Raise and safely support the vehicle.

16. Remove the right front and left rear transaxle-to-cradle bolts and the left stabilizer mount bolts. Remove the foremost cradle mount insulator bolt and the left cradle member, separate the right front corner first.

17. Remove the air injection reactor management valve/bracket assembly from the transaxle mount bracket and reposition the bracket to the transaxle stud bolts.

18. Lower the vehicle. Lower the transaxle to its normal position to gain access to the transaxle mounting bracket. Remove the mounting bracket.

19. Raise and safely support the vehicle. Remove the right rear transaxle mount-to-transaxle bracket. Remove the engine-to-transaxle brace bolts that pass into the transaxle VSS connector.

20. Mark the relationship between torque converter and flexplate for reassembly in the same position. Remove the flywheel covers, then, remove the torque converter bolts, rotating the crankshaft with a socket wrench as necessary to gain access. Position a jack under the transaxle to support it.

21. Remove the left and right bellhousing bolts; note the bolt lengths and positions.

NOTE: Access may be gained through the right wheelhouse opening to remove the bolt on the right side; use a 3 foot long socket extension to reach it.

22. Disconnect the oil cooler lines at the transaxle, drain them and plug the openings. Then, install halfshaft boot seal protectors and disconnect the halfshafts at the transaxle. Suspend the halfshafts aside and remove the transaxle.

To install:

23. Install the transaxle. Remove the halfshaft boot seal protectors and connect the halfshafts to the transaxle. Connect the oil cooler lines at the transaxle.

24. Install the left and right bellhousing bolts in their original locations. Tighten the bellhousing bolts to 55 ft. lbs. (75 Nm).

25. Connect the torque converter to the flywheel, observing the matchmarks made upon removal. Install the converter-to-flexplate bolts and tighten to 46 ft. lbs. (63 Nm). Install the flywheel covers.

26. Install the engine-to-transaxle brace bolts that pass into the transaxle VSS connector. Install the right rear transaxle mount-to-transaxle bracket. Lower the vehicle.

27. Install the air injection reactor management valve/bracket assembly from the transaxle mount bracket.

28. Install the foremost cradle mount insulator bolt and the left cradle member. Install the right front and left rear transaxle-to-cradle bolts and the left stabilizer mount bolts.

29. Install the engine mount and dampener-to-cradle attachments. Install the transaxle mount-to-cradle attachments. Install the wire loom clip

from the transaxle mount bracket and lower the vehicle.

30. Install the hose connections to the ends of the AIR pipes. Install the vacuum hoses and the wire loom to the clips at the front of the cradle.

31. Install the air conditioner splash shield and the mount cover for the forward most cradle insulator.

32. Install the ball joint cotter pins and nuts and press the ball joints to the steering knuckles. Tighten the ball joint nuts to 81 ft. lbs. (110 Nm). Install both front wheels, the right and left stabilizer link bolts.

33. Lower the vehicle.

34. Remove the engine support fixture.

35. Install the air injection reactor crossover pipe fitting and reposition the pipe. Install the radiator hose bracket and transaxle mount-to-bracket nuts.

36. Install the throttle valve cable support bracket and engine oil cooler line bracket. Install the bellhousing bolts. Tighten the bellhousing bolts to 55 ft. lbs. (75 Nm).

37. Install the vacuum modulator.

38. Install the fuel line bracket and connect the neutral safety switch connector.

39. Install the shift linkage bracket to the transaxle and the manual shift lever to the manual shift shaft.

40. Install the bracket for the engine oil cooler lines.

41. Install the cruise control servo and bracket assembly. Connect the electrical connectors going to the distributor, oil pressure sending unit and transaxle.

42. Install the air cleaner assembly. Disconnect the transaxle throttle valve cable. Connect the negative battery cable.

43. Adjust the transaxle valve cable and the shift linkage. Refill the transaxle to the proper level. Start engine and allow to come to normal operating temperature. Check transaxle fluid level and adjust as necessary.

1993 Allante

1. Disconnect the negative battery cable.

2. Remove the air cleaner and disconnect the range control cable and bracket at the transaxle.

3. Disconnect the manual shaft lever and the transaxle range switch.

4. Install an engine support fixture tool J28467 or equivalent, to the vehicle. Load the fixture so it begins to take the weight off the engine mounts.

5. Raise and safely support the vehicle.

6. Remove both front tires and wheels and remove both wheel opening splash shields.

7. Disconnect the electrical connectors at the 2 transaxle connectors, at the speed sensor connector and at the power steering gear connector.

8. Disconnect and plug the power steering pressure hose and return hose at the steering gear and the auxiliary cooler.

9. Rotate the steering shaft so the steering stub shaft clamp bolt is accessible from the left wheel opening. Remove the clamp bolt and disconnect the shaft from the steering gear.

NOTE: Do not turn the steering wheel after disconnecting the shaft from the steering gear. If the wheel is turned the SRS system may be disturbed.

10. Disconnect both front suspension sensors from the lower control arms and move them out of the way.

11. Remove both stabilizer links from the steering knuckles.

12. Remove the tie rod cotter pins and nuts and separate the tie rods from the steering knuckles.

13. Remove the lower ball joint cotter pins and nuts and separate the ball joints from the steering knuckles.

14. Remove the drive axle nuts and separate the drive axles from the hubs.

15. Remove the drive axles from the transaxle.

16. Remove the splash shield from the frame and remove the ABS modulator from the bracket and support it.

17. Remove the engine oil pan to transaxle bracket and remove the torque converter cover.

18. Mark the flywheel-to-converter positioning for assembly purposes. Remove the flywheel-to-converter bolts.

19. Disconnect the transaxle cooler lines from the transaxle.

20. Remove the left and right transaxle mount nuts and the right engine mount nuts at the frame.

21. Support the frame and remove the 6 frame mount bolts.

22. Lower the frame and/or raise the vehicle with steering gear intact.

23. Remove the left and right transaxle mounts and brackets from the transaxle.

24. Remove the engine-to-transaxle bracket.

25. Install a transmission jack to the transaxle.

26. Remove the engine-to-transaxle bolts and lower the transaxle out of the vehicle.

To install:

27. Raise the transmission jack until the transaxle is in place.

28. Install the engine to transaxle bolts and tighten the bolts to 35 ft. lbs. (47 Nm).

29. Install the right and left engine-to-transaxle brackets and mounts and tighten the bolts and nuts to 35 ft. lbs. (47 Nm).

30. Raise the frame and/or lower the vehicle while aligning the studs and the bolt holes.

31. Install the left side No. 2 bolt into the body and then the No. 1 bolt.

32. Install the remaining bolts and tighten all to 74 ft. lbs. (100 Nm).

33. Install the right and left transaxle mount nuts and right engine mount nuts at the frame. Torque the nuts to 35 ft. lbs. (47 Nm).

34. Connect the transaxle cooler pipe fittings to the transaxle. Tighten the fittings to 16 ft. lbs. (22 Nm).

35. Align the flywheel to it's proper position and tighten the flywheel-to-converter bolts to 35 ft. lbs. (47 Nm).

36. Install the torque converter cover and tighten the bolt to 106 in. lbs. (12 Nm).

37. Install the engine oil pan-to-transaxle bracket and tighten the bolts to 35 ft. lbs. (47 Nm).

38. Install the ABS modulator to the bracket and install the A/C splash shield to the frame.

39. Install both drive axles into the transaxle and into the hubs. Tighten both drive axle nuts to 110 ft. lbs. (145 Nm).

40. Install both lower ball joints into the steering knuckles and install both joint nuts and cotter pins.

41. Install both tie rods into the steering knuckles and install both tie rod nuts and cotter pins.

42. Install both stabilizer links to the steering knuckles and tighten the nuts to 49 ft. lbs. (65 Nm).

43. Connect both front suspension position sensors to the lower control arms.

44. Connect the steering intermediate shaft to the steering gear install the clamp bolt. Tighten the bolt to 35 ft. lbs. (47 Nm).

45. Connect the power steering return and pressure hoses. Tighten the pressure fitting to 20 ft. lbs. (27 Nm).

46. Connect the electrical connectors for the transaxle (2), for the speed sensor and for the power steering gear.

47. Install both front wheel shields and install both front wheels.

48. Lower the vehicle and remove the engine support fixture.

49. Connect the manual shaft lever and neutral start switch.

50. Adjust the transaxle range switch as needed.

51. Connect the range control cable and bracket at the transaxle. Tighten the bolts to 106 in. lbs. (12 Nm).

52. Install the air cleaner and connect the negative battery cable.

53. Check front suspension alignment and reset transaxle adapts.

54. Reset the transaxle oil life indicator.

SHIFT LINKAGE ADJUSTMENT

440-T4 Transaxle

1. Place the console shift lever in the **N** position.
2. Loosen the cable end pin nut at the transaxle lever arm.
3. Position the transaxle linkage lever arm in **N**. Locate the neutral position by rotating the transaxle lever arm clockwise from the **P** position, through **R** to **N**. Verify the console shift lever is in **N**.
4. Hold the shift lever in **N** and tighten the cable end pin nut. Tighten the nut to 20 ft. lbs. (27 Nm).

4T60 and 4T60E Transaxles

1. Move the shift lever to the **N** position. Neutral can be found by rotating the selector shaft clockwise from **P** through **R** to **N**.
2. Place the shift control assembly in **N**.
3. Push the cable adjuster tab to adjust the cable in the cable mounting bracket.

THROTTLE LINKAGE ADJUSTMENT

1. With the engine stopped, depress the accelerator pedal fully and have an assistant check the throttle body for wide open throttle.

NOTE: If the throttle body cannot achieve full throttle, repair the accelerator system.

2. At the engine end of the TV cable, depress and hold-down the metal readjust tab, move the slider until it stops against the fitting and release the readjustment tab.
3. Rotate the throttle lever, by hand, to it's full travel position.
4. The slider must move, ratchet, toward the lever when the lever is rotated to it's full travel position.

FRONT SUSPENSION

MacPherson Strut

REMOVAL & INSTALLATION

1. Disconnect the negative battery cable.
2. Remove nut(s) attaching top of strut assembly to body.

3. If equipped, disconnect electrical connector from top of strut.
4. Raise and safely support the vehicle.
5. Remove tire and wheel assembly.

NOTE: Whenever working near the halfshafts, care must be taken to prevent inner tri-pot joints from being overextended. Overextension of the joint could result in separation of internal components which could go undetected and result in failure of the joint.

Care should be taken to avoid scratching or cracking the spring coating when handling the front suspension coil spring. Damage to the spring coating could result in premature failure.

6. In order to reassemble the knuckle and strut in the same relationship, make the following scribe marks:
   a. Using a sharp tool, scribe the inboard surface of the strut along the upper knuckle radius.
   b. Scribe the knuckle along the lower curve of the strut.
   c. Scribe mark across the strut and knuckle interface.
7. Remove brake line bracket from strut.
8. Remove stabilizer link from strut.
9. Remove strut-to-knuckle bolts and support knuckle with wire.
10. Remove strut from vehicle.

To install:

11. Install strut while aligning scribe marks.
12. Install strut-to-knuckle bolts.
13. Install stabilizer link to strut.
14. Install brake line bracket to strut.
15. Install nuts attaching top of strut to body. Tighten stabilizer link nuts to 48 ft. lbs. (65 Nm). Tighten strut assembly-to-body nuts to 18 ft. lbs. (24 Nm). Tighten steering knuckle-to-strut nuts to 140 ft. lbs. (190 Nm).
16. Install tire and wheel assembly.
17. Lower vehicle.
18. Tighten wheel mounting nuts to 100 ft. lbs. (140 Nm).
19. If equipped, connect electrical connector to top of strut.
20. Connect negative battery cable.

Lower Ball Joints

INSPECTION

1. Raise and safely support the vehicle. Install jackstands under both lower control arms as far outboard as possible.
2. Lower the vehicle onto the jackstands so the downward tension

exerted by the stabilizer bar is relieved.
3. Install a dial indicator and clamp the assembly to the lower control arm.
4. Position the dial indicator plunger tip against the knuckle arm. Zero the dial indicator gauge.
5. Measure the axial travel of the knuckle arm with respect to the control arm, by raising and lowering the wheel using a prybar under the center of the tire.
6. During the measurement, if the axial travel of the control arm is 0.030 in. or more, relative to the knuckle arm, the ball joint should be replaced.

REMOVAL & INSTALLATION

1. Raise and safely support the vehicle.
2. Place jackstands under cradle and lower vehicle slightly so weight of the vehicle rests on the jackstands and not on the control arms.
3. Remove tire and wheel assembly.
4. Install a suitable outer CV-joint boot protector.
5. Remove stabilizer bar insulators, retainers, spacer and bolt.
6. Remove ball joint from knuckle.

NOTE: If equipped with anti-lock brakes, ensure that there is enough clearance between the ball joint stud and speed sensor ring. If not remove the halfshaft hub nut. Install special tool J–28733 or equivalent halfshaft remover. Tighten tool until halfshaft moves inboard enough to provide clearance for ball joint removal.

7. Drill out 3 rivets retaining ball joint starting with ¼ in. drill bit and finishing with ½ in. drill bit.
8. Remove ball joint.

To install:

9. Install new ball joint into control arm.
10. Install ball joint bolts.
11. Connect ball joint to knuckle. Tighten ball joint bolts to 50 ft. lbs. (68 Nm). Tighten ball joint nut to 7 ft. lbs. (10 Nm). Tighten nut an additional ½ turn (3 flats.)

NOTE: When tightening nut, a minimum torque of 48 ft. lbs. (65 Nm) must be obtained. If 48 ft. lbs. (65 Nm) is not obtained, inspect for stripped threads. If threads are satisfactory, replace ball joint and knuckle. If required, turn the nut up to an additional ⅛ of a turn to allow for installation of the cotter pin. Bend both ends of the cotter pin.

12. If removed, tighten the hub nut

to 183 ft. lbs. (245 Nm), to assure proper bearing clamp load.

13. Remove CV-joint boot protector.

14. Install tire and wheel assembly.

15. Raise vehicle enough to allow removal or jackstands.

16. Lower vehicle. Tighten wheel nuts to 100 ft. lbs. (140 Nm).

Lower Control Arms

REMOVAL & INSTALLATION

1. Raise and safely support the vehicle.

2. Place jackstands under cradle and lower vehicle slightly so weight of the vehicle rests on the jackstands and not the control arms.

3. Remove the tire and wheel assembly.

NOTE: Care must be taken not to overextend Tri-Pot joints. Overextension of the joint could result in separation of internal components which could go undetected and result in failure of the joint.

4. If equipped, disconnect the Road Sensing Suspension position sensor and install a suitable CV-joint boot protector.

5. Remove stabilizer shaft insulator, retainers, spacer and bolt to control arm.

6. Lower ball joint from knuckle.

7. Remove control arm bushing bolt and front nut, retainer and insulator.

8. Remove control arm from frame.

To install:

9. Connect control arm to frame.

10. Install control arm bushing bolt and front nut, retainer and insulator. Do not tighten at this time.

11. Connect lower ball joint to knuckle.

12. Install stabilizer shaft insulator, retainers, spacer and bolt. Tighten stabilizer shaft nut and bolt to 13 ft. lbs. (17 Nm).

NOTE: Tighten ball joint nut to 7 ft. lbs. (10 Nm). Tighten nut an additional ½ turn (3 flats). When tightening nut a minimum torque of 48 ft. lbs. (65 Nm) must be obtained. If 48 ft. lbs. (65 Nm) is not obtained, inspect for stripped threads. If threads are satisfactory, replace ball joint and knuckle. If required, turn the nut up to an additional ⅙ of a turn to allow for installation of the cotter pin. Bend both ends of the cotter pin.

13. Remove outer CV-joint boot protector and connect the Road Sensing Suspension position sensor.

14. Install tire and wheel assembly.

15. Raise vehicle slightly so weight of vehicle is supported by the control arms. Tighten control arm bushing bolt to 100 ft. lbs. (140 Nm) or nut to 91 ft. lbs. (123 Nm). Tighten retainer to 52 ft. lbs. (70 Nm).

16. Remove jackstands and lower vehicle.

17. Tighten wheel nuts to 100 ft. lbs. (140 Nm).

Sway Bar

REMOVAL & INSTALLATION

1. Disconnect the negative battery cable.

2. Raise and safely support the vehicle.

3. Place jackstands under cradle and lower vehicle slightly so the weight of the vehicle rests on the jackstands and not on the control arms.

4. Remove right side wheel assembly.

5. Remove left and right insulators, retainers, spacers and bolts.

6. Remove left and right bracket bolts, brackets and insulators.

7. Remove exhaust pipe from rear manifold and move pipe up.

8. Remove stabilizer shaft.

To install:

9. Install stabilizer shaft.

10. Install exhaust pipe to rear manifold.

11. Install left and right insulators, brackets and loosely install bolts.

12. Install left and right insulators, retainers, spacers and bolts.

13. Center stabilizer on frame and check clearance. Tighten bracket to frame bolts to 33 ft. lbs. (45 Nm). Tighten nuts to 13 ft. lbs. (17 Nm).

14. Raise vehicle enough to allow for removal of jackstands.

15. Lower vehicle. Tighten wheel nuts to 100 ft. lbs. (140 Nm).

REAR SUSPENSION

Shock Absorber

REMOVAL & INSTALLATION

1. Disconnect the negative battery cable.

2. Raise and safely support the vehicle.

3. Remove the wheel and tire from the vehicle.

4. Disconnect the shock absorber electrical connector from the rear suspension support.

5. Support the lower control arm to relieve the spring load.

6. Remove the shock absorber lower nut and bolt.

7. Remove the upper mounting nut, retainer and insulator.

8. Compress the shock absorber and remove through the upper control arm.

To install:

9. Position top of shock with the insulator attached into the suspension support.

10. Install the upper shock absorber insulator, retainer and nut.

11. Install the lower shock absorber nut and bolt. Tighten the upper nut to 55 ft. lbs. (75 Nm) and the lower nut to 75 ft. lbs. (102 Nm).

12. Connect the shock absorber electrical connector to the rear suspension support.

13. Install the wheel and tire, lower the vehicle and connect the negative battery cable.

MacPherson Strut

REMOVAL & INSTALLATION

1. Disconnect the negative battery cable.

2. Raise and safely support the vehicle.

3. Reinstall 2 wheel nuts to hold rotor on hub and bearing assembly.

4. Remove brake caliper and support with a length of wire.

NOTE: Do not allow caliper to hang by the brake hose unsupported.

5. Loosen knuckle pivot bolt on outboard end of control arm. Do not remove.

6. Remove upper strut rod cap, mounting nut, retainer and insulator.

7. Compress strut by hand and remove lower insulator.

8. Rotate strut and knuckle assembly outward by pivoting on knuckle pivot bolt.

9. Remove knuckle pinch bolt.

10. Remove strut from knuckle.

To install:

11. Position strut in knuckle. Strut must by fully seated in knuckle with tang on strut bottomed in knuckle slot.

12. Install knuckle pinch bolt. Tighten to 44 ft. lbs. (60 Nm).

13. Install lower insulator on strut and position strut rod in suspension support.

14. Install upper strut insulator, retainer and nut. Tighten upper strut nut to 65 ft. lbs. (88 Nm). Tighten knuckle pivot bolt to 59 ft. lbs. (80 Nm).

15. Install strut rod cap.

16. Install caliper and new caliper bracket mounting bolts.

17. Remove 2 wheel nuts previously installed to retain rotor.

18. Install wheel and tire assembly.

19. Lower vehicle. Tighten wheel nuts to 100 ft. lbs. (140 Nm).

Transverse-Mounted Leaf Spring

REMOVAL & INSTALLATION

NOTE: Removal and installation of the transverse-mounted rear spring requires disassembly of either the left or right suspension while leaving the other side intact. The spring may be removed from either side of the vehicle.

1. Disconnect the negative battery cable.

2. Raise and safely support the vehicle.

3. Remove tire and wheel assembly.

4. Disconnect height sensor link, if disassembling left control arm.

5. Remove stabilizer shaft mounting bolt at strut, if equipped with stabilizer.

6. Reinstall 2 wheel nuts to hold rotor on hub and bearing assembly.

7. Remove brake caliper and support with a length of wire.

NOTE: Do not allow caliper to hang by the brake hose unsupported.

8. Loosen knuckle pivot bolt on outboard end of control arm. Do not remove pivot bolt.

9. Support outboard end of control arm with a suitable lifting device to slightly compress spring.

10. Remove strut rod cap, mounting nut, retainer and upper insulator.

11. Slowly remove lifting device to relieve spring pressure.

12. Compress strut by hand and remove lower insulator.

13. Remove wheel speed sensor, if equipped with anti-lock brakes.

14. Remove inner control arm nuts.

15. While supporting the knuckle and control arm, remove inner control arm bolts and remove the control arm, knuckle, strut, hub and bearing and rotor from vehicle as an assembly.

16. Place a jackstand under the outboard end of spring.

17. Lower the vehicle so the weight loads the spring downward on jackstand.

18. Remove the 3 spring retainer bolts, retainer and lower insulator from retainer nearest the supported end of spring.

19. Slowly raise vehicle, allowing spring to deflect downward until spring no longer exerts force on the lifting device. Remove lifting device.

20. Remove spring retainer bolts, retainer and lower insulator from retainer on opposite side of vehicle.

21. Withdrawal spring from rear suspension support through disassembled side of vehicle suspension.

22. Remove upper spring insulators, as required.

NOTE: Inspect all spring insulators, insulator locating pads, retainers and control arm contact pads for cuts, cracks, tears or other damage. Replace worn or damaged parts.

To install:

23. Install spring insulators which were previously removed. Ensure that molded arrow on the insulator points toward the centerline of the vehicle when installing upper outboard insulators. Tighten center and upper outboard insulator nuts to 21 ft. lbs. (28 Nm).

NOTE: When positioning spring in suspension support, outboard and center insulator locating bands must be centered on spring insulators. Failure to position spring correctly may result in reduced vehicle handling characteristics.

24. With spring properly located, install lower insulator and spring retainer on side of vehicle opposite the disassembled portion of suspension.

25. Place suitable lifting device under free end of spring.

26. Lower vehicle, allowing weight to load spring and deflect free end of spring into position in suspension support.

27. Install lower insulator and spring retainer on disassembled side of suspension support. Tighten spring retainer bolts to 21 ft. lbs. (28 Nm).

28. Raise the vehicle and remove spring lifting device.

29. Position the assembled control arm, knuckle, strut, hub and bearing and rotor assembly in suspension support and install inner control arm bolts and nuts. Do not tighten at this time.

30. Connect wheel sensor, if equipped with anti-lock brakes.

31. Install lower strut insulator and position strut rod in suspension support assembly.

32. Position suitable lifting under outboard end of lower control arm to slightly compress spring.

33. Install strut insulator, retainer and nut. Tighten upper strut nut to 65 ft. lbs. (88 Nm). Tighten knuckle pivot bolt to 59 ft. lbs. (80 Nm). Tighten inner control arm bolts to 66 ft. lbs. (90 Nm).

34. Remove lifting device.

35. Install strut rod cap.

36. Install stabilizer shaft mounting bolt, if equipped with stabilizer. Tighten stabilizer shaft mounting bolt to 43 ft. lbs. (58 Nm).

37. Remove 2 wheel nuts previously installed to retain motor.

38. Install caliper and new caliper mounting bracket bolts. Tighten caliper mounting bracket bolts to 83 ft. lbs. (113 Nm).

39. Connect height sensor link, if left side of suspension was disassembled.

40. Install wheel and tire assembly.

41. Lower vehicle. Tighten wheel nuts to 100 ft. lbs. (140 Nm).

NOTE: Vehicle must have rear wheel alignment performed after removal and installation of rear spring.

Rear Control Arms

REMOVAL & INSTALLATION

Except 1993 Allante

1. Disconnect the negative battery cable.

2. Raise and safely support the vehicle.

3. Remove wheel and tire assembly.

4. If equipped with anti-lock brakes, remove speed sensor from knuckle.

5. Reinstall 2 wheel nuts to hold rotor on hub and bearing assembly.

6. Remove brake caliper and support with a length of wire.

NOTE: Do not allow caliper to hang by the brake hose unsupported.

7. Disconnect electrical connector from top of strut. Loosen knuckle pivot bolt on outboard end of control arm. Do not remove.

8. Support the outboard end of the control arm with a jackstand to slightly compress the spring.

9. Remove upper strut rod cap, mounting nut, retainer and insulator.

10. Slowly remove the jackstand to relieve the spring pressure.

11. Compress strut by hand and remove lower insulator.

12. While supporting the knuckle, remove knuckle pivot bolt and remove the knuckle, strut, hub, bearing and rotor from the vehicle as an assembly.

13. Remove both inner control arm bolts and remove control arm from vehicle.

To install:

14. Position control arm in vehicle and install both inner control arm bolts. Do not tighten bolts at this time.

15. Position the assembled knuckle,

strut, hub and bearing and rotor assembly in control arm and install knuckle pivot bolt. Do not tighten bolt at this time.

16. Install lower strut insulator and position strut rod in suspension support.

17. Position a jackstand under the outboard end of the lower control arm to slightly compress the spring.

18. Install upper strut insulator, retainer and nut. Tighten upper strut nut to 55 ft. lbs. (75 Nm). Tighten knuckle pivot bolt to 59 ft. lbs. (80 Nm). Tighten inner control arm bolts to 66 ft. lbs. (90 Nm).

19. Install strut rod cap.

20. Remove 2 wheel nuts previously installed to retain rotor.

21. Install caliper and new caliper bracket mounting bolts.

22. If equipped, install speed sensor to knuckle.

23. Install wheel and tire assembly.

24. Lower vehicle. Tighten wheel nuts to 100 ft. lbs. (140 Nm).

1993 Allante
LOWER

1. Raise and safely support the vehicle.

2. Remove the wheel and tire assembly.

3. Support the inboard end of the lower control arm with a jackstand.

4. Remove the stabilizer link lower attachment.

5. Disconnect the shock absorber lower attachment.

6. Remove the inboard lower control arm nuts and bolts.

7. Slowly lower the jackstand to relieve the spring pressure.

8. Pull lower control arm to remove the spring and remove the outboard bolt.

9. Remove the control arm from the vehicle.

To install:

10. Install the lower control arm to the vehicle and install the outboard control arm bolt and nut. Tighten the outer nut to 75 ft. lbs. (102 Nm).

11. Install the spring and the insulators and position the jackstand under the lower control arm. Raise the jackstand to slightly compress the spring.

12. Insert the inboard lower control arm bolts and nuts.

13. Install the shock absorber lower attachment and the stabilizer link lower attachment.

14. Remove the jackstand and place under the lower control arm to bring the suspension into the proper position.

15. Tighten the stabilizer link lower nut to 44 ft. lbs. (60 Nm), the shock absorber lower nut to 75 ft. lbs. (102 Nm)

and the lower control arm inner nuts to 75 ft. lbs. (102 Nm).

16. Install the wheel and lower the vehicle.

17. Rear wheel alignment must be done if control arm fasteners were loosened.

UPPER

1. Raise and safely support the vehicle.

2. Remove the wheel.

3. Disconnect the Road Sensing Suspension position sensor and bracket from the shock tower.

4. Remove the inner and outer control arm bolts.

5. Remove the control arm up and over the shock tower to remove from the vehicle.

To install:

6. Install the control arm over the shock tower.

7. Install the inner and outer control arm bolts.

8. Place a jackstand under the outboard end of the lower control arm to bring the suspension to the proper position.

9. Tighten the upper control arm inner and outer nuts to 42 ft. lbs. (57 Nm).

10. Connect the Road Sensing Suspension position sensor bracket and sensor.

11. Install the wheel and tire and lower the vehicle.

Rear Wheel Bearings

REMOVAL & INSTALLATION

1. Disconnect the negative battery cable.

2. Raise and safely support the vehicle.

3. Remove wheel and tire assembly.

4. If equipped with anti-lock brakes, remove speed sensor from knuckle.

5. Reinstall 2 wheel nuts to hold rotor on hub and bearing assembly.

6. Remove brake caliper and support with a length of wire.

NOTE: Do not allow caliper to hang by the brake hose unsupported.

7. Remove rotor.

8. Remove 4 hub mounting bolts.

9. Remove hub and bearing assembly.

To install:

10. Position hub and bearing assembly on knuckle.

11. Install 4 hub mounting bolts. Tighten to 52 ft. lbs. (70 Nm).

12. Install rotor.

13. Install caliper and new caliper bracket mounting bolts. Tighten to 83 ft. lbs. (113 Nm).

14. Install wheel and tire assembly.

15. Lower vehicle. Tighten wheel nuts to 100 ft. lbs. (140 Nm).

ADJUSTMENT

The hub and bearing are installed as an assembly. No periodic adjustment is required. If the bearing is found to have excessive play, the assembly must be replaced.

STEERING

Steering Wheel
— CAUTION —

Some vehicles are equipped with the Supplemental Inflatable Restraint (SIR) or air bag system. The SIR system must be disabled before performing service on or around SIR system components, steering column, instrument panel components, wiring and sensors. Failure to follow safety and disabling procedures could result in accidental air bag deployment, possible personal injury and unnecessary SIR system repairs.

REMOVAL & INSTALLATION

Rivera, Reatta, Tornado and Trofeo
1989

1. Disconnect the negative battery cable.

2. Remove the steering wheel-to-horn pad screws, located behind the steering wheel, and lift the pad from the steering wheel.

3. If the steering wheel is equipped with control buttons, disconnect the electrical connector(s).

4. Remove the steering wheel-to-shaft retainer, if equipped and nut.

5. Scribe an alignment mark on the steering wheel hub in line with the slash mark on the steering shaft.

6. Using the steering wheel puller, press the steering wheel from the steering shaft.

NOTE: If equipped with steering wheel controls, do not install steering wheel puller bolts beyond 5 turns as damage to electronic components behind the wheel may result.

To install:

7. Install the steering wheel to the shaft, observing the alignment mark made during removal.

8. Install the steering wheel-to-shaft retainer, if equipped and nut.

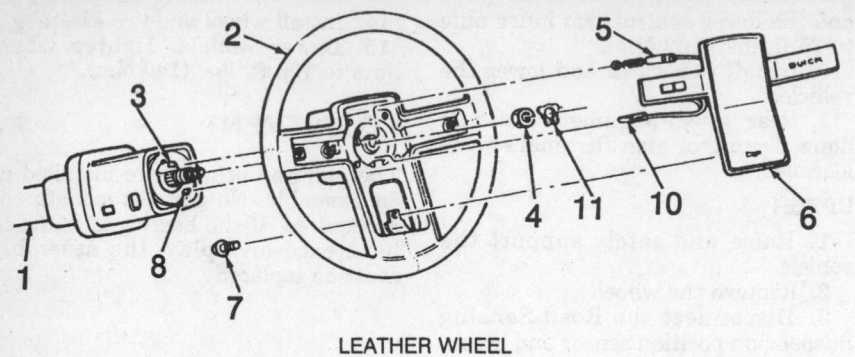

LEATHER WHEEL

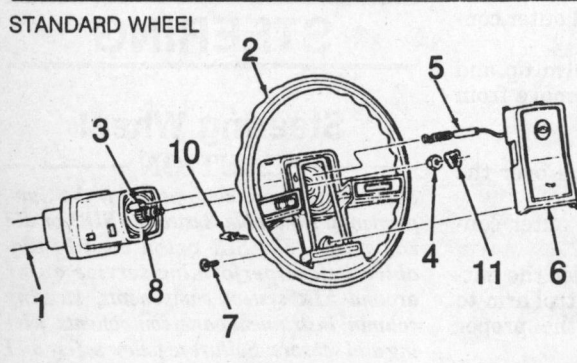

STANDARD WHEEL

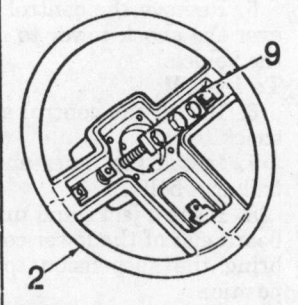

REMOVING STEERING WHEEL

1. Steering column
2. Steering wheel
3. Cam tower
4. Nut—35 ft. lbs.
5. Horn lead
6. Horn pad
7. Horn pad mounting screws—13 inch lbs.
8. Cruise control connector (column)
9. Steering Wheel Puller tool
10. Cruise control connector
11. Retainer

Exploded view of the steering wheel assembly—Reatta, Riviera, Toronado and Trofeo

Tighten the steering wheel-to-steering shaft nut to 35 ft. lbs. (47 Nm).

9. If the steering wheel is equipped with control buttons, connect the electrical connector(s).

10. Install the steering wheel-to-horn pad screws, located behind the steering wheel, and lift the pad from the steering wheel.

11. Connect the negative battery cable.

1990–93

1. Disconnect the negative battery cable. Ensure that ignition switch is in the **OFF** position.

2. Remove SIR fuse from fuse panel.

3. Remove left side sound insulator.

4. Remove left side courtesy light as required to ease removal of sound insulator.

5. Remove Connector Position Assurance (CPA) pin and yellow 2 way connector at the base of the steering column.

6. Loosen inflator module screws from back of steering wheel.

7. Remove horn contact by pushing slightly and twisting counterclockwise.

8. Remove Connector Position Assurance (CPA) pin and coil assembly connector from inflator module.

9. Remove steering column shaft nut.

10. Remove steering wheel using a suitable steering wheel puller.

To install:

11. Feed SIR coil assembly lead through slot in steering wheel.

12. Install steering wheel onto column shaft.

13. Install column shaft nut. Tighten to 30 ft. lbs. (41 Nm).

14. Install horn contact, coil assembly connector and CPA to inflator module.

15. Install inflator module onto steering wheel, securing with 4 screws behind steering wheel. Tighten to 27 inch lbs. (3 Nm).

16. Connect negative battery cable.

17. Connect yellow 2 way connector and CPA pin at the base of the steering column.

18. Install fuse in fuse panel.

19. Install left side sound insulator and connect courtesy light.

Allante, Eldorado and Seville

1989

1. Disconnect the negative battery cable.

2. For the Allante, pry the horn trim pad from the steering wheel. For the Eldorado and Seville, remove the steering wheel-to-horn pad screws, located behind the steering wheel, and the horn trim pad. Remove the horn contact wire, ground connector and cruise control wiring connector.

3. Remove the telescope locking lever assembly-to-adjuster screws. Unscrew and remove the telescoping adjuster from the steering shaft.

4. Remove the telescoping lever assembly. Scribe an alignment mark on the steering wheel hub-in-line with the slash mark on the steering shaft.

5. Remove the steering wheel-to-steering shaft locknut. Using the steering wheel puller, press the steering wheel from the steering shaft.

NOTE: When removing the steering wheel, be sure to remove the cruise control wire from it.

To install:

6. Feed the cruise control wire through the steering wheel, align the matchmark and install the steering wheel-to-steering shaft locknut. Tighten the steering wheel-to-steering shaft to 35 ft. lbs. (47 Nm).

NOTE: For ease of installation, fully extend the steering shaft and install the lock plate compressor screw tool, hand-tight; this will keep the shaft extended when installing the steering wheel. Feed the cruise control wire through the wheel.

7. Remove the tool and place the telescoping lever in the 5 o'clock position.

8. Thread the telescope adjuster assembly finger tight onto the shaft. Install the screws into the telescoping adjuster lever.

9. Move the adjuster lever all the way to the right. The steering wheel should move freely in and out. Move the adjuster lever to the left. The steering wheel should be locked in place with the telescope lever approximately ¼ in. from the left side of the shroud opening. The lever must not contact the shroud in the full locked position. Loosen and adjust the lever as required.

10. For the Allante, install the horn trim pad to the steering wheel. For the Eldorado and Seville, install the steering wheel-to-horn pad screws, located behind the steering wheel, and the

Steering Column

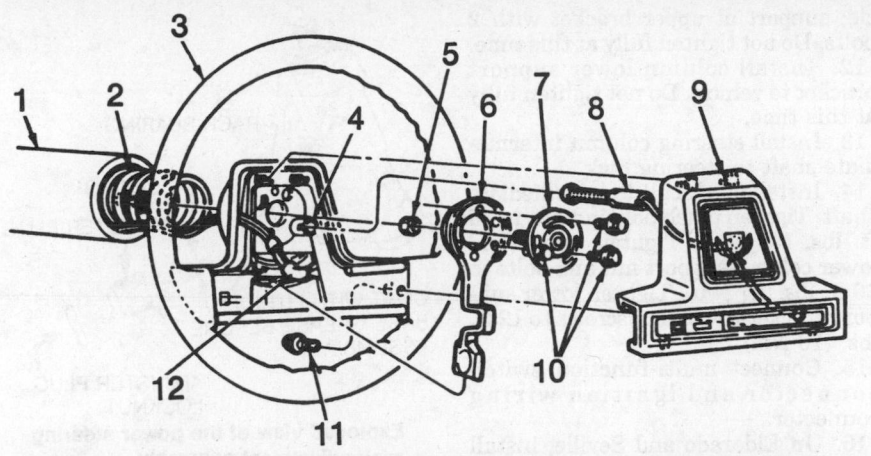

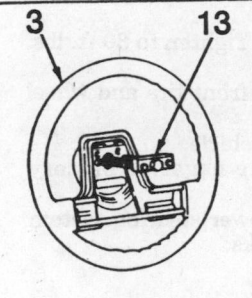
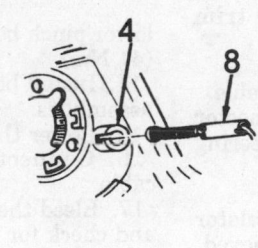
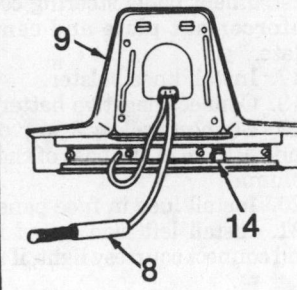

1.	Steering column	8.	Horn lead
2.	Telescoping spring	9.	Horn pad
3.	Steering wheel	10.	Telescope adjuster screws—13 inch lbs.
4.	Cam tower	11.	Horn pad mounting screws—13 inch lbs.
5.	Nut—35 ft. lbs.	12.	Cruise control connector (column)
6.	Telescope lever	13.	Steering Wheel Puller tool No. J-23072
7.	Telescope adjuster	14.	Cruise control connector

Exploded view of the steering wheel assembly—Eldorado and Seville shown

horn trim pad. Install the horn contact wire, ground connector and cruise control wiring connector.

11. Connect the negative battery cable.

1990–93

1. Disconnect the negative battery cable. Ensure that ignition switch is in the **OFF** position.
2. Remove SIR fuse from fuse panel.
3. Remove left side sound insulator.
4. Remove left side courtesy light, as required, to ease removal of sound insulator.
5. Remove Connector Position Assurance (CPA) pin and yellow 2 way connector at the base of the steering column.
6. Loosen inflator module screws from back of steering wheel.
7. Remove horn contact by pushing slightly and twisting counterclockwise.
8. Remove Connector Position As-

surance (CPA) pin and coil assembly connector from inflator module.
9. Remove steering column shaft nut.
10. Remove steering wheel using a suitable steering wheel puller.

To install:
11. Feed SIR coil assembly lead through slot in steering wheel.
12. Install steering wheel onto column shaft.
13. Install column shaft nut. Tighten to 30 ft. lbs. (41 Nm).
14. Install horn contact, coil assembly connector and CPA to inflator module.
15. Install inflator module onto steering wheel, securing with 4 screws behind steering wheel. Tighten to 27 inch lbs. (3 Nm).
16. Connect negative battery cable.
17. Connect yellow 2 way connector and CPA pin at the base of the steering column.
18. Install fuse in fuse panel.
19. Install left side sound insulator and connect courtesy light, if removed.

REMOVAL & INSTALLATION

1989

REATTA, RIVIERA, TORONADO AND TROFEO

1. Disconnect the negative battery cable.
2. Remove the left side sound insulator.
3. Remove the steering column trim cover.
4. Label and disconnect the electrical connectors from the steering column. Remove the wiring harness protector.
5. Remove the park lock cable from the ignition switch, if equipped.
6. Remove the lower column mounting bolts.

NOTE: On the Toronado, remove the pinch bolt.

7. If equipped with a column shifter, disconnect the shift linkage at the column.
8. Remove the upper steering column-to-instrument panel bolts and the column assembly from the vehicle.

To install:
9. Install the column assembly to the vehicle. Install the upper steering column-to-instrument panel bolts. Install the lower steering column-to-instrument panel bolts. Tighten the column bolts to 20 ft. lbs. (27 Nm).

NOTE: Failure to install the upper bolts first may result in a cracked lower bearing casting.

10. If equipped with a column shifter, connect the shift linkage to the column.
11 Install the lower column mounting bolts.

NOTE: On the Toronado, install the pinch bolt.

12. Install the park lock cable to the ignition switch, if equipped.
13. Connect the electrical connectors to the steering column. Install the wiring harness protector.
14. Install the steering column trim cover.
15. Install the left side sound insulator.
16. Connect the negative battery cable.

ALLANTE, ELDORADO AND SEVILLE

1. Disconnect the negative battery cable.
2. Remove left dash close-out panel.
3. Remove column wiring connector from left side hard shell grommet.

4. Remove park lock cable from ignition switch.

5. Remove bolt connecting steering shaft to intermediate shaft.

6. Remove bolts and nut connecting steering column to instrument panel bracket.

NOTE: When removing the steering column, the lower column bracket nut and bolts must be removed first. After removing lower bolts, remove upper column bracket bolts. Failure to remove lower nut and bolt first may result in a cracked lower bearing casting.

7. Remove column from the vehicle.

To install:

8. Install steering column mounting bolts and nut.

NOTE: When installing column, loosely install the upper column bracket bolts first. Before tightening upper bracket bolts, install lower column nuts and bolt. Failure to install upper bolts first may result in a cracked lower bearing casting.

9. Install intermediate shaft coupling to steering column shaft. Tighten intermediate shaft bolt to 35 ft. lbs. (47 Nm) and steering column bolts to 20 ft. lbs. (27 Nm).

10. Connect park lock cable to ignition switch.

11. Connect steering column wiring connector to left side hard shell grommet.

12. Install dash close-out panel.

13. Connect negative battery cable.

1990–93

1. Disconnect the negative battery cable. Ensure that ignition switch is in the **OFF** position.

2. Remove SIR fuse from fuse panel.

3. Remove left side sound insulator.

4. Remove left side courtesy light, as required, to ease removal of sound insulator.

5. Remove Connector Position Assurance (CPA) pin and yellow 2 way connector at the base of the steering column.

6. On Eldorado and Seville, remove center trim plate and instrument panel steering column reinforcing plate.

7. Remove knee bolster.

8. Disconnect ignition wiring connector and multi-function connector.

9. Remove pinch bolt from intermediate shaft.

10. Remove lower support bracket from vehicle. Remove upper column support from instrument panel and remove column from vehicle.

To install:

11. Install steering column into vehi-

cle; support at upper bracket with 2 bolts. Do not tighten fully at this time.

12. Install column lower support bracket to vehicle. Do not tighten fully at this time.

13. Install steering column intermediate shaft to steering rack.

14. Install pinch bolt to intermediate shaft. Tighten pinch bolt and nut to 35 ft. lbs. (47 Nm). Tighten upper and lower column support nut and bolts to 20 ft. lbs. (27 Nm). Tighten lower support bracket-to-column screws to 12 ft. lbs. (16 Nm).

15. Connect multi-function switch connector and ignition wiring connector.

16. On Eldorado and Seville, install instrument panel steering column reinforcement plate and center trim plate.

17. Install knee bolster.

18. Connect negative battery cable.

19. Connect yellow 2 way connector and CPA pin at the base of the steering column.

20. Install fuse in fuse panel.

21. Install left side sound insulator and connect courtesy light, if removed.

Power Rack and Pinion

REMOVAL & INSTALLATION

1. Disconnect the negative battery cable.

2. Raise and safely support the vehicle.

3. Remove both front tire and wheel assemblies.

4. Remove the intermediate shaft lower pinch bolt.

5. Remove the tie rod ends from the steering knuckles.

6. Remove the line retainer. Disconnect and plug the return and pressure hose from the steering rack and pinion.

7. Label and disconnect the electrical connection at the idle speed power steering switch.

8. Remove the rack and pinion assembly retaining bolts. Remove the rack and pinion assembly.

To install:

9. Install the rack and pinion assembly. Install the rack and pinion assembly attaching bolts. Tighten to 50 ft. lbs. (68 Nm).

10. Connect the electrical connection to the idle speed power steering switch.

11. Connect the return and pressure hose to the steering rack and pinion assembly. Install the line retainer.

12. Install the tie rod ends to the steering knuckles. Tighten nuts to 33 ft. lbs. (45 Nm).

13. Install the intermediate shaft

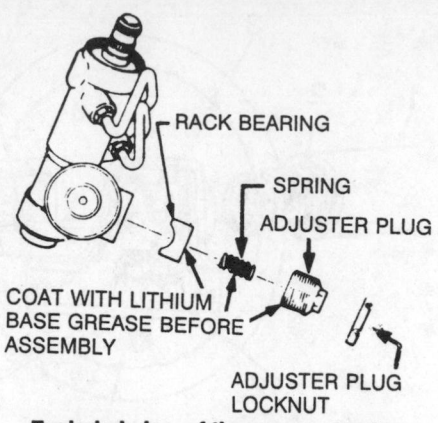

COAT WITH LITHIUM BASE GREASE BEFORE ASSEMBLY — RACK BEARING — SPRING — ADJUSTER PLUG — ADJUSTER PLUG LOCKNUT

Exploded view of the power steering rack adjustment assembly

lower pinch bolt. Tighten to 30 ft. lbs. (41 Nm).

14. Install both front tire and wheel assemblies.

15. Lower the vehicle.

16. Connect the negative battery cable.

17. Bleed the power steering system and check for leaks.

ADJUSTMENT

Rack Bearing Preload

NOTE: Make adjustment with front wheels raised and steering wheel centered. Be sure to check returnability of steering wheel to center after adjustment.

1. Disconnect the negative battery cable. Loosen the adjuster plug locknut.

2. Turn the adjuster plug clockwise until it bottoms and back it off 50–70 degrees.

3. While holding the adjuster plug, tighten the locknut to 50 ft. lbs. (70 Nm).

Power Steering Pump

REMOVAL & INSTALLATION

3.8L Engine

1. Disconnect the negative battery cable.

2. Remove the serpentine drive belt.

3. Raise and safely support the vehicle.

4. Disconnect and plug the pressure and return lines from the pump.

5. Remove the pump retaining bolts.

6. Remove the pump with the pulley.

To install:

7. Install the pump with the pulley and install the pump retaining bolts.

8. Connect the pressure and return lines to the pump.

9. Lower the vehicle.

10. Install the serpentine drive belt.

11. Connect the negative battery cable.

12. Refill the power steering pump reservoir. Bleed the power steering system.

4.5L, 4.6L and 4.9L Engines

1. Disconnect the negative battery cable.

2. Remove the serpentine drive belt, the power steering pump pulley.

3. Disconnect and plug the high pressure and feed lines from the pump.

4. Remove the power steering pump-to-bracket bolts and the pump.

To install:

5. Install the pump and the power steering pump-to-bracket bolts. Tighten to 30 ft. lbs. (41 Nm).

6. Connect the high pressure and feed lines to the pump.

7. Install the power steering pump pulley and the serpentine drive belt.

8. Connect the negative battery cable.

9. Refill the power steering pump reservoir. Bleed the power steering system.

BELT ADJUSTMENT

All accessories are driven by a single serpentine belt. The serpentine belt tension is maintained automatically by a spring tensioner. No adjustment is necessary or possible. If the belt tension is not within specification, replace the belt tensioner.

SYSTEM BLEEDING

1. Fill the fluid reservoir.

2. Let the fluid stand undisturbed for 2 minutes, crank the engine for about 2 seconds. Refill the reservoir, if necessary.

3. Repeat above steps until the fluid level remains constant after cranking the engine.

4. Raise and safely support the vehicle, until the wheels are off the ground. Start the engine and increase the engine speed to about 1500 rpm.

5. Turn the wheels lightly against the stops to the left and right, checking the fluid level and refilling, if necessary.

Outer Tie Rod Ends

REMOVAL & INSTALLATION

1. Disconnect the negative battery cable.

2. Raise and safely support the vehicle.

3. Remove cotter pin and hex slot- ted nut from outer tie rod assembly. Loosen jam nut.

4. Disconnect outer tie rod from steering knuckle using a suitable steering linkage separator tool.

5. Remove outer tie rod from inner tie rod.

To install:

6. Install outer tie rod assembly to inner tie rod. Do not tighten jam nut.

7. Connect outer tie rod to steering knuckle, hex slotted nut to outer tie rod stud. Tighten hex slotted nut to 35 ft. lbs. (50 Nm). Check for cotter pin slot alignment. Maximum torque is 45 ft. lbs. (60 Nm) to align slot. Do not back off for cotter pin insertion.

8. Install cotter pin into hole in tie rod stud.

9. Check toe and adjust by turning inner tie rod.

NOTE: Be sure rack and pinion boot is not twisted or puckered during toe adjustment.

10. Tighten jam nut against outer tie rod to 50 ft. lbs. (70 Nm).

BRAKES

Master Cylinder

REMOVAL & INSTALLATION

1. Disconnect the negative battery cable.

2. If equipped with ABS, relieve the brake system pressure.

3. If equipped with a fluid level sensor, disconnect the electrical connector.

4. Disconnect and plug hydraulic lines. Drain the master cylinder.

5. Remove the master cylinder-to-power brake booster nuts and the master cylinder.

To install:

6. Install the master cylinder. Install the master cylinder-to-power brake booster nuts. Tighten the mounting nuts to 26 ft. lbs. (35 Nm).

7. Connect the hydraulic lines to the master cylinder.

8. If equipped with a fluid level sensor, connect the electrical connector.

9. Refill the master cylinder and bleed the system.

10. Connect the negative battery cable.

Proportioning Valve

REMOVAL & INSTALLATION

Diagonal Split System

NOTE: Individual proportion- ing valves are installed on the master cylinder outlets.

1. Disconnect the negative battery cable. Disconnect and plug the fluid lines from the proportioning valves.

2. Remove the proportioning valves and O-rings from the master cylinder.

To install:

3. Replace the O-rings and install the proportioning valves. Tighten the proportioning valve-to-master cylinder to 18–30 ft. lbs. (24–41 Nm). Refill the master cylinder reservoir with clean brake fluid. Bleed the brake system.

Teves Anti-lock System

The Teves system uses a single proportioning valve located near the left rear wheel. The valve is not to be disassembled.

1. Disconnect the negative battery cable. Turn the ignition switch **OFF** throughout this procedure.

2. Using at least 50 lbs. (68 Nm) pressure on the brake pedal, depress the pedal at least 25 times; a noticeable change in pedal pressure will be noticed when the accumulator is discharged.

3. Disconnect the fluid lines from the proportioning valve and the valve from the vehicle.

To install:

4. Install the new proportioning valve and connect the brake fluid lines.

5. Bleed the brake system.

6. Connect the negative battery cable.

Bosch III System

The Bosch III system uses individual proportioning valves installed to the master cylinder. The valves are not to be disassembled.

1. Disconnect the negative battery cable. Turn the ignition switch **OFF** throughout this procedure.

2. Using at least 50 lbs. pressure on the brake pedal, depress the pedal at least 25 times; a noticeable change in pedal pressure will be noticed when the accumulator is discharged.

3. Disconnect and plug the fluid line(s) from the proportioning valve(s).

4. Remove the proportioning valve(s) from the hydraulic unit.

To install:

5. Install the proportioning valve(s) to the hydraulic unit. Tighten the proportioning valve(s)-to-hydraulic unit to 11 ft. lbs. (15 Nm).

6. Connect the fluid line(s) to the proportioning valve(s).

7. Bleed the brake system.

8. Connect the negative battery cable.

Bosch 2U Anti-lock System

The Bosch 2U system uses 2 proportioning valves located in-line on both sides of the vehicle. The valve is not to be disassembled.

1. Disconnect the negative battery cable. Turn the ignition switch **OFF** throughout this procedure.
2. Using at least 50 lbs. (68 Nm) pressure on the brake pedal, depress the pedal at least 25 times; a noticeable change in pedal pressure will be noticed when the accumulator is discharged.
3. Disconnect the fluid lines from the proportioning valves and the valves from the vehicle.

To install:

4. Install the new proportioning valves and connect the brake fluid lines.
5. Bleed the brake system.
6. Connect the negative battery cable.

Power Brake Booster

REMOVAL & INSTALLATION

1. Disconnect the negative battery cable. Remove the master cylinder-to-power booster nuts and move the master cylinder aside.
2. From inside the vehicle, detach the brake pushrod from the brake pedal.
3. Detach the vacuum hose at the vacuum cylinder.
4. Remove the nuts from the mounting studs which hold the unit to the dash panel. Remove the unit and clean it prior to installation.

To install:

5. Install the power brake booster and nuts to the mounting studs which hold the unit to the dash panel. Tighten the power booster-to-cowl nuts to 28 ft. lbs. (38 Nm).
6. Attach the vacuum hose to the vacuum cylinder.
7. From inside the vehicle, attach the brake pushrod to the brake pedal.
8. Install the master cylinder and master cylinder-to-power booster nuts. Tighten the master cylinder-to-power booster nuts to 28 ft. lbs. (38 Nm).
9. Connect the negative battery cable.
10. Bleed the brake system.

Brake Caliper

REMOVAL & INSTALLATION

Front

1. Remove ⅔ of brake fluid from master cylinder assembly.
2. Raise and safely support the vehicle. Mark the relationship of the wheel to axle flange.
3. Remove wheel. Reinstall 2 wheel nuts to retain rotor.
4. Remove bolt attaching inlet fitting. Plug openings in caliper and pipe to prevent fluid loss and contamination.
5. Remove mounting bolts.
6. Remove caliper from rotor and mounting bracket.

To install:

7. Install caliper over rotor in mounting bracket. Ensure that the bolt boots are in place.
8. Lubricate entire shaft of mounting bolts with silicone grease. For 1989–91 vehicles, tighten the mounting bolts to 63 ft. lbs. (85 Nm). For 1992–93 vehicles, tighten the mounting bolts to 38 ft. lbs. (51 Nm).
9. Connect inlet fitting and tighten to 24 ft. lbs. (32 Nm) for 1989–91 vehicles. Tighten fitting on 1992–93 vehicles to 33 ft. lbs. (45 Nm).
10. Remove wheel nuts securing rotor to hub. Install wheels and tires, aligning previous marks.
11. Lower vehicle.
12. Tighten wheel nuts to 100 ft. lbs. (140 Nm).
13. Fill master cylinder to proper level with clean brake fluid.
14. Bleed caliper.

Rear

1989–91 VEHICLES

1. Remove ⅔ of brake fluid from master cylinder assembly.
2. Raise and safely support the vehicle.
3. Mark the relationship of wheel to axle flange. Remove wheel and tire assembly. Reinstall 2 wheel nuts to retain rotor.
4. Loosen tension on parking brake cable at equalizer.
5. Remove retaining clip from lever.
6. Remove cable, return spring and damper from return spring.
7. Remove locknut while holding lever.
8. Remove lever, lever seal and anti-friction washer.
9. Compress bottom piston into caliper bore to provide clearance between linings and rotor.
10. Reinstall anti-friction washer, lever seal (sealing bead against housing), lever and nut.
11. Remove bolt attaching inlet fitting. Plug openings in caliper and pipe to prevent fluid loss and contamination.
12. Remove mounting bolts.
13. Remove caliper from rotor and mounting bracket.

To install:

14. Install caliper over rotor in mounting bracket, making sure boots are in place.
15. Lubricate entire shaft of mounting bolts with silicone grease.
16. Install mounting bolts and tighten to 63 ft. lbs. (85 Nm).
17. Connect inlet fittings and tighten to 15 ft. lbs. (20 Nm).

NOTE: Ensure that parking brake components are clean and free of corrosion. Parts found to be corroded should be replaced. Do not try to polish corrosion away.

18. Install anti-friction washer.
19. Install lever seal with sealing bead against caliper housing. Lubricate seal prior to installation.
20. Install lever on actuator screw hex, with lever pointing down.
21. Install nut while holding rotated lever toward front of vehicle and tighten to 35 ft. lbs. (48 Nm). Rotate lever back against stop on caliper.
22. Install damper and return spring.
23. Connect parking brake cable and adjust.
24. Install retaining clip on lever so it retains parking brake cable from sliding out of the slot in lever.
25. Remove 2 wheel nuts securing rotor to hub. Install wheel and tire assembly aligning previous marks.
26. Lower vehicle.
27. Tighten wheel nuts to 100 ft. lbs. (140 Nm).
28. Fill master cylinder to proper level with clean brake fluid.
29. Bleed caliper.

1992–93 VEHICLES

1. Raise and safely support the vehicle.
2. Remove wheel from the vehicle.
3. Disconnect the brake hose from the caliper. Plug the brake hose and the caliper.
4. Disconnect the parking brake cable from the lever.
5. Remove the bolt and washer that attach the cable support bracket to the caliper.
6. Remove the sleeve bolt and remove the caliper by sliding off of the pin.

To install:

7. Install caliper to original position. Make sure the boot and brake pads are in the proper position.
8. Install the sleeve bolt and tighten the bolt 20 ft. lbs. (27 Nm).
9. Install the cable support bracket and tighten the bolt to 32 ft. lbs. (43 Nm).
10. Connect the end of the brake cable to the lever.
11. Connect the brake hose to the caliper and bleed the system.
12. Install the wheels to the vehicle and lower the vehicle.

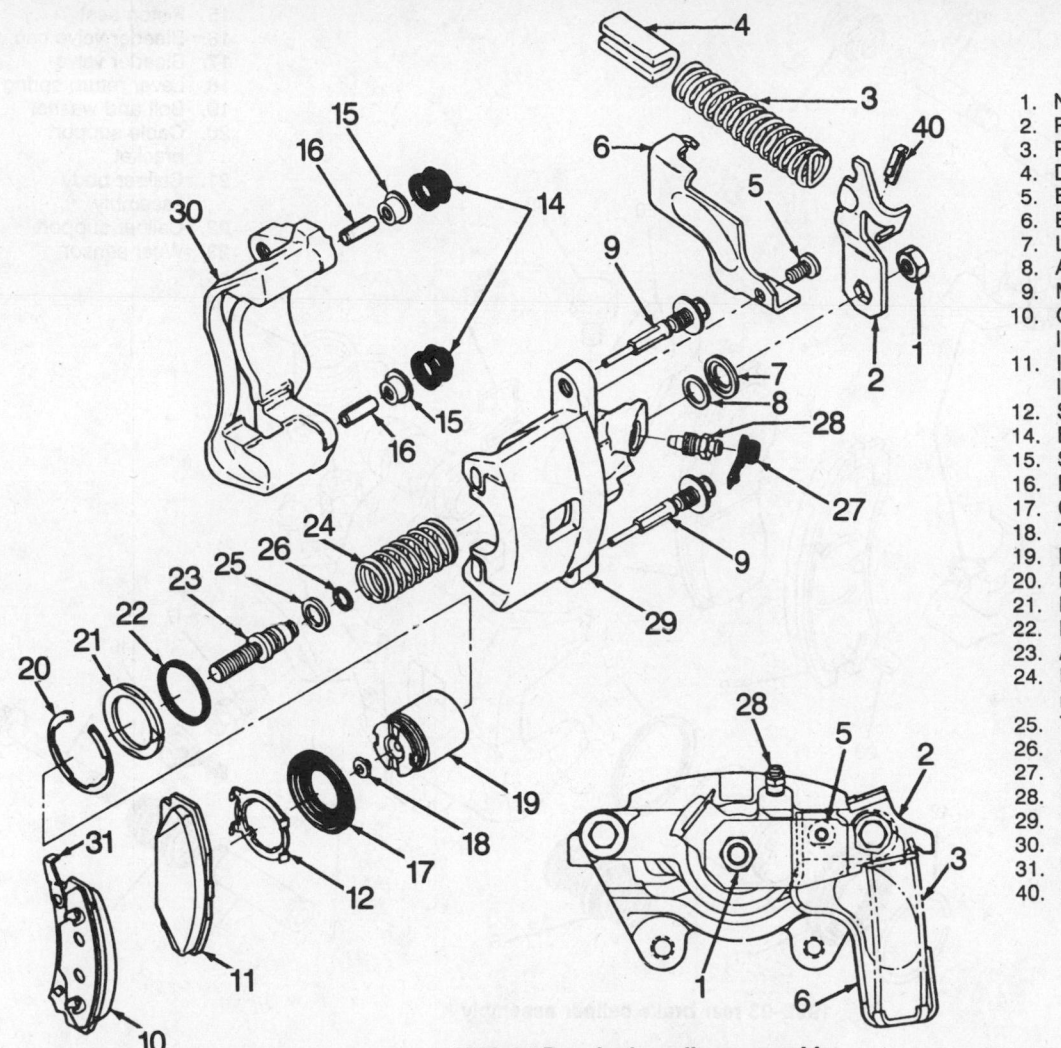

1. Nut
2. Park brake lever
3. Return spring
4. Damper
5. Bolt
6. Bracket
7. Lever seal
8. Anti-friction washer
9. Mounting bolt
10. Outboard shoe and lining
11. Inboard shoe and lining
12. Shoe retainer
14. Bolt boot
15. Support bushing
16. Bushing
17. Caliper piston boot
18. Two-way check valve
19. Piston assembly
20. Retainer
21. Piston locator
22. Piston seal
23. Actuator screw
24. Balance spring and retainer
25. Thrust washer
26. Shaft seal
27. Cap
28. Bleeder valve
29. Caliper housing
30. Bracket
31. Wear sensor
40. Retaining clip

1989–91 Rear brake caliper assembly

13. Pump the brakes 3 times to properly seat the brake pads.

Disc Brake Pads

REMOVAL & INSTALLATION

1. Remove disc brake caliper from mounting bracket and support with a length of wire or remove sleeve bolt and rotate caliper up and out of the way to remove shoes. Do not allow caliper to hang by the brake line unsupported.

2. Remove outboard shoe and lining. Use a suitable tool to disengage shoe springs from holes in caliper housing.

3. Remove inboard shoe and lining, unsnapping shoe spring from piston.

4. If installing new shoe and linings, bottom piston in caliper bore using large pliers. Take care not to damage piston or piston boot.

5. Remove bushings from mounting bolt holes in bracket.

To install:

6. Install new bushings to mounting bolt holes in bracket. Lubricate bushings with silicone grease before installation.

7. Install inboard shoe and lining by snapping shoe retainer spring into piston. Shoe retainer spring is already staked to the inboard shoe. Shoe must lay flat against piston.

8. Install outboard shoe and lining by snapping shoe springs into holes in caliper housing. Wear sensor should be at the trailing edge of shoe during forward wheel rotation. Back of shoe must lay flat against caliper.

9. Install caliper.

10. Apply approximately 175 lbs. (778 N) of force 3 times to brake pedal to seat linings.

Brake Rotor

REMOVAL & INSTALLATION

1. Remove disc brake caliper from mounting bracket and support with a length of mechanics wire. Do not allow caliper to hang by the brake line unsupported.

2. Remove 2 bolts retaining caliper mounting bracket, remove bracket and set aside.

3. Remove brake rotor taking care not to damage wheel nut threads.

To install:

4. Install the brake rotor.

5. Install the caliper mounting bracket and the 2 retaining bolts.

6. Install the caliper to the mounting bracket.

Parking Brake Cable

ADJUSTMENT

1. Lube the cables at the underbody rub points and at the equalizer hooks. Set and release the parking brake several times and check for free movement of all cables.

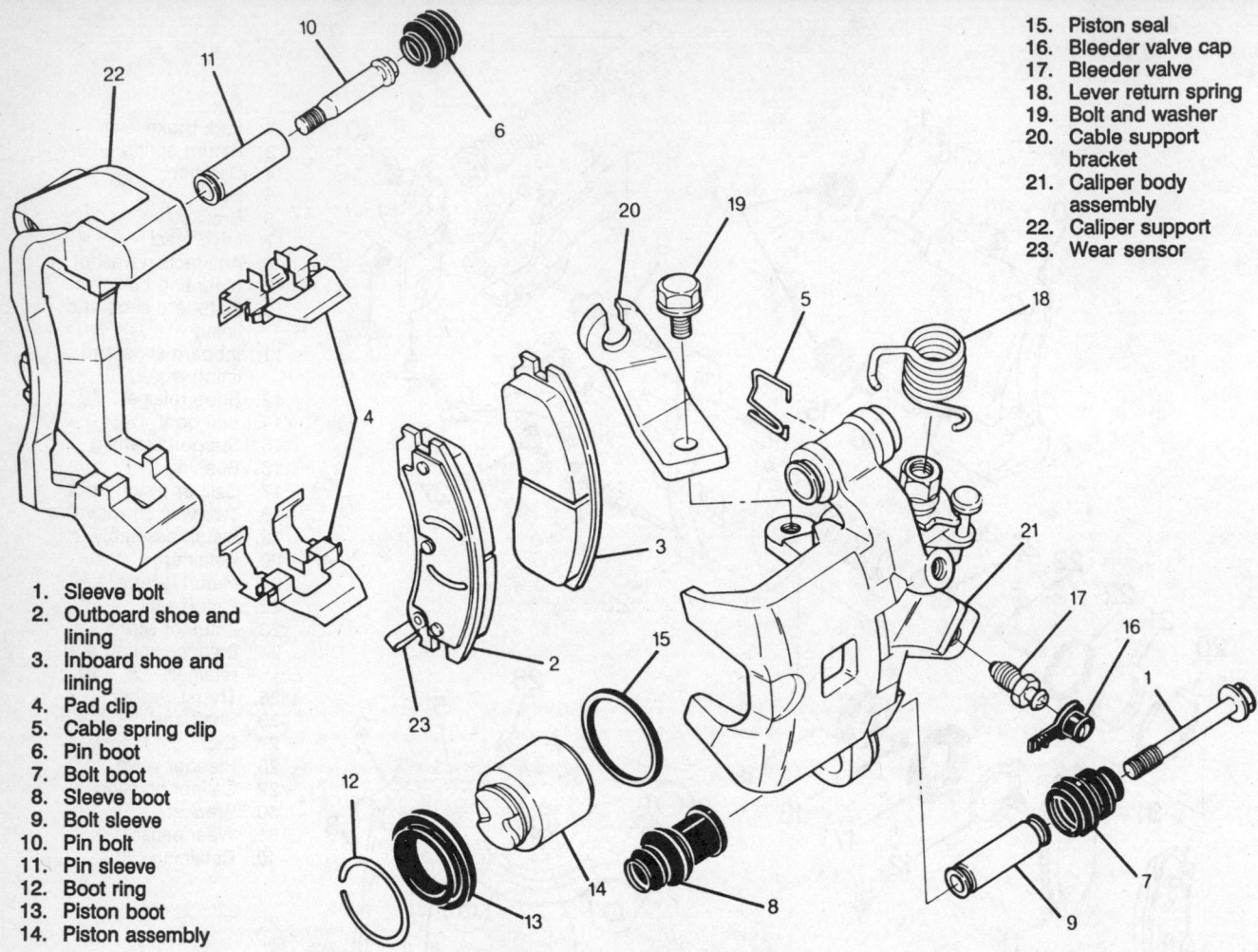

15. Piston seal
16. Bleeder valve cap
17. Bleeder valve
18. Lever return spring
19. Bolt and washer
20. Cable support bracket
21. Caliper body assembly
22. Caliper support
23. Wear sensor

1. Sleeve bolt
2. Outboard shoe and lining
3. Inboard shoe and lining
4. Pad clip
5. Cable spring clip
6. Pin boot
7. Bolt boot
8. Sleeve boot
9. Bolt sleeve
10. Pin bolt
11. Pin sleeve
12. Boot ring
13. Piston boot
14. Piston assembly

1992–93 rear brake caliper assembly

NOTE: With the ignition switch turned ON, the parking brake warning light should be OFF.

2. Set the parking brake pedal in the fully released position, raise and safely support the vehicle.

3. Hold the brake cable stud and tighten the equalizer nut until all cable slack is removed. Make sure the caliper levers are against the stops on the caliper housing; if not, loosen the cable until they are.

4. Operate the parking brake pedal several times to check the adjustment; the pedal should become firm after 3½ strokes.

5. Lower the vehicle and check that the caliper levers are still on their stops. If not, back off the parking brake adjuster until they are.

REMOVAL & INSTALLATION

The parking brake cable system consists of 4 separate cables: front, intermediate, left and right. The front and intermediate cables are joined at the adjuster screw. The left and right cables are joined to the intermediate cable through an equalizer.

1. Ensure that the parking brake is fully released.

2. Release the cable adjustment enough to allow removal of the desired cable(s).

NOTE: To prevent damage to threaded parking brake adjusting rod clean the exposed threads on each side of the nut and lubricate threads on the adjusting rod before turning the nut.

3. Remove old cable(s) and connect replacement cable(s).

4. Adjust new cable and check operation of parking brake.

Brake System Bleeding

DIAGONAL SPLIT SYSTEM

Master Cylinder

1. Refill the master cylinder reservoir.

2. Push the plunger several times to force fluid into the piston.

3. Continue pumping the plunger until the fluid is free of the air bubbles.

4. Plug the outlet ports and install the master cylinder.

System Bleeding

1. Fill the master cylinder with fresh brake fluid. Check the level often during the procedure.

2. Starting with the right rear wheel, remove the protective cap from the bleeder, if equipped, and place where it will not be lost. Clean the bleed screw.

— **CAUTION** —

When bleeding the brakes, keep face away from the brake area. Spewing fluid may cause facial and/or visual damage. Do not allow brake fluid to spill on the car's finish; it will remove the paint.

3. If the system is empty, the most efficient way to get fluid down to the wheel is to loosen the bleeder about ½–¾ turn, place a finger firmly over the bleeder and have a helper pump

the brakes slowly until fluid comes out the bleeder. Once fluid is at the bleeder, close it before the pedal is released inside the vehicle.

NOTE: If the pedal is pumped rapidly, the fluid will churn and create small air bubbles, which are difficult to remove from the system. These air bubbles will eventually congregate resulting in a spongy pedal.

4. Once fluid has been pumped to the caliper or wheel cylinder, open the bleed screw again, have the helper press the brake pedal to the floor, lock the bleeder and have the helper slowly release the pedal. Wait 15 seconds and repeat the procedure (including the 15 second wait) until no more air comes out of the bleeder upon application of the brake pedal. Remember to close the bleeder before the pedal is released inside the vehicle each time the bleeder is opened. If not, air will be induced into the system.

5. If a helper is not available, connect a small hose to the bleeder, place the end in a container of brake fluid and proceed to pump the pedal from inside the vehicle until no more air comes out the bleeder. The hose will prevent air from entering the system.

6. Repeat the procedure on remaining wheel cylinders in order:
   a. Left front
   b. Left rear
   c. Right front

7. Hydraulic brake systems must be totally flushed if the fluid becomes contaminated with water, dirt or other corrosive chemicals. To flush, bleed the entire system until all fluid has been replaced with the correct type of new fluid.

8. Install the bleeder cap(s) on the bleeder to keep dirt out. Always road test the vehicle after brake work of any kind is done.

TEVES ANTI-LOCK BRAKE SYSTEM

Front Brakes

1. Turn the ignition switch **OFF** throughout this procedure.

2. Using at least 50 lbs. pressure on the brake pedal, depress the pedal at least 25 times; a noticeable change in pedal pressure will be noticed when the accumulator is discharged.

3. Remove the reservoir cap. Check and/or refill the master cylinder reservoir.

4. Using the bleeder adapter tool, install it onto the fluid reservoir.

5. Attach a diaphragm type pressure bleeder to the adapter and charge the bleeder to 20 psi.

6. Using a transparent vinyl tube, connect it to either front wheel caliper and insert the other end in a beaker ½ full of clean brake fluid.

7. Open the bleeder valve ½–¾ turn and purge the caliper until bubble free fluid flows from the hose.

8. Tighten the bleeder screw and remove the bleeder equipment.

9. Turn the ignition switch **ON** and allow the pump to charge the accumulator.

10. After bleeding, inspect the pedal for sponginess and the brake warning light for unbalanced pressure; if either of the conditions exist, repeat the bleeding procedure.

Rear Brakes

1. Turn the ignition switch **OFF**.

2. Using at least 50 lbs. pressure on the brake pedal, depress the pedal at least 25 times; a noticeable change in pedal pressure will be noticed when the accumulator is discharged.

3. Check and/or refill the master cylinder reservoir.

4. Turn the ignition switch **ON** and allow the system to charge.

NOTE: The pump will turn OFF when the system is charged.

5. Using a transparent vinyl tube, connect it to a rear wheel bleeder valve and insert the other end in a beaker ½ full of clean brake fluid.

6. Open the bleeder valve ½–¾ turn and slightly depress the brake pedal for at least 10 seconds or until air is removed from the brake system. Close the bleeder valve.

NOTE: It is a good idea to check the fluid level several times during the bleeding operation. Remember, depressurize the system before checking the reservoir fluid.

7. Repeat the bleeding procedure for the other rear wheel.

8. After bleeding, inspect the pedal for sponginess and the brake warning light for unbalanced pressure; if either of the conditions exist, repeat the bleeding procedure.

BOSCH III ANTI-LOCK BRAKE SYSTEM

1. Turn the ignition switch **OFF**.

2. Using at least 50 lbs. pressure on the brake pedal, depress the pedal at least 25 times; a noticeable change in pedal pressure will be noticed when the accumulator is discharged.

3. Check and/or refill the reservoir to the full mark.

4. Using a transparent vinyl hose, connect it to a pump bleeder screw and insert the other end in a beaker ½ full of clean brake fluid.

5. Loosen the bleeder screw ½–¾ turn. Turn the ignition switch **ON**; the pump should run forcing fluid from the hose. When the fluid becomes bubble-free, turn the ignition switch **OFF**, tighten the bleeder screw.

6. Move the transparent vinyl hose to the hydraulic unit bleeder screw. Loosen the bleeder screw ½–¾ turn. Turn the ignition switch **ON**; the pump should run forcing fluid from the hose. When the fluid becomes bubble-free, turn the ignition switch **OFF**, tighten the bleeder screw.

7. Disconnect the bleeder hose.

8. Turn the ignition switch **ON** and allow the hydraulic unit to charge; the pump should turn **OFF** after 30 seconds.

BOSCH 2U ANTI-LOCK BRAKE SYSTEM

1. Turn the ignition switch **OFF**.

2. Using at least 50 lbs. pressure on the brake pedal, depress the pedal at least 25 times; a noticeable change in pedal pressure will be noticed when the accumulator is discharged.

3. Check and/or refill the reservoir to the full mark.

4. Using a transparent vinyl hose, connect it to a pump bleeder screw and insert the other end in a beaker ½ full of clean brake fluid.

5. Loosen the bleeder screw ½–¾ turn. Turn the ignition switch **ON**; the pump should run forcing fluid from the hose. When the fluid becomes bubble-free, turn the ignition switch **OFF**, tighten the bleeder screw.

6. Move the transparent vinyl hose to the hydraulic unit bleeder screw. Loosen the bleeder screw ½–¾ turn. Turn the ignition switch **ON**; the pump should run forcing fluid from the hose. When the fluid becomes bubble-free, turn the ignition switch **OFF**, tighten the bleeder screw.

7. Disconnect the bleeder hose.

8. Turn the ignition switch **ON** and allow the hydraulic unit to charge; the pump should turn **OFF** after 30 seconds.

Anti-Lock Brake System Service

PRECAUTIONS

Failure to observe the following precautions may result in system damage.

● Before performing electric arc welding on the vehicle, disconnect the Electronic Brake Control Module (EBCM) and the hydraulic modulator connectors.

● When performing painting work on the vehicle, do not expose the Electronic Brake Control Module (EBCM) to temperatures in excess of 185°F (85°C) for longer than 2 hrs. The system may be exposed to temperatures up to 200°F (95°C) for less than 15 min.

• Never disconnect or connect the Electronic Brake Control Module (EBCM) or hydraulic modulator connectors with the ignition switch ON.

• Never disassemble any component of the Anti-Lock Brake System (ABS) which is designated non-serviceable; the component must be replaced as an assembly.

• When filling the master cylinder, always use Delco Supreme 11 brake fluid or equivalent, which meets DOT-3 specifications; petroleum base fluid will destroy the rubber parts.

RELIEVING ANTI-LOCK BRAKE SYSTEM PRESSURE

NOTE: Unless otherwise specified, the hydraulic accumulator should be depressurized before disassembling any portion of the hydraulic system.

1. With the ignition switch in the OFF position, sensor block connector disconnected from the hydraulic unit or the negative battery cable disconnected, pump the brake pedal a minimum of 25 times using approximately 50 lbs. of pedal force. When a noticeable change in pedal feel occurs, the accumulator is discharged.

2. When a definite increase in pedal effort is felt, stroke the pedal a few additional times.

Hydraulic Modulator

REMOVAL & INSTALLATION

Teves System

NOTE: The hydraulic accumulator is under pressure and must be depressurized before attempting to dismantle the system.

1. Disconnect the negative battery cable.
2. Firmly apply the parking brake.
3. Using at least 50 lbs. pressure on the brake pedal, depress the pedal at least 20 times; a noticeable change in pedal pressure will be noticed when the accumulator is discharged.
4. Disconnect the electrical connectors from the hydraulic brake unit.
5. Remove the pump-to-hydraulic unit bolt and move the unit aside to gain access to the hydraulic lines.
6. Using a backup wrench, disconnect the hydraulic lines from the hydraulic unit.
7. From under the dash, disconnect the pushrod from the brake pedal.

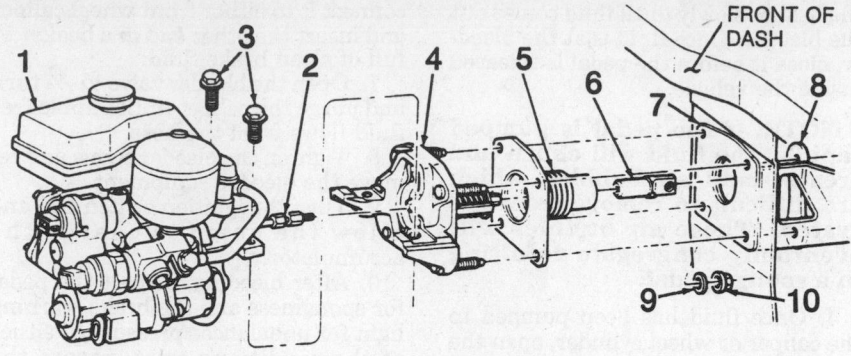

1. Hydraulic unit
2. Front pushrod half
3. Bolts — 37 ft. lbs.
4. Pushrod bracket assembly
5. Rubber boot
6. Rear pushrod half
7. Gasket
8. Reinforcement washer
9. Washer — used on lower right stud only
10. Nuts — 15 ft. lbs.

Exploded view of the anti-lock brake system hydraulic unit — Teves — except Allante

8. Move the dust boot forward, past the pushrod hex and unscrew both pushrod halves.
9. Remove the hydraulic unit-to-pushrod bracket bolts and separate the hydraulic unit from the pushrod bracket; half of the pushrod will remain locked in the hydraulic unit.
10. Disassemble the master cylinder from the hydraulic unit.

To install:
11. Assemble the master cylinder to the hydraulic unit.
12. Install the hydraulic unit to the pushrod bracket and install the hydraulic unit-to-pushrod bracket bolts. Tighten the hydraulic unit-to-pushrod bracket bolts to 37 ft. lbs. (50 Nm).
13. Install the pushrod halves and move the dust boot into position.
14. From under the dash, connect the pushrod to the brake pedal.
15. Using a backup wrench, connect the hydraulic lines to the hydraulic unit.
16. Install the hydraulic unit and pump-to-hydraulic unit bolt.
17. Connect the electrical connectors to the hydraulic brake unit. Bleed the brake system.
18. Release the parking brake.
19. Connect the negative battery cable.

Bosch III System

NOTE: The hydraulic accumulator is under pressure and must be depressurized before attempting to dismantle the system.

1. Disconnect the negative battery cable.
2. Firmly apply the parking brake.
3. Using at least 50 lbs. pressure on the brake pedal, depress the pedal at least 25 times; a noticeable change in pedal pressure will be noticed when the accumulator is discharged.

4. On Allante, remove the air intake duct from the air cleaner and the throttle body, as required.
5. Remove the cross brace.
6. Disconnect the electrical connectors from the hydraulic brake unit and the pump motor. Using a siphon, remove as much fluid from the reservoir as possible.
7. Remove the pressure hose fitting (banjo bolt) from the hydraulic unit; be careful not to drop the fitting washers. Disconnect the return hose from the reservoir fitting.
8. Using a backup wrench, disconnect the hydraulic lines from the hydraulic unit.
9. From under the dash, remove the driver's side sound insulator panel. From the pedal hub pin, remove the pushrod retainer and the foam washer.
10. From the engine compartment, remove the hydraulic unit-to-mounting adapter nuts.
11. Move the hydraulic unit to disengage the pushrod-to-pedal hub pin.
12. Remove the hydraulic unit from the vehicle.

To install:
13. Install the hydraulic unit to the vehicle.
14. Move the hydraulic unit to engage the pushrod-to-pedal hub pin.
15. Install the hydraulic unit-to-mounting adapter nuts. Tighten the hydraulic unit-to-mounting bracket nuts to 20 ft. lbs. (27 Nm).
16. From under the dash, install the pushrod retainer and the foam washer. Install the driver's side sound insulator panel.
17. From the engine compartment, connect the hydraulic lines to the hydraulic unit, using a backup wrench.
18. Install the pressure hose fitting (banjo bolt) to the hydraulic unit. Con-

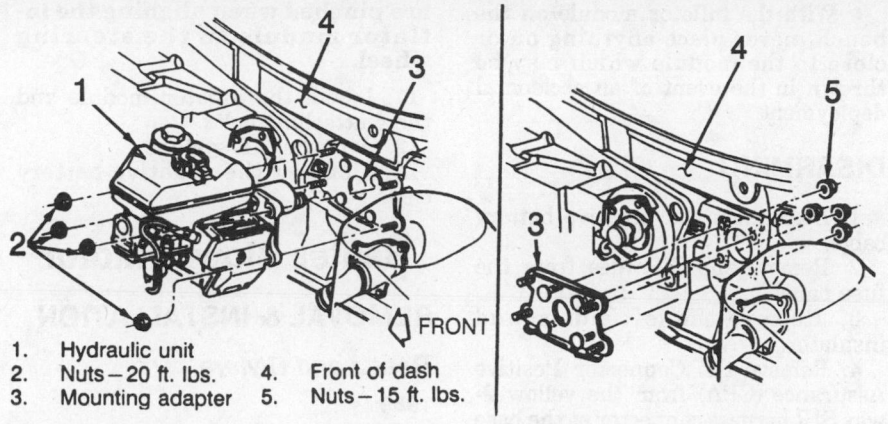

1. Hydraulic unit
2. Nuts — 20 ft. lbs.
3. Mounting adapter
4. Front of dash
5. Nuts — 15 ft. lbs.

View of the anti-lock brake system hydraulic unit and mounting bracket—Bosch III—Allante

nect the return hose to the reservoir fitting.

19. Connect the electrical connectors to the hydraulic brake unit and the pump motor.

20. Refill the reservoir to the **FULL** mark.

21. Turn the ignition **ON** and allow the pump to charge the hydraulic accumulator. Bleed the brake system.

22. Install the cross brace.

23. On Allante, install the air intake duct to the air cleaner and the throttle body, if removed.

24. Release the parking brake.

25. Connect the negative battery cable.

Bosch 2U System

NOTE: The hydraulic accumulator is under pressure and must be depressurized before attempting to dismantle the system.

1. Disconnect the negative battery cable.

2. Drain the brake fluid from the master cylinder.

3. Remove the left front radiator brace.

4. Remove the air cleaner intake hose.

5. Remove the ABS modulator relay cover.

6. Disconnect the 12-way connector and modulator ground strap.

7. Disconnect all brake lines from the modulator assembly.

8. Remove the modulator mounting nuts.

9. Remove the modulator from the mounting bracket; be careful not to drip fluid onto any painted surfaces.

10. Remove the mounting insulators from the modulator.

To install:

11. Install mounting insulators to the modulator.

12. Install the hydraulic modulator to the mounting bracket and install the mounting nuts.

13. Connect the brake lines to the modulator and connect the electrical connections.

14. Install the ABS modulator relay cover and air cleaner intake hose.

15. Install the left front radiator brace and refill brake master cylinder with fluid.

16. Connect the negative battery cable.

Wheel Speed Sensor

REMOVAL & INSTALLATION

Front Sensor

1. Disconnect sensor connector from underhood area near strut tower.

2. Raise and safely support the vehicle.

3. Disengage sensor cable grommet from wheel house pass-through hole and remove sensor cable from retainers.

4. Remove sensor mounting bolt and remove sensor from vehicle.

To install:

5. Route sensor cable and install retainers. Install wheelhouse pass-through grommet.

NOTE: Proper installation of wheel speed sensor cables is critical to continued system operation. Be sure cables are installed in retainers. Failure to install cables in retainers properly may result in contact with moving parts and/or over-extension of cables, resulting in circuit damage.

6. Position sensor in knuckle and install mounting bolt. Tighten mounting bolt to 9 ft. lbs. (12 Nm).

NOTE: If the wheel speed sensor is removed or replaced, the sensor body must be coated with a suitable anti-corrosion com-

pound where the sensor comes in contact with the knuckle.

7. Lower vehicle.

8. Connect wheel speed sensor connector underhood.

Rear Sensor

1. Raise and safely support the vehicle.

2. Disconnect sensor connector and remove sensor cable from retainer brackets.

3. Remove sensor mounting bolt and remove sensor from vehicle.

To install:

4. Position sensor in knuckle and install mounting bolt. Tighten to 9 ft. lbs. (12 Nm).

NOTE: If the wheel speed sensor is removed or replaced, the sensor body must be coated with a suitable anti-corrosion compound where the sensor comes in contact with the knuckle.

5. Install wheel speed sensor cable in retainers.

6. Connect wheel speed sensor connector.

7. Lower vehicle.

Electronic Brake Control Module (EBCM)

REMOVAL & INSTALLATION

Except Allante

1. Disconnect the negative battery cable.

2. Open trunk lid. Remove left trunk carpet trim.

3. Remove velcro-attached cover concealing the EBCM.

4. Disconnect EBCM connector.

5. Remove EBCM.

To install:

6. Install the EBCM.

7. Connect the EBCM connector.

8. Install the velcro-attached cover concealing the EBCM.

9. Install the left trunk carpet trim. Close the trunk lid.

10. Connect the negative battery cable.

Allante

1. Disconnect the negative battery cable.

2. Remove driver's side insulator panel.

3. Remove EBCM connector by disengaging retainer and rotating connector toward the driver's seat.

4. Remove EBCM retaining bolts.

5. Disengage EBCM from mounting bracket and remove from vehicle.

To install:

6. Position EBCM in mounting bracket and install retaining bolts.
7. Install EBCM connector.
8. Install driver's side sound insulator panel.
9. Connect negative battery cable.

CHASSIS ELECTRICAL

Air Bag
CAUTION

Some vehicles are equipped with the Supplemental Inflatable Restraint (SIR) or air bag system. The SIR system must be disabled before performing service on or around SIR system components, steering column, instrument panel components, wiring and sensors. Failure to follow safety and disabling procedures could result in accidental air bag deployment, possible personal injury and unnecessary SIR system repairs.

PRECAUTIONS

Several precautions must be observed when handling the inflator module to avoid accidental deployment and possible personal injury.

• Never carry the inflator module by the wires or connector on the underside of the module.

• When carrying a live inflator module, hold securely with both hands, and ensure that the bag and trim cover are pointed away.

• Place the inflator module on a bench or other surface with the bag and trim cover facing up.

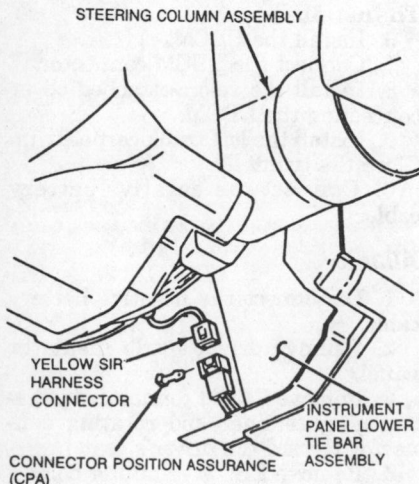

STEERING COLUMN ASSEMBLY

YELLOW SIR HARNESS CONNECTOR

CONNECTOR POSITION ASSURANCE (CPA)

INSTRUMENT PANEL LOWER TIE BAR ASSEMBLY

Yellow 2 way SIR harness connector

• With the inflator module on the bench, never place anything on or close to the module which may be thrown in the event of an accidental deployment.

DISARMING

1. Disconnect the negative battery cable.
2. Remove the SIR fuse from the fuse panel.
3. Remove the left side sound insulator.
4. Remove the Connector Positive Assurance (CPA) from the yellow 2-way SIR harness connector at the base of the steering column and separate the connector.

ARMING

1. Connect the yellow 2-way SIR connector at the base of the steering column and insert the Connect Positive Assurance (CPA).
2. Install the left side sound insulator.
3. Install the SIR fuse in the fuse panel.
4. Connect the negative battery cable.

REMOVAL & INSTALLATION

Inflator Module

1. Disconnect the negative battery cable.
2. Disarm the SIR system.

NOTE: Rotate the steering wheel so the access holes on the back of the steering wheel are at the 12 and 6 o'clock positions. This will allow tool access and reduce the possibility of marring the steering column cover.

3. Remove the 4 bolts from the back of the inflator module.
4. Remove the inflator module from the steering wheel.
5. Disconnect the horn contact by pushing slightly and twisting countercolockwise.
6. If equipped with steering wheel controls, disconnect the steering wheel switch assembly connector from the steering column coil connector.
7. Disconnect the coil assembly from the inflator module.
To install:
8. If equipped, with the ignition switch in the **OFF** position, connect the steering wheel switch assembly connector to the coil connector.
9. Connect the horn contact.
10. Connect the coil assembly connector.

NOTE: Ensure that no wires at the back of the inflator module

are pinched when aligning the inflator module to the steering wheel.

11. Install the inflator module and the 4 attaching bolts.
12. Arm the SIR system.
13. Connect the negative battery cable.

Heater Blower Motor

REMOVAL & INSTALLATION

Reatta and Riviera

1989

1. Disconnect the negative battery cable.
2. Remove the front of cowl shield(s).
3. Disconnect the electrical harness from the blower motor. Remove the harness from the retaining clips and move it aside.
4. Remove the cooling tube from the blower motor.
5. Remove the blower motor screws and the motor from the vehicle.
To install:
6. Install the blower motor to the housing and install the mounting screws.
7. Install the cooling tube to the blower motor.
8. Install the harness to the retaining clips. Connect the electrical harness to the blower motor.
9. Install the front of cowl shield(s).
10. Connect the negative battery cable.

1990–93

1. Disconnect the negative battery cable.
2. Remove cowl cross-tower brace; 2 nuts each side.
3. Remove both cowl relay center bracket nuts and position aside.
4. Remove blower motor electrical connector, cooling hose and mounting screws. Tilt blower motor in case and detach fan from motor.
5. Remove blower motor from case.
6. Remove fan from case.
To install:
7. Install fan to case.
8. Install blower motor to case.
9. Tilt blower motor in case and attach fan to motor. Install blower motor mounting screws, electrical connector and cooling hose.
10. Install both cowl relay center bracket nuts.
11. Install cowl cross-tower brace.
12. Connect the negative battery cable.

Allante

1. Disconnect the negative battery cable.

2. Remove the cross-tower brace.
3. Partially remove the upper intake manifold by performing the following procedures:
    a. Remove both right rear EGR pipe bolts.
    b. Remove the right rear transaxle dipstick bolt.
    c. Remove the right rear bracket bolt.
    d. Remove the right rear lower intake manifold nuts.
    e. Position the upper intake manifold aside.
4. Remove the electrical harness bracket and disconnect the electrical connector.
5. Remove the cooling hose, the mounting screws and the blower motor.

To install:
6. Install the blower motor, mounting screws and cooling hose.
7. Install the electrical harness bracket and connect the electrical connector.
8. Install the upper intake manifold by performing the following procedures:
    a. Place the upper intake manifold into position.
    b. Install the right rear lower intake manifold nuts.
    c. Install the right rear bracket bolt.
    d. Install the right rear transaxle dipstick bolt.
    e. Install both right rear EGR pipe bolts.
9. Install the cross-tower brace.
10. Connect the negative battery cable.

Eldorado and Seville

1. Disconnect the negative battery cable.
2. Remove the relay center bracket nuts and move the bracket aside.
3. Remove the air cleaner assembly and the cross-tower brace.
4. Disconnect the electrical harness support bracket.
5. On 1990–93 vehicles, remove the MAP sensor bracket.
6. Label and disconnect the electrical wiring connectors. Remove the cooling hose and mounting screws.
7. Tilt the blower motor in the case and remove the fan from the blower motor.

NOTE: Be careful not to bend the fan upon removal as a fan imbalance could result after reassembly.

8. Remove the blower motor and fan assembly from the vehicle.
To install:
9. Install the blower motor and fan assembly to the vehicle.

10. Tilt the blower motor in the case and install the fan to the blower motor.
11. Install the cooling hose and mounting screws. Connect the electrical wiring connectors.
12. On 1990–93 vehicles, install the MAP sensor bracket.
13. Connect the electrical harness support bracket.
14. Install the air cleaner assembly and the cross-tower brace.
15. Install the relay center bracket nuts.
16. Connect the negative battery cable.

Toronado and Trofeo
1989

1. Disconnect the negative battery cable.
2. Remove the front of the cowl shield.
3. Remove the bulkhead retaining screw and the bulkhead electrical connector.
4. Remove the Electronic Spark Control (ESC) module electrical connector.
5. Remove the ESC module and bracket assembly.
6. Remove the power steering pump bracket support.
7. Remove the coil bracket nuts. Label and disconnect the electrical connector from the coil.
8. Remove the plug wire guides. Remove the coil/bracket assembly and move it aside. Remove the wiring harness conduit.
9. Remove the blower motor cooling tube.
10. Label and disconnect the electrical connectors from the blower motor. Remove the blower motor mounting screws.
11. Remove the blower motor mounting screws and the blower motor.

To install:
12. Install blower motor fan to blower motor.
13. Install blower motor using strip caulk type sealing material between the motor and heater and air conditioning module.
14. Install blower motor mounting screws (5).
15. Install blower motor cooling tube.
16. Install blower motor electrical connector and wiring harness conduits.
17. Install plug wire guides (2).
18. Install coil electrical connector.
19. Install plug wires to coil (3).
20. Install coil bracket nuts (3).
21. Install power steering pump

bracket support and bracket support bolts.
22. Install ESC module and bracket assembly.
23. Install ESC module electrical connector.
24. Install bulkhead connector.
25. Install front of cowl shield.
26. Connect negative battery cable.

1990–93
1. Disconnect the negative battery cable.
2. Remove cowl cross-tower brace; 2 nuts each side.
3. Remove both cowl relay center bracket nuts and position aside.
4. Remove blower motor electrical connector, cooling hose and mounting screws. Tilt blower motor in case and detach fan from motor.
5. Remove blower motor from case.
6. Remove fan from case.
To install:
7. Install fan to case.
8. Install blower motor to case.
9. Tilt blower motor in case and attach fan to motor. Install blower motor mounting screws, electrical connector and cooling hose.
10. Install both cowl relay center bracket nuts.
11. Install cowl cross-tower brace.
12. Connect the negative battery cable.

Windshield Wiper Motor

REMOVAL & INSTALLATION

1. Disconnect the negative battery cable. Remove both wiper arms.
2. Remove the A/C pipe shroud if required.
3. Remove the cowl cover.
4. Remove the wiper arm drive link from the crank arm.
5. Disconnect the electrical connectors.
6. Remove the wiper motor-to-chassis bolts and the motor; guide the crank arm through the hole.
To install:
7. Guide the crank arm through the hole and install the wiper motor and the motor-to-chassis bolts.
8. If removed, install the air conditioning pipe shroud bracket.
9. Connect the electrical connectors.
10. Install the wiper arm drive link from the crank arm.
11. Install the cowl cover.
12. Connect the negative battery cable.
13. Verify proper wiper motor operation.

Windshield Wiper Switch

REMOVAL & INSTALLATION

1989 Reatta and Riviera
1989–93 Eldorado and Seville

The windshield wiper switch is attached to switch pod, located on the instrument panel to the right side of the steering wheel.

1. Disconnect the negative battery cable.
2. Remove the switch trim panel from the instrument panel.
3. Remove the switch-to-instrument panel screws.
4. Pull the switch outward and disconnect the electrical connectors from the rear of the switch.

To install:

5. Connect the electrical connectors to the rear of the switch and push the switch into position.
6. Install the switch-to-instrument panel screws.
7. Install the switch trim panel to the instrument panel
8. Connect the negative battery cable.

Allante

The windshield wiper switch is attached to switch pod, located on the instrument panel to the right side of the steering wheel.

1. Disconnect the negative battery cable.
2. Remove the bottom instrument panel trim plate.
3. Remove the switch pod-to-instrument panel screws, pull the pod outward and disconnect the electrical connectors. Remove the switch pod from the vehicle.

To install:

4. Connect the electrical connectors to the back of the pod and push the pod into position in the instrument panel.
5. Install the switch pod-to-instrument panel screws.
6. Install the bottom instrument panel trim plate.
7. Connect the negative battery cable.

1990–93 Reatta and Riviera
1989–92 Toronado and Trofeo

———— **CAUTION** ————

Replacing the windshield washer and wiper (pivot and pulse) switch necessitates removal of the steering wheel. If equipped with the Supplemental Inflatable Restraint (SIR) or air bag system, removing the steering wheel requires temporarily disabling the SIR system and removal of the inflator module. Failure to do so could result in accidental deployment of the air bag, possible personal injury and unnecessary SIR system repairs.

1. Disconnect the negative battery cable.
2. Place the ignition switch in the **LOCK** position to prevent uncentering of the coil assembly ring.
3. If equipped, disable the SIR system. Remove the inflator module.
4. Remove the steering wheel.
5. Remove coil assembly retaining ring.
6. Remove coil assembly from shaft end, allowing coil to hang freely.

NOTE: Coil assembly will become uncentered if the steering column is separated from steering gear and is allowed to rotate or if the centering spring is depressed, allowing hub to rotate while coil is removed from column.

7. Remove wave washer.
8. Remove shaft lock retaining ring using special tool J–23653–C to depress shaft lock.
9. Remove shaft lock.
10. Remove turn signal cancelling cam assembly.
11. Remove upper bearing spring, inner race seat and inner race.
12. Remove multi-function lever by performing the following:
    a. Ensure that the switch is in the **OFF** position before removing the access cover from steering wheel.
    b. Remove cruise control connector from lever. Note position of connector when installed in column.
    c. Pull lever straight out of switch.
13. Remove screws and signal switch arm.
14. Remove turn signal switch screws.
15. Remove screw from end of hazard knob assembly. Remove button spring and knob from switch cavity.
16. Remove turn signal switch assembly and allow to hang freely.
17. Remove wiring protector at base of steering column.
18. Disconnect wiring harness at the base of the steering column.
19. Gently pull wire harness through instrument panel bracket and column housing.
20. Remove the coil assembly by performing the following:
    a. Disconnect the yellow connector shroud from the black terminal connector.
    b. Remove the wiring protector.
    c. Attach a length of wire to the black terminal connector to aid in reassembly.
    d. Gently pull the wire through the instrument panel bracket and column housing.
21. Remove the key from the pass key lock cylinder set.
22. Remove the buzzer switch as-

sembly and buzzer switch retaining clip using a paper clip.
23. Reinsert the key in the pass key lock cylinder. Place the key in the **LOCK** position.
24. Remove the pass key lock cylinder by performing the following:
    a. Disconnect the terminal connector.
    b. Remove the wiring protector.
    c. Attach a length of wire to the terminal connector to aid in reassembly.
    d. Gently pull the wire through the instrument panel bracket and column housing.
25. Remove the lock housing cover screws. Remove the lock housing cover assembly.
26. Remove the tilt lever by gripping firmly and turning counterclockwise to remove from the steering column.
27. Remove the base plate and dimmer switch rod actuator.
28. Gently pull the pivot and pulse (wiper/washer) switch wire harness through the instrument panel bracket and column housing.
29. Remove the switch actuator pivot pin.
30. Remove the pivot and pulse switch assembly.

To install:

31. Install the pivot and pulse switch assembly to the cover.
32. Install the switch actuator pivot pin to the switch and cover.
33. Feed the pivot and pulse connector through the column housing and instrument panel bracket.
34. Connect the dimmer switch rod actuator to the base plate.
35. Install the base plate to the lock housing cover assembly.

NOTE: The bottom edge of the dimmer switch rod actuator should rest on the bend in the dimmer switch rod.

36. Install the lock housing cover assembly.
37. Install the multi-function lever by performing the following:
    a. Plug the multi-function lever connector and cruise control wire together and mount on the base plate.
    b. With the **WASH** paddle loose on the shaft, align the shaft with the switch notch and insert the shaft only.
    c. Rotate the **WASH** paddle into position and push into the switch
    d. Push on the knob to seat the lever into the switch.
38. Install the housing cover end cap. Install the screws and tighten the screw in the 12 o'clock position first, the screw in the 8 o'clock position second and the screw in the 3 o'clock position third. Tighten in the same sequence to 80 inch lbs. (9 Nm).
39. Install the pass key lock cylinder.

40. Install the lock retaining screw. Tighten to 22 inch lbs. (2.5 Nm).
41. Place the key in the **RUN** position.
42. Install the buzzer switch assembly and clip.
43. Route wiring assembly for the turn signal switch through column housing and instrument panel bracket.
44. Connect wiring assembly to connector at base of the steering column.
45. Connect coil assembly wire harness through column housing and instrument panel bracket. Allow coil to hang freely.
46. Install turn signal switch assembly and screws. Tighten to 30 inch lbs. (3.4 Nm).
47. Connect the yellow connector shroud to the black terminal connector.
48. Install wiring protector.
49. Install signal switch arm and screws. Tighten to 20.4 inch lbs. (2.3 Nm).
50. Install hazard knob, spring and button to hazard warning switch cavity. Install switch screw; drive in fully. Do not strip.
51. Install inner race, upper bearing inner race seat and upper bearing spring.
52. Install turn signal cancelling cam assembly.
53. Install shaft lock.

NOTE: Inspect shaft lock retaining ring for damage or deformation. If damaged or deformed, replace with new retaining ring.

54. Install shaft lock retaining ring. Align to block tooth on shaft using special tool J–23653–C to depress shaft lock. Ring must be firmly seated in groove on shaft.

NOTE: Set steering shaft so block teeth on upper steering shaft are at the 12 o'clock and 6 o'clock positions. The alignment mark at the end of the shaft should be at the 12 o'clock position and vehicle wheels straight-ahead. Set the ignition switch to the LOCK position to ensure no damage occurs to the coil assembly.

55. Ensure coil assembly hub is centered by performing the following:
    a. Hold coil assembly with clear bottom up to see coil ribbon.
    b. There are 2 styles of coils. One rotates clockwise and the other rotates counterclockwise. While holding coil assembly, depress spring lock to rotate hub in direction of arrow until it stops.
    c. The coil ribbon should be wound up snug against the center hub.

d. Rotate coil hub in opposite direction approximately 2½ turns. Release spring lock between locking tabs in front of arrow.

NOTE: If a new coil assembly is being installed, assemble the pre-centered coil assembly to column. Remove centering tab and dispose.

56. Install wave washer.
57. Install coil assembly using horn tower on cancelling cam assembly inner ring and projections on outer ring for alignment.
58. Install coil assembly retaining ring. Ring must be firmly seated in groove on shaft.

NOTE: Gently pull lower coil assembly wire to remove any wire kinks that may be inside column assembly.

59. Install steering wheel.
60. Install inflator module and enable SIR system.
61. Connect the negative battery cable.

Instrument Cluster

REMOVAL & INSTALLATION

Reatta and Riviera

1. Disconnect the negative battery cable.
2. Remove the center, left and right trim covers.
3. Remove the instrument cluster-to-dash screws, then, pull the cluster straight out of the housing.
To install:
4. Place the instrument cluster into position and install the instrument cluster-to-dash screws.
5. Install the center, left and right trim covers.
6. Connect the negative battery cable.

Allante

1. Disconnect the negative battery cable.
2. Remove the left and right switch pod trim plates.
3. Remove the cluster trim plate screws and remove the plate.
4. Remove the cluster assembly-to-dash screws, pull the cluster forward and disconnect the electrical connectors.
5. Remove the cluster assembly from the vehicle.
To install:
6. Install the cluster assembly to the vehicle.
7. Connect the electrical connectors. Install the instrument cluster assembly-to-dash screws.
8. Install the cluster trim plate.

9. Install the left and right switch pod trim plates.
10. Connect the negative battery cable.

Eldorado and Seville

1989–91

1. Disconnect the negative battery cable. Remove the screws located along the top and remove the instrument panel trim plate.
2. Remove the mounting screws and the filter lens.
3. Remove the warning light lens screws and the lens. Remove the trip odometer reset button.
4. Remove the instrument panel cluster screws. Pull the cluster off the electrical connections and remove it. Using a pair of pliers, hold the retaining tabs at either end of the cluster board and remove the board.
To install:
5. Align the instrument cluster with the electrical connectors, push it into the instrument panel. Install the instrument cluster-to-dash panel screws.
6. Install the filter lens and mounting screws.
7. Install the instrument panel trim plate and the screws located along the top of the panel.
8. Connect the negative battery cable.

1992–93

1. Disconnect the negative battery cable. Remove the **A5** and **B5** fuses from the rear fuse compartment. Remove the **A3** fuse from the engine fuse compartment.
2. Remove the upper trim panel.
3. Disconnect the 2 electrical connectors located on top of the instrument cluster.
4. Remove the 4 screws that secure the cluster to the panel.
5. If equipped with digital cluster, raise the cluster and remove the 2 screws that secure the PRNDL mechanism.
6. Remove the cluster.
To install:
7. Align the instrument cluster with the panel.
8. Install the 2 screws that secure the PRNDL mechanism. (Digital cluster only)
9. Install the 4 cluster retaining screws and connect the 2 electrical connectors at the top of the cluster.
10. Install the upper trim panel and replace the fuses. Connect the negative battery cable.

Toronado and Trofeo

1. Disconnect the negative battery cable.
2. Remove instrument panel cluster trim plate.

3. Remove screws retaining cluster to instrument panel.

4. Pull cluster out and disengage electrical connector.

To install:

5. Place the instrument cluster into position and engage the electrical connector.

6. Install the screws retaining the cluster to instrument panel.

7. Install the instrument cluster panel trim plate.

8. Connect the negative battery cable.

Radio

REMOVAL & INSTALLATION

Reatta and Riciera

The entertainment system on Reatta and Riviera vehicles consists of a remote radio receiver, an optional tape deck and an Electronic Control Center (ECC) monitor. The entertainment system is controlled by the Electronic Control Center (also known as CRT) through the use of "hard" and "soft" keys.

RADIO RECEIVER

1. Disconnect the negative battery cable.

2. Remove the gear selector handle, transaxle indicator assembly and storage compartment (lift lid) to reveal bolts retaining console assembly.

3. Remove 4 bolts retaining console assembly and remove assembly.

4. Disconnect antenna lead-in and radio harness connector from radio receiver.

5. Remove 2 bolts to radio support assembly top cover and remove radio receiver.

To install:

6. Install radio receiver and 2 bolts to radio support assembly top cover.

7. Connect radio harness connector and antenna lead-in to radio receiver.

8. Install console assembly and 4 retaining bolts.

9. Install storage compartment, transaxle indicator assembly and gear selector handle.

10. Connect negative battery cable.

Allante

The entertainment system on Allante vehicles consists of a remote radio receiver, a remote tape deck and a radio control head, below the Driver Information Center (DIC).

RADIO CONTROL HEAD AND COMBINATION PANEL

1. Disconnect the negative battery cable.

2. Remove pop-out air conditioner vent.

3. Remove 2 screws retaining the combination panel.

4. Remove left side sound insulation panel screws.

5. Remove left side sound insulation panel.

6. Remove 2 nuts and washers, at the back of tape player.

7. Remove combo panel.

8. Remove 3 electrical connectors, depress tabs, push in, then pull to release.

To install:

9. Connect electrical connectors.

10. Align combo panel.

11. Install 2 nuts and washers, at the back of the tape player.

12. Install left side sound insulation panel.

13. Install left side sound insulation panel screws.

14. Install 2 screws retaining combo panel.

15. Insert air conditioning vent.

TAPE PLAYER

1. Disconnect the negative battery cable.

2. Remove radio head/combo panel.

3. Remove 3 tape player retaining bolts, 1 on the side, 2 underneath.

4. Remove 3 bolts, open combo panel door.

5. Depress latch to open cassette door.

6. Release screw cover retaining tabs, access from inside cassette door.

7. Remove screw cover.

8. Remove 3 screws and washers.

9. Remove tape player door.

10. Remove 2 face plate retainer bolts.

11. Pull tape player out as far as it will go.

12. Disconnect 3 electrical connectors.

To install:

13. Install 3 electrical connectors.

14. Depress latch to open cassette door.

15. Slide tape player into place with door open.

16. Install 3 bolts retaining tape player in combo panel.

17. Close combo panel door and install 3 bolts.

18. Align face plate and install 2 bolts.

19. Align cassette door and install 3 screws.

20. Snap on screw cover.

21. Install radio head/combo panel.

22. Connect negative battery cable.

RADIO RECEIVER

1. Disconnect the negative battery cable.

2. Remove glove box assembly.

3. 2 screws and 1 nut and washer retaining the radio receiver.

4. Remove coaxial cable and 3 electrical connectors.

To install:

5. Install 3 electrical connectors and coaxial cable.

6. Install nut, washer and 3 screws retaining radio receiver.

7. Install glove box assembly.

8. Connect negative battery cable.

Eldorado and Seville

1. Disconnect the negative battery cable.

2. Remove radio trim plate.

3. Remove left side air conditioning vent.

4. Remove 7 screws attaching instrument panel trim plate.

5. Loosen lower 2 mounting nuts under radio; top 2 nuts do not have to be loosened.

6. Slide radio forward and disconnect electrical connectors.

7. Remove antenna lead-in.

To install:

8. Install antenna lead-in to radio.

9. Connect electrical connectors to radio.

10. Slide radio into instrument panel bracket and tighten lower mounting nuts.

11. Install instrument panel trim plate.

12. Install radio trim plate.

13. Install air conditioning vent.

14. Connect negative battery cable.

Toronado and Trofeo

RADIO HEAD

1. Disconnect the negative battery cable.

2. Remove driver's side lower hush panel.

3. Remove knee bolster.

4. Remove instrument panel trim panel.

5. Remove screws retaining radio/ECC bracket.

6. Remove nuts to remove radio bracket from radio.

7. Remove electrical connectors.

To install:

8. Install nuts attaching radio to mounting bracket.

9. Install electrical connections to radio and ECC.

10. Carefully reposition radio and mounting bracket to instrument panel.

NOTE: If the radio buttons operate unusually or intermittently, the condition may be due to poor alignment or uneven tightening of the radio or instrument panel trim panel screws. If this occurs, remove the trim panel, loosen the

radio mounting bolts and realign the radio unit.

11. Install trim plate and knee bolster.

12. Install lower hush panel.

13. Connect negative battery cable.

REMOTE RADIO RECEIVER

1. Disconnect the negative battery cable.

2. Open console storage tray and remove CD, cassette holder or phone handset, if equipped.

3. Remove T-15 Torx® screws and remove storage tray liner.

4. Remove electrical connectors to console seat controls and handset connector, if equipped.

5. Open ashtray and take out cigar lighter and ashtray bucket.

6. Set emergency brake, place shift lever in **N**.

7. Pull console trim plate up, console trim plate has clip tabs in area to right and left of top edge of shifter plate.

8. Disconnect bulb and cigar lighter electrical connectors and remove console trim plate.

9. The remote chassis will be visible towards the front end of the console.

10. Remove 10mm nuts retaining chassis to CRTC bracket.

11. Remove electrical connectors to remote chassis and coaxial lead-in connector.

12. Remove radio chassis.

To install:

13. Place radio chassis in top of CRTC bracket and install 10mm nuts. Make certain radio wiring is not trapped under radio receiver chassis.

14. Connect electrical connectors on left side of chassis.

15. Connect electrical connectors on right side of receiver. Best order is: lower white 4-pin, upper white 6-pin, lower black 6-pin and upper blue 4-pin.

16. Connect antenna coaxial lead-in.

17. Connect lower console trim plate over shift lever and reconnect electrical connectors to ashtray.

18. Carefully snap trim plate into place.

19. Return shift lever to park and release emergency brake.

20. Connect electrical connectors to remote chassis and coaxial lead-in connector.

21. Connect electrical connections to console mounted seat controls and connect phone handset connector, if equipped.

22. Connect lower console storage tray liner and fasten T-15 Torx® screws.

23. Reinsert CD/cassette bucket, handset, cigar lighter and ashtray.

24. Connect negative battery cable.

Concealed Headlights

MANUAL OPERATION

Reatta

1. Open the hood.

2. Turn the manual control knob in the direction of the arrow on the "Headlight Up" label. Turn the knob by hand until it stops.

3. Close the hood and check headlight operation.

Toronado and Trofeo

1. Disconnect 3-way headlight door actuator connector.

2. Remove protective cover from the knob.

3. Rotate the knob clockwise until the headlight doors open.

4. To close the doors, rotate the knob counterclockwise until the headlight doors close.

5. Install protective cover over knob.

6. Connect 3-way headlight door actuator connectors.

Headlight Switch

REMOVAL & INSTALLATION

The headlight switch is located on the left side of the instrument panel.

1. Remove the left trim plate screws and the trim plate, if equipped.

2. If equipped, remove the left air vent.

3. Remove the headlight switch screws, pull the switch forward and disconnect the electrical connectors or the fiber optic lead, if equipped.

4. Remove the headlight switch/switch pod.

To install:

5. Connect the electrical connectors or fiber optic lead, if equipped, to the headlight switch.

6. Push the switch/switch pod into position and install the headlight attaching screws.

7. Install the left air vent, if equipped.

8. Install the left trim plate and attaching screws.

Dimmer Switch

The dimmer switch is attached to the lower steering column jacket. It is activated by a rod attached to the multifunction lever.

REMOVAL & INSTALLATION

1. Disconnect the negative battery cable. Remove the left side sound insulator panel.

2. If necessary, remove the lower steering column trim cover.

3. Disconnect the electrical connector from the dimmer switch.

4. Remove the dimmer switch-to-steering column screws and the dimmer switch.

To install:

5. Position the actuator rod into the dimmer switch hole and install the dimmer switch-to-steering column screws.

6. Connect the electrical connector to the dimmer switch.

7. Adjust the dimmer switch by depressing the switch slightly and inserting a $\frac{3}{32}$ in. drill bit into the adjusting hole. Push the switch up to remove any play and tighten the dimmer switch adjusting screw.

8. If removed, install the lower steering column trim cover.

9. Install the left side sound insulator panel.

10. Connect the negative battery cable.

Turn Signal Switch

——— CAUTION ———

Replacing the turn signal switch requires removal of the steering wheel. If equipped with the Supplemental Inflatable Restraint (SIR) system, removing the steering wheel requires temporarily disabling the SIR system and removal of the inflator module. Failure to do so could result in accidental deployment of the air bag, possible personal injury and unnecessary SIR system repairs.

REMOVAL & INSTALLATION

1989

1. Disconnect the negative battery cable. Remove the steering wheel.

2. Remove the bumper and the carrier snapring retainer from the steering shaft.

3. Using the lock plate compressor screw tool, install in the upper steering shaft, tighten to 40 inch lbs., to keep the shaft from telescoping.

4. Using the lock plate compressor tool, install it on the upper steering shaft, tighten it to depress the shaft lock. Remove the shaft lock retainer, the compressor tool and the steering shaft lock.

5. Remove the turn signal cancelling cam assembly. Place the turn signal switch in the **N** position and remove the upper bearing spring.

6. Position the turn signal switch so the mounting screws can be removed through the holes in the switch and remove the turn signal lever.

7. Remove the turn signal switch-to-steering column screws and lift the turn signal switch. Remove the wire

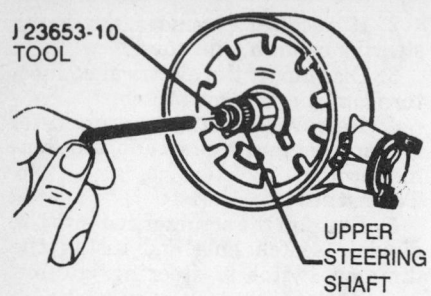

J 23653-10
TOOL

UPPER
STEERING
SHAFT

Installing the lock plate compressor screw

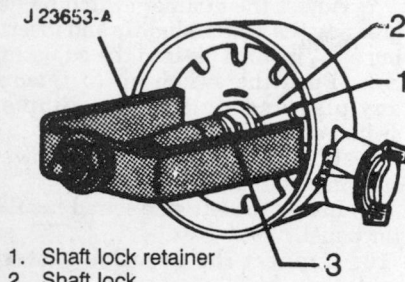

J 23653-A

1. Shaft lock retainer
2. Shaft lock
3. Upper steering shaft

Compressing the shaft lock

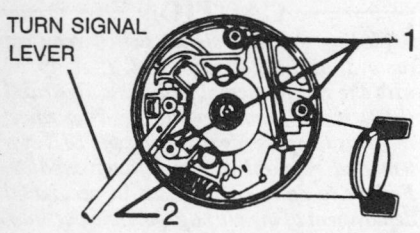

TURN SIGNAL
LEVER

1. Screw
2. Turn signal switch
   assembly

Positioning the turn signal lever to remove the turn signal switch screws

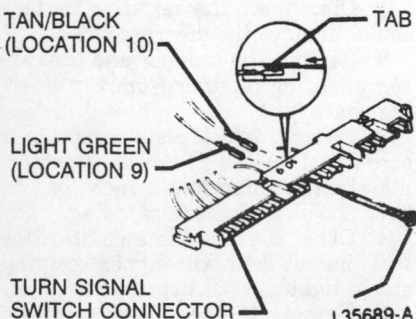

TAN/BLACK
(LOCATION 10)

TAB

LIGHT GREEN
(LOCATION 9)

TURN SIGNAL
SWITCH CONNECTOR

J 35689-A

Separating the buzzer switch wires from the turn signal electrical connector

protector and disconnect the turn signal switch connector.

8. Using the terminal remover tool, disconnect the buzzer switch wires from the turn signal switch connector. Using needle-nose pliers, remove the buzzer switch assembly.

9. Place the lock cylinder in the AC-CESSORY position, remove the lock retaining screw and the lock cylinder set.

10. Lifting the turn signal switch assembly, gently pull the wires through the steering column shroud.

To install:

11. Install turn signal connector through lock housing cover and steering column housing shroud.

12. Install steering column lock cylinder set while in **ACCESSORY** position.

13. Install lock retaining screw and tighten to 22 inch lbs. (2.5 Nm).

14. Install buzzer switch by pushing switch down into its retaining bore until bottomed with plastic tab covering lock retaining screw.

15. Install buzzer switch wires to turn signal switch connector: light green wire to location 9, tan/black wire to location 10.

NOTE: Wire terminal retainer must be removed and discarded from service buzzer switch wire.

16. Install wire connector retainer.
17. Install turn signal switch connector.
18. Install wire protector and turn signal switch. Install screws and tighten to 59 inch lbs. (6.8 Nm).

NOTE: Position turn signal switch so screws can be installed through openings in switch.

19. Install turn signal lever. Tighten screw to 53 inch lbs. (6 Nm).
20. Place turn signal switch in **OFF** position. Install upper bearing spring.
21. Install turn signal cancel cam assembly.
22. Install steering shaft lock.
23. Install shaft lock retainer to upper steering shaft using special tool J–23653–A to slightly depress shaft lock.
24. Install carrier snapring retainer. Install steering shaft bumper.
25. Extend shaft and lock in place. Install steering wheel and jam nut. Tighten to 30 ft. lbs. (41 Nm).
26. Remove lock plate compression screw J–23653–10.

1990–93

1. Disconnect the negative battery cable.
2. Place the ignition switch in the **LOCK** position to prevent uncentering of the coil assembly ring.
3. If equipped, disable the SIR system. Remove the inflator module.
4. Remove the steering wheel.
5. Remove coil assembly retaining ring.
6. Remove coil assembly from shaft end, allowing coil to hang freely.

NOTE: Coil assembly will be-

come uncentered if the steering column is separated from steering gear and is allowed to rotate or if the centering spring is depressed, allowing hub to rotate while coil is removed from column.

7. Remove wave washer.
8. Remove shaft lock retaining ring using special tool J–23653–C to depress shaft lock.
9. Remove shaft lock.
10. Remove turn signal cancelling cam assembly.
11. Remove upper bearing spring, inner race seat and inner race.
12. Remove multi-function lever by performing the following:
    a. Ensure that the switch is in the **OFF** position before access cover from steering wheel.
    b. Remove cruise control connector from lever. Note position of connector when installed in column.
    c. Pull lever straight out of switch.
13. Remove screws and signal switch arm.
14. Remove turn signal switch screws.
15. Remove screw from end of hazard knob assembly. Remove button spring and knob from switch cavity.
16. Remove turn signal switch assembly and allow to hang freely.
17. Remove wiring protector at base of steering column.
18. Disconnect wiring harness at the base of the steering column.
19. Gently pull wire harness through instrument panel bracket and column housing.

To install:

20. Route wiring assembly for new switch through column housing and instrument panel bracket.
21. Connect wiring assembly to connector at base of the steering column.
22. Connect coil assembly wire harness through column housing and instrument panel bracket. Allow coil to hang freely.
23. Install turn signal switch assembly and screws. Tighten to 30 inch lbs. (3.4 Nm).
24. Install wiring protector.
25. Install signal switch arm and screws. Tighten to 20.4 inch lbs. (2.3 Nm).
26. Install hazard knob, spring and button to hazard warning switch cavity. Install switch screw; drive in fully. Do not strip.
27. Install multi-function lever by performing the following:

NOTE: Ensure that the switch is in the OFF position before installation.

a. Install lever electrical connectors.

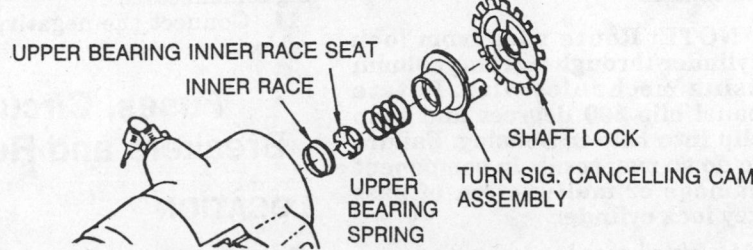

Removing shaft lock retaining ring

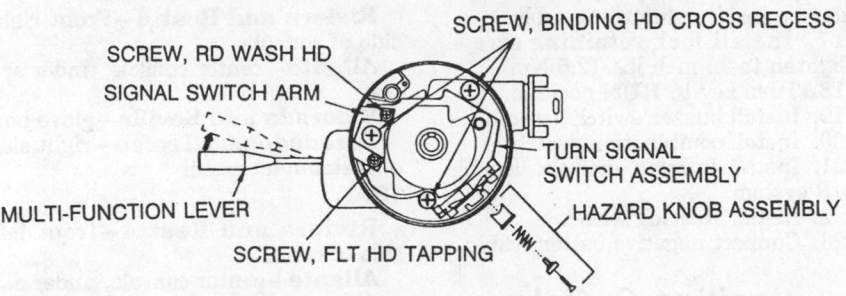

Removing upper shaft components

SCREW, BINDING HD CROSS RECESS
SCREW, RD WASH HD
SIGNAL SWITCH ARM
TURN SIGNAL SWITCH ASSEMBLY
MULTI-FUNCTION LEVER
HAZARD KNOB ASSEMBLY
SCREW, FLT HD TAPPING

Turn signal switch installed

b. With "WASH" paddle loose on the metal shaft, align shaft with the switch notch and insert shaft only.

c. Rotate "WASH" paddle into position and push into switch.

d. Push on the knob to seat lever into switch.

e. Install cruise control connector.

f. Install access cover onto steering column.

28. Install inner race, upper bearing inner race seat and upper bearing spring.

29. Install turn signal cancelling cam assembly.

30. Install shaft lock.

NOTE: Inspect shaft lock retaining ring for damage or deformation. If damaged or deformed, replace with new retaining ring.

31. Install shaft lock retaining ring. Align to block tooth on shaft using special tool J-23653-C to depress shaft lock. Ring must be firmly seated in groove on shaft.

NOTE: Set steering shaft so block teeth on upper steering

shaft are at the 12 o'clock and 6 o'clock positions. The alignment mark at the end of the shaft should be at the 12 o'clock position and vehicle wheels straight-ahead. Set the ignition switch to the LOCK position to ensure no damage occurs to the coil assembly.

32. Ensure coil assembly hub is centered by performing the following:

a. Hold coil assembly with clear bottom up to see coil ribbon.

b. There are 2 styles of coils. One rotates clockwise and the other rotates counterclockwise. While holding coil assembly, depress spring lock to rotate hub in direction of arrow until it stops.

c. The coil ribbon should be wound up snug against the center hub.

d. Rotate coil hub in opposite direction approximately 2½ turns. Release spring lock between locking tabs in front of arrow.

NOTE: If a new coil assembly is being installed, assemble the pre-centered coil assembly to column.

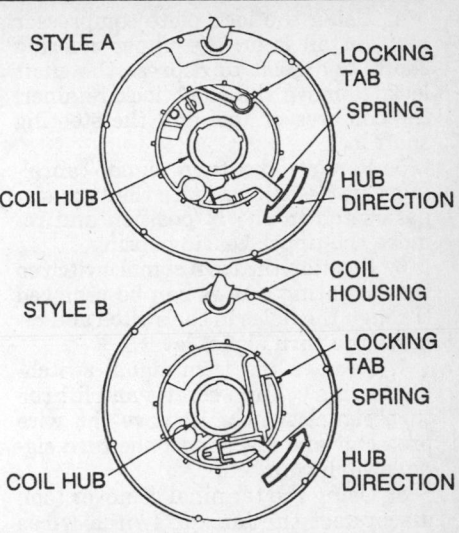

Removing pass key lock cylinder set

Remove centering tab and dispose.

33. Install wave washer.

34. Install coil assembly using horn tower on cancelling cam assembly inner ring and projections on outer ring for alignment.

35. Install coil assembly retaining ring. Ring must be firmly seated in groove on shaft.

NOTE: Gently pull lower coil assembly wire to remove any wire kinks that may be inside column assembly.

36. Install steering wheel.

37. Install inflator module and enable SIR system.

38. Connect the negative battery cable.

Ignition Lock
CAUTION
Replacing the ignition lock assembly necessitates removal of the steering wheel. If equipped with the Supplemental Inflatable Restraint (SIR) system, removing the steering wheel and inflator module requires temporarily disabling the SIR system and removal of the inflator module. Failure to do so could result in accidental deployment of the air bag and possible personal injury.

REMOVAL & INSTALLATION
1989

1. Disconnect the negative battery cable. Remove the steering wheel.

2. Remove the bumper and the carrier snapring retainer from the steering shaft.

3. Using the lock plate compressor screw tool, install it in the upper steering shaft, tighten to 40 inch lbs., to keep the shaft from telescoping.

4. Using the lock plate compressor tool, install it on the upper steering shaft, tighten it to depress the shaft lock. Remove the shaft lock retainer, the compressor tool and the steering shaft lock.

5. Remove the turn signal cancelling cam assembly. Place the turn signal switch in the **N** position and remove the upper bearing spring.

6. Position the turn signal switch so the mounting screws can be removed through the holes in the switch and remove the turn signal lever.

7. Remove the turn signal switch-to-steering column screws and lift the turn signal switch. Remove the wire protector and disconnect the turn signal switch connector.

8. Using the terminal remover tool, disconnect the buzzer switch wires from the turn signal switch connector. Using needle-nose pliers, remove the buzzer switch assembly.

9. Place the lock cylinder in the **ACC** position, remove the lock retaining screw and the lock cylinder set.

To install:

10. Reverse the removal procedures. Tighten the lock retaining screw to 22 inch lbs., the turn signal switch screws to 59 inch lbs. and the turn signal lever screw to 53 inch lbs.

11. Check the operation of the switches and the steering column.

1990–93

1. Disconnect the negative battery cable.

2. Place the ignition switch in the **LOCK** position to prevent uncentering of the coil assembly ring.

3. Disable the SIR system and remove the inflator module (air bag), if equipped.

4. Remove the steering wheel.

5. Remove the combination switch assembly and allow to hang freely. Do not remove wiring harness and connector from steering column.

6. Remove key from pass key lock cylinder set.

7. Disconnect buzzer switch assembly.

LOCK HOUSING COVER ASSEMBLY

ROUTE WIRE FROM LOCK CYLINDER AS SHOWN (DO NOT TWIST WIRES)

LOCK CYLINDER SET

ROTATE PANEL CLIP UP TO 360 DEGREES TO LOOP WIRE AWAY FROM SECTOR GEAR AND SNAP CLIP INTO HOLE IN LOCK HOUSING

Routing pass key wire harness

8. Reinsert key in pass key lock cylinder. Turn key to **LOCK** position.

9. Remove lock retaining screw.

10. Disconnect pass key lock cylinder terminal connector.

11. Remove wiring protector.

12. Attach a length of mechanics wire to terminal connector to aid in reassembly.

13. Gently pull wire through instrument panel bracket and column housing.

14. Remove pass key lock cylinder.

To install:

NOTE: **Route wire from lock cylinder through steering column using mechanics wire. Rotate panel clip 360 degrees and snap clip into hole in housing. Failure to do so may result in component damage or malfunction of pass key lock cylinder.**

15. Install pass key lock cylinder.

16. Gently pull lower lock cylinder wire to remove any wire kinks that may be inside column assembly.

17. Install lock retaining screw. Tighten to 22 inch lbs. (2.5 Nm).

18. Turn key to **RUN** position.

19. Install buzzer switch assembly.

20. Install combination switch.

21. Install inflator module. Enable SIR system.

22. Install steering wheel.

23. Connect negative battery cable.

Ignition Switch

REMOVAL & INSTALLATION

The ignition switch is hard-wired. The wiring harness with the column harness connector must be replaced with the ignition switch. Do not splice the new switch to the existing column wiring harness.

1. Disconnect the negative battery cable.

2. Remove the lower left sound insulator and the instrument panel steering column cover.

3. Remove the ignition switch wire protector and the switch-to-column screws.

4. Disconnect the ignition and turn signal switch column harness connectors from the dash connector.

5. Disconnect the turn signal harness connector from the column harness connector.

6. Remove the steering column bolts and nuts and gently lower steering column to the seat.

7. Remove the ignition switch assembly with the switch, harness and connector.

To install:

8. Install the ignition switch assembly with the harness and connector.

9. Raise the steering column into position and install the bolts and nuts.

10. Connect the turn signal harness connector to the column harness connector.

11. Connect the ignition and turn signal switch column harness connectors to the dash connector.

12. Install the ignition switch wire protector and the switch-to-column screws.

13. Install the lower left sound insulator and the instrument panel steering column cover.

14. Connect the negative battery cable.

Fuses, Circuit Breakers and Relays

LOCATION

Fuse Panels

1989

Riviera and Reatta—Front right side of console

Allante—center console, under ash tray

Eldorado and Seville—glove box

Toronado and Trofeo—right side of instrument panel

1990

Riviera and Reatta—front left side of console

Allante—center console, under ash tray

Eldorado and Seville—glove box

Toronado and Trofeo—right side of instrument panel

1991–92

Toronado and Trofeo—glove box

1991–93

Riviera and Reatta—front left side of console

Allante—center console, under ash tray

Eldorado and Seville—glove box

Circuit Breakers

A circuit breaker is an electrical switch which breaks the circuit during an electrical overload. Some circuit breakers are designed to automatically reset after a specified period of time. Others must be manually reset after the electrical malfunction causing the overload has been corrected.

The majority of circuit breakers can be found in the fuse panel. Some, however, are installed in-line near the device they are intended to protect.

Relays

Relays are generally mounted in the vicinity of the device(s) they are intended to control.

GM "F" Body
Rear Wheel Drive
CHEVROLET—Camaro PONTIAC—Firebird

SPECIFICATIONS

VEHICLE IDENTIFICATION CHART

It is important for servicing and ordering parts to be certain of the vehicle and engine identification. The VIN (vehicle identification number) is a 17 digit number visible through the windshield on the driver's side of the dash and contains the vehicle and engine identification codes. The tenth digit indicates model year and the eighth digit indicates engine code. It can be interpreted as follows:

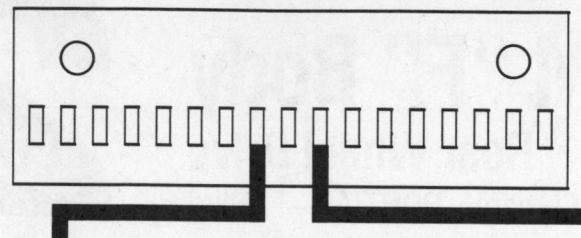

Engine Code

Code	Liters	Cu. In. (cc)	Cyl.	Fuel Sys.	Eng. Mfg.
S	2.8	173 (2837)	6	MFI	CPC
T	3.1	191 (3136)	6	MFI	CPC
F	5.0	305 (5011)	8	TPI	CPC
E	5.0	305 (5011)	8	TBI	CPC
8	5.7	350 (5733)	8	TPI	CPC
7	3.8	231 (3791)	6	SFI-Turbo	Buick

Model Year

Code	Year
K	1989
L	1990
M	1991
N	1992
P	1993

MFI—Multi Port Fuel Injection
SFI—Sequential Fuel Injection
TBI—Throttle Body Injection
TPI—Tuned Port Injection

ENGINE IDENTIFICATION

Year	Model	Engine Displacement Liter (cc)	Engine Series (ID/VIN)	Fuel System	No. of Cylinders	Engine Type
1989	Camaro	2.8 (2837)	S	MFI	6	OHV
	Firebird	2.8 (2837)	S	MFI	6	OHV
	Camaro	5.0 (5011)	F	TPI	8	OHV
	Firebird	5.0 (5011)	F	TPI	8	OHV
	Camaro	5.0 (5011)	E	TBI	8	OHV
	Firebird	5.0 (5011)	E	TBI	8	OHV
	Camaro	5.7 (5733)	8	TPI	8	OHV
	Firebird	5.7 (5733)	8	TPI	8	OHV
	Firebird	3.8 (3791)	7	SFI	6	OHV
1990	Camaro	3.1 (3136)	T	MFI	6	OHV
	Firebird	3.1 (3136)	T	MFI	6	OHV
	Camaro	5.0 (5011)	F	TPI	8	OHV
	Firebird	5.0 (5011)	F	TPI	8	OHV
	Camaro	5.0 (5011)	E	TBI	8	OHV
	Firebird	5.0 (5011)	E	TBI	8	OHV
	Camaro	5.7 (5733)	8	TPI	8	OHV
	Firebird	5.7 (5733)	8	TPI	8	OHV

ENGINE IDENTIFICATION

Year	Model	Engine Displacement Liter (cc)	Engine Series (ID/VIN)	Fuel System	No. of Cylinders	Engine Type
1991	Camaro	3.1 (3136)	T	MFI	6	OHV
	Firebird	3.1 (3136)	T	MFI	6	OHV
	Camaro	5.0 (5011)	F	TPI	8	OHV
	Firebird	5.0 (5011)	F	TPI	8	OHV
	Camaro	5.0 (5011)	E	TBI	8	OHV
	Firebird	5.0 (5011)	E	TBI	8	OHV
	Camaro	5.7 (5733)	8	TPI	8	OHV
	Firebird	5.7 (5733)	8	TPI	8	OHV
1992-93	Camaro	3.1 (3136)	T	MFI	6	OHV
	Firebird	3.1 (3136)	T	MFI	6	OHV
	Camaro	5.0 (5011)	F	TPI	8	OHV
	Firebird	5.0 (5011)	F	TPI	8	OHV
	Camaro	5.0 (5011)	E	TBI	8	OHV
	Firebird	5.0 (5011)	E	TBI	8	OHV
	Camaro	5.7 (5733)	8	TPI	8	OHV
	Firebird	5.7 (5733)	8	TPI	8	OHV

OHV—Overhead Valve
MFI—Mult-Port Fuel Injection
TBI—Throttle Body Injection
TPI—Tuned Port Injection
SFI—Sequential Fuel Injection

GENERAL ENGINE SPECIFICATIONS

Year	Engine ID/VIN	Engine Displacement Liter (cc)	Fuel System Type	Net Horsepower @ rpm	Net Torque @ rpm (ft. lbs.)	Bore × Stroke (in.)	Compression Ratio	Oil Pressure @ rpm
1989	S	2.8 (2837)	MFI	135 @ 5100	165 @ 3600	3.500 × 3.000	8.9:1	55 @ 2000
	F	5.0 (5011)	TPI	190 @ 4800	240 @ 3200	3.740 × 3.480	9.3:1	18 @ 2000
	E	5.0 (5011)	TBI	150 @ 4000	240 @ 3200	3.740 × 3.480	9.3:1	18 @ 2000
	8	5.7 (5733)	TPI	230 @ 4000	300 @ 3200	4.000 × 3.480	9.3:1	18 @ 2000
	7	3.8 (3791)	SFI-Turbo	235 @ 4400	330 @ 2800	3.800 × 3.400	8.5:1	60 @ 1850
1990	T	3.1 (3136)	MFI	140 @ 4400	180 @ 3600	3.503 × 3.312	8.8:1	55 @ 2000
	F	5.0 (5011)	TPI	230 @ 4400	300 @ 3200	3.740 × 3.480	9.3:1	18 @ 2000
	E	5.0 (5011)	TBI	170 @ 4000	255 @ 2400	3.740 × 3.480	9.3:1	18 @ 2000
	8	5.7 (5733)	TPI	240 @ 4400	345 @ 3200	4.000 × 3.480	9.3:1	18 @ 2000
1991	T	3.1 (3136)	MFI	140 @ 4400	180 @ 3600	3.503 × 3.312	8.5:1	8 @ 600
	F	5.0 (5011)	TPI	140 @ 4400	300 @ 3200	3.740 × 3.480	9.3:1	18 @ 2000
	E	5.0 (5011)	TPI	170 @ 4000	255 @ 2400	3.740 × 3.480	9.3:1	18 @ 2000
	8	5.7 (5733)	TPI	240 @ 4400	345 @ 3200	4.000 × 3.480	9.75:1	18 @ 2000
1992-93	T	3.1 (3136)	MFI	140 @ 4400	180 @ 3600	3.503 × 3.312	8.5:1	8 @ 600
	F	5.0 (5011)	TPI	140 @ 4400	300 @ 3200	3.740 × 3.480	9.3:1	18 @ 2000
	E	5.0 (5011)	TPI	170 @ 4000	255 @ 2400	3.740 × 3.480	9.3:1	18 @ 2000
	8	5.7 (5733)	TPI	240 @ 4400	345 @ 3200	4.000 × 3.480	9.75:1	18 @ 2000

NOTE: Horsepower and torque are SAE net figures. They are measured at the rear of the transmission with all accessories installed and operating. Since the figures vary when a given engine is installed in different models, some are representative rather than exact.
MFI—Multi-Port Fuel Injection
SFI—Sequential Fuel Injection
TBI—Throttle Body Injection
TPI—Tuned Port Injection

GASOLINE ENGINE TUNE-UP SPECIFICATIONS

Year	Engine ID/VIN	Engine Displacement Liter (cc)	Spark Plugs Gap (in.)	Ignition Timing (deg.) MT	Ignition Timing (deg.) AT	Fuel Pump (psi)	Idle Speed (rpm) MT	Idle Speed (rpm) AT	Valve Clearance In.	Valve Clearance Ex.
1989	S	2.8 (2837)	0.045	10	10	40–47	450	400	Hyd.	Hyd.
	F	5.0 (5011)	0.035	6	6	40–47	500	500	Hyd.	Hyd.
	E	5.0 (5011)	0.035	6	6	9.0–13.0	450	400	Hyd.	Hyd.
	8	5.7 (5733)	0.035	6	6	40–47	450	400	Hyd.	Hyd.
	7	3.8 (3791)	0.035	①	①	34–40	①	①	Hyd.	Hyd.
1990	T	3.1 (3136)	0.045	10	10	34–47	①	①	Hyd.	Hyd.
	F	5.0 (5011)	0.035	6	6	34–47	①	①	Hyd.	Hyd.
	E	5.0 (5011)	0.035	0	0	9.0–13.0	①	①	Hyd.	Hyd.
	8	5.7 (5733)	0.035	6	6	34–47	①	①	Hyd.	Hyd.
1991	T	3.1 (3136)	0.045	10	10	34–47	①	①	Hyd.	Hyd.
	F	5.0 (5011)	0.035	6	6	34–47	①	①	Hyd.	Hyd.
	E	5.0 (5011)	0.035	0	0	9.0–13.0	①	①	Hyd.	Hyd.
	8	5.7 (5733)	0.035	6	6	34–47	①	①	Hyd.	Hyd.
1992	T	3.1 (3136)	0.045	10	10	34–47	①	①	Hyd.	Hyd.
	F	5.0 (5011)	0.035	6	6	34–47	①	①	Hyd.	Hyd.
	E	5.0 (5011)	0.035	0	0	9.0–13.0	①	①	Hyd.	Hyd.
	8	5.7 (5733)	0.035	6	6	34–47	①	①	Hyd.	Hyd.
1993	REFER TO UNDERHOOD STICKER									

NOTE: The lowest cylinder pressure should be within 75% of the highest cylinder pressure reading. For example, if the highest cylinder is 134 psi, the lowest should be 101. Engine should be at normal operating temperature with throttle valve in the wide open position.

The underhood specifications sticker often reflects tune-up specification changes in production. Sticker figures must be used if they disagree with those in this chart.

Hyd.—Hydraulic

① See Underhood Emission Decal

FIRING ORDERS

NOTE: To avoid confusion, always replace spark plug wires one at a time.

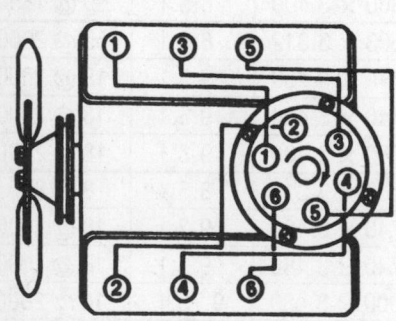

2.8L and 3.1L Engines
Engine Firing Order: 1–2–3–4–5–6
Distributor Rotation: Clockwise

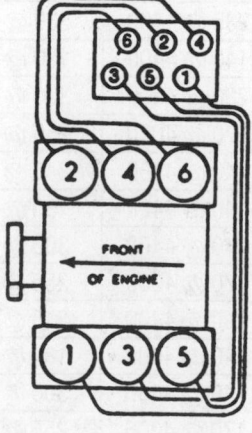

3.8L Engine
Engine Firing Order: 1–6–5–4–3–2
Distributorless Ignition System

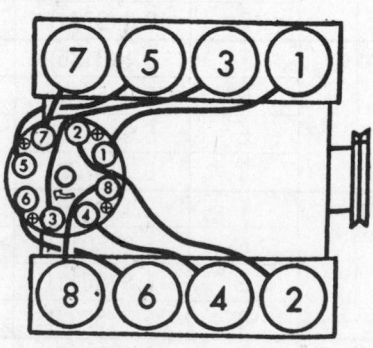

5.0L and 5.7L Engines
Engine Firing Order: 1–8–4–3–6–5–7–2
Distributor Rotation: Clockwise

CAPACITIES

Year	Model	Engine ID/VIN	Engine Displacement Liter (cc)	Engine Crankcase with Filter (qts.)	Transmission (pts.) 4-Spd	Transmission (pts.) 5-Spd	Transmission (pts.) Auto.	Drive Axle (pts.)	Fuel Tank (gal.)	Cooling System (qts.)
1989	Camaro	S	2.8 (2837)	4.0	—	6.6	8.5 ①	3.5	16	13
	Camaro	F	5.0 (5011)	5.0	—	6.6	8.5 ①	3.5	16	17
	Camaro	E	5.0 (5011)	5.0	—	6.6	8.5 ①	3.5	16	15.5
	Camaro	8	5.7 (5733)	5.0	—	6.6	8.5 ①	3.5	16	17
	Firebird	S	2.8 (2837)	4.0	—	6.6	8.5 ①	3.5	16	13
	Firebird	F	5.0 (5011)	5.0	—	6.6	8.5 ①	3.5	16	17
	Firebird	E	5.0 (5011)	5.0	—	6.6	8.5 ①	3.5	16	15.5
	Firebird	8	5.7 (5733)	5.0	—	6.6	8.5 ①	3.5	16	17
	Firebird	7	3.8 (3791)	—	—	—	10	3.5	15.5	16.5
1990	Camaro	T	3.1 (3136)	4.0	—	5.9	10	3.5	15.5	14.5
	Camaro	F	5.0 (5011)	5.0	—	5.9	10	3.5	15.5	17.5
	Camaro	E	5.0 (5011)	5.0	—	5.9	10	3.5	15.5	17.5
	Camaro	8	5.7 (5733)	5.0	—	5.9	10	3.5	15.5	16.5
	Firebird	T	3.1 (3136)	4.0	—	5.9	10	3.5	15.5	14.5
	Firebird	F	5.0 (5011)	5.0	—	5.9	10	3.5	15.5	17.5
	Firebird	E	5.0 (5011)	5.0	—	5.9	10	3.5	15.5	17.5
	Firebird	8	5.7 (5733)	5.0	—	5.9	10	3.5	15.5	16.5
1991	Camaro	T	3.1 (3136)	4.0	—	5.9	10	3.5	15.5	14.8
	Camaro	F	5.0 (5011)	5.0	—	5.9	10	3.5	15.5	18.0
	Camaro	E	5.0 (5011)	5.0	—	5.9	10	3.5	15.5	18.0
	Camaro	8	5.7 (5733)	5.0	—	5.9	10	3.5	15.5	16.7
	Firebird	T	3.1 (3136)	4.0	—	5.9	10	3.5	15.5	14.8
	Firebird	F	5.0 (5011)	5.0	—	5.9	10	3.5	15.5	18.0
	Firebird	E	5.0 (5011)	5.0	—	5.9	10	3.5	15.5	18.0
	Firebird	8	5.7 (5733)	5.0	—	5.9	10	3.5	15.5	16.7
1992-93	Camaro	T	3.1 (3136)	4.0	—	5.9	10	3.5	15.5	14.8
	Camaro	F	5.0 (5011)	5.0	—	5.9	10	3.5	15.5	18.0
	Camaro	E	5.0 (5011)	5.0	—	5.9	10	3.5	15.5	18.0
	Camaro	8	5.7 (5733)	5.0	—	5.9	10	3.5	15.5	16.7
	Firebird	T	3.1 (3136)	4.0	—	5.9	10	3.5	15.5	14.8
	Firebird	F	5.0 (5011)	5.0	—	5.9	10	3.5	15.5	18.0
	Firebird	E	5.0 (5011)	5.0	—	5.9	10	3.5	15.5	18.0
	Firebird	8	5.7 (5733)	5.0	—	5.9	10	3.5	15.5	16.7

① 10.0 if equipped with overdrive transmission

CAMSHAFT SPECIFICATIONS

All measurements given in inches.

Year	Engine ID/VIN	Engine Displacement Liter (cc)	Journal Diameter 1	Journal Diameter 2	Journal Diameter 3	Journal Diameter 4	Journal Diameter 5	Elevation In.	Elevation Ex.	Bearing Clearance	Camshaft End Play
1989	S	2.8 (2837)	1.8976–1.8996	1.8976–1.8996	1.8976–1.8996	1.8976–1.8996	—	0.2350	0.2660	NA	NA
	F	5.0 (5011)	1.8682–1.8692	1.8682–1.8692	1.8682–1.8692	1.8682–1.8692	1.8682–1.8692	0.2690	0.2760	NA	0.004–0.012

CAMSHAFT SPECIFICATIONS

All measurements given in inches.

Year	Engine ID/VIN	Engine Displacement Liter (cc)	Journal Diameter 1	2	3	4	5	Elevation In.	Ex.	Bearing Clearance	Camshaft End Play
	E	5.0 (5011)	1.8682–1.8692	1.8682–1.8692	1.8682–1.8692	1.8682–1.8692	1.8682–1.8692	0.2340	0.2570	NA	0.004–0.012
	8	5.7 (5733)	1.8682–1.8692	1.8682–1.8692	1.8682–1.8692	1.8682–1.8692	1.8682–1.8692	0.2730	0.2820	NA	0.004–0.012
	7	3.8 (3791)	1.7850–1.7860	1.7850–1.7860	1.7850–1.7860	1.7850–1.7860	—	NA	NA	①	NA
1990	T	3.1 (3136)	1.8678–1.8697	1.8678–1.8697	1.8678–1.8697	1.8678–1.8697	1.8678–1.8697	0.2626	0.2732	0.0010–0.0040	NA
	F	5.0 (5011)	1.8682–1.8692	1.8682–1.8692	1.8682–1.8692	1.8682–1.8692	1.8682–1.8692	0.2690	0.2760	NA	0.004–0.012
	E	5.0 (5011)	1.8682–1.8692	1.8682–1.8692	1.8682–1.8692	1.8682–1.8692	1.8682–1.8692	0.2340	0.2570	NA	0.004–0.012
	8	5.7 (5733)	1.8682–1.8692	1.8682–1.8692	1.8682–1.8692	1.8682–1.8692	1.8682–1.8692	0.2730	0.2820	NA	0.004–0.012
1991	T	3.1 (3136)	1.8678–1.8697	1.8678–1.8697	1.8678–1.8697	1.8678–1.8697	1.8678–1.8697	0.2626	0.2732	0.0010–0.0040	NA
	F	5.0 (5011)	1.8682–1.8692	1.8682–1.8692	1.8682–1.8692	1.8682–1.8692	1.8682–1.8692	0.2750	0.2850	NA	0.004–0.012
	E	5.0 (5011)	1.8682–1.8692	1.8682–1.8692	1.8682–1.8692	1.8682–1.8692	1.8682–1.8692	0.2340	0.2570	NA	0.004–0.012
	8	5.7 (5733)	1.8682–1.8692	1.8682–1.8692	1.8682–1.8692	1.8682–1.8692	1.8682–1.8692	0.2750	0.2850	NA	0.004–0.012
1992–93	T	3.1 (3136)	1.8678–1.8697	1.8678–1.8697	1.8678–1.8697	1.8678–1.8697	1.8678–1.8697	0.2626	0.2732	0.0010–0.0040	NA
	F	5.0 (5011)	1.8682–1.8692	1.8682–1.8692	1.8682–1.8692	1.8682–1.8692	1.8682–1.8692	0.2750	0.2850	NA	0.004–0.012
	E	5.0 (5011)	1.8682–1.8692	1.8682–1.8692	1.8682–1.8692	1.8682–1.8692	1.8682–1.8692	0.2340	0.2570	NA	0.004–0.012
	8	5.7 (5733)	1.8682–1.8692	1.8682–1.8692	1.8682–1.8692	1.8682–1.8692	1.8682–1.8692	0.2750	0.2850	NA	0.004–0.012

NA—Not available
① No. 1—0.0005–0.0025
No. 2, 3, 4—0.0005–0.0035

CRANKSHAFT AND CONNECTING ROD SPECIFICATIONS

All measurements are given in inches.

Year	Engine ID/VIN	Engine Displacement Liter (cc)	Crankshaft Main Brg. Journal Dia.	Main Brg. Oil Clearance	Shaft End-play	Thrust on No.	Connecting Rod Journal Diameter	Oil Clearance	Side Clearance
1989	S	2.8 (2837)	2.6473–2.6483	0.0017–0.0029	0.0019–0.0066	3	1.9980–1.9990	0.0014–0.0035	0.0060–0.0170
	F	5.0 (5011)	①	②	0.0020–0.0060	5	2.0980–2.0990	0.0018–0.0039	0.0080–0.0140
	E	5.0 (5011)	①	②	0.0020–0.0060	5	2.0980–2.0990	0.0018–0.0039	0.0080–0.0140
	8	5.7 (5733)	①	②	0.0020–0.0060	5	2.0980–2.0990	0.0013–0.0035	0.0060–0.0140
	7	3.8 (3791)	2.4995	0.0003–0.0018	0.0030–0.0110	2	2.2487–2.2495	0.0005–0.0026	0.0030–0.0150

CRANKSHAFT AND CONNECTING ROD SPECIFICATIONS

All measurements are given in inches.

Year	Engine ID/VIN	Engine Displacement Liter (cc)	Crankshaft Main Brg. Journal Dia.	Crankshaft Main Brg. Oil Clearance	Crankshaft Shaft End-play	Crankshaft Thrust on No.	Connecting Rod Journal Diameter	Connecting Rod Oil Clearance	Connecting Rod Side Clearance
1990	T	3.1 (3136)	2.6473–2.6483	③	0.0024–0.0083	3	1.9983–1.9994	0.0014–0.0036	0.0140–0.0290
	F	5.0 (5011)	①	②	0.0010–0.0070	5	2.0890–2.0990	0.0013–0.0035	0.0060–0.0140
	E	5.0 (5011)	①	②	0.0010–0.0070	5	2.0890–2.0990	0.0013–0.0035	0.0060–0.0140
	8	5.7 (5733)	①	②	0.0010–0.0070	5	2.0890–2.0990	0.0013–0.0035	0.0060–0.0140
1991	T	3.1 (3136)	2.6473–2.6483	④	0.0024–0.0083	3	1.9983–1.9994	0.0011–0.0033	0.0140–0.0290
	F	5.0 (5011)	①	②	0.0010–0.0070	5	2.0890–2.0990	0.0013–0.0035	0.0060–0.0140
	E	5.0 (5011)	①	②	0.0010–0.0070	5	2.0890–2.0990	0.0013–0.0035	0.0060–0.0140
	8	5.7 (5733)	①	②	0.0010–0.0070	5	2.0890–2.0990	0.0013–0.0035	0.0060–0.0140
1992–93	T	3.1 (3136)	2.6473–2.6483	④	0.0024–0.0083	3	1.9983–1.9994	0.0011–0.0033	0.0080–0.0170
	F	5.0 (5011)	①	②	0.0010–0.0070	5	2.0890–2.0990	0.0013–0.0035	0.0060–0.0140
	E	5.0 (5011)	①	②	0.0010–0.0070	5	2.0890–2.0990	0.0013–0.0035	0.0060–0.0140
	8	5.7 (5733)	①	②	0.0010–0.0070	5	2.0890–2.0990	0.0013–0.0035	0.0060–0.0140

① No. 1—2.4484-2.4493
Nos. 2, 3, 4—2.4481-2.4490
No. 5—2.4479-2.4488
② No. 1—0.0008-0.0020
Nos. 2, 3, 4—0.0011-0.0020
No. 5—0.0017-0.0032
③ Main Bearing Clearance—0.0012-0.0027
Main Thrust Bearing Clearance—0.0016-0.0027
④ Main Bearing Clearance—0.0012-0.0030
Main Thrust Bearing Clearance—0.0016-0.0030

VALVE SPECIFICATIONS

Year	Engine ID/VIN	Engine Displacement Liter (cc)	Seat Angle (deg.)	Face Angle (deg.)	Spring Test Pressure (lbs. @ in.)	Spring Installed Height (in.)	Stem-to-Guide Clearance (in.) Intake	Stem-to-Guide Clearance (in.) Exhaust	Stem Diameter (in.) Intake	Stem Diameter (in.) Exhaust
1989	S	2.8 (2837)	46	45	194 @ 1.18	1.57	0.0010–0.0027	0.0010–0.0027	NA	NA
	E	5.0 (5011)	46	45	194-206 @ 1.25	①	0.0010–0.0027	0.0010–0.0027	NA	NA
	F	5.0 (5011)	46	45	194-206 @ 1.25	①	0.0010–0.0027	0.0010–0.0027	NA	NA
	8	5.7 (5733)	46	45	194-206 @ 1.25	①	0.0010–0.0027	0.0010–0.0027	NA	NA
	7	3.8 (3791)	45	NA	185 @ 1.340	1.73	0.0015–0.0035	0.0015–0.0032	NA	NA

VALVE SPECIFICATIONS

Year	Engine ID/VIN	Engine Displacement Liter (cc)	Seat Angle (deg.)	Face Angle (deg.)	Spring Test Pressure (lbs. @ in.)	Spring Installed Height (in.)	Stem-to-Guide Clearance (in.)		Stem Diameter (in.)	
							Intake	Exhaust	Intake	Exhaust
1990	T	3.1 (3136)	46	45	190 @ 1.20	1.60	0.0014– 0.0025	0.0016– 0.0029	NA	NA
	F	5.0 (5011)	46	45	194-206 @ 1.25	①	0.0011– 0.0027	0.0011– 0.0027	NA	NA
	E	5.0 (5011)	46	45	194-206 @ 1.25	①	0.0011– 0.0027	0.0011– 0.0027	NA	NA
	8	5.7 (5733)	46	45	194-206 @1.25	①	0.0011– 0.0027	0.0011– 0.0027	NA	NA
1991	T	3.1 (3136)	46	45	190 @ 1.20	1.61	0.0014– 0.0025	0.0016– 0.0029	NA	NA
	F	5.0 (5011)	46	45	194-206 @ 1.25	①	0.0011– 0.0027	0.0011– 0.0027	NA	NA
	E	5.0 (5011)	46	45	194-206 @ 1.25	①	0.0011– 0.0027	0.0011– 0.0027	NA	NA
	8	5.7 (5733)	46	45	194-206 @1.25	①	0.0011– 0.0027	0.0011– 0.0027	NA	NA
1992–93	T	3.1 (3136)	46	45	190 @ 1.20	1.61	0.0014– 0.0025	0.0016– 0.0029	NA	NA
	F	5.0 (5011)	46	45	194-206 @ 1.25	1.70	0.0011– 0.0027	0.0011– 0.0027	NA	NA
	E	5.0 (5011)	46	45	194-206 @ 1.25	1.70	0.0011– 0.0027	0.0011– 0.0027	NA	NA
	8	5.7 (5733)	46	45	194-206 @1.25	1.70	0.0011– 0.0027	0.0011– 0.0027	NA	NA

NA—Not available   ① Intake—1.72   Exhaust—1.59

PISTON AND RING SPECIFICATIONS

All measurements are given in inches.

Year	Engine ID/VIN	Engine Displacement Liter (cc)	Piston Clearance	Ring Gap			Ring Side Clearance		
				Top Compression	Bottom Compression	Oil Control	Top Compression	Bottom Compression	Oil Control
1989	S	2.8 (2837)	0.0170– 0.0430	0.009– 0.019	0.009– 0.019	0.020– 0.055	0.0012– 0.0028	0.0015– 0.0037	0.0078 Max.
	F	5.0 (5011)	NA	0.010– 0.020	0.010– 0.025	0.015– 0.055	0.0012– 0.0032	0.0012– 0.0032	0.0020– 0.0070
	E	5.0 (5011)	0.0027	0.010– 0.020	0.010– 0.025	0.015– 0.055	0.0012– 0.0032	0.0012– 0.0032	0.0020– 0.0070
	8	5.7 (5733)	0.0027	0.010– 0.020	0.010– 0.025	0.015– 0.055	0.0012– 0.0032	0.0012– 0.0032	0.0020– 0.0070
	7	3.8 (3791)	0.0013 0.0035	0.010– 0.020	0.010– 0.020	0.015– 0.055	NA	NA	NA
1990	T	3.1 (3136)	0.0012– 0.0028	0.010– 0.020	0.010– 0.020	0.010– 0.030	0.0020– 0.0035	0.0020– 0.0035	0.0075 Max.
	F	5.0 (5011)	0.0007– 0.0021	0.010– 0.020	0.010– 0.025	0.015 0.055	0.0012– 0.0032	0.0012– 0.0032	0.0020– 0.0070
	E	5.0 (5011)	0.0007– 0.0021	0.010– 0.020	0.010– 0.025	0.015 0.055	0.0012– 0.0032	0.0012– 0.0032	0.0020– 0.0070
	8	5.7 (5733)	0.0007– 0.0021	0.010 0.020	0.018– 0.026	0.015 0.055	0.0012– 0.0032	0.0012– 0.0032	0.0020– 0.0070

PISTON AND RING SPECIFICATIONS

All measurements are given in inches.

| Year | Engine ID/VIN | Engine Displacement Liter (cc) | Piston Clearance | Ring Gap | | | Ring Side Clearance | | |
				Top Compression	Bottom Compression	Oil Control	Top Compression	Bottom Compression	Oil Control
1991	T	3.1 (3136)	0.0012–0.0028	0.010–0.020	0.020–0.028	0.010–0.030	0.0020–0.0035	0.0020–0.0035	0.0070 Max.
	F	5.0 (5011)	0.0007–0.0021	0.010–0.020	0.010–0.025	0.010 0.030	0.0012–0.0032	0.0012–0.0032	0.0020–0.0070
	E	5.0 (5011)	0.0007–0.0021	0.010–0.020	0.010–0.025	0.010 0.030	0.0012–0.0032	0.0012–0.0032	0.0020–0.0070
	8	5.7 (5733)	0.0007–0.0021	0.010 0.020	0.018–0.026	0.010 0.030	0.0012–0.0032	0.0012–0.0032	0.0020–0.0070
1992–93	T	3.1 (3136)	0.0012–0.0026	0.007–0.016	0.020–0.028	0.010–0.030	0.0020–0.0035	0.0020–0.0035	0.0070 Max.
	F	5.0 (5011)	0.0007–0.0021	0.010–0.020	0.018–0.026	0.010 0.030	0.0012–0.0032	0.0012–0.0032	0.0020–0.0070
	E	5.0 (5011)	0.0007–0.0021	0.010–0.020	0.018–0.026	0.010 0.030	0.0012–0.0032	0.0012–0.0032	0.0020–0.0070
	8	5.7 (5733)	0.0007–0.0021	0.010 0.020	0.018–0.026	0.010 0.030	0.0012–0.0032	0.0012–0.0032	0.0020–0.0070

NA—Not available

TORQUE SPECIFICATIONS

All readings in ft. lbs.

| Year | Engine ID/VIN | Engine Displacement Liter (cc) | Cylinder Head Bolts | Main Bearing Bolts | Rod Bearing Bolts | Crankshaft Damper Bolts | Flywheel Bolts | Manifold | | Spark Plugs | Lug Nut |
								Intake	Exhaust		
1989	S	2.8 (2837)	③	63–83	34–45	75	52	13–25	19–31	7–15	100
	F	5.0 (5011)	60–75	63–85	42–47	70	74	25–45	②	15–20	100
	E	5.0 (5011)	60–75	63–85	42–47	70	74	25–45	②	15–20	100
	8	5.7 (5733)	60–75	63–85	42–47	70	74	25–45	②	15–20	100
	7	3.8 (3791)	①	100	40	219	61	45	37	20	100
1990	T	3.1 (3136)	③	73	39	70	52	④	25	25	100
	F	5.0 (5011)	68	77	44	70	74	35	②	22	100
	E	5.0 (5011)	68	77	44	70	74	35	②	22	100
	8	5.7 (5733)	68	77	44	70	74	35	②	22	100
1991	T	3.1 (3136)	③	73	39	70	52	④	25	25	100
	F	5.0 (5011)	68	77	44	70	74	35	②	22	100
	E	5.0 (5011)	68	77	44	70	74	35	②	22	100
	8	5.7 (5733)	68	77	44	70	74	35	②	22	100
1992–93	T	3.1 (3136)	③	73	39	70	52	④	25	25	100
	F	5.0 (5011)	68	77	44	70	74	⑤	②	11	100
	E	5.0 (5011)	68	77	44	70	74	⑤	②	11	100
	8	5.7 (5733)	68	77	44	70	74	⑤	②	11	100

① Torque in 3 steps:
  1st step: Tighten to 2.5 ft. lbs.
  2nd step: Rotate wrench an additional 90 degrees.
  3rd step: Rotate wrench an additional 90 degrees.
  (Should 60 ft. lbs. be reached at any time in steps 2 & 3—STOP—do not turn any further)

② Outer bolts—26 ft. lbs.
  Center bolts—20 ft. lbs.

③ Torque in 2 steps:
  1st step: Tighten to 40 ft. lbs.
  2nd step: Rotate wrench an additional 90 degrees.

④ Lower intake manifold—19 ft. lbs.
  Center intake manifold—15 ft. lbs.

⑤ Torque in 2 steps:
  1st step: 89 inch lbs.
  2nd step: 35 ft. lbs.

BRAKE SPECIFICATIONS

All measurements in inches unless noted.

Year	Model	Master Cylinder Bore	Brake Disc Original Thickness	Brake Disc Minimum Thickness	Maximum Runout	Brake Drum Diameter Original Inside Diameter	Brake Drum Diameter Max. Wear Limit	Brake Drum Diameter Maximum Machine Diameter	Minimum Lining Thickness ④ Front	Minimum Lining Thickness ④ Rear
1989	Camaro	①	②	③	0.005	9.500	0.098	9.560	0.030	0.030
	Firebird	①	②	③	0.005	9.500	0.090	9.560	0.030	0.030
1990	Camaro	①	②	③	0.005	9.500	0.090	9.560	0.030	0.030
	Firebird	①	②	③	0.005	9.500	0.090	9.560	0.030	0.030
1991	Camaro	①	②	③	0.005	9.500	0.090	9.560	0.030	0.030
	Firebird	①	②	③	0.005	9.500	0.090	9.560	0.030	0.030
1992-93	Camaro	①	②	③	0.005	9.500	0.090	9.560	0.030	0.030
	Firebird	①	②	③	0.005	9.500	0.090	9.560	0.030	0.030

① Rear Drum—0.945
  Rear Disc—1.00
② Front—1.043
  Rear—0.744
③ Front—0.945
  Rear—0.724
④ Rear drum or disc

WHEEL ALIGNMENT

Year	Model	Caster Range (deg.)	Caster Preferred Setting (deg.)	Camber Range (deg.)	Camber Preferred Setting (deg.)	Toe-in (in.)	Steering Axis Inclination (deg.)
1989	Camaro	4³/₁₆P–5³/₁₆P	4¹¹/₁₆P	³/₁₆N–1³/₁₆P	⁵/₁₆P	0	NA
	Firebird	4³/₁₆P–5³/₁₆P	4¹¹/₁₆P	³/₁₆N–1³/₁₆P	⁵/₁₆P	0	NA
1990	Camaro	4³/₁₆P–5³/₁₆P	4¹¹/₁₆P	³/₁₆N–1³/₁₆P	⁵/₁₆P	0	NA
	Firebird	4³/₁₆P–5³/₁₆P	4¹¹/₁₆P	³/₁₆N–1³/₁₆P	⁵/₁₆P	0	NA
1991	Camaro	4⁵/₁₆P–5⁵/₁₆P	4¹³/₁₆P	³/₁₆N–1³/₁₆P	⁵/₁₆P	0	NA
	Firebird	4⁵/₁₆P–5⁵/₁₆P	4¹³/₁₆P	³/₁₆N–1³/₁₆P	⁵/₁₆P	0	NA
1992-93	Camaro	4⁵/₁₆P–5⁵/₁₆P	4¹³/₁₆P	³/₁₆N–1³/₁₆P	⁵/₁₆P	0	NA
	Firebird	4⁵/₁₆P–5⁵/₁₆P	4¹³/₁₆P	³/₁₆N–1³/₁₆P	⁵/₁₆P	0	NA

NA—Not available N—Negative P—Positive

ENGINE MECHANICAL

NOTE: Disconnecting the negative battery cable on some vehicles may interfere with the functions of the on board computer systems and may require the computer to undergo a relearning process.

Engine Assembly

REMOVAL & INSTALLATION

2.8L and 3.1L Engines

1. Disconnect the negative battery cable.

2. Remove the air cleaner duct on 3.1L engines or the air cleaner for 2.8L engines.

3. Mark the hood location on the hood supports and remove the hood.

4. Remove the serpentine belt.

5. Drain the radiator and remove the radiator hoses. Disconnect the heater hoses.

6. Remove the fan shroud, fan and radiator.

7. Disconnect the throttle linkage, including the cruise control detent cable.

8. Disconnect the air conditioning compressor and lay aside for 3.1L engines. For 2.8L engines, discharge the air conditioning system and disconnect the lines.

9. Remove the power steering pump and lay aside. Remove the vacuum brake booster line.

10. Remove the distributor cap and spark plug wires.

11. Disconnect the necessary electrical connections and hoses.

12. Raise and safely support the vehicle.

13. Disconnect the exhaust pipes at the exhaust manifolds. Disconnect the transmission oil cooler lines, for 3.1L engines at the oil pan clips.

14. Remove the flywheel cover and remove the converter bolts.

15. Disconnect the starter wire connections.

16. Remove the bellhousing and the motor mount through bolts.

17. Lower the vehicle.

18. Relieve the fuel system pressure. Disconnect the fuel lines and remove the wire from the rear left engine bracket

19. Support the transmission with a

suitable jack. Attach an engine lifting device.

20. Remove the engine assembly.

To install:

21. Position the engine assembly in the vehicle.

22. Attach the motor mount to engine brackets and lower the engine in place. Remove the engine lifting device and the transmission jack.

23. Raise and support the vehicle safely.

24. Install the motor mount through bolts and tighten the nuts to 50 ft. lbs. (68 Nm). Install the bellhousing bolts and tighten to 40 ft. lbs. (54 Nm).

25. On vehicles with automatic transmission, install the converter to flywheel attaching bolts to 46 ft. lbs. (63 Nm).

26. Install the flywheel splash shield and tighten to 89 inch lbs. (10 Nm).

27. Connect the starter wires and the fuel lines. Connect the transmission oil cooler lines.

28. Install the exhaust pipe on the exhaust manifold.

29. Lower the vehicle.

30. Install the power steering pump and the air conditioning compressor. If applicable, connect the air conditioning lines.

31. Connect the necessary wires and hoses. Connect the fuel lines and attach the wire to the bracket at the rear left of the engine.

32. Install the radiator, fan and fan shroud. Connect the radiator and heater hoses.

33. Connect the vacuum brake booster line, the throttle linkage and cruise control cable. Install the distributor cap and spark plug wires.

34. Fill the cooling system with the proper type and amount of coolant and the crankcase with the proper type of oil to the correct level.

35. Install the serpentine belt, the air cleaner or air cleaner duct and the hood.

36. Connect the negative battery cable, tighten the fuel filler cap and start the engine and check for leaks.

37. If applicable, charge the air conditioning system.

3.8L Engine

1. Disconnect the negative battery cable.

2. Mark the location of the hood on the hood hinges and remove the hood.

3. Drain the engine coolant.

4. Remove the fan, pulleys and belts. Remove the radiator hoses and the radiator and fan shroud.

5. Disconnect the power steering pump and air conditioning compressor from their mounting brackets and position aside.

6. Relieve the fuel system pressure. Disconnect the fuel line and the battery ground cable from the engine.

7. Disconnect the necessary hoses and wiring.

8. Disconnect the throttle cable.

9. Remove the alternator assembly.

10. Disconnect the engine to body ground straps at the engine.

11. Raise and safely support the vehicle.

12. Disconnect the crossover pipe from the exhaust manifolds.

13. Remove the flywheel cover and use a scribe to mark the relationship of the torque converter to the flywheel. Remove the covnerter to flywheel bolts.

14. Disconnect the starter wiring.

15. Remove the transmission to engine attaching bolts and the motor mount to frame bracket attaching bolts.

16. Lower the vehicle.

17. Support the transmission with a suitable jack and install and engine lifting device.

18. Remove the engine assembly.

To install:

19. Position the engine in the vehicle.

20. Install the transmission to engine attaching bolts and tighten to 35 ft. lbs. (48 Nm).

21. Raise and safely support the vehicle.

22. Install the motor mount to frame bracket attaching bolts and tighten to 48 ft. lbs. (65 Nm).

23. Install the converter to flywheel bolts making sure the scribed marks are aligned. Tighten the bolts to 46 ft. lbs. (63 Nm). Install the flywheel cover.

24. Connect the crossover pipe to the exhaust manifold.

25. Lower the vehicle.

26. Connect the engine to body ground straps and install the alternator.

27. Connect all necessary hoses and wiring.

28. Connect the throttle cable and the negative battery cable at the engine.

29. Connect the fuel lines.

30. Install the power steering pump and air conditioning compressor in their respective brackets.

31. Install the radiator, fan shroud, radiator and heater hoses and the fan, pulleys and belts.

32. Fill the cooling system with the proper type of quantity of coolant and the engine with the proper type of oil to the correct level.

33. Connect the negative battery cable, start the engine and check for leaks.

5.0L and 5.7L Engines

1. Disconnect the negative battery cable.

2. Mark the location of the hood on the hood hinges and remove the hood.

3. Remove the air cleaner.

4. Drain the cooling system.

5. Remove the radiator hoses.

6. Disconnect the electrical connectors and retaining clips at the fan, remove the fan mounting bolts and remove the fan and shroud.

7. Remove the radiator.

8. Remove the serpentine accessory drive belt.

9. Disconnect the throttle cable.

10. Remove the plenum extension screws and the plenum extension, if equipped.

11. Disconnect the spark plug wires at the distributor and remove the distributor. Remove the external coil, if equipped.

12. Disconnect the necessary vacuum hoses and wiring.

13. Disconnect the power steering and air conditioning compressors from their respective brackets and lay them aside.

14. Relieve the fuel system pressure. Disconnect the fuel lines.

15. Disconnect the negative battery cable at the engine block. Disconnect the AIR hoses and pipe.

16. Raise and safely support the vehicle.

17. Remove the exhaust pipes at the exhaust manifolds.

18. Remove the flywheel cover and remove the converter to flywheel bolts.

19. Disconnect the starter wires and remove the starter.

20. Disconnect the transmission oil cooler lines at the oil pan. Remove the motor mount through bolts.

21. Support the transmission with an adjustable lifting device and remove the crossmember bolts. Lower the transmission enough to remove the bellhousing bolts. Raise the transmission and install 2 crossmember bolts.

22. Remove the lifting device from the transmission. Lower the vehicle and Support the transmission with a suitable jack.

23. Remove the AIR/converter bracket and ground wires from the rear of the cylinder head.

24. Attach a suitable lifting device and remove the engine assembly.

To install:

25. Position the engine assembly in the vehicle.

26. Attach the motor mount to engine brackets and lower the engine into place. Attach the AIR/converter bracket and ground wires to the rear of the cylinder head.

27. Remove the engine lifting device and the transmission jack.

28. Raise and safely support the vehicle.

29. Install the motor mount through bolts and tighten to 50 ft. lbs. (68 Nm).

30. Install the bellhousing bolts and tighten to 35 ft. lbs. (47 Nm). Tighten the transmission crossmember bolts.

31. On vehicles with automatic transmission, install the converter to flywheel bolts. Tighten the bolts to 46 ft. lbs. (63 Nm). Install the flywheel cover and connect the transmission oil cooler lines to the clip at the oil pan.

32. Connect the starter wires and install the starter.

33. Connect the exhaust pipe at the exhaust manifold.

34. Lower the vehicle and connect the AIR hoses and pipe.

35. Connect the necessary wires, hoses and the fuel lines.

36. Install the power steering pump and air conditioning compressor in their respective brackets.

37. Install the distributor and spark plug wires. Install the external coil, if equipped.

38. Install the radiator, fan and fan shroud, radiator hoses and heater hoses.

39. Connect the cooling fan electrical connectors.

40. Install the plenum extension, if equipped. Connect the throttle cable.

41. Fill the cooling system with the proper type and quantity of coolant and the crankcase with the proper type of oil to the correct level.

42. Install the air cleaner and the hood.

43. Connect the negative battery cable to the engine block, install the serpentine belt and tighten the fuel filler cap.

44. Connect the negative battery and check all fluids. Start the engine, check for leaks and check timing.

Engine Mounts

REMOVAL & INSTALLATION

2.8L and 3.1L Engines

1. Disconnect the negative battery cable. Raise and support the vehicle safely.

2. Remove the engine mount through bolts and nuts.

3. Using a suitable engine lift, safely raise the front of the engine and remove the engine mount bolts, nuts and washers from the crossmember.

NOTE: Raise the engine only enough for sufficient clearance. Check for interference between the rear of the engine and the cowl panel which could cause distributor damage.

4. Remove the engine mount.
To install:

5. Install the engine bracket and mount. Tighten the crossmember-to-mount bolts to 30 ft. lbs. (41 Nm).

6. Carefully lower the engine and install the mount through bolts and nuts. Tighten the engine mount through bolt nuts to 50 ft. lbs. (68 Nm).

7. Connect the negative battery cable.

3.8L Engine

1. Disconnect the negative battery cable.

2. Raise and safely support the vehicle.

3. Support the weight of the engine at the forward edge of the oil pan.

4. Remove the mount to cylinder block bolts.

5. Raise the engine slightly and remove the mount to mount bracket bolt and nut. Remove the engine mount.

6. Installation is the reverse of the removal procedure. Tighten the mount to cylinder block bolts to 59 ft. lbs. (80 Nm) and the bolt and nut to 48 ft. lbs. (65 Nm).

5.0L and 5.7L Engines

1. Disconnect the negative battery cable.

2. Raise and support the vehicle safely.

3. Support the engine with a suitable jack to unload the engine mount. Remove the engine mount retaining bolt from below the frame mounting bracket.

NOTE: Do not use a jack under the oil pan, crankshaft pulley or any sheet metal when supporting the engine. Due to the small clearance between the oil pan and the oil pump screen, jacking against the oil pan may cause it to be bent against the pump screen, resulting in a damaged oil pickup.

4. Using a suitable engine lift, raise the front of the engine and remove the engine mount and bracket bolts and nuts. Remove the engine mount.

NOTE: Raise the engine only enough for sufficient clearance. Check for interference between the rear of the engine and the cowl panel which could cause distributor damage.

To install:

5. Install the bracket to the block and the mount to the crossmember. Tighten the mount and bracket bolts to 38 ft. lbs. (52 Nm) and the mount and bracket nuts to 30 ft. lbs. (41 Nm).

6. Carefully lower the engine and install the bracket through bolts. Tighten the through bolt nut to 50 ft. lbs. (68 Nm).

7. Lower the vehicle and connect the negative battery cable.

Cylinder Head

REMOVAL & INSTALLATION

2.8L and 3.1L Engines

1. Disconnect the negative battery cable.

2. Relieve the fuel system pressure and drain the engine coolant from the radiator into a suitable container.

3. Remove the intake manifold, the spark plugs and the dipstick tube with bracket.

4. Raise and support the vehicle safely. Drain the oil and remove the oil filter. Lower the vehicle.

5. Remove the exhaust manifold.

6. Remove the serpentine drive belt. Remove the air conditioning compressor with bracket and lay aside.

7. Remove the power steering pump with bracket and/or the alternator with bracket and lay aside.

8. Remove the ground cable from the rear of the cylinder head and, if equipped, remove the engine lift bracket.

9. Loosen the rocker arms and remove the pushrods.

10. Remove the cylinder head bolts and remove the cylinder heads.

To install:

11. Clean the gasket mating surfaces of all components. Be careful not to nick or scratch any surfaces as this will allow leak paths. Clean the bolt threads in the cylinder block and on the head bolts. Dirt will affect bolt torque.

12. Place the head gaskets in position over the dowel pins, with the note "This Side Up" showing.

13. Install the cylinder heads.

14. Coat the cylinder head bolts threads with GM sealer 1052080 or equivalent, and install the bolts. Tighten the bolts in the proper sequence. Tighten the head bolts in 2 steps, first tighten to 40 ft. lbs. (55 Nm), then turn each bolt in sequence an additional ¼ turn (90 degrees).

15. Install the pushrods and loosely retain them with the rocker arms. Make sure the lower ends of the pushrods are in the lifter seats.

16. Install the power steering pump bracket with pump, the air conditioning compressor bracket with compressor and/or the alternator with bracket.

17. Install the ground cable to the rear of the cylinder head, and if equipped, the engine lift bracket.

18. Install the exhaust manifold.

19. Install the dipstick tube and bracket.

20. Adjust the valve lash.

21. Install the intake manifold.

22. Install the serpentine drive belt.

23. Install the spark plugs.

24. Fill the cooling system with the

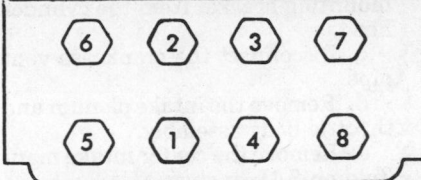

Cylinder head bolt torque sequence—
2.8L and 3.1L engines

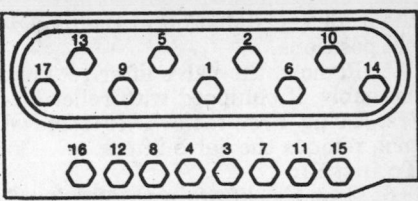

Cylinder head bolt torque sequence—
5.0L and 5.7L engines

proper type and quantity of coolant. Install a new oil filter and fill the crankcase with the proper type and quantity of oil.

25. Connect the negative battery cable, tighten the fuel filler cap, start the vehicle and check for leaks.

3.8L Engine

1. Disconnect the negative battery cable. Drain the cooling system and relieve the fuel system pressure.

2. Raise and support the vehicle safely. Drain the engine oil and remove the oil filter. Lower the vehicle.

3. Remove the accessory drive belt.

4. If removing the right cylinder head, remove the air conditioning compressor with the hoses attached, the alternator and the alternator bracket.

5. If removing the left cylinder head, remove the oil level indicator, power steering pump with the hoses connected and the power steering pump mounting bracket.

6. Remove the spark plug wires and the exhaust manifolds.

7. Remove the intake manifold, valve covers, rocker arm shafts, pushrods, cylinder head bolts and the cylinder heads.

To install:

8. Clean the gasket mating surfaces of all components. Be careful not to nick or scratch any surfaces at this will allow leak paths. Clean the bolt threads in the cylinder block and on the head bolts. Dirt will affect bolt torque.

9. Install the cylinder head gasket on the block and install the cylinder head.

10. Coat the head bolt threads with a suitable thread sealer and install. Tighten the head bolt in 3 steps as follows:

    a. Tighten in sequence to 25 ft. lbs. (34 Nm).

    b. Tighten in sequence an additional ¼ turn (90 degrees).

    c. Tighten in sequence an additional ¼ turn (90 degrees).

NOTE: If 60 ft. lbs. (81 Nm) is reached at any time in Steps b and c, stop at this point. Do not complete the balance of the 90 degree turn.

11. Install the exhaust manifolds, pushrods, rocker arm shaft, intake manifold, valve cover and spark plug wires.

12. When installing the right side cylinder head: install the alternator and it's mounting bracket and the air conditioning.

13. When installing the left side cylinder head: install the power steering pump and it's mounting bracket and the oil level indicator.

14. Install the accessory drive belt and fill the cooling system with the proper type and quantity of coolant.

15. Raise and safely support the vehicle. Install a new oil filter. Lower the vehicle and fill the crankcase with the proper type and quantity of engine oil.

16. Connect the negative battery cable, start the vehicle and check for leaks.

5.0L and 5.7L Engines

1. Disconnect the negative battery cable.

2. Drain the cooling system and relieve the fuel system pressure.

3. Remove the serpentine drive belt and the intake manifold.

4. Remove the power steering pump and alternator bracket or the air conditioning compressor mounting bracket, as necessary.

5. Remove the exhaust manifolds, the valve rocker covers and the ground strap.

6. Remove the rocker arms and pushrods.

7. Remove the diverter valve, if equipped.

8. Remove the cylinder head bolts, cylinder head and gasket.

To install:

9. Clean the gasket mating surfaces of all components. Be careful not to nick or scratch any surfaces as this will allow leak paths. Clean the bolt threads in the cylinder block and on the head bolts. Dirt will affect bolt torque.

NOTE: When using a steel gasket, coat both sides of the new gasket with a thin even coat of sealer.

If using a composition gasket, do not use any sealer.

10. Position the head gasket over the dowel pins with the head up. Install the cylinder head over the dowel pins and gasket.

11. Coat the threads of the head bolts with GM 1052080 thread sealer or equivalent. Install the head bolts and tighten in sequence to 68 ft. lbs. (92 Nm).

12. Install the exhaust manifolds.

13. Install the pushrods and rocker arms and adjust the valve lash. Install the valve covers.

14. Install the power steering pump and alternator bracket or air conditioning compressor mounting bracket, as necessary.

15. Connect the ground strap to the rear of the cylinder head.

16. Install the intake manifold and the serpentine drive belt.

17. Fill the cooling system with the proper type and amount of coolant.

18. Connect the negative battery cable and check fluid levels.

19. Start the engine, check for leaks and check the ignition timing.

Valve Lifters

REMOVAL & INSTALLATION

1. Disconnect the negative battery cable.

2. Drain the cooling system and relieve the fuel system pressure.

3. Remove the intake manifold assembly. Remove the valve rocker covers.

4. Remove the pushrods and rocker arms or rocker shafts, and arrange

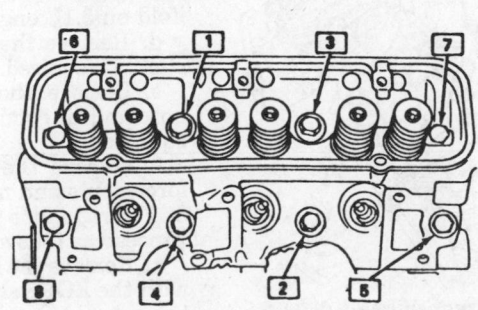

Cylinder head bolt torque sequence—3.8L engine

them for reinstallation in their original positions.

5. Remove the valve lifter retainer assembly, if equipped with roller lifters. Using a suitable lifter removal tool, remove the valve lifters.

To install:

6. Coat the lifters with Molykote® or its equivalent before installation. If installing the old lifters, make certain each lifter is inserted into the same lifter bore from which it was removed.

7. Install the valve lifter retainer assembly, if equipped, and the rocker arm/pushrod assemblies.

8. Install the intake manifold assembly.

9. Adjust the valve lash as necessary and install the valve rocker covers.

10. Fill the cooling system with proper type and amount of engine coolant.

11. Connect the negative battery cable, tighten the fuel filler cap, start the engine and check for leaks. Adjust the timing as necessary.

Valve Lash

ADJUSTMENT

3.8L Engine

Valve adjustment is not required, torque the rocker arms bolts to 28 ft. lbs. (38 Nm).

Except 3.8L Engine

1. Remove the valve covers.
2. Back each rocker arm nut until lash is felt at the pushrod.
3. Adjust the valves when the lifter is on the base circle of the camshaft lobe by cranking or slowly turning the engine until the mark on the vibration damper lines up with the center or 0 mark on the timing tab fastened to the crankcase front cover and the engine is in the No. 1 TDC firing position.

NOTE: The No. 1 TDC firing po-

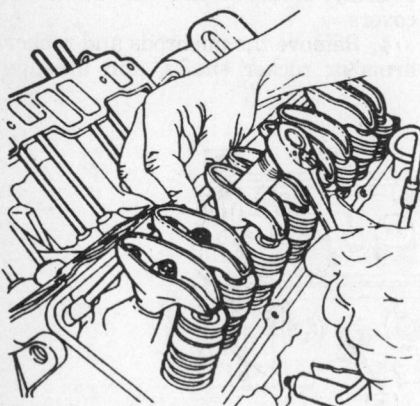

Valve adjustment procedure—5.0L and 5.7L engines

sition may be determined by placing a finger on the No. 1 valve as the mark on the damper comes near the 0 mark on the crankcase front cover. If the valves move as the mark comes up to the timing tab, the engine is in the No. 6 position on the V8 engine or No. 4 position on the V6 engine and should be turned 1 full turn to reach to No. 1 firing position.

4. With the engine in the No. 1 firing position, adjust the following valves:
   a. V8 engine—Exhaust—1, 3, 4, 8
   b. V8 engine—Intake—1, 2, 5, 7
   c. V6 engine—Exhaust—1, 5, 6
   d. V6 engine—Intake—1, 2, 3

5. Adjust the valve by turning in the adjusting nut until all lash is removed. This can be determined by rotating pushrod while turning adjusting nut. When play has been removed, turn adjusting nut down 1 full additional turn.

6. Crank or turn the engine 1 revolution until the pointer 0 mark and the vibration damper mark are again in alignment. This is the No. 6 position on the V8 engine or No. 4 position on the V6 engine.

7. With the engine in this position, adjust the following valves:
   a. V8 engine—Exhaust—2, 5, 6, 7
   b. V8 engine—Intake—3, 4, 6, 8
   c. V6 engine—Exhaust—2, 3, 4
   d. V6 engine—Intake—4, 5, 6

8. Install the valve covers.

9. Start the engine and adjust the idle speed as required.

Rocker Arms/Shafts

REMOVAL & INSTALLATION

2.8L and 3.1L Engines

1. Disconnect the negative battery cable.
2. For left side valve cover removal proceed as follows:
   a. Remove the accessory drive belt.
   b. Remove the intake plenum and throttle body assembly.
   c. Remove the center intake manifold on 3.1L engines.
   d. Remove the transmission dipstick, if required.
   e. Remove the air management hose and air conditioning bracket, if equipped.
   f. Remove the valve cover reinforcements and nuts.
3. For right side valve cover removal proceed as follows:
   a. Remove the EGR valve adapter with the EGR valve and shield from the exhaust manifold.
   b. Remove the coil and coil

mounting bracket from the cylinder head.
   c. Disconnect the crankcase vent pipe.
   d. Remove the intake plenum and throttle body assembly.
   e. Remove the center intake manifold on 3.1L engines.
   f. Disconnect the spark plug wire clips, if applicable.
   g. Remove the valve cover reinforcements and nuts.
4. Remove the valve cover by hand. Only if necessary, carefully pry until loose being careful not to distort the sealing flange.
5. Remove the rocker arm nuts, rocker arm balls, rocker arms and pushrods. Place the components in a rack for installation in the same location.

To install:

6. Install the pushrods and rocker arm assemblies in their original positions and adjust as necessary. If new rocker arms and/or balls are being used, coat bearing surfaces with Molykote® or its equivalent.

7. Carefully clean all gasket mating surfaces and make sure the valve cover flanges are not bent.

8. Place a ⅛ inch bead of RTV sealant 1052751 or equivalent at the intake manifold and cylinder head splitline. Install the new valve cover gasket over the studs in the manifold and cylinder head.

9. Install the valve covers, reinforcements and nuts. Tighten the nuts to 10 ft. lbs. or 120 inch lbs. (14 Nm).

10. Install components to the valve cover in reverse order of removal, as applicable.

11. Connect the negative battery cable.

3.8L Engine

1. Disconnect the negative battery cable.
2. Remove the valve cover as follows:
   a. Remove the PCV pipe to the air cleaner, all necessary computer command control hoses wire connectors and the hot air tube.
   b. Remove the spark plug wires and the accessory mounting brackets, as required.
   c. Remove the valve cover attaching bolts and remove the valve cover.
3. Remove the rocker arm shaft retaining bolts and the rocker arm shaft.
4. If the rocker arms are being replaced, remove the nylon rocker arm retainers and discard. Install the replacement rocker arm using a new nylon retainer. Install the nylon retainers with a suitable drift of least ½ inch diameter.

NOTE: Service rocker arms are stamped (R) for right and (L) for left. Ensure the rocker arms are installed on the rocker shaft in the correct sequence.

5. Installation is the reverse of the removal procedure. Ensure all gasket mating surfaces are clean before installation. Tighten the rocker arm shaft retaining bolts to 25 ft. lbs. (35 Nm).

5.0L and 5.7L Engines

1. Disconnect the negative battery cable.
2. Remove the air cleaner, if necessary.
3. To remove the right side valve rocker cover, perform the following:
   a. Remove the EGR pipe assembly, if necessary.
   b. Disconnect the electrical connections and wiring harnesses as necessary.
   c. Disconnect the spark plug wires from the distributor.
   d. Remove the crankcase vent hoses and valves.
   e. Remove the coil and disconnect the heater hose from the throttle body, if applicable.
   f. Remove the AIR control valve, check valve, pipes and hoses.
   g. Remove the valve rocker cover bolts, washers and the valve rocker cover. Discard the old gasket.
4. To remove the left side valve rocker cover, perform the following:
   a. Disconnect the electrical connections and the wiring harnesses, as necessary.
   b. Remove the alternator and disconnect the crankcase hoses and the PCV valve.
   c. Remove the valve rocker cover bolts, washers and the valve rocker cover. Discard the old gasket.
5. Remove the rocker arm balls, arms and pushrods. Place them in a rack so they may be reinstalled in the same location.
To install:
6. Install the pushrods and rocker arm assemblies in their original positions and adjust as necessary. If new rocker arms and/or balls are being used, coat bearing surfaces with Molykote® or its equivalent.
7. Carefully clean all gasket mating surfaces and make sure the valve cover flanges are not bent.
8. Install the new valve rocker cover gasket to the cylinder head.
9. Install the valve rocker covers, washers and bolts. Tighten the bolts to 96 inch lbs. (11 Nm) for 1991–93 engines or 89 inch lbs. (10 Nm) for 1989 engines.
10. Install components to the valve rocker cover in reverse order of removal, as applicable.
11. Connect the negative battery cable.

Intake Manifold

REMOVAL & INSTALLATION

2.8L and 3.1L Engines

1. Disconnect the negative battery cable.
2. Drain the cooling system and relieve the fuel system pressure.
3. Disconnect the air inlet duct at the throttle body and the crankcase vent pipe at the valve cover grommet.
4. Disconnect the vacuum harness connector from the throttle body.
5. Remove the throttle cable bracket bolt, the throttle body attaching bolts and remove the throttle body. Discard the throttle body gasket.
6. Remove the EGR transfer tube to plenum bolts and remove the EGR transfer tube. Discard the EGR transfer tube gasket.
7. Remove the air conditioning compressor to plenum bracket attaching hardware and the bracket.
8. Remove the plenum bolts/studs and the plenum. Discard the plenum gaskets.
9. Disconnect the fuel feed and return lines at the fuel rail. Discard the fuel line O-rings.
10. Disconnect the vacuum line at the pressure regulator and the injector electrical connectors.
11. Remove the fuel rail attaching bolts and the fuel rail assembly.
12. Remove the spark plug wires and the distributor cap. Mark the distributor position and remove the hold-down bracket and the distributor.
13. Remove the air management hose and bracket, if equipped.

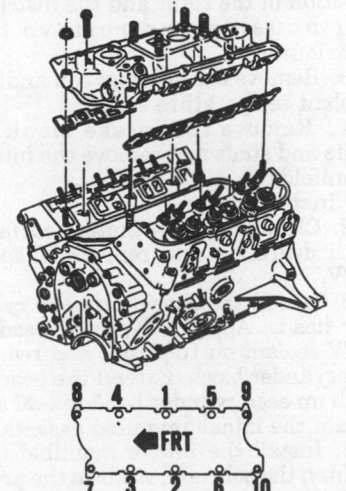

Intake manifold bolt tightening sequence—2.8L and 3.1L engines

14. Disconnect the emission canister hoses.
15. Remove the valve covers.
16. Remove the upper radiator hose at the manifold and disconnect the heater hose.
17. Disconnect the coolant switch sensors. Remove the transmission dipstick.
18. Remove the center intake manifold bolts and the center intake manifold. Remove and discard the gasket.
19. Remove the intake manifold bolts and the intake manifold. Remove and discard the gasket.

To install:
20. Ensure all gasket mating surfaces are clean and free of oil or water prior to installation.
21. Place a $\frac{3}{16}$ inch diameter bead of RTV sealer on each ridge. Install new gaskets on the cylinder heads and hold in place by extending the ridge RTV bead up ¼ inch onto the gasket ends. The new gaskets will have to be cut, where indicated, to install behind the pushrods. Cut only those areas that are necessary.
22. Install the intake manifold on the engine. Make sure the areas between the case ridges and intake are completely sealed.
23. Install the intake manifold retaining bolts and nuts and torque to 13–25 ft. lbs. (18–34 Nm) in the proper sequence on 1989 vehicles or to 19 ft. lbs. (26 Nm) for 1990–93 vehicles.
24. Install the center intake manifold and new gasket. Tighten bolts to 15 ft. lbs. (21 Nm).
25. Install the upper radiator hose and the valve covers and connect the heater hose and the coolant switch sensors.
26. Install the distributor, distributor cap and spark plug wires. Install the air management hose and bracket, if equipped.
27. Install the fuel rail assembly in the intake manifold. Tighten the attaching bolts to 18 ft. lbs. (25 Nm). Connect the injector electrical connectors and the vacuum line to the pressure regulator.
28. Install new O-rings on the fuel feed and return lines and connect the lines to the fuel rail. Tighten the fuel line nuts to 20 ft. lbs. (27 Nm).
29. Temporarily connect the negative battery cable. With the engine **OFF** and the ignition **ON**, check for fuel leaks. Disconnect the negative battery cable.
30. Install the plenum with a new gasket and install the bolts/studs. Tighten to 15 ft. lbs. (21 Nm).
31. Install the air conditioning compressor to plenum bracket and attaching hardware. Install the EGR transfer tube with a new gasket. Tighten

the attaching bolts to 19 ft. lbs. (26 Nm).

32. Install the throttle body with a new gasket and tighten the retaining bolts to 20 ft. lbs. (27 Nm).

33. Install the throttle cable bracket bolts and connect the vacuum harness connector to the throttle body.

34. Connect the air inlet duct to the throttle body and the crankcase vent pipe to the valve cover grommet.

35. Install the transmission dipstick and connect the necessary wires and hoses.

36. Connect the negative battery cable.

37. Fill the cooling system with the proper type and amount of coolant. Do not install the radiator cap.

38. Let the engine run until the upper radiator hose becomes hot (thermostat open). With the engine idling, add coolant to the radiator, if necessary, until the level reaches the bottom of the filler neck. Install the radiator cap, making sure the arrows on the cap line with the overflow tube.

39. Check and adjust the timing as necessary.

3.8L Engine

1. Disconnect the negative battery cable.

2. Drain the cooling system and relieve the fuel system pressure.

3. Remove the air inlet tube.

4. Disconnect the fuel line at the fuel rail and at the pressure regulator.

5. Disconnect the injector wiring harness connectors located just behind the coil.

6. Disconnect the coolant temperature sensor wire connectors located at the front of the manifold.

7. Disconnect the heater, bypass and upper radiator hoses, the vacuum lines and hoses from the EGR, fuel pressure regulator and PCV valve and the throttle, cruise control and TV cables from the throttle body.

8. Remove the EGR vacuum control valve and the ignition wires from the spark plugs.

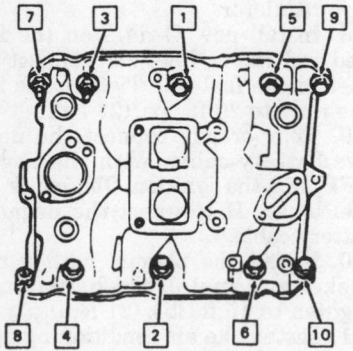

Intake manifold bolt tightening sequence – 3.8L engine

9. Remove the lower right side turbo mounting bracket to intake and bracket support to plenum. Remove the intake manifold bolts and remove the intake manifold.

10. Installation is the reverse of the removal procedure. Ensure all gasket mating surfaces are clean prior to installation. Torque the intake manifold bolts to 44 ft. lbs. (60 Nm) in the proper sequence.

5.0L TBI Engine

1. Disconnect the negative battery cable.

2. Drain the radiator, relieve the fuel system pressure and remove the air cleaner.

3. Disconnect the electrical connectors to the IAC valve, TPS and fuel injectors. Remove the injector wiring harness. Tag and disconnect the vacuum hoses, remove the vacuum hose bracket. Disconnect all wires and hoses as necessary.

4. Disconnect the throttle, transmission control and cruise control cables. Disconnect the fuel feed and return lines and discard the O-rings.

5. Remove the TBI unit attaching bolts and remove the TBI unit. Discard the old gasket.

6. Disconnect the ECM engine control harness and lay aside. Disconnect the upper radiator hose and heater hose at the manifold. Remove the EGR valve and solenoid and remove the thermostat housing and gasket.

7. Disconnect the fuel line clips and lines at the cylinder head and intake manifold. Disconnect the power brake vacuum pipe at the manifold.

8. Disconnect the throttle cable bracket.

9. Disconnect and tag the spark plug wires at the distributor cap and remove the distributor cap. Mark the position of the rotor and the distributor housing and remove the distributor.

10. Remove the external coil and the coolant temperature sensor.

11. Remove the intake manifold bolts and studs and remove the intake manifold.

To install:

12. Clean all gasket mating surfaces with degreaser and remove all loose RTV.

13. Install the gaskets on the cylinder heads. Apply a $\frac{3}{16}$ inch bead of RTV sealant on the front and rear of the cylinder block. Extend the bead $\frac{1}{2}$ inch up each cylinder head to seal and retain the intake manifold gaskets.

14. Install the intake manifold and tighten the bolts and studs in the proper 2-step sequence in order to obtain proper seal. On the first pass tighten the bolts and studs to 89 inch lbs. (10

Nm). For the final pass, tighten the bolts and studs to 35 ft. lbs. (47 Nm).

15. Install the ECM engine control harness and the coolant temperature sensor.

16. Align the rotor with the mark and install the distributor. Temporarily tighten the hold down clamp retaining bolt. Install the distributor cap, coil and spark plug wires.

17. Install the throttle cable bracket. Connect the fuel line clips and lines to the cylinder head and intake manifold. Connect the power brake vacuum pipe at the manifold.

18. Connect any remaining wires and hoses. Install the EGR valve and solenoid, the thermostat, housing and gasket, and the heater and radiator hoses.

19. Install the throttle body unit and a new gasket. Tighten the TBI attaching bolts to 16 ft. lbs. (22 Nm).

20. Install new O-rings on the fuel lines and connect the fuel feed and return lines. Tighten the fuel line nuts to 20 ft. lbs. (27 Nm). Connect the vacuum hoses and bracket.

21. Connect the throttle, transmission control and cruise control cables, as applicable. Make sure the throttle and cruise control cables do not hold the throttle open.

22. Connect the injectors wiring harness. Connect any remaining electrical connectors.

23. Add the proper type and amount of engine coolant, tighten the fuel filler cap and connect the negative battery cable.

24. Start the engine, check for leaks, check and adjust timing as necessary. If no timing adjustment is necessary, make sure the hold down clamp retaining bolt is tightened to specification.

5.0L and 5.7L TPI Engines

1. Disconnect the negative battery cable.

2. Drain the cooling system and relieve the fuel system pressure.

3. Disconnect the accelerator, TV and cruise control cables.

4. Remove the air intake duct.

5. Disconnect the heater hoses at the throttle body.

6. Disconnect the electrical connections at the throttle body and the intake manifold.

7. Disconnect the vacuum hoses and vent valve assembly.

8. Disconnect the fuel lines.

9. Disconnect the vapor pipe assembly.

10. Remove the plenum extension.

11. Remove the spark plug wires from the distributor cap. Mark the position of the rotor and the distributor housing and remove the distributor.

12. Remove the throttle body attach-

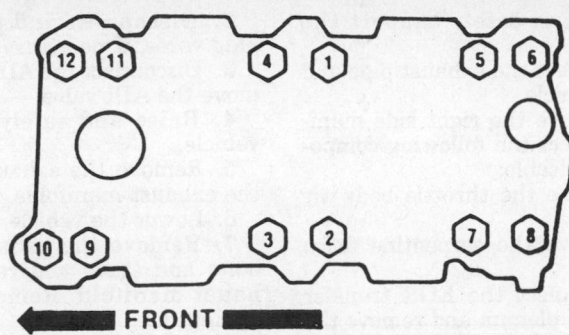

Intake manifold bolt tightening sequence—V8 engines

ing bolts and remove the throttle body. Discard the old gasket.

13. Disconnect the wiring harness from the fuel injectors and remove the harness from the manifold.

14. Disconnect the power brake vacuum hose at the plenum.

15. Remove the intake plenum bolts and disconnect the Manifold Absolute Pressure (MAP) sensor, if equipped.

16. Lift the plenum and disconnect the Manifold Air Temperature (MAT) sensor electrical connector, if equipped.

17. Remove the plenum and discard the plenum gaskets.

18. Remove the runner to manifold bolts, PCV valve and hose, EGR solenoid and the left and right side runners and gaskets. Discard the gaskets.

19. Remove the upper radiator hose.

Remove the fuel tube bracket bolt. Disconnect the fuel feed and return lines. Discard the fuel line O-rings..

21. Disconnect the vacuum line at the pressure regulator.

22. Remove the fuel rail attaching bolts and the fuel rail assembly.

23. Remove the ignition coil.

24. Remove the intake manifold bolts and studs and remove the intake manifold.

To install:

25. Clean gasket mating surfaces on the intake manifold, block and cylinder head with engine degreaser.

26. Install the intake manifold gaskets. Apply a $^3/_{16}$ inch bead of RTV sealant to the front and rear ridges of the cylinder case. Extend the RTV bead ½ inch up each cylinder head to

seal and retain the intake manifold gaskets.

27. Install the intake manifold and tighten the bolts and studs in the proper 2-step sequence in order to obtain proper seal. On the first pass tighten the bolts and studs to 89 inch lbs. (10 Nm). For the final pass, tighten the bolts and studs to 35 ft. lbs. (47 Nm).

28. Connect the electrical wires and the upper radiator hose.

29. Install the EGR valve and pipe and the ignition coil and EGR solenoid.

30. Lubricate new injector O-ring seals with engine oil and install on the injector.

NOTE: There are 2 injector part numbers used in production for the 5.0L engine and 2 different part numbers for the 5.7L engine. If replacing injectors, do not intermix injectors with different part numbers, as this will result in engine roughness and excessive emissions.

31. Install a new retainer clip onto the injector and install the injector into the fuel rail injector socket, with the electrical connector facing outward. Rotate the injector retainer clip to the locking position.

32. Install the fuel rail assembly in the intake manifold. Install the attaching bolts to 15 ft. lbs. (20 Nm). Install

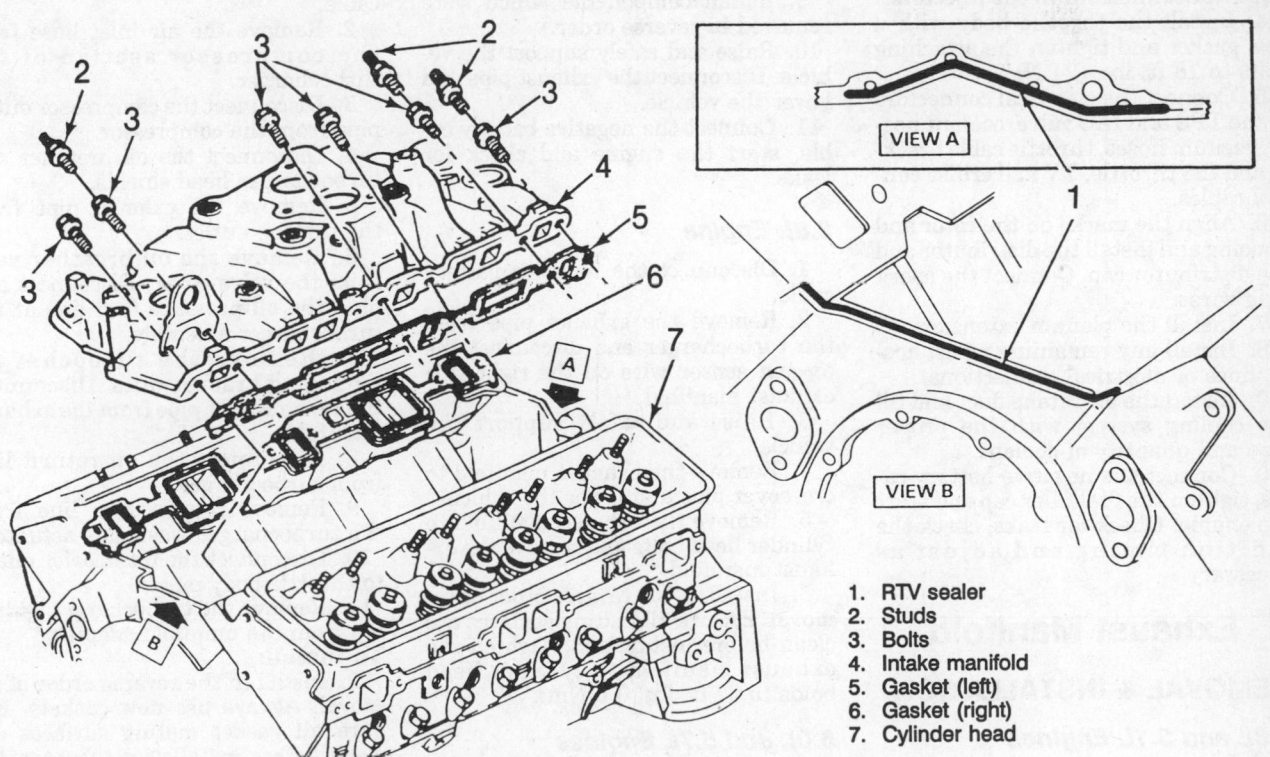

1. RTV sealer
2. Studs
3. Bolts
4. Intake manifold
5. Gasket (left)
6. Gasket (right)
7. Cylinder head

Intake manifold, bolt and gasket installation—V8 engines

the fuel tube bracket bolt and tighten to 25 ft. lbs. (34 Nm).

33. Connect the vacuum line to the pressure regulator.

34. Install new O-rings on the fuel feed and return lines and connect the fuel lines to the fuel rail. Tighten the fuel line nuts to 20 ft. lbs. (27 Nm).

35. Temporarily connect the negative battery cable. Turn the ignition switch **ON** for 2 seconds and then **OFF**. Again turn to the **ON** position and check for fuel leaks and turn the ignition **OFF**. Disconnect the negative battery cable.

36. Install new gaskets on the runners and manifold.

37. Install new gaskets, the runners and manifold to runner bolts to the intake manifold. Tighten the bolts to 25 ft. lbs. (34 Nm).

38. Install the right and left runner to manifold bolts finger tight only.

39. Support the plenum above the runners, connect the MAT sensor electrical connector, if equipped and lower the plenum into position. Start a few bolts to hold the plenum in position.

40. Connect the vacuum hoses and MAP sensor, if equipped.

41. Tighten all bolts to 25 ft. lbs. (34 Nm), starting in the center of the plenum/manifold and working outward.

42. Install the PCV valve and hose.

43. Connect the power brake vacuum hose to the fitting on the plenum, the left and right injector electrical harnesses, the attaching nuts and the electrical connectors to the injectors.

44. Install the throttle body with a new gasket and tighten the attaching bolts to 18 ft. lbs. (24 Nm).

45. Connect the electrical connectors to the TPS and IAC valve, coolant hoses, vacuum hoses, throttle cable bracket and the throttle, TV and cruise control cables.

46. Align the marks on the rotor and housing and install the distributor and the distributor cap. Connect the spark plug wires.

47. Install the plenum extension.

48. Install any remaining pipes, hoses, lines or electrical connections.

49. Install the air intake duct and fill the cooling system with the proper type and quantity of coolant.

50. Connect the negative battery cable, tighten the fuel filler cap and start the engine. Check for leaks, check the ignition timing and adjust as necessary.

Exhaust Manifold

REMOVAL & INSTALLATION

2.8L and 3.1L Engines

1. Disconnect the negative battery cable.

2. Raise and safely support the vehicle.

3. Disconnect the exhaust pipe and lower the vehicle.

4. To remove the right side manifold, disconnect the following components as applicable:

a. Remove the throttle body air duct.

b. Remove the serpentine drive belt.

c. Disconnect the EGR transfer tube at the plenum and remove the EGR valve adapter with the EGR valve and shield from the exhaust manifold.

d. Disconnect the vacuum line and the electrical connector from the diverter valve.

e. Remove the AIR pump bolt and AIR pump with diverter valve from the lower bracket. Remove the AIR pipe from the exhaust manifold.

f. Reomove the alternator brace nuts, bolts and brace.

5. To remove the left side manifold, remove the rear power steering pump bracket.

6. Remove the exhaust manifold bolts and nuts and remove the exhaust manifold.

To install:

7. Ensure all mating surfaces are clean before installation.

8. Position the exhaust manifold and install the manifold bolts and nuts. Tighten the exhaust manifold bolts and nuts to 25 ft. lbs. (34 Nm).

9. Install components which were removed in reverse order.

10. Raise and safely support the vehicle. Disconnect the exhaust pipe and lower the vehicle.

11. Connect the negative battery cable, start the engine and check for leaks.

3.8L Engine

1. Disconnect the negative battery cable.

2. Remove the exhaust pipe from the turbocharger and disconnect the oxygen sensor wire on the right side exhaust manifold.

3. Raise and safely support the vehicle.

4. Remove the exhaust manifold to crossover pipe and lower the vehicle.

5. Remove the exhaust manifold to cylinder head bolts and remove the exhaust manifold.

6. Install in the reverse order of removal. Ensure all mating surfaces are clean before installation. Tighten the exhaust manifold to cylinder head bolds to 37 ft. lbs. (50 Nm).

5.0L and 5.7L Engines

1. Disconnect the negative battery cable.

2. Disconnect and tag the spark plug wires, if necessary.

3. Disconnect the AIR pipes and remove the AIR valve.

4. Raise and safely support the vehicle.

5. Remove the exhaust pipes from the exhaust manifolds.

6. Lower the vehicle.

7. Remove the exhaust manifold bolts and studs and remove the exhaust manifold. Remove gasket, if equipped.

To install:

8. Make sure all mating surfaces are clean before installation. Install gasket, if equipped.

9. Install the exhaust manifold and Tighten the 4 outside exhaust manifold bolts and studs to 20 ft. lbs. (27 Nm) and the inside bolts to 26 ft. lbs. (35 Nm).

10. Raise and support the vehicle safely, connect the exhaust pipes, and lower the vehicle.

11. Install the AIR valve and connect the AIR pipes. If disconnected, reinstall the spark plug wires.

12. Connect the negative battery cable, start the engine and check for leaks.

Turbocharger

REMOVAL & INSTALLATION

1. Disconnect the negative battery cable.

2. Remove the air inlet hose from the compressor section of the turbocharger.

3. Disconnect the compressor outlet pipe from the compressor.

4. Disconnect the oil breather and turbocharger head shields.

5. Remove the exhaust pipe from the turbine outlet.

6. Remove the oil breather vent from the valve cover. Disconnect and plug the oil pressure feed line at the turbocharger assembly.

7. Remove the turbocharger mounting bracket nuts. Disconnect the turbine inlet pipe from the exhaust manifold.

8. Disconnect the oil return line from turbocharger.

9. Remove the vacuum line from the turbocharger wastegate actuator.

10. Disconnect the intercooler outlet to throttle body pipe.

11. Remove the turbocharger assembly from the manifold adapter.

To install:

12. Install in the reverse order of removal. Always use new gaskets. Ensure all gasket mating surfaces are clean before installation. Tighten the turbocharger bracket to cylinder head bolts to 37 ft. lbs. (50 Nm). Tighten the

turbocharger to bracket nuts to 20 ft. lbs. (27 Nm). Tighten the head shield retaining bolts to 20 ft. lbs. (27 Nm).

Timing Chain Front Cover

REMOVAL & INSTALLATION

2.8L and 3.1L Engines

1. Disconnect the negative battery cable.

2. Drain the cooling system into a suitable container and remove the serpentine drive belt. Disconnect the lower radiator hose at the front cover and heater hose at the water pump.

3. Raise and safely support the vehicle.

4. Drain the crankcase and remove the oil pan.

5. Lower the vehicle.

6. Remove the power steering pump with bracket and lay aside. Remove the power steering pump bracket.

7. Remove the water pump assembly.

8. Remove the vibration damper drive pulley and the damper retaining bolt. Using a suitable puller, remove the vibration damper.

9. Remove the front cover bolts and remove the front cover. Remove and discard the old gasket.

To install:

10. Ensure all gasket mating surfaces are clean before installation. Install a new gasket and the engine front cover. Tighten the front cover bolts to 15 ft. lbs. (21 Nm).

11. Install a vibration damper mounting tool onto the end of the crankshaft so at least 0.2 inch of thread engagement is obtained. Pull the vibration damper into position with the tool.

12. Install the drive pulley and the damper retaining bolt. Tighten the damper retaining bolt to 70 ft. lbs. (95 Nm).

13. Install the water pump assembly and the lower radiator hose.

14. Install the power steering pump with bracket.

15. Raise and support the vehicle safely. Install the oil pan, replacing gasket if necessary.

16. Lower the vehicles and add proper type and amount of engine oil.

17. Connect the negative battery cable and add engine coolant. Start engine and check for leaks.

3.8L Engine

1. Disconnect the negative battery cable.

2. Drain the radiator.

3. Disconnect the radiator hoses

and the heater return hose at the water pump.

4. Remove the fan assembly and pulleys.

5. Remove the crankshaft vibration damper.

6. Remove the alternator.

7. Remove the distributor, if equipped. If timing chain and sprockets are not going to be disturbed, note position of distributor rotor for reinstallation in same position.

8. Loosen and slide front clamp on thermostat bypass hose rearward.

9. Remove bolts attaching timing chain cover to cylinder block.

10. Remove 2 oil pan to timing chain cover bolts.

11. Remove timing chain cover assembly and gasket.

To install:

12. Thoroughly clean the cover, taking care not to damage to the gasket surface.

13. Installation is the reverse of the removal procedure.

14. Remove oil pump cover and pack the space around the oil pump gears completely full of petroleum jelly. There must be no air space left inside the pump. Reinstall cover using new gasket.

15. Tighten the front cover retaining bolts to 22 ft. lbs. (30 Nm) and the vibration damper bolt to 200 ft. lbs. (270 Nm).

5.0L and 5.7L Engines

1. Disconnect the negative battery cable.

2. Drain the cooling system and remove the serpentine drive belt and pulleys.

3. Remove the water pump.

4. Remove the crankshaft pulley retaining bolts and pulley. Remove the vibration damper retaining bolt and remove the vibration damper using a suitable puller.

5. Raise and safely support the vehicle.

6. Drain the crankcase and remove the oil pan assembly.

7. Remove the front cover bolts and the timing cover. Remove and discard the old gasket.

To install:

8. Ensure all gasket mating surfaces are clean prior to installation.

9. Install a new gasket and, if necessary, a new seal. Align the front cover dowel pins and loosely install the upper cover attaching bolts.

10. Tighten the upper bolts alternately and evenly while pressing downward on the cover to align the dowels with the cover holes. Do not force the cover over the dowels to the point where the flange or dowels become distorted.

11. Install the remaining cover bolts

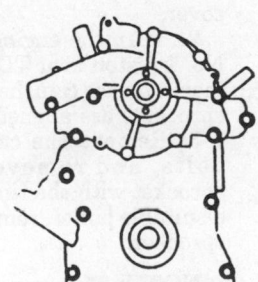

FRONT COVER BOLT LOCATION

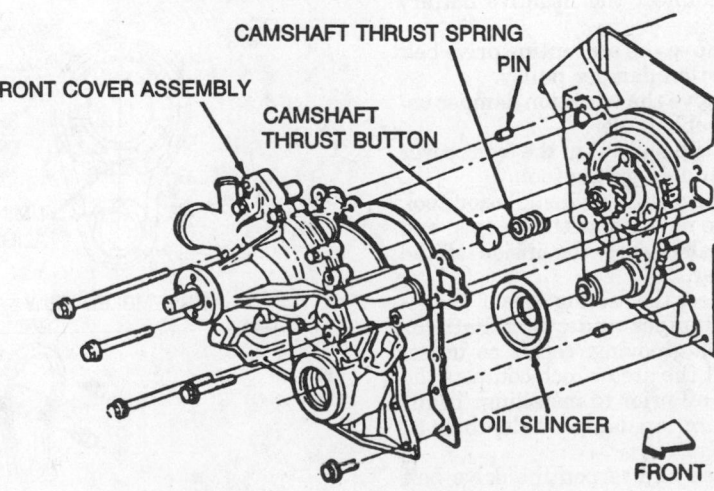

Timing chain front cover assembly—3.8L engine

and tighten the front cover bolts to 97 inch lbs. (11 Nm).

12. Coat the portion of the vibration damper which contacts the front cover seal with clean engine oil. Install a suitable damper installation tool fully onto the crankshaft end. Pull the damper into position using the installation tool.

13. Install the crankshaft pulley, the pulley retaining bolts and the vibration damper retaining bolt. Tighten the pulley bolts to 43 ft. lbs. (58 Nm) and the damper retaining bolt to 70 ft. lbs. (95 Nm).

14. Install the water pump.

15. Raise and safely support the vehicle. Install the oil pan assembly.

16. Lower the vehicle and add the proper type and amount of engine oil.

17. Connect the negative battery cable and add engine coolant. Start the engine and check for leaks.

Front Cover Oil Seal

REPLACEMENT

Except 3.8L Engine
FRONT COVER REMOVED

1. Using a suitable tool, pry the seal out from the front of the cover. Take care not to damage the cover while prying.

2. Using a suitable tool, install the new seal with the open end of the seal toward the inside of the front cover. Support the rear of the cover at the seal area while installing.

3. Inspect the sealing area of the vibration damper and crankshaft for damage or grooving, repair as necessary. Coat the area which contacts the seal with oil prior to installing. Tighten the vibration damper bolt to 70 ft. lbs. (95 Nm).

FRONT COVER INSTALLED

1. Disconnect the negative battery cable.

2. Remove the serpentine drive belt and vibration damper pulley.

3. Remove the vibration damper using a suitable puller.

4. Pry the seal out of the front cover with a suitable prying tool.

5. Using a suitable installation tool, install the new seal with the open end of the seal toward the inside of the front cover.

6. Inspect the sealing area of the vibration damper and crankshaft for damage or grooving, repair as necessary. Coat the area which contacts the seal with oil prior to installing. Tighten the vibration damper bolts to 70 ft. lbs. (95 Nm).

7. Install the serpentine drive belt and pulleys and connect the negative

battery cable. Start the engine and inspect for leaks.

3.8L Engine

1. Disconnect the negative battery cable.

2. Remove the front cover.

3. Use a suitable drift to drive out the old seal and shedder from the front toward the rear of the cover.

4. Coil new packing around the front cover opening so the ends of the packing are at the top.

5. Drive in the shedder using a suitable punch and stake the shedder in place at 3 locations.

6. Size the packing by rotating a suitable tool around the packing until the vibration damper hub can be inserted through the opening.

7. Installation is the reverse of the removal procedure. Inspect the sealing area of the vibration damper for damage or grooving and replace, as necessary. Coat the area which contacts the seal prior to installing. Tighten the vibration damper bolt to 200 ft. lbs. (270 Nm).

Timing Chain and Sprockets

REMOVAL & INSTALLATION

1. Disconnect the negative battery cable and remove the timing chain cover.

2. Turn the engine slowly until the No. 1 piston is at TDC and the timing marks on the camshaft and crankshaft sprockets are aligned.

3. Remove the camshaft sprocket bolts, and remove the camshaft sprocket with the timing chain. Using a suitable puller, remove the camshaft sprocket.

NOTE: The sprocket is a tight fit on the camshaft. If the sprock-

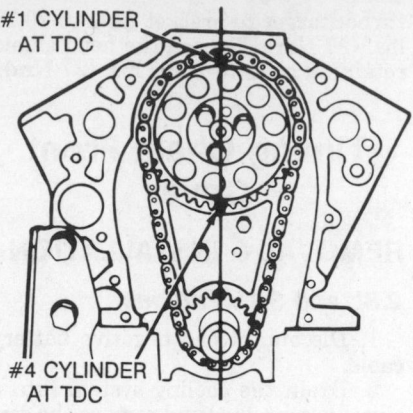

Timing mark alignment—2.8L and 3.1L engines

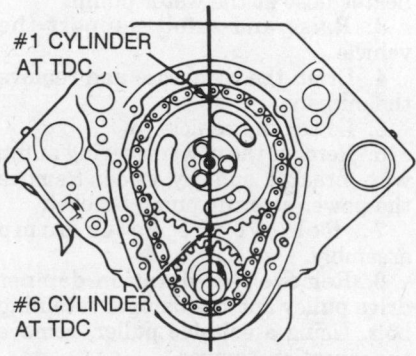

Timing mark alignment—5.0L and 5.7L engines

et does not come off easily, use a plastic mallet and strike the lower edge of the sprocket. This should dislodge the sprocket, allowing it to be removed from the shaft.

Once the timing chain has been removed, do not allow the crankshaft to turn or engine components may be damaged.

To install:

4. With the timing mark facing away from the engine, install the

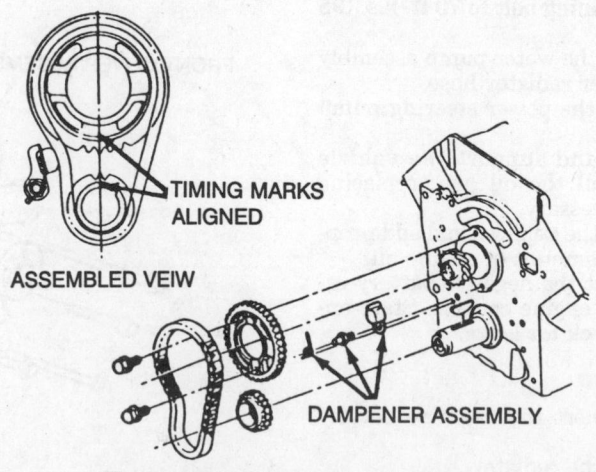

Timing mark alignment—3.8L engine

crankshaft sprocket using a suitable installation tool. Install the timing chain on the camshaft sprocket and lube the thrust surface with Molykote® or equivalent.

NOTE: The timing chains and sprockets should be replaced as an assembly. If a new chain or crankshaft sprocket is installed, replace the other parts as well.

5. Hold the sprocket vertically with the chain hanging down and align the marks on the camshaft and crankshaft sprockets.

6. Align the dowel in the camshaft with the dowel hole in the camshaft sprocket and install the sprocket on the camshaft.

7. Slowly and evenly draw the camshaft sprocket onto the camshaft using the mounting bolts and torque the bolts to 21 ft. lbs. (28 Nm) except 3.8L engine which is torqued to 31 ft. lbs. (42 Nm).

NOTE: Do not drive the sprocket onto the camshaft, this could cause the rear camshaft core plug to be dislodged.

8. Lubricate the timing chain with clean engine oil and install the timing chain cover.

9. Connect the negative battery cable and start the engine. Check and adjust the timing as necessary and inspect for leaks.

Camshaft

REMOVAL & INSTALLATION

2.8L and 3.1L EGNINES

1. Disconnect the negative battery cable. Relieve fuel pressure and drain the cooling system into a suitable container.

2. Remove the intake manifold and valve covers. Remove the rocker arm assemblies and pushrods.

3. Remove the valve lifters.

4. As required, remove the radiator, grille and air conditioning condenser.

5. Remove the front engine cover.

6. Remove the timing chain and sprockets. Carefully remove the camshaft.

To install:

7. Be sure to coat the camshaft lobes with GM EOS® or equivalent and the camshaft journals and lifters with clean engine oil before installation. It is recommended that all lifters be replaced to insure durability.

8. Carefully install the camshaft. Install the timing chain and sprockets.

9. Install the engine front cover. If removed, install the radiator, grille and/or air conditioning condenser.

10. Install the valve lifters, pushrods and rocker arm assemblies.

11. Install the intake manifold and valve covers.

12. Connect the negative battery cable, add engine coolant and tighten the fuel filler cap. Check and adjust engine timing as necessary.

3.8L Engine

1. Disconnect the negative battery cable, drain the cooling system, relieve the fuel system pressure and properly discharge the air conditioning system.

2. Remove the intake manifold.

3. Remove the valve covers.

4. Remove the rocker arm assemblies, pushrods and valve lifters, noting location.

5. Remove the radiator and the air condition condenser, as required.

6. Remove the timing chain cover, timing chain and sprocket.

7. Align the timing marks of camshaft and crankshaft sprocket. This avoids burring of the camshaft journals by the crankshaft during removal.

8. Slide the camshaft forward out of the engine carefully to avoid marring the bearing surfaces.

To install:

9. Reverse of the removal procedure to install.

10. Before installing the camshaft and the lifters, be sure to coat the camshaft lobes with Molykote® or equivalent, and the camshaft journals and lifters with clean engine oil.

11. Use new gaskets and seals, as required.

5.0L and 5.7L Engines

1. Disconnect the negative battery cable, relieve fuel pressure and drain the cooling system.

2. Remove the intake manifold, valve rocker covers, rocker arm assemblies and pushrods. Keep all parts in order for reinstallation.

3. Remove upper fan shroud and the serpentine drive belt. Remove all necessary wires and hoses.

4. Remove the radiator. Disconnect the transmission oil cooler lines.

5. Remove engine front cover and rotate the crankshaft slowly to align the timing marks. Remove the timing chain and the camshaft sprocket.

6. If necessary, purge the air conditioning system and remove the air conditioning condenser. Remove the grille supporting rods.

7. Remove the valve lifters.

8. Remove the camshaft retainer bolts and the camshaft retainer.

9. Install three $^5/_{16}$–18 x 4 inch bolts or equivalent, in the camshaft bolt holes and carefully pull the camshaft from the bearings. All camshaft are the same diameter and care must

be used to avoid damage to the bearings.

To install:

10. Lubricate the lobes of a new camshaft with Molykote®. Always lubricate the journals and lifters with a suitable engine oil, before installing the camshaft.

11. Carefully guide the camshaft into position and install the camshaft retainer. Tighten the retainer bolts to 106 inch lbs. (12 Nm).

12. Align the timing marks and install the timing chain and engine front cover assembly.

13. Install the valve lifters.

14. Install the grill support rods. Install and recharge the air conditioning condenser, if removed.

15. Install the radiator and the oil cooler lines.

16. Install the serpentine drive belt, all applicable hoses and the upper fan shroud.

17. Install the rocker arms and pushrods. Adjust as necessary.

18. Install the intake manifold and the valve rocker covers.

19. Connect any remaining wires and the negative battery cable.

20. Tighten the fuel filler cap and fill the cooling system with the proper type and amount of coolant.

Piston and Connecting Rod

POSITIONING

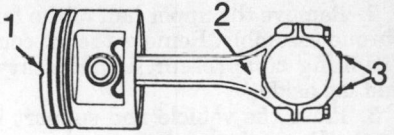

1. Notch on piston towards front of engine
2. Left bank: No. 1,3 and 5–2 bosses on rod towards rear of engine
   Right bank: No 2, 4 and 6–2 boses on rod towards front of engine
3. Left bank: Chamfered corners on rod cap towards front of engine
   Right bank: Chamfered corners on rod cap towars rear of engine

Piston and rod positioning—3.8L engine

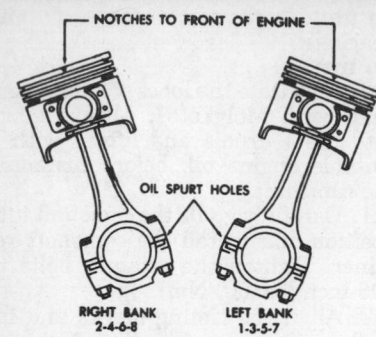

NOTCHES TO FRONT OF ENGINE

OIL SPURT HOLES

RIGHT BANK 2-4-6-8   LEFT BANK 1-3-5-7

Piston and rod notches facing forward— 5.0L and 5.7L engines

ENGINE LUBRICATION

Oil Pan

REMOVAL & INSTALLATION

1. Disconnect the negative battery cable. Remove the air cleaner assembly. Remove the plenum extension, if equipped. Remove the distributor cap and lay it aside.
2. Remove the upper half of the fan shroud assembly. Remove the air conditioning compressor, if necessary, and lay aside.
3. Raise the vehicle and support it safely. Drain the engine oil.
4. Remove the AIR hose at the catalytic convertor pipe and, if necessary the AIR pipe at the exhaust manifold. Remove the exhaust pipe at the manifolds.
5. Remove the torque converter dust shield. If equipped with manual transmission, it may be necessary to remove the oil filter in order to remove the dust shield. Disconnect the transmission oil cooler lines at the clips on the oil pan.
6. Remove the starter bolts, loosen the starter brace, then position the starter aside. If necessary, tag and disconnect the wires from the starter and remove the starter from the vehicle. On V8 engines, it may be necessary to remove the front starter brace.
7. Remove the engine mount through bolts.
8. Remove the oil pan nuts and

bolts, and if equipped, the reinforcement, retainers and brackets.
9. Lower the oil pan enough to determine whether the forward crankshaft throw and counterbalance weight are in the way of pan removal. If the front of the crankshaft prohibits removal of the pan, turn the crankshaft timing mark to the 6 o'clock position for V8 engines or 7 o'clock position for V6 engines.
10. Carefully raise the engine enough to provide sufficient clearance for oil pan removal. Be careful to watch the clearance between the engine and firewall so as not to damage components such as the distributor.
11. Remove the oil pan and gasket from the vehicle.
12. Remove all old RTV from the oil pan and engine block.

To install:
13. On V8 engines apply a small amount of RTV sealer, 1052914 or equivalent, to the front cover and cylinder block junction and to the rear seal retainer and cylinder block junction. Continue the bead of sealer for 1 inch in either direction of the radius cavity.
14. Install the new gasket on the oil pan and install the oil pan with the reinforcements, retainers and brackets as applicable. Tighten the retaining bolts, nuts and studs as follows:
  a. For the 2.8L and 3.1L engines, tighten the 2 rear oil pan retaining bolts to 18 ft. lbs. (25 Nm) and the rest of the retaining bolts and nuts to 89 inch lbs. (10 Nm).
  b. For the 3.8L engine, tighten the oil pan retaining bolts to 88 inch lbs. (10 Nm).
  c. For the 5.0L and 5.7L engines, tighten the oil pan retaining bolts to 101 inch lbs. (11 Nm) and the retaining nuts to 17 ft. lbs. (23 Nm).
15. Lower the engine and install the engine mount through bolts. Install the starter assembly. Connect the transmission oil cooler lines to the clips on the oil pan.
16. Install the torque converter dust shield and, if removed, the oil filter.
17. Install the the AIR hose to the catalytic convertor pipe, the AIR pipe to the exhaust manifold and the exhaust pipe to the manifolds, as applicable.
18. Lower the vehicle and fill the engine with the proper type of motor oil to the required level.
19. Install the air conditioning compressor and the upper half of the fan shroud assembly, if removed.
20. Install the distributor cap, the plenum extension if equipped, and the air cleaner assembly.
21. Connect the negative battery cable, start the engine and check for leaks.

Oil Pump

REMOVAL & INSTALLATION

Except 3.8L Engine

1. Disconnect the negative battery cable, drain the crankcase and remove the oil pan assembly.
2. Remove the oil pump attaching bolt from the rear main bearing cap.
3. Remove the oil pump with the extension shaft.
4. If necessary, remove the pickup screen and pipe as an assembly by placing the pump in a soft-jawed vise and extracting the pipe from the pump cover.

To install:
5. If the pickup screen and pipe was removed, it should be replaced as an assembly with a new part. Using a suitable tool, install a new pickup screen and pipe to the oil pump.
6. Prime the pump by turning it upside down and pouring clean oil into the pickup screen while turning the pump extension.
7. Align the slot or the hexagon head on the end of the shaft extension with the drive tang or the hexagon socket on the distributor shaft.
8. Tighten the oil pump bolt on 2.8L and 3.1L engines to 30 ft. lbs. (41 Nm) or to 65 ft. lbs. (88 Nm) on 5.0L and 5.7L engines.
9. Install the oil pan assembly and lower the vehicle.
10. Fill the crankcase with the proper amount and type of engine oil and connect the negative battery cable. Start the engine and check oil pressure.

3.8L Engine

NOTE: The oil pump is located on the left side of the timing chain cover. It is connected by a drilled passage in the cylinder crankcase, to an oil screen housing and stand pipe assembly.

1. Disconnect the negative battery cable.
2. Remove the oil filter.
3. Unbolt the pump cover assembly from the timing chain cover.
4. Remove the cover assembly and slide out the pump gears.
5. Remove the oil pressure relief valve cap, spring and valve. Do not remove the oil filter bypass valve and spring.
6. Check that the relief valve spring is not worn on the side, or collapsed.
7. Check that the relief valve is no more than an easy "slipfit" in the bore in the cover.

NOTE: If there is any perceptible side play in the relief valve, replace the valve. If there is still side play, replace the cover also.

8. Check the filter bypass valve for wear. Replace if necessary.

To install:

9. Lubricate and install the pressure relief valve and spring in the cover bore.

10. Install the gasket and cap, torquing the cap to 35 ft. lbs.

11. Install the gears and check that gear-to-cover end clearance is between 0.002–0.006 inch If the clearance is not as specified, check the timing cover gear pocket for wear. If the gear pocket is worn, the timing cover must be replaced.

12. Remove the gears and pack the gear pocket full of petroleum jelly. Don't use grease.

NOTE: Unless the pump is primed properly, the pump will not produce oil pressure when the engine is started.

13. Install the gears. Install a new gasket and the cover. Torque the bolts evenly to 10 ft. lbs. Replace the oil filter and check the oil level. Connect the negative battery cable.

CHECKING

NOTE: The oil pump housing on the 3.8L engine is part of the timing cover. If the housing is worn, the timing cover must be replaced. The oil pickup tube and screen are located in the oil pan.

1. Inspect pump housing and cover for cracks, scoring, casting imperfections and damaged threads.

2. Check idler gear shaft for play in pump body. If loose replace the oil pump except on 3.8L engine, where the engine timing cover should be replaced.

3. Check pressure regulator valve for sticking and pressure regulator spring for loss of tension.

4. Inspect the gears for chipping, galling or wear.

5. Inspect pickup screen and pipe assembly for broken wire mesh or looseness. The pickup screen and pipe are serviced as an assembly. If the assembly is removed for any reason a proper fit of the pipe to the oil pump housing cannot be assured and a new assembly must be installed.

Rear Main Bearing Oil Seal

REMOVAL & INSTALLATION

Except 3.8L Engine

1. Remove the transmission assembly.

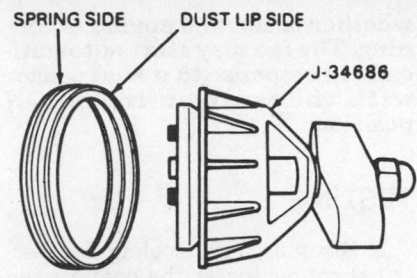

SEAL BORE TO SEAL SURFACE TO BE LUBRICATED WITH ENGINE OIL BEFORE ASSEMBLY

Rear main seal Installation tool—except 3.8L engine

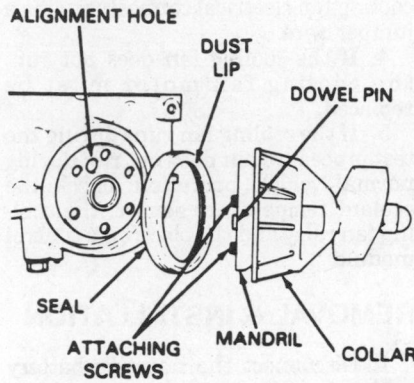

Installing rear main seal—except 3.8L engine

2. Remove the flywheel or flexplate.

3. Using a suitable prying tool, carefully pry the oil seal from the engine. Care should be taken not to nick the crankshaft sealing surface when removing the seal.

To install:

4. Coat the new seal completely with clean oil. Using tool J–35621 or equivalent main seal installer, press the new seal onto the crankshaft.

5. Install the flywheel or flexplate.

6. Install the transmission assembly.

3.8L Engine

NOTE: The following procedure is only to be used as an oil seal repair while the engine is in the vehicle. Whenever possible the crankshaft should be removed and a complete seal installed.

1. Disconnect the negative battery cable.

2. Drain the engine oil and remove the oil pan.

3. Remove the rear main bearing cap.

4. Insert packing tool J–21526–2 or equivalent, against 1 end of the seal in the cylinder block. Drive the old seal gently into the groove until it is packed tight. This will vary from 1/4 inch to 3/4 inch depending on the amount of pack required.

5. Repeat the procedure on the other end of the seal.

6. Measure the amount the seal was driven up on 1 side and add 1/16 inch. Using a suitable cutting tool, cut that length from the old seal removed from the rear main bearing cap. Repeat the procedure for the other side. Use the rear main bearing cap as a holding fixture when cutting the seal.

7. Install guide tool J–21526–1 or equivalent, onto the cylinder block.

8. Using the packing tool, work the short pieces cut in Step 6 into the guide tool and then pack into the cylinder block. The guide tool and packing tool are machined to provide a built in stop. Use this procedure for both sides. It may help to use oil on the short pieces of the rope seal when packing them into the cylinder block.

9. Remove the guide tool.

10. Apply Loctite 414 or equivalent, to the seal groove in the rear main bearing cap. Within 1 minute, insert a new seal into the groove and roll into place with a suitable tool until no more than 1/16 inch of the seal projects above the groove. Cut the excess seal materi-

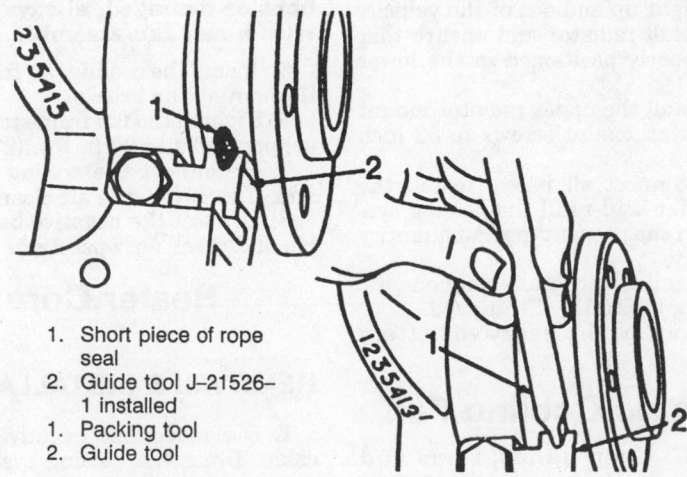

1. Short piece of rope seal
2. Guide tool J–21526–1 installed
1. Packing tool
2. Guide tool

Rear main seal Installation—3.8L engine

al with a sharp cutting tool at the bearing cap parting line.

11. Apply a thin film of chassis grease to the rope seal. Apply a thin film of RTV sealant on the bearing cap mating surface around the seal groove. Use the sealer sparingly.

12. Coat the side sealing strips for 5 minutes in light oil or kerosene. Install the sealing strips into the grooves along the sides of the main bearing cap. Install the rear main bearing cap and tighten to 100 ft. lbs. (135 Nm).

13. Install all remaining components.

ENGINE COOLING

Radiator

REMOVAL & INSTALLATION

1. Disconnect the negative battery cable.

2. Drain the cooling system into a suitable container.

3. Remove the intake duct, air duct bracket and air cleaner top, if equipped.

4. Remove the Mass Air Flow (MAF) sensor, if equipped.

5. Remove the engine cooling fan. If equipped with a fan clutch, the clutch should be set aside in an upright position to prevent seal leakage.

6. Disconnect the radiator hoses and heater hoses from the radiator.

7. If equipped with an automatic transmission, disconnect and plug the transmission cooler lines at the radiator.

8. Remove the upper radiator mount and screws, then lift the radiator straight up and out of the vehicle.

9. Install radiator and ensure that it is properly positioned in the lower cradle.

10. Install the upper radiator mount and tighten mount screws to 53 inch lbs.

11. Reconnect all hoses, install the cooling fan and refill the cooling system with the proper type and quantity of coolant.

12. Install all air intake components, including the MAF, if equipped.

13. Connect the negative battery cable.

Electric Cooling Fan

NOTE: Keep hands, tools and clothing away from cooling fan. Electric cooling fans can activate whether or not the engine is running. The fan may start automatically in response to a heat sensor with the ignition in the ON position.

TESTING

1. Disconnect the cooling fan electrical connector at the coolant fan from the wire harness.

2. Connect a 20 amp fused jumper wire from the positive terminal of the battery to 1 terminal of the cooling fan electrical connector.

3. Ground the other terminal of the cooling fan electrical connector using a jumper wire.

4. If the cooling fan does not run, the cooling fan motor must be replaced.

5. If the cooling fan runs during the test procedure but does not run during normal vehicle operation, check the coolant temperature sensor, the cooling fan relay and the electronic control module.

REMOVAL & INSTALLATION

1. Disconnect the negative battery cable.

2. Remove the air cleaner top, if equipped.

3. Remove the fan harness connector from the fan motor and frame.

4. Remove the fan frame to radiator support mounting bolts, remove the bracket if necessary, and remove the fan assembly.

To install:

NOTE: It is essential that fan assemblies remain in proper balance and proper balance cannot be assured once a fan assembly has been bent or damaged. Inspect the fan assembly prior to installation and if a fan blade is bent or damaged, always replace with a new fan assembly.

5. Install the cooling fan frame and, if removed, the bracket.

6. Tighten the fan frame to radiator support bolts to 20 ft. lbs. (27 Nm).

7. Reconnect the wiring harness and, if removed, the air cleaner top.

8. Connect the negative battery cable and check fan operation.

Heater Core

REMOVAL & INSTALLATION

1. Disconnect the negative battery cable. Drain the cooling system and disconnect the heater hoses.

2. Remove the right lower dash panels. Remove the instrument panel lower trim pad and the center console.

3. Remove the retaining screws from the top, bottom and right flanges of the rear heater case. Remove the rear case from the heater module.

4. Remove the core shroud screws and, if equipped, the clamp.

5. Remove the core shroud, heater core and mounting strap as an assembly.

6. Remove the core mounting strap and remove the heater core from the core shroud. If necessary, remove the shroud seal from the shroud and/or the heater core seal.

To install:

7. If removed, install the heater core seal and/or the shroud seal.

8. Install the heater core and mounting strap to the core shroud.

9. Carefully guide both heater core tubes into position at the holes in the dash panel and install the shroud assembly to the interior of the heater module.

10. Install the clamp, if equipped, and the shroud screws.

11. Replace the rear case flange sealer with fresh sealer and install the rear case to the heater module with the mounting screws.

12. Install the center console and instrument panels.

13. Connect the heater hoses and the negative battery cable. Fill the cooling system and operate the engine to check for leaks.

Water Pump

REMOVAL & INSTALLATION

1. Disconnect the negative battery cable and drain the cooling system into a suitable container.

2. Remove the air intake duct, if equipped.

3. Remove the drive belt.

4. Disconnect the radiator and heater hoses from the thermostat housing and water pump.

5. For V6 engines, remove the power steering pump bracket, if necessary.

6. For V8 engines, remove the water pump pulley bolts and water pump pulley.

7. Remove the water pump retaining bolts, the water pump and gaskets.

To install:

8. Clean all gasket mating surfaces and install new gaskets.

9. Install the water pump and bolts and tighten the water pump retaining bolts as follows:

a. 5.0L and 5.7L engines—30 ft. lbs. (41 Nm).

b. 3.8L engine—115 inch lbs. (13 Nm).

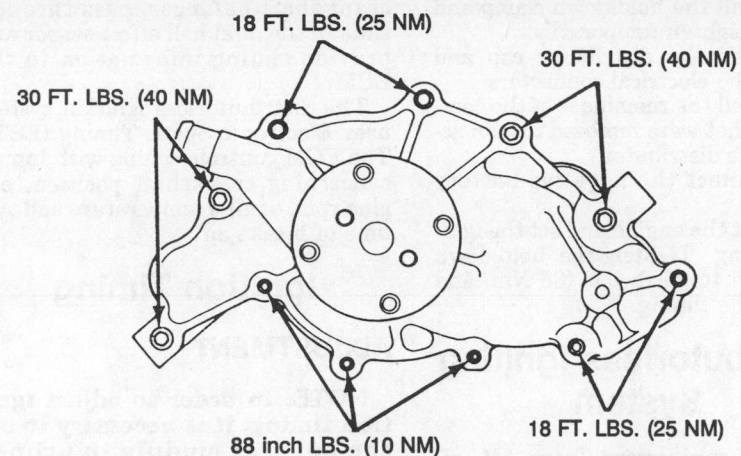

18 FT. LBS. (25 NM)
30 FT. LBS. (40 NM)
30 FT. LBS. (40 NM)
88 inch LBS. (10 NM)
18 FT. LBS. (25 NM)

Water pump torque specifications – 1991–93 3.1L engines

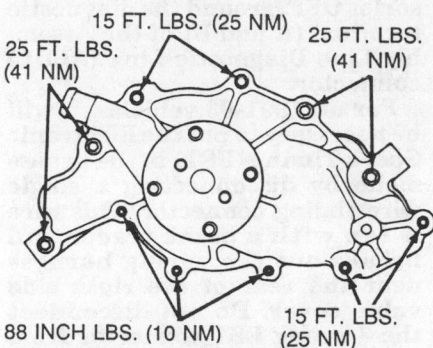

15 FT. LBS. (25 NM)
25 FT. LBS. (41 NM)
25 FT. LBS. (41 NM)
88 INCH LBS. (10 NM)
15 FT. LBS. (25 NM)

Water pump torque specifications – 1989 2.8L and 1990 3.1L engines

c. 2.8L and 3.1L engines – to specification.
10. Install the water pump pulley or the power steering pump bracket, as applicable. Tighten the water pump pulley bolts to 23 ft. lbs. (31 Nm).
11. Install the drive belt and connect all hoses.
12. Install the air duct and connect the negative battery cable.
13. Refill the cooling system with the proper type and quantity of coolant.

Thermostat

REMOVAL & INSTALLATION

1. Disconnect the negative battery cable.
2. Drain the cooling system to a level slightly below the thermostat.
3. Remove the air cleaner and intake duct, if required.
4. On some models it may be necessary to remove the throttle body and/or plenum, fuel lines and brackets.
5. Disconnect the radiator inlet hose.
6. Remove the thermostat housing retaining bolts and housing.
7. Remove the thermostat.

To install:

8. Make sure all gasket mating surfaces are clean before installation and replace the gasket as necessary. If upon removal of the thermostat housing the gasket remained attached to the housing, it is not necessary to replace the gasket.
9. Install the thermostat, then install the housing and tighten the retaining bolts as follows:
   a. 5.0L (VIN F) and 5.7L TPI engines – 25 ft. lbs. (34 Nm).
   b. 5.0L (VIN E) TBI engine – 21 ft. lbs. (28 Nm).
   c. 3.8L engine – 13 ft. lbs. (18 Nm).
   d. 2.8L and 3.1L engines – 15 ft. lbs. (21 Nm).
10. Connect the radiator inlet hose.
11. Install the throttle body and/or plenum, fuel lines and brackets, as applicable.
12. If removed, install the air cleaner and intake duct.
13. Connect the negative battery cable and refill the cooling system with the proper type and quantity of coolant.

Cooling System Bleeding

1. Drain the cooling system.
2. Fill the cooling system with a 50/50 mix of ethylene glycol antifreeze and water to a level just below the filler neck.
3. Fill the coolant recovery reservoir to the **COLD** fill mark and install the reservoir cap.
4. Run the engine with the radiator cap removed until the normal operating temperature is reached.

CAUTION

Ethylene glycol in engine coolant can be flammable under some conditions. Do not spill coolant on the exhaust system or on hot engine parts.

5. With the engine idling, add coolant to the radiator until the level reaches the bottom of the filler neck.
6. Install the radiator cap. The arrows on the cap must line up with the coolant recovery reservoir hose.

ENGINE ELECTRICAL

NOTE: Disconnecting the negative battery cable on some vehicles may interfere with the functions of the on board computer systems and may require the computer to undergo a relearning process once the negative battery cable is reconnected.

Distributor

All vehicles, except the 1989 20th anniversary special edition Firebird with the Buick 3.8L SFI engine, use a High Energy Ignition (HEI) distributor with Electronic Spark Timing (EST). The HEI system incorporates a distributor cap, rotor, ignition module, pole piece with internal teeth and pick-up coil. Vehicles use either an internally distributor mounted coil or an externally mounted ignition coil. Spark timing changes are controlled electronically by the Engine Control Module (ECM), which monitors various engine sensors, computes the desired spark timing and signals the distributor to change the timing accordingly.

REMOVAL

1. Disconnect the negative battery cable. Remove all the necessary components in order to gain access to the distributor assembly.
2. Disconnect and tag all electrical connections from the distributor.

NOTE: Use care when releasing the connector locking tabs on the distributor cap.

3. Remove the distributor cap and position it out of the way. Mark the position of the distributor housing and rotor in relation to the engine block.
4. Remove the distributor hold-down clamp and bolt.
5. Pull the distributor assembly up

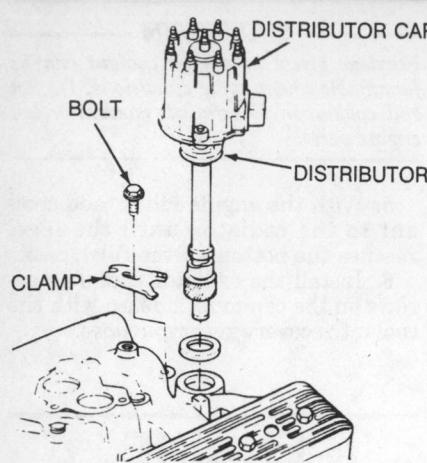

Typical HEI distributor assembly

from the engine, noting the position of the rotor as the distributor gear disengages from the camshaft.

INSTALLATION

Timing Not Disturbed

NOTE: To ensure correct ignition timing if the engine has not been disturbed, the distributor must be installed with the rotor in the same position as when removed.

1. Install the distributor, aligning the marks that were made during the removal procedure.
2. Install the distributor hold-down clamp and bolt and temporarily tighten.
3. Install the distributor cap and connect the electrical connectors.
4. Install the remainder of the components that were removed to gain access to the distributor.
5. Connect the negative battery cable.
6. Start the engine and set the ignition timing as necessary. Tighten the hold-down clamp bolt to 27 ft. lbs. (36 Nm) and recheck the timing.

Timing Distrubed

1. Remove the No. 1 spark plug. Place a finger over the spark plug hole and slowly rotate the engine in the normal direction of rotation, until compression is felt.
2. Place the No. 1 cylinder at TDC by aligning the timing mark on the crankshaft pulley to the **0** on the engine timing indicator by slowly rotating the engine in the same direction.
3. Position the rotor between No. 1 and No. 8 spark plug towers on the V8 engine or the No. 1 and No. 2 spark plug towers on the V6 engine.
4. Install the distributor in the engine.

5. Install the hold-down clamp and bolt and tighten temporarily.
6. Install the distributor cap and connect the electrical connectors.
7. Install the remainder of the components that were removed to gain access to the distributor.
8. Connect the negative battery cable.
9. Start the engine and set the ignition timing. Tighten the hold-down clamp bolt to 27 ft. lbs. (36 Nm) and recheck the timing.

Distributorless Ignition System

The 20th anniversary Trans AM, offered during the 1989 model year, is equipped with a 3.8L SFI turbocharged engine that features distributorless ignition system. This system uses a "waste spark" method of spark distribution. Each cylinder is paired with it's opposite in the firing order, so a cylinder on the compression stroke fires simultaneously with it's opposing cylinder on the exhaust stroke. The cylinder on the exhaust stroke requires very little voltage to fire it's plug, so most of the available voltage is used to fire the cylinder that is on the compression stroke.

The distributorless ignition system consists of a coil pack, the ignition module, a dual hall effect sensor, interrupter rings and the Electronic Control Module (ECM). The coil pack contains 3 separate ignition coils (1 for each pair of cylinders) enclosed in 1 housing and serviced as a unit. The ignition module is located under the coil pack and is connected to the ECM. The ignition module controls the primary circuit to the ignition coils and the spark timing below 400 rpm, if the ECM bypass circuit becomes open or grounded. The dual hall effect sensor is a combination camshaft and crankshaft sensor, mounted on the front cover behind the crankshaft balancer. Interrupter rings, mounted on the

crankshaft balancer, pass through slots in the dual hall effect sensor and provide timing information to the ECM.

The distributorless ignition system uses Electronic Spark Timing (EST). The ECM controls timing with inputs concerning crankshaft position, engine rpm, engine temperature and volume of intake air.

Ignition Timing

ADJUSTMENT

NOTE: In order to adjust ignition timing, it is necessary to set the control module in proper mode or to bypass the EST system. On 1989–90 vehicles, with the engine running and all accessories OFF, ground the diagnostic terminal (A and B) of the Assembly Line Diagnostic Link (ALDL) connector.

For all 1991–93 vehicles, it will be necessary to put the Electronic Spark Timing (EST) in the bypass mode by disconnecting a single wire timing connector. This wire is tan with a black tracer and breaks out the wiring harness near the rear of the right side valve cover. Do not disconnect the 4 prong EST connector from the distributor assembly.

1. Refer to the Vehicle Emission Information label, located on the radiator support panel, for the proper timing information.

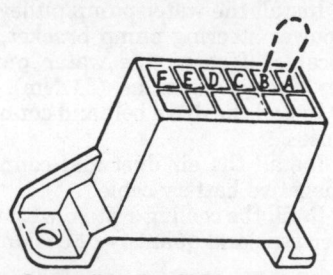

Grounding the ALDL terminals

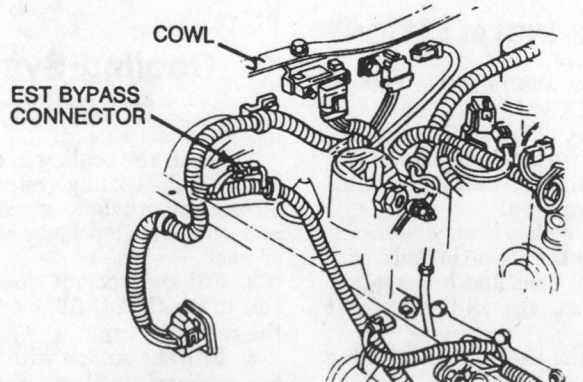

Electronic Spark Timing (EST) bypass connector location

2. With the ignition **OFF**, connect the pickup lead of an inductive timing light to the No. 1 spark plug wire. Connect the timing light power leads according to the manufacturers instructions.

3. Run the engine to normal operating temperature and with the engine running, disconnect the EST bypass mode connector or ground the diagnostic terminal of the ALDL connector, as applicable.

4. Check the timing, by aiming the timing light at the timing mark and harmonic balancer. If the engine timing requires adjustment, loosen the distributor holdown bolt and rotate the distributor slowly in either direction, to advance or retard the engine timing.

5. Tighten the hold-down bolt to 27 ft. lbs. (36 Nm) and recheck the engine timing.

6. With the engine still running, unground the diagnostic terminal or shut the engine **OFF** and reconnect the EST bypass mode connector, as applicable. On 1989–90 vehicles, if the ALDL connector ground was removed prior to turning the ignition **OFF**, no trouble code should be stored in Electronic Control Module (ECM) memory. A code may be set when the EST bypass connector is disconnected or if the ALDL diagnostic terminal is ungrounded after the engine is shut **OFF**.

7. If necessary, with the ignition **OFF**, clear the ECM code by disconnecting the negative battery cable for at least 30 seconds.

Alternator

PRECAUTIONS

Several precautions must be observed with alternator equipped vehicles to avoid damage to the unit.

- If the battery is removed for any reason, make sure it is reconnected with the correct polarity. Reversing the battery connections may result in damage to the 1-way rectifiers.
- When utilizing a booster battery as a starting aid, always connect the positive to positive terminals and the negative terminal from the booster battery to a good engine ground on the vehicle being started.
- Never use a fast charger as a booster to start vehicles.
- Disconnect the battery cables when charging the battery with a fast charger.
- Never attempt to polarize the alternator.
- Do not use test lights or more than 12 volts when checking diode continuity.

- Do not short across or ground any of the alternator terminals.
- The polarity of the battery, alternator and regulator must be matched and considered before making any electrical connections within the system.
- Never separate the alternator on an open circuit. Make sure all connection with the circuit are clean and tight.
- Disconnect the battery ground terminal when performing any service on electrical components.
- Disconnect the battery if arc welding is to be done on the vehicle.

BELT TENSION ADJUSTMENT

Serpentine belts are automatically adjusted by the tensioner on the engine. The tensioner should place enough tension on the belt so it can only be twisted 90 degrees at it's longest run.

If belt slippage occurs, check the belt length scale on the drive belt tensioner for the proper installed length and replace as necessary. If the drive belt tensioner is within it's operating range and the belt does not need replacement, check the belt tension as follows:

1. Run the engine for 5–10 minutes.
2. Shut OFF the engine and check the belt tension at the following locations using J–23600–B belt tension gauge or equivalent.

  a. V6 engines (except 3.8L engine): If without air conditioning, check the belt tension between the tensioner and the power steering pump pulley. If with air conditioning, check the belt tension between

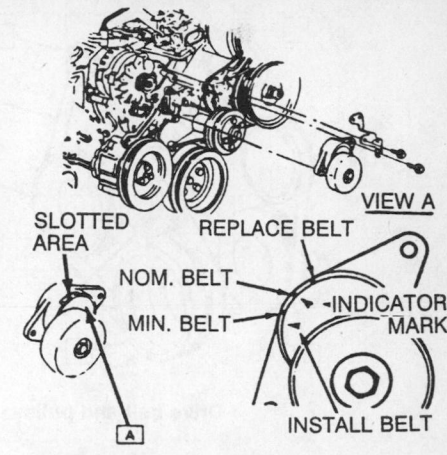

VIEW A

SLOTTED AREA — REPLACE BELT

NOM. BELT

MIN. BELT — INDICATOR MARK

INSTALL BELT

THE INDICATOR MARK ON THE MOVEABLE PORTION OF THE TENSIONER MUST BE WITHIN THE LIMITS OF THE SLOTTED AREA ON THE STATIOANRY PORTION OF THE TENSIONER. ANY READING OUTSIDE OF THESE LIMITS INDICATES EITHER A DEFECTIVE BELT OR TENSIONER.

Drive belt tensioner—2.8L and 3.1L engines

the tensioner and the air conditioner compressor pulley.

  b. V8 engine: Check the belt tension between any 2 pulleys.

3. Run the engine for 30 seconds and recheck the belt tension.

4. Repeat Step 3. The belt tension is the average of the 3 readings.

  a. V6 engine (except 3.8L engine): Belt tension should be 95–140 lbs. (422–623 N) if without air conditioning. If with air conditioning, the belt tension should be 85–110 lbs. (378–490 N).

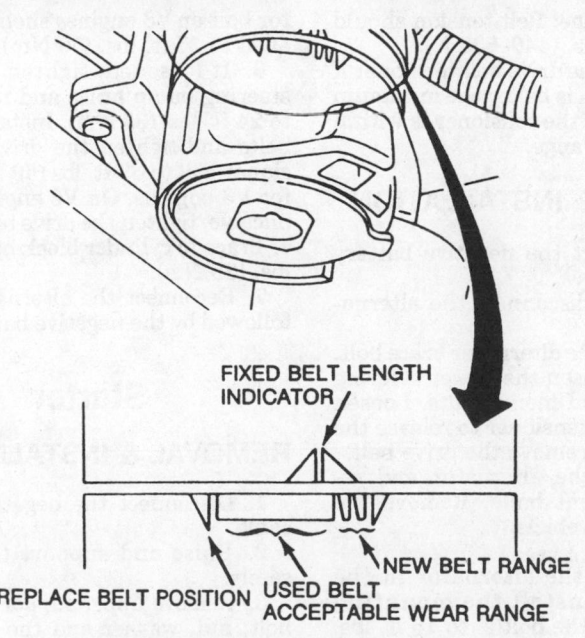

FIXED BELT LENGTH INDICATOR

NEW BELT RANGE

REPLACE BELT POSITION

USED BELT ACCEPTABLE WEAR RANGE

Drive belt tensioner—5.0L and 5.7L engines

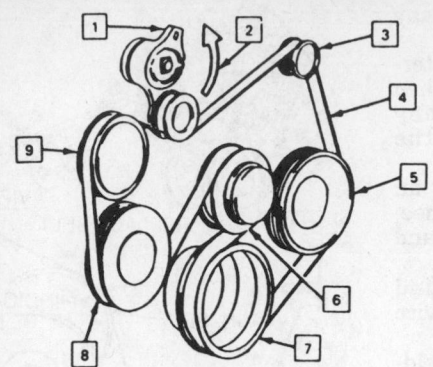

1. Tensioner assembly
2. Rotate tensioner in direction shown to install or remove belt
3. Alternator assembly
4. Accessory drive belt
5. Power steering pulley
6. Water pump
7. Crankshaft
8. AIR pump
9. Air conditioning compressor or belt idler

Drive belt and pulleys—5.0L and 5.7L engines

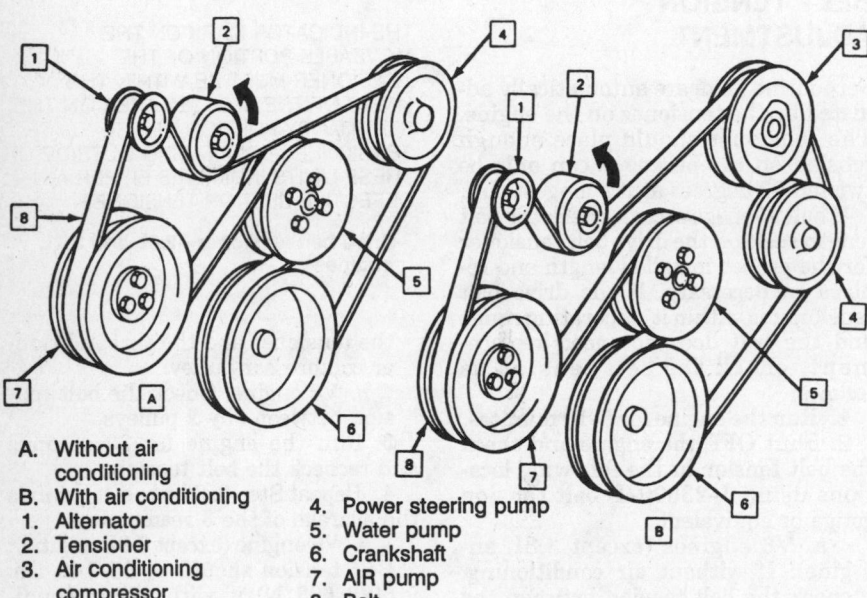

A. Without air conditioning
B. With air conditioning
1. Alternator
2. Tensioner
3. Air conditioning compressor
4. Power steering pump
5. Water pump
6. Crankshaft
7. AIR pump
8. Belt

Drive belt and pulleys—2.8L and 3.1L engines

b. V8 engine: Belt tension should be 99–121 lbs. (440–538 N).

5. Replace the drive belt tensioner if the belt tension is below the minimum specified and if the tensioner is within it's operating range.

REMOVAL & INSTALLATION

1. Disconnect the negative battery cable.
2. Tag and disconnect the alternator wiring.
3. Remove the alternator brace bolt. If required, loosen the power steering pump brace and mount nuts. Loosen and rotate the tensioner to release the drive belt and remove the drive belt.
4. Support the alternator and remove the mount bolts. Remove the unit from the vehicle.
To install:
5. Position the alternator in the bracket and install the mounting bolts. Tighten the bolt(s) to 18 ft. lbs. (25 Nm). The lower bracket to alterna-

tor bolt on V8 engines should be tightened to 37 ft. lbs. (50 Nm).

6. If loosened, tighten the power steering pump brace and mount nuts to 24 ft. lbs. (33 Nm). Install the drive belts and tighten the drive belt tensioner bolt to 37 ft. lbs (50 Nm) except for V6 engines. On V6 engines, as applicable, tighten the drive belt tensioner brace to cylinder block bolt to 18 ft. lbs. (25 Nm).

7. Reconnect the alternator wiring followed by the negative battery cable.

Starter

REMOVAL & INSTALLATION

1. Disconnect the negative battery cable.
2. Raise and support the vehicle safely.
3. Remove upper support attaching bolt, nut, washer and the bracket, if equipped.

4. Remove the flywheel housing cover.
5. Remove the starter mounting bolts and lower the starter enough to access wires.
6. Tag and disconnect the wiring, then remove starter.
To install:
7. Raise starter enough to connect the starter wiring.

NOTE: If shims were removed, they must be installed in their original location to assure proper drive pinion to flywheel engagement.

8. Hold starter in place, install starter mounting bolts and shims if equipped. Tighten mounting bolts to 35 ft. lbs. (37 Nm).
9. Check flywheel to pinion gear clearance and install flywheel housing cover.
10. Lower vehicle and connect the negative battery cable.

EMISSION CONTROLS

Due to the complex nature of modern electronic engine control systems, comprehensive diagnosis and testing procedures fall outside the confines of this repair manual. For complete information on diagnosis, testing and repair procedures concerning all modern engine and emission control systems, please refer to "Chilton's Guide to Fuel Injection and Electronic Engine Controls".

Emission Warning Lamps

RESETTING

The "Service Engine Soon" emission light located on the instrument panel and has 2 functions:
1. The light indicates to the driver when a problem has occurred and the vehicle should be taken for service as soon as reasonably possible.
2. The light is used by technicians to monitor "Trouble Codes" when the system is in the diagnostic mode.

To verify the bulb and wiring of the system is operating properly, the "Service Engine Soon" light will come ON with the key **ON** and the engine not running. When the engine is started, the "Service Engine Soon" light will turn OFF if the system is operating properly.

If the "Service Engine Soon" light remains ON, the self-diagnostic system has detected a problem. If the problem goes away, the light will go out in most cases after 10 seconds but a Trouble Code will remain in the ECM memory.

CLEARING TROUBLE CODES

After repairs are made to the faulty system(s) it is necessary to make sure the ECM memory is cleared of old trouble codes. Removing battery voltage to the ECM for 30 seconds will clear all stored trouble codes. This can be accomplished in various ways; by disconnecting the ECM harness from the positive battery pigtail with the ignition OFF, by removing the inline fuse that originates from the positive connection of the battery or by disconnecting the ECM fuse from the fuse holder. The negative battery cable may be disconnected but other on-board memory data, such as preset radio tuning, will also be deleted.

NOTE: To prevent ECM damage, the key must be OFF when disconnecting or reconnecting power to ECM (for example battery cable, ECM pigtail, ECM fuse, jumper cables, etc.).

ECM LEARNING ABILITY

The ECM has a "learning" ability which allows it to make corrections for minor variations in the fuel system in order to improve driveability. If the battery is disconnected to clear diagnostic codes or for repair, the "learning" process will reset and must begin again. A change may be noted in the vehicle's performance while the learning process begins. To "teach" the vehicle, make sure the vehicle is at operating temperature and drive at part throttle, with moderate acceleration and idle conditions, until normal performance returns.

FUEL SYSTEM

Fuel System Service Precautions

Safety is the most important factor when performing any type of maintenance but even more so when performing fuel system maintenance. Failure to conduct maintenance and repairs in a safe manner may result in serious personal injury or death. Maintenance and testing of the vehicle's fuel system components can be accomplished safely and effectively by adhering to the following rules and guidelines.

• To avoid the possibility of fire and personal injury, always disconnect the negative battery cable unless the repair or test procedure requires that battery voltage be applied.

• Always relieve the fuel system pressure prior to disconnecting any fuel system component (injector, fuel rail, pressure regulator, etc.), fitting or fuel line connection. Exercise extreme caution whenever relieving fuel system pressure to avoid exposing skin, face and eyes to fuel spray. Under pressure, fuel may penetrate the skin or any part of the body that it contacts.

• Always place a shop towel or cloth around the fitting or connection prior to loosening to absorb any excess fuel due to spillage. Ensure that all fuel spillage (should it occur) is quickly removed from engine surfaces and that all fuel soaked cloths or towels are deposited into a suitable waste container.

• Always keep a dry chemical (Class B) fire extinguisher near the work area.

• Do not allow fuel spray or fuel vapors to come into contact with a spark or open flame.

• Always use a backup wrench when loosening and tightening fuel line connection fittings. This will prevent unnecessary stress and torsion to fuel line piping. Always follow the proper torque specifications.

• Always replace worn fuel fitting O-rings with new. Do not substitute fuel hose or equivalent where fuel pipe is installed.

RELIEVING FUEL SYSTEM PRESSURE

Except TBI Engine

1. Disconnect the negative battery cable to prevent fuel discharge if the key is accidentally turned to the RUN position.
2. Loosen the fuel filler cap to relieve the tank pressure and do not tighten until service has been completed.
3. Connect J–34730–1 fuel pressure gauge or equivalent, to the fuel pressure valve. Wrap a shop cloth around the fitting while connecting the gauge to avoid spillage.
4. Place the end of the bleed hose into a suitable container and open the valve to relieve the fuel system pressure.

TBI Engine

1. Disconnect the negative battery cable to prevent fuel discharge if the key is accidentally turned to the RUN position.
2. Loosen the fuel filler cap to relieve the tank pressure and do not tighten until service has been completed.
3. Fuel system pressure is automatically relieved when the engine is turned OFF. No further action is necessary.

Fuel Tank

REMOVAL & INSTALLATION

1. Disconnect the negative battery cable, relieve fuel system pressure and drain the fuel tank.
2. Remove the fuel filler neck shield and attaching screws.
3. Raise and support vehicle safely.
4. Remove the rear axle assembly.
5. Disconnect the exhaust muffler and pipe. Remove the muffler heat shield and attaching screws.
6. Clean all fuel pipe connections and surrounding areas to prevent possible contamination of the fuel system, then disconnect the rear fuel pipe assembly and vapor return hose from the fuel sender assembly.
7. Disconnect the electrical connector.
8. With the aid of an assistant, support the fuel tank and remove the fuel tank straps and attaching bolts. Be careful not to bend the straps, as this may damage them.
9. Lower the fuel tank from the vehicle and place in a suitable work area.
To install:
10. Hook the rear end of the fuel tank straps into the underbody bracket.
11. With the aid of an assistant, raise the fuel tank into position and support it while connecting the fuel tank straps and attaching bolts. Tighten the attaching bolts to 25 ft. lbs. (34 Nm) on 1990–93 vehicles. For 1989 vehicles, tighten the front strap bolts to 26 ft. lbs. (35 Nm) and the rear strap bolts to 8 ft. lbs. (11 Nm).
12. Connect the electrical connector, the fuel feed pipe and the vapor return hose to the fuel sender assembly.
13. Install the muffler heat shield with the attaching screws, then connect the exhaust muffler and pipe.
14. Connect the rear axle assembly.
15. Lower the vehicle and connect the fuel filler neck shield and attaching screws.
16. Add fuel and tighten the filler cap.
17. Connect the negative battery cable.

18. Turn the ignition switch to the **ON** position for 2 seconds, **OFF** for 10 seconds, then to the **ON** position and check for fuel leaks.

19. If equipped with the 3.1L (VIN T) engine, the ECM will need to relearn Idle Air Control (IAC) valve pintle position following battery reconnection.

Fuel Filter

REMOVAL & INSTALLATION

1. Disconnect the negative battery cable.

2. Relieve the fuel system pressure.

3. Raise and safely support the vehicle.

4. Clean the fuel filter connections before disconnecting to prevent contamination of the fuel system. Disconnect the fuel lines from the fuel filter and plug the lines.

5. Remove the filter bracket screw and slide the fuel filter from the fuel filter bracket.

To install:

6. Check the fuel line O-rings for cuts, nicks, swelling or distortion and replace as necessary.

7. Position the replacement filter in the fuel filter bracket with the flow arrow pointing toward the engine.

8. Install the fuel filter bracket screw and and the fuel lines. Tighten the in-line fuel filter fittings to 20 ft. lbs. (27 Nm), using a backup wrench to prevent the filter from turning.

9. Lower the vehicle, connect the negative battery cable and tighten the fuel filler cap.

10. Turn the ignition switch to the **ON** position for 2 seconds, **OFF** for 10 seconds, then to the **ON** position and check for fuel leaks.

11. For vehicles equipped with the 3.1L (VIN T) engine, the ECM will need to relearn Idle Air Control (IAC) valve pintle position following battery reconnection.

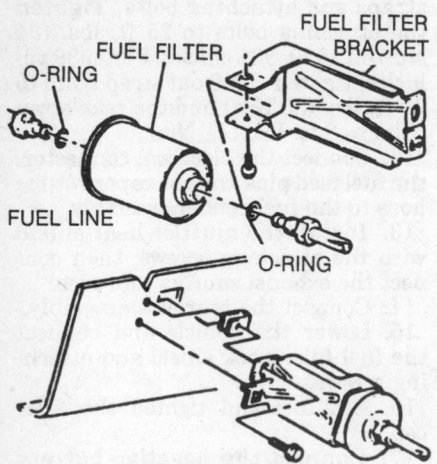

O-RING
FUEL FILTER
FUEL FILTER BRACKET
FUEL LINE
O-RING

Fuel filter assembly

Electric Fuel Pump

PRESSURE TESTING

5.0L TBI Engine

1. Relieve fuel system pressure and check that there is an adequate quantity of fuel in the tank.

2. Ensure the ignition switch is in the **OFF** position.

3. Connect a fuel pressure gauge to the fuel pump outlet line.

4. Using a 10 amp fused jumper wire, apply battery voltage to the fuel pump test connector located on the passenger side of the engine compartment.

5. Fuel pump pressure will drop immediately after the fuel pump stops running due to an controlled bleed in the fuel system.

6. The fuel pressure, with the pump running, should be 9–13 psi.

7. If there is no fuel pressure, listen for pump operation in tank.

8. If pump operation is heard, inspect lines and filter for restriction.

9. If there is no restriction, replace the fuel pump.

10. If pump is not heard running, inspect the fuel pump relay and wiring.

11. Disconnect the fuel pressure gauge and tighten the fuel filler cap.

Except 5.0L TBI Engine

1. Relieve fuel system pressure and check that there is an adequate quantity of fuel in the tank.

2. Connect a fuel pressure gauge to the fuel pump outlet line.

3. Make sure the ignition switch has been in the **OFF** position for at least 10 seconds and the all accessories are **OFF**.

4. Turn the ignition switch **ON**. The pump will run for about 2 seconds. The fuel pump pressure should be 34–47 psi.

NOTE: The ignition switch may have to be cycled to ON more than once to obtain maximum pressure. It is also normal for the pressure to drop slightly when the pump stops.

5. If fuel pressure is not as specified, verify that fuel pump operation is heard in the tank.

6. If fuel pump operation is not heard, inspect the fuel pump relay and wiring.

7. If fuel pump operation is heard, inspect filter and lines for restriction.

8. Start the engine and verify the pressure should decrease 3–10 psi.

9. If fuel pressure does not decrease, inspect pressure regulator and vacuum hose.

10. Disconnect the fuel pressure gauge and tighten the fuel filler cap.

REMOVAL & INSTALLATION

The electric fuel pump is part of the fuel sender assembly located inside the fuel tank.

1. Release the fuel pressure and disconnect the negative battery cable.

2. Raise and support the vehicle safely.

3. Remove the fuel tank from the vehicle.

4. Clean the area surrounding the sender assembly to prevent contamination of the fuel system.

5. Remove the fuel sender assembly from the tank as follows:

   a. For 1989 vehicles, turn the cam lock ring counterclockwise and carefully lift the assembly from the tank.

   b. For 1990 vehicles, remove the fuel feed and return pipe assemblies from the sender unit. Then with sending unit spanner wrench J-24187 or equivalent, remove the sender retaining cam, sender assembly and O-rings from the fuel tank. Discard the old O-ring.

   c. For 1991–93 vehicles, use tool J-24187 or equivalent to remove the fuel sender retaining cam, fuel sender assembly and O-rings, from the fuel tank. Discard the old O-ring.

6. If necessary, separate the fuel pump from the sending assembly.

To install:

7. If removed, install the fuel pump to the sending unit.

8. Inspect and clean the O-ring mating surfaces. Install the new O-ring in the groove around the tank opening, and if applicable, install a new O-ring on the fuel sender feed tube.

9. Install the fuel sender assembly as follows:

   a. For 1989–90 vehicles, carefully lower the assembly into the tank, taking care not to fold or twist the strainer which would restrict fuel flow. Also, ensure that the strainer does not block the full travel of the float arm.

   b. For 1991–93 vehicles, the fuel pump strainer must be in a horizontal position and when installed must not block the full travel of the float arm. Gently fold the fuel strainer over itself and slowly position the fuel sender assembly in the tank so the strainer is not damaged or trapped by sump walls.

10. Install assembly retainer cam using J-24187 or equivalent, on all vehicles except 1989. For 1989 vehicles install the cam lock over the sender assembly and lock by turning clockwise.

11. Install the fuel tank.

12. Lower the vehicle.

13. Fill the fuel tank, tighten the fuel filler cap and connect the negative battery cable.

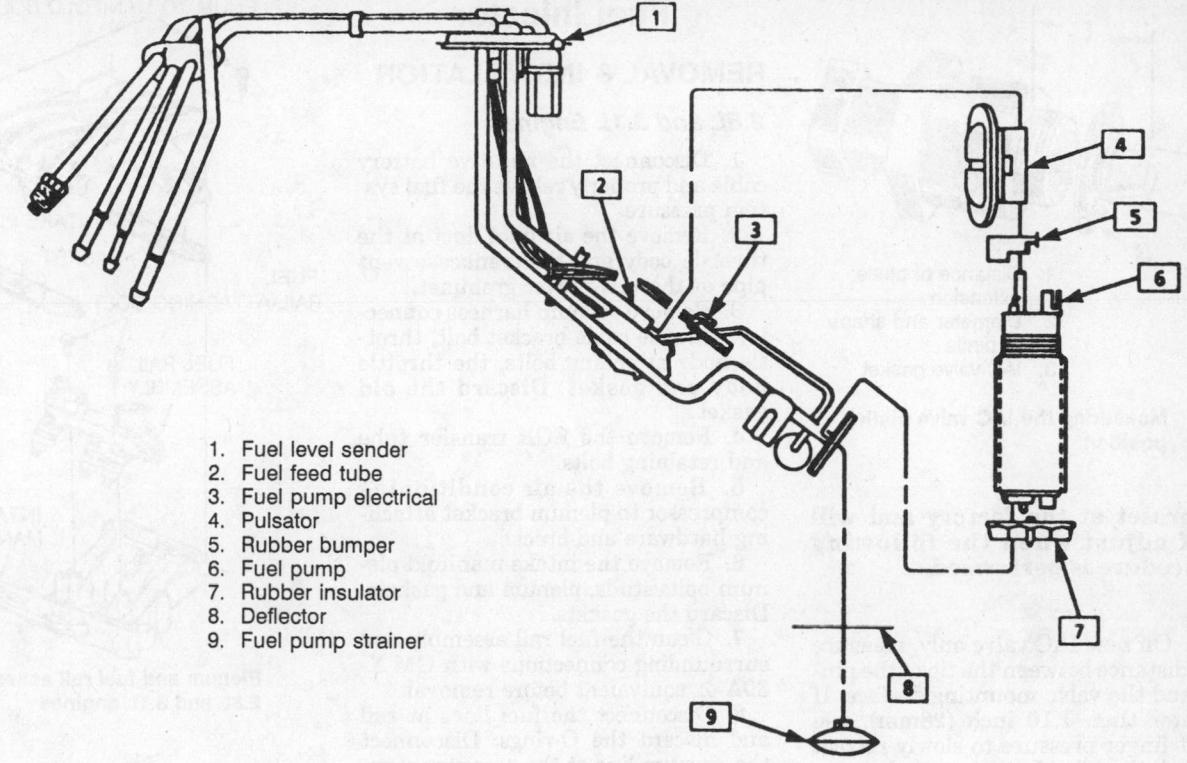

1. Fuel level sender
2. Fuel feed tube
3. Fuel pump electrical
4. Pulsator
5. Rubber bumper
6. Fuel pump
7. Rubber insulator
8. Deflector
9. Fuel pump strainer

Typical in-tank electric fuel pump assembly

14. Turn the ignition switch to the **ON** position for 2 seconds, **OFF** for 10 seconds, then to the **ON** position and check for fuel leaks.

15. If equipped with the 3.1L (VIN T) engine, the ECM will need to relearn Idle Air Control (IAC) valve pintle position following battery reconnection.

Fuel Injection

IDLE SPEED ADJUSTMENT

The idle speed and mixture are electronically controlled by the Electronic Control Module (ECM). All adjustments are preset at the factory and do not need periodic attention. Some throttle body units are equipped with a idle stop screw to allow adjustment of the minimum idle speed if the unit is used as a replacement. The only time the idle speed should need adjustment is when the throttle body assembly has been replaced.

1. Block the drive wheels and apply the parking brake. Remove the air cleaner assembly and/or air duct. Connect a scan tool to the ALDL connector.

2. For all engines except the 5.0L (VIN E), select the TPS voltage display on the scan tool and adjust the to obtain 0.46–0.62 volts.

3. For all engines, select the field service mode of the scan tool. Turn the

ignition **ON** and leave the engine **OFF**. Wait at least 45 seconds, this will allow the Idle Air Control (IAC) pintle to seat in the throttle body.

4. With the ignition switch in the **ON** position, the engine **OFF** and the scan tool in field service mode, disconnect the IAC valve electrical connector, exit field service mode and disconnect the distributor set-timing connector.

5. Connect a tachometer to the engine to monitor the engine speed.

6. Place the transmission in the **P** or **N** position and start the engine.

7. Run the engine until it reaches normal operating temperature or closed loop operation as indicated by the scan tool. It may be necessary to hold the throttle open slightly in order to maintain idle.

8. Be sure the throttle and cruise control cables do not hold the throttle open. Adjust the idle stop screw, if necessary, to obtain the correct specifications:
   2.8L engine:
   Automatic transmission—550 rpm in **D**.
   Manual transmission—650 rpm in **N**.
   3.8L engine—500 + 50 rpm in **D**.
   5.0L (VIN E) engine—450–500 rpm in **N**.
   5.0L (VIN F) engine—400 rpm in **N**.
   5.7L engine—450 rpm in **N**.

9. Turn the ignition **OFF** and reconnect the IAC valve electrical connector and the distributor set-timing connector.

10. For all engines except the 5.0L (VIN E) engine, turn the ignition **ON** and check TPS voltage on the scan tool. Adjust, if necessary, to obtain 0.46–0.62 volts.

11. Reset the Idle Air Control (IAC) valve pintle position.

12. Connect the air cleaner assembly, check and clear all ECM trouble codes.

IAC VALVE PINTLE ADJUSTMENT

Idle speed is controlled by the ECM through voltage pulses sent to the Idle Air Control (IAC) motor windings. Based on the number of voltage pulses received, the motor will move the IAC pintle in or out allowing more or less air through the throttle body. Whenever a new IAC valve is installed, the pintle must be adjusted to specification.

NOTE: If installing a new IAC valve measure and adjust the valve accordingly. If reinstalling a used IAC valve, do not push or pull on the pintle to adjust pintle length or damage to the IAC worm gear might occur. The valve

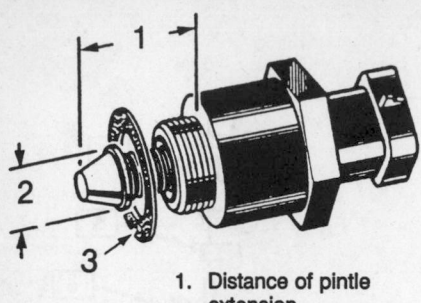

1. Distance of pintle extension
2. Diameter and shape of pintle
3. IAC valve gasket

Measuring the IAC valve pintle position.

is preset at the factory and will self adjust when the following procedure is performed.

1. On new IAC valve only, measure the distance between the tip of the pintle and the valve mounting surface. If greater than 1.10 inch (28mm), use light finger pressure to slowly retract the pintle. The force required to retract a new IAC valve will not damage the valve.
2. Install the IAC valve and gasket.
3. Connect the IAC valve wire connector.
4. Reset the IAC valve pintle position as follows:
  a. Depress the accelerator pedal slightly.
  b. Start the engine and run for 5 seconds.
  c. Turn the ignition **OFF** for 10 seconds.
  d. Restart the vehicle and check for proper idle operation.

IDLE LEARN PROCEDURE

Any time the battery is disconnected on vehicles equipped with the 3.1L engine, the programmed position of the IAC valve pintle is lost and replaced with a default value. To return the IAC valve pintle to the correct position, the idle learn procedure must be followed.
1. With the battery cables connected and the transmission in **P** or **N**, connect a suitable scan tool.
2. Select the IAC system, then select the Idle Learn portion of the Misc Test mode.
3. Proceed with the idle learn procedure as prompted by the scan tool.
4. The procedure should update ECM memory with the correct IAC valve pintle position and provide a stable idle speed.

Fuel Injector

REMOVAL & INSTALLATION

2.8L and 3.1L Engines

1. Disconnect the negative battery cable and properly relieve the fuel system pressure.
2. Remove the air inlet duct at the throttle body and the crankcase vent pipe at the valve cover grommet.
3. Remove vacuum harness connector, throttle cable bracket bolt, throttle body attaching bolts, the throttle body and gasket. Discard the old gasket.
4. Remove the EGR transfer tube and retaining bolts.
5. Remove the air conditioning compressor to plenum bracket attaching hardware and bracket.
6. Remove the intake manifold plenum bolts/studs, plenum and gaskets. Discard the gaskets.
7. Clean the fuel rail assembly and surrounding connections with GM X-30A or equivalent before removal.
8. Disconnect the fuel lines at rail and discard the O-rings. Disconnect the vacuum line at the pressure regulator and the injector electrical connections.
9. Disconnect the fuel rail attaching bolts and remove the assembly.

NOTE: Use care when handling the fuel rail assembly so as not to damage the injector connections or spray tips. Plug open lines and passages to prevent dirt and other contaminants from entering. Do not immerse fuel rail in liquid cleaning solvent.

10. Rotate the fuel injector retaining clip to the release position and remove the injector. Discard the injector retainer clip and O-rings.
To install:
11. Replace all O-rings, gaskets and retainer clips which were discarded. Carefully clean all gasket mating surfaces, taking care not to score or damage them with a sharp instrument.
12. Lubricate new fuel injector O-ring seals with engine oil and install on the injector. Connect new retainer clip and install fuel injector on fuel rail, rotate injector retainer clip to the lock position.
13. Tilt the rail assembly to install the injectors and install the assembly to the intake manifold.
14. Tighten the fuel rail attaching bolts to 18 ft. lbs. (25 Nm).
15. Connect the injector electrical connectors and the vacuum line.
16. Install new O-rings on the fuel lines and connect the fuel lines. Tighten fuel line nuts to 20 ft. lbs. (27 Nm).

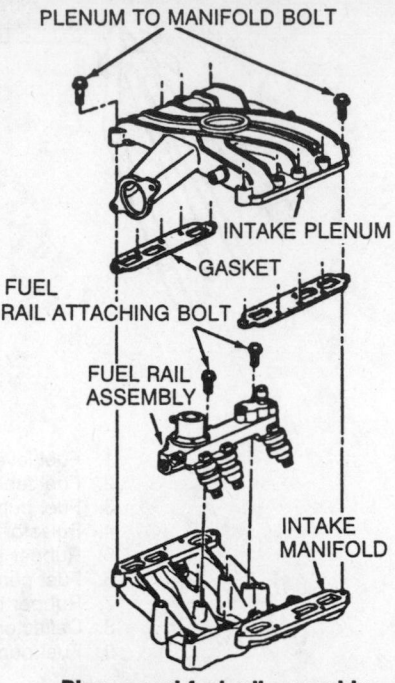

Plenum and fuel rail assembly— 2.8L and 3.1L engines

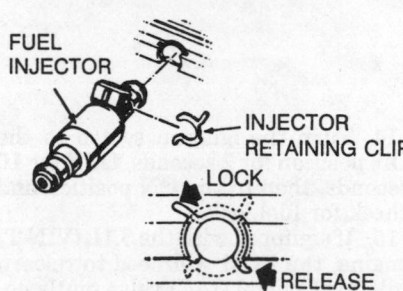

Fuel injector and retaining clip assembly

Temporarily connect the negative battery cable, and run the fuel pump to check for leaks, then disconnect the negative battery cable.
17. Install the new plenum gaskets, the plenum and attaching bolts/studs. Tighten bolts/studs to 15 ft. lbs. (21 Nm).
18. Install the air conditioning compressor bracket and hardware. Install the EGR transfer tube and bolts, tighten bolts to 19 ft. lbs. (26 Nm).
19. Install throttle body and new gasket. Tighten the attaching bolts to 20 ft. lbs. (27 Nm).
20. Install the throttle cable bracket bolt, the vacuum harness connector, the air inlet duct and the crankcase vent pipe.
21. Connect the negative battery cable and tighten the fuel filler cap.

3.8L Engine

1. Disconnect the negative battery cable.
2. Relieve the fuel system pressure.

3. Disconnect the electrical connectors from the fuel injectors.

4. Disconnect the vacuum hose from the pressure regulator.

5. Disconnect the fuel feed and return lines from the fuel rail.

6. Remove the fuel rail attaching bolts and remove the fuel rail and the fuel injectors.

7. Installation is the reverse of the removal procedure. Use new O-rings on the injectors and coat the O-rings with engine oil.

5.0L (VIN F) and 5.7L TPI Engines

1. Disconnect the negative battery cable.

2. Relieve the fuel system pressure.

3. Partially drain the cooling system so the coolant hoses at the throttle body can be removed.

4. Disconnect the throttle, TV and cruise control cables.

5. Disconnect the cable retaining bracket, air intake duct, vacuum hoses at the throttle body, coolant hoses and the electrical connectors from the Throttle Position Sensor (TPS) and the Idle Air Control (IAC) valve.

6. Remove the throttle body bolts and the throttle body assembly.

7. Disconnect the electrical connectors from the injectors, remove the left and right electrical harness attaching nuts and move the harnesses aside.

8. Disconnect the power brake vacuum hose at the plenum and remove the runner to plenum bolt attaching the Manifold Absolute Pressure (MAP) sensor. Disconnect the MAP sensor and vacuum hoses at the plenum.

9. Remove the remaining runner to plenum bolts. Lift the plenum and disconnect the Manifold Air Temperature (MAT) sensor electrical connector. Remove the plenum and discard the plenum gaskets.

10. Remove the runner to manifold bolts, PCV valve and hose, EGR solenoid and the left and right side runners and gaskets. Discard the gaskets.

11. Disconnect the fuel feed and return lines. Discard the fuel line O-rings.

12. Remove the fuel tube bracket bolt.

13. Disconnect the vacuum line at the pressure regulator.

14. Remove the fuel rail attaching bolts and the fuel rail assembly.

15. Rotate the injector retainer clip to the release position and remove the injector. Discard the O-rings and retainer clips.

To install:

NOTE: There are 2 injector part numbers used in production

for the 5.0L engine and 2 different part numbers for the 5.7L engine. Do not intermix injectors with different part numbers, as this will result in engine roughness and excessive emissions.

If the entire set of injectors are being replaced, either part number listed for that specific engine may be used.

16. Lubricate new injector O-ring seals with engine oil and install on the injector.

17. Install a new retainer clip onto the injector and install the injector into the fuel rail injector socket, with the electrical connector facing outward. Rotate the injector retainer clip to the locking positon.

18. Install the fuel rail assembly in the intake manifold. Install the attaching bolts to 15 ft. lbs. (20 Nm). Install the fuel tube bracket bolt and tighten to 25 ft. lbs. (34 Nm).

19. Connect the vacuum line to the pressure regulator.

20. Install new O-rings on the fuel feed and return lines and connect the fuel lines to the fuel rail. Tighten the fuel line nuts to 20 ft. lbs. (27 Nm).

21. Temporarily connect the negative battery cable. Turn the ignition switch to **ON** for 2 seconds and then to **OFF**. Again turn the ignition switch to the **ON** position and check for fuel leaks. Disconnect the negative battery cable.

22. Clean all plenum and runner gasket mating surfaces.

23. Install new gaskets, the runners and manifold to runner bolts to the intake manifold. Tighten the bolts to 25 ft. lbs. (34 Nm).

24. Install the EGR solenoid.

25. Install the right and left side hand runner to manifold bolts fingertight only.

26. Support the plenum above the runners, connect the MAT sensor electrical connector and lower the plenum into position. Start a few bolts to hold the plenum in position.

27. Connect the vacuum hoses and MAP sensor.

28. Tighten all bolts to 25 ft. lbs. (34 Nm), starting in the center of the plenum/manifold and working outward.

29. Install the PCV valve and hose.

30. Connect the power brake vacuum hose to the fitting on the plenum, the left and right injector electrical harnesses, the attaching nuts and the electrical connectors to the injectors.

31. Install the throttle body with a new gasket and tighten the attaching bolts to 18 ft. lbs. (24 Nm).

32. Connect the electrical connectors to the TPS and IAC valve, coolant hoses, vacuum hoses, throttle cable bracket and the throttle, TV and cruise control cables.

33. Refill the cooling system, tighten the fuel filler cap and connect the negative battery cable.

5.0L (VIN E) TBI Engine

1. Disconnect the negative battery cable.

2. Relieve the fuel system pressure.

3. Remove the air cleaner assembly.

4. Remove the electrical connectors from the fuel injectors by squeezing the plastic tabs and pulling straight up.

5. Remove the fuel meter cover attaching screws and remove the fuel meter cover assembly.

6. Remove the fuel meter outlet passage gasket and pressure regulator dust seal. If the fuel meter cover gasket is stuck to the fuel meter body, leave it in place. If it is stuck to the fuel meter cover, remove it and place it on the fuel meter body.

7. With the fuel meter cover gasket in place to protect the fuel meter body, use a suitable prybar and fulcrum to carefully pry out the injector.

8. Discard both injector O-rings and the fuel meter cover gasket.

To install:

NOTE: Be sure to replace the injector with an identical part. Injectors from other engines are calibrated for different flow rates. Service fuel injector packages may contain a fuel injector washer (spacer). The washer is not required for this application.

9. Lubricate a new upper (large) O-ring with engine oil and install in the fuel meter body cavity. Make sure the O-ring is seated properly and is flush with the top of the fuel meter body surface.

10. Lubricate a new lower (small) O-ring with engine oil and install on the nozzle end of the injector. Push the O-ring on far enough to contact the filter.

11. Install the injector by aligning the raised lug on the injector base with the notch in the fuel meter body cavity. Push down on the injector until it is fully seated in the fuel meter body.

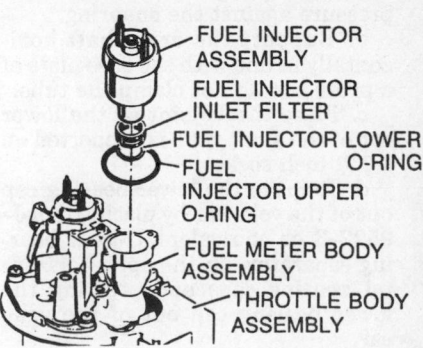

FUEL INJECTOR ASSEMBLY
FUEL INJECTOR INLET FILTER
FUEL INJECTOR LOWER O-RING
FUEL INJECTOR UPPER O-RING
FUEL METER BODY ASSEMBLY
THROTTLE BODY ASSEMBLY

Fuel Injector and O-rings—TBI

The electrical terminals of the injector should be parallel with the throttle shaft.

12. Install a new pressure regulator dust seal, fuel meter outlet gasket and cover gasket.

13. Install the fuel meter cover assembly. Apply Loctite 262 or equivalent, to the retaining screws and tighten to 27 inch lbs. (3 Nm).

14. Connect the electrical connectors to the fuel injectors, tighten the fuel filler cap and connect the negative battery cable.

15. Turn the ignition switch to the **ON** position for 2 seconds, then turn it to the **OFF** position for 5 seconds. Again, turn the switch to **ON** and check for fuel leaks.

16. Install the air cleaner assembly.

DRIVE AXLE

Driveshaft and U-Joints

REMOVAL & INSTALLATION

1. Raise and support the vehicle safely. Mark the rear axle pinion flange and driveshaft for assembly.

2. Remove the driveshaft strap bolts and remove the retaining straps.

3. Drop the driveshaft down at the rear, then carefully pull it backwards out from the transmission extension housing. The transmission housing should be plugged to prevent leakage. If the bearing caps are loose, tape them together to prevent dropping and losing the bearing rollers.

4. The U-joints will either be the nylon injected ring type or the snapring type. To replace the U-joints proceed as applicable:

    a. Remove the snaprings, if equipped. If the snapring does not readily come out, tap the end of the bearing cap lightly to relieve the pressure against the snapring.

    b. Support the driveshaft horizontally in line with the base plate of a press but do not clamp the tube.

    c. Place the U-joint so the lower ear of the shaft yoke is supported on a 1⅛ inch socket.

    d. Remove the lower bearing cap out of the yoke ear by placing tool J–9522–3 or equivalent U-joint bearing separator, on the open horizontal bearing caps and pressing the lower bearing cap out of the yoke ear.

NOTE: If the U-joint is a nylon

injected ring type, this will shear the nylon injector ring on the lower bearing cap. There are no bearing retainer grooves in the production bearing caps, therefore they cannot be reused. Replace nylon injected ring U-joints with external snapring type U-joints.

    e. If the bearing cap is not completely removed, lift tool J–9522–3 and insert tool J–9522–5 or equivalent between the bearing cap and seal and continue pressing the U-joint out of the yoke.

    f. Repeat the procedure for the opposite side.

    g. Remove the spider from the yoke.

To install:

5. When replacing U-joints always replace the entire assembly consisting of 1 pregreased spider, 4 bearing cap assemblies with seals, needle roller bearings, round and flat derlin washers, grease and 4 snaprings. Replace U-joints as follows:

    a. Install 1 bearing cap part way

into 1 side of the yoke. Turn this yoke ear to the bottom.

    b. Using tool J–9522–3 or equivalent, seat the trunnion into the bearing cap.

    c. Install the opposite bearing cap partially onto the trunnion.

    d. Ensure that both trunnions are straight and true in the bearing caps.

    e. Press the spider against the opposite bearing cap, while working the spider back and forth to ensure free movement of the trunnions in the bearings.

    f. If the trunnion is binding, one or more of the needle bearings have tipped under the end of the trunion.

    g. Stop pressing when 1 bearing cap clears the retainer groove inside the yoke.

    h. Install a snapring by pressing it into place.

    i. Repeat the procedure for the remaining bearing caps and u-joint.

6. Lubricate the spline with clean engine oil and install the slip yoke onto the transmission.

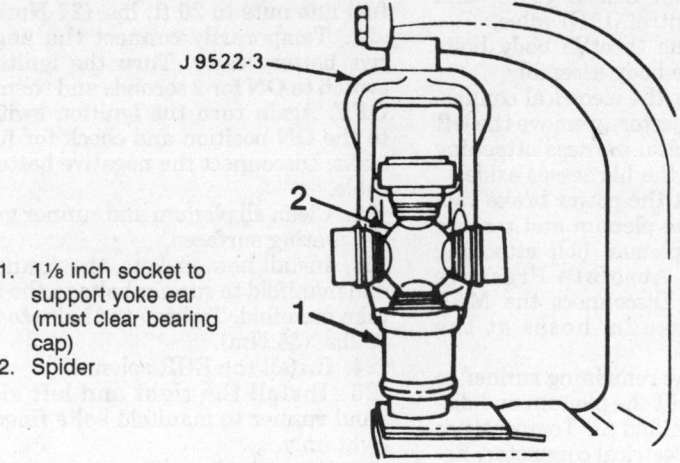

1. 1⅛ inch socket to support yoke ear (must clear bearing cap)
2. Spider

Universal joint removal and installation

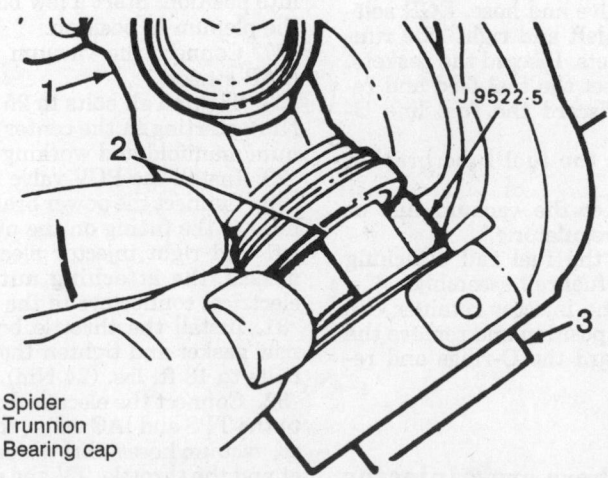

1. Spider
2. Trunnion
3. Bearing cap

Universal joint removal and installation

7. Align the marks and install the rear of the driveshaft with the rear U-joint to the pinion yoke making sure the bearing caps are properly seated.

8. Tighten the retaining strap bolts evenly to 16 ft. lbs. (22 Nm).

Rear Axle Shaft, Bearing and Seal

REMOVAL & INSTALLATION

Except Borg-Warner Rear Assembly

1. Raise and support the vehicle safely. Remove the rear wheels and drums or rotors.

2. Clean the carrier cover and surrounding area to prevent dirt or contamination from entering the housing. Remove the carrier cover and drain the gear oil into a suitable container.

3. Remove the rear axle pinion shaft lock screw and the rear axle pinion shaft.

4. Push the flanged end of the axle shaft into the axle housing and remove the C-clip from the opposite end of the shaft.

5. Remove the axle shaft from the axle housing.

6. Using a suitable tool, remove the oil seal from the axle housing. Be careful not to damage the housing.

7. Install tool J–22813–01 or equivalent axle bearing remover, into the bore of the axle housing and position it behind the bearing, ensure the tangs of the tool engage the outer race. Remove the bearing using a slide hammer.

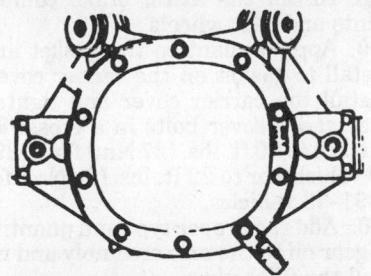

Rear axle identification—except Borg-Warner

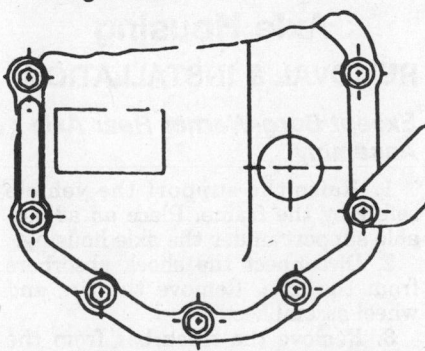

Rear axle identification—Borg-Warner

To install:

8. Lubricate the new bearing and sealing lips with gear lubricant and install the bearing with a suitable tool so the tool bottoms against the shoulder in axle housing.

9. Position seal on suitable tool and insert seal into the housing bore. Install seal into place, flush with the axle tube.

10. Taking care not to damage the seal, slide the axle shaft into place so the splines engage with the splines of the side gear.

11. Insert the C-lock into the bottom end of the axle shaft and push the shaft outward so the lock seats in the counterbore of the rear axle side gear.

12. Insert the rear axle pinion gear shaft through the differential case, thrust washer and pinion gears. Align the hole in the shaft with the lock screw hole.

13. Install the lock screw and tighten to 20 ft. lbs. (27 Nm) for 1989–90 vehicles or 27 ft. lbs. (36 Nm) for 1991–93 vehicles.

14. Clean the gasket mating surfaces of any old sealant. Apply a thin coat of 1052366 or equivalent sealant to the gasket and install the gasket onto the carrier cover.

15. Install the carrier cover and bolts. Tighten bolts in a crosswise pattern to 20 ft. lbs. (27 Nm) for 1989–90 vehicles or to 22 ft. lbs. (30 Nm) for 1991–93 vehicles.

16. Fill the carrier cover with the proper type and amount of axle lubricant and install the plug.

17. Install the rear brake assemblies and rear wheels. Lower the vehicle.

Borg-Warner Rear Assembly

NOTE: The Borg-Warner axle assembly can be quickly identified by checking the axle code. The Borg-Warner axle codes are BET, BEU and BEW on 1989 vehicles or 9EQ and 9ER on 1990 vehicles.

1. Raise the vehicle and support is safely.

2. Remove the rear wheels and as necessary, the brake components.

3. Remove the 4 nuts attaching the brake anchor plate and outer bearing retainer to the axle housing.

4. Remove the axle shaft and the wheel bearing assembly using axle shaft removal tool J–21579 and slide hammer J–2619 or equivalents.

5. To remove the inner bearing retainer and the bearing from the axle shaft, split the retainer with a chisel and remove it from the shaft. Using tool J–22912–01 or equivalent rear pinion bearing cone remover, press the bearing off the shaft. Discard the old cone, cup and seal.

6. Examine the old axle shaft, if it is in satisfactory condition it may be used again. Replace bearings and inner bearing retainers which have been removed from the shaft.

To install:

7. Install the outer bearing retainer onto the axle shaft.

NOTE: There are right (black banded) and left (gold banded) axle seals and they cannot be interchanged.

8. Lubricate the lips of the oil seal with a light coat of grease and install onto the axle shaft. Be sure the oil seal

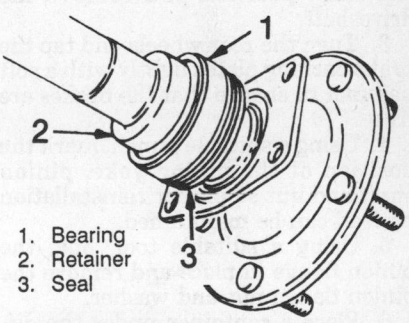

1. Bearing
2. Retainer
3. Seal

Axle shaft and bearing assembly—Borg-Warner

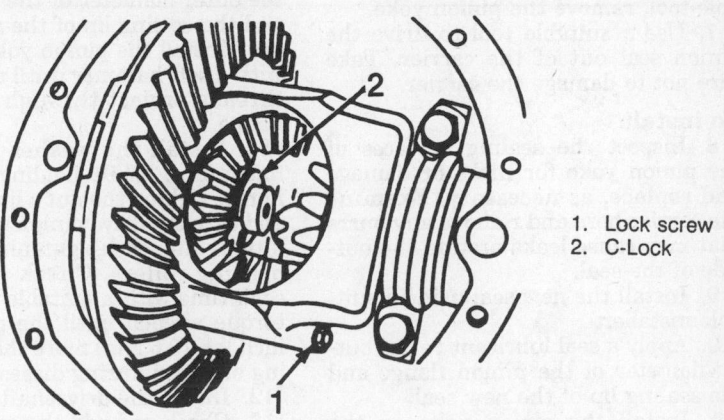

1. Lock screw
2. C-Lock

Pinion shaft lock screw and C-clip removal—except Borg-Warner

is installed with the spring side facing the center of the axle.

9. With a suitable installer, press the wheel bearing and inner bearing retainer hard against the bearing shoulder on the axle shaft. Be sure the retainer is tight against the bearing with the outer diameter chamfer toward the bearing.

10. Install the axle shaft through the brake anchor plate. Align the axle shaft and side gear splines.

11. Coat the outside diameter of the wheel bearing oil seal with a light coat of grease. Push the wheel bearing and oil seal into the housing.

12. Install the 4 backing plate bolts with new locknuts and tighten the bolts alternately to 36 ft. lbs. (48 Nm).

13. Install brake components, as necessary, and the rear wheels. Lower the vehicle.

Pinion Seal

REMOVAL & INSTALLATION

Except Borg-Warner Rear Axle Assembly

1. Release the parking brake. Raise and safely support the vehicle.

2. Mark the driveshaft and pinion yoke so they may be reassembled in the same position and remove the driveshaft.

3. Turn the rear wheels and tap the brake backing plates lightly with a soft hammer to ensure that the brakes are free

4. Using a suitable punch, mark the position of the pinion yoke, pinion shaft and nut so proper reinstallation preload can be maintained.

5. Using a suitable tool, hold the pinion flange in place and remove the pinion flange nut and washer.

6. Place a container under the differential to catch any fluid that may drain from the rear axle. Using a suitable tool, remove the pinion yoke.

7. Use a suitable tool to drive the pinion seal out of the carrier. Take care not to damage the carrier.

To install:

8. Inspect the sealing surfaces of the pinion yoke for nicks or damage and replace, as necessary. Examine the carrier bore and remove any burrs that may cause leaks around the outside of the seal.

9. Install the new seal using a suitable installer.

10. Apply a seal lubricant to the outer diameter of the pinion flange and the sealing lip of the new seal.

11. Install the pinion yoke on the drive pinion by taping with a soft-face hammer until a few pinion threads project through the pinion yoke.

12. Install the washer and pinion flange nut. While holding the pinion yoke, tighten the nut to the same position as marked earlier, then tighten an additional $\frac{1}{16}$ inch (1.59mm) turn beyond the marks.

13. Install the driveshaft, aligning the marks on the driveshaft and pinion yoke.

14. Check and add the correct lubricant, as necessary. Lower the vehicle and set the parking brake.

Borg-Warner Rear Axle Assembly

1. Raise and safely support the vehicle.

2. Mark the driveshaft and pinion yoke so they may be reassembled in the same position. Remove the driveshaft.

3. Using a suitable inch pound torque wrench on the pinion yoke nut, measure and record the preload at the pinion including the effects of drag from the pinion bearing, differential bearings, grease and the oil seal.

4. Using a suitable tool to hold the pinion yoke in place, remove the pinion yoke nut.

5. Place a suitable container under the differential to catch any fluid that may drain from the rear axle. Using a suitable tool, remove the pinion yoke.

6. Use a suitable tool to remove the pinion seal and discard the old seal.

To install:

7. Inspect the seal surface of the pinion flange for tool marks, nicks or damage and replace, as necessary. Examine the carrier bore and remove any burrs that might cause leaks around the outside of the seal.

8. Install the seal 0.010 inch (0.25mm) below the flange surface using a suitable seal installer.

9. Apply suitable seal lubricant to the outer diameter of the pinion yoke and the sealing lip of the new seal.

10. Install the pinion yoke by taping with a soft hammer until a few pinion threads project through the pinion flange.

11. Install the washer and pinion flange nut. While holding the pinion flange, tighten the nut a little at a time and turn the drive pinion several revolutions after each tightening, to set the bearing rollers. Check the preload each time with a suitable inch pound torque wrench until the preload is 5 inch lbs. (0.6 Nm) more then the reading obtained during disassembly.

12. Install the driveshaft.

13. Check and add the correct lubricant, as necessary. Lower the vehicle.

Differential Carrier

REMOVAL & INSTALLATION

1. Raise and safely support the vehicle.

2. Clean the area around the differential cover. Place a suitable container under the differential, remove the carrier cover and drain the gear oil.

3. Remove the tires, brake components and drive axles.

4. Mark the differential bearing caps **L** and **R** to make sure they will be reassembled in their original location. Remove the bearing cap bolts and caps.

5. Using a suitable tool, remove the differential carrier. Be careful not to damage the gasket sealing surface when removing the unit. Place the right and left bearing outer races of the side bearing assemblies and shims in sets with the marked differential bearings caps so they can be reinstalled in their original positions.

To install:

6. Inspect the differential carrier housing for foreign material. Check the ring and pinion for chipped teeth, excessive wear and scoring. Check the carrier bearings visually and by feel. Clean the differential housing and replace components, as necessary.

7. Install the differential carrier. Check the carrier bearing preload and ring and pinion backlash and adjust, as necessary. Tighten the differential bearing cap bolts to 55 ft. lbs. (75 Nm) except on Borg-Warner rear axles which should be tightened to 40 ft. lbs. (54 Nm).

8. Install the axles, brake components and rear wheels.

9. Apply sealant to the gasket and install to gasket on the carrier cover. Install the carrier cover and tighten the carrier cover bolts in a crosswise pattern to 20 ft. lbs. (27 Nm) for 1989–90 vehicles or to 22 ft. lbs. (20 Nm) for 1991–93 vehicles.

10. Add the proper type and quantity of gear oil to the axle assembly and install the filler plug.

11. Lower the vehicle.

Axle Housing

REMOVAL & INSTALLATION

Except Borg-Warner Rear Axle Assembly

1. Raise the support the vehicle safely by the frame. Place an adjustable support under the axle housing.

2. Disconnect the shock absorbers from the axle. Remove the tire and wheel assemblies.

3. Remove the track bar from the axle housing and body.

4. Remove the brake line junction block bolt at the axle housing. Disconnect and plug the brake lines at the junction block. Remove the brake lines from the housing clips.

5. Lower the rear axle assembly as needed and remove the springs.

6. Remove the axle shafts and the brake backing plates.

7. Disconnect the lower control arms and the torque arm from the axle housing.

8. Mark the driveshaft and pinion yoke, then disconnect the driveshaft and support aside.

9. Lower the rear axle assembly and remove it from the vehicle.

To install:

10. Raise the rear axle housing into position, align the driveshaft marks and install.

11. Connect the torque arm and the lower control arms to the axle. Tighten the torque arm bolts to 98 ft. lbs. (133 Nm) and loosely install the control arm bolts.

12. Install the brake backing plates and the axle shafts. Connect the brake lines to the under axle housing clips.

13. Lower the axle housing as needed, install the coil springs and raise the housing back into position.

14. Unplug and connect the brake lines to the junction block. Install the junction block bolt to the axle housing.

15. Install the track bar and the shock absorbers.

16. Check and add axle lubricant to the housing. Install the tire and wheel assemblies.

17. With the weight of the vehicle on the axle, tighten the control arm bolts to 85 ft. lbs. (115 Nm).

18. Remove the adjustable supports, lower the vehicle and bleed the brake system.

Borg Warner Rear Axle Assembly

1. Raise the support the vehicle safely by the frame. Place an adjustable support under the axle housing.

2. Remove the tire and wheel assemblies.

3. Loosen the parking brake cable adjuster and remove the parking brake cables from the adjuster and the body clips.

4. Disconnect the shock absorbers from the axle. Remove the track bar from the axle housing and body.

5. Mark the driveshaft and pinion yoke, then disconnect the driveshaft and support aside.

6. Remove the brake line junction block bolt at the axle housing. Disconnect and plug the brake lines at the wheel cylinders, if applicable. Release the brake lines from the clips.

7. Lower the rear axle sufficiently and remove the coil springs.

8. Remove the torque arm and the lower control arms from the rear axle.

9. If equipped, disconnect the brake calipers and lines, plug the lines and remove the rotors.

10. Lower the axle from the vehicle and remove the stabilizer bar from the axle.

To install:

11. Connect the stabilizer bar to the rear axle and raise the assembly into position.

12. Install the rotors and calipers, if equipped.

13. Install the lower control arms and the torque arm to the rear axle.

14. Lower the housing sufficiently, install the rear springs and raise the housing back into position.

15. Install the brake line junction block bolt to the housing, then unplug and connect the brake lines to the wheel cylinders or calipers. Bleed the brake system.

16. Align the marks and install the propeller shaft.

17. Install the stabilizer bushing and links to the axle. Install the shock absorbers.

18. Connect the parking brake cables to the body clips and to the adjuster. Adjust the parking brake as necessary.

19. Check and add axle lubricant to the axle housing as necessary. Install the tire and wheel assemblies.

20. Remove the adjustable supports and lower the vehicle.

MANUAL TRANSMISSION

For further information on transmission/transaxles, please refer to "Chilton's Guide to Transmission Repair".

Transmission Assembly

REMOVAL & INSTALLATION

1. Disconnect the negative battery cable.

2. For all vehicles except 1992–93, remove the shift control lever knob. For 1991–93 vehicles, the shift lever knob is threaded and bonded with an adhesive and should not be removed unless the shift lever is replaced.

3. For 1989–90 vehicles, remove the shift lever assembly by removing the center console, shift lever boot screws, shift lever boot, shift lever bolts and the shift control lever.

4. Raise and safely support the vehicle. Drain the transmission oil.

5. Safely support the left side of the rear axle to avoid damaging the brake lines and remove the driveshaft assembly.

NOTE: When the torque arm is disconnected from the rear axle, the pressure of the rear springs may cause the axle to twist and damage the vehicle. In order to avoid this the axle must be secured and the coil springs must removed before the torque arm is disconnected.

6. Remove the rear coil springs, the torque arm rear attaching bolts, front torque arm outer bracket and the torque arm.

7. Disconnect the speed sensor connector and the transmission wire connectors.

8. Remove the catalytic converter hanger, nuts and bolts.

9. Safely support the engine. Remove the transmission support nuts and bolts. Remove the support.

10. For 1991–93 vehicles, carefully lower the transmission with the aid of a helper enough to remove the shift control bolts and lever. Remove the shift control lever from the extension housing.

11. Remove the transmission-to-bellhousing bolts.

12. With the aid of a helper, remove the transmission assembly.

To install:

13. Clean sealing surfaces of transmission-to-shifter location. Place a continuos ⅛ inch bead of RTV or equivalent, to the shifter-to-transmission sealing surface.

14. Install the transmission and secure with attaching bolts to the bellhousing.

15. Torque the transmission-to-bellhousing bolts to 55 ft. lbs. (75 Nm).

16. For 1991–93 vehicles, install the shifter onto the transmission and torque the bolts to 13 ft. lbs. (17 Nm).

17. Install the transmission support and torque the transmission mount nuts to 35 ft. lbs. (47 Nm) and the support bolts to 40 ft. lbs. (54 Nm).

18. Install the catalytic converter hanger and torque the bolts to 30 ft. lbs. (40 Nm) for 1989–90 vehicles or 38 ft. lbs. (47 Nm) for 1991–93 vehicles.

19. Reconnect all electrical connectors.

20. Install torque arm, driveshaft assembly and the rear coil springs.

21. Tighten the front torque arm bracket to 20 ft. lbs. (27 Nm) for 1989–90 vehicles or 30 ft. lbs. (41 Nm) for 1991–93 vehicles. Tighten the rear torque arm nuts to 98 ft. lbs. (133 Nm). Remove the engine support and left rear axle support stand.

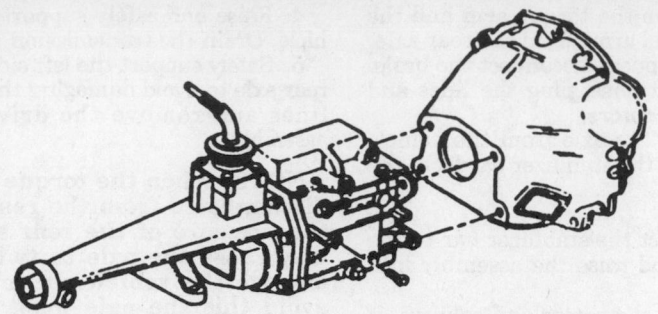

Transmission and bellhousing assembly

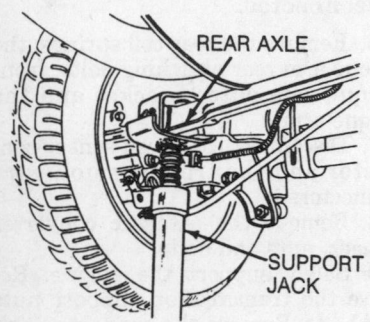

REAR AXLE

SUPPORT JACK

Supporting the rear axle during torque arm removal

22. Refill the transmission with Dexron® II or equivalent.

23. Lower the vehicle and connect the negative battery cable.

24. For 1989–90 vehicles, install the shift lever assembly.

25. Start the vehicle and inspect transmission for leaks and proper operation.

LINKAGE ADJUSTMENT

The M39, MK6 and MB1 5-speed manual transmissions are designed with an internal shift mechanism. Shifter control adjustments are not possible.

CLUTCH

Clutch Assembly

REMOVAL & INSTALLATION

1. Disconnect the negative battery cable.

2. Raise and safely support the vehicle.

3. Remove the transmission assembly.

4. Remove the clutch slave cylinder and heat shield assembly from the flywheel housing.

5. Remove the housing cover and the bolts attaching the flywheel housing to the engine. Remove the housing.

6. Remove the clutch release bearing. Slide the clutch fork from the ball stud and dust boot and remove the clutch fork with spring.

7. Install tool J–33169 for V6 engines, J-5824-01 for V8 engines, or equivalent clutch alignment arbor to support the clutch assembly during removal. Locate marks or a white painted letter on the clutch housing and an X mark on the flywheel. If the marks are not visible, place a mark on the flywheel and clutch cover for alignment during installation.

8. Loosen the clutch-to-flywheel bolts evenly 1 turn at a time until all spring pressure is released.

9. Remove the clutch and pressure plate assembly.

To install:

10. Inspect flywheel for heat stress, cracks or other defects and repair or replace as necesssary.

11. Inspect the clutch plate, disc, release bearing and fork for contamination, wear or heat stress, repair or replace as necessary.

12. Clean the pilot bearing then lubricate sparingly with machine oil.

13. Using the clutch alignment arbor, install the clutch pressure plate and disc onto the flywheel with the disc springs facing the transmission. The flywheel side is marked.

14. Align the marks on the flywheel with the mark on the pressure plate.

15. Install the pressure plate-to-flywheel bolts.

16. Alternately tighten the clutch assembly-to-flywheel bolts 1 turn at a time and then torque the bolts to 15 ft. lbs. (21 Nm) for the V6 engine or 30 ft. lbs. (40 Nm) for the V8 engine. Remove the clutch alignment tool.

17. Lubricate and install the clutch fork ball and clutch fork at the release bearing.

NOTE: If replacing the clutch fork, be sure to replace with the identical part number. Do not mix the V6 clutch fork with the V8 clutch or damage to the slave cylinder may result.

18. Install the dust boot, if removed.

19. Install the clutch release bearing onto the fork with the fork fingers and the retaining spring tabs installed into the release bearing grooves.

20. Install the clutch housing and torque the bolts to 35 ft. lbs. (47 Nm) for the V6 engine or 70 ft. lbs. (95 Nm) for the V8 engine.

21. Install the clutch housing cover and tighten the bolts to 53 inch lbs. (6 Nm).

22. Install the transmission, clutch slave cylinder and heat shield. Torque the slave cylinder bolts to 15 ft. lbs. (21 Nm).

23. Refill transmission with the proper type and quantity of oil. Lower the vehicle and check clutch operation.

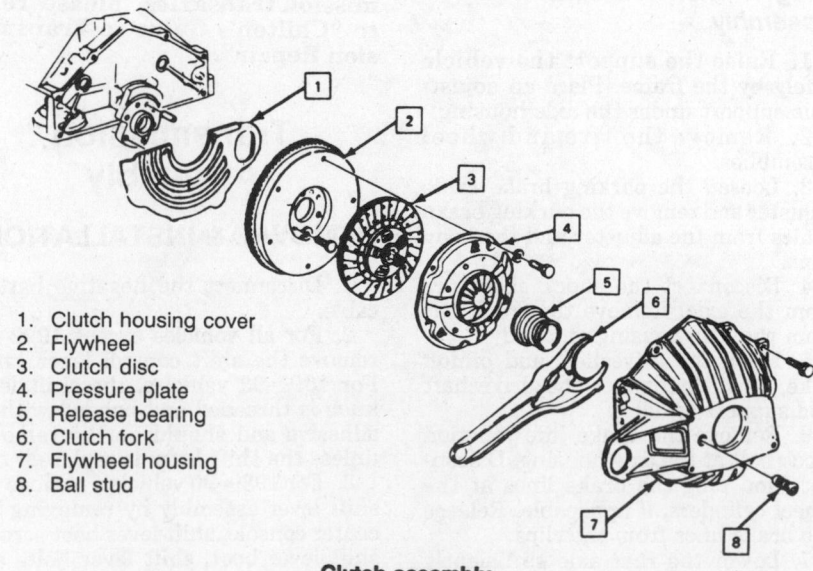

1. Clutch housing cover
2. Flywheel
3. Clutch disc
4. Pressure plate
5. Release bearing
6. Clutch fork
7. Flywheel housing
8. Ball stud

Clutch assembly

PEDAL HEIGHT/FREE-PLAY ADJUSTMENT

The hydraulic clutch system locates the clutch pedal height and provides automatic clutch adjustment. No adjustment of clutch linkage or pedal position is required.

Clutch Master Cylinder

REMOVAL & INSTALLATION

1. Disconnect the negative battery cable.
2. Remove the sound insulator or lower panel, as necessary, to gain access to the clutch pedal.
3. Disconnect the brake vacuum booster pushrod from the brake pedal. Remove the retainer and washer.
4. Disconnect the clutch master cylinder input rod from the pedal. Use a sharp cutting tool to cut the bushing retaining tabs.
5. Remove the clutch master cylinder-to-cowl nuts and the brake vacuum booster-to-cowl nuts.
6. Remove the hose clamp and the clutch fluid reservoir hose. Place a suitable drain pan under hose to catch the fluid leaking from the reservoir.
7. Pull the brake vacuum booster forward to gain access to the clutch master cylinder. Remove the clutch master cylinder with U-bolt from the cowl. Lower the master cylinder down to the clutch housing area.
8. Raise and safely support the vehicle.
9. Disconnect the high pressure hose and remove the clutch master cylinder.

To install:

10. Connect the high pressure hose and place the master cylinder up near the brake vacuum booster. Lower the vehicle.
11. Install the clutch master cylinder to the cowl with the U-bolt.
12. Install a new bushing to the pedal. Install the flat end of the bushing toward the pedal.
13. Install the clutch master cylinder input rod to the pedal. Install the retainer and washer.
14. Attach the brake vacuum booster to the cowl, connect the clutch fluid reservoir hose with the hose clamp and install the clutch master cylinder-to-cowl nuts. Tighten the nuts to 115 inch lbs. (13 Nm). Tighten the brake vacuum booster-to-cowl nuts to 15 ft. lbs. (21 Nm).
15. Replace the sound insulator or lower panel as necessary.
16. Connect the brake vacuum pushrod to the brake pedal.
17. Fill and bleed the clutch hydraulic system. Connect the negative battery cable.

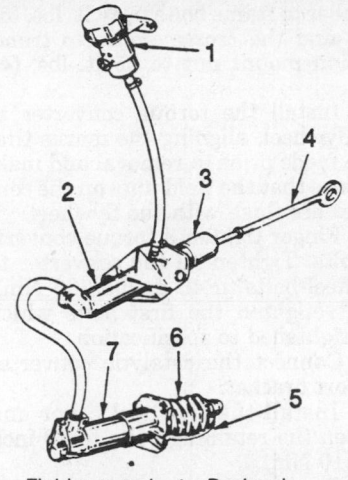

1. Fluid reservoir
2. Clutch master cylinder
3. Boot
4. Pushrod
5. Shipping strap
6. Boot
7. Clutch slave cylinder

Hydraulic clutch assembly

Clutch Slave Cylinder

REMOVAL & INSTALLATION

1. Disconnect the negative battery cable.
2. Remove the sound insulator panel to gain access to the clutch pedal.
3. Disconnect the clutch master cylinder input rod from the clutch pedal. Using a sharp cutting tool, cut the bushing retaining tabs.

NOTE: If the clutch master cylinder input rod is not disconnected, permanent damage to the slave cylinder will occur in the event that the clutch pedal is depressed while the slave cylinder is disconnected.

4. Raise and safely support the vehicle.
5. Disconnect the pressure hose and catch the leaking hydraulic fluid in a suitable container.
6. Remove the slave cylinder bolts, then remove the heat shield and slave cylinder.

To install:

7. Install the actuator and heat shield. Tighten the slave cylinder bolts to 15 ft. lbs. (21 Nm).
8. Install the pressure hose and lower the vehicle.
9. Install a new clutch pedal bushing with the flat side toward the clutch pedal.
10. Connect the clutch master cylinder input rod to the clutch pedal.
11. Install the sound insulator panel, bleed the hydraulic system and connect the negative battery cable.

Hydraulic Clutch System Bleeding

When bleeding the hydraulic clutch system always keep the reservoir filled with fresh clean brake fluid. Do not use fluid which has been bled from a system as it may contain moisture, air or other contaminants.

1. Clean all dirt and grease from the cap to make sure no foreign substances enter the system.
2. Remove the cap and diaphragm and fill the reservoir to the top with the approved DOT 3 brake fluid. Fully loosen the bleed screw which is in the slave cylinder body next to the inlet connection.
3. At this point, bubbles of air will appear at the bleed screw outlet. When the slave cylinder is full and a steady stream of fluid comes out of the slave cylinder bleeder, tighten the bleed screw to 18 inch lbs. (2 Nm).
4. Assemble the diaphragm and cap to the reservoir. Fluid in the reservoir should be level with the step. Exert a light load of about 20 lbs. to the slave cylinder piston by pushing the clutch fork towards the cylinder and loosening the bleed screw. Maintain a constant light load. Fluid and any air that is left will be expelled through the bleed port. Tighten the bleed screw when a steady flow of fluid and no air is being expelled.
5. Fill the reservoir fluid level back to normal capacity.
6. Exert a light load to the clutch fork, but do not open the bleeder screw. The piston in the slave cylinder will move slowly down the bore. Repeat this operation 2–3 times. The fluid movement will force any air left in the system into the reservoir. The hydraulic system should now be fully bled.
7. Check the operation of the clutch hydraulic system and repeat this procedure if necessary. Check the pushrod travel at the slave cylinder to insure the minimum travel is 0.43 inch for 2.8L and 3.1L engines or 0.57 in. for 5.0L and 5.7L engines.

AUTOMATIC TRANSMISSION

For further information on transmission/transaxles, please refer to "Chilton's Guide to Transmission Repair".

Transmission Assembly

REMOVAL & INSTALLATION

1. Disconnect the negative battery cable.
2. Remove the air cleaner assembly, if necessary.
3. Disconnect the Throttle Valve (TV) control cable at the throttle lever.
4. Remove the transmission oil dipstick. Unbolt and remove the dipstick tube.
5. Raise and support the vehicle safely, support the rear axle with adjustable lifting devices.
6. Remove the rear coil springs and the torque arm.
7. Mark the relationship between the driveshaft and the rear pinion flange so the driveshaft may be reinstalled in its original position. Remove the driveshaft from the vehicle.
8. Disconnect the speedometer cable or speed sensor, the electrical connectors and the shift linkage from the transmission.
9. Remove the flywheel cover, then mark the relationship between the torque converter and the flywheel.
10. Remove the torque converter to flywheel attaching bolts.
11. Disconnect the catalytic converter support bracket at the transmission.
12. Support the transmission with a jack, then remove the transmission mount to support nut.
13. Remove the transmission crossmember to frame bolts and, if used, insulators.
14. Lift the transmission slightly and remove the support. Slide the transmission support rearward.
15. Lower the transmission slightly. Disconnect the TV cable from the transmission. Disconnect and plug the oil cooler lines from the transmission.
16. Support the engine with a suitable tool. Remove the transmission to engine mounting bolts.
17. Attach a torque converter holding strap and remove the transmission from the vehicle. Keep the rear of the transmission lower then the front to avoid the possibility of the torque converter disengaging from the transmission.

To install:
18. Install the transmission in the vehicle.
19. Install and tighten the transmission to engine bolts to 35 ft. lbs. (47 Nm).
20. Connect the TV cable and oil cooler lines to the transmission.
21. Install the crossmember. Install and tighten the transmission cross-member to frame bolts to 40 ft. lbs. (54 Nm) and the crossmember to transmission mount nut to 35 ft. lbs. (47 Nm).
22. Install the torque converter to the flywheel, aligning the marks that were made prior to removal and making sure that the weld nuts on the converter are flush with the flywheel.
23. Finger tighten 3 torque converter bolts. Tighten all the converter to flywheel bolts to 46 ft. lbs. (63 Nm), then retighten the first bolts which was tightened to specification.
24. Connect the catalytic converter support bracket.
25. Install the flywheel cover and tighten the retaining bolts to 89 inch lbs. (10 Nm).
26. Connect the speedometer cable or speed sensor, the electrical connectors and the shift linkage control.
27. Install the driveshaft, aligning the marks that were made on the driveshaft and pinion flange prior to removal.
28. Install the torque arm and the rear coil springs.
29. Lower the vehicle.
30. Install the transmission dipstick and dipstick tube. Tighten the retaining bolt to 35 ft. lbs. (47 Nm) on V8 engines or to 55 ft. lbs. (75 Nm) for V6 engines.
31. Connect the TV control cable at the throttle lever.
32. Install the air cleaner assembly, if necessary, and connect the negative battery cable.

NOTE: **Transmission oil cooler flushing must be performed when a transmission is removed for service. The flushing should take place after the installation of the overhauled or replacement transmission assembly.**

33. With a suitable flushing tool and fluid, flush the transmission cooler and pipes.
34. Add the proper type and amount of transmission fluid, Start the engine and check the transmission fluid level. Adjust the TV cable and shift linkage, as necessary.

SHIFT CONTROL CABLE ADJUSTMENT

1. Raise and safely support the vehicle.
2. Loosen the shift control cable attachment at the shift lever.
3. Rotate the shift lever clockwise to the **P** detent and then back to the **N** detent.
4. Tighten the cable attaching nut to 11 ft. lbs. (15 Nm). The lever must be held out of **P** when tightening the nut. If applicable, tighten the shift cable bracket screws to 18 ft. lbs. (24 Nm).
5. Check cable adjustment by rotating the control lever through the detents.

THROTTLE VALVE CABLE ADJUSTMENT

NOTE: **Setting of the TV cable must be done by rotating the throttle lever at the throttle body. Do not use the accelerator pedal to rotate the throttle body lever.**

1. Ensure the engine is **OFF**.
2. Depress and hold-down the metal reset tab at the engine end of the TV cable.
3. Move the slider until it stops against the fitting.
4. Release the reset tab.
5. Rotate the throttle lever to it's full travel position.
6. The slider must move (ratchet) toward the lever when the lever is rotated to it's full travel position.
7. Ensure the cable moves freely. The cable may appear to function properly with the engine stopped and cold. Recheck after the engine is hot.

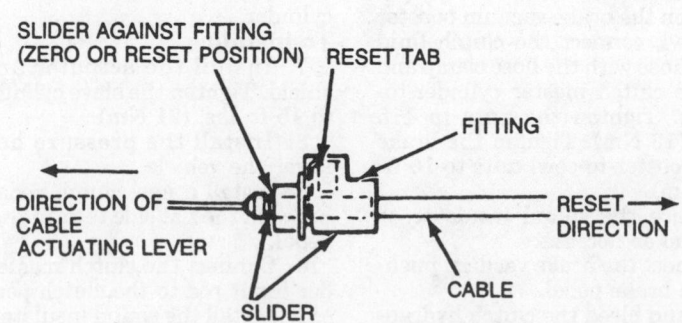

Throttle Valve (TV) cable adjustment

FRONT SUSPENSION

MacPherson Strut

REMOVAL & INSTALLATION

1. Raise and safely support the vehicle. Use a suitable device to support the lower control arm.
2. Mark and remove the wheel and tire assembly.
3. Remove the brake hose bracket.
4. Remove and discard the strut-to-knuckle bolts, washers and nuts.
5. Remove the cover from the upper mount assembly.
6. Remove the nut from the upper end of the strut.
7. Remove the strut and shield.

To install:

8. Install the strut and shield, attaching the nut to the upper end of the strut. Tighten the upper strut nut to 46 ft. lbs. (63 Nm) for 1989–91 vehicles or to 44 ft. lbs. (60 Nm) for 1992–93 vehicles.
9. Install the cover to the upper mount.
10. Install the new strut-to-knuckle bolts, washers and nuts. Tighten the strut-to-knuckle nuts to 125 ft. lbs. (170 Nm) followed by a 120 degree turn. Final torque must exceed 148 ft. lbs. (200 Nm).
11. Install the brake hose bracket.
12. Align the marks made earlier and install the tire and wheel assembly.
13. Lower the vehicle and check the front end alignment.

Coil Springs

REMOVAL & INSTALLATION

1. Raise and safely support the vehicle.
2. Mark and remove the wheel and tire assembly.
3. Remove the stabilizer link and bushings at the lower control arm.
4. Remove the cotter pin and nut from the tie rod end. Using a suitable tool, remove the tie rod ball joint stud from the steering knuckle.
5. Install a suitable spring compressor and compress the spring.
6. Loosen the lower control arm pivot bolts and pivot the lower control arm rearward.
7. Carefully remove the spring compressor and remove the spring.

To install:

8. Properly position the spring on the control arm, making sure the spring insulator is in place. The bottom of the spring is coiled helical and the top is coiled flat, with a gripper notch near the end of the wire. After assembly, the end of the spring coil must cover all or part of 1 inspection drain hole on the lower control arm. The other hole must be completely uncovered.
9. Carefully install the spring compressor and compress the spring.

NOTE: Take care not to damage the corrosion protection coating on the spring. If any of the coating is removed, it must be repaired.

10. Pivot the lower control arm forward into position in the frame.
11. Tighten the lower control arm pivot bolt/nuts to 66 ft. lbs. (90 Nm) for 1989–91 vehicles or to 61 ft. lbs. (83 Nm) for 1992–93 vehicles.
12. Remove the spring compressor.
13. Install the stabilizer linkage. Tighten the stabilizer link nut to 16 ft. lbs. (22 Nm) for 1989–91 vehicles or to 13 ft. lbs. (17 Nm) for 1992–93 vehicles.
14. Install the steering knuckle to the tie rod ball joint stud. Tighten the nut to 83 ft. lbs. (113 Nm) for 1989–91 vehicles or to 80 ft. lbs. (108 Nm) for 1992–93 vehicles.
15. Install a new cotter pin. If the hole in the stud does not line up with the slot in the nut, tighten the nut until it does. Do not back off the nut to install the cotter pin.
16. Align the marks made earlier and install the wheel and tire assembly. Lower the vehicle.

Lower Ball Joints

INSPECTION

1. Raise and safely support the vehicle. Use a suitable device to support the lower control arm in it's normal ride height position.
2. Grasp the wheel at the top and bottom. Alternately push and pull on the top and the bottom of the wheel in an attempt to move it toward and away from the vehicle. Check for any horizontal movement of the steering knuckle relative to the lower control arm. If there is any movement the ball joint must be replaced.
3. Check the ball joint when it is disconnected from the steering knuckle. If there is any looseness in the ball stud, if the ball stud can be twisted in it's socket using finger pressure or if there are any cuts or tears in the ball joint seal, replace the ball joint.
4. Visually inspect the ball joint seal for cuts and tears. Ball joints with cuts or tears in their seals must be replaced.

REMOVAL & INSTALLATION

1. Raise and safely support the vehicle. Support the lower control arm under the spring seat with a suitable jack which must remain in position throughout the procedure to retain the coil spring and control arm position.
2. Mark and remove the wheel and tire assembly.
3. Remove the cotter pin and loosen the lower ball joint nut. 4. Using a suitable tool, break the ball stud loose from the steering knuckle. Separate the lower control arm from the steering knuckle.
5. Remove the grease fittings and

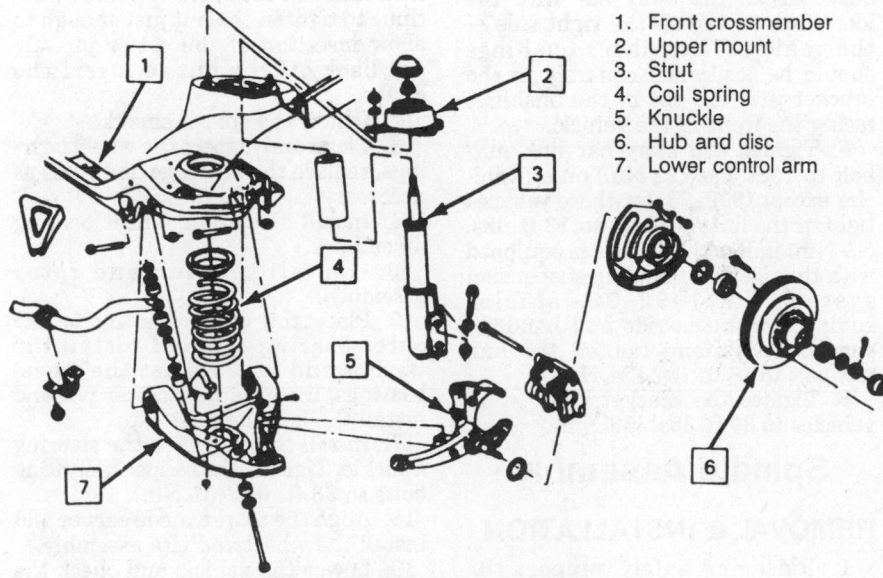

1. Front crossmember
2. Upper mount
3. Strut
4. Coil spring
5. Knuckle
6. Hub and disc
7. Lower control arm

Front suspension components

using suitable ball joint tools, press the ball joint from the lower control arm.

To install:

6. Position the new ball joint into the lower control arm and press into place using suitable ball joint installation tools. The ball joint must firmly press into the lower control arm, or the control arm may need to be replaced.

NOTE: When installing a new ball joint, position the purge vent on the rubber boot facing inward.

7. Connect the ball joint to the steering knuckle. Install the ball stud nut and tighten to 83 ft. lbs. (113 Nm) for 1989–91 vehicles or to 80 ft. lbs. (108 Nm) for 1992–93 vehicles. Then tighten again just enough to align the nut slot with the stud hold and install the cotter pin. Do not back off the nut to align the slot and hole.

8. Install and lubricate the ball joint fitting until grease appears at the seal.

9. Align the marks made earlier and install the wheel and tire assembly.

10. Lower the vehicle, check and adjust the front end alignment as necessary.

Lower Control Arms

REMOVAL & INSTALLATION

1. Raise and safely support the vehicle.

2. Mark and remove the wheel and tire assembly.

3. Remove the stabilizer link and bushings at the lower control arm.

4. Remove the cotter pin and nut from the tie rod end. Using a suitable tool, remove the steering knuckle from the tie rod ball joint stud.

5. Install a suitable spring compressor and compress the coil spring.

6. Remove the lower control arm pivot bolts.

7. Remove the control arm and spring.

To install:

8. Properly position the spring on the control arm, making sure the spring insulator is in place. The bottom of the spring is coiled helical and the top is coiled flat, with a gripper notch near the end of the wire. After assembly, the end of the spring coil must cover all or part of 1 inspection drain hole. The other hole must be completely uncovered.

9. Carefully install the spring compressor and compress the spring.

NOTE: Take care not to damage the corrosion protection coating on the spring. If any of the coating is removed, it must be repaired.

10. Install the lower control arm into position in the frame.

11. Install the bolts. The front bolt installs from front to rear first. Tighten the lower control arm pivot bolt/nuts to 66 ft. lbs. (90 Nm) for 1989–91 vehicles or to 61 ft. lbs. (83 Nm) for 1992–93 vehicles.

12. Remove the spring compressor.

13. Install the stabilizer linkage. Tighten the stabilizer link nut to 16 ft. lbs. (22 Nm) for 1989–91 vehicles or to 13 ft. lbs. (17 Nm) for 1992–93 vehicles.

14. Install the steering knuckle to the tie rod ball joint stud. Tighten the nut to 83 ft. lbs. (113 Nm) for 1989–91 vehicles or to 80 ft. lbs. (108 Nm) for 1992–93 vehicles.

15. Install a new cotter pin. If the hole in the stud does not line up with the slot in the nut, tighten the nut until it does. Do not back off the nut to install the cotter pin.

16. Align the marks made earlier and install the wheel and tire assembly. Lower the vehicle.

Sway Bar

REMOVAL & INSTALLATION

1. Raise and safely support the vehicle.

2. Remove each side of the sway bar linkage by removing the nut from the link bolt, pulling the bolt from the linkage and remove the retainers, grommets and spacer.

3. Remove the bracket-to-frame or body bolts and remove the sway bar, rubber bushings and brackets. Remove the lower structure brace if equipped.

To install:

4. Reverse of the removal procedure. Install the sway bar with the identification tag on the right side of the vehicle. The rubber bushings should be positioned squarely in the bracket with the slit in the bushings facing the front of the vehicle.

5. Tighten the sway bar link nut/bolt to 16 ft. lbs. (22 Nm) on all vehicles except 1992–93, for these vehicles tighten the link nut/bolt to 13 ft. lbs. (17 Nm) unless the vehicle is equipped with the ride and handling suspension system. For 1992–93 vehicles equipped with the ride and handling suspension system, tighten the link nut/bolt to 18 ft. lbs. (24 Nm).

6. Tighten the bracket bolts on all vehicles to 39 ft. lbs. (53 Nm).

Spindle Assembly

REMOVAL & INSTALLATION

1. Raise and safely support the vehicle.

2. Mark and remove the wheel and tire assembly.

3. Remove the caliper mounting bolts and remove the caliper. Support the caliper with mechanics wire. Do not let the caliper hang by the brake hose.

4. Remove the dust cap from the hub and remove the cotter pin, nut and washer from the spindle. Remove the hub and rotor assembly from the spindle. Remove the splash shield.

5. Remove the outer wheel bearing assembly from the hub. Using a suitable tool, pry out the inner bearing lip seal and remove the inner wheel bearing assembly.

6. Using a suitable tool, disconnect the tie rod from the spindle.

7. Support the lower control arm. Using a suitable tool, disconnect the ball joint from the spindle.

8. Remove and discard 2 bolts, washers and nuts attaching the strut to the spindle and remove the spindle.

To install:

9. Position the spindle to the strut. Install new strut-to-spindle bolts, washers and nuts to the strut. Tighten the 2 nuts to 125 ft. lbs. (170 Nm) followed by an additional 120 degree turn. The final torque must exceed 148 ft. lbs. (200 Nm).

10. Connect the ball joint stud and nut to the spindle. Tighten the castle nut to 83 ft. lbs. (113 Nm) and install a new cotter pin. If the hole in the stud does not line up with the slot in the castellated nut, continue to tighten the nut just enough to allow insertion of the cotter pin. Do not back off the nut to insert the cotter pin.

11. Connect the tie rod. Tighten the castellated nut to 35 ft. lbs. (47 Nm). If the hole in the stud does not line up with a slot in the castellated nut, continue to tighten the nut just enough to allow insertion of the cotter pin. Do not back off the nut to insert the cotter.

12. Install the splash shield.

13. Clean and inspect the wheel bearings, replace the bearings and races as necessary.

14. Install the inner wheel bearing assemblies.

15. Install the hub and rotor assembly.

16. Place the outer bearing in the outer bearing cup and install the washer and nut. Adjust the wheel bearings, install a new cotter pin and install the bearing dust cap.

17. Install the caliper to the steering knuckle. Tighten the caliper mounting bolts to 38 ft. lbs. (51 Nm).

18. Align the marks made earlier and install the wheel and tire assembly.

19. Lower the vehicle and check brake fluid level.

Front Wheel Bearings

ADJUSTMENT

1. Raise and safely support the vehicle.
2. Remove the wheel cover or center cap to expose the rotor dust cap.
3. Remove the dust cap from the hub.
4. Remove the cotter pin from the spindle nut.
5. Tighten the spindle nut to 12 ft. lbs. (16 Nm) while turning the wheel forward by hand to fully seat the bearings. This will remove any grease or burrs which could cause excessive wheel bearing play later.
6. Back off the nut to the just loose position.
7. Hand tighten the spindle nut. Loosen the spindle nut just enough that either hole in the spindle lines up with a slot in the nut, not more than ½ flat.
8. Install a new cotter pin. Bend the ends of the cotter pin against the nut and cut off the extra length to ensure the ends will not interfere with the dust cap.
9. Using a dial indicator, check the hub assembly. There should be 0.001–0.005 inch (0.03–0.13mm) endplay when properly adjusted.
10. Install the dust cap on the hub. Install the wheel cover or center cap.
11. Lower the vehicle.

REMOVAL & INSTALLATION

1. Raise and support the vehicle safely.
2. Mark and remove the wheel and tire assembly.
3. Remove the caliper assembly.
4. Remove the dust cap from the hub. Remove the cotter pin, nut and washer from the spindle.
5. Remove the hub and rotor assembly.
6. Remove the outer bearing assembly from the hub. The inner bearing assembly will remain in the hub and may be removed by prying out the inner seal with a suitable tool. Discard the seal after removal.
7. Remove the old bearing races from the hub with a suitable brass drift inserted behind the races in a recessed slot.
8. Clean all parts in clean solvent and air dry. Remove all old grease from the entire assembly. Do not mix greases as mixing may change grease properties and result in poor performance. Do not spin the bearing with compressed air while drying or the bearing may be damaged.
To install:
9. Inspect the bearings for cracked cages and worn or pitted rollers. Check the bearing races for cracks, scores or pitting condition. Replace as necessary.
10. If the races were removed, drive or press the races into the hub.
11. Apply a thin film of high temperature wheel bearing grease to the spindle at the outer bearing seat and at the inner bearing seat, shoulder and seal seat.
12. Put a small quantity of grease inboard of each bearing cup in the hub.
13. Pack the wheel bearings using a suitable bearing packer. If a bearing packer is not available, the bearings can be packed by hand. If hand packing is used, it is extremely important to work the grease thoroughly into the bearings between the rollers, cone and cage.
14. Place the inner bearing cone and roller assembly in the hub. Put an additional quantity of grease outboard of the bearing.
15. Install a new grease seal using a suitable tool until the seal is flush with the hub. Lubricate the seal lip with a thin layer of grease.
16. Carefully install the hub and rotor assembly. Place the outer bearing assembly in the outer bearing race. Install the washer and nut and tighten to 12 ft. lbs. (16 Nm).
17. Install caliper assembly, align the marks made earlier and install the wheel and tire assembly.
18. Adjust the wheel bearings and install the dust cap and the wheel cover or center cap as applicable. Lower the vehicle.

REAR SUSPENSION

Shock Absorbers

REMOVAL & INSTALLATION

1. Raise and support the vehicle safely at height which will allow access to both the upper and lower shock mounts. Support the rear axle with a jackstand.
2. Pull back the carpet in the rear hatch and remove the upper shock attaching nut.
3. Remove the lower shock mounting nut. Remove the shock absorber from the vehicle.

To install:
4. Position the shock absorber through the body mounting hole and loosely install the lower shock absorber mounting nut.
5. Install the upper shock absorber mounting nut and tighten the upper shock attaching nut to 13 ft. lbs. (17 Nm).
6. Tighten the lower attaching nut to 70 ft. lbs. (95 Nm) for 1989–91 vehicles or to 66 ft. lbs. (90 Nm) for 1992–93 vehicles.
7. Remove the rear axle support and lower the vehicle.

Coil Springs

REMOVAL & INSTALLATION

1. Raise and safely support the vehicle. Install an adjustable lifting device supporting the rear axle.
2. Remove the track bar mounting bolt at the axle assembly and loosen the track bar bolt at the body brace.
3. Disconnect the rear brake hose clip at the underbody to allow additional brake line play to lower axle.
4. Disconnect the right and left shock absorber lower attaching nuts.
5. Carefully lower the rear axle sufficiently to remove the coil springs and, if necessary, the insulators. Make certain that at no time is the rear axle suspended by the brake lines as damage to the hydraulic brake system may occur.
To install:
6. Position the springs and insulators properly in the spring seats. Be sure the spring is seated in the same position as before removal and raise the axle into place.
7. Install the shock absorbers to the rear axle. Tighten the shock mounting nuts to 70 ft. lbs. (95 Nm) for 1989–91 vehicles or to 66 ft. lbs. (90 Nm) for 1992–93 vehicles.
8. Clean and install the track bar mounting bolt and nut and the axle.
9. For 1989–91 vehicles, tighten the track bar mounting nut at the axle to 80 ft. lbs. (108 Nm), or to 76 ft. lbs. (103 Nm) for 1992–93 vehicles. Tighten the track bar bracket nut to 61 ft. lbs. (83 Nm).
10. Connect the rear brake line clip to the underbody.
11. Remove the adjustable lifting device and lower the vehicle.

Rear Control Arms

REMOVAL & INSTALLATION

NOTE: If both control arms are being replaced, remove and replace 1 control arm at a time to prevent the axle from rolling or slipping sideways and thus making replacement difficult or damaging components.

1. Raise and safely support the vehicle. Using a suitable jack, support the rear axle at the curb height position.
2. Remove the control arm-to-axle housing bolt and control arm-to-underbody bolt.
3. Remove the control arm.

To install:

4. Position the control arm and install the front and rear nuts and bolts.
5. Tighten the front and rear bolts to 85 ft. lbs. (115 Nm) for 1989–91 vehicles or to 80 ft. lbs. (108 Nm) for 1992–93 vehicles.
6. Remove the supports and lower the vehicle.

STEERING

Steering Wheel

REMOVAL & INSTALLATION

1989 Vehicles

1. Disconnect the negative battery cable.
2. Remove the horn pad.
3. Disconnect the horn contact lead.
4. Remove the retainer and steering wheel nut.
5. Using a suitable steering wheel puller, remove the steering wheel.

To install:

6. Position the steering wheel on the column and install the steering wheel nut. Tighten the steering wheel nut to 31 ft. lbs. (42 Nm) and install the retainer.
7. Connect the horn lead to the cam tower and install the horn pad.
8. Connect the negative battery cable.

1990–93 Vehicles

— **CAUTION** —

If equipped with a Supplemental Inflatable Restraint (SIR) system, follow the recommended disarming procedures before performing any work on or around the system. Failure to do so may result in possible deployment of the air bag and/or personal injury.

1. If equipped, disable the Supplemental Inflatable Restraint (SIR) system.
2. Disconnect the negative battery cable.
3. Loosen the screws and locknuts from the back of the steering wheel using a suitable Torx® driver or equiva-

lent, until the inflator module can be released from the steering wheel. Remove the inflator module from the steering wheel.

— **CAUTION** —

When carrying a live inflator module, ensure the bag and trim cover are pointed away from the body. Never carry the inflator module by the wires or connector on the underside of the module. This will minimize the chance of injury should the module accidentally deploy. When placing a live inflator module on a bench or other surface, always place the bag and trim cover up, away from the surface. This is necessary so a free space is provided to allow for air bag expansion in the unlikely event of accidental deployment.

4. Disconnect the coil assembly connector and CPA clip from the inflator module terminal.
5. Remove the steering wheel locking nut.
6. Using a suitable puller, remove the steering wheel and disconnect the horn contact. When attaching the steering wheel puller, use care to prevent threading the side screws into and thereby damaging the coil assembly.

To install:

7. Route the coil assembly connector through the steering wheel.
8. Connect the horn contact and install the steering wheel. When installing the steering wheel, align the block tooth on the steering wheel with the block tooth on the steering shaft within 1 female serration.
9. Install the steering wheel locking nut. Tighten the nut to 32 ft. lbs. (43 Nm).
10. Connect the coil assembly connector and CPA clip to the inflator module terminal.
11. Install the inflator module. Ensure the wiring is not exposed or trapped between the inflator module and the steering wheel. Tighten the inflator module screws to 25 inch lbs. (2.8 Nm).
12. Enable the SIR system, if equipped and connect the negative battery cable.

Steering Column

REMOVAL & INSTALLATION

1. Turn the wheels to the straight-ahead position. Turn the ignition to **LOCK** and disconnect the negative battery cable.
2. If equipped with air bag, disable the Supplemental Inflatable Restraint (SIR) system.
3. Remove the nut and bolt from the upper intermediate shaft coupling.

Separate the coupling from the lower end of the steering column.

4. Remove the steering wheel, if the column is to be replaced or repaired on the bench.
5. Remove the sound insulator panel and, if equipped, the knee bolster and bracket.
6. Remove the bolts attaching the toe plate to the cowl.
7. Disconnect the electrical connectors.
8. Remove the capsule nuts attaching the steering column support bracket to the instrument panel and carefully lower the column.
9. Disconnect the park lock cable from the ignition switch inhibitor, if equipped with automatic transmission.
10. Remove the steering column from the vehicle. Take care when handling the column assembly, it is extremely susceptible to damage. Leaning on the column, dropping it or exposing it to shock or stress could impair the column's collapsible design.

To install:

NOTE: If a replacement steering column is being installed, do not remove the anit-rotation pin until after the steering column has been connected to the steering gear. Removing the anit-rotation pin before the steering column is connected to the steering gear may damage the SIR coil assembly.

11. Position the steering column in the vehicle.
12. Connect the park lock cable to the ignition switch inhibitor on vehicles with automatic transmission.
13. Install the capsule nuts attaching the steering column support bracket to the instrument panel and tighten to 20 ft. lbs. (27 Nm).
14. Install the nut and bolt to the upper intermediate shaft coupling attaching the upper intermediate shaft to the steering column. Tighten the nut to 44 ft. lbs. (60 Nm) for 1989–91 vehicles or to 40 ft. lbs. (54 Nm) for 1992–93 vehicles.
15. Install the bolts attaching the toe plate to the cowl and tighten to 58 inch lbs. (6.5 Nm) for 1989–91 vehicles or to 37 inch lbs. (4.2 Nm) for 1992–93 vehicles.
16. Connect the electrical connectors.
17. Remove the anti-rotation pin if a service replacement steering column is being installed.
18. Install the knee bolster and bracket, if equipped and the sound insulator panel.
19. If a service replacement steering column is being installed, remove the

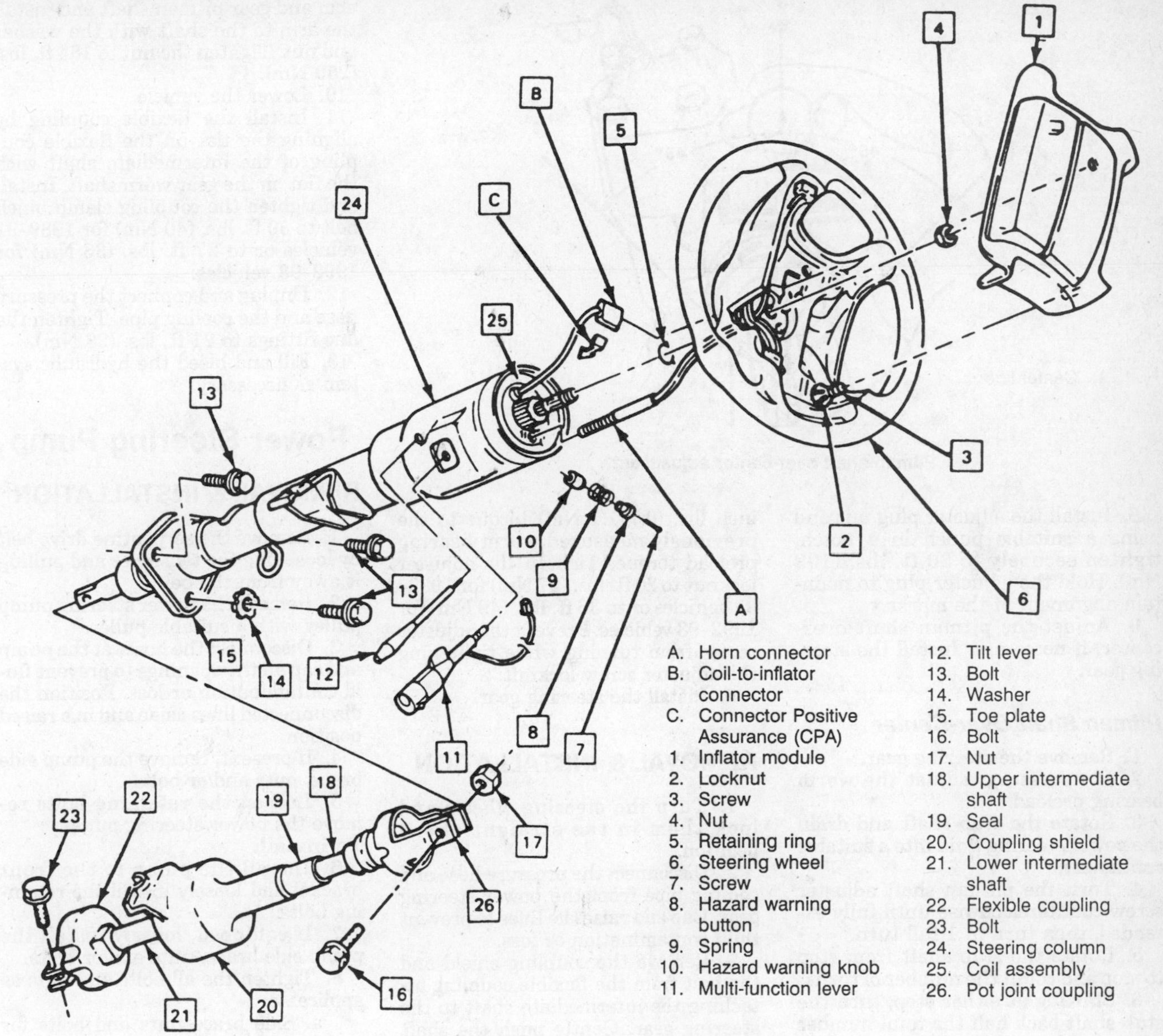

Steering column assembly with air bag

A. Horn connector
B. Coil-to-inflator connector
C. Connector Positive Assurance (CPA)
1. Inflator module
2. Locknut
3. Screw
4. Nut
5. Retaining ring
6. Steering wheel
7. Screw
8. Hazard warning button
9. Spring
10. Hazard warning knob
11. Multi-function lever
12. Tilt lever
13. Bolt
14. Washer
15. Toe plate
16. Bolt
17. Nut
18. Upper intermediate shaft
19. Seal
20. Coupling shield
21. Lower intermediate shaft
22. Flexible coupling
23. Bolt
24. Steering column
25. Coil assembly
26. Pot joint coupling

hexagon locking nut, the coil assembly shipping cover and disengage the connector from the cover.

NOTE: If SIR coil has become uncentered by turning of the steering wheel without the column connected to the steering gear, follow the proper centering procedure for the SIR coil assembly.

20. Install the steering wheel.
21. Enable the SIR system and connect the negative battery cable.

Power Steering Gear

ADJUSTMENT

NOTE: Adjust the worm bearing preload first, then proceed with the pitman shaft over-center adjustment.

Worm Bearing Preload

1. Remove the steering gear.
2. Rotate the stub shaft and drain the power steering fluid into a suitable container.
3. Mount the gear in a vise and remove the adjuster plug nut.
4. Turn the adjuster plug in (clockwise) using a suitable spanner wrench until the adjuster plug and thrust bearing are firmly bottomed in the housing. Tighten the adjuster plug to 20 ft. lbs. (27 Nm) for 1989–91 vehicles or to 22 ft. lbs. (30 Nm) for 1992–93 vehicles.
5. Place an index mark on the housing even with 1 of the holes in the adjuster plug.

6. Measure back counterclockwise ½ inch (13mm) from the mark and place a second mark on the housing.
7. Turn the adjuster plug counterclockwise until the hole in the adjuster plug is aligned with the second mark on the housing.

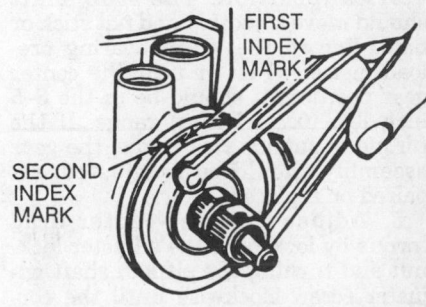

Adjusting the worm bearing preload

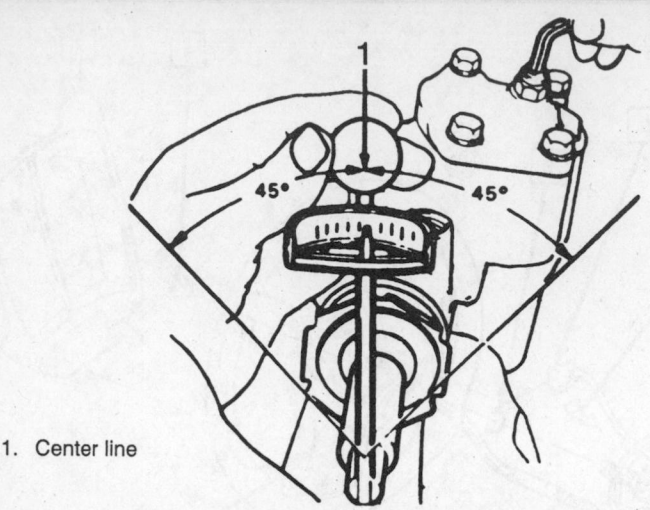

1. Center line

Pitman shaft over-center adjustment

8. Install the adjuster plug nut and using a suitable punch in a notch, tighten securely to 80 ft. lbs. (109 Nm). Hold the adjuster plug to maintain alignment of the marks.

9. Adjust the pitman shaft over-center, if necessary. Install the steering gear.

Pitman Shaft Over-Center

1. Remove the steering gear.
2. If necessary, adjust the worm bearing preload.
3. Rotate the stub shaft and drain the power steering fluid into a suitable container.
4. Turn the pitman shaft adjuster screw counterclockwise until fully extended, then turn in 1 full turn.
5. Rotate the stub shaft from stop to stop and count the number of turns.
6. Starting at either stop, turn the stub shaft back half the total number of turns. This is the "Center" position of the gear. When the gear is centered, the flat on the stub shaft should face upward and be parallel with the side cover and the master spline on the pitman shaft should be in line with the adjuster screw.
7. Rotate the stub shaft 45 degrees each side of the center using a suitable torque wrench with the handle in the vertical position. The stub shaft should move smoothly and not stick or bind. Record the worm bearing preload measured on or near the center gear position, it should be in the 6–5 inch lbs. (0.7–1.7 Nm) range. If the torque is outside this range, the gear assembly should be readjusted, repaired or replaced.
8. Adjust the over-center drag torque by loosening the adjuster locknut and turning the pitman shaft adjuster screw clockwise until the correct drag torque is obtained: Add 6–10

inch lbs. (0.7–1.1 Nm) torque to the previously measured worm bearing preload torque. Tighten the adjuster locknut to 20 ft. lbs. (27 Nm) for 1989–91 vehicles or to 36 ft. lbs. (49 Nm) for 1992–93 vehicles. Prevent the adjuster screw from turning while tightening the adjuster screw locknut.

9. Install the steering gear.

REMOVAL & INSTALLATION

1. Turn the steering wheels and lock them in the straight-ahead position.
2. Disconnect the pressure hose and cooling pipe from the power steering gear. Cap and raise the lines to prevent fluid contamination or loss.
3. Remove the coupling shield and the bolt from the flexible coupling attaching the intermediate shaft to the steering gear. Gently push the shaft assembly rearward to disengage the latch from the steering gear.
4. Raise and support the vehicle safely.
5. Remove the pitman arm nut and washer. Mark the position of the pitman arm in relation to the gear pitman shaft and remove the arm from the shaft with a suitable puller.
6. Remove the bolts and washers retaining the steering gear box to the side frame rail and remove the gear box from the vehicle.
To install:
7. Position the power steering gear to the frame and loosely install the washers and bolts. Adjust the gear so it aligns as straight as possible with the intermediate shaft.
8. Tighten the steering gear mounting bolts to 66 ft. lbs. (90 Nm) for 1989–91 vehicles or to 73 ft. lbs. (99 Nm) for 1992–93 vehicles.
9. Align the marks on the pitman

arm and gear pitman shaft and install the arm to the shaft with the washer and nut. Tighten the nut to 184 ft. lbs. (250 Nm).

10. Lower the vehicle.
11. Install the flexible coupling by aligning the flat on the flexible coupling of the intermediate shaft with the flat on the gear wormshaft. Install and tighten the coupling clamp pinch bolt to 30 ft. lbs. (40 Nm) for 1989–91 vehicles or to 27 ft. lbs. (36 Nm) for 1992–93 vehicles.
12. Unplug and connect the pressure hose and the cooling pipe. Tighten the line fittings to 21 ft. lbs. (28 Nm).
13. Fill and bleed the hydraulic system as necessary.

Power Steering Pump

REMOVAL & INSTALLATION

1. Remove the serpentine drive belt by loosening the tensioner and pulling it away from the belt.
2. Remove the power steering pump pulley with a suitable puller.
3. Disconnect the hoses at the pump and cap all the openings to prevent fluid contamination or loss. Position the disconnected lines aside and in a raised position.
4. If present, remove the pump side brace, nuts and/or bolts.
5. Loosen the retaining bolts remove the power steering pump.
To install:
6. Install the pump to the front bracket and loosely install the retaining bolts.
7. If equipped, loosely install the pump side brace, nuts and/or bolts.
8. Tighten the all bolts and nuts as applicable:
   a. Side brace nuts and bolts for the 2.8L or 3.1L engines to 18 ft. lbs. (25 Nm).
   b. Side brace to engine nut for the 5.0L or 5.7L engines to 24 ft. lbs. (33 Nm).
   c. Side brace to pump nut for the 5.0L or 5.7L engines to 37 ft. lbs. (50 Nm).
   d. Power steering pump retaining bolts to 37 ft. lbs. (50 Nm).
9. Uncap and connect the hoses to the pump. Tighten fittings to 21 ft. lbs. (28 Nm).
10. Using a suitable pulley installation tool, install the power steering pump pulley.
11. Install the serpentine drive belt.
12. Fill and bleed the hydraulic system as necessary.

BELT ADJUSTMENT

The power steering pump is driven by a serpentine belt. The serpentine belt is kept in adjustment by an automatic tensioner. No adjustment of the belt is required. If improper belt tension is suspected, refer to the serpentine belt tension check procedure under Alternator Belt Adjustment.

SYSTEM BLEEDING

1. With the engine **OFF**, raise and safely support the vehicle high enough to get the wheels off the ground.
2. Turn the wheels all the way to the left, add power steering fluid to the **COLD** mark on the fluid level indicator.
3. Start the engine and run at fast idle momentarily, shut the engine **OFF** and recheck the fluid level. If necessary, add fluid to bring level to the **COLD** mark.
4. Start the engine and bleed the system by turning the wheels from side to side without hitting the stops.
5. Return the wheels to the center position and keep the engine running for a few minutes.
6. Road test the vehicle and recheck the fluid level ensuring the level is up to the **HOT** mark.

Tie Rod Ends

REMOVAL & INSTALLATION

1. Raise and safely support the vehicle.
2. Remove the cotter pins from the ball studs and remove the castellated nuts.
3. Disconnect the tie rod end from the steering arm or knuckle with a tie rod joint separator.
4. Remove the inner ball stud from the intermediate rod with a puller.
5. Mark the tie rod end positions in relation to the adjuster tube. Loosen the clamp bolts and unscrew the ends from the adjuster tubes. Count the number of turns required to remove each tie rod end from the adjuster tube. If a force of more than 80 inch lbs. (9 Nm) is required to remove the ends after break away, the fasteners should be replaced.
To install:
6. Inspect the threads on the ball stud and castle nut for damage and the ball stud taper for nicks. Check the seal for damage. Replace components as necessary.
7. Lubricate the tie rod adjuster tube threads with chassis lube. Install the tie rod end into the tie rod adjuster tube, using the same number of turns counted during removal. This should align the marks made prior to removal of the ends from the adjuster.
8. Insert the inner balls stud to the intermediate rod and loosely attach the nut.
9. Install the tie rod end into the steering arm and install the castellated nut.
10. Tighten all nuts to 35 ft. lbs. (48 Nm) except for the inner ball attaching nut on 1991–93 vehicles which should be tightened to 40 ft. lbs. (54 Nm). Tighten all castellated the nuts again just enough to align the slot in the nut with the hole in the stud. Do not back off the nut to align the slot and hole.
11. Install new cotter pins on all castellated nuts.
12. Position the clamp on the adjuster tube with the bolt to the bottom of the tube and the nut to the front of the vehicle. Tighten the adjuster clamp nut to 15 ft. lbs. (20 Nm).
13. Lower the vehicle, check and adjust the toe setting as necessary.

BRAKES

Master Cylinder

REMOVAL & INSTALLATION

1. Disconnect the brake lines at the master cylinder.
2. Plug the lines to prevent fluid contamination or loss.
3. Remove the 2 master cylinder attaching nuts.
4. If equipped with a manual transmission, move the clutch master cylinder reservoir and bracket aside.
5. Move the combination valve aside.
6. Remove the master cylinder.
To install:
7. Install the master cylinder, combination valve and if applicable, the clutch master cylinder with bracket.
8. Install and tighten the 2 attaching nuts to 20 ft. lbs. (27 Nm) for 1989–90 vehicles, to 18 ft. lbs. (25 Nm) for 1991 vehicles or to 24 ft. lbs. (33 Nm) for 1992–93 vehicles.
9. Uncap and install the brake lines to the master cylinder. Tighten the fittings to 18 ft. lbs. (24 Nm).
10. Fill the master cylinder to the proper level with clean brake fluid and bleed the brake system.

Combination Valve

REMOVAL & INSTALLATION

1. Disconnect the negative battery cable.
2. Disconnect and the brake lines at the combination valve. Plug the lines to prevent fluid contamination or loss.
3. Disconnect the electrical connector from the combination valve switch terminal.
4. Remove the 2 nuts attaching the combination valve to the booster.
5. On vehicles with a manual transmission, move the clutch master cylinder and bracket aside.
6. Remove the combination valve.
To install:
7. Install the combination valve and if applicable, the clutch master cylinder with bracket.
8. Install the 2 attaching nuts and tighten to 20 ft. lbs. (27 Nm) for 1989–90 vehicles, to 18 ft. lbs. (25 Nm) for 1991 vehicles or to 24 ft. lbs. (33 Nm) for 1992–93 vehicles.
9. Uncap and install the brake lines to the master cylinder. Tighten the fittings to 18 ft. lbs. (24 Nm).
10. Connect the electrical connector to the combination valve switch terminal.
11. Connect the negative battery cable and bleed the brake system.

Power Brake Booster

REMOVAL & INSTALLATION

1. Disconnect the negative battery cable.
2. Disconnect the vacuum hose from the vacuum check valve.
3. Remove the 2 master cylinder attaching nuts.
4. On vehicles with manual transmission, remove the clutch master cylinder bracket with the clutch master cylinder reservoir and position aside.
5. Remove the combination valve with the attached combination valve bracket and position aside.
6. Remove the master cylinder from the booster.
7. Working inside the vehicle, remove the retainer and disconnect the booster pushrod from the brake pedal. Remove the booster attaching nuts.
8. Remove the power brake booster.
To install:
9. Install the power brake booster and tighten the attaching nuts to to 15 ft. lbs. (21 Nm) for 1989–91 vehicles or to 24 ft. lbs. (33 Nm) for 1992–93 vehicles.
10. Connect the booster pushrod and retainer to the brake pedal.
11. Install the master cylinder, combination valve and if applicable, the clutch master cylinder reservoir and bracket to the booster mounting studs.
12. Install the 2 master cylinder attaching nuts and tighten to 20 ft. lbs. (27 Nm) for 1989–90 vehicles, to 18 ft. lbs. (25 Nm) for 1991 vehicles or to 24 ft. lbs. (33 Nm) for 1992–93 vehicles.

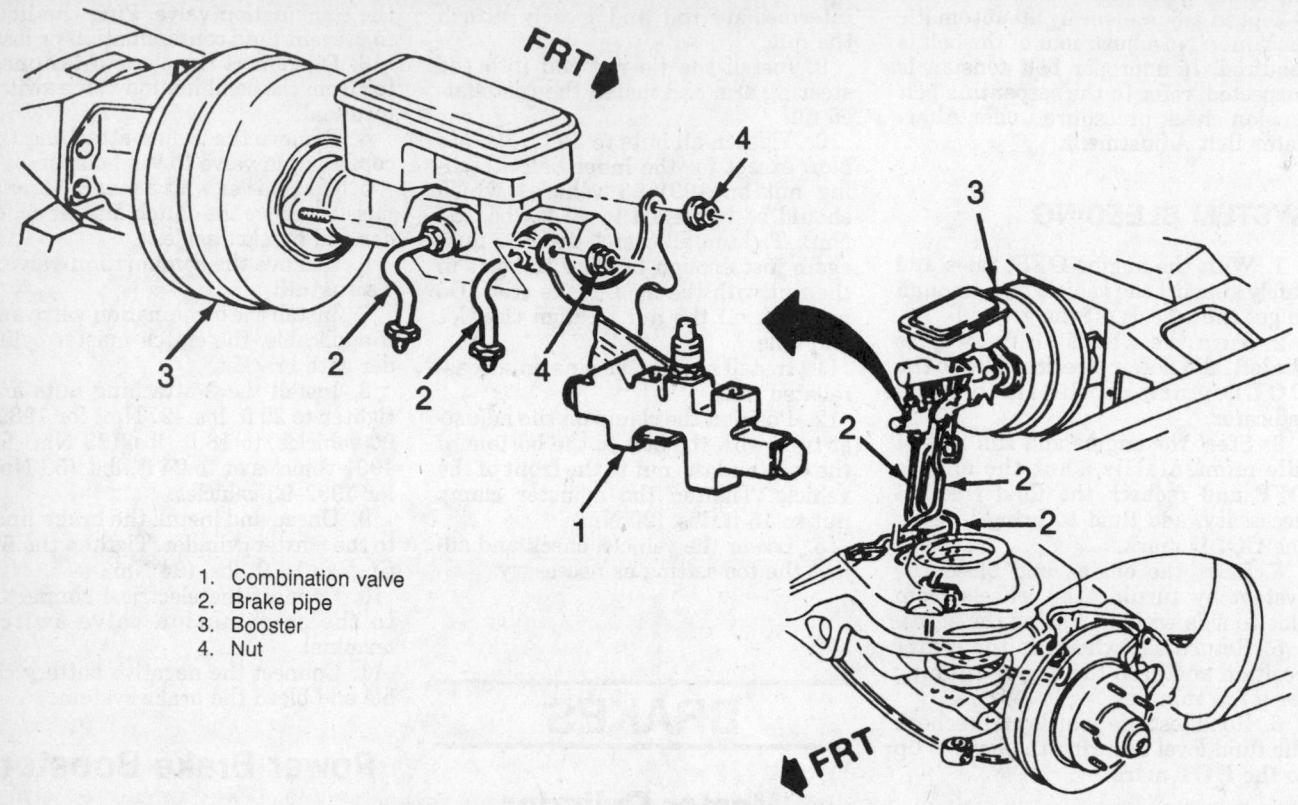

1. Combination valve
2. Brake pipe
3. Booster
4. Nut

Master cylinder and combination valve assembly

13. Connect the vacuum hose to the vacuum check valve.

14. Connect the negative battery cable and if brake lines were disconnected, bleed the hydraulic brake system.

Brake Caliper

REMOVAL & INSTALLATION

Front

SINGLE PISTON

1. Remove ⅔ of the brake fluid from the master cylinder.

2. Raise and safely support the vehicle.

3. Mark the relationship between the wheel and hub, then remove the wheel and tire assembly.

4. Position a suitable C-clamp over the outboard disc brake pad and the caliper housing. Using the C-clamp, bottom the piston into the caliper bore.

5. Remove the bolt, copper washers and inlet fitting from the caliper housing. Plug the openings in the inlet fitting and caliper housing to prevent fluid contamination and loss.

6. Remove the mounting bolts and sleeves.

7. Remove the caliper assembly from the rotor and bracket.

To install:

8. Inspect the mounting bolts and

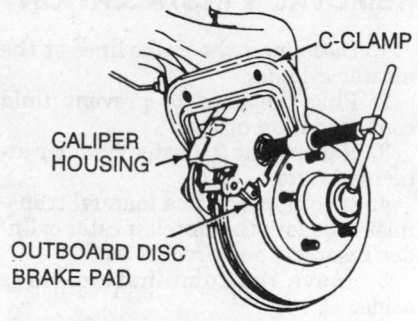

Compressing the front caliper housing

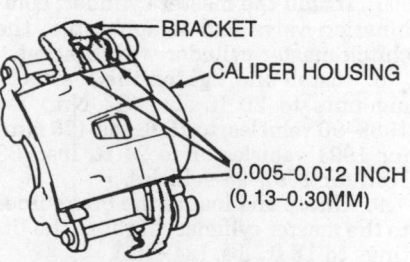

Front caliper housing to bracket clearance

sleeves for damage or corrosion and replace as necessary. Do not attempt to polish away corrosion. Ensure all caliper-to-bracket contact points are rust free and clean. Check the inlet fitting bolt for blockage.

9. Lubricate the sleeves, bushings and slide points with a suitable silicone grease.

10. Install the sleeves into the caliper housing. Install the caliper assembly onto the rotor and bracket. Install the mounting bolts and tighten to 37 ft. lbs. (50 Nm).

11. Measure the clearance between the caliper housing and the stops on the bracket. The clearance should be 0.005–0.012 inch (0.13–0.30mm). If necessary, remove the caliper assembly and file the ends of the stops on the bracket to provide proper clearance.

12. Install the bolt, new copper washers and the inlet fitting to the caliper housing. Tighten the bolt to 32 ft. lbs. (44 Nm).

13. Replace the brake fluid in the master cylinder and bleed the brake system.

14. Align the mark made earlier and install the wheel and tire assembly.

15. Lower the vehicle and with the engine running, pump the brake pedal slowly and firmly 3 times to seat the brake linings.

DUAL PISTON

1. Remove ⅔ of the brake fluid from the master cylinder.

2. Raise and support the vehicle safely.

3. Mark the relationship of the wheel and hub, then remove the wheel and tire assembly.

4. Remove the bolt, inlet fitting and

2 gaskets from the caliper housing. Plug the openings in the caliper housing and inlet fittings to prevent fluid contamination or loss.

5. Remove the circlip and retainer pin.

6. Remove the caliper housing from the rotor and mounting bracket.

To install:

7. Check the inlet fitting bolt for blockage, clear or replace as necessary.

8. Install the caliper housing over the rotor and onto the mounting bracket. Ensure the guiding surfaces on the inboard and outboard disc brake pads and mounting bracket are seated correctly.

9. Press the caliper housing down to compress the bias springs, slide a new retainer pin into position and install a new circlip.

10. Install the inlet fitting, bolt and 2 new gaskets. Tighten the bolt to 30 ft. lbs. (40 Nm).

11. Fill the master cylinder and bleed the brake system.

12. Align the marks made earlier and install the wheel and tire assembly.

13. Lower the vehicle and with the engine running, pump the brake pedal slowly and firmly 3 times to seat the brake pads.

Rear

1. Raise and safely support the vehicle.

2. Loosen the parking brake cable at the equalizer.

3. Mark the relationship between the wheel and hub, then remove the wheel and tire assembly. Install 2 wheel nuts to retain the rotor.

4. Remove the bolt, inlet fitting and 2 gaskets from the caliper housing. Plug the holes in the caliper housing and inlet fitting to prevent fluid contamination or loss.

5. Remove the caliper lever return spring only if it is defective. Discard the spring if the coils are opened.

6. Disconnect the parking brake cable from the caliper lever and caliper bracket.

7. Remove the 2 caliper guide pin holes.

8. Remove the caliper housing from the rotor and mounting bracket.

To install:

9. Inspect the guide pins and boots and replace if corroded, worn or damaged. Check the inlet fitting bolt for blockage, clear or replace as necessary.

10. Install the caliper housing over the rotor and into the mounting bracket. Install the 2 caliper guide pin bolts. Tighten the upper caliper guide pin bolt to 26 ft. lbs. (35 Nm) and the lower guide pin bolt to 16 ft. lbs. (22 Nm).

11. Connect the parking brake cable to the caliper bracket and caliper lever.

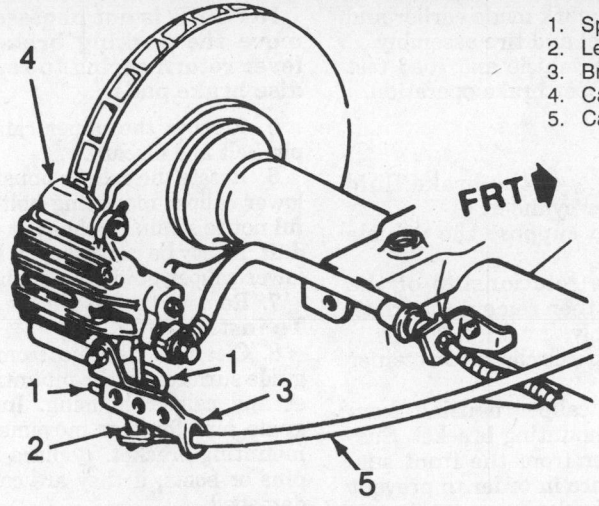

1. Spring
2. Lever
3. Bracket
4. Caliper housing
5. Cable

Rear caliper assembly

Install the caliper lever return spring, if removed.

12. Install the inlet fitting, bolt and 2 new gaskets to the caliper housing. Tighten the bolt to 30 ft. lbs. (40 Nm) for 1989–90 vehicles or to 22 ft. lbs. (30 Nm) for 1991–93 vehicles.

13. Bleed the brake system.

14. Adjust the parking brake free travel if the caliper was overhauled.

15. Lower the vehicle sufficiently and cycle the parking brake.

16. Raise and safely support the vehicle.

17. Inspect the caliper parking brake levers and ensure they are against the stops on the caliper housing. If the levers are not on their stops, check the parking brake adjustment.

18. Remove the 2 nuts securing the rotor, align the marks made earlier and install the wheel and tire assembly.

19. Lower the vehicle and with the engine running, pump the brake pedal slowly and firmly 3 times to seat the disc brake pads. Check the hydraulic system for leaks.

Disc Brake Pads

REMOVAL & INSTALLATION

Front

SINGLE PISTON

1. Remove ⅔ of the brake fluid from the master cylinder.

2. Raise and safely support the vehicle.

3. Mark the relationship between the wheel and hub, then remove the wheel and tire assembly.

4. Position a suitable C-clamp over the outboard disc brake pad and the caliper housing. Using the C-clamp, bottom the piston into the caliper bore and remove the C-clamp.

5. Remove the mounting bolts and sleeves.

6. Pivot the caliper off the rotor. Do not allow the caliper to hang by the brake hose, suspend it with a length of wire.

7. Remove the disc brake pads.

8. Remove the bushings from the mounting bolt holes and the pad retainer spring from the inboard pad.

To install:

9. Lubricate the bushings and sleeves with silicone grease. Install the bushings into the mounting bolt holes.

10. Install the retaining spring on the inboard pad in the correct position. Install the inboard pad into the caliper with the wear sensor at the leading edge of the pad during forward wheel rotation. Snap the retaining spring and pad into position. The pad must lay flat against the piston.

11. Install the outboard pad. The pad must lay flat against the caliper housing.

12. Pivot the caliper assembly onto the rotor and bracket. Install the mounting bolts and tighten to 37 ft. lbs. (50 Nm). Measure the clearance between the caliper housing and the stops on the bracket. The clearance should be 0.005–0.012 inch (0.13–0.30mm). If necessary, remove the caliper assembly and file the ends of the stops on the bracket to provide proper clearance.

13. Replace the brake fluid in the master cylinder and bleed the brake system. Pump the brake pedal slowly and firmly 3 times to seat the brake linings.

14. Clinch the outboard shoe retaining tabs to the caliper housing using a suitable tool, while a helper applies moderate pressure to the brake pedal. The outboard shoe should be locked in a fixed position.

15. Align the mark made earlier and install the wheel and tire assembly.

16. Lower the vehicle and road test to check for proper brake operation.

DUAL PISTON

1. Remove ⅔ of the brake fluid from the master cylinder.

2. Raise and support the vehicle safely.

3. Mark the relationship of the wheel and hub, then remove the wheel and tire assembly.

4. Remove the circlip and retainer pin.

5. Pivot the caliper housing from the rotor and mounting bracket. Suspend the caliper from the front suspension with wire in order to prevent damage to the brake line.

6. Position a C-clamp over the caliper housing and the center of the inboard disc brake pad. Compress the C-clamp until the pistons are bottomed.

7. Remove the disc brake pads.

To install:

8. Clean all residue from the mounting brackets and caliper pad contact surfaces.

9. Install the disc brake pads. The outboard disc brake pad with insulator is installed in the caliper housing. The inboard brake pad with wear sensor is pressed into the caliper pistons. Push the pads in firmly until they are flush and fully seated in the caliper housing.

10. Install the caliper housing over the rotor and onto the mounting bracket. Ensure the guiding surfaces on the inboard and outboard disc brake pads and mounting bracket are seated correctly.

11. Press the caliper housing down to compress the bias springs, slide a new retainer pin into position and install a new circlip.

12. Fill the master cylinder and bleed the brake system.

13. Align the marks made earlier and install the wheel and tire assembly.

14. Lower the vehicle and with the engine running, pump the brake pedal slowly and firmly 3 times to seat the brake pads.

Rear

1. Remove ⅔ of the brake fluid from the master cylinder reservoir.

2. Raise and safely support the vehicle.

3. Mark the relationship of the wheel to the axle flange and remove the wheel and tire assembly. Install 2 wheel nuts to retain the rotor.

4. Position a C-clamp and tighten until the piston bottoms in the base of the caliper housing. Make sure 1 end of the C-clamp rests on the inlet fitting bolt and the other against the outboard disc brake pad.

NOTE: It is not necessary to remove the parking brake caliper lever return spring to replace the disc brake pads.

5. Remove the upper caliper guide pin bolt and discard.

6. Rotate the caliper housing on the lower caliper mounting bolt. Be careful not to strain the hose or cable conduit. It may be necessary to loosen the lower caliper guide pin slightly.

7. Remove the disc brake pads.

To install:

8. Clean all residue from the pad guide surfaces on the mounting bracket and caliper housing. Inspect the guide pins for free movement in the mounting bracket. Replace the guide pins or boots, if they are corroded or damaged.

9. Install the disc brake pads. The outboard pad with insulator is installed toward the caliper housing. The inboard pad with the wear sensor is installed nearest the caliper piston. The wear sensor must be in the trailing position with forward wheel rotation.

10. Rotate the caliper housing into it's operating position. The springs on the outboard brake pad must not stick through the inspection hole in the caliper housing. If the springs are sticking through the inspection hole in the caliper housing, lift the caliper housing and make the necessary corrections to the outboard brake pad positions.

11. Install a new upper caliper guide pin bolt and tighten to 26 ft. lbs. (35 Nm). Ensure that the lower caliper guide bolt is tightened to 16 ft. lbs. (22 Nm).

12. With the engine running, pump the brake pedal slowly and firmly to seat the brake pads.

13. Check the caliper parking brake levers to make sure they are against the stops on the caliper housing. If the levers are not on their stops, check the parking brake adjustment.

14. Remove the 2 wheel nuts from the rotor and install the wheel and tire assembly.

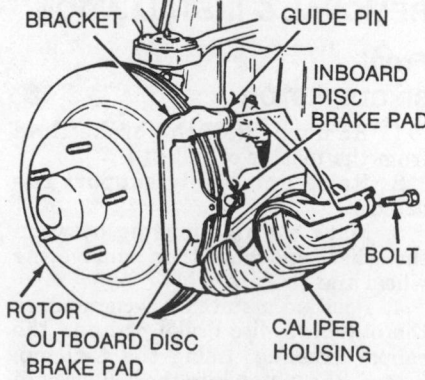

Rear disc pad installation

Labels: BRACKET, GUIDE PIN, INBOARD DISC BRAKE PAD, BOLT, CALIPER HOUSING, OUTBOARD DISC BRAKE PAD, ROTOR

15. Lower the vehicle, check the master cylinder fluid level and roadtest the vehicle.

Brake Rotor
REMOVAL & INSTALLATION
Front

1. Raise and support the vehicle safely.

2. Mark the relationship of the wheel and hub, then remove the wheel and tire assembly.

3. Follow the brake pad replacement procedure as necessary to disconnect and suspend the caliper assembly, with the brake pads installed, from the front suspension. For dual piston caliper assemblies, it may be necessary to remove the caliper bracket bolts and the bracket before removing the rotor.

4. Remove the dust cap from the hub. Remove the cotter pin, nut and washer from the spindle.

5. Carefully pull the hub and rotor assembly from the spindle.

To install:

6. Check the rotor for scoring or damage. Machine or replace the rotor assembly, as necessary. If machining is required, measure the rotor and check the minimum thickness specification.

7. Install the hub and rotor assembly. Adjust the wheel bearings as follows:

a. Tighten the spindle nut to 12 ft. lbs. (16 Nm) while turning the rotor forward by hand to fully seat the bearings.

b. Back off the nut to the just loose position.

c. Hand tighten the spindle nut. Loosen the spindle nut just enough that either hole in the spindle lines up with a slot in the nut, not more then ½ flat.

d. Install a new cotter pin and bend the ends of the pin against the nut. Cut off extra length to ensure ends will not interfere with the dust cap and install the dust cap.

e. Using a dial indicator, check the hub and rotor assembly. There should be 0.001–0.005 inch (0.03–0.13mm) endplay when properly adjusted.

8. Install caliper mounting bracket, if removed. Coat the threads of the mounting bracket bolts with suitable thread adhesive and tighten to 137 ft. lbs. (185 Nm). Recheck the torque immediately. Allow the adhesive to cure for 2 hours before moving the vehicle.

9. Install the caliper assembly.

10. Align the marks made earlier and install the wheel and tire assembly. Lower the vehicle and check the brake fluid.

Rear

1. Raise and support the vehicle safely.
2. Mark the relationship of the wheel to the axle flange and remove the wheel and tire assembly.
3. Remove the caliper assembly.
4. Remove the caliper mounting bracket and discard the bolts.
5. Remove the brake rotor.

To install:

6. Install the brake rotor and the mounting bracket.
7. Apply bolt adhesive to 2 new caliper mounting bracket bolts and tighten them to 70 ft. lbs. (95 Nm). Recheck the torque on both bolts immediately. Allow the bolt adhesive to dry for 2 hours before driving the vehicle.
8. Install the caliper assembly.
9. Align the marks made earlier and install the wheel and tire assembly.
10. Lower the vehicle and test. Remember to allow the mounting bracket bolt adhesive time to cure, if removed and reinstalled.

Brake Drums

REMOVAL & INSTALLATION

1. Raise and support the vehicle safely.
2. Mark the relationship of the wheel to the axle flange and remove the wheel and tire assembly.
3. Mark the relationship of the drum to the axle flange and remove the brake drum. If the brake drum is difficult to remove, try the following:
   a. Ensure the parking brake is released.
   b. Back off the parking brake cable adjustment.
   c. Remove the adjusting hole cover or knockout plate from the backing plate. Back off the adjusting screw, using suitable brake adjusting tools.
   d. Use a suitable rubber mallet to tap gently on the outer rim of the drum and/or around the inner drum diameter by the spindle. Be careful not to deform the drum by excessive use of force.

To install:

4. Install the drum, aligning the marks on the drum and the axle flange.
5. Install the wheel and tire assembly, aligning the marks on the wheel and axle flange.
6. Adjust the brakes as necessary.

Brake Shoes

REMOVAL & INSTALLATION

1. Raise and safely support the vehicle.

2. Mark the relationship of the wheel to the axle flange and remove the wheel and tire assembly.
3. Mark the relationship of the drum to the axle flange and remove the brake drum.
4. Remove the return springs using a suitable tool.
5. Remove the hold-down springs and pins. Remove the lever pivot.
6. Remove the actuator link while lifting up on the actuator lever.
7. Remove the actuator lever and lever return spring.
8. Remove the shoe guide, parking brake strut and strut spring.
9. Remove the brake shoes and disconnect the parking brake lever from the appropriate shoe.
10. Remove the adjusting screw assembly and spring.

To install:

NOTE: Any part or spring which are of doubtful strength due to discoloration from heat, overstress or wear should be replaced. Clean the adjusting screw threads with a wire brush and check the threads for smooth rotations. Replace as necessary.

11. Install the parking brake lever on the appropriate shoe by hooking the lever tab into the slot.
12. Install the adjusting screw and spring. Lubricate the adjusting screw with suitable brake grease.
13. Clean and lubricate the contact points of the backing plate and install the brake shoe assemblies and the parking brake cable.
14. Install the parking brake strut

and strut spring by spreading the shoes apart.
15. Install the shoe guide, actuator lever and lever return spring.
16. Install the hold-down pins, lever pivot and springs.
17. Install the actuator link on the anchor pin. Install the actuator link into the actuator lever while holding up on the lever.
18. Install the shoe return springs and adjust the brakes. When properly adjusted, the brake shoe linings will be approximately 0.050 inch (1.27 mm) less than the inner diameter of the brake drum.
19. Align and install the brake drum and the wheel and tire assembly.
20. Lower the vehicle and check the emergency brake for proper adjustment.

Wheel Cylinder

REMOVAL & INSTALLATION.

1. Raise and support the vehicle safely.
2. Mark and remove the tire and wheel assemblies and brake drums.
3. Remove the brake components, as required.
4. Clean the area around the wheel cylinder and brake line. Remove the brake line from the wheel cylinder and plug the brake line to prevent fluid contamination or loss.
5. Insert suitable awls, into the access slots between the wheel cylinder pilot and retainer locking tabs.
6. Bend both tabs away simultane-

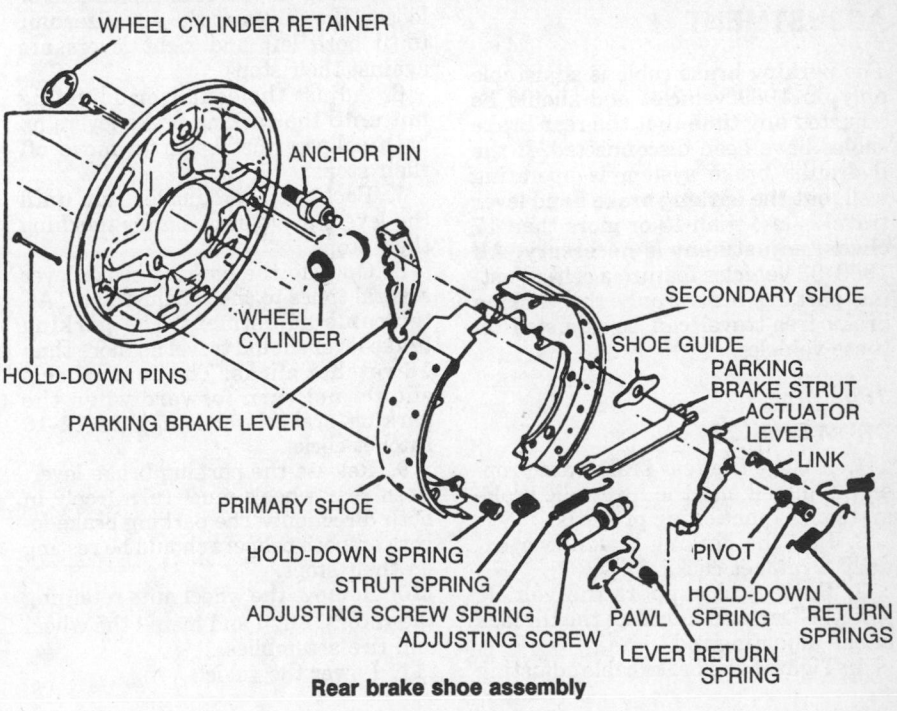

Rear brake shoe assembly

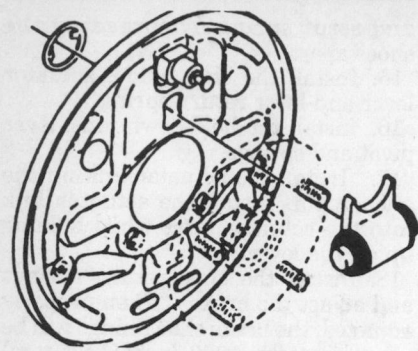

Wheel cylinder mounting

ously releasing the wheel cylinder. Discard the old retaining clip.

To install:

7. For ease of installation hold the wheel cylinder against the backing plate by inserting a block between the wheel cylinder and the axle shaft flange.

8. Position the wheel cylinder retainer clip so the tabs will be away from and in a horizontal position with the backing plate when installing.

9. Press the new retaining clip over the wheel cylinder abutment and into position using a 1⅛ inch 12-point socket. Make sure the retainer tabs are properly snapped under the abutment shoulder.

10. Install the brake components and the brake line. Tighten the brake line fitting to 11 ft. lbs. (15 Nm).

11. Align and install the brake drum; wheel and tire assembly. Be sure to bleed the brake system.

Parking Brake Cable

ADJUSTMENT

The parking brake cable is adjustable only on 1989 vehicles and should be adjusted any time that the rear brake cables have been disconnected. If the hydraulic brake system is operating well, but the parking brake hand lever travel is less than 13 or more than 17 clicks, adjustment is necessary. All 1990–93 vehicles feature a self-adjusting parking brake, only the parking brake free-travel can be adjusted on these vehicles.

1989

DRUM BRAKES

1. Ensure the rear brakes are properly adjusted and the hydraulic brake system is functioning properly.

2. Pull the parking brake lever exactly 2 ratchet clicks.

3. Raise and support the vehicle safely. Clean and lubricate the threads of the adjusting rod.

4. Tighten the brake cable adjusting

nut until the left rear wheel can just be turned rearward with both hands but locks when forward rotation is attempted.

5. Release the parking brake lever; both rear wheels must turn freely in either direction without brake drag. Be sure the parking brake cables are not adjusted too tightly causing the brakes to drag.

6. Lower the vehicle.

REAR DISC BRAKES

1. Apply the brake pedal 3 times with a pedal force of approximately 175 lbs. (778 N). Apply and release the parking brake 3 times.

2. Raise and safely support the vehicle.

3. Check the parking brake lever for full release:

a. Turn the ignition **ON** with the engine **OFF**.

b. The brake warning light should be **OFF**. If the brake warning light is still **ON** and the parking brake lever is completely released, pull downward on the front parking brake cable to remove slack from the lever assembly.

c. Turn the ignition switch **OFF**.

4. Mark the relationships of the wheels to the axle flanges and remove the rear wheels and tires. Reinstall 2 wheel nuts on each side to retain the brake rotors.

5. The parking brake levers on both calipers should be against the lever stops on the caliper housings. If the levers are not against the stops, check for binding in the rear cables and/or loosen the cables at the equalizer nut until both left and right levers are against their stops.

6. Adjust the equalizer adjusting nut until the parking brake levers on both calipers just begin to move off their stops.

7. Back off the adjuster nut until the levers move back, barely touching their stops.

8. Operate the parking brake lever several times to check adjustment. After cable adjustment, the parking brake lever should travel no more than 16 ratchet clicks. The rear wheels should not turn forward when the parking brake lever is applied 12–16 ratchet clicks.

9. Release the parking brake lever. Both rear wheels must turn freely in both directions. The parking brake levers on both calipers should be resting on their stops.

10. Remove the wheel nuts retaining the rotors. Align and install the wheel and tire assemblies.

11. Lower the vehicle.

Parking Brake Free-Travel

ADJUSTMENT

Parking brake free-travel should only be adjusted if the caliper has been taken apart. This adjustment will not correct a condition where the caliper levers will not return to their stops.

Rear Disc Brakes

NOTE: Disc brake pads must be new or parallel to within 0.006 inch (0.15mm). Parking brake adjustment is not valid with heavily tapered pads and may cause caliper/parking brake binding. Replace tapered brake pads.

1. Have an assistant apply a light brake pedal load, enough to stop the rotor from turning by hand. This takes up all clearances and ensures that components are correctly aligned.

2. Apply light pressure to the caliper lever.

3. Measure the free-travel between the caliper lever and the caliper housing. The free-travel must be 0.024–0.028 inch (0.6–0.7mm).

4. If the free-travel is incorrect, do the following:

a. Remove the adjuster screw.

b. Clean the thread adhesive residue from the threads.

c. Coat the threads with adhesive.

d. Screw in the adjuster screw far enough to obtain 0.024–0.028 inch (0.6–0.7mm) free-travel between the caliper lever and the caliper housing.

5. Have an assistant release the brake pedal, then apply the brake pedal firmly 3 times. Recheck the free-tavel and adjust as necessary.

REMOVAL & INSTALLATION

Front Cable

1989

1. Raise and safely support the vehicle.

2. Remove the adjusting nut at the equalizer and remove the front cable from the equalizer and bracket.

3. Lower the vehicle.

4. Remove the upper console and lower console rear screws. Lift the rear of the lower console to gain access to the parking brake control.

5. Remove the pin and retainer from the control assembly and front cable.

6. Use a ½ inch box end wrench to free the casing from the control assembly. Remove the cable and casing from the control assembly and bracket and

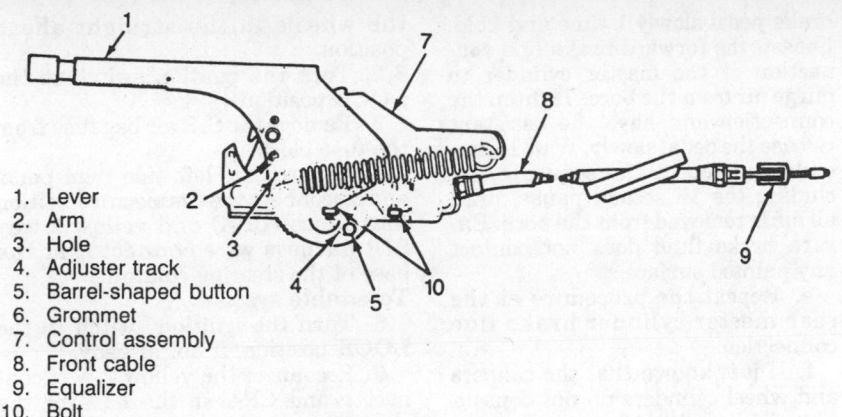

1. Lever
2. Arm
3. Hole
4. Adjuster track
5. Barrel-shaped button
6. Grommet
7. Control assembly
8. Front cable
9. Equalizer
10. Bolt

Parking brake control and front cable assembly—1990–93

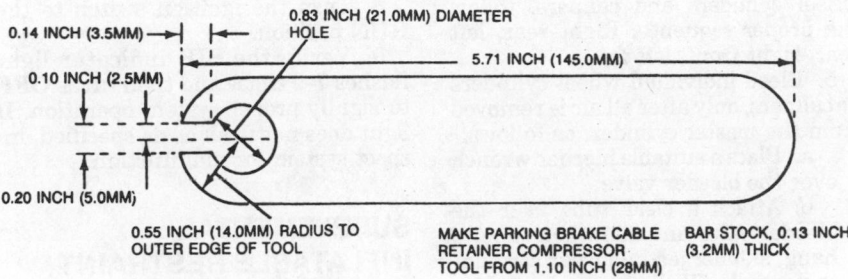

0.14 INCH (3.5MM)

0.83 INCH (21.0MM) DIAMETER HOLE

5.71 INCH (145.0MM)

0.10 INCH (2.5MM)

0.20 INCH (5.0MM)

0.55 INCH (14.0MM) RADIUS TO OUTER EDGE OF TOOL

MAKE PARKING BRAKE CABLE RETAINER COMPRESSOR TOOL FROM 1.10 INCH (28MM)

BAR STOCK, 0.13 INCH (3.2MM) THICK

Fabricated parking brake cable retainer compressor tool—1990–93

remove the cable and grommet from the vehicle.

To install:

7. Install the front cable and grommet in the vehicle. Seat the grommet in the floor pan.

8. Install the cable and casing to the control assembly and bracket. Install the pin and retainer to the control assembly and the cable.

9. Install the upper and lower console rear screws.

10. Raise and safely support the vehicle.

11. Connect the front cable to the equalizer and bracket. Install the adjusting nut at the equalizer and adjust the parking brake.

1990–93

1. Remove the carpet finish moulding.

2. Remove the console assembly.

3. With the parking brake lever in the down position, rotate the arm toward the front of the vehicle until a 3mm metal pin can be inserted into the hole. Insert the metal pin into the hole, locking out the self adjuster.

4. Raise and safely support the vehicle.

5. Disconnect the rear cables from the equalizer.

6. Remove the front cable from the bracket using a fabricated parking brake cable retainer compressor tool.

7. Remove the grommet from the hole.

8. Lower the vehicle.

9. Remove the barrel-shaped button from the adjuster track.

10. Remove the front cable and casing from the control assembly using a fabricated parking brake cable retainer compressor tool.

11. Remove the front cable from the floor pan.

To install:

12. Install the cable and seat the grommet in the floor pan.

13. Connect the cable casing to the control assembly.

14. Install the barrel-shaped button into the adjuster track.

15. Raise and support the vehicle safely.

16. Connect the rear cables to the equalizer and lower the vehicle.

17. Remove the metal pin from the hole, rotate the adjuster arm toward the rear of the vehicle and cycle lever.

18. Install the console and carpet finish molding.

Rear Cable

DRUM BRAKES

1. Raise and safely support the vehicle.

2. Remove the left and/or right rear cable from the equalizer as follows:

   a. For 1989 vehicles, loosen the adjusting nut at the equalizer to gain the necessary slack.

   b. For 1990–93 vehicles, pull the equalizer rearward to gain the necessary cable slack and insert a spacer to hold the equalizer in place.

3. Compress the retainer fingers on the casing and pull the left and/or right rear cable out of the seat belt plate.

4. On the left side, pull the left rear cable through the clip on the axle housing.

5. On the right side, remove the screw and clamp from the right rear cable.

6. Mark and remove the wheel and tire assemblies, as applicable.

7. Mark and remove the brake drum(s).

8. Disconnect the left and/or right rear cable from the brake shoe operating lever.

9. Compress the retainer fingers and pull the left and/or right cable from the backing plate.

To install:

10. Install the left and/or right cable to the backing plate and then to the shoe actuating lever.

11. Align the marks made earlier and install the brake drum(s) and the wheel and tire assemblies, as applicable.

12. On the right side, install the screw and clamp to the right rear cable.

13. On the left side, install the left cable through the clip on the axle housing.

14. Install the left and/or right cable into the seat belt plate and retainer.

15. Connect the left and/or right cable to the equalizer.

16. Adjust the parking brake on 1989 vehicles.

17. Lower the vehicle.

REAR DISC BRAKES

1. Raise and safely support the vehicle.

2. Remove the left and/or right rear cable from the equalizer as follows:

   a. For 1989 vehicles, loosen the adjusting nut at the equalizer to gain the necessary slack.

   b. For 1990–93 vehicles, pull the equalizer rearward to gain the necessary cable slack and insert a spacer to hold the equalizer in place.

3. Compress the retainer fingers on the casing and pull the left and/or right rear cable out of the seat belt plate.

4. On the left side, pull the left rear cable through the clip on the axle housing.

5. On the right side, remove the screw and clamp from the right rear cable.

6. Mark and remove the wheel and tire assemblies, as applicable.

7. Push forward on the caliper lever(s). Remove the left and/or right

rear cable from the tang on the caliper lever(s) and release the caliper lever(s).

8. Compress the retainer fingers on the cable casing and pull out of the bracket(s).

To install:

9. Push forward on the caliper lever(s). Install the left and/or right rear cable in the tang on the caliper lever(s) and release the lever(s).

10. Seat the finger retainers into the bracket.

11. Align the marks made earlier and install the tire assemblies, as applicable.

12. On the right side, install the screw and clamp to the right rear cable.

13. On the left side, install the left cable through the clip on the axle housing.

14. Install the left and/or right cable into the seat belt plate and retainer

15. Connect the left and/or right cable to the equalizer.

16. Adjust the parking brake on 1989 vehicles.

17. Lower the vehicle.

Brake System Bleeding

Whenever a hydraulic fitting is disconnected or air is somehow introduced into the brake system, bleeding is necessary to assure proper brake operation. Do not move a vehicle until a firm brake pedal is obtained. Air in the system can cause the loss of brake operation.

If air is introduced into the system at the master cylinder, it may be necessary to bled the entire system. If the disconnection of a fitting or pipe is the cause for air presence in the system, then only the wheel cylinder(s) or caliper(s) served by that component need to be bled.

1. Remove the vacuum reserve by applying the brakes several times, with the engine **OFF**.

2. Fill the master cylinder reservoir with brake fluid and keep it at least half full of fluid at all times during the bleeding operation.

3. If the master cylinder is known or suspected to have air in the bore, bleed the unit before wheel cylinders or calipers, in the following manner:

a. Disconnect the forward brake line connection at the master cylinder.

b. Allow brake fluid to fill the master cylinder bore until it begins to flow from the forward brake line port at the master cylinder.

c. Connect the forward brake line to the master cylinder and tighten.

d. Have an assistant depress the brake pedal slowly 1 time and hold. Loosen the forward brake line connection at the master cylinder to purge air from the bore. Tighten the connection and have the assistant release the pedal slowly. Wait 15 seconds and repeat the sequence, including the 15 second pause, until all air is removed from the bore. Ensure brake fluid does not contact any painted surface.

e. Repeat the procedure at the rear master cylinder brake line connection.

f. If it is known that the calipers and wheel cylinders do not contain any air, it will not be necessary to bleed them.

4. If it is necessary to bleed all of the wheel cylinders and calipers, follow the proper sequence: Right rear, left rear, right front, left front.

5. Bleed individual wheel cylinders or calipers, only after all air is removed from the master cylinder, as follows:

a. Place a suitable bleeder wrench over the bleeder valve.

b. Attach a clear tube over the bleeder valve and allow the tube to hang, submerged in a clear container partially filled with brake fluid.

c. Have an assistant depress the brake pedal slowly 1 time and hold. Loosen the bleeder valve to purge the air from the cylinder. Tighten the bleeder screw and have the assistant slowly release the pedal. Wait 15 seconds and repeat the sequence, including the 15 second pause, until all air is removed.

d. It may be necessary to repeat the sequence 10 or more times to remove all of the air.

NOTE: Rapid pumping of the brake pedal pushes the master cylinder secondary piston down the bore in a way that makes it difficult to bleed the rear side of the system.

6. Check the brake pedal for sponginess and the red brake warning light for an indication of unbalanced pressure. Repeat the bleeding procedure to correct either of these conditions.

CHASSIS ELECTRICAL

Air Bag

DISARMING

1. Turn the steering wheel to align the wheels in the straight-ahead position.

2. Turn the ignition switch to the **LOCK** position.

3. Remove the SIR air bag fuse from the fuse block.

4. Remove the left side trim panel and disconnect the Connector Position Assurance (CPA) and yellow 2-way SIR harness wire connector at the base of the steering column.

To enable system:

5. Turn the ignition switch to the **LOCK** position, if not already.

6. Reconnect the yellow 2-way connector and CPA at the base of the steering column.

7. Reinstall the SIR fuse and the left side trim panel.

8. Turn the ignition switch to the **RUN** position.

9. Verify the SIR indicator light flashes 7–9 times and then turns **OFF** to signify proper system operation. If light does not flash as as specified, inspect system for malfunction.

SUPPLEMENTAL INFLATABLE RESTRAINT (SIR) COIL ASSEMBLY

NOTE: After performing repairs on the internals of the steering column the coil assembly must be centered in order to avoid damaging the coil or accidental deployment of the air bag.

There are 2 different styles of coils, 1 rotates clockwise and the other rotates counterclockwise.

ADJUSTMENT

1. With the system properly disarmed and the wheels of the vehicle locked in the straight-ahead position, hold the coil assembly with the clear bottom up to see the coil ribbon.

2. While holding the coil assembly, depress the lock spring and rotate the hub in the direction of the arrow until it stops. The coil should now be wound up snug against the center hub.

3. Rotate the coil assembly in the opposite direction approximately 2½ turns and release the lock spring between the locking tabs in front of the arrow.

4. Install the coil assembly onto the steering shaft, enable the SIR system and watch the INFLATABLE RESTRAINT lamp to verify that the system is operating properly.

Heater Blower Motor

REMOVAL & INSTALLATION

1. Disconnect the negative battery

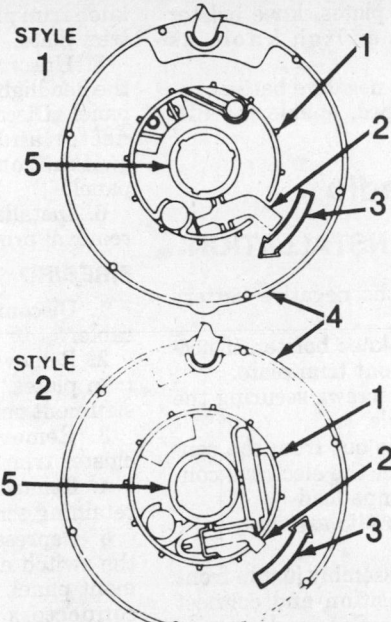

1. Locking tab
2. Spring
3. Hub direction
4. Coil housing
5. Coil hub

Centering the SIR coil assembly

cable. If necessary, remove the diagonal fender brace at the right rear corner of the engine compartment to gain access to the blower motor.

2. Disconnect the electrical wiring from the blower motor. If equipped with air conditioning, remove the blower relay and bracket as an assembly and swing them aside.

3. Remove the blower motor cooling tube.

4. Remove the blower motor retaining screws.

5. Remove the blower motor and fan as an assembly from the case. Be careful not to damage the blower fan.

To install:

6. Carefully guide the blower motor and fan into position being careful not to catch the fan on any protruding parts. Install the blower motor attaching screws and attach the blower motor cooling tube.

7. Connect the blower wiring and position the blower relay and bracket assembly into place. Install the bracket retaining screws and tighten to 13 inch lbs. (1.5 Nm).

8. If removed, install the diagonal fender brace and bolts.

9. Connect the negative battery cable and check blower operation.

Windshield Wiper Motor

REMOVAL & INSTALLATION

1. Disconnect the negative battery cable.

2. Remove the left and right wiper arms.

3. Remove the cowl panel assembly or the shroud vent grille, as applicable.

4. Loosen the motor drive link to crank arm retaining bolts. Remove the drive link from the motor crank arm.

5. Disconnect the electrical wiring from the motor assembly.

6. Remove the motor retaining bolts. Remove the windshield wiper motor while guiding the crank arm through the hole.

To install:

7. Install the wiper motor guiding crank arm through the hole. Be sure the motor is in the park position before assembling the crank arm to the drive link.

8. Install the wiper motor attaching nuts and tighten to 44 inch lbs. (5 Nm). Then, connect the drive link to the crank arm and tighten the retaining bolts to 35 inch lbs. (4 Nm).

9. Install the cowl panel assembly or shroud vent grille, as applicable and install the wiper arms.

10. Connect the negative battery cable and check wiper motor operation.

Windshield Wiper Switch

REMOVAL & INSTALLATION

NOTE: If equipped with an air bag, it is imperative that the disarming procedure is followed before repairs, and that the coil centering and rearming procedures are followed after repairs.

1. Disarm the air bag, if equipped, and disconnect the negative battery cable.

2. Remove the turn signal switch assembly.

3. Remove the SIR coil assembly from the column if necessary, as follows:

 a. Remove the connector shroud from the connector and remove the wiring protector.

 b. Attach a length of mechanics wire to the terminal connector to aid in reassembly.

 c. Carefully pull wire through the column.

4. Remove the lock cylinder set.

5. Remove the lock housing cover screws and housing cover end cap.

6. Remove the tilt lever, if equipped, by grasping and turning counterclockwise. Remove the lock housing cover.

7. Remove the housing cover base plate and the dimmer switch rod actuator.

8. Disconnect wiper switch connector from vehicle wire harness, attach a piece of mechanic's wire to the connector to aid in reinstallation and gently pull wire harness through column.

9. Remove the wiper switch actuator pivot pin and the switch.

To install:

10. Connect the wiper switch assembly to the lock housing cover assembly.

11. Attach the switch actuator pivot pin to the switch and cover.

12. Pull wiper switch wire connector through the steering column with the mechanic's wire and attach to the vehicle wire harness.

13. Attach the dimmer switch rod actuator to the housing cover base plate.

14. Connect base plate to lock housing cover assembly. The bottom edge of the dimmer switch rod actuator must rest on the bend in the dimmer switch rod.

15. Position lock housing cover in place and, if equipped, attach tilt lever by installing and turning clockwise.

16. Starting with the housing cover screw in the 12 o'clock position, then 8 o'clock and finally 3 o'clock positions, tighten the screws to 80 inch lbs. (9 Nm).

1. Lock housing cover
2. Switch actuator pivot pin
3. Windshield wiper switch

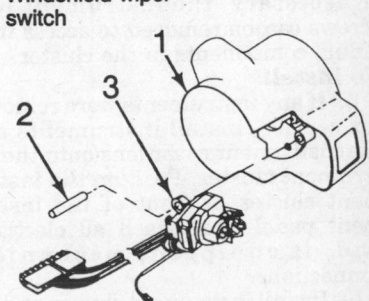

Wiper switch removal

17. Install the lock cylinder set.

18. Attach the SIR coil assembly, if necessary, by pulling wire connector through the steering column and reattaching the wire protector.

19. Install the turn signal assembly.

20. Be sure to center SIR coil assembly before reinstalling SIR inflator module and steering wheel.

21. Connect the negative battery cable and enable SIR system.

Instrument Cluster

REMOVAL & INSTALLATION

NOTE: If equipped with an air bag system, make certain to follow the recommended disarming procedures before, and rearming procedures after, repairs.

1. Disarm the SIR system and disconnect the negative battery cable.

2. Remove trim plates necessary to access the instrument cluster and lens:

a. On the 1989 Firebird, remove the right and left lower trim plates. Removal of the lower instrument panel covers is not required.

b. On the 1989 Camaro, remove the instrument cluster trim plates. Removal of the lower instrument panel cover is not required.

c. On the 1990–93 Firebird, remove the instrument panel knee bolster and the instrument panel cluster trim plate.

d. On 1990–93 Camaro, remove the instrument panel knee bolster and the headlight switch knob. Remove the cluster trim plate screws and pull the cluster trim plate forward. Disconnect the electrical connectors and remove the cluster trim plate.

3. Remove the retaining screws from the instrument cluster, pull the cluster back and disconnect the electrical connectors. Some 1989 vehicles are equipped with a mechanical speedometer, in these cases it is also necessary to disconnect the speedometer cable from the back of the instrument cluster.

4. Remove the instrument cluster. If necessary, the instrument lens screws can be removed to access individual components in the cluster.

To install:

5. If any instruments were removed for service, install instruments and the instrument cover lens onto the instrument cluster. Position the instrument cluster in front of the instrument panel and attach all electrical and, if equipped, mechanical connections.

6. Install instrument cluster and attaching screws.

7. Install trim plates, knee bolster and headlight switch knob, as applicable.

8. Connect the negative battery cable and, if equipped, enable the SIR system.

Radio

REMOVAL & INSTALLATION

1. Disconnect the negative battery cable.

2. Remove the knee bolster, if necessary, and the front trim plate.

3. Remove the screws securing the radio to the console.

4. Pull the radio out from the console and disconnect the electrical connections and antenna lead.

5. Remove the radio assembly.

To install:

6. Place radio assembly just in front of installation position and connect the electrical connections and antenna lead.

7. Slide radio into position and install with attaching screws.

8. Install front trim plate and attaching screws. Install the knee bolster, if removed.

9. Connect the negative battery cable.

Concealed Headlights

MANUAL OPERATION

The concealed headlights used on the Firebird are electrically operated. If an electrical failure involving the headlight actuators should occur, the headlights can be operated manually.

To raise the headlights, rotate the knob, located on the actuator, in a counterclockwise direction until the headlights are fully open. Lower the headlights by turning the actuator knob in a clockwise direction until the headlights are fully closed.

Headlight Switch

REMOVAL & INSTALLATION

1989

CAMARO

1. Disconnect the negative battery cable.

2. Remove the insulator screws and nut from under the instrument panel and remove the insulator.

3. Remove the headlight switch knob assembly by depressing the release button on the headlight switch from under the instrument panel.

4. Remove the headlight switch

knob trim plate screws and remove the trim plate.

5. Unscrew the retainer attaching the headlight switch to the instrument panel. Disconnect the electrical connector and remove the headlight switch from under the instrument panel.

6. Installation is the reverse of the removal procedure.

FIREBIRD

1. Disconnect the negative battery cable.

2. Remove the right and left lower trim plates. Removal of the lower instrument panel covers is not required.

3. Remove the instrument panel cluster trim plate.

4. Remove the 2 switch assembly retaining screws.

5. Depress the side tangs and pull the switch assembly from the instrument panel. Disconnect the electrical connectors and remove the switch assembly.

6. Installation is the reverse of the removal procedure.

1990–93

CAMARO

1. Disconnect the negative battery cable.

2. Remove the instrument panel knee bolster.

3. Remove the switch knob by depressing the release button on the switch from under the instrument panel.

4. Remove the retaining screws from the instrument panel cluster trim plate and pull it forward away from the instrument panel. Disconnect the electrical connectors and remove the cluster trim plate.

5. Remove the retaining nut from the headlight switch and lower the switch out through the bottom of the instrument panel.

6. Disconnect the electrical connectors and remove the switch.

To install:

7. Connect the electrical connectors and raise the switch up through the bottom of the instrument panel into place. Fasten the switch with the connecting nut.

8. Install the cluster trim plate and knee bolster.

9. Connect the negative battery cable.

FIREBIRD

1. Disconnect the negative battery cable.

2. Remove the instrument panel knee bolster and the instrument panel cluster trim plate.

3. Remove the headlight switch retaining screws.

5. Disconnect the electrical connectors and remove the switch assembly.
To install:

6. Install the electrical connectors and attach the switch assembly using the retaining screws. Tighten the switch retaining screws to 13 inch lbs. (1.5 Nm).

7. Install the instrument panel cluster trim plate and the knee bolster.

8. Connect the negative battery cable.

Dimmer Switch

REMOVAL & INSTALLATION

NOTE: If the vehicle is equipped with an air bag system, make certain to follow the recommended disarming procedure before, and rearming procedure after, repairs.

1. Disarm the SIR system, if equipped, and disconnect the negative battery cable.

2. Remove the steering column to instrument panel trim plates.

3. Carefully lower the steering column by loosening the toe plate retaining screws and remove the capsule nuts securing the steering column to the instrument panel. Support the column to prevent it from being damaged.

4. Remove the switch electrical connector and the retaining nut and/or screws, remove the dimmer switch.
To install:

5. Attach the dimmer switch to the steering column with the retaining

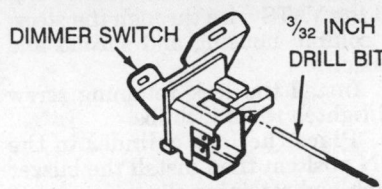

Dimmer switch adjustment

nut and/or screws. Adjust the dimmer switch by depressing the mechanism slightly to insert a ³⁄₃₂ inch drill bit. Move the switch to remove the lash.

6. Tighten the retaining nut and upper retaining screw to 35 inch lbs. (4 Nm), and/or the lower retaining screw to 22 inch lbs. (2.5 Nm).

7. Raise the steering column into place and secure to the instrument panel with the capsule securing nuts. Install the toe plate retaining screws.

8. Install the steering column to instrument panel trim plates.

9. Connect the negative battery cable and, if equipped, enable the SIR system.

Turn Signal Switch

REMOVAL & INSTALLATION

NOTE: If equipped with an air bag system, make certain to follow the recommended disarming procedure before and the rearming and coil centering procedures after repairs.

1. Properly disable the SIR air bag system, if equipped, and disconnect the negative battery cable.

2. Remove the inflator module, if equipped with an air bag.

─── **CAUTION** ───

To avoid personal injury when carrying a live inflator module, make sure the bag and trim cover are pointed away. Always face the air bag assembly up, and never carry the inflator module by the wires or connector, otherwise personal injury may result if the module should deploy.

3. Remove the steering wheel and, if necessary, the knee bolster.

4. Ensure the steering wheel is locked in the straight-ahead position and remove the coil assembly retaining ring on air bag equipped vehicles.

5. Pull the coil assembly out and allow it to hang.

6. Using a suitable tool, depress the lock plate to gain access to the retaining ring. Remove the ring and lockplate.

7. Remove the turn signal canceling cam, upper bearing spring, upper bearing inner race seat and inner race.

8. Push the multifunction lever up to the right turn position, disconnect any electrical connection and remove the lever by pulling straight out of the switch. Remove the retaining screw and the signal switch arm.

9. Remove the hazard warning knob assembly and the steering column wiring protector.

10. Remove the wiring protector. Disconnect the turn signal switch connector from the harness connector and attach a length of mechanic's wire to the signal switch connector to aid in reassembly.

1. Nut
2. Retaining ring
3. Coil assembly
4. Wave washer
5. Retaining ring
6. Shaft lock
7. Turn signal canceling cam
8. Upper bearing spring
9. Screw
10. Screw
11. Signal switch arm
12. Turn signal and hazard warning switch
13. Upper bearing inner race seat
14. Inner race
15. Screw
16. Buzzer switch
17. Buzzer switch retaining clip
18. Lock retaining screw
19. Lock housing cover
20. VATS lock cylinder set

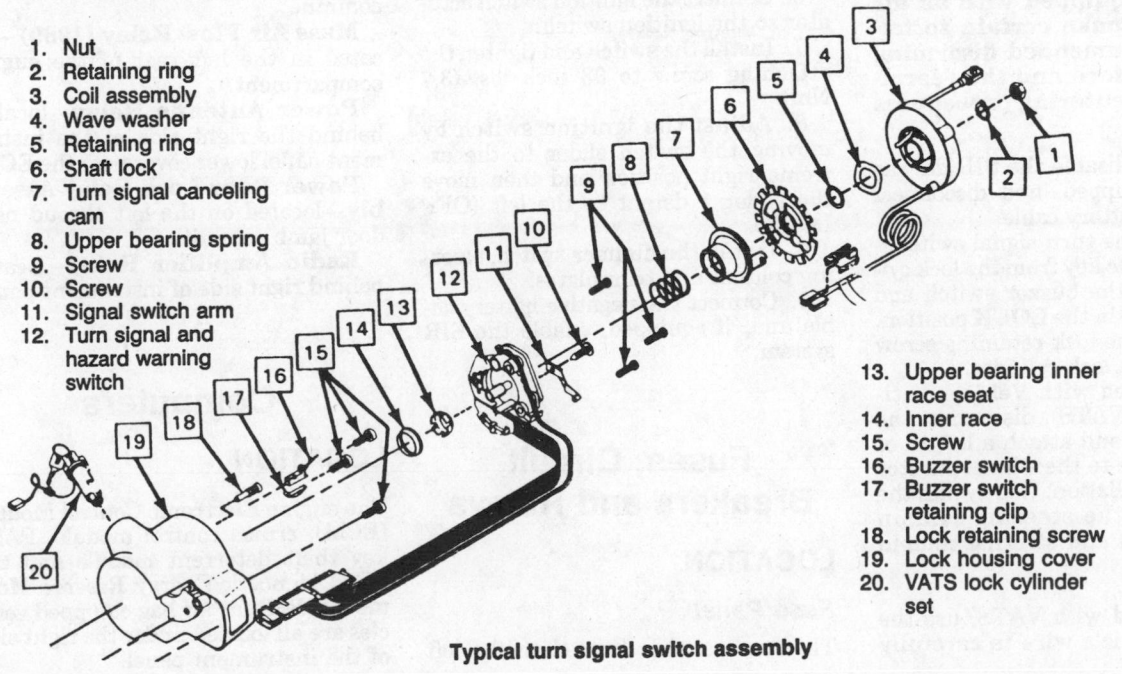

Typical turn signal switch assembly

11. Remove the switch retaining screws and remove the turn signal switch. Carefully pull the wire harness through the steering column housing and lock housing cover.

To install:

12. Using the mechanic's wire, gently pull the turn switch connector through the steering column, attach switch connector to the vehicle wire harness and install the wiring protector.

13. Install the turn switch assembly and screws. Tighten turn switch mounting screws to 30 inch lbs. (3.4 Nm).

14. Install the signal switch arm and retaining screw. Tighten screw to 20 inch lbs. (2.3 Nm).

15. Install the hazard knob assembly and multifunction lever.

16. Install the inner race, upper bearing race seat and upper bearing spring.

17. Install the canceling cam assembly.

18. Install shaft lock and new shaft lock retaining ring using tool J-23653-C or equivalent.

19. Install the wave washer.

20. Install and center the coil assembly and retaining ring.

21. Install the knee bolster, if removed.

22. Install steering wheel and locking nut.

23. Attach the inflator module.

24. Connect the negative battery cable and enable the SIR system.

Ignition Lock

REMOVAL & INSTALLATION

NOTE: If equipped with an air bag system, make certain to follow the recommended disarming procedure before and the rearming and coil centering procedures after repairs.

1. Properly disable the SIR air bag system, if equipped, and disconnect the negative battery cable.

2. Remove the turn signal switch.

3. Remove the key from the lock cylinder, remove the buzzer switch and reinsert the key in the **LOCK** position.

4. Remove the lock retaining screw and remove the lock cylinder.

5. If equipped with Vehicle Anti-Theft System (VATS), disconnect the wire connector and attach a length of mechanic's wire to the wire connector to aid in reinstallation. Gently pull the wire through the steering column housing shroud and steering column housing.

To install:

6. If equipped with VATS, use the length mechanic's wire to carefully

pull the VATS wire through the steering column housing and shroud and connect.

7. Install the lock retaining screw and tighten to 22 inch lbs.

8. Place the lock cylinder in the **RUN** position then install the buzzer switch and retaining clip.

9. Install the turn signal assembly.

10. Install and center the coil assembly, if equipped with SIR.

11. Connect the negative battery cable and, if equipped, enable the SIR system.

Ignition Switch

REMOVAL & INSTALLATION

NOTE: If equipped with an air bag system, make certain to follow the recommended disarming procedure before, and rearming procedure after, repairs.

1. Disarm the SIR system, if equipped, and disconnect the negative battery cable.

2. Remove the steering column to instrument panel trim plates.

3. Carefully lower the steering column by loosening the toe plate retaining screws and remove the capsule nuts securing the steering column to the instrument panel. Support the column to prevent it from being damaged.

4. Remove the dimmer switch.

5. Remove the switch electrical connector, retaining screw and the ignition switch.

To install:

6. Connect the ignition switch actuator to the ignition switch.

7. Install the switch and tighten the attaching screw to 33 inch lbs. (3.7 Nm).

8. Adjust the ignition switch by moving the switch slider to the extreme right position and then move the slider 1 detent to the left (OFF LOCK).

9. Install the dimmer switch, steering column and trim plates.

10. Connect the negative battery cable and, if equipped, enable the SIR system.

Fuses, Circuit Breakers and Relays

LOCATION

Fuse Panel

The fuse panel is located on the left

side of the vehicle, under the instrument panel assembly. In order to gain access to the fuse panel it may be necessary to first remove the under dash padding.

Circuit Breakers

The circuit breakers are located at the fuse panel.

RELAYS

All vehicles use a combination of the following electrical relays:

Air Conditioner/Heater Blower High Speed Relay—located near the blower module on the air conditioner module.

Air Conditioner Compressor Relay—located on the left side engine cowl on the relay bracket.

Burn-Off Relay (1989)—located behind the ECM.

Cooling Fan Relay—located on the left side of the engine cowl on the relay bracket.

Extend Relay—taped back to body rear harness near breakout to hatch pull-down/release unit.

Fog Light Relay (1989)—located in the left front corner of the engine compartment; **(1990)**—located in the left rear corner of the engine compartment; **(1991–93)**—located behind the left side instrument panel, near the fuse panel block.

Fuel Pump Relay—located on the left side of the engine cowl on the relay bracket.

Hatch Release Relay—located under the right side console, beside the gear selector.

Horn Relay—located in the convenience center, behind the instrument panel to the right of the steering column.

Mass Air Flow Relay (1989)—located in the left rear of the engine compartment.

Power Antenna Relay—located behind the right side of the instrument panel lower cover near the ECM.

Power Door Lock Relay Assembly—located on the left shroud near door jamb conduit.

Radio Amplifier Relay—located behind right side of instrument panel.

Computers

LOCATION

The engine Electronic Control Module (ECM), cruise control module, PASS key theft deterrent module and the SIR Diagnostic/Energy Reserve Module (DERM) for air bag equipped vehicles are all located under the right side of the instrument panel.

GM "J" Body
Front Wheel Drive
BUICK—Skyhawk **CHEVROLET**—Cavalier
PONTIAC—Sunbird

SPECIFICATIONS

VEHICLE IDENTIFICATION CHART

It is important for servicing and ordering parts to be certain of the vehicle and engine identification. The VIN (vehicle identification number) is a 17 digit number visible through the windshield on the driver's side of the dash and contains the vehicle and engine identification codes. The tenth digit indicates model year and the eighth digit indicates engine code. It can be interpreted as follows:

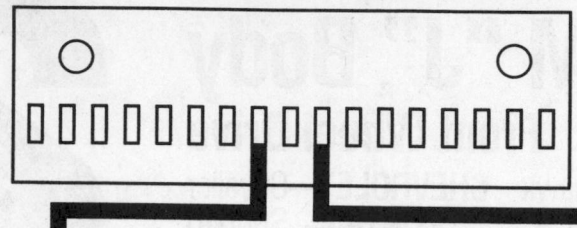

Engine Code

Code	Liters	Cu. In. (cc)	Cyl.	Fuel Sys.	Eng. Mfg.
M	2.0	121 (1983)	4	PFI Turbo	①
1	2.0	121 (1983)	4	TBI (HO)	Chevrolet
K	2.0	121 (1983)	4	TBI	①
G	2.2	134 (2196)	4	TBI	Chevrolet
H	2.0	121 (1983)	4	PFI	Pontiac
4	2.2	134 (2196)	4	PFI	Chevrolet
W	2.8	173 (2835)	6	PFI	Chevrolet
T	3.1	192 (3146)	6	PFI	Chevrolet

Model Year

Code	Year
K	1989
L	1990
M	1991
N	1992
P	1993

HO—High Output
PFI—Port Fuel Injection

TBI—Throttle Body Injection
① Chevrolet-Pontiac-GM of Canada

ENGINE IDENTIFICATION

Year	Model	Engine Displacement Liters (cc)	Engine Series (ID/VIN)	Fuel System	No. of Cylinders	Engine Type
1989	Cavalier	2.0 (1983)	1	TBI (HO)	4	OHV
	Cavalier	2.8 (2835)	W	PFI	6	OHV
	Sunbird	2.0 (1983)	K	TBI	4	OHC
	Sunbird	2.0 (1983)	M	PFI Turbo	4	OHC Turbo
	Skyhawk	2.0 (1983)	1	TBI (HO)	4	OHV
1990	Cavalier	2.2 (2196)	G	TBI	4	OHV
	Cavalier	3.1 (3146)	T	PFI	6	OHV
	Sunbird	2.0 (1983)	K	TBI	4	OHC
	Sunbird	2.0 (1983)	M	PFI Turbo	4	OHC Turbo
1991	Cavalier	2.2 (2196)	G	TBI	4	OHV
	Cavalier	3.1 (3146)	T	PFI	6	OHV
	Sunbird	2.0 (1983)	K	TBI	4	OHC
	Sunbird	3.1 (3146)	T	PFI	6	OHV
1992-93	Cavalier	2.2 (2196)	4	PFI	4	OHV
	Cavalier	3.1 (3146)	T	PFI	6	OHV
	Sunbird	2.0 (1983)	H	PFI	4	OHC
	Sunbird	3.1 (3146)	T	PFI	6	OHV

OHC—Overhead Cam
OHV—Overhead Valve

PFI—Port Fuel Injection
TBI—Throttle Body Injection

GENERAL ENGINE SPECIFICATIONS

Year	Engine ID/VIN	Engine Displacement Liters (cc)	Fuel System Type	Net Horsepower @ rpm	Net Torque @ rpm (ft. lbs.)	Bore × Stroke (in.)	Compression Ratio	Oil Pressure @ rpm
1989	M	2.0 (1983)	PFI-Turbo	160 @ 5600	160 @ 2800	3.38 × 3.38	8.0:1	65 @ 2500
	1	2.0 (1983)	TBI-HO	90 @ 5600	108 @ 3200	3.50 × 3.15	9.0:1	63–77 @ 1200
	K	2.0 (1983)	TBI	102 @ 5200	130 @ 2800	3.38 × 3.38	8.8:1	45 @ 2000
	W	2.8 (2835)	PFI	120 @ 4800	155 @ 3600	3.50 × 2.99	8.9:1	50 @ 2400
1990	K	2.0 (1983)	TBI	102 @ 5200	130 @ 2800	3.38 × 3.38	8.8:1	—
	M	2.0 (1983)	PFI-Turbo	160 @ 5600	160 @ 2800	3.38 × 3.38	8.0:1	—
	G	2.2 (2196)	TBI	95 @ 5200	120 @ 3200	3.50 × 3.46	9.0:1	56 @ 3000
	T	3.1 (3146)	PFI	140 @ 4500	180 @ 3600	3.50 × 3.31	8.8:1	—
1991	K	2.0 (1983)	TBI	96 @ 4800	130 @ 2800	3.38 × 3.38	8.8:1	—
	G	2.2 (2196)	TBI	95 @ 5200	120 @ 3200	3.50 × 3.46	9.0:1	56 @ 3000
	T	3.1 (3146)	PFI	140 @ 4500	180 @ 3600	3.50 × 3.31	8.8:1	—
1992–93	H	2.0 (1983)	PFI	111 @ 5200	125 @ 3600	3.38 × 3.38	9.2:1	—
	4	2.2 (2196)	PFI	110 @ 5200	130 @ 3200	3.50 × 3.46	9.0:1	56 @ 3000
	T	3.1 (3146)	PFI	140 @ 4200	185 @ 3200	3.50 × 3.31	8.8:1	—

NOTE: Horsepower and torque are SAE net figures. They are measured at the rear of the transmission with all accessories installed and operating. Since the figures vary when a given engine is installed in different models, some are representative rather than exact.
PFI—Port Fuel Injection
TBI—Throttle Body Injection

GASOLINE ENGINE TUNE-UP SPECIFICATIONS

Year	Engine ID/VIN	Engine Displacement Liters (cc)	Spark Plugs Gap (in.)	Ignition Timing (deg.) MT	AT	Fuel Pump (psi)	Idle Speed (rpm) MT	AT	Valve Clearance In.	Ex.
1989	M	2.0 (1983)	0.060	①	①	25–30	①	①	Hyd.	Hyd.
	1	2.0 (1983)	0.035	①	①	10–12	①	①	Hyd.	Hyd.
	K	2.0 (1983)	0.060	①	①	10	①	①	Hyd.	Hyd.
	W	2.8 (2835)	0.045	①	①	30–37	①	①	Hyd.	Hyd.
1990	K	2.0 (1983)	0.045	①	①	9–13	①	①	Hyd.	Hyd.
	M	2.0 (1983)	0.035	①	①	35–38	①	①	Hyd.	Hyd.
	G	2.2 (2196)	0.035	①	①	9–13	①	①	Hyd.	Hyd.
	T	3.1 (3146)	0.045	①	①	41–47②	①	①	Hyd.	Hyd.
1991	K	2.0 (1983)	0.045	①	①	9–13	①	①	Hyd.	Hyd.
	G	2.2 (2196)	0.035	①	①	9–13	①	①	Hyd.	Hyd.
	T	3.1 (3146)	0.045	①	①	41–47②	①	①	Hyd.	Hyd.
1992	H	2.0 (1983)	0.045	①	①	41–47②	①	①	Hyd.	Hyd.
	4	2.2 (2196)	0.045	①	①	41–47②	①	①	Hyd.	Hyd.
	T	3.1 (3146)	0.045	①	①	41–47②	①	①	Hyd.	Hyd.
1993	SEE UNDERHOOD SPECIFICATIONS STICKER									

NOTE: The lowest cylinder pressure should be within 75% of the highest cylinder pressure reading. For example, if the highest cylinder is 134 psi, the lowest should be 101. Engine should be at normal operating temperature with throttle valve in the wide open position.
The underhood specifications sticker often reflects tune-up specification changes in production. Sticker figures must be used if they disagree with those in this chart.
Hyd.—Hydraulic
① See underhood Vehicle Emission Control
   information label
② Full system pressure with engine not running;
   3–10 psi lower with engine at idle

FIRING ORDERS

NOTE: To avoid confusion, always replace spark plug wires one at a time.

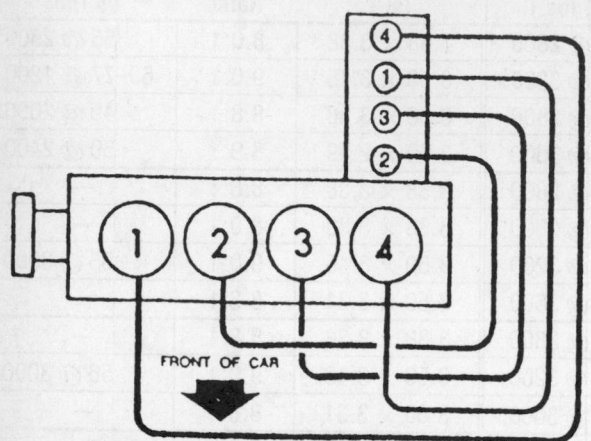

2.0L (VIN H and 1) and 2.2L Engines
Engine Firing Order: 1-3-4-2
Distributorless Ignition System

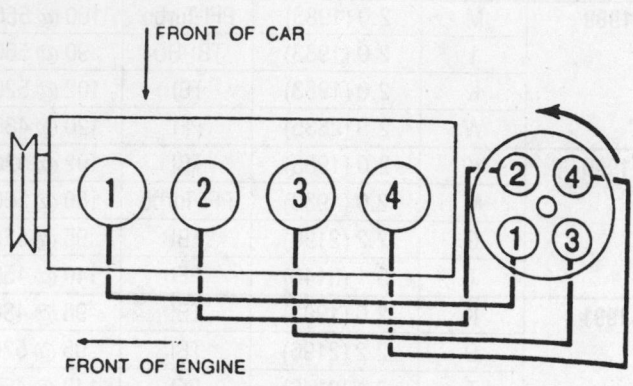

2.0L (VIN K and M) Engines
Engine Firing Order: 1-3-4-2
Distributor Rotation: Counterclockwise

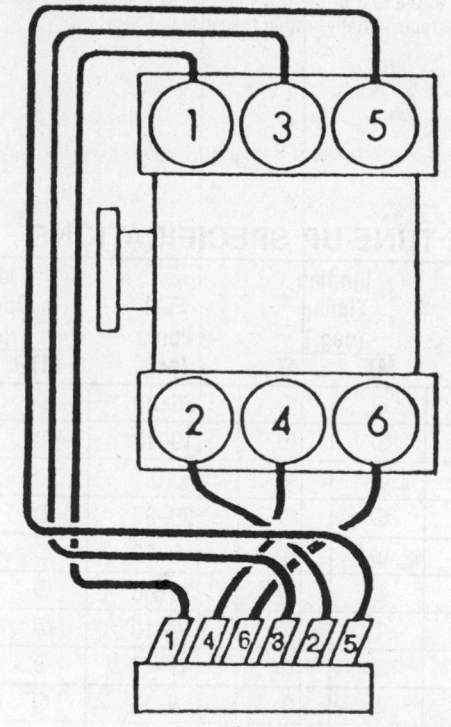

2.8L and 3.1L Engines
Engine Firing Order: 1-2-3-4-5-6
Distributorless Ignition System

CAPACITIES

Year	Model	Engine ID/VIN	Engine Displacement Liters (cc)	Engine Crankcase with Filter (qts.)	Transmission (pts.) 4-Spd	Transmission (pts.) 5-Spd	Transmission (pts.) Auto.	Transfer case (pts.)	Drive Axle Front (pts.)	Drive Axle Rear (pts.)	Fuel Tank (gal.)	Cooling System (qts.)
1989	Cavalier	1	2.0 (1983)	4①	—	4	8②	—	—	—	13.6	9.7
	Cavalier	W	2.8 (2835)	4①	—	4	8②	—	—	—	13.6	11.0
	Sunbird	K	2.0 (1983)	4①	—	4	8②	—	—	—	13.6	8.5
	Sunbird	M	2.0 (1983)	4①	—	4	8②	—	—	—	13.6	8.5
	Skyhawk	1	2.0 (1983)	4①	—	4	8②	—	—	—	13.6	9.7

CAPACITIES

Year	Model	Engine ID/VIN	Engine Displacement Liters (cc)	Engine Crankcase with Filter (qts.)	Transmission (pts.) 4-Spd	5-Spd	Auto.	Transfer case (pts.)	Drive Axle Front (pts.)	Rear (pts.)	Fuel Tank (gal.)	Cooling System (qts.)
1990	Cavalier	G	2.2 (2196)	4①	—	4	8②	—	—	—	13.6	8.5
	Cavalier	T	3.1 (3146)	4①	—	4	8②	—	—	—	13.6	11.0
	Sunbird	K	2.0 (1983)	4①	—	4	8②	—	—	—	13.6	8.5
	Sunbird	M	2.0 (1983)	4①	—	4	8②	—	—	—	13.6	8.5
1991	Cavalier	G	2.2 (2196)	4①	—	4	8②	—	—	—	13.6	8.5
	Cavalier	T	3.1 (3146)	4①	—	4	8②	—	—	—	13.6	11.0
	Sunbird	K	2.0 (1983)	4①	—	4	8②	—	—	—	13.6	8.5
	Sunbird	T	3.1 (3146)	4①	—	4	8②	—	—	—	13.6	11.0
1992–93	Cavalier	4	2.2 (2196)	4①	—	4	8②	—	—	—	13.6	8.5
	Cavalier	T	3.1 (3146)	4①	—	4	8②	—	—	—	13.6	11.0
	Sunbird	H	2.0 (1983)	4①	—	4	8②	—	—	—	13.6	8.5
	Sunbird	T	3.1 (3146)	4①	—	4	8②	—	—	—	13.6	11.0

① Check level after running engine
② Plus 4 pints when overhauling

CAMSHAFT SPECIFICATIONS

All measurements given in inches.

Year	Engine ID/VIN	Engine Displacement Liters (cc)	Journal Diameter 1	2	3	4	5	Elevation In.	Ex.	Bearing Clearance	Camshaft End Play
1989	M	2.0 (1983)	1.6714–1.6720	1.6812–1.6816	1.6911–1.6917	1.7009–1.7015	1.7108–1.7114	0.2409	0.2409	0.0008	0.0016–0.0063
	1	2.0 (1983)	1.8670–1.8690	1.8670–1.8690	1.8670–1.8690	1.8670–1.8690	1.8670–1.8690	0.2626	0.2626	0.0010–0.0039	NA
	K	2.0 (1983)	1.6714–1.6720	1.6812–1.6816	1.6911–1.6917	1.7009–1.7015	1.7108–1.7114	0.2409	0.2409	0.0008	0.0016–0.0063
	W	2.8 (2835)	1.8678–1.8815	1.8678–1.8815	1.8678–1.8815	1.8678–1.8815	1.8678–1.8815	0.2626	0.2732	0.0010–0.0040	NA
1990	K	2.0 (1983)	1.6706–1.6712	1.6812–1.6818	1.6911–1.6917	1.7009–1.7015	1.7100–1.7106	0.2366	0.2515	0.0011–0.0035	0.0016–0.0063
	M	2.0 (1983)	1.6714–1.6720	1.6812–1.6816	1.6911–1.6917	1.7009–1.7015	1.7108–1.7114	0.2625	0.2625	0.0011–0.0035	0.0016–0.0063
	G	2.2 (2196)	1.8670–1.8690	1.8670–1.8690	1.8670–1.8690	1.8670–1.8690	1.8670–1.8690	0.2590	0.2590	0.0010–0.0039	NA
	T	3.1 (3146)	1.8677–1.8815	1.8677–1.8815	1.8677–1.8815	1.8677–1.8815	1.8677–1.8815	0.2626	0.2732	0.0010–0.0040	NA
1991	K	2.0 (1983)	1.6706–1.6712	1.6812–1.6818	1.6911–1.6917	1.7009–1.7015	1.7100–1.7106	0.2366	0.2515	0.0011–0.0035	0.0016–0.0063
	G	2.2 (2196)	1.8670–1.8690	1.8670–1.8690	1.8670–1.8690	1.8670–1.8690	1.8670–1.8690	0.2590	0.2590	0.0010–0.0039	NA
	T	3.1 (3146)	1.8677–1.8815	1.8677–1.8815	1.8677–1.8815	1.8677–1.8815	1.8677–1.8815	0.2626	0.2732	0.0010–0.0040	NA
1992–93	H	2.0 (1983)	1.6706–1.6712	1.6812–1.6818	1.6911–1.6917	1.7009–1.7015	1.7100–1.7106	0.2626	0.2626	0.0011–0.0035	0.0016–0.0063
	4	2.2 (2196)	1.8670–1.8690	1.8670–1.8690	1.8670–1.8690	1.8670–1.8690	1.8670–1.8690	0.2590	0.2590	0.0010–0.0039	NA
	T	3.1 (3146)	1.8677–1.8815	1.8677–1.8815	1.8677–1.8815	1.8677–1.8815	1.8677–1.8815	0.2626	0.2732	0.0010–0.0040	NA

NA—Not available

CRANKSHAFT AND CONNECTING ROD SPECIFICATIONS

All measurements are given in inches.

Year	Engine ID/VIN	Engine Displacement Liters (cc)	Crankshaft				Connecting Rod		
			Main Brg. Journal Dia.	Main Brg. Oil Clearance	Shaft End-play	Thrust on No.	Journal Diameter	Oil Clearance	Side Clearance
1989	M	2.0 (1983)	①	0.0006–0.0016	0.0030–0.0120	3	1.9278–1.9286	0.0007–0.0024	0.0027–0.0095
	1	2.0 (1983)	2.4945–2.4954	0.0006–0.0019	0.0020–0.0080	4	1.9983–1.9994	0.0010–0.0031	0.0040–0.0150
	K	2.0 (1983)	①	0.0016–0.0016	0.0030–0.0120	3	1.9278–1.9286	0.0007–0.0024	0.0027–0.0095
	W	2.8 (2835)	2.6473–2.6482	0.0016–0.0033	0.0024–0.0083	3	1.9983–1.9994	0.0014–0.0037	0.0063–0.0173
1990	K	2.0 (1983)	2.2828–2.2833	0.0006–0.0016	0.0028–0.0118	3	1.9279–1.9287	0.0007–0.0025	0.0028–0.0095
	M	2.0 (1983)	2.2828–2.2833	0.0006–0.0016	0.0028–0.0118	3	1.9279–1.9287	0.0007–0.0025	0.0028–0.0095
	G	2.2 (2196)	2.4945–2.4954	0.0006–0.0019	0.0020–0.0070	4	1.9983–1.9994	0.0009–0.0031	0.0039–0.0149
	T	3.1 (3146)	2.6473–2.6483	0.0012–0.0030	0.0024–0.0083	3	1.9983–1.9994	0.0011–0.0034	0.0140–0.0270
1991	K	2.0 (1983)	2.2828–2.2833	0.0006–0.0016	0.0028–0.0118	3	1.9279–1.9287	0.0007–0.0025	0.0028–0.0095
	G	2.2 (2196)	2.4945–2.4954	0.0006–0.0019	0.0020–0.0070	4	1.9983–1.9994	0.0009–0.0031	0.0039–0.0149
	T	3.1 (3146)	2.6473–2.6483	0.0012–0.0030	0.0024–0.0083	3	1.9983–1.9994	0.0011–0.0034	0.0140–0.0270
1992–93	H	2.0 (1983)	2.2828–2.2833	0.0006–0.0016	0.0028–0.0118	3	1.9279–1.9287	0.0007–0.0025	0.0028–0.0095
	4	2.2 (2196)	2.4945–2.4954	0.0006–0.0019	0.0020–0.0070	4	1.9983–1.9994	0.0009–0.0031	0.0039–0.0149
	T	3.1 (3146)	2.6473–2.6483	0.0012–0.0030	0.0024–0.0083	3	1.9983–1.9994	0.0011–0.0034	0.0140–0.0270

① Bearings are identified by color:
Brown: 2.2830–2.3832;
Green: 2.2827–2.2830

VALVE SPECIFICATIONS

Year	Engine ID/VIN	Engine Displacement Liters (cc)	Seat Angle (deg.)	Face Angle (deg.)	Spring Test Pressure (lbs. @ in.)	Spring Installed Height (in.)	Stem-to-Guide Clearance (in.)		Stem Diameter (in.)	
							Intake	Exhaust	Intake	Exhaust
1989	M	2.0 (1983)	45	46	NA	NA	0.0006–0.0020	0.0010–0.0024	NA	NA
	1	2.0 (1983)	46	45	183 @ 1.33	1.60	0.0011–0.0026	0.0014–0.0030	0.0490–0.0560	0.0630–0.0750
	K	2.0 (1983)	45	46	NA	NA	0.0006–0.0020	0.0010–0.0024	NA	NA
	W	2.8 (2835)	46	45	195 @ 1.18	1.57	0.0010–0.0027	0.0010–0.0027	0.0610–0.0730	0.0670–0.0790

VALVE SPECIFICATIONS

Year	Engine ID/VIN	Engine Displacement Liters (cc)	Seat Angle (deg.)	Face Angle (deg.)	Spring Test Pressure (lbs. @ in.)	Spring Installed Height (in.)	Stem-to-Guide Clearance (in.)		Stem Diameter (in.)	
							Intake	Exhaust	Intake	Exhaust
1990	K	2.0 (1983)	45	46	165–197 @ 1.043	NA	0.0006–0.0017	0.0012–0.0024	0.2760–0.2755	0.2753–0.2747
	M	2.0 (1983)	45	46	165–197 @ 1.043	NA	0.0006–0.0017	0.0012–0.0024	0.2760–0.2755	0.2753–0.2747
	G	2.2 (2196)	46	45	208–222 @ 1.22	NA	0.0011–0.0026	0.0014–0.0030	NA	NA
	T	3.1 (3146)	46	45	215 @ 1.291	1.575	0.0010–0.0027	0.0010–0.0027	NA	NA
1991	K	2.0 (1983)	45	46	165–197 @ 1.043	NA	0.0006–0.0017	0.0012–0.0024	0.2760–0.2755	0.2753–0.2747
	G	2.2 (2196)	46	45	208–222 @ 1.22	NA	0.0011–0.0026	0.0014–0.0031	NA	NA
	T	3.1 (3146)	46	45	215 @ 1.291	1.575	0.0010–0.0027	0.0010–0.0027	NA	NA
1992–93	H	2.0 (1983)	45	46	165–197 @ 1.043	NA	0.0006–0.0017	0.0012–0.0024	0.2760–0.2755	0.2753–0.2747
	4	2.2 (2196)	46	45	225–233 @ 1.247	NA	0.0011–0.0026	0.0014–0.0031	NA	NA
	T	3.1 (3146)	46	45	215 @ 1.291	1.575	0.0010–0.0027	0.0010–0.0027	NA	NA

NA—Not available

PISTON AND RING SPECIFICATIONS

All measurements are given in inches.

Year	Engine ID/VIN	Engine Displacement Liters (cc)	Piston Clearance	Ring Gap			Ring Side Clearance		
				Top Compression	Bottom Compression	Oil Control	Top Compression	Bottom Compression	Oil Control
1989	M	2.0 (1983)	0.0012–0.0020	0.0120–0.0200	0.0120–0.0200	0.0160–0.0550	0.0020–0.0030	0.0010–0.0024	—
	1	2.0 (1983)	0.0009–0.0022	0.0100–0.0200	0.0100–0.0200	0.0100–0.0500	0.0010–0.0030	0.0010–0.0030	0.0006–0.0090
	K	2.0 (1983)	0.0004–0.0012	0.0120–0.0200	0.0120–0.0200	0.0160–0.0550	0.0020–0.0030	0.0010–0.0024	—
	W	2.8 (2835)	0.0022–0.0035	0.0100–0.0200	0.0100–0.0200	0.0100–0.0500	0.0020–0.0035	0.0020–0.0035	0.0080 Max.
1990	K	2.0 (1983)	0.0004–0.0012	0.0098–0.0177	0.0118–0.0197	NA	0.0024–0.0036	0.0019–0.0032	NA
	M	2.0 (1983)	0.0012–0.0020	0.0098–0.0177	0.0118–0.0197	NA	0.0024–0.0036	0.0019–0.0032	NA
	G	2.2 (2196)	0.0007–0.0017	0.0100–0.0200	0.0100–0.0200	0.0100–0.0500	0.0019–0.0027	0.0019–0.0027	0.0019–0.0082
	T	3.1 (3146)	0.0009–0.0022	0.0100–0.0200	0.0200–0.0280	0.0100–0.0300	0.0020–0.0035	0.0020–0.0035	0.0080 Max.
1991	K	2.0 (1983)	0.0004–0.0012	0.0098–0.0177	0.0118–0.0197	NA	0.0024–0.0036	0.0019–0.0032	NA
	G	2.2 (2196)	0.0007–0.0017	0.0100–0.0200	0.0100–0.0200	0.0100–0.0500	0.0019–0.0027	0.0019–0.0027	0.0019–0.0082
	T	3.1 (3146)	0.0009–0.0022	0.0100–0.0200	0.0200–0.0280	0.0100–0.0300	0.0020–0.0035	0.0020–0.0035	0.0080 Max.

PISTON AND RING SPECIFICATIONS

All measurements are given in inches.

Year	Engine ID/VIN	Engine Displacement Liters (cc)	Piston Clearance	Ring Gap			Ring Side Clearance		
				Top Compression	Bottom Compression	Oil Control	Top Compression	Bottom Compression	Oil Control
1992-93	H	2.0 (1983)	0.0004–0.0012	0.0098–0.0177	0.0118–0.0197	NA	0.0024–0.0036	0.0019–0.0032	NA
	4	2.2 (2196)	0.0007–0.0017	0.0100–0.0200	0.0100–0.0200	0.0100–0.0500	0.0019–0.0027	0.0019–0.0027	0.0019–0.0082
	T	3.1 (3146)	0.0009–0.0022	0.0100–0.0200	0.0200–0.0280	0.0100–0.0300	0.0020–0.0035	0.0020–0.0035	0.0080 Max.

NA—Not available

TORQUE SPECIFICATIONS

All readings in ft. lbs.

Year	Engine ID/VIN	Engine Displacement Liters (cc)	Cylinder Head Bolts	Main Bearing Bolts	Rod Bearing Bolts	Crankshaft Damper Bolts	Flywheel Bolts	Manifold		Spark Plugs	Lug Nut
								Intake	Exhaust		
1989	M	2.0 (1983)	②	44 ③	26 ④	20 ⑤	48 ⑥	16	16	15	100
	1	2.0 (1983)	⑦	63–77	34–43	68–89	63 ①	15–22	6–13	15	100
	K	2.0 (1983)	②	44 ③	26 ④	20 ⑤	48 ⑥	16	16	15	100
	W	2.8 (2835)	33 ⑧	63–83	34–45	66–84	45	18	14–22	15	100
1990	K	2.0 (1983)	②	44 ③	26 ④	114	⑮	16	⑫	15	100
	M	2.0 (1983)	②	44 ③	26 ④	114	⑮	16	⑫	15	100
	G	2.2 (2196)	⑩	70	38	85	⑬	18	⑪	7–15	100
	T	3.1 (3146)	33 ⑧	73	39	76	52	⑨	18	7–15	100
1991	K	2.0 (1983)	②	44 ③	26 ④	114	⑮	16	⑫	15	100
	G	2.2 (2196)	⑭	70	38	77	⑬	18	⑫	11	100
	T	3.1 (3146)	33 ⑧	73	39	76	52	⑨	18	11	100
1992-93	H	2.0 (1983)	②	44 ③	26 ④	114	⑮	16	⑫	15	100
	4	2.2 (2196)	⑭	70	38	77	⑬	18	⑫	11	100
	T	3.1 (3146)	33 ⑧	73	39	76	52	⑨	18	11	100

NOTE: Verify the correct original equipment engine is in the vehicle by referring to the VIN engine code before torquing any bolts.

① Auto. Trans.—45–59
② Step 1—18 ft. lbs.
   Step 2—Tighten additional 180 degrees in 3 steps of 60 degrees each
   Step 3—Warm engine—tighten bolts additional 30–50 degree turn
③ Plus additional 45–50 degree turn
④ Plus additional 45 degree turn
⑤ Crankshaft pulley to sprocket bolts
⑥ Plus additional 30 degree turn
⑦ Long bolts—73–83 ft. lbs.
   Short bolts—62–70 ft. lbs.
⑧ Coat thread with sealer an additional 90 degree turn
⑨ Tighten in sequence to 15 ft. lbs., then retighten to 24 ft. lbs.
⑩ Step 1—Tighten all bolts initially to 41 ft. lbs.
   Step 2—Tighten all bolts an additional 45 degrees in sequence
   Step 3—Tighten all bolts an additional 45 degrees in sequence
   Step 4—Tighten the long bolts—8, 4, 1, 5 and 9 an additional 20 degrees and tighten the short bolts—7, 3, 2, 6 and 10 an additional 10 degrees

⑪ Nuts—115 inch lbs.
   Studs—89 inch lbs.
⑫ 115 inch lbs.
⑬ Auto. trans.—52
   Manual trans.—55
⑭ Step 1—Tighten the long bolts—8, 4, 1, 5 and 9 to 46 ft. lbs.
   Tighten the short bolts—7, 3, 2, 6 and 10 to 43 ft. lbs.
   Step 2—Tighten all bolts an additional 90 degrees in sequence
⑮ Auto. trans.—48 ft. lbs.—can reuse bolts.
   Man. trans.—48 ft. lbs.—plus an additional 30 degrees—must use new bolts.

BRAKE SPECIFICATIONS

All measurements in inches unless noted.

Year	Model	Master Cylinder Bore	Brake Disc			Brake Drum Diameter			Minimum Lining Thickness	
			Original Thickness	Minimum Thickness	Maximum Runout	Original Inside Diameter	Max. Wear Limit	Maximum Machine Diameter	Front	Rear
1989	Cavalier	0.940	0.885	0.830①	0.004	7.879	7.899	7.929	1/8	1/8
	Sunbird	0.940	0.885	0.830①	0.004	7.879	7.899	7.929	1/8	1/8
	Skyhawk	0.940	0.885	0.830①	0.004	7.879	7.899	7.929	1/8	1/8
1990	Cavalier	0.874	0.885	0.830①	0.004	7.879	7.899	7.929	1/8	1/8
	Sunbird	0.874	0.885	0.830①	0.004	7.879	7.899	7.929	1/8	1/8
1991	Cavalier	0.874	0.885	0.830①	0.004	7.879	7.899	7.929	1/8	1/8
	Sunbird	0.874	0.885	0.830①	0.004	7.879	7.899	7.929	1/8	1/8
1992–93	Cavalier	0.874	0.806	0.796①	0.004	7.879	7.899	7.929	1/8	1/8
	Sunbird	0.874	0.806	0.796①	0.004	7.879	7.899	7.929	1/8	1/8

① Refinish thickness: minimum wear thickness is cast into the disc. Do not refinish disc to this, replace it if worn to this thickness.

WHEEL ALIGNMENT

Year	Model	Caster		Camber		Toe-in (in.)	Steering Axis Inclination (deg.)
		Range (deg.)	Preferred Setting (deg.)	Range (deg.)	Preferred Setting (deg.)		
1989	Cavalier	11/16P–2 11/16P	1 11/16P	3/16P–1 3/16P②	13/16P①	0	13 1/2
	Sunbird	11/16P–2 11/16P	1 11/16P	3/16P–1 3/16P	13/16P	0	13 1/2
	Skyhawk	11/16P–2 11/16P	1 11/16P	3/16P–1 3/16P	13/16P	0	13 1/2
1990	Cavalier	11/16P–2 11/16P	1 11/16P	3/16P–1 3/16P②	13/16P①	0	13 1/2
	Sunbird	11/16P–2 11/16P	1 11/16P	3/16P–1 3/16P	13/16P	0	13 1/2
1991	Cavalier	11/16P–2 11/16P	1 11/16P	3/16P–1 3/16P②	13/16P①	0	13 1/2
	Sunbird	11/16P–2 11/16P	1 11/16P	3/16P–1 3/16P	13/16P	0	13 1/2
1992–93	Cavalier	11/16P–2 11/16P	1 11/16P	3/16P–1 3/16P②	13/16P①	0	13 1/2
	Sunbird	11/16P–2 11/16P	1 11/16P	3/16P–1 3/16P	13/16P	0	13 1/2

N—Negative
P—Positive
① Z-24; 1N–P. Preferred setting is 0 camber
② If vehicle is equipped with P215-60R14 tires setting is 1/8 degree out

ENGINE MECHANICAL

NOTE: Disconnecting the negative battery cable on some vehicles may interfere with the functions of the on board computer systems and may require the computer to undergo a relearning process, once the negative battery cable is reconnected.

Engine Assembly

REMOVAL & INSTALLATION

2.0L (VIN 1) Engine

NOTE: Special tool J–24420 crankshaft pulley hub remover is required. The engine is removed from the top of vehicle.

1. Disconnect the negative battery cable and relieve the fuel system pressure.

2. Drain the cooling system.
3. Remove the air cleaner.
4. Disconnect the accelerator and TV cables.
5. Disconnect the ECM harness at engine.
6. Disconnect the necessary vacuum hoses.
7. Disconnect all of the cooling hoses at engine.
8. Remove the exhaust heat shield.
9. If equipped with air conditioning, remove the adjustment bolt at engine mount.

10. Disconnect engine wiring harness at bulkhead.
11. Remove the windshield washer bottle.
12. Remove the alternator and power steering belt.
13. Disconnect the fuel hoses.
14. Raise and safely support the vehicle. If equipped with air conditioning, remove the air conditioning brace.
15. Remove inner fender splash shield.
16. If equipped with air conditioning, remove the air conditioning compressor.
17. Remove flywheel splash shield.
18. Disconnect and the tag starter wires.
19. Disconnect the front starter brace.
20. Remove the starter.
21. Remove the 010993 converter bolts.
22. Remove the crankshaft pulley and hub using tool J–24420 or equivalent.
23. Remove the oil filter.
24. Disconnect the engine-to-transaxle bracket.
25. Disconnect the right rear mount.
26. Disconnect exhaust at manifold and center hanger.
27. Disconnect the TV and shift cable.
28. Remove the lower bellhousing bolts.
29. Lower the vehicle.
30. Remove the right front engine mount nuts.
31. Remove alternator and adjusting brace.
32. Disconnect the master cylinder and push it aside.
33. Install a suitable lifting device.
34. Remove the right front engine mount bracket.
35. Remove upper bellhousing bolts.
36. Remove the power steering pump while lifting engine.
37. Carefully remove the engine from the vehicle.
To install:
38. Install the engine mount alignment bolt M6X1X65 to ensure proper power train alignment.
39. Slowly lower the engine into the vehicle, leaving the lifting device attached.
40. Install the transaxle bracket. Install the mount to the side frame and secure with new bolts.
41. With the engine weight not on the mounts, tighten the transaxle bolts to 48–63 ft. lbs. (65–85 Nm).
42. Tighten the right front mount nuts.
43. Lower the engine weight onto the mounts. Remove the lifting device.
44. Install the power steering pump.
45. Install alternator and adjusting brace.

46. Install the right front engine mount nuts.
47. Connect the master cylinder.
48. Install the lower bellhousing bolts.
49. Connect the TV and shift cable.
50. Connect exhaust at manifold and center hanger.
51. Connect the right rear mount.
52. Connect the engine-to-transaxle bracket.
53. Install the oil filter.
54. Install the crankshaft pulley and hub using tool J–24420 or equivalent.
55. Install the torque converter bolts.
56. Install the starter.
57. Connect the front starter brace.
58. Connect the starter wires.
59. Install flywheel splash shield.
60. If equipped with air conditioning, install the air conditioning compressor. Install the air conditioning brace.
61. Install inner fender splash shield.
62. Connect the fuel hoses.
63. Install the alternator and power steering belts.
64. Install the windshield washer bottle.
65. Connect engine wiring harness at bulkhead.
66. If equipped with air conditioning, install the adjustment bolt at the engine mount.
67. Install the exhaust heat shield.
68. Connect all of the cooling hoses at engine.
69. Connect the vacuum hoses.
70. Connect the ECM harness at engine.
71. Connect the accelerator and TV cables.
72. Install the air cleaner.
73. Drain the cooling system.
74. Connect the negative battery cable.

2.0L (VIN H, K and M) and 2.2L Engines

NOTE: This procedure requires the use of a special powertrain alignment bolt M6X1X65. The engine is removed from the bottom of the vehicle.

1. Disconnect the negative battery cable and relieve fuel pressure.
2. Drain the cooling system into a clean container for reuse.
3. Remove the air cleaner assembly.
4. Remove the cooling fan.
5. Disconnect the engine electrical harness at bulkhead.
6. Disconnect the electrical connector at brake cylinder.
7. Disconnect the air conditioner relay cluster switches.
8. Disconnect the wiper motor electrical connector.
9. Disconnect the cooling fan, relay and ground.

10. Disconnect the ECM harness and pull harness through the bulkhead.
11. Disconnect the temperature switch at the thermostat housing.
12. Disconnect the EFI, MAP sensor and canister vacuum hoses.
13. Disconnect the cables from the throttle bracket and EFI, and shift control at the transaxle.
14. Disconnect the power steering return hose at the pump.
15. Raise and safely support the vehicle.
16. Disconnect the VSS connector or speedometer cable at the transaxle.
17. Disconnect the exhaust pipe at the exhaust manifold and exhaust hangers and swing aside.
18. Disconnect the hoses from the heater core.
19. Disconnect the fuel lines.
20. If equipped with automatic transaxle, disconnect the cooler lines from the radiator.
21. Remove the front wheels.
22. Remove the brake calipers and support using a length of wire.
23. Properly discharge and recover the refrigerant from the air conditioning system.
24. Disconnect the refrigerant lines from the compressor.

NOTE: Cap the refrigerant lines when opening the system to prevent the entry of dirt and moisture and the loss of refrigerant lubricant.

25. Remove the suspension support bolts as follows:
    a.rt.
29. Reposition the jack to the rear of the cowl with 4 × 4 × 6 in. timber spanning the vehicle width.
30. Raise the vehicle enough to remove the jackstands.
31. Position the dolly under the engine and transaxle with three 4 × 4 × 12 in. blocks as support.
32. Lower the vehicle onto the dolly lightly.
33. Remove the remaining bolt at each end of the right and left front suspension supports.
34. Remove the long mount-to-bracket bolt from the transaxle.
35. Remove the 2 mount-to-bracket bolts from the front engine mount.
36. Remove the 2 mount-to-bracket nuts and reinforcement bracket from the rear engine mount.
37. Carefully scribe the position of the strut on the hub to preserve the camber adjustment. Remove the 2 knuckle-to-strut bolts on each side.
38. Raise the vehicle leaving the engine, transaxle and suspension on the dolly.

39. Separate the engine and transaxle.

To install:

40. With the aid of an assistant, assemble the engine and transaxle. Tighten the engine-to-transaxle bolts to 85 ft. lbs. (75 Nm) for automatic transaxles or 60 ft. lbs. (75 Nm) for manual transaxles. Position the engine and transaxle assembly in the vehicle.

41. Install the 1 long mount-to-bracket bolt at the transaxle. Install the nut and tighten to 80 ft. lbs. (108 Nm).

42. Install the reinforcement bracket and 2 mount-to-bracket nuts at the rear engine mount. Tighten to 18 ft. lbs. (24 Nm).

43. Install the 2 mount-to-bracket bolts at the front engine mount. Tighten to 40 ft. lbs. (54 Nm).

44. Loosely install the bolt at each end of the right and left front suspension supports.

45. Install the knuckle-to-strut bolts. Align the scribe marks made during removal. Tighten the nuts to 133 ft. lbs. (180 Nm).

46. Raise the vehicle and remove the dolly. Using jackstands, remove the 6 in. timber and move the hoist to the front.

47. Install the remaining bolts in the right and left front suspension supports. Tighten to 65 ft. lbs. (88 Nm).

48. Connect the front and rear transaxle struts. Tighten to 50 ft. lbs. (68 Nm).

49. Connect the electrical connectors to the compressor.

50. Install the brake calipers.

51. Install the front wheels.

52. If equipped with automatic transaxle, connect the cooler lines to the radiator.

53. Connect the fuel lines.

54. Connect the hoses to the heater core.

55. Connect the exhaust pipe to the exhaust manifold and hangers.

56. Connect the speedometer cable or VSS connector at the transaxle.

57. Lower the vehicle.

58. Connect the power steering return hose to the pump.

59. Connect the power steering cutoff switch.

60. Connect the transaxle shift cable.

61. Connect the throttle cable to the bracket and EFI unit.

62. Connect the vacuum hoses to the MAP sensor, canister and EFI unit.

63. Connect the electrical connector to the temperature switch at the thermostat housing.

64. Pull the ECM harness through the bulkhead and connect the ECM connector.

65. Connect the air conditioner relay cluster switches.

66. Connect the wiper motor electrical connector.

67. Connect the cooling fan, relay and ground.

68. Connect the electrical connector to the brake cylinder.

69. Connect engine harness bulkhead connectors.

70. Connect the radiator hose.

71. Replace the compressor fitting O-rings. Lubricate the O-rings with refrigerant oil. Connect the air conditioner refrigerant lines.

72. Connect the negative battery cable.

73. Fill cooling system and check for leaks. Start the engine and allow to come to normal operating temperature. Recheck for leaks. Top-up coolant.

74. Evacuate, recharge and leak test the air conditioning system.

75. Recheck for coolant, fuel, oil and transaxle fluid leaks.

2.8L and 3.1L Engines

NOTE: Always release the fuel pressure before starting repair. The engine is removed from the top of the vehicle.

1. Disconnect the negative battery cable. Drain the cooling system and remove the air cleaner assembly. Mark the bolt location and remove the hood.

2. Remove the air flow sensor. Remove the exhaust crossover heat shield and remove the crossover pipe.

3. Remove the serpentine belt tensioner and belt.

4. Remove the power steering pump mounting bracket. Disconnect the heater pipe at the power steering pump mounting bracket.

5. Disconnect the radiator hoses from the engine.

6. Disconnect the accelerator and throttle valve cable at the throttle valve.

7. Remove the alternator. Tag and disconnect the wiring harness at the engine.

8. Relieve the fuel pressure and disconnect the fuel hose. Disconnect the coolant bypass and the over flow hoses at the engine.

9. Tag and remove the vacuum hoses to the engine.

10. Raise the vehicle and support it safely.

11. Remove the inner fender splash shield. Remove the harmonic balancer.

12. Remove the flywheel cover. Remove the starter bolts. Tag and disconnect the electrical connections to the starter. Remove the starter.

13. Disconnect the wires at the oil sending unit.

14. Remove the air conditioning compressor and related brackets.

15. Disconnect the exhaust pipe at the rear of the exhaust manifold.

16. Remove the flexplate-to-torque converter bolts.

17. Remove the transaxle-to-engine bolts. Remove the engine-to-rear mount frame nuts.

18. Disconnect the shift cable bracket at the transaxle. Remove the lower bellhousing bolts.

19. Lower the vehicle and disconnect the heater hoses at the engine.

NOTE: It may be necessary to remove the engine hood. Using an awl, scribe marks around the hood hinges to help aid correct hood alignment upon installation.

20. Install a suitable engine lifting device. While supporting the engine and transaxle, remove the upper bellhousing bolts.

21. Remove the front mounting bolts.

22. Remove the master cylinder from the booster.

23. Remove the engine assembly from the vehicle.

To install:

24. Install the engine in position in the vehicle.

25. Install the upper transaxle-to-engine bolts.

26. Raise and safely support the vehicle.

27. Install the lower transaxle-to-engine bolts.

28. Reconnect the shift cable bracket to the transaxle.

29. Install the engine mounts, tightening the front mount-to-frame bolts to 61 ft. lbs. (83 Nm) and the engine mount to bracket bolts to 50 ft. lbs. (68 Nm).

30. Install the flywheel to converter bolts.

31. Reconnect the exhaust pipe and install the air conditioning compressor. Install the flywheel cover.

32. Reconnect the coolant hoses and the fuel lines.

33. Install the wiring harness at the engine and install the alternator.

34. Lower the vehicle and install the accessory drive belt.

35. Refill all of the fluids and connect the negative battery cable.

36. Install the hood. Install the air cleaner assembly.

37. Road test the vehicle.

Engine Mounts

REMOVAL & INSTALLATION

Front

1. Disconnect the negative battery cable.

2. Raise the vehicle and support safely.

3. Using a suitable fixture, support the engine and remove the engine mount nuts.

4. Remove the inner fender shield.

5. Remove the engine mount bolts. The manufacturer recommends discarding the engine mount bolts and replacing with new bolts. Note the location and length of each bolt for reassembly.

6. Remove the engine mount.

To install:

7. Install the engine mount.

8. Install the engine mount bolts.

9. Install the inner fender shield.

10. Install the engine mount nuts. Remove the support fixture.

11. Lower the vehicle.

12. Connect the negative battery cable.

Rear

1. Disconnect the negative battery cable.

2. Raise and safely support the vehicle.

3. If equipped with manual transaxle, remove the oil filter in order to gain working clearance.

4. Using a suitable fixture, support the engine and remove the engine mounting nuts.

5. Remove the engine mounting bolts. Remove the engine mount.

To install:

6. Install the engine mount. Install the mounting bolts and nuts.

7. Remove the engine support fixture.

8. If equipped with manual transaxle, install the oil filter.

9. Lower the vehicle.

10. Connect the negative battery cable.

Cylinder Head

REMOVAL & INSTALLATION

2.0L (VIN 1) and 2.2L Engines

NOTE: The engine must be cold before removing the cylinder head. Always release the fuel pressure before starting repair.

1. Disconnect the negative battery cable.

2. Drain the cooling system.

3. Remove the TBI cover. Raise and safely support the vehicle.

4. Remove the exhaust shield. Disconnect the exhaust pipe.

5. Remove the heater hose from the intake manifold. Lower the vehicle.

6. Disconnect the accelerator and TV cable bracket.

7. Lower the vehicle.

8. Tag and disconnect the vacuum lines at the intake manifold and thermostat.

9. Disconnect the accelerator linkage at the throttle body and remove the linkage bracket.

10. Tag and disconnect all necessary wires. Remove the upper radiator hose at the thermostat.

11. Remove the serpentine belt.

12. Remove the power steering pump and lay it aside.

13. Make sure the fuel system pressure is released and disconnect and plug the fuel lines.

14. Remove the alternator. Remove the alternator brace from the head and remove the upper mounting bracket.

15. Remove the cylinder head cover. Remove the rocker arms and pushrods keeping all parts in order for correct installation.

16. Remove the cylinder head bolts. Remove the cylinder head with the throttle body, intake and exhaust manifolds still attached.

To install:

17. The gasket surfaces on both the head and the block must be clean of any foreign matter and free of any nicks or heavy scratches. Bolt threads in the block and the bolts must be clean.

18. Place a new cylinder head gasket in position over the dowel pins on the block. Carefully guide the cylinder head into position.

19. Coat the cylinder bolts with sealing compound and install them finger tight.

20. If equipped with a 2.0L engine, tighten the short bolts in sequence to 62–70 ft. lbs. (84–95 Nm) and tighten the long bolts in sequence to 73–83 ft. lbs. (99–113 Nm).

21. If equipped with a 2.2L engine, tighten the bolts in the following sequence:

   a. Tighten all bolts initially to 41 ft. lbs. (56 Nm).

   b. Tighten all bolts 45 degrees in sequence.

   c. Tighten all bolts an additional 45 degrees in sequence.

   d. Tighten the long bolts 8, 4, 1, 5 and 9 an additional 20 degrees.

   e. Tighten the short bolts 7, 3, 2, 6 and 10 an additional 10 degrees.

NOTE: The short bolts, exhaust side, should end up with a total rotation of 100 degrees and the long bolts, intake side, should end up with a total rotation of 110 degrees.

22. Reinstall the alternator. Install the power steering pump and brackets.

23. Reconnect the fuel lines and the hoses. Connect the exhaust pipe to the manifold.

24. Install the valve cover and connect the linkage at the throttle body. Install the air cleaner and fill all the fluids.

25. Connect the negative battery cable.

26. Start the engine and check for leaks.

2.0L (VIN H, K and M) Engines

NOTE: Cylinder head gasket replacement is necessary if camshaft carrier/cylinder head bolts are loosened. The head bolts should always be loosened when cold. New head bolts should be used every time camshaft carrier/cylinder head or gasket are replaced.

1. Disconnect the negative battery cable. Remove the air cleaner and relieve fuel pressure.

2. Drain the cooling system.

3. Remove the alternator and pivot bracket at the camshaft carrier housing.

4. Disconnect the power steering pump and bracket, lay it to one side.

5. Disconnect the ignition coil electrical connections and remove coil.

6. Disconnect the spark plug wires and distributor cap, remove the distributor.

7. Remove the throttle cable from the bracket at intake manifold.

8. Disconnect the throttle cable, downshift cable and TV cable from the EFI assembly.

9. Disconnect the ECM connectors from the EFI assembly.

10. Remove the vacuum brake hose at filter.

11. Disconnect the inlet and return fuel lines at flex joints.

12. Remove the water pump bypass

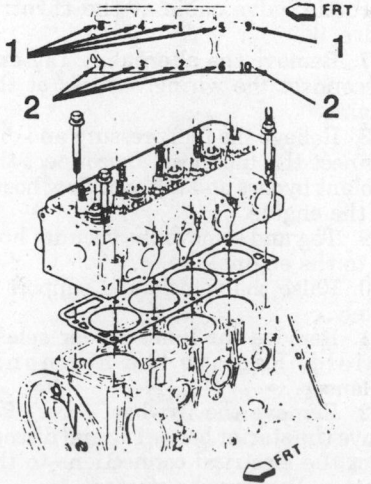

1. 73–83 ft. lbs.
2. 62–70 ft. lbs.

Cylinder head bolt torque sequence— 2.0L (VIN 1) and 2.2L engines

hose at the intake manifold and water pump.

13. Disconnect the ECM harness connectors at intake manifold.

14. Disconnect the heater hose from intake manifold.

15. Disconnect the exhaust pipe at exhaust manifold.

NOTE: On engine VIN M, remove the exhaust manifold to turbo connection and oxygen sensor connection.

16. Disconnect the breather hose at camshaft carrier.

17. Remove the upper radiator hose.

18. Disconnect the engine electrical harness and wires from thermostat housing.

19. Remove the timing cover.

20. Remove the timing probe holder.

21. Loosen the water pump retaining bolts and remove timing belt.

22. Loosen the camshaft carrier and cylinder head attaching bolts, a little at a time, in sequence.

23. Remove the camshaft carrier assembly.

24. Remove the cylinder head, intake manifold and exhaust manifold as an assembly.

To install:

25. Install a new cylinder head gasket in position on the block.

26. Apply a continuous bead of sealer to the cam carrier.

27. Install the cylinder head, reassembled with the intake and exhaust manifolds, if removed.

28. Install the camshaft carrier on the cylinder head and tighten the bolts, in following sequence, to the correct torque.

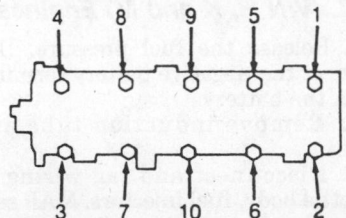

Camshaft carrier/cylinder head bolt loosening sequence—2.0L (VIN H, K and M) engines

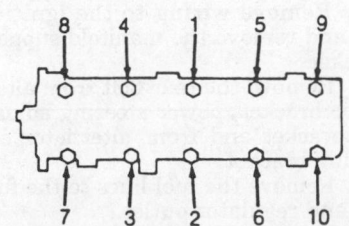

Camshaft carrier/cylinder head bolt torque sequence—2.0L (VIN H, K and M) engines

a. Tighten all bolts in sequence to 18 ft. lbs. (24 Nm).

b. Tighten all bolts an additional 180 degrees in 3 steps of 60 degrees each.

29. Install the timing belt.

30. Reconnect the electrical harness and the breather hose at the camshaft carrier.

31. Connect the exhaust pipe at the manifold and attach the heater hose to the intake manifold.

32. Connect the brake hose at the filter. Connect the throttle and TV cable.

33. Refill the cooling system and connect the negative battery cable.

34. Run the engine, until warm, thermostat open, and tighten all of the the cylinder head/cam carrier bolts an additional 30–50 degrees, in sequence. Check for leaks.

2.8L and 3.1L Engines

LEFT SIDE

1. Relieve the fuel system pressure and disconnect the negative battery cable. Drain the engine coolant into a clean container for reuse. Remove the rocker cover.

2. Remove the intake manifold. Disconnect the exhaust crossover at the right exhaust manifold.

3. Disconnect the oil level indicator tube bracket.

4. Loosen the rocker arms nuts enough to remove the pushrods.

5. Starting with the outer bolts, remove the cylinder head bolts. Remove the cylinder head with the exhaust manifold.

6. Clean and inspect the surfaces of the cylinder head, block and intake manifold. Clean the threads in the block and the threads on the bolts.

To install:

7. Align the new gasket over the dowels on the block with the note **THIS SIDE UP** facing the cylinder head.

8. Install the cylinder head and exhaust manifold crossover assembly on the engine.

9. Coat the cylinder head bolts with a proper sealer and install the bolts h and tight.

10. Tighten the bolts, in the correct sequence, to 33 ft. lbs. (45 Nm), then rotate an additional 90 degree (¼ turn).

11. Install the pushrods in the same order they were removed.

12. Install the rocker arms. Tighten to 18 ft. lbs. (24 Nm).

13. Install the intake manifold using a new gasket and following the correct sequence, tighten the bolts to the correct specification.

14. Connect the exhaust crossover at the right exhaust manifold.

15. Install the rocker cover.

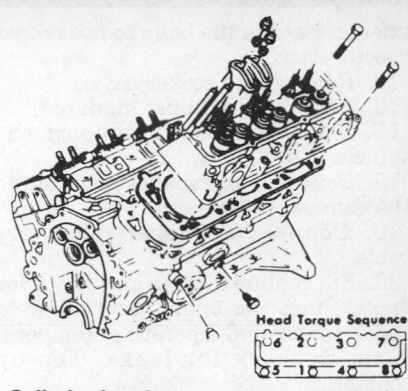

Cylinder head torque sequence—2.8L and 3.1L engines

16. Install the oil level dipstick tube.

17. Connect the negative battery cable.

18. Fill cooling system and check for leaks. Start the engine and allow to come to normal operating temperature. Recheck for leaks. Top-up coolant.

RIGHT SIDE

1. Disconnect the negative battery cable. Drain the engine coolant into a clean container for reuse.

2. Raise and safely support the vehicle. Disconnect the exhaust manifold from the exhaust pipe.

3. Lower the vehicle. Disconnect the exhaust manifold from the cylinder head and remove the manifold.

4. Remove the rocker cover. Remove the intake manifold.

5. Loosen the rocker arms enough so the pushrods can be removed. Note the position of the pushrods for assembly.

6. Starting with the outer bolts, remove the cylinder head bolts and remove the cylinder head.

7. Inspect and clean the surfaces of the cylinder head, engine block and intake manifold.

8. Clean the threads in the engine block and the threads on the cylinder head bolts.

To install:

9. Align the new gasket on the dowels on the engine block with the note **THIS SIDE UP** facing the cylinder head.

10. Install the cylinder head on the engine. Coat the head bolts with a proper sealer. Install and tighten the bolts h and tight.

11. Tighten the bolts, in sequence, to 33 ft. lbs. (45 Nm), then rotate an additional 90 degree (¼ turn).

12. Install the pushrods in the same order as they were removed.

13. Install the rocker arms. The correct rocker arm torque is 18 ft. lbs. (24 Nm).

14. Install the intake manifold using a new gasket. Following the correct se-

quence, tighten the bolts to the proper specification.
15. Remove the rocker cover.
16. Install the exhaust manifold.
17. Raise and safely support the vehicle.
18. Connect the exhaust manifold to the exhaust pipe.
19. Connect the negative battery cable.
20. Fill cooling system and check for leaks. Start the engine and allow to come to normal operating temperature. Recheck for leaks. Top-up coolant.

Valve Lifters

REMOVAL & INSTALLATION

1. Disconnect the negative battery cable.
2. If equipped with a 2.8L or 3.1L engine, remove the intake manifold.
3. Remove the rocker arm cover.
4. Loosen the rocker arm holding nut and move the rocker arm to the side.
5. Remove the pushrods.
6. Using a suitable tool, remove the valve lifter.
To install:
7. Fill lifter assembly with engine oil and lubricate the bottom of the valve lifter with Molykote® or equivalent. Install the valve lifter.
8. Install the pushrods.
9. Place the rocker arm into position. Tighten the rocker arm nut to 10 ft. lbs. (14 Nm) on a 2.0L engine, 14 ft. lbs. (19 Nm) on a 2.2L engine or 18 ft. lbs. (24 Nm) on a 2.8L or 3.1L engine.
10. Install the rocker arm cover.
11. If equipped with a 2.8L or 3.1L engine, install the intake manifold.
12. Connect the negative battery cable.

Rocker Arms

REMOVAL & INSTALLATION

2.0L (VIN H, K and M) Engines

1. Disconnect the negative battery cable. Remove camshaft carrier cover.
2. Hold the valves in place with compressed air, using air adapter tool J-22794 or equivalent, in spark plug hole.
3. Compress the valve springs with special tool J-33302-25 or equivalent.
4. Remove the rocker arms. Keep the rocker arms in order for reassembly.
To install:
5. Compress the valve springs with special tool J-33302-25 or equivalent.
6. If removed, install the valve lash compensators in original positions.

7. Install thrust pieces and rocker arms.
8. Install the camshaft carrier cover.
9. Connect the negative battery cable.

2.0L (VIN 1) and 2.2L Engines

1. Disconnect the negative battery cable. Remove the air cleaner. Remove the rocker cover.
2. Remove the rocker arm nut and ball. Lift the rocker arm off the stud and the pushrods from the engine. Always keep the valve system parts in order.
To install:
3. Coat the rocker arm balls with Molykote® or equivalent.
4. Install the pushrods in the order removed, making sure they seat properly in the lifter.
5. Install the rocker arms, balls and nuts in the order removed. Tighten to 11-18 ft. lbs. (15-24 Nm).
6. Install the rocker cover.
7. Install the air cleaner.
8. Connect the negative battery cable.

2.8L and 3.1L Engines

LEFT SIDE

1.
Disconnect the negative battery cable. Disconnect the bracket tube at the rocker cover.
2. Remove the spark plug wire cover. Drain the cooling system into a clean container for reuse and remove the heater hose at the filler neck.
3. Remove the rocker arm cover bolts and remove the rocker cover.
4. Remove the rocker arm nuts and remove the rocker arms. Note the order of removal for installation.
To install:
5. Install the rocker arms in the correct order. Tighten to 14-20 ft. lbs. (19-27 Nm).
6. Install the rocker arm cover. Connect the bracket tube at the rocker cover.
7. Install the spark plug wire cover.
8. Connect the heater hose to the filler neck.
9. Connect the negative battery cable.
10. Fill cooling system and check for leaks. Start the engine and allow to come to normal operating temperature. Recheck for leaks. Top-up coolant.

RIGHT SIDE

1. Disconnect the negative battery cable. Disconnect the brake booster vacuum line at the bracket.
2. Disconnect the cable bracket at the plenum.

3. Disconnect the vacuum line bracket at the cable bracket.
4. Disconnect the lines at the alternator brace stud.
5. Remove the rear alternator brace.
6. Remove the serpentine belt.
7. Remove the alternator and support it out of the way.
8. Remove the PCV valve.
9. Loosen the alternator bracket.
10. Remove the spark plug wires. Remove the rocker cover bolts and remove the rocker cover.
11. Remove the rocker arm nuts and remove the rocker arms. Note the order of removal for installation.
To install:
12. Install the rocker arms in the correct order. Tighten 14-20 ft. lbs. (19-27 Nm).
13. Install the rocker cover and attaching bolts. Install the spark plug wires.
14. Tighten the alternator bracket.
15. Install the PCV valve.
16. Install the alternator.
17. Install the serpentine belt.
18. Install the rear alternator brace.
19. Connect the lines at the alternator brace stud.
20. Connect the vacuum line bracket at the cable bracket.
21. Connect the cable bracket at the plenum.
22. Connect the brake booster vacuum line at the bracket. Connect the negative battery cable.

Intake Manifold

REMOVAL & INSTALLATION

2.0L (VIN H, K and M) Engines

1. Release the fuel pressure. Disconnect the negative battery terminal from the battery.
2. Remove induction tube and hoses.
3. Disconnect and tag wiring to throttle body, fuel injectors, MAP sensor and wastegate, if equipped.
4. Disconnect and tag PCV hose and vacuum hoses on the throttle body.
5. Remove the throttle cable and the cruise control cable, if equipped.
6. Remove wiring to the ignition coil and remove the manifold support bracket.
7. Remove the rear bolt from alternator bracket, power steering adjusting bracket and front alternator adjusting bracket.
8. Remove the fuel lines to the fuel rail and regulator outlet.
9. Remove the retaining nuts and washers and intake manifold.
To install:
10. Use a new gasket on the manifold

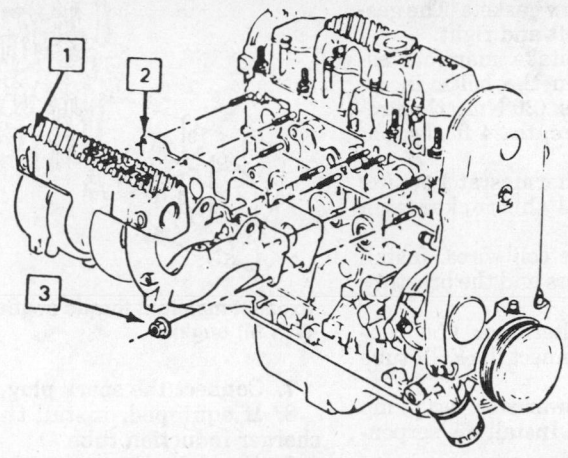

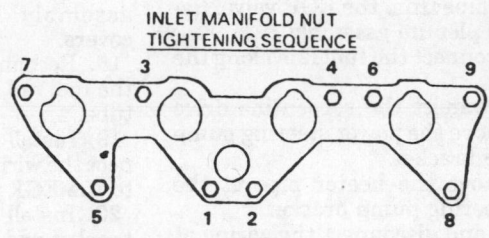

1. Intake manifold
2. Gasket
3. Nut (18 ft. lbs.)

Intake manifold torque sequence—2.0L (VIN H and M) engine

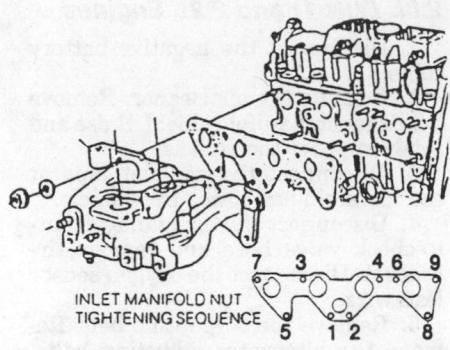

Intake manifold torque sequence—2.0L (VIN K) engine

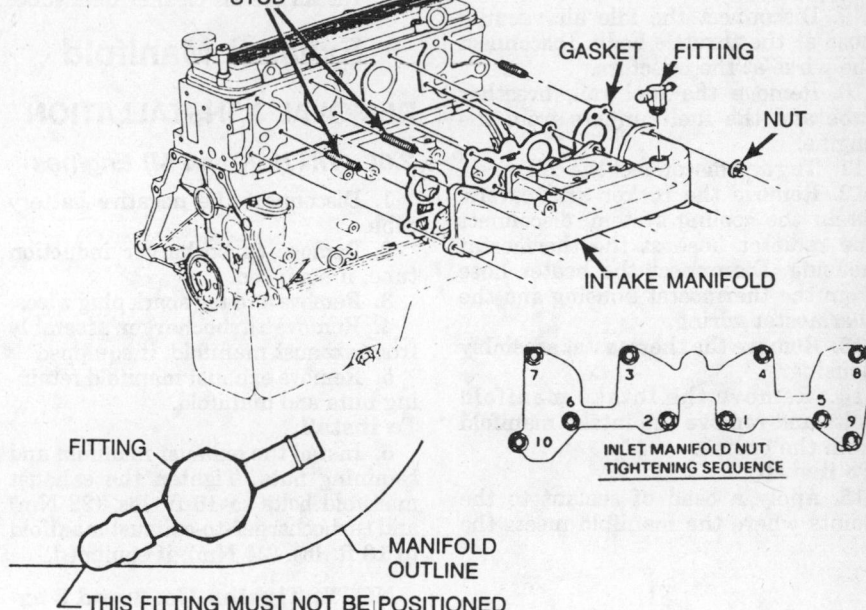

Intake manifold torque sequence—2.0L (VIN 1) and 2.2L engines

THIS FITTING MUST NOT BE POSITIONED OUTSIDE OF MANIFOLD OUTLINE

surface and mount the manifold in position.

11. Tighten the bolts to 16 ft. lbs. (22 Nm) for the VIN K engine or 18 ft. lbs. (24 Nm) for the VIN M engine, in the correct sequence.

12. Reconnect the fuel lines. Install the bolt for the power steering adjusting bracket and the alternator.

13. Connect the ignition coil wiring and connect the vacuum hoses.

14. Connect the induction tube and hoses.

15. Reconnect all of the electrical wiring and the battery cable.

2.0L (VIN 1) and 2.2L Engines

1. Disconnect the negative battery cable and relieve fuel pressure.

2. Remove the air cleaner assembly.

3. Drain the coolant.

4. Remove and tag the vacuum lines and wires as necessary.

5. Disconnect the fuel line, TBI linkage and remove the TBI unit.

6. Remove the power steering pump and lay aside.

7. Disconnect the coolant hose at the manifold.

8. Raise and support the vehicle safely.

9. Disconnect the coolant pipe retaining nut, located at the top of the DIS, and move the pipe rearward.

10. Disconnect the accelerator and TV cables and bracket.

11. Remove the lower intake manifold nuts.

12. Lower the vehicle, remove the remaining intake manifold bolts and nuts and remove the manifold.

To install:

13. Use a new gasket on the manifold surface and mount the manifold in position.

14. Install the upper manifold bolts.

15. Raise and safely support the vehicle.

16. Install the lower manifold bolts.

17. Tighten the nuts to 15–22 ft. lbs. (20–30 Nm) in the correct sequence.

18. Connect the accelerator and TV cables and bracket.

19. Move the coolant pipe located at the top of the DIS into position and install the retaining nut.

20. Lower the vehicle.

21. Connect the coolant hose at the manifold.

22. Install the power steering pump.

23. Install the TBI unit, TBI linkage and connect the fuel line.

24. Connect the vacuum lines and wires.

25. Install the air cleaner assembly.

26. Connect the negative battery cable.

27. Fill cooling system and check for leaks. Start the engine and allow to come to normal operating temperature. Recheck for leaks. Top-up coolant.

2.8L and 3.1L Engines

1. Disconnect the negative battery cable and relieve fuel pressure. Remove the air cleaner inlet tube.

2. Disconnect the accelerator cable bracket at the plenum.

3. Disconnect the throttle body and the EGR pipe from the EGR valve. Remove the plenum assembly.

4. Disconnect the fuel line along the fuel rail.

5. Disconnect the serpentine drive belt. Remove the power steering pump mounting bracket.

6. Remove the heater pipe at the power steering pump bracket.

7. Tag and disconnect the wiring at the alternator, remove the alternator.

8. Disconnect the wires from the cold start injector assembly. Remove the injector assembly from the intake manifold.

9. Disconnect the idle air vacuum hose at the throttle body. Disconnect the wires at the injectors.

10. Remove the fuel rail, breather tube and the fuel runners from the engine.

11. Tag and disconnect the coil wires.

12. Remove the rocker arm covers. Drain the cooling system, disconnect the radiator hose at the thermostat housing. Disconnect the heater hose from the thermostat housing and the thermostat wiring.

13. Remove the thermostat assembly housing.

14. Remove the intake manifold bolts and remove the intake manifold from the engine.

To install:

15. Apply a bead of sealant to the points where the manifold meets the block and install new gaskets. The gaskets are marked left and right.

16. Install the intake manifold assembly and tighten the bolts, in sequence, to 15 ft. lbs. (20 Nm), then retighten, in sequence, to 24 ft. lbs. (33 Nm).

17. Install the thermostat housing assembly. Install the rocker arm covers.

18. Reconnect the coil wires. Install the fuel rail, runners and the breather tube.

19. Install the alternator and connect the wiring. Connect the EGR tube to the EGR valve.

20. Install the power steering pump bracket and pump. Install the serpentine belt.

21. Connect the accelerator cable at the plenum and connect the negative battery cable.

22. Install the air cleaner inlet tube.

Exhaust Manifold

REMOVAL & INSTALLATION

2.0L (VIN H, K and M) Engines

1. Disconnect the negative battery cable.

2. Remove turbocharger induction tube, if equipped.

3. Remove and tag spark plug wires.

4. Remove turbocharger assembly from exhaust manifold, if equipped.

5. Remove exhaust manifold retaining nuts and manifold.

To install:

6. Install the exhaust manifold and retaining nuts. Tighten the exhaust manifold bolts to 16 ft. lbs. (22 Nm) and turbocharger-to-exhaust manifold to 18 ft. lbs. (24 Nm), if equipped.

NOTE: Tighten No. 2 and 3 exhaust manifold retaining nuts prior to No. 1 and 4.

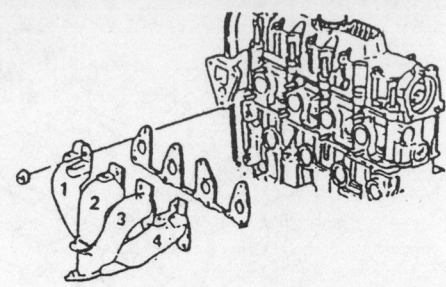

Exhaust manifold torque sequence–2.0L (VIN M) engine

7. Connect the spark plug wires.

8. If equipped, install the turbocharger induction tube.

9. Connect the negative battery cable.

2.0L (VIN 1) and 2.2L Engines

1. Disconnect the negative battery cable.

2. Remove the air cleaner. Remove the exhaust manifold shield. Raise and safely support the vehicle.

3. Disconnect the exhaust pipe at the manifold and lower the vehicle.

4. Disconnect the air management-to-check valve hose and remove the bracket. Disconnect the oxygen sensor lead wire.

5. Remove the serpentine belt. Remove the alternator adjusting bolts, loosen the pivot bolt and pivot the alternator upward.

6. Remove the alternator brace and the AIR pipes bracket bolt.

7. Unscrew the mounting bolts and remove the exhaust manifold. The manifold should be removed with the AIR plumbing as an assembly. If the manifold is to be replaced, transfer the plumbing to the new one.

To install:

8. Clean the mating surfaces on the manifold and the head.

1.
Tighten in proper sequence to 15 ft. lbs. (20Nm), then retighten to 24 ft. lbs. (33Nm)

⑦ ④ ③ ⑥
⑧ ① ② ⑤

2. Intake manifold
3. Gasket
4. Cylinder head
5. Sealer

Intake manifold torque sequence—2.8L and 3.1L engines

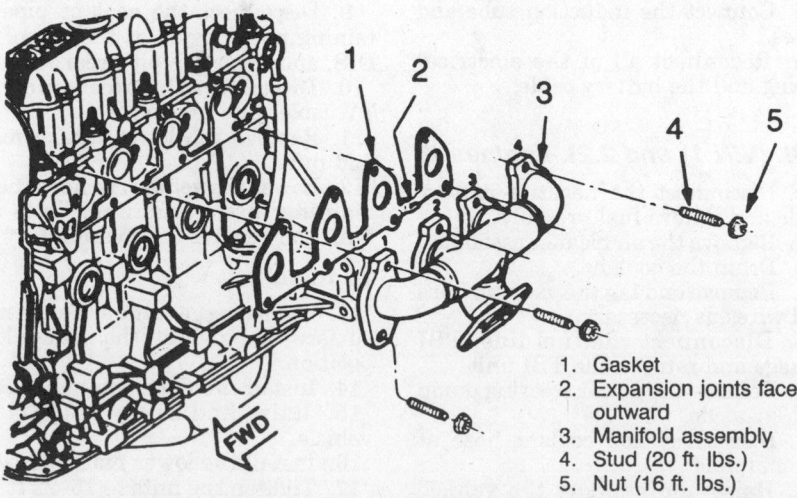

1. Gasket
2. Expansion joints face outward
3. Manifold assembly
4. Stud (20 ft. lbs.)
5. Nut (16 ft. lbs.)

Exhaust manifold installation torque sequence—2.0L (VIN H and K) engine

9. Install the manifold and tighten the nuts to 6–13 ft. lbs. (8–18 Nm) in the proper sequence.

10. Install the alternator brace and the AIR pipes bracket bolt.

11. Rotate the alternator into position and install the pivot bolt. Install the serpentine belt.

12. Connect the oxygen sensor lead wire. Install the air management-to-check valve bracket and connect the hose.

13. Raise and safely support the vehicle. Connect the exhaust pipe to the manifold.

14. Lower the vehicle. Install the exhaust manifold shield. Install the air cleaner.

15. Connect the negative battery cable.

2.8L and 3.1L Engines

LEFT SIDE

1. Disconnect the negative battery cable.

2. Remove the air cleaner assembly.

3. Remove the air flow sensor. Remove the engine heat shield.

4. Remove the crossover pipe at the manifold.

5. Remove the exhaust manifold bolts.

6. Remove the exhaust manifold.

To install:

7. Install the exhaust manifold.

8. Install the exhaust manifold bolts.

9. Install the crossover pipe at the manifold.

10. Install the engine heat shield. Install the air flow sensor.

11. Install the air cleaner assembly.

12. Connect the negative battery cable.

RIGHT SIDE

1. Disconnect the negative battery cable.

2. Remove the air cleaner assembly.

3. Remove the air flow sensor. Remove the engine heat shield.

4. Disconnect the crossover pipe at the manifold.

5. Disconnect the accelerator and throttle valve cable at the throttle lever and the plenum. Move aside to gain working clearance.

6. Disconnect the power steering line at the power steering pump.

7. Remove the EGR valve assembly.

8. Raise and safely support the vehicle.

9. Disconnect the exhaust pipe at the exhaust manifold.

10. Lower the vehicle.

11. Remove the manifold bolts. Remove the exhaust manifold.

To install:

12. Install the manifold and attaching bolts.

13. Raise and safely support the vehicle.

14. Connect the exhaust pipe at the exhaust manifold.

15. Lower the vehicle.

16. Install the EGR valve assembly.

17. Connect the power steering line at the power steering pump.

18. Connect the accelerator and throttle valve cable at the throttle lever and the plenum.

19. Connect the crossover pipe at the manifold.

20. Install the engine heat shield. Install the air flow sensor.

21. Install the air cleaner assembly.

22. Connect the negative battery cable.

Turbocharger

REMOVAL & INSTALLATION

1. Disconnect the negative battery cable.

2. Raise and safely support the vehicle.

3. Remove the lower fan retaining screws.

4. Disconnect the exhaust pipe at the turbocharger.

5. Remove air conditioning rear support bracket.

6. Remove the turbocharger support bracket from the engine.

7. Disconnect the oil drain and water return pipes at turbo.

8. Lower the vehicle and remove coolant recovery pipe.

9. Remove induction tube, coolant fan and oxygen sensor.

10. Disconnect the oil and water feed pipes.

11. Remove the air intake duct and vacuum hose at the actuator.

12. Remove the exhaust manifold retaining nuts, remove the turbocharger and manifold as an assembly.

13. Remove the turbocharger from exhaust manifold.

To install:

14. Install the turbocharger to the exhaust manifold and tighten the bolts to 18 ft. lbs. (24 Nm).

15. Install a new manifold gasket and install the manifold in position on the block. Tighten the bolts to 16 ft. lbs. (22 Nm).

16. Install the air intake duct and the vacuum hose actuator.

17. Install the induction tube and oxygen sensor. Install the coolant recovery tube.

18. Raise and safely support the vehicle. Connect the oil drain and water return pipe to the turbocharger.

19. Install the turbocharger support bracket. Connect the exhaust pipe to the turbocharger and install the rear air conditioning support bracket.

20. Install the lower fan retaining screws. Lower the vehicle and connect the negative battery cable. Check all fluid levels.

Turbocharger Wastegate Unit

REMOVAL & INSTALLATION

1. Disconnect the negative battery cable. Remove the induction tube.

2. Remove the clip attaching the wastegate linkage to the actuator rod.

3. Disconnect the vacuum hose. Remove the wastegate mounting bolts and remove the wastegate actuator.

To install:

4. Install the wastegate actuator and mounting bolts.

5. Connect the vacuum hose.

6. Install the clip attaching the wastegate linkage to the actuator rod.

7. Install the induction tube.

8. Connect the negative battery cable.

Timing Chain Front Cover

REMOVAL & INSTALLATION

2.0L (VIN 1) and 2.2L Engines

NOTE: The following procedure requires the use of a front cover centering tool J–35468 and crankshaft puller J–24420–B.

1. Disconnect the negative battery cable. Remove the serpentine belt.

2. Although not absolutely necessary, removal of the right front inner fender splash shield will facilitate access to the front cover.

3. Remove the center bolt from the crankshaft pulley and retaining bolts, remove the pulley. Using puller tool J–24420–B or equivalent, remove hub from the crankshaft.

4. Remove the alternator lower bracket.

5. Remove the oil pan-to-front cover bolts.

6. Remove the front cover-to-block bolts and remove the front cover. If the front cover is difficult to remove, use a rubber mallet to loosen it.

To install:

7. The surfaces of the block and front cover must be clean and free of oil. Apply a ⅛ in. bead of RTV sealant to the cover. The sealant must be wet to the touch when the bolts are torqued down.

NOTE: When applying RTV sealant to the front cover, be sure to keep it out of the bolt holes. When installing hub or pulley

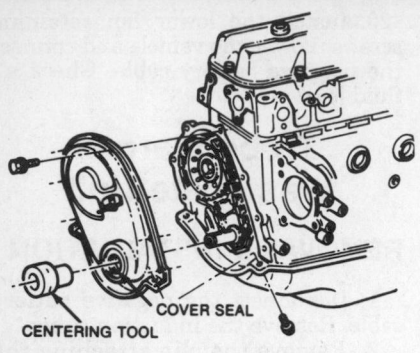

Front cover removal—2.0L (VIN 1) and 2.2L engines

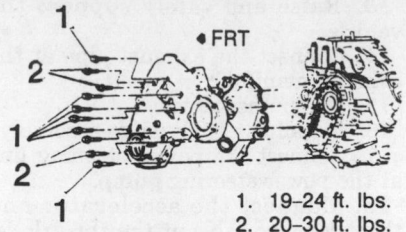

1. 19–24 ft. lbs.
2. 20–30 ft. lbs.

Front cover removal—2.8L and 3.1L engines

note position of key on crankshaft.

8. Position the front cover on the block using a centering tool J–35468 and tighten the screws.

9. Install the oil pan-to-front cover bolts.

10. Install the alternator lower bracket.

11. Using hub installer tool J–29113 or equivalent, install the crankshaft hub.

12. If removed, install the right front inner fender splash shield.

13. Install the serpentine belt.

14. Connect the negative battery cable.

2.8L and 3.1L Engines

1. Disconnect the negative battery cable.

2. Drain the cooling system and remove the coolant recovery tank from the vehicle.

3. Disconnect the MAP sensor and EGR sensor solenoids.

4. Remove the serpentine belt and adjusting pulley.

5. Tag and disconnect the heater hose at the power steering bracket.

6. Tag and disconnect the alternator wiring and remove the alternator.

7. Raise the vehicle and support it safely.

8. Remove the inner fender splash shield.

9. Remove the harmonic balancer with tool J–24420 or equivalent puller.

10. Remove the oil pan-to-block bolts and remove the oil pan. Remove the lower cover bolts.

11. Lower the vehicle and disconnect the radiator hoses at the water pump.

12. Remove the heater hose from the thermostat housing.

13. Disconnect the overflow hoses and the canister purge hose.

14. Remove the front cover.

To install:

15. Apply a bead of sealer to the front cover surface.

16. Install a new front cover gasket and front oil seal.

17. Install the front cover and tighten to 20–28 ft. lbs. (27–38 Nm).

18. Raise and safely support the vehicle. Install the oil pan and the lower front cover bolts.

19. Install the crankshaft balancer.

20. Install the inner splash shield and lower the vehicle.

21. Install the radiator hoses and the power steering pump.

22. Install the alternator and the accessory drive belt.

23. Refill the fluids and connect the negative battery cable.

Front Cover Oil Seal

REPLACEMENT

2.0L (VIN 1), 2.2L, 2.8L and 3.1L Engines

1. The oil seal can be replaced with the front cover either on or off the engine.

2. Although not absolutely necessary, removal of the right front inner fender splash shield will facilitate access to the front cover.

3. If the cover is on the engine, remove the crankshaft pulley and hub first.

4. Pry out the seal using a suitable tool, being careful not to distort the seal mating surfaces.

To install:

5. Install the new seal so the lip side, is towards the engine.

6. Press it into place with a seal driver.

7. Install the hub and pulley, if removed.

Timing Chain and Sprockets

REMOVAL & INSTALLATION

2.0L (VIN 1) and 2.2L Engines

1. Disconnect the negative battery cable. Remove the front cover.

2. Place the No. 1 piston at **TDC** of the compression stroke so the marks on the camshaft and crankshaft sprockets are in alignment.

3. Loosen the timing chain tensioner nut as far as possible, without actually removing it.

4. Remove the camshaft sprocket bolts and remove the sprocket and chain together. If the sprocket does not slide from the camshaft easily, a light blow with a soft tool at the lower edge of the sprocket will loosen it.

5. Use a gear puller J–22888–20 or equivalent, and remove the crankshaft sprocket.

To install:

6. Press the new crankshaft sprocket onto the crankshaft using crankshaft sprocket installer J–5590 or equivalent.

NOTE: Ensure that the sprocket is fully seated against the crankshaft.

7. Compress the tensioner spring. Insert a cotter pin or nail, into the hole to retain the tensioner.

8. Align the crankshaft and camshaft timing marks with the tabs on the chain tensioner.

9. Install the timing chain over the camshaft sprocket and around the crankshaft sprocket. Make sure the marks on the 2 sprockets are in alignment. Lubricate the thrust surface with Molykote® or equivalent.

10. Align the dowel in the camshaft with the dowel hole in the sprocket and install the sprocket onto the camshaft. Use the mounting bolt to draw the sprocket onto the camshaft and tighten to 77 ft. lbs. (105 Nm).

11. Lubricate the timing chain with clean engine oil. Remove the timing chain pin.

12. Install the front cover.

13. Connect the negative battery cable.

2.8L and 3.1L Engines

1. Disconnect the negative battery cable.

2. Remove the front cover.

3. Position the No. 1 piston at **TDC** with the marks on the crankshaft and camshaft sprockets aligned.

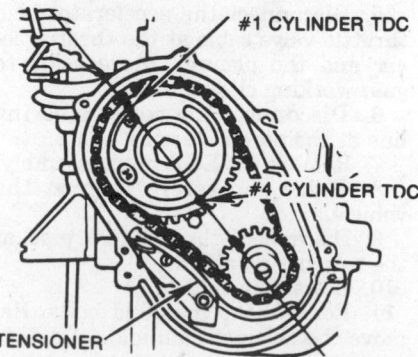

Timing mark alignment—2.0L (VIN 1) and 2.2L engines

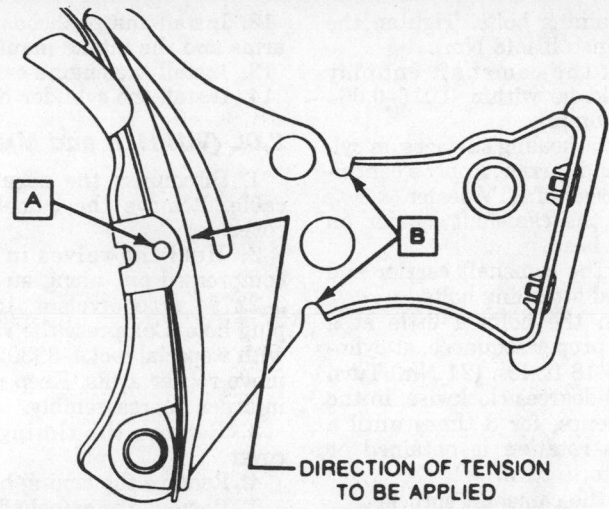

DIRECTION OF TENSION TO BE APPLIED

A INSERT PIN AFTER TENSION HAS BEEN APPLIED

B TABS, USED FOR CAMSHAFT AND CRANKSHAFT ALIGNMENT

Timing chain tensioner—2.0L (VIN 1) and 2.2L engines.

4. Remove the camshaft sprocket bolts.

5. Remove the camshaft sprocket and chain from the front of the engine.

NOTE: If the sprocket does not move freely from the camshaft, a light blow using a plastic tool on the lower edge of the sprocket should dislodge it.

6. Remove the crankshaft sprocket.
To install:

7. Install the crankshaft sprocket.

8. Apply Molykote® or equivalent, to the sprocket thrust surface.

9. Hold the sprocket with the chain hanging and align the timing marks on the camshaft and crankshaft sprockets.

10. Align the dowel in the camshaft with the dowel hole in the camshaft sprocket.

11. Draw the camshaft sprocket onto the camshaft using the mounting bolts. Tighten to 18 ft. lbs. (24 Nm).

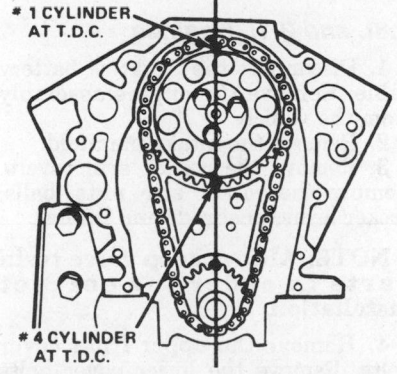

1 CYLINDER AT T.D.C.

4 CYLINDER AT T.D.C.

Timing mark alignment—2.8L and 3.1L engines

12. Lubricate the timing chain with engine oil.

13. Install the front cover.

14. Connect the negative battery cable.

Timing Belt Front Cover

REMOVAL & INSTALLATION

2.0L (VIN H, K and M) Engines

1. Disconnect the negative battery cable.

2. Remove the serpentine belt.

3. Remove the tensioner and bolt.

4. Remove the timing belt cover attaching bolts. Remove the cover.
To install:

5. Install the timing belt cover and attaching bolts. Tighten to 89 inch lbs. (11 Nm).

6. Install the serpentine belt. Tighten the timing belt tensioner to 40 ft. lbs. (54 Nm).

7. Connect the negative battery cable.

OIL SEAL REPLACEMENT

2.0L (VIN H, K and M) Engines

1. Remove the crankshaft sprocket.

2. Remove the crankshaft key and rear thrust washer.

3. Using a suitable prybar, pry out the front oil seal.
To install:

4. Place the protective sleeve of special tool set J–33083, seal installer or equivalent, onto the crankshaft.

5. Lubricate the lip of the new seal.

Using special tool J–33083, install the seal.

6. Remove the protective sleeve.

7. Install the rear thrust washer and key on the crankshaft.

8. Install the crankshaft sprocket.

Timing Belt and Tensioner

REMOVAL & INSTALLATION

2.0L (VIN H, K and M) Engines

1. Disconnect the negative battery cable.

2. Remove the serpentine belt and timing belt cover.

3. Loosen the water pump bolts and release tension with tool J–33039 or equivalent.

4. Raise and support the vehicle safely.

5. Remove the crankshaft pulley.

6. Lower the vehicle and remove the timing belt.
To install:

7. Turn the crankshaft and the camshaft gears clockwise to align the timing marks on the gears with the timing marks on the rear cover.

8. Install the timing belt, making sure the portion between the camshaft gear and crankcase gear is in tension.

9. Using tool J–33039 or equivalent, turn the water pump eccentric clockwise until the tensioner contacts the high torque stop. Tighten the water pump screws slightly.

10. Turn the engine by the crankshaft gear bolt 720 degrees to fully seat the belt into the gear teeth.

11. Turn the water pump eccentric counterclockwise until the hole in the tensioner arm is aligned with the hole in the base.

12. Tighten the water pump screws to 18 ft. lbs. (24 Nm) while checking that the tensioner holes remain as adjusted in the prior step.

13. Install the crankshaft pulley, timing belt cover and the serpentine drive belt.

Timing Sprockets

REMOVAL & INSTALLATION

Camshaft Sprocket

1. Disconnect the negative battery cable.

2. Remove the camshaft carrier cover.

3. Remove the timing belt.

4. Hold the camshaft with an open end wrench and remove the sprocket bolt, washer and and sprocket.
To install:

5. Install the sprocket, retaining

bolt and washer with the mark on the sprocket lined up with the mark on the rear timing belt cover. Tighten to 77 ft. lbs. (104 Nm) for 2.0L (VIN 1) and 2.2L engines or 34 ft. lbs. (46 Nm) for all others.

6. Install the timing belt.
7. Install the camshaft carrier cover.
8. Connect the negative battery cable.

Crankshaft Sprocket

1. Disconnect the negative battery cable.
2. Remove the timing belt.
3. Remove the crankshaft pulley.
4. Remove the bolt and retaining washer and remove the sprocket.

To install:

5. Install the sprocket over the key on the end of the crankshaft.
6. Install the thrust washer and attaching bolt and tighten to 114 ft. lbs. (155 Nm).
7. Install the crankshaft pulley and timing belt.
8. Connect the negative battery cable.

Camshaft Carrier

REMOVAL & INSTALLATION

2.0L (VIN H, K and M) Engines

NOTE: Whenever the camshaft carrier bolts are loosened, it is necessary to remove the cylinder head and replace the cylinder head gasket.

1. Disconnect the negative battery cable. Disconnect the crankcase ventilation hose from the camshaft carrier.
2. Mark and remove the distributor.
3. Remove the camshaft sprocket.
4. Loosen the camshaft carrier and cylinder head attaching bolts a little at a time in sequence.

NOTE: Camshaft carrier and cylinder head bolts should be loosened in sequence and only when the engine is cold.

5. Remove the camshaft carrier.
6. Remove the camshaft thrust plate from the rear of the camshaft carrier.
7. Slide the camshaft rearward and remove it from the carrier.
8. Remove the carrier front oil seal.

To install:

9. Install a new carrier front oil seal using tool J-33085.
10. Place the camshaft in the carrier.

NOTE: Take care not to damage the carrier front oil seal when installing the camshaft.

11. Install the camshaft thrust plate

and the retaining bolts. Tighten the bolts to 70 inch lbs. (8 Nm).
12. Check the camshaft endplay which should be within 0.016–0.064 in. (0.04–0.16mm).
13. Clean the sealing surfaces on cylinder head and carrier. Apply a continuous 3mm bead of RTV sealer.
14. Install the camshaft carrier on the cylinder head.
15. Install the camshaft carrier and cylinder head attaching bolts.
16. Tighten the bolts a little at a time, in the proper sequence, at cylinder head, to 18 ft. lbs. (24 Nm). Turn each bolt 60 degrees clockwise, in the proper sequence, for 3 times until a 180 degrees rotation is obtained or equivalent, to ½ turn.
17. Install the camshaft sprocket.
18. Install the distributor.
19. Connect the positive crankcase ventilation hose to the camshaft carrier.

NOTE: After remainder of installation is completed, start engine and let it run until the thermostat opens. Tighten all cylinder head bolts an additional 30–50 degrees in the proper sequence.

Camshaft

REMOVAL & INSTALLATION

2.0L (VIN 1) and 2.2L Engines

1. Remove the engine assembly.
2. Remove the intake manifold.
3. Remove the cylinder head cover, pivot the rocker arms to the sides and remove the pushrods, keeping them in order. Remove the valve lifters, keeping them in order.
4. Remove the front cover.
5. Remove the distributor.
6. Remove the fuel pump and its pushrod.
7. Remove the timing chain and sprocket.
8. Carefully pull the camshaft from the block, being sure the camshaft lobes do not contact the bearings.

To install:

9. Lubricate the camshaft journals with clean engine oil. Lubricate the lobes with Molykote® or equivalent. Install the camshaft into the engine, being extremely careful not to contact the bearings with the cam lobes.
10. Install the timing chain and sprocket. Install the fuel pump and pushrod. Install the timing cover. Install the distributor.
11. Install the valve lifters. If a new camshaft has been installed, new lifters should be used to ensure durability of the cam lobes.

12. Install the pushrods and rocker arms and the intake manifold.
13. Install the engine assembly.
14. Install the cylinder head cover.

2.0L (VIN H, K and M) Engines

1. Disconnect the negative battery cable. Remove the camshaft carrier cover.
2. Hold the valves in place with compressed air, using an air adapter J-22794 or equivalent, in the spark plug hole. Compress the valve springs with a special tool J-33302-25 and remove rocker arms. Keep rocker arms in order for reassembly.
3. Remove the timing belt front cover.
4. Remove the timing belt.
5. Remove the camshaft sprocket.
6. Mark and remove the distributor.
7. Remove the camshaft thrust plate from rear of camshaft carrier.
8. Slide the camshaft rearward and remove it from the carrier.

To install:

9. Install a new camshaft carrier front oil seal using tool J-33085 or equivalent.
10. Place the camshaft in the carrier.

NOTE: Take care not to damage the carrier front oil seal when installing the camshaft.

11. Install the camshaft thrust plate retaining bolts. Tighten bolts to 70 inch lbs. (8 Nm).
12. Check the camshaft endplay, which should be within 0.016–0.064 in.
13. Install the distributor.
14. Install the camshaft sprocket.
15. Install the timing belt.
16. Install the timing belt front cover.
17. Using an air adapter J-22794 or equivalent, in the spark plug hole to hold the valve closed and install valve train compressing fixture J-33302. Compress valve springs and replace rocker arms.
18. Install the camshaft carrier cover.

2.8L and 3.1L Engines

1. Disconnect the negative battery cable. Remove the engine assembly from the vehicle.
2. Remove the intake manifold.
3. Remove the rocker arm covers. Remove the rocker arm nuts, balls, rocker arms, pushrods and lifters.

NOTE: Always keep valve train parts in order for correct installation.

4. Remove the upper front cover bolts. Remove the lower cover bolts and the front cover.
5. Remove the camshaft sprocket

bolts, camshaft sprocket and timing chain.

6. Remove the camshaft by carefully sliding it out the front of the engine. Measure the camshaft bearing journals using a micrometer and replace the camshaft if the journals exceed 0.0009 in. (0.025mm) out of round.

To install:

NOTE: When installing a new camshaft, lubricate the camshaft lobes with GM Engine Oil Supplement (E.O.S.) 1052367 or equivalent.

7. Install the camshaft.
8. Install the timing chain and sprocket.
9. Install the intake manifold.
10. Install the crankcase front cover.
11. Install the lifters, pushrods, rocker arms, balls and rocker arm nuts. Install the valve covers.
12. Install the engine assembly to the vehicle.
13. Connect the negative battery cable.

Piston and Connecting Rod

POSITIONING

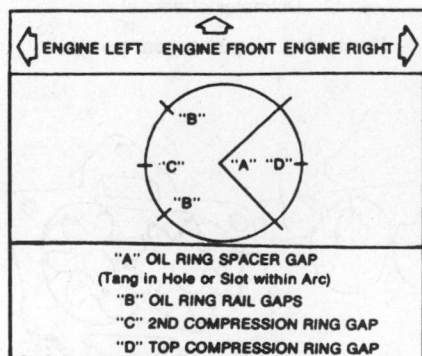

Piston ring gap locations

ENGINE LUBRICATION

Oil Pan

REMOVAL & INSTALLATION

2.0L (VIN 1) and 2.2L Engines

1. Disconnect the negative battery cable.
2. Raise and safely support the vehicle. Drain the crankcase.

3. Remove the air conditioning brace, if equipped.
4. Remove the exhaust shield and disconnect the exhaust pipe at the manifold.
5. Remove the starter motor and position it out of the way.
6. Remove the flywheel cover. Remove the oil pan retaining bolts and remove the oil pan.

To install:

NOTE: Prior to oil pan installation, check the sealing surfaces on the pan, cylinder block and front cover are clean and free of oil. If installing the old oil pan, be sure all old RTV has been removed.

7. Apply a ⅛ in. bead of RTV sealant to the oil pan sealing surface. Use a new oil pan rear seal and install the pan in place. Tighten the bolts to 9–13 ft. lbs. (12–18 Nm).
8. Install the flywheel cover and the starter.
9. Connect the exhaust pipe at the manifold.
10. Install the exhaust shield and install the air conditioning brace.
11. Connect the negative battery cable and run the vehicle to normal operating temperature. Refill and check for leaks.

2.0L (VIN H, K and M) Engines

1. Disconnect the negative battery cable.
2. Raise and safely support the vehicle.
3. Remove the right front wheel, as required.
4. If equipped, remove the front splash shield.
5. Drain the crankcase.
6. Remove the exhaust pipe from the manifold for the VIN K engine or wastegate for VIN M engine.
7. Remove the flywheel cover.
8. Remove the oil pan retaining bolts and remove the oil pan.
9. Remove the oil pump pick-up tube.
10. Remove the scraper and gasket.

To install:

11. Apply a bead of RTV sealant to the oil pan. Using a new gasket, install the oil scraper.
12. Install the pan and attaching bolts with Loctite®. Tighten the oil pan bolts to 44 inch lbs. (5 Nm).
13. Install the oil pan cover.
14. Install the flywheel cover.
15. Connect the exhaust pipe to the manifold for the VIN K engine or wastegate for the VIN M engine.
16. Lower the vehicle.
17. If equipped, install the splash shield.

18. If removed, install the right front wheel.
19. Lower the vehicle.
20. Fill the crankcase with oil.
21. Connect the negative battery cable.

2.8L and 3.1L Engines

1. Disconnect the negative battery cable.
2. Remove the serpentine belt and the tensioner.
3. Support the engine with tool J–28467 or equivalent.
4. Raise and safely support the vehicle. Drain the engine oil.
5. Remove the starter shield and the flywheel cover. Remove the starter.
6. Remove the engine to frame mount retaining nuts.
7. Lower the vehicle.
8. Support the engine using tool J–28467–A or equivalent, then raise and support the vehicle safely.
9. Remove the right tire and wheel assembly. Remove the right inner fender splash shield.
10. Remove the oil pan retaining bolts and nuts and remove the oil pan.

To install:

11. Clean the gasket mating surfaces.
12. Install a new gasket on the oil pan. Apply silicon sealer to the portion of the pan that contacts the rear of the block.
13. Install the oil pan retaining nuts. Tighten the nuts to 71 inch lbs. (8 Nm).
14. Install the oil pan retaining bolts. Tighten the rear bolts to 18 ft. lbs. (24 Nm) and the remaining bolts to 71 inch lbs. (8 Nm).
15. Install the right inner fender splash shield.
16. Lower the vehicle and remove the engine support tool.
17. Raise and support the vehicle safely.
18. Install the engine to frame mounting nuts.
19. Install the starter and splash shield. Install the flywheel shield.
20. Lower the vehicle and fill the crankcase with oil, install the belt tensioner and belt and connect the negative battery cable. Run the engine to normal operating temperature and check for leaks.

Oil Pump

REMOVAL & INSTALLATION

2.0L (VIN H, K and M) Engines

1. Disconnect the negative battery cable. Remove the crankshaft sprocket.

2. Remove the timing belt rear cover.

3. Disconnect the connector at oil pressure switch.

4. Raise and safely support the vehicle. Drain the engine oil and remove the oil pan.

5. Remove the oil filter.

6. Unbolt and remove the oil pickup tube.

7. Unbolt and remove the oil pump.

To install:

8. Install the pump using a new gasket. Tighten attaching bolts to 5 ft. lbs. (7 Nm).

9. Install the pickup tube and support with new O-ring.

10. Install the oil pan.

11. Use seal installer tool J–33083 or equivalent, to install new front oil seal.

12. Install a new oil filter.

13. Connect the oil pressure switch connector.

14. Install the rear timing belt cover.

15. Install the crankshaft sprocket.

16. Connect the negative battery cable.

2.0L (VIN 1) and 2.2L Engines

1. Disconnect the negative battery cable.

2. Raise and safely support the vehicle. Drain the engine oil and remove the engine oil pan.

3. Remove the pump attaching bolts and carefully lower the pump, extension shaft and retainer.

To install:

NOTE: Heat the retainer in hot water prior to assembling the extension shaft.

4. Install extension shaft to the oil pump.

NOTE: To ensure immediate oil pressure on start-up, the oil pump gear cavity should be packed with petroleum jelly.

5. Install the pump to the rear bearing cap and bolt. Tighten to 32 ft. lbs. (43 Nm).

6. Install the oil pan.

7. Lower the vehicle.

8. Fill the crankcase with oil.

9. Connect the negative battery cable.

2.8L and 3.1L Engines

1. Disconnect the negative battery cable.

2. Raise and safely support the vehicle. Drain the engine oil and remove the oil pan.

3. Remove the rear main bearing cap.

4. Remove the oil pump and extension shaft.

To install:

5. Install the oil pump and extension shaft.

6. Engage the drive shaft extension into the drive gear.

7. Install the pump to the rear bearing cap and install the bolt. Tighten to 30 ft. lbs. (41 Nm).

8. Install the oil pan.

9. Lower the vehicle.

10. Fill the crankcase with clean oil.

11. Connect the negative battery cable.

CHECKING

2.0L (VIN 1), 2.2L, 2.8L and 3.1L Engines

1. Drain the oil from the pump and remove the pump cover.

2. Measure the pump gear lash. It should be 0.0037–0.0077 in.

3. Measure the pump gear pocket. It should be as follows:

a. On pumps with aluminum body the depth should be 1.195–1.198 in. and the diameter should be 1.503–1.506 in.

b. On pumps with cast iron body the depth should be 1.202–1.205 in. and the diameter should be 1.504–1.506 in.

4. Measure the gear side clearance. It should be 0.003–0.004 in.

5. Measure the gear end clearance. It should be as follows:

a. On pumps with aluminum body the clearance should be 0.0016–0.0067 in.

b. On pumps with cast iron body, the clearance should be 0.002–0.006 in.

6. Lubricate all internal parts with engine oil during reassembly and install the pump gears.

7. Prime the engine oil galleries by removing the engine oil pump drive unit and rotate the oil pump using a drill motor and appropriate socket and extension.

8. Install the cover and gasket and tighten the pump cover bolts to 89 inch lbs. (10 Nm).

NOTE: Use only original equipment gaskets. The gasket thickness is critical to proper functioning of the pump.

Rear Main Bearing Oil Seal

REMOVAL & INSTALLATION

2.0L (VIN H, K and M) Engines

NOTE: The rear main bearing oil seal is a 1 piece unit and can be replaced without the removal of the oil pan or crankshaft.

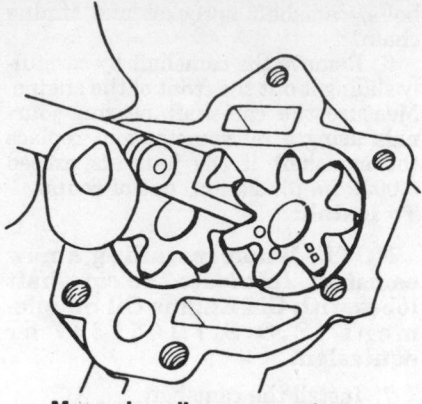

Measuring oil pump gear lash

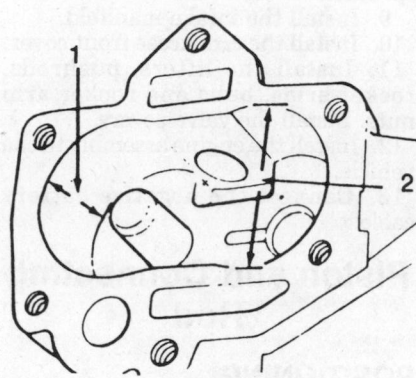

1. Depth of pocket
2. Diameter of pocket

Measuring oil pump gear pocket

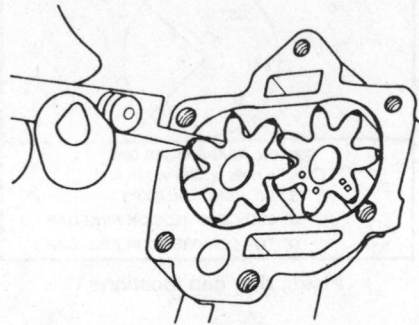

Measuring oil pump gear side clearance

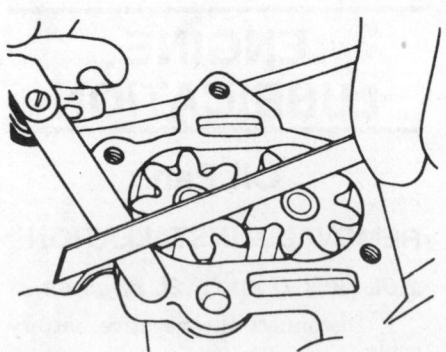

Measuring oil pump end clearance

1. Disconnect the negative battery cable. Raise and safely support the vehicle. Remove the transaxle.

2. If equipped with a manual transaxle, remove the pressure plate and clutch disc.

3. Remove the flywheel/flexplate-to-crankshaft bolts and the flywheel/flexplate. Discard the bolts.

NOTE: Flywheel bolts cannot be reused.

4. Using a medium prybar, pry out the old seal. Be careful not to scratch the crankshaft surface.

To install:

5. Clean the block and crankshaft-to-seal mating surfaces.

6. Using the seal installation tool no. J–36227 or equivalent, install the new rear seal into the seal retainer. Lubricate the outside of the seal to aid installation and press the seal in evenly with the tool.

7. If equipped with automatic transaxle, install the flexplate and attaching bolts. Tighten attaching bolts to 48 ft. lbs. (65 Nm). Flexplate bolts may be reused.

8. If equipped with manual transaxle, install the flywheel using new bolts. Tighten to 48 ft. lbs. (65 Nm), plus and additional 30 degrees.

9. If equipped with manual transaxle, install the pressure plate and disc.

10. Install the transaxle.

11. Lower the vehicle.

12. Connect the negative battery cable.

2.0L (VIN 1) and 2.2L Engines

1. Disconnect the negative battery cable. Raise and safely support the vehicle.

2. Remove the transaxle assembly.

3. Remove the flywheel/flexplate.

4. Remove the seal from the dust lip.

To install:

5. Clean the cylinder block and crankshaft sealing surface.

6. Inspect the crankshaft for damage. Coat the seal and engine mating surface with engine oil.

7. Install the new seal using seal installation tool J–34686 or equivalent.

8. Install the flywheel/flexplate.

9. Install the transaxle assembly.

10. Lower the vehicle.

11. Connect the negative battery cable.

2.8L and 3.1L Engines

NOTE: The rear main bearing oil seal is a 1 piece unit and can be replaced without the removal of the oil pan or crankshaft.

1. Disconnect the negative battery cable. Raise and safely support the vehicle.

2. Remove the transaxle assembly.

3. Remove the flywheel/flexplate.

4. Remove the seal from the dust lip.

NOTE: Care must be exercised during removal so as not to damage the crankshaft outside diameter area.

To install:

5. Clean the cylinder block and crankshaft sealing surface.

6. Inspect the crankshaft for nicks, burrs, scratches, etc.

7. Coat the seal and the engine mating surface with engine oil.

8. Install the new seal, using seal installation tool J–34686 or equivalent.

9. Install the flywheel/flexplate.

10. Install the transaxle assembly.

11. Lower the vehicle.

12. Connect the negative battery cable.

ENGINE COOLING

Radiator

REMOVAL & INSTALLATION

1. Disconnect the negative battery cable.

2. Drain the cooling system into a clean container for reuse.

3. Disconnect the electrical lead at the fan motor.

4. Remove the fan frame-to-radiator support bolts and remove the fan assembly.

5. Disconnect the upper and lower radiator hoses and the coolant recovery hose from the radiator.

6. Disconnect the transaxle oil cooler lines, on automatic transaxle equipped models, from the radiator and wire them out of the way.

7. Remove the radiator-to-radiator support attaching bolts and clamps. Remove the radiator.

To install:

8. Place the radiator in the vehicle so the bottom is located in the lower mounting pads. Tighten the attaching bolts and clamps.

9. In equipped with automatic transaxle, connect the transaxle oil cooler lines and tighten the bolts to 20 ft. lbs. (27 Nm).

10. Connect the upper and lower radiator hoses and the coolant recovery hose to the radiator.

11. Install the fan assembly and the fan frame-to-radiator support bolts.

12. Connect the fan motor electrical lead.

13. Connect the negative battery cable.

14. Fill cooling system and check for leaks. Start the engine and allow to come to normal operating temperature. Recheck for leaks. Top-up coolant.

Electric Cooling Fan

The coolant fan relay is activated by the Electronic Control Module (ECM) when the coolant temperature sensor recognizes temperature readings above 230°F (108°C) on 2.0L engine or 223°F (106°C) on all other engines. The coolant fan is also activated if a coolant temperature sensor failure is detected (Code 14 or 15) or if the ECM is in the backup mode. The ECM will also activate the cooling fan relay on 2.8L and 3.1L engines when the air conditioning pressure exceeds 200 psi. and on all engines when air conditioning is turned ON and the low pressure switch is closed.

NOTE: The ECM controls the cooling fan by grounding CKT 335 green/yellow wire. Once the ECM turns the fan relay on, it will keep fan on for a minimum of 30 seconds or until vehicle speed exceeds 70 mph on the 2.8L and 3.1L engine.

TESTING

NOTE: If the fan does not run while connected to the electrical wiring connector, inspect for a defective coolant temperature switch or air conditioning relay, if equipped. Always check body wiring for frayed or loose connections.

1. Disconnect the electrical wiring connector from the electric cooling fan.

2. Using a 14 gauge jumper wire, connect it between the fan and the positive battery terminal; the fan should run.

3. If the fan does not run when connected to the jumper wire, replace the fan assembly.

REMOVAL & INSTALLATION

1. Disconnect the negative battery cable.

2. Tag and disconnect the wiring harness from the fan frame and motor assembly.

3. Remove the fan assembly attaching bolts. Remove the fan and motor assembly from the vehicle.

To install:

4. Install the fan and motor assembly. Install the attaching bolts.

5. Connect the electrical connectors.

6. Connect the negative battery cable.

Heater Core

REMOVAL & INSTALLATION

Without Air Conditioning

1. Disconnect the negative battery cable and drain the cooling system.

2. Remove the heater hoses at the heater core.

3. Remove the heater outlet deflector.

4. Remove the heater core cover retaining screws. Remove the heater core cover.

5. Remove the heater core retaining straps and remove the heater core.

To install:

6. Install the new heater core and retaining straps.

7. Install the heater outlet deflector and heater core cover.

8. Connect the heater hoses to the core.

9. Fill and bleed the cooling system when finished. Check for leaks and the heater operation.

With Air Conditioning

1. Disconnect the negative battery cable and drain the cooling system.

2. Raise and safely support the vehicle.

3. Disconnect the drain tube from the heater case.

4. Remove the rear lateral transaxle support.

5. Remove the heater hoses and the drain tube from the housing.

6. Lower the vehicle. Remove the right and left hush panels, steering column trim cover, heater outlet duct and glove box.

7. Remove the heater core cover. Pull the cover straight to the rear so it does not damage the drain tube.

8. Remove the heater core clamps and remove the heater core.

To install:

9. Install the heater core and clamps.

10. Install the heater core cover using care not to damage the drain tube.

11. Install the glove box, heater outlet duct, steering column trim cover and hush panels.

12. Raise and support the vehicle safely.

13. Connect the heater hoses and the drain tube to the case. Install the rear transaxle lateral support.

14. Lower the vehicle, fill the cooling system and connect the negative battery cable.

15. Check the heater operation and bleed the cooling system. Check for leaks.

Water Pump

REMOVAL & INSTALLATION

2.0L (VIN 1), 2.2L, 2.8L and 3.1L Engines

1. Disconnect the negative battery cable.

2. Drain the cooling system into a clean container for reuse.

3. Remove all drive belts.

4. Remove the alternator.

5. Unscrew the water pump pulley mounting bolts and remove the pulley.

To install:

6. Place a 1/8 in. bead of RTV sealant on the water pump sealing surface. While the sealer is still wet, install the pump and tighten the bolts to 15–22 ft. lbs. (20–30 Nm) on 2.0L and 2.2L engines or 6–9 ft. lbs. (8–12 Nm) on 2.8L and 3.1L engines.

7. Install the water pump pulley and the mounting bolts.

8. Install the alternator.

9. Install all drive belts.

10. Connect the negative battery cable.

11. Fill cooling system and check for leaks. Start the engine and allow to come to normal operating temperature. Recheck for leaks. Top-up coolant.

2.0L (VIN M, H and K) Engines

1. Disconnect negative battery cable.

2. Drain cooling system into a clean container for reuse.

3. Remove timing belt.

4. Remove water pump retaining bolts, water pump and seal ring.

To install:

5. Install a new water pump seal ring, water pump and attaching bolts. Tighten the water pump bolts to 18 ft. lbs. (11 Nm).

6. Install the timing belt.

7. Connect the negative battery cable.

8. Fill cooling system and check for leaks. Start the engine and allow to come to normal operating temperature. Recheck for leaks. Top-up coolant.

Thermostat

REMOVAL & INSTALLATION

2.0L (VIN 1), 2.2L, 2.8L and 3.1L ENGINES

The thermostat is located inside a housing either on the cylinder head on 2.0L and 2.2L engines or in the thermostat housing on the intake manifold on 2.8L and 3.1L engines. It is not necessary to remove the radiator hose from the thermostat housing when removing the thermostat.

1. Disconnect the negative battery cable.

2. Drain the cooling system and remove the air cleaner.

3. Disconnect the AIR pipe at the upper check valve and the bracket at the water outlet.

4. Disconnect the electrical lead.

5. Remove the 2 retaining bolts from the thermostat housing and lift up the housing with the hose attached. Lift out the thermostat.

To install:

6. Insert the new thermostat, spring end down. Apply a thin bead of silicone sealer to the housing mating surface and install the housing while the sealer is still wet. Tighten the housing retaining bolts to 15–22 ft. lbs. (20–30 Nm) on 2.8L and 3.1L engines or 6–9 ft. lbs. (8–12 Nm) on 2.0L and 2.2L engines.

7. Connect the electrical lead.

8. Connect the AIR pipe at the upper check valve and the bracket at the water outlet.

9. Connect the negative battery cable.

10. Fill cooling system and check for leaks. Start the engine and allow to come to normal operating temperature. Recheck for leaks. Top-up coolant.

2.0L (VIN M, H and K) Engines

NOTE: The engine must be COLD for this procedure.

1. Disconnect the negative battery cable.

2. Remove the thermostat housing cap.

3. Grasp the handle of the thermostat assembly and gently pull upward.

4. Clean the thermostat housing and O-ring.

To install:

5. Apply a suitable lubricant to the O-ring. Install the thermostat into the housing, pushing down to ensure that the thermostat is firmly seated.

6. Replace the thermostat housing cap.

7. Connect the negative battery cable.

Cooling System Bleeding

After working on the cooling system, even to replace the thermostat, it must be bled. Air trapped in the system will prevent proper filling and leave the radiator coolant level low, causing a risk of overheating.

1. To bleed the system, start with the system cool, the radiator cap off and the radiator filled to about an inch below the filler neck.

2. Start the engine and run it at slightly above normal idle speed. This will insure adequate circulation. If air bubbles appear and the coolant level drops, fill the system with an anti-freeze/water mixture to bring the level back to the proper level.

3. Run the engine this way until the thermostat opens. When this happens, coolant will move abruptly across the top of the radiator and the temperature of the radiator will rise.

4. At this point, air is often expelled and the level may drop quite a bit. Keep refilling the system until the level is near the top of the radiator and remains constant.

5. If the vehicle has a coolant recovery tank, fill the radiator up to the filler neck then install the radiator cap and fill recovery tank to correct level.

ENGINE ELECTRICAL

NOTE: Disconnecting the negative battery cable on some vehicles may interfere with the functions of the on board computer systems and may require the computer to undergo a relearning process, once the negative battery cable is reconnected.

Distributor

REMOVAL

2.0L (VIN M and K) Engines

1. Disconnect the negative battery cable.

2. Tag the spark plug wires and remove the wires and ignition coil from the distributor.

3. Disconnect the wiring from the distributor.

4. Remove the 2 distributor hold-down nuts.

5. Mark the tang drive and camshaft for correct reassembly.

6. Remove the distributor.

INSTALLATION

Timing Not Disturbed

1. Align the tang drive according to the previous marking and install the distributor.

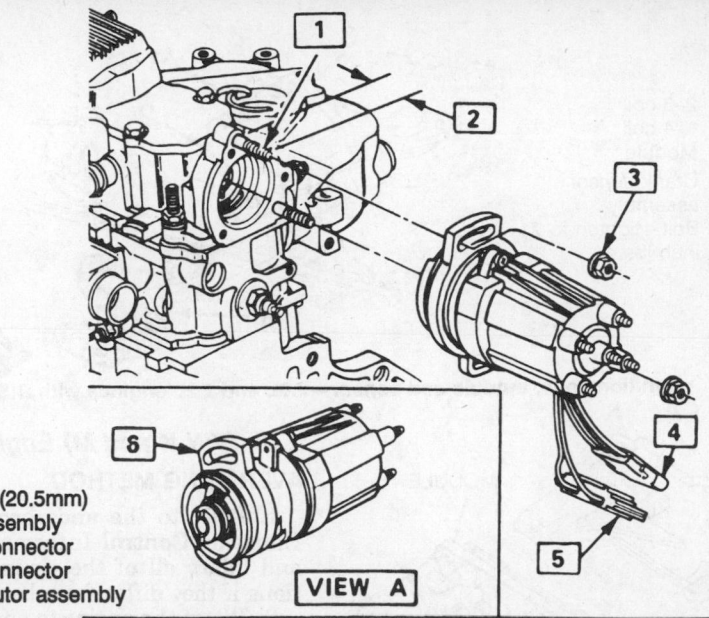

1. Stud
2. 0.8 in. (20.5mm)
3. Nut assembly
4. EST connector
5. Coil connector
6. Distributor assembly

VIEW A

Distributor removal on 2.0L (VIN K and M) engines

2. Tighten the hold-down nuts to 13 ft. lbs. (18 Nm).

3. Connect the wiring to the distributor.

4. Reconnect the cap and spark plug wires and connect the negative battery cable.

5. Check and/or adjust the ignition timing.

Timing Disturbed

1. Remove the No. 1 cylinder spark plug.

2. Place a finger over the spark plug hole while rotating the engine slowly by hand, until compression is felt.

3. Align the timing mark on the crankshaft pulley with the **0** degree mark on the timing scale on the front of the engine. This places the engine at TDC of the compression stroke for No. 1 cylinder.

4. Rotate the distributor shaft until the rotor points to the No. 1 spark plug tower on the distributor cap.

5. Install the distributor in the engine. Be sure to align the distributor-to-engine matchmarks.

6. Install and tighten the hold-down nuts to 13 ft. lbs. (18 Nm).

7. Connect all wiring to the distributor.

8. Start and run the engine.

9. Check and adjust the ignition timing.

Distributorless Ignition System

The Distributorless Ignition System (DIS) is used on the 2.0L (VIN 1 and H), 2.2L and V6 engines.

REMOVAL & INSTALLATION

DIS Assembly

1. Disconnect the negative battery cable.

2. Disconnect the electrical wires from the DIS assembly.

3. Mark the location of the spark plug wires on the DIS assembly and remove the wires.

4. Remove the DIS assembly mounting bolts and remove the assembly from the block.

NOTE: With the coil pack removed, the coils can each be removed and the ignition module can be removed as well.

To install:

5. Install the DIS assembly on the block.

6. Reconnect the plug wires to their original location.

7. Connect the DIS assembly wiring.

8. Connect the negative battery cable.

9. If equipped with PFI, perform the idle learn procedure to allow the ECM memory to be updated with the correct IAC valve pintle position and provide for a stable idle speed.

   a. Install a Tech 1 scan tool.

   b. Turn the ignition to the **ON** position, engine not running.

   c. Select **IAC SYSTEM**, then **IDLE LEARN** in the **MISC TEST** mode.

   d. Proceed with idle learn as directed by the scan tool.

Crankshaft Sensor

1. Disconnect the negative battery cable.

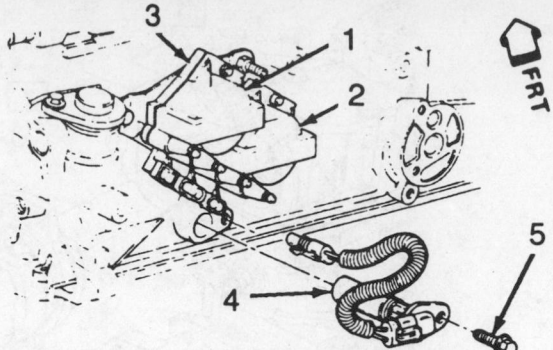

1. 2–3 coil
2. 1–4 coil
3. Module
4. Crank sensor assembly
5. Bolt—tighten to 71 inch lbs.

Ignition coils, module and sensor—2.0L and 2.2L engines with DIS

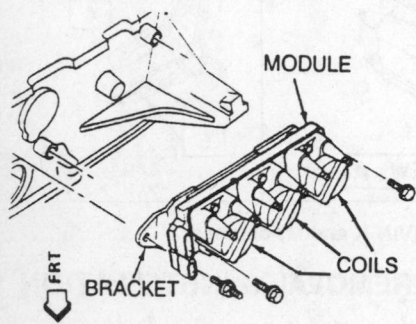

Ignition coil pack (DIS)—2.8L and 3.1L engines

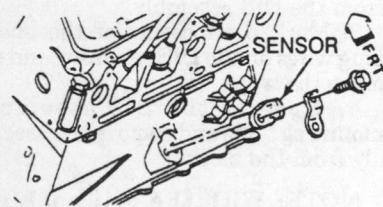

Crankshaft sensor removal—2.8L and 3.1L engines

2. Disconnect the sensor harness plug.

3. Remove the sensor-to-block bolt and remove the sensor from the engine.

4. To install the sensor, position the sensor in the block and install the sensor bolt. Tighten the sensor bolt to 71 inch lbs. (8 Nm).

5. Reconnect the sensor harness plug.

Ignition Timing

ADJUSTMENT

All DIS Engines

The ignition timing on engines with a distributorless ignition system is controlled by the Electronic Control Module (ECM). No adjustments are possible.

2.0L (VIN K and M) Engines
AVERAGING METHOD

1. Refer to the underhood Vehicle Emission Control Information label and follow all of the timing instructions if they differ from below.

2. Warm the engine to normal operating temperature.

3. Place the transmission in **N** or **P**. Apply the parking brake and block wheels.

4. Air conditioning, cooling fan and choke must be **OFF**. Do not remove the air cleaner, except as noted.

5. Ground the ALCL connector under the dash by installing a jumper wire between the **A** and **B** terminals. The Check Engine light should begin flashing.

6. Connect an inductive timing light to the No. 1 spark plug wire lead and record timing.

7. Connect an inductive timing light to the No. 4 spark plug wire lead and record timing.

8. Add the 2 timing numbers and divide by 2 to obtain "average timing".

NOTE: For example: No. 1 timing = 4 degrees and No. 4 timing = 8 degrees; 4 + 8 = 12 ÷ 2 = 6 degrees average timing. If a change is necessary, subtract the average timing from the timing specification to determine the amount of timing change to No. 1 cylinder. For example: if the timing specification is 8 degrees and the average timing is 6 degrees, advance the No. 1 cylinder 2 degrees to set the timing.

9. To correct the timing, loosen the distributor hold-down clamp, adjust the distributor and retighten the hold-down bolt.

10. Once the timing is properly set, remove the jumper wire from the ALCL connector.

11. If necessary to clear the ECM memory, disconnect the ECM harness from the positive battery pigtail for 10 seconds with the key in the **OFF** position.

Alternator

PRECAUTIONS

Several precautions must be observed with alternator equipped vehicles to avoid damage to the unit.

• If the battery is removed for any reason, make sure it is reconnected with the correct polarity. Reversing the battery connections may result in damage to the one-way rectifiers.

• When utilizing a booster battery as a starting aid, always connect the positive to positive terminals and the negative terminal from the booster battery to a good engine ground on the vehicle being started.

• Never use a fast charger as a booster to start vehicles.

• Disconnect the battery cables when charging the battery with a fast charger.

• Never attempt to polarize the alternator.

• Do not use test lamps of more than 12 volts when checking diode continuity.

• Do not short across or ground any of the alternator terminals.

• The polarity of the battery, alternator and regulator must be matched and considered before making any electrical connections within the system.

• Never operate the alternator on an open circuit. Make sure all connections within the circuit are clean and tight.

• Disconnect the battery ground terminal when performing any service on electrical components.

• Disconnect the battery if arc welding is to be done on the vehicle.

BELT TENSION ADJUSTMENT

V-Belts

If equipped with 2.0L (VIN K, H and M) engines, the air conditioner compressor is driven by a separate V-belt. Using a belt tension gauge, adjust the air conditioner belt, to 225 lbs. (1000 N) for a new belt or 115 lbs. (525 N) for a used belt.

Serpentine Belts

Serpentine belts are tensioned by loosening a bolt and rotating the belt tensioner. The correct belt tension is indicated on the indicator mark of the belt tensioner. If the indicator mark is not within specification, replace the belt or the tensioner.

NOTE: To remove or install the belt, push and rotate the tension-

er. Care should be taken to avoid twisting or bending the tensioner when applying torque.

REMOVAL & INSTALLATION

V-Belt Drive

1. Disconnect the negative battery cable.
2. Disconnect and tag the 2 terminal plug and the battery lead from the s.
6. Slip the drive belt over the pulley. Pull outward on the alternator and adjust the belt tension. Tighten the mounting and adjusting bolts.
7. Connect the electrical leads.
8. Connect the negative battery cable.

Serpentine Belt Drive

1. Disconnect the negative battery cable.
2. Disconnect and tag the alternator wiring at the rear of the alternator.
3. Loosen the belt tensioner pivot bolt and rotate the tensioner to remove the belt.
4. Support the alternator and remove the mounting bolts.
5. Remove the alternator from the engine.
To install:
6. Place the alternator in the mounts and install the bolts.
7. Install the serpentine belt and tighten the belt tensioner.
8. Connect the alternator wiring and negative battery cable.

Starter

REMOVAL & INSTALLATION

Except 2.0L (VIN K, H and M) Engines

1. Disconnect the negative battery cable. Raise and safely support the vehicle.
2. Disconnect and tag the solenoid wires and battery cable at the starter.
3. Remove the rear starter support bracket. Remove the air conditioning compressor support rod, if equipped.
4. Support the starter and remove the 2 starter-to-engine bolts.
5. Remove the starter. Note the location and number of any shims.
To install:
6. Install the starter, replacing the shims, if equipped, in the original location.
7. Tighten the mounting bolts to 25–37 ft. lbs. (34–50 Nm).
8. Install the support bracket and air conditioning compressor rod, if removed.

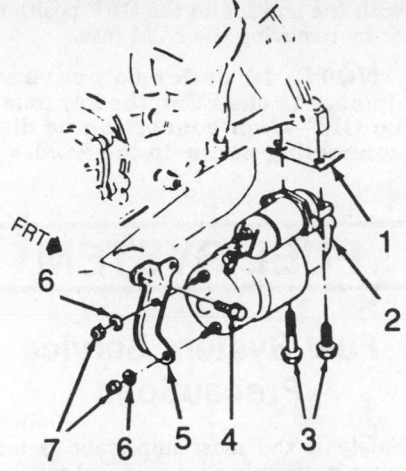

1. Shim
2. Starter
3. Bolt (32 ft. lbs.)
4. Bolt (9 ft. lbs.)
5. Bracket
6. Washer
7. Nut (24 ft. lbs.)

Starter mounting—2.0L (VIN 1) and 2.2L engines

9. Connect the starter wiring.
10. Connect the negative battery cable and check the starter operation.

2.0L (VIN K, H and M) Engines
MANUAL TRANSAXLE

1. Disconnect the negative battery cable.
2. Remove the wire loom strap from the upper starter bolt.
3. Disconnect the shift and selector level cables at the external selector lever.
4. Remove the upper and lower

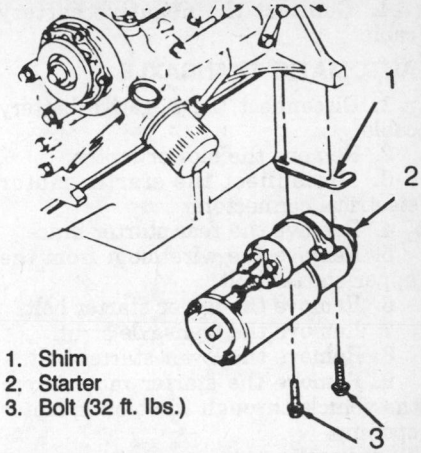

1. Shim
2. Starter
3. Bolt (32 ft. lbs.)

Starter mounting—2.8L and 3.1L engines

transaxle control lever cable bracket and cables.
5. Remove the drive axle support brace.
6. Disconnect the starter electrical connectors.
7. Remove the starter from the vehicle.
To install:
8. Install the starter.
9. Connect the starter electrical connectors.
10. Install the drive axle support brace.
11. Install the upper and lower transaxle control lever cable bracket and cables.
12. Connect the shift and selector lever cable bracket and cable.
13. Install the wire loom strap to the upper starter bolt.

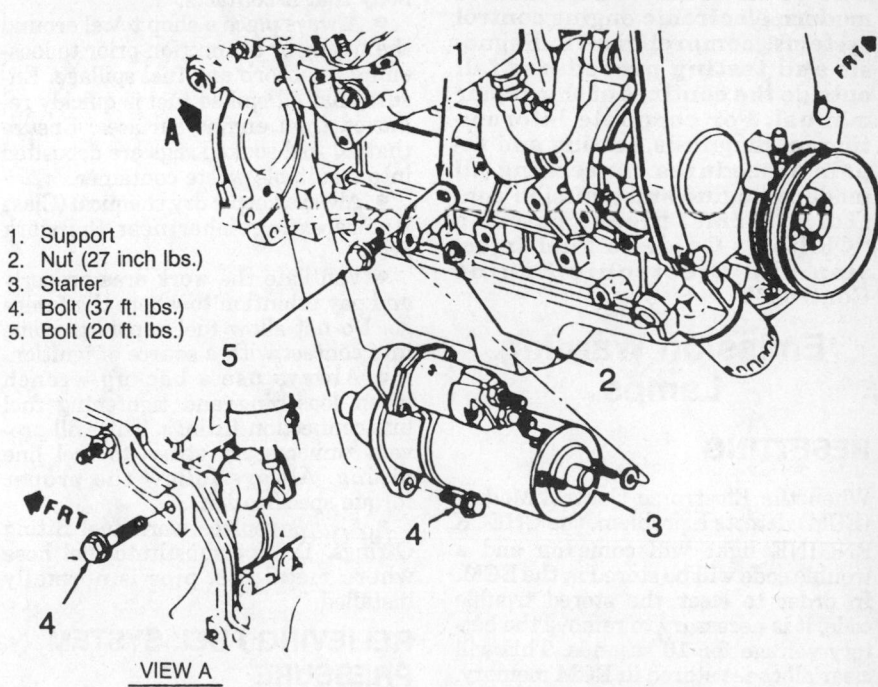

1. Support
2. Nut (27 inch lbs.)
3. Starter
4. Bolt (37 ft. lbs.)
5. Bolt (20 ft. lbs.)

VIEW A

Starter mounting—2.0L (VIN H, K and M) engines

14. Connect the negative battery cable.

AUTOMATIC TRANSAXLE

1. Disconnect the negative battery cable.
2. Remove the blower motor.
3. Disconnect the starter motor electrical connectors.
4. Remove the rear starter brace.
5. Remove the wire loom from the upper starter bolt.
6. Remove the upper starter bolt.
7. Remove the transaxle strut.
8. Remove the lower starter bolt.
9. Remove the starter motor from the vehicle through the blower motor opening.

To install:

10. Install the starter motor through the blower motor opening.
11. Install the lower starter bolt.
12. Install the transaxle strut.
13. With the help of an assistant, install the upper starter bolt.
14. Install the wire loom to the upper starter bolt.
15. Install the rear starter brace.
16. Connect the starter motor electrical connectors.
17. Install the blower motor.
18. Connect the negative battery cable.

EMISSION CONTROLS

Due to the complex nature of modern electronic engine control systems, comprehensive diagnosis and testing procedures fall outside the confines of this repair manual. For complete information on diagnosis, testing and repair procedures concerning all modern engine and emission control systems, please refer to "Chilton's Guide to Fuel Injection and Electronic Engine Controls".

Emission Warning Lamps

RESETTING

When the Electronic Control Module (ECM) detects a problem, the CHECK ENGINE light will come on and a trouble code will be stored in the ECM. In order to clear the stored trouble code, it is necessary to remove the battery voltage for 10 seconds. This will clear all codes stored in ECM memory. Do this by disconnecting the ECM harness from the positive battery cable

with the ignition in the **OFF** position or by removing the ECM fuse.

NOTE: In order to prevent damage to the ECM, the key must be OFF when connecting or disconnecting power to the ECM.

FUEL SYSTEM

Fuel System Service Precautions

Safety is the most important factor when performing not only fuel system maintenance but any type of maintenance. Failure to conduct maintenance and repairs in a safe manner may result in serious personal injury or death. Maintenance and testing of the vehicle's fuel system components can be accomplished safely and effectively by adhering to the following rules and guidelines.

• Always disconnect the negative battery cable before opening the fuel system fittings unless the repair or test procedure requires that battery voltage be applied.

• Always relieve the fuel system pressure prior to disconnecting any fuel system fitting or connection.

• Exercise extreme caution whenever relieving fuel system pressure to avoid exposing skin, face and eyes to fuel spray. Fuel under pressure may penetrate the skin or any part of the body that it contacts.

• Always place a shop towel around the fitting or connection prior to loosening to absorb any fuel spillage. Ensure that all spilled fuel is quickly removed from engine surfaces. Ensure that all fuel soaked rags are deposited into a suitable waste container.

• Always keep a dry chemical (Class B) fire extinguisher near the work area.

• Ventilate the work area properly and pay attention to where the fumes go. Do not allow fuel vapors to come into contact with a source of ignition.

• Always use a backup wrench when loosening and tightening fuel line connection fittings. This will prevent unnecessary stress to fuel line piping. Always follow the proper torque specifications.

• Always replace worn fuel fitting O-rings. Do not substitute fuel hose where metal fuel pipe is normally installed.

RELIEVING FUEL SYSTEM PRESSURE

The fuel delivery pipe is under high

pressure even after the engine is stopped. Direct removal of the fuel line, may result in dangerous fuel spray. Make sure to release the fuel pressure according to the following procedures:

2.0L (VIN 1) and 2.2L (VIN G) Engines

1. Disconnect the negative battery cable.
2. Release the fuel vapor pressure in the fuel tank by removing the fuel tank cap and reinstalling it.
3. The internal constant bleed feature of the TBI Models 700/220, relieves the fuel pump system pressure when the engine is turned **OFF** and no further pressure relive procedure is required.

2.0L (VIN H, K) and 2.2L (VIN 4) Engines

1. Release the fuel vapor pressure in the fuel tank by removing the fuel tank cap and reinstalling it.
2. Remove the fuel pump fuse from the fuse block.
3. Start the engine and allow it to run a few seconds until it runs out of fuel.
4. Once the engine is stopped, crank it a few times with the starter for about 3 seconds to dissipate the fuel in the lines.
5. If the fuel pressure can't be released in the above manner because the engine failed to run, disconnect the negative battery cable, cover the union bolt of the fuel line with a shop towel and loosen the union bolt slowly to release the fuel pressure gradually.

2.0L (VIN M) Engine

1. Disconnect the negative battery cable.
2. Disconnect the fuel filler cap.
3. Connect gauge J-34730-1 or equivalent, to the fuel pressure connection. Wrap a cloth around the fitting to absorb any fuel leakage.
4. Install the bleed hose into an approved container and open the valve to bleed system pressure.

2.8L and 3.1L Engines

1. Disconnect the negative battery cable.
2. Disconnect the fuel filler cap.
3. Connect gauge J-34730-1 or equivalent, to the fuel pressure connection. Wrap a cloth around the fitting to absorb any fuel leakage.
4. Install the bleed hose into an approved container and open the valve to bleed system pressure.

Fuel Filter

REMOVAL & INSTALLATION

The fuel filter is located under the rear of the vehicle near the fuel tank.

1. Relieve the fuel system pressure.
2. Disconnect the negative battery cable.
3. Raise and safely support the vehicle.
4. Disconnect the fuel lines from the filter.
5. Remove the filter retaining bolt and remove the filter from the vehicle.

To install:

6. Install the new filter in position, using new O-ring seals, and connect the fuel lines. Tighten the fuel lines to 20 ft. lbs. (27 Nm).
7. Lower the vehicle.

8. Connect the negative battery cable and run the engine. Check for leaks.

Electric Fuel Pump

PRESSURE TESTING

Throttle Body Injection

1. Relieve the fuel system pressure.
2. Remove the air cleaner and plug the thermal vacuum port on the throttle body unit.
3. Remove the steel fuel line from between the throttle body unit and the fuel filter.
4. Install a fuel pressure gauge with at least a 15 psi capacity between the throttle body and the filter.
5. Start the engine and observe the pressure reading. Pressure should be 9–13 psi. If the pressure is not within these limits, one or more of the following could be at fault:

    a. A short in the system
    b. A clogged fuel filter
    c. A shorted or defective oil pressure switch
    d. Defective fuel pump relay
    e. Defective fuel pump

NOTE: Check each of these components in turn to diagnose the problem before replacing the pump.

6. Follow the cautions at the start of this procedure to depressurize the system. Remove the pressure gauge and install the fuel line. Tighten the nuts to 19–25 ft. lbs. (26–34 Nm).
7. Start the engine and check for leaks.
8. Unplug the thermal vacuum port on the throttle body.

Port Fuel Injection

1. Release the fuel system pressure. Wrap a shop towel around fuel pressure connector on the fuel rail to absorb any leakage that may occur when installing gauge.
2. Install a fuel pressure gauge J–34730–1 or equivalent, to pressure connector.
3. With ignition **ON** pump pressure should be as follows:

    a. 40.5–47 psi on 2.0L (VIN H) and 2.2L (VIN 4) engines.
    b. 40.5–47 psi on 2.8L and 3.1L engines
    c. 35–38 psi on 2.0L (VIN M) Engine

4. When engine is idling, pressure should drop 25–30 psi on 2.0L (VIN M) engine or 3–10 psi on all other PFI engines.

NOTE: The application of vacuum to the pressure regulator should result in a fuel pressure drop.

5. Remove fuel pressure gauge J–34730–1 or equivalent, from pressure connector.

REMOVAL & INSTALLATION

The electric fuel pump is located in the fuel tank.

1. Relieve the fuel system pressure.
2. Disconnect the battery ground.
3. Raise and safely support the vehicle.
4. Remove the fuel filler cap.
5. Drain the fuel tank.
6. Disconnect the filler neck hose and the vent hose.
7. Remove the fuel tank strap rear support bolts and lower the tank on a jack, just enough, to disconnect the fuel feed line, return and vapor lines from the fuel meter.

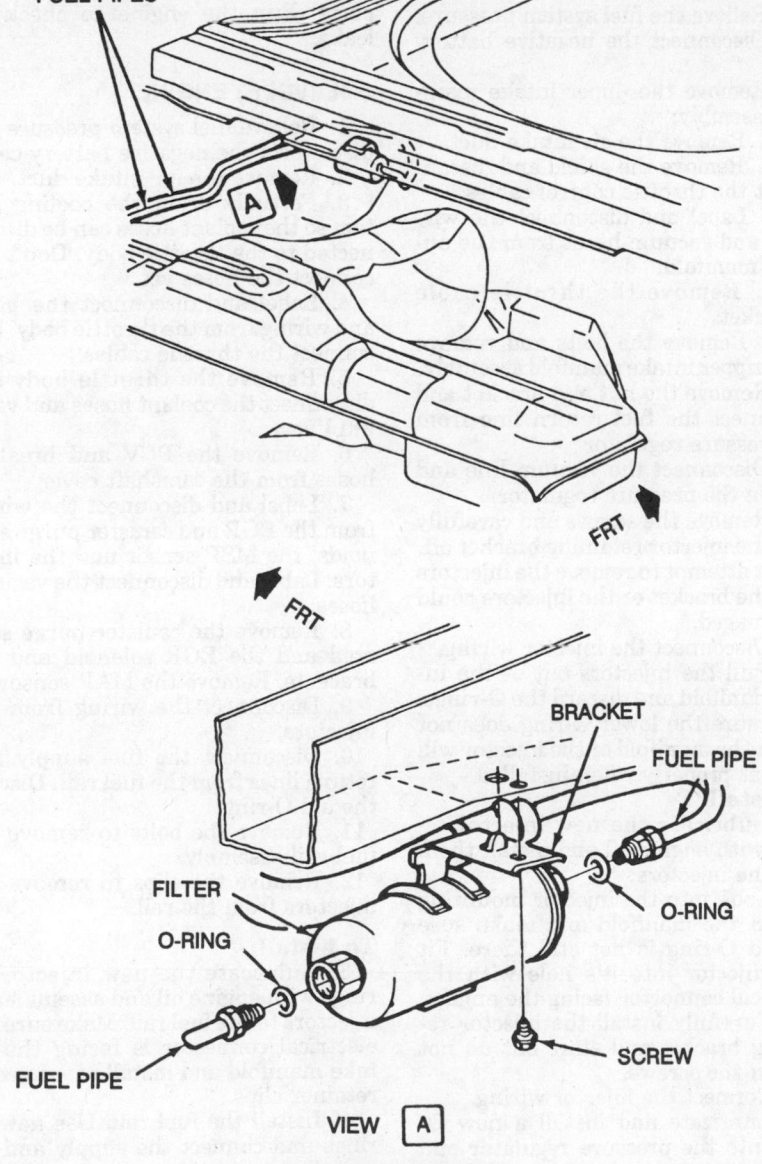

FUEL PIPES

A

FRT

FRT

BRACKET

FUEL PIPE

O-RING

FILTER

O-RING

FUEL PIPE

SCREW

VIEW A

Fuel filter installation

8. Remove the tank from the vehicle.

9. Remove the fuel meter/pump assembly by turning the cam lock ring counterclockwise. Lift the assembly from the tank and remove the pump from the meter.

10. Pull the pump up onto the attaching hose while pulling outward from the bottom support. Take care not to damage the rubber insulator and strainer. After the pump is clear of the bottom support pull it out of the rubber connector.

To install:

11. Install the pump to the fuel meter assembly.

12. Install the fuel meter/pump assembly into the tank. Install a new O-ring on the cam lock ring. Install the cam lock ring and tighten by turning clockwise.

13. Place the fuel tank into position.

14. Connect the fuel feed line, return and vapor lines to the fuel meter. Raise the tank and install the fuel tank strap rear support bolts.

15. Connect the filler neck hose and the vent hose.

16. Fill the fuel tank.

17. Install the fuel filler cap.

18. Lower the vehicle.

19. Connect the negative battery cable.

Fuel Injection

IDLE SPEED AND MIXTURE ADJUSTMENT

Idle speed and mixture are controlled by the Electronic Control Module (ECM). No adjustments are necessary.

Fuel Injector

REMOVAL & INSTALLATION

NOTE: Use care in removing injector to prevent damage to the electrical pins on top of the injector. The fuel injectors are an electrical component. Do not immerse in any type of cleaner.

Throttle Body Injection

1. Relieve the fuel pump pressure.

2. Disconnect the negative battery cable.

3. Remove the TBI cover and gasket.

4. Disconnect the electrical connector to fuel injector.

5. Remove the injector retainer.

6. Using a fulcrum, place a suitable tool under the ridge opposite the connector end and carefully pry injector out.

To install:

NOTE: Remove the upper and lower O-rings from injector body and in fuel injector cavity and replace with new O-rings before installing injector.

7. Install the injector.

8. Install the injector retainer.

9. Connect the electrical connector to fuel injector.

NOTE: Be sure the electrical connector end, on the injector is facing in the direction to the cut-out in the fuel meter body for the wire grommet to fit properly.

10. Install the TBI cover and gasket.

11. Connect the negative battery cable.

Port Fuel Injection

2.2L (VIN 4) ENGINE

1. Relieve the fuel system pressure.

2. Disconnect the negative battery cable.

3. Remove the upper intake manifold assembly:

　a. Remove the air intake duct.

　b. Remove the shield and disconnect the throttle control cables.

　c. Label and disconnect the wiring and vacuum hoses from the upper manifold.

　d. Remove the throttle cable bracket.

　e. Remove the bolts and remove the upper intake manifold assembly.

4. Remove the nut and bracket and disconnect the fuel return line from the pressure regulator.

5. Disconnect the vacuum line and remove the pressure regulator.

6. Remove the screws and carefully slide the injector retaining bracket off. Do not attempt to remove the injectors with the bracket or the injectors could be damaged.

7. Disconnect the injector wiring.

8. Pull the injectors out of the intake manifold and discard the O-rings. Make sure the lower O-ring does not stay in the manifold or the injector will not seat properly when installed.

To install:

9. Lubricate the new injector O-rings with engine oil and install them onto the injectors.

10. Look into the injector mounting hole in the manifold and make sure the old O-ring is not still there. Fit each injector into it's hole with the electrical connector facing the engine.

11. Carefully install the injector retaining bracket and start but do not tighten the screws.

12. Connect the injector wiring.

13. Lubricate and install a new O-ring onto the pressure regulator and install the regulator.

14. Apply thread locking compound to the injector bracket screws and the pressure regulator screws and torque them all to 31 inch lbs. (3.5 Nm).

15. Use a new gasket and install the upper intake manifold. Torque the bolts to 22 ft. lbs. (30 Nm).

16. Install the throttle cable bracket but do not tighten the bolts yet. To adjust the position of the bracket:

　a. If the bracket is equipped with a cross brace, no adjustment is required.

　b. Hold a steel rule against the throttle body bore with one end against the bracket.

　c. Adjust the gap between the bracket and the bore to ⅜ in. (10mm).

　d. Tighten the upper bracket bolt or nut first, then the remaining nuts.

17. Connect the throttle cables, wiring and hoses and install all remaining parts. Run the engine to check for leaks.

2.0L (VIN H) ENGINE

1. Relieve fuel system pressure and disconnect the negative battery cable.

2. Remove the air intake duct.

3. Partially drain the cooling system so the coolant hoses can be disconnected to the throttle body. Don't disconnect the hoses yet.

4. Label and disconnect the hoses and wiring from the throttle body. Disconnect the throttle cables.

5. Remove the throttle body and disconnect the coolant hoses and vacuum lines.

6. Remove the PCV and breather hoses from the camshaft cover.

7. Label and disconnect the wiring from the EGR and canister purge solenoids, the MSP sensor and the injectors. Label and disconnect the vacuum hoses.

8. Remove the canister purge solenoid and the EGR solenoid and the brackets. Remove the MAP sensor.

9. Disconnect the wiring from the injectors.

10. Disconnect the fuel supply and return lines from the fuel rail. Discard the old O-ring.

11. Remove the bolts to remove the fuel rail assembly.

12. Remove the clips to remove the injectors from the rail.

To install:

13. Lubricate the new injector O-rings with engine oil and assemble the injectors to the fuel rail. Make sure the electrical connector is facing the intake manifold and install new injector retainer clips.

14. Install the fuel rail. Use new O-rings and connect the supply and return lines.

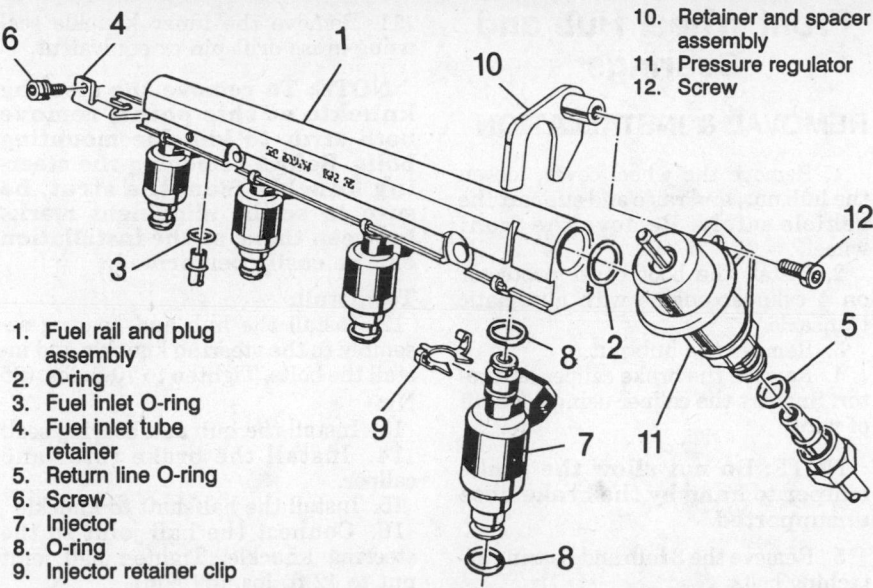

1. Fuel rail and plug assembly
2. O-ring
3. Fuel inlet O-ring
4. Fuel inlet tube retainer
5. Return line O-ring
6. Screw
7. Injector
8. O-ring
9. Injector retainer clip
10. Retainer and spacer assembly
11. Pressure regulator
12. Screw

Removing injectors from the fuel rail—2.0L (VIN H) engine

15. Connect the injector wiring.

16. Install the MAP sensor, EGR and purge valve solenoids. Connect the wiring and vacuum lines.

17. Connect the throttle body coolant hoses and vacuum lines and install the throttle body with a new gasket.

18. Connect the wiring and control cables.

19. Fill the cooling system and install all remaining components. Run the engine to check for leaks.

2.8L AND 3.1L ENGINES

NOTE: The fuel rail is removed as an assembly, then the injectors can be removed.

1. Disconnect the negative battery cable. Relieve the fuel system pressure.

2. Tag and disconnect the fuel injection electrical connections.

3. Remove the upper intake manifold plenum assembly. Remove the necessary components in order to gain access to the fuel rail retaining bolts.

4. Remove the fuel rail retaining bolts. Remove the fuel rail assembly.

5. Separate the fuel injector from the fuel rail.

To install:

6. Replace the O-rings when installing the injectors.

7. Install the fuel injector to the fuel rail.

8. Install the fuel rail assembly. Install the fuel rail retaining bolts.

9. Install the upper intake manifold plenum assembly.

10. Connect the fuel injector electrical connections.

11. Connect the negative battery cable.

DRIVE AXLE

Halfshaft

REMOVAL & INSTALLATION

NOTE: If equipped with tri-pot joints, care must be exercised not to allow joints to become overextended. Over extending the joint could result in separation of internal components.

1. Raise and safely support the vehicle. Do not support under lower control arms.

2. Remove the front wheels.

3. Remove the hub nut and washer.

4. Remove the caliper bolts and support caliper with a length of wire. Do not let the caliper hang by the brake hose unsupported.

5. Remove the rotor and lower ball joint nut.

6. Remove the stabilizer bolt from lower control arm.

NOTE: Install the halfshaft seal boot protectors J–34754 or equivalent, on the outer drive seal.

7. Install J–28733 or equivalent and press the halfshaft in and away from the hub. The halfshaft should only be pressed in until the press fit between the halfshaft and hub is loose.

8. Separate and remove the lower ball joint from the steering knuckle.

9. Install J–28468 or equivalent and slide hammer assembly. Remove the halfshaft.

To install:

10. To install the halfshaft, start the splines of the halfshaft into the transaxle and push halfshaft inward until it snaps into place.

11. Verify that the halfshaft is seated into the transaxle by grasping on the housing and pulling outboard.

12. Install the halfshaft to hub and bearing assembly.

13. Install the lower ball joint to the steering knuckle. Tighten the ball joint-to-steering knuckle nut to 41 ft. lbs. (56 Nm) with a minimum torque of 50 ft. lbs. (68 Nm). Tighten further to align the next cotter pin hole.

14. Install the washer and new driveshaft nut. Tighten the new axle shaft nut to 74 ft. lbs. (100 Nm).

15. Install the stabilizer bolt to lower control arm.

16. Install the rotor.

17. Install the caliper and attaching bolts.

18. Install the front wheels.

19. Lower the vehicle and apply a final torque to the axle shaft nut of 191 ft. lbs. (259 Nm).

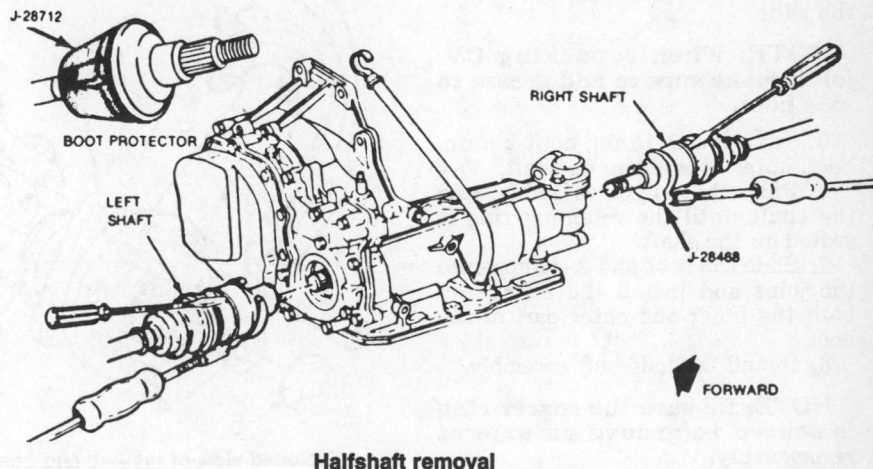

Halfshaft removal

CV-Boot

REMOVAL & INSTALLATION

Outer

1. Remove the halfshaft assembly.
2. Remove the steel deflector ring by using brass drift to tap it off. If the rubber ring is used, slide it off.
3. Cut the seal retaining clamps and lift the boot to gain access to retaining ring.
4. Using snapring pliers J–8059 or equivalent, spread the retaining ring inside the outer CV-joint and remove joint from shaft.
5. Slide the boot off shaft.

To install:

6. Clean the splines of the shaft and the CV-joint with solvent and repack the joint. Install a new retaining ring inside the joint.

NOTE: When repacking CV-joint, make sure to add grease to axle boot.

7. Install the inner boot clamp, boot, outer boot clamp on shaft.
8. Push the joint assembly onto the shaft until the ring is seated on the shaft.
9. Slide the boot and 2 clamps onto the joint and install the clamps on both the inner and outer part of the boot. Install deflector ring.
10. Install the halfshaft assembly.

Inner

1. Remove the halfshaft assembly.
2. Cut the seal retaining clamps and lift the boot to gain access to retaining ring for spider assembly.
3. Using snapring pliers J–8059 or equivalent, remove the retaining ring from shaft and remove the spider assembly. Slide the old boot off axle shaft.

To install:

4. Clean the splines of the shaft and the CV-joint with solvent and repack the joint.

NOTE: When repacking CV-joint, make sure to add grease to axle boot.

5. Install the inner boot clamp, boot, outer boot clamp on shaft.
6. Push the tri-pot assembly onto the shaft until the retaining ring is seated on the shaft.
7. Slide the boot and 2 clamps onto the joint and install the clamps on both the inner and outer part of the boot.
8. Install the halfshaft assembly.

NOTE: Be sure the spacer ring is seated in groove on axle at reassembly.

Front Wheel Hub and Bearings

REMOVAL & INSTALLATION

1. Remove the wheel cover, loosen the hub nut, and raise and support the vehicle safely. Remove the front wheel.
2. Install the boot cover protector on 4 cylinder engine with automatic transaxle.
3. Remove the hub nut.
4. Remove the brake caliper and rotor. Support the caliper using a length of wire.

NOTE: Do not allow the brake caliper to hang by the brake hose unsupported.

5. Remove the 3 hub and bearing attaching bolts.
6. Remove the splash shield.
7. Install special tool J–28733 or equivalent, and press the hub and bearing assembly off the halfshaft.
8. Disconnect the stabilizer link bolt at the lower control arm.
9. Separate the ball joint from steering knuckle.
10. Remove the halfshaft from knuckle and support out of the way.

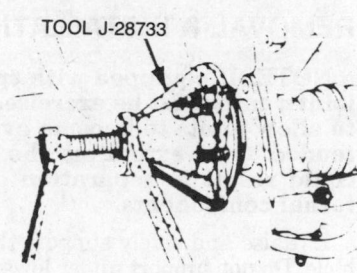

TOOL J-28733

Removing halfshaft from hub and bearing assembly

11. Remove the inner knuckle seal using brass drift pin or equivalent.

NOTE: To remove the steering knuckle at this point, remove both strut to knuckle mounting bolts. Before removing the steering knuckle from the strut, be sure to scribe alignment marks between them, so the installation can be easily performed.

To install:

12. Install the hub and bearing assembly to the steering knuckle and install the bolts. Tighten to 70 ft. lbs. (95 Nm).
13. Install the hub and bearing seal.
14. Install the brake rotor and caliper.
15. Install the halfshaft to knuckle.
16. Connect the ball joint to the steering knuckle. Tighten ball joint nut to 42 ft. lbs. (57 Nm).
17. Connect the stabilizer link bolt to the lower control arm. Tighten the steering knuckle-to-strut bolts to 133 ft. lbs. (181 Nm).
18. Install the splash shield.
19. Install the driveshaft nut.
20. Remove the boot cover protector on 4 cylinder engine with automatic transaxle.
21. Install the front wheel.
22. Lower the vehicle.
23. Apply a final torque to the hub and bearing nut to 185 ft. lbs. (251 Nm).
24. Install the wheel cover.

MANUAL TRANSAXLE

For further information on transmission/transaxles, please refer

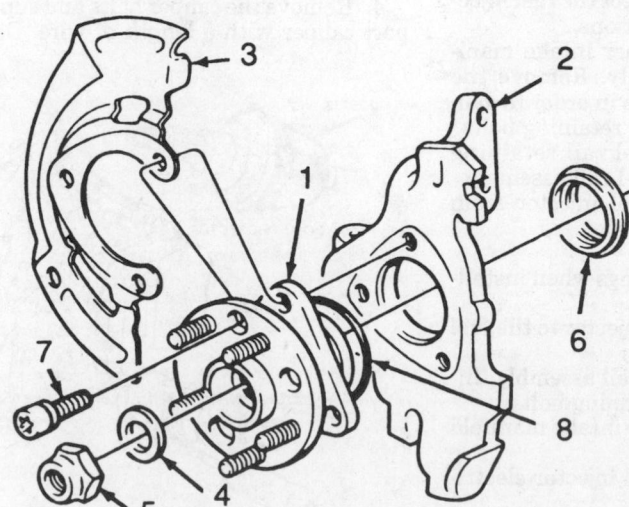

1. Hub and bearing assembly
2. Steering knuckle
3. Shield
4. Washer
5. Hub nut
6. Seal
7. Hub and bearing retaining bolt
8. O-ring

Exploded view of the hub and bearing attachment to the steering knuckle

to "Chilton's Guide to Transmission Repair".

Transaxle Assembly

REMOVAL & INSTALLATION

1. Disconnect the negative battery cable.

2. Install an engine holding bar so one end is supported on the cowl tray over the wiper motor and the other end rests on the radiator support. Use padding and be careful not to damage the paint or body work with the bar. Attach a lifting hook to the engine lift ring and to the bar and raise the engine enough to take the pressure off the motor mounts.

NOTE: If a lifting bar and hook is not available, a chain hoist can be used, however, during the procedure the vehicle must be raised, at which time the chain hoist must be adjusted to keep tension on the engine/transaxle assembly.

3. Remove the heater hose clamp at the transaxle mount bracket. Disconnect the electrical connector and remove the horn assembly.

4. Remove the transaxle mount attaching bolts. Discard the bolts attaching the mount to the side frame; new bolts must be used at installation.

5. Disconnect the clutch master cylinder pushrod from the clutch pedal and disconnect the clutch slave cylinder from the transaxle support bracket and move it aside.

6. Remove the transaxle mount bracket attaching bolts and nuts.

7. Disconnect the ground cables at the transaxle mounting stud.

8. Remove the 4 upper transaxle-to-engine mounting bolts.

9. Raise the vehicle and support it on stands. Remove the left front wheel.

10. Remove the left front inner splash shield. Remove the transaxle strut and bracket.

11. Remove the clutch housing cover bolts.

12. Disconnect the speedometer cable at the transaxle.

13. Disconnect the stabilizer bar at the left suspension support and control arm.

14. Disconnect the ball joint from the steering knuckle.

15. Remove the left suspension support attaching bolts and remove the support and control arm as an assembly.

16. Install boot protectors and disengage the halfshafts at the transaxle. Remove the left side shaft from the transaxle.

17. Position a jack under the transaxle case, remove the lower 2 transaxle-to-engine mounting bolts and remove the transaxle by sliding it towards the driver's side, away from the engine. Carefully lower the jack, guiding the right shaft out the transaxle.

To install:

18. Raise the transaxle into position and guide the right halfshaft into its bore as the transaxle is being raised. The right halfshaft can not be readily installed after the transaxle is connected to the engine.

19. Install the transaxle attaching bolts. Tighten the transaxle-to-engine bolts to 85 ft. lbs. (115 Nm).

20. Install the left side shaft to the transaxle. Remove the boot protectors.

21. Install the control arm as an assembly. Install the left suspension support and attaching bolts.

22. Connect the ball joint to the steering knuckle.

23. Connect the stabilizer bar to the left suspension support and control arm. Tighten the suspension support-to-body attaching bolts to 75 ft. lbs. (102 Nm).

24. Connect the speedometer cable to the transaxle.

25. Install the clutch housing cover and attaching bolts Tighten to 10 ft. lbs. (14 Nm).

26. Install the transaxle strut and bracket. Install the left front inner splash shield.

27. Install the left front wheel. Lower the vehicle.

28. Install the 4 upper transaxle-to-engine mounting bolts.

29. Connect the ground cables to the transaxle mounting stud.

30. Install the transaxle mount bracket attaching bolts and nuts. When installing the bolts attaching the mount-to-transaxle bracket, check the alignment bolt at the engine mount. If excessive effort is required to remove the alignment bolt, realign the powertrain components and tighten the bolts to 40 ft. lbs. (54 Nm) and remove the alignment bolt.

31. Connect the clutch slave cylinder to the transaxle support bracket and connect the clutch master cylinder pushrod to the clutch pedal.

32. Install the transaxle mount attaching bolts. Install new bolts attaching the mount to the side frame. Tighten the transaxle mount-to-side frame to 40 ft. lbs. (54 Nm).

33. Install the heater hose clamp to the transaxle mount bracket. Install the horn assembly and connect the electrical connector.

34. Remove the engine lifting fixture.

35. Connect the negative battery cable.

CLUTCH

Clutch Assembly

REMOVAL & INSTALLATION

—— **CAUTION** ——

The clutch plate contains asbestos, which has been determined to be a cancer causing agent. Never clean the clutch surfaces with compressed air. Avoid inhaling any dust from any clutch surface.

REMOVAL & INSTALLATION

1. Disconnect the negative battery cable. Raise and safely support the vehicle. Remove the transaxle.

2. Mark the pressure plate assembly and the flywheel so they can be assembled in the same position to maintain balance.

3. Loosen the attaching bolts 1 turn at a time until spring tension is relieved.

4. Support the pressure plate and remove the bolts. Remove the pressure plate and the clutch disc.

To install:

5. Inspect the flywheel, pressure plate, clutch disc, release bearing and the clutch fork for wear.

6. Clean the flywheel mating surfaces. Position the clutch disc and pressure plate into the installed position and support with a dummy shaft or clutch aligning tool.

NOTE: Clutch plate must be installed correctly. Clutch plate is marked INSTALL FLYWHEEL SIDE. Always replace clutch and pressure plate as a set.

7. Install the pressure plate-to-flywheel bolts. Tighten in a criss-cross pattern.

8. Lubricate the outside grooves and the inside recess of the release bearing with high temperature grease. Wipe off any excess. Install the release bearing.

9. Install the transaxle.

PEDAL HEIGHT/FREE-PLAY ADJUSTMENT

These vehicles use an hydraulic clutch system which provides automatic clutch adjustment. No adjustment of the clutch linkage or pedal height is required.

Clutch Master/Slave Cylinder

REMOVAL & INSTALLATION

NOTE: The clutch hydraulic system is serviced as a complete unit. Individual components of the system are not available separately.

1. Disconnect the negative battery cable.
2. Remove the left side sound insulator panel.

NOTE: If equipped with a 2.8L or 3.1L engine, remove the air cleaner, mass air flow sensor and air intake duct as an assembly. Disconnect electrical lead at the washer bottle and remove washer bottle from vehicle.

3. Disconnect the master cylinder pushrod from the clutch pedal.
4. Remove the master cylinder-to-cowl brace nuts and remove master cylinder.
5. Remove the slave cylinder retaining nuts at the transaxle and remove slave cylinder. Remove the hydraulic system as a unit from the vehicle.

To install:

6. Install the hydraulic system as a unit from the vehicle. Install the slave cylinder to the transaxle and install the attaching nuts.
7. Install the master cylinder and the master cylinder-to-cowl brace nuts.
8. Connect the master cylinder pushrod to the clutch pedal.

NOTE: If equipped with a 2.8L or 3.1L engine, install the air cleaner, mass air flow sensor and air intake duct as an assembly. Install the washer bottle. Connect the electrical lead to the washer bottle.

9. Install the left side sound insulator panel.
10. Connect the negative battery cable.
11. Bleed the hydraulic system.

NOTE: Do not remove the plastic pushrod retainer from the slave cylinder. The strap will break on the first clutch pedal application.

Hydraulic Clutch System Bleeding

1. Clean dirt and grease from the cap to ensure no foreign substances enter the system.
2. Fill reservoir to the top with approved brake fluid only.

NOTE: Brake fluid must be certified to DOT 3 specification.

3. Fully loosen the bleed screw which is in the slave cylinder body.
4. Fluid will now begin to move from the master cylinder, down the tube, to the slave cylinder. The reservoir must be kept full at all times.
5. When the slave cylinder is full, a steady stream of fluid will come from the slave outlet. At this point, tighten bleed screw.
6. Start the engine, push the clutch pedal to the floor and select reverse gear. There should be no grating of gears. If there is the system still contains air.

AUTOMATIC TRANSAXLE

For further information on transmission/transaxles, please refer to "Chilton's Guide to Transmission Repair".

Transaxle Assembly

NOTE: In September 1991, Hydra-matic changed the name of the THM 125C. The new name designation for this transaxle is Hydra-matic 3T40. On 1989–90 models, either name can be used when ordering parts. On later models, only the new name will be listed.

REMOVAL & INSTALLATION

1. Disconnect the negative terminal from the battery. Remove the air cleaner, bracket, Mass Air Flow (MAF) sensor and air tube as an assembly.
2. Disconnect the exhaust crossover from the right side manifold and remove the left side exhaust manifold, then, raise and support the manifold/crossover assembly.
3. Disconnect the TV cable from the throttle lever and the transaxle.
4. Remove the vent hose and the shift cable from the transaxle.
5. Remove the fluid level indicator and the filler tube.
6. Using the engine support fixture tool J–28467 or equivalent and the adapter tool J–35953 or equivalent, install them on the engine.
7. Remove the wiring harness-to-transaxle nut.
8. Label and disconnect the wires for the speed sensor, TCC connector and the neutral safety/back up light switch.
9. Remove the upper transaxle-to-engine bolts.

10. Remove the transaxle-to-mount through bolt, the transaxle mount bracket and the mount.
11. Raise and safely support the vehicle.
12. Remove the front wheel assemblies.
13. Disconnect the shift cable bracket from the transaxle.
14. Remove the left side splash shield.
15. Using a modified halfshaft seal protector tool J–34754 or equivalent, install one on each halfshaft to protect the seal from damage and the joint from possible failure.
16. Using care not to damage the halfshaft boots, disconnect the halfshafts from the transaxle.
17. Remove the torsional and lateral strut from the transaxle. Remove the left side stabilizer link pin bolt.
18. Remove the left frame support bolts and move it out of the way.
19. Disconnect the speedometer wire from the transaxle.
20. Remove the transaxle converter cover and matchmark the converter to the flywheel for assembly.
21. Disconnect and plug the transaxle cooler pipes.
22. Remove the transaxle-to-engine support.
23. Using a transmission jack, position and secure it to the transaxle and remove the remaining transaxle-to-engine bolts.
24. Make sure the torque converter does not fall out and remove the transaxle from the vehicle.

NOTE: The transaxle cooler and lines should be flushed any time the transaxle is removed for overhaul or to replace the pump, case or converter.

To install:

25. Put a small amount of grease on the pilot hub of the converter and make sure the converter is properly engaged with the pump.
26. Raise the transaxle to the engine while guiding the right-side halfshaft into the transaxle.
27. Install the lower transaxle mounting bolts, tighten to 55 ft. lbs. (75 Nm) and remove the jack.
28. Align the converter with the marks made previously on the flywheel and install the bolts h and tight.
29. Tighten the converter bolts to 46 ft. lbs. (62 Nm). Retorque the first bolt after the others.
30. Install the starter assembly. Install the left side halfshaft.
31. Install the converter cover, oil cooler lines and cover. Install the subframe assembly. Install the lower engine mount retaining bolts and the transaxle mount nuts.
32. Install the right and left ball

joints. Install the power steering rack, heat shield and cooler lines to the frame.

33. Install the right and left inner fender splash shields. Install the tire assemblies.

34. Lower the vehicle. Connect all electrical leads. Install the upper transaxle mount bolts, tighten to 55 ft. lbs. (75 Nm).

35. Attach the crossover pipe to the exhaust manifold. Connect the EGR tube to the crossover.

36. Connect the TV cable and the shift cable. Install the air cleaner and inlet tube.

37. Remove the engine support tool. Connect the negative battery cable.

SHIFT CONTROL CABLE ADJUSTMENT

1. Place the shift lever in the **N**.

NOTE: Neutral can be found by rotating the transaxle selector shaft counterclockwise from P through R to N.

2. Loosely attach the cable to the transaxle shift lever with a nut. Assemble the cable to the cable bracket and to shift lever. Tighten the cable to transaxle shift lever nut.

NOTE: The lever must be held out of P when torquing the nut.

Throttle Valve (TV) Cable Adjustment

Setting of the TV cable must be done by rotating the throttle lever at the carburetor or throttle body. Do not use the accelerator pedal to rotate the throttle lever.

1. With the engine OFF, depress and hold the reset tab at the engine end of the TV cable.

2. Move the slider until it stops against the fitting.

3. Release the rest tab.

4. Rotate the throttle lever to its full travel.

5. The slider must move (ratchet) toward the lever when the lever is rotated to its full travel position.

6. Recheck after the engine is hot and road test the vehicle.

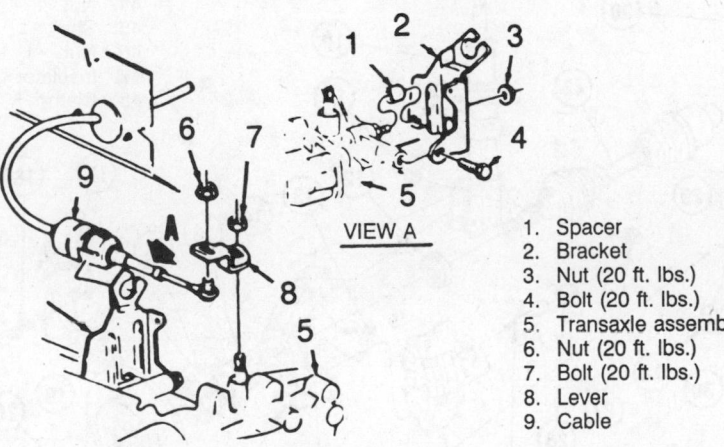

1.	Spacer
2.	Bracket
3.	Nut (20 ft. lbs.)
4.	Bolt (20 ft. lbs.)
5.	Transaxle assembly
6.	Nut (20 ft. lbs.)
7.	Bolt (20 ft. lbs.)
8.	Lever
9.	Cable

Engine compartment shift control cable

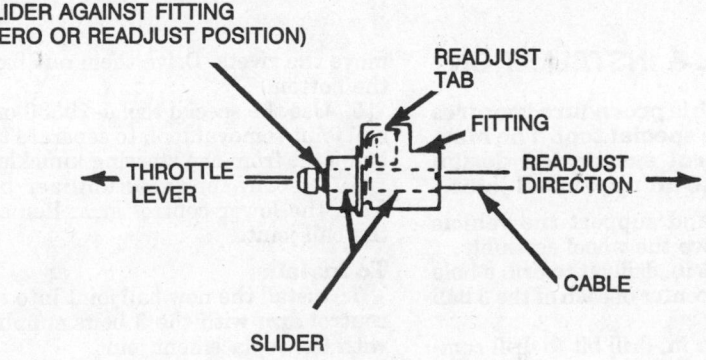

TV cable adjuster

FRONT SUSPENSION

MacPherson Strut

REMOVAL & INSTALLATION

NOTE: Before removing front suspension components, their positions should be marked so they may be assembled correctly.

1. Remove the 3 strut-to-body nuts.

2. Raise and safely support the vehicle.

3. Lower the vehicle slightly so the weight rests on jackstands at the frame and not on the control arms.

4. Remove the front wheel and tire assemblies. Remove the tie rod from the strut assembly using tool J–24319 or equivalent.

5. Some vehicles may use a silicone (gray) boot on the inboard axle joint. Use the boot protector tool J–33162 or equivalent, on these boots. All other boots are made from a thermoplastic material (black) and do not require the use of a boot seal protector.

6. Disconnect the brake line bracket from the strut assembly.

7. Remove the strut-to-steering knuckle bolts.

NOTE: Support steering knuckle to prevent tension from being applied to brake hose.

8. Remove the strut assembly from the vehicle. Care should be taken to avoid chipping or cracking the spring coating when handling the front suspension coil spring assembly.

To install:

9. Install the strut assembly to the vehicle.

10. Install the strut-to-steering knuckle bolts. Tighten to 133 ft. lbs. (184 Nm).

11. Connect the brake line bracket to the strut assembly.

12. If installed, remove the boot protector.

13. Connect the tie rod end to the strut assembly. Install the front wheel and tire assemblies.

14. Lower the vehicle.

15. Install the 3 strut-to-body nuts. Tighten to 18 ft. lbs. (24 Nm).

16. Check and/or adjust the front end alignment.

Lower Ball Joint

INSPECTION

1. Raise and safely support the ve-

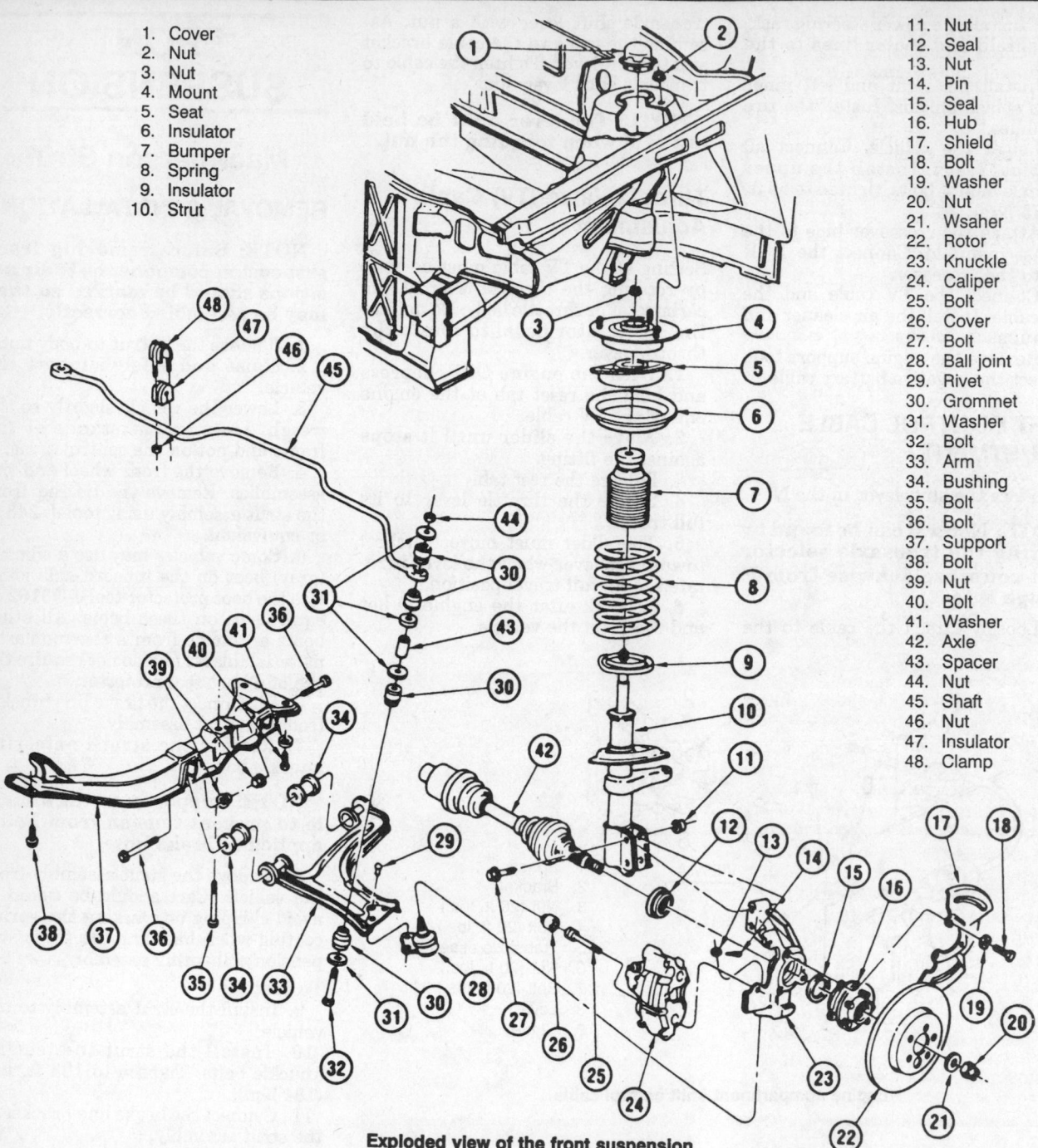

1. Cover
2. Nut
3. Nut
4. Mount
5. Seat
6. Insulator
7. Bumper
8. Spring
9. Insulator
10. Strut

11. Nut
12. Seal
13. Nut
14. Pin
15. Seal
16. Hub
17. Shield
18. Bolt
19. Washer
20. Nut
21. Wsaher
22. Rotor
23. Knuckle
24. Caliper
25. Bolt
26. Cover
27. Bolt
28. Ball joint
29. Rivet
30. Grommet
31. Washer
32. Bolt
33. Arm
34. Bushing
35. Bolt
36. Bolt
37. Support
38. Bolt
39. Nut
40. Bolt
41. Washer
42. Axle
43. Spacer
44. Nut
45. Shaft
46. Nut
47. Insulator
48. Clamp

Exploded view of the front suspension

hicle allowing the suspension to hang free.

2. Grasp the wheel at the top and bottom, shake it in an "in-and-out" motion. Check for any horizontal movement of the steering knuckle relative to the lower control arm. Replace the ball joint if such movement is noted.

3. If the ball stud is disconnected from the steering knuckle and any looseness is detected or if the ball stud can be twisted in its socket using finger pressure, replace the ball joint.

REMOVAL & INSTALLATION

NOTE: This procedure requires the use of a special tool. The MacPherson strut suspension design does not use an upper ball joint.

1. Raise and support the vehicle safely. Remove the wheel assembly.

2. Use a ⅛ in. drill bit to drill a hole through the center of each of the 3 ball joint rivets.

3. Use a ½ in. drill bit to drill completely through the rivet.

4. Use a hammer and punch to re-

move the rivets. Drive them out from the bottom.

5. Use the special tool J–29330 or a ball joint removal tool, to separate the ball joint from the steering knuckle.

6. Disconnect the stabilizer bar from the lower control arm. Remove the ball joint.

To install:

7. Install the new ball joint into the control arm with the 3 bolts supplied with the replacement joint.

8. Installation of the remaining components is in the reverse order of

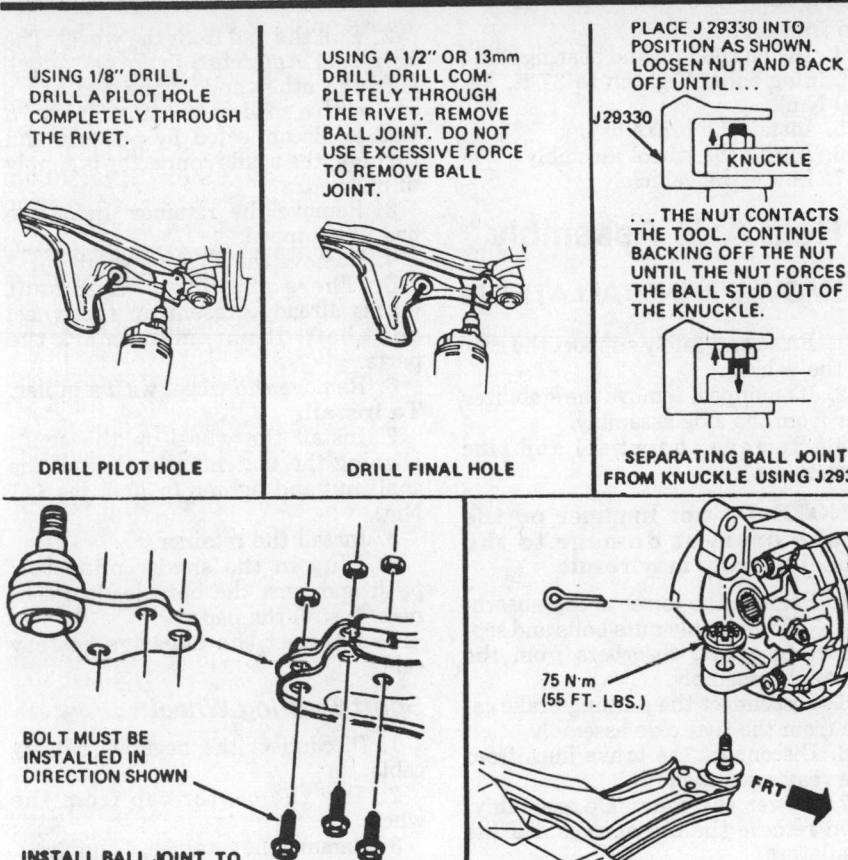

USING 1/8" DRILL, DRILL A PILOT HOLE COMPLETELY THROUGH THE RIVET.

DRILL PILOT HOLE

USING A 1/2" OR 13mm DRILL, DRILL COMPLETELY THROUGH THE RIVET. REMOVE BALL JOINT. DO NOT USE EXCESSIVE FORCE TO REMOVE BALL JOINT.

DRILL FINAL HOLE

PLACE J 29330 INTO POSITION AS SHOWN. LOOSEN NUT AND BACK OFF UNTIL...

J29330

KNUCKLE

...THE NUT CONTACTS THE TOOL. CONTINUE BACKING OFF THE NUT UNTIL THE NUT FORCES THE BALL STUD OUT OF THE KNUCKLE.

SEPARATING BALL JOINT FROM KNUCKLE USING J29330

BOLT MUST BE INSTALLED IN DIRECTION SHOWN

INSTALL BALL JOINT TO CONTROL ARM

75 N·m (55 FT. LBS.)

FRT

Ball joint removal and installation details

removal. Use a new cotter pin when installing the castellated nut on the ball joint.

9. Check the toe setting and adjust, as necessary.

Lower Control Arms

REMOVAL & INSTALLATION

1. Raise and support the vehicle safely. Remove the wheel assembly.
2. Disconnect the stabilizer bar from the control arm and/or support.
3. Separate the ball joint from the steering knuckle.
4. Remove the 2 control arm-to-support bolts and remove the control arm.
5. If control arm support bar removal is necessary, unscrew the 6 mounting bolts and remove the support.

To install:

6. If control arm support bar was removed, install the support and the 6 mounting bolts. Tighten the control arm support rail bolts, in sequence.
7. Install the control arm and 2 control arm-to-support bolts.
8. Connect the ball joint to the steering knuckle.
9. Connect the stabilizer bar to the control arm and/or support.

10. Install the wheel. Lower the vehicle.
11. Check the toe and adjust, as necessary.

Stabilizer Bar

REMOVAL & INSTALLATION

1. Raise and support the vehicle safely so the front suspension hang free.

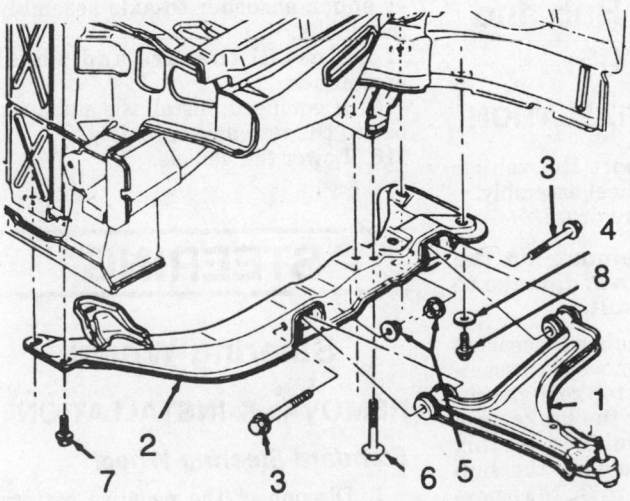

Lower control arm installation torque sequence

1. Control arm
2. Suspension support
3. Bolt (61 ft. lbs.)
4. Washer
5. Nut
6. Bolt (66 ft. lbs.) tighten first
7. Bolt (65 ft. lbs.) tighten second
8. Bolt (65 ft. lbs.) tighten third

2. Remove the left front wheel and tire.
3. Disconnect the stabilizer from the control arms.
4. Disconnect the stabilizer from the support assemblies.
5. Loosen the front bolts and remove the rear and center bolts from the support assemblies to lower them enough to remove the stabilizer shaft.
6. Remove the stabilizer shaft with grommets and insulators.

To install:

7. Install the stabilizer shaft with grommets and insulators.
8. Install the stabilizer shaft and tighten the front bolts and install the rear and center bolts to the support assemblies.
9. Connect the stabilizer to the support assemblies.
10. Connect the stabilizer to the control arms.
11. Install the left front wheel and tire.
12. Lower the vehicle.

REAR SUSPENSION

Shock Absorbers

REMOVAL & INSTALLATION

1. Open the hatch or trunk lid, remove the trim cover, if present, and remove the upper shock absorber nut.
2. Raise and support the vehicle safely to a convenient working height. It is not necessary to remove the weight of the vehicle from the shock absorbers, however, the vehicle can be left on the ground, if preferred.

3. Remove the lower attaching bolt and remove the shock.

To install:

4. If new shock absorbers are being installed, repeatedly compress them while inverted and extend them in their normal upright position. This will purge them of air.

5. Install the shocks in the reverse order of removal. Tighten the lower mount nut and bolt to 35 ft. lbs. (47 Nm) and the upper to 21 ft. lbs. (28 Nm).

Coil Springs

REMOVAL & INSTALLATION

――――――― CAUTION ―――――――

The coil springs are under a considerable amount of tension. Be very careful when removing or installing them; they can exert enough force to cause very serious injuries.

1. Raise and support the vehicle safely, use a jack under the axle to support it.

2. Support the axle so it can be raised and lowered.

3. Remove the brake hose attaching brackets both right and left, allowing the hoses to hang freely. Do not disconnect the hoses.

4. Remove both shock absorber lower attaching bolts from the axle.

5. Lower the axle. Remove the coil spring and insulator.

To install:

6. Position the spring and insulator on the axle.

7. The leg on the upper coil of the spring must be parallel to the axle, facing the left side of the vehicle.

8. Install the shock absorber bolts. Tighten to 35 ft. lbs. (47 Nm).

9. Install the brake line brackets. Tighten to 8 ft. lbs. (11 Nm).

10. Lower the vehicle.

Rear Wheel Hub and Bearings

REMOVAL & INSTALLATION

1. Raise and support the vehicle safely. Remove the wheel assembly.

2. Remove the brake drum.

NOTE: Do not hammer on the brake drum to remove; damage to the bearing will result.

3. Remove the 4 hub and bearing retaining bolts and remove the assembly from the axle. The top rear attaching bolt will not clear the brake shoe when removing the hub and bearing assembly. Partially remove the hub and bearing assembly prior to removing this bolt.

To install:

4. Install the hub and bearing and 4 retaining bolts. Tighten to 37 ft. lbs. (50 Nm).

5. Install the brake drum.

6. Install the wheel assembly.

7. Lower the vehicle.

Rear Axle Assembly

REMOVAL & INSTALLATION

1. Raise and safely support the rear of the vehicle.

2. If equipped, remove the stabilizer bar from the axle assembly.

3. Remove the wheel and tire assemblies.

NOTE: Do not hammer on the brake drum as damage to the wheel bearing may result.

4. Remove the lower shock absorber-to-axle assembly nuts/bolts and separate the shock absorbers from the rear axle assembly.

5. Disconnect the parking brake cable from the rear axle assembly.

6. Disconnect the brake lines from the rear axle assembly.

7. Lower the rear axle assembly, then remove the coil springs and the insulators.

8. Remove the rear axle assembly-to-chassis bolts and remove the axle assembly.

To install:

9. Install the rear axle assembly and the axle assembly-to-chassis bolts. Tighten to 37 ft. lbs. (50 Nm).

10. Install the coil springs and insulators and raise the rear axle assembly.

11. Connect the brake lines to the rear axle assembly.

12. Connect the parking brake cable to the rear axle assembly.

13. Connect the shock absorbers to the rear axle assembly. Install the lower shock absorber-to-axle assembly nuts/bolts.

14. Install the tire and wheel assemblies.

15. If equipped, install the stabilizer bar to the rear axle assembly.

16. Lower the vehicle.

STEERING

Steering Wheel

REMOVAL & INSTALLATION

Standard Steering Wheel

1. Disconnect the negative battery cable.

2. Pull the pad from the wheel. The horn lead is attached to the pad at one end; the other end of the pad has a wire with a spade connector. The horn lead is disconnected by pushing and turning; the spade connector is simply unplugged.

3. Remove the retainer under the pad, if equipped.

4. Remove the steering shaft nut.

5. There should be alignment marks already present on the wheel and shaft. If not, matchmark the parts.

6. Remove the wheel with a puller.

To install:

7. Install the wheel on the shaft, aligning the matchmarks. Install the shaft nut and tighten to 30 ft. lbs. (41 Nm).

8. Install the retainer.

9. Plug in the spade connector, push and turn the horn lead to connect. Install the pad.

10. Connect the negative battery cable.

Sport Steering Wheel

1. Disconnect the negative battery cable.

2. Pry the center cap from the wheel.

3. Remove the retainer, if equipped.

4. Remove the shaft nut.

5. If the wheel and shaft do not have factory alignment marks, matchmark the parts before removal of the wheel.

6. Install a puller and remove the wheel. A horn spring, eyelet and insulator are underneath.

To install:

7. Install the spring, eyelet and insulator into the tower in the column.

8. Align the matchmarks and install the wheel onto the shaft. Install the retaining nut and tighten to 30 ft. lbs. (41 Nm).

9. Install the retainer. Install the center cap. Connect the negative battery cable.

Steering Column

REMOVAL & INSTALLATION

NOTE: Once the steering column is removed from the vehicle, the column is extremely susceptible to damage. Dropping the column assembly on its end could collapse the steering shaft or loosen the plastic injections which maintain column rigidity. If it is necessary to remove the steering wheel, use a standard wheel puller. Under no condition should the end of the shaft be hammered upon, as hammering could loosen or break the plastic injection which maintains column rigidity.

1. Disconnect the negative battery cable.

2. If column repairs are to be made, remove the steering wheel.

3. Remove the sound insulator panels, as necessary, to gain access to the steering column retaining bolts.

4. Remove the nuts and bolts attaching the flexible coupling to the bottom of the steering column. Remove the safety strap and bolt, if equipped.

5. Remove the steering column trim shrouds and column covers.

6. Disconnect all wiring harness connectors. Remove the dust boot mounting screws and column mounting bracket bolts.

7. Remove the shift cable at the actuator and housing holder.

8. Lower the column to clear the mounting bracket and carefully remove from the vehicle.

To install:

9. Install the steering column in the vehicle.

10. Install the shift cable at the actuator and housing holder.

11. Connect all wiring harness connectors. Install the dust boot mounting screws and column mounting bracket bolts.

12. Install the steering column trim shrouds and column covers.

13. Install the nuts and bolts attaching the flexible coupling to the bottom of the steering column. Install the safety strap and bolt, if equipped.

14. If removed, install the sound insulator panels.

15. If column repairs were made, install the steering wheel.

NOTE: Some vehicles equipped with tilt steering columns may experience a squeaking noise when turning the steering wheel in a tilted position. This can be caused by insufficient grease in the tilting mechanism.

16. Disconnect the negative battery cable.

Power Steering Rack

REMOVAL & INSTALLATION

1. Disconnect the negative battery cable. Remove the air cleaner.

2. Raise and safely support the vehicle.

3. Remove both front wheel assemblies.

4. Remove the intermediate shaft lower pinch bolt at the steering gear. Remove the intermediate shaft from the stub shaft.

5. Disconnect the electrical lead at the power steering idle switch.

6. Separate the tie rod ends from

the knuckle assembly. Remove the rear sub-frame mounting bolts and lower the rear of the sub-frame approximately 4 in.

7. Remove the steering rack heat shield. Disconnect the pressure lines at the steering gear.

8. Remove the rack and pinion mounting bolts, remove the rack and pinion assembly through the left wheel opening.

To install:

9. Install the rack and pinion assembly through the left wheel opening. Tighten the mounting bolts to 59 ft. lbs. (80 Nm). Connect the pressure lines, tighten the fittings to 20 ft. lbs. (27 Nm).

10. Install the rack heat shield, tighten the retaining bolts to 53 inch lbs. (6 Nm). Attach the tie rod ends to the steering knuckle.

11. Connect the electrical lead to the power steering idle switch. Attach the intermediate shaft to the stub shaft, tighten the pinch bolt to 35 ft. lbs. (47 Nm).

12. Install both wheel assemblies. Lower the vehicle.

13. Install the air cleaner. Connect the negative battery cable. Fill and bleed the power steering system.

Power Steering Pump

REMOVAL & INSTALLATION

1. Disconnect the negative battery cable.

2. If equipped with V-belt, loosen the adjusting bolt and pivot bolt on the pump. Remove the pump drive belt.

3. Remove the 3 pump-to-bracket bolts and remove the adjusting bolt.

4. Remove the high pressure fitting from the pump.

5. Disconnect the reservoir-to-pump hose from the pump.

6. Remove the pump.

To install:

7. Install the pump.

8. Connect the reservoir-to-pump hose to the pump.

9. Install the high pressure fitting to the pump.

10. Install the adjusting bolt and the 3 pump-to-bracket bolts.

11. Install the drive belt. If equipped with V-belt, adjust belt tension and tighten the adjusting bolt and pivot bolt on the pump. Remove the pump drive belt.

12. Disconnect the negative battery cable.

13. Bleed the system.

BELT ADJUSTMENT

1. Loosen the adjustment nut and bolt in the slotted bracket. Slightly loosen the pivot bolt.

2. Pull the component outward to increase tension. Push inward to reduce tension. Tighten the adjusting nut, bolt and the pivot bolt.

3. Recheck the drive belt tension: it should be 135 lbs. on a new belt or 75 lbs. on a used belt. Readjust if necessary.

NOTE: On a serpentine belt the correct tension is indicated on the indicator mark of the belt tensioner. If the indicator mark is not within specification, replace the belt or tensioner.

SYSTEM BLEEDING

1. Raise the front of the vehicle and support safely.

2. With the wheels turned all the way to the left, add power steering fluid to the **COLD** mark on the fluid level indicator.

3. Start the engine and check the fluid level at fast idle. Add fluid, if necessary, to bring the level up to the **COLD** mark.

4. Bleed air from the system by turning the wheels from side-to-side without hitting the stops. Keep the fluid level just above the internal pump casting or at the **COLD** mark.

5. Return the wheels to the center position and continue running the engine for 2–3 minutes.

6. Road test the vehicle to check steering function and recheck the fluid level with the system at its normal operating temperature. Fluid should be at the **HOT** mark.

Tie Rod Ends

REMOVAL & INSTALLATION

1. Loosen both pinch bolts at the outer tie rod.

2. Remove the tie rod end from the strut assembly using a suitable removal tool.

3. Unscrew the outer tie rod end from the tie rod adjuster, counting the number of turns required before they are disconnected.

To install:

4. Install the new tie rod end, screwing it on the same number of turns as counted in Step 3.

5. When the tie rod end is installed, the tie rod adjuster must be centered between the tie rod and the tie rod end, with an equal number of threads exposed on both sides of the adjuster nut. Tighten the pinch bolts to 20 ft. lbs. (27 Nm).

6. Install the tie rod end to the strut assembly and tighten to 50 ft. lbs. (68 Nm). If the cotter pin cannot be installed, tighten the nut up to $1/16$ in.

further. Never back off the nut to align the holes for the cotter pin.

7. Check front end alignment.

BRAKES

Master Cylinder

REMOVAL & INSTALLATION

1. Disconnect the electrical connector from the master cylinder.

2. Place a container under the master cylinder to catch the brake fluid. Disconnect the brake tubes from the master cylinder; use a flare nut wrench if one is available. Plug the ends of the tubes.

NOTE: Brake fluid eats paint. Wipe up any spilled fluid immediately and flush the area with clear water.

3. Remove the 2 nuts attaching the master cylinder to the booster or firewall.

To install:

4. Attach the master cylinder to the booster with the nuts. Tighten to 22–30 ft. lbs. (30–41 Nm).

5. Remove the tape from the lines and connect to the master cylinder. Tighten to 10–15 ft. lbs. (14–20 Nm). Connect the electrical lead.

6. Bleed the brakes.

NOTE: When installing a master cylinder that mounts on an angle, attempts to bleed the system, with the cylinder installed, can allow air to enter the system. To remove air, it is necessary to raise the rear of the vehicle until the master cylinder bore is level.

Proportioning Valve

REMOVAL & INSTALLATION

There is a front and a rear proportioning valve located at the lower left side of the master cylinder.

1. Disconnect the brake lines from the valves. Disconnect the valves from the master cylinder and remove the O-rings.

2. Replace the old O-rings and proportioning valves with new ones and reinstall into the master cylinder.

3. Tighten the proportioning valves to 18–30 ft. lbs. (24–41 Nm).

Power Brake Booster

REMOVAL & INSTALLATION

1. Remove the master cylinder from the booster and set the master cylinder aside. It is not necessary to disconnect the lines from the master cylinder.

2. Disconnect the vacuum booster pushrod from the brake pedal inside the vehicle. It is retained by a bolt. A spring washer is under the bolt head and a flat washer goes on the other side of the pushrod eye, next to the pedal arm.

3. Remove the 4 attaching nuts from inside the vehicle. Remove the booster.

To install:

4. Install the booster on the firewall. Tighten the mounting nuts to 22–33 ft. lbs. (30–45 Nm).

5. Connect the pushrod to the brake pedal.

6. Install the master cylinder. Mounting torque is 22–33 ft. lbs. (30–45 Nm).

Brake Caliper

REMOVAL & INSTALLATION

1. Remove ⅔ of the brake fluid from the master cylinder.

2. Raise and safely support the vehicle.

3. Remove the wheel and tire and reinstall 2 nuts to retain the rotor.

4. Position a 12 inch adjustable pliers over the inboard brake shoe tab and inboard caliper housing to bottom the piston in the caliper bore. This provides clearance between the linings and rotor.

5. Remove the bolt attaching the inlet fitting, only if the caliper is to be removed from the vehicle for replacement or overhaul. Plug the fittings. If only shoe and linings are being replaced, proceed to next step.

6. Remove the boots, mounting bolts and sleeve assemblies.

7. Remove the caliper from the rotor and mounting bracket.

8. If only the shoe and linings are being replaced, suspend the caliper with a wire hook from the strut.

To install:

9. Liberally fill both cavities in the housing between the bushings with silicone grease.

10. Install the caliper over the rotor in the mounting bracket.

11. Install the mounting bolt and sleeve assemblies and tighten to 38 ft. lbs. (52 Nm).

12. Install the inlet fitting, if removed, and tighten to 33 ft. lbs. (45 Nm).

13. Remove the wheel nuts securing the rotor to the hub.

14. Install the wheel and tire, lower the vehicle and fill the master cylinder.

15. Bleed the system if the caliper inlet fitting was removed and recheck fluid level.

Disc Brake Pads

REMOVAL & INSTALLATION

1. Raise and safely support the vehicle.

2. Remove the wheel and tire assemblies.

3. Remove the caliper bolts.

4. Pivot the caliper off the rotor and suspend with a wire hook from the strut.

5. Remove the brake pads.

6. Remove the bushings from the mounting bolt holes.

To install:

7. Lubricate the bushings with silicone grease and install the bushings into the mounting bolt holes.

8. Install the inboard shoe into the caliper and snap the retaining spring into position. The shoe must lay flat against the piston. If it does not, use a large pair of pliers to compress the piston.

9. Install the outboard shoe with the wear sensor at the leading edge of the shoe.

10. Install the caliper onto the rotor. Tighten the mounting bolts to 38 ft. lbs. (52 Nm).

11. Apply the brake 3 times with approximately 175 lbs. (778 N) of force, this will seat the linings.

12. Clinch the outboard shoe retaining tabs using a small prybar to bend the tabs.

13. The outboard shoe should be locked in a fixed position.

14. Install the tire and wheel assemblies and lower the vehicle.

Brake Rotor

REMOVAL & INSTALLATION

1. Raise and safely support the vehicle.

2. Remove the wheel and tire assemblies.

3. Remove the caliper.

4. Pivot the caliper off the rotor and suspend with a wire hook from the strut.

5. Remove the rotor.

To install:

6. Reposition the rotor and install the caliper onto the rotor. Tighten the mounting bolts to 38 ft. lbs. (52 Nm).

7. Install the tire and wheel assemblies and lower the vehicle.

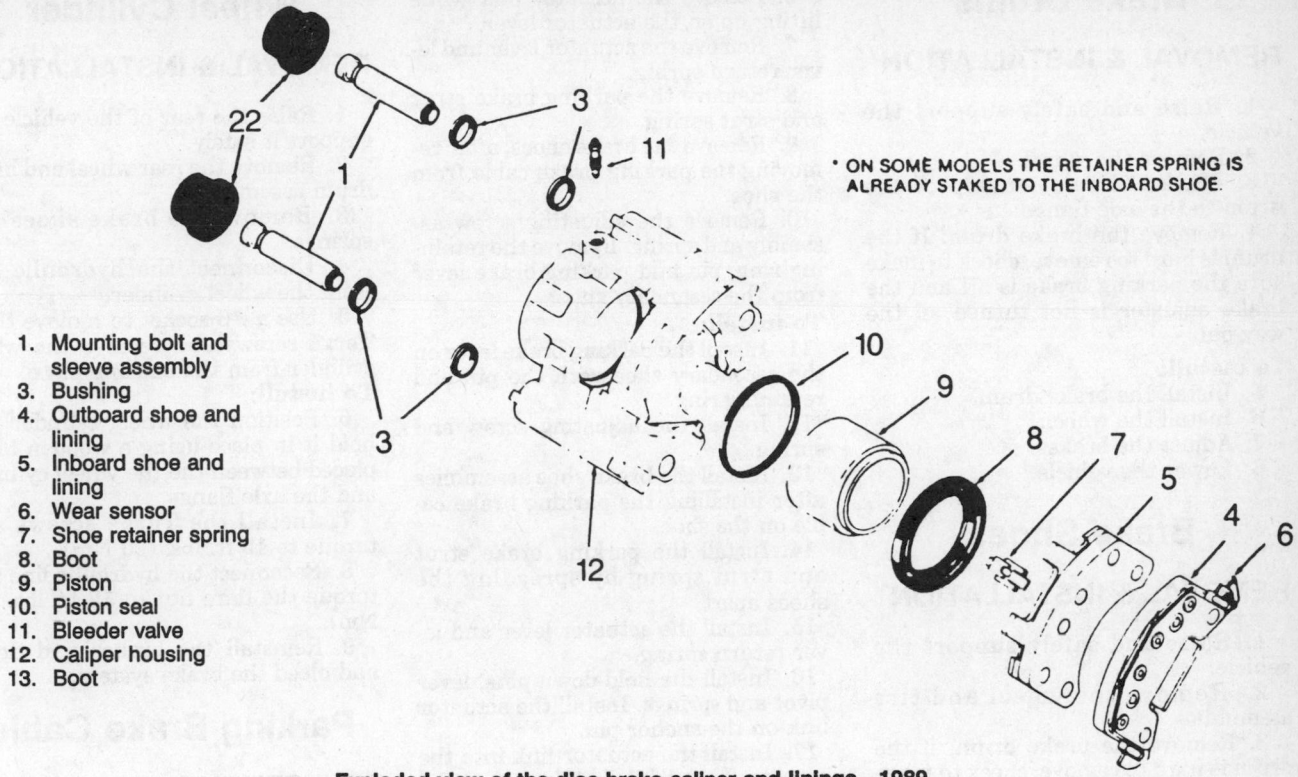

1. Mounting bolt and sleeve assembly
3. Bushing
4. Outboard shoe and lining
5. Inboard shoe and lining
6. Wear sensor
7. Shoe retainer spring
8. Boot
9. Piston
10. Piston seal
11. Bleeder valve
12. Caliper housing
13. Boot

* ON SOME MODELS THE RETAINER SPRING IS ALREADY STAKED TO THE INBOARD SHOE.

Exploded view of the disc brake caliper and linings—1989

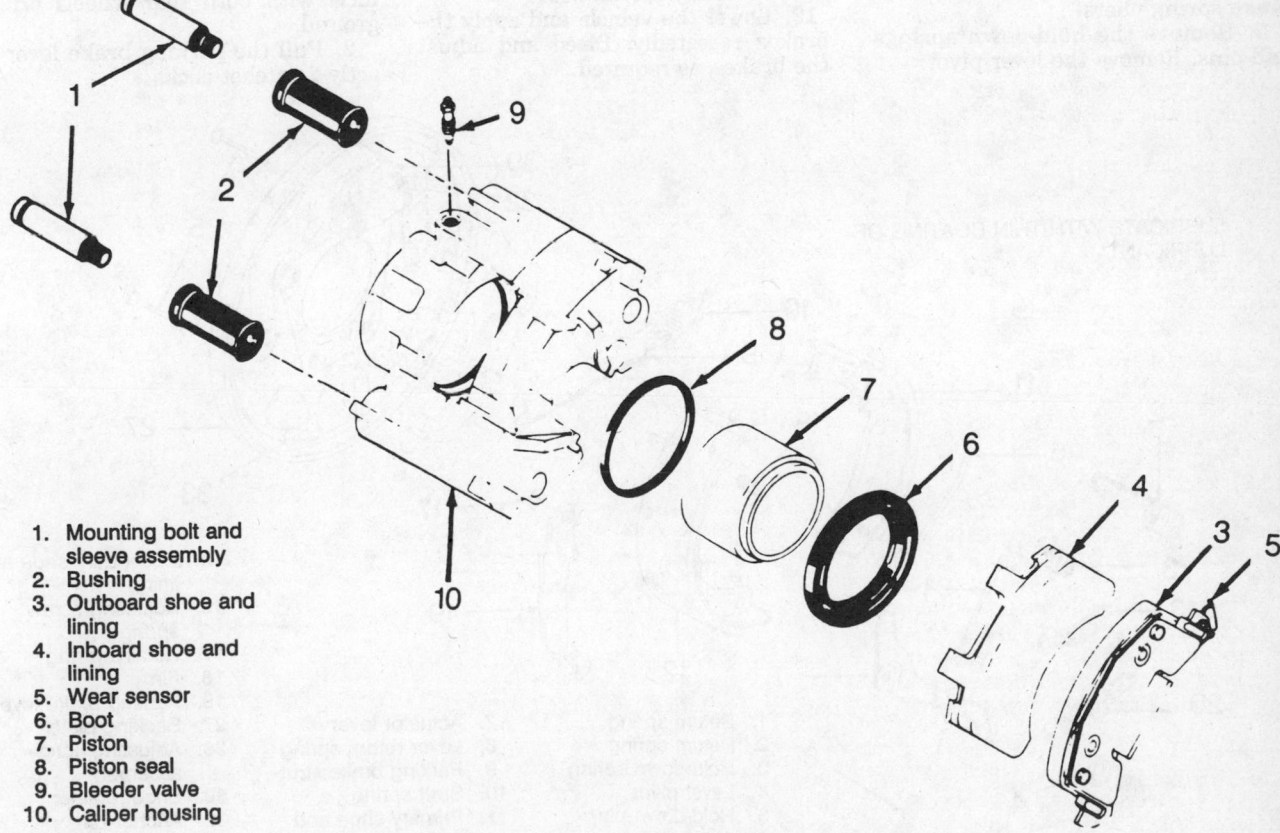

1. Mounting bolt and sleeve assembly
2. Bushing
3. Outboard shoe and lining
4. Inboard shoe and lining
5. Wear sensor
6. Boot
7. Piston
8. Piston seal
9. Bleeder valve
10. Caliper housing

Exploded view of the disc brake caliper and linings—1990–93

Brake Drums

REMOVAL & INSTALLATION

1. Raise and safely support the vehicle.
2. Remove the wheel.
3. Mark the relationship of the drum to the axle flange.
4. Remove the brake drum. If the drum is hard to remove, check to make sure the parking brake is off and the brake adjuster is not turned all the way out.

To install:

5. Install the brake drum.
6. Install the wheel.
7. Adjust the brakes.
8. Lower the vehicle.

Brake Shoes

REMOVAL & INSTALLATION

1. Raise and safely support the vehicle.
2. Remove the wheel and tire assemblies.
3. Remove the brake drum, if the drum is hard to remove, check to make sure the parking brake is off and the brake adjuster is not turned all the way out.
4. Remove the return springs, using brake spring pliers.
5. Remove the hold-down springs and pins. Remove the lever pivot.

6. Remove the actuator link while lifting up on the actuator lever.
7. Remove the actuator lever and lever return spring.
8. Remove the parking brake strut and strut spring.
9. Remove the brake shoes, after removing the parking brake cable from the shoe.
10. Remove the adjusting screw assembly and spring. Remove the retaining ring, pin and parking brake lever from the secondary shoe.

To install:

11. Install the parking brake lever on the secondary shoe with the pin and retaining ring.
12. Install the adjusting screw and spring.
13. Install the brake shoe assemblies after installing the parking brake cable on the shoe.
14. Install the parking brake strut and strut spring by spreading the shoes apart.
15. Install the actuator lever and lever return spring.
16. Install the hold-down pins, lever pivot and springs. Install the actuator link on the anchor pin.
17. Install the actuator link into the actuator lever while holding up on the lever.
18. Install the shoe return springs. Install the brake drum. Install the wheel and tire assemblies.
19. Lower the vehicle and apply the brakes repeatedly. Bleed and adjust the brakes, as required.

Wheel Cylinder

REMOVAL & INSTALLATION

1. Raise the rear of the vehicle and support it safely.
2. Remove the rear wheel and brake drum assembly.
3. Remove the brake shoes and springs.
4. Disconnect the hydraulic line from the wheel cylinder.
5. Use a #6 socket to remove the 2 Torx® screws and remove the wheel cylinder from the backing plate.

To install:

6. Position the wheel cylinder and hold it in place using a wooden block placed between the the wheel cylinder and the axle flange.
7. Install the Torx® screws and torque to 15 ft. lbs. (20 Nm).
8. Reconnect the hydraulic line and torque the flare nut to 12 ft. lbs. (16 Nm).
9. Reinstall the brakes and drum and bleed the brake system.

Parking Brake Cable

ADJUSTMENT

1. Disconnect the negative battery cable. Raise and safely support the vehicle with both rear wheels off the ground.
2. Pull the parking brake lever exactly 2 ratchet clicks.

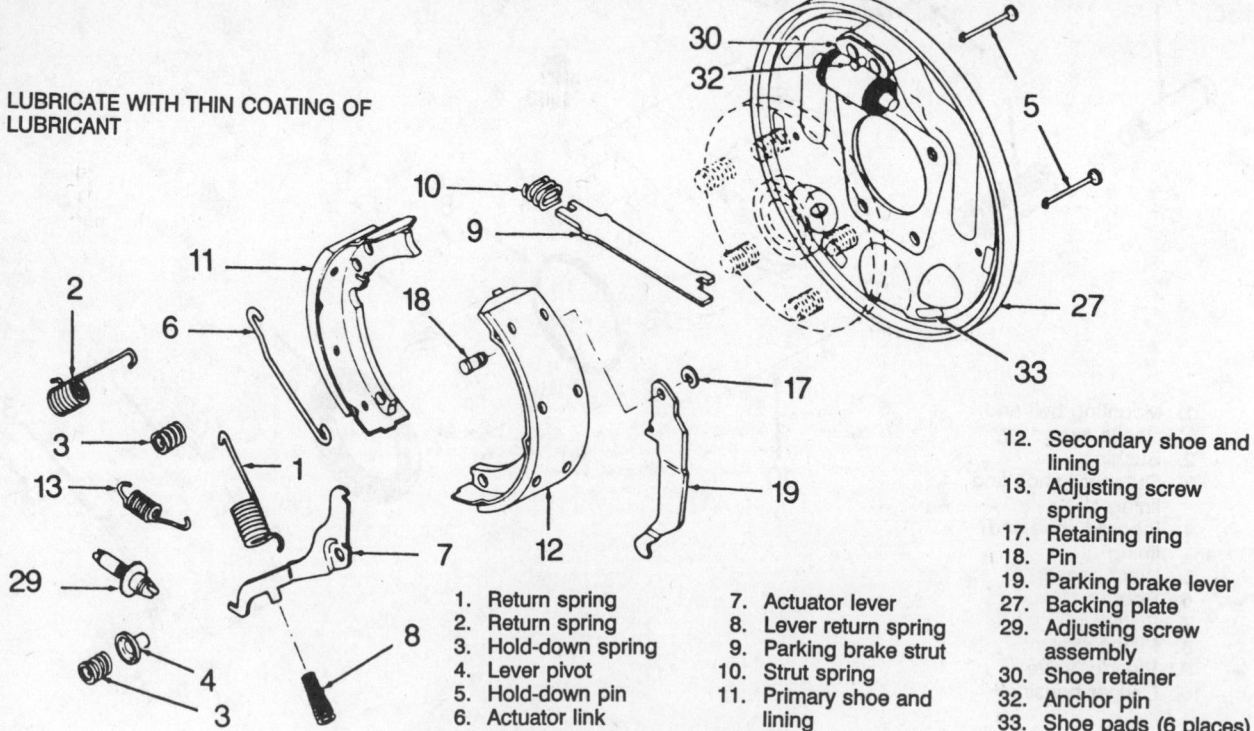

LUBRICATE WITH THIN COATING OF LUBRICANT

1. Return spring	7. Actuator lever
2. Return spring	8. Lever return spring
3. Hold-down spring	9. Parking brake strut
4. Lever pivot	10. Strut spring
5. Hold-down pin	11. Primary shoe and
6. Actuator link	lining

12. Secondary shoe and lining
13. Adjusting screw spring
17. Retaining ring
18. Pin
19. Parking brake lever
27. Backing plate
29. Adjusting screw assembly
30. Shoe retainer
32. Anchor pin
33. Shoe pads (6 places)

Exploded view of the drum brakes

NOTE: To prevent damage to the threaded adjusting rod, thoroughly clean and lubricate the threads before turning the adjusting nut.

3. Loosen the equalizer locknut and tighten the adjusting nut until the left rear wheel can just be turned backward using 2 hands but is locked in forward rotation.
4. Tighten the locknut.
5. Release the parking brake. Rotate the rear wheels, there should be no drag.
6. Lower the vehicle.

REMOVAL & INSTALLATION

Front

1. Place the gear selector in **N** and apply the parking brake.
2. Remove the center console.
3. Disconnect the parking brake cable from the lever.
4. Remove the cable retaining nut and the bracket securing the front cable to the floor panel.
5. Raise the vehicle and loosen the equalizer nut.
6. Loosen the catalytic converter shield and remove the parking brake cable from the body.
7. Disconnect the cable from the equalizer and remove the cable from the guide and the underbody clips.

To install:

8. Install the cable to the guide and the underbody clips and connect the cable to the equalizer.

9. Install the parking brake cable to the body tighten the catalytic converter shield.
10. Tighten the equalizer nut. Lower the vehicle.
11. Install the cable retaining nut and the bracket securing the front cable to the floor panel.
12. Connect the parking brake cable to the lever.
13. Install the center console.
14. Place the gear selector in **N** and apply the parking brake.
15. Adjust the parking brake.
16. Lower the vehicle.
17. Connect the negative battery cable.

Rear

1. Raise and safely support the rear of the vehicle.
2. Back off the equalizer nut until the cable tension is eliminated.
3. Remove the wheel assembly and brake drums.
4. Insert a small prybar or equivalent, between the brake shoe and the top part of the brake adjuster bracket. Push the bracket to the front and release the top brake adjuster rod.
5. Remove the rear hold-down spring. Remove the actuator lever and the lever return spring.
6. Remove the adjuster screw spring.
7. Remove the top rear brake shoe return spring.
8. Unhook the parking brake cable from the parking brake lever.
9. Depress the conduit fitting re-

taining tangs and remove the conduit fitting from the backing plate.
10. Remove the cable end button from the connector.
11. Depress the conduit fitting retaining tangs and remove the conduit fitting from the axle bracket.

To install:

12. Install the conduit fitting to the axle bracket.
13. Install the cable end button to the connector.
14. Install the conduit fitting to the backing plate.
15. Hook the parking brake cable to the parking brake lever.
16. Install the top rear brake shoe return spring.
17. Install the adjuster screw spring.
18. Install the actuator lever and the lever return spring. Install the rear hold-down spring.
19. Connect the top brake adjuster rod.
20. Install the wheel assembly and brake drums.
21. Adjust the parking brake.
22. Lower the vehicle.

Brake System Bleeding

The brake system must be bled when any brake line is disconnected or there is air in the system.

NOTE: Never bleed a wheel cylinder when a drum is removed.

9. Nut (21 ft. lbs.)
10. Equalizer
11. Adjuster nut
12. Retainer
13. Clevis
14. Parking brake cable

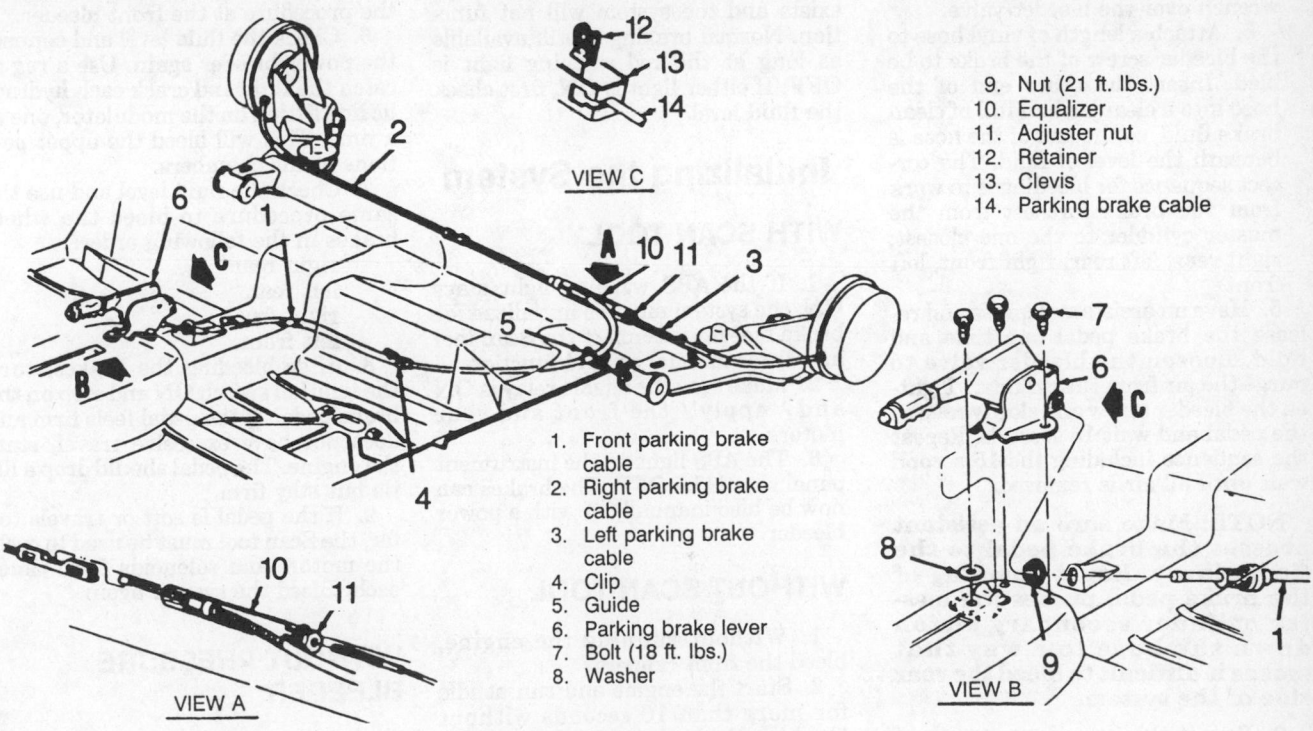

1. Front parking brake cable
2. Right parking brake cable
3. Left parking brake cable
4. Clip
5. Guide
6. Parking brake lever
7. Bolt (18 ft. lbs.)
8. Washer

Parking brake lever and cables

1. Clean the master cylinder of excess dirt and remove the cylinder cover and the diaphragm.

2. Fill the master cylinder to the proper level. Check the fluid level periodically during the bleeding process and replenish it, as necessary. Do not allow the master cylinder fall below ½ full.

3. If the master cylinder is suspected or known to have air in the bore, bleed it before any wheel cylinder or caliper as follows:

a. Disconnect the forward brake line connection at the master cylinder.

b. Allow brake fluid to fill the master cylinder bore until it begins to flow from the forward line connector port.

c. Connect the forward brake line to the master cylinder and tighten.

d. Have a helper depress the brake pedal slowly, one at a time, and hold. Loosen the forward brake line connection at the master cylinder to purge the air from the bore. Tighten the connection and have a helper release the brake pedal slowly. Wait 15 seconds and repeat the sequence. Repeat the sequence including the 15 second wait until all air is removed from the bore.

e. After all air is removed at the forward connection, repeat the above procedure for the rear connection at the master cylinder.

4. Bleed the individual wheel cylinders or calipers only after all air is removed from the master cylinder.

a. Attach the proper size box end wrench over the bleeder valve.

b. Attach a length of vinyl hose to the bleeder screw of the brake to be bled. Insert the other end of the hose into a clear jar half full of clean brake fluid, so the end of the hose is beneath the level of fluid. The correct sequence for bleeding is to work from the brake farthest from the master cylinder to the one closest; right rear, left rear, right front, left front.

5. Have an assistant depress and release the brake pedal one time and hold. Loosen the bleeder valve to purge the air from the cylinder. Tighten the bleeder screw and slowly release the pedal and wait 15 seconds. Repeat the sequence including the 15 second wait until all air is removed.

NOTE: Make sure an assistant presses the brake pedal to the floor slowly. Rapid pumping of the brake pedal pushes the master cylinder secondary piston down the bore in a way that makes it difficult to bleed the rear side of the system.

6. Repeat this procedure at each of the brakes. Remember to check the master cylinder level occasionally. Use only fresh fluid to refill the master cylinder, not the stuff bled from the system.

7. When the bleeding process is complete, refill the master cylinder, install its cover and diaphragm and discard the fluid bled from the brake system.

Anti-Lock Brake System Service

Beginning with the 1992 models, ABS-VI is available on Cavalier and Sunbird. When activated, the system minimumizes the chances of wheel lock-up by reducing hydraulic pressure to one or both front calipers and/or to both rear wheel cylinders as a pair. This is done by moving displacement pistons up or down to operate check valves in the modulator assembly. When the pistons are all the way up, the check valves are open and the system operates in normal braking mode. The pistons are operated by 3 motors and a gear train, all housed in the modulator assembly. This system does not include a hydraulic pump or high pressure chamber. It cannot increase hydraulic pressure above master cylinder pressure or apply the brakes by itself.

If the amber ABS warning light on the instrument panel is flashing while driving, ABS operation may still be possible but the system requires service. If the light stays **ON**, a problem exists and the system will not function. Normal braking is still available as long as the red warning light is **OFF**. If either light is **ON**, first check the fluid level.

Initializing the System

WITH SCAN TOOL

1. If the ABS warning light stays **ON**, the system must be initialized for brake bleeding. Connect the Scan tool and enter manual control function.

2. Make sure the enable relay is **ON** and "apply" the front and rear motors.

3. The ABS light on the instrument panel should be **OFF**. The brakes can now be bled manually or with a power bleeder.

WITHOUT SCAN TOOL

1. Without running the engine, bleed the front calipers.

2. Start the engine and run at idle for more than 10 seconds without touching the brake pedal.

3. If the ABS warning light turns **OFF**, the system is initialized. Bleed the entire system according to procedure. If the ABS warning light stays **ON**, there is another problem with the system that requires the help of diagnostic equipment.

Brake System Bleeding

NOTE: Bleeding the master cylinder/modulator requires initializing the system, setting the displacement pistons to the top of the modulator cylinders. If there is a problem with the system and the ABS warning light stays ON, the system cannot be bled.

WITH PRESSURE BLEEDER

1. Initialize the ABS modulator pistons and check the fluid level in the reservoir.

2. Connect a diaphragm type pressure bleeder and pressurize the system to 5–10 psi. (35–70 kPa) to check for leaks.

3. Increase the pressure to 30–35 psi. (205–240 kPa) and connect a clear tube to the rear modulator bleeder. Put the other end of the tube into a container of clean brake fluid.

4. Slowly open the bleeder. When no air is seen in the fluid flow, close the bleeder.

5. Check the fluid level and repeat the procedure at the front bleeder.

6. Check the fluid level and connect the power bleeder again. Use a rag to catch the fluid and crack each hydraulic line fitting on the modulator, one at a time. This will bleed the upper portions of the chambers.

7. Check the fluid level and use the same procedure to bleed the wheel brakes in the following order:
   right rear
   left rear
   right front
   left front

8. After bleeding the brakes, turn the ignition switch **ON** and step on the brake pedal. If the pedal feels firm and does not have excessive travel, start the engine. The pedal should drop a little but stay firm.

9. If the pedal is soft or travels too far, the Scan tool must be used to cycle the motors and solenoids 5–10 times each. Bleed the system again.

WITHOUT PRESSURE BLEEDER

1. Initialize the ABS modulator pis-

1. Right front wheel speed sensor
2. Engine compartment sensor wiring harness
3. Master cylinder
4. ABS relay
5. Electronic Brake Control Module (EBCM)
6. Body extension wiring harness
7. Rear body pass-through connector
8. Right rear wheel speed sensor
9. Rear axle wiring harness
10. Left rear wheel speed sensor
11. Body connector
12. Instrument panel wiring harness
13. Lamp driver module
14. Bulkhead connector
15. ABS motor/EMB connector
16. Engine compartment sensor wiring harness
17. Left front wheel speed sensor
18. ABS hydraulic modulator assembly
19. Isolation solenoids

Schematic of ABS VI available on 1992–93 models

tons and check the fluid level in the reservoir.

2. Connect a clear tube to the rear modulator bleeder. Put the other end of the tube into a container of clean brake fluid.

3. Open the bleeder and slowly press the brake pedal, then close the bleeder. Repeat until there is no air at the rear bleeder.

4. Check the fluid level and repeat the procedure at the front bleeder.

5. Check the fluid level. Place a rag to catch the fluid and crack each hydraulic line fitting on the modulator, one at a time, while pressing the pedal. This will bleed the upper portions of the chambers.

6. Check the fluid level and use the tube to bleed the wheel brakes in the following order:
   right rear
   left rear
   right front
   left front

7. After bleeding the brakes, turn the ignition switch **ON** and step on the brake pedal. If the pedal feels firm and does not have excessive travel, start the engine. The pedal should drop a little but stay firm.

8. If the pedal is soft or travels too far, the Scan tool must be used to cycle the motors and solenoids 5–10 times each. Bleed the system again.

Fluid Level Sensor

The sensor is mounted low on the left side of the reservoir and can be removed with needle-nose pliers

Front Wheel Speed Sensors

REMOVAL & INSTALLATION

1. The sensor is mounted to the steering knuckle. Disconnect the wiring from the sensor.

2. Remove the bolt to remove the sensor. If the locating pin on the sensor will not pull out of the locating hole easily, remove the brake rotor and carefully tap it out with a punch.

3. When installing the sensor, make sure the locating pin hole is clean and the sensor fits flush against the steering knuckle. Do not enlarge the pin hole.

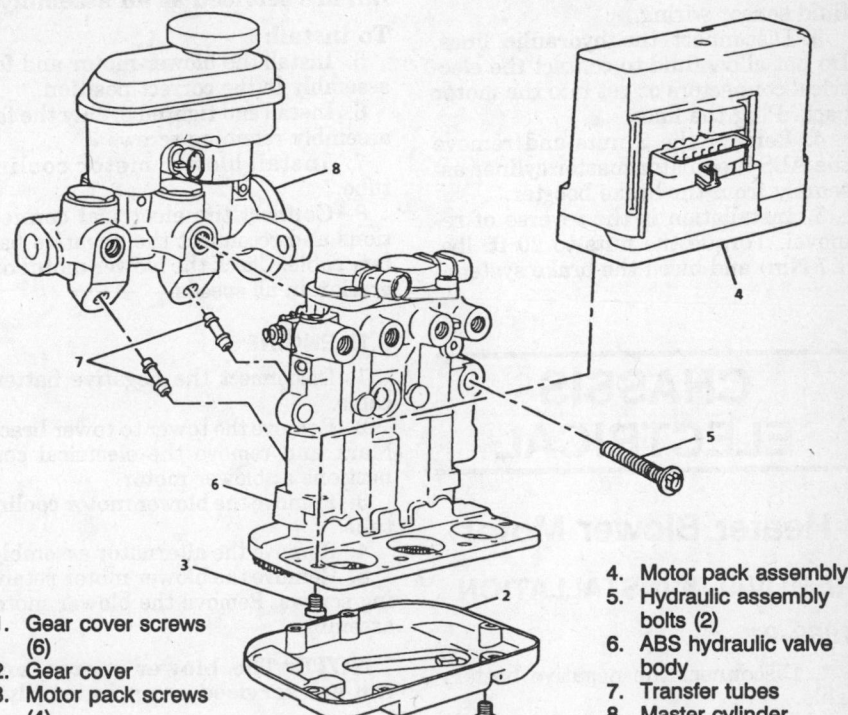

1. Gear cover screws (6)
2. Gear cover
3. Motor pack screws (4)
4. Motor pack assembly
5. Hydraulic assembly bolts (2)
6. ABS hydraulic valve body
7. Transfer tubes
8. Master cylinder

ABS hydraulic modulator and master cylinder assembly

Rear Wheel Speed Sensor

REMOVAL & INSTALLATION

1. The sensor, rear wheel hub and bearing are all a single assembly. Raise and safely support the vehicle and remove the rear wheel.
2. Remove the brake drum.
3. Remove the nuts and bolts to remove the rear hub assembly. The top bolt will not quite clear the brake shoe until the assembly is partially out.
4. Unplug the sensor connector. The backing plate is now held in place only by the metal brake line. Be careful not to damage the brake line.
5. Installation is the reverse of removal. Torque the bolts to 37 ft. lbs. (50 Nm).

ABS Modulator and Master Cylinder

REMOVAL & INSTALLATION

NOTE: There may be hydraulic pressure in the modulator due to gear tension in the system. Connect a Tech 1 Scan tool or equivalent and perform the gear tension relief procedure before disconnecting any hydraulic lines.

1. Relieve the gear system pressure in the modulator assembly.
2. Disconnect the modulator and fluid sensor wiring.
3. Disconnect the hydraulic lines. Do not allow fluid to contact the electrical connectors or get into the motor pack. Plug the lines.
4. Remove the 2 nuts and remove the ABS modulator/master cyliner assembly from the brake booster.
5. Installation is the reverse of removal. Torque the nuts to 20 ft. lbs. (27 Nm) and bleed the brake system.

CHASSIS ELECTRICAL

Heater Blower Motor

REMOVAL & INSTALLATION

1989–91

1. Disconnect the negative battery cable.
2. Disconnect the electrical connections at the blower motor and blower resistor.

NOTE: On the 3.1L engine remove the tower to tower brace assembly.

3. If equipped, remove the plastic water shield from the right side of the cowl.
4. Remove the blower motor retaining screws and remove the blower motor and cage.
5. Hold the blower motor cage and remove retaining nut from the blower motor shaft.
6. Remove the blower motor and cage.

To install:
7. Install the cage on the new motor.
8. Check that the retaining nut is on tight, the motor rotates and the fan cage is not interfering with the motor.
9. Install the motor in the heater assembly, connect the wiring and check the motor operation in all speeds.

1992

2.0L AND 2.2L ENGINES

1. Disconnect the negative battery cable.
2. Mark and remove the electrical connections at blower motor.
3. Remove the blower motor cooling tube.
4. Remove the blower motor retaining screws. Remove the blower motor fan.

NOTE: The blower motor and fan are serviced as an assembly.

To install:
5. Install the blower motor and fan assembly in the correct position.
6. Install and tighten evenly the fan assembly retaining screws.
7. Install blower motor cooling tube.
8. Connect the electrical connections and reconnect the negative battery cable. Check the blower motor operation in all speeds.

3.1L ENGINE

1. Disconnect the negative battery cable.
2. Remove the tower to tower brace. Mark and remove the electrical connections at blower motor.
3. Remove the blower motor cooling tube.
4. Remove the alternator assembly.
5. Remove the blower motor retaining screws. Remove the blower motor assembly.

NOTE: The blower motor and fan are serviced as an assembly.

To install:
5. Install the blower motor and fan assembly in the correct position.

6. Install and tighten evenly the fan assembly retaining screws.
7. Install the alternator assembly. Adjust the drive belt.
8. Install blower motor cooling tube.
9. Connect the electrical connections and install the tower to tower brace.
10. Reconnect the negative battery cable. Check the blower motor operation in all speeds.

Windshield Wiper Motor

REMOVAL & INSTALLATION

1. Disconnect the negative battery cable. Loosen, but do not remove the drive link-to-crank arm attaching nuts to detach the drive link from the motor crank arm.
2. Tag and disconnect all electrical leads from the wiper motor.
3. Unscrew the mounting bolts, rotate the motor up, outward and remove.

To install:
4. Guide the crank arm through the opening in the body and install the mounting bolts. Tighten to 48 inch lbs. (5 Nm).
5. Install the drive link to the crank arm with the motor in the park position.
6. Replace the shroud top vent grille and wiper arms.
7. Connect the negative battery cable.
8. Check the operation of the wiper system.

Windshield Wiper Switch

REMOVAL & INSTALLATION

1989–90

1. Disconnect the negative battery cable.
2. Remove the left side insulator panel. If equipped, remove the lower steering column cover.
3. Remove the steering wheel.
4. Remove the shaft lock cover by prying away from steering column housing.
5. Use lock plate compressor tools J–23653 and J–23653–4 to remove the shaft lock retaining ring. Install the tools to the steering column shaft and tighten the nut until the tool slightly depresses the shaft lock.
6. Remove the shaft lock retaining ring.
7. Remove the shaft lock.

8. Remove the cancelling cam assembly.

9. Remove the upper bearing spring.

10. If equipped with column-mounted dimmer control, remove the switch actuator arm assembly.

11. Disconnect the turn signal switch wiring harness connector at the base of the steering column and remove the wire protector. Remove the turn signal switch.

12. Turn the ignition switch to the **RUN** position and remove the key warning buzzer switch by depressing the tangs on the clip.

13. Remove the lock retaining screw. Remove the lock cylinder.

14. Remove the steering column cover attaching screws and remove the cover.

15. Disconnect the wiper switch electrical connector.

16. Remove the screws attaching the column housing to the mast jacket. Note the position of the dimmer switch actuator rod for reassembly. Remove the screws attaching the dimmer switch.

NOTE: Tilt and travel columns have a removable plastic cover on the column housing, providing access to the wiper switch without removing the entire column housing.

17. Remove the screws attaching the ignition switch.

18. Remove the column housing and switches as an assembly.

19. Remove the wiper switch actuator pin and remove the wiper switch.
To install:

20. Place the switch into the housing and install the pivot pin.

NOTE: Ensure that the bearing retainer, horn contact and upper bearing are positioned properly.

21. Position the housing onto the mast jacket and install the attaching screws.

22. Reconnect lower switch wiring connector. Install the wire protector.

23. Install and adjust the dimmer switch.

24. Install and adjust the ignition switch.

25. Install the lock cylinder.

26. Turn the lock to the **RUN** position and install the key warning buzzer switch, using a paper clip to aid installation.

27. Install the turn signal switch and connect the electrical connector at the base of the steering column.

28. If equipped with column-mounted dimmer control, install the switch actuator arm assembly.

29. Install the upper bearing spring.

30. Install the cancelling cam assembly.

31. Install the shaft lock.

32. Use lock plate compressor tools J–23653 and J–23653–4 to install the shaft lock retaining ring. Install the tools to the steering column shaft and tighten the nut until the tool slightly depresses the shaft lock. Install the shaft lock retaining ring.

33. Install the shaft lock to the steering column housing.

34. Install the steering wheel.

35. If equipped, install the lower steering column cover. Install the left side insulator panel.

36. Connect the negative battery cable.

1991–93
CAVALIER

1. Disconnect the negative battery cable.

2. Remove the steering wheel from the column.

3. Remove the upper steering column cover attaching screws. Remove the upper steering column.

4. Remove the lower steering column attaching screws. Remove the lower steering column cover.

5. Separate the rose bud fastener from the jacket assembly. The fastener is integral to the wire harness.

6. Remove the wash/wipe switch attaching screws.

7. Depress the locking tab and remove the wire harness connector from the wash/wipe switch.
To install:

8. Place the wash/wipe switch into position and connect the electrical connector.

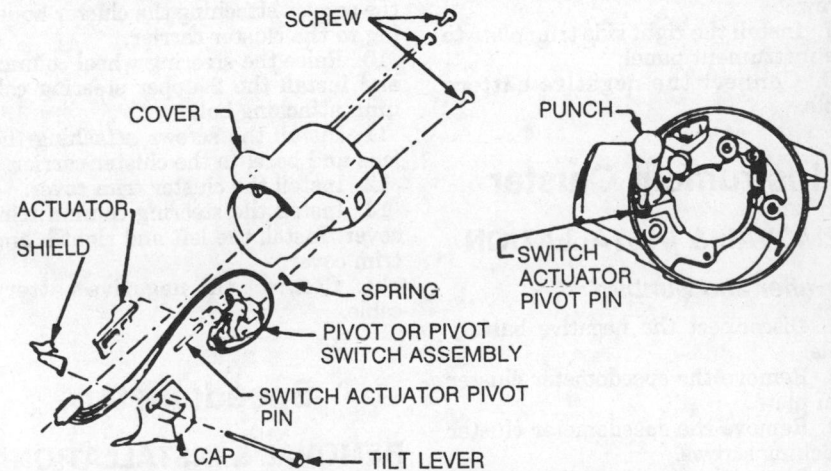

Wiper switch and related parts—adjustable steering column

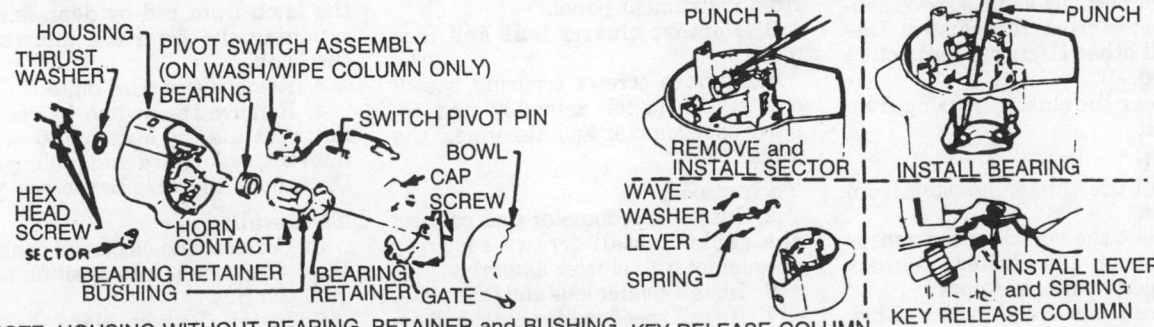

NOTE: HOUSING WITHOUT BEARING RETAINER and BUSHING HAS SPUN-IN BEARING. IF REPAIR IS NECESSARY, COMPLETE HOUSING ASSEMBLY REPLACEMENT IS NECESSARY.

Wiper switch and related parts—standard steering column

9. Install the wash/wipe switch attaching screws.

10. Connect the rose bud fastener to the jacket assembly.

11. Install the lower steering column cover and attaching screws. Tighten to 49 inch lbs. (6 Nm).

12. Install the upper steering column cover and attaching screws. Tighten to 49 inch lbs. (6 Nm).

13. Install the steering wheel onto the steering shaft. Install the hexagonal retaining nut and tighten to 30 ft. lbs. (41 Nm).

14. Connect the negative battery cable.

SUNBIRD

1. Disconnect the negative battery cable.

2. Remove the right side trim plate from the instrument panel.

3. Remove the windshield wiper switch attaching screw.

4. Disconnect the windshield wiper switch electrical connector.

To install:

5. Connect the windshield wiper switch electrical connector.

6. Position the switch on the instrument panel and install the attaching screw.

7. Install the right side trim plate to the instrument panel.

8. Connect the negative battery cable.

Instrument Cluster

REMOVAL & INSTALLATION

Cavalier and Sunbird

1. Disconnect the negative battery cable.

2. Remove the speedometer cluster trim plate.

3. Remove the speedometer cluster attaching screws.

4. Lower the steering column. Pull the cluster away from the instrument panel and disconnect the speedometer cable.

5. Disconnect the vehicle speed sensor connector from the cluster. Disconnect all other electrical connectors as required.

6. Remove the cluster housing from the vehicle.

To install:

7. Install the cluster housing from the vehicle.

8. Connect the vehicle speed sensor connector from the cluster. Connect all other electrical connectors.

9. Connect the speedometer cable. Push the instrument cluster into position on the instrument panel. Raise the steering column.

10. Install the speedometer cluster attaching screws.

11. Install the speedometer cluster trim plate.

12. Connect the negative battery cable.

Skyhawk

1. Disconnect the negative battery cable.

2. Remove the steering column trim cover. Remove the left and right h and trim cover.

3. Remove the cluster trim cover.

4. Remove the screws attaching the lens and bezel to the cluster carrier.

5. Lower the steering wheel column by removing the 2 upper steering column attaching bolts.

6. Remove the screws attaching the cluster housing to the cluster carrier. Pull the cluster out slightly from the instrument panel and disconnect the speedometer cable. Disconnect all others connectors.

7. Remove the cluster housing from the vehicle.

To install:

8. Install the cluster housing.

9. Connect the speedometer cable. Connect all others connectors. Install the screws attaching the cluster housing to the cluster carrier.

10. Raise the steering wheel column and install the 2 upper steering column attaching bolts.

11. Install the screws attaching the lens and bezel to the cluster carrier.

12. Install the cluster trim cover.

13. Install the steering column trim cover. Install the left and right h and trim cover.

14. Connect the negative battery cable.

Speedometer

REMOVAL & INSTALLATION

1. Disconnect the negative battery cable.

2. Remove speedometer cluster from instrument panel.

3. Remove cluster lens and face plate.

4. Remove screws securing speedometer to cluster assembly and remove speedometer and disconnect the cable.

To install:

5. Install speedometer and connect the cable. Install screws securing speedometer to cluster assembly.

6. Install cluster lens and face plate.

7. Install speedometer cluster from instrument panel.

8. Connect the negative battery cable.

Radio

REMOVAL & INSTALLATION

NOTE: Do not operate the radio with the speaker leads disconnected. Operating the radio without an electrical load will damage the output transistors.

1. Disconnect the negative battery cable.

2. Remove the center instrument panel trim plate.

3. Check the right side of the radio to determine whether a nut or a stud is used for side retention.

4. If a nut is used, remove the hush panel and loosen the nut from below, on vehicles without air conditioning. On vehicles with air conditioning, remove the hush panel, air conditioning duct and air conditioning control head for access to the nut. Do not remove the nut; loosen it just enough to pull the radio out. If a rubber stud is used, go to Step 5.

5. Remove the 2 radio bracket-to-instrument panel attaching screws. Pull the radio forward far enough to disconnect and tag the wiring and antenna. Remove the radio.

To install:

6. Connect the wiring and antenna. Place the radio into position and install the attaching screws.

7. If an attaching nut is used, install the nut and hush panel.

8. Install the center instrument panel trim plate.

9. Connect the negative battery cable.

Headlight Switch

REMOVAL & INSTALLATION

1989–90 Base Cavalier

1. Disconnect the negative battery cable.

2. Pull the knob out fully. Remove the knob from rod by depressing the retaining clip from the underside of the knob.

3. Remove the trim plate.

4. Remove the switch by removing nut, rotating the switch 180 degrees, then tilting forward and pulling it out. Disconnect the wire harness.

To install:

5. Connect the electrical connector. Place the switch into position and install the nut.

6. Install the trim plate.

7. Install the knob.

8. Connect the negative battery cable.

1991–93 Base Cavalier, Cavalier RS and Z24

1. Disconnect the negative battery cable.
2. Remove the steering wheel.
3. Remove the cover attaching screws.
4. Remove the upper steering column cover.
5. Remove the lower steering colum cover screws and remove the lower cover.
6. Separate the rose bud fastener (integral to the wire harness) from the jacket assembly.
7. Remove the switch mounting screws and remove the turn signal switch.
8. Depress the locking tabs and disconnect the wire harness connectors from the turn signal switch assembly.

To install:

9. Connect the wire harness connectors to the turn signal switch assembly.
10. Install the switch and install the attaching screws. Tighten to 49 inch lbs. (6 Nm).
11. Connect the rose bud fastener (integral to the wiring harness) to the jacket assembly.
12. Install the lower steering column cover and attaching screws. Tighten to 49 inch lbs. (6 Nm).
13. Install the upper steering column cover and attaching screws. Tighten to 49 inch lbs. (6 Nm).
14. Install the steering wheel on the steering shaft with the hexagon nut. Tighten to 30 ft. lbs. (41 Nm).
15. Connect the negative battery cable.

1989–93 Sunbird
1989–90 Cavalier RS and Z24

1. Disconnect the negative battery cable.
2. Remove the left side trim plate.
3. Remove the attaching screw from the headlight switch housing.
4. Disconnect the headlight switch electrical connector.

To install:

5. Connect the headlight switch electrical connector.
6. Install the headlight switch into the housing.
7. Install the attaching screw.
8. Install the left side trim plate.
9. Connect the negative battery cable.

Skyhawk

1. Disconnect the negative battery cable.
2. Remove the left side trim cover.
3. Remove the screws attaching the headlight switch to the instrument panel.

4. Pull the switch rearward in order to release the locking tabs and remove the switch from the vehicle.

To install:

5. Connect the electrical connector.
6. Place the switch into position and install the attaching screws.
7. Install the left side trim panel.
8. Connect the negative battery cable.

Dimmer Switch

REMOVAL & INSTALLATION

1. Disconnect the negative battery cable. Remove the steering wheel. Remove the trim cover.
2. Remove the turn signal switch assembly.
3. Remove the ignition switch stud and screw. Remove the ignition switch.
4. Remove the dimmer switch actuator rod by sliding it from the switch assembly.
5. Remove the dimmer switch bolts and the dimmer switch.

To install:

6. Install the dimmer switch and attaching bolts.
7. Connect the dimmer switch actuator rod.
8. Adjust the dimmer switch by depressing the switch slightly and inserting a $\frac{3}{32}$ in. drill bit into the adjusting hole. Push the switch up to remove any play and tighten the dimmer switch adjusting screw.
9. Install the turn signal switch assembly.
10. Install the trim cover.
11. Install the steering wheel.
12. Connect the negative battery cable.

Turn Signal Switch

REMOVAL & INSTALLATION

NOTE: Before removing the turn signal switch, be sure the lever is in the OFF or CENTER position.

1. Disconnect the negative battery cable. Remove the steering wheel. Remove the trim cover.
2. Pry the cover from the steering column.
3. Position a U-shaped lockplate compressing tool on the end of the steering shaft nut clockwise. Pry the wire snapring on the shaft groove off.
4. Remove the tool and lift the lockplate off the shaft.
5. Slip the cancelling cam, upper bearing preload spring and thrust washer off the shaft.
6. Remove the turn signal lever.

a. Make sure the switch is in the center or **OFF** position.
b. Pull the lever straight out of the turn signal switch.
c. If equipped with cruise control, attach the connector to mechanic's wire and pull the harness through the column.
7. Remove the hazard flasher button retaining screw and remove the button, spring and knob.
8. Pull the switch connector out of the mast jacket and tape the upper part to facilitate switch removal. Attach a long piece of wire to the turn signal switch connector. When installing the turn signal switch, feed this wire through the column first and then use this wire to pull the switch connector into position. On tilt columns, place the turn signal and shifter housing in **LOW** position and remove the harness cover.
9. Remove the 3 switch mounting

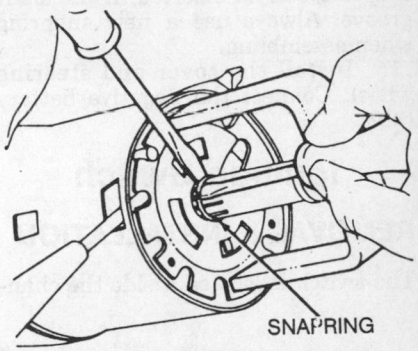

Using the lock plate depressing tool to remove the snapring

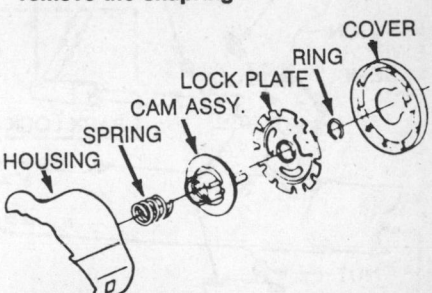

Remove these parts for removal of the turn signal switch

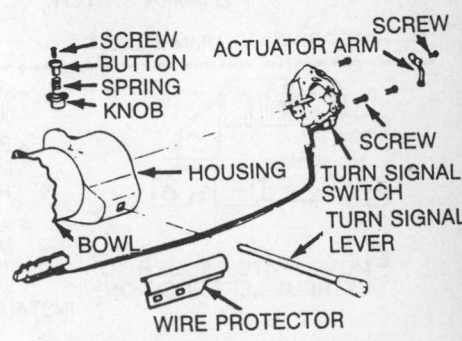

Turn signal switch removal details

screws. Remove the switch by pulling it straight up while guiding the wire harness cover through the column.

To install:

10. Install the replacement switch by working the connector and cover down through the housing and under the bracket. If equipped with tilt steering, the connector is worked down through the housing, under the bracket and then the cover is installed on the harness.

11. Install the switch mounting screws and the connector on the mast jacket bracket. Install the column-to-dash trim plate.

12. Install the flasher knob and turn the signal lever.

13. With the turn signal lever in middle position and the flasher knob out, slide the thrust washer, upper bearing preload spring and cancelling cam onto the shaft.

14. Position the lock plate on the shaft and press it down until a new snapring can be inserted in the shaft groove. Always use a new snapring when assembling.

15. Install the cover and steering wheel. Connect the negative battery cable.

Ignition Switch

REMOVAL & INSTALLATION

The switch is located inside the chan-

nel section of the brake pedal support and is completely inaccessible without first lowering the steering column. The switch is actuated by a rod and rack assembly. A gear on the end of the lock cylinder engages the toothed upper end of the rod.

1. Disconnect the negative battery cable.

2. Lower the steering column; be sure to properly support it.

3. Place the switch in the **OFF-LOCKED** position. With the cylinder removed, the rod is in **OFF-UN-LOCKED** position when it is in the next to the upper most detent.

4. Remove the 2 switch screws and remove the switch assembly.

To install:

5. Prior to installation, move the slider on the switch to the following positions:

    a. Key release columns—Leave the slider to the extreme left.

    b. Park lock columns—Move slider 1 detent to the right in the **OFF-LOCK** position.

    c. All other columns—Move the slider 2 detents to the right in the **OFF-UNLOCKED** position.

6. Install the activating rod into the switch and assemble the switch on the column. Tighten the mounting screws. Use only the specified screws, since over length screws could impair the effectiveness of the column to collapse.

7. Install the steering column.

8. Connect the negative battery cable.

Ignition Lock Cylinder

REMOVAL & INSTALLATION

Standard Steering Column

1. Disconnect the negative battery cable.

2. Remove the steering wheel.

3. Turn the ignition key to the **RUN** position.

4. Remove the lock plate, turn signal or combination switch and the key warning buzzer switch. The warning buzzer switch is pulled out with small tool.

5. Remove the lock cylinder retaining screw and lock cylinder.

NOTE: If the retaining screw is dropped during removal, it could fall into the column, requiring complete column disassembly to retrieve the screw.

To install:

6. Rotate the cylinder clockwise to align the cylinder key with the keyway in the housing.

7. Push the lock all the way in.

8. Install the screw. Tighten to 15 inch lbs. (2 Nm).

9. Install the key warning switch. Turn the lock to **RUN** position and

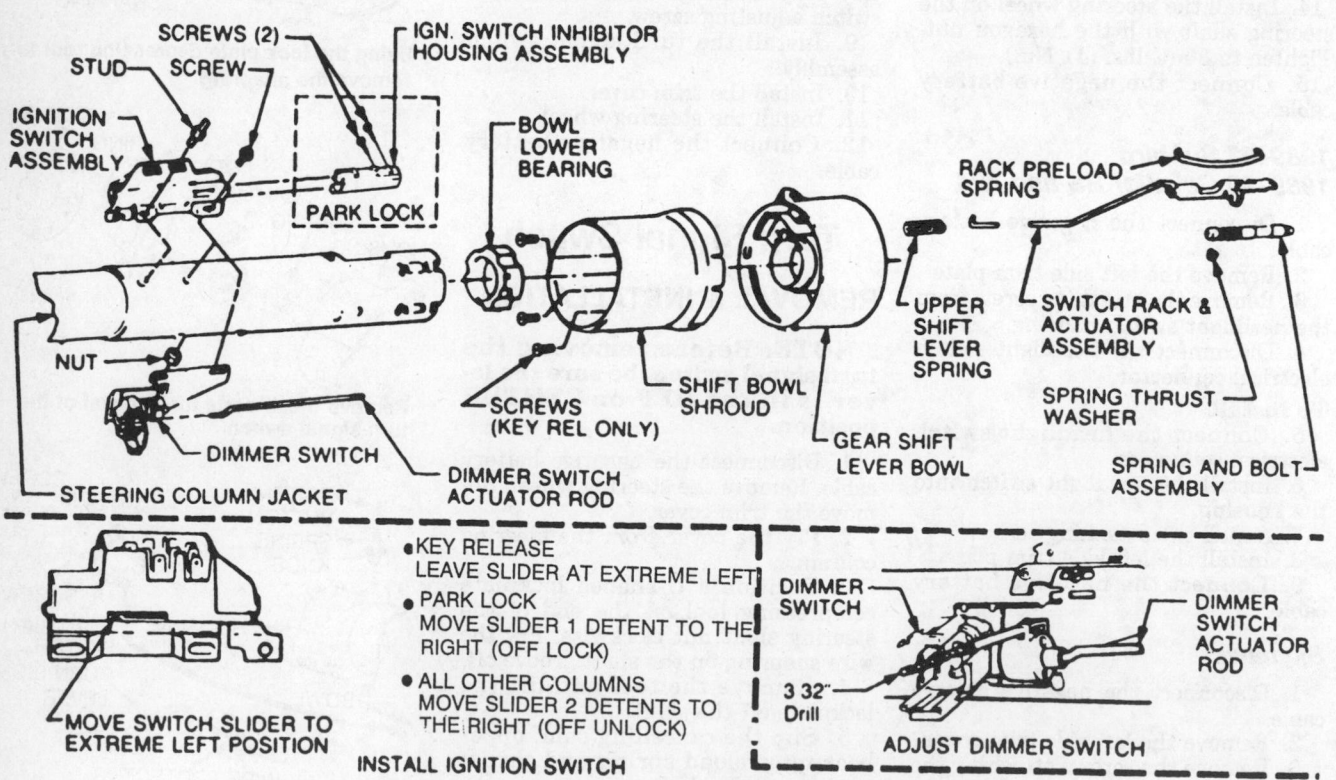

Ignition switch and dimmer switch removal and installation—standard column

GM "N" Body
Front Wheel Drive
BUICK—Skylark   OLDSMOBILE—Achieva • Calais   PONTIAC—Grand Am

YEAR IDENTIFICATION

VEHICLE IDENTIFICATION CHART

It is important for servicing and ordering parts to be certain of the vehicle and engine identification. The VIN (vehicle identification number) is a 17 digit number visible through the windshield on the driver's side of the dash and contains the vehicle and engine identification codes. The tenth digit indicates model year and the eighth digit indicates engine code. It can be interpreted as follows:

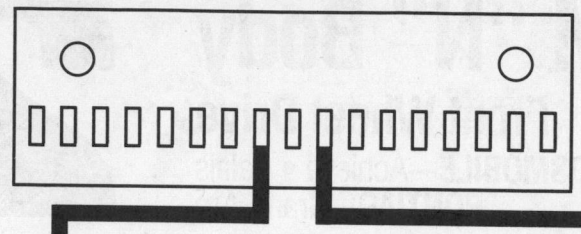

Engine Code					
Code	Liters	Cu. In. (cc)	Cyl.	Fuel Sys.	Eng. Mfg.
M	2.0	122 (2000)	4	Turbo	Pontiac
A	2.3 HO	138 (2262)	4	PFI	Oldsmobile
D	2.3	138 (2262)	4	PFI	Oldsmobile
U	2.5	151 (2475)	4	TBI	Pontiac
N	3.3	204 (3344)	6	PFI	Buick
3	2.3	138 (2262)	4	PFI	Oldsmobile

Model Year	
Code	Year
K	1989
L	1990
M	1991
N	1992
P	1993

HO—High Output
PFI—Port Fuel Injection
TBI—Throttle Body Injection

ENGINE IDENTIFICATION

Year	Model	Engine Displacement Liters (cc)	Engine Series (ID/VIN)	Fuel System	No. of Cylinders	Engine Type
1989	Grand Am	2.0 (2000)	M	Tubo	4	OHC Turbo
	Grand Am	2.3 (2262)	D	PFI	4	DOHC
	Grand Am	2.3 (2262)	A	PFI	4	DOHC-HO
	Grand Am	2.5 (2475)	U	TBI	4	OHV
	Calais	2.3 (2262)	D	PFI	4	DOHC
	Calais	2.3 (2262)	A	PFI	4	DOHC-HO
	Calais	2.5 (2475)	U	TBI	4	OHV
	Calais	3.3 (3344)	N	PFI	6	OHV
	Skylark	2.3 (2262)	D	PFI	4	DOHC
	Skylark	2.5 (2475)	U	TBI	4	OHV
	Skylark	3.3 (3344)	N	PFI	6	OHV
1990	Grand Am	2.3 (2262)	D	PFI	4	DOHC
	Grand Am	2.3 (2262)	A	PFI	4	DOHC-HO
	Grand Am	2.5 (2475)	U	TBI	4	OHV
	Calais	2.3 (2262)	D	PFI	4	DOHC
	Calais	2.3 (2262)	A	PFI	4	DOHC-HO
	Calais	2.5 (2475)	U	TBI	4	OHV
	Calais	3.3 (3344)	N	PFI	6	OHV

ENGINE IDENTIFICATION

Year	Model	Engine Displacement Liters (cc)	Engine Series (ID/VIN)	Fuel System	No. of Cylinders	Engine Type
1990	Skylark	2.3 (2262)	D	PFI	4	DOHC
	Skylark	2.5 (2475)	U	TBI	4	OHV
	Skylark	3.3 (3344)	N	PFI	6	OHV
1991	Grand Am	2.3 (2262)	D	PFI	4	DOHC
	Grand Am	2.3 (2262)	A	PFI	4	DOHC-HO
	Grand Am	2.5 (2475)	U	TBI	4	OHV
	Calais	2.3 (2262)	D	PFI	4	DOHC
	Calais	2.3 (2262)	A	PFI	4	DOHC-HO
	Calais	2.5 (2475)	U	TBI	4	OHV
	Calais	3.3 (3344)	N	PFI	6	OHV
	Skylark	2.3 (2262)	D	PFI	4	DOHC
	Skylark	2.5 (2475)	U	TBI	4	OHV
	Skylark	3.3 (3344)	N	PFI	6	OHV
1992-93	Grand Am	2.3 (2262)	D	PFI	4	DOHC
	Grand Am	2.3 (2262)	A	PFI	4	DOHC-HO
	Grand Am	2.3 (2262)	3	PFI	4	DOHC
	Grand Am	3.3 (3344)	N	PFI	6	OHV
	Achieva	2.3 (2262)	D	PFI	4	DOHC
	Achieva	2.3 (2262)	A	PFI	4	DOHC-HO
	Achieva	2.3 (2262)	3	PFI	4	DOHC
	Achieva	3.3 (3344)	N	PFI	6	OHV
	Skylark	2.3 (2262)	3	PFI	4	DOHC
	Skylark	3.3 (3344)	N	PFI	6	OHV

DOHC—Double Overhead Cam
HO—High Output
OHC—Overhad Cam
OHV—Overhad Valve
PFI—Port Fuel Injection
TBI—Throttle Body Injection

GENERAL ENGINE SPECIFICATIONS

Year	Engine ID/VIN	Engine Displacement Liters (cc)	Fuel System Type	Net Horsepower @ rpm	Net Torque @ rpm (ft. lbs.)	Bore × Stroke (in.)	Compression Ratio	Oil Pressure @ rpm
1989	M	2.0 (2000)	Turbo	167 @ 4500	175 @ 4000	3.40 × 3.40	8.0:1	NA
	A	2.3 (2262)	PFI	180 @ 6200	160 @ 5200	3.62 × 3.35	10.0:1	30 @ 2000
	D	2.3 (2262)	PFI	160 @ 6200	155 @ 5200	3.62 × 3.35	9.5:1	30 @ 2000
	U	2.5 (2475)	TBI	110 @ 5200	135 @ 3200	4.00 × 3.00	8.3:1	37 @ 2000
	N	3.3 (3344)	PFI	160 @ 5200	185 @ 3200	3.70 × 3.16	9.0:1	45 @ 2000
1990	A	2.3 (2262)	PFI	180 @ 6200	160 @ 5200	3.62 × 3.35	10.0:1	30 @ 2000
	D	2.3 (2262)	PFI	160 @ 6200	155 @ 5200	3.62 × 3.35	9.5:1	30 @ 2000
	U	2.5 (2475)	TBI	110 @ 5200	135 @ 3200	4.00 × 3.00	8.3:1	37 @ 2000
	N	3.3 (3344)	PFI	160 @ 5200	185 @ 3200	3.70 × 3.16	9.0:1	45 @ 2000
1991	A	2.3 (2262)	PFI	180 @ 6200	160 @ 5200	3.62 × 3.35	10.0:1	30 @ 2000
	D	2.3 (2262)	PFI	160 @ 6200	155 @ 5200	3.62 × 3.35	9.5:1	30 @ 2000
	U	2.5 (2475)	TBI	110 @ 5200	135 @ 3200	4.00 × 3.00	8.3:1	26 @ 800
	N	3.3 (3344)	PFI	160 @ 5200	185 @ 3200	3.70 × 3.16	9.0:1	60 @ 1850

GENERAL ENGINE SPECIFICATIONS

Year	Engine ID/VIN	Engine Displacement Liters (cc)	Fuel System Type	Net Horsepower @ rpm	Net Torque @ rpm (ft. lbs.)	Bore × Stroke (in.)	Compression Ratio	Oil Pressure @ rpm
1992–93	A	2.3 (2262)	PFI	180 @ 6200	160 @ 5200	3.62 × 3.35	10.0:1	30 @ 2000
	D	2.3 (2262)	PFI	160 @ 6200	155 @ 5200	3.62 × 3.35	9.5:1	30 @ 2000
	3	2.3 (2262)	PFI	120 @ 5200	140 @ 3200	3.62 × 3.35	9.5:1	30 @ 2000
	N	3.3 (3344)	PFI	160 @ 5200	185 @ 2000	3.70 × 3.16	9.0:1	60 @ 1850

NA—Not available
PFI—Port Fuel Injection
TBI—Throttle Body Injection

GASOLINE ENGINE TUNE-UP SPECIFICATIONS

Year	Engine ID/VIN	Engine Displacement Liters (cc)	Spark Plugs Gap (in.)	Ignition Timing (deg.) MT	Ignition Timing (deg.) AT	Fuel Pump (psi)	Idle Speed (rpm) MT	Idle Speed (rpm) AT	Valve Clearance In.	Valve Clearance Ex.
1989	M	2.0 (2000)	0.035	①	①	35–38	④	④	Hyd.	Hyd.
	A	2.3 (2262)	0.035	③	③	②	④	④	Hyd.	Hyd.
	D	2.3 (2262)	0.035	③	③	②	④	④	Hyd.	Hyd.
	U	2.5 (2475)	0.060	③	③	9–13	④	④	Hyd.	Hyd.
	N	3.3 (3344)	0.060	—	①	②	—	④	Hyd.	Hyd.
1990	A	2.3 (2262)	0.035	③	③	②	④	④	Hyd.	Hyd.
	D	2.3 (2262)	0.035	③	③	②	④	④	Hyd.	Hyd.
	U	2.5 (2475)	0.060	③	③	9–13	④	④	Hyd.	Hyd.
	N	3.3 (3344)	0.060	—	③	②	—	④	Hyd.	Hyd.
1991	A	2.3 (2262)	0.035	③	③	②	④	④	Hyd.	Hyd.
	D	2.3 (2262)	0.035	③	③	②	④	④	Hyd.	Hyd.
	U	2.5 (2475)	0.060	③	③	9–13	④	④	Hyd.	Hyd.
	N	3.3 (3344)	0.060	—	③	②	—	④	Hyd.	Hyd.
1992	A	2.3 (2262)	0.035	③	③	②	④	④	Hyd.	Hyd.
	D	2.3 (2262)	0.035	③	③	②	④	④	Hyd.	Hyd.
	3	2.3 (2262)	0.035	③	③	②	④	④	Hyd.	Hyd.
	N	3.3 (3344)	0.060	—	③	②	—	④	Hyd.	Hyd.
1993	SEE UNDERHOOD SPECIFICATIONS STICKER									

NOTE: The lowest cylinder pressure should be within 75% of the highest cylinder pressure reading. For example, if the highest cylinder is 134 psi, the lowest should be 101. Engine should be at normal operating temperature with throttle valve in the wide open position.
The underhood specifications sticker often reflects tune-up specification changes in production. Sticker figures must be used if they disagree with those in this chart.
Hyd.—Hydraulic
① See Underhood Specifications sticker
② 1—Connect fuel pressure guage, engine at
   normal operating temperature.
   2—Turn ignition switch on.
   3—After approx. 2 seconds; pressure should
   read 41–47 psi and hold steady.
   4—Start engine and idle; pressure should drop
   3–10 psi from static pressure.
③ Ignition timing is controlled by the ECM and is
   not adjustable
④ Idle speed is controlled by the ECM and is not
   adjustable

FIRING ORDERS

NOTE: To avoid confusion, always replace spark plug wires one at a time.

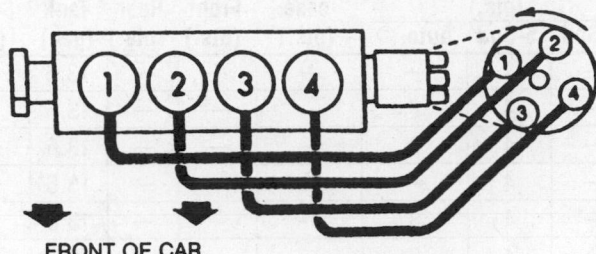

2.0L Engine
Engine Firing Order: 1–3–4–2
Distributor Rotation: Counterclockwise

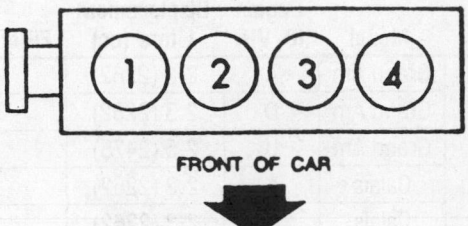

FRONT OF CAR

2.3L Engine
Engine Firing Order: 1–3–4–2
Distributorless Ignition System

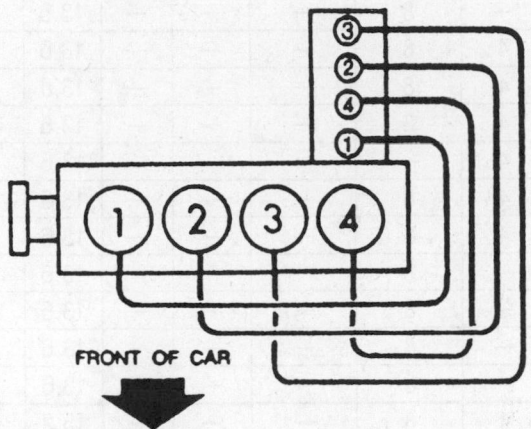

FRONT OF CAR

2.5L Engine
Engine Firing Order: 1–3–4–2
Distributorless Ignition System

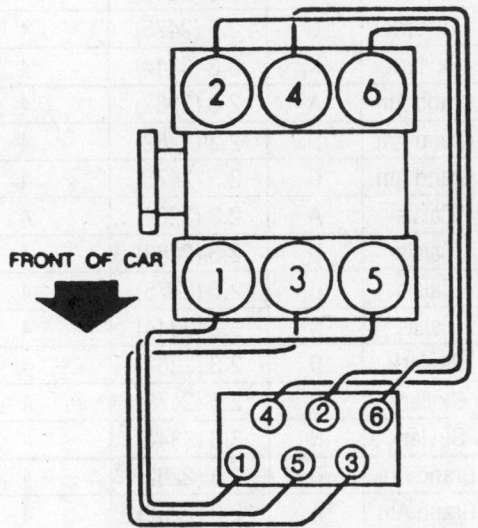

FRONT OF CAR

3.3L Engine
Engine Firing Order: 1–6–5–4–3–2
Distributorless Ignition System

CAPACITIES

Year	Model	Engine ID/VIN	Engine Displacement Liters (cc)	Engine Crankcase with Filter (qts.) ①	Transmission (pts.)			Transfer case (pts.)	Drive Axle		Fuel Tank (gal.)	Cooling System (qts.)
					4-Spd	5-Spd	Auto. ②		Front (pts.)	Rear (pts.)		
1989	Grand Am	M	2.0 (2000)	4	—	4	8	—	—	—	13.6	8
	Grand Am	A	2.3 (2262)	4	—	4	—	—	—	—	13.6	8
	Grand Am	D	2.3 (2262)	4	—	4	8	—	—	—	13.6	8
	Grand Am	U	2.5 (2475)	4	—	4	8	—	—	—	13.6	8
	Calais	A	2.3 (2262)	4	—	4	—	—	—	—	13.6	8
	Calais	D	2.3 (2262)	4	—	4	8	—	—	—	13.6	8
	Calais	U	2.5 (2475)	4	—	4	8	—	—	—	13.6	8
	Calais	N	3.3 (3344)	4	—	—	8	—	—	—	13.6	10
	Skylark	D	2.3 (2262)	4	—	—	8	—	—	—	13.6	8
	Skylark	U	2.5 (2475)	4	—	—	8	—	—	—	13.6	8
	Skylark	N	3.3 (3344)	4	—	—	8	—	—	—	13.6	10

CAPACITIES

Year	Model	Engine ID/VIN	Engine Displacement Liters (cc)	Engine Crankcase with Filter (qts.)①	Transmission (pts.) 4-Spd	5-Spd	Auto.②	Transfer case (pts.)	Drive Axle Front (pts.)	Rear (pts.)	Fuel Tank (gal.)	Cooling System (qts.)
1990	Grand Am	A	2.3 (2262)	4	—	4	—	—	—	—	13.6	8
	Grand Am	D	2.3 (2262)	4	—	4	8	—	—	—	13.6	8
	Grand Am	U	2.5 (2475)	4	—	4	8	—	—	—	13.6	8
	Calais	A	2.3 (2262)	4	—	4	—	—	—	—	13.6	8
	Calais	D	2.3 (2262)	4	—	4	8	—	—	—	13.6	8
	Calais	U	2.5 (2475)	4	—	4	8	—	—	—	13.6	8
	Calais	N	3.3 (3344)	4	—	—	8	—	—	—	13.6	10
	Skylark	D	2.3 (2262)	4	—	—	8	—	—	—	13.6	8
	Skylark	U	2.5 (2475)	4	—	—	8	—	—	—	13.6	8
	Skylark	N	3.3 (3344)	4	—	—	8	—	—	—	13.6	10
1991	Grand Am	A	2.3 (2262)	4	—	4	8	—	—	—	13.6	10.4
	Grand Am	D	2.3 (2262)	4	—	4	8	—	—	—	13.6	10.4
	Grand Am	U	2.5 (2475)	4	—	4	8	—	—	—	13.6	10.7
	Calais	A	2.3 (2262)	4	—	4	—	—	—	—	13.6	10.4
	Calais	D	2.3 (2262)	4	—	4	8	—	—	—	13.6	10.4
	Calais	U	2.5 (2475)	4	—	4	8	—	—	—	13.6	10.7
	Calais	N	3.3 (3344)	4	—	—	8	—	—	—	13.6	12.7
	Skylark	D	2.3 (2262)	4	—	—	8	—	—	—	13.6	10.4
	Skylark	U	2.5 (2475)	4	—	—	8	—	—	—	13.6	10.7
	Skylark	N	3.3 (3344)	4	—	—	8	—	—	—	13.6	12.7
1992–93	Grand Am	D	2.3 (2262)	4	—	4	8	—	—	—	15.2	9.5
	Grand Am	A	2.3 (2262)	4	—	4	8	—	—	—	15.2	9.5
	Grand Am	3	2.3 (2262)	4	—	4	8	—	—	—	15.2	9.5
	Grand Am	N	3.3 (3344)	4	—	—	8	—	—	—	15.2	12.7
	Achieva	D	2.3 (2262)	4	—	4	8	—	—	—	15.2	9.5
	Achieva	A	2.3 (2262)	4	—	4	8	—	—	—	15.2	9.5
	Achieva	3	2.3 (2262)	4	—	4	8	—	—	—	15.2	9.5
	Achieva	N	3.3 (3344)	4	—	—	8	—	—	—	15.2	9.5
	Skylark	3	2.3 (2262)	4	—	—	8	—	—	—	15.2	9.5
	Skylark	N	3.3 (3344)	4	—	—	8	—	—	—	15.2	12.7

① When changing the oil filter, additional oil may be needed to fill the crankcase.
② Drain and refill capacity shown. Dry capacity is 12 pts.

CAMSHAFT SPECIFICATIONS

All measurements given in inches.

Year	Engine ID/VIN	Engine Displacement Liters (cc)	Journal Diameter 1	2	3	4	5	Elevation In.	Ex.	Bearing Clearance	Camshaft End Play
1989	M	2.0 (2000)	1.6706–1.6712	1.6812–1.6818	1.6911–1.6917	1.7009–1.7015	1.7100–1.7106	0.2625	0.2625	0.0011–0.0035	0.0016–0.0064
	D	2.3 (2262)	1.3751–1.3760	1.3751–1.3760	1.3751–1.3760	1.3751–1.3760	1.3751–1.3760	0.3400	0.3500	0.0019–0.0043	0.0060–0.0140
	A	2.3 (2262)	1.3751–1.3760	1.3751–1.3760	1.3751–1.3760	1.3751–1.3760	1.3751–1.3760	0.4100	0.4100	0.0019–0.0043	0.0060–0.0140

CAMSHAFT SPECIFICATIONS

All measurements given in inches.

Year	Engine ID/VIN	Engine Displacement Liters (cc)	Journal Diameter					Elevation		Bearing Clearance	Camshaft End Play
			1	2	3	4	5	In.	Ex.		
1989	U	2.5 (2475)	1.8690	1.8690	1.8690	1.8690	1.8690	0.2480	0.2480	0.0007–0.0027	0.0014–0.0050
	N	3.3 (3344)	1.7850–1.7860	1.7850–1.7860	1.7850–1.7860	1.7850–1.7860	—	0.2500	0.2550	0.0005–0.0035	NA
1990	D	2.3 (2262)	1.5720–1.5728	1.3751–1.3760	1.3751–1.3760	1.3751–1.3760	1.3751–1.3760	0.3400	0.3500	0.0019–0.0043	0.0060–0.0140
	A	2.3 (2262)	1.5720–1.5728	1.3751–1.3760	1.3751–1.3760	1.3751–1.3760	1.3751–1.3760	0.4100	0.4100	0.0019–0.0043	0.0060–0.0140
	U	2.5 (2475)	1.8690	1.8690	1.8690	1.8690	1.8690	0.2480	0.2480	0.0007–0.0027	0.0020–0.0090
	N	3.3 (3344)	1.7850–1.7860	1.7850–1.7860	1.7850–1.7860	1.7850–1.7860	—	0.2500	0.2550	0.0005–0.0035	NA
1991	D	2.3 (2262)	1.5720–1.5728	1.3751–1.3760	1.3751–1.3760	1.3751–1.3760	1.3751–1.3760	0.3750	0.3750	0.0019–0.0043	0.0009–0.0088
	A	2.3 (2262)	1.5720–1.5728	1.3751–1.3760	1.3751–1.3760	1.3751–1.3760	1.3751–1.3760	0.4100	0.4100	0.0019–0.0043	0.0009–0.0088
	U	2.5 (2475)	1.8690	1.8690	1.8690	1.8690	1.8690	0.2480	0.2480	0.0007–0.0027	0.0020–0.0090
	N	3.3 (3344)	1.7850–1.7860	1.7850–1.7860	1.7850–1.7860	1.7850–1.7860	—	0.2500	0.2550	0.0005–0.0035	NA
1992-93	D	2.3 (2262)	1.5720–1.5728	1.3751–1.3760	1.3751–1.3760	1.3751–1.3760	1.3751–1.3760	0.3750	0.3750	0.0019–0.0043	0.0009–0.0088
	A	2.3 (2262)	1.5720–1.5728	1.3751–1.3760	1.3751–1.3760	1.3751–1.3760	1.3751–1.3760	0.4100	0.4100	0.0019–0.0043	0.0009–0.0088
	3	2.3 (2262)	1.5720–1.5728	1.3751–1.3760	1.3751–1.3760	1.3751–1.3760	1.3751–1.3760	0.4100	0.4100	0.0019–0.0043	0.0009–0.0088
	N	3.3 (3344)	1.7850–1.7860	1.7850–1.7860	1.7850–1.7860	1.7850–1.7860	—	0.2500	0.2550	0.0005–0.0035	NA

NA—Not Available

CRANKSHAFT AND CONNECTING ROD SPECIFICATIONS

All measurements are given in inches.

Year	Engine ID/VIN	Engine Displacement Liters (cc)	Crankshaft				Connecting Rod		
			Main Brg. Journal Dia.	Main Brg. Oil Clearance	Shaft End-play	Thrust on No.	Journal Diameter	Oil Clearance	Side Clearance
1989	M	2.0 (2000)	2.2828–2.2833	0.0006–0.0016	0.0028–0.0118	3	1.9279–1.9287	0.0007–0.0025	0.0028–0.0095
	A	2.3 (2262)	2.0470–2.0480	0.0005–0.0023	0.0034–0.0095	3	1.8887–1.8897	0.0005–0.0020	0.0059–0.0177
	D	2.3 (2262)	2.0470–2.0480	0.0005–0.0023	0.0034–0.0095	3	1.8887–1.8897	0.0005–0.0020	0.0059–0.0177
	U	2.5 (2475)	2.3000	0.0005–0.0020	0.0060–0.0110	5	2.0000	0.0005–0.0030	0.0060–0.0240
	N	3.3 (3344)	2.4988–2.4998	0.0003–0.0018	0.0030–0.0110	2	2.2487–2.2499	0.0003–0.0026	0.0030–0.0150

CRANKSHAFT AND CONNECTING ROD SPECIFICATIONS

All measurements are given in inches.

Year	Engine ID/VIN	Engine Displacement Liters (cc)	Crankshaft				Connecting Rod		
			Main Brg. Journal Dia.	Main Brg. Oil Clearance	Shaft End-play	Thrust on No.	Journal Diameter	Oil Clearance	Side Clearance
1990	A	2.3 (2262)	2.0470–2.0480	0.0005–0.0023	0.0034–0.0095	3	1.8887–1.8897	0.0005–0.0020	0.0059–0.0177
	D	2.3 (2262)	2.0470–2.0480	0.0005–0.0023	0.0034–0.0095	3	1.8887–1.8897	0.0005–0.0020	0.0059–0.0177
	U	2.5 (2475)	2.3000	0.0005–0.0020	0.0060–0.0110	5	2.0000	0.0005–0.0030	0.0060–0.0240
	N	3.3 (3344)	2.4988–2.4998	0.0003–0.0018	0.0030–0.0110	2	2.2487–2.2499	0.0003–0.0026	0.0030–0.0150
1991	A	2.3 (2262)	2.0470–2.0480	0.0005–0.0023	0.0034–0.0095	3	1.8887–1.8897	0.0005–0.0020	0.0059–0.0177
	D	2.3 (2262)	2.0470–2.0480	0.0005–0.0023	0.0034–0.0095	3	1.8887–1.8897	0.0005–0.0020	0.0059–0.0177
	U	2.5 (2475)	2.3000	0.0005–0.0022	0.0060–0.0110	5	2.0000	0.0005–0.0030	0.0060–0.0240
	N	3.3 (3344)	2.4988–2.4998	0.0003–0.0018	0.0030–0.0110	2	2.2487–2.2499	0.0003–0.0026	0.0030–0.0150
1992–93	A	2.3 (2262)	2.0470–2.0480	0.0005–0.0023	0.0034–0.0095	3	1.8887–1.8897	0.0005–0.0020	0.0059–0.0177
	D	2.3 (2262)	2.0470–2.0480	0.0005–0.0023	0.0034–0.0095	3	1.8887–1.8897	0.0005–0.0020	0.0059–0.0177
	3	2.3 (2262)	2.0470–2.0480	0.0005–0.0023	0.0034–0.0095	3	1.8887–1.8897	0.0005–0.0020	0.0059–0.0177
	N	3.3 (3344)	2.4988–2.4998	0.0003–0.0018	0.0030–0.0110	2	2.2487–2.2499	0.0008–0.0022	0.0030–0.0150

VALVE SPECIFICATIONS

Year	Engine ID/VIN	Engine Displacement Liters (cc)	Seat Angle (deg.)	Face Angle (deg.)	Spring Test Pressure (lbs. @ in.)②	Spring Installed Height (in.)	Stem-to-Guide Clearance (in.)		Stem Diameter (in.)	
							Intake	Exhaust	Intake	Exhaust
1989	M	2.0 (2000)	45	46	165–179 @ 1.043 in.	NA	0.0006–0.0017	0.0010–0.0024	0.2755–0.2760	0.2747–0.2753
	A	2.3 (2262)	45	①	188–202 @ 1.043 in.	1.42–1.44	0.0009–0.0027	0.0015–0.0032	0.2744–0.2751	0.2740–0.2747
	D	2.3 (2262)	45	①	159–173 @ 1.043 in.	1.42–1.44	0.0009–0.0027	0.0015–0.0032	0.2744–0.2751	0.2740–0.2747
	U	2.5 (2475)	46	45	173 @ 1.24 in.	1.68	0.0010–0.0026	0.0013–0.0041	NA	NA
	N	3.3 (3344)	45	45	200–220 @ 1.315 in.	1.69–1.75	0.0015–0.0035	0.0015–0.0032	NA	NA
1990	A	2.3 (2262)	45	①	193–207 @ 1.043 in.	1.42–1.44	0.0009–0.0027	0.0015–0.0032	0.2744–0.2751	0.2740–0.2747
	D	2.3 (2262)	45	①	193–207 @ 1.043 in.	1.42–1.44	0.0009–0.0027	0.0015–0.0032	0.2744–0.2751	0.2740–0.2747
	U	2.5 (2475)	46	45	173 @ 1.24 in.	1.68	0.0010–0.0026	0.0013–0.0041	NA	NA
	N	3.3 (3344)	45	45	200–220 @ 1.315 in.	1.69–1.75	0.0015–0.0035	0.0015–0.0032	NA	NA

VALVE SPECIFICATIONS

Year	Engine ID/VIN	Engine Displacement Liters (cc)	Seat Angle (deg.)	Face Angle (deg.)	Spring Test Pressure (lbs. @ in.)②	Spring Installed Height (in.)	Stem-to-Guide Clearance (in.)		Stem Diameter (in.)	
							Intake	Exhaust	Intake	Exhaust
1991	A	2.3 (2262)	45	44	193–207 @ 1.043 in.	0.98–③ 1.00	0.0010–0.0027	0.0015–0.0032	0.2744–0.2751	0.2740–0.2747
	D	2.3 (2262)	45	44	193–207 @ 1.043 in.	0.98–③ 1.00	0.0010–0.0027	0.0015–0.0032	0.2744–0.2751	0.2740–0.2747
	U	2.5 (2475)	46	45	173 @ 1.24 in.	1.68	0.0010–0.0026	0.0013–0.0041	NA	NA
	N	3.3 (3344)	45	45	210 @ 1.315 in.	1.69–1.75	0.0015–0.0035	0.0015–0.0032	NA	NA
1992–93	A	2.3 (2262)	45	44	193–207 @ 1.043 in.	0.98–③ 1.00	0.0010–0.0027	0.0015–0.0032	0.2744–0.2751	0.2740–0.2747
	D	2.3 (2262)	45	44	193–207 @ 1.043 in.	0.98–③ 1.00	0.0010–0.0027	0.0015–0.0032	0.2744–0.2751	0.2740–0.2747
	3	2.3 (2262)	45	44	193–207 @ 1.043 in.	0.98–③ 1.00	0.0010–0.0027	0.0015–0.0032	0.2744–0.2751	0.2740–0.2747
	N	3.3 (3344)	45	45	210 @ 1.315 in.	1.69–1.75	0.0015–0.0035	0.0015–0.0032	NA	NA

NA—Not Available
① Intake: 44°
  Exhaust: 44.5°
② Load—open
③ Measured from top of valve stem to top of camshaft housing mounting surface

PISTON AND RING SPECIFICATIONS

All measurements are given in inches.

Year	Engine ID/VIN	Engine Displacement Liters (cc)	Piston Clearance	Ring Gap			Ring Side Clearance		
				Top Compression	Bottom Compression	Oil Control	Top Compression	Bottom Compression	Oil Control
1989	M	2.0 (2000)	0.0012–0.0020	0.010–0.020	0.012–0.020	0.016–0.055	0.002–0.004	0.002–0.003	NA
	A	2.3 (2262)	0.0007–0.0020	0.014–0.024	0.016–0.026	0.016–0.055	0.002–0.004	0.002–0.003	NA
	D	2.3 (2262)	0.0007–0.0020	0.014–0.024	0.016–0.026	0.016–0.055	0.002–0.004	0.002–0.003	NA
	U	2.5 (2475)	0.0014–0.0022	0.010–0.020	0.010–0.020	0.020–0.060	0.002–0.003	0.001–0.003	0.015–0.055
	N	3.3 (3344)	0.0004–0.0022	0.010–0.025	0.010–0.025	0.010–0.040	0.001–0.003	0.001–0.003	0.001–0.008
1990	A	2.3 (2262)	0.0007–0.0020	0.014–0.024	0.016–0.026	0.016–0.055	0.003–0.005	0.002–0.003	NA
	D	2.3 (2262)	0.0007–0.0020	0.014–0.024	0.016–0.026	0.016–0.055	0.002–0.004	0.002–0.003	NA
	U	2.5 (2475)	0.0014–0.0022	0.010–0.020	0.010–0.020	0.020–0.060	0.002–0.003	0.001–0.003	0.015–0.055
	N	3.3 (3344)	0.0004–0.0022	0.010–0.025	0.010–0.025	0.010–0.040	0.001–0.003	0.001–0.003	0.001–0.008

PISTON AND RING SPECIFICATIONS

All measurements are given in inches.

Year	Engine ID/VIN	Engine Displacement Liters (cc)	Piston Clearance	Ring Gap Top Compression	Ring Gap Bottom Compression	Ring Gap Oil Control	Ring Side Clearance Top Compression	Ring Side Clearance Bottom Compression	Ring Side Clearance Oil Control
1991	A	2.3 (2262)	0.0007–0.0020	0.014–0.024	0.016–0.026	0.016–0.055	0.003–0.005	0.002–0.003	NA
	D	2.3 (2262)	0.0007–0.0020	0.014–0.024	0.016–0.026	0.016–0.055	0.002–0.004	0.002–0.003	NA
	U	2.5 (2475)	0.0014–0.0022	0.010–0.020	0.010–0.020	0.020–0.060	0.002–0.003	0.001–0.003	0.015–0.055
	N	3.3 (3344)	0.0004–①0.0022	0.010–0.025	0.010–0.025	0.010–0.040	0.001–0.003	0.001–0.003	0.001–0.008
1992–93	A	2.3 (2262)	0.0007–0.0020	0.014–0.024	0.016–0.026	0.016–0.055	0.003–0.005	0.002–0.003	NA
	D	2.3 (2262)	0.0007–0.0020	0.014–0.024	0.016–0.026	0.016–0.055	0.002–0.004	0.002–0.003	NA
	3	2.3 (2262)	0.0007–0.0020	0.014–0.024	0.016–0.026	0.016–0.055	0.002–0.004	0.002–0.003	NA
	N	3.3 (3344)	0.0004–①0.0022	0.010–0.025	0.010–0.025	0.015–0.055	0.001–0.003	0.001–0.003	0.001–0.008

NA—Not Available

① Measured 1.8 in. (44mm) down from top of piston

TORQUE SPECIFICATIONS

All readings in ft. lbs.

Year	Engine ID/VIN	Engine Displacement Liters (cc)	Cylinder Head Bolts	Main Bearing Bolts	Rod Bearing Bolts	Crankshaft Damper Bolts	Flywheel Bolts	Manifold Intake	Manifold Exhaust	Spark Plugs	Lug Nut
1989	M	2.0 (2000)	①	44②	26②	20	63②	18	10	15	100
	A	2.3 (2262)	④	15⑤	18⑬	74⑤	22②	18	27	17	100
	D	2.3 (2262)	④	15⑤	18⑬	74⑤	22②	18	27	17	100
	U	2.5 (2475)	⑫	65	29	162	⑨	25	⑩	15	100
	N	3.3 (3344)	⑭	90	20②	219	61	7	30	20	100
1990	A	2.3 (2262)	⑮	15⑤	18⑬	74⑤	22②	18	⑦	17	100
	D	2.3 (2262)	⑮	15⑤	18⑬	74⑤	22②	18	⑦	17	100
	U	2.5 (2475)	⑫	65	29	162	⑨	25	⑩	15	100
	N	3.3 (3344)	⑭	90	20②	219	61	7	30	20	100
1991	A	2.3 (2262)	⑮	15⑤	18⑬	74⑤	22②	18	⑦	17	100
	D	2.3 (2262)	⑮	15⑤	18⑬	74⑤	22②	18	⑦	17	100
	U	2.5 (2475)	⑫	65	29	162	⑨	25	⑩	15	100
	N	3.3 (3344)	⑭	26⑯	20②	105⑰	89⑧⑤	89⑧	41	20	100

TORQUE SPECIFICATIONS
All readings in ft. lbs.

Year	Engine ID/VIN	Engine Displacement Liters (cc)	Cylinder Head Bolts	Main Bearing Bolts	Rod Bearing Bolts	Crankshaft Damper Bolts	Flywheel Bolts	Manifold Intake	Manifold Exhaust	Spark Plugs	Lug Nut
1992–93	A	2.3 (2262)	⑱	15 ⑤	18 ⑬	74 ⑤	22 ②	18	⑦	17	100
	D	2.3 (2262)	⑱	15 ⑤	18 ⑬	74 ⑤	22 ②	18	⑦	17	100
	3	2.3 (2262)	⑱	15 ⑤	18 ⑬	74 ⑤	22 ②	18	⑦	17	100
	N	3.3 (3344)	⑭	26 ③	20 ③	110 ⑥	11 ③	88 ⑧ ⑪	38	12	100

① Step 1: 18 ft. lbs.
  Step 2: 3 rounds of 60° turns in sequence
  Step 3: An additional 30–50° turn after engine warm up
② Plus an additional 40–50° turn
③ Plus an addition 50° turn
④ Short bolts: 26 ft. lbs. plus an additional 80° turn
  Long bolts: 26 ft. lbs. plus an additional 90° turn
⑤ Plus an additional 90° turn
⑥ Plus an additional 75° turn

⑦ Nuts: 27 ft. lbs.
  Studs: 106 inch lbs.
⑧ Inch lbs.
⑨ Manual transaxle: 69 ft. lbs.
  automatic transaxle: 55 ft. lbs.
⑩ Outer bolts: 26 ft. lbs.
  Inner bolts: 37 ft. lbs.
⑪ Upper intake manifold to lower: 22 ft. lbs.
⑫ Step 1: 18 ft. lbs.
  Step 2: 26 ft. lbs., except front bolt/stud
  Step 3: Front bolt/stud to 18 ft. lbs.
  Step 4: An additional 90° turn

⑬ Plus an additional 80° turn
⑭ Step 1: 35 ft. lbs.
  Step 2: An additional 130° turn
  Step 3: An additional 30° turn on center 4 bolts
⑮ Short bolts: 26 ft. lbs. plus an additional 100° turn
  Long bolts: 26 ft. lbs. plus an additional 110° turn
⑯ Plus an additional 45° turn
⑰ Plus an additional 56° turn
⑱ Bolts 1 through 6: 26 ft. lbs. + 90° turn
  Bolts 7 and 8: 15 ft. lbs. + 90° turn
  Bolts 9 through 10: 22 ft. lbs. + 90° turn

BRAKE SPECIFICATIONS
All measurements in inches unless noted

Year	Model	Master Cylinder Bore	Brake Disc Original Thickness	Brake Disc Minimum Thickness	Brake Disc Maximum Runout	Brake Drum Diameter Original Inside Diameter	Brake Drum Diameter Max. Wear Limit	Brake Drum Diameter Maximum Machine Diameter	Minimum Lining Thickness Front	Minimum Lining Thickness Rear
1989	All	0.874	0.885	0.830	0.004	7.879	7.929	7.899	0.06	0.06
1990	All	0.874	0.885	0.830	0.004	7.879	7.929	7.899	0.06	0.06
1991	All	0.874	0.806	0.786	0.003	7.879	7.929	7.899	0.06	0.06
1992–93	All	0.874	0.796	0.736	0.003	7.879	7.929	7.899	0.06	0.06

WHEEL ALIGNMENT

Year	Model		Caster Range (deg.)	Caster Preferred Setting (deg.)	Camber Range (deg.)	Camber Preferred Setting (deg.)	Toe-in (in.)	Steering Axis Inclination (deg.)
1989	Calais	front	11/16P–2 11/16P	1 11/16P	1/8P–1 1/2P ②	13/16P ①	0	13 1/2
		rear	—	—	3/4N–1/4P	1/4N	1/4	—
	Grand Am	front	11/16P–2 11/16P	1 11/16P	1/8P–1 1/2P ②	13/16P ①	0	13 1/2
		rear	—	—	3/4N–1/4P	1/4N	1/4	—
	Skylark	front	11/16P–2 11/16P	1 11/16P	1/8P–1 1/2P	13/16P	0	13 1/2
		rear	—	—	1/4N–1/4P	1/4N	1/4	—
1990	Calais	front	11/16P–2 11/16P	1 11/16P	1/8P–1 1/2P ②	13/16P ①	0	13 1/2
		rear	—	—	3/4N–1/4P	1/4N	1/4	—
	Grand Am	front	11/16P–2 11/16P	1 11/16P	1/8P–1 1/2P ②	13/16P ①	0	13 1/2
		rear	—	—	3/4N–1/4P	1/4N	1/4	—
	Skylark	front	11/16P–2 11/16P	1 11/16P	1/8P–1 1/2P ②	13/16P ①	0	13 1/2
		rear	—	—	3/4N–1/4P	1/4N	1/4	—

WHEEL ALIGNMENT

Year	Model		Caster Range (deg.)	Caster Preferred Setting (deg.)	Camber Range (deg.)	Camber Preferred Setting (deg.)	Toe-in (in.)	Steering Axis Inclination (deg.)
1991	Calais	front	$^{11}/_{16}$P–2$^{11}/_{16}$P	1$^{11}/_{16}$P	$^{11}/_{16}$N–$^{11}/_{16}$P	0	0	13½
		rear	—	—	$^{13}/_{16}$N–$^{5}/_{16}$P	¼N	⅛	—
	Grand Am	front	$^{11}/_{16}$P–2$^{11}/_{16}$P	1$^{11}/_{16}$P	$^{11}/_{16}$N–$^{11}/_{16}$P	0	0	13½
		rear	—	—	$^{13}/_{16}$N–$^{5}/_{16}$P	¼N	⅛	—
	Skylark	front	$^{11}/_{16}$P–2$^{11}/_{16}$P	1$^{11}/_{16}$P	$^{11}/_{16}$N–$^{11}/_{16}$P	0	0	13½
		rear	—	—	$^{3}/_{4}$N–$^{1}/_{2}$P	¼N	⅛	—
1992–93	Achieva	front	$^{11}/_{16}$P–2$^{11}/_{16}$P	1$^{11}/_{16}$P	$^{11}/_{16}$N–$^{11}/_{16}$P	0	0	13½
		rear	—	—	$^{13}/_{16}$N–$^{5}/_{16}$P	¼N	¼	—
	Grand Am	front	$^{11}/_{16}$P–2$^{11}/_{16}$P	1$^{11}/_{16}$P	$^{11}/_{16}$N–$^{11}/_{16}$P	0	0	13½
		rear	—	—	$^{13}/_{16}$N–$^{5}/_{16}$P	¼N	¼	—
	Skylark	front	$^{11}/_{16}$P–2$^{11}/_{16}$P	1$^{11}/_{16}$P	$^{11}/_{16}$N–$^{11}/_{16}$P	0	0	13½
		rear	—	—	$^{13}/_{16}$N–$^{5}/_{16}$P	¼N	¼	—

N—Negative
P—Positive
① with 16 in. wheels: 0
② with 16 in. wheels: $^{11}/_{16}$N–$^{11}/_{16}$P

ENGINE MECHANICAL

NOTE: Disconnecting the negative battery cable on some vehicles may interfere with the functions of the on board computer systems and may require the computer to undergo a relearning process, once the negative battery cable is reconnected.

Engine Assembly

REMOVAL & INSTALLATION
2.0L and 2.5L Engines

1. Relieve the fuel system pressure.
2. Disconnect both battery cables and ground straps.
3. Drain the cooling system and remove the cooling fan.
4. Remove the air cleaner assembly.
5. Disconnect the ECM connections and feed harness through the bulkhead. Lay the harness across the engine.
6. Label and disconnect the engine wiring harness and all engine-related connectors and lay across the engine.
7. Label and disconnect the radiator hoses and vacuum lines. Disconnect and plug the fuel lines.
8. On 2.5L engine, remove the air conditioning compressor from the engine and lay it aside, without disconnecting the refrigerant lines. Remove the transaxle struts.
9. If equipped with power steering, remove the power steering pump from its mount and lay it aside. Remove the power steering pump bracket from the engine.
10. If equipped with a manual transaxle, disconnect the clutch and transaxle linkage. Remove the throttle cable from the throttle body.
11. If equipped with an automatic transaxle, disconnect the transaxle cooler lines, shifter linkage, downshift cable and throttle cable from the throttle body.
12. Raise and safely support the vehicle.
13. Disconnect all wiring from the transaxle.
14. On 2.0L engine, properly discharge the air conditioning system and remove the compressor. Remove the transaxle strut(s).
15. Disconnect the exhaust pipe from the exhaust manifold and hangers.
16. Disconnect the heater hoses from the heater core tubes and plug them.
17. Remove the front wheels. Remove the calipers and wire them up aside. Remove the brake rotors.
18. Matchmark and remove the knuckle-to-strut bolts.
19. Remove the body-to-cradle bolts at the lower control arms. Loosen the remaining body-to-cradle bolts. Remove a bolt at each cradle side, leaving 1 bolt per corner.
20. Using the proper equipment, support the vehicle under the radiator frame support.
21. Position a jack to the rear of the body pan with a 4 inch × 4 inch × 6 ft. timber support spanning the vehicle.
22. Raise the vehicle enough to remove the support equipment.
23. Position a dolly under the engine/transaxle assembly with 3 blocks of wood for additional support.
24. Lower the vehicle slightly, allowing the engine/transaxle assembly to rest on the dolly.
25. Remove all engine and transaxle mount bolts and brackets. Remove the remaining cradle-to-body bolts.
26. Raise the vehicle, leaving engine and transaxle assembly with the suspension on the dolly.
27. Separate the engine and transaxle.

To install:
28. Assemble the engine and transaxle assembly and position on the dolly.
29. Raise and safely support the vehicle. Roll the assembly to the installation position and lower the vehicle over the assembly.
30. Install all engine, transaxle and suspension mounting bolts. Tighten all cradle mounting bolts to 65 ft. lbs. (88 Nm). Connect the wiring to the transaxle.
31. Install the knuckle-to-strut bolts and assemble the brakes.
32. Connect the exhaust pipe to the exhaust manifold and hangers.

33. Connect the heater hoses to the heater core tubes.

34. If equipped with the 2.0L engine, install the air conditioning compressor.

35. Install the wheels and lower the vehicle.

36. If equipped with the 2.5L engine, install the air conditioning compressor.

37. Install the power steering pump and related parts.

38. If equipped with a manual transaxle, connect the clutch and transaxle linkage. Connect the throttle cable to the throttle body.

39. If equipped with an automatic transaxle, connect the transaxle cooler lines, shifter linkage, downshift cable and throttle cable to the throttle body.

40. Connect the radiator hoses, vacuum lines and fuel lines.

41. Connect the engine wiring harness and all engine-related connectors. Feed the ECM connections through the bulkhead and connect.

42. Install the air cleaner assembly.

43. Fill all fluids to their proper levels.

44. Connect the battery cables, start the engine and set the timing, if necessary. Check for leaks.

2.3L Engine

1. Relieve the fuel system pressure.

2. Disconnect both battery cables and ground straps from the front engine mount bracket and the transaxle.

3. Drain the cooling system and remove the cooling fan.

4. Remove the air cleaner duct.

5. Disconnect the heater and radiator hoses from the thermostat housing.

6. Properly discharge the air conditioning system and disconnect the hoses from the compressor.

7. Remove the upper radiator support.

8. Disconnect the 2 vacuum hoses from the front of the engine.

9. Label and disconnect all electrical connectors from engine and transaxle mounted devices.

10. Disconnect the wires at the starter solenoid.

11. Disconnect the power brake vacuum hose from the throttle body.

12. Disconnect the throttle cable and remove the bracket.

13. Remove the power steering pump bracket and lay the pump aside with the lines attached.

14. Disconnect and plug the fuel lines.

15. If equipped with a manual transaxle, disconnect the shifter cables and the clutch actuator cylinder.

16. If equipped with an automatic transaxle, disconnect the shift and TV cables.

17. Disconnect the transaxle and engine oil cooler pipes, if equipped.

18. Remove the exhaust manifold and heat shield.

19. Remove the lower radiator hose and front engine mount.

20. Install engine support fixture tool J–28467–A or equivalent.

21. Raise and safely support the vehicle.

22. Remove the wheels, right side splash shield and radiator air deflector.

23. Separate the ball joints from the steering knuckles.

24. Using the proper equipment, support the suspension supports, crossmember and stabilizer shaft. Remove the attaching bolts and remove as an assembly.

25. Disconnect the heater hose from the radiator outlet pipe.

26. Remove the halfshafts from the transaxle.

27. Remove the nut from the transaxle mount through bolt.

28. Remove the nut from the rear engine mount through bolt.

29. Remove the rear engine mount body bracket.

30. Position a suitable support fixture below the engine/transaxle assembly and lower the vehicle so the weight of the engine/transaxle assembly is on the support fixture.

31. Remove the transaxle mount through bolt.

32. Mark the threads on fixture tool J–28467–A so the setting can be duplicated when installing the engine/transaxle assembly. Remove the fixture.

33. Move the engine/transaxle assembly rearward and slowly raise the vehicle from the engine/transaxle assembly.

NOTE: **Many of the bell housing bolts are of different lengths; note their locations before removing. It is imperative that these bolts go back in their original locations when assembling the engine and transaxle or engine damage could result.**

34. Separate the engine from the transaxle.

To install:

35. Assemble the engine to the transaxle. If equipped with an automatic transaxle, thoroughly clean and dry the torque converter bolts and bolt holes, apply thread locking compound to the threads and tighten the bolts to 46 ft. lbs. (63 Nm). If equipped with a manual transaxle, tighten the clutch cover bolts to 22 ft. lbs. (30 Nm).

36. Raise and safely support the vehicle. Position the engine/transaxle assembly and lower the vehicle over the assembly until the transaxle mount is indexed, then install the bolt.

37. Install the engine support fixture and adjust to previously indexed setting. Raise the vehicle off the support fixture.

38. Install the rear mount to body bracket and tighten the bolts to 55 ft. lbs. (75 Nm).

39. Install the rear mount nut and tighten to 55 ft. lbs. (75 Nm).

40. Install the transaxle mount through bolt and tighten the nut to 55 ft. lbs. (75 Nm). Tighten so equal gaps are maintained.

41. Install the halfshafts.

42. Connect the heater hose to the the radiator outlet pipe.

43. Install the suspension supports, crossmember and stabilizer shaft assembly. Tighten the center bolts first, then front, then rear, to 65 ft. lbs. (90 Nm).

44. Install the ball joints and tighten the nuts to a maximum of 50 ft. lbs. (68 Nm).

45. Install the radiator air deflector and splash shield.

46. Install the wheels and lower the vehicle.

47. Install the front engine mount nut and tighten to 41 ft. lbs. (56 Nm). Remove the engine support fixture. Connect the lower radiator hose.

48. Install the exhaust manifold and heat shield.

49. Connect the transaxle and engine oil cooler pipes, if equipped.

50. If equipped with a manual transaxle, connect the shifter cables and the clutch actuator cylinder.

51. If equipped with an automatic transaxle, connect the shift and TV cables.

52. Connect the fuel lines.

53. Install the power steering pump and related parts.

54. Connect the throttle cable and install the bracket.

55. Connect the power brake vacuum hose to the throttle body.

56. Connect the starter wires.

57. Connect all electrical connectors and cables to the proper engine and transaxle-mounted devices.

58. Connect the 2 vacuum hoses at the front of the engine.

59. Install the upper radiator support.

60. Using new seals, connect the air conditioning hoses to the compressor.

61. Connect the heater and radiator hoses at the thermostat housing.

62. Install the air cleaner duct.

63. Fill all fluids to their proper levels.

64. Connect the battery cables, start the engine and check for leaks.

3.3L Engine

1989–91

1. Disconnect the negative battery cable. Relieve the fuel pressure.
2. Matchmark the hinge-to-hood position and remove the hood.
3. Drain the cooling system. Disconnect and label all electrical connectors from the engine, alternator and fuel injection system, vacuum hoses, and engine ground straps. Remove the alternator.
4. Remove the coolant hoses from the radiator and engine. Remove the radiator and cooling fan assembly.
5. Remove the air intake duct. Disconnect the fuel lines from the fuel rail. Disconnect the throttle, TV and cruise control cables from the throttle body.
6. Raise and safely support the vehicle. Drain the engine oil. Disconnect the exhaust pipe from the exhaust manifold.
7. Remove the air conditioning compressor mounting bolts, and position it aside.
8. Disconnect the heater hoses.
9. Remove the transaxle inspection cover, matchmark the converter to the flexplate and remove the torque converter bolts.
10. Remove the rear engine mount bolts.
11. Remove the lower bell housing bolts. Label and disconnect the starter motor wiring and remove the starter motor from the engine.
12. Lower the vehicle. Remove the power steering pump mounting bolts and set the pump aside.
13. Support the transaxle with a floor jack or equivalent. Attach an engine lifting device to the engine.
14. Remove the upper bell housing bolts.
15. Remove the front engine mount bolts.
16. Lift and remove the engine from the vehicle. If the master cylinder is preventing removal, remove it and plug the brake lines.

To install:

17. Lower the engine into the engine compartment. Align the engine mounts and install the bolts. Tighten the bolts to their proper values:
    Front engine mount bracket to block—66 ft. lbs. (90 Nm)
    Front engine mount to underbody—54 ft. lbs. (73 Nm)
    Front engine mount to engine bracket—15 ft. lbs. (20 Nm)
    Rear engine mount to bracket—18 ft. lbs. (24 Nm)
    Rear engine mount bracket to underbody—41 ft. lbs. (56 Nm)
    Rear engine mount to engine bracket—40 ft. lbs. (54 Nm)
18. Install the upper transaxle-to-engine mounting bolts and tighten to 55 ft. lbs. (75 Nm). Remove the engine lifting fixture from the engine.
19. Raise and safely support the vehicle.
20. Align the converter marks, install the torque converter bolts and tighten to 46 ft. lbs. (63 Nm). Install the transaxle inspection cover.
21. Connect the exhaust pipe to the exhaust manifold. Install the starter motor and connect the wiring.
22. Install the air conditioning compressor. Connect the heater hoses.
23. Lower the vehicle. Install the power steering pump.
24. Install the alternator and belt.
25. Connect all vacuum hoses and electrical connectors to the engine.
26. Connect the fuel lines and all cables to the throttle body. Install the air intake duct.
27. Install the radiator and fan assembly. Connect the fan motor wiring. Connect the radiator hoses and refill the cooling system.
28. Fill all fluids to their proper levels.
29. Connect the battery cables, start the engine and check for leaks.

1992–93

1. Remove the hood from the vehicle and cover the fenders.
2. Install engine support/lift device J-28467-A or equivalent to the engine.
3. Depressurize the fuel system and disconnect the fuel lines from the fuel rail.
4. Disconnect the negative battery cable.
5. Drain the cooling system.
6. Disconnect the radiator and heater hoses.
7. Remove the cooling fan assembly.
8. Remove the air intake duct from the throttle body.
9. Disconnect the vacuum lines from the brake power booster and from the evaporative purge canister.
10. Disconnect the cable bracket and the cables from the throttle body.
11. Remove the accessory drive belt.
12. Remove the power steering pump bolts and place the pump aside, out of the way.
13. Disconnect all electrical connectors.
14. Remove the upper transaxle-to-engine bolts.
15. Raise and safely support the vehicle.
16. Remove the A/C compressor bolts and position aside, out of the way.
17. Remove the right engine mount and the torque strut.
18. Remove the flywheel dust cover. Use a scribe to mark the relationship of the flywheel to the converter and remove the flywheel-to-converter bolts.
19. Remove the lower engine to transaxle bolts.
20. Lower the vehicle away from the engine.

To install:

21. Lower the engine into the engine compartment. Align the engine mounts and install the bolts. Tighten the bolts to their proper values:
    Front engine mount strut to support—89 ft. lbs. (120 Nm)
    A/C compressor bracket assembly bolts—66 ft. lbs. (90 Nm)
    Engine mount strut bracket to A/C compressor bracket—37 ft. lbs. (50 Nm)
22. Align the flywheel to the converter and install the bolts. Tighten the bolts twice to 46 ft. lbs. (63 Nm).
23. Install the flywheel dust cover.
24. Install the right engine mount and torque strut.
25. Install the A/C compressor.
26. Lower the vehicle and install the upper engine to transaxle bolts.
27. Connect the electrical connections.
28. Install the power steering pump and accessory drive belt.
29. Connect the cable bracket and cables to the throttle body.
30. Connect the vacuum lines and install the air intake duct.
31. Install the cooling fan and radiator and heater hoses.
32. Refill the cooling system with the proper coolant and connect the fuel lines.
33. Connect the negative battery cable and install the hood.

Engine Mounts
REMOVAL & INSTALLATION

1. Disconnect the negative battery cable.
2. Matchmark the engine mount to its mounting location.
3. Raise and safely support the vehicle, as required. Using the proper equipment, support the weight of the engine.
4. Remove all bolts and nuts that attach the mount to the engine, transaxle or body and remove the mount assembly from the vehicle.
5. Remove the through bolt and separate the insulator from the bracket, as required.
6. The installation is the reverse of the removal procedure. Make sure the matchmarks are aligned before tightening bolts.

Cylinder Head
REMOVAL & INSTALLATION

2.0L Engine

NOTE: Cylinder head gasket replacement is necessary if camshaft carrier/cylinder head bolts are loosened. **The head bolts should only be loosened when the engine is cold and should never be reused.**

1. Relieve the fuel system pressure. Disconnect the negative battery cable.
2. Drain the coolant. Remove the induction tube.
3. Remove the alternator and bracket.
4. Remove the ignition coil.
5. Matchmark the rotor to the distributor housing and the distributor housing to the cam carrier. Remove the distributor and spark plug wires.
6. Disconnect all cables from the throttle body.
7. Disconnect and tag all electrical connections from the throttle body and intake manifold.
8. Disconnect all vacuum lines and heater hoses.
9. Disconnect and plug the fuel lines.
10. Remove the breather from the camshaft carrier.
11. Remove the upper radiator support.
12. Disconnect the exhaust manifold from the turbocharger and disconnect the oxygen sensor.
13. Label and disconnect wiring at engine harness and thermostat housing.
14. Remove the timing belt.
15. Remove the camshaft carrier/cylinder head bolts in the reverse order of the installation sequence.
16. Remove camshaft carrier, rocker arms and valve lifters.
17. Remove cylinder head and manifolds as an assembly. Remove the head gasket.

To install:

18. Thoroughly clean and dry the mating surfaces and bolt holes. Apply a continuous bead of RTV sealant to the sealing surface of camshaft carrier.
19. Install a new head gasket and position the head on the engine block. Tighten the new head bolts in sequence as follows:

Step 1—Tighten to 18 ft. lbs. (25 Nm).
Step 2—Using a torque angle meter, tighten an additional 60 degrees.
Step 3—Tighten another additional 60 degrees.
Step 4—Tighten a third additional 60 degrees.
Step 5—Tighten and additional 30–50 degrees turn after engine warm up.
20. Install the rear cover and timing belt.
21. Connect all wiring to the engine harness and thermostat housing.
22. Install the exhaust manifold to turbo connection and connect the oxygen sensor.
23. Install the upper radiator support.
24. Install the breather on the camshaft carrier.
25. Connect all vacuum and fuel lines.
26. Connect the heater hoses.
27. Connect all electrical connectors to the throttle body and intake manifold.
28. Connect all cables to the throttle body.
29. Install the distributor and spark plug wires, aligning the matchmarks.
30. Install the ignition coil.
31. Install the alternator and bracket.
32. Fill all fluids to their proper levels.
33. Connect the battery cable, start the engine and check for leaks.
34. Tighten all head bolts another additional 30–50 degrees, in sequence, after full engine warm up.

2.3L Engine

1. Relieve the fuel system pressure. Disconnect the negative battery cable and drain cooling system.
2. Disconnect heater inlet and throttle body heater hoses from water outlet. Disconnect the upper radiator hose from the water outlet.
3. Remove the exhaust manifold.
4. Remove the intake and exhaust camshaft housings.
5. Remove the oil cap and dipstick.

Pull oil fill tube upward to unseat from block.
6. Label and disconnect the injector harness electrical connector.
7. Disconnect the throttle body air intake duct. Disconnect the cables and bracket and position aside.
8. Remove the throttle body from the intake manifold.
9. Matchmark and disconnect the vacuum hose from intake manifold.
10. Remove intake manifold bracket to block bolt.
11. Disconnect the coolant sensor connectors.
12. Remove the cylinder head bolts in reverse order of the installation sequence.
13. Remove the cylinder head and gasket. Inspect the oil flow check valve for freedom of movement.

To install:

14. Thoroughly clean and dry all bolts, bolt holes and mating surfaces. Inspect the head bolts for any damage and replace, if necessary.
15. Install the cylinder head gasket to the cylinder block and carefully position the cylinder head in place.
16. Coat the head bolt threads with clean engine oil and allow the oil to drain off before installing.
17. On 1989 engines, tighten the cylinder head bolts in sequence as follows:

Step 1—Tighten all head bolts to 26 ft. lbs. (35 Nm).
Step 2—Using a torque angle meter, tighten the short bolts an addi-

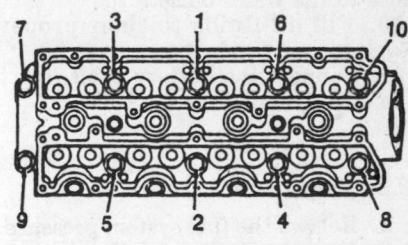

▲ FRONT OF ENGINE

Cylinder head bolt torque sequence— 1989–91 2.3L engine

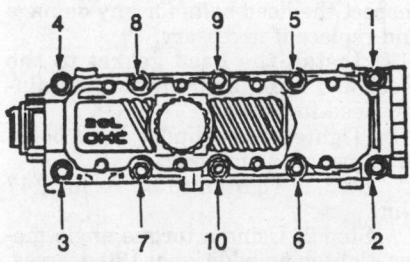

Camshaft carrier/cylinder head bolt torque sequence—2.0L engine

◀ FRONT OF ENGINE

Engine cylinder head torque sequence—1992–93 2.3L engine

tional 80 degrees and the long bolts an additional 90 degrees.

18. On 1990–91 engines, tighten the cylinder head bolts in sequence as follows:

Step 1—Tighten all head bolts to 26 ft. lbs. (35 Nm).

Step 2—Using a torque angle meter, tighten the short bolts an additional 100 degrees and the long bolts an additional 110 degrees.

19. On 1992–93 engines, tighten the cylinder head bolts in sequence as follows:

Step 1—Tighten head bolts 1 through 6 to 26 ft. lbs. (35 Nm).

Step 2—Tighten head bolts 7 and 8 to 15 ft. lbs. (20 Nm).

Step 3—Tighten head bolts 9 and 10 to 22 ft. lbs. (30 Nm).

20. Install the intake manifold bracket.

21. Connect the MAP sensor vacuum hose to the intake manifold.

22. Install the throttle body to the intake manifold.

23. Connect the throttle body air intake duct. Install the throttle cable and bracket.

24. Connect the injector harness electrical connector.

25. Connect the 2 coolant sensor connections.

26. Install the oil cap and dipstick. Install the oil fill tube into the block.

27. Install the exhaust and intake camshaft housings.

28. Install the exhaust manifold.

29. Connect the heater inlet and throttle body heater hoses to the water outlet. Connect the upper radiator hose to the water outlet.

30. Fill all fluids to their proper levels.

31. Connect the battery cable, start the engine and check for leaks.

2.5L Engine

1. Relieve the fuel system pressure.
2. Disconnect the negative battery cable.
3. Drain the coolant and remove the oil dipstick tube.
4. Remove the air cleaner assembly.
5. Raise and safely support the vehicle. Disconnect the exhaust pipe from the manifold.
6. Lower the vehicle.
7. Label and disconnect the electrical wiring and throttle linkage from the throttle body assembly.
8. Disconnect the heater hose from the intake manifold.
9. Remove the ignition coil. Label and disconnect the electrical wiring connectors from the intake manifold and the cylinder head. Remove the alternator.
10. If equipped with a top-mounted

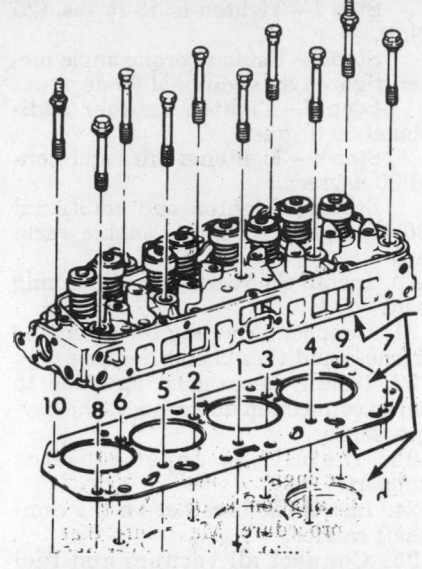

Cylinder head bolt torque sequence— 2.5L engine

air conditioning compressor, remove the compressor and lay it aside.

11. If equipped with power steering, remove the upper bracket from the power steering pump.

12. Remove the radiator hoses from the engine.

13. Remove the valve cover. Label and remove the rocker arms and pushrods.

14. Remove the cylinder head bolts in reverse order of the installation sequence and remove the cylinder head.

To install:

15. Thoroughly clean and dry all bolts, bolt holes and mating surfaces. Inspect the head bolts for any damage and replace if necessary.

16. Install the head gasket to the block and carefully position the cylinder head in place.

17. Tighten the cylinder head bolts in sequence as follows:

Step 1: Tighten all bolts to 18 ft. lbs. (25 Nm).

Step 2: Tighten to 26 ft. lbs. (35 Nm), except front bolt/stud.

Step 3: Tighten front bolt/stud to 18 ft. lbs. (25 Nm).

Step 4: Using a torque angle meter, tighten all bolts an additional 90 degrees.

18. Install the pushrods and rocker arms in their original positions. Install the valve cover with a new gasket.

19. Install the radiator hoses. Install the power steering pump and upper bracket.

20. Install the air conditioning compressor, if removed.

21. Install the ignition coil and connect the electrical wiring connectors to the intake manifold and the cylinder head.

22. Install the alternator.

23. Install the heater hose to the intake manifold.

24. Connect the electrical wiring and throttle linkage to the throttle body assembly.

25. Raise and safely support the vehicle.

26. Install the exhaust pipe to the manifold.

27. Install the air cleaner assembly.

28. Adjust all belt tensions and fill all fluids to their proper levels.

29. Connect the battery cable, start the engine and check for leaks.

3.3L Engine

1. Relieve the fuel system pressure.
2. Disconnect the negative battery cable and drain the coolant.
3. Remove the mass air flow sensor and the air intake duct.
4. Remove C^3I ignition module and wiring.
5. Remove the serpentine drive belt, the alternator and bracket.
6. Label and remove all necessary vacuum lines and electrical connections.
7. Remove the fuel lines, the fuel rail and the spark plug wires.
8. Remove the heater/radiator hoses from the throttle body and intake manifold. Remove the cooling fan and the radiator.
9. Remove the intake manifold.
10. Remove the valve covers. Label and remove the rocker arms, pedestals and pushrods.
11. Remove the left side exhaust manifold.
12. Remove the power steering pump. Remove the dipstick and dipstick tube.
13. Remove the left side head bolts in reverse order of the installation sequence and lift the left cylinder head from the engine.
14. Raise and safely support the vehicle. Remove the right exhaust manifold-to-engine bolts.
15. Remove the right cylinder head-to-engine bolts in reverse of the installation sequence and lift the right cylinder head from the engine.

To install:

16. Thoroughly clean and dry all bolts, bolt holes and mating surfaces. Inspect the head bolts for any damage and replace if necessary.

17. Install the head gasket to the block and carefully position the cylinder head in place.

18. Tighten the cylinder head bolts, in sequence, as follows:

Step 1: Tighten to 35 ft. lbs. (47 Nm).

Step 2: Using a torque angle meter, tighten an additional 130 degrees.

Step 3: Tighten the 4 center bolts an additional 30 degrees.

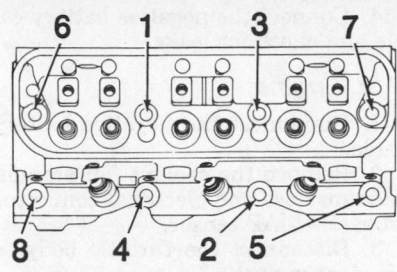

Cylinder head bolt torque sequence—3.3L engine

19. Install the intake manifold. Raise and safely support the vehicle. Install the exhaust manifold. Lower the vehicle.
20. Install the power steering pump. Install the dipstick and dipstick tube.
21. Install new valve cover gaskets and install the valve covers.
22. Install the rocker arms, pedestals and bolts. Tighten pedestal bolts to 28 ft. lbs. (38 Nm).
23. Install the intake manifold assembly.
24. Install the heater and radiator hoses to the throttle body and intake manifold.
25. Install the cooling fan and the radiator.
26. Install the fuel lines, the fuel rail and the spark plug wires.
27. Install all vacuum lines and electrical connections.
28. Install the serpentine drive belt, the alternator and bracket.
29. Install the C³I ignition module and wiring.
30. Install the mass air flow sensor and the air intake duct.
31. Fill all fluids to their proper levels.
32. Connect the battery cable, start the engine and check for leaks.

Valve Lifters

REMOVAL & INSTALLATION

2.0L Engine

1. Disconnect the negative battery cable. Remove the camshaft carrier cover.
2. Hold the valves in place with compressed air, using an air adapter in the spark plug hole.
3. Compress the valve springs using a valve spring compressor.
4. Remove rocker arms; keep them in order for reassembly.
5. Remove the lifters.
6. The installation is the reverse of the removal procedure. Soak the lifters in clean engine oil prior to installation.
7. Connect the negative battery ca-

ble and check the lifters for proper operation.

2.3L Engine

1. Disconnect the negative battery cable.
2. Remove the camshafts.
3. Remove the lifters from their bores.
4. The installation is the reverse of the removal procedure. Soak the lifters in clean engine oil prior to installation.
5. Connect the negative battery cable and check the lifters for proper operation.

2.5L Engine

1. Relieve the fuel system pressure.
2. Disconnect the negative battery cable.
3. Remove the valve cover and intake manifold.
4. Remove the side pushrod cover.
5. Loosen the rocker arms in pairs and rotate them in order to clear the pushrods.
6. Remove the pushrods, retainer and guide from each cylinder.
7. Remove the valve lifters.
8. The installation is the reverse of the removal procedure. Soak the lifters in clean engine oil prior to installation.
9. Connect the negative battery cable and check the lifters for proper operation.

3.3L Engine

1. Relieve the fuel system pressure.
2. Disconnect the negative battery terminal.
3. Disconnect and remove the fuel rail and the throttle body from the intake manifold.
4. Drain the cooling system.
5. Remove valve covers and the intake manifold.
6. Remove the rocker arms, pedestals and pushrods. Keep these components in order for proper installation.
7. Remove the valve lifters.
To install:
8. Soak the lifters in clean engine oil prior to installation.
9. Clean all gasket surfaces and valve train parts.
10. Assemble the lifters, guides, retainers, pushrods and rocker arms.
11. Apply a thread locking compound to the rocker arm bolts and tighten to 28 ft. lbs. (38 Nm).
12. Install the intake manifold and gaskets.
13. Install the valve covers and gaskets.
14. Install the fuel rail assembly.
15. Refill the coolant to the proper level and connect the negative battery cable.

Rocker Arms

REMOVAL & INSTALLATION

2.0L Engine

1. Disconnect the negative battery cable. Remove the camshaft carrier cover.
2. Hold the valves in place with compressed air, using an air adapter in the spark plug hole.
3. Compress the valve springs using a suitable valve spring compressor.
4. Remove rocker arms. Keep them in order if they are being reused.
5. The installation is the reverse of the removal procedure.
6. Connect the negative battery cable and check for proper operation.

2.5L Engine

1. Relieve the fuel system pressure.
2. Disconnect the negative battery cable.
3. Remove the valve cover and intake manifold.
4. Remove the rocker arm bolts and remove the rocker arms.
5. The installation is the reverse of the removal procedure. Tighten the attaching bolts to 20 ft. lbs. (27 Nm).
6. Connect the negative battery cable and check for proper operation.

3.3L Engine

LEFT/FRONT HEAD

1. Relieve the fuel system pressure.
2. Disconnect the negative battery cable.
3. Disconnect all electrical components and vacuum hoses which prevent access to the valve cover bolts.
4. Remove the serpentine drive belt.
5. Remove the alternator brace bolt and remove the alternator belt.
6. Remove the spark plug wire harness.
7. Remove the valve cover.
8. Remove the rocker arm pedestal-to-cylinder head bolts, the rocker arm and pedestal assembly.
To install:
9. Install the rocker arm and pedestal assembly. Apply a thread locking compound to the bolt threads and tighten the rocker arm pedestal bolts to 28 ft. lbs. (38 Nm).
10. Install the valve cover and spark plug wire harness.
11. Install the alternator belt and tighten the brace bolt.
12. Install the serpentine drive belt.
13. Connect any vacuum lines and electrical connectors that were disconnected.
14. Connect the negative battery cable and check for proper operation.

RIGHT/REAR HEAD

1. Relieve the fuel system pressure.
2. Disconnect the negative battery terminal.
3. Remove the serpentine drive belt.
4. Loosen the power steering pump bolts and slide the pump forward.
5. Remove the power steering braces.
6. Remove the spark plug wires from the spark plugs.
7. Remove the valve cover.
8. Remove the rocker arm pedestal-to-cylinder head bolts. Remove the rocker arm and pedestal assembly.

To install:

9. Install the rocker arm and pedestal assembly.
10. Apply a thread locking compound to the bolt threads and tighten the rocker arm pedestal bolts to 28 ft. lbs. (38 Nm).
11. Install the valve cover and connect the spark plug wires to the spark plugs.
12. Install the power steering pump to it's proper position and tighten the bolts. Install the power steering brace.
13. Install the serpentine drive belt.
14. Refill the cooling system. Connect the battery cable and check for proper operation.

Intake Manifold

REMOVAL & INSTALLATION

2.0L Engine

1. Relieve the fuel system pressure. Disconnect the negative battery cable.
2. Remove induction tube and hoses.
3. Label and disconnect the wiring to throttle body, fuel injectors, MAP sensor and wastegate.
4. Disconnect the PCV and vacuum hoses on the throttle body.
5. Disconnect the throttle and cruise control cables, if equipped.
6. Remove the fuel return line from the throttle cable support bracket.
7. Disconnect the wiring to the ignition coil.
8. Remove the vacuum hoses from the rear of the manifold.
9. Remove the transaxle fill tube bracket.
10. Remove the manifold support bracket.
11. Remove the heater tube support bracket on the lower side of the manifold.
12. Disconnect the wires from the injectors.
13. Drain and remove the coolant recovery tank.
14. Remove the serpentine drive belt.
15. Remove the rear bolt from alternator bracket, the power steering ad-

justing bracket and front alternator adjusting bracket.
16. Remove the alternator.
17. Disconnect the fuel lines to fuel rail and regulator outlet.
18. Remove the attaching nuts and washers and remove the intake manifold.

To install:

19. Thoroughly clean and dry the mating surfaces. Install new gaskets and place the intake manifold in position.
20. Tighten the intake manifold attaching nuts to 18 ft. lbs. (24 Nm), starting from the middle and working outward.
21. Connect the fuel return line to the regulator outlet.
22. Install the power steering pump bracket and alternator and power steering pump adjusting brackets.
23. Install the alternator and belt.
24. Install the coolant recovery tank.
25. Connect the injector wiring.
26. Install the heater tube support, manifold support and transaxle fill tube brackets.
27. Connect the vacuum hoses at the rear of the bracket.
28. Install the ignition coil with its bracket.
29. Install the fuel supply line to the throttle cable support bracket.
30. Connect the cables, hoses and connectors to the throttle body.
31. Connect the wiring to the wastegate and MAP sensor.
32. Install the induction tube and hoses.
33. Fill all fluids to the proper levels.

Intake manifold bolt torque sequence—1989–90 2.3L engine

34. Connect the negative battery cable and check for leaks.

2.3L Engine

1. Disconnect the negative battery cable.
2. Remove the coolant fan shroud, vacuum hose and electrical connector from the MAP sensor.
3. Disconnect the throttle body to air cleaner duct.
4. Remove the throttle cable bracket.
5. Remove the power brake vacuum hose, including the attaching bracket to power steering bracket and position it aside.
6. Remove the throttle body from the intake manifold with electrical harness, coolant hoses, vacuum hoses and throttle cable attached. Position these components aside.
7. Remove the oil/air separator bolts and hoses. Leave the hoses attached to the separator, disconnect from the oil fill, chain housing and the intake manifold. Remove as an assembly.
8. Remove the oil fill cap and oil level indicator stick.
9. Pull the oil tube fill upward to unseat from block and remove.
10. Disconnect the injector harness connector.
11. Remove the fill tube, rotating as necessary to gain clearance for the oil/air separator nipple between the intake tubes and fuel rail electrical harness.
12. Remove the intake manifold support bracket bolts and nut. Remove the intake manifold attaching nuts and bolts.
13. Remove the intake manifold.

To install:

14. Thoroughly clean and dry the mating surfaces. Install new gaskets and place the intake manifold in position.
15. Tighten the intake manifold bolts/nuts, in sequence, to 18 ft. lbs. (25 Nm). Tighten intake manifold brace and retainers hand tight. Tighten to specifications in the following order:

a. Nut to stud bolt—18 ft. lbs. (25 Nm).

b. Bolt to intake manifold—40 ft. lbs. (55 Nm).

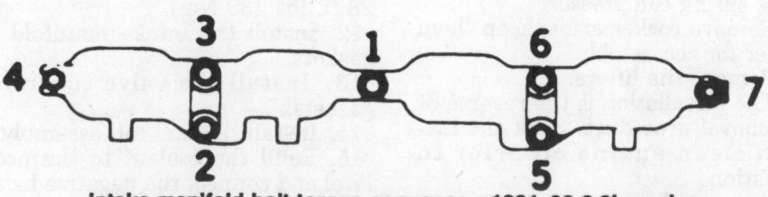

Intake manifold bolt torque sequence—1991–93 2.3L engine

c. Bolt to cylinder block—40 ft. lbs. (55 Nm).

16. Lubricate a new oil fill tube ring seal with engine oil and install tube between No. 1 and 2 intake tubes. Rotate as necessary to gain clearance for oil/air separator nipple on fill tube.

17. Locate the oil fill tube in its cylinder block opening. Align the fill tube so it is approximately in its installed position. Press straight down to seat fill tube and seal into cylinder block.

18. Lubricate the hoses and install the oil/air separator assembly. Install the throttle body to intake manifold using a new gasket.

19. Install the power brake vacuum hose and the attaching bracket to power steering bracket.

20. Install the throttle cable bracket.

21. Connect the throttle body to air cleaner duct.

22. Install the coolant fan shroud, vacuum hose and electrical connector to the MAP sensor.

23. Fill all fluids to their proper levels.

24. Connect the negative battery cable and check for leaks.

2.5L Engine

1. Relieve the system fuel pressure. Disconnect the negative battery cable.

2. Drain the coolant. Remove the air cleaner, PCV valve and hose.

3. Disconnect and plug the vacuum lines and fuel lines. Disconnect the wiring and linkages from the throttle body.

4. Disconnect the throttle linkage and bell crank; position the assembly aside for clearance.

5. Disconnect the heater hoses. If equipped with power steering, disconnect and remove the upper power steering pump bracket.

6. If equipped with cruise control, disconnect the servo cable. Remove the ignition coil.

7. Remove the intake manifold mounting bolts and remove the intake manifold.

To install:

8. Install the intake manifold with the new gasket.

NOTE: Make sure the stamped numbers on the gasket are facing the manifold surface.

9. Install the retaining bolts and washers. Tighten the bolts in sequence. Tighten the outside bolts to 26 ft. lbs. (35 Nm) and the inside bolts to 37 ft. lbs. (50 Nm).

10. Lubricate a new oil fill tube O-ring with clean engine oil and install the tube down through the intake manifold and press tube into position in the engine block.

11. Install the oil/air separator assembly and intall the oil fill tube bolt/screw.

12. Install the throttle body to the intake manifold with a new gasket.

13. Connect the coolant lines and power brake vacuum hose to the throttle body.

14. Install the throttle cable bracket and the vacuum hoses to the intake manifold.

15. Install the hose from the fuel regulator and purge solenoid to the power steering bracket.

16. Connect the electrical connectors to the MAP sensor, MAT sensor, purge solenoid and fuel injector harness.

17. Install the coolant recovery tank and fill the coolant to the proper level.

18. Connect the negative battery cable.

3.3L Engine

1. Relieve the fuel system pressure.

2. Disconnect the negative battery cable.

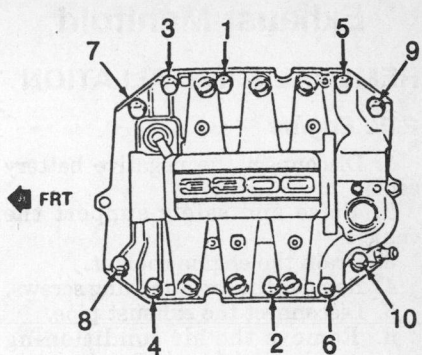

FRT

Intake manifold bolt torque sequence—3.3L engine

3. Drain the coolant and remove the air intake duct.

4. Remove the serpentine drive belt, alternator and bracket.

5. Remove the power steering pump braces and the coolant bypass hose.

6. Label and remove all the necessary vacuum and electrical wiring connectors.

7. Remove the throttle, cruise control and TV cables from the throttle body assembly.

8. Disconnect the heater hoses from the throttle body.

9. Remove the upper radiator hose from the intake manifold.

10. Remove the fuel lines, the fuel rail and the fuel injectors. Label and disconnect the spark plug wires.

11. Remove the intake manifold mounting bolts and remove the intake manifold.

To install:

12. Thoroughly clean and dry all mating surfaces. Apply sealer to the 4 head-to-block corners.

13. Apply thread lock compound to the threads and tighten to 88 inch lbs. (10 Nm).

14. Install the fuel injectors, rail and lines. Connect the spark plug wires.

15. Connect the heater hoses to the throttle body.

16. Install the upper radiator hose to the intake manifold.

17. Connect the throttle, cruise control and TV cables to the throttle body assembly.

18. Connect all remaining vacuum and electrical wiring connectors.

19. Install the power steering pump braces.

20. Install the alternator, bracket and serpentine drive belt.

21. Connect the mass air flow sensor, if equipped. Install the air intake duct.

22. Fill all fluids to their proper levels.

23. Connect the negative battery cable and check for leaks.

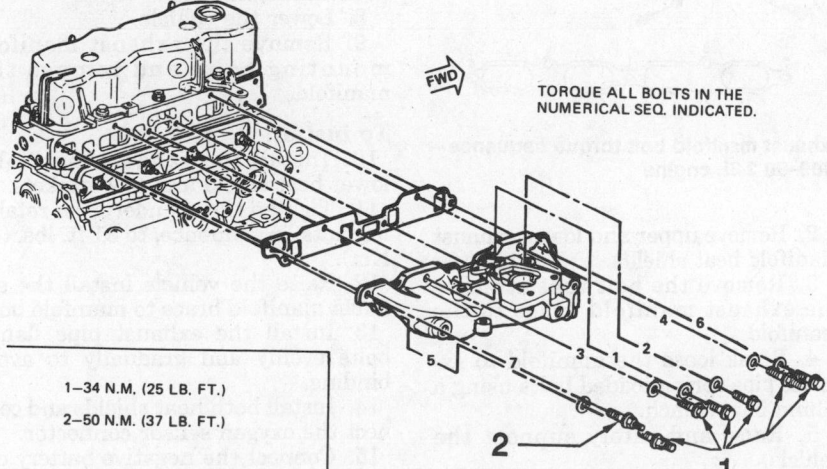

FWD

TORQUE ALL BOLTS IN THE NUMERICAL SEQ. INDICATED.

1—34 N.M. (25 LB. FT.)
2—50 N.M. (37 LB. FT.)

Intake manifold bolt torque sequence—2.5L engine

Exhaust Manifold

REMOVAL & INSTALLATION

2.0L Engine

1. Disconnect the negative battery cable.
2. Raise and safely support the vehicle.
3. Drain the engine coolant.
4. Remove the fan attaching screws.
5. Disconnect the exhaust pipe.
6. Remove the air conditioning compressor rear support bracket.
7. Remove turbocharger support bracket to engine.
8. Disconnect and plug the oil drain pipe at turbocharger.
9. Disconnect water return pipe at turbocharger.
10. Lower vehicle and remove coolant recovery pipe.
11. Remove the air induction tube, coolant fan, oxygen sensor.
12. Disconnect the oil and water feed pipes.
13. Remove air intake duct and vacuum hose at actuator.
14. Remove the exhaust manifold attaching nuts and remove turbocharger and manifold as an assembly.
15. Remove turbocharger from exhaust manifold.

To install:

16. Assemble the turbocharger and exhaust manifold.
17. Clean the exhaust manifold and cylinder head mating surfaces.
18. Install a new gasket and install the manifold/turbocharger assembly to the engine. Tighten No. 2 and 3 manifold runner nuts first, then Nos. 1 and 4, to 18 ft. lbs. (24 Nm).
19. Connect the oil and water feed and return lines.
20. Connect the oxygen sensor.
21. Install the air intake duct and connect the vacuum hose to the actuator.
22. Install the cooling fan.
23. Install the induction tube and coolant recovery tube.
24. Raise and safely support the vehicle.
25. Install the rear turbocharger support bolt.
26. Install the compressor support bracket.
27. Install the oil drain hose.
28. Connect the exhaust pipe.
29. Connect the negative battery cable and check the turbocharger for proper operation and the assembly for leaks.

2.3L Engine

1. Disconnect the negative battery cable and oxygen sensor connector.

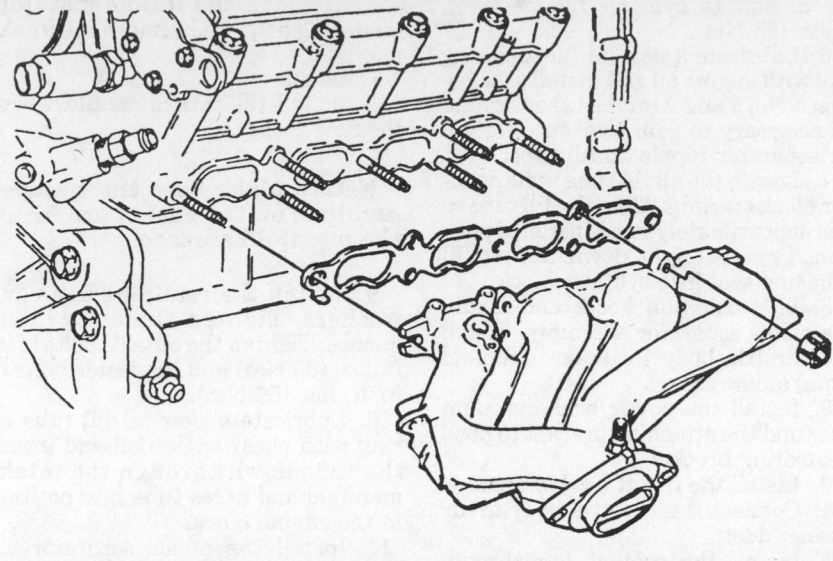

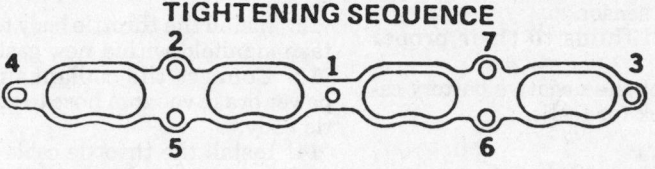

TIGHTENING SEQUENCE

Exhaust manifold bolt torque sequence—1991–93 2.3L engine

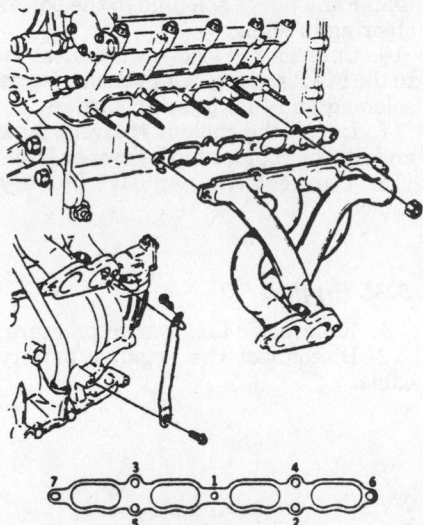

Exhaust manifold bolt torque sequence—1989–90 2.3L engine

2. Remove upper and lower exhaust manifold heat shields.
3. Remove the bolt that attaches the exhaust manifold brace to the manifold.
4. Break loose the manifold to exhaust pipe spring loaded bolts using a 13mm box wrench.
5. Raise and safely support the vehicle.

NOTE: It is necessary to relieve

the spring pressure from 1 bolt prior to removing the second bolt. If the spring pressure is not relieved it will cause the exhaust pipe to twist and bind up the bolt as it is removed.

6. Remove the manifold to exhaust pipe bolts from the exhaust pipe flange as follows:
   a. Unscrew either bolt clockwise 4 turns.
   b. Remove the other bolt.
   c. Remove the first bolt.
7. Pull down and back on the exhaust pipe to disengage it from the exhaust manifold bolts.
8. Lower the vehicle.
9. Remove the exhaust manifold mounting bolts and remove the manifold.

To install:

10. Install the exhaust manifold, lower heat shield and new gaskets.
11. Tighten the cylinder head retaining nuts, in sequence, to 31 ft. lbs. (42 Nm).
12. Raise the vehicle install the exhaust manifold brace to manifold bolt.
13. Install the exhaust pipe flange bolts evenly and gradually to avoid binding.
14. Install both heat shields and connect the oxygen sensor connector.
15. Connect the negative battery cable, start the engine and check for exhaust leaks.

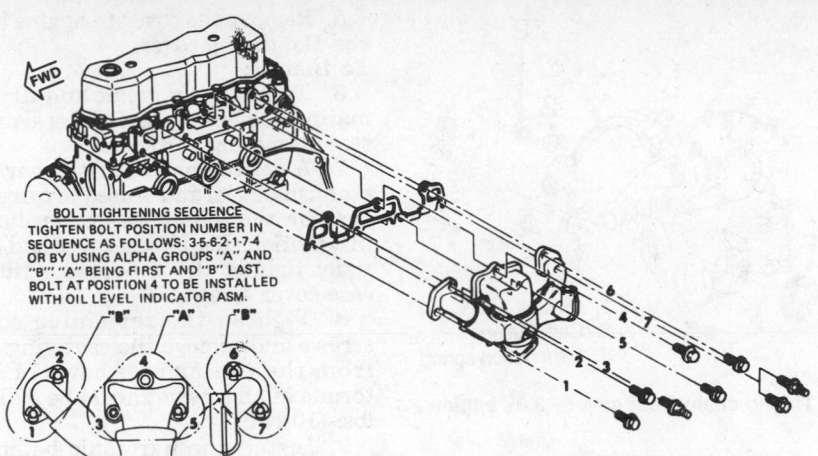

BOLT TIGHTENING SEQUENCE
TIGHTEN BOLT POSITION NUMBER IN
SEQUENCE AS FOLLOWS: 3-5-6-2-1-7-4
OR BY USING ALPHA GROUPS "A" AND
"B". "A" BEING FIRST AND "B" LAST.
BOLT AT POSITION 4 TO BE INSTALLED
WITH OIL LEVEL INDICATOR ASM.

Exhaust manifold bolt torque sequence—2.5L engine

2.5L Engine

1. Disconnect the negative battery cable and oxygen sensor connector. Remove the air cleaner assembly.
2. Remove the upper alternator mount and position the unit to one side.
3. Raise and safely support the vehicle.
4. Disconnect the exhaust pipe-to-exhaust manifold bolts and lower the exhaust pipe.
5. Lower the vehicle.
6. Remove the exhaust manifold mounting bolts and lift the exhaust manifold from the engine.
7. The installation is the reverse of the removal procedure. Tighten the exhaust manifold bolts, in sequence, to 32 ft. lbs. (43 Nm).
8. Connect the negative battery cable and check for leaks.

3.3L Engine

LEFT/FRONT MANIFOLD

1. Disconnect the negative battery cable.
2. Disconnect air cleaner mounting bolts.
3. Remove the bolts attaching the exhaust crossover pipe to the manifold.
4. Disconnect the spark plug wires.
5. Remove the cooling fan.
6. Remove the mounting bolts and remove the manifold.

NOTE: The oil dipstick tube may have to be removed to provide access to the manifold bolts.

7. The installation is the reverse of the removal procedure. Tighten the mounting bolts to 30 ft. lbs. (41 Nm) and the nuts to 19 ft. lbs. (26 Nm).
8. Connect the negative battery cable and check for leaks.

RIGHT/REAR MANIFOLD

1. Disconnect the negative battery cable.
2. Remove the 2 bolts attaching exhaust pipe to manifold.
3. Disconnect oxygen sensor wire.
4. Disconnect and tag spark plug wires.
5. Remove 2 nuts attaching crossover pipe to manifold.
6. Remove serpentine belt.
7. Remove power steering pump.
8. Remove heater hose from tube, heat shield and C^3I bracket nuts, if necessary.
9. Remove the bolts attaching the manifold to cylinder head.

To install:
10. Install the manifold to the cylinder head and tighten the mounting bolts to 30 ft. lbs. (41 Nm) and the nuts to 19 ft. lbs. (26 Nm).
11. Install the heater hose to the tube, if removed and install the power steering pump.
12. Install the serpentine belt and install the 2 nuts that secure the crossover pipe to the exhaust manifold.
13. Install the spark plug wires to the spark plugs and connect the oxygen sensor wire.
14. Install the 2 bolts that secure the exhaust pipe to the manifold and connect the negative battery cable.
15. Start the engine and check for leaks.

Turbocharger

REMOVAL & INSTALLATION

1. Disconnect the negative battery cable.
2. Raise and safely support the vehicle.
3. Drain the engine coolant.
4. Remove the fan attaching screws.
5. Disconnect the exhaust pipe.

6. Remove the air conditioning compressor rear support bracket.
7. Remove turbocharger support bracket to engine.
8. Disconnect and plug the oil drain pipe at turbocharger.
9. Disconnect water return pipe at turbocharger.
10. Lower vehicle and remove coolant recovery pipe.
11. Remove the air induction tube, coolant fan, oxygen sensor.
12. Disconnect the oil and water feed pipes.
13. Remove air intake duct and vacuum hose at actuator.
14. Remove the exhaust manifold attaching nuts and remove turbocharger and manifold as an assembly.
15. Remove turbocharger from exhaust manifold.

To install:
16. Assemble the turbocharger and exhaust manifold.
17. Clean the exhaust manifold and cylinder head mating surfaces.
18. Install a new gasket and install the manifold/turbocharger assembly to the engine. Tighten the Nos. 2 and 3 manifold runner nuts first, then Nos. 1 and 4, to 18 ft. lbs. (24 Nm).
19. Connect the oil and water feed and return lines.
20. Connect the oxygen sensor.
21. Install the air intake duct and connect the vacuum hose to the actuator.
22. Install the cooling fan.
23. Install the induction tube and coolant recovery tube.
24. Raise and safely support the vehicle.
25. Install the rear turbocharger support bolt.
26. Install the compressor support bracket.
27. Install the oil drain hose.
28. Connect the exhaust pipe.
29. Connect the negative battery cable and check the turbocharger for proper operation and the assembly for leaks.

Timing Chain Front Cover

REMOVAL & INSTALLATION

2.3L Engine

1. Disconnect the negative battery cable. Remove the coolant recovery reservoir.
2. Remove the serpentine drive belt using a 13mm wrench that is at least 24 in. long.
3. Remove upper cover fasteners.
4. Raise and safely support the vehicle.
5. Remove the right front wheel assembly and lower splash shield.

6. Remove the crankshaft balancer assembly.

NOTE: Do not install an automatic transaxle-equipped engine balancer on a manual-transaxle equipped engine or vice-versa.

7. Remove lower cover fasteners and lower the vehicle.
8. Remove the front cover.
9. The installation is the reverse of the removal procedure. Tighten the balancer attaching bolt to 74 ft. lbs. (100 Nm).

2.5L Engine

1990–91

1. Disconnect the negative battery cable.
2. Remove the belts. Remove the power steering pump mounting bolts and position it aside.
3. Raise and safely support the vehicle. Remove the inner fender splash shield.
4. Remove the harmonic balancer.
5. Remove the timing case cover-to-engine bolts and the timing case cover.

To install:

6. Thoroughly clean and dry all mating surfaces. Use RTV sealant to seal all mating surfaces.
7. A centering tool fits over the crankshaft seal and is used to correctly position the timing case cover during installation. Install the cover and partially tighten the 2 opposing timing case cover screws.
8. Tighten the remaining cover screws and remove the centering tool from the timing case cover. Tighten to 89 inch lbs. (10 Nm).
9. Install the harmonic balancer and tighten the bolt to 162 ft. lbs. (220 Nm). Install the belts and the power steering pump.
10. Install the splash shield.
11. Connect the negative battery cable and check for leaks.

3.3L Engine

1. Disconnect the negative battery cable and drain the engine coolant.
2. Remove the accessory drive belt and remove the heater pipes.
3. Remove the lower radiator hose and coolant bypass hose from the cover.
4. Raise and safely support the vehicle. Remove the right front wheel assembly and the right inner fender splash shield.
5. Remove the torque converter cover.
6. Hold the flywheel in place, using a flywheel holding device J-37096 or equivalent, and remove the balancer bolt and balancer assembly.
7. Remove the crankshaft sensor

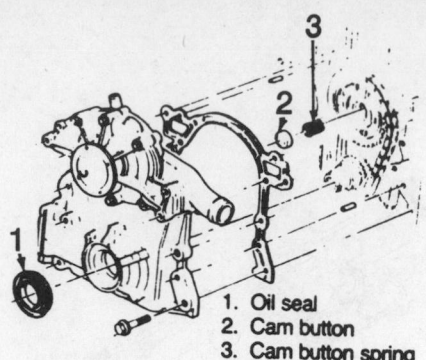

1. Oil seal
2. Cam button
3. Cam button spring

Timing chain front cover—3.3L engine

shield and disconnect the following electrical connectors:

    Crankshaft sensor
    Camshaft sensor
    Oil pressure sender

8. Remove the oil pan to the front cover bolts.
9. Remove the front cover attaching bolts and remove the cover.

To install:

10. Install the gasket to the cylinder block and install the front cover and attaching bolts. Apply thread locking compound to the bolts and tighten the bolts to 22 ft. lbs. (30 Nm).
11. Install the oil pan to front cover bolts and tighten to 88 inch lbs. (10 Nm).
12. Connect the electrical connections.
13. If necessary, adjust the crankshaft sensor.
14. Install the crankshaft sensor shield.
15. Install the crankshaft balancer and bolt and tighten to 110 ft. lbs. (150 Nm) plus 76 degrees.
16. Install the torque converter cover and inner fender splash shield.
17. Install the right front wheel to the vehicle and lower the vehicle.
18. Install the coolant bypass hose, lower radiator hose and heater pipes.
19. Install the accessory drive belt and fill the cooling system.
20. Connect the negative battery cable and check for leaks.

Timing Gear Front Cover

REMOVAL & INSTALLATION

1989 2.5L Engine

1. Disconnect the negative battery cable.
2. Remove the belts.
3. Raise and safely support the vehicle. Remove the inner fender splash shield.
4. Remove the harmonic balancer.

5. Remove the cover-to-engine bolts and the timing cover.

To install:

6. Thoroughly clean and dry all mating surfaces. Use RTV sealant to seal all mating surfaces.
7. A centering tool fits over the crankshaft seal and is used to correctly position the timing case cover during installation. Install the cover and partially tighten the 2 opposing timing case cover screws.
8. Tighten the remaining cover screws and remove the centering tool from the timing case cover. Final torque of all screws should be 89 inch lbs. (10 Nm).
9. Install the harmonic balancer and tighten the bolt to 162 ft. lbs. (220 Nm). Install the belts and the power steering pump.
10. Install the splash shield.
11. Connect the negative battery cable and check for leaks.

Front Cover Oil Seal

REPLACEMENT

1. Disconnect the negative battery cable.
2. Remove the front cover.
3. Using a small prybar, pry out the old oil seal.

NOTE: Use care to avoid damage to seal bore or seal contact surfaces.

4. Thoroughly clean and dry the oil seal mounting surface.
5. Use the appropriate installation tool and drive the oil seal into the front cover.
6. Lubricate balancer and seal lip with clean engine oil.
7. The installation is the reverse of the removal procedure.
8. Connect the negative battery cable and check for leaks.

Timing Chain and Sprockets

REMOVAL & INSTALLATION

2.3L Engine

NOTE: It is recommended that the entire procedure be reviewed before attempting to service the timing chain.

1. Disconnect the negative battery cable.
2. Remove the front timing chain cover and crankshaft oil slinger.
3. Looking from the front of the engine, rotate the crankshaft clockwise, (normal rotation) until the camshaft sprocket's timing dowel pin holes align

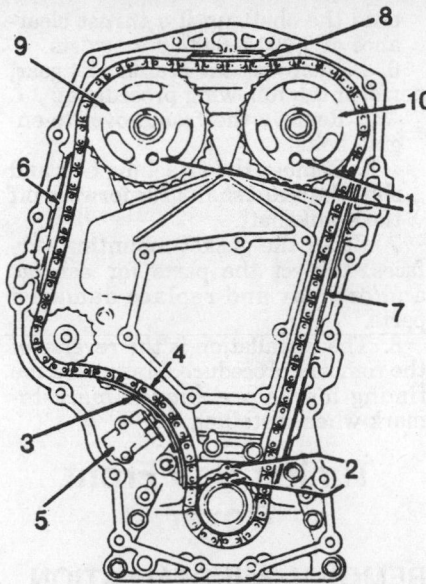

1. Camshaft timing marks
2. Crankshaft timing mark
3. Tensioner shoe assembly
4. Timing chain
5. Tensioner
6. R/H guide
7. L/H guide
8. Upper guide
9. Exhaust camshaft sprocket
10. Intake camshaft sprocket

Timing chain installation—2.3L engine

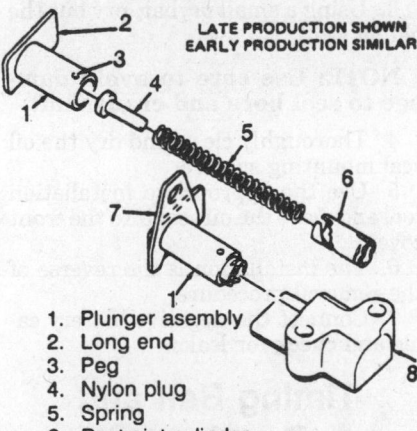

LATE PRODUCTION SHOWN
EARLY PRODUCTION SIMILAR

1. Plunger asembly
2. Long end
3. Peg
4. Nylon plug
5. Spring
6. Restraint cylinder
7. J–36589 anti-release devise
8. Tensioner body

Exploded view of the timing chain tensioner—2.3L engine. Versions may differ slightly with year.

with the holes in the timing chain housing. The mark on the crankshaft sprocket should align with the mark on the cylinder block. The crankshaft

sprocket keyway should point upwards and align with the centerline of the cylinder bores. This is the normal timed position.

4. Remove the timing chain guides.
5. Raise and safely support the vehicle.
6. Gently pry off timing chain tensioner spring retainer and remove spring.

NOTE: Two styles of tensioner are used. Early production engines will have a spring post and late production ones will not. Both styles are identical in operation and are interchangeable.

7. Remove the timing chain tensioner shoe retainer.
8. Make sure all the slack in the timing chain is above the tensioner assembly; remove the chain tensioner shoe. The timing chain must be disengaged from the wear grooves in the tensioner shoe in order to remove the shoe. Slide a prybar under the timing chain while pulling shoe outward.
9. If difficulty is encountered removing chain tensioner shoe, proceed as follows:
   a. Lower the vehicle.
   b. Hold the intake camshaft sprocket with a holding tool and remove the sprocket bolt and washer.
   c. Remove the washer from the bolt and re-thread the bolt back into the camshaft by hand, the bolt provides a surface to push against.
   d. Remove intake camshaft sprocket using a 3-jaw puller in the 3 relief holes in the sprocket. Do not attempt to pry the sprocket off the camshaft or damage to the sprocket or chain housing could occur.
10. Remove the tensioner assembly attaching bolts and the tensioner.

—— **CAUTION** ——

The tensioner piston is spring loaded and could fly out causing personal injury.

11. Remove the chain housing to block stud, which is actually the timing chain tensioner shoe pivot.
12. Remove the timing chain.
To install:
13. Tighten intake camshaft sprocket attaching bolt and washer, while holding the sprocket with tool J–36013, if removed.
14. Install the special tool through holes in camshaft sprockets into holes in timing chain housing. This positions the camshafts for correct timing.
15. If the camshafts are out of position and must be rotated more than ⅛ turn in order to install the alignment dowel pins:
   a. The crankshaft must be rotated 90 degrees clockwise off TDC in

order to give the valves adequate clearance to open.
   b. Once the camshafts are in position and the dowels installed, rotate the crankshaft counterclockwise back to TDC. Do not rotate the crankshaft clockwise to TDC or valve and piston damage could occur.
16. Install the timing chain over the exhaust camshaft sprocket, around the idler sprocket and around the crankshaft sprocket.
17. Remove the alignment dowel pin from the intake camshaft. Using a dowel pin remover tool, rotate the intake camshaft sprocket counterclockwise enough to slide the timing chain over the intake camshaft sprocket. Release the camshaft sprocket wrench. The length of chain between the 2 camshaft sprockets will tighten. If properly timed, the intake camshaft alignment dowel pin should slide in easily. If the dowel pin does not fully index, the camshafts are not timed correctly and the procedure must be repeated.
18. Leave the alignment dowel pins installed.
19. With slack removed from chain between intake camshaft sprocket and crankshaft sprocket, the timing marks on the crankshaft and the cylinder block should be aligned. If marks are not aligned, move the chain 1 tooth forward or rearward, remove slack and recheck marks.
20. Tighten the chain housing to block stud. The stud is installed under the timing chain. Tighten to 19 ft. lbs. (26 Nm).
21. Reload timing chain tensioner assembly to its position as follows:
   a. Assemble restraint cylinder, spring and nylon plug into plunger. Index slot in restraint cylinder with peg in plunger. While rotating the restraint cylinder clockwise, push the restraint cylinder into the plunger until it bottoms. Keep rotating the restraint cylinder clockwise but allow the spring to push it out of the plunger. The pin in the plunger will lock the restraint in the loaded position.
   b. Install tool J–36589 or equivalent, onto plunger assembly.
   c. Install plunger assembly into tensioner body with the long end toward the crankshaft when installed.
22. Install the tensioner assembly to the chain housing. Recheck plunger assembly installation. It is correctly installed when the long end is toward the crankshaft.
23. Install and tighten timing chain tensioner bolts and tighten to 10 ft. lbs. (14 Nm).
24. Install the tensioner shoe and tensioner shoe retainer. Remove spe-

cial tool J–36589 and squeeze plunger assembly into the tensioner body to unload the plunger assembly.

25. Lower vehicle and remove the alignment dowel pins. Rotate crankshaft clockwise 2 full rotations. Align crankshaft timing mark with mark on cylinder block and reinstall alignment dowel pins. Alignment dowel pins will slide in easily if engine is timed correctly.

NOTE: If the engine is not correctly timed, severe engine damage could occur.

26. Install 3 timing chain guides and crankshaft oil slinger.
27. Install the timing chain front cover.
28. Connect the negative battery cable and check for leaks.

3.3L and 1990–91 2.5L Engines

1. Disconnect the negative battery cable.
2. Drain the cooling system. Disconnect the cooling hose from the water pump.
3. Raise and safely support the vehicle.
4. Remove the inner fender splash shield.
5. Remove the serpentine drive belt.
6. Remove the crankshaft pulley bolt and slide the pulley from the crankshaft.
7. Remove the front cover.
8. Rotate the crankshaft to align the timing marks on the sprockets. Remove the chain dampener assembly.
9. Remove the camshaft sprocket-to-camshaft bolt(s), remove the camshaft sprocket and chain and thrust bearing.
10. Remove the crankshaft gear by sliding it forward.
11. Clean the gasket mounting surfaces. Inspect the timing chain and the sprockets for damage and/or wear and replace damaged parts.

To install:
12. Position the crankshaft so the No. 1 piston is at TDC of its compression stroke. Install the thrust bearing on 2.5L engine.
13. Temporarily install the gear on the camshaft and position the camshaft so the timing mark on the gear is pointing straight down.
14. Assemble the timing chain to the gears so the timing marks are aligned, mark-to-mark.
15. Install the camshaft sprocket attaching bolt(s).
16. Install the camshaft thrust bearing, if not already done.
17. Install the timing chain dampener.
18. Install the front cover and all related parts.

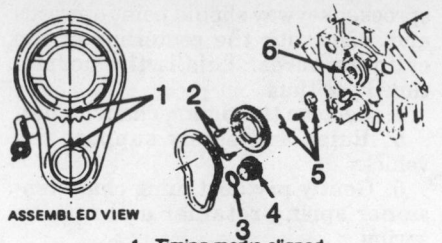

ASSEMBLED VIEW

1. Timing marks aligned
2. 22 ft. lbs. (30 Nm)
3. Seal
4. Crankshaft gear
5. Dampener assembly
6. Camshaft

Timing chain and timing mark alignment—3.3L engine

19. Connect the negative battery cable and check for leaks.

Timing Gears

REMOVAL & INSTALLATION

1989 2.5L Engine

NOTE: If the camshaft gear is to be replaced, the engine must be removed from the vehicle. The crankshaft gear may be replaced with the engine in the vehicle.

1. Disconnect the negative battery cable.
2. Raise and safely support the vehicle.
3. Remove the inner fender splash shield.
4. Remove the accessory drive belts. Remove the crankshaft pulley-to-crankshaft pulley bolt and slide the pulley from the crankshaft.
5. If replacing the camshaft gear, perform the following procedures:
   a. Remove the engine from the vehicle and secure it onto a suitable holding fixture.
   b. Remove the camshaft from the engine.
   c. Using an arbor press, press the camshaft gear from the camshaft.
   d. To install the camshaft gear onto the camshaft, press the gear

Aligning the timing marks—1989 2.5L engine

onto the shaft until a thrust clearance of 0.0015–0.0050 in. exists.
6. If removing the crankshaft gear, perform the following procedures:
   a. Remove the front cover-to-engine bolts.
   b. Remove the attaching bolt and slide the crankshaft gear forward off the crankshaft.
7. Clean the gasket mounting surfaces. Inspect the parts for damage and/or wear and replace damaged parts.
8. The installation is the reverse of the removal procedure. Make sure the timing marks are aligned mark-to-mark when installing.

Timing Belt Front Cover

REMOVAL & INSTALLATION

2.0L Engine

1. Disconnect negative battery cable.
2. Remove tensioner and bolt.
3. Remove serpentine belt.
4. Unsnap upper and lower cover.
5. The installation is the reverse of the removal procedure.

OIL SEAL REPLACEMENT

1. Disconnect the negative battery cable.
2. Remove the timing belt sprockets and the inner cover. Remove the crankshaft key and thrust washer.
3. Using a small prybar, pry out the old oil seal.

NOTE: Use care to avoid damage to seal bore and crankshaft.

4. Thoroughly clean and dry the oil seal mounting surface.
5. Use the appropriate installation tool and drive the oil seal into the front cover.
6. The installation is the reverse of the removal procedure.
7. Connect the negative battery cable and check for leaks.

Timing Belt and Tensioner

ADJUSTMENT

2.0L Engine

1. Disconnect the negative battery cable. Remove the timing belt cover.
2. Make sure the portion of the belt between the camshaft and crankshaft has no slack.
3. Adjust the timing belt using tool J-33039 to turn the water pump ec-

centric clockwise until the tensioner contacts the high torque stop. Temporarily tighten the water to prevent movement.

4. Turn the engine 2 revolutions.

5. Turn the water pump eccentric counterclockwise until the hole in the tensioner arm is aligned with the hole in the base.

6. Tighten the water pump bolts to 19 ft. lbs. (25 Nm), making sure the tensioner hole remains aligned.

7. Install the timing belt cover and all related parts.

8. Connect the negative battery cable and road test the vehicle.

REMOVAL & INSTALLATION

2.0L Engine

1. Disconnect the negative battery cable.

2. Remove the timing belt cover.

3. Remove the crankshaft pulley.

4. Loosen the water pump mounting bolts and relieve the tension using tool J–33039.

5. Remove the timing belt.

To install:

6. Position the camshaft and crankshaft so the marks on their sprockets aligns with the marks on the rear cover.

7. Install the timing belt so the portion between the camshaft and crankshaft has no slack.

8. Adjust the timing belt using tool J–33039 to turn the water pump eccentric clockwise until the tensioner contacts the high torque stop. Temporarily tighten the water to prevent movement.

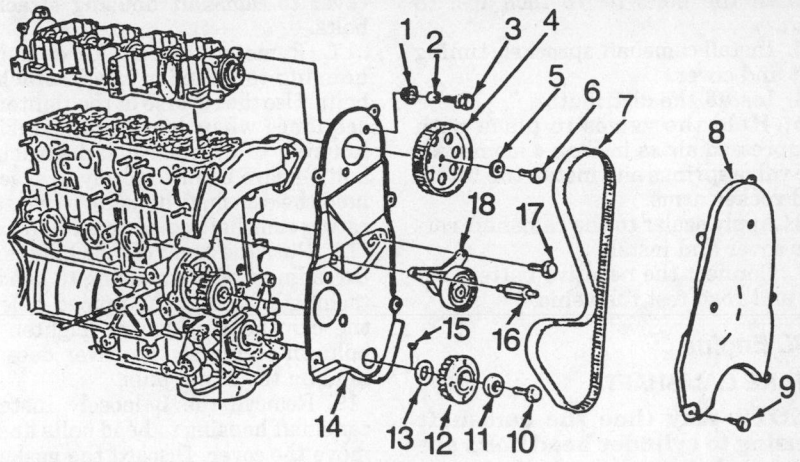

1. Grommet	7. Timing belt	13. Washer
2. Sleeve	8. Front cover	14. Rear cover
3. Bolt	9. Bolt	15. Key
4. Camshaft sprocket	10. Bolt	16. Stud
5. Washer	11. Washer	17. Bolt
6. Bolt	12. Crankshaft sprocket	18. Tensioner

Timing belt and related parts—1989 2.0L engine

9. Turn the engine 2 revolutions to fully seat the belt into the gear teeth.

10. Turn the water pump eccentric counterclockwise until the hole in the tensioner arm is aligned with the hole in the base.

11. Tighten the water pump bolts to 19 ft. lbs. (25 Nm), making sure the tensioner hole remains aligned as in Step 10.

12. Install the timing belt cover and all related parts.

13. Install the crankshaft pulley.

14. Install the timing belt cover and all related parts.

15. Connect the negative battery cable and road test the vehicle.

Timing Sprockets

REMOVAL & INSTALLATION

1. Disconnect the negative battery cable.

2. If removing the camshaft sprocket, remove the camshaft carrier cover.

3. Remove the timing belt cover.

4. Position the engine so the timing marks are aligned for belt installation.

5. Remove the timing belt.

6. If removing the camshaft sprocket, hold the camshaft with an open-end wrench.

7. Remove the camshaft or crankshaft sprocket attaching bolt, washer and the sprocket.

8. The installation is the reverse of the removal procedure. Tighten the camshaft sprocket bolt to 34 ft. lbs. (45 Nm). Tighten the crankshaft sprocket bolt to 114 ft. lbs. (155 Nm).

9. Connect the negative battery cable and road test the vehicle.

Camshaft

REMOVAL & INSTALLATION

2.0L Engine

1. Relieve the fuel system pressure.

2. Disconnect the negative battery cable.

3. Remove the camshaft carrier cover.

4. Hold the valves in place with compressed air, using air adapters in the spark plug holes.

5. Compress the valve springs with the special valve spring compressing tool.

6. Remove the rocker arms and lifters and keep them in order for reassembly. Hold the camshaft with an open-end wrench and remove the camshaft sprocket. Try to keep the valve timing by using a rubber cord, if possible. If the timing cannot be kept intact, the timing belt will have to be reset.

7. Matchmark and remove the distributor.

8. Remove the camshaft thrust plate from the rear of the carrier.

9. Remove the camshaft by sliding it toward the rear. Remove the front carrier seal.

To install:

10. Install a new carrier seal.

11. Thoroughly lubricate the camshaft and journals with clean oil and install the camshaft.

12. Install the rear thrust plate and

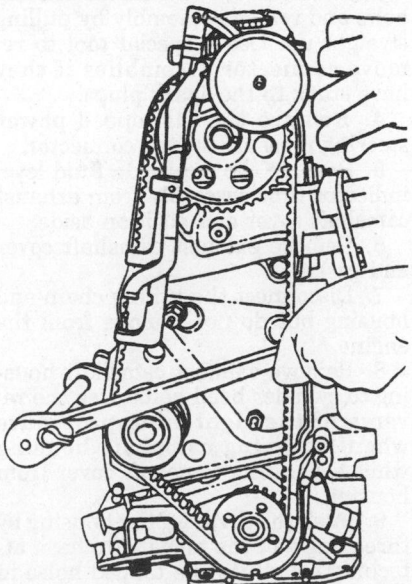

Adjusting the timing belt tension—2.0L engine

tighten the bolts to 70 inch lbs. (8 Nm).

13. Install camshaft sprocket, timing belt and cover.

14. Install the distributor.

15. Hold the valves in place with compressed air as in Step 4, compress the valve springs and install the lifters and rocker arms.

16. Apply sealer to the camshaft carrier cover and install.

17. Connect the negative battery cable and road test the vehicle.

2.3L Engine

INTAKE CAMSHAFT

NOTE: Any time the camshaft housing to cylinder head bolts are loosened or removed, the camshaft housing to cylinder head gasket must be replaced.

1. Relieve the fuel system pressure. Disconnect the negative battery cable.

2. Label and disconnect the ignition coil and module assembly electrical connections.

3. Remove the ignition coil and module assembly to camshaft housing bolts and remove assembly by pulling straight up. Use a special spark plug boot wire remover tool to remove connector assemblies, if they have stuck to the spark plugs.

4. Remove the idle speed power steering pressure switch connector.

5. Loosen 3 power steering pump pivot bolts and remove drive belt.

6. Disconnect the 2 rear power steering pump bracket to transaxle bolts.

7. Remove the front power steering pump bracket to cylinder block bolt.

8. Disconnect the power steering pump assembly and position aside.

9. Using the special tool, remove the power steering pump drive pulley from the intake camshaft.

10. Remove oil/air separator bolts and hoses. Leave the hoses attached to the separator, disconnect from the oil fill, chain housing and intake manifold. Remove as an assembly.

11. Remove vacuum line from fuel pressure regulator and disconnect the fuel injector harness connector.

12. Disconnect fuel line attaching clamp from bracket on top of intake camshaft housing.

13. Remove fuel rail to camshaft housing attaching bolts.

14. Remove the fuel rail from the cylinder head. Cover injector openings in cylinder head and cover injector nozzles. Leave fuel lines attached and position fuel rail aside.

15. Disconnect the timing chain and housing but do not remove from the engine.

16. Remove intake camshaft housing

cover to camshaft housing attaching bolts.

17. Remove the intake camshaft housing to cylinder head attaching bolts. Use the reverse of the tightening sequence when loosening camshaft housing to cylinder head attaching bolts. Leave 2 bolts loosely in place to hold the camshaft housing while separating camshaft cover from housing.

18. Push the cover off the housing by threading 4 of the housing to head attaching bolts into the tapped holes in the cam housing cover. Tighten the bolts in evenly so the cover does not bind on the dowel pins.

19. Remove the 2 loosely installed camshaft housing to head bolts and remove the cover. Discard the gaskets.

20. Note the position of the chain sprocket dowel pin for reassembly. Remove the camshaft carefully; do not damage the camshaft oil seal.

21. Remove intake camshaft oil seal from camshaft and discard seal. This seal must be replaced any time the housing and cover are separated.

22. Remove the camshaft carrier from the cylinder head and remove the gasket.

To install:

23. Thoroughly clean the mating surfaces of the camshaft carrier and the cylinder head, bolts and bolt holes. Install a new gasket and place the housing on the head. Install 1 bolt loosely to hold in place.

24. Install the lifters into their bores. If the camshaft is being replaced, the lifters must also be replaced. Lubricate camshaft lobes, journals and lifters with camshaft and lifter prelube. The camshaft lobes and journals must be adequately lubricated or engine damage could occur upon start up.

25. Install the camshaft in the same position as when removed. The timing chain sprocket dowel pin should be straight up and align with the centerline of the lifter bores.

26. Install new camshaft housing to camshaft housing cover seals into cover; do not use sealer. Make sure the correct color seal is placed in each groove. Install the cover to the housing.

27. Apply thread locking compound to the camshaft housing and cover attaching bolt threads.

28. Install bolts and tighten to 11 ft. lbs. (15 Nm). Rotate the bolts, except the 2 rear bolts that hold the fuel pipe to the camshaft housing, an additional 75 degrees, in sequence. Tighten the excepted bolts to 16 ft. lbs. (15 Nm), then rotate an additional 25 degrees.

29. Install timing chain housing and timing chain.

30. Uncover fuel injectors and install new fuel injector O-ring seals lubricated with oil. Install the fuel rail.

31. Install the fuel line attaching clamp and retainer to bracket on top of the intake camshaft housing.

32. Connect the vacuum line to the fuel pressure regulator.

33. Connect the fuel injectors harness connector.

34. Install the oil/air separator assembly.

35. Lubricate the inner sealing surface of the intake camshaft seal with oil and install the seal to the housing.

36. Install the power steering pump pulley onto the intake camshaft.

37. Install the power steering pump assembly and drive belt.

38. Connect the idle speed power steering pressure switch connector.

39. Clean any loose lubricant that is present on the ignition coil and module assembly to camshaft housing bolts. Apply Loctite or equivalent, onto the ignition coil and module assembly to camshaft housing bolts. Install the bolts and tighten to 13 ft. lbs. (18 Nm).

40. Connect the electrical connectors to ignition coil and module assembly.

41. Connect the negative battery cable and road test the vehicle. Check for leaks.

EXHAUST CAMSHAFT

NOTE: Any time the camshaft housing to cylinder head bolts are loosened or removed the camshaft housing to cylinder head gasket must be replaced.

1. Relieve the fuel system pressure. Disconnect the negative battery cable.

2. Label and disconnect the ignition coil and module assembly electrical connections.

3. Remove the ignition coil and module assembly to camshaft housing bolts and remove assembly by pulling straight up. Use a special tool to remove connector assemblies if they have stuck to the spark plugs.

4. Remove the idle speed power steering pressure switch connector.

5. Remove the transaxle fluid level indicator tube assembly from exhaust camshaft cover and position aside.

6. Remove exhaust camshaft cover and gasket.

7. Disconnect the timing chain and housing but do not remove from the engine.

8. Remove exhaust camshaft housing to cylinder head bolts. Use the reverse of the tightening procedure when loosening camshaft housing while separating camshaft cover from housing.

9. Push the cover off the housing by threading 4 of the housing to head attaching bolts into the tapped holes in the camshaft cover. Tighten the bolts in evenly so the cover does not bind on the dowel pins.

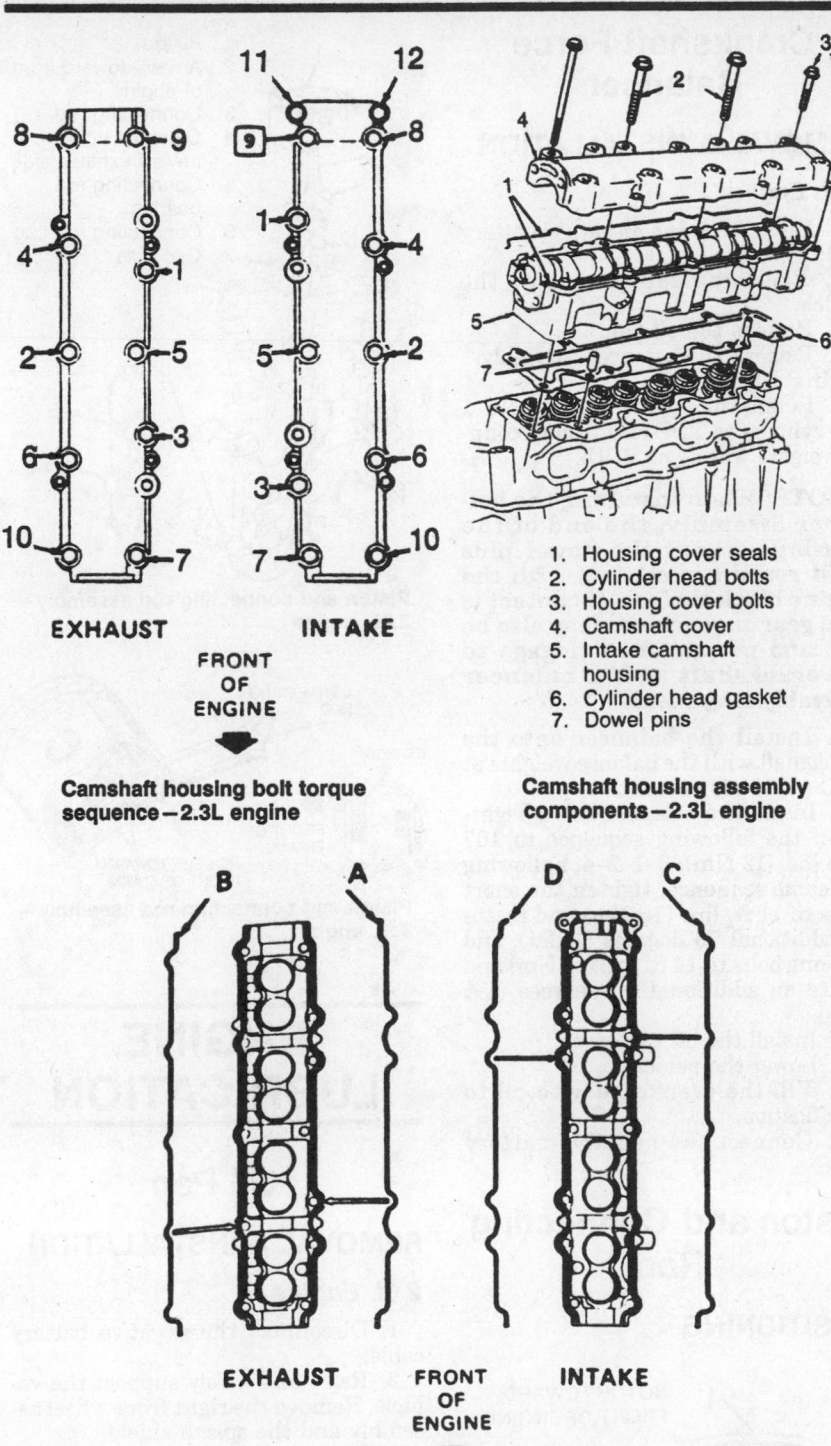

EXHAUST   INTAKE

FRONT
OF
ENGINE

Camshaft housing bolt torque sequence—2.3L engine

1. Housing cover seals
2. Cylinder head bolts
3. Housing cover bolts
4. Camshaft cover
5. Intake camshaft housing
6. Cylinder head gasket
7. Dowel pins

Camshaft housing assembly components—2.3L engine

B   A   D   C

EXHAUST   FRONT OF ENGINE   INTAKE

A. Seal—inner (exhaust—red)
B. Seal—outer (exhaust—red)
C. Seal—outer (intake—blue)
D. Seal—inner (intake—blue)

Camshaft housing cover seal identification—2.3L engine

10. Remove the 2 loosely installed camshaft housing to cylinder head bolts and remove cover, discard gaskets.

11. Loosely reinstall 1 camshaft housing to cylinder head bolt to retain the housing during camshaft and lifter removal.

12. Note the position of the chain sprocket dowel pin for reassembly. Remove camshaft being careful not to damage the camshaft or journals.

13. Remove the camshaft carrier from the cylinder head and remove the gasket.

To install:

14. Thoroughly clean the mating surfaces of the camshaft carrier and the cylinder head, bolts and bolt holes. Install a new gasket and place the housing on the head. Install 1 bolt loosely to hold in place.

15. Install the lifters into their bores. If the camshaft is being replaced, the lifters must also be replaced. Lubricate camshaft lobes, journals and lifters with camshaft and lifter prelube. The camshaft lobes and journals must be adequately lubricated or engine damage could occur upon start up.

16. Install camshaft in same position as when removed. The timing chain sprocket dowel pin should be straight up and align with the centerline of the lifter bores.

17. Install new camshaft housing to camshaft housing cover seals into cover; do not use sealer. Make sure the correct color seal is placed in each groove. Install the cover to the housing.

18. Apply thread locking compound to the camshaft housing and cover attaching bolt threads.

19. Install bolts and tighten, in sequence, to 11 ft. lbs. (15 Nm). Then rotate the bolts an additional 75 degrees, in sequence.

20. Install timing chain housing and timing chain.

21. Install the transaxle fluid level indicator tube assembly to exhaust camshaft cover.

22. Connect the idle speed power steering pressure switch connector.

23. Clean any loose lubricant that is present on the ignition coil and module assembly to camshaft housing bolts. Apply Loctite® or equivalent, onto the ignition coil and module assembly to camshaft housing bolts. Install the bolts and tighten to 13 ft. lbs. (18 Nm).

24. Connect the electrical connectors to ignition coil and module assembly.

25. Connect the negative battery cable and road test the vehicle. Check for leaks.

2.5L Engine

1. Disconnect the negative battery cable. Relieve the fuel system pressure before disconnecting any fuel lines. Remove the engine from the vehicle and secure to a suitable holding fixture.

2. Remove the valve cover, rocker arms and pushrods. Keep all parts in order for reassembly.

3. Remove the distributor, spark plug wires and plugs.

4. Remove the pushrod cover, the

gasket and the lifters. Keep all parts in order for reassembly.

5. Remove the alternator, alternator lower bracket and the front engine mount bracket assembly.

6. Remove the oil pump driveshaft and gear assembly.

7. Remove the crankshaft pulley and front cover Remove the timing chain and gears, if equipped.

8. Remove the 2 camshaft thrust plate screws by working through the holes in the gear.

9. Remove the camshaft, and gear assembly, if gear driven by pulling it through the front of the block. Take care not to damage the bearings while removing the camshaft.

To install:

10. The installation is the reverse of the removal procedure. Coat all parts with a liberal amount of clean engine oil supplement before installing.

11. Fill all fluids to their proper levels.

12. Connect the negative battery cable and check for leaks.

3.3L Engine

1. Disconnect the negative battery cable. Relieve the fuel system pressure before disconnecting any fuel lines. Remove the engine from the vehicle and secure to a suitable holding fixture.

2. Remove the intake manifold.

3. Remove the valve covers, rocker arm assemblies, pushrods and lifters. Keep all parts in order for reassembly.

4. Remove the crankshaft balancer from the crankshaft.

5. Remove the crankshaft sensor shield and the front cover.

6. Rotate the crankshaft to align the timing marks on the timing sprockets. Remove the camshaft sprocket and the timing chain.

7. Remove the camshaft retainer bolts/thrust plate and slide the camshaft forward out of the engine. Take care not to damage the bearings while removing the camshaft.

To install:

8. Install the camshaft to the engine and install the retainer bolts/thrust plate. Coat all parts with a liberal amount of clean engine oil supplement before installing.

9. Install the timing chain and sprockets.

10. Install the front cover and crankshaft sensor shield.

11. Install the crankshaft balancer and valve lifters.

12. Install the push rods, rocker arms and the valve covers.

13. Install the intake manifold.

14. Install the engine to the vehicle.

15. Connect the negative battery cable and check for leaks.

Crankshaft Force Balancer

REMOVAL & INSTALLATION

2.5L Engine

1. Disconnect the negative battery cable.

2. Raise and safely support the vehicle.

3. Remove the oil pan.

4. Remove the balancer assembly.

To install:

5. Rotate the engine to bring No. 1 or 4 cylinder to TDC (crankshaft counterweights will be at BDC).

NOTE: When installing the balancer assembly, the end of the housing without the dowel pins must remain in contact with the engine block surface. If contact is lost, gear engagement may also be lost and permanent damgage to the crankshaft and/or balancer assembly may result.

6. Install the balancer onto the crankshaft with the balance weights at BDC (± ½ gear tooth).

7. Install the balancer bolts. Tighten in the following sequence to 107 inch lbs. (12 Nm): 3–1–2–4. Following the same sequence, tighten the short bolts to 11 ft. lbs. (15 Nm) and rotate an additional 75 degrees (1 flat), and the long bolts to 11 ft. lbs. (15 Nm) and rotate an additional 90 degrees (1½ flats).

8. Install the oil pan.

9. Lower the vehicle.

10. Fill the crankcase with oil to specification.

11. Connect the negative battery cable.

Piston and Connecting Rod

POSITIONING

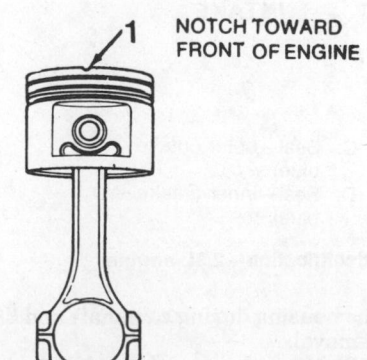

Piston and connecting rod assembly— 2.0L and 2.5L engines

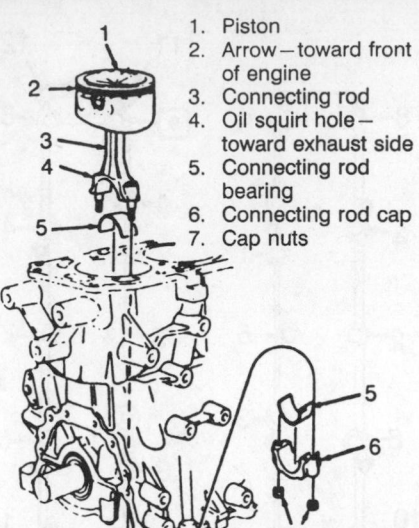

1. Piston
2. Arrow—toward front of engine
3. Connecting rod
4. Oil squirt hole— toward exhaust side
5. Connecting rod bearing
6. Connecting rod cap
7. Cap nuts

Piston and connecting rod assembly— 2.3L engine

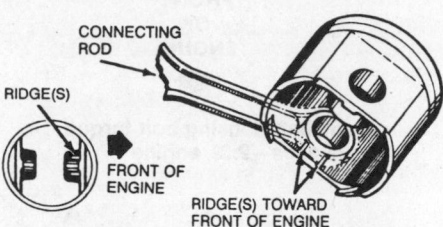

Piston and connecting rod assembly— 3.3L engine

ENGINE LUBRICATION

Oil Pan

REMOVAL & INSTALLATION

2.0L Engine

1. Disconnect the negative battery cable.

2. Raise and safely support the vehicle. Remove the right front wheel assembly and the splash shield.

3. Drain the engine oil.

4. Remove the exhaust pipe from the turbocharger.

5. Remove the flywheel inspection cover.

6. Remove the oil pan attaching bolts and remove the oil pan, scraper and gasket.

7. The installation is the reverse of the removal procedure. Use a new gasket and apply sealant at the 4 engine block seams. Use thread locking compound on the bolt threads and tighten to 4 ft. lbs. (6 Nm), starting from the middle and working outward.

8. Fill the crankcase with oil to specification.

9. Connect the negative battery cable and check for leaks.

2.3L Engine

1. Disconnect the negative battery cable. Raise and safely support the vehicle.

2. Remove the flywheel inspection cover.

3. Remove the splash shield-to-suspension support bolt. Remove the exhaust manifold brace, if equipped.

4. Remove the radiator outlet pipe-to-oil pan bolt.

5. Remove the transaxle-to-oil pan nut and stud using a 7mm socket.

6. Gently pry the spacer out from between oil pan and transaxle.

7. Remove the oil pan bolts. Rotate the crankshaft, if necessary, and remove the oil pan and gasket from the engine.

8. Inspect the silicone strips across the top of the aluminum carrier at the oil pan-cylinder block-seal housing 3-way joint. If damaged, these strips must be repaired with silicone sealer. Use only enough sealer to restore the strips to their original dimension; too much sealer could cause leakage.

To install:

9. Thoroughly clean and dry the mating surfaces, bolts and bolt holes. Install the oil pan with a new gasket; do not uses sealer on the gasket. Loosely install the pan bolts.

10. Place the spacer in its approximate installed position but allow clearance to tighten the pan bolt above it.

11. Tighten the pan to block bolts to

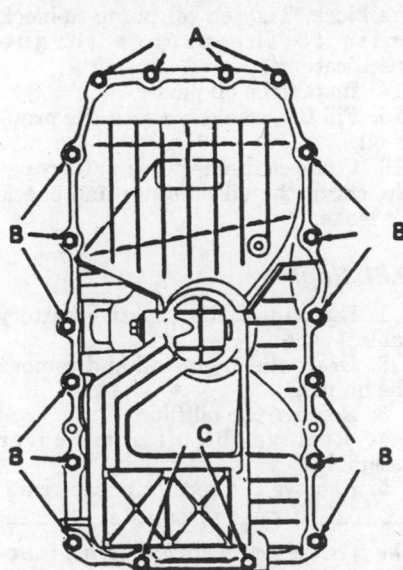

A. Chain housing bolts
B. Block bolts
C. Carrier seal bolts

Oil pan mounting bolts—1989–90 2.3L engine

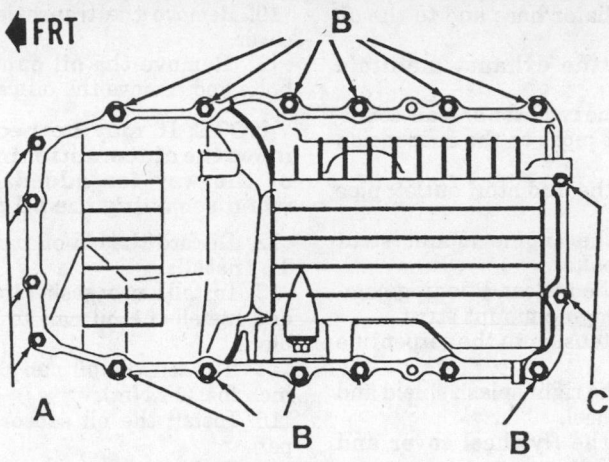

Oil pan—1991–93 2.3L Engine

17 ft. lbs. (24 Nm) and the remaining bolts to 106 inch lbs. (12 Nm).

12. Install the spacer and stud.

13. Install the oil pan transaxle nut and bolt.

14. Install the slash shield to suspension support.

15. Install the radiator outlet pipe bolt.

16. Install the exhaust manifold brace, if removed.

17. Install the flywheel inspection cover.

18. Fill the crankcase with the proper oil.

19. Connect the negative battery cable and check for leaks.

2.5L Engine

1989–90

1. Disconnect the negative battery cable.

2. Raise and safely support the vehicle. Drain the engine oil.

3. Disconnect the exhaust pipe and hangers from the exhaust manifold and allow it to swing aside.

4. Disconnect electrical connectors from the starter. Remove the starter-to-engine bolts, the starter and the flywheel housing inspection cover from the engine.

5. Remove the oil pan-to-engine bolts and the oil pan.

To install:

6. Thoroughly clean the mating surfaces, bolts and bolt holes.

7. Apply sealant to the oil pan flange, surrounding all bolt holes. Also, apply sealant to the engine at the front and rear seams.

8. Install the oil pan and tighten the bolts to 89 inch lbs. (10 Nm).

9. Install the flywheel housing cover and exhaust pipe.

10. Fill the crankcase with oil to specification.

11. Connect the negative battery cable and check for leaks.

1991–93

1. Disconnect the negative battery cable.

2. Raise and safely support the vehicle.

3. Drain the engine oil and the cooling system.

4. Remove the flywheel cover and the right wheel.

5. Remove the right splash shield.

6. Release the serpentine drive belt tension.

7. Remove the engine mount strut from the strut bracket.

8. Remove the air conditioning compressor from the bracket and support it out of the way.

9. Remove the engine mount strut bracket bolts and move the bracket out of the way.

10. Remove the radiator outlet pipe bolts.

11. Disconnect the radiator and air conditioning outlet pipes from the suspension supports.

12. Remove the exhaust manifold brace.

13. Remove the oil pan-to-flywheel cover nut and bolt and remove the flywheel cover stud.

14. Remove the radiator outlet pipe from the lower radiator hose and oil pan.

15. Disconnect the oil level sensor wire.

16. Remove the oil pan bolts and remove the oil pan from the vehicle.

To install:

17. Install the oil pan complete with a new gasket and loosely install the oil pan bolts.

18. Tighten bolts A and C to 106 inch lbs. (12 Nm) and bolt B to 17 ft. lbs. (24 Nm).

19. Install the oil pan studs and tighten to 19 ft. lbs. (26 Nm).

20. Connect the oil level sensor wire.

21. Install the radiator outlet pipe to

the lower radiator hose and to the oil pan.

22. Install the exhaust manifold brace.

23. Install the radiator and air conditioning outlet pipes to the suspension supports.

24. Install the radiator outlet pipe bolts.

25. Install the engine mount strut bracket and bolts.

26. Install the air conditioning compressor and engine mount strut.

27. Release tension to the serpentine drive belt.

28. Install the right splash shield and right front wheel.

29. Install the flywheel cover and lower the vehicle.

30. Fill the crankcase and fill the cooling system.

31. Start the engine and check for leaks.

3.3L Engine

1989–91

1. Disconnect the negative battery cable.

2. Raise and safely support the vehicle.

3. Drain the engine oil and remove the oil filter.

4. Remove the flywheel cover and the starter.

5. Remove the oil pan, tensioner spring and formed rubber gasket.

6. The installation is the reverse of the removal procedure. Tighten the oil pan-to-engine bolts to 124 inch lbs. (14 Nm).

7. Fill the crankcase with the proper oil.

8. Connect the negative battery cable and check for leaks.

1992–93

1. Disconnect the negative battery cable.

2. Raise and safely support the vehicle.

3. Drain the engine oil and remove the oil filter.

4. Remove the lower flap and the splash shield.

5. Remove the crankshaft pulley and the crank sensor cover.

6. Disconnect the air conditioning compressor electrical connector and remove the compressor from the bracket and support the compressor off to the side.

7. Remove the bolts from the right front suspension support.

8. Loosen all the remaining suspension support bolts to the point that the supports actually drop 1.5 inches (38mm).

9. Disconnect the oil level sensor from the oil pan, if equipped.

10. Remove the transaxle converter cover.

11. Remove the oil pan retaining bolts and remove the oil pan.

NOTE: It may be necessary to move the air conditioning line out of the way for added clearance when removing the oil pan.

12. Discard the old oil pan gasket.

To install:

13. Install a new gasket to the oil pan and install the oil pan to the engine block.

14. Tighten the oil pan bolts to 124 inch lbs. (14 Nm).

15. Install the oil sensor to the oil pan.

16. Tighten the suspension support bolts and install the right front support bolts.

17. Install the air conditioning compressor and hose support.

18. Connect the compressor electrical connector.

19. Install the crank sensor cover and the crankshaft pulley.

20. Install the lower flap, splash shield and the transaxle converter cover.

21. Lower the vehicle, refill the engine with oil and connect the negative battery cable.

Oil Pump

REMOVAL & INSTALLATION

2.0L Engine

1. Disconnect negative battery cable.

2. Remove the timing belt and crankshaft sprocket.

3. Remove the rear timing belt cover.

4. Disconnect oil pressure sending unit connector.

5. Raise and safely support the vehicle.

6. Drain the engine oil.

7. Remove the oil pan and oil filter.

8. Remove the oil pump mounting bolts and remove the pump and pickup tube.

To install:

9. Prime the pump by pouring fresh oil into the pump intake and turning the driveshaft until oil comes out the pressure port. Repeat a few times until no air bubbles are present.

10. The installation is the reverse of the removal procedure. Use a new gasket and seal and tighten the oil pump bolts to 5 ft. lbs. (7 Nm). Use a new ring for the pickup tube.

11. Fill the crankcase with the proper oil.

12. Connect the negative battery cable, check the oil pressure and check for leaks.

2.3L Engine

1. Disconnect the negative battery cable.

2. Raise and safely support the vehicle.

3. Drain the engine oil and remove the oil pan.

4. Remove the oil pump attaching bolts and nut.

5. Remove the oil pump assembly, shims if equipped, and screen.

To install:

6. With the oil pump assembly off the engine, remove 3 attaching bolts and separate the driven gear cover and screen assembly from the oil pump.

7. Install the oil pump on the block using the original shims, if equipped. Tighten the bolts for 1989–90 vehicles to 33 ft. lbs. (45 Nm) or for the 1991–93 vehicles to 40 ft. lbs. (54 Nm).

8. Mount a dial indicator assembly to measure backlash between oil pump to drive gear.

9. Record oil pump drive to driven gear backlash. Proper backlash is 0.010–0.018 in. When measuring, do not allow the crankshaft to move.

10. If equipped with shims, remove shims to decrease clearance and add shims to increase clearance. If no shims were present, replace the assembly if proper backlash cannot be obtained.

11. When the proper clearance is reached, rotate crankshaft ½ turn and recheck clearance.

12. Remove oil pump from block, fill the cavity with petroleum jelly and reinstall driven gear cover and screen assembly to pump. Tighten the bolts to 106 inch lbs. (13 Nm).

13. Reinstall the pump assembly to the block. Tighten oil pump-to-block bolts to the proper torque specifications.

14. Install the oil pan.

15. Fill the crankcase with the proper oil.

16. Connect the negative battery cable, check the oil pressure and check for leaks.

2.5L Engine

1. Disconnect the negative battery cable.

2. Drain the engine oil and remove the oil pan.

3. Remove the oil filter.

4. Remove the oil pump cover assembly.

5. Remove the gerotor pump gears.

--- **CAUTION** ---

The pressure regulator valve spring is under pressure. Exercise caution when removing the pin or personal injury may result.

6. Remove the pressure regulator pin, spring and valve.

To install:

7. Lubricate all internal parts with clean engine oil and fill all pump cavities with petroleum jelly.

8. Install the pressure regulator valve, spring and secure the pin.

9. Install the gerotor gears.

10. Install the pump cover and tighten the screws to 10 ft. lbs. (14 Nm).

11. Install the oil filter.

12. Install the oil pan.

13. Fill the crankcase with oil to specification.

14. Connect the negative battery cable, check the oil pressure and check for leaks.

3.3L Engine

1. Disconnect the negative battery cable.

2. Remove the timing chain front cover.

3. Raise and safely support the vehicle.

4. Drain the engine oil. Lower the vehicle.

5. Remove the oil filter adapter, the pressure regulator valve and the valve spring.

6. Remove the oil pump cover-to-oil pump screws and remove the cover.

7. Remove the oil pump gears.

To install:

8. Lubricate the oil pump gears with clean engine oil.

9. Pack the pump cavity with petroleum jelly.

10. Install the oil pump cover screws using a new gasket and tighten to 97 inch lbs. (11 Nm).

11. Install the pressure regulator spring and valve.

12. Install the oil filter adaptor using a new gasket. Tighten the oil filter adapter-to-engine bolts to 24 ft. lbs. (33 Nm).

13. Install the timing chain front cover to the engine.

14. Fill the crankcase with clean engine oil.

15. Connect the negative battery cable, check the oil pressure and check for leaks.

CHECKING

2.0L Engine

1. Inspect all components carefully for physical damage of any type and replace worn parts.

2. Check the gear pocket depth. The specification is 0.395–0.397 in. (10.03–10.08mm).

3. Check the gear pocket diameter. The specification is 3.230–3.235 in. (82.02–82.15mm).

4. Check the diameter of the gears. The specifications are 0.014–0.018 in. (0.35–0.45mm) for the drive gear and

0.004–0.007 in. (0.11–0.19mm) for the idler gear.

5. Check the side clearance. The specifications are 2.317–2.319 in. (58.85–58.90mm) for the drive gear and 3.225–3.227 in. (81.91–81.96mm) for the idler gear.

6. Check the end clearance below the pump housing. The specification is 0.001–0.004 in. (0.03–0.10mm).

2.3L Engine

1. Inspect all components carefully for physical damage of any type and replace worn parts.

2. Check the gerotor cavity depth. The specification is 0.674–0.676 in. (17.11–17.16mm).

3. Check the gerotor cavity diameter. The specification is 2.127–2.129 in. (53.95–54.00mm).

4. Check the inner gerotor tip clearance. The maximum clearance is 0.006 in. (15mm).

5. Check the outer gerotor diameter clearance. The specification is 0.010–0.014 in. (0.254–0.354mm).

2.5L Engine

1. Inspect all components carefully for physical damage of any type and replace worn parts.

2. Check the gerotor cavity depth. The specification is 0.514–0.516 in. (13.05–13.10mm).

3. Check the gear lash. The specification is 0.009–0.015 in. (0.23–0.38mm).

4. Check the clearance of both gears. The maximum clearance is 0.004 in. (0.10mm).

3.3L Engine

1. Inspect all components carefully for physical damage of any type and replace worn parts.

2. Check the gear pocket depth. The specification is 0.461–0.463 in. (11.71–11.75mm).

3. Check the gear pocket diameter. The specification is 3.508–3.512 in. (89.10–89.20mm).

4. Check the inner gear tip clearance. The maximum clearance is 0.006 in. (0.152mm).

5. Check the outer gear diameter clearance. The specification is 0.008–0.015 in. (0.025–0.089mm).

Rear Main Bearing Oil Seal

REMOVAL & INSTALLATION

2.0L and 2.5L Engines

1. Disconnect the negative battery cable.

2. Remove the transaxle.

3. If equipped with a manual transaxle, remove the pressure plate and clutch disc.

4. Remove the flywheel-to-crankshaft bolts and the flywheel.

5. Using a medium prybar, pry out the old seal; be careful not to scratch the crankshaft surface.

6. Clean the block and crankshaft-to-seal mating surfaces.

7. Using the appropriate seal installation tool, install the new rear seal into the block. Lubricate the outside of the seal to aid installation and press the seal in evenly with the tool.

8. The installation is the reverse of the removal procedure.

9. Connect the negative battery cable and check for leaks.

2.3L Engine

1. Disconnect the negative battery cable.

2. Remove the transaxle.

3. If equipped with a manual transaxle, remove the pressure plate and clutch disc.

4. Remove the flywheel-to-crankshaft bolts and the flywheel.

5. Remove the oil pan-to-seal housing bolts and the block-to-seal housing bolts.

6. Remove the seal housing from the engine.

7. Place 2 blocks of equal thickness on a flat surface and position the seal housing on the 2 blocks. Remove the seal from the housing.

To install:

8. Press the new seal into the housing, using tool J36005 or equivalent.

9. Position the new seal housing to the block over the dowel alignment pins.

10. Lube the lip of the crankshaft seal with engine oil and install the seal housing assembly.

11. Tighten the seal housing-to-block bolts to 106 inch lbs. (12 Nm).

12. Tighten the oil pan-to-seal housing bolts to 106 inch lbs. (12 Nm).

13. Install the flywheel. Tighten the bolts evenly to specification.

14. If equipped with manual transaxle, install the clutch, pressure plate and clutch cover.

15. Install the transaxle to the vehicle and connect the negative battery cable.

16. Start the engine and check for leaks.

3.3L Engine

1989–90

NOTE: If replacing the entire 2-piece seal, the engine must be removed in order to remove the crankshaft. Use the following if only replacing the lower half of the seal.

1. Disconnect the negative battery cable. Raise and safely support the vehicle.

2. Drain the oil and remove the oil pan.

3. Remove the rear main bearing cap-to-engine bolts and the bearing cap from the engine.

4. Remove the old seal from the bearing cap.

To install:

5. Using a seal packing tool, insert it against one end of the seal in the cylinder block. Pack the old seal into the groove until it is packed tightly. Repeat the procedure on the other end of the seal.

6. Measure the amount the seal was driven up and add approximately $\frac{1}{16}$ in. Cut this length from the old seal removed from the lower bearing cap, repeat for the other side.

NOTE: When cutting the seal into short lengths, use a double edged blade and the lower bearing cap as a holding fixture.

7. Using a seal packer guide, install it onto the cylinder block.

8. Using the packing tool, work the short pieces into the guide tool and pack into the cylinder block until the tool hits the built-in stop.

NOTE: It may help to use oil on the short seal pieces when packing into the block.

9. Repeat steps 7 and 8 for the other side.

10. Remove the guide tool.

11. Install a new rope seal into the lower bearing cap.

12. Install the lower main bearing cap and tighten the main bearing cap bolts to 90 ft. lbs. (122 Nm).

13. Install the oil pan.

14. Fill the crankcase with the proper engine oil.

15. Connect the negative battery cable and check for leaks.

1991-93

1. Disconnect the negative battery cable.

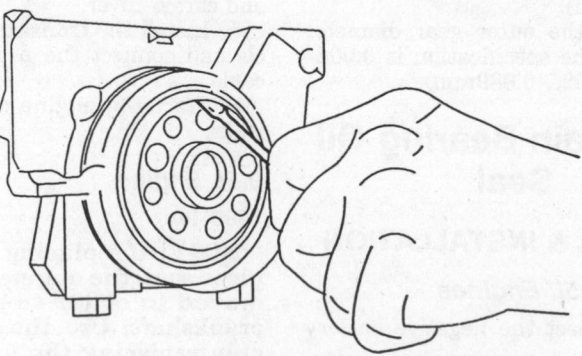

Removal of rear main seal—1991–93 3.3L engine

2. Raise and safely support the vehicle and remove the transaxle from the vehicle.

3. Remove the flywheel from the vehicle.

4. Carefully pry the seal out using a flat bladed prybar.

5. Inspect the inside diameter of the bore for nicks, burrs or scratches.

To install:

6. Apply clean engine oil to outside diameter of the new seal.

7. Using a rear seal installation tool J-38196 or equivalent, install the seal.

8. Install the flywheel and install the transaxle.

9. Lower the vehicle and connect the negative battery cable.

ENGINE COOLING

Radiator

REMOVAL & INSTALLATION

1989-91

1. Disconnect the negative battery cable.

2. Drain the coolant. Disconnect the the engine strut brace at the radiator, loosen the engine side bolt and swing aside, if equipped.

3. Matchmark and remove the hood latch from the radiator support.

4. Remove the upper hose and coolant reserve tank hose from the radiator.

5. Disconnect the forward light harness connector and fan connector. Remove the electric cooling fan.

6. Raise and safely support the vehicle. Remove the lower hose from the radiator.

7. Disconnect the automatic transaxle cooler hoses, if equipped, and plug them. Lower the vehicle.

8. If equipped with air conditioning,

remove the radiator to condenser bolts. Remove the refrigerant line clamp bolt.

9. Remove the mounting bolts and clamps and carefully lift the radiator out of the engine compartment.

To install:

10. Lower the radiator into position.

11. Install the mounting clamps and bolts, including those associated with air conditioning parts.

12. Raise and safely support the vehicle. Connect the automatic transaxle cooler lines, if equipped.

13. Connect the lower hose. Lower the vehicle.

14. Install the electric cooling fan and connect the connectors.

15. Connect the upper hose and coolant reserve tank hose.

16. Install the hood latch and strut brace.

17. Fill the system with coolant.

18. Connect the negative battery cable, run the vehicle until the thermostat opens, fill the radiator and recovery tank completely and check the automatic transaxle fluid level.

19. Once the vehicle has cooled, recheck the coolant level.

1992-93

1. Disconnect the negative battery cable.

2. Drain the cooling system into a proper container.

3. Remove the air intake duct assembly.

4. Disconnect the upper transaxle cooler line and the upper radiator hose.

5. Remove the lower transaxle cooler line.

6. Disconnect the cooling fan electrical connector and remove the fan.

7. Remove the splash shield from below the lower radiator hose and remove the lower radiator hose.

8. Remove the condenser line retaining clip and remove the condenser to radiator bolts.

9. Remove the coolant surge tank hose.

10. Remove the radiator retaining bolts and remove the radiator from the vehicle.

To install:

11. Install the radiator to the vehicle and install the retaining bolts. Tighten the bolts to 90 inch lbs. (10 Nm).

12. Install the coolant surge tank hose.

13. Install the condenser to radiator bolts and install the condenser line retaining clip.

14. Install the lower radiator hose to the radiator.

15. Install the splash guard below the lower radiator hose.

16. Install the cooling fan and retain-

ing bolt(s). Connect the fan electrical connector.

17. Install the lower transaxle cooler line, upper radiator hose and the upper transaxle cooler line.

18. Install the air intake duct assembly.

19. Fill the cooling system to the proper level and inspect for leaks.

20. Connect the negative battery cable and run the vehicle until the thermostat opens.

21. After engine has cooled, check the coolant level.

Electric Cooling Fan

CAUTION

The cooling fan can turn ON at any time. To avoid personal injury, ensure the ignition key is in the OFF position and use caution when working on or near the electric cooling fan.

TESTING

1. Check fuse or circuit breaker for power to cooling fan motor.

2. Remove connector(s) at cooling fan motor(s). Connect jumper wires to the connector on the cooling fan: 1 to a solid ground and the other to the positive battery terminal. The motor should run.

3. Using an ohmmeter, check for continuity in cooling fan motor.

NOTE: Remove the cooling fan connector at the fan motor before performing continuity checks. Perform continuity check of the motor windings only. The cooling fan control circuit is connected electrically to the ECM through the cooling fan relay. Ohmmeter battery voltage must not be applied to the ECM.

4. Ensure continuity of cooling fan motor ground circuit at chassis ground connector.

REMOVAL & INSTALLATION

1989–91

ALL EXCEPT 2.3L (VIN D) ENGINE

1. Disconnect the negative battery cable.

2. Unplug the connector.

3. Remove the mounting screws.

4. Remove the fan assembly from the vehicle.

5. Installation is the reverse of the removal procedure.

2.3L (VIN D) ENGINE

1. Disconnect the negative battery cable.

2. Remove the air cleaner to throttle body duct.

3. Disconnect the electrical connectors from the TPS, IAC and MAP sensor and position the harness aside.

4. Disconnect the vacuum harness from the throttle body and position the harness aside.

5. Disconnect the MAP sensor vacuum hose from the intake manifold.

6. Remove the coolant fan shroud retaining bolts and remove the shroud with the MAP sensor from the vehicle.

7. Remove the coolant fan to upper radiator support bolt and the remaining upper radiator support bolt. Remove the upper radiator support.

8. Disconnect the coolant fan electrical connector.

9. Lift the fan assembly out of the 2 lower supports and rotate the assembly so the lower legs point up. Remove the fan by guiding it up carefully past the radiator.

To install:

10. Position the fan so the 2 lower legs are pointing upward.

11. Carefully slide the fan between the radiator and the throttle body.

12. Rotate the fan assembly and install the 2 lower legs into their respective brackets.

13. Connect the fan electrical connector.

14. Install the upper radiator support.

15. Install the fan shroud.

16. Install the coolant fan to upper radiator support mounting bolt.

17. Connect the vacuum lines and the electrical connectors.

18. Install the air cleaner duct.

19. Connect the negative battery cable.

1992–93

2.3L ENGINE

1. Disconnect the negative battery cable.

2. Remove the air intake duct assembly.

3. Remove the coolant fan mounting bolt and disconnect the coolant fan electrical connector.

4. Remove the fan assembly through the bottom.

5. Installation is the reverse of the removal procedure. Tighten the coolant fan mounting bolt to 8 ft. lbs. (11 Nm).

3.3L (VIN N) Engine

1. Disconnect the negative battery cable.

2. Remove the air intake duct to the air cleaner assembly.

3. Partially drain the cooling system.

4. Remove the top radiator hose from the vehicle.

5. Disconnect the wiring harness from the motor and from the fan frame.

6. Remove the fan guard and the hose support, if necessary.

7. Remove the fan assembly from the vehicle.

To install:

8. Install the fan to the radiator support.

9. Install the fan guard and hose support, if removed.

10. Connect the wiring harness and install the top radiator hose to the radiator.

11. Fill the cooling system to the proper level.

12. Install the air intake duct assembly.

13. Connect the negative battery cable.

Heater Core

REMOVAL & INSTALLATION

1. Disconnect the negative battery cable.

2. Drain the engine coolant into a clean container for reuse.

3. Raise and safely support the vehicle.

4. Remove the rear lateral transaxle strut mount, if necessary.

5. Remove the drain tube and disconnect the heater hoses from the core tubes. Lower the vehicle.

6. Remove the sound insulators, console, console extensions and/or steering column filler, as required.

7. Remove the floor or console outlet ductwork and hoses.

8. Remove the heater core cover.

9. Remove the heater core mounting clamps and remove the heater core.

To install:

10. Install the heater core and clamps.

11. Install the heater core cover.

12. Install the outlet hoses and ducts.

13. Install the sound insulators, console, console extensions and/or steering column filler.

14. Raise and safely support the vehicle. Install the drain tube and connect the heater hoses to the core tubes.

15. Install the rear lateral transaxle strut mount, if removed. Lower the vehicle.

16. Connect the negative battery cable.

17. Fill cooling system and check for leaks. Start the engine and allow to come to normal operating temperature. Recheck for leaks. Top-up coolant.

Water Pump

REMOVAL & INSTALLATION

2.0L Engine

1. Disconnect the negative battery cable.
2. Drain the engine coolant into a clean container for reuse.
3. Remove the timing belt.
4. Remove the water pump attaching bolts, water pump and seal ring.
To install:
5. Thoroughly clean and dry the mounting surfaces, bolts and bolt holes.
6. Using a new sealing ring, install the water pump to the engine and tighten the bolts by hand.
7. Install the timing belt and properly adjust the tension.
8. Tighten the water pump bolts to 18 ft. lbs. (24 Nm).
9. Install the timing belt cover and related parts.
10. Connect the negative battery cable.
11. Fill cooling system and check for leaks. Start the engine and allow to come to normal operating temperature. Recheck for leaks. Top-up coolant.

2.3L Engine

1. Disconnect the negative battery cable and oxygen sensor connector.
2. Drain the engine coolant into a clean container for reuse. Remove the heater hose from the thermostat housing for more complete coolant drain.

3. Remove upper and lower exhaust manifold heat shields.
4. Remove the bolt that attaches the exhaust manifold brace to the manifold.
5. Break loose the manifold to exhaust pipe spring loaded bolts using a 13mm box wrench.
6. Raise and safely support the vehicle.

NOTE: It is necessary to relieve the spring pressure from 1 bolt prior to removing the second bolt. If the spring pressure is not relieved, it will cause the exhaust pipe to twist and bind up the bolt as it is removed.

7. Remove the manifold to exhaust pipe bolts from the exhaust pipe flange as follows:
    a. Unscrew either bolt clockwise 4 turns.
    b. Remove the other bolt.
    c. Remove the first bolt.
8. Pull down and back on the exhaust pipe to disengage it from the manifold bolts.
9. Remove the radiator outlet pipe from the oil pan and transaxle. If equipped with a manual transaxle, remove the exhaust manifold brace. Leave the lower radiator hose attached and pull down on the outlet pipe to remove it from the water pump.
10. Lower the vehicle.
11. Remove the exhaust manifold, seals and gaskets.
12. Loosen and reposition the rear engine mount and bracket for clearance, as required.
13. Remove the water pump mount-

ing bolts and nuts. Remove the water pump and cover assembly and separate the 2 pieces.
To install:
14. Thoroughly clean and dry all mounting surfaces, bolts and bolt holes. Using a new gasket, install the water pump to the cover and tighten the bolts finger-tight.
15. Lubricate the splines of the water pump with clean grease and install the assembly to the engine using new gaskets. Install the mounting bolts and nuts finger-tight.
16. Lubricate the radiator outlet pipe O-ring with antifreeze and install to the water pump with the bolts finger tight.
17. With all gaps closed, tighten the bolts, in the following sequence, to the proper values:
    a. Pump assembly to chain housing nuts—19 ft. lbs. (26 Nm).
    b. Pump cover to pump assembly—106 inch lbs. (12 Nm).
    c. Cover to block, bottom bolt first—19 ft. lbs. (26 Nm).
    d. Radiator outlet pipe assembly to pump cover—125 inch lbs. (14 Nm).
18. Install the exhaust manifold.
19. Raise and safely support the vehicle.
20. Install the exhaust pipe flange bolts evenly and gradually to avoid binding.
21. Connect the radiator outlet pipe to the transaxle and oil pan. Install the exhaust manifold brace, if removed. Lower the vehicle.
22. Install the bolt that attaches the exhaust manifold brace to the manifold.
23. Install the heat shields.
24. Connect the oxygen sensor connector.
25. Fill the radiator with coolant until it comes out the heater hose outlet at the thermostat housing. Then connect the heater hose.
26. Connect the negative battery cable, run the vehicle until the thermostat opens, fill the radiator and recovery tank completely.
27. Once the vehicle has cooled, recheck the coolant level.

2.5L Engine

1. Disconnect the negative battery cable.
2. Drain the engine coolant into a clean container for reuse.
3. Remove the drive belts, alternator and air conditioning compressor, as required.
4. Remove the water pump mounting bolts and remove the water pump from the vehicle.
To install:
5. Transfer the water pump pulley

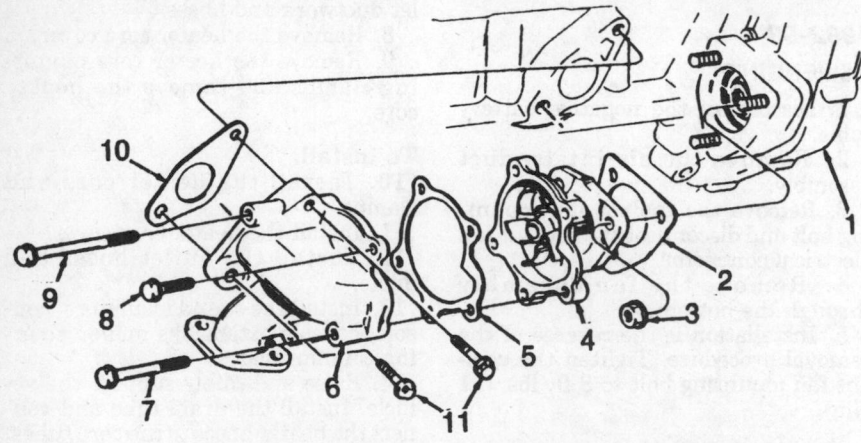

1. Timing chain housing
2. Water pump to timing chain housing gasket
3. Nut
4. water pump
5. Water pump body cover gasket
6. Water pump cover
7. Bolt
8. Bolt
9. Bolt
10. Water pump gasket cover to block gasket
11. water pump cover bolts

Water pump assembly—2.3L engine

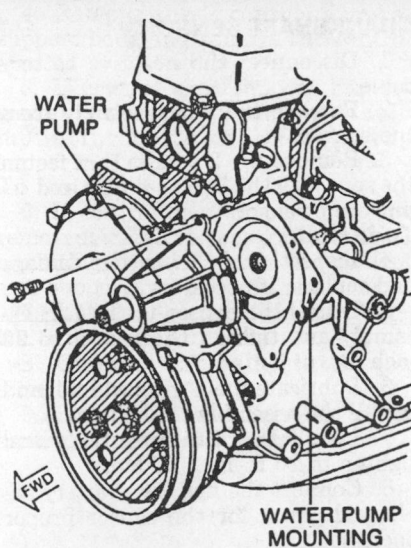

Water pump assembly—2.5L engine

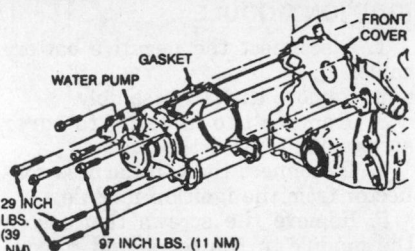

Water pump assembly—3.3L engine

to the new pump using the proper pulley removal and installation tools.

6. Thoroughly clean and dry the mounting surfaces, bolts and bolt holes. Place a 1/8 in. bead of RTV sealant on the pump's sealing surface.

7. Install the pump to the engine and coat the bolt threads with sealant as they are installed. Tighten the bolts to 25 ft. lbs. (34 Nm).

8. Install the alternator and/or air conditioning compressor. Install and adjust the drive belts.

9. Connect the negative battery cable.

10. Fill cooling system and check for leaks. Start the engine and allow to come to normal operating temperature. Recheck for leaks. Top-up coolant.

3.3L Engine

1. Disconnect the negative battery cable.

2. Drain the engine coolant into a clean container for reuse.

3. Remove the serpentine belt.

4. Remove the idler pulley bolt.

5. Remove the water pump pulley bolts and remove the pulley.

6. Remove the water pump mounting bolts and remove the pump.

To install:

7. Thoroughly clean and dry the mounting surfaces, bolts and bolt holes.

8. Using a new gasket, install the water pump to the engine and tighten pump to front cover bolts to 97 inch lbs. (11 Nm) and the pump to block bolts to 29 ft. lbs. (39 Nm).

9. Install the water pump pulley and tighten the bolts to 115 inch lbs. (13 Nm).

10. Install the idler pulley bolt.

11. Install the serpentine belt.

12. Fill the system with coolant.

13. Connect the negative battery cable, run the vehicle until the thermostat opens, fill the radiator and recovery tank completely.

14. Once the vehicle has cooled, recheck the coolant level.

Thermostat

REMOVAL & INSTALLATION

Except 2.0L Engine

1. Disconnect the negative battery cable. Drain the coolant down to thermostat level or below.

2. Remove the air cleaner assembly, as required. Disconnect the coolant sensor on 1989–91 2.3L engine.

3. Disconnect the hose(s) and remove the thermostat housing.

4. Remove the thermostat and discard the gasket.

5. Clean the housing mating surfaces and use a new gasket.

To install:

6. Install the thermostat with new gasket and the thermostat housing.

7. Connect the heater, throttle body and radiator hoses.

8. Connect the electrical connector and fill the system with coolant.

9. Connect the negative battery cable, run the vehicle until the thermostat opens, fill the radiator and recovery tank completely.

2.0L Engine

1. Disconnect the negative battery cable.

2. Remove the thermostat housing cap.

3. Remove the thermostat and discard the gasket.

4. Clean the housing mating surfaces and use a new gasket.

5. The installation is the reverse of the removal procedure.

ENGINE ELECTRICAL

NOTE: Disconnecting the nega- tive battery cable on some vehicles may interfere with the functions of the on board computer systems and may require the computer to undergo a relearning process, once the negative battery cable is reconnected.

Distributor

REMOVAL

2.0L Engine

1. Disconnect the negative battery cable.

2. Disconnect the coil and Electronic Spark Timing (EST) connectors.

3. Remove the coil wire. Unscrew the distributor cap hold-down screws and lift off the distributor cap with all ignition wires still connected.

4. Matchmark the rotor to the distributor housing and the distributor housing to the cam carrier.

NOTE: Do not crank the engine during this procedure. If the engine is cranked, the rotor's matchmark must be disregarded.

5. Remove the hold-down nuts.

6. Remove the distributor from the engine.

INSTALLATION

Timing Not Disturbed

1. Install a new distributor housing O-ring.

2. Install the distributor in the cam carrier so the rotor is aligned with the matchmark on the housing and the housing is aligned with the matchmark on the cam carrier. Make sure the distributor is fully seated and the distributor tang drive is fully engaged.

3. Install the hold-down nuts.

4. Install the distributor cap and attaching screws. Install the coil wire.

5. Connect the coil and EST connectors.

6. Connect the negative battery cable.

7. Adjust the ignition timing and tighten the hold-down nuts.

Timing Disturbed

1. Install a new distributor housing O-ring.

2. Position the engine so the No. 1 piston is at TDC of the compression stroke and the mark on the vibration damper is aligned with **0** on the timing indicator.

3. Install the distributor in the cam carrier so the rotor is aligned with the matchmark on the housing and the housing is aligned with the

matchmark on the cam carrier. Make sure the distributor is fully seated and the distributor tang drive is fully engaged.

4. Install the hold-down nuts.

5. Install the distributor cap and attaching screws. Install the coil wire.

6. Connect the coil and EST connectors.

7. Connect the negative battery cable.

8. Adjust the ignition timing and tighten the hold-down nuts.

Distributorless Ignition System

REMOVAL & INSTALLATION

2.3L Engine

INTEGRATED DIRECT IGNITION (IDI) ASSEMBLY

1. Disconnect the negative battery cable.

2. Disconnect IDI harness connector.

3. Remove the bolts that fasten the assembly to the camshaft housing.

4. Remove the IDI assembly. If the boots adhere to the spark plugs, remove them by twisting and pulling up on the retainers.

To install:

5. Install the boots and retainers to the housing, if they were separated during removal.

6. Align the spark plug boots with the plugs and place the assembly on the camshaft housing.

7. Install the mounting bolts and tighten to 15 ft. lbs. (20 Nm).

8. Connect the harness connector.

9. Connect the negative battery cable and check for proper operation.

IGNITION COILS

1. Disconnect the negative battery cable.

2. Remove the IDI assembly.

3. Remove the housing to cover screws and remove the cover.

4. Disconnect the coil harness connectors.

5. Remove the coil(s), contact(s) and seal(s) from the cover.

To install:

6. Install the coil(s) to the cover and connect the connectors.

7. Install new seal(s) to the housing. Using petroleum jelly to retain, install the contact(s) to the housing.

8. Assemble the cover to the housing, install the screws and tighten to 35 inch lbs. (4 Nm).

9. Install the IDI assembly.

10. Connect the negative battery cable and check for proper operation.

IGNITION MODULE

1. Disconnect the negative battery cable.

2. Remove the IDI assembly.

3. Remove the housing to cover screws and remove the cover.

4. Disconnect the coil harness connector from the ignition module.

5. Remove the screws that fasten the module to the cover and remove the module from the cover. Do not wipe the heat-protective grease away from the module if it is being reused.

To install:

6. If a new module is used, spread the grease included with the package on the metal face of the module and on the module's seat on the cover.

7. Install the module to the cover and connect the harness connector.

8. Assemble the cover to the housing, install the screws and tighten to 35 inch lbs. (4 Nm).

9. Install the IDI assembly.

10. Connect the negative battery cable and check for proper operation.

CRANKSHAFT SENSOR

1. Disconnect the negative battery cable.

2. Disconnect the connector from the sensor.

3. Remove the attaching bolt and remove the sensor from the engine.

To install:

4. Inspect the O-ring for damage and replace, if necessary.

5. Lubricate the O-ring with oil and install the sensor to its bore in the engine.

6. Install the attaching bolt and tighten to 88 inch lbs. (10 Nm).

7. Connect the sensor electrical connector.

8. Connect the negative battery cable and check the sensor for proper operation.

2.5L Engine

DISTRIBUTORLESS IGNITION SYSTEM (DIS) ASSEMBLY

1. Disconnect the negative battery cable.

2. Disconnect the connectors from the DIS assembly, located at the rear of the engine.

3. Label and remove the spark plug wires from the assembly.

4. Remove the 3 mounting bolts and remove the assembly from the engine.

To install:

5. Inspect the O-ring for damage and replace, if necessary.

6. Lubricate the O-ring with oil and install the assembly to the engine.

7. Install the attaching bolts and tighten to 20 ft. lbs. (27 Nm).

8. Connect the connectors.

9. Connect the negative battery cable and check for proper operation.

CRANKSHAFT SENSOR

1. Disconnect the negative battery cable.

2. Remove the DIS assembly from the engine.

3. Remove the 2 screws that fasten the sensor to the DIS assembly and remove the sensor.

To install:

4. Inspect the O-ring for damage and replace, if necessary.

5. Install the sensor to the DIS assembly and tighten the screws to 20 inch lbs. (2 Nm).

6. Lubricate the O-ring with oil and install the assembly to the engine.

7. Install the attaching bolts and tighten to 20 ft. lbs. (27 Nm).

8. Connect the negative battery cable and check for the sensor proper operation.

IGNITION COILS

1. Disconnect the negative battery cable.

2. Remove the DIS assembly.

3. Remove the coils attaching nuts and remove the coil(s) from the assembly.

4. The installation is the reverse of the removal procedure.

5. Connect the negative battery cable and check the proper operation.

IGNITION MODULE

1. Disconnect the negative battery cable.

2. Remove the DIS assembly.

3. Remove the coils attaching nuts and remove the coils from the assembly.

4. Remove the module from the assembly plate.

5. The installation is the reverse of the removal procedure.

6. Connect the negative battery cable and check the proper operation.

3.3L Engine

C³I COILS AND MODULE ASSEMBLY

1. Disconnect the negative battery cable.

2. Disconnect the 14-way connector from the module.

3. Label and remove the spark plug wires from the assembly.

4. Remove the fasteners securing the assembly to its mounting bracket and remove the assembly.

To install:

5. Install the assembly to the bracket and install the fasteners.

6. Connect the spark plug wires and the harness connector.

7. Connect the negative battery cable and check the for proper operation.

IGNITION COILS

1. Disconnect the negative battery cable.

2. Disconnect the spark plug wires.

3. Remove the screws and remove the coil(s) or coil pack from the ignition module. Disconnect the coil to module connector, if equipped.

To install:

4. Connect the harness connector.

5. Install the coil(s) or coil pack to the ignition module and install the attaching screws.

6. Connect the spark plug wires.

7. Connect the negative battery cable and check for proper operation.

CRANKSHAFT SENSOR

1. Disconnect the negative battery cable.

2. Remove the serpentine belt.

3. Raise and safely support the vehicle.

4. Remove the right front wheel and splash shield.

5. Remove the harmonic balancer.

6. Disconnect the sensor electrical connector.

7. Remove the sensor and pedestal from the engine and remove the sensor from the pedestal.

To install:

8. Loosely install the sensor to the pedestal.

9. Attach special aligning tool J–37089 or equivalent, to the assembly. Slide the tool over the crankshaft and tighten the pedestal to engine screws to 22 ft. lbs. (30 Nm). Tighten the pedestal pinch bolt to 30–35 inch lbs. (3–4 Nm).

10. Remove tool J-37089 from the crankshaft and place on the harmonic balancer and turn. If any vane of the harmonic balancer touches the tool, replace the balancer assembly.

11. Install the harmonic balancer to the crankshaft and tighten the attaching bolt to 219 ft. lbs. (300 Nm).

12. Connect the connector.

13. Install the splash shield and wheel.

14. Lower the vehicle and install the serpentine belt.

15. Connect the negative battery cable and check the sensor for proper operation.

Ignition Timing

ADJUSTMENT

NOTE: Distributorless ignition systems do not give provisions for setting ignition timing; only the timing on the 2.0L engine can be set. Follow all instructions on the Vehicle Emission Control Information label if they are not consistent with these procedures.

1989

1. Start the engine, set the parking brake and run the engine until at normal operating temperature. Keep all lights and accessories OFF.

2. Connect the red lead of a tachometer to the terminal of the coil labeled **TACH** and connect the black lead to a good ground.

3. If a magnetic timing unit is available, insert the probe into the receptacle near the timing scale.

4. If a magnetic timing unit is not available, connect a conventional power timing light to the No. 1 cylinder spark plug wire.

5. With parking brake safely set, place automatic transaxle in **D** or leave manual transaxle in neutral.

6. Ground the ALDL connector under the dash by installing a jumper wire between the **A** and **B** terminals. The check engine light should begin flashing.

7. Aim the timing light at the timing scale or read the magnetic timing unit. Record the reading.

8. Repeat Steps 3–6 using the No. 4 spark plug wire. Record the reading.

9. Use the average of the 2 readings to derive an average timing value.

10. Loosen the distributor hold-down nuts so the distributor can be rotated.

11. Using the average timing value, turn the distributor in the proper direction until the specified timing according to the Vehicle Emission Control Information label is reached.

12. Tighten the hold-down nuts and recheck the timing values.

13. Remove the jumper wire from the ALDL connector. To clear the ECM memory, disconnect the ECM harness from the positive battery pigtail for 10 seconds with the key in the OFF position.

Alternator

PRECAUTIONS

Several precautions must be observed with alternator-equipped vehicles to avoid damage to the unit.

• If the battery is removed for any reason, make sure it is reconnected with the correct polarity. Reversing the battery connections may result in damage to the rectifiers.

• When utilizing a booster battery as a starting aid, always connect the positive to positive terminals and the negative terminal from the booster battery to a good engine ground on the vehicle being started.

• Never use a fast charger as a booster to start vehicles.

• Disconnect the battery cables when charging the battery with a fast charger.

• Never attempt to polarize the alternator.

• Do not use a tester of of greater than 12 volts when checking diode continuity.

• Do not short across or ground any of the alternator terminals.

• The polarity of the battery, alternator and regulator must be matched and considered before making any electrical connections within the system.

• Never separate the alternator on an open circuit. Make sure all connections within the circuit are clean and tight.

• Disconnect the battery ground terminal when performing any service on electrical components.

• Disconnect the battery if arc welding is to be done on the vehicle.

• Never disconnect the battery with the engine running.

BELT TENSION ADJUSTMENT

V-Belt

1. Disconnect the negative battery cable.

2. Loosen the alternator mounting bolts.

3. Using a standard belt tension gauge, install it to the center of the longest span of the drive belt.

4. Use a medium prybar or the adjustment lug on the alternator housing to move the alternator. When the drive belt tension is 90–100 lbs. for a used belt or 165–175 lbs. for a new belt, tighten the alternator mounting bolts.

5. Connect the negative battery cable.

Serpentine Belt

A single serpentine belt may be used to drive engine-mounted accessories. Drive belt tension is maintained by a spring loaded tensioner. The drive belt tensioner can control belt tension over a broad range belt lengths, however, there are limits to the tensioner's ability to compensate.

1. Disconnect the negative battery cable.

2. Inspect tensioner markings to see if the belt is within operating lengths. Replace the belt if the belt is excessively worn or is outside of the tensioner's operating range.

3. Run the engine until operating temperature is reached. Be sure all accessories are OFF. Turn the engine OFF and read the belt tension using a belt tension gauge tool placed halfway between the alternator and the air conditioning compressor. If not equipped with air conditioning, read the tension between the power steer-

ing pump and crankshaft pulley. Remove the tool.

4. Run the engine for 15 seconds and turn it OFF. Using a box-end wrench, apply clockwise force to tighten to the tensioner pulley bolt. Release the force and immediately take a tension reading without disturbing belt tensioner position.

5. Using the same wrench, apply a counterclockwise force to the tensioner pulley bolt and raise the pulley to its fully raised position. Slowly lower the pulley to engage the belt. Take a tension reading without disturbing the belt tensioner position.

6. Average the 3 readings. If their average is lower than specifications, replace the tensioner:

2.0L and 2.3L engines—50 lbs.
3.3L engine—67 lbs.

REMOVAL & INSTALLATION

Except 2.3L Engine

1. Disconnect the negative battery cable.

2. Label and disconnect the wiring from the back of the alternator.

3. On the 2.5L engine, loosen the adjusting bolts and remove the alternator belt. If equipped with a serpentine belt, loosen the serpentine belt tensioner and rotate it counterclockwise to remove the drive belt.

4. Remove the alternator attaching bolts and remove the alternator from the vehicle.

5. Installation is the reverse of the removal procedure.

6. Check and/or adjust the belt tension.

7. Connect the negative battery cable and check the alternator for proper operation.

2.3L Engine

1. Disconnect the negative battery cable.

2. Using a 13mm wrench that is at least 24 in. long, loosen the tensioner pulley bolt, rotate the tensioner counterclockwise and remove the belt from the alternator pulley.

3. Label and disconnect the vacuum lines at the front of engine and remove the attaching bracket.

4. Label and disconnect the injector harness and alternator connectors.

5. Remove the 2 rear alternator mounting bolts.

6. Remove the front alternator bolt and engine harness clip.

NOTE: Care must be taken during removal and installation not to damage the air conditioning hoses.

7. Remove the alternator by manipulating it between the engine lift-

ing eyelet and the air conditioning hoses.

To install:

8. Position the alternator on the engine.

9. Install the front mounting bolt loosely and install the clip.

10. Install the 2 rear mounting bolts and tighten to 37 ft. lbs. (50 Nm).

11. Tighten the front mounting bolt to 20 ft. lbs. (26 Nm).

12. Connect the injector harness and alternator connectors.

13. Connect the vacuum lines and install the bracket.

14. Install the belt.

15. Connect the negative battery cable and check the alternator for proper operation.

Starter

REMOVAL & INSTALLATION

Except 2.3L Engine

1. Disconnect the negative battery cable.

2. Raise and safely support the vehicle. Disconnect the electrical wiring from the starter.

3. Remove the dust cover bolts and pull the dust cover back to gain access to the front starter bolt and remove the front starter bolt.

4. Remove the rear support bracket.

5. Pull the rear dust cover back to gain access to the rear starter bolt and remove the rear bolt.

6. Note the number and location of any shims.

7. Push the dust cover back into place and remove the starter from the vehicle.

8. The installation is the reverse of the removal procedure.

9. Tighten the starter bolts to 30–35 ft. lbs. (41–47 Nm).

2.3L Engine

1989 (VIN D) ENGINE

1. Disconnect the negative battery cable.

2. Remove the air cleaner to throttle body duct.

3. Label and disconnect the TPS, IAC and MAP sensor connectors.

4. Remove vacuum harness assembly from intake and position aside.

5. Remove cooling fan shroud attaching bolts and remove the shroud.

6. Remove upper radiator support.

7. Disconnect the connector from the cooling fan and remove the fan assembly. Do not damage the lock tang on the TPS with the fan bracket.

8. Remove the starter mounting bolts.

9. Tilt the rear of starter towards

the radiator, pull the starter out and rotate solenoid towards the radiator to gain access to the electrical connections.

NOTE: If present, do not to damage the crank sensor mounted directly to the rear of the starter.

10. Disconnect the connectors from the solenoid.

11. Move the starter toward the driver's side of the vehicle and remove.

To install:

12. Lower the starter and connect the solenoid connectors.

13. Rotate the starter into installation position, properly install any shims that were removed and install the mounting bolts. Tighten to 74 ft. lbs. (100 Nm).

14. Install the fan, support and shroud.

15. Install the vacuum harness assembly and connect the TPS, IAC and MAP sensor connectors.

16. Install the air cleaner to throttle body duct.

17. Connect the negative battery cable and check the starter for proper operation.

1990–93 (VIN D), 1989–93 (VIN A) AND 1992–93 (VIN 3) ENGINES

1. Disconnect the negative battery cable. Remove the air induction tube, if necessary.

2. Remove the cooling fan assembly.

3. Remove the oil filter, if necessary.

4. Remove the intake manifold brace, if equipped.

5. Remove the mounting bolts; some engines may have 3 starter mounting bolts. Pull the starter out of the hole and move toward the front of the vehicle.

6. Disconnect the wiring from the starter.

7. Remove the starter by lifting it between the intake manifold and the radiator.

To install:

8. Lower the starter between the intake manifold and the radiator and connect the wiring to the solenoid.

9. Rotate the starter into installation position and install the mounting bolts. Tighten to 74 ft. lbs. (100 Nm).

10. Install the intake manifold brace and oil filter.

11. Install the cooling fan assembly and air induction tube, if removed.

12. Connect the negative battery cable and check the starter for proper operation.

EMISSION CONTROLS

Due to the complex nature of modern electronic engine control systems, comprehensive diagnosis and testing procedures fall outside the confines of this repair manual. For complete information on diagnosis, testing and repair procedures concerning all modern engine and emission control systems, please refer to "Chilton's Guide to Fuel Injection and Electronic Engine Controls".

FUEL SYSTEM

Fuel System Service Precautions

Safety is the most important factor when performing not only fuel system maintenance but any type of maintenance. Failure to conduct maintenance and repairs in a safe manner may result in serious personal injury or death. Maintenance and testing of the vehicle's fuel system components can be accomplished safely and effectively by adhering to the following rules and guidelines.

- To avoid the possibility of fire and personal injury, always disconnect the negative battery cable unless the repair or test procedure requires that battery voltage be applied.
- Always relieve the fuel system pressure prior to disconnecting any fuel system component (injector, fuel rail, pressure regulator, etc.), fitting or fuel line connection. Exercise extreme caution whenever relieving fuel system pressure to avoid exposing skin, face and eyes to fuel spray. Please be advised that fuel under pressure may penetrate the skin or any part of the body that it contacts.
- Always place a shop towel or cloth around the fitting or connection prior to loosening to absorb any excess fuel due to spillage. Ensure that all fuel spillage (should it occur) is quickly removed from engine surfaces. Ensure that all fuel soaked cloths or towels are deposited into a suitable waste container.
- Always keep a dry chemical (Class B) fire extinguisher near the work area.
- Do not allow fuel spray or fuel vapors to come into contact with a spark or open flame.

- Always use a backup wrench when loosening and tightening fuel line connection fittings. This will prevent unnecessary stress and torsion to fuel line piping. Always follow the proper torque specifications.
- Always replace worn fuel fitting O-rings with new. Do not substitute fuel hose or equivalent where fuel pipe is installed.

RELIEVING FUEL SYSTEM PRESSURE

2.5L and 1992–93 2.3L Engines

1. Loosen the fuel filler cap.
2. Remove the fuse marked fuel pump from the fuse block or disconnect the harness connector at the tank.
3. Start the engine and run at idle until it stalls.
4. Crank the engine for an additional 3 seconds to make sure all of the fuel pressure is exhausted from the fuel lines.
5. Turn the ignition switch OFF, disconnect the negative battery cable and reinstall the fuel pump fuse or connect the connector at the tank.
6. Tighten the filler cap.

Except 2.5L and 1992–93 2.3L Engines

1. Disconnect the negative battery cable.
2. Loosen the fuel filler cap.
3. Install a fuel pressure gauge to the fuel pressure connection on the fuel pressure regulator assembly. Wrap a shop towel around the connection to avoid any fuel spray.
4. Install the bleed hose into an approved container and open the valve to bleed the fuel pressure.
5. Drain any residual fuel in the gauge into the container.
6. Tighten the filler cap.

Fuel Tank

REMOVAL & INSTALLATION

1. Disconnect the negative battery cable.
2. Drain the fuel tank into a proper container.
3. Raise and safely support the vehicle.
4. Disconnect the fuel sender connector.
5. Remove the ground wire screw and the muffler hanger bolt.
6. Remove the rubber exhaust hangers and allow the exhaust pipe to rest against the rear axle.
7. Disconnect all hoses at the fuel tank.
8. With the aid of an assistant, support the fuel tank and disconnect the 2 fuel tank retaining straps.
9. Lower the tank away from the vehicle. Make sure all hoses and electrical connectors are disconnected.
To install:
10. With the aid of an assistant raise the fuel tank up and into position.
11. Install the fuel tank retaining straps and tighten the bolts to 25 ft. lbs. (33 Nm).
12. Connect the hoses and connectors to the fuel tank.
13. Install the rubber exhaust hangers and install the muffler hanger bolt.
14. Connect the ground lead to the underbody.
15. Connect the fuel tank sender electrical connector.
16. Lower the vehicle and refill the fuel tank.
17. Connect the negative battery cable.
18. Turn the ignition to ON for 2 seconds and then OFF for 10 seconds. Repeat the procedure and then inspect fuel system for leaks.
19. Turn the ignition ON and check fuel guage operation.

Fuel Filter

The fuel filter is located near the rear of the vehicle, forward of the fuel tank.

REMOVAL & INSTALLATION

1. Relieve the fuel system pressure.
2. Raise and safely support the vehicle.
3. Using a backup wrench, remove the fuel line fittings from the fuel filter.
4. Remove the fuel filter mounting screws and remove the filter from the vehicle.
5. The installation is the reverse of the removal procedure. Replace the O-rings. Tighten the fuel line to filter connectors to 22 ft. lbs. (30 Nm).

Electric Fuel Pump

PRESSURE TESTING

1. Relieve the fuel system pressure.
2. Connect an appropriate fuel pressure gauge to the pressure connection on the fuel pressure regulator assembly, if equipped. If there is no valve, install in-line to the pressure line.
3. Wrap a clean shop towel around the fitting to catch any fuel leakage.
4. Turn the ignition ON and read the pressure on the gauge.
5. If not within specifications, inspect the system for clogs, collapsed hoses, kinks or a faulty pump. The fuel pressure can be measured at different

points in the system to locate the problem area.

6. Relieve the fuel system pressure and disconnect the gauge.

REMOVAL & INSTALLATION

1989–91

1. Relieve the fuel system pressure.
2. Raise and safely support the vehicle.
3. Using the proper approved equipment, drain the fuel tank.
4. Disconnect all wiring and hoses from the tank.
5. Place a transmission jack under the center of the tank and apply slight pressure. Remove the tank straps.
6. Remove the fuel tank from the vehicle.
7. Using a hammer and a brass drift, turn the lock ring counterclockwise to release the pump/sending unit assembly.
8. Disassemble the unit to separate the pump itself from the assembly.
To install:
9. Push the fuel pump onto the attaching hose and install the filter on the end of the pump.
10. Install a new tank seal O-ring to the pump.
11. Install the pump into the tank and install the lock ring with a hammer and brass punch turning the ring clockwise.
12. Install the fuel tank.
13. Connect the negative battery cable, start the engine and check for leaks.

1992–93

1. Relieve the fuel system pressure.
2. Raise and safely support the vehicle.
3. Using the proper approved equipment, drain the fuel tank.
4. Disconnect all wiring and hoses from the tank.
5. Place a transmission jack under the center of the tank and apply slight pressure. Remove the tank straps.
6. Remove the fuel tank from the vehicle.
7. Remove the snapring from the top of the pump/sending unit assembly and remove the assembly.
8. Disassemble the unit to separate the pump itself from the assembly.
To install:
9. Push the fuel pump onto the attaching hose and install the filter on the end of the pump.
10. Install a new tank seal O-ring to the pump.
11. Install the pump into the tank and install the snapring.
12. Install the fuel tank.
13. Connect the negative battery ca-

ble, start the engine and check for leaks.

Fuel Injection

IDLE SPEED ADJUSTMENT

The idle speed is controlled by the ECM, which receives data from various sensors and switches within the fuel injection system. Adjustments are preset at the factory and not adjustable.

Fuel Injector

REMOVAL & INSTALLATION

Except 2.5L Engine

NOTE: Injector removal does not necessitate complete fuel rail removal on the 2.0L or 2.3L engine. Use only exact replacements according to the part number inscribed on the injector; some injectors may look identical but each is specifically calibrated for its application.

1. Relieve the fuel system pressure.
2. If equipped with the 2.0L or 2.3L engine, remove the crankcase ventilation oil/air separator and the fuel pipe clamp bolt.
3. Disconnect the vacuum hose from the pressure regulator.
4. Disconnect the fuel pressure and return hoses, if removing the fuel rail from the vehicle.
5. Remove the fuel rail attaching bolts and separate the fuel rail assembly from the cylinder head.
6. Disconnect the connector(s) from the injector(s).
7. Remove the injector retainer clip and remove the injector from the fuel rail assembly.
To install:
8. Lubricate the new injector O-rings with clean engine oil and install to the injector.
9. Install a new retainer clip to the injector so the opening of the clip faces the injector's terminals.
10. Install the injector assembly to the fuel rail with the terminals facing outward. Make sure the injector is pushed in far enough to fully engage the retainer clip with the machined slots on the rail socket.
11. Install the fuel rail assembly to the engine and connect the vacuum hose and fuel hoses, if removed.
12. Install the fuel pipe clamp bolt and the crankcase ventilation oil/air separator, if removed.
13. Connect the negative battery cable, start the engine and check for fuel leaks.

2.5L Engine

1. Relieve the fuel system pressure.
2. Disconnect the negative battery cable.
3. Remove the air cleaner.
4. Disconnect the electrical connector from the fuel injector.
5. Remove the injector retainer screw and the retainer.
6. Position a small prybar and a fulcrum on the side of the injector opposite the terminals. Carefully lift the injector out of its cavity in the throttle body.
7. Remove the O-rings from the injector.
To install:
8. Lubricate the O-rings with clean engine oil. Place the upper O-ring in its groove and the lower 1 flush against the filter.
9. Push the fuel injector straight into the throttle body cavity so the terminals facing the wire grommet cut out.
10. Install the retainer, apply thread locking compound on the threads of the attaching screw and tighten to 27 inch lbs. (3 Nm).
11. Connect the connector and install the air cleaner.
12. Connect the negative battery cable, start the engine and check for fuel leaks.

DRIVE AXLE

Halfshaft

REMOVAL & INSTALLATION

NOTE: If equipped with tri-pot joints, care must be exercised not to allow joints to become overextended. Overextending the joint could result in separation of internal components.

1. Disconnect the negative battery cable.
2. Raise and safely support the vehicle.
3. Remove the wheels.
4. Install the halfshaft seal protector on the outer joint.
5. Remove the shaft nut and washer.
6. Remove the ball joint attaching nut and separate the control arm from the steering knuckle. Remove the stabilizer shaft, if necessary.
7. Pull out on lower knuckle area. Using a plastic or rubber mallet, strike

the end of the halfshaft to disengage it from the hub and bearing assembly.

8. Separate the halfshaft from the hub and bearing assembly and move the strut assembly rearward.

9. Remove the inner joint from the transaxle or intermediate shaft using the slide hammer tool.

10. To remove the intermediate shaft, remove the rear engine mount through bolt. Then remove the intermediate shaft bracket bolts and remove the assembly.

To install:

11. Install the seal protector to the transaxle. Install the intermediate shaft, if removed. Tighten the bracket bolts to 35 ft. lbs. (47 Nm).

12. Drive the halfshaft into the transaxle or intermediate shaft by placing a suitable tool into the groove on the joint housing and tapping until seated. Be careful not to damage the axle seal or spring. Verify that the axle is seated by grasping the inner joint housing and pulling outboard.

13. Install the axle to the hub and bearing assembly.

14. Install the washer and nut and tighten to 185 ft. lbs. (260 Nm).

15. Install the ball joint to the steering knuckle. Install the stabilizer shaft, if removed.

16. Remove the seal protectors.

17. Install the wheels.

18. Connect the negative battery cable and check for proper operation.

CV-Boot

REMOVAL & INSTALLATION

1. Disconnect the negative battery cable. Raise and safely support the vehicle. Remove the halfshaft assembly.

2. Remove the steel deflector ring by using brass drift to tap it off. If rubber ring is used, slide it off.

3. Cut the seal's retaining clamps and lift the boot up to gain access to retaining ring.

4. Remove the snapring and remove the joint from the shaft.

5. Slide the boot off shaft.

To install:

6. Clean the splines of the shaft and the CV-joint.

7. Install the clamp and boot onto the shaft. Fill the boot with amount of grease specified.

8. Install the joint to the shaft and install a new retaining ring.

9. Crimp the outer clamp securely in the groove.

10. Install the steel deflector ring or rubber ring.

11. Install the halfshaft assembly.

12. Connect the negative battery cable and check for proper operation.

Front Wheel Hub, Knuckle and Bearing

REMOVAL & INSTALLATION

1. Raise and safely support the vehicle.

2. Remove the front wheel assemblies.

3. Install a halfshaft boot seal protector tool on the outer CV-joints and a halfshaft boot seal protector tool on the inner tri-pot joints.

4. Insert a long punch through the caliper and into a rotor vent to keep it from turning.

5. Clean the shaft threads and lubricate them with a thread lubricant.

6. Remove the hub nut and washer.

7. Remove the caliper-to-steering knuckle bolts and support the caliper on a wire aside.

8. Remove the rotor.

9. Remove the halfshaft from the hub and bearing assembly.

10. Remove the 3 hub bolts, the shield and the hub and bearing assembly. Remove the bearing seal from the knuckle.

11. To remove the steering knuckle, perform the following procedures:

   a. At the ball joint-to-steering knuckle and the tie-rod-to-steering knuckle intersections, remove the cotter pins and nuts.

   b. Using a ball joint removal tool, separate the ball joint and the tie-rod end from the steering knuckle.

   c. Matchmark the strut to the knuckle. While supporting the steering knuckle, remove the steering knuckle-to-strut bolts and the steering knuckle from the vehicle.

To install:

12. Install the steering knuckle and all attaching bolts. Tighten the bolts to their proper torques:

   a. Align the matchmarks and tighten the steering knuckle-to-strut bolts to 140 ft. lbs. (190 Nm).

   b. Tighten the ball joint-to-steering knuckle nut to 55–65 ft. lbs. (75–88 Nm) and install a new cotter pin.

   c. Tighten the tie-rod-to-steering knuckle nut to 35 ft. lbs. (47 Nm) and install a new cotter pin.

13. Install a new seal to the knuckle.

14. If reinstalling the original assembly, replace the O-ring. Install the hub and bearing assembly, shield and bolts. Tighten the bolts to 70 ft. lbs. (95 Nm).

15. Install the halfshaft and brake parts.

16. Install the wheels.

17. Check and adjust front end alignment, as required.

MANUAL TRANSAXLE

For further information on transmission/transaxles, please refer to "Chilton's Guide to Transmission Repair".

Transaxle Assembly

REMOVAL & INSTALLATION

1. Disconnect the negative battery cable from the battery and transaxle. Remove air ducts and tubes, etc. to gain access to transaxle mounting bolts.

2. Remove the power steering pump and brackets and position aside, if necessary.

3. Attach an engine support fixture to the engine and raise the engine enough to take the pressure off the engine mounts.

NOTE: If a lifting bar is not available, a chain hoist can be used. However, during the removal procedure the vehicle must be raised and the chain hoist adjusted to keep tension on the engine/transaxle assembly.

4. Remove the left side steering column opening filler from inside the vehicle.

5. Disconnect the clutch master cylinder pushrod from the clutch pedal.

6. Disconnect the clutch slave cylinder from the transaxle support bracket and move it aside.

7. Remove the transaxle mount-to-transaxle bolts. Discard the bolts attaching the mount to the side frame. New bolts must be used upon installation.

8. Remove the transaxle mount bracket attaching bolts and nuts. Remove the upper transaxle to engine bolts.

9. Remove the transaxle vent tube and disconnect the reverse light switch.

10. Disconnect the shift cables and retaining clips from the transaxle.

11. Raise and safely support the vehicle.

12. Remove the left front wheel assembly.

13. Remove the left front inner splash shield. Drain the transaxle oil.

14. Remove the transaxle strut and bracket, if equipped.

15. Remove the flywheel housing cover bolts.

16. Disconnect the speedometer cable or sensor from the transaxle.

17. If equipped with a 2.3L engine, remove the radiator outlet pipe support bolt from transaxle.

18. Disconnect the stabilizer bar from the left suspension support and control arm.

19. Disconnect the ball joint-to-steering knuckle nut and separate the ball joint from the steering knuckle.

20. Remove the left suspension support attaching bolts, the support and control arm as an assembly.

21. Use boot protectors and disengage the halfshafts from the transaxle. Remove the left halfshaft from the transaxle.

22. Remove engine mount components and remaining transaxle mount bolts, as required.

23. Position a transmission jack under and secure to the transaxle case. Remove the remaining transaxle-to-engine mounting bolts.

24. Remove the transaxle by sliding it toward the driver's side, away from the engine. Carefully lower the jack, guiding the right or intermediate shaft out of the transaxle. Lower the engine to aid the operation, if necessary.

To install:

25. Install the transaxle into position. As the transaxle is being installed, guide the right halfshaft into place. Lower the engine to its installation position.

26. Connect the negative battery cable to the transaxle case.

27. Install engine mount components and remaining transaxle mount bolts. Install the flywheel cover(s).

28. Remove the support jack when the transaxle is securely mounted.

29. Install the left halfshaft.

30. Install the left suspension support.

31. Install the engine mount crossmember nuts, if removed.

32. Connect the stabilizer bar to the left suspension support and control arm.

33. Install the radiator outlet pipe support bolt, if equipped.

34. Connect the speedometer cable or sensor.

35. Install the transaxle bracket and strut, if equipped.

36. Install the splash shield and wheel. Lower the vehicle.

37. Connect the shift cables and install the retaining clips.

38. Install the transaxle vent tube and connect the reverse light switch connector.

39. Install the upper transaxle to engine bolts. Install the transaxle mount bracket attaching bolts and nuts.

40. Install the new transaxle mount-to-transaxle bolts.

41. Connect the clutch slave cylinder to the support bracket.

42. Connect the clutch master cylinder pushrod to the clutch pedal.

43. Install the steering column opening filler panel.

44. Remove the engine support tool.

45. Install the power steering pump and brackets, if they were removed.

46. Install air ducts, etc. that were removed.

47. Fill the transaxle with the proper fluid.

48. Connect the negative battery cable and check the transaxle for proper operation.

CLUTCH

Clutch Assembly

REMOVAL & INSTALLATION

1. Disconnect the negative battery cable.

2. Remove the sound insulator panel from inside of the vehicle and disconnect the clutch master cylinder pushrod from the clutch pedal.

3. Remove the transaxle from the vehicle.

4. If reinstalling old parts, matchmark the clutch/pressure plate cover and flywheel. Insert a clutch plate alignment tool into the clutch disc hub.

5. Loosen the flywheel to pressure plate bolts gradually and evenly to avoid warpage.

6. Remove the pressure plate/clutch assembly from the flywheel.

7. Inspect the flywheel for excessive scores or cracks and replace if damaged. If the flywheel appears to be OK, sand the flywheel.

8. Sparingly apply anti-seize compound to the input shaft and clutch disc splines. Install a new release bearing.

To install:

9. Install the clutch disc and the pressure plate. Align with a clutch disc alignment tool and loosely tighten the pressure plate bolts to center the disc.

10. Tighten bolts 1, 2 and 3 to 12 ft. lbs. (16 Nm) and then bolts 4, 5 and 6 to 12 ft. lbs. (16 Nm).

11. Tighten all the bolts in order to 15 ft. lbs. (20 Nm) plus an additional 30 degrees.

12. Install the transaxle.

13. Connect the pushrod to the clutch pedal and install the sound insulator.

14. Connect the negative battery cable and check the clutch and reverse lights for proper operation.

Clutch Master and Slave Cylinders

REMOVAL & INSTALLATION

1. Disconnect the negative battery cable.

2. Remove the steering column opening filler/sound insulator from inside the vehicle.

3. Disconnect the clutch master cylinder pushrod from the clutch pedal.

4. Remove the clutch master cylinder attaching nuts at the front of the dash and disconnect the remote fluid reservoir, if equipped.

5. Remove the actuator cylinder attaching nuts at the transaxle.

6. Remove the hydraulic actuating system as an assembly.

To install:

7. Bleed the system, if necessary.

8. Install the actuator cylinder to the transaxle, aligning the pushrod

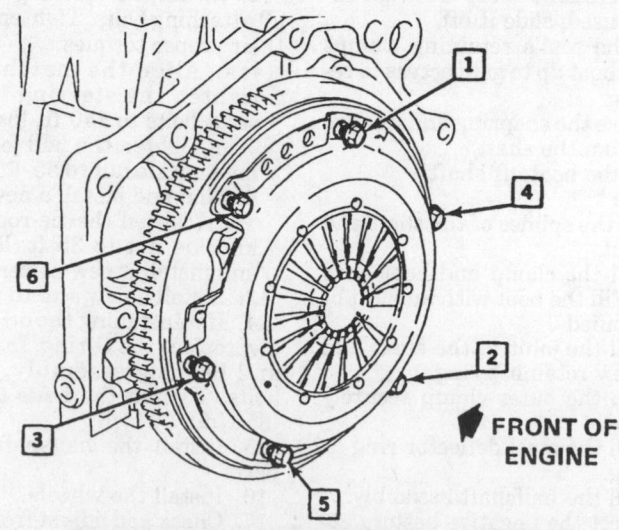

Clutch pressure plate bolt tightening sequence

into the pocket on the lever. Tighten the attaching nuts evenly to prevent damage.

NOTE: New actuators are packaged with plastic straps to retain the pushrod. Do not break the strap off; it will break upon the first clutch application.

9. Install the master cylinder. Tighten the attaching nuts evenly to prevent damage. Connect the remote fluid reservoir, if equipped. If equipped with a bleed screw and bleeding is necessary, bleed the system.
10. Remove the pushrod restrictor from the master cylinder pushrod. Lubricate the bushing on the clutch pedal. Connect the pushrod to the pedal and install the retaining clip. Make sure the cruise control switch is operating properly.

NOTE: When adjusting the cruise control switch, do not use a force of more than 20 lbs. to pull the pedal and nut, or damage to the master cylinder pushrod retaining ring could result.

11. Install the steering column opening filler from inside the vehicle.
12. Push the clutch pedal down a few times. This will break the plastic straps on the actuator.
13. Connect the negative battery cable and check for proper operation.

ADJUSTMENT

The hydraulic system used provides automatic clutch adjustment, therefore no adjustment to any portion of the system is required.

Hydraulic Clutch System Bleeding

With Bleed Screw

1. Make sure the reservoir is full of DOT 3 fluid and is kept topped off throughout this procedure.
2. Loosen the bleed screw, located on the actuator cylinder body next to the inlet connection.
3. When a steady stream of fluid comes out the bleeder, tighten it to 17 inch lbs. (2 Nm).
4. Refill the fluid reservoir.
5. To check the system, start the engine and wait 10 seconds.
6. Depress the clutch pedal and shift into Reverse. If there is any gear clash, air may still be present.

Without Bleed Screw

1. Remove the actuator cylinder from the transaxle.

2. Loosen the master cylinder attaching nuts to the ends of the studs.
3. Remove the reservoir cap and diaphragm.
4. Depress the actuator cylinder pushrod about ¾ in. into its bore and hold the position.
5. Install the reservoir diaphragm and cap while holding the actuator pushrod.
6. Release the pushrod when the diaphragm and cap are properly installed.
7. With the actuator lower than the master cylinder, hold the actuator vertically with the pushrod end facing the ground.
8. Press the actuator pushrod into its bore with ½ in. strokes. Check the reservoir for bubbles. Continue until no bubbles enter the reservoir.
9. Install the master cylinder and actuator.
10. Refill the fluid reservoir.
11. To check the system, start the engine and wait 10 seconds.
12. Depress the clutch pedal and shift into reverse. If there is any gear clash, air may still be present.

AUTOMATIC TRANSAXLE

For further information on transmission/transaxles, please refer to "Chilton's Guide to Transmission Repair".

Transaxle Assembly

REMOVAL & INSTALLATION

1. Disconnect the negative battery cable. If necessary, drain the coolant and disconnect the heater core hoses.
2. Remove the air cleaner assembly. If equipped with a 3.3L engine, remove the mass air flow sensor and air intake duct.
3. Disconnect the throttle valve cable from the throttle lever and the transaxle.
4. If equipped with a 2.3L engine, remove the power steering pump and bracket and position it aside.
5. Remove the transaxle dipstick and tube.
6. Install an engine support tool. Insert a ¼ × 2 inch bolt in the hole at the front right motor mount to maintain driveline alignment.
7. Remove the wiring harness-to-transaxle nut. Disconnect the wiring connectors from the speed sensor,

TCC connector, neutral safety switch and reverse light switch.
8. Disconnect the shift linkage from the transaxle.
9. Remove the upper 2 transaxle-to-engine bolts and the upper left transaxle mount along with the bracket assembly.
10. Remove the rubber hose from the transaxle vent pipe. Remove the remaining upper engine-to-transaxle bolts.
11. Raise and safely support the vehicle. Remove both front wheels.
12. If equipped with a 2.3L engine, remove both lower ball joints and stabilizer shafts links.
13. Drain the transaxle fluid.
14. Remove the shift linkage bracket from the transaxle.
15. Install a halfshaft boot seal protector on the inner seals.

NOTE: Some vehicles may use a gray silicone boot on the inboard axle joint. Use boot protector tool on these boots. All other boots are made from a black thermo-plastic material and do not require the use of a boot seal protector.

16. Remove both ball joint-to-control arm nuts and separate the ball joints from the control arms.
17. Remove both halfshafts and support them with a cord or wire.
18. Remove the transaxle mounting strut/brace.
19. Remove the left stabilizer bar link pin bolt, left frame bushing clamp nuts and left frame support assembly.
20. Remove the torque converter cover. Matchmark the flexplate and torque converter for installation purposes. Remove the torque converter-to-flexplate bolts.
21. Disconnect and plug the transaxle oil cooler lines.
22. Remove the transaxle-to-engine support bracket and install the transaxle removal jack.
23. Remove the remaining transaxle-to-engine attaching bolts and the transaxle from the vehicle.
To install:
24. Secure the transaxle to the jack.
25. Apply a small amount of grease on the torque converter hub and seat in the oil pump.
26. Position the transaxle in the vehicle and install the lower engine to transaxle bolts.
27. Install the transaxle to engine support bracket. Once the transaxle is securely held in place, remove the jack. Connect the cooler lines.
28. Install the torque converter bolts and tighten to specification.
29. Install the torque converter cover.
30. Install the left frame support assembly.

31. Install the left stabilizer shaft frame busing nuts and link pin bolt.

32. Install the transaxle mounting strut.

33. Install the halfshafts. Install the ball joints.

34. Install the shift linkage bracket to the transaxle.

35. Install the wheels and lower the vehicle.

36. Install the upper transaxle to engine bolts.

37. Install the left side transaxle mount.

38. Connect the shift linkage to the transaxle.

39. Connect the wiring connectors to their switches on the transaxle.

40. Remove the ¼ × 2 in. bolt that was placed in the hole at the front right motor mount to maintain driveline alignment. Remove an engine support tool.

41. Replace the O-ring, lubricate it and install the dipstick tube and dipstick.

42. Install the TV cable and rubber vent tube.

43. Install the air cleaner assembly and air tubes.

44. Connect the heater hoses, if disconnected.

45. Fill all fluids to their proper levels. Adjust cables as required.

46. Connect the negative battery cable and check the transaxle for proper operation and leaks.

TV CABLE ADJUSTMENT

Except 2.3L Engine

1. Disconnect the negative battery cable.

2. Depress and hold the adjustment tap at the TV cable adjuster.

3. Release the throttle lever by hand to its full travel position. On the 2.5L engine, press the accelerator pedal to the full travel position.

4. The slider must move toward the lever when the lever is rotated to the full travel position or when the accelerator pedal is pressed to the full travel position on the 2.5L engine.

5. Inspect the cable for freedom of movement. The cable may appear to function properly with the engine stopped and cold. Recheck the cable after the engine is warm.

6. Road test the vehicle and check for proper shifting.

2.3L Engine

1. Disconnect the negative battery cable.

2. Rotate the TV cable adjuster body at the transaxle 90 degrees and pull the cable conduit out until the slider mechanism contacts the stop.

3. Rotate the adjuster body back to the original position.

4. Using a torque wrench, rotate the TV cable adjuster until 75 inch lbs. (9 Nm) is reached.

5. Road test the vehicle and check for proper shifting.

SHIFT CABLE ADJUSTMENT

1. Place the selector in the **N** detent.

2. Raise the locking tab on the cable adjuster.

3. Place the shift control assembly on the transaxle in the neutral position.

4. Push the locking tab back into position.

FRONT SUSPENSION

MacPherson Strut

REMOVAL & INSTALLATION

1. Remove the mounting nuts from the shock tower under the hood.

2. Raise and safely support the vehicle. Remove the wheel.

3. Place jackstands under the front suspension to support the vehicle's weight.

NOTE: Do not allow the tri-pot joints from becoming overextended or they can get separated and damaged.

1. Strut assembly
2. Steering knuckle
3. Bolts
4. Nuts
5. Suspension support
6. Cover
7. Mounting nut

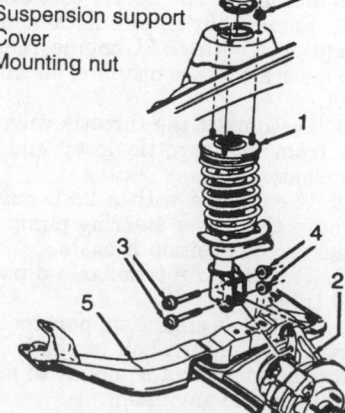

MacPherson strut assembly

4. Matchmark the lower strut mount to the knuckle and remove the strut to knuckle bolts and nuts.

5. While the strut is off the vehicle, the lower mounting hole may be elongated for alignment purposes. Paint any exposed metal afterward to prevent rusting.

To install:

6. Install the strut into position and install the 3 nuts.

7. Align the steering knuckle with the strut flange scribe marks and install the bolts and nuts. Tighten the nuts to 133 ft. lbs. (180 Nm).

8. Install the tie rod end to the strut assembly and install the bolt and cotter pin. Tighten the tie rod end bolt to 55 ft. lbs. (75 Nm).

9. Tighten the upper mounting strut nuts to 18 ft. lbs. (25 Nm).

10. Raise the vehicle and remove the jackstands.

11. Install the tire/wheel(s) and check the front end alignment.

Lower Ball Joints

INSPECTION

1. Raise the vehicle safely so the front suspension hangs free.

2. Grasp the tire at the top and bottom and move with an in-and-out motion.

3. If any horizontal movement is detected from the knuckle, relative to the control arm, replace the ball joint.

4. Shake the wheel and feel for movement of the stud end or castellated nut at the knuckle boss.

5. Check the nut for loose torque. A loose nut may indicate a bent stud or expanded hole in the knuckle.

6. Replace all parts found to be worn or damaged.

REMOVAL & INSTALLATION

1. Raise and safely support the vehicle.

2. The control arms must not be supporting the vehicle's weight.

NOTE: Do not allow the tri-pot joints from becoming overextended or they can get separated and damaged.

3. Remove the wheel.

4. Install inner drive joint seal protector J34754 or equivalent.

5. Remove the cotter pin and remove the ball joint nut.

6. Using the proper tools, separate the ball joint from the steering knuckle.

7. Use a ⅛ in. drill bit, drill a pilot hole through the attaching rivets. Finish the drilling with a ½ in. drill bit.

8. Loosen the stabilizer shaft bush-

ing assembly nut and remove the ball joint from the control arm.

To install:

9. Install the ball joint to the control arm.

10. Install the 3 special ball joint bolts and nuts as shown in the instruction sheet included with the replacement kit and tighten to the torque specified.

11. Install the ball stud to the steering knuckle. Install the nut and tighten to 40–50 ft. lbs. (55–65 Nm). Install a new cotter pin.

12. Install the stabilizer link/stabilizer shaft nut. If equipped without direct acting stabilizer system, tighten the nut to 13 ft. lbs. (17 Nm). If equipped with direct acting stabilizer system, tighten the nut to 70 ft. lbs. (95 Nm).

13. Install the wheel.

14. Perform a front end alignment and road test the vehicle.

Lower Control Arms

REMOVAL & INSTALLATION

1. Raise and safely support the vehicle. Remove the tire and wheel assembly.

2. Remove the nut attaching the stabilizer shaft to the stabilizer link and the nuts attaching the stabilizer shaft clamp to the suspension support. Remove the stabilizer shaft.

NOTE: Do not allow the tri-pot joints from becoming overextended or they can get separated and damaged.

3. Remove the ball joint stud attaching nut.

4. Pry the lower control arm from the steering knuckle.

5. Remove the control arm to suspension support bolts and nuts.

6. Remove the control arm from the vehicle.

7. Transfer reusable parts to the new control arm.

To install:

8. Install the control arm to the vehicle and loosely install the attaching bolts.

9. Install the suspension support into position and guide the ball joint into position. Loosely install the bolts.

10. Install the nuts attaching the stabilizer shaft clamp to the suspension support. Tighten the nuts to 17 ft. lbs. (23 Nm).

11. Install the ball joint to steering knuckle nut and tighten to 26 ft. lbs. (35 Nm) plus 60 degrees.

12. Install the stabilizer link to stabilizer shaft nut and tighten the nut as follows:

a. If equipped with direct acting

stabilizer system, tighten nut to 70 ft. lbs. (95 Nm).

b. If not equipped with direct acting stabilizer system, tighten nut to 13 ft. lbs. (17 Nm).

13. Install the tire/wheel assembly and lower the vehicle so the full weight of the vehicle is on the ground.

14. Torque the suspension support bolts as follows:

a. Tighten the center bolts to 66 ft. lbs. (90 Nm).

b. Tighten the front bolts to 65 ft. lbs. (88 Nm).

c. Tighten the rear bolts to 65 ft. lbs. (88 Nm).

15. Tighten the control arm attaching bolts to 61 ft. lbs. (83 Nm).

16. Perform a front end alignment.

Stabilizer Link

REMOVAL & INSTALLATION

1. Remove the stabilizer link to the stabilizer shaft nut.

2. If vehicle equipped with direct acting stabilizer system, remove the stabilizer link to the strut bracket nut, and remove the stabilizer link.

3. Remove the bolt, insulators, spacer and washers from vehicles not equipped with direct acting stabilizer system, and remove the stabilizer link.

To install:

4. Installation is the reverse of removal.

5. If vehicle is equipped with the direct acting suspension system, tighten the nut to 70 ft. lbs. (95 Nm).

6. If not equipped with the direct acting suspension system, tighten the nut to 13 ft. lbs. (17 Nm).

7. Tighten the stabilizer link to strut bracket nut to 70 ft. lbs. (95 Nm).

Stabilizer Shaft

REMOVAL & INSTALLATION

1. Raise and safely support the vehicle.

2. Remove the front tire/wheel assemblies.

3. Remove the nuts attaching the stabilizer shafts to the stabilizer links.

4. Support the suspension with jackstands and remove the clamps attaching the stabilizer shaft to the stabilizer links.

5. Remove the rear and center suspension support assemblies and loosen the front bolts.

6. Remove the stabilizer shaft with the insulators.

To install:

7. Install the stabilizer shaft with the insulators. Install the clamps and hand tighten.

8. Install the suspension support

assemblies into position and hand tighten the bolts. Remove the jackstands.

9. Install the nuts that attach the stabilizer shaft to the stabilizer links. Tighten the nuts as follows:

a. If equipped with direct acting stabilizer system, tighten nut to 70 ft. lbs. (95 Nm).

b. If not equipped with direct acting stabilizer system, tighten nut to 13 ft. lbs. (17 Nm).

10. Torque the suspension support bolts as follows:

a. Tighten the center bolts to 66 ft. lbs. (90 Nm).

b. Tighten the front bolts to 65 ft. lbs. (88 Nm).

c. Tighten the rear bolts to 65 ft. lbs. (88 Nm).

d. Tighten the stabilizer shaft to the support assembly nuts to 16 ft. lbs. (22 Nm).

e. Tighten the stabilizer shaft to control arm nuts to 13 ft. lbs. (17 Nm).

f. Tighten the clamp nuts to 17 ft. lbs. (23 Nm).

11. Install the front wheel/tire assemblies.

12. Check the front end alignment.

REAR SUSPENSION

Shock Absorbers

REMOVAL & INSTALLATION

1. Disconnect the negative battery cable.

2. Open the deck lid and remove the trim cover.

3. Remove the upper shock attaching nut. Remove 1 shock at a time if removing both.

4. Raise and safely support the vehicle.

5. Remove the lower mounting bolt.

6. Remove the shock from the vehicle.

7. The installation is the reverse of the removal procedure.

Coil Springs

REMOVAL & INSTALLATION

1. Raise and safely support the vehicle.

2. Using the proper equipment, support the weight of the rear axle. Disconnect the brake lines from the rear axle.

3. Remove the bolts that attach the shock to the lower mounting bracket.

4. Lower the axle and remove the coil spring from the vehicle.

5. The installation is the reverse of the removal procedure.

Rear Wheel Bearings

REMOVAL & INSTALLATION

1. Raise and safely support the vehicle.

2. Remove the wheel assembly.

3. Remove the brake drum.

4. Remove the 4 hub/bearing assembly-to-rear axle assembly nuts/bolts and the hub/bearing assembly from the axle.

NOTE: The top rear attaching bolt will not clear the brake shoe when removing the hub and bearing assembly. Partially remove the hub prior to removing this bolt.

5. The installation is the reverse of the removal procedure. Tighten the hub/bearing assembly-to-rear axle assembly nuts/bolts to 39 ft. lbs. (53 Nm).

ADJUSTMENT

The rear wheel bearing assembly is non-adjustable and is serviced by replacement only.

Rear Axle Assembly

REMOVAL & INSTALLATION

1. Raise the vehicle safely under the control arms.

2. If equipped, remove the stabilizer bar from the axle assembly.

3. Remove the wheel assemblies and support the rear axle with jackstands.

4. Remove the lower shock absorber-to-axle assembly nuts/bolts and separate the shock absorbers from the rear axle assembly.

5. Disconnect the parking brake cable at the equalizer and at the right rear wheel assembly.

6. Disconnect the ABS wiring connector, if equipped with anti-lock brakes, along with the clip, located near the fuel tank.

7. Disconnect the brake lines from the rear axle assembly; be sure the assembly is not suspended by the brake lines.

8. Lower the rear axle assembly and remove the coil spring. Transfer all reusable parts to the new assembly.

To install:

9. Install the rear axle and loosely install the attaching bolts.

10. Connect the right and left brake lines.

11. Connect the ABS wiring connector and mount clip.

12. Connect the parking brake cable.

13. Install the upper and lower insulators.

14. Install both springs and raise the axle assembly into place.

15. Install the lower shock absorber mount bolts and nuts and tighten to 35 ft. lbs. (47 Nm).

16. Install the left and right side brake line bracket mount bolts and tighten the screws to 8 ft. lbs. (11 Nm).

17. Install the tire/wheel assemblies and remove the jackstands from under the axle.

18. Lower the vehicle and bleed the rear brake system.

19. Adjust the parking brake if neccessary.

STEERING

Steering Wheel

REMOVAL & INSTALLATION

1. Disconnect the negative battery cable.

2. Remove the 2 screws that retain the steering pad, if equipped.

3. Disconnect the horn lead and remove the horn pad.

4. Remove the retainer, nut and dampener, if equipped.

5. Matchmark the steering wheel to the shaft and remove the steering wheel from the vehicle.

6. The installation is the reverse of the removal procedure. Tighten the attaching nut to 30 ft. lbs. (41 Nm).

Steering Column

REMOVAL & INSTALLATION

1. Disconnect the negative battery cable.

2. Remove the steering wheel.

3. Remove the steering column-to-intermediate shaft coupling pinch bolt. Remove the safety strap and bolt, if equipped.

4. Remove the steering column trim shrouds and column covers.

5. If equipped, remove the tilt lever.

6. Disconnect all wiring harness connectors. Remove the dust boot mounting screws and steering column-to-dash bracket bolts.

7. Lower the column to clear the mounting bracket and carefully remove from the vehicle.

To install:

8. Install the column assembly and install the column bracket support bolts and the upper pinch bolt.

9. Tighten the column braket support bolts to 22 ft. lbs. (30 Nm) and the upper pinch bolt to 29 ft. lbs. (40 Nm).

10. Connect the park lock/brake transmission shift interlock cable to the ignition switch.

11. Connect the electrical connectors.

12. Install the upper and lower steering column covers and install the tilt lever, if equipped.

13. Install the steering wheel and the horn pad.

14. Install the lower steering column filler and left sound insulator.

15. Connect the negative battery cable and check all column mounted switches, accessories and the vehicle's steering mechanism for proper operation.

Power Rack and Pinion Steering Gear

ADJUSTMENT

Rack Bearing Preload

1. Center the steering wheel. Raise and safely support the vehicle.

2. Loosen the locknut and turn the adjuster plug clockwise until it bottoms in the housing. Then back off about ⅛ turn and tighten the locknut while holding the position of the adjuster plug.

3. Check the steering for ability to return to center after the adjustment has been completed.

REMOVAL & INSTALLATION

1. Disconnect the negative battery cable. Remove the left side sound insulator.

2. Disconnect the upper pinch bolt on the steering coupling assembly.

3. Disconnect the clamp nuts.

4. Raise and safely support the vehicle. Remove both front wheel assemblies.

5. Remove the clamp nut and the fluid line retainer.

6. Remove the tie rod end-to-steering knuckle cotter pin and castle nut. Using a puller tool, disconnect the tie rod ends from the steering knuckles.

7. Lower the vehicle.

8. Disconnect and plug the fluid lines from the power steering rack.

9. Remove the mounting clamps. Move the steering rack forward and remove the lower pinch bolt on the coupling assembly.

10. Disconnect the coupling from the steering rack.

11. Remove the rack and pinion assembly with the dash seal through the left wheel opening.

To install:

12. If the studs were removed with the mounting clamps, reinstall the studs into the cowl. If the stud is being reused, use Loctite® to secure the threads.

13. Slide the rack and pinion assembly through the left side wheel housing opening and secure the dash seal.

14. Move the assembly forward and install the coupling.

15. Install the lower pinch bolt and tighten to 29 ft. lbs. (40 Nm).

16. Connect the fluid lines.

17. Install the clamp nuts. Tighten the left side clamp first, then tighten the right side. Raise and safely support the vehicle.

18. Connect the tie rod ends to the steering knuckle, tighten the nut to 35 ft. lbs. (47 Nm) and install a new cotter pin. Install the wheels.

19. Install the line retainer and lower the vehicle.

20. Install the upper pinch bolt on the coupling assembly. Tighten to 29 ft. lbs. (40 Nm).

21. Install the sound insulator.

22. Fill the power steering pump with fluid and bleed the system.

23. Connect the negative battery cable and check the rack for proper operation and leaks.

24. Check and adjust front end alignment, as required.

Power Steering Pump

REMOVAL & INSTALLATION

2.3L Engine

1. Disconnect the negative battery cable.

2. Disconnect the pressure and return lines from the pump.

3. Remove the rear bracket to pump bolts.

4. Remove the drive belt and position aside.

5. Remove the rear bracket to transaxle bolts.

6. Remove the front bracket to engine bolt.

7. Remove the pump and bracket as an assembly.

8. Transfer pulley and bracket, as necessary.

9. The installation is the reverse of the removal procedure.

10. Fill the power steering pump with fluid and bleed the system.

11. Connect the negative battery cable and check the pump for proper operation and leaks.

2.5L Engine

1. Disconnect the negative battery cable.

2. Remove the drive belt.

3. Disconnect and plug the pressure tubes from the power steering pump.

4. Remove the front adjustment bracket-to-rear adjustment bracket bolt.

5. Remove the front adjustment bracket-to-engine bolt and spacer.

6. Remove the pump with the front adjustment bracket.

7. If installing a new pump, transfer the pulley and front adjustment bracket to the new pump.

To install:

8. The installation is the reverse of the removal procedure.

9. Adjust the drive belt tension.

10. Fill the power steering pump with fluid and bleed the system.

11. Connect the negative battery cable and check the pump for proper operation and leaks.

2.0L and 3.3L Engines

1. Disconnect the negative battery cable.

2. Remove the serpentine drive belt.

3. Remove the power steering pump-to-engine bolts.

4. Pull the pump forward and disconnect the pressure lines.

5. Remove the pump and transfer the pulley, as necessary.

To install:

6. Connect the power steering lines to the pump.

7. Install the pump to the bracket and install the bolts. Tighten the bolts to 18 ft. lbs. (25 Nm).

8. Install the belt and adjust the drive belt tension.

9. Fill the power steering pump with fluid and bleed the system.

10. Connect the negative battery cable and check the pump for proper operation and leaks.

BELT ADJUSTMENT

NOTE: Serpentine belt driven power steering pumps do not require adjustment. If the belt is stretched beyond usable limits, replace it.

1. Place the appropriate gauge on the belt and measure the tension. The specifications are:

2.3L engine, new and used belt—110 lbs.

2.5L engine, used belt—100 lbs; new belt—180 lbs.

2. If the tension is not at specifications, loosen the mounting bolts and move the pump or turn the adjustment stud.

3. Tighten the mounting bolts while holding the adjusted position of the pump.

4. Run the engine for 2 minutes and recheck the tension.

SYSTEM BLEEDING

1. Raise the vehicle so the wheels are off the ground. Turn the wheels all the way to the left. Add power steering fluid to the **COLD** or **FULL COLD** mark on the fluid level indicator.

2. Start the engine and check the fluid level at fast idle. Add fluid, if necessary to bring the level up to the mark.

3. Bleed air from the system by turning the wheels from side-to-side without hitting the stops. Keep the fluid level at the **COLD** or **FULL COLD** mark. Fluid with air in it has a tan appearance.

4. Return the wheels to the center position and continue running the engine for 2–3 minutes.

5. Lower the vehicle and road test to check steering function and recheck the fluid level with the system at its normal operating temperature. Fluid should be at the **HOT** mark when finished.

Tie Rod Ends

REMOVAL & INSTALLATION

Inner Tie Rod

1. Disconnect the negative battery cable. Remove the rack and pinion gear from the vehicle.

2. Remove the lock plate from the inner tie rod bolts.

3. If removing both tie rods, remove both bolts, the bolt support plate and 1 of the tie rod assemblies. Reinstall the removed tie rod's bolt to keep inner parts of the rack aligned. Remove the remaining tie rod.

4. If only removing 1 tie rod, slide the assembly out from between the support plate and the center housing cover washer.

To install:

5. Install the center housing cover washer fitted into the rack and pinion boot.

6. Install the inner tie rod bolts through the holes in the bolt support plate, inner pivot bushing, center housing cover washer, rack housing and into the threaded holes.

7. Tighten the bolts to 65 ft. lbs. (90 Nm).

8. Install a new lock plate with its notches over the bolt flats.

9. Install the rack and pinion gear.

10. Fill the power steering pump with fluid and bleed the system.

11. Connect the negative battery ca-

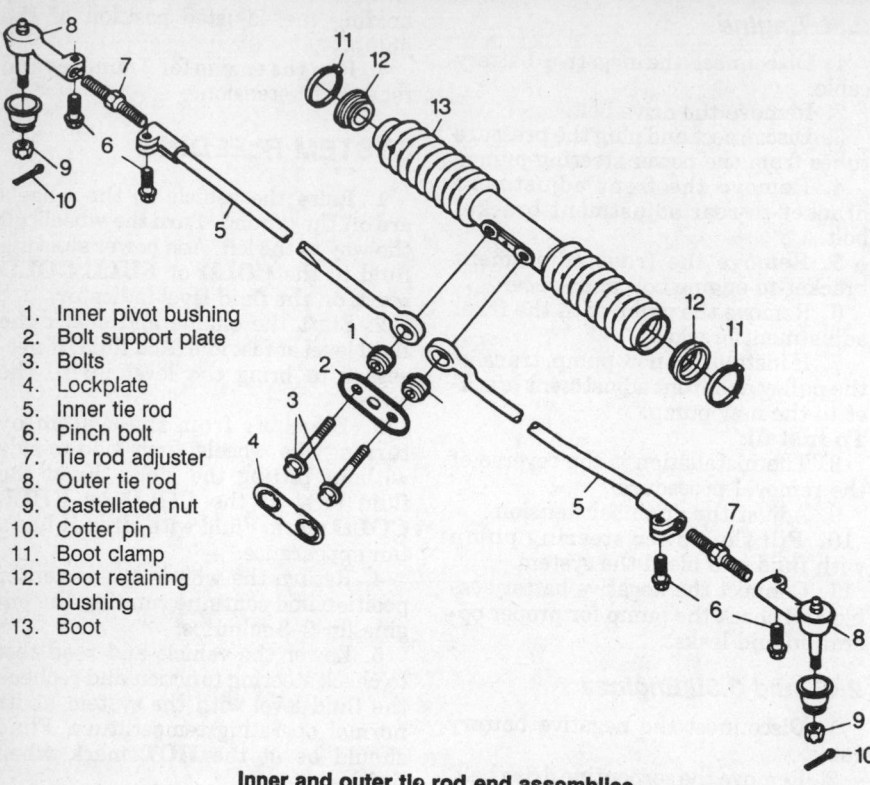

1. Inner pivot bushing
2. Bolt support plate
3. Bolts
4. Lockplate
5. Inner tie rod
6. Pinch bolt
7. Tie rod adjuster
8. Outer tie rod
9. Castellated nut
10. Cotter pin
11. Boot clamp
12. Boot retaining bushing
13. Boot

Inner and outer tie rod end assemblies

ble and check the rack for proper operation and leaks.

Outer Tie Rod

1. Disconnect the negative battery cable.
2. Remove the cotter pin and the nut from the tie rod ball stud at the steering knuckle.
3. Loosen the pinch bolts.
4. Using the proper tools, separate the tie rod taper from the steering knuckle.
5. Remove the tie rod from the adjuster.
6. The installation is the reverse of the removal procedure.
7. Perform a front end alignment.

BRAKES

Master Cylinder

REMOVAL & INSTALLATION

1989–91

1. Disconnect the negative battery cable. Unplug the fluid level sensor connector.
2. Disconnect and plug the brake lines from the master cylinder.

3. Remove the nuts attaching the master cylinder to the power booster.
4. Remove the master cylinder from the mounting studs.
5. Remove the retaining roll pins and remove the fluid reservoir from the cylinder, if necessary.

To install:

6. Replace the reservoir O-rings and bench bleed the master cylinder.
7. Install to the booster and install the nuts.
8. Install the brake lines to the master cylinder.
9. Fill the reservoir with brake fluid.
10. Connect the negative battery cable and check the brakes for proper operation.

1992–93

1. Disconnect the negative cable and the electrical connector from the fluid level sensor.
2. Disconnect the electrical connectors from both solenoids.
3. Disconnect the 3-pin and 6-pin motor pack electrical connectors.
4. Disconnect the brake pipe tube nuts from the master cylinder and from the modulator assembly.
5. Plug the brake lines to prevent brake fluid loss.
6. Remove the master cylinder mounting nuts.
7. Remove the master cylinder and the modulator assembly.

To install:

8. Install the master cylinder and the modulator assembly to the power booster.
9. Tighten the master cylinder and modulator assembly mounting nuts to 20 ft. lbs. (27 Nm).
10. Connect the brake lines to the master cylinder and to the modulator assembly. Tighten the nuts to 15 ft. lbs. (20 Nm).
11. Connect the electrical connectors to the fluid level sensor and to both solenoids.
12. Connect the 3-pin and 6-pin electrical connectors to the motor pack.
13. Refill the master cylinder with brake fluid and bleed the system if necessary.
14. Connect the negative battery cable.

Proportioner Valves

REMOVAL & INSTALLATION

1. Disconnect the negative battery cable.
2. Remove the retaining roll pins and remove the fluid reservoir from the cylinder, if necessary.
3. Remove the proportioner valve cap assemblies.
4. Remove the O-rings.
5. Remove the springs.
6. Carefully remove the proportioner valve pistons.
7. Remove the seals from the pistons.

To install:

8. Thoroughly clean and dry all parts.
9. Lubricate the new piston seals with the silicone grease included in the repair kit or brake assembly fluid. Install to the pistons with the seal lips facing upward toward the cap assembly.
10. Lubricate the stem of the pistons and install to their bores.
11. Install the springs.
12. Lubricate and install the new O-rings in their grooves in the cap assemblies.
13. Install the caps to the master cylinder and tighten to 20 ft. lbs. (27 Nm).
14. Install the reservoir, if removed.
15. Fill the reservoir with brake fluid.
16. Connect the negative battery cable and check the brakes for proper operation.

Power Brake Booster

REMOVAL & INSTALLATION

1. Disconnect the negative battery cable.

2. Disconnect the vacuum hose(s) from the booster.

3. Remove the master cylinder and if equipped, remove the modulator assembly.

4. From inside of the vehicle, remove the booster pushrod from the brake pedal.

5. Remove the nuts that attach the booster to the dash panel and remove it from the vehicle.

6. Transfer the necessary parts to the new booster.

7. The installation is the reverse of the removal procedure.

8. Connect the negative battery cable and check the brakes for proper operation.

Brake Caliper

REMOVAL & INSTALLATION

1. Raise and safely support the vehicle.

2. Remove the tire and wheel assembly.

3. Push the piston completely into its bore for clearance.

4. Remove the bolt that attaches the brake hose from the caliper. Plug the hose and the caliper to prevent fluid loss.

5. Remove the caliper mounting bolt and sleeve assemblies.

6. Lift the caliper off the rotor.

To install:

7. Install the brake hose to the caliper using new copper washers.

8. Position the caliper over the rotor so the caliper engages the adaptor correctly. Lubricate and install the sleeves and bolts. Tighten to 38 ft. lbs. (51 Nm).

9. Connect the brake line inlet fitting and tighten the fitting to 33 ft. lbs. (45 Nm).

10. Install the tire and wheel assembly.

11. Fill the master cylinder and bleed the brakes.

Disc Brake Pads

REMOVAL & INSTALLATION

1. Remove some of the fluid from the master cylinder. Raise and safely support the vehicle.

2. Remove the tire and wheel assembly.

3. Bottom the piston in its bore for clearance.

4. Remove the caliper mounting bolt and sleeve assemblies.

5. Lift the caliper off the rotor.

6. Remove the pads from the caliper.

To install:

7. Use a large C-clamp to compress the piston back into the caliper bore.

8. Install the pads and anti-rattle clip to the caliper. Adjust the bent-over tabs for a tight fit.

9. Position the caliper over the rotor so the caliper engages the adaptor correctly. Lubricate and install the sleeves and bolts. Tighten to 38 ft. lbs. (51 Nm).

10. Install the tire and wheel assembly.

11. Fill the master cylinder and check the brakes for proper operation.

Brake Rotor

REMOVAL & INSTALLATION

1. Raise and safely support the vehicle. Remove the tire and wheel assembly.

2. Remove the caliper and brake pads.

3. Remove the rotor from the hub.

4. The installation is the reverse of the removal procedure.

Brake Drums

REMOVAL & INSTALLATION

1. Raise and safely support the vehicle.

2. Remove the wheel and tire assembly.

3. Remove the drum. If the drum is difficult to remove, remove the plug from the rear of the backing plate and push the self-adjuster lever away from the star wheel. Rotate the star wheel to retract the shoes.

4. The installation is the reverse of the removal procedure.

5. Adjust the brakes as required.

Brake Shoes

NOTE: If unsure of spring positioning, finish one side before starting the other and use the untouched side as a guide.

REMOVAL & INSTALLATION

1. Remove the wheels and drums. Remove the primary and secondary shoe return springs from the anchor pin but leave them installed on the shoes.

2. Lift on the adjuster lever and remove the adjuster cable. Remove the actuating lever link and pawl return spring.

3. Remove the hold-down pin return springs and cups. Remove the parking brake strut and spring. Remove the actuating lever and pawl.

4. Remove the shoes, held together by the lower spring, while separating the parking brake actuating lever from the shoe with a twisting motion.

5. Lift the wheel cylinder dust boots and inspect for fluid leakage.

6. Thoroughly clean and dry the backing plate.

To install:

7. Remove, clean and dry all parts still on the old shoes. Lubricate the star wheel shaft threads and transfer all the parts to the new shoes in their proper locations.

8. To prepare the backing plate, lubricate the bosses, anchor pin and parking brake actuating lever pivot surface lightly with the brake-compatible lubricant.

9. Spread the shoes apart, engage the parking brake actuating lever and position them on the backing plate so the wheel cylinder pins engage properly and the anchor pin holds the shoes up.

10. Install the parking brake strut and the hold-down pin assemblies. Install the actuating lever with the hold-down pin assembly.

11. Install the anchor plate. Lubricate the sliding surface of the adjuster cable plate and install the adjuster cable.

12. Install the shoe return spring opposite the cable, then the remaining spring. Install the actuating lever link, the shoe return springs and assemble the pawl and return spring.

13. Adjust the star wheel.

14. Remove any grease from the linings and install the drum.

15. Complete the brake adjustment with the wheels installed and adjust the parking brake cable.

Wheel Cylinder

REMOVAL & INSTALLATION

1. Raise and safely support the vehicle.

2. Remove the wheel, drum and brake shoes.

3. Remove and plug the brake line from the wheel cylinder.

4. Remove the wheel cylinder bolts and remove the cylinder from the backing plate.

To install:

5. Apply a very thin coating of silicone sealer to the cylinder mounting surface, install the cylinder to the backing plate and install the attaching bolts.

6. Connect the brake line to the wheel cylinder.

7. Install all brake parts that were removed.

8. Install the tire and wheel assembly.

9. Bleed the brakes.

Parking Brake Cable

ADJUSTMENT

1. Adjust the rear brake shoes.
2. Depress the parking brake pedal exactly 3 ratchet clicks.
3. Raise and safely support the vehicle.
4. Check that the equalizer nut groove is liberally lubricated with chassis lube. Tighten the adjusting nut until the right rear wheel can just be turned to the rear with both hands but is locked when forward rotation is attempted.
5. With the mechanism totally disengaged, both rear wheels should turn freely in either direction with no brake drag. Do not adjust the parking brake so tightly as to cause brake drag.

REMOVAL & INSTALLATION

Front Cable

1. Disconnect the negative battery cable. Raise and safely support the vehicle.
2. Loosen and remove the equalizer nut. Lower the vehicle.
3. Remove the console.
4. Disconnect the parking brake cable from the lever.
5. Remove the nut that secures the front cable to the floor pan.
6. Loosen the catalytic converter shield and the parking brake cable from the body, if necessary.
7. Remove the cable from the equalizer, guide and underbody clips.
8. The installation is the reverse of the removal procedure.
9. Adjust the cable.
10. Connect the negative battery cable and check the parking brakes for proper operation.

Rear Cables

1. Disconnect the negative battery cable. Raise and safely support the vehicle.
2. Loosen or remove the equalizer nut.
3. Remove the wheel(s) and drum(s).
4. Insert a suitable tool between the brake shoe and the top part of the brake adjuster bracket. Push the bracket to the front and release the top adjuster bracket rod.
5. Remove the hold-down spring, actuator lever and lever return spring.
6. Remove the adjuster screw spring.
7. Remove the top rear brake shoe return spring.
8. Disconnect the parking brake cable from the actuating lever.
9. Pull the cable through the back-ing plate while depressing the retaining tangs.
10. On the right side, remove the cable end button from the connector.
11. Remove the conduit fitting from the axle bracket while depressing the retaining tangs.

To install:

12. Install the conduit fitting into the axle bracket, securing the retaining tangs.
13. Install the cable end button to the connector, if working on the right side.
14. Click the cable assembly into the backing plate.
15. Connect the cable to the actuating lever.
16. Assemble the rear brake components.
17. Install the drum(s) and wheel(s).
18. Adjust the rear brakes and parking brake cable.
19. Connect the negative battery cable and check the parking brakes for proper operation.

Brake System Bleeding

Except Anti-Lock Brakes

NOTE: If using a pressure bleeder, follow the instructions furnished with the unit and choose the correct adaptor for the application. Do not substitute an adapter that "almost fits" as it will not work and could be dangerous.

MASTER CYLINDER

If the master cylinder is off the vehicle it can be bench bled.

1. Connect 2 short pieces of brake line to the outlet fittings, bend them until the free end is below the fluid level in the master cylinder reservoirs.
2. Fill the reservoir with fresh brake fluid. Pump the piston slowly until no more air bubbles appear in the reservoirs.
3. Disconnect the 2 short lines, refill the master cylinder and securely install the cylinder caps.
4. If the master cylinder is on the vehicle, it can still be bled, using a flare nut wrench.
5. Open the brake lines slightly with the flare nut wrench while pressure is applied to the brake pedal by a helper inside the vehicle.
6. Be sure to tighten the line before the brake pedal is released.
7. Repeat the process with both lines until no air bubbles come out.

CALIPERS AND WHEEL CYLINDERS

1. Fill the master cylinder with fresh brake fluid. Check the level often during the procedure.
2. Starting with the right rear wheel, remove the protective cap from the bleeder, if equipped, and place where it will not be lost. Clean the bleed screw.

CAUTION

When bleeding the brakes, keep face away from the brake area. Spewing fluid may cause facial and/or visual damage. Do not allow brake fluid to spill on the car's finish; it will remove the paint.

---

3. If the system is empty, the most efficient way to get fluid down to the wheel is to loosen the bleeder about ½–¾ turn, place a finger firmly over the bleeder and have a helper pump the brakes slowly until fluid comes out the bleeder. Once fluid is at the bleeder, close it before the pedal is released inside the vehicle.

NOTE: If the pedal is pumped rapidly, the fluid will churn and create small air bubbles, which are almost impossible to remove from the system. These air bubbles will eventually congregate and a spongy pedal will result.

4. Once fluid has been pumped to the caliper or wheel cylinder, open the bleed screw again, have the helper press the brake pedal to the floor, lock the bleeder and have the helper slowly release the pedal. Wait 15 seconds and repeat the procedure (including the 15 second wait) until no more air comes out of the bleeder upon application of the brake pedal. Remember to close the bleeder before the pedal is released inside the vehicle each time the bleeder is opened. If not, air will be induced into the system.
5. If a helper is not available, connect a small hose to the bleeder, place the end in a container of brake fluid and proceed to pump the pedal from inside the vehicle until no more air comes out the bleeder. The hose will prevent air from entering the system.
6. Repeat the procedure on remaining wheel cylinders in order:
   a. Left front
   b. Left rear
   c. Right front
7. Hydraulic brake systems must be totally flushed if the fluid becomes contaminated with water, dirt or other corrosive chemicals. To flush, bleed the entire system until all fluid has been replaced with the correct type of new fluid.
8. Install the bleeder cap(s), if equipped, on the bleeder to keep dirt out. Always road test the vehicle after brake work of any kind is done.

Anti-Lock Brakes
BRAKE CONTROL ASSEMBLY

NOTE: Only use brake fluid from a sealed container which meets DOT 3 specifications.

1. Clean the area around the master cylinder cap.
2. Check fluid level in master cylinder reservoir and top-up, as necessary. Check fluid level frequently during bleeding procedure.
3. Attach a bleeder hose to the rear bleeder valve on the brake control assembly. Slowly open the bleeder valve.
4. Depress the brake pedal slowly until fluid begins to flow.
5. Close the valve and release the brake pedal.
6. Repeat for the front bleeder valve on the brake control assembly.

NOTE: When fluid flows from both bleeder valves, the brake control assembly is sufficiently full of fluid. However, it may not be completely purged of air. Bleed the individual wheel calipers/cylinders and return to the control assembly to purge the remaining air.

WHEEL CALIPERS/CYLINDERS

NOTE: Prior to bleeding the rear brakes, the rear displacement cylinder must be returned to the top-most position. This can be accomplished using the Tech I Scan tool, T-100 (CAMS) or equivalent, by entering the manual control function and applying the rear motor.

If a Tech I or T-100 are unavailable, bleed the front brakes. Ensure the pedal is firm. Carefully drive the vehicle to a speed above 4 mph to cause the ABS system to initialize. This will return the rear displacement cylinder to the top-most position.

1. Clean the area around the master cylinder cap.
2. Check fluid level in master cylinder reservoir and top-up, as necessary. Check fluid level frequently during bleeding procedure.
3. Raise and safely support the vehicle.
4. Attach a bleeder hose to the bleeder valve of the right rear wheel and submerge the opposite hose in a clean container partially filled with brake fluid.
5. Open the bleeder valve.
6. Slowly depress the brake pedal.
7. Close the bleeder valve and release the brake pedal.
8. Wait 5 seconds.
9. Repeat Steps 5–8 until the pedal begins to feel firm and no air bubbles appear in the bleeder hose.

10. Repeat Steps 5–9, until the pedal is firm and no air bubbles appear in the brake hose, for the remaining wheels in the following order:
   a. Left rear
   b. Right front
   c. Left front.
11. Lower the vehicle.

Anti-Lock Brake System Service

PRECAUTION

Failure to observe the following precautions may result in system damage.

● Before performing electric arc welding on the vehicle, disconnect the Electronic Brake Control Module (EBCM) and the hydraulic modulator connectors.

● When performing painting work on the vehicle, do not expose the Electronic Brake Control Module (EBCM) to temperatures in excess of 185°F (85°C) for longer than 2 hrs. The system may be exposed to temperatures up to 200°F (95°C) for less than 15 min.

● Never disconnect or connect the Electronic Brake Control Module (EBCM) or hydraulic modulator connectors with the ignition switch ON.

● Never disassemble any component of the Anti-Lock Brake System (ABS) which is designated non-serviceable; the component must be replaced as an assembly.

● When filling the master cylinder, always use Delco Supreme 11 brake fluid or equivalent, which meets DOT-3 specifications; petroleum base fluid will destroy the rubber parts.

ABS Hydraulic Modulator Assembly

REMOVAL & INSTALLATION

—— CAUTION ——
To avoid personal injury, use the Tech I Scan tool to relieve the gear tension in the hydraulic modulator. This procedure must be performed prior to removal of the brake control and motor assembly.

1. Disconnect the negative battery cable.
2. Disconnect the 2 solenoid electrical connectors and the fluid level sensor connector.
3. Disconnect the 6-pin and 3-pin motor pack electrical connectors.
4. Wrap a shop towel around the hydraulic brake lines and disconnect the 4 brake lines from the modulator.

NOTE: Cap the disconnected

lines to prevent the loss of fluid and the entry of moisture and contaminants.

5. Remove the 2 nuts attaching the ABS hydraulic modulator assembly to the vacuum booster.
6. Remove the ABS hydraulic modulator assembly from the vehicle.
To install:
7. Install the ABS hydraulic modulator assembly to the vehicle. Install the 2 attaching nuts and tighten to 20 ft. lbs. (27 Nm).
8. Connect the 4 brake pipes to the modulator assembly. Tighten to 13 ft. lbs. (17 Nm).
9. Connect the 6-pin and 3-pin electrical connectors and the fluid level sensor connector.
10. Properly bleed the system.
11. Connect the negative battery cable.

Brake Control Solenoid Assembly

REMOVAL & INSTALLATION

1. Disconnect the negative battery cable.
2. Disconnect the solenoid electrical connector.
3. Remove the Torx® head bolts.
4. Remove the solenoid assembly.
To install:
5. Lubricate the O-rings on the new solenoid with clean brake fluid.
6. Position the solenoid so the connectors face each other.
7. Press down firmly by hand until the solenoid assembly flange seats on the modulator assembly.
8. Install the Torx® head bolts. Tighten to 39 inch lbs. (5 Nm).
9. Connect the solenoid electrical connector.
10. Properly bleed the brake system.
11. Connect the negative battery cable.

Front Wheel Speed Sensor

REMOVAL & INSTALLATION

1. Disconnect the negative battery cable.
2. Raise and safely support the vehicle.
3. Disconnect the front sensor electrical connector.
4. Remove the Torx® bolt.
5. Remove the front wheel speed sensor.
To install:
6. Install the front wheel speed sensor on the mounting bracket.

NOTE: Ensure the front wheel speed sensor is properly aligned and lays flat against the bracket bosses.

7. Install the Torx® bolt. Tighten to 106 inch lbs. (12 Nm).

8. Connect the front sensor electrical connector.

9. Lower the vehicle.

10. Connect the negative battery cable.

Rear Wheel Bearing and Speed Sensor Assembly

REMOVAL & INSTALLATION

NOTE: The rear integral wheel bearing and sensor assembly must be replaced as a unit.

1. Disconnect the negative battery cable.

2. Raise and safely support the vehicle.

3. Remove the rear wheel.

4. Remove the brake drum.

5. Disconnect the rear sensor electrical connector.

6. Remove the bolts and nuts attaching the rear wheel bearing and speed sensor assembly to the backing plate.

NOTE: With the rear wheel bearing and speed sensor attaching bolts and nuts removed, the drum brake assembly is supported only by the brake line connection. To avoid bending or damage to the brake line, do not bump or exert force on the assembly.

7. Remove the rear wheel bearing and speed sensor assembly.
To install:

8. Install the rear wheel bearing and speed sensor assembly by aligning the bolt hoses in the wheel bearing and speed sensor assembly, drum brake assembly and rear suspension bracket. Install the attaching bolts and nuts. Tighten to 37 ft. lbs. (50 Nm).

9. Connect the rear speed sensor electrical connector.

10. Install the brake drum.

11. Install the rear wheel.

12. Lower the vehicle.

13. Connect the negative battery cable.

CHASSIS ELECTRICAL

Heater Blower Motor

REMOVAL & INSTALLATION

1989–91

1. Disconnect negative battery cable.

2. Remove the serpentine belt and/or the power steering pressure hose, as required.

3. Disconnect the connector to the blower motor and remove the cooling tube.

4. Remove the attaching screws and remove the blower from the case.

5. If necessary, remove the fan from the blower motor.

6. The installation is the reverse of the removal procedure.

7. Connect the negative battery cable and check the blower motor for proper operation.

1992–93

1. Disconnect the negative battery cable.

2. If equipped with the 3.3L (VIN N) engine, remove the power steering retaining pump bolts and position the pump out of the way.

3. Disconnect the electrical connectors from the blower motor.

4. Cut the blower case following the marks indicated on the case.

NOTE: Cover is ⅛ inch (2mm) thick. Do not cut much deeper or damage may result to the cooling tube.

5. Swing the cut portion of the cover down and disconnect the blower motor cooling tube.

6. Remove the blower motor retaining screws and remove the blower motor.
To install:

7. Install the blower motor and the mounting screws.

8. Install the blower motor cooling tube.

9. Install the blower motor cover and secure with retaining clips.

10. Connect the electrical connectors to the blower motor.

11. Install the power steering pump to the 3.3L (VIN L) engine.

12. Connect the negative battery cable.

Windshield Wiper Motor

REMOVAL & INSTALLATION

1. Disconnect the negative battery cable.

2. Remove the wiper arm assembly(s) and cowl cover/panel, if necessary.

3. Remove the wiper arm drive link from the crank arm.

4. Disconnect the connectors from the motor.

5. Remove the wiper motor attaching bolts.

6. Remove the wiper motor and crank arm by guiding the assembly through the access hole in the upper shroud panel.
To install:

7. Install the wiper motor while guiding the crank arm through the hole.

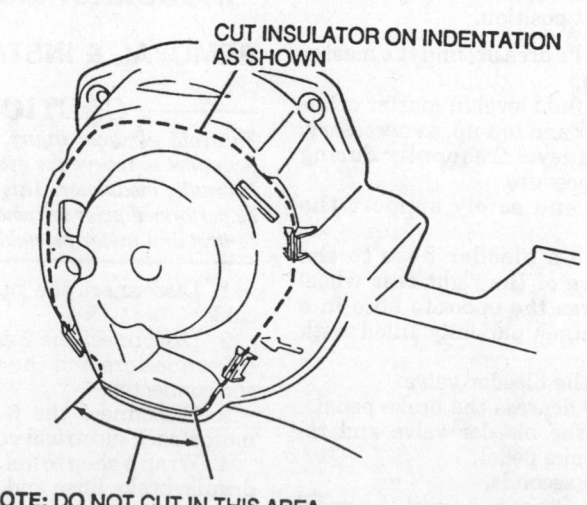

CUT INSULATOR ON INDENTATION AS SHOWN

NOTE: DO NOT CUT IN THIS AREA

N30036-1A-N

Blower motor case cut diagram—1992–93 vehicles

8. Install the wiper motor attaching bolts and tighten to 80 inch lbs. (9 Nm)

9. Connect the electrical connectors.

10. Connect the wiper arm drive link to the motor crank arm.

11. Install the cowl cover/panel assembly.

12. Install the wiper arm/blade assemblies and connect the negative battery cable.

Windshield Wiper Switch

REMOVAL & INSTALLATION

All Except Skylark

1989–91

1. Disconnect the negative battery cable.

2. Remove the cluster trim, instrument panel trim or wiper switch trim screws, as required.

3. Remove the wiper switch attaching screws.

4. Pull the switch out, unplug the connectors and remove the switch assembly.

5. The installation is the reverse of the removal procedure.

6. Connect the negative battery cable and check the wipers and washers for proper operation.

Skylark

1989–91

1. Disconnect the negative battery cable.

2. Remove the lower instrument panel sound insulator, trim pad and steering column trim collar.

3. Straighten the steering wheel so the tires are pointing straight-ahead.

4. Remove the steering wheel.

5. Remove the plastic wire protector from under the steering column.

6. Disconnect the turn signal switch, wiper switch and cruise control connectors, if equipped.

7. To disassemble the top of the column:

   a. Remove the shaft lock cover.

   b. If equipped with telescope steering, remove the first set of spacers, bumper, second set of spacers and carrier snapring retainer.

   c. Depress the lockplate with the proper depressing tool and remove the retaining ring from its groove.

   d. Remove the tool, retaining ring, lockplate, cancelling cam and spring.

8. Pull the turn signal lever straight out of the wiper switch.

9. Remove the 3 screws and remove the turn signal switch and actuator lever.

10. Remove the ignition key light.

11. Place the key in the **RUN** position and use a thin suitable tool to remove the buzzer switch.

12. Remove the key lock cylinder attaching screw and remove the lock cylinder.

13. Remove the 3 housing cover screws and remove the housing cover assembly.

14. Remove the wiper switch pivot pin and remove the switch.

To install:

15. Run the wiring through the opening and down the steering column, position the switch and install the wiper switch pivot pin.

16. Install the housing cover assembly, making sure the dimmer switch actuator is properly aligned.

17. Install the key lock cylinder and place in the **RUN** position. Install the buzzer switch and key light.

18. Install the turn signal switch and lever.

19. To assemble the top end of the column:

   a. Install the spring, cancelling cam, lockplate and retaining ring on the steering shaft.

   b. Depress the plate with the depressing tool and install the ring securely in the groove. Remove the tool slowly.

   c. If equipped with telescope steering, install the carrier snapring retainer, lower set of spacers, bumper and upper set of spacers.

   d. Install the shaft lock cover.

20. Connect the turn signal switch, wiper switch and cruise control connectors. Install the wire protector.

21. Install and steering wheel.

22. Install the steering column trim collar, lower instrument panel trim pad and sound insulator.

23. Connect the negative battery cable and check the key lock cylinder, wiper and washer, cruise control, turn signal switch and dimmer switch for proper operation.

All Vehicles

1992–93

1. Disconnect the negative battery cable.

2. Remove the horn pad and the steering wheel from the vehicle.

3. Remove the tilt lever from the column, if equipped. This can be done by turning the lever counterclockwise and pulling outward with locking pliers.

4. Remove the upper and lower steering column covers.

5. Remove the dampener assembly.

6. Remove the multi-function switch screw and remove the switch assembly.

7. Remove the turn signal switch assembly.

To install:

8. Install the turn signal and headlight switches.

9. Install the dampener assembly.

10. Install the upper and lower steering column covers.

11. If equipped with tilt wheel, install the tilt lever to the column.

12. Install the steering wheel and install the horn pad.

13. Connect the negative battery cable.

Instrument Cluster

REMOVAL & INSTALLATION

Achieva

1. Disconnect the negative battery cable.

2. Remove the instrument cluster trim plate screws.

3. Remove the cluster trim plate by pulling rearward to disengage the clips.

4. Remove the 4 screws fastening the cluster to the instrument panel, pull the cluster out to unplug all connectors and remove the cluster.

5. The installation is the reverse of the removal procedure. Tighten the screws to 17 inch lbs. (2 Nm).

6. Connect the negative battery cable and check all cluster-related components for proper operation.

Calais

1. Disconnect the negative battery cable.

2. Remove the steering column collar.

3. Remove the steering column and cluster trim plates.

4. Lower the steering column.

5. Remove the screws fastening the cluster to the instrument panel pad, pull the cluster out to unplug all connectors and remove the cluster.

6. Remove the lens and applique, if necessary, to gain access to the speedometer or gauges attaching screws and remove the speedometer or gauges.

7. The installation is the reverse of the removal procedure.

8. Connect the negative battery cable and check all cluster-related components for proper operation.

Grand Am

1989–91

1. Disconnect the negative battery cable.

2. Remove the 3 screws at the lower edge of the cluster and remove the trim plate.

3. Remove the steering column cover and lower the column.

4. Remove the screws fastening the cluster to the instrument panel pad, pull the cluster out to unplug all connectors and remove the cluster.

5. Remove the lens and gauge trim plate to gain access to the speedometer assembly or gauges attaching screws and remove the speedometer or gauges. If equipped with digital dash, replace it as an assembly.

6. The installation is the reverse of the removal procedure.

7. Connect the negative battery cable and check all cluster-related components for proper operation.

1992–93

1. Disconnect the negative battery cable.

2. Remove the left sound insulator from below the dashboard.

3. Remove the steering column filler.

4. Remove the driver's side air deflectors by gently pulling rearward.

5. Remove the instrument panel cover by alternately prying upward on the left and right retaining clips.

6. Remove the fuse cover and remove the left instrument panel trim plate screws. Remove the left side trim plate.

7. Remove the upper glove compartment by opening the compartment door and removing the attaching screws.

8. Remove the lower glove compartment by removing the compartment door and then removing the attaching screws.

9. Remove the right side instrument panel cluster trim plate screws and pull trim plate rearward to disengage the clips. Remove the trim plate.

10. Remove the cluster mounting screws and pull cluster out to disconnect the electrical connectors.

11. Remove the cluster from the vehicle.

To install:

12. Install the instrument cluster to the vehicle and tighten the screws to 17 inch lbs. (2 Nm).

13. Install the right side instrument panel trim plate.

14. Install the upper and lower glove compartments.

15. Install the left side instrument panel trim plate.

16. Install the instrument panel cover.

17. Install the steering column filler.

18. Install the left sound insulator.

19. Connect the negative battery cable.

Skylark

1989

1. Disconnect the negative battery cable.

2. Remove the cluster trim plate, headlight and wiper switch trim plates and the switches.

3. Remove the screws fastening the cluster to the instrument panel pad, pull the cluster out to unplug all connectors and remove the cluster.

4. Remove the lens and gauge trim plate to gain access to the speedometer assembly attaching screws and remove the speedometer or gauges. If equipped with digital gauges, replace them as an assembly.

5. The installation is the reverse of the removal procedure.

6. Connect the negative battery cable and check all cluster-related components for proper operation.

1990–91

1. Disconnect the negative battery cable.

2. Remove the steering column opening filler.

3. Remove the cluster trim plate.

4. If equipped with a column-mounted shifter, disconnect the PRNDL cable clip from the shift collar on the column.

5. Remove the screws fastening the cluster to the instrument panel pad, pull the cluster out to unplug all connectors and remove the cluster.

6. Remove the lens and gauge trim plate to gain access to the speedometer assembly attaching screws and remove the speedometer or gauges. If equipped with digital dash, replace it as an assembly.

7. The installation is the reverse of the removal procedure.

8. Connect the negative battery cable and check all cluster-related components for proper operation.

1992–93

1. Disconnect the negative battery cable.

2. Remove the instrument cluster trim plate screws.

3. Remove the cluster trim plate by pulling rearward to disengage the clips.

4. Remove the 4 screws fastening the cluster to the instrument panel, pull the cluster out to unplug all connectors and remove the cluster.

5. The installation is the reverse of the removal procedure. Tighten the screws to 17 inch lbs. (2 Nm).

6. Connect the negative battery cable and check all cluster-related components for proper operation.

Radio

REMOVAL & INSTALLATION

Console Mounted

NOTE: If equipped with a compact disc player, removal and installation procedures are the same as for the radio.

1. Disconnect the negative battery cable.

2. Remove the console bezel.

3. Remove the screws that attach the radio to the console.

4. Pull the radio out, disconnect the connectors, ground cable and antenna and remove the radio.

5. The installation is the reverse of the removal procedure.

6. Connect the negative battery cable and check the radio for proper operation.

Dash Mounted

1. Disconnect the negative battery cable.

2. Remove the instrument panel extension bezel.

3. Remove the radio bracket.

4. Remove the screws/nuts that attach the radio to the instrument panel.

5. Pull the radio out, disconnect the connectors, ground cable and antenna and remove the radio.

6. The installation is the reverse of the removal procedure.

7. Connect the negative battery cable and check the radio for proper operation.

Headlight Switch

REMOVAL & INSTALLATION

1989–91

1. Disconnect the negative battery cable.

2. Remove the cluster trim, instrument panel trim or headlight switch trim screws, as required.

3. Remove the headlight switch attaching screws.

4. Pull the switch out, unplug the connectors and remove the switch assembly.

5. The installation is the reverse of the removal procedure.

6. Connect the negative battery cable and check the headlight switch for proper operation.

1992–93

NOTE: The headlight switch is incorporated into the combination switch assembly which includes the dimmer switch, turn signal switch and if equipped, the cruise control switch. For removal and installation, refer to Combination Switch section.

Dimmer Switch

REMOVAL & INSTALLATION

1989–91

1. Disconnect the negative battery cable.
2. Remove the lower steering column cover.
3. Unplug the switch, located on the lower portion of the steering column.
4. Hold the actuating rod against its upper seat, remove the screw and nut that attaches the switch to the column and remove the switch.
5. The installation is the reverse of the removal procedure. To adjust the switch:
   a. Depress the switch slightly and insert a $^3/_{32}$ in. drill.
   b. Force the switch up to remove the lash.
   c. Tighten the screw and nut.
6. Connect the negative battery cable and check the switch for proper operation.

1992–93

NOTE: The dimmer switch is incorporated into the combination switch assembly which includes the headlight switch, turn signal switch and if equipped, the cruise control switch. For removal and installation, refer to Combination Switch section.

Turn Signal Switch

REMOVAL & INSTALLATION

1989–91

1. Disconnect the negative battery cable.
2. Remove the lower instrument panel sound insulator, trim pad and steering column trim collar.
3. Straighten the steering wheel so the tires are pointing straight-ahead.
4. Remove the steering wheel.
5. Remove the plastic wire protector from under the steering column.
6. Disconnect the turn signal switch connector at the bottom of the column.
7. To disassemble the top of the column:
   a. Remove the shaft lock cover.
   b. If equipped with telescope steering, remove the first set of spacers, bumper, second set of spacers and carrier snapring retainer.
   c. Depress the lockplate with the proper depressing tool and remove the retaining ring from its groove.
   d. Remove the tool, ring, lockplate, cancelling cam and spring.
8. Remove the 3 screws, the turn signal switch and actuator lever.

To install:
9. Install the turn signal switch and lever.
10. To assemble the top end of the column:
   a. Install the spring, cancelling cam, lockplate and retaining ring on the steering shaft.
   b. Depress the plate with the depressing tool and install the ring securely in the groove. Remove the tool slowly.
   c. If equipped with telescope steering, install the carrier snapring retainer, lower set of spacers, bumper and upper set of spacers.
   d. Install the shaft lock cover.
11. Connect the turn signal switch connector and install the wire protector.
12. Install the steering wheel.
13. Install the steering column trim collar, lower instrument panel trim pad and sound insulator.
14. Connect the negative battery cable and check the turn signal switch for proper operation.

1992–93

NOTE: The turn signal switch is incorporated into the combination switch assembly which includes the headlight switch, dimmer switch and if equipped, the cruise control switch. For removal and installation, refer to Combination Switch section.

Combination Switch

REMOVAL & INSTALLATION

1992–93

1. Disconnect the negative battery cable.
2. Remove the horn pad and the steering wheel from the vehicle.
3. Remove the tilt lever from the column, if equipped. This can be done by turning the lever counterclockwise and pulling outward with locking pliers.
4. Remove the upper and lower steering column covers.
5. Remove the dampener assembly.
6. Remove the combination switch screw and remove the switch assembly.

To install:
7. Install the combination switch.
8. Install the dampener assembly.
9. Install the upper and lower steering column covers.
10. If equipped with tilt wheel, install the tilt lever to the column.
11. Install the steering wheel and install the horn pad.
12. Connect the negative battery cable.

Ignition Lock Cylinder

REMOVAL & INSTALLATION

1989–91

1. Disconnect the negative battery cable.
2. Remove the lower instrument panel sound insulator, trim pad and steering column trim collar.
3. Straighten the steering wheel so the tires are pointing straight ahead.
4. Remove the steering wheel.
5. Remove the plastic wire protector from under the steering column.
6. Disconnect the turn signal switch.
7. To disassemble the top of the column:
   a. Remove the shaft lock cover.
   b. If equipped with telescope steering, remove the first set of spacers, bumper, second set of spacers and carrier snapring retainer.
   c. Depress the lock plate with the proper depressing tool and remove the retaining ring from its groove.
   d. Remove the tool, retaining ring, lockplate, cancelling cam and spring.
8. Remove the 3 screws and pull the turn signal switch out from its mount as far as possible.
9. Place the key in the RUN position and use a thin suitable tool to remove the buzzer switch.
10. Remove the key lock cylinder attaching screw and remove the lock cylinder.

To install:
11. Install the key lock cylinder and place in the RUN position. Install the buzzer switch and key light.
12. Install the turn signal switch and lever.
13. To assemble the top end of the column:
   a. Install the spring, cancelling cam, lock plate and retaining ring on the steering shaft.
   b. Depress the plate with the depressing tool and install the ring securely in the groove. Remove the tool slowly.
   c. If equipped with telescope steering, install the carrier snapring retainer, lower set of spacers, bumper and upper set of spacers.
   d. Install the shaft lock cover.
14. Connect the turn signal switch connector. Install the wire protector.
15. Install the steering wheel.
16. Install the steering column trim collar, lower instrument panel trim pad and sound insulator.
17. Connect the negative battery cable and check the key lock cylinder and turn signal switch for proper operation.

1992–93

1. Disconnect the negative battery cable.
2. Remove the left side instrument panel sound insulator from below the dashboard.
3. Remove the lower steering column filler panel.
4. Remove the horn pad and remove the steering wheel.
5. Remove the tilt lever, if equipped.
6. Remove the upper and lower steering column covers.
7. Disconnect the headlight and windshield wiper switch electrical connectors.
8. Disconnect the park lock/brake transmission shift interlock cable from the ignition switch.
9. Remove the upper flexible column bolt and the column bracket support bolts.
10. Disconnect the attaching electrical connectors and remove the steering column from the vehicle.
11. Turn the key to the **RUN** position and shift the shifter into **PARK**.
12. Using a ¼ inch (6.5mm) drill bit, drill off the heads of the shear bolts that attach the lock cylinder housing.
13. Remove the lock cylinder housing from the vehicle.
14. Remove the remainder of the shear bolts from the housing.

To install:

15. Install the lock cylinder and install the shear bolts. Tighten the shear bolts until the heads seperate.
16. Install the steering column to the vehicle. Tighten the bracket support bolts to 22 ft. lbs. (30 Nm) and the upper pinch bolt to 29 ft. lbs. (40 Nm).
17. Install the park lock/brake transmission shift interlock cable to the ignition switch.
18. Connect the headlamp switch connector and the windshield wiper switch connector.
19. Install the upper and lower steering column covers. Install the tilt lever, if equipped.
20. Install the steering wheel and the horn pad.
21. Install the lower steering column filler panel and the left side sound insulator.
22. Connect the negative battery cable.

Ignition Switch

REMOVAL & INSTALLATION

1989–91

1. Disconnect the negative battery cable.
2. Remove the left instrument panel insulator.
3. Remove the left instrument panel trim pad and the steering column trim collar.
4. Remove the steering column upper support bracket bolts and remove the support bracket.
5. Lower the steering column and support it safely.
6. Disconnect the wiring from the ignition switch.
7. Remove the ignition switch-to-steering column screws. Remove the ignition from the steering column.

To install:

8. Before installing, place the slider in the proper position (switch viewed with the terminals pointing up), according to the steering column and accessories:
   a. Standard column with key release—extreme left detent.
   b. Standard column with PARK/LOCK—1 detent from extreme left.
   c. All other standard columns—2 detents from extreme left.
   d. Tilt column with key release—extreme right detent.
   e. Tilt column with PARK/LOCK—1 detent from extreme right.
   f. All other tilt columns—2 detents from extreme right.
9. Install the activating rod into the switch and install the switch to the column. Do not use oversized screws as they could impair the collapsibility of the column.
10. Connect the wiring to the ignition switch. Adjust the switch, as required.
11. Install the steering column.
12. Install the steering column trim collar, instrument panel trim pad and insulator.
13. Connect the negative battery cable and check the ignition switch for proper operation.

1992–93

1. Disconnect the negative battery cable.
2. Remove the steering wheel pad and remove the steering wheel.
3. Place the vehicle in **PARK** and remove the key.
4. Remove the steering wheel covers.
5. Remove the ignition switch screws and remove the switch.
6. Disconnect the electrical connector from the switch.

To install:

7. Connect the electrical connector to the switch.
8. Install the ignition switch to the lock cylinder housing and secure with the screws. Tighten the screws to 21 inch lbs. (2.4 Nm).
9. Install the steering wheel, horn pad and the steering wheel covers.
10. Connect the negative battery cable.

Stoplight Switch

REMOVAL & INSTALLATION

1. Disconnect the negative battery cable.
2. Remove the left sound insulator.
3. Disconnect the wiring from the switch.
4. Pull the switch out of the retainer in the bracket.

To install:

5. Install the retainer in the bracket, at the underside of the bracket.
6. Depress the brake pedal and insert the switch into the retainer until the switch seats. Allow the pedal to return.
7. Connect the connector.
8. To adjust the switch, pull the pedal up against the switch until no more clicks are heard. The switch will automatically move up in the retainer providing adjustment. Repeat a few times to ensure that the switch is properly adjusted.
9. Connect the negative battery cable and check the switch for proper operation.

Fuses, Circuit Breakers and Relays

LOCATION

Fuses and Circuit Breakers

The fuse block, which contains the fuses and also the circuit breakers for power accessories, is located on the lower left side of the instrument panel, behind an access door.

Flashers

LOCATION

Turn Signal

The turn signal flasher is clipped to the instrument panel near the fuse block.

Hazard

On all vehicles except 1989–91 Grand Am, the hazard flasher is in the convenience center, located near the fuse block. On the 1989–91 Grand Am, the hazard flasher is clipped to the console front extension bracket.

Computer

LOCATION

The ECM is located on the right side of the instrument panel, near the glove box.

GM "W" Body
Front Wheel Drive
BUICK—Regal **CHEVROLET**—Lumina
OLDSMOBILE—Cutlass Supreme **PONTIAC**

26

SPECIFICATIONS

VEHICLE IDENTIFICATION CHART

It is important for servicing and ordering parts to be certain of the vehicle and engine identification. The VIN (vehicle identification number) is a 17 digit number visible through the windshield on the driver's side of the dash and contains the vehicle and engine identification codes. The tenth digit indicates model year and the eighth digit indicates engine code. It can be interpreted as follows:

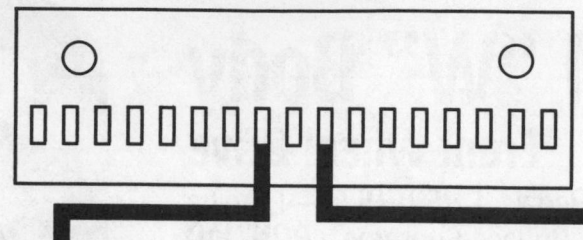

Engine Code

Code	Liters	Cu. In. (cc)	Cyl.	Fuel Sys.	Eng. Mfg.
A ①	2.3	138 (2300)	4	MPFI	BOC
D	2.3	138 (2300)	4	MPFI	BOC
R	2.5	151 (2500)	4	TBI	CPC
W	2.8	173 (2835)	6	MPFI	CPC
V ②	3.1	191 (3100)	6	MPFI	CPC
T	3.1	191 (3100)	6	MPFI	CPC
X	3.4	204 (3400)	6	MPFI	CPC
L	3.8	231 (3800)	6	TPI	BOC

Model Year

Code	Year
K	1989
L	1990
M	1991
N	1992
P	1993

CPC—Chevrolet/Pontiac/Canada
BOC—Buick/Oldsmobile/Cadillac
TBI—Throttle Body Injection
TPI—Tuned Port Injection
MPFI—Multi-Port Fuel Injection
① Supercharged Engine
② Turbocharged Engine

ENGINE IDENTIFICATION

Year	Model	Engine Displacement Liters (cc)	Engine Series (ID/VIN)	Fuel System	No. of Cylinders	Engine Type
1989	Grand Prix	2.8 (2835)	W	MPFI	6	OHV
	Grand Prix	3.1 (3100)	T	MPFI	6	OHV
	Cutlass Supreme	2.8 (2835)	W	MPFI	5	OHV
	Cutlass Supreme	3.1 (3100)	T	MPFI	6	OHV
	Regal	2.8 (2835)	W	MPFI	6	OHV
	Regal	3.1 (3100)	T	MPFI	6	OHV
1990	Grand Prix	2.3 (2300)	D	MPFI	4	DOHC
	Grand Prix	3.1 (3100)	T	MPFI	6	OHV
	Grand Prix	3.1 (3100)	V ①	MPFI	6	OHV
	Cutlass Supreme	2.3 (2300)	A ②	MPFI	4	DOHC
	Cutlass Supreme	2.3 (2300)	D	MPFI	4	DOHC
	Cutlass Supreme	3.1 (3100)	T	MPFI	6	OHV
	Regal	3.1 (3100)	T	MPFI	6	OHV
	Regal	3.8 (3800)	L	TPI	6	OHV
	Lumina	2.5 (2500)	R	TBI	4	OHV
	Lumina	3.1 (3100)	T	MPFI	6	OHV

ENGINE IDENTIFICATION

Year	Model	Engine Displacement Liters (cc)	Engine Series (ID/VIN)	Fuel System	No. of Cylinders	Engine Type
1991	Grand Prix	2.3 (2300)	D	MPFI	4	DOHC
	Grand Prix	3.1 (3100)	T	MPFI	6	OHV
	Grand Prix	3.4 (3400)	X	MPFI	6	DOHC
	Cutlass Supreme	2.3 (2300)	D	MPFI	4	DOHC
	Cutlass Supreme	3.1 (3100)	T	MPFI	6	OHV
	Cutlass Supreme	3.4 (3400)	X	MPFI	6	DOHC
	Regal	3.1 (3100)	T	MPFI	6	OHV
	Regal	3.8 (3800)	L	TPI	6	OHV
	Lumina	2.5 (2500)	R	TBI	4	OHV
	Lumina	3.1 (3100)	T	MPFI	6	OHV
	Lumina	3.4 (3400)	X	MPFI	6	DOHC
1992–93	Grand Prix	3.1 (3100)	T	MPFI	6	OHV
	Grand Prix	3.4 (3400)	X	MPFI	6	DOHC
	Cutlass Supreme	3.1 (3100)	T	MPFI	6	OHV
	Cutlass Supreme	3.4 (3400)	X	MPFI	6	DOHC
	Regal	3.1 (3100)	T	MPFI	6	OHV
	Regal	3.8 (3800)	L	TPI	6	OHV
	Lumina	2.5 (2500)	R	TBI	4	OHV
	Lumina	3.1 (3100)	T	MPFI	6	OHV
	Lumina	3.4 (3400)	X	MPFI	6	DOHC

DOHC—Double Overhead Camshaft
MPFI—Multi-Port Fuel Injection
OHV—Overhead Valve
TBI—Throttle Body Injection
TPI—Tuned Port Injection
① Turbocharged Engine
② Supercharged Engine

GENERAL ENGINE SPECIFICATIONS

Year	Engine ID/VIN	Engine Displacement Liters (cc)	Fuel System Type	Net Horsepower @ rpm	Net Torque @ rpm (ft. lbs.)	Bore × Stroke (in.)	Compression Ratio	Oil Pressure @ rpm
1989	W	2.8 (2835)	MPFI	125 @ 4500	160 @ 3600	3.500 × 2.990	8.9:1	15 @ 1100
	T	3.1 (3100)	MPFI	140 @ 4200	185 @ 3600	3.500 × 3.310	8.8:1	15 @ 1100
1990	D	2.3 (2300)	MPFI	160 @ 6200	155 @ 5200	3.620 × 3.350	9.5:1	30 @ 2000
	A①	2.3 (2300)	MPFI	180 @ 6200	160 @ 5200	3.620 × 3.350	10.0:1	30 @ 2000
	R	2.5 (2500)	TBI	105 @ 4800	135 @ 3200	4.000 × 3.000	8.3:1	26 @ 800
	T	3.1 (3100)	MPFI	140 @ 4200	185 @ 3600	3.500 × 3.310	8.8:1	15 @ 1100
	V②	3.1 (3100)	MPFI	205 @ 4800	220 @ 3000	3.500 × 3.310	8.9:1	15 @ 1100
	L	3.8 (3800)	TPI	170 @ 4800	220 @ 3200	3.800 × 3.400	8.5:1	60 @ 1850
1991	D	2.3 (2300)	MPFI	160 @ 6200	155 @ 5200	3.620 × 3.350	9.5:1	30 @ 2000
	R	2.5 (2500)	TBI	105 @ 4800	135 @ 3200	4.000 × 3.000	8.3:1	26 @ 800
	T	3.1 (3100)	MPFI	140 @ 4200	185 @ 3600	3.500 × 3.310	8.8:1	15 @ 1100
	X	3.4 (3400)	MPFI	210 @ 5200	215 @ 4000	3.620 × 3.310	9.25:1	15 @ 1100
	L	3.8 (3800)	TPI	170 @ 4800	220 @ 3200	3.800 × 3.400	8.5:1	60 @ 1850

GENERAL ENGINE SPECIFICATIONS

Year	Engine ID/VIN	Engine Displacement Liters (cc)	Fuel System Type	Net Horsepower @ rpm	Net Torque @ rpm (ft. lbs.)	Bore × Stroke (in.)	Com-pression Ratio	Oil Pressure @ rpm
1992–93	R	2.5 (2500)	TBI	105 @ 4800	135 @ 3200	4.000 × 3.000	8.3:1	26 @ 800
	T	3.1 (3100)	MPFI	140 @ 4200	185 @ 3600	3.500 × 3.310	8.8:1	15 @ 1100
	X	3.4 (3400)	MPFI	210 @ 5200	215 @ 4000	3.620 × 3.310	9.25:1	15 @ 1100
	L	3.8 (3800)	TPI	170 @ 4800	220 @ 3200	3.800 × 3.400	8.5:1	60 @ 1850

MPFI—Multi-Port Fuel Injection
TBI—Throttle Body Injection
TPI—Tuned Port Injection
① High Output Engine
② Turbocharged Engine

GASOLINE ENGINE TUNE-UP SPECIFICATIONS

Year	Engine ID/VIN	Engine Displacement Liters (cc)	Spark Plugs Gap (in.)	Ignition Timing (deg.) MT	Ignition Timing (deg.) AT	Fuel Pump ① (psi)	Idle Speed (rpm) MT	Idle Speed (rpm) AT	Valve Clearance In.	Valve Clearance Ex.
1989	W	2.8 (2835)	0.045	①	①	40–47	①	①	Hyd.	Hyd.
	T	3.1 (3100)	0.045	①	①	40–47	①	①	Hyd.	Hyd.
1990	D	2.3 (2300)	0.035	①	①	40–47	①	①	Hyd.	Hyd.
	A①	2.3 (2300)	0.035	①	①	40–47	①	①	Hyd.	Hyd.
	R	2.5 (2500)	0.060	①	①	26–32	①	①	Hyd.	Hyd.
	T	3.1 (3100)	0.045	①	①	41–47	①	①	Hyd.	Hyd.
	V②	3.1 (3100)	0.045	①	①	41–47	①	①	Hyd.	Hyd.
	L	3.8 (3800)	0.045	①	①	41–47	①	①	Hyd.	Hyd.
1991	D	2.3 (2300)	0.035	①	①	41–47	①	①	Hyd.	Hyd.
	R	2.5 (2500)	0.060	①	①	26–32	①	①	Hyd.	Hyd.
	T	3.1 (3100)	0.045	①	①	41–47	①	①	Hyd.	Hyd.
	X	3.4 (3400)	0.045	①	①	41–47	①	①	Hyd.	Hyd.
	L	3.8 (3800)	0.060	①	①	40–47	①	①	Hyd.	Hyd.
1992	R	2.5 (2500)	0.060	①	①	26–32	①	①	Hyd.	Hyd.
	T	3.1 (3100)	0.045	①	①	41–47	①	①	Hyd.	Hyd.
	X	3.4 (3400)	0.045	①	①	41–47	①	①	Hyd.	Hyd.
	L	3.8 (3800)	0.060	①	①	40–47	①	①	Hyd.	Hyd.
1993	SEE UNDERHOOD SPECIFICATIONS STICKER									

NOTE: The lowest cylinder pressure should be within 75% of the highest cylinder pressure reading. For example, if the highest cylinder is 134 psi, the lowest should be 101. Engine should be at normal operating temperature with throttle valve in the wide open position.
The underhood specifications sticker often reflects tune-up specification changes in production. Sticker figures must be used if they disagree with those in this chart.
Hyd.—Hydraulic
① Ignition timing and engine speed are controlled by the Electronic Control Module. No adjustment is necessary.

FIRING ORDERS

NOTE: To avoid confusion, always replace spark plug wires one at a time.

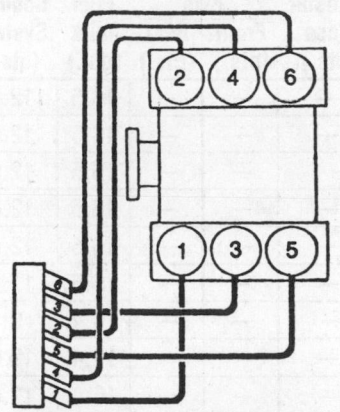

2.8L, 3.1L and 3.4L Engines
Engine Firing Order: 1–2–3–4–5–6
Distributorless Ignition System

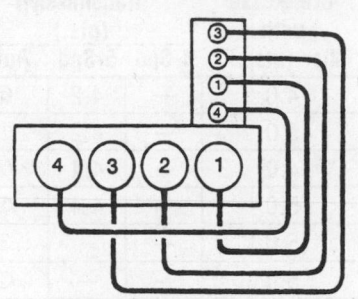

2.5L Engine
Engine Firing Order: 1–3–4–2
Distributorless Ignition System

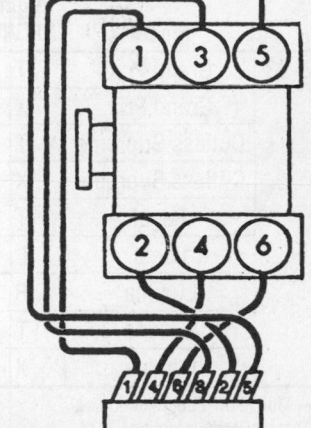

3.8L Engine
Engine Firing Order: 1–2–3–4–5–6
Distributorless Ignition System

CAPACITIES

Year	Model	Engine ID/VIN	Engine Displacement Liters (cc)	Engine Crankcase with Filter (qts.)②	Transmission (pts.) 4-Spd	5-Spd	Auto.	Transfer Case (pts.)	Drive Axle Front (pts.)	Rear (pts.)	Fuel Tank (gal.)	Cooling System (qts.)
1989	Grand Prix	W	2.8 (2835)	4.0	—	5	12.0①	—	—	—	16.0	12.6
	Grand Prix	T	3.1 (3100)	4.0	—	5	12.0①	—	—	—	16.0	12.6
	Cutlass Supreme	W	2.8 (2835)	4.0	—	5	12.0①	—	—	—	16.0	12.6
	Cutlass Supreme	T	3.1 (3100)	4.0	—	5	12.0①	—	—	—	16.0	12.6
	Regal	W	2.8 (2835)	4.0	—	5	12.0①	—	—	—	16.0	12.6
	Regal	T	3.1 (3100)	4.0	—	5	12.0①	—	—	—	16.0	12.6
1990	Grand Prix	D	2.3 (2300)	4.0	—	4.2	③	—	—	—	16.5	9.2
	Grand Prix	T	3.1 (3100)	4.0	—	4.2	③	—	—	—	16.5	12.5
	Grand Prix	V	3.1 (3100)	4.0	—	4.2	③	—	—	—	16.5	13.2
	Cutlass Supreme	A	2.3 (2300)	4.0	—	4.4	③	—	—	—	16.5	8.9
	Cutlass Supreme	D	2.3 (2300)	4.0	—	4.4	③	—	—	—	16.5	9.2
	Cutlass Supreme	T	3.1 (3100)	4.0	—	4.4	③	—	—	—	16.5	12.5
	Regal	T	3.1 (3100)	4.0	—	—	③	—	—	—	16.5	12.5
	Regal	L	3.8 (3800)	4.0	—	—	③	—	—	—	16.5	11.1
	Lumina	R	2.5 (2500)	4.0	—	—	③	—	—	—	16.0	9.4
	Lumina	T	3.1 (3100)	4.0	—	—	③	—	—	—	16.0	12.6
1991	Grand Prix	D	2.3 (2300)	4.0	—	4.2	③	—	—	—	16.5	9.2
	Grand Prix	T	3.1 (3100)	4.0	—	4.2	③	—	—	—	16.5	12.5
	Grand Prix	X	3.4 (3400)	5.0	—	4.0	③	—	—	—	16.5	12.7
	Cutlass Supreme	D	2.3 (2300)	4.0	—	4.4	③	—	—	—	16.5	9.2
	Cutlass Supreme	T	3.1 (3100)	4.0	—	4.4	③	—	—	—	16.5	12.5
	Cutlass Supreme	X	3.4 (3400)	5.0	—	4.0	③	—	—	—	16.5	12.7
	Regal	T	3.1 (3100)	4.0	—	—	③	—	—	—	16.5	12.5
	Regal	L	3.8 (3800)	4.0	—	—	③	—	—	—	16.5	11.1
	Lumina	R	2.5 (2500)	4.0	—	—	③	—	—	—	16.0	9.4
	Lumina	T	3.1 (3100)	4.0	—	—	③	—	—	—	16.0	12.6
	Lumina	X	3.4 (3400)	5.0	—	—	③	—	—	—	16.5	12.7

CAPACITIES

Year	Model	Engine ID/VIN	Engine Displacement Liters (cc)	Engine Crankcase with Filter (qts.)②	Transmission (pts.) 4-Spd	5-Spd	Auto.	Transfer Case (pts.)	Drive Axle Front (pts.)	Rear (pts.)	Fuel Tank (gal.)	Cooling System (qts.)
1992–93	Grand Prix	T	3.1 (3100)	4.0	—	4.2	③	—	—	—	16.5	12.6
	Grand Prix	X	3.4 (3400)	5.0	—	4.2	③	—	—	—	16.5	12.6
	Cutlass Supreme	T	3.1 (3100)	4.0	—	4.4	③	—	—	—	16.5	12.6
	Cutlass Supreme	X	3.4 (3400)	5.0	—	4.4	③	—	—	—	16.5	12.6
	Regal	T	3.1 (3100)	5.0	—	—	③	—	—	—	16.5	12.6
	Regal	L	3.8 (3800)	5.0	—	—	③	—	—	—	16.5	11.1
	Lumina	R	2.5 (2500)	4.0	—	—	③	—	—	—	16.4	9.1
	Lumina	T	3.1 (3100)	4.0	—	—	③	—	—	—	16.4	12.6
	Lumina	X	3.4 (3400)	5.0	—	4.2	③	—	—	—	16.4	12.6

MPFI—Multi-Port Fuel Injection
TBI—Throttle Body Injection
TPI—Tuned Port Injection
① Drain and refill only. Complete overhaul—16 pts.

② Add fluid as required to fill to the appropriate level.
③ 3T40: drain and refill only—8 pts., overhaul—14 pts.
4T60: drain and refill only—12 pts., overhaul—16 pts.
4T60E: drain and refill only—14.8 pts., overhaul—20 pts.

CAMSHAFT SPECIFICATIONS

All measurements given in inches.

Year	Engine ID/VIN	Engine Displacement Liters (cc)	Journal Diameter 1	2	3	4	5	Elevation In.	Ex.	Bearing Clearance	Camshaft End Play
1989	W	2.8 (2835)	1.867–1.881	1.867–1.881	1.867–1.881	1.867–1.881	—	0.262	0.273	0.0010–0.0040	—
	T	3.1 (3100)	1.867–1.881	1.867–1.881	1.867–1.881	1.867–1.881	—	0.262	0.273	0.0010–0.0040	—
1990	D	2.3 (2300)	1.572–1.573	1.375–1.376	1.375–1.376	1.375–1.376	1.375–1.376	0.375	0.375	0.0019–0.0043	0.0009–0.0088
	A	2.3 (2300)	1.572–1.573	1.375–1.376	1.375–1.376	1.375–1.376	1.375–1.376	0.410	0.410	0.0019–0.0043	0.0009–0.0088
	R	2.5 (2500)	1.869	1.869	1.869	1.869	—	0.248	0.248	0.0007–0.0027	0.0014–0.0050
	T	3.1 (3100)	1.868–1.882	1.868–1.882	1.868–1.882	1.868–1.882	—	0.262	0.273	0.0010–0.0040	—
	V	3.1 (3100)	1.868–1.882	1.868–1.882	1.868–1.882	1.868–1.882	—	0.262	0.273	0.0010–0.0040	—
	L	3.8 (3800)	1.785–1.786	1.785–1.786	1.785–1.786	1.785–1.786	—	0.250	0.255	0.0005–0.0035	—
1991	D	2.3 (2300)	1.572–1.573	1.375–1.376	1.375–1.376	1.375–1.376	1.375–1.376	0.375	0.375	0.0019–0.0043	0.0009–0.0088
	R	2.5 (2500)	1.869	1.869	1.869	1.869	—	0.248	0.248	0.0007–0.0027	0.0014–0.0050
	T	3.1 (3100)	1.868–1.882	1.868–1.882	1.868–1.882	1.868–1.882	—	0.262	0.273	0.0010–0.0040	—
	X	3.4 (3400)	2.165–2.166	2.165–2.166	2.165–2.166	2.165–2.166	—	0.370	0.370	0.0015–0.0035	—
	L	3.8 (3800)	1.785–1.786	1.785–1.786	1.785–1.786	1.785–1.786	—	0.250	0.255	0.0005–0.0035	—

CAMSHAFT SPECIFICATIONS

All measurements given in inches.

Year	Engine ID/VIN	Engine Displacement Liters (cc)	Journal Diameter					Elevation		Bearing Clearance	Camshaft End Play
			1	2	3	4	5	In.	Ex.		
1992-93	R	2.5 (2500)	1.869	1.869	1.869	1.869	—	0.248	0.248	0.0007–0.0027	0.0009–0.0088
	T	3.1 (3100)	1.868–1.882	1.868–1.882	1.868–1.882	1.868–1.882	—	0.262	0.273	0.0010–0.0040	0.0014–0.0050
	X	3.4 (3400)	2.165–2.166	2.165–2.166	2.165–2.166	2.165–2.166	—	0.370	0.370	0.0015–0.0035	—
	L	3.8 (3800)	1.785–1.786	1.785–1.786	1.785–1.786	1.785–1.786	—	0.250	0.255	0.0005–0.0035	—

CRANKSHAFT AND CONNECTING ROD SPECIFICATIONS

All measurements are given in inches.

Year	Engine ID/VIN	Engine Displacement Liters (cc)	Crankshaft				Connecting Rod		
			Main Brg. Journal Dia.	Main Brg. Oil Clearance	Shaft End-play	Thrust on No.	Journal Diameter	Oil Clearance	Side Clearance
1989	W	2.8 (2835)	2.6473–2.6483	0.0012–0.0027	0.0024–0.0083	3	1.9983–1.9994	0.0014–0.0036	0.0140–0.0270
	T	3.1 (3100)	2.6473–2.6483	0.0024–0.0027	0.0012–0.0083	3	1.9983–1.9994	0.0014–0.0036	0.0140–0.0270
1990	D	2.3 (2300)	2.0470–2.0480	0.0005–0.0023	0.0034–0.0095	3	1.8887–1.8897	0.0005–0.0020	0.0054–0.0177
	A	2.3 (2300)	2.0470–2.0480	0.0005–0.0023	0.0034–0.0095	3	1.8887–1.8897	0.0005–0.0020	0.0054–0.0177
	R	2.5 (2500)	2.3000	0.0005–0.0022	0.0005–0.0180	5	2.0000	0.0005–0.0030	0.0060–0.0240
	T	3.1 (3100)	2.6473–2.6483	0.0024–0.0027	0.0012–0.0083	3	1.9983–1.9994	0.0014–0.0036	0.0140–0.0270
	V	3.1 (3100)	2.6473–2.6483	0.0024–0.0027	0.0012–0.0083	3	1.9983–1.9994	0.0014–0.0036	0.0140–0.0270
	L	3.8 (3800)	2.4988–2.4998	0.0018–0.0030	0.0003–0.0110	3	2.2487–2.2499	0.0003–0.0026	0.0030–0.0150
1991	D	2.3 (2300)	2.0470–2.0480	0.0005–0.0023	0.0034–0.0095	3	1.8887–1.8897	0.0005–0.0020	0.0054–0.0177
	R	2.5 (2500)	2.3000	0.0005–0.0022	0.0005–0.0180	5	2.0000	0.0005–0.0030	0.0060–0.0240
	T	3.1 (3100)	2.6473–2.6483	0.0024–0.0027	0.0012–0.0083	3	1.9983–1.9994	0.0014–0.0036	0.0140–0.0270
	X	3.4 (3400)	2.6473–2.6479	0.0013–0.0030	0.0024–0.0083	3	1.9987–1.9994	0.0011–0.0032	0.0140–0.0250
	L	3.8 (3800)	2.4988–2.4998	0.0018–0.0030	0.0003–0.0110	3	2.2487–2.2499	0.0003–0.0026	0.0030–0.0150
1992-93	R	2.5 (2500)	2.3000	0.0005–0.0022	0.0005–0.0180	5	2.0000	0.0005–0.0030	0.0060–0.0240
	T	3.1 (3100)	2.6473–2.6483	0.0024–0.0027	0.0012–0.0083	3	1.9983–1.9994	0.0014–0.0036	0.0140–0.0270
	X	3.4 (3400)	2.6473–2.6479	0.0013–0.0030	0.0024–0.0083	3	1.9987–1.9994	0.0011–0.0032	0.0140–0.0250
	L	3.8 (3800)	2.4988–2.4998	0.0018–0.0030	0.0003–0.0110	3	2.2487–2.2499	0.0003–0.0026	0.0030–0.0150

VALVE SPECIFICATIONS

Year	Engine ID/VIN	Engine Displacement Liters (cc)	Seat Angle (deg.)	Face Angle (deg.)	Spring Test Pressure (lbs. @ in.)	Spring Installed Height (in.)	Stem-to-Guide Clearance (in.) Intake	Stem-to-Guide Clearance (in.) Exhaust	Stem Diameter (in.) Intake	Stem Diameter (in.) Exhaust
1989	W	2.8 (2835)	46	45	90 @ 1.70	1.57	0.0010–0.0027	0.0010–0.0027	NA	NA
	T	3.1 (3100)	46	45	90 @ 1.70	1.57	0.0010–0.0027	0.0010–0.0027	NA	NA
1990	D	2.3 (2300)	45	①	76 @ 1.43	NA	0.0010–0.0027	0.0010–0.0027	NA	NA
	A	2.3 (2300)	45	①	76 @ 1.43	NA	0.0010–0.0027	0.0010–0.0027	NA	NA
	R	2.5 (2500)	45	46	75 @ 1.68	1.68	0.0010–0.0026	0.0013–0.0041	NA	NA
	T	3.1 (3100)	46	45	90 @ 1.70	1.57	0.0010–0.0027	0.0010–0.0027	NA	NA
	V	3.1 (3100)	46	45	90 @ 1.70	1.57	0.0010–0.0027	0.0010–0.0027	NA	NA
	L	3.8 (3800)	46	45	80 @ 1.70	1.70	0.0015–0.0032	0.0015–0.0032	NA	NA
1991	D	2.3 (2300)	45	①	76 @ 1.43	NA	0.0010–0.0027	0.0010–0.0027	NA	NA
	R	2.5 (2500)	45	46	75 @ 1.68	1.68	0.0010–0.0026	0.0013–0.0041	NA	NA
	T	3.1 (3100)	46	45	90 @ 1.70	1.57	0.0010–0.0027	0.0010–0.0027	NA	NA
	X	3.4 (3400)	46	45	75 @ 1.40	1.40	0.0011–0.0026	0.0014–0.0031	NA	NA
	L	3.8 (3800)	46	45	80 @ 1.75	1.70	0.0015–0.0032	0.0015–0.0032	NA	NA
1992–93	R	2.5 (2500)	45	46	75 @ 1.68	1.68	0.0010–0.0026	0.0013–0.0041	NA	NA
	T	3.1 (3100)	46	45	90 @ 1.70	1.57	0.0010–0.0027	0.0010–0.0027	NA	NA
	X	3.4 (3400)	46	45	75 @ 1.40	1.40	0.0011–0.0026	0.0014–0.0031	NA	NA
	L	3.8 (3800)	46	45	80 @ 1.70	1.70	0.0015–0.0032	0.0015–0.0032	NA	NA

NA—Not available
① Intake—44 degrees; Exhaust—44.5 degrees

PISTON AND RING SPECIFICATIONS

All measurements are given in inches.

Year	Engine ID/VIN	Engine Displacement Liters (cc)	Piston Clearance	Ring Gap Top Compression	Ring Gap Bottom Compression	Ring Gap Oil Control	Ring Side Clearance Top Compression	Ring Side Clearance Bottom Compression	Ring Side Clearance Oil Control
1989	W	2.8 (2835)	0.0009–0.0022	0.010–0.020	0.010–0.020	0.020–0.055	0.002–0.003	0.002–0.003	0.001–0.008
	T	3.1 (3100)	0.0009–0.0022	0.010–0.020	0.010–0.020	0.020–0.055	0.002–0.003	0.002–0.003	0.001–0.008

PISTON AND RING SPECIFICATIONS

All measurements are given in inches.

| Year | Engine ID/VIN | Engine Displacement Liters (cc) | Piston Clearance | Ring Gap | | | Ring Side Clearance | | |
				Top Compression	Bottom Compression	Oil Control	Top Compression	Bottom Compression	Oil Control
1990	D	2.3 (2300)	0.0007–0.0020	0.013–0.023	0.015–0.025	0.015–0.055	0.002–0.003	0.001–0.003	0.002–0.003
	A	2.3 (2300)	0.0007–0.0020	0.013–0.023	0.015–0.025	0.015–0.055	0.002–0.004	0.001–0.004	0.002–0.003
	R	2.5 (2500)	0.0014–0.0022	0.010–0.020	0.010–0.020	0.020–0.060	0.002–0.003	0.001–0.003	0.002–0.006
	T	3.1 (3100)	0.0009–0.0022	0.010–0.020	0.010–0.028	0.010–0.030	0.002–0.003	0.002–0.003	0.001–0.008
	V	3.1 (3100)	0.0009–0.0022	0.010–0.020	0.010–0.028	0.010–0.030	0.002–0.003	0.002–0.003	0.001–0.008
	L	3.8 (3800)	0.0004–0.0022	0.010–0.025	0.010–0.025	0.015–0.055	0.001–0.003	0.001–0.003	0.001–0.008
1991	D	2.3 (2300)	0.0007–0.0020	0.013–0.023	0.015–0.025	0.015–0.055	0.002–0.003	0.001–0.003	0.002–0.003
	R	2.5 (2500)	0.0014–0.0022	0.010–0.020	0.010–0.020	0.020–0.060	0.002–0.003	0.001–0.003	0.002–0.006
	T	3.1 (3100)	0.0009–0.0022	0.010–0.020	0.010–0.028	0.010–0.030	0.002–0.003	0.002–0.003	0.001–0.008
	X	3.4 (3400)	0.0009–0.0023	0.012–0.022	0.019–0.029	0.010–0.030	0.002–0.004	0.002–0.004	0.002–0.008
	L	3.8 (3800)	0.0004–0.0022	0.010–0.025	0.010–0.025	0.015–0.055	0.001–0.003	0.001–0.003	0.001–0.008
1992–93	R	2.5 (2500)	0.0014–0.0022	0.010–0.020	0.010–0.020	0.020–0.060	0.002–0.003	0.001–0.003	0.002–0.006
	T	3.1 (3100)	0.0009–0.0022	0.010–0.020	0.010–0.028	0.010–0.030	0.002–0.003	0.002–0.003	0.001–0.008
	X	3.4 (3400)	0.0009–0.0023	0.012–0.022	0.019–0.029	0.010–0.030	0.002–0.004	0.002–0.004	0.002–0.008
	L	3.8 (3800)	0.0004–0.0022	0.010–0.025	0.010–0.025	0.015–0.055	0.001–0.003	0.001–0.003	0.001–0.008

TORQUE SPECIFICATIONS

All readings in ft. lbs.

| Year | Engine ID/VIN | Engine Displacement Liters (cc) | Cylinder Head Bolts | Main Bearing Bolts | Rod Bearing Bolts | Crankshaft Damper Bolts | Flywheel Bolts | Manifold | | Spark Plugs | Lug Nut |
								Intake	Exhaust		
1989	W	2.8 (2835)	①	70	37	76	46	③	18	18	100
	T	3.1 (3100)	①	70	37	76	46	③	18	18	100
1990	D	2.3 (2300)	⑤	⑥	⑦	⑧	⑨	18	27	17	100
	A	2.3 (2300)	⑤	⑥	⑦	⑧	⑨	18	27	17	100
	R	2.5 (2500)	②	65	29	162	55	25	④	18	100
	T	3.1 (3100)	①	73	39	76	60	③	18	18	100
	V	3.1 (3100)	①	73	39	76	60	③	18	18	100
	L	3.8 (3800)	⑩	⑪	⑫	⑬	⑭	⑮	41	20	100

TORQUE SPECIFICATIONS

All readings in ft. lbs.

Year	Engine ID/VIN	Engine Displacement Liters (cc)	Cylinder Head Bolts	Main Bearing Bolts	Rod Bearing Bolts	Crankshaft Damper Bolts	Flywheel Bolts	Manifold Intake	Manifold Exhaust	Spark Plugs	Lug Nut
1991	D	2.3 (2300)	⑤	⑥	⑦	⑧	⑨	18	27	17	100
	R	2.5 (2500)	②	65	29	162	55	25	④	11	100
	T	3.1 (3100)	①	73	39	76	60	③	18	11	100
	X	3.4 (3400)	⑯	⑰	39	78	61	18	⑱	11	100
	L	3.8 (3800)	⑩	⑪	⑫	⑬	⑭	⑮	41	20	100
1992-93	R	2.5 (2500)	②	65	29	162	55	25	④	11	100
	T	3.1 (3100)	①	73	39	76	44	③	18	11	100
	X	3.4 (3400)	⑯	⑰	39	78	61	18	⑱	11	100
	L	3.8 (3800)	⑩	⑪	⑫	⑬	⑭	⑮	41	20	100

① Torque in 2 steps:
  1st step—33 ft. lbs.
  2nd step—Turn an additional 90 degrees (¼ turn)

② Torque in 3 steps:
  1st step—18 ft. lbs.
  2nd step—Bolts "A" through "J" except "I" to 26 ft. lbs. Tighten bolt "I" to 18 ft lbs.
  3rd step—Turn an additional 90 degrees (¼) turn

③ Torque in 2 steps:
  1st step—15 ft. lbs.
  2nd step—24 ft. lbs.

④ Torque inner bolts to 37 ft. lbs. and outer bolts to 26 ft. lbs.

⑤ Torque in 2 steps:
  1st step—Torque all bolts in sequence to 26 ft. lbs.
  2nd step—Torque in sequence bolts number 7 and 9 an additional 100 degrees and the remaining bolts 110 degrees

⑥ 15 ft. lbs. plus an additional 90 degree turn

⑦ 18 ft. lbs. plus an additional 80 degree turn

⑧ 74 ft. lbs. plus an additional 90 degree turn

⑨ 22 ft. lbs. plus an additional 45 degree turn

⑩ Torque in 3 steps:
  1st step—Tighten all bolts in sequence to 35 ft. lbs.
  2nd step—Tighten all bolts in sequence an additional 130 degrees
  3rd step—Tighten the center 4 bolts an additional 30 degrees

⑪ 26 ft. lbs. plus an additional 45 degree turn

⑫ 20 ft. lbs. plus an additional 50 degree turn

⑬ 105 ft. lbs. plus an additional 56 degree turn

⑭ 89 inch lbs. plus an additional 90 degree turn

⑮ Intake manifold to cylinder head (lower)— 89 inch lbs.

⑯ Torque in 2 steps:
  1st step—Torque all bolts in sequence to 37 ft. lbs.
  2nd step—Turn an additional 90 degrees (¼ turn)

⑰ 37 ft. lbs. plus an additional 75 degree turn

⑱ Torque to 115 inch lbs.

BRAKE SPECIFICATIONS

All measurements in inches unless noted.

Year	Model		Master Cylinder Bore	Brake Disc Original Thickness	Brake Disc Minimum Thickness	Brake Disc Maximum Runout	Brake Drum Diameter Original Inside Diameter	Brake Drum Diameter Max. Wear Limit	Brake Drum Diameter Maximum Machine Diameter	Minimum Lining Thickness Front	Minimum Lining Thickness Rear
1989	Grand Prix	Front	0.945	1.040	0.972	0.004	—	—	—	0.003	0.003
		Rear	—	0.492	0.429	0.004	—	—	—	0.003	0.003
	Cutlass Supreme	Front	0.945	1.040	0.972	0.004	—	—	—	0.003	0.003
		Rear	—	0.492	0.429	0.004	—	—	—	0.003	0.003
	Regal	Front	0.945	1.040	0.972	0.004	—	—	—	0.003	0.003
		Rear	—	0.492	0.429	0.004	—	—	—	0.003	0.003
1990	Grand Prix	Front	0.945	1.040	0.972	0.004	—	—	—	0.003	0.003
		Rear	—	0.492	0.429	0.004	—	—	—	0.003	0.003
	Cutlass Supreme	Front	0.945	1.040	0.972	0.004	—	—	—	0.003	0.003
		Rear	—	0.492	0.429	0.004	—	—	—	0.003	0.003
	Regal	Front	0.945	1.040	0.972	0.004	—	—	—	0.003	0.003
		Rear	—	0.492	0.429	0.004	—	—	—	0.003	0.003
	Lumina	Front	0.945	1.040	0.972	0.004	—	—	—	0.003	0.003
		Rear	—	0.492	0.429	0.004	—	—	—	0.003	0.003

BRAKE SPECIFICATIONS
All measurements in inches unless noted.

Year	Model		Master Cylinder Bore	Brake Disc Original Thickness	Brake Disc Minimum Thickness	Brake Disc Maximum Runout	Brake Drum Diameter Original Inside Diameter	Brake Drum Diameter Max. Wear Limit	Brake Drum Diameter Maximum Machine Diameter	Minimum Lining Thickness Front	Minimum Lining Thickness Rear
1991	Grand Prix	Front	0.945	1.040	0.972	0.004	—	—	—	0.003	0.003
		Rear	—	0.492	0.429	0.004	—	—	—	0.003	0.003
	Cutlass Supreme	Front	0.945	1.040	0.972	0.004	—	—	—	0.003	0.003
		Rear	—	0.492	0.429	0.004	—	—	—	0.003	0.003
	Regal	Front	0.945	1.040	0.972	0.004	—	—	—	0.003	0.003
		Rear	—	0.492	0.429	0.004	—	—	—	0.003	0.003
	Lumina	Front	0.945	1.040	0.972	0.004	—	—	—	0.003	0.003
		Rear	—	0.492	0.429	0.004	—	—	—	0.003	0.003
1992-93	Grand Prix	Front	0.945	1.040	0.972	0.004	—	—	—	0.003	0.003
		Rear	—	0.492	0.429	0.004	—	—	—	0.003	0.003
	Cutlass Supreme	Front	0.945	1.040	0.972	0.004	—	—	—	0.003	0.003
		Rear	—	0.492	0.429	0.004	—	—	—	0.003	0.003
	Regal	Front	0.945	1.040	0.972	0.004	—	—	—	0.003	0.003
		Rear	—	0.492	0.429	0.004	—	—	—	0.003	0.003
	Lumina	Front	0.945	1.040	0.972	0.004	—	—	—	0.003	0.003
		Rear	—	0.492	0.429	0.004	—	—	—	0.003	0.003

WHEEL ALIGNMENT

Year	Model	Caster Range (deg.)	Caster Preferred Setting (deg.)	Camber Range (deg.)	Camber Preferred Setting (deg.)	Toe-in (in.)	Steering Axis Inclination (deg.)
1989	Cutlass Supreme	1⁵/₁₆P-2⁵/₁₆P	1¹³/₁₆P	³/₁₆P-1³/₁₆P	¹¹/₁₆P	³/₃₂N-³/₃₂P	NA
	Grand Prix	1⁵/₁₆P-2⁵/₁₆P	1¹³/₁₆P	³/₁₆P-1³/₁₆P	¹¹/₁₆P	³/₃₂N-³/₃₂P	NA
	Regal	1½P-2½P	2P	³/₁₆P-1³/₁₆P	¹¹/₁₆P	³/₃₂N-³/₃₂P	NA
1990	Cutlass Supreme	1½P-2½P	2P	³/₁₆P-1³/₁₆P	¹¹/₁₆P	³/₃₂N-³/₃₂P	NA
	Grand Prix	1⁵/₁₆P-2⁵/₁₆P	1¹³/₁₆P	³/₁₆P-1³/₁₆P	¹¹/₁₆P	³/₃₂N-³/₃₂P	NA
	Regal	1½P-2½P	2P	³/₁₆P-1³/₁₆P	¹¹/₁₆P	³/₃₂N-³/₃₂P	NA
	Lumina	1½P-2½P	2P	³/₁₆P-1³/₁₆P	¹¹/₁₆P	³/₃₂N-³/₃₂P	NA
1991	Cutlass Supreme	1½P-2½P	2P	³/₁₆P-1³/₁₆P	¹¹/₁₆P	³/₃₂N-³/₃₂P	NA
	Grand Prix	1⁵/₁₆P-2⁵/₁₆P	1¹³/₁₆P	³/₁₆P-1³/₁₆P	¹¹/₁₆P	³/₃₂N-³/₃₂P	NA
	Regal	1½P-2½P	2P	³/₁₆P-1³/₁₆P	¹¹/₁₆P	³/₃₂N-³/₃₂P	NA
	Lumina	1½P-2½P	2P	³/₁₆P-1³/₁₆P	¹¹/₁₆P	³/₃₂N-³/₃₂P	NA
1992-93	Cutlass Supreme	1½P-2½P	2P	³/₁₆P-1³/₁₆P	¹¹/₁₆P	³/₃₂N-³/₃₂P	NA
	Grand Prix	1⁵/₁₆P-2⁵/₁₆P	1¹³/₁₆P	³/₁₆P-1³/₁₆P	¹¹/₁₆P	³/₃₂N-³/₃₂P	NA
	Regal	1½P-2½P	2P	³/₁₆P-1³/₁₆P	¹¹/₁₆P	³/₃₂N-³/₃₂P	NA
	Lumina	1½P-2½P	2P	³/₁₆P-1³/₁₆P	¹¹/₁₆P	³/₃₂N-³/₃₂P	NA

NA—Not available
N—Negative
P—Positive

ENGINE MECHANICAL

NOTE: Disconnecting the negative battery cable on some vehicles may interfere with the functions of the on board computer systems and may require the computer to undergo a relearning process, once the negative battery cable is reconnected.

Engine Assembly

REMOVAL & INSTALLATION

2.3L Engine

1. Release the fuel system pressure.
2. Disconnect the negative battery cable.
3. Mark the position of the hood hinges to aid in installation. Remove the hood hinge bolts and the hood with aid from an assistant.
4. Drain the engine coolant into drain pan.
5. Remove the heater hoses at the heater core and thermostat housing. Remove the radiator upper hose.
6. Remove the air cleaner and inlet hose from the vehicle.
7. If equipped with air conditioning, discharge the system using the appropriate equipment. Remove the air conditioning compressor and condenser hose at the compressor.
8. Disconnect and label all engine vacuum lines.
9. Disconnect the power brake vacuum hose and throttle cable.
10. Label and disconnect the electrical connectors from the alternator, air conditioning compressor, fuel injection harness, starter solenoid, engine ground strap, ignition assembly, coolant sensor, oil pressure sensor, knock sensor, oxygen sensor, Idle Air Control (IAC) valve and Throttle Position Sensor (TPS). The last 2 sensors are located at the throttle body.
11. Remove the power steering pump and position aside. Do not remove the pump hoses, unless necessary.
12. Release the fuel pressure, if not already done and remove the fuel lines from the fuel rail.
13. If equipped with automatic transaxle, remove the transaxle fill tube.
14. Remove the engine torque strut mounts.
15. Raise the vehicle and support it safely.
16. Remove the exhaust heat shield and exhaust pipe from the engine manifold.

17. Remove the exhaust to transaxle mounting brace.
18. Remove the remaining lower transaxle-to-engine retaining bolts.
19. Remove the lower radiator hose.
20. Remove the flywheel or converter cover.
21. Scribe a mark on the torque converter and flywheel. Remove the torque converter to driveplate fasteners. Push the converter back into the transaxle bellhousing as far as possible.
22. Remove the transaxle-to-engine bracket.
23. Lower the vehicle. Support the transaxle assembly using the appropriate equipment.
24. Remove the upper transaxle-to-engine bolts.
25. Install the engine lifting fixture and remove the remaining engine mounting bolts.
26. Remove the engine from the vehicle.

To install:

NOTE: Make sure all the engine mounting bolts are in their correct location to prevent transaxle and engine damage.

27. Install the engine to a lifting fixture and position the engine in the vehicle. With the aid of an assistant, align the engine-to-transaxle.
28. Install the engine mounting bolts and the upper transaxle to engine mounting bolts.
29. With the engine and transaxle secured in the vehicle, raise the vehicle and support it safely.
30. Install the transaxle-to-engine bracket and bolts. Torque the engine-to-transaxle bolts as follows:
   a. Positions No. 2, 3, 4, 5, 6 – 71 ft. lbs. (96 Nm).
   b. Positions No. 7, 8 – 41 ft. lbs. (56 Nm).
31. Apply thread locking compound and install the torque converter-to-flywheel bolts. Torque the bolts to 46 ft. lbs. (63 Nm). Install the flywheel inspection cover.
32. At the right side of the vehicle, install the engine mount bolt.
33. Install the lower radiator hose and engine ground wires.
34. Install the air conditioning compressor and condensor hose, using new O-rings at the couplings. Connect the compressor and alternator electrical harnesses.
35. Install the heater hoses at the heater core and throttle body.
36. Install the exhaust-to-transaxle bracket.
37. Lower the vehicle.
38. Install the exhaust pipe-to-manifold and heat shield. Torque the exhaust bolts to 22 ft. lbs. (30 Nm).

39. Install the upper engine mounts.
40. Connect the fuel lines to the fuel rail making sure to use new O-rings at the fitting connections.
41. Install the power steering pump, lines and drive belt.
42. Install the throttle cable and power brake vacuum hose.
43. Connect the electrical connectors to the oxygen sensor, knock sensor, oil pressure sensor, coolant sensor, ignition assembly, TPS sensor, IAC sensor and starter solenoid.
44. Connect all engine vacuum hoses.
45. Install the upper radiator hose and fill the radiator with the specified amount of antifreeze.
46. Refill the engine with the specified amount of engine oil.
47. Evacuate and recharge the air conditioning system.
48. Install the air cleaner and inlet hose.
49. Install the hood assembly with the help of an assistant.
50. Recheck all procedures for completion of repair.
51. Recheck all fluid levels.
52. Connect the negative battery cable. Start the engine and check for fluid leaks.

2.5L Engine

1. Disconnect the negative battery cable.
2. Place drain pan under the radiator drain valve and drain the engine coolant.
3. Remove the air cleaner assembly. Release fuel system pressure.
4. Mark the hood hinges with a scribe and remove the hood assembly.
5. Mark and remove all engine wiring. Place all the wire assemblies out of the way.
6. Remove the vacuum, heater and radiator hoses labeling for location.
7. Remove the air conditioning compressor from the engine and place to the side with a piece of rope or wire. Do not disconnect the hoses from the compressor.
8. Remove the alternator and bracket.
9. Remove the engine torque strut.
10. Remove the throttle and transaxle linkage.
11. Remove the transaxle-to-engine bolts except the 2 upper bolts.
12. Raise the vehicle and support it safely.
13. Remove the engine mount-to-frame bolts.
13. Remove the exhaust pipe from the manifold.
14. Remove the torque converter-to-flywheel bolts.
15. Remove the starter motor.
16. Remove the power steering pump

and attach to the inner fender with a piece of rope or wire. Do not disconnect the hoses.

17. Release fuel pressure, if not done prior, and remove the fuel lines at the throttle body assembly.

18. Remove the rear engine support bracket.

19. Support the transaxle assembly with a transaxle holding fixture.

20. Disconnect the transaxle from the engine and support with a jack.

21. Attach an appropriate engine lifting device securely to the engine.

22. Remove the engine assembly. Use care not to get under the engine assembly in case of lift failure.

23. Place the engine on a workstand.

To install:

24. Place the engine assembly onto an appropriate lifting device.

25. With the aid of an assistant, install the engine into the vehicle.

26. Position the engine into the engine mounts and engage the transaxle with the engine.

27. Remove the engine lifting device.

28. Install the torque converter bolts and engine-to-transaxle mounting bolts. Torque the torque converter bolts to 55 ft. lbs. (75 Nm).

29. Remove the transaxle holding fixture.

30. Install the rear support bracket bolts.

31. Install the engine mount nuts and torque to 32 ft. lbs. (43 Nm).

32. Install the rear transaxle mount bracket bolts and torque to 35 ft. lbs. (47 Nm).

33. Install the fuel lines to the throttle body assembly.

34. Install the power steering pump.

35. Install the starter motor assembly.

36. Install the flywheel cover plate.

37. Install the exhaust pipe-to-manifold.

38. Install the engine torque strut.

39. Install the alternator and bracket.

40. Install the air conditioning compressor.

41. Install the heater, radiator and vacuum hoses.

42. Install the throttle and transaxle linkages.

43. Install and reconnect all engine wiring harnesses.

44. Install the hood assembly to its original position with an assistant.

45. Refill the cooling system with engine coolant.

46. Reconnect the negative battery cable.

47. Install the air cleaner assembly.

48. Inspect for proper fluid levels.

49. Recheck every procedure for proper reinstallation.

50. Start the vehicle and check for fluid leaks.

2.8L, 3.1L and 3.4L Engines

1. Remove the air cleaner and duct assembly.

2. Disconnect the negative battery cable.

3. Mark the hood hinges to ensure proper reinstallation. With the help of an assistant, remove the hood retaining bolt and remove hood from the vehicle.

4. Mark and remove all necessary engine wiring and place the harnesses out of the way.

5. Remove the throttle, TV and cruise control cables, if equipped, from the throttle body assembly.

6. Release the fuel pressure and remove the fuel lines at engine.

7. Remove the AIR pump and serpentine belt.

8. Position drain pan under the radiator drain valve and drain the engine coolant. Remove coolant recovery tank. Remove the cooling fans.

9. Remove the upper and lower radiator hoses and heater hose quick connect at intake manifold.

10. Discharge the air conditioning system using the appropriate equipment. Remove the air conditioning compressor mounting bolts at the front mounting bracket.

11. Remove the power steering pump and move to the side. Attach to the body with a piece of wire or rope. Do not disconnect the pump hoses.

12. Remove the heater hoses from the engine and move out of the way.

13. Remove the brake booster vacuum hose.

14. Remove the EGR hose from the exhaust manifold. Remove pipe from EGR valve, if equipped.

15. Raise the vehicle and support it safely.

16. Remove the air conditioning compressor from the engine and attach to the body with a piece of rope or wire. The factory recommends removal of the air conditioning manifold from compressor.

17. Remove the right front tire and wheel. Remove the right front splash shield.

18. Disconnect right ball joint nut and separate from control arm.

19. Remove halfshaft assembly. Disconnect any remaining electrical connectors at the back of the engine.

20. Remove the flywheel cover, starter motor and torque converter bolts. Matchmark the converter to driveplate to aid installation.

21. Remove the transaxle bracket and front engine mount nuts.

22. Remove the exhaust pipe and converter assembly from manifold.

23. Lower the vehicle.

24. Remove the torque struts.

25. Remove the exhaust crossover.

26. Disconnect the bulkhead electrical connector and quick connects near Electronic Control Module (ECM).

27. Disconnect the electrical connectors at the alternator assembly.

28. Support the transaxle with floor jack or equivalent.

29. Remove the remaining transaxle-to-engine bolts.

30. Attach an engine lifting device and remove the engine from the vehicle. Check for connected wires and hoses as the engine is coming out of the body.

31. Place the engine on a workstand.

To install:

32. With an assistant, install a lifting device onto the engine and position into the vehicle.

33. Remove the lifting device.

34. Install the transaxle-to-engine bolts.

35. Remove the transaxle support.

36. Reconnect the right crossover pipe-to-manifold clamp.

37. Reconnect the bulkhead electrical connector.

38. Reconnect electrical connector at ECM.

39. Install the left crossover pipe-to-manifold clamp.

40. Install the coolant recovery bottle and torque struts.

41. Raise the vehicle and support it safely.

42. Reinstall halfshaft assembly.

43. Reconnect ball joint to control arm.

44. Reinstall tire and wheel. Torque to 100 ft. lbs.

45. Reconnect ABS electrical connector if equipped.

46. Install the crossover pipe and converter assembly.

47. Install the front engine mount retaining nuts and torque to 32 ft. lbs. (43 Nm).

48. Install the transaxle bracket, torque converter bolts and starter motor.

49. Install the flywheel cover.

50. Install the air conditioning compressor to engine.

51. Lower the vehicle.

52. Install the EGR pipe and hose to valve.

53. Reconnect the brake booster vacuum supply, heater hoses and power steering pump.

54. Install the air conditioning compressor front mounting bracket bolts.

55. Install the radiator hoses and fans, serpentine and AIR pump belts. Recharge as required.

56. Reconnect the fuel lines. Install coolant recovery tank.

57. Install the throttle, TV and cruise control linkage to the throttle body.

58. Reconnect all necessary engine electrical and ground wiring.

59. Install the hood assembly with an assistant.

60. Reconnect the battery cables.

61. Turn the ignition ON for 3 seconds and then return to OFF position. Check for fuel leaks. Repeat this procedure a second time.

62. Install the air cleaner and duct assembly.

63. Recheck all procedures for proper reinstallation and correct if necessary.

64. Refill the engine with engine oil, coolant and transaxle fluid, if needed.

65. Inspect vehicle for fluid leaks before and after starting the engine.

66. Road test the vehicle and recheck for fluid leaks.

3.8L Engine

1. Disconnect the negative battery cable.

2. Remove the air cleaner assembly.

3. Release the fuel system pressure.

4. Disconnect the fuel lines from the rail and mounting brackets.

5. Drain the engine coolant and remove the recovery bottle.

6. Remove the inner fender electrical cover and the fuel injector sight cover.

7. Disconnect the throttle cables from the throttle body and mounting bracket.

8. Remove the rear heat shield from the crossover pipe.

9. Remove the throttle cable mounting bracket and vacuum line as an assembly.

10. Disconnect the exhaust crossover from the manifolds.

11. Disconnect the engine torque strut bolt and strut from the engine.

12. Remove the right side engine cooling fan.

13. Disconnect the vacuum line to the transaxle module.

14. Remove the serpentine belt.

15. Remove the power steering pump and alternator assemblies.

16. Tag and disconnect all electrical connections from the engine.

17. Disconnect the upper and lower radiator, and heater hoses from the engine.

18. Remove the transaxle to engine bolts and ground wire harness.

19. Raise and support the vehicle safely.

20. Remove the right front wheel and inner splash shield.

21. Remove the flywheel cover, scribe a mark on the torque converter and flywheel and remove the flywheel to torque converter bolts.

22. Disconnect the wire harness clamps from the frame near the radiator.

23. Remove the air conditioner compressor from the bracket, lay aside and secure to the frame.

24. Disconnect the wires and remove the starter motor assembly.

25. Safely support the transaxle and remove the transaxle to engine bolt, through the wheel well, using a long extension.

26. Attach a lifting device and remove the engine mount to frame nuts.

27. Drain the engine oil and remove the oil filter.

28. Disconnect the oil cooler pipes from the hose connections.

29. Disconnect the exhaust pipe from the manifold.

30. Lower the vehicle and remove the engine assembly from the vehicle.

To install:

31. With an assistant, install a lifting device onto the engine and position into the vehicle.

32. Support the transaxle, install the transaxle-to-engine bolts and ground wire harness and torque to 46 ft. lbs. (62 Nm).

33. Install the heater and upper and lower radiator hoses to the engine.

34. Install all electrical connections to the engine.

35. Install the alternator, power steering pump and serpentine belt.

36. Install the vacuum line to the transaxle module.

37. Install the engine torque strut and bolt and torque to 41 ft. lbs. (56 Nm).

38. Install the exhaust crossover pipe.

39. Install the throttle cable mounting bracket and vacuum lines.

40. Install the heat shield to the crossover pipe and the throttle cables to the throttle body and mounting bracket.

41. Install the inner fender electrical cover and the coolant recovery bottle.

42. Install the fuel hoses to the fuel rail and mounting brackets.

43. Raise and support the vehicle safely.

44. Connect the front exhaust pipe to the manifold.

45. Install the oil filter and oil cooler pipes.

46. Install the engine mount nuts to the frame and torque to 32 ft. lbs. (43 Nm).

47. Install the transaxle to engine bolt through the wheel well and torque to 46 ft. lbs. (62 Nm).

48. Install the starter motor assembly and connect the electrical connectors.

49. Install the air conditioner compressor to the bracket.

50. Install the wire harness clamps to the frame near the radiator.

51. Align the scribe marks, install the torque converter to flywheel bolts and torque to 46 ft. lbs. (62 Nm).

52. Install the flywheel cover and the inner fender splash shield.

53. Install the right front wheel assembly and lower the vehicle.

54. Refill the cooling system and bleed the power steering system.

55. Install the right side cooling fan.

56. Install the fuel injector sight shield and the air cleaner assembly.

57. Connect the negative battery cable and install the hood.

58. Check and add fluids as required. Test drive vehicle and recheck for leaks and correct levels.

Cylinder Head

REMOVAL & INSTALLATION

2.3L Engine

1. Disconnect the negative battery cable.

2. Drain the cooling system.

3. Remove the heater inlet and throttle body heater hoses from the water inlet.

4. Remove the exhaust manifold.

5. Remove the intake and exhaust camshaft housing.

6. Remove the oil fill cap, tube and retainer. Pull the tube up and out of the block.

7. Disconnect and move the fuel injector harness.

8. Release the fuel system pressure.

9. Remove the throttle body and air inlet tube with the hoses and cables still connected. Position the assembly out of the way.

10. Remove the power brake booster hose and throttle cable bracket.

11. Remove the MAP sensor vacuum hose and all electrical connectors from the intake manifold and cylinder head.

12. Remove the radiator inlet hose and coolant sensor connectors.

13. In the reveres order of installation, remove the cylinder head-to-block retaining bolts.

14. Gently tap the outer edges of the cylinder head with a rubber hammer to dislodge the head gasket. Do not pry a screwdriver between the 2 surfaces.

15. Remove the cylinder head and intake manifold as an assembly.

To install:

16. Clean all gasket mating surfaces with a plastic scraper and solvent. Remove all dirt from the bolts with a wire brush.

17. Clean and inspect the oil flow check valve but do not remove the valve.

18. Check the cylinder head mating surface for flatness using a straightedge and a feeler gauge. Resurface the head, if the warpage exceeds 0.010 inch (0.25mm).

19. Check to see if the dowel pins are installed properly, replace, if necessary.

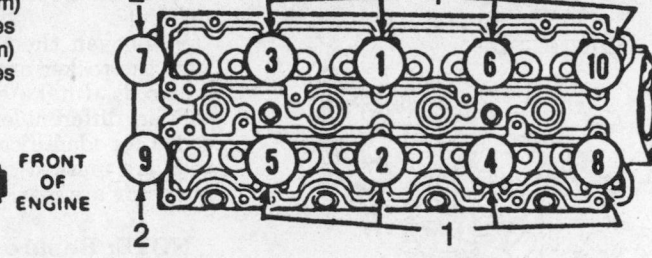

1. 26 ft. lbs. (35 Nm) plus 110 degrees
2. 26 ft. lbs (35 Nm) plus 100 degrees

FRONT OF ENGINE

Cylinder head bolt tightening sequence—2.3L Engine

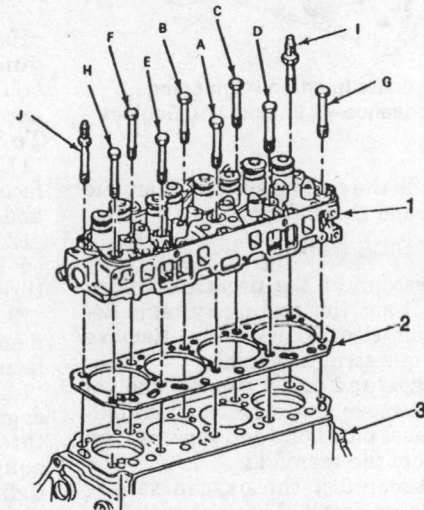

1. Cylinder head
2. Gasket
3. Cylinder block
4. NOTE: Tighten all bolts in proper sequence to 18 ft. lbs. (25 Nm). Tighten bolts "A" through "J" (except "I") again to 26 ft. lbs. (35 Nm) and Bolt "I" to 18 ft. lbs. (25 Nm). Tighten all bolts in proper sequence an additional ¼ turn or 90 degrees.

Cylinder head bolt tightening sequence—2.5L Engine

NOTE: To avoid damage, install new spark plugs after the cylinder head has been installed on the engine. In the mean time, plug the holes to prevent dirt from entering the combustion chamber during reinstallation.

20. Do not use any sealing compounds on the new cylinder head gasket. Match the new gasket with the old one to ensure a perfect match.
21. Install the cylinder head and camshaft housing covers.
22. Torque all bolts to 26 ft. lbs. (35 Nm) following the proper sequence. Now, in the appropriate order, tighten bolts No. 7 and 9 an additional 100 degrees and all other bolts an additional 110 degrees.
23. Install the throttle body heater hoses, upper radiator hose and intake manifold bracket.
24. Install cylinder head and intake manifold electrical connectors and vacuum hoses.
25. Install the throttle body-to-intake manifold with a new gasket. Install the throttle cable, MAP sensor vacuum hose and air cleaner duct.
26. Lubricate the new oil fill tube O-ring and install the fill tube. Make sure the tube is fully seated in the block.

27. Install and torque the exhaust manifold.
28. Fill the radiator with the specified amount of engine coolant.
29. Recheck all procedures to ensure completion of repair.
30. Connect the negative battery cable, start the engine and check for fluid leaks.

2.5L Engine

1. Disconnect the negative battery cable.
2. Drain the cooling system.
3. Raise and safely support the vehicle.
4. Remove the exhaust pipe and oxygen sensor.
5. Lower the vehicle.
6. Remove the oil level indicator tube and auxiliary ground cable.
7. Remove the air cleaner assembly.
8. Disconnect the EFI electrical connections and vacuum hoses.
9. Release the fuel pressure. Remove the wiring connectors, throttle linkage and fuel lines.
10. Remove the heater hose from the intake manifold.
11. Remove the wiring connectors from the manifold and cylinder head.
12. Remove the vacuum hoses, serpentine belt and alternator bracket.

13. Remove the radiator hoses.
14. Remove the rocker arm cover.
15. Loosen the rocker arm nuts and move the rocker arms to the side enough to remove the pushrods.
16. Mark each pushrod and remove from the engine.

NOTE: Mark each valve train component to ensure that they are installed in the same location as removed.

17. Remove the cylinder head bolts.
18. Tap the sides of the cylinder head with a plastic hammer to dislodge the gasket. Remove the cylinder head with the intake and exhaust manifold still attached.
19. If the cylinder head has to be serviced or replaced, remove the intake manifold, exhaust manifold and remaining hardware.

To install:

20. Before installing, clean the gasket surfaces of the head and block.
21. Check the cylinder head for warpage using a straightedge.
22. Match up the old head gasket with the new one to ensure the holes are exact. Install a new gasket over the dowel pins in the cylinder block.
23. Install the cylinder head in place over the dowel pins.
24. Coat the cylinder head bolt threads with sealing compound and install finger-tight.
25. Torque the cylinder head bolts, in sequence, in 3 steps.
    a. Torque all bolts to 18 ft. lbs. (26 Nm).
    b. Torque bolts "A" through "J" except "I" to 26 ft. lbs. (35 Nm). Torque bolt "I" to 18 ft. lbs. (24 Nm).
    c. Turn all bolts an additional 90 degree (¼ turn).
26. Install the pushrods, rocker arms and nuts (or bolts) in the same location as removed. Tighten the nuts (or bolts) to 24 ft. lbs. (32 Nm).
27. Install the rocker arm cover.
28. Install the radiator hoses, alternator bracket and serpentine belt.
29. Connect all intake manifold and cylinder head wiring.
30. Install the vacuum hoses and heater hose at manifold.
31. Install the wiring, throttle linkage and fuel lines to the throttle body assembly.
32. Install the oil level indicator tube-to-exhaust manifold.
33. Install the air cleaner assembly and refill the cooling system.
34. Raise and safely support the vehicle.
35. Install the exhaust pipe and oxygen sensor.
36. Lower the vehicle and connect the negative battery cable.

37. Start the engine and check for leaks.

2.8L and 3.1L Engines
LEFT SIDE (FRONT)

1. Disconnect the negative battery cable. Drain the cooling system. Remove the rocker cover.

2. Remove the intake manifold-to-cylinder head bolts and the intake manifold.

3. Disconnect the exhaust crossover and manifold bolts and remove left exhaust manifold.

4. Disconnect the oil level indicator tube bracket.

5. Loosen the rocker arms nuts, turn the rocker arms and remove the pushrods. Intake and exhaust pushrods are different lengths and are color coded for identification; intake pushrods are marked orange and exhaust pushrods are marked blue in color.

NOTE: Be sure to keep the parts in order for installation purposes.

6. Remove spark plug wires.

7. Remove the cylinder head-to-engine bolts; start with the outer bolts and work toward the center. Remove the cylinder head with the exhaust manifold as an assembly.

To install:

8. Clean the gasket mounting surfaces. Inspect the surfaces of the cylinder head, block and intake manifold for damage or warpage. Clean the threaded holes in the block and the cylinder head bolt threads.

9. Use new gaskets, align the new cylinder head gasket over the dowels on the block with the note **THIS SIDE UP** facing the cylinder head.

10. Install the cylinder head and exhaust manifold crossover assembly on the engine.

11. Using GM sealant 1052080 or equivalent, coat the cylinder head bolts and install the bolts hand-tight.

12. Using the correct sequence, torque the bolts to 33 ft. lbs. (45 Nm). After all bolts are torqued to 33 ft. lbs. (45 Nm), rotate the torque wrench another 90 degrees or ¼ turn. This will apply the correct torque to the bolts.

13. Install the pushrods in the same order that they were removed. Torque the rocker arm nuts to 14–20 ft. lbs. (19–27 Nm).

14. Install the intake manifold using a new gasket and following the correct sequence, torque the bolts to the correct specification.

15. Install the oil level indicator tube and install the rocker cover. Install the air inlet tube and spark plug wires.

16. Reinstall engine strut bracket and exhaust manifold.

17. Connect the negative battery ca-

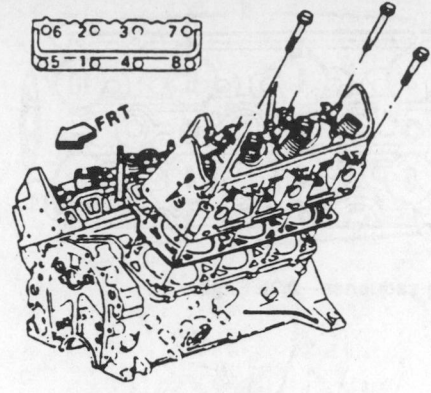

Cylinder head bolt tightening sequence—2.8L and 3.1L Engines

ble. Refill the cooling system. Start the engine and check for leaks.

RIGHT SIDE (REAR)

1. Disconnect the negative battery cable. Drain the cooling system. Remove air cleaner assembly. Remove the torque strut at engine.

2. Raise and safely support the vehicle. Remove the exhaust manifold-to-exhaust pipe bolts and separate the pipe from the manifold.

3. Disconnect the oxygen sensor harness connector. Lower the vehicle. Remove coolant recovery tank.

4. If more clearance is required, rotate the engine as follows:
   a. Put the transaxle in **N**.
   b. Remove the air cleaner.
   c. Disconnect the negative battery cable.
   d. Remove the torque strut to engine bracket bolt and swing strut aside.
   e. Replace the passenger side torque strut to engine bracket bolt in engine bracket.
   f. Place a prybar in the bracket so it contacts the bracket and the bolt.
   g. Rotate the engine by pulling forward on the prybar. Align the slave hole in the driver side torque strut to the engine bracket hole.
   h. Retain the engine in this position using the torque strut to engine bracket bolt.

NOTE: To prevent shearing of the rubber bushing, loosen the bolts on the engine strut before swinging the struts.

5. Remove the exhaust manifold-to-cylinder head bolts and the exhaust manifold from the engine.

6. Remove exhaust crossover heat shield and crossover pipe at right exhaust manifold.

7. Remove right side spark plug wires at cylinder head.

8. Remove the rocker arm cover. Remove the intake manifold-to-cylin-

der head bolts and the intake manifold.

9. Loosen the rocker arms nuts, turn the rocker arms and remove the pushrods. Intake and exhaust pushrods are different lengths and are color coded for identification; intake pushrods are marked orange and exhaust pushrods are marked blue in color.

NOTE: Be sure to keep the components in order for reassembly purposes.

10. Remove the cylinder head-to-engine bolts, starting with the outer bolts and working toward the center and the cylinder head.

To install:

11. Clean the gasket mounting surfaces. Inspect the parts for damage and/or warpage.

12. Clean the engine block's threaded holes and the cylinder head bolt threads.

13. Install new gasket on the alignment dowels with **THIS SIDE UP** facing the cylinder head.

14. Install the cylinder head onto the engine. Coat the cylinder head bolt threads with GM sealant 1052080 or equivalent, and install bolts hand-tight.

15. Following the proper torque sequence, tighten bolts to 33 ft. lbs. (45 Nm). After all bolts are torqued to 33 ft. lbs. (45 Nm), rotate the torque wrench an additional 90 degrees or ¼ turn. This will apply the correct torque to the bolts.

16. Install the pushrods in the same order as they were removed. Torque the rocker arm nuts to 14–20 ft. lbs. (19–27 Nm).

17. Follow the torquing sequence, use a new gasket and install the intake manifold.

18. Return the engine to normal resting position as follows:
   a. Pull forweard on the prybar to take the weight off the torque strut to engine bracket bolt.
   b. Remove bolt from the strut slave hole and engine bracket.
   c. Install engine torque strut and tighten the strut to engine bracket bolt to 32 ft. lbs. (43 Nm).

19. Install spark plug wires to cylinder head.

20. Install right side exhaust crossover pipe, heat shield and manifold.

21. Install exhaust pipe to manifold. Connect the oxygen sensor harness connector.

22. Install the oil level indicator tube and install the rocker cover. Install the air inlet tube.

23. Install coolant recovery tank. Refill the cooling system. Start the engine, allow it to reach normal operating temperatures and check for leaks.

3.4L Engine

LEFT SIDE (FRONT)

1. Disconnect the negative battery cable.

2. Drain cooling system. Remove intake manifold.

3. Remove left side cam carrier as follows:

   a. Disconnect oil/air breather hose from cam carrier cover. Remove spark plug wires from plugs and remove rear spark plug wire cover.

   b. Remove cam carrier cover bolts and lift off cover. Remove gasket and O-rings from cover.

   c. Remove secondary timing belt by removing secondary timing belt actuator and tensioner assembly and sliding belt from pulleys.

   d. Install 6 sections of fuel line hoses under camshaft and between lifters. This will hold lifters in the carrier. For this procedure use $3/16$ inch fuel line hose for exhaust valves and $5/32$ inch fuel line hose for the intake valves.

   e. Remove exhaust crossover pipe and torque strut.

   f. Remove torque strut bracket at engine.

   g. Remove cam carrier mounting bolts and nuts and remove cam carrier.

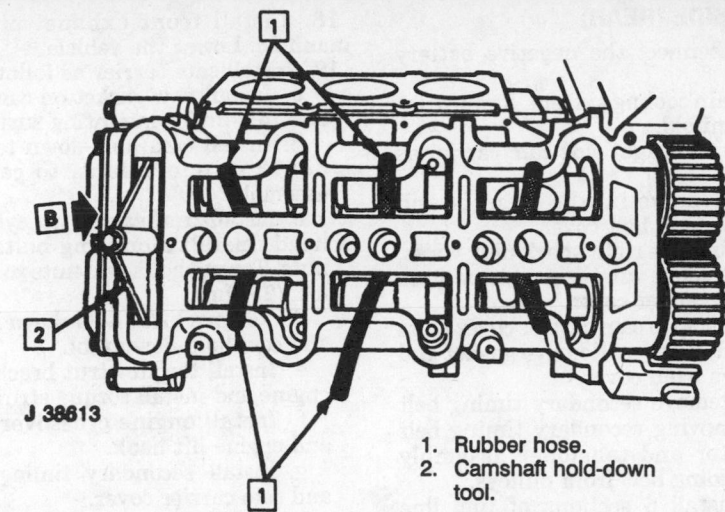

J 38613

1. Rubber hose.
2. Camshaft hold-down tool.

Cam carrier with lifter hold-down hoses in place

   h. Remove cam carrier gasket from cylinder head.

4. Remove front air hose on manual transaxle only.

5. Remove right cooling fan.

6. Remove exhaust mounting bolts and manifold.

7. Remove oil level indicator tube bolt and tube.

8. Disconnect electrical connector from temperature sending unit.

9. Remove cylinder head bolts and remove cylinder head.

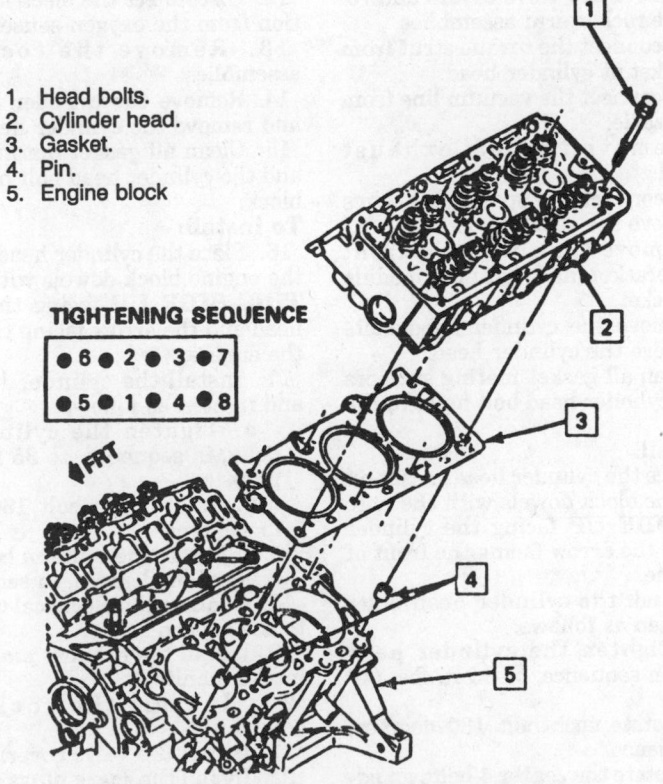

1. Head bolts.
2. Cylinder head.
3. Gasket.
4. Pin.
5. Engine block

TIGHTENING SEQUENCE

```
● 6   ● 2   ● 3   ● 7
● 5   ● 1   ● 4   ● 8
```

◄ FRT

Cylinder head torque sequence—3.4L Engine

To install:

10. Clean the gasket mounting surfaces. Inspect the parts for damage or warpage.

11. Clean the engine block threaded holes and the cylinder head bolt threads. Remove oil from threaded holes in block.

12. Install new cylinder head gasket to block with tabs between cylinders facing up.

13. Install cylinder head and bolts and torque in proper sequence. Tighten bolts to 33 ft. lbs. (45 Nm) plus an additional ¼ turn.

14. Connect electrical connector to coolant temperature sending unit.

15. Install oil level tube and bolt. Tighten to 89 inch lbs. (10 Nm).

16. Install exhaust manifold and nuts. Tighten to 116 inch lbs. (13 Nm).

17. Install front air pipe, manual transaxle. Install cooling fan.

18. Install cam carrier following these steps:

    a. Install new gasket on cam carrier to cylinder mounting surface.

    b. Install cam hold-down tool J-38613 or equivalent, to carrier assembly.

    c. Install cam carrier to cylinder head. Install mounting bolts and nuts. Torque bolts and nuts to 18 ft. lbs. (24 Nm).

    d. Remove lifter hold-down hoses and cam hold-down tool.

    e. Install torque strut bracket to engine and install torque strut.

    f. Install engine crossover pipe.

    g. Install secondary timing belt and cam carrier cover.

19. Install intake manifold. Tighten bolts to 18 ft. lbs. (25 Nm).

20. Refill fluid levels as required. Connect negative battery cable.

21. Start vehicle and check for fluid leaks.

RIGHT SIDE (REAR)

1. Disconnect the negative battery cable.

2. Drain cooling system. Remove intake manifold.

3. Remove right side cam carrier as follows:

   a. Remove intake plenum and right timing belt cover.

   b. Remove right spark plug wires.

   c. Remove air/oil separator hose at cam carrier cover.

   d. Remove cam carrier cover bolts and lift of cover. Remove gasket and O-rings from cover.

   e. Remove secondary timing belt by removing secondary timing belt actuator and tensioner assembly and sliding belt from pulleys.

   f. Install 6 sections of fuel line hoses under camshaft and between lifters. This will hold lifters in carrier. For this procedure use $3/16$ inch fuel line hose for exhaust valves and $5/32$ inch fuel line hose for the intake valves.

   g. Remove exhaust crossover pipe and torque strut.

   h. Remove torque strut bracket at engine. Remove front engine lift hook.

   i. Remove cam carrier mounting bolts and nuts and remove cam carrier.

   j. Remove cam carrier gasket from cylinder head.

4. Raise and support vehicle safely.

5. Remove front exhaust pipe at manifold.

6. Remove rear air hose from air pipe on manual transaxle only.

7. Lower vehicle and disconnect electrical connector from oxygen sensor.

8. Remove rear timing belt tensioner bracket.

9. Remove cylinder head bolts and remove cylinder head.

To install:

10. Clean the gasket mounting surfaces. Inspect the parts for damage and/or warpage.

11. Clean the engine block threaded holes and the cylinder head bolt threads. Remove oil from threaded holes in block.

12. Install new cylinder head gasket to block with tabs between cylinders facing up.

13. Install cylinder head and bolts and torque in proper sequence. Tighten bolts to 33 ft. lbs. (45 Nm) plus an additional ¼ turn.

14. Install rear timing belt tensioner bracket.

15. Connect electrical connector to oxygen sensor.

16. Raise vehicle and support safely.

17. Connect rear air hose to air pipe for manual transaxle.

18. Install front exhaust pipe to manifold. Lower the vehicle.

19. Install cam carrier as follows:

   a. Install new gasket on cam carrier to cylinder mounting surface.

   b. Install cam hold-down tool J–38613 or equivalent, to carrier assembly.

   c. install cam carrier to cylinder head. Install mounting bolts and nuts. Torque bolts and nuts to 18 ft. lbs. (25 Nm).

   d. Remove lifter hold-down hoses and cam hold-down tool.

   e. Install torque strut bracket to engine and install torque strut.

   f. Install engine crossover pipe and engine lift hook.

   g. Install secondary timing belt and cam carrier cover.

   h. Install spark plug wires and cover.

20. Install intake manifold. Torque bolts to 18 ft. lbs. (25 Nm).

21. Refill fliud levels as required. Connect negative battery cable.

22. Start vehicle and check for fluid leaks.

3.8L Engine

LEFT SIDE (FRONT)

1. Disconnect the negative battery cable and remove the air cleaner assembly.

2. Drain the cooling system and remove the intake manifold.

3. Remove the valve covers and remove the rocker arm assemblies.

4. Disconnect the torque strut from the bracket at cylinder head.

5. Disconnect the vacuum line from the transaxle.

6. Remove the left exhaust manifold.

7. Disconnect the spark plug wires and remove the spark plugs.

8. Remove the alternator front mount bracket and ignition module with bracket.

9. Remove the cylinder head bolts and remove the cylinder head.

10. Clean all gasket mating surfaces and the cylinder head bolt holes in the block.

To install:

11. Place the cylinder head gasket on the engine block dowels with the note **THIS SIDE UP** facing the cylinder head and the arrow facing the front of the engine.

12. Install the cylinder head bolts and tighten as follows:

   a. Tighten the cylinder head bolts, in sequence, to 35 ft. lbs. (47 Nm).

   b. Rotate each bolt 130 degrees, in sequence.

   c. Rotate the center 4 bolts an additional 30 degrees, in sequence.

13. Install the rocker arm assemblies and valve covers.

14. Install the intake and exhaust manifolds.

15. Install the alternator front mount bracket and ignition module with bracket and torque the bolts to 37 ft. lbs. (50 Nm).

16. Install the spark plugs and wires.

17. Install the torque strut to the bracket, at the head and torque to 41 ft. lbs. (56 Nm).

18. Fill the cooling system, connect the negative battery cable and install the air cleaner assembly.

RIGHT SIDE (REAR)

1. Disconnect the negative battery cable and remove the air cleaner assembly.

2. Drain the cooling system and disconnect the exhaust crossover pipe.

3. Remove the intake manifold.

4. Raise and support the vehicle safely.

5. Disconnect the front exhaust pipe from the manifold.

6. Remove the valve covers.

7. Remove the belt tensioner pulley.

8. Disconnect the heater hose from the engine.

9. Remove the power steering pump mounting bracket and lay the pump aside.

10. Remove the spark plug wires and remove the spark plugs.

11. Disconnect the exhaust manifold and leave in place.

12. Disconnect the electrical connection from the oxygen sensor.

13. Remove the rocker arm assemblies.

14. Remove the cylinder head bolts and remove the cylinder head.

15. Clean all gasket mating surfaces and the cylinder head bolt holes in the block.

To install:

16. Place the cylinder head gasket on the engine block dowels with the note **THIS SIDE UP** facing the cylinder head and the arrow facing the front of the engine.

17. Install the cylinder head bolts and tighten as follows:

   a. Tighten the cylinder head bolts, in sequence, to 35 ft. lbs. (47 Nm).

   b. Rotate each bolt 130 degrees, in sequence.

   c. Rotate the center 4 bolts an additional 30 degrees, in sequence.

18. Connect the electrical connection to the oxygen sensor.

19. Install the exhaust manifold and intake manifold.

20. Install the rocker arm assemblies.

21. Install the valve cover.

22. Install the spark plugs and wires.

23. Install the power steering pump

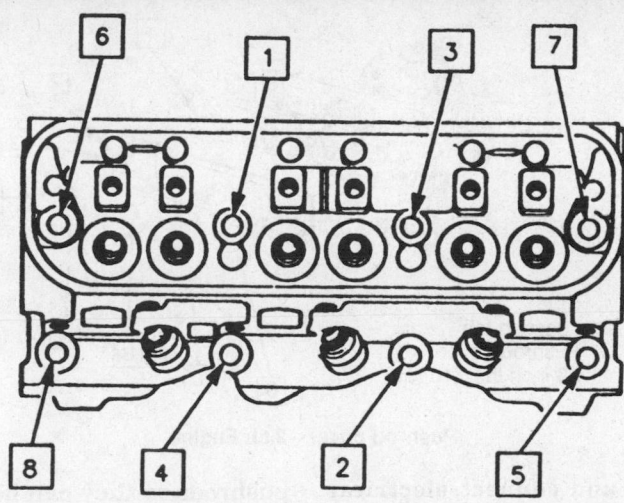

Cylinder head bolt tightening sequence—3.8L Engine

bracket and torque the bolts to 37 ft. lbs. (50 Nm).

24. Install the belt tensioner pulley.

25. Install the heater hose to the engine.

26. Install the exhaust crossover pipe.

27. Raise and support the vehicle safely.

28. Install the front exhaust pipe to the manifold and lower the vehicle.

29. Fill the cooling system, connect the negative battery cable and install the air cleaner assembly.

Valve Lifters

REMOVAL & INSTALLATION

2.3L Engine

INTAKE CAMSHAFT AND LIFTERS

1. Disconnect the negative battery cable.

2. Remove the ignition coil and module assembly electrical connections.

3. Remove the ignition coil and module from engine.

4. Remove idle speed power steering pressure switch connector.

5. Remove power steering drive belt and remove power steering pump as required.

6. Remove oil/air separator hose, fuel harness connector, vacuum hose to fuel regulator and fuel rail as required. Position fuel rail out of the way leaving fuel rail attached to fuel lines.

7. Disconnect timing chain housing but do not remove from vehicle. Install 2 bolts in timing chain housing to hold into place.

8. Remove intake cam housing cover to housing bolts.

9. Remove intake cam housing to

cylinder head retaining bolts using the reverse of the tightening sequence.

10. Remove the cover off the housing by threading 4 of the housing to head bolts into the tapped holes in the camshaft cover. Tighten bolts in evenly so not to bind the cover on the dowel pins.

11. Remove 2 loosely installed bolts in cover and remove cover. Discard gasket from cover.

12. Note position of chain sprocket dowel pin for reassembly. Remove camshaft.

13 Remove valve lifters keeping in order of removal.

To install:

14. Install lifters into bores. Used lifters must be returned to their original position. Replace all lifters if new camshaft is being installed.

15. Prelube camshaft lobes and journals and install into same position as when removed.

16. Install new camshaft housing to camshaft housing cover seals into cover. Remove bolts holding housing into place and install cover and retaining bolts. Coat housing and cover retaining bolts with pipe sealer prior to installing. Torque bolts 82A, in proper sequence, to 11 ft. lbs. plus an additional 75 degrees; on 82B bolts, torque to 11 ft. lbs. plus an additional 25 degrees.

17. Install timing chain and housing.

18. Install new O-rings on injectors and install fuel rail into cylinder head. Install fuel rail to camshaft housing bolts and tighten to 19 ft. lbs. (26 Nm).

19. Install injector wiring harness, vacuum hose to fuel pressure regulator and oil/air separator assembly.

20. Lube inner sealing surface of intake camshaft seal with clean engine oil and install seal into housing using tool J–36009 or equivalent.

21. Install drive pulley onto intake camshaft using tool J–36015 or equivalent.

22. Install power steering pump and drive belt.

23. Install idle speed power steering switch connector.

24. Install ignition module and coil

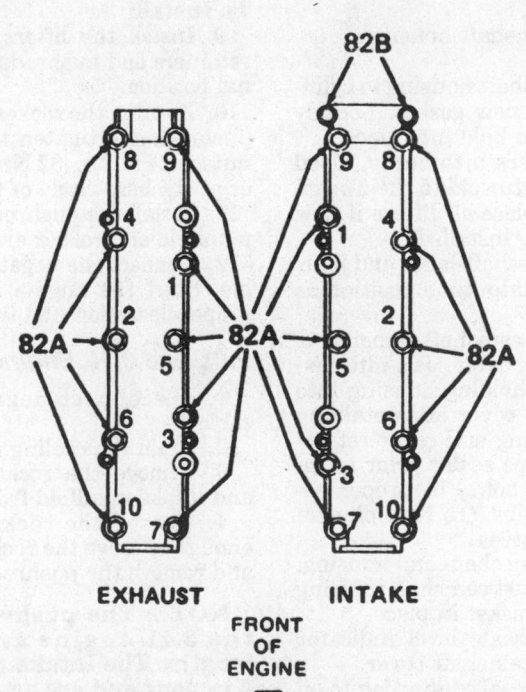

Camshaft housing bolt tightening sequence—2.3L Engine

assembly with retainer bolts and re-connect electrical connector.

25. Connect negative battery cable, start engine and check for oil leaks.

EXHAUST CAMSHAFT AND LIFTERS

1. Disconnect the negative battery cable.

2. Disconnect electrical connection from ignition coil and module assembly.

3. Remove ignition coil and module assembly from camshaft housing.

4. Disconnect electrical connector from oil pressure switch.

5. Remove transaxle fluid level indicator tube from exhaust camshaft cover and set aside for automatic transaxle only.

6. Remove exhaust camshaft cover and gasket.

7. Disconnect timing chain housing but do not remove from vehicle.

8. Remove exhaust housing to cylinder head bolts reversing the order of tightening. Leave 2 bolts loosely in place while removing cover from housing.

9. Remove the cover off the housing by threading 4 of the housing to head retaining bolts into the tapped holes in the camshaft cover. Tighten bolts in evenly so not to bind the cover on the dowel pins.

10. Remove 2 loosely installed bolts in cover and remove cover.

11. Note position of chain sprocket dowel pin for reassembly. Remove camshaft.

12. Remove valve lifters keeping in order of removal.

13. Remove camshaft housing.

To install:

14. Install camshaft housing to cylinder head with a new gasket. Loosely install one bolt to hold into place.

15. Install lifters into bores. Used lifters must be returned to their original position. Replace all lifters if new camshaft is being installed.

16. Prelube camshaft lobes and journals and install into same position as removed.

17. Install new camshaft housing to camshaft housing cover seals into cover. Remove bolt holding housing into place and install cover and retaining bolts. Coat housing and cover retaining bolts with pipe sealer prior to installing. Torque bolts, in proper sequence, to 11 ft. lbs. (15 Nm) plus an additional 75 degrees.

18. Install timing chain and housing.

19. Install exhaust camshaft housing cover with new gasket in place.

20. Install transaxle level indicator tube to exhaust camshaft cover.

21. Install electrical connection to oil pressure switch.

22. Install ignition coil and module

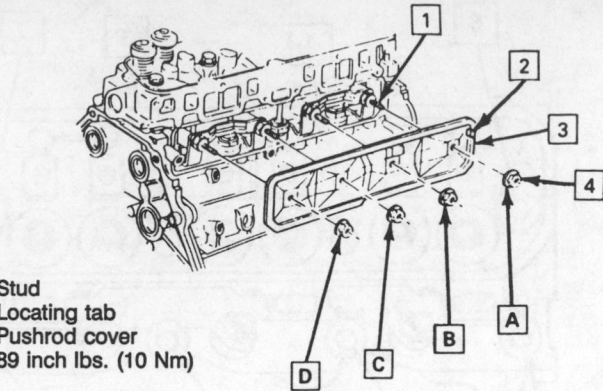

1. Stud
2. Locating tab
3. Pushrod cover
4. 89 inch lbs. (10 Nm)

Pushrod cover—2.5L Engine

assembly and connect electrical connector.

23. Install negative battery cable and start vehicle. Inspect for leaks.

2.5L Engine

1. Disconnect the negative battery cable.

2. Remove the rocker arm cover.

3. Remove the intake manifold.

4. Remove the pushrod cover.

5. Loosen the rocker arms, rotate to clear the pushrods and move to the side.

6. Mark and remove the pushrods, retainer and lifter guides.

7. Mark and remove the lifters.

NOTE: Mark each valve component location for reassembly.

8. Lubricate all bearing surfaces and lifters with clean engine oil.
To install:

9. Install the lifters, lifter guides, retainers and pushrods in their original position.

10. Position the rocker arms over the pushrods and tighten the rocker arm nuts to 24 ft. lbs. (32 Nm) with the lifter at the base circle of the camshaft.

11. Install the pushrod cover, intake manifold and rocker arm cover.

12. Connect the negative battery cable. Start the engine and check for proper operation and fluid leaks.

2.8L and 3.1L Engines

1. Disconnect negative battery cable.

2. Drain the cooling system.

3. Remove the rocker arm covers and intake manifold from the engine.

4. Loosen the rocker arms nuts enough to move the rocker arms aside and remove the pushrods.

NOTE: The pushrods used on the 3.1L engine are different lengths. The intake pushrods are 6 in. long and are orange in color. The exhaust pushrods are blue in color and are 6⅜ in. long. Label

pushrods so they can be installed in their original position during assembly.

Some 3.1L engines may contain oversized lifters. Where oversized lifters are used, the cylinder case will be marked with white paint or 0.25mm will be stamped on the lifter boss. If replacement of the lifter is required, use the correct size lifters with a narrow flat ground along the lower ¾ of lifter. This flat will allow for additional oil to flow to the cam lobe and the lifter surfaces.

5. Remove the lifters from the engine keeping in order or removal. If original lifter is being reused, it is essential that they be installed in their original position.
To install:

6. Using Molykote® or equivalent, coat the base of the new lifters and install them into the engine.

7. Position the pushrods and the rocker arms correctly into their original positions. Torque the rocker arm nuts to 18 ft. lbs. (25 Nm).

8. Install the intake manifold and tighten the intake manifold-to-cylinder head bolts to specification following the torque sequence.

9. Install the rocker cover.

10. Connect the negative battery cable and fill the cooling system. Start the engine, check for proper operation and fluid leaks.

3.4L Engine

LEFT SIDE (FRONT)

1. Disconnect the negative battery cable. Drain the cooling system.

2. Remove left side cam carrier as follows:

a. Disconnect oil/air breather hose from cam carrier cover. Remove spark plug wires from plugs and remove rear spark plug wire cover.

b. Remove cam carrier cover bolts

and lift off cover. Remove gasket and O-rings from cover.

c. Remove secondary timing belt by removing secondary timing belt actuator and tensioner assembly and sliding belt from pulleys.

d. Install 6 sections of fuel line hoses under cam shaft and between lifters. This will hold lifters in the carrier. For this procedure use $3/16$ in. fuel line hose for exhaust valves and $5/32$ in. fuel line hose for the intake valves.

e. Remove exhaust crossover pipe and torque strut.

f. Remove torque strut bracket at engine.

g. Remove cam carrier mounting bolts and nuts and remove cam carrier.

h. Remove cam carrier gasket from cylinder head.

3. Remove the 6 lifter hold-down hoses. Remove the lifters.

NOTE: Valve lifters must be kept in order so they can be installed in their original position.

To install:

4. Lubricate lifters with clean engine oil and install lifters into original position.

5. Install lifter hold-down hoses to cam carrier.

6. Install cam carrier following these steps:

a. Install new gasket on cam carrier to cylinder mounting surface.

b. Install cam hold-down tool J–38613 or equivalent, to carrier assembly.

c. Install cam carrier to cylinder head. Install mounting bolts and nuts. Torque bolts and nuts to 18 ft. lbs.

d. Remove lifter hold-down hoses and cam hold-down tool.

e. Install torque strut bracket to engine and install torque strut.

f. Install engine crossover pipe.

g. Install secondary timing belt and cam carrier cover.

h. Reconnect spark plug cover and wires.

i. Connect breather hose to cam carrier cover.

7. Add fluids as required, reconnect negative battery cable. Start engine and recheck for leaks.

RIGHT SIDE (REAR)

1. Disconnect the negative battery cable. Drain cooling system.

2. Remove right side cam carrier as follows:

a. Remove intake plenum and right timing belt cover.

b. Remove right spark plug wires.

c. Remove air/oil separator hose at cam carrier cover.

d. Remove cam carrier cover bolts

and lift of cover. Remove gasket and O-rings from cover.

e. Remove secondary timing belt by removing secondary timing belt actuator and tensioner assembly and sliding belt from pulleys.

f. Install 6 sections of fuel line hoses under cam shaft and between lifters. This will hold lifters in carrier. For this procedure use $3/16$ in. fuel line hose for exhaust valves and $5/32$ in. fuel line hose for the intake valves.

g. Remove exhaust crossover pipe and torque strut.

h. Remove torque strut bracket at engine. Remove front engine lift hook.

i. Remove cam carrier mounting bolts and nuts and remove cam carrier.

j. Remove cam carrier gasket from cylinder head.

3. Remove 6 lifter hold-down hoses.

4. Remove lifters keeping in order of removal.

NOTE: Valve lifters must be kept in order so they can be installed in their original position.

To install:

5. Lubricate lifters with clean engine oil and install lifters into original position.

6. Install lifter hold-down hoses to cam carrier.

7. Install cam carrier following these steps:

a. Install new gasket on cam carrier to cylinder mounting surface.

b. Install cam hold-down tool J–38613 or equivalent, to carrier assembly.

c. Install cam carrier to cylinder head. Install mounting bolts and nuts. Torque bolts and nuts to 18 ft. lbs.

d. Remove lifter hold-down hoses and cam hold-down tool.

e. Install torque strut bracket to engine and install torque strut.

f. Install engine crossover pipe and engine lift hook.

g. Install secondary timing belt and cam carrier cover.

h. Install spark plug wires and cover.

8. Add fluids as required. Connect negative battery cable. Start engine and check for fluid leaks.

3.8L Engine

1. Disconnect negative battery cable.

2. Drain the cooling system.

3. Remove the rocker arm covers and intake manifold.

4. Remove the rocker arm assemblies.

5. Remove the guide retainer bolts and retainer.

NOTE: Be sure to keep all valve train components in order so they can be reinstalled in their original locations and with the same mating surfaces as when removed.

6. Remove the valve lifter guides and the valve lifters keeping in order of removal.

To install:

7. Prelube (dip) the valve lifters with oil before installation.

8. Install the lifter guides, guide retainers and bolts and torque to 22 ft. lbs. (30 Nm).

9. Install the rocker arm assemblies, intake manifold and valve covers.

10. Fill the cooling system and connect the negative battery cable. Start the engine and check for proper operation and fluid leaks.

Valve Lash

ADJUSTMENT

All engines use hydraulic valve lifters. No adjustment is necessary.

Rocker Arms

REMOVAL & INSTALLATION

2.5L Engine

1. Disconnect the negative battery cable.

2. Remove the rocker arm cover.

3. Remove the rocker arm bolt and ball.

4. Remove the rocker arm and guide.

NOTE: Mark all valve components so they are reinstalled in their original location. The pushrods are of different lenghts and must be installed in their original locations.

5. If removed, install the pushrod through the cylinder head and into the lifter seat.

6. Install the guide, rocker arm, ball and bolt. Tighten the rocker arm bolts to 24 ft. lbs. (32 Nm)

7. Install the rocker arm cover and connect the negative battery cable.

2.8L and 3.1L Engines

LEFT SIDE

1. Disconnect the negative battery cable. Remove the air cleaner assembly.

2. Remove the ignition wire clamps

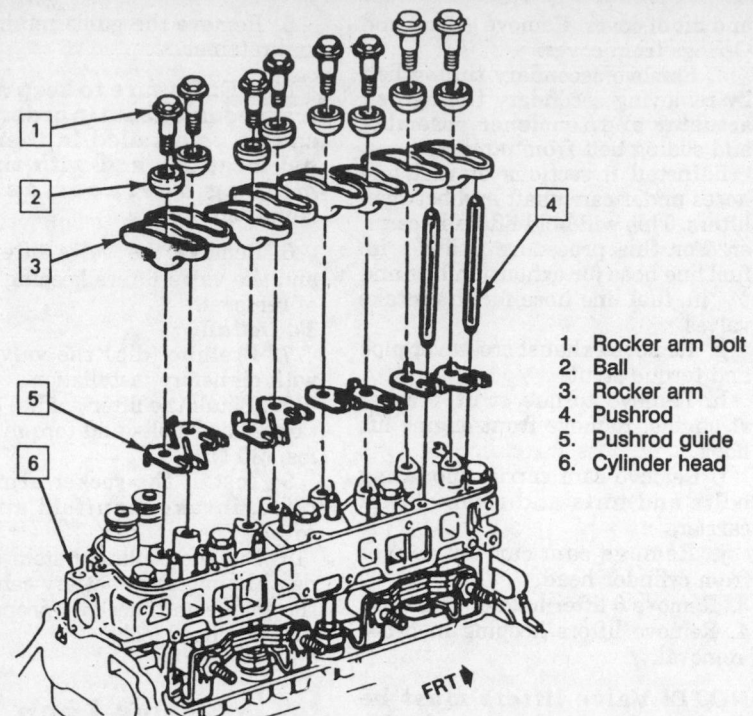

1. Rocker arm bolt
2. Ball
3. Rocker arm
4. Pushrod
5. Pushrod guide
6. Cylinder head

Rocker arms, pushrods and guides—2.5L Engine

from coolant tube. Disconnect the bracket tube from the rocker cover.

3. Remove the spark plug wire cover. Drain the cooling system and remove the heater hose from the filler neck. Remove the coolant hose at the coolant pump and the coolant tube.

4. On 2.5L engine, remove the EGR valve.

5. Remove the rocker arm cover-to-cylinder head bolts and the rocker cover.

NOTE: If the rocker arm cover will not lift off the cylinder head easily, strike the end with the palm of the hand or a rubber mallet.

6. Remove the rocker arm nuts and remove the rocker arms, keep the components in order for installation purposes.

7. Clean the gasket mounting surfaces.

8. To install rocker arms torque the rocker arm nuts to 18–20 ft. lbs. (25–27 Nm).

9. To install new rocker cover gaskets apply a bead of sealant, GM 1052917 or equivalent, to the rocker cover and position on head.

10. Install the spark plug wire cover. Install EGR valve, if removed.

11. Attach the heater hose to the filler neck. Attach the coolant hose at the coolant pump. Fill the cooling system.

12. Install negative battery cable and air cleaner assembly. Start vehicle and check for leaks.

RIGHT SIDE

1. Disconnect the negative battery cable. Disconnect the brake booster vacuum line from the bracket.

2. Disconnect the cable bracket from the plenum. Disconnect throttle, cruise control and transaxle cable from throttle body.

3. Drain cooling system and remove coolant hose at throttle body. Remove coolant recovery tank.

4. Remove serpentine belt. Remove

EGR tube at crossover pipe and disconnect crossover pipe from exhaust pipe.

5. Disconnect the vacuum line bracket from the cable bracket.

6. Disconnect the lines from the alternator brace stud.

7. Remove the rear alternator brace and the serpentine drive belt.

8. Remove the alternator and position aside.

9. Remove the PCV valve.

10. Loosen the alternator bracket.

11. Disconnect the spark plug wires from the spark plugs. Remove the rocker cover-to-cylinder head bolts and the rocker cover.

NOTE: If the rocker arm cover will not lift off the cylinder head easily, strike the end with the palm of the hand or a rubber mallet.

12. Remove the rocker arm nuts and the rocker arms; be sure to keep the components in order for installation purposes.

To install:

13. Clean the gasket mounting surfaces.

14. Install rocker assembly and torque nuts to 18 ft. lbs. (25 Nm).

15. To install, use new rocker cover gaskets apply a bead of sealant, GM 1052917 or equivalent, to the rocker cover and torque cover bolts to 89 inch lbs. (10 Nm).

16. Install the spark plug wire cover and attach the heater hose to the filler neck. Install coolant recovery tank and hose at throttle body. Fill the cooling system.

17. Reconnect exhaust crossover pipe and exhaust pipe.

1. Cylinder head
2. Hydraulic valve lifter
3. Lifter guide
4. Valve lifter pushrod guide
5. Rocker arms
6. 28 ft. lbs.
7. Pushrod

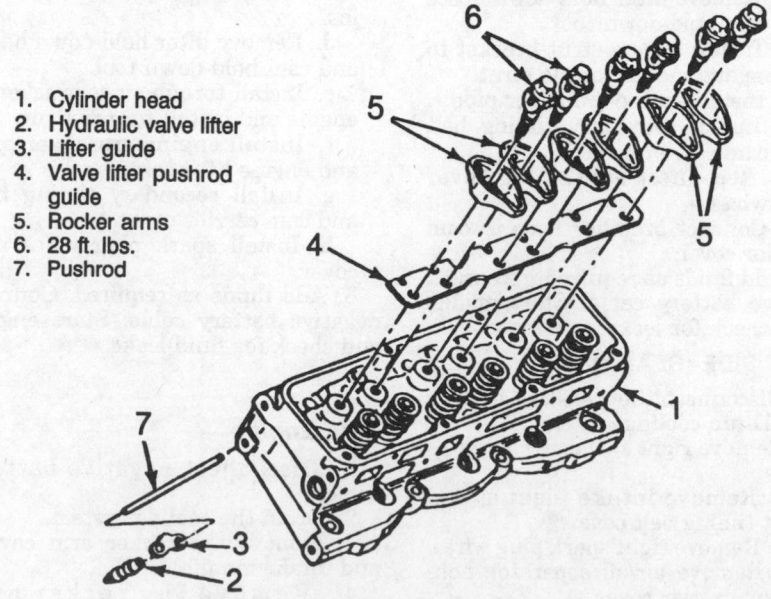

Rocker arm installation—3.8L Engine

18. install serpentine belt.

19. Install throttle, transaxle and cruise control cables to throttle body and resecure cable bracket.

20. Refasten all electrical and vacuum connection.

21. Install negative battery cable and air cleaner assembly and start engine. Check for fluid leaks.

3.8L Engine

1. Disconnect the negative battery cable.

2. Remove the valve cover.

3. Remove the rocker arm pedestal retaining bolts and remove the pedestal and rocker arm assembly.

4. Remove the pushrods keeping in order of removal.

NOTE: Store components in order so they can reassembled in the same location.

To install:

5. Install the pushrods and make sure they seat in the lifter.

6. Apply a thread lock compound to the bolt threads before reasssembly.

7. Install the pedestal and rocker arm assemblies and tighten the retaining bolts to 28 ft. lbs. (38 Nm).

8. Install the valve covers and connect the negative battery cable.

9. Start engine and check for fliud leaks.

Intake Manifold

REMOVAL & INSTALLATION

2.3L Engine

1. Disconnect the negative battery cable. Drain the cooling system.

2. Remove the coolant fan shroud. Disconnect the vacuum hoses and electrical connectors from the MAP and MAT sensors and purge solenoid.

3. Disconnect the throttle body to air cleaner duct.

4. Remove the throttle cable bracket.

5. Remove the power brake vacuum hose, including the retaining bracket to power steering bracket and position aside.

6. Remove the throttle body from the intake manifold with electrical harness, coolant hoses, vacuum hoses and throttle cable attached. Position these components aside.

7. Remove the oil/air separator bolts and hoses. Leave the hoses attached to the separator, disconnect from the oil fill, chain housing and the intake manifold. Remove as an assembly.

8. Remove the oil fill cap and oil level indicator stick.

9. Remove the oil fill tube retainer bolt. Pull the oil tube fill upward to unseat from block and remove.

10. Disconnect the injector harness connectors from each injector.

11. Remove the fill tube, rotating as necessary to gain clearance for the oil/air separator nipple between the intake tubes and fuel rail electrical harness.

12. Remove the intake manifold support bracket bolts and nut. Remove the intake manifold retaining nuts and bolts.

13. Remove the intake manifold from the engine.

To install:

14. Thoroughly clean and dry the mating surfaces. Install new gaskets and place the intake manifold in position.

NOTE: When installing new intake manifold gaskets, make sure the numbers stamped on the surface of the gasket face toward the manifold surface.

15. Tighten the intake manifold bolts/nuts, in sequence, to 18 ft. lbs. (25 Nm). Tighten intake manifold brace and retainers hand-tight. Tighten brace retainers to specifications in the following order:

a. Nut to stud bolt—18 ft. lbs. (25 Nm)

b. Bolt to intake manifold—40 ft. lbs. (55 Nm)

c. Bolt to cylinder block—40 ft. lbs. (55 Nm)

16. Lubricate a new oil fill tube ring seal with engine oil and install tube between No. 1 and 2 intake tubes. Rotate as necessary to gain clearance for oil/air separator nipple on fill tube.

17. Locate the oil fill tube in its cylinder block opening. Align the fill tube so it is approximately in its installed position. Press straight down to seat fill tube and seal into cylinder block.

18. Lubricate the hoses and install the oil/air separator assembly.

19. Install throttle body to intake manifold using a new gasket. Instal the coolant hoses to the throttle body.

20. Install the power brake vacuum hose and the retaining bracket to power steering bracket.

21. Install the throttle cable bracket.

22. Connect the throttle body to air cleaner duct.

23. Install the coolant fan shroud, vacuum hoses and electrical connectors to the appropriate sensors and fittings.

24. Drain and replace the engine oil and replace the oil filter. Fill the remaining fluids to the proper levels.

25. Connect the negative battery cable, start the engine and check for leaks.

2.5L Engine

1. Disconnect the negative battery cable.

2. Remove the air cleaner assembly.

3. Remove the PCV valve and hose at the throttle body assembly.

4. Drain the engine coolant at the radiator.

5. Release the fuel pressure and remove the fuel lines from the throttle body.

6. Remove the vacuum lines and brake booster hose from the throttle body.

7. Remove all linkage and wiring from the TBI assembly.

8. Remove the power steering pump and position aside.

9. Remove the heater hose.

10. Remove the 7 intake manifold retaining bolts and the manifold.

To install:

11. Clean all gasket surfaces on the cylinder head and intake manifold.

12. Install the intake manifold with a new gasket.

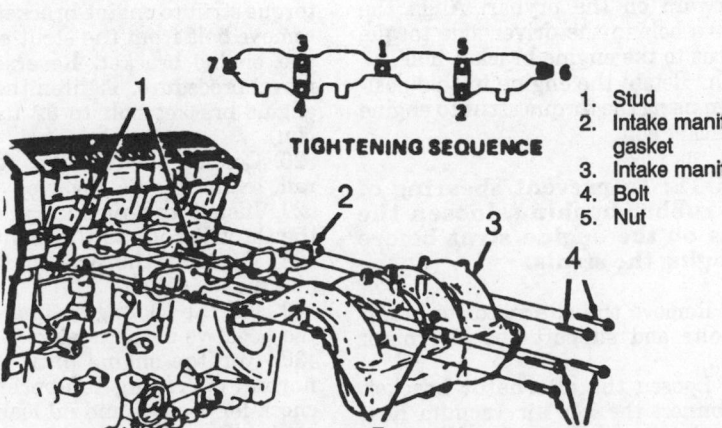

TIGHTENING SEQUENCE

1. Stud
2. Intake manifold gasket
3. Intake manifold
4. Bolt
5. Nut

Intake manifold Installation—2.3L Engine

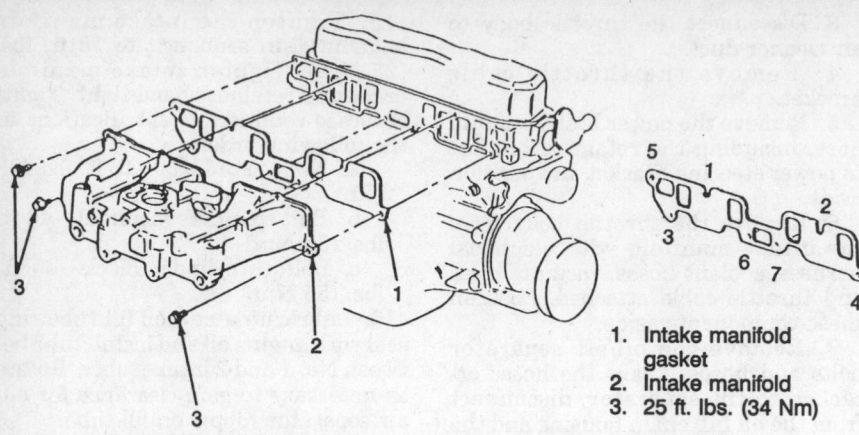

1. Intake manifold gasket
2. Intake manifold
3. 25 ft. lbs. (34 Nm)

Intake manifold Installation and torque sequence—2.5L Engine

13. Install all the retaining bolts and washers hand-tight.

14. Tighten the bolts, in proper sequence, to 25 ft. lbs. (34 Nm)

15. Install power steering pump assembly and tighten bolts to 20 ft. lbs. (27 Nm).

16. Install all heater hoses, vacuum hoses, throttle linkages and wiring.

17. Install the fuel lines using new O-rings at each connection.

18. Install the PCV valve and hose to the TBI assembly.

19. Refill the engine coolant.

20. Install the air cleaner assembly and connect the negative battery cable.

21. Start the engine and check for fluid leaks.

2.8L and 3.1L Engines

1. Disconnect the negative battery

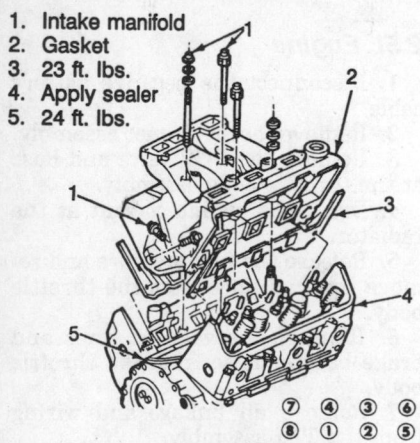

1. Intake manifold
2. Gasket
3. 23 ft. lbs.
4. Apply sealer
5. 24 ft. lbs.

Intake manifold Installation—
2.8L and 3.1L Engines

FRONT ⑦ ④ ③ ⑥
← ⑧ ① ② ⑤

Intake manifold torque sequence—
2.8L and 3.1L Engines

cable. Drain the cooling system. Relieve fuel system pressure.

2. Disconnect the TV and accelerator cables from the plenum.

3. Remove the throttle body-to-plenum bolts and the throttle body. Remove the EGR valve.

4. Remove the plenum-to-intake manifold bolts and the plenum. Disconnect and plug the fuel lines and return pipes at the fuel rail.

5. Remove the serpentine drive belt. Remove the power steering pump-to-bracket bolts and support the pump out of the way; do not disconnect the pressure hoses.

6. Rotate the engine as follows:
   a. Put the transaxle in **N**.
   b. Remove the air cleaner.
   c. Disconnect the negative battery cable.
   d. Remove the torque strut to engine bracket bolt and swing strut aside.
   e. Replace the passenger side torque strut to engine bracket bolt in engine bracket.
   f. Place a prybar in the bracket so it contacts the bracket and the bolt.
   g. Rotate the engine by pulling forward on the prybar. Align the slave hole in the driver side torque strut to the engine bracket hole.
   h. Retain the engine in this position using the torque strut to engine bracket bolt.

NOTE: To prevent shearing of the rubber bushing, loosen the bolts on the engine strut before swinging the struts.

7. Remove the alternator-to-bracket bolts and support the alternator aside.

8. Loosen the alternator bracket. Disconnect the idle air vacuum hose from the throttle body.

9. Label and disconnect the electrical connectors from the fuel injectors. Remove the fuel rail.

10. Remove the breather tube. Disconnect the runners.

11. Remove both rocker arm cover-to-cylinder head bolts and the covers. Remove the radiator hose from the thermostat housing.

12. Label and disconnect the electrical connectors from the coolant temperature sensor and oil pressure sending unit. Remove the coolant sensor.

13. Remove the bypass hose from the filler neck and cylinder head. Remove top radiator hose.

14. Remove the intake manifold-to-cylinder head bolts and the manifold.

15. Loosen the rocker arm nuts, turn them 90 degrees and remove the pushrods; be sure to keep the components in order for installation purposes.

16. Clean all of the gasket mounting surfaces.

To install:

17. Place a bead of RTV sealer or equivalent on each ridge where the intake manifold and block meet. Install the intake manifold gasket in place on the block.

18. Install the pushrods and reposition the rocker arms, tighten the rocker arm nuts to 18 ft. lbs. (25 Nm).

19. Mount the intake manifold on the engine and tighten the bolts to 23 ft. lbs. (29 Nm) following the tightening sequence.

20. Connect the heater inlet pipe to the manifold. Install and connect the coolant sensor.

21. Attach the radiator hoses. Connect the wire at the oil sending switch.

22. Install the rocker covers, tighten the retaining bolts to 90 inch lbs. (10 Nm).

23. Install the runners, breather tube, fuel rail and connect the wires at the fuel injectors.

24. Install the alternator bracket and the alternator. Install the power steering pump.

25. After repairs, pull forward on the prybar to take the weight off of the torque strut to engine bracket bolt and remove bolt from the strut slave hole and engine bracket. Reverse the removal procedure. Tighten the strut to engine bracket bolt to 32 ft. lbs. (43 Nm).

26. Connect the fuel lines to the fuel rail. Install the EGR valve.

27. Install the plenum and mount the throttle body to the plenum.

28. Connect the accelerator cable and the TV cable.

29. Fill the cooling system. Connect the negative battery cable.

30. Run the engine until it reaches normal operating temperature and check for coolant and oil leaks.

3.4L Engine

1. Relieve fuel system pressure and disconnect negative battery cable.

2. Drain the cooling system.
3. Remove the intake plenum as follows:

   a. Remove the air cleaner assembly.

   b. Remove the control cables from the throttle body.

   c. Remove the fuel rail cover bolts and the fuel rail from the engine.

   d. Disconnect the fuel supply and return lines at the fuel rail.

   e. Disconnect the heater hose from the intake manifold. Disconnect the vacuum hose from the PCV valve and the throttle body. Disconnect the vacuum hose tee on the plunum.

   f. Disconnect the electrical harness connectors at the AIR solenoid, EGR valve, canister purge valve, MAP sensor and the Throttle Position Sensor (TPS).

   g. Remove the EGR mounting bolts and separate the valve from the manifold.

   h. Remove the throttle heater hose at the plenum. Remove the fuel line bracket at the throttle body plenum.

   i. Remove the nuts from the plenum support bracket. Remove the plenum mounting bolts and the intake plenum from the engine.
4. Remove fuel rail from the engine.
5. Remove the radiator hose from

1. Bolt torque to 18 ft. lbs.
2. Intake manifold
3. Gasket
4. Cylinder head

FRT

Intake manifold—3.4L Engine

the thermostat housing. Disconnect the electrical connector at the temperature sensor.

6. Remove the heater pipe nut at the throttle body.
7. Remove intake manifold mount-

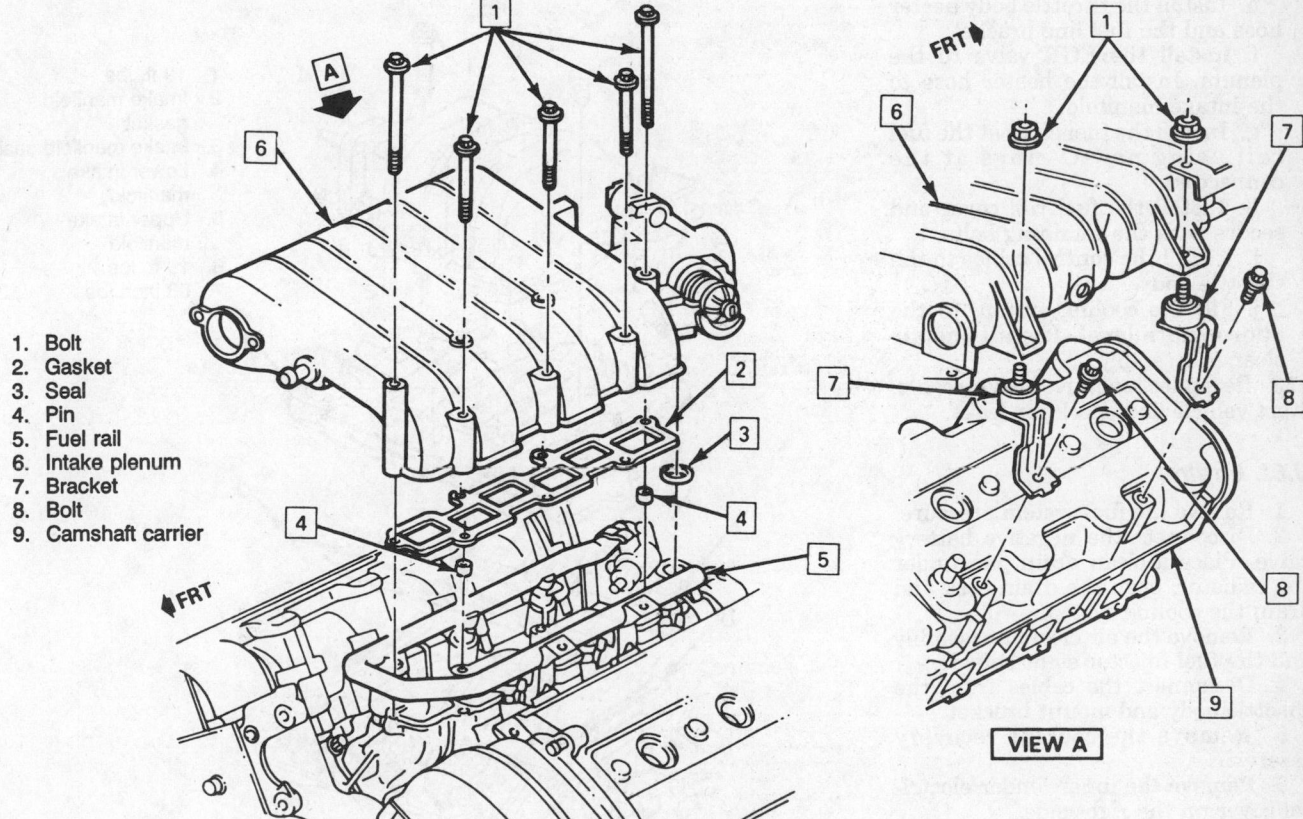

1. Bolt
2. Gasket
3. Seal
4. Pin
5. Fuel rail
6. Intake plenum
7. Bracket
8. Bolt
9. Camshaft carrier

FRT

VIEW A

Intake plenum—3.4L Engine

ing bolts and manifold from the engine.

To install:

8. Clean mating surfaces and install new gaskets.

9. Install intake manifold. Insert rubber isolators into manifold flange. Draw manifold in place by tightening bolts gradually, starting with the center bolts and working outward in a circular pattern. Tighten mounting bolts to 18 ft. lbs. (25 Nm). Start with center bolts and work in a circular pattern.

10. Install the heater hose pipe nut at the throttle body.

11. Connect the electrical connector at the temperature sensor.

12. Install the radiator hose to the throttle body.

13. Install the fuel rail to the engine.

14. Install the intake plenum as follows:

a. Clean gasket material from all mating surfaces. Install the intake plenum with new gaskets in place. Tighten the plenum retainer bolts to 89 inch lbs. (10 Nm).

b. Install the nut at the plenum support bracket and tighten to 18 ft. lbs. (25 nm).

c. Install the wire loom bracket for the rear spark plugs. Install the vacuum hoses the tee on the plenum.

d. Connect all harness connectors to the appropriate components.

e. Install the throttle body heater hose and the fuel line bracket.

f. Install the EGR valve to the plenum. Install the heater hose to the intake manifold.

g. Install the fuel pipes at the fuel rail using new O-rings at the connectors.

h. Install the fuel rail cover and secure with the retaining bolts.

i. Install the control cables to the throttle body.

j. Fill the cooling system to the appropriate level. Install the air cleaner assembly.

15. Reconnect negative battery cable, start vehicle and check for leaks.

3.8L Engine

1. Relieve the fuel system pressure.

2. Disconnect the negative battery cable. Place a clean drain pan under the radiator, open the drain cock and drain the cooling system.

3. Remove the air cleaner assembly and the fuel injector sight shield.

4. Disconnect the cables from the throttle body and mount bracket.

5. Remove the coolant recovery reservoir.

6. Remove the inner fender electrical cover on the right side.

7. Remove the right rear crossover pipe heat shield.

8. Disconnect the fuel lines from the fuel rail and from the cable bracket.

9. Remove the alternator and brace and position aside.

10. Remove the throttle body cable mounting bracket with the vacuum lines and disconnect the vacuum lines.

11. Tag and disconnect the electrical connections at the throttle body and both banks of fuel injectors.

12. Disconnect the vacuum hoses from the canister purge solenoid valve, transaxle module and intake connection.

13. Disconnect the power steering pump and move forward. Remove the belt tensioner pulley from the mounting bracket.

14. Disconnect the spark plug wires and lay aside.

15. Disconnect the coolant bypass hose from the intake manifold.

16. Disconnect the solenoid valve mounting bracket and power steering support brace from the intake manifold.

17. Disconnect the heater pipes from the intake and front cover.

18. Disconnect the alternator support brace from the intake.

19. Disconnect the upper radiator hose from the housing.

20. Remove the thermostat housing and thermostat from the intake.

21. Disconnect the electrical connector from the temperature sensor and sensor switch.

22. Remove the intake manifold bolts and manifold as an assembly from the vehicle.

23. Remove the upper intake manifold as follows:

a. Remove the fuel injectors from the manifold.

b. Remove the coolant sensor switch.

c. Remove the manifold end covers.

d. Remove the upper intake manifold and the throttle body from the manifold.

To install:

24. Clean all gasket material from the manifold mating surfaces.

25. Apply a $\frac{1}{15}$ in. bead of Loctite® Instalnt Gasket Eliminator or equivalent, to the lower manifold mating surfaces making sure to circle all bolt holes.

26. Install upper intake manifold onto the lower manifold and install bolts tightening to 22 ft. lbs. (30 Nm).

27. Install the manifold end cap covers and the coolant sensor switch.

28. Install the fuel injectors and rail to the manifold.

29. Install intake manifold gaskets to the engine. Apply sealer to ends of in-

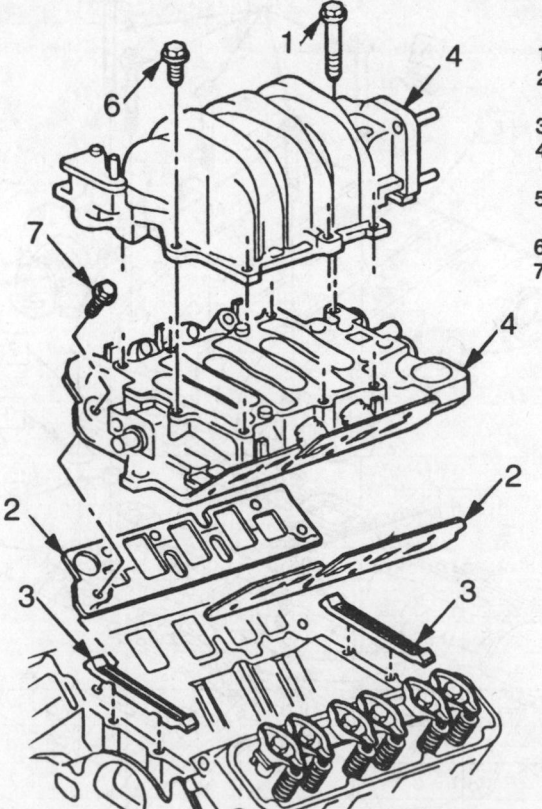

1. 19 ft. lbs.
2. Intake manifold gasket
3. Intake manifold seal
4. Lower intake manifold
5. Upper intake manifold
6. 19 ft. lbs.
7. 88 inch lbs.

Intake manifold installation—3.8L Engine

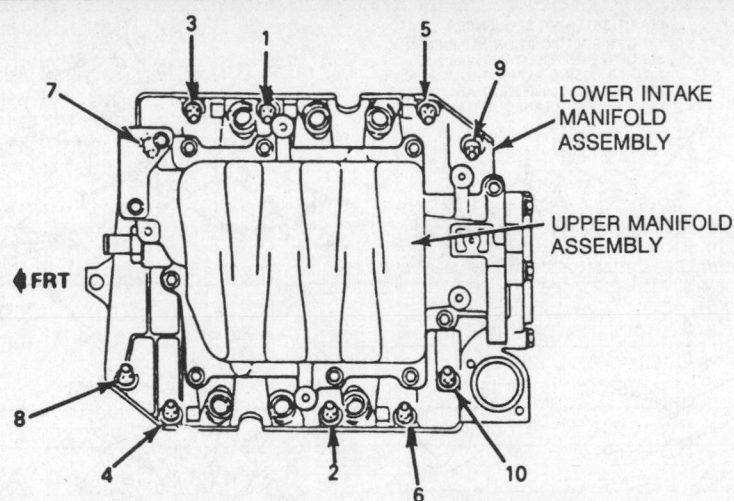

Intake manifold torque sequence—3.8L Engine

take manifold seals. Install intake manifold assembly.

30. Apply thread lock compound to the intake manifold bolt threads and install. Tighten the manifold bolts to 88 inch lbs. (10 Nm), twice following the torque sequence.

31. Install the electrical connector at the temperature sensor switch at intake.

32. Install the thermostat housing and thermostat with a new gasket.

33. Connect the alternator support brace to the intake.

34. Connect the solenoid valve mounting bracket and power steering support brace to the intake manifold.

35. Connect the heater pipes to the intake and front cover.

36. Connect the coolant bypass hose to the intake manifold.

37. Install the power steering pump support bracket and torque to 37 ft. lbs.

38. Install the spark plug wires on both sides.

39. Install the belt tensioner pulley and tighten to 33 ft. lbs.

40. Install the power steering pump.

41. Connect the vacuum hoses to the canister purge solenoid valve and transaxle module and intake connection.

42. Connect the electrical connections at the throttle body and both banks of fuel injectors.

43. Install the alternator and brace.

44. Connect the throttle body cable

mounting bracket with the vacuum lines.

45. Install the right rear crossover pipe heat shield.

46. Install the cables to the throttle body.

47. Connect the fuel lines to the fuel rail and mount bracket.

48. Install the inner fender electrical cover on the right side.

49. Install the coolant recovery reservoir and upper radiator hose. Fill the cooling system.

50. Install the air cleaner assembly and the fuel injector sight shield.

51. Connect the negative battery cable.

Exhaust Manifold

REMOVAL & INSTALLATION

2.3L Engine

1. Disconnect the negative battery cable and oxygen sensor connector.

2. Remove upper and lower exhaust manifold heat shields.

3. Remove the bolt that attaches the exhaust manifold brace to the manifold.

4. Break loose the manifold to exhaust pipe spring loaded bolts using a 13mm box wrench.

5. Raise the vehicle and support safely.

NOTE: It is necessary to relieve the spring pressure from 1 bolt prior to removing the second bolt. If the spring pressure is not relieved it will cause the exhaust pipe to twist and bind up the bolt as it is removed.

6. Remove the manifold to exhaust pipe bolts from the exhaust pipe flange as follows:
    a. Unscrew either bolt clockwise 4 turns.
    b. Remove the other bolt.
    c. Remove the first bolt.

7. Pull down and back on the exhaust pipe to disengage it from the exhaust manifold bolts.

8. Lower the vehicle.

9. Remove the exhaust manifold mounting bolts and remove the manifold.

To install:

10. Install the exhaust manifold to engine with new gasket in place. Install retaining nuts and tighten to specifications following the torque sequence.

11. Tighten the exhaust manifold to cylinder head nuts to 27 ft. lbs. (376 Nm) and the exhaust manifold to cylinder head studs to 106 inch lbs. (12 Nm).

12. Install the exhaust manifold

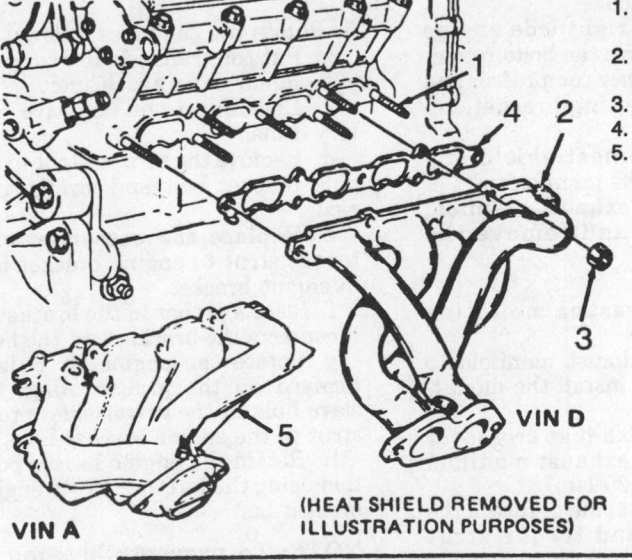

1. Exhaust manifold to cylinder head stud
2. Manifold assembly (VIN D)
3. Nut
4. Gasket
5. Manifold assembly (VIN A)

(HEAT SHIELD REMOVED FOR ILLUSTRATION PURPOSES)

Exhaust manifold installation and torque sequence—2.3L Engine

1. Gasket
2. Exhaust manifold
3. Lock
4. 26 ft. lbs. (35 Nm)
5. 26 ft. lbs. (35 Nm)
6. 37 ft. lbs. (50 Nm)
7. 37 ft. lbs. (50 Nm)

8. Note: When installing the lock tabs on the exhaust manifold, one tab must be bent against a flat of the hex to prevent rotation.

BOLT TIGHTENING SEQUENCE
TIGHTEN BOLT POSITION NUMBER IN SEQUENCE AS FOLLOWS: 3-5-6-2-1-7-4 OR BY USING ALPHA GROUPS "A" AND "B". "A" BEING FIRST AND "B" LAST. OR SIMULTANEOUS GANG DRIVE.

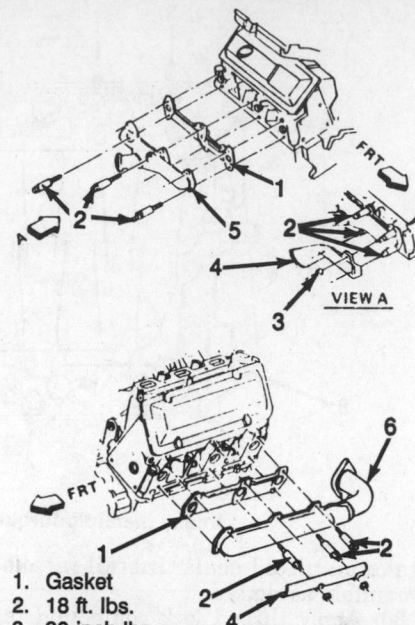

VIEW A

VIEW B

Exhaust manifold installation and torque sequence—2.5L Engine

1. Gasket
2. 18 ft. lbs.
3. 90 inch lbs.
4. Heat shield
5. Right exhaust manifold
6. Left exhaust manifold

Exhaust manifold installation— 2.8L and 3.1L Engines

brace to manifold bolt. Raise and safely support the vehicle.

13. Install the exhaust pipe to the manifold and secure with the spring loaded nuts. Turn both nuts in evenly to avoid cocking the exhaust pipe and binding the nuts. Turn nuts in until fully seated.

14. Lower the vehicle. Install the heat shields and connect the electrical harness to the oxygen sensor.

15. Connect the negative battery and start the engine. Check for exhaust leaks.

2.5L Engine

1. Disconnect the negative battery cable.

2. Remove the torque strut bolts at the radiator panel and cylinder head.

3. Remove the oxygen sensor and the oil level indicator tube.

4. Raise and safely support the vehicle.

5. Remove the exhaust pipe from the manifold and lower the vehicle.

6. Bend rocking tabs away from the bolts and remove the retaining bolts and washers.

7. Remove the exhaust manifold and gasket.

To install:

8. Clean the sealing surfaces of the cylinder head and manifold.

9. Lubricate the bolt threads with anti-seize compound and install the exhaust manifold with a new gasket.

10. Tighten the bolts in sequence to the appropriate torque.

11. Bend the locking tabs against the bolts.

12. Raise and support the vehicle safely.

13. Install the exhaust pipe to the manifold and lower the vehicle.

14. Install the oil level indicator

tube, oxygen sensor and torque rod bracket at the cylinder head and radiator support.

15. Connect the negative battery cable.

2.8L and 3.1L Engines

LEFT SIDE

1. Disconnect the negative battery cable.

2. Remove the coolant recovery bottle.

3. Relieve the accessory drive belt tension and remove the belt.

4. Remove the air conditioner compressor mounting bolts and support the compressor aside.

5. Remove the right side engine torque strut. Remove the bolts retaining the air conditioner compressor and torque strut mounting bracket, remove the bracket.

6. Remove the heat shield and crossover pipe at the manifold.

7. Remove the exhaust manifold mounting bolts and remove the manifold.

To install:

8. Clean the gasket mounting surfaces.

9. Install the exhaust manifold to the engine, loosely install the mounting bolts.

10. Install the exhaust crossover pipe. Tighten the exhaust manifold bolts to 18 ft. lbs. (25 Nm)

11. Attach the heat shield. Install the air conditioner and torque strut mounting bracket.

12. Install the torque strut. Mount the air conditioner compressor and install the accessory drive belt.

13. Install the coolant recovery bottle and connect the negative battery cable.

RIGHT SIDE

1. Disconnect the negative battery cable.

2. Raise and safely support the vehicle.

3. Remove the exhaust pipe at the crossover. Lower the vehicle.

4. Remove the coolant recovery bottle.

5. Rotate the engine as follows:

a. Put the transaxle in N.

b. Remove the air cleaner.

c. Disconnect the negative battery cable.

d. Remove the torque strut to engine bracket bolt and swing strut aside.

e. Replace the passenger side torque strut to engine bracket bolt in engine bracket.

f. Place a prybar in the bracket so it contacts the bracket and the bolt.

g. Rotate the engine by pulling forward on the prybar. Align the slave hole in the driver side torque strut to the engine bracket hole.

h. Retain the engine in this position using the torque strut to engine bracket bolt.

NOTE: To prevent shearing of the rubber bushing, loosen the bolts on the engine strut before swinging the struts.

6. Remove the air cleaner, breather, mass air flow sensor and heat shield.

7. Remove the crossover at the

manifold. Disconnect the accelerator and TV cables.

8. Remove the manifold mounting bolts and remove the manifold. Clean the manifold mounting surfaces.

To install:

9. Install the exhaust manifold and loosely install the mounting bolts.

10. Attach the crossover at the manifold. Tighten the manifold mounting bolts to 18 ft. lbs. (25 Nm).

11. Connect the accelerator and TV cables.

12. Attach the air cleaner, breather and mass air flow sensor.

13. Position the engine in it's normal resting position as follows:

    a. Pull forward on the prybar to take the weight off the torque strut to engine bracket bolt.

    b. Remove bolt from the strut slave hole and engine bracket.

    c. Position the strut to the engine and tighten the strut to engine bracket bolt to 32 ft. lbs. (43 Nm).

14. Install the coolant recovery bottle.

15. Raise and safely support the vehicle. Install the exhaust pipe to the crossover.

16. Lower the vehicle. Connect the negative battery cable.

3.4L Engine

LEFT SIDE (FRONT)

1. Remove air cleaner assembly. Disconnect the negative battery cable.

2. Remove exhaust crossover .

3. Remove the engine torque strut bracket at frame and position out of the way.

4. Remove upper radiator shroud. Remove the cooling fan assembly.

5. Remove front hose from air pipe for manual transaxle only.

6. Remove exhaust retaining nuts

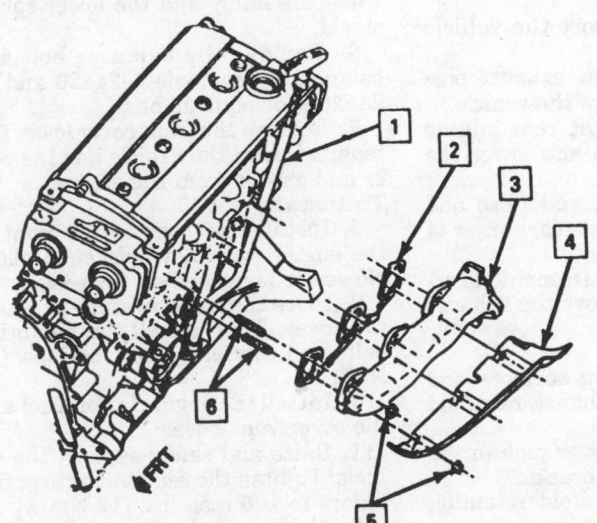

1. Oil level indicator.
2. Gasket.
3. Left exhaust manifold.
4. Heat shield.
5. Nuts torqued to 115 inch lbs.
6. Studs torqued to 13 ft. lbs.

Left side exhaust manifold—3.4L Engine

1. Gasket.
2. Stud to 13 ft. lbs.
3. Right exhaust manifold. (automatic transaxle)
4. Right heat shield (automatic transaxle)
5. Nut to 116 inch lbs.
6. Right heat shield. (manual transaxle)
7. Right exhaust manifold (manual transaxle)

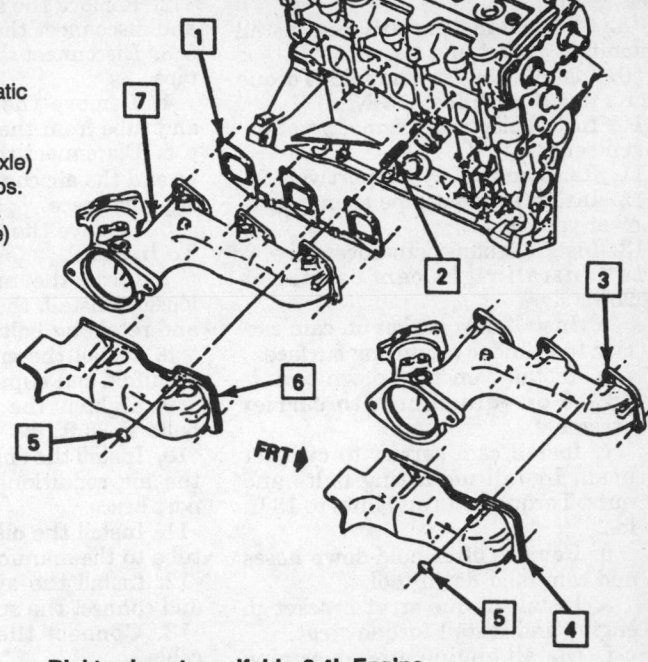

Right exhaust manifold—3.4L Engine

and manifold. Remove old gasket and disgard.

To install:

7. Install a new gasket, manifold and heat shields onto the engine.

8. Install manifold nuts and torque to 115 inch lbs. (13 Nm).

9. Install cooling fan, radiator shroud and torque strut into position and secure.

10. Install exhaust crossover. Install negative battery cable and air cleaner assembly.

RIGHT SIDE (REAR) WITH AUTOMATIC TRANSAXLE

1. Disconnect the negative battery cable.

2. Remove right side cam carrier as follows:

    a. Remove intake plenum and right timing belt cover.

    b. Remove right spark plug wires.

    c. Remove air/oil separator hose at cam carrier cover.

    d. Remove cam carrier cover bolts and lift of cover. Remove gasket and O-rings from cover.

    e. Remove secondary timing belt by removing secondary timing belt actuator and tensioner assembly and sliding belt from pulleys.

    f. Install 6 sections of fuel line hoses under cam shaft and between lifters. This will hold lifters in carrier. For this procedure use $3/16$ inch fuel line hose for exhaust valves and $5/32$ inch fuel line hose for the intake valves.

    g. Remove exhaust crossover pipe and torque strut.

    h. Remove torque strut bracket at engine. Remove front engine lift hook.

    i. Remove cam carrier mounting bolts and nuts and remove cam carrier.

    j. Remove cam carrier gasket from cylinder head.

3. Remove exhaust manifold to crossover pipe nuts and the crossover pipe.

4. Raise and safely support vehicle.

5. Remove front exhaust pipe at manifold. Lower vehicle.

6. Remove electrical connector from oxygen sensor.

7. Remove exhaust manifold nuts, heat shield and manifold.

To install:

8. Clean all mating surfaces, install manifold gasket and heat shields.

9. Install exhaust manifold. Torque nuts to 116 inch lbs. (13 Nm).

10. Install electrical connector at oxygen sensor.

11. Raise and safely support vehicle.

12. Install exhaust pipe at manifold. Lower vehicle.

13. Install exhaust crossover pipe.

14. Install right cam carrier as follows:

a. Install new gasket on cam carrier to cylinder mounting surface.

b. Install cam hold-down tool J–38613 or equivalent, to carrier assembly.

c. Install cam carrier to cylinder head. Install mounting bolts and nuts. Torque bolts and nuts to 18 ft. lbs.

d. Remove lifter hold-down hoses and cam hold-down tool.

e. Install torque strut bracket to engine and install torque strut.

f. Install engine crossover pipe and engine lift hook.

g. Install secondary timing belt and cam carrier cover and gasket.

h. Install spark plug wires and cover.

15. Reconnect negative battery cable.

RIGHT SIDE (REAR) WITH MANUAL TRANSAXLE

1. Disconnect the negative battery cable. Remove the air cleaner assembly.

2. Remove exhaust crossover.

3. Raise and safely support vehicle.

4. Remove exhaust pipe and converter assembly. Remove oxygen sensor connector.

5. Remove EGR pipe at manifold and manifold heat shields.

6. Remove exhaust manifold retaining nuts, manifold and gasket from the engine.

To install:

7. Install gasket and manifold to the engine. Torque retaining nuts to 116 inch lbs. (13 Nm).

8. Install EGR pipe and heat shields to exhaust manifold.

9. Install electrical connector at oxygen sensor.

10. Install exhaust pipe to manifold and lower vehicle.

11. Install exhaust crossover and negative battery cable.

12. Start the engine and check for leaks.

3.8L Engine

LEFT SIDE (FRONT)

1. Disconnect the negative battery cable.

2. Remove the air cleaner assembly and disconnect the spark plug wires.

3. Disconnect the exhaust crossover pipe.

4. Remove the oil level indicator and tube from the manifold.

5. Disconnect the engine lift bracket and the air conditioner compressor support brace.

6. Remove the exhaust manifold.

To install:

7. Clean the mating surfaces and loosely install the exhaust manifold and retaining bolts.

8. Install the crossover pipe to the manifold and support bracket.

9. Tighten the manifold retaining bolts to 38 ft. lbs. (52 Nm).

10. Install the engine lift bracket and the air conditioner compressor support brace.

11. Install the oil level indicator and tube to the manifold.

12. Install the air cleaner assembly and connect the spark plug wires.

13. Connect the negative battery cable.

RIGHT SIDE (REAR)

1. Disconnect the negative battery cable. Remove the fuel injector sight shield.

2. Remove the coolant recovery reservoir. Disconnect the exhaust crossover pipe.

3. Remove the air cleaner assembly and disconnect the spark plug wires.

4. Remove the oil level indicator and tube from the manifold.

5. Disconnect the oxygen sensor electrical connector.

6. Disconnect the engine torque strut and bolt from the engine.

7. Remove the engine lift bracket from the engine.

8. Remove the spark plugs from the right side rear bank.

9. Raise and support the vehicle safely.

10. Remove the front exhaust pipe and the converter from the vehicle.

11. Remove the right rear engine mount to frame nuts and lower the engine.

12. Use a floor jack and raise and support safely the right rear corner of the engine for access.

13. Remove the exhaust manifold retaining bolts and remove the exhaust manifold.

To install:

14. Clean the mating surfaces and loosely install the exhaust manifold and retaining bolts.

15. Install the crossover pipe to the manifold and support bracket.

16. Tighten the manifold retaining bolts to 38 ft. lbs. (52 Nm).

17. Lower the engine and remove the floor jack.

18. Raise and support the vehicle safely.

19. Install the front exhaust pipe and the converter.

20. Install the right rear engine mount to frame nuts and lower the engine.

21. Tighten the crossover bolts.

22. Install the spark plugs to the right side rear bank.

23. Install the engine lift bracket to the engine.

24. Connect the oxygen sensor electrical connector.

25. Connect the engine torque strut and bolt to the engine and torque to 35 ft. lbs. (47 Nm).

26. Install the oil level indicator and tube to the manifold.

27. Install the air cleaner assembly, injector sight shield and connect the spark plug wires.

28. Connect the negative battery cable.

Timing Chain/Gear Front Cover

REMOVAL & INSTALLATION

2.3L Engine

1. Disconnect the negative battery cable. Remove the coolant recovery reservoir.

2. Remove the serpentine drive belt using a 13mm wrench that is at least 24 in. long.

3. Remove the upper cover fasteners.

4. Remove the cover vent hose and the engine lift bracket.

5. Raise and safely support the vehicle. Remove the right front tire and wheel assembly and the lower splash shield.

6. Remove the balancer bolt and balancer using tools J–24420 and J–24420B, or equivalent.

7. Remove the front cover lower fasteners. Lower the vehicle and the cover and gasket from the engine.

To install:

8. Install the cover to the front of the engine with new gasket in place. No sealer is needed on the gasket.

9. Place the nuts on studs to retain the cover. Then install the mounting bolts and tighten to 106 inch lbs. (12 Nm).

10. Install the engine lift bracket and the cover vent hose.

11. Raise and safely support the vehicle. Tighten the remaining cover fasteners to 106 inch lbs. (12 Nm).

12. Lubricate the front crankshaft seal and the front sealing surface of the crankshaft balancer with chassis

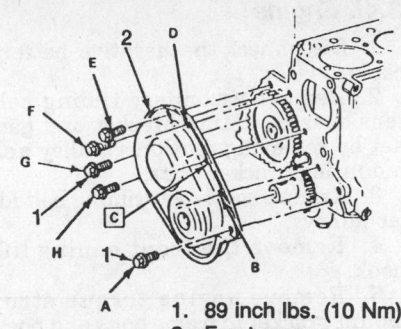

1. 89 inch lbs. (10 Nm)
2. Front cover

**Timing case cover assembly—
1990 2.5L Engine**

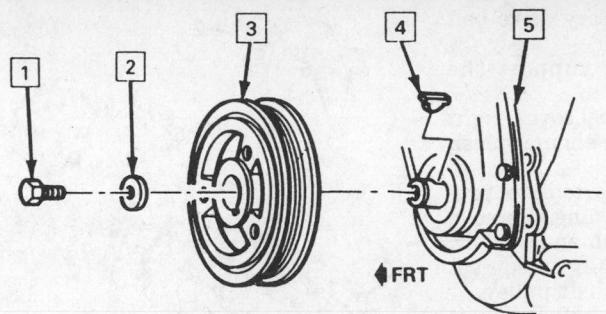

1. 162 ft. lbs. (220 Nm)
2. Washer
3. Crankshaft pulley
4. Key
5. Front cover

Crankshaft pulley assembly—2.5L Engine

grease. Install the crankshaft balancer assembly.

13. Install the right front tire and wheel assembly.

14. Lower the vehicle. Install the accessory drive belt using tool J–37059 or equivalent.

15. Install the coolant recovery tank. Add coolant to fill the system to the appropriate system.

16. Connect the negative battery cable. Start the engine and check for leaks.

2.5L Engine

1990

1. Disconnect the negative battery cable.

2. Remove the torque strut bolt at the cylinder head bracket and move the strut out of the way.

3. Remove the serpentine belt.

4. Install the engine support fixture tool J–28467–A and J–36462.

5. Raise and safely support the vehicle.

6. Remove the right front tire assembly.

7. Disconnect the right lower ball joint from the knuckle.

8. Remove the 2 right frame attaching bolts.

9. Loosen the 2 left frame attaching bolts but do not remove.

10. Lower the vehicle.

11. Lower the engine on the right side. Raise and safely support the vehicle.

12. Remove the engine vibration dampener using a dampener puller.

13. Remove the timing cover retaining bolts and cover.

To install:

14. Clean all gasket mating surfaces with solvent and a gasket scraper.

15. Apply a 3/8 in. wide by $^{3}/_{16}$ in. thick bead of RTV sealer to the joint at the oil pan and timing cover.

16. Apply a ¼ in. wide by ⅛ in. thick bead of RTV sealer to the timing cover at the block mating surface.

17. Install a new timing cover oil seal using a timing cover seal installer tool J–34995 or equivalent.

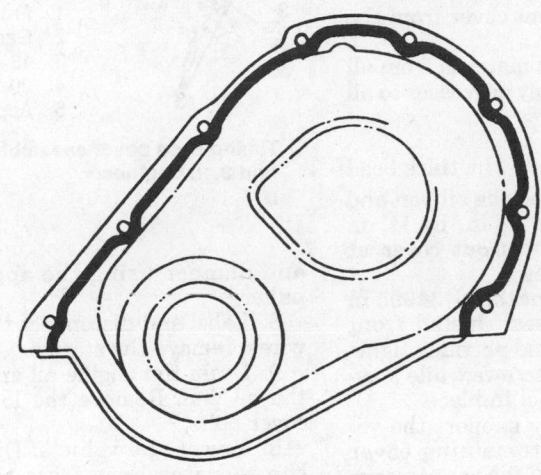

Front cover sealer application—2.5L Engine

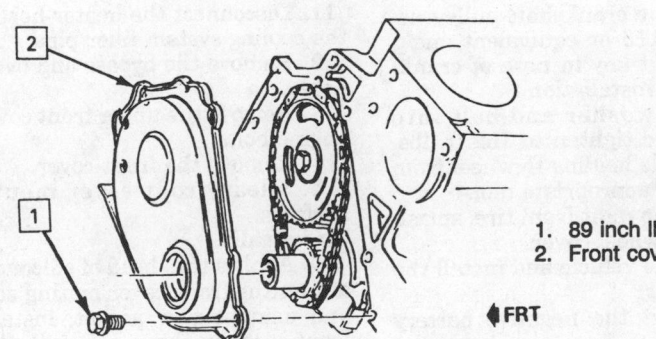

1. 89 inch lbs. (10 Nm)
2. Front cover

Front cover—2.5L Engine

18. Install the cover onto the block and install the retaining bolts loosely.

19. Install the timing cover seal installer tool J–34995 to align the timing cover.

20. Tighten the opposing bolts to hold the cover in place.

21. Torque the bolts in sequence to 89 inch lbs. (10 Nm). Remove the timing cover oil seal installation tool.

22. Install the crankshaft vibration dampener and torque the bolt to 162 ft. lbs. (220 Nm).

23. Lower the vehicle.

24. Raise the engine to its proper position using the support fixture.

25. Raise and safely support the vehicle.

26. Raise the frame and install the

removed frame bolts. Torque the bolts to 103 ft. lbs. (140 Nm).

27. Install the right ball joint and tighten the nut.

28. Install the right front tire, torque the lug nuts to 100 ft. lbs. (136 Nm) and lower the vehicle.

29. Remove the engine support fixture.

30. Install the torque strut and bolt to the cylinder head bracket.

31. Install the serpentine belt, connect the negative battery cable and check for oil leaks.

1991–93

1. Disconnect negative battery cable.

2. Remove the accessory drive belt and tensioner.

3. Raise and safely support the vehicle.

4. Remove the flywheel cover, right front tire and right side engine splash shield.

5. Install appropriate tool to prevent flywheel from turning. Remove the crankshaft pulley bolt and washer.

6. Using tool J–24420B or equivalent, remove the crankshaft pulley.

7. Remove the crankshaft key so it won't get lost. Remove the front cover retaining screws. Lower the vehicle.

8. Remove the front cover from the engine.

9. Clean all gasket material from all mating surfaces. Apply degreaser to all sealing surfaces.

To install:

10. Apply a ⅜ in. by 3/16 in. thick bead of sealer to the joint at the oil pan and front cover. Apply a ¼ in. by ⅛ in. bead of sealer to the front cover at block mating surfaces.

11. Install alignment tool J–34995 in the front cover oil seal. Install front cover to the engine and partially tighten 2 opposing cover screws while leaving the alignment tool in place.

12. Raise and safely support the vehicle. Tighten the remaining cover bolts to 89 inch lbs. (10 Nm). Remove the alignment tool.

13. Install the crankshaft pulley using tool J–29113 or equivalent, making sure to put key in nose of crankshaft prior to installation.

14. Install washer and bolt into crankshaft and tighten to 162 ft. lbs. (220 Nm) while holding flywheel from turning using appropriate tool.

15. Install the right front tire, splash shield and flywheel cover.

16. Lower the vehicle and install the serpentine belt.

17. Reconnect the negative battery cable.

2.8L and 3.1L Engines

1. Disconnect the negative terminal from the battery. Drain the cooling system.

2. Remove the serpentine belt and the belt tensioner.

3. Remove the alternator-to-bracket bolts and remove the alternator, with the wires attached, support it out of the way.

4. Remove the power steering pump-to-bracket bolts and support it out of the way. Do not disconnect the pressure hoses.

5. Raise and safely support the vehicle.

6. Remove the right side inner fender splash shield. Remove the flywheel dust cover.

7. Remove the crankshaft pulley

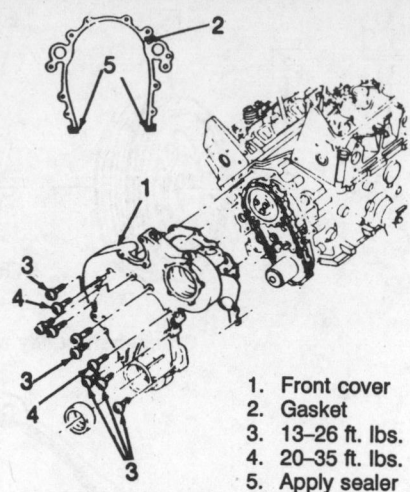

1. Front cover
2. Gasket
3. 13–26 ft. lbs.
4. 20–35 ft. lbs.
5. Apply sealer

Timing case cover assembly—2.8L and 3.1L Engines

and damper using the appropriate puller.

8. Label and disconnect the starter wires, remove the starter.

9. Drain the engine oil and remove the oil pan. Remove the lower front cover bolts.

10. Lower the vehicle. Disconnect the radiator hose from the water pump.

11. Disconnect the heater hose from the cooling system filler pipe.

12. Remove the bypass and overflow hoses.

13. Remove the upper front cover-to-engine bolts.

14. Remove the front cover.

15. Clean front cover mounting surfaces.

To install:

16. Apply a thin bead of silicone sealant on the front cover mating surface and using a new gasket, install the front cover on the engine with the top bolts to hold it in place.

17. Raise and safely support the vehicle.

18. Install the oil pan. Install the lower front cover bolts, tighten all of the front cover bolts to 26–35 ft. lbs. (35–48 Nm).

19. Install the serpentine belt and idler pulley. Install the damper on the engine using tool J–29113 or equivalent. Install the starter.

20. Install the inner fender splash shield. Lower the vehicle.

21. Attach the radiator hose too the water pump and attach the heater hoses.

22. Install the power steering pump and the alternator.

23. Attach the spark plug wire shield. Fill the cooling system.

24. Connect the negative battery cable. Check for coolant and oil leaks.

3.4L Engine

1. Disconnect the negative battery cable.

2. Remove secondary timing belt tensioner mounting bracket and gasket by removing tensioner pulley and mounting bracket bolts.

3. Remove secondary timing belt idler pulleys.

4. Remove the front engine lift hook.

5. Remove engine torque strut mount bracket to frame bolts and position strut out of the way.

6. Remove the upper radiator support, cooling fan bolts and cooling fans.

7. Drain cooling system and remove lower radiator hose from coolant pump inlet pipe. Remove both cooling fans.

8. Remove coolant hoses at the water pump and the heater pipe bracket retainer bolts at frame.

9. If equipped with manual transaxle, remove the air hose at the front exhaust pipe.

10. Remove the heater pipe retaining screws at the frame.

11. Raise and safely support vehicle. Remove right front tire and wheel assembly. Remove right splash shield.

12. Remove crankshaft pulley and damper. Remove oil filter.

13. Remove air conditioner compressor mounting bracket bolts. Remove the air conditioning compressor and set compressor aside.

14. Remove the starter motor and position aside.

15. Remove the torsional damper.

16. Remove the alternator and position aside. Remove the rear alternator bracket. Lower vehicle.

17. Disconnect and relocate the engine oil cooler assembly as required.

18. Remove the front oil pan retainer bolts and nuts. Loosen the remaining oil pan mounting bolts.

19. Remove the lower front cover mounting bolts.

20. Remove the timing belt drive sprocket retaining bolt and extract sprocket using tool J–38616 or equivalent.

21. Remove the forward lamp relay center screw and position relay center aside.

22. Remove coolant pump pulley.

23. Remove upper front cover bolts and the front cover. Remove the old gasket and clean mating surfaces of front cover and block.

To install:

24. Apply GM sealer 1052080 or equivalent, to lower edges of the sealing surface of the front cover and install. Apply thread sealant to large bolts and tighten cover into place.

25. Install coolant pump pulley. In-

1. Front cover
2. Sealer
3. Gasket
4. Locating pins
5. Engine block
6. Bolts to 35 ft. lbs.
7. Bolt to 18 ft. lbs.
8. Front cover oil seal

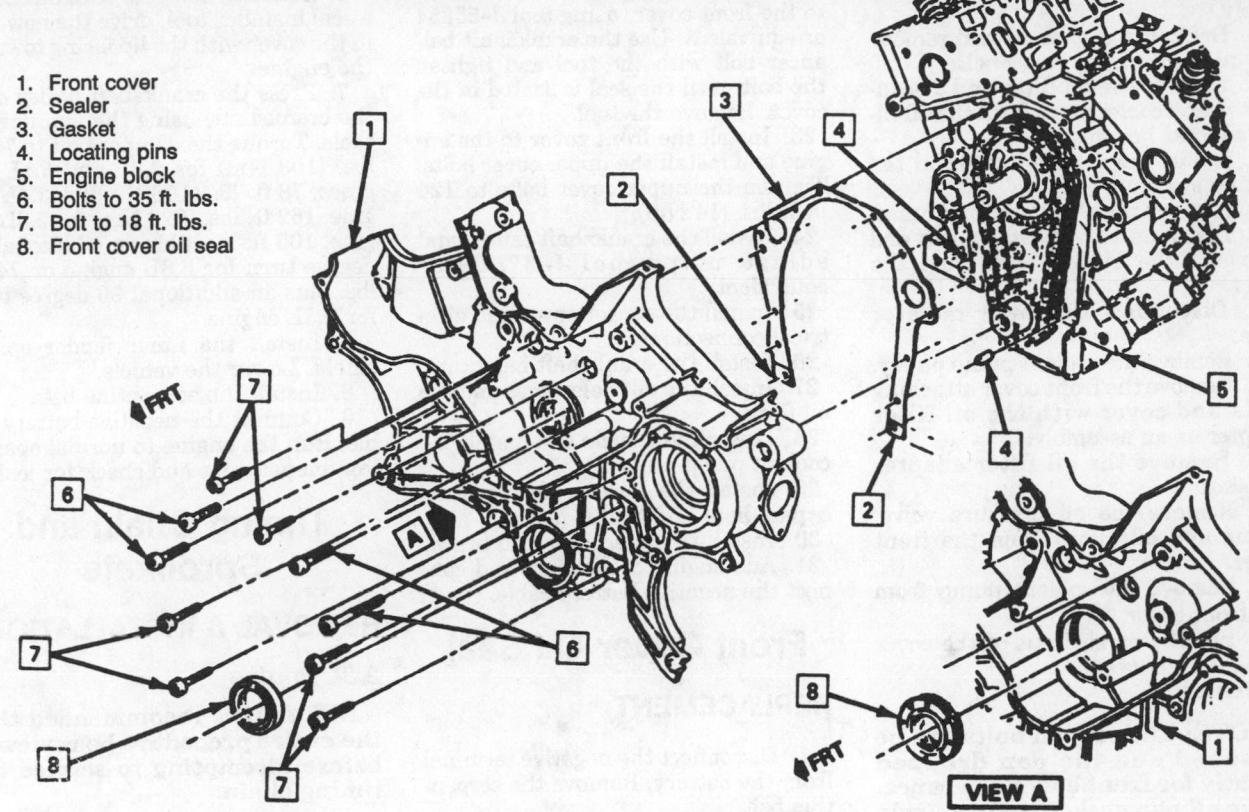

Front cover and oil seal—3.4L Engine

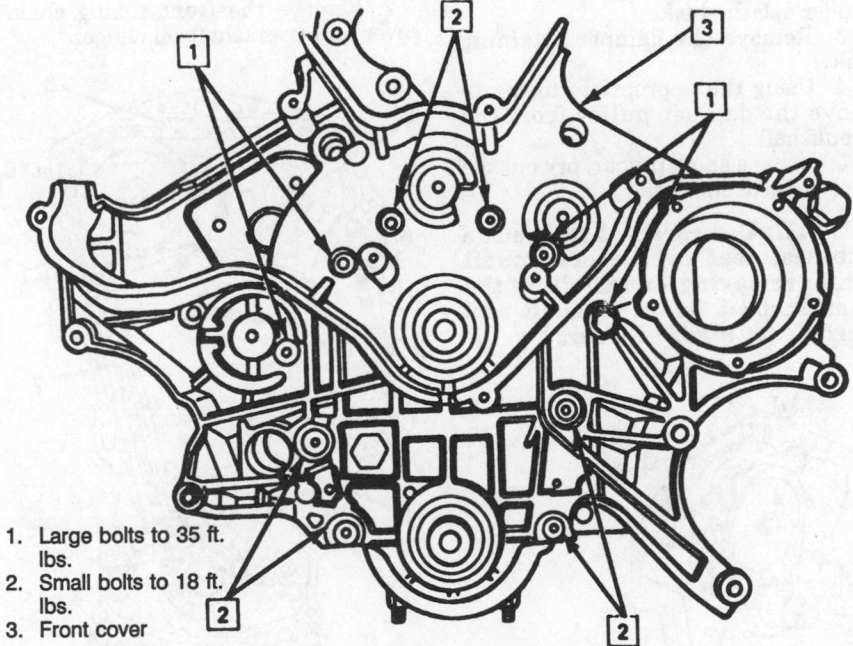

1. Large bolts to 35 ft. lbs.
2. Small bolts to 18 ft. lbs.
3. Front cover

Front cover bolt locations—3.4L Engine

stall oil cooler coolant hose to front cover.

26. Install forward light relay center and upper alternator retaining bolts.

27. Install the drive belt sprocket and retaining bolt.

28. Raise and safely support vehicle.

29. Install starter motor.

30. Reinstall halfshaft and rear alternator bracket.

31. Install lower front cover bolts. Tighten lower cover bolts to 18 ft. lbs.

(25 Nm). Install air conditioning compressor mounting bolts.

32. Install oil filter, crankshaft damper and crankshaft pulley.

33. Install right side splash shield and wheel assembly. Lower vehicle.

34. Tighten upper front cover small bolts to 18 ft. lbs. (25 Nm) and the front cover large bolts to 35 ft. lbs. (47 Nm).

35. Install heater hoses at front cover, lower radiator hose to coolant pump and add coolant to correct level.

36. Install retainer screws into heater pipe bracket.

37. Install both radiator fans, upper radiator support and torque strut to frame bolts.

38. Install front engine lift hook and secondary timing belt idler pulley.

39. Install secondary timing belt tensioner mounting bracket tightening bolts to 37 ft. lbs. (50 Nm).

40. Reconnect negative battery cable.

3.8L Engine

1. Disconnect the negative battery cable.

2. Remove the crankshaft balancer.

3. Remove the crankshaft sensor cover.

4. Disconnect the electrical connections at the camshaft, crankshaft and oil pressure sensors.

5. Raise and support the vehicle safely.

6. Drain the engine oil and remove the oil pan to front cover bolts.

7. Remove the oil filter and disconnect the oil cooler pipes from the oil filter adapter housing.

8. Lower the vehicle and drain the cooling system.

9. Remove the alternator and brace.

10. Disconnect the heater hoses and pipe and the bypass hose from the cover.

11. Disconnect the lower radiator hose.

12. Remove the coolant pump pulley.

13. Remove the front cover attaching bolts and cover with the oil filter adapter as an assembly.

14. Remove the oil filter adapter housing.

15. Remove the oil pressure valve, spring and oil pump from the front cover.

16. Remove the coolant pump from the front cover.

17. Pry the oil seal out of the cover using a prying tool.

To install:

NOTE: **The oil pan bolts can be loosened and the pan dropped slightly for front cover clearance. If the oil pan gasket is excessively swollen, the oil pan must be removed and the gasket replaced.**

18. Clean the mating surfaces of the front cover and cylinder block with a degreaser.

19. Install the oil filter and adapter housing with the oil pressure valve and spring to the cover. Tighten the bolts to 24 ft. lbs. (33 Nm).

20. Install the oil pump assembly to the cover.

21. Use a new gasket, apply sealer to the bolt threads and install the coolant pump to the front cover.

22. Lubricate a new front cover oil seal with clean engine oil and install it to the front cover, using tool J–35354 or equivalent. Use the crankshaft balancer bolt with the tool and tighten the bolt until the seal is seated in the cover. Remove the tool.

23. Install the front cover to the engine and install the upper cover bolts. Tighten the upper cover bolts to 124 inch lbs. (14 Nm).

24. Install the crankshaft sensor and adjust, using tool J–37089 or equivalent.

25. Install the sensor cover and electrical connections.

26. Install the crankshaft balancer.

27. Install the oil cooler lines and the oil filter.

28. Lower the vehicle and install the coolant pump pulley.

29. Install the lower radiator hose, bypass hose and heater hoses.

30. Install the alternator and brace.

31. Add engine coolant, oil and connect the negative battery cable.

Front Cover Oil Seal

REPLACEMENT

1. Disconnect the negative terminal from the battery. Remove the serpentine belt.

2. Raise and safely support the vehicle. Remove the right side inner fender splash shield.

3. Remove the damper retaining bolt.

4. Using the appropriate tools, remove the damper pulley from the crankshaft.

5. Using a small prybar, pry out the seal in the front cover.

NOTE: **Use care not to damage the seal seat or the crankshaft while removing or installing the seal. Inspect the crankshaft seal surface for signs of wear.**

6. Coat the new seal with oil. Using a seal installer tool, drive the new seal in the cover with the lip facing towards the engine.

7. Press the crankshaft pulley onto the crankshaft, using the appropriate tools. Torque the damper bolt to 76 ft. lbs. (103 Nm) for 2.8L and 3.1L engines, 78 ft. lbs (106 Nm) for 3.4L engine, 162 ft. lbs. (220 Nm) for 2.5L engine, 105 ft. lbs. plus an additional 56 degree turn for 3.8L engine or 74 ft. lbs. plus an additional 90 degree turn for 2.3L engine.

8. Install the inner fender splash shield. Lower the vehicle.

9. Install the serpentine belt.

10. Connect the negative battery cable. Run the engine to normal operating temperature and check for leaks.

Timing Chain and Sprockets

REMOVAL & INSTALLATION

2.3L Engine

NOTE: **It is recommended that the entire procedure be reviewed before attempting to service the timing chain.**

1. Disconnect the negative battery cable.

2. Remove the front timing chain cover and crankshaft oil slinger.

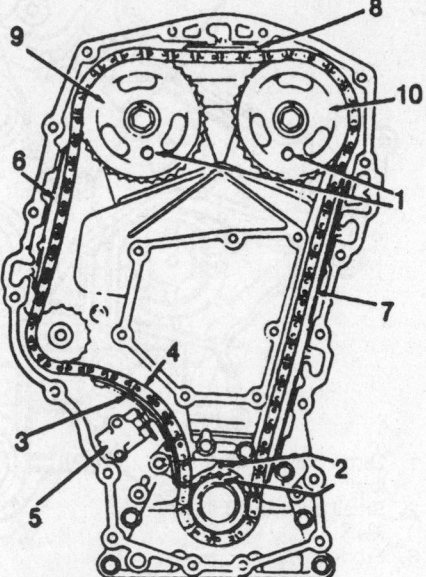

1. Camshaft timing marks
2. Crankshaft timing marks
3. Tensioner shoe assembly
4. Timing chain
5. Tensioner
6. R/H guide
7. L/H guide
8. Upper guide
9. Exhaust camshaft sprocket
10. Intake camshaft sprocket

Timing chain installation—2.3L Engine

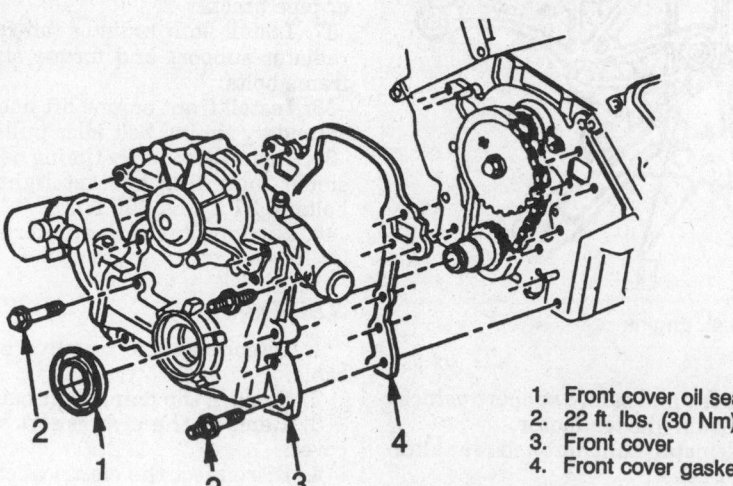

1. Front cover oil seal
2. 22 ft. lbs. (30 Nm)
3. Front cover
4. Front cover gasket

Timing chain cover installation—3.8L Engine

3. Rotate the crankshaft clockwise, as viewed from front of engine (normal rotation) until the camshaft sprocket's timing dowel pin holes line up with the holes in the timing chain housing. The mark on the crankshaft sprocket should line up with the mark on the cylinder block. The crankshaft sprocket keyway should point upwards and line up with the centerline of the cylinder bores. This is the normal timed position.

4. Remove the 3 timing chain guides.

5. Raise the vehicle and support safely.

6. Gently pry off timing chain tensioner spring retainer and remove spring.

NOTE: Two styles of tensioner are used. Early production engines will have a spring post and late production ones will not. Both styles are identical in operation and are interchangeable.

7. Remove the timing chain tensioner shoe retainer.

8. Make sure all the slack in the timing chain is above the tensioner assembly; remove the chain tensioner shoe. The timing chain must be disengaged from the wear grooves in the tensioner shoe in order to remove the shoe. Slide a prybar under the timing chain while pulling shoe outward.

9. If difficulty is encountered removing chain tensioner shoe, proceed as follows:

a. Lower the vehicle.

b. Hold the intake camshaft sprocket with a holding tool and remove the sprocket bolt and washer.

c. Remove the washer from the bolt and thread the bolt back into the camshaft by hand, the bolt provides a surface to push against.

d. Remove intake camshaft sprocket using a 3-jaw puller in the 3 relief holes in the sprocket. Do not attempt to pry the sprocket off the camshaft or damage to the sprocket or chain housing could occur.

10. Remove the tensioner assembly retaining bolts and the tensioner.

--- **CAUTION** ---

The tensioner piston is spring loaded and could fly out causing personal injury.

11. Remove the chain housing to block stud (timing chain tensioner shoe pivot).

12. Remove the timing chain.

To install:

13. Tighten intake camshaft sprocket retaining bolt and washer while holding the sprocket with tool J–36013, if removed.

14. Install the special tool through holes in camshaft sprockets into holes in timing chain housing. This positions the camshafts for correct timing.

15. If the camshafts are out of position and must be rotated more than ⅛ turn in order to install the alignment dowel pins:

a. The crankshaft must be rotated 90 degrees clockwise off TDC in order to give the valves adequate clearance to open.

b. Once the camshafts are in position and the dowels installed, rotate the crankshaft counterclockwise back to top dead center. Do not rotate the crankshaft clockwise to TDC, or valve or piston damage could occur.

16. Install the timing chain over the exhaust camshaft sprocket, around the idler sprocket and around the crankshaft sprocket.

17. Remove the alignment dowel pin from the intake camshaft. Using a dowel pin remover tool, rotate the intake camshaft sprocket counterclockwise enough to slide the timing chain over the intake camshaft sprocket. Release the camshaft sprocket wrench. The length of chain between the 2 camshaft sprockets will tighten. If properly timed, the intake camshaft alignment dowel pin should slide in easily. If the dowel pin does not fully index, the camshafts are not timed correctly and the procedure must be repeated.

18. Leave the alignment dowel pins installed.

19. With slack removed from chain between intake camshaft sprocket and crankshaft sprocket, the timing marks on the crankshaft and the cylinder block should be aligned. If marks are not aligned, move the chain 1 tooth forward or rearward, remove slack and recheck marks.

20. Tighten the chain housing to block stud (timing chain tensioner shoe pivot). the stud is installed under the timing chain. Tighten to 19 ft. lbs. (26 Nm).

21. Reload timing chain tensioner assembly to its **0** position as follows:

a. Assemble restraint cylinder, spring and nylon plug into plunger. Index slot in restraint cylinder with peg in plunger. While rotating the restraint cylinder clockwise, push the restraint cylinder into the plunger until it bottoms. Keep rotating the restraint cylinder clockwise but allow the spring to push it out of the plunger. The pin in the plunger will lock the restraint in the loaded position.

b. Install tool J–36589 or equivalent, onto plunger assembly.

c. Install plunger assembly into tensioner body with the long end toward the crankshaft when installed.

22. Install the tensioner assembly to the chain housing. Recheck plunger assembly installation. It is correctly installed when the long end is toward the crankshaft.

23. Install and tighten timing chain tensioner bolts and tighten to 10 ft. lbs. (14 Nm).

24. Install the tensioner shoe and tensioner shoe retainer.

25. Remove special tool J–36589 and squeeze plunger assembly into the tensioner body to unload the plunger assembly.

26. Lower vehicle and remove the alignment dowel pins. Rotate crankshaft clockwise 2 full rotations. Align crankshaft timing mark with mark on cylinder block and reinstall alignment dowel pins. Alignment dowel pins will slide in easily if engine is timed correctly.

NOTE: If the engine is not correctly timed, severe engine damage could occur.

27. Install the 3 timing chain guides and crankshaft oil slinger.

28. Install the timing chain front cover.

29. Connect the negative battery cable and check for leaks.

2.5L Engine

1991–93

1. Disconnect negative battery cable.

2. Remove the front cover as follows:

a. Remove the accessory drive belt and tensioner.

b. Raise and safely support the vehicle. Remove the flywheel cover, right front tire and right side engine splash shield.

c. Install appropriate tool to prevent flywheel from turning. Remove the crankshaft pulley bolt and washer. Using tool J–24420B or equivalent, remove the crankshaft pulley.

d. Remove the crankshaft key so it won't get lost. Remove the front cover retaining screws. Lower the vehicle.

e. Remove the front cover from the engine.

3. Position the engine at TDC so timing marks on the camshaft and crankshaft are in alignment.

4. Retract the timing chain tensioner and hold it in retract position with an appropriate size cotter pin or rivet.

5. Remove the camshaft bolt. Remove the timing chain and sprocket from the front of the engine.

6. Clean timing chain and sprocket and check for damage or excess wear, replace components as required.

To install:

7. Install timing chain and sprocket making sure timing marks on both the

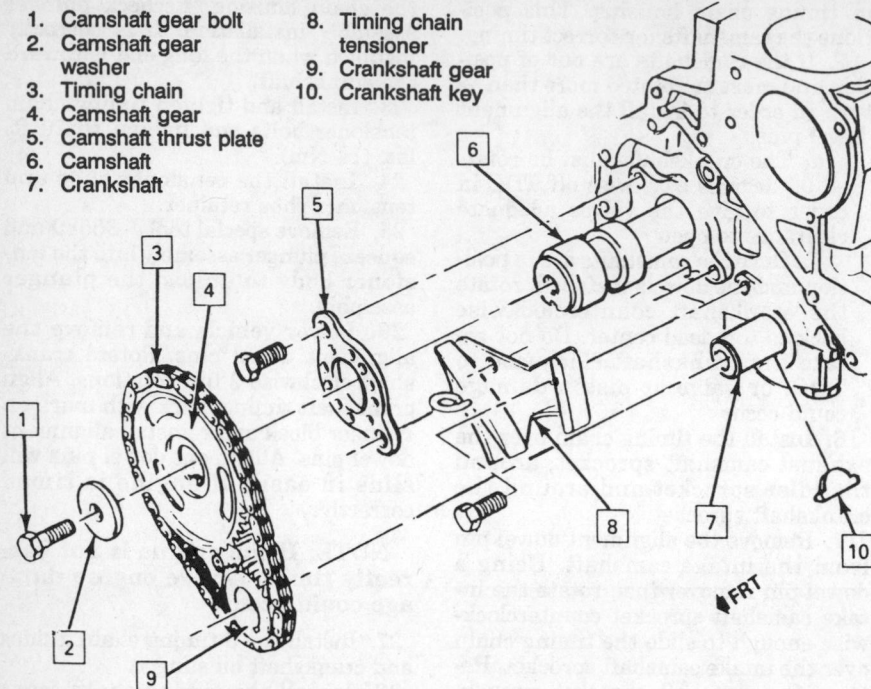

1. Camshaft gear bolt
2. Camshaft gear washer
3. Timing chain
4. Camshaft gear
5. Camshaft thrust plate
6. Camshaft
7. Crankshaft
8. Timing chain tensioner
9. Crankshaft gear
10. Crankshaft key

Timing chain and gears—2.5L Engine

camshaft and the crankshaft are in alignment.

8. Install the camshaft gear retainer bolt and washer. Tighten the bolt to 43 ft. lbs. (58 Nm).

9. Remove the cotter pin or rivet holding the tensioner in the retracted position.

10. Install the front cover to the engine as follows:

a. Apply a ⅜ in. by ³⁄₁₆ in. thick bead of sealer to the joint at the oil pan and front cover. Apply a ¼ in. by ⅛ in. bead of sealer to the front cover at block mating surfaces.

b. Install alignment tool J-34995 in the front cover oil seal. Install front cover to the engine and partially tighten 2 opposing cover screws while leaving the alignment tool in place.

c. Raise and safely support the vehicle. Tighten the remaining cover bolts to 89 inch lbs. (10 Nm). Remove the alignment tool.

d. Install the crankshaft pulley using tool J-29113 or equivalent, making sure to put key in nose of crankshaft prior to installation.

e. Install washer and bolt into crankshaft and tighten to 162 ft. lbs. (220 Nm) while holding flywheel from turning using appropriate tool.

f. Install the right front tire, splash shield and flywheel cover.

g. Lower the vehicle and install the serpentine belt tensioner and belt.

h. Reconnect the negative battery cable.

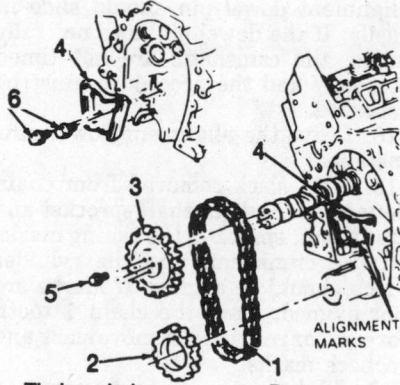

1. Timing chain
2. Crank sprocket
3. Camshaft sprocket
4. Damper
5. 15–20 ft. lbs.
6. 13–18 ft. lbs.

Timing chain and sprockets—2.8L and 3.1L Engines

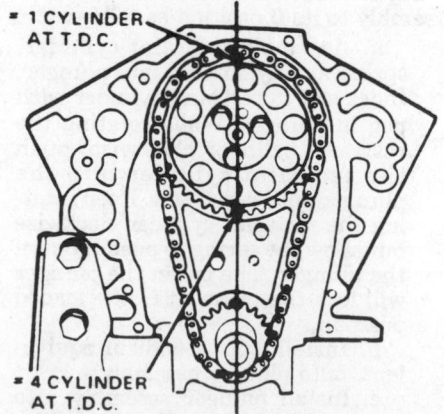

= 1 CYLINDER AT T.D.C.

= 4 CYLINDER AT T.D.C.

Engine timing mark alignment—2.8L and 3.1L Engines

11. Start the engine and check for leaks.

2.8L and 3.1L Engines

1. Disconnect the negative battery cable.

2. Remove the front cover assembly.

3. Place the No. 1 piston at TDC with the marks on the crankshaft and the camshaft aligned.

4. Remove the camshaft sprocket and the timing chain.

NOTE: If the camshaft sprocket does not come off easily, a light blow on the lower edge of the sprocket with a rubber mallet should loosen the sprocket.

5. Remove the crankshaft sprocket using a prybar.
To install:

6. Install the crankshaft sprocket. Apply a coat of Molykote® or equivalent, to the sprocket thrust surface.

7. Hold the camshaft sprocket with the chain hanging down and align the marks on the camshaft and crankshaft sprockets.

8. Align the dowel in the camshaft with the dowel hole in the camshaft sprocket. Install the camshaft sprocket and chain, use the camshaft sprocket bolts to draw the sprocket on to the camshaft. Tighten the sprocket bolts to 18 ft. lbs. (25 Nm).

9. Lubricate the timing chain with engine oil. Install the front cover assembly.

3.4L Engine

1. Disconnect the negative battery cable. On 1991 vehicles, the factory recommends removal of the engine for this procedure.

2. Remove the engine front cover.

3. Mark the position of the crankshaft and the intermediate shaft sprockets on the timing chain.

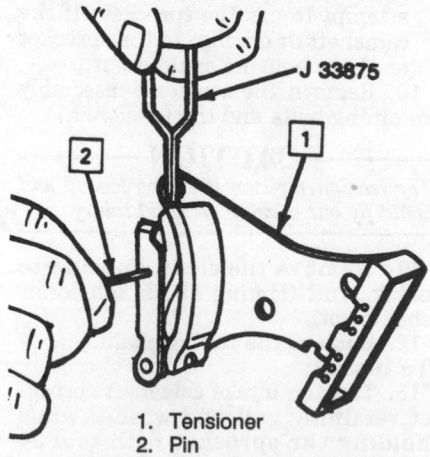

1. Tensioner
2. Pin

Retracting timing chain tensioner—3.4L Engine

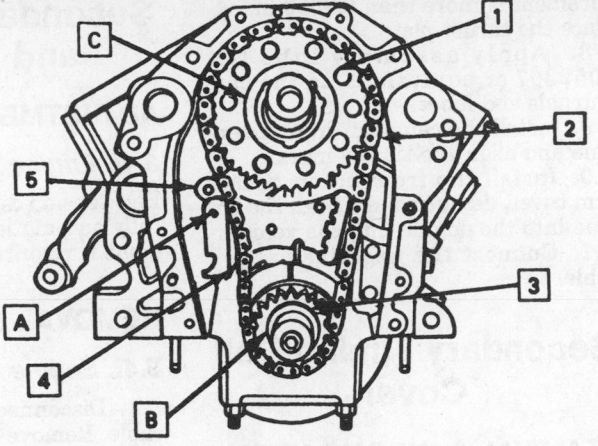

1. Intermediate shaft sprocket
2. Timing chain.
3. Crankshaft sprocket
4. Timing chain tensioner
5. 18 ft. lbs.
A. Spring pin hole
B. Chamfer and counter bore inward
C. Sprockets outward

Timing chain assembly—3.4L Engine

4. Remove the timing chain tensioner bolts and tensioner from the engine.

5. Raise and safely support the vehicle. Retract timing chain tensioner shoe by using J–33875 or equivalent, on both sides of the tensioner and pulling on the thru pin in the tensioner arm to retract the spring. While spring is retracted, insert a cotter pin or rivet into hole in tensioner to hold in this position.

6. Remove the timing chain, crankshaft sprocket and intermediate shaft sprocket as an assembly using tool J–8433 and J–38611 or equivalent, on the crankshaft sprocket. If intermediate gear does not slide off easily with the timing chain assembly, rotate the crankshaft back and forth to help loosen the fit.

7. Inspect the crankshaft alignment key for burrs or marks that could affect assembly.

To install:

8. Make sure the crankshaft key is installed and fully seated. Retract the chain tensioner by compressing the spring in the retractor assembly and inserting a cotter pin or rivet into the hole to hold in this position.

NOTE: The large chamfer and counterbore of the crankshaft sprocket are installed towards the crankshaft. The intermediate sprocket spline sockets are installed away from the case.

9. Slip both sprockets and chain over proper shaft and engage slot in key. Intermediate shaft may move against the rear cover. Slide sprocket and chain assembly on shafts maintaining parallel alignment of sprockets. Make sure the snubber or tensioner blade do not become caught, misaligned or dislodged. For the final 8mm, press the crankshaft sprocket on crankshaft using J–38612 or equivalent.

10. Verify timing of the engine was maintained.

11. Pull the retainer pin from the tensioner.

1. Key
2. Damper assembly
3. Crankshaft sprocket
4. 52 ft. lbs. (70 Nm) plus 110 degrees
5. Timing chain
6. Camshaft sprocket
7. Balance shaft drive gear

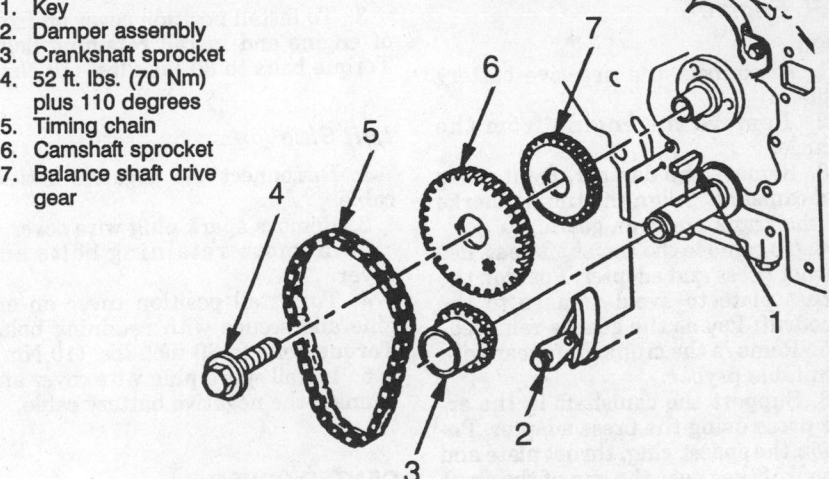

Timing chain and sprocket installation—3.8L Engine

12. Install the front cover.

13. Reconnect the negative battery cable.

3.8L Engine

1. Disconnect the negative battery cable.

2. Remove the front cover assembly.

3. Align the timing marks on the sprockets and remove the timing chain damper.

4. Remove the camshaft sprocket bolts, camshaft sprocket and chain.

5. Remove the crankshaft sprocket by applying a light blow on the lower edge of the sprocket with a plastic mallet.

To install:

6. If the pistons have been moved in the engine, do the following:

a. Turn the crankshaft so the No. 1 piston is at Top Dead Center (TDC).

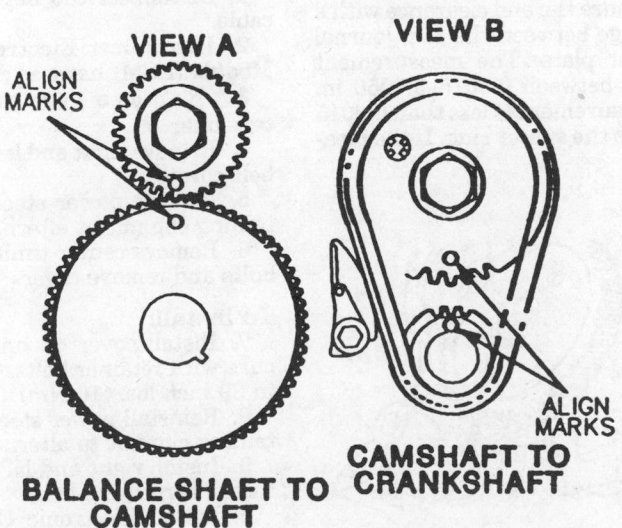

VIEW A

ALIGN MARKS

BALANCE SHAFT TO CAMSHAFT

VIEW B

ALIGN MARKS

CAMSHAFT TO CRANKSHAFT

Timing balancer shaft and camshaft marks—3.8L Engine

b. Turn the camshaft with the sprocket temporarily installed, so timing mark is straight down.

7. Assemble the timing chain on the sprockets with the timing marks facing each other.

8. Install the timing chain and sprockets and tighten the camshaft sprocket bolts to 52 ft. lbs. plus an additional 110 degree turn on 1990–91 engine or 74 ft. lbs. (100 Nm) plus an additional 105 degree turn on 1992–93 engine.

9. Install the timing chain damper and tighten the bolt to 14 ft. lbs. (19 Nm).

10. Rotate the engine 2 revolutions and make sure the marks are aligned correctly.

11. Install the front cover assembly.

12. Connect the negative battery cable.

Timing Gears

REMOVAL & INSTALLATION

2.5L Engine

1990

1. Disconnect the negative battery cable.

2. Remove the engine from the vehicle.

3. Remove the damper, front cover and camshaft. Align the timing marks on the crank and cam gears.

4. To remove the camshaft gear, use a arbor press and adapter. Position the thrust plate to avoid damage to the Woodruff key as the gear is removed.

5. Remove the crankshaft gear with a suitable prybar.

6. Support the camshaft in the arbor press using the press adapter. Position the spacer ring, thrust plate and Woodruff key over the end of the shaft and press the gear onto the camshaft.

7. Measure the end clearance with a feeler gauge between the cam journal and thrust plate. The measurement should be between 0.0015–0.0050 in. If the measurement is less than 0.0015 in., replace the spacer ring. If the mea-

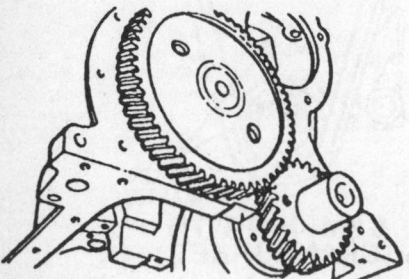

Engine timing mark alignment—1990 2.5L Engine

surement is more than 0.0050 in., replace the thrust plate.

8. Apply assembly lube GM 1052367 or equivalent, to the cam journals and lobes.

9. Install the camshaft into the engine and align the timing marks.

10. Install the front cover, rocker arm cover, damper and install the engine into the engine into the vehicle.

11. Connect the negative battery cable.

Secondary Timing Belt Cover

REMOVAL & INSTALLATION

3.4L ENGINE

RIGHT SIDE

1. Disconnect negative battery cable.

2. Remove retaining bolts and remove cover.

3. To install position cover on front of engine and install retaining bolts. Torque bolts to 89 inch lbs. (10 Nm).

Left Side

1. Disconnect the negative battery cable.

2. Remove spark plug wire cover.

3. Remove retaining bolts and cover.

4. To install position cover on engine and secure with retaining bolts. Torque bolts to 89 inch lbs. (10 Nm).

5. Install spark plug wire cover and connect the negative battery cable.

CENTER COVER

1. Disconnect the negative battery cable.

2. Disconnect Electronic Control Module (ECM) harness cover.

3. Remove serpentine belt tensioner.

4. Remove right and left side timing belt covers.

5. Remove power steering pipe retaining clip nut at alternator stud.

6. Remove center timing belt cover bolts and remove cover.

To install:

7. Install cover on engine and secure with retainer bolts. Torque bolts to 89 inch lbs. (10 Nm).

8. Reinstall power steering pipe retaining clip nut to alternator stud.

9. Install right and left side covers. Install serpentine belt.

10. Install Electronic Control Module (ECM) harness cover. Reconnect negative battery cable.

Secondary Timing Belt and Tensioner

ADJUSTMENT

3.4L Engine

Belt tension is set and maintained by fully automatic tensioners. No adjustment is required.

REMOVAL & INSTALLATION

3.4L Engine

1. Disconnect the negative battery cable. Remove the serpentine belt.

2. Remove secondary timing belt actuator as follows:

a. Remove the power steering pump and set aside. If more clearance is required, siphon the fluid from the pump and remove pump from the vehicle.

b. Remove the center secondary timing belt cover.

c. Turn the crankshaft to position No. 1 cylinder at TDC. In this position all timing marks should be in alignment.

d. Loosely clamp the 2 cam sprockets on each side of the engine together using clamping pliers or equivalent. Hold the belt to the right hand exhaust sprocket with a C-clamp and a wide pad on belt. Do not mar cam sprockets with clamping device.

e. Remove the tensioner side plate retainer bolts from the tensioner and remove the side plate from the actuator and base.

f. Rotate actuator assembly around the arm pivot and out of the mounting base. Removal of the tensioner from the base allows it to extend to its maximum travel.

g. Set the actuator on table in vertical position to allow oil to drain to boot end for at least 5 minutes prior to refilling.

NOTE: The actuator assembly uses a tapered bushing between the actuator and mounting base. Do not loosen or damage the bushing when removing the tensioner assembly.

h. Straighten out a standard paper clip to a minimum straight length of 1.85 in. (47mm). Form a double loop in the bent end of the paper clip.

i. Remove the rubber end plug from the rear of the tensioner assembly. Oil may escape the tensioner. Hold tensioner in hand at vertical position with the plug end at the top and the tip pointing down. Do not remove the vent plug.

j. Push the paper clip through the center hole in the vent plug and into the pilot hole. Insert a small screwdriver into the screw slot inside the end of the tensioner.

k. Retract the tensioner plunger by rotating the screw in a clockwise direction while pushing the rod tip against a table top, until fully retracted.

l. Rotate the screw slot to align with the vent hole and push the straight section of wire into the screw slot to retain the plunger in the retracted position.

m. If tensioner oil has been lost, fill the tensioner with SAE 5W30 Mobil 1 or equivalent engine oil through the end hole. Fill to bottom of plug hole only when the plunger is fully retracted and the lock pin is installed.

3. If the secondary timing belt is to be reused, mark direction of rotation for reference during installation.

4. Remove tensioner and pulley arm assembly.

5. Remove timing belt by sliding it off the pulleys. Do not bend, twist or kink belt or damage to the belt may occur.

To install:

6. Make sure the timing reference marks on all sprockets are properly aligned.

7. Install the actuator and side plate as follows:

a. Install the rubber end plug to the rear of the actuator assembly, if not already done. The cap will snap into place and be flush against the case.

b. Install the actuator bushing into the side plate. Install the actuator assembly into the mounting base by inserting tapered trunnion of tensioner into machined hole of the bushing in the bracket and installing the side plate bolts. Tighten the side plate bolts to 18 ft. lbs. (25 Nm).

8. Position the timing belt onto the engine by routing it around all sprockets and idlers as follows:

a. Start with the intermediate cam sprocket and work counterclockwise.

b. Make sure the belt is installed in the direction of rotation.

c. Engage teeth into all sprockets, place rubber hose behind belt at intermediate sprocket and accumulate slack at the tensioner.

9. Install tension pulley to mounting base. Use tape or cup plug to hold pivot tube in pulley or pivot may fall out. After starting pivot bolt, rotate arm counterclockwise to position the square lug at the 6 o'clock position. Tighten the bolt to 37 ft. lbs. (50 Nm). Inspect the actuator assembly to as-

1. Exhaust camshaft sprocket
2. Bolt
3. Intake camshaft sprocket
4. Lock ring

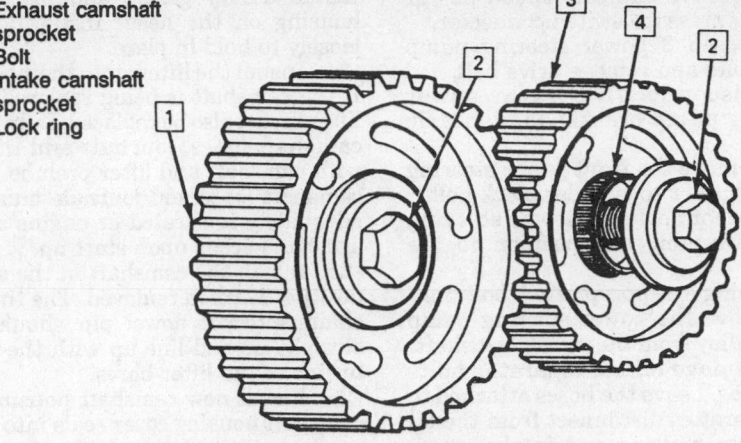

Cam sprockets and locking rings—3.4L Engine

sure it is free and will rotate under its own weight.

NOTE: The arm busing and pivot must be clean and not lubricated.

10. Gently rotate the tensioner pulley counterclockwise into the belt using the cast square lug on body and engage ball end of the actuator into socket on pulley arm.

11. Remove tensioner lock pin allowing tensioner shaft to extend and the pulley to move into the belt. Remove any belt holding devices still in place.

12. Rotate the tensioner pulley counterclockwise applying 12–15 ft. lbs. torque. This will set the initial tension on the belt.

13. Rotate the engine in direction of rotation, clockwise, 3 times to seat belt. Check the sprocket reference marks during final rotation to TDC. Do not allow crankshaft to spring back or reverse direction of rotation.

14. Install the secondary timing belt covers.

15. Install the power steering pump and serpentine belt.

16. Reconnect the negative battery cable.

Camshaft Sprocket

REMOVAL & INSTALLATION

3.4L Engine

1. Release the fuel system pressure. Disconnect negative battery cable.

2. Remove the front and rear camshaft covers. Remove the secondary timing belt.

3. Rotate the camshaft so the flats on the cam to be serviced are face up. Remove oil from cam hold down tool hole in the carrier and install tool J–38616 or equivalent, tightening the bolt to 22 ft. lbs. (30 Nm).

4. Remove the camshaft sprocket bolt and washer while holding the

camshaft from turning using tool J–38613 and J–38614 or equivalent.

5. Remove the sprocket using tool J–38616. Remove flat ring from the sprocket bore.

To install:

6. Install new flat ring to large bore of sprocket. Wipe the nose of the camshaft with a light coat of oil.

7. Install the sprocket onto the camshaft. Lightly oil new lock ring and insert ring far enough into the sprocket to minimize tipping.

8. Lightly oil the camshaft sprocket bolt threads and washer before using. Thread bolt and washer into the camshaft finger-tight, then loosen bolt ½ turn.

9. Check sprocket for binding by rotating it around the shaft. If binding occurs, check for foreign material or burrs.

10. Install secondary timing belt and set cam shaft timing.

Camshaft

REMOVAL & INSTALLATION

2.3L Engine

INTAKE CAMSHAFT

NOTE: Any time the camshaft housing to cylinder head bolts are loosened or removed, the camshaft housing to cylinder head gasket must be replaced.

1. Relieve the fuel system pressure. Disconnect the negative battery cable.

2. Label and disconnect the ignition coil and module assembly electrical connections.

3. Remove 4 ignition coil and module assembly to camshaft housing bolts and remove assembly by pulling straight up. Use a spark plug boot wire remover tool to remove connector assemblies if they have stuck to the spark plugs.

4. Remove the idle speed power steering pressure switch connector.

5. Loosen 3 power steering pump pivot bolts and remove drive belt.

6. Disconnect the 2 rear power steering pump bracket to transaxle bolts.

7. Remove the front power steering pump bracket to cylinder block bolt.

8. Disconnect the power steering pump assembly and position to the side.

9. Using an appropriate 3 bolt puller, remove the power steering pump drive pulley from the intake camshaft.

10. Remove oil/air separator bolts and hoses. Leave the hoses attached to the separator, disconnect from the oil fill, chain housing and intake manifold. Remove as an assembly.

11. Remove vacuum line from fuel pressure regulator and disconnect the fuel injector harness connector.

12. Disconnect fuel line retaining clamp from bracket on top of intake camshaft housing.

13. Remove fuel rail to camshaft housing retaining bolts.

14. Remove the fuel rail from the cylinder head. Cover injector openings in cylinder head and cover injector nozzles. Leave fuel lines attached and position fuel rail aside.

15. Disconnect the timing chain and housing but do not remove from the engine.

16. Remove intake camshaft housing cover to camshaft housing retaining bolts.

17. Remove the intake camshaft housing to cylinder head retaining bolts. Use the reverse of the tightening sequence when loosening camshaft housing to cylinder head retaining bolts. Leave 2 bolts loosely in place to hold the camshaft housing while separating camshaft cover from housing.

18. Push the cover off the housing by threading 4 of the housing to head retaining bolts into the tapped holes in the cam housing cover. Tighten the bolts in evenly so the cover does not bind on the dowel pins.

19. Remove the 2 loosely installed camshaft housing to head bolts and remove the cover. Discard the gaskets.

20. Note the position of the chain sprocket dowel pin for reassembly. Remove the camshaft carefully; do not damage the camshaft oil seal.

21. Remove intake camshaft oil seal from camshaft and discard seal. This seal must be replaced any time the housing and cover are separated.

22. Remove the camshaft carrier from the cylinder head and remove the gasket.

To install:

23. Thoroughly clean the mating surfaces of the camshaft carrier and the cylinder head, bolts and bolt holes.

Install a new gasket and place the housing on the head. Install 1 bolt loosely to hold in place.

24. Install the lifters into their bores. If the camshaft is being replaced, the lifters must also be replaced. Lubricate camshaft lobes, journals and lifters with camshaft and lifter prelube. The camshaft lobes and journals must be adequately lubricated or engine damage could occur upon start up.

25. Install the camshaft in the same position as when removed. The timing chain sprocket dowel pin should be straight up and line up with the centerline of the lifter bores.

26. Install new camshaft housing to camshaft housing cover seals into cover; do not use sealer. Make sure the correct color seal is placed in each groove. Install the cover to the housing.

27. Apply thread locking compound to the camshaft housing and cover retaining bolt threads.

28. Install bolts and torque to 11 ft. lbs. (15 Nm). Rotate the bolts (except the 2 rear bolts that hold fuel pipe to camshaft housing) an additional 75 degrees in sequence. Rotate the excepted bolts an additional 25 degrees.

29. Install timing chain housing and timing chain.

30. Uncover fuel injectors and install new fuel injector ring seals lubricated with oil. Install the fuel rail.

31. Install the fuel line retaining clamp and retainer to bracket on top of the intake camshaft housing.

32. Connect the vacuum line to the fuel pressure regulator.

33. Connect the fuel injectors harness connector.

34. Install the oil/air separator assembly.

35. Lubricate the inner sealing surface of the intake camshaft seal with oil and install the seal to the housing.

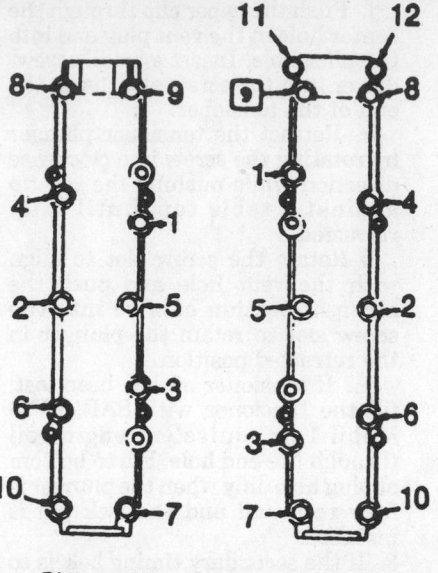

EXHAUST　　　**INTAKE**

FRONT OF ENGINE

Camshaft housing bolt torque sequence—2.3L Engine

36. Install the power steering pump pulley onto the intake camshaft.

37. Install the power steering pump assembly and drive belt.

38. Connect the idle speed power steering pressure switch connector.

39. Clean any loose lubricant that is present on the ignition coil and module assembly to camshaft housing bolts. Apply Loctite® 592 or equivalent, onto the ignition coil and module assembly to camshaft housing bolts. Install the bolts and torque to 13 ft. lbs. (18 Nm).

40. Connect the electrical connectors to ignition coil and module assembly.

41. Connect the negative battery ca-

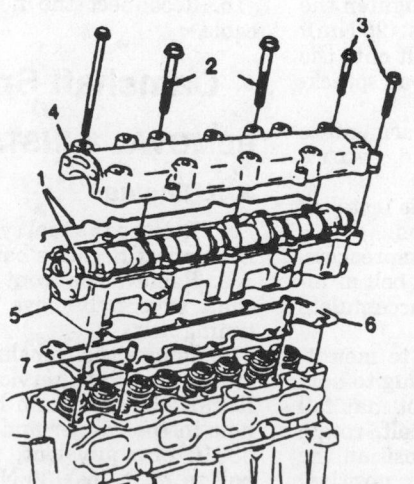

1. Housing cover seals
2. Cylinder head bolts
3. Housing cover bolts
4. Camshaft cover
5. Intake camshaft housing
6. Cylinder head gasket
7. Dowel pins

Camshaft housing assembly—2.3L Engine

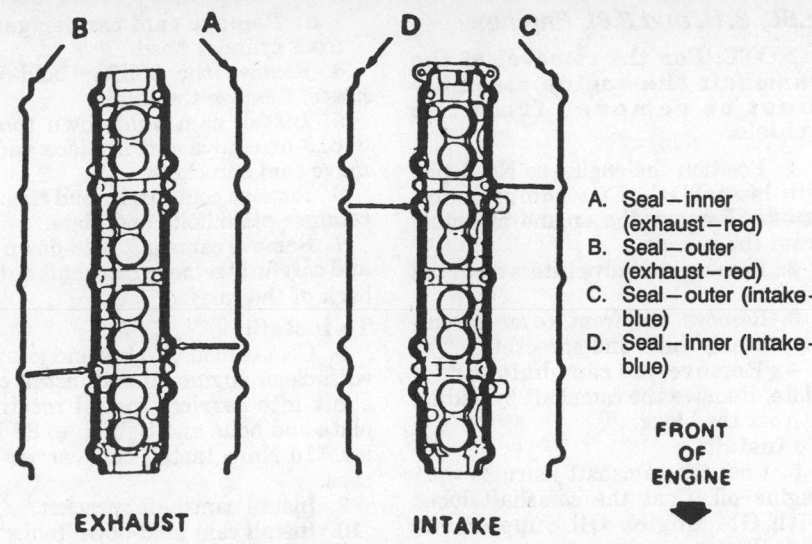

A. Seal—inner (exhaust—red)
B. Seal—outer (exhaust—red)
C. Seal—outer (intake—blue)
D. Seal—inner (Intake—blue)

FRONT OF ENGINE

EXHAUST   INTAKE

Camshaft cover assembly—2.3L Engine

ble and road test the vehicle. Check for leaks.

EXHAUST CAMSHAFT

NOTE: Any time the camshaft housing to cylinder head bolts are loosened or removed the camshaft housing to cylinder head gasket must be replaced.

1. Relieve the fuel system pressure. Disconnect the negative battery cable.
2. Label and disconnect the ignition coil and module assembly electrical connections.
3. Remove 4 ignition coil and module assembly to camshaft housing bolts and remove assembly by pulling straight up. Use a special tool to remove connector assemblies if they have stuck to the spark plugs.
4. Remove the idle speed power steering pressure switch connector.
5. Remove the transaxle fluid level indicator tube assembly from exhaust camshaft cover and position aside.
6. Remove exhaust camshaft cover and gasket.
7. Disconnect the timing chain and housing but do not remove from the engine.
8. Remove exhaust camshaft housing to cylinder head bolts. Use the reverse of the tightening procedure when loosening camshaft housing while separating camshaft cover from housing.
9. Push the cover off the housing by threading 4 of the housing to head retaining bolts into the tapped holes in the camshaft cover. Tighten the bolts evenly so the cover does not bind on the dowel pins.
10. Remove the 2 loosely installed camshaft housing to cylinder head bolts and remove cover, discard gaskets.

11. Loosely install 1 camshaft housing to cylinder head bolt to retain the housing during camshaft and lifter removal.
12. Note the position of the chain sprocket dowel pin for reassembly. Remove camshaft being careful not to damage the camshaft or journals.
13. Remove the camshaft carrier from the cylinder head and remove the gasket.

To install:
14. Thoroughly clean the mating surfaces of the camshaft carrier and the cylinder head, bolts and bolt holes. Install a new gasket and place the housing on the head. Install 1 bolt loosely to hold in place.
15. Install the lifters into their bores. If the camshaft is being replaced, the lifters must also be replaced. Lubricate camshaft lobes, journals and lifters with camshaft and lifter prelube. The camshaft lobes and journals must be adequately lubricated or engine damage could occur upon start up.
16. Install camshaft in same position as when removed. The timing chain sprocket dowel pin should be straight up and align with the centerline of the lifter bores.
17. Install new camshaft housing to camshaft housing cover seals into cover; do not use sealer. Make sure the correct color seal is placed in each groove. Install the cover to the housing.
18. Apply thread locking compound to the camshaft housing and cover retaining bolt threads.
19. Install bolts and torque in sequence to 11 ft. lbs. (15 Nm). Then rotate the bolts an additional 75 degrees, in sequence.
20. Install timing chain housing and timing chain.

21. Install the transaxle fluid level indicator tube assembly to exhaust camshaft cover.
22. Connect the idle speed power steering pressure switch connector.
23. Clean any loose lubricant that is present on the ignition coil and module assembly to camshaft housing bolts. Apply Loctite® 592 or equivalent, onto the ignition coil and module assembly to camshaft housing bolts. Install the bolts and torque to 13 ft. lbs. (18 Nm).
24. Connect the electrical connectors to ignition coil and module assembly.
25. Connect the negative battery cable and road test the vehicle. Check for leaks.

2.5L Engine

1989–90

NOTE: For the removal of the camshaft, the engine assembly must be removed from the vehicle.

1. Disconnect the negative battery cable.
2. Remove the engine assembly from the vehicle.
3. Remove the rocker arm cover and pushrods.
4. Remove the pushrod cover and valve lifters.
5. Remove the serpentine belt, crankshaft pulleys and vibration dampener.
6. Remove the front cover.
7. Remove the camshaft thrust plate screws.

NOTE: The camshaft journals are the same diameter. Care must be taken when removing the camshaft to avoid damage to the cam bearings.

8. Carefully slide the camshaft and gear through the front of the block.
9. To remove the camshaft gear, use a arbor press and adapter.
10. Old and new camshafts should be cleaned with solvent and compressed air before being installed.

To install:
11. Install the camshaft gear onto the camshaft with an arbor press.
12. Measure the end clearance with a feeler gauge between the cam journal and thrust plate. The measurement should be between 0.0015–0.0050 in. If the measurement is less than 0.0015 in., replace the spacer ring. If the measurement is more than 0.0050 in., replace the thrust plate.

NOTE: Always apply assembly lube, GM Engine Oil Supplement (E.O.S) or equivalent, to the cam journals and lobes. If this procedures is not done, cam damage may result.

13. Lubricate the camshaft journals with EOS and carefully install the camshaft into the engine block by rotating and pushing forward until seated.

14. Install the thrust plate screws and torque to 89 inch lbs. (10 Nm).

15. Install the front cover, vibration dampener and serpentine belt.

16. Install the valve lifter and pushrod cover.

17. Install the pushrods and rocker arm cover.

18. Install the engine into the vehicle.

19. Refill all necessary fluids.

20. Start the engine and check for leaks.

1991–93

NOTE: For the removal of the camshaft, the engine assembly must be removed from the vehicle.

1. Disconnect the negative battery cable.

2. Remove the engine assembly from the vehicle.

3. Remove the rocker arm cover and pushrods.

4. Remove the pushrod cover and valve lifters.

5. Remove the serpentine belt, crankshaft pulleys and vibration dampener.

6. Remove the front cover.

7. Remove the timing chain and sprockets from the engine.

8. Remove the camshaft thrust plate.

NOTE: The camshaft journals are the same diameter. Care must be taken when removing the camshaft to avoid damage to the cam bearings.

9. Carefully slide the camshaft and gear through the front of the block.

To install:

10. Lubricate the camshaft journals with Engine Oil Supplement (E.O.S) or equivalent, and carefully install the camshaft into the engine block by rotating and pushing forward until seated.

11. Install the camshaft thrust plate and tighten bolts to 89 inch lbs. (10 Nm).

12. Install the timing chain and sprockets. Tighten the camshaft sprocket to 43 ft. lbs. (58 Nm).

13. Install the pushrod cover and the valve lifters.

14. Install the rocker arm cover and pushrods.

15. Install the engine into the vehicle.

16. Refill all necessary fluids.

17. Start the engine and check for leaks.

2.8L, 3.1L and 3.8L Engines

NOTE: For the removal of the camshaft the engine assembly must be removed from the vehicle.

1. Position the engine so No. 1 piston is at TDC of its compression stroke. Remove the engine assembly from the vehicle.

2. Remove the valve lifters from the engine.

3. Remove the front cover assembly, timing chain and sprockets.

4. Remove the camshaft thrust plate. Remove the camshaft by sliding it from the block.

To install:

5. Coat the camshaft journals with engine oil. Coat the camshaft lobes with GM Engine Oil Supplement (E.O.S) or equivalent.

6. Slide the camshaft into the block. Install the thrust plate and tighten the bolts to 11 ft. lbs. (15 Nm).

7. Install the timing chain and sprockets making sure to align the timing marks.

8. Install the front cover assembly. Install the valve lifters.

9. Install the engine assembly into the vehicle. Fill all fluids to the appropriate levels.

10. Run the engine and check for leaks.

3.4L Engine

LEFT SIDE

1. Disconnect the negative battery cable.

2. Drain cooling system.

3. Remove left side cam carrier as follows:

   a. Disconnect oil/air breather hose from cam carrier cover. Remove spark plug wires from plugs and remove rear spark plug wire cover.

   b. Remove cam carrier cover bolts and lift off cover. Remove gasket and O-rings from cover.

   c. Remove secondary timing belt by removing secondary timing belt actuator and tensioner assembly and sliding belt from pulleys.

   d. Install 6 sections of fuel line hoses under cam shaft and between lifters. This will hold lifters in the carrier. For this procedure use $\frac{3}{16}$ inch fuel line hose for exhaust valves and $\frac{5}{32}$ inch fuel line hose for the intake valves.

   e. Remove exhaust crossover pipe and torque strut.

   f. Remove torque strut bracket at engine.

   g. Remove cam carrier mounting bolts and nuts and remove cam carrier.

   h. Remove cam carrier gasket from cylinder head.

4. Remove the 6 lifter hold-down hoses. Remove the lifters.

5. Install cam hold-down tool J–38613 or equivalent, in place and remove cam sprockets.

6. Remove cam carrier end caps and retainer plate bolts and plate.

7. Remove camshaft hold-down tool and carefully remove camshaft out the back of the carrier.

To install:

8. Coat camshaft lobes and journals with clean engine oil and install camshaft into carrier. Install retaining plate and bolts and tighten to 89 inch lbs. (10 Nm). Install cam carrier end caps.

9. Install camshaft sprocket.

10. Install cam hold-down tool.

11. Lubricate lifters with clean engine oil and install lifters into original position.

12. Install lifter hold-down hoses to cam carrier. Adjust cam timing.

13. Install cam carrier following these steps:

   a. Install new gasket on cam carrier to cylinder mounting surface.

   b. Install cam hold-down tool J–38613 or equivalent, to carrier assembly.

   c. Install cam carrier to cylinder head. Install mounting bolts and nuts. Torque bolts and nuts to 18 ft. lbs. (25 Nm).

   d. Remove lifter hold-down hoses and cam hold-down tool.

   e. Install torque strut bracket to engine and install torque strut.

   f. Install engine crossover pipe.

   g. Install secondary timing belt and cam carrier cover.

   h. Reconnect spark plug cover and wires.

   i. Connect breather hose to cam carrier cover.

14. Add fluids as required and reconnect negative battery cable. Start engine and recheck for leaks.

RIGHT SIDE (REAR)

1. Disconnect the negative battery cable. Drain cooling system.

2. Remove right side cam carrier as follows:

   a. Remove intake plenum and right timing belt cover.

   b. Remove right spark plug wires.

   c. Remove air/oil separator hose at cam carrier cover.

   d. Remove cam carrier cover bolts and lift of cover. Remove gasket and O-rings from cover.

   e. Remove secondary timing belt by removing secondary timing belt actuator and tensioner assembly and sliding belt from pulleys.

   f. Install 6 sections of fuel line hoses under cam shaft and between lifters. This will hold lifters in carrier. For this procedure use ³/₁₆ inch fuel line hose for exhaust valves and ⁵/₃₂ inch fuel line hose for the intake valves.

g. Remove exhaust crossover pipe and torque strut.

h. Remove torque strut bracket at engine. Remove front engine lift hook.

i. Remove cam carrier mounting bolts and nuts and remove cam carrier.

j. Remove cam carrier gasket from cylinder head.

3. Remove 6 lifter hold-down hoses.

4. Remove lifters.

5. Install cam hold-down tool J–38613 or equivalent, and remove cam sprocket.

6. Remove cam carrier end caps and retainer plate. Remove cam hold-down tool and slide cam shaft out rear of carrier.

To install

7. Lubricate camshaft lobes and journals with clean engine oil and slide into cam carrier.Install retainer plate and bolts and tighten bolts to 89 inch lbs. (10 Nm).

8. Install cam carrier end caps and cam sprockets.

9. Install cam shaft carrier hold-down tool and adjust cam timing.

10. Lubricate lifters with clean engine oil and install lifters into original position.

11. Install lifter hold-down hoses to cam carrier.

12. Install cam carrier following these steps:

a. Install new gasket on cam carrier to cylinder mounting surface.

b. Install cam hold-down tool J–38613 or equivalent, to carrier assembly.

c. Install cam carrier to cylinder head. Install mounting bolts and nuts. Torque bolts and nuts to 18 ft. lbs.

d. Remove lifter hold-down hoses and cam hold-down tool.

e. Install torque strut bracket to engine and install torque strut.

f. Install engine crossover pipe and engine lift hook.

g. Install secondary timing belt and cam carrier cover.

h. Install spark plug wires and cover.

13. Add fluids as required and connect negative battery cable. Start engine and check for fluid leaks.

Balance Shaft/ Intermediate Shaft

REMOVAL & INSTALLATION

3.4L Engine

INTERMEDIATE SHAFT

1. Disconnect the negative battery cable.

2. Remove engine from vehicle.

3. Remove right side cylinder head and oil pump drive assembly.

4. Remove the timing chain assembly.

5. Remove thrust plate screws and plate.

6. Remove the intermediate shaft using care not to damage journals or bearings.

To install:

7. Lubricate intermediate shaft journals and gear with engine oil. Install shaft, thrust plate and retainer screws. Tighten screws to 89 inch lbs. (10 Nm).

8. Replace O-ring after sprocket is installed and install timing chain and gear assembly.

9. Install oil pump drive assembly and cylinder head onto the cylinder block.

10. Install engine assembly into the vehicle. Fill fluids to the appropriate level, start the engine and check for leaks.

3.8L Engine

BALANCE SHAFT

1. Disconnect the negative battery cable. Remove the engine and secure to workstand.

2. Remove the flywheel-to-crankshaft bolts and the flywheel from the engine.

3. Remove the intake manifold from the engine.

4. Remove the lifter guide retainer bolt and retainer.

5. Remove the engine front cover.

6. Remove the balance shaft drive gear bolt.

7. Remove the camshaft sprocket and timing chain.

8. Remove the balance shaft retainer bolts, retainer and gear.

9. Using tool J–6125B, remove the balance shaft from the engine.

10. If replacing the rear balance shaft bearing, perform the following procedures:

a. Drive the rear plug from the engine.

b. Using the camshaft remover/installer tool, press the rear bearing from the rear of the engine.

NOTE: The balance shaft and bearings are serviced as a complete package.

To install:

11. Dip bearing in clean engine oil and install into the engine using tool J–36995–5. Make sure the bearing with the rolled edge faces into the engine and the manufacturer's markings face the flywheel side.

12. Dip the front balance shaft bearing in clean engine oil. Install the balance shaft into the engine block using tool J–36996. Torque the balance shaft retainer-to-engine bolts to 27 ft. lbs. (37 Nm).

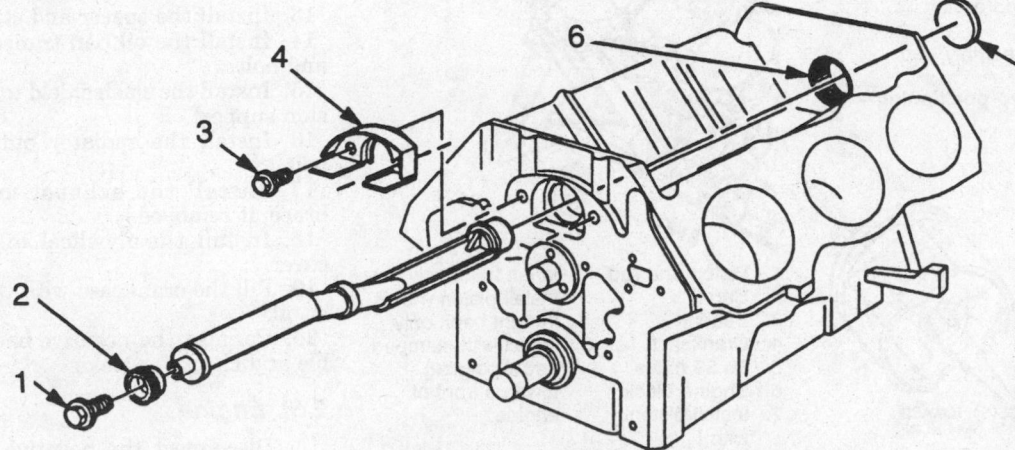

1. 14 ft. lbs. (20 Nm) plus 35 degrees
2. Balance shaft gear
3. 22 ft. lbs. (30 Nm)
4. Retainer
5. Plug
6. Bearing

Balance shaft Installation–3.8L Engine

13. Coat the threads of the balance shaft drive gear bolt with thread lock compound. Install the balance shaft drive gear and bolt and tighten to 15 ft. lbs. (20 Nm). Then rotate the bolt an additional 35 degrees.

14. Install the balance shaft rear plug.

15. Align the marks on the balance shaft gear and the camshaft gear by turning the balance shaft. Turn the crankshaft so the No. 1 piston is at TDC. Install the timing chain and sprocket.

16. Replace the balance shaft front bearing retainer and bolts. Tighten the bolts to 26 ft. lbs. (35 Nm).

17. Install the front timing cover and lifter guide retainer. Tighten the lifter guide retainer bolts to 22 ft. lbs. (35 Nm).

18. Install the intake manifold and flywheel assembly. Tighten the flywheel bolts to 11 ft. lbs., plus an additional 50 degrees.

19. Install the engine assembly into the vehicle and connect the negative battery cable. Start the engine and check for leaks.

Piston and Connecting Rod

POSITIONING

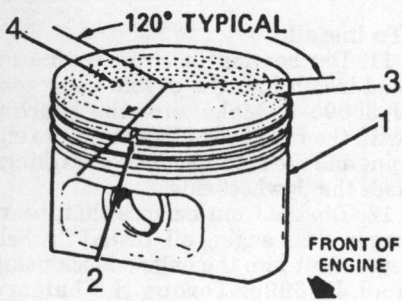

1. Piston
2. Upper compression ring gap
3. Lower compression ring gap
4. Oil ring assembly gap

Piston ring end gap positioning— 2.3L Engine

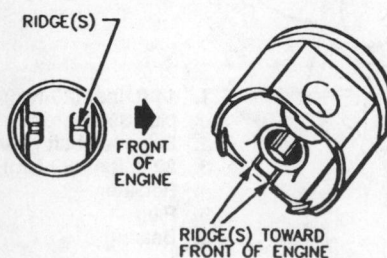

Piston positioning—3.8L Engine

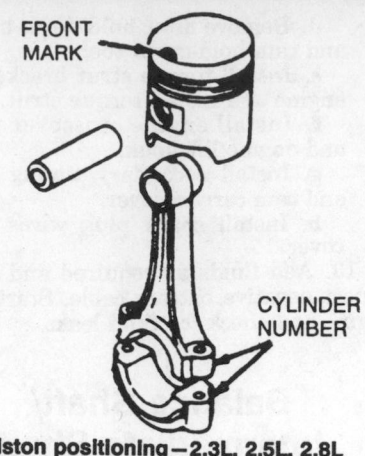

Piston positioning—2.3L, 2.5L, 2.8L and 3.1L Engines

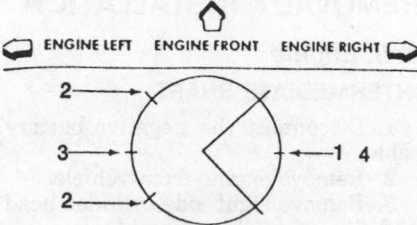

1. Oil ring spacer gap (tang in hole or slot with arc)
2. Oil ring rail gaps
3. Second compression ring gap
4. Top compression ring gap

Piston ring end gap positioning—2.5L, 2.8L, 3.1L, 3.4L and 3.8L Engines

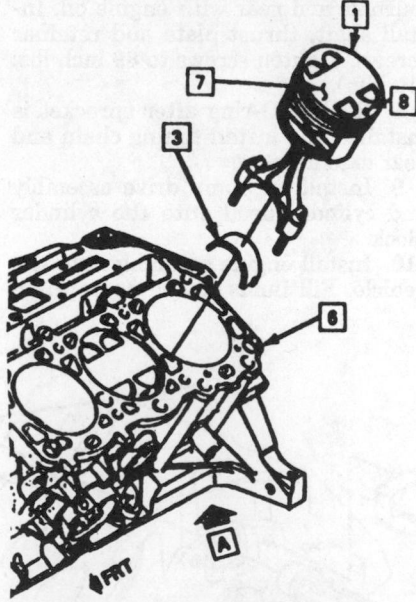

1. Piston and rod
2. Cap
3. Bearing
4. Crankshaft
5. To 39 ft. lbs.
6. Engine block
7. Install piston with L

in left bank only. Install piston with R in right bank only.

8. Install with stamped arrow pointing towards front of engine.

Piston and connecting rod assembly

ENGINE LUBRICATION

Oil Pan

REMOVAL & INSTALLATION

2.3L Engine

1. Disconnect the negative battery cable.

2. Raise and support the vehicle safely.

3. Remove the flywheel inspection cover.

4. Remove the splash shield-to-suspension support bolt. Remove the exhaust manifold brace, if equipped.

5. Remove the radiator outlet pipe-to-oil pan bolt.

6. Remove the transaxle-to-oil pan nut and stud using a 7mm socket.

7. Gently pry the spacer out from between oil pan and transaxle.

8. Remove the oil pan bolts. Rotate the crankshaft if necessary and remove the oil pan and gasket from the engine.

9. Inspect the silicone strips across the top of the aluminum carrier at the oil pan-cylinder block-seal housing 3-way joint. If damaged, the strips must be repaired with silicone sealer. Use only enough sealer to restore the strips to their original dimension; too much sealer could cause leakage.

To install:

10. Thoroughly clean and dry the mating surfaces, bolts and bolt holes. Install the oil pan with a new gasket; do not uses sealer on the gasket. Loosely install the pan bolts.

11. Place the spacer in its approximate installed position but allow clearance to tighten the pan bolt above it.

12. Torque the pan to block bolts to 17 ft. lbs. (24 Nm) and the remaining bolts to 106 inch lbs. (12 Nm).

13. Install the spacer and stud.

14. Install the oil pan transaxle nut and bolt.

15. Install the slash shield to suspension support.

16. Install the radiator outlet pipe bolt.

17. Install the exhaust manifold brace, if removed.

18. Install the flywheel inspection cover.

19. Fill the crankcase with the proper oil.

20. Connect the negative battery cable and check for leaks.

2.5L Engine

1. Disconnect the negative battery cable.

2. Remove the coolant recovery bottle, engine torque strut, air cleaner and the air inlet.

3. Remove the serpentine belt, loosen and move the air conditioning compressor from the bracket.

4. Remove the oil level indicator and fill tube.

5. Support the engine using an engine support tool J–28467–A and J–36462.

6. Raise and safely support the vehicle, drain the engine oil and remove the oil filter.

7. Remove the starter motor and flywheel cover. Turn the front wheels to full right travel.

8. Remove the engine wiring harness retainers under the oil pan on the right and left sides.

9. Remove the right engine splash shield, front engine mount bracket bolts and nuts.

10. Remove the transaxle mount nuts.

11. Using the engine support fixture tool J–28467–A and J–36462, raise the engine about 2 in.

12. Remove the front engine mount, bracket and loosen the frame bolts.

13. Remove the oil pan retaining bolts and oil pan.

To install:

14. Clean all gasket surfaces and apply RTV sealer to the oil pan and engine surfaces.

15. Install the oil pan and retaining bolts and tighten to 89 inch lbs. (10 Nm).

16. Install the frame bolts and tighten to 103 ft. lbs. (140 Nm).

17. Install the engine mount, bracket, lower the engine into position and install the transaxle mount nuts.

18. Install the engine mount nuts and bracket bolts.

19. Install the engine splash shield, wiring harness to the oil pan, flywheel cover and the starter motor.

20. Lower the vehicle and remove the engine support fixtures.

21. Install the oil level indicator and tube assembly.

22. Reinstall the air conditioning compressor to original location and serpentine belt.

23. Install the air inlet, air cleaner, torque strut and coolant recovery bottle.

24. Connect the negative battery cable and fill the engine with oil.

25. Start the engine and allow to reach normal operating temperature. Check for leaks.

2.8L and 3.1L Engines

1. Disconnect the negative battery cable.

2. Remove the serpentine belt and the tensioner.

3. Support the engine with tool J–28467 or equivalent.

4. Raise and safely support the vehicle. Drain the engine oil.

5. Remove the right tire and wheel assembly. Remove the right inner fender splash shield.

6. Remove the steering gear pinch bolt. Remove the transaxle mount retaining bolts.

NOTE: Failure to disconnect intermediate shaft from rack and pinion stub shaft can result in damage to the steering gear and/or intermediate shaft. This could cause a loss of steering control which could result in personal injury.

7. Remove the engine-to-cradle mounting nuts. Remove the front engine collar bracket from the block.

8. Remove the starter shield and the flywheel cover. Remove the starter.

9. Loosen, but do not remove the

rear engine cradle bolts. Remove electrical connector at DIS sensor.

10. Remove the front cradle bolts and lower front of frame. Remove the oil pan retaining bolts and nuts. Remove the oil pan.

To install:

11. Clean the gasket mating surfaces.

12. Install a new gasket on the oil pan. Apply silicon sealer to the portion of the pan that contacts the rear of the block.

13. Install the oil pan, nuts and retaining bolts. Tighten rear bolts to 18 ft. lbs. (18–25 Nm) and remaining nuts and bolts to 89 inch lbs. (10 Nm).

14. Install the frame to the vehicle and loosely install new mounting bolts. Align the frame by inserting 2 pins 0.74 in. (19mm) in diameter by 8.0 in. (203mm) long in the alignment holes on the right side of the frame. Tighten the right side bolts with alignment pins in place to 103 ft. lbs. (140 Nm). Then tighten the remaining bolts to the same torque. Install and tighten the engine to engine bracket bolts.

15. Connect the DIS connector. Install the starter and the heat shield. Install the flywheel inspection cover.

16. Install the steering pinch bolt. Install the right inner fender splash shield and tire assembly. Lower the vehicle.

17. Once engine is securely fastened in the vehicle, remove the engine support tool. Install the serpentine belt and tensioner.

18. Fill the crankcase to the correct level. Connect the negative battery cable. Run the engine to normal operating temperature and check for leaks.

3.4L Engine

1. Disconnect the negative battery cable.

2. Raise and safely support vehicle. Drain engine oil.

3. Remove right front wheel assembly and steering gear heat shield.

4. Remove steering gear retaining bolts and support steering gear to body.

5. Separate right and left lower ball joints from the lower control arms.

6. Disconnect power steering cooler line clamps at frame.

7. Support frame and remove engine mount nuts at frame. Remove the engine oil filter.

8. Remove frame retaining bolts and remove frame assembly.

9. Remove the oil filter, starter assembly and flywheel cover. Disconnect the fluid lines at the oil cooler.

10. Remove the oil pan retaining nuts and bolts. Remove the oil pan from the vehicle.

11. Clean all gasket material from

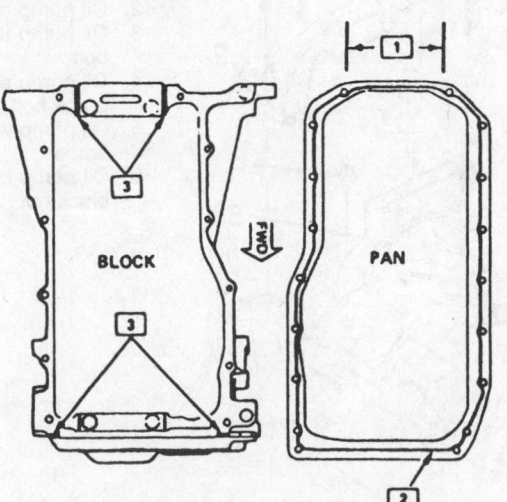

Apply RTV Sealant as specified:
1. ⅜ inch wide x ³⁄₁₆ inch thick
2. ³⁄₈ inch wide x ⅛ inch thick
3. ⅛ inch bead in areas shown

Oil pan sealer locations—2.5L Engine

the oil pan flanges, oil pan rail, front cover, rear main bearing cap and threaded holes.

To install:

12. Install new gasket adding sealer next to the rear main bearing cap. Install the oil pan to the block and secure using the retainers. Tighten the rear bolts to 18 ft. lbs. (25 Nm), the nuts to 89 inch lbs. (10 Nm) and the remaining bolts to 89 inch lbs. (10 Nm).

13. Install flywheel cover and starter motor.

14. Install frame assembly and secure all bolts.

15. Install engine mount nuts at frame. Remove frame support.

16. Install power steering cooler lines at frame.

17. Install lower ball joints. Install steering gear to steering gear mounts.

18. Install steering gear retainer bolts and heat shield.

19. Install tire assembly and lower vehicle.

20. Connect negative battery cable and add engine oil.

21. Start vehicle and check for leaks.

3.8L Engine

1. Disconnect the negative battery cable.

2. Disconnect the engine torque strut from the engine.

3. Raise and support the vehicle safely.

4. Disconnect the front exhaust pipe from the manifold.

5. Remove the right front wheel and inner fender splash shield.

6. Drain the engine oil and remove the oil filter.

7. Disconnect the oil cooler pipes and allow to hang loose for access.

8. Remove both front engine mounts from frame.

9. Remove the flywheel cover.

10. Raise the engine assembly slightly using the proper equipment and remove the oil pan retaining bolts.

11. Lower the oil pan and disconnect the oil pump screen assembly.

12. Remove the oil pan and pump screen assembly.

To install:

13. Clean the gasket mating surfaces.

14. Use a new oil pan gasket and install the oil pan and screen assembly to the engine.

NOTE: If the rear main bearing cap is being installed, then RTV sealant must be placed on the oil pan gasket tabs that insert into the gasket groove of the outer surface on the rear main bearing cap.

15. Tighten the screen assembly bolts to 115 inch lbs. and the oil pan

retaining bolts to 124 inch lbs. (13 Nm). Do not overtighten.

16. Lower the engine and install the transaxle converter cover.

17. Install the engine mount nuts to the frame and tighten to 32 ft. lbs. (44 Nm).

18. Install the oil cooler pipes and oil filter.

19. Install the inner fender splash shield and wheel assembly.

20. Install the front exhaust pipe to the manifold.

21. Lower the vehicle and install the engine torque strut to the engine.

22. Fill with engine oil and connect the negative battery cable.

Oil Pump

REMOVAL & INSTALLATION

2.3L Engine

1. Disconnect the negative battery cable.

2. Raise and support the vehicle safely.

3. Drain the engine oil and remove the oil pan.

4. Remove the oil pump retaining bolts and nut.

5. Remove the oil pump assembly, shims, if equipped, and screen.

To install:

6. With oil pump assembly off engine, remove 3 retaining bolts and separate the driven gear cover and screen assembly from the oil pump.

7. Install the oil pump on the block using the original shims, if equipped. Tighten the bolts to 33 ft. lbs. (45 Nm).

8. Mount a dial indicator assembly

to measure backlash between oil pump to drive gear.

9. Record oil pump drive to driven gear backlash. Proper backlash is 0.010–0.018 in. When measuring, do not allow the crankshaft to move.

10. If equipped with shims, remove shims to decrease clearance and add shims to increase clearance. If no shims were present, replace the assembly if proper backlash cannot be obtained.

11. When the proper clearance is reached, rotate crankshaft ½ turn and recheck clearance.

12. Remove oil pump from block, fill the cavity with petroleum jelly and reinstall driven gear cover and screen assembly to pump. Tighten the bolts to 106 inch lbs. (13 Nm).

13. Reinstall the pump assembly to the block. Torque oil pump-to-block bolts 33 ft. lbs. (45 Nm).

14. Install the oil pan.

15. Fill the crankcase with oil to the proper level.

16. Connect the negative battery cable, check the oil pressure and check for leaks.

2.5L, 2.8L, 3.1L and 3.4L Engines

NOTE: On the 2.5L engine, the force balancer assembly does not have to be removed to service the oil pump or pressure regulator assemblies.

1. Disconnect the negative battery cable.

2. Raise and safely support the vehicle.

3. Drain the engine oil.

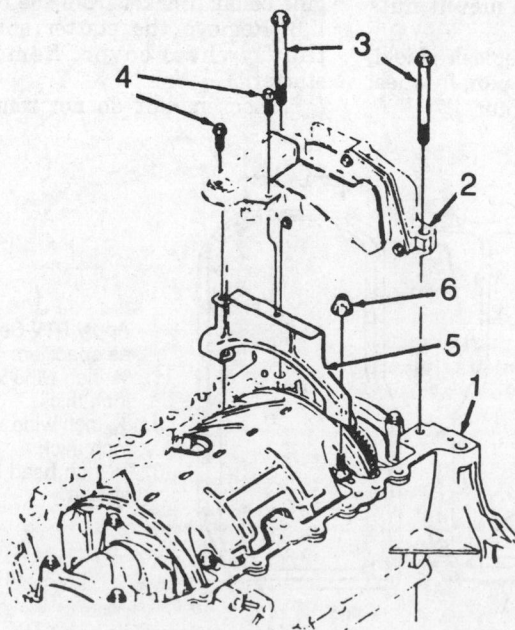

1. Cylinder block
2. Oil pump assembly
3. Oil pump to block bolt
4. Oil pump screen to brace bolt
5. Oil pump to block brace
6. Oil pump brace to block nut

Oil pump Installation—2.3L Engine

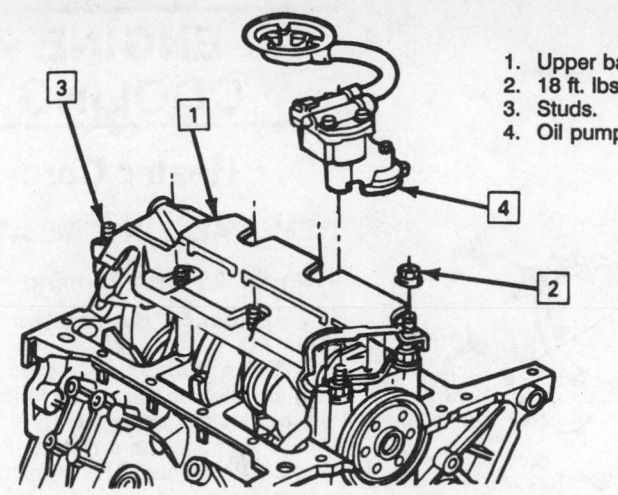

1. Upper baffle.
2. 18 ft. lbs.
3. Studs.
4. Oil pump.

Oil pan baffle—3.4L Engine

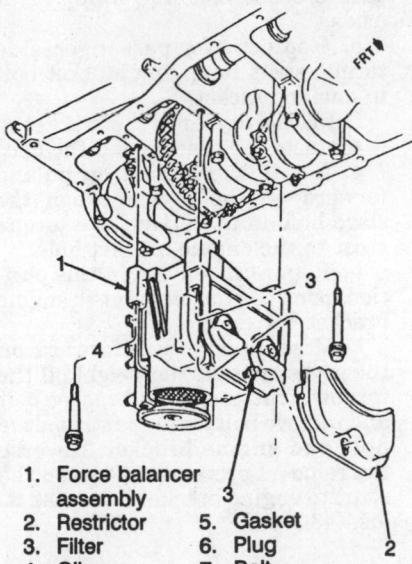

1. Force balancer assembly
2. Restrictor
3. Filter
4. Oil pan
5. Gasket
6. Plug
7. Bolt

Oil pump/force balancer assembly—2.5L Engine

4. Remove the oil pan.

5. On 3.4L engine, remove the oil pan baffle by extracting the nuts and rotating the oil pickup tube out of the way.

6. Remove the oil pump retaining bolts and remove the oil pump and pump driveshaft.

To install:

7. Install the oil pump and pump driveshaft. Tighten the oil pump mounting bolts to 30 ft. lbs. (41 Nm) for the 2.8L and 3.1L engines, 40 ft. lbs. (54 Nm) for 3.4L engine or to 89 inch lbs. (10 Nm) for 2.5L engine.

8. Install oil pan baffle, if equipped, and tighten nuts to 18 ft. lbs. (24 Nm). Install oil pan. Lower the vehicle.

9. Fill the crankcase to the correct level with oil. Run the vehicle and check for leaks.

3.8L Engine

1. Disconnect the negative battery cable.

2. Raise and safely support the vehicle.

3. Drain the engine oil.

4. Remove the front cover assembly.

5. Remove the oil filter adapter, pressure regulator valve and spring.

6. Remove the oil pump cover attaching screws and remove the cover.

7. Remove the oil pump gears.

To install:

8. Lubricate the gears with petroleum jelly and install the gears into the housing.

9. Pack the gear cavity with petroleum jelly after the gears have been installed in the housing.

10. Install the oil pump cover and screws and tighten to 97 inch lbs. (11 Nm).

11. Install the oil filter adapter with new gasket, pressure regulator valve and spring.

12. Install the front cover assembly.

13. Fill with clean engine oil and test oil pressure.

NOTE: Running the engine without measurable oil pressure will cause extensive damage.

CHECKING

2.3L Engine

1. Inspect all components carefully for physical damage of any type and replace worn parts.

2. Check the gerotor cavity depth. The specification is 0.674–0.676 in. (17.11–17.16mm).

3. Check the gerotor cavity diameter. The specification is 2.127–2.129 in. (53.95–54.00mm).

4. Check the inner gerotor tip clearance. The maximum clearance is 0.006 in. (15mm).

5. Check the outer gerotor diameter clearance. The specification is 0.010–0.014 in. (0.254–0.354mm).

2.5L Engine

1. Inspect all components carefully for physical damage of any type and replace worn parts.

2. Check the gerotor cavity depth. The specification is 0.514–0.516 in. (13.05–13.10mm).

3. Check the gear lash. The specification is 0.009–0.015 in. (0.23–0.38mm).

4. Check the clearance of both gears. The maximum clearance is 0.004 in. (0.10mm).

2.8L, 3.1L and 3.4L Engines

1. Inspect all components carefully for physical damage of any type and replace worn parts.

2. Check the gear pocket depth. The specification is 1.195–1.198 in. (30.36–30.44mm).

3. Check the gear pocket diameter. The specification is 1.503–1.506 in. (38.18–38.25mm).

4. Check the gear length. The measurement is 1.199–1.200 in. (30.45–30.48mm).

5. Check the outer gear diameter clearance. The specification is 1.498–1.500 in. (38.05–38.10mm).

6. The pressure regulator valve-to-bore clearance should be 0.0015–0.0035 in. (0.038–0.089mm).

3.8L Engine

1. Inspect all components carefully for physical damage of any type and replace worn parts.

2. The inner tip clearance should be 0.006 in.

3. The outer gear diameter clearance should be 0.008–0.015 in.

4. The gear end clearance or the drop in the housing should be 0.001–0.0035 in.

5. The pressure regulator valve-to-bore clearance should be 0.0015–0.003 in.

Rear Main Bearing Oil Seal

REMOVAL & INSTALLATION

2.3L Engine

1. Disconnect the negative battery cable. Remove the transaxle from the vehicle.

2. Remove the flywheel. Remove the oil pan-to-seal housing bolts and the block-to-seal housing bolts.

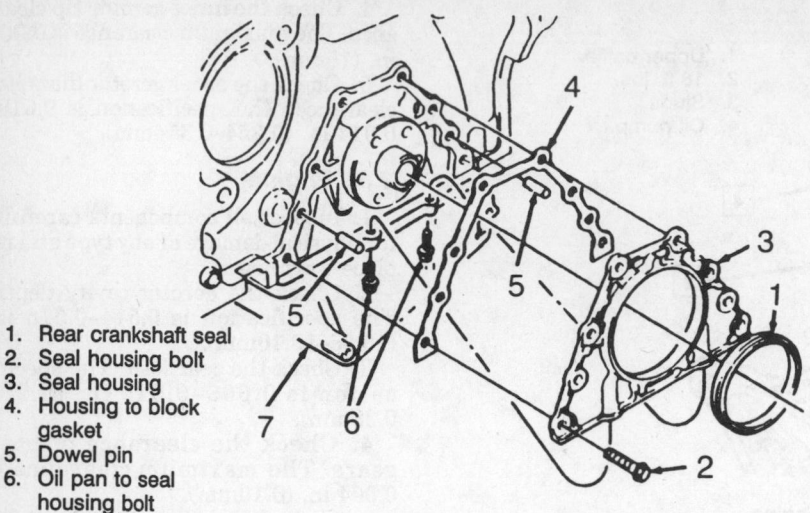

1. Rear crankshaft seal
2. Seal housing bolt
3. Seal housing
4. Housing to block gasket
5. Dowel pin
6. Oil pan to seal housing bolt
7. Oil pan

Rear crankshaft seal Installation—2.3L Engine

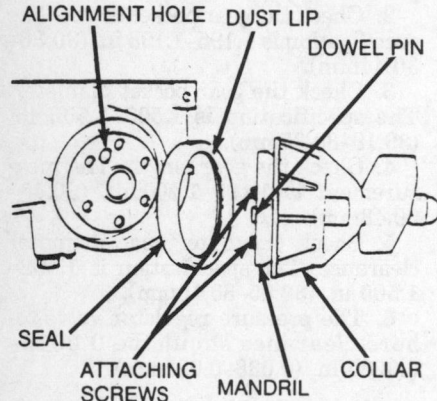

ALIGNMENT HOLE   DUST LIP
DOWEL PIN
SEAL
ATTACHING SCREWS   MANDRIL   COLLAR

Rear main seal replacement—2.8L, 3.1L, 3.4L and 3.8L Engines

3. Remove the seal housing from the engine.
4. Place 2 blocks of equal thickness on a flat surface and position the seal housing on the 2 blocks. Remove the seal from the housing.
5. The installation is the reverse of the removal procedure. Use new gaskets when installing.

2.5L Engine

1. Disconnect the negative battery cable. Remove the transaxle assembly.
2. Remove the flywheel from the vehicle.
3. Carefully pry out the seal, using prying tool.

To install:
4. Clean the the block and crankshaft to seal mating surfaces.

5. Apply engine oil to the inside and outside diameter of the new seal.
6. Press the new seal evenly into place, using tool J–34924–A or equivalent.
7. Install the flywheel and transaxle and check for leaks.

2.8L, 3.1L, 3.4L and 3.8L Engines

NOTE: These engines use a round rear oil seal that requires removal of the transaxle and flywheel.

1. Support the engine with tool J–28467 or equivalent. Raise and safely support the vehicle.
2. Remove the transaxle assembly. Remove the flywheel.
3. Using a small prybar or equivalent, insert it through the dust lip at an angle and pry the old seal from the block.
4. Inspect the seal bore and the crankshaft end for any damage.
5. Coat the inside lip of the seal with engine oil and install on the seal installation tool J–34686 or equivalent.
6. Align the dowel pin of the tool with the dowel pin of the crankshaft. Install the tool on the crankshaft and turn the wing nut until the tool and seal are fully seated on the crankshaft.
7. Loosen the wing nut and remove the tool. Check the seal to make sure it is properly seated.
8. Install the flywheel and the transaxle.
9. Remove the engine support tool. Run the engine and check for leaks.

ENGINE COOLING

Heater Core

REMOVAL & INSTALLATION

Without Air Conditioning

1. Disconnect the negative battery cable.
2. Drain the cooling system.
3. Rotate the engine as follows:
   a. Put the transaxle in N.
   b. Remove the air cleaner.
   c. Disconnect the negative battery cable.
   d. Remove the torque strut to engine bracket bolt and swing strut aside.
   e. Replace the passenger side torque strut to engine bracket bolt in engine bracket.
   f. Place a prybar in the bracket so it contacts the bracket and the bolt.
   g. Rotate the engine by pulling forward on the prybar. Align the slave hole in the driver side torque strut to the engine bracket hole.
   h. Retain the engine in this position using the torque strut to engine bracket bolt.
   i. After repairs, pull forward on the prybar to take the weight off the torque strut to engine bracket bolt and remove bolt from the strut slave hole and engine bracket. Reverse the removal procedure. Tighten the strut to engine bracket bolt to 32 ft. lbs. (43 Nm).

NOTE: To prevent shearing of the rubber bushing, loosen the bolts on the engine strut before swinging the struts.

4. Remove heater hose retaining nuts and the heater hoses from core after loosening mubea clamps using tool J–38543 or equivalent.
5. Remove the right sound insulator panel and rear seat duct adapter.
6. Remove heater floor duct and lower left sound insulator panel.
7. Remove core cover screws and cover.
8. Remove core retaining bolts and core.

To install:
9. Install core and retaining bolts.
10. Install core cover and attaching screws.
11. Install lower left sound insulator panel, heater floor duct and rear seat adapter.
12. Reinstall right sound insulator panel.
13. Install heater hoses to core using

mubea clamps and tool J–38543 or equivalent.

14. Reinstall heater hose retaining bracket nuts.

15. Refill with coolant using the proper delution and reconnect negative battery cable.

With Air Conditioning

1. Disconnect the negative battery cable.

2. Drain the cooling system.

3. Rotate the engine as follows:

   a. Put the transaxle in **N**.

   b. Remove the air cleaner.

   c. Disconnect the negative battery cable.

   d. Remove the torque strut to engine bracket bolt and swing strut aside.

   e. Replace the passenger side torque strut to engine bracket bolt in engine bracket.

   f. Place a prybar in the bracket so it contacts the bracket and the bolt.

   g. Rotate the engine by pulling forward on the prybar. Align the slave hole in the driver side torque strut to the engine bracket hole.

   h. Retain the engine in this position using the torque strut to engine bracket bolt.

   i. After repairs, pull forward on the prybar to take the weight off the torque strut to engine bracket bolt and remove bolt from the strut slave hole and engine bracket. Reverse the removal procedure. Tighten the strut to engine bracket bolt to 32 ft. lbs. (43 Nm).

NOTE: To prevent shearing of the rubber bushing, loosen the bolts on the engine strut before swinging the struts.

4. Remove the upper firewall weatherstrip. Remove the upper secondary cowl and lower secondary cowl upper retaining nut.

5. Remove the heater hoses from the core.

6. Remove the heater core cover and remove the heater core.

To install:

7. Install the heater core and the heater core cover.

8. Install the sound insulator.

9. Attach the heater hoses to the core. Install the lower secondary cowl upper nut, the upper cowl and the weatherstrip.

10. Fill the cooling system and check for leaks. Connect the negative battery cable.

Water Pump

REMOVAL & INSTALLATION

2.3L Engine

1. Disconnect the negative battery cable.

2. Disconnect the upper engine torque strut and rotate the engine rearward.

3. Disconnect and remove the oxygen sensor, as required.

4. Remove the exhaust heat shield and EGR valve, if equipped.

5. Remove the exhaust pipe from manifold.

6. Remove the exhaust manifold.

7. Partially drain the engine coolant.

8. Remove the coolant return hose and lower coolant pipe from the pump.

9. Remove the pump retaining bolts and pump.

To install:

10. Clean the gasket mating surfaces.

11. Install the pump, retaining bolts and torque to 19 ft. lbs. (26 Nm).

12. Install the lower coolant pipe and torque to 124 inch lbs. (14 Nm).

13. Install the coolant return hose.

14. Install the exhaust manifold and pipe, oxygen sensor, EGR valve and heat shield.

15. Return the engine to its proper position and install the torque strut.

16. Refill the engine with coolant, connect the negative battery cable, start the engine and check for coolant leaks.

2.5L Engine

1. Disconnect the negative battery cable.

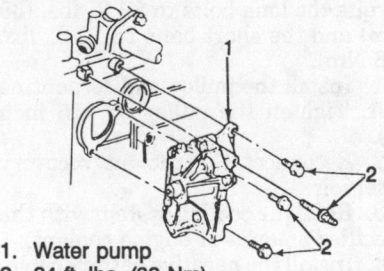

1. Water pump
2. 24 ft. lbs. (33 Nm)

Water pump mounting—2.5L Engine

2. Remove the alternator.

3. Remove the convenience center heat shield.

4. Drain about a gallon of engine coolant from the radiator. Enough to be below the water pump level.

5. Remove water pump-to-engine attaching bolts.

6. Remove the water pump and gasket.

7. Remove the pulley from the old pump, as required.

To install:

8. Clean the water pump mating surfaces.

9. Install the pump and pulley assembly onto the engine with a new gasket in place.

10. Install the water pump attaching bolts and torque to 24 ft. lbs. (33 Nm).

11. Apply sealer to the pump inlet and install. Install coolant pump inlet bolts and coolant pump hoses.

12. Install the convenience center heat shield, alternator and negative battery cable.

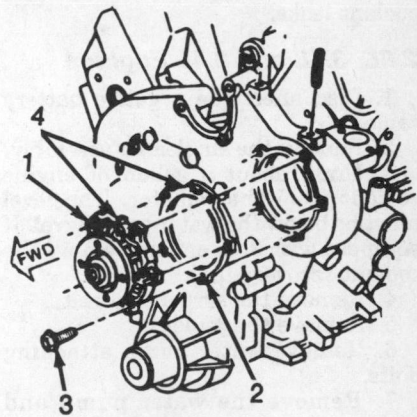

1. Water pump
2. Gasket
3. Mounting bolts
4. Pump locator—must be vertical

Water pump mounting—2.8L and 3.1L Engines

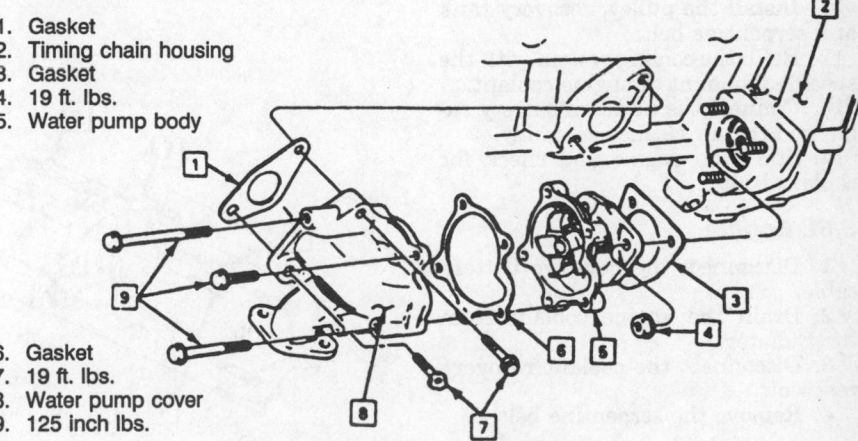

1. Gasket
2. Timing chain housing
3. Gasket
4. 19 ft. lbs.
5. Water pump body
6. Gasket
7. 19 ft. lbs.
8. Water pump cover
9. 125 inch lbs.

Water pump mounting—2.3L Engine

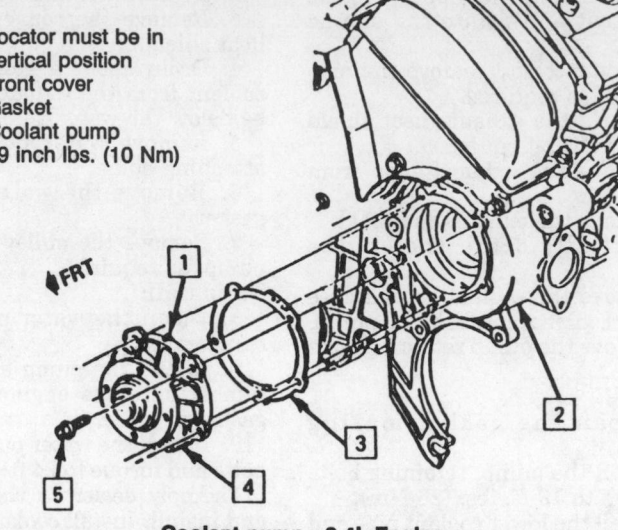

1. Locator must be in vertical position
2. Front cover
3. Gasket
4. Coolant pump
5. 89 inch lbs. (10 Nm)

Coolant pump—3.4L Engine

13. Refill the cooling system with the specified amount of engine coolant.

14. Start the engine and check for coolant leaks.

2.8L, 3.1L and 3.4L Engines

1. Disconnect the negative battery cable.

2. Remove the air cleaner assembly.

3. Drain about a gallon of engine coolant from the radiator. The level must be below the water pump level. If equipped with 3.4L engine, remove the coolant recovery tank.

4. Remove the serpentine belt.

5. Remove the pulley.

6. Remove water pump attaching bolts.

7. Remove the water pump and gasket.

To install:

8. Clean the water pump mounting surfaces.

9. Install the water pump with a new gasket in place.

10. Install the attaching bolts and torque to 89 inch lbs. (10 Nm).

11. Install the pulley, recovery tank and serpentine belt.

12. Refill the cooling system with specified amount of engine coolant.

13. Connect the negative battery cable and the air cleaner assembly.

14. Start the engine and check for coolant leaks.

3.8L Engine

1. Disconnect the negative battery cable.

2. Drain the engine coolant from the radiator.

3. Disconnect the coolant recovery reservoir.

4. Remove the serpentine belt.

NOTE: If more access is need-

ed, remove the inner fender electrical cover.

5. Remove the pulley.

6. Remove water pump attaching bolts.

7. Remove the water pump and gasket.

To install:

8. Clean the water pump mounting surfaces.

9. Install the water pump with a new gasket.

10. Install the attaching bolts and torque the long bolts to 22 ft. lbs. (30 Nm) and the short bolts to 13 ft. lbs. (18 Nm).

11. Install the pulley and serpentine belt. Tighten the pulley to 115 inch lbs.

12. Reconnect the coolant recovery reservoir.

13. Refill the cooling system with the specified amount of engine coolant.

14. Install the negative battery cable.

15. Start the engine and check for coolant leaks.

Thermostat

REMOVAL & INSTALLATION

2.3L Engine

1. Disconnect the negative battery cable.

2. Remove the air cleaner assembly and partially drain the engine coolant into a drain pan.

3. Remove the radiator and heater hoses from the coolant outlet.

4. Remove the electrical connectors from the coolant outlet.

5. Remove the pipe and retaining bolts from the outlet.

6. Remove the outlet and thermostat.

To install:

7. Clean the gasket mating surfaces.

8. Using a new gasket and RTV sealant, install the thermostat and outlet.

9. Torque the bolts to 19 ft. lbs. (26 Nm).

10. Install the pipe, electrical connectors and hoses to the coolant outlet.

11. Refill the radiator with the specified amount of engine coolant, connect the negative battery cable and install the air cleaner.

12. Start the engine and check for leaks.

2.5L Engine

1. Partially drain engine coolant from the radiator. Disconnect negative battery cable.

2. Remove the thermostat housing cap.

3. Remove the thermostat by using the wire handle to lift it out of the housing.

To install:

4. Insert the thermostat and seal into the housing.

5. Install the thermostat housing cap and refill the engine with the prop-

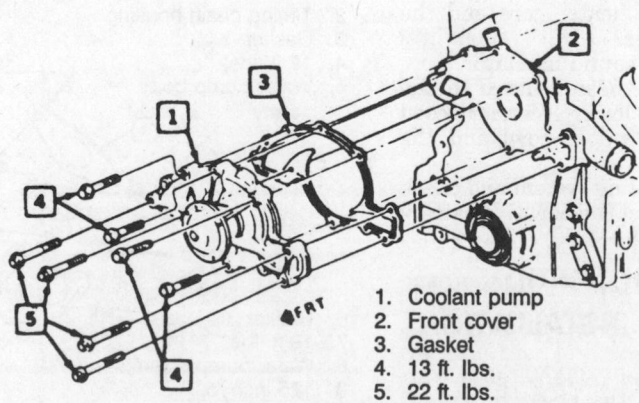

1. Coolant pump
2. Front cover
3. Gasket
4. 13 ft. lbs.
5. 22 ft. lbs.

Water pump mounting—3.8L Engine

er amount of engine coolant. Reconnect negative battery cable.

6. Start engine and check for leaks.

2.8L, 3.1L and 3.4L Engines

1. Disconnect the negative battery cable. Drain 1 gallon of engine coolant from the radiator.

2. Remove the radiator hose from the water outlet.

3. Remove the water outlet attaching bolts and water outlet.

4. Remove the thermostat.

5. Clean the manifold water inlet and water outlet mating surfaces.

To install:

6. Position the thermostat into the inlet manifold.

7. Apply a 0.125 inch (3mm) bead of RTV sealer to the thermostat housing.

8. Install the water outlet to the inlet manifold. Torque the attaching bolts to 18 ft. lbs. (25 Nm).

9. Install the radiator hose to the water outlet housing.

10. Refill the engine with the specified engine coolant. Reconnect negative battery cable, start the engine and check for coolant leaks.

3.8L Engine

1. Drain about a ½ gallon of engine coolant from the radiator. Disconnect negative battery cable.

2. Remove the radiator hose from the water outlet.

3. Disconnect the electrical connections from the throttle body assembly.

4. Remove the water outlet attaching bolts and water outlet.

5. Remove the thermostat.

6. Clean the manifold water inlet and water outlet mating surfaces.

To install:

7. Position the thermostat into the intake manifold with a new gasket.

8. Install the water outlet to the intake manifold with RTV sealer. Torque the attaching bolts to 20 ft. lbs. (27 Nm).

9. Install the radiator hose to the water outlet housing.

10. Connect the electrical connections to the throttle body assembly.

11. Refill the engine with the specified engine coolant. Connect the negative battery cable, start the engine and check for coolant leaks.

Cooling System Bleeding

To insure complete filling of the cooling system, it is necessary to bleed the system.

1. Disconnect the negative battery cable.

2. Park vehicle on level surface.

3. Remove thermostat housing cap and thermostat or open bleed vents:

a. On 2.5L engine, remove the thermostat housing cap and thermostat.

b. On 2.3L and 2.8L engines open bleed valve on thermostat housing 2–3 turns.

c. On 3.1L engine, open the air bleed vents on the thermostat housing and the throttle body return pipe above coolant pump. Open vents 2–3 turns.

d. On 3.4L engine, open the air bleed vents on the thermostat housing and the heater coolant inlet pipe by the master brake cylinder. Open vents 2–3 turns.

e. On 3.8L engine, open air bleed vent on thermostat housing. Open 2–3 turns.

4. Fill cooling system with coolant to base of radiator neck .

5. Reinstall or replace the thermostat and housing and close air vents.

6. Fill coolant reservoir to proper level with ethylene glycol/water mixture.

7. Reconnect negative battery cable. Start vehicle and let engine reach operating temperature adding coolant as needed. Check the cooling system for leaks.

ENGINE ELECTRICAL

NOTE: Disconnecting the negative battery cable on some vehi- cles may interfere with the functions of the on board computer systems and may require the computer to undergo a relearning process, once the negative battery cable is reconnected.

Distributorless Ignition System

REMOVAL & INSTALLATION

Ignition CoiL

2.3L ENGINE

1. Disconnect the negative battery cable.

2. Disconnect the 11-pin (IDI) harness connector at the ignition cover.

3. Remove the 4 ignition system assembly-to-camshaft housing bolts.

4. Remove the ignition assembly from the vehicle.

5. Remove the 4 coil housing-to-cover screws.

NOTE: Be careful not to damage the module terminals when pulling the coil assemblies from the module. Pull slowly and carefully away from the ignition assembly.

6. Disconnect the coil harness connectors.

7. Remove the coils, contacts and seals from the cover.

NOTE: If the spark plug boots stick, use a spark plug connector removing tool J-36011 or equivalent, to remove with a twisting motion.

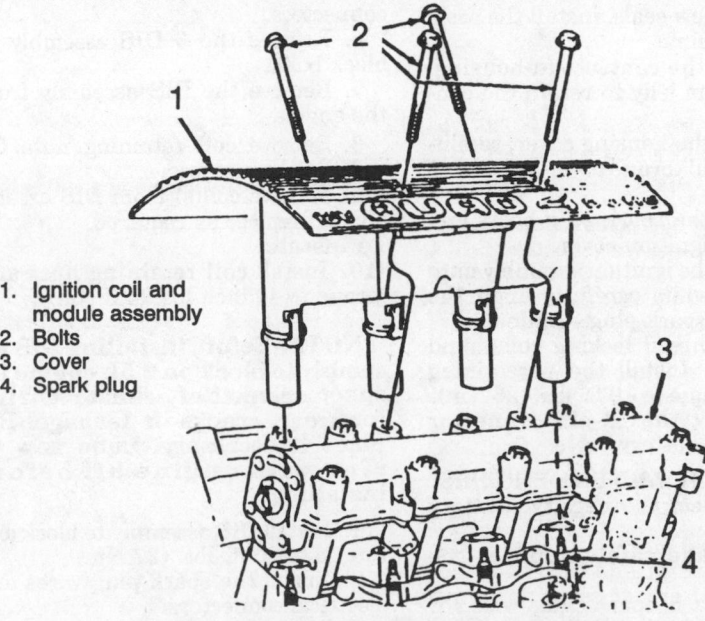

1. Ignition coil and module assembly
2. Bolts
3. Cover
4. Spark plug

Ignition coil and module assembly – 2.3L Engine

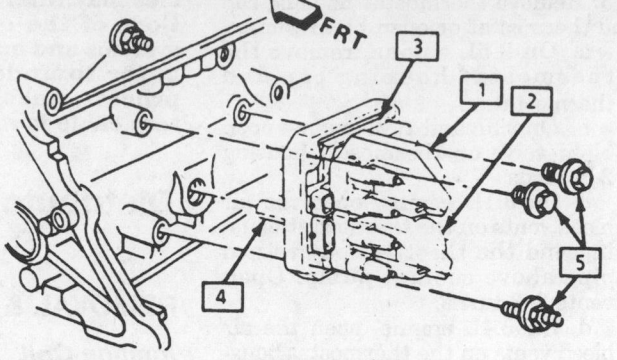

1. No. 2–3 ignition coil
2. No. 1–4 ignition coil
3. Ignition module
4. Crankshaft sensor
5. Bolt (20 ft. lbs.)

Ignition coils, module and sensor—2.5L Engine

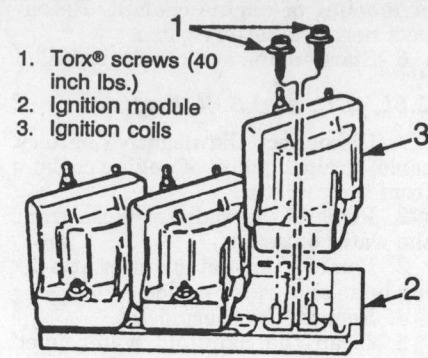

1. Torx® screws (40 inch lbs.)
2. Ignition module
3. Ignition coils

Ignition coil mounting—3.8L Engine

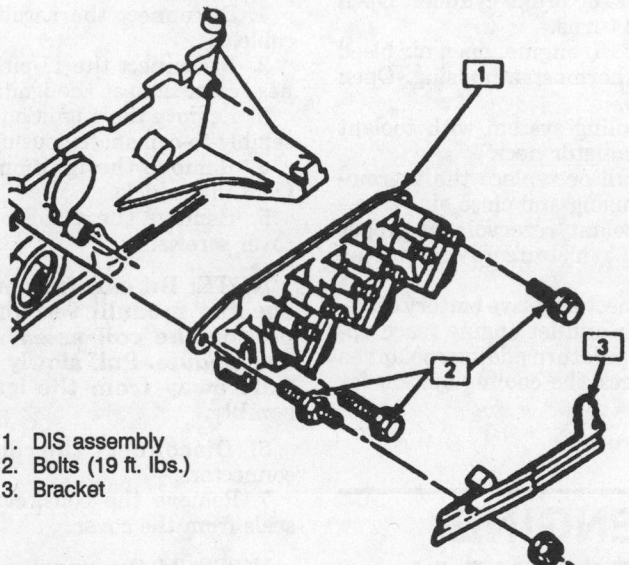

1. DIS assembly
2. Bolts (19 ft. lbs.)
3. Bracket

Coil and module assembly mounting—2.8L and 3.1L Engines

To install:
8. Install the coils to the cover.
9. Connect the coil harness.
10. Using new seals, install the seals into the housing.
11. Install the contacts-to-housing. Use petroleum jelly to retain the contact in place.
12. Install the housing cover, retaining screws and torque to 35 inch lbs. (4 Nm).
13. Install the spark plug boots and retainers-to-ignition cover.
14. Install the ignition assembly onto the engine while carefully align the boots to the spark plug terminals.
15. Apply thread locking compound to the bolts. Install the 4 retaining bolts and torque to 19 ft. lbs. (26 Nm).
16. Connect the 11-pin connector and negative battery cable.

2.5L, 2.8L, 3.1L AND 3.4L ENGINES
1. Disconnect the negative battery cable.
2. Raise and safely support the vehicle.
3. Label each spark plug wire for proper installation.

4. Remove the spark plug wires from the ignition coils.
5. Remove the DIS electrical connectors.
6. Remove the 3 DIS assembly to block bolts.
7. Remove the DIS assembly from the engine.
8. Remove coil retaining nuts for coil(s) to be replaced.
9. Remove coil(s) from DIS assembly and replace as required.
To install:
10. Install coil retaining nuts and torque to 40 inch lbs. (4.5 Nm).

NOTE: Befofe installing DIS assembly to block on 2.5L engine inspect crankshaft sensor O-ring for wear, cracks or leakage. Replace if necessary. Lube new O-ring with engine oil before installing.

11. Install DIS assembly to block and torque to 20 ft. lbs. (27 Nm).
12. Install the spark plug wires and electrical connectors.
13. Reconnect negative battery cable.

3.8L ENGINE
1. Disconnect negative battery cable.
2. Label and disconnect spark plug wires.
3. Remove 2 screws securing coil to ignition module.
4. Remove coil(s) from module.
5. Install coil using 2 screws, torque to 40 inch lbs.
6. Reconnect spark plug wires and negative battery cable.

Ignition Module

2.3L ENGINE
1. Disconnect the negative battery cable.
2. Disconnect the 11 pin IDI electrical harness connector. Remove the 4 ignition system assembly retaining bolts and the ignition cover assembly from the engine.
3. Remove the 4 housing screws, coil housing and coil harness connectors.
4. Remove the 3 module-to-housing cover screws and module.
To install:
5. If replacing the module or a coil, the new unit should come with a package of silicone grease, if not, purchase a tube at your local parts distributor. Spread the grease on the metal face of the module and on the cover where the module seats. The grease is used for module cooling.
6. Install the module-to-cover, module screws and torque to 35 inch lbs. (4 Nm).
7. Install the coil harness-to-module and housing cover screws. Torque the screws to 35 inch lbs. (4 Nm).
8. Install the spark plug boots and retainers to the housing.
9. Install the ignition system to the engine while carefully aligning the spark plug boots with the terminals.
10. Apply thread locking compound to the bolts. Install the 4 retaining bolts and torque to 19 ft. lbs. (26 Nm).
11. Connect the 11-pin connector and negative battery cable.

2.5L ENGINE

1. Disconnect the negative battery cable.
2. Label each spark plug wire for proper installation.
3. Remove the spark plug and module electrical connectors from the DIS assembly.
4. Remove the 3 DIS assembly-to-engine attaching bolts.

NOTE: Be careful not to damage the crankshaft sensor and module terminals when pulling the DIS assemblies from the engine. Pull slowly and carefully away from the engine.

5. Remove the DIS assembly from the engine.
6. Remove the coils from the DIS assembly.
7. Remove the module from assembly plate.
To install:
8. Carefully engage the sensor to module terminals and install module assembly to plate.
9. Reinstall coils, torque screws to 45 inch lbs. (5 Nm).
10. Install the DIS assembly and torque bolts to 20 ft. lbs. (27 Nm).
11. Reconnect the spark plugs and module electrical connectors to their original positions.

3.1L AND 3.4L ENGINES

1. Disconnect the negative battery cable.
2. Raise the vehicle and support safely.
3. Label each spark plug wire for proper installation.
4. Remove the spark plug and module electrical connectors from the DIS assembly.
5. Remove the 3 DIS assembly attaching bolts.
6. Remove the DIS assembly from the engine.
7. Remove the coils from the DIS assembly. Remove the module from assembly plate.
To install:
8. Install the module to the assembly plate.
9. Install the coil assemblies to the module and torque the screws to 45 inch lbs. (5 Nm).
10. Install the DIS assembly and attaching bolts to the engine and torque to 20 ft. lbs. (27 Nm).
11. Reconnect the spark plug and module electrical connectors to their original positions.
12. Reconnect the negative battery cable.

3.8L ENGINE

1. Disconnect the negative battery cable.

2. Disconnect the 14-way connector at the ignition module.
3. Disconnect and label the spark plug wires.
4. Remove the 6 screws securing the coil assemblies to the ignition module and disconnect the coils from the module.
5. Remove the 3 nuts and washers securing the ignition module assembly to the bracket and remove the module.
To install:
6. Install the coils onto the module and tighten the 6 retaining screws to 40 inch lbs.
7. Install the 3 nuts and washers securing the ignition module assembly to the bracket and tighten to 70 inch lbs.
8. Connect the spark plug wires.
9. Connect the 14-way connector to the ignition module.
10. Reconnect negative battery cable.

Ignition Timing

ADJUSTMENT

Because the reluctor is an integral part of the crankshaft and the crankshaft sensor is mounted in a fixed position, timing adjustment is not possible.

Alternator

PRECAUTIONS

Several precautions must be observed with alternator equipped vehicles to avoid damage to the unit.

- If the battery is removed for any reason, make sure it is reconnected with the correct polarity. Reversing the battery connections may result in damage to the 1-way rectifiers.
- When utilizing a booster battery as a starting aid, always connect the positive to positive terminals and the negative terminal from the booster battery to a good engine ground on the vehicle being started.
- Never use a fast charger as a booster to start vehicles.
- Disconnect the battery cables when charging the battery with a fast charger.
- Never attempt to polarize the alternator.
- Do not use test lights of more than 12 volts when checking diode continuity.
- Do not short across or ground any of the alternator terminals.
- The polarity of the battery, alternator and regulator must be matched and considered before making any electrical connections within the system.

- Never separate the alternator on an open circuit. Make sure all connections within the circuit are clean and tight.
- Disconnect the battery ground terminal when performing any service on electrical components.
- Disconnect the battery if arc welding is to be done on the vehicle.

BELT TENSION ADJUSTMENT

A single serpentine belt is used to drive all engine mounted components. Drive belt tension is maintained by a spring loaded tensioner.

NOTE: The drive belt tensioner can control the belt tension over a wide range of belt lengths; however, there are limits to the tensioners ability to compensate for various belt lengths. Installing the wrong size belt and using the tensioner outside of its operating range can result in poor tension control and damage to the tensioner, drive belt and driven components.

REMOVAL & INSTALLATION

2.3L Engine

1. Disconnect the negative battery cable.
2. Remove the electrical center fuse block shield.
3. Remove the serpentine belt, by removing the belt guard, and lifting or rotating the tensioner, using a breaker bar.
4. Label and remove the alternator electrical connectors.
5. Remove the alternator brace bolt, rear bolt and front bolt.

NOTE: Use extreme care when removing the alternator, not to damage the air conditioning compressor and condensor hose.

6. Lift the alternator out between the engine lifting eyelet and the air conditioning compressor.
To install:
7. Install the alternator to the engine. Install the front, rear and brace retaining bolts.
8. Torque the long bolt to 40 ft. lbs. (54 Nm), the short bolt to 19 ft. lbs. (26 Nm) and the brace bolt to 18 ft. lbs. (25 Nm).
9. Connect the alternator electrical connectors, serpentine belt and fuse block shield.
10. Connect the negative battery cable and check for proper operation.

2.5L Engine

1. Disconnect the negative battery cable.
2. Remove the serpentine belt.
3. Remove the electrical connectors from the back of the alternator.
4. Remove the rear attaching bolt first, then the front attaching bolt and heat shield.
5. Remove the alternator assembly carefully making sure all wires are disconnected.

To install:

6. Position the alternator into the mounting bracket.
7. Install the front and rear mounting bolts but do not tighten.
8. Install the heat shield with the rear mounting bolts.
9. Install the electrical connectors and tighten the battery cable nut.
10. Torque the mounting bolts to 18 ft. lbs. (25 Nm).
11. Install the serpentine belt.
12. Reconnect the negative battery cable.

2.8L and 3.1L Engines

1. Disconnect the negative battery cable. Remove the air cleaner assembly.
2. Remove the serpentine belt.
3. Remove the electrical connectors from the back of the alternator.
4. Remove the rear and front attaching bolts and the bolt from brace to alternator.
5. Remove the alternator assembly carefully making sure all wires are disconnected.

NOTE: If alternator brace is removed, studs must be retightened before installation or damage to the brace may result.

To install:

6. Position the alternator into the mounting bracket.
7. Install brace to alternator bolt but do not tighten.
8. Install the front and rear mounting bolts. Torque the mounting bolts as follows:
   a. Long bolt to 35 ft. lbs. (47 Nm)
   b. Short bolt to 18 ft. lbs. (25 Nm)
   c. Bracket bolt to 18 ft. lbs. (25 Nm)
9. Check that tightening of the brace bolts did not bind alternator.
10. Install the electrical connectors and tighten the battery cable nut.
11. Install the serpentine belt.
12. Install the air cleaner and negative battery cable.

3.4L Engine

1. Disconnect the negative battery cable.
2. Remove air cleaner assembly.

3. Remove coolant recovery reservoir and set aside.
4. Remove serpentine belt.
5. Raise and safely support vehicle.
6. Remove power steering pipe retaining clip nut from upper alternator stud and remove alternator stud.
7. Remove right front tire and wheel assembly.
8. Separate lower ball joint from lower control arm.
9. Remove halfshaft from transaxle.
10. Remove right hand engine splash shield.
11. Disconnect connectors and wires from alternator.
12. Remove brace bolt from alternator and loosen brace at engine block.
13. Remove alternator lower mounting bolt and alternator.

To install:

14. Install alternator and loosely install all mounting bolts.
If replacement alternator does not fit into mounts, remove adhesive-backed shim from rear of alternator bracket.
15. Tighten alternator lower mounting bolts to 61 ft. lbs. (83 Nm).
16. Install connectors and wires to alternator.
17. Install right hand engine splash shield.
18. Reinstall halfshaft.
19. Install lower ball joint to lower control arm.
20. Reinstall tire and wheel assembly and lower vehicle.
21. Install upper alternator stud and power steering pipe retaining clip nut.
22. Reinstall serpentine belt and coolant recovery reservoir.
23. Reinstall negative battery cable.
24. Install air cleaner assembly.

3.8L Engine

1. Disconnect the negative battery cable. Remove the serpentine belt.
2. Remove the electrical connectors from the back of the alternator.
3. Remove the nut and the positive battery connector from the **BAT** terminal.
4. Remove the alternator mounting bolts and remove the alternator from the vehicle.

To install:

5. Installation is the reverse of removal. Tighten all mounting bolts to 20 ft. lbs. using the following sequence:
   a. Alternator attaching bolt to the direct fire mounting bracket/ rear brace.
   b. Alternator attaching bolt to the power steering and tensioner pulley bracket.
   c. Alternator brace bolt to engine.

NOTE: Make sure tightening bolts do not bind alternator.

Starter

REMOVAL & INSTALLATION

2.3L Engine

1. Disconnect the negative battery cable.
2. Remove the air cleaner and inlet hose from the throttle body.
3. Remove and plug the coolant reservoir hose at the radiator filler neck.
4. Remove the coolant reservoir.
5. Remove the intake manifold brace bolts.
6. Place a drain pan under the oil filter and remove the filter.
7. Remove the starter retaining bolts, lower the starter onto the frame member and disconnect the starter electrical connectors.

To install:

8. Position the starter into the vehicle, connect the electrical connectors and torque the retaining bolts to 32 ft. lbs. (43 Nm).
9. Install a new oil filter. Add engine oil as needed, to fill to the proper level.
10. Install the intake manifold brace, coolant reservoir and hoses.
11. Add coolant, if needed.
12. Install the air cleaner and inlet hose.
13. Connect the negative battery cable and check for proper operation.

2.5L Engine

1. Disconnect the negative battery cable.
2. Raise and support the vehicle safely.
3. Remove the flywheel inspection cover bolts and cover.
4. Remove the stud from the starter support bracket.
5. Remove the 2 starter mounting bolts and shim, if equipped.
6. Remove the starter motor. Be careful not to damage the starter wires by letting the starter hang.
7. While holding the starter motor, disconnect the starter electrical connectors from the starter solenoid.
8. Remove the starter from the rear bracket.

To install:

9. Install the support bracket to the starter.
10. Install the starter adjustment shims, if equipped.
11. Position the starter to the engine mounting flange and torque the bolts to 32 ft. lbs. (43 Nm).
12. Install the bracket-to-engine and torque the stud to 18 ft. lbs. (25 Nm).
13. Install the inspection cover.
14. Lower the vehicle and connect the starter electrical wires. Reconnect the negative battery cable.

2.8L, 3.1L and 3.4L Engines

1. Remove the air cleaner.
2. Disconnect the negative battery cable.
3. Raise the vehicle and support it safely. Disconnect the electrical connectors from the DIS module and the engine oil pressure sensor.
4. If equipped with an engine oil cooler, position a drain pan under the engine and remove the engine oil and oil filter. Remove the oil cooler adapter stud and position the oil cooler aside.

NOTE: It is not necessary to open the cooling system to position the oil cooler out of the way.

5. If equipped with 3.1L engine, remove the nut from the brace at the air conditioning compressor, nut from the brace at the engine and the brace.
6. Remove the flywheel inspection cover.
7. Remove the starter bolts and shims, if equipped. Do not let the starter hang from the starter wires.
8. Remove the starter wires from the solenoid and remove the starter.
To install:
9. While supporting the starter, connect the starter wires at the solenoid.
10. Install the starter motor-to-engine mount with the shims, if equipped, and the mounting bolts. Torque the bolts to 32 ft. lbs. (43 Nm).
11. If equipped with an engine oil cooler, reposition the hose next to the starter motor, install the oil filter and refill the engine with the proper amount of engine oil.
12. Install the flywheel inspection cover and tighten the bolts.
13. Install the starter support brace to the air conditioning compressor and torque the nut to 23 ft. lbs. (31 Nm).
14. Lower the vehicle, reconnect the negative battery cable and install the air cleaner assembly.

3.8L Engine

1. Disconnect the negative battery cable.
2. If necessary, remove the right side cooling fan.
3. Remove the serpentine drive belt.
4. Disconnect the air conditioning compressor upper support brace and lay the compressor in the fan opening.
5. Raise and support the vehicle safely.
6. Disconnect the engine oil cooler lines at the flex connector.
7. Remove the flywheel inspection cover.
8. Remove the starter motor retaining bolts and remove the starter motor and shims, if used.
9. Disconnect the starter motor wir-

ing and remove the starter from the vehicle.
To install:
10. Position the starter motor and shims, if used, to the engine and tighten the mounting bolts to 32 ft. lbs. (43 Nm).
11. Connect the electrical connectors to the starter terminals and tighten the battery nut to 80 inch lbs. and the S terminal nut to 27 inch lbs. (3 Nm).
12. Install the flywheel inspection cover. Tighten to 89 inch lbs. (10 Nm).
13. Connect the engine oil cooler lines at the flex connector.
14. Lower the vehicle and install the air conditioner compressor.
15. Install the serpentine drive belt, cooling fan and negative battery cable.

EMISSION CONTROLS

Due to the complex nature of modern electronic engine control systems, comprehensive diagnosis and testing procedures fall outside the confines of this repair manual. For complete information on diagnosis, testing and repair procedures concerning all modern engine and emission control systems, please refer to "Chilton's Guide to Fuel Injection and Electronic Engine Controls".

FUEL SYSTEM

Fuel System Service Precautions

Safety is the most important factor when performing not only fuel system maintenance but any type of maintenance. Failure to conduct maintenance and repairs in a safe manner may result in serious personal injury or death. Maintenance and testing of the vehicle's fuel system components can be accomplished safely and effectively by adhering to the following rules and guidelines.

● To avoid the possibility of fire and personal injury, always disconnect the negative battery cable unless the repair or test procedure requires that battery voltage be applied.

● Always relieve the fuel system pressure prior to disconnecting any fuel system component (injector, fuel rail, pressure regulator, etc.), fitting or fuel line connection. Exercise extreme caution whenever relieving fuel system pressure to avoid exposing skin, face and eyes to fuel spray. Please be advised that fuel under pressure may penetrate the skin or any part of the body that it contacts.

● Always place a shop towel or cloth around the fitting or connection prior to loosening to absorb any excess fuel due to spillage. Ensure that all fuel spillage (should it occur) is quickly removed from engine surfaces. Ensure that all fuel soaked cloths or towels are deposited into a suitable waste container.

● Always keep a dry chemical (Class B) fire extinguisher near the work area.

● Do not allow fuel spray or fuel vapors to come into contact with a spark or open flame.

● Always use a backup wrench when loosening and tightening fuel line connection fittings. This will prevent unnecessary stress and torsion to fuel line piping. Always follow the proper torque specifications.

● Always replace worn fuel fitting O-rings with new. Do not substitute fuel hose or equivalent where fuel pipe is installed.

RELIEVING FUEL SYSTEM PRESSURE

2.5L Engine

1. Remove the fuel filler cap.
2. Raise and safely support the vehicle.
3. Disconnect the fuel pump harness connector at the fuel pump electrical connector.
4. Lower the vehicle.
5. Start the engine and run until the engine stops due to the lack of fuel.
6. Crank the engine for 3 seconds to ensure all pressure is relieved.
7. Reconnect the fuel pump harness connector.
8. Disconnect the negative battery cable to prevent the build of fuel pressure in the event that the key accidentally is turned ON.

Except 2.5L Engine

1. Disconnect the negative battery cable. Loosen fuel filler cap.
2. Connect fuel pressure gauge J-34730-1 or equivalent, to the fuel pressure connection.
3. Wrap a shop cloth around the fitting while connecting the gauge to catch any leaking fuel.
4. Install the bleed hose into an ap-

proved container and open the valve. Connect the negative battery cable.

5. When the repair to the fuel system is complete check all of the fittings for leaks.

Fuel Filter

REMOVAL & INSTALLATION

With Quick–Connect Fitting

1. Relieve fuel system pressure.
2. Disconnect the negative battery cable.
3. Raise and support the vehicle safely.
4. Remove the filter bracket attaching screws and the filter bracket.
5. Disconnect the quick-connect fittings as follows:
   a. Grasp the filter and fuel line fitting. Twist the quick-connect fitting ¼ turn in each direction to loosen any dirt within the fitting.

NOTE: Saftey glasses should be worn when using compressed air or working with the fuel system, as flying dirt particles or fuel spray may cause eye injury.

   b. Using compressed air, blow the dirt from the quick-connect fittings. Clean the filter connection and surrounding area before disconnecting to prevent possible contamination of the system.
   c. Squeeze plastic tab on male end of connector and pull connection apart.
6. To reduce fuel spillage, place a shop towel over the fuel lines before disconnecting. Disconnect the fuel feed pipe nut from the fuel filter. Drain any fuel remaining in the filter into an approved gasoline container.
7. Inspect the fuel pipe O-ring for cuts, nicks or swelling and replace if necessary.
To install:
8. Apply a few drops of clean engine oil to the male tube end of the filter. Install a new plastic connector retainer on filter inlet.
9. Push the connectors together to cause the retaining tabs to snap into place. Once installed, pull on both ends of each connection to make sure they are secure.
10. Align the fuel filter on the frame and install the filter bracket attaching screws.
11. Install and tighten the fuel filter outlet nut to 22 ft. lbs. (30 Nm). Install and tighten the fuel filler cap.
12. Connect the negative battery cable. Turn the ignition ON for 2 seconds and then turn to OFF for 10 seconds. Again turn the key ON and check for fuel leaks.
13. If equipped with the 3.1L or 3.4L

engine, perform the Idle Learn procedure to allow the ECM memory to be updated with the correct IAC valve pintle position for a stable idle speed.
   a. Install a Tech 1 scan tool.
   b. Turn the ignition to the ON position, engine not running.
   c. Select IAC SYSTEM, then IDLE LEARN in the MISC TEST mode.
   d. Proceed with idle learn as directed by the scan tool.

Except Quick Connect Fitting

1. Relieve fuel system pressure.
2. Disconnect the negative battery cable.
3. Raise and support the vehicle safely.
4. Disconnect the fuel lines from the filter.
5. Remove the clamp and filter from the vehicle.
To install:
6. Loosely install the new filter. Using new O-ring seals, install the fuel lines to the filter.
7. Use a backup wrench to prevent the filter from turning and O-ring damage. Torque the fittings to 16 ft. lbs. (22 Nm).
7. Secure the filter to the vehicle. Tighten fuel filler cap.
8. Reconnect the negative battery cable. Lower the vehicle and start the engine to check for fuel leaks.

Electric Fuel Pump

PRESSURE TESTING

2.5L Engine

1. With the ignition OFF, release the fuel pressure and check for fuel in the tank.
2. Connect a fuel pressure gauge J–29658–B or equivalent, to the service fitting. Jump the fuel pump test terminal to 12 volts using a fused jumper wire.
3. With the key in the ON position and engine NOT running, the pressure should be 26–32 psi (179–220 kPa).
4. Listen to the pump running in the tank. If the pump is running, check for obstructed fuel filter, lines or pressure regulator.

Except 2.5L Engine

1. Release the fuel system pressure. Wrap a shop towel around fuel pressure connector on the fuel rail to absorb any leakage that may occur when installing gauge.
2. Connect a fuel pressure gauge J–34730–1 or equivalent, to the service fitting.
3. With the ignition switch ON and

engine NOT running, the fuel pump pressure should be 40–47 psi (280–325 kPa) and hold steady when the engine is turned OFF.

REMOVAL & INSTALLATION

1. Release the fuel system pressure. Disconnect the negative battery cable.
2. Drain all fuel from the fuel tank.
3. Raise and safely support the vehicle. Support the fuel tank and remove the retaining straps.
4. Lower the fuel tank slightly and disconnect the fuel lines, hoses and the sending unit electrical connectors.
5. Remove the tank from the vehicle.
6. Remove the sending unit retaining cam using tool J–35731 or equivalent and remove the sending unit assembly from the tank.
7. Support the pump with 1 hand and grasp the strainer with the other hand. Rotate the strainer in 1 direction and pull off pump.
8. Disconnect the fuel pump electrical connector. Place the sender assembly upside down on a bench. Pull the fuel pump downward to remove from the mounting bracket, then tilt pump outward and remove from fuel pulse dampener.
9. Inspect the pump strainer. If the strainer is contaminated, the fuel tank must be flushed.
To install:
10. Install the rubber bumper and insulator onto the fuel pump, if removed. Position the fuel pump sender assembly upside down. Install the fuel pump between the fuel pulse dampener and mounting bracket. Connect the fuel pump electrical connector.

NOTE: Always install a new pump strainer when installing fuel pump.

11. Position new pump strainer on fuel pump and push on outer edge of ferrule until fully seated.
12. Install the sender assembly retainer cam using tool J–35731 or equivalent.
13. Replace O-ring on pump assembly and install the unit into the tank.
14. Raise the tank into position and attach all fuel lines, hoses and electrical connectors to the tank.

NOTE: If equipped with quick-connect fittings, lubricate the male tube ends with clean engine oil prior to connecting line fittings. This will insure proper reconnection and prevent a possible fuel leak.

15. Install the retaining straps. Tighten the tank retaining strap bolts to 35 ft. lbs. (47 Nm).

16. Lower the vehicle and refill the tank. Connect the negative battery cable.

17. Turn the ignition **ON** for 2 seconds, then turn ignition **OFF** and check for leaks. Start vehicle and recheck for leaks.

18. If equipped with the 3.1L or 3.4L engine, perform the Idle Learn procedure to allow the ECM memory to be updated with the correct IAC valve pintle position for a stable idle speed.

Fuel Injection

IDLE SPEED ADJUSTMENT

Idle speed and mixture are electronically controlled by the ECM. No adjustments are possible.

DRIVE AXLE

Halfshaft

REMOVAL & INSTALLATION

Vehicles equipped with a manual transaxle use an intermediate shaft connecting the transaxle assembly and the right halfshaft. The right halfshaft inner CV–joint uses a female spline that will be installed over the intermediate axle shaft.

NOTE: Do not attempt to move the vehicle with the with the drive axle(s) removed from the vehicle. Wheel(s) could fall off, dropping vehicle to the ground causing personal injury or damage to the vehicle.

1. With the weight of the vehicle on the tires, loosen the hub nut 1 revolution.
2. Raise and safely support the vehicle.
3. Remove the tire and wheel asssembly.
4. Remove the brake caliper and rotor assembly. Do not separate the brake hose from the caliper and tie aside using wire.
5. If equipped with ABS, remove the ABS sensor mounting bolt and position the sensor aside.
6. Remove the hub/bearing to strut housing bolts. Pull the hub/bearing out of the strut bracket.
7. Remove the right halfshaft from the transaxle using removal tool J–

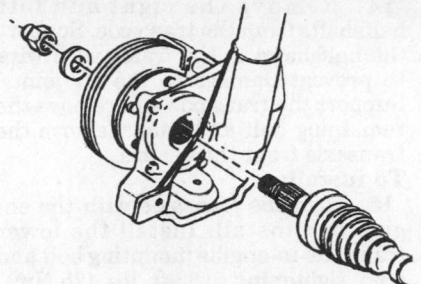

Removing the halfshaft from the hub/knuckle assembly

33008 or equivalent and the extension tool J–29794 or equivalent.

8. If equipped with 3T40 transaxle, saparate the halfshaft from the transaxle assembly using removal tool J–33008 or equivalent and the extension tool J–29794 or equivalent.

9. If equipped with 4T60 or 4T60–E transaxles, using the frame for leverage, separate the drive axle from the transaxle assembly using a prybar in the groove provided on the inner joint.

10. Remove the hub nut, if not already done. Pull the axle and hub assembly through the strut housing. Using a spindle remover tool J–28733 or equivalent, remove the halfshaft from the hub and bearing.

To install:

11. Install tool J–37292–A to the right side of the transaxle in a position so it can be removed after axle is installed, approximately between 5 and 7 o'clock position.

12. Install the axle assembly into the transaxle and remove tool J–37292–A.

13. Properly position the ABS sensor and install the retainer bolt, if removed.

14. Loosely secure the bearing to knuckle bolts.

15. Seat the axle into the transaxle using prybar in the groove provided on the inner joint. Pry against the frame or lower control arm.

16. Verify that the snapring is seated by tapping on the inner groove. Also grasp the inner housing and pull outward. If correctly seated, the axle will remain in place. Do not pull on the shaft.

17. Install the hub and bearing assembly to the shaft using new drive axle nut and washer. Tighten the drive axle nut but do not torque.

18. Install the brake rotor ad caliper assembly. Install the tire and wheel.

19. Lower the vehicle. With the weight of the vehicle on the suspension, tighten the axle nut to 184 ft. lbs. (250 Nm).

20. Inspect the transaxle fluid and add as required. Pump the brakes until a firm pedal is obtained. Test drive the vehicle.

Front Wheel Hub and Bearing

The vehicles are equipped with sealed hub and bearing assemblies. The hub and bearing assemblies are non-serviceable. If the assembly is damaged, the complete unit must be replaced.

REMOVAL & INSTALLATION

1. Disconnect the negative battery cable.
2. Loosen the drive axle shaft nut and washer 1 turn.
3. Raise the vehicle and support it safely.
4. Remove the tire and wheel assembly, caliper, bracket and rotor.
5. Remove the halfshaft nut and washer.
6. Loosen the 4 hub/bearing-to-knuckle attaching bolts.
7. Using tool J–28733–A or equivalent, push the halfshaft splines back out of the hub/bearing.
8. Remove the ABS sensor, if equipped, and position out of the way.
9. Protect the halfshaft boots, remove the hub/bearing assembly attaching bolts and remove the hub/bearing assembly.

To install:

10. Install the hub/bearing assembly onto the knuckle. Install the 4 attaching bolts and torque to 52 ft. lbs. (70 Nm).
11. Install the ABS sensor, if equipped.
12. Install the rotor, caliper and bracket.
13. Install the tire and wheel assembly. Torque the lug nut to 100 ft. lbs. (135 Nm).
14. Lower the vehicle and torque the hub nut to 184 ft. lbs. (250 Nm).

MANUAL TRANSAXLE

For further information on transmission/transaxles, please refer to "Chilton's Guide to Transmission Repair".

Transaxle Assembly

REMOVAL & INSTALLATION

NOTE: Before performing any maintenance that requires the removal of the slave cylinder, transaxle or clutch housing, the clutch master cylinder pushrod must

first be disconnected from the clutch pedal. Failure to disconnect the pushrod will result in permanent damage to the slave cylinder if the clutch pedal is depressed with the slave cylinder disconnected.

1. Disconnect the negative battery cable.

2. Install the engine support tool J–28467 or equivalent.

3. Remove the air cleaner housing and intake tube. Disconnect the clutch slave cylinder from the transaxle.

4. Disconnect the electrical connection at the speed sensor assembly. Disconnect the clutch and shift cables from the transaxle.

5. Remove the exhaust crossover pipe at the left manifold and remove the EGR tube from the crossover.

6. Loosen the crossover-to-right exhaust manifold clamp and move the crossover pipe to gain access to the transaxle bolts for V6 engine.

7. Remove the 2 upper transaxle mounting bolts and remove the 2 upper mounting studs. Leave 1 bottom bolt and stud attached.

8. Disconnect the electrical connection at the backup light switch. Raise and safely support the vehicle. Disconnect the speed sensor wire harness.

9. Drain the transaxle fluid. Remove the clutch housing cover. Remove both front tire assemblies.

10. Remove the inner fender splash shields from both side of the vehicle. Disconnect the power steering lines from the frame.

11. Remove the rack and pinion heat shield and remove the rack and pinion from the frame.

12. Disconnect the right and left ball joints. Remove the upper transaxle mount retaining bolts. Remove the lower engine mount retaining nuts.

13. Remove the sub-frame retaining bolts and remove the sub-frame from the vehicle. Remove the starter and support it aside.

14. Remove the right and left halfshafts from the transaxle. Support the halfshafts to the frame with wire to prevent damage to the CV-joints. Support the transaxle and remove the remaining bolt and stud. Remove the transaxle from the vehicle.

To install:

15. Align the transaxle with the engine and install. Install the lower transaxle-to-engine mounting bolt and stud, tightening to 55 ft. lbs. (75 Nm).

16. Install the starter assembly. Install the left and right halfshaft.

17. Install the sub-frame and retaining bolts. Install the lower engine mount retaining nuts.

18. Install the upper transaxle retaining bolts, tightening to 55 ft. lbs. (75 Nm). Install the right and left ball joints to the steering knuckles.

19. Install the rack and pinion, heat shield and lines to the frame. Install the right and left inner fender splash shields.

20. Install the clutch housing cover, tighten the screws to 115 inch lbs. (13 Nm). Lower the vehicle.

21. Attach the crossover pipe to the manifolds and attach the EGR pipe to the crossover.

22. Attach the shift and clutch cables to the transaxle. Connect all of the electrical connectors. Install the air cleaner housing and tube. Remove the engine support tool.

23. Fill the transaxle with fluid. Connect the negative battery cable.

CLUTCH

Clutch Assembly

REMOVAL & INSTALLATION

NOTE: Before any service that requires removal of the slave cylinder, the master cylinder pushrod must be disconnected from the clutch pedal and the connection in the hydraulic lines must be separated using tool J–36221 or equivalent. If not disconnected, permanent damage to the slave cylinder will occur if the clutch pedal is depressed while the system is not resisted by clutch loads.

1. Disconnect the negative terminal from the battery.

2. From inside the vehicle, remove the sound insulator panel.

3. Disconnect the clutch master cylinder pushrod from the clutch pedal and disconnect the quick connect fitting in the hydraulic line. Remove the actuator from the transaxle housing.

4. Remove the transaxle.

5. With the transaxle removed, matchmark the pressure plate and flywheel assembly to insure proper balance during reassembly.

6. Loosen the pressure plate-to-flywheel bolts, a few turns at a time, until the spring pressure is removed.

7. Support the pressure plate and remove the bolts.

8. Remove the pressure plate and disc assembly; be sure to note the flywheel side of the clutch disc.

To install:

9. Clean and inspect the clutch assembly, flywheel, release bearing, clutch fork and pivot shaft for signs of wear. Replace any necessary parts.

10. Position the clutch disc and pressure plate in the appropriate position, support the assembly with the appropriate alignment tools.

NOTE: Make sure the clutch disc is facing the same direction it was removed. If the same pressure plate is being reused, align the marks made during removal and install, install the pressure plate retaining bolts and tighten them gradually and evenly.

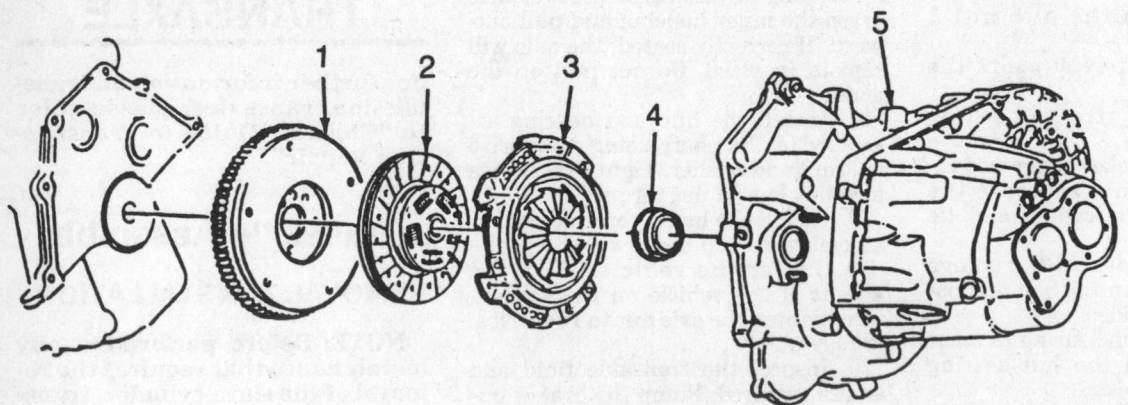

1. Flywheel
2. Driven plate assembly
3. Clutch cover assembly
4. Clutch release bearing
5. Transaxle

Exploded view of the clutch assembly

11. With the alignment tool installed, tighten the clutch plate assembly mounting bolts until the plate contacts the flywheel. At this point the plate position can still adjusted.

12. Gradually turn each bolt down about ½ turn at a time tightening in an alternating sequence.

13. Using tool J–36660, torque the bolts to 15 ft. lbs. (20 Nm) in an alternating sequence. Then rotate the bolts an additional 30 degrees in the same tightening sequence. Remove the alignment tool.

14. Lightly lubricate the clutch fork ends. Fill the recess ends of the release bearing with grease. Lubricate the input shaft with a light coat of grease.

15. Install the transaxle assembly into the vehicle.

16. Install the clutch master cylinder pushrod and install the sound insulator panel.

NOTE: The clutch lever must not be moved towards the flywheel until the transaxle is bolted to the engine. Damage to the transaxle, release bearing and clutch fork could occur if this is not followed.

17. Connect the negative battery cable. Bleed the clutch system and check the clutch operation.

PEDAL HEIGHT/FREE-PLAY ADJUSTMENT

The clutch system is a hydraulic linkage system that provides automatic clutch adjustment and determines the clutch pedal position. No adjustment of clutch linkage or pedal position is required or possible.

Clutch Master Cylinder, Actuator and Reservoir

REMOVAL & INSTALLATION

NOTE: The factory hydraulic system is serviced as a single assembly. Replacement hydraulic assemblies are pre-filled with fluid and do not require bleeding. Individual components of the system are not available separately. Check with an aftermarket part supplier to see if individual components can be purchased separately.

1. Disconnect the negative battery cable.

2. Remove the sound insulator inside the vehicle and disconnect the master cylinder pushrod at the clutch pedal.

3. Remove the left upper secondary cowl panel.

4. Remove the 2 master cylinder reservoir-to-strut tower retaining nuts.

5. Remove the anti-rotation screw located next to the master cylinder flange at the pedal support plate.

6. Using wrench flats on the front end of the master cylinder body, twist the cylinder counterclockwise to release the twist lock attachment-to-plate. Do not torque on the hose connection on top of the cylinder body, damage may occur.

7. Remove the 2 actuator-to-transaxle retaining nuts and actuator assembly.

8. Pull the master cylinder with the pushrod attached forward out of the pedal plate. Lift the reservoir off the strut tower studs and remove the 3 components as a complete assembly.
To install:

9. Install the master cylinder into the opening in the pedal plate and rotate 45 degrees by applying torque on the wrench flats only.

10. Install the anti-rotation screw.

11. Install the fluid reservoir-to-strut tower and torque the retaining nuts to 36 inch lbs. (4 Nm).

12. Install a new pushrod bushing and lubricate before installation.

13. Install the master cylinder pushrod-to-clutch pedal.

14. Install the clutch actuator-to-transaxle.

15. Press the clutch pedal down several times to ensure proper operation. Adjust cruise control switch if equipped.

16. Install the left upper secondary cowl panel, sound insulator and connect the negative battery cable.

Clutch Slave Cylinder

REMOVAL & INSTALLATION

1. Disconnect the negative battery cable.

2. Remove the sound insulator inside the vehicle and disconnect the master cylinder pushrod at the clutch pedal.

3. Remove 2 bolts holding canister to transaxle. Remove 2 actuator retainer nuts and remove actuator from transaxle housing.
To install:

4. Position canister mounting bracket and bolts to transaxle assembly and secure retaining bolts to 28 ft. lbs. (38 Nm).

5. Install actuator to housing studs with pushrods centered in pocket of lever in housing. Install actuator retainer nuts to 18 ft. lbs. (25 Nm).

6. Install a new pushrod bushing and lubricate before installation.

7. Install the master cylinder pushrod-to-clutch pedal.

8. Install the clutch actuator-to-transaxle.

9. Press the clutch pedal down several times to ensure proper operation. Adjust cruise control switch if equipped.

10. Install the left upper secondary cowl panel, sound insulator and connect the negative battery cable.

Hydraulic Clutch System Bleeding

1. Disconnect the negative battery cable.

2. Disconnect quick connect fittings in clutch hydraulic line. Insert J–36221 or equivalent hydraulic line separator tool and depress plastic sleeve to separate connection.

3. Remove cap and diaphragm and fill reservoir with DOT 3 brake fluid.

4. Remove left hand upper secondary cowl.

5. Remove air from supply hose by squeezing it until no more air bubbles are seen in reservoir.

6. Pump clutch pedal slowly until slight pressure is observed. Hold pressure on pedal and depress internal valve on quick connect fitting.

7. Repeat Step 6 until pedal is firm and no bubbles are seen.

8. Reconnect clutch hydraulic line. Refill clutch system and replace reservoir cap. Reconnect battery cable.

AUTOMATIC TRANSAXLE

For further information on transmission/transaxles, please refer to "Chilton's Guide to Transmission Repair".

Transaxle Assembly

NOTE: On September 1, 1991, Hydra-matic changed the name designations of the THM 125C and THM 440–R4 automatic transaxle. The new name designations are Hydra-matic 3T40 and 4T60. Transaxles built between 1989–1990 will serve as transitional years in which a dual system, made up of the old designation and the new designation will be in effect.

REMOVAL & INSTALLATION

1. Disconnect the negative battery cable. Remove the air cleaner, coolant reservoir, Mass Air Flow (MAF) sensor and air tube as an assembly.

2. Disconnect both torque struts from the engine. Remove the left torque strut bracket. Disconnect the oil cooler lines at the transaxle.

3. Disconnect the shift control cable, TV cable from the throttle lever and the transaxle.

4. Remove the vent hose from the transaxle. Remove the fluid level indicator and the filler tube.

5. Using a engine support fixture tool J–28467 or equivalent and the adapter tool J–35953 or equivalent, install them on the engine.

6. Remove the wiring harness-to-transaxle nut.

7. Label and disconnect the wires for the speed sensor, TCC connector and the neutral safety/backup light switch.

8. Remove the upper transaxle-to-engine bolts.

9. Remove the transaxle-to-mount through bolt, the transaxle mount bracket and the mount.

10. Raise and safely support the vehicle. Remove the front wheel assemblies.

11. Disconnect the shift cable bracket from the transaxle. Remove the transaxle fill tube.

12. Remove the caliper assemblies and the rotors from the vehicle.

13. Disconnect both lower ball joint studs from the lower control arms.

14. Remove both lower engine splash shields. Remove the ground cable at the transaxle.

15. Using a modified halfshaft seal protector tool J–34754 or equivalent, install 1 on each halfshaft to protect the seal from damage and the joint from possible failure. Remove both halfshafts from the transaxle and support the halfshafts to the body to prevent CV-joint damage. Take care not to damage the halfshaft boots.

16. Remove the torsional and lateral strut from the transaxle.

17. Remove the left side stabilizer link pin bolt.

18. Remove the rack and pinion heat shield and electrical connector, if equipped.

19. Disconnect the speedometer wire from the transaxle. Remove the starter motor.

20. Remove the transaxle converter cover and matchmark the converter to the flywheel for assembly.

21. Remove the bolt holding the wiring harness to the transaxle case and position aside.

22. Remove the bolts holding the power steering lines to the frame.

23. Position and secure a transmission jack under the transaxle. Remove the remaining transaxle-to-engine bolts.

24. Make sure the torque converter does not fall out and remove the transaxle from the vehicle.

To install:

25. Put a small amount of grease on the pilot hub of the converter and make sure the converter is properly engaged with the pump.

26. Raise the transaxle to the engine while guiding the right side halfshaft into the transaxle.

27. Install the lower transaxle mounting bolts, tighten to 55 ft. lbs. (75 Nm) and remove the jack.

28. Align the converter with the marks made on the flywheel and install the bolts hand-tight.

29. Torque the converter bolts to 46 ft. lbs. (61 Nm). Retorque the first bolt after the others.

30. Install the starter assembly. Install both halfshafts.

31. Install the converter cover, oil cooler lines and cover. Install the subframe assembly. Install the lower engine mount retaining bolts and the transaxle mount nuts.

32. Install the right and left ball joints. Install the power steering rack, heat shield and cooler lines to the frame.

33. Install the right and left inner fender splash shields. Install the tire assemblies.

34. Lower the vehicle. Connect all electrical leads. Install the upper transaxle mount bolts, tighten to 55 ft. lbs. (75 Nm).

35. Attach the crossover pipe to the exhaust manifold. Connect the EGR tube to the crossover.

36. Connect the TV cable and the shift cable. Install the air cleaner and inlet tube.

37. Remove the engine support tool. Connect the negative battery cable.

FRONT SUSPENSION

MacPherson Strut/Knuckle

REMOVAL & INSTALLATION

—— CAUTION ——

Do not remove the strut cartridge nut without compressing the coil spring first. This procedure must be followed because it keeps the coil spring compressed. Use care to support the strut assembly adequately because the coil spring is under heavy load, if released too quickly personal injury could result. Never remove the center strut nuts unless the spring is compressed with a MacPherson strut spring compressor tool J–26584 or equivalent. The vehicle weight can be used when the strut assembly is still in the vehicle and only the strut cartridge is going to be replaced.

1. Disconnect the negative battery cable.

2. Loosen the cover plate bolts.

3. Loosen the wheel nuts. Raise and safely support the vehicle.

4. Remove the tire and wheel assembly. Remove the brake caliper and bracket assembly, hang the caliper aside. Do not hang the caliper by the brake lines.

5. Remove the brake rotor. Remove the hub and bearing attaching bolts.

6. Remove the halfshaft. Remove the tie rod attaching nut. Using tool J–35917 or equivalent, separate the tie rod from the steering knuckle.

7. Remove the lower ball joint attaching nut and separate the lower ball from the lower control arm.

8. Remove the hub and bearing attaching bolts and hub assembly.

9. Remove the cover plate bolts and remove the strut from the vehicle.

To install:

10. Install the strut mount cover plate, tighten the nuts after lowering the vehicle. Install the lower ball joint and torque to specifications. Install new cotter pin.

11. Install the tie rod and torque to 40 ft. lbs. (54 Nm) to line up the cotter pin hole. Install new cotter pin.

12. Install the halfshaft and install the hub and bearing-to-knuckle attaching bolts and tighten to 52 ft. lbs. (70 Nm).

13. Install the brake rotor and caliper assembly.

14. Install the wheel assembly, tighten the wheel lug nuts to 100 ft. lbs. (136 Nm).

15. Lower the vehicle, tighten the strut cover bolts to 17 ft. lbs. (24 Nm) and tighten the wheel nuts.

16. Connect the negative battery cable.

Lower Ball Joint

INSPECTION

1. Raise and safely support the vehicle, allowing the front suspension to hang freely.

2. Grasp and shake the wheel at the top and bottom to feel if there is any in and out movement.

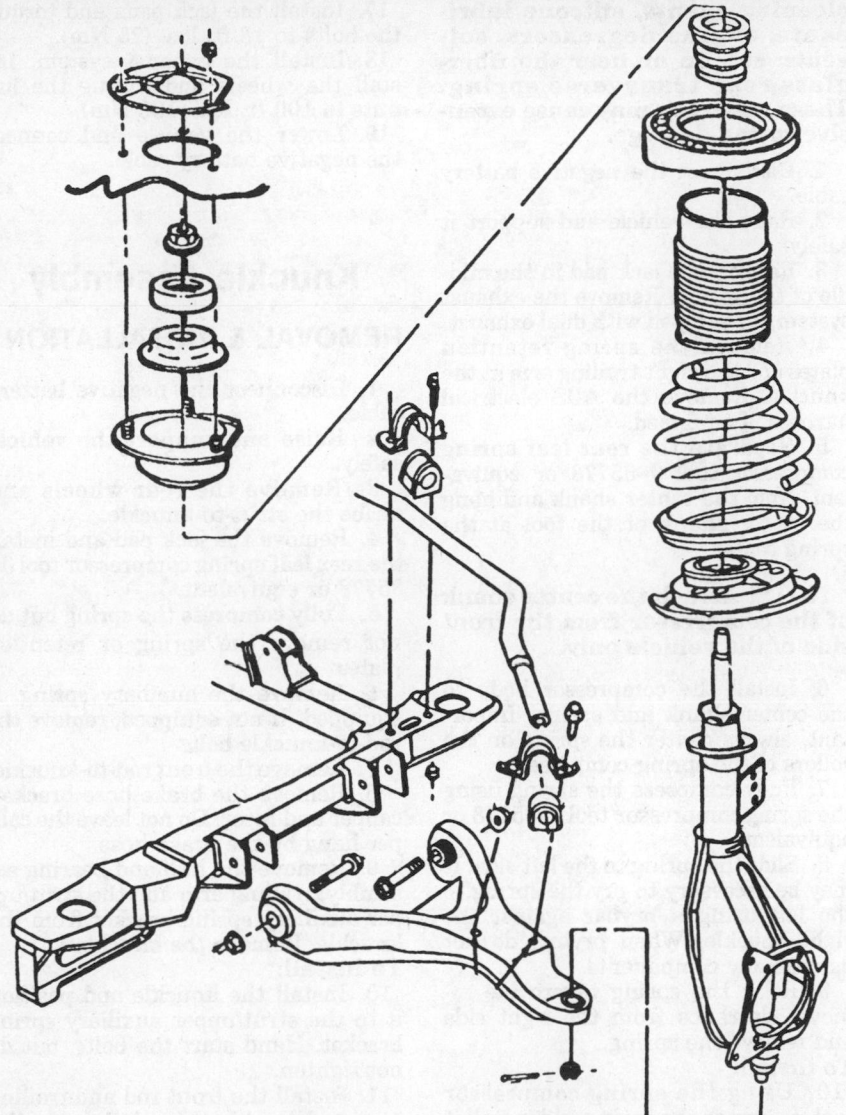

Exploded view of the front suspension

3. Replace the ball joint if any movement is detected.

4. When the ball joint is disconnected from the knuckle, check for any looseness or if the ball joint can be twisted freely in the socket by hand.

REMOVAL & INSTALLATION

1. Raise and safely support the vehicle.

2. Remove the wheel assembly.

3. Remove the ball joint heat shield retaining nuts and remove the heat shield.

4. Remove the ball joint cotter pin and nut.

5. Loosen, but do not remove, the stabilizer bar bushing bolts.

6. Using tool J–35917 or equivalent, remove the ball joint from the lower control arm.

7. Using an ⅛ in. drill bit, make a pilot hole in each of the rivets retaining the ball joint to the lower control arm. Using a ½ in. drill bit, drill the rivets out and remove the ball joint.

To install:

8. Install the ball joint to the lower control arm, install the retaining nut hand-tight.

9. Install the ball joint to the steering knuckle. Install the 4 ball joint retaining nuts and bolts, supplied with the replacement joint.

10. Tighten the stabilizer bushing bar bushing bolts to 35 ft. lbs. (48 Nm). Tighten the ball joint retaining nut as follows:

1989–90 – 89 inch lbs. (10 Nm) plus 120 degrees (2 flats).

1991 – 15 ft. lbs. (20 Nm) plus 90 degrees (1½ flats).

1992–93 – 63 ft. lbs. (85 Nm).

NOTE: Once torque specifica- tion has been obtained, tighten nut as little as possible to align cotter pin holes. Do not at any time loosen the ball joint nut to align it when installing the cotter pin.

11. Install a new cotter pin and bend against nut flats to lock in place.

12. Install the ball joint heat shield and tighten the retaining bolts to 89 inch lbs. (10 Nm).

13. Install tire and wheel assembly and lower the vehicle.

Lower Control Arms

REMOVAL & INSTALLATION

1. Raise and safely support the vehicle.

2. Remove the tire and wheel assembly from the vehicle. If equipped with 3.4L engine, remove the splash shield from the vehicle.

3. Remove the stabilizer shaft-to-lower control arm bolts. Remove the ball joint retaining nut and cotter pin.

4. Using tool J–35917 or equivalent, separate the ball joint from the control arm.

5. Remove the lower control arm-to-frame attaching nuts and bolts. Remove the lower control arm from the vehicle.

To install:

6. Install the lower control arm to the frame and pivot it to the ball joint.

7. Tighten the lower control arm bolts to 56 ft. lbs. (75 Nm). Tighten the ball joint nut to specifications and install a new cotter pin.

8. Install the stabilizer shaft to the lower control arm, tighten the bolts to 35 ft. lbs. (48 Nm). Install the splash shield, if removed.

9. Install the tire and wheel assembly and lower the vehicle. Tighten the wheel nuts to 100 ft. lbs. (136 Nm).

Front Wheel Bearings

The hub and bearing assemblies are not serviced independently. If the assembly is damaged, the complete unit must be replaced. Refer to the "Drive Axle" section for the procedure.

REAR SUSPENSION

The rear suspension features a lightweight composite fiberglass mono-leaf transverse spring. Each wheel is mounted to a tri-link independent suspension system. The 3 links consist of an inverted U–channel trailing arm and tubular front and rear rods.

MacPherson Strut

REMOVAL & INSTALLATION

1. Disconnect the negative battery cable.
2. Raise and support the vehicle safely.
3. Remove the rear wheel assembly.
4. Scribe the strut-to-knuckle for proper installation.
5. Remove the auxiliary spring, if equipped.
6. Remove the jack pad.
7. Install a rear leaf spring compressor tool J–35778 or equivalent.
8. Fully compress the spring but do not remove the retention plates or the spring.
9. Remove the 2 strut-to-body bolts.
10. Remove the brake hose from the strut.
11. Remove the strut and auxiliary spring upper bracket from the knuckle.

To install:
12. Position the strut to the body and knuckle bracket.
13. Install the strut-to-body bolts and torque to 34 ft. lbs. (46 Nm).
14. Install the strut-to-knuckle, align the scribe marks and torque the bolts to 133 ft. lbs. (180 Nm).
15. Install the brake hose bracket and remove the spring compressing tool.
16. Install the jack pad and torque the bolts to 18 ft. lbs. (25 Nm).
17. Install the auxiliary spring, if so equipped.
18. Install the wheel and torque the lug nuts to 100 ft. lbs. (136 Nm).
19. Lower the vehicle and connect the negative battery cable.

NOTE: The rear strut assembly is not serviceable. The assembly is replaced as a complete unit.

Transverse Spring Assembly

REMOVAL & INSTALLATION

——————— CAUTION ———————

Do not disconnect any rear suspension components until the transverse spring has been compressed using a rear spring compressor tool J–35778 or equivalent. Failure to follow this procedure may result in personal injury.

——————————————————

NOTE: Do not use any corrosive cleaning agents, silicone lubricants, engine degreasers, solvents, etc. on or near the fiberglass rear transverse spring. These materials may cause extensive spring damage.

1. Disconnect the negative battery cable.
2. Raise the vehicle and support it safely.
3. Remove the jack pad in the middle of the spring. Remove the exhaust system, if equipped with dual exhaust.
4. Remove the spring retention plates and the right trailing arm at the knuckle. Remove the ABS electrical harness, if equipped.
5. Separate the rear leaf spring compressor tool J–35778 or equivalent, from the center shank and hang the center shank of the tool at the spring center.

NOTE: Attach the center shank of the compressor from the front side of the vehicle only.

6. Install the compressor body to the center shank and spring. Important, always center the spring on the rollers of the spring compressor.
7. Fully compress the spring using the spring compressor tool J–35778 or equivalent.
8. Slide the spring to the left side. It may be necessary to pry the spring to the left using a prybar against the right knuckle. When prying, do not damage any components.
9. Relax the spring to provide removal clearance from the right side and remove the spring.

To install:
10. Using the spring compressor tool, compress the spring and install it through the left knuckle. Slide towards the left side as far as possible and raise the right side of the spring as far as possible.
11. Compress the spring fully and install it into right knuckle.

NOTE: The rear spring retention plates are designed with tabs on 1 end. The tabs must be aligned with the support assembly to prevent damage to the fuel tank.

12. Center the spring to align the holes for the spring retention plate bolts.
13. Install the spring retention plates and bolts. Do not tighten at this time.
14. Position the trailing arm and install the bolt. Torque the bolt to 192 ft. lbs. (260 Nm).
15. Install the ABS electrical harness, if equipped.
16. Remove the spring compressor tool J–35778. Torque the spring retention plate bolts to 15 ft. lbs. (20 Nm).

17. Install the jack pads and torque the bolts to 18 ft. lbs. (25 Nm).
18. Install the exhaust system. Install the wheels and torque the lug nuts to 100 ft. lbs. (136 Nm).
19. Lower the vehicle and connect the negative battery cable.

Knuckle Assembly

REMOVAL & INSTALLATION

1. Disconnect the negative battery cable.
2. Raise and support the vehicle safely.
3. Remove the rear wheels and scribe the strut-to-knuckle.
4. Remove the jack pad and install the rear leaf spring compressor tool J–35778 or equivalent.
5. Fully compress the spring but do not remove the spring or retention plates.
6. Remove the auxiliary spring, if equipped. If not equipped, remove the rod-to-knuckle bolt.
7. Remove the front rod-to-knuckle.
8. Remove the brake hose bracket, caliper and rotor. Do not leave the caliper hang by the brake hose.
9. Remove the hub and bearing assembly, trailing arm and the strut/upper auxiliary spring bracket from the knuckle. Remove the knuckle.

To install:
10. Install the knuckle and position it to the strut/upper auxiliary spring bracket. Hand start the bolts, but do not tighten.
11. Install the front rod and trailing arm-to-knuckle. Hand-tighten the bolts.
12. Torque the trailing arm bolt and nut to 192 ft. lbs. (260 Nm).
13. Install the hub/bearing assembly and torque the bolts to 52 ft. lbs. (70 Nm).
14. Install the rotor and caliper.
15. Align the scribe marks to ensure proper alignment. Torque the strut-to-knuckle attaching bolts to 133 ft. lbs. (180 Nm).
16. Remove the rear leaf spring compressor.
17. Install the jack pad, auxiliary spring, if equipped, and rod-to-knuckle bolt. Apply thread locking compound to the knuckle bolts.
18. Torque the rod-to-knuckle bolts to 66 ft. lbs. (90 Nm), plus 90 degree turn.
19. Install the rear wheels and torque the lug nuts to 100 ft. lbs. (136 Nm).
20. Check for completion of repair, lower the vehicle and connect the negative battery cable.

Rear Wheel Bearings

The hub and bearing assemblies are sealed units and are non-serviceable. If the assembly is damaged, the complete unit must be replaced.

REMOVAL & INSTALLATION

1. Disconnect the negative battery cable.
2. Raise and support the vehicle safely.
3. Remove the rear wheel, caliper, bracket and rotor.
4. Loosen the 4 hub/bearing-to-knuckle attaching bolts.
5. Remove the hub/bearing assembly.

To install:

6. Install the hub/bearing assembly onto the knuckle. Install the 4 attaching bolts and torque to 52 ft. lbs. (70 Nm).
7. Install the rotor, caliper and bracket.
8. Install the rear wheel and torque the lug nut to 100 ft. lbs. (135 Nm).
9. Lower the vehicle and connect the negative battery cable.

STEERING

Steering Wheel

REMOVAL & INSTALLATION

1. Disconnect the negative battery cable.
2. Remove the screws holding the pad, if equipped. Push down and turn the horn pad and remove retainer.
3. Disconnect the horn electrical lead from the cancelling cam tower.
4. Turn the ignition switch to the **ON** position.
5. Scribe an alignment mark on the steering wheel hub in line with the slash mark on the steering shaft.

NOTE: When removing the steering wheel from a vehicle with redundant accessory control switches on the pad careful and proper use of puller J-1859-03 or equivalent, must be adhered to. Do not screw the bolts of the puller more than 5 turns or contact may be made with the electronic components in the hub.

6. Loosen the steering shaft nut and position the nut at the end of the threads. Install steering wheel puller J-1859-03 or equivalent, and pull the steering wheel free of the shaft. Re-

move the steering wheel nut and the steering wheel.

7. Align the matchmarks on the wheel hub and shaft and install the steering wheel. Tighten the steering shaft nut to 30 ft. lbs. (41 Nm).
8. Connect the horn electrical lead and install the horn pad.
9. Connect the negative battery cable.

Power Rack and Pinion

REMOVAL & INSTALLATION

1. Disconnect the negative battery cable. Remove the air cleaner assembly.
2. Raise and safely support the vehicle.
3. If equipped with 3.4L engine, disconnect the front exhaust pipe at the exhaust manifold.
4. Remove both front tire and wheel assemblies.

NOTE: Failure to disconnect the intermediate shaft from the rack and pinion stub shaft can result in damage to the steering gear or intermediate shaft. This damage can cause loss of steering control which could result in personal injury.

5. Remove the intermediate shaft lower pinch bolt at the steering gear. Remove the intermediate shaft from the stub shaft.
6. Disconnect the electrical lead at the power steering idle switch.
7. Separate the tie rod ends from the knuckle assembly.
8. Support the frame at center rear using appropriate equipment. Remove the sub-frame mounting bolts and lower the rear of the sub-frame approximately 4 in.
9. Remove the steering rack heat shield. Disconnect the pressure lines at the steering rack.
10. Remove the steering rack mounting bolts, remove the rack and pinion through the left wheel opening.

To install:

11. Install the rack and pinion through the left wheel opening. Tighten the mounting bolts to 59 ft. lbs. (81 Nm).

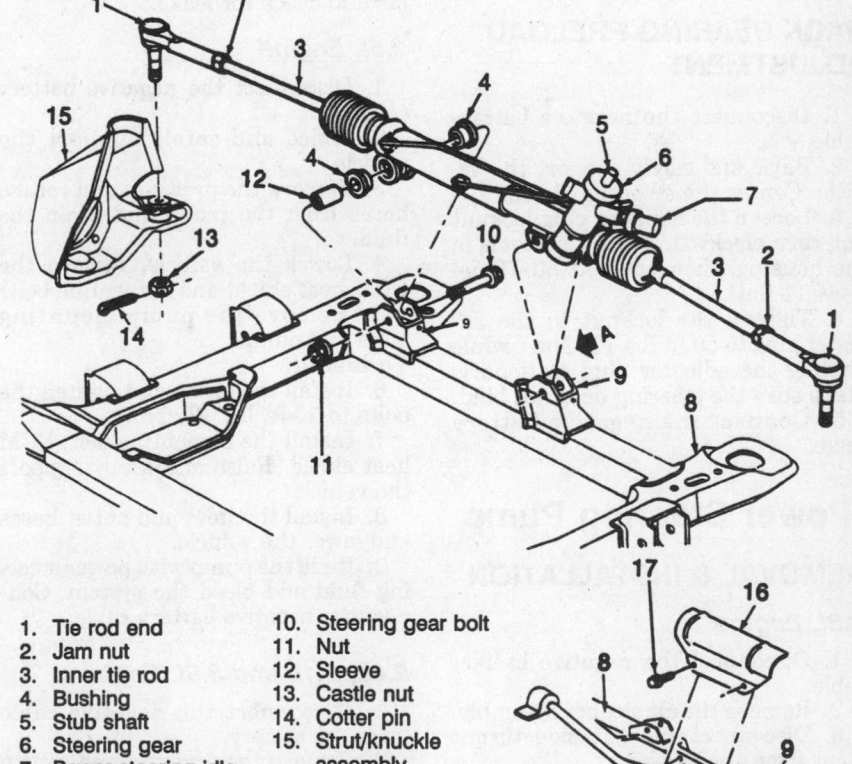

1. Tie rod end
2. Jam nut
3. Inner tie rod
4. Bushing
5. Stub shaft
6. Steering gear
7. Power steering idle speed switch
8. Frame
9. Steering gear mount
10. Steering gear bolt
11. Nut
12. Sleeve
13. Castle nut
14. Cotter pin
15. Strut/knuckle assembly
16. Heat shield
17. Screw

Power rack assembly mounting

12. Connect the pressure lines, tighten the fittings to 20 ft. lbs. (27 Nm).

13. Install the rack heat shield, tighten the retaining bolts to 53 inch lbs. (6 Nm).

14. Raise the frame assembly and align the steering gear stub shaft to the intermediate steering shaft. Install the frame retaining bolts and secure frame in place. Remove the support at the frame.

15. Connect the electrical lead to the power steering idle switch. Attach the intermediate shaft to the stub shaft, tighten the pinch bolt to 35 ft. lbs. (48 Nm).

16. Install the intermediate steering shaft pinch bolt at the steering gear and tighten to 35 ft. lbs. (47 Nm).

17. Install the exhaust pipe and converter assembly to the exhaust manifold, if removed.

18. Connect the tie rod ends to the steering knuckle and secure.

19. Install both wheel assemblies, tighten lug nuts to 100 ft. lbs. (136 Nm) and lower the vehicle.

20. Install the air cleaner. Connect the negative battery cable. Fill and bleed the power steering system.

21. Inspect and adjust the front suspension toe setting as required.

RACK BEARING PRELOAD ADJUSTMENT

1. Disconnect the negative battery cable.

2. Raise and safely support the vehicle. Center the steering wheel.

3. Loosen the adjuster plug locknut and turn clockwise until it bottoms in the housing, then back off 50–70 degrees (1 flat).

4. Tighten the locknut to the adjuster plug to 50 ft. lbs. (70 Nm), while holding the adjuster plug stationary. Make sure the steering does not bind.

5. Connect the negative battery cable.

Power Steering Pump

REMOVAL & INSTALLATION

2.3L Engine

1. Disconnect the negative battery cable.

2. Remove the air cleaner assembly.

3. Disconnect the left side torque strut from the engine.

4. Separate the throttle cable bracket from the engine torque strut bracket and set aside. Do not remove cables.

5. Remove the engine torque strut bracket.

6. Disconnect the hydraulic pump lines.

7. Remove the rear bracket to pump bolts.

8. Remove the drive belt and lay aside.

9. Remove the rear bracket to transaxle bolts.

10. Remove the front bracket to engine bolt and remove the pump with bracket.

11. Transfer the pulley and bracket, as necessary.

To install:

12. Install the pump, pulley and bracket.

13. Install the front bracket to engine bolt.

14. Install the rear bracket to transaxle bolts.

15. Install the rear bracket to pump bolts.

16. Install the drive belt.

17. Connect the hydraulic pump lines.

18. Install the engine torque strut bracket.

19. Install the throttle cable bracket to the engine torque strut bracket.

20. Connect the left side torque strut to the engine.

21. Install the air cleaner assembly.

22. Fill with fluid and bleed the air from the system.

23. Connect the negative battery cable and check for leaks.

2.5L Engine

1. Disconnect the negative battery cable.

2. Raise and safely support the vehicle.

3. Remove the pressure and return hoses from the pump and drain the fluid.

4. Lower the vehicle, remove the ECM heat shield and serpentine belt.

5. Remove the pump mounting bolts and pump.

To install:

6. Install the pump and tighten the bolts to 20 ft. lbs. (27 Nm).

7. Install the serpentine belt, ECM heat shield. Raise and safely support the vehicle.

8. Install the inlet and outlet hoses and lower the vehicle.

9. Refill the pump with power steering fluid and bleed the system. Connect the negative battery cable.

2.8L, 3.1L and 3.8L Engines

1. Disconnect the negative cable from the battery.

2. Remove the pressure and return hoses from the pump and drain the system into an appropriate container.

3. Cap the fittings at the pump.

4. Remove the serpentine belt.

5. Locate the pump attaching bolts through the pulley and remove the bolts.

6. Remove the pump assembly.

To install:

7. Install the pump and torque the mounting bolts to 25 ft. lbs. (34 Nm) for the 2.8L and 3.1L engines or 20 ft. lbs. (27 Nm), in sequence, top bolt first, bottom bolt second, for the 3.8L engine.

8. Reconnect the hoses to the pump and install the serpentine belt.

9. Refill the power steering pump reservoir and bleed the system. Connect the negative battery cable.

3.4L Engine

1. Disconnect the negative battery cable.

2. Remove the air cleaner assembly and the coolant recovery reservoir.

3. Siphon as much fluid from the reservoir as possible. Power steering fluid will damage the secondary timing belt if contact is made.

4. Remove the serpentine drive belt from the engine. Remove the steering line bracket from the cover.

5. Disconnect the lines from the power steering pump. Plug the lines and the connections at the pump housing to prevent dirt from entering.

6. Remove the pump mounting bolts and remove the pump.

To install:

7. Connect the power steering lines at the pump.

8. Install the power steering pump to mounting bracket and tighten attaching bolts to 25 ft. lbs. (34 Nm).

9. Install the serpentine belt, coolant recovery tank and air cleaner assembly.

10. Fill the reservoir with fluid and bleed the system. Inspect the power steering system for leaks.

BELT ADJUSTMENT

Except 2.3L Engine

Serpentine belt tension is maintained by the tensioner and is not adjustable.

2.3L Engine

1. Place belt tension gauge J–36018 or equivalent, on the belt.

2. Loosen the 2 pump housing to rear bracket adjustment bolts. Loosen the engine to front bracket bolt.

3. Torque the engine to front bracket bolt to 44 inch lbs. (5 Nm).

4. Insert a ½ in. drive handle into the pump adjustment tab and pull until the tension gauge reads 110 lbs. (500 N). Hold that adjustment while torquing the pump adjustment bolts to 19 ft. lbs. (26 Nm).

5. If installing a new belt, set the tension to the rating listed above, run the engine for a minimum of 5 minutes and reset the tension to the specification.

SYSTEM BLEEDING

NOTE: Automatic transmission fluid is not compatible with the seals and hoses of the power steering system. Under no circumstances should automatic transmission be used in place of power steering fluid in this system.

1. With the engine turned OFF, turn the wheels all the way to the left.
2. Fill the reservoir with power steering fluid until the level is at the FULL COLD mark on the reservoir.
3. Raise the front wheels off the ground.
4. Turn the steering way from side to side without touching the stops. Keep the fluid level and the FULL COLD mark.
5. Start the engine. With the engine at idle, check the fluid level and add as required to bring fluid to FULL COLD.
6. Continue to run the vehicle and allow to idle for 3 minutes. Recheck the fluid level and add as required.

Tie Rod Ends

REMOVAL & INSTALLATION

Outer

1. Disconnect the negative battery cable.
2. Remove the cotter pin and hex slotted nut from the outer tie rod assembly.
3. Loosen the jam nut and remove the tie rod from the steering knuckle using a steering linkage removing tool J–35917 or equivalent.
4. Holding the inner tie rod stationary, count number of turns to remove the outer tie rod.

To install:

5. Lubricate the inner rod threads with anti-seize compound and install the outer tie rod the same amount of turns that it took to remove.
6. Install the outer tie rod-to-knuckle and install the slotted nut. Torque the nut to 35 ft. lbs. (50 Nm) and to 45 ft. lbs. (60 Nm) maximum to align the cotter pin slot. Do not back off to align the cotter pin.
7. Install a new cotter pin and bend over. Torque the jam nut to 50 ft. lbs. (70 Nm) and connect the negative battery cable.

Inner

1. Disconnect the negative battery cable.
2. Remove the rack and pinion assembly from the vehicle.
3. Remove the outer tie rod end.
4. Remove the jam nut, boot clamps

and boot. Use side cutters to cut the boot clamps.
5. Remove the shock dampener from the inner tie rod and slide back on the rack.

NOTE: Do not let the rack slide out of the rack housing while the tie rods are moved.

6. Place wrenches on the flats of the rack and inner tie rod assemblies.
7. Rotate the housing counterclockwise until the inner rod separates from the rack.

To install:

8. Install the inner tie rod end onto the rack and torque to 70 ft. lbs. (95 Nm).
9. Support the rack assembly in a vise.
10. Stake both sides of the inner tie rod housing to the flats on the rack.
11. Slide the shock dampener over the housing until it engages.
12. Install the boot and new boot clamps. Do not tighten the clamps at this time.
13. Apply grease to the inner tie rod, housing and boot.
14. Align the breather tube with the boot, making sure it is not twisted.
15. Crimp the boot clamps with keystone clamp pliers, tool J–22610 or equivalent.
16. Install the jam nut and outer tie rod end.
17. Install the rack and pinion assembly into the vehicle.

BRAKES

Master Cylinder

REMOVAL & INSTALLATION

NOTE: On vehicles equipped with ABS, to help avoid personal injury due to a retained load on the ABS Hydraulic Modulator assembly, the gear tension relief function of the TECH I Scan tool must be performed prior to removal of the brake control and modulator assembly.

1. If equipped with Anti-lock Brakes, depressurize the ABS brake system as follows:
   a. With the ignition key **OFF**, firmly apply and release the brake pedal a minimum of 40 times.
   b. A noticeable change in the pedal feel will occur when the accumulator is completely discharged (a hard pedal).
   c. Do not turn the ignition key **ON** after depressurizing the system.

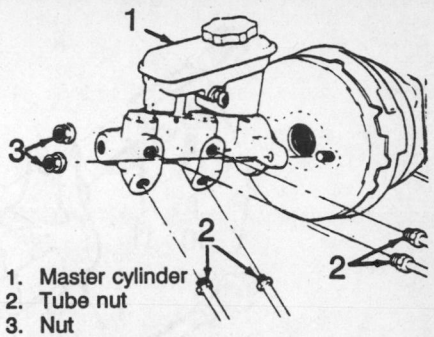

1. Master cylinder
2. Tube nut
3. Nut

Master cylinder mounting

2. Using the TECH I Scan tool, perform the gear tension relief function. Remove the ABS hydraulic modulator assembly, if equipped with ABS brakes.
3. Disconnect the electrical harness connector from the fluid level sensor on the master cylinder.
4. Using a flare nut wrench, remove the brake lines from the master cylinder. Plug the lines to prevent fluid loss and contamination.
5. Remove the 2 master cylinder-to-brake power booster retaining nuts and remove master cylinder.

To install:

6. Install the master cylinder and torque the retaining nuts to 20 ft. lbs. (27 Nm).
7. Install the brake lines and torque to 15 ft. lbs. (20 Nm), using a flare nut wrench.
8. Connect the fluid level sensor electrical wire.
9. Install the ABS hydraulic modulator assembly, if removed.
10. Fill the master cylinder to the proper level with new brake fluid meeting DOT 3 specifications.
11. Bleed the hydraulic system and recheck the fluid level. Do not move the vehicle until a firm brake pedal is obtained.

Brake Caliper

REMOVAL & INSTALLATION

Front

1. Remove ⅔ of the brake fluid from the brake reservoir using a syringe.
2. Raise and support the vehicle safely.
3. Mark the relationship of the wheel-to-hub and bearing assembly.
4. Remove the tire and wheel. Install 2 lug nuts to retain the rotor.
5. If the caliper is going to be removed, disconnect and plug the brake hose.
6. Remove the caliper mounting

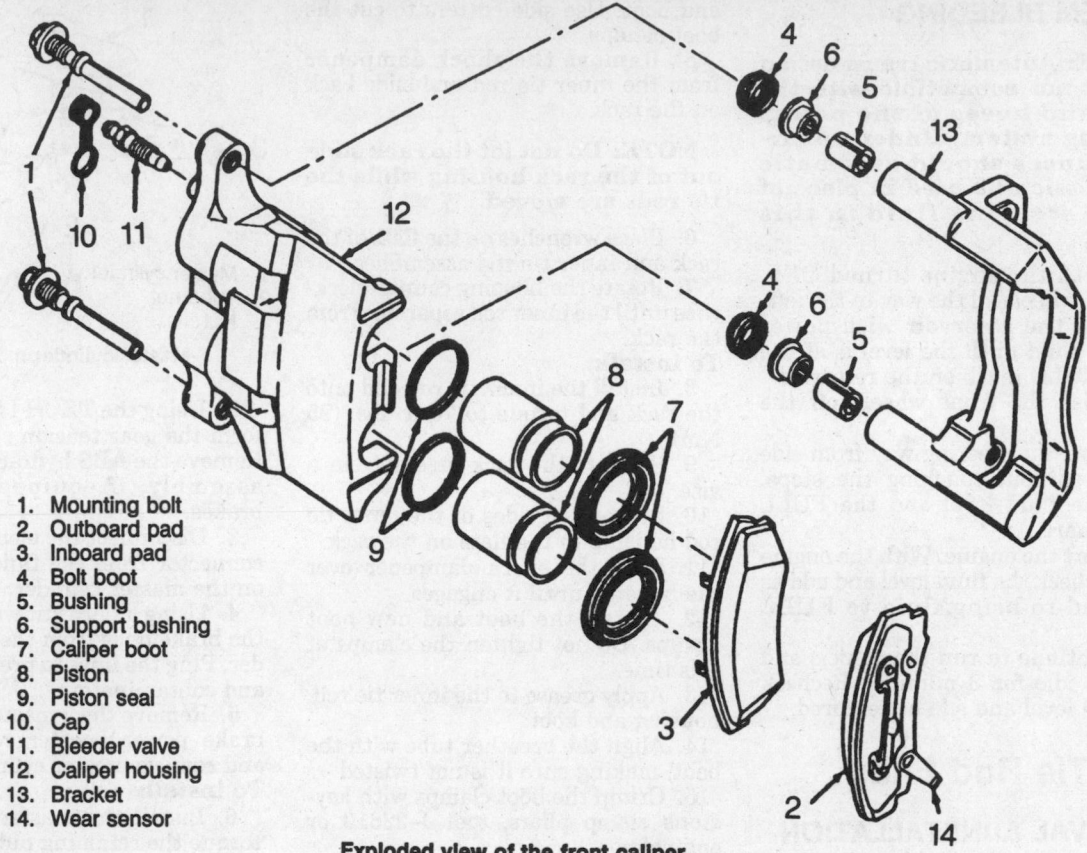

1. Mounting bolt
2. Outboard pad
3. Inboard pad
4. Bolt boot
5. Bushing
6. Support bushing
7. Caliper boot
8. Piston
9. Piston seal
10. Cap
11. Bleeder valve
12. Caliper housing
13. Bracket
14. Wear sensor

Exploded view of the front caliper

bolts and pull the caliper from the mounting bracket and rotor. Support the caliper with wire if not removing.
To install:

7. Inspect the bolt boots and support bushings for cuts or damage, replace if necessary. Inspect the bolts and bushings for corrosion, replace if any corrosion is found. Do not attempt to polish away the corrosion.

8. Install the caliper over the rotor into the mounting bracket. Make sure the bolt boots are in place.

9. Lubricate the entire shaft of the mounting bolts and cavities with silicone grease.

10. Install the mounting bolts and torque to 79 ft. lbs. (107 Nm).

11. Install the brake hose, using new copper washers and torque to 32 ft. lbs. (44 Nm).

12. Remove the 2 wheel lugs, install the wheels and torque the lug nuts to 100 ft. lbs. (136 Nm).

13. Lower the vehicle.

14. Fill the master cylinder and bleed the front brake calipers.

15. Check for hydraulic leaks. Pump the brake pedal a few times before moving the vehicle.

Rear

1. Remove ⅔ of the brake fluid from the reservoir with a syringe.

2. Raise and support the vehicle safely.

3. Remove the rear wheel assembly and install 2 lug nuts to retain the rotor.

4. Remove the brake shield assembly.

5. Loosen the tension on the parking brake cable at the equalizer.

6. Remove the parking cable and return spring from the lever.

7. Hold the cable lever and remove the lock nut, lever and seal.

8. Push the piston into the caliper bore using 2 adjustable pliers over the inboard pad tabs.

NOTE: Do not allow pliers to contact the actuator screw. Protect the piston so the contact surface does not get damaged.

9. Reinstall the lever seal with the sealing bead against the caliper housing, lever and locknut.

10. Remove and plug the brake hose inlet fitting only if the caliper is going to be removed from the vehicle.

11. Remove the bolt and bracket to gain access to the upper mounting bolt.

12. Remove the caliper mounting bolts, caliper and hang from the suspension with a piece of wire to prevent brake hose damage.

To install:

13. Inspect all brake parts for damage and deterioration. Replace any parts, if necessary.

14. Push the caliper sleeves inward. Install the caliper to the adapter bracket.

15. Install the caliper-to-mounting bracket bolts. Torque the mounting bolts to 92 ft. lbs. (125 Nm).

16. Install the bracket and bolt after the mounting bolts have been torqued.

17. Install the brake hose inlet with new copper washers, if removed. Torque the hose bolt to 32 ft. lbs. (44 Nm).

18. Remove the locknut, lever and seal. Lubricate the lever seal and lever shaft.

19. Install the seal and lever with the lever facing down.

20. Hold the lever back against the stop and torque the lock nut to 35 ft. lbs. (47 Nm).

21. Install the return spring and parking brake cable and adjust.

22. Install the brake shield and rear wheel assembly. Torque the lug nuts to 100 ft. lbs. (136 Nm).

23. Lower the vehicle.

24. Fill the brake reservoir with DOT 3 brake fluid.

25. Bleed the brake caliper, if removed.

26. Inspect the brake system for fluid leaks.

27. Pump the brakes until a firm pedal is achieved, prior to moving the vehicle. This will seat the brake pads against the rotors.

Disc Brake Pads

REMOVAL & INSTALLATION

Front

1. Disconnect the negative battery cable.

2. Raise and support the vehicle safely.

3. Remove the wheel and tire assembly.

4. Remove the 2 caliper mounting bolts, caliper and hang from the suspension with a piece of wire. Do not hang by the brake hose.

5. Using a prybar, lift the outboard pad retaining spring to clear the center lug.

6. Remove the inboard pad by unsnapping from the pistons.

To install:

7. Remove about ⅔ of the fluid from the brake reservoir with a syring.

8. Bottom the pistons in the caliper bore using a C-clamp and the old inboard brake pad.

9. Install the new inboard brake pad. Make sure both inboard pad tangs are inside the piston cavity.

10. Install the outboard pad by snapping the pad retainer spring over the housing center lug and into the housing slot.

11. Make sure both pads remain free of grease or oil. The wear sensor should be at the trailing edge of the pad during rotation.

12. Install the caliper assembly, wheels assembly and lower the vehicle.

13. Fill the master cylinder to the **FULL** mark and pump the brakes until a firm pedal is obtained.

14. Connect the negative battery cable.

Rear

1. Raise and support the vehicle safely.

2. Remove the rear wheel assemblies.

3. Remove the rear caliper and hang by the suspension with a piece of wire to prevent brake hose damage.

4. Using a prybar, disengage the buttons on the outboard pad from the holes in the caliper housing.

5. Press in on the edge of the inboard pad and tilt outward to release the pad from the pad retainer.

6. Remove the plug from the end of the caliper piston using a small prybar.

To install:

NOTE: **Do not allow pliers to contact the actuator screw. Protect the piston so the contact surface does not get damaged.**

7. Bottom the piston into the caliper bore by positioning a twelve inch adjustable pliers over the caliper housing and piston surface.

8. Lubricate a new plug and install it into the end of the piston.

9. Install the inboard brake pad. Engage the pad edge in the retainer tabs closest to the caliper bridge. Press down and snap the tabs at the open side of the caliper. The wear sensor should be at the leading edge of the pad during wheel rotation. The back of the pad must lay flat against the piston. The button on the back of the pad must engage the D-shaped notch in the piston.

NOTE: **If the piston will not align or retract into the bore. Turn the piston clockwise using a piston turning tool J-7624 or equivalent.**

10. Install the outboard brake pad. Snap the pad retainer spring into the slots in the caliper housing. The back of the pad must lay flat against the caliper.

11. Install the caliper onto the mounting bracket.

12. Apply force to the brake pedal until a firm pedal is obtained, prior to moving the vehicle. This will seat the brake pads against the rotors.

13. Install the rear wheels and torque the lug nuts to 100 ft. lbs. (136 Nm).

14. Lower the vehicle and check for fluid leaks.

Brake Rotor

REMOVAL & INSTALLATION

1. Raise and support the vehicle safely.

2. Remove the wheel and tire assembly.

3. Remove the brake caliper and support with a wire to the body.

4. Slide the rotor off the hub assembly.

To install:

5. Install the brake rotor over the hub assembly.

6. Install the brake caliper.

7. Install the wheel and tire assembly. Torque the lug nuts to 100 ft. lbs. (136 Nm).

8. Lower the vehicle. Pump the brakes until a firm pedal is obtained, prior to moving the vehicle.

Parking Brake Cable

ADJUSTMENT

1. Apply the parking brake pedal 3 times with heavy force.

2. Do not apply the main brake pedal during this step. Fully apply and release the parking brake 3 times.

3. Raise and support the vehicle safely. Mark the relationship of the wheel to the hub and bearing asembly.

4. Make sure the parking brake is fully released.

5. Remove the rear wheel assemblies and install 2 lug nuts to retain the rotors.

6. The parking brake levers at the calipers should be against the lever stop on the caliper housing. If not against the stops, check the cables for binding.

7. Tighten the parking brake cable at the adjuster until the clearance between either the right or left lever and their respective stop is 0.02–0.08 in.(0.5–2.mm).

8. Operate the parking brake several times to check adjustments. A firm pedal should be present.

9. Remove the 2 wheel lugs, install the rear wheels and lower the vehicle.

Brake System Bleeding

Standard System

1. Fill the master cylinder reservoir with brake fluid and keep the reservoir at least half full during the bleeding operation.

2. If the master cylinder has air in the bore, it must be removed before bleeding the calipers. Bleed the master cylinder as follows:

a. Fill the reservoir with clean brake fluid. Do not allow brake fluid to contact painted surfaces, it will damage the finish.

b. Loosen the brake tubes at the master cylinder and slowly depress the brake pedal. While holding the brake pedal to the floor, tighten the brake tubes. Wait 15 seconds and repeat until all air is removed from the master cylinder.

3. Bleed the brakes in the following order:

    Right rear caliper
    Left front caliper
    Left rear caliper
    Right front caliper

4. Install a box end wrench over the bleeder valve and connect a clear tube onto the valve. Place the other end of the tube into a container of new brake fluid. The end of the tube must be submerged in brake fluid.

5. Depress the brake pedal slowly 1 time and hold. Loosen the bleeder valve to purge the air from the caliper. Close the valve and release the pedal. Wait 15 seconds. Repeat the procedure until all air is removed from the brake fluid. It may take 10 repetitions or more to completely purge the system of air.

6. Do not pump the brake pedal rapidly, this causes the secondary master cylinder piston to push to the end of the bore and make bleeding difficult.

7. After the calipers have been bled, check the brake pedal for sponginess and the **BRAKE** warning lamp for unbalanced pressure.

8. Repeat the bleeding operation if a spongy pedal is felt and fill the reservoir to the **MAX** line.

Anti-Lock Brake System (ABS)

1989–91

— **CAUTION** —

Use only clean DOT 3 brake fluid from a sealed container in the anti-lock brake system. Any other type of fluid may cause severe damage to the internal components causing brake failure and personal injury.

1. Make sure the vehicle ignition is **OFF**.

2. Disconnect the negative battery cable.

3. Depressurize the Powermaster III unit as follows:

  a. With the ignition key **OFF**, firmly apply and release the brake pedal a minimum of 40 times.

  b. A noticeable change in the pedal feel will occur when the accumulator is completely discharged (a hard pedal).

  c. Do not turn the ignition key **ON** after depressurizing the system unless instructed to do so.

4. Clean and remove the reservoir cap.

5. Fill the reservoir with DOT 3 brake fluid.

6. Raise the vehicle and support the vehicle safely.

7. Bleed the right front wheel by attaching a clean hose to the bleeder valve and submerge the other end into a container of partially filled brake fluid.

8. Open the valve and slowly depress the brake pedal.

9. Tap lightly on the brake caliper with a rubber mallet to dislodge the air bubbles.

10. Close the valve and release the brake pedal. Repeat until all air is removed.

11. Repeat steps 7–10 on the left front wheel.

12. Connect the negative battery cable and turn the ignition key to the **RUN** position without starting the vehicle. Allow the pump to run to pressurize the accumulator.

13. Bleed the right rear brake by installing a bleeder hose and container, open the valve, with the ignition **ON** slowly depress the pedal part way until the fluid begins to flow from the bleeder valve and allow the fluid to flow for 15 seconds. Do not fully depress the brake pedal.

14. Close the valve and release the brake pedal.

15. Fill the reservoir with fluid to 1 inch below the FULL mark.

16. Repeat Steps 13–16 for the left rear wheel.

17. Lower the vehicle and bleed the Powermaster III isolation valves (at the master cylinder) as follows:

  a. Attach a clear hose and container to the Powermaster III inboard bleeder valves.

  b. With the ignition in the **ON** position, apply the pedal, slowly open the valve and allow fluid to flow until no air bubbles are seen.

  c. Close the valve and repeat the steps to the outboard bleeder valve until no air bubbles are present.

18. Bleed the accumulator as follows.

  a. Turn the ignition key to the **OFF** position, depressurize the system and wait 2 minutes.

NOTE: Never check the brake fluid level without fully derpressurizing the Powermaster III Unit or overfilling will result.

  b. Remove the reservoir cover and check the fluid level. Add if necessary.

  c. Install the reservoir cap.

  d. Turn the ignition key to the **RUN** position but do not start the engine.

  e. When the pump has stopped, depress the brake pedal and repeat the **OFF/RUN** procedures 10 times to cycle the solenoids.

19. Apply the brake pedal and note the pedal feel and travel.

20. If the pedal feels firm and smooth without excessive travel, the system is properly bled. Connect the negative battery cable.

1992–93

If pressure bleeding the system, the equipment must be of the diaphragm type. It must have a rubber diaphragm between the air supply and the brake fluid to prevent air, moisture and other containants from entering the system. Follow the specific instructions that are supplied with the pressure bleeder.

— **CAUTION** —

Use only clean DOT 3 brake fluid from a sealed container in the anti-lock brake system. Any other type of fluid may cause severe damage to the internal components causing brake failure and personal injury.

Prior to bleeding the brakes, the front and the rear displacement cylinder pistons must be returned to the top most position.

1. Position the front and the rear displacement cylinder pistons at the top most position as follows:

  a. Using a Tech I or T–100 (CAMS), enter the manual control function and apply the front and rear motors. Be sure the relay is ON.

  b. If Tech I or T–100 (CAMS) is not available, bleed the front brakes. Start the engine and allow to run for at least 10 seconds. This will cause the ABS system to initialize itself and return the front and the rear displacement cylinders to the top position.

  c. At this point, the entire brake system should be rebled.

2. Clean and remove the reservoir cover.

3. Inspect the fluid level in the reservoir and add as required to correct level.

4. Prime the ABS modulator and master cylinder assembly as follows:

  a. Attach bleeder hose to the rearward bleeder valve and submerge the opposite end of hose in container partially filled with clean brake fluid.

  b. Slowly open the rearward bleeder valve ½ turn. Depress the brake pedal until fluid begins to flow.

  c. Close the valve and release the brake pedal. Repeat this procedure for forward bleeder valve until fluids begins to flow.

5. Remove the reservoir cover and inspect the fluid level and add fluid as required.

6. Bleed the wheels in the following sequence:

  Right rear
  Left rear
  Right front
  Left front

7. Raise and support the vehicle safely.

8. Bleed the wheel in the sequence listed above by attaching a clean hose to the bleeder valve and submerge the other end into a container of partially filled brake fluid.

9. Open the valve and slowly depress the brake pedal.

10. Tap lightly on the brake caliper with a rubber mallet to dislodge the air bubbles.

11. Close the valve and release the brake pedal. Wait 5 seconds and repeat until all air is removed.

12. Repeat Steps 5–8 until all wheels are bled. Lower the vehicle.

13. Remove the reservoir cover and inspect the fluid level. Add brake fluid as required to correct the level.

Anti-Lock Brake System Service

PRECAUTION

Failure to observe the following precautions may result in system damage.

- The brake system uses a hydraulic accumulator which when fully charged, contains brake fluid at high pressure. Before disconnecting any hydraulic lines, hoses or fittings, be sure the accumulator is fully depressurized.
- Never disassemble any component of the Anti-Lock Brake System (ABS) which is designated non-servicable; the component must be replaced as an assembly.
- Replace all components included in repair kits used to service the system.
- When filling the master cylinder, always use Delco Supreme 11 brake fluid or equivalent, which meets DOT-3 specifications; petroleum base fluid will destroy the rubber parts.
- Avoid spilling brake fluid on the vehicles painted surfaces, wiring, cables or electrical connectors. Brake fluid will damage paint and electrical connections.

RELIEVING ANTI-LOCK BRAKE SYSTEM PRESSURE

1989–91

> CAUTION
> *Failure to fully depressurize the system before performing service operations could result in personal injury from a high pressure spray of brake fluid.*

1. With the ignition key **OFF**, firmly apply and release the brake pedal a minimum of 40 times.

2. A noticeable change in the pedal feel will occur when the accumulator is completely discharged (a hard pedal).

3. Do not turn the ignition key **ON** after depressurizing the system.

Powermaster III Unit

REMOVAL & INSTALLATION

1. Depressurize the ABS brake system as follows:
   a. With the ignition key **OFF**, firmly apply and release the brake pedal a minimum of 40 times.
   b. A noticeable change in the pedal feel will occur when the accumulator is completely discharged (a hard pedal).
   c. Do not turn the ignition key **ON** after depressurizing the system.

2. Disconnect the negative battery cable.

3. Disconnect the 3 Powermaster III electrical connectors and move out of the way.

4. Remove and plug the 3 metal brake lines using flare nut wrenches. Plug the lines to prevent fluid loss and contamination.

5. Remove the hair pin clip from inside the vehicle at the brake pedal.

6. Remove the 2 ABS unit-to-cowl retaining nuts.

7. Remove the ABS unit. Make sure none of the electrical connectors are still connected.

To install:

8. Lightly lubricate the entire outer surface of the pushrod with silicone grease.

9. Position the ABS unit into the vehicle. Loosely install the retaining nuts and pushrod.

10. Install the pushrod hair pin clip and torque the 2 retaining nuts to 15–25 ft. lbs. (20–34 Nm).

11. Install the 3 brake pipes using flare nut wrenches. Torque the pipes to 11 ft. lbs. (20 Nm).

12. Install the ABS unit electrical connectors.

13. Adjust the stoplight switch.

14. Bleed the ABS system. Reconnect the negative battery cable.

CHASSIS ELECTRICAL

Heater Blower Motor

REMOVAL & INSTALLATION

1. Disconnect negative battery cable.

2. Remove the mounting screws and the sound insulator from under right side of the instrument panel.

3. Remove the convenience center rear screws, loosen the front screws and slide the convenience center out of the vehicle.

4. Grasp the carpet at the top side and pull forward.

5. Disconnect the electrical connections from the blower motor and resistor.

6. Remove the plastic water shield from the right side of the cowl, if equipped.

7. Remove the blower motor-to-chassis screws and the blower motor.

8. Remove the cage retaining nut and the cage (old style).

NOTE: Some of the new style blower cages are plastic welded to the motor shaft. Use a hot knife to cut a slot in the cage shaft sleeve in 3 places. Cut through the plastic material from the dome to the end of the shaft until the cage splits from the shaft.

To install:

9. Install the cage on the new blower motor with the opening facing away from the motor.

10. Install the blower motor and screws. Install the sound insulator and connect the electrical leads to the motor and resistor.

11. Install the water shield to the cowl. Reinstall the carpet at the cowl.

12. Install the convenience center and secure retainer screws.

13. Install the sound insulator panel and connect the negative battery cable.

Windshield Wiper Motor

REMOVAL & INSTALLATION

1991 Lumina

1. Disconnect the negative battery cable.

2. Remove the left and the right wiper arms.

3. Remove the top vent screen shroud.

4. Remove the wiper arm drive link from the crank arm.

5. Disconnect the electrical connectors. Remove the wiper motor attaching bolts.

6. Remove the wiper arm drive link from the crank arm.

7. Remove the wiper motor while guiding the crank arm through the hole.

8. Remove the crank arm from the motor as required.

To install:

9. Install the crank arm to the motor. Install the wiper motor while guiding the crank arm through the hole.

10. Install the wiper motor attaching bolts.

11. Connect the electrical connectors and the wiper linkage to the crank arm.

12. Install the top vent screen shroud. Install both side wiper arms.

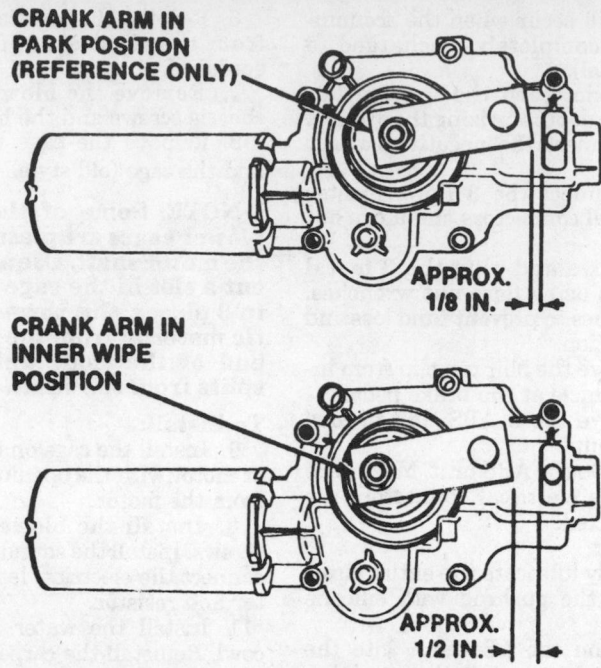

CRANK ARM IN
PARK POSITION
(REFERENCE ONLY)

APPROX.
1/8 IN.

CRANK ARM IN
INNER WIPE
POSITION

APPROX.
1/2 IN.

Crank arm in inner wipe and park position

13. Reconnect the negative battery cable.

Except 1991 Lumina

1. Disconnect the negative battery cable.
2. Remove wiper module from vehicle, if equipped, as follows:

a. Raise the hood. Disconnect the washer hoses and remove protective cap and nut from each wiper arm. Lift each wiper arm and insert a pin or pop rivet completely through the 2 holes located next to the pivot of arm. Then lift the arm off transmission shaft using a rocking motion.

NOTE: Remove metal shavings from knurls of transmission linkage shaft using a wire brush.

b. Remove the screws retaining the cowl cover. Lower the hood partially and remove the cowl cover.
c. Remove the air inlet panel and underhood light switch, if equipped.

NOTE: Attach holding wire to upper portion of switch before removing retaining nut or switch will fall between panels.

d. Disconnect 2 wiring harness connectors from motor, and washer hose at firewall.
e. Position crank arm to inner wipe position, remove 3 screws from bellcrank housing, lower transmission and remove.
3. Remove crank arm from motor.

NOTE: Do not remove the crank arm from the transmission because the factory has preset the adjustment. The crank arm must be removed from the motor only.

4. Remove 3 screws retaining the motor and remove the motor.
To install:
5. Attach the motor to the module assembly.
6. Install the crank arm and nut. Tighten to 25–38 ft. lbs. (34–51 Nm).
7. Attach the bellcrank to module assembly and install the wire connectors washer hose, air inlet panel and light switch.
8. Install cowl cover, wiper arms, washer hoses and nuts with protective caps.
9. Connect the negative battery cable and check the operation of the wiper motor.

Windshield Wiper Switch

REMOVAL & INSTALLATION

The wiper/washer switch is mounted on the steering column.
1. Disconnect the negative battery cable.
2. Remove the steering wheel horn pad, wheel retaining nut and steering wheel.
3. Remove the turn signal cancelling cam assembly, if required.
4. Remove the wiring protector around the instrument panel opening and the switch retaining screws.
5. To aid in switch removal, pull the bottom of the switch rearward first and then remove. Disconnect the electrical connector.
To install:
6. Install the switch assembly. Install the wiring protector around the instrument panel opening, covering all wires.
7. Install the steering column housing cover and torque the screws to 35 inch lbs. (4 Nm).
8. Install the hazard knob and lubricate the bottom side of the cancelling cam with lithium grease.
9. Install the steering wheel and torque the shaft nut to 30 ft. lbs. (41 Nm).
10. Connect the negative battery cable and check steering column operations.

Instrument Cluster

REMOVAL & INSTALLATION

Cutlass Supreme

1. Remove the air cleaner assembly. Disconnect the negative battery cable.
2. Remove screws at top of the trim plate.
3. Pull the bottom of the trim plate out to release the spring clips and remove panel from the vehicle.
4. Disconnect the **PRNDL** cable, if equipped.
5. Remove the screws retaining the instrument cluster and pull the cluster forward slightly. Disconnect the electrical connectors.
6. Remove the cluster assembly from the instrument panel.
To install:
7. Position the cluster at the instrument panel and connect the electrical harness connectors. Install the cluster assembly into the carrier.
8. Connect the **PRNDL** cable, if equipped.
9. Secure cluster in place with the retainer bolts tightened to 18 inch lbs. (2 Nm).

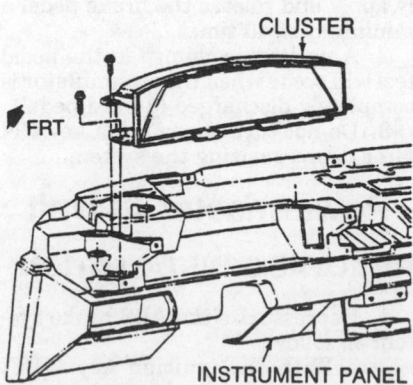

CLUSTER

FRT

INSTRUMENT PANEL

Removing the instrument cluster—Grand Prix

Saturn Corp.
Front Wheel Drive
SATURN—Coupe • Sedan

SPECIFICATIONS

VEHICLE IDENTIFICATION CHART

It is important for servicing and ordering parts to be certain of the vehicle and engine identification. The VIN (vehicle identification number) is a 17 digit number visible through the windshield on the driver's side of the dash and contains the vehicle and engine identification codes. The tenth digit indicates model year and the eighth digit indicates engine code. It can be interpreted as follows:

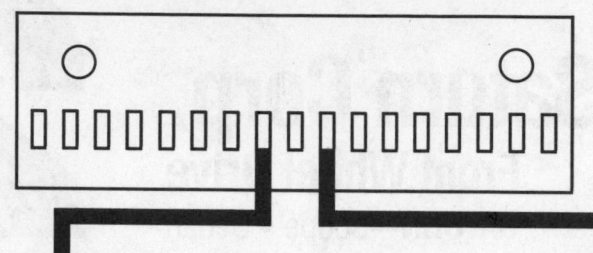

		Engine Code					Model Year	
Code	Liters	Cu. In. (cc)	Cyl.	Fuel Sys.	Eng. Mfg.		Code	Year
7	1.9	116 (1901)	4	MFI	Saturn		M	1991
9	1.9	116 (1901)	4	TBI	Saturn		N	1992
							P	1993

MFI—Multi-Point Fuel Injection
TBI—Throttle Body Injection

ENGINE IDENTIFICATION

Year	Model	Engine Displacement Liters (cc)	Engine Series Identification (ID/VIN)	Fuel System	No. of Cylinders	Engine Type
1991	Sedan	1.9 (1901)	7	MFI	4	DOHC
	Sedan	1.9 (1901)	9	TBI	4	SOHC
	Coupe	1.9 (1901)	7	MFI	4	DOHC
1992	Sedan	1.9 (1901)	7	MFI	4	DOHC
	Sedan	1.9 (1901)	9	TBI	4	SOHC
	Coupe	1.9 (1901)	7	MFI	4	DOHC
1993	Wagon	1.9 (1901)	7	MFI	4	DOHC
	Wagon	1.9 (1901)	9	TBI	4	SOHC
	Sedan	1.9 (1901)	7	MFI	4	DOHC
	Sedan	1.9 (1901)	9	TBI	4	SOHC
	Coupe	1.9 (1901)	9	TBI	4	SOHC
	Coupe	1.9 (1901)	7	MFI	4	DOHC

DOHC—Dual Overhead Cam
SOHC—Single Overhead Cam
MFI—Multi-Point Fuel Injection
TBI—Throttle Body Injection

GENERAL ENGINE SPECIFICATIONS

Year	Engine ID/VIN	Engine Displacement Liters (cc)	Fuel System Type	Net Horsepower @ rpm	Net Torque @ rpm (ft. lbs.)	Bore × Stroke (in.)	Compression Ratio	Oil Pressure @ rpm
1991	7	1.9 (1901)	MFI	124 @ 5600	122 @ 4800	3.23 × 3.54	9.5:1	36 @ 2000
	9	1.9 (1901)	TBI	85 @ 5000	107 @ 2400	3.23 × 3.54	9.3:1	36 @ 2000
1992	7	1.9 (1901)	MFI	124 @ 5600	122 @ 4800	3.23 × 3.54	9.5:1	36 @ 2000
	9	1.9 (1901)	TBI	85 @ 5000	107 @ 2400	3.23 × 3.54	9.3:1	36 @ 2000

GENERAL ENGINE SPECIFICATIONS

Year	Engine ID/VIN	Engine Displacement Liters (cc)	Fuel System Type	Net Horsepower @ rpm	Net Torque @ rpm (ft. lbs.)	Bore × Stroke (in.)	Compression Ratio	Oil Pressure @ rpm
1993	7	1.9 (1901)	MFI	124 @ 5600	122 @ 4800	3.23 × 3.54	9.5:1	36 @ 2000
	9	1.9 (1901)	TBI	85 @ 5000	107 @ 2400	3.23 × 3.54	9.3:1	36 @ 2000

MFI—Multi Point Fuel Injection
TBI—Throttle Body Injection

ENGINE TUNE-UP SPECIFICATIONS

Year	Engine ID/VIN	Engine Displacement Liters (cc)	Spark Plugs Gap (in.)	Ignition Timing (deg.) MT	Ignition Timing (deg.) AT	Fuel Pump (psi)	Idle Speed (rpm)② MT	Idle Speed (rpm)② AT	Valve Clearance In.	Valve Clearance Ex.
1991	7	1.9 (1901)	0.040	①	①	31–44	850	750	Hyd.	Hyd.
	9	1.9 (1901)	0.040	①	①	26–31	750	650	Hyd.	Hyd.
1992	7	1.9 (1901)	0.040	①	①	31–44	850	750	Hyd.	Hyd.
	9	1.9 (1901)	0.040	①	①	26–31	750	650	Hyd.	Hyd.
1993				SEE UNDERHOOD SPECIFICATIONS STICKER						

NOTE: The lowest cylinder pressure should be within 75% of the highest cylinder pressure reading. For example, if the highest cylinder is 134 psi, the lowest should be 101. Engine should be at normal operating temperature with throttle valve in the wide open position.
The underhood specifications sticker often reflects tune-up specification changes in production. Sticker figures must be used if they disagree with those in this chart.
Hyd.—Hydraulic
① These engines are equipped with Distributorless Ignition System (DIS), therefore the ignition timing is not adjustable.
② Manual speed with transmission in N
Automatic speed with transmission in D

FIRING ORDERS

NOTE: To avoid confusion, always replace spark plug wires one at a time.

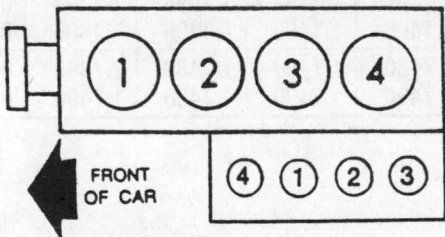

1.9L Engine
Engine Firing Order: 1–3–4–2
Distributorless Ignition System

CAPACITIES

Year	Model	Engine ID/VIN	Engine Displacement Liters (cc)	Engine Crankcase with Filter (qts.)	Transmission (pts.) 4-Spd	Transmission (pts.) 5-Spd	Transmission (pts.) Auto.	Drive Axle (pts.)	Fuel Tank (gal.)	Cooling System (qts.)
1991	Sedan	7	1.9 (1901)	4.0	—	5.2	7.5	—	12.8	7.0
	Sedan	9	1.9 (1901)	4.0	—	5.2	7.5	—	12.8	7.0
	Coupe	7	1.9 (1901)	4.0	—	5.2	7.5	—	12.8	7.0

CAPACITIES

Year	Model	Engine ID/VIN	Engine Displacement Liters (cc)	Engine Crankcase with Filter (qts.)	Transmission (pts.) 4-Spd	5-Spd	Auto.	Drive Axle (pts.)	Fuel Tank (gal.)	Cooling System (qts.)
1992	Sedan	7	1.9 (1901)	4.0	—	5.2	7.5	—	12.8	7.0
	Sedan	9	1.9 (1901)	4.0	—	5.2	7.5	—	12.8	7.0
	Coupe	7	1.9 (1901)	4.0	—	5.2	7.5	—	12.8	7.0
1993	Wagon	7	1.9 (1901)	4.0	—	5.2	7.5	—	12.8	7.0
	Wagon	9	1.9 (1901)	4.0	—	5.2	7.5	—	12.8	7.0
	Sedan	7	1.9 (1901)	4.0	—	5.2	7.5	—	12.8	7.0
	Sedan	9	1.9 (1901)	4.0	—	5.2	7.5	—	12.8	7.0
	Coupe	7	1.9 (1901)	4.0	—	5.2	7.5	—	12.8	7.0
	Coupe	9	1.9 (1901)	4.0	—	5.2	7.5	—	12.8	7.0

CAMSHAFT SPECIFICATIONS

All measurements given in inches.

Year	Engine ID/VIN	Engine Displacement Liters (cc)	Journal Diameter 1	2	3	4	5	Elevation In.	Ex.	Bearing Clearance	Camshaft End Play
1991	7	1.9 (1901)	1.1398–1.1406	1.1398–1.1406	1.1398–1.1406	1.1398–1.1406	1.1398–1.1406	0.3528–0.3559	0.3409–0.3441	0.0012–0.0030	0.0020–0.0080
	9	1.9 (1901)	1.7480–1.7490	1.7480–1.7490	1.7480–1.7490	1.7480–1.7490	1.7480–1.7490	0.2531–0.2556	0.2531–0.2556	0.0020–0.0040	0.0028–0.0079
1992	7	1.9 (1901)	1.1398–1.1406	1.1398–1.1406	1.1398–1.1406	1.1398–1.1406	1.1398–1.1406	0.3528–0.3559	0.3409–0.3441	0.0012–0.0030	0.0020–0.0080
	9	1.9 (1901)	1.7480–1.7490	1.7480–1.7490	1.7480–1.7490	1.7480–1.7490	1.7480–1.7490	0.2531–0.2556	0.2531–0.2556	0.0020–0.0040	0.0028–0.0079
1993	7	1.9 (1901)	1.1398–1.1406	1.1398–1.1406	1.1398–1.1406	1.1398–1.1406	1.1398–1.1406	0.3528–0.3559	0.3409–0.3441	0.0012–0.0030	0.0020–0.0080
	9	1.9 (1901)	1.7480–1.7490	1.7480–1.7490	1.7480–1.7490	1.7480–1.7490	1.7480–1.7490	0.2531–0.2556	0.2531–0.2556	0.0020–0.0040	0.0028–0.0079

CRANKSHAFT AND CONNECTING ROD SPECIFICATIONS

All measurements are given in inches.

Year	Engine ID/VIN	Engine Displacement Liters (cc)	Crankshaft Main Brg. Journal Dia.	Main Brg. Oil Clearance	Shaft End-play	Thrust on No.	Connecting Rod Journal Diameter	Oil Clearance	Side Clearance
1991	7	1.9 (1901)	2.2438–2.2444	0.0002–0.0020	0.002–0.008	3	0.8500–0.8508	0.0004–0.0025	0.0065–0.1713
	9	1.9 (1901)	2.2438–2.2444	0.0002–0.0020	0.002–0.008	3	0.8500–0.8508	0.0004–0.0025	0.0065–0.1713
1992–93	7	1.9 (1901)	2.2438–2.2444	0.0002–0.0020	0.002–0.008	3	0.8500–0.8508	0.0004–0.0025	0.0065–0.1713
	9	1.9 (1901)	2.2438–2.2444	0.0002–0.0020	0.002–0.008	3	0.8500–0.8508	0.0004–0.0025	0.0065–0.1713

VALVE SPECIFICATIONS

Year	Engine ID/VIN	Engine Displacement Liters (cc)	Seat Angle (deg.)	Face Angle (deg.)	Spring Test Pressure (lbs. @ in.)	Spring Installed Height (in.)	Stem-to-Guide Clearance (in.) Intake	Exhaust	Stem Diameter (in.) Intake	Exhaust
1991	7	1.9 (1901)	44.5–45.5	45.0–45.5	163–180 @ 0.984	1.6100	0.0010–0.0025	0.0015–0.0032	0.2736–0.2740	0.2729–0.2736
	9	1.9 (1901)	44.5–45.5	45.0–45.5	202–211 @ 1.280	1.8898–1.9134	0.0010–0.0025	0.0015–0.0032	0.2736–0.2741	0.2736–0.2740
1992–93	7	1.9 (1901)	44.5–45.5	45.0–45.5	163–180 @ 0.984	1.6100	0.0010–0.0025	0.0015–0.0032	0.2736–0.2740	0.2729–0.2736
	9	1.9 (1901)	44.5–45.5	45.0–45.5	202–211 @ 1.280	1.8898–1.9134	0.0010–0.0025	0.0015–0.0032	0.2736–0.2741	0.2736–0.2740

PISTON AND RING SPECIFICATIONS

All measurements are given in inches.

Year	Engine ID/VIN	Engine Displacement Liters (cc)	Piston Clearance	Ring Gap Top Compression	Bottom Compression	Oil Control	Ring Side Clearance Top Compression	Bottom Compression	Oil Control
1991	7	1.9 (1901)	①	0.0098–0.0197	0.0098–0.0197	0.0098–0.0492	0.0016–0.0035	0.0012–0.0031	Snug
	9	1.9 (1901)	①	0.0098–0.0197	0.0098–0.0197	0.0098–0.0492	0.0016–0.0035	0.0012–0.0031	Snug
1992–93	7	1.9 (1901)	①	0.0098–0.0197	0.0098–0.0197	0.0098–0.0492	0.0016–0.0035	0.0012–0.0031	Snug
	9	1.9 (1901)	①	0.0098–0.0197	0.0098–0.0197	0.0098–0.0492	0.0016–0.0035	0.0012–0.0031	Snug

① Bore 1, 2, 3: 0.0002–0.0017
Bore 4: 0.0006–0.0021

TORQUE SPECIFICATIONS

All readings in ft. lbs.

Year	Engine ID/VIN	Engine Displacement Liters (cc)	Cylinder Head Bolts	Main Bearing Bolts	Rod Bearing Bolts	Crankshaft Damper Bolts	Flywheel Bolts	Manifold Intake	Exhaust	Spark Plugs	Lug Nut
1991	7	1.9 (1901)	②	37	33	159	59	22③	23③	20	103
	9	1.9 (1901)	①	37	33	159	59	15③	16③	20	103
1992–93	7	1.9 (1901)	②	37	33	159	59	22③	23③	20	103
	9	1.9 (1901)	①	37	33	159	59	15③	16③	20	103

① 1st step: 22 ft. lbs.
2nd step: 33 ft. lbs.
3rd step: 90 degrees torquing angle
② 1st step: 22 ft. lbs.
2nd step: 37 ft. lbs.
3rd step: 90 degrees torquing angle
③ Studs—106 inch lbs.

BRAKE SPECIFICATIONS

All measurements in inches unless noted.

Year	Model	Master Cylinder Bore	Brake Disc Original Thickness	Minimum Thickness	Maximum Runout	Brake Drum Diameter Original Inside Diameter	Max. Wear Limit	Maximum Machine Diameter	Minimum Lining Thickness Front	Rear
1991	All	NA	0.710①	0.633②	0.005	7.87	7.93	7.90	³⁄₃₂	³⁄₃₂

BRAKE SPECIFICATIONS

All measurements in inches unless noted.

Year	Model	Master Cylinder Bore	Brake Disc Original Thickness	Brake Disc Minimum Thickness	Maximum Runout	Brake Drum Diameter Original Inside Diameter	Max. Wear Limit	Maximum Machine Diameter	Minimum Lining Thickness Front	Rear
1992–93	All	NA	0.710①	0.633②	0.005	7.87	7.93	7.90	3/32	3/32

NA—Not available
① Rear Disc: 0.430
② Rear Disc: 0.370
NOTE: Both front and rear disc specifications are minimums to which the rotors may be machined. The discard wear limit is 0.625 for front discs and 0.350 for rear discs.

WHEEL ALIGNMENT

Year	Model	Caster Range (deg.)	Caster Preferred Setting (deg.)	Camber Range (deg.)	Camber Preferred Setting (deg.)	Toe-in (in.)	Steering Axis Inclination (deg.)
1991	All models	1.20P–2.30P	1.70P	1.00N–0.65P①	0.00	0.20P②	NA
1992–93	All models	1.20P–2.30P	1.70P	1.00N–0.65P①	0.00	0.20P②	NA

NA—Not available
N—Negative
P—Positive
① Rear 1.40N–0.00
   Preferred 0.60N
② Specification is total toe front or rear

ENGINE MECHANICAL

NOTE: Disconnecting the negative battery cable on some vehicles may interfere with the functions of the on board computer systems and may require the computer to undergo a relearning process, once the negative battery cable is reconnected.

Engine Assembly

REMOVAL & INSTALLATION

NOTE: The manufacturer recommends that the engine and transaxle be removed as a complete unit. Disconnect the cradle and lower the entire assembly instead of lifting the assembly out of the vehicle.

1. Properly disable the SIR system, if equipped. Disconnect the negative and then the positive battery cable.
2. Properly drain the engine coolant.
3. Properly relieve the fuel system pressure.
4. Remove the air cleaner or air intake duct.
5. Disconnect and label all accessible electrical connectors and vacuum hoses from the engine and transaxle.
6. Disconnect the 2 ground connectors from the transaxle attachment studs at the rear side of the cylinder block.
7. Disconnect the accelerator cable assembly.
8. Using service tool SA9157E or equivalent, disconnect the fuel supply and return lines at the connectors. Plug the lines to prevent fuel contamination or loss. The lines may be tied to the master cylinder lines to help prevent fuel spillage.
9. Disconnect the upper radiator hose and the cylinder head outlet and the the deareation hose at the engine.
10. Remove the serpentine drive belt and if equipped, remove the air conditioning compressor from its brackets with the hoses attached. Support the compressor from the front crossbar.
11. If equipped, disconnect the automatic transaxle cooler lines at the transaxle. Plug the lines to prevent fluid loss or contamination.
12. Disconnect the automatic transaxle shifter cable or the manual shifter cables from the transaxle.
13. If equipped with manual transaxles, remove the 2 hydraulic damper retaining nuts, then slide the damper and bracket assembly from the studs. Rotate the clutch actuator ¼ turn counterclockwise while pushing toward the housing to disengage the bayonet connector and remove from the clutch housing. Support the clutch hydraulic system to the battery tray making sure not to kink or pinch the hydraulic lines.
14. Using appropriate wire, tie the radiator, condenser and fan to the front crossbar. Route the wire around the 2 fan shroud supports and the crossbar.
15. Raise and support the vehicle safely.
16. Remove the front wheels and disconnect the side and front fender shields from the cradle.
17. Remove the brake brackets attaching bolts and hang the caliper assemblies from the body using wire. Do not hang by the brake hose. The springs and shocks will remain with the body.
18. Disconnect the struts from the knuckles on both sides. The knuckle and hub assembly will remain with the cradle. The stabilizer bar will remain attached to the cradle and the lower control arms.
19. Disconnect the lower radiator

and heater return hoses from the engine. Disconnect the heater inlet hose at the front of the dash or the engine.

20. Disconnect the steering shaft and pressure switch connectors at the gear, as applicable.

21. Disconnect the exhaust pipe at the manifold, catalytic converter and powertrain stiffening bracket.

22. For 1991 vehicles, remove the powertrain stiffening bracket bolts, except the 3 bolts holding the torque resistor bracket to the transaxle.

23. Remove the flywheel cover and torque converter bolts, if equipped.

24. Remove the alternator and starter shields.

25. Disconnect and label all remaining electrical connectors, vacuum hoses, cables and hoses that are accessible from underneath. Plug all open hoses or lines.

26. Unclip the brake lines from the rear side of the cradle.

27. Carefully remove the electrical harness from the engine and transaxle, then lay the electrical harness on top of the underhood junction block and battery cover.

28. For 1992–93 vehicles with a torque axis mount system, place a 1 inch × 1 inch × 2 inch long block of wood between the torque strut and cradle for ease of torque mount removal and installation. Remove the 3 right side upper engine torque axis to front cover nuts and the 2 mount to midrail bracket nuts, allowing the powertrain to rest on the block of wood.

29. Place a powertrain support dolly under the cradle. Use two 4 inch × 4 inch × 36 inch pieces of wood to support the cradle on the dolly.

30. Remove the 2 right side front engine mount, torque strut brackets to cradle nuts.

31. Remove the 4 cradle attaching bolts and carefully lower the complete powertrain assembly from the vehicle. Verify all components are disconnected before complete removal.

32. Attach the 2 washers located between the cradle and body to the cradle. They must be repositioned and installed during cradle installation.

33. Disconnect the spark plug wires at the ignition module.

34. If applicable, remove the power steering pump and bracket. Support the assembly from the cradle or the steering gear in an upright position.

35. Install a suitable engine lifting device to the service support brackets.

36. Remove the front mount assembly and disconnect the motion restrictor bracket, if applicable.

37. Place a ½ inch × 1 inch × 3 inch block of wood under the axle shaft and remove the starter support bracket bolt, intake manifold support brace (on DOHC engines), and 3 axle shaft

bracket support bolts. Allow the bracket to rotate rearward. Lift the engine slightly for clearance, as necessary.

38. For 1991 vehicles, remove the front engine mount assembly and disconnect the motion restrictor cable used with the DOHC engine and manual transaxle.

39. For 1992–93 vehicles with a torque axis mount system, place a 4 inch × 4 inch × 6 inch long block of wood under the transaxle housing for support.

40. For 1992–93 vehicles, remove the engine strut bracket and torque strut as an assembly. Lift the engine slightly as necessary for removal.

41. Remove the 4 transaxle attaching bolts and separate the assembly. Manual transaxles will require the engine to be moved about 4 inches (100mm) forward in the cradle to disengage the input shaft.

42. Lift the engine off the cradle.

To install:

43. If installing a manual transaxle, align the yellow dot on the clutch pressure plate near the mark on the flywheel. Use SA9145T or an equivalent clutch alignment tool to align the disk and input shaft, then tighten the pressure plate bolts to 19 ft. lbs. (25 Nm).

44. If installing an automatic transaxle the yellow dot on the torque converter must be in the 6 o'clock position when the first flexplate to torque converter bolt is tightened.

45. Position the engine on the cradle aligning it with the transaxle and then install the 4 transaxle attaching bolts and the stiffening bracket fastener. Tighten the lower bolts to 96 ft. lbs. (130 Nm), the upper bolts to 66 ft. lbs. (90 Nm) and the stiffening bracket to powertrain fastener to 40 ft. lbs. (54 Nm). If applicable, remove the 4 inch × 4 inch × 6 inch block of wood from under the transaxle housing.

46. Install the front engine mount assembly to the engine and tighten to 41 ft. lbs. (55 Nm). For the 1991 DOHC engine with manual transaxle, install the motion restrictor bracket and tighten to 40 ft. lbs. (54 Nm).

47. For 1991 vehicles, install the front engine mount to cradle nut and tighten to 52 ft. lbs. (70 Nm).

48. For 1992–93 vehicles, install the engine strut bracket and torque strut assembly, if removed. Hand-tighten the cradle nuts, but do not torque until the upper midrail mount in installed.

49. For 1992–93 vehicles, install the 1 inch × 1 inch × 2 inch long block of wood between the torque strut and cradle for ease of torque mount installation.

50. Attach the axle shaft and starter bracket. Tighten the axle shaft fasten-

ers to 41 ft. lbs. (55 Nm) and the starter bracket to 80 inch lbs. (9 Nm).

51. Position the powertrain and cradle assembly onto the dolly.

52. Carefully lift the powertrain and cradle into position. Make sure the radiator grommets are correctly aligned and that the 2 washers are reinstalled between the cradle and body at each rear cradle attachment position. Tighten the cradle to body fasteners to 151 ft. lbs. (205 Nm).

53. Attach the brake lines to the cradle and install the steering shaft U-joint. Tighten the U-joint bolt to 35 ft. lbs. (47 Nm).

54. Position the electrical harness around the engine and connect all electrical connections which are accessible from underneath.

55. Install the engine stiffening bracket bolts, as applicable and tighten to 35 ft. lbs. (47 Nm).

56. Install new gaskets and the exhaust front pipe. Tighten the pipe to manifold fasteners to 23 ft. lbs. (31 Nm), the pipe to stiffener bracket fasteners to 35 ft. lbs. (47 Nm), the pipe to support bracket fasteners to 23 ft. lbs. (31 Nm) and the pipe to catalytic converter fasteners to 35 ft. lbs. (48 Nm).

57. Connect the heater, lower radiator and coolant fill hoses, then remove the radiator assembly support wires.

58. Install the cylinder block drain plug and tighten to 27 ft. lbs. (36 Nm), then close the radiator drain.

59. Install the knuckle to strut attachment bolts, tighten the bolts to 148 ft. lbs. (200 Nm).

60. Install the brake caliper assemblies and tighten the bolts to 81 ft. lbs. (110 Nm).

61. Install the shift cables, with new retainers.

62. Install any remaining vacuum hoses, cables or connections accessible from underneath, then lower the vehicle.

63. Install the hydraulic clutch slave cylinder, damper and shift cables, if applicable and tighten the nuts to 19 ft. lbs. (25 Nm).

64. If equipped, install the automatic transaxle cooler lines and/or the air conditioning compressor assembly. Tighten the compressor to front bracket bolts to 40 ft. lbs. (54 Nm) and the compressor to rear bracket bolts to 22 ft. lbs. (30 Nm).

65. Install the serpentine drive belt, making sure the belt is properly aligned in the grooves.

66. For 1992–93 vehicles equipped with a torque axis mount system, install the 2 engine mounts to midrail bracket nuts and tighten to 52 ft. lbs. (70 Nm). Next install the 3 mount to front cover nuts, tighten them uniformly to 52 ft. lbs. (70 Nm) in order to

prevent front cover damage. Then remove the block of wood from under the torque strut.

67. For 1992–93 vehicles with 2 torque strut bracket to cradle nuts, tighten the nuts to 52 ft. lbs. (70 Nm).

68. If equipped, install the automatic transaxle torque converter to flexplate bolts. Tighten the bolts to 52 ft. lbs. (70 Nm). Install the dust cover and tighten to 89 inch lbs. (10 Nm).

69. Install the tires and splash shields.

70. Attach all remaining electrical connections and vacuum hoses.

71. Install the accelerator cable and attach the fuel lines.

72. Install the upper radiator and deareation hoses.

73. Check the upper cooling module grommets for binding or misalignment. The module retaining pins must be centered in the grommets supported by the brackets. If the grommets are pinched, loosen the brackets and reposition them. It is extremely important that the cooling module be able to move freely.

74. Install the air induction system, PCV valve and fresh air hoses.

75. For 1991 vehicles, verify proper powertrain alignment and adjust the engine mounts as necessary.

76. Connect the battery cables and if equipped, enable the SIR system. Check all engine and transaxle fluids, add or fill as necessary.

77. Prime the fuel system, start the engine and check for leaks.

78. Peform a road test and check the engine again for leaks.

Engine Mounts

REMOVAL & INSTALLATION

1991

1. Disconnect the negative battery cable.

2. For DOHC vehicles with a manual transaxle, remove the cross-car duct to front tie bar bolts, disconnect the air temperature sensor and remove the duct. Remove the engine motion restrictor to engine cradle fastener and tape the restrictor stud plate in place on the cradle.

3. Raise and support the vehicle safely.

4. Remove the right tire and inner fender shield.

5. Remove the engine mount nuts.

6. Place a screw jack under the engine oil pan with a block of wood to protect the pan and unload the engine mount.

7. Remove the 4 engine mount bracket-to-engine bolts.

8. Raise the engine enough to remove the mount and bracket.

9. Remove the mount assembly from the vehicle.

To install:

10. Install the mount assembly into the vehicle, then install and tighten the 4 bolts to 40 ft. lbs. (54 Nm).

11. Carefully lower the engine and engage the mount stud with the cradle. Be sure the mount stud threads are not damaged.

12. Install the mount nut and tighten to 66 ft. lbs. (90 Nm).

13. Install the inner fender splash shield.

14. Remove all rust from the wheel mounting surfaces and brake rotors or drums to assure proper wheel lug tightening, then install the wheel assembly onto the hub.

15. Lower the vehicle.

16. For DOHC vehicles, install the engine motion restrictor mount onto the cradle and tighten the nut to 35 ft. lbs. (48 Nm). Connect the air temperature sensor electrical connector and install the cross-car duct with fasteners.

17. Align the powertrain as follows:

  a. Loosen the rear axle mount through-bolt and rock the powertrain to make sure it is free.

  b. The rear transaxle mount bracket should move vertically ¼–½ inch (6.35–12.70mm) when measured at the through-bolt hole slot.

  c. If the powertrain cannot be rocked, loosen the transaxle front mount to transaxle bolts, bounce the powertrain and wait 30 minutes to allow the powertrain to settle into the proper position.

  d. Verify the front transaxle mount housing is parallel both horizontally and vertically with the transaxle housing.

  e. If mount orientation is not correct, remove the 2 rearward lower radiator splash shield pushpins and lower the rear of the shield. Verify that the transaxle mount housing and rubber insert are parallel vertically and horizontally.

  f. If the vertical alignment of the mount housing and insert is not correct, remove the cradle nuts and 2 bolts attaching the cradle to the transaxle, then inspect the surfaces for debris under the mount. Repair or replace as necessary.

  g. If the horizontal alignment of the mount housing and insert is not correct, loosen both transaxle front mount to cradle attachment nuts ¼. Continue loosening the nuts in ¼ turn increments until the housing straightens.

  h. Hold the mount in place, then tighten the 2 nuts and the mount to transaxle bolts to 35 ft. lbs. (48 Nm).

  i. If proper alignment cannot be

achieved, the mount assembly must be replaced.

  j. Tighten the rear mount pivot bolt to 52 ft. lbs. (70 Nm), but do not pull downward on the mount bolt or nut while tightening as this will preload the mount's rubber insert.

18. Lower the vehicle and connect the negative battery cable.

1992–93

1. Properly disable the SIR system, if equipped and disconnect the negative battery cable.

2. Raise and support the vehicle safely.

3. Remove the right wheel assembly and wheelhouse panel.

4. Lower the vehicle sufficiently to allow underhood access to the engine mount.

5. Remove the 2 engine mount to midrail bracket nuts.

6. Position a suitable floor jack and a block of wood under the engine oil pan, then raise the powertrain slightly to unload the mount.

7. Remove the 3 engine mount to engine front cover nuts, then remove the engine mount.

8. If the engine midrail bracket removal is required, remove the 4 midrail to bracket bolts from the engine side of the bracket. Then, from the wheelhouse side of the bracket, remove the 3 bracket to midrail bolts and remove the bracket.

To install:

9. If removed, position the bracket to the midrail and hand tighten all 7 bolts. Tighten all bolts to 22 ft. lbs. (30 Nm).

10. Position the engine mount to the front cover and install the 3 nuts. Tighten the nuts to 52 ft. lbs. (70 Nm).

11. Carefully lower the powertrain, guiding the mount over the midrail studs to prevent thread damage. Remove the jack and the block of wood.

12. Install the 2 mount to bracket nuts and tighten to 52 ft. lbs. (70 Nm).

13. Install the wheelhouse cover and the wheel assembly.

14. Lower the vehicle and connect the negative battery cable.

15. If equipped, properly enable the SIR system.

Cylinder Head

REMOVAL & INSTALLATION

NOTE: Remove the cylinder head when the engine is cold. Warpage may result if removed hot.

1. Disconnect the negative battery cable and properly drain the engine coolant.

```
┌─────────────────────────────┐
│        INTAKE SIDE          │
│                             │
│    3   7   10   6   2       │
│                             │
│    4   8   9    5   1       │
│                             │
│        EXHAUST SIDE         │
└─────────────────────────────┘
```

Cylinder head bolt removal sequence—all engines

```
┌─────────────────────────────┐
│        INTAKE SIDE          │
│                             │
│    8   4   1   5   9        │
│                             │
│    7   3   2   6   10       │
│                             │
│        EXHAUST SIDE         │
└─────────────────────────────┘
```

Cylinder head bolt torque sequence—all engines

2. Remove the air cleaner assembly and air inlet duct. For SOHC engines, disconnect the PCV valve and fresh air hose. For DOHC engines, disconnect the camshaft cover air hose at the cover.

3. Disconnect the accelerator cable from the throttle body and the bracket from the intake manifold.

4. Properly relieve the fuel system pressure.

5. Label and disconnect the electrical connectors from the cylinder head assembly. Long nose pliers are necessary to disconnect the coolant temperature connectors. Position the electrical harness over the underhood junction block.

6. Label and disconnect all necessary vacuum hoses from the area around the cylinder head assembly.

7. Disconnect the upper radiator hose at the cylinder head outlet, the heater hose at the intake manifold and the deareation hose next to the TBI assembly or at the intake manifold.

8. Remove the bolt which retains the fuel lines to the intake manifold assembly. Disconnect the fuel feed and return lines from the fuel rail or throttle body, as applicable. For SOHC engines, remove the lower intake manifold support bracket stud. For DOHC engines, disconnect the fuel return line from the regulator, then remove the upper intake manifold support bracket bolt.

9. For 1992–93 vehicles with a torque axis mount system, unclip the lower splash shield. Place a 1 inch × 1 inch × 2 inch block of wood between the torque strut and cradle prior to mount removal for ease of installation.

10. For 1992–93 vehicles, remove the 3 right side upper engine mount to en-gine front cover nuts and the 2 mount to midrail bracket nuts allowing the engine to rest on the block of wood.

11. Remove the serpentine drive belt and belt tensioner. It is not necessary to remove the water pump pulley, however, for 1992–93 vehicles it will be necessary to remove the idler pulley to access the engine front cover.

12. For SOHC engines, disconnect the deareation line at the cylinder head water outlet and from the support bracket.

13. Remove the camshaft cover, then inspect the cover silicone insulators for cracks or deterioration and replace as necessary. Be sure to cover the valve train area to prevent foreign debris from entering the engine.

14. If equipped, remove the power steering pump bracket attaching bolts and position the assembly next to the right side front of the dash panel away from the intake manifold and cylinder head. It is not necessary to remove the water pump pulley.

15. If equipped, remove the 3 air conditioning compressor front bracket bolts attached to the cylinder head and block, then remove the rear bracket bolts from the compressor. Do not discharge the system or disconnect the refrigerant lines. Support the compressor aside from the vehicle front support bar.

16. Raise the and support vehicle safely, then drain the engine oil.

17. Remove the right side tire and splash shield.

18. For DOHC engines, remove the intake manifold support brace bolt attached to the intake manifold next to the alternator.

19. Remove the crankshaft damper/pulley assembly. Use a strap wrench or a block of wood wedged between the pulley spoke and the rear lower side of the front cover to hold the assembly while removing the bolt. Then use a 3 jaw puller on the jaw slots cast into the pulley and remove the assembly.

20. Disconnect the exhaust from the manifold.

21. Install crankshaft gear retainer tool SA9104E or equivalent and properly remove the engine front cover.

22. Rotate the crankshaft clockwise so the timing mark and keyway align with the main bearing cap split line. This will make sure pistons will not contact the valves upon assembly.

23. Remove the timing chain, tensioner, guides, camshaft sprocket(s) and chain. Use a 7/8 inch (21mm) wrench to hold the camshaft when removing the sprocket bolts.

24. For the SOHC engine, remove the throttle body assembly and cover the intake manifold opening.

25. Use a 6 point socket to remove the 10 cylinder head bolts in several passes of the proper sequence. Failure to follow the proper sequence or removal of the head when hot could result in head warpage or cracking. Also, the use of a 12 point socket on the cylinder head bolts may round the bolt heads.

26. Lift the cylinder head from the dowels. Be careful not to damage the sealing surfaces if prying is necessary to remove the head from the block.

27. If necessary, remove the intake manifold or the exhaust manifold by loosening the mounting nuts in the proper sequence. If any cylinder head studs come out, the threads should be cleaned, the studs carefully installed and then tightened to 106 inch lbs. (12 Nm).

To install:

28. If removed, install the intake manifold and/or the exhaust manifold and new gasket(s). Tighten to specification in the proper sequence.

29. Clean the gasket mating surfaces. Be careful not to damage the aluminum components. Make sure the block bolt holes are clean of any residual sealer, oil or foreign matter.

30. Check that the cylinder liners are flush or do not deviate more than 0.0005 in. (0.013mm).

31. Install the cylinder head gasket and carefully guide the head into place over the dowels.

32. If the head bolts or the block were replaced, install the bolts and tighten in sequence to 48 ft. lbs. (65 Nm) to insure proper clamp load, then remove the bolts.

33. Coat the cylinder head bolts with clean engine oil and thread the bolts by hand until finger-tight. Tighten the bolts in sequence to 22 ft. lbs. (30 Nm).

34. Tighten the cylinder head bolts again, in sequence to 33 ft. lbs. (45 Nm) for SOHC engines or to 37 ft. lbs. (50 Nm) for DOHC engines. Install Snap-on® tool 360 or equivalent torque angle gauge and calibrate the gauge to 0. Tighten each cylinder head bolt an additional 90 degrees, in sequence.

35. Install the timing chain, sprockets, guides and tensioner.

36. Install the front cover assembly and connect the exhaust manifold to the exhaust pipe.

37. Install the crankshaft damper/pulley assembly and tighten the bolt to 158 ft. lbs. (214 Nm).

38. For DOHC vehicles, install the intake manifold support brace bolts next to the alternator, then tighten the bracket to block bolt to 33 ft. lbs. (45 Nm) and tighten the bracket to manifold bolt to 22 ft. lbs. (30 Nm).

39. Apply a small drop of RTV accross the cylinder head and front cover T-joints. Inspect the old cam-

shaft cover gasket and replace if damaged. Install the gasket and the camshaft cover. Tighten the fasteners uniformly to 22 ft. lbs. (30 Nm) for SOHC vehicles or in proper sequence to 89 inch lbs. (10 Nm) for DOHC vehicles.

40. Install the drive belt tensioner and tighten the bolt to 22 ft. lbs. (30 Nm). For 1992–93 vehicles, install the idler pulley and tighten the fasteners to 33 ft. lbs. (45 Nm).

41. If not done during removal, drain the engine oil and change the filter, then install the drain plug and tighten to 26 ft. lbs. (35 Nm).

42. If removed, verify the gaps on all spark plugs and install. Tighten to 20 ft. lbs. (27 Nm).

43. If applicable, install a new gasket and the TBI assembly. Tighten the assembly retainers to 24 ft. lbs. (33 Nm).

44. If equipped, install the power steering pump assembly to the bracket, then tighten the bolts to 22 ft. lbs. (30 Nm).

45. If equipped, install the air conditioning compressor and bolts. Tighten the rear bracket to the compressor and tighten the bolts to 19 ft. lbs. (25 Nm), then tighten the front bracket bolts to 40 ft. lbs. (54 Nm).

46. Install the accessory drive belt making sure the belt is properly aligned on the pulley.

47. For 1992–93 vehicles with a torque axis mounting, install the 2 mount to midrail bracket nuts and tighten to 52 ft. lbs. (70 Nm). Install the 3 upper mount to engine front cover nuts and tighten them uniformly to 52 ft. lbs. (70 Nm). Remove the support block of wood after the assembly is installed.

48. Install the splash shield, then install the wheel assembly.

49. Position the wiring harness and connect all wire connectors.

50. Connect all vacuum hoses disconnected during removal.

51. Install the accelerator cable bracket and tighten the fastener to 19 ft. lbs. (25 Nm). Connect the cable, then verify that it is properly routed and not binding.

52. Connect all coolant hoses which were disconnected during removal.

53. Connect the fuel feed and return lines to the throttle body and tighten the fittings to 19 ft. lbs. (25 Nm) or to the fuel rail and pressure regulator and tighten the fittings to 133 inch lbs. (15 Nm). Install fuel bracket retaining bolts, as applicable.

54. Install the air cleaner and intake duct assembly.

55. Add engine oil and properly fill the engine cooling system.

56. Connect the negative battery cable.

57. Prime the fuel system, start the engine and check for leaks.

Valve Lifters

REMOVAL & INSTALLATION

SOHC Engine

1. Disconnect the negative battery cable.

2. Remove the rocker arm cover, then inspect the cover silicone insulators for cracks or deterioration and replace as necessary.

3. Turn the crankshaft until the **0** mark on the crankshaft pulley is in alignment with the pointer and No. 1 cylinder is at TDC of the compression stroke.

4. Uniformly remove the rocker arm assembly bolts and remove the 2 rocker arm shafts.

5. Remove the retainers, guide plates and lifters. Mark all components to assure installation in their original locations.

To install:

6. Oil the lifters and install into the cylinder head bores.

7. Rotate the lifters until the flats are parallel with the intake and exhaust sides of cylinder head, then install the guide plates. Make sure the plates are properly seated with the retaining spring slot upwards and all lifters fit squarely in the guide plate.

8. Install the rocker arm shaft assemblies. Make sure the rocker arm tangs are squarely seated on the lifter and the retaining spring is positioned in the guide plate slot.

9. Torque the rocker arm bolts to 19 ft. lbs. (25 Nm) in a uniform sequence.

10. Apply a small drop of RTV to each cylinder head and front cover T-joint. Inspect the rocker arm cover gasket and replace if necessary. Install the gasket and rocker arm cover, then tighten the fasteners uniformly to 22 ft. lbs. (30 Nm).

11. Connect the negative battery cable, start the engine and check for leaks.

DOHC Engine

1. Disconnect the negative battery cable.

2. Remove the camshaft cover.

3. Remove the camshafts.

4. Remove the valve lifters from their bores. Be sure to place all lifters in a rack or label them to assure installation in their original locations. Store lifters with their camshaft contact face down.

To install:

5. Lubricate the lifters and install them in their proper locations.

6. Properly align and install the intake and exhaust camshafts.

7. Apply a small drop of RTV across the cylinder head and front cover T-joints. Inspect the old camshaft cover gasket and replace if damaged. Install the gasket and the camshaft cover. Tighten the fasteners in the proper sequence to 89 inch lbs. (10 Nm).

8. Connect the negative battery cable, start the engine and check for leaks.

Valve Lash

ADJUSTMENT

All engines in this section use hydraulic valve lifters. There is no adjustment needed or possible.

Rocker Arms/Shafts

REMOVAL & INSTALLATION

SOHC Engine

1. Disconnect the negative battery cable.

2. Remove the rocker arm cover, then inspect the cover silicone insulators for cracks or deterioration and replace as necessary.

3. Turn the crankshaft until the 0 mark on the crankshaft pulley is in alignment with the pointer and No. 1 cylinder is at TDC of the compression stroke.

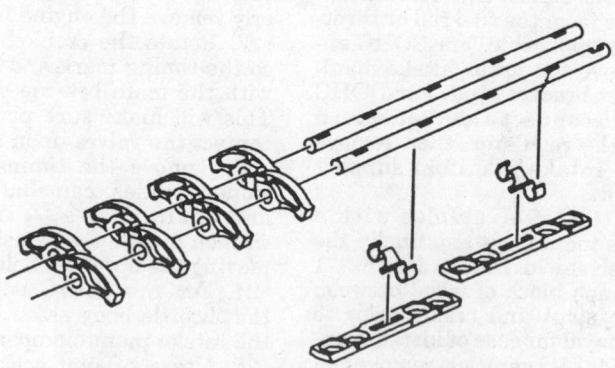

Lifter guide plate positioning—SOHC engine

4. Uniformly remove the rocker arm assembly bolts and the 2 rocker arm shafts.

5. If necessary, disassemble the rocker arms from the shafts.

To install:

6. If removed, oil the rocker arm shafts and install the rocker arms onto the shafts.

7. Snap 1 end of each lifter guide plate retaining spring onto the rocker arm shaft between No. 1–No. 2 and the No. 3–No. 4 cylinder rocker arms.

8. Install the rocker arm shaft assemblies. To prevent valve or piston damage, be sure the rocker arm tangs are squarely seated on the lifter and the retaining spring is positioned in the guide plate slot.

9. Tighten the 5 rocker arm bolts on each shaft to 18 ft. lbs. (25 Nm) in a uniform sequence. Verify the proper position and seating of all rocker components.

10. Apply a small drop of RTV to each cylinder head and front cover T-joint. Inspect the rocker arm cover gasket and replace if necessary. Install the gasket and rocker arm cover, then tighten the fasteners uniformly to 22 ft. lbs. (30 Nm).

11. Connect the negative battery cable, start the engine and check for leaks.

Intake Manifold

REMOVAL & INSTALLATION

SOHC Engine

1. Disconnect the negative battery cable and drain the engine coolant.

2. Remove the air cleaner and the fresh air tube at the rocker cover. Remove the PCV tube and hose.

3. Properly relieve the fuel system pressure at the test port, then disconnect the fuel supply and return lines at the connectors using service tool SA9157E or equivalent. Plug the lines to prevent system contamination.

5. Disconnect the throttle cable from the throttle body, then remove the throttle cable bracket attaching nuts and position the assembly aside.

6. Label and disconnect all wiring and vacuum hoses from the intake manifold. Lay the harness away from the manifold onto the fuel relay.

7. Remove the coolant hoses from the intake manifold and position hoses aside.

8. Remove the intake manifold support bracket bolt located next to the starter and attached to the block. If necessary, the bolt can be removed from below the vehicle.

9. Remove the serpentine drive belt, then remove the power steering pump from the bracket and support the

Intake manifold torque sequence— SOHC engine

```
UPPER SIDE
8  4  1  5
7  3  2  6  9
LOWER SIDE
```

pump next to the right side dash panel sufficiently away from the intake manifold and cylinder head.

10. Remove the manifold retaining nuts, then remove the manifold and throttle body assembly. If necessary the lower manifold nuts can be accessed from under the vehicle.

To install:

11. Thoroughly clean all gasket mating surfaces. Be careful not to damage or score the aluminum surface. If replaced, use Loctite® 290 or equivalent to seal the new PCV valve inlet tube into the manifold.

12. Position the new gasket, then install the manifold and retaining nuts. Tighten the nuts in sequence to 22 ft. lbs. (30 Nm).

13. Install the power steering pump and tighten the fasteners to 27 ft. lbs. (38 Nm).

14. Install the serpentine drive belt.

15. Connect the coolant hoses to the manifold assembly, then install the manifold support bracket bolt. Tighten the bolt to 22 ft. lbs. (30 Nm).

16. Connect the fuel supply and return lines to the TBI and tighten the fittings to 19 ft. lbs. (25 Nm).

17. Reposition the wiring harness and connect the wiring and vacuum hoses to their original location. The harness leads to the TPS and EGR solenoid must be routed between the intake manifold runners.

18. Install the air cleaner and frsh air tubes, then install the PCV valve hose.

19. Connect the negative battery cable and properly fill the engine cooling system.

20. Prime the fuel system, start the engine and check for leaks.

DOHC Engine

1. Disconnect the negative battery cable and drain the engine coolant.

2. Remove the air inlet tube and resonator, then remove the PCV tube.

3. Properly relieve the fuel system pressure at the test port.

4. Remove the fuel line bracket bolt and disconnect the lines from the fuel rail. Disconnect the fuel lines from the connectors using service tool SA9157E or equivalent. Plug the openings to prevent fuel system contamination.

5. Disconnect the throttle cable from the throttle body, then remove

Intake manifold torque sequence— DOHC engine

```
UPPER SIDE
5  2  3
7  4  1  6
LOWER SIDE
```

the cable bracket assembly and position aside.

6. Label and disconnect all electrical connectors and vacuum hoses from the intake manifold. Disconnect all coolant hoses from the manifold.

7. Position the wiring harness over the brake master cylinder, then remove the intake manifold support bracket bolt attached to the manifold next to the brake master cylinder.

8. Remove the serpentine drive belt. Remove the power steering pump assembly with the support bracket, then remove the upper pump bracket attachment bolts and position the pump away from the manifold and cylinder head, near the right dash panel. Remove the lower power steering pump bracket brace.

9. Remove the 3 upper intake manifold attachment nuts, then raise and support the vehicle safely.

10. Remove the lower power steering unit support bracket. Remove the intake manifold support bracket bolt located next to the alternator, then loosen the lower bracket bolt and rotate the bracket out of the way.

11. If not already disconnected, remove the canister purge solenoid and brake booster vacuum hose.

12. Remove the intake manifold attaching stud and lower the vehicle.

13. Remove the intake manifold assembly, then remove and discard the old gasket.

To install:

14. Thoroughly clean the gasket mating surfaces. Be careful not to score or damage the aluminum sealing surfaces. If installing a new coolant deareation tube elbow into the manifold use Loctite® 290 or equivalent to seal.

15. Position the new gasket, then install the intake manifold and retaining nuts. Torque the nuts in sequence to 22 ft. lbs. (30 Nm).

16. Install the power steering pump and brackets. Tighten the fasteners to 28 ft. lbs. (38 Nm).

17. Install the serpentine drive belt making sure the belt is properly aligned on the pulleys.

18. Connect the coolant hoses to the manifold.

19. Position the manifold support

brackets and install the bolts. Tighten the right bolt to block to 41 ft. lbs. (55 Nm), then tighten the left block bolt and the support bracket to intake manifold bolts to 22 ft. lbs. (30 Nm).

20. Lubricate the male fuel supply and return connects, then install.

21. Connect the throttle cable to the throttle body and install the support bracket. Tighten the bracket retaining bolts to 19 ft. lbs. (25 Nm). Verify that the cable locking tangs are fully engaged when assembled.

22. Position the wiring harness and connect all electrical connectors and vacuum hoses in their original locations.

23. Install the PCV hose, the air inlet tube and resonator.

24. Connect the negative battery cable and properly fill the engine cooling system.

25. Prime the fuel system, start the engine and check for leaks.

Exhaust Manifold

REMOVAL & INSTALLATION

1. Disconnect the negative battery cable, then raise and support the vehicle safely.

2. Remove the pipe-to-manifold nuts and lower the pipe, then remove the old gasket and discard.

3. Lower the vehicle.

4. Remove the the air conditioning compressor and bracket and position to the side. Do not disconnect the refrigerant lines.

5. Disconnect the oxygen sensor connector. If necessary, use a 19mm, 6 point, crows foot to remove the oxygen sensor.

6. Remove the manifold retaining nuts and remove the manifold. Remove and discard the old gasket.

To install:

7. Thoroughly clean the gasket mating surfaces, be careful not to score or damage the aluminum surface.

8. Install the new gasket with the smooth side facing the manifold, then install the manifold and attaching nuts. Tighten the nuts in sequence to 16 ft. lbs. (22 Nm) for the SOHC Engine or to 23 ft. lbs. (31 Nm) for the DOHC engine.

9. If replacing the oxygen sensor, coat the threads with nickel based anti-seize compound and tighten to 18 ft. lbs. (25 Nm). Connect the oxygen sensor electrical connector.

10. Install the air conditioning compressor and brackets. Tighten all fasteners except the front bracket to compressor fasteners to 19 ft. lbs. (25 Nm). Tighten the front bracket to compressor fasteners to 40 ft. lbs. (54 Nm).

```
┌─────────────────────────┐
│        UPPER SIDE       │
│                         │
│   8    4    1    5      │
│                         │
│   7    3    2    6      │
│                         │
│        LOWER SIDE       │
│        SOHC ENGINE      │
└─────────────────────────┘

┌─────────────────────────┐
│        UPPER SIDE       │
│                         │
│        2    3           │
│                         │
│   4    1    5           │
│                         │
│        LOWER SIDE       │
│        DOHC ENGINE      │
└─────────────────────────┘
```

Exhaust manifold torque sequence

11. Raise and support the vehicle safely, then install a new gasket onto the studs between the pipe and manifold.

12. Connect the pipe and manifold and tighten the fasteners in a crosswise pattern to 23 ft. lbs. (31 Nm), then lower the vehicle.

13. Connect the negative battery cable, start the engine and check for leaks.

Timing Chain Front Cover

REMOVAL & INSTALLATION

1. Disconnect the negative battery cable and drain the engine oil.

2. Raise and support the vehicle safely, then remove the right wheel and splash shield.

3. For 1992–93 vehicles with a torque axis mount system, remove the engine mount and midrail bracket.

4. Remove the serpentine drive belt and belt tensioner. It is not necessary to remove the water pump pulley, however, for 1992–93 vehicles the idler pulley must be removed to access the engine front cover.

5. Remove the power steering pump and position the assembly aside.

6. Remove the rocker or camshaft cover. Be sure to protect the valve train assemblies from foreign debris or dirt.

7. Using a strap wrench or a piece of wood wedged between the damper spoke and the lower side of the engine front cover, hold the damper and remove the bolt. With a suitable 3 jaw puller and the slots cast into the damper, pull the crankshaft damper/pulley assembly from the crankshaft.

8. Install the special tool SA9104E or equivalent, to make sure the front crankshaft timing sprocket is held firmly in place and prevent guide damage. Install with the flat side towards the crankshaft sprocket.

9. Remove the front 4 oil pan bolts, then using a suitable RTV cutting tool, cut the front seal away from the front cover.

10. Spray the 2 dowel pin holes with penetrating oil to facilitate front cover removal from the dowel pins.

11. Remove the front cover bolts. For 1992–93 vehicles, 1 bolt is located above the serpentine drive belt pulley, under the torque axis mount flange.

12. Using a small suitable tool, carefully pry the cover away from the cylinder block at the pry locations tabs which are provided and remove the cover.

To install:

13. Make sure the oil galleys are clear. Carefully clean the gasket mating surfaces with a scraper or wire brush and carburetor solvent, brake clean or alcohol. Use a 3/16 inch drill bit and tap handle to clean the front cover holes.

NOTE: If the engine front cover casting or assembly is replaced on 1992–93 vehicles, the 3 torque

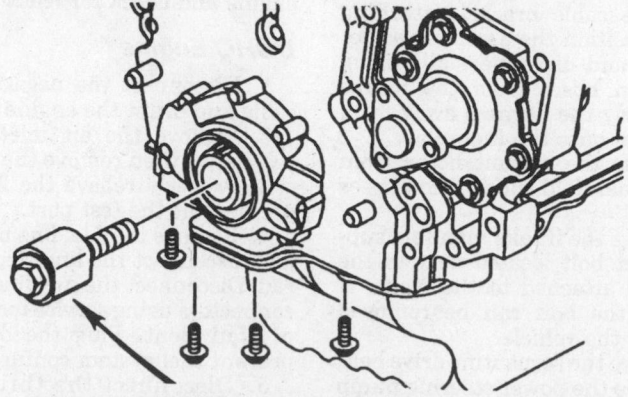

Using tool SA9104E to hold the timing sprocket in place

axis mount studs should also be replaced. Tighten the studs to 19 ft. lbs. (25 Nm).

14. Apply a 0.16 inch (4mm) bead of RTV sealer on the along the vertical sealing surfaces of the front cover to the inside of the bolt holes and to the front of the oil pan. Extra sealer is necessary at the oil pan and cylinder head joints. For DOHC engines apply a thin bead around the 1 center cover bolt hole on 1991 vehicles or the 2 inner cover bolt holes on 1992–93 vehicles. Be sure to assemble the front cover to the engine within 3 minutes of application.

15. Install the crankshaft gear retaining tool and position the front cover to the engine and install the bolts. Tighten the perimeter bolts starting at the center and working outwards on both sides to 19 ft. lbs. (25 Nm) for SOHC engines or to 22 ft. lbs. (30 Nm) for DOHC engines.

16. Install and tighten the front cover center or inner bolts to 89 inch lbs. (10 Nm), then install the 4 oil pan front bolts and tighten to 80 inch lbs. (9 Nm).

17. After front cover installation, spray 6–12 squirts of oil though the front oil seal drain back hole to verify it is not plugged.

18. Apply a thin film of RTV between the damper/pulley assembly flange and washer only, the washer and bolt head flange are designed to prevent oil leakage.

19. Remove the crankshaft retaining tool and position the crankshaft damper/pulley assembly, then secure as accomplished during removal while tightening the bolt to 159 ft. lbs. (215 Nm).

20. Apply a small drop of RTV accross the cylinder head and front cover T-joints. Inspect the old camshaft cover gasket and replace if damaged. Install the gasket and the camshaft cover. Tighten the fasteners uniformly to 22 ft. lbs. (30 Nm) for SOHC vehicles or in proper sequence to 89 inch lbs. (10 Nm) for DOHC vehicles.

21. Install the power steering pump assembly.

22. Install the idler pulley if removed, then install the belt tensioner and the serpentine drive belt.

23. For 1992–93 vehicles, install the engine mount and midrail assembly.

24. Install the splash shield and the wheel assembly, then lower the vehicle.

25. Properly fill the engine crankcase and connect the negative battery cable.

26. Start the engine and check for leaks.

```
             INTAKE SIDE

               6   8   9
      12
            3    1    2    4
      11
            5    7    10

             EXHAUST SIDE
```

Camshaft cover fastener torque sequence — DOHC engine

Front Cover Oil Seal

REPLACEMENT

With Front Cover Installed

1. Disconnect the negative battery cable and drain the engine oil.
2. Raise the vehicle and support safely, then remove the right wheel and splash shield.
3. For 1992–93 vehicles with a torque axis mount system, remove the engine mount and midrail bracket, as necessary.
4. Using a strap wrench or a piece of wood wedged between the damper spoke and the lower side of the engine front cover, hold the damper and remove the bolt. With a suitable 3 jaw puller and the slots cast into the damper, pull the crankshaft damper/pulley assembly from the crankshaft.
5. Use a suitable prytool to carefully pry the front oil seal from the front cover. Be careful not to damage the front cover or crankshaft.
6. Clean the seal bore and oil drain back passage.

To install:

7. Make sure the oil drain back is free of contamination. Position the oil seal and thread service seal installer tool SA9104E or equivalent onto the end of the crankshaft. Use the tool to draw the seal into position. Never tap on the seal or the seal install with a hammer.
8. Apply a thin film of clean engine oil to the new seal lip.
9. Position the crankshaft damper/pulley assembly, then secure as accomplished during removal while tightening the bolt to 159 ft. lbs. (215 Nm).
10. If removed, install the engine mount and midrail assembly.
11. Install the splash shield and the wheel assembly, then lower the vehicle.
12. Properly fill the engine crankcase and connect the negative battery cable.
13. Start the engine and check for leaks.

With Front Cover Removed

1. Use a suitable prytool to carefully pry the front oil seal from the front cover. Be careful not to damage the front cover or crankshaft.
2. Clean the seal bore and oil drain back passage.
3. Place the engine front cover on the base of a suitable arbor press.
4. Position the seal to the front cover and place tool SA9104E, or equivalent installation tool, over the seal.
5. Press the seal into the engine front cover approximately 0.04 inch (1mm) further into the engine front cover than the factory seal removed earlier.
6. Install the timing chain front cover.

Timing Chain and Sprockets

REMOVAL & INSTALLATION

SOHC Engine

1. Disconnect the negative battery cable.
2. Remove the timing chain front cover.

NOTE: Position the crankshaft 90 degrees off TDC to make sure the pistons will not contact the valves upon assembly.

3. Carefully rotate the crankshaft clockwise so the timing mark on the crankshaft sprocket and keyway align with the main bearing cap split line.
4. Remove the timing guides and tensioner.
5. Remove the camshaft sprocket bolt, using a $7/8$ in. (21mm) wrench to hold the camshaft. Then remove the timing chain and camshaft sprocket. Remove the crankshaft sprocket, if necessary.

To install:

6. Inspect the chain for wear and damage. Check the inside diameter of the chain, it should be no more than 16.77 in. (426mm). Inspect the chain guides for wear or cracks and the timing gears for teeth or key wear. Replace components as necessary.
7. Verify that the crankshaft is positioned 90 degrees clockwise past TDC from the keyway (keyway at 3 o'clock).
8. Bring the camshaft up to No. 1 TDC by loosely installing the sprocket and rotating the sprocket until the timing pin can be installed. The camshaft contains wrench flats to assist in turning the shaft. The dowel pin should be at 12 o'clock when No. 1 is at TDC and a timing pin ($3/16$ inch drill bit) should then install at about the 8 o'clock position.
9. Rotate the crankshaft counterclockwise 90 degrees up to No. 1 TDC (keyway at 12 o'clock).

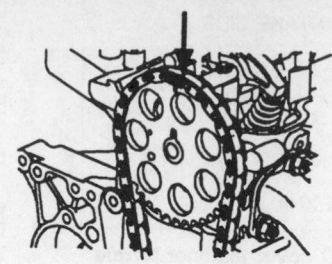

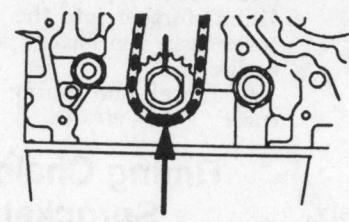

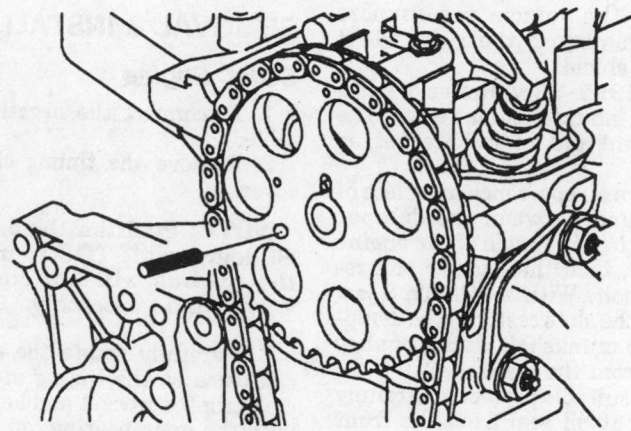

Timing chain and sprocket alignment marks—SOHC engine

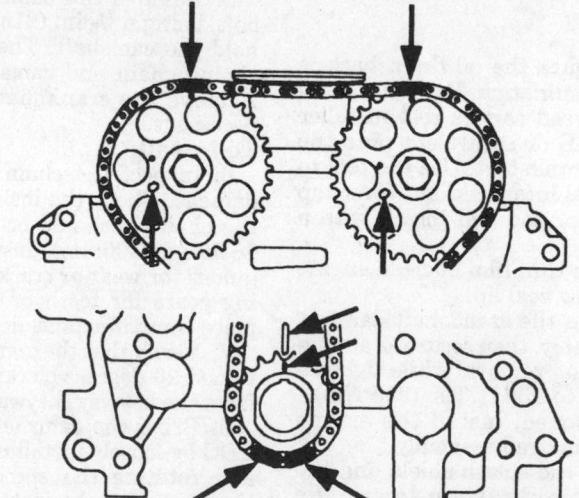

Timing chain and sprocket alignment marks—DOHC engine

away from the cylinder head and excess chain slack should be located on the tensioner side of the block.

11. Tighten the sprocket bolt to 75 ft. lbs. (102 Nm). Again, use an wrench on the camshaft wrench flats to hold the shaft in position while tightening the bolt. Do not allow the camshaft retaining bolt to torque against the timing pin or cylinder head damage will result.

12. Install the chain guides with the words FRONT facing out. Install the fixed guide first and verify the chain is snug against the guide, then install the pivot guide. Tighten the bolts to 19 ft. lbs. (26 Nm) and verify that the pivot guide moves freely.

13. Retract the tensioner plunger and pin the ratchet lever using a 1/8 in. No. 31 drill bit inserted in the alignment hole. Install the tensioner and tighten the bolts to 14 ft. lbs. (19 Nm), then remove the drill bit.

14. Make sure all alignment pins are removed and install the timing chain front cover.

15. Connect the negative battery cable, start the engine and check for leaks.

DOHC Engine

1. Disconnect the negative battery cable.

2. Remove the timing chain front cover.

NOTE: Position the crankshaft 90 degrees off TDC to make sure the pistons will not contact the valves upon assembly.

3. Carefully rotate the crankshaft clockwise so the timing mark on the crankshaft sprocket and keyway align with the main bearing cap split line.

4. Remove the timing guides and tensioner.

5. Remove the camshaft sprocket bolt, using a 7/8 in. (21mm) wrench to hold the camshaft. Then remove the timing chain and camshaft sprocket. Remove the crankshaft sprocket, if necessary.

To install:

6. Inspect the chain for wear and damage. Check the inside diameter of the chain, it should be no more than 23.15 in. (588mm). Inspect the chain guides for wear or cracks and the timing gears for teeth or key wear. Replace components as necessary.

7. Verify that the crankshaft is positioned 90 degrees clockwise past TDC. The crankshaft keyway should be at 3 o'clock aligned with the main bearing cap split line to prevent piston and valve damage.

8. Install the camshaft gears, retaining bolts and washers. Make sure the letters FRT on the gears face forward, away from the cylinder block.

10. Position the crankshaft sprocket into the chain, place the chain over the camshaft sprocket and slide the crankshaft sprocket into position. Install the timing chain and the crankshaft sprockets so the 1 silver link plate aligns with the pip mark on the camshaft sprocket and the other aligns with the downward tooth at the 6 o'clock position on the crankshaft sprocket. The letters FRT on the camshaft sprocket must face forward,

Use the wrench flats provided on the camshafts to hold the shaft and tighten the bolts to 75 ft. lbs. (102 Nm).

9. Bring the camshafts up to No. 1 TDC. The dowel pin should be at 12 o'clock. Install a $^3/_{16}$ in. drill bit into the hole in the sprocket about 8 o'clock.

10. Rotate the crankshaft up to No. 1 TDC (keyway at 12 o'clock).

11. Position the crankshaft sprocket into the timing chain. Install the timing chain over the camshaft sprockets so the 2 silver link plates align with the pip marks on the camshaft sprockets and the other 2 plates align with the downward tooth (at 6 o'clock position) on the crankshaft sprocket. Install the crankshaft sprocket. Excess chain slack should be located on the tensioner side of the cylinder block.

12. Verify that the crankshaft pip mark aligns with the cylinder block mark at 12 o'clock and that the timing pin holes are aligned at about the 8 o'clock position. Remove the timing pins from the camshaft sprockets.

13. Install the timing chain fixed guide to the right of the block face toward the water pump. Tighten the bolts to 21 ft. lbs. (28 Nm) and verify the chain is snug against the guide.

14. Install the pivoting chain guide and check for clearance between the block and head. Tighten the bolt to 19 ft. lbs. (26 Nm) and verify the guide pivots freely.

15. Retract the tensioner plunger and pin the ratchet lever using a 1/8 in. No. 31 drill bit inserted in the alignment hole. Install the tensioner and tighten the bolts to 14 ft. lbs. (19 Nm), then remove the drill bit.

16. Make sure all alignment pins are removed and install the timing chain front cover.

17. Connect the negative battery cable, start the engine and check for leaks.

Camshaft

REMOVAL & INSTALLATION

SOHC Engine

1. Disconnect the negative battery cable.

2. Remove the timing chain front cover.

3. Remove the timing chain and camshaft sprocket.

4. Remove the rocker arm cover and rocker assemblies.

5. Remove the lifters and label of position for assembly in their original locations.

6. Remove the battery cover and battery.

7. Drive the camshaft plug inward, then remove it from the cylinder head with a magnet.

8. Carefully pull the camshaft from the rear of the cylinder head though the oversized camshaft plug hole.

To install:

9. Lubricate the camshaft and install into the cylinder head.

10. Coat a new rear cylinder head plug with Loctite® 242 or equivalent and install it using a standard bushing driver.

11. Install the battery and tighten the battery hold-down nut and screw to 80 inch lbs. (9 Nm). Connect the positive battery cable only, at this time.

12. Install the valve lifters into their original bores.

13. Install the rocker arm shaft assemblies.

14. Install the timing chain and camshaft sprocket.

15. Install the timing chain front cover.

16. Connect the negative battery cable, start the engine and check for leaks.

DOHC Engine

1. Disconnect the negative battery cable and remove the serpentine drive belt.

2. Disconnect the spark plug wires from the plugs, remove the EGR valve solenoid attachment screw and remove the PCV fresh air hose.

3. Remove the camshaft cover, then inspect the cover silicone insulators for cracks or deterioration and replace as necessary.

4. Turn the crankshaft until the **0** mark on the crankshaft pulley is in alignment with the pointer and No. 1 cylinder is at TDC of the compression stroke. Both camshaft dowel pins will be at the 12 o'clock position and the timing pin holes will be aligned when the No. 1 cylinder is at TDC. If necessary, the right wheel and splash shield may be removed to help observe the timing marks.

5. Carefully remove each camshaft sprocket's retaining bolts. Use a $^7/_8$ inch (21mm) open end wrench to hold the camshaft from turning while removing the bolts.

6. For 1992–93 vehicles, position the front angled support fixture in front of the camshaft sprockets.

7. Attach the camshaft sprocket adapters to the end of each camshaft using the pilot bolts, but do not tighten the bolts. For 1992–93 vehicles, the pilot bolts should be started from outside of the front angled support.

8. Remove the upper timing chain guide and both front camshaft bearing caps.

9. For 1991 vehicles, position the front support fixture.

10. Secure the support fixture using $^3/_8$ inch bolts/blocks and align the 2 holes in each camshaft sprocket, adapter and the front support fixture. Install the 4 nuts, but do not tighten. The steel blocks should be installed against the rearward side of the camshaft sprocket. Tighten the sprocket pilot bolts to 19 ft. lbs. (25 Nm) while holding the camshafts from turning with an open end wrench.

11. Move each camshaft sprocket off the end of the camshaft by rocking the sprocket forward or by carefully prying between the end of the camshaft and the sprocket. Then tighten the 4 nuts and bolts with blocks from the side of the support fixture to 19 ft. lbs. (25 Nm).

12. Install the 2 bolts retaining the support fixture to the engine front cover and tighten the bolts to 89 inch lbs. (10 Nm). Then remove each camshaft sprocket pilot bolt while holding the camshafts with a wrench.

13. Carefully pry between the sprocket and the end of the camshaft to move the camshaft rearward. Pry only enough to remove its end from inside the sprocket pilot otherwise camshaft or lifter damage may occur.

14. Uniformly loosen and remove the remaining camshaft bearing cap bolts. To prevent bolt/cap damage, do not use power tools and make several passes. Then remove each camshaft. Position the caps for installation in their original locations.

To install:

15. Oil the camshaft and install with the **IN** camshaft on the intake side and **EX** camshaft on the exhaust side.

NOTE: The dowel pin in each camshaft must be located at the 12 o'clock position during installation to prevent valve and piston damage.

16. Install all bearing caps, except for the forward pair, in their original positions. Uniformly tighten the cap bolts to 124 inch lbs. (14 Nm).

17. Install 1 camshaft sprocket pilot bolt in each camshaft and tighten to 124 inch lbs. (14 Nm) in order to pull the camshaft fully forward and align the sprocket support for installation of the sprocket onto the camshaft.

18. Remove the 4 sprocket support bolt/blocks and nuts. Then for 1991 vehicles, remove the front angled support fixture. The torque axis mount system of the 1992–93 vehicles requires the fixture to remain in place longer.

19. Verify that the camshafts are fully positioned forward and install the 2 forward bearing caps and the up-

per chain guide. The caps are marked E1 or I1 for exhaust or intake and must be positioned with their arrows pointing towards the sprockets. Tighten the cap bolts to 124 inch lbs. (14 Nm).

20. Make sure the camshaft dowel pin aligns with the slot in each camshaft sprocket. If necessary, rotate the camshaft slightly (1–2 degrees) and move each sprocket from the adapter onto the end of the camshaft. Fully seat each sprocket on the end of each camshaft.

21. Remove the 2 sprocket pilot bolts and adapters while using a wrench on the camshaft flats to assure the camshaft cannot move.

22. For 1992–93 vehicles, remove the support angled fixture.

23. Install the camshaft sprocket retaining bolts and washers. Hold the camshafts and tighten the bolts to 76 ft. lbs. (103 Nm).

24. Verify all visible timing marks and holes are in alignment. Turn the crankshaft clockwise until the mark on the crankshaft pulley aligns with the mark on the front cover. Insert $^3/_{16}$ inch drill bits through the camshaft sprocket alignment holes, into the cylinder head. If the alignment pins cannot be inserted, turn the crankshaft 360 degrees clockwise and repeat. If the pins cannot be inserted within 1–2 degrees of either TDC position, the camshafts are not properly timed. Do not start the engine until the camshafts are timed.

25. Apply a small drop of RTV across the cylinder head and front cover T-joints. Inspect the old camshaft cover gasket and replace if damaged. Install the gasket and the camshaft cover. Tighten the fasteners in proper sequence to 89 inch lbs. (10 Nm).

26. Install the right splash shield and wheel, if removed to observe the timing marks.

27. Install the PCV and fresh air hoses, the EGR valve solenoid attaching screw and the spark plug wires.

28. Install the serpentine drive belt and connect the negative battery cable.

29. Start the engine and check for leaks.

Piston and Connecting Rod

POSITIONING

NOTE: Only the top ring on the DOHC engine and the second ring on both engines have pip marks. The top ring on the SOHC engine can be installed with either side up.

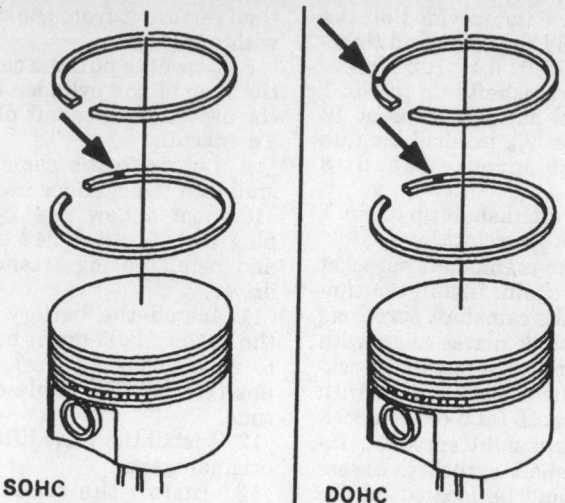

Piston ring positioning—do not align ring gaps, rings should be rotated 90–120 degrees from each other

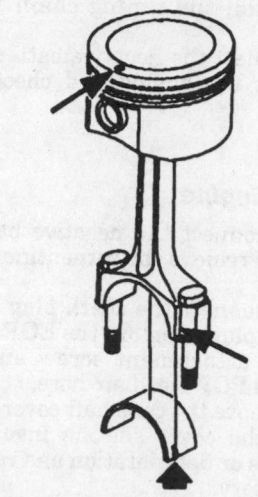

Piston and connecting rod positioning—align the mark on top of the piston with the front of the engine. Assemble the connecting rod to the piston with the bearing tang slots directed toward the exhaust manifold side

ENGINE LUBRICATION

Oil Pan

REMOVAL & INSTALLATION

1. Raise and support the vehicle safely, then drain the engine oil.
2. Remove the front exhaust pipe.
3. For 1991 vehicles, remove the engine stiffening bracket and the flywheel cover.
4. Remove the right wheel and splash shield, then loosen the 4 front motor mount bolts. Back the bolts out about ½ inch (12mm).
5. Remove all the oil pan bolts. For vehicles with a manual transaxle, an 8mm flex socket may be used to access the rear oil pan bolts next to the flywheel.
6. Using SA9123E, or an equivalent RTV cutter tool, separate the oil pan from the engine. Drive the tool around the pan to shear the RTV seam, then tap the pan sideways with a rubber mallet to loosen.
7. Pry the engine mount away from the engine as necessary and remove the oil pan.

To install:

8. Carefully clean the gasket mating surfaces with a scraper and solvent.
9. Apply a 0.16 inch (4mm) bead of RTV sealer to the pan flange, to the inside of the bolt holes.
10. Install the oil pan within 3 minutes and tighten the bolts to 80 inch lbs. (9 Nm).
11. Tighten the front mount bolts to 40 ft. lbs. (54 Nm).
12. Install the right splash shield and wheel.
13. For 1991 vehicles, install the engine stiffening bracket and the flywheel cover.
14. Install the exhaust pipe. Tighten the pipe to manifold nuts in a crosswise pattern to 23 ft. lbs. (31 Nm) and the pipe to converter bolts to 33 ft. lbs. (45 Nm).
15. Lower the vehicle and properly fill the engine crankcase.
16. Start the engine and check for leaks.

Oil Pump
REMOVAL & INSTALLATION

1. Disconnect the negative battery cable and drain the engine oil.

2. Remove the timing chain front cover.

3. Remove the oil pump cover Torx® bolts using a suitable impact driver. Because the pump cover screws are coated with a sealant to prevent oil leakage, they must be replaced when removed.

4. Remove the driven and drive gears.

5. If necessary, remove the relief valve using tool SA9103E or equivalent, to pull the valve from the bore. Because the puller jaws will damage the relief valve sealing seat, the valve cannot be used again.

To install:

6. If removed, install a new relief valve into the cover bore. Coat the valve with clean engine oil and tap it into the bore using a hammer and SA9103E or an equivalent installer tool.

NOTE: Whenever the oil pump

is installed, the assembly must be packed with petroleum jelly in order to prime the pump.

7. Install the driven and drive gears into the pump with the chamfer toward the front oil seal.

8. Install the pump body cover and secure with new bolts. Tighten the bolts to 97 inch lbs. (11 Nm).

9. Install the timing chain front cover.

10. Properly fill the engine crankcase, start the engine and check for leaks.

CHECKING

1. With the timing chain front cover and the oil pump body cover removed, use a feeler gauge to measure the clearance between the driven gear and pump body. Clearance should not exceed 0.0042 in. (0.105mm).

2. Use a feeler gauge and measure

the clearance between the both gear tips. Clearance should not exceed 0.006 in. (0.150mm).

3. Using Plastigage®, install the pump cover to measure the gerotor-to-cover clearance. Clearance should not exceed 0.005 in. (0.128mm).

Rear Main Bearing Oil Seal

REMOVAL & INSTALLATION

Both engines use a 1-piece round seal.

1. Disconnect the negative battery cable.

2. Remove the transaxle assembly from the vehicle.

3. Remove the flywheel assembly.

4. Use the prying tangs provided in the carrier to remove the seal with a small suitable prybar and hammer. Be careful not to damage the crankshaft oil seal lip contact surface.

To install:

5. Clean the carrier and crankshaft with solvent and shop rag to prevent damage during installation. Check for scores or damage to the sealing surfaces.

6. Oil the seal install using a seal installer SA9121E or equivalent. The tool is designed to prevent seal lip from rolling during installation and will seat the seal 0.04 inch (1mm) lower than the factory seal. Never tap on the seal or seal installer with a hammer.

7. Install the flywheel assembly.

8. Install the transaxle assembly into the vehicle.

9. Connect the negative battery cable, start the engine and check for leaks.

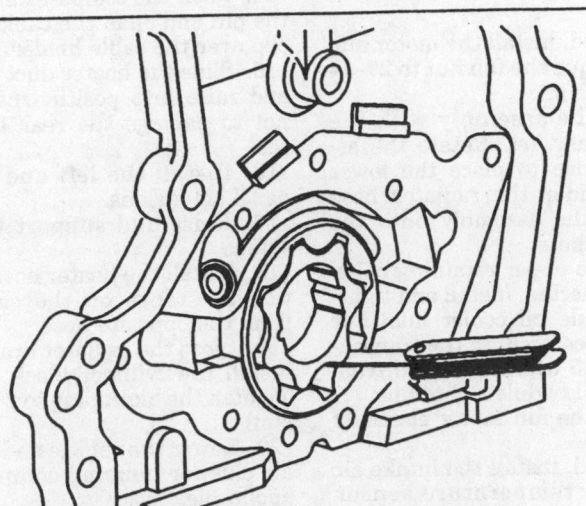

Checking oil pump body and tip clearance

ENGINE COOLING

Radiator

REMOVAL & INSTALLATION

1. Disconnect the negative battery cable and drain the engine coolant.

2. Remove the air intake ducts and for the DOHC engine, remove the air cleaner housing.

3. Disconnect the temperature sensor connector.

4. Remove the upper radiator hose and, if equipped with an automatic transaxle, disconnect the upper transaxle cooler line. Plug the line to prevent fluid contamination or loss.

5. Remove the electric cooling fan assembly.

6. Remove the lower radiator hose.

7. Raise and support the vehicle safely.

8. Remove the lower splash shield, then if applicable, disconnect and plug the lower transaxle cooler line.

9. Remove the 4 condenser bracket-to-radiator bolts. Wire the condenser to the frame assembly so it stays in place, then lower the vehicle.

10. Remove the upper radiator nuts and brackets. If equipped the air conditioning, remove the upper radiator seal.

11. Remove the radiator from the vehicle.

To install:

12. Install the radiator into the vehicle.

13. Install the upper seal, if applicable, then install the brackets and retaining nuts. Be sure the brackets do not pinch the radiator locating pins and the radiator moves freely in the grommets.

14. Raise and support the vehicle safely.

15. Install the condenser bracket bolts, and if applicable, install the lower transaxle cooler line.

16. Install the lower splash shield and lower the vehicle.

17. Install the lower radiator hose with the clamp tangs positioned at 1 o'clock.

18. Install the cooling fan assembly.

19. For 1991 vehicles with an automatic transaxle, connect the upper transaxle cooler line and tighten. For 1992–93 vehicles with an automatic transaxle, connect the upper transaxle cooler line at a 35 degree angle inward from vertical and hold while tightening.

20. Install the upper radiator hose with the clamp tangs at 12 o'clock.

21. For the DOHC engine, install the air cleaner housing.

22. Install the intake air ducts and connect the air temperature sensor connector.

23. Close the radiator drain plug and install the cylinder block drain plug. Tighten the block plug to 26 ft. lbs. (35 Nm).

24. Connect the negative battery cable and properly fill the engine cooling system.

Electric Cooling Fan

TESTING

When conducting tests on the electric cooling fan and circuit use of a high impedance Digital Volt Ohm Meter (DVOM) is necessary. If the cooling fan is inoperative, test the system as follows:

1. Check the 30 amp cooling fan maxifuse in the underhood junction block.

2. If the fuse is OK, disconnect the cooling fan motor connector and connect a DVOM from terminal B (BLK/RED) wire to ground.

3. Start the engine and turn the air conditioning **ON**. If there is voltage at the B wire, check for open at terminal A (BLK) wire to ground.

4. Check the fan motor by jumping 12 volts to the 2 wires (A = negative, B = positive).

5. Replace if necessary.

REMOVAL & INSTALLATION

1. Disconnect the negative battery cable.

2. For vehicles equipped with the DOHC engine, remove the air intake ducts and temperature sensor connector.

3. Disconnect the motor electrical connector.

4. Remove the top fan motor assembly bolts.

5. It may be necessary to loosen the top automatic transaxle cooler line, if equipped with air conditioning, and move it aside.

6. Lift the fan assembly off the lower mounting brackets. Move the assembly to the left and rotate counterclockwise lifting the right side up past the radiator hose, then remove the assembly from the vehicle.

7. If necessary, remove the fan blade from the shaft and remove the motor from the housing.

To install:

8. If removed, install the motor and fan blade. Torque the fan nut to 27–44 inch lbs. (3–5 Nm).

9. Install the assembly with the lower left corner 1st. Rotate the assembly clockwise to place the lower left mount under the radiator hose and position the assembly onto the mounting brackets.

10. Install the upper retaining bolts.

11. If disconnected, install and tighten the transaxle oil cooler line. For 1992–93 vehicles position the transaxle cooler line 35 degrees inward from vertical and hold while tightening.

12. Connect the fan motor electrical connector.

13. If removed, install the intake air ducts and the temperature sensor connector.

14. Connect the negative battery cable.

Heater Core

REMOVAL & INSTALLATION

1. Disconnect the negative battery cable and drain the engine coolant.

2. Raise and support the vehicle safely.

3. Move the heater core clamps up the hoses and off the fittings, then lower the vehicle.

4. For the DOHC engine, remove the air cleaner housing cover and disconnect the air induction hose at the intake manifold. For the SOHC engine, remove the air cleaner housing.

5. Remove the hoses from the heater core.

6. Remove the left and right lower trim lower trim panel extensions by disconnecting the velcro and pulling them out of the upper retaining clips.

7. Remove the retaining screws and lower the heater duct straight down. Carefully slide the duct to the side and out.

8. Push down on the cable and lift the plastic tab to release the temperature cable hold down clip, then disconnect the temperature cable by squeezing the valve pin and pulling the cable straight off.

9. Remove the heater core side cover and retaining screws.

10. Remove the lower heater core cover and screws, then remove the screw and pipe clamp.

11. Remove the core retainer and the heater core.

To install:

12. Install the core being careful not to damage the pipe seal. Use a coating of petroleum jelly to ease installation of the pipes through the cowl.

13. Install the heater core retainer, pipe clamp, lower and side covers.

14. Push the temperature cable over the pin and snap the cable hold down clip over the cable holder.

15. Slide the heater duct in sideways and raise into position being careful not to damage the rear floor heater seal.

16. Install the left and right trim panel extensions.

17. Raise and support the vehicle safely.

18. Install the heater hoses and position the tangs on the clamps away from the opposite hose.

19. Close the radiator drain plug and install the cylinder block drain plug. Tighten the block plug to 26 ft. lbs. (35 Nm).

20. Lower the vehicle and replace the air cleaner housing components, as applicable.

21. Connect the negative battery cable and properly fill the engine cooling system.

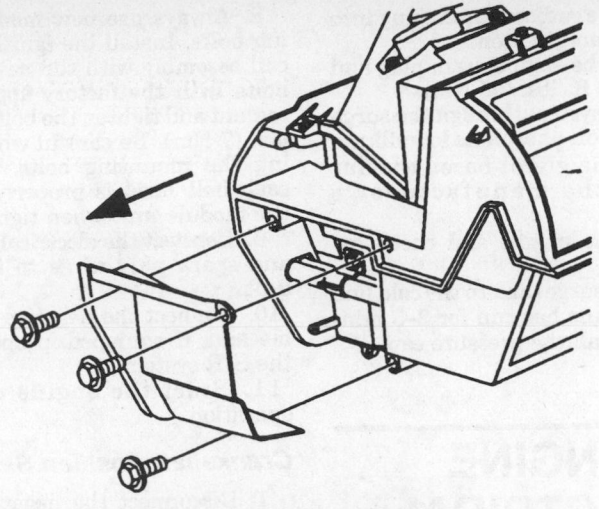

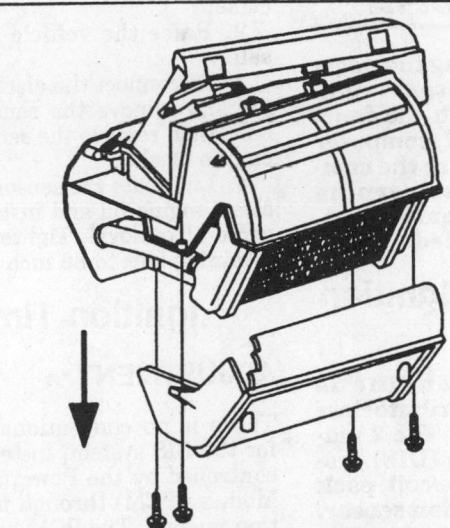

Heater core removal

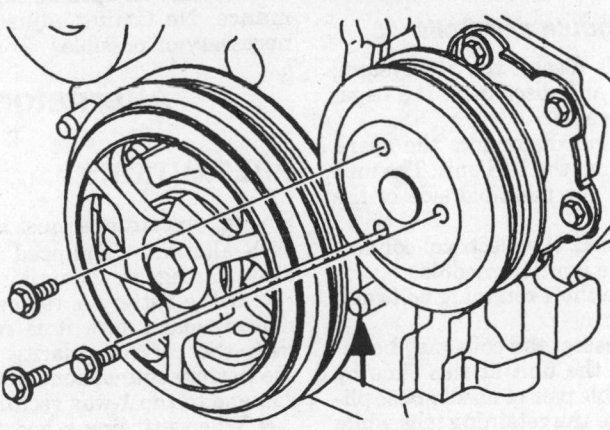

Water pump pulley

Water Pump
REMOVAL & INSTALLATION

1. Disconnect the negative battery cable and drain the engine coolant.

2. Remove the serpentine drive belt.

3. Raise the vehicle and support safely. Remove the right front tire and inner wheel well splash shield.

4. If top access is desired, remove the air conditioning compressor bolts and position the compressor aside with the refrigerant lines intact.

5. Spray the water pump hub with penetrating oil to loosen the pulley and prevent damage during pump removal.

6. Remove the water pump pulley bolts and allow the pulley to hang freely on the hub. A 1 inch (25.4mm) block of wood may be wedged between the pump pulley and crankshaft to hold the pulley while loosening the retaining bolts.

7. Move the pulley outward or remove as necessary for access and remove the 6 water pump flange bolts. Carefully pull the pump and pulley assembly away from the engine and remove the assembly from the vehicle. If necessary, a gasket scrapper may be inserted under the flange, but be careful not to damage the aluminum block sealing surface.

To install:

8. Thoroughly clean the gasket mating surface of all old gasket material. Apply a small amount of gasket sealant at the outer edges of the bolt holes to hold that gasket in place and install onto the water pump assembly.

9. Install the pump assembly with the small bump located next to 1 of the attaching bolts in the 11 o'clock position. Install and tighten the bolts in a criss-cross sequence to 22 ft. lbs. (30 Nm).

10. Install or reposition the pump pulley, as applicable and tighten the bolts to 19 ft. lbs. (25 Nm). If the pump hub exposed through the pulley is rusty, clean it with a wire brush and apply a thin coat of primer to prevent the pulley from rusting onto the hub.

11. Install the serpentine drive belt, splash shield and tire.

12. If repositioned, install the air conditioning compressor.

13. Close the radiator drain plug and install the cylinder block drain plug. Tighten the block plug to 26 ft. lbs. (35 Nm).

14. Connect the negative battery cable and properly fill the engine cooling system.

Thermostat

REMOVAL & INSTALLATION

1. Drain the engine coolant.

2. Disconnect the lower radiator hose at the thermostat housing.

3. Remove the 2 bolts at the water inlet housing, then remove the housing, thermostat and O-ring assembly.

4. Remove the thermostat from the housing using the tool provided with the replacement thermostat element.

To install:

NOTE: The thermostat will not

function correctly if it has been contacted by oil. If oil is found in the cooling system, the thermostat cartridge must be replaced and the cooling system must be flushed.

5. Install the replacement thermostat using the tool provided. Make sure the element's retaining tangs are properly seated in the 2 legs and the element piston is correctly positioned in the inlet housing.

6. Install a new O-ring and position the housing to the engine. Tighten the retaining bolts to 22 ft. lbs. (30 Nm).

7. Close the radiator drain plug and install the cylinder block drain plug. Tighten the block plug to 26 ft. lbs. (35 Nm).

8. Install the hose to the inlet housing.

9. Connect the negative battery cable and properly fill the engine cooling system.

Cooling System Bleeding

The Saturn cooling system a pressure coolant surge tank and an inlet side thermostat. Coolant is added through the pressure cap in the surge tank and fills the engine cylinder block, radiator, heater core and hoses. The system therefore, does not require any bleeding.

DRAINING ENGINE COOLING SYSTEM

1. With the engine cool and the vehicle parked on a level surface, remove the surge tank pressure cap and position a drain pan with a minimum 2 gallon capacity below the engine and radiator.

2. Unscrew the drain plug on the radiator and carefully pry the plug out of the housing. If necessary for replacement, pinch the housing tabs closed and remove the housing from the radiator by pulling straight out.

3. Remove the cylinder block drain plug located at the right front of the engine below the thermostat housing and allow the coolant to drain from the openings.

REFILLING ENGINE COOLING SYSTEM

1. If removed, install the drain plug housing by pinching the tabs and inserting into the hole. Once the housing is in the hole, release the tabs and push the housing until it snaps into place. Be careful not to push the housing through the hole into the radiator.

2. Push the radiator drain plug into the housing and tighten.

3. Install the engine drain plug and tighten to 26 ft. lbs. (35 Nm).

4. Fill the system through the surge tank with a non-phosphate low silicate base ethylene glycol-based coolant mixed to the manufacturer's instructions.

5. Start the engine and check for leaks.

6. Fill the surge tank to the cold line after the engine has run for 2–3 minutes and install the pressure cap.

ENGINE ELECTRICAL

NOTE: Disconnecting the negative battery cable on some vehicles may interfere with the functions of the on board computer systems and may require the computer to undergo a relearning process, once the negative battery cable is reconnected.

Distributorless Ignition System

NOTE: The 1.9L engine is equipped with a Distributorless Ignition System (DIS). The 2 major components of the (DIS) system are a DIS module/coil pack and a crankshaft position sensor.

REMOVAL & INSTALLATION

Ignition Module and Coils

1. Properly disable the SIR system, if equipped, and disconnect the negative battery cable.

2. Label and disconnect the spark plug wires from the DIS unit. The unit is located at the manifold side of the bellhousing.

3. Disconnect the electrical connectors from the ignition module.

4. Remove the 4 retaining bolts and the DIS unit.

5. If necessary, the coils may be removed from the unit at this time by using a suitable pair of needle-nose pliers to squeeze the retaining tabs while pulling the coils upward.
To install:

6. If removed, install the coils to the ignition module.

7. Run a 6 × 1.0mm tap through the module mounting holes to remove remaining thread sealant residue and verify that the module and bellhousing mating surfaces are clean and free from grit or dirt.

8. Always use new module mounting bolts. Install the ignition module/coil assembly with the new mounting bolts with the factory applied yellow sealant and tighten the bolts to 61 inch lbs. (7 Nm). Be careful when tightening the mounting bolts, verify that each bolt head is properly seated on the module unit when tightened.

9. Connect the electrical connectors and spark plug wires to the module unit.

10. Connect the negative battery cable and, if equipped, properly enable the SIR system.

11. Start the engine and check operation.

Crankshaft Position Sensor

1. Disconnect the negative battery cable.

2. Raise the vehicle and support safely.

3. Disconnect the electrical connector and remove the sensor retaining bolt, then remove the sensor from the engine block.

4. Lubricate the sensor O-ring with clean engine oil and install in the reverse of removal. Tighten the sensor retaining bolt to 80 inch lbs. (9 Nm).

Ignition Timing

ADJUSTMENT

There is no conventional distributor for the DIS system. Instead, timing is controlled by the Powertrain Control Module (PCM) through the DIS ignition module. The PCM has the ability to advance or retard ignition timing, as necessary for optimal engine performance. No timing adjustments are necessary or possible.

Alternator

PRECAUTIONS

Several precautions must be observed with alternator equipped vehicles to avoid damage to the unit.

• If the battery is removed for any reason, make sure it is reconnected with the correct polarity. Reversing the battery connections may result in damage to the 1-way rectifiers.

• When utilizing a booster battery as a starting aid, always connect the positive to positive terminals and the negative terminal from the booster battery to a good engine ground on the vehicle being started.

• Never use a fast charger as a booster to start vehicles.

• Disconnect the battery cables when charging the battery with a fast charger.

- Never attempt to polarize the alternator.
- Do not use test lights of more than 12 volts when checking diode continuity.
- Do not short across or ground any of the alternator terminals.
- The polarity of the battery, alternator and regulator must be matched and considered before making any electrical connections within the system.
- Never separate the alternator on an open circuit. Make sure all connections within the circuit are clean and tight.
- Disconnect the battery ground terminal when performing any service on electrical components.
- Disconnect the battery if arc welding is to be done on the vehicle.

BELT TENSION ADJUSTMENT

The belt is automatically adjusted using a spring loaded automatic tensioner. The marking on the tensioner arm must fall within the operating range (2 marks) on the tensioner body. If the tensioner falls outside the operating range, the serpentine drive belt must be replaced.

REMOVAL & INSTALLATION

1. Disconnect the negative battery cable and remove the serpentine drive belt.
2. Remove the power steering pump assembly, to access the alternator attaching bolts.
3. Remove the alternator splash shield attaching bolt and unclip the shield from the alternator.
4. Disconnect the alternator electrical connections.
5. Remove the upper and lower alternator attaching bolts. If necessary, remove the vehicle passenger's side tire and splash shield to access the lower alternator bolt.
6. Lift the alternator through the opening between the shock tower and the intake manifold and remove the alternator from the vehicle.

To install:

7. Install a new wiring harness-to-generator fastener to be sure of proper electrical contact.
8. Position the alternator in the vehicle and install the lower attaching bolt.
9. Install the upper attaching bolt and the 2 wiring harness connectors.
10. Tighten the alternator attaching bolts to 27 ft. lbs. (37 Nm) and the alternator positive terminal to 89 inch lbs. (10 Nm).

11. If removed, install the vehicle passenger's side tire and splash shield.
12. Install the alternator splash shield and tighten the fastener bolt to 89 inch lbs. (10 Nm).
13. Install the power steering pump assembly.
14. Connect the negative battery cable.

Serpentine Drive Belt

REMOVAL & INSTALLATION

1. Depress the tensioner arm using Snap-on® tool S-8190A, or an equivalent $^9/_{16}$ in. (14mm) wrench.
2. Remove the belt off the idler or air conditioning compressor.
3. Remove the drive belt from the vehicle.

To install:

4. Install the belt around the pulleys, except for the front cover idler or air conditioning compressor.
5. Depress the tensioner arm and slip the belt over the idler or air conditioning compressor pulley. Make sure the belt ribs are properly aligned on the pulleys.
6. If the tensioner idler pulley retaining bolt is loose, remove the bolt and apply Loctite® 242 or equivalent to the bolt threads. Install the bolt and tighten to 22 ft. lbs. (30 Nm).

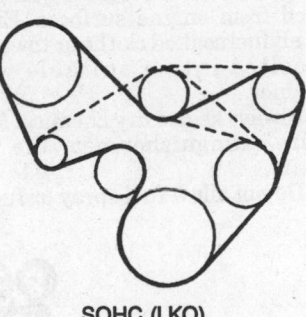

SOHC (LKO)

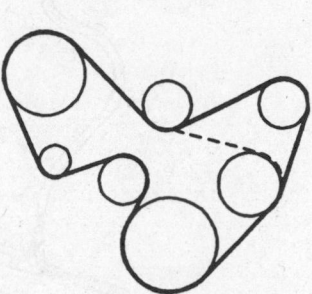

DOHC (LLO)

Accessory drive belt routing

Starter

REMOVAL & INSTALLATION

1. Disconnect the negative battery cable.
2. Remove the air inlet tube and fresh air hose. For the DOHC engine, the resonator must be lifted for disengagement from the engine support bracket.
3. Remove the upper starter bolts using the access hole provided next to the intake manifold support. If necessary, remove the intake support bracket for ease of removal.
4. Raise and support the vehicle safely.
5. Remove the starter shield pin by pulling on it with pliers. Lift and release it from the solenoid.
6. It is very important that the solenoid electrical connection nuts and studs are sprayed with penetrating oil prior to removal to avoid damage to the solenoid end cap.
7. Carefully loosen the bolts and disconnect the starter electrical connectors.
8. Remove the lower starter bolt.
9. Remove the rear starter support bracket attaching bolt.
10. Rotate the starter until the bracket misses the axle shaft support bracket. Pull the starter rearward and toward the left side of the vehicle to remove.

To install:

11. Install the rear starter support bracket and shield to the starter. Tighten the bracket nuts to 80 inch lbs. (9 Nm).
12. Guide the starter into the bellhousing and rotate the assembly until the lower bolt hole in the starter aligns.
13. Verify that the bracket is properly aligned and loosely install the bracket and bolt, then loosely install the housing bolts.
14. Raise the vehicle, support it safely and install the upper bolt.
15. Torque the mounting bolts to 26 ft. lbs. (37 Nm) and the bracket bolt to 22 ft. lbs. (30 Nm).
16. Reconnect the electrical connectors and install the nuts. Be careful not to overtighten the nuts and crack the solenoid end cap. Tighten the starter positive terminal to 89 inch lbs. (10 Nm) and the solenoid terminal to 44 inch lbs. (5 Nm).
17. Install the shield and push pin, being careful that the pin is positioned for possible future removal.
18. Lower the vehicle and if removed, install the intake manifold support bracket.
19. Install the air intake tube and

fresh air hose. For the DOHC engine, verify the resonator button is properly located in the service bracket.

20. Connect the negative battery cable.

EMISSION CONTROLS

Due to the complex nature of modern electronic engine control systems, comprehensive diagnosis and testing procedures fall outside the confines of this repair manual. For complete information on diagnosis, testing and repair procedures concerning all modern engine and emission control systems, please refer to "Chilton's Guide to Fuel Injection and Electronic Engine Controls".

Emission Warning Lamps

The Service Engine Soon light serves multiple functions. It informs a driver that the PCM has detected a problem and the vehicle should be taken in for service as soon as reasonably possible. It displays trouble codes stored by the PCM and it indicates if the engine is in OPEN LOOP or CLOSED LOOP operation.

The light will come ON with the key ON and engine not running. When the engine is started, the light will turn OFF. If the light stays ON, the self-diagnostic system has detected a problem. In most cases, should a fault disappear during operation, the light will turn OFF approximately 10 seconds after the fault disappears. A code will be stored in memory even if the light extinguishes.

When a fault has been detected by the PCM a code will set in 2 places, general information and malfunction history. Both memories can be cleared with the use of the Saturn PDT or an equivalent scan tool. If no scan tool is available, general information can be cleared if the A and B terminals are of the ALDL are grounded 3 times in 5 seconds with the ignition ON.

General information will also clear if the problem is absent for 50 ignition ON/OFF cycles or if the battery supply to the PCM is interrupted. Malfunction history can only be cleared with aid of a scan tool.

FUEL SYSTEM

Fuel System Service Precaution

Safety is the most important factor when performing any type of maintenance, but even more so when working on the fuel system. Failure to conduct maintenance and repairs in a safe manner may result in serious personal injury or death. Maintenance and testing of the vehicle's fuel system components can be accomplished safely and effectively by adhering to the following rules and guidelines.

• To avoid the possibility of fire and personal injury, always disconnect the negative battery cable unless the repair or test procedure requires that battery voltage be applied.

• Always relieve the fuel system pressure prior to disconnecting any fuel system component (injector, fuel rail, pressure regulator, etc.), fitting or fuel line connection. Exercise extreme caution whenever relieving fuel system pressure to avoid exposing skin, face and eyes to fuel spray. Under pressure, fuel may penetrate the skin or any part of the body that it contacts.

• Always place a shop towel or cloth around the fitting or connection prior to loosening to absorb any excess fuel due to spillage. Ensure that all fuel spillage (should it occur) is quickly removed from engine surfaces. Ensure that all fuel soaked cloths or towels are deposited into a suitable waste container.

• Always keep a dry chemical (Class B) fire extinguisher near the work area.

• Do not allow fuel spray or fuel vapors to come into contact with a spark or open flame.

• Always use a backup wrench when loosening and tightening fuel line connection fittings. This will prevent unnecessary stress and torsion to fuel line piping. Always follow the proper torque specifications.

• Always replace worn fuel fitting O-rings with new. Do not substitute fuel hose or equivalent where fuel pipe is installed.

RELIEVING FUEL SYSTEM PRESSURE

1. Unless battery voltage is needed for testing, disconnect the negative battery cable.
2. Remove the air cleaner or air intake duct, as applicable.
3. Wrap a shop rag around the fuel test port fitting, remove the cap and connect the pressure gauge tool SA9127E or equivalent.
4. Install the bleed hose into an approved container and open the valve to bleed the system pressure.
5. After the system pressure is bled, remove the gauge from the pressure test port and recap it.
6. Install the air cleaner or intake duct, unless the procedure requires its removal.
7. After repairs are completed, connect the negative battery cable and prime the fuel system as follows:

   a. Turn the ignition **ON** for 5 seconds and then **OFF** for 10 seconds.

   b. Repeat the ON/OFF cycle 2 more times.

   c. Crank the engine until it starts.

   d. If it does not start, repeat Steps a–c.

   e. Run the engine and check for leaks.

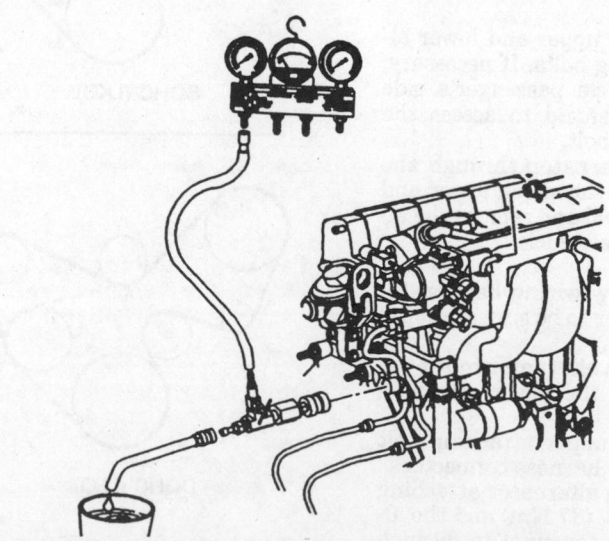

Relieving fuel system pressure—DOHC engine shown, SOHC engine similar

Fuel Tank

REMOVAL & INSTALLATION

—————— CAUTION ——————

Whenever the fuel tank requires removal, the fuel level should not be more than ¾ full. If the tank is more than ¾ full, use extreme care when removing the hoses.

1. Disconnect the negative battery cable.
2. Properly relieve fuel system pressure.
3. Remove the fuel cap, then raise the rear of the vehicle approximately 28 inches to allow the fuel in the tank to flow away from the filler neck. Be sure to support the vehicle safely.
4. Clean the area surrounding the filler neck to avoid fuel system contamination, then position an appropriate container with a minimum 12 inch (300mm) in diameter opening under the filler neck to catch fluid. Loosen the filler neck tube clamp at the rear of the tank, wrap a shop towel around the neck tube and slowly remove the tube from the fuel tank.
5. Use the large round end of a ½ in. socket extension which is approximately 18 inches in length to push the filler neck check ball into the tank.
6. Drain the tank into an approved container using a suitable pump or siphon.
7. Remove the filler neck bracket fastener at the left side of the frame rail and loosen the fuel vent hose retaining clamp.

NOTE: It is easier to remove hoses from the tank than to pull them from the steel vent and fill tubes.

8. Disconnect the fuel pressure and return line quick connects by pinching the 2 plastic tangs together. Grasp both ends of 1 fuel line connection and twist ¼ turn in each direction while pulling them apart. Disconnect the fuel vent hose by holding the line and by pushing on the rubber connector with a small open end wrench.
9. With the aid of an assistant, remove the 2 support strap fasteners at the rear of the tank.
10. Lower the tank and support panel approximately 8 inches to disconnect the electrical connector from the top of the tank. Remove the tank from the vehicle.

To install:
11. Clean the area surrounding the fuel pump and spray the lockring tangs with penetrating oil to loosen the fitting. Remove the fuel pump assembly by turning the lockring counterclockwise using tool SA9156E or equivalent.

12. Remove the filler neck check ball from inside the tank and inspect for cracks or holes. Reinstall or replace the check ball, as applicable. The check ball must be installed from the inside of the tank by reaching through the fuel pump opening. Install the fuel pump.
13. With the aid of an assistant, raise the tank into position and connect the electrical connectors.
14. The filler neck and fuel tank must be properly aligned during installation. Install the tank support and the 2 retaining straps, then tighten the nuts to 35 ft. lbs. (47 Nm).

NOTE: The fuel line steel clamps are specially designed to prevent hoses damage and must be replaced with original equipment parts.

15. Align the fuel fill neck and tank. Attach the fill line and tighten the clamp to 18 inch lbs. (2 Nm). Install the fill tube and bracket bolt, then tighten the bolt to 53 inch lbs. (6 Nm).
16. Insert the vent line into the rubber boot until the white marks on the tube align with the side of the boot. Tighten the vent hose clamp at the tank to 18 inch lbs. (2 Nm).
17. Apply a few drops of clean engine oil to the male ends of the fuel pressure and return lines. Push the connectors together until the retaining tabs snap into place, then pull on opposite ends of each connection to verify that the connection is secure.
18. Lower the vehicle, add fuel and tighten the fuel filler cap.
19. Connect the negative battery cable and prime the fuel system.
20. Run the engine and check for leaks.

Fuel Filter

REMOVAL & INSTALLATION

1. Disconnect the negative battery cable.
2. Remove the air intake duct or air cleaner, as applicable.
3. Properly relieve the fuel system pressure.
4. Disconnect the large underhood fuel line connection located near the intake manifold support brace on the left side of the vehicle using the tool supplied with the replacement filter, SA9157E or equivalent. It may be necessary to clean the female end of the quick connect fittings by spraying them with penetrating oil prior to disconnection.
5. Raise and support the vehicle safely.
6. Disengage the quick connect at the fuel filter inlet by pinching the 2

plastic tangs together and pulling on the supply line.
7. Loosen the fuel filter band clamp nut, but do not completely remove.
8. Carefully push or pull the filter out of the assembly and discard the filter in an appropriate container.

To install:
9. If the band clamp was removed, clip the fuel return and vapor lines in place and install 2 new band clamp nuts. Make sure all lines are in place and will not interfere with or be damaged by filter installation and tighten the bracket nuts to 27 inch lbs. (3 Nm).
10. Clean the female end of the filter inlet quick connect fitting by holding the line facing downward and spraying penetrating oil up into the fitting. Be careful not to bend of kink the line.
11. If not already installed, insert a new snap lock retainer into the female end of the filter inlet quick connect fitting.
12. Route the filter's nylon outlet line through the band clamp and insert the filter fan enough into the band clamp to connect the outlet line to the engine fuel line attachment. Lubricate the male end of the connector with clean engine oil, snap the connector together and pull on the line to verify proper fitting.
13. Position the filter in the band clamp assembly with the filter's upper edge located ¼ inch (6.35mm) from the top of the band clamp.
14. Lubricate the male end of the fuel supply line with clean engine oil. Snap the line to the fuel filter and pull back to verify the fitting is secure. Tighten the band clamp nut to 89 inch lbs. (10 Nm).
15. Lower the vehicle and install the air cleaner or intake duct, as applicable.
16. Connect the negative battery cable and prime the fuel system.
17. Run the engine and check for leaks.

Electric Fuel Pump

PRESSURE TESTING

1. Remove the air intake duct.
2. Connect a fuel gauge SA9127E or equivalent, to the fuel pressure test port below the throttle body.
3. Close the gauge shut off valve and start the engine.
4. The fuel pressure should read as follows:
   a. SOHC at idle and 3000 rpm— 26–31 psi.
   b. DOHC at idle—31–36 psi.
   c. DOHC key ON engine OFF— 38–44 psi.
   d. DOHC at idle with the vacuum

line disconnected from the pressure regulator—6–10 psi variation.

5. Replace the pressure regulator if the pressure reading does not change when the vacuum line is disconnected.

6. Remove the pressure gauge and reconnect the pressure line, if applicable.

7. Install the air intake duct, start the engine and check for leaks.

REMOVAL & INSTALLATION

The fuel pump module is located in the fuel tank. The tank must be removed to access the pump/sender assembly.

1. Disconnect the negative battery cable and properly relieve fuel system pressure.

2. Drain the tank into a suitable container and remove the tank from the vehicle.

3. Clean the area surrounding the fuel pump module and spray the cam lockring tangs with a suitable penetrating oil to loosen the fitting.

4. Using a fuel module lockring removing tool SA9156E or equivalent, and a ½ inch breaker bar of approximately 18 inches in length, remove the fuel pump lockring.

5. Carefully lift the fuel module from the tank at a 45 degree angle to prevent float arm damage. Discard the large module O-ring.

6. The sending unit is the only portion of the module which may be serviced. The filter may be cleaned with mineral spirits but must be replaced as an assembly with the module. If necessary, remove the sending unit from the module as follows:

   a. Remove the 2 electrical connectors with needle-nose pliers or by pressing down the locking tab and pulling the connectors from the terminals.

   b. Use a small suitable tool to push in on the sender assembly attaching tang, lift up and remove the sender.

To install:

7. If removed, install the sending unit to the fuel module as follows:

   a. Position the sending unit tang in the locator slot and snap into place.

   b. Install the 2 electrical connectors.

   c. Gently pull on the connectors without pressing the tab to verify the connector is secure.

8. Inspect the fuel tank for debris or metal chips. If necessary, remove all contaminants and replace the fuel filter.

9. Install the fuel tank check ball from inside the tank by reaching through the tank module opening.

10. Clean any debris from the O-ring mating surface and position a new O-ring onto the tank.

11. Carefully install the fuel module at a 45 degree angle to prevent damaging the sending unit and float arm. The filter and float arm must face toward the front of the tank and the module tabs must align with the tank slots.

12. Install the cam lockring using the service tool.

13. Install the fuel tank assembly.

14. Lower the vehicle, connect the negative battery cable and fill the fuel tank.

15. Prime the fuel system, start the engine and check for leaks.

Fuel Injection

IDLE SPEED ADJUSTMENT

NOTE: The minimum idle speed adjustment is preset at the factory and requires no periodic adjustments. Adjustments should be performed ONLY when the throttle body has been replaced and/or proper idle speed can not be obtained. The engine should be at normal operating temperature, the A/C and cooling fans should be OFF when making adjustments.

1. Before making any adjustments, clean the throttle body bore with a shop towel and carburetor cleaner that does not contain methyl ethyl keytone. Then check the idle speed to be sure adjustment is necessary. Proper idle speeds are as follows:

   a. SOHC with manual or automatic transaxle in N—700–800 rpm.

   b. SOHC with automatic transaxle in D—600–700 rpm.

   c. SOHC with automatic transaxle in D and A/C ON—725–825 rpm.

   d. DOHC with manual transaxle in N—800–900 rpm.

   e. DOHC with automatic transaxle in D—700–800 rpm.

2. If adjustment is necessary, block the wheels and apply the parking brake.

3. Connect the IAC tester SA9195E or equivalent, to the IAC valve at the throttle body.

4. Remove the idle stop screw plug by piercing it with an awl and applying leverage for SOHC engines. On DOHC engines, remove the idle stop screw cover.

5. Insert the IAC air plug in the throttle body; use SA9196E for TBI or SA9106E for MFI or equivalent.

6. Connect the Saturn Portable Diagnostic Tool (PDT) or equivalent to the Assembly Line Diagnostic Link (ALDL), start the engine and check the minimum idle speed. Minimun idle speed should be 450–650 rpm for all engines.

7. If not within specification adjust the idle screw to obtain an minimum idle speed of 500–600 rpm.

8. Turn the ignition OFF and reconnect the IAC electrical connector.

9. Using the Saturn PDT or equivalent scan tool, check the TPS voltage. Do not replace the TPS unless setting is not between 0.35–0.70 volts.

10. Remove the IAC air plug and install the idle stop plug or cover.

11. Start the engine and check for proper idle operation.

12. Shut the engine OFF and remove the PDT or scan tool.

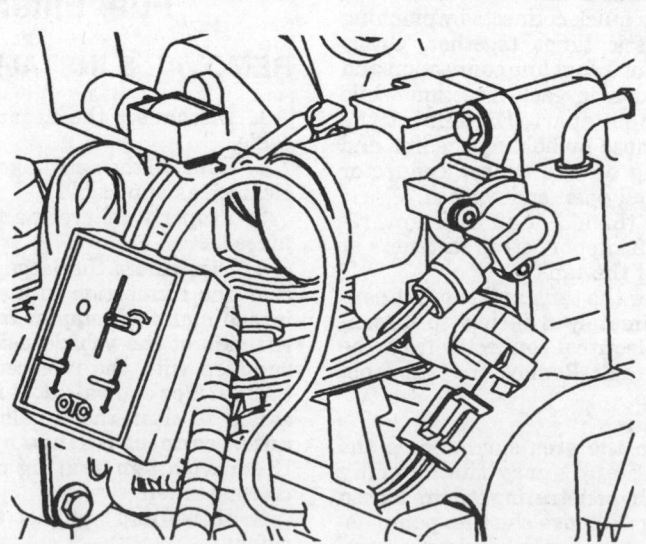

Connecting the IAC connector to the throttle body

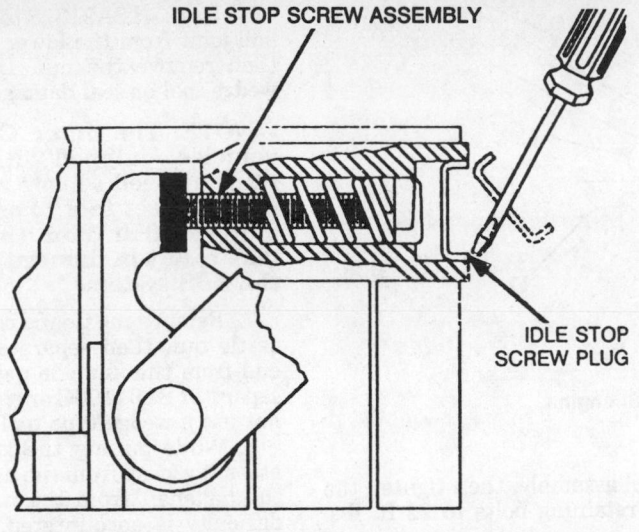

IDLE STOP SCREW ASSEMBLY

IDLE STOP SCREW PLUG

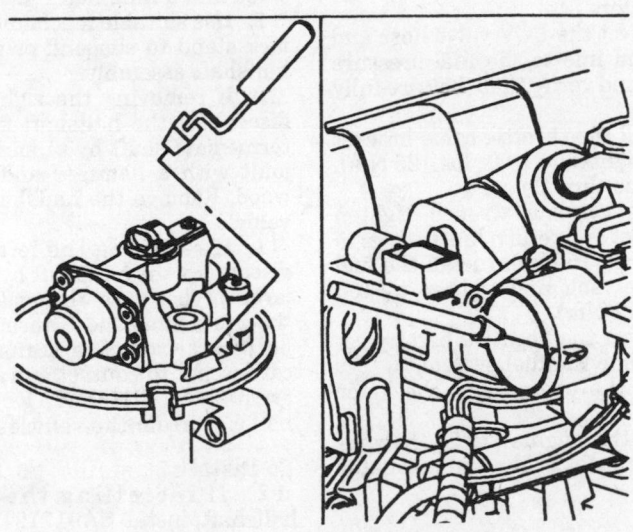

Removing idle screw plug and covering the IAC air plug

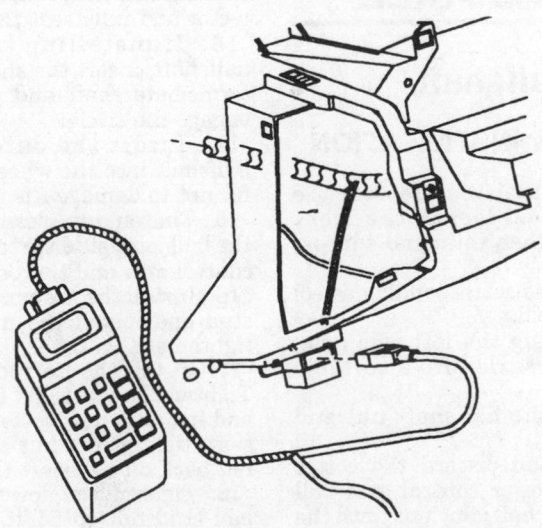

Connecting the Saturn diagnostic unit

IDLE MIXTURE ADJUSTMENT

The idle mixture is controlled by the Powertrain Control Module (PCM) and is not adjustable.

Fuel Injector

REMOVAL & INSTALLATION

Throttle Body Injection (TBI)

1. Disconnect the negative battery cable.
2. Remove the air cleaner assembly.
3. Properly relieve fuel system pressure.
4. Disconnect the injector electrical connector.
5. Remove the injector retaining screw and bracket.
6. Using a fulcrum and prybar, carefully pry the injector out of the throttle body. Make sure the electrical connector and injector nozzle are protected from damage.

To install:

7. Remove the upper and lower O-rings and inspect the injector for dirt or contamination. The injector may be cleaned using safety glasses and compressed air, but the screen may not be removed from the injector. If injector replacement is necessary, be sure to use an identical part.
8. Install new O-rings and lubricate with clean engine oil. Be sure the upper O-ring is in the groove on the injector and the lower ring is properly installed in the fuel meter body cavity.
9. Install the injector, pushing it straight into the injector cavity with the electrical connector facing toward the fuel pressure regulator.
10. Install the retaining bracket. Coat the screw with Loctite® 242 or equivalent, then install and tighten the screw to 35 inch lbs. (3 Nm).
11. Reconnect the injector connector and the negative battery cable.
12. Prime the fuel system, start the engine and check for leaks.
13. Shut the engine **OFF** and install the air cleaner assembly.

Multi-Port Fuel Injection (MFI)

1. Disconnect the negative battery cable.
2. Remove the air intake tube with resonator and fresh air tube.
3. Properly relieve fuel system pressure.
4. Remove the fuel line bracket bolt and disconnect the fuel pressure and return lines. Be sure to use a $^{15}/_{16}$ inch (24mm) backup wrench to prevent inlet port or bracket damage. If necessary, remove the fuel line bolts and rotate the rail slightly for wrench access.

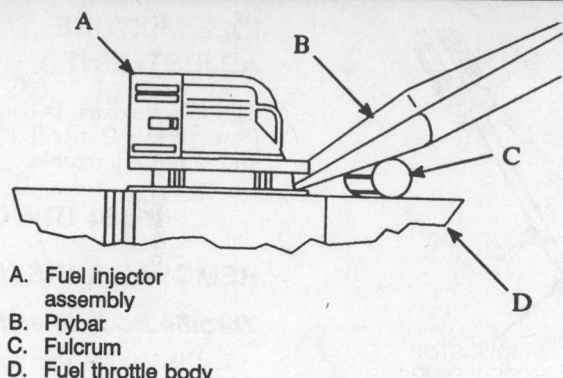

A. Fuel injector
   assembly
B. Prybar
C. Fulcrum
D. Fuel throttle body

Removing the fuel injector—TBI engine

Remove the old O-rings from the lines with a suitable tool and discard.

5. Disconnect the pressure regulator vacuum hose.

6. Remove the throttle cable bracket bolts and disconnect the cable from the throttle lever. Lay the cable over the intake manifold.

7. Disconnect the fuel injector electrical connectors and remove the fuel rail retaining bolts.

8. Remove the fuel rail assembly by carefully pulling the rail back and upward to pull the injectors from the manifold ports. Be careful not to damage the injector spray tips and electrical connectors. Rotate the rail so the injectors point downward, then lift the rail end opposite of the fuel connections to remove the rail from between the camshaft cover and intake manifold.

9. Make sure the rails and injectors are clean and free of dirt. If injector removal is required, slide the injector retaining clip off the injector and pull the injector from the fuel rail. Remove the old injector O-rings with a suitable seal removal tool or brass seal pick and discard.

To install:

10. If removed, lubricate the new injector O-rings with engine oil and install with the injector assembly into the fuel rail. Install the retaining clip.

11. Lubricate the new fuel inlet and return line O-rings, then install the O-rings into the fuel outlet of the pressure regulator and inlet of the fuel rail.

12. With the pressure regulator end first and the injectors pointing downward, guide the fuel rail assembly through the passage between the camshaft cover and the intake manifold from the power steering pump side of the engine. Align the injectors with their respective port holes and carefully push the injectors into the holes.

13. Verify the injectors have properly seated on the intake manifold. Loosely connect the fuel inlet and return lines to the rail assembly, then tighten the fuel rail retaining bolts to 22 ft. lbs. (30 Nm).

14. Connect the fuel injector electrical connectors.

15. Connect the PCV valve hose and the vacuum line to the fuel pressure regulator and verify that they are fully seated.

16. Install the throttle cable bracket bolts and tighten to 19 ft. lbs. (25 Nm). Connect the throttle cable.

17. Using a backup wrench, tighten the fuel inlet and return line fittings to 133 inch lbs. (15 Nm). Install the fuel line bracket bolt and tighten to 106 inch lbs. (12 Nm).

19. Connect the negative battery cable and prime the fuel system.

20. Start the engine and check for leaks.

21. Shut the engine **OFF**, then install the air intake tube and resonator assembly.

DRIVE AXLE

Halfshaft

REMOVAL & INSTALLATION

1. Have an assistant depress the brake pedal and loosen the front halfshaft nut, then raise and support the vehicle safely.

2. Remove the corresponding wheel and splash shield.

3. If removing the left side axle, drain the transaxle into a suitable container.

4. Remove the halfshaft nut and washer.

5. Remove and discard the cotter pin from the lower control arm ball joints. Back the ball joint nut until the top of the nut is even with the top of the threads.

6. Use tool SA9132S to separate the ball joint from the lower control arm, then remove the nut. Do not use a wedge tool or seal damage may occur.

NOTE: The outer CV-joint for vehicles equipped with ABS contains a speed sensor ring. Use of an incorrect tool to separate the control arm from the knuckle may result in damage and loss of the ABS system.

7. Remove the tie rod cotter pin and castle nut, then separate the tie rod end from the knuckle using a tie rod separator SA91100C or equivalent. Do not use a wedge-type tool.

8. While pulling the knuckle/strut assembly away from the halfshaft, pull the halfshaft from the wheel hub. If difficulty is encountered, tap on the end of the halfshaft using a block of wood and a hammer.

9. Use suitable mechanic's wire or a jack stand to suspend or support the halfshaft assembly.

10. If removing the right halfshaft, disconnect the halfshaft from the intermediate shaft by tapping the inner joint with a hammer and a block of wood. Remove the halfshaft from the vehicle.

11. If removing the left halfshaft, disconnect the halfshaft by inserting a large prybar into the space between the inner joint and transaxle. Pry the halfshaft from the transaxle being careful not to contact and damage the transaxle oil seal. Remove the halfshaft from the vehicle.

To install:

12. If installing the left side halfshaft, install SA91112T or equivalent transaxle seal protector. Install the halfshaft into the transaxle, after the splines have safely passed the transaxle oil seal, remove the seal protector and fully seat the halfshaft.

13. If installing the right side halfshaft, insert the shaft onto the intermediate shaft and push firmly to engage the circlip.

14. Insert the outer end of the halfshaft into the wheel hub. Be careful not to damage the CV-joint boot.

15. Thoroughly clean and lubricate the ball joint stud threads of the lower control arm and tie rod end.

16. Install the lower control arm ball stud and install the nut, but do not tighten at this time.

17. Install the tie rod end and nut. Tighten the nut to 33 ft. lbs. (45 Nm) and install a new cotter pin. If necessary, tighten the nut additionally, do not back off to insert the cotter pin.

18. Tighten the lower control arm ball stud nut to 55 ft. lbs. (75 Nm), tighten additionally if necessary and install a new cotter pin.

19. Install the washer and a new halfshaft nut, then tighten the nut to 145 ft. lbs. (200 Nm).
20. Install the inner splash shield and wheel.
21. Lower the vehicle and properly fill the transaxle.
22. Check and adjust the alignment as necessary.

Front Wheel Hub, Knuckle/Spindle and Bearings

REMOVAL & INSTALLATION

1. If equipped with ABS, disconnect the negative battery cable.
2. Have an assistant depress the brake pedal and loosen the front halfshaft nut, then raise and support the vehicle safely.
3. Remove the wheel assembly.
4. Remove the brake caliper mounting bracket bolts and suspend the assembly from the strut spring with wire.
5. Loosen the strut-to-knuckle bolts, but do not remove at this time.
6. Remove the rotor, axle nut and washer.
7. Remove and discard the cotter pin from the lower control arm ball joints. Back the ball joint nut until the top of the nut is even with the top of the threads.
8. Use tool SA9132S to separate the ball joint from the lower control arm, then remove the nut. Do not use a wedge tool or seal damage may occur.

NOTE: The outer CV-joint for vehicles equipped with ABS contains a speed sensor ring. Use of an incorrect tool to separate the control arm from the knuckle may result in damage and loss of the ABS system.

9. Remove the tie rod cotter pin and castle nut, then separate the tie rod end from the knuckle using a tie rod separator SA91100C or equivalent. Do not use a wedge-type tool.
10. If equipped, disconnect the ABS wheel speed sensor electrical connector.
11. Suspend the halfshaft from the body with wire, then remove the knuckle/hub fasteners and remove the knuckle/hub assembly from the vehicle. If necessary, position a block of wood on the end of the halfshaft and tap on the wood with a hammer to free the hub assembly.
12. If necessary, disassemble the knuckle hub assembly as follows:
    a. For 1991 vehicles, remove the 3 dust shield fasteners and separate the shield from the assembly.

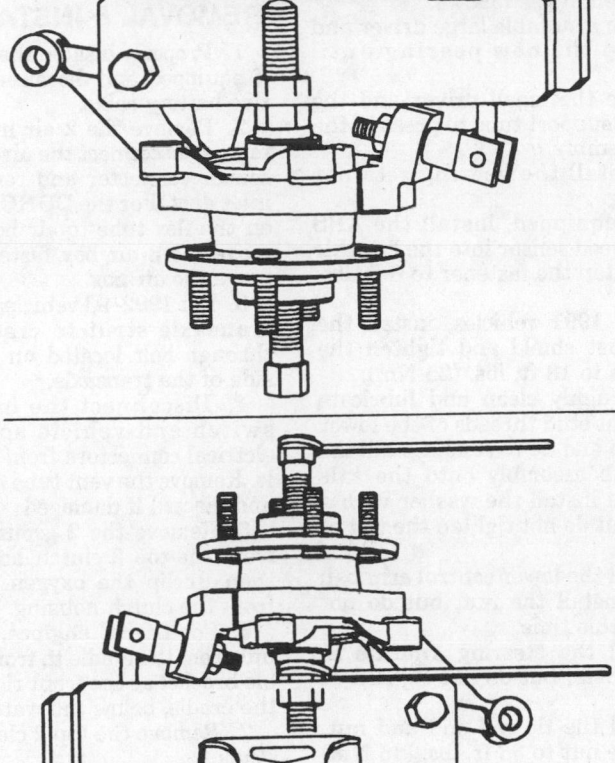

Front wheel bearing and seal removal

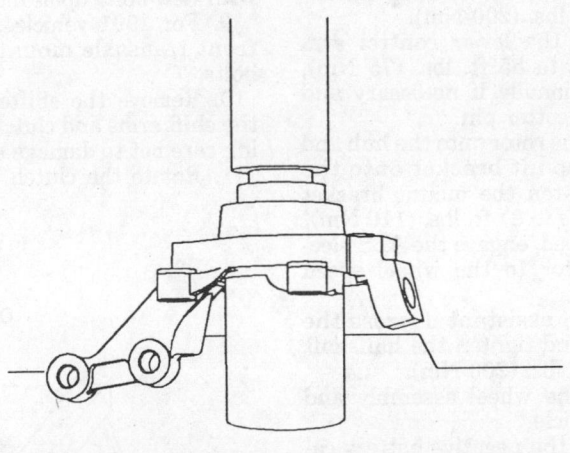

Pressing the wheel bearing from the knuckle.

b. If equipped, remove the ABS wheel speed sensor from the knuckle.
c. Install wheel bearing removing tools SA9159S or equivalent, to the knuckle and secure the assembly in a vise.
d. Hold the hub driver with a wrench and tighten the hub driver screw to remove the hub. If the in-

ner bearing race is pulled out with the hub, remove the race with a bearing race remover.
e. Remove the assembly from the vice and remove the wheel hub removal tools.
f. Position the knuckle in a shop press on a knuckle support tube and press the bearing from the knuckle with a suitable small driver.

To install:

13. If necessary, assemble the knuckle hub assembly as follows:

    a. Use a suitable large driver and press in the new bearing until seated.

    b. Use the small driver and the knuckle support tube to press in the hub assembly.

    c. Install the bearing retainer snapring.

    d. If equipped, install the ABS wheel speed sensor into the knuckle and tighten the fastener to 6 ft. lbs. (8 Nm).

    e. For 1991 vehicles, install the brake dust shield and tighten the fasteners to 18 ft. lbs. (25 Nm).

14. Thoroughly clean and lubricate the ball joint stud threads of the lower control arm and tie rod end. Install the knuckle/hub assembly onto the axle shaft. Then install the washer with a new nut, but do not tighten the nut at this time.

15. Install the lower control arm ball stud and install the nut, but do not tighten at this time.

16. Install the steering knuckle to strut fasteners, but do not tighten at this time.

17. Install the tie rod end and nut. Tighten the nut to 33 ft. lbs. (45 Nm) and install a new cotter pin. If necessary, tighten the nut additionally, do not back off to insert the cotter pin.

18. Push inward on the bottom of the strut and tighten the knuckle fasteners to 148 ft. lbs. (200 Nm).

19. Tighten the lower control arm ball stud nut to 55 ft. lbs. (75 Nm), tighten additionally if necessary and install a new cotter pin.

20. Install the rotor onto the hub and the calper mount bracket onto the knuckle. Tighten the mount bracket assembly bolts to 81 ft. lbs. (110 Nm).

21. If equipped, engage the ABS electrical connector to the wheel speed sensor.

22. Have an assistant depress the brake pedal and tighten the halfshaft nut to 148 ft. lbs. (200 Nm).

23. Install the wheel assembly and lower the vehicle.

24. Connect the negative battery cable, check and adjust the alignment, as necessary.

MANUAL TRANSAXLE

For further information on transmission/transaxles, please refer to "Chilton's Guide to Transmission Repair".

Transaxle Assembly

REMOVAL & INSTALLATION

1. Properly disable the SIR system, if equipped and disconnect the negative battery cable.

2. Remove the 2 air inlet duct fasteners, disconnect the air temperature sensor connector and remove the air inlet duct. For the DOHC engine, loosen the flex tube to air box clamp, remove the 3 air box fasteners and remove the air box.

3. For 1992–93 vehicles, remove the transaxle strut to cradle bracket through bolt located on the radiator side of the transaxle.

4. Disconnect the backup light switch and vehicle speed sensor elctrical connectors from the transaxle. Remove the vent tube retaining clip and discard if damaged.

5. Remove the 2 ground terminals from the top 2 clutch housing studs, then unclip the oxygen sensor wire from the clutch housing.

6. For DOHC engines, remove the nut from the cradle to front engine cable bracket at the front right corner of the cradle, below the water pump.

7. Remove the top 2 clutch housing studs.

8. Remove the 4 DIS coil to clutch housing bolts, then wire the coil to the cylinder head coolant outlet. Discard the old coil retaining bolts and replace with new bolts upon installation.

9. For 1991 vehicles, loosen the 2 front transaxle mount to transaxle bolts.

10. Remove the shifter cables from the shift arms and clutch housing taking care not to damage the cable boot.

11. Rotate the clutch slave cylinder ¼ turn counterclockwise while pushing into the clutch housing, then remove the cylinder from the housing. Remove the 2 clutch hydraulic damper to clutch housing bolts, then wire the hydraulic assembly to the battery tray.

12. Wire the radiator to the upper radiator support to hold the assembly in place when the cradle is removed.

13. Install SA9105E or an equivalent engine support bar assembly.

14. Raise and support the vehicle safely, then remove the drain plug from the lower center of the housing and drain the transaxle fluid.

15. Remove the front wheels and engine splash shields from the vehicle. For coupes, remove the left and right lower facia braces.

16. For 1992–93 vehicles, remove the front engine strut cradle bracket to cradle nuts from below the cradle.

17. Remove the transaxle mount to cradle nut from under the cradle.

18. Remove the front exhaust pipe nuts at the manifold, then disconnect the pipe from the support bracket.

19. Remove the front pipe to catalytic converter bolts and lower the pipe from the vehicle.

20. Remove the engine to transaxle stiffening bracket bolts and remove the bracket. For 1991 vehicles, remove the rear transxle mount bracket to transaxle bolt, then loosen the mount bolt and allow the bracket to hang out of the way.

21. Remove the clutch housing dust cover. Remove the steering rack to cradle bolts and wire the gear for support when cradle is removed. Remove the brake line and retainer from the cradle.

22. Remove and discard the cotter pin from the lower ball joints. Back the

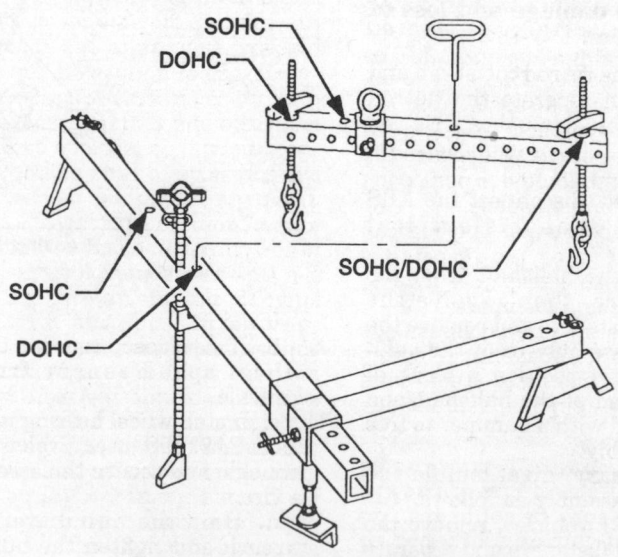

Engine support bar assembly SA9105E.

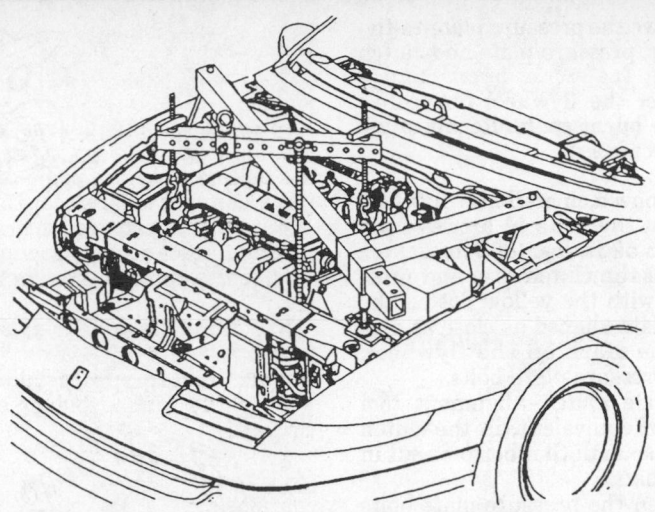

Position the support brackets on the shock towers and the threaded stabilizer on the block. Connect the bar hooks to the engine bracket.

ball joint nut until the top of the nut is even with the top of the threads.

23. Use tool SA9132S to separate the ball joint from the lower control arm, then remove the nut. Do not use a wedge tool or seal damage may occur.

NOTE: The outer CV-joint for vehicles equipped with ABS contains a speed sensor ring. Use of an incorrect tool to separate the control arm from the knuckle may result in damage and loss of the ABS system.

24. For 1991 vehicles, remove the front transaxle mount to cradle nuts and the engine lower mount to cradle nuts. Nuts are all located under the front or side cradle members.

25. Position two 4 inch × 4 inch × 36 inch pieces of wood onto a powertrain support dolley and position the dolley under the vehicle.

26. Remove the 4 cradle to body bolts and carefully lower the cradle from the vehicle with the support dolley. Tape or wire the 2 large washers from the rear cradle to body attachments in position to prevent loss.

27. Support the transaxle securely with a suitable jack.

28. Use an appropriate prybar to separate the left side axle from the transaxle. Remove the axle sufficiently to install SA91112T or an equivalent seal proctector around the axle and into the seal to prevent the seal from being cut by the shaft spline.

29. Remove the 2 bottom clutch housing to engine bolts and install a guide bolt into the bottom rear clutch housing bolt hole from the side of the engine block.

30. Carefully separate the transaxle from the engine enough to clear the in-termediate shaft and lower the transaxle from the vehicle.

To install:

31. Place the transaxle assembly securely onto the jack and position under the vehicle.

32. Install axle seal protectors into seals on both sides, then place the transaxle in any gear.

33. Raise the transaxle into the vehicle guiding the unit onto the intermediate shaft. While guiding the transaxle onto the shaft, rotate the shaft back and forth to align the splines. When aligned, continue to rotate the intermediate shaft until the input shaft splines are aligned with the clutch.

34. Verify that the intermediate shaft splines line up with the differential side gear spline, then install the 2 lower clutch housing to engine bolts and tighten to 96 ft. lbs. (130 Nm). The bolts should not be used to draw the transaxle to the engine.

35. Install the left side axle into the transaxle and remove the seal protectors. Lower the transaxle jack.

36. Clean and lubricate the ball joint threads, then raise the cradle up on the support dolley and place the ball joints into the knuckles.

37. Verify the correct positioning of the lower control arm bar studs to knuckle, the cooling module support bushings, the engine strut bracket and the transaxle mount.

38. Insert $9/16$ inch round steel rods into the cradle to body alignment holes near the front cradle to body fastener holes. Guide the cradle into position making sure all mount studs are properly guided into their holes.

39. Make sure the washers are in place and install the 2 rear cradle to body bolts. Verify proper cradle posi-tioning and install the 2 front cradle bolts. Tighten the 4 cradle bolts to 151 ft. lbs. (205 Nm).

40. Remove the support dolley and lower the vehicle sufficiently for underhood access. Remove the engine support bar assembly.

41. For 1992–93 vehicles, install the transaxle strut to cradle bracket through bolt and nut, then tighten the fasteners to 52 ft. lbs. (70 Nm).

42. Remove the radiator assembly support wire.

43. Use a 6 × 1.0mm tap to clean the sealant from the ignition module mounting holes in the transaxle. In-stall the ignition module and the new bolts with sealant. Use extreme cau-tion to assure proper bolt installation. Tighten the bolts to 61 inch lbs. (7 Nm) and verify that the bolt heads are properly seated on the ignition module.

44. Install the 2 top clutch housing to engine studs and tighten to 74 ft. lbs. (100 Nm). Connect the 2 ground ter-minals to the studs and tighten to 18 ft. lbs. (25 Nm).

45. Connect the vehicle speed sensor and backup light switch electrical con-nectors to the transaxle.

46. Install the vent hose clip and the oxygen sensor wire clip to the housings.

47. Connect the shift control cables to the shift arms and the clutch hous-ing, then install the cable retainers.

48. Remove the support wire from the battery tray, position the damper, then install the 2 slave damper to clutch housing nuts and tighten to 18 ft. lbs. (25 Nm). Push the actuator into the clutch housing and rotate ¼ turn clockwise, then install the retaining clip. Check that the master cylinder at front of dash connection is locked in place.

49. For 1991 vehicles, check and properly align the engine mounts.

50. For DOHC vehicles, install the air box and tighten the fasteners to 89 inch lbs. (10 Nm). Connect the flex tube to the air box, align the arrows and tighten the clamp.

51. Install the air inlet duct and fas-teners, then connect the air tempera-ture sensor electrical connector.

52. Raise and support the vehicle safely.

53. For 1992–93 vehicles, install the transaxle mount to cradle nut and the 2 engine strut cradle bracket to cradle nuts from under the cradle, then tight-en the nuts to 52 ft. lbs. (70 Nm).

54. For 1991 vehicles, tighten the front transaxle mount to transaxle bolts and install the front transaxle mount cradle nuts. Tighten the fasten-ers to 35 ft. lbs. (48 Nm). Then install the right side mount to cradle nuts and tighten to 40 ft. lbs. (54 Nm).

55. Remove the steering gear support wire and position the gear to the cradle. Install the gear bolts and nuts, then tighten the fasteners to 40 ft. lbs. (54 Nm). Connect the brake line and retainer to the cradle.

56. Install the clutch housing dust cover and tighten the fasteners to 89 inch lbs. (10 Nm).

57. For 1991 vehicles, install the rear pitch restrictor to transaxle bolts and tighten to 40 ft. lbs. (55 Nm). Then install the powertrain stiffening bracket and tighten the bracket to powertrain bolts to 35 ft. lbs. (47 Nm).

58. Position the exhaust manifold front pipe into the vehicle and install the manifold retaining nuts. Tighten the nuts in a crosswise pattern to 23 ft. lbs. (31 Nm). Install the front pipe to the catalytic converter and tighten the bolts to 33 ft. lbs. (45 Nm). Finally, install the front pipe to the transaxle support bracket and tighten the fasteners to 23 ft. lbs. (31 Nm).

NOTE: If the converter flange threads are damaged use the Saturn 21010753 converter fastener kit in place of the self tapping screws to provide proper clamp load and prevent exhaust leaks.

59. Install the nuts onto the ball joint studs and tighten to 55 ft. lbs. (75 Nm). Continue to tighten the nuts as necessary and install new cotter pins.

60. Install the center and both wheel splash shields.

61. For coupes, install the right left lower facia braces, J-nuts and fasteners. Tighten the fasteners to 89 inch lbs. (10 Nm).

62. Install the tire and wheel assemblies, then lower the vehicle.

63. Connect the negative battery cable and fill the transaxle with Dexron® IIE (preferred), Dexron® II or equivalent fluid.

64. Properly enable the SIR system, if equipped.

65. Check the vehicle alignment and adjust as necessary.

CLUTCH

Clutch Assembly

REMOVAL & INSTALLATION

1. Properly disable the SIR system, if equipped, and disconnect the negative battery cable.

2. Remove the transaxle from the vehicle.

3. Unsnapping the release fork from the ball stud, then remove the fork and bearing from the vehicle. Slide the bearing from the fork.

4. Remove the pressure plate-to-flywheel bolts, pressure plate and clutch disc.

5. Inspect the flywheel for scores, warpage or burnt spots. Repair or replace as necessary.
To install:

6. If removed, install the flywheel and tighten the bolts in a criss-cross sequence to 59 ft. lbs. (80 Nm).

7. Install the clutch disc and pressure plate with the yellow dot on the pressure plate aligned as close as possible to the mark on the flywheel. Start the pressure plate bolts.

8. Install a clutch alignment tool SA9145T or equivalent, in the clutch disc and push in until it bottoms out in the crankshaft.

9. Tighten the pressure plate bolts using multiple passes of a criss-cross sequence to 18 ft. lbs. (25 Nm) and remove the alignment tool.

10. Lube the fork pivot point with high temperature grease and install the release bearing to the fork. Do not lube the release bearing or bearing quill.

11. Snap the release bearing and fork onto the ball stud.

12. Lube the splines of the input shaft lightly with a high temperature grease.

13. Install the transaxle assembly.

14. Connect the negative battery cable and if equipped, properly enable the SIR system.

PEDAL HEIGHT/FREE PLAY ADJUSTMENT

The clutch release system is adjusted automatically. No adjustment is necessary or possible.

Clutch Master and Slave Cylinder Assembly

REMOVAL & INSTALLATION

NOTE: The master cylinder, pipes and slave cylinder are a complete assembly and must be replaced as a signle unit.

1. Block the clutch pedal to prevent it from being depressed while the slave cylinder is remove from the transaxle.

2. Remove the air intake duct.

3. Rotate the slave cylinder about ¼ turn counterclockwise while pushing toward the bellhousing in order to disengage the connector and remove the cylinder from the clutch housing. Remove the slave cylinder bracket retaining nuts and pull the assembly from the studs.

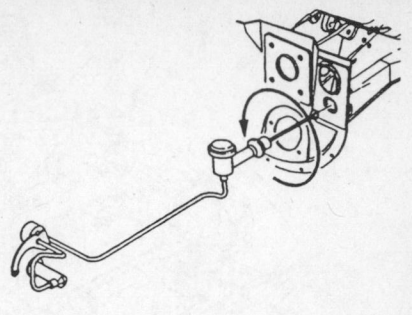

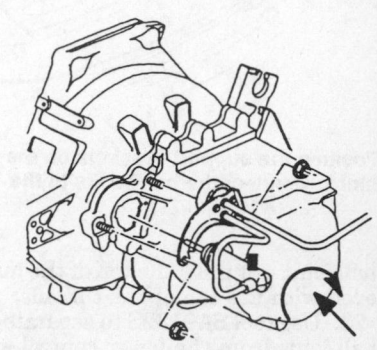

Clutch release system installation, removal is in opposite direction

4. Remove the master cylinder pushrod retaining clip and disconnect the pushrod from the pedal.

5. Turn the clutch cylinder about ⅛ turn clockwise and remove from the instrument panel.
To install:

6. Position the master cylinder to the dash with the reservoir leaning toward the driver's fender. Install and turn about ⅛ turn counterclockwise to lock in position.

7. Slide the slave cylinder onto the clutch housing studs, install the nuts and tighten to 18 ft. lbs. (25 Nm).

NOTE: When installing a new assembly, the plastic retainer straps should remain in place on the slave cylinder to ensure the actuator rod seats on the release fork pocket upon installation.
If reinstalling an assembly, be sure to position a new plastic retainer strap onto the end of the pushrod and attach the straps to the cylinder.

8. Insert the slave cylinder into the housing with the bleeder screw facing forward and rotate about ¼ turn clockwise while pushing into the housing.

9. Lube the clutch pedal pin with silicone grease, then connect the pushrod to the clutch pedal and install the retaining clip.

10. Install the air inlet duct assembly

and connect the negative battery cable.

11. Remove the block from behind the clutch pedal and if equipped, properly enable the SIR system.

12. Start the engine and check the pedal for proper operation.

Hydraulic Clutch System Bleeding

The clutch hydraulic assembly is serviced as a complete unit which has been filled with fluid and bled of air at the factory. The unit does not require periodic checking. The system is full when the reservoir is half full.

Only DOT 3 brake fluid should be added to the system. If fluid levels drop, inspect the system, including the slave cylinder, for leakage. A slight wetting of the slave cylinder surface is normal. Should an assembly have air in the system and not require replacement, bleed the assembly as follows:

1. Fill the clutch master cylinder reservoir with brake fluid. Be careful not to spill brake fluid on the painted surface of the vehicle.

2. Fit a vinyl bleeder tube over the bleeder screw at the front of the slave cylinder and place the other end in a clean jar half filled with brake fluid.

3. Have an assistant depress the clutch pedal several times. Loosen the bleeder screw and allow the fluid to flow into the jar.

4. Tighten the screw and have the assistant release the clutch pedal.

5. Repeat bleeding procedure until no air bubbles are present in the fluid. Make sure the master cylinder is kept full during the procedure.

NOTE: If the master cylinder is run dry during the bleeding procedure, the entire system must be re-bled.

6. Refill the master cylinder to the specified level.

AUTOMATIC TRANSAXLE

For further information on transmission/transaxles, please refer to "Chilton's Guide to Transmission Repair".

Transaxle Assembly

REMOVAL & INSTALLATION

1. Properly disable the SIR system, if equipped and disconnect the negative battery cable.

2. Remove the 2 air inlet duct fasteners, disconnect the air temperature sensor connector and remove the air inlet duct. For the DOHC engine, loosen the flex tube to air box clamp, remove the 3 air box fasteners and remove the air box.

3. For 1992–93 vehicles, remove the transaxle strut to cradle bracket through bolt located on the radiator side of the transaxle.

4. Disconnect the vehicle and turbine speed sensor, transaxle temperature sensor, selector switch and actuator connectors from the transaxle.

5. Remove the 2 ground terminals from the top 2 converter housing studs.

6. Remove the ground wire from the neutral (selector) switch and unclip the oxygen sensor wire retainer from the converter housing.

7. Remove the top 2 converter housing studs.

8. Remove the 4 DIS coil to converter housing bolts, then wire the coil to the cylinder head coolant outlet. Discard the old coil retaining bolts and replace with new bolts upon installation.

9. For 1991 vehicles, loosen the 2 front transaxle mount to transaxle fasteners.

10. Wire the radiator to the upper radiator support to hold the assembly in place when the cradle is removed.

11. Install SA9105E or an equivalent engine support bar assembly.

12. Raise and support the vehicle safely.

13. Remove the drain plug from the transaxle housing and drain the transaxle fluid. The drain plug is on the lower cowl side of the housing and is inserted from the engine side of the vehicle.

14. Remove the front wheels and engine splash shields from the vehicle. For coupes, remove the left and right lower facia braces.

15. For 1992–93 vehicles, remove the front engine strut cradle bracket to cradle nuts from below the cradle.

16. Remove the transaxle mount to cradle nut from under the cradle.

17. Remove and discard the cotter pin from the lower ball joints. Back the ball joint nut until the top of the nut is even with the top of the threads.

18. Use tool SA9132S to separate the ball joint from the lower control arm, then remove the nut. Do not use a wedge tool or seal damage may occur.

NOTE: The outer CV-joint for

vehicles equipped with ABS contains a speed sensor ring. Use of an incorrect tool to separate the control arm from the knuckle may result in damage and loss of the ABS system.

19. Remove the front exhaust pipe nuts at the manifold, then disconnect the pipe from the support bracket.

20. Remove the front pipe to catalytic converter bolts and lower the pipe from the vehicle.

21. Remove the engine to transaxle stiffening bracket bolts and remove the bracket. For 1991 vehicles, remove the rear transaxle mount bracket to transaxle bolts, then loosen the mount bolt and allow the bracket to hang out of the way.

22. Remove the steering rack to cradle bolts and wire the gear for support when the cradle is removed. Remove the brake line and retainer from the cradle.

23. Remove the clutch housing dust cover, then remove the torque converter to flywheel bolts.

24. For 1991 vehicles, remove the front transaxle mount to cradle nuts and the engine lower mount to cradle nuts. Nuts are all located under the front or side cradle members.

25. Position two 4 inch × 4 inch × 36 inch pieces of wood onto a powertrain support dolly and position the dolly under the vehicle.

26. Remove the 4 cradle to body bolts and carefully lower the cradle from the vehicle with the support dolly. Tape or wire the 2 large washers from the rear cradle to body attachments in position to prevent loss.

27. Squeeze the plastic tabs at the transaxle cooler line connectors and pull the lines out of the connectors. The plastic retainer should remain on the lines. Connect 1 end of a $\frac{3}{8}$ inch rubber hose over each cooler line to prevent fluid contamination or loss.

28. If necessary for the transaxle to clear the body, lower the vehicle enough to adjust the engine support assembly and lower the transaxle side of the assembly until the valve body cover clears the frame.

29. Raise and support the vehicle safely, then support the transaxle securely with a suitable jack.

30. Use an appropriate pry bar to separate the left side axle from the transaxle. Remove the axle sufficiently to install SA91112T or an equivalent seal proctector around the axle and into the seal to prevent the seal from being cut by the shaft spline.

31. Remove the 2 bottom converter housing to engine bolts and lower the transaxle sufficiently to reach the shifter cable.

32. Disconnect the transaxle shifter

cable and remove the cable from the converter housing.

33. Carefully lower the transaxle from the vehicle. Use SA9165T or an equivalent transaxle cooler cleaning tool to clean the cooler and lines.

To install:

34. Place the transaxle assembly securely onto the jack and position under the vehicle. Install axle seal protectors into seals on both sides.

35. Raise the transaxle sufficiently and connect the shifter cable to the gear selector lever and to the converter housing.

36. Raise the transaxle into the vehicle and verify that the intermediate shaft splines line up with the differential side gear spline, then install the 2 lower clutch housing to engine bolts and tighten to 96 ft. lbs. (130 Nm). The bolts should not be used to draw the transaxle to the engine.

37. Install the axle into the transaxle. After the splines clear the seal, but before the axle snaps into place remove the seal protectors. Push the axle all of the way into the transaxle and install the snapring. Remove the transaxle jack.

38. Clean and lubricate the ball joint threads, then raise the cradle up on the support dolley and place the ball joints into the knuckles. Verify the correct positioning of the lower control arm bar studs to knuckle, the cooling module support bushings, the engine strut bracket and the transaxle mount.

39. Insert $^9/_{16}$ inch round steel rods into the cradle to body alignment holes near the front cradle to body fastener holes. Guide the cradle into position making sure all mount studs are properly guided into their holes.

40. Make sure the washers are in place and install the 2 rear cradle to body bolts. Verify proper cradle positioning and install the 2 front cradle bolts. Tighten the 4 cradle bolts to 151 ft. lbs. (205 Nm).

41. Remove the support dolley and lower the vehicle sufficiently for underhood access. Remove the engine support bar assembly.

42. For 1992–93 vehicles, install the transaxle strut to cradle bracket through bolt and nut, then tighten the fasteners to 52 ft. lbs. (70 Nm).

43. Remove the radiator assembly support wire.

44. Use a 6 × 1.0mm tap to clean the sealant from the ignition module mounting holes in the transaxle. Install the ignition module, then secure using the new bolts with sealant. Use extreme caution to assure proper bolt installation. Tighten the bolts to 61 inch lbs. (7 Nm) and verify that the bolt heads are properly seated on the ignition module.

45. For 1991 vehicles, install the front transaxle mount to transaxle fasteners and tighten to 35 ft. lbs. (48 Nm).

46. Install the 2 top converter housing to engine studs and tighten to 74 ft. lbs. (100 Nm). Connect the 2 ground terminals to the studs and tighten to 18 ft. lbs. (25 Nm).

47. Connect the actuator circuit connector and tighten to 35 inch lbs. (4 Nm). Connect the vehicle and turbine speed sensors and tighten to 124 inch lbs. (14 Nm). Connect the transaxle oil temperature sensor and the selector switch connectors.

48. Connect the ground wire to the neutral (selector) switch and clip the oxygen sensor wire to the converter housing.

49. Unplug the transaxle cooler lines and press them into the transaxle connectors until they bottom out.

50. Adjust the shifter cable, then for DOHC vehicles, install the air box and tighten the fasteners to 89 inch lbs. (10 Nm). Connect the flex tube to the air box, align the arrows and tighten the clamp.

51. Install the air inlet duct and fasteners, then connect the air temperature sensor electrical connector.

52. Raise and support the vehicle safely.

53. For 1992–93 vehicles, install the transaxle mount to cradle nut and the 2 engine strut cradle bracket to cradle nuts from under the cradle, then tighten the nuts to 52 ft. lbs. (70 Nm).

54. For 1991 vehicles, install the front transaxle mount cradle nuts and tighten the nuts to 35 ft. lbs. (48 Nm). Then install the right side mount to cradle nuts and tighten to 40 ft. lbs. (54 Nm).

55. Remove the steering gear support wire and position the gear to the cradle. Install the gear bolts and nuts, then tighten the fasteners to 40 ft. lbs. (54 Nm). Connect the brake line and retainer to the cradle.

56. Install the torque converter to flexplate bolts and tighten to 52 ft. lbs. (70 Nm). Install the converter housing dust cover and tighten the bolts to 89 inch lbs. (10 Nm).

57. For 1991 vehicles, install the rear pitch restrictor to transaxle bolts and tighten to 40 ft. lbs. (55 Nm). Then install the powertrain stiffening bracket and tighten the bracket to powertrain bolts to 35 ft. lbs. (47 Nm).

58. Position the exhaust manifold front pipe into the vehicle and install the manifold retaining nuts. Tighten the nuts in a crosswise pattern to 23 ft. lbs. (31 Nm). Install the front pipe to the catalytic converter and tighten the bolts to 33 ft. lbs. (45 Nm). Finally, install the front pipe to the transaxle support bracket and tighten the fasteners to 23 ft. lbs. (31 Nm).

NOTE: If the converter flange threads are damaged use the Saturn 21010753 converter fastener kit in place of the self tapping screws to provide proper clamp load and prevent exhaust leaks.

59. Install the nuts onto the ball joint studs and tighten to 55 ft. lbs. (75 Nm). Continue to tighten the nuts as necessary and install new cotter pins.

60. Install the center and both wheel splash shields.

61. For coupes, install the right left lower facia braces, J-nuts and fasteners. Tighten the fasteners to 89 inch lbs. (10 Nm).

62. Install the tire and wheel assemblies, then lower the vehicle.

63. Connect the negative battery cable and fill the transaxle with Dexron® II or equivalent fluid.

64. Properly enable the SIR system, if equipped.

65. Warm the engine and check the transaxle fluid. Check and adjust vehicle alignment, as necessary.

FRONT SUSPENSION

MacPherson Strut

REMOVAL & INSTALLATION

—— **CAUTION** ——

The MacPherson strut is under extreme spring pressure. Do not remove the strut shaft center support nut at the top without using an approved spring compressor. Personal injury may result if this caution is not followed.

1. If equipped wtih ABS, disconnect the negative battery cable, then raise and support the vehicle safely.

2. Remove the front wheel.

3. If equipped, disconnect the ABS wiring from the strut wring bracket. If the strut is being replaced, drill the rivet head retaining the ABS wiring bracket to the strut and remove the bracket.

4. Loosen the 2 steering knuckle-to-strut housing bolts, but do not remove them at this time.

5. Lower the vehicle sufficiently and remove the 3 upper strut-to-body nuts.

6. Place a rag over the CV-joint seal to protect it from damage, then remove the 2 steering knuckle-to-strut housing bolts.

7. Remove the strut assembly from the vehicle.

To install:

8. Position the strut and install 3 new upper mount nuts. Tighten the nuts to 21 ft. lbs. (29 Nm).

9. Install the knuckle bolts with new nuts. Push the bottom of the strut inward while tightening the fasteners to 148 ft. lbs. (200 Nm).

10. If the strut was replaced, install the ABS wiring bracket to the strut using a new rivet. Connect the ABS wiring to the bracket.

11. Install the wheel assembly and lower the vehicle.

12. Connect the negative battery cable, check and adjust the alignment as necessary.

Lower Ball Joints

INSPECTION

There should be no axial movement in the lower ball joint. The ball joint is an integral part of the lower control arm and can not be serviced separately.

Lower Control Arms

REMOVAL & INSTALLATION

1. Raise and support the vehicle safely. Remove the wheel and splash shield.

2. Remove and discard the cotter pin from the lower control arm ball joints. Back the ball joint nut until the top of the nut is even with the top of the threads.

3. Use tool SA9132S to separate the ball joint from the lower control arm, then remove the nut. Do not use a wedge tool or seal damage may occur.

NOTE: The outer CV-joint for vehicles equipped with ABS contains a speed sensor ring. Use of an incorrect tool to separate the control arm from the knuckle may result in damage and loss of the ABS system.

4. Remove the control arm-to-cradle bolt, then remove the sway bar-to-control arm nut and remove the control arm from the vehicle.

To install:

5. Position the control arm and install the arm onto the sway bar without the fastener, then place the end of the arm into the cradle. Install the cradle nut and bolt. Tighten the cradle bolt to 92 ft. lbs. (125 Nm), then tighten the cradle nut to 74 ft. lbs. (100 Nm).

6. Install the sway bar nut and tighten to 106 ft. lbs. (144 Nm).

7. Thoroughly clean and lubricate the ball joint stud threads, then install the lower control arm ball stud into the steering knuckle. Install the nut and tighten the lower control arm ball stud nut to 55 ft. lbs. (75 Nm), tighten additionally if necessary and install a new cotter pin.

8. Install the splash shield and the wheel assembly.

9. Lower the vehicle, check and adjust the alignment as necessary.

REAR SUSPENSION

MacPherson Strut

REMOVAL & INSTALLATION

—— CAUTION ——
The MacPherson strut is under extreme spring pressure. Do not remove the strut shaft support nut at the top center of the assembly without using an approved spring compressor. Personal injury may result if this caution is not followed.

1. On coupes, remove the rear seat cushion bottom, left or right rocker panel interior moldings and left or right rear sail interior panels.

2. On sedans, remove the left or right C-pillar interior moulding.

3. Fold down the rear seat backs and remove the rear seat side bolsters from the vehicle.

4. On coupes, remove the rear deck package shelf screws attaching the shelf to the side of the cargo area.

5. Remove the speaker grill speaker grills and fasteners from the shelf, then remove the seatbelt bezel and separate the seat belts from the shelf. Remove the rear package shelf carpeting.

6. If equipped with ABS, disconnect the negative battery cable.

7. Raise and support the vehicle safely, then remove the appropriate rear wheel.

8. If equipped, disconnect the ABS wiring from the strut wiring bracket. If the strut is being replaced, drill the rivet head retaining the ABS wiring bracket to the strut and remove the bracket.

9. Loosen the 2 strut to knuckle bolts; but do not remove at this time.

10. Lower the vehicle sufficiently and place a floor jack under the rear knuckle, then raise the jack enough to support the knuckle.

11. Remove the 3 upper strut-to-body nuts.

12. Slowly raise the hoist, lowering the strut from the body.

13. Remove the strut to knuckle bolts and remove the strut assembly from the vehicle.

To install:

14. Install 3 new strut to upper mount nuts and tighten the nuts to 21 ft. lbs. (29 Nm).

15. Install the knuckle bolts with new nuts, then push the bottom of the strut inward and tighten the fasteners to 148 ft. lbs. (200 Nm).

16. If the strut was replaced, install the ABS wiring bracket to the strut using a new rivet. Connect the ABS wiring to the bracket.

17. Install the wheel assembly and lower the vehicle.

18. Install the interior components.

19. Connect the negative battery cable, check and adjust the rear alignment as necessary.

Rear Control Arms

REMOVAL & INSTALLATION

Lateral Links

If the front lateral link is to be replaced, remove the fuel tank.

1. Raise and support the vehicle safely, then remove the rear wheel(s).

2. If removing the front lateral link, remove the fuel tank.

3. Remove the lateral links-to-knuckle bolt, then remove the crossmember bolt(s).

4. Remove the link or links from the vehicle.

To install:

5. Install the link(s) into the crossmember with the fastener(s), but do not tighten at this time.

6. Install the link(s) to the knuckle with the knuckle-to-links bolt, but do not tighten at this time.

7. Tighten the crossmember bolts as applicable. Tighten the front link bolt to 126 ft. lbs. (170 Nm) and/or the rear link bolt to 89 ft. lbs. (120 Nm). Then tighten the knuckle bolt to 122 ft. lbs. (165 Nm).

8. If the front lateral link was removed, install the fuel tank.

9. Install the rear wheel(s) and lower the vehicle, then check and adjust the rear alignment as necessary.

Trailing Arm

1. Raise and support the vehicle safely, then remove the rear wheels.

2. Remove the trailing arm-to-knuckle nut, then remove the trailing arm body bolts.

3. Slide the trailing arm from the knuckle.

To install:

4. Install the trailing arm into the knuckle and torque the nut to 106 ft. lbs. (144 Nm).

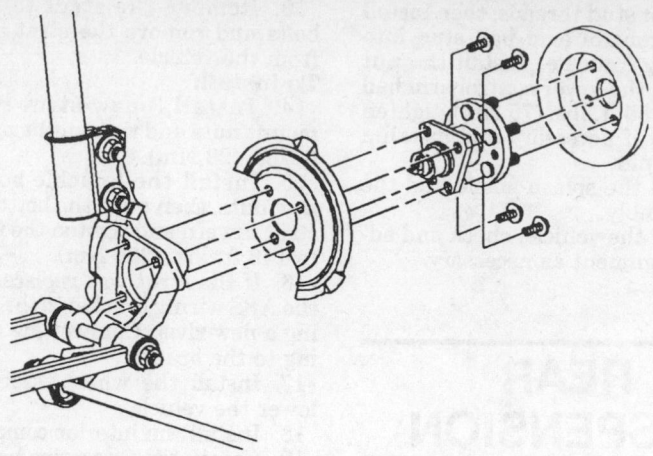

Rear wheel hub/bearing assembly—vehicles with rear disc. Rear drum vehicles similar

5. Position the arm to the body, install and tighten the body bolts to 89 ft. lbs. (120 Nm).

6. Install the rear wheels and lower the vehicle, check and adjust the rear alignment, as necessary.

Rear Wheel Hub/ Bearing Assembly

REMOVAL & INSTALLATION

1. If equipped with ABS, disconnect the negative battery cable. Raise and support the vehicle safely, then remove the rear wheel.

2. Disconnect the ABS speed sensor connector, if equipped.

3. On disc brake equipped models, remove and support the caliper with a wire from the strut. Remove the rotor.

4. On drum brake equipped models, remove the brake drum.

5. Remove the 4 hub/bearing-to-knuckle bolts and remove the assembly from the vehicle.

To install:

6. Install the brake backing plate, hub/bearing assembly and retaining bolts. Tighten the bolts to 63 ft. lbs. (85 Nm).

7. Install the brake drum or rotor and caliper. If applicable, tighten the caliper retaining bolts to 63 ft. lbs. (85 Nm).

8. Connect the ABS speed sensor connector, if equipped.

9. Install the wheel assembly and lower the vehicle. If applicable, connect the negative battery cable.

ADJUSTMENT

The rear hub/bearing assembly is a sealed assembly, requiring no periodic maintenance. No adjustments are necessary or possible.

Rear Knuckle Assembly

REMOVAL & INSTALLATION

1. Raise and support the vehicle safely.

2. Remove the hub/bearing assembly.

3. If equipped with rear drum brakes, suspend the brake assembly clear of the knuckle.

4. Loosen the lateral link-to-knuckle bolts, but do not remove at this time.

5. Remove the trailing arm knuckle nut and body bolts.

6. Slide the trailing arm out of the knuckle.

7. Remove the lateral link and remove the strut-to-knuckle bolts, then remove the knuckle from the vehicle.

To install:

8. Place the knuckle in the strut and install the bolts, but do not tighten at this time.

9. Install the lateral links and trailing arm.

10. Tighten the trailing arm-to-body bolts to 89 ft. lbs. (120 Nm), trailing arm-to-knuckle nut to 106 ft. lbs. (144 Nm) and the lateral link-to-knuckle bolts to 122 ft. lbs. (165 Nm). Push inward on the bottom of the strut and tighten the strut-to-knuckle bolts to 148 ft. lbs. (200 Nm).

11. Install the hub/bearing assembly.

12. Lower the vehicle, then check and adjust the rear alignment as necessary.

STEERING

Steering Wheel

REMOVAL & INSTALLATION

Without Air Bag

1. Disconnect the negative battery cable.

2. Remove the horn pad by pulling on the edge of the pad firmly, disconnect the wires and remove the horn pad from the vehicle.

3. Remove the clip on the end of the steering column shaft and remove the retaining nut.

4. Note the position of the steering wheel locating notch for reassembly purposes.

5. Install a suitable steering wheel puller and remove the steering wheel from the steering column.

To install:

6. Route the wires through the wheel and position the steering wheel making sure to properly align the locating notch. If the locating notch is not properly positioned, any attempt to install the steering wheel will damage the wheel and column beyond repair.

7. Install a new steering wheel nut. Tighten the nut to 30 ft. lbs. (40 Nm) and install a new clip on the end of the column.

8. Connect the wires to the horn pad and press the pad firmly into position on the wheel.

9. Connect the negative battery cable.

With Air Bag

— **CAUTION** —

When the vehicle is equipped with a Supplemental Inflatable Restraint (SIR) system, follow the recommended disarming procedures before performing any work on or around the system. Failure to do so may result in possible deployment of the air bag and/or personal injury.

1. Properly disable the SIR system and disconnect the negative battery cable.

2. Loosen the fasteners from the back of the steering wheel and release the inflator module from the steering wheel. Disconnect any electrical connections and remove the inflator module from the steering wheel.

— **CAUTION** —

When carrying a live inflator module, ensure the bag and trim cover are pointed away from the body. Never carry the inflator module by the wires or connector on the underside of the module. This will mini-

mize the chance of injury should the module accidentally deploy.

When placing a live inflator module on a bench or other surface, always place the bag and trim cover up, away from the surface. This is necessary so a free space is provided to allow for air bag expansion in the unlikely event of accidental deployment.

3. Remove the clip on the end of the steering column shaft and remove the retaining nut.

4. Note the position of the steering wheel locating notch for reassembly purposes.

5. Install a suitable steering wheel puller and remove the steering wheel from the steering column.

To install:

6. Route the SIR wire and connections through the wheel and position the steering wheel making sure to properly align the locating notch. If the locating notch is not properly positioned, any attempt to install the steering wheel will damage the wheel and column beyond repair.

7. Install a new steering wheel nut. Tighten the nut to 30 ft. lbs. (40 Nm) and install a new clip on the end of the column.

8. Position and connect the SIR electrical connection on the steering wheel and to the inflator module. Secure the module with the fasteners.

9. Connect the negative battery cable and properly enable the SIR system.

Manual Rack and Pinion

REMOVAL & INSTALLATION

1. Disconnect the negative battery cable, then raise and support the vehicle safely.

2. Remove the front tires and the left inner splash shield.

3. Remove and discard the tie rod cotter pins, then remove the castle nuts. Disconnect the tie rod ends using SA91100C or an equivalent separator tool. Do not use a wedge-type tool or seal damage may occur.

4. Loosen the intermediate shaft cover from the steering gear and move up enough to access the pinch bolt. Remove the pinch bolt.

5. Remove the steering gear fasteners and remove the gear through the left fenderwell.

To install:

6. Install the steering gear and torque the steering gear-to-cradle bolts to 52 ft. lbs. (70 Nm).

7. Position the intermediate steering shaft to the gear and tighten the pinch bolt to 35 ft. lbs. (47 Nm).

8. Thoroughly clean and lubricate the threads of the tie rod ends, then install the ends into the steering knuckles. Install the castle nuts and tighten to 33 ft. lbs. (45 Nm). Install new cotter pins. If necessary, tighten the nut additionally to install the pin, do not back off.

9. Install the left inner splash shield and install the front wheels.

10. Lower the vehicle and connect the negative battery cable.

11. Check alignment and adjust vehicle toe, as necessary.

ADJUSTMENT

Steering gear bearing preload adjustment is the same for both manual and power rack and pinion units.

Power Rack and Pinion

REMOVAL & INSTALLATION

1. Disconnect the negative battery cable, then raise and support the vehicle safely.

2. Remove both front tires and the left inner splash shield.

3. Remove and discard the tie rod cotter pins, then remove the castle nuts. Disconnect the tie rod ends using SA91100C or an equivalent separator tool. Do not use a wedge-type tool or seal damage may occur.

4. Loosen the intermediate shaft cover from the steering gear and move up enough to access the pinch bolt. Remove the pinch bolt.

5. For 1991 vehicles, disconnect the power steering pressure switch electrical connector at the steering gear.

6. Place a suitable container under the steering assembly. Disconnect the pressure and return lines at the steering gear and allow the system to drain.

7. Remove the steering gear fasteners and remove the gear through the left fenderwell.

To install:

8. Install the steering gear and tighten the steering gear-to-cradle bolts to 52 ft. lbs. (70 Nm).

9. Position the intermediate steering shaft to the gear and tighten the pinch bolt to 35 ft. lbs. (47 Nm).

10. Connect the pressure and return hoses, then tighten the fittings to 20 ft. lbs. (27.5 Nm).

11. For 1991 vehicles, connect the power steering pressure switch electrical connector.

12. Thoroughly clean and lubricate the threads of the tie rod ends, then install the ends into the steering knuckles. Install the castle nuts and tighten to 33 ft. lbs. (45 Nm). Install new cot-

ter pins. If necessary, tighten the nut additionally to install the pin, do not back off.

13. Install the left inner splash shield and install the front wheels.

14. Lower the vehicle and connect the negative battery cable.

15. Check alignment and adjust vehicle toe, as necessary.

16. Bleed the power steering system.

Power Steering Pump

REMOVAL & INSTALLATION

1. Disconnect the negative battery cable.

2. Remove the reservoir fill cap.

3. Raise and support the vehicle safely.

4. Place a suitable container under the power steering hoses, then remove the hoses from the steering gear and allow the system to drain.

NOTE: Once the hoses have been removed from the steering gear, do not rotate the steering wheel or additional fluid will be forced from the gear.

5. Lower the vehicle sufficiently for underhood access. Use a box end wrench to relieve the spring tension from the accessory drive belt tensioner and remove the belt from the steering pump pulley.

6. For DOHC engines, remove the pump-to-intake and pump-to-block fasteners and brackets.

7. Remove the 3 pump to block bolts and raise the pump far enough to disconnect the electrical connector from the pump.

8. Remove the pump, with the hoses connected, from the vehicle. If necessary, remove the pressure and return hoses from the pump.

To install:

9. If removed, replace the O-ring seals and install the pressure and return hoses. Tighten the fittings to 20 ft. lbs. (27.5 Nm).

10. Position the pump to the block and connect the electrical connector. Install the 3 retaining bolts and tighten the bolts to 28 ft. lbs. (38 Nm).

11. For DOHC engines, install the pump-to-intake and pump-to-block brackets and fasteners. Tighten the fasteners to 22 ft. lbs. (30 Nm).

12. Install the drive belt to the steering pump pulley.

13. Raise and support the vehicle safely. Connect the pressure and return hoses to the steering gear, then tighten the fittings to 20 ft. lbs. (27.5 Nm). Route the return hose, then the pressure hose into the retaining clip.

14. Lower the vehicle and fill the

power steering reservoir with clean fluid.

15. Connect the negative battery cable and bleed the power steering system.

BELT ADJUSTMENT

The belt is automatically adjusted by a self-tensioning device. Adjustment is not needed or possible.

SYSTEM BLEEDING

1. Raise and support the vehicle safely.
2. Fill the reservoir to the full mark.
3. Bleed the system by turning the wheels from side-to-side without hitting the stops. It may take several cycles to bleed the system.
4. Keep the reservoir to the full mark during the procedure.
5. Start the engine and check the fluid level with the engine idling. If necessary, add to bring the level to the full mark.
6. Road test the vehicle and check for proper operation. Recheck the fluid level and make sure it is at or slightly above the full mark after the system has stabilized at normal operating temperature.

Tie Rod Ends

REMOVAL & INSTALLATION

Outer

1. Raise and support the vehicle safely.
2. Remove the front wheel and if necessary, remove the splash shield.
3. Remove the cotter pin and nut from the tie rod end.
4. Separate the tie rod end from the knuckle with separator tool SA91100C or equivalent. Do not use a wedge-type tool or the seal may be damaged.
5. Mark the threaded portion of the steering arm for installation purposes.
6. Loosen the tie rod jam nut and thread the tie rod end off the steering shaft. Count the number of turns necessary to remove.
To install:
7. Clean the threads and grease before installation.
8. Install the tie rod end using the same number of turns as counted during removal. Align the tie rod end to the marked location.
9. Install the tie rod to the knuckle. Install the castle nut and tighten to 33 ft. lbs. (45 Nm) and install a new cotter pin. If necessary, tighten the nut additionally, do not back off to insert the cotter pin.
10. Tighten the tie rod jam nut to 74 ft. lbs. (100 Nm).

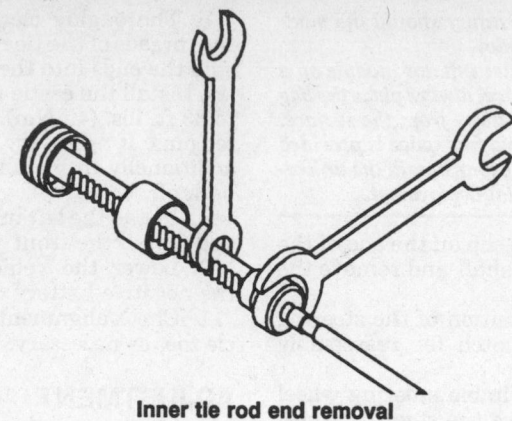

Inner tie rod end removal

11. Install the splash shield, if removed, then install the wheel assembly.
12. Lower the vehicle, check and adjust toe as necessary.

Inner

1. Remove the rack and pinion assembly from the vehicle.
2. Place the assembly in a holding fixture and loosen the outer tie rod jam nut.
3. Unthread the outer tie rod from the inner tie rod. Count the number of turns necessary or mark for realignment.
4. Remove the outer tie rod jam nut, then remove the steering gear boot.
5. Slide the shock damper toward the steering gear and off the inner tie rod.
6. Remove the inner tie rod assembly from the steering gear. To prevent damage, place a shop cloth over the gear teeth and hold the teeth with a suitable open end wrench. If removing the right inner tie rod, the left side boot must be removed to access the teeth.

To install:
7. Remove the old Loctite® from the rack and inner tie rod threads. Then, apply an even coat of Loctite® 262 to the inner tie rod threads.
8. Slide the shock damper onto the steering gear.
9. Properly hold the gear teeth and install the inner tie rod assembly onto the steering gear. Tighten the inner rod to 70 ft. lbs. (95 Nm).
10. Slide the shock damper up against the inner tie rod assembly and install the steering boot onto the gear.
11. Thread the outer tie rod jam nut onto the inner tie rod, then install the outer tie rod to the assembly. Use the same number or turns or align the marks made earlier and tighten the jam nut to 74 ft. lbs. (100 Nm).
12. Install the rack and pinion assembly to the vehicle.

13. Align the front end and bleed the power steering, as necessary.

BRAKES

Master Cylinder

REMOVAL & INSTALLATION

Without Anti-Lock Brakes

1. Disconnect the negative battery cable, then disconnect the fluid level connector at the reservoir.
2. Remove the hydraulic pipes from the master cylinder using a suitable wrench. Plug the pipes to prevent fluid contamination or loss.
3. Remove the 2 master cylinder retaining nuts and remove the master cylinder from the vehicle.
To install:
4. Install the master cylinder onto the brake booster studs, then install the retaining nuts and tighten to 20 ft. lbs. (27 Nm).
5. Connect the hydraulic brake pipe to the master cylinder and tighten the fittings to 18 ft. lbs. (24 Nm).
6. Properly bleed the hydraulic brake system.
7. Connect the brake fluid level electrical connector.
8. Connect the negative battery cable and start the engine. Have an assistant depress the brake pedal and check for leaks.

With Anti-Lock Brakes

The master cylinder for ABS equipped vehicles is attached to and removed with the ABS control assembly.

Brake Caliper

REMOVAL & INSTALLATION

Front

1. Raise and support the vehicle safely, then remove the front wheel.

2. Disconnect the brake hose from the caliper. Plug the openings to prevent fluid contamination or loss.

3. Remove the lock pin, guide pin.

4. Remove the caliper from the support, being careful not to damage the pin boots. If necessary, remove the pin boots from the caliper support.

To install:

5. Make sure the piston is bottomed in the bore.

6. If removed, install the brake pads to the caliper support.

7. Lubricate the pin boots and guide pins with silicone grease. If removed, install the pin boots into the caliper support and the caliper body.

8. Position the caliper, then lubricate the non-threaded portion of the guide and lock pins. Install the pins and tighten to 27 ft. lbs. (36 Nm).

9. Make sure the brake line is properly routed with loop to the rear, then install the brake hose with new washers. Tighten the fitting to 36 ft. lbs. (49 Nm).

10. Properly bleed the hydraulic brake system.

11. Install the wheel assembly and lower the vehicle.

Rear

1. Raise and support the vehicle safely, then remove the rear wheel.

2. Disconnect the brake hose from the caliper. Plug the openings to prevent fluid contamination or loss.

3. Slip the end of the parking cable off the parking brake lever, then remove the cable outer housing from the cable bracket with SA9151BR or an equivalent cable release tool.

4. Remove the lock pin and guide pin.

5. Remove the caliper from the support, being careful not to damage the pin boots. If necessary, remove the pin boots from the caliper support.

To install:

6. Make sure the piston is bottomed in the bore.

7. If removed, install the brake pads to the caliper support.

8. Lubricate the pin boots and guide pins with silicone grease. If removed, install the pin boots into the caliper support and the caliper body.

9. Position the caliper, then lubricate the non-threaded portion of the guide and lock pins. Install the pins and tighten to 27 ft. lbs. (36 Nm).

10. Install the brake hose with new washers, the tighten the fitting to 36 ft. lbs. (49 Nm).

11. Connect the parking brake cable.

12. Properly bleed the hydraulic brake system.

13. Install the wheel assembly and lower the vehicle.

Disc Brake Pads

REMOVAL & INSTALLATION

Front

NOTE: Always replace the brake pads in sets, both front or both rear axle assemblies.

1. Raise and support the vehicle safely and remove the front wheels.

2. Remove the lower caliper lock pin.

3. Pivot the caliper up on the guide pin, then remove the 2 brake pads and the the pad clips from the caliper support. Discard the old pad clips.

4. Check the caliper pins, pin boots and the piston boot for deterioration or damage.

To install:

5. Using a C-clamp, bottom the piston all the way into the caliper bore.

6. Carefully lift the inner edge of the piston boot to release any trapped air.

7. Install new pad clips into the caliper support.

8. Install the inner and outer brake pads into the support.

9. Pivot the caliper body on the upper guide pin into position.

10. Lubricate the lower lock pin with silicone grease, then install the pin and tighten to 27 ft. lbs. (36 Nm).

11. Repeat the procedure for the opposite side brake pads.

12. Install the front wheel assemblies and lower the vehicle.

13. Prior to operating the vehicle, depress the brake pedal a few times until the brake pads are seated against the rotor.

Rear

NOTE: Always replace the brake pads in sets, both front or both rear axle assemblies.

1. Raise and support the vehicle safely, then remove the rear wheels.

2. Remove the caliper guide pins.

3. Remove the caliper from the support, being careful not to damage the pin boots and suspend the caliper from a wire.

4. Remove the brake pads from the support.

To install:

5. Using SA9158BR or an equivalent piston driver tool, bottom the piston by rotating it clockwise into the caliper bore; do not use a C-clamp to press the piston into the bore.

6. Align the piston slots so the slots run horizontal to the mounting bracket.

7. Carefully lift the inner edge of the piston boot to release any trapped air.

8. Install new pad clips into the caliper support.

9. Install the inner and outer brake pads into the clips on the support. The pad with the wear sensor should be located outboard. The piston indentation slots should be positioned to correctly accept the brake pads.

10. Position the caliper body onto the support. Lubricate the non-threaded portion of the guide and lock pins, then install the pins and tighten to 27 ft. lbs. (36 Nm).

11. Check the position of the pad clips. If necessary, use a small suitable tool to re-seat or center the pad clips on the support. Repeat the procedure for the opposite side brake pads.

12. Install the rear wheel assemblies and lower the vehicle.

13. Prior to operating the vehicle, depress the brake pedal a few times until the brake pads are seated against the rotor.

Brake Rotor

REMOVAL & INSTALLATION

1. Raise and support the vehicle safely, then remove the wheel assembly.

2. Remove the brake caliper from the support bracket and hang it from the suspension with wire to prevent brake line damage.

3. Remove the 2 caliper support brackets mounting bolts.

4. Remove the rotor from the vehicle. If it is difficult to remove the rotor from the hub, insert two M8 × 1.25 self tapping bolts into the holes provided on the rotor and drive it from the hub.

To install:

5. Install the rotor and caliper support bracket. Tighten the bolts to 81 ft. lbs. (110 Nm) for front caliper brackets or to 63 ft. lbs. (85 Nm) for rear caliper brackets.

6. Unwire and install the caliper.

7. Install the wheel assembly and lower the vehicle.

Brake Drums

REMOVAL & INSTALLATION

1. Release the parking brake, then raise and support the vehicle safely.

2. Remove the rear wheel and remove the brake drum.

3. If necessary, turn the star wheel of the brake adjuster assembly to loosen the brake shoes and allow for drum removal.

Brake Shoes

REMOVAL & INSTALLATION

NOTE: Brake shoes must be replaced as axle sets.

1. Raise and support the vehicle, then remove the wheels and brake drums.
2. Remove the lower return and adjuster spring using a universal brake spring remover.
3. Remove the leading brake shoe hold-down cup, spring and pin.
4. Pull the leading shoe towards the front of the vehicle and remove the adjuster assembly and lever. It may be necessary to turn the adjuster star wheel to shorten its length.
5. Remove the leading shoe by twisting the shoe out of engagement with the upper return spring.
6. Remove the upper return spring from the park brake shoe. Remove the shoe hold-down cup, spring and pin. Push the park brake lever into the cable spring while disengaging the cable from the end lever and remove the parking brake shoe, lever and cable spring.
7. Remove the parking brake lever retainer and wave washer from the brake shoe.

To install:

8. Lubricate the adjuster assembly, the backing plate brake shoe raised contact pads, the brake lever pin and brake shoe webs with brake lubricant.
9. Install the park brake lever onto the pin on the brake shoe and secure with the wave washer and retainer clip. Crimp the ends of the retainer to secure the brake lever.
10. Install the cable spring into the cage on the park brake lever, then install the cable through the spring and onto the lever.
11. Install the brake shoes, hold-down pin, spring and cup. Use a universal spring cup remover/installer tool.
12. Install the long straight end of the upper return spring into the back hole in the park brake shoe, then install the other end of the spring into the back of the leading brake shoe.
13. Pull the lead shoe toward the front of the vehicle and install the adjuster between the park and leading brake shoes. Verify that the adjuster notches properly engage the brake shoe notches.
14. Install the adjuster lever and adjuster spring. Make sure the notch on the lever engages the pin on the park shoe and the notch on the adjusting socket. The lower leg of the lever should engage the teeth of the star wheel adjuster assembly.

15. Install the adjuster spring to the upper side of the brake shoes with the short end to the lead shoe and the long end to the park shoe. Then install the lower return spring into the lower holes of the shoes.
16. Verify the correct location of all brake components, if necessary, use the other side brake assembly for comparison.
17. Using a suitable drum clearance gauge, measure the inner diameter of the brake drum and adjust the outside diameter of the brake shoes to 0.02 inch (0.50mm) less than the inner diameter of the drum.
18. Repeat the procedure for the opposite brake shoes. If the wheel cylinders have been replaced, bleed the hydraulic brake system.
19. Install the brake drums and wheel assemblies.
20. Lower the vehicle and apply the brake pedal 20 times to allow the adjuster to properly position the brake shoes.
21. Check and adjust the parking brake cable, as necessary.

Brake System Bleeding

EXCEPT ANTI-LOCK BRAKES

Make sure the master cylinder contains clean DOT 3 brake fluid at all times during the procedure.

1. The master cylinder must be bled first if it is suspected to contain air. Bleed the master cylinder as follows:

a. Loosen the front brake line at the master cylinder and allow the fluid to flow from the front port.

b. Connect the line and tighten to 18 ft. lbs. (24 Nm).

c. Have an assistant depress the brake pedal slowly one time, loosen the front line and expel air from the master cylinder. Tighten the line and release the brake pedal. Repeat until all air is removed from the master cylinder.

d. Tighten the brake line to 18 ft. lbs. (24 Nm) when finished.

2. If a pipe or fitting was the only hydraulic line disconnected, then only the caliper(s) or wheel cylinder(s) affected by that line must be bled. If the master cylinder required bleeding, then all calipers and wheel cyliders must be bled in the proper sequence:

a. Right rear
b. Left front
c. Left rear
d. Right front

3. Bleed the individual calipers or wheel cylinders as follows:

a. Place a suitable wrench over

the bleeder screw and attach a clear plastic hose over the screw end.

b. Submerge the other end in a transparent container of brake fluid.

c. Loosen the bleed screw, then have an assistant apply the brake pedal slowly and hold. Tighten the bleed screw to 97 inch lbs. (11 Nm) and release the brake pedal. Repeat the sequence until all air is expelled from the caliper or cylinder.

d. Tighten the bleed screw to 97 inch lbs. (11 Nm) when finished.

4. Check the pedal for a hard feeling with the engine not running. If the pedal is soft, repeat the bleeding procedure until a firm pedal is obtained.

Anti-Lock Brake System Service

RELIEVING ANTI-LOCK BRAKE SYSTEM PRESSURE

Connect 1 end of a thin plastic tube to the bleeder screw on the ABS control unit and place the other end into a suitable container, then SLOWLY loosen the bleeder ½–¾ of a turn until the pressure is released.

Electronic Brake Control Module (EBCM)

REMOVAL & INSTALLATION

The EBCM is located under the instrument panel, to the left of the steering column. The module is outboard of the Powertrain Control Module (PCM) and closest to the left kick panel.

NOTE: If replacing the EBCM with a service replacement, the EE PROM of the new module must be programmed by the Saturn Service Stall or equivalent system.

1. Disconnect the negative battery cable.
2. Remove the CPA connector locking pin and disconnect the 2-way connector form the EBCM.
3. Disconnect the 32-way electrical connector from the EBCM.
4. Turn the module retaining screw ¼ turn and remove the module by pulling downward. Be careful not to snag the wiring.

To install:

5. Position the EBCM into the bracket, taking care not to snag the wiring.

6. Seat the retaining screw by pushing upward 2 clicks.

7. Connect the wiring and insert the CPA locking pin onto the 2-way connector.

8. If necessary, programm the EE PROM.

CHASSIS ELECTRICAL

Air Bag

DISARMING

1. Align the steering wheel so the vehicle wheels are pointing in the straight-ahead position.

2. Turn the ignition switch to the **OFF** position.

3. Remove the SIR fuse from the fuse block.

4. Remove the Connector Position Assurance (CPA) and disconnect the yellow 2-way SIR harness wire connector at the base of the steering column.

To enable system:

5. Verify that the ignition switch is in the **OFF** position.

6. Cconnect the yellow 2-way connector at the base of the steering column and install the CPA.

7. Install the SIR fuse.

8. Turn the ignition switch to the **RUN** position.

9. Verify the SIR indicator light flashes 7–9 times and then turns **OFF** to signify proper system operation. If light does not flash as specified, inspect system for malfunction.

Heater Blower Motor

REMOVAL & INSTALLATION

1. Disconnect the negative battery cable.

2. Disconnect the blower motor connectors under the glove compartment.

3. Remove the blower motor mounting screws and motor assembly.

4. Install the motor in the reverse order and check operation.

Windshield Wiper Motor

REMOVAL & INSTALLATION

1. Verify that the wipers are in the **PARK** position and disconnect the negative battery cable.

2. Remove the wiper arm finish cap and wiper arm fastening nut. Lift the blade away from the windshield and remove. Repeat for the other blade.

3. Remove the cowl trim panel fasteners at the windshield edge of the panel, open the hood and remove the remaining fasteners. Carefully remove the cowl trim panel.

4. Remove the instrument panel top cover screw caps and screws. Carefully remove the cover by lifting at the rear edge to disengage the retaining clips and sliding the panel out of the windshield clips.

5. Disconnect the defroster duct from the heating and air conditioning module and reposition it towards the glove box to expose the wiper module rear fasteners.

6. Remove the wiper module fasteners and reposition the module to disconnect the wiring from the motor and module frame. Carefully remove the wiper module and motor assembly making sure not to contact or damage the windshield.

7. Remove the crank arm nut and disconnect the arm from the motor shaft, then remove the wiper motor attaching screws and remove the motor from the module.

To install:

8. Verify that the motor is in the **PARK** position. If necessary, temporarily connect the motor wiring and the negative battery cable, turn the wiper control **ON** then **OFF** and the motor will move to the correct position.

9. Install the motor to the module. Position the motor crank arm to the 9 o'clock position and install the arm onto the motor shaft. Install a new retaining nut and tighten to 21 ft. lbs. (28 Nm).

10. Position the wiper module assembly into the vehicle and connect the wiring to the wiper motor and to the module frame.

11. Install the module retaining bolts and tighten to 89 inch lbs. (10 Nm).

12. Install the cowl trim panel.

13. Install the wiper arm assemblies using new nuts and tighten the nuts to 21 ft. lbs. (28 Nm).

14. Position the heating and air conditioning module and connect the defroster duct.

15. Install the instrument panel top cover and screws. Insert the panel cover screw caps.

16. Connect the negative battery cable and verify proper system operation.

Instrument Cluster Assembly

REMOVAL & INSTALLATION

1. Properly disable the SIR system, if equipped, and disconnect the negative battery cable.

2. Remove the 2 instrument panel top cover screw caps and screws. Carefully remove the cover by lifting at the rear edge to disengage the retaining clips and by sliding the panel out of the windshield clips.

3. Carefully remove the center radio finish panel and air outlet assembly by pulling outward at the clip locations. Start at the bottom and move upward. Do not use tools that might damage the trim panel.

4. Open the glove box and remove the 4 cluster trim panel attaching screws.

5. Carefully pull the cluster trim panel upward to disengage it from the retainers, then remove the CPA and disconnect the electrical connectors from the instrument panel lighting and rear window defogger switches. Remove the panel from the vehicle.

6. Remove the instrument cluster retaining screws, pull the cluster out far enough to disconnect the electrical connectors. Disconnect the connectors by depressing the retainer legs and remove the assembly.

To install:

7. Connect the electrical connectors to the instrument cluster assembly.

8. Verify that the connectors for the cluster trim panel lighting and rear window defogger switches are properly positioned and install the instrument cluster assembly and retaining screws.

9. Position the cluster trim panel and connect the electrical connectors to the panel lighting and the rear defogger switches, then install the CPA.

10. Install the cluster trim panel into the retainers, then install and tighten the retaining screws.

11. Push the center radio finish panel and air outlet assembly into the clip locations.

12. Install the rear of the instrument panel top cover into the windshield clips and snap the panel into position. Install the upper panel cover screws and screw caps.

13. Connect the negative battery cable and, if equipped, properly enable the SIR system.

Combination Switch

REMOVAL & INSTALLATION

1. Properly disable the SIR system, if equipped, and disconnect the negative battery cable.

2. Remove the steering wheel.

3. Remove the 2 retaining screws and the upper steering column cover from the steering column.

4. Remove the ignition lock bezel,

then remove the 2 retaining screws and the lower steering column cover.

5. Disconnect the velcro fasteners, then remove the left and right lower trim panel extensions by pulling them out of the 2 upper fasteners on each side.

6. Carefully remove the center radio finish panel and air outlet assembly by pulling outward at the clip locations. Start at the bottom and move upward. Do not use tools that might damage the trim panel.

7. If necessary, remove the trim panel extension strip by pulling out at the fastener locations.

8. Remove the 2 instrument panel top cover screw caps and screws. Carefully remove the cover by lifting at the rear edge to disengage the retaining clips and by sliding the panel out of the windshield clips.

9. Remove the 4 cluster trim panel attaching screws. Carefully pull the cluster trim panel upward to disengage it from the retainers.

10. Remove the CPA and disconnect the electrical connectors from the instrument panel lighting and rear window defogger switches. Remove the cluster trim panel from the vehicle.

11. Remove the 6 screws attaching the steering column opening filler assembly, then carefully remove the assembly. Protect the console from the damage when removing the assembly.

12. Remove the CPA and disconnect the wires from the lever control switch.

13. Remove the retaining bolts and remove the combination switch assembly from the steering column.

To install:

14. Install the combination switch and retaining bolts. Tighten the lower mounting bolt first to assure proper location and seating, then connect the switch electrical connectors and insert the CPA.

15. Install the steering column opening filler and attaching screws.

16. Position the cluster trim panel and connect the electrical connectors to the panel lighting and the rear defogger switches, then install the CPA. Install the cluster trim panel into the retainers, then install and tighten the retaining screws

17. Install the rear of the instrument panel top cover into the windshield clips and snap the panel into position. If necessary, replace the 6 rearward clips. Install the upper panel cover screws and screw caps.

18. Install the trim panel extension strip and push the center radio finish panel and air outlet assembly into the clip locations.

19. Install the lower left and right trim panel extensions.

20. Install the steering column covers and the ignition bezel.

21. Install the steering wheel.

22. Connect the negative battery cable and, if equipped, properly enable the SIR system.

Fuses, Circuit Breakers and Relays

LOCATION
Underhood Junction Block

The block is located next to the battery on the left inner fender. It houses maxifuses, minifuses, relays and 1 circuit breaker. There are two 30 amp maxifuses for the ignition and 1 each for the battery, ABS and cooling fan. The circuit breaker is a 30 amp unit for the power windows and/or sunroof.

The horn, air conditioning control, cooling fan and automatic transaxle relays are located in the underhood junction block.

Instrument Panel Junction Block

The block is located under the instrument panel, behind the center console. It houses minifuses and relays. The relays for the power window, fuel pump, flasher, rear defogger and blower motor are located in the block.